HORNSEY
HAMSTED
HAKENEY
PARS
LONDON
HAMERSMITH
SOUTHVARK
CAMENVEL
STRETHAM

the complete works of shakespeare

MIDDEL
SEXIAE
HARMSWORTH
HESTON
HOWNSLEY
ASHFORD

preface to the revised edition

Although I never had the good fortune to study under Hardin Craig, I know from several friends who have done so that he was a gifted teacher—generous, enthusiastic, learned. His fondness for Shakespeare was catching, and a number of his students have gone on to distinguished careers in Craig's own footsteps. Craig's edition of Shakespeare has commanded the same sort of affectionate respect, both from his students and from many who never met him. The book is commonly referred to as a "standby," a landmark in the teaching of literature since an early version of it first appeared in 1931. In many important ways it has set a standard for later texts of Shakespeare, with its interpretive notes, its glossary and bibliographies, and its extensive general introduction on Shakespeare's age and theatre.

In revising a work that has enjoyed undiminished popularity for more than forty years of use, I have attempted to bring it up to date without changing the book's essential and enduring character. Much of the critical material has been rewritten, since scholarship and criticism have made significant advances in recent years, but the subjects covered in this present edition are basically the same as in previous editions, and the proportions of the volume remain unaltered. I have always thought that Craig's arrangement of the plays—in chronological order and yet grouped by genre within each chronological period—is the most suitable for a text of this sort. The plays remain in their familiar order in this new edition, organized into the four periods of Shakespeare's development. The volume as a whole tries to elucidate that development of Shakespeare's artistry with which Craig was so concerned. The general introduction is of approximately the same length and scope as in the previous edition, and most of the section headings and subheadings are unchanged. The individual play introductions are entirely rewritten from a critical point of view, but the historical information on text, dating, sources, and stage history supplied by Craig's introductions has been retained in a new set of appendices. The notes are basically Craig's, and the text is still based on the Globe edition though carefully reviewed throughout and brought up to date in certain particulars. (Craig had already introduced a number of significant alterations into the Globe text.) Here are some details about the revisions in this edition, so that the reader will know as precisely as possible what work is Craig's and what is mine.

The General Introduction. The amount of revision varies from section to section. Craig's discussion of "Shakespeare's English" remains virtually unchanged; I have added only a paragraph on rhetorical figures such as parison and isocolon. The section called "A Note on Doubtful and Lost Plays" is basically Craig's, although rearranged and rephrased to some extent. In the various sections on "Shakespeare's Life and Work" that precede the four chronological periods of the book, I have retained most of Craig's biographical data, contemporary allusions, and ordering of topics, but I have for the most part rewritten these sections. Similarly, the sections on "The Drama before Shakespeare," "London Theatres and Dramatic Companies," and "The Order of Shakespeare's Plays" follow Craig's order of events and retain many of his observations, but on the whole are updated and rewritten. "Life in Shakespeare's England" is for the most part new, though aimed at informing the reader on the topics covered in earlier editions. "Shakespeare Criticism" and "Editions and Editors of Shakespeare" should be considered as entirely new.

The Play Introductions. These are new, and are designed to fulfill a different purpose from that envisaged by Craig. His chief aim was to provide factual and historical material about dating, early texts, sources, stage history, and the like. This present volume provides instead an interpretative essay on each play that takes dating and sources into account, but strives to present a critical view of the play touching upon those points that Shakespeare critics have found most fascinating. Hopefully, such essays can serve as a point of departure for classroom discussion of the plays. The essays also devote considerable attention to Shakespeare's development as a dramatist, pointing up thematic and technical similarities among the Roman plays, for example, or the late romances. Readers who wish to learn more on factual matters of dating, early texts, and the like, are referred to the new appendices at the end of the volume in which these matters are discussed in detail (see below).

The Notes. These notes are basically Craig's. I have, however, assisted by a panel of consultants whose names appear below, gone over all the notes and have revised where necessary. Notes in which Craig commented on the characters in the plays have generally been removed to make room for more glosses on difficult words and phrases. The glosses on sexual double entendres in this edition are virtually all new; like other editors of his generation, Craig was silent on such matters. Revision of the notes is more extensive in the major and later plays than in the early plays, although even in the late plays the large percentage of notes is still Craig's. His occasional textual notes have been retained, since they constitute his record of the changes he introduced into the Globe edition. Most of Craig's citations from earlier editors and critics have also been retained, though I have not tried to emulate this "Variorum" feature with citations from more recent criticism. Virtually all the notes have been reset.

Text. Although many casual users of Craig's Shakespeare have assumed that his text was simply a reprint of the Globe text of 1864 (see Craig's Preface), such was by no means the case. After all, textual scholarship has made enormous advances in the last century, and Craig was himself a textual scholar. In effect he reedited the whole of *Titus Andronicus*, as he certainly needed to do, since a hitherto unknown quarto edition of that play had come to light in 1905 and had proved to be superior as a textual authority to the Folio text on which the Globe editors had based their work. Craig also introduced corrected readings throughout the volume, and recorded these changes in the notes.

I have continued this modernizing process. Because the Globe editors based their edition of *Richard III* on the first quarto of 1597 rather than on the Folio text (now widely regarded as the superior copy text), I have in effect reedited this play. Although the entire text of *Richard III* has been reset, however, most of the changes are of a relatively minor sort (substituting "liege" for "lord," "betwixt" for "between," and the like) that do not disturb line numbering or meaning. The changes will not, I believe, interfere with the reference value of the Globe text. In some other plays I have also corrected the Globe's tendency to be "eclectic" when dealing with two early texts—for example, to choose unsystematically between the readings of the 1608 quarto and the Folio texts of *King Lear*, first from one and then from the other. Modern bibliographical theory has shown the unlikelihood that such a method can recover what Shakepeare actually wrote; the more systematic method is to determine which early text is closest to Shakespeare's composition, and then to stay conservatively close to that copy text. Accordingly, I have moved the texts of *King Lear* and *Othello* somewhat closer to their respective Folio originals. Three other plays are now more conservatively based on the quarto editions that have been shown to be the best copy texts: *Romeo and Juliet* (Q2, 1599), *2 Henry IV* (Q of 1600), and *Hamlet* (Q2, 1604-1605). These changes are generally not extensive, and do not interfere with the lineation of the Globe text.

Other individual changes are to be found scattered throughout the volume, as in Craig's revision of the Globe text. Virtually all of my changes are restorations of the original textual reading; that is, I have rejected a number of emendations adopted by the Globe editors. Some of these restorations deal with simple grammatical matters: for example, I have resisted the Globe editors' tendency to regularize or "improve" Shakespeare's use of *further* and *farther*, *show'd* and *shown*, *does* and *doth*, *seemeth* and *seems*, and the like. In most such cases I have simply followed the original Folio or quarto text. I have also restored a few characters' names as they appear in the original texts where it is quite clear that the printer's copy must consistently have used such a spelling, notably Berowne (not Biron) in *Love's Labour's Lost*, Sir John Falstaff (not Fastolfe) in *1 Henry VI*, Lavatch and Lafew (not Lavache and Lafeu) in *All's Well that Ends Well*, and Thidias and Decretas (not Thyreus and Dercetas) in *Antony and Cleopatra*. In general I have held to the view that glossing of unfamiliar words should occur in the notes rather than by revising the text, and so I have restored *mushrump* for *mushroom*, *Bristow* for *Bristol*, *whe'r* for *whether*, *strond* for *strand*, *wrack* for *wreck*, *moe* for *more*, and the like. These changes have been enumerated in the textual notes, so that the book can continue to be used as a Globe text for purposes of reference.

In addition I have introduced a number of nonsubstantive changes. Most important among these concerns elision. The Globe editors were not consistent in their use of elision. Although they adopted the system of eliding the *e* in a word like *enjoy'd*, as in the First Folio and quartos, to indicate that the word has two syllables rather than three, they often left words such as *loved* unelided even though the scansion and the original copy text both demanded an elision. I have reviewed all such elisions, and have followed the original copy texts in elision as conservatively as possible. I have also followed the original copy in such words as *fall'n*, *t' account*, *scatt'red*, *suff'ring*, *y' are*, *th' art*, *th' abhorr'd*, *spak'st*, *'a* (for *he*), and so on. I have not entered most such changes in the prose, however, since the Globe text adopted the common system of differentiating between prose (in which the elisions in the original text are in any case quite inconsistent) and verse (in which elision is crucial to proper scansion of the lines).

I have also followed the original texts faithfully on stage directions, and have employed square brackets to indicate editorial additions to the original stage directions (including indications of act and scene). In adopting this system, which preserves Shakespeare's own language in many cases, I have altered the language of the Globe stage directions as little as possible. The indications of place for each scene, through enclosed in square brackets, are with very few exceptions as they appear in the Globe text. The Globe-supplied lists of *dramatis personae* have similarly been placed in square brackets; those lists of characters not in square brackets, as in the case of *The Tempest*, *Othello*, and others, are from the original texts.

These various textual changes have involved a fair amount of resetting of lines and other presswork, but most of the changes will be scarcely visible even to readers who have used the previous edition. Most importantly, the lineation and line numbers of the Globe text have been preserved in all but a very few instances (as in *Richard III*, IV, v, where some lines are transposed). Rarely have I changed the forms of the speech prefixes, the spelling, the punctuation, or the appearance on the page of Craig's version of the Globe text. Hopefully the text will seem thoroughly familiar to users even though it incorporates a large number of small improvements in accuracy. I will be genuinely grateful to anyone who points out to me any new errors that have crept into this edition.

Glossary. With one insignificant alteration, this glossary is as Craig wrote it.

Appendices. The three appendices are new, and are intended to provide further reference for students wishing to learn more about textual problems, dating, sources, and stage history. Appendix I provides a literal transcript of all the title pages of the relevant early texts, a feature contained in the play introductions of Craig's previous editions. Appendix II contains summaries of Shakespeare's sources, a new feature and not found in most texts of Shakespeare today. Appendix III is an essay on stage history from Shakespeare's time to the present, in place of the notes on the stage history of individual plays found in Craig's previous editions.

Bibliographies. These lists of suggestions for further reading and research are new. Those for the individual plays are based on suggestions submitted by the consultants. The various lists also contain the names of many books to which I am personally indebted for information and ideas used in writing the introductions and other critical materials for this volume.

Index. The index has of course been revised, but retains many headings and classifications found in Craig's earlier editions.

I take pleasure in acknowledging the generous assistance I have received in preparing this volume. A group of scholarly consultants read and criticized early drafts of the general introduction and the individual play introductions. These consultants also made up lists of recommended reading for the individual plays, carefully reviewed the notes, offered helpful ideas on the editing of the text, and assisted in many needful ways. Their names are as follows: for the general introduction, John Wasson of Washington State University (Pullman) and Michael Houlahan of North Park College; for the comedies, Neil Rudenstine of Princeton University; for the history plays, John Elliott of the University of California (Santa Barbara) and Charles Forker of Indiana University; for the poems and sonnets, Cyrus Hoy of the University of Rochester; for the early tragedies, George Williams of Duke University; for the remainder of the tragedies, Howard Felperin of Yale University; and for the late romances, Arthur Kirsch of the University of Virginia. I have also received valuable advice on the project as a whole from Madeleine Doran of the University of Wisconsin (Madison) and from C. L. Barber of the University of California (Santa Cruz). Two admirable students, David Kastan and John Cox, with whom I have discussed most of Shakespeare's plays, have read over the proofs of the introductions and appendices and have rescued me from a number of errors and inconsistencies. In addition, my wife Peggy and my mother Helen Bevington, both of them expert teachers and stylists, have commented on portions of the manuscript. Editors Amanda Clark and Stanley Stoga, picture editor Denise Tamayo, production editors Helen Scott and Anne Gwash, and designer Susan Kearney, of the editorial staff at Scott, Foresman, have been unfailing in their energy and attention to detail. My children, to whom this edition is dedicated, have been wonderfully patient and even interested in what has kept me so long at my desk instead of playing softball.

David Bevington

preface to the first edition

In order fully to understand and appreciate Shakespeare, it is necessary to see him as a whole. It is not enough to read individual passages, scenes, and plays as independent units; they should be studied in their relation to the development of Shakespeare's powers as a dramatist, to the drama itself, and to Renaissance literature. The student who would know Shakespeare needs to know the temper of the Elizabethan age. As the student comes to understand better the meaning that Shakespeare had in his own day he will at the same time, the editor believes, develop a richer appreciation of the qualities of Shakespeare's genius that have given his work meaning in all ages.

The aim of this complete edition of Shakespeare has been, as far as was possible in one volume, to provide the reader or student with the information he normally needs in order to understand and appreciate Shakespeare. The editor has tried to present the most important background materials and at the same time to digest and make available to the student the most authoritative critical and textual work offered by Shakespeare scholars. By and large, the general objective of this complete edition of Shakespeare's works is the same as that of the editor's *Shakespeare: A Historical and Critical Study with Annotated Texts of Twenty-one Plays*, published by Scott, Foresman and Company in 1931. This, however, is a new edition throughout and carries over from the older book only those materials in the introductions and notes that the editor regards as still valid, still representative of the best information and judgment he could bring to bear upon the subject.

The plays and poems are arranged in the order in which most scholars believe they were written.

The text used is that of the widely known Globe, edited by William George Clark and William Aldis Wright (first printed in 1864) on the basis of the so-called Cambridge Shakespeare by these same editors (7 volumes, 1863-1866). The Globe was the first reliable edition of Shakespeare in convenient form and on modern lines. It appeared at a time when it was available for use in the large number of Shakespearean reference works that were published toward the end of the nineteenth century—dictionaries, concordances, studies of meter and words, comparative considerations of text, and so on. The result was that the Globe Shakespeare with the Cambridge line numbering attained a wide currency. Later conservative editions of Shakespeare, such as those of W. J. Craig, W. A. Neilson, and G. L. Kittredge, do not differ greatly from the Globe in their handling of the text—its punctuation, format, line numbering, and the placing of such things as act and scene divisions, names of speakers, stage directions, entrances and exits.

The Globe text is a good one, conservative and sensible, and it has been faithfully followed in this edition. However, more recent scholarship has shown a number of readings in which the Globe is clearly in error. It sometimes, as in the case of *King Lear* and *Richard III*, gives preference to what have since been proved inferior texts. In this edition, the Globe readings have been replaced in cases where the editor thought they were wrong. In order not to destroy the value for purposes of reference of the Globe text, all such changes have been carefully recorded in the notes. The dagger (†) placed by the Globe editors in front of lines which they considered corrupt has been retained, since that symbol still serves the reader as a warning and has come to be a ready and easy way of locating cruxes in the text.

Because almost all references to Shakespeare follow the line numbers in the Globe edition, care has been taken to reproduce these numbers in the present text. Uninterrupted lines of verse will, of course, have the same numbers in any edition, but in prose passages, owing to differences in column width and type used, the actual number of lines in a given passage does not always correspond exactly with that in the Globe or any other edition. This merely means that the reader must make some allowance for these differences when he is counting lines of prose to locate a particular word or sentence.

In the footnotes to the plays and poems, annotated words and passages are designated by the numbers of the lines in which they occur; and for every change of act and scene, a new paragraph is begun in the footnotes. The notes for facing pages are arranged in even blocks below the text.

For instruction in Shakespeare's language there is provided in the General Introduction (pp. 59-64) an account of "Shakespeare's English." There is also a glossary of the most frequently used Shakespearean words and meanings. This avoids tiresome repetition in the notes. Such words and meanings are, however, introduced into the notes and defined there in at least their first two occurrences in the plays and poems.

An attempt to supply a key to the wide range of information in this volume has been made in the index. Although limiting itself strictly to introductions and notes, the index records the names of plays and characters, with comments both general and specific; the names of persons, places, and literary works which are discussed or cited; and, under general headings, references to drama, literature, manners and customs, current beliefs, learned opinions, and the ideals of the age. Bibliographies are listed in the index, but not the books, articles, and authors which are included in these bibliographies.

In order to save space one great group of names has been omitted from the index: the names of commentators and critics who are referred to in the footnotes of the plays. In this edition the greatest care has been exercised to give exact credit to every commentator whose words or ideas have been followed. This has ordinarily been done by putting the surname of the authority in parentheses after the citation. For example, (Malone) after a statement or definition means that the authority for that note is the eighteenth-century scholar Edmund Malone. A list of these editors, textual critics, and commentators appears on the page immediately preceding the [textual notes]. In addition, the names of some forty-five general editors of Shakespeare are recorded in the section of the General Introduction called ["Editions and Editors of Shakespeare"] (pp. 51-58). These names do not occur in the index unless these editors are specifically mentioned in the introductory materials in connection with some opinion or achievement.

The illustrations reproduced in the book have been chosen for their suggestive portrayal of the life and spirit, the beliefs and practices of the Renaissance. They have been gathered from many sources, and it is hoped that they will introduce an element of variety into the illustration of Shakespeare texts.

The editor was fortunate in having in the early stages of this work the painstaking and scholarly assistance of Dr. Sina Spiker, now of the University of Wisconsin Press. He wishes to express his gratitude to her. He wishes also to thank Miss Josephine Pearce of the English Department of the University of Missouri for her assistance in the latest stages of his editorial work. Professor Carroll Camden of the Rice Institute was kind enough to supply a number of valuable notes, particularly on *Othello*, *King Lear*, and *Macbeth*. Professor Madeleine Doran of the University of Wisconsin read all of the introductions and editorial material in this edition while they were in galley proof. The editor feels that his book was improved by her criticisms and suggestions. Finally, the editor wishes to express on his own behalf and on that of the publishers, gratitude to Miss Dorothy Bowen and other members of the staff of the Henry E. Huntington Library and to Dr. James G. McManaway and Dr. Giles E. Dawson of the Folger Library for assistance in collecting materials to be used for illustration.

Hardin Craig

CONTENTS

the period of tragedies

the period of romances

Shakespeare as an English Dramatist

LIFE IN SHAKESPEARE'S ENGLAND

England during Shakespeare's lifetime (1564–1616) was a proud nation with a strong sense of national identity, but she was also a small nation by modern standards. Probably not more than five million people lived in the whole of England, considerably fewer than now live in London. England's territories in France were no longer extensive, as they had been during the fourteenth century and earlier; in fact, by the end of Queen Elizabeth's reign (1558–1603), England had virtually retired from her once-great empire on the continent. Her overseas empire in America had scarcely begun. Scotland was not yet a part of Great Britain; union with Scotland would not take place until 1707, despite the fact that King James VI of Scotland assumed the English throne in 1603 as James I of England. Ireland, although declared a kingdom under English rule in 1541, was more a source of trouble than of economic strength. The last years of Elizabeth's reign, especially from 1597 to 1601, were plagued by the rebellion of the Irish under Hugh O'Neill, Earl of Tyrone. Thus, England of the sixteenth and early seventeenth centuries was both small and isolated.

THE SOCIAL AND ECONOMIC BACKGROUND

By and large, England was a rural land. Much of the kingdom was still wooded, though timber was being used increasingly in manufacturing and shipbuilding. The area of the midlands, today heavily industrialized, was still at that time a region of great trees, green fields, and clear streams. England's chief means of livelihood was agriculture. This part of the economy was generally in a bad way, however, and Englishmen who lived off the land did not share in the prosperity of many Londoners. A problem throughout the sixteenth century was that of "enclosure": the conversion by rich landowners of crop lands into pasturage. Farmers and peasants complained bitterly that they were being dispossessed and starved for the benefit of livestock. Rural uprisings and food riots were common, to the dismay of the authorities. The agrarian poor of Oxfordshire arose in 1596, threatening to massacre the gentry and march on London; other riots had occurred in 1586 and 1591, provoking memories of the infamous May Day riots of 1517. Although the government did what it could to inhibit enclosure, the economic forces at work were too massive and too inadequately understood to be curbed by governmental fiat. Pasture was more profitable than crop land; it used large areas with greater efficiency than in crop farming, and required far less labor. The wool produced by the pasturing of sheep was needed in ever-increasing amounts for the manufacture of cloth.

The wool industry also experienced occasional economic difficulties, to be sure; overexpansion in the early years of the sixteenth century created a glutted market that had collapsed disastrously in 1551, creating widespread unemployment. Despite such fluctuations and reversals, however, the wool industry continued on the whole to expand and to provide handsome profits for landowners and middlemen. Mining and manufacture in coal, iron, tin, copper, and lead, although insignificant by modern standards, were also expanding at an enormous rate. Trading companies exploited the rich new resources of the Americas, as well as of Eastern Europe and the Orient. Queen Elizabeth aided economic development by keeping England out of war with her continental enemies as long as possible, despite provocations from those powers and despite the eagerness of some of her advisers to retaliate.

The new economic prosperity was not evenly distributed. Especially during Shakespeare's first years in London, in the late 1580's and the 1590's, the gap between rich and poor grew more and more extreme. Elizabeth's efforts at peacemaking were no longer able to prevent years of war with the Catholic powers of the Continent. Taxation grew heavier, and inflation proceeded at an unusually rapid rate during this period. A succession of bad harvests compounded the miseries of those who dwelled on the land. When the hostilities on the Continent ceased for a time in about 1597, a wave of returning veterans added to unemployment and crime. The rising prosperity experienced by Shakespeare and other fortunate Londoners was undeniably real, but it was not universal. No-

This illustration by Claes Janszoon de Visscher in the year of Shakespeare's death shows the London of 1616 as a thriving metropolis. The various boats on the Thames are evidence of the vital role the river played in the city's emergence as a center for international as well as national trade.

where was the contrast between rich and poor more visible than in London.

London

Sixteenth-century London was at once more attractive and less attractive than twentieth-century London. It was full of trees and gardens; meadows and cultivated lands reached in some places to its very walls. Today we can perhaps imagine the way in which it bordered clear streams and green fields, when we approach from a distance some uncommercial provincial city such as Lincoln, York, or Hereford. Surrounded by its ancient wall, London was by no means a large metropolis. Although its population had expanded into the surrounding area in all directions, the city proper stretched along the north bank of the Thames River from the old Tower of London on the east to St. Paul's Cathedral and the Fleet Ditch on the west—a distance of little more than a mile. A visitor approaching London from the south bank of the Thames (the bankside), and crossing London Bridge, could see virtually all of this exciting city lying before him. London Bridge itself was one of the major attractions of the city, lined with shops and richly decorated on occasion for the triumphal entry of a king or queen.

Yet London had its grim and ugly side as well. On London Bridge could sometimes be seen the heads of executed traitors. The city's houses were generally small and crowded; its streets were often narrow and filthy. In the absence of sewers, open ditches in the streets served to collect and carry off refuse. Frequent epidemics of the bubonic plague were the inevitable result of unsanitary conditions and medical ignorance. Lighting of the streets at night was generally nonexistent, and the constabulary was notoriously unreliable. Shakespeare gives us unforgettable satires of night watchmen and bumbling police officials in *Much Ado about Nothing* (Dogberry and the night watch) and *Measure for Measure* (Constable Elbow). Prostitution thrived in the suburbs, conveniently located although beyond the reach of the London authorities. Again, we are indebted to Shakespeare for a memorable portrayal in *Measure for Measure* of just such a demimonde (Mistress Overdone the bawd, Pompey her pimp, and various customers). Houses of prostitution were often to be found in the vicinity of

THE FOLGER SHAKESPEARE LIBRARY

the public theatres, since the theatres also took advantage of suburban locations to escape the stringent regulations imposed by London's Lord Mayor and Council of Aldermen. The famous Globe Theatre, for example, was on the south bank of the Thames, a short distance to the west of London Bridge. Another theatrical building (called simply "The Theatre") used earlier by Shakespeare and the Lord Chamberlain's players was located in Finsbury Fields, a short distance across Moorfields from London's northeast corner. The suburbs also housed various con games and illegal operations, some of them brilliantly illustrated (and no doubt exaggerated) in Ben Jonson's *The Alchemist* (1610).

London's population stood at perhaps one hundred thousand people within the walls and as many more in the suburbs. The royal palace of Whitehall, Westminster Abbey (then known as the Abbey Church of St. Peter), the Parliament House, and Westminster Hall were well outside London, two miles or so to the west on the Thames River. They remain today in the same location, in Westminster, although the metropolis of London has long since surrounded these official buildings.

Travel

Travel was still extremely painful and slow because of the unimproved condition of the roads. It was also dangerous on account of highway robbers, as we can see from Shakespeare's celebrated portrayal of the robbery at Gads Hill, in *1 Henry IV*. (This robbery occurs on the main road between London and Canterbury.) English inns seem to have been good, however, certainly much better than the inns of the Continent. Travel on horseback was the most common method, and probably the most comfortable, since coachbuilding was a new and imperfect art. Coaches of state, some of which we see in prints and pictures of the era, were lumbering affairs, no doubt handsome enough in processions, but springless, unwieldy, and hard to transport. Carts and wagons were used for carrying merchandise, but packsaddles were safer and quicker. Under such difficulties, no metropolitan area such as London could possibly have thrived in the interior. London depended for its commercial greatness upon the Thames River and its access to the North Sea.

Commerce

When Elizabeth came to the English throne in 1558, England's chief foreign trade was with Antwerp, Bruges, and other Belgian cities. Antwerp was an especially important market for England's export of wool cloth. This market was a seriously threatened one, however, since the Low Countries were under the domination of the Catholic King of Spain, Philip II. When Philip shortsightedly undertook to punish his

THE FOLGER SHAKESPEARE LIBRARY

London Bridge, lined with shops and over 100 houses, was a picturesque route for those traveling between the north bank of the Thames and the south, where many Elizabethan theatres were located, including the Globe.

Protestant subjects in the Low Countries for their religious heresy, many of Elizabeth's counselors and subjects urged her to come to the defense of England's Protestant neighbors and trading allies. Elizabeth prudently held back. Philip's armies attacked Antwerp in 1576 and again in 1585, putting to an end the commercial ascendancy of that great northern European metropolis. Perhaps as many as one third of Antwerp's merchants and artisans settled in London, bringing with them their expert knowledge of commerce and manufacture. The influx of so many skilled workmen and merchants into London produced problems of unemployment and overcrowding, but contributed nevertheless to London's emergence as a leading port of trade.

English ships assumed a dominant position in Mediterranean trade, formerly carried on mainly by the Venetians. In the Baltic Sea, England captured trade that had previously been controlled by the Hanseatic League. Bristol thrived on commerce with Ireland and subsequently on trade with the Western Hemisphere. Boston and Hull increased their business with Scandinavian ports. The Russia Company was founded in 1555; the Levant Company became the famous East India Company in 1600; and the Virginia Company opened up trade with the New World in the Western Hemisphere. Fisheries were developed in the North Sea, in the waters north of Ireland, and off the banks of Newfoundland. Elizabeth and her ministers wisely encouraged this commercial expansion.

The Poor Laws and Apprenticeship

Despite the new prosperity experienced by many Elizabethans, especially in London, unemployment remained a serious problem. The suppression of the monasteries in 1536–1539, as part of Henry VIII's reformation of the Catholic Church, had dispossessed a large class of persons who were not easily reemployed. Other causes of unemployment, such as the periodic collapses of the wool trade, dispossession of farm workers by enclosure of land, the sudden influx of skilled artisans from Antwerp, and the return of army veterans, have already been mentioned. Elizabethan Parliaments attempted to cope with the problem of unemployment, but did so in ways that seem unduly harsh today. In 1572 an act of Parliament made the mayors, magistrates, and county officials responsible for the care of their local poor and for the enforcement of stern measures against vagabonds. Under this act, vagabonds were arrested and sent back to their own parishes and there compelled to work. This localization of responsibility laid the basis for what has been known historically as the "poor rate" (a local tax levied for the support of the poor) and for that sinister institution, the workhouse. The provisions of the act of 1572 remained in force for centuries.

Regulations for apprentices were no less strict. An

act of Parliament of 1563, known as the Statute of Artificers, gave the craft trades of England—still organized as medieval guilds—virtually complete authority over the young persons apprenticed to a trade. Apprenticeship usually began at the age of fourteen to seventeen, and lasted for a period of not less than seven years. During this time the young worker lived with the family of his master. Without such an extensive apprenticeship, entry into the skilled crafts was virtually impossible. Acting companies, such as the company Shakespeare joined, were similarly organized as guilds and took on boy actors in an apprenticeship role. We do not know, however, whether Shakespeare actually served such an indenture before becoming a full member of his acting company.

Social Change

The opportunities for rapid economic advance in Elizabethan England, though by no means available to all, did produce social change and a quality of restlessness in English society. "New men" at court were an increasing phenomenon under the Tudor monarchs, who tended to rely on loyal counselors of humble origin rather than on the once-too-powerful nobility. Cardinal Wolsey, for example, rose from obscurity to become the most mighty subject of Henry VIII's realm, with a newly built residence (Hampton Court) rivaling the splendor of the king's own palaces. He was detested as an upstart by old aristocrats such as the Duke of Norfolk, and his sudden fall was as spectacular as had been his rise to power. The Earl of Leicester, Queen Elizabeth's first favorite, was a descendant of the Edmund Dudley who had risen from unpretentious beginnings to great eminence under Henry VII, Queen Elizabeth's grandfather. Such new and influential families were numerous. Conversely, the ancient families discovered that they were no longer entrusted with positions of highest authority. To be sure, the aristocracy remained vitally important as the apex of England's social structure. New aspirants to power emulated the aristocracy by purchasing land and building splendid residences, rather than defining themselves as a rich new "middle class." Bourgeois status was something the new men put behind them as quickly as they could. Moreover, social mobility could work in both directions, both upward and downward. Many men were quickly ruined by the costly and competitive business of seeking favor at the Tudor court. Nonetheless, the Elizabethan era was one of greater opportunity for rapid social and economic advancement than England had heretofore known.

Increased economic contacts with the outside world inevitably led to the importation of new styles of living. Such new fashions, together with the rapid changes now possible in social position, produced a reaction of dismay from those who feared the destruction of traditional English values. Italy was particularly reviled, both as the home of the Catholic Church and as the originator of many supposedly decadent fashions. The word "Italianate" connoted a whole range of villainous practices, including diabolical methods of torture and revenge: poisoned books of devotion which would kill the unsuspecting victims who kissed them, ingeniously contrived chairs that would close upon the person who sat in them, and the like. The revenge plays of Shakespeare's contemporaries, such as *Antonio's Revenge* by John Marston, *The Revenger's Tragedy* perhaps by Cyril Tourneur or Thomas Middleton, and *The White Devil* by John Webster, offer spectacular caricatures of the so-called Italianate style in murder. The name of Italy was also associated with licentiousness, immorality, and outlandish fashions in clothes. France, too, was accused of encouraging such extravagances in dress as ornamented headdresses, stiffly pleated ruffs, padded doublets, puffed or double sleeves, and richly decorated hose. Rapid changes in fashion added to the costliness of being up to date, and thereby increased the outcry against vanity in dress. Fencing, dicing, the use of cosmetics, the smoking of tobacco, the drinking of imported wines, and almost every vice known to man were attributed by angry moralists to the corrupting influence from abroad.

Not all Englishmen deplored continental fashion, of course. Persons of advanced taste saw the importation of European styles as a culturally liberating process. Fashion thus became a subject of debate between moral traditionalists and those who welcomed the new styles. The controversy was a bitter one, with religious overtones, in which the reformers' angry accusations became increasingly extreme. This attack on changing fashion was in fact an integral part of the Puritan movement. It therefore stressed the sinfulness not only of extravagance in clothing but of the costli-

COURTESY OF THE TRUSTEES, THE BRITISH MUSEUM

The wealthy felt little obligation to relieve the widespread poverty and unemployment of the times.

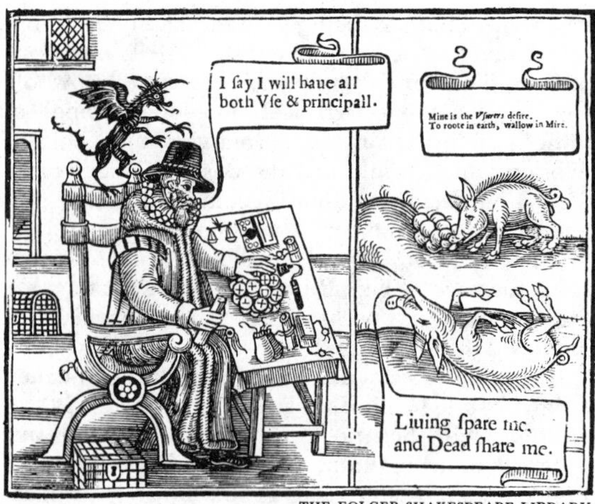

I ſay I will haue all
both Vſe & principall.
Mine is the *Vſurers* deſire.
To roote in earth, wallow in Mire.
Liuing ſpare me,
and Dead ſhare me.

THE FOLGER SHAKESPEARE LIBRARY

The English usurer was seen by many as a most disreputable fellow: an unsavory outcast, piglike in his greed.

ness in building great houses and other such worldly pursuits. Those whose sympathies were Puritan became more and more disaffected with the cultural values represented by the court, and thus English society drifted further and further toward irreconcilable conflict.

Shakespeare's personal views on this controversy are hard to determine and do not bear importantly on his achievement as an artist. Generally, however, we can observe that his many references to changes in fashion cater neither to the avant-garde nor to reactionary traditionalists. Shakespeare's audience was after all a broadly national one. It included many ordinary Londoners who viewed "Italianate" fashion neither with enthusiasm nor with alarm, but with satiric laughter. Such spectators would certainly have seen the point, for example, in Mercutio's witty diatribe at the expense of the new French style in fencing. The object of his scorn is Tybalt, who, according to Mercutio, "fights as you sing prick-song" and fancies himself to be "the very butcher of a silk button." "Is not this a lamentable thing," asks Mercutio rhetorically, "that we should be thus afflicted with these strange flies, these fashion-mongers, these perdonami's, who stand so much on the new form, that they cannot sit at ease on the old bench?" (*Romeo and Juliet*, II,iv). In a similar vein, Shakespeare's audience would have appreciated the joking in *The Merchant of Venice* about England's servile imitation of continental styles in clothes. "What say you, then, to Falconbridge, the young baron of England?" asks Nerissa of her mistress Portia concerning one of Portia's many suitors. Portia replies, "How oddly he is suited! I think he bought his doublet in Italy, his round hose in France, his bonnet in Germany and his behaviour everywhere" (I,ii). Court butterflies in Shakespeare's plays who bow and scrape and fondle their plumed headgear, like Le Beau in *As You Like It* and Osric in *Hamlet*, are the objects of ridicule. Hotspur in *1 Henry IV*, though flawed by aristocratic pride, contrasts favorably with the effeminate courtier, "perfumed like a milliner," who has come from King Henry to discuss the question of prisoners (I,iii). Throughout Shakespeare's plays, the use of cosmetics generally has the negative connotation of artificial beauty used to conceal inward corruption, as in Claudius' reference to "the harlot's cheek, beautied with plast'ring art" (*Hamlet*, III,i). Yet Shakespeare's treatment of newness in fashion is never shrill in tone. Nor does he fail in his dramas to give an honorable place to the ceremonial use of wealth and splendid costuming. His plays thus avoid both extremes in the controversy over changing fashions, though they give plentiful evidence as to the liveliness and currency of the topic.

Shakespeare also reflects a contemporary interest in the problem of usury, especially in *The Merchant of Venice*. Although usury was becoming more and more of a necessity, emotional attitudes toward it changed only slowly. The traditional moral view condemned usury as forbidden by Christian teaching; on the other hand, European governments of the sixteenth century found themselves increasingly obliged to borrow large sums of money. The laws against usury were alternatively relaxed and enforced, according to the economic exigencies of the moment. Shakespeare's plays capture the Elizabethan ambivalence of attitude toward this feared but necessary practice (see Introduction to *The Merchant of Venice*). Similarly, most Englishmen had contradictory attitudes toward what we today would call the law of supply and demand in the marketplace. Conservative moralists complained bitterly when merchants exploited the scarcity of some commodity by forcing up prices; the practice was denounced as excessive profit-taking and declared to be sinful, like usury. In economic policy, then, as in matters of changing fashion or increased social mobility, the old-fashioned and disappearing world of late medieval England exerted a strong emotional appeal.

Elizabethan Houses

Those fortunate Englishmen who grew wealthy in the reign of Elizabeth took special pleasure in building themselves fine new houses. Chimneys were increasingly common, so that smoke no longer had to escape through a hole in the roof. Pewter, or even silver dishes, took the place of the wooden spoon and trencher. Beds and even pillows became common. Carpets were replacing rushes as covering for the floors; wainscoting, tapestries or hangings, and pictures appeared on the walls; and glass began to be used extensively for windows.

Despite the warnings of those moralists who preached against the vanity of worldly acquisition, domestic comfort made considerable progress in Elizabethan England. Many splendid Tudor mansions stand today, testifying to the important social changes that had taken place between the strife-torn fifteenth century and the era of relative peace under Elizabeth. The battlement, the moat, the fortified gate, and the narrow window used for archery or firearms generally disappeared in favor of handsome gardens and terraces. On a lower social scale, the peasant enjoyed greater physical security, and no longer needed to bring his cows, pigs, and poultry into his house at night in order to protect them from thieves. City houses, of which many exist today, were often large and imposing structures, three or four stories in height, and framed usually of strong oak with the walls filled in with brick and plaster. Although the frontage on the streets of London was usually narrow, many houses had trees and handsome gardens at the rear.

With these finer houses, too, came features of privacy that had been virtually unknown to previous generations. Life in the household of a medieval lord had generally focused on the great hall, which could serve variously as the kitchen, dining hall, and sitting room for the entire family and its retainers. The men drank in the hall in the evenings and slept there at night. The new dwellings of prosperous Elizabethans, on the other hand, featured private chambers into which the family and the chief guests could retire.

The Elizabethans built well. Not only do we still admire their houses, but we can see from their oriel windows and stained glass, their broad staircases, their jewels, and their costumes, that they treasured the new beauty of their lives made possible by the culture of the Renaissance. Although the graphic and plastic arts did not thrive in England to the same extent as in Italy, France, and the Low Countries, England made lasting achievements in architecture as well as in music, drama, and all forms of literature.

THE POLITICAL AND RELIGIOUS BACKGROUND

England under the Tudor kings suffered from almost unceasing religious conflict. The battle over religion affected every aspect of life, none more so than politics. At the very beginning of the Tudor reign, to be sure, England's problem was not religious but dynastic. Henry VII, the first of the Tudor kings, brought an end to the devastating civil wars of the fifteenth cen-

PHOTOGRAPH BY HERSCHEL LEVIT

In contrast to the fortresslike structures of an earlier, more tumultous era, the Tudor house was usually a comfortable plaster-and-timber dwelling—evidence of the relative peace and prosperity of the times.

ENGLAND'S MONARCHS, 1377–1649

The House of Plantagenet	
Richard II	1377–1399
The House of Lancaster	
Henry IV	1399–1413
Henry V	1413–1422
Henry VI	1422–1461
The House of York	
Edward IV	1461–1483
Edward V	1483
Richard III	1483–1485
The House of Tudor	
Henry VII	1485–1509
Henry VIII	1509–1547
Edward VI	1547–1553
Mary	1553–1558
Elizabeth I	1558–1603
The House of Stuart	
James I	1603–1625
Charles I	1625–1649

For further details, see Genealogical Tables on pp. 1394–1395.

tury by his overthrow of Richard III at the battle of Bosworth Field in 1485. The civil wars thus ended were the so-called Wars of the Roses, between the Lancastrian House of Henry VI (symbolized by the red rose) and the Yorkist House of Edward IV (symbolized by the white rose). Shakespeare chose these eventful struggles as the subject for his first series of English history plays, from *Henry VI* in three parts to *Richard III.* The House of Lancaster drew its title from John of Gaunt, Duke of Lancaster, father of Henry IV and great-grandfather of Henry VI; the House of York drew its title from Edmund Langley, Duke of York, great-grandfather of Edward IV and Richard III. Because John of Gaunt and Edmund Langley had been brothers, virtually all the noble contestants in this War of the Roses were cousins of one another, caught in a senseless dynastic struggle for control of the English crown. Many of them lost their lives in the fighting. By 1485, England was exhausted from civil conflict. Although Henry VII's own dynastic claim to the throne was weak, he managed to suppress factional opposition and to give England the respite from war she so desperately needed. His son, Henry VIII, inherited a throne in 1509 that was more secure than it had been in nearly a century.

Henry VIII's notorious marital difficulties, however, soon brought an end to dynastic security and civil accord. Because he divorced his first wife, Katharine of Aragon, in 1530 without the consent of Rome, he was excommunicated from the Catholic Church; his response in 1534 was to have himself proclaimed "Protector and only Supreme Head of the Church and Clergy of England." This decisive act signaled the beginning of the Reformation in England, not many years after Martin Luther's momentous break with the Papacy in 1517 and the consequent beginning of Lutheran Protestantism on the Continent. In England, Henry's act of defiance split the church and the nation. Many men chose Sir Thomas More's path of martyrdom rather than submit to Henry's new title as supreme head of the English church. Henry's later years did witness a period of retrenchment in religion, after the downfall of Thomas Cromwell in 1540, and indeed Henry's break with Rome had had its origin in political and marital rivalries rather than in matters of dogma and liturgy. Nevertheless, the establishment of an Anglican church was now an accomplished fact. The accession of Henry's ten-year-old son Edward VI, in 1547, gave reformers an opportunity to bring about rapid changes in English Protestantism. Archbishop Cranmer's forty-two articles of religion (1551), and his prayer book, laid the basis for the Anglican church of the sixteenth century.

The death of the sickly Edward VI in 1553 brought with it an intense crisis in religious politics, and a temporary reversal of England's religious direction. For five years England returned to Catholicism under the rule of Edward's elder sister Mary, daughter of the Catholic Queen Katharine of Aragon. The crisis accompanying such changes of government during this midcentury period was greatly exacerbated by the fact that all three of Henry VIII's living children were considered illegitimate by one faction or another of the English people. In Protestant eyes, Mary was the daughter of the divorced Queen Katharine, whose marriage to Henry had never been valid because she had previously been the spouse of Henry VIII's older brother Arthur. This Arthur had died at a young age, in 1502, shortly after his state marriage to the Spanish princess. If, as the Protestants insisted, Arthur had consummated the marriage, then Katharine's subsequent union with her deceased husband's brother was invalid, and Henry was free instead to marry Anne Boleyn—the mother-to-be of Elizabeth. In Catholic eyes, however, both Elizabeth and her brother Edward VI (son of Jane Seymour, Henry VIII's third wife) were the bastard issue of Henry's bigamous marriages; Henry's one and only true marriage in the Catholic faith was that to Katharine of Aragon. Edward and Elizabeth were regarded by many Catholics, at home and abroad, not only as illegitimate children but as illegitimate rulers, to be disobeyed and even overthrown by force. Thus, dynastic and marital conflicts became matters of grave political consequence.

Because of these struggles, Elizabeth's accession to the throne in 1558 remained an uncertainty until the last moment. Once she actually became ruler, however, England returned once more to the Protestant faith. Even then, tact and moderation were required to prevent open religious war. Elizabeth's genius at compromise prompted her to seek a middle position for her church, one that combined an episcopal form of church government (owing no allegiance to the Pope) with an essentially traditional form of liturgy and dogma. As much as was practicable, she left matters up to individual conscience; she drew the line, however, where matters of conscience tended to "exceed their bounds and grow to be matter of faction." In practice this meant that she did not tolerate avowed Catholics on the religious right, or Brownists and Unitarians (who denied the doctrine of the Trinity) on the religious left. The foundation for this so-called Elizabethan compromise was the thirty-nine articles, adopted in 1563 and based in many respects upon the forty-two articles of 1551. The compromise did not please everyone, of course, but it did achieve a remarkable degree of consensus during Elizabeth's long reign.

Queen Elizabeth and Tudor Absolutism

Elizabeth had to cope with a religiously divided nation and with extremists of both right and left who wished her downfall. She was a woman, in an age openly skeptical of women's ability or right to rule. Her success in dealing with such formidable odds was in large measure the result of her personal style as a monarch. Her combination of imperious will and femininity and her brilliant handling of her many contending male admirers have become legendary. She remained unmarried throughout her life, in part at least because marriage would have upset the delicate balance she maintained among rival groups, both foreign and domestic. Marriage would have committed her irretrievably to either one foreign nation or to one constituency at home. She chose instead to bestow her favor on certain courtiers, notably Robert Dudley (whom she elevated to be the Earl of Leicester) and, after Leicester's death in 1588, Robert Devereux, second Earl of Essex. Her relationship with these men, despite her partiality to them, was marked by her outbursts of tempestuous jealousy. In addition, she relied on the staid counsel of her hard-working ministers: Lord Burghley, Sir Francis Walsingham, Burghley's son Robert Cecil, and a few others.

In theory, at least, Tudor England was an absolutist monarchy in an age when many of England's greatest rivals—France, Spain, the Holy Roman Empire—were also under absolutist rule. The rise of absolutism throughout Renaissance Europe was the result of an increase of centralized national power and a corresponding decrease in autonomous baronial influence. Henry VII's strong assertion of his royal authority at the expense of the feudal lords corresponded roughly in time with the ascendancy of Francis I of France (1515) and Charles V of the Holy Roman Empire (1519). Yet England had long enjoyed a tradition of rule by consensus. When Elizabeth came to the throne, England was already in some ways a "limited" monarchy. Parliament, and especially the members of the House of Commons, claimed prerogatives of their own and were steadily gaining in both experience and power. In the mid-1560's, for example, the Commons made repeated attempts to use their tax-levying authority as a means of obliging Elizabeth to name a Protestant successor to the throne. The attempt, despite its failure to achieve its immediate goal, was significant; the Commons had shown that they were a force to be reckoned with. Even though Elizabeth made skillful rhetorical use of the theory of absolutism, portraying herself as God's appointed deputy on earth, her idea of absolutism should not be confused with despotism. She needed all her considerable diplomatic skills in dealing with her Parliaments and with the English people, self-reliant and proud of their reputation for independence. Elizabeth had more direct authority over her Privy Council, since she could appoint its members herself; still, she consulted faithfully with them on virtually everything she did. Nor were her closest advisers reluctant to offer her advice. Many vocal leaders in her government, including Walsingham and Leicester, urged the queen during the 1570's and 1580's to undertake a more active military role on the Continent against the Catholic powers. So did her later favorite, the Earl of Essex. With remarkable tact, she managed to retain the loyalty of her militant and sometimes exasperated counselors, and yet to keep England out of war with Spain until that country actually launched an invasion attempt in 1588 (the Great Armada).

Catholic Opposition

During her early years, Elizabeth sought through her religious compromise to ease the divisions of her kingdom, and attempted to placate her enemies abroad (notably Philip of Spain) rather than involve England in a costly war. For about twelve years, while England's economy gained much-needed strength, this policy of temporizing succeeded. Yet Elizabeth's more extreme Catholic opponents at home and abroad could never be reconciled to the daughter of that Protestant "whore," Anne Boleyn. England's period of relative accommodation came to an end in 1569 and 1570, with Catholic uprisings in the north and with Papal excommunication of the English queen. As a declared heretic, Elizabeth's very life was in danger; her Catholic subjects were enjoined by Rome to disobey her and to seek means for her violent overthrow.

Conspirators did in fact make attempts on the queen's life, notably in the so-called Babington conspiracy of 1586. This plot, brought to light by Secretary of State Walsingham, sought to place Mary Queen of Scots on the English throne in Elizabeth's stead. Mary was Elizabeth's kinswoman; Mary's

NATIONAL GALLERY OF SCOTLAND, SCOTTISH NATIONAL PORTRAIT GALLERY OF SCOTTISH NATIONAL GALLERY OF MODERN ART

The 1587 beheading of Mary Queen of Scots, shown holding a crucifix and surrounded by official witnesses in this contemporary watercolor, virtually ended any serious Catholic challenge to Elizabeth's throne.

grandmother, sister to Henry VIII, had been married to James IV of Scotland. So long as Elizabeth remained childless, Mary was a prominent heir to the English throne. Catholics pinned their hopes on her succession, by force if necessary; Protestant leaders urged Elizabeth to marry and give birth to a Protestant heir, or at least name a Protestant successor. Mary had abdicated the Scottish throne in 1567, after the sensational murder of her Catholic counselor David Rizzio, the murder of Mary's husband the Earl of Darnley (in which Mary was widely suspected to have taken part), and her subsequent marriage to Darnley's slayer, the Earl of Bothwell. Taking refuge in England, Mary remained a political prisoner and the inevitable focus of Catholic plotting against Elizabeth for approximately two decades. All that long while Elizabeth resisted demands from her Protestant advisers that she execute her kinswoman and thereby end a constant threat to the throne. Finally, Mary's clear involvement in the Babington conspiracy led to her execution in 1587. By that time, Spain was mounting an invasion against England, and Elizabeth's temporizing tactics were no longer feasible. The long years of peace had done their work, however, and England was considerably stronger and more resolute than she had been thirty years before. With Elizabeth's tacit approval, Sir Francis Drake and other naval commanders carried the fighting to Spain's very shore and to her American colonies. In 1585, Elizabeth had permitted troops under the command of the Earl of Leicester to aid the Dutch against Spain. The war with Spain continued from 1588 until about 1597.

Protestant Opposition

The threat from the religious left was no less worrisome than that from the right. Protestant reformers had experienced their first taste of power at the time of Henry VIII's break with Rome in 1534. Under Thomas Cromwell, Cardinal Wolsey's successor as the king's chief minister, the monasteries were suppressed and William Tyndale's English Bible was authorized. The execution of Cromwell introduced a period of conservative retrenchment, but the accession of Edward VI in 1547 brought reform once more into prominence. Thereafter Mary's Catholic reign drove most of the reformers into continental exile. When they returned after 1558, many had been made more radical by their continental experience.

To be sure, reform covered a wide spectrum from moderation to radicalism. Some preferred to work within the existing hierarchical structure of church and state, whereas others were religious separatists. Only the more radical groups, such as the Brownists and Anabaptists, endorsed ideas of equality and communal living. The abusive epithet "Puritan," applied indiscriminately to all shades of reforming activity, tended to obscure the wide range of differences in the reform movement. The reformers were to some extent united by a dislike for formal ritual and ecclesiastical garments, by a preference for a simple and pious manner of living, and by a belief in the literal word of the Bible rather than the patristic teachings of the church. They stressed personal responsibility in religion and were Calvinist in their emphasis on human depravity and the need for grace through election. Yet at first only the more radical were involved in a movement to establish an entirely separate church.

The radicals on the religious left, even if they represented at first only a minority of the religious reformers, posed a serious threat to Elizabeth's government. Their program bore an ironic resemblance to that of the Catholic opposition on the religious right. In their theoretical writings, the extreme reformers justified overthrow of what they considered to be tyrannical rule, just as Catholic spokesmen had absolved Elizabeth's subjects of obedience to her on the grounds that she was illegitimate. Both extremes appealed to disobedience in the name of a higher religious law. Among the reforming theoreticians was John Ponet, whose *Shorte Treatise of Politike Power* (1556) argued that a monarch is subject to a social contract and must rule according to laws that are equally subscribed to by Parliament, the clergy, and the people.

The Doctrine of Passive Obedience

Elizabeth's government countered such assaults on its authority, from both the right and the left, with many arguments, of which perhaps the most central was that of passive obedience. This doctrine condemned rebellion under virtually all circumstances. Its basic assumption was that the king is God's appointed deputy on earth. To depose such a monarch must therefore be an act of disobedience against God's will. Since God is all-wise and all-powerful, his placing of an evil ruler in power must proceed from some divine intention such as the punishment of a wayward people. Rebellion against God's "scourge" merely displays further disobedience to God's will. A people suffering under a tyrant must wait patiently for God to remove the burden, which he will surely do when the proper time arrives.

This doctrine was included in the official book of homilies of the Church of England, and was read from the pulpit at regular intervals. The best-known such homily was entitled *Against Disobedience and Wilful Rebellion.* Shakespeare heard it often, and he expresses its ideas through several of his characters such as John of Gaunt in *Richard II* (I,ii). This is not to say that he endorses such ideas, however, for he sets them in dramatic opposition to other and more heterodox concepts. We can say, nevertheless, that Shakespeare's audience would have recognized in Gaunt's speeches a clear expression of a familiar and officially correct position.

The Political Ideas of Machiavelli

The orthodoxies of the Elizabethan establishment were under attack not only from the Catholic right and the Protestant left, but also from a new and revolutionary point of view that set aside all criteria of religious morality. Tudor defense of order was based, as we have seen, on the assumption that the monarch rules in accord with a divine plan, a higher Law of Nature to which every just ruler is attuned. Political morality must be at one with religious morality. Catholic and Protestant critiques of the Tudor establishment made similar assumptions, even though they appealed to revolution in the name of that religious morality. To Niccolò Machiavelli, however, politics was a manipulative science best governed by the dictates of social expediency. His philosophy did not, as many accusingly charged, lead necessarily to the cynical promotion of mere self-interest. Nevertheless, he did argue, in his *Discourses* and *The Prince*, that survival and political stability are the first obligations of any ruler. Machiavelli regarded religion as a tool of the enlightened ruler rather than as a morally absolute guide. He extolled in his ideal leader the quality of *virtù*—a mixture of cunning and forcefulness. He saw history as a subject offering practical lessons in the kind of pragmatic statecraft he proposed.

Machiavelli was a hated name in England, and his works were never available in an English printed edition during Shakespeare's lifetime. Nevertheless, his writings were available in Italian, French, and Latin editions, and in manuscript English translations. His ideas certainly had a profound impact on the England of the 1590's. Marlowe caricatures the Italian writer in his *The Jew of Malta*, but he clearly was fascinated by what Machiavelli had to say. Shakespeare too reveals a complex awareness. However much he may lampoon the type of conscienceless villain in Richard III, he shows us more plausible pragmatists in *Richard II* and *1 Henry IV*. Conservative theories of the divine right of kings are set in debate with the more heterodox ambitions of Henry Bolingbroke and his associates. Bolingbroke is not a very attractive figure, but he does succeed politically where Richard has failed.

Shakespeare thus reveals himself as less a defender of the established order than as a great dramatist able to give sympathetic expression to the aspirations of all sides in a tense political struggle. His history plays have been variously interpreted as defenses of monarchy and as subtle pleas for rebellion, but the consensus today is that they are plays about human conflict. Perhaps the plays do stress the painful consequences of disorder, and perhaps they present an admiring view of monarchy (especially in *Henry V*) despite the manifest limitations of that institution. Certainly we can sense that Shakespeare's history plays were written for a generation of Englishmen who had experienced political crisis, and who could perceive issues of statecraft in Shakespeare's plays that were relevant to England's struggles in the 1580's and the 1590's. The play of *King John*, for example, deals with a king whose uncertain claim to the throne is challenged by the Catholic powers of France and the Papacy in the name of John's nephew, Arthur; Elizabeth faced a similar situation in her dilemma over her kinswoman, Mary Queen of Scots. Elizabeth also bitterly acknowledged the cogency of a popular analogy comparing her reign with that of King Richard II; and when Shakespeare's play about Henry IV's overthrow of Richard was apparently revived for political purposes shortly before the Earl of Essex' abortive rebellion against Elizabeth, Shakespeare's acting company had some explaining to do to the authorities (see Introduction to *Richard II*). Nevertheless, Shakespeare's attitudes toward the issues of his own day are ultimately unknowable and unimportant, since his main concern seems to have been with the dramatization of conflict rather than with the urging of a controversial position.

Shakespeare on Religion

Our impressions of Shakespeare's personal sympathies in religion are similarly obscured by his refusal to use his art for polemical purposes. Although various attempts have been made to prove him a Catholic sympathizer or a loyal moderate Anglican, we see in his plays a spectrum of religious attitudes portrayed with an extraordinary range of insight. Some Catholic prelates are schemers, like Pandulph in *King John*. Ordinarily, however, Shakespeare's satirical digs at ecclesiastical pomposity and hypocrisy have little to do with the Catholic question. Cardinal Beaufort in *1 Henry VI* is a political maneuverer, but so are many of his secular rivals. Cardinal Wolsey in *Henry VIII* is motivated by personal ambition rather than by any sinister conspiracy of the international church. Many of Shakespeare's nominally Catholic clerics, such as Friar Laurence in *Romeo and Juliet* or Friar Francis in *Much Ado about Nothing*, are gentle and well-intentioned people even if occasionally bumbling. We can certainly say that Shakespeare consistently avoids the chauvinistic anti-Catholic baiting so often found in the plays of his contemporaries.

The same avoidance of extremes can be seen in his portrayal of Protestant reformers, though the instances in this case are very few in number. Malvolio in *Twelfth Night* is fleetingly compared with a "Puritan," although Shakespeare insists that no extensive analogy can be made. Angelo in *Measure for Measure* is sometimes thought to be a critical portrait of the Puritan temperament. Even if so, Shakespeare's satire is extremely indirect compared with the lampoons written by his contemporaries Ben Jonson and Thomas Dekker.

Stuart Absolutism

Queen Elizabeth's successor, James I of the Scottish house of Stuarts, reigned from 1603 to 1625. Like Elizabeth, he was a strong believer in the divine right of kings. He did not possess Elizabeth's tact, however, in dealing with the heterogeneous and antagonistic forces that she had kept in precarious balance through the sheer force of her personality. At the Hampton Court Conference of 1604, James totally alienated the Puritan wing of the church and drove even its more moderate members into the arms of the separatists. He similarly antagonized an increasingly radical group in the House of Commons. In the widening rift between the absolutists and those who defended the supremacy of Parliament, James' court moved toward the right. Catholic sympathies at court became common. Open civil war and the beheading of King Charles I (James' son) would not occur until the 1640's, but throughout James' reign the sense of estrangement between the right and the left was becoming more and more extreme. The infamous Gunpowder Plot of 1605, in which Guy Fawkes and other Catholic conspirators were accused of having plotted to blow up the houses of Parliament, raised hysteria to a new level of intensity. Penal laws against papists were harshly enforced. The Parliament of 1614 included in its membership John Pym, Thomas Wentworth, and John Eliot, men who were to become turbulent spokesmen against taxes imposed without parliamentary grant, imprisonment without the stating of specific criminal charges, and other abuses of royal prerogative. The polarization of English society naturally affected the London theatres. Popular London audiences (often Puritan in sympathy) grew disaffected with the stage, while even the popular acting companies came under the increasing domination of the court. Shakespeare's late plays reflect the increasing influence of a courtly audience.

THE INTELLECTUAL BACKGROUND

Renaissance Cosmology

In learning, as in politics and religion, Shakespeare's England was a time of conflict and excitement. Medieval ideas of a hierarchical and ordered creation were under attack but were still widely prevalent, and were used to justify a hierarchical order in society itself. According to the so-called Ptolemaic system of the universe, formulated by Ptolemy of Alexandria in the second century A.D., the earth stood at the center of creation. Around it moved in nine concentric spheres the heavenly bodies of the visible universe, in order as follows (from the earth outward): the moon, Mercury, Venus, the sun, Mars, Jupiter, Saturn, the fixed stars on a single plane, and lastly the *primum mobile* imparting motion to the whole system. Some medieval commentators proposed alternate arrangements or speculated as to the existence of one or two additional spheres, in particular a "crystalline sphere" between the fixed stars and the *primum mobile*, but they did not challenge the concept of an earth-centered cosmos.

The *primum mobile* was thought to turn the entire universe around the earth once every twenty-four hours. Simultaneously, the individual heavenly bodies moved more slowly around the earth on their individual spheres, constantly changing position with respect to the fixed stars. The moon, being the only heavenly body that seemed subject to change in its monthly waxing and waning, was thought to represent the boundary between the unchanging universe and the incessantly changing world. Beneath the moon, in the "sublunary" sphere, all creation was subject to death as a result of Adam's fall from grace; beyond the moon lay perfection. Hell was imagined to exist deep within the earth, as in Dante's *Inferno*, or else outside the *primum mobile* and far below the created universe in the realm of chaos, as in Milton's *Paradise Lost*.

Heaven or the Empyrean stood, according to most Ptolemaic systems, at the top of the universe. Between heaven and earth dwelled the nine angelic orders, each associated with one of the nine concentric spheres. According to a work attributed to Dionysius the Areopagite, *On the Heavenly Hierarchy* (fifth century A.D.), the nine angelic orders consisted of three hierarchies. Closest to God were the contemplative orders of Seraphim, Cherubim, and Thrones; next, the intermediate orders of Dominations, Powers, and Virtues; and finally the active orders of Principalities, Archangels, and Angels. These last served as God's messengers and intervened from time to time in the affairs of mortals. Ordered life among men, although manifestly imperfect when compared with the eternal bliss of the angelic orders, still modeled itself on that Platonic idea of perfect harmony. Thus the state, the church, and the family all resembled one another because they resembled (however distantly) the kingdom of God. An eloquent expression of the order of creation is to be found in Richard Hooker's *Of the Laws of Ecclesiastical Polity* (1594–1597).

The devils of hell were fallen angels, with Satan as their leader. Such evil spirits might assume any number of shapes as demons, goblins, wizards, or witches. Believers in evil spirits generally made no distinction between orthodox Christian explanations of evil and the more primitive folklore of witchcraft. Belief in witchcraft was widespread indeed; King James I took the matter very seriously. On the other hand, a book like Reginald Scot's *Discoverie of Witchcraft* (1584) attempted to confute what the author regarded as ignorant superstition. Throughout Shakespeare's lifetime, belief and skepticism about such matters existed side by side.

A similar ambiguity pertained to belief in the Ptolemaic universe itself. All major poets of the Renaissance, including Shakespeare, Spenser, and Milton (who completed *Paradise Lost* after 1660), represented the universe in cosmic terms essentially as described by Ptolemy. Yet Nicolaus Copernicus' *De revolutionibus orbium coelestium* had been published in 1543, and Galileo Galilei (who adopted the Copernican theory

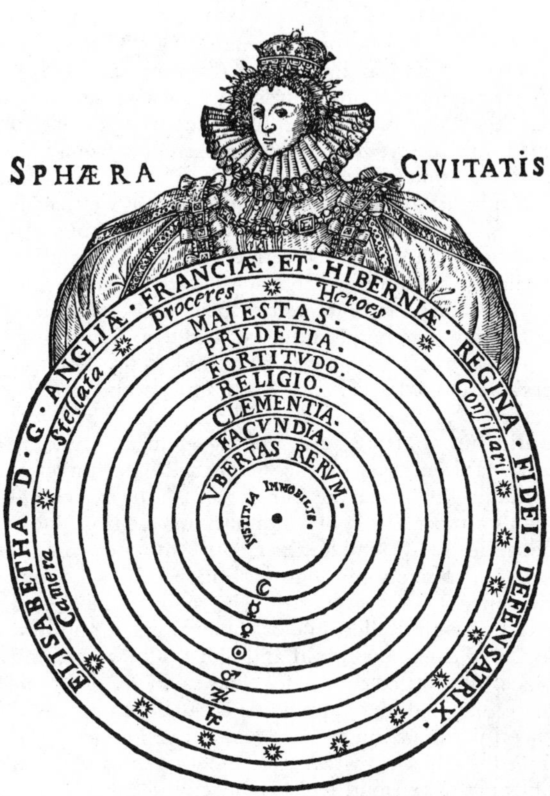

THE HUNTINGTON LIBRARY, SAN MARINO, CALIFORNIA

In this graphic analogy to a Ptolemaic universe, Elizabeth is shown as the primum mobile, *responsible for uniting and imparting motion to the spheres of state.*

of a sun-centered system, though he was reluctant to speak out), published the results of his telescopic examinations of the moon in 1610. John Donne lamented in 1611–1612 that the "new philosophy" (i.e., the new science) "calls all in doubt." Skeptical uncertainty about the cosmos was on the rise. The poetic affirmations in Renaissance art of traditional ideas of the cosmos can best be understood as a response to uncertainty, a statement of faith in an age of increasing doubt.

Alchemy and Medicine

In all areas of Renaissance learning, the new and the old science were confusedly juxtaposed. Alchemy, for example, made important contributions to learning despite its superstitious character. Its chief goal was the transformation of base metals into gold, on the assumption that all metals were ranked on a hierarchical scale and could be raised from lower to higher positions on that scale by means of certain alchemical techniques. Other aims of alchemy included the discovery of a universal cure for diseases, and of a means for preserving life indefinitely. Such aims encouraged quackery and prompted various exposés, such as

Chaucer's "The Canon's Yeoman's Tale" (late fourteenth century) and Jonson's *The Alchemist* (1610). Yet many of the procedures used in alchemy were essentially chemical procedures, and the science of chemistry received an invaluable impetus from constant experimentation.

In physics, medicine, and psychology, as well, older concepts vied with new. Traditional learning apportioned all physical matter into four elements, earth, air, fire, and water. Each of these was thought to be a different combination of the four "qualities" of the universe, hot, cold, moist, and dry. Earth combined cold and dry, air hot and moist, fire hot and dry, water cold and moist. Earth and water were the baser or lower elements, confined to the physical world; fire and air were aspiring elements, tending upward. Man, as a microcosm of the larger universe, contained in himself the four elements. The individual man's temperament, or "humour" or "complexion," depended on which "humour" predominated in him. The four humours in man corresponded to the four elements of physical matter. The blood was hot and moist, like air; yellow bile or choler was hot and dry, like fire; phlegm was cold and moist, like water; and black bile was cold and dry, like earth. A predominance of blood in an individual created a sanguine or cheerful temperament (or humour), yellow bile produced a choleric or irascible temperament, phlegm a phlegmatic or stolid temperament, and black bile a melancholic temperament. Diet could affect the balance among these humours, since an excess of a particular food would stimulate overproduction of one humour. The stomach and the liver, which converted food into humours, were regarded as the seat of human passions. A common remedy in medicine for illness was to let blood and thereby purge the body of unwanted humours.

THE FOLGER SHAKESPEARE LIBRARY

One Renaissance belief was that the useful exercise of knowledge gained through study was the only permanent thing in this life—all else was subject to Death's grip.

The traditional name associated with such theories was that of Galen, the most celebrated of ancient writers on medicine (c. 130 A.D.). A more revolutionary name was that of Paracelsus, a famous German physician (c. 1493–1541), who attacked the Aristotelianism of his time and urged a more unfettered pragmatic research into pharmacy and medicine. Such experimentalism bore fruit in the anatomical research of Vesalius and in William Harvey's investigations of the circulation of the blood (c. 1616). Nevertheless, the practice of medicine in Renaissance times remained under the influence of the "humours" theory until quite late, and its ideas are to be found throughout Shakespeare's plays.

THE BODLEIAN LIBRARY

Alchemists employed relatively sophisticated equipment in their futile search for the "philosopher's stone."

Learning

In learning generally, and in theories of education, new ideas conflicted with old. The curriculum of schools and colleges in the Renaissance was inherited largely from the Middle Ages and displayed many traditional characteristics. The curriculum consisted of the seven Liberal Arts: a lower division called the trivium, comprised of grammar, rhetoric, and logic, and an upper division called the quadrivium, comprised of arithmetic, geometry, astronomy, and music. In addition there were the philosophical studies, associated chiefly with Aristotle: natural philosophy, ethics, and metaphysics.

Aristotle's name had a towering influence in medieval times, and remained important to the Renaissance as well. Even among his Renaissance admirers, however, Aristotle proved more compelling in practical matters than in the abstract scholastic reasoning associated with his name in the Middle Ages. The Italian Aristotelians whose work made its way into England were interested primarily in the science of human behavior. Aristotelian ethics was for them a practical subject, telling men how to live usefully and well and how to govern themselves politically. Rhetoric was the science of persuasion, enabling men to use eloquence for socially useful goals. Poetry was a kind of rhetoric, a language of persuasion which dramatists too might use for morally pragmatic ends.

At the same time, new thinkers were daring to attack Aristotle by name as a symbol of traditional medieval thought. The attack was not always fair to Aristotle himself, whose work had been bent to the *a priori* purposes of much medieval scholasticism. Nevertheless, his name had assumed such symbolic importance that he had to be confronted directly. The Huguenot logician Petrus Ramus (1515–1572), defiantly proclaiming that "everything that Aristotle taught is false," argued for rules of logic as derived from observation. He urged, for example, that his students learn about rhetoric from observing in detail Cicero's effect on his listeners, rather than by the rote practice of syllogism. Actually, Ramus' thought was less revolutionary in its concepts of logic than in the tremendous ferment of opinion caused by his iconoclastic teaching.

A basic issue at stake in the anti-Aristotelian movement was that of traditional authority versus independent observation. How does man best acquire true knowledge, through the teachings of his predecessors or through his own discovery? The issue had profound implications for religious truth as well: should the individual heed the collective wisdom of the earthly church, or read the Bible with his individual perceptions as his guide? Is "reason" an accretive wisdom handed down by authority or a quality of the individual soul? Obviously a middle ground exists between the two extremes, and no new thinker of the Renaissance professed to abandon entirely the use of ancient authority. For men like Henricus Agrippa (1486–1535) and Sir Francis Bacon (1561–1626), however, the weight of scholastic tradition had exerted its

RADIO TIMES HULTON PICTURE LIBRARY

This guide graphically setting forth the ideals to which every English gentlemen and gentlewoman should aspire illustrates the Renaissance concept that outward deportment and accomplishments correctly and invariably mirror a person's inner nature. Compare the different standards for each sex.

oppressive influence far too long. Authority needed to be examined critically and scientifically. Bacon, in his *The Advancement of Learning* (1605), fought against the blind acceptance of ancient wisdom, and argued that "knowledge derived from Aristotle, and exempted from liberty of examination, will not rise again higher than the knowledge of Aristotle." Sir Walter Ralegh and others joined in the excited new search for what human "reason" could discover when set free from scholastic restraint. The new learning did not seem to trouble these men in their religious faith, although a tension between scientific observation and faith in miracles was to become plentifully evident in the seventeenth century.

The Nature of Man

Another challenge to established concepts of thought came from Michel de Montaigne, Shakespeare's great French contemporary. In his "Apology for Raymond Sebond" and other of his essays, Montaigne questioned the assumption of man's superiority to the rest of the animal kingdom. That assumption rested on biblical and patristic teachings about the hierarchy of creation, in which man stood at the apex of physical creation nearest God and the angels. Man was thus supreme on earth in the so-called chain of being. His human reason, though subject to error because of his sinfulness, enabled man to aspire toward divinity. Man was, in the view of medieval philosophers, the great amphibian as well as the microcosm of the universe, part bestial and part immortal, doomed by Adam's fall to misery and death in this life but promised eternal salvation through Christ's atonement. Right reason, properly employed, could lead man to the truths of revealed Christianity and thus give him a glimpse of the heavenly perfection one day to be his.

Renaissance neo-Platonism, as expounded, for example, in Castiglione's *The Courtier* (translated by Sir Thomas Hoby, 1561), offered man a vision of a Platonic ladder extending from the perception of a woman's beauty to the experiencing of God's transcendent love.

Montaigne, on the other hand, gave Shakespeare a fundamentally different way to consider the nature of man—a way that reflects itself, for example, in Hamlet's observations on man as a "quintessence of dust." Montaigne stressed man's arrogance, vanity, and frailty. He was unconvinced of man's purported moral superiority to the animals, and argued that animals are no less endowed with a soul. Montaigne destroyed, in other words, the hierarchy in which man was the unquestioned master of the physical world, just as Copernican science overturned the earth-centered cosmos and Machiavelli's political system dismissed as an improbable fiction the divinely constituted hierarchy of the state. Montaigne was not alone in his skepticism about man's nature: his ideas had much in common with Bernardino Telesio's *De Rerum Natura* and with the writings of the Italian Giordano Bruno. Montaigne was followed in the seventeenth century by that overpowering iconoclast, Thomas Hobbes, who extended the concept of mechanical laws governing human society and human psychology. Hobbes postdates Shakespeare, to be sure, but one has only to consider Iago's philosophy of the assertive individual will (in *Othello*), or Edmund's contempt for his father Gloucester's astrological pieties (in *King Lear*), to see the enormous impact on Shakespeare of the new heterodoxies of his age. Shakespeare customarily puts such insidious philosophies in the mouths of his villains, and affirms more traditional values through contrastingly virtuous characters; nevertheless, the challenge to the older cosmos in a play like *King Lear* is profound.

THE DRAMA BEFORE SHAKESPEARE

At some time between 1585 and 1592 William Shakespeare left Stratford-upon-Avon and established himself, apparently in a position of relative importance, in the theatre in London. The theatre was even then an important institution and was of such complexity that it is necessary for us to inquire into its origin and growth in order to understand the opportunity that it offered Shakespeare and the power, both personal and literary, that it enabled him to achieve. We must consider the origin of the Elizabethan drama as an artistic form, the gradual provision of an adequate physical equipment for the theatre and the stage, and the assemblage and organization of the personnel, under proper leadership, into licensed companies of players with effective business management.

The Liturgical Drama

The sixth-century Catholic Church had been largely responsible for closing down the late Roman theatre, with its bloody gladiatorial contests and its pervasive moral decadence. Thereafter, for about four centuries the theatre officially did not exist in Western Europe. Paradoxically, it was the church in the tenth century that sponsored the beginnings of a new dramatic form within the liturgy (the prescribed form of worship) of the church itself. This dramatic activity began as an insertion into the regular service of a "trope" or musical composition designed to be sung antiphonally by members of a religious community. The earliest of these may have been composed for Easter morning, at the supremely important moment of Christ's resurrection. The Mass itself had long displayed semidramatic characteristics, and the first Easter expansions must not have seemed particularly revolutionary to anyone involved. The simplest of the early tropes (though not necessarily the first), composed at St. Gall in Switzerland some time early in the tenth century, consists merely of a chanted interrogation, *Quem quaeritis in sepulchro, Christicolae?* ("Whom do you seek in the sepulchre, O followers of Christ?"), and a chanted response, *Jesum Nazarenum crucifixum, o caelicolae* ("Jesus of Nazareth who was crucified, O heaven-dwellers"), followed by an announcement that Christ is risen as he had predicted. From other early texts of this sort, we can guess that this simple antiphon was accompanied by some stylized semidramatic assignment of roles to members of the religious community as the three Marys visiting Christ's tomb, and as the angels guarding the tomb. At any rate, tenth-century tropes of Easter soon included use of simple costume, physical movement toward the tomb, and appropriate gestures.

Other actions were appropriate to such a dramatic representation of the resurrection: the visit of the disciples to the sepulchre, the appearance of Christ as a gardener to Mary Magdalene, and his appearance to the disciples on the road to Emmaus. Moreover, other seasons of the year afforded similar opportunities, especially Christmas; the crèche was already a venerable custom, and Christmas tropes may have originated as early as Easter tropes or possibly even earlier.

In any event, Christmas liturgical dramatic activity grew apace, perhaps more rapidly than at Easter because of the sacred inhibitions associated with the resurrection. By the twelfth century, Christmas liturgical drama had become lengthy and complex, including not only the visit of the shepherds and the Magi but also the slaughter of the innocents and the flight into Egypt. Simultaneously, liturgical plays were developed for other festivals in the liturgical calendar. Some were in the vernacular: by the end of the twelfth century, an Anglo-Norman poet had written a play of Adam featuring the creation of man, the expulsion from the garden of Eden, the slaughter of Abel by Cain, and a lengthy procession of prophets announcing the advent of Christ. Such early vernacular plays may well have influenced the development of Latin liturgical drama. The twelfth century also saw a play about Daniel in the lions' den, various Saint Nicholas plays in which that popular saint performed miracles, a play at Tegernsee about the Antichrist, a play about the conversion of Saint Paul, and many others. In other words, by 1200 or thereabouts the liturgical drama had produced plays of considerable length and complexity for numerous religious festivals throughout the year. Montecassino in Italy had a complex passion play by this date. The thirteenth century saw the performance at Benedicktbauern in Germany of the impressive "Carmina Burana" plays for Easter and Christmas.

The Corpus Christi Play

Although one might suppose that these liturgical plays would be gathered together into larger cycles of the divine history of the world, compilations of this sort do not seem generally to have taken place. The liturgical plays continued to be performed individually at the appropriate times in the church calendar. Most religious communities proudly owned and produced one or two such plays year after year, but no communities owned or produced very many such plays. The plays were numerous but scattered throughout Western Europe.

What appears to have happened instead is that the various craft guilds of certain towns, especially in England, banded together with the ecclesiastical authorities to produce a summer festival that would be both civic and religious in nature. One impetus was the institution of the feast of Corpus Christi in the early fourteenth century. The feast was designed to honor the Eucharist (the reenactment of Christ's Last Supper) in a joyous mood, uninhibited by the somber reflections on Christ's crucifixion that are appropriate to Passion Week. The date chosen, the Thursday after Trinity Sunday, came during a slack period in the liturgical calendar in very late spring. In May or June the days of the year are longest, and the English weather generally cooperative. The cycles that thus originated were performed on other festivals of the early summer season besides Corpus Christi day, but that festival has given its name to the genre.

The feast of Corpus Christi regularly featured elaborate processions through town, and indeed these processions may have preceded the plays themselves. Each guild in town was normally assigned an event in the divine history of the world for which it had to prepare and maintain a pageant wagon. The plays written for such guilds had to be numerous in most towns, since there were many guilds: the York cycle, for example, had forty-eight plays, the Towneley cycle (probably acted at Wakefield) thirty-two, the so-called N-Town or *Ludus Coventriae* cycle (probably acted in the vicinity of Lincoln) forty-three. The texts were evidently not translations from the Latin liturgical drama but were English compositions often based on medieval narrative accounts of the divine history of the world. Such versions contained much patristic and legendary material as well as straightforward biblical narrative: for example, the account of Christ's harrowing of hell had become an accepted part of the story, even though the Bible does not specifically mention it. The cycles varied somewhat as to contents, but they tended to choose many of the same traditional stories embodied in church liturgy. The main figures in these favorite stories—Abel, Noah, Abraham and Isaac—were often seen as "typological," that is, prefiguring by their piety and suffering the advent of Christ himself.

The common core of most cycles included the fol-

COURTESY OF THE TRUSTEES, THE BRITISH MUSEUM

This scene from a mystery play acted on a stationary scaffold in Coventry's town square depicts Christ's appearance before Pilate.

lowing: the creation, the fall of Adam and expulsion from Paradise, Cain's slaying of Abel, Noah's flood, Abraham and Isaac, Moses, the prophets, the annunciation, the visit of the shepherds and the Magi, the flight into Egypt, the slaughter of the innocents, the baptism, the temptation in the wilderness, the raising of Lazarus, the entry into Jerusalem and the entire passion sequence, the burial and resurrection, the harrowing of hell, Christ's appearances to the disciples, his ascension, and the day of doom. Other subjects were often added, such as the day of Pentecost, the assumption of the blessed Virgin Mary, and the coming of Antichrist.

Sometimes these medieval "pageants" were acted on pageant wagons before a series of audiences gathered at fixed locales throughout the town. Recent investigations have shown, however, the almost insuperable difficulties involved in performing a complete cycle of plays in narrow streets, with each pageant having to wait in line until the preceding pageant had finished. Street processions remained common but may often have involved displays in *tableau vivant* rather than full performance of each play. Certainly in many towns the plays themselves were acted not on pageant wagons but in the round, in arena theatres with several scaffolds on the periphery or even in the center of the acting area. Scaffolds variously represented Heaven and hell, Pilate's judgment hall, the house of the Last Supper, and the like. In the market place at Wakefield and in the cathedral close at Lincoln, the pageants may have been ranged in order about the open space so that the spectators themselves could move from scene to scene. Multiple-place staging certainly existed in London and in the south of England, and was the regular form of the mystery-play stage on the Continent. (The Corpus Christi plays are sometimes called "mystery" plays since they were acted by the "mystery" or trade guilds.)

Each subject or group of subjects in the Corpus Christi play was assigned to a particular company of artisans or to certain associated companies, who had their own playbook and pageant, and even pageant-house in which to store the pageant-wagon. For example, at Coventry the shearmen and tailors for a long time acted the scenes of the nativity, the shepherds, the visit of the Magi, the flight into Egypt, and the slaughter of the innocents. The weavers acted the story of the presentation of Jesus in the temple and the disputation of Jesus with the Jewish doctors. The texts of both of these plays are preserved. In the former, the *Shearmen and Taylors Pageant*, Herod is a comic character who acts what Bottom in *A Midsummer Night's Dream* calls "a part to tear a cat in." At the point where the Magi, warned by an angel to depart into their own country by another way, escape Herod's clutches, a stage direction in the play says, "Here Erode ragis in the pagond and in the strete also," a detail which indicates what Hamlet means when he says, "it out-herods Herod." The rich mercers' company of Coventry, able to supply clothes and hangings in abundance, acted the magnificent pageant of the assumption of the blessed Virgin Mary. In some other places we find the goldsmiths' company presenting the play of the Magi or "The Three Kings of Cologne," apparently because they were able to supply the necessary crowns and jewels. At Coventry the drapers' company presented the play of the Last Judgment and each year made provision for three "worlds" to be burnt. They had also an earthquake "with a barrel for the same." Among their characters were God, two demons, three white souls, three black souls, two spirits, four angels, three patriarchs, two worms of conscience, a prologue, two "clarks" for singing (one to sing bass), and a Pharisee. Unfortunately the text of this pageant, as well as that of the mercers, has been lost.

The annual Corpus Christi play was a source of municipal pride at Coventry and elsewhere, and of profit also, since it drew crowds of spectators. Royal persons and great noblemen frequently attended. It is recorded, for example, that King Richard III, being at Kenilworth in 1484, came to Coventry at Corpus Christi-tide to see the pageants. There were possibly as many as twenty full-scope plays, mostly of the Corpus Christi type, in the kingdom, though the complete texts of only four have been preserved. The York, Towneley, and N-Town cycles have already been mentioned; a fourth extant cycle was acted at Chester. In addition, two fragments exist of a cycle acted at Coventry, one each from Norwich and Newcastle-on-Tyne, and several other single scenes from places not located.

There is also preserved, in the now extinct Celtic language of Cornwall, an example of another type of religious drama, a great passion play of the form common on the Continent. The passion play, which seems also to have been the type acted at London and in the south of England, centers on the theme of man's redemption and does not contain the scenes dealing with the nativity. The Cornish cycle includes Old Testament subjects, a circumstance not unusual in the continental passion plays.

The Saints' Play

Saints' plays were also widely current in England, although few examples survive today. These dramas resembled the Corpus Christi cycles in their staging and their panoramic religious spectacle, but differed from the cycles in that they told about the lives and miracles of saints and martyrs rather than about personages from the Old and New Testament. Some individual cases, to be sure, blurred this seemingly clear distinction between saints' plays and Corpus Christi plays. The story of Mary Magdalene, for example, was derived in part from the biblical accounts of her meetings with Christ, but the narrative had been enormously expanded to include legendary reports of her travels and miraculous deeds as a saint. St. Paul was another biblical figure whose sudden conversion and subsequent travels gave to his story the characteristics of a typical saint's life. As a group, however, saints' plays offered more emphasis on miraculous conversion from sin to grace, and on the wondrous intervention of saints in the lives of ordinary men, than did the Corpus Christi cycles.

According to English historical records, a considerable number of plays dealing with St. Katharine, St. Laurence, St. Nicholas, and other saints existed at one time. As it happens, however, the only three surviving texts in English are not typical. The Croxton *Play of the Sacrament* (1461–1500) tells of five Jews who desecrate the Holy Sacrament and discover that Christ is truly present in it. Although no saint's life is told, the story is one of conversion by the greatest of all miracles. The Digby *Mary Magdalene* (c. 1480–1520) is a composite saint's life and biblical drama combining scenes from the life of Christ, moral allegory, and a romantic narrative of travel drawn from the *Legenda Aurea* or Golden Legend of the lives of the saints. The Digby *Conversion of St. Paul* (c. 1480–1520) centers on the conversion of Saul or Paul from sinfulness to a life of faith in Christ. These plays are especially interesting for their staging; *Mary Magdalene*, for example, seems to have been staged in the round, like some of the Corpus Christi cycles, with acting scaffolds on the periphery of a *platea* or open acting area. Despite their importance to later English drama, however, these few surviving English saints' plays are not really typical. To know what went on dramatically in honor of the saints one must study the many saints' plays preserved in French, including the *Miracles de Nôtre Dame*.

The Morality Play

Still another important genre in the religious drama of the late Middle Ages was the morality play. Its distinctive mode was the allegorical rendition of man's spiritual journey through life, his preparation for death, and his standing in judgment before God. Allegory was certainly not unknown in the cycles or in the saints' plays, but the morality play made extensive use of it. A number of fifteenth-century morality plays, such as *The Castle of Perseverance*, *Mankind*, and *Everyman*, are still in existence. The morality play survived late into the sixteenth century, late enough indeed to have made a significant impact on late Elizabethan drama—including that of Shakespeare and Ben Jonson. The morality told a story of spiritual struggle and eventual triumph over sin not unlike that of the cycles and saints' plays, but it did so in a way that could be adapted to the religious and social controversies of the era. The Corpus Christi cycles and saints' plays were,

Four morality players personifying Contemplation, Perseverance, Imagination, and Free Will.

after all, tied to biblical or legendary event; when Reformation authorities sought to suppress the "idolatrous" representation of God on stage, or banned worship of the Virgin Mary and the saints, the cycles and saints' plays were doomed. Even though they were occasionally staged late enough in the sixteenth century for Shakespeare to have seen performances, they belonged to an earlier, pre-Reformation era. The morality play, on the other hand, thrived on controversy. Its simple plot of soul struggle between the forces of good and evil for the allegiance of Mankind or Everyman, and his wavering progress toward eventual salvation, could and did frequently serve as a vehicle for portraying many social phenomena of the sixteenth century.

In John Skelton's political morality play called *Magnificence* (1515–1518), for example, Mankind has become a representative king-figure who must choose between evil counselors urging fiscal extravagance on the one hand, and wise counselors urging fiscal prudence on the other hand. The plot, telling of the king's temptation and his choosing of the wrong path before he is finally awakened to his folly, is essentially that of earlier nonpolitical morality plays such as *Hickescorner* or *Youth* (c. 1513–1520), in which the mankind figure inevitably succumbs to temptation but is eventually rescued through divine guidance. The issues in Skelton's play have become secular, but the simple story line and the dramatic structure have remained virtually unchanged. The transition to the study of a "historical" type, in this case a king, enables such a play to comment on contemporary history and yet appeal simultaneously to a universal moral pattern. Skelton's play alludes to the fiscal recklessness of Henry VIII under Cardinal Wolsey's persuasive tutelage, but it discusses fiscal responsibility in general terms that also apply to any king—or to any man. Shakespeare's English history plays, especially the early plays about Henry VI and Richard III, owe an important debt to the tradition of the political morality as exemplified by *Magnificence*.

In a similar vein, Shakespeare's history play of *King John* studies a king who had actually been the subject of one of the most important of political moralities, *King Johan* by John Bale (1538, later revised). Although Shakespeare may not have consulted Bale's play directly, Bale had still made an impressive contribution to the English history play by demonstrating how the morality structure could be used in the analysis of political crises. His play is an avowedly Protestant tract in the guise of a morality play, depicting its historical protagonist as a victim of Catholic duplicity and hence an example of what sixteenth-century England had to fear from its Catholic enemies. Later popular plays combining a morality structure with a passionate interest in history and contemporary political theory include Thomas Preston's *Cambises* (1560–1561) and John Pickering's *Horestes* (1567).

During the Reformation, the morality play was used polemically by both the Protestant and Catholic sides. Dramatists were often commissioned by governmental authorities to write plays for public performance by touring actors, as weapons of ideological persuasion. In Protestant plays such as *Lusty Juventus* (c. 1547–1553) or *New Custom* (c. 1570), the villainous Vices were depicted as Catholic tempters; in Catholic plays such as *Respublica* (1553, during the reign of Queen Mary), the Vices were Protestant. The protean flexibility of the morality formula enabled it to adapt itself to many different situations in this way. Polemical drama put ideology ahead of artistic concern, to be sure, but constant experimentation with new forms provided the popular drama of mid-century England with much-needed practical experience. One permutation of the Reformation morality play, for example, proved of considerable importance to the development of English tragedy. In some Protestant morality plays that Calvinistically stress man's innate depravity, such as William Wager's *Enough Is as Good as a Feast* (c. 1559–1570) and Nathaniel Woodes' *The Conflict of Conscience* (1570–1581), spiritual struggle ends in failure rather than in triumph for the mankind protagonist. Among the great English tragedies of the late sixteenth century, Marlowe's *Doctor Faustus* (c. 1588) is most obviously indebted to such dramatic renditions of spiritual despair, but Shakespeare's *Macbeth* and other plays may also have learned something from a native homiletic tradition in tragedy.

In staging and acting, as well, the morality play served as an important transition from late medieval religious drama to the drama of the late sixteenth century. In its origins, as seen, for example, in *The Castle of Perseverance* (early fifteenth century), the morality play had been staged like many of the cycles or saints' plays such as *Mary Magdalene:* that is, in the round, with an open acting area surrounded by acting scaffolds on the periphery. The morality play developed great flexibility in its staging, however, just as it had developed flexibility in its approach to contemporary political or social issues. *Mankind* (c. 1471) required only an acting platform, raised probably on trestles to a height of four or five feet, and a curtain backdrop through which the actors could enter and exit. A stage of this simplicity could be carried anywhere in England and set up at a moment's notice—on a village green, in town hall, or in the banqueting hall of a lord's manor. The troupe acting *Mankind* was vastly more efficient and transportable than the company of twenty-two or more actors required for *The Castle of Perseverance; Mankind* required only six actors.

Troupes of four or five men and one boy apprentice (for women's roles) were quite standard in early Tudor England. They traveled the length and breadth of the country, and dominated the field of popular entertainment from the late fifteenth century until Shakespeare's day. They were, in fact, the professional ancestors of the Shakespearean acting company. Under the direction of their leading player, who often acted the part of Vice since it was usually the choice role of the morality play, the actors were organized as repertory companies able to perform a number of plays on short notice and to present a remarkably large number of roles by the doubling of parts. They grew slowly in size as they prospered, but they retained their traditional organization. The best of the troupes gravitated to London, where, in 1576, a troupe of perhaps six or eight men and two boys founded England's first permanent theatre. Shakespeare's company, the Lord Chamberlain's men (later the King's men), was only slightly larger than this, with perhaps ten actors who were partners or "sharers" in the company, two or more boys, and a few hired hands. Shakespeare's early plays, moreover, were sometimes structured for presentation by just such a company, much as earlier popular plays had been structured, with considerable doubling of parts, and with a multiplicity of episodes allowing for the sequential presentation of numerous minor roles. The early history plays about Henry VI and Richard III are especially illustrative of this structural tradition.

Shakespeare's awareness of medieval religious drama, including the morality play, can be seen in his many allusions to it. When Hamlet addresses the visiting players on the subject of correct and incorrect styles of acting, for example, he cites ranting Herod and Termagent as illustrations of the worst kind of histrionic exaggeration (*Hamlet*, III,ii,14–16). Herod was the familiar tyrant of the Corpus Christi cycle, raging because he had failed to destroy Christ along with the slaughtered innocents; Termagent was a Saracen deity of ferocious mien who appeared in medieval drama and romance. Although these allusions may at first sound uncomplimentary to the older drama, the cycle plays themselves invite laughter at the expense of Herod's bombastic style; Shakespeare's reference is both friendly and familiar. In a similar vein, Prince Hal jestingly caricatures Falstaff as "that roasted Manningtree ox with the pudding in his belly, that reverend vice, that grey iniquity, that father ruffian, that vanity in years . . . that old white-bearded Satan" (*1 Henry IV*, II,iv,498–509). Manningtree in Essex appears to have been renowned for its annual fair at which plays were acted and great-sized oxen were roasted; the Vice, as we have seen, was the chief comic tempter of most morality plays. Falstaff himself refers to the Vice's traditional dagger of lath in his contemptuous remarks about Justice Shallow: "And now is this Vice's dagger become a squire" (*2 Henry IV*, III,ii,343). The Porter scene in *Macbeth* (II,iii) contains several allusions to the harrowing of hell, which Shakespeare's audience would have easily recognized, owing to their familiarity with dramatic representations of the harrowing of hell in the Corpus Christi cycles.

Shakespeare's specific references to late medieval drama are less important, however, than his larger indebtedness to it. His use of a structural tradition of episodic multiplicity, especially in the early history plays, has already been suggested. Of equal significance is his indebtedness to the Vice, the comic tempter of the morality play whose sinister but fascinating techniques of evil persuasion had become an enduring part of Tudor popular drama. The Vice's boastful and chortling brand of villainy is still clearly recognizable, though transmuted into superb poetry, in the insinuations of Richard III, Aaron the Moor (in *Titus Andronicus*), Iago (in *Othello*), and Edmund (in *King Lear*). As Bernard Spivack has argued, in his *Shakespeare and the Allegory of Evil*, Shakespeare's poetic vision of the contest between good and evil for men's souls owes much to the morality tradition.

Early Tudor Humanist Drama

The development of the morality play, briefly sketched in the preceding section, tells only one part of the story of sixteenth-century drama. The trend we have observed in morality drama, toward the depiction of contemporary English life, manifested itself also in other kinds of plays that were not so plainly derived from the religious drama of the middle ages. A new influence was that of classical and neoclassical drama, from the ancient classical world and from Renaissance Europe. Important too were the secular kinds of dramatic entertainment that had flourished in the English court even before the advent of neoclassicism. Early Tudor drama for courtly and well-

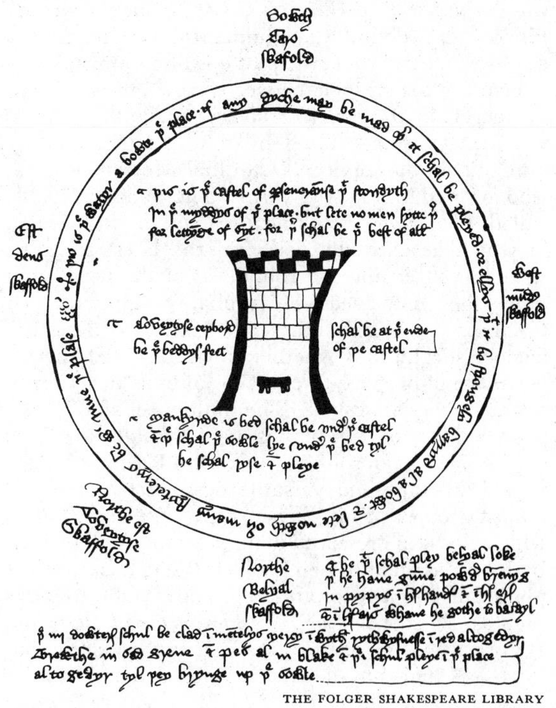

THE FOLGER SHAKESPEARE LIBRARY

A fifteenth-century diagram for a presentation of The Castle of Perseverance *shows the scaffolds surrounding the open acting area with the castle at the center.*

educated audiences was heterogeneous because it reflected so many diverse impulses: the intensified renewal of classical learning that had come about through the activities of the new humanists, the ferment of ideologies introduced by the Reformation, the increase in social mobility in the Tudor court, and the like. In varying proportions, the courtly and intellectual drama of the period borrowed from the English morality play, from courtly pastimes such as the "disguising" (a kind of masque) and the dialogue or *débat*, from secular farce and romance, from classical and neoclassical literature, and even from the Corpus Christi cycles and saints' plays. The mixture, experimental and often uneven, was nonetheless stimulating because it attempted to fuse English culture with that of neoclassical Europe.

The dramatists who associated themselves with the great humanist Sir Thomas More and with his patron Cardinal Morton shared many humanist ideals that can be seen in their plays. Henry Medwall, chaplain to Cardinal Morton, wrote a morality play called *Nature* (c. 1490–1501) that reveals an interest in Aristotelian ethics as well as in traditional Christian ideas of salvation. Medwall also wrote *Fulgens and Lucrece* (c. 1497), the earliest extant play in England to use an ancient Roman setting and a secular romantic love plot. The heroine, Lucrece, chooses the love of a virtuous but untitled "new" man at court, in preference to a haughty and degenerate aristocrat. This *débat* was derived from *De Vera Nobilitate* by Buonaccorso of Pistoia, an ardent Italian humanist. Despite its ancient setting and romantic plot it is also unmistakably relevant to the struggle between "new" men and old aristocrats in the court of Henry VII. Both of Medwall's plays were printed by John Rastell, another humanist in the service of Cardinal Morton. Rastell, who married More's sister, wrote a humanist interlude called *The Nature of the Four Elements* (c. 1517–1518), in which he excitedly discussed the latest scientific theories concerning the roundness of the world and other such new ideas. He probably also wrote *Of Gentleness and Nobility* (c. 1527–1530), a play that iconoclastically asks whether monarchy and the inheritance of property are not social evils that ideally ought to be abolished. The influence of Thomas More's *Utopia* on this play is unmistakable.

John Heywood, son-in-law of John Rastell, was the most important and versatile dramatist of the humanist group. All his plays except *Witty and Witless*, which has been preserved in manuscript, were printed by John Rastell or his son William Rastell. Heywood's plays fall into two groups: the courtly disputations such as *The Play of Love*, *The Play of the Weather*, and *Witty and Witless* (c. 1525–1533), and the more popular farces that may have been intended for popular audiences as well, such as *The Pardoner and the Friar*, *The Four PP*, and *John John the Husband* (c. 1513–1533). In the first group, *Weather* reveals a characteristic attention to humanist and courtly themes. In an obvious analogy to the Tudor concept of an absolutist yet benevolent monarchy, the various petitioners of the play complain to Jupiter about the weather but are finally persuaded to be grateful for the mixed weather that is provided them. Heywood is suggesting, in other words, that the English monarchy must bestow its favors impartially on all classes of men, and that all subjects ought to recognize the essential soundness of the social order as it presently exists. Heywood's second group of plays, however, eschews such courtly and political themes for a broader slapstick comedy in the vein of Chaucerian fabliau and French farce.

In addition to these humanist plays written by members of the Sir Thomas More circle, the learned drama of early Tudor England included many plays written for schoolboys or for the choristers attached to royal and noble households. The plays written under such auspices tended to reveal a much stronger interest in classical and neoclassical drama than did the plays written for popular audiences. Schoolmasters wrote dramatic texts derived from the classics for educational purposes; at court, sophisticated audiences were interested in the latest dramatic fashions from Italy or France. Ancient Greek drama did not receive nearly so much attention, however, as the Latin drama of Terence, Plautus, and Seneca. These Latin authors had long been used as schoolboys' texts, though they were frequently expurgated or allegorized into the terms of Christian morality in order to render them suitable for schoolboys' sensibilities. This academic tradition, on the Continent and in England, produced a number of imitative plays that could be acted by boys as part of their training in classical languages. Some plays, such as Palsgrave's *Acolastus* (1540), were intended to be read rather than acted. Many others were Latin biblical plays in classical guise, such as Thomas Watson's *Absalom* (c. 1535–1544) and George Buchanan's *Jephthes* (1540–1545).

At court and in noble households, choristers were becoming noted for their acting ability. They performed chiefly during seasons of revels, such as in the Christmas season. They did not appear commercially before public audiences during the early Tudor period, as did the players of moralities and popular interludes. The Children of the Royal Chapel are known to have presented plays as early as 1506. The boys of St. Paul's School acted before King Henry VIII in 1528. Later, in the 1570's and 1580's, these children's groups were organized into professional acting companies. Children's plays were generally written by schoolmasters or choirmasters. The plays were heavily influenced by continental traditions, and often depicted themes—such as that of the Prodigal Son—that were congenial to boys of school age. *Nice Wanton* (1547–1553) offers an instance of this sort. Biblical themes were common, and were sometimes used to urge a political lesson in the presence of a courtly audience. *Godly Queen Hester* (1525–1529), for example, seems to defend the cause of Katharine of Aragon and denounce the machinations of Cardinal

Wolsey. *Jacob and Esau* (1547–1553) draws an unflattering comparison between the unregenerate Esau and those who refuse to abandon the Catholic faith. Classical subjects were of course much in demand, as in *Appius and Virginia* (1559–1567) and in Richard Edwards' *Damon and Pythias* (c. 1565).

Early Comedy

Schoolboys' drama was also vitally important in the development of classical or "regular" comedy on the English stage. Native morality drama was often highly comic, to be sure, especially in its depiction of the resourceful and scheming Vice: but English drama still had much to learn from classical example about play construction and about the presentation of various types of characters. Perhaps the two most famous early English "regular" comedies were *Ralph Roister Doister* and *Gammer Gurton's Needle.*

Ralph Roister Doister, by Nicholas Udall, at one time headmaster of Eton, was acted probably between 1552 and 1554 by boy actors. Its staging is essentially that of Latin comedy, with two houses facing onto a street. The play employs a classical five-act structure and preserves the unities of time and place. (According to classical and neoclassical theory, a play's action should be limited to one location—a city, for example—and to a single day.) Stock comic types include the *miles gloriosus* or braggart soldier, and the parasite. At the same time, Udall has transformed his heroine, usually a courtesan in Plautus' racy comedies, into a winsomely pious Englishwoman named Christian Custance. Ralph Roister Doister, the braggardly type for whom the play is named, is foiled in his mean-spirited determination to win Christian Custance away from her true love, Gawin Goodluck. Almost all the characters virtuously conspire to expose Ralph for his effrontery and pretended bravery; even Matthew Merrygreek, the fun-loving parasite, proves ultimately to be on the side of decency and fair play. Throughout, Udall has adapted Roman comedy to English customs and mores.

Gammer Gurton's Needle, written by William Stevenson, fellow of Christ's College, Cambridge, at about the same time as *Roister Doister*, is similarly designed for student acting. Stock Roman characters are transformed into hearty English types. Diccon the Bedlam, who engineers the farcical action of the lost needle, resembles not only the Roman parasite but also the English natural fool or zany. To some extent he also reminds us of the mischievous and inventive Vice of the morality play. Other characters are even less purely Roman in their origin: Hodge, the clownish servant, Dame Chat, the shrewish neighbor, and Dr. Rat, the impoverished and ill-trained clergyman who spends most of his time drinking and complaining about his wretched lot. The play is an educated college man's indulgent laugh at his country neighbors. Yet the play is, like *Ralph Roister Doister*, classically structured into five acts with a single stage setting that preserves the unities of time and place.

In 1566, the members of Gray's Inn saw a production of George Gascoigne's *Supposes*, translated from the Italian of Ariosto (1509). Because it was a translation and not an English adaptation, this play preserves essentially in their original form the stock character types of neoclassical comedy: the parasite, the pantaloon or miserly aged rival in love, the overly watchful father, the clever servant, the bawdy nurse, and so on. The heroine, though no longer a Roman courtesan as in Plautus, is nonetheless a self-possessed and sophisticated young woman who conducts a secret affair for some time without being detected by her father. The mores of this continental play must have seemed challengingly cosmopolitan to its fashionable courtly and intellectual audience. Just as importantly, the play offered graceful prose language as its medium, rather than the homely English verse of *Ralph Roister Doister* and *Gammer Gurton's Needle. Supposes* provided a racy new model for neoclassical comedy, and was to become (with some of its continental morality anglicized) a source for Shakespeare's *The Taming of the Shrew.* Indeed, Shakespeare learned much about play construction, dialogue, and characterization from neoclassical comedies of this sort; perhaps his earliest comedy, *The Comedy of Errors*, owes a great deal to Plautus and to neoclassical imitators of that Latin comic writer. Another important early Italian comedy in English, *The Bugbears*, was adapted from Grazzini's *La Spiritata* and acted in about 1563–1565 by boy actors.

Early Tragedy

In early English tragedy, as in early comedy, native and neoclassical traditions coalesced and sometimes

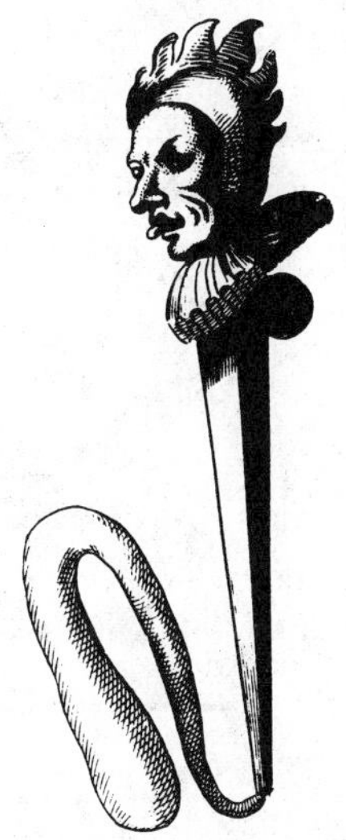

THE HUNTINGTON LIBRARY, SAN MARINO, CALIFORNIA

The slapstick was used in early farce by the prankster figures to create loud noises and to pummel one another.

clashed. Native traditions of tragedy had partly originated in two great medieval commonplaces, the "wheel of fortune" and the "fall of princes." Both were incorporated in Chaucer's "The Monk's Tale" and its source, Boccaccio's *De Casibus Virorum Illustrium*. Chaucer had defined tragedy as the story of a great person "that stood in greet prosperitee, And is yfallen out of heigh degree Into myserie, and endeth wrecchedly." His examples, taken from Boccaccio, included Lucifer, Adam, Samson, Hercules, Julius Caesar, and others. These were men or evil beings who had either fallen through sinful pride or had been brought low through the inevitable turn of fortune's wheel. Both types of tragedy illustrated to the medieval mind the folly of trusting to worldly expectations. The "fall of princes" tradition was extended into Elizabethan times through Lydgate's Chaucerian imitation, *The Fall of Princes*, and its sequel in *A Myrroure for Magistrates* (1559, with many subsequent revisions and enlargements). The morality play contributed a pattern similar to that of Satan's tragic fall through pride; and, although the mankind figure of early morality plays invariably was recovered to God's grace by the end of the play, some early Elizabethan Calvinistic moralities (such as *Enough Is as Good as a Feast* or *The Longer Thou Livest the More Fool Thou Art*) featured human protagonists who were eternally damned. As we have already seen, Elizabethan moralities of this sort anticipated the tragic pattern of Marlowe's *Doctor Faustus*.

Native traditions of tragedy evolved quite independent of classical tragic drama, and were in some ways strikingly different from it. Christian morality often served as a major explanation of the cause of tragic fall in medieval tragedy. Moreover, the focus was broad and cosmic, often embracing the protagonist's whole life (as in *Doctor Faustus*). Comedy was often made an integral part of stories ending tragically, especially in the morality plays. Classical tragedy, on the other hand, usually focused on a moment of crisis in the protagonist's life, and presented this crisis in its full tragic intensity without the undercutting of comic effect. In classical tragedy generally, narrative interest was subordinated to dramatic or lyrical interest. Unity of action, as understood by Renaissance theorists of drama, necessarily included unity of time and place. Thus the gap between native and classical tragedy was potentially vast.

Perhaps the earliest classical tragedy in England was Thomas Norton and Thomas Sackville's *Gorboduc*, presented before Queen Elizabeth at Whitehall on January 18, 1562. Although Sir Philip Sidney later complained about the play's violation of the unities in the fifth act, he praised it otherwise as "an exact

THE FOLGER SHAKESPEARE LIBRARY

Human destiny was thought to be controlled by the inscrutable caprices of Dame Fortune, depicted here as two-faced and multi-handed, and by the inexorable turns of the Wheel of Fortune.

model of all tragedies." To be sure, native concepts of tragedy are observable in *Gorboduc*, especially in its use of an ancient British setting and in its moral and Christian explanations of the causes of tragedy. Nevertheless, the classical element predominates.

This classical element is basically Senecan. Ancient Greek tragedy was relatively unknown to Elizabethan England except through Seneca's Roman adaptations. Seneca's ten plays were all translated into English by 1581, and had long been read in the schools as models of rhetoric (just as Terence and Plautus were also read). Seneca's plays were in fact closet dramas, intended to be recited rather than acted. Seneca provided *Gorboduc* with a model for its long declamatory speeches, its occasional passages of stichomythia (rapid one-line exchange of dialogue), its five-act structure punctuated by dumb shows, and its supernatural agents prognosticating doom. Moreover, *Gorboduc's* blank verse, created to approximate the Latin meters of Seneca, set a style for blank verse tragedy that dominated the English stage throughout Shakespeare's career. (Blank verse had been used shortly before *Gorboduc* by the Earl of Surrey in his translations from *The Aeneid*, but never before in drama.) *Gorboduc* also made an important contribution to the English history play by its use of chronicle materials in a tragic setting.

Other Senecan plays followed, written at first for gentlemanly audiences of the universities and the Inns of Court rather than for the popular stage. In 1588 eight gentlemen of Gray's Inn, including Thomas Hughes and Francis Bacon, presented before the queen a drama similar in form to *Gorboduc*, namely, *The Misfortunes of Arthur*. This tragedy borrows from Seneca not only chorus, messengers, and machinery, but ideas, sentiments, and words. Like *Gorboduc*, *The Misfortunes of Arthur* is somewhat free with the classical unities. Also, it is based upon the chronicle history of Britain, which was to become one of the chief sources of subject matter for English tragedy.

Another principal source of tragic themes was the Italian short story, which, because it was also impassioned and serious, offered to writers of tragedy many themes. *Gismond of Salerne* dramatizes a well-known Italian tale, and, like *Gorboduc* and *The Misfortunes of Arthur*, is Senecan in form and nature. It was acted before the queen in 1566 or 1568. In the same magazine of narrative, Shakespeare was later to find his sources for *Romeo and Juliet* and *Othello* as well as for such tragicomic comedies as *The Merchant of Venice* and *Measure for Measure*.

Sir Philip Sidney as Dramatic Critic

The kind of tragedy that Shakespeare and other popular dramatists wrote in the late sixteenth and early seventeenth centuries is not rigorously classical. It preserves many of the elements of English tragedy already enumerated: a broad narrative focus, frequent violations or total ignoring of the classical unities of time and place, the inclusion of comedy, and the like. Because of its freedom from the classical rules, the term "romantic tragedy" is sometimes applied to this characteristically English type of Renaissance drama.

Romantic tragedy might never have developed in England to so high a point or been accepted as the prevailing form of tragedy but for two things: in the first place, few Elizabethan dramatists learned their craft by studying the classical rules; and, in the second, the Elizabethan audience, with a taste for native English drama, demanded new, varied, and sensational plots accompanied by vaudeville clownage and songs. Such popular drama was often condemned by those critics who were familiar with classical literature, but to have made English tragedy conform with classical rules would have meant changing its nature. In France, where in Shakespeare's time the drama came under the control of the court and the learned classes, tragedy developed according to classical rules into the drama of Corneille and Racine; but in England, fortunately for the world, Shakespeare and his fellows created the new form of romantic tragedy.

The most famous classical critic of the age, Sir Philip Sidney, took vigorous exception to the kind of tragedy in vogue during the 1580's. His views are set forth in *The Defence of Poesie*, written in 1581 or slightly later:

> Our tragedies and comedies not without cause cried out against, observing rules neither of honest civility nor skilful poetry, excepting *Gorboduc*—again I say of those that I have seen. Which not withstanding as it is full of stately speeches and well-sounding phrases, climbing to the height of Seneca his style, and as full of notable morality, which it doth most delightfully teach, and so obtain the very end of poesy; yet in truth it is very defectious in the circumstances, which grieves me, because it might not remain as an exact model of all tragedies. For it is faulty both in place and time, the two necessary companions of all corporal actions. For where the stage should alway represent but one place, and the uttermost time presupposed in it should be, both by Aristotle's precept and common reason, but one day; there is both many days and many places inartificially imagined.
>
> But if it be so in *Gorboduc*, how much more in all the rest? where you shall have Asia of the one side and Afric of the other, and so many other under-kingdoms, that the player, when he comes in, must ever begin with telling where he is, or else the tale will not be conceived. Now you shall have three ladies walk to gather flowers, and then we must believe the stage to be a garden. By and by we hear news of shipwrack in the same place; then we are to blame if we accept it not for a rock. Upon the back of that comes out a hideous monster with fire and smoke, and then the miserable beholders are bound to take it for a cave. While in the meantime two armies fly in, represented with four swords and bucklers, and then what hard heart will not receive it for a pitched field?
>
> Now of time they are much more liberal. For

ordinary it is that two young princes fall in love; after many traverses she is got with child, delivered of a fair boy; he is lost, groweth a man, falleth in love, and is ready to get another child,—and all this in two hours space; which how absurd it is in sense even sense may imagine, and art hath taught, and all ancient examples justified, and at this day the ordinary players in Italy will not err in. . . .

Later he tells us that English plays are "neither right tragedies nor right comedies," but that they mingle clowns and kings with "neither decency nor discretion."

This merrily written criticism presents an excellent picture of the conditions prevailing upon the English stage when Sidney wrote, and, as criticism from a strictly classical point of view, it is perfectly just. To popular audiences of the time, however, it must have seemed just as easy to imagine the lapse of a period of twenty years with its concomitant changes as to imagine the lapse of a period of two hours. And if such an audience is willing so far to grant any author "that willing suspension of disbelief for the moment which constitutes poetic faith," as Coleridge puts it, that they will believe one scene in the theatre to be in Asia instead of London, they will be equally willing to believe in the same way that another scene following it is in Africa. English dramatists discovered, moreover, that human emotion is sufficiently mobile to switch itself quickly from a serious to a comic theme and back again. In human emotion the comic, the pathetic, the grotesque, and the tragic often blend and reinforce each other in the most inexplicable ways, so that Shakespeare and his fellows seem to have had nature as well as native bias on their side. No doubt the steady and monotonous pressure of an emotion born of fear, as in classical French tragedy, will finally break through the deadness which it generates and triumph over its victim; but certainly there is another and a quicker road to emotional intensification. The effect of alternately making and breaking the line of suspense, whether by a frustrated hope of escape or by mere diversion, usually results, not in annoyance or in loss of interest, but in heightened or heightening feeling. In other words, recurrence is more poignant than continued strain.

John Lyly

In facing the problem of understanding just what Elizabethan drama was and how it became what it was, we are forced to recognize that the classification of drama into comedy and tragedy by the ancients does not tell the whole story. Even when we add the history or chronicle play to these two divisions of drama, we have at best a rough classification which leaves out a great deal and implies that these three forms were sharply discriminated. In point of fact Elizabethan drama is, generally speaking, a blend of many elements. Nearly all Elizabethan tragedies have in them comic scenes and by-plots; most comedies have in them serious issues, which might conceivably result in disaster; and history plays are often, to all intents and purposes, capable of being classified as comedies or as tragedies. It seems well, therefore, to consider the varied works of a number of dramatists whose practice was successful on the stage and who influenced Shakespeare and his immediate contemporaries. Of these, John Lyly is one of the most important.

John Lyly (1554?–1606), an Oxford man who also studied at Cambridge, acquired fame by a single stroke—by the publication in 1578 of the famous and influential book *Euphues, The Anatomy of Wyt.* One of the curiosities of literature, it stands as the most sensational and brilliant effort in the struggle of English prose to acquire a conscious artistic manner. The style, as far as the author could achieve such a thing, is made up wholly of devices. He makes use of antithesis, personification, rhetorical question, metaphor and simile, and above all of balance reinforced by alliteration. *Euphues, The Anatomy of Wyt* and its sequel, *Euphues and his England*, which came out in 1580, were ardently followed by dozens of writers, including Robert Greene and Thomas Lodge, and seem to have set a new fashion of smart speech in the court of Queen Elizabeth. "Euphuism" itself had a vast influence on the style of the drama and other literature both in poetry and in prose.

Euphues and its sequel are made up of the slight adventures and the interminable discussions and letters of a seeker after true education and culture. They borrow facts, illustrations, and ideas from Plutarch, Pliny, Guevera, and many other writers, and may be said to embody the materials of Renaissance culture in the form of a handbook for the courtier, the lover, the traveler, and the statesman. They served to make the favorite ideas of the Renaissance current among ordinary educated men and women, and the expression of them conscious and adequate. As for the actual fad of euphuistic speech, Shakespeare joins with those who ridiculed it; but, nonetheless, there are qualities in *Love's Labour's Lost*, *A Midsummer Night's Dream*, *As You Like It*, and elsewhere which could not have been as they are but for Lyly. (For amusing examples of Shakespeare's parodying of the euphuistic style, see Falstaff's speech in *1 Henry IV*, II,iv,440 f., beginning "for though the camomile, the more it is trodden on the faster it grows, yet youth, the more it is wasted the sooner it wears"; or Don Armado's love letter in *Love's Labour's Lost*, IV,i,60 f.: "Shall I command thy love? I may: shall I enforce thy love? I could: shall I entreat thy love? I will," and so on.)

Lyly also influenced drama directly, since he was the author of at least eight comedies. They were written to suit the taste of the court and were possibly all acted before the queen by the children of the Chapel Royal or of St. Paul's School. The plays are often courtly debates in the tradition of Medwall's *Fulgens and Lucrece*, with much wit combat and philosophical argument. These comedies are also sufficiently Plautine to indicate that the characteristic features of Latin comedy had by this time (1580–1590) become naturalized on the English stage. *Mother Bombie*, like Shakespeare's *The Comedy of Errors*, is a fairly close adaptation of Latin comedy. The stock figures of Latin comedy, such as the pedant, the rascally servant, the duped parent, the parasite, and the aged lover, are there; but usually in the comic parts of all Lyly's plays he reminds us not so much of the Latin comedy as of the earlier English rough clownage.

However much Lyly may recall classical Latin comedy, he is most important as the inventor of a gay and fanciful type of comedy which found its high point in such plays as Shakespeare's *A Midsummer Night's Dream* and *As You Like It*. Lyly's *Sapho and Phao*, *Endymion*, and *Midas* have romantic plots derived from Ovidian mythology, made more delightful to Elizabeth's court by the embodiment of topical allegory. Three others, *Gallathea*, *Love's Metamorphosis*, and *The Woman in the Moon*, are pastoral comedies—that is, comedies whose characters are shepherds and shepherdesses after the tradition of the ancient Arcadia. *Gallathea* has the realistic sort of pastoralism. The scene is laid in Lincolnshire, just as one suspects that the scene of *As You Like It* is laid in Warwickshire. Two maidens are disguised as boys, and a good deal of the mythology, like that in *A Midsummer Night's Dream*, is manufactured for the occasion.

The Woman in the Moon is written in verse; all the rest of Lyly's plays are in prose, which is, of course, euphuistic. Yet this euphuistic style is turned to a purpose; it brightens the plays. The style is suited to dialogue and gives it a pungency and even a naturalness as dramatic conversation which the drama had hitherto lacked. It has been thought that Lyly learned something about the true sound of dialogue from the *Colloquies* of Erasmus, a much used schoolbook for Latin classes; and it is also possible that he may have learned a great deal of the new comic method he followed from the *Dialogues* of Lucian, which he knew. In any case, Lyly's followers in the drama learned much from him about the writing of dialogue.

George Peele

Another author who contributed to the romantic and poetic tone of Shakespearean comedy was George Peele (1558?–1597), whose *Arraignment of Paris*, written about 1581 in varied and brilliant blank verse, is one of the most delightful things of its time. Peele follows Virgil, as Lyly followed Ovid, and connects himself with the spirit of Spenser's *Shepheardes Calender*. He shows knowledge of the famous French group of poets headed by Clement Marot and known as the Plèiade. Fortunately Shakespeare, as the immediate follower of Lyly and Peele, and subjected to the same influences as they, began his work early enough to catch the fine imaginative fervor of the poets and dramatists of the decade from 1580 to 1590.

Peele was one of those "University Wits" who had to live by writing, and he turned to many styles of drama. *The Arraignment of Paris* was a courtly entertainment for Elizabeth, but his other plays were designed for the rapidly burgeoning popular stage. *Edward I* (1590–1593) is typical of the new genre of English history plays; it is jingoistically anti-Spanish, and features a popular folk-hero king who understands and respects the proud local customs of his people. *The Battle of Alcazar* (1588–1589) revels in the exotic world of Africa and the Middle East, in the vaunting heroic vein of Marlowe's *Tamburlaine*. *The Old Wives' Tale* (c. 1588–1594) is a seemingly naive but actually skillful medley of folk legends in the spirit of popular romance.

Robert Greene

Another of the striking figures of this decade is Robert Greene (1558–1592), a man whose dissolute and yet romantic impatience with the ways of the world became his own destruction. His undoubted talent and immense energy expressed themselves in a dozen love stories in euphuistic prose, largely based on the Greek novel. (Shakespeare too was influenced by the Greek novel, especially in his late "romances" such as *Pericles*, *The Winter's Tale*, and *Cymbeline;* the plot of *The Winter's Tale* came to Shakespeare by way of Greene's *Pandosto*.) The Greek novel comes not from the great times of the Greek drama and Greek philosophy, but mainly from the second, third, and fourth centuries A.D., when the Greeks had been long under Roman rule and were scattered round the shores of the Mediterranean. The Greeks were the merchants, traders, sailors, and schoolmasters of the Roman Empire, and this earliest form of the prose romance reflects the adventurous life which they lived. Such romances, as written by Heliodorus, Achilles Tatius, and others, are made up of a succession of strange and often improbable adventures, chance meetings, piracies, children exposed in infancy and restored grown and beautiful to their parents, families separated and reunited, indistinguishable twins, and many of the plot devices rendered familiar to us in the literature of the Renaissance; for the Renaissance, in its thirst for antiquity, did not distinguish between this kind of sensationalism and the real classics.

From the Greek novel, and also no doubt from his own experience in life, Greene got the new conception of woman which the world has learned from Shakespeare. The society depicted by the Greek novel gave women great liberty, and like them Greene's heroines are independent, witty, resourceful, and boylike, though at the same time feminine. Greene's dramas are almost the first modern productions in which woman is in any degree represented as assuming a relatively dignified station as the friend and companion of man.

The Greek novel itself had a large element of the pastoral, and here again we find a parallel in Greene.

COURTESY OF THE TRUSTEES, THE BRITISH MUSEUM

A crude woodcut from one of Robert Greene's pamphlets on cony-catching (1591) shows some methods of London sharpers in swindling their conies (or dupes), usually depicted as rabbits.

His plays, particularly *James IV* and *Friar Bacon and Friar Bungay* (c. 1589–1592), give us that blend of the pastoral and the romantic which the world has enjoyed in *As You Like It* and *Love's Labour's Lost.* Greene must be regarded as the first great master of plot in English comedy.

Greene may also have written *George a Greene, the Pinner of Wakefield* (1587–1593), a play that exalts the virtues of England's yeoman class in defiance of the aristocracy and all foreign foes. The hero, George, is a patriot, a scorner of hereditary titles, and a representative of the common people against vested interests. As a new breed of English folk-hero, he is so invincible that even Robin Hood must yield to his authority. The appeal of this dream of power to the artisans and yeomen in Greene's popular audiences must have been heady indeed.

Shortly before he fell victim to the notorious debaucheries of his bohemian existence (he was reported to have died from a surfeit of pickled herring and Rhenish wine), Greene wrote many pamphlets, some about London roguery, some about his own hard usage at the hands of the world. In one of the latter, *Groats-worth of Wit Bought with a Million of Repentance* (1592), he gave us our first personal reference to Shakespeare, a circumstance which must engage our attention later. It should be pointed out that it was not only Shakespeare who felt the influence of Greene, but Munday, Dekker, and most of the popular dramatists of the next decade.

Thomas Kyd

While romantic comedy was being shaped and developed in the hands of Lyly, Peele, and Greene, the Senecan tradition was finding its proponents on the popular stage. The greatest genius in adapting Senecan action to the English theatre was Thomas Kyd (1558–1594). His influence on his contemporaries and on later dramatists was immense; *The Spanish Tragedy* (c. 1583–1587) was probably acted more times during the sixteenth century than any other English play, and became a pattern for subsequent revenge drama. Kyd caught the unabashed brutality and horror of Senecan story and revealed it openly. Instead of having the action reported as taking place off the stage, as in Seneca and in most classical tragedy, he presented it directly. For tales of Greek mythology he substituted a modern story of love, conspiracy, murder, and political intrigue. He retained the Senecan ghost, the revenge motive, the spirit of stoicism, and a modified form of the chorus. He tells the tale of the revenge of Hieronimo, whose son, Horatio, had been seized and hanged in the garden of his father's house by Balthazar, his rival in love, and Lorenzo, his political enemy. Hieronimo feigns insanity and waits for his revenge. Ultimately, in a masque which he had written for the entertainment of the court, Hieronimo plays a part and in deadly earnest stabs his enemies, who likewise were actors in the tragic masque. Probably Kyd is also the author of the first dramatic version of the story of Hamlet, an important circumstance to be treated later.

Christopher Marlowe

Kyd's work gave rise to a series of revenge plays not only in his own time, but later, in 1600 and the years following, when the revenge tragedy again became fashionable. Moreover, Kyd seems to have had a shaping influence on Greene and on Christopher Marlowe (1564–1593). *The Spanish Tragedy* probably preceded Marlowe's *Tamburlaine,* which is conjecturally dated 1587. In blank-verse style Kyd was, therefore, the forerunner of Marlowe, whose *Jew of Malta* (c. 1589) in its extravagance and sensational intrigue seems to follow *The Spanish Tragedy.*

Nevertheless, however much Kyd may have contributed in matters of style and form, the fact remains that Marlowe became the leader in the great romantic type of Elizabethan tragedy. He is the one who shaped the genre subsequently perfected by Shakespeare. This he achieved by giving the English drama a hero more striking even than Hieronimo and by centering dramatic interest in personality and character. The aspiring spirit of the Renaissance finds expression in Marlowe's heroes. Tamburlaine has a thirst for world conquest; Dr. Faustus would go to the utmost bounds of knowledge and the power which knowledge gives; and Barabas in *The Jew of Malta* sets no limit to his longing for wealth.

Structurally, *Tamburlaine* is a good deal closer to the English popular morality play than to classical drama. Each of the play's two parts consists of a linear sequence of conquests by the humbly born but seemingly invincible Tamburlaine, until at last death ends his glory. Because many characters appear in one episode only, the cast is large and yet within the capacities of an Elizabethan acting company. Doubling of parts, as in Shakespeare's early history plays, is both common and necessary. Structural unity is achieved through thematic repetition rather than through a narrowing of the narrative focus. At the same time, the language of *Tamburlaine* is rich and new in its vibrant appeal to limitless human aspiration. The Elizabethan playgoer is invited to forget moral considerations in evaluating the play's ruthless hero, and to revel instead in the intoxicating spectacle of a baseborn shepherd "threat'ning the world with high astounding terms."

A profound ambivalence permeates all of Marlowe's plays, and gives them a restless brilliant energy that is characteristic of the times for which they were written. Tamburlaine is both a remorseless butcher of his enemies and a superhuman quester. He is fierce, mysterious, oriental, exotic, unknowable; as the projection of a universal human dream of aspiration, he is to be both admired and feared. Barabas in *The Jew of Malta* is at once colossally rich and colossally evil. Similarly, the protagonist of *Doctor Faustus* (c. 1588) is both a sinner who falls from grace and a noble but doomed Overreacher (as Harry Levin describes him) daring like Icarus to fly toward the sun. In medieval and Christian orthodox terms, Faustus is guilty of pride, the deadliest of the Deadly Sins; but in Renaissance terms he at least fleetingly resembles Prometheus, challenging the hierarchy of an oppressive and outmoded universe. In its free mixture of comedy and tragedy, and its wholesale disregard of the classical unities, *Doctor Faustus* brilliantly demonstrates what the native and homiletic tradition of tragedy had to offer Shakespeare.

Edward II, perhaps Marlowe's last play (1591–1593), is ambivalent toward its paired central figures, Edward and Mortimer Junior. At first the effeminate king seems chiefly in the wrong, while his baronial opponents lament England's decline. Toward the end of the play, however, the king becomes the sympathetic victim of a power-mad and Machiavellian Mortimer. Queen Isabella also changes radically from a long-suffering neglected wife into a scheming adultress. This shift in sympathy from the barons to King Edward is structurally much like that of Shakespeare's *Richard II*, and unquestionably Marlowe's history play had a profound effect on Shakespeare. Yet Marlowe's tone, as in his other plays, remains one of naturalistic amorality. He wryly regards England's political struggles as one more manifestation of the restlessness and ambition afflicting all mortal endeavors. His world is one of constant turmoil in which men of insatiable will must assert themselves and rise to the top, at whatever cost to themselves and to society. Shakespeare's world is basically different, even though he learned a great deal from Marlowe's tragic vision.

Marlowe first gave to English tragedy its realization of character and still more its dignity and seriousness. Educated at Cambridge, Marlowe was a good scholar and a born poet. He endowed English drama with the spirit of aspiration. Shakespeare was to be followed by a group of realists and satirists, but fortunately—let it be said again—he was early enough in his appearance to catch the enthusiasm for beauty which Spenser and Marlowe had. Not the least among Marlowe's gifts to English drama is a new and more flexible blank-verse style. In the following familiar lines which constitute the prologue to *Tamburlaine the Great*, Part I, it will be seen that Marlowe does not treat each blank-verse line as a separate unit, but runs the sense on from line to line and produces what might be described as a blank-verse paragraph, a thing most necessary to drama if it was to represent widely varying emotions, thoughts, and characters:

From jigging veins of rhyming mother wits,
And such conceits as clownage keeps in pay,
We'll lead you to the stately tent of war,
Where you shall hear the Scythian Tamburlaine
Threat'ning the world with high astounding terms,
And scourging kingdoms with his conquering sword.
View but his picture in this tragic glass,
And then applaud his fortunes as you please.

This is not only the pronunciamento of tragic seriousness; it is also, in spite of its elevated style, one of the first examples in English tragedy of vigorous, natural, straightforward expression. Tamburlaine in his ut-

The title page of the 1624 edition of Doctor Faustus *shows Faustus' temptation by the devil, here conventionally hideous, yet strangely docile and unthreatening.*

terances is a typical Renaissance poet on the themes of both love and war; and the following lines, almost as familiar to students of the English drama as those just quoted, will express the insatiable quality of Marlowe's aspiration:

> If all the pens that ever poets held
> Had fed the feeling of their masters' thoughts,
> And every sweetness that inspir'd their hearts,
> Their minds, and muses on admired themes;
> If all the heavenly quintessence they still
> From their immortal flowers of poesy,
> Wherein, as in a mirror, we perceive
> The highest reaches of a human wit;
> If these had made one poem's period,
> And all combin'd in beauty's worthiness,
> Yet should there hover in their restless heads
> One thought, one grace, one wonder, at the least,
> Which into words no virtue can digest.
>
> —*Tamburlaine*, Pt. I, V,ii,98–110

One feels that but for Marlowe Shakespeare might not have written so eloquently about "the young-ey'd cherubins" or the "lights that do mislead the morn."

Shakespeare's Dramatic Heritage

Shakespeare as an English Dramatist

Shakespearean tragedy began, roughly speaking, as a combination of Marlowe and Kyd: poetry, character, and style from Marlowe; motive, plot, and tragic intensity from Kyd. It was for Shakespeare himself in some of his great plays, such as *Richard II*, *Julius Caesar*, *Othello*, and *King Lear*, to make tragic action spring from tragic motive. No evidence suggests that Shakespeare was ever particularly aware of, or influenced by, Aristotelian theories of tragedy. He was holding "the mirror up to nature" and showing "virtue her own feature, scorn her own image, and the very age and body of the time his form and pressure" (*Hamlet*, III,ii,25–27). Sometimes in telling a story of universal human significance he approximated Aristotelian ideals in his plays (most nearly, perhaps, in *Othello*, *Macbeth*, and *Coriolanus*), but not by conscious design. Nor was he a slavish borrower from Marlowe and Kyd, even in his early tragedies such as *Titus Andronicus*. Greene and many others sought to imitate Marlowe in tragedy with but indifferent success. Shakespeare was Marlowe's only successful imitator, and he bettered Marlowe by humanizing him and rendering more natural those very qualities for which he was indebted to him.

Likewise the elements of Shakespearean comedy are in part derivative from Lyly, Peele, and Greene. The contributions of Lyly and Peele were those of style, setting, and movement. Greene, primarily a writer of romance, an adapter of the Greek novel, furnished the element of love and adventure which makes so many Elizabethan plays delightful merely as stories; and, although there are not many women in comedy and tragedy who illustrate the type, one acknowledges that it was Greene who put upon the stage the witty, independent-minded woman, usually in boy's clothes, who gives point and naturalness to love intrigue whether in serious drama or in comedy. Not only did Shakespeare, who was a far greater genius than any of them, combine the elements of the comedies of these men and better the instruction, but, as his career went on, he realized on a broad scale the possibilities of the comic point of view in the representation of human life and character. Atmosphere in his comedies reinforces plot, and plot gives rise to character. Even the simple episodic clownage of his predecessors becomes organic in his hands and contributes to the total artistic effect he chooses to produce.

All in all, we find Shakespeare falling heir to a form which through three centuries of religious drama had become endeared to the tastes of the popular mind, and which had, in the early sixteenth-century drama, undergone a process of development at the hands of conscious creators. This traditional pattern, improved by the skill of the later dramatists and infused with new spirit by his immediate predecessors, offered to Shakespeare an instrument which under his touch became a transcendent artistic medium for the depiction of human emotions and experiences. Shakespeare became not only the greatest of renaissance dramatists, but the greatest of dramatists.

SOME IMPORTANT PLAYS BY SHAKESPEARE'S PREDECESSORS

The Wakefield Corpus Christi Play c. 1390–1410
The Castle of Perseverance c. 1405–1425
Mankind c. 1471
The Digby *Mary Magdalene* c. 1480–1520
Everyman c. 1495–1500
H. Medwall, *Fulgens and Lucrece* c. 1497
J. Skelton, *Magnificence* c. 1515–1518
J. Heywood, *The Four PP* c. 1520–1522
J. Heywood, *The Play of the Weather* c. 1525–1533
J. Bale, *King Johan* 1538, later rev.
N. Udall, *Ralph Roister Doister* c. 1552–1554
W. Stevenson, *Gammer Gurton's Needle* c. 1552–1563
T. Preston, *Cambises* 1560–1561
Norton and Sackville, *Gorboduc* 1562
G. Gascoigne, *Supposes* 1566
J. Pickering, *Horestes* 1567
G. Peele, *The Arraignment of Paris* c. 1581–1584
T. Kyd, *The Spanish Tragedy* c. 1583–1587
J. Lyly, *Endymion* 1588
C. Marlowe, *Tamburlaine* 1587–1588
C. Marlowe, *Doctor Faustus* c. 1588
C. Marlowe, *The Jew of Malta* c. 1589
R. Greene, *Friar Bacon and Friar Bungay* c. 1589–1592
C. Marlowe, *Edward II* c. 1591–1593

LONDON THEATRES AND DRAMATIC COMPANIES

Throughout Shakespeare's life the propriety of acting any plays at all was a matter of bitter controversy. Indeed, when one considers the power and earnestness of the opposition, one is surprised that there could come into being such a wealth of dramatic excellence, and that Shakespeare's plays should reflect so little the bitterness of the controversy waged in his time.

Religious and Moral Opposition to the Theatre

From the 1570's onward, and even earlier, the city fathers of London revealed an ever-increasing distrust of the public performance of plays. They fretted about the dangers of plague and of riotous assembly. They objected to the fact that apprentices idly wasted their time instead of working in their shops. And always the municipal authorities suspected immorality. Thus, by an order of the Common Council of London, dated December 6, 1574, the players were put under severe restrictions.

The order cites the reasons. The players, it was charged, had been acting in the innyards of the city, which in consequence were haunted by great multitudes of people, especially youths. These gatherings had been the occasions of frays and quarrels, "evil practices of incontinency in great inns"; the players published "uncomely and unshamefast speeches and doings," withdrew the queen's subjects from divine service on Sundays and holidays, wasted the money of "poor and fond persons," gave opportunity to pickpockets, uttered "busy and seditious matters," and injured and maimed people by engines, by the falling of their scaffolds, and by weapons and powder used in plays. The order goes on to state the Common Council's fear that if the plays, which had been forbidden on account of the plague, should be resumed, God's wrath would manifest itself by an increase of the infection. Therefore, no innkeeper, tavernkeeper, or other person, might cause or suffer to be openly played "any play, interlude, comedy, tragedy, matter, or show" which had not been first licensed by the mayor and the court of aldermen.

The mayor and aldermen did not always state their case plainly, because Queen Elizabeth was a patron of the players, and because the players had friends and patrons in the Privy Council and among the nobility; sometimes, however, they did so quite boldly. One sees the case against plays stated syllogistically in the following words of Thomas White, a preacher at Paul's Cross in 1577:

> Looke but vppon the common playes of London, and see the multitude that flocketh to them and followeth them: beholde the sumptuous Theater houses, a continuall monument of London prodigalitie and folly. But I vnderstande they are now forbidden bycause of the plague. I like the pollicye well if it hold still, for a disease is but bodged or patched vp that is not cured in the cause, and the cause of plagues is sinne, if you looke to it well: and the cause of sinne are playes: therefore the cause of plagues are playes.
> (From *A Sermon preached at Paules Cross . . . in the time of the Plague*, 1578.)

Moved, no doubt, by the prohibition of the Common Council, James Burbage, with a company of actors under the patronage of the Earl of Leicester, leased a site in Shoreditch, a London suburb in Middlesex, beyond the immediate jurisdiction of the official enemies in the Common Council, whose authority extended only to the city limits. By 1576 he had completed the Theatre. He could call it "the Theatre" because there was no other; Burbage erected England's first permanent commercial theatrical

THE FOLGER SHAKESPEARE LIBRARY

Because of restrictions placed on London street players such as these, England's first permanent theatre was erected for the Earl of Leicester's men in 1576.

building. In general, the building combined features of the innyard and the animal-baiting house, having a central and probably paved courtyard open to the sky (like an innyard) and surrounding galleries on all sides (like an animal-baiting house). Burbage erected a stage at one side of the circular arena, and put dressing rooms in back of it. His Theatre became the model for other public playhouses such as the Curtain, the Swan, and the Globe which were constructed later.

Burbage had in this manner availed himself of that immunity from the enforcement of law which arises from indirect jurisdiction. The city fathers could not suppress plays nor control them with perfect success if they were performed in Middlesex or on the famous Bankside across the Thames in Surrey. In order to get at them in these suburban regions it was necessary to petition the queen's Privy Council to give orders to the magistrates and officers of the law in these counties. The queen's Privy Council, although always on the most polite terms with the Lord Mayor and his brethren of the city and always open to the argument that the assemblage of crowds caused the spread of the plague, were to a much less degree in sympathy with the moral scruples of the city. There were, moreover, current arguments for the plays, derived from the works of scholars, poets, and playwrights; namely, that there was precedent in antiquity for dramatic spectacles; that by drawing a true picture of both the bad and the good in life, plays enabled men to choose the good; that the people should have wholesome amusement; and that plays provided livelihood for loyal subjects of the queen.

Of these arguments the Privy Council made little use, resting the case for plays on what was no doubt an unanswerable argument—that, since the players were to appear before Her Majesty, the players needed practice in order to prepare themselves to please the royal taste. There was a good deal of politic fencing over the whole matter, and, so far as orders, complaints, and denunciations were concerned, the reforming opposition had much the better of it. The preachers thundered against plays. Pamphleteers denounced all matters pertaining to the stage: Stephen Gosson in *The Schoole of Abuse, Containing a pleasaunt invective against Poets, Pipers, Plaiers, Iesters and such like Caterpillers of a Commonwelth* (1579) and other works; Philip Stubbes in *The Anatomie of Abuses* (1583); and finally and most furiously of all, William Prynne in *Histrio-Mastix: the Players Scourge or Actors Tragedy* (1633). Gosson spoke of plays as "the inventions of the devil, the offerings of idolatry, the pomp of worldlings, the blossoms of vanity, the root of apostacy, food of iniquity, riot and adultery." "Detest them," he warns. "Players are masters of vice, teachers of wantonness, spurs to impurity, the sons of idleness."

Still, such diatribes represented an extreme reforming opinion that obviously was not shared at first by a majority of London viewers. They kept coming to plays, and the public theatres continued to flourish, until the early reign of James I (1603–1625) when the rift between the Puritans and the court erupted into irreconcilable antagonism. After about 1604, when James openly alienated the Puritans at the Hampton Court Conference, popular London audiences fell away increasingly from the theatre. The acting companies, whether through choice or necessity, moved toward the precinct of the court. Opposition to the stage, which had become increasingly Puritan in character, forced the total closing of the theatres in 1642.

The Public Theatres

A year or more after Burbage built the Theatre in 1576, the Curtain was put up near it by Philip Henslowe, or possibly by Henry Laneman, or Lanman. About ten years later Henslowe built the Rose, the first playhouse on the Bankside (the southern bank of the Thames River). The Swan was built there in 1594. In 1599 Richard and Cuthbert Burbage, sons of James Burbage, the former being the great actor of Shakespeare's heroes, tore down the Theatre because of trouble about the lease of the land and rebuilt it as the Globe on the Bankside. This Globe was the theatre that burned June 29, 1613, from cannon wadding which set fire to the roof after the discharge of ordnance during the acting of a play called *All is True*, thought to be identical with Shakespeare's *Henry VIII*. The Globe was rebuilt, probably in its original polygonal form—that is, essentially round with a large number of sides. In 1600 Henslowe built the Fortune, specifications for which have been preserved at Dulwich College with the other invaluable papers of the old theatre manager. This college, it may be said in passing, was founded by the munificence of the great actor Edward Alleyn, who had married Henslowe's stepdaughter.

Henslowe's Fortune Theatre was apparently a countermove to the activities of the Burbage group, who constituted a joint stock company for the support of the king's company, whereas Henslowe operated as theatre proprietor. He managed the Lord Admiral's men and secured, we may be sure, a large part of the profits of their activities. The contract for building the Fortune was let to the same contractor who had built the new Globe, and, since it was specified that it should be like the Globe in all its main features, except that it was to be square instead of polygonal, we may gain from these specifications an idea of the Globe. There is also preserved a drawing of the Swan, a Bankside theatre, which accompanies a description of the playhouse by Johannes De Witt, who visited London in 1596. The drawing, which was discovered in the University Library at Utrecht, is the work of one Van Buchell and may be based on drawings by De Witt himself. Besides these there are two or three little pictures of the Elizabethan public stage on the title pages of published plays, the most important being that on the title page of William Alabaster's *Roxana* (1632).

From these documents and pictures and from scattered references to the theatres, as well as from extended studies of stage directions and scenic conditions in plays themselves, we have a fairly clear idea of the public stage. Its features are these: a pit about 70 feet in diameter, usually circular and open to the sky; surrounding this, galleries in three tiers, where were the most expensive seats; and a rectangular stage, about 43 by 27 feet, wider than it was deep, raised about 5½ feet above the surface of the yard, sometimes built on trestles so that it could be removed if the house was also customarily used for bearbaiting and bullbaiting. The flat open stage usually contained one trap door. Part of the stage was roofed over by a wooden cover supported by posts, which might constitute "the heavens." Above this roof was a "hut" perhaps containing suspension gear for ascents and descents.

At the back of the stage was a partition wall, the "tiring-house façade," with at least two doors opening out of the actors' dressing rooms or "tiring house." Some theatres appear to have had no more than two doors, left and right, as shown in the Swan drawing; other theatres may have had a third door in the center. The arrangement of the Globe Theatre in this important matter cannot be finally determined, although some particular scenes from Shakespeare's plays seem to demand a third door. In any case, the so-called inner stage, long supposed to have stood at the rear of the Elizabethan stage, almost certainly did not exist. A more modest "discovery space" could be provided at one of the curtained doors when needed, as for example when Ferdinand and Miranda are suddenly "discovered" at their game of chess by Prospero in *The Tempest*. Such scenes never called for extensive action within the discovery space, however, and indeed the number of such discoveries in Elizabethan plays is very few. Well-to-do spectators who may have been seated in the gallery above the rear of the stage could not see into the discovery space. Accordingly it was used sparingly for brief visual effects. Otherwise, the actors performed virtually all their scenes on the open stage. Sometimes curtains were hung over the tiring-house façade between the doors to facilitate scenes of concealment, as when Polonius and Claudius eavesdrop on Hamlet and Ophelia.

An upper station was sometimes used as an acting space, but not nearly so often as was once supposed. The gallery seats above the stage, sometimes known as the "Lord's room," were normally sold to well-to-do spectators. (We can see such spectators in the Swan drawing and in Alabaster's *Roxana.*) Occasionally these box seats could be used by the actors, as when Juliet appears at her window (it is never called a balcony). In military sequences, as in the *Henry VI* plays, the tiring-house façade could represent the walls of a besieged city, with the city's defenders appearing "on the walls" (i.e., in the gallery above the stage) in order to parley with the besieging enemy standing below on the main stage. Such scenes were relatively infrequent, however, and usually required only a small number of persons to be aloft. A music room, when needed, could be located in one of the gallery boxes over the stage; but public theatres did not emulate the private stages with music rooms and entr' act music until some time around 1609.

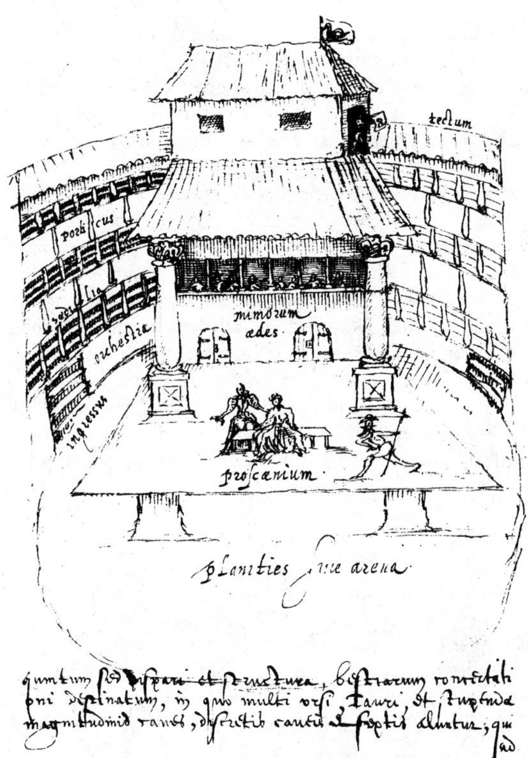

UTRECHT UNIVERSITY LIBRARY

The only extant illustration of the Swan; by Van Buchell (c. 1596), it may be based on several by De Witt.

The use of scenery was almost wholly unknown on the Elizabethan public stage, although we do find occasional hints of the use of labels to designate a certain door or area as a fixed location (as, perhaps, in *The Comedy of Errors*). For the most part, the scene was unlimited and the concept of space extremely fluid. No proscenium arch or curtain stood between the actors and audience, so the action could not be easily interrupted. Only belatedly did the public companies adopt the private-theatre practice of entr' act music, as we have seen. Most popular Elizabethan plays were written to be performed nonstop. Five-act structure had little currency, especially at first, and the divisions in Shakespeare's text of this kind are nonauthorial. Acting tempo was brisk. The Prologue of *Romeo and Juliet* speaks of "the two hours' traffic of our stage." Plays were performed in the afternoons, and had to be completed by dark in order to allow the audience to return safely to London. During the winter season playing time was severely restricted.

A capacity audience for the popular theatres came to about 3000 persons. The spectators represented a broad national cross-section, from the small shopkeepers and artisans who stood in the pit or yard for a penny, to the more substantial citizens who paid two pence or three pence for gallery seats, to the lords who occupied the elegant twelve-penny rooms. These spectators were lively, demanding, and intelligent. Although Shakespeare does allow Hamlet to refer disparagingly on one occasion to the "groundlings" who "for the most part are capable of nothing but inexplicable dumbshows and noise" (*Hamlet*, III,ii), Shakespeare wrote to please every level of his audience simultaneously, and thereby achieved a breadth of vision seldom found in continental courtly drama of the same period. The vitality and financial success of the Elizabethan public theatre is without parallel in English history. The city of London itself had only about 100,000 inhabitants, yet throughout Shakespeare's career several companies were competing simultaneously for this audience and constantly producing new plays. Most new plays ran for only a few performances, so that the acting companies were always in rehearsal with new shows. The actors needed phenomenal memories and a gift of improvisation as well. Their acting seems to have been of a high caliber despite the speed with which they worked. Among other things, many of them were expert fencers and singers.

The London public stage inherited many of its practices from native and medieval traditions. The fluid, open stage with spectators on four sides recalled the arena staging of many early Corpus Christi cycles, saints' plays, and moralities. The adult professional companies were, as we have seen, descended from the itinerant troupes who had taken their portable booth stages to every part of England, setting up in innyards, street corners, noble houses, and palaces. The Elizabethan tiring-house façade and platform stage owed much to the simple curtained booth stage and trestle platform of the itinerant troupes, set up against one wall of an innyard or animal-baiting house. Yet when those same itinerant actors had set up their plays in noblemen's banqueting halls or at court, they encountered another structure that had an important influence on their concept of a stage: the Tudor hall screen. We must next examine the significance of this indoor theatrical setting.

The Tudor Hall

According to Richard Hosley, Richard Southern, and others, the Tudor banqueting hall and its hall screen played a major part in the staging of much early Tudor drama. Medwall's *Fulgens and Lucrece*, one of the earliest such plays, was written to be performed during the intervals of a state banquet. The patrician guests were seated at tables, while servingmen bustled to and fro or stood crowded together at the doors in the hall "screen." This screen or partition traversed the lower end of the rectangular hall, providing a passageway to the kitchens and to the outside. Its doors—often two, sometimes three—were normally curtained to prevent drafts. This arrangement of the doors anticipated that of many playhouses in late Elizabethan England, both public and private. Moreover, hall screens and passageways were normally surmounted by a gallery where musicians could play —an architectural feature markedly resembling the upper galleries of late Elizabethan theatres. The Tudor hall screen, then, provided a natural façade for dramatic action, with curtained doorways for entrances and exits. The actors of *Fulgens and Lucrece* clearly made use of those doorways, sometimes joking

THE FOLGER SHAKESPEARE LIBRARY

A drawing of the gallery seats or "Lord's room" (third row, second panel), from the title page of Roxana *(1632).*

with the servingmen as the actors pushed their way into the hall. Heywood's *Play of the Weather* calls for a similar *mise en scène*. The actors normally performed on the floor in front of the screen, among the spectators' tables. Although this ready-made "stage" sufficed for most Tudor plays, the actors sometimes provided additional stage structures; *Weather*, for example, calls for a throne-room into which Jupiter can retire without leaving the hall. Similar structures could represent a shop, an orchard, a mountain, or what have you.

Although both medieval and continental drama offered traditions of multiple staging, in which a series of simultaneously visible and adjacent structures would represent as fixed locations all the playing areas needed for the performance of a play, Tudor indoor staging seems to have made less use of this method than was once supposed. Nor did the various indoor theatres of Tudor England make extensive use of neoclassical staging from Italy, with its street scene in perspective created by means of lath-and-canvas stage "houses." Italian scenery of this sort came into use sooner in the court masque than in regular drama. Nevertheless, we do find in the Tudor indoor theatre a neoclassical tendency toward fixation of locale in preference to the unlimited open stage. *Gammer Gurton's Needle*, for example, acted probably in a university hall, seems to have used one stage structure, or possibly one door, to represent Gammer's house throughout the action, and another to represent Dame Chat's house. Shakespeare may well have been influenced by this kind of fixed-locale staging in his early neoclassical plays, especially *The Comedy of Errors*.

The Private Stage

Despite such influences on the public stage, the most significant contribution of the Tudor hall and its hall screen was to the so-called private stage of the late Elizabethan period. In the 1570's, choir boys began performing professionally to courtly and intellectual audiences in London. The choir boys had long performed plays for the royal and noble households to which they were attached, but in the 1570's they were in effect organized into professional acting companies. Sebastian Westcote and the Children of Paul's may have originated this enterprise. Their theatre was apparently some indoor hall in the vicinity of St. Paul's in London, outfitted much like the typical domestic Tudor hall to which the boys had grown accustomed. Comparable indoor "private" theatres soon followed at Blackfriars and Whitefriars.

At some point a low stage was constructed in front of the hall screen, and seats were provided for all the spectators. Many of these seats were in the "pit," or what we would call the "orchestra," facing toward the stage at one end of the rectangular room. Other seats were in galleries along both sides of the room; these were quite elaborate in the so-called Second Blackfriars of 1596, and provided two or three tiers of seats. Elegant box seats stood at either side of the stage it-

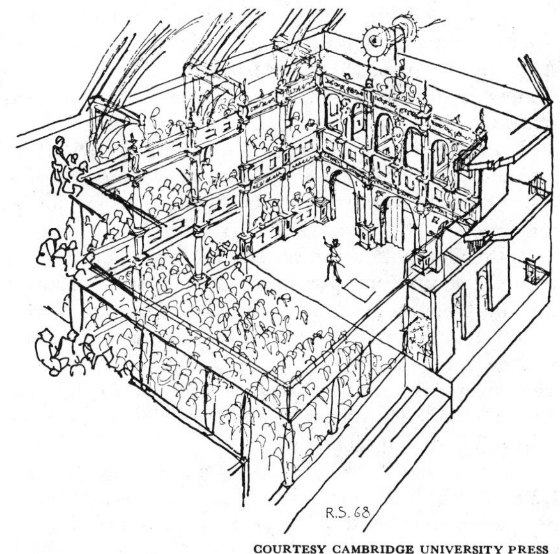

COURTESY CAMBRIDGE UNIVERSITY PRESS

A reconstruction of the Second Blackfriars shows it to be much like our modern theatres.

self. The Second Blackfriars had a permanently built tiring house to the rear of the stage, modeled on the Tudor hall screen with probably three doors. Above it was a gallery used variously as a lord's room, a music room, and an upper station for occasional acting.

The private theatre flourished during the 1580's and again after 1598–1599, having been closed down during most of the 1590's because of its satirical activities. Although a commercial theatre, it was "private" in its clientele because its high price of admission (sixpence) excluded those who could stand in the yards of the "public" theatres for a penny (roughly the equivalent of an hour's wage for a skilled worker). Plays written for the more select audiences of the "private" theatres tended to be more satirical and oriented to courtly values than those written for the "public" theatres, although the distinction is not absolute.

London Private Theatres

The important private theatres of Shakespeare's London were two in the precinct, or "liberty," of Blackfriars, an early one in Whitefriars about which little is known, a later one there, and a theatre at Paul's, the exact location and nature of which is not known. In the thirteenth century, the mother house in the Dominican friars, or Blackfriars, was established on the sloping ground between St. Paul's Cathedral and the river. It was a sizeable institution, which ultimately covered about five acres of ground. It stood on the very border of the city, and, after the custom of the time, was made a liberty; that is to say, it had its own local government and was removed from the immediate jurisdiction of the city of London. After the suppression of the friary and the confiscation of its lands, the jealousy existing between the Privy Council, representing the crown, and the mayor and aldermen, representing the city and probably also the rights of property holders, prevented the district of the Blackfriars from losing its political independence of the municipality. It was still a liberty and, therefore, offered a fair chance for the encroachments of play-lovers upon those who regarded theatres as sinful abominations. Also Blackfriars no doubt gathered into its precincts many persons whose activities were slightly beyond the pale of the law; but there were also aristocratic residents in the region who demanded protection, and the crown had certain rights still in its control.

From 1576 to 1584 the Children of the Queen's Chapel, one of the two most important companies of boy actors, had used a hall in the precinct of Blackfriars in which to act their plays. Here were acted some, at least, of Lyly's plays. In 1596 James Burbage purchased property in this precinct and seems to have spent a good deal of money in its adaptation for use as an indoor theatre (the so-called Second Blackfriars). He probably appreciated its advantages over Cripplegate or the Bankside, particularly for use in winter. But the aristocratic residents of the Blackfriars by petition to the Privy Council prevented him from making use of his theatre. Plays within the city proper had only recently been finally and successfully prohibited, and the petitioners no doubt objected to their intrusion into Blackfriars on the grounds that they and their crowds were a nuisance.

Burbage's new indoor theatre may have lain idle from the time of its preparation until 1600; but, in any case, in that year it became the scene of many plays. It was let by lease to a group of men for the use of the Children of the Chapel, who in 1604 became the Children of the Queen's Revels. These theatre managers brought into their service a number of new dramatists, Jonson, Marston, Chapman, and later Webster; the vogue of the plays acted by the Children of the Chapel was so great as to damage the patronage of the established companies and to compel them to go on the road. Out of this rivalry between the children and the adult actors arose that "War of the Theatres" alluded to in *Hamlet* (II,ii). In 1608 the Burbage interests secured the evacuation of the lease, so that the theatre in Blackfriars became the winter playhouse of Shakespeare's company from that time forward.

System of Patronage

In 1572 common players of interludes, along with minstrels, bearwards, and fencers, were included within the hard terms of the act for the punishment of vagabonds, provided that such common players were not enrolled as the servants of a baron of the realm or of some honorable person of greater degree. The result was the system of patronage of theatrical companies in Elizabethan and Jacobean times, according to which players became the "servants" of some nobleman or of some member of the royal family.

There were in existence before Shakespeare came to London more than a dozen of these companies, some of them long antedating the passage of the act of 1572. In the provincial records of the visits of players to various towns and cities it is sometimes difficult, however, to tell whether we have to do with actors or with acrobats, since other public performers, as well as players, were similarly organized. At any rate, we may say that there were in London about the time that Shakespeare arrived there companies of players under the patronage of the queen, the Earl of Worcester, the Earl of Leicester, the Earl of Oxford, the Earl of Sussex, the Lord Admiral, and Charles, Lord Howard of Effingham. The companies were gradually to be very greatly reduced in number, so that there were usually only three adult companies acting in London during Shakespeare's prime. In addition to these were the children's companies, privately controlled, acting intermittently, but at times very successfully. The most important of these were the Children of the Chapel and Queen's Revels and the Children of Paul's; but there were also boy players of Windsor, Eton College, The Merchant Taylors, Westminster, and other schools.

Shakespeare and the London Theatrical Companies

We know that by 1592 Shakespeare had arrived in London and had achieved sufficient notice as a young playwright to arouse the resentment of a rival dramatist, Robert Greene. In that year, shortly before he died, Greene—or possibly his editor after Greene's death—lashed out at an "vpstart Crow, beautified with our feathers," who had had the audacity to fancy himself "the onely Shake-scene in a countrey" (*Groatsworth of Wit*). This petulant outburst was plainly directed at Shakespeare, since Greene included in his remarks a parody of some lines from *3 Henry VI*. As a university man and an established dramatist, Greene seems to have resented the intrusion into his profession of a mere player who was not university trained. This "vpstart Crow" was achieving a very real success on the London stage. Shakespeare had probably already written *The Comedy of Errors*, *Love's Labour's Lost*, *The Two Gentlemen of Verona*, the *Henry VI* plays, and *Titus Andronicus*, and perhaps also *Richard III* and *The Taming of the Shrew*.

For what acting company or companies had he written these plays, however? By 1594 we know that Shakespeare was an established member of the Lord Chamberlain's company, important enough in fact to have been named along with Will Kempe and Richard Burbage as payee for court performances on December 26 and 28 of 1594. But when had he joined the Chamberlain's men, and for whom had he written and acted previously? These are the problems of the so-called dark years during which Shakespeare came to London (presumably around 1587) and got started on his career.

One prestigious acting company he could have joined was the Earl of Leicester's company, led by James Burbage, father of Shakespeare's later colleague Richard Burbage. Leicester was a favorite minister of Queen Elizabeth until his death in 1588, and his company of actors received from the queen in 1574 an extraordinary patent to perform plays anywhere in England despite all local prohibitions, provided that the plays were approved beforehand by the master of the Queen's Revels. Since an act of 1572 had outlawed all unlicensed troupes, Leicester's men and a few similar companies attached to important noblemen were given a virtual monopoly over public acting. In 1576 Burbage built the Theatre for his company in the northeast suburbs of London. This group also toured the provinces. Conceivably Shakespeare served an apprenticeship in this company, though no evidence exists to prove a connection. Leicester's company had lost some of its prominence in 1583, when several of its best men joined the newly formed Queen's men with Richard Tarleton as its most famous actor. The remaining members of Leicester's company disbanded in 1588 upon the death of the earl, and many of its principal actors ultimately became part of Lord Strange's company. These probably included George Bryan, Will Kempe, and Thomas Pope, all of whom subsequently went on to become Lord Chamberlain's men.

Lord Strange's (The Earl of Derby's) Men

Besides Leicester's men and the Queen's men, other prominent companies of the 1580's and early 1590's included Lord Strange's men, the Lord Admiral's men, the Earl of Pembroke's men, and the Earl of Sussex' men. Scholars have long speculated that Shakespeare may have joined the company of Ferdinando Stanley, Lord Strange (who in 1593 became the Earl of Derby). As we have seen, many of the leading actors of Leicester's disbanded company, including George Bryan, Will Kempe, and Thomas Pope, joined Lord Strange's company. Their names appear on a roster of 1593, along with those of John Heminges and Augustine Phillips. All these men later became part of the Lord Chamberlain's company, most of them when it was first formed in 1594. Shakespeare's name does not appear on the 1593 Lord Strange's list (which was a license for touring in the provinces), but he may possibly have stayed in London to attend to his writing while the company toured. Certainly an important number of his later associates belonged to this group.

From about 1590 to 1594, Lord Strange's men formed an amalgamation with the Admiral's men, including the famous Edward Alleyn. This impressive

THE FOLGER SHAKESPEARE LIBRARY

The most famous comic of the time was Will Kempe of the Lord Chamberlain's men, for whom Shakespeare created several roles.

combination of talents enjoyed a successful season in 1591–1592, with six performances at court. Alleyn's father-in-law, Philip Henslowe, recorded in his *Diary* the performances of the combined players in early 1592, probably at the Rose Theatre. Their repertory included a *Harey the vj* and a *Titus & Vespacia*. The latter play is, however, no longer thought to have any connection with Shakespeare's *Titus Andronicus;* and the *Harey the vj* may or may not have been Shakespeare's, since *3 Henry VI* was (according to its 1595 title page) acted by Pembroke's men rather than Lord Strange's men. If Shakespeare was a member of the Strange-Admiral's combination in 1591–1592, we are at a loss to explain why Henslowe's 1592 list records so many performances of plays by Marlowe, Greene, Kyd, and others, and none that are certainly by Shakespeare. On the other hand, the *Harey the vj* may be his, and the title page of the 1594 quarto of *Titus Andronicus* does list the Earl of Derby's men as performers of the play in addition to the Earl of Pembroke's and the Earl of Sussex' men. (Lord Strange's men became officially known as the Earl of Derby's men when Lord Strange was made an earl in September of 1593.) At any rate, the company disbanded when the earl died in April of 1594, leaving them without a patron. The connection with the Admiral's men was discontinued, with Alleyn returning to the Admiral's and the rest of the group forming a new company under the patronage of Henry Carey, first Lord Hunsdon, the Lord Chamberlain.

The Earl of Pembroke's Men

The other company to which Shakespeare is most likely to have belonged prior to 1594 is the Earl of Pembroke's company. This group came to grief in 1593–1594, evidently as a result of virulent outbursts of the plague which had kept the theatres closed dur-

DULWICH COLLEGE PICTURE GALLERY

Richard Burbage, instrumental in the early success of the Lord Chamberlain's men, became its chief tragedian.

ing most of 1592 and 1593. Pembroke's men were forced to tour the provinces and then to sell a number of their best plays to the booksellers. Henslowe wrote to Alleyn in September of 1593 of the extreme financial plight of Pembroke's company: "As for my lorde a Penbrockes [men], which you desier to knowe wheare they be, they ar all at home and hausse ben this v or sixe weackes, for they cane not saue ther carges [charges, expenses] with trauell, as I heare, & weare fayne to pane ther parell [pawn their apparel] for ther carge." Soon thereafter this company disbanded.

Pembroke's men were associated with a significant number of Shakespeare's early plays. Among the playbooks they evidently sold in 1593–1594 were *The Taming of A Shrew* and *The True Tragedy of Richard Duke of York*. The first of these was published in 1594 with the assertion that it had been "sundry times acted by the Right honorable the Earle of Pembrook his seruants." Although the text of this quarto is not Shakespeare's play as we know it but instead an anonymous version, most scholars now feel certain that it was an imitation of Shakespeare's play and that the work performed by Pembroke's men was in fact Shakespeare's. The same conclusion pertains to a performance in 1594 of "*the Tamynge of A Shrowe*" at Newington Butts, a playhouse south of London bridge. Henslowe's *Diary* informs us that the actors on this occasion were either the Lord Chamberlain's or the Lord Admiral's men. The probability, then, is that Shakespeare's *The Taming of the Shrew* passed from Pembroke's men to the Chamberlain's men when Pembroke's company collapsed in 1593–1594.

The True Tragedy of Richard Duke of York, published in 1595, was a "bad" quarto of Shakespeare's *3 Henry VI*. Its title page declared that it had been "sundrie times acted by the Right Honourable the Earle of Pembrooke his seruants." Probably they acted *2 Henry VI* as well, to which part three was a sequel. In addition, the 1594 quarto of *Titus Andronicus* mentions on its title page the Earl of Pembroke's servants, although the Earl of Derby's and the Earl of Sussex' men are named there as well. Thus, Pembroke's men performed as many as four of Shakespeare's early plays, more than we can assign to any other known company. Nevertheless, their claim to Shakespeare remains uncertain. We simply do not know who acted several of Shakespeare's earliest plays, such as *The Comedy of Errors*, *Love's Labour's Lost*, and *The Two Gentlemen of Verona*. Lord Strange's (Derby's) men did act something called *Harey the vj*, and are named on the 1594 title page of *Titus Andronicus*. Sussex' men may conceivably have owned for a time some early Shakespearean plays that later went to the Lord Chamberlain's, such as *Titus Andronicus*. The Queen's men, although associated with no known Shakespeare play, other than the old *King Lear* (acted jointly with Sussex' men in 1593), were a leading company during the years in question. All we can say for sure is that the plague difficulties of 1592–1593, and the death of the Earl of Derby in 1594, led to a major reshuffling of the London acting companies. From this reshuffling emerged in 1594 the Lord Chamberlain's company, with Shakespeare and Richard Burbage (whose earlier history is also difficult to trace) as two of its earliest and most prominent members.

THE ORDER OF SHAKESPEARE'S PLAYS: HIS DRAMATIC DEVELOPMENT

The plays of Shakespeare in the first collected edition (the First Folio, published in 1623) are arranged in three groups—Comedies, Histories, and Tragedies—with no recognition of the order of their composition. The first comedy is *The Tempest*, which is known to be one of the very latest plays; the second is *The Two Gentlemen of Verona*, one of the very earliest. The Histories are arranged in order of the English kings whose reigns they treat, although it is obvious that Shakespeare did not write them in this order. There is no discoverable order in the arrangement of the tragedies. If we are to understand Shakespeare's dramatic development, we must have some better knowledge of the order in which he wrote his plays.

External Evidence

Eighteen of the thirty-six plays in the First Folio had been previously published singly at various dates in quarto form. The remaining eighteen were published for the first time in the First Folio. *Pericles* was not included in the First Folio, but existed only as a quarto until its inclusion in the Third Folio of 1663–1664. All the quarto editions, except *Romeo and Juliet* and *Love's Labour's Lost*, appear in the Register of the Stationers' Company of London; and two, *As You Like It* (S.R. 1600) and *Antony and Cleopatra* (S.R. 1608), which were not printed in quarto, are entered there, this step having been taken, possibly, to forestall publication by printers who had no right to them. The date of entry of a play in the register indicates that at least by that time the play was in existence. The quarto editions have also certain information on their title pages regarding date, author, and publisher, and sometimes tell what theatrical company had acted the play.

Such information about dating is usually called "external" evidence, that is, derived from outside the play. Other kinds of external evidence include references to Shakespeare's plays in diaries, journals, or accounts of the period, and quotations from his plays in the literary works of Elizabethan and Jacobean writers. Allusions in Shakespeare's plays themselves to contemporary events may be considered as partly external and partly internal evidence. Evidence of this kind, though abundant, is often uncertain because of the difficulty in determining whether Shakespeare is actually alluding to some historical event or is instead describing a typical situation that happens to fit some historical circumstance. See Appendix I, at the end of this volume, for a detailed discussion on "Canon, Dates, and Early Texts" of each of Shakespeare's plays.

Internal Evidence

Once Shakespeare's plays have been arranged in approximate chronological order on the basis of the kinds of external evidence already described, we can perceive that his style underwent a continuous development from his earliest years to the end of his career as a dramatist. In fact, Shakespeare's development in the use of certain types of images, of rhymes, of run-on lines, of weak or feminine endings, and the like, is so remarkably consistent that various verse "tests" can actually be employed as additional evidence about dating of the plays. Such evidence is, by its nature, internal evidence.

Certain difficulties are inevitable in the use of verse tests, and limit the extent to which we may rely on them for precise dating. In some instances, Shakespeare may have revised his own work, imposing a relatively late style on an early style. Theories of revision are not argued as extensively as they once were; but *Love's Labour's Lost*, for example, is still thought by some scholars to have been written as early as 1588–1589 and revised some eight years later. Again, Shakespeare may have collaborated with other writers, or rewritten the work of earlier dramatists. Although collaboration theories are also generally out of favor today, multiple authorship cannot be entirely ruled out as a possibility in the case of a play like *Henry VIII*. The texts of some plays, notably that of *Pericles*, are corrupt and may not represent exactly what Shakespeare wrote. Shakespeare may well have chosen on certain occasions to write in a deliberately "old-fashioned" style, as in the First Player's recitation about the slaying of Priam (*Hamlet*, II,ii) or in "The Murder of Gonzago" performed before King Claudius (*Hamlet*, III,ii). Conversely, Shakespeare may at times have anticipated his later style. If we make sufficient allowance for certain variations in detail, however, we can still discover a consistency in the overall pattern that is surprisingly clear. The very fact of this consistency lends support to one's impression of Shakespeare's extraordinary artistic growth.

The specific kinds of verse tests that can be applied to the dating of Shakespeare's plays are discussed in the following sections. Taken as a whole, they reveal a movement toward ever greater freedom in the use of both verse and prose. Shakespeare increasingly abandons rhyme for prose, and formal end-stopped blank verse for a fluid and often conversational style. He introduces more and more pauses in the middle of lines, and uses hypermetric lines containing more or less than the ten syllables of the conventional iambic pattern. Speeches end in the middle of lines with greater frequency. Shakespeare uses feminine, light, and weak endings in ever-increasing numbers. By the end of his career, his style has virtually been transformed from one of formal and rhetorical regularity to one of vast flexibility and range.

Mixture of Prose and Blank Verse

Statistically, not much can be determined as to the date of a play merely on the basis of its percentage of lines in prose or in blank verse; at best, these tests give only an approximation of date. Nevertheless, we can make several observations as to Shakespeare's habitual use of prose and blank verse. In his early plays he seldom uses prose except in the speeches of clowns, servants, and rustics. On the other hand, he uses blank verse often in his early plays, more so than in his later career. Blank verse is his common vehicle of expression in speeches of heightened oratory or dramatic seriousness, as in the early history plays. Blank verse remains of course important throughout Shakespeare's poetic career, but in terms of percentages it is especially prominent during his early years. Marlowe, the originator of the "mighty line" in blank verse, was an important influence, and a rival until his death in 1593. During the plays of Shakespeare's so-called lyric period, c. 1594–1596, rhymed verse often takes the place of blank verse; see, for example, *Romeo and Juliet*, *A Midsummer Night's Dream*, and *Richard II*.

The use of prose is striking in several mature comedies of the later 1590's, especially *Much Ado about Nothing* and *The Merry Wives of Windsor*. Thereafter, prose is always essential to Shakespeare's comic world, and is no longer limited to buffoonish types as in some early comedies. Prose also serves a vital function in *Hamlet* and other great tragedies; and, as the verse grows more free, the alternations between verse and prose are no longer so formally distinguished as they were in the writings of the early Shakespeare.

Rhyme

The amount of rhyme is statistically more significant than that of blank verse. Early plays and those of the lyric period, such as *A Midsummer Night's Dream* and *Romeo and Juliet*, use a great deal of rhyme, whereas late plays such as *The Tempest* use practically none. The commonest form of rhyme is the iambic pentameter measure rhymed in couplet; as when Phebe, quoting Marlowe's *Hero and Leander*, says in *As You Like It* (III,v,81–82),

> Dear shepherd, now I find thy saw of might,
> 'Who ever lov'd that lov'd not at first sight?'

Shakespeare does not limit his use of rhyme to the couplet, however. *Romeo and Juliet* and *Love's Labour's Lost* each contain a number of complete sonnets, as well as rhymed sequences made up of a quatrain followed by a couplet, and a good deal of alternate rhyme. Doggerel appears in some of the early plays.

One quite formal use of the rhymed couplet does not conform to the statistical pattern that we observe generally in the use of rhyme. Because the Elizabethan theatre lacked a front curtain to mark a pause between scenes in a play, Elizabethan dramatists often gave emphasis to a scene ending by means of a rhymed couplet. Possibly the device served also as a cue to those actors backstage who were waiting to begin the next scene. At any rate, the use of scene-ending couplets is common in some plays that otherwise make little use of rhyme. For example, Act I, scene v of *Hamlet* ends with the following concluding statement by the protagonist:

> The time is out of joint: O cursed spite,
> That ever I was born to set it right!

Apart from this convention, however, use of rhyme in Shakespeare is normally indicative of early style. His lovers in the early plays often speak in rhyme; later, they tend to use prose.

Blank Verse Tests

Although the actual percentage of blank verse in Shakespeare's plays is not always statistically revealing, a number of tests can be applied to the blank verse that are meaningfully consistent. Throughout his career, Shakespeare's blank verse moves gradually but steadily toward greater freedom. Completely regular blank verse, invariably consisting of ten syllables to each unrhymed line with an accent falling on every other syllable, soon becomes monotonous. This iambic pattern can, however, be varied by a number of subtle changes. Extra syllables, accented or unaccented, can be added to the line, or a line may occasionally be short by one or more syllables. The regular alternation of accented and unaccented syllables, which produces the effect of five iambic "feet" in each line (each foot consisting of an unaccented and an accented syllable), can be interrupted by the occasional inversion of a foot. Pauses, or caesuras, may occur at several points in the line. Most importantly, the line can be "end-stopped"—with a strong pause at the end of the line—or "run on" without interruption into the next line. Variations of this sort can transform blank verse from a formal and rhetorical vehicle into one that is highly conversational, almost proselike.

Blank verse before Marlowe's time was usually quite formal, regular, and end-stopped. One of Marlowe's contributions was to provide for greater continuity in thought and style, by means of what has been called the "verse paragraph." His verses, though prevailingly end-stopped, are so constructed that they flow into each other. They have, in other words, somewhat the effect of run-on lines. Marlowe also varied the measure by breaking up the regularity in the forms of the individual feet within the line, sometimes substituting for the regular iambic a trochaic foot (consisting of a stressed followed by an unstressed syllable). The shifting of the medial pause, or caesura, was his chief means of rendering the verse sufficiently flexible to be used in dialogue.

Still, Marlowe's experimentations with blank verse came to an end with his death in 1593; Shakespeare carried the movement toward stylistic freedom a great distance further. The "Marlovian" Shakespeare, as in *Richard III*, is still insistent upon metrical regularity. By means of rhetorical devices, such as parallelism or antithesis, he often groups his lines of blank verse into pairs or four-line units as though they were parts of a formal sonnet. He runs on past the ends of lines with relative infrequency. In his late years, contrastingly, perhaps influenced by the new styles in blank verse of John Fletcher and other Jacobean dramatists, Shakespeare employs far greater flexibility. We find many more hypermetric lines containing more or fewer than ten syllables. And, as the chart on page 42 reveals, the percentage of run-on lines in his plays increases more or less steadily from the early to the late period.

The following passage from Clarence's description of his dream in *Richard III* (I,iv,21–23) may be taken as an example of Shakespeare's earlier blank verse style. Note that there is a pause at the end of every line except the ninth:

O Lord! methought, what pain it was to drown!
What dreadful noise of water in mine ears!
What sights of ugly death within mine eyes!
Methoughts I saw a thousand fearful wracks;
A thousand men that fishes gnaw'd upon;
Wedges of gold, great anchors, heaps of pearl,
Inestimable stones, unvalued jewels,
All scatt'red in the bottom of the sea:
Some lay in dead men's skulls; and, in the holes
Where eyes did once inhabit, there were crept,
As 'twere in scorn of eyes, reflecting gems,
That woo'd the slimy bottom of the deep,
And mock'd the dead bones that lay scatt'red by.

As an example of the latest manner, consider Prospero's description of his magic in *The Tempest* (V,i, 33–50) where only the first, fifth, eighth, and tenth lines are end-stopped:

Ye elves of hills, brooks, standing lakes and groves,
And ye that on the sands with printless foot
Do chase the ebbing Neptune and do fly him
When he comes back; you demi-puppets that
By moonshine do the green sour ringlets make,
Whereof the ewe not bites, and you whose pastime
Is to make midnight mushrumps, that rejoice
To hear the solemn curfew; by whose aid,
Weak masters though ye be, I have bedimm'd
The noontide sun, call'd forth the mutinous winds,
And 'twixt the green sea and the azur'd vault
Set roaring war: to the dread rattling thunder
Have I given fire and rifted Jove's stout oak
With his own bolt; the strong-bas'd promontory
Have I made shake and by the spurs pluck'd up
The pine and cedar: graves at my command
Have wak'd their sleepers, op'd, and let 'em forth
By my so potent art.

These two passages have been chosen for comparison in part because they are both set speeches, rich in formal characteristics. Yet a comparison of more informal speeches from early and late plays ought to reveal no less clearly the shift in Shakespeare's style away from rhetorical balance toward a freedom from verse restraint, a deliberate syncopation of blank verse rhythms, and a complication of syntax.

The Speech-Ending Test

A verse freedom somewhat akin to Shakespeare's use of run-on rather than end-stopped lines is his growing tendency to divide a line between two speakers, or even among several speakers. The practice of dividing a line of verse in this fashion increases steadily from *The Comedy of Errors*, where there are almost none, to *The Winter's Tale*, where eighty-seven percent of the speeches end in the middle of a line. The speech-ending test might be even more impressive in its consistency were it not for the likelihood that some texts have been cut for acting (*Macbeth*, for instance) or otherwise tampered with in such a way as to alter the author's original intention.

Feminine or "Double" Endings

Another variation in the composition of blank verse has to do with the fifth foot at the end of the line. In early Shakespearean end-stopped blank verse, with its emphasis on the completion of each line of verse, the final syllable naturally tends to be stressed with great regularity. In the passage from *Richard III* quoted above, for example, every line except possibly the seventh ends in an accented syllable. As a means of breaking away from this regular and monotonous partition of the sense, Shakespeare introduces more and more frequently an extra unaccented syllable at the ends of lines, thus making the line consist of eleven instead of ten syllables. Even in the blank verse of *Richard III* and other early plays of Shakespeare, we find a good many more extra-syllable or "double" endings than in the blank verse of Marlowe.

To some Elizabethans this stylistic variation seemed sweeter and less abrupt than the regular pattern; for that reason, the extra unaccented syllable was called a "feminine" ending in contrast to the accented or "masculine" ending. The relative number of masculine and feminine endings forms another test of the time of composition, since feminine endings increase as Shakespeare's development progresses. A similar tendency also causes the introduction, more and more, of extra syllables before the pauses within the lines.

Light and Weak Endings

One other among the various tests is of major importance. Early in his career Shakespeare almost never ended lines with conjunctions, prepositions, auxiliary verbs, possessive pronouns, and other lightly stressed words. After 1600, however, he used such endings with increasing freedom. There are more than a hundred such lines each in *Coriolanus* and *Cymbeline*. In *The Comedy of Errors* and *The Two Gentlemen of Verona* there are none at all. We have, therefore, the light- and weak-ending test. A line ending in an unstressed word, such as a pronoun or an auxiliary verb, is said to have a light ending. A weak ending carries the process still further and seems to forbid any vocal stress at all. Prepositions and conjunctions, such as *in, to, and, if, or*, produce this effect.

Imagery

Another highly useful study that reveals a chronological pattern in the evolution of Shakespeare's style, although not tabulated in the accompanying chart, is Wolfgang Clemen's *The Development of Shakespeare's Imagery* (1951). As Clemen convincingly demon-

Table of Metrical Tests Applied to Shakespeare's Plays

Name of Play	*No. of Lines*	*Prose*	*Blank Verse*	*5-Foot Rhymes*	*Run-on Lines %*	*Double Endings*	*Speech Ending %*	*No. Light Weak End.*	*Probable Dates*
Com. Er.	1778	240	1150	380	12.9	137	0.6	0	c. 1589–1593
L. L. L.	2789	1086	579	1028	18.4	9	10.0	3	c. 1588–1589 rev. 1596–97(?)
Two Gent.	2294	409	1510	116	12.4	203	5.8	0	c. 1590–1594
Tit. And.	2523	43	2338	144	9.5	154	2.5	5	c. 1589–1591
1 Hen. VI	2677	0	2379	314	10.4	140	0.5	4	c. 1589–1592
2 Hen. VI	3162	448	2562	122	11.4	255	1.1	3	c. 1589–1592
3 Hen. VI	2904	0	2749	155	9.5	346	0.9	3	c. 1589–1592
Rich. III	3619	55(?)	3374	170	13.1	570	2.9	4	c. 1591–1594
Tam. Shrew.	2649	516	1971	169	8.1	260	3.6	14(?)	c. 1592–1594
Mids. Dream.	2174	441	878	731	13.2	29	17.3	1	c. 1594–1595
R. & J.	3052	405	2111	486	14.2	118	14.9	7	c. 1594–1596
K. John	2570	0	2403	150	17.7	54	12.7	7	c. 1594–1595
Rich. II	2756	0	2107	537	19.9	148	7.3	4	c. 1595–1596
Mer. Ven.	2660	673	1896	93	21.5	297	22.2	7	c. 1594–1598
1 Hen. IV	3176	1464	1622	84	22.8	60	14.2	7	c. 1596–1598
2 Hen. IV	3446	1860	1417	74	21.4	203	16.8	1	c. 1596–1598
Much Ado	2826	2106	643	40	19.3	129	20.7	2	c. 1598–1599
A. Y. L. I.	2857	1681	925	71	17.1	211	21.6	2	c. 1598–1600
Henry V	3380	1531	1678	101	21.8	291	18.3	2	c. 1599
J. C.	2478	165	2241	34	19.3	369	20.3	10	c. 1599
Merry Wives	3018	2703	227	69	20.1	32	20.5	1	c. 1597–1601
12th Night	2690	1741	763	120	14.7	152	36.3	4	c. 1600–1602
Hamlet	3931	1208	2490	81	23.1	508	51.6	8	c. 1599–1601
T. & C.	3496	1186	2025	196	27.4	441	31.3	6	c. 1601–1602
All's Well	2966	1453	1234	280	28.4	223	74.4	13	c. 1601–1604
Meas. Meas.	2821	1134	1574	73	23.0	338	51.4	7	c. 1603–1604
Othello	3316	541	2672	86	19.5	646	41.4	2	c. 1603–1604
K. Lear	3334	903	2238	74	29.3	567	60.9	6	c. 1605
Tim. of Ath.	2373	596	1560	184	32.5	257	62.8	30	c. 1605–1608
Macbeth	2108	158	1588	118	36.6	399	77.2	23	c. 1606–1607
A. &. C.	3063	255	2761	42	43.3	613	77.5	99	c. 1606–1607
Pericles	2389	418	1436	225	18.2	120	71.0	82	c. 1606–1608
Coriolanus	3410	829	2521	42	45.9	708	79.0	104	c. 1608
Cymbeline	3339	638	2585	107	46.0	726	85.0	130	c. 1608–1610
Wint. Tale	3075	844	1825	0	37.5	639	87.6	100	c. 1610–1611
Tempest	2064	458	1458	2	41.5	476	84.5	67	c. 1610–1611
Henry VIII	2822	67(?)	2613	16	46.3	1195	72.4	82	c. 1613

strates, Shakespeare uses figures of speech for decoration and amplification in his early style, and learns only gradually to integrate these figures into a presentation of theme, subject, and individual character. In Shakespeare's later work, simile is often transformed into metaphor, and assumes an organic function in relation to the entire play.

The Periods of Shakespeare's Creativity

Critics once spoke of the periods of Shakespeare's creative life in biographical terms, as in Edward Dowden's fanciful evocation of the experimental years "In the Workshop" (1590–1594), the years of happy success at writing comedy and history "In the World" (1595–1601), the tragic period "De Profundis" or "Out of the Depths" (1602–1608), and the final years of serene resignation "On the Heights" (1608–1612). Such implicitly biographical explanations are now regarded with great skepticism. Still, most critics would agree that Shakespeare developed from phase to phase with extraordinary artistic consistency. Although we talk now in terms of genres rather than of Shakespeare's changing spiritual mood, we nevertheless generally recognize four discernible phases in his career.

1. The Early Period. Shakespeare's experimentalism is plainly evident in *The Comedy of Errors*, based chiefly on Plautus' *Menaechmi*, and in *Titus Andronicus*, a revenge play inspired partly by Thomas Kyd's *The Spanish Tragedy*. When he wrote *Love's Labour's Lost*, Shakespeare seems to have been especially impressed by John Lyly. The *Henry VI* plays and *Richard III* owe a lot to Marlowe and Peele. Shakespeare's genius is evident everywhere in these plays, but he has not yet developed fully his most distinctive genres. *The Two Gentlemen of Verona*, for example, is a romantic comedy containing many of the features Shakespeare later used to such marvelous effect—maidens disguised as young men, banishment to a forest, outlaws—and yet the lovers of this play do not achieve the poetic insights into the nature of love that we come to expect from Shakespeare's mature comedies.

2. The Period of Comedies and Histories. The greatest comedies and history plays were virtually all written between 1595 and 1601, beginning perhaps with *A Midsummer Night's Dream* and *Richard II* and continuing through *The Merchant of Venice*, *Much Ado about Nothing*, *As You Like It*, *Twelfth Night*, *Henry IV*, and *Henry V*. Shakespeare wrote virtually no tragedies during the entire first half of his career; we have only the early and experimental *Titus Andronicus*, and the exquisitely comic and touching *Romeo and Juliet*. Shakespeare may have had several reasons for concentrating so on the perfection of two genres only, romantic comedy and patriotic English history. For one thing, these genres were very much in vogue on the stage for which he wrote. The Spanish Armada victory of 1588 had helped launch the history play as an expression of England's jubilantly patriotic mood during much of the 1590's. By the time of Queen Elizabeth's death in 1603, however, the mood had shifted to doubt and uncertainty. Perhaps also the popular appetite for patriotic drama had simply been satiated. The children's companies, reopening in 1598–1599 after having been closed for most of the 1590's, were wholly uninterested in patriotic history drama; they preferred satires and revenge tragedies, following the new vogue. Shakespeare's *Henry V* in 1599 was not only his last history play except for the late and uncharacteristic *Henry VIII* (1613), but was one of the last popular history plays written by any Elizabethan dramatist. The genre came to an end, almost as abruptly as it had started. Similar changes in fashion affected romantic comedy. Shakespeare's masterpieces in the genre, composed from 1595 to 1601, coincided with the great age of romantic comedy in the Elizabethan theatre. Greene and Peele had preceded Shakespeare in this genre; Thomas Heywood, Thomas Dekker, and others were his contemporaries. In about 1600–1601 this genre too began to decline, partly because the great Puritan-leaning popular audiences of London were on the verge of renouncing the theatre.

3. The Period of Tragedies. The 1600's thus saw the theatres gravitate more and more to the tastes of courtly and intellectual audiences. Shakespeare's tragic period is characterized not only by the great tragedies of *Hamlet*, *Othello*, *King Lear*, and *Macbeth*, but also by the more ironic and iconoclastic Roman or classical plays: *Julius Caesar*, *Troilus and Cressida*, *Timon of Athens*, *Antony and Cleopatra*, *Coriolanus*. *Troilus and Cressida* seems to have been Shakespeare's experiment with avant-garde satire. He wrote perhaps two comedies during the tragic period, *All's Well* and *Measure for Measure*, but they are so affected by the dark preoccupations of Shakespeare's tragic period that they are often referred to as "problem comedies" or "problem plays."

4. The Period of Romances. Shakespeare's final phase was a return to comedy of a sort, but comedy with such leanings toward tragicomedy and miraculous circumstance that the final plays are often called romances to distinguish them from the earlier "festive" comedies. Here again Shakespeare both reflects and contributes to a shift in the artistic movements of his era; other dramatists such as Beaumont and Fletcher were showing a new interest in tragicomedy. Most of the late romances were evidently written with sophisticated Blackfriars audiences in mind, although these plays continued to be performed at the Globe Theatre as well.

SHAKESPEARE CRITICISM

In his own time, Shakespeare achieved a reputation for immortal greatness that is astonishing when we consider the low regard in which playwrights were then generally held. Francis Meres compared him to Ovid, Plautus, and Seneca, and proclaimed Shakespeare to be England's most excellent writer in both comedy and tragedy. John Weever spoke of "Honie-tong'd *Shakespeare*." The number of such praising allusions is high. Even Ben Jonson, the opinionated literary dictator of his age, lauded Shakespeare as "a Moniment without a tombe," England's best poet exceeding Chaucer, Spenser, Beaumont, Kyd, and Marlowe. In tragedy, Jonson compared Shakespeare with Aeschylus, Euripides, and Sophocles; in comedy he insisted Shakespeare had no rival even in "insolent *Greece* or haughtie *Rome*." This tribute appeared in Jonson's commendatory poem written for the Shakespearean Folio of 1623.

To be sure, Jonson had more critical things to say about Shakespeare. Even in the Folio commendatory poem, Jonson could not resist a dig at Shakespeare's "small *Latine*, and lesse *Greeke*." To William Drummond of Hawthornden he objected that Shakespeare "wanted Arte" because in a play (*The Winter's Tale*) he "brought in a number of men saying they had suffered Shipwrack in Bohemia, wher ther is no Sea neer by some 100 Miles." In *Timber, or Discoveries,* Jonson chided Shakespeare for his unrestrained facility in writing. "The Players have often mentioned it as an honour to *Shakespeare,* that in his writing, (whatsoever he penn'd) hee never blotted out [a] line. My answer hath beene, would he had blotted a thousand." In a preface to his own play, *Every Man in His Humour* (1616 edition), Jonson satirized English history plays (such as Shakespeare's) that "with three rustie swords, And helpe of some few foot-and-halfe-foote words, Fight ouer *Yorke,* and *Lancasters* long iarres: And in the tyring-house bring wounds, to scarres." He also jeered at plays lacking unity of time in which children grow to the age of sixty or older, and at nonsensical romantic plays featuring fireworks, thunder, and a chorus that "wafts you ore the seas."

These criticisms are all of a piece. As a classicist himself, Jonson held in high regard the classical unities. He deplored much English popular drama, including some of Shakespeare's plays, for their undisciplined mixture of comedy and tragedy. Measured against his cherished ideals of classical decorum and refinement of language, Shakespeare's histories and late romances seemed irritatingly naive and loose-jointed. Yet Jonson knew that Shakespeare had an incomparable genius, superior even to Jonson's own. Jonson's affection and respect for Shakespeare seem to have been quite unforced. In the midst of his critical remarks in *Timber,* he freely conceded that "I lov'd the man, and doe honour his memory (on this side Idolatry) as much as any. Hee was (indeed) honest, and of an open, and free nature: had an excellent *Phantsie;* brave notions, and gentle expressions."

NATIONAL PORTRAIT GALLERY, LONDON

Chief dramatic rival for public acclaim during Shakespeare's later years was Ben Jonson, poet, playwright, critic, and literary high priest.

The Age of Dryden and Pope

Jonson's attitude toward Shakespeare lived on into the Restoration period of the late seventeenth century. A commonplace of that age held it proper to "admire" Ben Jonson but to "love" Shakespeare. Jonson was the more correct poet, the better model for imitation. Shakespeare often had to be rewritten according to the sophisticated tastes of the Restoration (see Appendix III for an account of Restoration stage adaptations of Shakespeare), but he was also regarded as a natural genius. Dryden reflected this view in his *Essay of Dramatic Poesy* (1668) and his *Essay on the Dramatic Poetry of the Last Age* (1672). Dryden condemned *The Winter's Tale, Pericles,* and several other plays for "the lameness of their plots" and for their "ridiculous incoherent story" which is usually "grounded on impossibilities." Not only Shakespeare, he charged, but several of his contemporaries "neither understood correct plotting, nor that which they call *the decorum of the stage.*" Had Shakespeare lived in the Restoration, Dryden believed, he would doubtless have written "more correctly" under the influence of a language that had become more "courtly" and a wit that had grown more "refined." Shakespeare, he thought, had limitless "fancy" but sometimes lacked "judgment." Dryden regretted that Shakespeare had been forced to write in "ignorant" times and for audiences who "knew no better." Like Jonson, nevertheless, Dryden had the magnanimity to perceive that Shakespeare transcended his limitations. Shakespeare, said Dryden, was "the Man who of all Modern, and perhaps Ancient Poets, had the largest and most comprehensive soul." From a classical writer, this was high praise indeed.

Alexander Pope's edition of Shakespeare (1725) was based upon a similar estimate of Shakespeare as an untutored genius. Pope freely "improved" Shakespeare's language, rewriting lines and excising those parts he considered vulgar, in order to rescue Shakespeare from the barbaric circumstances of his Elizabethan milieu. Other critics of the Restoration and early eighteenth century who stressed Shakespeare's "natural" genius and imaginative powers were John Dennis, Joseph Addison, and the editors Nicholas Rowe and Lewis Theobald.

The Age of Johnson

Shakespeare was not without his detractors during the late seventeenth and early eighteenth centuries; after all, classical criticism tended to distrust imagination and fancy. Notable among the harsher critics of the Restoration period was Thomas Rymer, whose *Short View of Tragedy* (1692) included a famous attack on *Othello* for making too much out of Desdemona's handkerchief. In the eighteenth century, Voltaire spoke out sharply against Shakespeare's violation of the classical unities, though Voltaire also had some admiring things to say.

The most considered answer to such criticism in the later eighteenth century was that of Dr. Samuel Johnson, in his edition of Shakespeare's plays and its great preface (1765). Shakespeare, said Johnson, is the poet of nature who "holds up to his readers a faithful mirror of manners and of life. His characters are not modified by the customs of particular places, unpractised by the rest of the world. . . . In the writings of other poets a character is too often an individual; in those of Shakespeare it is commonly a species." Johnson's attitudes were essentially classical in that he praised Shakespeare for being universal, for having provided a "just representation of general nature," for having stood the test of time. Yet Johnson also magnanimously praised Shakespeare for having transcended the classical rules. Johnson triumphantly vindicated the mixture of comedy and tragedy in Shakespeare's plays and the supposed indecorum of his characters.

Of course Johnson did not praise everything he saw. He objected to Shakespeare's loose construction of plot, careless huddling together of the ends of his plays, licentious humor, and above all the punning wordplay. He deplored Shakespeare's failure to satisfy the demands of poetic justice, especially in *King Lear*, and he regretted that Shakespeare seemed more anxious to please than to instruct. Still, Johnson did much to free Shakespeare from the constraint of an overly restrictive classical approach to criticism.

The Age of Coleridge

With the beginning of the Romantic period, in England and on the Continent, Shakespeare criticism increasingly turned away from classical precept in favor of a more spontaneous and enthusiastic approach to Shakespeare's creative genius. The new Shakespeare became indeed a rallying cry for those who now deplored such "regular" dramatic poets as Racine and Corneille. Shakespeare became a seer, a bard with mystic powers of insight into the human condition. Goethe, in *Wilhelm Meister* (1796), conceived of Hamlet as the archetypal "Romantic" poet, melancholic, delicate, unable to act.

Critical trends in England moved toward similar conclusions. Maurice Morgann, in his *Essay on the Dramatic Character of Sir John Falstaff* (1777), glorified Falstaff into a rare individual of courage, dignity, and —yes—honor. To do so, Morgann had to suppress much evidence as to Falstaff's overall function in the *Henry IV* plays. Dramatic structure in fact did not interest him; his passion was "character," and his study of Falstaff reflected a new Romantic preoccupation with character analysis. Like other character critics who followed him, Morgann tended to move away from the play itself and into a world where the dramatic personage being considered might lead an independent existence. What would it have been like to know Falstaff as a real person? How would he have behaved on occasions other than those reported by Shakespeare? Such questions fascinated Morgann and others because they led into grand speculations about human psychology and philosophy. Shakespeare's incomparably penetrating insights into character prompted further investigations of the human psyche.

Other late eighteenth-century works devoted to the study of character included Lord Kames' *Elements of Criticism* (1762), Thomas Whately's *Remarks on Some of the Characters of Shakespeare* (published 1785), William Richardson's *Philosophical Analysis and Illustration of Some of Shakespeare's Remarkable Characters* (1774), and William Jackson's *Thirty Letters on Various Subjects* (1782). Morgann spoke for this school of critics when he insisted, "it may be fit to consider them [Shakespeare's characters] rather as Historic than Dramatic beings; and, when occasion requires, to account for their conduct from the *whole* of character, from general principles, from latent motives, and from policies not avowed."

Samuel Taylor Coleridge, the greatest of the English Romantic critics, was profoundly influenced by character criticism, both English and continental. He himself made important contributions to the study of character. His conception of Hamlet, derived in part from Goethe and Hegel, as one who "vacillates from sensibility, and procrastinates from thought, and loses the power of action in the energy of resolve," was to dominate nineteenth-century interpretations of Hamlet. His insight into Iago's evil nature—"the motive-hunting of a motiveless malignity"—was also influential.

Nevertheless, Coleridge did not succumb to the temptation, as did so many character critics, of ignoring the unity of an entire play. Quite to the contrary, he affirmed in Shakespeare an "organic form" or "innate" sense of shape, developed from within, that gave new meaning to Shakespeare's fusion of comedy and tragedy, his seeming anachronisms, his improbable fictions, and his supposedly rambling plots. Coleridge heaped scorn on the eighteenth-century idea of Shakespeare as a "natural" but untaught genius. He praised Shakespeare not for having mirrored life, as Dr. Johnson had said, but for having created an imaginative world attuned to its own internal harmonies. He saw Shakespeare as an inspired but deliberate artist who fitted together the parts of his imaginative world with consummate skill. "The judgement of Shakespeare is commensurate with his genius."

In all this Coleridge was remarkably close to his German contemporary and rival, August Wilhelm Schlegel, who insisted that Shakespeare was "a profound artist, and not a blind and wildly luxuriant genius." In Shakespeare's plays, said Schlegel, "the Fancy lays claim to be considered as an independent mental power governed according to its own laws." Between them, Coleridge and Schlegel utterly inverted the critical values of the previous age, substituting "sublimity" and "imagination" for universality and trueness to nature.

Other Romantic critics included William Hazlitt (*Characters of Shakespear's Plays*, 1817), Charles Lamb (*On the Tragedies of Shakespeare*, 1811), and Thomas De Quincey (*On the Knocking at the Gate in Macbeth*, 1823). Keats also had some penetrating things to say in his letters. As a whole the Romantics were enthusiasts for Shakespeare, sometimes even idolaters. Yet they consistently refused to recognize him as a man of the theatre. Lamb wrote, "It may seem a paradox, but I cannot help being of opinion that the plays of Shakespeare are less calculated for performance on a stage, than those of almost any other dramatist whatever." Hazlitt similarly observed, "We do not like to see our author's plays acted, and least of all, *Hamlet*. There is no play that suffers so much in being transferred to the stage." These hostile attitudes toward the theatre reflected in part the condition of the stage in nineteenth-century England. In part, however, these attitudes were the inevitable result of character criticism, or what Lamb called the desire "to know the internal workings and movements of a great mind, of an Othello or a Hamlet for instance, the *when* and the *why* and the *how far* they should be moved." This fascination with character swept everything before it during the Romantic period.

A. C. Bradley

The tendency of nineteenth-century criticism, as we have seen, was to exalt Shakespeare as a poet and philosopher rather than playwright, and as a creator of immortal characters whose "lives" might be studied as though existing independent of a dramatic text. Not infrequently, this critical approach led to a biographical interpretation of Shakespeare through his plays, on the assumption that what he wrote was his own spiritual autobiography and a key to his own fascinating character. Perhaps the most famous critical studies in this line were Edward Dowden's *Shakspere: A Critical Study of His Mind and Art* (1875) and his *Shakespeare Primer* (1877), in which he traced a progression from Shakespeare's early exuberance and passionate involvement through brooding pessimism to a final philosophical calm.

At the same time, the nineteenth century also saw the rise of a more factual and methodological scholarship, especially in the German universities. Dowden in fact reflected this trend as well, for one of the achievements of philological study was to establish with some accuracy the dating of Shakespeare's plays and thus make possible an analysis of his artistic development. Hermann Ulrici's *Über Shakespeares dramatische Kunst* (1839) and Gottfried Gervinus' edition of 1849 were among the earliest studies to interest themselves in Shakespeare's chronological development.

The man who best summed up the achievement of nineteenth-century Shakespeare criticism was A. C. Bradley, in his *Shakespearean Tragedy* (1904) and other studies. *Shakespearean Tragedy* dealt with the four "great" tragedies, *Hamlet*, *Othello*, *King Lear*, and *Macbeth*. Bradley revealed his Romantic tendencies in his focus on psychological analysis of character, but he also brought to his work a scholarly awareness of the text that had been missing in some earlier character critics. His work continues to have considerable influence today, despite modern tendencies to rebel against nineteenth-century idealism. To Bradley, Shakespeare's tragic world was ultimately explicable and profoundly moral. Despite the overwhelming impression of tragic waste in *King Lear*, he argued, we as audience experience a sense of compensation and completion that implies an ultimate pattern in human life. "Good, in the widest sense, seems thus to be the principle of life and health in the world; evil, at least in these worst forms, to be a poison. The world reacts against it violently, and, in the struggle to expel it, is driven to devastate itself." Man must suffer because of his fatal tendency to pursue some extreme passion, but man learns through suffering about himself and the nature of his world. We as audience are reconciled to our existence through purgative release; we smile through our tears. Cordelia is wantonly destroyed, but the fact of her transcendent goodness is eternal. Although in one sense she fails, said Bradley, she is "in another sense superior to the world in which [she] appears; is, in some way which we do not seek to define, untouched by the doom that overtakes [her]; and is rather set free from life than deprived of it."

Historical Criticism

The first major twentieth-century reaction against character criticism was that of the so-called historical critics. These critics insisted on a more hardheaded and skeptical appraisal of Shakespeare through better understanding of his historical milieu: his theatre, his audience, his political and social environment. In good part, this movement was the result of a new professionalism of Shakespearean studies in the twentieth century. Whereas earlier critics—Dryden, Pope, Johnson, Coleridge—had generally been literary amateurs in the best sense, early twentieth-century criticism became increasingly the province of those who taught in universities. Historical research became a professional activity. Bradley himself was Professor of English Literature at Liverpool and Oxford, and did much to legitimize the incorporation of Shakespeare into the humanities curriculum. German scholarship produced the first regular periodical devoted to Shakespeare studies, *Shakespeare-Jahrbuch*, to be followed in due course in England and America by *Shakespeare Survey* (beginning in 1948), *Shakespeare Quarterly* (1950), and *Shakespeare Studies* (1965).

From the start, historical criticism took a new look at Shakespeare as a man of the theatre. Sir Walter Raleigh (Professor of English Literature at Oxford, not to be confused with his Elizabethan namesake) rejected the Romantic absorption in psychology and turned his attention instead to the artistic methods by which plays affect theatre-going spectators. The poet Robert Bridges insisted that Shakespeare had often sacrificed consistency and logic for primitive theatrical effects designed to please his vulgar audience. Bridges' objections were often based on serious lack of information about Shakespeare's stage, but they had a healthy iconoclastic effect nonetheless on the scholarship of his time. In Germany, Levin Schücking pursued a similar line of reasoning in his *Character Problems in Shakespeare's Plays* (1917, translated into English in 1922). Schücking argued that Shakespeare had disregarded coherent structure and had striven instead for vivid dramatic effect ("episodic intensification") in his particular scenes. Schücking's *The Meaning of Hamlet* (1937) explained the strange contradictions of that play as resulting from its primitive and brutal Germanic source materials which Shakespeare had not fully assimilated.

A keynote for historical critics of the early twentieth century was the concept of artifice or convention in the construction of a play. Perhaps the leading spokesman for this approach was E. E. Stoll, a student of G. L. Kittredge of Harvard University, himself a leading force in historical scholarship in America. Stoll vigorously insisted, in such works as *Othello: An Historical and Comparative Study* (1915), *Hamlet: An Historical and Comparative Study* (1919), and *Art and Artifice in Shakespeare* (1933), that a critic must never be sidetracked by moral, psychological, or biographical interpretations. A play, he argued, is an artifice arising out of its historical milieu. Its conventions are implicit agreements between playwright and spectator. They alter with time, and a modern reader who is ignorant of Elizabethan conventions is all too apt to be misled by his own post-Romantic preconceptions. For example, a calumniator like Iago in *Othello* is conventionally supposed to be believed by the other characters on stage. We do not need to speculate about the "realities" of Othello's being duped, and in fact we are likely to be led astray by such Romantic speculations. Stoll went so far as to affirm, in fact, that Shakespearean drama intentionally distorts reality through its theatrical conventions in order to fulfill its own existence as artifice. *Hamlet* is not a play about delay but a revenge story of a certain length, deriving many of its circumstances from Shakespeare's sources; delay is a conventional device needed to continue the story to its conclusion.

Stoll's zeal led to excessive claims for historical criticism, as one might expect in the early years of a pioneering movement. At its extreme, historical criticism came close to implying that Shakespeare was a mere product of his environment. Indeed, the movement owed many of its evolutionist assumptions to the supposedly scientific "social Darwinism" of Thomas Huxley and other late nineteenth-century social philosophers. In more recent years, however, the crusading spirit has given way to a more moderate historical criticism that continues to be an important part of Shakespearean scholarship.

Alfred Harbage, for example, in *As They Liked It* (1947) and *Shakespeare and the Rival Traditions* (1952), has analyzed the audience for which Shakespeare wrote, and the rivalry between popular and elite theatres in the London of his day. Harbage sees Shakespeare as a popular dramatist writing for a highly intelligent, enthusiastic, and socially diversified audience. G. E. Bentley has amassed an invaluable storehouse of information about *The Jacobean and Caroline Stage* (1941–1968), just as E. K. Chambers had earlier collected documents and data on *The Elizabethan Stage* (1923). Other studies by these historical scholars include Chambers' *William Shakespeare: A Study of Facts and Problems* (1930), and Bentley's *Shakespeare and His Theatre* (1964) and *The Profession of Dramatist in Shakespeare's Time* (1971). T. W. Baldwin exemplifies the historical scholar who like Stoll claims too much for the method; nevertheless, much information on Shakespeare's schooling, reading, and professional theatrical life is available in such works as *William Shakspere's Small Latine and Lesse Greeke* (1944) and *The Organization and Personnel of the Shakespearean Company* (1927). Hardin Craig uses historical method in *An Interpretation of Shakespeare* (1948).

Historical criticism has contributed greatly to our knowledge of the staging of Shakespeare's plays. George Pierce Baker, in *The Development of Shakespeare as a Dramatist* (1907), continued the line of investigation begun by Walter Raleigh. Harley Granville-Barker brought to his *Prefaces to Shakespeare* (1930, 1946) a wealth of professional theatrical experience of his own. Ever since his time, the new theatrical method of interpreting Shakespeare has been based to an ever-increasing extent on a genuine revival of interest in Shakespearean production. John Dover Wilson shows an awareness of the stage in *What Happens in Hamlet* (1935) and *The Fortunes of Falstaff* (1943). At its best, as in John Russell Brown's *Shakespeare's Plays in Performance* (1966), this critical method reveals many insights into the text that are hard to obtain without an awareness of theatrical technique.

Supporting this theatrical criticism, historical research has learned a great deal about the physical nature of Shakespeare's stage. J. C. Adams' well-known model of the Globe Playhouse, as presented in

Irwin Smith's *Shakespeare's Globe Playhouse: A Modern Reconstruction* (1956), is now generally discredited in favor of a simpler building as reconstructed by C. Walter Hodges (*The Globe Restored*, 1953), Bernard Beckerman (*Shakespeare at the Globe*, 1962), Richard Hosley ("The Playhouses and the Stage" in *A New Companion to Shakespeare Studies*, ed. K. Muir and S. Schoenbaum, 1971, and several other good essays), T. J. King (*Shakespearean Staging, 1599–1642*, 1971), and others. Information on the private theatres such as the Blackfriars, where Shakespeare's plays were also performed, appears in William Armstrong, *The Elizabethan Private Theatres* (1958), Richard Hosley, "A Reconstruction of the Second Blackfriars" (*The Elizabethan Theatre*, 1969), Glynne Wickham, *Early English Stages* (1959–1972), and others.

A related pursuit of historical criticism has been the better understanding of Shakespeare through his dramatic predecessors and contemporaries. Willard Farnham, in *The Medieval Heritage of Elizabethan Tragedy* (1936), traces the evolution of native English tragedy through the morality plays of the early Tudor period. J. M. R. Margeson's *The Origins of English Tragedy* (1967) broadens the pattern to include still other sources for Elizabethan ideas on dramatic tragedy. Bernard Spivack, in *Shakespeare and the Allegory of Evil* (1958), sees Iago, Edmund, Richard III, and other boasting villains in Shakespeare as descendants of the morality Vice. In *Shakespeare and the Idea of the Play* (1962), Anne Righter traces the device of the play-within-the-play and the metaphor of the world as a stage back to medieval and classical ideas of dramatic illusion. Irving Ribner's *The English History Play in the Age of Shakespeare* (1959, rev. 1965) examines Shakespeare's plays on English history in the context of the popular Elizabethan genre to which they belonged. Many other studies of this sort could be cited, including Glynne Wickham's *Shakespeare's Dramatic Heritage* (1969), Oscar J. Campbell's *Shakespeare's Satire* (1943), M. C. Bradbrook's *Themes and Conventions of Elizabethan Tragedy* (1935), and S. L. Bethell's *Shakespeare and the Popular Dramatic Tradition* (1944).

Another important concern of historical criticism has been the relationship between Shakespeare and the ideas of his age—cosmological, philosophical, political. Among the first scholars to study Elizabethan cosmology were Hardin Craig, in *The Enchanted Glass* (1936), and A. O. Lovejoy in *The Great Chain of Being* (1936). As their successor, E. M. W. Tillyard provided in *The Elizabethan World Picture* (1943) a definitive view of the conservative and hierarchical values which Elizabethans were supposed to have espoused. In *Shakespeare's History Plays* (1944), Tillyard extended his essentially conservative view of Shakespeare's philosophical outlook to the histories, arguing that they embody a "Tudor myth" and thereby lend support to the Tudor state. Increasingly, however, critics have disputed the extent to which Shakespeare in fact endorsed the "establishment" values of the Elizabethan world picture. Theodore Spencer, in *Shakespeare and the Nature of Man* (1942), discusses the impact on Shakespeare of radical new thinkers like Machiavelli, Montaigne, and Copernicus. In political matters, Henry A. Kelly's *Divine Providence in the England of Shakespeare's Histories* (1970) has challenged the existence of a single "Tudor myth" and has argued that Shakespeare's history plays reflect contrasting political philosophies set dramatically in conflict with one another. M. M. Reese's *The Cease of Majesty* (1961) also offers a graceful corrective to Tillyard's lucid but occasionally one-sided interpretations.

Historical criticism has also yielded many profitable specialized studies, in which Shakespeare is illuminated by a better understanding of various sciences of his day. Lily Bess Campbell approaches Shakespearean tragedy through Renaissance psychology in *Shakespeare's Tragic Heroes: Slaves of Passion* (1930). Paul Jorgensen uses Elizabethan documents on the arts of war and generalship in his study of *Shakespeare's Military World* (1956). Many similar studies examine Shakespeare in relation to law, medicine, and other professions.

"New" Criticism

As we have seen, historical criticism is still an important part of Shakespeare criticism; for better and for worse, it is the stuff of many research-oriented universities and their Ph.D. programs. Since its beginning, however, historical criticism has had to face a critical reaction generated in part by its own utilitarian and fact-gathering tendencies. The suggestions urged by Stoll and others, that Shakespeare was the product of his cultural and theatrical environment, tended to obscure his achievement as a poet. Amassing of information about Shakespeare's reading or his theatrical company often seemed to inhibit the scholar from responding to the power of words and images.

Such at any rate was the rallying cry of the *Scrutiny* group in England, centered around F. R. Leavis, L. C. Knights, and Derek Traversi, and the "new" critics in America such as Cleanth Brooks. The new critics demanded close attention to the poetry without the encumbrance of historical research. Especially at first, the new critics were openly hostile to any criticism distracting readers from the text. The satirical force of the movement can perhaps best be savored in L. C. Knights' "How Many Children Had Lady Macbeth?" (1933), prompted by the learned appendices in Bradley's *Shakespearean Tragedy:* "When was the murder of Duncan first plotted? Did Lady Macbeth really faint? Duration of the action in *Macbeth*. Macbeth's age. 'He has no children.' "

In part, the new critical movement was (and still is) a pedagogical movement, a protest against the potential dryness of historical footnoting and an insistence that classroom study of Shakespeare ought to focus on a response to his language. Cleanth Brooks' "The Naked Babe and the Cloak of Manliness" (in *The Well Wrought Urn*, 1947), offers to the teacher a model of close reading that focuses on imagery and yet attempts to see a whole vision of the play through its language. G. Wilson Knight concentrates on imagery and verbal texture in his *The Wheel of Fire* (1930), *The Imperial Theme* (1931), *The Shakespearian Tempest* (1932), *The Crown of Life* (1947), and others. William Empson is best known for his *Seven Types of Ambiguity* (1930) and *Some Versions of Pastoral* (1935). Derek Traversi's works include *An Approach to Shakespeare* (1938), *Shakespeare: The Last Phase* (1954), *Shakespeare: From Richard II to Henry V* (1957), and *Shakespeare: The Roman Plays* (1963). Perhaps the greatest critic of this school has been L. C. Knights, whose books include *Explorations* (1946), *Some Shakespearean Themes* (1959), *An Approach to Hamlet* (1960), and *Further Explorations* (1965). T. S. Eliot's perceptive and controversial observations have also had an important influence on critics of this school. Other studies making good use of the new critical method include Robert Heilman's *This Great Stage* (1948) and *Magic in the Web* (1956). Many of these critics are concerned not only with language but with the larger moral and structural implications of Shakespeare's plays as discovered through a sensitive reading of the text.

More specialized studies of Shakespearean imagery and language include Caroline Spurgeon's *Shakespeare's Imagery and What It Tells Us* (1935). Its classifications are now recognized to be overly statistical and restricted in definition, but the work has nonetheless prompted valuable further study. Among later works are Sister Miriam Joseph's *Shakespeare's Use of the Arts of Language* (1947, partly reprinted in *Rhetoric in Shakespeare's Time*, 1962), Wolfgang Clemen's *The Development of Shakespeare's Imagery* (1951), Maurice Charney's *Style in Hamlet* (1969) and *Shakespeare's Roman Plays* (1961), and M. M. Mahood's *Shakespeare's Wordplay* (1957). The study of prose has not received as much attention as that of poetry, although Brian Vickers' *The Artistry of Shakespeare's Prose* (1968) and Milton Crane's *Shakespeare's Prose* (1951) make significant contributions.

Psychological Criticism

In a sense, Freudian and other psychological criticism continues the "character" criticism of the nineteenth century. Freudian critics sometimes follow a character into a world outside the text, analyzing Hamlet (for instance) as though he were a real person whose childhood traumas can be inferred from the symptoms he displays. The most famous work in this vein is *Hamlet and Oedipus* (1910, revised 1949), by Freud's disciple Ernest Jones. According to Jones, Hamlet's delay is caused by an oedipal trauma. Hamlet's uncle, Claudius, has done exactly what Hamlet himself incestuously and subconsciously wished to do: kill his father and marry his mother. Because he cannot articulate these forbidden impulses to himself, Hamlet is paralyzed into inactivity. Jones' critical analysis thus assumes, as did Romantic critics such as Coleridge, that the central problem of *Hamlet* is one of character and motivation: why does Hamlet delay? (Many modern critics would deny that this is a problem, or would insist at least that by setting such a problem Jones has limited the number of possible answers.) Psychological criticism sometimes also reveals its affinities with nineteenth-century character criticism in its attempt to analyze Shakespeare's personality through his plays, as though the works constituted a spiritual autobiography. The terminology of psychological criticism is suspect to some readers because it is at least superficially anachronistic when dealing with a Renaissance writer. The terminology is also sometimes overburdened with technical jargon.

Nonetheless, psychological criticism has afforded many insights into Shakespeare not readily available through other modes of perception. Jones' book makes clear the intensity of Hamlet's revulsion toward women as a result of his mother's inconstancy. At a mythic level, Hamlet's story certainly resembles that of Oedipus, and Freudian criticism is often at its best when it shows us this universal aspect of the human psyche. Freudian terminology need not be anachronistic when it deals with timeless truths. Psychological criticism can reveal to us Shakespeare's preoccupation with certain types of women in his plays, such as the domineering and threatening masculine type (Joan of Arc, Margaret of Anjou) or conversely the long-suffering and patient heroine (Helena in *All's Well*, Hermione in *The Winter's Tale*). Psychological criticism is perhaps most useful in studying family relationships in Shakespeare. It also has much to say about the psychic or sexual connotations of symbol. Influential books include Norman O. Brown's *Life Against Death: The Psychoanalytical Meaning of History* (1959), and Norman Holland's *Psychoanalysis and Shakespeare* (1966) and *The Shakespearean Imagination* (1964).

Mythological Criticism

Related to psychological criticism is the search for archetypal myth in literature, as an expression of the "collective unconscious" of the human race. Behind such an approach lie the anthropological and psychological assumptions of Jung and his followers. One of the earliest studies of this sort was Gilbert Murray's *Hamlet and Orestes* (1914), analyzing the archetype of revenge for a murdered father. Clearly this custom goes far back into tribal prehistory, and emerges in varying but interrelated forms in many different societies. This anthropological universality enables us to look at *Hamlet* as the heightened manifestation of an incredibly basic story. *Hamlet* gives shape to urgings that are a part of our innermost social being. However civilized we may think ourselves, we are formed by our past; the struggle between the civilized and the primitive goes on in us as in the play of *Hamlet*.

The vast interdisciplinary character of myth criticism leaves it vulnerable to charges of speculativeness and glib theorizing. At its best, however, myth criticism can illuminate the nature of our responses as audience to a work of art. Northrop Frye argues, in *A Natural Perspective* (1965), that we respond to mythic patterns by imagining ourselves participating in them communally. The Greek drama emerged, after all, from Dionysiac ritual. All drama celebrates in one form or another the primal myths of vegetation, from the death of the year to the renewal or resurrection of life. In his most influential book, *Anatomy of Criticism* (1957), Frye argues that mythic criticism presents a universal scheme for the investigation of all literature, or all art, since art is itself the ordering of our most primal stirrings. Frye sees in drama (as in other literature) a fourfold correspondence to the cyclical pattern of the year: comedy is associated with spring, romance with summer, tragedy with autumn, and satire with winter. Historically, civilization moves through a recurrent cycle from newness and flourishing to decadence and decay; this cycle expresses itself culturally in a progression from epic and romance to tragedy, to social realism, and finally to irony and satire before the cycle renews itself. Thus, according to Frye, the genres of dramatic literature (and of other literary forms as well) have an absolute and timeless relationship to myth and cultural history. That is why we as audience respond so deeply to form and meaning as contained in genre. C. L. Barber, in *Shakespeare's Festive Comedy* (1959), makes a similar argument: our enjoyment of comedy arises from our intuitive appreciation for such "primitive" social customs as Saturnalian revels, May games, and fertility rites. John Holloway offers an anthropological study of Shakespeare's tragedies in *The Story of the Night* (1961).

Frye's critical system has not been without its detractors. For example, Frederick Crews (*Psychoanalysis and Literary Process*, 1970), argues that Frye's system is too self-contained in its ivory tower, too much an abstract artifact of the critical mind, to be "relevant" to the social purposes of art. Nevertheless, Frye continues to be one of the most influential critics of the late twentieth century.

Typological Criticism

Another controversy of the later twentieth century has to do with the Christian interpretation of Shakespeare. Do the images and allusions of Shakespeare's plays show him to be deeply immersed in a Christian culture inherited from the Middle Ages? Does he reveal a typological cast of mind, so common in medieval literature, whereby a story can suggest through analogy a universal religious archetype? For example, does the mysterious duke in *Measure for Measure* suggest to us a God-figure, hovering unseen throughout the play to test men's wills and then to present them with an omniscient but merciful judgment? Is the wanton slaughter of the good Cordelia in *King Lear* reminiscent of the Passion of Christ? Can Portia in *The Merchant of Venice* be seen as an angelic figure descending from Belmont into the fallen human world of Venice? Often the operative question we must ask is, how far should such analogy be pursued? Richard II unquestionably likens himself to Christ betrayed by the disciples, and at times the play evokes images of Adam banished from Paradise; but do these allusions coalesce into a sustained analogy?

Among the most enthusiastic searchers after Christian meaning are J. A. Bryant in *Hippolyta's View* (1961) and Roy Battenhouse in *Shakespearean Tragedy: Its Art and Christian Premises* (1969). Their efforts have encountered stern opposition, however. One notable dissenter is Roland M. Frye, whose *Shakespeare and Christian Doctrine* (1963) argues that Shakespeare cannot be shown to have known much Renaissance theology, and that in any case his plays are concerned with human drama rather than with otherworldly questions of damnation or salvation. Frye's argument stresses the incompatibility of Christianity and tragedy, as does also D. G. James' *The Dream of Learning* (1951) and Clifford Leech's *Shakespeare's Tragedies and Other Studies in Seventeenth-Century Drama* (1950). Virgil Whitaker's *The Mirror Up to Nature* (1965) sees religion as an essential element in Shakespeare's plays, but argues that Shakespeare uses the religious knowledge of his audience as a shortcut to characterization and meaning rather than as an ideological weapon. The controversy will doubtless long continue, even though the typological critics have had to assume a defensive posture.

Eclectic Criticism

In the increasingly diverse world of Shakespeare criticism, several other "schools" certainly ought to be mentioned. A group of critics at the University of Chicago, including R. S. Crane, Richard McKeon, Elder Olson, and Norman Maclean, has espoused a formal or structural approach to criticism using Aristotle as its point of departure. Crane is reacting to the "new" critics who, in his view, have restricted the kinds of answers they could obtain by limiting themselves to one methodology. Critics hostile to the "Chicago" school have responded, however, that Crane's own approach has tended to produce its own dogmatism. Another controversial brand of criticism is the existentialist approach of Jan Kott, whose *Shakespeare: Our Contemporary* (1964, translated from the Polish) sees Shakespeare as a dramatist of the absurd and the grotesque. In this view, Shakespearean plays are often close to "black" comedy or comedy of the absurd. Indeed, Kott has inspired productions that expose traditional values to skepticism and ridicule. Portia and Bassanio in *The Merchant of Venice* become scheming adventurers; Henry V becomes a priggish warmonger. This sardonic undercutting brings Shakespeare closer to modern theatre and indeed to the modern world, but often at the expense of the language of Shakespeare's plays.

At its best, however, late twentieth-century criticism transcends the splintering effect of a heterogeneous critical tradition to achieve a synthesis that is at once unified and multiform in its vision. The eclectic approach aims at overall balance and a reinforcement of one critical approach through the methodology of another. Many of the works already cited in this introduction refuse to be constricted by methodological boundaries. The best historical criticism makes use of close explication of the text where appropriate; image patterns can certainly reinforce mythological patterns; typological interpretation, when sensibly applied, serves the cause of image study. Some fine books are so eclectic in their method that one hesitates to apply the label of any one critical school. Among such works are Maynard Mack's *King Lear in Our Time* (1965), David Young's *Something of Great Constancy: The Art of A Midsummer Night's Dream* (1966), R. G. Hunter's *Shakespeare and the Comedy of Forgiveness* (1965), and Paul Jorgensen's *Our Naked Frailties: Sensational Art and Meaning in Macbeth* (1971).

EDITIONS AND EDITORS OF SHAKESPEARE

The earliest complete edition of Shakespeare's plays was the so-called First Folio of 1623, sponsored by Shakespeare's theatrical colleagues John Heminges and Henry Condell. (A "folio" book was one in which the printing sheets were folded only once, each producing two "leaves" or four rather large printed pages of about 13½ x 8¼ inches. In a "quarto" book the sheets were folded twice, producing eight pages half the folio size.) The First Folio brought together eighteen plays that had previously been published in single quarto volumes, and eighteen plays that had never before been published. It did not include Shakespeare's nondramatic poetry, of which *Venus and Adonis* and *The Rape of Lucrece* had been published in 1593–1594 and the sonnets in 1609. Nor did it include *Pericles*.

The nature of the early printed texts, and their relationship to what Shakespeare actually wrote, is a complex subject requiring some understanding of the physical process by which Elizabethan plays were written, prepared for staging, licensed, and printed. What sorts of manuscripts lie behind the various printed early editions we have, and how were those manuscripts modified successively by scribes, governmental officials, theatrical producers, actors, editors, compositors, proofreaders, and editors of subsequent editions? Let us start at the beginning, with the manuscripts themselves.

Manuscripts: "Foul Papers"

Most often, Elizabethan dramatic companies obtained a play by commissioning a known professional dramatist to write a new play, to revise an old one, or to collaborate with another author. Usually the company paid the dramatist a flat fee. Shakespeare, on the other hand, was a "sharer" in the Chamberlain's (later the King's) company—that is, he was part owner and took a share of the profits. He seems to have written plays not for a fee but as his chief contribution to the company's activities. Whatever the financial arrangement between author and company, in any case, the play became the property of the acting company and the author gave up his individual right to sell it elsewhere. Moreover, he ordinarily wrote the play with a view not to publication but to performance. Occasionally, a literary-minded author like Ben Jonson would see his plays through the press (and be scoffed at for his pretentiousness). Shakespeare, however, almost certainly did not do this. The quarto texts of his plays that appeared during his lifetime show no trace of having been prepared for the reader. They are playhouse documents.

When Shakespeare had finished writing a play, he presumably submitted a readable manuscript to his acting company. This draft in his handwriting, or any earlier draft, went by the name of "foul papers," as distinguished from "fair papers" or a clean copy that might be prepared by the author or a playhouse scribe. Actually, the foul papers need not have been especially messy, although a certain amount of deletion, interlineation, inconsistency, and illegibility was inevitable. These foul papers were usually preserved by the acting company and were often turned over to the printer when the company decided to sell its rights in a play. The company usually preferred to hold on to its prompt-book copy of the play (see below), and to dispose of the foul papers as of little further value. A manuscript of this sort naturally posed some difficulties for the compositor.

Among the Shakespearean quarto texts thought to have been based on foul papers are the first quartos of *Titus Andronicus*, *Love's Labour's Lost*, *A Midsummer Night's Dream*, *Richard II*, *The Merchant of Venice*, *Much Ado about Nothing*, and *1* and *2 Henry IV*, and the second quartos of *Romeo and Juliet* and *Hamlet*. Three more first quartos—*Troilus and Cressida*, *Othello*, and *King Lear*—were also based apparently on foul papers, although each is an anomalous case. In addition, the First Folio contains several newly printed plays based on foul papers or a transcript thereof, including *The Comedy of Errors*, *The Taming of the Shrew*, *All's Well that Ends Well*, *Timon of Athens*, *Coriolanus*, and *Henry VIII*. Two more Folio plays are based on transcripts of foul papers by the scrivener Ralph Crane: *Measure for Measure* and *The Winter's Tale*. The text of *King John* seems to have been based on foul papers also, but with some reference to a prompt-book in the final two acts.

At their best, foul papers are close to what Shakespeare wrote, but they are also potentially laden with error. Some foul-paper texts preserve Shakespeare's work in an early state of composition: *Timon of Athens*, for example, seems never to have been finished by Shakespeare, since the text we have retains glaring inconsistencies and redundancies that he presumably would have straightened out in a final version. *Love's Labour's Lost* contains uncanceled duplicatory passages. On the other hand, *The Merchant of Venice*, *Richard II*, and the *Henry IV* plays are very good texts, and *Much Ado* is almost ready for stage production; the names of two actors appear among the speech-prefixes, although other irregularities suggest that the manuscript was in the last stages of authorial revision. Foul papers therefore represent a whole spectrum of states from unrevised manuscript to a text that has been thoroughly worked over.

Unfortunately, no manuscript of a regular Shakespearean play has survived today. Other early dramatic manuscripts have survived, however, enabling textual scholars to determine when a printed text has been based upon foul papers. The telltale characteristics are these: vagueness in specifying the number of supernumeraries needed for a scene, lack of precision in the marking of entrances and especially exits, authorial stage-directions that tend to describe stage business or the emotional states of the characters more than a businesslike prompt-book would require, speech prefixes that inconsistently refer to a character both by his personal name and his generic title, and so on. Thus, in *Love's Labour's Lost*, Navarre, Armado, and Holofernes are at times referred to as King, Braggart, and Pedant; Navarre is also called Ferdinand. See Appendix I at the end of this volume for a play-by-play summary of the kind of manuscript thought to lie behind each of Shakespeare's plays and poems.

Licensing for Performance

Before a Shakespearean play could go into production, it had to be licensed by the Master of the Revels, an officer of the royal household responsible for supervising court entertainments. Since the beginning of Elizabeth's reign, and even earlier, dramatic performances throughout England had been made subject to governmental control. Elizabeth had authorized municipal and other local governments to scrutinize plays performed within their jurisdictions. In the vicinity of London, however, where municipal hostility toward the theatre was particularly strong, she took the unusual step in 1581 of transferring licensing power to her own Master of the Revels. Since many public plays came to court, as we have seen, Elizabeth was inclined to protect the players against the city authorities in this way, and to adopt the useful fiction that public performances were rehearsals of plays intended for her ultimate benefit.

The Master of the Revels did occasionally censor Shakespeare's plays. For example, the scene of Richard II's deposition, omitted from the three earliest quarto editions of the play, seems to have been disallowed for acting during Elizabeth's lifetime. (She was sensitive to a widespread and libelous analogy comparing her with Richard.) More often, one suspects, the mere threat of censorship was sufficient to keep the London dramatic companies in line. The Tudor establishment had no intention of tolerating openly seditious criticism in the drama. Generally, the Master of the Revels was more concerned with questions of religion and politics than with morals. Edmund Tilney served as Master of the Revels from 1579 to 1610, when he was succeeded by his deputy, Sir George Buc. In 1622 the office passed to Sir Henry Herbert.

The Prompt-Book

The document on which the Master of the Revels affixed his seal of approval was the prompt-book or prompt-copy or playbook—that is, the version prepared by the acting company for use in actual production. Usually this version was a fair copy of the manuscript, readied for stage performance—that is, with the technical inconsistencies weeded out and with more businesslike stage directions added. Occasionally the author's last draft might be converted into a prompt-book, if it was legible enough. Whatever manuscript was thus used, the prompt-copy would be sure to normalize any inconsistent speech prefixes (such as those already noted in *Love's Labour's Lost*), in order to avoid confusion for actors and stage managers. Stage directions would tend to concentrate on technical matters such as entrances, exits, and occasional specific effects. In *Julius Caesar*, for example, we find such stage directions as "Enter Brutus in his orchard," "Thunder and lightning. Enter Julius Caesar in his nightgown," and "Brutus goes into the pulpit."

Comparatively few of Shakespeare's texts are derived from prompt-books, actually, since the prompt-book, bearing the official license of the Master of the Revels, was an invaluable document if the play was ever to be revived. Of the nineteen Shakespearean plays published in quarto prior to 1623, not one was printed from a prompt-book. The author's foul papers were far more expendable once the prompt-book had been prepared. Nevertheless, the First Folio does contain a few plays printed from prompt-books or transcripts of prompt-books, including *As You Like It*, *Twelfth Night*, *Julius Caesar*, and *Macbeth* (in a cut version). Two more plays, *The Two Gentlemen of Verona* and *The Merry Wives of Windsor*, were printed from transcriptions by Ralph Crane of prompt-books. Four additional plays seem to have been set from Shakespeare's drafts (or transcriptions of the drafts) that had already been annotated by the stage adapter, although not yet actually made into prompt-books: *1 Henry VI*, *Antony and Cleopatra*, perhaps *Cymbeline*, and *The Tempest* (in a transcription by Ralph Crane).

Prompt-books are not as likely to correspond with the author's intentions as his own papers, and indeed some prompt-books probably reflect changes occurring in the theatre over a period of years. A prompt-book might be altered for the revival of an old favorite, or might even represent a cut performance intended to be taken on tour—as perhaps in the case of *Macbeth.* Such a text might incorporate non-Shakespearean material; *Macbeth* seems to contain songs and lines attributed to Thomas Middleton.

Prompt-books were also used to copy out individual parts for each actor. Although such actors' "rolls," as they were called, could conceivably have been used to assemble a printed text, no Shakespearean play is known to have been printed in this fashion. A few plays, such as *The Two Gentlemen of Verona* and *The Winter's Tale,* were once thought to have been made up out of actors' rolls, since the texts of these plays generally omit stage directions and group characters' names at the head of each scene; but these traits are now known to be the identifying characteristics of the professional scrivener named Ralph Crane. Apparently, Crane was employed to prepare a number of fair copies (also including *The Tempest, The Merry Wives of Windsor,* and *Measure for Measure*) for the printers of the First Folio.

The Bad Quartos

An acting company did not normally like to see its plays in print. On occasion, to be sure, a company might disband and sell its plays, or experience financial difficulties and sell some older plays for ready money, but ordinarily the company regarded its plays as the very key to its economic prosperity. Popular plays that enjoyed long runs, and could later be revived, were especially valuable. Hence the company guarded carefully its authorial manuscripts and prompt-books, and did not usually permit other copies to be made or circulated.

By the same token, however, the temptation for some unscrupulous bookseller to pirate an edition of a popular play was obviously great. And, unfortunately, no copyright law protected the acting companies from such piracy. If a bookseller could obtain a dramatic text in any way, all he had to do was to present his book at Stationers' Hall and enter it in the Stationers' Register, or official record book of the London Company of Stationers (i.e., booksellers). By paying a fee, usually sixpence, he reserved the right to publish the work he had thus entered. This right had considerable legal force. Although authors and acting companies could not copyright their plays, the stationers or booksellers enjoyed a tight monopoly. Their London Company of Stationers had a patent from the crown to restrict the number of presses operating in London, the number of books that could be printed, and so on. Legal safeguards were all on the side of the booksellers.

To protect themselves, the acting companies sometimes formed friendly relationships with cooperative booksellers and entered agreements with them designed to forestall the piratical activities of less scrupulous publishers. The acting company might allow a friendly bookseller or printer to register a play for later publication. For example, on July 22, 1598, the printer James Roberts entered in the Stationers' Register "a booke of the Marchaunt of Venyce, or otherwise called the Jewe of Venyce, Prouided, that yt bee not prynted by the said James Robertes or anye other whatsoeuer without lycence first had from the Right honorable the lord Chamberlen." This is what is generally known as a "staying entry," since Roberts agrees to "stay" or withhold publication pending further authorization from the acting company's patron. Such an entry would have prevented publication of *The Merchant of Venice* by an unauthorized publisher. Similar entries occur in August of 1600 for *Much Ado about Nothing, As You Like It,* and *Henry V.* The stratagem did not always work—an unauthorized quarto of *Henry V* appeared in August of 1600—but it did sometimes achieve its purpose.

Despite all precautions, unauthorized or "bad" quartos were fairly common. After all, the plays were publicly performed; a would-be pirate had easy access to repeated performances. Heminges and Condell, in their prefatory letter "To the great Variety of Readers" of the First Folio, complain about "diuerse stolne and surreptitious copies, maimed, and deformed by the frauds and stealthes of iniurious impostors." Thomas Heywood similarly protests against pirated editions of his plays, which "haue (vnknowen to me, and without any of my direction) accidentally come into the Printers handes, and therefore so corrupt and mangled, (coppied onely by the eare) that I haue bene vnable to know them" (Preface to *The Rape of Lucrece,* 1608).

How were such pirated texts obtained? Heywood says they were "coppied onely by the eare." Elsewhere, in *Pleasant Dialogues and Dramas* (1637), he complains about the pirating of one of his plays "by Stenography." The stenographic hypothesis is not now widely accepted, however, chiefly because the systems of shorthand available in Shakespeare's day were inadequate and because attempts at shorthand reporting might well have been detected by an alert acting company. Besides, the pirated texts we have seem to rely heavily on the use of memory.

Textual scholarship now generally supports the findings of W. W. Greg that most pirated texts were put together by "memorial reconstruction." The usual culprits seem to have been one or more actors, in league with an unscrupulous printer. Most pirates were temporary actors hired to perform minor roles, rather than actor-sharers having a vested interest in the acting company and its stock of plays. Possibly one or more such minor actors got together and slowly recited what they could remember of a play, while a scribe took down what they recited. The reporter or reporters of a pirated text can sometimes tentatively be identified by the relative accuracy of certain roles. For example, the actor who perhaps doubled the minor parts of Marcellus and Lucianus in *Hamlet* may have helped in the memorial reconstruction of the bad quarto of that play.

A bad quarto put together by memorial reconstruction can be identified with some accuracy by modern textual methods. Such a text tends to give a fairly accurate rendition of the overall plot, but garbles some speeches, transfers or misplaces lines of dialogue or even whole scenes, borrows scraps of phrases from other plays in which the actor-reporters may have acted, mislineates blank verse or crudely versifies passages of prose, ad-libs freely in half-remembered parts of the play, and so on. A bad quarto is always shorter than the regular version. Visual impressions are often vivid, since the actor-reporters are remembering things they have seen on stage. The stage directions tend to be more frequent and more detailed than in either an author's manuscript or a prompt-book.

Seven bad quartos have been identified. An unregistered and memorially reconstructed quarto of *Romeo and Juliet*, published in 1597, was answered two years later by an authorized second quarto, "Newly corrected, augmented, and amended." (A similar phrase, "Newly corrected and augmented," appears in the title of the 1598 quarto of *Love's Labour's Lost*, suggesting that a now-lost bad quarto of that play had appeared prior to 1598.) The famous bad quarto of *Hamlet* appeared in 1603, containing apparently some echoes of the lost pre-Shakespearean *Hamlet* known to have been in existence by 1589. Other bad quartos include *Henry V* (1600), *The Merry Wives of Windsor* (1602), and *Pericles* (1609—the only substantive text we have of this play). In addition, the quartos published in 1594 and 1595 as *The First part of the Contention betwixt the two famous Houses of Yorke and Lancaster* and *The true Tragedie of Richard Duke of Yorke* are now generally recognized to have been the memorially reconstructed bad quartos of *2* and *3 Henry VI.*

A few texts seem to have been put together by unusual circumstances that somewhat resemble memorial reconstruction. *The Taming of the Shrew* was not printed until the Folio of 1623, but a quarto did appear in 1594 of a very similar play called *The Taming of A Shrew.* Its place names and characters' names are different from those of the Folio version, and the language differs throughout. Some scholars still regard the play as a source for Shakespeare. Nevertheless, the generally held view today is that *A Shrew* is a special kind of pirated text, one in which a rival dramatist has changed the language and the names of the characters to make the work seem his own. A different sort of anomaly is seen in *Richard III.* The 1597 quarto shows many unmistakable signs of memorial reconstruction, and yet the text is much more accurate and full than in most bad quartos. Shakespeare's own company may have collaborated on this memorial reconstruction, perhaps while they were on tour and had no prompt-book with them. A somewhat similar circumstance occurs in the case of *King Lear:* the quarto of 1608 seems to have been based on a draft to which Shakespeare's company somehow contributed.

The Good Quartos

Despite their general unwillingness to see their plays in print, acting companies did sometimes sell texts to the printers for ready cash or to correct bad quartos that had already appeared (as in the case of the good quartos of *Romeo and Juliet*, 1599, *Hamlet*, 1604–1605, and probably *Love's Labour's Lost*, 1598). The good quartos were based generally on Shakespeare's own drafts, or transcripts of them. Good first quartos include *Titus Andronicus* (1594), *Richard II* (1597), *1 Henry IV* (1598), *2 Henry IV* (1600), *A Midsummer Night's Dream* (1600), *The Merchant of Venice* (1600), *Much Ado about Nothing* (1600), *Troilus and Cressida* (1609, printed seemingly without permission of Shakespeare's company), and the late first quarto of *Othello* (1622). This is a short list and is sporadic in its time schedule; Shakespeare's company did not regularly dispose of its plays to the printers. Once a play had appeared in print, however, it was apt to be reprinted. *Richard III* went through six quartos before the Folio of 1623. At the other extreme we have *2 Henry IV*, issued in only one quarto prior to 1623; possibly the printers ran off a large number of copies in anticipation of heavy sales. Some quarto texts continued to appear after the Folio of 1623.

Before a play could be printed, it had to be licensed for performance. The licensing agency responsible for printed matter was a panel of London clergymen known as the "correctors of the press," operating under the authority of the Privy Council, the Bishop of London, the Archbishop of Canterbury, and the Lord Chamberlain. In 1606, Parliament passed a law forbidding references to the Deity in the texts of plays.

The Pavier Collection of 1619

A few years before the Shakespearean Folio appeared in 1623, a bookseller named Thomas Pavier and a printer named William Jaggard made an apparent attempt to collect Shakespeare's plays. Pavier already owned the publishing rights to *Henry V*, for in August of 1600 he had received assignment of rights to the bad quarto of the play published in that year. He brought out a second quarto of *Henry V* in 1602, and a third (printed by Jaggard) in 1619 as part of his anthologizing project. In 1602 Pavier had also obtained the rights to *The First part of the Contention* and *The true Tragedie of Richard Duke of Yorke*, now generally regarded as the bad quartos of *2* and *3 Henry VI.* Pavier issued them in 1619 under the combined title *The Whole Contention betweene the two Famous Houses, Lancaster and Yorke*, printed by Jaggard. Pavier also included in his collection two pseudo-Shakespearean plays to which he owned the rights, *A Yorkshire Tragedy* and *Sir John Oldcastle*, and five Shakespearean plays to which he may have obtained rights or which he considered to be unowned: *A Midsummer Night's Dream*, *The Merchant of Venice*, *The Merry Wives of Windsor*, *King Lear*, and *Pericles*.

Pavier's evident intention was to publish these ten plays in a single volume, and indeed one such copy exists today in the Folger Library. His scheme was frustrated, however, seemingly by the Lord Chamberlain at the instigation of Shakespeare's company. Pavier chose the expedient of publishing his plays separately, some with fraudulently early dates and names of publishers in an apparent attempt to obscure the fact of new publication. None of Pavier's texts provides any independent textual authority, for all were copied from earlier quartos.

Publishing Rights for the 1623 Folio

Pavier's dubious and abortive undertaking may possibly have given impetus to a more legitimate edition of Shakespeare's collected plays, although Shakespeare's company may already have been contemplating such an honor to its famous playwright. Ben Jonson's folio collection of plays in 1616 had established a major precedent for such a volume, despite the scorn of those who regarded all plays as subliterary. The large and tomelike folio format, normally reserved for edifying religious works and the like, might now be used also for a collection of plays.

The first task facing the supervisors of the Folio collection, Heminges and Condell, was the assembling of publishing rights to those eighteen Shakespearean plays that had already appeared in print. The most efficient means of doing so was to form a syndicate of publishers who already owned the rights to a large number of the plays. The colophon at the very end of the First Folio names those who took part: "Printed at the Charges of W. Jaggard, Ed. Blount, I. Smithweeke, and W. Aspley, 1623." William Jaggard had succeeded to the printing business of James Roberts in 1608. Despite Jaggard's part in the printing of the Pavier quartos of 1619, he evidently remained on good terms with Shakespeare's company and became (together with his son Isaac) the printer of the 1623 Folio. (William Jaggard died in November of 1623, but his son carried on the business.) Edward Blount had registered *Antony and Cleopatra* and *Pericles* in 1608, though he seems to have overlooked the fact, for *Antony* was re-registered in 1623, and *Pericles* never appeared in the Folio. John Smethwick had received from Nicholas Ling the rights to *Love's Labour's Lost*, *Romeo and Juliet*, and *Hamlet* in 1607. William Aspley owned the rights to *Much Ado about Nothing* and *2 Henry IV*. One other previously published play, *A Midsummer Night's Dream*, was "derelict" or no longer assigned to a publisher.

Some further negotiations must still have been necessary, with Richard Bonian and Henry Walley for *Troilus and Cressida*, with Nathaniel Butter for *King Lear*, with Thomas Pavier for *2* and *3 Henry VI*, *Titus Andronicus*, and *Henry V*, perhaps also with Edward White for *Titus Andronicus*, with Matthew Law for *Richard III*, *Richard II*, and *1 Henry IV*, with Thomas Heyes for *The Merchant of Venice*, with Arthur Johnson for *The Merry Wives of Windsor*, and with Thomas Walkley for *Othello*. The last-minute inclusion of *Troilus and Cressida* between the histories and the tragedies with incomplete pagination may suggest that Bonian and Walley held out for a long time.

Eighteen plays had never before been printed. To secure rights to these plays, Messrs. Blount and Isaac Jaggard caused the following entry to be made in the Stationers' Register on November 8, 1623:

> Mr Blounte Isaak Jaggard. Entred for their Copie vnder the hands of Mr Doctor Worrall and Mr Cole, warden, Mr William Shakspeers Comedyes Histories, and Tragedyes soe manie of the said Copies as are not formerly entred to other men. vizt. Comedyes. The Tempest. The two gentlemen of Verona. Measure for Measure. The Comedy of Errors. As you Like it. All's well that ends well. Twelft night. The winters tale. Histories. The thirde parte of Henry the sixt. Henry the eight. Coriolanus. Timon of Athens. Julius Caesar. Tragedies. Mackbeth. Anthonie and Cleopatra. Cymbeline.

The Stationers' Register list includes only sixteen names, since *The Taming of the Shrew* and *King John* were considered to have been published previously: *The Taming of A Shrew* and *The Troublesome Reign of King John*, now generally regarded as a bad quarto and a source respectively, had appeared in print in 1594 and 1591. Two plays on the list had actually been registered previously, *As You Like It* and *Antony and Cleopatra*. "The thirde parte of Henry the sixt" refers to *1 Henry VI*, since the other two *Henry VI* plays had already been published as bad quartos.

The Texts Used for the 1623 Folio

In addition to securing publishing rights, Heminges and Condell and their associates had the further task of selecting copy from which the printers were to set up their work. In the case of the eighteen as yet unpublished plays, the editors selected the best manuscripts they could find: author's drafts for *The Comedy of Errors*, *All's Well*, and others, prompt-books for *As You Like It*, *Twelfth Night*, and so on. Apparently the editors planned at first to give the printers clean new transcriptions of such plays, for the first four plays in the Folio—*The Tempest*, *The Two Gentlemen of Verona*, *The Merry Wives of Windsor*, and *Measure for Measure*—were all printed from copies made by the professional scribe Ralph Crane. If the editors had planned to continue this practice throughout the volume, however, they abandoned it after the fourth play and turned instead to a variety of sorts of copy.

The complicated choices involved plays that had already been published. Printers, then as now, preferred to work from printed copy because of its legibility. Yet some published Shakespearean plays were bad quartos, the "stolne and surreptitious copies" that Heminges and Condell had vowed to replace with more perfect copies. Although one might suppose that Heminges and Condell would have set aside bad quartos entirely, they did not always do so, perhaps because the manuscript alternatives were illegible or defective. In other cases, the editors had to make a more subtle choice between a "good" quarto and a still better manuscript. What the editors sometimes did in such cases was to use the inferior printed text but to annotate it by reference to a superior manuscript. This process of annotation might vary widely in its degree of thoroughness.

The use of bad quartos as copy was, to be sure, unusual. Yet it did sometimes happen. The Folio text of *Henry V* seems to have been set from pages of the second and third quartos, which were derived from the pirated quarto of 1600; fortunately, those pages had been conscientiously corrected by reference to a manuscript source—probably Shakespeare's own papers—and hence provided a fairly reliable text. The Folio texts of *2* and *3 Henry VI* may similarly have been set from pages of the second and third quartos of the pirated texts of those plays, as corrected by reference to independent manuscript sources. Even in these questionable cases, an attempt seems to have been made to overcome the limitations of the bad quarto copy.

More often, one of the good quartos was corrected by checking it against a manuscript source. The Folio text of *Titus Andronicus*, for example, was evidently derived from a copy of the third quarto, but that copy may have been corrected by reference to an annotated copy of the second quarto which had been used as a prompt-book. In any case, a portion of Act III that is missing from all the early quartos must have been derived from some manuscript source. Other texts of this kind include *Richard III*, *Richard II*, *Troilus and Cressida*, *Othello* and *King Lear;* disputed cases include *Hamlet* and *2 Henry IV*. See Appendix I for statements on the texts of each play.

The Printing of the 1623 Folio

The printing of the 1623 Folio continued from April of 1621 to December of 1623 in the printing shop of William and Isaac Jaggard. The compositors who actually set the type were, according to Charlton Hinman (*The Printing and Proof-Reading of the First Folio of Shakespeare*, 2 vols., 1963), five in number. For convenient reference they are designated as compositors A through E. A and B were the principal workmen. E was evidently an inept apprentice, unfortunately brought into the project just in time to work on several of the tragedies.

Compositors had to rely on their ability to memorize whole lines of verse at a time, since they needed to look at the type they were setting manually. Hence, they were apt to make mistakes based on imperfect remembering. Less skillful compositors not infrequently introduced errors by transposing words in a line, substituting a new word for what was in the copy, or maiming the scansion of a line of verse by adding or subtracting syllables.

Compositors were largely responsible for the "pointing" or punctuation of the text. They also usually imposed their own normalized spelling practices on their copy. Since no copy editor went over the materials first to normalize spelling, the compositors did what they could. Elizabethan spelling was in any case chaotic by our standards. The modern textual business of identifying compositors relies mainly on discovering the characteristic spelling habits of each.

Rather than setting their pages in numbered sequence right through an entire play, as we would assume, the compositors of the Folio used a system known as "casting off": that is, they estimated the amount of copy needed to fill a page of type, and divided the whole text up into portions of the estimated correct length. They could then set page twelve right after they had set page one, and immediately start printing these two pages side by side on the same "forme" or side of a sheet. (When three large sheets are folded once and gathered together, the result is a "quire" of twelve pages with pages one and twelve printed on the outer side or "forme" of the outermost sheet, pages two and eleven on the inner forme of that same sheet, pages three and ten on the outer forme of the middle sheet, and so on.) Since type was expensive and in limited supply in a printing shop, the type had to be redistributed into the fonts as soon as the requisite number of copies of any forme had been run off. Casting off enabled the printers to print and redistribute the type of pages one and twelve without having to wait for all the intervening pages to be set up also. (The reappearance of distributed type is in fact the clue by which Hinman was able to discover that the Folio had been set up throughout by casting off rather than by printing in sequence.)

Despite the advantages of flexibility, casting off had its disadvantages. If a compositor discovered he had been given too little copy for a page of text, he had to stretch his material by heavy "leading." If, on the other hand, he discovered he had been given too much copy for a page, he had to crowd his lines, print verse as prose, or even eliminate words and lines. Knowledge of this sort of printing information is useful to a modern editor, since it enables him to determine when the compositors may have interfered with the text that Shakespeare wrote.

When a compositor had completed one entire forme, consisting of two pages of text to be printed on one side of a large printing sheet, the forme went into the press and the requisite number of copies was run off by hand. One side of the sheet, either the inner or outer forme, was printed at a time. Proofreading, or "press correction," took place while the printing continued. At first, a number of sides of the sheet would be printed in their uncorrected state, that is,

THE FOLGER SHAKESPEARE LIBRARY

Although printing in Shakespeare's time was a cumbersome and time-consuming process usually conducted by press-operators more interested in profit than in accuracy and consistency, the printers of the First Folio seem to have been more conscientious and skilled than most.

entirely unproofread. When the press corrector found errors, the presses would be stopped in order that the errors might be corrected, after which printing would continue. Such interruptions might occur several times. Uncorrected or partially corrected sheets were not destroyed, however; paper was too costly for that. Later, when the stack of sheets printed on one side were printed on the other side, errors would again be corrected as printing continued. Ultimately, when the sheets were gathered by three's into a quire of twelve pages and then sewn into a complete volume, no single copy of the Folio was apt to be exactly like another. In fact, the many copies of the First Folio extant today differ from one another in their press variants. Even though we might regard this as evidence of carelessness, Jaggard's work on the First Folio seems to have been scrupulous when judged by the standards of the day.

About 1200 copies of the First Folio were printed and sold for twenty shillings. Approximately 230 copies survive today, of which 80 are to be found in the collection of the Folger Library, Washington, D.C.

The Later Folios

When after nine years the first edition of the Folio had been sold out, a second edition was printed in 1632 by Thomas Cotes. He had succeeded to the Jaggards' business after the death of Isaac in 1627. The Second Folio merely reprinted the text of the First Folio together with a considerable number of editorial emendations. These have no independent textual authority, although some of the more commonsense suggestions have since been adopted by modern editors. A third edition appeared in 1663, based on the second. A second issue of this same third edition in 1664 included seven new plays: *Pericles*, *The London Prodigal*, *Thomas Lord Cromwell*, *Sir John Oldcastle*, *The Puritan*, *A Yorkshire Tragedy*, and *Locrine*. Of these, only *Pericles* has gained general acceptance in the Shakespeare canon (see Appendix I and the play introduction). A fourth edition of the Folio in 1685, based on the third, also included the seven new plays. Like the second and third editions, this fourth edition offered many emendations or new errors not based on any textual authority.

Later Editions

The first editor of Shakespeare in the modern sense of the term was Nicholas Rowe. His seven-volume edition of 1709 (reissued in nine volumes in 1714) was based on the Fourth Folio, to which the publisher Jacob Tonson had acquired the rights. Rowe began many practices we now regard as standard for a reader's edition. He provided a complete list of *dramatis personae* for each play, whereas the earlier folios had done so only sporadically. He similarly extended the practice of announcing the locale at the beginning of a scene. He marked entrances and exits with more care than in the folios, and provided more extensive division of the plays into acts and scenes. Although he did not consult Shakespeare's early texts, Rowe did offer a number of textual emendations. He also modernized spelling and punctuation.

Alexander Pope was Shakespeare's next editor. Pope's text, completed in 1725 in six volumes (reissued in 1728), was printed from a copy of Rowe's edition with Pope's annotations. Pope excluded *Pericles* and the spurious plays that had been added to the Third Folio. He completed Rowe's task of indicating locale for each of the scenes, and also completed the division of the text into acts and scenes. In fact, Pope used the "continental" system of marking a new scene whenever a major character comes on stage, so that his text contained many more scenes than did other editions. Most importantly, Pope extensively rewrote Shakespeare. Although he claimed to have consulted the early quartos, Pope regarded Shakespeare's text as something to be "improved" because it had been written in a barbaric age for ignorant spectators. He excised parts of Shakespeare's text that he considered vulgar, regularized lines that struck him as defective, eliminated anachronisms he regarded as indecorous, and the like. Pope's edition reflected the "refined" eighteenth-century view of Shakespeare as a very rough diamond in need of polishing. As a result, Pope removed Shakespearean editing far indeed from any serious attempt to recover what Shakespeare had actually written.

A corrective was in order. Lewis Theobald took up the challenge, though he was to be rewarded for his pains by being crowned the King of Dullness in Pope's *The Dunciad* (1728 version). Theobald's edition appeared in 1733 and was later reissued several times. He was the first editor to consult the folios and quartos. He did not, however, wholly recognize the textual value of those quartos. He also failed to base his text directly on the earliest substantive texts; instead, he annotated a copy of Pope's edition, just as Pope had annotated Rowe and Rowe had annotated the Fourth Folio. Despite his consultation of the early texts and his occasional brilliance as an emender, therefore, Theobald inevitably perpetuated more errors than he eliminated from the Rowe-Pope tradition.

The convention of relying on one's predecessor's edition continued to afflict eighteenth-century editing of Shakespeare. Robert Walker (whose edition appeared in 1734–1735) Sir Thomas Hanmer (1744), and Thomas Warburton (1747) contributed little that was new. (This Warburton is not, however, the John Warburton whose cook is said to have burned a number of now-lost early editions of plays by using them to line pie-plates.) Even Dr. Johnson (1765), who set an admirable standard of conservatism in admitting emendations to the Shakespearean text, based his edition on an annotated copy of Warburton's edition.

Only with Edward Capell (1768) did an eighteenth-century editor finally base his text on the original Folio and quartos. Capell amassed an admirable collection of quartos and was the first to recognize that they might sometimes be preferred as copy text to the Folio itself. Unlike his eighteenth-century predecessors, who generally dismissed the quartos as based on prompt-books and hence contaminated by theatrical revision, Capell saw that they usually represented Shakespeare's own drafts. Capell's work heavily influenced George Steevens' 1773 revision of Dr. Johnson's text.

Edmund Malone, at first a collaborator with Steevens and later his rival, issued an eleven-volume edition in 1790. Malone reintroduced *Pericles*, which Pope and subsequent editors had eliminated along with the spurious plays of the Third Folio. Malone brought to his editing an extensive knowledge of Elizabethan documents such as the Stationers' Register, Henslowe's *Diary*, and the records of the Master of the Revels. He left uncompleted a variorum edition recording all textual variants; this edition was finished in 1821 by James Boswell, son of Dr. Johnson's biographer, and became known as the Third Variorum because Isaac Reed's earlier editions (1803, 1813) had called themselves the First and Second Variorums. The so-called New Variorum Shakespeare continued this tradition under Henry Howard Furness, beginning in 1871.

Nineteenth-century editions were numerous. One of the most famous and influential was the "bowdlerized" or expurgated *Family Shakespeare* of the Rev. Thomas Bowdler, first appearing in 1804 and 1818 and soon extending throughout the English-speaking world. Other editions included those of William Harness (1825), S. W. Singer (1826, 1856), John Payne Collier (1841–1844), Charles Knight (1838–1842), Alexander Dyce (1857), Howard Staunton (1858–1860), Nikolaus Delius (1854–1861), H. N. Hudson (1851–1856), and J. O. Halliwell-Phillips (1853–1861).

The outstanding scholarly edition of the nineteenth century was the so-called Cambridge Shakespeare of William George Clark and William Aldis Wright, 1863–1866, issued in 1864 in a single volume known as the Globe text. Although its choice of copy texts has been challenged in two or three instances by twentieth-century bibliographical research, the Globe text was soundly edited and soon established itself as definitive. Its act and scene divisions and its line numbering became standards of reference for concordances, works of literary criticism, and the like. It forms the basis for this present edition, and is still widely in use elsewhere.

Later nineteenth- and early twentieth-century editions included those of W. J. Rolfe (1871–1896), Appleton Morgan (1888), F. A. Marshall and others (The Henry Irving Shakespeare, 1888–1890), Sir Israel Gollancz (The Temple Shakespeare, 1894–1895), W. J. Craig (1892), C. H. Herford (1899), and Helen Porter and Charlotte Clarke (1903–1914). Influential American editions included those of W. A. Neilson (1906) and George Lyman Kittredge (1936).

The twentieth century has seen an enormous increase in the information available on bibliographical matters: memorial reconstruction of texts, printing-house procedures, the mechanics of book production, watermarks, printer's ornaments, Elizabethan handwriting, spelling, punctuation, and the like. Some pioneering studies include A. W. Pollard's *Shakespeare's Folios and Quartos* (1909) and *Shakespeare's Hand in the Play of Sir Thomas More* (1923), R. B. McKerrow's *An Introduction to Bibliography for Literary Students* (1927) and *Prolegomena for the Oxford Shakespeare* (1939), W. W. Greg's *Principles of Emendation in Shakespeare* (1928) and *The Editorial Problem in Shakespeare* (third edition, 1954), and E. K. Chambers' *William Shakespeare: A Study of Facts and Problems* (1930). No less important are Alice Walker's *Textual Problems of the First Folio* (1953) and Fredson Bowers' *Bibliography and Textual Criticism* (1964). Significant studies have also appeared on individual plays, such as that of Peter Alexander on the *Henry VI* plays and *Richard III*, Madeleine Doran also on *Henry VI*, J. Dover Wilson on *Hamlet*, George Williams on *Romeo and Juliet*, and G. I. Duthie on *King Lear*.

These bibliographical studies have led to new twentieth-century editions of Shakespeare in which the textual method has been measurably advanced. Among the most significant are the New Cambridge Shakespeare of Sir Arthur Quiller-Couch and J. Dover Wilson, and the still-continuing Arden Shakespeare under a succession of general editors including W. J. Craig, R. H. Case, Una Ellis-Fermor, and Harold Jenkins and Harold Brooks. Two old-spelling critical editions are in progress under the direction of Alice Walker (continuing the unfinished work of McKerrow) and J. Leeds Barroll at the University of South Carolina. College editions reedited from original texts include the Pelican Shakespeare under the general editorship of Alfred Harbage (1956–1969), the revision of Kittredge's edition by Irving Ribner (1971), and the Signet Classic Shakespeare under the general editorship of Sylvan Barnet (1972). This present edition, though based on the Globe text, has been revised on the basis of a study of the First Folio and early quartos. Other new texts are forthcoming from Houghton Mifflin and W. W. Norton.

Norton has also issued its Norton *Facsimile of The First Folio of Shakespeare*, prepared by Charlton Hinman from the Folios of the Folger Library (1968). Older facsimiles of the Folio are available in libraries, such as that prepared by Sidney Lee (1902) and J. Dover Wilson (in separate plays), but the Norton facsimile unquestionably sets a new standard of excellence. Facsimiles of the quartos are also available. Xerox copies of early printed books such as Shakespearean quartos are to be found in many libraries through the S.T.C. (Short Title Catalogue) series of University Microfilms. Photographic copies of early texts are also frequently available on microfilm.

The most extensive collection of Shakespearean documents today are to be found in the British Museum, the Bodleian Library at Oxford, the Folger Shakespeare Library in Washington, D.C., and the Henry E. Huntington Library in San Marino, California. Other important collections include Cambridge University Library (Sandars Collection), the library of Trinity College, Cambridge (Capell Collection), the Victoria and Albert Museum in London (Dyce Collection), Edinburgh University Library (Drummond and Halliwell Collections), the Shakespeare Birthplace Library and the Shakespeare Memorial Libraries in Stratford-upon-Avon, the Birmingham (England) Public Library, Harvard University Library (White Collection), the Boston Public Library (Pierpont Collection), the John Carter Brown Library in Providence, R.I., and the Pierpont Morgan Library in New York. Many smaller collections also exist in private hands.

SHAKESPEARE'S ENGLISH

We could probably understand the spoken English of Shakespeare's time; but the speaker, even when his words were just the ones we would use, would seem to us to be speaking a strange dialect. This is because spoken English, mainly in the pronunciation of vowel sounds, has undergone many striking changes. Some authorities have claimed that the original pronunciation adds something to the melody of Shakespeare's verse and to the vividness of his speech, so that the experiment of learning it may be worth trying. One can, however, indicate only approximately what the pronunciation was, because local dialects seem then to have been far more commonly used by educated persons than they are now and because several of the commonest vowel sounds were in a state of transition and are, therefore, difficult to fix definitely.

We know that Sir Walter Ralegh spoke his native

Devonshire dialect, and it may be that Shakespeare's oral utterance was colored by the Warwickshire dialect. A few Warwickshire words and expressions occur in his plays. The London dialect had become even more dominant than it was in Chaucer's time, but because of a wider national intercourse London speech had taken in a large admixture of northern, eastern, and southern forms.

Pronunciation

Consonants were in general pronounced as they are now. There were, however, a few differences. The *k* and *g* were pronounced in such words as *knife* and *gnaw*, and *l* was sounded in *should, would, folk*, etc. The *-tion* and *-sion* endings were usually pronounced as two syllables and were not yet given the sounds of *sh* and *zh*. The letter *r* was clearly pronounced, but was probably losing its trilled quality.

The short vowels *a, e*, and *i* were pronounced as at present, although short *a* was in transition from *a* in *Colorado* (*o* in *folly*) to *a* in *that*. Short *o* was probably more distinctly an *o*-sound than it is with us; that is, it was like the *o* in *folk* rather than the *o* in *hot*. A greater number of the short *u*'s had the genuine *u*-sound, rather than the lax vowel we now hear in many words; that is, *brush* rhymed exactly with *push*, and *dull* with *pull*. Long *a* in words like *state* was an open sound like the *a* in *hat* prolonged and diphthongized. Open and close long *e* were discriminated; that is, *seam* and *seem* were not sounded alike, the former being somewhat like *same* only more open (*a* in *hat* prolonged), and the latter pretty much as it is now. Long *i* was in a transitional state and was variously uttered. Henry Bradley, in his article on "Shakespeare's English" (*Shakespeare's England*, 1904, II, 543), expresses the opinion that it usually had the sound of *i* in *pin* followed by the consonantal *y*. Long open *o* (like the *oa* in *broad*) still had its proper sound, so that a word like *old* was pronounced *auld*. Long close *o* had probably completed its change from the long *o*-sound to the *oo*-sound. Long *u* was approximately short *i* followed by *w*, so that *tiwn* and *riwl* represent the pronunciation of *tune* and *rule*. The change which gave us our pronunciation of *blue, rue*, and *jury* did not occur until the eighteenth century. Perhaps *ai* and *ay* were usually pronounced like our long *i;* that is, *day* was like our word *die*. The diphthong *oi* (*oy*) may be represented by *ooi*. The sound of *ou* and *ow* varied, as it still does, according to descent. When the sound came from Old English long *u* or French *ou*, it was like *oo* in *boot;* when it came from Old English *ag, ah, aw*, or *ow* with a long vowel, it was sounded like *au* in *autumn;* for example, *house* was pronounced *hoos*, and *soul, know*, and *own*, as *saul, knaw*, and *awn*, respectively.

A matter of more practical importance than phonetic changes is that of differences in Shakespeare's English and ours in the accentuation of syllables. There are many cases of variable stress in Shakespeare, in which he seems to have been at liberty to accent the word in two different ways; in other cases words were customarily accented on a different syllable from that in current speech. For example, the following accentuations are either usual or frequent: *aspect', charac'ter, com'mendable, com'plete, con'ceal'd, con'fessor, consort'* (n.), *contract'* (n.), *de'testable, dis'tinct, envy', for'lorn, hu'mane, instinct', ob'scure, persev'er, pi'oner, ple'beians, portents', pur'sue, record'* (n.), *reven'ue, se'cure, sinis'ter, welcome'*.

Not only are *-tion* and *-sion* regularly pronounced as two syllables, but the same situation causes other words in which *e* or *i* stand before vowels to be uttered in Shakespeare's language with one more syllable than in ours; for example, *oce-an, courti-er, marri-age*. We may even have *cre-ature, tre-asure*, and *venge-ance*. Nasals and liquids are frequently pronounced as if an extra vowel were introduced between them and a preceding letter. We accordingly have *wrest(e)ler, Eng(e)land, as-semb(e)ly*, and *ent(e)rance*, as well as *de-ar, you(e)r*, and *mo-re*. Final *-er* often has a greater syllabic importance than it ever has in later poetry, as in the line: "And thére / upón, / gíve me / your daúgh / tér" (*Henry V*, V,ii,375). Final *-(e)s* in the genitive singular and the plural of nouns not ending in an *s*- sound may constitute a separate syllable; for example, "To show his teeth as white as wha-*le's* bone" (*Love's Labour's Lost*, V,ii,332).

An idea of the spelling and of the pronunciation of the Shakespearean language may be gained from the following passage (*King Lear*, IV,vi,11–24), which is reproduced, first, in the text of the First Folio and, secondly, in Vietor's transcription of the English of the First Folio in the International Phonetic Alphabet as he employed it. The transcribed passage has the punctuation of the Globe text.[1]

How fearefull
And dizie 'tis to cast ones eyes so low,
The Crowes and Choughes, that wing the midway ayre
Shew scarce so grosse as Beetles. Halfe way downe
Hangs one that gathers Sampire: dreadfull Trade:
Me thinkes he seemes no bigger then his head.
The Fishermen, that walke vpon the beach
Appeare like Mice: and yond tall Anchoring Barke,
Diminish'd to her Cocke: her Cocke, a Buoy
Almost too small for sight. The murmering Surge,
That on th'vnnumbred idle Pebble chafes
Cannot be heard so high. Ile looke no more,
Least my braine turne, and the deficient sight
Topple downe headlong.

huw fe:rful
ænd dizi tiz, tu kæst o:nz ijz so: lo:!

[1] Key: The symbol is given first, then the key-word in Modern English. Explanations are in parentheses. æ:, *name* (*a* in *hat* prolonged); æ, *hat;* æi, *day* (*a* in *hat* followed by *e* in *be*); a:, *saw;* e:, *there;* e, *get;* eu, *few* (*e* in *get* followed by *oo* in *too*); i:, *be;* i, *bit;* ij, *by* (slightly prolonged in pronunciation); iu, *mute;* o, *folk;* o:, *saw* (slightly less open); oi, *boy* (first element of the sound slightly closer to long *o*); ou, *own* (slightly closer to *ow* in *gown*); u:, *too;* u, *full;* uw, *too* (*oo* followed by *w*); ŋ, *sing;* ð, *the;* θ, *thin;* ʃ, *shall;* ʒ, *urge*.

ðe krouz ænd tʃufs ðæt wiŋ ðe midwæi æir
ʃo:skærs so gro:s æz bi:t,lz : ha:f wæi duwn
hæŋz o:n ðæt gæðerz sæmpijr, dre(:)dful træ:d!
mi θinks hi si:mz no biger ðen hiz hed:
ðe fiʃermen, ðæt wa:k upon ðe be:tʃ,
æpe:r lijk mijs; ænd jond ta:l ænk(o)riŋ bærk,
diminiʃt tu her kok : her kok, æ bwoi
a:lmo:st tu sma:l for sijt : ðe murm(u)riŋ surdʒ,
ðæt on ðunnumbred ijd,l peb,l, tʃae:fs,
kænot bi hærd so hij. ijl lu:k no mo:r;
le(:)st mij bræin turn, ænd ðe defisient sijt
top,l duwn hedloŋ.

There thus arises in the reading and scansion of Shakespeare a problem as to how many syllables the poet intended a given word to have, for as compared to current English a Shakespearean word (a) may have an additional syllable or (b) may have one fewer syllables, or (c) two adjoining syllables in different words may coalesce. The difficulty is that such differences may or may not appear in the spelling of words. The following lines and words will illustrate these situations.

(a) I do wander every where,
Swifter than the moon's̈ sphere.
(*A Midsummer Night's Dream*, II,i,6–7)
O me! You jugglër! You canker-blössom.
(*A Midsummer Night's Dream*, III,ii,282)
After the prompter: for our entrance.
(*Romeo and Juliet*, I,iv,8)
Mislike me not for my complexïon.
(*The Merchant of Venice*, II,i,1)

The words *captain*, *monstrous*, *esperancë*, *this* (*this is*), *Georgë* (*Richard III*, V,v,9), *valiant*, *villain*, *jealous*, have extra syllables in pronunciation.

(b) Good mother, do not marry me to yond fool.
(*The Merry Wives of Windsor*, III,iv,87)

The words *lineal*, *journeying*, *carrion*, *celestial*, *herald*, *royal*, *malice*, *absolute*, *perjury*, *madame*, *needle*, *taken*, *gentleman*, *unpeople*, *forward*, *gather*, *innocent*, *violet*, *Africa*, *eagle*, *listen*, *venomous*, have usually one fewer syllables than in current English.

(c) Why should I joy in any‿abortive birth?
(*Love's Labour's Lost*, I,i,104)
He was paid for‿that. (*Cymbeline*, IV,ii,246)
The lover,‿all as frantic.
(*A Midsummer Night's Dream*, V,i,10)
Romans, do‿me right. (*Titus Andronicus*, I,i,203)

Differences in accentuation and lengthening of words, of course, have great importance in the reading and scanning of Shakespeare's verse, as also do the various ways by which words are shortened. Shortening of words by elision or by slurring is, of course, very common in Shakespeare, but in this matter the modern practice forms a good guide. Syllables ending in vowels are not infrequently elided before words beginning with a vowel, as in "How cáme / *we as*hóre" (*The Tempest*, I,ii,158) and "too hárd / a knót / for mé / *to un*tie" (*Twelfth Night*, II,ii,42). Syncopation, or the omission of a syllable, often occurs in words with *r*, as "I wár-*ran*t / it wíll" (*Hamlet*, I,ii,243); and in final *-er*, *-el*, and *-le*, as "Tráv*el* you / far ón" (*The Taming of the Shrew*, IV,ii,73) and "I am / a gént*le* / mán of / a cóm / paný" (*Henry V*, IV,i,39). The following words and other similar ones may be treated as monosyllabic in Shakespeare's verse: *whether*, *ever*, *hither*, *other*, *father*, *evil*, *having*. Almost any unaccented syllable of a polysyllabic word (especially if it contains an *i*) may be softened and ignored; this syncopation is frequent in polysyllabic words and proper names; as "Thoughts spéc*u* / latíve" (*Macbeth*, V,iv,19) and "Did sláy / this Fór*tinbras;* / who, bý / a seál'd / compáct" (*Hamlet*, I,i,86). Other occasions for slurring, as listed by Abbott in his *Shakespearian Grammar*, are light vowels preceded by heavy vowels, as *pow*er, *dy*ing, etc.; plurals and possessives of nouns ending in an *s*-sound, final *-ed* following *d* or *t*, as "you háve / exceéd*ed* / all prómise" (*As You Like It*, I,ii,256); and the *-est* of superlatives (pronounced *-st*) after dentals and liquids, as "the stérn'st / good-níght" (*Macbeth*, II,ii,4) and "thy éld'st / son's són" (*King John*, II,i,177).

Grammar

Shakespeare's grammar presents but few differences in forms from the grammar of current modern English. The *-eth* ending in the third person singular of the present tense, indicative mood, was very commonly used, especially in serious prose. Shakespeare frequently uses the older form, especially *hath*, *doth*, and *saith*, but seems to prefer the form in *-s* or *-es*. There are also a few cases in which he seems to use the old northern plural in *-s* or *-es* in the third person of the present indicative; as ". . . at those springs On chalic'd flow'rs that *lies*" (*Cymbeline*, II,iii,24–25). He does not always agree with modern usage in the forms of the past tenses and the perfect participles of the verbs that he employs. He retains some lost forms of the strong verbs, sometimes confuses the past tense with the perfect participle, or vice versa, and treats some verbs as weak (or regular) which are now strong (or irregular). For example, he uses *arose* for *arisen*, *swam* for *swum*, *foughten* for *fought*, *gave* for *given*, *took* for *taken*, *sprung* for *sprang*, *writ* for *wrote*. He has *blowed* for *blew*, *weaved* for *wove*, *shaked* for *shaken*. Forms like *degenerate* for *degenerated* and *exhaust* for *exhausted* are especially common. There are a few cases of the archaic *y-* with the past participle, as in *yclad*. The regular form of the possessive case of the neuter personal pronoun *it* was *his*. This is Shakespeare's usual form; but he has also a possessive form *it*, and in the First Folio, published seven years after Shakespeare's death, there are several occurrences of the new form *its*. Shakespeare uses the old form *moe* as the plural of *many*, and the form *enow* as the plural of *enough*. *Near* and *next* are employed, along with *nearer* and *nearest*, as the comparative and superlative of *nigh*. These are the most obvious of the formal differences between Shakespeare's grammar and our own.

The functional differences are more considerable. Elizabethan language exercised an extraordinary freedom, even for English, in the use of one part of speech for another. Shakespeare uses verbs, adjectives, adverbs, and pronouns as nouns. He makes verbs out of nouns and adjectives, and, of course, uses nouns as adjectives, for this is a distinguishing characteristic of English speech; but he uses also adverbs, verbs, and prepositional phrases as adjectives. Almost any adjective may be freely used as an adverb. He makes active words, both adjectives and adverbs, discharge a passive function; as "the sightless [invisible] couriers of the air" (*Macbeth*, I,vii,23) and "this aspect of mine Hath fear'd the valiant," i.e., caused the valiant to be afraid (*The Merchant of Venice*, II,i,8–9). There is a wider use in Shakespeare of the infinitive as a verbal noun or as a gerundive participle than in our language; as "This to be true, I do engage my life" (*As You Like It*, V,iv,171–172), "My operant powers their functions leave to do" (*Hamlet*, III,ii,184), "Nor do I now make moan to be abridg'd" (*The Merchant of Venice*, I,i,126), and "you might have saved me my pains, to have taken [by having taken] it away yourself" (*Twelfth Night*, II,ii,6). The functions of prepositions in Elizabethan English were so various that one can only refer the student to the notes to the text or to a dictionary.

In certain other features, however, Shakespeare's language is as restricted and conventional as ours is at formal levels, or even more so. *Shall* is regularly used in Shakespeare to express something inevitable in future time, and is, therefore, the usual future tense for all persons. *Will*, which originally expressed intention, determination, or willingness, was, however, beginning to encroach on *shall* for the expression of futurity in the second and third persons; but in its use there is usually a consciousness of its original meaning. *Should* and *would* had their original senses of obligation and volition, respectively, and had other peculiarities, then as now, of considerable difficulty. The subjunctive mood was not only vital in Shakespeare but was used carefully. It expressed condition, doubt, concession, and command. It was used to express wish or desire and in dependent clauses to express indefiniteness, purpose, or sometimes simple futurity. Note the following examples:

But if my father *had* not scanted me . . .
Yourself, renowned prince, then *stood* as fair.
(*The Merchant of Venice*, II,i,17,20)

Live a thousand years,
I *shall* not find myself so apt to die.
(*Julius Caesar*, III,i,159–160)

Lest your retirement *do amaze* your friends.
(*1 Henry IV*, V,iv,6)

'*Twere* best he speak no harm of Brutus here.
(*Julius Caesar*, III,ii,73)

Melt Egypt into Nile! and kindly creatures
Turn all to serpents! (*Antony and Cleopatra*, II,v,78–79)

Yet were it true
To say this boy *were* like me.
(*The Winter's Tale*, I,ii,134–135)

And may direct his course as *please* himself.
(*Richard III*, II,ii,129)

The following minor features of Shakespeare's grammar deserve notice: he often omits the relative pronoun; often uses the nominative case of the pronoun for the accusative case, and vice versa; uses *him*, *her*, *me*, and *them* as true reflexives to mean *himself*, *herself*, *myself*, and *themselves;* employs double negatives and double comparatives and superlatives; shows a consciousness in the use of *thee* and *thou* of their application to intimates and inferiors and of their insulting quality when addressed to strangers (e.g., "If thou thouest him some thrice, it shall not be amiss," *Twelfth Night*, III,ii,48); employs *which* to refer to both persons and things; and does not discriminate closely between *ye*, nominative, and *you*, objective. Finally, he makes frequent use of the dative constructions, i.e., the objective forms of the pronouns, *me*, *thee*, *you*, *him*, *her*, etc., without prepositions where the meaning is "by me," "for me," "with me," "to me," "of me," etc. For example:

I am appointed *him* [by him] to murder you.
(*The Winter's Tale*, I,ii,412)

She looks *us* [to us] like
A thing made more of malice than of duty.
(*Cymbeline*, III,v,32–33)

Particular mention should be made of the ethical dative, a construction in which the pronoun is used to indicate the person interested in the statement. In *King John* (III,iv,146) we have "John lays *you* plots," i.e., "plots which you may profit by." In the following, *me* means "to my detriment" or "to my disadvantage":

See how this river comes *me* cranking in,
And cuts *me*, from the best of all my land,
A huge half moon. (*1 Henry IV*, III,i,98–100)

"Whip *me* such honest knaves" (*Othello*, I,i,49) means "In my judgment such knaves should be whipped." In Quickly's description of Mistress Page, the dative *you* is equivalent to "mark you," "take notice":

. . . a civil modest wife, and one, I tell you, that will not miss *you* morning nor evening prayer, as any is in Windsor. (*The Merry Wives of Windsor*, II,ii,100–103)

Of the forms and figures of rhetoric there are in Shakespeare, as in other poets, innumerable instances. He is very fond, for example, of using the abstract for the concrete, as in the words addressed by Surrey to Cardinal Wolsey, "Thou scarlet sin" (*Henry VIII*, III,ii,255). Transpositions are numerous, as are inversions, ellipses, and broken or confused constructions, as in the following examples:

That thing you speak of,
I took it for a man = absolute construction.
(*King Lear*, IV,vi,77–78)

Souls and bodies hath he divorced three = transposition of adjective. (*Twelfth Night*, III,iv,260)

A happy gentleman in blood and lineaments = transposition of adjectival phrase. (*Richard II*, III,i,9)

Your state of fortune and your due of birth = transposition of pronoun. (*Richard III*, III,vii,120)

She calls me proud, and [says] that she could not love me = ellipsis. (*As You Like It*, IV,iii,16)

Returning were as tedious as [to] go o'er = ellipsis.
(*Macbeth*, III,iv,138)

They call him Doricles; and boasts himself
To have a worthy feeding = ellipsis of nominative.
(*The Winter's Tale*, IV,iv,168–169)

Of all men else I have avoided thee = confusion of two constructions. (*Macbeth*, V,viii,4)

The venom of such looks, we fairly hope,
Have lost their quality = confusion of number arising from proximity. (*Henry V*, V,ii,18–19)

Rather proclaim it, Westmoreland, through my host,
That he which hath no stomach to this fight,
Let him depart = construction changed by change of thought. (*Henry V*, IV,iii,34–36)

For always I am Cæsar = inversion of adverb.
(*Julius Caesar*, I,ii,212)

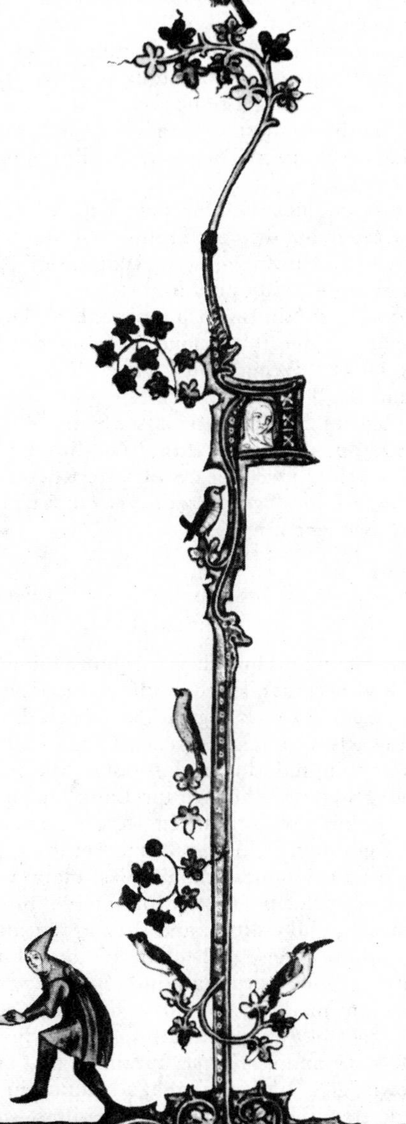

Shakespeare often uses rhetorical figures for symmetrical effects, especially in the early, ornamental style of *Richard III* and the nondramatic poems. Following are definitions of some of the most popular figures he uses, with illustrations from *Venus and Adonis:*

(1) *Parison*, the symmetrical repetition of words in grammatically parallel phrases: "How love makes young men thrall, and old men dote."

(2) *Isocolon*, the symmetrical repetition of sounds and words in phrases of equal length, as in the previous example, and in this: "Or as the wolf doth grin before he barketh, Or as the berry breaks before it staineth." Parison and isocolon are frequently combined.

(3) *Anaphora*, the symmetrical repetition of a word at the beginning of a sequence of clauses or sentences,

THE BODLEIAN LIBRARY

In the plays are several allusions to the Morris Dance, a rural amusement (which Shakespeare would have been familiar with) in which the participants frolicked to the accompaniment of a fife and drum.

often at the beginning of lines. Anaphora is frequently combined with parison and isocolon, as in the second example already given, and in this: " 'Give me my hand,' saith he. 'Why dost thou feel it?' 'Give me my heart,' saith she, 'and thou shalt have it.' "

(4) *Antimetabole*, the symmetrical repetition of words in inverted order: "She clepes him king of graves, and grave for kings."

(5) *Anadiplosis*, the beginning of a phrase with the final words of the previous phrase: "O, thou didst kill me, kill me once again!"

(6) *Epanalepsis*, the symmetrical repetition of a word or words at the beginning and ending of a line: "He sees his love, and nothing else he sees."

(7) *Ploce*, the insistent repetition of a word within the same line or phrase: "Then why not lips on lips, since eyes in eyes?"

(8) *Epizeuxis*, an intensified form of ploce, repeating the word without another intervening word: " 'Ay me!' she cries, and twenty times, 'Woe, woe!' And twenty echoes twenty times cry so."

(9) *Antanaclasis*, the shifting of a repeated word from one meaning to another: "My love to love is love but to disprove it," or " 'Where did I leave?' 'No matter where,' quoth he, 'Leave me.' "

For other figures and illustrations, see Sister Miriam Joseph, *Shakespeare's Use of the Arts of Language* (1947) and Brian Vickers, "Shakespeare's Use of Rhetoric," in *A New Companion to Shakespeare Studies*, ed. Kenneth Muir and S. Schoenbaum (1971).

The Shakespearean Vocabulary

With reference to words and their meanings the spirit of the Renaissance manifested itself in England in very great hospitality to foreign importations. Large numbers of words were taken directly from Latin. In fact there was an inundation of classicism, for it was a fashion among writers to pillage the Latin language. Many of the words so introduced were naturalized and served to enrich the language, its power to express thought, and its rhythmical capabilities; many were discarded. The principal borrowings were in the realm of learning and culture, and they were usually employed with distinct recollection of their Latin sense. Sometimes such words have not replaced native words of the same meaning, so that we have such pairs of synonyms as *acknowledge* and *confess;* just as Shakespeare had *wonder* and *admiration.* It follows that even a slight knowledge of Latin is a great advantage in the correct understanding of Elizabethan writers, since many Latin borrowings have taken on since the sixteenth century a different shade of meaning from that in which they were borrowed. The Latin sense of *aggravate* still struggles for recognition; but *apparent* no longer means primarily *visible* or *evident*, and *intention* does not convey the idea of *intentness*.

Latin words were often taken over in their Latin forms, as *objectum* and *subjectum*, *statua* and *aristocratia*, and later were made to conform to English spelling and accentuation, though a few, such as *decorum*, still have a Latin form. French continued to be drawn upon and sometimes caused a new Latin borrowing to be adopted in a French form; just as, on the other hand, such words as *adventure* were supplied with a *d* to make them conform to Latin spelling. This principle is illustrated in the pedantry of Holofernes when he objects (*Love's Labour's Lost*, V,i,25) to "det" as the pronunciation of "debt." Spanish, Italian, and Dutch were made to supply many terms. Spanish gave words having to do with commerce, religion, and the New World, such as *mosquito*, *alligator*, *ambuscado*, and *grandee*. From Italian came terms of art, learning, and dueling: *bandetto*, *portico*, *canto*, *stoccato*. The Dutch contributed many nautical and oriental words.

These foreign borrowings were a part of what might be called the linguistic ambition of the age, a desire for forcible expression. Language was in a plastic state, so that it had an unparalleled freedom in both vocabulary and form; and with this came a consequent confusion, since there were in Elizabethan times few efforts at grammatical precision. Such efforts were made by the age of Dryden and the Royal Society, who felt that English was too vague and irregular for use as a means of scientific expression. Indeed the task of rendering the language more precise has been the object of the learned part of the population ever since the sixteenth century, and yet it must be acknowledged that English could never have been as great a language as it is without its Renaissance expansion and its subsequent absorption with Shakespeare and the English Bible. It gained, for example, an increased facility in the making of compounds. Shakespeare, with his *cloud-capp'd towers* and his *home-keeping wits*, was a genius at this. Likewise from Shakespeare's time came the English power in the use of prefixes, such as *dis-*, *re-*, *en-*, and of suffixes, such as *-ful*, *-less*, *-ness*, *-hood*.

Obsolete words, however, and words employed by Shakespeare in entirely different meanings give the student little trouble. The difficulty arises from the innumerable cases in which the student is able to get without effort an idea fairly close to Shakespeare's meaning, so that he constantly understands Shakespeare imperfectly. He is thus liable to miss the exact shade of meaning and consequently the tone of Shakespeare's feeling. In Othello's account to the Venetian senators of the circumstances of his courtship of Desdemona (*Othello*, I,iii,158–166) he says:

My story being done,
She gave me for my pains a world of sighs: . . .
She wish'd she had not heard it, yet she wish'd
That heaven had made her such a man; she thank'd
me,
And bade me, if I had a friend that lov'd her,
I should but teach him how to tell my story,
And that would woo her. Upon this *hint* I spake.

The word *hint* means *occasion* or *opportunity;* it does not mean *invitation* or *suggestion by covert allusion*. To understand the word in the contemporary sense changes subtly the meaning of the passage.

The real secret of Shakespeare's language is to learn the attitude toward speech accepted by him and his contemporaries. Speech was traditionally and piously regarded as God's final and consummate gift to man, and speech in the thought of the Elizabethans was ultimately powerful. Truth, if truly uttered, was bound to prevail. To have heard truth and to have rejected it was an unnatural thing. It showed that Satan had entered the obdurate heart and caused it to reject God's truth. Christians were bound to preach the Word, and, when the Word had been uttered clearly and rejected, the heretic or culprit should be destroyed. Hence, the struggle to excel in utterance, the practice, the sincerity, and the eloquence.

A NOTE ON DOUBTFUL AND LOST PLAYS

In his edition of *The Shakespeare Apocrypha* (Oxford, 1908, 1918), Tucker Brooke enumerates some forty-two plays, other than those included in the First Folio, which at one time or another have been ascribed to Shakespeare. (The word "apocrypha," as in the case of the Apocryphal Books of the Bible, signifies works whose place in the accepted canon is disputed.) The First Folio itself contains thirty-six plays which seem to have been selected with great care by Shakespeare's friends and professional associates, John Heminges and Henry Condell. So conscientious was their work, in fact, that recent studies of the Shakespearean canon and of the First Folio have tended to confirm their judgment and to rule against the possibility that they made serious omissions. *Pericles* has, to be sure, gained virtually universal inclusion in the canon along with the thirty-six plays edited by Heminges and Condell. *The Two Noble Kinsmen* is now regarded by most scholars as the result of a collaboration between Shakespeare and John Fletcher, though the major portion of the play is usually given to Fletcher. Recently a noteworthy attempt has been made to establish Shakespeare's authorship of certain scenes in *Sir Thomas More*. Beyond this point, however, no claim has been established with anything approaching certainty. Of the forty-two plays mentioned by Tucker Brooke, indeed, only about fifteen deserve serious discussion.

The Two Noble Kinsmen

"A Tragi Comedy called the two noble kinsmen by John Fletcher and William Shakespeare" was first entered in the Stationers' Register in 1634 by the publisher John Waterson. A quarto appeared in that same year, entitled "*The Two Noble Kinsmen: Presented at the Black-friers by the Kings Maiesties servants, with great applause: Written by the memorable Worthies of their time; Mr. John Fletcher, and Mr. William Shakespeare, Gent.* Tho. Cotes for John Watterson." The date of composition is pretty certainly 1613.

The Stationers' Register entry and title page of 1634 have some authority. Waterson was a reputable publisher with close ties to Shakespeare's and Fletcher's acting company, the King's men. The text published by Waterson seems to have been a theatrical prompt-copy. Shakespeare and Fletcher may well have had occasion to work together, since Shakespeare was on the verge of retiring in 1613 from the King's company, and Fletcher had already become his chief successor. The two men may also have collaborated in 1613 on *Henry VIII*, although that hypothesis remains seriously in doubt (see Play Introduction).

Certainly *The Two Noble Kinsmen* gives the impression of two contrasting styles, one flowing and casual in a characteristically Fletcherian manner, and one densely elliptical in a way that reminds us of the late Shakespeare (as, for example, in Leontes' soliloquies in *The Winter's Tale*). Those who are convinced of Shakespeare's authorship in *The Two Noble Kinsmen* usually give him the following scenes on the basis of style: I,i-iii; II,i, the very beginning; III,i; and V,i and iii-iv. Sometimes scenes iv and v of Act I are tentatively added to the list. Shakespeare's purported contributions are thus most prominent at the beginning and ending of the play. According to this theory, he seems to have begun the work and made contributions later on, but left to Fletcher the development of the action and the final fitting together of the parts. The overall impression, then, is of a Fletcherian play to which Shakespeare may have contributed some important scenes.

Whether the result of Shakespeare's authorship or not, the play is heavily influenced by the conventions of tragicomedy and romance that were so prominent in plays of the period. Like many of Shakespeare's late plays and Fletcher's early plays, *The Two Noble Kinsmen* was acted at the indoor Blackfriars theatre. (Shakespeare's late plays were also acted at the Globe, a public theatre, but it burned to the ground in 1613.) For its source, *The Two Noble Kinsmen* turns to Chaucer's "The Knight's Tale" in *The Canterbury Tales*. In the chivalric world of Theseus' court, the noble cousins Palamon and Arcite vie with one another for the hand of the fair Emilia. As in many romance plays, men's destinies are controlled by the will of the gods: the rivalry between Palamon and Arcite is, on a broader scale, a contest between Venus and Mars. Although the gods do not appear directly on stage, their altars are prominently visible in Act V. So is that of Diana, to whom Emilia prays for aid. Otherworldly musical effects, riddles, and oracles attest to the invisible cosmic presence of the three deities. The ending, in which Arcite triumphs in the tourney but then dies, leaving Emilia to Palamon, gives a symbolic victory to both Venus and Mars; love and chivalry have been perenially affirmed. Diana too shares in the ending, for Emilia's chastity is preserved in an honorable marriage. The play throughout is courtly in tone, with its debates on love versus friendship and the vanity of worldly striving. Even the comedy is strongly affected by courtly traditions of the masque and the pastoral.

Despite the affinities to Shakespearean romance, the play as a whole is considerably more Fletcherian than Shakespearean. For this reason, and because of uncertainties in the authorship question, the play was not included in the Globe Shakespeare and is omitted from this present edition. Indeed, the play contrasts markedly with Shakespeare's late romances in a way that *Henry VIII* does not. Implausible secondary love plots (such as that of the Jailer's Daughter for Palamon) playfully exaggerate the love theme into the sort of titillating and "campy" mannerism we associate with Fletcher. Serious themes lose their dramatic seriousness in an atmosphere of ingeniously contrived situation. The mad scene of the Jailer's Daughter reads like a travesty of that of Ophelia. The self-aware artifice of the play does resemble a tendency in the late Shakespeare, and may hint at the direction he might have taken had he continued to write. Just as plausibly, however, *The Two Noble Kinsmen* may be an essentially Fletcherian work that gives an erroneous impression if considered as Shakespeare's last play.

Additions to the Third Folio

Many anonymous plays were attributed to Shakespeare during his lifetime and afterward. Often this may have been nothing more than a device on the part of unscrupulous printers to increase sales by featuring Shakespeare's name or initials on the title page of some play in quarto. Seven such plays deserve special consideration, however, since they were included in the second printing of the Third Folio of 1664: *Pericles Prince of Tyre*, *The London Prodigal*, *The History of Thomas Lord Cromwell*, *Sir John Oldcastle Lord Cobham*, *The Puritan or the Widow of Watling Street*, *A Yorkshire Tragedy*, *The Tragedy of Locrine*.

Of this group, *Pericles* has been accepted since the time of Malone as at least in large part the work of Shakespeare.

The London Prodigal was published in 1605 by Nathaniel Butter (who published *King Lear*), "As it was plaied by the Kings Maiesties seruants. By William Shakespeare." It is a lively comedy of London life, full of humours and manners, but unlike anything known to have been written by Shakespeare. Thomas Dekker has been proposed as the author.

Thomas Lord Cromwell was printed for William Jones in 1602, "As it hath beene sundrie times publikely Acted by the Right Honorable the Lord Chamberlaine his Seruants. Written by W.S." It is an undistinguished specimen of the biographical history play. There seem to be no grounds for attributing it to Shakespeare, since even the initials "W.S." may have been intended to designate some other author.

Sir John Oldcastle, ascribed to Shakespeare in a quarto of 1600, is known from Henslowe's *Diary* to have been written for the Lord Admiral's company by Drayton, Hathway, Munday, and Wilson.

The Puritan, a comedy of manners, was printed by G. Eld in 1607, as "Acted by the Children of Paules. Written by W.S." Brooke points out certain resemblances between this play and *Eastward Hoe!* and suggests tentatively that Marston had a hand in it. Thomas Middleton's name has also been seriously suggested. There seems no reason to connect the play with Shakespeare.

A Yorkshire Tragedy is on better ground. Shakespeare's name appears both in the entry in the Stationers' Register and on the title page of the quarto of 1608. In the latter place it is also stated that the play was "Acted by his Maiesties Players at the Globe." So far as the use of Shakespeare's name is concerned, however, it may well have been due to the desire of the notorious piratical publisher, Thomas Pavier, to make dishonest gain. *A Yorkshire Tragedy* is a murder play, belonging to the genre of homiletic or "domestic" tragedy. The Calverly murder, which it dramatizes, had occurred in 1605, and Shakespeare's company had no doubt taken immediate advantage of the sensation to prepare and present the play. It is hard to think that Shakespeare at such a time in his career could have been employed on such a job; but, since there are prose passages in the play of profound psychological knowledge and insight and of breathless intensity, many critics have thought that they show the touch of his hand. George Wilkins is now thought to have had at least a major share in the play.

Locrine is a tragedy of an early type, like *Gorboduc* and *The Misfortunes of Arthur;* and, since it resembles *Alphonsus, King of Aragon* by Robert Greene and *Selimus* (probably also by Greene), Brooke argues strongly that *Locrine* is Greene's work and earlier than either of those mentioned. Another possible author is George Peele. The play was printed by Thomas Creed in 1595 as "Newly set foorth, ouerseene and corrected, By W.S." This "W.S." may again have been some author besides Shakespeare.

The Charles II Group

In addition to the Shakespeare apocrypha of the Third Folio, another seventeenth-century collection of Elizabethan plays ascribed to Shakespeare was found in the library of no less a person than King Charles II of England. This collection consisted of three quarto plays—*Fair Em*, *Mucedorus*, and *The Merry Devil of Edmonton*—all bound together and collectively entitled "Shakespeare, Vol. I." The binding and labeling in this fashion do not offer any real evidence that the plays were in fact by Shakespeare, however. All had been printed anonymously and were popular dramas dating from Shakespeare's lifetime. The collection may simply reflect a tendency to ascribe to Shakespeare any popular Elizabethan plays not known to have been written by some other dramatist.

Fair Em was printed first without date (as acted by Lord Strange's servants) and later, in 1631, for John Wright. Because its romanticized view of English life somewhat resembles that of *Friar Bacon and Friar Bungay* (c. 1589–1592) by Robert Greene, and also that of *George a Greene, the Pinnner of Wakefield*, probably by Greene, the comedy has sometimes been attributed to that dramatist. R. Wilson is also a plausible contender for authorship. *Fair Em* was seemingly written around 1590.

Mucedorus was one of the most popular plays of the age. It appeared in at least seventeen quarto editions, the third of which (1610) states that it is "Amplified with new additions, as it was acted before the Kings Maiestie at White-hall on Shrove-Sunday night. By his Highness Seruants usually playing at the Globe." The first edition was in 1598. No one seriously attributes the original play to Shakespeare; but, since the "new additions" referred to on the title page of the third quarto are superior to the rest of the play, they have sometimes been regarded as Shakespeare's. Robert Greene has again been regarded without sufficient warrant as original author.

The text of *The Merry Devil of Edmonton*, a better play than either of the others, looks as if the play had been worn by much acting and many alterations. The suspected Revels Accounts of Peter Cunningham connect it with Shakespeare's company, as does the title page of the first quarto, printed for Arthur Johnson in 1608. The play was again entered in the Stationers' Register to Humphrey Moseley, the bookseller, in 1653, this time with Shakespeare's name as author. *The Merry Devil of Edmonton* was a popular play and was early connected with Shakespeare's name. There is no other probability of its being his play, and but little of his having revised it; but it would do him no discredit. Possibly it was by Thomas Dekker.

Other Attributions

A play called *The Birth of Merlin*, first published by Francis Kirkman in 1662, is said on the title page to have been "Written by William Shakespear and William Rowley." Kirkman, an unreliable publisher, also attributed the tragicomedy of *The Birth of Merlin* to Shakespeare and Rowley in his catalogues. The play seems to date from the reign of King James. Recent critics have been unimpressed by Kirkman's wholly unsupported and implausible claim.

Arden of Feversham, an early bourgeois "domestic" tragedy about a murder, was published without attribution of authorship by Edward White in 1592. Edward Jacob, a citizen of Feversham, printed the play in 1770 and attributed it to Shakespeare. His grounds for doing so were inadequate, nor have any valid grounds been found since. The story is of a murder done at Feversham in 1551, the account of which is embodied in Holinshed's *Chronicles*. The play remains anonymous, although Kyd has been suggested as a likely author.

Edward III is another anonymous play assigned to Shakespeare on the basis of a seventeenth-century attribution. It was first printed by Cuthbert Burby in 1596 and first attributed to Shakespeare in a bookseller's leaflet in 1654. The Shakespearean scholar Edward Capell edited it in 1760 and argued that it was by Shakespeare. Ever since then, the play has continued to receive serious consideration—more so, probably, than any other candidate for the Shakespearean canon other than *Pericles*, *The Two Noble Kinsmen*, and *Sir Thomas More*. The play is an English history play dealing with the period of later medieval English history dramatized by Shakespeare, Thomas Heywood, Peele, Marlowe, and others. Its moderate political stance, its unhysterical depiction of Catholics and foreign foes, and its concern with the ethical responsibilities of war remind us more of Shakespeare than of any rival dramatist. More significantly, *Edward III* uses image patterns in a way that is strikingly reminiscent of *Richard II*. The play even alludes to Shakespeare's own writings, as in this quotation from Sonnet 94: "Lilies that fester smell far worse than weeds." Shakespeare does not habitually quote himself, however, and *Edward III* may be the work of some admiring and talented imitator. Another possibility is that Shakespeare had a hand in the play but was not responsible for all of it. Unfortunately, the argument must rest on stylistic considerations, which are too often subjective.

Sir Thomas More

The last serious contender for the Shakespearean canon is *Sir Thomas More*. The play exists in Harleian Ms. 7368 in the British Museum, labeled "The Booke of Sir Thomas Moore." It was first edited for the Shakespeare Society by Alexander Dyce in 1844. In 1871 the Shakespeare scholars Richard Simpson and James Spedding put forward the idea that certain scenes in this play were not only the work of Shakespeare but were written in his own hand. Simpson rested his case mainly on literary evidence and the "Shakespearian flavor."

The play is a biographical chronicle made up of three main episodes, or groups of scenes. The first of these describes a famous riot against alien workers that took place on the "ill May-Day" of 1517, and introduces Sir Thomas More, sheriff of London, in the act of pacifying the anti-alien rioters by his oratory. Because popular uprisings of a similar nature were greatly feared in the London of about 1595, the authorities were naturally unwilling to have these scenes performed. The play shows evidence, therefore, of having been heavily cut by the censor, Edmund Tilney, who bade the players leave the insurrection out completely. The result of his censorship is the disappearance of two long passages. The play seems to have been originally written by Anthony Munday. Perhaps in anticipation of the objections of the censor, however, another hand was employed to rewrite these scenes of the mob in a style not calculated to give offense. Three sheets of the manuscript, containing a total of 147 lines, make up these revisions. In them, the rioters express attitudes much like those we find in the mob scenes of *Julius Caesar*, or the Cade Rebellion of *2 Henry VI.* Thomas More's appeals to the mob point out the blessings of peace and order and the godlike authority of the king. In 1916 Sir E. Maunde Thompson, the paleographer, reasserted Shakespeare's authorship of these three sheets dealing with the "ill May-Day" mob. He attempted to prove by comparison with the handwriting of the six unquestioned signatures of Shakespeare that these sheets were indeed written in Shakespeare's hand. Since that time the matter has remained in dispute, although the weight of opinion today favors assigning the inserted portion of the manuscript to Shakespeare. (For a comprehensive and lucid review of the scholarship, see R. C. Bald, "*The Booke of Sir Thomas More* and Its Problems," *Shakespeare Survey 2* [1949], 44–61.) The play is dated by various critics from 1592 to 1601.

Lost Plays

A drama called *The History of Cardenio* was entered in the Stationers' Register, but apparently never printed, by Humphrey Moseley on September 9, 1653, as "by Mr. Fletcher and Shakespeare." Since a play called *Cardenno* or *Cardenna* had in fact been twice acted before King James by Shakespeare's company in 1612–1613, the obvious implication is that these various references are to a single play. Evidently it was based on an episode in Cervantes' *Don Quixote* (Part I, chs. xxiii-xxxvii). The play, though lost, has an intriguing subsequent history. In 1728 Lewis Theobald, the editor of Shakespeare, published a play based on the story of Cardenio entitled *The Double Falsehood, or the Distrest Lovers.* Theobald described his work as "written originally by W. Shakespeare, and now revised and adapted to the stage by Mr. Theobald." He claimed to have in his possession three manuscripts of the original; and, although those purported manuscripts have never been found, and Theobald has often been suspected of having written *The Double Falsehood* himself, he was not ordinarily given to creating forgeries. Moreover, the play does recall Fletcher's style: Possibly, then, we have still one more hint of a collaboration between Shakespeare and Fletcher in 1613.

At the same time that Moseley entered *The History of Cardenio* in the Stationers' Register, he also entered *The Merry Devil of Edmonton,* which he ascribed to Shakespeare, and "*Henry ye first, & Hen: ye 2d* by Shakespeare, & Dauenport." On June 29, 1660, he entered "*The History of King Stephen; Duke Humphrey, a Tragedy; Iphis & Iantha or a marriage without a man,* a Comedy, by Will. Shakespeare."

Among the manuscript plays burned by Warburton's cook were "*Henry ye 1st* by Will. Shakespear & Rob. Davenport, *Duke Humphrey* [*by*] Will. Shakespear," and "A Play by Will. Shakespear." John Warburton (1682–1759), antiquary and book collector, got into his possession a body of manuscripts of rare Elizabethan and Jacobean plays most of which were, he said, through his own "carelessness and the ignorance" of Betsy Baker, his servant, "unluckily burnd or put under pye bottoms."

How great was the world's loss in the plays mentioned by Moseley and Warburton we do not know. An obvious and tantalizing speculation is that Shakespeare may have written more history plays treating the early period to which *King John* belongs, perhaps a cycle of them.

A seventeenth-century watercolor based on de Visscher's View of London *shows the Globe theatre on the south bank of the Thames, a short distance west of London Bridge. In the vicinity were the competing Rose and Swan, making this area a leading theatre district of London.*

GLOBE . SOUTHWARKE.

K
O
L
M
Q
O
J
E
E
N
H
G
F
C.WALTER
HODGES
A

The (Second) Globe Playhouse, 1614-1644.

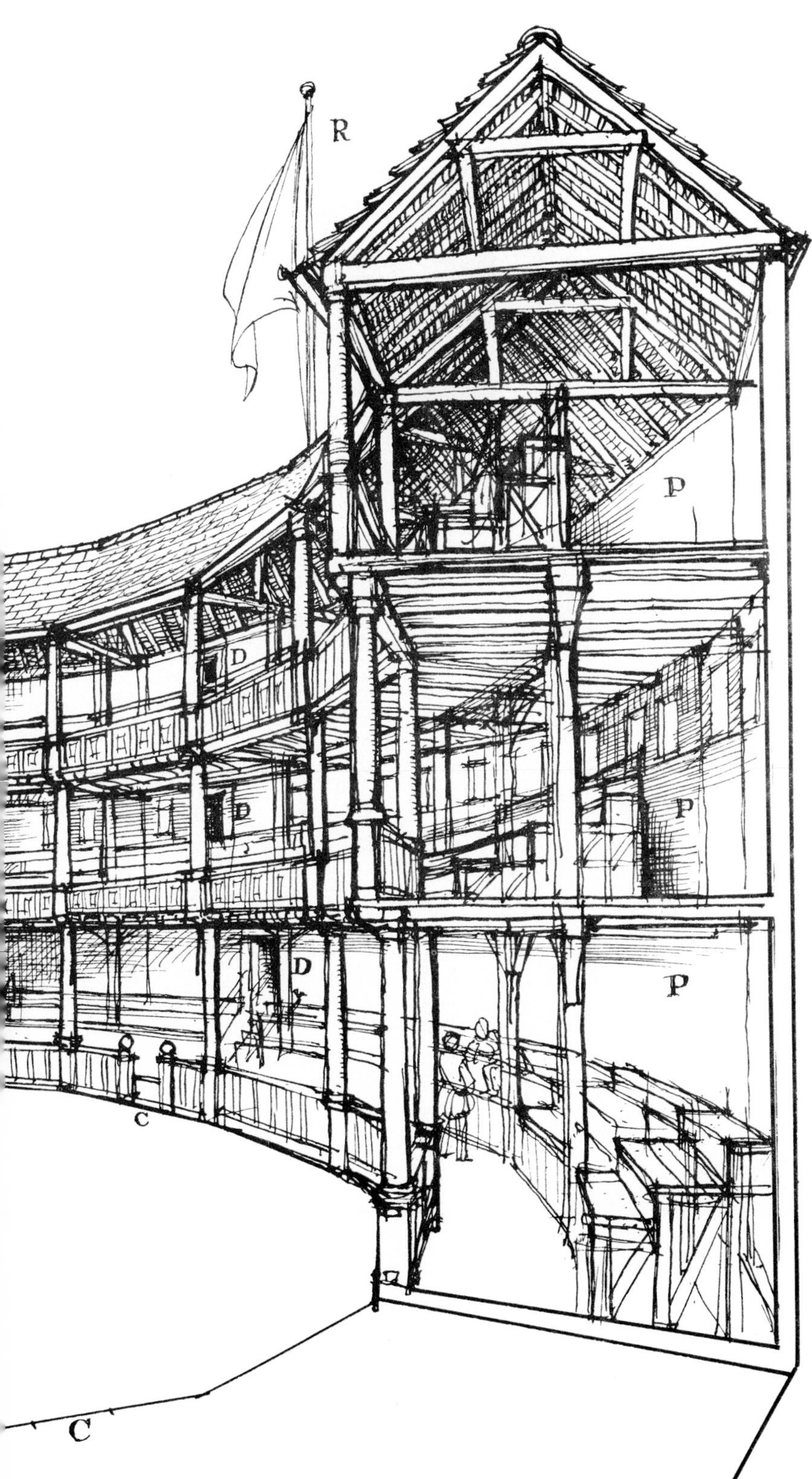

Key.

AA.	*Main entrances to auditorium.*
B.	*Yard for standing spectators.*
CC.	*Entrances to lowest gallery.*
DD.	*Entrances to staircase leading to upper galleries.*
EE.	*"Gentlemen's Rooms."*
F.	*The stage.*
G.	*The stage trap (leading from the "Hell" beneath the stage).*
H.	*Curtained space for "discovery" scenes.*
J.	*Upper stage.*
K.	*The "Heavens." (This area probably often covered across with a stretched canopy painted to represent the sky.)*
L.	*Backing painted with clouds. A shutter is here shown open to allow a god's throne to travel forward. (c.f. "Cymbeline," Act V sc. IV)*
M.	*The throne about to descend to the stage.*
N.	*Backstage area (or "Tiring-house").*
O.	*Wardrobe and dressing-rooms.*
P.	*Spectator galleries.*
Q.	*"Fly" gallery in the Heavens.*
R.	*Playhouse flag (reached from top landing of staircase, and raised to denote performance days).*

The second Globe Theatre, built in 1613 after a fire had destroyed the first Globe during a performance of Shakespeare's Henry VIII. *This building generally resembled its predecessor in the size of the stage and the "yard" for spectators, the location of stage doors and of a curtained area backstage for discovery scenes, etc. The upper acting station in this second Globe Theatre may, however, have been somewhat more elaborate than in the first Globe where spectators often sat above the stage (see p. 33). In neither theatre was the upper acting station used extensively for dramatic presentation.*

ORIGINAL ILLUSTRATION COURTESY C. WALTER HODGES

THE FOLGER SHAKESPEARE LIBRARY

Euterpe:
4
Euterpe, She is the Muſe that with ſwett Sounds an
Mellodye deliteth men, and hath her name of Euterpo,
which ſignifyeth to delyte:

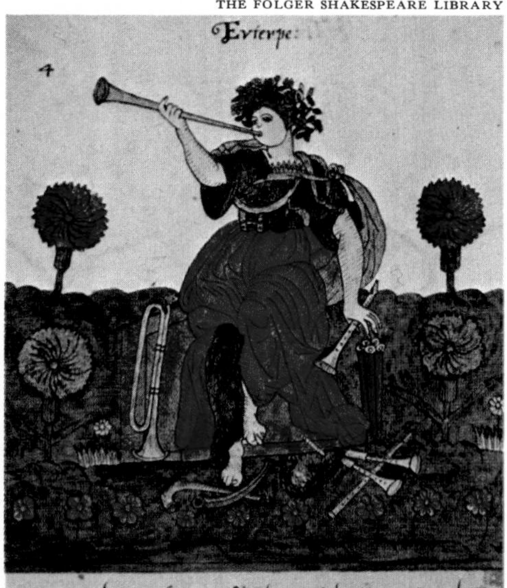

Throughout the ages, Euterpe, the muse of music, has been courted by lyric poets, with varying degrees of success.

A simplified map of the London of Shakespeare's time shows the prominent landmarks, as well as the theatres and other places where plays were performed.

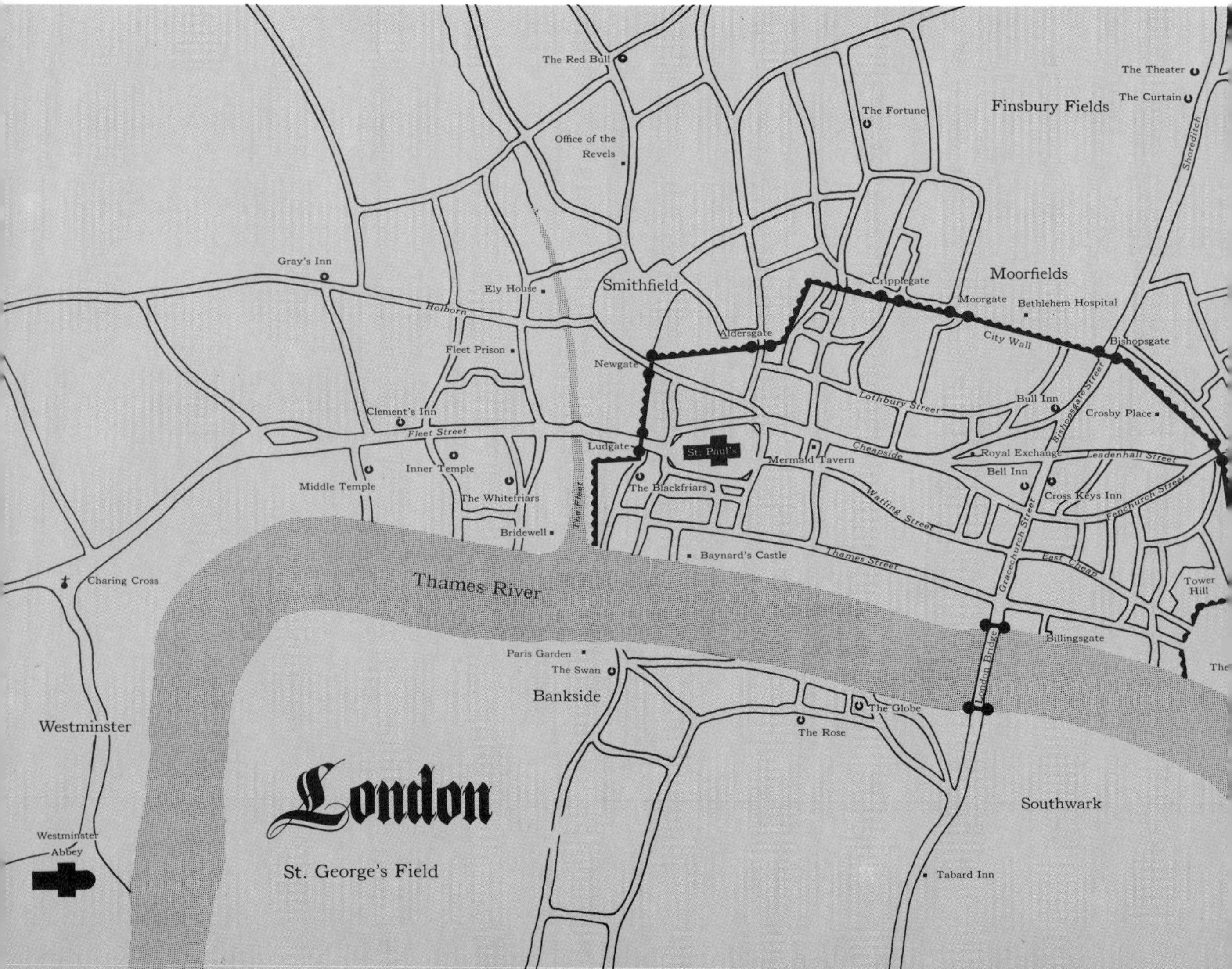

London
The Red Bull
The Theater
The Curtain
The Fortune
Finsbury Fields
Shoreditch
Office of the Revels
Gray's Inn
Ely House
Smithfield
Cripplegate
Moorfields
Moorgate
Bethlehem Hospital
Holborn
Aldersgate
City Wall
Bishopsgate
Fleet Prison
Newgate
Lothbury Street
Bull Inn
Bishopsgate Street
Crosby Place
Clement's Inn
Fleet Street
Ludgate
St. Paul's
Cheapside
Royal Exchange
Leadenhall Street
Inner Temple
Mermaid Tavern
Middle Temple
The Blackfriars
Bell Inn
The Whitefriars
Cross Keys Inn
Fenchurch Street
Watling Street
Bridewell
The Fleet
Baynard's Castle
Thames Street
Gracechurch Street
East Cheap
Charing Cross
Thames River
Tower Hill
Billingsgate
Paris Garden
The Swan
London Bridge
Bankside
The Globe
The Rose
Westminster
Southwark
Westminster Abbey
St. George's Field
Tabard Inn

In 1623, *John Heminges and Henry Condell collected thirty-six of Shakespeare's plays into the First Folio;* Troilus and Cressida *was omitted from the original table of contents.*

A CATALOGVE

of the ſeuerall Comedies, Hiſtories, and Tragedies contained in this Volume.

COMEDIES.

THe Tempeſt.	Folio 1.
The two Gentlemen of Verona.	20
The Merry Wiues of Windſor.	38
Meaſure for Meaſure.	61
The Comedy of Errours.	85
Much adoo about Nothing.	101
Loues Labour loſt.	122
Midſommer Nights Dreame.	145
The Merchant of Venice.	163
As you Like it.	185
The Taming of the Shrew.	208
All is well, that Ends well.	230
Twelfe-Night, or what you will.	255
The Winters Tale.	304

HISTORIES.

The Life and Death of King John.	Fol. 1.
The Life & death of Richard the ſecond.	23
The Firſt part of King Henry the fowrth.	46
The Second part of K. Henry the fourth.	74
The Life of King Henry the Fift.	69
The Firſt part of King Henry the Sixt.	96
The Second part of King Hen. the Sixt.	120
The Third part of King Henry the Sixt.	147
The Life & Death of Richard the Third.	173
The Life of King Henry the Eight.	205

TRAGEDIES.

The Tragedy of Coriolanus.	Fol. 1.
Titus Andronicus.	31
Romeo and Juliet.	53
Timon of Athens.	80
The Life and death of Julius Cæſar.	109
The Tragedy of Macbeth.	131
The Tragedy of Hamlet.	152
King Lear.	283
Othello, the Moore of Venice.	310
Anthony and Cleopater.	346
Cymbeline King of Britaine.	369

COURTESY OF THE TRUSTEES, THE BRITISH MUSEUM

Martin Droeshout's engraving on the title page of the First Folio is one of only two authentic likenesses of Shakespeare in existence.

Inigo Jones, a brilliant costumer and stage designer, created this costume for one of Ben Jonson's masques.

DEVONSHIRE COLLECTION CHATSWORTH. REPRODUCED BY PERMISSION OF THE TRUSTEES OF THE CHATSWORTH SETTLEMENT.

With London providing the background in this painting from about 1590, an elaborate Elizabethan wedding feast, complete with bakers, musicians, and elegantly attired guests, is about to begin.

HATFIELD HOUSE. HERTFORDSHIRE. BY PERMISSION OF THE MARQUESS OF SALISBURY

VICTORIA AND ALBERT MUSEUM. CROWN COPYRIGHT

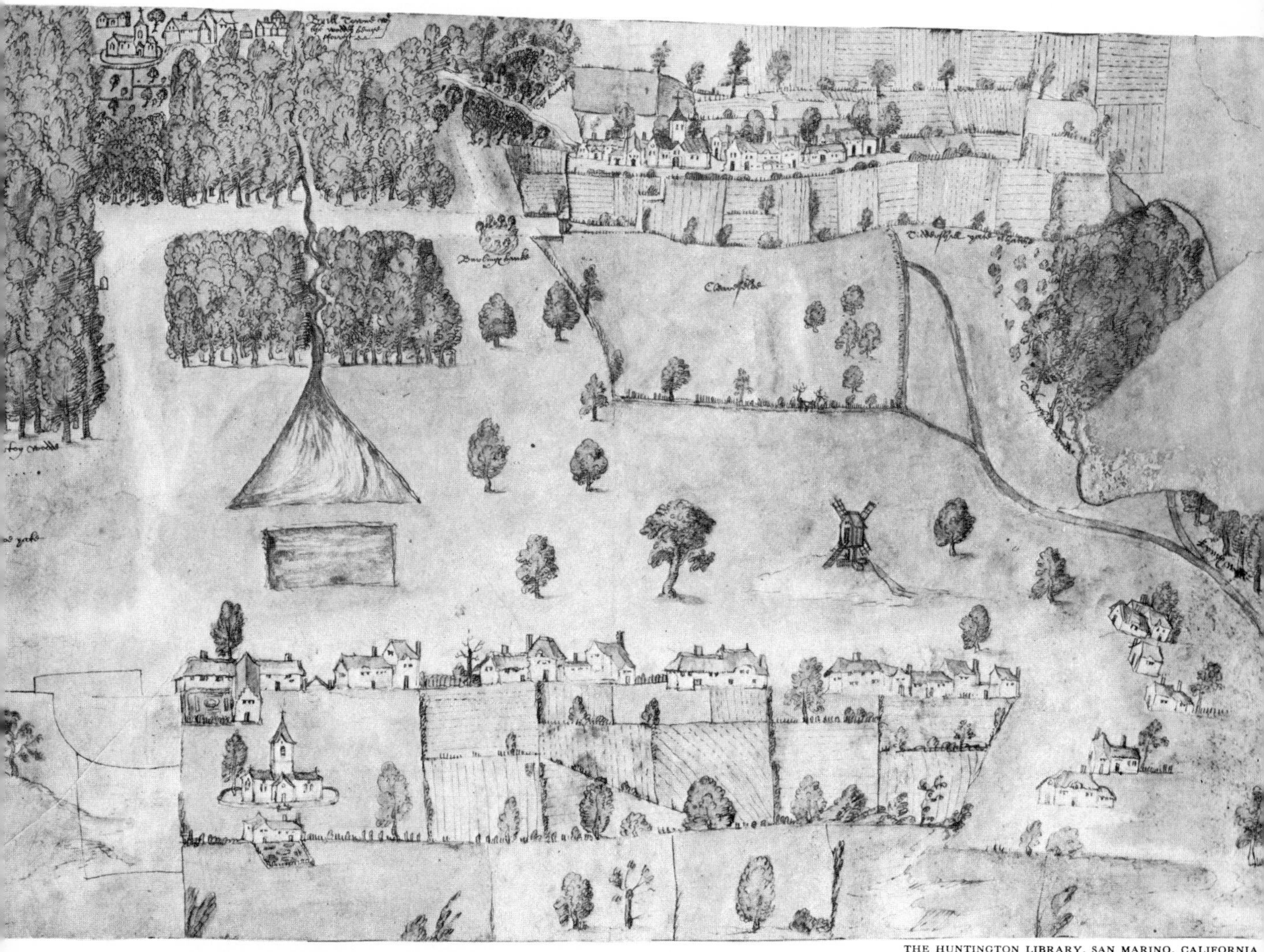

THE HUNTINGTON LIBRARY, SAN MARINO, CALIFORNIA

A watercolor of the rural district of Buckinghamshire in about 1575, with neatly arranged villages and well-tended fields, reflects a bucolic serenity that sharply contrasts with the political and religious turmoil of the times.

diversions in this early tapestry reflect c life at its idyllic best: well-kept ·ges, fruitful vegetation, eager hounds uing abundant game, and a pair of ·ly lovers.

SCENES FROM SHAKESPEARE'S PLAYS

THE TATE GALLERY, LONDON

PHOTOGRAPH: MAX WALDMAN, NEW YORK

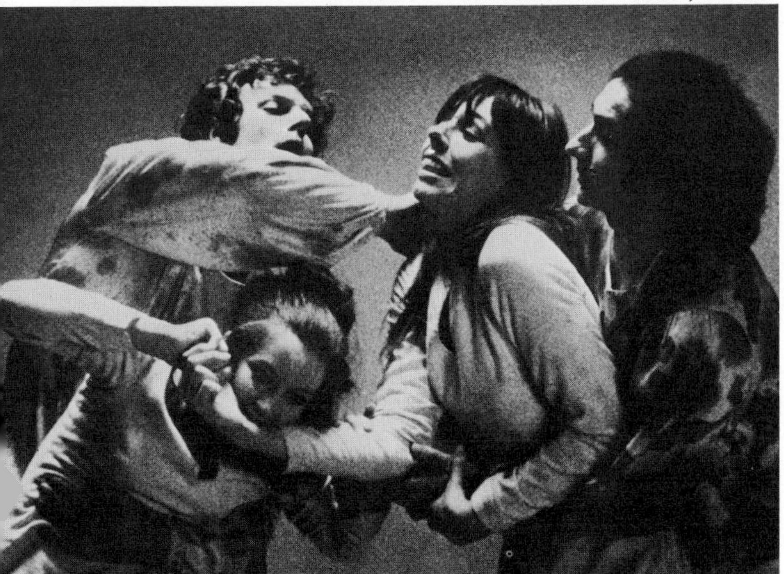

COURTESY OF THE NEWBERRY LIBRARY, CHICAGO

Three sharply contrasting conceptions of A Midsummer Night's Dream *attests to the play's continuously wide appeal through the years. At the top, the eighteenth-century poet, William Blake, catches the fanciful and dreamlike flavor of the play in his rendering of the meeting of Oberon, Titania, Puck, and attendant fairies; above, an engraving from about 1800 shows a scene in Act III—the buffoonish craftsmen surround Bottom the Weaver who wears the ass's head magically placed there by the mischievous Puck during their rehearsal of "Pyramus and Thisbe"; left, a scene of the squabbling lovers from Peter Brook's controversial British production reflects a contemporary interpretation of the play.*

ıonarchs have ever influenced an age so pervasively and left their stamp on it so ıently as did Elizabeth I during her reign from 1558 to 1603.

.D HOUSE. HERTFORDSHIRE. BY PERMISSION OF THE MARQUESS OF SALISBURY. PHOTOGRAPH: J. R. FREEMAN & CO.

Mid nineteenth-century America and England acclaimed the Cushman sisters in Romeo and Juliet*— Charlotte as Romeo and Susan as Juliet.*

THE FOLGER SHAKESPEARE LIBRARY

In the Induction to The Taming of the Shrew*, Christophero Sly, a drunken tinker, is jokingly attired in finery and attended by servants preparatory to his witnessing of the play itself.*

THE FOLGER SHAKESPEARE LIBRARY

LONGLEAT, WILTSHIRE. BY PERMISSION OF THE MARQUESS OF BATH. PHOTOGRAPH: COURTAULD INSTITUTE

Two contemporary illustrations of several scenes from Titus Andronicus, *Shakespeare's early attempt at revenge tragedy: above, Queen Tamora begs for the life of her sons; below, their eventual slaughter and Titus' grisly banquet.*

THE FOLGER SHAKESPEARE LIBRARY

The eighteenth-century London stage was dominated by David Garrick, theatre manager, director, author, and consummate actor, depicted here as Richard III.

THE FOLGER SHAKESPEARE LIBRARY

George Cruikshank's watercolor of a scene in Twelfth Night *shows Olivia's foppish steward, Malvolio, affecting gentlemanly airs.*

COLLECTION OF DR. LOUIS MARDER, UNIVERSITY OF ILLINOI

THE FOLGER SHAKESPEARE LIBRARY

METRO-GOLDWYN-MAYER INC.

Marlon Brando as Marc Antony in a 1953 film version of Julius Caesar, *a fairly successful Hollywood adaptation of Shakespeare.*

THE FOLGER SHAKESPEARE LIBRARY

In two scenes from The Merry Wives of Windsor, *Falstaff is the object of comic humiliation: left, opposite page, disguised as an old woman, he is beaten by an irate husband; near left, to escape the same fate he is hidden in a clothes basket by the merry wives.*

THE FOLGER SHAKESPEARE LIBRARY

Rising from amid the vapors of the steaming cauldrons, the three "secret, black, and midnight hags" prophesy Macbeth's ominous future in this romanticized nineteenth-century illustration.

HARVARD THEATRE COLLECTION

Right: Sarah Bernhardt as Hamlet contemplating the skull of Yoric—a stylized pose that unfortunately has become hackneyed and humorously associated with ham actors attempting the role. Below: John Everett Millais' "Ophelia" (1851) is a Pre-Raphaelite conception of her drowning.

THE TATE GALLERY, LONDON

THE FOLGER SHAKESPEARE LIBRARY

Henry VIII and Anne Bullen are entertained by a contemplative Cardinal Wolsey in an eighteenth-century painting by William Hogarth.

An eighteenth-century charcoal drawing by George Romney shows Shylock of The Merchant of Venice *as unusually fierce.*

THE FOLGER SHAKESPEARE LIBRARY

In this painting by Fuseli from the Boydell edition of Shakespeare (1803), King Lear fiercely denounces Cordelia while Regan and Goneril watch, thus setting the stage for his eventual tragic end.

COLLECTION OF DR. LOUIS MARDER, UNIVERSITY OF ILLINOIS

THE FOLGER SHAKESPEARE LIBRARY

Right: the frontispiece of Nicholas Rowe's 1709 edition of The Tempest *shows Ariel and other spirits churning up the seas which results in the travelers landing on Prospero's enchanted island; below, Fuseli's 1803 version of Prospero, Miranda, Caliban, and Ariel.*

COLLECTION OF DR. LOUIS MARDER, UNIVERSITY OF ILLINOIS

The early period

Before we attempt to give a connected account of Shakespeare's life and work, we should consider briefly the kinds of information that are available about him. The sources for a biography of Shakespeare fall into two large classes: documents and traditions. Formal written documents are impersonal, often official, and usually reliable. No motive for falsification existed in the making of the legal and commercial records that concerned Shakespeare. Yet such records, because they often give us only the insignificant and routine features of his life, remain dead and dry. Tradition, on the other hand, is likely to be fanciful, even false, arising as it does, for the most part, from posterity's craving for personal detail and anecdote.

Documents

Manuscripts of some of Shakespeare's plays and many documents containing personal information about him must have perished in the great fire of London in 1666. The records of Stratford, however, where he spent his first and his last years, still remain to give us many vital biographical statistics. Dates for his birth and death are determined from the baptismal and burial registers of Stratford-upon-Avon. The *Episcopal Register* of the Diocese of Worcester records the issuing of his marriage license and of the marriage bond. At Somerset House in London, a British government building which contains a depository of legal documents, is to be found his will, dated March 25, 1616. Other records, such as those of the land that he bought and sold, the lawsuits to which he was a party, and the tax returns which listed his property for taxation, indicate his financial resources and his activities as a man of the world. From these purely official documents one can usually learn where Shakespeare happened to be living at a particular time of his life, and often something about his activities at such times.

Documentary information about Shakespeare still continues to gather slowly, even after some three hundred years of collecting and setting down facts about his life. In 1910, for example, C. W. Wallace discovered in the Public Record Office in London a legal document pertaining to a suit in Chancery from the year 1612, in which Shakespeare was called as a witness. Shakespeare's signature to his deposition in this case added a sixth authentic signature to those previously known. His testimony in the lawsuit showed that he had been, possibly for some years after 1602, a lodger in the house of a Huguenot tiremaker (i.e., a maker of women's ornamental headdresses) named Mountjoy, at the corner of Muggle and Silver streets in London. He thus may have been for a considerable time in contact with a French-speaking household.

No letter written by Shakespeare exists today, and only one short letter addressed to him has been preserved. In it a Stratford neighbor, Richard Quiney, asked Shakespeare for the loan of thirty pounds. Other letters do exist that mention Shakespeare's name, mainly in connection with his activities as a citizen of Stratford. In addition to correspondence of this sort, a few diaries of the time have been discovered to contain personal anecdotes about him. Because he acted with his company at court, his name frequently appears in the official records of court performances, that is, in the accounts of the Office of Revels. He is several times mentioned as one of the principal members of his company to whom payment was made.

First publications of Shakespeare's works furnish a great deal of information about him. The famous First Folio of 1623 was edited by his fellow actors, John Heminges and Henry Condell, whose names are signed to a dedicatory epistle and to an epistle "To the great Variety of Readers." The book contains, besides other laudatory verses, a poetic eulogy of Shakespeare by his celebrated contemporary Ben Jonson. The title pages and dedicatory epistles of the two poems *Venus and Adonis* (1593) and *The Rape of Lucrece* (1594), the title pages of various plays issued singly before the collected edition of 1623, and the entries of plays in the register of the Stationers' Company of London furnish information as to Shakespeare's claims to courtly patronage, his association with printers and dramatic companies, and approximate dates of composition of some of his works.

Quotations from Shakespeare and allusions to his work are an important source of biographical information. Some references of this sort have been found in commonplace books and poems even from his earliest years as a dramatist. Of the many allusions that have been found, the most valuable are those that are chronologically close to his time and unmistakably clear in their referring to Shakespeare. Probably the best known source of allusions is Francis Meres' *Palladis Tamia*, or *Wit's Treasury*, a slender volume on contemporary literature and art which would never be remembered today except for its valuable listing of most of Shakespeare's works prior to 1598.

Traditions

Although documentary information about Shakespeare is more extensive than for any other Elizabethan playwright except Ben Jonson, this information is still austerely statistical and tantalizing in its lack of personal details. Posterity has had to satisfy its craving for a more intimate knowledge of Shakespeare by turning instead to various traditions about him. Such traditions, usually written down fairly late, are often inconsistent with one another and with knowledge we have from documentary sources. Although they may in some instances contain important elements of truth and are certainly appealing, these traditions must be approached with caution.

The seventeenth century provides most of our anecdotes about Shakespeare's life. Although he was not yet regarded as deserving a full-scale biography, various men of letters jotted down what they had heard about him. Thomas Fuller wrote a not very informative sketch in his *Lives of the Worthies* (1662). John Aubrey includes Shakespeare in his *Lives of Eminent Men* (compiled between 1669 and 1696, though not published until 1813), where he records matters derived from the actor and theatre manager, William Beeston, whose father had almost certainly been an associate of Shakespeare's. The Reverend John Ward, vicar of Stratford, the Reverend William Fulman, the Reverend Richard Davies, and other persons collected local traditions and examined some records. All of these accounts, except Aubrey's, were gathered up and used by the first modern editor of Shakespeare, Nicholas Rowe, who prefixed a life of the dramatist to his edition of the plays in 1709.

Unfortunately, the collecting of information about Shakespeare had begun rather late—not until the end of the seventeenth century. Too many generations had passed since Shakespeare had lived, and the fire of London in 1666 had done its work. Those who had seen his plays were virtually all dead, and so were his direct descendants. Biographers in quest of personal details about Shakespeare had therefore to rely on oral traditions, handed down as stories from those who had claimed to know something about Shakespeare. Oral traditions of this sort were still widely in circulation in the second half of the eighteenth century, at the time of the great Shakespeare editors Samuel Johnson and Edmund Malone.

Late traditions sometimes seem implausible because they do not fit into what is known from more reliable sources; others, though questionable or even false in some details, seem authentically to confirm what we know or would expect. Consider, for example, the two following popular traditions. The first is set down in the *Lives of the Poets* attributed to Theophilus Cibber (1753). According to this report, Shakespeare's first employment in the theatre after he came to London was as a holder of horses for the gentlemen who rode to the playhouse to see the plays. Shakespeare is also supposed to have organized the boys of the neighborhood into a company of horseholders known as "Will's Boys." William Davenant and Thomas Betterton, both important persons in the Restoration theatre, are cited as authorities for this story. Such men would have been in a position to have learned a great deal of lore about the theatre in Shakespeare's time. Nevertheless, this particular story does not jibe with what we know about the actual conditions of entry into the acting profession in the 1580's and 1590's.

The second tradition comes through William Oldys, who, in about 1750–1760, wrote that one of Shakespeare's younger brothers, "who lived to a good old age, even some years, as I compute, after the restora-

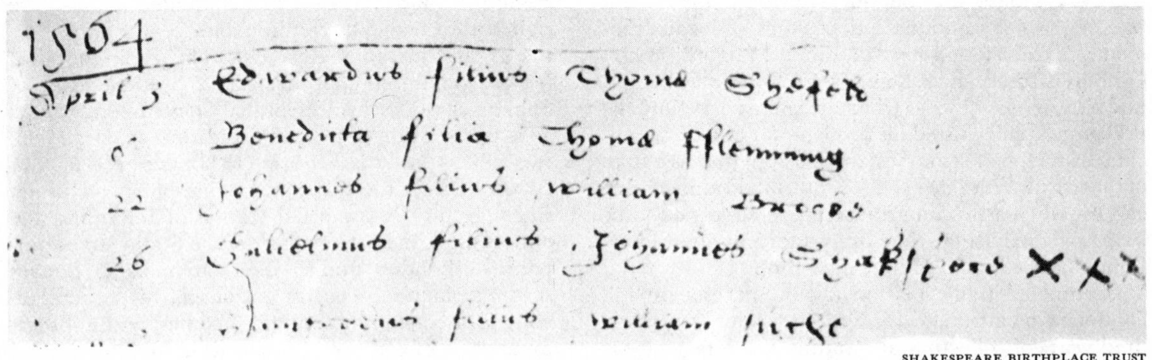

SHAKESPEARE BIRTHPLACE TRUST

"Gulielmus filius Johannes Shakspere"—the earliest written reference to William Shakespeare is this record of his christening at Stratford, April 26, 1564, traditionally assumed to have been entered three days after his birth.

tion of *King Charles II.*," came, on more than one occasion, to London to see his brother act in plays. When he was asked at a later time what parts his brother played he "was so stricken in years, and possibly his memory so weakened with infirmities (which might make him the easier pass for a man of weak intellects) that he could give them but little light into their enquiries; and all that could be recollected from him of his brother *Will*, in that station was, the faint, general, and almost lost ideas he had of having once seen him act a part in one of his own comedies, wherein being to personate a decrepit old man, he wore a long beard, and appeared so weak and drooping and unable to walk, that he was forced to be supported and carried by another person to a table, at which he was seated among some company, who were eating, and one of them sung a song." Actually, none of Shakespeare's brothers lived past Shakespeare's own death in 1616, so that the ascription of this later anecdote to a brother is impossible. Yet the recollection here by some aged person of the part of Adam in *As You Like It* does sound authentic. It lends some strength perhaps to other uncertain hints that Shakespeare may have acted old men's parts, including that of Adam. The tradition remains doubtful and yet fascinating, like so many late stories about him.

Stratford-upon-Avon

About Shakespeare's place of birth, Stratford-upon-Avon, there is no doubt. He spent his childhood there and returned periodically throughout his life. During most or all of his long professional career in London, his wife and children lived in Stratford. He acquired property and took some interest in local affairs. He retired to Stratford and chose to be buried there. Its Warwickshire surroundings lived in his poetic imagination.

The Stratford of Shakespeare's day was a small market town of perhaps two thousand inhabitants, with fairly broad streets and half-timbered houses roofed with thatch. It could boast of a long history and an attractive setting on the river Avon. A bridge of fourteen arches, built in 1496 by Sir Hugh Clopton, Lord Mayor of London, spanned the river. Beside the Avon stood Trinity Church, built on the site of a Saxon monastery. The chapel of the Guild of the Holy Trinity, dating from the thirteenth century, and an old King Edward VI grammar school, were buildings of note. Stratford had maintained a grammar school at least since 1424 and probably long before that. It was a town without the domination of clergy, aristocracy, or great wealth, where simple, honest people plied their trades and occupied their own positions of honor in the local society.

Warwickshire

Warwickshire, in which Stratford lies, is a midland county just south of the center of England and almost as far inland as one can get in that country. On the north side is Staffordshire, on the south Gloucestershire and Oxfordshire, on the east Leicestershire and Northampton, and on the west Worcestershire. It is an agricultural region broken by rich valleys of the Avon, the Stour, and the Thames. The northern part of the county was once occupied by the Forest of Arden, but even in Shakespeare's day almost the whole county was under cultivation. In his time the famous industrial city of Birmingham was inconspicuous. Coventry, which is now a manufacturing center, was a neat, clean, progressive borough devoted to varied cottage industries and noted for its active community life.

Warwick, the county seat, where the great Warwick Castle still stands, and Kenilworth, whose royal castle was destroyed by Oliver Cromwell, are on the road between Stratford and Coventry, the total distance between these places being about fourteen miles. Warwickshire, in the reign of Queen Elizabeth, was a rich county in which the standard of living was relatively high. Families and towns were more or less independent and self-supporting units, and agriculture was the basic occupation.

The Shakespeares

The family which bore the name of Shakespeare was well distributed throughout England, but was especially numerous in Warwickshire. A name "Saquespee," in various spellings, is found in Normandy at an early date. It means, according to J. Q. Adams, "to draw out the sword quickly." That name, in the form "Sakspee," with many variants, is found in England; also the name "Saksper," varying gradually to the form "Shakespeare." It may have been wrought into that form by the obvious military meaning of "one who shakes the spear."

Our first substantial records of the family begin with Richard Shakespeare, who was in all probability Shakespeare's grandfather, a farmer living in the village of Snitterfield four miles from Stratford. He was a tenant on the property of Robert Arden of Wilmcote, a wealthy man with the social status of gentleman. Richard Shakespeare died about 1561 possessed of an estate valued at the very respectable sum of £38 17s.

John Shakespeare

No doubt the prosperity of Richard laid the basis for the fortunes of John, the poet's father. John Shakespeare, who is the first of the family to become in any way conspicuous, was a man about whom considerable information has been collected. He made a great step forward in the world by his marriage with Mary Arden, daughter of his father's landlord. John Shakespeare had some property of his own and through his wife acquired a good deal more. He moved from Snitterfield to Stratford at some date before 1552. He rose to great local importance in Stratford and bought several houses, among them the one on Henley Street traditionally identified as Shakespeare's birthplace. William Shakespeare was born in 1564 and was baptized on April 26. The exact date of his birth is not known, but traditionally we celebrate it on April 23,

SHAKESPEARE BIRTHPLACE TRUST

The probable birthplace of Shakespeare on Henley Street in Stratford. Its size attests to John Shakespeare's prominent social standing in the town.

the feast day of St. George, England's patron saint. The house in which Shakespeare was probably born, though changed in various and unknown ways during the years which have intervened since Shakespeare's birth, still stands. It is of considerable size, having four rooms on the ground floor, and must, therefore, have been an important business house in the Stratford of those days. John Shakespeare's occupation seems to have been that of a tanner and glover—that is, he cured skins, made gloves and some other leather goods, and sold them in his shop. He was also a dealer in wool, grain, malt, and other farm produce.

The long story, beginning in 1552, of John Shakespeare's success and misfortunes in Stratford is attested by many borough records. He held various city offices. He was ale taster (inspector of bread and malt), burgess (petty constable), affeeror (assessor of fines), city chamberlain (treasurer), alderman, and high bailiff of the town—the highest municipal office in Stratford. At some time around 1576 he applied to the Herald's office for the right to bear arms and style himself a gentleman. This petition was later to be renewed and successfully carried through to completion by his famous son. In 1577 or 1578, however, when William was as yet only thirteen or fourteen years old, John Shakespeare's fortunes began a sudden and mysterious decline. He absented himself from council meetings. He had to mortgage his wife's property and showed other signs of being in financial difficulty. He became involved in serious litigation and was assessed heavy fines. Although he kept his position on the corporation council until 1586 or 1587, he was finally replaced as alderman because of his failure to attend. Conceivably John Shakespeare's sudden difficulties were the result of persecution for Catholic faith, since John's wife's family had remained loyal to Catholicism, and the old faith was being attacked with new vigor in the Warwickshire region in 1577 and afterwards. This hypothesis is unsubstantial, however, and we have little evidence as to John Shakespeare's religious faith or as to the reasons for his sudden reversal of fortune.

Our only tentative personal glimpse of John Shakespeare comes from a note in the Memoranda of Archdeacon Plume of Rochester, written about 1656. This note purports to describe John Shakespeare in his later years as one who thought well of his own wit and was willing to match it at any time against that of his famous son:

> He [Shakespeare] was a glovers son. Sir John Mennis saw once his old Father in his shop—a merry Cheekd old man that said, "Will was a good Honest Fellow, but he [John Shakespeare] durst have crackt a jeast with him at any time."

This tradition may contain some element of truth, even though the name of Sir John Mennes cannot be accurate: Mennes was not born until 1599, two years before the death of Shakespeare's father.

The family of Shakespeare's mother could trace its ancestry back to the time of William the Conqueror; and Shakespeare's father, in spite of his troubles, was a citizen of importance. John Shakespeare made his mark instead of writing his name, but so did other men of the time who we know could read and write. His offices, particularly that of chamberlain, and the various public functions he discharged, indicate that he must have had some education.

Shakespeare in School

Nicholas Rowe, who published in 1709 the first extensive biographical account of Shakespeare, reports the tradition that Shakespeare studied "for some time at a Free-School." Although the list of students who actually attended the King's New School at Stratford-upon-Avon in the late sixteenth century has not survived, we cannot doubt that Rowe is reporting accurately. Shakespeare's father, as a leading citizen of Stratford, would scarcely have spurned the benefits of one of Stratford's most prized institutions. The town had had a free school since the thirteenth century, at first under the auspices of the church. During the reign of King Edward VI (1547–1553), the church lands were expropriated by the crown and the town of Stratford was granted a corporate charter. At this time the school was reorganized as the King's New School, named in honor of the reigning monarch. It prospered. Its teachers or "masters" regularly held degrees from Oxford during Shakespeare's childhood and received salaries that were superior to those of most comparable schools.

Much has been learned about the curriculum of such a school. A child would first learn the rudiments of reading and writing English by spending two or three years in a "petty" or elementary school. The child learned to read from his "hornbook," a single sheet of paper mounted on a board and protected by a thin transparent layer of horn, on which was usually printed the alphabet in small and capital letters and the Lord's Prayer. The child would also practice his ABC book with catechism. When he had demonstrated the ability to read satisfactorily, he was admitted, at about the age of seven, to the grammar school proper. Here the day was a rigorous one, usually extending from 6 A.M. in the summer or 7 A.M. in the winter until 5 P.M. Intervals for food or brief recreation came at midmorning, noon, and midafternoon. Holidays occurred at Christmas, Easter, and Whitsuntide (usually late May and June), comprising perhaps forty days in all through the year. Discipline was strict and physical punishment was common.

Latin formed the basis of the grammar school curriculum. The scholars studied grammar, read ancient writers, recited, and learned to write in Latin. A standard text was the *Grammatica Latina* by William Lilly or Lyly, father of the later Elizabethan dramatist John Lyly. The scholars also became familiar with the *Disticha de Moribus* (moral proverbs) attributed to Cato, *Aesop's Fables*, the *Eclogues* of Baptista Spagnuoli Mantuanus or Mantuan (alluded to in *Love's Labour's Lost*), the *Eclogues* and *Aeneid* of Virgil, the comedies of Plautus or Terence (sometimes performed in Latin by the children), Ovid's *Metamorphoses* and other of his works, and possibly some Horace and Seneca.

Shakespeare plentifully reveals in his dramatic writings an awareness of many of these authors, especially Plautus (in *The Comedy of Errors*), Ovid (in *A Midsummer Night's Dream* and elsewhere), and Seneca (in *Titus Andronicus*). Although he often consulted translations of these authors, he seems to have known the originals as well. He had, in Ben Jonson's learned estimation, "small Latine and lesse Greeke"; the tone is condescending, but the statement does concede that Shakespeare had some of both. He would have acquired some Greek in the last years of his grammar schooling. By twentieth-century standards, Shakespeare had a fairly comprehensive amount of training in the ancient classics, certainly enough to account for the general if unscholarly references we find in the plays themselves.

The Anti-Stratfordian Movement

What we know of Shakespeare's life so far is really quite considerable. The information we have is just the kind one would expect. It hangs together and refers to one man and one career. Though lacking in the personal details we should like to have, it is both adequate and plausible. Yet the past hundred years or so have seen the growth of a tendency to doubt Shakespeare's authorship of the plays and poems ascribed to him. The phenomenon is sometimes called the "anti-Stratfordian" movement, since its attack is leveled at the literary credentials of the man who was born in Stratford and later became an actor in London. Although based on no reliable evidence, the

SHAKESPEARE BIRTHPLACE TRUST

In Stratford's Grammar School, Shakespeare's undoubtedly prodigious curiosity must have been further sharpened, despite dulling pedagogical techniques.

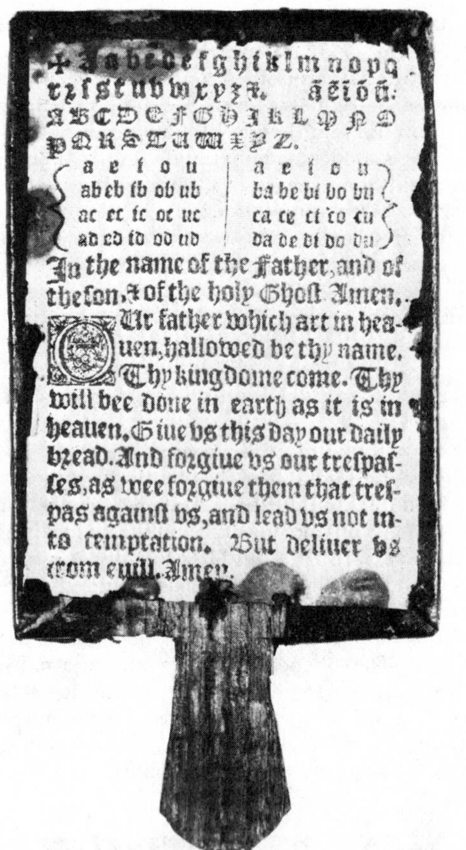

THE FOLGER SHAKESPEARE LIBRARY

Memorization seasoned with inspiration: the ABC's and the Lord's Prayer on an early English hornbook.

movement has persisted long enough to become a kind of myth. It also has the appeal of a mystery thriller: who really wrote Shakespeare's plays? A brief account must be made here of the origins of the anti-Stratfordian movement.

Beginning in the late eighteenth century, and especially in the mid nineteenth century, a few admirers of Shakespeare began to be troubled by the scantiness of information about England's greatest author. As we have already seen, good reasons exist for that scarcity: the great London fire of 1666 that destroyed many records, the relatively low social esteem accorded to popular dramatists during the Elizabethan period, and the like. Also, we do actually know more about Shakespeare than about most of his contemporaries in the theatre, despite the difficulties imposed by the passage of time. Still, some nineteenth-century readers saw only that they knew far less about Shakespeare than about many authors of more recent date.

Moreover, the impressions of the man did not seem to square with his unparalleled literary greatness. William Shakespeare had been brought up in a small country town; were his parents cultured folk, or even literate? No record of his schooling has been preserved; was Shakespeare himself able to read and write, much less write immortal plays and poems? The anti-Stratfordians did not deny the existence of a man called Shakespeare from Stratford-upon-Avon, but they found it incredible that such a person should be connected with the works ascribed to him. Mark Twain, himself an anti-Stratfordian, was fond of joking that the plays were not by Shakespeare but by another person of the same name. Beneath the humor in this remark lies a deep-seated mistrust: how could a simple country boy have written so knowledgeably and eloquently about the lives of kings and queens? Where could such a person have learned so much about the law, about medicine, about the art of war, about heraldry? The puzzle seemed a genuine one, even though no one until the late eighteenth century had thought to question Shakespeare's authorship of the plays—least of all his colleagues and friends, such as Ben Jonson, who admitted that Shakespeare's classical learning was "small," but insisted that Shakespeare was an incomparable genius.

The first candidate put forward as the "real" author of the plays was Sir Francis Bacon, a reputable Elizabethan writer with connections at court and considerable cultural attainments. Yet the ascription of the plays to Bacon was based on no documentary evidence. It relied instead on the essentially snobbish argument that Bacon was better born and purportedly better educated than Shakespeare—an argument that appealed strongly to the nineteenth century in which a university education was becoming more and more a distinctive mark of the cultivated person. The assertion of Bacon's authorship was also based on a conspiratorial theory of history. That is, its believers had to assume the existence of a mammoth conspiracy in Elizabethan times in which Shakespeare would allow his name to be used by Bacon as a *nom de plume*, and in which Shakespeare's friends such as Ben Jonson would take part. (Jonson knew Shakespeare too well, after all, to have been duped for a period of almost twenty years.) The motive for such an arrangement, presumably, was that Bacon did not deign to lend his dignified name to the writing of popular plays (since they were considered subliterary) and so chose a common actor named Shakespeare to serve as his alter ego. This theory of an elaborate hoax involving England's greatest literary giant has proved powerfully attractive to modern writers like Mark Twain, who sometimes refer to themselves as rebels against the cultural "Establishment" of their own times.

Bacon's claim to have written Shakespeare was soon challenged by that of other prominent Elizabethans: the Earl of Oxford, the Earl of Southampton, Anthony Bacon, the Earl of Rutland, the Earl of Devonshire, Christopher Marlowe, and others. Since Bacon's documentary claims to Shakespearean greatness were nonexistent, other Elizabethans could be proposed to fill his role just as satisfactorily as Bacon himself. The anti-Stratfordian movement gained momentum and came to include several prominent persons including Delia Bacon and Sigmund Freud as well as Mark Twain. One of the appeals of the anti-Stratfordian movement in recent years has proved to be a kind of amateur sleuthing or scholarship carried on by professional lawyers, doctors, and the like, who have explored Shakespeare's interest in law and medicine as a hobby and have convinced themselves that Shakespeare's wisdom in these subjects entitles him to claim a better birth than that of a glover's son from Stratford. Absurdly ingenious efforts at "deciphering" hidden meanings in the works have been adduced to prove some authorship claim or other. The academic "Establishments" of modern universities have been accused of perpetuating Shakespeare's name out of mere vested self-interest: Shakespeare scholarship is an industry, and its busy workers need to preserve their source of income.

We must ask in all seriousness, however, whether such assertions are not offering answers to nonexistent questions. Responsible recent scholarship has admirably dispelled the seeming mystery of Shakespeare's humble beginnings. T. W. Baldwin, for example, in *William Shakspere's Petty School* (1943) and *William Shakspere's Small Latine and Lesse Greeke* (1944) has shown just what sort of classical training Shakespeare almost surely received in the free grammar school of Stratford. It is precisely the sort of training that would have enabled him to use classical authors as he does, with the familiarity of one who likes to read. His Latin and Greek were passable but not strong; he often consulted modern translations as well as classical originals. Just as importantly, Shakespeare's social background was in fact typical of many of the greatest writers of the English Renaissance. He earned his living by his writing, and thus had one of the strongest of motives for success. So did his contemporaries Marlowe (who came from a shoemakers' family) and Jonson (whose stepfather was a brickmason). Greene, Peele, Nashe, and many others sold plays and other writings for a livelihood. Although a few well-born persons such as Bacon and Sir Philip Sidney also made exceptional contributions to literature, and although a number of courtiers emulated Henry VIII and Elizabeth as gifted amateurs in the arts, the court was not the direct or major source of England's literary greatness. Most courtiers were not, like Shakespeare, professional writers. A man like Bacon lacked Shakespeare's connection with a commercial acting company. Surely the theatre was a more relevant "university" for Shakespeare than Oxford or Cambridge, where most of his studies would have been in ancient languages and in divinity.

Shakespeare's Marriage

When Shakespeare was eighteen years old, he married Anne Hathaway, a woman eight years his senior. (The inscription on her grave states that she was sixty-seven when she died in August of 1623.) The bishop's register of Worcester, the central city of the diocese, shows for November 27, 1582, the issue of a bishop's license for the marriage of William Shakespeare and Anne Hathaway. She has been identified with all reasonable probability as Agnes (or Anne) Hathaway, daughter of the then recently deceased Richard Hathaway of the hamlet of Shottery, a short distance from Stratford.

The obtaining of a license was not normally required for a marriage. William Shakespeare and Anne Hathaway seem to have applied for a license on this occasion because they wished to be married after only one reading of the banns rather than the usual three. (The reading of the banns, or announcement in church of a forthcoming marriage, usually on three successive Sundays, enabled any party to object to the marriage if he knew of any legal impediment.) Since the reading of all banns was suspended for long periods during Advent (before Christmas) and Lent (before Easter), a couple intending to marry shortly before Christmas might have had to wait until April before the banns could be read thrice. Accordingly, the bishop not uncommonly granted a license permitting couples to marry during the winter season with only one reading of the banns. To obtain such a license, two friends of the bride's family had to sign a bond obligating themselves to pay the bishop up to forty pounds, should any impediment to the marriage result in a legal action against the bishop for having issued the license.

The actual record of the marriage in a parish register has not survived, but presumably the couple were joined in matrimony shortly after obtaining the license. They may have been married in Temple Grafton, where Anne had relatives. The couple took up residence in Stratford. Anne was already pregnant at the time of the marriage, for she gave birth to a daughter, Susanna, on May 26, 1583. The birth of a child six months after the wedding may explain the need for haste the previous November. These circumstances, and Anne's considerable seniority in age to William, have given rise to much speculation about matters that can never be satisfactorily resolved. We do know that a formal betrothal in the presence of witnesses could legally validate a binding relationship, enabling a couple to consummate their love without social stigma. We know also that Shakespeare dramatized the issue of premarital contract and pregnancy in *Measure for Measure*. Whether Shakespeare entered into such a formal relationship with Anne is, however, undiscoverable.

On February 2, 1585, Shakespeare's only other children, the twins Hamnet and Judith, were baptized in Stratford Church. The twins seem to have been named after Shakespeare's friends and neighbors, Hamnet Sadler, a baker, and his wife, Judith.

The Seven "Dark" Years

From 1585, the year in which his twins were baptized, until 1592, when he is first referred to as an actor and dramatist of growing importance in London, Shakespeare's activities are wholly unknown. Presumably at some time during this period he made his way to London and entered its theatrical world, but otherwise we can only record traditions and guesses as to what he did between the ages of 21 and 28.

One of the oldest and most intriguing suggestions comes from John Aubrey, who, in collecting information about actors and dramatists for his "Minutes of Lives," sought the help of one William Beeston. John Dryden believed Beeston to be "the chronicle of the stage," and Aubrey seems also to have had a high opinion of Beeston's theatrical knowledge. In his manuscript, Aubrey made a note to himself: "W. Shakespeare—quære [i.e., inquire of] Mr. Beeston, who knows most of him." Aubrey then cites Beeston as his authority for this tradition about Shakespeare:

> Though, as Ben: Johnson sayes of him, that he had but little Latine and lesse Greeke, He understood Latine pretty well: for he had been in his younger yeares a Schoolmaster in the Countrey.

Beeston had been a theatrical manager all his life. He was the son of the actor Christopher Beeston, who had been a member of Shakespeare's company probably from 1596 until 1602 and who therefore had occasion to know Shakespeare well.

Shakespeare's own grammar school education would not have qualified him to be the master of a school, but he could have served as "usher" or assistant to the master. The idea that Shakespeare may have taught in this way is not unattractive. Although, as we have seen, he had some acquaintance with Plautus, Ovid, and other classical writers through his own grammar school reading, a stint as schoolmaster would have made these authors more familiar and readily accessible to him when he began writing his plays and nondramatic poems. His earliest works—*The Comedy of Errors*, *Love's Labour's Lost*, *Titus Andronicus*, *Venus and Adonis*, *The Rape of Lucrece*—show most steadily and directly the effect of his classical reading. Schoolteaching experience might have encouraged his ambitions to be a writer, like Marlowe or Greene, who went to London not to be actors but to try their hands at poetry and playwriting. All in all, however, it seems more probable that Shakespeare became a young actor rather than a schoolteacher.

Another tradition about the years from 1585 to 1592 asserts that Shakespeare served part of an apprenticeship in Stratford. This suggestion comes to us from one John Dowdall who, traveling through Warwickshire in 1693, heard the story from an old parish clerk who was showing him around the town of Stratford. According to this parish clerk, Shakespeare had been bound as apprentice to a butcher, but ran away from his master to London where he was received into a playhouse as "serviture." John Aubrey records a similar tradition: "when he [Shakespeare] was a boy he exercised his father's Trade." Aubrey believed this trade to have been that of a butcher. Moreover, says Aubrey, "when he kill'd a Calfe, he would doe it in a *high style*, & make a Speech." No other evidence confirms, however, that Shakespeare was a runaway apprentice. The allusion to "killing a calf" may instead refer to an ancient rural amusement in which the slaughter of a calf was staged behind a curtain for the entertainment of visitors at county fairs. Conceivably Shakespeare's participation in such a game during his youth may have given rise to the tradition that he had been a butcher's apprentice.

Deerstealing a Doubtful Tradition

Another legend, that of Shakespeare's deerstealing, has enjoyed wide currency. We are indebted for this story to the Reverend Richard Davies who, some time between 1688 and 1709, jotted down some gossipy interpolations in the manuscripts of the Reverend William Fulman. (Fulman himself was an antiquarian who had collected a number of notes about Shakespeare and Stratford.) According to Davies, Shakespeare was "much given to all unluckinesse in stealing venison & Rabbits, particularly from Sir ——— Lucy, who had him oft whipt & sometimes Imprisoned & at last made Him fly his Native Country, to his great Advancement."

This tradition was seized upon and augmented in 1709 by Nicholas Rowe, who saw a possible connection between Sir Thomas Lucy of Charlecote Hall, near Stratford, and Justice Shallow of *2 Henry IV* and *The Merry Wives of Windsor*. Shallow, observed Rowe, is a caricature of the rural magistrate and country squire. The dozen white "luces" in Justice Shallow's coat of arms may therefore, Rowe speculated, be intended as a slurring reference to the three white luces in the Lucy family's coat of arms. Rowe attempted to bolster his case by noting that Shallow in *The Merry Wives* is irate at Falstaff for the very offense that Sir Thomas Lucy is supposed to have charged against the young Shakespeare: deerstealing (I,i,114). Rowe even went so far as to suppose that Shakespeare composed a satirical ballad—his first poetic composition—for the occasion:

> He had, by a Misfortune common enough to young Fellows, fallen into ill Company; and amongst them, some that made a frequent practice of Deer-stealing, engag'd him with them more than once in robbing a Park that belong'd to Sir *Thomas Lucy* of *Cherlecot*, near *Stratford*. For this he was prosecuted by that Gentleman, as he thought, somewhat too severely; and in order to revenge that ill Usage, he made a Ballad upon him. And tho' this, probably the first Essay of his Poetry, be lost, yet it is said to have been so very bitter, that it redoubled the Prosecution against him to that degree, that he was oblig'd to leave his Business and Family in *Warwickshire*, for some time, and shelter himself in *London*.

In fact, however, the ballad is not lost, and it proves to have been written considerably later than Rowe supposed. Recently, moreover, Leslie Hotson has argued that Shallow is a hit not at Thomas Lucy at all but at Justice William Gardiner of Surrey (see Play Introduction to *The Merry Wives*). Neither explanation of Shakespeare's satiric treatment of Justice Shallow has received unanimous critical endorsement. We have no sure way of knowing whether Shakespeare's personal experience had anything whatsoever to do with his artistic creation in this instance, or even whether the purported incident actually took place. The deerstealing episode makes interesting fiction but unreliable biography.

Shakespeare's Arrival in London

Because of the total absence of reliable information concerning the seven years from 1585 to 1592, we do not know how Shakespeare got his start in the theatrical world. He may have joined one of the touring companies that came to Stratford, and then accompanied the players to London. Edmund Malone offered the unsupported statement (in 1780) that Shakespeare's "first office in the theatre was that as prompter's attendant." Presumably a young man from the country would have had to begin at the bottom. Shakespeare's later work certainly reveals an intimate and practical acquaintance with technical matters of stagecraft. In any case, his rise to eminence as an actor and writer seems to have been rapid. He was fortunate also in having at least one prosperous acquaintance in London, Richard Field, formerly of Stratford and the son of an associate of Shakespeare's father. Field was a printer, and in 1593 and 1594 he published two handsome editions of Shakespeare's first serious poems, *Venus and Adonis* and *The Rape of Lucrece*.

"The Onely Shake-scene in a Countrey"

The first allusion to Shakespeare after his Stratford days is a vitriolic attack on him. It occurs in *Greene's Groats-worth of Wit Bought with a Million of Repentance*, written by Robert Greene during the last months of his wretched existence (he died in poverty in September of 1592). A famous passage in this work lashes out at the actors of the public theatres for having deserted Greene and for bestowing their favor instead on a certain upstart dramatist. The passage warns three fellow dramatists and University Wits, Christopher Marlowe, Thomas Nashe, and George Peele, to abandon the writing of plays before they fall prey to a similar ingratitude. The diatribe runs as follows:

> . . . Base minded men all three of you, if by my miserie you be not warnd: for vnto none of you (like mee) sought those burres to cleaue: those Puppets (I meane) that spake from our mouths, those Anticks garnisht in our colours. Is it not strange, that I, to whom they all haue beene beholding: is it not like that you, to whome they all have beene beholding, shall (were yee in that case as I am now) bee both at once of them forsaken? Yes trust them not: for there is an vpstart Crow, beautified with our feathers, that with his *Tygers hart wrapt in a Players hyde*, supposes he is as well able to bombast out a blanke verse as the best of you: and beeing an absolute *Iohannes fac totum*, is in his owne conceit the onely Shake-scene in a countrey.

The "burres" here referred to are the actors who have forsaken Greene in his poverty for the rival playwright "Shake-scene"—an obvious hit at Shakespeare. The sneer at a "Johannes fac totum" suggests another dig at Shakespeare for being a Jack-of-all-trades—actor, playwright, poet, and theatrical handyman in the directing and producing of plays. The most unmistakable reference to Shakespeare, however, is to be found in the burlesque line, "Tygers hart wrapt in a Players hyde," modeled after "O tiger's heart wrapt in a woman's hide!" from *3 Henry VI* (I,iv,137). Shakespeare's success as a dramatist has led to an envious outburst from an older, disappointed rival.

Chettle's Apology

Shakespeare may understandably have resented this attack on his professional reputation. Marlowe, too, had cause for grievance, since Greene had accused him in the same pamphlet of atheism. Greene died soon after he wrote *Groats-worth of Wit*, but some of his fellow dramatists were suspected of having had a hand in the libel. Thomas Nashe vigorously denied any responsibility. So did Henry Chettle, the man who saw Greene's manuscript through the press, although Chettle is even today under suspicion for having written the attack on Shakespeare and Marlowe himself. Whether or not Chettle was guilty, he quickly protected himself by denying in his *Kind-Harts Dreame* that he had done anything more than act as Greene's literary executor:

> . . . I had onely in the copy this share: it was il written, as sometime *Greenes* hand was none of the best; licensd it must be, ere it could bee printed, which could neuer be if it might not be read. To be breife, *I* writ it ouer; and as neare as *I* could, followed the copy; onely in that letter *I* put something out, but in the whole booke not a worde in: for I protest it was all *Greenes*, not mine nor Maister Nashes, as some vniustly haue affirmed.

Chettle professes not to have known Marlowe personally, and insists he has no desire to make the acquaintance of so notorious a person; but toward Shakespeare he expresses genuine concern and regret that the publishing incident took place:

> The other, whome at that time I did not so much spare, as since I wish I had, for that as I haue moderated the heate of liuing writers, and might have vsde my owne discretion (especially in such a case) the Author beeing dead, that I did not, I am as sory as if the originall fault had beene my fault, because my selfe haue seene his demeanor no lesse ciuill than he exelent in the qualitie he professes: Besides, diuers of worship haue reported his uprightnes of dealing, which argues his honesty, and his facetious grace in writting, that approoues his Art.

This handsome apology reveals the young Shakespeare in a most attractive light. It suggests that Chettle, though not having known Shakespeare previously, has been impressed by Shakespeare's civility. Chettle also praises the young dramatist as "exelent in the qualitie he professes," that is, excellent as an actor. Chettle notes with approval that Shakespeare enjoys the favor of certain persons of importance, some of whom have borne witness to his uprightness in dealing. By "diuers of worship" Chettle does not mean actors or theatrical people, but persons of gentle blood. *Groats-worth of Wit,* then, with its rancorous attack on Shakespeare, has served paradoxically to reveal the fact that in 1592 Shakespeare was regarded as a man of pleasant demeanor, honest reputation, and acknowledged skill as an actor and writer.

Dramatic Apprenticeship

By the end of the year 1594, when after the long plague the theatrical companies were again permitted to act before London audiences, we find Shakespeare a member of the Lord Chamberlain's company. He had already written *The Comedy of Errors, Love's Labour's Lost, The Two Gentlemen of Verona,* the *Henry VI* plays, and *Titus Andronicus.* (*A Love's Labour's Won,* mentioned by Francis Meres in 1598, is possibly either a lost play or an alternate title for one of the extant comedies.) He may also have completed *The Taming of the Shrew, A Midsummer Night's Dream, Richard III, King John,* and *Romeo and Juliet.* Although a few scholars still question his authorship in part or all of *Titus* and the *Henry VI* plays, no one questions that they are from the period around 1590.

Shakespeare's early development is hard to follow because of difficulties in exact dating of the early plays and because some of the texts (such as *Love's Labour's Lost*) may have been later revised. As a learner making rapid progress in the skill of his art, Shakespeare was also subjected to outside influences which can only partly be determined. Among these influences, we may be sure, were the plays of his contemporary dramatists. If we could define these influences and form an idea of the kinds of plays acceptable on the stage during Shakespeare's early period, we could better understand the milieu in which he began his work.

Fortunately, we know a fair amount concerning the dramatic repertory in London during Shakespeare's early years. Henslowe's *Diary,* for example, records the daily performances of plays by the Lord Strange's men, in conjunction with the Admiral's men, from 19 February to 22 June 1592. Many of their plays unfortunately are lost, but enough of them are preserved to indicate the sorts of drama then in vogue. The Strange-Admiral's repertory included Christopher Marlowe's *The Jew of Malta,* Robert Greene's *Orlando Furioso* and *Friar Bacon and Friar Bungay, A Looking Glass for London and England* by Greene and Thomas Lodge, Thomas Kyd's *The Spanish Tragedy,* the anonymous *A Knack to Know a Knave,* and possibly George Peele's *The Battle of Alcazar* and Shakespeare's *1 Henry VI.* We find, in other words, a tragedy with a villain hero, a romantic comedy masquerading as a heroic play, a love comedy featuring a lot of magic, a biblical moral, England's first great revenge tragedy, a popular satiric comedy aimed at dissolute courtiers and usurers, a history play about Portugal's African empire, and an English history play. The titles of other works now lost suggest a similar amalgam of widely differing genres.

Comparatively few plays may have been written during the period when plays were forbidden because of the long plague of 1592–1594. When the Lord Chamberlain's men and the Lord Admiral's men acted under Henslowe's management at the suburban theatre of Newington Butts from June 3 to 13, 1594, their repertories seem to have consisted largely of old plays. In this brief period, they are thought to have acted *Titus Andronicus, Hamlet* (the pre-Shakespearean version), *The Taming of A Shrew* (quite possibly Shakespeare's version), *The Jew of Malta,* a lost play called *Hester and Ahasuerus,* and others.

The Lord Admiral's men probably moved soon afterwards in 1594 to the Rose on the Bankside, across the river Thames from the city of London, where they continued to play under Henslowe's management until 1603. During the years 1594–1597 Henslowe kept in his *Diary* a careful record of their plays and of the sums of money taken. This circumstance enables us to know a great deal more about the repertory of Shakespeare's rival company than we can ever know about his own. When the Lord Admiral's men began again in 1594, they had five of Marlowe's plays. They seem also to have had Peele's *Edward I,* Kyd's *The Spanish Tragedy,* and a Henry V play. They may also have had plays by both Greene and Peele (Henslowe's chaotic spelling makes it hard to determine), although some of the principal dramas of these two authors had probably ceased to be acted.

We do not know the repertory of the Lord Chamberlain's company as a whole as we do that of the Lord Admiral's. We know enough of it, however, to be sure that in 1594, both companies were acting the same sorts of plays that had been on the boards in 1592. We have, therefore, grounds for assuming that, in spite of the loss of many plays (some of which may have been important), the chief contemporary influences upon Shakespeare during his early period were those of Marlowe, Greene, Peele, and Kyd. As an actor possibly in Lord Strange's company or the Earl of Pembroke's company, he would have been familiar with their plays.

Shakespeare learned also from Lyly, though perhaps more from reading than from actually seeing or performing in Lyly's plays. The boy actors for whom Lyly wrote were forced by the authorities to suspend acting in about 1591 because of their tendency toward controversial satire, and a number of Lyly's plays were printed at that time. As a theatrical figure, therefore, Lyly belonged really to the previous decade.

The Early Plays

Although Shakespeare's genius manifests itself in his early work, his indebtedness to contemporary dramatists and to classical writers is also more plainly evident than in his later writings. His first tragedy, *Titus Andronicus* (c. 1589–1591), is more laden with quotations and classical references than any other tragedy he wrote. Its genre owes much to the revenge play that had been made so popular by Thomas Kyd. Like Kyd, Shakespeare turns to Seneca but also reveals on stage a considerable amount of sensational violence in a manner that is distinctly not classical. For his first villain, Aaron the Moor, Shakespeare borrows some motifs from the morality play and its gleefully sinister tempter, the Vice. Shakespeare may also have had in mind the boastful antics of Marlowe's Vicelike Barabas, in *The Jew of Malta*. Certainly Shakespeare reveals an extensive debt in his early works to Ovid and to the vogue of Ovidian narrative poetry in the early 1590's, as for example in his repeated allusions to the story of Philomela and Tereus (in *Titus Andronicus*) and in his Ovidian poems, *Venus and Adonis* and *The Rape of Lucrece* (1593, 1594).

Shakespeare was still questing for a suitable genre in tragedy, and was discovering that the English drama of the 1590's offered no single clear model. His only other early tragedy, *Romeo and Juliet* (c. 1594–1596), proved to be as different a tragedy from *Titus Andronicus* as could be imagined. Revenge is still prominent as a theme in *Romeo and Juliet*, but revenge in this play is overwhelmed and destroyed by sacrificial love. Shakespeare's source is not Senecan or Kydian revenge drama, but a romantic love narrative derived from the fiction of Renaissance Italy. Elements of comedy so predominate in the play's first half that one senses a closer affinity to *A Midsummer Night's Dream* than to *The Spanish Tragedy*.

Shakespeare discovered his true bent more quickly in comedy than in tragedy. Again, however, he experimented with a wide range of models and genres. *The Comedy of Errors* (c. 1589–1593) brings together elements of two plots from the Latin drama of Plautus. The character types and situation are partly derivative, but Shakespeare still reveals an impressive skill in plot construction. The characters too are given a human warmth and decency not often found in the original. *Love's Labour's Lost* (c. 1588–1589, perhaps later revised) is Shakespeare's most Lylyan early comedy, with its witty debates and its amicable war between the sexes. Yet the play also features refreshingly vulgar clowns and country sluts who help to undercut the preciousness of the courtiers' mannered ways. *The Two Gentlemen of Verona* (c. 1590–1594) and *The Taming of the Shrew* (c. 1592–1594) are derived from Italianate romantic comedy. In both, Shakespeare reveals great architectonic skill by combining simultaneous plots that offer contrasting views on love and friendship. (*The Taming of the Shrew* also makes effective use of a "frame" plot involving a group of characters who serve as audience for the rest of the play.) *A Midsummer Night's Dream* (c. 1594–1595), with its four brilliantly interwoven actions involving court figures, lovers, fairies, and Athenian tradesmen, shows us Shakespeare already at the height of his powers in play construction, even though the comic emphasis on love's irrationality in this play is still in keeping with Shakespeare's early style. The early comedies are all "happy" comedies, almost untouched as yet by the social dilemmas of *The Merchant of Venice*, the narrowly averted catastrophe of *Much Ado about Nothing*, or the melancholy vein of *As You Like It* and *Twelfth Night*. On stage, early comedies such as *The Comedy of Errors* and *The Taming of the Shrew* are as hilariously funny as anything Shakespeare ever wrote.

Shakespeare's early history plays show a marked affinity to those of Marlowe, Peele, and Greene. Yet today Shakespeare is given more credit for pioneering in the genre of the English history play than he once was. If all the *Henry VI* plays (c. 1589–1592) are basically his, as scholars now generally allow, he had more imitators in this genre than predecessors. He scored a huge early success with the heroic character of Lord Talbot in *1 Henry VI;* and, by the time Richard Duke of Gloucester had emerged from the *Henry VI* plays to become King Richard III, Shakespeare's fame as a dramatist was assured. He had, of course, learned much from Marlowe's "mighty line" in *Tamburlaine* (1587–1588) and perhaps from Peele's *The Battle of Alcazar* (1588–1589). The anonymous *Famous Victories of Henry V* (1583–1588) must have preceded and influenced his work. Even so, Shakespeare had done much more than simply "beautify" himself with the "feathers" of earlier dramatists, as Greene (or Chettle) enviously charged. Even in his earliest work, Shakespeare already displayed an extraordinary ability to transcend the models from which he learned.

THE COMEDY OF ERRORS

The Comedy of Errors is a superb illustration of Shakespeare's "apprenticeship" in comedy. It is more imitative of classical comedy, especially of Plautus, than is Shakespeare's mature work. Its verbal humor, including the scatological jokes about breaking wind, the bawdy jests about cuckold's horns, and the overly ingenious chop-logic banter (as in II,ii) is at times adolescent. The play abounds in the farcical slapstick humor of physical abuse, so endearing to children of all ages. It is perhaps the most uncomplicatedly funny of all Shakespeare's plays. Yet the softening touches of Shakespeare's maturity are unmistakably present as well. Shakespeare frames his farce of mistaken identity with old Ægeon's tragicomic story of separation, threatened death, and eventual reunion. He adds characters to the Plautine original in order to enhance the love interest and to reconcile Plautus with English moral conventions. He touches upon themes of illusion, madness, and Saturnalian inversion that are to figure prominently in *A Midsummer Night's Dream* and in *Twelfth Night*, a later comedy of mistaken identity. In these respects, *The Comedy of Errors* is both a fascinating prelude to Shakespeare's later development and a rich achievement in its own right. On stage, it has not attracted the greatest Shakespearean actors since it offers no complex or dominating roles, but it has seldom failed to delight audiences.

We cannot be sure precisely how early the play was written. A performance took place on December 28, 1594, at Gray's Inn, before an unruly assembly of lawyers, law students, and their guests. This was probably not the first performance, however. Topical allusions offer possible hints of an earlier date. When Dromio of Syracuse speaks of France as "armed and reverted, making war against her heir" (III,ii), Dromio clearly refers to the Catholic League's opposition to Henry of Navarre, who was the apparent heir to the French throne until 1593, when he became king. Another allusion, to Spain's sending "whole armadoes of caracks," would possibly have lost its comic point soon after the Invincible Armada of 1588. The play's style, characterization, and imitative construction are all consistent with a date between 1589 and 1593.

Whatever the exact date, Shakespeare's youthful fascination with Plautus is manifest. Shakespeare's command of Latin, though sneered at by Ben Jonson, was undoubtedly good enough to have let him read Plautus with pleasure. He must have been drilled in Latin for years as a student in the town of Stratford-upon-Avon, and, if John Aubrey is right, went on to teach Latin as a country schoolmaster before becoming an actor. Indeed, the influence not only of Plautus but of Ovid and Seneca (together with touches of Horace, Catullus, etc.) is a prominent feature of Shakespeare's early work, dramatic and nondramatic. Shakespeare may have consulted Plautus both in the original and in a contemporary translation, as was frequently his custom with non-English sources. From Renaissance Latin editions of Plautus he apparently took the odd designation "Antipholus Sereptus" (i.e., "serruptus," snatched away), which appears in the Folio text in a stage direction at II,i to indicate the twin who was separated from his father. On the other hand, a translation by "W. W." (William Warner), published in 1595, was registered in 1594 and might have been available earlier to Shakespeare in manuscript.

Plautus had much to offer Shakespeare and his fellow dramatists, especially in the way of tightly organized and complex plot construction. Native English drama of the sixteenth century tended to be episodic and panoramic in its design. Shakespeare's apprenticeship in neoclassical form can be seen in his precise observation of the unities of time and place—those unities which he openly disregarded in some of his later plays. At the play's beginning, Ægeon is informed that he has until sundown to raise his ransom money, and the play then moves toward that point in time with periodic observations that it is now noon, now 2 o'clock, and so on. (At one point time even seems to go backwards, but that is part of the illusion of madness.) The action is restricted to the city of Ephesus; events that have happened elsewhere, at an earlier time (such as the separation of the Antipholus family), are told to us by persons in the play such as old Ægeon. Although Shakespeare's company did not employ the sort of painted scenery drawn in perspective used by continental neoclassicists, with fixed locations for houses facing on a street, the original production of this play may nonetheless have used one stage "house" or door to represent the dwelling of Antipholus of Ephesus (the Phoenix) throughout the drama. The entire play can be staged as if all the action occurs in the vicinity of this single "house," with the Abbey near at hand. Seldom again does Shakespeare utilize such a neoclassical stage.

These unities of time and place are mechanical matters, but they do also harmonize with a more essential unity of action. The story moves, as though in perfect accord with neoclassical five-act theory, from exposition and complication to climax, anagnoresis (discovery), and peripeteia (reversal of fortune). The brilliance of the plotting is decidedly Plautine. Shakespeare pushes to its limit the interweaving of comic misunderstandings only to unravel all these seemingly tightly woven knots with effortless ease. Yet the imitation of Plautus, even in matters of construction, is by no means slavish, for Shakespeare borrows both from Plautus' farce on the mistaken identity of twins (*The Menaechmi*) and from Plautus' best-known comedy (*Amphitruo*), in which a husband and his servant are excluded from their own house while a disguised visitor usurps the master's role within. Such ingenious adaptations and rearrangements were common among neoclassical dramatists like Ariosto; and, although Shakespeare seems not to have used any of the sixteenth-century analogues that have been found to this play, he does reveal an acquaintance with neoclassical comedy as a whole, and an ability to compete with the best that Europe had to offer in this vein. Such versatility is astonishing in a young dramatist who was to reveal himself in time as far less of a neoclassicist than a native English writer. Moreover, even if his self-imposed neoclassical training was only an apprenticeship, it was to prove ultimately invaluable to Shakespeare. Despite his later tendency toward "romantic" plotting—toward the depiction of multiple actions extending over widely separated spaces and extended periods of time—Shakespeare's greatest comedies continue to point toward the same gratifying resolution of dramatic conflict in a single and well-structured denouement.

For all its Plautine skill of design, however, *The Comedy of Errors* is quite far removed from *The Menaechmi* in tone and spirit. Gone are the cynicism, the satirical hardness, and the indifference to moral issues of the Roman original. The characters, though still recognizable as types, are humanized. The familiar Plautine parasite is excluded entirely. The usual clever servant happily becomes the Dromio Twins. Plautus' quack Doctor, Medicus, is hilariously transmuted into Dr. Pinch, a pedantic schoolmaster. The Courtezan's role is no longer prominent. Instead Shakespeare creates Luciana, the virtuous sister of Adriana, who pleads the cause of patient forbearance in marriage and who eventually becomes the bride of Antipholus of Syracuse. *The Comedy of Errors* does not end, as do most of Shakespeare's later comedies, with a parade of couples to the altar, but the marriage of Antipholus and Luciana is at least one important step in that direction. Besides, we are told of yet another marriage still to come—that of Dromio of Ephesus to Luce, the fat kitchen wench. This belowstairs parody of wedded affection is thoroughly English in character, and recalls a similar rivalry between two servants for a maid in Medwall's *Fulgens and Lucrece* (c. 1497). The motif is not sufficiently stressed to threaten the unity of the main plot, but the potentiality for double plotting is unmistakable.

An even more significant contrast to Plautine farce is to be found in the romantic saga of old Ægeon and his long-lost wife, the Abbess. Their story is one not of mistaken identity (though that contributes to the denouement) but of painful separation, wandering, and reunion. Indeed, the note struck at the beginning of the play might seem tragic, were we not already attuned to the conventional romantic expectation that separated members of a family are likely to be restored to one another again. Ægeon, threatened with immediate execution, unfolds to us a narrative of wedded bliss interrupted by the malignancy of Fortune. In contrast to the tightly controlled unity of time of the farcical action, the romantic narrative extends (by recollection) over many years of error and suffering. Ægeon's tragicomic story of testing and of patient endurance is very much like that of Apollonius of Tyre, a popular tale used by Shakespeare in his late romance *Pericles* (c. 1606–1608). The conventions of this sort of romance, ultimately Greek in origin, stress improbability: identical twins who can be told apart only by birthmarks, a storm at sea splitting a vessel in half and neatly dividing the family, and so on. The sea is emblematic of unpredictable Fortune, taking away with one hand and restoring with the other. The wife who is lost at sea, like her counterpart in *Apollonius* or *Pericles*, takes to a life of cloistered devotion, suggesting a pattern of symbolic death, healing, and ultimate rebirth. The ending of *The Comedy of Errors* has just a hint of death restored mysteriously to life: "After so long grief, such Nativity!"

Ægeon's story of endurance counterpoints the farce in yet another way. His arraignment before the Duke of Ephesus introduces into the play a "tragic" world of law, punishment, and death. Ægeon's date with the executioner is not illusory. His predicament is the result of the bitter "mortal and intestine jars" between two cities caught in a frenzy of economic reprisals. The law cannot be merciful, even though the unfairness of Ægeon's plight is manifest to everyone, including the Duke. These potentially tragic factors must not be overstressed, for the first scene is brief and we are reassured by the play's hilarious tone (and by our surmising that Ægeon is father of the Antipholus twins) that all will be well. Still, Shakespeare's addition of this romance plot suggests his restlessness with pure farce. As in his later comedies, which are virtually all threatened by catastrophes, the denouement of *The Comedy of Errors* is deepened into something approaching miraculous recovery. Moreover, the backdrop of a near-tragic world of genuine suffering heightens our appreciation of comic unreality in the self-contained world of Plautine farce, and stresses the illusory nature of the dilemmas arising out of purely mistaken identity. Such delusions are all the more comic because they are the delusions that supposedly sane people suffer: contentiousness and jealousy in marriage, concern for respectable appearances among one's neighbors, and the suspicion that one is always being cheated in money matters. These are the chimeras which, by being made to look so plausible and yet so patently insane, are farcically exploited in Shakespeare's comic device: the inversion of madness and sanity, dreaming and waking, illusion and reality.

What happens when the behavior of one twin is mistaken for that of the other? The situation is of course amusing in itself, but it also serves as a test of the other characters, to discover what mad hypotheses they will construct. Adriana, faced with her husband's seeming refusal to come home to dinner, launches into a jealous tirade against husbands who neglect their wives for courtesans. The illusory situation, in other words, brings out her latent fears. We understand better now why she acts shrewishly: she fears rejection and the fading of her beauty, and imagines that her fading beauty may be the cause of her husband's neglect. In point of fact, her absent husband is dutifully making arrangements about a chain he means to give Adriana; but, when subsequently he is locked out of his own house, and jumps to the conclusion that Adriana is being faithless, he resolves in his fury to bestow the chain on a courtesan in order to "spite my wife." He would actually do so, did not benign providence in the guise of mistaken identity deliver the chain into the hands of his twin. Once again, illusion has prompted a character to assume the worst, to reveal his suspicions of a plot against him. And so it goes when Antipholus of Ephesus is arrested for nonpayment of the chain (he assumes that all merchants are thieves) or is denied his bail money by the servant he thinks he sent to fetch it (he assumes that all servants are thieves). We laugh at the endless capacity of the human mind for distortions of this self-punishing sort.

The metaphor used most often to convey this sense of bewilderment, even a confusion about one's own identity, is that of metamorphosis or transformation. All have drunk of Circe's cup (V,i) and have turned into animals—most of them into asses. All have hearkened to the mermaid's song, and are enchanted. Ephesus, they conclude, must be haunted by sorcerers, witches, goblins, and spirits (IV,iii). In such a mad world the characters assume a license to embark on Saturnalian holiday. The experience of transformation thus leads to various forms of "release" from ordinary social behavior, but the experience is also disturbing, and continually reminds the characters of exorcism, hell, and devils. The characters can explain their inverted world only by assuming that all men are lunatic, all honest women whores, and all true men thieves. "Do you know me, sir? . . . Am I myself?" "Am I in earth, or heaven, or in hell? Sleeping or waking? mad or well advis'd?" It is both reassuring and hilariously anticlimactic that these questionings can finally be dispelled by the most mundane of explanations: there are two Antipholuses and two Dromios.

This playfulness about illusion should not be overemphasized, for the play expends most of its energies on the farcical level. The Dromios, with their incessant drubbings, are often the center of interest in performance, and rightly so. Shakespeare employs no behind-the-scenes manipulator of illusion, such as Puck in *A Midsummer Night's Dream* or the Duke in *Measure for Measure*. His interest in the metaphor of the world as a stage is discernible only as the foreshadowing of greatness to come. Nevertheless, Shakespeare's alterations of Plautus amply reveal the philosophic and idealistic direction that his subsequent comedy is to take.

THE COMEDY OF ERRORS

[*Dramatis Personae*

SOLINUS, *Duke of Ephesus.*
ÆGEON, *a merchant of Syracuse.*
ANTIPHOLUS of Ephesus, } *twin brothers, and*
ANTIPHOLUS of Syracuse, } *sons to Ægeon and Æmilia.*
DROMIO of Ephesus, } *twin brothers, and at-*
DROMIO of Syracuse, } *tendants on the two Antipholuses.*
BALTHAZAR, *a merchant.*
ANGELO, *a goldsmith.*
First Merchant, *friend to Antipholus of Syracuse.*
Second Merchant, *to whom Angelo is a debtor.*
PINCH, *a schoolmaster.*

ÆMILIA, *wife to Ægeon, an abbess at Ephesus.*
ADRIANA, *wife to Antipholus of Ephesus.*
LUCIANA, *her sister.*
LUCE, *servant to Adriana.*
A Courtezan.

Gaoler, Officers, *and* other Attendants.

SCENE: *Ephesus.*]

ACT I.

SCENE I. [*A hall in the* DUKE'S *palace.*]

Enter the DUKE *of Ephesus, with* [ÆGEON] *the Merchant of Syracuse,* Gaoler, *and other* Attendants.

Æge. Proceed, Solinus, to procure my fall
And by the doom of death end woes and all.
Duke. Merchant of Syracusa, plead no more;
I am not partial to infringe our laws:
The enmity and discord which of late
Sprung from the rancorous outrage of your duke
To merchants, our well-dealing countrymen,
Who wanting guilders to redeem their lives
Have seal'd his rigorous statutes with their bloods,
Excludes all pity from our threat'ning looks.
For, since the mortal and intestine jars
'Twixt thy seditious countrymen and us,
It hath in solemn synods been decreed,
Both by the Syracusians and ourselves,
To admit no traffic to our adverse towns:
Nay, more,
If any born at Ephesus be seen
At any Syracusian marts and fairs;
Again: if any Syracusian born
Come to the bay of Ephesus, he dies,
His goods confiscate to the duke's dispose,
Unless a thousand marks be levied,
To quit the penalty and to ransom him.
Thy substance, valued at the highest rate,

Cannot amount unto a hundred marks;
Therefore by law thou art condemn'd to die.
Æge. Yet this my comfort: when your words are done,
My woes end likewise with the evening sun.
Duke. Well, Syracusian, say in brief the cause
Why thou departed'st from thy native home
And for what cause thou cam'st to Ephesus.
Æge. A heavier task could not have been impos'd
Than I to speak my griefs unspeakable:
Yet, that the world may witness that my end
Was wrought by nature, not by vile offence,
I'll utter what my sorrow gives me leave.
In Syracusa was I born, and wed
Unto a woman, happy but for me,
And by me, had not our hap been bad.
With her I liv'd in joy; our wealth increas'd
By prosperous voyages I often made
To Epidamnum; till my factor's death
And the great care of goods at random left
Drew me from kind embracements of my spouse:
From whom my absence was not six months old
Before herself, almost at fainting under
The pleasing punishment that women bear,
Had made provision for her following me
And soon and safe arrived where I was.
There had she not been long but she became
A joyful mother of two goodly sons;
And, which was strange, the one so like the other
As could not be distinguish'd but by names.
That very hour and in the self-same inn
A meaner woman was delivered
Of such a burden, male twins, both alike:
Those, for their parents were exceeding poor,
I bought and brought up to attend my sons.
My wife, not meanly proud of two such boys,
Made daily motions for our home return:
Unwilling I agreed; alas! too soon
We came aboard.
A league from Epidamnum had we sail'd,
Before the always wind-obeying deep
Gave any tragic instance of our harm:
But longer did we not retain much hope;
For what obscured light the heavens did grant
Did but convey unto our fearful minds
A doubtful warrant of immediate death;
Which though myself would gladly have embrac'd,
Yet the incessant weepings of my wife,
Weeping before for what she saw must come,
And piteous plainings of the pretty babes,
That mourn'd for fashion, ignorant what to fear,
Forc'd me to seek delays for them and me.
And this it was, for other means was none:
The sailors sought for safety by our boat,
And left the ship, then sinking-ripe, to us:
My wife, more careful for the latter-born,
Had fast'ned him unto a small spare mast,
Such as seafaring men provide for storms;
To him one of the other twins was bound,
Whilst I had been like heedful of the other:
The children thus dispos'd, my wife and I,
Fixing our eyes on whom our care was fix'd,
Fast'ned ourselves at either end the mast;
And floating straight, obedient to the stream,
Was carried towards Corinth, as we thought.
At length the sun, gazing upon the earth,
Dispers'd those vapours that offended us;
And, by the benefit of his wished light,
The seas wax'd calm, and we discovered
Two ships from far making amain to us,
Of Corinth that, of Epidaurus this:
But ere they came,—O, let me say no more!
Gather the sequel by that went before.
Duke. Nay, forward, old man; do not break off so;
For we may pity, though not pardon thee.
Æge. O, had the gods done so, I had not now
Worthily term'd them merciless to us!
For, ere the ships could meet by twice five leagues,
We were encount'red by a mighty rock;
Which being violently borne upon,
Our helpful ship was splitted in the midst;
So that, in this unjust divorce of us,
Fortune had left to both of us alike
What to delight in, what to sorrow for.
Her part, poor soul! seeming as burdened
With lesser weight but not with lesser woe,
Was carried with more speed before the wind;
And in our sight they three were taken up
By fishermen of Corinth, as we thought.
At length, another ship had seiz'd on us;
And, knowing whom it was their hap to save,
Gave healthful welcome to their shipwrack'd guests;
And would have reft the fishers of their prey,
Had not their bark been very slow of sail;
And therefore homeward did they bend their course.
Thus have you heard me sever'd from my bliss,
That by misfortunes was my life prolong'd,
To tell sad stories of my own mishaps.
Duke. And, for the sake of them thou sorrowest for,
Do me the favour to dilate at full
What hath befall'n of them and thee till now.
Æge. My youngest boy, and yet my eldest care,
At eighteen years became inquisitive
After his brother: and importun'd me

ACT I. SCENE I. *Stage Direction:* ***A hall in the* Duke's *palace.*** The New Cambridge editors (*The Works of Shakespeare*, edited by Sir Arthur Quiller-Couch and John Dover Wilson, Cambridge University Press, *in progress*) limit the settings of the entire play to two. Considering the play as preserved to have been prepared for acting on the dais of a hall with three rear doors, they suggest two localities: (*a*) an open space before the house of Antipholus with a priory on one side and a street exit on the other; and (*b*) the Mart with Courtesan's house in the center and street exits on each side, one of them leading to the bay. The setting for the first scene is (*a*). 2. **doom,** judgment. 4. **partial,** predisposed, biased. 8. **guilders,** money; the guilder was a Dutch silver coin worth about 1s. 8d. English; also a gold coin used in the Netherlands, and parts of Germany. 9. **seal'd,** ratified; see glossary. 11. **mortal,** deadly; see glossary. **intestine.** The usual meaning is "civil" or "internal"; used with *mortal* it emphasizes the idea of "deadly civil war." **jars,** quarrels; see glossary. 21. **confiscate,** confiscated; accent on second syllable. **dispose,** disposal; see glossary. 22. **marks.** A mark was the sum of 13s. 4d. 23. **quit,** pay or clear off; see glossary. 24. **rate,** estimate; see glossary. 35. **nature,** i.e., by natural affection, which prompted him to seek his son at Ephesus. 42. **factor's,** agent's. 44. **kind,** affectionate; see glossary. 53. **As,** that they; see glossary. 55. **meaner,** i.e., of lower rank; see *mean* in glossary. 59. **meanly,** in a slight degree. 60. **motions,** proposals. 65. **instance,** proof, sign; see glossary. 69. **doubtful,** ominous; see glossary. 73. **plainings,** wailings. 78. **sinking-ripe,** ready to sink. 79. **careful,** attentive; see glossary. **latter-born.** Cf. line 125, from which we learn that the younger of the twins was saved with the father. 84. **dispos'd,** stowed; see glossary. 93. **amain,** with might and main. 94. **Epidaurus,** a town in Argolis on the Saronic Gulf. 96. **that,** that which. 104. **helpful.** Rowe's conjecture *helpless* is unnecessary; the word may refer to the masts after the wreck (ll. 80-86) or to the general quality of the ship while she held together. 105. **unjust,** unjustified; see glossary. 115. **healthful,** implying, perhaps, *recovery* from the sufferings of shipwreck (Cuningham). 123. **dilate,** relate.

That his attendant—so his case was like,
Reft of his brother, but retain'd his name—
Might bear him company in the quest of him:
Whom whilst I laboured of a love to see,
I hazarded the loss of whom I lov'd.
Five summers have I spent in furthest Greece,
Roaming clean through the bounds of Asia,
And, coasting homeward, came to Ephesus;
Hopeless to find, yet loath to leave unsought
Or that or any place that harbours men.
But here must end the story of my life;
And happy were I in my timely death,
Could all my travels warrant me they live.
Duke. Hapless Ægeon, whom the fates have mark'd
To bear the extremity of dire mishap!
Now, trust me, were it not against our laws,
Against my crown, my oath, my dignity,
Which princes, would they, may not disannul,
My soul should sue as advocate for thee.
But, though thou art adjudged to the death
And passed sentence may not be recall'd
But to our honour's great disparagement,
Yet I will favour thee in what I can.
Therefore, merchant, I'll limit thee this day
To seek thy life by beneficial help:
Try all the friends thou hast in Ephesus;
Beg thou, or borrow, to make up the sum,
And live; if no, then thou art doom'd to die.
Gaoler, take him to thy custody.
Gaol. I will, my lord.
Æge. Hopeless and helpless doth Ægeon wend,
But to procrastinate his lifeless end. *Exeunt.*

[SCENE II. *The Mart.*]

Enter ANTIPHOLUS [*of Syracuse*], [the First] Merchant, *and* DROMIO [*of Syracuse*].

First Mer. Therefore give out you are of Epidamnum,
Lest that your goods too soon be confiscate.
This very day a Syracusian merchant
Is apprehended for arrival here;
And not being able to buy out his life
According to the statute of the town
Dies ere the weary sun set in the west.
There is your money that I had to keep.
Ant. S. Go bear it to the Centaur, where we host,
And stay there, Dromio, till I come to thee.
Within this hour it will be dinner-time:
Till that, I'll view the manners of the town,
Peruse the traders, gaze upon the buildings,
And then return and sleep within mine inn,
For with long travel I am stiff and weary.
Get thee away.
Dro. S. Many a man would take you at your word,
And go indeed, having so good a mean. *Exit Dro.*
Ant. S. A trusty villain, sir, that very oft,
When I am dull with care and melancholy,
Lightens my humour with his merry jests.
What, will you walk with me about the town,
And then go to my inn and dine with me?
First Mer. I am invited, sir, to certain merchants,
Of whom I hope to make much benefit;
I crave your pardon. Soon at five o'clock,
Please you, I'll meet with you upon the mart
And afterward consort you till bed-time:
My present business calls me from you now.
Ant. S. Farewell till then: I will go lose myself
And wander up and down to view the city.
First Mer. Sir, I commend you to your own content. *Exit.*
Ant. S. He that commends me to mine own content
Commends me to the thing I cannot get.
I to the world am like a drop of water
That in the ocean seeks another drop,
Who, falling there to find his fellow forth,
Unseen, inquisitive, confounds himself:
So I, to find a mother and a brother,
In quest of them, unhappy, lose myself.

Enter DROMIO of Ephesus.

Here comes the almanac of my true date.
What now? how chance thou art return'd so soon?
Dro. E. Return'd so soon! rather approach'd too late:
The capon burns, the pig falls from the spit,
The clock hath strucken twelve upon the bell;
My mistress made it one upon my cheek:
She is so hot because the meat is cold;
The meat is cold because you come not home;
You come not home because you have no stomach;
You have no stomach having broke your fast;
But we that know what 'tis to fast and pray
Are penitent for your default to-day.
Ant. S. Stop in your wind, sir: tell me this, I pray:
Where have you left the money that I gave you?
Dro. E. O,—sixpence, that I had a Wednesday last
To pay the saddler for my mistress' crupper?
The saddler had it, sir; I kept it not.
Ant. S. I am not in a sportive humour now:
Tell me, and dally not, where is the money?
We being strangers here, how dar'st thou trust
So great a charge from thine own custody?
Dro. E. I pray you, jest, sir, as you sit at dinner:
I from my mistress come to you in post;
If I return, I shall be post indeed,
For she will score your fault upon my pate.
Methinks your maw, like mine, should be your clock
And strike you home without a messenger.
Ant. S. Come, Dromio, come, these jests are out of season;

128. **so his case was like.** In *Menaechmi* of Plautus one twin takes the name of his stolen brother Menaechmus; in a similar way in this play Shakespeare has taken it for granted that the twin slave has taken the name of his lost brother Dromio (cf. l. 53). 131. **of,** i.e., out of, impelled by; see glossary. 134. **clean,** entirely. 137. **Or . . . or,** either . . . or; see glossary. 139. **timely,** early, speedy. 140. **travels,** "travails" as well as *travels*. **warrant,** assure. 145. **disannul,** annul. 147. **the death,** i.e., death by judicial sentence. 152. **life**. F: *helpe*, possibly for *helthe* meaning "welfare."

SCENE II. 8. **keep,** guard, care for; see glossary. 9. **host,** lodge, put up. 13. **Peruse,** observe. 18. **mean,** opportunity, money; see glossary. 19. **villain,** used good-humoredly, or as a term of endearment. 21. **humour,** mood, disposition, vagary; see glossary. 26. **Soon at,** about. 28. **consort,** attend. 29. **present,** immediate; see glossary. 37. **fellow,** companion; see glossary. **forth,** out. 38. **confounds,** mingles indistinguishably; see glossary. 40. *Stage Direction:* **Enter Dromio of Ephesus.** Shakespeare's technique resembles that of *Amphitruo* rather than that of *Menaechmi*, which he definitely follows in his plot. *Menaechmi* begins with a true situation which is followed by a false situation; *Amphitruo*, like *The Comedy of Errors*, begins with a false situation to be followed by a true situation. The confusion is, therefore, more bewildering and interesting because of this method. 41. **al-**

Reserve them till a merrier hour than this.
Where is the gold I gave in charge to thee?
Dro. E. To me, sir? why, you gave no gold to me.
Ant. S. Come on, sir knave, have done your foolishness
And tell me how thou hast dispos'd thy charge.
Dro. E. My charge was but to fetch you from the mart
Home to your house, the Phœnix, sir, to dinner:
My mistress and her sister stays for you.
Ant. S. Now, as I am a Christian, answer me
In what safe place you have bestow'd my money,
Or I shall break that merry sconce of yours
That stands on tricks when I am undispos'd:
Where is the thousand marks thou hadst of me?
Dro. E. I have some marks of yours upon my pate,
Some of my mistress' marks upon my shoulders,
But not a thousand marks between you both.
If I should pay your worship those again,
Perchance you will not bear them patiently.
Ant. S. Thy mistress' marks? what mistress, slave, hast thou?
Dro. E. Your worship's wife, my mistress at the Phœnix;
She that doth fast till you come home to dinner
And prays that you will hie you home to dinner.
Ant. S. What, wilt thou flout me thus unto my face,
Being forbid? There, take you that, sir knave.
Dro. E. What mean you, sir? for God's sake, hold your hands!
Nay, an you will not, sir, I'll take my heels. *Exit Dro.*
Ant. S. Upon my life, by some device or other
The villain is o'er-raught of all my money.
They say this town is full of cozenage,
As, nimble jugglers that deceive the eye,
Dark-working sorcerers that change the mind,
Soul-killing witches that deform the body,
Disguised cheaters, prating mountebanks,
And many such-like liberties of sin:
If it prove so, I will be gone the sooner.
I'll to the Centaur, to go seek this slave:
I greatly fear my money is not safe. *Exit.*

ACT II.

[SCENE I. *The house of* ANTIPHOLUS of Ephesus.]

Enter ADRIANA, *Wife to Antipholus* [*of Ephesus*], *with* LUCIANA, *her Sister.*

Adr. Neither my husband nor the slave return'd,
That in such haste I sent to seek his master!
Sure, Luciana, it is two o'clock.
Luc. Perhaps some merchant hath invited him
And from the mart he 's somewhere gone to dinner.
Good sister, let us dine and never fret:
A man is master of his liberty:
Time is their master, and when they see time
They'll go or come: if so, be patient, sister.
Adr. Why should their liberty than ours be more?
Luc. Because their business still lies out o' door.
Adr. Look, when I serve him so, he takes it ill.
Luc. O, know he is the bridle of your will.
Adr. There 's none but asses will be bridled so.
Luc. Why, headstrong liberty is lash'd with woe.
There 's nothing situate under heaven's eye
But hath his bound, in earth, in sea, in sky:
The beasts, the fishes and the winged fowls
Are their males' subjects and at their controls:
Men, more divine, the masters of all these,
Lords of the wide world and wild wat'ry seas,
Indued with intellectual sense and souls,
Of more pre-eminence than fish and fowls,
Are masters to their females, and their lords:
Then let your will attend on their accords.
Adr. This servitude makes you to keep unwed.
Luc. Not this, but troubles of the marriage-bed.
Adr. But, were you wedded, you would bear some sway.
Luc. Ere I learn love, I'll practise to obey.
Adr. How if your husband start some other where?
Luc. Till he come home again, I would forbear.
Adr. Patience unmov'd! no marvel though she pause;
They can be meek that have no other cause.
A wretched soul, bruis'd with adversity,
We bid be quiet when we hear it cry;
But were we burd'ned with like weight of pain,
As much or more we should ourselves complain:
So thou, that hast no unkind mate to grieve thee,
With urging helpless patience wouldst relieve me;
But, if thou live to see like right bereft,
This fool-begg'd patience in thee will be left.
Luc. Well, I will marry one day, but to try.
Here comes your man; now is your husband nigh.

Enter DROMIO of Ephesus.

Adr. Say, is your tardy master now at hand?
Dro. E. Nay, he 's at two hands with me, and that my two ears can witness.
Adr. Say, didst thou speak with him? know'st thou his mind?
Dro. E. Ay, ay, he told his mind upon mine ear:
Beshrew his hand, I scarce could understand it.
Luc. Spake he so doubtfully, thou couldst not feel his meaning?
Dro. E. Nay, he struck so plainly, I could too well feel his blows; and withal so doubtfully that I could scarce understand them.
Adr. But say, I prithee, is he coming home?
It seems he hath great care to please his wife.
Dro. E. Why, mistress, sure my master is horn-mad.
Adr. Horn-mad, thou villain!
Dro. E. I mean not cuckold-mad;
But, sure, he is stark mad.

manac . . . date, i.e., being born in the same hour, Dromio serves as an almanac by which Antipholus can see his age; see *date* in glossary. 45. **twelve.** The usual dinner hour was half after eleven. 49. **stomach,** appetite; see glossary. 52. **penitent,** undergoing punishment. 53. **wind,** words. 63. **post,** haste; see glossary. 64. **post,** doorpost of a tavern used for keeping reckonings. 66. **maw,** stomach; applied to animals. 75. **Phœnix,** the sign of his master's shop. 76. **stays,** waits; see glossary. 78. **bestow'd,** deposited. 79. **sconce,** head. 80. **stands on,** concerns or troubles itself about. 96. **o'er-raught,** overreached, cheated. 97. **cozenage,** cheating. 99. 100. **Dark-working, Soul-killing.** It was Johnson's idea that these epithets should be interchanged. 102. **liberties of sin,** persons allowed improper freedom to sin.

ACT II. SCENE I. 7. **A man . . . liberty.** With this line begins the formal issue between the two women. It presents the theme of the shrew and the patient wife. 11. **still,** always; see glossary. 15. **lash'd,** scourged, castigated; possibly used for "leash'd." 22. **sense,** mental faculty; see glossary. 30. **some other where,** somewhere else. 39. **helpless,** unavailing, unprofitable. 41. **fool-begg'd,** made foolish by asking (me to be patient). 47. **mind,** thoughts; see glossary. 49. **Beshrew,** "bad luck to"; see glossary. **understand,** stand under. 57. **horn-mad,** mad as a horned beast, with a quibble on the sense of "rage at being made a cuckold."

When I desir'd him to come home to dinner,
He ask'd me for a thousand marks in gold:
' 'Tis dinner-time,' quoth I; 'My gold!' quoth he:
'Your meat doth burn,' quoth I; 'My gold!' quoth he:
'Will you come home?' quoth I; 'My gold!' quoth he,
'Where is the thousand marks I gave thee, villain?'
'The pig,' quoth I, 'is burn'd;' 'My gold!' quoth he:
'My mistress, sir,' quoth I; 'Hang up thy mistress!
I know not thy mistress; out on thy mistress!'

Luc. Quoth who?

Dro. E. Quoth my master:
'I know,' quoth he, 'no house, no wife, no mistress.'
So that my errand, due unto my tongue,
I thank him, I bare home upon my shoulders;
For, in conclusion, he did beat me there.

Adr. Go back again, thou slave, and fetch him home.

Dro. E. Go back again, and be new beaten home?
For God's sake, send some other messenger.

Adr. Back, slave, or I will break thy pate across.

Dro. E. And he will bless that cross with other beating:
Between you I shall have a holy head.

Adr. Hence, prating peasant! fetch thy master home.

Dro. E. Am I so round with you as you with me,
That like a football you do spurn me thus?
You spurn me hence, and he will spurn me hither:
If I last in this service, you must case me in leather.
[*Exit.*]

Luc. Fie, how impatience loureth in your face!

Adr. His company must do his minions grace,
Whilst I at home starve for a merry look.
Hath homely age th' alluring beauty took
From my poor cheek? then he hath wasted it:
Are my discourses dull? barren my wit?
If voluble and sharp discourse be marr'd,
Unkindness blunts it more than marble hard:
Do their gay vestments his affections bait?
That 's not my fault; he 's master of my state:
What ruins are in me that can be found,
By him not ruin'd? then is he the ground
Of my defeatures. My decayed fair
A sunny look of his would soon repair:
But, too unruly deer, he breaks the pale
And feeds from home; poor I am but his stale.

Luc. Self-harming jealousy! fie, beat it hence!

Adr. Unfeeling fools can with such wrongs dispense.
I know his eye doth homage otherwhere;
Or else what lets it but he would be here?
Sister, you know he promis'd me a chain;
Would that alone, alone he would detain,
So he would keep fair quarter with his bed!
I see the jewel best enamelled
Will lose his beauty; yet the gold bides still,
That others touch, and often touching will
†Wear gold: and no man that hath a name,
By falsehood and corruption doth it shame.
Since that my beauty cannot please his eye,
I'll weep what 's left away, and weeping die.

Luc. How many fond fools serve mad jealousy!
Exit [*with Adriana*].

[SCENE II. *A public place.*]

Enter ANTIPHOLUS [of Syracuse].

Ant. S. The gold I gave to Dromio is laid up
Safe at the Centaur; and the heedful slave
Is wand'red forth, in care to seek me out
By computation and mine host's report.
I could not speak with Dromio since at first
I sent him from the mart. See, here he comes.

Enter DROMIO of Syracuse.

How now, sir! is your merry humour alter'd?
As you love strokes, so jest with me again.
You know no Centaur? you receiv'd no gold?
Your mistress sent to have me home to dinner?
My house was at the Phœnix? Wast thou mad,
That thus so madly thou didst answer me?

Dro. S. What answer, sir? when spake I such a word?

Ant. S. Even now, even here, not half an hour since.

Dro. S. I did not see you since you sent me hence,
Home to the Centaur, with the gold you gave me.

Ant. S. Villain, thou didst deny the gold's receipt
And told'st me of a mistress and a dinner;
For which, I hope, thou felt'st I was displeas'd.

Dro. S. I am glad to see you in this merry vein:
What means this jest? I pray you, master, tell me.

Ant. S. Yea, dost thou jeer and flout me in the teeth?
Think'st thou I jest? Hold, take thou that, and that.
Beats Dromio.

Dro. S. Hold, sir, for God's sake! now your jest is earnest:
Upon what bargain do you give it me?

Ant. S. Because that I familiarly sometimes
Do use you for my fool and chat with you,
Your sauciness will jest upon my love
And make a common of my serious hours.
When the sun shines let foolish gnats make sport,
But creep in crannies when he hides his beams.
If you will jest with me, know my aspect
And fashion your demeanour to my looks,
Or I will beat this method in your sconce.

Dro. S. Sconce call you it? so you would leave battering, I had rather have it a head: an you use these blows long, I must get a sconce for my head and insconce it too; or else I shall seek my wit in my shoulders. But, I pray, sir, why am I beaten?

Ant. S. Dost thou not know?

Dro. S. Nothing, sir, but that I am beaten.

Ant. S. Shall I tell you why?

72. **due unto my tongue,** i.e., instead of committing to me a message that I might deliver (with my tongue), he gave me one to bear home on my shoulders (i.e., a beating). 79. **bless,** consecrate; also, beat. 80. **holy,** with quibble on the sense "full of holes." 82. **round,** spherical, with pun on the sense of "plain-spoken"; see glossary. 86. **loureth,** frowns. 87. **minions,** paramours, darlings; see glossary. **grace,** honor; see glossary. 91. **discourses,** conversations; see glossary. 94. **affections,** passions; see glossary. **bait,** entice. 95. **state,** outward display, i.e., clothes; see glossary. 97. **ground,** cause. 98. **defeatures,** disfigurements. **decayed,** impaired, perished; see glossary. **fair,** beauty; see glossary. 101. **stale.** She is stale to him, he dear (*deer*) to her; a *stale* is a lover made into a dupe, or a laughingstock. 103. **dispense,** pardon, condone by dispensation. 105. **lets,** hinders; see glossary. 107. **detain,** withhold. 108. **keep fair quarter,** be on good terms. 109-113. **I see . . . shame.** This is a difficult passage, possibly corrupt. Herford explains: "The best enameled jewel tarnishes, but the gold setting keeps its luster; however, it may be worn by the touch. Similarly, a man of assured reputation can commit domestic infidelity without blasting it." 112. **Wear,** so Theobald; F: *Where.* 116. **fond,** doting; see glossary.

SCENE II. *Stage Direction:* ***A public place.*** New Cambridge: *The Mart of Ephesus.* 22. **in the teeth,** to my face. 24. **earnest,** money paid

Dro. S. Ay, sir, and wherefore; for they say every why hath a wherefore.

Ant. S. Why, first,—for flouting me; and then, wherefore,—
For urging it the second time to me.

Dro. S. Was there ever any man thus beaten out of season,
When in the why and the wherefore is neither rhyme nor reason?
Well, sir, I thank you.

Ant. S. Thank me, sir! for what?

Dro. S. Marry, sir, for this something that you gave me for nothing.

Ant. S. I'll make you amends next, to give you nothing for something. But say, sir, is it dinner-time?

Dro. S. No, sir: I think the meat wants that I have.

Ant. S. In good time, sir; what 's that?

Dro. S. Basting.

Ant. S. Well, sir, then 'twill be dry.

Dro. S. If it be, sir, I pray you, eat none of it.

Ant. S. Your reason?

Dro. S. Lest it make you choleric and purchase me another dry basting.

Ant. S. Well, sir, learn to jest in good time: there 's a time for all things.

Dro. S. I durst have denied that, before you were so choleric.

Ant. S. By what rule, sir?

Dro. S. Marry, sir, by a rule as plain as the plain bald pate of father Time himself.

Ant. S. Let 's hear it.

Dro. S. There 's no time for a man to recover his hair that grows bald by nature.

Ant. S. May he not do it by fine and recovery?

Dro. S. Yes, to pay a fine for a periwig and recover the lost hair of another man.

Ant. S. Why is Time such a niggard of hair, being, as it is, so plentiful an excrement?

Dro. S. Because it is a blessing that he bestows on beasts; and what he hath scanted men in hair he hath given them in wit.

Ant. S. Why, but there 's many a man hath more hair than wit.

Dro. S. Not a man of those but he hath the wit to lose his hair.

Ant. S. Why, thou didst conclude hairy men plain dealers without wit.

Dro. S. The plainer dealer, the sooner lost: yet he loseth it in a kind of jollity.

Ant. S. For what reason?

Dro. S. For two; and sound ones too.

Ant. S. Nay, not sound, I pray you.

Dro. S. Sure ones then.

Ant. S. Nay, not sure, in a thing falsing.

Dro. S. Certain ones then.

Ant. S. Name them.

Dro. S. The one, to save the money that he spends in tiring; the other that at dinner they should not drop in his porridge.

Ant. S. You would all this time have proved there is no time for all things.

Dro. S. Marry, and did, sir; namely, e'en no time to recover hair lost by nature.

Ant. S. But your reason was not substantial, why there is no time to recover.

Dro. S. Thus I mend it: Time himself is bald and therefore to the world's end will have bald followers.

Ant. S. I knew 'twould be a bald conclusion: But, soft! who wafts us yonder?

Enter ADRIANA *and* LUCIANA.

Adr. Ay, ay, Antipholus, look strange and frown:
Some other mistress hath thy sweet aspects;
I am not Adriana nor thy wife.
The time was once when thou unurg'd wouldst vow
That never words were music to thine ear,
That never object pleasing in thine eye,
That never touch well welcome to thy hand,
That never meat sweet-savour'd in thy taste,
Unless I spake, or look'd, or touch'd, or carv'd to thee.
How comes it now, my husband, O, how comes it,
That thou art thus estranged from thyself?
Thyself I call it, being strange to me,
That, undividable, incorporate,
Am better than thy dear self's better part.
Ah, do not tear away thyself from me!
For know, my love, as easy mayst thou fall
A drop of water in the breaking gulf
And take unmingled thence that drop again,
Without addition or diminishing,
As take from me thyself and not me too.
How dearly would it touch thee to the quick,
Shouldst thou but hear I were licentious
And that this body, consecrate to thee,
By ruffian lust should be contaminate!
Wouldst thou not spit at me and spurn at me
And hurl the name of husband in my face
And tear the stain'd skin off my harlot-brow
And from my false hand cut the wedding-ring
And break it with a deep-divorcing vow?
I know thou canst; and therefore see thou do it.
I am possess'd with an adulterate blot;
My blood is mingled with the crime of lust:
For if we two be one and thou play false,
I do digest the poison of thy flesh,
Being strumpeted by thy contagion.
Keep then fair league and truce with thy true bed;
I live distain'd, thou undishonoured.

Ant. S. Plead you to me, fair dame? I know you not:
In Ephesus I am but two hours old,
As strange unto your town as to your talk;
Who, every word by all my wit being scann'd,
Want wit in all one word to understand.

as an installment to secure a bargain, with quibble on the meaning "serious"; see glossary. 28. **jest upon,** trifle with. 29. **common,** public playground. 32. **aspect,** look, expression; also, favor or disfavor of a heavenly body. 34. **sconce,** head; fort (l. 35); helmet (l. 38). 37. **use,** make a practice of; see glossary. 38. **insconce,** to shelter behind or within a *sconce*, or fortification. 39. **seek . . . shoulders,** run away, show my back (Cuningham); but Dromio probably means that his head will be beaten into his shoulders. 57. **wants,** lacks; see glossary. **that,** what. 58. **In good time,** indeed. 63. **choleric.** Hot or dry food would produce or aggravate the choleric humor. 64. **dry basting,** hard beating. 70. **Marry,** an oath by the Virgin Mary; see glossary. 75. **fine and recovery,** legal procedure; Schmidt: "finery and recovery." 79. **excrement,** outgrowth (of hair). 84. **more . . . wit,** a proverbial phrase. 85-86. **he . . . hair,** a reference to the venereal diseases in which loss of hair was a symptom. 90. **jollity.** This word and *sound* and *falsing* (ll. 93, 95) continue the reference to disease. 95. **falsing,** deceptive. 99. **tiring,** dressing the hair. 110. **bald,** senseless. 111. **wafts,** beckons. 112. **strange,** estranged, unfriendly; see glossary. 125. **better part,** i.e., soul, spirit. 127. **fall,** i.e., let fall; see glossary. 145. **digest,** assimilate; see glossary. 146. **strumpeted,** made a strumpet. 148. **distain'd.** Dyce interprets as "I, as a wife, receive the *stain* of your present conduct, while you, as a husband, suffer no loss of honour."

Luc. Fie, brother! how the world is chang'd with you!
When were you wont to use my sister thus?
She sent for you by Dromio home to dinner.
Ant. S. By Dromio?
Dro. S. By me?
Adr. By thee; and this thou didst return from him,
That he did buffet thee and in his blows
Denied my house for his, me for his wife.
Ant. S. Did you converse, sir, with this gentlewoman?
What is the course and drift of your compact?
Dro. S. I, sir? I never saw her till this time.
Ant. S. Villain, thou liest; for even her very words
Didst thou deliver to me on the mart.
Dro. S. I never spake with her in all my life.
Ant. S. How can she thus then call us by our names?
Unless it be by inspiration.
Adr. How ill agrees it with your gravity
To counterfeit thus grossly with your slave,
Abetting him to thwart me in my mood!
Be it my wrong you are from me exempt,
But wrong not that wrong with a more contempt.
Come, I will fasten on this sleeve of thine:
Thou art an elm, my husband, I a vine,
Whose weakness married to thy stronger state
Makes me with thy strength to communicate:
If aught possess thee from me, it is dross,
Usurping ivy, brier, or idle moss;
Who, all for want of pruning, with intrusion
Infect thy sap and live on thy confusion.
Ant. S. [*Aside*] To me she speaks; she moves me for her theme:
What, was I married to her in my dream?
Or sleep I now and think I hear all this?
What error drives our eyes and ears amiss?
Until I know this sure uncertainty,
I'll entertain the offer'd fallacy.
Luc. Dromio, go bid the servants spread for dinner.
Dro. S. O, for my beads! I cross me for a sinner.
This is the fairy land: O spite of spites!
We talk with goblins, owls and sprites:
If we obey them not, this will ensue,
They'll suck our breath or pinch us black and blue.
Luc. Why prat'st thou to thyself and answer'st not?
Dromio, thou drone, thou snail, thou slug, thou sot!
Dro. S. I am transformed, master, am I not?
Ant. S. I think thou art in mind, and so am I.
Dro. S. Nay, master, both in mind and in my shape.
Ant. S. Thou hast thine own form.
Dro. S. No, I am an ape.
Luc. If thou art chang'd to aught, 'tis to an ass.
Dro. S. 'Tis true; she rides me and I long for grass.
'Tis so, I am an ass; else it could never be
But I should know her as well as she knows me.
Adr. Come, come, no longer will I be a fool,
To put the finger in the eye and weep,
Whilst man and master laugh my woes to scorn.
Come, sir, to dinner. Dromio, keep the gate.
Husband, I'll dine above with you to-day
And shrive you of a thousand idle pranks.
Sirrah, if any ask you for your master,
Say he dines forth and let no creature enter.
Come, sister. Dromio, play the porter well.
Ant. S. Am I in earth, in heaven, or in hell?
Sleeping or waking? mad or well-advis'd?
Known unto these, and to myself disguis'd!
I'll say as they say and persever so
And in this mist at all adventures go.
Dro. S. Master, shall I be porter at the gate?
Adr. Ay; and let none enter, lest I break your pate.
Luc. Come, come, Antipholus, we dine too late.
[*Exeunt.*]

ACT III.

SCENE I. [*Before the house of* ANTIPHOLUS of Ephesus.]

Enter ANTIPHOLUS of Ephesus, *his Man* DROMIO, ANGELO *the Goldsmith, and* BALTHAZAR *the Merchant.*

Ant. E. Good Signior Angelo, you must excuse us all;
My wife is shrewish when I keep not hours:
Say that I linger'd with you at your shop
To see the making of her carcanet
And that to-morrow you will bring it home.
But here 's a villain that would face me down
He met me on the mart and that I beat him
And charg'd him with a thousand marks in gold
And that I did deny my wife and house.
Thou drunkard, thou, what didst thou mean by this?
Dro. E. Say what you will, sir, but I know what I know;
That you beat me at the mart, I have your hand to show:
If the skin were parchment and the blows you gave were ink,
Your own handwriting would tell you what I think.
Ant. E. I think thou art an ass.
Dro. E. Marry, so it doth appear
By the wrongs I suffer and the blows I bear.
I should kick, being kick'd; and, being at that pass,
You would keep from my heels and beware of an ass.
Ant. E. Y' are sad, Signior Balthazar: pray God our cheer
May answer my good will and your good welcome here.
Bal. I hold your dainties cheap, sir, and your welcome dear.
Ant. E. O, Signior Balthazar, either at flesh or fish,
A table full of welcome makes scarce one dainty dish.
Bal. Good meat, sir, is common; that every churl affords.
Ant. E. And welcome more common; for that 's nothing but words.

163. **compact,** plot. 172. **mood,** anger, displeasure. 173. **exempt,** separated. 180. **idle,** unprofitable. 182. **confusion,** overthrow, ruin; see glossary. 183. **moves,** appeals to; see glossary. **theme,** subject, i. e., trouble. 186. **error.** Cf. I, ii, 97, *this town is full of cozenage;* Antipholus and Dromio continue in their belief in the witchery of Ephesus. 188. **entertain,** accept; see glossary. **fallacy,** delusive notion, error. 190. **beads,** rosary. 194. **suck . . . breath.** This piece of folklore was perhaps connected with the old idea that the breath of man was his soul. 196. **sot,** fool. 209. **dine above.** Elizabethans customarily dined on an upper floor. 210. **shrive,** to hear a person's confession and give him absolution. 211. **Sirrah,** customary form of address to servants; see glossary. 212. **forth,** out. 215. **well-advis'd,** in my right mind.

ACT III. SCENE I. 4. **carcanet,** necklace of jewels. 6. **face me down,** maintain to my face that. 8. **with,** i.e., with possession of. 9. **deny,** disown; see glossary. 11 ff. Note the appearance of doggerel at this point and in the following lines. Balthazar appears here only; Luce is elsewhere known as Nell; the conversation of the Dromios seemingly points to some textual inconsistency. 12. **hand,** quibble on "handwriting." 19. **sad,** serious; see glossary. 20. **answer,** agree with; see glossary. 24. **churl,** one of mean station. 28. **cates,** dainties. 31. **Gillian, Ginn,** Juliana, Jenny (?) 32. **Mome,** dolt, blockhead. **malt-**

Bal. Small cheer and great welcome makes a merry feast.
Ant. E. Ay to a niggardly host and more sparing guest:
But though my cates be mean, take them in good part;
Better cheer may you have, but not with better heart.
But, soft! my door is lock'd. Go bid them let us in.
Dro. E. Maud, Bridget, Marian, Cicely, Gillian, Ginn!
Dro. S. [*Within*] Mome, malt-horse, capon, coxcomb, idiot, patch!
Either get thee from the door or sit down at the hatch.
Dost thou conjure for wenches, that thou call'st for such store,
When one is one too many? Go get thee from the door.
Dro. E. What patch is made our porter? My master stays in the street.
Dro. S. [*Within*] Let him walk from whence he came, lest he catch cold on 's feet.
Ant. E. Who talks within there? ho, open the door!
Dro. S. [*Within*] Right, sir; I'll tell you when, an you'll tell me wherefore.
Ant. E. Wherefore? for my dinner: I have not din'd to-day.
Dro. S. [*Within*] Nor to-day here you must not; come again when you may.
Ant. E. What art thou that keep'st me out from the house I owe?
Dro. S. [*Within*] The porter for this time, sir, and my name is Dromio.
Dro. E. O villain! thou hast stol'n both mine office and my name.
The one ne'er got me credit, the other mickle blame.
If thou hadst been Dromio to-day in my place,
Thou wouldst have chang'd thy face for a name or thy name for an ass.
Luce. [*Within*] What a coil is there, Dromio? who are those at the gate?
Dro. E. Let my master in, Luce.
Luce. [*Within*] Faith, no; he comes too late;
And so tell your master.
Dro. E. O Lord, I must laugh!
Have at you with a proverb—Shall I set in my staff?
Luce. [*Within*] Have at you with another; that 's—When? can you tell?
Dro. S. [*Within*] If thy name be call'd Luce,—Luce, thou hast answer'd him well.
Ant. E. Do you hear, you minion? you'll let us in, I hope?
Luce. [*Within*] I thought to have ask'd you.
Dro. S. [*Within*] And you said no.
Dro. E. So, come, help: well struck! there was blow for blow.
Ant. E. Thou baggage, let me in.
Luce. [*Within*] Can you tell for whose sake?
Dro. E. Master, knock the door hard.
Luce. [*Within*] Let him knock till it ache.
Ant. E. You'll cry for this, minion, if I beat the door down.
Luce. [*Within*] What needs all that, and a pair of stocks in the town?
Adr. [*Within*] Who is that at the door that keeps all this noise?
Dro. S. [*Within*] By my troth, your town is troubled with unruly boys.
Ant. E. Are you there, wife? you might have come before.
Adr. [*Within*] Your wife, sir knave! go get you from the door.
Dro. E. If you went in pain, master, this 'knave' would go sore.
Ang. Here is neither cheer, sir, nor welcome: we would fain have either.
Bal. In debating which was best, we shall part with neither.
Dro. E. They stand at the door, master; bid them welcome hither.
Ant. E. There is something in the wind, that we cannot get in.
Dro. E. You would say so, master, if your garments were thin.
Your cake there is warm within; you stand here in the cold:
It would make a man mad as a buck, to be so bought and sold.
Ant. E. Go fetch me something: I'll break ope the gate.
Dro. S. [*Within*] Break any breaking here, and I'll break your knave's pate.
Dro. E. A man may break a word with you, sir, and words are but wind,
Ay, and break it in your face, so he break it not behind.
Dro. S. [*Within*] It seems thou want'st breaking: out upon thee, hind!
Dro. E. Here 's too much 'out upon thee!' I pray thee, let me in.
Dro. S. [*Within*] Ay, when fowls have no feathers and fish have no fin.
Ant. E. Well, I'll break in: go borrow me a crow.
Dro. E. A crow without feather? Master, mean you so?
For a fish without a fin, there 's a fowl without a feather:
If a crow help us in, sirrah, we'll pluck a crow together.
Ant. E. Go get thee gone; fetch me an iron crow.
Bal. Have patience, sir; O, let it not be so!
Herein you war against your reputation
And draw within the compass of suspect
Th' unviolated honour of your wife.
Once this,—your long experience of her wisdom,
Her sober virtue, years and modesty,

horse, brewer's horse; stupid person. **patch,** fool, clown. 33. **hatch,** a wicket or half door. 42. **owe,** own; see glossary. 45 **mickle,** much. 47. **face for a name.** New Cambridge editors suggest pun "face for an aim," when he was beaten by Antipholus and Adriana; otherwise unexplained. 48. **Luce [*Within*].** New Cambridge editors suggest that Luce and Adriana in this scene are on the upper stage, not able to see Antipholus and Dromio of Ephesus at rear door under the balcony. The Folio stage directions have Luce enter at l. 48, Adriana at l. 61. **coil,** noise, disturbance; see glossary. 51. **Have at,** let me at; see glossary. **Shall I set in my staff,** i.e., take up my abode. 52. **When . . . tell,** a proverbial expression used to turn aside a question. 54. **hope.** Theobald read *trow*, making a triple rhyme. Malone thought that a line had been dropped out; if so, it would account for the obscurity of the next two lines. 67. **debating,** discussing; see glossary. **part,** depart; see glossary. 72. **buck,** i.e., in rutting time. **bought and sold,** imposed upon. 77. **hind,** slave; see glossary. 83. **pluck a crow together,** to pick a bone together, settle accounts; suggested by *crow* meaning "crowbar." 87. **draw . . . suspect,** bring under suspicion. 89. **Once this,** to be brief, in short. 90. **virtue,** merit, general excellence; see glossary.

Plead on her part some cause to you unknown;
And doubt not, sir, but she will well excuse
Why at this time the doors are made against you.
Be rul'd by me: depart in patience,
And let us to the Tiger all to dinner,
And about evening come yourself alone
To know the reason of this strange restraint.
If by strong hand you offer to break in
Now in the stirring passage of the day,
A vulgar comment will be made of it,
And that supposed by the common rout
Against your yet ungalled estimation
That may with foul intrusion enter in
And dwell upon your grave when you are dead;
For slander lives upon succession,
For ever hous'd where it gets possession.
Ant. E. You have prevail'd: I will depart in quiet,
And, in despite of mirth, mean to be merry.
I know a wench of excellent discourse,
Pretty and witty, wild and yet, too, gentle:
There will we dine. This woman that I mean,
My wife—but, I protest, without desert—
Hath oftentimes upbraided me withal:
To her will we to dinner. [*To Ang.*] Get you home
And fetch the chain; by this I know 'tis made:
Bring it, I pray you, to the Porpentine;
For there 's the house: that chain will I bestow—
Be it for nothing but to spite my wife—
Upon mine hostess there: good sir, make haste.
Since mine own doors refuse to entertain me,
I'll knock elsewhere, to see if they'll disdain me.
Ang. I'll meet you at that place some hour hence.
Ant. E. Do so. This jest shall cost me some expense.
Exeunt.

[SCENE II. *The same.*]

Enter LUCIANA *with* ANTIPHOLUS of Syracuse.

Luc. And may it be that you have quite forgot
A husband's office? shall, Antipholus,
Even in the spring of love, thy love-springs rot?
Shall love, in building, grow so ruinate?
If you did wed my sister for her wealth,
Then for her wealth's sake use her with more kindness:
Or if you like elsewhere, do it by stealth;
Muffle your false love with some show of blindness:
Let not my sister read it in your eye;
Be not thy tongue thy own shame's orator;
Look sweet, speak fair, become disloyalty;
Apparel vice like virtue's harbinger;
Bear a fair presence, though your heart be tainted;
Teach sin the carriage of a holy saint;
Be secret-false: what need she be acquainted?
What simple thief brags of his own attaint?
'Tis double wrong, to truant with your bed
And let her read it in thy looks at board:
Shame hath a bastard fame, well managed;
Ill deeds is doubled with an evil word.
Alas, poor women! make us but believe,
Being compact of credit, that you love us;
Though others have the arm, show us the sleeve;
We in your motion turn and you may move us.
Then, gentle brother, get you in again;
Comfort my sister, cheer her, call her wife:
'Tis holy sport to be a little vain,
When the sweet breath of flattery conquers strife.
Ant. S. Sweet mistress,—what your name is else, I know not,
Nor by what wonder you do hit of mine,—
Less in your knowledge and your grace you show not
Than our earth's wonder, more than earth divine.
Teach me, dear creature, how to think and speak;
Lay open to my earthy-gross conceit,
Smoth'red in errors, feeble, shallow, weak,
The folded meaning of your words' deceit.
Against my soul's pure truth why labour you
To make it wander in an unknown field?
Are you a god? would you create me new?
Transform me then, and to your pow'r I'll yield.
But if that I am I, then well I know
Your weeping sister is no wife of mine,
Nor to her bed no homage do I owe:
Far more, far more to you do I decline.
O, train me not, sweet mermaid, with thy note,
To drown me in thy sister's flood of tears:
Sing, siren, for thyself and I will dote:
Spread o'er the silver waves thy golden hairs,
And as a bed I'll take them and there lie,
And in that glorious supposition think
He gains by death that hath such means to die:
Let Love, being light, be drowned if she sink!
Luc. What, are you mad, that you do reason so?
Ant. S. Not mad, but mated; how, I do not know.
Luc. It is a fault that springeth from your eye.
Ant. S. For gazing on your beams, fair sun, being by.
Luc. Gaze where you should, and that will clear your sight.
Ant. S. As good to wink, sweet love, as look on night.
Luc. Why call you me love? call my sister so.
Ant. S. Thy sister's sister.
Luc. That 's my sister.
Ant. S. No;
It is thyself, mine own self's better part,
Mine eye's clear eye, my dear heart's dearer heart,
My food, my fortune and my sweet hope's aim,
My sole earth's heaven and my heaven's claim.
Luc. All this my sister is, or else should be.
Ant. S. Call thyself sister, sweet, for I am thee.
Thee will I love and with thee lead my life:
Thou hast no husband yet nor I no wife.
Give me thy hand.
Luc. O, soft, sir! hold you still:
I'll fetch my sister, to get her good will. *Exit.*

Enter DROMIO of Syracuse.

92. **excuse,** justify; see glossary. 93. **made,** fastened. 98. **offer,** venture; see glossary. 99. **passage,** people passing by. 100. **vulgar,** public. 102. **ungalled,** uninjured. 105. **slander . . . succession,** i.e., one slander grows out of another. 108. **in . . . mirth,** in despite of mirth, which has abandoned me. Theobald suggested *wrath* for *mirth*. 112. **desert,** my deserving it. 115. **this,** this time. 116. **Porpentine,** name of an inn; the word means "porcupine."

SCENE II. 1. **may,** can; see glossary. 3. **love-springs,** tender "shoots" of love. 11. **fair,** courteously; see glossary. **become disloyalty,** carry falseness gracefully. 14. **carriage,** demeanor, behavior. 16. **attaint,** stain, dishonor; or possibly, conviction of crime. 18. **board,** table. 19. **fame,** reputation; see glossary. 22. **compact of credit,** made up of credulity. 27. **vain,** false. 30. **hit of,** hit upon, guess. 32. **earth's wonder.** Douce sees in this a reference to Queen Elizabeth. 34. **conceit,** wit, mental faculty; see glossary. 36. **folded,** concealed. 44. **decline,** incline, lean toward. 45. **train,** entice, allure; see glossary. 52. **light,** buoyant, with quibble on the sense of "wanton." The idea is that *Love* cannot possibly sink. 53. **reason,**

Ant. S. Why, how now, Dromio! where runn'st thou so fast?

Dro. S. Do you know me, sir? am I Dromio? am I your man? am I myself?

Ant. S. Thou art Dromio, thou art my man, thou art thyself.

Dro. S. I am an ass, I am a woman's man and besides myself.

Ant. S. What woman's man? and how besides thyself?

Dro. S. Marry, sir, besides myself, I am due to a woman; one that claims me, one that haunts me, one that will have me.

Ant. S. What claim lays she to thee?

Dro. S. Marry, sir, such claim as you would lay to your horse; and she would have me as a beast: not that, I being a beast, she would have me; but that she, being a very beastly creature, lays claim to me.

Ant. S. What is she?

Dro. S. A very reverent body; ay, such a one as a man may not speak of without he say 'Sir-reverence.' I have but lean luck in the match, and yet is she a wondrous fat marriage.

Ant. S. How dost thou mean a fat marriage?

Dro. S. Marry, sir, she 's the kitchen wench and all grease; and I know not what use to put her to but to make a lamp of her and run from her by her own light. I warrant, her rags and the tallow in them will burn a Poland winter: if she lives till doomsday, she'll burn a week longer than the whole world.

Ant. S. What complexion is she of?

Dro. S. Swart, like my shoe, but her face nothing like so clean kept: for why, she sweats; a man may go over shoes in the grime of it.

Ant. S. That 's a fault that water will mend.

Dro. S. No, sir, 'tis in grain; Noah's flood could not do it.

Ant. S. What 's her name?

Dro. S. Nell, sir; but her name and three quarters, that 's an ell and three quarters, will not measure her from hip to hip.

Ant. S. Then she bears some breadth?

Dro. S. No longer from head to foot than from hip to hip; she is spherical, like a globe; I could find out countries in her.

Ant. S. In what part of her body stands Ireland?

Dro. S. Marry, sir, in her buttocks: I found it out by the bogs.

Ant. S. Where Scotland?

Dro. S. I found it by the barrenness; hard in the palm of the hand.

Ant. S. Where France?

Dro. S. In her forehead; armed and reverted, making war against her heir.

Ant. S. Where England?

Dro. S. I looked for the chalky cliffs, but I could find no whiteness in them; but I guess it stood in her chin, by the salt rheum that ran between France and it.

Ant. S. Where Spain?

Dro. S. Faith, I saw it not; but I felt it hot in her breath.

Ant. S. Where America, the Indies?

Dro. S. Oh, sir, upon her nose, all o'er embellished with rubies, carbuncles, sapphires, declining their rich aspect to the hot breath of Spain; who sent whole armadoes of caracks to be ballast at her nose.

Ant. S. Where stood Belgia, the Netherlands?

Dro. S. Oh, sir, I did not look so low. To conclude, this drudge, or diviner, laid claim to me; called me Dromio; swore I was assured to her; told me what privy marks I had about me, as, the mark of my shoulder, the mole in my neck, the great wart on my left arm, that I amazed ran from her as a witch:
And, I think, if my breast had not been made of faith and my heart of steel,
She had transform'd me to a curtal dog and made me turn i' th' wheel.

Ant. S. Go hie thee presently, post to the road:
An if the wind blow any way from shore,
I will not harbour in this town to-night:
If any bark put forth, come to the mart,
Where I will walk till thou return to me.
If every one knows us and we know none,
'Tis time, I think, to trudge, pack and be gone.

Dro. S. As from a bear a man would run for life,
So fly I from her that would be my wife. *Exit.*

Ant. S. There 's none but witches do inhabit here;
And therefore 'tis high time that I were hence.
She that doth call me husband, even my soul
Doth for a wife abhor. But her fair sister,
Possess'd with such a gentle sovereign grace,
Of such enchanting presence and discourse,
Hath almost made me traitor to myself:
But, lest myself be guilty to self-wrong,
I'll stop mine ears against the mermaid's song.

Enter ANGELO *with the chain.*

Ang. Master Antipholus,—

Ant. S. Ay, that 's my name.

Ang. I know it well, sir: lo, here is the chain.
I thought to have ta'en you at the Porpentine:
The chain unfinish'd made me stay thus long.

Ant. S. What is your will that I shall do with this?

Ang. What please yourself, sir: I have made it for you.

Ant. S. Made it for me, sir! I bespoke it not.

Ang. Not once, nor twice, but twenty times you have.
Go home with it and please your wife withal;
And soon at supper-time I'll visit you
And then receive my money for the chain.

Ant. S. I pray you, sir, receive the money now,
For fear you ne'er see chain nor money more.

Ang. You are a merry man, sir: fare you well. *Exit.*

Ant. S. What I should think of this, I cannot tell:
But this I think, there 's no man is so vain
That would refuse so fair an offer'd chain.
I see a man here needs not live by shifts,

talk. 54. **mated,** amazed, confounded, with quibble on the sense of "matched with a wife." 56. **being by,** i.e., being near you. 58. **wink,** close the eyes in sleep; see glossary. 64. **My . . . claim,** i.e., my heaven on earth and my claim on heaven hereafter. 93. **'Sir-reverence,'** i.e., save your reverence, an expression used in apology for the remark that follows it. **lean,** poor, meager. 104. **Swart,** swarthy, dark. 108. **in grain,** indelible, ineradicable. 123. **barrenness.** New Cambridge editors print *barren-nesses*, indicating a pun on *ness*, a promontory. 126. **armed and reverted.** See Introduction for explanation of reference to the French war. 130. **them,** i.e., her teeth. 140. **armadoes of caracks,** fleets of galleons. 141. **ballast,** loaded, freighted. 142. **Netherlands,** with bawdy double meaning. 144. **diviner,** sorceress. 145. **assured,** affianced. 151. **curtal dog,** dog with docked tail, of no service in the chase. **turn . . . wheel.** Dogs, by running in a wheel, turned the spit. 152. **presently,** at once; see glossary. **post,** hasten; see glossary. **road,** harbor, roadstead. 158. **pack,** depart; see glossary. 165. **Possess'd with,** having possession of; see *possess* in glossary. 168. **to,** of. 187. **shifts,** stratagems, tricks; see glossary.

When in the streets he meets such golden gifts.
I'll to the mart and there for Dromio stay:
If any ship put out, then straight away. *Exit.*

ACT IV.

SCENE I. [*A public place.*]

Enter a [Second] Merchant, *Goldsmith* [ANGELO], *and an* Officer.

Sec. Mer. You know since Pentecost the sum is due,
And since I have not much importun'd you;
Nor now I had not, but that I am bound
To Persia and want guilders for my voyage:
Therefore make present satisfaction,
Or I'll attach you by this officer.
Ang. Even just the sum that I do owe to you
Is growing to me by Antipholus,
And in the instant that I met with you
He had of me a chain: at five o'clock
I shall receive the money for the same.
Pleaseth you walk with me down to his house,
I will discharge my bond and thank you too.

Enter ANTIPHOLUS of Ephesus [*and*] DROMIO [of Ephesus] *from the courtezan's.*

Off. That labour may you save: see where he comes.
Ant. E. While I go to the goldsmith's house, go thou
And buy a rope's end: that will I bestow
Among my wife and her confederates,
For locking me out of my doors by day.
But, soft! I see the goldsmith. Get thee gone;
Buy thou a rope and bring it home to me.
Dro. E. I buy a thousand pound a year: I buy a rope. *Exit Dromio.*
Ant. E. A man is well holp up that trusts to you:
I promised your presence and the chain;
But neither chain nor goldsmith came to me.
Belike you thought our love would last too long,
If it were chain'd together, and therefore came not.
Ang. Saving your merry humour, here 's the note
How much your chain weighs to the utmost carat,
The fineness of the gold and chargeful fashion,
Which doth amount to three odd ducats more
Than I stand debted to this gentleman:
I pray you, see him presently discharg'd,
For he is bound to sea and stays but for it.
Ant. E. I am not furnish'd with the present money;
Besides, I have some business in the town.
Good signior, take the stranger to my house
And with you take the chain and bid my wife
Disburse the sum on the receipt thereof:
Perchance I will be there as soon as you.
Ang. Then you will bring the chain to her yourself?
Ant. E. No; bear it with you, lest I come not time enough.
Ang. Well, sir, I will. Have you the chain about you?
Ant. E. An if I have not, sir, I hope you have;
Or else you may return without your money.
Ang. Nay, come, I pray you, sir, give me the chain:
Both wind and tide stays for this gentleman,
And I, to blame, have held him here too long.
Ant. E. Good Lord! you use this dalliance to excuse
Your breach of promise to the Porpentine.
I should have chid you for not bringing it,
But, like a shrew, you first begin to brawl.
Sec. Mer. The hour steals on; I pray you, sir, dispatch.
Ang. You hear how he importunes me;—the chain!
Ant. E. Why, give it to my wife and fetch your money.
Ang. Come, come, you know I gave it you even now.
Either send the chain or send me by some token.
Ant. E. Fie, now you run this humour out of breath,
Come, where 's the chain? I pray you, let me see it.
Sec. Mer. My business cannot brook this dalliance.
Good sir, say whe'r you'll answer me or no:
If not, I'll leave him to the officer.
Ant. E. I answer you! what should I answer you?
Ang. The money that you owe me for the chain.
Ant. E. I owe you none till I receive the chain.
Ang. You know I gave it you half an hour since.
Ant. E. You gave me none: you wrong me much to say so.
Ang. You wrong me more, sir, in denying it:
Consider how it stands upon my credit.
Sec. Mer. Well, officer, arrest him at my suit.
Off. I do; and charge you in the duke's name to obey me.
Ang. This touches me in reputation.
Either consent to pay this sum for me
Or I attach you by this officer.
Ant. E. Consent to pay thee that I never had!
Arrest me, foolish fellow, if thou dar'st.
Ang. Here is thy fee; arrest him, officer.
I would not spare my brother in this case,
If he should scorn me so apparently.
Off. I do arrest you, sir: you hear the suit.
Ant. E. I do obey thee till I give thee bail.
But, sirrah, you shall buy this sport as dear
As all the metal in your shop will answer.
Ang. Sir, sir, I shall have law in Ephesus,
To your notorious shame; I doubt it not.

Enter DROMIO of Syracuse, *from the bay.*

Dro. S. Master, there 's a bark of Epidamnum
That stays but till her owner comes aboard
And then, sir, she bears away. Our fraughtage, sir,
I have convey'd aboard and I have bought
The oil, the balsamum and aqua-vitæ.
The ship is in her trim: the merry wind
Blows fair from land: they stay for nought at all
But for their owner, master, and yourself.
Ant. E. How now! a madman! Why, thou peevish sheep,

190. **straight,** immediately; see glossary.
ACT IV. SCENE I. *Stage Direction:* ***A public place.*** New Cambridge: *Place in the Mart.* 6. **attach,** arrest, seize; see glossary. 8. **growing,** due, accruing. 16. **bestow,** employ. 21. **buy a thousand pound a year,** doubtfully explained as "a thousand pounds (blows) a year"; possibly, "I'll buy a rope as gladly as I would buy," etc. 22. **holp,** helped; see glossary. 29. **chargeful,** expensive. 31. **debted,** indebted. 56. **send . . . token,** i.e., send me with some sign authorizing me to receive payment. 59. **brook,** endure; see glossary. 68. **stands upon,** concerns. 87. **fraughtage,** freight. 89. **balsamum, aqua-vitæ,** balm, ardent spirits. 90. **in her trim,** rigged and ready to sail. 93. **peevish,** silly, senseless; see glossary. **sheep,** a pun; pronounced much like "ship." 95. **waftage,** conveyance by ship. 98. **rope's end,** a hangman's noose. 101. **list,** listen to; see glossary. 110. **Dowsabel,** used ironically for *Nell;* from *douce et belle.*
SCENE II. 2. **austerely,** i.e., not being affected by his pleas. 6. **meteors,** changes of color and expression. 7ff. Note the use of stichomythia, dialogue in which each speech consists of a single line; much used in classical drama. 8. **spite,** vexation. 14. **honest,** honorable; see glossary. 20. **shapeless,** misshapen. 22. **Stigmatical,** crooked, or

What ship of Epidamnum stays for me?
Dro. S. A ship you sent me to, to hire waftage.
Ant. E. Thou drunken slave, I sent thee for a rope
And told thee to what purpose and what end.
Dro. S. You sent me for a rope's end as soon:
You sent me to the bay, sir, for a bark.
Ant. E. I will debate this matter at more leisure
And teach your ears to list me with more heed.
To Adriana, villain, hie thee straight:
Give her this key, and tell her, in the desk
That 's cover'd o'er with Turkish tapestry
There is a purse of ducats; let her send it:
Tell her I am arrested in the street
And that shall bail me: hie thee, slave, be gone!
On, officer, to prison till it come.
Exeunt [*Sec. Merchant, Angelo, Officer, and Ant. E.*].
Dro. S. To Adriana! that is where we din'd,
Where Dowsabel did claim me for her husband:
She is too big, I hope, for me to compass.
Thither I must, although against my will,
For servants must their masters' minds fulfil. *Exit.*

[SCENE II. *The house of* ANTIPHOLUS of Ephesus.]

Enter ADRIANA *and* LUCIANA.

Adr. Ah, Luciana, did he tempt thee so?
Mightst thou perceive austerely in his eye
That he did plead in earnest? yea or no?
Look'd he or red or pale, or sad or merrily?
What observation mad'st thou in this case
Of his heart's meteors tilting in his face?
Luc. First he denied you had in him no right.
Adr. He meant he did me none; the more my spite.
Luc. Then swore he that he was a stranger here.
Adr. And true he swore, though yet forsworn he were.
Luc. Then pleaded I for you.
Adr. And what said he?
Luc. That love I begg'd for you he begg'd of me.
Adr. With what persuasion did he tempt thy love?
Luc. With words that in an honest suit might move.
First he did praise my beauty, then my speech.
Adr. Didst speak him fair?
Luc. Have patience, I beseech.
Adr. I cannot, nor I will not, hold me still;
My tongue, though not my heart, shall have his will.
He is deformed, crooked, old and sere,
Ill-fac'd, worse bodied, shapeless everywhere;
Vicious, ungentle, foolish, blunt, unkind,
Stigmatical in making, worse in mind.
Luc. Who would be jealous then of such a one?
No evil lost is wail'd when it is gone.
Adr. Ah, but I think him better than I say,
And yet would herein others' eyes were worse.
Far from her nest the lapwing cries away:
My heart prays for him, though my tongue do curse.

Enter DROMIO of Syracuse.

Dro. S. Here! go; the desk, the purse! sweet, now, make haste.
Luc. How hast thou lost thy breath?
Dro. S. By running fast.
Adr. Where is thy master, Dromio? is he well?
Dro. S. No, he 's in Tartar limbo, worse than hell.
†A devil in an everlasting garment hath him;
One whose hard heart is button'd up with steel;
A fiend, a fury, pitiless and rough;
A wolf, nay, worse, a fellow all in buff;
A back-friend, a shoulder-clapper, one that countermands
The passages of alleys, creeks and narrow lands;
A hound that runs counter and yet draws dry-foot well;
One that before the judgement carries poor souls to hell.
Adr. Why, man, what is the matter?
Dro. S. I do not know the matter: he is 'rested on the case.
Adr. What, is he arrested? Tell me at whose suit.
Dro. S. I know not at whose suit he is arrested well:
But he's in a suit of buff which 'rested him, that can I tell.
Will you send him, mistress, redemption, the money in his desk?
Adr. Go fetch it, sister. *(Exit Luciana.)* This I wonder at,
That he, unknown to me, should be in debt.
Tell me, was he arrested on a band?
Dro. S. Not on a band, but on a stronger thing;
A chain, a chain! Do you not hear it ring?
Adr. What, the chain?
Dro. S. No, no, the bell: 'tis time that I were gone:
It was two ere I left him, and now the clock strikes one.
Adr. The hours come back! that did I never hear.
Dro. S. O, yes: if any hour meet a sergeant, 'a turns back for very fear.
Adr. As if Time were in debt! how fondly dost thou reason!
Dro. S. Time is a very bankrupt and owes more than he 's worth to season.
Nay, he 's a thief too: have you not heard men say,
That Time comes stealing on by night and day?
If 'a be in debt and theft, and a sergeant in the way,
Hath he not reason to turn back an hour in a day?

Enter LUCIANA [*with a purse*].

Adr. Go, Dromio; there 's the money, bear it straight,
And bring thy master home immediately.
Come, sister: I am press'd down with conceit—
Conceit, my comfort and my injury. *Exeunt.*

[SCENE III. *A public place.*]

Enter ANTIPHOLUS of Syracuse.

branded with deformity. **making,** form. 32. **Tartar limbo,** Tartarus or pagan hell, worse than Christian hell. 33. **everlasting garment,** leather used as the attire of police officers; reference to *buff* (l. 36). 37. **back-friend,** a false friend; the police officer who comes up behind and claps one on the back. **countermands,** prohibits, forbids. 38. **creeks,** narrow or winding passages. **narrow lands,** possible reference to strips into which agricultural lands were anciently divided (New Cambridge). 39. **runs counter,** follows a trail in a direction opposite to that which the game has taken, with quibble on *counter*, a prison. **draws dry-foot,** follows game by mere scent of the foot. 40. **judgement,** quibble on "day of judgment" and "legal decision." **hell,** debtor's prison. 42. **case,** form of procedure, "action on the case," with quibble on *case* meaning "the container of *matter*." 46. **mistress, redemption.** New Cambridge editors read *Mistress Redemption*, with F_4, as suggestive of morality plays alluded to in *judgement*, etc., above. 49. **band,** bond; also, manacle, leash for a dog; see glossary. 56. **'a,** he (it); see glossary. 58. **season,** opportunity.

SCENE III. *Stage Direction:* **A public place.** New Cambridge: *The Mart.*

Ant. S. There 's not a man I meet but doth salute me
As if I were their well-acquainted friend;
And every one doth call me by my name.
Some tender money to me; some invite me;
Some other give me thanks for kindnesses;
Some offer me commodities to buy:
Even now a tailor call'd me in his shop
And show'd me silks that he had bought for me
And therewithal took measure of my body.
Sure, these are but imaginary wiles
And Lapland sorcerers inhabit here.

Enter DROMIO of Syracuse.

Dro. S. Master, here 's the gold you sent me for. What, have you got the picture of old Adam new-apparelled?

Ant. S. What gold is this? what Adam dost thou mean?

Dro. S. Not that Adam that kept the Paradise, but that Adam that keeps the prison: he that goes in the calf's skin that was killed for the Prodigal; he that came behind you, sir, like an evil angel, and bid you forsake your liberty.

Ant. S. I understand thee not.

Dro. S. No? why, 'tis a plain case: he that went, like a bass-viol, in a case of leather; the man, sir, that, when gentlemen are tired, gives them a sob and 'rests them; he, sir, that takes pity on decayed men and gives them suits of durance; he that sets up his rest to do more exploits with his mace than a morris-pike.

Ant. S. What, thou meanest an officer?

Dro. S. Ay, sir, the sergeant of the band; he that brings any man to answer it that breaks his band; one that thinks a man always going to bed and says 'God give you good rest!'

Ant. S. Well, sir, there rest in your foolery. Is there any ship puts forth to-night? may we be gone?

Dro. S. Why, sir, I brought you word an hour since that the bark Expedition put forth to-night; and then were you hindered by the sergeant, to tarry for the hoy Delay. Here are the angels that you sent for to deliver you.

Ant. S. The fellow is distract, and so am I;
And here we wander in illusions:
Some blessed power deliver us from hence!

Enter a Courtezan.

Cour. Well met, well met, Master Antipholus.
I see, sir, you have found the goldsmith now:
Is that the chain you promis'd me to-day?

Ant. S. Satan, avoid! I charge thee, tempt me not.

Dro. S. Master, is this Mistress Satan?

Ant. S. It is the devil.

Dro. S. Nay, she is worse, she is the devil's dam; and here she comes in the habit of a light wench: and thereof comes that the wenches say 'God damn me;' that 's as much to say 'God make me a light wench.' It is written, they appear to men like angels of light: light is an effect of fire, and fire will burn; ergo, light wenches will burn. Come not near her.

Cour. Your man and you are marvellous merry, sir.
Will you go with me? We'll mend our dinner here?

Dro. S. Master, if you do, expect spoon-meat; or bespeak a long spoon.

Ant. S. Why, Dromio?

Dro. S. Marry, he must have a long spoon that must eat with the devil.

Ant. S. Avoid then, fiend! what tell'st thou me of supping?
Thou art, as you are all, a sorceress:
I conjure thee to leave me and be gone.

Cour. Give me the ring of mine you had at dinner,
Or, for my diamond, the chain you promis'd,
And I'll be gone, sir, and not trouble you.

Dro. S. Some devils ask but the parings of one's nail,
A rush, a hair, a drop of blood, a pin,
A nut, a cherry-stone;
But she, more covetous, would have a chain.
Master, be wise: and if you give it her,
The devil will shake her chain and fright us with it.

Cour. I pray you, sir, my ring, or else the chain:
I hope you do not mean to cheat me so.

Ant. S. Avaunt, thou witch! Come, Dromio, let us go.

Dro. S. 'Fly pride,' says the peacock: mistress, that you know. *Exit* [*with Antipholus*].

Cour. Now, out of doubt Antipholus is mad,
Else would he never so demean himself.
A ring he hath of mine worth forty ducats,
And for the same he promis'd me a chain:
Both one and other he denies me now.
The reason that I gather he is mad,
Besides this present instance of his rage,
Is a mad tale he told to-day at dinner,
Of his own doors being shut against his entrance.
Belike his wife, acquainted with his fits,
On purpose shut the doors against his way.
My way is now to hie home to his house,
And tell his wife that, being lunatic,
He rush'd into my house and took perforce
My ring away. This course I fittest choose;
For forty ducats is too much to lose. [*Exit.*]

[SCENE IV. *A street.*]

Enter ANTIPHOLUS of Ephesus *with a* Gaoler.

Ant. E. Fear me not, man; I will not break away:
I'll give thee, ere I leave thee, so much money,
To warrant thee, as I am 'rested for.
My wife is in a wayward mood to-day,
And will not lightly trust the messenger.
That I should be attach'd in Ephesus,
I tell you, 'twill sound harshly in her ears.

Enter DROMIO of Ephesus *with a rope's-end.*

Here comes my man; I think he brings the money.
How now, sir! have you that I sent you for?

Dro. E. Here 's that, I warrant you, will pay them all.

Ant. E. But where 's the money?

11. **Lapland sorcerers.** Lapland was said to surpass all nations in the practice of witchcraft and sorcery. 14. **old Adam.** This is taken to mean, "Have you got rid of the picture of old Adam, namely, the sergeant dressed in buff, as Adam was dressed in skins" (Genesis 3:21). 18-19. **calf's . . . Prodigal.** Cf. Luke 15:23. 25. **sob,** breathing space. 27. **durance,** a kind of long-wearing cloth like buff, as well as prison. **sets . . . rest,** stakes his all; metaphor from the game of primero. 28. **mace,** staff of office carried by a sergeant. **morris-pike,** Moorish pike. 40. **hoy,** a small coasting vessel. 41. **angels,** gold coins worth about 10s.; good angels this time, sent by Mistress Redemption (New Cambridge). 42. **distract,** distracted. 49. **Mistress Satan,** yet another character in Dromio's miracle play (New Cambridge). 52. **habit,** demeanor, manner; see glossary. 53. **light,** wanton. 56. **angels of light.** Cf. II Corinthians 11:14. 58. **will burn,** i.e., are diseased. 60. **mend,** supplement, complete. 61. **spoon-meat,** food for infants, hence, delicacies; but the sense is obscure. 72-77. **Some . . . it.** F prints this as prose, which fact, with the broken line at 74, suggests revision or abridgment (New Cambridge). 81. **'Fly . . . peacock.**

Dro. E. Why, sir, I gave the money for the rope.
Ant. E. Five hundred ducats, villain, for a rope?
Dro. E. I'll serve you, sir, five hundred at the rate.
Ant. E. To what end did I bid thee hie thee home?
Dro. E. To a rope's-end, sir; and to that end am I return'd.
Ant. E. And to that end, sir, I will welcome you. [*Beating him.*]
Off. Good sir, be patient.
Dro. E. Nay, 'tis for me to be patient; I am in adversity.
Off. Good now, hold thy tongue.
Dro. E. Nay, rather persuade him to hold his hands.
Ant. E. Thou whoreson, senseless villain!
Dro. E. I would I were senseless, sir, that I might not feel your blows.
Ant. E. Thou art sensible in nothing but blows, and so is an ass.
Dro. E. I am an ass, indeed; you may prove it by my long ears. I have served him from the hour of my nativity to this instant, and have nothing at his hands for my service but blows. When I am cold, he heats me with beating; when I am warm, he cools me with beating: I am waked with it when I sleep; raised with it when I sit; driven out of doors with it when I go from home; welcomed home with it when I return: nay, I bear it on my shoulders, as a beggar wont her brat; and, I think, when he hath lamed me, I shall beg with it from door to door.

Enter ADRIANA, LUCIANA, Courtezan, *and a Schoolmaster called* PINCH.

Ant. E. Come, go along; my wife is coming yonder.
Dro. E. Mistress, 'respice finem,' respect your end; or rather, †the prophecy like the parrot, 'beware the rope's end.'
Ant. E. Wilt thou still talk? *Beats Dromio.*
Cour. How say you now? is not your husband mad?
Adr. His incivility confirms no less.
Good Doctor Pinch, you are a conjurer;
Establish him in his true sense again,
And I will please you what you will demand.
Luc. Alas, how fiery and how sharp he looks!
Cour. Mark how he trembles in his ecstasy!
Pinch. Give me your hand and let me feel your pulse.
Ant. E. There is my hand, and let it feel your ear. [*Striking him.*]
Pinch. I charge thee, Satan, hous'd within this man,
To yield possession to my holy prayers
And to thy state of darkness hie thee straight:
I conjure thee by all the saints in heaven!
Ant. E. Peace, doting wizard, peace! I am not mad.
Adr. O, that thou wert not, poor distressed soul!
Ant. E. You minion, you, are these your customers?
Did this companion with the saffron face
Revel and feast it at my house to-day,
Whilst upon me the guilty doors were shut
And I denied to enter in my house?
Adr. O husband, God doth know you din'd at home;
Where would you had remain'd until this time,
Free from these slanders and this open shame!
Ant. E. Din'd at home! Thou villain, what sayest thou?
Dro. E. Sir, sooth to say, you did not dine at home.
Ant. E. Were not my doors lock'd up and I shut out?
Dro. E. Perdie, your doors were lock'd and you shut out.
Ant. E. And did not she herself revile me there?
Dro. E. Sans fable, she herself revil'd you there.
Ant. E. Did not her kitchen-maid rail, taunt and scorn me?
Dro. E. Certes, she did; the kitchen-vestal scorn'd you.
Ant. E. And did not I in rage depart from thence?
Dro. E. In verity you did; my bones bear witness,
That since have felt the vigour of his rage.
Adr. Is 't good to soothe him in these contraries?
Pinch. It is no shame: the fellow finds his vein
And yielding to him humours well his frenzy.
Ant. E. Thou hast suborn'd the goldsmith to arrest me.
Adr. Alas, I sent you money to redeem you,
By Dromio here, who came in haste for it.
Dro. E. Money by me! heart and good-will you might;
But surely, master, not a rag of money.
Ant. E. Went'st not thou to her for a purse of ducats?
Adr. He came to me and I deliver'd it.
Luc. And I am witness with her that she did.
Dro. E. God and the rope-maker bear me witness
That I was sent for nothing but a rope!
Pinch. Mistress, both man and master is possess'd;
I know it by their pale and deadly looks:
They must be bound and laid in some dark room.
Ant. E. Say, wherefore didst thou lock me forth to-day?
And why dost thou deny the bag of gold?
Adr. I did not, gentle husband, lock thee forth.
Dro. E. And, gentle master, I receiv'd no gold;
But I confess, sir, that we were lock'd out.
Adr. Dissembling villain, thou speak'st false in both.
Ant. E. Dissembling harlot, thou art false in all
And art confederate with a damned pack
To make a loathsome abject scorn of me:
But with these nails I'll pluck out these false eyes
That would behold in me this shameful sport.

Enter three or four, and offer to bind him. He strives.

Adr. O, bind him, bind him! let him not come near me.
Pinch. More company! The fiend is strong within him.
Luc. Ay me, poor man, how pale and wan he looks!
Ant. E. What, will you murder me? Thou gaoler, thou,

The accusation of dishonesty coming from this woman, whom Dromio takes to be dishonest, seems to him as out of place as a warning against pride given by the peacock. 83. **demean,** conduct. 88. **rage,** madness; see glossary. 95. **perforce,** forcibly; see glossary.

SCENE IV. 22. **Good now,** pray thee. 28. **sensible,** sensitive; see glossary. 40. **wont,** i.e., is wont to carry. 44. **'respice finem.'** *Respice funem,* "consider the hangman's rope," was a jesting variant of this expression. 46. **'beware the rope's end,'** i.e., beware the halter; possibly a phrase taught by sailors to parrots. 50. **conjurer.** Being able to speak Latin, Pinch could conjure spirits. 52. **please,** pay. **demand,** request; see glossary. 54. **ecstasy,** madness; see glossary. 63. **customers,** guests (in a bad sense). 64. **companion,** fellow; see glossary. **saffron,** yellow. 74. **Perdie,** oath from *par Dieu.* 76. **Sans,** without; see glossary. 78. **kitchen-vestal,** her charge being like that of the vestal virgins, to keep the fire burning (Johnson). 82. **soothe,** encourage, humor. 89. **rag,** scrap. 96. **deadly,** death-like. 97. **bound . . . room,** the regular treatment for lunacy in Shakespeare's day.

I am thy prisoner: wilt thou suffer them
To make a rescue?
Off. Masters, let him go:
He is my prisoner, and you shall not have him.
Pinch. Go bind this man, for he is frantic too.
[*They offer to bind Dro. E.*]
Adr. What wilt thou do, thou peevish officer?
Hast thou delight to see a wretched man
Do outrage and displeasure to himself?
Off. He is my prisoner: if I let him go,
The debt he owes will be requir'd of me.
Adr. I will discharge thee ere I go from thee:
Bear me forthwith unto his creditor
And, knowing how the debt grows, I will pay it.
Good master doctor, see him safe convey'd
Home to my house. O most unhappy day!
Ant. E. O most unhappy strumpet!
Dro. E. Master, I am here ent'red in bond for you.
Ant. E. Out on thee, villain! wherefore dost thou mad me?

Dro. E. Will you be bound for nothing? be mad, good master: cry 'The devil!'

Luc. God help, poor souls, how idly do they talk!
Adr. Go bear him hence. Sister, go you with me.
Exeunt. Mane[*n*]*t Officer, Adriana, Luciana, Courtezan.*
Say now, whose suit is he arrested at?
Off. One Angelo, a goldsmith: do you know him?
Adr. I know the man. What is the sum he owes?
Off. Two hundred ducats.
Adr. Say, how grows it due?
Off. Due for a chain your husband had of him.
Adr. He did bespeak a chain for me, but had it not.
Cour. When as your husband all in rage to-day
Came to my house and took away my ring—
The ring I saw upon his finger now—
Straight after did I meet him with a chain.
Adr. It may be so, but I did never see it.
Come, gaoler, bring me where the goldsmith is:
I long to know the truth hereof at large.

Enter ANTIPHOLUS of Syracuse *with his rapier drawn, and* DROMIO of Syracuse.

Luc. God, for thy mercy! they are loose again.
Adr. And come with naked swords.
Let's call more help to have them bound again.
Off. Away! they'll kill us. *Run all out.*
Exeunt omnes, as fast as may be, frighted.
Ant. S. I see these witches are afraid of swords.
Dro. S. She that would be your wife now ran from you.
Ant. S. Come to the Centaur; fetch our stuff from thence:
I long that we were safe and sound aboard.

Dro. S. Faith, stay here this night; they will surely do us no harm: you saw they speak us fair, give us gold: methinks they are such a gentle nation that, but for the mountain of mad flesh that claims marriage of me, I could find in my heart to stay here still and turn witch.

Ant. S. I will not stay to-night for all the town;
Therefore away, to get our stuff aboard. *Exeunt.*

ACT V.

SCENE I. [*A street before a Priory.*]

Enter the [Second] Merchant *and* [ANGELO] *the Goldsmith.*

Ang. I am sorry, sir, that I have hind'red you;
But, I protest, he had the chain of me,
Though most dishonestly he doth deny it.
Sec. Mer. How is the man esteem'd here in the city?
Ang. Of very reverend reputation, sir,
Of credit infinite, highly belov'd,
Second to none that lives here in the city:
His word might bear my wealth at any time.
Sec. Mer. Speak softly: yonder, as I think, he walks.

Enter ANTIPHOLUS [of Syracuse] *and* DROMIO [of Syracuse] *again.*

Ang. 'Tis so; and that self chain about his neck
Which he forswore most monstrously to have.
Good sir, draw near to me, I'll speak to him.
Signior Antipholus, I wonder much
That you would put me to this shame and trouble;
And, not without some scandal to yourself,
With circumstance and oaths so to deny
This chain which now you wear so openly:
Beside the charge, the shame, imprisonment,
You have done wrong to this my honest friend,
Who, but for staying on our controversy,
Had hoisted sail and put to sea to-day:
This chain you had of me; can you deny it?
Ant. S. I think I had; I never did deny it.
Sec. Mer. Yes, that you did, sir, and forswore it too.
Ant. S. Who heard me to deny it or forswear it?
Sec. Mer. These ears of mine, thou know'st, did hear thee.
Fie on thee, wretch! 'tis pity that thou liv'st
To walk where any honest men resort.
Ant. S. Thou art a villain to impeach me thus:
I'll prove mine honour and mine honesty
Against thee presently, if thou dar'st stand.
Sec. Mer. I dare, and do defy thee for a villain.
They draw.

Enter ADRIANA, LUCIANA, [*the*] Courtezan, *and others.*

Adr. Hold, hurt him not, for God's sake! he is mad.
Some get within him, take his sword away:
Bind Dromio too, and bear them to my house.
Dro. S. Run, master, run; for God's sake, take a house!
This is some priory. In, or we are spoil'd!
Exeunt [*Ant. S. and Dro. S.*] *to the Priory.*

Enter [*the*] Lady Abbess.

Abb. Be quiet, people. Wherefore throng you hither?
Adr. To fetch my poor distracted husband hence.
Let us come in, that we may bind him fast
And bear him home for his recovery.

126, 127. **unhappy,** fatal; miserable; see glossary. 139. **bespeak,** order. 140. **When as,** when. 146. **at large,** in full, in detail; see *large* in glossary. 150. *Stage Direction:* ***Run all out,*** etc. F prints *Runne all out* after line 149, and *Exeunt omnes as fast as may be, frighted,* after line 150. *Exeunt omnes* was the original stage direction, the rest being written in the margin of the manuscript (New Cambridge). 153. **stuff,** goods, baggage.

ACT V. SCENE I. *Stage Direction: A street before a Priory.* New Cambridge: *The square before the house of Antipholus.* 8. **might bear,** is worth. 11. **forswore,** repudiated on oath or with strong words. 12. **to me.** Hudson conjectures *with me.* 16. **circumstance,** details, particulars; see glossary. 32. **defy,** challenge; see glossary. 34. **within him,**

Ang. I knew he was not in his perfect wits.
Sec. Mer. I am sorry now that I did draw on him.
Abb. How long hath this possession held the man?
Adr. This week he hath been heavy, sour, sad,
And much different from the man he was;
But till this afternoon his passion
Ne'er brake into extremity of rage.
Abb. Hath he not lost much wealth by wrack of sea?
Buried some dear friend? Hath not else his eye
Stray'd his affection in unlawful love?
A sin prevailing much in youthful men,
Who give their eyes the liberty of gazing.
Which of these sorrows is he subject to?
Adr. To none of these, except it be the last;
Namely, some love that drew him oft from home.
Abb. You should for that have reprehended him.
Adr. Why, so I did.
Abb. Ay, but not rough enough.
Adr. As roughly as my modesty would let me.
Abb. Haply, in private.
Adr. And in assemblies too.
Abb. Ay, but not enough.
Adr. It was the copy of our conference:
In bed he slept not for my urging it;
At board he fed not for my urging it;
Alone, it was the subject of my theme;
In company I often glanced it;
Still did I tell him it was vile and bad.
Abb. And thereof came it that the man was mad:
The venom clamours of a jealous woman
Poisons more deadly than a mad dog's tooth.
It seems his sleeps were hind'red by thy railing,
And thereof comes it that his head is light.
Thou say'st his meat was sauc'd with thy upbraidings:
Unquiet meals make ill digestions;
Thereof the raging fire of fever bred;
And what 's a fever but a fit of madness?
Thou sayest his sports were hind'red by thy brawls:
Sweet recreation barr'd, what doth ensue
But moody and dull melancholy,
Kinsman to grim and comfortless despair,
And at her heels a huge infectious troop
Of pale distemperatures and foes to life?
In food, in sport and life-preserving rest
To be disturb'd, would mad or man or beast:
The consequence is then thy jealous fits
Have scar'd thy husband from the use of wits.
Luc. She never reprehended him but mildly,
When he demean'd himself rough, rude and wildly.
Why bear you these rebukes and answer not?
Adr. She did betray me to my own reproof.
Good people, enter and lay hold on him.
Abb. No, not a creature enters in my house.
Adr. Then let your servants bring my husband forth.
Abb. Neither: he took this place for sanctuary,
And it shall privilege him from your hands
Till I have brought him to his wits again,
Or lose my labour in assaying it.
Adr. I will attend my husband, be his nurse,
Diet his sickness, for it is my office,
And will have no attorney but myself;
And therefore let me have him home with me.
Abb. Be patient; for I will not let him stir
Till I have us'd the approved means I have,
With wholesome syrups, drugs and holy prayers,
To make of him a formal man again:
It is a branch and parcel of mine oath,
A charitable duty of my order.
Therefore depart and leave him here with me.
Adr. I will not hence and leave my husband here:
And ill it doth beseem your holiness
To separate the husband and the wife.
Abb. Be quiet and depart: thou shalt not have him. [*Exit.*]
Luc. Complain unto the duke of this indignity.
Adr. Come, go: I will fall prostrate at his feet
And never rise until my tears and prayers
Have won his grace to come in person hither
And take perforce my husband from the abbess.
Sec. Mer. By this, I think, the dial points at five:
Anon, I'm sure, the duke himself in person
Comes this way to the melancholy vale,
The place of death and sorry execution,
Behind the ditches of the abbey here.
Ang. Upon what cause?
Sec. Mer. To see a reverend Syracusian merchant,
Who put unluckily into this bay
Against the laws and statutes of this town,
Beheaded publicly for his offence.
Ang. See where they come: we will behold his death.
Luc. Kneel to the duke before he pass the abbey.

Enter the DUKE of Ephesus *and* [ÆGEON] *the Merchant of Syracuse, barehead, with the* Headsman *and other* Officers.

Duke. Yet once again proclaim it publicly,
If any friend will pay the sum for him,
He shall not die; so much we tender him.
Adr. Justice, most sacred duke, against the abbess!
Duke. She is a virtuous and a reverend lady:
It cannot be that she hath done thee wrong.
Adr. May it please your grace, Antipholus my husband,
Whom I made lord of me and all I had,
At your important letters,—this ill day
A most outrageous fit of madness took him;
That desp'rately he hurried through the street,—
With him his bondman, all as mad as he,—
Doing displeasure to the citizens
By rushing in their houses, bearing thence
Rings, jewels, any thing his rage did like.
Once did I get him bound and sent him home,
Whilst to take order for the wrongs I went
That here and there his fury had committed.
Anon, I wot not by what strong escape,
He broke from those that had the guard of him;
And with his mad attendant and himself,
Each one with ireful passion, with drawn swords,
Met us again and madly bent on us
Chas'd us away, till raising of more aid
We came again to bind them. Then they fled
Into this abbey, whither we pursu'd them:

under his guard. 36. **take,** repair to for refuge; see glossary. 51. **Stray'd,** led astray. 57 ff. **reprehended him,** etc. Note the shrewdness of the Abbess in bringing out the true quality of Adriana's behavior, and the dramatic irony of the dialogue. 62. **copy,** topic, theme. 66. **glanced,** alluded to. 82. **distemperatures,** physical disorders, illness. 100. **attorney,** agent, deputy. 105. **formal,** normal. 106. **parcel,** part, portion. 121. **sorry,** exciting sorrow, sad. 132. **so much,** i.e., so much consideration. 138. **important,** urgent, pressing. **letters.** Adriana would seem to have been ward to the duke. 144. **rage,** madness, insanity; see glossary. 146. **order for,** measures for settling. 148. **wot,** know; see glossary. **strong,** violent.

And here the abbess shuts the gates on us
And will not suffer us to fetch him out,
Nor send him forth that we may bear him hence.
Therefore, most gracious duke, with thy command
Let him be brought forth and borne hence for help.
Duke. Long since thy husband serv'd me in my wars,
And I to thee engag'd a prince's word,
When thou didst make him master of thy bed,
To do him all the grace and good I could.
Go, some of you, knock at the abbey-gate
And bid the lady abbess come to me.
I will determine this before I stir.

Enter a [*Servant as*] Messenger.

Serv. O mistress, mistress, shift and save yourself!
My master and his man are both broke loose,
Beaten the maids a-row and bound the doctor,
Whose beard they have sing'd off with brands of fire;
And ever, as it blaz'd, they threw on him
Great pails of puddled mire to quench the hair:
My master preaches patience to him and the while
His man with scissors nicks him like a fool,
And sure, unless you send some present help,
Between them they will kill the conjurer.
Adr. Peace, fool! thy master and his man are here.
And that is false thou dost report to us.
Serv. Mistress, upon my life, I tell you true:
I have not breath'd almost since I did see it.
He cries for you and vows, if he can take you,
To scorch your face and to disfigure you. *Cry within.*
Hark, hark! I hear him, mistress: fly, be gone!
Duke. Come, stand by me; fear nothing. Guard with halberds!
Adr. Ay me, it is my husband! Witness you,
That he is borne about invisible:
Even now we hous'd him in the abbey here;
And now he 's there, past thought of human reason.

Enter ANTIPHOLUS [of Ephesus] *and* DROMIO of Ephesus.

Ant. E. Justice, most gracious duke, O, grant me justice!
Even for the service that long since I did thee,
When I bestrid thee in the wars and took
Deep scars to save thy life; even for the blood
That then I lost for thee, now grant me justice.
Æge. Unless the fear of death doth make me dote,
I see my son Antipholus and Dromio.
Ant. E. Justice, sweet prince, against that woman there!
She whom thou gav'st to me to be my wife,
That hath abused and dishonoured me
Even in the strength and height of injury!
Beyond imagination is the wrong
That she this day hath shameless thrown on me.
Duke. Discover how, and thou shalt find me just.
Ant. E. This day, great duke, she shut the doors upon me,
While she with harlots feasted in my house.
Duke. A grievous fault! Say, woman, didst thou so?
Adr. No, my good lord: myself, he and my sister
To-day did dine together. So befall my soul
As this is false he burdens me withal!
Luc. Ne'er may I look on day, nor sleep on night,
But she tells to your highness simple truth!
Ang. O perjur'd woman! They are both forsworn:
In this the madman justly chargeth them.
Ant. E. My liege, I am advised what I say,
Neither disturbed with the effect of wine,
Nor heady-rash, provok'd with raging ire,
Albeit my wrongs might make one wiser mad.
This woman lock'd me out this day from dinner:
That goldsmith there, were he not pack'd with her,
Could witness it, for he was with me then;
Who parted with me to go fetch a chain,
Promising to bring it to the Porpentine,
Where Balthazar and I did dine together.
Our dinner done, and he not coming thither,
I went to seek him: in the street I met him
And in his company that gentleman.
There did this perjur'd goldsmith swear me down
That I this day of him receiv'd the chain,
Which, God he knows, I saw not: for the which
He did arrest me with an officer.
I did obey, and sent my peasant home
For certain ducats: he with none return'd.
Then fairly I bespoke the officer
To go in person with me to my house.
By th' way we met
My wife, her sister, and a rabble more
Of vile confederates. Along with them
They brought one Pinch, a hungry lean-fac'd villain,
A mere anatomy, a mountebank,
A threadbare juggler and a fortune-teller,
A needy, hollow-ey'd, sharp-looking wretch,
A living-dead man: this pernicious slave,
Forsooth, took on him as a conjurer,
And, gazing in mine eyes, feeling my pulse,
And with no face, as 'twere, outfacing me,
Cries out, I was possess'd. Then all together
They fell upon me, bound me, bore me thence
And in a dark and dankish vault at home
There left me and my man, both bound together;
Till, gnawing with my teeth my bonds in sunder,
I gain'd my freedom and immediately
Ran hither to your grace; whom I beseech
To give me ample satisfaction
For these deep shames and great indignities.
Ang. My lord, in truth, thus far I witness with him,
That he din'd not at home, but was lock'd out.
Duke. But had he such a chain of thee or no?
Ang. He had, my lord: and when he ran in here,
These people saw the chain about his neck.
Sec. Mer. Besides, I will be sworn these ears of mine
Heard you confess you had the chain of him
After you first forswore it on the mart:
And thereupon I drew my sword on you;
And then you fled into this abbey here,
From whence, I think, you are come by miracle.

162. **engag'd,** pledged; see glossary. 170. **a-row,** one after another. 175. **nicks him like a fool.** Fools or professional jesters were accustomed to shave their heads like monks. 192. **bestrid,** stood over to defend him when fallen in battle. 199. **abused,** maltreated; see glossary. 203. **Discover,** reveal; see glossary. 205. **harlots,** probably, vagabonds, rascals. 209. **burdens,** charges. **withal,** with; see glossary. 214. **am advised,** know very well. 219. **pack'd with,** in conspiracy with; see *pack* in glossary. 231. **peasant,** servant. 233. **fairly,** civilly; see glossary. 238. **mere,** absolute, pure; see glossary. **anatomy,** skeleton. **mountebank,** quack, charlatan. 242. **took . . . as,** pretended to be. 269. **impeach,** charge, accusation. 270. **Circe's cup,** the poisoned cup, a draft of which turned men into beasts. 272. **coldly,** calmly.

Ant. E. I never came within these abbey-walls,
Nor ever didst thou draw thy sword on me:
I never saw the chain, so help me Heaven!
And this is false you burden me withal.
Duke. Why, what an intricate impeach is this!
I think you all have drunk of Circe's cup.
If here you hous'd him, here he would have been;
If he were mad, he would not plead so coldly:
You say he din'd at home; the goldsmith here
Denies that saying. Sirrah, what say you?
Dro. E. Sir, he din'd with her there, at the Porpentine.
Cour. He did, and from my finger snatch'd that ring.
Ant. E. 'Tis true, my liege; this ring I had of her.
Duke. Saw'st thou him enter at the abbey here?
Cour. As sure, my liege, as I do see your grace.
Duke. Why, this is strange. Go call the abbess hither.
I think you are all mated or stark mad.
Exit one to the Abbess.
Æge. Most mighty duke, vouchsafe me speak a word:
Haply I see a friend will save my life
And pay the sum that may deliver me.
Duke. Speak freely, Syracusian, what thou wilt.
Æge. Is not your name, sir, call'd Antipholus?
And is not that your bondman, Dromio?
Dro. E. Within this hour I was his bondman, sir,
But he, I thank him, gnaw'd in two my cords:
Now am I Dromio and his man unbound.
Æge. I am sure you both of you remember me.
Dro. E. Ourselves we do remember, sir, by you;
For lately we were bound, as you are now.
You are not Pinch's patient, are you, sir?
Æge. Why look you strange on me? you know me well.
Ant. E. I never saw you in my life till now.
Æge. O, grief hath chang'd me since you saw me last.
And careful hours with time's deformed hand
Have written strange defeatures in my face:
But tell me yet, dost thou not know my voice?
Ant. E. Neither.
Æge. Dromio, nor thou?
Dro. E. No, trust me, sir, nor I.
Æge. I am sure thou dost.
Dro. E. Ay, sir, but I am sure I do not; and whatsoever a man denies, you are now bound to believe him.
Æge. Not know my voice! O time's extremity,
Hast thou so crack'd and splitted my poor tongue
In seven short years, that here my only son
Knows not my feeble key of untun'd cares?
Though now this grained face of mine be hid
In sap-consuming winter's drizzled snow
And all the conduits of my blood froze up,
Yet hath my night of life some memory,
My wasting lamps some fading glimmer left,
My dull deaf ears a little use to hear:
All these old witnesses—I cannot err—
Tell me thou art my son Antipholus.
Ant. E. I never saw my father in my life.
Æge. But seven years since, in Syracusa, boy,
Thou know'st we parted: but perhaps, my son,
Thou sham'st to acknowledge me in misery.
Ant. E. The duke and all that know me in the city
Can witness with me that it is not so:
I ne'er saw Syracusa in my life.
Duke. I tell thee, Syracusian, twenty years
Have I been patron to Antipholus,
During which time he ne'er saw Syracusa:
I see thy age and dangers make thee dote.

Enter the Abbess, *with* ANTIPHOLUS of Syracuse *and* DROMIO of Syracuse.

Abb. Most mighty duke, behold a man much wrong'd. *All gather to see them.*
Adr. I see two husbands, or mine eyes deceive me.
Duke. One of these men is Genius to the other;
And so of these, which is the natural man,
And which the spirit? who deciphers them?
Dro. S. I, sir, am Dromio: command him away.
Dro. E. I, sir, am Dromio: pray, let me stay.
Ant. S. Ægeon art thou not? or else his ghost?
Dro. S. O, my old master! who hath bound him here?
Abb. Whoever bound him, I will loose his bonds
And gain a husband by his liberty.
Speak, old Ægeon, if thou be'st the man
That hadst a wife once call'd Æmilia
That bore thee at a burden two fair sons:
O, if thou be'st the same Ægeon, speak,
And speak unto the same Æmilia!
Duke. Why, here begins his morning story right:
These two Antipholuses, these two so like,
And these two Dromios, one in semblance,—
Besides her urging of her wrack at sea,—
These are the parents to these children,
Which accidentally are met together.
Æge. If I dream not, thou art Æmilia:
If thou art she, tell me where is that son
That floated with thee on the fatal raft?
Abb. By men of Epidamnum he and I
And the twin Dromio all were taken up;
But by and by rude fishermen of Corinth
By force took Dromio and my son from them
And me they left with those of Epidamnum.
What then became of them I cannot tell;
I to this fortune that you see me in.
Duke. Antipholus, thou cam'st from Corinth first?
Ant. S. No, sir, not I; I came from Syracuse.
Duke. Stay, stand apart; I know not which is which.
Ant. E. I came from Corinth, my most gracious lord,—
Dro. E. And I with him.
Ant. E. Brought to this town by that most famous warrior,
Duke Menaphon, your most renowned uncle.
Adr. Which of you two did dine with me to-day?
Ant. S. I, gentle mistress.
Adr. And are not you my husband?
Ant. E. No; I say nay to that.

294. **Pinch's patient.** Dromio refers to the binding, evidently the feature of Pinch's treatment which most impressed him. 298. **deformed,** deforming. 307. **Not know my voice.** Genuine feeling comes out in the speech of Aegeon, a feature of this play which aligns it with Shakespeare's romantic comedies. 310. **my . . . cares,** the whole tone of my voice which is altered by sorrow. 311. **grained,** lined, furrowed.

315. **lamps,** eyes. 332. **Genius,** attendant spirit. 333. So F; Globe places period after *these*. 343. **burden,** birth. 348. **semblance,** trisyllabic; likewise *children* in line 350. 356-361. Globe follows Capell and places these lines after line 345. Text follows F.

Ant. S. And so do I; yet did she call me so:
And this fair gentlewoman, her sister here,
Did call me brother. [*To Luc.*] What I told you then,
I hope I shall have leisure to make good;
If this be not a dream I see and hear.
Ang. That is the chain, sir, which you had of me.
Ant. S. I think it be, sir; I deny it not.
Ant. E. And you, sir, for this chain arrested me.
Ang. I think I did, sir; I deny it not.
Adr. I sent you money, sir, to be your bail,
By Dromio; but I think he brought it not.
Dro. E. No, none by me.
Ant. S. This purse of ducats I receiv'd from you
And Dromio my man did bring them me.
I see we still did meet each other's man,
And I was ta'en for him, and he for me,
And thereupon these errors are arose.
Ant. E. These ducats pawn I for my father here.
Duke. It shall not need; thy father hath his life.
Cour. Sir, I must have that diamond from you.
Ant. E. There, take it; and much thanks for my good cheer.
Abb. Renowned duke, vouchsafe to take the pains
To go with us into the abbey here
And hear at large discoursed all our fortunes:
And all that are assembled in this place,
That by this sympathized one day's error
Have suffer'd wrong, go keep us company,
And we shall make full satisfaction.
Thirty-three years have I but gone in travail
Of you, my sons; and till this present hour
My heavy burthen ne'er delivered.
The duke, my husband and my children both,
And you the calendars of their nativity,
Go to a gossips' feast, and go with me;
After so long grief, such nativity!
Duke. With all my heart, I'll gossip at this feast.
Exeunt omnes. Mane[n]t the two Dromios and two Brothers.
Dro. S. Master, shall I fetch your stuff from shipboard?
Ant. E. Dromio, what stuff of mine hast thou embark'd?
Dro. S. Your goods that lay at host, sir, in the Centaur.
Ant. S. He speaks to me. I am your master, Dromio:
Come, go with us; we'll look to that anon:
Embrace thy brother there; rejoice with him.
Exit [with Antipholus of Ephesus].
Dro. S. There is a fat friend at your master's house,
That kitchen'd me for you to-day at dinner:
She now shall be my sister, not my wife.
Dro. E. Methinks you are my glass, and not my brother:
I see by you I am a sweet-fac'd youth.
Will you walk in to see their gossiping?
Dro. S. Not I, sir; you are my elder.
Dro. E. That 's a question: how shall we try it?
Dro. S. We'll draw cuts for the senior: till then lead thou first.
Dro. E. Nay, then, thus:
We came into the world like brother and brother;
And now let 's go hand in hand, not one before another.
Exeunt.

397. **sympathized,** shared in by all equally. 404. **calendars . . . nativity,** the Dromios. 405. **gossips' feast.** A gossip is the godparent to one's child. 407. **gossip,** i.e., be a gossip, in the sense of boon companion, familiar acquaintance. 410. **lay at host,** were put up. 415. **kitchen'd,** entertained in the kitchen. 419. **gossiping,** merrymaking.

LOVE'S LABOUR'S LOST

In much the same way that *The Comedy of Errors* is Shakespeare's apprenticeship to Plautus and neoclassical comedy, *Love's Labour's Lost* is his apprenticeship to John Lyly's courtly drama of the 1580's, to the court masque, and to conventions of Petrarchan lyric poetry. The play is word-conscious and stylistically mannered to an extent that is unusual even for the pun-loving Shakespeare. The humor abounds in the pert repartee for which juvenile actors were especially fitted, and an extraordinarily high percentage of roles are assigned to boys: four women and a diminutive page (Moth) among seventeen named roles. The social setting is patrician, the entertainments aristocratic, the attitude toward commoners generally condescending. (The lower classes are there, nominally at least, to amuse their betters.) Very little happens in *Love's Labour's Lost*, especially if one compares its events with those of *The Comedy of Errors.* Fast-moving plot is replaced by a structure that includes a series of debates on courtly topics reminiscent of John Lyly: love versus honor, the flesh versus the spirit, pleasure versus instruction. The songs and sonnets composed by the courtiers for the ladies (IV,iii) gracefully caricature the excesses of the Petrarchan love-convention: the lovers are "sick to death" with unrequited passion, they catalogue the charms of their proud mistresses, they express their exquisitely tortured emotions through elaborate poetical "conceits" or metaphors, and so on. Stage movements are often masquelike; characters group themselves and then pair off two by two as in a formal dance. Actual masques and pageants, presented by the courtiers or devised for their amusement, are essential ingredients of the spectacle.

Yet beneath the brightly polished surfaces of this Lylyan courtesy-book comedy, we often catch glimpses of a candor and a simplicity that offset the tinsel and glitter. The wits ultimately disclaim (with some qualification) their wittiness, and the ladies confess they have tried too zealously to put down the men; both sides disavow the excessively Petrarchan postures they have striven so to maintain. The clowns, though deflated by mocking laughter for their naiveté and pomposity, deflate the courtiers in turn for lack of compassion. From this interplay among various forms of courtly wit, Petrarchism, pedantry, and rustic speech emerges a "recommended style" that is witty but not irresponsibly so, courtly yet sincere, polished and yet free of affectation or empty verbal ornament. This new harmony is expressed most aptly by Berowne and Rosaline, whose witty quest for self-understanding in love foreshadows that of Benedick and Beatrice in *Much Ado about Nothing*.

Like *The Comedy of Errors*, *Love's Labour's Lost* may either be a very early play or just an early play. It was published in quarto in 1598 "as it was presented before her Highnes this last Christmas" (1597). The text also purports to be "newly corrected and augmented," though we know of no earlier published version. Perhaps a play that was already several years old may have seemed in need of stylistic revision. Act IV does in fact contain two long duplicatory passages, suggesting that a certain amount of rewriting did take place. (See Appendix I.) The revisions alter the meaning only slightly, however, and give little support to the widely held notion that Shakespeare must have reworked the ending of his play. The abrupt ending, in which no marriages take place and in which the Princess' territorial claims to Aquitaine are left unresolved, should probably be regarded not as unfinished but as highly imaginative and indeed indispensable. The title after all assures us that "love's labours" will be lost.

Equally inconclusive are theories that the play was a topical satire written for a special audience, or that it was a comparatively late play of Shakespeare's "lyric" period, 1594–1595. Topical hypotheses arise from the quest for sources. Since the plot of *Love's Labour's Lost* is derived from no known literary source, may it have been drawn instead from the Elizabethan contemporary scene, poking fun at the pretentiousness of literary figures and intellectuals such as John Florio, Thomas Nashe, Gabriel Harvey, Sir Walter Ralegh, and George Chapman? Or should we seek topical meaning in the undoubted currency of such names as Navarre (Henry of Navarre, King Henry IV of France), Berowne (Biron, Henry IV's general), Dumaine (De Mayenne, brother of the Catholic Guise), and others? From the point of view of dating the play, however, such names would have been distastefully controversial in a courtly comedy after 1589. That date saw the beginning in France of a bitter civil conflict between the Catholic Guise and Protestant Navarre, continuing until Henry abjured Protestantism in 1593 and assumed the French throne. In the 1580's, on the other hand, the tiny kingdom of Navarre would have seemed charmingly appropriate as a setting for Shakespeare's play. Such an early date, although by no means certain, would also help explain the Lylyan tone of the comedy and its early techniques of versification: the high percentage of rhymed lines in couplets and quatrains, the end-stopped blank verse, the use of various sonnet forms and of seven-stress (septenary) couplets, and the like. Possibly, then, the play was first written in about 1588–1589 for a boys' company, and revised for Shakespeare's company in about 1596–1597.

The world of *Love's Labour's Lost*, as compared with that of most of Shakespeare's comedies, is not only uneventful but is remarkably unthreatened by danger or evil. The characters are menaced by nothing worse than teasing, and stand to lose nothing more serious than their dignity. In such an artificial world, however, the preservation of one's self-esteem assumes undue importance. Using the criteria of wit and self-awareness, Moth and Boyet, as manipulators and choric figures, show us how to laugh at folly in love and pomposity in language. They present to us variations on a theme of courtly behavior, creating in effect a scale of manners ranging from the most aristocratic (the King and the Princess, Berowne and Rosaline) to the most absurdly pretentious (Armado, Holofernes). Nearly all the characters are mocked, but those at the lower end of the scale are also humiliated because they are grossly unself-aware and hence unteachable.

The King and his companions deserve to be mocked because of the transparent hypocrisy and futility of their vows against love. As Berowne concedes from the start, such defiance of love is at odds with a fundamental natural rhythm that cannot ultimately be thwarted—a rhythm that provides a counterpoint and corrective to the frequently artificial rhythms of courtly life. This natural rhythm asserts itself throughout the play until it becomes starkly insistent in the death of the Princess' royal father and in the resulting twelve-month delay of all marriages.

Hypocritical defiance of love is doomed to comic failure and satirical punishment. The basic devices used to expose this hypocrisy are misdirected love letters and overhearings, both devices of unmasking. Appropriately the young ladies administer their most amusing comeuppance to the men by seeing through their Muscovite masks. The code governing this merry conflict is one of "mock for mock," and "sport by sport o'erthrown" (V,ii). Love is metaphorically a war, a siege, a battle of the sexes in which the women come off virtually unscathed. The language of love is that of parry and thrust (with occasional bawdy overtones). The men naturally are chagrined to be put down by the ladies, but ultimately are cured, laughing at their own pretentiousness and somewhat hyperbolically vowing to cast aside all "affectation" and "maggot ostentation" in favor of "russet yeas and honest kersey noes."

The clownish types are generally more victimized by their affectations. The fantastical Don Armado, as lover of Jaquenetta the country wench, apes the courtly conventions of the aristocrats to whose company he aspires. Enervated by base passion, penning wretched love letters, and worshiping a dairy-maid as though she were an unapproachable goddess, he is a caricature of the Petrarchan lover. Generally, however, the affectations of the comic characters have to do with language rather than love. Armado himself is known as a phrase-maker, "a plume of feathers," a "weathercock": "Did you ever hear better?" (IV,i). His letter to Jaquenetta, read aloud for the Princess' amusement, is an exquisite spoof of John Lyly's exaggeratedly mannered style called Euphuism: "Shall I command thy love? I may. Shall I enforce thy love? I could. Shall I entreat thy love? I will. What shalt thou exchange for rags? Robes. For tittles? Titles. For thyself? Me." Here we see the repeated antitheses, the balanced structure (reflected also in the structure of the play), and the alliterative effects that so intoxicated literary sophisticates of the 1580's. In a similar spirit, other comic types are distinguished by their verbal habits: Constable Dull by his malapropisms (anticipating Dogberry and Elbow), Holofernes by his Latinisms, his philological definitions, and his varied epithets, Nathaniel by his deference to Holofernes as a fellow "book-man," Costard by his amiable but unlettered confusion over such grandiose terms as "remuneration" and "guerdon." The word-conscious humor of the play gives us parodies of excruciatingly bad verse (as in Holofernes' "extemporal epitaph on the death of the deer"), teeth-grating puns (enfranchise, en-Frances), and the longest Latin word in existence (*honorificabilitudinitatibus*).

A little of this sort of thing goes a long way, and occasional scenes of verbal sparring are as tedious as anything Shakespeare ever wrote. He tries to have it both ways, reveling in Lylyan mannerism while laughing at its excesses. Yet the self-possessed characters do at least come to a realization that verbal overkill, like Petrarchan posturing, must be cast aside in favor of decorum and frankness in speech. The comic characters at their best help emphasize this same point. Costard especially is blessed with a pragmatic folk wisdom and simplicity that enable him to stand up unflinchingly to the ladies and gentlemen. He does not hesitate to tell the Princess that she is the "thickest and the tallest" of the ladies, for "Truth is truth." His forebearing description of Nathaniel as "a little o'erparted" in the role of Alexander serves as a gentle rebuke to the wits, whose caustic observations on "The Nine Worthies" have gotten out of hand. Even Holofernes justly chides, before retiring in confusion as Judas Maccabaeus, that "This is not generous, not gentle, not humble" (V,ii).

Above all, however, it is the play's unexpected ending that introduces an invaluable new insight on the courtiers' brittle war of wits. The death of the Princess' father brings everyone back to reality, to sober responsibility, to an awareness that marriage requires thoughtful decision. Devouring Time has entered the never-never land of Navarre's park. The song at the end, appropriately cast in the form of a dialogue or debate, gives us the two voices of Spring and Winter, love and death, Carnival and Lent, to remind us that human happiness and self-understanding are complex and perishable.

LOVE'S LABOUR'S LOST

[*Dramatis Personae*

FERDINAND, *King of Navarre.*
BEROWNE, LONGAVILLE, DUMAINE, *lords attending on the King.*
BOYET, MARCADE, *lords attending on the Princess of France.*
DON ADRIANO DE ARMADO, *a fantastical Spaniard.*
SIR NATHANIEL, *a curate.*
HOLOFERNES, *a schoolmaster.*
DULL, *a constable.*
COSTARD, *a clown.*
MOTH, *page to Armado.*
A Forester.

The PRINCESS of France.
ROSALINE, MARIA, KATHARINE, *ladies attending on the Princess.*
JAQUENETTA, *a country wench.*

Lords, Attendants, *&c.*

SCENE: *Navarre.*]

[ACT I.

SCENE I. *The King of Navarre's park.*]

Enter FERDINAND, KING of Navarre, BEROWNE, LONGAVILLE, *and* DUMAINE.

King. Let fame, that all hunt after in their lives,
Live regist'red upon our brazen tombs
And then grace us in the disgrace of death;
When, spite of cormorant devouring Time,
Th' endeavour of this present breath may buy
That honour which shall bate his scythe's keen edge
And make us heirs of all eternity.
Therefore, brave conquerors,—for so you are,
That war against your own affections
And the huge army of the world's desires,—
Our late edict shall strongly stand in force:
Navarre shall be the wonder of the world;
Our court shall be a little Academe,
Still and contemplative in living art.
You three, Berowne, Dumaine, and Longaville,
Have sworn for three years' term to live with me
My fellow-scholars and to keep those statutes
That are recorded in this schedule here:
Your oaths are pass'd; and now subscribe your names,
That his own hand may strike his honour down
That violates the smallest branch herein:
If you are arm'd to do as sworn to do,
Subscribe to your deep oaths, and keep it too.
Long. I am resolved; 'tis but a three years' fast:

The mind shall banquet, though the body pine:
Fat paunches have lean pates, and dainty bits
Make rich the ribs, but bankrout quite the wits.
Dum. My loving lord, Dumaine is mortified:
The grosser manner of these world's delights
He throws upon the gross world's baser slaves:
To love, to wealth, to pomp, I pine and die;
With all these living in philosophy.
Ber. I can but say their protestation over;
So much, dear liege, I have already sworn,
That is, to live and study here three years.
But there are other strict observances;
As, not to see a woman in that term,
Which I hope well is not enrolled there;
And one day in a week to touch no food
And but one meal on every day beside,
The which I hope is not enrolled there;
And then, to sleep but three hours in the night,
And not be seen to wink of all the day—
When I was wont to think no harm all night
And make a dark night too of half the day—
Which I hope well is not enrolled there:
O, these are barren tasks, too hard to keep,
Not to see ladies, study, fast, not sleep!
King. Your oath is pass'd to pass away from these.
Ber. Let me say no, my liege, an if you please:
I only swore to study with your grace
And stay here in your court for three years' space.
Long. You swore to that, Berowne, and to the rest.
Ber. By yea and nay, sir, then I swore in jest.
What is the end of study? let me know.
King. Why, that to know, which else we should not know.
Ber. Things hid and barr'd, you mean, from common sense?
King. Ay, that is study's god-like recompense.
Ber. Come on, then; I will swear to study so,
To know the thing I am forbid to know:
As thus,—to study where I well may dine,
When I to feast expressly am forbid;
Or study where to meet some mistress fine,
When mistresses from common sense are hid;
Or, having sworn too hard a keeping oath,
Study to break it and not break my troth.
If study's gain be thus and this be so,
Study knows that which yet it doth not know:
Swear me to this, and I will ne'er say no.
King. These be the stops that hinder study quite
And train our intellects to vain delight.
Ber. Why, all delights are vain; but that most vain,
Which with pain purchas'd doth inherit pain:
As, painfully to pore upon a book
To seek the light of truth; while truth the while
Doth falsely blind the eyesight of his look:
Light seeking light doth light of light beguile:
So, ere you find where light in darkness lies,
Your light grows dark by losing of your eyes.
Study me how to please the eye indeed
By fixing it upon a fairer eye,
Who dazzling so, that eye shall be his heed
And give him light that it was blinded by.
Study is like the heaven's glorious sun
That will not be deep-search'd with saucy looks:
Small have continual plodders ever won
Save base authority from others' books.
These earthly godfathers of heaven's lights
That give a name to every fixed star
Have no more profit of their shining nights
Than those that walk and wot not what they are.
Too much to know is to know nought but fame;
And every godfather can give a name.
King. How well he 's read, to reason against reading!
Dum. Proceeded well, to stop all good proceeding!
Long. He weeds the corn and still lets grow the weeding.
Ber. The spring is near when green geese are a-breeding.
Dum. How follows that?
Ber. Fit in his place and time.
Dum. In reason nothing.
Ber. Something then in rhyme.
King. Berowne is like an envious sneaping frost
That bites the first-born infants of the spring.
Ber. Well, say I am; why should proud summer boast
Before the birds have any cause to sing?
Why should I joy in any abortive birth?
At Christmas I no more desire a rose
Than wish a snow in May's new-fangled shows;
But like of each thing that in season grows.
So you, to study now it is too late,
Climb o'er the house to unlock the little gate.
King. Well, sit you out: go home, Berowne: adieu.

ACT I. SCENE I. 2. **brazen,** brass. 3. **grace,** honor; see glossary. **disgrace,** disfigurement. 4. **cormorant,** ravenous, rapacious. 6. **bate,** abate, blunt; see glossary. 9. **affections,** emotions, feelings; see glossary. 13. **Academe,** academy, from the name of the grove near Athens where Plato and his followers gathered. 14. **living art,** that art of which we shall give a living proof (Furness, who finds an antithesis between *still* and *living*); the phrase is a probable adaptation of *ars vitae* or *ars vivendi* (the art of life, the art of living), phrases familiar to Renaissance men through their study of the Stoic philosophers. 15. **Berowne,** accent on second syllable; it rhymes with *moon*. 18. **schedule,** slip of paper or scroll containing writing. 19. **pass'd,** pledged; see glossary. 28. **mortified,** deprived of feeling. Dumaine's extravagant oath suggests almost its literal sense; cf. l. 31. 29. **manner,** kind, sort. 32. **With . . . philosophy,** i.e., the pleasure afforded by these I find in philosophy. 43. **wink,** close the eyes; see glossary. **of all the day,** during the day; see *of* in glossary; cf. *Hamlet*, I, v, 60, *of the afternoon;* also the expression still current, "of a sudden." 44-45. **no . . . day,** no harm to sleep all night and half the day. 47. **barren,** dull, pointless. 50. **an if,** if; see glossary. 54. **By yea and nay,** an oath biblical in its connotation. Berowne assumes mock seriousness, an attitude by which the Puritans were often ridiculed. 57. **barr'd,** excluded. **common sense,** common observation or knowledge; see *sense* in glossary. 65. **too . . . oath,** an oath too hard to keep. 70. **stops,** obstacles. 71. **train,** allure, entice; see glossary. 73. **pain,** labor, effort, with quibble on the meaning "suffering"; see glossary. **purchas'd,** acquired; see glossary. 74. **As,** that is; see glossary. 76. **falsely,** treacherously; see glossary. **his,** its; see glossary; the antecedent is *eyesight*. **look,** power to see; see glossary. 77. **light,** multiple quibble on the meanings "the eye," "knowledge," and "vision" or "power to see"; i.e., the eye (*light*) by study (*seeking light*) beguiles or deprives itself of power to see (*light*). 80. **me,** probably, for me, by my advice; i.e., I would have you study thus. The pronoun is what is known as the ethical dative, an old construction that survives today in but a very few phrases. Cf. Abbott, 220, where the English dative is explained and amply illustrated; cf. also the General Introduction, the section on Shakespeare's English. 82. **Who dazzling so,** the man who is thus dazzled. **heed,** guard, means of safety. 85. **deep-search'd,** scrutinized. 86. **Small,** used substantively, little. 88. **earthly godfathers,** astronomers; alluding to the custom in baptism of having the godparents pronounce the name of the child. 91. **wot,** know; see glossary. 92. **fame,** report. 95. **Proceeded,** the academic sense of taking a university degree. 97. **green geese,** young geese born the previous autumn, and sold at green-goose fair, a season of merriment, held on Whitmonday. 99. **reason . . . rhyme.** Cf. the saying, "neither rhyme nor reason." 100. **envious,** malignant, malicious; see glossary. **sneaping,** biting. 101. **infants . . . spring,** flower buds. 106. **shows,** so QF; Globe: *mirth*. 107. **like of,** approve of. 108-109. **So . . . gate,** i.e., you are beginning at the wrong end—doing now what you should have done as boys. 110. **sit you out,** a term from card playing.

Ber. No, my good lord; I have sworn to stay with you:
And though I have for barbarism spoke more
Than for that angel knowledge you can say,
Yet confident I'll keep what I have swore
And bide the penance of each three years' day.
Give me the paper; let me read the same;
And to the strict'st decrees I'll write my name.
King. How well this yielding rescues thee from shame!
Ber. [*reads*]. 'Item, That no woman shall come within a mile of my court:' Hath this been proclaimed?

Long. Four days ago.

Ber. Let 's see the penalty. [*Reads*] 'On pain of losing her tongue.' Who devised this penalty?

Long. Marry, that did I.

Ber. Sweet lord, and why?

Long. To fright them hence with that dread penalty.

Ber. A dangerous law against gentility!
[*Reads*] 'Item, If any man be seen to talk with a woman within the term of three years, he shall endure such public shame as the rest of the court can possibly devise.'
This article, my liege, yourself must break;
For well you know here comes in embassy
The French king's daughter with yourself to speak—
A maid of grace and complete majesty—
About surrender up of Aquitaine
To her decrepit, sick and bedrid father:
Therefore this article is made in vain,
Or vainly comes th' admired princess hither.
King. What say you, lords? why, this was quite forgot.
Ber. So study evermore is overshot:
While it doth study to have what it would
It doth forget to do the thing it should,
And when it hath the thing it hunteth most,
'Tis won as towns with fire, so won, so lost.
King. We must of force dispense with this decree;
She must lie here on mere necessity.
Ber. Necessity will make us all forsworn
Three thousand times within this three years' space;
For every man with his affects is born,
Not by might mast'red but by special grace:
If I break faith, this word shall speak for me;
I am forsworn on 'mere necessity.'
So to the laws at large I write my name: [*Subscribes.*]
And he that breaks them in the least degree
Stands in attainder of eternal shame:
Suggestions are to other as to me;
But I believe, although I seem so loath,
I am the last that will last keep his oath.
But is there no quick recreation granted?
King. Ay, that there is. Our court, you know, is haunted
With a refined traveller of Spain;
A man in all the world's new fashion planted,
That hath a mint of phrases in his brain;
One who the music of his own vain tongue
Doth ravish like enchanting harmony;
A man of complements, whom right and wrong
Have chose as umpire of their mutiny:
This child of fancy that Armado hight
For interim to our studies shall relate
In high-born words the worth of many a knight
From tawny Spain lost in the world's debate.
How you delight, my lords, I know not, I;
But, I protest, I love to hear him lie
And I will use him for my minstrelsy.
Ber. Armado is a most illustrious wight,
A man of fire-new words, fashion's own knight.
Long. Costard the swain and he shall be our sport;
And so to study, three years is but short.

Enter [DULL,] *a Constable, with* COSTARD, *with a letter.*

Dull. Which is the duke's own person?

Ber. This, fellow: what wouldst?

Dull. I myself reprehend his own person, for I am his grace's farborough: but I would see his own person in flesh and blood.

Ber. This is he.

Dull. Signior Arme–Arme–commends you. There's villany abroad: this letter will tell you more.

Cost. Sir, the contempts thereof are as touching me.

King. A letter from the magnificent Armado.

Ber. How low soever the matter, I hope in God for high words.

Long. A high hope for a low heaven: God grant us patience!

Ber. To hear? or forbear hearing?

Long. To hear meekly, sir, and to laugh moderately; or to forbear both.

Ber. Well, sir, be it as the style shall give us cause to climb in the merriness.

Cost. The matter is to me, sir, as concerning Jaquenetta. The manner of it is, I was taken with the manner.

Ber. In what manner?

Cost. In manner and form following, sir; all those three: I was seen with her in the manor-house, sitting with her upon the form, and taken following her into the park; which, put together, is in manner and form following. Now, sir, for the manner,—it is the manner of a man to speak to a woman: for the form,—in some form.

Ber. For the following, sir?

Cost. As it shall follow in my correction and God defend the right!

112. **barbarism,** ignorance; opposed to *knowledge* (l. 113). 114. **confident,** used adverbially. 115. **bide,** endure. **each . . . day,** every day of the three years. 126. **Marry,** a mild interjection equivalent to "Indeed!"; originally an oath by the Virgin Mary; see glossary. 135. **in embassy,** as an ambassador. 137. **complete,** fully endowed; see glossary. 141. **admired,** exciting wonder; see glossary. 148. **of force,** necessarily. 149. **lie,** reside; see glossary. 152. **affects,** natural tendencies. 153. **grace,** divine favor; see glossary. 155. **mere,** absolute, pure; see glossary. 156. **at large,** as a whole, in general; see *large* in glossary. 158. **attainder,** dishonoring accusation. 159. **Suggestions,** temptations; see glossary. 162. **quick,** lively; see glossary. 163. **haunted,** frequented, visited. 167. **who,** so QF; Globe: *whom. Who* in the objective position is frequent in Shakespeare; see Abbott, 274. 169. **complements,** those formal manners which go to complete a gentleman; cf. Armado's words below (I, ii, 46-47), *the varnish of a complete man.* 170. **mutiny,** discord. 171. **child of fancy,** fantastic or grotesque creature; see *fancy* in glossary. 172. **interim,** interlude. 174. **tawny,** probably a reference to the complexion of the people. 175. **How you delight,** what delights you, how you are delighted. 180. **Costard.** The name means a large apple; the term is frequently applied humorously or derisively to the head; cf. III, i, 71. **swain,** young man in love; especially a rustic. 183. **fellow,** customary form of address to a servant; see glossary. 184. **reprehend,** represent. We have in this play Shakespeare's first employment of the comic device of malapropism, which he brought to such perfection in characterizing the constable of *Much Ado about Nothing*. 185. **farborough,** so Q; Dull means *tharborough* (the Globe reading), a common variant of "thirdborough," a petty officer. 193. **magnificent,** boastful. 198. **hearing,** so QF; Globe,

King. Will you hear this letter with attention?

Ber. As we would hear an oracle.

Cost. Such is the simplicity of man to hearken after the flesh.

King [*reads*]. 'Great deputy, the welkin's vicegerent and sole dominator of Navarre, my soul's earth's god, and body's fostering patron.'

Cost. Not a word of Costard yet.

King [*reads*]. 'So it is,'—

Cost. It may be so: but if he say it is so, he is, in telling true, but so.

King. Peace!

Cost. Be to me and every man that dares not fight!

King. No words!

Cost. Of other men's secrets, I beseech you.

King [*reads*]. 'So it is, besieged with sable-coloured melancholy, I did commend the black-oppressing humour to the most wholesome physic of thy health-giving air; and, as I am a gentleman, betook myself to walk. The time when? About the sixth hour; when beasts most graze, birds best peck, and men sit down to that nourishment which is called supper: so much for the time when. Now for the ground which; which, I mean, I walked upon: it is ycleped thy park. Then for the place where; where, I mean, I did encounter that obscene and most preposterous event, that draweth from my snow-white pen the ebon-coloured ink, which here thou viewest, beholdest, surveyest, or seest: but to the place where; it standeth north-north-east and by east from the west corner of thy curious-knotted garden: there did I see that low-spirited swain, that base minnow of thy mirth,'—

Cost. Me?

King [*reads*]. 'that unlettered small-knowing soul,'—

Cost. Me?

King [*reads*]. 'that shallow vassal,'—

Cost. Still me?

King [*reads*]. 'which, as I remember. hight Costard,'—

Cost. O, me!

King [*reads*]. 'sorted and consorted, contrary to thy established proclaimed edict and continent canon, which with,—O, with—but with this I passion to say wherewith,'—

Cost. With a wench.

King [*reads*]. 'with a child of our grandmother Eve, a female; or, for thy more sweet understanding, a woman. Him I, as my ever-esteemed duty pricks me on, have sent to thee, to receive the meed of punishment, by thy sweet grace's officer, Anthony Dull; a man of good repute, carriage, bearing, and estimation.'

Dull. Me, an 't shall please you; I am Anthony Dull.

King [*reads*]. 'For Jaquenetta,—so is the weaker vessel called which I apprehended with the aforesaid swain,—I keep her as a vessel of thy law's fury; and shall, at the least of thy sweet notice, bring her to trial. Thine, in all compliments of devoted and heart-burning heat of duty. DON ADRIANO DE ARMADO.'

Ber. This is not so well as I looked for, but the best that ever I heard.

King. Ay, the best for the worst. But, sirrah, what say you to this?

Cost. Sir, I confess the wench.

King. Did you hear the proclamation?

Cost. I do confess much of the hearing it, but little of the marking of it.

King. It was proclaimed a year's imprisonment, to be taken with a wench.

Cost. I was taken with none, sir: I was taken with a damsel.

King. Well, it was proclaimed 'damsel.'

Cost. This was no damsel neither, sir; she was a virgin.

King. It is so varied too; for it was proclaimed 'virgin.'

Cost. If it were, I deny her virginity: I was taken with a maid.

King. This maid will not serve your turn, sir.

Cost. This maid will serve my turn, sir.

King. Sir, I will pronounce your sentence: you shall fast a week with bran and water.

Cost. I had rather pray a month with mutton and porridge.

King. And Don Armado shall be your keeper.
My Lord Berowne, see him delivered o'er:
And go we, lords, to put in practice that
Which each to other hath so strongly sworn.
[*Exeunt King, Longaville, and Dumaine.*]

Ber. I'll lay my head to any good man's hat,
These oaths and laws will prove an idle scorn.
Sirrah, come on.

Cost. I suffer for the truth, sir; for true it is, I was taken with Jaquenetta, and Jaquenetta is a true girl; and therefore welcome the sour cup of prosperity! Affliction may one day smile again; and till then, sit thee down, sorrow! *Exeunt.*

[SCENE II. *The same.*]

Enter ARMADO *and* MOTH, *his Page.*

Arm. Boy, what sign is it when a man of great spirit grows melancholy?

Moth. A great sign, sir, that he will look sad.

Arm. Why, sadness is one and the self-same thing, dear imp.

Moth. No, no; O Lord, sir, no.

Arm. How canst thou part sadness and melancholy, my tender juvenal?

Moth. By a familiar demonstration of the working, my tough senior.

following Capell and others: *laughing*. 201. **style,** quibble on "stile," which gives point to *climb* (l. 202). 205. **with the manner,** with the stolen goods; an Anglo-French law term *mainoure* (from *manœuvre*). 209. **form,** bench or long seat. 215. **correction,** punishment. 221. **welkin's**, sky's, heaven's; see glossary. 227. **but so,** indifferent; cf. the modern phrase "so, so." 234-235. **black-oppressing humour,** i.e., black choler or melancholy; see *humour* in glossary. 235. **physic,** medicine, medical treatment; see glossary. 242. **ycleped,** called (archaic); an affectation on Armado's part. 244. **obscene,** disgusting. 245. **snow-white pen,** i.e., the white goose quill. 249. **curious-knotted,** delicately or intricately designed; see *curious* in glossary. 251. **minnow,** contemptible little person. 256. **vassal,** base slave. 261. **sorted and consorted,** associated. 262-263. **continent canon,** restraint enforced by law; note the affectation of legal language. 264. **passion,** grieve; see glossary. 283. **sirrah,** ordinary form of address to inferiors; see glossary. 287, 288. **hearing, marking.** This may be an echo of the collect for the second Sunday in Advent: "hear, read, mark, learn, and inwardly digest." 300. **serve your turn,** answer your purpose; see *serve* in glossary. 304. **mutton,** possible glance at the meaning "prostitute." 310. **lay,** wager. **good man's,** probably should be read *goodman's*, i.e., citizen's, husband's.

SCENE II. 5. **imp,** child. 8. **juvenal,** youth, with possible reference here to the classical satirist, Juvenal. Those who find treatment in this play of the Harvey-Nashe quarrel think this an allusion to Nashe's satirical vein. 9. **familiar,** plain, easily understood; see glossary.

Arm. Why tough senior? why tough senior?

Moth. Why tender juvenal? why tender juvenal?

Arm. I spoke it, tender juvenal, as a congruent epitheton appertaining to thy young days, which we may nominate tender.

Moth. And I, tough senior, as an appertinent title to your old time, which we may name tough.

Arm. Pretty and apt.

Moth. How mean you, sir? I pretty, and my saying apt? or I apt, and my saying pretty?

Arm. Thou pretty, because little.

Moth. Little pretty, because little. Wherefore apt?

Arm. And therefore apt, because quick.

Moth. Speak you this in my praise, master?

Arm. In thy condign praise.

Moth. I will praise an eel with the same praise.

Arm. What, that an eel is ingenious?

Moth. That an eel is quick.

Arm. I do say thou art quick in answers: thou heatest my blood.

Moth. I am answered, sir.

Arm. I love not to be crossed.

Moth. [*Aside*] He speaks the mere contrary; crosses love not him.

Arm. I have promised to study three years with the duke.

Moth. You may do it in an hour, sir.

Arm. Impossible.

Moth. How many is one thrice told?

Arm. I am ill at reckoning; it fitteth the spirit of a tapster.

Moth. You are a gentleman and a gamester, sir.

Arm. I confess both: they are both the varnish of a complete man.

Moth. Then, I am sure, you know how much the gross sum of deuce-ace amounts to.

Arm. It doth amount to one more than two.

Moth. Which the base vulgar do call three.

Arm. True.

Moth. Why, sir, is this such a piece of study? Now here is three studied, ere ye'll thrice wink: and how easy it is to put 'years' to the word 'three,' and study three years in two words, the dancing horse will tell you.

Arm. A most fine figure!

Moth. [*Aside*] To prove you a cipher.

Arm. I will hereupon confess I am in love: and as it is base for a soldier to love, so am I in love with a base wench. If drawing my sword against the humour of affection would deliver me from the reprobate thought of it, I would take Desire prisoner, and ransom him to any French courtier for a new-devised courtesy. I think scorn to sigh: methinks I should outswear Cupid. Comfort me, boy: what great men have been in love?

Moth. Hercules, master.

Arm. Most sweet Hercules! More authority, dear boy, name more; and, sweet my child, let them be men of good repute and carriage.

Moth. Samson, master: he was a man of good carriage, great carriage, for he carried the town-gates on his back like a porter: and he was in love.

Arm. O well-knit Samson! strong-jointed Samson! I do excel thee in my rapier as much as thou didst me in carrying gates. I am in love too. Who was Samson's love, my dear Moth?

Moth. A woman, master.

Arm. Of what complexion?

Moth. Of all the four, or the three, or the two, or one of the four.

Arm. Tell me precisely of what complexion.

Moth. Of the sea-water green, sir.

Arm. Is that one of the four complexions?

Moth. As I have read, sir; and the best of them too.

Arm. Green indeed is the colour of lovers; but to have a love of that colour, methinks Samson had small reason for it. He surely affected her for her wit.

Moth. It was so, sir; for she had a green wit.

Arm. My love is most immaculate white and red.

Moth. Most maculate thoughts, master, are masked under such colours.

Arm. Define, define, well-educated infant.

Moth. My father's wit and my mother's tongue, assist me!

Arm. Sweet invocation of a child; most pretty and pathetical!

Moth. If she be made of white and red,
Her faults will ne'er be known,
For blushing cheeks by faults are bred
And fears by pale white shown:
Then if she fear, or be to blame,
By this you shall not know,
For still her cheeks possess the same
Which native she doth owe.

A dangerous rhyme, master, against the reason of white and red.

Arm. Is there not a ballad, boy, of the King and the Beggar?

Moth. The world was very guilty of such a ballad some three ages since: but I think now 'tis not to be found; or, if it were, it would neither serve for the writing nor the tune.

Arm. I will have that subject newly writ o'er, that I may example my digression by some mighty precedent. Boy, I do love that country girl that I took in the park with the rational hind Costard: she deserves well.

Moth. [*Aside*] To be whipped; and yet a better love than my master.

Arm. Sing, boy; my spirit grows heavy in love.

Moth. And that 's great marvel, loving a light wench.

Arm. I say, sing.

27. **condign,** worthily deserved. 32. **thou . . . blood,** you make me angry; see *blood* in glossary. 36. **crosses,** coins, so called because many of them were impressed with crosses. 41. **told,** counted; see *tell* in glossary. 43. **tapster,** proverbially a very ignorant person. 57. **dancing horse,** a famous trained horse named Morocco, frequently mentioned in the literature of the time. 58. **figure,** used in rhetorical sense. 66. **new-devised courtesy,** any new fashion. 83. **four** (*complexions*), i.e., sanguine, choleric, phlegmatic, and melancholy, the four recognized dispositions or habits of mind, supposed to be determined by the relative proportions of the four humors; see *complexion* and *humour* in glossary. 90. **Green,** the color of hope and rejoicing; possible quibble on an older notion that green denoted inconstancy. 92. **affected,** loved; see glossary. 94. **green wit,** possible allusion to the seven green withes with which Samson was bound (Judges 16:7-8). 95. **white and red,** possible allusion to cosmetics. 97. **maculate,** stained, polluted. 98. **colours,** used with quibble on the meaning "pretexts"; see glossary. 111. **native,** naturally. **owe,** own; see glossary. 114-115. **ballad . . . Beggar,** a reference to the popular ballad of King Cophetua and the beggar maid (cf. IV, i, 66). 121. **example,** give an example of. **digression,** waywardness. 123. **rational hind,** intelligent rustic or clown; see *hind* in glossary. 133. **keep,** confine, imprison; see glossary. 134. **penance,** perhaps a malapropism for "pleasance." **a',** he; see glossary. 136. **day-woman,** dairy woman. 145. **With that face?** So Q; F: *With what face?* All editors follow Q. The phrase was taken by Steevens, and others after him, for slang; explained by Hart as equivalent to "You don't mean it!" Furness argues that F may be right, adducing as support the phrase from the longer exhortation of the Communion Service in the *Book of Common Prayer* (1552): "With what face, then, or with

Moth. Forbear till this company be past.

Enter [COSTARD *the*] *Clown,* [DULL *the*] *Constable, and* [JAQUENETTA, *a*] *Wench.*

Dull. Sir, the duke's pleasure is, that you keep Costard safe: and you must suffer him to take no delight nor no penance; but 'a must fast three days a week. For this damsel, I must keep her at the park: she is allowed for the day-woman. Fare you well.

Arm. I do betray myself with blushing. Maid!
Jaq. Man?
Arm. I will visit thee at the lodge.
Jaq. That 's hereby.
Arm. I know where it is situate.
Jaq. Lord, how wise you are!
Arm. I will tell thee wonders.
Jaq. With that face?
Arm. I love thee.
Jaq. So I heard you say.
Arm. And so, farewell.
Jaq. Fair weather after you!
Dull. Come, Jaquenetta, away!
Exeunt [*Dull and Jaquenetta*].

Arm. Villain, thou shalt fast for thy offences ere thou be pardoned.

Cost. Well, sir, I hope, when I do it, I shall do it on a full stomach.

Arm. Thou shalt be heavily punished.

Cost. I am more bound to you than your fellows, for they are but lightly rewarded.

Arm. Take away this villain; shut him up.

Moth. Come, you transgressing slave; away!

Cost. Let me not be pent up, sir: I will fast, being loose.

Moth. No, sir; that were fast and loose: thou shalt to prison.

Cost. Well, if ever I do see the merry days of desolation that I have seen, some shall see.

Moth. What shall some see?

Cost. Nay, nothing, Master Moth, but what they look upon. It is not for prisoners to be too silent in their words; and therefore I will say nothing: I thank God I have as little patience as another man; and therefore I can be quiet. *Exit* [*with Moth*].

Arm. I do affect the very ground, which is base, where her shoe, which is baser, guided by her foot, which is basest, doth tread. I shall be forsworn, which is a great argument of falsehood, if I love. And how can that be true love which is falsely attempted? Love is a familiar; Love is a devil: there is no evil angel but Love. Yet was Samson so tempted, and he had an excellent strength; yet was Solomon so seduced, and he had a very good wit. Cupid's butt-shaft is too hard for Hercules' club; and therefore too much odds for a Spaniard's rapier. The first and second cause will not serve my turn; the passado he respects not, the duello he regards not: his disgrace is to be called boy; but his glory is to subdue men. Adieu, valour! rust, rapier! be still, drum! for your manager is in love; yea, he loveth. Assist me, some extemporal god of rhyme, for I am sure I shall turn sonnet. Devise, wit; write, pen; for I am for whole volumes in folio. *Exit.*

[ACT II.

SCENE I. *The same.*]

Enter the PRINCESS of France, *with three attending* Ladies [ROSALINE, MARIA, KATHARINE] *and three* Lords [*one being* BOYET].

Boyet. Now, madam, summon up your dearest spirits:
Consider who the king your father sends,
To whom he sends, and what 's his embassy:
Yourself, held precious in the world's esteem,
To parley with the sole inheritor
Of all perfections that a man may owe,
Matchless Navarre; the plea of no less weight
Than Aquitaine, a dowry for a queen.
Be now as prodigal of all dear grace
As Nature was in making graces dear
When she did starve the general world beside
And prodigally gave them all to you.

Prin. Good Lord Boyet, my beauty, though but mean,
Needs not the painted flourish of your praise:
Beauty is bought by judgement of the eye,
Not utter'd by base sale of chapmen's tongues:
I am less proud to hear you tell my worth
Than you much willing to be counted wise
In spending your wit in the praise of mine.
But now to task the tasker: good Boyet,
You are not ignorant, all-telling fame
Doth noise abroad, Navarre hath made a vow,
Till painful study shall outwear three years,
No woman may approach his silent court:
Therefore to 's seemeth it a needful course,
Before we enter his forbidden gates,
To know his pleasure; and in that behalf,
Bold of your worthiness, we single you
As our best-moving fair solicitor.
Tell him, the daughter of the King of France,
On serious business, craving quick dispatch,
Importunes personal conference with his grace:
Haste, signify so much; while we attend,
Like humble-visag'd suitors, his high will.

Boyet. Proud of employment, willingly I go.

Prin. All pride is willing pride, and yours is so.
Exit Boyet.

what countenance [i.e., effrontery] shal ye heare these words?" 151. **Villain,** quibble on "servant" and "rascal." 151-154. **fast . . . on a full stomach,** probably a quibble on the idea of "full-stomached," meaning "with good courage"; see *stomach* in glossary. 157. **lightly,** i.e., only slightly. 162. **fast and loose,** a cheating or gambling trick executed with a stick and a cord or belt. The phrase was very early applied metaphorically to matters of conduct with the meaning "inconstant, tricky, slippery." Shakespeare so used it in *King John*, III, i, 242. 177. **familiar,** attendant spirit; see glossary. 181. **butt-shaft,** unbarbed arrow used in archery practice; applied to Cupid's darts because, although they hit hard, they were easily extracted. 183-184. **first . . . cause.** Cf. *The Booke of Honor and Armes* (1590): ". . . the causes of a quarrell wherevpon it behoueth to vse the triall of Armes, may be reduced into two. . . . Wherefore whensoeuer one man doth accuse another of such a crime as meriteth death, in that case the Combat ought to be graunted. The second cause of Combat is Honor, because among persons of reputation, Honor is preferred before life." (*Modern Language Review*, II, 76-77.) 184. **passado,** forward thrust with the sword, one foot being advanced at the same time. 185. **respects,** heeds; see glossary. **duello,** established code of duelists. 189. **extemporal,** impromptu.

ACT II. SCENE I. 1. **dearest,** best. 9, 10. **dear,** quibble on the meanings "beloved," "cherished," and "bearing a high price"; see glossary. 13. **mean,** average, moderate; see glossary. 15. **Beauty . . . eye,** i.e., the buyer's judgment, not the merchant's advertising, is the determinant. 16. **chapmen's,** merchants'. 20. **task,** lay a task upon. 25. **to 's,** to us. 28. **Bold of,** confident of. 29. **best-moving,** most eloquent. **fair,** just; see glossary.

Who are the votaries, my loving lords,
That are vow-fellows with this virtuous duke?
First Lord. Lord Longaville is one.
Prin. Know you the man?
Mar. I know him, madam: at a marriage-feast,
Between Lord Perigort and the beauteous heir
Of Jaques Falconbridge, solemnized
In Normandy, saw I this Longaville:
A man of sovereign parts he is esteem'd;
Well fitted in arts, glorious in arms:
Nothing becomes him ill that he would well.
The only soil of his fair virtue's gloss,
If virtue's gloss will stain with any soil,
Is a sharp wit match'd with too blunt a will;
Whose edge hath power to cut, whose will still wills
It should none spare that come within his power.
Prin. Some merry mocking lord, belike; is 't so?
Mar. They say so most that most his humours know.
Prin. Such short-liv'd wits do wither as they grow.
Who are the rest?
Kath. The young Dumaine; a well-accomplish'd youth,
Of all that virtue love for virtue lov'd:
Most power to do most harm, least knowing ill;
For he hath wit to make an ill shape good,
And shape to win grace though he had no wit.
I saw him at the Duke Alençon's once;
And much too little of that good I saw
Is my report to his great worthiness.
Ros. Another of these students at that time
Was there with him, if I have heard a truth.
Berowne they call him; but a merrier man,
Within the limit of becoming mirth,
I never spent an hour's talk withal:
His eye begets occasion for his wit;
For every object that the one doth catch
The other turns to a mirth-moving jest,
Which his fair tongue, conceit's expositor,
Delivers in such apt and gracious words
That aged ears play truant at his tales
And younger hearings are quite ravished;
So sweet and voluble is his discourse.
Prin. God bless my ladies! are they all in love,
That every one her own hath garnished
With such bedecking ornaments of praise?
First Lord. Here comes Boyet.

Enter BOYET.

Prin. Now, what admittance, lord?
Boyet. Navarre had notice of your fair approach;
And he and his competitors in oath
Were all address'd to meet you, gentle lady,
Before I came. Marry, thus much I have learnt:
He rather means to lodge you in the field,
Like one that comes here to besiege his court,
Than seek a dispensation for his oath,
To let you enter his unpeopled house.

Enter [KING of] Navarre, LONGAVILLE, DUMAINE, *and* BEROWNE [,*with* Attendants].

Here comes Navarre.
King. Fair princess, welcome to the court of Navarre.
Prin. 'Fair' I give you back again; and 'welcome' I have not yet: the roof of this court is too high to be yours; and welcome to the wide fields too base to be mine.
King. You shall be welcome, madam, to my court.
Prin. I will be welcome, then: conduct me thither.
King. Hear me, dear lady; I have sworn an oath.
Prin. Our Lady help my lord! he'll be forsworn.
King. Not for the world, fair madam, by my will.
Prin. Why, will shall break it; will and nothing else.
King. Your ladyship is ignorant what it is.
Prin. Were my lord so, his ignorance were wise,
Where now his knowledge must prove ignorance.
I hear your grace hath sworn out house-keeping:
'Tis deadly sin to keep that oath, my lord,
And sin to break it.
But pardon me, I am too sudden-bold:
To teach a teacher ill beseemeth me.
Vouchsafe to read the purpose of my coming,
And suddenly resolve me in my suit.
King. Madam, I will, if suddenly I may.
Prin. You will the sooner, that I were away;
For you'll prove perjur'd if you make me stay.
Ber. Did not I dance with you in Brabant once?
Ros. Did not I dance with you in Brabant once?
Ber. I know you did.
Ros. How needless was it then to ask the question!
Ber. You must not be so quick.
Ros. 'Tis 'long of you that spur me with such questions.
Ber. Your wit 's too hot, it speeds too fast, 'twill tire.
Ros. Not till it leave the rider in the mire.
Ber. What time o' day?
Ros. The hour that fools should ask.
Ber. Now fair befall your mask!
Ros. Fair fall the face it covers!
Ber. And send you many lovers!
Ros. Amen, so you be none.
Ber. Nay, then will I be gone.
King. Madam, your father here doth intimate
The payment of a hundred thousand crowns;
Being but the one half of an entire sum
Disbursed by my father in his wars.
But say that he or we, as neither have,
Receiv'd that sum, yet there remains unpaid
A hundred thousand more; in surety of the which,
One part of Aquitaine is bound to us,
Although not valued to the money's worth.
If then the king your father will restore
But that one half which is unsatisfied,
We will give up our right in Aquitaine,

37. **votaries,** those who have taken vows. 44. **sovereign parts,** excellent qualities. 46. **would well,** wants to do well. 47. **virtue's gloss,** appearance of general excellence; see *virtue* and *gloss* in glossary. 49. **too blunt a will,** i.e., too insensitive to the feelings of others. 56-60. **The . . . wit.** Dumaine, a highly accomplished young nobleman, esteemed for his virtue by all who love virtue; one who, by his talent and graceful person, has the utmost power of doing the greatest harm by the ill employment of those qualities, is nevertheless ignorant of evil (Halliwell). 72. **conceit's expositor,** interpreter of fanciful ideas: see *conceit* in glossary. 76. **discourse,** art of conversing; see glossary. 82. **competitors,** associates. 88. **unpeopled,** so F; Q: *vnpeeled,* which probably represents an Elizabethan pronunciation. 104. **sworn out,** renounced. **house-keeping,** hospitality. 107. **sudden-bold,** rashly bold. 110. **resolve,** answer; see glossary. 119. **'long of,** on account of; see glossary. 124. **fair befall,** an optative expression frequent in Elizabethan literature, equivalent to "Good luck!" 125. **fall,** befall; see glossary. 129-149. **your . . . is.** Cf. I, i, 138-139. The French king offers to discharge but half his debt to Navarre, for which Aquitaine has been the surety. The king of Navarre objects, insisting that Aquitaine, weakened as it is, is insufficient security for the 100,000 crowns that would still be owing. He holds out for payment in full. 147. **depart withal,** part with; see *depart* and *withal* in glossary. 149.

And hold fair friendship with his majesty.
But that, it seems, he little purposeth,
For here he doth demand to have repaid
A hundred thousand crowns; and not demands,
On payment of a hundred thousand crowns,
To have his title live in Aquitaine;
Which we much rather had depart withal
And have the money by our father lent
Than Aquitaine so gelded as it is.
Dear princess, were not his requests so far
From reason's yielding, your fair self should make
A yielding 'gainst some reason in my breast
And go well satisfied to France again.
Prin. You do the king my father too much wrong
And wrong the reputation of your name,
In so unseeming to confess receipt
Of that which hath so faithfully been paid.
King. I do protest I never heard of it;
And if you prove it, I'll repay it back
Or yield up Aquitaine.
Prin. We arrest your word.
Boyet, you can produce acquittances
For such a sum from special officers
Of Charles his father.
King. Satisfy me so.
Boyet. So please your grace, the packet is not come
Where that and other specialties are bound:
To-morrow you shall have a sight of them.
King. It shall suffice me: at which interview
All liberal reason I will yield unto.
Meantime receive such welcome at my hand
As honour without breach of honour may
Make tender of to thy true worthiness:
You may not come, fair princess, within my gates;
But here without you shall be so receiv'd
As you shall deem yourself lodg'd in my heart,
Though so denied fair harbour in my house.
Your own good thoughts excuse me, and farewell:
To-morrow shall we visit you again.
Prin. Sweet health and fair desires consort your grace!
King. Thy own wish wish I thee in every place!
Exit [with Longaville and Dumaine].
Ber. Lady, I will commend you to mine own heart.
Ros. Pray you, do my commendations; I would be glad to see it.
Ber. I would you heard it groan.
Ros. Is the fool sick?
Ber. Sick at the heart.
Ros. Alack, let it blood.
Ber. Would that do it good?
Ros. My physic says 'ay.'
Ber. Will you prick 't with your eye?
Ros. No point, with my knife.
Ber. Now, God save thy life!
Ros. And yours from long living!
Ber. I cannot stay thanksgiving. *Exit.*

Enter Dumaine.
Dum. Sir, I pray you, a word: what lady is that same?
Boyet. The heir of Alençon, Katharine her name.
Dum. A gallant lady. Monsieur, fare you well. *Exit.*
[Enter Longaville.]
Long. I beseech you a word: what is she in the white?
Boyet. A woman sometimes, an you saw her in the light.
Long. Perchance light in the light. I desire her name.
Boyet. She hath but one for herself; to desire that were a shame.
Long. Pray you, sir, whose daughter?
Boyet. Her mother's, I have heard.
Long. God's blessing on your beard!
Boyet. Good sir, be not offended.
She is an heir of Falconbridge.
Long. Nay, my choler is ended.
She is a most sweet lady.
Boyet. Not unlike, sir, that may be. *Exit Long.*
Enter Berowne.
Ber. What 's her name in the cap?
Boyet. Rosaline, by good hap.
Ber. Is she wedded or no?
Boyet. To her will, sir, or so.
Ber. You are welcome, sir: adieu.
Boyet. Farewell to me, sir, and welcome to you.
Exit Berowne.
Mar. That last is Berowne, the merry mad-cap lord:
Not a word with him but a jest.
Boyet. And every jest but a word.
Prin. It was well done of you to take him at his word.
Boyet. I was as willing to grapple as he was to board.
Mar. Two hot sheeps, marry.
Boyet. And wherefore not ships?
No sheep, sweet lamb, unless we feed on your lips.
Mar. You sheep, and I pasture: shall that finish the jest?
Boyet. So you grant pasture for me.
[Offering to kiss her.]
Mar. Not so, gentle beast:
My lips are no common, though several they be.
Boyet. Belonging to whom?
Mar. To my fortunes and me.
Prin. Good wits will be jangling; but, gentles, agree:
This civil war of wits were much better used
On Navarre and his book-men; for here 'tis abused.
Boyet. If my observation, which very seldom lies,
By the heart's still rhetoric disclosed with eyes,
Deceive me not now, Navarre is infected.
Prin. With what?
Boyet. With that which we lovers entitle affected.
Prin. Your reason?
Boyet. Why, all his behaviours did make their retire

gelded, weakened. 156. **unseeming,** i.e., apparently unwilling. 160. **arrest,** take as security. 165. **specialties,** special contracts for payment of money. 168. **liberal,** becoming a gentleman; see glossary. 172. **within,** so Q; Globe, following F: *in.* 178. **consort,** attend, accompany. 181. **do my commendations,** convey my greetings (i.e., to your heart). 186. **let it blood,** bleed it; a reference to the medical practice of drawing blood. 190. **No point,** not at all; with quibble; cf. V, ii, 277. 193. **stay thanksgiving,** stay long enough to thank you properly. 199. **light in the light,** wanton when her conduct is known (brought to light). 203. **God's . . . beard.** The Yale editors think this a recognition of Boyet's years, with which his remarks are not in keeping. Hart points out that any reference to one's beard was dangerous or unmannerly. 214. **welcome to you,** you are welcome to go. 218. **grapple, board,** tactics of sea warfare. 219. **sheeps, ships.** Cf. *Two Gentlemen of Verona*, I, i, 72, 73, note. 223. **common,** common land. **several,** private enclosed land, with quibble on the meaning, "more than one"; see glossary. 227. **abused,** misapplied; see glossary. 229. **still,** silent, mute; see glossary. 234. **retire,** retirement. 235. **thorough,** through; see glossary. 236. **agate,** an allusion to small figures cut in agate.

To the court of his eye, peeping thorough desire:
His heart, like an agate, with your print impressed,
Proud with his form, in his eye pride expressed:
His tongue, all impatient to speak and not see,
Did stumble with haste in his eyesight to be;
All senses to that sense did make their repair,
To feel only looking on fairest of fair:
Methought all his senses were lock'd in his eye,
As jewels in crystal for some prince to buy;
Who, tend'ring their own worth from where they were glass'd,
Did point you to buy them, along as you pass'd:
His face's own margent did quote such amazes
That all eyes saw his eyes enchanted with gazes.
I'll give you Aquitaine and all that is his,
An you give him for my sake but one loving kiss.

Prin. Come to our pavilion: Boyet is dispos'd.

Boyet. But to speak that in words which his eye hath disclos'd.
I only have made a mouth of his eye,
By adding a tongue which I know will not lie.

Ros. Thou art an old love-monger and speakest skilfully.

Mar. He is Cupid's grandfather and learns news of him.

Ros. Then was Venus like her mother, for her father is but grim.

Boyet. Do you hear, my mad wenches?

Mar. No.

Boyet. What then, do you see?

Ros. Ay, our way to be gone.

Boyet. You are too hard for me. *Exeunt omnes.*

[ACT III.

SCENE I. *The same.*]

Enter [ARMADO *the*] *Braggart and* [MOTH,] *his Boy.*

Arm. Warble, child; make passionate my sense of hearing.

Moth. Concolinel. [*Singing.*]

Arm. Sweet air! Go, tenderness of years; take this key, give enlargement to the swain, bring him festinately hither: I must employ him in a letter to my love.

Moth. Master, will you win your love with a French brawl?

Arm. How meanest thou? brawling in French?

Moth. No, my complete master: but to jig off a tune at the tongue's end, canary to it with your feet, humour it with turning up your eye-lids, sigh a note and sing a note, sometime through the throat, as if you swallowed love with singing love, sometime through the nose, as if you snuffed up love by smelling love; with your hat penthouse-like o'er the shop of your eyes; with your arms crossed on your thin-belly doublet like a rabbit on a spit; or your hands in your pocket like a man after the old painting; and keep not too long in one tune, but a snip and away. These are complements, these are humours; these betray nice wenches, that would be betrayed without these; and make them men of note—do you note? men—that most are affected to these.

Arm. How hast thou purchased this experience?

Moth. By my penny of observation.

Arm. But O,—but O,—

Moth. 'The hobby-horse is forgot.'

Arm. Callest thou my love 'hobby-horse'?

Moth. No, master; the hobby-horse is but a colt, and your love perhaps a hackney. But have you forgot your love?

Arm. Almost I had.

Moth. Negligent student! learn her by heart.

Arm. By heart and in heart, boy.

Moth. And out of heart, master: all those three I will prove.

Arm. What wilt thou prove?

Moth. A man, if I live; and this, by, in, and without, upon the instant: by heart you love her, because your heart cannot come by her; in heart you love her, because your heart is in love with her; and out of heart you love her, being out of heart that you cannot enjoy her.

Arm. I am all these three.

Moth. And three times as much more, and yet nothing at all.

Arm. Fetch hither the swain: he must carry me a letter.

Moth. A message well sympathized; a horse to be ambassador for an ass.

Arm. Ha, ha! what sayest thou?

Moth. Marry, sir, you must send the ass upon the horse, for he is very slow-gaited. But I go.

Arm. The way is but short: away!

Moth. As swift as lead, sir.

Arm. The meaning, pretty ingenious?
Is not lead a metal heavy, dull, and slow?

Moth. Minimè, honest master; or rather, master, no.

Arm. I say lead is slow.

Moth. You are too swift, sir, to say so:
Is that lead slow which is fir'd from a gun?

Arm. Sweet smoke of rhetoric!
He reputes me a cannon; and the bullet, that's he:
I shoot thee at the swain.

Moth. Thump then and I flee. [*Exit.*]

Arm. A most acute juvenal; volable and free of grace!
By thy favour, sweet welkin, I must sigh in thy face:
Most rude melancholy, valour gives thee place.
My herald is return'd.

Enter [MOTH *the*] *Page and* [COSTARD *the*] *Clown.*

Moth. A wonder, master! here's a costard broken in a shin.

Arm. Some enigma, some riddle: come, thy l'envoy; begin.

---

240. **repair,** resort. 246. **margent,** margin of a page of a book; hence, commentary; often used of the eyes, as here, as commenting upon or illuminating the countenance. **quote,** indicate, a figurative application of the meaning "to give a reference." **amazes,** extreme astonishment. 250. **dispos'd,** inclined to be merry; see glossary.

ACT III. SCENE I. 1. **passionate,** sorrowful. 3. **Concolinel.** There are many guesses as to what the word signifies; it is probably the burden or refrain of a song. 5. **enlargement,** release from confinement. 6. **festinately,** hastily. 9. **French brawl,** a kind of dance. 12. **canary,** dance. 16. **sometime,** from time to time; see glossary. 17. **penthouse-like,** i.e., a reference to the Elizabethan custom of building shops and houses with the second story projecting out over the street door. The meaning here is that his hat is worn over his eyes. 21. **old painting,** apparently a reference to some well-known picture. 24. **nice,** wanton; see glossary. 25-26. **men of note,** men of distinction, of importance. 25-26. **note—do you note? men—that.** So the New Cambridge editors punctuate; QF: *note: do you note men that;* Globe, following Hanmer: *note—do you note me?—that.* 28. **penny.** So Globe following Hanmer; Q: *penne.* 30. **hobby-horse,** figure of a horse made of light material and fastened over the torso and head of a morris dancer.

Cost. No egma, no riddle, no l'envoy; no salve †in the mail, sir: O, sir, plantain, a plain plantain! no l'envoy, no l'envoy; no salve, sir, but a plantain!

Arm. By virtue, thou enforcest laughter; thy silly thought my spleen; the heaving of my lungs provokes me to ridiculous smiling. O, pardon me, my stars! Doth the inconsiderate take salve for l'envoy, and the word l'envoy for a salve?

Moth. Do the wise think them other? is not l'envoy a salve?

Arm. No, page: it is an epilogue or discourse, to make plain
Some obscure precedence that hath tofore been sain.
I will example it:
 The fox, the ape and the humble-bee,
 Were still at odds, being but three.
There 's the moral. Now the l'envoy.

Moth. I will add the l'envoy. Say the moral again.

Arm. The fox, the ape, the humble-bee,
 Were still at odds, being but three.

Moth. Until the goose came out of door,
 And stay'd the odds by adding four.
Now will I begin your moral, and do you follow with my l'envoy.
 The fox, the ape and the humble-bee,
 Were still at odds, being but three.

Arm. Until the goose came out of door,
 Staying the odds by adding four.

Moth. A good l'envoy, ending in the goose: would you desire more?

Cost. The boy hath sold him a bargain, a goose, that 's flat.
Sir, your pennyworth is good, an your goose be fat.
To sell a bargain well is as cunning as fast and loose:
Let me see; a fat l'envoy; ay, that 's a fat goose.

Arm. Come hither, come hither. How did this argument begin?

Moth. By saying that a costard was broken in a shin.
Then call'd you for the l'envoy.

Cost. True, and I for a plantain: thus came your argument in;
Then the boy's fat l'envoy, the goose that you bought;
And he ended the market.

Arm. But tell me; how was there a costard broken in a shin?

Moth. I will tell you sensibly.

Cost. Thou hast no feeling of it, Moth: I will speak that l'envoy:
I Costard, running out, that was safely within,
Fell over the threshold, and broke my shin.

Arm. We will talk no more of this matter.

Cost. Till there be more matter in the shin.

Arm. Sirrah Costard, I will enfranchise thee.

Cost. O, marry me to one Frances: I smell some l'envoy, some goose, in this.

Arm. By my sweet soul, I mean setting thee at liberty, enfreedoming thy person: thou wert immured, restrained, captivated, bound.

Cost. True, true; and now you will be my purgation and let me loose.

Arm. I give thee thy liberty, set thee from durance; and, in lieu thereof, impose on thee nothing but this: bear this significant [*giving a letter*] to the country maid Jaquenetta: there is remuneration; for the best ward of mine honour is rewarding my dependents. Moth, follow. [*Exit.*]

Moth. Like the sequel, I. Signior Costard, adieu. *Exit.*

Cost. My sweet ounce of man's flesh! my incony Jew!
Now will I look to his remuneration. Remuneration! O, that 's the Latin word for three farthings: three farthings—remuneration. 'What 's the price of this inkle?'—'One penny.'—'No, I'll give you a remuneration:' why, it carries it. Remuneration! why, it is a fairer name than French crown. I will never buy and sell out of this word.

Enter BEROWNE.

Ber. O, my good knave Costard! exceedingly well met.

Cost. Pray you, sir, how much carnation ribbon may a man buy for a remuneration?

Ber. What is a remuneration?

Cost. Marry, sir, halfpenny farthing.

Ber. Why, then, three-farthing worth of silk.

Cost. I thank your worship: God be wi' you!

Ber. Stay, slave; I must employ thee:
As thou wilt win my favour, good my knave,
Do one thing for me that I shall entreat.

Cost. When would you have it done, sir?

Ber. This afternoon.

Cost. Well, I will do it, sir: fare you well.

Ber. Thou knowest not what it is.

Cost. I shall know, sir, when I have done it.

Ber. Why, villain, thou must know first.

Cost. I will come to your worship to-morrow morning.

Ber. It must be done this afternoon.
Hark, slave, it is but this:
The princess comes to hunt here in the park,
And in her train there is a gentle lady;
When tongues speak sweetly, then they name her name,
And Rosaline they call her: ask for her;
And to her white hand see thou do commend
This seal'd-up counsel. There 's thy guerdon; go.
 [*Giving him a shilling.*]

Cost. Gardon, O sweet gardon! better than remuneration, a 'leven-pence farthing better: most sweet gardon! I will do it, sir, in print. Gardon! Remuneration! *Exit.*

Ber. And I, forsooth, in love! I, that have been love's whip;
A very beadle to a humorous sigh;
A critic, nay, a night-watch constable;
A domineering pedant o'er the boy;

Lines 29-30 are probably a fragment of a popular song; cf. *Hamlet*, III, ii, 144-145. 33. **hackney,** prostitute. 52. **sympathized,** matched. 61. **Minimè,** not at all. 66. **Thump,** representing the sound of cannon. 67. **volable,** quick-witted. 68. **favour,** good will, leave; see glossary. 72. **l'envoy,** a postscript attached to a composition, sometimes a commendatory statement to the reader. 73-75. **egma . . . plantain.** Costard mistakes these strange names for kinds of salve for his broken shin; he wants instead the old-fashioned plantain, an herb whose leaves had cooling properties. Although it is questionable if the pronunciations were identical, *salve* is used with a quibble on the Latin *salve*, i.e., greeting, strictly speaking, the antithesis of *l'envoy*, a parting; apparently, however, a *salve* was a parting also; cf. ll. 79-82. 74. **mail,** pouch, bag; possibly a reference to the mountebank's bag. 77. **spleen,** seat of emotions and passions, held to be the organ which controlled excessive mirth or anger; see glossary. 110-111. **goose . . . market,** an allusion to the proverb, "Three women and a goose make a market." 121. **enfranchise,** release from confinement. 131. **significant,** token; applied here bombastically to a letter. 136. **incony,** rare, delicate. 140. **inkle,** kind of tape. 169. **commend,** entrust. 170. **counsel,** private or secret communication. **guerdon,** reward. 173. **in print,** most exactly.

Than whom no mortal so magnificent!
This wimpled, whining, purblind, wayward boy;
This senior-junior, giant-dwarf, Dan Cupid;
Regent of love-rhymes, lord of folded arms,
Th' anointed sovereign of sighs and groans,
Liege of all loiterers and malcontents,
Dread prince of plackets, king of codpieces,
Sole imperator and great general
Of trotting 'paritors:—O my little heart!—
And I to be a corporal of his field,
And wear his colours like a tumbler's hoop!
What? I love! I sue! I seek a wife!
A woman, that is like a German clock,
Still a-repairing, ever out of frame,
And never going aright, being a watch,
But being watch'd that it may still go right!
Nay, to be perjur'd, which is worst of all;
And, among three, to love the worst of all;
A whitely wanton with a velvet brow,
With two pitch-balls stuck in her face for eyes;
Ay, and, by heaven, one that will do the deed
Though Argus were her eunuch and her guard:
And I to sigh for her! to watch for her!
To pray for her! Go to; it is a plague
That Cupid will impose for my neglect
Of his almighty dreadful little might.
Well, I will love, write, sigh, pray, sue, groan:
Some men must love my lady and some Joan. [*Exit.*]

[ACT IV.

SCENE I. *The same.*]

Enter the PRINCESS, *a* Forester, *her* Ladies, *and her* Lords.

Prin. Was that the king, that spurr'd his horse so hard
Against the steep uprising of the hill?
Boyet. I know not; but I think it was not he.
Prin. Whoe'er 'a was, 'a show'd a mounting mind.
Well, lords, to-day we shall have our dispatch:
On Saturday we will return to France.
Then, forester, my friend, where is the bush
That we must stand and play the murderer in?
For. Hereby, upon the edge of yonder coppice;
A stand where you may make the fairest shoot.
Prin. I thank my beauty, I am fair that shoot,
And thereupon thou speak'st the fairest shoot.
For. Pardon me, madam, for I meant not so.
Prin. What, what? first praise me and again say no?
O short-liv'd pride! Not fair? alack for woe!
For. Yes, madam, fair.
Prin. Nay, never paint me now:
Where fair is not, praise cannot mend the brow.
Here, good my glass, take this for telling true:
Fair payment for foul words is more than due.
For. Nothing but fair is that which you inherit.
Prin. See, see, my beauty will be sav'd by merit!
O heresy in fair, fit for these days!
A giving hand, though foul, shall have fair praise.
But come, the bow: now mercy goes to kill,
And shooting well is then accounted ill.
Thus will I save my credit in the shoot:
Not wounding, pity would not let me do 't;
If wounding, then it was to show my skill,
That more for praise than purpose meant to kill.
And out of question so it is sometimes,
Glory grows guilty of detested crimes,
When, for fame's sake, for praise, an outward part,
We bend to that the working of the heart;
As I for praise alone now seek to spill
The poor deer's blood, that my heart means no ill.
Boyet. Do not curst wives hold that self-sovereignty
Only for praise sake, when they strive to be
Lords o'er their lords?
Prin. Only for praise: and praise we may afford
To any lady that subdues a lord.

Enter [COSTARD *the*] *Clown.*

Boyet. Here comes a member of the commonwealth.
Cost. God dig-you-den all! Pray you, which is the head lady?
Prin. Thou shalt know her, fellow, by the rest that have no heads.
Cost. Which is the greatest lady, the highest?
Prin. The thickest and the tallest.
Cost. The thickest and the tallest! it is so; truth is truth.
An your waist, mistress, were as slender as my wit,
One o' these maids' girdles for your waist should be fit.
Are not you the chief woman? you are the thickest here.
Prin. What's your will, sir? what's your will?
Cost. I have a letter from Monsieur Berowne to one Lady Rosaline.
Prin. O, thy letter, thy letter! he 's a good friend of mine:
Stand aside, good bearer. Boyet, you can carve;
Break up this capon.
Boyet. I am bound to serve.
This letter is mistook, it importeth none here;
It is writ to Jaquenetta.
Prin. We will read it, I swear.
Break the neck of the wax, and every one give ear.
Boyet [*reads*]. 'By heaven, that thou art fair, is most infallible; true, that thou art beauteous; truth itself, that thou art lovely. More fairer than fair, beautiful

181. **wimpled,** blindfold. 188. **'paritors,** apparitors, summoners of ecclesiastical courts. 189. **corporal of his field,** a superior officer of the army in the 16th and 17th centuries, who acted as assistant to the sergeant major (*NED*); cf. IV, iii, 86, note. 191. **What?** So QF; Globe: *What, I!* 193. **Still,** always; see glossary. **a-repairing,** needing repair. 198. **whitely,** pale, sallow; so New Cambridge editors, following Q: *whitley;* F: *whitly;* Globe: *wightly*, i.e., nimble. 201. **Argus,** a fabulous monster with a hundred eyes, some of which were always awake; he was charmed to sleep and slain by Hermes. 202. **watch,** lose sleep; see glossary. 206. **sue, groan.** QF: *shue, groan;* Globe: *sue and groan.* 207. **my lady . . . Joan,** a common antithesis made familiar through the proverb, "Joan's as good as my lady." Joan was a name proverbial for servant girls; cf. *King John*, I, i, 184.

ACT IV. SCENE I. 10. **stand,** flat-roofed building erected for the purpose of giving the hunter a better aim. 16. **paint,** flatter. 18. **good my glass.** The princess' speech embodies a Renaissance commonplace concerning the relation between the ruler and his courtiers. Most to be abhorred was the flatterer, and most valued was the honest counselor who appraised his sovereign truthfully. The princess amuses herself with these ideas, much to the Forester's discomfort. The figure of the honest counselor as a mirror wherein the prince saw himself as he was is frequent. 20. **inherit,** have in possession. 36. **curst,** shrewish; see glossary. 41. **member of the commonwealth,** possibly one of the common folk; perhaps a derisive reference to Navarre's newly ordered court. 42. **God dig-you-den,** God give you good even. 47. **thickest, tallest,** probably a humorous allusion to the stature of the boy who played the part. 56. **Break . . . capon.** Like the French *poulet*, *capon* designates figuratively a love letter. *Break up* is a technical phrase in carving; cf. *break the neck of the wax*, l. 59. 66-67. **king . . . Zenelophon,** another reference to the king and the beggar; cf. I, ii, 114-115. 69. **annothanize,** explain, interpret; probably for "anatomize." 77. **catastrophe,** technical dramatic term, the conclusion of a drama or that which brings about the conclusion. 86. **tittles,** points or dots; specifically applied to the dots commonly printed at the end of the alphabet than beauteous, truer than truth itself, have commiseration on thy heroical vassal! The magnanimous and most illustrate king Cophetua set eye upon the pernicious and indubitate beggar Zenelophon; and he it was that might rightly say, Veni, vidi, vici; which to annothanize in the vulgar,—O base and obscure vulgar!—videlicet, He came, saw, and overcame: he came, one; saw, two; overcame, three. Who came? the king: why did he come? to see: why did he see? to overcome: to whom came he? to the beggar: what saw he? the beggar: who overcame he? the beggar. The conclusion is victory: on whose side? the king's. The captive is enriched: on whose side? the beggar's. The catastrophe is a nuptial: on whose side? the king's: no, on both in one, or one in both. I am the king; for so stands the comparison: thou the beggar; for so witnesseth thy lowliness. Shall I command thy love? I may: shall I enforce thy love? I could: shall I entreat thy love? I will. What shalt thou exchange for rags? robes; for tittles? titles; for thyself? me. Thus, expecting thy reply, I profane my lips on thy foot, my eyes on thy picture, and my heart on thy every part. Thine, in the dearest design of industry,

DON ADRIANO DE ARMADO.'

Thus dost thou hear the Nemean lion roar
'Gainst thee, thou lamb, that standest as his prey.
Submissive fall his princely feet before,
And he from forage will incline to play:
But if thou strive, poor soul, what art thou then?
Food for his rage, repasture for his den.

Prin. What plume of feathers is he that indited this letter?
What vane? what weathercock? did you ever hear better?

Boyet. I am much deceived but I remember the style.

Prin. Else your memory is bad, going o'er it erewhile.

Boyet. This Armado is a Spaniard, that keeps here in court;
A phantasime, a Monarcho, and one that makes sport
To the prince and his bookmates.

Prin. Thou fellow, a word:
Who gave thee this letter?

Cost. I told you; my lord.

Prin. To whom shouldst thou give it?

Cost. From my lord to my lady.

Prin. From which lord to which lady?

Cost. From my lord Berowne, a good master of mine,
To a lady of France that he call'd Rosaline.

Prin. Thou hast mistaken his letter. Come, lords, away.
[*To Ros.*] Here, sweet, put up this: 'twill be thine another day. [*Exeunt Princess and train.*]

Boyet. Who is the suitor? who is the suitor?

Ros. Shall I teach you to know?

Boyet. Ay, my continent of beauty.

Ros. Why, she that bears the bow.
Finely put off!

Boyet. My lady goes to kill horns; but, if thou marry,
Hang me by the neck, if horns that year miscarry.
Finely put on!

Ros. Well, then, I am the shooter.

Boyet. And who is your deer?

Ros. If we choose by the horns, yourself come not near.
Finely put on, indeed!

Mar. You still wrangle with her, Boyet, and she strikes at the brow.

Boyet. But she herself is hit lower: have I hit her now?

Ros. Shall I come upon thee with an old saying, that was a man when King Pepin of France was a little boy, as touching the hit it?

Boyet. So I may answer thee with one as old, that was a woman when Queen Guinover of Britain was a little wench, as touching the hit it.

Ros. Thou canst not hit it, hit it, hit it,
Thou canst not hit it, my good man.

Boyet. An I cannot, cannot, cannot,
An I cannot, another can.

Exit [*Ros. with Kath.*]

Cost. By my troth, most pleasant: how both did fit it!

Mar. A mark marvellous well shot, for they both did hit it.

Boyet. A mark! O, mark but that mark! A mark, says my lady!
Let the mark have a prick in 't, to mete at, if it may be.

Mar. Wide o' the bow hand! i' faith, your hand is out.

Cost. Indeed, 'a must shoot nearer, or he'll ne'er hit the clout.

Boyet. An if my hand be out, then belike your hand is in.

Cost. Then will she get the upshoot by cleaving the pin.

Mar. Come, come, you talk greasily; your lips grow foul.

Cost. She 's too hard for you at pricks, sir: challenge her to bowl.

Boyet. I fear too much rubbing. Good night, my good owl. [*Exeunt Boyet and Maria.*]

Cost. By my soul, a swain! a most simple clown!
Lord, Lord, how the ladies and I have put him down!
O' my troth, most sweet jests! most incony vulgar wit!
When it comes so smoothly off, so obscenely, as it were, so fit.
Armado o' th' one side,—O, a most dainty man!

in horn books. 87. **profane,** desecrate, pollute; a frequent complimentary closing in letters to ladies was, "I kiss your hand." 89. **industry,** zeal; i.e., in her service; hence, gallantry. 90-95. **Thus . . . den.** These lines represent the sonnet which Armado was devising above (I, ii, 190). 90. **Nemean lion.** One of Hercules' labors was to strangle the lion which infested the region of Nemea. 93. **forage,** raging, ravening; i.e., foraging. 95. **repasture,** food. 96. **What plume of feathers,** what kind of bird. 101. **Monarcho,** title assumed by an insane Italian who fancied himself the emperor of the world; hence applied to one who is the object of ridicule for his absurd pretensions (Onions). 110. **suitor,** a play on *shooter*, line 116, archer; the pronunciation was probably identical. The pun, a frequent one, gains point from Cupid's being an archer. 111. **continent,** summary, sum; see glossary. 119. **strikes . . . brow,** takes good aim; i.e., strikes at the brow, antler. 120. **hit lower,** i.e., in the heart. 121. **come upon thee.** Rosaline continues the metaphor from hunting and marksmanship, which is the basis for much of the word-play of this passage. 122. **King Pepin,** a French king of the eighth century; Rosaline refers to the staleness of the saying. 123. **hit it,** catch or round to be sung dancing. 125-126. **Queen Guinover . . . wench.** The name was not a respectable one because of this queen's liaison with Lancelot; there is a probable quibble in *wench* on the meanings "a young girl" and "a prostitute." 127-130. **Thou . . . can,** words of the "hit it" mentioned above. Chappell gives the tune in his *Popular Music of the Olden Time*. 134. **prick,** spot in the center of the target, the bull's eye (with sexual double entendre, as throughout this passage). **mete at,** measure with the eye; i.e., aim at. 135. **Wide . . . hand,** wide of the mark on the left side; i.e., too far to the left. **out,** aimed the wrong way; see glossary. 136. **clout,** nail marking the center of the target. 139. **greasily,** grossly. 141. **rubbing,** the striking together of the bowling balls (with sexual double entendre). 145. **obscenely,** another of Costard's malapropisms. 146. **dainty,** refined, elegant see glossary.

To see him walk before a lady and to bear her fan!
To see him kiss his hand! and how most sweetly 'a
will swear!
And his page o' t'other side, that handful of wit!
Ah, heavens, it is a most pathetical nit!
Sola, sola! *Shout within.*
Exit [Costard, running].

[SCENE II. *The same.*]

Enter DULL, HOLOFERNES *the Pedant, and* NATHANIEL.

Nath. Very reverend sport, truly; and done in the testimony of a good conscience.

Hol. The deer was, as you know, sanguis, in blood; ripe as the pomewater, who now hangeth like a jewel in the ear of caelo, the sky, the welkin, the heaven; and anon falleth like a crab on the face of terra, the soil, the land, the earth.

Nath. Truly, Master Holofernes, the epithets are sweetly varied, like a scholar at the least: but, sir, I assure ye, it was a buck of the first head.

Hol. Sir Nathaniel, haud credo.

Dull. 'Twas not a haud credo; 'twas a pricket.

Hol. Most barbarous intimation! yet a kind of insinuation, as it were, in via, in way, of explication; facere, as it were, replication, or rather, ostentare, to show, as it were, his inclination, after his undressed, unpolished, uneducated, unpruned, untrained, or rather, unlettered, or ratherest, unconfirmed fashion, to insert again my haud credo for a deer.

Dull. I said the deer was not a haud credo; 'twas a pricket.

Hol. Twice-sod simplicity, bis coctus!
O thou monster Ignorance, how deformed dost thou
look!

Nath. Sir, he hath never fed of the dainties that are
bred in a book;
he hath not eat paper, as it were; he hath not drunk ink: his intellect is not replenished; he is only an animal, only sensible in the duller parts:
And such barren plants are set before us, that we
thankful should be,
Which we of taste and feeling are, for those parts that
do fructify in us more than he.
For as it would ill become me to be vain, indiscreet,
or a fool,
So were there a patch set on learning, to see him in a
school:
But omne bene, say I; being of an old father's mind,
Many can brook the weather that love not the wind.

Dull. You two are book-men: can you tell me by
your wit
What was a month old at Cain's birth, that 's not five
weeks old as yet?

Hol. Dictynna, goodman Dull; Dictynna, goodman
Dull.

Dull. What is Dictynna?

Nath. A title to Phœbe, to Luna, to the moon.

Hol. The moon was a month old when Adam was
no more,
And raught not to five weeks when he came to five-
score.
The allusion holds in the exchange.

Dull. 'Tis true indeed; th' collusion holds in the
exchange.

Hol. God comfort thy capacity! I say, th' allusion holds in the exchange.

Dull. And I say, the pollusion holds in the exchange; for the moon is never but a month old: and I say beside that, 'twas a pricket that the princess killed.

Hol. Sir Nathaniel, will you hear an extemporal epitaph on the death of the deer? And, to humour the ignorant, call I the deer the princess killed a pricket.

Nath. Perge, good Master Holofernes, perge; so it shall please you to abrogate scurrility.

Hol. I will something affect the letter, for it argues facility.

The preyful princess pierc'd and prick'd a pretty
pleasing pricket;
Some say a sore; but not a sore, till now made sore
with shooting.
The dogs did yell; put L to sore, then sorel jumps from
thicket;
Or pricket sore, or else sorel; the people fall
a-hooting.
If sore be sore, then L to sore makes fifty sores one
sorel.
Of one sore I an hundred make by adding but one
more L.

Nath. A rare talent!

Dull. [*Aside*] If a talent be a claw, look how he claws him with a talent.

Hol. This is a gift that I have, simple, simple; a foolish extravagant spirit, full of forms, figures, shapes, objects, ideas, apprehensions, motions, revolutions: these are begot in the ventricle of memory, nourished in the womb of pia mater, and delivered upon the mellowing of occasion. But the gift is good in those in whom it is acute, and I am thankful for it.

Nath. Sir, I praise the Lord for you: and so may my parishioners; for their sons are well tutored by you, and their daughters profit very greatly under you: you are a good member of the commonwealth.

Hol. Mehercle, if their sons be ingenuous, they shall want no instruction; if their daughters be capable, I

150. **nit,** egg of a small insect; hence, anything very small, often contemptuously applied.

SCENE II. 4. **pomewater,** a kind of apple, large and juicy. 11. **haud credo,** I cannot believe it. 12. **pricket,** buck in its second year, or, as Nathaniel has already said, *a buck of the first head.* 23. **Twice-sod,** sodden. **bis coctus,** twice cooked, insipid. 28. **sensible,** capable of perception; see glossary. 32. **patch,** fool, dolt; i.e., setting a fool to learn. 33. **omne bene,** all is well. **mind,** opinion; see glossary. 34. **Many . . . wind,** apparently a current but unidentified proverb. **brook,** endure; see glossary. 37, 39. **Dictynna, Phœbe, Luna.** classical names for the moon. The first is uncommon and is appropriate to the pedant. It occurs in Golding's Ovid, a book which Shakespeare knew. 41. **raught,** attained; an old past tense of "reach." 42. **allusion,** likening, application; or perhaps, jest—an obsolete meaning. **exchange,** change; the riddle usually appeared with Adam instead of Cain. 54. **Perge,** proceed. 56. **something,** somewhat; see glossary. **affect the letter,** use alliteration. 59. **sore,** a buck in its fourth year. 60. **sorel,** a buck in its third year. 66. **claws,** flatters. 69. **motions,** impulses; see glossary. 71. **pia mater,** the brain. 80. **Mehercle,** a mild oath; probably a corruption of "By Hercules." 81. **want,** lack; see glossary. 82. **capable,** intelligent; see glossary. 82-83. **vir . . . loquitur,** he is a wise man who speaks little. 85, 86, 89. **pers-on, pierced, piercing.** The pronunciation of the root syllables was probably identical. These are sometimes taken as allusions to Nashe's *Pierce Penniless, His Supplication to the Devil*, a fantastic satire in which the author, in the character of Pierce, comments on the vices of the times; also to Harvey's answer, *Pierce's Supererogation.* In the latter Pierce is referred to as "the hogges-head of witt"; cf. l. 89. 89-90. **lustre of conceit,** gleam of the intelligence. 95-97. **Fauste . . . Mantuan,** "I pray thee, Faustus, while the cattle chew their cud in the cool shade. . . ." This is the first line of the first eclogue of the Renaissance poet, Mantuan. It was no doubt familiar to every schoolboy. QF have *Facile* will put it to them: but vir sapit qui pauca loquitur; a soul feminine saluteth us.

Enter JAQUENETTA *and* [COSTARD] *the Clown.*

Jaq. God give you good morrow, master Parson.

Hol. Master Parson, quasi pers-on. An if one should be pierced, which is the one?

Cost. Marry, master schoolmaster, he that is likest to a hogshead.

Hol. Of piercing a hogshead! a good lustre of conceit in a turf of earth; fire enough for a flint, pearl enough for a swine: 'tis pretty; it is well.

Jaq. Good master Parson, be so good as read me this letter: it was given me by Costard, and sent me from Don Armado: I beseech you, read it.

Hol. Fauste, precor gelida quando pecus omne sub umbra Ruminat,—and so forth. Ah, good old Mantuan! I may speak of thee as the traveller doth of Venice;

Venetia, Venetia,
Chi non ti vede non ti pretia.

Old Mantuan, old Mantuan! who understandeth thee not, loves thee not. Ut, re, sol, la, mi, fa. Under pardon, sir, what are the contents? or rather, as Horace says in his—What, my soul, verses?

Nath. Ay, sir, and very learned.

Hol. Let me hear a staff, a stanze, a verse; lege, domine.

Nath. [*reads*]
If love make me forsworn, how shall I swear to love?
Ah, never faith could hold, if not to beauty vow'd!
Though to myself forsworn, to thee I'll faithful prove;
Those thoughts to me were oaks, to thee like osiers bow'd.
Study his bias leaves and makes his book thine eyes,
Where all those pleasures live that art would comprehend:
If knowledge be the mark, to know thee shall suffice;
Well learned is that tongue that well can thee commend,
All ignorant that soul that sees thee without wonder;
Which is to me some praise that I thy parts admire:
Thy eye Jove's lightning bears, thy voice his dreadful thunder,
Which, not to anger bent, is music and sweet fire.
Celestial as thou art, O, pardon love this wrong,
That sings heaven's praise with such an earthly tongue.

Hol. You find not the apostraphas, and so miss the accent: let me supervise the canzonet. Here are only numbers ratified; but, for the elegancy, facility, and golden cadence of poesy, caret. Ovidius Naso was the man: and why, indeed, Naso, but for smelling out the odoriferous flowers of fancy, the jerks of invention? Imitari is nothing: so doth the hound his master, the ape his keeper, the tired horse his rider. But, damosella virgin, was this directed to you?

Jaq. Ay, sir, from one Monsieur Berowne, one of the strange queen's lords.

Hol. I will overglance the superscript: 'To the snow-white hand of the most beauteous Lady Rosaline.' I will look again on the intellect of the letter, for the nomination of the party writing to the person written unto: 'Your ladyship's in all desired employment, BEROWNE.' Sir Nathaniel, this Berowne is one of the votaries with the king; and here he hath framed a letter to a sequent of the stranger queen's, which accidentally, or by the way of progression, hath miscarried. Trip and go, my sweet; deliver this paper into the royal hand of the king: it may concern much. Stay not thy compliment; I forgive thy duty: adieu.

Jaq. Good Costard, go with me. Sir, God save your life!

Cost. Have with thee, my girl. *Exit* [*with Jaq.*].

Nath. Sir, you have done this in the fear of God, very religiously; and, as a certain father saith,—

Hol. Sir, tell not me of the father; I do fear colourable colours. But to return to the verses: did they please you, Sir Nathaniel?

Nath. Marvellous well for the pen.

Hol. I do dine to-day at the father's of a certain pupil of mine; where, if, before repast, it shall please you to gratify the table with a grace, I will, on my privilege I have with the parents of the foresaid child or pupil, undertake your ben venuto; where I will prove those verses to be very unlearned, neither savouring of poetry, wit, nor invention: I beseech your society.

Nath. And thank you too; for society, saith the text, is the happiness of life.

Hol. And, certes, the text most infallibly concludes it. [*To Dull*] Sir, I do invite you too; you shall not say me nay: pauca verba. Away! the gentles are at their game, and we will to our recreation. *Exeunt.*

[SCENE III. *The same.*]

Enter BEROWNE, *with a paper in his hand, alone.*

Ber. The king he is hunting the deer; I am coursing myself: they have pitched a toil; I am toiling in a pitch,—pitch that defiles: defile! a foul word. Well, set thee down, sorrow! for so they say the fool said, and so say I, and I the fool: well proved, wit! By the Lord, this love is as mad as Ajax: it kills sheep; it kills me, I a sheep: well proved again o' my side! I will not love: if I do, hang me; i' faith, I will not. O, but her eye,—by this light, but for her eye, I would

for *Fauste*, which was corrected by Theobald. The correction is adopted by most editors, although some retain the misquotation, thus impugning the pedant's Latin. 99-100. **Venetia . . . pretia.** Venice, Venice, who sees thee not esteems thee not. 102. **Ut . . . fa.** If Holofernes intends here to sing the hexachord, he displays his ignorance. 108. **lege, domine,** read, Master. 109-122. **If . . . tongue.** These lines were printed in *The Passionate Pilgrim* (1599), a collection of poems by various authors but attributed to Shakespeare. Two others of the volume are from this play, that read by Longaville (IV, iii, 60-73) and that by Dumaine (IV, iii, 101-120). 113. **bias,** inclination or bent; i.e., the student leaves his special study; see glossary. 123. **apostrophas,** apostrophes, punctuation marks used to indicate omitted vowels and shortened pronunciation of a word. 124. **supervise,** glance over, peruse. 125. **only numbers ratified,** i.e., merely language made metrical, or perhaps merely conventional verse. The author of the "extemporal epitaph on the death of the deer" is criticizing Berowne's lines for their lack of genuine poetic feeling. 127. **caret,** it is wanting. **Naso,** from Latin *nasus*, nose. 129. **invention,** the creative faculty; see glossary. **Imitari,** to imitate. 134. **strange,** foreign; see glossary. 135. **superscript,** address. 137. **intellect,** meaning, import; hence, contents. 142. **sequent,** follower, attendant. 143-144. **by . . . progression,** in process of delivery. 151. **Have with thee,** I'll go with you; see glossary. 156. **colourable colours,** plausible pretexts; probably a quibbling allusion to the "colors" of rhetoric; see glossary. 164. **ben venuto,** welcome. 171. **pauca verba,** few words. 172. **gentles,** gentle folk.

SCENE III. 2. **coursing,** pursuing. **pitched a toil,** set a snare. 3. **toiling . . . pitch,** generally taken as a quibbling reference to Rosaline's eyes, which he has earlier (III, i, 199) called *two pitch-balls*. 7. **mad as Ajax,** an allusion to the fable of Ajax, who, maddened by his failure in a contest for Achilles' armor, attacked a flock of sheep, supposing them to be a hostile army.

not love her; yes, for her two eyes. Well, I do nothing in the world but lie, and lie in my throat. By heaven, I do love: and it hath taught me to rhyme and to be melancholy; and here is part of my rhyme, and here my melancholy. Well, she hath one o' my sonnets already: the clown bore it, the fool sent it, and the lady hath it: sweet clown, sweeter fool, sweetest lady! By the world, I would not care a pin, if the other three were in. Here comes one with a paper: God give him grace to groan! *He stands aside.*

The KING *entereth* [*with a paper*].

King. Ay me!

Ber. [*Aside*] Shot, by heaven! Proceed, sweet Cupid: thou hast thumped him with thy bird-bolt under the left pap. In faith, secrets!

King [*reads*].

So sweet a kiss the golden sun gives not
To those fresh morning drops upon the rose,
As thy eye-beams, when their fresh rays have smote
The night of dew that on my cheeks down flows:
Nor shines the silver moon one half so bright
Through the transparent bosom of the deep,
As doth thy face through tears of mine give light;
Thou shin'st in every tear that I do weep:
No drop but as a coach doth carry thee;
So ridest thou triumphing in my woe.
Do but behold the tears that swell in me,
And they thy glory through my grief will show:
But do not love thyself; then thou wilt keep
My tears for glasses, and still make me weep.
O queen of queens! how far dost thou excel,
No thought can think, nor tongue of mortal tell.
How shall she know my griefs? I'll drop the paper:
Sweet leaves, shade folly. Who is he comes here?

Enter LONGAVILLE [*with a paper*]. *The* KING *steps aside.*

What, Longaville! and reading! listen, ear.

Ber. Now, in thy likeness, one more fool appear!

Long. Ay me, I am forsworn!

Ber. Why, he comes in like a perjure, wearing papers.

King. In love, I hope: sweet fellowship in shame!

Ber. One drunkard loves another of the name.

Long. Am I the first that have been perjur'd so?

Ber. I could put thee in comfort. Not by two that I know:
Thou makest the triumviry, the corner-cap of society,
The shape of Love's Tyburn that hangs up simplicity.

Long. I fear these stubborn lines lack power to move.
O sweet Maria, empress of my love!
These numbers will I tear, and write in prose.

Ber. O, rhymes are guards on wanton Cupid's hose:
Disfigure not his shop.

Long. This same shall go.

He reads the sonnet.

Did not the heavenly rhetoric of thine eye,
'Gainst whom the world cannot hold argument,
Persuade my heart to this false perjury?
Vows for thee broke deserve not punishment.
A woman I forswore; but I will prove,
Thou being a goddess, I forswore not thee:
My vow was earthly, thou a heavenly love;
Thy grace being gain'd cures all disgrace in me.
Vows are but breath, and breath a vapour is:
Then thou, fair sun, which on my earth dost shine,
Exhal'st this vapour-vow; in thee it is:
If broken then, it is no fault of mine:
If by me broke, what fool is not so wise
To lose an oath to win a paradise?

Ber. This is the liver-vein, which makes flesh a deity,
A green goose a goddess: pure, pure idolatry.
God amend us, God amend! we are much out o' th' way.

Enter DUMAINE [*with a paper*].

Long. By whom shall I send this?—Company! stay. [*Steps aside.*]

Ber. All hid, all hid; an old infant play.
Like a demigod here sit I in the sky,
And wretched fools' secrets heedfully o'er-eye.
More sacks to the mill! O heavens, I have my wish!
Dumaine transform'd! four woodcocks in a dish!

Dum. O most divine Kate!

Ber. O most profane coxcomb!

Dum. By heaven, the wonder in a mortal eye!

Ber. By earth, she is not, corporal, there you lie.

Dum. Her amber hair for foul hath amber quoted.

Ber. An amber-colour'd raven was well noted.

Dum. As upright as the cedar.

Ber. Stoop, I say;
Her shoulder is with child.

Dum. As fair as day.

Ber. Ay, as some days; but then no sun must shine.

Dum. O that I had my wish!

Long. And I had mine!

King. And I mine too, good Lord!

Ber. Amen, so I had mine: is not that a good word?

Dum. I would forget her; but a fever she
Reigns in my blood and will rememb'red be.

Ber. A fever in your blood! why, then incision
Would let her out in saucers: sweet misprision!

Dum. Once more I'll read the ode that I have writ.

Ber. Once more I'll mark how love can vary wit.

Dumaine reads his sonnet.

On a day—alack the day!—
Love, whose month is ever May,
Spied a blossom passing fair
Playing in the wanton air:
Through the velvet leaves the wind,
All unseen, can passage find;
That the lover, sick to death,
Wish himself the heaven's breath.

47. **perjure,** perjurer. 48. **wearing papers,** an allusion to the custom of attaching to a felon's breast a description of his offense; there is a glance here at the poem Longaville is carrying. 54. **Tyburn,** a reference to the triangular gallows at Tyburn hill. 58. **guards,** embroideries. 59. **shop,** slang for codpiece, a baggy pouch at the fly of a man's "hose," or breeches. 60-73. **Did . . . paradise.** Cf. IV, ii, 109-122, note. 74. **liver-vein,** the vein or style of a lover, since the liver was assumed to be the seat of the passions. 75. **green goose.** Cf. I, i, 97, note. 81. **More . . . mill,** a proverbial expression, "there's more to come." 82. **woodcocks,** birds typifying stupidity. 85. **mortal,** human; see glossary.

86. **she . . . corporal.** Several explanations have been offered. Theobald emended to *she is but corporal*, a reading adopted by several editors. The New Cambridge editors define *corporal* as "champion," adding that in the sixteenth century there were four "corporals of the field" in every regiment. Note that in III, i, 189, Berowne refers to himself as corporal of Cupid's field. 87. **quoted,** designated. 89. **Stoop,** usually taken as the antithesis of *upright* in the preceding speech. Berowne means that Dumaine's language is too lofty. 90. **shoulder . . . child,** i.e., describing her posture, which is not as Dumaine has said, *upright as the cedar*. 94. **is . . . word?** Is that not kind of me? (Hart). 97. **incision,** letting

Air, quoth he, thy cheeks may blow;
Air, would I might triumph so!
But, alack, my hand is sworn
Ne'er to pluck thee from thy thorn;
Vow, alack, for youth unmeet,
Youth so apt to pluck a sweet!
Do not call it sin in me,
That I am forsworn for thee;
Thou for whom Jove would swear
Juno but an Ethiope were;
And deny himself for Jove,
Turning mortal for thy love.
This will I send and something else more plain,
That shall express my true love's fasting pain.
O, would the king, Berowne, and Longaville,
Were lovers too! Ill, to example ill,
Would from my forehead wipe a perjur'd note;
For none offend where all alike do dote.
Long. [*advancing*]. Dumaine, thy love is far from charity,
That in love's grief desir'st society:
You may look pale, but I should blush, I know,
To be o'erheard and taken napping so.
King [*advancing*]. Come, sir, you blush; as his your case is such;
You chide at him, offending twice as much;
You do not love Maria! Longaville
Did never sonnet for her sake compile,
Nor never lay his wreathed arms athwart
His loving bosom to keep down his heart!
I have been closely shrouded in this bush
And mark'd you both and for you both did blush:
I heard your guilty rhymes, observ'd your fashion,
Saw sighs reek from you, noted well your passion:
Ay me! says one; O Jove! the other cries;
One, her hairs were gold, crystal the other's eyes:
[*To Long.*] You would for paradise break faith and troth;
[*To Dum.*] And Jove, for your love, would infringe an oath.
What will Berowne say when that he shall hear
Faith so infringed, which such zeal did swear?
How will he scorn! how will he spend his wit!
How will he triumph, leap and laugh at it!
For all the wealth that ever I did see,
I would not have him know so much bv me.
Ber. Now step I forth to whip hypocrisy. [*Advancing.*]
Ah, good my liege, I pray thee, pardon me!
Good heart, what grace hast thou, thus to reprove
These worms for loving, that art most in love?
Your eyes do make no coaches; in your tears
There is no certain princess that appears;
You'll not be perjur'd, 'tis a hateful thing;
Tush, none but minstrels like of sonneting!
But are you not ashamed? nay, are you not,
All three of you, to be thus much o'ershot?
You found his mote; the king your mote did see;
But I a beam do find in each of three.
O, what a scene of fool'ry have I seen,
Of sighs, of groans, of sorrow and of teen!
O me, with what strict patience have I sat,
To see a king transformed to a gnat!
To see great Hercules whipping a gig,
And profound Solomon to tune a jig,
And Nestor play at push-pin with the boys,
And critic Timon laugh at idle toys!
Where lies thy grief, O, tell me, good Dumaine?
And, gentle Longaville, where lies thy pain?
And where my liege's? all about the breast:
A caudle, ho!
King. Too bitter is thy jest.
Are we betray'd thus to thy over-view?
Ber. Not you to me, but I betray'd by you:
I, that am honest; I, that hold it sin
To break the vow I am engaged in;
I am betray'd, by keeping company
†With men like you, men of inconstancy.
When shall you see me write a thing in rhyme?
Or groan for love? or spend a minute's time
In pruning me? When shall you hear that I
Will praise a hand, a foot, a face, an eye,
A gait, a state, a brow, a breast, a waist,
A leg, a limb?
King. Soft! whither away so fast?
A true man or a thief that gallops so?
Ber. I post from love: good lover, let me go.

Enter JAQUENETTA *and* [COSTARD *the*] *Clown.*

Jaq. God bless the king!
King. What present hast thou there?
Cost. Some certain treason.
King. What makes treason here?
Cost. Nay, it makes nothing, sir.
King. If it mar nothing neither,
The treason and you go in peace away together.
Jaq. I beseech your grace, let this letter be read:
Our parson misdoubts it; 'twas treason, he said.
King. Berowne, read it over.
He [*Berowne*] *reads the letter.*
Where hadst thou it?
Jaq. Of Costard.
King. Where hadst thou it?
Cost. Of Dun Adramadio, Dun Adramadio.
[*Berowne tears the letter.*]
King. How now! what is in you? why dost thou tear it?
Ber. A toy, my liege, a toy: your grace needs not fear it.
Long. It did move him to passion, and therefore let 's hear it.
Dum. It is Berowne's writing, and here is his name.
[*Gathering up the pieces.*]
Ber. [*To Costard*] Ah, you whoreson loggerhead! you were born to do me shame.
Guilty, my lord, guilty! I confess, I confess.
King. What?
Ber. That you three fools lack'd me fool to make up the mess:

blood. 98. **saucers,** saucerfuls. **misprision,** mistake. 101-120. **On . . . love.** Cf. IV, ii, 109-122, note. 124. **example ill,** furnish a bad example. 135-136. **wreathed . . . bosom,** a conventional pose of the lover. 140. **passion,** amorous disposition. 145. **when that,** when. 155. **coaches,** an allusion to the king's sonnet, where this conceit is employed (l. 34). 160. **o'ershot,** wide of the mark; i.e., in error. 164. **teen,** affliction, grief. 169. **Nestor,** a Greek chieftain in the Trojan War. The reference here is to his extreme old age and to his reputation for sagacity. 170. **Timon,** a citizen of Athens in the fifth century B.C., notorious for his misanthropy. He is the central figure of Shakespeare's play, *Timon of Athens.* **toys,** trifles; see glossary. 174. **caudle,** warm drink given to sick people. 178. **engaged in,** sworn to; see *engage* in glossary. 180. **men like you, men,** *you* omitted in QF; a corrupt phrase for which there are many conjectures: *men-like men; moon-like men;* etc. 183. **pruning,** preening; i.e., trimming, dressing up. 188. **post,** hasten; see glossary. 190. **makes treason,** has treason to do; see *make* in glossary. 194. **misdoubts,** suspects; see glossary.

He, he, and you, and you, my liege, and I,
Are pick-purses in love, and we deserve to die.
O, dismiss this audience, and I shall tell you more.
Dum. Now the number is even.
Ber. True, true; we are four.
Will these turtles be gone?
King. Hence, sirs; away!
Cost. Walk aside the true folk, and let the traitors stay. [*Exeunt Costard and Jaquenetta.*]
Ber. Sweet lords, sweet lovers, O, let us embrace!
As true we are as flesh and blood can be:
The sea will ebb and flow, heaven show his face;
Young blood doth not obey an old decree:
We cannot cross the cause why we were born;
Therefore of all hands must we be forsworn.
King. What, did these rent lines show some love of thine?
Ber. Did they, quoth you? Who sees the heavenly Rosaline,
That, like a rude and savage man of Ind,
At the first opening of the gorgeous east,
Bows not his vassal head and strucken blind
Kisses the base ground with obedient breast?
What peremptory eagle-sighted eye
Dares look upon the heaven of her brow,
That is not blinded by her majesty?
King. What zeal, what fury hath inspir'd thee now?
My love, her mistress, is a gracious moon;
She an attending star, scarce seen a light.
Ber. My eyes are then no eyes, nor I Berowne:
O, but for my love, day would turn to night!
Of all complexions the cull'd sovereignty
Do meet, as at a fair, in her fair cheek,
Where several worthies make one dignity,
Where nothing wants that want itself doth seek.
Lend me the flourish of all gentle tongues,—
Fie, painted rhetoric! O, she needs it not:
To things of sale a seller's praise belongs,
She passes praise; then praise too short doth blot.
A wither'd hermit, five-score winters worn,
Might shake off fifty, looking in her eye:
Beauty doth varnish age, as if new-born,
And gives the crutch the cradle's infancy:
O, 'tis the sun that maketh all things shine.
King. By heaven, thy love is black as ebony.
Ber. Is ebony like her? O wood divine!
A wife of such wood were felicity.
O, who can give an oath? where is a book?
That I may swear beauty doth beauty lack,
If that she learn not of her eye to look:
No face is fair that is not full so black.
King. O paradox! Black is the badge of hell,
The hue of dungeons and the school of night;
And beauty's crest becomes the heavens well.
Ber. Devils soonest tempt, resembling spirits of light.
O, if in black my lady's brows be deck'd,
It mourns that painting and usurping hair
Should ravish doters with a false aspect;
And therefore is she born to make black fair.
Her favour turns the fashion of the days,
For native blood is counted painting now;
And therefore red, that would avoid dispraise,
Paints itself black, to imitate her brow.
Dum. To look like her are chimney-sweepers black.
Long. And since her time are colliers counted bright.
King. And Ethiopes of their sweet complexion crack.
Dum. Dark needs no candles now, for dark is light.
Ber. Your mistresses dare never come in rain,
For fear their colours should be wash'd away.
King. 'Twere good, yours did; for, sir, to tell you plain,
I'll find a fairer face not wash'd to-day.
Ber. I'll prove her fair, or talk till doomsday here.
King. No devil will fright thee then so much as she.
Dum. I never knew man hold vile stuff so dear.
Long. Look, here's thy love: my foot and her face see. [*Showing his shoe.*]
Ber. O, if the streets were paved with thine eyes,
Her feet were much too dainty for such tread!
Dum. O vile! then, as she goes, what upward lies
The street should see as she walk'd overhead.
King. But what of this? are we not all in love?
Ber. Nothing so sure; and thereby all forsworn.
King. Then leave this chat; and, good Berowne, now prove
Our loving lawful, and our faith not torn.
Dum. Ay, marry, there; some flattery for this evil.
Long. O, some authority how to proceed;
Some tricks, some quillets, how to cheat the devil.
Dum. Some salve for perjury.
Ber. O! 'tis more than need.
Have at you, then, affection's men at arms.
Consider what you first did swear unto,
To fast, to study, and to see no woman;
Flat treason 'gainst the kingly state of youth.
Say, can you fast? your stomachs are too young;
And abstinence engenders maladies.
And where that you have vow'd to study, lords,
In that each of you have forsworn his book,
Can you still dream and pore and thereon look?
For when would you, my lord, or you, or you,
Have found the ground of study's excellence
Without the beauty of a woman's face?
[From women's eyes this doctrine I derive;
They are the ground, the books, the academes
From whence doth spring the true Promethean fire.]
Why, universal plodding poisons up
The nimble spirits in the arteries,
As motion and long-during action tires
The sinewy vigour of the traveller.
Now, for not looking on a woman's face,

222. **Ind,** usually written "Inde," a very common name in the sixteenth century for India. 231. **scarce . . . light,** a light scarcely to be seen. 234. **cull'd,** chosen; i.e., the others are culls. 236. **worthies,** excellencies. 241. **praise . . . blot,** inadequate praise detracts. 255. **school,** as in QF. Many emendations have been proposed: *scowl*, *stole*, *soul*, *soil*, *scroll*, *shroud*, *seal*, etc. Some of those disposed to retain the original reading think it may have a contemporary reference to an actual group of poets or scholars known as the School of Night. 256. **beauty's crest,** i.e., brightness. 262. **favour,** countenance; see glossary. 288. **quillets,** verbal niceties, subtle distinctions; see glossary. 290. **Have at you,** I come at you, i.e., listen to me; see glossary. 293. **state,** majesty; see glossary. 302-304. These lines seem out of place and repetitive; regarded as evidence of revision. 304. **Promethean fire,** divine fire, from the legend that Prometheus stole fire from heaven and gave it to mankind; cf. *Othello*, V, ii, 12. 305. **poisons,** so Globe, following QF; Theobald: prisons. 324. **entirely,** without intermission. 329. **elements,** i.e., earth, air, fire, and water. 336. **head of theft**, i.e., ears of a thief. 354. **aught,** anything. 370. **glozes**, sophistries. 375. **attach,** seize; see glossary. 383. **Allons!** Let's be going! 384. **measure,** proportion; see glossary. 385. **Light,** frivolous, merry; also

You have in that forsworn the use of eyes
And study too, the causer of your vow;
For where is any author in the world
Teaches such beauty as a woman's eye?
Learning is but an adjunct to ourself
And where we are our learning likewise is:
Then when ourselves we see in ladies' eyes,
Do we not likewise see our learning there?
O, we have made a vow to study, lords,
And in that vow we have forsworn our books.
For when would you, my liege, or you, or you,
In leaden contemplation have found out
Such fiery numbers as the prompting eyes
Of beauty's tutors have enrich'd you with?
Other slow arts entirely keep the brain;
And therefore, finding barren practisers,
Scarce show a harvest of their heavy toil:
But love, first learned in a lady's eyes,
Lives not alone immured in the brain;
But, with the motion of all elements,
Courses as swift as thought in every power,
And gives to every power a double power,
Above their functions and their offices.
It adds a precious seeing to the eye;
A lover's eyes will gaze an eagle blind;
A lover's ear will hear the lowest sound,
When the suspicious head of theft is stopp'd:
Love's feeling is more soft and sensible
Than are the tender horns of cockled snails;
Love's tongue proves dainty Bacchus gross in taste:
For valour, is not Love a Hercules,
Still climbing trees in the Hesperides?
Subtle as Sphinx; as sweet and musical
As bright Apollo's lute, strung with his hair;
And when Love speaks, the voice of all the gods
Make heaven drowsy with the harmony.
Never durst poet touch a pen to write
Until his ink were temp'red with Love's sighs;
O, then his lines would ravish savage ears
And plant in tyrants mild humility.
From women's eyes this doctrine I derive:
They sparkle still the right Promethean fire;
They are the books, the arts, the academes,
That show, contain and nourish all the world:
Else none at all in aught proves excellent.
Then fools you were these women to forswear,
Or keeping what is sworn, you will prove fools.
For wisdom's sake, a word that all men love,
Or for love's sake, a word that loves all men,
Or for men's sake, the authors of these women,
Or women's sake, by whom we men are men,
Let us once lose our oaths to find ourselves,
Or else we lose ourselves to keep our oaths.
It is religion to be thus forsworn,
For charity itself fulfils the law,
And who can sever love from charity?

King. Saint Cupid, then! and, soldiers, to the field!

Ber. Advance your standards, and upon them, lords;
Pell-mell, down with them! but be first advis'd,
In conflict that you get the sun of them.

Long. Now to plain-dealing; lay these glozes by:
Shall we resolve to woo these girls of France?

King. And win them too: therefore let us devise
Some entertainment for them in their tents.

Ber. First, from the park let us conduct them thither;
Then homeward every man attach the hand
Of his fair mistress: in the afternoon
We will with some strange pastime solace them,
Such as the shortness of the time can shape;
For revels, dances, masks and merry hours
Forerun fair Love, strewing her way with flowers.

King. Away, away! no time shall be omitted
That will betime, and may by us be fitted.

Ber. Allons! allons! Sow'd cockle reap'd no corn;
And justice always whirls in equal measure:
Light wenches may prove plagues to men forsworn;
If so, our copper buys no better treasure. [*Exeunt*.]

[ACT V.

SCENE I. *The same.*]

Enter [HOLOFERNES] *the Pedant*, [NATHANIEL] *the Curate, and* DULL [*the Constable*].

Hol. Satis quid sufficit.

Nath. I praise God for you, sir: your reasons at dinner have been sharp and sententious: pleasant without scurrility, witty without affection, audacious without impudency, learned without opinion, and strange without heresy. I did converse this quondam day with a companion of the king's, who is intituled, nominated, or called, Don Adriano de Armado.

Hol. Novi hominem tanquam te: his humour is lofty, his discourse peremptory, his tongue filed, his eye ambitious, his gait majestical, and his general behaviour vain, ridiculous, and thrasonical. He is too picked, too spruce, too affected, too odd, as it were, too peregrinate, as I may call it.

Nath. A most singular and choice epithet.

Draw out his table-book.

Hol. He draweth out the thread of his verbosity finer than the staple of his argument. I abhor such fanatical phantasimes, such insociable and point-devise companions; such rackers of orthography, as to speak dout, fine, when he should say doubt; det, when he should pronounce debt,—d, e, b, t, not d, e, t: he clepeth a calf, cauf; half, hauf; neighbour vocatur nebour; neigh abbreviated ne. This is abhominable,—which he would call abbominable: it insinuateth †me of insanie: ne intelligis, domine? to make frantic, lunatic.

Nath. Laus Deo, bene intelligo.

wanton, with quibble.

ACT V. SCENE I. 1. **quid,** so QF; Globe, following Rowe and others in correcting the pedant's faulty Latin: *quod*. The phrase is the equivalent of the proverb, "Enough is as good as a feast." 6. **opinion,** self-conceit, arrogance; see glossary. 7. **this quondam,** the other. 10. **Novi . . . te,** I know the man as well as I know you. 11. **peremptory,** positive, overbearing. 12. **filed,** polished. 14. **thrasonical,** boastful. 15. **peregrinate,** having the manner of one who has traveled. 17. *Stage Direction:* ***table-book,*** notebook. 21. **point-devise,** extremely precise. **companions,** fellows (used contemptuously); see glossary. 21-22. **rackers of orthography.** Holofernes' tirade represents a conscious attempt of Renaissance educators to conform the English spelling and pronunciation of certain borrowed words more nearly to their Latin originals. 22. **fine,** mincingly. 26. **abhominable.** Here Holofernes' pedantry has run aground; the word is derived from the Latin *ab* + *omen* (a foreboding) and not from *ab* + *homine*. 28. **ne,** so QF; Globe: *anne*. **ne . . . domine?** Do you understand, Master? 30. **Laus . . . intelligo,** praise God, I understand well.

Hol. Bon, bon, fort bon! Priscian a little scratched, 'twill serve.

Enter [Armado *the*] *Braggart,* [Moth, *his*] *Boy* [, *and* Costard].

Nath. Videsne quis venit?

Hol. Video, et gaudeo.

Arm. Chirrah! [*To Moth.*]

Hol. Quare chirrah, not sirrah?

Arm. Men of peace, well encountered.

Hol. Most military sir, salutation.

Moth. [*Aside to Costard*] They have been at a great feast of languages, and stolen the scraps.

Cost. O, they have lived long on the alms-basket of words. I marvel thy master hath not eaten thee for a word; for thou art not so long by the head as honorificabilitudinitatibus: thou art easier swallowed than a flap-dragon.

Moth. Peace! the peal begins.

Arm. [*To Hol.*] Monsieur, are you not lettered?

Moth. Yes, yes; he teaches boys the horn-book. What is a, b, spelt backward, with the horn on his head?

Hol. Ba, pueritia, with a horn added.

Moth. Ba, most silly sheep with a horn. You hear his learning.

Hol. Quis, quis, thou consonant?

Moth. The third of the five vowels, if you repeat them; or the fifth, if I.

Hol. I will repeat them,—a, e, i,—

Moth. The sheep: the other two concludes it,—o, u.

Arm. Now, by the salt wave of the Mediterraneum, a sweet touch, a quick venue of wit! snip, snap, quick and home! it rejoiceth my intellect: true wit!

Moth. Offered by a child to an old man; which is wit-old.

Hol. What is the figure? what is the figure?

Moth. Horns.

Hol. Thou disputes like an infant: go, whip thy gig.

Moth. Lend me your horn to make one, and I will whip about your infamy circum circa,—a gig of a cuckold's horn.

Cost. An I had but one penny in the world, thou shouldst have it to buy gingerbread: hold, there is the very remuneration I had of thy master, thou halfpenny purse of wit, thou pigeon-egg of discretion. O, an the heavens were so pleased that thou wert but my bastard, what a joyful father wouldst thou make me! Go to; thou hast it ad dunghill, at the fingers' ends, as they say.

Hol. O, I smell false Latin; dunghill for unguem.

Arm. Arts-man, preambulate, we will be singuled from the barbarous. Do you not educate youth at the charge-house on the top of the mountain?

Hol. Or mons, the hill.

Arm. At your sweet pleasure, for the mountain.

Hol. I do, sans question.

Arm. Sir, it is the king's most sweet pleasure and affection to congratulate the princess at her pavilion in the posteriors of this day, which the rude multitude call the afternoon.

Hol. The posterior of the day, most generous sir, is liable, congruent and measurable for the afternoon: the word is well culled, chose, sweet and apt, I do assure you, sir, I do assure.

Arm. Sir, the king is a noble gentleman, and my familiar, I do assure ye, very good friend: for what is inward between us, let it pass. I do beseech thee, remember thy courtesy; I beseech thee, apparel thy head: and among other importunate and most serious designs, and of great import indeed, too, but let that pass: for I must tell thee, it will please his grace, by the world, sometime to lean upon my poor shoulder, and with his royal finger, thus, dally with my excrement, with my mustachio; but, sweet heart, let that pass. By the world, I recount no fable: some certain special honours it pleaseth his greatness to impart to Armado, a soldier, a man of travel, that hath seen the world; but let that pass. The very all of all is,—but, sweet heart, I do implore secrecy,—that the king would have me present the princess, sweet chuck, with some delightful ostentation, or show, or pageant, or antique, or firework. Now, understanding that the curate and your sweet self are good at such eruptions and sudden breaking out of mirth, as it were, I have acquainted you withal, to the end to crave your assistance.

Hol. Sir, you shall present before her the Nine Worthies. Sir Nathaniel, as concerning some entertainment of time, some show in the posterior of this day, to be rendered by our assistance, the king's command, and this most gallant, illustrate, and learned gentleman, before the princess; I say none so fit as to present the Nine Worthies.

Nath. Where will you find men worthy enough to present them?

Hol. †Joshua, yourself; myself and this gallant gentleman, Judas Maccabæus; this swain, because of his great limb or joint, shall pass Pompey the Great; the page, Hercules,—

Arm. Pardon, sir; error: he is not quantity enough for that Worthy's thumb: he is not so big as the end of his club.

Hol. Shall I have audience? he shall present Hercules in minority: his enter and exit shall be strangling a snake; and I will have an apology for that purpose.

Moth. An excellent device! so, if any of the audience

31. **Bon . . . Priscian.** QF: *Bome boon for boon prescian.* There are several suggested emendations. Theobald's *Bone? bone for bene* calls for emending *bene* to *bone* in the preceding speech. This reading has been favored by some editors. **Priscian,** a grammarian; Holofernes means, "Your Latin is a little faulty." 33. **Videsne quis venit?** Do you see who comes? 34. **Video, et gaudeo,** I see and I rejoice. This trivial Latin dialogue is after the manner of schoolboys' exercises. 36. **Quare,** why. 44. **honorificabilitudinitatibus,** reputably the longest known word. It is an inflected form of a genuine medieval Latin word, meaning something like "honorableness." 45. **flap-dragon,** the raisin or plum in burning brandy to be snapped with the mouth in the game of snapdragon. 52. **pueritia,** boyhood. 55. **Quis,** who. 62. **venue,** a thrust in fencing. 63. **home,** effectually, to the quick; see glossary. 66. **wit-old,** mentally feeble, with quibble on "wittol," a cuckold. 69. **disputes,** reasonest; see glossary. 72. **circum circa,** round and round; Theobald's emendation of QF *vnum cita,* which has not been satisfactorily explained. Perhaps Furness is right in assuming that it is a fragment of schoolboy nonsense rhyme. 84. **unguem.** *Ad unguem* (to a nicety, perfectly) were the last words of a proverbial expression used of a lesson well learned; probably recited to schoolboys by their masters. It is not unlikely that we have in *ad dunghill* a schoolboys' perversion of the phrase. 85. **singuled,** singled out. 87. **charge-house,** a reference not identified. Hart suggests that it may mean a school where children were taught at the expense of the parish, or merely a school for their charge or care. 91. **sans,** without; see glossary. 105. **importunate,** so Q_2Ff; Globe: *important,* following Capell's rendering of Q_1: *importunt.* 109. **excrement,** outgrowth (of hair). 117. **chuck,** i.e., chick, a term of endearment. 118. **pageant,** spectacular entertainment; see glossary. 124. **Nine Worthies,** a conventional subject familiar to Shakespeare's audience in poems, pageants, and tapestries. The nine were three pagans, Hector of Troy, Alexander the Great, and Julius Caesar; three Jews, Joshua, David, and

hiss, you may cry 'Well done, Hercules! now thou crushest the snake!' that is the way to make an offence gracious, though few have the grace to do it.

Arm. For the rest of the Worthies?—

Hol. I will play three myself.

Moth. Thrice-worthy gentleman!

Arm. Shall I tell you a thing?

Hol. We attend.

Arm. We will have, if this fadge not, an antique. I beseech you, follow.

Hol. Via, goodman Dull! thou hast spoken no word all this while.

Dull. Nor understood none neither, sir.

Hol. Allons! we will employ thee.

Dull. I'll make one in a dance, or so; or I will play
On the tabor to the Worthies, and let them dance the hay.

Hol. Most dull, honest Dull! To our sport, away!
Exeunt.

[SCENE II. *The same.*]

Enter the Ladies [*the* PRINCESS, KATHARINE, ROSALINE, *and* MARIA].

Prin. Sweet hearts, we shall be rich ere we depart,
If fairings come thus plentifully in:
A lady wall'd about with diamonds!
Look you what I have from the loving king.

Ros. Madame, came nothing else along with that?

Prin. Nothing but this! yes, as much love in rhyme
As would be cramm'd up in a sheet of paper,
Writ o' both sides the leaf, margent and all,
That he was fain to seal on Cupid's name.

Ros. That was the way to make his godhead wax,
For he hath been five thousand years a boy.

Kath. Ay, and a shrewd unhappy gallows too.

Ros. You'll ne'er be friends with him; a' kill'd your sister.

Kath. He made her melancholy, sad, and heavy;
And so she died: had she been light, like you,
Of such a merry, nimble, stirring spirit,
She might ha' been a grandam ere she died:
And so may you; for a light heart lives long.

Ros. What 's your dark meaning, mouse, of this light word?

Kath. A light condition in a beauty dark.

Ros. We need more light to find your meaning out.

Kath. You'll mar the light by taking it in snuff;
Therefore I'll darkly end the argument.

Ros. Look, what you do, you do it still i' th' dark.

Kath. So do not you, for you are a light wench.

Ros. Indeed I weigh not you, and therefore light.

Kath. You weigh me not? O, that 's you care not for me.

Ros. Great reason; for 'past cure is still past care.'

Prin. Well bandied both; a set of wit well play'd.
But, Rosaline, you have a favour too:
Who sent it? and what is it?

Ros. I would you knew:
An if my face were but as fair as yours,
My favour were as great; be witness this.
Nay, I have verses too, I thank Berowne:
The numbers true; and, were the numb'ring too,
I were the fairest goddess on the ground:
I am compar'd to twenty thousand fairs.
O, he hath drawn my picture in his letter!

Prin. Any thing like?

Ros. Much in the letters; nothing in the praise.

Prin. Beauteous as ink; a good conclusion.

Kath. Fair as a text B in a copy-book.

Ros. 'Ware pencils, ho! let me not die your debtor,
My red dominical, my golden letter:
O that your face were not so full of O's!

Kath. A pox of that jest! and I beshrew all shrows.

Prin. But, Katharine, what was sent to you from fair Dumaine?

Kath. Madam, this glove.

Prin. Did he not send you twain?

Kath. Yes, madam, and moreover
Some thousand verses of a faithful lover,
A huge translation of hypocrisy,
Vilely compil'd, profound simplicity.

Mar. This and these pearls to me sent Longaville:
The letter is too long by half a mile.

Prin. I think no less. Dost thou not wish in heart
The chain were longer and the letter short?

Mar. Ay, or I would these hands might never part.

Prin. We are wise girls to mock our lovers so.

Ros. They are worse fools to purchase mocking so.
That same Berowne I'll torture ere I go:
O that I knew he were but in by th' week!
How I would make him fawn and beg and seek
And wait the season and observe the times
And spend his prodigal wits in bootless rhymes
And shape his service wholly to my hests
And make him proud to make me proud that jests!
†So perttaunt-like would I o'ersway his state
That he should be my fool and I his fate.

Prin. None are so surely caught, when they are catch'd,
As wit turn'd fool: folly, in wisdom hatch'd,
Hath wisdom's warrant and the help of school
And wit's own grace to grace a learned fool.

Ros. The blood of youth burns not with such excess
As gravity's revolt to wantonness.

Mar. Folly in fools bears not so strong a note
As foolery in the wise, when wit doth dote;
Since all the power thereof it doth apply

Judas Maccabaeus; and three Christians, Arthur, Charlemagne, and Godfrey of Bouillon. Shakespeare does not adhere to this list but introduces Pompey and Hercules. 130. **present,** represent; see glossary. 142. **strangling a snake.** According to legend, Hercules as an infant displayed his great strength by strangling two serpents sent by the envious Juno to destroy him in his cradle. 154. **fadge,** fit, be suitable. 156. **Via,** an interjection of encouragement, used by commanders to their troops and by riders to their horses. 161. **the hay,** a country dance.

SCENE II. 2. **fairings,** complimentary gifts. 10. **wax,** increase, with quibble on the noun. 12. **shrewd,** bad; see glossary. **unhappy,** ill-fated; see glossary. **gallows,** one deserving to be hanged. 19. **mouse,** term of endearment. 20. **condition,** disposition, temperament; see glossary. 22. **taking . . . snuff,** taking offense, with quibble on *snuff*, a burning candlewick. 44. **dominical,** from the Latin *dies dominica* (Lord's day). It is customary in ecclesiastical calendars (see, for example, the *Book of Common Prayer*) to designate the day in January on which the first Sunday falls by one of the first seven letters of the alphabet—*A* when it falls on New Year's Day, *B* when it falls on the second, etc., up to *G*. This is called the dominical letter for the year. It was often printed in red and gold on church calendars to denote Sundays. Here it refers quibblingly to Katharine's fair complexion. 46. **beshrew,** curse, blame; see glossary. **shrows,** shrews. 57. **Ay . . . part.** This speech is probably accompanied by some stage business with the chain that Maria is handling. 61. **in . . . week,** caught, trapped; contemporary uses of the phrase indicate that it may imply conditions of servitude or imprisonment. (See Furness Variorum.) 67. **perttaunt-like,** so Q; of the many emendations suggested, *planet-like* (New Cambridge) is the most convincing; Hanmer's *portent-like* deserves consideration. As it stands, it probably means, like one holding a winning hand (pair-taunt) in the card game of "post and pair."

To prove, by wit, worth in simplicity.

Enter BOYET.

Prin. Here comes Boyet, and mirth is in his face.
Boyet. O, I am stabb'd with laughter! Where 's her grace?
Prin. Thy news, Boyet?
Boyet. Prepare, madam, prepare!
Arm, wenches, arm! encounters mounted are
Against your peace: Love doth approach disguis'd,
Armed in arguments; you'll be surpris'd:
Muster your wits; stand in your own defence;
Or hide your heads like cowards, and fly hence.
Prin. Saint Denis to Saint Cupid! What are they
That charge their breath against us? say, scout, say.
Boyet. Under the cool shade of a sycamore
I thought to close mine eyes some half an hour;
When, lo! to interrupt my purpos'd rest,
Toward that shade I might behold addrest
The king and his companions: warily
I stole into a neighbour thicket by,
And overheard what you shall overhear;
That, by and by, disguis'd they will be here.
Their herald is a pretty knavish page,
That well by heart hath conn'd his embassage:
Action and accent did they teach him there;
'Thus must thou speak,' and 'thus thy body bear:'
And ever and anon they made a doubt
Presence majestical would put him out;
'For,' quoth the king, 'an angel shalt thou see;
Yet fear not thou, but speak audaciously.'
The boy replied, 'An angel is not evil;
I should have fear'd her had she been a devil.'
With that, all laugh'd and clapp'd him on the shoulder,
Making the bold wag by their praises bolder:
One rubb'd his elbow thus, and fleer'd and swore
A better speech was never spoke before;
Another, with his finger and his thumb,
Cried, 'Via! we will do 't, come what will come;'
The third he caper'd, and cried, 'All goes well;'
The fourth turn'd on the toe, and down he fell.
With that, they all did tumble on the ground,
With such a zealous laughter, so profound,
That in this spleen ridiculous appears,
To check their folly, passion's solemn tears.
Prin. But what, but what, come they to visit us?
Boyet. They do, they do; and are apparell'd thus,
Like Muscovites or Russians, as I guess.
Their purpose is to parle, to court and dance;
And every one his love-feat will advance
Unto his several mistress, which they'll know
By favours several which they did bestow.
Prin. And will they so? the gallants shall be task'd;
For, ladies, we will every one be mask'd;
And not a man of them shall have the grace,
Despite of suit, to see a lady's face.
Hold, Rosaline, this favour thou shalt wear,
And then the king will court thee for his dear;
Hold, take thou this, my sweet, and give me thine,
So shall Berowne take me for Rosaline.
And change you favours too; so shall your loves
Woo contrary, deceiv'd by these removes.
Ros. Come on, then; wear the favours most in sight.
Kath. But in this changing what is your intent?
Prin. The effect of my intent is to cross theirs:
They do it but in mockery-merriment;
And mock for mock is only my intent.
Their several counsels they unbosom shall
To loves mistook, and so be mock'd withal
Upon the next occasion that we meet,
With visages display'd, to talk and greet.
Ros. But shall we dance, if they desire us to 't?
Prin. No, to the death, we will not move a foot;
Nor to their penn'd speech render we no grace,
But while 'tis spoke each turn away her face.
Boyet. Why, that contempt will kill the speaker's heart,
And quite divorce his memory from his part.
Prin. Therefore I do it; and I make no doubt
The rest will ne'er come in, if he be out.
There 's no such sport as sport by sport o'erthrown,
To make theirs ours and ours none but our own:
So shall we stay, mocking intended game,
And they, well mock'd, depart away with shame.
Sound trumpet.
Boyet. The trumpet sounds: be mask'd; the maskers come. [*The Ladies mask.*]

Enter Blackamoors with music; [MOTH] *the Boy, with a speech, and* [*the* KING, BEROWNE, *and*] *the rest of the* Lords *disguised* [*in Russian habits*].

Moth. All hail, the richest beauties on the earth!—
Boyet. Beauties no richer than rich taffeta.
Moth. A holy parcel of the fairest dames
The Ladies turn their backs to him.
That ever turn'd their—backs—to mortal views!
Ber. [*Aside to Moth*] Their eyes, villain, their eyes.
Moth. That ever turn'd their eyes to mortal views!—
Out—
Boyet. True; out indeed.
Moth. Out of your favours, heavenly spirits, vouchsafe
Not to behold—
Ber. [*Aside to Moth*] Once to behold, rogue.
Moth. Once to behold with your sun-beamed eyes,
——with your sun-beamed eyes—
Boyet. They will not answer to that epithet;
You were best call it 'daughter-beamed eyes.'
Moth. They do not mark me, and that brings me out.
Ber. Is this your perfectness? be gone, you rogue!
[*Exit Moth.*]
Ros. What would these strangers? know their minds, Boyet:
If they do speak our language, 'tis our will
That some plain man recount their purposes:
Know what they would.
Boyet. What would you with the princess?
Ber. Nothing but peace and gentle visitation.

82. **encounters,** encounterers. **mounted,** raised; the figure implied is of an artillery attack; cf. *charge,* l. 88. 87. **Saint Denis,** patron saint of France. 92. **might,** could; see *may* in glossary. **addrest,** approaching. 95. **overhear,** hear over again. 98. **embassage,** message. 101. **made a doubt,** were apprehensive; see *doubt* in glossary. 117. **spleen ridiculous,** excess of mirth. 121. **Muscovites or Russians,** costumes not uncommon in court masquerades. 122. **parle,** parley; see glossary. 126. **task'd,** tried, tested. 129. **suit,** petition, entreaty. 135. **removes,** removals, changes; see glossary. 136. **most in sight,** conspicuously. 139. **mockery-merriment,** so Q; Globe, following F: *mocking merriment.* 141. **counsels,** private intentions, secret purposes. 144. **greet,** be amicably together (Schmidt). 152. **if . . . out,** if he be confused or annoyed. 159. **taffeta,** i.e., their masks of taffeta. 160. **parcel,** small party or company. 174. **What would,** etc. Rosaline, masked as the princess, presides over the occasion. 184. **measur'd,** traversed, with quibble; see glossary. 200. **accompt,** reckoning. 206. **eyne,** eyes;

Ros. What would they, say they?
Boyet. Nothing but peace and gentle visitation.
Ros. Why, that they have; and bid them so be gone.
Boyet. She says, you have it, and you may be gone.
King. Say to her, we have measur'd many miles
To tread a measure with her on this grass.
Boyet. They say, that they have measur'd many a mile
To tread a measure with you on this grass.
Ros. It is not so. Ask them how many inches
Is in one mile: if they have measur'd many,
The measure then of one is eas'ly told.
Boyet. If to come hither you have measur'd miles,
And many miles, the princess bids you tell
How many inches doth fill up one mile.
Ber. Tell her, we measure them by weary steps.
Boyet. She hears herself.
Ros. How many weary steps,
Of many weary miles you have o'ergone,
Are numb'red in the travel of one mile?
Ber. We number nothing that we spend for you:
Our duty is so rich, so infinite,
That we may do it still without accompt.
Vouchsafe to show the sunshine of your face,
That we, like savages, may worship it.
Ros. My face is but a moon, and clouded too.
King. Blessed are clouds, to do as such clouds do!
Vouchsafe, bright moon, and these thy stars, to shine,
Those clouds remov'd, upon our watery eyne.
Ros. O vain petitioner! beg a greater matter;
Thou now requests but moonshine in the water.
King. Then, in our measure do but vouchsafe one change.
Thou bid'st me beg: this begging is not strange.
Ros. Play, music, then! Nay, you must do it soon.
[*Music plays.*]
Not yet! no dance! Thus change I like the moon.
King. Will you not dance? How come you thus estranged?
Ros. You took the moon at full, but now she 's changed.
King. Yet still she is the moon, and I the man.
The music plays; vouchsafe some motion to it.
Ros. Our ears vouchsafe it.
King. But your legs should do it.
Ros. Since you are strangers and come here by chance,
We'll not be nice: take hands. We will not dance.
King. Why take we hands, then?
Ros. Only to part friends:
Curtsy, sweet hearts; and so the measure ends.
King. More measure of this measure; be not nice.
Ros. We can afford no more at such a price.
King. Price you yourselves: what buys your company?
Ros. Your absence only.
King. That can never be.
Ros. Then cannot we be bought: and so, adieu;
Twice to your visor, and half once to you.
King. If you deny to dance, let 's hold more chat.
Ros. In private, then.
King. I am best pleas'd with that.
[*They converse apart.*]
Ber. White-handed mistress, one sweet word with thee.
Prin. Honey, and milk, and sugar; there is three.
Ber. Nay then, two treys, and if you grow so nice,
Metheglin, wort, and malmsey: well run, dice!
There 's half-a-dozen sweets.
Prin. Seventh sweet, adieu:
Since you can cog, I'll play no more with you.
Ber. One word in secret.
Prin. Let it not be sweet.
Ber. Thou grievest my gall.
Prin. Gall! bitter.
Ber. Therefore meet. [*They converse apart.*]
Dum. Will you vouchsafe with me to change a word?
Mar. Name it.
Dum. Fair lady,—
Mar. Say you so? Fair lord,—
Take that for your fair lady.
Dum. Please it you,
As much in private, and I'll bid adieu.
[*They converse apart.*]
Kath. What, was your vizard made without a tongue?
Long. I know the reason, lady, why you ask.
Kath. O for your reason! quickly, sir; I long.
Long. You have a double tongue within your mask,
And would afford my speechless vizard half.
Kath. Veal, quoth the Dutchman. Is not 'veal' a calf?
Long. A calf, fair lady!
Kath. No, a fair lord calf.
Long. Let 's part the word.
Kath. No, I'll not be your half:
Take all, and wean it; it may prove an ox.
Long. Look, how you butt yourself in these sharp mocks!
Will you give horns, chaste lady? do not so.
Kath. Then die a calf, before your horns do grow.
Long. One word in private with you, ere I die.
Kath. Bleat softly then; the butcher hears you cry.
[*They converse apart.*]
Boyet. The tongues of mocking wenches are as keen
As is the razor's edge invisible,
Cutting a smaller hair than may be seen,
Above the sense of sense; so sensible
Seemeth their conference; their conceits have wings
Fleeter than arrows, bullets, wind, thought, swifter things.
Ros. Not one word more, my maids; break off, break off.
Ber. By heaven, all dry-beaten with pure scoff!
King. Farewell, mad wenches; you have simple wits.
Exeunt [*King, Lords, and Blackamoors*].
Prin. Twenty adieus, my frozen Muscovits.
Are these the breed of wits so wondered at?
Boyet. Tapers they are, with your sweet breaths puff'd out.

archaic plural. 208. **moonshine in the water,** proverbial expression for a waste of time. 209. **change,** round in dancing (Schmidt). 227. **Twice . . . you.** Rosaline means her courtesy is not given to the king, for whom she has none to spare; but to the mask which is identical with Berowne's (Hart). 228. **deny,** refuse; see glossary. 233. **Metheglin,** a spiced drink made from herbs and honey. **wort,** sweet unfermented beer. **malmsey,** a strong sweet wine. 235. **cog,** cheat; see glossary. 247. **Veal,** quibble on the Dutch pronunciation of "well" and the meaning "calf" (Schmidt); also, possibly, "dunce"; the Cambridge editors took *Dutchman* to mean German and *veal* to be equivalent to German *viel,* i.e., much. The word is introduced irrelevantly for the sake of the subsequent word-play. 259. **Above . . . sense,** quibble on the meanings "mental" and "physical perception"; see *sense* in glossary. 263. **dry-beaten,** beaten soundly without blood drawn. 264. **simple,** common, not distinguished by any excellence.

Ros. Well-liking wits they have; gross, gross; fat, fat.
Prin. O poverty in wit, kingly-poor flout!
Will they not, think you, hang themselves to-night?
Or ever, but in vizards, show their faces?
This pert Berowne was out of count'nance quite.
Ros. O, they were all in lamentable cases!
The king was weeping-ripe for a good word.
Prin. Berowne did swear himself out of all suit.
Mar. Dumaine was at my service, and his sword:
No point, quoth I; my servant straight was mute.
Kath. Lord Longaville said, I came o'er his heart;
And trow you what he call'd me?
Prin. Qualm, perhaps.
Kath. Yes, in good faith.
Prin. Go, sickness as thou art!
Ros. Well, better wits have worn plain statute-caps.
But will you hear? the king is my love sworn.
Prin. And quick Berowne hath plighted faith to me.
Kath. And Longaville was for my service born.
Mar. Dumaine is mine, as sure as bark on tree.
Boyet. Madam, and pretty mistresses, give ear:
Immediately they will again be here
In their own shapes; for it can never be
They will digest this harsh indignity.
Prin. Will they return?
Boyet. They will, they will, God knows,
And leap for joy, though they are lame with blows:
Therefore change favours; and, when they repair,
Blow like sweet roses in this summer air.
Prin. How blow? how blow? speak to be understood.
Boyet. Fair ladies mask'd are roses in their bud;
Dismask'd, their damask sweet commixture shown,
Are angels vailing clouds, or roses blown.
Prin. Avaunt, perplexity! What shall we do,
If they return in their own shapes to woo?
Ros. Good madam, if by me you 'll be advis'd,
Let 's mock them still, as well known as disguis'd:
Let us complain to them what fools were here,
Disguis'd like Muscovites, in shapeless gear;
And wonder what they were and to what end
Their shallow shows and prologue vilely penn'd
And their rough carriage so ridiculous,
Should be presented at our tent to us.
Boyet. Ladies, withdraw: the gallants are at hand.
Prin. Whip to our tents, as roes run o'er land.
Exeunt [*Princess, Rosaline, Katharine, and Maria*].

Enter the KING *and the rest* [BEROWNE, LONGAVILLE, *and* DUMAINE, *in their proper habits*].

King. Fair sir, God save you! Where 's the princess?
Boyet. Gone to her tent. Please it your majesty
Command me any service to her thither?
King. That she vouchsafe me audience for one word.
Boyet. I will; and so will she, I know, my lord. *Exit.*
Ber. This fellow pecks up wit as pigeons pease,
And utters it again when God doth please:
He is wit's pedler, and retails his wares
At wakes and wassails, meetings, markets, fairs;
And we that sell by gross, the Lord doth know,
Have not the grace to grace it with such show.
This gallant pins the wenches on his sleeve;
Had he been Adam, he had tempted Eve;
'A can carve too, and lisp: why, this is he
That kiss'd his hand away in courtesy;
This is the ape of form, monsieur the nice,
That, when he plays at tables, chides the dice
In honourable terms: nay, he can sing
A mean most meanly; and in ushering
Mend him who can: the ladies call him sweet;
The stairs, as he treads on them, kiss his feet:
This is the flower that smiles on every one,
To show his teeth as white as whale's bone;
And consciences, that will not die in debt,
Pay him the due of honey-tongu'd Boyet.
King. A blister on his sweet tongue, with my heart,
That put Armado's page out of his part!

Enter the Ladies [*with* BOYET].

Ber. See where it comes! Behaviour, what wert thou
Till this madman show'd thee? and what art thou now?
King. All hail, sweet madam, and fair time of day!
Prin. 'Fair' in 'all hail' is foul, as I conceive.
King. Construe my speeches better, if you may.
Prin. Then wish me better; I will give you leave.
King. We came to visit you, and purpose now
To lead you to our court; vouchsafe it then.
Prin. This field shall hold me; and so hold your vow:
Nor God, nor I, delights in perjur'd men.
King. Rebuke me not for that which you provoke:
The virtue of your eye must break my oath.
Prin. You nickname virtue: vice you should have spoke;
For virtue's office never breaks men's troth.
Now by my maiden honour, yet as pure
As the unsullied lily, I protest,
A world of torments though I should endure,
I would not yield to be your house's guest;
So much I hate a breaking cause to be
Of heavenly oaths, vow'd with integrity.
King. O, you have liv'd in desolation here,
Unseen, unvisited, much to our shame.
Prin. Not so, my lord; it is not so, I swear;
We have had pastimes here and pleasant game:
A mess of Russians left us but of late.
King. How, madam! Russians!
Prin. Ay, in truth, my lord:
Trim gallants, full of courtship and of state.
Ros. Madam, speak true. It is not so, my lord:
My lady, to the manner of the days,
In courtesy gives undeserving praise.
We four indeed confronted were with four
In Russian habit: here they stay'd an hour,
And talk'd apace; and in that hour, my lord,
They did not bless us with one happy word.
I dare not call them fools; but this I think,

268. **Well-liking,** in good condition, plump. 269. **kingly-poor flout,** poor mockery of a king (Schmidt); the New Cambridge editors see here a reversal of *Well-liking* in Rosaline's speech (l. 268): king-ly-poor, not well-ly-king. 274. **weeping-ripe,** ready to weep. 277. **No point,** quibble on the meaning "sword's point" and the French negative *ne point* (not at all); cf. II, i, 190. **straight,** immediately; see glossary. 279. **trow you,** would you believe; see glossary. **Qualm,** pronounced as "calm," with quibble; *came* in the preceding line probably approximated the same pronunciation. 281. **statute-caps,** woolen caps ordered by act of Parliament (1571) to be worn "upon the Saboth and Holy Daye," by "all and every person and persons above Thage of syxe yeres," except women and certain officials (Onions). Hart thinks the *plain statute-caps* were those worn by London apprentices. 289. **digest,** put up with; see glossary. 292. **repair,** return. 297. **vailing,** letting fall, lowering; see glossary. The line has caused some perplexity because *vailing* (French *avaler*) has been confused with "veiling." Johnson paraphrased: Ladies unmasked are like angels vailing clouds, or letting those clouds which obscured their brightness sink from before them.

When they are thirsty, fools would fain have drink.
Ber. This jest is dry to me. Fair gentle sweet,
Your wits makes wise things foolish: when we greet,
With eyes best seeing, heaven's fiery eye,
By light we lose light: your capacity
Is of that nature that to your huge store
Wise things seem foolish and rich things but poor.
Ros. This proves you wise and rich, for in my eye,—
Ber. I am a fool, and full of poverty.
Ros. But that you take what doth to you belong,
It were a fault to snatch words from my tongue.
Ber. O, I am yours, and all that I possess!
Ros. All the fool mine?
Ber. I cannot give you less.
Ros. Which of the vizards was it that you wore?
Ber. Where? when? what vizard? why demand you this?
Ros. There, then, that vizard; that superfluous case
That hid the worse and show'd the better face.
King. We were descried; they'll mock us now downright.
Dum. Let us confess and turn it to a jest.
Prin. Amaz'd, my lord? why looks your highness sad?
Ros. Help, hold his brows! he'll swoon! Why look you pale?
Sea-sick, I think, coming from Muscovy.
Ber. Thus pour the stars down plagues for perjury.
Can any face of brass hold longer out?
Here stand I: lady, dart thy skill at me;
Bruise me with scorn, confound me with a flout;
Thrust thy sharp wit quite through my ignorance;
Cut me to pieces with thy keen conceit;
And I will wish thee never more to dance,
Nor never more in Russian habit wait.
O, never will I trust to speeches penn'd,
Nor to the motion of a schoolboy's tongue,
Nor never come in vizard to my friend,
Nor woo in rhyme, like a blind harper's song!
Taffeta phrases, silken terms precise,
Three-pil'd hyperboles, spruce affectation,
Figures pedantical; these summer-flies
Have blown me full of maggot ostentation:
I do forswear them; and I here protest,
By this white glove,—how white the hand, God knows!—
Henceforth my wooing mind shall be express'd
In russet yeas and honest kersey noes:
And, to begin, wench,—so God help me, la!—
My love to thee is sound, sans crack or flaw.
Ros. Sans sans, I pray you.
Ber. Yet I have a trick
Of the old rage: bear with me, I am sick;
I'll leave it by degrees. Soft, let us see:
Write, 'Lord have mercy on us' on those three;
They are infected; in their hearts it lies;
They have the plague, and caught it of your eyes;
These lords are visited; you are not free,
For the Lord's tokens on you do I see.
Prin. No, they are free that gave these tokens to us.
Ber. Our states are forfeit: seek not to undo us.
Ros. It is not so; for how can this be true,
That you stand forfeit, being those that sue?
Ber. Peace! for I will not have to do with you.
Ros. Nor shall not, if I do as I intend.
Ber. Speak for yourselves; my wit is at an end.
King. Teach us, sweet madam, for our rude transgression
Some fair excuse.
Prin. The fairest is confession.
Were not you here but even now disguis'd?
King. Madam, I was.
Prin. And were you well advis'd?
King. I was, fair madam.
Prin. When you then were here,
What did you whisper in your lady's ear?
King. That more than all the world I did respect her.
Prin. When she shall challenge this, you will reject her.
King. Upon mine honour, no.
Prin. Peace, peace! forbear:
Your oath once broke, you force not to forswear.
King. Despise me, when I break this oath of mine.
Prin. I will: and therefore keep it. Rosaline,
What did the Russian whisper in your ear?
Ros. Madam, he swore that he did hold me dear
As precious eyesight, and did value me
Above this world; adding thereto moreover
That he would wed me, or else die my lover.
Prin. God give thee joy of him! the noble lord
Most honourably doth uphold his word.
King. What mean you, madam? by my life, my troth,
I never swore this lady such an oath.
Ros. By heaven, you did; and to confirm it plain,
You gave me this: but take it, sir, again.
King. My faith and this the princess I did give:
I knew her by this jewel on her sleeve.
Prin. Pardon me, sir, this jewel did she wear;
And Lord Berowne, I thank him, is my dear.
What, will you have me, or your pearl again?
Ber. Neither of either; I remit both twain.
I see the trick on 't: here was a consent,
Knowing aforehand of our merriment,
To dash it like a Christmas comedy:
Some carry-tale, some please-man, some slight zany,
Some mumble-news, some trencher-knight, some Dick,
That smiles his cheek in years and knows the trick
To make my lady laugh when she 's dispos'd,
Told our intents before; which once disclos'd,
The ladies did change favours: and then we,
Following the signs, woo'd but the sign of she.
Now, to our perjury to add more terror,
We are again forsworn, in will and error.
Much upon this it is: and might not you [*To Boyet.*]
Forestall our sport, to make us thus untrue?

303. **shapeless,** unshapely, ugly. **gear,** apparel; see glossary. 309. **Whip,** move quickly. 315. **pease,** plural of "pea." 319. **by gross,** by wholesale. 323. **carve,** show courtesy and affability. 328. **mean,** a middle voice. **meanly,** moderately well. **ushering,** introducing, as a forerunner or harbinger. 329. **Mend,** improve on. 337. **it,** contemptuous reference to Boyet. 349. **nickname,** mention by mistake. 368. **habit,** costume; see glossary. 374. **wits,** so QF; Globe: *wit*. **greet,** regard, look on. 386. **demand,** inquire; see glossary. 389. **were,** so Q; Globe: *are*. **descried,** spied upon, discovered. 395. **face of brass,** brazen manner. 397. **confound,** destroy; see glossary. 400. **wish,** entreat. 405. **blind harper's,** a proverbial expression. 409. **blown,** filled with eggs, made foul. 413. **russet,** simple, homespun. **kersey,** plain, homely. 416. **Sans sans,** without *sans;* i.e., without affection of foreign phrases; see glossary. 417. **rage,** fever, affliction. 425. **undo,** ruin; see glossary. 434. **well advis'd,** in one's right mind. 440. **force,** attach force or importance to, think of the consequences; hence, hesitate. 464. **trencher-knight,** serving man at table. **Dick.** Cf. the current expression, "Tom, Dick and Harry."

Do not you know my lady's foot by th' squier,
And laugh upon the apple of her eye?
And stand between her back, sir, and the fire,
Holding a trencher, jesting merrily?
You put our page out: go, you are allow'd;
Die when you will, a smock shall be your shroud.
You leer upon me, do you? there 's an eye
Wounds like a leaden sword.

Boyet. Full merrily
Hath this brave manage, this career, been run.

Ber. Lo, he is tilting straight! Peace! I have done.

Enter [COSTARD *the*] *Clown.*

Welcome, pure wit! thou part'st a fair fray.

Cost. O Lord, sir, they would know
Whether the three Worthies shall come in or no.

Ber. What, are there but three?

Cost. No, sir; but it is vara fine,
For every one pursents three.

Ber. And three times thrice is nine.

Cost. Not so, sir; under correction, sir; I hope it is not so.
You cannot beg us, sir, I can assure you, sir; we know what we know:
I hope, sir, three times thrice, sir,—

Ber. Is not nine.

Cost. Under correction, sir, we know whereuntil it doth amount.

Ber. By Jove, I always took three threes for nine.

Cost. O Lord, sir, it were pity you should get your living by reckoning, sir.

Ber. How much is it?

Cost. O Lord, sir, the parties themselves, the actors, sir, will show whereuntil it doth amount: for mine own part, I am, as they say, but to parfect one man in one poor man, Pompion the Great, sir.

Ber. Art thou one of the Worthies?

Cost. It pleased them to think me worthy of Pompion the Great: for mine own part, I know not the degree of the Worthy, but I am to stand for him.

Ber. Go, bid them prepare.

Cost. We will turn it finely off, sir; we will take some care. *Exit.*

King. Berowne, they will shame us: let them not aproach.

Ber. We are shame-proof, my lord: and 'tis some policy
To have one show worse than the king's and his company.

King. I say they shall not come.

Prin. Nay, my good lord, let me o'errule you now:
That sport best pleases that doth least know how:
†Where zeal strives to content, and the contents
Dies in the zeal of that which it presents:
Their form confounded makes most form in mirth,
When great things labouring perish in their birth.

Ber. A right descrition of our sport, my lord.

Enter [ARMADO *the*] *Braggart.*

Arm. Anointed, I implore so much expense of thy royal sweet breath as will utter a brace of words.

[*Converses apart with the King, and delivers him a paper.*]

Prin. Doth this man serve God?

Ber. Why ask you?

Prin. 'A speaks not like a man of God his making.

Arm. That is all one, my fair, sweet, honey monarch; for, I protest, the schoolmaster is exceeding fantastical; too too vain, too too vain: but we will put it, as they say, to fortuna della guerra. I wish you the peace of mind, most royal couplement! *Exit.*

King. Here is like to be a good presence of Worthies. He presents Hector of Troy; the swain, Pompey the Great; the parish curate, Alexander; Armado's page, Hercules; the pedant, Judas Maccabæus:
And if these four Worthies in their first show thrive,
These four will change habits, and present the other five.

Ber. There is five in the first show.

King. You are deceived; 'tis not so.

Ber. The pedant, the braggart, the hedge-priest, the fool and the boy:—
†Abate throw at novum, and the whole world again
Cannot pick out five such, take each one in his vein.

King. The ship is under sail, and here she comes amain.

Enter [COSTARD, *for*] *Pompey.*

Cost. I Pompey am,—

Boyet. You lie, you are not he.

Cost. I Pompey am,—

Boyet. With libbard's head on knee.

Ber. Well said, old mocker: I must needs be friends with thee.

Cost. I Pompey am, Pompey surnam'd the Big,—

Dum. The Great.

Cost. It is, 'Great', sir:—
Pompey surnam'd the Great;
That oft in field with targe and shield, did make my foe to sweat:
And travelling along this coast. I here am come by chance,
And lay my arms before the legs of this sweet lass of France.
If your ladyship would say, 'Thanks, Pompey,' I had done.

Prin. Great thanks, great Pompey.

Cost. 'Tis not so much worth; but I hope I was perfect: I made a little fault in 'Great.'

474. **squier,** foot rule. 477. **trencher,** wooden dish or plate; see glossary. 479. **smock,** woman's undergarment; see glossary; here a sign of effeminacy. 481. **leaden sword,** mock weapon (used figuratively). 482. **brave,** fine; see glossary. **manage,** maneuver on horseback. 487. **vara,** dialect pronunciation of "very." 503. **parfect,** Costard's malapropism for, probably, "perform" or "present." 513. **policy,** stratagem. 518-519. **Where . . . presents.** The lines have been variously explained, depending on the interpretation of *contents:* where the unintelligent zeal of the actors strives to content the audience, and the gist (*contents*) of the entertainment is destroyed by this very zeal in performance (Yale); where zeal strives to give contentment, and the contentment (*contents*) dies in the zeal for that sport which zeal presents (Furness). Most explanations incline toward one or the other of these two paraphrases. 528. **'A,** so Q; Globe, following F: *He.* **God his,** so Q; Globe, following F: *God's.* 533-534. **fortuna della guerra,** the fortune of war. 533. **della,** Globe: *de la.* 535. **couplement,** couple. 536. **presence,** assembly. 545. **hedge-priest,** illiterate, rural priest. 547. **Abate,** leave out of count; see glossary. **novum,** the game *novum quinque,* so called from the principal throws of the dice—nine and five. The line is obscure and several emendations have been suggested. Malone's *Abate a throw,* etc., has been most generally adopted. The Yale editors paraphrase: Except for a rare throw at dice. A quibble is observable here on the notion of Nine Worthies being presented by five players. 551. **libbard's,** leopard's; an allusion to the ornaments occasionally worn on knees or elbows of garments. 568-569. **Your . . . knight.** These remarks refer to reputed physical peculiarities of Alexander—a wry neck, which would make his features stand not *right* but obliquely, and a sweet breath and a bodily

Ber. My hat to a halfpenny, Pompey proves the best Worthy.

Enter [NATHANIEL *the*] *Curate, for Alexander.*

Nath. When in the world I liv'd, I was the world's commander;
By east, west, north, and south, I spread my conquering might:
My scutcheon plain declares that I am Alisander,—

Boyet. Your nose says, no, you are not; for it stands too right.

Ber. Your nose smells 'no' in this, most tender-smelling knight.

Prin. The conqueror is dismay'd. Proceed, good Alexander.

Nath. When in the world I liv'd, I was the world's commander,—

Boyet. Most true, 'tis right; you were so, Alisander.

Ber. Pompey the Great,—

Cost. Your servant, and Costard.

Ber. Take away the conqueror, take away Alisander.

Cost. [*To Sir Nath.*] O, sir, you have overthrown Alisander the conqueror! You will be scraped out of the painted cloth for this: your lion, that holds his poll-axe sitting on a close-stool, will be given to Ajax: he will be the ninth Worthy. A conqueror, and afeard to speak! run away for shame, Alisander. [*Nath. retires.*] There, an 't shall please you; a foolish mild man; an honest man, look you, and soon dashed. He is a marvellous good neighbour, faith, and a very good bowler: but, for Alisander,—alas, you see how 'tis,—a little o'erparted. But there are Worthies a-coming will speak their mind in some other sort.

Prin. Stand aside, good Pompey.

Enter [HOLOFERNES *the*] *Pedant, for Judas, and* [MOTH] *the Boy, for Hercules.*

Hol. Great Hercules is presented by this imp,
Whose club kill'd Cerberus, that three-headed canus;
And when he was a babe, a child, a shrimp,
Thus did he strangle serpents in his manus.
Quoniam he seemeth in minority,
Ergo I come with this apology.
Keep some state in thy exit, and vanish. *Exit Boy.*
Judas I am,—

Dum. A Judas!

Hol. Not Iscariot, sir.
Judas I am, ycliped Maccabæus.

Dum. Judas Maccabæus clipt is plain Judas.

Ber. A kissing traitor. How art thou proved Judas?

Hol. Judas I am,—

Dum. The more shame for you, Judas.

Hol. What mean you, sir?

Boyet. To make Judas hang himself.

Hol. Begin, sir; you are my elder.

Ber. Well followed: Judas was hanged on an elder.

Hol. I will not be put out of countenance.

Ber. Because thou hast no face.

Hol. What is this?

Boyet. A cittern-head.

Dum. The head of a bodkin.

Ber. A Death's face in a ring.

Long. The face of an old Roman coin, scarce seen.

Boyet. The pommel of Cæsar's falchion.

Dum. The carved-bone face on a flask.

Ber. Saint George's half-cheek in a brooch.

Dum. Ay, and in a brooch of lead.

Ber. Ay, and worn in the cap of a tooth-drawer.
And now forward; for we have put thee in countenance.

Hol. You have put me out of countenance.

Ber. False; we have given thee faces.

Hol. But you have out-faced them all.

Ber. An thou wert a lion, we would do so.

Boyet. Therefore, as he is an ass, let him go.
And so adieu, sweet Jude! nay, why dost thou stay?

Dum. For the latter end of his name.

Ber. For the ass to the Jude; give it him:—Jud-as, away!

Hol. This is not generous, not gentle, not humble.

Boyet. A light for Monsieur Judas! it grows dark, he may stumble. [*Hol. retires.*]

Prin. Alas, poor Maccabæus, how hath he been baited!

Enter [ARMADO *the*] *Braggart* [*for Hector*].

Ber. Hide thy head, Achilles: here comes Hector in arms.

Dum. Though my mocks come home by me, I will now be merry.

King. Hector was but a Troyan in respect of this.

Boyet. But is this Hector?

King. I think Hector was not so clean-timbered.

Long. His leg is too big for Hector's.

Dum. More calf, certain.

Boyet. No; he is best indued in the small.

Ber. This cannot be Hector.

Dum. He 's a god or a painter; for he makes faces.

Arm. The armipotent Mars, of lances the almighty,
Gave Hector a gift,—

Dum. A gilt nutmeg.

Ber. A lemon.

Long. Stuck with cloves.

Dum. No, cloven.

Arm. Peace!—
The armipotent Mars, of lances the almighty,
Gave Hector a gift, the heir of Ilion;
A man so breath'd, that certain he would fight; yea
From morn till night, out of his pavilion.
I am that flower,—

odor of "marvellous good savour." The details would be familiar to Shakespeare from North's Plutarch. 579. **scraped . . . cloth,** an allusion to the frequent representation of the Nine Worthies painted on an arras or tapestry. 579-581. **your lion . . . close-stool.** Theobald found in Gerard Leigh's *Accidens of Armorie* (1591) a description of the armorial emblems of the Nine Worthies, where Alexander's is described as "a lion or [gold] seiante [sitting] in a chayer, holding a battle-ax." 581. **Ajax,** quibble on "a jakes," a latrine. This unsavory pun is not infrequent. 588. **o'erparted,** having a part too difficult. 591. **Stand . . . Pompey.** After this line the early texts have a stage direction: Q: *Exit Curat;* F_1: *Exit Cu.;* F_{2-4}: *Exit Clo.* Costard probably left the stage at this point. His absence during the remainder of the entertainment motivates his conduct later at line 678. 593. **Cerberus,** three-headed dog at the entrance to Hades, the capturing of which was one of Hercules' twelve labors. **canus,** for *canis*, dog. 595. **manus,** hands. 596. **Quoniam,** since. 613. **What is this.** Holofernes points to his face, provoking the quips which follow. 614. **cittern,** cithern, guitar. The head was usually grotesquely carved. 615. **bodkin,** long, jeweled pin for a lady's hair. 618. **falchion,** curved sword. 620. **half-cheek,** profile. **brooch,** any jeweled ornament. 640. **Troyan,** Trojan; term of contempt. 642. **clean-timbered,** clean-limbed. 647. **indued,** endowed. **small,** part of the leg below the calf. 649. **a god or a painter,** a proverbial expression. 650. **armipotent,** powerful in arms; an epithet commonly applied to Mars. 652. **gilt,** an old cookery term—glazed with egg yolk, saffron, etc. There are several contemporary references to gilded nutmegs. The gilding may have been a preservative. 659. **so breathed,** i.e., in good condition, valiant. 660. **pavilion,** tent or camp, whither the combatant retired when not engaged in a fight.

Dum. That mint.
Long. That columbine.

Arm. Sweet Lord Longaville, rein thy tongue.

Long. I must rather give it the rein, for it runs against Hector.

Dum. Ay, and Hector 's a greyhound.

Arm. The sweet war-man is dead and rotten; sweet chucks, beat not the bones of the buried: when he breathed, he was a man. But I will forward with my device. [*To the Princess*] Sweet royalty, bestow on me the sense of hearing.

Prin. Speak, brave Hector: we are much delighted.

Arm. I do adore thy sweet grace's slipper.

Boyet. [*Aside to Dum.*] Loves her by the foot.

Dum. [*Aside to Boyet*] He may not by the yard.

Arm. This Hector far surmounted Hannibal,—

Cost. The party is gone, fellow Hector, she is gone; she is two months on her way.

Arm. What meanest thou?

Cost. Faith, unless you play the honest Troyan, the poor wench is cast away: she 's quick; the child brags in her belly already: 'tis yours.

Arm. Dost thou infamonize me among potentates? thou shalt die.

Cost. Then shall Hector be whipped for Jaquenetta that is quick by him and hanged for Pompey that is dead by him.

Dum. Most rare Pompey!

Boyet. Renowned Pompey!

Ber. Greater than great, great, great, great Pompey! Pompey the Huge!

Dum. Hector trembles.

Ber. Pompey is moved. More Ates, more Ates! stir them on! stir them on!

Dum. Hector will challenge him.

Ber. Ay, if 'a have no more man's blood in 's belly than will sup a flea.

Arm. By the north pole, I do challenge thee.

Cost. I will not fight with a pole, like a northern man: I'll slash; I'll do it by the sword. I bepray you, let me borrow my arms again.

Dum. Room for the incensed Worthies!

Cost. I'll do it in my shirt.

Dum. Most resolute Pompey!

Moth. Master, let me take you a button-hole lower. Do you not see Pompey is uncasing for the combat? What mean you? You will lose your reputation.

Arm. Gentlemen and soldiers, pardon me; I will not combat in my shirt.

Dum. You may not deny it: Pompey hath made the challenge.

Arm. Sweet bloods, I both may and will.

Ber. What reason have you for 't?

Arm. The naked truth of it is, I have no shirt; I go woolward for penance.

Boyet. True, and it was enjoined him in Rome for want of linen: since when, I'll be sworn, he wore none but a dishclout of Jaquenetta's, and that 'a wears next his heart for a favour.

Enter a Messenger, Monsieur MARCADE.

Mar. God save you, madam!

Prin. Welcome, Marcade;
But that thou interrupt'st our merriment.

Mar. I am sorry, madam; for the news I bring
Is heavy in my tongue. The king your father—

Prin. Dead, for my life!

Mar. Even so; my tale is told.

Ber. Worthies, away! the scene begins to cloud.

Arm. For mine own part, I breathe free breath. I have seen the day of wrong through the little hole of discretion, and I will right myself like a soldier.
Exeunt Worthies.

King. How fares your majesty?

Prin. Boyet, prepare; I will away to-night.

King. Madam, not so; I do beseech you, stay.

Prin. Prepare, I say. I thank you, gracious lords,
For all your fair endeavours; and entreat,
Out of a new-sad soul, that you vouchsafe
In your rich wisdom to excuse or hide
The liberal opposition of our spirits,
If over-boldly we have borne ourselves
In the converse of breath: your gentleness
Was guilty of it. Farewell, worthy lord!
A heavy heart bears not a humble tongue:
Excuse me so, coming too short of thanks
For my great suit so easily obtain'd.

King. The extreme parts of time extremely forms
All causes to the purpose of his speed,
And often at his very loose decides
That which long process could not arbitrate:
And though the mourning brow of progeny
Forbid the smiling courtesy of love
The holy suit which fain it would convince,
Yet, since love's argument was first on foot,
Let not the cloud of sorrow justle it
From what it purpos'd; since, to wail friends lost
Is not by much so wholesome-profitable
As to rejoice at friends but newly found.

Prin. I understand you not: my griefs are double.

Ber. Honest plain words best pierce the ear of grief;
And by these badges understand the king.
For your fair sakes have we neglected time,
Play'd foul play with our oaths: your beauty, ladies,
Hath much deform'd us, fashioning our humours
Even to the opposed end of our intents:
And what in us hath seem'd ridiculous,—
As love is full of unbefitting strains,
All wanton as a child, skipping and vain,
Form'd by the eye and therefore, like the eye,
Full of strange shapes, of habits and of forms,
Varying in subjects as the eye doth roll
To every varied object in his glance:

670. QF have a stage direction here: *Berowne steppes forth.* The stage business at this point probably had something to do with Costard's conduct immediately below. 678. **The . . . gone.** QF print these words as part of Armado's speech, as do the New Cambridge editors, who think they have something to do with the stage direction just noted. 694. **Ates,** incitements to mischief. Ate was the goddess of discord. 706-707. **Master . . . lower,** help remove your doublet, with a quibble on the proverbial "take down a hole"; i.e., humiliate. 717. **woolward,** with woolen clothing next to the skin; i.e., instead of linen or silk, suggesting the hair shirt of the penitent. 743. **liberal opposition,** too-free antagonism. 745. **converse of breath,** conversation. 747. **humble,** civil, complimentary; so QF; Globe, following Theobald: *nimble.* 750-753. **The . . . arbitrate,** i.e., much is accomplished in the last minutes after a long period of dallying. The observation is not an uncommon one although the expression here is obscure. The difficulty of the passage is due in part to lack of agreement between the grammatical subject *parts*, its verbs *forms* and *decides*, and its pronoun *he.* The actual subject is *time.* Capell so paraphrases it: Time in his extreme parts, or drawing to his extreme, etc. Such grammatical usage is not un-Shakespearean. The word *loose* (l. 752) is an archery term, the discharge of an arrow; *at his very loose*, at the last moment. The New Cambridge editors, finding the passage corrupt, would emend *parts* to *pulse*

Which parti-coated presence of loose love
Put on by us, if, in your heavenly eyes,
Have misbecom'd our oaths and gravities,
Those heavenly eyes, that look into these faults,
Suggested us to make. Therefore, ladies,
Our love being yours, the error that love makes
Is likewise yours: we to ourselves prove false,
By being once false for ever to be true
To those that make us both,—fair ladies, you:
And even that falsehood, in itself a sin,
Thus purifies itself and turns to grace.
Prin. We have receiv'd your letters full of love;
Your favours, the ambassadors of love;
And, in our maiden council, rated them
At courtship, pleasant jest and courtesy
As bombast and as lining to the time:
But more devout than this in our respects
Have we not been; and therefore met your loves
In their own fashion, like a merriment.
Dum. Our letters, madam, show'd much more than jest.
Long. So did our looks.
Ros. We did not quote them so.
King. Now, at the latest minute of the hour,
Grant us your loves.
Prin. A time, methinks, too short
To make a world-without-end bargain in.
No, no, my lord, your grace is perjur'd much,
Full of dear guiltiness; and therefore this:
If for my love, as there is no such cause,
You will do aught, this shall you do for me:
Your oath I will not trust; but go with speed
To some forlorn and naked hermitage,
Remote from all the pleasures of the world;
There stay until the twelve celestial signs
Have brought about the annual reckoning.
If this austere insociable life
Change not your offer made in heat of blood;
If frosts and fasts, hard lodging and thin weeds
Nip not the gaudy blossoms of your love,
But that it bear this trial and last love;
Then, at the expiration of the year,
Come challenge me, challenge me by these deserts,
And, by this virgin palm now kissing thine,
I will be thine; and till that instant shut
My woeful self up in a mourning house,
Raining the tears of lamentation
For the remembrance of my father's death.
If this thou do deny, let our hands part,
Neither intitled in the other's heart.
King. If this, or more than this, I would deny,
To flatter up these powers of mine with rest,
The sudden hand of death close up mine eye!
Hence hermit then my heart is in thy breast.
[*Ber.* And what to me, my love? and what to me?
Ros. You must be purged too, your sins are rack'd,
You are attaint with faults and perjury:
Therefore if you my favour mean to get,
A twelvemonth shall you spend, and never rest,
But seek the weary beds of people sick.]
Dum. But what to me, my love? but what to me?
A wife?
Kath. A beard, fair health, and honesty;
With three-fold love I wish you all these three.
Dum. O, shall I say, I thank you, gentle wife?
Kath. Not so, my lord; a twelvemonth and a day
I'll mark no words that smooth-fac'd wooers say:
Come when the king doth to my lady come;
Then, if I have much love, I'll give you some.
Dum. I'll serve thee true and faithfully till then.
Kath. Yet swear not, lest ye be forsworn again.
Long. What says Maria?
Mar. At the twelvemonth's end
I'll change my black gown for a faithful friend.
Long. I'll stay with patience; but the time is long.
Mar. The liker you; few taller are so young.
Ber. Studies my lady? mistress, look on me;
Behold the window of my heart, mine eye,
What humble suit attends thy answer there:
Impose some service on me for thy love.
Ros. Oft have I heard of you, my Lord Berowne,
Before I saw you; and the world's large tongue
Proclaims you for a man replete with mocks,
Full of comparisons and wounding flouts,
Which you on all estates will execute
That lie within the mercy of your wit.
To weed this wormwood from your fruitful brain,
And therewithal to win me, if you please,
Without the which I am not to be won,
You shall this twelvemonth term from day to day
Visit the speechless sick and still converse
With groaning wretches; and your task shall be,
With all the fierce endeavour of your wit
To enforce the pained impotent to smile.
Ber. To move wild laughter in the throat of death?
It cannot be; it is impossible:
Mirth cannot move a soul in agony.
Ros. Why, that 's the way to choke a gibing spirit,
Whose influence is begot of that loose grace
Which shallow laughing hearers give to fools:
A jest's prosperity lies in the ear
Of him that hears it, never in the tongue
Of him that makes it: then, if sickly ears,
Deaf'd with the clamours of their own dear groans,
Will hear your idle scorns, continue then,
And I will have you and that fault withal;
But if they will not, throw away that spirit,
And I shall find you empty of that fault,
Right joyful of your reformation.
Ber. A twelvemonth! well; befall what will befall,
I'll jest a twelvemonth in an hospital.
Prin. [*To the King*] Ay, sweet my lord; and so I take my leave.
King. No, madam; we will bring you on your way.

(sixteenth-century spelling, *pouls*). 776-777. **Which . . . if,** an instance of a Latinism common in Renaissance English in which the relative serves the double function of coordinating conjunction and substantive, equivalent here to "and if this presence," etc., after the Latin construction *qui si* (Abbott, 418). 776. **parti-coated,** dressed like a fool, in motley. **loose,** unrestrained. 780. **Suggested,** tempted; see glossary. 789. **rated,** computed, estimated; see glossary. 791. **bombast,** a loosely made fabric used for padding or stuffing garments. 792. **respects,** considerations; see glossary. 796. **quote,** interpret. 807. **twelve celestial signs,** signs of the zodiac. 811. **thin weeds,** probably garments, although Hart suggests a reference to fasting, i.e., unnourishing herbs and roots; see *weed* in glossary. 816. **palm . . . thine,** an image frequent in referring to clasping of hands, particularly those of lovers; cf. *Romeo and Juliet,* I, v, 102. 826. **hermit,** so New Cambridge and Arden editions; Q: *herrite,* F: *euer.* 827-832. Regarded as evidence of imperfect cancellation; see Introduction. 828. **rack'd,** extended "to the top of their bent" (Malone); Rowe's emendation *rank* is adopted by many editors. Steevens noted the appropriateness of this emendation, citing *Hamlet,* III, iii, 36. See, however, *rack* and *rank* in glossary. 854. **comparisons,** i.e., witty, sarcastic comparisons. 855. **all estates,** all classes of people. 861. **converse,** associate with; see glossary. 869. **influence,** an astronomical metaphor; see glossary.

Ber. Our wooing doth not end like an old play;
Jack hath not Jill: these ladies' courtesy
Might well have made our sport a comedy.
King. Come, sir, it wants a twelvemonth and a day,
And then 'twill end.
Ber. That 's too long for a play.

Enter [ARMADO *the*] *Braggart*.

Arm. Sweet majesty, vouchsafe me,—
Prin. Was not that Hector?
Dum. The worthy knight of Troy.

Arm. I will kiss thy royal finger, and take leave. I am a votary; I have vowed to Jaquenetta to hold the plough for her sweet love three years. But, most esteemed greatness, will you hear the dialogue that the two learned men have compiled in praise of the owl and the cuckoo? it should have followed in the end of our show.

King. Call them forth quickly; we will do so.
Arm. Holla! approach.

Enter all [HOLOFERNES, NATHANIEL, MOTH, COSTARD, *and others*].

This side is Hiems, Winter, this Ver, the Spring; the one maintained by the owl, the other by the cuckoo. Ver, begin.

THE SONG.

[SPRING.]

When daisies pied and violets blue
And lady-smocks all silver-white
And cuckoo-buds of yellow hue
Do paint the meadows with delight,
The cuckoo then, on every tree,
Mocks married men; for thus sings he,
Cuckoo;
Cuckoo, cuckoo: O word of fear,
Unpleasing to a married ear!

When shepherds pipe on oaten straws
And merry larks are ploughmen's clocks,
When turtles tread, and rooks, and daws,
And maidens bleach their summer smocks,
The cuckoo then, on every tree,
Mocks married men; for thus sings he,
Cuckoo;
Cuckoo, cuckoo: O word of fear,
Unpleasing to a married ear!

WINTER.

When icicles hang by the wall
And Dick the shepherd blows his nail
And Tom bears logs into the hall
And milk comes frozen home in pail,
When blood is nipp'd and ways be foul,
Then nightly sings the staring owl,
Tu-whit;
Tu-who, a merry note,
While greasy Joan doth keel the pot.
When all aloud the wind doth blow
And coughing drowns the parson's saw
And birds sit brooding in the snow
And Marian's nose looks red and raw,
When roasted crabs hiss in the bowl,
Then nightly sings the staring owl,
Tu-whit;
Tu-who, a merry note,
While greasy Joan doth keel the pot.

[*Arm*.] The words of Mercury are harsh after the songs of Apollo. [You that way: we this way. *Exeunt*.]

893. **hold the plough,** become a farmer, a rustic. 905. **lady-smocks,** cuckoo flowers, the *cardamine pratensis;* probably for "our Lady's smock." 906. **cuckoo-buds of yellow,** a flower not positively identified; perhaps buttercup or crowfoot. 912. **Unpleasing,** i.e., because the cuckoo suggests cuckoldry; the latter word is derived from the former, from the popular notion that the cuckoo laid its eggs in other birds' nests. 930. **keel,** skim and stir. 932. **saw,** maxim, moral observation. 935. **crabs,** crab apples. 940. **words of Mercury.** The reference is to Mercury as the god of eloquence in antithesis to Apollo as the god of music.

THE TWO GENTLEMEN OF VERONA

If by "romantic comedy" we mean a love story in which the lovers overcome parental obstacles, jealousies, separations, and dangers to be united at last in married bliss, then *The Two Gentlemen of Verona* is perhaps Shakespeare's first. Although *The Comedy of Errors* may be an earlier play, it is a farce of mistaken identity with only a secondary interest in marriage, whereas *Love's Labour's Lost* is a courtly confection ending in the postponement of all marriages. No mention of *The Two Gentlemen of Verona* occurs until Francis Meres' list of 1598, but the play is often dated around 1590–1594 on the basis of style: rhymed couplets, end-stopped verse, passages of excessive wit-combat, and the like. *The Taming of the Shrew* (c. 1592–1594) is often dated a little later than *The Two Gentlemen,* although admittedly the two plays are much alike and perhaps ought to share the credit and the blame for Shakespeare's first experimentation with romantic comedy. In any event, this was to be the genre of Shakespeare's best-known "festive" comedies from *A Midsummer Night's Dream* to *Twelfth Night*.

The Two Gentlemen of Verona, then, is Shakespeare's apprenticeship to the romantic fiction of Italy and other southern European countries, whence he later derived so many plots of threatened love. He locates his story in Italy and gives his characters Italian names. He uses the conventional plot devices of romantic fiction: inconstancy in love and in friendship, the disguise of the heroine as a page, the overhearing of false vows, banishment, elopement, capture by outlaws, and so on. Virtually all the characters have a recognizable ancestry, not only in continental fiction but in neoclassical drama as well: Lucetta is the usual female confidante, Thurio is the rich but unwelcome rival wooer (the pantaloon), Antonio and the Duke are typically strong-willed fathers opposing the romantic marriages of their children, Speed and Launce are at least supposed to be the clever servants who deliver messages and arrange rendezvous, and the four young lovers are the romantic protagonists.

Even in this early apprenticeship, to be sure, Shakespeare departs from the neoclassical norm of his continental sources. The setting remains nominally Italian, but the tone is often heartily English. Lucetta is a true friend of Julia and a virtuous counselor in love; the jest about her being a "broker" or a go-between reminds us how unlike a bawdy duenna she really is. Thurio, Antonio, and the Duke are all portrayed with such amiable forbearance that they often seem inadequately motivated as the opponents of romantic happiness. Most of all, Speed and Launce have cast loose from their traditional roles as comic manipulators to become vaudeville jokesters.

Despite these liberties, however, the conventions of continental fiction retain much of their force, and indeed create problems of interpretation for modern readers not attuned to such conventions. What are we to make of the inconstant Proteus, who rejects his faithful Julia the moment he is away from her, tries instead to win the lady-fair of his dearest friend Valentine, informs the Duke of Valentine's plan to elope with Silvia, and then attempts a violent assault on Silvia's chastity? What sort of romantic hero is this, and why should he be rewarded by being forgiven and restored to his Julia? Most puzzling of all, is it credible that Valentine should respond to all this perfidy by offering to relinquish Silvia to Proteus? By the same token, isn't it absurd that the outlaws in the forest near Mantua should turn out to be gentlemen in exile, and that they should offer command of their group to Valentine, whom they have just captured? Isn't the Duke's forgiveness of his eloped daughter Silvia rather sudden and unconvincing? These problems, which have troubled many readers of the play (though they generally seem less formidable to spectators of an actual production), can perhaps best be analyzed in two ways: as a result of Shakespeare's having combined two sources with conflicting conventions, and as a result of Shakespeare's conscious interest in the theme of unexpected forgiveness for his erring protagonist.

Using a device of plotting that was to become customary in his romantic comedies, Shakespeare combines two fictional sources and thereby sets up a dramatic tension between the two. His chief source appears to have been *Diana*, a popular pastoral romance in Spanish by the Portuguese Jorge de Montemayor (1520–1561). Its heroine, Felismena (corresponding to Julia), is wooed by Don Felix (Proteus), whose father (Antonio) disapproves of the match and sends Don Felix away to court. Felismena, following after him disguised as a page, stops at an inn and is invited by the host to listen to some music, whereupon she overhears Don Felix protesting his love to a new lady, Celia (Silvia). At this point the resemblance between *Diana* and Shakespeare's play breaks off. Even thus far, despite several striking resemblances, the story provides no counterpart for Valentine, Proteus' best friend and the faithful lover of Silvia. Montemayor's romance is solely concerned with inconstancy in love.

For the motif of true friendship, Shakespeare may have turned to the story of Titus and Gisippus, as told by Thomas Elyot in *The Governour* (1531). Here Gisippus, upon learning that his dear friend Titus has fallen in love with Gisippus' lady-love, not only relinquishes the lady to Titus but actually smuggles him into bed with her, all unbeknownst to the lady. The point of this story, as of other well-known treatises on friendship such as John Lyly's *Euphues* (1578) and *Endymion* (1588), or Richard Edwards' *Damon and Pythias* (1565), is that friendship is a higher form of human affection than erotic love since it is disinterested, Platonically pure, and capable of teaching selflessness to others. Such a tale of perfect friendship provides, however, no counterpart for Julia, the lady abandoned by Proteus. Shakespeare has neatly dovetailed the two stories, making a quartet of lovers out of two triangular situations. The false lover of the first story becomes also the false friend of the second —only to be overwhelmed at the end by the generosity of his true friend.

The difficulty of combining these two stories is that they arouse different expectations. The one is dedicated to the virtue of constancy in love, the other to friendship. Valentine's ultimate function is to demonstrate the triumph of selfless friendship over love, and yet his function in the plot of love-rivalry is to demonstrate true loyalty to his Silvia. His relinquishing of her to Proteus seems inconsistent with his vows as a lover. Conversely, Proteus' double perfidy, toward his lover Julia and his friend Valentine, seems to render him unworthy of the generous action Valentine bestows on him. Proteus' very name is synonymous with inconstancy; his namesake in *The Odyssey* was infamous for his ability to change shapes at will. (Valentine's name, on the other hand, betokens constancy in love.) The coupling of the two plots simultaneously intensifies Proteus' guilt and Valentine's magnanimity.

Yet Shakespeare makes a virtue out of the seeming lack of credibility. Paradoxically, the more unlikely Valentine's actions seem, the more transcendent and wondrous they appear. Shakespeare prepares for his climactic scene of forgiveness in several ways. First, he presents Proteus as an essentially noble person who has fallen through a single fault. Proteus is well-born, accomplished, handsome. The worthy Julia loves him for his good qualities, and he responds with sincerity and passion. He is equally ardent as a friend to Valentine. Only when he sees Silvia does Proteus become helpless, "metamorphosed." He cannot completely be blamed for being overwhelmed by passion, for the other lovers are no less obedient to love's command. According to the Petrarchism that infuses this play, love cannot choose its object. Proteus' unhappy fate is to love Silvia. His self-hatred increases as he turns flatterer, liar, betrayer, and finally would-be rapist. Like Angelo in *Measure for Measure*, Proteus is compulsively driven to abhorrent sin. The psychological insight of that later dark comedy is lacking—the soliloquies do not create the suffocating atmosphere of a nightmare—but the pattern of a guilty fall is still manifest.

This pattern may in turn clarify Valentine's role as the selfless friend. The very implausibility of his offer to relinquish Silvia accentuates the nobility of the gesture. We are surprised, because we don't expect such selflessness in human nature; but if friendship is to be seen as a supreme achievement of the human spirit, it must transcend man's all-too-common penchant for rivalry and ingratitude. Valentine's generosity is not achieved without inner struggle. In the climactic scene of attempted rape, his first natural reaction is angry denunciation. What changes his mind is the depth and earnestness of Proteus' confession and desire for forgiveness: "If hearty sorrow Be a sufficient ransom for offence, I tender 't here." Valentine responds in the name of mercy and at the prompting of divine example: "By penitence th' Eternal's wrath's appeas'd." The more undeserved the pardon, the more selfless the act of him who pardons. Only by conquering his desire for Silvia can Valentine teach his friend selflessness and thus reunite all four lovers in perfect joy. The pattern of *The Two Gentlemen* is thus one of a comedy of forgiveness, anticipating later plays in which the romantic protagonist is equally culpable and yet equally forgiven: *Much Ado about Nothing*, *Measure for Measure*, *All's Well that Ends Well*, *Cymbeline*, and others (see R. G. Hunter's *Shakespeare and the Comedy of Forgiveness*).

Forgiveness of Proteus must proceed no less from Julia than from Valentine. She too has much to pardon; as Proteus contritely observes, "O heaven, were man But constant, he were perfect!" Julia initiates a line of Shakespearean heroines, including Hero, Isabella, Helena, and Imogen in the plays already named, who must similarly cure inconstancy by their constancy. Like many Shakespearean heroines Julia is plucky, resourceful, modest yet witty, patiently obedient in love and yet coyly flirtatious, a true friend of her confidante, and long-suffering. Disguised as a page, she overhears her lover's infidelity and yet never loses her faith in him. She patiently delivers Proteus' messages to her rival (like Viola in *Twelfth Night*) and gently acts as conscience to her erring master.

The repeated device of overhearing, as in later comedies, provides a test for the protagonists' intentions. Thinking themselves unobserved, they reveal their true natures for better or for worse. In the ingeniously devised climactic scene (V,iv), Proteus as would-be ravisher is overheard by both his rejected mistress and his betrayed friend. Conversely, Silvia proves loyal and chaste whenever she is silently observed by Julia (disguised as Sebastian) or by Valentine in the forest scenes. These overhearings suggest not only that men's good and evil deeds are witnessed, but that a beneficent providence will protect the virtuous. Valentine's unseen presence assures that Silvia will be saved from rape, and that Proteus will be prevented from committing an actual crime of violence. As in later comedies of this sort, forgiveness is possible because the guilt remains one of intent only.

These happy resolutions of conflict take place in a forest near Mantua, the first of what Northrop Frye calls Shakespeare's "green worlds." Although sketchily presented, this forest does anticipate the forest of Arden and other sylvan restorative landscapes. Its inhabitants are banished men protesting the injustice of society at court, or fugitives from unkind love. Valentine learns to prefer "unfrequented woods" to "flourishing peopled towns." His "wild faction" of outlaws desist from attacking "silly women or poor passengers," and appropriately swear "By the bare scalp of Robin Hood's fat friar" (IV,i). They are charmingly suited to their role of threatening and then reuniting the lovers, providentially capturing Silvia just as she is on her way to find Valentine. Their actions are highly improbable, but then so are Valentine's forgiveness of Proteus and the Duke's sudden reconciliation with his prospective son-in-law Valentine. Like Arden, this forest is a strange place in which such changes of heart are expected to occur. The aura of improbability may also explain the play's carelessness about social distinctions and the realities of geography: the Duke is sometimes called the Emperor, and at one point Valentine sets sail from Verona to Milan (both located inland).

The buffoonish comedy of Launce and Speed performs a function similar to that of romantic improbability by undercutting the Petrarchan seriousness of the love story. How can we worry long over Valentine's banishment when Launce bursts out, "Sir, there is a proclamation that you are vanished"? Or how can we fret about Proteus' courtship of Silvia when the love-token he sends her turns out to be Launce's odiferous dog? This sort of absurd anticlimax occurs at every turn. Launce's first soliloquy, about the dog's refusal to mourn their departure from Verona (II,iii), is a brilliant example of what we would call vaudeville or "stand-up" comic joking, but it also comments on the immediately preceding scene of Proteus' tearful farewell to Julia. Launce's friendship for Speed, and especially his friendship for the dog, delightfully blaspheme the play's serious interest in true friendship. In Launce's funniest scene (IV,iv), he describes how he has selflessly taken on himself the punishment meted out to the dog for urinating on Silvia's farthingale. Similarly, the spectacle of Launce in love, cataloguing his mistress' virtues and vices, insures us against too deep an involvement in the hazards of Cupid. The play continually reminds us of the folly of love without denying its exquisite joys or its highest potential for selflessness.

THE TWO GENTLEMEN OF VERONA

The Names of All the Actors.

Duke [of Milan], *father to Silvia.*
Valentine, } *the two Gentlemen.*
Proteus, }
Antonio, *father to Proteus.*
Thurio, *a foolish rival to Valentine.*
Eglamour, *agent for Silvia in her escape.*
Host, *where Julia lodges.*
Outlaws, *with Valentine.*
Speed, *a clownish servant to Valentine.*
Launce, *the like to Proteus.*
Panthino, *servant to Antonio.*

Julia, *beloved of Proteus.*
Silvia, *beloved of Valentine.*
Lucetta, *waiting-woman to Julia.*

[Servants, Musicians.

Scene, *Verona; Milan; the frontiers of Mantua.*]

ACT I.

scene i. [*Verona. An open place.*]

[*Enter*] Valentine [*and*] Proteus.

Val. Cease to persuade, my loving Proteus:
Home-keeping youth have ever homely wits.
Were 't not affection chains thy tender days
To the sweet glances of thy honour'd love,
I rather would entreat thy company
To see the wonders of the world abroad
Than, living dully sluggardiz'd at home,
Wear out thy youth with shapeless idleness.
But since thou lov'st, love still and thrive therein,
Even as I would when I to love begin.
Pro. Wilt thou be gone? Sweet Valentine, adieu!
Think on thy Proteus, when thou haply seest
Some rare note-worthy object in thy travel:
Wish me partaker in thy happiness
When thou dost meet good hap; and in thy danger,
If ever danger do environ thee,
Commend thy grievance to my holy prayers,
For I will be thy beadsman, Valentine.
Val. And on a love-book pray for my success?
Pro. Upon some book I love I'll pray for thee.
Val. That 's on some shallow story of deep love:
How young Leander cross'd the Hellespont.
Pro. That 's a deep story of a deeper love;
For he was more than over shoes in love.
Val. 'Tis true; for you are over boots in love,
And yet you never swum the Hellespont.
Pro. Over the boots? nay, give me not the boots.
Val. No, I will not, for it boots thee not.
Pro. What?
Val. To be in love, where scorn is bought with groans;
Coy looks with heart-sore sighs; one fading moment's mirth
With twenty watchful, weary, tedious nights:
If haply won, perhaps a hapless gain;
If lost, why then a grievous labour won;
However, but a folly bought with wit,
Or else a wit by folly vanquished.
Pro. So, by your circumstance, you call me fool.
Val. So, by your circumstance, I fear you'll prove.
Pro. 'Tis love you cavil at: I am not Love.
Val. Love is your master, for he masters you:
And he that is so yoked by a fool,
Methinks, should not be chronicled for wise.
Pro. Yet writers say, as in the sweetest bud
The eating canker dwells, so eating love
Inhabits in the finest wits of all.
Val. And writers say, as the most forward bud
Is eaten by the canker ere it blow,
Even so by love the young and tender wit
Is turn'd to folly, blasting in the bud,
Losing his verdure even in the prime
And all the fair effects of future hopes.
But wherefore waste I time to counsel thee
That art a votary to fond desire?
Once more adieu! my father at the road
Expects my coming, there to see me shipp'd.
Pro. And thither will I bring thee, Valentine.
Val. Sweet Proteus, no; now let us take our leave.
To Milan let me hear from thee by letters
Of thy success in love and what news else
Betideth here in absence of thy friend;
And I likewise will visit thee with mine.
Pro. All happiness bechance to thee in Milan!
Val. As much to you at home! and so, farewell. *Exit.*
Pro. He after honour hunts, I after love:
He leaves his friends to dignify them more;
I leave myself, my friends and all, for love.
Thou, Julia, thou hast metamorphos'd me,
Made me neglect my studies, lose my time,
War with good counsel, set the world at nought;
Made wit with musing weak, heart sick with thought.

[*Enter*] Speed.

Speed. Sir Proteus, save you! Saw you my master?
Pro. But now he parted hence, to embark for Milan.

Act i. scene i. 3. **affection,** passion, love; see glossary. 9. **still,** always, constantly; see glossary. 18. **beadsman,** one engaged to pray for others. 19. **on a love-book,** i.e., instead of a prayer book. 20 ff. The puns and conceits throughout this and following dialogues are characteristic of Shakespeare's early style. As Shakespeare matures, such passages, when they occur, are more and more closely integrated into the substance of scene or character and have less the effect of a mere *tour de force.* Here the style sets the artificial tone which permeates the play. 27. **give me not the boots,** don't fool with me; don't be so flippant. 28. **boots,** avails, profits; see glossary. 29-30. **To . . . mirth,** typical Renaissance chatter in discussions of love. These are conventional details frequently attributed to lovers. Cf. ll. 65-69 and II, i, 17-33, below. 36, 37. **circumstance,** in the first instance, "detailed discourse," or "circumlocution"; in the second, "condition," or "state of affairs"; see glossary. 42-50. **Yet . . . hopes.** This passage offers an early instance of what is to become a characteristic of Shakespeare's felicitous style; that is, the repetition of phrases and images with infinite variety in treatment and substance. The best known example is *As You Like It,* II, vii, 113-226. 52. **fond,** foolish; see glossary. 57. **To Milan.** Today one does not travel from Verona to Milan by ship. In the sixteenth century this may have been the easier route. 58. **success,** outcome; see glossary. 64. **dignify,** i.e., by leaving them for self-improvement he will add luster to them. 71. **parted,** departed; see glossary.

Speed. Twenty to one then he is shipp'd already,
And I have play'd the sheep in losing him.
Pro. Indeed, a sheep doth very often stray,
An if the shepherd be a while away.
Speed. You conclude that my master is a shepherd then and I a sheep?
Pro. I do.
Speed. Why then, my horns are his horns, whether I wake or sleep.
Pro. A silly answer and fitting well a sheep.
Speed. This proves me still a sheep.
Pro. True; and thy master a shepherd.
Speed. Nay, that I can deny by a circumstance.
Pro. It shall go hard but I'll prove it by another.
Speed. The shepherd seeks the sheep, and not the sheep the shepherd; but I seek my master, and my master seeks not me: therefore I am no sheep.
Pro. The sheep for fodder follow the shepherd; the shepherd for food follows not the sheep: thou for wages followest thy master; thy master for wages follows not thee: therefore thou art a sheep.
Speed. Such another proof will make me cry 'baa.'
Pro. But, dost thou hear? gavest thou my letter to Julia?
Speed. Ay, sir: I, a lost mutton, gave your letter to her, a laced mutton, and she, a laced mutton, gave me, a lost mutton, nothing for my labour.
Pro. Here 's too small a pasture for such store of muttons.
Speed. If the ground be overcharged, you were best stick her.
Pro. Nay: in that you are astray, 'twere best pound you.
Speed. Nay, sir, less than a pound shall serve me for carrying your letter.
Pro. You mistake; I mean the pound,—a pinfold.
Speed. From a pound to a pin? fold it over and over,
'Tis threefold too little for carrying a letter to your lover.
Pro. But what said she?
Speed. [*First nodding*] Ay.
Pro. Nod—Ay—why, that 's noddy.
Speed. You mistook, sir; I say, she did nod: and you ask me if she did nod; and I say, 'Ay.'
Pro. And that set together is noddy.
Speed. Now you have taken the pains to set it together, take it for your pains.
Pro. No, no; you shall have it for bearing the letter.
Speed. Well, I perceive I must be fain to bear with you.
Pro. Why, sir, how do you bear with me?
Speed. Marry, sir, the letter, very orderly; having nothing but the word 'noddy' for my pains.
Pro. Beshrew me, but you have a quick wit.
Speed. And yet it cannot overtake your slow purse.
Pro. Come, come, open the matter in brief: what said she?
Speed. Open your purse, that the money and the matter may be both at once delivered.
Pro. Well, sir, here is for your pains. What said she?
Speed. Truly, sir, I think you'll hardly win her.
Pro. Why, couldst thou perceive so much from her?
Speed. Sir, I could perceive nothing at all from her; no, not so much as a ducat for delivering your letter: and being so hard to me that brought your mind, I fear she'll prove as hard to you in telling your mind. Give her no token but stones; for she 's as hard as steel.
Pro. What said she? nothing?
Speed. No, not so much as 'Take this for thy pains.' To testify your bounty, I thank you, you have testerned me; in requital whereof, henceforth carry your letters yourself: and so, sir, I'll commend you to my master.
Pro. Go, go, be gone, to save your ship from wrack,
Which cannot perish having thee aboard,
Being destin'd to a drier death on shore. [*Exit Speed.*]
I must go send some better messenger:
I fear my Julia would not deign my lines,
Receiving them from such a worthless post. *Exit.*

SCENE II. [*The same. Garden of* JULIA'S *house.*]

Enter JULIA *and* LUCETTA.

Jul. But say, Lucetta, now we are alone,
Wouldst thou then counsel me to fall in love?
Luc. Ay, madam, so you stumble not unheedfully.
Jul. Of all the fair resort of gentlemen
That every day with parle encounter me,
In thy opinion which is worthiest love?
Luc. Please you repeat their names, I'll show my mind
According to my shallow simple skill.
Jul. What think'st thou of the fair Sir Eglamour?
Luc. As of a knight well-spoken, neat and fine;
But, were I you, he never should be mine.
Jul. What think'st thou of the rich Mercatio?
Luc. Well of his wealth; but of himself, so so.
Jul. What think'st thou of the gentle Proteus?
Luc. Lord, Lord! to see what folly reigns in us!
Jul. How now! what means this passion at his name?
Luc. Pardon, dear madam: 'tis a passing shame
That I, unworthy body as I am,
Should censure thus on lovely gentlemen.
Jul. Why not on Proteus, as of all the rest?
Luc. Then thus: of many good I think him best.
Jul. Your reason?
Luc. I have no other but a woman's reason; I think him so because I think him so.
Jul. And wouldst thou have me cast my love on him?
Luc. Ay, if you thought your love not cast away.

72, 73. **shipp'd, sheep.** Elizabethan pronunciation doubtless made the pun obvious. 75. **An if,** though, even if; see glossary. 101, 102. **lost, laced.** As with *shipp'd, sheep,* above, the Elizabethan pronunciation of the two words was similar. 102. **laced mutton,** a courtesan. 108. **stick,** stab, with bawdy suggestion. 119. **noddy,** a simpleton. The New Cambridge editors suggest a quibble with "nothing." 130. **Marry,** mild oath, equivalent to "Indeed!" See glossary. 132. **Beshrew,** curse; see glossary. 141. **hardly,** with difficulty; see glossary. 145. **ducat,** silver coin worth about 3s. 6d. 147. **mind,** desires, intentions; see glossary. 153. **testerned,** given (me) a testern, a sixpence. 157-158. **Which . . . shore,** an allusion to the proverb, "He that is born to be hanged shall never be drowned." Cf. *The Tempest,* I, i, 31-32. 161. **post,** messenger; see glossary.

SCENE II. 4. **resort,** persons resorting to, or visiting (often by way of courtship). 5. **parle,** talk; see glossary. 7. **repeat their names.** Shakespeare uses this expository device with more point and greater effectiveness in *The Merchant of Venice,* where Portia has Nerissa recount the names of her suitors as a means of informing the audience. 9. **Sir Eglamour,** not to be identified with Silvia's friend of the same name. The New Cambridge editors suggest that in an earlier version of the play they were the same person. 16. **passion,** passionate outburst; see glossary. 17. **passing,** surpassing; see glossary. 19. **censure,** pass sentence; see glossary. 25-32. **And wouldst . . . their love.** This artificial style of speaking, in which the dialogue alternates line by line between two characters, is called stichomythia. It is a device from classical drama that Shakespeare employed occasionally in his

Jul. Why he, of all the rest, hath never mov'd me.
Luc. Yet he, of all the rest, I think, best loves ye.
Jul. His little speaking shows his love but small.
Luc. Fire that 's closest kept burns most of all.
Jul. They do not love that do not show their love.
Luc. O, they love least that let men know their love.
Jul. I would I knew his mind.
Luc. Peruse this paper, madam. [*Gives letter.*]
Jul. 'To Julia.' Say, from whom?
Luc. That the contents will show.
Jul. Say, say, who gave it thee?
Luc. Sir Valentine's page; and sent, I think, from Proteus.
He would have given it you; but I, being in the way,
Did in your name receive it: pardon the fault, I pray.
Jul. Now, by my modesty, a goodly broker!
Dare you presume to harbour wanton lines?
To whisper and conspire against my youth?
Now, trust me, 'tis an office of great worth
And you an officer fit for the place.
There, take the paper: see it be return'd;
Or else return no more into my sight.
Luc. To plead for love deserves more fee than hate.
Jul. Will ye be gone?
Luc. That you may ruminate. *Exit.*
Jul. And yet I would I had o'erlooked the letter:
It were a shame to call her back again
And pray her to a fault for which I chid her.
What 'fool is she, that knows I am a maid,
And would not force the letter to my view!
Since maids, in modesty, say 'no' to that
Which they would have the profferer construe 'ay.'
Fie, fie, how wayward is this foolish love
That, like a testy babe, will scratch the nurse
And presently all humbled kiss the rod!
How churlishly I chid Lucetta hence,
When willingly I would have had her here!
How angerly I taught my brow to frown,
When inward joy enforc'd my heart to smile!
My penance is to call Lucetta back
And ask remission for my folly past.
What ho! Lucetta!

[*Enter* LUCETTA.]

Luc. What would your ladyship?
Jul. Is 't near dinner-time?
Luc. I would it were,
That you might kill your stomach on your meat
And not upon your maid.
Jul. What is 't that you took up so gingerly?
Luc. Nothing.
Jul. Why didst thou stoop, then?
Luc. To take a paper up that I let fall.
Jul. And is that paper nothing?
Luc. Nothing concerning me.
Jul. Then let it lie for those that it concerns.
Luc. Madam, it will not lie where it concerns,
Unless it have a false interpreter.
Jul. Some love of yours hath writ to you in rhyme.
Luc. That I might sing it, madam, to a tune.
Give me a note: your ladyship can set.
Jul. As little by such toys as may be possible.
Best sing it to the tune of 'Light o' love.'
Luc. It is too heavy for so light a tune.
Jul. Heavy! belike it hath some burden then?
Luc. Ay, and melodious were it, would you sing it.
Jul. And why not you?
Luc. I cannot reach so high.
Jul. Let 's see your song. How now, minion!
Luc. Keep tune there still, so you will sing it out:
And yet methinks I do not like this tune.
Jul. You do not?
Luc. No, madam; it is too sharp.
Jul. You, minion, are too saucy.
Luc. Nay, now you are too flat
And mar the concord with too harsh a descant:
There wanteth but a mean to fill your song.
Jul. The mean is drown'd with your unruly bass.
Luc. Indeed, I bid the base for Proteus.
Jul. This babble shall not henceforth trouble me.
Here is a coil with protestation! [*Tears the letter.*]
Go get you gone, and let the papers lie:
You would be fing'ring them, to anger me.
Luc. She makes it strange; but she would be best pleas'd
To be so ang'red with another letter. [*Exit.*]
Jul. Nay, would I were so ang'red with the same!
O hateful hands, to tear such loving words!
Injurious wasps, to feed on such sweet honey
And kill the bees that yield it with your stings!
I'll kiss each several paper for amends.
Look, here is writ 'kind Julia.' Unkind Julia!
As in revenge of thy ingratitude,
I throw thy name against the bruising stones,
Trampling contemptuously on thy disdain.
And here is writ 'love-wounded Proteus.'
Poor wounded name! my bosom as a bed
Shall lodge thee till thy wound be throughly heal'd;
And thus I search it with a sovereign kiss.
But twice or thrice was 'Proteus' written down.
Be calm, good wind, blow not a word away
Till I have found each letter in the letter,
Except mine own name: that some whirlwind bear
Unto a ragged fearful-hanging rock
And throw it thence into the raging sea!
Lo, here in one line is his name twice writ,
'Poor forlorn Proteus, passionate Proteus,
To the sweet Julia:' that I'll tear away.
And yet I will not, sith so prettily
He couples it to his complaining names.
Thus will I fold them one upon another:
Now kiss, embrace, contend, do what you will.

earlier plays. 27. **mov'd,** made a proposal to, appealed or applied to; see glossary. 41. **broker,** agent, intermediary (particularly in love affairs). 53. **What 'fool,** so F; Globe: *What a fool.* 68. **stomach,** a quibble on the meanings "appetite" and "angry temper"; see glossary. **meat,** pronounced more nearly like "mate," punning on *maid* in the next line. 80-97. **That . . . Proteus.** The quibbles on musical terms here are obvious enough in themselves; but their rapid succession, probably accompanied by gestures and stage business, makes the passage difficult to follow in reading. 81. **note,** a quibbling reference to Proteus' letter. **set,** i.e., set to music, with quibble on "writing a letter." 82. **toys,** trifles; see glossary. 83. **'Light o' love,'** an air well known at the time. Cf. *Much Ado about Nothing,* III, iv, 44, where it is mentioned as here with a quibble on *burden.* 85. **burden,** bass accompaniment to a melody. 87. **reach so high.** Proteus' rank is too high for Lucetta to aspire to. 88. **minion,** saucy woman; see glossary. 89. **tune,** temper, mood. 91, 93. **sharp, flat.** The New Cambridge editors suggest a pinch and a slap as accompanying stage business. 94. **descant,** improvised harmony accompanying a melody. 95. **mean,** tenor part; a reference to Proteus; see glossary. 97. **bid the base,** a challenge in the game of prisoner's base. 99. **coil,** commotion, fuss. **protestation,** solemn declaration or promise. 102. **makes it strange,** pretends indifference or ignorance; see *strange* in glossary. 108. **several,** separate; see glossary. 109. **Unkind,** unnatural, cruel; see glossary. 116. **search,** probe, as a wound. 126. **sith,** since; see glossary.

[*Enter* LUCETTA.]

Luc. Madam,
Dinner is ready, and your father stays.
Jul. Well, let us go.
Luc. What, shall these papers lie like telltales here?
Jul. If you respect them, best to take them up.
Luc. Nay, I was taken up for laying them down:
Yet here they shall not lie, for catching cold.
Jul. I see you have a month's mind to them.
Luc. Ay, madam, you may say what sights you see;
I see things too, although you judge I wink.
Jul. Come, come; will 't please you go? *Exeunt.*

SCENE III. [*The same.* ANTONIO's *house.*]

Enter ANTONIO *and* PANTHINO.

Ant. Tell me, Panthino, what sad talk was that
Wherewith my brother held you in the cloister?
Pan. 'Twas of his nephew Proteus, your son.
Ant. Why, what of him?
Pan. He wond'red that your lordship
Would suffer him to spend his youth at home,
While other men, of slender reputation,
Put forth their sons to seek preferment out:
Some to the wars, to try their fortune there;
Some to discover islands far away;
Some to the studious universities.
For any or for all these exercises
He said that Proteus your son was meet,
And did request me to importune you
To let him spend his time no more at home,
Which would be great impeachment to his age,
In having known no travel in his youth.
Ant. Nor need'st thou much importune me to that
Whereon this month I have been hammering.
I have consider'd well his loss of time
And how he cannot be a perfect man,
Not being tried and tutor'd in the world:
Experience is by industry achiev'd
And perfected by the swift course of time.
Then tell me, whither were I best to send him?
Pan. I think your lordship is not ignorant
How his companion, youthful Valentine,
Attends the emperor in his royal court.
Ant. I know it well.
Pan. 'Twere good, I think, your lordship sent him thither:
There shall he practise tilts and tournaments,
Hear sweet discourse, converse with noblemen,
And be in eye of every exercise
Worthy his youth and nobleness of birth.
Ant. I like thy counsel; well hast thou advis'd:
And that thou mayst perceive how well I like it
The execution of it shall make known.
Even with the speediest expedition
I will dispatch him to the emperor's court.
Pan. To-morrow, may it please you, Don Alphonso
With other gentlemen of good esteem
Are journeying to salute the emperor
And to commend their service to his will.
Ant. Good company; with them shall Proteus go:
And, in good time! now will we break with him.

[*Enter*] PROTEUS.

Pro. Sweet love! sweet lines! sweet life!
Here is her hand, the agent of her heart;
Here is her oath for love, her honour's pawn.
O, that our fathers would applaud our loves,
To seal our happiness with their consents!
O heavenly Julia!
Ant. How now! what letter are you reading there?
Pro. May 't please your lordship, 'tis a word or two
Of commendations sent from Valentine,
Deliver'd by a friend that came from him.
Ant. Lend me the letter; let me see what news.
Pro. There is no news, my lord, but that he writes
How happily he lives, how well belov'd
And daily graced by the emperor;
Wishing me with him, partner of his fortune.
Ant. And how stand you affected to his wish?
Pro. As one relying on your lordship's will
And not depending on his friendly wish.
Ant. My will is something sorted with his wish.
Muse not that I thus suddenly proceed;
For what I will, I will, and there an end.
I am resolv'd that thou shalt spend some time
With Valentinus in the emperor's court:
What maintenance he from his friends receives,
Like exhibition thou shalt have from me.
To-morrow be in readiness to go:
Excuse it not, for I am peremptory.
Pro. My lord, I cannot be so soon provided:
Please you, deliberate a day or two.
Ant. Look what thou want'st shall be sent after thee:
No more of stay! to-morrow thou must go.
Come on, Panthino: you shall be employ'd
To hasten on his expedition. [*Exeunt Ant. and Pan.*]
Pro. Thus have I shunn'd the fire for fear of burning,
And drench'd me in the sea, where I am drown'd.
I fear'd to show my father Julia's letter,
Lest he should take exceptions to my love;
And with the vantage of mine own excuse
Hath he excepted most against my love.
O, how this spring of love resembleth
The uncertain glory of an April day,
Which now shows all the beauty of the sun,
And by and by a cloud takes all away!

[*Enter* PANTHINO.]

Pan. Sir Proteus, your father calls for you:
He is in haste; therefore, I pray you, go.
Pro. Why, this it is: my heart accords thereto,
And yet a thousand times it answers 'no.' *Exeunt.*

---

131. **stays,** waits; see glossary; cf. note to II, ii, 13, below. 134. **respect,** prize, esteem; see glossary. 137. **month's mind,** inclination, liking. 139. **wink,** have the eyes closed; see glossary.

SCENE III. 1. **sad,** serious; see glossary. 4-16. **He . . . youth.** These lines reflect some Renaissance customs in the education of young gentlemen; cf. ll. 30-32, below. 6. **slender reputation,** i.e., men of lower station than yourself. 7. **Put . . . sons,** send their sons away from home. **out,** abroad; see glossary. 15. **impeachment . . . age,** detriment or cause for reproach to him in his mature years. 18. **hammering,** beating (an idea) into shape; cf. *Richard II*, V, v, 5. 27. **emperor,** i.e., the duke of Milan, not the ruler of the Holy Roman Empire. 30. **practise,** perform, take part in; see glossary. 31. **discourse,** conversation; see glossary. **converse,** associate with; see glossary. 44. **break with,** reveal, disclose (it to him). 49. **seal,** conclude, ratify; see glossary. 58. **graced,** favored; see glossary. 60. **affected,** disposed, inclined; see glossary. 63. **something,** somewhat; see glossary. **sorted,** adapted, made to agree. 69. **exhibition,** allowance of money. 71. **Excuse,** decline, offer no excuses; see glossary. 82. **vantage,** ad-

ACT II.

SCENE I. [*Milan. The* DUKE's *palace.*]

Enter VALENTINE [*and*] SPEED.

Speed. Sir, your glove.
Val. Not mine; my gloves are on.

Speed. Why, then, this may be yours, for this is but one.

Val. Ha! let me see: ay, give it me, it 's mine:
Sweet ornament that decks a thing divine!
Ah, Silvia, Silvia!

Speed. Madam Silvia! Madam Silvia!

Val. How now, sirrah?

Speed. She is not within hearing, sir.

Val. Why, sir, who bade you call her?

Speed. Your worship, sir; or else I mistook.

Val. Well, you'll still be too forward.

Speed. And yet I was last chidden for being too slow.

Val. Go to, sir: tell me, do you know Madam Silvia?

Speed. She that your worship loves?

Val. Why, how know you that I am in love?

Speed. Marry, by these special marks: first, you have learned, like Sir Proteus, to wreathe your arms, like a malecontent; to relish a love-song, like a robin-redbreast; to walk alone, like one that had the pestilence; to sigh, like a schoolboy that had lost his A B C; to weep, like a young wench that had buried her grandam; to fast, like one that takes diet; to watch, like one that fears robbing; to speak puling, like a beggar at Hallowmas. You were wont, when you laughed, to crow like a cock; when you walked, to walk like one of the lions; when you fasted, it was presently after dinner; when you looked sadly, it was for want of money: and now you are metamorphosed with a mistress, that, when I look on you, I can hardly think you my master.

Val. Are all these things perceived in me?

Speed. They are all perceived without ye.

Val. Without me? they cannot.

Speed. Without you? nay, that 's certain, for, without you were so simple, none else would: but you are so without these follies, that these follies are within you and shine through you like the water in an urinal, that not an eye that sees you but is a physician to comment on your malady.

Val. But tell me, dost thou know my lady Silvia?

Speed. She that you gaze on so as she sits at supper?

Val. Hast thou observed that? even she, I mean.

Speed. Why, sir, I know her not.

Val. Dost thou know her by my gazing on her, and yet knowest her not?

Speed. Is she not hard-favoured, sir?

Val. Not so fair, boy, as well-favoured.

Speed. Sir, I know that well enough.

Val. What dost thou know?

Speed. That she is not so fair as, of you, well favoured.

Val. I mean that her beauty is exquisite, but her favour infinite.

Speed. That 's because the one is painted and the other out of all count.

Val. How painted? and how out of count?

Speed. Marry, sir, so painted, to make her fair, that no man counts of her beauty.

Val. How esteemest thou me? I account of her beauty.

Speed. You never saw her since she was deformed.

Val. How long hath she been deformed?

Speed. Ever since you loved her.

Val. I have loved her ever since I saw her; and still I see her beautiful.

Speed. If you love her, you cannot see her.

Val. Why?

Speed. Because Love is blind. O, that you had mine eyes; or your own eyes had the lights they were wont to have when you chid at Sir Proteus for going ungartered!

Val. What should I see then?

Speed. Your own present folly and her passing deformity: for he, being in love, could not see to garter his hose, and you, being in love, cannot see to put on your hose.

Val. Belike, boy, then, you are in love; for last morning you could not see to wipe my shoes.

Speed. True, sir; I was in love with my bed: I thank you, you swinged me for my love, which makes me the bolder to chide you for yours.

Val. In conclusion, I stand affected to her.

Speed. I would you were set, so your affection would cease.

Val. Last night she enjoined me to write some lines to one she loves.

Speed. And have you?

Val. I have.

Speed. Are they not lamely writ?

Val. No, boy, but as well as I can do them. Peace! here she comes.

Speed. [*Aside*] O excellent motion! O exceeding puppet! Now will he interpret to her.

[*Enter*] SILVIA.

Val. Madam and mistress, a thousand good-morrows.

Speed. [*Aside*] O, give ye good even! here 's a million of manners.

Sil. Sir Valentine and servant, to you two thousand.

Speed. [*Aside*] He should give her interest, and she gives it him.

Val. As you enjoin'd me, I have writ your letter
Unto the secret nameless friend of yours;
Which I was much unwilling to proceed in
But for my duty to your ladyship. [*Gives letter.*]

Sil. I thank you, gentle servant: 'tis very clerkly done.

Val. Now trust me, madam, it came hardly off;
For being ignorant to whom it goes
I writ at random, very doubtfully.

Sil. Perchance you think too much of so much pains?

vantage; i.e., by my excuse I have given him the advantage whereby he makes my love to suffer most; see glossary.

ACT II. SCENE I. 14. **Go to,** an expression of remonstrance; see glossary. 19. **wreathe . . . malecontent,** allusion to the posture of an unhappy malcontent. 23. **A B C,** ABC book, primer. 25. **watch,** lie awake, sit up at night; see glossary. 26-27. **a beggar at Hallowmas,** a reference to a custom of begging alms on All Saints' Day. 30. **presently,** immediately; see glossary. 60. **favour,** charm, kindness; see glossary. 62. **out . . . count,** incalculable. 65. **counts,** makes account of. 70. **deformed,** i.e., the lover's distorted vision alters his lady's true appearance. 91. **set,** seated, as opposed to *stand* in the preceding line, with a quibble on the meaning "concluded." 100, 101. **motion, puppet, interpret.** In a puppet show (called *motion*), the voice speaking for the puppet is said to *interpret. Motion* and *puppet* refer to Silvia, probably splendidly dressed. 106. **servant,** a term of gallantry, denoting a man devoted to serving a lady. 113. **duty,** obedience, submission; see glossary. 114. **clerkly,** in a scholarly manner.

Val. No, madam; so it stead you, I will write,
Please you command, a thousand times as much;
And yet—
Sil. A pretty period! Well, I guess the sequel;
And yet I will not name it; and yet I care not;
And yet take this again; and yet I thank you,
Meaning henceforth to trouble you no more.
Speed. [*Aside*] And yet you will; and yet another 'yet.'
Val. What means your ladyship? do you not like it?
Sil. Yes, yes: the lines are very quaintly writ;
But since unwillingly, take them again.
Nay, take them. [*Gives back the letter.*]
Val. Madam, they are for you.
Sil. Ay, ay: you writ them, sir, at my request;
But I will none of them; they are for you;
I would have had them writ more movingly.
Val. Please you, I'll write your ladyship another.
Sil. And when it 's writ, for my sake read it over,
And if it please you, so; if not, why, so.
Val. If it please me, madam, what then?
Sil. Why, if it please you, take it for your labour:
And so, good morrow, servant. *Exit Sil.*
Speed. O jest unseen, inscrutable, invisible,
As a nose on a man's face, or a weathercock on a steeple!
My master sues to her, and she hath taught her suitor,
He being her pupil, to become her tutor.
O excellent device! was there ever heard a better,
That my master, being scribe, to himself should write the letter?

Val. How now, sir? what are you reasoning with yourself?

Speed. Nay, I was rhyming: 'tis you that have the reason.

Val. To do what?
Speed. To be a spokesman from Madam Silvia.
Val. To whom?
Speed. To yourself: why, she wooes you by a figure.
Val. What figure?
Speed. By a letter, I should say.
Val. Why, she hath not writ to me?

Speed. What need she, when she hath made you write to yourself? Why, do you not perceive the jest?

Val. No, believe me.

Speed. No believing you, indeed, sir. But did you perceive her earnest?

Val. She gave me none, except an angry word.
Speed. Why, she hath given you a letter.
Val. That 's the letter I writ to her friend.

Speed. And that letter hath she delivered, and there an end.

Val. I would it were no worse.
Speed. I'll warrant you, 'tis as well:
For often have you writ to her, and she, in modesty,
Or else for want of idle time, could not again reply;
Or fearing else some messenger that might her mind discover,
Herself hath taught her love himself to write unto her lover.
All this I speak in print, for in print I found it.
Why muse you, sir? 'tis dinner-time.
Val. I have dined.

Speed. Ay, but hearken, sir; though the chameleon Love can feed on the air, I am one that am nourished by my victuals and would fain have meat. O, be not like your mistress; be moved, be moved. *Exeunt.*

SCENE II. [*Verona.* JULIA'S *house.*]

Enter PROTEUS [*and*] JULIA.

Pro. Have patience, gentle Julia.
Jul. I must, where is no remedy.
Pro. When possibly I can, I will return.
Jul. If you turn not, you will return the sooner.
Keep this remembrance for thy Julia's sake.
[*Giving a ring.*]
Pro. Why, then, we'll make exchange; here, take you this.
Jul. And seal the bargain with a holy kiss.
Pro. Here is my hand for my true constancy;
And when that hour o'erslips me in the day
Wherein I sigh not, Julia, for thy sake,
The next ensuing hour some foul mischance
Torment me for my love's forgetfulness!
My father stays my coming; answer not;
The tide is now: nay, not thy tide of tears;
That tide will stay me longer than I should.
Julia, farewell! [*Exit Julia.*]
What, gone without a word?
Ay, so true love should do: it cannot speak;
For truth hath better deeds than words to grace it.

[*Enter*] PANTHINO.

Pan. Sir Proteus, you are stay'd for.
Pro. Go: I come, I come.
Alas! this parting strikes poor lovers dumb. *Exeunt.*

SCENE III. [*The same. A street.*]

Enter LAUNCE [*leading a dog*].

Launce. Nay, 'twill be this hour ere I have done weeping; all the kind of the Launces have this very fault. I have received my proportion, like the prodigious son, and am going with Sir Proteus to the Imperial's court. I think Crab my dog be the sourest-natured dog that lives: my mother weeping, my father wailing, my sister crying, our maid howling, our cat wringing her hands, and all our house in a great perplexity, yet did not this cruel-hearted cur shed one tear: he is a stone, a very pebblestone, and has no more pity in him than a dog: a Jew would have wept to have seen our parting; why, my grandam, having no eyes, look you, wept herself blind at my parting. Nay, I'll show you the manner of it. This shoe is my father: no, this left shoe is my father: no, no, this left shoe is my mother: nay, that cannot be so neither: yes, it is so, it is so, it hath the worser sole. This shoe,

119. **stead,** help; be of use to; see glossary. 154. **figure,** device, ruse, perhaps with a quibble on the rhetorical sense. 163. **earnest,** quibble between "seriousness" and "money paid as an installment to secure a bargain"; see glossary. 175. **speak in print,** i.e., he has memorized the verse.

SCENE II. 2. **where,** where there; an instance of a type of ellipsis frequent in Elizabethan English in which the conjunctive serves a double function. 13. **stays,** waits for; so likewise *stay'd for* (l. 19 below), where modern usage employs the active, "they wait for you"; see glossary.

SCENE III. 2. **kind,** kindred, race; see glossary. 3. **proportion,** portion, allotment; see glossary. 30-31. **a wood woman.** F: *a would-woman.* The emendation is Theobald's and is accepted by all modern editors; *wood* meaning "mad," with quibble on "wooden shoe." The New with the hole in it, is my mother, and this my father; a vengeance on 't! there 'tis: now, sir, this staff is my sister, for, look you, she is as white as a lily and as small as a wand: this hat is Nan, our maid: I am the dog: no, the dog is himself, and I am the dog—Oh! the dog is me, and I am myself; ay, so, so. Now come I to my father; Father, your blessing: now should not the shoe speak a word for weeping: now should I kiss my father; well, he weeps on. Now come I to my mother: O, that she could speak now like a wood woman! Well, I kiss her; why, there 'tis; here 's my mother's breath up and down. Now come I to my sister; mark the moan she makes. Now the dog all this while sheds not a tear nor speaks a word; but see how I lay the dust with my tears.

[*Enter*] PANTHINO.

Pan. Launce, away, away, aboard! thy master is shipped and thou art to post after with oars. What 's the matter? why weepest thou, man? Away, ass! you'll lose the tide, if you tarry any longer.

Launce. It is no matter if the tied were lost; for it is the unkindest tied that ever any man tied.

Pan. What 's the unkindest tide?

Launce. Why, he that 's tied here, Crab, my dog.

Pan. Tut, man, I mean thou 'lt lose the flood, and, in losing the flood, lose thy voyage, and, in losing thy voyage, lose thy master, and, in losing thy master, lose thy service, and, in losing thy service,—Why dost thou stop my mouth? 51

Launce. For fear thou shouldst lose thy tongue.

Pan. Where should I lose my tongue?

Launce. In thy tale.

Pan. In my tail!

Launce. Lose the tide, and the voyage, and the master, and the service, and the tied! Why, man, if the river were dry, I am able to fill it with my tears; if the wind were down, I could drive the boat with my sighs.

Pan. Come, come away, man; I was sent to call thee.

Launce. Sir, call me what thou darest.

Pan. Wilt thou go?

Launce. Well, I will go. *Exeunt.*

SCENE IV. [*Milan. The* DUKE'S *palace.*]

Enter VALENTINE, SILVIA, THURIO, [*and*] SPEED.

Sil. Servant!

Val. Mistress?

Speed. Master, Sir Thurio frowns on you.

Val. Ay, boy, it 's for love.

Speed. Not of you.

Val. Of my mistress, then.

Speed. 'Twere good you knocked him. [*Exit.*]

Sil. Servant, you are sad.

Val. Indeed, madam, I seem so.

Thu. Seem you that you are not?

Val. Haply I do.

Thu. So do counterfeits.

Val. So do you.

Thu. What seem I that I am not?

Val. Wise.

Thu. What instance of the contrary?

Val. Your folly.

Thu. And how quote you my folly?

Val. I quote it in your jerkin.

Thu. My jerkin is a doublet.

Val. Well, then, I'll double your folly.

Thu. How?

Sil. What, angry, Sir Thurio! do you change colour?

Val. Give him leave, madam; he is a kind of chameleon.

Thu. That hath more mind to feed on your blood than live in your air.

Val. You have said, sir.

Thu. Ay, sir, and done too, for this time.

Val. I know it well, sir; you always end ere you begin.

Sil. A fine volley of words, gentlemen, and quickly shot off.

Val. 'Tis indeed, madam; we thank the giver.

Sil. Who is that, servant?

Val. Yourself, sweet lady; for you gave the fire. Sir Thurio borrows his wit from your ladyship's looks, and spends what he borrows kindly in your company.

Thu. Sir, if you spend word for word with me, I shall make your wit bankrupt.

Val. I know it well, sir; you have an exchequer of words, and, I think, no other treasure to give your followers, for it appears, by their bare liveries, that they live by your bare words.

Sil. No more, gentlemen, no more: here comes my father.

[*Enter*] DUKE.

Duke. Now, daughter Silvia, you are hard beset.
Sir Valentine, your father 's in good health:
What say you to a letter from your friends
Of much good news?

Val. My lord, I will be thankful
To any happy messenger from thence.

Duke. Know ye Don Antonio, your countryman?

Val. Ay, my good lord, I know the gentleman
To be of worth and worthy estimation
And not without desert so well reputed.

Duke. Hath he not a son?

Val. Ay, my good lord; a son that well deserves
The honour and regard of such a father.

Duke. You know him well?

Val. I know him as myself; for from our infancy
We have convers'd and spent our hours together:
And though myself have been an idle truant,
Omitting the sweet benefit of time
To clothe mine age with angel-like perfection,
Yet hath Sir Proteus, for that 's his name,
Made use and fair advantage of his days;
His years but young, but his experience old;
His head unmellowed, but his judgement ripe;
And, in a word, for far behind his worth

Cambridge editors see a possible misreading by the compositor of *a nould* (i.e., an old) *woman*, and suggest another possibility, *a wold-woman*, i.e., a country woman. 37. **post,** hasten; see glossary. 55. **my,** so Hanmer; Globe, following F: *thy*.

SCENE IV. 16. **instance,** proof; see glossary. 18. **quote,** notice, observe. 19. **jerkin,** close-fitting jacket, frequently of leather. 20. **doublet,** close-fitting garment with or without sleeves; possible quibble on the sense of "duplicity." 38-40. **Sir Thurio . . . company,** i.e., what he borrows from you he naturally (*kindly*) spends in your company. 49. **hard,** much. The New Cambridge editors suspect a cut here because of the abruptness of the remark.

Comes all the praises that I now bestow,
He is complete in feature and in mind
With all good grace to grace a gentleman.
Duke. Beshrew me, sir, but if he make this good,
He is as worthy for an empress' love
As meet to be an emperor's counsellor.
Well, sir, this gentleman is come to me,
With commendation from great potentates;
And here he means to spend his time awhile:
I think 'tis no unwelcome news to you.
Val. Should I have wish'd a thing, it had been he.
Duke. Welcome him then according to his worth.
Silvia, I speak to you, and you, Sir Thurio;
For Valentine, I need not cite him to it:
I will send him hither to you presently. [*Exit*.]
Val. This is the gentleman I told your ladyship
Had come along with me, but that his mistress
Did hold his eyes lock'd in her crystal looks.
Sil. Belike that now she hath enfranchis'd them
Upon some other pawn for fealty.
Val. Nay, sure, I think she holds them prisoners still.
Sil. Nay, then he should be blind; and, being blind,
How could he see his way to seek out you?
Val. Why, lady, Love hath twenty pair of eyes.
Thu. They say that Love hath not an eye at all.
Val. To see such lovers, Thurio, as yourself:
Upon a homely object Love can wink.
Sil. Have done, have done; here comes the gentleman. [*Exit Thurio*.]

[*Enter*] PROTEUS.

Val. Welcome, dear Proteus! Mistress, I beseech you,
Confirm his welcome with some special favour.
Sil. His worth is warrant for his welcome hither,
If this be he you oft have wish'd to hear from.
Val. Mistress, it is: sweet lady, entertain him
To be my fellow-servant to your ladyship.
Sil. Too low a mistress for so high a servant.
Pro. Not so, sweet lady: but too mean a servant
To have a look of such a worthy mistress.
Val. Leave off discourse of disability:
Sweet lady, entertain him for your servant.
Pro. My duty will I boast of; nothing else.
Sil. And duty never yet did want his meed:
Servant, you are welcome to a worthless mistress.
Pro. I'll die on him that says so but yourself.
Sil. That you are welcome?
Pro. That you are worthless.

[*Enter* THURIO.]

Thu. Madam, my lord your father would speak with you.
Sil. I wait upon his pleasure. Come, Sir Thurio,
Go with me. Once more, new servant, welcome:
I'll leave you to confer of home affairs;
When you have done, we look to hear from you.
Pro. We'll both attend upon your ladyship.
[*Exeunt Silvia and Thurio*.]
Val. Now, tell me how do all from whence you came?
Pro. Your friends are well and have them much commended.
Val. And how do yours?
Pro. I left them all in health.
Val. How does your lady? and how thrives your love?
Pro. My tales of love were wont to weary you;
I know you joy not in a love-discourse.
Val. Ay, Proteus, but that life is alter'd now:
I have done penance for contemning Love,
Whose high imperious thoughts have punish'd me
With bitter fasts, with penitential groans,
With nightly tears and daily heart-sore sighs;
For in revenge of my contempt of love,
Love hath chas'd sleep from my enthralled eyes
And made them watchers of mine own heart's sorrow.
O gentle Proteus, Love 's a mighty lord
And hath so humbled me as I confess
There is no woe to his correction
Nor to his service no such joy on earth.
Now no discourse, except it be of love;
Now can I break my fast, dine, sup and sleep,
Upon the very naked name of love.
Pro. Enough; I read your fortune in your eye.
Was this the idol that you worship so?
Val. Even she; and is she not a heavenly saint?
Pro. No; but she is an earthly paragon.
Val. Call her divine.
Pro. I will not flatter her.
Val. O, flatter me; for love delights in praises.
Pro. When I was sick, you gave me bitter pills,
And I must minister the like to you.
Val. Then speak the truth by her; if not divine,
Yet let her be a principality,
Sovereign to all the creatures on the earth.
Pro. Except my mistress.
Val. Sweet, except not any;
Except thou wilt except against my love.
Pro. Have I not reason to prefer mine own?
Val. And I will help thee to prefer her too:
She shall be dignified with this high honour—
To bear my lady's train, lest the base earth
Should from her vesture chance to steal a kiss
And, of so great a favour growing proud,
Disdain to root the summer-swelling flow'r
And make rough winter everlastingly.
Pro. Why, Valentine, what braggardism is this?
Val. Pardon me, Proteus: all I can is nothing
To her whose worth makes other worthies nothing;
She is alone.
Pro. Then let her alone.
Val. Not for the world: why, man, she is mine own,
And I as rich in having such a jewel
As twenty seas, if all their sand were pearl,
The water nectar and the rocks pure gold.
Forgive me that I do not dream on thee,
Because thou see'st me dote upon my love.
My foolish rival, that her father likes
Only for his possessions are so huge,
Is gone with her along, and I must after,
For love, thou know'st, is full of jealousy.
Pro. But she loves you?

73. **complete,** perfect; see glossary. **feature,** shape or form of body; see glossary. 90. **Belike that,** perhaps. 104. **entertain,** take into one's service; see glossary. 112. **want,** lack, be without; see glossary. **his,** its; see glossary. 135. **watchers of,** those who stay awake with; cf. *watch,* II, i, 25. 137. **as,** that; see glossary. 156, 157. **prefer,** in the first instance, the modern sense; in the second, "advance." 165. **can,** know; see glossary. 196. **eye,** not in F or Globe. **Valentine's** (pronounced with four syllables). 198. **reasonless,** without justification, wrongly. 207. **advice,** deliberation, reflection; see glossary. 213. **check,** restrain; see glossary.

Val. Ay, and we are betroth'd: nay, more, our marriage-hour,
With all the cunning manner of our flight,
Determin'd of; how I must climb her window,
The ladder made of cords, and all the means
Plotted and 'greed on for my happiness.
Good Proteus, go with me to my chamber,
In these affairs to aid me with thy counsel.
Pro. Go on before; I shall inquire you forth:
I must unto the road, to disembark
Some necessaries that I needs must use,
And then I'll presently attend you.
Val. Will you make haste? *Exit.*
Pro. I will.
Even as one heat another heat expels,
Or as one nail by strength drives out another,
So the remembrance of my former love
Is by a newer object quite forgotten.
†Is it mine eye, or Valentine's praise,
Her true perfection, or my false transgression,
That makes me reasonless to reason thus?
She is fair; and so is Julia that I love—
That I did love, for now my love is thaw'd;
Which, like a waxen image 'gainst a fire,
Bears no impression of the thing it was.
Methinks my zeal to Valentine is cold,
And that I love him not as I was wont.
O, but I love his lady too too much,
And that 's the reason I love him so little.
How shall I dote on her with more advice,
That thus without advice begin to love her!
'Tis but her picture I have yet beheld,
And that hath dazzled my reason's light;
But when I look on her perfections,
There is no reason but I shall be blind.
If I can check my erring love, I will:
If not, to compass her I'll use my skill. *Exit.*

SCENE V. [*The same. A street.*]

Enter SPEED *and* LAUNCE [*severally*].

Speed. Launce! by mine honesty, welcome to Milan!

Launce. Forswear not thyself, sweet youth, for I am not welcome. I reckon this always, that a man is never undone till he be hanged, nor never welcome to a place till some certain shot be paid and the hostess say 'Welcome!'

Speed. Come on, you madcap, I'll to the alehouse with you presently; where, for one shot of five pence, thou shalt have five thousand welcomes. But, sirrah, how did thy master part with Madam Julia?

Launce. Marry, after they closed in earnest, they parted very fairly in jest.

Speed. But shall she marry him?

Launce. No.

Speed. How then? shall he marry her?

Launce. No, neither.

Speed. What, are they broken?

Launce. No, they are both as whole as a fish.

Speed. Why, then, how stands the matter with them?

Launce. Marry, thus; when it stands well with him, it stands well with her.

Speed. What an ass art thou! I understand thee not.

Launce. What a block art thou, that thou canst not! My staff understands me.

Speed. What thou sayest?

Launce. Ay, and what I do too: look thee, I'll but lean, and my staff understands me.

Speed. It stands under thee, indeed.

Launce. Why, stand-under and under-stand is all one.

Speed. But tell me true, will 't be a match?

Launce. Ask my dog: if he say ay, it will; if he say no, it will; if he shake his tail and say nothing, it will.

Speed. The conclusion is then that it will.

Launce. Thou shalt never get such a secret from me but by a parable.

Speed. 'Tis well that I get it so. But, Launce, how sayest thou, that my master is become a notable lover?

Launce. I never knew him otherwise.

Speed. Than how?

Launce. A notable lubber, as thou reportest him to be.

Speed. Why, thou whoreson ass, thou mistakest me.

Launce. Why, fool, I meant not thee; I meant thy master.

Speed. I tell thee, my master is become a hot lover.

Launce. Why, I tell thee, I care not though he burn himself in love. If thou wilt, go with me to the alehouse; if not, thou art an Hebrew, a Jew, and not worth the name of a Christian.

Speed. Why?

Launce. Because thou hast not so much charity in thee as to go to the ale with a Christian. Wilt thou go?

Speed. At thy service. *Exeunt.*

SCENE VI. [*The same. The* DUKE'S *palace.*]

Enter PROTEUS *solus.*

Pro. To leave my Julia, shall I be forsworn;
To love fair Silvia, shall I be forsworn;
To wrong my friend, I shall be much forsworn;
And ev'n that pow'r which gave me first my oath
Provokes me to this threefold perjury;
Love bade me swear and Love bids me forswear.
O sweet-suggesting Love, if thou hast sinn'd,
Teach me, thy tempted subject, to excuse it!
At first I did adore a twinkling star,
But now I worship a celestial sun.
Unheedful vows may heedfully be broken,
And he wants wit that wants resolved will
To learn his wit t' exchange the bad for better.
Fie, fie, unreverend tongue! to call her bad,
Whose sovereignty so oft thou hast preferr'd
With twenty thousand soul-confirming oaths.
I cannot leave to love, and yet I do;
But there I leave to love where I should love.
Julia I lose and Valentine I lose:
If I keep them, I needs must lose myself;

SCENE V. 2. **Milan.** F: *Padua.* Other errors in place names occur at III, i, 81 and V, iv, 129. 5. **undone,** ruined; see glossary. 7. **shot,** fee; tavern reckoning. 11. **sirrah,** ordinary form of address to inferiors; see glossary. 13. **closed,** came to terms. 14. **fairly,** kindly, gently; see glossary. 23. **stands,** with a bawdy pun. 41. **parable,** enigmatical talk. 61. **ale,** church ale or festival.

SCENE VI. 7. **sweet-suggesting,** sweetly seductive. 13. **learn,** teach; see glossary. 15. **preferr'd,** introduced, recommended. 17. **leave to love,** cease loving.

If I lose them, thus find I by their loss
For Valentine myself, for Julia Silvia.
I to myself am dearer than a friend,
For love is still most precious in itself;
And Silvia—witness Heaven, that made her fair!—
Shows Julia but a swarthy Ethiope.
I will forget that Julia is alive,
Rememb'ring that my love to her is dead;
And Valentine I'll hold an enemy,
Aiming at Silvia as a sweeter friend.
I cannot now prove constant to myself,
Without some treachery us'd to Valentine.
This night he meaneth with a corded ladder
To climb celestial Silvia's chamber-window,
Myself in counsel, his competitor.
Now presently I'll give her father notice
Of their disguising and pretended flight;
Who, all enrag'd, will banish Valentine;
For Thurio, he intends, shall wed his daughter;
But, Valentine being gone, I'll quickly cross
By some sly trick blunt Thurio's dull proceeding.
Love, lend me wings to make my purpose swift,
As thou hast lent me wit to plot this drift! *Exit.*

SCENE VII. [*Verona.* JULIA'S *house.*]

Enter JULIA *and* LUCETTA.

Jul. Counsel, Lucetta; gentle girl, assist me;
And ev'n in kind love I do conjure thee,
Who art the table wherein all my thoughts
Are visibly character'd and engrav'd,
To lesson me and tell me some good mean
How, with my honour, I may undertake
A journey to my loving Proteus.
Luc. Alas, the way is wearisome and long!
Jul. A true-devoted pilgrim is not weary
To measure kingdoms with his feeble steps;
Much less shall she that hath Love's wings to fly,
And when the flight is made to one so dear,
Of such divine perfection, as Sir Proteus.
Luc. Better forbear till Proteus make return.
Jul. O, know'st thou not his looks are my soul's food?
Pity the dearth that I have pined in,
By longing for that food so long a time.
Didst thou but know the inly touch of love,
Thou wouldst as soon go kindle fire with snow
As seek to quench the fire of love with words.
Luc. I do not seek to quench your love's hot fire,
But qualify the fire's extreme rage,
Lest it should burn above the bounds of reason.
Jul. The more thou damm'st it up, the more it burns.
The current that with gentle murmur glides,
Thou know'st, being stopp'd, impatiently doth rage;
But when his fair course is not hindered,
He makes sweet music with th' enamell'd stones,
Giving a gentle kiss to every sedge
He overtaketh in his pilgrimage,
And so by many winding nooks he strays
With willing sport to the wild ocean.
Then let me go and hinder not my course:
I'll be as patient as a gentle stream
And make a pastime of each weary step,
Till the last step have brought me to my love;
And there I'll rest, as after much turmoil
A blessed soul doth in Elysium.
Luc. But in what habit will you go along?
Jul. Not like a woman; for I would prevent
The loose encounters of lascivious men:
Gentle Lucetta, fit me with such weeds
As may beseem some well-reputed page.
Luc. Why, then, your ladyship must cut your hair.
Jul. No, girl; I'll knit it up in silken strings
With twenty odd-conceited true-love knots.
To be fantastic may become a youth
Of greater time than I shall show to be.
Luc. What fashion, madam, shall I make your breeches?
Jul. That fits as well as 'Tell me, good my lord,
What compass will you wear your farthingale?'
Why ev'n what fashion thou best likes, Lucetta.
Luc. You must needs have them with a codpiece, madam.
Jul. Out, out, Lucetta! that will be ill-favour'd.
Luc. A round hose, madam, now 's not worth a pin,
Unless you have a codpiece to stick pins on.
Jul. Lucetta, as thou lov'st me, let me have
What thou think'st meet and is most mannerly.
But tell me, wench, how will the world repute me
For undertaking so unstaid a journey?
I fear me, it will make me scandaliz'd.
Luc. If you think so, then stay at home and go not.
Jul. Nay, that I will not.
Luc. Then never dream on infamy, but go.
If Proteus like your journey when you come,
No matter who's displeas'd when you are gone:
I fear me, he will scarce be pleas'd withal.
Jul. That is the least, Lucetta, of my fear:
A thousand oaths, an ocean of his tears
And instances of infinite of love
Warrant me welcome to my Proteus.
Luc. All these are servants to deceitful men.
Jul. Base men, that use them to so base effect!
But truer stars did govern Proteus' birth;
His words are bonds, his oaths are oracles,
His love sincere, his thoughts immaculate,
His tears pure messengers sent from his heart,
His heart as far from fraud as heaven from earth.
Luc. Pray heaven he prove so, when you come to him!
Jul. Now, as thou lov'st me, do him not that wrong
To bear a hard opinion of his truth:
Only deserve my love by loving him;
And presently go with me to my chamber,
To take a note of what I stand in need of,
To furnish me upon my longing journey.
All that is mine I leave at thy dispose,

35. **competitor,** associate, partner. 43. **drift,** scheme, plot.
SCENE VII. 3. **table,** tablet; see glossary. 4. **character'd,** engraved, inscribed; see glossary. 10. **measure,** traverse; see glossary. 18. **inly,** inward. 22. **qualify,** control, moderate. 40. **prevent,** forestall; see glossary. 42. **weeds,** garments; see glossary. 46. **odd-conceited,** strangely devised. 48. **of greater time,** of greater years, older. 51. **compass,** circumference; i.e., its fullness or width around the bottom. **farthingale,** hooped petticoat. 53. **codpiece,** a bagged appendage to the front of close-fitting hose or breeches worn by men from the fifteenth to the seventeenth century, often conspicuous and ornamented. 54. **Out,** an expression of reproach or indignation; see glossary. 60. **unstaid,** unbecoming. 67. **withal,** with it; see glossary. 70. **infinite,** infinity. 85. **furnish,** fit out; see glossary. **longing,** prompted by longing. 86. **dispose,** disposal; see glossary.
ACT III. SCENE I. 1. **give us leave,** a polite form of dismissal. 4. **discover,** reveal; see glossary. 5. **The law of friendship.** Violation

My goods, my lands, my reputation;
Only, in lieu thereof, dispatch me hence.
Come, answer not, but to it presently!
I am impatient of my tarriance. *Exeunt.*

ACT III.

SCENE I. [*Milan. The* DUKE'S *palace.*]

Enter DUKE, THURIO, [*and*] PROTEUS.

Duke. Sir Thurio, give us leave, I pray, awhile;
We have some secrets to confer about. [*Exit Thu.*]
Now, tell me, Proteus, what 's your will with me?
Pro. My gracious lord, that which I would discover
The law of friendship bids me to conceal;
But when I call to mind your gracious favours
Done to me, undeserving as I am,
My duty pricks me on to utter that
Which else no worldly good should draw from me.
Know, worthy prince, Sir Valentine, my friend,
This night intends to steal away your daughter:
Myself am one made privy to the plot.
I know you have determin'd to bestow her
On Thurio, whom your gentle daughter hates;
And should she thus be stol'n away from you,
It would be much vexation to your age.
Thus, for my duty's sake, I rather chose
To cross my friend in his intended drift
Than, by concealing it, heap on your head
A pack of sorrows which would press you down,
Being unprevented, to your timeless grave.
Duke. Proteus, I thank thee for thine honest care;
Which to requite, command me while I live.
This love of theirs myself have often seen,
Haply when they have judg'd me fast asleep,
And oftentimes have purpos'd to forbid
Sir Valentine her company and my court:
But fearing lest my jealous aim might err
And so unworthily disgrace the man,
A rashness that I ever yet have shunn'd,
I gave him gentle looks, thereby to find
That which thyself hast now disclos'd to me.
And, that thou mayst perceive my fear of this,
Knowing that tender youth is soon suggested,
I nightly lodge her in an upper tow'r,
The key whereof myself have ever kept;
And thence she cannot be convey'd away.
Pro. Know, noble lord, they have devis'd a mean
How he her chamber-window will ascend
And with a corded ladder fetch her down;
For which the youthful lover now is gone
And this way comes he with it presently;
Where, if it please you, you may intercept him.
But, good my lord, do it so cunningly
That my discovery be not aimed at;
For love of you, not hate unto my friend,
Hath made me publisher of this pretence.
Duke. Upon mine honour, he shall never know
That I had any light from thee of this.
Pro. Adieu, my lord; Sir Valentine is coming. [*Exit.*]

[*Enter*] VALENTINE.

Duke. Sir Valentine, whither away so fast?
Val. Please it your grace, there is a messenger
That stays to bear my letters to my friends,
And I am going to deliver them.
Duke. Be they of much import?
Val. The tenour of them doth but signify
My health and happy being at your court.
Duke. Nay then, no matter; stay with me awhile;
I am to break with thee of some affairs
That touch me near, wherein thou must be secret.
'Tis not unknown to thee that I have sought
To match my friend Sir Thurio to my daughter.
Val. I know it well, my lord; and, sure, the match
Were rich and honourable; besides, the gentleman
Is full of virtue, bounty, worth and qualities
Beseeming such a wife as your fair daughter:
Cannot your grace win her to fancy him?
Duke. No, trust me; she is peevish, sullen, froward,
Proud, disobedient, stubborn, lacking duty,
Neither regarding that she is my child
Nor fearing me as if I were her father;
And, may I say to thee, this pride of hers,
Upon advice, hath drawn my love from her;
And, where I thought the remnant of mine age
Should have been cherish'd by her child-like duty,
I now am full resolv'd to take a wife
And turn her out to who will take her in:
Then let her beauty be her wedding-dow'r;
For me and my possessions she esteems not.
Val. What would your grace have me to do in this?
Duke.†There is a lady in Verona here
Whom I affect; but she is nice and coy
And nought esteems my aged eloquence:
Now therefore would I have thee to my tutor—
For long agone I have forgot to court;
Besides, the fashion of the time is chang'd—
How and which way I may bestow myself
To be regarded in her sun-bright eye.
Val. Win her with gifts, if she respect not words:
Dumb jewels often in their silent kind
More than quick words do move a woman's mind.
Duke. But she did scorn a present that I sent her.
Val. A woman sometimes scorns what best contents her.
Send her another; never give her o'er;
For scorn at first makes after-love the more.
If she do frown, 'tis not in hate of you,
But rather to beget more love in you:
If she do chide, 'tis not to have you gone;
For why, the fools are mad, if left alone.
Take no repulse, whatever she doth say;
For 'get you gone,' she doth not mean 'away!'
Flatter and praise, commend, extol their graces;
Though ne'er so black, say they have angels' faces.
That man that hath a tongue, I say, is no man,

of this law—a well-formalized code in the Renaissance period—is Proteus' crime. See Introduction for a discussion of the importance of this code to an understanding of the play. 22. **honest,** decent, proper; see glossary. 28. **aim,** conjecture, guess. 34. **suggested,** tempted; see glossary. 45. **aimed at,** guessed. 64. **Were,** would be; subjunctive. 65. **virtue,** good accomplishments; see glossary. **qualities,** gifts, attainments; see glossary. 68. **peevish,** obstinate; see glossary. 81. **Verona,** so F; an obvious error, due to possible revision. The fact that *Verona* makes the line metrical whereas "Milan" does not, indicates that the former may have been the reading in the original. A similar error occurs at V, iv, 129; cf. II, v, 1, note. 82. **affect,** am fond of; see glossary. **nice,** shy; see glossary. 87. **bestow,** behave, conduct. 90. **kind,** manner, fashion; see glossary. 93-101. **A woman . . . 'away.'** This is the courtship code observed earlier in the play (I, ii) by Julia when she received Proteus' letter. 99. **For why,** because; see glossary.

If with his tongue he cannot win a woman.
Duke. But she I mean is promis'd by her friends
Unto a youthful gentleman of worth,
And kept severely from resort of men,
That no man hath access by day to her.
Val. Why, then, I would resort to her by night.
Duke. Ay, but the doors be lock'd and keys kept safe,
That no man hath recourse to her by night.
Val. What lets but one may enter at her window?
Duke. Her chamber is aloft, far from the ground,
And built so shelving that one cannot climb it
Without apparent hazard of his life.
Val. Why then, a ladder quaintly made of cords,
To cast up, with a pair of anchoring hooks,
Would serve to scale another Hero's tow'r,
So bold Leander would adventure it.
Duke. Now, as thou art a gentleman of blood,
Advise me where I may have such a ladder.
Val. When would you use it? pray, sir, tell me that.
Duke. This very night; for Love is like a child,
That longs for every thing that he can come by.
Val. By seven o'clock I'll get you such a ladder.
Duke. But, hark thee; I will go to her alone:
How shall I best convey the ladder thither?
Val. It will be light, my lord, that you may bear it
Under a cloak that is of any length.
Duke. A cloak as long as thine will serve the turn?
Val. Ay, my good lord.
Duke. Then let me see thy cloak:
I'll get me one of such another length.
Val. Why, any cloak will serve the turn, my lord.
Duke. How shall I fashion me to wear a cloak?
I pray thee, let me feel thy cloak upon me.
What letter is this same? What 's here? 'To Silvia'!
And here an engine fit for my proceeding.
I'll be so bold to break the seal for once. [*Reads*.]
'My thoughts do harbour with my Silvia nightly,
And slaves they are to me that send them flying:
O, could their master come and go as lightly,
Himself would lodge where senseless they are lying!
My herald thoughts in thy pure bosom rest them;
While I, their king, that hither them importune,
Do curse the grace that with such grace hath bless'd them,
Because myself do want my servants' fortune:
I curse myself, for they are sent by me,
That they should harbour where their lord would be.'
What 's here?
'Silvia, this night I will enfranchise thee.'
'Tis so; and here 's the ladder for the purpose.
Why, Phaethon,—for thou art Merops' son,—
Wilt thou aspire to guide the heavenly car
And with thy daring folly burn the world?
Wilt thou reach stars, because they shine on thee?
Go, base intruder! overweening slave!
Bestow thy fawning smiles on equal mates,
And think my patience, more than thy desert,
Is privilege for thy departure hence:
Thank me for this more than for all the favours
Which all too much I have bestow'd on thee.
But if thou linger in my territories
Longer than swiftest expedition
Will give thee time to leave our royal court,
By heaven! my wrath shall far exceed the love
I ever bore my daughter or thyself.
Be gone! I will not hear thy vain excuse;
But, as thou lov'st thy life, make speed from hence.
[*Exit*.]
Val. And why not death rather than living torment?
To die is to be banish'd from myself;
And Silvia is myself: banish'd from her
Is self from self: a deadly banishment!
What light is light, if Silvia be not seen?
What joy is joy, if Silvia be not by?
Unless it be to think that she is by
And feed upon the shadow of perfection.
Except I be by Silvia in the night,
There is no music in the nightingale;
Unless I look on Silvia in the day,
There is no day for me to look upon;
She is my essence, and I leave to be,
If I be not by her fair influence
Foster'd, illumin'd, cherish'd, kept alive.
I fly not death, to fly his deadly doom:
Tarry I here, I but attend on death:
But, fly I hence, I fly away from life.

[*Enter* PROTEUS *and*] LAUNCE.

Pro. Run, boy, run, run, and seek him out.
Launce. Soho, soho!
Pro. What seest thou?
Launce. Him we go to find: there 's not a hair on 's head but 'tis a Valentine.
Pro. Valentine?
Val. No.
Pro. Who then? his spirit?
Val. Neither.
Pro. What then?
Val. Nothing.
Launce. Can nothing speak? Master, shall I strike?
Pro. Who wouldst thou strike?
Launce. Nothing.
Pro. Villain, forbear.
Launce. Why, sir, I'll strike nothing: I pray you,—
Pro. Sirrah, I say, forbear. Friend Valentine, a word.
Val. My ears are stopt and cannot hear good news,
So much of bad already hath possess'd them.
Pro. Then in dumb silence will I bury mine,
For they are harsh, untuneable and bad.
Val. Is Silvia dead?
Pro. No, Valentine.
Val. No Valentine, indeed, for sacred Silvia.
Hath she forsworn me?
Pro. No, Valentine.
Val. No Valentine, if Silvia have forsworn me.
What is your news?
Launce. Sir, there is a proclamation that you are vanished.

113. **lets,** hinders; see glossary. 116. **apparent,** plain, evident; see glossary. 119-120. **Hero's . . . Leander,** a reference to the story of Hero and Leander, two lovers who lived on the opposite shores of the Hellespont. See I, i, 22 ff. 131. **serve the turn,** answer the purpose; see *serve* in glossary. 138. **engine,** mechanical contrivance; see glossary. 143. **lying,** dwelling; see *lie* in glossary. 146. **grace . . . grace,** good fortune . . . charm, favor; see glossary. 151. **enfranchise,** release from confinement. 153. **Phaethon, Merops'.** Phaethon was the son of Phoebus and Clymene, lawful wife of Merops. A possible play on "ropes" has been suggested. Another suggestion is that the duke wishes to plague Valentine with the taunt of inferior birth. The story of Phaethon's attempt to drive the chariot of the sun was familiar to Shakespeare from his acquaintance with Golding's Ovid. 157. **overweening,** arrogant, presumptuous. 177. **shadow,** image; see glossary. 182. **leave to be,** die, cease to be. 183. **influence,** metaphorical reference to an ethereal fluid supposed to flow from the stars and to have power over the destinies of men; see glossary. 185. **I . . . doom.** I shall not escape death by flying from it, for if I do, I shall die at once. 189. **Soho,** hunting cry used when a hare is descried. 192. **Valentine,** token of true love; cf. l. 211 below. 216, 217. **you, thou.**

Pro. That thou art banished—O, that 's the news!—
From hence, from Silvia and from me thy friend.
Val. O, I have fed upon this woe already,
And now excess of it will make me surfeit.
Doth Silvia know that I am banished?
Pro. Ay, ay; and she hath offer'd to the doom—
Which, unrevers'd, stands in effectual force—
A sea of melting pearl, which some call tears:
Those at her father's churlish feet she tender'd;
With them, upon her knees, her humble self;
Wringing her hands, whose whiteness so became
them
As if but now they waxed pale for woe:
But neither bended knees, pure hands held up,
Sad sighs, deep groans, nor silver-shedding tears,
Could penetrate her uncompassionate sire;
But Valentine, if he be ta'en, must die.
Besides, her intercession chaf'd him so,
When she for thy repeal was suppliant,
That to close prison he commanded her,
With many bitter threats of biding there.
Val. No more; unless the next word that thou
speak'st
Have some malignant power upon my life:
If so, I pray thee, breathe it in mine ear,
As ending anthem of my endless dolour.
Pro. Cease to lament for that thou canst not help,
And study help for that which thou lament'st.
Time is the nurse and breeder of all good.
Here if thou stay, thou canst not see thy love;
Besides, thy staying will abridge thy life.
Hope is a lover's staff; walk hence with that
And manage it against despairing thoughts.
Thy letters may be here, though thou art hence;
Which, being writ to me, shall be deliver'd
Even in the milk-white bosom of thy love.
The time now serves not to expostulate:
Come, I'll convey thee through the city-gate;
And, ere I part with thee, confer at large
Of all that may concern thy love-affairs.
As thou lov'st Silvia, though not for thyself,
Regard thy danger, and along with me!
Val. I pray thee, Launce, an if thou seest my boy,
Bid him make haste and meet me at the North-gate.
Pro. Go, sirrah, find him out. Come, Valentine.
Val. O my dear Silvia! Hapless Valentine!
[*Exeunt Val. and Pro.*]

Launce. I am but a fool, look you; and yet I have the wit to think my master is a kind of a knave: but that 's all one, if he be but one knave. He lives not now that knows me to be in love; yet I am in love; but a team of horse shall not pluck that from me; nor who 'tis I love; and yet 'tis a woman; but what woman, I will not tell myself; and yet 'tis a milkmaid; yet 'tis not a maid, for she hath had gossips; yet 'tis a maid, for she is her master's maid, and serves for wages. She hath more qualities than a water-spaniel; which is much in a bare Christian. [*Pulling out a paper.*] Here is the cate-log of her condition. 'Imprimis: She can fetch and carry.' Why, a horse can do no more: nay, a horse cannot fetch, but only carry; therefore is she better than a jade. 'Item: She can milk;' look you, a sweet virtue in a maid with clean hands.

[*Enter*] Speed.

Speed. How now, Signior Launce! what news with your mastership?

Launce. With my master's ship? why, it is at sea.

Speed. Well, your old vice still; mistake the word. What news, then, in your paper?

Launce. The blackest news that ever thou heardest.

Speed. Why, man, how black?

Launce. Why, as black as ink.

Speed. Let me read them.

Launce. Fie on thee, jolt-head! thou canst not read.

Speed. Thou liest; I can.

Launce. I will try thee. Tell me this: who begot thee?

Speed. Marry, the son of my grandfather.

Launce. O illiterate loiterer! it was the son of thy grandmother: this proves that thou canst not read.

Speed. Come, fool, come; try me in thy paper.

Launce. There; and Saint Nicholas be thy speed!

Speed. [*Reads*] 'Imprimis: She can milk.'

Launce. Ay, that she can.

Speed. 'Item: She brews good ale.'

Launce. And thereof comes the proverb: 'Blessing of your heart, you brew good ale.'

Speed. 'Item: She can sew.'

Launce. That 's as much as to say, Can she so?

Speed. 'Item: She can knit.'

Launce. What need a man care for a stock with a wench, when she can knit him a stock?

Speed. 'Item: She can wash and scour.'

Launce. A special virtue; for then she need not be washed and scoured.

Speed. 'Item: She can spin.'

Launce. Then may I set the world on wheels, when she can spin for her living.

Speed. 'Item: She hath many nameless virtues.'

Launce. That 's as much as to say, bastard virtues; that, indeed, know not their fathers and therefore have no names.

Speed. 'Here follow her vices.'

Launce. Close at the heels of her virtues.

Speed. 'Item: She is not to be kissed fasting, in respect of her breath.'

Launce. Well, that fault may be mended with a breakfast. Read on.

Speed. 'Item: She hath a sweet mouth.'

Launce. That makes amends for her sour breath.

Speed. 'Item: She doth talk in her sleep.'

Launce. It 's no matter for that, so she sleep not in her talk.

Speed. 'Item: She is slow in words.'

Launce. O villain, that set this down among her vices! To be slow in words is a woman's only virtue: I pray thee, out with 't, and place it for her chief virtue.

Speed. 'Item: She is proud.'

Observe that Launce addresses Valentine as *you*, the polite form of pronoun used in addressing one's superiors, whereas Proteus uses the familiar *thou* because of both their social equality and their intimacy. This distinction is commonly maintained by Shakespeare and his contemporaries. 222. **doom,** verdict, sentence. 234. **repeal,** recall from exile. 235. **close,** enclosed; see glossary. 236. **biding,** permanently dwelling. 242. **study,** be intent upon, devise. 247. **manage,** wield, handle (as a weapon). 253. **confer at large,** discuss at length; see *large* in glossary. 269. **gossips,** godparents to a child of hers. 273. **cate-log.** Although this is an early spelling of "catalog," most editors retain the old form, believing a mispronunciation is intended. The New Cambridge editors think that it is no more than a common Shakespearean spelling which editors have mistaken for a joke. **condition,** qualities; see glossary. 277. **jade,** ill-conditioned horse; also a term of contempt for a woman. 290. **jolt-head,** blockhead. 300. **Saint Nicholas,** the patron saint of schoolboys. 301. **speed,** protection; see glossary. 311. **stock,** dowry. 312. **stock,** stocking. 317. **set . . . wheels,** take life easy. 330. **sweet mouth,** sweet tooth, with a wanton sense.

Launce. Out with that too; it was Eve's legacy, and cannot be ta'en from her.

Speed. 'Item: She hath no teeth.'

Launce. I care not for that neither, because I love crusts.

Speed. 'Item: She is curst.'

Launce. Well, the best is, she hath no teeth to bite.

Speed. 'Item: She will often praise her liquor.'

Launce. If her liquor be good, she shall: if she will not, I will; for good things should be praised.

Speed. 'Item: She is too liberal.'

Launce. Of her tongue she cannot, for that 's writ down she is slow of; of her purse she shall not, for that I'll keep shut: now, of another thing she may, and that cannot I help. Well, proceed.

Speed. 'Item: She hath more hair than wit, and more faults than hairs, and more wealth than faults.'

Launce. Stop there; I'll have her: she was mine, and not mine, twice or thrice in that last article. Rehearse that once more.

Speed. 'Item: She hath more hair than wit,'—

Launce. More hair than wit? It may be: I'll prove it. The cover of the salt hides the salt, and therefore it is more than the salt; the hair that covers the wit is more than the wit, for the greater hides the less. What 's next?

Speed. 'And more faults than hairs,'—

Launce. That 's monstrous: O, that that were out!

Speed. 'And more wealth than faults.'

Launce. Why, that word makes the faults gracious. Well, I'll have her: and if it be a match, as nothing is impossible,—

Speed. What then?

Launce. Why, then will I tell thee—that thy master stays for thee at the North-gate.

Speed. For me?

Launce. For thee! ay, who art thou? he hath stayed for a better man than thee.

Speed. And must I go to him?

Launce. Thou must run to him, for thou hast stayed so long that going will scarce serve the turn.

Speed. Why didst not tell me sooner? pox of your love-letters! [*Exit.*]

Launce. Now will he be swinged for reading my letter; an unmannerly slave, that will thrust himself into secrets! I'll after, to rejoice in the boy's correction. *Exit.*

SCENE II. [*The same. The* DUKE'S *palace.*]

Enter DUKE [*and*] THURIO.

Duke. Sir Thurio, fear not but that she will love you,
Now Valentine is banish'd from her sight.
Thu. Since his exile she hath despis'd me most,
Forsworn my company and rail'd at me,
That I am desperate of obtaining her.
Duke. This weak impress of love is as a figure
Trenched in ice, which with an hour's heat
Dissolves to water and doth lose his form.
A little time will melt her frozen thoughts
And worthless Valentine shall be forgot.

[*Enter*] PROTEUS.

How now, Sir Proteus! Is your countryman
According to our proclamation gone?
Pro. Gone, my good lord.
Duke. My daughter takes his going grievously.
Pro. A little time, my lord, will kill that grief.
Duke. So I believe; but Thurio thinks not so.
Proteus, the good conceit I hold of thee—
For thou hast shown some sign of good desert—
Makes me the better to confer with thee.
Pro. Longer than I prove loyal to your grace
Let me not live to look upon your grace.
Duke. Thou know'st how willingly I would effect
The match between Sir Thurio and my daughter.
Pro. I do, my lord.
Duke. And also, I think, thou art not ignorant
How she opposes her against my will.
Pro. She did, my lord, when Valentine was here.
Duke. Ay, and perversely she persevers so.
What might we do to make the girl forget
The love of Valentine and love Sir Thurio?
Pro. The best way is to slander Valentine
With falsehood, cowardice and poor descent,
Three things that women highly hold in hate.
Duke. Ay, but she'll think that it is spoke in hate.
Pro. Ay, if his enemy deliver it:
Therefore it must with circumstance be spoken
By one whom she esteemeth as his friend.
Duke. Then you must undertake to slander him.
Pro. And that, my lord, I shall be loath to do:
'Tis an ill office for a gentleman,
Especially against his very friend.
Duke. Where your good word cannot advantage him,
Your slander never can endamage him;
Therefore the office is indifferent,
Being entreated to it by your friend.
Pro. You have prevail'd, my lord: if I can do it
By aught that I can speak in his dispraise,
She shall not long continue love to him.
But say this weed her love from Valentine,
It follows not that she will love Sir Thurio.
Thu. Therefore, as you unwind her love from him,
Lest it should ravel and be good to none,
You must provide to bottom it on me;
Which must be done by praising me as much
As you in worth dispraise Sir Valentine.
Duke. And, Proteus, we dare trust you in this kind,
Because we know, on Valentine's report,
You are already Love's firm votary
And cannot soon revolt and change your mind.
Upon this warrant shall you have access
Where you with Silvia may confer at large;
For she is lumpish, heavy, melancholy,
And, for your friend's sake, will be glad of you;
Where you may temper her by your persuasion
To hate young Valentine and love my friend.
Pro. As much as I can do, I will effect:

347. **curst,** perverse, shrewish; see glossary. 358. **another thing** (with bawdy suggestion, playing on "purse"). 392. **swinged,** thrashed.

SCENE II. 3. **Since his exile.** This would indicate that some days have elapsed since Valentine's departure. It is evident, however, from lines 11-12 that this is not so. Later in the play (IV, i, 21) Valentine says he has been away from Verona sixteen months, an unduly long period for the requirements of the plot. The New Cambridge editors believe the discrepancies to be due to revision and abridgment. 5. **That,** so that. 6. **impress of love,** impression made by love. 17. **conceit,** opinion, estimate; see glossary. 19. **the better,** the rather; i.e., more willingly. 26. **opposes her,** contends. 42. **advantage,** profit; see glossary. 44. **indifferent,** neither good nor bad. 49. **weed.** *Wean* (Rowe) and *wend* (New Cambridge) have been suggested as emendations. 53. **bottom,** wind, as a skein of thread; a weaver's term. 62.

But you, Sir Thurio, are not sharp enough;
You must lay lime to tangle her desires
By wailful sonnets, whose composed rhymes
Should be full-fraught with serviceable vows.
Duke. Ay,
Much is the force of heaven-bred poesy.
Pro. Say that upon the altar of her beauty
You sacrifice your tears, your sighs, your heart:
Write till your ink be dry, and with your tears
Moist it again, and frame some feeling line
That may discover such integrity:
For Orpheus' lute was strung with poets' sinews,
Whose golden touch could soften steel and stones,
Make tigers tame and huge leviathans
Forsake unsounded deeps to dance on sands.
After your dire-lamenting elegies,
Visit by night your lady's chamber-window
With some sweet consort; to their instruments
Tune a deploring dump: the night's dead silence
Will well become such sweet-complaining grievance.
This, or else nothing, will inherit her.
Duke. This discipline shows thou hast been in love.
Thu. And thy advice this night I'll put in practice.
Therefore, sweet Proteus, my direction-giver,
Let us into the city presently
To sort some gentlemen well skill'd in music.
I have a sonnet that will serve the turn
To give the onset to thy good advice.
Duke. About it, gentlemen!
Pro. We'll wait upon your grace till after supper,
And afterward determine our proceedings.
Duke. Even now about it! I will pardon you. *Exeunt.*

ACT IV.

SCENE I. [*The frontiers of Mantua. A forest.*]

Enter certain Outlaws.

First Out. Fellows, stand fast; I see a passenger.
Sec. Out. If there be ten, shrink not, but down with 'em.

[*Enter*] VALENTINE [*and*] SPEED.

Third Out. Stand, sir, and throw us that you have about ye:
If not, we'll make you sit and rifle you.
Speed. Sir, we are undone; these are the villains
That all the travellers do fear so much.
Val. My friends,—
First Out. That 's not so, sir: we are your enemies.
Sec. Out. Peace! we'll hear him.
Third Out. Ay, by my beard, will we, for he is a proper man.
Val. Then know that I have little wealth to lose:
A man I am cross'd with adversity;
My riches are these poor habiliments,
Of which if you should here disfurnish me,
You take the sum and substance that I have.
Sec. Out. Whither travel you?
Val. To Verona.
First Out. Whence came you?
Val. From Milan.
Third Out. Have you long sojourn'd there?
Val. Some sixteen months, and longer might have stay'd,
If crooked fortune had not thwarted me.
First Out. What, were you banish'd thence?
Val. I was.
Sec. Out. For what offence?
Val. For that which now torments me to rehearse:
I kill'd a man, whose death I much repent;
But yet I slew him manfully in fight,
Without false vantage or base treachery.
First Out. Why, ne'er repent it, if it were done so.
But were you banish'd for so small a fault?
Val. I was, and held me glad of such a doom.
Sec. Out. Have you the tongues?
Val. My youthful travel therein made me happy,
Or else I often had been miserable.
Third Out. By the bare scalp of Robin Hood's fat friar,
This fellow were a king for our wild faction!
First Out. We'll have him. Sirs, a word.
Speed. Master, be one of them; it 's an honourable kind of thievery.
Val. Peace, villain!
Sec. Out. Tell us this: have you any thing to take to?
Val. Nothing but my fortune.
Third Out. Know, then, that some of us are gentlemen,
Such as the fury of ungovern'd youth
Thrust from the company of awful men:
Myself was from Verona banished
For practising to steal away a lady,
An heir, and near allied unto the duke.
Sec. Out. And I from Mantua, for a gentleman,
Who, in my mood, I stabb'd unto the heart.
First Out. And I for such like petty crimes as these.
But to the purpose—for we cite our faults,
That they may hold excus'd our lawless lives;
And partly, seeing you are beautified
With goodly shape and by your own report
A linguist and a man of such perfection
As we do in our quality much want—
Sec. Out. Indeed, because you are a banish'd man,
Therefore, above the rest, we parley to you:
Are you content to be our general?
To make a virtue of necessity
And live, as we do, in this wilderness?
Third Out. What say'st thou? wilt thou be of our consort?
Say ay, and be the captain of us all:
We'll do thee homage and be rul'd by thee,
Love thee as our commander and our king.
First Out. But if thou scorn our courtesy, thou diest.
Sec. Out. Thou shalt not live to brag what we have offer'd.
Val. I take your offer and will live with you,
Provided that you do no outrages
On silly women or poor passengers.
Third Out. No, we detest such vile base practices.

lumpish, dull. 68. **lime,** birdlime, a sticky substance smeared on twigs of trees to ensnare small birds. 84. **consort,** a company of musicians; so F; Globe: *concert.* 85. **dump,** mournful melody or song. 87. **inherit,** put you in possession of. 92. **sort,** choose. 94. **onset,** beginning.
ACT IV. SCENE I. 10. **proper,** good-looking; see glossary. 14. **disfurnish,** deprive. 21. **sixteen months.** Cf. III, ii, 3, note. 22. **crooked,** perverse, malignant. 27. **I kill'd a man.** There is no obvious motive for Valentine's giving a false reason for his banishment. 33. **the tongues,** foreign languages. 37. **faction,** band, set (of persons); see glossary. 46. **awful,** law-abiding. 51. **mood,** anger, displeasure. 64. **consort,** fellowship, company. 72. **silly,** helpless, defenseless.

Come, go with us, we'll bring thee to our crews,
And show thee all the treasure we have got;
Which, with ourselves, all rest at thy dispose. *Exeunt.*

SCENE II. [*Milan. Outside the* DUKE'S *palace, under* SILVIA'S *chamber.*]

Enter PROTEUS.

Pro. Already have I been false to Valentine
And now I must be as unjust to Thurio.
Under the colour of commending him,
I have access my own love to prefer:
But Silvia is too fair, too true, too holy,
To be corrupted with my worthless gifts.
When I protest true loyalty to her,
She twits me with my falsehood to my friend;
When to her beauty I commend my vows,
She bids me think how I have been forsworn
In breaking faith with Julia whom I lov'd:
And notwithstanding all her sudden quips,
The least whereof would quell a lover's hope,
Yet, spaniel-like, the more she spurns my love,
The more it grows and fawneth on her still.
But here comes Thurio: now must we to her window,
And give some evening music to her ear.

[*Enter*] THURIO [*and*] Musicians.

Thu. How now, Sir Proteus, are you crept before us?
Pro. Ay, gentle Thurio: for you know that love
Will creep in service where it cannot go.
Thu. Ay, but I hope, sir, that you love not here.
Pro. Sir, but I do; or else I would be hence.
Thu. Who? Silvia?
Pro. Ay, Silvia; for your sake.
Thu. I thank you for your own. Now, gentlemen,
Let 's tune, and to it lustily awhile.

[*Enter, at a distance,*] Host, [*and*] JULIA [*in boy's clothes*].

Host. Now, my young guest, methinks you're allycholly: I pray you, why is it?

Jul. Marry, mine host, because I cannot be merry.

Host. Come, we'll have you merry: I'll bring you where you shall hear music and see the gentleman that you asked for.

Jul. But shall I hear him speak?

Host. Ay, that you shall.

Jul. That will be music. [*Music plays.*]

Host. Hark, hark!

Jul. Is he among these?

Host. Ay: but, peace! let 's hear 'em.

SONG.

Who is Silvia? what is she,
  That all our swains commend her?
Holy, fair and wise is she;
  The heaven such grace did lend her,
That she might admired be.

Is she kind as she is fair?
  For beauty lives with kindness.
Love doth to her eyes repair,
  To help him of his blindness,
And, being help'd, inhabits there.

Then to Silvia let us sing,
  That Silvia is excelling;
She excels each mortal thing
  Upon the dull earth dwelling:
To her let us garlands bring.

Host. How now! are you sadder than you were before? How do you, man? the music likes you not.

Jul. You mistake; the musician likes me not.

Host. Why, my pretty youth?

Jul. He plays false, father.

Host. How? out of tune on the strings?

Jul. Not so; but yet so false that he grieves my very heart-strings.

Host. You have a quick ear.

Jul. Ay, I would I were deaf; it makes me have a slow heart.

Host. I perceive you delight not in music.

Jul. Not a whit, when it jars so.

Host. Hark, what fine change is in the music!

Jul. Ay, that change is the spite.

Host. You would have them always play but one thing?

Jul. I would always have one play but one thing.
But, host, doth this Sir Proteus that we talk on
Often resort unto this gentlewoman?

Host. I tell you what Launce, his man, told me: he loved her out of all nick.

Jul. Where is Launce?

Host. Gone to seek his dog; which tomorrow, by his master's command, he must carry for a present to his lady.

Jul. Peace! stand aside: the company parts.
Pro. Sir Thurio, fear not you: I will so plead
That you shall say my cunning drift excels.
Thu. Where meet we?
Pro. At Saint Gregory's well.
Thu. Farewell.
[*Exeunt Thu. and Musicians.*]

[*Enter*] SILVIA [*above*].

Pro. Madam, good ev'n to your ladyship.
Sil. I thank you for your music, gentlemen.
Who is that that spake?
Pro. One, lady, if you knew his pure heart's truth,
You would quickly learn to know him by his voice.
Sil. Sir Proteus, as I take it.
Pro. Sir Proteus, gentle lady, and your servant.
Sil. What 's your will?
Pro. That I may compass yours.
Sil. You have your wish; my will is even this:
That presently you hie you home to bed.
Thou subtle, perjur'd, false, disloyal man!
Think'st thou I am so shallow, so conceitless,
To be seduced by thy flattery,
That hast deceiv'd so many with thy vows?
Return, return, and make thy love amends.
For me, by this pale queen of night I swear,
I am so far from granting thy request
That I despise thee for thy wrongful suit,

74. **crews,** bands.

SCENE II. 2. **unjust,** dishonest; see glossary. 3. **colour,** pretext; see glossary. 12. **quips,** sharp, sarcastic remarks. 18. **crept,** moved unnoticed. 20. **creep,** move slowly, as if disabled. **go,** walk at an ordinary pace. 27. **allycholly,** mallycholly, an old form of *melancholy.* 43. **admired,** wondered at; see glossary. 56. **likes,** pleases, with quibble on the modern sense in the following speech; see glossary. 67. **jars,** is discordant; see glossary. 68. **change,** modulation, a musical term. In the next speech Julia quibbles on it with reference to Proteus' inconstancy. 76. **out of all nick,** beyond all reckoning. 83.

And by and by intend to chide myself
Even for this time I spend in talking to thee.
Pro. I grant, sweet love, that I did love a lady;
But she is dead.
Jul. [*Aside*] 'Twere false, if I should speak it;
For I am sure she is not buried.
Sil. Say that she be; yet Valentine thy friend
Survives; to whom, thyself art witness,
I am betroth'd: and art thou not asham'd
To wrong him with thy importunacy?
Pro. I likewise hear that Valentine is dead.
Sil. And so suppose am I; for in his grave
Assure thyself my love is buried.
Pro. Sweet lady, let me rake it from the earth.
Sil. Go to thy lady's grave and call hers thence,
Or, at the least, in hers sepulchre thine.
Jul. [*Aside*] He heard not that.
Pro. Madam, if your heart be so obdurate,
Vouchsafe me yet your picture for my love,
The picture that is hanging in your chamber;
To that I'll speak, to that I'll sigh and weep:
For since the substance of your perfect self
Is else devoted, I am but a shadow;
And to your shadow will I make true love.
Jul. [*Aside*] If 'twere a substance, you would, sure, deceive it,
And make it but a shadow, as I am.
Sil. I am very loath to be your idol, sir;
But since your falsehood shall become you well
To worship shadows and adore false shapes,
Send to me in the morning and I'll send it:
And so, good rest.
Pro. As wretches have o'ernight
That wait for execution in the morn.
[*Exeunt Pro. and Sil. severally.*]
Jul. Host, will you go?
Host. By my halidom, I was fast asleep.
Jul. Pray you, where lies Sir Proteus?
Host. Marry, at my house. Trust me, I think 'tis almost day.
Jul. Not so; but it hath been the longest night
That e'er I watch'd and the most heaviest. [*Exeunt.*]

SCENE III. [*The same.*]

Enter EGLAMOUR.

Egl. This is the hour that Madam Silvia
Entreated me to call and know her mind:
There 's some great matter she 'ld employ me in.
Madam, madam!

[*Enter*] SILVIA [*above*].

Sil. Who calls?
Egl. Your servant and your friend;
One that attends your ladyship's command.
Sil. Sir Eglamour, a thousand times good morrow.
Egl. As many, worthy lady, to yourself:
According to your ladyship's impose,
I am thus early come to know what service
It is your pleasure to command me in.
Sil. O Eglamour, thou art a gentleman—
Think not I flatter, for I swear I do not—
Valiant, wise, remorseful, well accomplish'd:
Thou art not ignorant what dear good will
I bear unto the banish'd Valentine,
Nor how my father would enforce me marry
Vain Thurio, whom my very soul abhors.
Thyself hast lov'd; and I have heard thee say
No grief did ever come so near thy heart
As when thy lady and thy true love died,
Upon whose grave thou vow'dst pure chastity.
Sir Eglamour, I would to Valentine,
To Mantua, where I hear he makes abode;
And, for the ways are dangerous to pass,
I do desire thy worthy company,
Upon whose faith and honour I repose.
Urge not my father's anger, Eglamour,
But think upon my grief, a lady's grief,
And on the justice of my flying hence,
To keep me from a most unholy match,
Which heaven and fortune still rewards with plagues.
I do desire thee, even from a heart
As full of sorrows as the sea of sands,
To bear me company and go with me:
If not, to hide what I have said to thee,
That I may venture to depart alone.
Egl. Madam, I pity much your grievances;
Which since I know they virtuously are plac'd,
I give consent to go along with you,
Recking as little what betideth me
As much I wish all good befortune you.
When will you go?
Sil. This evening coming.
Egl. Where shall I meet you?
Sil. At Friar Patrick's cell,
Where I intend holy confession.
Egl. I will not fail your ladyship. Good morrow, gentle lady.
Sil. Good morrow, kind Sir Eglamour.
Exeunt [*severally*].

SCENE IV. [*The same.*]

Enter LAUNCE [*with his Dog*].

Launce. When a man's servant shall play the cur with him, look you, it goes hard: one that I brought up of a puppy; one that I saved from drowning, when three or four of his blind brothers and sisters went to it. I have taught him, even as one would say precisely, 'thus I would teach a dog.' I was sent to deliver him as a present to Mistress Silvia from my master; and I came no sooner into the dining-chamber but he steps me to her trencher and steals her capon's leg: O, 'tis a foul thing when a cur cannot keep himself in all companies! I would have, as one should say, one that takes upon him to be a dog indeed, to be, as it were, a dog at all things. If I had not had more wit than he, to take a fault upon me that he did, I think verily he had been hanged for 't; sure as I live, he had suffered for 't: you shall judge. He thrusts me himself into the company of three or four gentlemanlike dogs, under

drift, scheme. 96. **conceitless,** witless. 112. **importunacy,** importunity. 130. **become,** befit. 136. **By my halidom,** originally an oath on the holy relics; subsequently a weak asseveration. 141. **heaviest,** most grievous.

SCENE III. 8. **impose,** injunction. 13. **remorseful,** compassionate. 37. **grievances,** trouble, distress. 40. **Recking,** caring for, heeding.

SCENE IV. 3. **of,** from; see glossary. 9. **steps me,** i.e., to my injury, to my detriment; the ethical dative; cf. *thrusts me,* l. 18. 10. **trencher,** wooden dish or plate; see glossary. 11. **keep,** restrain; see glossary.

the duke's table: he had not been there—bless the mark!—a pissing while, but all the chamber smelt him. 'Out with the dog!' says one: 'What cur is that?' says another: 'Whip him out' says the third: 'Hang him up' says the duke. I, having been acquainted with the smell before, knew it was Crab, and goes me to the fellow that whips the dogs: 'Friend,' quoth I, 'you mean to whip the dog?' 'Ay, marry, do I,' quoth he. 'You do him the more wrong,' quoth I; ''twas I did the thing you wot of.' He makes me no more ado, but whips me out of the chamber. How many masters would do this for his servant? Nay, I'll be sworn, I have sat in the stocks for puddings he hath stolen, otherwise he had been executed; I have stood on the pillory for geese he hath killed, otherwise he had suffered for 't. Thou thinkest not of this now. Nay, I remember the trick you served me when I took my leave of Madam Silvia: did not I bid thee still mark me and do as I do? when didst thou see me heave up my leg and make water against a gentlewoman's farthingale? didst thou ever see me do such a trick?

[*Enter*] Proteus [*and*] Julia [*in boy's clothes*].

Pro. Sebastian is thy name? I like thee well
And will employ thee in some service presently.
Jul. In what you please: I'll do what I can.
Pro. I hope thou wilt. [*To Launce*] How now, you whoreson peasant!
Where have you been these two days loitering?

Launce. Marry, sir, I carried Mistress Silvia the dog you bade me.

Pro. And what says she to my little jewel?

Launce. Marry, she says your dog was a cur, and tells you currish thanks is good enough for such a present.

Pro. But she received my dog?

Launce. No, indeed, did she not: here have I brought him back again.

Pro. What, didst thou offer her this from me?

Launce. Ay, sir; the other squirrel was stolen from me by the hangman boys in the market-place: and then I offered her mine own, who is a dog as big as ten of yours, and therefore the gift the greater.

Pro. Go get thee hence, and find my dog again,
Or ne'er return again into my sight.
Away, I say! stayest thou to vex me here? [*Exit Launce.*]
A slave, that still an end turns me to shame!
Sebastian, I have entertained thee,
Partly that I have need of such a youth
That can with some discretion do my business,
For 'tis no trusting to yond foolish lout,
But chiefly for thy face and thy behaviour,
Which, if my augury deceive me not,
Witness good bringing up, fortune and truth:
Therefore know thou, for this I entertain thee.
Go presently and take this ring with thee,
Deliver it to Madam Silvia:
She lov'd me well deliver'd it to me.
Jul. It seems you lov'd not her, to leave her token.
She is dead, belike?
Pro. Not so; I think she lives.
Jul. Alas!
Pro. Why dost thou cry 'alas'?
Jul. I cannot choose
But pity her.
Pro. Wherefore shouldst thou pity her?
Jul. Because methinks that she lov'd you as well
As you do love your lady Silvia:
She dreams on him that has forgot her love;
You dote on her that cares not for your love.
'Tis pity love should be so contrary;
And thinking on it makes me cry 'alas!'
Pro. Well, give her that ring and therewithal
This letter. That 's her chamber. Tell my lady
I claim the promise for her heavenly picture.
Your message done, hie home unto my chamber,
Where thou shalt find me, sad and solitary. [*Exit.*]
Jul. How many women would do such a message?
Alas, poor Proteus! thou hast entertain'd
A fox to be the shepherd of thy lambs.
Alas, poor fool! why do I pity him
That with his very heart despiseth me?
Because he loves her, he despiseth me;
Because I love him, I must pity him.
This ring I gave him when he parted from me,
To bind him to remember my good will;
And now am I, unhappy messenger,
To plead for that which I would not obtain,
To carry that which I would have refus'd,
To praise his faith which I would have disprais'd.
I am my master's true-confirmed love;
But cannot be true servant to my master,
Unless I prove false traitor to myself.
Yet will I woo for him, but yet so coldly
As, heaven it knows, I would not have him speed.

[*Enter*] Silvia [*attended*].

Gentlewoman, good day! I pray you, be my mean
To bring me where to speak with Madam Silvia.
Sil. What would you with her, if that I be she?
Jul. If you be she, I do entreat your patience
To hear me speak the message I am sent on.
Sil. From whom?
Jul. From my master, Sir Proteus, madam.
Sil. O, he sends you for a picture.
Jul. Ay, madam.
Sil. Ursula, bring my picture there.
Go give your master this: tell him from me,
One Julia, that his changing thoughts forget,
Would better fit his chamber than this shadow.
Jul. Madam, please you peruse this letter.—
Pardon me, madam; I have unadvis'd
Deliver'd you a paper that I should not:
This is the letter to your ladyship.
Sil. I pray thee, let me look on that again.
Jul. It may not be; good madam, pardon me.
Sil. There, hold!
I will not look upon your master's lines:
I know they are stuff'd with protestations
And full of new-found oaths; which he will break
As easily as I do tear his paper.
Jul. Madam, he sends your ladyship this ring.

30. **wot of,** know about; see glossary. 59. **squirrel,** a contemptuous reference to the little dog which Proteus asked him to deliver to Silvia. 60. **hangman,** i.e., fit for the hangman. 90. **therewithal,** in addition to that, at the same time. 98. **fool,** term of pity and endearment; see glossary. 112. **speed,** succeed; see glossary. 115. **if that,** if. 126-129. **Madam . . . ladyship.** This reference to a letter in Julia's possession is without motive. It suggests that the play has been revised or abridged. 159. **starv'd,** caused to die; see glossary. 161. **black,** of a dark complexion. 164. **pageants of delight,** delightful entertainment; see *pageants* in glossary. 170. **agood,** in earnest. 172. **Ariadne,** daughter of Minos, king of Crete. She fell in love with one of her father's captives, Theseus, an Athenian hero. When he was shut up in the labyrinth, she gave him a clue of thread by which he was able to find his way among the intricate passages. He escaped, carried her

Sil. The more shame for him that he sends it me;
For I have heard him say a thousand times
His Julia gave it him at his departure.
Though his false finger have profan'd the ring,
Mine shall not do his Julia so much wrong.
Jul. She thanks you.
Sil. What say'st thou?
Jul. I thank you, madam, that you tender her.
Poor gentlewoman! my master wrongs her much.
Sil. Dost thou know her?
Jul. Almost as well as I do know myself:
To think upon her woes I do protest
That I have wept a hundred several times.
Sil. Belike she thinks that Proteus hath forsook her.
Jul. I think she doth; and that 's her cause of sorrow.
Sil. Is she not passing fair?
Jul. She hath been fairer, madam, than she is:
When she did think my master lov'd her well,
She, in my judgement, was as fair as you;
But since she did neglect her looking-glass
And threw her sun-expelling mask away,
The air hath starv'd the roses in her cheeks
And pinch'd the lily-tincture of her face,
That now she is become as black as I.
Sil. How tall was she?
Jul. About my stature; for at Pentecost,
When all our pageants of delight were play'd,
Our youth got me to play the woman's part,
And I was trimm'd in Madam Julia's gown,
Which served me as fit, by all men's judgements,
As if the garment had been made for me:
Therefore I know she is about my height.
And at that time I made her weep agood,
For I did play a lamentable part:
Madam, 'twas Ariadne passioning
For Theseus' perjury and unjust flight;
Which I so lively acted with my tears
That my poor mistress, moved therewithal,
Wept bitterly; and would I might be dead
If I in thought felt not her very sorrow!
Sil. She is beholding to thee, gentle youth.
Alas, poor lady, desolate and left!
I weep myself to think upon thy words.
Here, youth, there is my purse; I give thee this
For thy sweet mistress' sake, because thou lov'st her.
Farewell. [*Exit Silvia, with attendants.*]
Jul. And she shall thank you for 't, if e'er you know her.
A virtuous gentlewoman, mild and beautiful!
I hope my master's suit will be but cold,
Since she respects my mistress' love so much.
Alas, how love can trifle with itself!
Here is her picture: let me see; I think,
If I had such a tire, this face of mine
Were full as lovely as is this of hers:
And yet the painter flatter'd her a little,
Unless I flatter with myself too much.
Her hair is auburn, mine is perfect yellow:
If that be all the difference in his love,
I'll get me such a colour'd periwig.
Her eyes are grey as glass, and so are mine:
Ay, but her forehead 's low, and mine 's as high.
What should it be that he respects in her
But I can make respective in myself,
If this fond Love were not a blinded god?
Come, shadow, come, and take this shadow up,
For 'tis thy rival. O thou senseless form,
Thou shalt be worshipp'd, kiss'd, lov'd and ador'd!
And, were there sense in his idolatry,
My substance should be statue in thy stead.
I'll use thee kindly for thy mistress' sake,
That us'd me so; or else, by Jove I vow,
I should have scratch'd out your unseeing eyes,
To make my master out of love with thee! *Exit.*

ACT V.

SCENE I. [*Milan. An abbey.*]

Enter EGLAMOUR.

Egl. The sun begins to gild the western sky;
And now it is about the very hour
That Silvia, at Friar Patrick's cell, should meet me.
She will not fail, for lovers break not hours,
Unless it be to come before their time;
So much they spur their expedition.
See where she comes.

[*Enter*] SILVIA.

Lady, a happy evening!
Sil. Amen, amen! Go on, good Eglamour,
Out at the postern by the abbey-wall:
I fear I am attended by some spies.
Egl. Fear not: the forest is not three leagues off;
If we recover that, we are sure enough. *Exeunt.*

SCENE II. [*The same. The* DUKE's *palace.*]

Enter THURIO, PROTEUS, [*and*] JULIA.

Thu. Sir Proteus, what says Silvia to my suit?
Pro. O, sir, I find her milder than she was;
And yet she takes exceptions at your person.
Thu. What, that my leg is too long?
Pro. No; that it is too little.
Thu. I'll wear a boot, to make it somewhat rounder.
Jul. [*Aside*] But love will not be spurr'd to what it loathes.
Thu. What says she to my face?
Pro. She says it is a fair one.
Thu. Nay then, the wanton lies; my face is black.
Pro. But pearls are fair; and the old saying is,
Black men are pearls in beauteous ladies' eyes.
Jul. [*Aside*] 'Tis true; such pearls as put out ladies' eyes;
For I had rather wink than look on them.
Thu. How likes she my discourse?
Pro. Ill, when you talk of war.
Thu. But well, when I discourse of love and peace?

away, and married her. Later, when he forsook her, she hanged herself. passioning, sorrowing, grieving. 178. **beholding,** indebted. 190. **tire,** headdress, attire. 194. **auburn,** brownish white. **perfect yellow,** the color of Queen Elizabeth's hair; hence the fashionable color. 202. **Come . . . up,** i.e., the shadow of myself takes up this shadow of my rival—Silvia's picture; see *shadow* in glossary. **take up,** i.e., in the hostile sense of accepting a challenge. 205. **sense,** rational meaning; see glossary.

ACT V. SCENE I. 9. **postern,** small back or side door. 12. **recover,** get to, reach, arrive at.

SCENE II. 3. **takes exceptions at,** disapproves, finds fault with. 7. **spurr'd,** incited; a quibble on *boot* (i.e., riding boot) in the preceding line.

Jul. [*Aside*] But better, indeed, when you hold your peace.
Thu. What says she to my valour?
Pro. O, sir, she makes no doubt of that.
Jul. [*Aside*] She needs not, when she knows it cowardice.
Thu. What says she to my birth?
Pro. That you are well derived.
Jul. [*Aside*] True; from a gentleman to a fool.
Thu. Considers she my possessions?
Pro. O, ay; and pities them.
Thu. Wherefore?
Jul. [*Aside*] That such an ass should owe them.
Pro. That they are out by lease.
Jul. Here comes the duke.

[*Enter*] DUKE.

Duke. How now, Sir Proteus! how now, Thurio!
Which of you saw Sir Eglamour of late?
Thu. Not I.
Pro. Nor I.
Duke. Saw you my daughter?
Pro. Neither.
Duke. Why then,
She 's fled unto that peasant Valentine;
And Eglamour is in her company.
'Tis true; for Friar Laurence met them both,
As he in penance wander'd through the forest;
Him he knew well, and guess'd that it was she,
But, being mask'd, he was not sure of it;
Besides, she did intend confession
At Patrick's cell this even; and there she was not;
These likelihoods confirm her flight from hence.
Therefore, I pray you, stand not to discourse,
But mount you presently and meet with me
Upon the rising of the mountain-foot
That leads toward Mantua, whither they are fled:
Dispatch, sweet gentlemen, and follow me. [*Exit.*]
Thu. Why, this it is to be a peevish girl,
That flies her fortune when it follows her.
I'll after, more to be reveng'd on Eglamour
Than for the love of reckless Silvia. [*Exit.*]
Pro. And I will follow, more for Silvia's love
Than hate of Eglamour that goes with her. [*Exit.*]
Jul. And I will follow, more to cross that love
Than hate for Silvia that is gone for love. *Exit.*

SCENE III. [*The frontiers of Mantua. The forest.*]

[*Enter*] SILVIA, [*led by*] Outlaws.

First Out. Come, come,
Be patient; we must bring you to our captain.
Sil. A thousand more mischances than this one
Have learn'd me how to brook this patiently.
Sec. Out. Come, bring her away.
First Out. Where is the gentleman that was with her?
Third Out. Being nimble-footed, he hath outrun us,
But Moyses and Valerius follow him.
Go thou with her to the west end of the wood;
There is our captain: we'll follow him that 's fled;
The thicket is beset; he cannot 'scape.
First Out. Come, I must bring you to our captain's cave:
Fear not; he bears an honourable mind,
And will not use a woman lawlessly.
Sil. O Valentine, this I endure for thee! *Exeunt.*

SCENE IV. [*Another part of the forest.*]

Enter VALENTINE.

Val. How use doth breed a habit in a man!
This shadowy desert, unfrequented woods,
I better brook than flourishing peopled towns:
Here can I sit alone, unseen of any,
And to the nightingale's complaining notes
Tune my distresses and record my woes.
O thou that dost inhabit in my breast,
Leave not the mansion so long tenantless,
Lest, growing ruinous, the building fall
And leave no memory of what it was!
Repair me with thy presence, Silvia;
Thou gentle nymph, cherish thy forlorn swain!
What halloing and what stir is this to-day?
These are my mates, that make their wills their law,
Have some unhappy passenger in chase.
They love me well; yet I have much to do
To keep them from uncivil outrages.
Withdraw thee, Valentine: who 's this comes here?

[*Enter*] PROTEUS, SILVIA, [*and*] JULIA.

Pro. Madam, this service I have done for you,
Though you respect not aught your servant doth,
To hazard life and rescue you from him
That would have forc'd your honour and your love;
Vouchsafe me, for my meed, but one fair look;
A smaller boon than this I cannot beg
And less than this, I am sure, you cannot give.
Val. [*Aside*] How like a dream is this I see and hear!
Love, lend me patience to forbear awhile.
Sil. O miserable, unhappy that I am!
Pro. Unhappy were you, madam, ere I came;
But by my coming I have made you happy.
Sil. By thy approach thou mak'st me most unhappy.
Jul. [*Aside*] And me, when he approacheth to your presence.
Sil. Had I been seized by a hungry lion,
I would have been a breakfast to the beast,
Rather than have false Proteus rescue me.
O, Heaven be judge how I love Valentine,
Whose life 's as tender to me as my soul!
And full as much, for more there cannot be,
I do detest false perjur'd Proteus.
Therefore be gone; solicit me no more.
Pro. What dangerous action, stood it next to death,
Would I not undergo for one calm look!
O, 'tis the curse in love, and still approv'd,
When women cannot love where they're belov'd!

23. **derived,** descended, which gives point for the modern reader to Julia's aside; see glossary. 26. **pities,** despises. 28. **owe,** own; see glossary.

SCENE III. 4. **brook,** endure, tolerate; see glossary.

SCENE IV. 1. **use,** custom; see glossary. **habit,** demeanor, bearing, manner; see glossary. 9. **growing ruinous,** brought to ruin. 12. **cherish,** treat with kindness. 23. **Vouchsafe,** etc. Silvia is wearing a mask. 42. **undergo,** undertake; see glossary. 61. **fashion,** kind, sort. 62. **common,** as opposed to extraordinary. 73. **confounds,** ruins; see glossary. 77. **commit,** sin. 82-83. **And . . . thee.** This passage has provoked much critical comment. Bond finds the lines to be intentionally ambiguous in order to motivate Julia's swooning, paraphrasing it as, "All the love that I felt in Silvia's case I extend to thee." 86-90. **Why, boy . . . done.** These lines present a crux of some difficulty. A number of editors attempt to make blank verse of them. In F they appear as prose. Julia's words here contradict preceding action and dia-

Sil. When Proteus cannot love where he's belov'd.
Read over Julia's heart, thy first best love,
For whose dear sake thou didst then rend thy faith
Into a thousand oaths; and all those oaths
Descended into perjury, to love me.
Thou hast no faith left now, unless thou 'dst two;
And that 's far worse than none; better have none
Than plural faith which is too much by one:
Thou counterfeit to thy true friend!
Pro. In love
Who respects friend?
Sil. All men but Proteus.
Pro. Nay, if the gentle spirit of moving words
Can no way change you to a milder form,
I'll woo you like a soldier, at arms' end,
And love you 'gainst the nature of love,—force ye.
Sil. O heaven!
Pro. I'll force thee yield to my desire.
Val. Ruffian, let go that rude uncivil touch,
Thou friend of an ill fashion!
Pro. Valentine!
Val. Thou common friend, that 's without faith or love,
For such is a friend now; treacherous man!
Thou hast beguil'd my hopes; nought but mine eye
Could have persuaded me: now I dare not say
I have one friend alive; thou wouldst disprove me.
Who should be trusted, when one's right hand
Is perjured to the bosom? Proteus,
I am sorry I must never trust thee more,
But count the world a stranger for thy sake.
The private wound is deepest: O time most accurst,
'Mongst all foes that a friend should be the worst!
Pro. My shame and guilt confounds me.
Forgive me, Valentine: if hearty sorrow
Be a sufficient ransom for offence,
I tender 't here; I do as truly suffer
As e'er I did commit.
Val. Then I am paid;
And once again I do receive thee honest.
Who by repentance is not satisfied
Is nor of heaven nor earth, for these are pleas'd.
By penitence th' Eternal's wrath 's appeas'd:
And, that my love may appear plain and free,
All that was mine in Silvia I give thee.
Jul. O me unhappy! [*Swoons.*]
Pro. Look to the boy.
Val. Why, boy! why, wag! how now! what 's the matter? Look up; speak.
Jul. O good sir, my master charged me to deliver a ring to Madam Silvia, which, out of my neglect, was never done.
Pro. Where is that ring, boy?
Jul. Here 'tis; this is it. [*Gives ring.*]
Pro. How! let me see:
Why, this is the ring I gave to Julia.
Jul. O, cry you mercy, sir, I have mistook: This is the ring you sent to Silvia. [*Shows another ring.*]
Pro. But how cam'st thou by this ring? At my depart
I gave this unto Julia.
Jul. And Julia herself did give it me;
And Julia herself hath brought it hither.
Pro. How! Julia!
Jul. Behold her that gave aim to all thy oaths,
And entertain'd 'em deeply in her heart.
How oft hast thou with perjury cleft the root!
O Proteus, let this habit make thee blush!
Be thou asham'd that I have took upon me
Such an immodest raiment, if shame live
In a disguise of love:
It is the lesser blot, modesty finds,
Women to change their shapes than men their minds.
Pro. Than men their minds! 'tis true. O heaven! were man
But constant, he were perfect. That one error
Fills him with faults; makes him run through all th' sins:
Inconstancy falls off ere it begins.
What is in Silvia's face, but I may spy
More fresh in Julia's with a constant eye?
Val. Come, come, a hand from either:
Let me be blest to make this happy close;
'Twere pity two such friends should be long foes.
Pro. Bear witness, Heaven, I have my wish for ever.
Jul. And I mine.

[*Enter*] Duke [*and*] Thurio, [*led by*] Outlaws.

Outlaws. A prize, a prize, a prize!
Val. Forbear, forbear, I say! it is my lord the duke.
Your grace is welcome to a man disgrac'd,
Banished Valentine.
Duke. Sir Valentine!
Thu. Yonder is Silvia; and Silvia 's mine.
Val. Thurio, give back, or else embrace thy death;
Come not within the measure of my wrath;
Do not name Silvia thine; if once again,
†Verona shall not hold thee. Here she stands:
Take but possession of her with a touch:
I dare thee but to breathe upon my love.
Thu. Sir Valentine, I care not for her, I:
I hold him but a fool that will endanger
His body for a girl that loves him not:
I claim her not, and therefore she is thine.
Duke. The more degenerate and base art thou,
To make such means for her as thou hast done
And leave her on such slight conditions.
Now, by the honour of my ancestry,
I do applaud thy spirit, Valentine,
And think thee worthy of an empress' love:
Know then, I here forget all former griefs,
Cancel all grudge, repeal thee home again,
Plead a new state in thy unrival'd merit,
To which I thus subscribe: Sir Valentine,
Thou art a gentleman and well deriv'd;
Take thou thy Silvia, for thou hast deserv'd her.
Val. I thank your grace; the gift hath made me happy.
I now beseech you, for your daughter's sake,

logue; cf. IV, iv, 139-142. These observations, taken with Silvia's inexplicable silence from this point on, support the hypothesis for revision and abridgment. 86. **wag,** boy. The New Cambridge editors think it unlikely that Valentine would use such familiar address to a page he had not seen before. 94. **cry you mercy,** beg your pardon; see glossary. 101. **gave aim,** was the object of. 104. **this habit,** i.e., her page's costume. 113. **falls off,** withdraws from allegiance. 115. **constant,** steady, loyal. 117. **close,** conclusion, union. 129. **Verona,** for *Milan*; cf. III, i, 81, note. 144. **a new state,** a new standing for myself (Neilson). Bond suggests emending to *a new statute*, i.e., a new order of things; as an alternative he conjectures *Plant* for *Plead*, i.e., establish a new order, alluding to Valentine's union with Silvia. Steevens placed a period after the preceding line and made *Plead* an imperative, i.e., "Put in a plea for reinstatement."

To grant one boon that I shall ask of you.
Duke. I grant it, for thine own, whate'er it be.
Val. These banish'd men that I have kept withal
Are men endu'd with worthy qualities:
Forgive them what they have committed here
And let them be recall'd from their exile:
They are reformed, civil, full of good
And fit for great employment, worthy lord.
Duke. Thou hast prevail'd; I pardon them and thee:
Dispose of them as thou know'st their deserts.
Come, let us go: we will include all jars
With triumphs, mirth and rare solemnity.
Val. And, as we walk along, I dare be bold
With our discourse to make your grace to smile.
What think you of this page, my lord?
Duke. I think the boy hath grace in him; he blushes.
Val. I warrant you, my lord, more grace than boy.
Duke. What mean you by that saying?
Val. Please you, I'll tell you as we pass along,
That you will wonder what hath fortuned.
Come, Proteus; 'tis your penance but to hear
The story of your loves discovered:
That done, our day of marriage shall be yours;
One feast, one house, one mutual happiness. *Exeunt.*

160. **include,** conclude.

THE TAMING OF THE SHREW

Like other early comedies, *The Taming of the Shrew* (c. 1592–1594) looks forward to Shakespeare's mature comic drama in several ways. By skillfully juxtaposing two plots and an "Induction," or framing plot, it offers contrasting views on the battle of the sexes. This debate on the nature of the love relationship continues through many later comedies, somewhat in the manner of Chaucer's "Marriage Group." Moreover, the play adroitly manipulates the device of mistaken identity, as in *The Comedy of Errors*, inverting appearance and reality, dream and awakening, and the master-servant relationship in order to create a transformed Saturnalian world anticipating that of *A Midsummer Night's Dream* and *Twelfth Night*.

The Induction sets up the theme of illusion, using an old motif known as "The Sleeper Awakened" (as found for example in *The Arabian Nights*). This device "frames" the main action of the play, giving to it an added perspective. *The Taming of the Shrew* purports in fact to be a play within a play, an entertainment devised by a witty nobleman as a practical joke on a drunken tinker, Christophero Sly. The jest is to convince Sly that he is not Sly at all, but an aristocrat suffering delusions. Outlandishly dressed in new finery, Sly is invited to witness a play from the gallery over the stage. In a version of the play called *The Taming of a Shrew*, printed in 1594 and now generally thought to be an imitation of Shakespeare's play by a rival dramatist (who relied chiefly on memory and who liberally changed the characters' names and setting), the framing plot concludes by actually putting Sly back out on the street in front of the alehouse where he was found. He awakes, recalls the play as a dream, and proposes to put the vision to good use by taming his own wife. Whether this ending reflects an epilogue now lost from the text of Shakespeare's play cannot be said, but it does reinforce the idea of the play as Sly's fantasy. Like Puck at the end of *A Midsummer Night's Dream*, urging us to dismiss what we have seen as the product of our own slumbering, Sly continually reminds us that the play is only an illusion or shadow.

With repeated daring, Shakespeare calls attention to the contrived nature of his artifact, the play. When, for example, Sly is finally convinced that he is in fact a noble lord recovering from madness, and lustily proposes to hasten off to bed with his long-neglected wife, we are comically aware that the wife or "lady" is an impostor, a young page in disguise. Yet this counterfeiting of roles is no more unreal than the employment of Elizabethan boy-actors for the parts of Katharina and Bianca in the "real" play. As we watch Sly watching a play, levels of meaning interplay in this evocative fashion. Again, the paintings offered to Sly by his new attendants call attention to art's ability to confound illusion and reality. In one painting, Cytherea is hidden by water-rushes "Which seem to move and wanton with her breath Even as the waving sedges play with wind," and in another painting Io appears "As lively painted as the deed was done." Sly's function, then, is that of the naive observer who inverts illusion and reality in his mind, concluding that his whole previous life of tinkers and alehouses and Cicely Hackets has been unreal. As his attendants explain to him, "These fifteen years you have been in a dream; Or when you wak'd, so wak'd as if you slept." We laugh at Sly's naiveté, and yet we too are moved and even transformed by an artistic vision that we know to be illusory.

Like Sly, many characters in the main action of the play are persuaded, or nearly persuaded, to be what they are not. Lucentio and Tranio exchange roles of master and servant. Bianca's supposed tutors are in fact her wooers, using their lessons to disguise messages of love. Katharina is prevailed upon by her husband, Petruchio, to declare that the sun is the moon and that an old gentleman (Vincentio) is a fair young maiden. Vincentio is publicly informed that he is an impostor, and that the "real" Vincentio (the Pedant) is at that very moment looking at him out of the window of his son Lucentio's house. This last ruse does not fool the real Vincentio, but it nearly succeeds in fooling everyone else. Baptista Minola is about to commit Vincentio to jail for the infamous slander of asserting that the supposed Lucentio is only a servant in disguise. Vincentio, as the newly arrived stranger, is able to see matters as they really are; but the dwellers of Padua have grown so accustomed to the mad and improbable fictions of their life that they are not easily awakened to reality.

Shakespeare multiplies these devices of illusion by combining two entirely distinct plots, each concerned at least in part with the comic inversion of appearance and reality: the shrew-taming plot involving Petruchio and Kate, and the more conventional romantic plot involving Lucentio and Bianca. The latter plot is derived from the *Supposes* of George Gascoigne, a play first presented at Gray's Inn in 1566 as translated from Ariosto's neoclassical comedy *I Suppositi*, 1509. (Ariosto's work was based in turn upon Terence's *Eunuchus* and Plautus' *Captivi*.) The "Supposes" are mistaken identities or misunderstandings, the kind of hilarious farcical mix-ups Shakespeare had already experimented with in *The Comedy of Errors*. Shakespeare has, as usual, both romanticized his source and moralized it in a characteristically English way. The heroine, who in classical "new" comedy would have been a courtesan, and who in *Supposes* is made pregnant by her clandestine lover, remains thoroughly chaste in Shakespeare's comedy. Consequently she has no need for a pander or go-between, such as the bawdy Duenna or Nurse of *Supposes*. The satire directed at the heroine's unwelcome old wooer is far less savage than in *Supposes*, where the "pantaloon," Dr. Cleander, is a villainously corrupt lawyer epitomizing the depravity of "respectable" society. Despite Shakespeare's modifications, however, the basic plot involves an effort to foil parental authority, using a "trick to catch the old one." The young lovers, choosing one another for romantic reasons, must fend off the materialistic calculations of their parents.

Because this comic situation is "stock" or conventional, the character types in this plot are also conventional. Gremio, the aged wealthy wooer, is actually labeled a "pantaloon" in the text (III,i) to stress his neoclassical ancestry. (Lean and foolish old wooers of this sort were customarily dressed in pantaloons, slippers, and spectacles on the Italian stage.) Gremio is typically "the greybeard," and Baptista Minola is "the narrow-prying father" (III,ii). Even though Shakespeare renders these "blocking" characters, or *alazons*, far less unattractive than in *Supposes*, their worldly behavior still invites reprisal from the young. Since Baptista Minola insists on selling his daughter Bianca to the highest bidder, it is fitting that her wealthiest suitor (the supposed Lucentio) should turn out in the end to be a penniless servant (Tranio) disguised as a man of affluence and position. In his traditional role as the clever servant of neoclassical comedy, Tranio skillfully apes the mannerisms of respectable society. He can deal in mere surfaces, or clothes, or reputation, out of which a man's social importance is created, and can even furnish himself with a rich father. Gremio and Baptista deserve to be foiled because they accept the illusion of respectability as real.

Even the romantic lovers of this borrowed plot are largely conventional. To be sure, Shakespeare emphasizes their virtuous qualities and their sincerity. He adds Hortensio (not in *Supposes*) to provide Lucentio with a genuine rival and Bianca with a real choice. Lucentio and Bianca deserve their romantic triumph; they are self-possessed, witty, and steadfast to one another. Yet we know very little about them, nor have they seen deeply into one another. Lucentio's love-talk is laden with conventional Petrarchan images in praise of Bianca's dark eyes and scarlet lips. He discovers to his surprise, at the play's end, that she can be willful, even disobedient. Has her appearance of virtue concealed something from him and from us? Because the relationship between these lovers is superficial, they are appropriately destined to a superficial marriage as well. The passive Bianca becomes the proud and unmanageable wife.

By contrast, Petruchio and Kate are the more interesting lovers whose courtship involves mutual self-discovery. Admittedly, we must not overstate the case. Especially at first, these lovers are also stock types: the shrew-tamer and his proverbially shrewish wife. Although Shakespeare seems not to have used any single source for this plot, he was well acquainted with crude antifeminist stories demonstrating the need for putting women in their place. In a ballad called *A Merry Jest of a Shrewde and Curste Wyfe, Lapped in Morrelles Skin* (printed c. 1550), for example, the husband tames his shrewish spouse by flaying her bloody with birch rods and then wrapping her in the freshly salted skin of a plough-horse named Morel. (This shrewish wife, like Kate, has an obedient and gentle younger sister who is their father's favorite.) Other features of Shakespeare's plot can be found in similar tales: the tailor scolded for devising a gown of outlandish fashion (Gerard Legh's *Accidence of Armory*, 1562), the wife obliged to agree with her husband's assertion of some patent falsehood (Don Juan Manuel's *El Conde Lucanor*, c. 1350), and the three husbands' wager on their wives' obedience (*The Book of the Knight of La Tour-Landry*, printed 1484). In the raw spirit of this antifeminist tradition, so unlike the refined Italianate sentiment of his other plot, Shakespeare introduces Petruchio as a man of reckless bravado who is ready to marry the ugliest or sharpest-tongued woman alive so long as she is rich. However much he may be later attracted by Kate's fiery spirit, his first attraction to her is crassly financial. Kate is, moreover, a thoroughly disagreeable young woman at first, described by those who know her as "intolerable curst And shrewd and froward," aggressive in her bullying of Bianca. She and Petruchio meet as grotesque comic counterparts. Even at the play's end, the traditional pattern of male dominance and female acquiescence is still of course prominent. Kate achieves peace only by yielding to a divinely ordained hierarchical framework in which a husband is the princely ruler of his subservient wife.

Within this male-oriented frame of reference, however, Petruchio and Kate are surprisingly like Benedick and Beatrice of *Much Ado about Nothing*. Petruchio, for all his rant, is increasingly drawn to Kate by her spirit. As wit-combatants they are worthy of one another's enmity—or love. No one else in the play is a fit match for either of them. Kate too is attracted to Petruchio, despite her war of words. Her guise of hostility is part defensive protection, part testing of his sincerity. If she is contemptuous of the wooers she has seen till now, she has good reason to be so. We share her condescension toward the aged Gremio or the laughably inept Hortensio. She rightly fears that her father wishes to dispose of her so that he may auction off Bianca to the wealthiest competitor. Kate's jaded view of such marriage-broking is entirely defensible. Not surprisingly she first views Petruchio, whose professed intentions are far from reassuring, as another mere gamester in love. She is impressed by his "line" in wooing her, but needs to test his constancy and sincerity. Quite possibly, then, she is a woman who has always wanted to be possessed, but only by a man she can respect. She puts most men down with a shrewish manner that challenges their very masculinity; Petruchio is the first to be man enough to "board" her. He senses that she really longs to be mastered, even though she resists. His "schooling" is therefore curative. Having wooed and partly won her, he tests her with his late arrival at the marriage, his unconventional dress, and his crossing all her desires. In this display of willfulness, he shows her an ugly picture of what she herself is like. Most of all, however, he succeeds because he insists on what she too desires: subordination tempered by mutual respect and love. Kate is visibly a happier person at the play's end. Her closing speech, with its fine blend of irony and self-conscious hyperbole, together with its seriousness of concern, expresses beautifully the way in which Kate's independence of spirit and her newfound satisfaction in submissiveness are successfully fused.

THE TAMING OF THE SHREW

[*Dramatis Personae*

A Lord.
CHRISTOPHERO SLY, *a tinker*.
Hostess, Page, Players, Huntsmen, *and* Servants.
} *Persons in the Induction.*

BAPTISTA, *a rich gentleman of Padua.*
VINCENTIO, *an old gentleman of Pisa.*
LUCENTIO, *son to Vincentio, in love with Bianca.*
PETRUCHIO, *a gentleman of Verona, a suitor to Katharina.*
GREMIO, HORTENSIO, } *suitors to Bianca.*
TRANIO, BIONDELLO, } *servants to Lucentio.*
GRUMIO, CURTIS, } *servants to Petruchio.*
A Pedant.

KATHARINA, *the shrew*, BIANCA, } *daughters to Baptista.*
Widow.

Tailor, Haberdasher, *and* Servants attending on Baptista and Petruchio.

SCENE: *Padua, and Petruchio's country house.*]

[INDUCTION]

SCENE I. [*Before an alehouse on a heath.*]

Enter Beggar (CHRISTOPHERO SLY) *and* Hostess.

Sly. I'll pheeze you, in faith.

Host. A pair of stocks, you rogue!

Sly. Ye are a baggage: the Slys are no rogues; look in the chronicles; we came in with Richard Conqueror. Therefore paucas pallabris; let the world slide: sessa!

Host. You will not pay for the glasses you have burst?

Sly. No, not a denier. Go by, Jeronimy: go to thy cold bed, and warm thee.

Host. I know my remedy; I must go fetch the third-borough. [*Exit.*]

Sly. Third, or fourth, or fifth borough, I'll answer him by law: I'll not budge an inch, boy: let him come, and kindly. *Falls asleep.*

Wind horns. Enter a Lord *from hunting, with his train.*

Lord. Huntsman, I charge thee, tender well my hounds:
†Brach Merriman, the poor cur is emboss'd;
And couple Clowder with the deep-mouth'd brach.
Saw'st thou not, boy, how Silver made it good

At the hedge-corner, in the coldest fault?
I would not lose the dog for twenty pound.
First Hun. Why, Belman is as good as he, my lord;
He cried upon it at the merest loss
And twice to-day pick'd out the dullest scent:
Trust me, I take him for the better dog.
Lord. Thou art a fool: if Echo were as fleet,
I would esteem him worth a dozen such.
But sup them well and look unto them all:
To-morrow I intend to hunt again.
First Hun. I will, my lord.
Lord. What 's here? one dead, or drunk? See, doth he breathe?
Sec. Hun. He breathes, my lord. Were he not warm'd with ale,
This were a bed but cold to sleep so soundly.
Lord. O monstrous beast! how like a swine he lies!
Grim death, how foul and loathsome is thine image!
Sirs, I will practise on this drunken man.
What think you, if he were convey'd to bed,
Wrapp'd in sweet clothes, rings put upon his fingers,
A most delicious banquet by his bed,
And brave attendants near him when he wakes,
Would not the beggar then forget himself?
First Hun. Believe me, lord, I think he cannot choose.
Sec. Hun. It would seem strange unto him when he wak'd.
Lord. Even as a flatt'ring dream or worthless fancy.
Then take him up and manage well the jest:
Carry him gently to my fairest chamber
And hang it round with all my wanton pictures:
Balm his foul head in warm distilled waters
And burn sweet wood to make the lodging sweet:
Procure me music ready when he wakes,
To make a dulcet and a heavenly sound;
And if he chance to speak, be ready straight
And with a low submissive reverence
Say 'What is it your honour will command?'
Let one attend him with a silver basin
Full of rose-water and bestrew'd with flowers;
Another bear the ewer, the third a diaper,
And say 'Will 't please your lordship cool your hands?'
Some one be ready with a costly suit
And ask him what apparel he will wear;
Another tell him of his hounds and horse,
And that his lady mourns at his disease:
Persuade him that he hath been lunatic;
†And when he says he is, say that he dreams,
For he is nothing but a mighty lord.
This do and do it kindly, gentle sirs:
It will be pastime passing excellent,
If it be husbanded with modesty.
First Hun. My lord, I warrant you we will play our part,
As he shall think by our true diligence
He is no less than what we say he is.
Lord. Take him up gently and to bed with him;
And each one to his office when he wakes.
[*Some bear out Sly.*] *Sound trumpets.*
Sirrah, go see what trumpet 'tis that sounds:
[*Exit Servingman.*]
Belike, some noble gentleman that means,
Travelling some journey, to repose him here.

Enter Servingman.

How now! who is it?
Serv. An 't please your honour, players
That offer service to your lordship.
Lord. Bid them come near.

Enter Players.

Now, fellows, you are welcome.
Players. We thank your honour.
Lord. Do you intend to stay with me tonight?
A Player. So please your lordship to accept our duty.
Lord. With all my heart. This fellow I remember,
Since once he play'd a farmer's eldest son:
'Twas where you woo'd the gentlewoman so well:
I have forgot your name; but, sure, that part
Was aptly fitted and naturally perform'd.
A Player. I think 'twas Soto that your honour means.
Lord. 'Tis very true: thou didst it excellent.
Well, you are come to me in happy time;
The rather for I have some sport in hand
Wherein your cunning can assist me much.
There is a lord will hear you play to-night:
But I am doubtful of your modesties;
Lest over-eyeing of his odd behaviour,—
For yet his honour never heard a play—
You break into some merry passion
And so offend him; for I tell you, sirs,
If you should smile he grows impatient.
A Player. Fear not, my lord: we can contain ourselves,
Were he the veriest antic in the world.
Lord. Go, sirrah, take them to the buttery,
And give them friendly welcome every one:
Let them want nothing that my house affords.
Exit one with the Players.
Sirrah, go you to Barthol'mew my page,
And see him dress'd in all suits like a lady:
That done, conduct him to the drunkard's chamber;
And call him 'madam,' do him obeisance.
Tell him from me, as he will win my love,

INDUCTION. SCENE I. 1. **pheeze,** beat; possibly an echo of the Hostess' threat (Bond). 5. **paucas pallabris,** a blunder for Spanish *pocas palabras*, few words. 6. **sessa,** an interjection of doubtful import (Onions); Spanish *cessa* (Theobald); French *cessez* (Halliwell), i.e., be quiet; German *sa sa* (Schmidt), a term of applause or encouragement; an exhortation to swift running (Bond, citing *King Lear*, III, iv, 104; III, vi, 77). 9. **denier,** French coin, the twelfth of a *sou*. **Go by, Jeronimy,** a phrase from Kyd's *Spanish Tragedy*. 12. **third-borough,** constable. 16. **tender,** treat with tenderness. 17. **Brach,** female of the hound kind, here used as an epithet to Merriman; so F; the New Cambridge editors emend to *Broach* (early spelling probably *Broch*), explaining as "bleed," a probable veterinarian remedy in the sixteenth century for an *emboss'd* hound. Other conjectures and emendations: *Trash, Leech, Bathe, Brace*. Gollancz proposed that *Brach* be taken to mean "mate, couple," hardly agreeable to the context. **emboss'd,** foaming at the mouth from exhaustion. 18. **brach,** kind of hound that hunts by scent, especially a female hound. 20. **fault,** loss of scent. 23. **cried upon it,** bayed, gave mouth. **merest loss,** i.e., no scent or trace at all; see *mere* in glossary. 35. **image,** likeness; see glossary. 36. **practise on,** play a joke on; see glossary. 40. **brave,** finely arrayed, showy; see glossary. 44. **fancy,** flight of imagination; see glossary. 50. **me,** the ethical dative. 57. **diaper,** towel. 64. **And . . . is,** i.e., and when he says what he really is. 67. **passing,** surpassingly; see glossary. 82. **duty,** expression of respect; see glossary. 88. **Soto,** a character in Fletcher's *Woman Pleased* (1620). The New Cambridge editors point out the alternatives that this reference is a late non-Shakespearean insertion or that the Fletcher play is based on an earlier production which belonged to the Shakespearean company. The latter they find to be the more probable. 94. **doubtful,** apprehensive; see glossary. **your modesties,** i.e., lest the players stare rudely at Sly. 97. **merry passion,** outburst of laughter; see *passion* in glossary. 101. **antic,** buffoon. 104. **want,** lack; see glossary. 106. **in all suits,** in every detail.

He bear himself with honourable action,
Such as he hath observ'd in noble ladies
Unto their lords, by them accomplished:
Such duty to the drunkard let him do
With soft low tongue and lowly courtesy,
And say 'What is 't your honour will command,
Wherein your lady and your humble wife
May show her duty and make known her love?'
And then with kind embracements, tempting kisses,
And with declining head into his bosom,
Bid him shed tears, as being overjoy'd
To see her noble lord restor'd to health,
Who for this seven years hath esteemed him
No better than a poor and loathsome beggar:
And if the boy have not a woman's gift
To rain a shower of commanded tears,
An onion will do well for such a shift,
Which in a napkin being close convey'd
Shall in despite enforce a watery eye.
See this dispatch'd with all the haste thou canst:
Anon I'll give thee more instructions.
Exit a Servingman.
I know the boy will well usurp the grace,
Voice, gait and action of a gentlewoman:
I long to hear him call the drunkard husband,
And how my men will stay themselves from laughter
When they do homage to this simple peasant.
I'll in to counsel them; haply my presence
May well abate the over-merry spleen
Which otherwise would grow into extremes. [*Exeunt.*]

[SCENE II. *A bedchamber in the* Lord's *house.*]

Enter aloft the Drunkard [SLY], *with* Attendants; *some with apparel, basin and ewer and other appurtenances; and* Lord.

Sly. For God's sake, a pot of small ale.

First Serv. Will 't please your lordship drink a cup of sack?

Sec. Serv. Will 't please your honour taste of these conserves?

Third Serv. What raiment will your honour wear to-day?

Sly. I am Christophero Sly; call not me 'honour' nor 'lordship:' I ne'er drank sack in my life; and if you give me any conserves, give me conserves of beef: ne'er ask me what raiment I'll wear; for I have no more doublets than backs, no more stockings than legs, nor no more shoes than feet; nay, sometime more feet than shoes, or such shoes as my toes look through the over-leather.

Lord. Heaven cease this idle humour in your honour!
O, that a mighty man of such descent,
Of such possessions and so high esteem,
Should be infused with so foul a spirit!

Sly. What, would you make me mad? Am not I Christopher Sly, old Sly's son of Burton-heath, by birth a pedlar, by education a card-maker, by transmutation a bear-herd, and now by present profession a tinker? Ask Marian Hacket, the fat ale-wife of Wincot, if she know me not: if she say I am not fourteen pence on the score for sheer ale, score me up for the lyingest knave in Christendom. What! I am not bestraught: here 's—

Third Serv. O, this it is that makes your lady mourn!

Sec. Serv. O, this is it that makes your servants droop!

Lord. Hence comes it that your kindred shuns your house,
As beaten hence by your strange lunacy.
O noble lord, bethink thee of thy birth,
Call home thy ancient thoughts from banishment
And banish hence these abject lowly dreams.
Look how thy servants do attend on thee,
Each in his office ready at thy beck.
Wilt thou have music? hark! Apollo plays *Music.*
And twenty caged nightingales do sing:
Or wilt thou sleep? we'll have thee to a couch
Softer and sweeter than the lustful bed
On purpose trimm'd up for Semiramis.
Say thou wilt walk; we will bestrew the ground:
Or wilt thou ride? thy horses shall be trapp'd,
Their harness studded all with gold and pearl.
Dost thou love hawking? thou hast hawks will soar
Above the morning lark: or wilt thou hunt?
Thy hounds shall make the welkin answer them
And fetch shrill echoes from the hollow earth.

First Serv. Say thou wilt course; thy greyhounds are as swift
As breathed stags, ay, fleeter than the roe.

Sec. Serv. Dost thou love pictures? we will fetch thee straight
Adonis painted by a running brook,
And Cytherea all in sedges hid,
Which seem to move and wanton with her breath,
Even as the waving sedges play with wind.

Lord. We'll show thee Io as she was a maid,
And how she was beguiled and surpris'd,
As lively painted as the deed was done.

Third Serv. Or Daphne roaming through a thorny wood,
Scratching her legs that one shall swear she bleeds,
And at that sight shall sad Apollo weep,
So workmanly the blood and tears are drawn.

Lord. Thou art a lord and nothing but a lord:
Thou hast a lady far more beautiful
Than any woman in this waning age.

First Serv. And till the tears that she hath shed for thee
Like envious floods o'er-run her lovely face,
She was the fairest creature in the world;

122. **him,** i.e., himself. 126. **for . . . shift,** to serve a purpose; see *shift* in glossary. 127. **napkin,** handkerchief; see glossary. 130. **Anon,** presently; see glossary. 134. **stay,** withhold; see glossary. 137. **abate,** lessen; see glossary. **spleen,** supposed seat of the passions; see glossary.

SCENE II. 2. **sack,** sweet Spanish wine; see glossary. 11. **sometime,** sometimes; see glossary. 14. **humour,** whim; see glossary. 19. **Burton-heath.** Sir Sidney Lee considered this an allusion to Barton-on-the-Heath, where Shakespeare's aunt lived. It was about sixteen miles from Stratford. 21. **bear-herd,** keeper of a tame bear. 23. **Marian . . . Wincot,** another local allusion. There was a small village of Wincot about four miles from Stratford; the parish register shows that there were Hackets living there in 1591. 26-27. **Christendom . . . here 's—.** The New Cambridge editors, following a suggestion from Bond, insert after *Christendom* the stage direction, *a servant brings him a pot of ale*, and at the end of the speech, *he drinks*. Sly had called for ale at the beginning of the scene. 28. **O, this,** etc. To this point the servants' speeches in F have been *1 Ser.*, *2 Ser.*, etc.; they appear from this point on to the end of the scene as *1 Man*, *2 Man*, etc. The New Cambridge editors find this change coincides with a change in the style of the play, remarking that Sly begins to speak blank verse. The implication is that we have to do with revision here. Sly's taking to blank verse, however, may be humorously intentional; he is so thoroughly convinced of his lordly station that he begins to speak like a lord. 41. **Semiramis,** legendary queen of Assyria famous for her voluptuousness. 47. **welkin,** the sky, the heavens; see glossary. 50. **breathed,**

And yet she is inferior to none.
Sly. Am I a lord? and have I such a lady?
Or do I dream? or have I dream'd till now?
I do not sleep: I see, I hear, I speak;
I smell sweet savours and I feel soft things:
Upon my life, I am a lord indeed
And not a tinker nor Christophero Sly.
Well, bring our lady hither to our sight;
And once again, a pot o' th' smallest ale.
Sec. Serv. Will 't please your mightiness to wash your hands?
O, how we joy to see your wit restor'd!
O, that once more you knew but what you are!
These fifteen years you have been in a dream;
Or when you wak'd, so wak'd as if you slept.
Sly. These fifteen years! by my fay, a goodly nap.
But did I never speak of all that time?
First Serv. O, yes, my lord, but very idle words:
For though you lay here in this goodly chamber,
Yet would you say ye were beaten out of door;
And rail upon the hostess of the house;
And say you would present her at the leet,
Because she brought stone jugs and no seal'd quarts:
Sometimes you would call out for Cicely Hacket.
Sly. Ay, the woman's maid of the house.
Third Serv. Why, sir, you know no house nor no such maid,
Nor no such men as you have reckon'd up,
As Stephen Sly and old John Naps of Greece
And Peter Turph and Henry Pimpernell
And twenty more such names and men as these
Which never were nor no man ever saw.
Sly. Now Lord be thanked for my good amends!
All. Amen.

Enter [*the* Page *as a*] *lady, with* Attendants.

Sly. I thank thee: thou shalt not lose by it.
Page. How fares my noble lord?
Sly. Marry, I fare well; for here is cheer enough.
Where is my wife?
Page. Here, noble lord: what is thy will with her?
Sly. Are you my wife and will not call me husband?
My men should call me 'lord:' I am your goodman.
Page. My husband and my lord, my lord and husband;
I am your wife in all obedience.
Sly. I know it well. What must I call her?
Lord. Madam.
Sly. Al'ce madam, or Joan madam?
Lord. 'Madam,' and nothing else: so lords call ladies.
Sly. Madam wife, they say that I have dream'd
And slept above some fifteen year or more.
Page. Ay, and the time seems thirty unto me,
Being all this time abandon'd from your bed.
Sly. 'Tis much. Servants, leave me and her alone.
Madam, undress you and come now to bed.
Page. Thrice-noble lord, let me entreat of you
To pardon me yet for a night or two,
Or, if not so, until the sun be set:
For your physicians have expressly charg'd,
In peril to incur your former malady,
That I should yet absent me from your bed:
I hope this reason stands for my excuse.

Sly. Ay, it stands so that I may hardly tarry so long. But I would be loath to fall into my dreams again: I will therefore tarry in despite of the flesh and the blood.

Enter a Messenger.

Mess. Your honour's players, hearing your amendment,
Are come to play a pleasant comedy;
For so your doctors hold it very meet,
Seeing too much sadness hath congeal'd your blood,
And melancholy is the nurse of frenzy:
Therefore they thought it good you hear a play
And frame your mind to mirth and merriment,
Which bars a thousand harms and lengthens life.

Sly. Marry, I will, let them play it. Is not a comonty a Christmas gambold or a tumbling-trick?

Page. No, my good lord; it is more pleasing stuff.
Sly. What, household stuff?
Page. It is a kind of history.

Sly. Well, we'll see 't. Come, madam wife, sit by my side and let the world slip: we shall ne'er be younger. *Flourish.*

[ACT I.

SCENE I. *Padua. A public place.*]

Enter LUCENTIO *and his man* TRANIO.

Luc. Tranio, since for the great desire I had
To see fair Padua, nursery of arts,
I am arriv'd for fruitful Lombardy,
The pleasant garden of great Italy;
And by my father's love and leave am arm'd
With his good will and thy good company,
My trusty servant, well approv'd in all,
Here let us breathe and haply institute
A course of learning and ingenious studies.
Pisa renowned for grave citizens
Gave me my being and my father first,
A merchant of great traffic through the world,
Vincentio, come of the Bentivolii.
Vincentio's son brought up in Florence
It shall become to serve all hopes conceiv'd,
To deck his fortune with his virtuous deeds:
And therefore, Tranio, for the time I study,
Virtue and that part of philosophy
Will I apply that treats of happiness

accustomed to violent exercise. 53. **Cytherea,** one of the names for Venus, goddess of love. 56. **Io,** one of Jupiter's paramours. Juno in a jealous rage changed her into a heifer. 59. **Daphne,** a wood nymph beloved by Apollo. When he pursued her, Diana changed her into a laurel tree in order to preserve her from assault. 67. **envious,** spiteful; see glossary. 83. **fay,** faith. 89. **leet,** special court of record which the lords of certain manors were empowered to hold yearly or half-yearly. 90. **seal'd quarts,** officially stamped as of that capacity. Malone noted that sale of liquors in sealed or unsealed measures was matter for inquiry in a leet (Kitchen's *Courts*, 1663). 95. **Stephen Sly and old John Naps of Greece.** There was a genuine Stephen Sly who was in the dramatist's day a self-assertive citizen of Stratford; and 'Greece,' whence 'old John Naps' derived his cognomen, is an obvious misreading of Greet, a hamlet by Winchmere in Gloucestershire, not far removed from Shakespeare's native town (Sir Sidney Lee, *Life*, 1904, 167). 127. **stands,** a bawdy pun. 140-141. **comonty, gambold,** Sly's blunders for "comedy" and "gambol."

ACT I. SCENE I. 2. **Padua . . . arts,** one of the most renowned of universities during Shakespeare's time. 2, 3. **Padua, Lombardy.** Shakespeare's geography here is inaccurate. From subsequent mentions in the play (e.g., I. 42) it is evident that he thought of Padua as a seaport. It is in the province of Venetia, a few miles inland from Venice. 3. **for,** at (Perry); for a stay (Bond). 7. **well . . . all,** i.e., he has proved himself trustworthy in all things. 8. **institute,** begin. 9. **ingenious,** pertaining to the wits, intellectual. 15. **all hopes conceiv'd,** i.e., the hopes entertained for me by my friends.

By virtue specially to be achiev'd.
Tell me thy mind; for I have Pisa left
And am to Padua come, as he that leaves
A shallow plash to plunge him in the deep
And with satiety seeks to quench his thirst.

Tra. Mi perdonato, gentle master mine,
I am in all affected as yourself;
Glad that you thus continue your resolve
To suck the sweets of sweet philosophy.
Only, good master, while we do admire
This virtue and this moral discipline,
Let 's be no stoics nor no stocks, I pray;
Or so devote to Aristotle's checks
As Ovid be an outcast quite abjur'd:
Balk logic with acquaintance that you have
And practise rhetoric in your common talk;
Music and poesy use to quicken you;
The mathematics and the metaphysics,
Fall to them as you find your stomach serves you;
No profit grows where is no pleasure ta'en:
In brief, sir, study what you most affect.

Luc. Gramercies, Tranio, well dost thou advise.
If, Biondello, thou wert come ashore,
We could at once put us in readiness,
And take a lodging fit to entertain
Such friends as time in Padua shall beget.
But stay a while: what company is this?

Tra. Master, some show to welcome us to town.

Enter BAPTISTA *with his two Daughters* KATHARINA *and* BIANCA, GREMIO *a Pantaloon,* [*and*] HORTENSIO *suitor to* BIANCA. LUCENTIO [*and*] TRANIO *stand by.*

Bap. Gentlemen, importune me no farther,
For how I firmly am resolv'd you know;
That is, not to bestow my youngest daughter
Before I have a husband for the elder:
If either of you both love Katharina,
Because I know you well and love you well,
Leave shall you have to court her at your pleasure.

Gre. [*Aside*] To cart her rather: she 's too rough for me.
There, there, Hortensio, will you any wife?

Kath. I pray you, sir, is it your will
To make a stale of me amongst these mates?

Hor. Mates, maid! how mean you that? no mates for you,
Unless you were of gentler, milder mould.

Kath. I' faith, sir, you shall never need to fear:
I wis it is not half way to her heart;
But if it were, doubt not her care should be
To comb your noddle with a three-legg'd stool
And paint your face and use you like a fool.

Hor. From all such devils, good Lord deliver us!

Gre. And me too, good Lord!

Tra. Hush, master! here 's some good pastime toward:
That wench is stark mad or wonderful froward.

Luc. But in the other's silence do I see
Maid's mild behaviour and sobriety.
Peace, Tranio!

Tra. Well said, master; mum! and gaze your fill.

Bap. Gentlemen, that I may soon make good
What I have said, Bianca, get you in:
And let it not displease thee, good Bianca,
For I will love thee ne'er the less, my girl.

Kath. A pretty peat! it is best
Put finger in the eye, an she knew why.

Bian. Sister, content you in my discontent.
Sir, to your pleasure humbly I subscribe:
My books and instruments shall be my company,
On them to look and practise by myself.

Luc. Hark, Tranio! thou may'st hear Minerva speak.

Hor. Signior Baptista, will you be so strange?
Sorry am I that our good will effects
Bianca's grief.

Gre. Why will you mew her up,
Signior Baptista, for this fiend of hell,
And make her bear the penance of her tongue?

Bap. Gentlemen, content ye; I am resolv'd:
Go in, Bianca: [*Exit Bianca.*]
And for I know she taketh most delight
In music, instruments and poetry,
Schoolmasters will I keep within my house,
Fit to instruct her youth. If you, Hortensio,
Or Signior Gremio, you, know any such,
Prefer them hither; for to cunning men
I will be very kind, and liberal
To mine own children in good bringing up:
And so farewell. Katharina, you may stay;
For I have more to commune with Bianca. *Exit.*

Kath. Why, and I trust I may go too, may I not? What, shall I be appointed hours; as though, belike, I knew not what to take, and what to leave, ha? *Exit.*

Gre. You may go to the devil's dam: your gifts are so good, here 's none will hold you. Their love is not so great, Hortensio, but we may blow our nails together, and fast it fairly out: our cake 's dough on both sides. Farewell: yet, for the love I bear my sweet Bianca, if I can by any means light on a fit man to teach her that wherein she delights, I will wish him to her father.

Hor. So will I, Signior Gremio: but a word, I pray. Though the nature of our quarrel yet never brooked parle, know now, upon advice, it toucheth us both, that we may yet again have access to our fair mistress and be happy rivals in Bianca's love, to labour and effect one thing specially.

Gre. What 's that, I pray?

Hor. Marry, sir, to get a husband for her sister.

Gre. A husband! a devil.

Hor. I say, a husband.

Gre. I say, a devil. Thinkest thou, Hortensio, though her father be very rich, any man is so very a fool to be married to hell?

Hor. Tush, Gremio, though it pass your patience and mine to endure her loud alarums, why, man, there be good fellows in the world, an a man could

23. **plash,** pool. 25. **Mi perdonato,** pardon me. 26. **affected,** disposed; see glossary. 31. **stocks,** devoid of feeling. 32. **devote,** devoted. **checks,** restraints; see glossary. Blackstone's suggestion that this is an error for "ethics" has much to recommend it. 33. **Ovid,** a Latin love poet. The antithesis is between serious study, as typified by Aristotle, and preoccupation with lighter entertainment, as typified by Ovid. 34. **Balk logic,** argue, bandy words (Onions). 38. **stomach,** inclination, disposition; see glossary. 40. **what . . . affect,** what pleases you most; see *affect* in glossary. 55. **cart,** carry in a cart through the streets by way of punishment or public exposure. 58. **stale,** laughing-stock, with play on the meaning "harlot." **mates,** rude fellows. 68. **toward,** about to take place; see glossary. 78. **peat,** darling, pet. 87. **mew her up,** coop her up; see *mew* in glossary. 108. **Their,** so F. The antecedent has been variously explained: women in general; Baptista and Bianca (for her suitors); Katharina and Bianca (for each other); Baptista and Bianca (for each other). The New Cambridge editors adopt the reading of the 1631 Q: *There loue*, punctuating *There-love*, etc. 109. **blow . . . together,** equivalent to the modern expression "twirl our thumbs." **fairly,** handsomely (used contemptuously); see glossary. 117. **brooked,** endured, tolerated; see glossary. **parle,** con-

light on them, would take her with all faults, and money enough.

Gre. I cannot tell; but I had as lief take her dowry with this condition, to be whipped at the high cross every morning.

Hor. Faith, as you say, there 's small choice in rotten apples. But come; since this bar in law makes us friends, it shall be so far forth friendly maintained till by helping Baptista's eldest daughter to a husband we set his youngest free for a husband, and then have to 't afresh. Sweet Bianca! Happy man be his dole! He that runs fastest gets the ring. How say you, Signior Gremio?

Gre. I am agreed; and would I had given him the best horse in Padua to begin his wooing that would thoroughly woo her, wed her and bed her and rid the house of her! Come on. *Exeunt ambo. Mane[n]t Tranio and Lucentio.*

Tra. I pray, sir, tell me, is it possible
That love should of a sudden take such hold?
Luc. O Tranio, till I found it to be true,
I never thought it possible or likely;
But see, while idly I stood looking on,
I found the effect of love in idleness:
And now in plainness do confess to thee,
That art to me as secret and as dear
As Anna to the queen of Carthage was,
Tranio, I burn, I pine, I perish, Tranio,
If I achieve not this young modest girl.
Counsel me, Tranio, for I know thou canst;
Assist me, Tranio, for I know thou wilt.
Tra. Master, it is no time to chide you now;
Affection is not rated from the heart:
If love have touch'd you, nought remains but so,
'Redime te captum quam queas minimo.'
Luc. Gramercies, lad, go forward; this contents:
The rest will comfort, for thy counsel's sound.
Tra. Master, you look'd so longly on the maid,
Perhaps you mark'd not what 's the pith of all.
Luc. O yes, I saw sweet beauty in her face,
Such as the daughter of Agenor had,
That made great Jove to humble him to her hand,
When with his knees he kiss'd the Cretan strand.
Tra. Saw you no more? mark'd you not how her sister
Began to scold and raise up such a storm
That mortal ears might hardly endure the din?
Luc. Tranio, I saw her coral lips to move
And with her breath she did perfume the air:
Sacred and sweet was all I saw in her.
Tra. Nay, then, 'tis time to stir him from his trance.
I pray, awake, sir: if you love the maid,
Bend thoughts and wits to achieve her. Thus it stands:
Her elder sister is so curst and shrewd
That till the father rid his hands of her,
Master, your love must live a maid at home;
And therefore has he closely mew'd her up,
Because she will not be annoy'd with suitors.
Luc. Ah, Tranio, what a cruel father 's he!
But art thou not advis'd, he took some care
To get her cunning schoolmasters to instruct her?
Tra. Ay, marry, am I, sir; and now 'tis plotted.
Luc. I have it, Tranio.
Tra. Master, for my hand,
Both our inventions meet and jump in one.
Luc. Tell me thine first.
Tra. You will be schoolmaster
And undertake the teaching of the maid:
That 's your device.
Luc. It is: may it be done?
Tra. Not possible; for who shall bear your part,
And be in Padua here Vincentio's son,
Keep house and ply his book, welcome his friends,
Visit his countrymen and banquet them?
Luc. Basta; content thee, for I have it full.
We have not yet been seen in any house,
Nor can we be distinguish'd by our faces
For man or master; then it follows thus;
Thou shalt be master, Tranio, in my stead,
Keep house and port and servants, as I should:
I will some other be, some Florentine,
Some Neapolitan, or meaner man of Pisa.
'Tis hatch'd and shall be so: Tranio, at once
Uncase thee; take my colour'd hat and cloak:
When Biondello comes, he waits on thee;
But I will charm him first to keep his tongue.
Tra. So had you need.
In brief, sir, sith it your pleasure is,
And I am tied to be obedient;
For so your father charg'd me at our parting,
'Be serviceable to my son,' quoth he,
Although I think 'twas in another sense;
I am content to be Lucentio,
Because so well I love Lucentio.
Luc. Tranio, be so, because Lucentio loves.
And let me be a slave, t' achieve that maid
Whose sudden sight hath thrall'd my wounded eye.

Enter BIONDELLO.

Here comes the rogue. Sirrah, where have you been?

Bion. Where have I been! Nay, how now! where are you? Master, has my fellow Tranio stolen your clothes? Or you stolen his? or both? pray, what 's the news?

Luc. Sirrah, come hither: 'tis no time to jest,
And therefore frame your manners to the time.
Your fellow Tranio here, to save my life,
Puts my apparel and my count'nance on,
And I for my escape have put on his;
For in a quarrel since I came ashore
I kill'd a man and fear I was descried:
Wait you on him, I charge you, as becomes,
While I make way from hence to save my life:
You understand me?
Bion. I, sir! ne'er a whit.
Luc. And not a jot of Tranio in your mouth:
Tranio is chang'd into Lucentio.

ference; see glossary. **advice,** reflection; see glossary. 137. **high cross,** cross set on a pedestal in a market place or center of a town. 144. **dole,** portion in life, destiny; i.e., may it be his dole to be called "Happy man!" (Onions). 145. **the ring,** an allusion to the sport of riding at the ring, with quibble on "wedding ring." 156. **love in idleness,** the flower heartsease, pansy, to which was attributed magical power in love. 159. **Anna . . . Carthage.** Anna was the confidante of her sister, Dido, queen of Carthage. 165. **rated,** driven away by chiding; see glossary. 167. **'Redime . . . minimo,'** buy yourself out of bondage for as little as you can. 173. **daughter of Agenor,** Europa; the story is related in Ovid's *Metamorphoses.* 185. **curst,** shrewish; see glossary. **shrewd,** ill-natured; see glossary. 192. **cunning,** skillful. 195. **inventions,** plans; see glossary. **jump,** tally, agree; see glossary. 203. **Basta,** enough. 208. **port,** state, social station; see glossary. 210. **meaner,** of a lower social class; see *mean* in glossary. 216. **sith,** since; see glossary. 225. **Whose sudden sight,** i.e., the sudden sight of whom. 226. **Sirrah,** ordinary form of addressing servants; see glossary.

Bion. The better for him: would I were so too!
Tra. So could I, faith, boy, to have the next wish after,
That Lucentio indeed had Baptista's youngest daughter.
But, sirrah, not for my sake, but your master's, I advise
You use your manners discreetly in all kind of companies:
When I am alone, why, then I am Tranio;
But in all places else your master Lucentio.

Luc. Tranio, let 's go: one thing more rests, that thyself execute, to make one among these wooers: if thou ask me why, sufficeth, my reasons are both good and weighty. *Exeunt.*

The presenters above speak.

First Serv. My lord, you nod; you do not mind the play.

Sly. Yes, by Saint Anne, do I. A good matter, surely: comes there any more of it?

Page. My lord, 'tis but begun.

Sly. 'Tis a very excellent piece of work, madam lady: would 'twere done! *They sit and mark.*

[SCENE II. *Padua. Before* HORTENSIO'S *house.*]

Enter PETRUCHIO *and his man* GRUMIO.

Pet. Verona, for a while I take my leave,
To see my friends in Padua, but of all
My best beloved and approved friend,
Hortensio; and I trow this is his house.
Here, sirrah Grumio; knock, I say.

Gru. Knock, sir! whom should I knock? is there any man has rebused your worship?

Pet. Villain, I say, knock me here soundly.

Gru. Knock you here, sir! why, sir, what am I, sir, that I should knock you here, sir?

Pet. Villain, I say, knock me at this gate
And rap me well, or I'll knock your knave's pate.

Gru. My master is grown quarrelsome. I should knock you first,
And then I know after who comes by the worst.

Pet. Will it not be?
Faith, sirrah, an you'll not knock, I'll ring it;
I'll try how you can sol, fa, and sing it.
He wrings him by the ears.

Gru. Help, masters, help! my master is mad.

Pet. Now, knock when I bid you, sirrah villain!

Enter HORTENSIO.

Hor. How now! what 's the matter? My old friend Grumio! and my good friend Petruchio! How do you all at Verona?

Pet. Signior Hortensio, come you to part the fray?
'Con tutto il cuore, ben trovato,' may I say.

Hor. 'Alla nostra casa ben venuto, molto honorato signor mio Petruchio.'
Rise, Grumio, rise: we will compound this quarrel.

Gru. Nay, 'tis no matter, sir, what he 'leges in Latin. If this be not a lawful cause for me to leave his service, look you, sir, he bid me knock him and rap him soundly, sir: well, was it fit for a servant to use his master so, being perhaps, for aught I see, two and thirty, a pip out?
Whom would to God I had well knock'd at first,
Then had not Grumio come by the worst.

Pet. A senseless villain! Good Hortensio,
I bade the rascal knock upon your gate
And could not get him for my heart to do it.

Gru. Knock at the gate! O heavens! Spake you not these words plain, 'Sirrah, knock me here, rap me here, knock me well, and knock me soundly'? And come you now with, 'knocking at the gate'?

Pet. Sirrah, be gone, or talk not, I advise you.

Hor. Petruchio, patience; I am Grumio's pledge:
Why, this 's a heavy chance 'twixt him and you,
Your ancient, trusty, pleasant servant Grumio.
And tell me now, sweet friend, what happy gale
Blows you to Padua here from old Verona?

Pet. Such wind as scatters young men through the world
To seek their fortunes farther than at home
Where small experience grows. But in a few,
Signior Hortensio, thus it stands with me:
Antonio, my father, is deceas'd;
And I have thrust myself into this maze,
Haply to wive and thrive as best I may:
Crowns in my purse I have and goods at home,
And so am come abroad to see the world.

Hor. Petruchio, shall I then come roundly to thee
And wish thee to a shrewd ill-favour'd wife?
Thou 'ldst thank me but a little for my counsel:
And yet I'll promise thee she shall be rich
And very rich: but th' art too much my friend,
And I'll not wish thee to her.

Pet. Signior Hortensio, 'twixt such friends as we
Few words suffice; and therefore, if thou know
One rich enough to be Petruchio's wife,
As wealth is burden of my wooing dance,
Be she as foul as was Florentius' love,
As old as Sibyl and as curst and shrewd
As Socrates' Xanthippe, or a worse,
She moves me not, or not removes, at least,
Affection's edge in me, were she as rough
As are the swelling Adriatic seas:
I come to wive it wealthily in Padua;
If wealthily, then happily in Padua.

Gru. Nay, look you, sir, he tells you flatly what his mind is: why, give him gold enough and marry him to a puppet or an aglet-baby; or an old trot with ne'er a tooth in her head, though she have as many diseases as two and fifty horses: why, nothing comes amiss, so money comes withal.

Hor. Petruchio, since we are stepp'd thus far in,
I will continue that I broach'd in jest.

250. **rests,** remains to be done. 251. **execute,** undertake. **make one,** i.e., make yourself one. 252. **sufficeth,** it suffices that. 253. *Stage Direction:* ***presenters,*** those who present the Induction. 254. **mind,** attend; see glossary.

SCENE II. 4. **trow,** believe; see glossary. 8, 11, 12. **me,** the ethical dative. 16. **an,** if; see glossary. 17. **I'll . . . it.** Petruchio wants to hear him howl; possibly Grumio had been singing. 24. **'Con . . . trovato,'** with all my heart, well met. 25-26. **'Alla . . . Petruchio,'** welcome to our house, my much honored Petruchio. 27. **compound,** settle; see glossary. 28. **'leges,** alleges, with quibble on Latin *leges,* meaning "you read." 33. **two . . . out,** not quite up to the mark; a possible reference to Petruchio's age; refers to the old card game of one-and-thirty or bone-ace, in which the ace of diamonds was the highest and took half the bone, or stake; a pip was a spot on a card. 59. **roundly,** plainly, without ceremony; see glossary. 68. **burden,** musical accompaniment. 69. **Florentius' love,** an allusion to Gower's version in *Confessio Amantis* of the fairy tale of the knight who promised to marry an ugly old woman if she solved the riddle he must answer. After the fulfillment of all promises, she became young and beautiful. Another version of this story is Chaucer's *Tale of the Wife of Bath.*

I can, Petruchio, help thee to a wife
With wealth enough and young and beauteous,
Brought up as best becomes a gentlewoman:
Her only fault, and that is faults enough,
Is that she is intolerable curst
And shrewd and froward, so beyond all measure
That, were my state far worser than it is,
I would not wed her for a mine of gold.

Pet. Hortensio, peace! thou know'st not gold's effect:
Tell me her father's name and 'tis enough;
For I will board her, though she chide as loud
As thunder when the clouds in autumn crack.

Hor. Her father is Baptista Minola,
An affable and courteous gentleman:
Her name is Katharina Minola,
Renown'd in Padua for her scolding tongue.

Pet. I know her father, though I know not her;
And he knew my deceased father well.
I will not sleep, Hortensio, till I see her;
And therefore let me be thus bold with you
To give you over at this first encounter,
Unless you will accompany me thither.

Gru. I pray you, sir, let him go while the humour lasts. A my word, an she knew him as well as I do, she would think scolding would do little good upon him: she may perhaps call him half a score knaves or so: why, that 's nothing; an he begin once, he'll rail in his rope-tricks. I'll tell you what, sir, an she stand him but a little, he will throw a figure in her face and so disfigure her with it that she shall have no more eyes to see withal than a cat. You know him not, sir.

Hor. Tarry, Petruchio, I must go with thee,
For in Baptista's keep my treasure is:
He hath the jewel of my life in hold,
His youngest daughter, beautiful Bianca,
And her withholds from me and other more,
Suitors to her and rivals in my love,
Supposing it a thing impossible,
For those defects I have before rehears'd,
That ever Katharina will be woo'd;
Therefore this order hath Baptista ta'en,
That none shall have access unto Bianca
Till Katharine the curst have got a husband.

Gru. Katharine the curst!
A title for a maid of all titles the worst.

Hor. Now shall my friend Petruchio do me grace,
And offer me disguis'd in sober robes
To old Baptista as a schoolmaster
Well seen in music, to instruct Bianca;
That so I may, by this device, at least
Have leave and leisure to make love to her
And unsuspected court her by herself.

Enter GREMIO, *and* LUCENTIO *disguised.*

Gru. Here 's no knavery! See, to beguile the old folks, how the young folks lay their heads together! Master, master, look about you: who goes there, ha?

Hor. Peace, Grumio! it is the rival of my love.
Petruchio, stand by a while. [*They stand aside.*]

Gru. A proper stripling and an amorous!

Gre. O, very well; I have perus'd the note.
Hark you, sir; I'll have them very fairly bound:
All books of love, see that at any hand;
And see you read no other lectures to her:
You understand me: over and beside
Signior Baptista's liberality,
I'll mend it with a largess. Take your paper too,
And let me have them very well perfum'd:
For she is sweeter than perfume itself
To whom they go to. What will you read to her?

Luc. Whate'er I read to her, I'll plead for you
As for my patron, stand you so assur'd,
As firmly as yourself were still in place:
Yea, and perhaps with more successful words
Than you, unless you were a scholar, sir.

Gre. O this learning, what a thing it is!

Gru. O this woodcock, what an ass it is!

Pet. Peace, sirrah!

Hor. Grumio, mum! God save you, Signior Gremio.

Gre. And you are well met, Signior Hortensio.
Trow you whither I am going? To Baptista Minola.
I promis'd to inquire carefully
About a schoolmaster for the fair Bianca:
And by good fortune I have lighted well
On this young man, for learning and behaviour
Fit for her turn, well read in poetry
And other books, good ones, I warrant ye.

Hor. 'Tis well; and I have met a gentleman
Hath promis'd me to help me to another,
A fine musician to instruct our mistress;
So shall I no whit be behind in duty
To fair Bianca, so belov'd of me.

Gre. Belov'd of me; and that my deeds shall prove.

Gru. [*Aside*] And that his bags shall prove.

Hor. Gremio, 'tis now no time to vent our love:
Listen to me, and if you speak me fair,
I'll tell you news indifferent good for either.
Here is a gentleman whom by chance I met,
Upon agreement from us to his liking,
Will undertake to woo curst Katharine,
Yea, and to marry her, if her dowry please.

Gre. So said, so done, is well.
Hortensio, have you told him all her faults?

Pet. I know she is an irksome brawling scold:
If that be all, masters, I hear no harm.

Gre. No, say'st me so, friend? What countryman?

Pet. Born in Verona, old Antonio's son:
My father dead, my fortune lives for me;
And I do hope good days and long to see.

Gre. O sir, such a life, with such a wife, were strange!
But if you have a stomach, to 't a God's name:
You shall have me assisting you in all.
But will you woo this wild-cat?

Pet. Will I live?

Gru. [*Aside*] Will he woo her? ay, or I'll hang her.

70. **Sibyl,** prophetess of Cumae to whom Apollo gave as many years of life as she held grains of sand in her hand. 71. **Xanthippe,** the philosopher's notoriously shrewish wife. 78. **mind,** intention; see glossary. 79. **aglet-baby,** small figure carved on the tag of a lace. 80. **trot,** old woman. 82. **withal,** with it; see glossary. 95. **board,** accost. 105. **give you over,** desert you. 112. **rope-tricks,** variously explained: Grumio's blunder for "rhetoric," borne out by his use of *figure* below; tricks deserving a halter—i.e., hanging (Perry); Bond recalls the nurse in *Romeo and Juliet* (II, iv, 154) characterizing Mercutio's remarks as *ropery,* and suspects similar coarse allusions here.

113. **stand,** withstand. 114. **figure,** figure of speech. 131. **do me grace,** do me a favor; see *grace* in glossary. 134. **Well seen,** well skilled. 144. **proper,** handsome (used facetiously); see glossary. Grumio is alluding to the old Gremio, not to Lucentio. 147. **at any hand,** in any case. 151. **largess,** free gift of money. 161. **woodcock,** a bird easily caught; frequently used to indicate a simpleton. 180. **fair,** civilly, courteously; see glossary. 181. **indifferent,** equally. 183. **Upon . . . liking,** on terms agreeable to him. A few lines below (215-216) we learn that Bianca's suitors will *bear his charge of wooing.*

Pet. Why came I hither but to that intent?
Think you a little din can daunt mine ears?
Have I not in my time heard lions roar?
Have I not heard the sea puff'd up with winds
Rage like an angry boar chafed with sweat?
Have I not heard great ordnance in the field,
And heaven's artillery thunder in the skies?
Have I not in a pitched battle heard
Loud 'larums, neighing steeds, and trumpets' clang?
And do you tell me of a woman's tongue,
That gives not half so great a blow to hear
As will a chestnut in a farmer's fire?
Tush, tush! fear boys with bugs.
Gru. For he fears none.
Gre. Hortensio, hark:
This gentleman is happily arriv'd,
My mind presumes, for his own good and ours.
Hor. I promis'd we would be contributors
And bear his charge of wooing, whatsoe'er.
Gre. And so we will, provided that he win her.
Gru. [*Aside*] I would I were as sure of a good dinner.

Enter TRANIO *brave, and* BIONDELLO.

Tra. Gentlemen, God save you. If I may be bold,
Tell me, I beseech you, which is the readiest way
To the house of Signior Baptista Minola?
Bion. He that has the two fair daughters: is 't he you mean?
Tra. Even he, Biondello.
Gre. Hark you, sir; you mean not her to—
Tra. Perhaps, him and her, sir: what have you to do?
Pet. Not her that chides, sir, at any hand, I pray.
Tra. I love no chiders, sir. Biondello, let 's away.
Luc. [*Aside*] Well begun, Tranio.
Hor. Sir, a word ere you go;
Are you a suitor to the maid you talk of, yea or no?
Tra. And if I be, sir, is it any offence?
Gre. No; if without more words you will get you hence.
Tra. Why, sir, I pray, are not the streets as free
For me as for you?
Gre. But so is not she.
Tra. For what reason, I beseech you?
Gre. For this reason, if you'll know,
That she 's the choice love of Signior Gremio.
Hor. That she 's the chosen of Signior Hortensio.
Tra. Softly, my masters! if you be gentlemen,
Do me this right; hear me with patience.
Baptista is a noble gentleman,
To whom my father is not all unknown;
And were his daughter fairer than she is,
She may more suitors have and me for one.
Fair Leda's daughter had a thousand wooers;
Then well one more may fair Bianca have:
And so she shall; Lucentio shall make one,
Though Paris came in hope to speed alone.
Gre. What! this gentleman will out-talk us all.
Luc. Sir, give him head: I know he'll prove a jade.
Pet. Hortensio, to what end are all these words?
Hor. Sir, let me be so bold as ask you,
Did you yet ever see Baptista's daughter?
Tra. No, sir; but hear I do that he hath two,
The one as famous for a scolding tongue
As is the other for beauteous modesty.
Pet. Sir, sir, the first 's for me; let her go by.
Gre. Yea, leave that labour to great Hercules;
And let it be more than Alcides' twelve.
Pet. Sir, understand you this of me in sooth:
The youngest daughter whom you hearken for
Her father keeps from all access of suitors,
And will not promise her to any man
Until the elder sister first be wed:
The younger then is free and not before.
Tra. If it be so, sir, that you are the man
Must stead us all and me amongst the rest,
And if you break the ice and do this feat,
Achieve the elder, set the younger free
For our access, whose hap shall be to have her
Will not so graceless be to be ingrate.
Hor. Sir, you say well and well you do conceive;
And since you do profess to be a suitor,
You must, as we do, gratify this gentleman,
To whom we all rest generally beholding.
Tra. Sir, I shall not be slack: in sign whereof,
Please ye we may contrive this afternoon,
And quaff carouses to our mistress' health,
And do as adversaries do in law,
Strive mightily, but eat and drink as friends.
Gru. Bion. O excellent motion! Fellows, let 's be gone.
Hor. The motion 's good indeed and be it so,
Petruchio, I shall be your ben venuto. *Exeunt.*

[ACT II.

SCENE I. *Padua. A room in* BAPTISTA'S *house.*]

Enter KATHARINA *and* BIANCA [*with her hands tied*].

Bian. Good sister, wrong me not, nor wrong yourself,
To make a bondmaid and a slave of me;
That I disdain: but for these other gawds,
Unbind my hands, I'll pull them off myself,
Yea, all my raiment, to my petticoat;
Or what you will command me will I do,
So well I know my duty to my elders.
Kath. Of all thy suitors, here I charge thee, tell
Whom thou lov'st best: see thou dissemble not.
Bian. Believe me, sister, of all the men alive
I never yet beheld that special face
Which I could fancy more than any other.
Kath. Minion, thou liest. Is 't not Hortensio?
Bian. If you affect him, sister, here I swear
I'll plead for you myself, but you shall have him.
Kath. O then, belike, you fancy riches more:
You will have Gremio to keep you fair.
Bian. Is it for him you do envy me so?
Nay then you jest, and now I well perceive
You have but jested with me all this while:
I prithee, sister Kate, untie my hands.

204. **ordnance,** cannon. 211. **fear . . . bugs,** frighten children with bugbears; see *fear* in glossary. 244. **Fair Leda's daughter,** Helen of Troy. 247. **speed,** succeed; see glossary. 249. **prove a jade,** tire like an ill-conditioned horse. 258. **Alcides',** son of Alcaeus, i.e., Hercules, who, noted for the achievement of the twelve great labors, is the only one capable of conquering Katharina. 270. **graceless,** rude, with play on the meaning "ungrateful." **ingrate,** ungrateful; cf. *gratify* (l. 273). 273. **gratify,** requite. 276. **contrive,** spend, pass (time); see glossary. 280. **motion,** suggestion, proposal; see glossary. 282. **ben venuto,** welcome; Hortensio is host to Petruchio.

ACT II. SCENE I. 3. **gawds,** ornaments, articles of jewelry. 13. **Minion,** saucy woman; see glossary. 17. **fair,** resplendent with finery;

Kath. If that be jest, then all the rest was so.
Strikes her.

Enter BAPTISTA.

Bap. Why, how now, dame! whence grows this insolence?
Bianca, stand aside. Poor girl! she weeps.
Go ply thy needle; meddle not with her.
For shame, thou hilding of a devilish spirit,
Why dost thou wrong her that did ne'er wrong thee?
When did she cross thee with a bitter word?
Kath. Her silence flouts me, and I'll be reveng'd.
Flies after Bianca.
Bap. What, in my sight? Bianca, get thee in.
[*Exit Bianca.*
Kath. What, will you not suffer me? Nay, now I see
She is your treasure, she must have a husband;
I must dance bare-foot on her wedding day
And for your love to her lead apes in hell.
Talk not to me: I will go sit and weep
Till I can find occasion of revenge. [*Exit.*]
Bap. Was ever gentleman thus griev'd as I?
But who comes here?

Enter GREMIO, LUCENTIO *in the habit of a mean man;* PETRUCHIO, *with* [HORTENSIO *as a musician; and*] TRANIO, *with his Boy* [BIONDELLO] *bearing a lute and books.*

Gre. Good morrow, neighbour Baptista.
Bap. Good morrow, neighbour Gremio. God save you, gentlemen!
Pet. And you, good sir! Pray, have you not a daughter
Call'd Katharina, fair and virtuous?
Bap. I have a daughter, sir, call'd Katharina.
Gre. You are too blunt: go to it orderly.
Pet. You wrong me, Signior Gremio: give me leave.
I am a gentleman of Verona, sir,
That, hearing of her beauty and her wit,
Her affability and bashful modesty,
Her wondrous qualities and mild behaviour,
Am bold to show myself a forward guest
Within your house, to make mine eye the witness
Of that report which I so oft have heard.
And, for an entrance to my entertainment,
I do present you with a man of mine,
[*Presenting Hortensio.*]
Cunning in music and the mathematics,
To instruct her fully in those sciences,
Whereof I know she is not ignorant:
Accept of him, or else you do me wrong:
His name is Licio, born in Mantua.
Bap. Y' are welcome, sir; and he, for your good sake.
But for my daughter Katharine, this I know,
She is not for your turn, the more my grief.
Pet. I see you do not mean to part with her,
Or else you like not of my company.
Bap. Mistake me not; I speak but as I find.
Whence are you, sir? what may I call your name?
Pet. Petruchio is my name; Antonio's son,
A man well known throughout all Italy.
Bap. I know him well: you are welcome for his sake.
Gre. Saving your tale, Petruchio, I pray,
Let us, that are poor petitioners, speak too:
Baccare! you are marvellous forward.
Pet. O, pardon me, Signior Gremio; I would fain be doing.
Gre. I doubt it not, sir; but you will curse your wooing.
Neighbour, this is a gift very grateful, I am sure of it. To express the like kindness, myself, that have been more kindly beholding to you than any, freely give unto you this young scholar [*presenting Lucentio*], that hath been long studying at Rheims; as cunning in Greek, Latin, and other languages, as the other in music and mathematics: his name is Cambio; pray, accept his service.
Bap. A thousand thanks, Signior Gremio. Welcome, good Cambio. [*To Tranio*] But, gentle sir, methinks you walk like a stranger: may I be so bold to know the cause of your coming?
Tra. Pardon me, sir, the boldness is mine own,
That, being a stranger in this city here,
Do make myself a suitor to your daughter,
Unto Bianca, fair and virtuous.
Nor is your firm resolve unknown to me,
In the preferment of the eldest sister.
This liberty is all that I request,
That, upon knowledge of my parentage,
I may have welcome 'mongst the rest that woo
And free access and favour as the rest:
And, toward the education of your daughters,
I here bestow a simple instrument,
And this small packet of Greek and Latin books:
If you accept them, then their worth is great.
Bap. Lucentio is your name; of whence, I pray?
Tra. Of Pisa, sir; son to Vincentio.
Bap. A mighty man of Pisa; by report
I know him well: you are very welcome, sir. [*To Hor.*]
Take you the lute, and you the set of books; [*To Luc.*]
You shall go see your pupils presently.
Holla, within!

Enter a Servant.

Sirrah, lead these gentlemen
To my daughters; and tell them both,
These are their tutors: bid them use them well.
[*Exit Servant, with Lucentio and Hortensio, Biondello following.*]
We will go walk a little in the orchard,
And then to dinner. You are passing welcome,
And so I pray you all to think yourselves.
Pet. Signior Baptista, my business asketh haste.
And every day I cannot come to woo.
You knew my father well, and in him me,
Left solely heir to all his lands and goods,
Which I have bettered rather than decreas'd:
Then tell me, if I get your daughter's love,
What dowry shall I have with her to wife?
Bap. After my death the one half of my lands,
And in possession twenty thousand crowns.

see glossary. 18. **envy,** hate; see glossary. 26. **hilding,** good-for-nothing person. 33. **dance bare-foot,** an allusion to the popular belief that an unmarried elder sister might avoid spinsterhood by dancing barefoot at her younger sister's wedding; hence a proverbial expression for being an old maid. 34. **lead apes in hell,** popularly supposed to be the fate of women who died unmarried. 50. **qualities,** accomplishments, gifts; see glossary. 63. **not for your turn.** Cf. the phrase "serve your turn," i.e., suit you. 73. **Baccare!** Stand back! 98. **favour,** leave, permission, i.e., to go and come; see glossary. 108. **presently,** immediately; see glossary. 123. **in possession,** i.e., immediate possession.

Pet. And, for that dowry, I'll assure her of
Her widowhood, be it that she survive me,
In all my lands and leases whatsoever:
Let specialties be therefore drawn between us,
That covenants may be kept on either hand.
Bap. Ay, when the special thing is well obtain'd,
That is, her love; for that is all in all.
Pet. Why, that is nothing; for I tell you, father,
I am as peremptory as she proud-minded;
And where two raging fires meet together
They do consume the thing that feeds their fury:
Though little fire grows great with little wind,
Yet extreme gusts will blow out fire and all:
So I to her and so she yields to me;
For I am rough and woo not like a babe.
Bap. Well mayst thou woo, and happy be thy speed!
But be thou arm'd for some unhappy words.
Pet. Ay, to the proof; as mountains are for winds,
That shake not, though they blow perpetually.

Enter HORTENSIO, *with his head broke.*

Bap. How now, my friend! why dost thou look so pale?
Hor. For fear, I promise you, if I look pale.
Bap. What, will my daughter prove a good musician?
Hor. I think she'll sooner prove a soldier:
Iron may hold with her, but never lutes.
Bap. Why, then thou canst not break her to the lute?
Hor. Why, no; for she hath broke the lute to me.
I did but tell her she mistook her frets,
And bow'd her hand to teach her fingering;
When, with a most impatient devilish spirit,
'Frets, call you these?' quoth she; 'I'll fume with them:'
And, with that word, she struck me on the head,
And through the instrument my pate made way;
And there I stood amazed for a while,
As on a pillory, looking through the lute;
While she did call me rascal fiddler
And twangling Jack; with twenty such vile terms,
As had she studied to misuse me so.
Pet. Now, by the world, it is a lusty wench;
I love her ten times more than e'er I did:
O, how I long to have some chat with her!
Bap. Well, go with me and be not so discomfited:
Proceed in practice with my younger daughter;
She 's apt to learn and thankful for good turns.
Signior Petruchio, will you go with us,
Or shall I send my daughter Kate to you?
Pet. I pray you do. *Exeunt. Manet Petruchio.*
I'll attend her here,
And woo her with some spirit when she comes.
Say that she rail; why then I'll tell her plain
She sings as sweetly as a nightingale:
Say that she frown; I'll say she looks as clear
As morning roses newly wash'd with dew:
Say she be mute and will not speak a word;
Then I'll commend her volubility,
And say she uttereth piercing eloquence:
If she do bid me pack, I'll give her thanks,
As though she bid me stay by her a week:
If she deny to wed, I'll crave the day
When I shall ask the banns and when be married.
But here she comes; and now, Petruchio, speak.

Enter KATHARINA.

Good morrow, Kate; for that 's your name, I hear.
Kath. Well have you heard, but something hard of hearing:
They call me Katharine that do talk of me.
Pet. You lie, in faith; for you are call'd plain Kate,
And bonny Kate and sometimes Kate the curst;
But Kate, the prettiest Kate in Christendom,
Kate of Kate Hall, my super-dainty Kate,
For dainties are all Kates, and therefore, Kate,
Take this of me, Kate of my consolation;
Hearing thy mildness prais'd in every town,
Thy virtues spoke of, and thy beauty sounded,
Yet not so deeply as to thee belongs,
Myself am mov'd to woo thee for my wife.
Kath. Mov'd! in good time: let him that mov'd you hither
Remove you hence: I knew you at the first
You were a moveable.
Pet. Why, what 's a moveable?
Kath. A join'd-stool.
Pet. Thou hast hit it: come, sit on me.
Kath. Asses are made to bear, and so are you.
Pet. Women are made to bear, and so are you.
Kath. No such jade as you, if me you mean.
Pet. Alas! good Kate, I will not burden thee;
For, knowing thee to be but young and light—
Kath. Too light for such a swain as you to catch;
And yet as heavy as my weight should be.
Pet. Should be! should—buzz!
Kath. Well ta'en, and like a buzzard.
Pet. O slow-wing'd turtle! shall a buzzard take thee?
Kath. Ay, for a turtle, as he takes a buzzard.
Pet. Come, come, you wasp; i' faith, you are too angry.
Kath. If I be waspish, best beware my sting.
Pet. My remedy is then, to pluck it out.
Kath. Ay, if the fool could find it where it lies.
Pet. Who knows not where a wasp does wear his sting? In his tail.
Kath. In his tongue.
Pet. Whose tongue?
Kath. Yours, if you talk of tails: and so farewell.
Pet. What, with my tongue in your tail? nay, come again,
Good Kate; I am a gentleman.
Kath. That I'll try. *She strikes him.*
Pet. I swear I'll cuff you, if you strike again.

125. **widowhood,** i.e., as long as she remains a widow. 127. **specialties,** terms of contract. 140. **unhappy,** evil; see glossary. 141. **to the proof,** i.e., in armor, proof against her shrewishness; see *proof* in glossary. 147. **hold with,** hold out against. 150. **frets,** metal or ivory ridges across the finger boards of stringed instruments, such as the lute, to indicate where the string is to be shortened for raising the tone. 153. **Frets . . . fume,** an echo of the alliterative pair, fume and fret. 165. **practice,** exercises for instruction; see glossary. 178. **pack,** be gone; see glossary. 180. **deny,** refuse; see glossary. 184. **heard, hard,** pronounced nearly alike. **something,** somewhat; see glossary. 189. **Kate Hall,** taken by the New Cambridge editors to allude to "a dining-house at Katharine Hall," a place where Elizabeth stopped on a progress through the south of England in 1591; also taken by some to allude to St. Catherine's Hall at Cambridge. 190. **all Kates,** quibble on "cates," confections. 191. **of,** from; see glossary. 196. **in good time,** indeed. 200. **bear,** a bawdy pun, as also in *asses*, *tail*, etc. 205. **swain,** young man in love, usually indicating a rustic. 206. **And . . . be.** The New Cambridge editors take this as an allusion to catch-weights in horse racing, i.e., the weight of a contestant as he happens or chooses to be, instead of as fixed by rule. 207. **Should . . . buzz.** There are several puns here to give the passage point. Petruchio implies a double understanding of Katharina's lightness (l. 205); *buzz* implies a pun on *be* and is itself a quibble on the verb and the interjection. 207, 208, 209. **buzzard,** an inferior kind of hawk, useless in

Kath. So may you lose your arms:
If you strike me, you are no gentleman;
And if no gentleman, why then no arms.
Pet. A herald, Kate? O, put me in thy books!
Kath. What is your crest? a coxcomb?
Pet. A combless cock, so Kate will be my hen.
Kath. No cock of mine; you crow too like a craven.
Pet. Nay, come, Kate, come; you must not look so sour.
Kath. It is my fashion, when I see a crab.
Pet. Why, here 's no crab; and therefore look not sour.
Kath. There is, there is.
Pet. Then show it me.
Kath. Had I a glass, I would.
Pet. What, you mean my face?
Kath. Well aim'd of such a young one.
Pet. Now, by Saint George, I am too young for you.
Kath. Yet you are wither'd.
Pet. 'Tis with cares.
Kath. I care not.
Pet. Nay, hear you, Kate: in sooth you scape not so.
Kath. I chafe you, if I tarry: let me go.
Pet. No, not a whit: I find you passing gentle.
'Twas told me you were rough and coy and sullen,
And now I find report a very liar;
For thou art pleasant, gamesome, passing courteous,
But slow in speech, yet sweet as spring-time flowers:
Thou canst not frown, thou canst not look askance,
Nor bite the lip, as angry wenches will,
Nor hast thou pleasure to be cross in talk,
But thou with mildness entertain'st thy wooers,
With gentle conference, soft and affable.
Why does the world report that Kate doth limp?
O sland'rous world! Kate like the hazel-twig
Is straight and slender and as brown in hue
As hazel nuts and sweeter than the kernels.
O, let me see thee walk: thou dost not halt.
Kath. Go, fool, and whom thou keep'st command.
Pet. Did ever Dian so become a grove
As Kate this chamber with her princely gait?
O, be thou Dian, and let her be Kate;
And then let Kate be chaste and Dian sportful!
Kath. Where did you study all this goodly speech?
Pet. It is extempore, from my mother-wit.
Kath. A witty mother! witless else her son.
Pet. Am I not wise?
Kath. Yes; keep you warm.
Pet. Marry, so I mean, sweet Katharine, in thy bed:
And therefore, setting all this chat aside,
Thus in plain terms: your father hath consented
That you shall be my wife; your dowry 'greed on;
And, will you, nill you, I will marry you.
Now, Kate, I am a husband for your turn;
For, by this light, whereby I see thy beauty,
Thy beauty, that doth make me like thee well,
Thou must be married to no man but me;

Enter BAPTISTA, GREMIO, [*and*] TRANIO.

For I am he am born to tame you, Kate,
And bring you from a wild Kate to a Kate
Conformable as other household Kates.
Here comes your father: never make denial;
I must and will have Katharine to my wife.
Bap. Now, Signior Petruchio, how speed you with my daughter?
Pet. How but well, sir? how but well?
It were impossible I should speed amiss.
Bap. Why, how now, daughter Katharine! in your dumps?
Kath. Call you me daughter? now, I promise you,
You have show'd a tender fatherly regard,
To wish me wed to one half lunatic;
A mad-cap ruffian and a swearing Jack,
That thinks with oaths to face the matter out.
Pet. Father, 'tis thus: yourself and all the world,
That talk'd of her, have talk'd amiss of her:
If she be curst, it is for policy,
For she 's not froward, but modest as the dove;
She is not hot, but temperate as the morn;
For patience she will prove a second Grissel,
And Roman Lucrece for her chastity:
And to conclude, we have 'greed so well together,
That upon Sunday is the wedding-day.
Kath. I'll see thee hang'd on Sunday first.
Gre. Hark, Petruchio; she says she'll see thee hang'd first.
Tra. Is this your speeding? nay, then, good night our part!
Pet. Be patient, gentlemen; I choose her for myself:
If she and I be pleas'd, what's that to you?
'Tis bargain'd 'twixt us twain, being alone,
That she shall still be curst in company.
I tell you, 'tis incredible to believe
How much she loves me: O, the kindest Kate!
She hung about my neck; and kiss on kiss
She vied so fast, protesting oath on oath,
That in a twink she won me to her love.
O, you are novices! 'tis a world to see,
How tame, when men and women are alone,
A meacock wretch can make the curstest shrew.
Give me thy hand, Kate: I will unto Venice,
To buy apparel 'gainst the wedding-day.
Provide the feast, father, and bid the guests;
I will be sure my Katharine shall be fine.
Bap. I know not what to say: but give me your hands;
God send you joy, Petruchio! 'tis a match.
Gre. Tra. Amen, say we: we will be witnesses.
Pet. Father, and wife, and gentlemen, adieu;
I will to Venice; Sunday comes apace:
We will have rings and things and fine array;
And kiss me, Kate, we will be married a Sunday.
Exeunt Petruchio and Katharine [*severally*].

falconry; also a type of stupidity. Most editors regard Katharina's remarks as quibbling on these two meanings. Onions suggests a third quibble on the meaning "a buzzing insect," which offers a play on *wasp* (l. 210). 208. **turtle,** turtle dove. 224. **no arms,** no coat of arms. 225. **thy books,** the official records of the college of heralds, with quibble on the phrase "to be in a person's books," i.e., to be in good standing with a person. 228. **craven,** a cock that is not "game" (Onions). 230. **crab,** crab apple. 238. **too young,** too strong (New Cambridge); perhaps, too nimble-witted. 245. **coy,** disdainful. 259. **whom thou keep'st,** i.e., those whom you employ—your servants; see *keep* in glossary. 260. **Dian,** goddess of the hunt and of chastity. 263. **sportful,** amorous. 267-268. **wise . . . warm,** an allusion to the proverbial phrase "enough wit to keep oneself warm." 273. **nill,** will not. 279. **wild Kate,** a quibble on "wildcat." Theobald saw a similar pun in *household Kates* in the next line. 294. **policy,** cunning, i.e., she has some motive for assuming this pose; see glossary. 297. **second Grissel,** an allusion to the story of Patient Griselda, the epitome of wifely patience and devotion. The story was told by Chaucer in *The Clerk's Tale* and earlier by Boccaccio and Petrarch. 298. **Roman Lucrece,** an allusion to the story of Lucretia, a Roman lady who took her own life after her chastity had been violated by the Tarquin prince, Sextus. Shakespeare told the story in *The Rape of Lucrece*. 315. **meacock,** effeminate, cowardly.

Gre. Was ever match clapp'd up so suddenly?
Bap. Faith, gentlemen, now I play a merchant's part,
And venture madly on a desperate mart.
Tra. 'Twas a commodity lay fretting by you:
'Twill bring you gain, or perish on the seas.
Bap. The gain I seek is, quiet in the match.
Gre. No doubt but he hath got a quiet catch.
But now, Baptista, to your younger daughter:
Now is the day we long have looked for:
I am your neighbour, and was suitor first.
Tra. And I am one that love Bianca more
Than words can witness, or your thoughts can guess.
Gre. Youngling, thou canst not love so dear as I.
Tra. Greybeard, thy love doth freeze.
Gre. But thine doth fry.
Skipper, stand back: 'tis age that nourisheth.
Tra. But youth in ladies' eyes that flourisheth.
Bap. Content you, gentlemen: I will compound this strife:
'Tis deeds must win the prize; and he of both
That can assure my daughter greatest dower
Shall have my Bianca's love.
Say, Signior Gremio, what can you assure her?
Gre. First, as you know, my house within the city
Is richly furnished with plate and gold;
Basins and ewers to lave her dainty hands;
My hangings all of Tyrian tapestry;
In ivory coffers I have stuff'd my crowns;
In cypress chests my arras counterpoints,
Costly apparel, tents, and canopies,
Fine linen, Turkey cushions boss'd with pearl,
Valance of Venice gold in needlework,
Pewter and brass and all things that belong
To house or housekeeping: then, at my farm
I have a hundred milch-kine to the pail,
Sixscore fat oxen standing in my stalls,
And all things answerable to this portion.
Myself am struck in years, I must confess;
And if I die to-morrow, this is hers,
If whilst I live she will be only mine.
Tra. That 'only' came well in. Sir, list to me:
I am my father's heir and only son:
If I may have your daughter to my wife,
I'll leave her houses three or four as good,
Within rich Pisa walls, as any one
Old Signior Gremio has in Padua;
Besides two thousand ducats by the year
Of fruitful land, all which shall be her jointure.
What, have I pinch'd you, Signior Gremio?
Gre. Two thousand ducats by the year of land!
My land amounts not to so much in all:
That she shall have; besides an argosy
That now is lying in Marseilles' road.
What, have I chok'd you with an argosy?
Tra. Gremio, 'tis known my father hath no less
Than three great argosies; besides two galliases,
And twelve tight galleys: these I will assure her,
And twice as much, whate'er thou off'rest next.
Gre. Nay, I have off'red all, I have no more;
And she can have no more than all I have:
If you like me, she shall have me and mine.
Tra. Why, then the maid is mine from all the world,
By your firm promise: Gremio is out-vied.
Bap. I must confess your offer is the best;
And, let your father make her the assurance,
She is your own; else, you must pardon me,
If you should die before him, where 's her dower?
Tra. That 's but a cavil: he is old, I young.
Gre. And may not young men die, as well as old?
Bap. Well, gentlemen,
I am thus resolv'd: on Sunday next you know
My daughter Katharine is to be married:
Now, on the Sunday following, shall Bianca
Be bride to you, if you make this assurance;
If not, to Signior Gremio:
And so, I take my leave, and thank you both. *Exit.*
Gre. Adieu, good neighbour.—Now I fear thee not:
Sirrah young gamester, your father were a fool
To give thee all, and in his waning age
Set foot under thy table: tut, a toy!
An old Italian fox is not so kind, my boy. *Exit.*
Tra. A vengeance on your crafty withered hide!
Yet I have fac'd it with a card of ten.
'Tis in my head to do my master good:
I see no reason but suppos'd Lucentio
Must get a father, call'd 'suppos'd Vincentio;'
And that's a wonder: fathers commonly
Do get their children; but in this case of wooing,
A child shall get a sire, if I fail not of my cunning. *Exit.*

ACT III.

[SCENE I. *Padua.* BAPTISTA'S *house.*]

Enter LUCENTIO, HORTENSIO, *and* BIANCA.

Luc. Fiddler, forbear; you grow too forward, sir:
Have you so soon forgot the entertainment
Her sister Katharine welcom'd you withal?
Hor. But, wrangling pedant, this is
The patroness of heavenly harmony:
Then give me leave to have prerogative;
And when in music we have spent an hour,
Your lecture shall have leisure for as much.
Luc. Preposterous ass, that never read so far
To know the cause why music was ordain'd!
Was it not to refresh the mind of man
After his studies or his usual pain?
Then give me leave to read philosophy,
And while I pause, serve in your harmony.
Hor. Sirrah, I will not bear these braves of thine.
Bian. Why, gentlemen, you do me double wrong,
To strive for that which resteth in my choice:
I am no breeching scholar in the schools;
I'll not be tied to hours nor 'pointed times,
But learn my lessons as I please myself.

330. **lay.** The subject is "which," understood. **fretting,** said of goods such as cloth destroyed by moth or grain infested by weevil, with quibble on the more obvious meaning. 341. **Skipper,** flighty fellow. 344. **he of both,** i.e., the one of you two. 353. **arras,** tapestried. **counterpoints,** counterpanes. 355. **boss'd,** embossed. 359. **milch-kine . . . pail,** cows whose milk is not going to their calves (New Cambridge). 376. **That she shall have,** i.e., all of my land. **argosy,** merchant vessel of the largest size. 380. **galliases,** heavy, low-built vessels. 381. **tight,** not leaking, sound. 402. **were,** subjunctive, which implies Gremio's disbelief of the pretended Lucentio's resources. 404. **toy,** nonsense. 407. **fac'd . . . ten,** brazened it out with only a ten-spot of cards.

ACT III. SCENE I. 6. **prerogative,** precedence. 9. **Preposterous,** used here in its literal sense of inverting the natural order of things (Herford). 14. **serve in,** i.e., as if music were an after-dinner trifle (New Cambridge). 18. **breeching scholar,** schoolboy liable to be whipped. 24. **in tune,** used here and in the next line with quibble on the meaning "in good temper" (New Cambridge). 28-29. **'Hic . . .**

And, to cut off all strife, here sit we down:
Take you your instrument, play you the whiles;
His lecture will be done ere you have tun'd.

Hor. You'll leave his lecture when I am in tune?

Luc. That will be never: tune your instrument.

Bian. Where left we last?

Luc. Here, madam:
'Hic ibat Simois; hic est Sigeia tellus;
Hic steterat Priami regia celsa senis.'

Bian. Conster them.

Luc. 'Hic ibat,' as I told you before, 'Simois,' I am Lucentio, hic est,' son unto Vincentio of Pisa, 'Sigeia tellus,' disguised thus to get your love; 'Hic steterat,' and that Lucentio that comes a-wooing, 'Priami,' is my man Tranio, 'regia,' bearing my port, 'celsa senis,' that we might beguile the old pantaloon.

Hor. Madam, my instrument 's in tune.

Bian. Let 's hear. O fie! the treble jars.

Luc. Spit in the hole, man, and tune again.

Bian. Now let me see if I can conster it: 'Hic ibat Simois,' I know you not, 'hic est Sigeia tellus,' I trust you not; 'Hic steterat Priami,' take heed he hear us not, 'regia,' presume not, 'celsa senis,' despair not.

Hor. Madam, 'tis now in tune.

Luc. All but the base.

Hor. The base is right; 'tis the base knave that jars.
[*Aside*] How fiery and forward our pedant is!
Now, for my life, the knave doth court my love:
Pedascule, I'll watch you better yet.

Bian. In time I may believe, yet I mistrust.

Luc. Mistrust it not; for, sure, Æacides
Was Ajax, call'd so from his grandfather.

Bian. I must believe my master; else, I promise you,
I should be arguing still upon that doubt:
But let it rest. Now, Licio, to you:
Good masters, take it not unkindly, pray,
That I have been thus pleasant with you both.

Hor. You may go walk, and give me leave a while:
My lessons make no music in three parts.

Luc. Are you so formal, sir? well, I must wait,
[*Aside*] And watch withal; for, but I be deceiv'd,
Our fine musician groweth amorous.

Hor. Madam, before you touch the instrument,
To learn the order of my fingering,
I must begin with rudiments of art;
To teach you gamut in a briefer sort,
More pleasant, pithy and effectual,
Than hath been taught by any of my trade:
And there it is in writing, fairly drawn.

Bian. Why, I am past my gamut long ago.

Hor. Yet read the gamut of Hortensio.

Bian. [*Reads*] " 'Gamut' I am, the ground of all accord,
'A re,' to plead Hortensio's passion;
'B mi,' Bianca, take him for thy lord,
'C fa ut,' that loves with all affection:
'D sol re,' one clef, two notes have I:
'E la mi,' show pity, or I die."
Call you this gamut? tut, I like it not:
Old fashions please me best; I am not so nice,
To change true rules for old inventions.

Enter a [Servant *as*] *Messenger.*

Serv. Mistress, your father prays you leave your books
And help to dress your sister's chamber up:
You know to-morrow is the wedding-day.

Bian. Farewell, sweet masters both; I must be gone.
[*Exeunt Bianca and Servant.*]

Luc. Faith, mistress, then I have no cause to stay.
[*Exit.*]

Hor. But I have cause to pry into this pedant:
Methinks he looks as though he were in love:
Yet if thy thoughts, Bianca, be so humble
To cast thy wand'ring eyes on every stale,
Seize thee that list: if once I find thee ranging,
Hortensio will be quit with thee by changing. *Exit.*

[SCENE II. *Padua. Before* BAPTISTA'S *house.*]

Enter BAPTISTA, GREMIO, TRANIO, KATHARINE, BIANCA, [LUCENTIO,] *and* others, attendants.

Bap. [*To Tranio*] Signior Lucentio, this is the 'pointed day
That Katharine and Petruchio should be married,
And yet we hear not of our son-in-law.
What will be said? what mockery will it be,
To want the bridegroom when the priest attends
To speak the ceremonial rites of marriage!
What says Lucentio to this shame of ours?

Kath. No shame but mine: I must, forsooth, be forc'd
To give my hand oppos'd against my heart
Unto a mad-brain rudesby full of spleen;
Who woo'd in haste and means to wed at leisure.
I told you, I, he was a frantic fool,
Hiding his bitter jests in blunt behaviour:
And, to be noted for a merry man,
He'll woo a thousand, 'point the day of marriage,
Make feasts, invite friends, and proclaim the banns;
Yet never means to wed where he hath woo'd.
Now must the world point at poor Katharine,
And say, 'Lo, there is mad Petruchio's wife,
If it would please him come and marry her!'

Tra. Patience, good Katharine, and Baptista too.
Upon my life, Petruchio means but well,
Whatever fortune stays him from his word:
Though he be blunt, I know him passing wise;
Though he be merry, yet withal he 's honest.

Kath. Would Katharine had never seen him though! *Exit weeping* [*followed by Bianca and others*].

Bap. Go, girl; I cannot blame thee now to weep;
For such an injury would vex a very saint,
Much more a shrew of thy impatient humour.

Enter BIONDELLO.

senis,' here flowed the river Simois, here is the Sigeian land; here stood the lofty palace of old Priam (Ovid, *Heroides*, I, 33). 30. **Conster,** construe. 37. **old pantaloon,** enfeebled old man, old fool; at Gremio's first entrance (I, i, 47) the stage direction in F is *Enter . . . Gremio a Pantelowne*. The pantaloon was a stock character in Italian comedy. 39. **jars,** is discordant; see glossary. 40. **Spit in the hole,** i.e., to make the peg stick. 50. **Pedascule,** a word contemptuously coined by Hortensio, the vocative of *pedasculus*, little pedant. 52-53. **Æacides . . . grandfather,** a pointless remark to mislead Hortensio. 67. **gamut,** the scale, from the alphabet name (*gamma*) of the first note plus *ut*, its syllable name, now commonly called *do*. The *gamut* of Hortensio begins on G instead of on C, the first note of the natural scale. 80. **nice,** fastidious. 91. **thee,** frequently used for the nominative with imperatives; see Abbott, 212. **list,** desire, with probable quibble on "strip of cloth" (a contemptuous reference to Lucentio in the disguise of a pedant); see glossary. **ranging,** inconstant; see glossary. 92. **quit,** quits; see glossary. **by changing,** i.e., by loving another.

SCENE II. 10. **rudesby,** unmannerly fellow.

Bion. Master, master! news, old news, and such news as you never heard of!

Bap. Is it new and old too? how may that be?

Bion. Why, is it not news, to hear of Petruchio's coming?

Bap. Is he come?

Bion. Why, no, sir.

Bap. What then?

Bion. He is coming.

Bap. When will he be here?

Bion. When he stands where I am and sees you there.

Tra. But say, what to thine old news?

Bion. Why, Petruchio is coming in a new hat and an old jerkin, a pair of old breeches thrice turned, a pair of boots that have been candle-cases, one buckled, another laced, an old rusty sword ta'en out of the town-armoury, with a broken hilt, and chapeless; with two broken points: his horse hipped with an old mothy saddle and stirrups of no kindred; besides, possessed with the glanders and like to mose in the chine; troubled with the lampass, infected with the fashions, full of windgalls, sped with spavins, rayed with the yellows, past cure of the fives, stark spoiled with the staggers, begnawn with the bots, swayed in the back and shoulder-shotten; near-legged before and with a half-cheeked bit and a head-stall of sheep's leather which, being restrained to keep him from stumbling, hath been often burst and now repaired with knots; one girth six times pieced and a woman's crupper of velure, which hath two letters for her name fairly set down in studs, and here and there pieced with packthread.

Bap. Who comes with him?

Bion. O, sir, his lackey, for all the world caparisoned like the horse; with a linen stock on one leg and a kersey boot-hose on the other, gartered with a red and blue list; an old hat and 'the humour of forty fancies' pricked in 't for a feather: a monster, a very monster in apparel, and not like a Christian footboy or a gentleman's lackey.

Tra. 'Tis some odd humour pricks him to this fashion;
Yet oftentimes he goes but mean-apparell'd.

Bap. I am glad he 's come, howsoe'er he comes.

Bion. Why, sir, he comes not.

Bap. Didst thou not say he comes?

Bion. Who? that Petruchio came?

Bap. Ay, that Petruchio came.

Bion. No, sir; I say his horse comes, with him on his back.

Bap. Why, that 's all one.

Bion. Nay, by Saint Jamy,
I hold you a penny,
A horse and a man
Is more than one,
And yet not many.

Enter PETRUCHIO *and* GRUMIO.

Pet. Come, where be these gallants? who 's at home?

Bap. You are welcome, sir.

Pet. And yet I come not well.

Bap. And yet you halt not.

Tra. Not so well apparell'd
As I wish you were.

Pet. Were it better, I should rush in thus.
But where is Kate? where is my lovely bride?
How does my father? Gentles, methinks you frown:
And wherefore gaze this goodly company,
As if they saw some wondrous monument,
Some comet or unusual prodigy?

Bap. Why, sir, you know this is your wedding-day:
First were we sad, fearing you would not come;
Now sadder, that you come so unprovided.
Fie, doff this habit, shame to your estate,
An eye-sore to our solemn festival!

Tra. And tell us, what occasion of import
Hath all so long detain'd you from your wife,
And sent you hither so unlike yourself?

Pet. Tedious it were to tell, and harsh to hear:
Sufficeth, I am come to keep my word,
Though in some part enforced to digress;
Which, at more leisure, I will so excuse
As you shall well be satisfied withal.
But where is Kate? I stay too long from her:
The morning wears, 'tis time we were at church.

Tra. See not your bride in these unreverent robes:
Go to my chamber; put on clothes of mine.

Pet. Not I, believe me: thus I'll visit her.

Bap. But thus, I trust, you will not marry her.

Pet. Good sooth, even thus; therefore ha' done with words:
To me she 's married, not unto my clothes:
Could I repair what she will wear in me,
As I can change these poor accoutrements,
'Twere well for Kate and better for myself.
But what a fool am I to chat with you,
When I should bid good morrow to my bride,
And seal the title with a lovely kiss!

Exit [with Grumio].

Tra. He hath some meaning in his mad attire:
We will persuade him, be it possible,
To put on better ere he go to church.

Bap. I'll after him, and see the event of this.

Exit [with Gremio, and attendants].

Tra. But to her love concerneth us to add
Her father's liking: which to bring to pass,
As I before imparted to your worship,
I am to get a man,—whate'er he be,
It skills not much, we'll fit him to our turn,—
And he shall be Vincentio of Pisa;
And make assurance here in Padua
Of greater sums than I have promised.
So shall you quietly enjoy your hope,
And marry sweet Bianca with consent.

45. **candle-cases,** i.e., discarded and used to contain candle ends. 48. **chapeless,** without the chape, the metal plate or mounting of a scabbard, especially that which covers the point. 49. **points,** tagged laces for attaching hose to doublet. **hipped,** lamed in the hip. Bond notes that almost all the diseases here named are described in Gervase Markham's *How to chuse, ride, trayne, and dyet, both Hunting Horses and Running Horses. . . . Also a Discourse of Horsemanship,* probably first published in 1593. 51. **mose . . . chine,** suffer from glanders; *mose,* not found elsewhere, is taken by the New Cambridge editors to be a misprint for *pose,* a form of glanders; mourn of the chine, i.e., backbone, is, however, a common expression for the nasal discharge of horses with glanders. 52. **lampass.** Bond quotes Markham: ". . . a thicke spongie fleshe growing ouer a Horses vpper teeth, hindering the coniunction of his Chappes in such sorte that he can hardlye eate." 53. **fashions,** a corruption of "farcin," a disease closely allied to glanders. **windgalls,** a soft tumor or swelling generally found on the fetlock joint, so called from having been supposed to contain air. **spavins,** a disease of the hock, marked by a small bony enlargement inside the leg. 54. **yellows,** jaundice. **fives,** avives, a glandular disease. 56. **bots,** a disease from parasitic worms. **shoulder-shotten,** sprained in the shoulder. 57. **near-legged before,** with forelegs close together, knock-kneed. **half-cheeked bit,** one to which the bridle is attached half-way up the cheek or sidepiece so as not to give sufficient control over the horse. 58. **head-stall,** part of the bridle over the head. **sheep's**

Luc. Were it not that my fellow-schoolmaster
Doth watch Bianca's steps so narrowly,
'Twere good, methinks, to steal our marriage;
Which once perform'd, let all the world say no,
I'll keep mine own, despite of all the world.
Tra. That by degrees we mean to look into,
And watch our vantage in this business:
We'll over-reach the greybeard, Gremio,
The narrow-prying father, Minola,
The quaint musician, amorous Licio;
All for my master's sake, Lucentio.

Enter GREMIO.

Signior Gremio, came you from the church?
Gre. As willingly as e'er I came from school.
Tra. And is the bride and bridegroom coming home?
Gre. A bridegroom say you? 'tis a groom indeed,
A grumbling groom, and that the girl shall find.
Tra. Curster than she? why, 'tis impossible.
Gre. Why, he 's a devil, a devil, a very fiend.
Tra. Why, she 's a devil, a devil, the devil's dam.
Gre. Tut, she 's a lamb, a dove, a fool to him!
I'll tell you, Sir Lucentio: when the priest
Should ask, if Katharine should be his wife,
'Ay, by gogs-wouns,' quoth he; and swore so loud,
That, all-amaz'd, the priest let fall the book;
And, as he stoop'd again to take it up,
This mad-brain'd bridegroom took him such a cuff
That down fell priest and book and book and priest:
'Now take them up,' quoth he, 'if any list.'
Tra. What said the wench when he rose again?
Gre. Trembled and shook; for why, he stamp'd and swore,
As if the vicar meant to cozen him.
But after many ceremonies done,
He calls for wine: 'A health!' quoth he, as if
He had been aboard, carousing to his mates
After a storm; quaff'd off the muscadel
And threw the sops all in the sexton's face;
Having no other reason
But that his beard grew thin and hungerly
And seem'd to ask him sops as he was drinking.
This done, he took the bride about the neck
And kiss'd her lips with such a clamorous smack
That at the parting all the church did echo:
And I seeing this came thence for very shame;
And after me, I know, the rout is coming.
Such a mad marriage never was before:
Hark, hark! I hear the minstrels play. *Music plays.*

Enter PETRUCHIO, KATE, BIANCA, HORTENSIO, BAPTISTA [, GRUMIO, *and train*].

Pet. Gentlemen and friends, I thank you for your pains:
I know you think to dine with me to-day,
And have prepar'd great store of wedding cheer;
But so it is, my haste doth call me hence,
And therefore here I mean to take my leave.
Bap. Is 't possible you will away to-night?
Pet. I must away to-day, before night come:
Make it no wonder; if you knew my business,
You would entreat me rather go than stay.
And, honest company, I thank you all,
That have beheld me give away myself
To this most patient, sweet and virtuous wife:
Dine with my father, drink a health to me;
For I must hence; and farewell to you all.
Tra. Let us entreat you stay till after dinner.
Pet. It may not be.
Gre. Let me entreat you.
Pet. It cannot be.
Kath. Let me entreat you.
Pet. I am content.
Kath. Are you content to stay?
Pet. I am content you shall entreat me stay;
But yet not stay, entreat me how you can.
Kath. Now, if you love me, stay.
Pet. Grumio, my horse.
Gru. Ay, sir, they be ready: the oats have eaten the horses.
Kath. Nay, then,
Do what thou canst, I will not go to-day;
No, nor to-morrow, not till I please myself.
The door is open, sir; there lies your way;
You may be jogging whiles your boots are green;
For me, I'll not be gone till I please myself:
'Tis like you'll prove a jolly surly groom,
That take it on you at the first so roundly.
Pet. O Kate, content thee; prithee, be not angry.
Kath. I will be angry: what hast thou to do?
Father, be quiet: he shall stay my leisure.
Gre. Ay, marry, sir, now it begins to work.
Kath. Gentlemen, forward to the bridal dinner:
I see a woman may be made a fool,
If she had not a spirit to resist.
Pet. They shall go forward, Kate, at thy command.
Obey the bride, you that attend on her;
Go to the feast, revel and domineer,
Carouse full measure to her maidenhead,
Be mad and merry, or go hang yourselves:
But for my bonny Kate, she must with me.
Nay, look not big, nor stamp, nor stare, nor fret;
I will be master of what is mine own:
She is my goods, my chattels; she is my house,
My household stuff, my field, my barn,
My horse, my ox, my ass, my any thing;
And here she stands, touch her whoever dare;
I'll bring mine action on the proudest he
That stops my way in Padua. Grumio,
Draw forth thy weapon, we are beset with thieves;
Rescue thy mistress, if thou be a man.
Fear not, sweet wench, they shall not touch thee, Kate:

leather. Pigskin was used for strongest harness; hence of inferior quality. 59. **restrained,** drawn back. 61. **crupper,** leather loop passing under the horse's tail and fastened to the saddle. 62. **velure,** velvet, used sometimes on horses ridden by ladies. 67. **stock,** stocking. 68. **kersey boot-hose,** overstocking of coarse material. 70. **'the humour . . . fancies,'** probably the title of a pamphlet book of songs or ballads. 101. **unprovided,** ill-equipped. 102. **estate,** position, station, as in the modern phrase, "man's estate." 125. **seal,** confirm, ratify; see glossary. 129. **event,** outcome; see glossary. 134. **skills not,** makes no difference. 146. **vantage,** opportunity, advantage; see glossary. 154. **a groom indeed,** i.e., a serving man. 159. **fool,** term of endearment and pity; see glossary. 162. **gogs-wouns,** God's wounds, a common oath. 165. **took,** struck; see *take* in glossary. 169. **for why,** because; see glossary. 170. **cozen,** cheat, i.e., by not performing the ceremony with all regularity. 173. **aboard,** i.e., aboard ship. 175. **sops,** pieces of cake soaked in wine. 183. **rout,** wedding party. 193. **Make,** consider; see glossary. 195. **honest,** kind; see glossary. 213. **whiles . . . green,** i.e., new; proverbial for "getting an early start," with a sarcastic allusion to his unseemly attire. 215. **jolly,** arrogant. 226. **domineer,** feast riotously. 230. **big,** threatening. 234. **ox . . . any thing.** This catalog of a man's possessions is from the Tenth Commandment.

I'll buckler thee against a million.
Exeunt Petruchio, Katharina [*, and Grumio*].
Bap. Nay, let them go, a couple of quiet ones.
Gre. Went they not quickly, I should die with laughing.
Tra. Of all mad matches never was the like.
Luc. Mistress, what 's your opinion of your sister?
Bian. That, being mad herself, she 's madly mated.
Gre. I warrant him, Petruchio is Kated.
Bap. Neighbours and friends, though bride and bridegroom wants
For to supply the places at the table,
You know there wants no junkets at the feast.
Lucentio, you shall supply the bridegroom's place;
And let Bianca take her sister's room.
Tra. Shall sweet Bianca practise how to bride it?
Bap. She shall, Lucentio. Come, gentlemen, let 's go.
Exeunt.

[ACT IV.

SCENE I. PETRUCHIO'S *country house.*]

Enter GRUMIO.

Gru. Fie, fie on all tired jades, on all mad masters, and all foul ways! Was ever man so beaten? was ever man so rayed? was ever man so weary? I am sent before to make a fire, and they are coming after to warm them. Now, were not I a little pot and soon hot, my very lips might freeze to my teeth, my tongue to the roof of my mouth, my heart in my belly, ere I should come by a fire to thaw me: but I, with blowing the fire, shall warm myself; for, considering the weather, a taller man than I will take cold. Holla, ho! Curtis.

Enter CURTIS.

Curt. Who is that calls so coldly?

Gru. A piece of ice: if thou doubt it, thou mayst slide from my shoulder to my heel with no greater a run but my head and my neck. A fire, good Curtis.

Curt. Is my master and his wife coming, Grumio?

Gru. O, ay, Curtis, ay: and therefore fire, fire; cast on no water.

Curt. Is she so hot a shrew as she 's reported?

Gru. She was, good Curtis, before this frost: but, thou knowest, winter tames man, woman and beast; for it hath tamed my old master and my new mistress and myself, fellow Curtis.

Curt. Away, you three-inch fool! I am no beast.

Gru. Am I but three inches? why, thy horn is a foot; and so long am I at the least. But wilt thou make a fire, or shall I complain on thee to our mistress, whose hand, she being now at hand, thou shalt soon feel, to thy cold comfort, for being slow in thy hot office?

Curt. I prithee, good Grumio, tell me, how goes the world?

Gru. A cold world, Curtis, in every office but thine; and therefore fire: do thy duty, and have thy duty; for my master and mistress are almost frozen to death.

Curt. There 's fire ready; and therefore, good Grumio, the news.

Gru. Why, 'Jack boy! ho! boy!' and as much news as wilt thou.

Curt. Come, you are so full of cony-catching!

Gru. Why, therefore fire; for I have caught extreme cold. Where 's the cook? is supper ready, the house trimmed, rushes strewed, cobwebs swept; the servingmen in their new fustian, their white stockings, and every officer his wedding-garment on? Be the jacks fair within, the jills fair without, the carpets laid, and every thing in order?

Curt. All ready; and therefore, I pray thee, news.

Gru. First, know, my horse is tired; my master and mistress fallen out.

Curt. How?

Gru. Out of their saddles into the dirt; and thereby hangs a tale.

Curt. Let 's ha 't, good Grumio.

Gru. Lend thine ear.

Curt. Here.

Gru. There. [*Strikes him.*]

Curt. This is to feel a tale, not to hear a tale.

Gru. And therefore 'tis called a sensible tale: and this cuff was but to knock at your ear, and beseech listening. Now I begin: Imprimis, we came down a foul hill, my master riding behind my mistress,—

Curt. Both of one horse?

Gru. What 's that to thee?

Curt. Why, a horse.

Gru. Tell thou the tale: but hadst thou not crossed me, thou shouldst have heard how her horse fell and she under her horse; thou shouldst have heard in how miry a place, how she was bemoiled, how he left her with the horse upon her, how he beat me because her horse stumbled, how she waded through the dirt to pluck him off me, how he swore, how she prayed, that never prayed before, how I cried, how the horses ran away, how her bridle was burst, how I lost my crupper, with many things of worthy memory, which now shall die in oblivion and thou return unexperienced to thy grave.

Curt. By this reckoning he is more shrew than she.

Gru. Ay; and that thou and the proudest of you all shall find when he comes home. But what talk I of this? Call forth Nathaniel, Joseph, Nicholas, Philip, Walter, Sugarsop and the rest: let their heads be sleekly combed, their blue coats brushed and their garters of an indifferent knit; let them curtsy with their left legs and not presume to touch a hair of my master's horse-tail till they kiss their hands. Are they all ready?

Curt. They are.

Gru. Call them forth.

Curt. Do you hear, ho? you must meet my master to countenance my mistress.

Gru. Why, she hath a face of her own.

Curt. Who knows not that?

Gru. Thou, it seems, that calls for company to countenance her.

Curt. I call them forth to credit her.

Gru. Why, she comes to borrow nothing of them.

241. **buckler,** shield, defend. 250. **junkets,** sweetmeats.
ACT IV. SCENE I. 3. **rayed,** dirtied, fouled. 6. **a little . . . hot,** a proverbial expression; Grumio refers to his small stature. 11. **taller,** finer, better; see glossary. 27. **three-inch fool,** another reference to Grumio's size. 27-28. **I am no beast.** Grumio has paralleled himself with *beast* (l. 25) and has then called Curtis *fellow*. 43. **'Jack . . . boy,'** the first line of a song. 45. **cony-catching,** cheating. 48. **rushes strewed.** Floors were strewn with green rushes on ceremonial occasions. 49. **fustian,** coarse cloth of cotton and flax. 51, 52. **jacks, jills,** drinking measures of one-half and one-fourth pints (used quibblingly). 66. **sensible,** capable of sensation, with quibble on the current meaning; see glossary. 68. **Imprimis,** in the first place. 77. **bemoiled,** befouled

Enter four or five Serving-men.

Nath. Welcome home, Grumio!

Phil. How now, Grumio!

Jos. What, Grumio!

Nich. Fellow Grumio!

Nath. How now, old lad?

Gru. Welcome, you;—how now, you;—what, you; —fellow, you;—and thus much for greeting. Now, my spruce companions, is all ready, and all things neat?

Nath. All things is ready. How near is our master?

Gru. E'en at hand, alighted by this; and therefore be not—Cock's passion, silence! I hear my master.

Enter PETRUCHIO *and* KATE.

Pet. Where be these knaves? What, no man at door
To hold my stirrup nor to take my horse!
Where is Nathaniel, Gregory, Philip?

All Serv. Here, here, sir; here, sir.

Pet. Here, sir! here, sir! here, sir! here, sir!
You logger-headed and unpolish'd grooms!
What, no attendance? no regard? no duty?
Where is the foolish knave I sent before?

Gru. Here, sir; as foolish as I was before.

Pet. You peasant swain! you whoreson malt-horse drudge!
Did I not bid thee meet me in the park,
And bring along these rascal knaves with thee?

Gru. Nathaniel's coat, sir, was not fully made,
And Gabriel's pumps were all unpink'd i' th' heel;
There was no link to colour Peter's hat,
And Walter's dagger was not come from sheathing:
There were none fine but Adam, Ralph, and Gregory;
The rest were ragged, old, and beggarly;
Yet, as they are, here are they come to meet you.

Pet. Go, rascals, go, and fetch my supper in.
Exeunt Servants.
[*Singing*] Where is the life that late I led—
Where are those—Sit down, Kate, and welcome.—
Soud, soud, soud, soud!

Enter Servants *with supper.*

Why, when, I say? Nay, good sweet Kate, be merry.
Off with my boots, you rogues! you villains, when?
[*Sings*] It was the friar of orders grey,
As he forth walked on his way:—
Out, you rogue! you pluck my foot awry:
Take that, and mend the plucking off the other.
[*Strikes him.*]
Be merry, Kate. Some water, here; what, ho!

Enter one with water.

Where's my spaniel Troilus? Sirrah, get you hence,
And bid my cousin Ferdinand come hither:
One, Kate, that you must kiss, and be acquainted with.
Where are my slippers? Shall I have some water?
Come, Kate, and wash, and welcome heartily.
You whoreson villain! will you let it fall? [*Strikes him.*]

Kath. Patience, I pray you; 'twas a fault unwilling.

Pet. A whoreson beetle-headed, flap-ear'd knave!
Come, Kate, sit down; I know you have a stomach.
Will you give thanks, sweet Kate; or else shall I?
What 's this? mutton?

First Serv. Ay.

Pet. Who brought it?

Peter. I.

Pet. 'Tis burnt; and so is all the meat.
What dogs are these! Where is the rascal cook?
How durst you, villains, bring it from the dresser,
And serve it thus to me that love it not?
There, take it to you, trenchers, cups, and all:
[*Throws the meat, &c. at them. They run out.*]
You heedless joltheads and unmanner'd slaves!
What, do you grumble? I'll be with you straight.

Kath. I pray you, husband, be not so disquiet:
The meat was well, if you were so contented.

Pet. I tell thee, Kate, 'twas burnt and dried away;
And I expressly am forbid to touch it,
For it engenders choler, planteth anger;
And better 'twere that both of us did fast,
Since, of ourselves, ourselves are choleric,
Than feed it with such over-roasted flesh.
Be patient; to-morrow 't shall be mended,
And, for this night, we'll fast for company:
Come, I will bring thee to thy bridal chamber. *Exeunt.*

Enter Servants *severally.*

Nath. Peter, didst ever see the like?

Peter. He kills her in her own humour.

Enter CURTIS.

Gru. Where is he?

Curt. In her chamber, making a sermon of continency to her;
And rails, and swears, and rates, that she, poor soul,
Knows not which way to stand, to look, to speak,
And sits as one new-risen from a dream.
Away, away! for he is coming hither. [*Exeunt.*]

Enter PETRUCHIO.

Pet. Thus have I politicly begun my reign,
And 'tis my hope to end successfully.
My falcon now is sharp and passing empty;
And till she stoop she must not be full-gorg'd,
For then she never looks upon her lure.
Another way I have to man my haggard,
To make her come and know her keeper's call,
That is, to watch her, as we watch these kites
That bate and beat and will not be obedient.
She eat no meat to-day, nor none shall eat;
Last night she slept not, nor to-night she shall not;
As with the meat, some undeserved fault
I'll find about the making of the bed;
And here I'll fling the pillow, there the bolster,
This way the coverlet, another way the sheets:
Ay, and amid this hurly I intend
That all is done in reverend care of her;
And in conclusion she shall watch all night:
And if she chance to nod I'll rail and brawl
And with the clamour keep her still awake.
This is a way to kill a wife with kindness;

with mire. 121. **Cock's,** a perversion of "God's"; used in oaths. 136. **unpink'd,** not scalloped. 137. **link,** torch, material from which was used as blackening. 145. **Soud,** a nonsense song; or perhaps "food." 150. **Out,** exclamation of anger or reproach; see glossary. 168. **trenchers,** wooden dishes or plates; see glossary. 169. **joltheads,** blockheads. 170. **with you,** i.e., even with you (Hart). **straight,** immediately; see glossary. 178. **feed it,** partake of food. 196. **man,** tame, accustom to the presence of men; a term of falconry. **haggard,** wild female hawk; hence, an intractable woman. 198. **watch her,** keep her watching, i.e., awake; see glossary. 199. **bate,** beat the wings impatiently and flutter away from the hand or perch. **beat,** flap the wings; the pronunciation of *bate* and *beat* was somewhat alike.

And thus I'll curb her mad and headstrong humour.
He that knows better how to tame a shrew,
Now let him speak: 'tis charity to show. *Exit.*

[SCENE II. *Padua. Before* BAPTISTA'S *house.*]

Enter TRANIO *and* HORTENSIO.

Tra. Is 't possible, friend Licio, that Mistress Bianca
Doth fancy any other but Lucentio?
I tell you, sir, she bears me fair in hand.
Hor. Sir, to satisfy you in what I have said,
Stand by and mark the manner of his teaching.

Enter BIANCA [*and* LUCENTIO].

Luc. Now, mistress, profit you in what you read?
Bian. What, master, read you? first resolve me that.
Luc. I read that I profess, the Art to Love.
Bian. And may you prove, sir, master of your art!
Luc. While you, sweet dear, prove mistress of my heart! [*They stand aside.*]
Hor. Quick proceeders, marry! Now, tell me, I pray,
You that durst swear that your mistress Bianca
Lov'd none in the world so well as Lucentio.
Tra. O despiteful love! unconstant womankind!
I tell thee, Licio, this is wonderful.
Hor. Mistake no more: I am not Licio,
Nor a musician, as I seem to be;
But one that scorn to live in this disguise,
For such a one as leaves a gentleman,
And makes a god of such a cullion:
Know, sir, that I am call'd Hortensio.
Tra. Signior Hortensio, I have often heard
Of your entire affection to Bianca;
And since mine eyes are witness of her lightness,
I will with you, if you be so contented,
Forswear Bianca and her love for ever.
Hor. See, how they kiss and court! Signior Lucentio,
Here is my hand, and here I firmly vow
Never to woo her more, but do forswear her,
As one unworthy all the former favours
That I have fondly flatter'd her withal.
Tra. And here I take the like unfeigned oath,
Never to marry with her though she would entreat:
Fie on her! see, how beastly she doth court him!
Hor. Would all the world but he had quite forsworn!
For me, that I may surely keep mine oath,
I will be married to a wealthy widow,
Ere three days pass, which hath as long lov'd me
As I have lov'd this proud disdainful haggard.
And so farewell, Signior Lucentio.
Kindness in women, not their beauteous looks,
Shall win my love: and so I take my leave,
In resolution as I swore before. [*Exit.*]
Tra. Mistress Bianca, bless you with such grace
As 'longeth to a lover's blessed case!
Nay, I have ta'en you napping, gentle love,
And have forsworn you with Hortensio.
Bian. Tranio, you jest: but have you both forsworn me?
Tra. Mistress, we have.
Luc. Then we are rid of Licio.
Tra. I' faith, he'll have a lusty widow now,
That shall be woo'd and wedded in a day.
Bian. God give him joy!
Tra. Ay, and he'll tame her.
Bian. He says so, Tranio.
Tra. Faith, he is gone unto the taming-school.
Bian. The taming-school! what, is there such a place?
Tra. Ay, mistress, and Petruchio is the master;
That teacheth tricks eleven and twenty long,
To tame a shrew and charm her chattering tongue.

Enter BIONDELLO.

Bion. O master, master, I have watch'd so long
That I am dog-weary: but at last I spied
†An ancient angel coming down the hill,
Will serve the turn.
Tra. What is he, Biondello?
Bion. Master, a mercatante, or a pedant,
I know not what; but formal in apparel,
In gait and countenance surely like a father.
Luc. And what of him, Tranio?
Tra. If he be credulous and trust my tale,
I'll make him glad to seem Vincentio,
And give assurance to Baptista Minola,
As if he were the right Vincentio.
Take in your love, and then let me alone.
[*Exeunt Lucentio and Bianca.*]

Enter a Pedant.

Ped. God save you, sir!
Tra. And you, sir! you are welcome.
Travel you far on, or are you at the farthest?
Ped. Sir, at the farthest for a week or two:
But then up farther, and as far as Rome;
And so to Tripoli, if God lend me life.
Tra. What countryman, I pray?
Ped. Of Mantua.
Tra. Of Mantua, sir? marry, God forbid!
And come to Padua, careless of your life?
Ped. My life, sir! how, I pray? for that goes hard.
Tra. 'Tis death for any one in Mantua
To come to Padua. Know you not the cause?
Your ships are stay'd at Venice, and the duke,
For private quarrel 'twixt your duke and him,
Hath publish'd and proclaim'd it openly:
'Tis marvel, but that you are but newly come,
You might have heard it else proclaim'd about.
Ped. Alas! sir, it is worse for me than so;
For I have bills for money by exchange
From Florence and must here deliver them.
Tra. Well, sir, to do you courtesy,
This will I do, and this I will advise you:
First, tell me, have you ever been at Pisa?
Ped. Ay, sir, in Pisa have I often been,
Pisa renowned for grave citizens.
Tra. Among them know you one Vincentio?
Ped. I know him not, but I have heard of him;
A merchant of incomparable wealth.
Tra. He is my father, sir; and, sooth to say,
In count'nance somewhat doth resemble you.
Bion. [*Aside*] As much as an apple doth an oyster, and all one.

SCENE II. 7. **resolve,** answer; see glossary. 8. **Art to Love,** Ovid's *Ars amandi.* 11. **proceeders,** candidates for degrees, suggested by the phrase *master of your art* (l. 9), with quibble on the ordinary sense. 20. **cullion,** base creature. 50. **lusty,** merry, pleasant. 57. **eleven and twenty,** an allusion to the card game, one-and-thirty; cf. note to I, ii, 33. 61. **ancient angel,** generally explained as a fellow of the good old stamp, i.e., the stamp of the archangel on the coin as distinguished from the debased coinage of the day. 62. **serve the turn.**

Tra. To save your life in this extremity,
This favour will I do you for his sake;
And think it not the worst of all your fortunes
That you are like to Sir Vincentio.
His name and credit shall you undertake,
And in my house you shall be friendly lodg'd:
Look that you take upon you as you should;
You understand me, sir: so shall you stay
Till you have done your business in the city:
If this be court'sy, sir, accept of it.
Ped. O sir, I do; and will repute you ever
The patron of my life and liberty.
Tra. Then go with me to make the matter good.
This, by the way, I let you understand;
My father is here look'd for every day,
To pass assurance of a dow'r in marriage
'Twixt me and one Baptista's daughter here:
In all these circumstances I'll instruct you:
Go with me to clothe you as becomes you. *Exeunt.*

[SCENE III. *A room in* PETRUCHIO'S *house.*]

Enter KATHARINA *and* GRUMIO.

Gru. No, no, forsooth; I dare not for my life.
Kath. The more my wrong, the more his spite appears:
What, did he marry me to famish me?
Beggars, that come unto my father's door
Upon entreaty have a present alms;
If not, elsewhere they meet with charity:
But I, who never knew how to entreat,
Nor never needed that I should entreat,
Am starv'd for meat, giddy for lack of sleep,
With oaths kept waking and with brawling fed:
And that which spites me more than all these wants,
He does it under name of perfect love;
As who should say, if I should sleep or eat,
'Twere deadly sickness or else present death.
I prithee go and get me some repast;
I care not what, so it be wholesome food.
Gru. What say you to a neat's foot?
Kath. 'Tis passing good: I prithee let me have it.
Gru. I fear it is too choleric a meat.
How say you to a fat tripe finely broil'd?
Kath. I like it well: good Grumio, fetch it me.
Gru. I cannot tell; I fear 'tis choleric.
What say you to a piece of beef and mustard?
Kath. A dish that I do love to feed upon.
Gru. Ay, but the mustard is too hot a little.
Kath. Why then, the beef, and let the mustard rest.
Gru. Nay then, I will not: you shall have the mustard,
Or else you get no beef of Grumio.
Kath. Then both, or one, or any thing thou wilt.
Gru. Why then, the mustard without the beef.
Kath. Go, get thee gone, thou false deluding slave, *Beats him.*
That feed'st me with the very name of meat:
Sorrow on thee and all the pack of you,
That triumph thus upon my misery!
Go, get thee gone, I say.

Enter PETRUCHIO *and* HORTENSIO *with meat.*

Pet. How fares my Kate? What, sweeting, all amort?
Hor. Mistress, what cheer?
Kath. Faith, as cold as can be.
Pet. Pluck up thy spirits; look cheerfully upon me.
Here, love; thou see'st how diligent I am
To dress thy meat myself and bring it thee:
I am sure, sweet Kate, this kindness merits thanks.
What, not a word? Nay, then thou lov'st it not;
And all my pains is sorted to no proof.
Here, take away this dish.
Kath. I pray you, let it stand.
Pet. The poorest service is repaid with thanks;
And so shall mine, before you touch the meat.
Kath. I thank you, sir.
Hor. Signior Petruchio, fie! you are to blame.
Come, Mistress Kate, I'll bear you company.
Pet. [*Aside*] Eat it up all, Hortensio, if thou lovest me.
Much good do it unto thy gentle heart!
Kate, eat apace: and now, my honey love,
Will we return unto thy father's house
And revel it as bravely as the best,
With silken coats and caps and golden rings,
With ruffs and cuffs and fardingales and things;
With scarfs and fans and double change of brav'ry,
With amber bracelets, beads and all this knav'ry.
What, hast thou din'd? The tailor stays thy leisure,
To deck thy body with his ruffling treasure.

Enter Tailor.

Come, tailor, let us see these ornaments:
Lay forth the gown.

Enter Haberdasher.

What news with you, sir?
Hab. Here is the cap your worship did bespeak.
Pet. Why, this was moulded on a porringer;
A velvet dish: fie, fie! 'tis lewd and filthy:
Why, 'tis a cockle or a walnut-shell,
A knack, a toy, a trick, a baby's cap:
Away with it! Come, let me have a bigger.
Kath. I'll have no bigger: this doth fit the time,
And gentlewomen wear such caps as these.
Pet. When you are gentle, you shall have one too,
And not till then.
Hor. [*Aside*] That will not be in haste.
Kath. Why, sir, I trust I may have leave to speak;
And speak I will; I am no child, no babe:
Your betters have endur'd me say my mind,
And if you cannot, best you stop your ears.
My tongue will tell the anger of my heart,
Or else my heart concealing it will break,
And rather than it shall, I will be free
Even to the uttermost, as I please, in words.
Pet. Why, thou say'st true; it is a paltry cap,
A custard-coffin, a bauble, a silken pie:
I love thee well, in that thou lik'st it not.
Kath. Love me or love me not, I like the cap;
And it I will have, or I will have none.
[*Exit Haberdasher.*]
Pet. Thy gown? why, ay: come, tailor, let us see 't.

answer the purpose; see *serve* in glossary. 63. **mercatante,** merchant. 119. **circumstances,** details; see glossary.
SCENE III. 5. **present,** immediate, prompt; see glossary. 17. **neat,** any cattle of the ox kind. 36. **all amort,** dejected, dispirited. 43. **sorted to no proof,** proved to be to no purpose (Schmidt). 54. **bravely,** splendidly dressed. 56. **fardingales,** hooped petticoats. 64. **porringer,** porridge bowl. 66. **cockle,** scallop shell. 82. **custard-coffin,** crust over a custard, with quibble on "costard" meaning "head."

O mercy, God! what masquing stuff is here?
What 's this? a sleeve? 'tis like a demi-cannon:
What, up and down, carv'd like an apple-tart?
Here's snip and nip and cut and slish and slash,
Like to a censer in a barber's shop:
Why, what, a devil's name, tailor, call'st thou this?
Hor. [*Aside*] I see she's like to have neither cap nor gown.
Tai. You bid me make it orderly and well,
According to the fashion and the time.
Pet. Marry, and did; but if you be rememb'red,
I did not bid you mar it to the time.
Go, hop me over every kennel home,
For you shall hop without my custom, sir:
I'll none of it: hence! make your best of it.
Kath. I never saw a better-fashion'd gown,
More quaint, more pleasing, nor more commendable:
Belike you mean to make a puppet of me.
Pet. Why, true; he means to make a puppet of thee.
Tai. She says your worship means to make a puppet of her.
Pet. O monstrous arrogance! Thou liest, thou thread, thou thimble,
Thou yard, three-quarters, half-yard, quarter, nail!
Thou flea, thou nit, thou winter-cricket thou!
Brav'd in mine own house with a skein of thread?
Away, thou rag, thou quantity, thou remnant;
Or I shall so be-mete thee with thy yard
As thou shalt think on prating whilst thou liv'st!
I tell thee, I, that thou hast marr'd her gown.
Tai. Your worship is deceiv'd; the gown is made
Just as my master had direction:
Grumio gave order how it should be done.
Gru. I gave him no order; I gave him the stuff.
Tai. But how did you desire it should be made?
Gru. Marry, sir, with needle and thread.
Tai. But did you not request to have it cut?
Gru. Thou hast faced many things.
Tai. I have.
Gru. Face not me: thou hast braved many men; brave not me; I will neither be faced nor braved. I say unto thee, I bid thy master cut out the gown; but I did not bid him cut it to pieces: ergo, thou liest.
Tai. Why, here is the note of the fashion to testify.
Pet. Read it.
Gru. The note lies in 's throat, if he say I said so.
Tai. [*Reads*] 'Imprimis, a loose-bodied gown:'
Gru. Master, if ever I said loose-bodied gown, sew me in the skirts of it, and beat me to death with a bottom of brown thread: I said a gown.
Pet. Proceed.
Tai. [*Reads*] 'With a small compassed cape:'
Gru. I confess the cape.
Tai. [*Reads*] 'With a trunk sleeve:'
Gru. I confess two sleeves.
Tai. [*Reads*] 'The sleeves curiously cut.'
Pet. Ay, there 's the villany.
Gru. Error i' the bill, sir; error i' the bill. I commanded the sleeves should be cut out and sewed up again; and that I'll prove upon thee, though thy little finger be armed in a thimble.
Tai. This is true that I say: an I had thee in place where, thou shouldst know it.
Gru. I am for thee straight: take thou the bill, give me thy mete-yard, and spare not me.
Hor. God-a-mercy, Grumio! then he shall have no odds.
Pet. Well, sir, in brief, the gown is not for me.
Gru. You are i' the right, sir: 'tis for my mistress.
Pet. Go, take it up unto thy master's use.
Gru. Villain, not for thy life: take up my mistress' gown for thy master's use!
Pet. Why, sir, what 's your conceit in that?
Gru. O, sir, the conceit is deeper than you think for: Take up my mistress' gown to his master's use! O, fie, fie, fie!
Pet. [*Aside*] Hortensio, say thou wilt see the tailor paid.
Go take it hence; be gone, and say no more.
Hor. Tailor, I'll pay thee for thy gown to-morrow:
Take no unkindness of his hasty words:
Away! I say; commend me to thy master. *Exit Tailor.*
Pet. Well, come, my Kate; we will unto your father's
Even in these honest mean habiliments:
Our purses shall be proud, our garments poor;
For 'tis the mind that makes the body rich;
And as the sun breaks through the darkest clouds,
So honour peereth in the meanest habit.
What is the jay more precious than the lark,
Because his feathers are more beautiful?
Or is the adder better than the eel,
Because his painted skin contents the eye?
O, no, good Kate; neither art thou the worse
For this poor furniture and mean array,
If thou account'st it shame, lay it on me;
And therefore frolic: we will hence forthwith,
To feast and sport us at thy father's house.
Go, call my men, and let us straight to him;
And bring our horses unto Long-lane end;
There will we mount, and thither walk on foot.
Let 's see; I think 'tis now some seven o'clock,
And well we may come there by dinner-time.
Kath. I dare assure you, sir, 'tis almost two;
And 'twill be supper-time ere you come there.
Pet. It shall be seven ere I go to horse:
Look, what I speak, or do, or think to do,
You are still crossing it. Sirs, let 't alone:
I will not go to-day; and ere I do,
It shall be what o'clock I say it is.
Hor. [*Aside*] Why, so this gallant will command the sun. [*Exeunt.*]

[SCENE IV. *Padua. Before* BAPTISTA'S *house.*]

Enter TRANIO, *and the* Pedant *dressed like* VINCENTIO.

Tra. Sir, this is the house: please it you that I call?
Ped. Ay, what else? and but I be deceived
Signior Baptista may remember me,
Near twenty years ago, in Genoa,
Where we were lodgers at the Pegasus.

89. **up and down,** all over, exactly. 91. **censer,** perfuming pan having an ornamented lid. 96. **Marry,** mild interjection; see glossary. 109. **nail,** measure of length for cloth—two and one-fourth inches. 111. **Brav'd,** defied; see glossary. 112. **quantity,** fragment. 113. **be-mete,** measure. 123. **faced,** bullied, with quibble on the meaning "trim." 135. **loose-bodied,** a quibble on the notion, "loose woman." 138. **bottom,** ball wound from a skein. 162. **conceit,** idea.

SCENE IV. 2. **and but,** unless. 5. **the Pegasus,** an inn. 11. **throughly,** thoroughly; see glossary. 17. **hold . . . drink,** i.e., giving him a tip. 18. *Stage Direction:* **booted and bareheaded,** i.e., the Pedant puts on a show of just arriving and greeting. 21. **good father,** quibble on "godfather." 36. **curious,** overly particular. 49. **affied,** betrothed.

Tra. 'Tis well; and hold your own, in any case,
With such austerity as 'longeth to a father.

Enter BIONDELLO.

Ped. I warrant you. But, sir, here comes your boy;
'Twere good he were school'd.
Tra. Fear you not him. Sirrah Biondello,
Now do your duty throughly, I advise you:
Imagine 'twere the right Vincentio.
Bion. Tut, fear not me.
Tra. But hast thou done thy errand to Baptista?
Bion. I told him that your father was at Venice,
And that you look'd for him this day in Padua.
Tra. Th' art a tall fellow: hold thee that to drink.
Here comes Baptista: set your countenance, sir.

Enter BAPTISTA *and* LUCENTIO. PEDANT *booted and bareheaded.*

Signior Baptista, you are happily met.
[*To the Pedant*] Sir, this is the gentleman I told you of:
I pray you, stand good father to me now,
Give me Bianca for my patrimony.
Ped. Soft, son!
Sir, by your leave: having come to Padua
To gather in some debts, my son Lucentio
Made me acquainted with a weighty cause
Of love between your daughter and himself:
And, for the good report I hear of you
And for the love he beareth to your daughter
And she to him, to stay him not too long,
I am content, in a good father's care,
To have him match'd; and if you please to like
No worse than I, upon some agreement
Me shall you find ready and willing
With one consent to have her so bestow'd;
For curious I cannot be with you,
Signior Baptista, of whom I hear so well.
Bap. Sir, pardon me in what I have to say:
Your plainness and your shortness please me well.
Right true it is, your son Lucentio here
Doth love my daughter and she loveth him,
Or both dissemble deeply their affections:
And therefore, if you say no more than this,
That like a father you will deal with him
And pass my daughter a sufficient dower,
The match is made, and all is done:
Your son shall have my daughter with consent.
Tra. I thank you, sir. Where then do you know best
We be affied and such assurance ta'en
As shall with either part's agreement stand?
Bap. Not in my house, Lucentio; for, you know,
Pitchers have ears, and I have many servants:
Besides, old Gremio is heark'ning still;
And happily we might be interrupted.
Tra. Then at my lodging, an it like you:
There doth my father lie; and there, this night,
We'll pass the business privately and well.
Send for your daughter by your servant here;
My boy shall fetch the scrivener presently.
The worst is this, that, at so slender warning,
You are like to have a thin and slender pittance.
Bap. It likes me well. Cambio, hie you home,
And bid Bianca make her ready straight;
And, if you will, tell what hath happened,
Lucentio's father is arriv'd in Padua,
And how she 's like to be Lucentio's wife. [*Exit Luc.*]
Bion. I pray the gods she may with all my heart! *Exit.*
Tra. Dally not with the gods, but get thee gone.
Signior Baptista, shall I lead the way?
Welcome! one mess is like to be your cheer:
Come, sir; we will better it in Pisa.
Bap. I follow you. *Exeunt* [*Tranio, Pedant, and Baptista*].

Enter LUCENTIO *and* BIONDELLO.

Bion. Cambio!
Luc. What sayest thou, Biondello?
Bion. You saw my master wink and laugh upon you?
Luc. Biondello, what of that?
Bion. Faith, nothing; but has left me here behind, to expound the meaning or moral of his signs and tokens.
Luc. I pray thee, moralize them.
Bion. Then thus. Baptista is safe, talking with the deceiving father of a deceitful son.
Luc. And what of him?
Bion. His daughter is to be brought by you to the supper.
Luc. And then?
Bion. The old priest of Saint Luke's church is at your command at all hours.
Luc. And what of all this?
Bion. I cannot tell; expect they are busied about a counterfeit assurance: take you assurance of her, 'cum privilegio ad imprimendum solum:' to the church; take the priest, clerk, and some sufficient honest witnesses:
If this be not that you look for, I have no more to say,
But bid Bianca farewell for ever and a day.
Luc. Hearest thou, Biondello?
Bion. I cannot tarry: I knew a wench married in an afternoon as she went to the garden for parsley to stuff a rabbit; and so may you, sir: and so, adieu, sir. My master hath appointed me to go to Saint Luke's, to bid the priest be ready to come against you come with your appendix. *Exit.*
Luc. I may, and will, if she be so contented:
She will be pleas'd; then wherefore should I doubt?
Hap what hap may, I'll roundly go about her:
It shall go hard if Cambio go without her. *Exit.*

[SCENE V. *A public road.*]

Enter PETRUCHIO, KATE, HORTENSIO [, *and* Servants].

Pet. Come on, a God's name; once more toward our father's.
Good Lord, how bright and goodly shines the moon!
Kath. The moon! the sun: it is not moonlight now.
Pet. I say it is the moon that shines so bright.
Kath. I know it is the sun that shines so bright.
Pet. Now, by my mother's son, and that 's myself,

53. **hearkening still,** continually listening. 54. **happily,** haply, perhaps. 55. **like,** please; see glossary. 56. **lie,** lodge; see glossary. 59. **scrivener,** notary, one to draw up contracts. 62. **Cambio,** so F; Globe: *Biondello.* Evidently Lucentio, addressed as "Cambio," exits at l. 66, followed by Biondello. 66. **like,** likely. 70. **mess,** dish, course of food. **cheer,** welcome, entertainment. 92. **assurance,** betrothal. 93. **'cum . . . solum,'** with exclusive copyright, here jokingly applied to the actual marriage; the phrase appeared often on the title pages of books. 104. **appendix,** i.e., your bride. 108. **go hard,** a bawdy quibble.

It shall be moon, or star, or what I list,
Or ere I journey to your father's house.
Go on, and fetch our horses back again.
Evermore cross'd and cross'd; nothing but cross'd!
Hor. Say as he says, or we shall never go.
Kath. Forward, I pray, since we have come so far,
And be it moon, or sun, or what you please:
An if you please to call it a rush-candle,
Henceforth I vow it shall be so for me.
Pet. I say it is the moon.
Kath. I know it is the moon.
Pet. Nay, then you lie: it is the blessed sun.
Kath. Then, God be bless'd, it is the blessed sun:
But sun it is not, when you say it is not;
And the moon changes even as your mind.
What you will have it nam'd, even that it is;
And so it shall be so for Katharine.
Hor. Petruchio, go thy ways; the field is won.
Pet. Well, forward, forward! thus the bowl should run,
And not unluckily against the bias.
But, soft! company is coming here.

Enter VINCENTIO.

[*To Vincentio*] Good morrow, gentle mistress: where away?
Tell me, sweet Kate, and tell me truly too,
Hast thou beheld a fresher gentlewoman?
Such war of white and red within her cheeks!
What stars do spangle heaven with such beauty,
As those two eyes become that heavenly face?
Fair lovely maid, once more good day to thee.
Sweet Kate, embrace her for her beauty's sake.
Hor. 'A will make the man mad, to make a woman of him.
Kath. Young budding virgin, fair and fresh and sweet,
Whither away, or where is thy abode?
Happy the parents of so fair a child;
Happier the man, whom favourable stars
Allot thee for his lovely bed-fellow!
Pet. Why, how now, Kate! I hope thou art not mad:
This is a man, old, wrinkled, faded, withered,
And not a maiden, as thou say'st he is.
Kath. Pardon, old father, my mistaking eyes,
That have been so bedazzled with the sun
That everything I look on seemeth green:
Now I perceive thou art a reverend father;
Pardon, I pray thee, for my mad mistaking.
Pet. Do, good old grandsire; and withal make known
Which way thou travellest: if along with us,
We shall be joyful of thy company.
Vin. Fair sir, and you my merry mistress,
That with your strange encounter much amaz'd me,
My name is call'd Vincentio; my dwelling Pisa;
And bound I am to Padua; there to visit
A son of mine, which long I have not seen.
Pet. What is his name?
Vin. Lucentio, gentle sir.
Pet. Happily met; the happier for thy son.
And now by law, as well as reverend age,
I may entitle thee my loving father:
The sister to my wife, this gentlewoman,
Thy son by this hath married. Wonder not,
Nor be not griev'd: she is of good esteem,
Her dowry wealthy, and of worthy birth;
Beside, so qualified as may beseem
The spouse of any noble gentleman.
Let me embrace with old Vincentio,
And wander we to see thy honest son,
Who will of thy arrival be full joyous.
Vin. But is this true? or is it else your pleasure,
Like pleasant travellers, to break a jest
Upon the company you overtake?
Hor. I do assure thee, father, so it is.
Pet. Come, go along, and see the truth hereof;
For our first merriment hath made thee jealous.
Exeunt [*all but Hortensio*].
Hor. Well, Petruchio, this has put me in heart.
Have to my widow! and if she be froward,
Then hast thou taught Hortensio to be untoward.
Exit.

[ACT V.

SCENE I. *Padua. Before* LUCENTIO'S *house.*]

Enter BIONDELLO, LUCENTIO, *and* BIANCA. GREMIO *is out before.*

Bion. Softly and swiftly, sir; for the priest is ready.

Luc. I fly, Biondello: but they may chance to need thee at home; therefore leave us.

Bion. Nay, faith, I'll see the church a your back; and then come back to my master's as soon as I can.
[*Exeunt Lucentio, Bianca, and Biondello.*]

Gre. I marvel Cambio comes not all this while.

Enter PETRUCHIO, KATE, VINCENTIO, GRUMIO, *with* Attendants.

Pet. Sir, here 's the door, this is Lucentio's house:
My father's bears more toward the marketplace;
Thither must I, and here I leave you, sir.
Vin. You shall not choose but drink before you go:
I think I shall command your welcome here,
And, by all likelihood, some cheer is toward. *Knock.*

Gre. They 're busy within; you were best knock louder.

Pedant *looks out of the window.*

Ped. What 's he that knocks as he would beat down the gate?

Vin. Is Signior Lucentio within, sir?

Ped. He 's within, sir, but not to be spoken withal.

Vin. What if a man bring him a hundred pound or two, to make merry withal?

Ped. Keep your hundred pounds to yourself: he shall need none, so long as I live.

Pet. Nay, I told you your son was well beloved in Padua. Do you hear, sir? To leave frivolous circum-

SCENE V. 8. **Or ere,** before; see *or* in glossary. 12. **Forward, I pray,** etc. In the resolving of this merry and complicated plot, nothing is so artistically pleasing as the resolution of the strife between Petruchio and Katharina, where we see the shrew emerge as a witty, sanguine person, none the less spirited for all her taming. The turn in her character occurs when she is able to see and to make a joke. 14. **rush-candle,** a rush dipped into tallow; hence a very feeble light. 25. **against the bias,** contrary to the normal tendency; see *bias* in glossary. 35. **'A,** he; see glossary. 47. **green,** young and fresh. 76. **jealous,** suspicious. 79. **untoward,** unmannerly.

ACT V. SCENE I. *Stage Direction:* **Gremio is out before.** The New Cambridge editors give the scene and directions as follows: *The square in* stances, I pray you, tell Signior Lucentio that his father is come from Pisa and is here at the door to speak with him.

Ped. Thou liest: his father is come from Padua and here looking out at the window.

Vin. Art thou his father?

Ped. Ay, sir; so his mother says, if I may believe her.

Pet. [*To Vincentio*] Why, how now, gentleman! why, this is flat knavery, to take upon you another man's name.

Ped. Lay hands on the villain: I believe 'a means to cozen somebody in this city under my countenance.

Enter BIONDELLO.

Bion. I have seen them in the church together: God send 'em good shipping! But who is here? mine old master Vincentio! now we are undone and brought to nothing.

Vin. [*Seeing Biondello*] Come hither, crack-hemp.

Bion. I hope I may choose, sir.

Vin. Come hither, you rogue. What, have you forgot me?

Bion. Forgot you! no, sir: I could not forget you, for I never saw you before in all my life.

Vin. What, you notorious villain, didst thou never see thy master's father, Vincentio?

Bion. What, my old worshipful old master? yes, marry, sir: see where he looks out of the window.

Vin. Is 't so, indeed? *He beats Biondello.*

Bion. Help, help, help! here's a madman will murder me. [*Exit.*]

Ped. Help, son! help, Signior Baptista!

[*Exit from above.*]

Pet. Prithee, Kate, let 's stand aside and see the end of this controversy. [*They retire.*]

Enter [*below*] Pedant *with* Servants, BAPTISTA, [*and*] TRANIO [*as Lucentio*].

Tra. Sir, what are you that offer to beat my servant?

Vin. What am I, sir! nay, what are you, sir? O immortal gods! O fine villain! A silken doublet! a velvet hose! a scarlet cloak! and a copatain hat! O, I am undone! I am undone! while I play the good husband at home, my son and my servant spend all at the university.

Tra. How now! what 's the matter?

Bap. What, is the man lunatic?

Tra. Sir, you seem a sober ancient gentleman by your habit, but your words show you a madman. Why, sir, what 'cerns it you if I wear pearl and gold? I thank my good father, I am able to maintain it.

Vin. Thy father! O villain! he is a sailmaker in Bergamo.

Bap. You mistake, sir, you mistake, sir. Pray, what do you think is his name?

Vin. His name! as if I knew not his name: I have brought him up ever since he was three years old, and his name is Tranio.

Ped. Away, away, mad ass! his name is Lucentio; and he is mine only son, and heir to the lands of me, Signior Vincentio.

Vin. Lucentio! O, he hath murdered his master! Lay hold on him, I charge you, in the duke's name. O, my son, my son! Tell me, thou villain, where is my son Lucentio?

Tra. Call forth an officer.

[*Enter one with an Officer.*]

Carry this mad knave to the gaol. Father Baptista, I charge you see that he be forthcoming.

Vin. Carry me to the gaol!

Gre. Stay, officer: he shall not go to prison.

Bap. Talk not, Signior Gremio: I say he shall go to prison.

Gre. Take heed, Signior Baptista, lest you be cony-catched in this business: I dare swear this is the right Vincentio.

Ped. Swear, if thou darest.

Gre. Nay, I dare not swear it.

Tra. Then thou wert best say that I am not Lucentio.

Gre. Yes, I know thee to be Signior Lucentio.

Bap. Away with the dotard! to the gaol with him!

Enter BIONDELLO, LUCENTIO, *and* BIANCA.

Vin. Thus strangers may be haled and abused: O monstrous villain!

Bion. O! we are spoiled and—yonder he is: deny him, forswear him, or else we are all undone.

Exeunt Biondello, Tranio, and Pedant, as fast as may be.

Luc. Pardon, sweet father. *Kneel.*

Vin. Lives my sweet son?

Bian. Pardon, dear father.

Bap. How hast thou offended?
Where is Lucentio?

Luc. Here 's Lucentio,
Right son to the right Vincentio;
That have by marriage made thy daughter mine,
While counterfeit supposes blear'd thine eyne.

Gre. Here 's packing, with a witness, to deceive us all!

Vin. Where is that damned villain Tranio,
That fac'd and brav'd me in this matter so?

Bap. Why, tell me, is not this my Cambio?

Bian. Cambio is chang'd into Lucentio.

Luc. Love wrought these miracles. Bianca's love
Made me exchange my state with Tranio,
While he did bear my countenance in the town;
And happily I have arrived at the last
Unto the wished haven of my bliss.
What Tranio did, myself enforc'd him to;
Then pardon him, sweet father, for my sake.

Vin. I'll slit the villain's nose, that would have sent me to the gaol.

Bap. But do you hear, sir? have you married my daughter without asking my good will?

Vin. Fear not, Baptista; we will content you, go to: but I will in, to be revenged for this villany. *Exit.*

Bap. And I, to sound the depth of this knavery. *Exit.*

Luc. Look not pale, Bianca; thy father will not frown. *Exeunt* [*Lucentio and Bianca*].

Gre. My cake is dough; but I'll in among the rest,

Padua. Gremio seated under the trees, nodding; the door of Baptista's house opens softly; Biondello, Lucentio (in his proper habit) and Bianca (muffled) steal forth. 43. **good shipping,** bon voyage. 44. **undone,** ruined; see glossary. 46. **crack-hemp,** gallows bird. 48. **I hope . . . sir,** allow me, sir; spoken to a disagreeable person who bars one's path (New Cambridge). 69. **copatain hat,** high, sugar-loaf hat. 71. **good husband,** good provider, manager. 111. **abused,** maltreated; see glossary. 120. **supposes,** substitutions; an allusion to Gascoigne's *Supposes*, an adaptation of *I Suppositi* by Ariosto, from which Shakespeare took the Lucentio-Bianca plot of intrigue. Hart notes that *supposes* was the name for a social pastime familiar to the age. 128. **state,** station; see glossary.

Out of hope of all, but my share of the feast. [*Exit.*]
Kath. Husband, let 's follow, to see the end of this ado.
Pet. First kiss me, Kate, and we will.
Kath. What, in the midst of the street?
Pet. What, art thou ashamed of me?
Kath. No, sir, God forbid; but ashamed to kiss.
Pet. Why, then let 's home again. [*To Grumio*] Come, sirrah, let 's away.
Kath. Nay, I will give thee a kiss: now pray thee, love, stay. [*Kisses him.*]
Pet. Is not this well? Come, my sweet Kate:
Better once than never, for never too late. *Exeunt.*

[SCENE II. *Padua:* LUCENTIO'S *house.*]

Enter BAPTISTA, VICENTIO, GREMIO, *the Pedant,* LUCENTIO, *and* BIANCA; [PETRUCHIO, KATE, HORTENSIO,] TRANIO, BIONDELLO, GRUMIO, *and* Widow; *the Serving-men with Tranio bringing in a banquet.*

Luc. At last, though long, our jarring notes agree:
And time it is, when raging war is done,
To smile at scapes and perils overblown.
My fair Bianca, bid my father welcome,
While I with self-same kindness welcome thine.
Brother Petruchio, sister Katharina,
And thou, Hortensio, with thy loving widow,
Feast with the best, and welcome to my house:
My banquet is to close our stomachs up,
After our great good cheer. Pray you, sit down;
For now we sit to chat as well as eat. [*They sit.*]
Pet. Nothing but sit and sit, and eat and eat!
Bap. Padua affords this kindness, son Petruchio.
Pet. Padua affords nothing but what is kind.
Hor. For both our sakes, I would that word were true.
Pet. Now, for my life, Hortensio fears his widow.
Wid. Then never trust me, if I be afeard.
Pet. You are very sensible, and yet you miss my sense:
I mean, Hortensio is afeard of you.
Wid. He that is giddy thinks the world turns round.
Pet. Roundly replied.
Kath. Mistress, how mean you that?
Wid. Thus I conceive by him.
Pet. Conceives by me! How likes Hortensio that?
Hor. My widow says, thus she conceives her tale.
Pet. Very well mended. Kiss him for that, good widow.
Kath. 'He that is giddy thinks the world turns round:'
I pray you, tell me what you meant by that.
Wid. Your husband, being troubled with a shrew,
Measures my husband's sorrow by his woe:
And now you know my meaning.
Kath. A very mean meaning.
Wid. Right, I mean you.
Kath. And I am mean indeed, respecting you.
Pet. To her, Kate!
Hor. To her, widow!
Pet. A hundred marks, my Kate does put her down.
Hor. That 's my office.
Pet. Spoke like an officer: ha' to thee, lad!
Drinks to Hortensio.
Bap. How likes Gremio these quick-witted folks?
Gre. Believe me, sir, they butt together well.
Bian. Head, and butt! an hasty-witted body
Would say your head and butt were head and horn.
Vin. Ay, mistress bride, hath that awakened you?
Bian. Ay, but not frighted me; therefore I'll sleep again.
Pet. Nay, that you shall not: since you have begun,
Have at you for a bitter jest or two!
Bian. Am I your bird? I mean to shift my bush;
And then pursue me as you draw your bow.
You are welcome all.
Exit Bianca [*with Kate and Widow*].
Pet. She hath prevented me. Here, Signior Tranio,
This bird you aim'd at, though you hit her not;
Therefore a health to all that shot and miss'd.
Tra. O, sir, Lucentio slipp'd me like his greyhound,
Which runs himself and catches for his master.
Pet. A good swift simile, but something currish.
Tra. 'Tis well, sir, that you hunted for yourself:
'Tis thought your deer does hold you at a bay.
Bap. O ho, Petruchio! Tranio hits you now.
Luc. I thank thee for that gird, good Tranio.
Hor. Confess, confess, hath he not hit you here?
Pet. 'A has a little gall'd me, I confess;
And, as the jest did glance away from me,
'Tis ten to one it maim'd you two outright.
Bap. Now, in good sadness, son Petruchio,
I think thou hast the veriest shrew of all.
Pet. Well, I say no: and therefore for assurance
Let 's each one send unto his wife;
And he whose wife is most obedient
To come at first when he doth send for her,
Shall win the wager which we will propose.
Hor. Content. What is the wager?
Luc. Twenty crowns.
Pet. Twenty crowns!
I'll venture so much of my hawk or hound,
But twenty times so much upon my wife.
Luc. A hundred then.
Hor. Content.
Pet. A match! 'tis done.
Hor. Who shall begin?
Luc. That will I.
Go, Biondello, bid your mistress come to me.
Bion. I go. *Exit.*
Bap. Son, I'll be your half, Bianca comes.
Luc. I'll have no halves; I'll bear it all myself.

Enter BIONDELLO.

How now! what news?
Bion. Sir, my mistress sends you word
That she is busy and she cannot come.
Pet. How! she is busy and she cannot come!
Is that an answer?
Gre. Ay, and a kind one too:
Pray God, sir, your wife send you not a worse.

SCENE II. 9. **banquet,** dessert. **stomachs,** used with quibble on the meaning "quarrels." 17. **afeard,** suspicious. 29. **Measures,** judges; see glossary. 32. **mean,** used quibblingly; see glossary. **respecting,** compared to. 45. **Have at,** I shall come at; see glossary. 58. **gird,** sharp, biting jest. 63. **sadness,** seriousness; see glossary. 99. **holidame,** halidom; cf. *The Two Gentlemen of Verona,* IV, ii, 136, note. 104. **Swinge,** thrash. **me,** the ethical dative. 109. **awful rule,** i.e., authority respected; see *awful* in glossary. 140. **Confounds,** ruins; see

Pet. I hope, better.
Hor. Sirrah Biondello, go and entreat my wife
To come to me forthwith. *Exit Bion.*
Pet. O, ho! entreat her!
Nay, then she must needs come.
Hor. I am afraid, sir,
Do what you can, yours will not be entreated.

Enter BIONDELLO.

Now, where 's my wife?
Bion. She says you have some goodly jest in hand:
She will not come; she bids you come to her.
Pet. Worse and worse; she will not come! O vile,
Intolerable, not to be endur'd!
Sirrah Grumio, go to your mistress;
Say, I command her come to me. *Exit* [*Grumio*].
Hor. I know her answer.
Pet. What?
Hor. She will not.
Pet. The fouler fortune mine, and there an end.

Enter KATHARINA.

Bap. Now, by my holidame, here comes Katharina!
Kath. What is your will, sir, that you send for me?
Pet. Where is your sister, and Hortensio's wife?
Kath. They sit conferring by the parlour fire.
Pet. Go, fetch them hither: if they deny to come,
Swinge me them soundly forth unto their husbands:
Away, I say, and bring them hither straight.
[*Exit Katharina.*]
Luc. Here is a wonder, if you talk of a wonder.
Hor. And so it is: I wonder what it bodes.
Pet. Marry, peace it bodes, and love and quiet life,
And awful rule and right supremacy;
And, to be short, what not, that 's sweet and happy?
Bap. Now, fair befal thee, good Petruchio!
The wager thou hast won; and I will add
Unto their losses twenty thousand crowns;
Another dowry to another daughter,
For she is chang'd, as she had never been.
Pet. Nay, I will win my wager better yet
And show more sign of her obedience,
Her new-built virtue and obedience.

Enter KATE, BIANCA, *and* Widow.

See where she comes and brings your froward wives
As prisoners to her womanly persuasion.
Katharine, that cap of yours becomes you not:
Off with that bauble, throw it under-foot.
Wid. Lord, let me never have a cause to sigh,
Till I be brought to such a silly pass!
Bian. Fie! what a foolish duty call you this?
Luc. I would your duty were as foolish too:
The wisdom of your duty, fair Bianca,
Hath cost me an hundred crowns since suppertime.
Bian. The more fool you, for laying on my duty.
Pet. Katharine, I charge thee, tell these headstrong women
What duty they do owe their lords and husbands.
Wid. Come, come, you 're mocking: we will have no telling.
Pet. Come on, I say; and first begin with her.
Wid. She shall not.
Pet. I say she shall: and first begin with her.
Kath. Fie, fie! unknit that threatening unkind brow,
And dart not scornful glances from those eyes,
To wound thy lord, thy king, thy governor:
It blots thy beauty as frosts do bite the meads,
Confounds thy fame as whirlwinds shake fair buds,
And in no sense is meet or amiable.
A woman mov'd is like a fountain troubled,
Muddy, ill-seeming, thick, bereft of beauty;
And while it is so, none so dry or thirsty
Will deign to sip or touch one drop of it.
Thy husband is thy lord, thy life, thy keeper,
Thy head, thy sovereign; one that cares for thee,
And for thy maintenance commits his body
To painful labour both by sea and land,
To watch the night in storms, the day in cold,
Whilst thou li'st warm at home, secure and safe;
And craves no other tribute at thy hands
But love, fair looks and true obedience;
Too little payment for so great a debt.
Such duty as the subject owes the prince
Even such a woman oweth to her husband;
And when she is froward, peevish, sullen, sour,
And not obedient to his honest will,
What is she but a foul contending rebel
And graceless traitor to her loving lord?
I am asham'd that women are so simple
To offer war where they should kneel for peace,
Or seek for rule, supremacy and sway,
When they are bound to serve, love and obey.
Why are our bodies soft and weak and smooth,
Unapt to toil and trouble in the world,
But that our soft conditions and our hearts
Should well agree with our external parts?
Come, come, you froward and unable worms!
My mind hath been as big as one of yours,
My heart as great, my reason haply more,
To bandy word for word and frown for frown;
But now I see our lances are but straws,
Our strength as weak, our weakness past compare,
That seeming to be most which we indeed least are.
Then vail your stomachs, for it is no boot,
And place your hands below your husband's foot:
In token of which duty, if he please,
My hand is ready; may it do him ease.
Pet. Why, there 's a wench! Come on, and kiss me, Kate.
Luc. Well, go thy ways, old lad; for thou shalt ha 't.
Vin. 'Tis a good hearing when children are toward.
Luc. But a harsh hearing when women are froward.
Pet. Come, Kate, we'll to bed.
We three are married, but you two are sped.
[*To Luc.*] 'Twas I won the wager, though you hit the white;
And, being a winner, God give you good night!
Exit Petruchio [*and Kate*].
Hor. Now, go thy ways; thou hast tam'd a curst shrew.
Luc. 'Tis a wonder, by your leave, she will be tamed so. [*Exeunt.*]

glossary. **fame,** reputation; see glossary. 142. **mov'd,** angry; see glossary. 157. **peevish,** obstinate; see glossary. 167. **conditions,** qualities; see glossary. 176. **vail,** lower; see glossary. **boot,** profit, advantage; see glossary. 179. **do . . . ease,** give pleasure or assistance; see *ease* in glossary. 186. **white,** the center of the target, with quibble on the name of Bianca, which in Italian means "white."

A MIDSUMMER NIGHT'S DREAM

A *Midsummer Night's Dream* (c. 1594–1595) belongs to the period of transition from Shakespeare's experimental, imitative comedy to his mature, romantic, philosophical, "festive" vein. The play resembles Shakespeare's earlier attempts in its lighthearted presentation of love's tribulations. The two sets of lovers, scarcely distinguishable one from the other, are conventional figures. In them we find no hint of the profound self-discovery experienced by Beatrice and Benedick (*Much Ado about Nothing*) or Rosalind and Orlando (*As You Like It*). At the same time, this play develops the motif of love as an imaginative journey from reality into a fantasy world created by the artist, ending in return to a reality that has itself been partly transformed by the experience of the journey. (Shakespeare gives us an earlier hint of such an imaginary silvan landscape in *The Two Gentleman of Verona.*) This motif, with its contrasting worlds of social order and imaginative escape, remained an enduring vision for Shakespeare to the very last.

In construction, *A Midsummer Night's Dream* is a skillful interweaving of four plots involving four groups of characters: the court party of Duke Theseus, the four young lovers, the fairies, and the "rude mechanicals" or would-be actors. Mendelssohn's nineteenth-century incidental music evokes the contrasting textures of the various groups: Theseus' hunting horns and ceremonial wedding marches, the lovers' soaring and throbbing melodies, the fairies' pianissimo staccato, the tradesmen's clownish bassoon. Moreover, each plot is derived from its own set of source materials. The action involving Theseus and Hippolyta, for example, owes several details to Thomas North's translation (1579) of Plutarch's *Lives of the Noble Grecians and Romanes*, to Chaucer's *Knight's Tale* and perhaps his *Legend of Good Women*, and to Ovid's *Metamorphoses* (in the Latin text or in Golding's popular Elizabethan translation). The lovers' story, meanwhile, is Italianate and Ovidian in tone, and also in the broadest sense follows the conventions of plot in Plautus' and Terence's Roman comedies, although no particular source is known. Shakespeare's rich fairy lore, by contrast, is part folk tradition and part "learned." Although he certainly needed no books to tell him about mischievous spirits that could prevent churned milk from turning to butter, for instance, Shakespeare might have borrowed Oberon's name either from the French romance *Huon of Bordeaux* (translated into English by 1540), or from Greene's play *James IV* (c. 1591), or from Spenser's *The Fairie Queene*, II,i,8 (1590). Similarly, he may have taken Titania's name from the *Metamorphoses*, where it is used as an epithet for both Diana and Circe. Finally, for Bottom the Weaver and company, Shakespeare's primary inspiration was doubtless his own theatrical experience, although even here he is indebted to Ovid for the story of Pyramus and Thisbe, and probably to Apuleius' *Golden Ass* (translated by William Adlington, 1566) for Bottom's transformation.

Each of the four main plots in *A Midsummer Night's Dream* contains one or more pairs of lovers whose happiness has been frustrated by misunderstanding or parental opposition. Theseus and Hippolyta, once enemies in battle, become husband and wife; and their court marriage, constituting the "overplot" of the play, provides a framework for other dramatic actions that similarly oscillate between conflict and harmony. Theseus' actions are in fact instrumental in setting in motion and finally resolving the tribulations of the other characters. In the beginning of the play, for example, the lovers flee from Theseus' Athenian law; at the end, they are awakened by him from their dream. The king and queen of fairies come to Athens to celebrate Theseus' wedding, but quarrel with one another because Oberon has long been partial to Hippolyta, and Titania partial to Theseus. The Athenian tradesmen go off into the forest to rehearse their performance of "Pyramus and Thisbe" in anticipation of the wedding festivities.

The tragic love story of Pyramus and Thisbe, although it seems absurdly ill-suited for a wedding, simply reinforces by contrast the universal accord reuniting the other couples. Theseus, who originally won the Amazonian Hippolyta with his sword, doing her injuries, finally becomes the devoted husband. Hippolyta, legendary figure of woman's self-assertive longing to dominate the male, emerges as the happily submissive wife. The reconciliation of Oberon and Titania, meanwhile, reinforces this hierarchy of male over female. Having taught Titania a lesson concerning the changeling boy she tried to keep from him, Oberon relents and eventually frees Titania from her enchantment. Thus, the occasion of Theseus' wedding both initiates and brings to an end the difficulties that have beset the drama's various couples.

Despite Theseus' cheerful preoccupation with marriage, his court embodies at first a stern attitude toward young love. As administrator of the law, Theseus must accede to the remorseless demands of Hermia's father, Egeus. The inflexible Athenian law sides with parentage, age, wealth, and position against youth and romantic choice in love. The penalties are harsh: death, or perpetual virginity—and virginity is presented in this comedy (despite the nobly chaste examples of Christ, St. Paul, and Queen Elizabeth) as a fate worse than death. Egeus is a "blocking" or "heavy" character, the enemy of festival, the *alazon* of Plautus' or Terence's Latin versions of Grecian New Comedy. Indeed, the lovers' story is distantly derived from that New Comedy, which conventionally celebrated the triumph of young love over the machinations of age and wealth. Lysander reminds us that "the course of true love never did run smooth," and he sees its enemies as being chiefly external: the conflicting interests of parents or friends, or mismating in respect of years and blood, or war, or death, or sickness (I,i). This description clearly applies to "Pyramus and Thisbe," and it is tested by the action of *A Midsummer Night's Dream* as a whole (as well as by other early Shakespearean plays, such as *Romeo and Juliet*). The archetypal story, whether ending happily or sadly, is an evocation of love's difficulties in the face of social hostility and indifference.

While Shakespeare uses several "New Comedy" elements in setting up the basic conflicts of his drama, however, he also introduces important modifications from the very beginning. For example, he discards one conventional confrontation of classical and neoclassical comedy in which the heroine must choose between an old, wealthy suitor supported by her family, and the young but impecunious darling of her heart. Lysander is equal to his rival in social position, income, and attractiveness. Egeus' demand, therefore—that Hermia marry Demetrius rather than Lysander—seems simply arbitrary and unjust. Shakespeare emphasizes in this way the irrationality of Egeus' harsh insistence on being obeyed, and Theseus' rather complacent acceptance of the law's inequity. Spurned by an unfeeling social order, Lysander and Hermia are compelled to elope. To be sure, Egeus proves at the last to be no formidable threat; even he must admit the logic of permitting the lovers to couple as they ultimately desire. Thus, the obstacles to love are from the start seen as fundamentally superficial and indeed almost whimsical. Egeus is as "heavy" a villain as we are likely to find in this *jeu d'esprit*. Moreover, the very irrationality of his position paves the way for an ultimate resolution of the conflict. Nevertheless, by the end of Act I the supposedly rational world of conformity and duty has, by its customary insensitivity to youthful happiness, set in motion a temporary escape to a fantasy world where the law cannot reach.

In the forest, all the lovers—including Titania and Bottom—undergo a transforming experience engineered by the mischievous Puck. This experience demonstrates the universal power of love, which can overcome the queen of fairies as readily as the lowliest of men. It also suggests the irrational nature of love and its affinity to enchantment, witchcraft, and even madness. Love is seen as an affliction taken in through the frail senses, particularly the eyes. When it strikes, the victim cannot choose but to embrace the object of his dotage. By his amusing miscalculations, Puck shuffles the four interchangeable lovers through various permutations with mathematical predictability. First, two gentlemen compete for one lady, leaving the second lady sadly unrequited in love; then everything is at cross-purposes, with each gentleman pursuing the lady who is in love with the other man; then the two gentlemen compete for the lady they both previously ignored. Finally, of course, Jack shall have his Jill—whom else should he have? The couples are properly united, as they evidently were at some time prior to the commencement of the play when Demetrius had made love to Helena, and Lysander and Hermia had preferred one another.

We sense that Puck is by no means unhappy about his knavish errors. "Lord, what fools these mortals be!" Along with the other fairies in this play, Puck takes his being and his complex motivation from many denizens of the invisible world. As the agent of all-powerful love, Puck compares himself to Cupid. The love-juice he administers comes from Cupid's flower, "love-in-idleness." Like Cupid, Puck acts at the behest of the gods, and yet he wields a power that the chiefest gods themselves cannot resist. Essentially, however, Puck is less a classical love deity than a prankish folk spirit, such as we find in every folklore: gremlin, leprechaun, hobgoblin, and the like. Titania's fairies recognize Puck as one who, for example, can deprive a beer barrel of its yeast so that it spoils rather than ferments. Puck characterizes himself as a practical joker, pulling stools out from behind old ladies.

Folk wisdom imagines the inexplicable and unaccountable events in life to be caused by invisible forces who laugh at man's discomfiture and mock him for mere sport. Puck is related to such mysterious forces dwelling in nature, who must be placated with gifts and ceremonies. Although Shakespeare restricts Puck to a benign sportive role in dealing with the lovers or with Titania, the actual folk legends about Puck mentioned in this play are frequently disquieting. Puck is known to "mislead night-wanderers, laughing at their harm"; indeed, he demonstrates as much with Demetrius and Lysander, engineering a confrontation that greatly oppresses the lovers even though we perceive the sportful intent. At the play's end, Puck links himself and his fellows with the ghoulish apparitions of death and night: wolves howling at the moon, screech-owls, shrouds, gaping graves. Associations of this sort go beyond mere sportiveness to the witchcraft and demonology practiced by spirits rising from the dead. Even Oberon's assurance that the fairies will bless all the marriages of this play, shielding their progeny against mole, harelip, or other birth defects, carries the implication that such misfortunes can be caused by offended spirits. The magic of this play is thus explicitly related to deep irrational powers and forces capable of doing great harm, although of course the spirit of comedy keeps such veiled threats safely at a distance in *A Midsummer Night's Dream*.

Oberon and Titania, in their view of the relationship between gods and men, reflect yet another aspect of the fairies' spiritual ancestry—one more nearly related to the gods and goddesses of the world of Greek mythology. The king and queen of fairies assert that, because they are immortal, their regal quarrels in love must inevitably have dire consequences on earth, either in the love relationship of Theseus and Hippolyta or in the management of the weather. Floods, storms, diseases, and sterility abound, "And this same progeny of evils comes From our debate, from our dissension; We are their parents and original" (II,i). Even though this motif of the gods' quarreling over human affairs is Homeric or Virgilian in conception, however, the motif in this lighthearted play is more nearly mock-epic than truly epic. The consequences of the gods' anger are simply mirth-provoking, most of all in Titania's love affair with Bottom the Weaver.

The "Bottom" incident is recognizably a "metamorphosis" in a playfully classical mode, a love affair between a god and an earthly creature, underscoring man's dual nature. Bottom is himself half man and half beast, although he is ludicrously unlike the centaurs, mermaids, and other half-human beings of classical mythology. Whereas the head should be the aspiring part of him and his body the bestial part, Bottom wears an ass's knoll on his shoulders. His very name suggests the solid nature of his fleshly being ("bottom" is also appropriately a weaving term). He and Titania represent the opposites of flesh and spirit, miraculously yoked for a time in a twofold vision of man's absurd and ethereal nature.

A play bringing together fairies and mortals inevitably raises questions of illusion and reality. These questions reach their greatest intensity in the presentation of "Pyramus and Thisbe." This play within a play focuses our attention on the familiarly Shakespearean metaphor of art as illusion, and of the world itself as a stage on which men and women are merely players. As Theseus observes, apologizing for the ineptness of the tradesmen's performance, "the best in this kind are but shadows." That is, Shakespeare's own play is of the same order of reality as Bottom's play. Puck too, in his epilogue, enjoins any spectator offended by Shakespeare's play to dismiss it as a mere dream—as, indeed, the play's very title suggests. Theseus goes even further, linking dream to the essence of imaginative art, although he does so in a clearly critical and rather patronizing way. The artist, he says, is like the madman or the lover in his frenzy of inspiration, giving "to airy nothing A local habitation and a name" (V,i). Artistic achievements are too unsubstantial for Theseus; from his point of view they are the products of mere fantasy and irrationality, mere myths or fairy stories or old wives' tales. Behind this critical persona defending the "real" world of his court, however, we can hear Shakespeare's characteristically self-effacing. defense of "dreaming."

"Pyramus and Thisbe," like the larger play surrounding it, attempts to body forth "the forms of things unknown." The play within the play gives us personified moonshine, a speaking wall, and an apologetic lion. Of course it is an absurdly bad play, full of lame epithets, bombastic alliteration, and bathos. In part Shakespeare is here satirizing the abuses of a theatre he had helped reform. The players' chosen method of portraying imaginative matters is ridiculous, and calls forth deliciously wry comments from the courtly spectators on stage: "Would you desire lime and hair to speak better?" At the same time, those spectators on stage are actors in our play. Their sarcasms render them less sympathetic in our eyes; we see that their kind of sophistication is as restrictive as it is illuminating. Bottom and his friends have conceived moonshine and lion as they did because these simple men are so responsive to the terrifying power of art. A lion might frighten the ladies and get them all hanged. Theirs is a primitive faith, naive but strong, and in this sense it contrasts favorably with the jaded rationality of the court party. Theseus' valuable reminder, that all art is only "illusion," is thus juxtaposed with Bottom's insistence that imaginative art has a reality of its own.

Theseus above all embodies the sophistication of the court in his description of art as a frenzy of seething brains. Genially scoffing at "These antic fables" and "these fairy toys," he is unmoved by the lovers' account of their dreamlike experience. Limited by his own skepticism, Theseus has never experienced the enchantment of the forest. Even Bottom can claim more than that, for he has been lover of the queen of fairies; and, although his language cannot adequately describe the experience, Bottom will see it made into a ballad called "Bottom's Dream." Shakespeare leaves the status of his fantasy world deliberately complex; Theseus' lofty denial of dreaming is too abrupt. Even if the Athenian forest world can be made only momentarily substantial in the artifact of Shakespeare's play, we as audience respond to its tantalizing vision. We emerge back into our lives wondering if the fairies were "real," that is, puzzled by the relationship of these artistic symbols to the tangible concreteness of our daily existence. Unless our perceptions have been thus enlarged by sharing in the author's "dream," we have not surrendered to the imaginative experience.

A MIDSUMMER NIGHT'S DREAM

[*Dramatis Personae*

THESEUS, Duke of Athens.
EGEUS, *father to Hermia.*
LYSANDER, } *in love with Hermia.*
DEMETRIUS, }
PHILOSTRATE, *master of the revels to Theseus.*

QUINCE, *a carpenter.*
SNUG, *a joiner.*
BOTTOM, *a weaver.*
FLUTE, *a bellows-mender.*
SNOUT, *a tinker.*
STARVELING, *a tailor.*

HIPPOLYTA, *queen of the Amazons, betrothed to Theseus.*
HERMIA, *daughter to Egeus, in love with Lysander.*
HELENA, *in love with Demetrius.*

OBERON, *king of the fairies.*
TITANIA, *queen of the fairies.*
PUCK, *or Robin Goodfellow.*
PEASEBLOSSOM, }
COBWEB, } *fairies.*
MOTH, }
MUSTARDSEED, }
Other fairies attending their king and queen.

Attendants on Theseus and Hippolyta.

SCENE: *Athens, and a wood near it.*]

[ACT I.

SCENE I. *Athens. The palace of* THESEUS.]

Enter THESEUS, HIPPOLYTA, [PHILOSTRATE,] *with others.*

The. Now, fair Hippolyta, our nuptial hour
Draws on apace; four happy days bring in
Another moon: but, O, methinks, how slow
This old moon wanes! she lingers my desires,
Like to a step-dame or a dowager
Long withering out a young man's revenue.
Hip. Four days will quickly steep themselves in night;
Four nights will quickly dream away the time;
And then the moon, like to a silver bow
New-bent in heaven, shall behold the night
Of our solemnities.
The. Go, Philostrate,
Stir up the Athenian youth to merriments;
Awake the pert and nimble spirit of mirth:
Turn melancholy forth to funerals;
The pale companion is not for our pomp.
[*Exit Philostrate.*]
Hippolyta, I woo'd thee with my sword,
And won thy love, doing thee injuries;
But I will wed thee in another key,
With pomp, with triumph and with revelling.

Enter EGEUS *and his Daughter* HERMIA, *and* LYSANDER, *and* DEMETRIUS.

Ege. Happy be Theseus, our renowned duke!
The. Thanks, good Egeus: what 's the news with thee?
Ege. Full of vexation come I, with complaint
Against my child, my daughter Hermia.
Stand forth, Demetrius. My noble lord,
This man hath my consent to marry her.
Stand forth, Lysander: and, my gracious duke,
This man hath bewitch'd the bosom of my child:
Thou, thou, Lysander, thou hast given her rhymes
And interchang'd love-tokens with my child:
Thou hast by moonlight at her window sung
With feigning voice verses of feigning love,
And stol'n the impression of her fantasy
With bracelets of thy hair, rings, gawds, conceits,
Knacks, trifles, nosegays, sweetmeats, messengers
Of strong prevailment in unhardened youth:
With cunning hast thou filch'd my daughter's heart,
Turn'd her obedience, which is due to me,
To stubborn harshness: and, my gracious duke,
Be it so she will not here before your grace
Consent to marry with Demetrius,
I beg the ancient privilege of Athens,
As she is mine, I may dispose of her:
Which shall be either to this gentleman
Or to her death, according to our law
Immediately provided in that case.
The. What say you, Hermia? be advis'd, fair maid:
To you your father should be as a god;
One that compos'd your beauties, yea, and one
To whom you are but as a form in wax
By him imprinted and within his power
To leave the figure or disfigure it.
Demetrius is a worthy gentleman.
Her. So is Lysander.
The. In himself he is;
But in this kind, wanting your father's voice,
The other must be held the worthier.
Her. I would my father look'd but with my eyes.
The. Rather your eyes must with his judgement look.
Her. I do entreat your grace to pardon me.
I know not by what power I am made bold,
Nor how it may concern my modesty,
In such a presence here to plead my thoughts;
But I beseech your grace that I may know
The worst that may befall me in this case,

ACT I. SCENE I. 5. **step-dame,** stepmother. **dowager,** widow with a jointure or dower. 13. **pert,** lively, brisk. 19. **triumph,** public festivity. 27. **bosom,** here thought of as the seat of the passions. 32. **And . . . fantasy,** made her fall in love with you (imprinting your image on her fancy) by dishonest means; see *fantasy* in glossary. 33. **gawds,** playthings. 34. **Knacks,** knickknacks. 35. **prevailment,** power to persuade. 45. **Immediately,** expressly. 51. **disfigure,** obliterate. 54. **kind,** respect; see glossary. **voice,** authority, approval. 60. **concern,** befit.

If I refuse to wed Demetrius.
The. Either to die the death or to abjure
For ever the society of men.
Therefore, fair Hermia, question your desires;
Know of your youth, examine well your blood,
Whether, if you yield not to your father's choice,
You can endure the livery of a nun,
For aye to be in shady cloister mew'd,
To live a barren sister all your life,
Chanting faint hymns to the cold fruitless moon.
Thrice-blessed they that master so their blood,
To undergo such maiden pilgrimage;
But earthlier happy is the rose distill'd,
Than that which withering on the virgin thorn
Grows, lives and dies in single blessedness.
Her. So will I grow, so live, so die, my lord,
Ere I will yield my virgin patent up
Unto his lordship, whose unwished yoke
My soul consents not to give sovereignty.
The. Take time to pause; and, by the next new moon—
The sealing-day betwixt my love and me,
For everlasting bond of fellowship—
Upon that day either prepare to die
For disobedience to your father's will,
Or else to wed Demetrius, as he would;
Or on Diana's altar to protest
For aye austerity and single life.
Dem. Relent, sweet Hermia: and, Lysander, yield
Thy crazed title to my certain right.
Lys. You have her father's love, Demetrius;
Let me have Hermia's: do you marry him.
Ege. Scornful Lysander! true, he hath my love,
And what is mine my love shall render him.
And she is mine, and all my right of her
I do estate unto Demetrius.
Lys. I am, my lord, as well deriv'd as he,
As well possess'd; my love is more than his;
My fortunes every way as fairly rank'd,
If not with vantage, as Demetrius';
And, which is more than all these boasts can be,
I am belov'd of beauteous Hermia:
Why should not I then prosecute my right?
Demetrius, I'll avouch it to his head,
Made love to Nedar's daughter, Helena,
And won her soul; and she, sweet lady, dotes,
Devoutly dotes, dotes in idolatry,
Upon this spotted and inconstant man.
The. I must confess that I have heard so much,
And with Demetrius thought to have spoke thereof;
But, being over-full of self-affairs,
My mind did lose it. But, Demetrius, come;
And come, Egeus; you shall go with me,
I have some private schooling for you both.
For you, fair Hermia, look you arm yourself
To fit your fancies to your father's will;
Or else the law of Athens yields you up—
Which by no means we may extenuate—
To death, or to a vow of single life.
Come, my Hippolyta: what cheer, my love?
Demetrius and Egeus, go along:
I must employ you in some business
Against our nuptial and confer with you
Of something nearly that concerns yourselves.
Ege. With duty and desire we follow you.
Exeunt [*all but Lysander and Hermia*].
Lys. How now, my love! why is your cheek so pale?
How chance the roses there do fade so fast?
Her. Belike for want of rain, which I could well
Beteem them from the tempest of my eyes.
Lys. Ay me! for aught that I could ever read,
Could ever hear by tale or history,
The course of true love never did run smooth;
But, either it was different in blood,—
Her. O cross! too high to be enthrall'd to low.
Lys. Or else misgraffed in respect of years,—
Her. O spite! too old to be engag'd to young.
Lys. Or else it stood upon the choice of friends,—
Her. O hell! to choose love by another's eyes.
Lys. Or, if there were a sympathy in choice,
War, death, or sickness did lay siege to it,
Making it momentany as a sound,
Swift as a shadow, short as any dream;
Brief as the lightning in the collied night,
That, in a spleen, unfolds both heaven and earth,
And ere a man hath power to say 'Behold!'
The jaws of darkness do devour it up:
So quick bright things come to confusion.
Her. If then true lovers have been ever cross'd,
It stands as an edict in destiny:
Then let us teach our trial patience,
Because it is a customary cross,
As due to love as thoughts and dreams and sighs,
Wishes and tears, poor fancy's followers.
Lys. A good persuasion: therefore, hear me, Hermia.
I have a widow aunt, a dowager
Of great revenue, and she hath no child:
From Athens is her house remote seven leagues;
And she respects me as her only son.
There, gentle Hermia, may I marry thee;
And to that place the sharp Athenian law
Cannot pursue us. If thou lovest me then,
Steal forth thy father's house to-morrow night;
And in the wood, a league without the town,
Where I did meet thee once with Helena,
To do observance to a morn of May,
There will I stay for thee.
Her. My good Lysander!
I swear to thee, by Cupid's strongest bow,
By his best arrow with the golden head,
By the simplicity of Venus' doves,
By that which knitteth souls and prospers loves,
And by that fire which burn'd the Carthage queen,
When the false Troyan under sail was seen,
By all the vows that ever men have broke,

69. **Whether,** one syllable, like "where." 71. **mew'd,** shut in (as used of a hawk); see glossary. 74. **blood,** supposed source of passions; see glossary. 76. **earthlier happy,** happier as respects this world. 80. **patent,** privilege. 89. **protest,** vow. 92. **crazed,** unsound. 98. **estate unto,** settle or bestow upon. 99. **deriv'd,** descended, i.e., as well born; see glossary. 100. **As well possess'd,** possessed of as much wealth; see *possess* in glossary. 101. **fairly,** handsomely; see glossary. 102. **vantage,** superiority; see glossary. 106. **avouch . . . head,** declare it to his face. 117. **look,** take care; see glossary. 118. **fancies,** likings, thoughts of love. 120. **extenuate,** mitigate. 125. **Against,** in preparation for. 126. **nearly that,** that closely. 127. **duty,** reverence; see glossary. 130. **Belike,** very likely. 131. **Beteem,** grant. 137. **misgraffed,** badly matched. 143. **momentany,** lasting but a moment. 145. **collied,** blackened, darkened. 146. **spleen,** swift impulse. **unfolds,** discloses; see glossary. 149. **confusion,** ruin, destruction; see glossary. 150. **ever cross'd,** always tormented. 155. **fancy's,** amorous passion's; see glossary. 160. **respects,** regards, considers; see glossary. 167. **do . . . May,** perform the ceremonies of May Day. 171-251. **By the simplicity,** etc. The style here shifts to the rhymed couplet. While Theseus was on the scene and the business was serious, the play was

In number more than ever women spoke,
In that same place thou hast appointed me,
To-morrow truly will I meet with thee.
Lys. Keep promise, love. Look, here comes Helena.

Enter HELENA.

Her. God speed fair Helena! whither away?
Hel. Call you me fair? that fair again unsay.
Demetrius loves your fair: O happy fair!
Your eyes are lode-stars; and your tongue 's sweet air
More tuneable than lark to shepherd's ear,
When wheat is green, when hawthorn buds appear.
Sickness is catching: O, were favour so,
Yours would I catch, fair Hermia, ere I go;
My ear should catch your voice, my eye your eye,
My tongue should catch your tongue's sweet melody.
Were the world mine, Demetrius being bated,
The rest I 'ld give to be to you translated.
O, teach me how you look, and with what art
You sway the motion of Demetrius' heart.
Her. I frown upon him, yet he loves me still.
Hel. O that your frowns would teach my smiles such skill!
Her. I give him curses, yet he gives me love.
Hel. O that my prayers could such affection move!
Her. The more I hate, the more he follows me.
Hel. The more I love, the more he hateth me.
Her. His folly, Helena, is no fault of mine.
Hel. None, but your beauty: would that fault were mine!
Her. Take comfort: he no more shall see my face;
Lysander and myself will fly this place.
Before the time I did Lysander see,
Seem'd Athens as a paradise to me:
O, then, what graces in my love do dwell,
That he hath turn'd a heaven unto a hell!
Lys. Helen, to you our minds we will unfold:
To-morrow night, when Phœbe doth behold
Her silver visage in the wat'ry glass,
Decking with liquid pearl the bladed grass,
A time that lovers' flights doth still conceal,
Through Athens' gates have we devis'd to steal.
Her. And in the wood, where often you and I
Upon faint primrose-beds were wont to lie,
Emptying our bosoms of their counsel sweet,
There my Lysander and myself shall meet;
And thence from Athens turn away our eyes,
To seek new friends and stranger companies.
Farewell, sweet playfellow: pray thou for us;
And good luck grant thee thy Demetrius!
Keep word, Lysander: we must starve our sight
From lovers' food till morrow deep midnight.
Lys. I will, my Hermia. *Exit Herm.*
Helena, adieu:
As you on him, Demetrius dote on you! *Exit Lys.*
Hel. How happy some o'er other some can be!
Through Athens I am thought as fair as she.
But what of that? Demetrius thinks not so;
He will not know what all but he do know:
And as he errs, doting on Hermia's eyes,
So I, admiring of his qualities:
Things base and vile, holding no quantity,
Love can transpose to form and dignity:
Love looks not with the eyes, but with the mind;
And therefore is wing'd Cupid painted blind:
Nor hath Love's mind of any judgement taste;
Wings and no eyes figure unheedy haste:
And therefore is Love said to be a child,
Because in choice he is so oft beguil'd.
As waggish boys in game themselves forswear,
So the boy Love is perjur'd every where:
For ere Demetrius look'd on Hermia's eyne,
He hail'd down oaths that he was only mine;
And when this hail some heat from Hermia felt,
So he dissolv'd, and show'rs of oaths did melt.
I will go tell him of fair Hermia's flight:
Then to the wood will he to-morrow night
Pursue her; and for this intelligence
If I have thanks, it is a dear expense:
But herein mean I to enrich my pain,
To have his sight thither and back again. *Exit.*

[SCENE II. *Athens*. QUINCE'S *house*.]

Enter QUINCE *the Carpenter*, *and* SNUG *the Joiner*, *and* BOTTOM *the Weaver*, *and* FLUTE *the Bellows Mender*, *and* SNOUT *the Tinker*, *and* STARVELING *the Tailor*.

Quin. Is all our company here?

Bot. You were best to call them generally, man by man, according to the scrip.

Quin. Here is the scroll of every man's name, which is thought fit, through all Athens, to play in our interlude before the duke and the duchess, on his wedding-day at night.

Bot. First, good Peter Quince, say what the play treats on, then read the names of the actors, and so grow to a point.

Quin. Marry, our play is, The most lamentable comedy, and most cruel death of Pyramus and Thisby.

Bot. A very good piece of work, I assure you, and a merry. Now, good Peter Quince, call forth your actors by the scroll. Masters, spread yourselves.

Quin. Answer as I call you. Nick Bottom, the weaver.

Bot. Ready. Name what part I am for, and proceed.

Quin. You, Nick Bottom, are set down for Pyramus.

Bot. What is Pyramus? a lover, or a tyrant?

Quin. A lover, that kills himself most gallant for love.

Bot. That will ask some tears in the true performing of it: if I do it, let the audience look to their eyes; I will move storms, I will condole in some measure. To the rest: yet my chief humour is for a tyrant: I

in blank verse. The transition indicates the lighter import of the conversation of the lovers. 173, 174. **Carthage queen, false Troyan.** According to Virgil (*Aeneid* iv.) Dido, queen of Carthage, slew herself after desertion by the Trojan hero Aeneas. 182. **fair,** beauty; see glossary. 183. **lode-stars,** stars of guidance. 184. **tuneable,** tuneful. 186. **favour,** appearance; or, affection. 190. **bated,** excepted; see glossary. 193. **motion,** impulse; see glossary. 194-201. **I . . . mine.** Each character speaks one line of the dialogue. This artificiality of style is called stichomythia; it is characteristic of classical drama. 197. **affection,** passion; see glossary. **move,** arouse; see glossary. 209. **Phœbe,** Diana, the moon. 215. **faint,** pale. 231. **admiring of,** wondering at; see glossary. 237. **figure,** are a symbol of. 242. **eyne,** eyes; old form of plural. 249. **a dear expense,** a thing which will be costly to me; see *dear* in glossary.

SCENE II. 2. **generally,** Bottom's blunder for "severally." 3. **scrip,** writing, written list. 10. **grow to,** come to. 11. **Marry,** a mild oath; see glossary. 29. **condole,** grieve; here in some blundering sense. 30. **humour,** inclination, whim; see glossary.

could play Ercles rarely, or a part to tear a cat in, to make all split.

The raging rocks
And shivering shocks
Shall break the locks
  Of prison gates;
And Phibbus' car
Shall shine from far
And make and mar
  The foolish Fates.

This was lofty! Now name the rest of the players. This is Ercles' vein, a tyrant's vein; a lover is more condoling.

Quin. Francis Flute, the bellows-mender.

Flu. Here, Peter Quince.

Quin. Flute, you must take Thisby on you.

Flu. What is Thisby? a wandering knight?

Quin. It is the lady that Pyramus must love.

Flu. Nay, faith, let not me play a woman; I have a beard coming.

Quin. That 's all one: you shall play it in a mask, and you may speak as small as you will.

Bot. An I may hide my face, let me play Thisby too, I'll speak in a monstrous little voice, 'Thisne, Thisne;' 'Ah Pyramus, my lover dear! thy Thisby dear, and lady dear!'

Quin. No, no; you must play Pyramus: and, Flute, you Thisby.

Bot. Well, proceed.

Quin. Robin Starveling, the tailor.

Star. Here, Peter Quince.

Quin. Robin Starveling, you must play Thisby's mother. Tom Snout, the tinker.

Snout. Here, Peter Quince.

Quin. You, Pyramus' father: myself, Thisby's father. Snug, the joiner; you, the lion's part: and, I hope, here is a play fitted.

Snug. Have you the lion's part written? pray you, if it be, give it me, for I am slow of study.

Quin. You may do it extempore, for it is nothing but roaring.

Bot. Let me play the lion too: I will roar, that I will do any man's heart good to hear me; I will roar, that I will make the duke say 'Let him roar again, let him roar again.'

Quin. An you should do it too terribly, you would fright the duchess and the ladies, that they would shriek; and that were enough to hang us all.

All. That would hang us, every mother's son.

Bot. I grant you, friends, if that you should fright the ladies out of their wits, they would have no more discretion but to hang us: but I will aggravate my voice so that I will roar you as gently as any sucking dove; I will roar you an 'twere any nightingale.

Quin. You can play no part but Pyramus; for Pyramus is a sweet-faced man; a proper man, as one shall see in a summer's day; a most lovely gentleman-like man: therefore you must needs play Pyramus.

Bot. Well, I will undertake it. What beard were I best to play it in?

Quin. Why, what you will.

Bot. I will discharge it in either your straw-colour beard, your orange-tawny beard, your purple-in-grain beard, or your French-crown-colour beard, your perfect yellow.

Quin. Some of your French crowns have no hair at all, and then you will play barefaced. But, masters, here are your parts: and I am to entreat you, request you and desire you, to con them by to-morrow night; and meet me in the palace wood, a mile without the town, by moonlight; there will we rehearse, for if we meet in the city, we shall be dogged with company, and our devices known. In the meantime I will draw a bill of properties, such as our play wants. I pray you, fail me not.

Bot. We will meet; and there we may rehearse most obscenely and courageously. Take pains; be perfect: adieu.

Quin. At the duke's oak we meet.

Bot. Enough; hold or cut bow-strings. *Exeunt.*

[ACT II.

SCENE I. *A wood near Athens.*]

Enter a Fairy *at one door, and* Robin Goodfellow [Puck] *at another.*

Puck. How now, spirit! whither wander you?

Fai. Over hill, over dale,
    Thorough bush, thorough brier,
  Over park, over pale,
    Thorough flood, thorough fire,
  I do wander every where,
  Swifter than the moon's sphere;
  And I serve the fairy queen,
  To dew her orbs upon the green.
  The cowslips tall her pensioners be:
  In their gold coats spots you see;
  Those be rubies, fairy favours,
  In those freckles live their savours:
I must go seek some dewdrops here
And hang a pearl in every cowslip's ear.
Farewell, thou lob of spirits; I'll be gone:
Our queen and all her elves come here anon.

Puck. The king doth keep his revels here to-night:
Take heed the queen come not within his sight;
For Oberon is passing fell and wrath,
Because that she as her attendant hath
A lovely boy, stolen from an Indian king;
She never had so sweet a changeling;
And jealous Oberon would have the child
Knight of his train, to trace the forests wild;

31. **Ercles,** Hercules, a popular character in Tudor drama. From Seneca's *Hercules Furens* had come the tradition of ranting in this part, as in the case of Herod in the mystery plays. **tear a cat,** proverbial for "rant." 32. **make all split,** proverbial for "cause a commotion." 37. **Phibbus',** Phoebus'. 47. **wandering knight,** knight-errant. 54. **An,** if; see glossary. 84. **aggravate,** Bottom's blunder for "diminish." 88. **proper,** handsome; see glossary. 95. **discharge,** perform. 97. **purple-in-grain,** very deep red. **French-crown-colour,** color of a French crown; a gold coin. 99. **crowns,** heads bald from syphilis, the "French disease." 103. **con,** learn by heart. 107. **devices,** plans. 111. **obscenely,** Bottom's blunder for "obscurely" (?) 114. **hold . . . bow-strings,** an archer's expression not definitely explained, but easy to understand; Chambers suggests, "keep your promises, or give up the play."

Act II. scene I. 3. **Thorough,** through; see glossary. 9. **orbs,** fairy rings. 10. **pensioners,** bodyguards of the sovereign; possible allusion to Queen Elizabeth's fifty gentlemen pensioners. 13. **savours,** sweet smells. 16. **lob,** country bumpkin. 17. **anon,** at once; see glossary. 20. **passing fell,** exceedingly angry; see *passing* in glossary. **wrath,** wrathful. 23. **changeling,** child left by fairies in exchange for one stolen; here, the stolen child. 26. **perforce,** forcibly; see glossary. 30. **square,** quarrel. 33. **shrewd,** mischievous; see glossary. 34. **Robin Goodfellow,** a mischievous household spirit of very ancient folklore; Shakespeare associates him with fairies. 35. **villagery,** villages or villagers collectively. 36. **quern,** handmill. 38. **sometime,** at times; see glossary. **barm,** yeast, froth. 47. **gossip's bowl,** drink of gossiping women. 48. **crab,** crab apple. 50. **dewlap,** loose skin on neck.

But she perforce withholds the loved boy,
Crowns him with flowers and makes him all her joy:
And now they never meet in grove or green,
By fountain clear, or spangled starlight sheen,
But they do square, that all their elves for fear
Creep into acorn-cups and hide them there.

Fai. Either I mistake your shape and making quite,
Or else you are that shrewd and knavish sprite
Call'd Robin Goodfellow: are not you he
That frights the maidens of the villagery;
Skim milk, and sometimes labour in the quern
And bootless make the breathless housewife churn;
And sometime make the drink to bear no barm;
Mislead night-wanderers, laughing at their harm?
Those that Hobgoblin call you and sweet Puck,
You do their work, and they shall have good luck:
Are you not he?

Puck. Thou speakest aright;
I am that merry wanderer of the night.
I jest to Oberon and make him smile
When I a fat and bean-fed horse beguile,
Neighing in likeness of a filly foal:
And sometime lurk I in a gossip's bowl,
In very likeness of a roasted crab,
And when she drinks, against her lips I bob
And on her withered dewlap pour the ale.
The wisest aunt, telling the saddest tale,
Sometime for three-foot stool mistaketh me;
Then slip I from her bum, down topples she,
And 'tailor' cries, and falls into a cough;
And then the whole quire hold their hips and laugh,
And waxen in their mirth and neeze and swear
A merrier hour was never wasted there.
But, room, fairy! here comes Oberon.

Fai. And here my mistress. Would that he were gone!

Enter [OBERON] *the King of Fairies at one door, with his train; and* [TITANIA] *the Queen at another, with hers.*

Obe. Ill met by moonlight, proud Titania.

Tita. What, jealous Oberon! Fairy, skip hence:
I have forsworn his bed and company.

Obe. Tarry, rash wanton: am not I thy lord?

Tita. Then I must be thy lady: but I know
When thou hast stolen away from fairy land,
And in the shape of Corin sat all day,
Playing on pipes of corn and versing love
To amorous Phillida. Why art thou here,
Come from the farthest steep of India?
But that, forsooth, the bouncing Amazon,
Your buskin'd mistress and your warrior love,
To Theseus must be wedded, and you come
To give their bed joy and prosperity.

Obe. How canst thou thus for shame, Titania,
Glance at my credit with Hippolyta,
Knowing I know thy love to Theseus?
Didst thou not lead him through the glimmering night
From Perigenia, whom he ravished?
And make him with fair Ægles break his faith,
With Ariadne and Antiopa?

Tita. These are the forgeries of jealousy:
And never, since the middle summer's spring,
Met we on hill, in dale, forest or mead,
By paved fountain or by rushy brook,
Or in the beached margent of the sea,
To dance our ringlets to the whistling wind,
But with thy brawls thou hast disturb'd our sport.
Therefore the winds, piping to us in vain,
As in revenge, have suck'd up from the sea
Contagious fogs; which falling in the land
Have every pelting river made so proud
That they have overborne their continents:
The ox hath therefore stretch'd his yoke in vain,
The ploughman lost his sweat, and the green corn
Hath rotted ere his youth attain'd a beard;
The fold stands empty in the drowned field,
And crows are fatted with the murrion flock;
The nine men's morris is fill'd up with mud,
And the quaint mazes in the wanton green
For lack of tread are undistinguishable:
The human mortals want their winter here;
No night is now with hymn or carol blest:
Therefore the moon, the governess of floods,
Pale in her anger, washes all the air,
That rheumatic diseases do abound:
And thorough this distemperature we see
The seasons alter: hoary-headed frosts
Fall in the fresh lap of the crimson rose,
And on old Hiems' thin and icy crown
An odorous chaplet of sweet summer buds
Is, as in mockery, set: the spring, the summer,
The childing autumn, angry winter, change
Their wonted liveries, and the mazed world,
By their increase, now knows not which is which:
And this same progeny of evils comes
From our debate, from our dissension;
We are their parents and original.

Obe. Do you amend it then; it lies in you:
Why should Titania cross her Oberon?
I do but beg a little changeling boy,
To be my henchman.

Tita. Set your heart at rest:
The fairy land buys not the child of me.
His mother was a vot'ress of my order:
And, in the spiced Indian air, by night,
Full often hath she gossip'd by my side,
And sat with me on Neptune's yellow sands,
Marking th' embarked traders on the flood,
When we have laugh'd to see the sails conceive
And grow big-bellied with the wanton wind;

51. **aunt,** old woman. 54. **'tailor' cries,** allusion obscure; *NED* suggests that *tailor* (corruption of *tailard*), means "one with a tail." 56. **neeze,** sneeze. 66, 68. **Corin, Phillida,** names of pastoral lovers. 67. **pipes of corn,** tubular wind instruments made of straw. 69. **steep,** mountain range; so F; Globe, following Q_1: *steppe.* 71. **buskin'd,** shod with half boots. 75. **Glance at,** hit at, reflect upon. 78. **Perigenia,** Perigouna (Grant White), daughter of the robber Sinnis; a story from Plutarch. 79. **Ægles,** a nymph beloved by Theseus, for whom he deserted Ariadne; QF: *Eagles,* corrected by Rowe; form should be *Aegles* as in Plutarch's *Life of Theseus,* from which Shakespeare took the names in this passage. 80. **Ariadne,** daughter of Minos, king of Crete; by her aid Theseus slew the Minotaur and escaped from the labyrinth. **Antiopa,** queen of the Amazons and wife of Theseus, elsewhere called Hippolyta. 82. **middle summer's spring,** beginning of midsummer. 85. **in,** on. **margent,** edge, border. 86. **ringlets.** See *orbs* above, line 9. 91. **pelting,** paltry. 92. **continents,** i.e., banks that contain them; see glossary. 97. **murrion,** murrain (plague); here, diseased. 98. **nine men's morris,** rustic game played on a board or on squares laid out on the village green with nine pebbles or pegs. 99. **quaint,** ingeniously wrought; see glossary. **mazes,** figures marked out on the village green for sports. **wanton,** luxuriant or sportive. 101. **want,** lack; see glossary. 106. **distemperature,** disturbance in nature. 109. **Hiems'.** Hiems is the god of winter. 112. **childing,** fruitful. 113. **mazed,** bewildered. 117. **original,** origin. 121. **henchman,** attendant, page.

Which she, with pretty and with swimming gait
Following,—her womb then rich with my young squire,—
Would imitate, and sail upon the land,
To fetch me trifles, and return again,
As from a voyage, rich with merchandise.
But she, being mortal, of that boy did die;
And for her sake do I rear up her boy,
And for her sake I will not part with him.

Obe. How long within this wood intend you stay?

Tita. Perchance till after Theseus' wedding-day.
If you will patiently dance in our round
And see our moonlight revels, go with us;
If not, shun me, and I will spare your haunts.

Obe. Give me that boy, and I will go with thee.

Tita. Not for thy fairy kingdom. Fairies, away!
We shall chide downright, if I longer stay.

Exeunt [Titania with her train].

Obe. Well, go thy way: thou shalt not from this grove
Till I torment thee for this injury.
My gentle Puck, come hither. Thou rememb'rest
Since once I sat upon a promontory,
And heard a mermaid on a dolphin's back
Uttering such dulcet and harmonious breath
That the rude sea grew civil at her song
And certain stars shot madly from their spheres,
To hear the sea-maid's music.

Puck I remember.

Obe. That very time I saw, but thou couldst not,
Flying between the cold moon and the earth,
Cupid all arm'd: a certain aim he took
At a fair vestal throned by the west,
And loos'd his love-shaft smartly from his bow,
As it should pierce a hundred thousand hearts;
But I might see young Cupid's fiery shaft
Quench'd in the chaste beams of the wat'ry moon,
And the imperial vot'ress passed on,
In maiden meditation, fancy-free.
Yet mark'd I where the bolt of Cupid fell:
It fell upon a little western flower,
Before milk-white, now purple with love's wound,
And maidens call it love-in-idleness.
Fetch me that flow'r; the herb I shew'd thee once:
The juice of it on sleeping eye-lids laid
Will make or man or woman madly dote
Upon the next live creature that it sees.
Fetch me this herb; and be thou here again
Ere the leviathan can swim a league.

Puck. I'll put a girdle round about the earth
In forty minutes. *[Exit.]*

Obe. Having once this juice,
I'll watch Titania when she is asleep,
And drop the liquor of it in her eyes.
The next thing then she waking looks upon,
Be it on lion, bear, or wolf, or bull,
On meddling monkey, or on busy ape,
She shall pursue it with the soul of love:
And ere I take this charm from off her sight,
As I can take it with another herb,
I'll make her render up her page to me.
But who comes here? I am invisible;
And I will overhear their conference.

Enter DEMETRIUS, HELENA *following him.*

Dem. I love thee not, therefore pursue me not.
Where is Lysander and fair Hermia?
The one I'll slay, the other slayeth me.
Thou told'st me they were stol'n unto this wood;
And here am I, and wode within this wood,
Because I cannot meet my Hermia.
Hence, get thee gone, and follow me no more.

Hel. You draw me, you hard-hearted adamant;
But yet you draw not iron, for my heart
Is true as steel: leave you your power to draw,
And I shall have no power to follow you.

Dem. Do I entice you? do I speak you fair?
Or, rather, do I not in plainest truth
Tell you, I do not, nor I cannot love you?

Hel. And even for that do I love you the more.
I am your spaniel; and, Demetrius,
The more you beat me, I will fawn on you:
Use me but as your spaniel, spurn me, strike me,
Neglect me, lose me; only give me leave,
Unworthy as I am, to follow you.
What worser place can I beg in your love,—
And yet a place of high respect with me,—
Than to be used as you use your dog?

Dem. Tempt not too much the hatred of my spirit,
For I am sick when I do look on thee.

Hel. And I am sick when I look not on you.

Dem. You do impeach your modesty too much,
To leave the city and commit yourself
Into the hands of one that loves you not;
To trust the opportunity of night
And the ill counsel of a desert place
With the rich worth of your virginity.

Hel. Your virtue is my privilege: for that
It is not night when I do see your face,
Therefore I think I am not in the night;
Nor doth this wood lack worlds of company,
For you in my respect are all the world:
Then how can it be said I am alone,
When all the world is here to look on me?

Dem. I'll run from thee and hide me in the brakes,
And leave thee to the mercy of wild beasts.

Hel. The wildest hath not such a heart as you.
Run when you will, the story shall be chang'd:
Apollo flies, and Daphne holds the chase;
The dove pursues the griffin; the mild hind
Makes speed to catch the tiger; bootless speed,
When cowardice pursues and valour flies.

Dem. I will not stay thy questions; let me go:
Or, if thou follow me, do not believe
But I shall do thee mischief in the wood.

Hel. Ay, in the temple, in the town, the field,
You do me mischief. Fie, Demetrius!
Your wrongs do set a scandal on my sex:
We cannot fight for love, as men may do;
We should be woo'd and were not made to woo.

[Exit Dem.]

I'll follow thee and make a heaven of hell,

148-168. **Thou . . . love-in-idleness.** This famous passage contains an allusion to Queen Elizabeth and probably to some entertainment in her honor at Kenilworth in 1575, or more probably at Elvetham in 1591. 151. **breath,** voice, notes. 157. **all,** fully. 161. **might,** could; see glossary. 168. **love-in-idleness,** pansy, heartsease. 174. **leviathan,** sea monster. 176. **forty,** used indefinitely. 192. **wode,** mad; usual form, wood. 195. **adamant,** very hard stone; here lodestone. 197. **leave,** give up. 199. **fair,** courteously; see glossary. 220. **virtue,** goodness or power to attract. **privilege,** safeguard, warrant. **for that,** because. 224. **in my respect,** as far as I am concerned; or, in my opinion. 231. **Apollo . . . chase,** allusion to the story of Apollo's pursuit of Daphne; here Daphne *holds the chase*, or pursues, instead of Apollo. 232. **griffin,** a fabulous monster with the head of an eagle and the body of a lion. **hind,** female deer. 235. **stay,** wait for; see glossary. **questions,** talk or argu-

To die upon the hand I love so well. [*Exit.*]
Obe. Fare thee well, nymph: ere he do leave this grove,
Thou shalt fly him and he shall seek thy love.

Enter PUCK.

Hast thou the flower there? Welcome, wanderer.
Puck. Ay, there it is.
Obe. I pray thee, give it me.
I know a bank where the wild thyme blows,
Where oxlips and the nodding violet grows,
†Quite over-canopied with luscious woodbine,
With sweet musk-roses and with eglantine:
There sleeps Titania sometime of the night,
Lull'd in these flowers with dances and delight;
And there the snake throws her enamell'd skin,
Weed wide enough to wrap a fairy in:
And with the juice of this I'll streak her eyes,
And make her full of hateful fantasies.
Take thou some of it, and seek through this grove:
A sweet Athenian lady is in love
With a disdainful youth: anoint his eyes;
But do it when the next thing he espies
May be the lady: thou shalt know the man
By the Athenian garments he hath on.
Effect it with some care that he may prove
More fond on her than she upon her love:
And look thou meet me ere the first cock crow.
Puck. Fear not, my lord, your servant shall do so.
Exeunt.

[SCENE II. *Another part of the wood.*]

Enter TITANIA, *Queen of Fairies, with her train.*

Tita. Come, now a roundel and a fairy song;
Then, for the third part of a minute, hence;
Some to kill cankers in the musk-rose buds,
Some war with rere-mice for their leathern wings,
To make my small elves coats, and some keep back
The clamorous owl that nightly hoots and wonders
At our quaint spirits. Sing me now asleep;
Then to your offices and let me rest.

Fairies sing.

You spotted snakes with double tongue,
Thorny hedgehogs, be not seen;
Newts and blind-worms, do no wrong,
Come not near our fairy queen.
Philomel, with melody
Sing in our sweet lullaby;
Lulla, lulla, lullaby, lulla, lulla, lullaby:
Never harm,
Nor spell nor charm,
Come our lovely lady nigh;
So, good night, with lullaby.

First F. Weaving spiders, come not here;
Hence, you long-legg'd spinners, hence!
Beetles black, approach not near;
Worm nor snail, do no offence.
Philomel, with melody, &c.

Sec. F. Hence, away! now all is well:
One aloof stand sentinel.
[*Exeunt Fairies. Titania sleeps.*]

Enter OBERON [*and squeezes the flower on Titania's eyelids*].

Obe. What thou seest when thou dost wake,
Do it for thy true-love take,
Love and languish for his sake:
Be it ounce, or cat, or bear,
Pard, or boar with bristled hair,
In thy eye that shall appear
When thou wak'st, it is thy dear:
Wake when some vile thing is near. [*Exit.*]

Enter LYSANDER *and* HERMIA.

Lys. Fair love, you faint with wand'ring in the wood;
And to speak troth, I have forgot our way:
We'll rest us, Hermia, if you think it good,
And tarry for the comfort of the day.
Her. Be it so, Lysander: find you out a bed;
For I upon this bank will rest my head.
Lys. One turf shall serve as pillow for us both;
One heart, one bed, two bosoms and one troth.
Her. Nay, good Lysander; for my sake, my dear,
Lie further off yet, do not lie so near.
Lys. O, take the sense, sweet, of my innocence!
Love takes the meaning in love's conference.
I mean, that my heart unto yours is knit
So that but one heart we can make of it;
Two bosoms interchained with an oath;
So then two bosoms and a single troth.
Then by your side no bed-room me deny;
For lying so, Hermia, I do not lie.
Her. Lysander riddles very prettily:
Now much beshrew my manners and my pride,
If Hermia meant to say Lysander lied.
But, gentle friend, for love and courtesy
Lie further off; in human modesty,
Such separation as may well be said
Becomes a virtuous bachelor and a maid,
So far be distant; and, good night, sweet friend:
Thy love ne'er alter till thy sweet life end!
Lys. Amen, amen, to that fair prayer, say I;
And then end life when I end loyalty!
Here is my bed: sleep give thee all his rest!
Her. With half that wish the wisher's eyes be press'd!
[*They sleep.*]

Enter PUCK.

Puck. Through the forest have I gone,
But Athenian found I none,
On whose eyes I might approve
This flower's force in stirring love.
Night and silence.—Who is here?
Weeds of Athens he doth wear:
This is he, my master said,
Despised the Athenian maid;
And here the maiden, sleeping sound,
On the dank and dirty ground.
Pretty soul! she durst not lie

ment. 244. **upon,** by. 250. **oxlips,** flowers resembling cowslip and primrose. 251. **woodbine,** honeysuckle. 252. **eglantine,** sweetbriar. 254. **dances and delight,** delightful dances. 255. **throws . . . skin,** sloughs off her enamel-like skin. 256. **Weed,** garment; see glossary. 257. **streak,** stroke, touch softly. 266. **fond on,** doting on; see *fond* in glossary.

SCENE II. 1. **roundel,** dance in a ring. 3. **cankers,** cankerworms. 4. **rere-mice,** bats. 11. **Newts,** lizards. 13. **Philomel,** nightingale; Philomela, daughter of Pandion, was transformed into a nightingale in a familiar story in Ovid, *Metamorphoses*, vi. 30. **ounce,** lynx. 31. **Pard,** panther or leopard. 36. **troth,** truth. 42. **troth,** faith, troth-plight. 45. **sense,** import; see glossary. 51. **deny,** refuse; see glossary. 54. **beshrew,** curse (but mildly meant). 57. **human,** humane, courteous. 68. **approve,** test, prove.

Near this lack-love, this kill-courtesy.
Churl, upon thy eyes I throw
All the power this charm doth owe.
When thou wak'st, let love forbid
Sleep his seat on thy eyelid:
So awake when I am gone;
For I must now to Oberon. *Exit.*

Enter DEMETRIUS *and* HELENA, *running.*

Hel. Stay, though thou kill me, sweet Demetrius.
Dem. I charge thee, hence, and do not haunt me thus.
Hel. O, wilt thou darkling leave me? do not so.
Dem. Stay, on thy peril: I alone will go. [*Exit.*]
Hel. O, I am out of breath in this fond chase!
The more my prayer, the lesser is my grace.
Happy is Hermia, wheresoe'er she lies;
For she hath blessed and attractive eyes.
How came her eyes so bright? Not with salt tears:
If so, my eyes are oft'ner wash'd than hers.
No, no, I am as ugly as a bear;
For beasts that meet me run away for fear:
Therefore no marvel though Demetrius
Do, as a monster, fly my presence thus.
What wicked and dissembling glass of mine
Made me compare with Hermia's sphery eyne?
But who is here? Lysander! on the ground!
Dead? or asleep? I see no blood, no wound.
Lysander, if you live, good sir, awake.
Lys. [*Awaking*] And run through fire I will for thy sweet sake.
Transparent Helena! Nature shows art,
That through thy bosom makes me see thy heart.
Where is Demetrius? O, how fit a word
Is that vile name to perish on my sword!
Hel. Do not say so, Lysander; say not so.
What though he love your Hermia? Lord, what though?
Yet Hermia still loves you: then be content.
Lys. Content with Hermia! No; I do repent
The tedious minutes I with her have spent.
Not Hermia but Helena I love:
Who will not change a raven for a dove?
The will of man is by his reason sway'd;
And reason says you are the worthier maid.
Things growing are not ripe until their season:
So I, being young, till now ripe not to reason;
And touching now the point of human skill,
Reason becomes the marshal to my will
And leads me to your eyes, where I o'erlook
Love's stories written in love's richest book.
Hel. Wherefore was I to this keen mockery born?
When at your hands did I deserve this scorn?
Is 't not enough, is 't not enough, young man,
That I did never, no, nor never can,
Deserve a sweet look from Demetrius' eye,
But you must flout my insufficiency?
Good troth, you do me wrong, good sooth, you do,
In such disdainful manner me to woo.
But fare you well: perforce I must confess
I thought you lord of more true gentleness.
O, that a lady, of one man refus'd,
Should of another therefore be abus'd! *Exit.*
Lys. She sees not Hermia. Hermia, sleep thou there:
And never mayst thou come Lysander near!
For as a surfeit of the sweetest things
The deepest loathing to the stomach brings,
Or as the heresies that men do leave
Are hated most of those they did deceive,
So thou, my surfeit and my heresy,
Of all be hated, but the most of me!
And, all my powers, address your love and might
To honour Helen and to be her knight! *Exit.*
Her. [*Awaking*] Help me, Lysander, help me! do thy best
To pluck this crawling serpent from my breast!
Ay me, for pity! what a dream was here!
Lysander, look how I do quake with fear:
Methought a serpent eat my heart away,
And you sat smiling at his cruel prey.
Lysander! what, remov'd? Lysander! lord!
What, out of hearing? gone? no sound, no word?
Alack, where are you? speak, an if you hear;
Speak, of all loves! I swoon almost with fear.
No? then I well perceive you are not nigh:
Either death or you I'll find immediately. *Exit.*

[ACT III.

SCENE I. *The wood. Titania lying asleep.*]

Enter the Clowns [QUINCE, SNUG, BOTTOM, FLUTE, SNOUT, *and* STARVELING].

Bot. Are we all met?

Quin. Pat, pat; and here 's a marvellous convenient place for our rehearsal. This green plot shall be our stage, this hawthorn-brake our tiring-house; and we will do it in action as we will do it before the duke.

Bot. Peter Quince,—

Quin. What sayest thou, bully Bottom?

Bot. There are things in this comedy of Pyramus and Thisby that will never please. First, Pyramus must draw a sword to kill himself; which the ladies cannot abide. How answer you that?

Snout. By 'r lakin, a parlous fear.

Star. I believe we must leave the killing out, when all is done.

Bot. Not a whit: I have a device to make all well. Write me a prologue; and let the prologue seem to say, we will do no harm with our swords and that Pyramus is not killed indeed; and, for the more better assurance, tell them that I Pyramus am not Pyramus, but Bottom the weaver: this will put them out of fear.

Quin. Well, we will have such a prologue; and it shall be written in eight and six.

Bot. No, make it two more; let it be written in eight and eight.

Snout. Will not the ladies be afeard of the lion?

Star. I fear it, I promise you.

79. **owe,** own; see glossary. 86. **darkling,** in the dark. 89. **grace,** favor I obtain; see glossary. 90. **lies,** dwells; see glossary. 99. **sphery eyne,** starlike eyes. 103. **run through fire,** proverbial for any hard task. 118. **ripe,** usually understood as a verb in this passage meaning "grow ripe." 133. **of,** by; see glossary. 134. **abus'd,** maltreated; see glossary. 150. **prey,** act of preying upon. 154. **of all loves,** for all love's sake.

ACT III. SCENE I. 5. **tiring-house,** dressing room. 8. **bully,** term of companionship. 14. **By 'r lakin,** by our ladykin, i.e., the Virgin Mary. **parlous,** perilous. 25. **eight and six,** alternate lines of eight and six syllables, ballad measure. 32. **lion among ladies.** Malone called attention to a pamphlet (*Somers' Tracts*, ii, 179) which tells how at the christening of Prince Henry, eldest son of King James I, then James VI of Scotland, a "blackmoor" instead of a lion drew the triumphal chariot, since the lion's presence might have "brought some fear to the nearest." 33. **fearful,** fear-inspiring; see glossary. 40. **de-**

Bot. Masters, you ought to consider with yourselves: to bring in—God shield us!—a lion among ladies, is a most dreadful thing; for there is not a more fearful wild-fowl than your lion living; and we ought to look to 't.

Snout. Therefore another prologue must tell he is not a lion.

Bot. Nay, you must name his name, and half his face must be seen through the lion's neck: and he himself must speak through, saying thus, or to the same defect, —'Ladies,'—or 'Fair ladies,—I would wish you,'—or 'I would request you,'—or 'I would entreat you,—not to fear, not to tremble: my life for yours. If you think I come hither as a lion, it were pity of my life: no, I am no such thing; I am a man as other men are;' and there indeed let him name his name, and tell them plainly he is Snug the joiner.

Quin. Well, it shall be so. But there is two hard things; that is, to bring the moonlight into a chamber; for, you know, Pyramus and Thisby meet by moonlight.

Snout. Doth the moon shine that night we play our play?

Bot. A calendar, a calendar! look in the almanac; find out moonshine, find out moonshine.

Quin. Yes, it doth shine that night.

Bot. Why, then may you leave a casement of the great chamber window, where we play, open, and the moon may shine in at the casement.

Quin. Ay; or else one must come in with a bush of thorns and a lanthorn, and say he comes to disfigure, or to present, the person of Moonshine. Then, there is another thing: we must have a wall in the great chamber; for Pyramus and Thisby, says the story, did talk through the chink of a wall.

Snout. You can never bring in a wall. What say you, Bottom?

Bot. Some man or other must present Wall: and let him have some plaster, or some loam, or some rough-cast about him, to signify wall; and let him hold his fingers thus, and through that cranny shall Pyramus and Thisby whisper.

Quin. If that may be, then all is well. Come, sit down, every mother's son, and rehearse your parts. Pyramus, you begin: when you have spoken your speech, enter into that brake: and so every one according to his cue.

Enter ROBIN [PUCK].

Puck. What hempen home-spuns have we
swagg'ring here,
So near the cradle of the fairy queen?
What, a play toward! I'll be an auditor;
An actor too perhaps, if I see cause.

Quin. Speak, Pyramus. Thisby, stand forth.

Bot. Thisby, the flowers of odious savours sweet,—

Quin. Odours, odours.

Bot. —— odours savours sweet:
So hath thy breath, my dearest Thisby dear.
But hark, a voice! stay thou but here awhile,
And by and by I will to thee appear. *Exit.*

Puck. A stranger Pyramus than e'er played here.
[*Exit.*]

Flu. Must I speak now?

Quin. Ay, marry, must you; for you must understand he goes but to see a noise that he heard, and is to come again.

Flu. Most radiant Pyramus, most lily-white of hue,
Of colour like the red rose on triumphant brier,
Most brisky juvenal and eke most lovely Jew,
As true as truest horse that yet would never tire.
I'll meet thee, Pyramus, at Ninny's tomb.

Quin. 'Ninus' tomb,' man: why, you must not speak that yet; that you answer to Pyramus: you speak all your part at once, cues and all. Pyramus enter: your cue is past; it is, 'never tire.'

Flu. O,—As true as truest horse, that yet would
never tire.

[*Enter* PUCK, *and* PYRAMUS *with the ass head.*]

Bot. If I were fair, Thisby, I were only thine.

Quin. O monstrous! O strange! we are haunted.
Pray, masters! fly, masters! Help!
[*Exeunt Quince, Snug, Flute, Snout, and Starveling.*]

Puck. I'll follow you, I'll lead you about a round,
Through bog, through bush, through brake,
through brier:
Sometime a horse I'll be, sometime a hound,
A hog, a headless bear, sometime a fire;
And neigh, and bark, and grunt, and roar, and burn,
Like horse, hound, hog, bear, fire, at every turn. *Exit.*

Bot. Why do they run away? this is a knavery of them to make me afeard.

Enter SNOUT.

Snout. O Bottom, thou art changed! what do I see on thee?

Bot. What do you see? you see an ass-head of your own, do you? [*Exit Snout.*]

Enter QUINCE.

Quin. Bless thee, Bottom! bless thee! thou art translated. *Exit.*

Bot. I see their knavery: this is to make an ass of me; to fright me, if they could. But I will not stir from this place, do what they can: I will walk up and down here, and I will sing, that they shall hear I am not afraid. [*Sings.*]

The ousel cock so black of hue,
With orange-tawny bill,
The throstle with his note so true,
The wren with little quill,—

Tita. [*Awaking*] What angel wakes me from my
flow'ry bed?

Bot. [*Sings*]
The finch, the sparrow and the lark,
The plain-song cuckoo gray,
Whose note full many a man doth mark,
And dares not answer nay;—
for, indeed, who would set his wit to so foolish a bird?

fect, Bottom's blunder for "effect." 44. **pity of my life,** i.e., my life would be in jeopardy. 61. **bush of thorns.** According to legend, the man in the moon was a person who had been banished there for gathering firewood on Sundays. 62. **disfigure,** blunder for "prefigure." **present,** represent; see glossary. 71. **rough-cast,** a mixture of lime and gravel used to plaster the outside of buildings. 81. **toward,** about to take place; see glossary. 97. **brisky juvenal,** brisk juvenile or youth. **Jew,** probably an absurd repetition of the first syllable of *juvenal*. 100. **'Ninus,'** mythical founder of Babylon, at which place the scene of the story of Pyramus and Thisby is laid. 106. *Stage Direction:* **Pyramus . . . ass head.** As in F; indicates a particular stage property. 122. **translated,** transformed. 128. **ousel,** blackbird. 134. **plain-song,** melody without variations; here used as an adjective.

who would give a bird the lie, though he cry 'cuckoo' never so?

Tita. I pray thee, gentle mortal, sing again:
Mine ear is much enamoured of thy note;
So is mine eye enthralled to thy shape;
And thy fair virtue's force perforce doth move me
On the first view to say, to swear, I love thee.

Bot. Methinks, mistress, you should have little reason for that: and yet, to say the truth, reason and love keep little company together now-a-days; the more the pity that some honest neighbours will not make them friends. Nay, I can gleek upon occasion.

Tita. Thou art as wise as thou art beautiful.

Bot. Not so, neither: but if I had wit enough to get out of this wood, I have enough to serve mine own turn.

Tita. Out of this wood do not desire to go:
Thou shalt remain here, whether thou wilt or no.
I am a spirit of no common rate:
The summer still doth tend upon my state;
And I do love thee: therefore, go with me;
I'll give thee fairies to attend on thee,
And they shall fetch thee jewels from the deep,
And sing while thou on pressed flowers dost sleep:
And I will purge thy mortal grossness so
That thou shalt like an airy spirit go.
Peaseblossom! Cobweb! Moth! and Mustardseed!

Enter four Fairies [PEASEBLOSSOM, COBWEB, MOTH, *and* MUSTARDSEED].

Peas. Ready.
Cob. And I.
Moth. And I.
Mus. And I.
All. Where shall we go?

Tita. Be kind and courteous to this gentleman;
Hop in his walks and gambol in his eyes;
Feed him with apricocks and dewberries,
With purple grapes, green figs, and mulberries;
The honey-bags steal from the humble-bees,
And for night-tapers crop their waxen thighs
And light them at the fiery glow-worm's eyes,
To have my love to bed and to arise;
And pluck the wings from painted butterflies
To fan the moonbeams from his sleeping eyes:
Nod to him, elves, and do him courtesies.

Peas. Hail, mortal!
Cob. Hail!
Moth. Hail!
Mus. Hail!

Bot. I cry your worships mercy, heartily: I beseech your worship's name.

Cob. Cobweb.

Bot. I shall desire you of more acquaintance, good Master Cobweb: if I cut my finger, I shall make bold with you. Your name, honest gentleman?

Peas. Peaseblossom.

Bot. I pray you, commend me to Mistress Squash, your mother, and to Master Peascod, your father. Good Master Peaseblossom, I shall desire you of more acquaintance too. Your name, I beseech you, sir?

Mus. Mustardseed.

Bot. Good Master Mustardseed, I know your patience well: that same cowardly, giant-like ox-beef hath devoured many a gentleman of your house: I promise you your kindred hath made my eyes water ere now. I desire you of more acquaintance, good Master Mustardseed.

Tita. Come wait upon him; lead him to my bower.
The moon methinks looks with a wat'ry eye;
And when she weeps, weeps every little flower,
Lamenting some enforced chastity.
Tie up my lover's tongue, bring him silently. *Exeunt.*

[SCENE II. *Another part of the wood.*]

Enter [OBERON,] *King of Fairies.*

Obe. I wonder if Titania be awak'd;
Then, what it was that next came in her eye,
Which she must dote on in extremity.

[*Enter*] ROBIN GOODFELLOW [PUCK].

Here comes my messenger.
How now, mad spirit!
What night-rule now about this haunted grove?

Puck. My mistress with a monster is in love.
Near to her close and consecrated bower,
While she was in her dull and sleeping hour,
A crew of patches, rude mechanicals,
That work for bread upon Athenian stalls,
Were met together to rehearse a play
Intended for great Theseus' nuptial-day.
The shallowest thick-skin of that barren sort,
Who Pyramus presented, in their sport
Forsook his scene and ent'red in a brake:
When I did him at this advantage take,
An ass's nole I fixed on his head:
Anon his Thisby must be answered,
And forth my mimic comes. When they him spy,
As wild geese that the creeping fowler eye,
Or russet-pated choughs, many in sort,
Rising and cawing at the gun's report,
Sever themselves and madly sweep the sky,
So, at his sight, away his fellows fly;
And, at our stamp, here o'er and o'er one falls;
He murder cries and help from Athens calls.
Their sense thus weak, lost with their fears thus strong,
Made senseless things begin to do them wrong;
For briers and thorns at their apparel snatch;
Some sleeves, some hats, from yielders all things catch.
I led them on in this distracted fear,
And left sweet Pyramus translated there:
When in that moment, so it came to pass,
Titania wak'd and straightway lov'd an ass.

Obe. This falls out better than I could devise.
But hast thou yet latch'd the Athenian's eyes
With the love-juice, as I did bid thee do?

Puck. I took him sleeping,—that is finish'd too,—
And the Athenian woman by his side;
That, when he wak'd, of force she must be ey'd.

143. **thy fair virtue's force,** the power of thy beauty. 150. **gleek,** scoff, jest. 154. **serve . . . turn,** answer my purpose; see glossary. 157. **rate,** rank. 158. **still,** ever, always; see glossary. 191. **Squash,** unripe pea pod. 197. **patience,** what you have endured. 205. **enforced,** forced, violated.

SCENE II. 2. **next,** nearest, first. 3. **in extremity,** to the utmost degree. 5. **night-rule,** regular diversion for the night. 9. **patches,** clowns, fools. **mechanicals,** artisans, workingmen. 13. **barren sort,** stupid company or crew. 17. **nole,** head. 19. **mimic,** burlesque actor. 21. **choughs,** probably, jackdaws; Clarendon Press reads *russet-patted,* meaning "red-legged," to refer to the Cornish chough. 36. **latch'd,** caught and held fast as by a charm. 40. **of force,** perforce. 45. **use,** treat; see glossary. 57. **dead,** deadly. 65. **Out,** expression of impatience; see glossary. 70. **brave touch,** noble exploit. 71. **worm,**

Enter DEMETRIUS *and* HERMIA.

Obe. Stand close: this is the same Athenian.
Puck. This is the woman, but not this the man.
Dem. O, why rebuke you him that loves you so?
Lay breath so bitter on your bitter foe.
Her. Now I but chide; but I should use thee worse,
For thou, I fear, hast given me cause to curse.
If thou hast slain Lysander in his sleep,
Being o'er shoes in blood, plunge in the deep,
And kill me too.
The sun was not so true unto the day
As he to me: would he have stolen away
From sleeping Hermia? I'll believe as soon
This whole earth may be bor'd and that the moon
May through the centre creep and so displease
Her brother's noontide with th' Antipodes.
It cannot be but thou hast murd'red him;
So should a murderer look, so dead, so grim.
Dem. So should the murdered look, and so should I,
Pierc'd through the heart with your stern cruelty:
Yet you, the murderer, look as bright, as clear,
As yonder Venus in her glimmering sphere.
Her. What 's this to my Lysander? where is he?
Ah, good Demetrius, wilt thou give him me?
Dem. I had rather give his carcass to my hounds.
Her. Out, dog! out, cur! thou driv'st me past the bounds
Of maiden's patience. Hast thou slain him, then?
Henceforth be never numb'red among men!
O, once tell true, tell true, even for my sake!
Durst thou have look'd upon him being awake,
And hast thou kill'd him sleeping? O brave touch!
Could not a worm, an adder, do so much?
An adder did it; for with doubler tongue
Than thine, thou serpent, never adder stung.
Dem. You spend your passion on a mispris'd mood:
I am not guilty of Lysander's blood;
Nor is he dead, for aught that I can tell.
Her. I pray thee, tell me then that he is well.
Dem. An if I could, what should I get therefore?
Her. A privilege never to see me more.
And from thy hated presence part I so:
See me no more, whether he be dead or no. *Exit.*
Dem. There is no following her in this fierce vein:
Here therefore for a while I will remain.
So sorrow's heaviness doth heavier grow
For debt that bankrout sleep doth sorrow owe;
Which now in some slight measure it will pay,
If for his tender here I make some stay.
Lie down [and sleep].
Obe. What hast thou done? thou hast mistaken quite
And laid the love-juice on some true-love's sight:
Of thy misprision must perforce ensue
Some true love turn'd and not a false turn'd true.
Puck. Then fate o'er-rules, that, one man holding troth,
A million fail, confounding oath on oath.
Obe. About the wood go swifter than the wind,
And Helena of Athens look thou find:
All fancy-sick she is and pale of cheer,
With sighs of love, that costs the fresh blood dear:
By some illusion see thou bring her here:
I'll charm his eyes against she do appear.
Puck. I go, I go; look how I go,
Swifter than arrow from the Tartar's bow. [*Exit.*]
Obe. Flower of this purple dye,
Hit with Cupid's archery,
Sink in apple of his eye.
When his love he doth espy,
Let her shine as gloriously
As the Venus of the sky.
When thou wak'st, if she be by,
Beg of her for remedy.

Enter PUCK.

Puck. Captain of our fairy band,
Helena is here at hand;
And the youth, mistook by me,
Pleading for a lover's fee.
Shall we their fond pageant see?
Lord, what fools these mortals be!
Obe. Stand aside: the noise they make
Will cause Demetrius to awake.
Puck. Then will two at once woo one;
That must needs be sport alone;
And those things do best please me
That befal prepost'rously.

Enter LYSANDER *and* HELENA.

Lys. Why should you think that I should woo in scorn?
Scorn and derision never come in tears:
Look, when I vow, I weep; and vows so born,
In their nativity all truth appears.
How can these things in me seem scorn to you,
Bearing the badge of faith, to prove them true?
Hel. You do advance your cunning more and more.
When truth kills truth, O devilish-holy fray!
These vows are Hermia's: will you give her o'er?
Weigh oath with oath, and you will nothing weigh:
Your vows to her and me, put in two scales,
Will even weigh, and both as light as tales.
Lys. I had no judgement when to her I swore.
Hel. Nor none, in my mind, now you give her o'er.
Lys. Demetrius loves her, and he loves not you.
Dem. [*Awaking*] O Helen, goddess, nymph, perfect, divine!
To what, my love, shall I compare thine eyne?
Crystal is muddy. O, how ripe in show
Thy lips, those kissing cherries, tempting grow!
That pure congealed white, high Taurus' snow,
Fann'd with the eastern wind, turns to a crow
When thou hold'st up thy hand: O, let me kiss
This princess of pure white, this seal of bliss!
Hel. O spite! O hell! I see you all are bent
To set against me for your merriment:
If you were civil and knew courtesy,
You would not do me thus much injury.
Can you not hate me, as I know you do,
But you must join in souls to mock me too?
If you were men, as men you are in show,

serpent. 74. **passion,** violent feelings; see glossary. **misprised,** mistaken. 86-87. **Which . . . stay,** i.e., if he waits until sleep "tenders" itself, he will derive some relief for his sorrow. 90. **misprision,** mistake. 93. **confounding . . . oath,** i.e., invalidating one oath with another; see *confound* in glossary. 96. **fancy-sick,** lovesick. **cheer,** face. 97. **sighs . . . blood,** allusion to the physiological theory that each sigh cost the heart a drop of blood. 101. **Tartar's bow.** Tartars were famed for their skill with the bow. 114. **fond pageant,** foolish exhibition; see *fond* and *pageant* in glossary. 121. **prepost'rously,** in inverted order. 124-125. **vows . . . appears,** i.e., vows made by one who is weeping give evidence thereby of their sincerity. 135. **mind,** opinion; see glossary. 141. **Taurus',** a lofty mountain range in Asia Minor. 144. **seal,** pledge, covenant.

You would not use a gentle lady so;
To vow, and swear, and superpraise my parts,
When I am sure you hate me with your hearts.
You both are rivals, and love Hermia;
And now both rivals, to mock Helena:
A trim exploit, a manly enterprise,
To conjure tears up in a poor maid's eyes
With your derision! none of noble sort
Would so offend a virgin and extort
A poor soul's patience, all to make you sport.
Lys. You are unkind, Demetrius; be not so;
For you love Hermia; this you know I know:
And here, with all good will, with all my heart,
In Hermia's love I yield you up my part;
And yours of Helena to me bequeath,
Whom I do love and will do till my death.
Hel. Never did mockers waste more idle breath.
Dem. Lysander, keep thy Hermia; I will none:
If e'er I lov'd her, all that love is gone.
My heart to her but as guest-wise sojourn'd,
And now to Helen is it home return'd,
There to remain.
Lys. Helen, it is not so.
Dem. Disparage not the faith thou dost not know,
Lest, to thy peril, thou aby it dear.
Look, where thy love comes; yonder is thy dear.

Enter HERMIA.

Her. Dark night, that from the eye his function takes,
The ear more quick of apprehension makes;
Wherein it doth impair the seeing sense,
It pays the hearing double recompense.
Thou art not by mine eye, Lysander, found;
Mine ear, I thank it, brought me to thy sound.
But why unkindly didst thou leave me so?
Lys. Why should he stay, whom love doth press to go?
Her. What love could press Lysander from my side?
Lys. Lysander's love, that would not let him bide,
Fair Helena, who more engilds the night
Than all yon fiery oes and eyes of light.
Why seek'st thou me? could not this make thee know,
The hate I bear thee made me leave thee so?
Her. You speak not as you think: it cannot be.
Hel. Lo, she is one of this confederacy!
Now I perceive they have conjoin'd all three
To fashion this false sport, in spite of me.
Injurious Hermia! most ungrateful maid!
Have you conspir'd, have you with these contriv'd
To bait me with this foul derision?
Is all the counsel that we two have shar'd,
The sisters' vows, the hours that we have spent,
When we have chid the hasty-footed time
For parting us,—O, is it all forgot?
All school-days' friendship, childhood innocence?
We, Hermia, like two artificial gods,
Have with our needles created both one flower,
Both on one sampler, sitting on one cushion,
Both warbling of one song, both in one key,
As if our hands, our sides, voices and minds,
Had been incorporate. So we grew together,
Like to a double cherry, seeming parted,
But yet an union in partition;
Two lovely berries moulded on one stem;
So, with two seeming bodies, but one heart;
Two of the first, like coats in heraldry,
Due but to one and crowned with one crest.
And will you rent our ancient love asunder,
To join with men in scorning your poor friend?
It is not friendly, 'tis not maidenly:
Our sex, as well as I, may chide you for it,
Though I alone do feel the injury.
Her. I am amazed at your passionate words.
I scorn you not: it seems that you scorn me.
Hel. Have you not set Lysander, as in scorn,
To follow me and praise my eyes and face?
And made your other love, Demetrius,
Who even but now did spurn me with his foot,
To call me goddess, nymph, divine and rare,
Precious, celestial? Wherefore speaks he this
To her he hates? and wherefore doth Lysander
Deny your love, so rich within his soul,
And tender me, forsooth, affection,
But by your setting on, by your consent?
What though I be not so in grace as you,
So hung upon with love, so fortunate,
But miserable most, to love unlov'd?
This you should pity rather than despise.
Her. I understand not what you mean by this.
Hel. Ay, do, persever, counterfeit sad looks,
Make mouths upon me when I turn my back;
Wink each at other; hold the sweet jest up:
This sport, well carried, shall be chronicled.
If you have any pity, grace, or manners,
You would not make me such an argument.
But fare ye well: 'tis partly my own fault;
Which death or absence soon shall remedy.
Lys. Stay, gentle Helena; hear my excuse:
My love, my life, my soul, fair Helena!
Hel. O excellent!
Her. Sweet, do not scorn her so.
Dem. If she cannot entreat, I can compel.
Lys. Thou canst compel no more than she entreat:
Thy threats have no more strength than her weak prayers.
Helen, I love thee; by my life, I do:
I swear by that which I will lose for thee,
To prove him false that says I love thee not.
Dem. I say I love thee more than he can do.
Lys. If thou say so, withdraw, and prove it too.
Dem. Quick, come!
Her. Lysander, whereto tends all this?
Lys. Away, you Ethiope!
Dem. †No, no; he'll . . .
Seem to break loose; take on as you would follow,
But yet come not: you are a tame man, go!
Lys. Hang off, thou cat, thou burr! vile thing, let loose,
Or I will shake thee from me like a serpent!
Her. Why are you grown so rude? what change is this?

153. **superpraise,** overpraise. **parts,** qualities. 157. **trim,** pretty; used ironically. 169. **will none,** i.e., of her. 175. **aby,** pay for. 177. **his,** its; see glossary. 188. **oes,** general word for "circles" and "orbs." 195. **Injurious,** insulting. 196. **contriv'd,** plotted; see glossary. 203. **artificial,** skilled in art. 208. **incorporate,** united in one body. 213. **Two of the first,** i.e., two bodies, referred to like colors in the description of a coat-of-arms. "The first" is the color first mentioned.

237. **persever,** persevere; accented on the second syllable. **sad,** grave, serious; see glossary. 238. **Make mouths upon,** make faces at. 240. **carried,** managed; see glossary. 242. **argument,** subject for a story; see glossary. 257. **No, no; he'll.** Q: *No, no: heele.* F: *No, no, Sir;* text apparently corrupt. We may understand that Demetrius first addresses Helena and breaks off, then turns to chide Lysander. 260. **Hang off,** let go. 272. **what news?** What is the matter? 274.

Sweet love,—
Lys. Thy love! out, tawny Tartar, out!
Out, loathed med'cine! O hated potion, hence!
Her. Do you not jest?
Hel. Yes, sooth; and so do you.
Lys. Demetrius, I will keep my word with thee.
Dem. I would I had your bond, for I perceive
A weak bond holds you: I'll not trust your word.
Lys. What, should I hurt her, strike her, kill her dead?
Although I hate her, I'll not harm her so.
Her. What, can you do me greater harm than hate?
Hate me! wherefore? O me! what news, my love!
Am not I Hermia? are not you Lysander?
I am as fair now as I was erewhile.
Since night you lov'd me; yet since night you left me:
Why, then you left me—O, the gods forbid!—
In earnest, shall I say?
Lys. Ay, by my life;
And never did desire to see thee more.
Therefore be out of hope, of question, of doubt;
Be certain, nothing truer; 'tis no jest
That I do hate thee and love Helena.
Her. O me! you juggler! you cankerblossom!
You thief of love! what, have you come by night
And stol'n my love's heart from him?
Hel. Fine, i' faith!
Have you no modesty, no maiden shame,
No touch of bashfulness? What, will you tear
Impatient answers from my gentle tongue?
Fie, fie! you counterfeit, you puppet, you!
Her. Puppet? why so? ay, that way goes the game.
Now I perceive that she hath made compare
Between our statures; she hath urg'd her height;
And with her personage, her tall personage,
Her height, forsooth, she hath prevail'd with him.
And are you grown so high in his esteem,
Because I am so dwarfish and so low?
How low am I, thou painted maypole? speak;
How low am I? I am not yet so low
But that my nails can reach unto thine eyes.
Hel. I pray you, though you mock me, gentlemen,
Let her not hurt me: I was never curst;
I have no gift at all in shrewishness;
I am a right maid for my cowardice:
Let her not strike me. You perhaps may think,
Because she is something lower than myself,
That I can match her.
Her. Lower! hark, again.
Hel. Good Hermia, do not be so bitter with me.
I evermore did love you, Hermia,
Did ever keep your counsels, never wrong'd you;
Save that, in love unto Demetrius,
I told him of your stealth unto this wood.
He followed you; for love I followed him;
But he hath chid me hence and threat'ned me
To strike me, spurn me, nay, to kill me too:
And now, so you will let me quiet go,
To Athens will I bear my folly back
And follow you no further: let me go:
You see how simple and how fond I am.
Her. Why, get you gone: who is 't that hinders you?
Hel. A foolish heart, that I leave here behind.
Her. What, with Lysander?
Hel. With Demetrius.
Lys. Be not afraid; she shall not harm thee, Helena.
Dem. No, sir, she shall not, though you take her part.
Hel. O, when she 's angry, she is keen and shrewd!
She was a vixen when she went to school;
And though she be but little, she is fierce.
Her. 'Little' again! nothing but 'low' and 'little'!
Why will you suffer her to flout me thus?
Let me come to her.
Lys. Get you gone, you dwarf;
You minimus, of hind'ring knot-grass made;
You bead, you acorn.
Dem. You are too officious
In her behalf that scorns your services.
Let her alone: speak not of Helena;
Take not her part; for, if thou dost intend
Never so little show of love to her,
Thou shalt aby it.
Lys. Now she holds me not;
Now follow, if thou dar'st, to try whose right,
Of thine or mine, is most in Helena. [*Exit.*]
Dem. Follow! nay, I'll go with thee, cheek by jowl. [*Exit, following Lysander.*]
Her. You, mistress, all this coil is 'long of you:
Nay, go not back.
Hel. I will not trust you, I,
Nor longer stay in your curst company.
Your hands than mine are quicker for a fray,
My legs are longer though, to run away. [*Exit.*]
Her. I am amaz'd, and know not what to say. *Exit.*
Obe. This is thy negligence: still thou mistak'st,
Or else committ'st thy knaveries wilfully.
Puck. Believe me, king of shadows, I mistook.
Did not you tell me I should know the man
By the Athenian garments he had on?
And so far blameless proves my enterprise,
That I have 'nointed an Athenian's eyes;
And so far am I glad it so did sort
As this their jangling I esteem a sport.
Obe. Thou see'st these lovers seek a place to fight:
Hie therefore, Robin, overcast the night;
The starry welkin cover thou anon
With drooping fog as black as Acheron,
And lead these testy rivals so astray
As one come not within another's way.
Like to Lysander sometime frame thy tongue,
Then stir Demetrius up with bitter wrong;
And sometime rail thou like Demetrius;
And from each other look thou lead them thus,
Till o'er their brows death-counterfeiting sleep
With leaden legs and batty wings doth creep:
Then crush this herb into Lysander's eye;
Whose liquor hath this virtuous property,
To take from thence all error with his might,
And make his eyeballs roll with wonted sight.
When they next wake, all this derision
Shall seem a dream and fruitless vision,
And back to Athens shall the lovers wend,

erewhile, just now. 288. **puppet.** This word, *Ethiope* (l. 257), and *dwarfish* (l. 295) indicate that Hermia is short and dark. 300. **curst,** shrewish; see glossary. 302. **right,** true. 304. **something,** somewhat; see glossary. 310. **stealth,** stealing away. 329. **minimus,** diminutive creature. **knot-grass,** a weed (*polygonum aviculare*), an infusion of which was thought to stunt the growth. 333. **intend,** give sign of. 338. **cheek by jowl,** side by side. 339. **coil,** turmoil, dissension; see glossary. **'long of you,** on account of you; see glossary. 347. **king of shadows.** Note the suggestion in this and other passages of a larger aspect of Oberon's power. 352. **sort,** turn out. 356. **welkin,** sky; see glossary. 357. **Acheron,** river of hell, which Shakespeare seems to have thought of as a pit or lake. 359. **As,** so that; see glossary. 370. **derision,** four syllables.

With league whose date till death shall never end.
Whiles I in this affair do thee employ,
I'll to my queen and beg her Indian boy;
And then I will her charmed eye release
From monster's view, and all things shall be peace.
Puck. My fairy lord, this must be done with haste,
For night's swift dragons cut the clouds full fast,
And yonder shines Aurora's harbinger;
At whose approach, ghosts, wand'ring here and there,
Troop home to churchyards: damned spirits all,
That in crossways and floods have burial,
Already to their wormy beds are gone;
For fear lest day should look their shames upon,
They wilfully themselves exile from light
And must for aye consort with black-brow'd night.
Obe. But we are spirits of another sort:
I with the morning's love have oft made sport,
And, like a forester, the groves may tread,
Even till the eastern gate, all fiery-red,
Opening on Neptune with fair blessed beams,
Turns into yellow gold his salt green streams.
But, notwithstanding, haste; make no delay:
We may effect this business yet ere day. [*Exit.*]
Puck. Up and down, up and down,
I will lead them up and down:
I am fear'd in field and town:
Goblin, lead them up and down.
Here comes one.

Enter LYSANDER.

Lys. Where art thou, proud Demetrius? speak thou now.
Puck. Here, villain; drawn and ready. Where art thou?
Lys. I will be with thee straight.
Puck. Follow me, then,
To plainer ground. [*Exit Lysander, as following the voice.*]

Enter DEMETRIUS.

Dem. Lysander! speak again:
Thou runaway, thou coward, art thou fled?
Speak! In some bush? Where dost thou hide thy head?
Puck. Thou coward, art thou bragging to the stars,
Telling the bushes that thou look'st for wars,
And wilt not come? Come, recreant; come, thou child,
I'll whip thee with a rod: he is defil'd
That draws a sword on thee.
Dem. Yea, art thou there?
Puck. Follow my voice: we'll try no manhood here.
Exeunt.

[*Enter* LYSANDER.]

Lys. He goes before me and still dares me on:
When I come where he calls, then he is gone.
The villain is much lighter-heel'd than I:
I followed fast, but faster he did fly;
That fallen am I in dark uneven way,
And here will rest me. [*Lies down.*] Come, thou gentle day!
For if but once thou show me thy grey light,
I'll find Demetrius and revenge this spite. [*Sleeps.*]

[*Enter*] ROBIN [PUCK] *and* DEMETRIUS.

Puck. Ho, ho, ho! Coward, why com'st thou not?
Dem. Abide me, if thou dar'st; for well I wot
Thou runn'st before me, shifting every place,
And dar'st not stand, nor look me in the face.
Where art thou now?
Puck. Come hither: I am here.
Dem. Nay, then, thou mock'st me. Thou shalt buy this dear,
If ever I thy face by daylight see:
Now, go thy way. Faintness constraineth me
To measure out my length on this cold bed.
By day's approach look to be visited.
[*Lies down and sleeps.*]

Enter HELENA.

Hel. O weary night, O long and tedious night,
Abate thy hours! Shine comforts from the east,
That I may back to Athens by daylight,
From these that my poor company detest:
And sleep, that sometimes shuts up sorrow's eye,
Steal me awhile from mine own company.
[*Lies down and*] *sleep*[*s*].
Puck. Yet but three? Come one more;
Two of both kinds makes up four.
Here she comes, curst and sad:
Cupid is a knavish lad,
Thus to make poor females mad.

[*Enter* HERMIA.]

Her. Never so weary, never so in woe,
Bedabbled with the dew and torn with briers,
I can no further crawl, no further go;
My legs can keep no pace with my desires.
Here will I rest me till the break of day.
Heavens shield Lysander, if they mean a fray!
[*Lies down and sleeps.*]
Puck. On the ground
Sleep sound:
I'll apply
To your eye,
Gentle lover, remedy.
[*Squeezing the juice on Lysander's eyes.*]
When thou wak'st,
Thou tak'st
True delight
In the sight
Of thy former lady's eye:
And the country proverb known,
That every man should take his own,
In your waking shall be shown:
Jack shall have Jill;
Nought shall go ill;
The man shall have his mare again, and all shall be well. [*Exit.*]

---

373. **date,** term of existence; see glossary. 379. **dragons,** supposed by Shakespeare to be yoked to the car of the goddess of night. 380. **Aurora's harbinger,** the morning star. 383. **crossways . . . burial.** Those who had committed suicide were buried at crossways, with a stake driven through them; those drowned, i.e., buried in floods or great waters, would be condemned to wander disconsolate for want of burial rites. 389. **morning's love,** Cephalus, a beautiful youth beloved by Aurora; sometimes taken to refer to the goddess herself. 402. **drawn,** with drawn sword. 403. **straight,** immediately; see glossary. 409. **recreant,** cowardly wretch; see glossary. 422. **wot,** know; see glossary. 432. **Abate,** lessen; see glossary.

ACT IV. SCENE I. 2. **coy,** caress. 20. **neaf,** fist. 21. **leave your courtesy,** put on your hat. 25. **Cavalery,** cavalero, gentleman; form of address. 31. **tongs . . . bones,** instruments for rustic music, the

[ACT IV.

SCENE I. *The same.* LYSANDER, DEMETRIUS, HELENA, *and* HERMIA *lying asleep.*]

Enter [TITANIA,] *Queen of Fairies, and* [BOTTOM *the*] *Clown, and* Fairies; *and* [OBERON,] *the King, behind them.*

Tita. Come, sit thee down upon this flow'ry bed,
While I thy amiable cheeks do coy,
And stick musk-roses in thy sleek smooth head,
And kiss thy fair large ears, my gentle joy.

Bot. Where 's Peaseblossom?

Peas. Ready.

Bot. Scratch my head, Peaseblossom. Where 's Mounsieur Cobweb?

Cob. Ready.

Bot. Mounsieur Cobweb, good mounsieur, get you your weapons in your hand, and kill me a red-hipped humble-bee on the top of a thistle; and, good mounsieur, bring me the honey-bag. Do not fret yourself too much in the action, mounsieur; and, good mounsieur, have a care the honey-bag break not; I would be loath to have you overflown with a honey-bag, signior. Where 's Mounsieur Mustardseed?

Mus. Ready.

Bot. Give me your neaf, Mounsieur Mustardseed. Pray you, leave your courtesy, good mounsieur.

Mus. What 's your will?

Bot. Nothing, good mounsieur, but to help Cavalery Cobweb to scratch. I must to the barber's, mounsieur; for methinks I am marvellous hairy about the face; and I am such a tender ass, if my hair do but tickle me, I must scratch.

Tita. What, wilt thou hear some music, my sweet love?

Bot. I have a reasonable good ear in music. Let 's have the tongs and the bones.

Tita. Or say, sweet love, what thou desirest to eat.

Bot. Truly, a peck of provender: I could munch your good dry oats. Methinks I have a great desire to a bottle of hay: good hay, sweet hay, hath no fellow.

Tita. I have a venturous fairy that shall seek
The squirrel's hoard, and fetch thee new nuts.

Bot. I had rather have a handful or two of dried peas. But, I pray you, let none of your people stir me: I have an exposition of sleep come upon me.

Tita. Sleep thou, and I will wind thee in my arms.
Fairies, be gone, and be all ways away. [*Exeunt fairies.*]
So doth the woodbine the sweet honeysuckle
Gently entwist; the female ivy so
Enrings the barky fingers of the elm.
O, how I love thee! how I dote on thee! [*They sleep.*]

Enter ROBIN GOODFELLOW [PUCK].

Obe. [*Advancing*] Welcome, good Robin. See'st thou this sweet sight?
Her dotage now I do begin to pity:
For, meeting her of late behind the wood,
Seeking sweet favours for this hateful fool,
I did upbraid her and fall out with her;
For she his hairy temples then had rounded
With coronet of fresh and fragrant flowers;
And that same dew, which sometime on the buds
Was wont to swell like round and orient pearls,
Stood now within the pretty flouriets' eyes
Like tears that did their own disgrace bewail.
When I had at my pleasure taunted her
And she in mild terms begg'd my patience,
I then did ask of her her changeling child;
Which straight she gave me, and her fairy sent
To bear him to my bower in fairy land.
And now I have the boy, I will undo
This hateful imperfection of her eyes:
And, gentle Puck, take this transformed scalp
From off the head of this Athenian swain;
That, he awaking when the other do,
May all to Athens back again repair
And think no more of this night's accidents
But as the fierce vexation of a dream.
But first I will release the fairy queen.
Be as thou wast wont to be;
See as thou wast wont to see:
Dian's bud o'er Cupid's flower
Hath such force and blessed power.
Now, my Titania; wake you, my sweet queen.

Tita. My Oberon! what visions have I seen!
Methought I was enamour'd of an ass.

Obe. There lies your love.

Tita. How came these things to pass?
O, how mine eyes do loathe his visage now!

Obe. Silence awhile. Robin, take off this head.
Titania, music call; and strike more dead
Than common sleep of all these five the sense.

Tita. Music, ho! music, such as charmeth sleep! [*Music.*]

Puck. Now, when thou wak'st, with thine own fool's eyes peep.

Obe. Sound, music! Come, my queen, take hands with me,
And rock the ground whereon these sleepers be. [*Dance.*]
Now thou and I are new in amity
And will to-morrow midnight solemnly
Dance in Duke Theseus' house triumphantly
And bless it to all fair prosperity:
There shall the pairs of faithful lovers be
Wedded, with Theseus, all in jollity.

Puck. Fairy king, attend, and mark:
I do hear the morning lark.

Obe. Then, my queen, in silence sad,
Trip we after night's shade:
We the globe can compass soon,
Swifter than the wand'ring moon.

Tita. Come, my lord, and in our flight
Tell me how it came this night
That I sleeping here was found
With these mortals on the ground. *Exeunt.*

Wind horn [*within*].

Enter THESEUS *and all his train* [; HIPPOLYTA, EGEUS].

The. Go, one of you, find out the forester;
For now our observation is perform'd;

former described as an instrument played like the triangle; the latter are bones held between the fingers and used as clappers. 35. **bottle,** bundle (of hay). 36. **fellow,** equal; see glossary. 42. **exposition,** Bottom's word for "disposition." 44. **all ways,** in all directions. 52. **favours,** i.e., nosegays of flowers. 57. **orient pearls,** i.e., the most beautiful of all pearls, those coming from the Orient. 58. **flouriets',** flowerets'. 69. **other,** others. 76. **Dian's bud,** sometimes defined as *agnus castus* or chaste-tree, which could preserve chastity; perhaps simply invented by Shakespeare to correspond to Cupid's flower. 85. **these five,** i.e., the four lovers and Bottom. 100. **night's,** dissyllable. 108. **observation,** i.e., *observance to a morn of May* (I, i, 167).

And since we have the vaward of the day,
My love shall hear the music of my hounds.
Uncouple in the western valley; let them go:
Dispatch, I say, and find the forester. [*Exit an Attendant.*]
We will, fair queen, up to the mountain's top
And mark the musical confusion
Of hounds and echo in conjunction.

Hip. I was with Hercules and Cadmus once,
When in a wood of Crete they bay'd the bear
With hounds of Sparta: never did I hear
Such gallant chiding; for, besides the groves,
The skies, the fountains, every region near
Seem'd all one mutual cry: I never heard
So musical a discord, such sweet thunder.

The. My hounds are bred out of the Spartan kind,
So flew'd, so sanded, and their heads are hung
With ears that sweep away the morning dew;
Crook-knee'd, and dew-lapp'd like Thessalian bulls;
Slow in pursuit, but match'd in mouth like bells,
Each under each. A cry more tuneable
Was never holla'd to, nor cheer'd with horn,
In Crete, in Sparta, nor in Thessaly:
Judge when you hear. But, soft! what nymphs are these?

Ege. My lord, this is my daughter here asleep;
And this, Lysander; this Demetrius is;
This Helena, old Nedar's Helena:
I wonder of their being here together.

The. No doubt they rose up early to observe
The rite of May, and, hearing our intent,
Came here in grace of our solemnity.
But speak, Egeus; is not this the day
That Hermia should give answer of her choice?

Ege. It is, my lord.

The. Go, bid the huntsmen wake them with their horns.

Shout within. They all start up. Wind horns.

Good morrow, friends. Saint Valentine is past:
Begin these wood-birds but to couple now?

Lys. Pardon, my lord. [*They kneel.*]

The. I pray you all, stand up.
I know you two are rival enemies:
How comes this gentle concord in the world,
That hatred is so far from jealousy,
To sleep by hate, and fear no enmity?

Lys. My lord, I shall reply amazedly,
Half sleep, half waking: but as yet, I swear,
I cannot truly say how I came here;
But, as I think,—for truly would I speak,
And now I do bethink me, so it is,—
I came with Hermia hither: our intent
Was to be gone from Athens, where we might,
Without the peril of the Athenian law.

Ege. Enough, enough, my lord; you have enough:
I beg the law, the law, upon his head.
They would have stol'n away; they would, Demetrius,
Thereby to have defeated you and me,
You of your wife and me of my consent,
Of my consent that she should be your wife.

Dem. My lord, fair Helen told me of their stealth,
Of this their purpose hither to this wood;
And I in fury hither followed them,
Fair Helena in fancy following me.
But, my good lord, I wot not by what power,—
But by some power it is,—my love to Hermia,
Melted as the snow, seems to me now
As the remembrance of an idle gawd
Which in my childhood I did dote upon;
And all the faith, the virtue of my heart,
The object and the pleasure of mine eye,
Is only Helena. To her, my lord,
Was I betroth'd ere I saw Hermia:
But, like in sickness, did I loathe this food;
But, as in health, come to my natural taste,
Now I do wish it, love it, long for it,
And will for evermore be true to it.

The. Fair lovers, you are fortunately met:
Of this discourse we more will hear anon.
Egeus, I will overbear your will;
For in the temple, by and by, with us
These couples shall eternally be knit:
And for the morning now is something worn,
Our purpos'd hunting shall be set aside.
Away with us to Athens; three and three,
We'll hold a feast in great solemnity.
Come, Hippolyta.

[*Exeunt Theseus, Hippolyta, Egeus, and train.*]

Dem. These things seem small and undistinguishable,
Like far-off mountains turned into clouds.

Her. Methinks I see these things with parted eye,
When every thing seems double.

Hel. So methinks:
And I have found Demetrius like a jewel,
Mine own, and not mine own.

Dem. Are you sure
That we are awake? It seems to me
That yet we sleep, we dream. Do not you think
The duke was here, and bid us follow him?

Her. Yea; and my father.

Hel. And Hippolyta.

Lys. And he did bid us follow to the temple.

Dem. Why, then, we are awake: let 's follow him;
And by the way let us recount our dreams. [*Exeunt.*]

Bot. [*Awaking*] When my cue comes, call me, and I will answer: my next is, 'Most fair Pyramus.' Heigh-ho! Peter Quince! Flute, the bellows-mender! Snout, the tinker! Starveling! God 's my life, stolen hence, and left me asleep! I have had a most rare vision. I have had a dream, past the wit of man to say what dream it was: man is but an ass, if he go about to expound this dream. Methought I was—there is no man can tell what. Methought I was,—and methought I had,—but man is but a patched fool, if he will offer to say what methought I had. The eye of man hath not heard, the ear of man hath not seen, man's hand is not able to taste, his tongue to conceive, nor his heart to report, what my dream was. I

109. **vaward,** vanguard, i.e., earliest part. 116-122. **I was . . . thunder.** This reminiscence, which brings such unlikely huntsmen into the field together, is probably of Shakespeare's invention. Hounds of Crete and of Sparta were alike celebrated, the Spartan the more famous. 124. **flew'd,** with large overhanging jaws. **sanded,** of sandy color. 127. **mouth,** voice (of hounds). 128. **Each under each,** with differing notes. **cry,** pack of hounds. 138. **solemnity,** i.e., solemnization of their marriage. 143. **Saint Valentine.** Birds were supposed to choose their mates on St. Valentine's Day. 156. **where,** wherever. 157. **Without,** outside of, beyond. 158. **Enough,** i.e., evidence to convict him. 161. **defeated,** ruined, thwarted; see glossary. 212. **go about,** attempt. 216. **patched,** wearing motley, i.e., a dress of various colors. **offer,** venture. 226. **her,** Thisby's (?).

SCENE II. 4. **transported,** carried off, or possibly, transformed. 20. **sixpence a day,** i.e., as a royal pension. 26. **hearts,** good fellows. 27. **courageous,** used blunderingly. 29. **discourse,** relate; see glossary. 38. **presently,** immediately; see glossary. 40. **preferred,** selected for consideration.

will get Peter Quince to write a ballad of this dream: it shall be called Bottom's Dream, because it hath no bottom; and I will sing it in the latter end of a play, before the duke: peradventure, to make it the more gracious, †I shall sing it at her death. *Exit.*

[SCENE II. *Athens.* QUINCE'S *house.*]

Enter QUINCE, FLUTE [, SNOUT, *and* STARVELING].

Quin. Have you sent to Bottom's house? is he come home yet?

Star. He cannot be heard of. Out of doubt he is transported.

Flu. If he come not, then the play is marred: it goes not forward, doth it?

Quin. It is not possible: you have not a man in all Athens able to discharge Pyramus but he.

Flu. No, he hath simply the best wit of any handicraft man in Athens.

Quin. Yea, and the best person too; and he is a very paramour for a sweet voice.

Flu. You must say 'paragon:' a paramour is, God bless us, a thing of naught.

Enter SNUG *the Joiner.*

Snug. Masters, the duke is coming from the temple, and there is two or three lords and ladies more married: if our sport had gone forward, we had all been made men.

Flu. O sweet bully Bottom! Thus hath he lost sixpence a day during his life; he could not have 'scaped sixpence a day: an the duke had not given him sixpence a day for playing Pyramus, I'll be hanged; he would have deserved it: sixpence a day in Pyramus, or nothing.

Enter BOTTOM.

Bot. Where are these lads? where are these hearts?

Quin. Bottom! O most courageous day! O most happy hour!

Bot. Masters, I am to discourse wonders: but ask me not what; for if I tell you, I am not true Athenian. I will tell you every thing, right as it fell out.

Quin. Let us hear, sweet Bottom.

Bot. Not a word of me. All that I will tell you is, that the duke hath dined. Get your apparel together, good strings to your beards, new ribbons to your pumps; meet presently at the palace; every man look o'er his part; for the short and the long is, our play is preferred. In any case, let Thisby have clean linen; and let not him that plays the lion pare his nails, for they shall hang out for the lion's claws. And, most dear actors, eat no onions nor garlic, for we are to utter sweet breath; and I do not doubt but to hear them say, it is a sweet comedy. No more words: away! go, away! [*Exeunt.*]

[ACT V.

SCENE I. *Athens. The palace of* THESEUS.]

Enter THESEUS, HIPPOLYTA, *and* PHILOSTRATE [, Lords, *and* Attendants].

Hip. 'Tis strange, my Theseus, that these lovers speak of.
The. More strange than true: I never may believe
These antique fables, nor these fairy toys.
Lovers and madmen have such seething brains,
Such shaping fantasies, that apprehend
More than cool reason ever comprehends.
The lunatic, the lover and the poet
Are of imagination all compact:
One sees more devils than vast hell can hold,
That is, the madman: the lover, all as frantic,
Sees Helen's beauty in a brow of Egypt:
The poet's eye, in a fine frenzy rolling,
Doth glance from heaven to earth, from earth to heaven;
And as imagination bodies forth
The forms of things unknown, the poet's pen
Turns them to shapes and gives to airy nothing
A local habitation and a name.
Such tricks hath strong imagination,
That, if it would but apprehend some joy,
It comprehends some bringer of that joy;
Or in the night, imagining some fear,
How easy is a bush suppos'd a bear!
Hip. But all the story of the night told over,
And all their minds transfigur'd so together,
More witnesseth than fancy's images
And grows to something of great constancy;
But, howsoever, strange and admirable.

Enter lovers: LYSANDER, DEMETRIUS, HERMIA, *and* HELENA.

The. Here come the lovers, full of joy and mirth.
Joy, gentle friends! joy and fresh days of love
Accompany your hearts!
Lys. More than to us
Wait in your royal walks, your board, your bed!
The. Come now; what masques, what dances shall we have,
To wear away this long age of three hours
Between our after-supper and bed-time?
Where is our usual manager of mirth?
What revels are in hand? Is there no play,
To ease the anguish of a torturing hour?
Call Philostrate.
Phil. Here, mighty Theseus.
The. Say, what abridgement have you for this evening?
What masque? what music? How shall we beguile
The lazy time, if not with some delight?
Phil. There is a brief how many sports are ripe:
Make choice of which your highness will see first.
[*Giving a paper.*]

ACT V. SCENE I. 2. **may,** can; see glossary. 3. **antique,** strange, grotesque. **toys,** trifles; see glossary. 4-22. **Lovers . . . bear.** These lines furnish a probable illustration of the discoveries of the bibliographical students of Shakespeare. If lines 4-6, 9-11, and 18-22 are read consecutively without paying attention to the lines omitted, it will be found that they make complete sense, and that they refer only to the madman and the lover. The other lines, which refer to the poet, are found in the earliest printed texts of the play to be slightly deranged in verse form. It is inferred that Shakespeare's first draft introduced only the figures of the lover and the madman, and that he subsequently expanded them in his happiest vein with the lines referring to the poet, writing the new lines on the margin. The printers, working from the original playbook, were unable to get them exactly correct in the alignment of the verse. 8. **compact,** formed, composed. 11. **Helen's,** i.e., Helen of Troy, pattern of beauty. **brow of Egypt,** i.e., the face of a gypsy. 21. **fear,** object of fear; see glossary. 25. **images,** creations of the imagination; see glossary. 26. **constancy,** certainty. 39. **abridgement,** pastime. 42. **brief,** short written statement.

The. [*Reads*] 'The battle with the Centaurs, to be sung
By an Athenian eunuch to the harp.'
We'll none of that: that have I told my love,
In glory of my kinsman Hercules.
[*Reads*] 'The riot of the tipsy Bacchanals,
Tearing the Thracian singer in their rage.'
That is an old device; and it was play'd
When I from Thebes came last a conqueror.
[*Reads*] 'The thrice three Muses mourning for the death
Of Learning, late deceas'd in beggary.'
That is some satire, keen and critical,
Not sorting with a nuptial ceremony.
[*Reads*] 'A tedious brief scene of young Pyramus
And his love Thisby; very tragical mirth.'
Merry and tragical! tedious and brief!
That is, hot ice and wondrous strange snow.
How shall we find the concord of this discord?
Phil. A play there is, my lord, some ten words long,
Which is as brief as I have known a play;
But by ten words, my lord, it is too long,
Which makes it tedious; for in all the play
There is not one word apt, one player fitted:
And tragical, my noble lord, it is;
For Pyramus therein doth kill himself.
Which, when I saw rehears'd, I must confess,
Made mine eyes water; but more merry tears
The passion of loud laughter never shed.
The. What are they that do play it?
Phil. Hard-handed men that work in Athens here,
Which never labour'd in their minds till now,
And now have toil'd their unbreathed memories
With this same play, against your nuptial.
The. And we will hear it.
Phil. No, my noble lord;
It is not for you: I have heard it over,
And it is nothing, nothing in the world;
Unless you can find sport in their intents,
Extremely stretch'd and conn'd with cruel pain,
To do you service.
The. I will hear that play;
For never anything can be amiss,
When simpleness and duty tender it.
Go, bring them in: and take your places, ladies.
[*Exit Philostrate.*]
Hip. I love not to see wretchedness o'er-charg'd
And duty in his service perishing.
The. Why, gentle sweet, you shall see no such thing.
Hip. He says they can do nothing in this kind.
The. The kinder we, to give them thanks for nothing.
Our sport shall be to take what they mistake:
And what poor duty cannot do, noble respect
†Takes it in might, not merit.
Where I have come, great clerks have purposed
To greet me with premeditated welcomes;
Where I have seen them shiver and look pale,
Make periods in the midst of sentences,
Throttle their practis'd accent in their fears
And in conclusion dumbly have broke off,
Not paying me a welcome. Trust me, sweet,
Out of this silence yet I pick'd a welcome;
And in the modesty of fearful duty
I read as much as from the rattling tongue
Of saucy and audacious eloquence.
Love, therefore, and tongue-tied simplicity
In least speak most, to my capacity.

[*Enter* PHILOSTRATE.]

Phil. So please your grace, the Prologue is address'd.
The. Let him approach. [*Flourish of trumpets.*]

Enter the Prologue [QUINCE].

Pro. If we offend, it is with our good will.
That you should think, we come not to offend,
But with good will. To show our simple skill,
That is the true beginning of our end.
Consider then we come but in despite.
We do not come as minding to content you,
Our true intent is. All for your delight
We are not here. That you should here repent you,
The actors are at hand and by their show
You shall know all that you are like to know.
The. This fellow doth not stand upon points.

Lys. He hath rid his prologue like a rough colt; he knows not the stop. A good moral, my lord: it is not enough to speak, but to speak true.

Hip. Indeed he hath played on his prologue like a child on a recorder; a sound, but not in government.

The. His speech was like a tangled chain; nothing impaired, but all disordered. Who is next?

Enter PYRAMUS *and* THISBY, *and* WALL, *and* MOONSHINE, *and* LION.

Pro. Gentles, perchance you wonder at this show;
But wonder on, till truth make all things plain.
This man is Pyramus, if you would know;
This beauteous lady Thisby is certain.
This man, with lime and rough-cast, doth present
Wall, that vile Wall which did these lovers sunder;
And through Wall's chink, poor souls, they are content
To whisper. At the which let no man wonder.
This man, with lanthorn, dog, and bush of thorn,
Presenteth Moonshine; for, if you will know,
By moonshine did these lovers think no scorn
To meet at Ninus' tomb, there, there to woo.
This grisly beast, which Lion hight by name,
The trusty Thisby, coming first by night,
Did scare away, or rather did affright;
And, as she fled, her mantle she did fall,
Which Lion vile with bloody mouth did stain.
Anon comes Pyramus, sweet youth and tall,
And finds his trusty Thisby's mantle slain:
Whereat, with blade, with bloody blameful blade,
He bravely broach'd his boiling bloody breast;

44. **battle with the Centaurs,** probably refers to the battle of the Centaurs and the Lapithae, as narrated in Ovid, *Metamorphoses*, Bk. xii. 47. **kinsman.** Plutarch's *Life of Theseus* states that Hercules and Theseus were near kinsmen. 48-49. **tipsy . . . singer.** This was the story of the death of Orpheus, as told in *Metamorphoses*, Bk. xi. 52-53. **'The . . . beggary.'** These two lines were long thought to have some reference to Spenser's *Teares of the Muses* (1591) and were connected by Knight with the death in poverty of the learned poet, Robert Greene. The editors of the New Cambridge Shakespeare see in the lines following, which describe the piece as a satire, a mild retaliation on Shakespeare's part for Greene's attack on Shakespeare as "an upstart crow"; see Shakespeare's Life and Work, Early Period. 55. **Not sorting with,** not befitting. 74. **unbreathed,** unexercised. 80. **stretch'd,** strained. 92. **Takes . . . merit,** values it for the effort made rather than for the excellence achieved (?). 93. **clerks,** learned men. 96. **periods,** full stops. 100. **I pick'd a welcome.** In the kindly speech of Theseus we are probably to see a tribute to the graciousness of Queen Elizabeth. Attempts have been made to see in the passage a reference to a particular occasion. 105. **to my capacity,** as far as I am able to understand. 106. **Prologue,** speaker of the Prologue. **address'd,** ready. 108-117. **If . . . to know.** The humor of the passage is in the blunders of its punctuation. There is a similar piece in *Ralph Roister Doister*, which is

And Thisby, tarrying in mulberry shade,
His dagger drew, and died. For all the rest,
Let Lion, Moonshine, Wall, and lovers twain
At large discourse, while here they do remain.
Exeunt Lion, Thisby, and Moonshine.

The. I wonder if the lion be to speak.

Dem. No wonder, my lord: one lion may, when many asses do.

Wall. In this same interlude it doth befall
That I, one Snout by name, present a wall;
And such a wall, as I would have you think,
That had in it a crannied hole or chink,
Through which the lovers, Pyramus and Thisby,
Did whisper often very secretly.
This loam, this rough-cast and this stone doth show
That I am that same wall; the truth is so:
And this the cranny is, right and sinister,
Through which the fearful lovers are to whisper.

The. Would you desire lime and hair to speak better?

Dem. It is the wittiest partition that ever I heard discourse, my lord.

[PYRAMUS *comes forward.*]

The. Pyramus draws near the wall: silence!

Pyr. O grim-look'd night! O night with hue so black!
O night, which ever art when day is not!
O night, O night! alack, alack, alack,
I fear my Thisby's promise is forgot!
And thou, O wall, O sweet, O lovely wall,
That stand'st between her father's ground and mine!
Thou wall, O wall, O sweet and lovely wall,
Show me thy chink, to blink through with mine eyne! [*Wall holds up his fingers.*]
Thanks, courteous wall: Jove shield thee well for this!
But what see I? No Thisby do I see.
O wicked wall, through whom I see no bliss!
Curs'd be thy stones for thus deceiving me!

The. The wall, methinks, being sensible, should curse again.

Pyr. No, in truth, sir, he should not. 'Deceiving me' is Thisby's cue: she is to enter now, and I am to spy her through the wall. You shall see, it will fall pat as I told you. Yonder she comes.

Enter THISBY.

This. O wall, full often hast thou heard my moans,
For parting my fair Pyramus and me!
My cherry lips have often kiss'd thy stones,
Thy stones with lime and hair knit up in thee.

Pyr. I see a voice: now will I to the chink,
To spy an I can hear my Thisby's face.
Thisby!

This. My love thou art, my love I think.

Pyr. Think what thou wilt, I am thy lover's grace;
And, like Limander, am I trusty still.

This. And I like Helen, till the Fates me kill.

Pyr. Not Shafalus to Procrus was so true.

This. As Shafalus to Procrus, I to you.

Pyr. O, kiss me through the hole of this vile wall!

This. I kiss the wall's hole, not your lips at all.

Pyr. Wilt thou at Ninny's tomb meet me straightway?

This. 'Tide life, 'tide death, I come without delay.
[*Exeunt Pyramus and Thisby.*]

Wall. Thus have I, Wall, my part discharged so;
And, being done, thus Wall away doth go. [*Exit.*]

The. Now is the mural down between the two neighbours.

Dem. No remedy, my lord, when walls are so wilful to hear without warning.

Hip. This is the silliest stuff that ever I heard.

The. The best in this kind are but shadows; and the worst are no worse, if imagination amend them.

Hip. It must be your imagination then, and not theirs.

The. If we imagine no worse of them than they of themselves, they may pass for excellent men. Here come two noble beasts in, a man and a lion.

Enter LION *and* MOONSHINE.

Lion. You, ladies, you, whose gentle hearts do fear
The smallest monstrous mouse that creeps on floor,
May now perchance both quake and tremble here,
When lion rough in wildest rage doth roar.
Then know that I, as Snug the joiner, am
A lion fell, nor else no lion's dam;
For, if I should as lion come in strife
Into this place, 'twere pity on my life.

The. A very gentle beast, and of a good conscience.

Dem. The very best at a beast, my lord, that e'er I saw.

Lys. This lion is a very fox for his valour.

The. True; and a goose for his discretion.

Dem. Not so, my lord; for his valour cannot carry his discretion; and the fox carries the goose.

The. His discretion, I am sure, cannot carry his valour; for the goose carries not the fox. It is well: leave it to his discretion, and let us listen to the moon.

Moon. This lanthorn doth the horned moon present;—

Dem. He should have worn the horns on his head.

The. He is no crescent, and his horns are invisible within the circumference.

Moon. This lanthorn doth the horned moon present;
Myself the man i' th' moon do seem to be.

The. This is the greatest error of all the rest: the man should be put into the lanthorn. How is it else the man i' the moon?

Dem. He dares not come there for the candle; for, you see, it is already in snuff.

Hip. I am aweary of this moon: would he would change!

quoted in Wilson's *Arte of Rhetoric*, which Shakespeare probably knew. 113. **minding,** intending; see glossary. 118. **not stand upon points,** quibbling upon the two meanings (1) "to be overscrupulous" and (2) "to mind his stops in reading." 123. **recorder,** a wind instrument like a flute or flageolet. 124. **government,** control. 140. **hight,** is called. 143. **fall,** let fall; see glossary. 145. **tall,** courageous. 148. **broach'd,** stabbed; used rantingly. 152. **At large,** in full; see *large* in glossary. 164. **sinister,** left. 168. **partition,** wall, and section of a learned book. 171. **grim-look'd,** grim-looking. 183. **sensible,** capable of feeling; see glossary. 198-199. **Limander . . . Helen,** blunders for "Leander" and "Hero." 201. **Shafalus to Procrus,** blunder for "Cephalus" to "Procris," also famous lovers. 205. **'Tide life, 'tide death,** whether life or death betide. 213. **shadows,** likenesses, representations; see glossary. 214. **if imagination amend them.** The idea in this passage is fundamental in art and recurs so frequently in Shakespeare as to be a recognizable article of his faith. 227. **lion fell,** fierce lion (with pun on *fell,* skin). 244. **horns on his head,** the customary jest about the horns of the cuckold. 253. **for,** because of. 254. **in snuff,** pun on the meanings "to be offended" and "to be in need of snuffing."

The. It appears, by his small light of discretion, that he is in the wane; but yet, in courtesy, in all reason, we must stay the time.

Lys. Proceed, Moon.

Moon. All that I have to say, is, to tell you that the lanthorn is the moon; I, the man in the moon; this thorn-bush, my thorn-bush; and this dog, my dog.

Dem. Why, all these should be in the lanthorn; for all these are in the moon. But, silence! here comes Thisby.

Enter THISBY.

This. This is old Ninny's tomb. Where is my love?

Lion. [*Roaring*] Oh—— [*Thisby runs off.*]

Dem. Well roared, Lion.

The. Well run, Thisby.

Hip. Well shone, Moon. Truly, the moon shines with a good grace.

[*The Lion shakes Thisby's mantle, and exit.*]

The. Well moused, Lion.

Dem. And then came Pyramus.

Lys. And so the lion vanished.

Enter PYRAMUS.

Pyr. Sweet Moon, I thank thee for thy sunny beams;
I thank thee, Moon, for shining now so bright;
For, by thy gracious, golden, glittering gleams,
I trust to take of truest Thisby sight.
But stay, O spite!
But mark, poor knight,
What dreadful dole is here!
Eyes, do you see?
How can it be?
O dainty duck! O dear!
Thy mantle good,
What, stain'd with blood!
Approach, ye Furies fell!
O Fates, come, come,
Cut thread and thrum;
Quail, crush, conclude, and quell!

The. This passion, and the death of a dear friend, would go near to make a man look sad.

Hip. Beshrew my heart, but I pity the man.

Pyr. O wherefore, Nature, didst thou lions frame?
Since lion vile hath here deflower'd my dear:
Which is—no, no—which was the fairest dame
That liv'd, that lov'd, that lik'd, that look'd with cheer.
Come, tears, confound;
Out, sword, and wound
The pap of Pyramus;
Ay, that left pap,
Where heart doth hop: [*Stabs himself.*]
Thus die I, thus, thus, thus.
Now am I dead,
Now am I fled;
My soul is in the sky:
Tongue, lose thy light;
Moon, take thy flight: [*Exit Moonshine.*]
Now die, die, die, die, die. [*Dies.*]

Dem. No die, but an ace, for him; for he is but one.

Lys. Less than an ace, man; for he is dead; he is nothing.

The. With the help of a surgeon he might yet recover, and prove an ass.

Hip. How chance Moonshine is gone before Thisby comes back and finds her lover?

The. She will find him by starlight. Here she comes; and her passion ends the play.

[*Enter* THISBY.]

Hip. Methinks she should not use a long one for such a Pyramus: I hope she will be brief.

Dem. A mote will turn the balance, which Pyramus, which Thisby, is the better; he for a man, God warrant us; she for a woman, God bless us.

Lys. She hath spied him already with those sweet eyes.

Dem. And thus she means, videlicet:—

This. Asleep, my love?
What, dead, my dove?
O Pyramus, arise!
Speak, speak. Quite dumb?
Dead, dead? A tomb
Must cover thy sweet eyes.
These lily lips,
This cherry nose,
These yellow cowslip cheeks,
Are gone, are gone:
Lovers, make moan:
His eyes were green as leeks.
O Sisters Three,
Come, come to me,
With hands as pale as milk;
Lay them in gore,
Since you have shore
With shears his thread of silk.
Tongue, not a word:
Come, trusty sword;
Come, blade, my breast imbrue: [*Stabs herself.*]
And, farewell, friends;
Thus Thisby ends:
Adieu, adieu, adieu. [*Dies.*]

The. Moonshine and Lion are left to bury the dead.

Dem. Ay, and Wall too.

Bot. [*Starting up*] No, I assure you; the wall is down that parted their fathers. Will it please you to see the epilogue, or to hear a Bergomask dance between two of our company?

The. No epilogue, I pray you; for your play needs no excuse. Never excuse; for when the players are all dead, there need none to be blamed. Marry, if he that writ it had played Pyramus and hanged himself in Thisby's garter, it would have been a fine tragedy: and so it is, truly; and very notably discharged. But, come, your Bergomask; let your epilogue alone.

[*A dance.*]

283. **dole,** grief. 291. **thread and thrum,** the warp in weaving and the loose end of the warp; Bottom was a weaver. 292. **Quail,** overpower. **quell,** kill, destroy. 299. **cheer,** countenance. 312. **ace,** the side of the die containing the single pip, or spot. 330. **means,** moans, laments. 343. **Sisters Three,** the Fates. 347. **shore,** shorn. 351. **imbrue,** stain with blood. 360. **Bergomask dance,** dance named from Bergamo, a province in the state of Venice, noted for the rusticity of its manners. The New Cambridge edition points out that this rustic dance is the antimasque, or grotesque contrasting measure, to the dance of the fairies that is to follow. 363. **excuse,** seek to extenuate (a fault); see glossary. 370. **told,** counted; see *tell* in glossary. 374. **palpable-gross,** palpably gross, obviously crude. 381. **fordone,** exhausted. 391. **triple Hecate's.** Hecate ruled in three capacities: as Luna or Cynthia in heaven, as Diana on earth, and as Proserpina in hell. 394. **frolic,** merry. 397. **sweep the dust behind the door,** i.e., where it would not show. Robin Goodfellow was a household spirit and helped good housemaids and punished lazy ones. 398-407. **Through . . . place.** The editors of the New Cambridge Shakespeare find

The iron tongue of midnight hath told twelve:
Lovers, to bed; 'tis almost fairy time.
I fear we shall out-sleep the coming morn
As much as we this night have overwatch'd.
This palpable-gross play hath well beguil'd
The heavy gait of night. Sweet friends, to bed.
A fortnight hold we this solemnity,
In nightly revels and new jollity. *Exeunt.*

Enter PUCK.

Puck. Now the hungry lion roars,
And the wolf behowls the moon;
Whilst the heavy ploughman snores,
All with weary task fordone.
Now the wasted brands do glow,
Whilst the screech-owl, screeching loud,
Puts the wretch that lies in woe
In remembrance of a shroud.
Now it is the time of night
That the graves all gaping wide,
Every one lets forth his sprite,
In the church-way paths to glide:
And we fairies, that do run
By the triple Hecate's team,
From the presence of the sun,
Following darkness like a dream,
Now are frolic: not a mouse
Shall disturb this hallowed house:
I am sent with broom before,
To sweep the dust behind the door.

Enter [OBERON *and* TITANIA,] *King and Queen of Fairies, with all their train.*

Obe. Through the house give glimmering light,
By the dead and drowsy fire:
Every elf and fairy sprite
Hop as light as bird from brier;
And this ditty, after me,
Sing, and dance it trippingly.
Tita. First, rehearse your song by rote,
To each word a warbling note:
Hand in hand, with fairy grace,
Will we sing, and bless this place. [*Song and dance.*]
Obe. Now, until the break of day,
Through this house each fairy stray.
To the best bride-bed will we,
Which by us shall blessed be;
And the issue there create
Ever shall be fortunate.
So shall all the couples three
Ever true in loving be;
And the blots of Nature's hand
Shall not in their issue stand;
Never mole, hare lip, nor scar,
Nor mark prodigious, such as are
Despised in nativity,
Shall upon their children be.
With this field-dew consecrate,
Every fairy take his gait;
And each several chamber bless,
Through this palace, with sweet peace;
And the owner of it blest
Ever shall in safety rest.
Trip away; make no stay;
Meet me all by break of day.
Exeunt [*Oberon, Titania, and train*].
Puck. If we shadows have offended,
Think but this, and all is mended,
That you have but slumb'red here
While these visions did appear.
And this weak and idle theme,
No more yielding but a dream,
Gentles, do not reprehend:
If you pardon, we will mend:
And, as I am an honest Puck,
If we have unearned luck
Now to 'scape the serpent's tongue,
We will make amends ere long;
Else the Puck a liar call:
So, good night unto you all.
Give me your hands, if we be friends,
And Robin shall restore amends. [*Exit.*]

in this passage evidence that the play was written for performance in the great chamber of some private house on the occasion of the celebration of a marriage. Theseus and the court leave the stage; the lights are extinguished, all but one; the fairies enter, kindle their torches at the remaining flame, place them on their heads and exhibit their dance; then depart as if to bless the bridal chamber. 412. **create,** created. 419. **prodigious,** monstrous, unnatural. 422. **consecrate,** consecrated. 424. **several,** separate; see glossary. 432. **That . . . here,** i.e., that it is a "midsummer-night's dream." 440. **serpent's tongue,** hissing. 444. **Give . . . hands,** applaud by clapping.

THE HENRY THE SIXTH PLAYS

Throughout much of the fifteenth century, England had suffered the ravages of civil war. From the long struggles between the Lancastrians and the Yorkists, the so-called Wars of the Roses, the country had emerged in 1485 shaken but united at last under the strong rule of the Tudors. To Elizabethan Englishmen, this period of civil war was a still-recent event that had tested and almost destroyed England's nationhood. Elizabethans were, moreover, still troubled by political and dynastic uncertainties of their own. Queen Elizabeth, granddaughter of the first Tudor king, Henry VII, was unmarried and aging, her successor unchosen. Her Catholic enemies at home and abroad plotted a return to the ancient faith renounced by Henry VIII in his reformation of the church. Spain had attempted an invasion of England with her great Armada in 1588, perhaps two years before Shakespeare began writing his *Henry VI* plays. It was in such an era of crisis and patriotic excitement that the *Henry VI* plays first appeared. Moreover, they helped to establish the vogue of the English history play, which was to flourish throughout the decade of the 1590's. England's civil wars could be studied and analyzed now, from a perspective of over one hundred years later, as a key to the present time. At hand was a new edition of Holinshed's chronicles, 1587, along with the earlier chronicle writings of Fabyan, Stow, Grafton, Edward Hall's *Union of the Two Noble and Illustre Famelies of Lancastre and Yorke*, John Foxe's *Actes and Monuments of Martyrs*, and *A Myrroure for Magistrates*.

How had these wars begun? Elizabethan Englishmen searched for an answer not in economic or social terms, but in religious and moral ones. According to a traditional and government-sponsored explanation, formulated most comprehensively by Edward Hall and familiar to Shakespeare whether he accepted it fully or not, the Wars of the Roses were a manifestation of God's wrath, a divine punishment inflicted on the English people for their wayward behavior. The people and their rulers had brought civil war on themselves by self-serving ambition, arrogance, and disloyalty. King Henry VI's grandfather, Henry IV, had come to the throne in 1399 by deposing and then executing his own cousin Richard II (a momentous event to be portrayed by Shakespeare in a later history play). Henry VI was himself an infant when he succeeded to the throne in 1422, owing to the untimely death of his father Henry V. Too young at first to rule, and never blessed with his father's ability to act decisively, Henry VI was utterly unable to halt the struggle for power that developed among members of his large but discordant family. Ultimately, his very title to the throne was challenged by his kinsman Richard Plantagenet, Duke of York, who claimed to be rightful king by virtue of his descent from Henry IV's older brother Lionel, Duke of Clarence. The Yorkist faction marched to battle against Henry VI's Lancastrian faction (so named because for generations the family had been possessors of the dukedom of Lancaster), and the war was on.

All these harrowing misfortunes were the result, according to Tudor historians, of God's anger toward a rebellious people. The outcome of the war confirmed this pattern: universal devastation and the deaths of those most responsible for the conflict led eventually to appeasement of God's anger and a restoration of order. Richard Plantagenet died in the struggle, as did Henry VI, Henry's son Edward, and much of the English nobility. Richard's son Edward survived to become Edward IV; but his manner of obtaining the throne was so manifestly offensive to Providence that (according to the theory) he suffered a retributive death at the hands of an angry God and was succeeded by his younger brother, Richard III. This last Yorkist ruler governed only two years, 1483–1485, and it was through Richard's insane vengeance that God finally settled all his scores against the wayward English people. Having completed this purgation, God chose as his instrument of a new order Henry Tudor, Earl of Richmond, Henry VII. Although Henry's return to England and defeat of Richard at the battle of Bosworth Field might outwardly resemble Henry IV's seizure of power from Richard II, the difference was crucial to Tudor historians. Richard III had to be seen not as a flawed legitimate monarch but as a mad usurper and tyrant; his defeat was not the disobedient act of one man but a rising up of the entire English nation at the prompting of divine command. Henry VII's accession to power was to be viewed not as a precedent for further rebellion but as a manifestation of divine will without parallel in human history.

The essence of this "Tudor myth," as it has been called, was thus the revelation in human history of divine retribution and eventual reconciliation. The theory of course served the interests of the Tudor state, and was in part a propaganda weapon calculatedly employed by the ruling class. Shakespeare's commitment to it should not be taken for granted, and indeed a number of recent studies have expressed a profound skepticism toward the "Tudor myth" as the basis of Shakespeare's dramaturgy. Especially in his later tetralogy or four-play series from *Richard II* to *Henry V*, Shakespeare reveals considerably more interest in the clash of personalities than in patterns of divine retribution. Shakespeare does not one-sidedly endorse the orthodox view that Bolingbroke's seizure of the throne is a violation of divine purpose for which he and England must be humbled; instead, Shakespeare portrays the issues as many-sided and subject to varying interpretations. Even in his earlier tetralogy from *1 Henry VI* to *Richard III*, Shakespeare seldom returns all the way to the deposition of Richard II in order to explain the misfortunes of England's civil wars. Most of the prophecies that are grimly fulfilled in these plays are the result of men's evil actions during the Wars of the Roses. Nevertheless, a pattern of divine anger, retribution, and eventual appeasement is manifestly evident throughout this earlier tetralogy. Such a pattern is in harmony with the chronicles of Edward Hall and others, written in part to glorify the Tudor state and to give thanks for its having ended the prolonged anarchy of the fifteenth century. This is not to say that Shakespeare was an apologist for the Tudor state, but that he gave expression to a widely felt distrust of political chaos. The pattern of divine wrath and appeasement provided a causal explanation for England's darkest hour of suffering. Moreover, with its overriding cosmic irony stressing the gulf between human folly and the inscrutable intentions of providence, the pattern offered itself as a potentially stirring subject for drama.

Shakespeare wrote his first tetralogy, from *1 Henry VI* to *Richard III*, some time between 1589 and 1594. Just how much of this first tetralogy may have been planned out when Shakespeare began work is hard to say. In fact the very order of composition has long been in dispute. Despite the commonsense pleading of Dr. Johnson that Part II follows from Part I as a logical consequence, some scholars argue that Part I was composed last. One piece of evidence is that a corrupt version of Part II was published in quarto version in 1594 as *The First part of the Contention betwixt the two famous Houses of Yorke and Lancaster*, and a corrupt version of Part III in octavo in 1595 as *The true Tragedie of Richard Duke of Yorke*. Part I had to await publication in the Folio of 1623, and was registered for publication at that time as "The thirde parte of Henry the sixt." It seems odd, moreover, that Parts II and III make no mention of Lord Talbot, so prominent in Part I. If, however, as seems likely, the early printed versions of Parts II and III were memorial reconstructions without the authority of the official prompt book, the claim of Part II to have been written first may be unsubstantial. The very fact of prior publication of Parts II and III could explain why Part I was called "The thirde parte" in 1623. Although Talbot is not mentioned in Parts II and III, these texts do recall important aspects of Part I. It is certainly possible that Shakespeare wrote all three parts in normal order.

Equally vexing is the question of authorship. Many Elizabethan plays were written by teams of authors, and Shakespeare might have collaborated, especially at the beginning of his career. Perhaps he rewrote older works by such writers as Nashe, Greene, and Marlowe. Yet the theories of multiple authorship, once a commonplace of scholarship, are now generally in disfavor. Greene's famous resentment toward Shakespeare as the "vpstart crow beautified with our feathers" seems more the envy of a lesser talent than the righteous indignation of one who has been plagiarized. The chief criteria used to "disintegrate" the plays into the hands of various supposed contributors are those of taste and style: for example, the low comic scenes of Joan of Arc were long held to be too coarse for Shakespeare's genius. Today most critics see a consistency of view throughout the *Henry VI* plays despite minor inconsistencies of fact that might be the result of simple error or of using multiple sources, and find nothing in these plays inimical to Shakespeare's budding genius. This belief confirms the judgment of Heminges and Condell, Shakespeare's fellow actors and editors of the 1623 Folio, who placed all the *Henry VI* plays among Shakespeare's collected works in their historical order.

If Shakespeare was at least chiefly responsible for the *Henry VI* series, he may also have been an important innovator in the new genre of the history play. Only the anonymous *Famous Victories of Henry V* is certainly earlier in dealing with recent English history. There were, to be sure, plays about legendary British history such as *Gorboduc* or *The Misfortunes of Arthur*, or about far-off lands such as *Cambises* or Marlowe's *Tamburlaine*. All these plays had analogously explored political questions fascinating to Elizabethan England, and *Tamburlaine*'s immense success had certainly established a vogue for grand scenes of military conquest. Still, the English history play as a recognizable form came into being with *Henry VI*. The success was evidently tremendous, and established Shakespeare as a major playwright.

1 Henry VI, like all the plays in this first tetralogy, comprises a large number of episodes, a sizeable cast of characters, and a wide geographical range. The subject is England's loss of her French territories because of political division at home. The structure of the play is one of sequential action displayed in great variety and in alternating scenes that are thematically juxtaposed and contrasted with one another. In the rapid shifting back and forth between the English and French court, for example, Shakespeare displays contrasting scenes of epic martial seriousness and debased sexual frivolity, and establishes by this means his first paradoxical theme: France triumphs in England's weakness, not in her own strength. The English are naturally superior but are torn apart by internal dissension, by a "jarring discord of nobility" and a "shouldering of each other in the court" among those attempting to take advantage of Henry VI's weak minority rule and his vulnerable genealogical claim. Two of young Henry's kinsmen jockeying for position are Humphrey, Duke of Gloucester, and the Bishop of Winchester. Humphrey's intentions are virtuous, but he is unable to prevent the opportunistic scheming of his rival. Winchester, despite his ecclesiastical calling, is a man of evil ambition and corrupt life, wholly intent on destroying the rightminded Gloucester. Shakespeare employs derisive anticlerical humor against Winchester, and enlists the Protestant sympathies of his Elizabethan audience against the meddling Catholic church attempting to exploit England's weak kingship for its own ulterior purposes.

Even so, the menace threatening England is not seen as a Catholic conspiracy throughout; Winchester is only one opportunist fishing in troubled waters. Of greater danger in the long run is Richard Plantagenet, scion of the Yorkist claim. From the start, Shakespeare portrays him as cunning, able to ingratiate himself and bide his time, ultimately ruthless. In these qualities he ominously foreshadows his youngest son and namesake, Richard III. In this play, Plantagenet's strategy is to allow England to wear herself down by the various conflicts at court and military losses abroad; once the situation is reduced to anarchy, Plantagenet will be able to move in. The strategy works only too well.

Chief defender of England's military might in France, and eventual victim of the bickering on the home front, is Lord Talbot. He is the great heroic figure of this play with whom Elizabethan audiences identified. He pleads for political and military unity against the French, and demonstrates that with such unity England would be invincible. Talbot is "the terror of the French," able to hold off a troop of French soldiers with his bare fists, reputed to twist bars of steel. As the embodiment of chivalry, he delivers a richly deserved rebuke to Sir John Falstaff (historically "Fastolfe," but called "Falstaff" in the Folio text of this play), the cowardly soldier who foreshadows the fat knight of *1 Henry IV*. In *1 Henry VI*, cowardice and honor are rendered in black and white extremes. Talbot is a model general, illustrating all the qualities of great leadership advocated by the textbooks of the age: he is a stirring orator, fearless, witty, and concerned with a proper lasting fame. In the touching scenes with his son, Talbot rises triumphantly above his death to become the immortal incarnation of brave soldiership. His unnecessary death offers a devastating comment on the weak leadership that has allowed authority in France to be divided among political rivals.

The relations between men and women in this play are also used to create thematic contrasts. Talbot's chief military rival in France is Joan of Arc; and, although many earlier scholars have wanted to deny Shakespeare's authorship of the Joan of Arc scenes, their thematic function is central. As a woman in armor, Joan is the embodiment of the domineering Amazonian woman to whom the effete and self-indulgent dauphin, Charles, weakly capitulates. The sexual roles have been reversed; Venus triumphs over Mars. Joan also attempts to practice her witchcraft on Talbot and his son, but in vain. Talbot's sense of duty never succumbs to Circean voluptuousness. In his encounter with the Countess of Auvergne, Talbot resourcefully outwits another woman who, like Joan, seeks to entrap him by subterfuge. The Countess finally submits to Talbot's courteous but firm authority, thereby reestablishing the right relationship of male and female. Talbot stands for every kind of decency and order that ought to prevail, but is senselessly destroyed through England's political squabbling.

The last woman introduced in the play, Margaret of Anjou, is also a domineering female. Her adulterous relationship with the fleshly Suffolk, and her ascendancy over the weak Henry VI, are to be of fateful consequence in the ensuing plays. Her scenes, although once dismissed as an afterthought linking *1 Henry VI* with the following plays, in fact recapitulate the motifs of female dominance with great dramatic effect. Young Henry VI is no Talbot; inexperienced in love and highly impressionable, he surrenders to the mere description of a woman he has not even seen, and refuses a politically advantageous match arranged by Duke Humphrey in order that he may marry a dowryless and conniving Frenchwoman. The marriage also anticipates that of Edward IV (in *3 Henry VI*), in which Edward spurns a political alliance with France urged by Warwick in order to wed a penniless widow who has caught his roving eye. Such dismal triumphs of passion over reason are emblematic of the general decay among the English aristocracy. Despite Henry's weakness, he is the central character of this play after all, and his enervating surrender in love is a fitting anticlimax with which to end the first installment of England's decline.

2 Henry VI picks up where the first play ends (in the year 1445) and continues down to the very eve of actual civil war at the Battle of St. Albans (1455). The major events portrayed are the downfall of Humphrey, Duke of Gloucester, and the angry stirrings of the commons leading finally to Jack Cade's rebellion. Popular agitation brings about the death of the Duke of Suffolk, thereby claiming the life of one of those most cynically responsible for England's troubles. The villainous Cardinal of Winchester also dies a horrible and edifying death, suggesting that divine retribution is beginning to reveal its inexorable force. Yet throughout this declining action we witness as countermovement the ominous rise of Richard Plantagenet, Duke of York.

Richard's strategy, like that of his namesake in *Richard III*, is to exploit antagonisms at the English court, turning feuding nobles against one another until his potential rivals for power have destroyed themselves. In particular, he takes advantage of the animosity between the new Queen Margaret of Anjou and Duke Humphrey. Margaret is a consort in the autocratic European style. She haughtily insists on the privileges of her exalted rank, and spurns those who govern in the name of justice. "Is this the guise, Is this the fashion in the court of England?" she incredulously inquires of Suffolk, her lover and political ally (I,iii). Suffolk is an apt mate for Margaret, since he too oppresses the commons. A petition "against the Duke of Suffolk, for enclosing the commons of Melford" is one of many heartfelt grievances brought to the attention of the throne by the common people. Margaret naturally resents the moderate and fair-minded counsel of Duke Humphrey, who urges King

Henry to remedy the distress of the commons. Richard of York has no inherent admiration for Suffolk and Margaret, but cynically backs them as a way of destroying the good Duke of Gloucester. He advises his partners Salisbury and Warwick, "Wink at the Duke of Suffolk's insolence, At Beaufort's pride, at Somerset's ambition, At Buckingham and all the crew of them, Till they have snar'd the shepherd of the flock, That virtuous prince, the good Duke Humphrey" (II,ii). Regrettably, Humphrey has a fatal weakness through which he can be pulled down: the ambition of his wife, Eleanor. Intent on being first lady of the land, Eleanor comes into inevitable conflict with the remorseless Queen Margaret. Winchester and Suffolk, knowing Eleanor's self-blinding pride, find it pathetically easy to plant spies in her household who will encourage her penchant for witchcraft. Humphrey is never contaminated personally by his wife's pride, but is doomed nonetheless. King Henry knows of Humphrey's goodness but cannot save him. This dismaying fall of a courageous moderate, highlighted in the title of the 1594 quarto text ("with the death of the good Duke Humphrey"), singles Humphrey out as the most prominent victim of the second play, like Talbot in Part I. He is cut down by an insincere and temporary alliance of extremists from both sides: those like Margaret and Suffolk who cling to despotic privilege, and those like York who wish to stir up the commons for their own ulterior purposes. In times of confrontation the middle position is inherently vulnerable, and its destruction leads to escalating polarization.

As York both foresees and desires, the commons are indeed unruly when deprived of Humphrey's moderating leadership. Shakespeare has already shown that they tend to ape the quarrels of their elders (as in the ludicrous duels between Horner the Armorer and his man Peter Thump), and are superstitiously gullible (as in the episode of Simpcox the fraudulent blind man). Now, no longer able to petition through channels, their voice becomes importunate. "The commons, like an angry hive of bees That want their leader, scatter up and down And care not who they sting in his revenge" (III,ii). At first their grievances are plausible and their wrath directed at guilty objects. They suspect rightly that their hero, Humphrey, has been destroyed by Suffolk and the Cardinal, and they demand Suffolk's banishment. The request is laudable, but the new note of ultimatum suggests that the people are beginning to feel their own political power. Unless Suffolk is banished, they warn, they will take him by force from the palace. Poor King Henry, lamenting the lost conciliatory authority of Humphrey, aptly points up the central issue of royal prerogative: "And had I not been cited so by them, Yet did I purpose as they do entreat" (III,ii). It is unfortunate in the viewpoint of this play that Henry has to appear to yield to popular force, but he has no alternative. Equally lamentable is the execution of Suffolk by private citizens taking justice into their own hands. However much this despot deserved to be condemned, his lynching is an affront to justice. Servant has turned against master; the commons have tasted blood.

The popular rebellion itself, Cade's uprising, makes a grotesque travesty of popular longings for social justice, and suggests that any movement of this sort is bound to end in absurdity. Shakespeare, for all his deeply appreciative depiction of individual commoners, never credits them with collective political sagacity once they are demonstrating for their rights. In fact Shakespeare unhistorically brings together the worst excesses of the Cade rebellion itself and the famous Peasants' Revolt of 1381 in order to exaggerate the dangers of popular agitation. The Cade scenes abound in the degrading comedy of grandiose pretentiousness. We laugh at the contrast between Cade's professed Utopian notions of abundant food and drink for all, and his petty ambition to be king. He kills those who refer to him as Jack Cade rather than by his pretended title of Lord Mortimer. His movement is fiercely anti-intellectual. Yet the sour joke does not indict the commons alone. Cade's insolent pretentions and his claptrap genealogical claims are a recognizable parody of aristocratic behavior. Even more importantly, we remember that Cade was whetted on to his rebellion by the demagogic York. That schemer has "seduced" Cade to make commotion while York himself raises a huge personal army and advances his fortunes in Ireland. "This devil here shall be my substitute" (III,i). The commons can indeed prove irresponsible when goaded, but throughout *2 Henry VI* feuding aristocrats must bear the chief blame for causing popular discontent.

Prophecy assumes a structural importance in *2 Henry VI* that is to be accentuated in later plays of the tetralogy. The convention holds true that prophecies are always fulfilled. Accordingly, they enable the audience to foresee consequences of present ill-advised action. A spirit appears to the Duchess of Gloucester, predicting that Suffolk will die "by water" and that Somerset should "shun castles." Suffolk's nemesis is a man named Walter (pronounced "water"), whereas Somerset dies at the castle of St. Albans, at the play's end. More importantly, the spirit predicts that "The duke yet lives that Henry shall depose; But him outlive, and die a violent death" (I,iv). Such riddling statements emphasize the cosmic irony of Providence's indirect but inevitable course. Time will confirm that Edward IV and Henry will in turn depose one another, but that Edward will outlive Henry only to die a retributive death. In such prophecy there is already the concept of an eye for an eye, a Lancastrian for a Yorkist, through which Providence will impose its penalty on a rebellious people.

3 Henry VI, because it represents the entire military phase of the civil war, is the most crowded and bustling play of the series. Historically it covers the period from the battles of Wakefield and second St. Albans (1460–1461) to the decisive Yorkist victories at Barnet and Tewkesbury (1471). These and other battles are actually represented on stage. The conventional method of representing armed conflict is by means of alarums and excursions, employing as many soldiers as the acting company could muster, with martial music and numerous entrances and exits in rapid succession. Battles are usually preceded by florid boastful rhetorical exchanges, or *flytings*, between the combatants. The military contests focus on heroic confrontations between individual leaders. Staging of battles often uses the Elizabethan playhouse to its physical capacity, with appearances "on the walls" of some town (i.e., from the upper gallery), scaling operations, sieges, and the like. *3 Henry VI* abounds in spectacular deaths, often performed as gruesome rituals. Young Rutland is dragged from his tutor by the implacable Clifford, and Richard of York is mocked with a paper crown by Queen Margaret; Clifford dies with an arrow in his neck and Warwick the kingmaker dies lamenting the vanity of all earthly achievement; King Henry dies in the tower, a defenseless prisoner in the hands of Richard of Gloucester. The play is perhaps confusing to the reader, but breathes with violent energy on stage.

The action lacks a central character. The title of the 1595 octavo edition pairs the deaths of Richard of York and of King Henry as the play's most memorable episodes; and in this dual focus we see the dominant motif of reciprocity, a Yorkist death for a Lancastrian death. This pattern will continue into *Richard III*, for *3 Henry VI* ends with an ominous amount of unfinished business; Clarence, for example, later sees that he must atoningly die for his part in the slaughter of Edward, the Lancastrian Prince of Wales. Just as the deaths are balanced and contrasted with one another, the military action also seesaws back and forth. Both Henry VI and Edward IV are at times imprisoned. The wheel of fortune elevates one side and then the other. Political alliances shift the balance of power one way and then the other. The action is painfully indecisive, the carnage pointlessly leading only to further violence. The spectacle is made infinitely more agonizing by the realization that all this is a family quarrel. The commons suffer accordingly: we witness the grief of a father who has mistakenly killed his son in battle, and a son who has killed his father (II,v). The people, seldom seen, are no longer political troublemakers but mere victims, waiting patiently for an end. A recurrent emblem used to convey the utter futility of this war is the molehill. York is mockingly crowned before his execution on a molehill, and King Henry retires from a battle to a molehill in order to meditate on the happy contemplative life he has been denied. The molehill suggests the ironic perversity of man's quest for worldly power, whereby those who possess power are incapable of exercising it wisely, and those who burn with ambition are denied legitimate opportunity.

As in earlier plays of the series, the relationships between men and women echo the discord of the English nation, and contribute in turn to further discord. Margaret of Anjou, the remorseless defender of her son Edward's claim, acts with increasingly masculine authority while her ineffectual husband abdicates responsibility. She is the Lancastrian general, resourceful in battle and often victorious, implacable in vengeance. This inversion of male and female roles is reflected on the Yorkist side by Edward IV's disastrous marriage with Lady Elizabeth Grey. She is the widow of a Lancastrian soldier with no family position or political power to bring to the marriage—nothing, in fact, but her ambition on behalf of her kinsmen. Edward's attraction to her is fleshly indulgence in defiance of more prudent considerations. Indeed, to make matters much worse, Warwick is at that very moment negotiating a highly favorable alliance with the King of France. Edward IV thus unconsciously apes the earlier willfulness of his counterpart, Henry VI. Edward IV's snubbing of Warwick leads to the defection of that powerful leader, and through him the defection of Edward's brother Clarence who has succumbed to the charms of Warwick's daughter Isabel. And although *1 Henry VI* at least counterbalances the uxoriousness of Henry with the positive example of Lord Talbot, *3 Henry VI* fails to discover any such noble character. (Briefly, to be sure, we are introduced to the young Earl of Richmond, who is to be Henry VII, but only as the merest glimpse of a distant future.) The almost total lack of any distinctly virtuous character throughout the play gives to *3 Henry VI* its predominantly dismaying and helpless mood. The heroes have been destroyed.

Richard of Gloucester alone seems to profit from England's decline. Like his father York, his strategy has been to let England flay herself into anarchic vulnerability. Once the father York has disappeared from the scene, young Richard's malevolent character becomes increasingly apparent. No longer merely one of York's brave sons, Richard is the new genius of discord. His bravura soliloquy in III,ii is often included in performances of *Richard III*, for it yields rich clues to his emerging character: he is ambitious, ruthless, deformed from birth, and above all a consummate deceiver. To the audience he boasts of his ability, claiming that as a hypocrite he will excel the combined talents of Nestor, Ulysses, Sinon, Proteus, and Machiavelli. The superb self-assurance is arresting, the utter heartless consistency admirable even though we must detest his intention. In a second soliloquy, virtually at the end of the play, having already dispatched Henry VI and his son Edward, Richard confides to the audience that Clarence is to be his next victim. And although Richard pledges fealty to his young nephew Edward, the Yorkist crown prince, at the Yorkist victory celebration with which the play ends, we know that Richard's kiss of peace is no more trustworthy than Judas' kissing of Christ. All those standing between Richard and the throne are to be eliminated. Clearly, the pious longings for peace expressed by King Edward IV are to be cruelly violated.

THE FIRST PART OF KING HENRY THE SIXTH

[*Dramatis Personae*

KING HENRY the Sixth.
DUKE OF GLOUCESTER, *uncle to the King, and* Protector.
DUKE OF BEDFORD, *uncle to the King, and* Regent of France.
THOMAS BEAUFORT, Duke of Exeter, *great-uncle to the King.*
HENRY BEAUFORT, *great-uncle to the King,* Bishop of Winchester, *and afterwards* Cardinal.
JOHN BEAUFORT, Earl, *afterwards* Duke, of Somerset.
RICHARD PLANTAGENET, *son of Richard late Earl of Cambridge, afterwards* Duke of York.
EARL OF WARWICK.
EARL OF SALISBURY.
EARL OF SUFFOLK.
LORD TALBOT, *afterwards* Earl of Shrewsbury.
JOHN TALBOT, *his son.*
EDMUND MORTIMER, Earl of March.
SIR JOHN FALSTAFF.
SIR WILLIAM LUCY.
SIR WILLIAM GLANSDALE.
SIR THOMAS GARGRAVE.
Mayor of London.
WOODVILE, *Lieutenant of the Tower.*
VERNON, *of the White-Rose or York faction.*
BASSET, *of the Red-Rose or Lancaster faction.*
A Lawyer. Mortimer's Keepers.

CHARLES, Dauphin, *and afterwards* King, of France.
REIGNIER, Duke of Anjou, *and titular* King of Naples.
DUKE OF BURGUNDY.
DUKE OF ALENÇON.
BASTARD OF ORLEANS.
Governor of Paris.
Master-Gunner of Orleans, *and* his Son.
General of the French forces in Bourdeaux.
A French Sergeant. A Porter.
An old Shepherd, father to Joan la Pucelle.

MARGARET, *daughter to Reignier, afterwards married to King Henry.*
COUNTESS OF AUVERGNE.
JOAN LA PUCELLE, *commonly called* Joan of Arc.

Lords, Warders of the Tower, Heralds, Officers, Soldiers, Messengers, *and* Attendants.

Fiends appearing to La Pucelle.

SCENE: *Partly in England, and partly in France.*]

ACT I.

SCENE I. [*Westminster Abbey.*]

Dead March. Enter the Funeral of KING HENRY the Fifth, *attended on by the* DUKE OF BEDFORD, *Regent of France; the* DUKE OF GLOUCESTER, *Protector; the* DUKE OF EXETER, [*the* EARL OF] WARWICK, *the* BISHOP OF WINCHESTER, *and the* DUKE OF SOMERSET [, Heralds, *&c.*].

Bed. Hung be the heavens with black, yield day to night!
Comets, importing change of times and states,
Brandish your crystal tresses in the sky,
And with them scourge the bad revolting stars
That have consented unto Henry's death!
King Henry the Fifth, too famous to live long!
England ne'er lost a king of so much worth.
Glou. England ne'er had a king until his time.
Virtue he had, deserving to command:
His brandish'd sword did blind men with his beams:
His arms spread wider than a dragon's wings;
His sparkling eyes, replete with wrathful fire,
More dazzled and drove back his enemies
Than mid-day sun fierce bent against their faces.
What should I say? his deeds exceed all speech:
He ne'er lift up his hand but conquered.
Exe. We mourn in black: why mourn we not in blood?
Henry is dead and never shall revive:
Upon a wooden coffin we attend,
And death's dishonourable victory
We with our stately presence glorify,
Like captives bound to a triumphant car.
What! shall we curse the planets of mishap
That plotted thus our glory's overthrow?
Or shall we think the subtle-witted French
Conjurers and sorcerers, that afraid of him
By magic verses have contriv'd his end?
Win. He was a king bless'd of the King of kings.
Unto the French the dreadful judgement-day
So dreadful will not be as was his sight.
The battles of the Lord of hosts he fought:
The church's prayers made him so prosperous.
Glou. The church! where is it? Had not churchmen pray'd,
His thread of life had not so soon decay'd:
None do you like but an effeminate prince,
Whom, like a school-boy, you may over-awe.
Win. Gloucester, whate'er we like, thou art protector
And lookest to command the prince and realm.
Thy wife is proud; she holdeth thee in awe,
More than God or religious churchmen may.
Glou. Name not religion, for thou lov'st the flesh,

ACT I. SCENE I. 1. **Hung . . . black,** a metaphor from the theatrical practice of draping the stage in black when a tragedy was to be performed. (*Shakespeare's England*, II, 280.) 2. **Comets.** That comets boded evil to princes and to the state was a widespread popular belief; cf. *King John*, III, iv, 153-159; *Julius Caesar*, II, ii, 30-31. 3. **crystal,** bright, shining; the epithet was frequently applied to astral phenomena. 8. **England ne'er had a king,** etc. This speech and others in the scene reflect the traditional opinion of King Henry v, who was a national hero of the English for centuries. 9. **Virtue,** excellence; see glossary. 10. **his,** its; see glossary. 16. **lift,** lifted. 19. **wooden,** probably a quibble on the meanings "dull, dead, as the sound of wood when struck" and "senseless." 21. **our stately presence,** the stately funeral procession. 33. **pray'd,** with pun on *prey'd*. 34. **decay'd,** been destroyed; see glossary. 39. **Thy wife is proud,** a reference to Gloucester's ambitious wife, Elinor, whose inordinate desire for greatness is depicted in *2 Henry VI*.

And ne'er throughout the year to church thou go'st
Except it be to pray against thy foes.
Bed. Cease, cease these jars and rest your minds in peace:
Let 's to the altar: heralds, wait on us:
Instead of gold, we'll offer up our arms;
Since arms avail not now that Henry 's dead.
Posterity, await for wretched years,
When at their mothers' moist'ned eyes babes shall suck,
Our isle be made a nourish of salt tears,
And none but women left to wail the dead.
Henry the Fifth, thy ghost I invocate:
Prosper this realm, keep it from civil broils,
Combat with adverse planets in the heavens!
A far more glorious star thy soul will make
Than Julius Cæsar or bright——

Enter a Messenger.

Mess. My honourable lords, health to you all!
Sad tidings bring I to you out of France,
Of loss, of slaughter and discomfiture:
Guienne, Champagne, Rheims, Orleans,
Paris, Guysors, Poictiers, are all quite lost.
Bed. What say'st thou, man, before dead Henry's corse?
Speak softly, or the loss of those great towns
Will make him burst his lead and rise from death.
Glou. Is Paris lost? is Rouen yielded up?
If Henry were recall'd to life again,
These news would cause him once more yield the ghost.
Exe. How were they lost? what treachery was us'd?
Mess. No treachery; but want of men and money.
Amongst the soldiers this is muttered,
That here you maintain several factions,
And whilst a field should be dispatch'd and fought,
You are disputing of your generals:
One would have ling'ring wars with little cost;
Another would fly swift, but wanteth wings;
A third thinks, without expense at all,
By guileful fair words peace may be obtain'd
Awake, awake, English nobility!
Let not sloth dim your honours new-begot:
Cropp'd are the flower-de-luces in your arms;
Of England's coat one half is cut away. [*Exit.*]
Exe. Were our tears wanting to this funeral,
These tidings would call forth her flowing tides.
Bed. Me they concern; Regent I am of France.
Give me my steeled coat. I'll fight for France.
Away with these disgraceful wailing robes!
Wounds will I lend the French instead of eyes,
To weep their intermissive miseries.

Enter to them another Messenger.

Mess. Lords, view these letters full of bad mischance.
France is revolted from the English quite,
Except some petty towns of no import:
The Dauphin Charles is crowned king in Rheims;
The Bastard of Orleans with him is join'd;
Reignier, Duke of Anjou, doth take his part;
The Duke of Alençon flieth to his side. *Exit.*
Exe. The Dauphin crowned king! all fly to him!
O, whither shall we fly from this reproach?
Glou. We will not fly, but to our enemies' throats.
Bedford, if thou be slack, I'll fight it out.
Bed. Gloucester, why doubt'st thou of my forwardness?
An army have I muster'd in my thoughts,
Wherewith already France is overrun.

Enter another Messenger.

Mess. My gracious lords, to add to your laments,
Wherewith you now bedew King Henry's hearse,
I must inform you of a dismal fight
Betwixt the stout Lord Talbot and the French.
Win. What! wherein Talbot overcame? is 't so?
Mess. O, no; wherein Lord Talbot was o'erthrown:
The circumstance I'll tell you more at large.
The tenth of August last this dreadful lord,
Retiring from the siege of Orleans,
Having full scarce six thousand in his troop,
By three and twenty thousand of the French
Was round encompassed and set upon.
No leisure had he to enrank his men;
He wanted pikes to set before his archers;
Instead whereof sharp stakes pluck'd out of hedges
They pitched in the ground confusedly,
To keep the horsemen off from breaking in.
More than three hours the fight continued;
Where valiant Talbot above human thought
Enacted wonders with his sword and lance:
Hundreds he sent to hell, and none durst stand him;
Here, there, and every where, enrag'd he slew:
The French exclaim'd, the devil was in arms;
All the whole army stood agaz'd on him:
His soldiers spying his undaunted spirit
A Talbot! a Talbot! cried out amain
And rush'd into the bowels of the battle.
Here had the conquest fully been seal'd up,
If Sir John Falstaff had not play'd the coward:
He, being in the vaward, plac'd behind
With purpose to relieve and follow them,
Cowardly fled, not having struck one stroke.
Hence grew the general wrack and massacre;
Enclosed were they with their enemies:
A base Walloon, to win the Dauphin's grace,
Thrust Talbot with a spear into the back,
Whom all France with their chief assembled strength
Durst not presume to look once in the face.
Bed. Is Talbot slain? then I will slay myself,

44. **jars,** discords; usually applied to music; see glossary. 50. **nourish,** nurse; early spelling "nourice." 54. **adverse planets,** an allusion to the supposed influence exerted on human and terrestrial affairs by celestial bodies. 60. **Champagne,** the city of Compiegne. 64. **lead,** leaden coffin. 71. **factions,** groups, sets of persons; see glossary. 73. **of,** about. 80. **flower-de-luces,** the *fleurs-de-lis*, or iris, national emblem of France. According to the Treaty of Troyes, 1420, the crown of France was ceded to England but was nominally to belong to the French king, Charles VI, as long as he lived. Henry V's title was designated "King of England and Heir of France." At his death this title passed to Henry VI; but within two months after this took place, Charles VI died and his son Charles VII was proclaimed king. The loss of the French crown would deprive the English king of the right to display the *fleur-de-lis* in his coat of arms. 82. **wanting,** lacking; see glossary. 87-88. **Wounds . . . weep,** i.e., he will make them shed blood instead of weep tears. 88. **intermissive,** intermittent; having a short intermission (Warburton and others). 105. **dismal,** ill-boding, sinister. 109. **circumstance,** particulars; see glossary. **at large,** in full detail; see *large* in glossary. 116. **pikes,** ironbound stakes sharpened at the ends and set in the ground in front of archers as protection against cavalry charges. 125. **exclaim'd,** protested; see glossary. 126. **agazed,** astounded. 128. **amain,** with full force. 130. **seal'd up,** completed; see *seal* in glossary. 131. **Sir John Falstaff.** "Fastolfe" in the chronicles; but the Shakespearean spelling used here shows us the origin of the name used in the *Henry IV* plays. 132. **vaward,** vanguard. 137. **Walloon,** an inhabitant of that province, now a part of southern Belgium. 146. **Lord Scales, Lord Hungerford,** English lords who participated in the wars in France. Both are mentioned in Holinshed. 154. **Saint George's feast,**

For living idly here in pomp and ease,
Whilst such a worthy leader, wanting aid,
Unto his dastard foemen is betray'd.
Mess. O no, he lives; but is took prisoner,
And Lord Scales with him and Lord Hungerford:
Most of the rest slaughter'd or took likewise.
Bed. His ransom there is none but I shall pay:
I'll hale the Dauphin headlong from his throne:
His crown shall be the ransom of my friend;
Four of their lords I'll change for one of ours.
Farewell, my masters; to my task will I;
Bonfires in France forthwith I am to make,
To keep our great Saint George's feast withal:
Ten thousand soldiers with me I will take,
Whose bloody deeds shall make all Europe quake.
Mess. So you had need; for Orleans is besieg'd;
The English army is grown weak and faint:
The Earl of Salisbury craveth supply,
And hardly keeps his men from mutiny,
Since they, so few, watch such a multitude. [*Exit.*]
Exe. Remember, lords, your oaths to Henry sworn,
Either to quell the Dauphin utterly,
Or bring him in obedience to your yoke.
Bed. I do remember it; and here take my leave,
To go about my preparation. *Exit Bedford.*
Glou. I'll to the Tower with all the haste I can,
To view th' artillery and munition;
And then I will proclaim young Henry king. *Exit Glou.*
Exe. To Eltham will I, where the young king is,
Being ordain'd his special governor,
And for his safety there I'll best devise. *Exit.*
Win. Each hath his place and function to attend:
I am left out; for me nothing remains.
But long I will not be Jack out of office:
The king from Eltham I intend to steal
And sit at chiefest stern of public weal. *Exit.*

[SCENE II. *France. Before Orleans.*]

Sound a flourish. Enter CHARLES, ALENÇON, *and* REIGNIER, *marching with drum and Soldiers.*

Char. Mars his true moving, even as in the heavens
So in the earth, to this day is not known:
Late did he shine upon the English side;
Now we are victors; upon us he smiles.
What towns of any moment but we have?
At pleasure here we lie near Orleans;
Otherwhiles the famish'd English, like pale ghosts,
Faintly besiege us one hour in a month.
Alen. They want their porridge and their fat bull-beeves:
Either they must be dieted like mules
And have their provender tied to their mouths
Or piteous they will look, like drowned mice.
Reig. Let 's raise the siege: why live we idly here?
Talbot is taken, whom we wont to fear:
Remaineth none but mad-brain'd Salisbury;
And he may well in fretting spend his gall,
Nor men nor money hath he to make war.
Char. Sound, sound alarum! we will rush on them.
Now for the honour of the forlorn French!
Him I forgive my death that killeth me
When he sees me go back one foot or fly. *Exeunt.*

Here alarum; they are beaten back by the English with great loss. Enter CHARLES, ALENÇON, *and* REIGNIER.

Char. Who ever saw the like? what men have I!
Dogs! cowards! dastards! I would ne'er have fled,
But that they left me 'midst my enemies.
Reig. Salisbury is a desperate homicide;
He fighteth as one weary of his life.
The other lords, like lions wanting food,
Do rush upon us as their hungry prey.
Alen. Froissart, a countryman of ours, records,
England all Olivers and Rowlands bred
During the time Edward the Third did reign.
More truly now may this be verified;
For none but Samsons and Goliases
It sendeth forth to skirmish. One to ten!
Lean raw-bon'd rascals! who would e'er suppose
They had such courage and audacity?
Char. Let 's leave this town; for they are hare-brain'd slaves,
And hunger will enforce them to be more eager:
Of old I know them; rather with their teeth
The walls they'll tear down than forsake the siege.
Reig. I think, by some odd gimmors or device
Their arms are set like clocks, still to strike on;
Else ne'er could they hold out so as they do.
By my consent, we'll even let them alone.
Alen. Be it so.

Enter the BASTARD *of Orleans.*

Bast. Where 's the Prince Dauphin ? I have news for him.
Char. Bastard of Orleans, thrice welcome to us.
Bast. Methinks your looks are sad, your cheer appall'd:
Hath the late overthrow wrought this offence?
Be not dismay'd, for succour is at hand:
A holy maid hither with me I bring,
Which by a vision sent to her from heaven
Ordained is to raise this tedious siege
And drive the English forth the bounds of France.
The spirit of deep prophecy she hath,
Exceeding the nine sibyls of old Rome:
What 's past and what 's to come she can descry.

---

the twenty-third of April. St. George was the patron saint of England. To celebrate his day in a foreign land would be a boastful, chauvinistic action. 167. **the Tower.** The Tower of London, ancient palace-fortress, later a prison for persons of eminence, was begun by William the Conqueror and enlarged at different times by his successors. 175. **Jack out of office,** an unimportant fellow with nothing to do. 177. **at chiefest stern,** in a position of supreme control.

SCENE II. *Stage Direction:* ***flourish,*** fanfare of trumpets; see glossary. 1. **Mars . . . moving.** The ordinary man during Shakespeare's time seems to have had some knowledge of the astronomers' perplexity regarding the eccentricity of the orbit of Mars; cf. *All's Well that Ends Well,* I, i, 206-210. (*Shakespeare's England,* I, 448-449.) 9. **fat bull-beeves,** food supposed to confer courage (Hart). 16. **spend,** expend, waste. **gall,** bitterness of spirit. 28. **hungry prey,** hungry for prey; a transferred epithet. 29. **Froissart,** a fourteenth-century French chronicler who wrote of recent and contemporary events of Flanders, France, Spain, and England. 30. **Olivers and Rowlands,** paladins in the Charlemagne legends, the most famous of the twelve for their daring exploits. 33. **Samsons, Goliases,** Biblical characters typifying great physical strength. 35. **rascals,** young, lean, or inferior deer of a herd. 41. **gimmors,** gimmals, joints or connecting parts for transmitting motion. 48. **appall'd,** made pale. 56. **nine . . . Rome,** inspired women of the ancient world, not of Rome. The phrase here is probably due to a confusion with the sibyl who came to Tarquin with nine prophetic books. 57. **descry,** discover, discern.

Speak, shall I call her in? Believe my words,
For they are certain and unfallible.
Char. Go, call her in. [*Exit Bastard.*] But first, to try her skill,
Reignier, stand thou as Dauphin in my place:
Question her proudly; let thy looks be stern:
By this means shall we sound what skill she hath.

Enter [*the* BASTARD of Orleans, *with*] JOAN [LA] PUCELLE.

Reig. Fair maid, is 't thou wilt do these wondrous feats?
Puc. Reignier, is 't thou that thinkest to beguile me?
Where is the Dauphin? Come, come from behind;
I know thee well, though never seen before.
Be not amaz'd, there 's nothing hid from me:
In private will I talk with thee apart.
Stand back, you lords, and give us leave awhile.
Reig. She takes upon her bravely at first dash.
Puc. Dauphin, I am by birth a shepherd's daughter,
My wit untrain'd in any kind of art.
Heaven and our Lady gracious hath it pleas'd
To shine on my contemptible estate:
Lo, whilst I waited on my tender lambs,
And to sun's parching heat display'd my cheeks,
God's mother deigned to appear to me
And in a vision full of majesty
Will'd me to leave my base vocation
And free my country from calamity:
Her aid she promis'd and assur'd success:
In complete glory she reveal'd herself;
And, whereas I was black and swart before,
With those clear rays which she infus'd on me
That beauty am I bless'd with which you may see.
Ask me what question thou canst possible,
And I will answer unpremeditated:
My courage try by combat, if thou dar'st,
And thou shalt find that I exceed my sex.
Resolve on this, thou shalt be fortunate,
If thou receive me for thy warlike mate.
Char. Thou hast astonish'd me with thy high terms:
Only this proof I'll of thy valour make,
In single combat thou shalt buckle with me,
And if thou vanquishest, thy words are true;
Otherwise I renounce all confidence.
Puc. I am prepar'd: here is my keen-edg'd sword,
Deck'd with five flower-de-luces on each side;
The which at Touraine, in Saint Katharine's churchyard,
Out of a great deal of old iron I chose forth.
Char. Then come, a God's name; I fear no woman.
Puc. And while I live, I'll ne'er fly from a man.
Here they fight, and Joan La Pucelle overcomes.
Char. Stay, stay thy hands! thou art an Amazon
And fightest with the sword of Deborah.
Puc. Christ's mother helps me, else I were too weak.
Char. Whoe'er helps thee, 'tis thou that must help me:
Impatiently I burn with thy desire;
My heart and hands thou hast at once subdu'd.
Excellent Pucelle, if thy name be so,
Let me thy servant and not sovereign be:
'Tis the French Dauphin sueth to thee thus.
Puc. I must not yield to any rites of love,
For my profession 's sacred from above:
When I have chased all thy foes from hence,
Then will I think upon a recompense.
Char. Meantime look gracious on thy prostrate thrall.
Reig. My lord, methinks, is very long in talk.
Alen. Doubtless he shrives this woman to her smock;
Else ne'er could he so long protract his speech.
Reig. Shall we disturb him, since he keeps no mean?
Alen. He may mean more than we poor men do know:
These women are shrewd tempters with their tongues.
Reig. My lord, where are you? what devise you on?
Shall we give o'er Orleans, or no?
Puc. Why, no, I say, distrustful recreants!
Fight till the last gasp; I will be your guard.
Char. What she says I'll confirm; we'll fight it out.
Puc. Assign'd am I to be the English scourge.
This night the siege assuredly I'll raise:
Expect Saint Martin's summer, halcyon days,
Since I have entered into these wars.
Glory is like a circle in the water,
Which never ceaseth to enlarge itself
Till by broad spreading it disperse to nought.
With Henry's death the English circle ends;
Dispersed are the glories it included.
Now am I like that proud insulting ship
Which Cæsar and his fortune bare at once.
Char. Was Mahomet inspired with a dove?
Thou with an eagle art inspired then.
Helen, the mother of great Constantine,
Nor yet Saint Philip's daughters, were like thee.
Bright star of Venus, fall'n down on the earth,
How may I reverently worship thee enough?
Alen. Leave off delays, and let us raise the siege.
Reig. Woman, do what thou canst to save our honours;
Drive them from Orleans and be immortaliz'd.
Char. Presently we'll try: come, let's away about it:
No prophet will I trust, if she prove false. *Exeunt.*

[SCENE III. *London. Before the Tower.*]

Enter [*the* DUKE OF] GLOUCESTER, *with his* Serving-men [*in blue coats*].

71. **takes . . . bravely,** plays her part well. 83. **complete,** perfect in quality; see glossary. 84. **black and swart,** probably alluding to her complexion, tanned and roughened by exposure. 94. **proof,** trial, test; see glossary. 95. **buckle,** join in close combat (with bawdy suggestion). 98-101. **my keen-edg'd . . . iron.** Holinshed: ". . . from saint Katharins church of Fierbois in Touraine, (where she neuer had beene and knew not,) in a secret place there among old iron, appointed she hir sword to be sought out and brought hir, (that with fiue floure delices was grauen on both sides,) wherewith she fought and did manie slaughters by hir owne hands." 105. **Deborah,** Hebrew prophetess who "judged" Israel in the fourteenth century B.C. She led an army against the Canaanite oppressors, whom she overcame. (Judges 4, 5.) 119. **shrives,** hears confession and gives absolution. **to her smock,** i.e., completely; see *smock* in glossary. 121. **keeps no mean,** observes no middle position, is immoderate. 123. **shrewd,** cunning; see glossary. 124. **devise,** decide. 126. **recreants,** cowards; see glossary. 131. **Saint Martin's summer,** i.e., Indian summer; St. Martin's Day is November 11. **halcyon days.** The halcyon is the kingfisher, which, according to fable, nested at midwinter; it had the virtue of calming the waves. 138-139. **that . . . once,** an allusion to a story in Plutarch which relates how Caesar, encountering a storm at sea, said to the mariners, "Fear not, for thou hast Caesar and his fortune with thee." (Hart). 142. **Helen . . . Constantine,** famous among other things for having visions. She is said to have discovered the holy cross and sepulcher of the Lord. 143. **Saint Philip's daughters,** the four daughters of Philip the Evangelist, said in Acts 21:9 to have the power of prophecy. 149. **Presently,** at once; see glossary.

SCENE III. This scene depicts the rivalry between Gloucester and the bishop of Winchester. As the nearest relative of the infant king, Gloucester would normally have been made regent; but by the bishop's instigation, the Council refused to recognize him as such, conferring

Glou. I am come to survey the Tower this day:
Since Henry's death, I fear, there is conveyance.
Where be these warders, that they wait not here?
Open the gates; 'tis Gloucester that calls.
First Warder. [*Within*] Who 's there that knocks so imperiously?
First Serv. It is the noble Duke of Gloucester.
Second Warder. [*Within*] Whoe'er he be, you may not be let in.
First Serv. Villains, answer you so the lord protector?
First Warder. [*Within*] The Lord protect him! so we answer him:
We do no otherwise than we are will'd.
Glou. Who willed you? or whose will stands but mine?
There 's none protector of the realm but I.
Break up the gates, I'll be your warrantize:
Shall I be flouted thus by dunghill grooms?

Gloucester's men rush at the Tower Gates, and Woodvile the Lieutenant speaks within.

Woodv. What noise is this? what traitors have we here?
Glou. Lieutenant, is it you whose voice I hear?
Open the gates; here 's Gloucester that would enter.
Woodv. Have patience, noble duke; I may not open;
The Cardinal of Winchester forbids:
From him I have express commandement
That thou nor none of thine shall be let in.
Glou. Faint-hearted Woodvile, prizest him 'fore me?
Arrogant Winchester, that haughty prelate,
Whom Henry, our late sovereign, ne'er could brook?
Thou art no friend to God or to the king:
Open the gates, or I'll shut thee out shortly.
Serving-men. Open the gates unto the lord protector,
Or we'll burst them open, if that you come not quickly.

Enter to the Protector at the Tower Gates WINCHESTER *and his men in tawny coats.*

Win. How now, ambitious Humphrey! what means this?
Glou. Peel'd priest, dost thou command me to be shut out?
Win. I do, thou most usurping proditor,
And not protector, of the king or realm.
Glou. Stand back, thou manifest conspirator,
Thou that contrivedst to murder our dead lord;
Thou that giv'st whores indulgences to sin:
I'll canvass thee in thy broad cardinal's hat,
If thou proceed in this thy insolence.
Win. Nay, stand thou back; I will not budge a foot:
This be Damascus, be thou cursed Cain,
To slay thy brother Abel, if thou wilt.
Glou. I will not slay thee, but I'll drive thee back:
Thy scarlet robes as a child's bearing-cloth
I'll use to carry thee out of this place.
Win. Do what thou dar'st; I beard thee to thy face.
Glou. What! am I dar'd and bearded to my face?
Draw, men, for all this privileged place;
Blue coats to tawny coats. Priest, beware your beard;
I mean to tug it and to cuff you soundly:
Under my feet I stamp thy cardinal's hat:
In spite of pope or dignities of church,
Here by the cheeks I'll drag thee up and down.
Win. Gloucester, thou wilt answer this before the pope.
Glou. Winchester goose, I cry, a rope! a rope!
Now beat them hence; why do you let them stay?
Thee I'll chase hence, thou wolf in sheep's array.
Out, tawny coats! out, scarlet hypocrite!

Here Gloucester's men beat out the Cardinal's men, and enter in the hurly-burly the Mayor of London *and his* Officers.

May. Fie, lords! that you, being supreme magistrates,
Thus contumeliously should break the peace!
Glou. Peace, mayor! thou know'st little of my wrongs:
Here 's Beaufort, that regards nor God nor king,
Hath here distrain'd the Tower to his use.
Win. Here 's Gloucester, a foe to citizens,
One that still motions war and never peace,
O'ercharging your free purses with large fines,
That seeks to overthrow religion,
Because he is protector of the realm,
And would have armour here out of the Tower,
To crown himself king and suppress the prince.
Glou. I will not answer thee with words, but blows.

Here they skirmish again.

May. Nought rests for me in this tumultuous strife
But to make open proclamation:
Come, officer; as loud as e'er thou canst
Cry.
[*Off.*] All manner of men assembled here in arms this day against God's peace and the king's, we charge and command you, in his highness' name, to repair to your several dwelling-places; and not to wear, handle, or use any sword, weapon, or dagger, henceforward, upon pain of death.
Glou. Cardinal, I'll be no breaker of the law:
But we shall meet, and break our minds at large.
Win. Gloucester, we will meet; to thy cost, be sure:
Thy heart-blood I will have for this day's work.
May. I'll call for clubs, if you will not away.
This cardinal's more haughty than the devil.
Glou. Mayor, farewell: thou dost but what thou mayst.
Win. Abominable Gloucester, guard thy head;

on him instead the title Lord Protector, with powers granted "by consent of the Council." In the fourth year of Henry VI's reign, Gloucester presented to the Parliament articles of accusation against the bishop, the first of which was that Gloucester had been refused admission to the Tower "by the Commaundement of my saied Lord of Winchester." 2. **conveyance,** trickery. 10. **will'd,** commanded. 13. **warrantize,** guarantee. 24. **brook,** endure; see glossary. 26. **I'll . . . shortly,** i.e., he will take possession shortly and shut Woodvile out. 30. **Peel'd,** shaven, tonsured. 31. **proditor,** traitor. 34. **Thou . . . lord.** Gloucester, in his bill of particulars against Winchester, charged that the latter had suborned someone to hide in Henry V's bedchamber and to slay the king in his bed. 36. **canvass,** deal with severely; a metaphor from tossing someone in a canvas or blanket as sport or punishment. 39. **Damascus,** a city reputed to have been built on the site of Cain's quarrel with Abel. 40. **thy brother.** Winchester was Gloucester's uncle; see the Genealogical Table. 42. **bearing-cloth,** christening robe. 44. **beard,** openly defy. 46. **privileged place.** The Tower, as a royal residence, was one of the precincts where drawing of weapons was forbidden by the law of arms; cf. II, iv, 86, note. 47. **Blue coats,** customarily worn by serving men. **tawny coats,** worn by attendants on a church dignitary. 52. **answer,** render an account of; see glossary. 56. **out, scarlet,** referring to the cardinal's red cassock. An exclamation of reproach; see *out* in glossary. 58. **contumeliously,** arrogantly, contemptuously. 61. **distrain'd,** confiscated. 63. **still,** always, continuously; see glossary. **motions,** proposes. 64. **O'ercharging . . . purses,** overburdening you with excessive taxation. 79. **pain,** punishment; see glossary. 81. **break our minds,** reveal our purposes; with a pun on "cracking of heads."

For I intend to have it ere long.

Exeunt [*, severally, Gloucester and Winchester with their Serving-men*].

May. See the coast clear'd, and then we will depart.
Good God, these nobles should such stomachs bear!
I myself fight not once in forty year. *Exeunt*.

[SCENE IV. *Orleans*.]

Enter the Master Gunner *of Orleans and his* Boy.

M. Gun. Sirrah, thou know'st how Orleans is besieg'd,
And how the English have the suburbs won.

Boy. Father, I know; and oft have shot at them,
Howe'er unfortunate I miss'd my aim.

M. Gun. But now thou shalt not. Be thou rul'd by me:
Chief master-gunner am I of this town;
Something I must do to procure me grace.
The prince's espials have informed me
How the English, in the suburbs close intrench'd,
Wont through a secret grate of iron bars
In yonder tower to overpeer the city
And thence discover how with most advantage
They may vex us with shot or with assault.
To intercept this inconvenience,
A piece of ordnance 'gainst it I have plac'd;
And even these three days have I watch'd,
If I could see them.
Now do thou watch, for I can stay no longer.
If thou spy'st any, run and bring me word;
And thou shalt find me at the governor's. *Exit*.

Boy. Father, I warrant you; take you no care;
I'll never trouble you, if I may spy them. *Exit*.

Enter SALISBURY *and* TALBOT *on the turrets, with* [SIR WILLIAM GLANSDALE, SIR THOMAS GARGRAVE, *and*] *others*.

Sal. Talbot, my life, my joy, again return'd!
How wert thou handled being prisoner?
Or by what means gots thou to be releas'd?
Discourse, I prithee, on this turret's top.

Tal. The Duke of Bedford had a prisoner
Call'd the brave Lord Ponton de Santrailles;
For him was I exchang'd and ransomed.
But with a baser man of arms by far
Once in contempt they would have barter'd me:
Which I disdaining scorn'd and craved death
Rather than I would be so vile-esteem'd.
In fine, redeem'd I was as I desir'd.
But, O! the treacherous Falstaff wounds my heart,
Whom with my bare fists I would execute,
If I now had him brought into my power.

Sal. Yet tell'st thou not how thou wert entertain'd.

Tal. With scoffs and scorns and contumelious taunts.
In open market-place produc'd they me,
To be a public spectacle to all:
Here, said they, is the terror of the French,
The scarecrow that affrights our children so.
Then broke I from the officers that led me,
And with my nails digg'd stones out of the ground,
To hurl at the beholders of my shame:
My grisly countenance made others fly;
None durst come near for fear of sudden death.
In iron walls they deem'd me not secure;
So great fear of my name 'mongst them were spread
That they suppos'd I could rend bars of steel
And spurn in pieces posts of adamant:
Wherefore a guard of chosen shot I had
That walk'd about me every minute while;
And if I did but stir out of my bed,
Ready they were to shoot me to the heart.

Enter the Boy *with a linstock*.

Sal. I grieve to hear what torments you endur'd,
But we will be reveng'd sufficiently.
Now it is supper-time in Orleans:
Here, through this grate, I count each one
And view the Frenchmen how they fortify:
Let us look in; the sight will much delight thee.
Sir Thomas Gargrave, and Sir William Glansdale,
Let me have your express opinions
Where is best place to make our batt'ry next.

Gar. I think, at the north gate; for there stands lords.

Glan. And I, here, at the bulwark of the bridge.

Tal. For aught I see, this city must be famish'd,
Or with light skirmishes enfeebled.

Here they shoot, and Salisbury [*and Gargrave*] *fall down*.

Sal. O Lord, have mercy on us, wretched sinners!

Gar. O Lord, have mercy on me, woful man!

Tal. What chance is this that suddenly hath cross'd us?
Speak, Salisbury; at least, if thou canst speak:
How far'st thou, mirror of all martial men?
One of thy eyes and thy cheek's side struck off!
Accursed tower! accursed fatal hand
That hath contriv'd this woful tragedy!
In thirteen battles Salisbury o'ercame;
Henry the Fifth he first train'd to the wars;
Whilst any trump did sound, or drum struck up,
His sword did ne'er leave striking in the field.
Yet liv'st thou, Salisbury? though thy speech doth fail,
One eye thou hast, to look to heaven for grace:
The sun with one eye vieweth all the world.
Heaven, be thou gracious to none alive,
If Salisbury wants mercy at thy hands!
Bear hence his body; I will help to bury it.
Sir Thomas Gargrave, hast thou any life?
Speak unto Talbot; nay, look up to him.
Salisbury, cheer thy spirit with this comfort;
Thou shalt not die whiles—
He beckons with his hand and smiles on me,
As who should say 'When I am dead and gone,
Remember to avenge me on the French.'
Plantagenet, I will; and like thee,
Play on the lute, beholding the towns burn:

90. **stomachs,** angry tempers; see glossary.

SCENE IV. 1. **Sirrah,** customary form of address to an inferior; see glossary. 7. **do . . . grace,** reflect credit on; see glossary. 8. **espials,** spies. 14. **inconvenience,** mischief. 26. **Discourse,** tell it; see glossary. 34. **In fine,** finally; see *fine* in glossary. 47. **grisly,** grim, horrible. 52. **spurn,** kick. 53. **chosen shot,** excellent marksmanship. 56. *Stage Direction:* **linstock,** staff about three feet long having a forked head to hold a lighted match for firing cannon. 69. *Stage Direction: Here they shoot,* i.e., the French (probably off stage). 95. **Plantagenet.** The Earl of Salisbury was Thomas Montacute; he was descended from the Plantagenet Edward I. **like thee.** Salisbury is being compared to Nero, who played music while Rome burned. 100. **gather'd head,** drawn their forces together. 107. **puzzel,** drab, slut. **dolphin.** The English spelling is retained here for the sake of the pun; this is the usual spelling in F. 110. **me,** the ethical dative.

SCENE V. 12. **high-minded,** arrogant. 14. **go victual,** proceed to supply with provisions. 21. **like Hannibal,** i.e., by stratagem rather than by force of arms. 22. **lists,** pleases; see glossary. 30. **treacherous,**

Wretched shall France be only in my name.
Here an alarum, and it thunders and lightens.
What stir is this? what tumult 's in the heavens?
Whence cometh this alarum and the noise?

Enter a Messenger.

Mess. My lord, my lord, the French have gather'd head:
The Dauphin, with one Joan la Pucelle join'd,
A holy prophetess new risen up,
Is come with a great power to raise the siege.
Here Salisbury lifteth himself up and groans.
Tal. Hear, hear how dying Salisbury doth groan!
It irks his heart he cannot be reveng'd.
Frenchmen, I'll be a Salisbury to you:
Pucelle or puzzel, dolphin or dogfish,
Your hearts I'll stamp out with my horse's heels,
And make a quagmire of your mingled brains.
Convey me Salisbury into his tent,
And then we'll try what these dastard Frenchmen dare. *Alarum. Exeunt.*

[SCENE V. *The same.*]

Here an alarum again: and TALBOT *pursueth the* DAUPHIN, *and driveth him: then enter* JOAN LA PUCELLE, *driving Englishmen before her [and exit after them]: then [re-]enter* TALBOT.

Tal. Where is my strength, my valour, and my force?
Our English troops retire, I cannot stay them;
A woman clad in armour chaseth them.

Enter [LA] PUCELLE.

Here, here she comes, I'll have a bout with thee;
Devil or devil's dam, I'll conjure thee:
Blood will I draw on thee, thou art a witch,
And straightway give thy soul to him thou serv'st.
Puc. Come, come, 'tis only I that must disgrace thee.
Here they fight.
Tal. Heavens, can you suffer hell so to prevail?
My breast I'll burst with straining of my courage
And from my shoulders crack my arms asunder,
But I will chastise this high-minded strumpet.
They fight again.
Puc. Talbot, farewell; thy hour is not yet come:
I must go victual Orleans forthwith.
A short alarum: then enter the town with soldiers.
O'ertake me, if thou canst; I scorn thy strength.
Go, go, cheer up thy hungry-starved men;
Help Salisbury to make his testament:
This day is ours, as many more shall be. *Exit.*
Tal. My thoughts are whirled like a potter's wheel;
I know not where I am, nor what I do:
A witch, by fear, not force, like Hannibal,
Drives back our troops and conquers as she lists:
So bees with smoke and doves with noisome stench
Are from their hives and houses driven away.
They call'd us for our fierceness English dogs;
Now, like to whelps, we crying run away.
A short alarum.
Hark, countrymen! either renew the fight,
Or tear the lions out of England's coat;
Renounce your soil, give sheep in lions' stead:
Sheep run not half so treacherous from the wolf,
Or horse or oxen from the leopard,
As you fly from your oft-subdued slaves.
Alarum. Here another skirmish.
It will not be: retire into your trenches:
You all consented unto Salisbury's death,
For none would strike a stroke in his revenge.
Pucelle is ent'red into Orleans,
In spite of us or aught that we could do.
O, would I were to die with Salisbury!
The shame hereof will make me hide my head.
Exit Talbot. Alarum; retreat; flourish.

[SCENE VI. *The same.*]

Enter, on the walls, [LA] PUCELLE, DAUPHIN [CHARLES], REIGNIER, ALENÇON, *and Soldiers.*

Puc. Advance our waving colours on the walls;
Rescu'd is Orleans from the English:
Thus Joan la Pucelle hath perform'd her word.
Char. Divinest creature, Astræa's daughter,
How shall I honour thee for this success?
Thy promises are like Adonis' gardens
That one day bloom'd and fruitful were the next.
France, triumph in thy glorious prophetess!
Recover'd is the town of Orleans:
More blessed hap did ne'er befall our state.
Reig. Why ring not out the bells aloud throughout the town?
Dauphin, command the citizens make bonfires
And feast and banquet in the open streets,
To celebrate the joy that God hath given us.
Alen. All France will be replete with mirth and joy,
When they shall hear how we have play'd the men.
Char. 'Tis Joan, not we, by whom the day is won;
For which I will divide my crown with her,
And all the priests and friars in my realm
Shall in procession sing her endless praise.
A statelier pyramis to her I'll rear
Than Rhodope's or Memphis' ever was:
In memory of her when she is dead,
Her ashes, in an urn more precious
Than the rich-jewel'd coffer of Darius,
Transported shall be at high festivals
Before the kings and queens of France.
No longer on Saint Denis will we cry,
But Joan la Pucelle shall be France's saint.
Come in, and let us banquet royally,
After this golden day of victory. *Flourish. Exeunt.*

ACT II.

SCENE I. [*Before Orleans.*]

Enter a Sergeant *of a band, with two* Sentinels.

cowardly.

SCENE VI. 1. **Advance,** lift up. 4. **Astraea,** goddess of Justice. 6. **Adonis' gardens.** Tucker Brooke's note: "What these were in classic literature has been acrimoniously disputed, but a beautiful and extended description, which perhaps inspired the present line, is given by Spenser, *Faerie Queen*, III, iv." 16. **play'd the men,** proved ourselves courageous. 21. **pyramis,** pyramid. 22. **Rhodope's.** Rhodope was a Greek courtesan who became the wife of the king of Egypt. A legend was current that she built the third pyramid. **Memphis'.** Memphis is an ancient city of Egypt near which stand the pyramids of Rameses II. 25. **Darius,** king of Persia, conquered by Alexander the Great. The latter, according to legend, used Darius' *rich-jewel'd coffer* to carry about the poems of Homer. The passage has a parallel in Puttenham's *Art of English Poesie*. 28. **Saint Denis,** patron saint of France.

Serg. Sirs, take your places and be vigilant:
If any noise or soldier you perceive
Near to the walls, by some apparent sign
Let us have knowledge at the court of guard.
First Sent. Sergeant, you shall. [*Exit Sergeant.*] Thus are poor servitors,
When others sleep upon their quiet beds,
Constrain'd to watch in darkness, rain and cold.

Enter TALBOT, BEDFORD, BURGUNDY, [*and forces,*] *with scaling-ladders, their drums beating a dead march.*

Tal. Lord Regent, and redoubted Burgundy,
By whose approach the regions of Artois,
Wallon and Picardy are friends to us,
This happy night the Frenchmen are secure,
Having all day carous'd and banqueted:
Embrace we then this opportunity
As fitting best to quittance their deceit
Contriv'd by art and baleful sorcery.
Bed. Coward of France! how much he wrongs his fame,
Despairing of his own arm's fortitude,
To join with witches and the help of hell!
Bur. Traitors have never other company.
But what 's that Pucelle whom they term so pure?
Tal. A maid, they say.
Bed. A maid! and be so martial!
Bur. Pray God she prove not masculine ere long,
If underneath the standard of the French
She carry armour as she hath begun.
Tal. Well, let them practise and converse with spirits:
God is our fortress, in whose conquering name
Let us resolve to scale their flinty bulwarks.
Bed. Ascend, brave Talbot; we will follow thee.
Tal. Not all together: better far, I guess,
That we do make our entrance several ways;
That, if it chance that one of us do fail,
The other yet may rise against their force.
Bed. Agreed: I'll to yond corner.
Bur. And I to this.
Tal. And here will Talbot mount, or make his grave.
Now, Salisbury, for thee, and for the right
Of English Henry, shall this night appear
How much in duty I am bound to both.
Sent. Arm! arm! the enemy doth make assault!
Cry: 'St. George,' 'A Talbot.'

The French leap o'er the walls in their shirts. Enter, several ways, [*the*] BASTARD [of Orleans], ALENÇON, [*and*] REIGNIER, *half ready, and half unready.*

Alen. How now, my lords! what, all unready so?
Bast. Unready! ay, and glad we 'scap'd so well.
Reig. 'Twas time, I trow, to wake and leave our beds,
Hearing alarums at our chamber-doors.
Alen. Of all exploits since first I follow'd arms,
Ne'er heard I of a warlike enterprise
More venturous or desperate than this.
Bast. I think this Talbot be a fiend of hell.
Reig. If not of hell, the heavens, sure, favour him.
Alen. Here cometh Charles: I marvel how he sped.
Bast. Tut, holy Joan was his defensive guard.

Enter CHARLES *and* JOAN [LA PUCELLE].

Char. Is this thy cunning, thou deceitful dame?
Didst thou at first, to flatter us withal,
Make us partakers of a little gain,
That now our loss might be ten times so much?
Puc. Wherefore is Charles impatient with his friend?
At all times will you have my power alike?
Sleeping or waking must I still prevail,
Or will you blame and lay the fault on me?
Improvident soldiers! had your watch been good,
This sudden mischief never could have fall'n.
Char. Duke of Alençon, this was your default,
That, being captain of the watch to-night,
Did look no better to that weighty charge.
Alen. Had all your quarters been as safely kept
As that whereof I had the government,
We had not been thus shamefully surpris'd.
Bast. Mine was secure.
Reig. And so was mine, my lord.
Char. And, for myself, most part of all this night,
Within her quarter and mine own precinct
I was employ'd in passing to and fro,
About relieving of the sentinels:
Then how or which way should they first break in?
Puc. Question, my lords, no further of the case,
How or which way: 'tis sure they found some place
But weakly guarded, where the breach was made.
And now there rests no other shift but this;
To gather our soldiers, scatter'd and dispers'd,
And lay new platforms to endamage them.

Alarum. Enter a[*n English*] Soldier, *crying 'A Talbot! a Talbot!' They fly, leaving their clothes behind.*

Sold. I'll be so bold to take what they have left.
The cry of Talbot serves me for a sword;
For I have loaden me with many spoils,
Using no other weapon but his name. *Exit.*

[SCENE II. *Orleans. Within the town.*]

Enter TALBOT, BEDFORD, BURGUNDY [, *a* Captain, *and others*].

Bed. The day begins to break, and night is fled,
Whose pitchy mantle over-veil'd the earth.
Here sound retreat, and cease our hot pursuit.
Retreat [*sounded*].
Tal. Bring forth the body of old Salisbury,
And here advance it in the market-place,
The middle centre of this cursed town.
Now have I paid my vow unto his soul;
For every drop of blood was drawn from him
There hath at least five Frenchmen died tonight.
And that hereafter ages may behold

ACT II. SCENE I. 3. **apparent,** plain; see glossary. 7. *Stage Direction:* **Burgundy.** The presence of the duke of Burgundy among the English is explained by the fact that the duchy of Burgundy, which included the provinces of Artois, Wallon, and Picardy, was under the English crown in accordance with terms of the Treaty of Troyes (cf. I, i, 80, note); its allegiance was further secured by the Treaty of Amiens, 1423, negotiated by the Duke of Bedford. **a dead march,** i.e., for Salisbury (?). Probably the stage direction for a dead march belongs at II, ii. 14. **quittance,** requite. 16. **Coward of France,** i.e., the Dauphin. **fame,** reputation; see glossary. 25. **practice,** scheme, plot; see glossary. **converse,** hold intercourse; see glossary. ,30. **several ways,** i.e., on ladders at different points; see *several* in glossary. 37. **duty,** obedience; see glossary. 38. *Stage Direction:* **The French . . . shirts.** The details of the hasty flight of the French, i.e., *in their shirts*, are recorded in Holinshed's account of the battle of Le Mans, where Talbot had a leading part. Historically Talbot was not present at Orleans. 39. **unready,** not fully clothed. 41. **trow,** believe; see glossary. 48. **sped,** fared; see glossary. 68. **her,** i.e., Joan's (with a bawdy suggestion). 75. **shift,** strategy; see glossary. 77. **platforms,** plans.

SCENE II. 8. **was,** which was. 19. **muse,** wonder; see glossary. 20.

What ruin happened in revenge of him,
Within their chiefest temple I'll erect
A tomb, wherein his corpse shall be interr'd:
Upon the which, that every one may read,
Shall be engrav'd the sack of Orleans,
The treacherous manner of his mournful death
And what a terror he had been to France.
But, lords, in all our bloody massacre,
I muse we met not with the Dauphin's grace,
His new-come champion, virtuous Joan of Arc,
Nor any of his false confederates.
Bed. 'Tis thought, Lord Talbot, when the fight began,
Rous'd on the sudden from their drowsy beds,
They did amongst the troops of armed men
Leap o'er the walls for refuge in the field.
Bur. Myself, as far as I could well discern
For smoke and dusky vapours of the night,
Am sure I scar'd the Dauphin and his trull,
When arm in arm they both came swiftly running,
Like to a pair of loving turtle-doves
That could not live asunder day or night.
After that things are set in order here,
We'll follow them with all the power we have.

Enter a Messenger.

Mess. All hail, my lords! Which of this princely train
Call ye the warlike Talbot, for his acts
So much applauded through the realm of France?
Tal. Here is the Talbot: who would speak with him?
Mess. The virtuous lady, Countess of Auvergne,
With modesty admiring thy renown,
By me entreats, great lord, thou wouldst vouchsafe
To visit her poor castle where she lies,
That she may boast she hath beheld the man
Whose glory fills the world with loud report.
Bur. Is it even so? Nay, then, I see our wars
Will turn unto a peaceful comic sport,
When ladies crave to be encount'red with.
You may not, my lord, despise her gentle suit.
Tal. Ne'er trust me then; for when a world of men
Could not prevail with all their oratory,
Yet hath a woman's kindness over-rul'd:
And therefore tell her I return great thanks,
And in submission will attend on her.
Will not your honours bear me company?
Bed. No, truly; it is more than manners will:
And I have heard it said, unbidden guests
Are often welcomest when they are gone.
Tal. Well then, alone, since there 's no remedy,
I mean to prove this lady's courtesy.
Come hither, captain. *(Whispers.)* You perceive my mind?
Capt. I do, my lord, and mean accordingly. *Exeunt.*

[SCENE III. *Auvergne. The* COUNTESS's *castle.*]

Enter [*the*] COUNTESS [*and her* Porter].

Count. Porter, remember what I gave in charge;
And when you have done so, bring the keys to me.
Port. Madam, I will. *Exit.*
Count. The plot is laid: if all things fall out right,
I shall as famous be by this exploit
As Scythian Tomyris by Cyrus' death.
Great is the rumour of this dreadful knight,
And his achievements of no less account:
Fain would mine eyes be witness with mine ears,
To give their censure of these rare reports.

Enter Messenger *and* TALBOT.

Mess. Madam,
According as your ladyship desir'd,
By message crav'd, so is Lord Talbot come.
Count. And he is welcome. What! is this the man?
Mess. Madam, it is.
Count. Is this the scourge of France?
Is this the Talbot, so much fear'd abroad
That with his name the mothers still their babes?
I see report is fabulous and false:
I thought I should have seen some Hercules,
A second Hector, for his grim aspect,
And large proportion of his strong-knit limbs.
Alas, this is a child, a silly dwarf!
It cannot be this weak and writhled shrimp
Should strike such terror to his enemies.
Tal. Madam, I have been bold to trouble you;
But since your ladyship is not at leisure,
I'll sort some other time to visit you. [*Going.*]
Count. What means he now? Go ask him whither he goes.
Mess. Stay, my Lord Talbot; for my lady craves
To know the cause of your abrupt departure.
Tal. Marry, for that she 's in a wrong belief,
I go to certify her Talbot 's here.

Enter Porter *with keys.*

Count. If thou be he, then art thou prisoner.
Tal. Prisoner! to whom?
Count. To me, blood-thirsty lord;
And for that cause I train'd thee to my house.
Long time thy shadow hath been thrall to me,
For in my gallery thy picture hangs:
But now the substance shall endure the like,
And I will chain these legs and arms of thine,
That hast by tyranny these many years
Wasted our country, slain our citizens
And sent our sons and husbands captivate.
Tal. Ha, ha, ha!
Count. Laughest thou, wretch? thy mirth shall turn to moan.
Tal. I laugh to see your ladyship so fond
To think that you have aught but Talbot's shadow
Whereon to practise your severity.
Count. Why, art not thou the man?
Tal. I am indeed.
Count. Then have I substance too.
Tal. No, no, I am but shadow of myself:

virtuous Joan of Arc, spoken contemptuously. 28. **trull,** strumpet; contemptuous reference to Joan of Arc. 39. **admiring,** wondering at; see glossary. 41. **lies,** dwells; see glossary. 45. **comic,** ludicrous, merry; used in antithesis to "tragic"—as war is tragic. 58. **prove,** put to test; see glossary.

SCENE III. 6. **Scythian Tomyris,** tribal queen of the Messagetae, who slew Cyrus the Great when he invaded her territory. The epithet *Scythian* is used to suggest her savagery. 10. **censure,** critical opinion; see glossary. 19, 20. **Hercules, Hector,** types of great physical strength. 21. **proportion,** size; see glossary. 22. **child, dwarf.** These words may be merely contemptuous and not actually descriptive of Talbot's size. 23. **writhled,** wrinkled. Talbot was eighty years old when he was killed in battle (1453). 31. **Marry,** mild interjection; see glossary. **for that,** because; see glossary. 35. **train'd,** lured, enticed; see glossary. 36. **shadow,** image, likeness; see glossary. **thrall,** enslaved. 37. **thy picture.** The countess may mean that she was practicing witchcraft on his image. 45. **fond,** foolish; see glossary.

You are deceiv'd, my substance is not here;
For what you see is but the smallest part
And least proportion of humanity:
I tell you, madam, were the whole frame here,
It is of such a spacious lofty pitch,
Your roof were not sufficient to contain 't.

Count. This is a riddling merchant for the nonce;
He will be here, and yet he is not here:
How can these contrarieties agree?

Tal. That will I show you presently.

Winds his horn. Drums strike up: a peal of ordnance. Enter Soldiers.

How say you, madam? are you now persuaded
That Talbot is but shadow of himself?
These are his substance, sinews, arms and strength,
With which he yoketh your rebellious necks,
Razeth your cities and subverts your towns
And in a moment makes them desolate.

Count. Victorious Talbot! pardon my abuse:
I find thou art no less than fame hath bruited
And more than may be gathered by thy shape.
Let my presumption not provoke thy wrath;
For I am sorry that with reverence
I did not entertain thee as thou art.

Tal. Be not dismay'd, fair lady; nor misconster
The mind of Talbot, as you did mistake
The outward composition of his body.
What you have done hath not offended me;
Nor other satisfaction do I crave,
But only, with your patience, that we may
Taste of your wine and see what cates you have;
For soldiers' stomachs always serve them well.

Count. With all my heart, and think me honoured
To feast so great a warrior in my house. *Exeunt.*

[SCENE IV. *London. The Temple-garden.*]

Enter RICHARD PLANTAGENET, WARWICK, SOMERSET, [WILLIAM DE LA] POLE [EARL OF SUFFOLK, VERNON], *and others* [*including a* Lawyer].

Plan. Great lords and gentlemen, what means this silence?
Dare no man answer in a case of truth?

Suf. Within the Temple-hall we were too loud;
The garden here is more convenient.

Plan. Then say at once if I maintain'd the truth;
Or else was wrangling Somerset in th' error?

Suf. Faith, I have been a truant in the law,
And never yet could frame my will to it;
And therefore frame the law unto my will.

Som. Judge you, my Lord of Warwick, then, between us.

War. Between two hawks, which flies the higher pitch;
Between two dogs, which hath the deeper mouth;
Between two blades, which bears the better temper:
Between two horses, which doth bear him best;
Between two girls, which hath the merriest eye;
I have perhaps some shallow spirit of judgement;
But in these nice sharp quillets of the law,
Good faith, I am no wiser than a daw.

Plan. Tut, tut, here is a mannerly forbearance:
The truth appears so naked on my side
That any purblind eye may find it out.

Som. And on my side it is so well apparell'd,
So clear, so shining and so evident
That it will glimmer through a blind man's eye.

Plan. Since you are tongue-tied and so loath to speak,
In dumb significants proclaim your thoughts:
Let him that is a true-born gentleman
And stands upon the honour of his birth,
If he suppose that I have pleaded truth,
From off this brier pluck a white rose with me.

Som. Let him that is no coward nor no flatterer,
But dare maintain the party of the truth,
Pluck a red rose from off this thorn with me.

War. I love no colours, and without all colour
Of base insinuating flattery
I pluck this white rose with Plantagenet.

Suf. I pluck this red rose with young Somerset
And say withal I think he held the right.

Ver. Stay, lords and gentlemen, and pluck no more,
Till you conclude that he upon whose side
The fewest roses are cropp'd from the tree
Shall yield the other in the right opinion.

Som. Good Master Vernon, it is well objected:
If I have fewest, I subscribe in silence.

Plan. And I.

Ver. Then for the truth and plainness of the case,
I pluck this pale and maiden blossom here,
Giving my verdict on the white rose side.

Som. Prick not your finger as you pluck it off,
Lest bleeding you do paint the white rose red
And fall on my side so, against your will.

Ver. If I, my lord, for my opinion bleed,
Opinion shall be surgeon to my hurt
And keep me on the side where still I am.

Som. Well, well, come on: who else?

Law. Unless my study and my books be false,
The argument you held was wrong in you;
[*To Somerset.*]
In sign whereof I pluck a white rose too.

Plan. Now, Somerset, where is your argument?

Som. Here in my scabbard, meditating that
Shall dye your white rose in a bloody red.

55. **pitch,** height; see glossary. 56. **roof,** house; an instance of metonymy. 57. **riddling merchant,** dealer in riddles. 67. **abuse,** error; also, deception. 68. **bruited,** reported, rumored. 79. **cates,** delicacies, dainty confections.

SCENE IV. *Stage Direction:* ***Temple-garden.*** The Temple was a district of London which took its name from the Knights Templars, who owned it during the twelfth and thirteenth centuries. It was leased to law students and converted into Inns of Court (the Inner Temple and the Middle Temple) in the fourteenth century. This scene placed in the garden has no basis in history. 12. **mouth,** voice. 16. **shallow . . . judgement,** superficial ability to judge. 17. **quillets,** verbal niceties, subtle distinctions; see glossary. 18. **daw,** jackdaw; a type of foolishness. 21. **purblind,** dimsighted. 26. **significants,** tokens, signs. 30. **white rose,** badge of the house of York. 32. **party,** part, side; cf. l. 123; see glossary. 33. **red rose,** badge of the house of Lancaster. 34. **colours,** colour, pretexts, appearance; see glossary. 36. **Plantagenet.** This was the nickname of Geoffrey of Anjou, father of Henry II, founder of the dynasty. None of Geoffrey's descendants assumed the name until Richard Duke of York adopted it in order to proclaim his superior right to the crown. The name first appears in the rolls of Parliament for 1460. 53. **Opinion,** public opinion, i.e., my reputation; see glossary. 57. **argument,** reason; see glossary. 60. **that,** that which. 70. **his,** its; the antecedent is *rose* (l. 69). 76. **peevish,** sullen; see glossary. 79. **I'll . . . throat,** he will throw the lies or slanders back into the throat from which they proceeded. 80. **William de la Pole,** the name of the duke of Suffolk. 81. **grace,** do honor to; see glossary. **yeoman,** a small freeholder, to be contrasted with a landed gentleman; cf. *crestless yeoman* (l. 85). 83. **His . . . Clarence.** Lionel was Richard's maternal great-great-grandfather; Edmund Duke of York was his paternal grandfather, whose estates and title Richard inherited from his father's brother, Edward (see the Genealogical Table). His blood was "corrupted" because of his father's treason. Warwick appears here to be

Plan. Meantime your cheeks do counterfeit our roses;
For pale they look with fear, as witnessing
The truth on our side.
Som. No, Plantagenet,
'Tis not for fear but anger that thy cheeks
Blush for pure shame to counterfeit our roses,
And yet thy tongue will not confess thy error.
Plan. Hath not thy rose a canker, Somerset?
Som. Hath not thy rose a thorn, Plantagenet?
Plan. Ay, sharp and piercing, to maintain his truth;
Whiles thy consuming canker eats his falsehood.
Som. Well, I'll find friends to wear my bleeding roses,
That shall maintain what I have said is true,
Where false Plantagenet dare not be seen.
Plan. Now, by this maiden blossom in my hand,
I scorn thee and thy fashion, peevish boy.
Suf. Turn not thy scorns this way, Plantagenet.
Plan. Proud Pole, I will, and scorn both him and thee.
Suf. I'll turn my part thereof into thy throat.
Som. Away, away, good William de la Pole!
We grace the yeoman by conversing with him.
War. Now, by God's will, thou wrong'st him, Somerset;
His grandfather was Lionel Duke of Clarence,
Third son to the third Edward King of England;
Spring crestless yeomen from so deep a root?
Plan. He bears him on the place's privilege,
Or durst not, for his craven heart, say thus.
Som. By him that made me, I'll maintain my words
On any plot of ground in Christendom.
Was not thy father, Richard Earl of Cambridge,
For treason executed in our late king's days?
And, by his treason, stand'st not thou attainted,
Corrupted, and exempt from ancient gentry?
His trespass yet lives guilty in thy blood;
And, till thou be restor'd, thou art a yeoman.
Plan. My father was attached, not attainted,
Condemn'd to die for treason, but no traitor;
And that I'll prove on better men than Somerset,
Were growing time once ripened to my will.
For your partaker Pole and you yourself,
I'll note you in my book of memory,
To scourge you for this apprehension:
Look to it well and say you are well warn'd.
Som. Ah, thou shalt find us ready for thee still;
And know us by these colours for thy foes,
For these my friends in spite of thee shall wear.
Plan. And, by my soul, this pale and angry rose,
As cognizance of my blood-drinking hate,
Will I for ever and my faction wear,
Until it wither with me to my grave
Or flourish to the height of my degree.
Suf. Go forward and be chok'd with thy ambition!
And so farewell until I meet thee next. *Exit.*
Som. Have with thee, Pole. Farewell, ambitious Richard. *Exit.*
Plan. How I am brav'd and must perforce endure it!
War. This blot that they object against your house
Shall be wip'd out in the next parliament
Call'd for the truce of Winchester and Gloucester;
And if thou be not then created York,
I will not live to be accounted Warwick.
Meantime, in signal of my love to thee,
Against proud Somerset and William Pole,
Will I upon thy party wear this rose:
And here I prophesy: this brawl to-day,
Grown to this faction in the Temple-garden,
Shall send between the red rose and the white
A thousand souls to death and deadly night.
Plan. Good Master Vernon, I am bound to you,
That you on my behalf would pluck a flower.
Ver. In your behalf still will I wear the same.
Law. And so will I.
Plan. Thanks, gentle sir.
Come, let us four to dinner: I dare say
This quarrel will drink blood another day. *Exeunt.*

[SCENE V. *The Tower of London.*]

Enter MORTIMER, *brought in a chair, and* Gaolers.

Mor. Kind keepers of my weak decaying age,
Let dying Mortimer here rest himself.
Even like a man new haled from the rack,
So fare my limbs with long imprisonment;
And these grey locks, the pursuivants of death,
Nestor-like aged in an age of care,
Argue the end of Edmund Mortimer.
These eyes, like lamps whose wasting oil is spent,
Wax dim, as drawing to their exigent;
Weak shoulders, overborne with burthening grief,
And pithless arms, like to a withered vine
That droops his sapless branches to the ground:
Yet are these feet, whose strengthless stay is numb,
Unable to support this lump of clay,
Swift-winged with desire to get a grave,
As witting I no other comfort have.
But tell me, keeper, will my nephew come?
First Gaol. Richard Plantagenet, my lord, will come:
We sent unto the Temple, unto his chamber;
And answer was return'd that he will come.
Mor. Enough: my soul shall then be satisfied.
Poor gentleman! his wrong doth equal mine.
Since Henry Monmouth first began to reign,

urging Richard's *ancient gentry* because of his maternal inheritance. It was through the maternal line that his claim to the throne was advanced. 84. **Third son.** Edward III's second son, William, died young. 86. **bears him,** presumes. **place's privilege.** Engaging in quarrels with drawn weapons was prohibited in certain precincts—the universities, the Inns of Court, and official residences of the sovereign. 92. **attainted,** convicted and condemned. According to law, the heirs of a person so attainted were deprived of all the rights and titles of their forebears; their blood was pronounced "corrupted"; cf. II, v, 128. The attainder of the Earl of Cambridge was reversed by Parliament in 1461 at the first triumph of the Yorkists. 96. **attached,** arrested; see glossary. 99. **Were,** conditional subjunctive. 100. **partaker,** supporter. 102. **apprehension,** conception. 114. **Have with,** I'll go along with you. 115. **brav'd,** defied; see glossary. **perforce,** necessarily; see glossary. 116-117. **This . . . parliament.** Cf. l. 92, note. 118. **the truce.** Cf. note at I, iii. 121. **signal,** token. 123. **upon thy party,** in your behalf.

SCENE V. 5. **pursuivants,** heralds. 6. **Nestor-like,** i.e., extremely old. Nestor, the oldest of the Greek chieftains at the siege of Troy, came to represent a type of old age. 9. **exigent,** end; i.e., the last strait or emergency. 23-25. **Since . . . had.** The chroniclers, according to Boswell-Stone, confused Edmund Mortimer with his cousin, Sir John Mortimer. The latter suffered a series of imprisonments and was executed in 1424. Hall and Holinshed represent the character in this play as having been imprisoned for years. Historically, however, he appears never to have lost his liberties for any long period. He enjoyed favors from Henry V, to whom he was loyal. The conspiracy for which Richard Plantagenet's father suffered was to advance Edmund's claim to the crown. The latter, however, in loyalty to Henry, himself revealed the conspiracy. The identification of Mortimer is further complicated by Shakespeare's apparent confusion of this Earl of March with his father's brother, Edmund; cf. note to the latter in the Genealogical Table; cf. ll. 73-75 below. 23. **Henry Monmouth,** Henry V.

Before whose glory I was great in arms,
This loathsome sequestration have I had;
And even since then hath Richard been obscur'd,
Depriv'd of honour and inheritance.
But now the arbitrator of despairs,
Just death, kind umpire of men's miseries,
With sweet enlargement doth dismiss me hence:
I would his troubles likewise were expir'd,
That so he might recover what was lost.

Enter RICHARD [PLANTAGENET].

First Gaol. My lord, your loving nephew now is come.
Mor. Richard Plantagenet, my friend, is he come?
Plan. Ay, noble uncle, thus ignobly us'd,
Your nephew, late despised Richard, comes.
Mor. Direct mine arms I may embrace his neck,
And in his bosom spend my latter gasp:
O, tell me when my lips do touch his cheeks,
That I may kindly give one fainting kiss.
And now declare, sweet stem from York's great stock,
Why didst thou say, of late thou wert despis'd?
Plan. First, lean thine aged back against mine arm;
And, in that ease, I'll tell thee my disease.
This day, in argument upon a case,
Some words there grew 'twixt Somerset and me;
Among which terms he us'd his lavish tongue
And did upbraid me with my father's death:
Which obloquy set bars before my tongue,
Else with the like I had requited him.
Therefore, good uncle, for my father's sake,
In honour of a true Plantagenet
And for alliance sake, declare the cause
My father, Earl of Cambridge, lost his head.
Mor. That cause, fair nephew, that imprison'd me
And hath detain'd me all my flow'ring youth
Within a loathsome dungeon, there to pine,
Was cursed instrument of his decease.
Plan. Discover more at large what cause that was,
For I am ignorant and cannot guess.
Mor. I will, if that my fading breath permit
And death approach not ere my tale be done.
Henry the Fourth, grandfather to this king,
Depos'd his nephew Richard, Edward's son,
The first-begotten and the lawful heir
Of Edward king, the third of that descent:
During whose reign the Percies of the north,
Finding his usurpation most unjust,
Endeavour'd my advancement to the throne:
The reason mov'd these warlike lords to this
Was, for that—young King Richard thus remov'd,
Leaving no heir begotten of his body—
I was the next by birth and parentage;
For by my mother I derived am
From Lionel Duke of Clarence, third son
To King Edward the Third; whereas he
From John of Gaunt doth bring his pedigree,
Being but fourth of that heroic line.
But mark: as in this haughty great attempt
They laboured to plant the rightful heir,
I lost my liberty and they their lives.
Long after this, when Henry the Fifth,
Succeeding his father Bolingbroke, did reign,
Thy father, Earl of Cambridge, then deriv'd
From famous Edmund Langley, Duke of York,
Marrying my sister that thy mother was,
Again in pity of my hard distress
Levied an army, weening to redeem
And have install'd me in the diadem:
But, as the rest, so fell that noble earl
And was beheaded. Thus the Mortimers,
In whom the title rested, were suppress'd.
Plan. Of which, my lord, your honour is the last.
Mor. True; and thou seest that I no issue have
And that my fainting words do warrant death:
Thou art my heir; the rest I wish thee gather:
But yet be wary in thy studious care.
Plan. Thy grave admonishments prevail with me:
But yet, methinks, my father's execution
Was nothing less than bloody tyranny.
Mor. With silence, nephew, be thou politic:
Strong-fixed is the house of Lancaster
And like a mountain, not to be remov'd.
But now thy uncle is removing hence;
As princes do their courts, when they are cloy'd
With long continuance in a settled place.
Plan. O, uncle, would some part of my young years
Might but redeem the passage of your age!
Mor. Thou dost then wrong me, as that slaughterer doth
Which giveth many wounds when one will kill.
Mourn not, except thou sorrow for my good;
Only give order for my funeral:
And so farewell, and fair be all thy hopes
And prosperous be thy life in peace and war! *Dies.*
Plan. And peace, no war, befall thy parting soul!
In prison hast thou spent a pilgrimage
And like a hermit overpass'd thy days.
Well, I will lock his counsel in my breast;
And what I do imagine let that rest.
Keepers, convey him hence, and I myself
Will see his burial better than his life.
Exeunt [*Gaolers, bearing out the body of Mortimer*].
Here dies the dusky torch of Mortimer,
Chok'd with ambition of the meaner sort:
And for those wrongs, those bitter injuries,
Which Somerset hath offer'd to my house,
I doubt not but with honour to redress;
And therefore haste I to the parliament,
Either to be restored to my blood,
Or make my will th' advantage of my good. *Exit.*

ACT III

SCENE I. [*London. The Parliament-house.*]

Flourish. Enter KING, EXETER, GLOUCESTER, WIN-

30. **enlargement,** release from confinement. 38. **latter,** last. 44. **disease,** trouble, grievance. 47. **us'd . . . tongue,** used his tongue lavishly. 59. **Discover,** make known. 64. **nephew,** cousin. 67. **Percies,** the Percy family of Northumberland. They figure prominently in *1 Henry IV* as antagonists to the king. 70. **mov'd,** i.e., which moved. 73-75. **I . . . Clarence.** Shakespeare identifies the speaker with his uncle, Edmund Mortimer, second son of Lionel's daughter Philippa. 74. **derived,** descended; see glossary. 76. **he.** The reference is to *this king*, line 63, i.e., Henry VI. 82-91. **when . . . beheaded.** The incident is dramatized in *Henry V*, II, ii, where Cambridge is treated unsympathetically by Shakespeare. 88. **weening,** hoping imaginatively. 96. **gather,** infer. 97. **studious,** diligent. 104. **thy . . . hence,** i.e., himself, about to die. 105. **cloy'd,** satiated. 115. **parting,** departing; see glossary. 123. **meaner sort,** those whose claim to the throne was inferior to his. 128. **restored . . . blood.** Cf. II, iv, 92, note. 129. **Or . . . good,** or make my will-power the means of achieving my ambition.

ACT III. SCENE I. On the historical aspects of this scene see the note at I, iii. 2. **studiously,** carefully. 5. **invention,** premeditated design, in antithesis to *extemporal speech;* see glossary. 7. **object,** urge, present. 8. **this place.** Gloucester, as protector of the realm, opened Parliament. 10. **preferr'd,** put forward. 13. **method . . . pen,** what I have written. 23. **at London bridge.** Gloucester's articles of accusation against

CHESTER, WARWICK, SOMERSET, SUFFOLK, RICH PLANTAGENET [*, and others*]. GLOUCESTER *offers to put up a bill;* WINCHESTER *snatches it,* [*and*] *tears it.*

Win. Com'st thou with deep premeditated lines,
With written pamphlets studiously devis'd,
Humphrey of Gloucester? If thou canst accuse,
Or aught intend'st to lay unto my charge,
Do it without invention, suddenly;
As I with sudden and extemporal speech
Purpose to answer what thou canst object.
Glou. Presumptuous priest! this place commands my patience,
Or thou shouldst find thou hast dishonour'd me.
Think not, although in writing I preferr'd
The manner of thy vile outrageous crimes,
That therefore I have forg'd, or am not able
Verbatim to rehearse the method of my pen:
No, prelate; such is thy audacious wickedness,
Thy lewd, pestiferous and dissentious pranks,
As very infants prattle of thy pride.
Thou art a most pernicious usurer,
Froward by nature, enemy to peace;
Lascivious, wanton, more than well beseems
A man of thy profession and degree;
And for thy treachery, what 's more manifest?
In that thou laid'st a trap to take my life,
As well at London bridge as at the Tower.
Beside, I fear me, if thy thoughts were sifted,
The king, thy sovereign, is not quite exempt
From envious malice of thy swelling heart.
Win. Gloucester, I do defy thee. Lords, vouchsafe
To give me hearing what I shall reply.
If I were covetous, ambitious or perverse,
As he will have me, how am I so poor?
Or how haps it I seek not to advance
Or raise myself, but keep my wonted calling?
And for dissension, who preferreth peace
More than I do?—except I be provok'd.
No, my good lords, it is not that offends;
It is not that that hath incens'd the duke:
It is, because no one should sway but he;
No one but he should be about the king;
And that engenders thunder in his breast
And makes him roar these accusations forth.
But he shall know I am as good—
Glou. As good!
Thou bastard of my grandfather!
Win. Ay, lordly sir; for what are you, I pray,
But one imperious in another's throne?
Glou. Am I not protector, saucy priest?
Win. And am not I a prelate of the church?
Glou. Yes, as an outlaw in a castle keeps
And useth it to patronage his theft.
Win. Unreverent Gloster!
Glou. Thou art reverent
Touching thy spiritual function, not thy life.
Win. Rome shall remedy this.
War. Roam thither, then.
Som. My lord, it were your duty to forbear.
War. Ay, see the bishop be not overborne.
Som. Methinks my lord should be religious
And know the office that belongs to such.
War. Methinks his lordship should be humbler;
It fitteth not a prelate so to plead.
Som. Yes, when his holy state is touch'd so near.
War. State holy or unhallow'd, what of that?
Is not his grace protector to the king?
Plan. [*Aside*] Plantagenet, I see, must hold his tongue,
Lest it be said 'Speak, sirrah, when you should;
Must your bold verdict enter talk with lords?'
Else would I have a fling at Winchester.
King. Uncles of Gloucester and of Winchester,
The special watchmen of our English weal,
I would prevail, if prayers might prevail,
To join your hearts in love and amity.
O, what a scandal is it to our crown,
That two such noble peers as ye should jar!
Believe me, lords, my tender years can tell
Civil dissension is a viperous worm
That gnaws the bowels of the commonwealth.
A noise within, 'Down with the tawny-coats!'
What tumult 's this?
War. An uproar, I dare warrant,
Begun through malice of the bishop's men.
A noise again, 'Stones! stones!'

Enter Mayor.

May. O, my good lords, and virtuous Henry,
Pity the city of London, pity us!
The bishop and the Duke of Gloucester's men,
Forbidden late to carry any weapon,
Have fill'd their pockets full of pebble stones
And banding themselves in contrary parts
Do pelt so fast at one another's pate
That many have their giddy brains knock'd out:
Our windows are broke down in every street
And we for fear compell'd to shut our shops.

Enter [Serving-men], *in skirmish with bloody pates.*

King. We charge you, on allegiance to ourself,
To hold your slaught'ring hands and keep the peace.
Pray, uncle Gloucester, mitigate this strife.
First Serv. Nay, if we be forbidden stones, we'll fall to it with our teeth.
Sec. Serv. Do what ye dare, we are as resolute.
Skirmish again.
Glou. You of my household, leave this peevish broil
And set this unaccustom'd fight aside.
Third Serv. My lord, we know your grace to be a man
Just and upright; and, for your royal birth,
Inferior to none but to his majesty:
And ere that we will suffer such a prince,
So kind a father of the commonweal,

Winchester presented to the Parliament stated that the latter had "set men of armes and archers, at thende of London bridge next Southwerke," to prevent Gloucester's going to Eltham to interfere with the bishop's plans regarding the young king. 26. **envious,** wicked; see glossary. **swelling,** inflated with pride. 30. **how am I so poor.** Historically, Winchester was extremely rich. 42. **Thou bastard.** Winchester—son of John of Gaunt and Catherine Swynford before their marriage—was, with his two brothers and one sister, legitimatized by act of Parliament in Richard II's reign. 47. **keeps,** dwells; see glossary. 53. **overborne,** prevailed over. 58. **state,** degree, rank. **touch'd so near,** so closely concerned. 70. **jar,** quarrel. 71. **my tender years.** The king was actually five years old at the time of this episode. 73. *Stage Direction:* **tawny-coats.** Cf. I, iii, 47, note. 78-85. **The . . . shops.** Boswell-Stone finds an account to parallel this scene in Fabyan's Chronicle: "Proclamacyons were made, that men shulde leue theyr Swerdes & other wepeyns in theyr Innys, the people toke great battes & stauys in theyr neckes, and so folowed theyr lordes and maisters vnto the Parliament. And whan that wepyn was Inhybyted theym, then they toke stonys & plummettes of lede, & trussyed them secretely in theyr sleuys & bosomys." 96. **Inferior . . . majesty.** The serving-man alludes to the close kinship of Gloucester with the young king.

To be disgraced by an inkhorn mate,
We and our wives and children all will fight
And have our bodies slaught'red by thy foes.
First Serv. Ay, and the very parings of our nails
Shall pitch a field when we are dead. *Begin again.*
Glou. Stay, stay, I say!
And if you love me, as you say you do,
Let me persuade you to forbear awhile.
King. O, how this discord doth afflict my soul!
Can you, my Lord of Winchester, behold
My sighs and tears and will not once relent?
Who should be pitiful, if you be not?
Or who should study to prefer a peace,
If holy churchmen take delight in broils?
War. Yield, my lord protector; yield, Winchester;
Except you mean with obstinate repulse
To slay your sovereign and destroy the realm.
You see what mischief and what murder too
Hath been enacted through your enmity;
Then be at peace, except ye thirst for blood.
Win. He shall submit, or I will never yield.
Glou. Compassion on the king commands me stoop;
Or I would see his heart out, ere the priest
Should ever get that privilege of me.
War. Behold, my Lord of Winchester, the duke
Hath banish'd moody discontented fury,
As by his smoothed brows it doth appear:
Why look you still so stern and tragical?
Glou. Here, Winchester, I offer thee my hand.
King. Fie, uncle Beaufort! I have heard you preach
That malice was a great and grievous sin;
And will not you maintain the thing you teach,
But prove a chief offender in the same?
War. Sweet king! the bishop hath a kindly gird.
For shame, my Lord of Winchester, relent!
What, shall a child instruct you what to do?
Win. Well, Duke of Gloucester, I will yield to thee;
Love for thy love and hand for hand I give.
Glou. [*Aside*] Ay, but, I fear me, with a hollow heart.—
See here, my friends and loving countrymen,
This token serveth for a flag of truce
Betwixt ourselves and all our followers:
So help me God, as I dissemble not!
Win. [*Aside*] So help me God, as I intend it not!
King. O loving uncle, kind Duke of Gloucester,
How joyful am I made by this contract!
Away, my masters! trouble us no more;
But join in friendship, as your lords have done.
First Serv. Content: I'll to the surgeon's.
Sec. Serv. And so will I.
Third Serv. And I will see what physic the tavern affords. *Exeunt* [*Serving-men, Mayor, &c.*].
War. Accept this scroll, most gracious sovereign,
Which in the right of Richard Plantagenet
We do exhibit to your majesty.
Glou. Well urg'd, my Lord of Warwick: for, sweet prince,
An if your grace mark every circumstance,
You have great reason to do Richard right;
Especially for those occasions
At Eltham Place I told your majesty.
King. And those occasions, uncle, were of force:
Therefore, my loving lords, our pleasure is
That Richard be restored to his blood.
War. Let Richard be restored to his blood;
So shall his father's wrongs be recompens'd.
Win. As will the rest, so willeth Winchester.
King. If Richard will be true, not that alone
But all the whole inheritance I give
That doth belong unto the house of York,
From whence you spring by lineal descent.
Plan. Thy humble servant vows obedience
And humble service till the point of death.
King. Stoop then and set your knee against my foot;
And, in reguerdon of that duty done,
I gird thee with the valiant sword of York:
Rise, Richard, like a true Plantagenet,
And rise created princely Duke of York.
Plan. And so thrive Richard as thy foes may fall!
And as my duty springs, so perish they
That grudge one thought against your majesty!
All. Welcome, high prince, the mighty Duke of York!
Som. [*Aside*] Perish, base prince, ignoble Duke of York!
Glou. Now will it best avail your majesty
To cross the seas and to be crown'd in France:
The presence of a king engenders love
Amongst his subjects and his loyal friends,
As it disanimates his enemies.
King. When Gloucester says the word, King Henry goes;
For friendly counsel cuts off many foes.
Glou. Your ships already are in readiness.
Sennet. Flourish. Exeunt. Manet Exeter.
Exe. Ay, we may march in England or in France,
Not seeing what is likely to ensue.
This late dissension grown betwixt the peers
Burns under feigned ashes of forg'd love
And will at last break out into a flame:
As fest'red members rot but by degree,
Till bones and flesh and sinews fall away,
So will this base and envious discord breed.
And now I fear that fatal prophecy
Which in the time of Henry nam'd the Fifth
Was in the mouth of every sucking babe;
That Henry born at Monmouth should win all
And Henry born at Windsor lose all:
Which is so plain that Exeter doth wish
His days may finish ere that hapless time. *Exit.*

SCENE II. [*France. Before Rouen.*]

Enter [LA] PUCELLE *disguised, with four* Soldiers *with sacks upon their backs.*

Puc. These are the city gates, the gates of Rouen,

99. **inkhorn mate,** scribbler. 102-103. **the . . . dead,** i.e., our zest for Gloucester's cause is such that we shall prepare for battle barehanded even after we are dead; typical extravagant boasting of servants. 131. **kindly,** appropriate; see glossary. **gird,** rebuke. 147. **physic,** remedy; see glossary. 153. **An if,** if; see glossary. 155. **occasions,** reasons. 170. **reguerdon,** reward. 183. **disanimates,** discourages. 186. *Stage Direction:* **Sennet,** set of notes played on a trumpet as a signal for the approach and departure of processions; see glossary. 195. **fatal prophecy.** Cf. Holinshed: "This yeare, at Windsore, on the daie of saint Nicholas, in December, the queene was deliuered of a sonne named Henrie. . . . The king, being certified hereof, as he laie at seige before Meaux, gaue God thanks. . . . But, when he heard reported the place of his natiuitie, were it that he [was] warned by some prophesie, or had some foreknowledge, or else iudged himselfe of his sonnes fortune, he said vnto the lord Fitz Hugh, his trustie chamberleine, these words: 'My lord, I *Henrie, borne at Monmouth,* shall small time reigne, & much get; *and Henrie, borne at Windsore,* shall long reigne, and *all loose:* but, as God will, so be it.'"

Through which our policy must make a breach:
Take heed, be wary how you place your words;
Talk like the vulgar sort of market men
That come to gather money for their corn.
If we have entrance, as I hope we shall,
And that we find the slothful watch but weak,
I'll by a sign give notice to our friends,
That Charles the Dauphin may encounter them.

First Sol. Our sacks shall be a mean to sack the city,
And we be lords and rulers over Rouen;
Therefore we'll knock. *Knock.*

Watch. [*Within*] Qui est là?

Puc. Paysans, pauvres gens de France;
Poor market folks that come to sell their corn.

Watch. Enter, go in; the market bell is rung.

Puc. Now, Rouen, I'll shake thy bulwarks to the ground. *Exeunt.*

Enter CHARLES, [*the*] BASTARD [of Orleans], ALENÇON [, REIGNIER, *and forces*].

Char. Saint Denis bless this happy stratagem!
And once again we'll sleep secure in Rouen.

Bast. Here ent'red Pucelle and her practisants;
Now she is there, how will she specify
Where is the best and safest passage in?

Reig. By thrusting out a torch from yonder tower;
Which, once discern'd, shows that her meaning is,
No way to that, for weakness, which she ent'red.

Enter [LA] PUCELLE *on the top, thrusting out a torch burning.*

Puc. Behold, this is the happy wedding torch
That joineth Rouen unto her countrymen,
But burning fatal to the Talbotites! [*Exit.*]

Bast. See, noble Charles, the beacon of our friend;
The burning torch in yonder turret stands.

Char. Now shine it like a comet of revenge,
A prophet to the fall of all our foes!

Reig. Defer no time, delays have dangerous ends;
Enter, and cry 'The Dauphin!' presently,
And then do execution on the watch. *Alarum.* [*Exeunt.*]

An alarum. [*Enter*] TALBOT *in an excursion.*

Tal. France, thou shalt rue this treason with thy tears,
If Talbot but survive thy treachery.
Pucelle, that witch, that damned sorceress,
Hath wrought this hellish mischief unawares,
That hardly we escap'd the pride of France. *Exit.*

An alarum: excursions. BEDFORD, *brought in sick in a chair. Enter* TALBOT *and* BURGUNDY *without: within* [LA] PUCELLE, CHARLES, BASTARD, [ALENÇON,] *and* REIGNIER, *on the walls.*

Puc. Good morrow, gallants! want ye corn for bread?
I think the Duke of Burgundy will fast
Before he'll buy again at such a rate:
'Twas full of darnel; do you like the taste?

Bur. Scoff on, vile fiend and shameless courtezan!
I trust ere long to choke thee with thine own
And make thee curse the harvest of that corn.

Char. Your grace may starve perhaps before that time.

Bed. O, let no words, but deeds, revenge this treason!

Puc. What will you do, good grey-beard? break a lance,
And run a tilt at death within a chair?

Tal. Foul fiend of France, and hag of all despite,
Encompass'd with thy lustful paramours!
Becomes it thee to taunt his valiant age
And twit with cowardice a man half dead?
Damsel, I'll have a bout with you again,
Or else let Talbot perish with this shame.

Puc. Are ye so hot, sir? yet, Pucelle, hold thy peace;
If Talbot do but thunder, rain will follow.
They [*the English*] *whisper together in council.*
God speed the parliament! who shall be the speaker?

Tal. Dare ye come forth and meet us in the field?

Puc. Belike your lordship takes us then for fools,
To try if that our own be ours or no.

Tal. I speak not to that railing Hecate,
But unto thee, Alençon, and the rest;
Will ye, like soldiers, come and fight it out?

Alen. Signior, no.

Tal. Signior, hang! base muleters of France!
Like peasant foot-boys do they keep the walls
And dare not take up arms like gentlemen.

Puc. Away, captains! let 's get us from the walls;
For Talbot means no goodness by his looks.
God b' uy, my lord! we came but to tell you
That we are here. *Exeunt from the walls.*

Tal. And there will we be too, ere it be long,
Or else reproach be Talbot's greatest fame!
Vow, Burgundy, by honour of thy house,
Prick'd on by public wrongs sustain'd in France,
Either to get the town again or die:
And I, as sure as English Henry lives
And as his father here was conqueror,
As sure as in this late-betrayed town
Great Cœur-de-lion's heart was buried,
So sure I swear to get the town or die.

Bur. My vows are equal partners with thy vows.

Tal. But, ere we go, regard this dying prince,
The valiant Duke of Bedford. Come, my lord,
We will bestow you in some better place,
Fitter for sickness and for crazy age.

Bed. Lord Talbot, do not so dishonour me:
Here will I sit before the walls of Rouen
And will be partner of your weal or woe.

Bur. Courageous Bedford, let us now persuade you.

Bed. Not to be gone from hence; for once I read
That stout Pendragon in his litter sick
Came to the field and vanquished his foes:
Methinks I should revive the soldiers' hearts,
Because I ever found them as myself.

Tal. Undaunted spirit in a dying breast!

SCENE II. 2. **policy,** stratagem; see glossary. 10. **a mean,** means; see glossary. 16. **market bell,** bell rung to announce the opening of a market. 20. **practisants,** plotters, conspirators. 25. **No . . . ent'red,** i.e., it is not comparable in weakness to that by which she entered. 35. *Stage Direction:* ***excursion,*** stage battle or skirmish; see glossary. 40. *Stage Direction:* **Bedford . . .** ***sick.*** There are two alterations of history in this scene: Bedford outlived Joan of Arc three years; moreover, at his death he was still comparatively young. 44. **darnel,** injurious weed. 64. **Hecate,** goddess of night and of magic. 68. **muleters,** mule drivers (contemptuously). 83. **Great . . . heart.** According to Holinshed, Richard Coeur-de-Lion (king of England 1189-1199) had willed that "his heart be conueied vnto Rouen, and there buried; in testimonie of the loue which he had eur borne vnto that citie. . . ." 95. **Pendragon,** an allusion to the legend—attributed to the Welsh chieftain, Uther Pendragon, by Geoffrey of Monmouth, but to his brother by Holinshed —that "euen sicke as he was, [he] caused himselfe to be caried forth *in a litter;* with whose presence his people were so incouraged, that incountring with the Saxons, they wan the victorie. . . ."

Then be it so: heavens keep old Bedford safe!
And now no more ado, brave Burgundy,
But gather we our forces out of hand
And set upon our boasting enemy.
Exeunt [all but Bedford and Attendants].

An alarum: excursions. Enter SIR JOHN FALSTAFF *and a* Captain.

Cap. Whither away, Sir John Falstaff, in such haste?
Fal. Whither away! to save myself by flight:
We are like to have the overthrow again.
Cap. What! will you fly, and leave Lord Talbot?
Fal. Ay,
All the Talbots in the world, to save my life. *Exit.*
Cap. Cowardly knight! ill fortune follow thee! *Exit.*

Retreat: excursions. [LA] PUCELLE, ALENÇON, *and* CHARLES *fly.*

Bed. Now, quiet soul, depart when heaven please,
For I have seen our enemies' overthrow.
What is the trust or strength of foolish man?
They that of late were daring with their scoffs
Are glad and fain by flight to save themselves.
Bedford dies, and is carried in by two in his chair.

An alarum. Enter TALBOT, BURGUNDY, *and the rest.*

Tal. Lost, and recovered in a day again!
This is a double honour, Burgundy:
Yet heavens have glory for this victory!
Bur. Warlike and martial Talbot, Burgundy
Enshrines thee in his heart and there erects
Thy noble deeds as valour's monuments.
Tal. Thanks, gentle duke. But where is Pucelle now?
I think her old familiar is asleep:
Now where 's the Bastard's braves, and Charles his gleeks?
What, all amort? Rouen hangs her head for grief
That such a valiant company are fled.
Now will we take some order in the town,
Placing therein some expert officers,
And then depart to Paris to the king,
For there young Henry with his nobles lie.
Bur. What wills Lord Talbot pleaseth Burgundy.
Tal. But yet, before we go, let 's not forget
The noble Duke of Bedford late deceas'd,
But see his exequies fulfill'd in Rouen:
A braver soldier never couched lance,
A gentler heart did never sway in court;
But kings and mightiest potentates must die,
For that 's the end of human misery. *Exeunt.*

SCENE III. [*The plains near Rouen.*]

Enter CHARLES, [*the*] BASTARD [of Orleans], ALENÇON, [LA] PUCELLE [*, and forces*].

Puc. Dismay not, princes, at this accident,
Nor grieve that Rouen is so recovered:
Care is no cure, but rather corrosive,
For things that are not to be remedied.
Let frantic Talbot triumph for a while
And like a peacock sweep along his tail;
We'll pull his plumes and take away his train,
If Dauphin and the rest will be but rul'd.
Char. We have been guided by thee hitherto
And of thy cunning had no diffidence:
One sudden foil shall never breed distrust.
Bast. Search out thy wit for secret policies,
And we will make thee famous through the world.
Alen. We'll set thy statue in some holy place,
And have thee reverenc'd like a blessed saint:
Employ thee then, sweet virgin, for our good.
Puc. Then thus it must be; this doth Joan devise:
By fair persuasions mix'd with sug'red words
We will entice the Duke of Burgundy
To leave the Talbot and to follow us.
Char. Ay, marry, sweeting, if we could do that,
France were no place for Henry's warriors;
Nor should that nation boast it so with us,
But be extirped from our provinces.
Alen. For ever should they be expuls'd from France
And not have title of an earldom here.
Puc. Your honours shall perceive how I will work
To bring this matter to the wished end.
Drum sounds afar off.
Hark! by the sound of drum you may perceive
Their powers are marching unto Paris-ward.

Here sound an English march. [*Enter, and pass over at a distance,* TALBOT *and his forces.*]

There goes the Talbot, with his colours spread,
And all the troops of English after him.

French march. [*Enter the* DUKE OF BURGUNDY *and forces.*]

Now in the rearward comes the duke and his:
Fortune in favour makes him lag behind.
Summon a parley; we will talk with him.
Trumpets sound a parley.
Char. A parley with the Duke of Burgundy!
Bur. Who craves a parley with the Burgundy?
Puc. The princely Charles of France, thy countryman.
Bur. What say'st thou, Charles? for I am marching hence.
Char. Speak, Pucelle, and enchant him with thy words.
Puc. Brave Burgundy, undoubted hope of France!
Stay, let thy humble handmaid speak to thee.
Bur. Speak on; but be not over-tedious.
Puc. Look on thy country, look on fertile France,
And see the cities and the towns defac'd
By wasting ruin of the cruel foe.
As looks the mother on her lowly babe
When death doth close his tender dying eyes,
See, see the pining malady of France;
Behold the wounds, the most unnatural wounds,
Which thou thyself hast given her woful breast.
O, turn thy edged sword another way;
Strike those that hurt, and hurt not those that help.
One drop of blood drawn from thy country's bosom

122. **familiar,** demon; see glossary. 123. **gleeks,** gibes, jests. 124. **all amort,** sick to death, dispirited. 133. **exequies,** funeral rites. 135. **sway in court,** exercise power and influence in court.

SCENE III. 10. **diffidence,** distrust, suspicion. 11. **foil,** repulse, defeat. 24. **extirped,** rooted out. 34. **in favour,** benevolently, i.e., in our favor; see *favour* in glossary. 41. **undoubted,** fearless. 60. **exclaims on,** denounces, accuses. 85. **Done . . . again.** This aside, spoken out of character, is addressed to the prejudice of the English audience, for whom the inconstancy of the French was a common subject of satire. It was suggested by Warburton that this might allude to the conversion of Henry of Navarre to Catholicism in 1593. 91. **prejudice,** i.e., devise his overthrow.

Should grieve thee more than streams of foreign gore:
Return thee therefore with a flood of tears,
And wash away thy country's stained spots.
Bur. Either she hath bewitch'd me with her words,
Or nature makes me suddenly relent.
Puc. Besides, all French and France exclaims on thee,
Doubting thy birth and lawful progeny.
Who join'st thou with but with a lordly nation
That will not trust thee but for profit's sake?
When Talbot hath set footing once in France
And fashion'd thee that instrument of ill,
Who then but English Henry will be lord
And thou be thrust out like a fugitive?
Call we to mind, and mark but this for proof,
Was not the Duke of Orleans thy foe?
And was he not in England prisoner?
But when they heard he was thine enemy,
They set him free without his ransom paid,
In spite of Burgundy and all his friends.
See, then, thou fight'st against thy countrymen
And join'st with them will be thy slaughter-men.
Come, come, return; return, thou wandering lord;
Charles and the rest will take thee in their arms.
Bur. I am vanquished; these haughty words of hers
Have batt'red me like roaring cannon-shot,
And made me almost yield upon my knees.
Forgive me, country, and sweet countrymen,
And, lords, accept this hearty kind embrace:
My forces and my power of men are yours:
So farewell, Talbot; I'll no longer trust thee.
Puc. [*Aside*] Done like a Frenchman: turn, and turn again!
Char. Welcome, brave duke! thy friendship makes us fresh.
Bast. And doth beget new courage in our breasts.
Alen. Pucelle hath bravely play'd her part in this,
And doth deserve a coronet of gold.
Char. Now let us on, my lords, and join our powers,
And seek how we may prejudice the foe. *Exeunt*.

SCENE IV. [*Paris. The palace*.]

Enter the KING, GLOUCESTER, WINCHESTER, [RICHARD DUKE OF] YORK, SUFFOLK, SOMERSET, WARWICK, EXETER [, VERNON, BASSET, *and others*]. *To them with his* Soldiers, TALBOT.

Tal. My gracious prince, and honourable peers,
Hearing of your arrival in this realm,
I have awhile given truce unto my wars,
To do my duty to my sovereign:
In sign whereof, this arm, that hath reclaim'd
To your obedience fifty fortresses,
Twelve cities and seven walled towns of strength,
Beside five hundred prisoners of esteem,
Lets fall his sword before your highness' feet,
And with submissive loyalty of heart
Ascribes the glory of his conquest got
First to my God and next unto your grace. [*Kneels*.]
King. Is this the Lord Talbot, uncle Gloucester,
That hath so long been resident in France?
Glou. Yes, if it please your majesty, my liege.
King. Welcome, brave captain and victorious lord!
When I was young, as yet I am not old,
I do remember how my father said
A stouter champion never handled sword.
Long since we were resolved of your truth,
Your faithful service and your toil in war;
Yet never have you tasted our reward,
Or been reguerdon'd with so much as thanks,
Because till now we never saw your face:
Therefore, stand up; and, for these good deserts,
We here create you Earl of Shrewsbury;
And in our coronation take your place.
Sennet. Flourish. Exeunt. Mane[n]t Vernon and Basset.
Ver. Now, sir, to you, that were so hot at sea,
Disgracing of these colours that I wear
In honour of my noble Lord of York:
Dar'st thou maintain the former words thou spak'st?
Bas. Yes, sir; as well as you dare patronage
The envious barking of your saucy tongue
Against my lord the Duke of Somerset.
Ver. Sirrah, thy lord I honour as he is.
Bas. Why, what is he? as good a man as York.
Ver. Hark ye; not so: in witness, take ye that. *Strikes him*.
Bas. Villain, thou knowest the law of arms is such
That whoso draws a sword, 'tis present death,
Or else this blow should broach thy dearest blood.
But I'll unto his majesty, and crave
I may have liberty to venge this wrong;
When thou shalt see I'll meet thee to thy cost.
Ver. Well, miscreant, I'll be there as soon as you;
And, after, meet you sooner than you would. *Exeunt*.

ACT IV.

SCENE I. [*Paris. A hall of state*.]

Enter KING, GLOUCESTER, WINCHESTER, [RICHARD DUKE OF] YORK, SUFFOLK, SOMERSET, WARWICK, TALBOT, EXETER, Governor [of Paris, *and others*].

Glou. Lord bishop, set the crown upon his head.
Win. God save King Henry, of that name the sixth!
Glou. Now, governor of Paris, take your oath,
That you elect no other king but him;
Esteem none friends but such as are his friends,
And none your foes but such as shall pretend
Malicious practices against his state:
This shall ye do, so help you righteous God!

Enter [SIR JOHN] FALSTAFF.

Fal. My gracious sovereign, as I rode from Calais,
To haste unto your coronation,
A letter was deliver'd to my hands,
Writ to your grace from th' Duke of Burgundy.
Tal. Shame to the Duke of Burgundy and thee!
I vow'd, base knight, when I did meet thee next,
To tear the garter from thy craven's leg, [*Plucking it off*.]
Which I have done, because unworthily

SCENE IV. 18. **I . . . said.** Henry VI was an infant of nine months at his father's death. 20. **resolved,** convinced; see glossary. 28. **so hot at sea.** The details of this quarrel are recited below, IV, i, 89-97. 38. **the law of arms.** Cf. I, iii, 46, note. 39. **present,** instant; see glossary. 40. **broach,** tap, draw. **dearest,** i.e., life blood; see glossary.

ACT IV. SCENE I. 4. **elect,** acknowledge. 6. **pretend,** purpose, intend. 7. **practices,** stratagems; see glossary. 15. **garter,** badge of the Knights of the Garter, a ribbon of blue velvet edged and buckled with gold, worn below the left knee.

Thou wast installed in that high degree.
Pardon me, princely Henry, and the rest:
This dastard, at the battle of Patay,
When but in all I was six thousand strong
And that the French were almost ten to one,
Before we met or that a stroke was given,
Like to a trusty squire did run away:
In which assault we lost twelve hundred men;
Myself and divers gentlemen beside
Were there surpris'd and taken prisoners.
Then judge, great lords, if I have done amiss;
Or whether that such cowards ought to wear
This ornament of knighthood, yea or no.
Glou. To say the truth, this fact was infamous
And ill beseeming any common man,
Much more a knight, a captain and a leader.
Tal. When first this order was ordain'd, my lords,
Knights of the garter were of noble birth,
Valiant and virtuous, full of haughty courage,
Such as were grown to credit by the wars;
Not fearing death, nor shrinking for distress,
But always resolute in most extremes.
He then that is not furnish'd in this sort
Doth but usurp the sacred name of knight,
Profaning this most honourable order,
And should, if I were worthy to be judge,
Be quite degraded, like a hedge-born swain
That doth presume to boast of gentle blood.
King. Stain to thy countrymen, thou hear'st thy doom!
Be packing, therefore, thou that wast a knight:
Henceforth we banish thee, on pain of death.
[*Exit Falstaff*.]
And now, my lord protector, view the letter
Sent from our uncle Duke of Burgundy.
Glou. What means his grace, that he hath chang'd his style?
No more but, plain and bluntly, 'To the king!'
Hath he forgot he is his sovereign?
Or doth this churlish superscription
Pretend some alteration in good will?
What 's here? [*Reads*] 'I have, upon especial cause,
Mov'd with compassion of my country's wrack,
Together with the pitiful complaints
Of such as your oppression feeds upon,
Forsaken your pernicious faction
And join'd with Charles, the rightful King of France.'
O monstrous treachery! can this be so,
That in alliance, amity and oaths,
There should be found such false dissembling guile?
King. What! doth my uncle Burgundy revolt?
Glou. He doth, my lord, and is become your foe.
King. Is that the worst this letter doth contain?
Glou. It is the worst, and all, my lord, he writes.
King. Why, then, Lord Talbot there shall talk with him
And give him chastisement for this abuse.
How say you, my lord? are you not content?
Tal. Content, my liege! yes, but that I am prevented,
I should have begg'd I might have been employ'd.
King. Then gather strength and march unto him straight:
Let him perceive how ill we brook his treason
And what offence it is to flout his friends.
Tal. I go, my lord, in heart desiring still
You may behold confusion of your foes. [*Exit*.]

Enter VERNON *and* BASSET.

Ver. Grant me the combat, gracious sovereign.
Bas. And me, my lord, grant me the combat too.
York. This is my servant: hear him, noble prince.
Som. And this is mine: sweet Henry, favour him.
King. Be patient, lords; and give them leave to speak.
Say, gentlemen, what makes you thus exclaim?
And wherefore crave you combat? or with whom?
Ver. With him, my lord; for he hath done me wrong.
Bas. And I with him; for he hath done me wrong.
King. What is that wrong whereof you both complain?
First let me know, and then I'll answer you.
Bas. Crossing the sea from England into France,
This fellow here, with envious carping tongue,
Upbraided me about the rose I wear;
Saying, the sanguine colour of the leaves
Did represent my master's blushing cheeks,
When stubbornly he did repugn the truth
About a certain question in the law
Argu'd betwixt the Duke of York and him;
With other vile and ignominious terms:
In confutation of which rude reproach
And in defence of my lord's worthiness,
I crave the benefit of law of arms.
Ver. And that is my petition, noble lord:
For though he seem with forged quaint conceit
To set a gloss upon his bold intent,
Yet know, my lord, I was provok'd by him;
And he first took exceptions at this badge,
Pronouncing that the paleness of this flower
Bewray'd the faintness of my master's heart.
York. Will not this malice, Somerset, be left?
Som. Your private grudge, my Lord of York, will out,
Though ne'er so cunningly you smother it.
King. Good Lord, what madness rules in brainsick men,
When for so slight and frivolous a cause
Such factious emulations shall arise!
Good cousins both, of York and Somerset,
Quiet yourselves, I pray, and be at peace.
York. Let this dissension first be tried by fight,
And then your highness shall command a peace.
Som. The quarrel toucheth none but us alone;
Betwixt ourselves let us decide it then.
York. There is my pledge; accept it, Somerset.
Ver. Nay, let it rest where it began at first.
Bas. Confirm it so, mine honourable lord.
Glou. Confirm it so! Confounded be your strife!

23. **trusty squire,** used contemptuously. 30. **fact,** deed; see glossary. 35. **haughty,** exalted. 39. **furnish'd,** endowed; see glossary. 43. **hedge-born,** lowly born; cf. *2 Henry VI*, IV, ii, 55. 46. **packing,** departing; see glossary. 54. **Pretend,** import. 64. **my uncle,** a reference to the alliance of the Lancastrian and Burgundian houses by the marriage of the duke of Bedford, the king's uncle, to Anne, sister of the duke of Burgundy. 71. **prevented,** forestalled, anticipated; see glossary. 73. **straight,** immediately; see glossary. 77. **confusion,** destruction; see glossary. 78. **the combat,** permission to fight; cf. I, iii, 46, note. 90. **fellow,** an insulting form of reference or address; see glossary. 94. **repugn,** oppose, resist. 100. **benefit . . . arms,** right to protect one's honor in a duel. 102. **quaint,** carefully elaborated; see glossary. **conceit,** device, fanciful design; see glossary. 103. **gloss,** speciously fair appearance; see glossary. 107. **Bewray'd,** revealed. 113. **emulations,** contentions between rivals. 114. **cousins,** any relatives not of one's immediate family; see glossary. 123. **Con-**

And perish ye, with your audacious prate!
Presumptuous vassals, are you not asham'd
With this immodest clamorous outrage
To trouble and disturb the king and us?
And you, my lords, methinks you do not well
To bear with their perverse objections;
Much less to take occasion from their mouths
To raise a mutiny betwixt yourselves:
Let me persuade you take a better course.

Exe. It grieves his highness: good my lords, be friends.

King. Come hither, you that would be combatants:
Henceforth I charge you, as you love our favour,
Quite to forget this quarrel and the cause.
And you, my lords, remember where we are;
In France, amongst a fickle wavering nation:
If they perceive dissension in our looks
And that within ourselves we disagree,
How will their grudging stomachs be provok'd
To wilful disobedience, and rebel!
Beside, what infamy will there arise,
When foreign princes shall be certified
That for a toy, a thing of no regard,
King Henry's peers and chief nobility
Destroy'd themselves, and lost the realm of France!
O, think upon the conquest of my father,
My tender years, and let us not forego
That for a trifle that was bought with blood!
Let me be umpire in this doubtful strife.
I see no reason, if I wear this rose, [*Putting on a red rose.*]
That any one should therefore be suspicious
I more incline to Somerset than York:
Both are my kinsmen, and I love them both:
As well they may upbraid me with my crown,
Because, forsooth, the king of Scots is crown'd.
But your discretions better can persuade
Than I am able to instruct or teach:
And therefore, as we hither came in peace,
So let us still continue peace and love.
Cousin of York, we institute your grace
To be our regent in these parts of France:
And, good my Lord of Somerset, unite
Your troops of horsemen with his bands of foot;
And, like true subjects, sons of your progenitors,
Go cheerfully together and digest
Your angry choler on your enemies.
Ourself, my lord protector and the rest
After some respite will return to Calais;
From thence to England; where I hope ere long
To be presented, by your victories,
With Charles, Alençon and that traitorous rout.

Flourish. Exeunt. Mane[n]t York, Warwick, Exeter [and] Vernon.

War. My Lord of York, I promise you, the king
Prettily, methought, did play the orator.

York. And so he did; but yet I like it not,
In that he wears the badge of Somerset.

War. Tush, that was but his fancy, blame him not;
I dare presume, sweet prince, he thought no harm.

York. An if I wist he did,—but let it rest;
Other affairs must now be managed.

Exeunt. Manet Exeter.

Exe. Well didst thou, Richard, to suppress thy voice;
For, had the passions of thy heart burst out,
I fear we should have seen decipher'd there
More rancorous spite, more furious raging broils,
Than yet can be imagin'd or suppos'd.
But howsoe'er, no simple man that sees
This jarring discord of nobility,
This shouldering of each other in the court,
This factious bandying of their favourites,
But that it doth presage some ill event.
'Tis much when sceptres are in children's hands;
But more when envy breeds unkind division;
There comes the ruin, there begins confusion. *Exit.*

[SCENE II. *Before Bourdeaux.*]

Enter TALBOT, *with trump and drum, before Bourdeaux.*

Tal. Go to the gates of Bourdeaux, trumpeter;
Summon their general unto the wall.

[*Trumpet*] *sounds. Enter* General [*and others*], *aloft.*

English John Talbot, captains, calls you forth,
Servant in arms to Harry King of England;
And thus he would: Open your city gates;
Be humble to us; call my sovereign yours,
And do him homage as obedient subjects;
And I'll withdraw me and my bloody power:
But, if you frown upon this proffer'd peace,
You tempt the fury of my three attendants,
Lean famine, quartering steel, and climbing fire;
Who in a moment even with the earth
Shall lay your stately and air-braving towers,
If you forsake the offer of their love.

Gen. Thou ominous and fearful owl of death,
Our nation's terror and their bloody scourge!
The period of thy tyranny approacheth.
On us thou canst not enter but by death;
For, I protest, we are well fortified
And strong enough to issue out and fight:
If thou retire, the Dauphin, well appointed,
Stands with the snares of war to tangle thee:
On either hand thee there are squadrons pitch'd,
To wall thee from the liberty of flight;
And no way canst thou turn thee for redress,
But death doth front thee with apparent spoil
And pale destruction meets thee in the face.
Ten thousand French have ta'en the sacrament
To rive their dangerous artillery
Upon no Christian soul but English Talbot.
Lo, there thou stand'st, a breathing valiant man,
Of an invincible unconquer'd spirit!
This is the latest glory of thy praise
That I, thy enemy, due thee withal;
For ere the glass, that now begins to run,
Finish the process of his sandy hour,
These eyes, that see thee now well coloured,

founded, spent, wasted; see glossary. 129. **objections,** charges, accusations. 144. **certified,** informed. 145. **toy,** trifle; see glossary. 167. **digest,** disperse, dissipate; see glossary. 191. **event,** outcome; see glossary. 193. **unkind,** unnatural; see glossary.

SCENE II. 10. **my three attendants.** Cf. Hall's *Chronicle*, Seventh Year of Henry v: "The Goddess of warre . . . hath these three handmaydes, euer of necessitie to attend vpon her, that is, blood, fyre and famine"; cf. *Henry V*, Prologue, 7. 15. **fearful,** exciting fear; see glossary. **owl of death.** The call of the owl was regarded as a prognostication of death; cf. *Macbeth*, II, ii, 3-4. 17. **period,** termination. 21. **appointed,** equipped. 23. **thee,** i.e., of thee; dative of reference; see Abbott, 220. 26. **spoil,** destruction; see glossary. 28. **ta'en the sacrament,** i.e., taken the most solemn oaths. 29. **rive,** burst, fire. 34. **due,** endue, invest. 37. **well coloured,** in health.

Shall see thee withered, bloody, pale and dead.
Drum afar off.
Hark! hark! the Dauphin's drum, a warning bell,
Sings heavy music to thy timorous soul;
And mine shall ring thy dire departure out.
Exit [with his men].
Tal. He fables not; I hear the enemy:
Out, some light horsemen, and peruse their wings.
O, negligent and heedless discipline!
How are we park'd and bounded in a pale,
A little herd of England's timorous deer,
Maz'd with a yelping kennel of French curs!
If we be English deer, be then in blood;
Not rascal-like, to fall down with a pinch,
But rather, moody-mad and desperate stags,
Turn on the bloody hounds with heads of steel
And make the cowards stand aloof at bay:
Sell every man his life as dear as mine,
And they shall find dear deer of us, my friends.
God and Saint George, Talbot and England's right,
Prosper our colours in this dangerous fight! [*Exeunt.*]

[SCENE III. *Plains in Gascony.*]

Enter a Messenger *that meets* YORK. *Enter* YORK *with trumpet and many* Soldiers.

York. Are not the speedy scouts return'd again,
That dogg'd the mighty army of the Dauphin?
Mess. They are return'd, my lord, and give it out
That he is march'd to Bourdeaux with his power,
To fight with Talbot: as he march'd along,
By your espials were discovered
Two mightier troops than that the Dauphin led,
Which join'd with him and made their march for Bourdeaux.
York. A plague upon that villain Somerset,
That thus delays my promised supply
Of horsemen, that were levied for this siege!
Renowned Talbot doth expect my aid,
And I am lowted by a traitor villain
And cannot help the noble chevalier:
God comfort him in this necessity!
If he miscarry, farewell wars in France.

Enter another Messenger [SIR WILLIAM LUCY].

Lucy. Thou princely leader of our English strength,
Never so needful on the earth of France,
Spur to the rescue of the noble Talbot,
Who now is girdled with a waist of iron
And hemm'd about with grim destruction:
To Bourdeaux, warlike duke! to Bourdeaux, York!
Else, farewell Talbot, France, and England's honour.
York. O God, that Somerset, who in proud heart
Doth stop my cornets, were in Talbot's place!
So should we save a valiant gentleman
By forfeiting a traitor and a coward.
Mad ire and wrathful fury makes me weep,
That thus we die, while remiss traitors sleep.
Lucy. O, send some succour to the distress'd lord!
York. He dies, we lose; I break my warlike word;
We mourn, France smiles; we lose, they daily get;
All 'long of this vile traitor Somerset.
Lucy. Then God take mercy on brave Talbot's soul;
And on his son young John, who two hours since
I met in travel toward his warlike father!
This seven years did not Talbot see his son;
And now they meet where both their lives are done.
York. Alas, what joy shall noble Talbot have
To bid his young son welcome to his grave?
Away! vexation almost stops my breath,
That sund'red friends greet in the hour of death.
Lucy, farewell: no more my fortune can,
But curse the cause I cannot aid the man.
Maine, Blois, Poictiers, and Tours, are won away,
'Long all of Somerset and his delay.
Exit [with his soldiers].
Lucy. Thus, while the vulture of sedition
Feeds in the bosom of such great commanders,
Sleeping neglection doth betray to loss
The conquest of our scarce cold conqueror,
That ever living man of memory,
Henry the Fifth: whiles they each other cross,
Lives, honours, lands and all hurry to loss.

[SCENE IV. *Plains in Gascony.*]

Enter SOMERSET, *with his army* [; *a* Captain *of* TALBOT'S *with him*].

Som. It is too late; I cannot send them now:
This expedition was by York and Talbot
Too rashly plotted: all our general force
Might with a sally of the very town
Be buckled with: the over-daring Talbot
Hath sullied all his gloss of former honour
By this unheedful, desperate, wild adventure:
York set him on to fight and die in shame,
That, Talbot dead, great York might bear the name.
Cap. Here is Sir William Lucy, who with me
Set from our o'ermatch'd forces forth for aid.

[SIR WILLIAM LUCY *comes forward.*]

Som. How now, Sir William! whither were you sent?
Lucy. Whither, my lord? from bought and sold Lord Talbot;
Who, ring'd about with bold adversity,
Cries out for noble York and Somerset,
To beat assailing death from his weak legions:
And whiles the honourable captain there
Drops bloody sweat from his war-wearied limbs,
And, in advantage ling'ring, looks for rescue,
You, his false hopes, the trust of England's honour,
Keep off aloof with worthless emulation.
Let not your private discord keep away
The levied succours that should lend him aid,
While he, renowned noble gentleman,
Yields up his life unto a world of odds:
Orleans the Bastard, Charles, Burgundy,
Alençon, Reignier, compass him about,
And Talbot perisheth by your default.
Som. York set him on; York should have sent him aid.
Lucy. And York as fast upon your grace exclaims;
Swearing that you withhold his levied host,

43. **peruse,** survey, inspect. 49. **rascal-like.** Cf. I, ii, 35, note. 55. **Saint George.** Cf. I, i, 154, note.
SCENE III. 13. **lowted,** made a fool of, mocked. 25. **cornets,** cavalry units, so called from their long, horn-shaped standards. 33. **'long of,** on account of; see glossary. 47-48. **vulture . . . bosom,** allusion to Zeus' punishment of Prometheus.
SCENE IV. 4. **the very town,** i.e., the mere garrison, unsupported by the relieving armies (Tucker Brooke). 5. **Be buckled with,** be joined in combat. 19. **in advantage ling'ring,** protracting his resistance by the advantage of a strong post (Johnson); making the most of every

Collected for this expedition.
Som. York lies; he might have sent and had the horse;
I owe him little duty, and less love;
And take foul scorn to fawn on him by sending.
Lucy. The fraud of England, not the force of France,
Hath now entrapp'd the noble-minded Talbot:
Never to England shall he bear his life;
But dies, betray'd to fortune by your strife.
Som. Come, go; I will dispatch the horsemen straight:
Within six hours they will be at his aid.
Lucy. Too late comes rescue: he is ta'en or slain;
For fly he could not, if he would have fled;
And fly would Talbot never, though he might.
Som. If he be dead, brave Talbot, then adieu!
Lucy. His fame lives in the world, his shame in you.
Exeunt.

[SCENE V. *The English camp near Bourdeaux.*]

Enter TALBOT *and his son* [JOHN].

Tal. O young John Talbot! I did send for thee
To tutor thee in stratagems of war,
That Talbot's name might be in thee reviv'd
When sapless age and weak unable limbs
Should bring thy father to his drooping chair.
But, O malignant and ill-boding stars!
Now thou art come unto a feast of death,
A terrible and unavoided danger:
Therefore, dear boy, mount on my swiftest horse;
And I'll direct thee how thou shalt escape
By sudden flight: come, dally not, be gone.
John. Is my name Talbot? and am I your son?
And shall I fly? O, if you love my mother,
Dishonour not her honourable name,
To make a bastard and a slave of me!
The world will say, he is not Talbot's blood,
That basely fled when noble Talbot stood.
Tal. Fly, to revenge my death, if I be slain.
John. He that flies so will ne'er return again.
Tal. If we both stay, we both are sure to die.
John. Then let me stay; and, father, do you fly:
Your loss is great, so your regard should be;
My worth unknown, no loss is known in me.
Upon my death the French can little boast;
In yours they will, in you all hopes are lost.
Flight cannot stain the honour you have won;
But mine it will, that no exploit have done:
You fled for vantage, every one will swear;
But, if I bow, they'll say it was for fear.
There is no hope that ever I will stay,
If the first hour I shrink and run away.
Here on my knee I beg mortality,
Rather than life preserv'd with infamy.
Tal. Shall all thy mother's hopes lie in one tomb?
John. Ay, rather than I'll shame my mother's womb.
Tal. Upon my blessing, I command thee go.
John. To fight I will, but not to fly the foe.
Tal. Part of thy father may be sav'd in thee.
John. No part of him but will be shame in me.
Tal. Thou never hadst renown, nor canst not lose it.
John. Yes, your renowned name: shall flight abuse it?
Tal. Thy father's charge shall clear thee from that stain.
John. You cannot witness for me, being slain.
If death be so apparent, then both fly.
Tal. And leave my followers here to fight and die?
My age was never tainted with such shame.
John. And shall my youth be guilty of such blame?
No more can I be severed from your side,
Than can yourself yourself in twain divide:
Stay, go, do what you will, the like do I;
For live I will not, if my father die.
Tal. Then here I take my leave of thee, fair son,
Born to eclipse thy life this afternoon.
Come, side by side together live and die;
And soul with soul from France to heaven fly. *Exeunt.*

[SCENE VI. *A field of battle.*]

Alarum: excursions, wherein TALBOT'S Son *is hemmed about, and* TALBOT *rescues him.*

Tal. Saint George and victory! fight, soldiers, fight:
The regent hath with Talbot broke his word
And left us to the rage of France his sword.
Where is John Talbot? Pause, and take thy breath;
I gave thee life and rescu'd thee from death.
John. O, twice my father, twice am I thy son!
The life thou gav'st me first was lost and done,
Till with thy warlike sword, despite of fate,
To my determin'd time thou gav'st new date.
Tal. When from the Dauphin's crest thy sword struck fire,
It warm'd thy father's heart with proud desire
Of bold-fac'd victory. Then leaden age,
Quicken'd with youthful spleen and warlike rage,
Beat down Alençon, Orleans, Burgundy,
And from the pride of Gallia rescued thee.
The ireful bastard Orleans, that drew blood
From thee, my boy, and had the maidenhood
Of thy first fight, I soon encountered,
And interchanging blows I quickly shed
Some of his bastard blood; and in disgrace
Bespoke him thus; 'Contaminated, base
And misbegotten blood I spill of thine,
Mean and right poor, for that pure blood of mine
Which thou didst force from Talbot, my brave boy:'
Here, purposing the Bastard to destroy
Came in strong rescue. Speak, thy father's care,
Art thou not weary, John? how dost thou fare?
Wilt thou yet leave the battle, boy, and fly,
Now thou art seal'd the son of chivalry?
Fly, to revenge my death when I am dead:
The help of one stands me in little stead.
O, too much folly is it, well I wot,
To hazard all our lives in one small boat!
If I to-day die not with Frenchmen's rage,
To-morrow I shall die with mickle age:
By me they nothing gain an if I stay;

desperate chance (Tucker Brooke).
SCENE V. 22. **regard,** heed for yourself. 28. **vantage,** advantage, i.e., for some military strategy; see glossary.
SCENE VI. 2. **The regent,** the Duke of York; cf. IV, i, 162-163. 3. **France his,** France's. 9. **date,** termination, i.e., postponed my hour of death; see glossary. 13. **spleen,** courage, ardor. 15. **Gallia,** France. 25. **purposing,** as I purposed. 32. **wot,** know; see glossary. 35. **mickle age,** great old age.

'Tis but the short'ning of my life one day:
In thee thy mother dies, our household's name,
My death's revenge, thy youth, and England's fame:
All these and more we hazard by thy stay;
All these are sav'd if thou wilt fly away.
John. The sword of Orleans hath not made me smart;
These words of yours draw life-blood from my heart:
On that advantage, bought with such a shame,
To save a paltry life and slay bright fame,
Before young Talbot from old Talbot fly,
The coward horse that bears me fall and die!
And like me to the peasant boys of France,
To be shame's scorn and subject of mischance!
Surely, by all the glory you have won,
An if I fly, I am not Talbot's son:
Then talk no more of flight, it is no boot;
If son to Talbot, die at Talbot's foot.
Tal. Then follow thou thy desp'rate sire of Crete,
Thou Icarus; thy life to me is sweet:
If thou wilt fight, fight by thy father's side;
And, commendable prov'd, let's die in pride. *Exeunt.*

[SCENE VII. *Another part of the field.*]

Alarum: excursions. Enter old TALBOT *led* [*by a* Servant].

Tal. Where is my other life? mine own is gone;
O, where 's young Talbot? where is valiant John?
Triumphant death, smear'd with captivity,
Young Talbot's valour makes me smile at thee:
When he perceiv'd me shrink and on my knee,
His bloody sword he brandish'd over me,
And, like a hungry lion, did commence
Rough deeds of rage and stern impatience;
But when my angry guardant stood alone,
Tend'ring my ruin and assail'd of none,
Dizzy-ey'd fury and great rage of heart
Suddenly made him from my side to start
Into the clust'ring battle of the French;
And in that sea of blood my boy did drench
His over-mounting spirit, and there died,
My Icarus, my blossom, in his pride.

Enter [Soldiers], *with* JOHN TALBOT, *borne.*

Serv. O my dear lord, lo, where your son is borne!
Tal. Thou antic death, which laugh'st us here to scorn,
Anon, from thy insulting tyranny,
Coupled in bonds of perpetuity,
Two Talbots, winged through the lither sky,
In thy despite shall 'scape mortality.
O thou, whose wounds become hard-favoured Death,
Speak to thy father ere thou yield thy breath!
Brave Death by speaking, whether he will or no;
Imagine him a Frenchman and thy foe.
Poor boy! he smiles, methinks, as who should say,
Had Death been French, then Death had died to-day.
Come, come and lay him in his father's arms:
My spirit can no longer bear these harms.
Soldiers, adieu! I have what I would have,
Now my old arms are young John Talbot's grave. *Dies.*

Enter CHARLES, ALENÇON, BURGUNDY, BASTARD, *and* [LA] PUCELLE [, *and forces*].

Char. Had York and Somerset brought rescue in,
We should have found a bloody day of this.
Bast. How the young whelp of Talbot's, raging-wood,
Did flesh his puny sword in Frenchmen's blood!
Puc. Once I encount'red him, and thus I said:
'Thou maiden youth, be vanquish'd by a maid:'
But, with a proud majestical high scorn,
He answer'd thus: 'Young Talbot was not born
To be the pillage of a giglot wench:'
So, rushing in the bowels of the French,
He left me proudly, as unworthy fight.
Bur. Doubtless he would have made a noble knight:
See, where he lies inhearsed in the arms
Of the most bloody nurser of his harms!
Bast. Hew them to pieces, hack their bones asunder,
Whose life was England's glory, Gallia's wonder.
Char. O, no, forbear! for that which we have fled
During the life, let us not wrong it dead.

Enter [SIR WILLIAM] LUCY [*attended;* Herald *of the* French *preceding*].

Lucy. Herald, conduct me to the Dauphin's tent,
To know who hath obtain'd the glory of the day.
Char. On what submissive message art thou sent?
Lucy. Submission, Dauphin! 'tis a mere French word;
We English warriors wot not what it means.
I come to know what prisoners thou hast ta'en
And to survey the bodies of the dead.
Char. For prisoners ask'st thou? hell our prison is.
But tell me whom thou seek'st.
Lucy. But where 's the great Alcides of the field,
Valiant Lord Talbot, Earl of Shrewsbury,
Created, for his rare success in arms,
Great Earl of Washford, Waterford and Valence;
Lord Talbot of Goodrig and Urchinfield,
Lord Strange of Blackmere, Lord Verdun of Alton,
Lord Cromwell of Wingfield, Lord Furnival of Sheffield,
The thrice-victorious Lord of Falconbridge;
Knight of the noble order of Saint George,
Worthy Saint Michael and the Golden Fleece;
Great marshal to Henry the Sixth
Of all his wars within the realm of France?
Puc. Here is a silly stately style indeed!
The Turk, that two and fifty kingdoms hath,
Writes not so tedious a style as this.
Him that thou magnifi'st with all these titles
Stinking and fly-blown lies here at our feet.
Lucy. Is Talbot slain, the Frenchmen's only scourge,

48. **like me,** liken me. 52. **boot,** profit; see glossary. 55. **Thou Icarus,** an allusion to the story of Daedalus, sire of Crete, and his son Icarus, who escaped from the Labyrinth by means of wings that the father's ingenuity had devised. As they flew across the sea, Icarus mounted too high, the sun's heat melted the wax by which his wings were attached, and he fell into the sea (hence, called the Icarian Sea) and was lost.

SCENE VII. 3. **smear'd,** disgraced. 9. **guardant,** guardian. 10. **Tend'ring,** being concerned for. 13. **battle,** army; see glossary. 18. **Thou antic death,** one of the personifications of death suggested, probably, by the grotesque pictorial representations of the Middle Ages and early Renaissance, such as the Dance of Death; cf. *Richard II*, III, ii, 162. 19. **Anon,** soon; see glossary. 21. **lither,** yielding. 23. **become . . . death,** make death, otherwise hideous, beautiful. 35. **raging-wood,** furiously mad. 36. **flesh,** use for the first time in battle; see glossary. 41. **giglot,** lewd, wanton. 54. **mere,** pure, absolute; see glossary. 60. **Alcides,** Hercules, son of Alcaeus. 61-67. **Valiant . . . Falconbridge.** These titles of Lord Talbot are in the epitaph fixed on his tomb in Rouen. They appear first to have been reproduced in print in Cotton's *An Armor of Proofe* (1596), where occurs the form *Washford*, more commonly Wexford. These observations suggest that Shakespeare may have revised the play after 1596. 73. **The Turk,**

Your kingdom's terror and black Nemesis?
O, were mine eye-balls into bullets turn'd,
That I in rage might shoot them at your faces!
O, that I could but call these dead to life!
It were enough to fright the realm of France:
Were but his picture left amongst you here,
It would amaze the proudest of you all.
Give me their bodies, that I may bear them hence
And give them burial as beseems their worth.
Puc. I think this upstart is old Talbot's ghost,
He speaks with such a proud commanding spirit.
For God's sake, let him have 'em; to keep them here,
They would but stink, and putrefy the air.
Char. Go, take their bodies hence.
Lucy. I'll bear them hence; but from their ashes shall be rear'd
A phœnix that shall make all France afeard.
Char. So we be rid of them, do with 'em what thou wilt.
And now to Paris, in this conquering vein
All will be ours, now bloody Talbot 's slain. *Exeunt.*

[ACT V.]

SCENE [I. *London. The palace.*]

Sennet. Enter KING, GLOUCESTER, *and* EXETER.

King. Have you perus'd the letters from the pope,
The emperor and the Earl of Armagnac?
Glou. I have, my lord: and their intent is this:
They humbly sue unto your excellence
To have a godly peace concluded of
Between the realms of England and of France.
King. How doth your grace affect their motion?
Glou. Well, my good lord; and as the only means
To stop effusion of our Christian blood
And stablish quietness on every side.
King. Ay, marry, uncle; for I always thought
It was both impious and unnatural
That such immanity and bloody strife
Should reign among professors of one faith.
Glou. Beside, my lord, the sooner to effect
And surer bind this knot of amity,
The Earl of Armagnac, near knit to Charles,
A man of great authority in France,
Proffers his only daughter to your grace
In marriage, with a large and sumptuous dowry.
King. Marriage, uncle! alas, my years are young!
And fitter is my study and my books
Than wanton dalliance with a paramour.
Yet call th' ambassadors; and, as you please,
So let them have their answers every one:
I shall be well content with any choice
Tends to God's glory and my country's weal.

Enter WINCHESTER [*in Cardinal's habit*], *and three* Ambassadors [*one a* Legate].

Exe. What! is my Lord of Winchester install'd,
And call'd unto a cardinal's degree?
Then I perceive that will be verified
Henry the Fifth did sometime prophesy,
'If once he come to be a cardinal,
He'll make his cap co-equal with the crown.'
King. My lords ambassadors, your several suits
Have been consider'd and debated on.
Your purpose is both good and reasonable;
And therefore are we certainly resolv'd
To draw conditions of a friendly peace;
Which by my Lord of Winchester we mean
Shall be transported presently to France.
Glou. And for the proffer of my lord your master,
I have inform'd his highness so at large
As liking of the lady's virtuous gifts,
Her beauty and the value of her dower,
He doth intend she shall be England's queen.
King. In argument and proof of which contract,
Bear her this jewel, pledge of my affection.
And so, my lord protector, see them guarded
And safely brought to Dover; where inshipp'd
Commit them to the fortune of the sea.
Exeunt [all but Winchester and Legate].
Win. Stay, my lord legate: you shall first receive
The sum of money which I promised
Should be delivered to his holiness
For clothing me in these grave ornaments.
Leg. I will attend upon your lordship's leisure.
Win. [*Aside*] Now Winchester will not submit, I trow,
Or be inferior to the proudest peer.
Humphrey of Gloucester, thou shalt well perceive
That, neither in birth or for authority,
The bishop will be overborne by thee:
I'll either make thee stoop and bend thy knee,
Or sack this country with a mutiny. *Exeunt.*

SCENE [II. *France. Plains in Anjou.*]

Enter CHARLES, BURGUNDY, ALENÇON, BASTARD, REIGNIER, *and* JOAN [LA PUCELLE, *with forces*].

Char. These news, my lords, may cheer our drooping spirits:
'Tis said the stout Parisians do revolt
And turn again unto the warlike French.
Alen. Then march to Paris, royal Charles of France,
And keep not back your powers in dalliance.
Puc. Peace be amongst them, if they turn to us;
Else, ruin combat with their palaces!

Enter Scout.

Scout. Success unto our valiant general,
And happiness to his accomplices!
Char. What tidings send our scouts? I prithee, speak.
Scout. The English army, that divided was
Into two parties, is now conjoin'd in one

used as equivalent of *Islam.* **two and fifty kingdoms,** an instance of hyperbole. 93. **phœnix,** fabulous bird, the only one of its kind, which every five hundred years built itself a funeral pile and died upon it; from the ashes a new phoenix arose.

ACT V. SCENE I. 1-2. **pope . . . Armagnac.** During the year 1434 efforts were made by the emperor and other potentates to effect a peace. The marriage proposal of the king to the Earl of Armagnac's daughter, however, was made nine years later. 7. **affect,** incline toward; see glossary. **motion,** proposal; see glossary. 9. **effusion,** shedding (of blood); cf. Hall's *Chronicle:* ". . . all christendom lamented . . . the effusion of so muche Christen bloud." 13. **immanity,** atrocious savagery. 17. **knit,** i.e., by ties of kinship. 27. **Tends,** which tends. 31-33. **Henry . . . crown.** The prophecy is recorded in Hall and Holinshed, Fifth Year of Henry VI: "whiche degree, kyng Henry the fifth knowyng the haute corage, and the ambicious mynde of the man, prohibited hym on his allegeaunce once, either to sue for or to take, meanyng that cardinalles Hattes should not presume to be egall with Princes." 31. **sometime,** at one time; see glossary. 41. **my lord your master,** addressed to the ambassadors. 49. **inshipp'd,** embarked.

SCENE II. 7. **Else . . . palaces!** Otherwise, let ruin destroy their palaces!

And means to give you battle presently.
Char. Somewhat too sudden, sirs, the warning is;
But we will presently provide for them.
Bur. I trust the ghost of Talbot is not there:
Now he is gone, my lord, you need not fear.
Puc. Of all base passions, fear is most accurs'd.
Command the conquest, Charles, it shall be thine,
Let Henry fret and all the world repine.
Char. Then on, my lords; and France be fortunate!
Exeunt.

[SCENE III. *Before Angiers.*]

Alarum. Excursions. Enter JOAN LA PUCELLE.

Puc. The regent conquers, and the Frenchmen fly.
Now help, ye charming spells and periapts;
And ye choice spirits that admonish me
And give me signs of future accidents. *Thunder.*
You speedy helpers, that are substitutes
Under the lordly monarch of the north,
Appear and aid me in this enterprise.

Enter Fiends.

This speedy and quick appearance argues proof
Of your accustom'd diligence to me.
Now, ye familiar spirits, that are cull'd
Out of the powerful regions under earth,
Help me this once, that France may get the field.
They walk, and speak not.
O, hold me not with silence over-long!
Where I was wont to feed you with my blood,
I'll lop a member off and give it you
In earnest of a further benefit,
So you do condescend to help me now.
They hang their heads.
No hope to have redress? My body shall
Pay recompense, if you will grant my suit.
They shake their heads.
Cannot my body nor blood-sacrifice
Entreat you to your wonted furtherance?
Then take my soul, my body, soul and all,
Before that England give the French the foil.
They depart.
See, they forsake me! Now the time is come
That France must vail her lofty-plumed crest
And let her head fall into England's lap.
My ancient incantations are too weak,
And hell too strong for me to buckle with:
Now, France, thy glory droopeth to the dust. *Exit.*

Excursions. BURGUNDY *and* YORK *fight hand to hand. French fly.* [LA PUCELLE *is taken.*]

York. Damsel of France, I think I have you fast:
Unchain your spirits now with spelling charms
And try if they can gain your liberty.
A goodly prize, fit for the devil's grace!
See, how the ugly witch doth bend her brows,
As if with Circe she would change my shape!
Puc. Chang'd to a worser shape thou canst not be.
York. O, Charles the Dauphin is a proper man;
No shape but his can please your dainty eye.
Puc. A plaguing mischief light on Charles and thee!
And may ye both be suddenly surpris'd
By bloody hands, in sleeping on your beds!
York. Fell banning hag, enchantress, hold thy tongue!
Puc. I prithee, give me leave to curse awhile.
York. Curse, miscreant, when thou comest to the stake. *Exeunt.*

Alarum. Enter SUFFOLK, *with* MARGARET *in his hand.*

Suf. Be what thou wilt, thou art my prisoner.
Gazes on her.
O fairest beauty, do not fear nor fly!
For I will touch thee but with reverent hands;
I kiss these fingers for eternal peace,
And lay them gently on thy tender side.
Who art thou? say, that I may honour thee.
Mar. Margaret my name, and daughter to a king,
The King of Naples, whosoe'er thou art.
Suf. An earl I am, and Suffolk am I call'd.
Be not offended, nature's miracle,
Thou art allotted to be ta'en by me:
So doth the swan her downy cygnets save,
Keeping them prisoner underneath her wings.
Yet, if this servile usage once offend,
Go and be free again as Suffolk's friend. *She is going.*
O, stay! [*Aside*] I have no power to let her pass;
My hand would free her, but my heart says no.
As plays the sun upon the glassy streams,
Twinkling another counterfeited beam,
So seems this gorgeous beauty to mine eyes.
Fain would I woo her, yet I dare not speak:
I'll call for pen and ink, and write my mind.
Fie, de la Pole! disable not thyself;
Hast not a tongue? is she not here?
Wilt thou be daunted at a woman's sight?
Ay, beauty's princely majesty is such,
Confounds the tongue and makes the senses rough.
Mar. Say, Earl of Suffolk—if thy name be so—
What ransom must I pay before I pass?
For I perceive I am thy prisoner.
Suf. How canst thou tell she will deny thy suit,
Before thou make a trial of her love?
Mar. Why speak'st thou not? what ransom must I pay?
Suf. She 's beautiful and therefore to be woo'd;
She is a woman, therefore to be won.
Mar. Wilt thou accept of ransom? yea, or no.
Suf. Fond man, remember that thou hast a wife;
Then how can Margaret be thy paramour?
Mar. I were best to leave him, for he will not hear.
Suf. There all is marr'd; there lies a cooling card.
Mar. He talks at random; sure, the man is mad.
Suf. And yet a dispensation may be had.
Mar. And yet I would that you would answer me.
Suf. I'll win this Lady Margaret. For whom?
Why, for my king: tush, that 's a wooden thing!
Mar. He talks of wood: it is some carpenter.

15. **provide for,** get ready for.
SCENE III. 1. **The regent,** i.e., the Duke of York. 2. **periapts,** amulets. 3. **admonish,** inform. 4. **accidents,** occurrences. 6. **north.** Evil spirits were frequently associated with the north. 14. **feed . . . blood,** a reference to the belief that witches fed their "familiars" with their own blood. 16. **earnest,** partial payment; see glossary. 25. **vail,** lower; see glossary. 31. **spirits,** i.e., the demons—"familiars"—attending on Joan; cf. l. 10. **spelling charms,** charms that cast a spell. 35. **Circe,** sorceress celebrated for her power to change men into swine. 37. **proper,** handsome; see glossary. 38. **dainty,** particular; see glossary. 42. **Fell,** fierce, cruel. **banning,** cursing. 44. **miscreant,** base villain. 63. **Twinkling,** causing to twinkle. 75.

Suf. Yet so my fancy may be satisfied,
And peace established between these realms.
But there remains a scruple in that too;
For though her father be the King of Naples,
Duke of Anjou and Maine, yet is he poor,
And our nobility will scorn the match.
Mar. Hear ye, captain, are you not at leisure?
Suf. It shall be so, disdain they ne'er so much:
Henry is youthful and will quickly yield.—
Madam, I have a secret to reveal.
Mar. [*Aside*] What though I be enthrall'd? he seems a knight,
And will not any way dishonour me.
Suf. Lady, vouchsafe to listen what I say.
Mar. Perhaps I shall be rescu'd by the French;
And then I need not crave his courtesy.
Suf. Sweet madam, give me hearing in a cause—
Mar. Tush, women have been captivate ere now.
Suf. Lady, wherefore talk you so?
Mar. I cry you mercy, 'tis but Quid for Quo.
Suf. Say, gentle princess, would you not suppose
Your bondage happy, to be made a queen?
Mar. To be a queen in bondage is more vile
Than is a slave in base servility;
For princes should be free.
Suf. And so shall you,
If happy England's royal king be free.
Mar. Why, what concerns his freedom unto me?
Suf. I'll undertake to make thee Henry's queen,
To put a golden sceptre in thy hand
And set a precious crown upon thy head,
If thou wilt condescend to be my—
Mar. What?
Suf. His love.
Mar. I am unworthy to be Henry's wife.
Suf. No, gentle madam; I unworthy am
To woo so fair a dame to be his wife
And have no portion in the choice myself.
How say you, madam, are ye so content?
Mar. An if my father please, I am content.
Suf. Then call our captains and our colours forth.
And, madam, at your father's castle walls
We'll crave a parley, to confer with him.

Sound [*a parley*]. *Enter* REIGNIER *on the walls.*

See, Reignier, see, thy daughter prisoner!
Reig. To whom?
Suf. To me.
Reig. Suffolk, what remedy?
I am a soldier and unapt to weep
Or to exclaim on fortune's fickleness.
Suf. Yes, there is remedy enough, my lord:
Consent, and for thy honour give consent,
Thy daughter shall be wedded to my king;
Whom I with pain have woo'd and won thereto;
And this her easy-held imprisonment
Hath gain'd thy daughter princely liberty.
Reig. Speaks Suffolk as he thinks?
Suf. Fair Margaret knows
That Suffolk doth not flatter, face, or feign.
Reig. Upon thy princely warrant, I descend
To give thee answer of thy just demand.
[*Exit from the walls.*]
Suf. And here I will expect thy coming.

Trumpets sound. Enter REIGNIER [*below*].

Reig. Welcome, brave earl, into our territories:
Command in Anjou what your honour pleases.
Suf. Thanks, Reignier, happy for so sweet a child,
Fit to be made companion with a king:
What answer makes your grace unto my suit?
Reig. Since thou dost deign to woo her little worth
To be the princely bride of such a lord;
Upon condition I may quietly
Enjoy mine own, the country Maine and Anjou,
Free from oppression or the stroke of war,
My daughter shall be Henry's, if he please.
Suf. That is her ransom; I deliver her;
And those two counties I will undertake
Your grace shall well and quietly enjoy.
Reig. And I again, in Henry's royal name,
As deputy unto that gracious king,
Give thee her hand, for sign of plighted faith.
Suf. Reignier of France, I give thee kingly thanks,
Because this is in traffic of a king.
[*Aside*] And yet, methinks, I could be well content
To be mine own attorney in this case.—
I'll over then to England with this news,
And make this marriage to be solemniz'd.
So farewell, Reignier: set this diamond safe
In golden palaces, as it becomes.
Reig. I do embrace thee, as I would embrace
The Christian prince, King Henry, were he here.
Mar. Farewell, my lord: good wishes, praise and prayers
Shall Suffolk ever have of Margaret. *She is going.*
Suf. Farewell, sweet madam: but hark you, Margaret;
No princely commendations to my king?
Mar. Such commendations as becomes a maid,
A virgin and his servant, say to him.
Suf. Words sweetly plac'd and modestly directed.
But, madam, I must trouble you again;
No loving token to his majesty?
Mar. Yes, my good lord, a pure unspotted heart,
Never yet taint with love, I send the king.
Suf. And this withal. *Kiss her.*
Mar. That for thyself: I will not so presume
To send such peevish tokens to a king.
[*Exeunt Reignier and Margaret.*]
Suf. O, wert thou for myself! But, Suffolk, stay;
Thou mayest not wander in that labyrinth;
There Minotaurs and ugly treasons lurk.
Solicit Henry with her wondrous praise:
Bethink thee on her virtues that surmount,
And natural graces that extinguish art;
Repeat their semblance often on the seas,
That, when thou com'st to kneel at Henry's feet,
Thou mayest bereave him of his wits with wonder.
Exit.

deny, refuse; see glossary. 84. **cooling card,** apparently a term of some lost card game; figuratively, something that cools one's ardor (Onions); card played by an adversary which dashes one's hope (Tucker Brooke). 89. **wooden thing,** awkward business (Steevens); expressionless, insensible thing, referring to the king (Hart). 109. **cry you mercy,** beg your pardon; see glossary. **Quid for Quo,** tit for tat. 142. **face,** show a false face. 164. **traffic,** business. 188. **labyrinth,** a structure built by Daedalus consisting of intricate passageways where the Minotaur—a monster born from the union of the Cretan king's wife with a bull—was confined.

[SCENE IV. *Camp of the* DUKE OF YORK *in Anjou.*]

Enter YORK, WARWICK, Shepherd, [*and* LA] PUCELLE [*guarded*].

York. Bring forth that sorceress condemn'd to burn.
Shep. Ah, Joan, this kills thy father's heart outright!
Have I sought every country far and near,
And, now it is my chance to find thee out,
Must I behold thy timeless cruel death?
Ah, Joan, sweet daughter Joan, I'll die with thee!
Puc. Decrepit miser! base ignoble wretch!
I am descended of a gentler blood:
Thou art no father nor no friend of mine.
Shep. Out, out! My lords, an please you, 'tis not so;
I did beget her, all the parish knows:
Her mother liveth yet, can testify
She was the first fruit of my bach'lorship.
War. Graceless! wilt thou deny thy parentage?
York. This argues what her kind of life hath been,
Wicked and vile; and so her death concludes.
Shep. Fie, Joan, that thou wilt be so obstacle!
God knows thou art a collop of my flesh;
And for thy sake have I shed many a tear:
Deny me not, I prithee, gentle Joan.
Puc. Peasant, avaunt! You have suborn'd this man,
Of purpose to obscure my noble birth.
Shep. 'Tis true, I gave a noble to the priest
The morn that I was wedded to her mother.
Kneel down and take my blessing, good my girl.
Wilt thou not stoop? Now cursed be the time
Of thy nativity! I would the milk
Thy mother gave thee when thou suck'dst her breast,
Had been a little ratsbane for thy sake!
Or else, when thou didst keep my lambs a-field,
I wish some ravenous wolf had eaten thee!
Dost thou deny thy father, cursed drab?
O, burn her, burn her! hanging is too good. *Exit.*
York. Take her away; for she hath liv'd too long,
To fill the world with vicious qualities.
Puc. First, let me tell you whom you have condemn'd:
Not me begotten of a shepherd swain,
But issued from the progeny of kings;
Virtuous and holy; chosen from above,
By inspiration of celestial grace,
To work exceeding miracles on earth.
I never had to do with wicked spirits:
But you, that are polluted with your lusts,
Stain'd with the guiltless blood of innocents,
Corrupt and tainted with a thousand vices,
Because you want the grace that others have,
You judge it straight a thing impossible
To compass wonders but by help of devils.
No, misconceived! Joan of Arc hath been
A virgin from her tender infancy,
Chaste and immaculate in very thought;
Whose maiden blood, thus rigorously effus'd,
Will cry for vengeance at the gates of heaven.
York. Ay, ay: away with her to execution!
War. And hark ye, sirs; because she is a maid,
Spare for no faggots, let there be enow:
Place barrels of pitch upon the fatal stake,
That so her torture may be shortened.
Puc. Will nothing turn your unrelenting hearts?
Then, Joan, discover thine infirmity,
That warranteth by law to be thy privilege.
I am with child, ye bloody homicides:
Murder not then the fruit within my womb,
Although ye hale me to a violent death.
York. Now heaven forfend! the holy maid with child!
War. The greatest miracle that e'er ye wrought:
Is all your strict preciseness come to this?
York. She and the Dauphin have been juggling:
I did imagine what would be her refuge.
War. Well, go to; we'll have no bastards live;
Especially since Charles must father it.
Puc. You are deceiv'd; my child is none of his:
It was Alençon that enjoy'd my love.
York. Alençon! that notorious Machiavel!
It dies, an if it had a thousand lives.
Puc. O, give me leave, I have deluded you:
'Twas neither Charles nor yet the duke I nam'd,
But Reignier, king of Naples, that prevail'd.
War. A married man! that 's most intolerable.
York. Why, here 's a girl! I think she knows not well,
There were so many, whom she may accuse.
War. It 's sign she hath been liberal and free.
York. And yet, forsooth, she is a virgin pure.
Strumpet, thy words condemn thy brat and thee:
Use no entreaty, for it is in vain.
Puc. Then lead me hence; with whom I leave my curse:
May never glorious sun reflex his beams
Upon the country where you make abode;
But darkness and the gloomy shade of death
Environ you, till mischief and despair
Drive you to break your necks or hang yourselves!
Exit [*guarded*].
York. Break thou in pieces and consume to ashes,
Thou foul accursed minister of hell!

Enter CARDINAL [BEAUFORT, Bishop of Winchester, *attended*].

Car. Lord regent, I do greet your excellence
With letters of commission from the king.
For know, my lords, the states of Christendom,
Mov'd with remorse of these outrageous broils,
Have earnestly implor'd a general peace
Betwixt our nation and the aspiring French;
And here at hand the Dauphin and his train
Approacheth, to confer about some matter.
York. Is all our travail turn'd to this effect?
After the slaughter of so many peers,
So many captains, gentlemen and soldiers,
That in this quarrel have been overthrown
And sold their bodies for their country's benefit,
Shall we at last conclude effeminate peace?
Have we not lost most part of all the towns,
By treason, falsehood and by treachery,
Our great progenitors had conquered?
O, Warwick, Warwick! I foresee with grief

SCENE IV. 4. **find thee out,** discover you. 5. **timeless,** premature. 17. **obstacle,** stubborn. 18. **collop,** slice of meat; figuratively applied to offspring. 23. **noble,** coin worth 6s. 8d. 29. **ratsbane,** rat poison. 32. **drab,** whore. 35. **qualities,** arts, tricks; see glossary. 49. **misconceived,** having a wrong idea. 65. **forfend,** forbid; see glossary. 74. **Machiavel,** an allusion to the Elizabethan conception of Niccolo Machiavelli, an Italian political philosopher who advocated the practice of expediency regardless of the ethics involved. To the Elizabethan he symbolized crafty and ruthless ambition. 82. **liberal,** unrestrained, licentious; see glossary. 86. **whom.** The antecedent is in the understood subject of the imperative verb *lead*. 96. **states of Christendom.** Cf. Hall's *Chronicle*, Twenty-second Year of Henry VI: ". . . all the

The utter loss of all the realm of France.
War. Be patient, York: if we conclude a peace,
It shall be with such strict and severe covenants
As little shall the Frenchmen gain thereby.

Enter CHARLES, ALENÇON, BASTARD, REIGNIER [*, and others*].

Char. Since, lords of England, it is thus agreed
That peaceful truce shall be proclaim'd in France,
We come to be informed by yourselves
What the conditions of that league must be.
York. Speak, Winchester; for boiling choler chokes
The hollow passage of my poison'd voice,
By sight of these our baleful enemies.
Car. Charles, and the rest, it is enacted thus:
That, in regard King Henry gives consent,
Of mere compassion and of lenity,
To ease your country of distressful war,
And suffer you to breathe in fruitful peace,
You shall become true liegemen to his crown:
And, Charles, upon condition thou wilt swear
To pay him tribute, and submit thyself,
Thou shalt be plac'd as viceroy under him,
And still enjoy thy regal dignity.
Alen. Must he be then as shadow of himself?
Adorn his temples with a coronet,
And yet, in substance and authority,
Retain but privilege of a private man?
This proffer is absurd and reasonless.
Char. 'Tis known already that I am possess'd
With more than half the Gallian territories,
And therein reverenc'd for their lawful king:
Shall I, for lucre of the rest unvanquish'd,
Detract so much from that prerogative,
As to be call'd but viceroy of the whole?
No, lord ambassador, I'll rather keep
That which I have than, coveting for more,
Be cast from possibility of all.
York. Insulting Charles! hast thou by secret means
Us'd intercession to obtain a league,
And, now the matter grows to compromise,
Stand'st thou aloof upon comparison?
Either accept the title thou usurp'st,
Of benefit proceeding from our king
And not of any challenge of desert,
Or we will plague thee with incessant wars.
Reig. My lord, you do not well in obstinacy
To cavil in the course of this contract:
If once it be neglected, ten to one
We shall not find like opportunity.
Alen. To say the truth, it is your policy
To save your subjects from such massacre
And ruthless slaughters as are daily seen
By our proceeding in hostility;
And therefore take this compact of a truce,
Although you break it when your pleasure serves.
War. How say'st thou, Charles? shall our condition stand?
Char. It shall;
Only reserv'd, you claim no interest
In any of our towns of garrison.
York. Then swear allegiance to his majesty,
As thou art knight, never to disobey
Nor be rebellious to the crown of England,
Thou, nor thy nobles, to the crown of England.
So, now dismiss your army when ye please;
Hang up your ensigns, let your drums be still,
For here we entertain a solemn peace. *Exeunt.*

[SCENE V. *London. The palace.*]

Enter SUFFOLK *in conference with the* KING, GLOUCESTER *and* EXETER.

King. Your wondrous rare description, noble earl,
Of beauteous Margaret hath astonish'd me:
Her virtues graced with external gifts
Do breed love's settled passions in my heart:
And like as rigour of tempestuous gusts
Provokes the mightiest hulk against the tide,
So am I driven by breath of her renown
Either to suffer shipwreck or arrive
Where I may have fruition of her love.
Suf. Tush, my good lord, this superficial tale
Is but a preface of her worthy praise;
The chief perfections of that lovely dame,
Had I sufficient skill to utter them,
Would make a volume of enticing lines,
Able to ravish any dull conceit:
And, which is more, she is not so divine,
So full-replete with choice of all delights,
But with as humble lowliness of mind
She is content to be at your command;
Command, I mean, of virtuous chaste intents,
To love and honour Henry as her lord.
King. And otherwise will Henry ne'er presume.
Therefore, my lord protector, give consent
That Marg'ret may be England's royal queen.
Glou. So should I give consent to flatter sin.
You know, my lord, your highness is betroth'd
Unto another lady of esteem:
How shall we then dispense with that contract,
And not deface your honour with reproach?
Suf. As doth a ruler with unlawful oaths;
Or one that, at a triumph having vow'd
To try his strength, forsaketh yet the lists
By reason of his adversary's odds:
A poor earl's daughter is unequal odds,
And therefore may be broke without offence.
Glou. Why, what, I pray, is Margaret more than that?
Her father is no better than an earl,
Although in glorious titles he excel.
Suf. Yes, my lord, her father is a king,
The King of Naples and Jerusalem;
And of such great authority in France
As his alliance will confirm our peace
And keep the Frenchmen in allegiance.
Glou. And so the Earl of Armagnac may do,
Because he is near kinsman unto Charles.
Exe. Beside, his wealth doth warrant a liberal dower,
Where Reignier sooner will receive than give.

princes of Christendom, so muche labored and trauailed, by their orators and Ambassadors, that the frostie hartes of bothe the parties wer somewhat mollified, and their indurate stomackes greatly asswaged." 97. **remorse of,** compassion on account of; see glossary. 114. **covenants,** clauses or articles of a contract. 120. **choler,** red bile, humor dominant in angry tempers; see *humour* in glossary. 150. **comparison,** quibbling rhetoric (Tucker Brooke); satirical or scoffing similes (Onions). 156. **cavil,** raise frivolous or fault-finding objections. 165. **condition,** treaty, contract; see glossary. 168. **towns of garrison,** fortified towns.

SCENE V. 4. **settled,** fixed, rooted. 31. **triumph,** tournament. 35. **broke,** i.e., negotiations may be broken off.

Suf. A dow'r, my lords! disgrace not so your king,
That he should be so abject, base and poor,
To choose for wealth and not for perfect love.
Henry is able to enrich his queen
And not to seek a queen to make him rich:
So worthless peasants bargain for their wives,
As market-men for oxen, sheep, or horse.
Marriage is a matter of more worth
Than to be dealt in by attorneyship;
Not whom we will, but whom his grace affects,
Must be companion of his nuptial bed:
And therefore, lords, since he affects her most,
It most of all these reasons bindeth us,
In our opinions she should be preferr'd.
For what is wedlock forced but a hell,
An age of discord and continual strife?
Whereas the contrary bringeth bliss,
And is a pattern of celestial peace.
Whom should we match with Henry, being a king,
But Margaret, that is daughter to a king?
Her peerless feature, joined with her birth,
Approves her fit for none but for a king:
Her valiant courage and undaunted spirit,
More than in women commonly is seen,
Will answer our hope in issue of a king;
For Henry, son unto a conqueror,
Is likely to beget more conquerors,
If with a lady of so high resolve
As is fair Margaret he be link'd in love.
Then yield, my lords; and here conclude with me
That Margaret shall be queen, and none but she.

King. Whether it be through force of your report,
My noble Lord of Suffolk, or for that
My tender youth was never yet attaint
With any passion of inflaming love,
I cannot tell; but this I am assur'd,
I feel such sharp dissension in my breast,
Such fierce alarums both of hope and fear,
As I am sick with working of my thoughts.
Take, therefore, shipping; post, my lord, to France;
Agree to any covenants, and procure
That Lady Margaret do vouchsafe to come
To cross the seas to England and be crown'd
King Henry's faithful and anointed queen:
For your expenses and sufficient charge,
Among the people gather up a tenth.
Be gone, I say; for, till you do return,
I rest perplexed with a thousand cares.
And you, good uncle, banish all offence:
If you do censure me by what you were,
Not what you are, I know it will excuse
This sudden execution of my will.
And so, conduct me where, from company,
I may revolve and ruminate my grief. *Exit*.

Glou. Ay, grief, I fear me, both at first and last.
Exit Gloucester [*with Exeter*].

Suf. Thus Suffolk hath prevail'd; and thus he goes,
As did the youthful Paris once to Greece,
With hope to find the like event in love,
But prosper better than the Trojan did.
Margaret shall now be queen, and rule the king;
But I will rule both her, the king and realm. *Exit*.

56. **by attorneyship,** by an attorney, by proxy. 68. **feature,** figure; see glossary. 81. **attaint.** infected. 87. **post,** hasten; see glossary. 93. **gather up a tenth,** levy a tax of ten per cent. 95. **rest,** remain. 97. **censure,** judge; see glossary. 100. **from company,** i.e., alone.

THE SECOND PART OF KING HENRY THE SIXTH

[*Dramatis Personae*

KING HENRY the Sixth.
HUMPHREY, Duke of Gloucester, *his uncle.*
CARDINAL BEAUFORT, Bishop of Winchester, *great-uncle to the King.*
RICHARD PLANTAGENET, Duke of York.
EDWARD *and* RICHARD, *his sons.*
DUKE OF SOMERSET.
DUKE OF SUFFOLK.
DUKE OF BUCKINGHAM.
LORD CLIFFORD.
Young CLIFFORD, *his son.*
EARL OF SALISBURY.
EARL OF WARWICK.
LORD SCALES.
LORD SAY.
SIR HUMPHREY STAFFORD, *and* WILLIAM STAFFORD, *his brother.*
SIR JOHN STANLEY.
VAUX.
MATTHEW GOFFE.
A Lieutenant, Master, *and* Master's-Mate, *and* WALTER WHITMORE.
Two Gentlemen, *prisoners with Suffolk.*
JOHN HUME *and* JOHN SOUTHWELL, *priests.*
BOLINGBROKE, *a conjurer.*
THOMAS HORNER, *an armourer.* PETER, *his man.*
Clerk of Chatham. Mayor of Saint Alban's.
SIMPCOX, *an impostor.*
ALEXANDER IDEN, *a Kentish gentleman.*
JACK CADE, *a rebel.*
GEORGE BEVIS, JOHN HOLLAND, DICK *the butcher,* SMITH *the weaver,* MICHAEL, *&c., followers of Cade.*
Two Murderers.

MARGARET, *Queen to King Henry.*
ELEANOR, Duchess of Gloucester.
MARGARET JOURDAIN, *a witch.*
Wife to Simpcox.

Lords, Ladies, *and* Attendants, Petitioners, Aldermen, a Herald, a Beadle, Sheriff, *and* Officers, Citizens, 'Prentices, Falconers, Guards, Soldiers, Messengers, *&c.*

A Spirit.

SCENE: *England.*]

ACT I.

SCENE I. [*London. The palace.*]

Flourish of trumpets: then hautboys. Enter [*the*] KING, DUKE HUMPHREY [of GLOUCESTER], SALISBURY, WARWICK, *and* [CARDINAL] BEAUFORT, *on the one side;* the QUEEN, SUFFOLK, YORK, SOMERSET, *and* BUCKINGHAM, *on the other.*

Suf. As by your high imperial majesty
I had in charge at my depart for France,
As procurator to your excellence,
To marry Princess Margaret for your grace,
So, in the famous ancient city Tours,
In presence of the Kings of France and Sicil,
The Dukes of Orleans, Calaber, Bretagne and Alençon,
Seven earls, twelve barons and twenty reverend bishops,
I have perform'd my task and was espous'd:
And humbly now upon my bended knee,
In sight of England and her lordly peers,
Deliver up my title in the queen
To your most gracious hands, that are the substance
Of that great shadow I did represent;
The happiest gift that ever marquess gave,
The fairest queen that ever king receiv'd.

King. Suffolk, arise. Welcome, Queen Margaret:
I can express no kinder sign of love
Than this kind kiss. O Lord, that lends me life,
Lend me a heart replete with thankfulness!
For thou hast given me in this beauteous face
A world of earthly blessings to my soul,
If sympathy of love unite our thoughts.

Queen. Great King of England and my gracious lord,
The mutual conference that my mind hath had,
By day, by night, waking and in my dreams,
In courtly company or at my beads,
With you, mine alder-liefest sovereign,
Makes me the bolder to salute my king
With ruder terms, such as my wit affords
And over-joy of heart doth minister.

King. Her sight did ravish; but her grace in speech,
Her words y-clad with wisdom's majesty,
Makes me from wond'ring fall to weeping joys;
Such is the fulness of my heart's content.
Lords, with one cheerful voice welcome my love.

All (kneeling). Long live Queen Margaret, England's happiness!

Queen. We thank you all. *Flourish.*

Suf. My lord protector, so it please your grace,
Here are the articles of contracted peace
Between our sovereign and the French king Charles,
For eighteen months concluded by consent.

Glou. (Reads) 'Imprimis, It is agreed between the French king Charles, and William de la Pole, Mar-

ACT I. SCENE I. *Stage Direction:* **hautboys,** double-reed wind instruments, oboes. 2. **I . . . France.** Cf. *1 Henry VI*, V, iii, and V, v, where Suffolk negotiates with the duke Reignier for the marriage of his daughter to the English king. **depart,** departure. 3. **procurator,** agent, proxy. The language of the play here follows Hall and Holinshed: "The marquesse of Suffolke, as procurator to king Henrie, espoused the said ladie in the church of saint Martins. At the which mariage were present the father and mother of the bride: the French king himselfe, which was vncle to the husband; and the French queene also, which was aunt to the wife. There were also the dukes of Orleance, of Calabre, of Alanson, and of Britaine, seauen earles, twelue barons, twentie bishops, besides knights and gentlemen." 6. **Sicil,** Sicily, of which Margaret's father was titular king. 14. **shadow,** image, i.e., of royalty; see glossary. 18. **kinder**, more natural; see *kind* in glossary. 28. **alder-liefest,** most loved. 30. **ruder**, less elegant. 33. **y-clad,** clothed. 43. **Imprimis,** in the first place.

quess of Suffolk, ambassador for Henry King of England, that the said Henry shall espouse the Lady Margaret, daughter unto Reignier King of Naples, Sicilia and Jerusalem, and crown her Queen of England ere the thirtieth of May next ensuing. Item, that the duchy of Anjou and the county of Maine shall be released and delivered to the king her father'—

[*Lets the paper fall.*]

King. Uncle, how now!
Glou. Pardon me, gracious lord;
Some sudden qualm hath struck me at the heart
And dimm'd mine eyes, that I can read no further.
King. Uncle of Winchester, I pray, read on.

Car. [*Reads*] 'Item, It is further agreed between them, that the duchies of Anjou and Maine shall be released and delivered over to the king her father, and she sent over of the King of England's own proper cost and charges, without having any dowry.'

King. They please us well. Lord marquess, kneel down:
We here create thee the first duke of Suffolk,
And gird thee with the sword. Cousin of York,
We here discharge your grace from being regent
I' th' parts of France, till term of eighteen months
Be full expir'd. Thanks, uncle Winchester,
Gloucester, York, Buckingham, Somerset,
Salisbury, and Warwick;
We thank you all for this great favour done,
In entertainment to my princely queen.
Come, let us in, and with all speed provide
To see her coronation be perform'd.

Exeunt King, Queen, and Suffolk. Manet the rest.

Glou. Brave peers of England, pillars of the state,
To you Duke Humphrey must unload his grief,
Your grief, the common grief of all the land.
What! did my brother Henry spend his youth,
His valour, coin and people, in the wars?
Did he so often lodge in open field,
In winter's cold and summer's parching heat,
To conquer France, his true inheritance?
And did my brother Bedford toil his wits,
To keep by policy what Henry got?
Have you yourselves, Somerset, Buckingham,
Brave York, Salisbury, and victorious Warwick,
Receiv'd deep scars in France and Normandy?
Or hath mine uncle Beaufort and myself,
With all the learned council of the realm,
Studied so long, sat in the council-house
Early and late, debating to and fro
How France and Frenchmen might be kept in awe,
And had his highness in his infancy
Crowned in Paris in despite of foes?
And shall these labours and these honours die?
Shall Henry's conquest, Bedford's vigilance,
Your deeds of war and all our counsel die?
O peers of England, shameful is this league!
Fatal this marriage, cancelling your fame,
Blotting your names from books of memory,
Razing the characters of your renown,
Defacing monuments of conquer'd France,
Undoing all, as all had never been!
Car. Nephew, what means this passionate discourse,
This peroration with such circumstance?
For France, 'tis ours; and we will keep it still.
Glou. Ay, uncle, we will keep it, if we can;
But now it is impossible we should:
Suffolk, the new-made duke that rules the roast,
Hath given the duchy of Anjou and Maine
Unto the poor King Reignier, whose large style
Agrees not with the leanness of his purse.
Sal. Now, by the death of Him that died for all,
These counties were the keys of Normandy.
But wherefore weeps Warwick, my valiant son?
War. For grief that they are past recovery:
For, were there hope to conquer them again,
My sword should shed hot blood, mine eyes no tears.
Anjou and Maine! myself did win them both;
Those provinces these arms of mine did conquer:
And are the cities, that I got with wounds,
Deliver'd up again with peaceful words?
Mort Dieu!
York. For Suffolk's duke, may he be suffocate,
That dims the honour of this warlike isle!
France should have torn and rent my very heart,
Before I would have yielded to this league.
I never read but England's kings have had
Large sums of gold and dowries with their wives;
And our King Henry gives away his own,
To match with her that brings no vantages.
Glou. A proper jest, and never heard before,
That Suffolk should demand a whole fifteenth
For costs and charges in transporting her!
She should have stay'd in France and starv'd in France,
Before—
Car. My Lord of Gloucester, now ye grow too hot:
It was the pleasure of my lord the king.
Glou. My Lord of Winchester, I know your mind;
'Tis not my speeches that you do mislike,
But 'tis my presence that doth trouble ye.
Rancour will out: proud prelate, in thy face
I see thy fury: if I longer stay,
We shall begin our ancient bickerings.
Lordings, farewell; and say, when I am gone,
I prophesied France will be lost ere long. *Exit Hum.*
Car. So, there goes our protector in a rage.
'Tis known to you he is mine enemy,
Nay, more, an enemy unto you all,
And no great friend, I fear me, to the king.
Consider, lords, he is the next of blood,
And heir apparent to the English crown:
Had Henry got an empire by his marriage,

51. **released,** surrendered. 61. **proper,** exclusive; see glossary. 67. **term . . . months,** i.e., the period of the truce between England and France. 78. **Henry,** Henry V. 83-87. **And . . . Normandy.** The absence of any mention of Talbot's exploits suggests that this play was written independently of *1 Henry VI*. 84. **policy,** prudent management; see glossary. 91. **debating,** discussing; see glossary. 101. **characters,** records; see glossary. 105. **peroration,** rhetorical discourse. **circumstance,** elaborate talk; detail. 106. **still,** always; see glossary. 109. **rules the roast,** has the lead, domineers. 111-112. **large . . . purse.** A similar antithesis is in Holinshed: "King Reiner hir father, for all his long stile, had too short a pursse to send his daughter honorablie to the King hir spouse." **large,** lavish; see glossary. 127. **league,** friendly alliance. 131. **vantages,** benefits, profits; see glossary. 133. **a whole fifteenth,** i.e., the tax levy granted by the Commons consisting of one-fifteenth of the produce of lands and industry; felt as excessive; see *1 Henry VI*, V, v, 92-93. The phrase is in Holinshed: ". . . and, for the fetching of hir, the marquesse of Suffolke demanded a whole fifteenth in open parliament." Cf. *1 Henry VI*, V, v, 92-93. 139. **mind,** thoughts; see glossary. 144. **our ancient bickerings.** The rivalry between Gloucester and Winchester during Henry's minority and their outward reconciliation are chronicled by Hall and Holinshed (Fourth Year of Henry VI); cf. *1 Henry VI*, I, i, 33-34; III, i. 154. **the wealthy . . . west,** possibly an anachronistic reference to New World possessions. 159. **good . . . Gloucester.** Gloucester's

And all the wealthy kingdoms of the west,
There 's reason he should be displeas'd at it.
Look to it, lords; let not his smoothing words
Bewitch your hearts; be wise and circumspect.
What though the common people favour him,
Calling him 'Humphrey, the good Duke of Gloucester,'
Clapping their hands, and crying with loud voice,
'Jesu maintain your royal excellence!'
With 'God preserve the good Duke Humphrey!'
I fear me, lords, for all this flattering gloss,
He will be found a dangerous protector.

Buck. Why should he, then, protect our sovereign,
He being of age to govern of himself?
Cousin of Somerset, join you with me,
And all together, with the Duke of Suffolk,
We'll quickly hoise Duke Humphrey from his seat.

Car. This weighty business will not brook delay;
I'll to the Duke of Suffolk presently. *Exit Car.*

Som. Cousin of Buckingham, though Humphrey's pride
And greatness of his place be grief to us,
Yet let us watch the haughty cardinal:
His insolence is more intolerable
Than all the princes in the land beside:
If Gloucester be displac'd, he'll be protector.

Buck. Or thou or I, Somerset, will be protector,
Despite Duke Humphrey or the cardinal.

Exeunt Buckingham and Somerset.

Sal. Pride went before, ambition follows him.
While these do labour for their own preferment,
Behoves it us to labour for the realm.
I never saw but Humphrey Duke of Gloucester
Did bear him like a noble gentleman.
Oft have I seen the haughty cardinal,
More like a soldier than a man o' th' church,
As stout and proud as he were lord of all,
Swear like a ruffian and demean himself
Unlike the ruler of a commonweal.
Warwick, my son, the comfort of my age,
Thy deeds, thy plainness and thy housekeeping,
Hath won the greatest favour of the commons,
Excepting none but good Duke Humphrey:
And, brother York, thy acts in Ireland,
In bringing them to civil discipline,
Thy late exploits done in the heart of France,
When thou wert regent for our sovereign,
Have made thee fear'd and honour'd of the people:
Join we together, for the public good,
In what we can, to bridle and suppress
The pride of Suffolk and the cardinal,
With Somerset's and Buckingham's ambition;
And, as we may, cherish Duke Humphrey's deeds,
While they do tend the profit of the land.

War. So God help Warwick, as he loves the land,
And common profit of his country!

York. [*Aside*] And so says York, for he hath greatest cause.

Sal. Then let 's make haste away, and look unto the main.

War. Unto the main! O father, Maine is lost;
That Maine which by main force Warwick did win,
And would have kept so long as breath did last!
Main chance, father, you meant; but I meant Maine,
Which I will win from France, or else be slain.

Exeunt Warwick and Salisbury. Manet York.

York. Anjou and Maine are given to the French;
Paris is lost; the state of Normandy
Stands on a tickle point, now they are gone:
Suffolk concluded on the articles,
The peers agreed, and Henry was well pleas'd
To change two dukedoms for a duke's fair daughter.
I cannot blame them all: what is 't to them?
'Tis thine they give away, and not their own.
Pirates may make cheap pennyworths of their pillage
And purchase friends and give to courtezans,
Still revelling like lords till all be gone;
While as the silly owner of the goods
Weeps over them and wrings his hapless hands
And shakes his head and trembling stands aloof,
While all is shar'd and all is borne away,
Ready to starve and dare not touch his own:
So York must sit and fret and bite his tongue,
While his own lands are bargain'd for and sold.
Methinks the realms of England, France and Ireland
Bear that proportion to my flesh and blood
As did the fatal brand Althæa burn'd
Unto the prince's heart of Calydon.
Anjou and Maine both given unto the French!
Cold news for me, for I had hope of France,
Even as I have of fertile England's soil.
A day will come when York shall claim his own;
And therefore I will take the Nevils' parts
And make a show of love to proud Duke Humphrey,
And, when I spy advantage, claim the crown,
For that 's the golden mark I seek to hit:
Nor shall proud Lancaster usurp my right,
Nor hold the sceptre in his childish fist,
Nor wear the diadem upon his head,
Whose church-like humours fits not for a crown.
Then, York, be still awhile, till time do serve:
Watch thou and wake when others be asleep,
To pry into the secrets of the state;
Till Henry, surfeiting in joys of love,
With his new bride and England's dear-bought queen,
And Humphrey with the peers be fall'n at jars:
Then will I raise aloft the milk-white rose,
With whose sweet smell the air shall be perfum'd;
And in my standard bear the arms of York,
To grapple with the house of Lancaster;
And, force perforce, I'll make him yield the crown,

popularity is recorded in the chronicles, where he is represented as "an vpright and politike gouernour." 163. **gloss,** specious talk. 169. **hoise,** remove. 170. **brook,** endure; see glossary. 171. **presently,** immediately; see glossary. 172. **Cousin,** any relative not of one's immediate family; see glossary. 180. **Pride,** i.e., Winchester. **ambition,** i.e., Buckingham and Somerset. 191. **housekeeping,** hospitality. 208. **the main,** important business; also, main chance. 216. **tickle,** easily shifted, insecure. 222. **cheap pennyworths,** bargains. 234. **Althæa,** mother of Meleager, at whose birth the three Fates were present and bestowed gifts—courage, strength, and duration of life only as long as a brand, at the time burning on the fire, remained unconsumed. When the three had departed, the infant's mother snatched the brand, extinguished it, and put it in safe keeping. Years later, when Meleager quarreled with Althæa's brothers and slew them, she resentfully threw the fatal brand into the fire, and as it was reduced to ashes Meleager died. 240. **the Nevils'.** York's wife was Cecille Nevil, sister to the earl of Salisbury and aunt to the earl of Warwick. 242. **advantage,** opportunity; see glossary. 247. **humours,** temperament, cast of mind; see glossary. 248. **do serve,** is favorable; see *serve* in glossary. 253. **jars,** discords (as in music); see glossary. 258. **force perforce,** by violent compulsion; see *perforce* in glossary.

Whose bookish rule hath pull'd fair England down.
Exit York.

[SCENE II. *The* DUKE OF GLOUCESTER'S *house.*]

Enter DUKE HUMPHREY *and his wife* ELEANOR.

Duch. Why droops my lord, like overripen'd corn,
Hanging the head at Ceres' plenteous load?
Why doth the great Duke Humphrey knit his brows,
As frowning at the favours of the world?
Why are thine eyes fix'd to the sullen earth,
Gazing on that which seems to dim thy sight?
What seest thou there? King Henry's diadem,
Enchas'd with all the honours of the world?
If so, gaze on, and grovel on thy face,
Until thy head be circled with the same.
Put forth thy hand, reach at the glorious gold.
What, is 't too short? I'll lengthen it with mine;
And, having both together heav'd it up,
We'll both together lift our heads to heaven,
And never more abase our sight so low
As to vouchsafe one glance unto the ground.
Glou. O Nell, sweet Nell, if thou dost love thy lord,
Banish the canker of ambitious thoughts.
And may that thought, when I imagine ill
Against my king and nephew, virtuous Henry,
Be my last breathing in this mortal world!
My troublous dream this night doth make me sad.
Duch. What dream'd my lord? tell me, and I'll requite it
With sweet rehearsal of my morning's dream.
Glou. Methought this staff, mine office-badge in court,
Was broke in twain; by whom I have forgot,
But, as I think, it was by th' cardinal;
And on the pieces of the broken wand
Were plac'd the heads of Edmund Duke of Somerset,
And William de la Pole, first duke of Suffolk.
This was my dream: what it doth bode, God knows.
Duch. Tut, this was nothing but an argument
That he that breaks a stick of Gloucester's grove
Shall lose his head for his presumption.
But list to me, my Humphrey, my sweet duke:
Methought I sat in seat of majesty
In the cathedral church of Westminster,
And in that chair where kings and queens are crown'd;
Where Henry and dame Margaret kneel'd to me
And on my head did set the diadem.
Glou. Nay, Eleanor, then must I chide outright:
Presumptuous dame, ill-nurtur'd Eleanor,
Art thou not second woman in the realm,
And the protector's wife, belov'd of him?
Hast thou not worldly pleasure at command,
Above the reach or compass of thy thought?
And wilt thou still be hammering treachery,
To tumble down thy husband and thyself
From top of honour to disgrace's feet?
Away from me, and let me hear no more!
Duch. What, what, my lord! are you so choleric
With Eleanor, for telling but her dream?
Next time I'll keep my dreams unto myself,
And not be check'd.
Glou. Nay, be not angry; I am pleas'd again.

Enter Messenger.

Mess. My lord protector, 'tis his highness' pleasure
You do prepare to ride unto Saint Alban's,
Where as the king and queen do mean to hawk.
Glou. I go. Come, Nell, thou wilt ride with us?
Duch. Yes, my good lord, I'll follow presently.
Exit Humphrey [with Messenger].
Follow I must; I cannot go before,
While Gloucester bears this base and humble mind.
Were I a man, a duke, and next of blood,
I would remove these tedious stumbling-blocks
And smooth my way upon their headless necks;
And, being a woman, I will not be slack
To play my part in Fortune's pageant.
Where are you there? Sir John! nay, fear not, man,
We are alone; here 's none but thee and I.

Enter HUME.

Hume. Jesus preserve your royal majesty!
Duch. What say'st thou? majesty! I am but grace.
Hume. But, by the grace of God, and Hume's advice,
Your grace's title shall be multiplied.
Duch. What say'st thou, man? hast thou as yet conferr'd
With Margery Jourdain, the cunning witch,
With Roger Bolingbroke, the conjurer?
And will they undertake to do me good?
Hume. This they have promised, to show your highness
A spirit rais'd from depth of under-ground,
That shall make answer to such questions
As by your grace shall be propounded him.
Duch. It is enough; I'll think upon the questions:
When from Saint Alban's we do make return,
We'll see these things effected to the full.
Here, Hume, take this reward; make merry, man,
With thy confederates in this weighty cause.
Exit Eleanor.
Hume. Hume must make merry with the duchess' gold;
Marry, and shall. But, how now, Sir John Hume!
Seal up your lips, and give no words but mum:
The business asketh silent secrecy.
Dame Eleanor gives gold to bring the witch:
Gold cannot come amiss, were she a devil.
Yet have I gold flies from another coast;
I dare not say, from the rich cardinal
And from the great and new-made Duke of Suffolk,
Yet I do find it so; for, to be plain,
They, knowing Dame Eleanor's aspiring humour,
Have hired me to undermine the duchess
And buz these conjurations in her brain.
They say 'A crafty knave does need no broker;'
Yet am I Suffolk and the cardinal's broker.

259. **bookish,** scholarly and ineffectual.
SCENE II. 2. **Ceres',** goddess of the harvest. 8. **Enchas'd,** adorned as with gems. 21. **mortal,** i.e., as distinguished from the next world. 32. **argument,** proof, evidence. 42. **Presumptuous dame.** Cf. Winchester's words, *1 Henry VI,* I, i, 39-40. 47. **hammering,** devising. 67. **pageant,** spectacular entertainment; see glossary. 68. **Sir John,** common nickname for a priest. 71. **I am but grace.** "Your grace" is the appropriate address to a duchess. 88. **Marry,** mild interjection; see glossary. 93. **flies,** i.e., that flies. 106. **attainture,** disgrace.
SCENE III. 3-4. **in the quill,** simultaneously (Hart); in a body (Onions); possibly, "in writing." 7. **'a,** he; see glossary. 11. **fellow,** contemptuous or condescending form of address; see glossary. 24. **enclosing the commons,** the action of a lord of a manor in enclosing or converting into private property lands formerly undivided and used by

Hume, if you take not heed, you shall go near
To call them both a pair of crafty knaves.
Well, so it stands; and thus, I fear, at last
Hume's knavery will be the duchess' wrack,
And her attainture will be Humphrey's fall:
Sort how it will, I shall have gold for all. *Exit.*

[SCENE III. *The palace.*]

Enter three or four Petitioners, [PETER,] *the Armourer's man, being one.*

First Petit. My masters, let 's stand close: my lord protector will come this way by and by, and then we may deliver our supplications in the quill.

Sec. Petit. Marry, the Lord protect him, for he 's a good man! Jesu bless him!

Enter SUFFOLK *and* QUEEN.

Peter. Here 'a comes, methinks, and the queen with him. I'll be the first, sure.

Sec. Petit. Come back, fool; this is the Duke of Suffolk, and not my lord protector.

Suf. How now, fellow! wouldst any thing with me?

First Petit. I pray, my lord, pardon me; I took ye for my lord protector.

Queen. [*Reading*] 'To my Lord Protector!' Are your supplications to his lordship? Let me see them: what is thine?

First Petit. Mine is, an 't please your grace, against John Goodman, my lord cardinal's man, for keeping my house, and lands, and wife and all, from me.

Suf. Thy wife too! that 's some wrong, indeed. What 's yours? What 's here! [*Reads*] 'Against the Duke of Suffolk, for enclosing the commons of Melford.' How now, sir knave!

Sec. Petit. Alas, sir, I am but a poor petitioner of our whole township.

Peter. [*Giving his petition*] Against my master, Thomas Horner, for saying that the Duke of York was rightful heir to the crown.

Queen. What say'st thou? did the Duke of York say he was rightful heir to the crown?

Peter. That my master was? no, forsooth: my master said that he was, and that the king was an usurper.

Suf. Who is there? *(Enter Servant.)* Take this fellow in, and send for his master with a pursuivant presently: we'll hear more of your matter before the king.

Exit [*Servant with Peter*].

Queen. And as for you, that love to be protected
Under the wings of our protector's grace,
Begin your suits anew, and sue to him.

Tear the supplication.

Away, base cullions! Suffolk, let them go.

All. Come, let 's be gone. *Exeunt.*

Queen. My Lord of Suffolk, say, is this the guise,
Is this the fashion in the court of England?
Is this the government of Britain's isle,
And this the royalty of Albion's king?
What, shall King Henry be a pupil still
Under the surly Gloucester's governance?
Am I a queen in title and in style,
And must be made a subject to a duke?
I tell thee, Pole, when in the city Tours
Thou ran'st a tilt in honour of my love
And stol'st away the ladies' hearts of France,
I thought King Henry had resembled thee
In courage, courtship and proportion:
But all his mind is bent to holiness,
To number Ave-Maries on his beads;
His champions are the prophets and apostles,
His weapons holy saws of sacred writ,
His study is his tilt-yard, and his loves
Are brazen images of canonized saints.
I would the college of the cardinals
Would choose him pope and carry him to Rome,
And set the triple crown upon his head:
That were a state fit for his holiness.

Suf. Madam, be patient: as I was cause
Your highness came to England, so will I
In England work your grace's full content.

Queen. Beside the haughty protector, have we Beaufort
The imperious churchman, Somerset, Buckingham,
And grumbling York; and not the least of these
But can do more in England than the king.

Suf. And he of these that can do most of all
Cannot do more in England than the Nevils:
Salisbury and Warwick are no simple peers.

Queen. Not all these lords do vex me half so much
As that proud dame, the lord protector's wife.
She sweeps it through the court with troops of ladies,
More like an empress than Duke Humphrey's wife:
Strangers in court do take her for the queen:
She bears a duke's revenues on her back,
And in her heart she scorns our poverty:
Shall I not live to be aveng'd on her?
Contemptuous base-born callet as she is,
She vaunted 'mongst her minions t'other day,
The very train of her worst wearing gown
Was better worth than all my father's lands,
Till Suffolk gave two dukedoms for his daughter.

Suf. Madam, myself have lim'd a bush for her,
And plac'd a quire of such enticing birds,
That she will light to listen to the lays,
And never mount to trouble you again.
So, let her rest: and, madam, list to me;
For I am bold to counsel you in this.
Although we fancy not the cardinal,
Yet must we join with him and with the lords,
Till we have brought Duke Humphrey in disgrace.
As for the Duke of York, this late complaint
Will make but little for his benefit.
So, one by one, we'll weed them all at last,
And you yourself shall steer the happy helm.

Sound a sennet. Enter the KING, DUKE HUMPHREY [of Gloucester], CARDINAL [BEAUFORT], BUCKINGHAM,

the community as a whole. 37. **pursuivant,** officer-at-arms. 43. **cullions,** base fellows. 48. **Albion's king,** Albion is a poetic name for England. 57. **courtship,** court manners. **proportion,** carriage, build; see glossary. 58-61. **to holiness . . . writ.** The pious and idealistic character of the king is touched upon in *1 Henry VI*, III, i, and IV, i. 76. **the Nevils.** Cf. I, i, 240, note. This mention prepares for the important role played by Warwick later in the Henry VI cycle. 86. **callet,** lewd woman. 87. **minions,** followers, with quibble on the meaning "saucy women"; see glossary. 91. **lim'd a bush,** set a trap; a metaphor from the practice of catching birds by liming twigs of trees. 93. **lays,** songs. 103. *Stage Direction: sennet,* set of notes played on a trumpet as a signal for the approach or departure of processions; see glossary.

YORK, [SOMERSET,] SALISBURY, WARWICK, *and the* DUCHESS [OF GLOUCESTER].

King. For my part, noble lords, I care not which;
Or Somerset or York, all 's one to me.
York. If York have ill demean'd himself in France,
Then let him be denay'd the regentship.
Som. If Somerset be unworthy of the place,
Let York be regent; I will yield to him.
War. Whether your grace be worthy, yea or no,
Dispute not that: York is the worthier.
Car. Ambitious Warwick, let thy betters speak.
War. The cardinal 's not my better in the field.
Buck. All in this presence are thy betters, Warwick.
War. Warwick may live to be the best of all.
Sal. Peace, son! and show some reason, Buckingham,
Why Somerset should be preferr'd in this.
Queen. Because the king, forsooth, will have it so.
Glou. Madam, the king is old enough himself
To give his censure: these are no women's matters.
Queen. If he be old enough, what needs your grace
To be protector of his excellence?
Glou. Madam, I am protector of the realm;
And, at his pleasure, will resign my place.
Suf. Resign it then and leave thine insolence.
Since thou wert king—as who is king but thou?—
The commonwealth hath daily run to wrack;
The Dauphin hath prevail'd beyond the seas;
And all the peers and nobles of the realm
Have been as bondmen to thy sovereignty.
Car. The commons hast thou rack'd; the clergy's bags
Are lank and lean with thy extortions.
Som. Thy sumptuous buildings and thy wife's attire
Have cost a mass of public treasury.
Buck. Thy cruelty in execution
Upon offenders hath exceeded law
And left thee to the mercy of the law.
Queen. Thy sale of offices and towns in France,
If they were known, as the suspect is great,
Would make thee quickly hop without thy head.
Exit Humphrey. [*The Queen drops her fan*.]
Give me my fan: what, minion! can ye not?
She gives the Duchess a box on the ear.
I cry you mercy, madam; was it you?
Duch. Was 't I! yea, I it was, proud Frenchwoman:
Could I come near your beauty with my nails,
I 'ld set my ten commandments in your face.
King. Sweet aunt, be quiet; 'twas against her will.
Duch. Against her will! good king, look to 't in time;
She'll hamper thee, and dandle thee like a baby:
Though in this place most master wear no breeches,
She shall not strike Dame Eleanor unreveng'd.
Exit Eleanor.
Buck. Lord cardinal, I will follow Eleanor,
And listen after Humphrey, how he proceeds:
She 's tickled now; her fume needs no spurs,
She'll gallop far enough to her destruction. *Exit Buck*.

Enter HUMPHREY.

Glou. Now, lords, my choler being over-blown
With walking once about the quadrangle,
I come to talk of commonwealth affairs.
As for your spiteful false objections,
Prove them, and I lie open to the law:
But God in mercy so deal with my soul,
As I in duty love my king and country!
But, to the matter that we have in hand:
I say, my sovereign, York is meetest man
To be your regent in the realm of France.
Suf. Before we make election, give me leave
To show some reason, of no little force,
That York is most unmeet of any man.
York. I'll tell thee, Suffolk, why I am unmeet:
First, for I cannot flatter thee in pride;
Next, if I be appointed for the place,
My Lord of Somerset will keep me here,
Without discharge, money, or furniture,
Till France be won into the Dauphin's hands:
Last time, I danc'd attendance on his will
Till Paris was besieg'd, famish'd, and lost.
War. That can I witness; and a fouler fact
Did never traitor in the land commit.
Suf. Peace, headstrong Warwick!
War. Image of pride, why should I hold my peace?

Enter [HORNER, *the*] *Armourer, and his man* [PETER, *guarded*].

Suf. Because here is a man accus'd of treason:
Pray God the Duke of York excuse himself!
York. Doth any one accuse York for a traitor?
King. What mean'st thou, Suffolk; tell me, what are these?
Suf. Please it your majesty, this is the man
That doth accuse his master of high treason:
His words were these: that Richard Duke of York
Was rightful heir unto the English crown
And that your majesty was an usurper.
King. Say, man, were these thy words?

Hor. An 't shall please your majesty, I never said nor thought any such matter: God is my witness, I am falsely accused by the villain.

Pet. By these ten bones, my lords, he did speak them to me in the garret one night, as we were scouring my Lord of York's armour.

York. Base dunghill villain and mechanical,
I'll have thy head for this thy traitor's speech.
I do beseech your royal majesty,
Let him have all the rigour of the law.

Hor. Alas, my lord, hang me, if ever I spake the words. My accuser is my 'prentice; and when I did correct him for his fault the other day, he did vow upon his knees he would be even with me: I have good witness of this; therefore I beseech your majesty, do not cast away an honest man for a villain's accusation.

King. Uncle, what shall we say to this in law?
Glou. This doom, my lord, if I may judge:
Let Somerset be regent o'er the French,
Because in York this breeds suspicion:

105. **Or . . . or,** whether . . . or. 107. **denay'd,** denied. 120. **censure,** opinion; see glossary. 131. **rack'd,** strained beyond the capacity to endure; see glossary. 135-136. **Thy . . . law.** The charge is recorded in the chronicles that Gloucester "had caused men adjudged to die, to be put to other execution than the law of the land assigned." Gloucester's enemies repeat the charge in III, i, 58-59. 139. **suspect,** suspicion. 142. **cry you mercy,** beg your pardon; see glossary. 145. **my ten commandments,** i.e., marks of her ten fingers. 148. **dandle,** rock on the knee, fondle. 153. **tickled,** vexed, irritated. 161. **duty,** reverence; see glossary. 163. **meetest,** answering the purpose best, fittest. 172. **discharge,** payment of what is owed. **furniture,** equipment. 176. **fact,** deed; see glossary. 181. **excuse,** vindicate; see glossary. 192. **falsely,** treacherously; see glossary. 193. **bones,** fingers. 196. **mechanical,** common workman. 211. **these,** i.e., Peter and Horner. 212. **single combat,** fight between two, duel. 214-216. **Then be . . . the French.** These two lines, omitted from the Globe text, are not in F; they are supplied from the quarto of *The Contention*. 222. **Sirrah,** customary form of address to servants.

And let these have a day appointed them
For single combat in convenient place,
For he hath witness of his servant's malice:
This is the law, and this Duke Humphrey's doom.
King. Then be it so. My lord of Somerset,
We make your grace lord regent o'er the French.
Som. I humbly thank your royal majesty.
Hor. And I accept the combat willingly.
Pet. Alas, my lord, I cannot fight; for God's sake, pity my case. The spite of man prevaileth against me. O Lord, have mercy upon me! I shall never be able to fight a blow. O Lord, my heart!
Glou. Sirrah, or you must fight, or else be hang'd.
King. Away with them to prison; and the day of combat shall be the last of the next month. Come, Somerset, we'll see thee sent away. *Flourish. Exeunt.*

[SCENE IV. GLOUCESTER'S *garden*.]

Enter [MARGERY JOURDAIN] *the Witch, the two Priests* [HUME *and* SOUTHWELL], *and* BOLINGBROKE.

Hume. Come, my masters; the duchess, I tell you, expects performance of your promises.
Boling. Master Hume, we are therefore provided: will her ladyship behold and hear our exorcisms?
Hume. Ay, what else? fear you not her courage.
Boling. I have heard her reported to be a woman of an invincible spirit: but it shall be convenient, Master Hume, that you be by her aloft, while we be busy below; and so, I pray you, go, in God's name, and leave us. *(Exit Hume.)* Mother Jourdain, be you prostrate and grovel on the earth; John Southwell, read you; and let us to our work.

Enter [DUCHESS] ELEANOR *aloft* [, HUME *following*].

Duch. Well said, my masters; and welcome all. To this gear the sooner the better.
Boling. Patience, good lady; wizards know their times:
Deep night, dark night, the silent of the night,
The time of night when Troy was set on fire;
The time when screech-owls cry and ban-dogs howl
And spirits walk and ghosts break up their graves,
That time best fits the work we have in hand.
Madam, sit you and fear not: whom we raise,
We will make fast within a hallow'd verge.

Here [*they*] *do the ceremonies belonging, and make the circle: Bolingbroke or Southwell reads.* Conjuro te, &c. *It thunders and lightens terribly; then the Spirit riseth.*

Spir. Adsum.
M. Jourd. Asmath,
By the eternal God, whose name and power
Thou tremblest at, answer that I shall ask;
For, till thou speak, thou shalt not pass from hence.
Spir. Ask what thou wilt. That I had said and done!
Boling. 'First of the king: what shall of him become?'
[*Reading out of a paper*.]
Spir. The duke yet lives that Henry shall depose;
But him outlive, and die a violent death.
[*As the Spirit speaks, Southwell writes the answer*.]
Boling. 'What fates await the Duke of Suffolk?'
Spir. By water shall he die, and take his end.
Boling. 'What shall befall the Duke of Somerset?'
Spir. Let him shun castles;
Safer shall he be upon the sandy plains
Than where castles mounted stand.
Have done, for more I hardly can endure.
Boling. Descend to darkness and the burning lake!
False fiend, avoid! *Thunder and lightning. Exit Spirit.*

Enter the DUKE OF YORK *and the* DUKE OF BUCKINGHAM *with their* Guard *and break in*.

York. Lay hands upon these traitors and their trash.
Beldam, I think we watch'd you at an inch.
What, madam, are you there? the king and commonweal
Are deeply indebted for this piece of pains:
My lord protector will, I doubt it not,
See you well guerdon'd for these good deserts.
Duch. Not half so bad as thine to England's king,
Injurious duke, that threatest where 's no cause.
Buck. True, madam, none at all: what call you this?
Away with them! let them be clapp'd up close,
And kept asunder. You, madam, shall with us.
Stafford, take her to thee.
[*Exeunt above Duchess and Hume, guarded*.]
We'll see your trinkets here all forthcoming.
All, away! *Exit* [*guard with Jourdain, Southwell, &c.*].
York. Lord Buckingham, methinks, you watch'd her well:
A pretty plot, well chosen to build upon!
Now, pray, my lord, let 's see the devil's writ.
What have we here? *Reads.*
'The duke yet lives, that Henry shall depose;
But him outlive, and die a violent death.'
Why, this is just
'Aio te, Æacida, Romanos vincere posse.'
Well, to the rest:
'Tell me what fate awaits the Duke of Suffolk?
By water shall he die, and take his end.
What shall betide the Duke of Somerset?
Let him shun castles;
Safer shall he be upon the sandy plains
Than where castles mounted stand.'
Come, come, my lords;
These oracles are hardly attain'd,
And hardly understood.
The king is now in progress towards Saint Alban's,
With him the husband of this lovely lady:
Thither go these news, as fast as horse can carry them:
A sorry breakfast for my lord protector.
Buck. Your grace shall give me leave, my Lord of York,
To be the post, in hope of his reward.
York. At your pleasure, my good lord. Who 's within there, ho!

SCENE IV. 5. **exorcisms,** conjurations, calling up spirits. 6. **fear,** doubt; see glossary. 17. **gear,** business; see glossary. 21. **ban-dogs,** watchdogs. 25. **hallow'd verge,** magic circle. *Stage Direction:* ***the ceremonies belonging,*** i.e., the "hocus-pocus" necessary to conjure spirits, such as drawing a magic circle and reciting a formula. 26. **Adsum,** I am here. 27. **Asmath,** probably "Asmenoth, guider of the North" in Greene's *Friar Bacon* (Hart); cf. *1 Henry VI*, V, iii, 6; or, *Asnath*, anagram for Sathan. 33-34. **The . . . death.** The first line of the prophecy, as is characteristic of such utterances, is capable of a double construction. The second line is fulfilled in *3 Henry VI* in the death of York. 45. **at an inch,** closely. 47. **piece of pains,** example of trouble undergone (used ironically). 56. **trinkets,** trifles, rubbish. 65. **'Aio . . . posse,'** ambiguous answer given by the Delphic oracle to Pyrrhus, quoted from Ennius by Cicero (*De divinatione* II, lvi): "I say that thou, Aeacides, canst conquer the Romans, or that the Romans can conquer thee." 74. **hardly,** with difficulty; see glossary. 76. **progress,** state journey made by a sovereign. 81. **post,** messenger; see glossary.

Enter a Servingman.

Invite my Lords of Salisbury and Warwick
To sup with me to-morrow night. Away! *Exeunt.*

[ACT II.

SCENE I. *Saint Alban's.*]

Enter the KING, QUEEN, PROTECTOR [GLOUCESTER], CARDINAL, *and* SUFFOLK, *with* Falconers *halloing.*

Queen. Believe me, lords, for flying at the brook,
I saw not better sport these seven years' day:
Yet, by your leave, the wind was very high;
And, ten to one, old Joan had not gone out.
King. But what a point, my lord, your falcon made,
And what a pitch she flew above the rest!
To see how God in all his creatures works!
Yea, man and birds are fain of climbing high.
Suf. No marvel, an it like your majesty,
My lord protector's hawks do tow'r so well;
They know their master loves to be aloft
And bears his thoughts above his falcon's pitch.
Glou. My lord, 'tis but a base ignoble mind
That mounts no higher than a bird can soar.
Car. I thought as much; he would be above the clouds.
Glou. Ay, my lord cardinal? how think you by that?
Were it not good your grace could fly to heaven?
King. The treasury of everlasting joy.
Car. Thy heaven is on earth; thine eyes and thoughts
Beat on a crown, the treasure of thy heart;
Pernicious protector, dangerous peer,
That smooth'st it so with king and commonweal!
Glou. What, cardinal, is your priesthood grown peremptory?
Tantæne animis cœlestibus iræ?
Churchmen so hot? good uncle, hide such malice;
With such holiness can you do it?
Suf. No malice, sir; no more than well becomes
So good a quarrel and so bad a peer.
Glou. As who, my lord?
Suf. Why, as you, my lord,
An 't like your lordly lord-protectorship.
Glou. Why, Suffolk, England knows thine insolence.
Queen. And thy ambition, Gloucester.
King. I prithee, peace, good queen,
And whet not on these furious peers;
For blessed are the peacemakers on earth.
Car. Let me be blessed for the peace I make,
Against this proud protector, with my sword!
Glou. [*Aside to Car.*] Faith, holy uncle, would 'twere come to that!
Car. [*Aside to Glou.*] Marry, when thou dar'st.
Glou. [*Aside to Car.*] Make up no factious numbers for the matter;
In thine own person answer thy abuse.
Car. [*Aside to Glou.*] Ay, where thou dar'st not peep: an if thou dar'st,
This evening, on the east side of the grove.
King. How now, my lords!
Car. Believe me, cousin Gloucester,
Had not your man put up the fowl so suddenly,
We had had more sport. [*Aside to Glou.*] Come with thy two-hand sword.
Glou. True, uncle.
Car. [*Aside to Glou.*] Are ye advis'd? the east side of the grove?
Glou. [*Aside to Car.*] Cardinal, I am with you.
King. Why, how now, uncle Gloucester!
Glou. Talking of hawking; nothing else, my lord.
[*Aside to Car.*] Now, by God's mother, priest, I'll shave your crown for this,
Or all my fence shall fail.
Car. [*Aside to Glou.*] Medice, teipsum—
Protector, see to 't well, protect yourself.
King. The winds grow high; so do your stomachs, lords.
How irksome is this music to my heart!
When such strings jar, what hope of harmony?
I pray, my lords, let me compound this strife.

Enter one [*a* Townsman *of Saint Alban's*] *crying* 'A miracle!'

Glou. What means this noise?
Fellow, what miracle dost thou proclaim?
Towns. A miracle! a miracle!
Suf. Come to the king and tell him what miracle.
Towns. Forsooth, a blind man at Saint Alban's shrine,
Within this half-hour, hath receiv'd his sight;
A man that ne'er saw in his life before.
King. Now, God be prais'd, that to believing souls
Gives light in darkness, comfort in despair!

Enter the Mayor *of Saint Alban's and his brethren, bearing the man* [SIMPCOX], *between two in a chair* [, SIMPCOX's Wife *following*].

Car. Here comes the townsmen on procession,
To present your highness with the man.
King. Great is his comfort in this earthly vale,
Although by his sight his sin be multiplied.
Glou. Stand by, my masters: bring him near the king;
His highness' pleasure is to talk with him.
King. Good fellow, tell us here the circumstance,
That we for thee may glorify the Lord.
What, hast thou been long blind and now restor'd?
Simp. Born blind, an 't please your grace.
Wife. Ay, indeed, was he.
Suf. What woman is this?
Wife. His wife, an 't like your worship.
Glou. Hadst thou been his mother, thou couldst have better told.
King. Where wert thou born?
Simp. At Berwick in the north, an 't like your grace.

ACT II. SCENE I. 1. **flying . . . brook,** hawking for waterfowl. 2. **these . . . day,** in seven years' time. 4. **old Joan,** name of a hawk. **had not,** would not have. 5. **point,** advantageous position from which the hawk attacks the bird. 6. **pitch,** height to which a hawk soars before descending on its prey; see glossary. 8. **of,** as regards; cf. the modern expression "desirous of"; see glossary. 9. **an,** if; see glossary. **like,** please; see glossary. 22. **smooth'st,** flatterest, humorest. 24. **Tantæne . . . iræ?** Is there such resentment in the minds of the gods? (Virgil, *Aeneid* I, 13.) 41. **abuse,** offense, insult; see glossary. 47. **Are ye advis'd?** Do you understand? 52. **fence,** defense. 53. **Medice, teipsum,** physician, heal thyself (see Luke 4:23). 55. **stomachs,** tempers; see glossary. 58. **compound,** settle; see glossary. *Stage Direction:* **Enter one** [**a Townsman,** etc. This scene serves dramatically to illustrate Gloucester's perspicacity and his efficiency as an administrator. 63. **Saint Alban's shrine.** St. Alban, the first Christian martyr in Britain, was executed under the edicts of Diocletian in the third century for

King. Poor soul, God's goodness hath been great to thee:
Let never day nor night unhallowed pass,
But still remember what the Lord hath done.
Queen. Tell me, good fellow, cam'st thou here by chance,
Or of devotion, to this holy shrine?
Simp. God knows, of pure devotion; being call'd
A hundred times and oftener, in my sleep,
By good Saint Alban; who said, 'Simon, come,
Come, offer at my shrine, and I will help thee.'
Wife. Most true, forsooth; and many time and oft
Myself have heard a voice to call him so.
Car. What, art thou lame?
Simp. Ay, God Almighty help me!
Suf. How cam'st thou so?
Simp. A fall off of a tree.
Wife. A plum-tree, master.
Glou. How long hast thou been blind?
Simp. O, born so, master.
Glou. What, and wouldst climb a tree?
Simp. But that in all my life, when I was a youth.
Wife. Too true; and bought his climbing very dear.
Glou. Mass, thou lov'dst plums well, that wouldst venture so.
Simp. Alas, good master, my wife desir'd some damsons,
And made me climb, with danger of my life.
Glou. A subtle knave! but yet it shall not serve.
Let me see thine eyes: wink now: now open them:
In my opinion yet thou see'st not well.
Simp. Yes, master, clear as day, I thank God and Saint Alban.
Glou. Say'st thou me so? What colour is this cloak of?
Simp. Red, master; red as blood.
Glou. Why, that 's well said. What colour is my gown of?
Simp. Black, forsooth: coal-black as jet.
King. Why, then, thou know'st what colour jet is of?
Suf. And yet, I think, jet did he never see.
Glou. But cloaks and gowns, before this day, a many.
Wife. Never, before this day, in all his life.
Glou. Tell me, sirrah, what 's my name?
Simp. Alas, master, I know not.
Glou. What 's his name?
Simp. I know not.
Glou. Nor his?
Simp. No, indeed, master.
Glou. What 's thine own name?
Simp. Saunder Simpcox, an if it please you, master.

Glou. Then, Saunder, sit there, the lyingest knave in Christendom. If thou hadst been born blind, thou mightst as well have known all our names as thus to name the several colours we do wear. Sight may distinguish of colours, but suddenly to nominate them all, it is impossible. My lords, Saint Alban here hath done a miracle; and would ye not think his cunning to be great, that could restore this cripple to his legs again?

Simp. O master, that you could!

Glou. My masters of Saint Alban's, have you not beadles in your town, and things called whips?

May. Yes, my lord, if it please your grace.

Glou. Then send for one presently.

May. Sirrah, go fetch the beadle hither straight.
Exit [an Attendant].

Glou. Now fetch me a stool hither by and by. Now, sirrah, if you mean to save yourself from whipping, leap me over this stool and run away.

Simp. Alas, master, I am not able to stand alone:
You go about to torture me in vain.

Enter a Beadle *with whips*.

Glou. Well, sir, we must have you find your legs. Sirrah beadle, whip him till he leap over that same stool.

Bead. I will, my lord. Come on, sirrah; off with your doublet quickly.

Simp. Alas, master, what shall I do? I am not able to stand.

After the Beadle hath hit him once, he leaps over the stool and runs away; and they follow and cry, 'A miracle!'

King. O God, seest Thou this, and bearest so long?
Queen. It made me laugh to see the villain run.
Glou. Follow the knave; and take this drab away.
Wife. Alas, sir, we did it for pure need.

Glou. Let them be whipped through every market-town, till they come to Berwick, from whence they came. *Exit [Wife, with Beadle, Mayor, & c.]*.

Car. Duke Humphrey has done a miracle to-day.
Suf. True; made the lame to leap and fly away.
Glou. But you have done more miracles than I;
You made in a day, my lord, whole towns to fly.

Enter BUCKINGHAM.

King. What tidings with our cousin Buckingham?
Buck. Such as my heart doth tremble to unfold.
A sort of naughty persons, lewdly bent,
Under the countenance and confederacy
Of Lady Eleanor, the protector's wife,
The ringleader and head of all this rout,
Have practis'd dangerously against your state,
Dealing with witches and with conjurers:
Whom we have apprehended in the fact;
Raising up wicked spirits from under ground,
Demanding of King Henry's life and death,
And other of your highness' privy-council;
As more at large your grace shall understand.
Car. [*Aside to Glou.*] And so, my lord protector, by this means
Your lady is forthcoming yet at London.
This news, I think, hath turn'd your weapon's edge;
'Tis like, my lord, you will not keep your hour.
Glou. Ambitious churchman, leave to afflict my heart:
Sorrow and grief have vanquish'd all my powers;
And, vanquish'd as I am, I yield to thee,
Or to the meanest groom.
King. O God, what mischiefs work the wicked ones,

sheltering a Christian priest. He was put to death on a hill overlooking the ancient city of Verulam, the ruins of which are across the river Ver from the modern city of St. Albans. 68. **comes.** The present tense, third person plural verb in *s* is not uncommon in Shakespeare; see Abbott, 333. 71. **his sin be multiplied,** i.e., he may now be guilty of the sins of seeing; a probable allusion to this category of sins in the confessional rubric (see John 9:41). 91. **Simon,** a variant of Simpcox. 101. **Mass,** by the Mass (oath). 105. **wink,** close the eyes; see glossary.

130. **nominate,** call by name. 137. **beadles,** inferior parish officers who might punish petty offenses. 140. **straight,** immediately; see glossary. 142. **by and by,** at once, presently. 144. **me,** the ethical dative. 166. **unfold,** disclose; see glossary. 167. **sort,** lot. **naughty,** wicked; see glossary. 175. **Demanding,** inquiring about. 179. **forthcoming,** ready to appear (in court). 182. **leave to afflict,** cease afflicting. 185. **meanest,** of lowest degree; see glossary.

Heaping confusion on their own heads thereby!
Queen. Gloucester, see here the tainture of thy nest,
And look thyself be faultless, thou wert best.
Glou. Madam, for myself, to heaven I do appeal,
How I have lov'd my king and commonweal:
And, for my wife, I know not how it stands;
Sorry I am to hear what I have heard:
Noble she is, but if she have forgot
Honour and virtue and convers'd with such
As, like to pitch, defile nobility,
I banish her my bed and company
And give her as a prey to law and shame,
That hath dishonoured Gloucester's honest name.
King. Well, for this night we will repose us here:
To-morrow toward London back again,
To look into this business thoroughly
And call these foul offenders to their answers
And poise the cause in justice' equal scales,
Whose beam stands sure, whose rightful cause prevails. *Flourish. Exeunt.*

[SCENE II. *London. The* DUKE OF YORK'S *garden.*]

Enter YORK, SALISBURY, *and* WARWICK.

York. Now, my good Lords of Salisbury and Warwick,
Our simple supper ended, give me leave
In this close walk to satisfy myself,
In craving your opinion of my title,
Which is infallible, to England's crown.
Sal. My lord, I long to hear it at full.
War. Sweet York, begin: and if thy claim be good,
The Nevils are thy subjects to command.
York. Then thus:
Edward the Third, my lords, had seven sons:
The first, Edward the Black Prince, Prince of Wales;
The second, William of Hatfield, and the third,
Lionel Duke of Clarence; next to whom
Was John of Gaunt, the Duke of Lancaster;
The fifth was Edmund Langley, Duke of York;
The sixth was Thomas of Woodstock, Duke of Gloucester;
William of Windsor was the seventh and last.
Edward the Black Prince died before his father
And left behind him Richard, his only son,
Who after Edward the Third's death reign'd as king;
Till Henry Bolingbroke, Duke of Lancaster,
The eldest son and heir of John of Gaunt,
Crown'd by the name of Henry the Fourth,
Seiz'd on the realm, depos'd the rightful king,
Sent his poor queen to France, from whence she came,
And him to Pomfret; where, as all you know,
Harmless Richard was murdered traitorously.
War. Father, the duke hath told the truth;
Thus got the house of Lancaster the crown.
York. Which now they hold by force and not by right;
For Richard, the first son's heir, being dead,
The issue of the next son should have reign'd.
Sal. But William of Hatfield died without an heir.
York. The third son, Duke of Clarence, from whose line
I claim the crown, had issue, Philippe, a daughter,
Who married Edmund Mortimer, Earl of March:
Edmund had issue, Roger Earl of March;
Roger had issue, Edmund, Anne and Eleanor.
Sal. This Edmund, in the reign of Bolingbroke,
As I have read, laid claim unto the crown;
And, but for Owen Glendower, had been king,
Who kept him in captivity till he died.
But to the rest.
York. His eldest sister, Anne,
My mother, being heir unto the crown,
Married Richard Earl of Cambridge; who was son
To Edmund Langley, Edward the Third's fifth son.
By her I claim the kingdom: she was heir
To Roger Earl of March, who was the son
Of Edmund Mortimer, who married Philippe,
Sole daughter unto Lionel Duke of Clarence:
So, if the issue of the elder son
Succeed before the younger, I am king.
War. What plain proceeding is more plain than this?
Henry doth claim the crown from John of Gaunt,
The fourth son; York claims it from the third.
Till Lionel's issue fails, his should not reign:
It fails not yet, but flourishes in thee
And in thy sons, fair slips of such a stock.
Then, father Salisbury, kneel we together;
And in this private plot be we the first
That shall salute our rightful sovereign
With honour of his birthright to the crown.
Both. Long live our sovereign Richard, England's king!
York. We thank you, lords. But I am not your king
Till I be crown'd and that my sword be stain'd
With heart-blood of the house of Lancaster;
And that 's not suddenly to be perform'd,
But with advice and silent secrecy.
Do you as I do in these dangerous days:
Wink at the Duke of Suffolk's insolence,
At Beaufort's pride, at Somerset's ambition,
At Buckingham and all the crew of them,
Till they have snar'd the shepherd of the flock,
That virtuous prince, the good Duke Humphrey:
'Tis that they seek, and they in seeking that
Shall find their deaths, if York can prophesy.
Sal. My lord, break we off; we know your mind at full.
War. My heart assures me that the Earl of Warwick
Shall one day make the Duke of York a king.
York. And, Nevil, this I do assure myself:
Richard shall live to make the Earl of Warwick
The greatest man in England but the king. *Exeunt.*

[SCENE III. *A hall of justice.*]

Sound trumpets. Enter the KING *and State* [*the* QUEEN,

187. **confusion,** destruction; see glossary. 188. **tainture,** defilement. 189. **look,** take care; see glossary. 195. **convers'd,** had to do with; see glossary.

SCENE II. 42. **till he died.** This historical error is repeated from the chronicles; cf. *1 Henry VI,* II, v, 1. 56. **fails,** dies out; see glossary. 62. **birthright,** right by primogeniture.

SCENE III. 4. **by God's book,** a reference to the commandments in the Bible against witches (Exodus 22:18) and enchantments (Leviticus 19:26). 13. **With . . . Stanley,** an error for Sir Thomas Stanley, the Duchess' custodian (and the Lord Stanley of *Richard III*). 21. **would,** would have; *would* here has the force of Old English "willan," to wish. 23. **staff.** Cf. I, ii, 25, where Gloucester calls his staff *mine office-badge in*

Gloucester, York, Suffolk, Salisbury, *and others*], *with Guard, to banish the* Duchess [of Gloucester, *who is brought on under guard with* Southwell, Hume, *and* Bolingbroke].

King. Stand forth, Dame Eleanor Cobham, Gloucester's wife:
In sight of God and us, your guilt is great:
Receive the sentence of the law for sins
Such as by God's book are adjudg'd to death.
You four, from hence to prison back again;
From thence unto the place of execution:
The witch in Smithfield shall be burn'd to ashes,
And you three shall be strangled on the gallows.
You, madam, for you are more nobly born,
Despoiled of your honour in your life,
Shall, after three days' open penance done,
Live in your country here in banishment,
With Sir John Stanley, in the Isle of Man.

Duch. Welcome is banishment; welcome were my death.

Glou. Eleanor, the law, thou see'st, hath judged thee:
I cannot justify whom the law condemns.
[*Exeunt Duchess and other prisoners, guarded.*]
Mine eyes are full of tears, my heart of grief.
Ah, Humphrey, this dishonour in thine age
Will bring thy head with sorrow to the ground!
I beseech your majesty, give me leave to go;
Sorrow would solace and mine age would ease.

King. Stay, Humphrey Duke of Gloucester: ere thou go,
Give up thy staff: Henry will to himself
Protector be; and God shall be my hope,
My stay, my guide and lantern to my feet:
And go in peace, Humphrey, no less belov'd
Than when thou wert protector to thy king.

Queen. I see no reason why a king of years
Should be to be protected like a child.
God and King Henry govern England's realm.
Give up your staff, sir, and the king his realm.

Glou. My staff? here, noble Henry, is my staff:
As willingly do I the same resign
As e'er thy father Henry made it mine;
And even as willingly at thy feet I leave it
As others would ambitiously receive it.
Farewell, good king: when I am dead and gone,
May honourable peace attend thy throne! *Exit Glou.*

Queen. Why, now is Henry king, and Margaret queen;
And Humphrey Duke of Gloucester scarce himself,
That bears so shrewd a maim; two pulls at once;
His lady banish'd, and a limb lopp'd off.
This staff of honour raught, there let it stand
Where it best fits to be, in Henry's hand.

Suf. Thus droops this lofty pine and hangs his sprays;
Thus Eleanor's pride dies in her youngest days.

York. Lords, let him go. Please it your majesty,
This is the day appointed for the combat;
And ready are the appellant and defendant,
The armourer and his man, to enter the lists,
So please your highness to behold the fight.

Queen. Ay, good my lord; for purposely therefore
Left I the court, to see this quarrel tried.

King. A God's name, see the lists and all things fit:
Here let them end it; and God defend the right!

York. I never saw a fellow worse bested,
Or more afraid to fight, than is the appellant,
The servant of this armourer, my lords.

Enter at one door, the Armourer [Horner] *and his* Neighbours, *drinking to him so much that he is drunk; and he enters with a drum before him and his staff with a sand-bag fastened to it; and at the other door his man* [Peter], *with a drum and sand-bag, and* 'Prentices *drinking to him.*

First Neigh. Here, neighbour Horner, I drink to you in a cup of sack: and fear not, neighbour, you shall do well enough.

Sec. Neigh. And here, neighbour, here 's a cup of charneco.

Third Neigh. And here 's a pot of good double beer, neighbour: drink, and fear not your man.

Hor. Let it come, i' faith, and I'll pledge you all; and a fig for Peter!

First 'Pren. Here, Peter, I drink to thee: and be not afraid.

Sec. 'Pren. Be merry, Peter, and fear not thy master: fight for credit of the 'prentices.

Peter. I thank you all: drink, and pray for me, I pray you; for I think I have taken my last draught in this world. Here, Robin, an if I die, I give thee my apron: and, Will, thou shalt have my hammer: and here, Tom, take all the money that I have. O Lord bless me! I pray God! for I am never able to deal with my master, he hath learnt so much fence already.

Sal. Come, leave your drinking, and fall to blows. Sirrah, what 's thy name?

Peter. Peter, forsooth.

Sal. Peter! what more?

Peter. Thump.

Sal. Thump! then see thou thump thy master well.

Hor. Masters, I am come hither, as it were, upon my man's instigation, to prove him a knave and myself an honest man: and touching the Duke of York, I will take my death, I never meant him any ill, nor the king, nor the queen: and therefore, Peter, have at thee with a downright blow!

York. Dispatch: this knave's tongue begins to double.
Sound, trumpets, alarum to the combatants!
[*Alarum.*] *They fight, and Peter strikes him down.*

Hor. Hold, Peter, hold! I confess, I confess treason. [*Dies.*]

York. Take away his weapon. Fellow, thank God, and the good wine in thy master's way.

Peter. O God, have I overcome mine enemy in this presence? O Peter, thou hast prevailed in right!

King. Go, take hence that traitor from our sight;
For by his death we do perceive his guilt:
And God in justice hath reveal'd to us
The truth and innocence of this poor fellow,
Which he had thought to have murder'd wrongfully.

court. 41. **shrewd,** grievous, severe; see glossary. **maim,** mutilation. **pulls,** pluckings (of feathers); i.e., has suffered two mutilations. 43. **raught,** attained, seized. 45. **lofty pine,** an emblem adopted by Henry IV, Gloucester's father. 46. **her youngest days.** *Her* may refer to Eleanor's ambition or pride (Hart); or it may refer to Eleanor, *youngest* meaning "last." 49. **appellant,** challenger. 56. **bested,** i.e., bestead, situated. 60. **sack,** generic term for Spanish and Canary wines; see glossary. 63. **charneco,** a kind of wine. 79. **fence,** skill in fencing. 90. **take my death,** i.e., take an oath on my death. 92. **have at,** let me at; see glossary. 94. **double,** thicken, as an intoxicated person's.

Come, fellow, follow us for thy reward.
Sound a flourish. *Exeunt.*

[SCENE IV. *A street.*]

Enter DUKE HUMPHREY [OF GLOUCESTER] *and his Men in mourning cloaks.*

Glou. Thus sometimes hath the brightest day a cloud;
And after summer evermore succeeds
Barren winter, with his wrathful nipping cold:
So cares and joys abound, as seasons fleet.
Sirs, what 's o'clock?
Serv. Ten, my lord.
Glou. Ten is the hour that was appointed me
To watch the coming of my punish'd duchess:
Uneath may she endure the flinty streets,
To tread them with her tender-feeling feet.
Sweet Nell, ill can thy noble mind abrook
The abject people gazing on thy face,
With envious looks, laughing at thy shame,
That erst did follow thy proud chariot-wheels
When thou didst ride in triumph through the streets.
But, soft! I think she comes; and I'll prepare
My tear-stain'd eyes to see her miseries.

Enter the DUCHESS [OF GLOUCESTER] *in a white sheet, and a taper burning in her hand; with the* Sheriff *and* Officers [*and* SIR JOHN STANLEY].

Serv. So please your grace, we'll take her from the sheriff.
Glou. No, stir not, for your lives; let her pass by.
Duch. Come you, my lord, to see my open shame?
Now thou dost penance too. Look how they gaze!
See how the giddy multitude do point,
And nod their heads, and throw their eyes on thee!
Ah, Gloucester, hide thee from their hateful looks,
And, in thy closet pent up, rue my shame,
And ban thine enemies, both mine and thine!
Glou. Be patient, gentle Nell; forget this grief.
Duch. Ah, Gloucester, teach me to forget myself!
For whilst I think I am thy married wife
And thou a prince, protector of this land,
Methinks I should not thus be led along,
Mail'd up in shame, with papers on my back,
And follow'd with a rabble that rejoice
To see my tears and hear my deep-fet groans.
The ruthless flint doth cut my tender feet,
And when I start, the envious people laugh
And bid me be advised how I tread.
Ah, Humphrey, can I bear this shameful yoke?
Trowest thou that e'er I'll look upon the world,
Or count them happy that enjoy the sun?
No; dark shall be my light and night my day;
To think upon my pomp shall be my hell.
Sometime I'll say, I am Duke Humphrey's wife,
And he a prince and ruler of the land:
Yet so he rul'd and such a prince he was
As he stood by whilst I, his forlorn duchess,
Was made a wonder and a pointing-stock
To every idle rascal follower.
But be thou mild and blush not at my shame,
Nor stir at nothing till the axe of death
Hang over thee, as, sure, it shortly will;
For Suffolk, he that can do all in all
With her that hateth thee and hates us all,
And York and impious Beaufort, that false priest,
Have all lim'd bushes to betray thy wings,
And, fly thou how thou canst, they'll tangle thee:
But fear not thou, until thy foot be snar'd,
Nor never seek prevention of thy foes.
Glou. Ah, Nell, forbear! thou aimest all awry;
I must offend before I be attainted;
And had I twenty times so many foes,
And each of them had twenty times their power,
All these could not procure me any scathe,
So long as I am loyal, true and crimeless.
Wouldst have me rescue thee from this reproach?
Why, yet thy scandal were not wip'd away,
But I in danger for the breach of law.
Thy greatest help is quiet, gentle Nell:
I pray thee, sort thy heart to patience;
These few days' wonder will be quickly worn.

Enter a Herald.

Her. I summon your grace to his majesty's parliament,
Holden at Bury the first of this next month.
Glou. And my consent ne'er ask'd herein before!
This is close dealing. Well, I will be there. [*Exit Herald.*]
My Nell, I take my leave: and, master sheriff,
Let not her penance exceed the king's commission.
Sher. An 't please your grace, here my commission stays,
And Sir John Stanley is appointed now
To take her with him to the Isle of Man.
Glou. Must you, Sir John, protect my lady here?
Stan. So am I given in charge, may 't please your grace.
Glou. Entreat her not the worse in that I pray
You use her well: the world may laugh again;
And I may live to do you kindness if
You do it her: and so, Sir John, farewell!
Duch. What, gone, my lord, and bid me not farewell!
Glou. Witness my tears, I cannot stay to speak.
Exit Gloucester [*with his Men*].
Duch. Art thou gone too? all comfort go with thee!
For none abides with me: my joy is death;
Death, at whose name I oft have been afear'd,
Because I wish'd this world's eternity.
Stanley, I prithee, go, and take me hence;
I care not whither, for I beg no favour,
Only convey me where thou art commanded.
Stan. Why, madam, that is to the Isle of Man;
There to be us'd according to your state.
Duch. That 's bad enough, for I am but reproach:
And shall I then be us'd reproachfully?
Stan. Like to a duchess, and Duke Humphrey's lady;
According to that state you shall be us'd.

SCENE IV. 8. **Uneath,** with difficulty. 10. **abrook,** endure. 11. **abject,** lowly born. 12. **envious,** full of malice; see glossary. 13. **erst,** formerly. 24. **closet,** private room. 25. **ban,** curse. 31. **Mail'd up,** enveloped (a hawking term). She refers to the white sheet, the garment she was required to wear while doing public penance. **papers on my back,** i.e., a schedule pinned to her back containing a description of the sin for which she is doing the penance. 33. **deep-fet,** fetched from the depths. 35. **start,** startle, wince. 38. **Trow'st,** believest; see glossary. 57. **prevention,** forestalling. 62. **scathe,** injury. 68. **sort,** adapt. 69. **wonder,** surprise, astonishment. 73. **close,** secret; see glossary. 76. **stays,** stops; see glossary. 96. **I . . . reproach,** I am the embodiment of reproach or disgrace. 100. **better than I fare,** may you fare better than I. 101. **conduct,** conductor.

ACT III. SCENE I. 1. **muse,** wonder; see glossary. 2. **wont,** custom,

Duch. Sheriff, farewell, and better than I fare,
Although thou hast been conduct of my shame.
Sher. It is my office; and, madam, pardon me.
Duch. Ay, ay, farewell; thy office is discharg'd.
Come, Stanley, shall we go?
Stan. Madam, your penance done, throw off this sheet,
And go we to attire you for our journey.
Duch. My shame will not be shifted with my sheet:
No, it will hang upon my richest robes
And show itself, attire me how I can.
Go, lead the way; I long to see my prison. *Exeunt.*

[ACT III.

SCENE I. *The Abbey at Bury St. Edmund's.*]

Sound a sennet. Enter KING, QUEEN, CARDINAL [BEAUFORT], SUFFOLK, YORK, BUCKINGHAM, SALISBURY *and* WARWICK *to the Parliament.*

King. I muse my Lord of Gloucester is not come:
'Tis not his wont to be the hindmost man,
Whate'er occasion keeps him from us now.
Queen. Can you not see? or will ye not observe
The strangeness of his alter'd countenance?
With what a majesty he bears himself,
How insolent of late he is become,
How proud, how peremptory, and unlike himself?
We know the time since he was mild and affable,
And if we did but glance a far-off look,
Immediately he was upon his knee,
That all the court admir'd him for submission:
But meet him now, and, be it in the morn,
When every one will give the time of day,
He knits his brow and shows an angry eye
And passeth by with stiff unbowed knee,
Disdaining duty that to us belongs.
Small curs are not regarded when they grin;
But great men tremble when the lion roars;
And Humphrey is no little man in England.
First note that he is near you in descent,
And should you fall, he is the next will mount.
Me seemeth then it is no policy,
Respecting what a rancorous mind he bears
And his advantage following your decease,
That he should come about your royal person
Or be admitted to your highness' council.
By flattery hath he won the commons' hearts,
And when he please to make commotion,
'Tis to be fear'd they all will follow him.
Now 'tis the spring, and weeds are shallow-rooted;
Suffer them now, and they'll o'ergrow the garden
And choke the herbs for want of husbandry.
The reverent care I bear unto my lord
Made me collect these dangers in the duke.
If it be fond, call it a woman's fear;
Which fear if better reasons can supplant,
I will subscribe and say I wrong'd the duke.
My Lord of Suffolk, Buckingham, and York,
Reprove my allegation, if you can;
Or else conclude my words effectual.
Suf. Well hath your highness seen into this duke;
And, had I first been put to speak my mind,
I think I should have told your grace's tale.
The duchess by his subornation,
Upon my life, began her devilish practices:
Or, if he were not privy to those faults,
Yet, by reputing of his high descent,
As next the king he was successive heir,
And such high vaunts of his nobility,
Did instigate the bedlam brain-sick duchess
By wicked means to frame our sovereign's fall.
Smooth runs the water where the brook is deep;
And in his simple show he harbours treason.
The fox barks not when he would steal the lamb.
No, no, my sovereign; Gloucester is a man
Unsounded yet and full of deep deceit.
Car. Did he not, contrary to form of law,
Devise strange deaths for small offences done?
York. And did he not, in his protectorship,
Levy great sums of money through the realm
For soldiers' pay in France, and never sent it?
By means whereof the towns each day revolted.
Buck. Tut, these are petty faults to faults unknown,
Which time will bring to light in smooth Duke Humphrey.
King. My lords, at once: the care you have of us,
To mow down thorns that would annoy our foot,
Is worthy praise: but, shall I speak my conscience,
Our kinsman Gloucester is as innocent
From meaning treason to our royal person
As is the sucking lamb or harmless dove:
The duke is virtuous, mild and too well given
To dream on evil or to work my downfall.
Queen. Ah, what 's more dangerous than this fond affiance!
Seems he a dove? his feathers are but borrow'd,
For he 's disposed as the hateful raven:
Is he a lamb? his skin is surely lent him,
For he 's inclin'd as is the ravenous wolves.
Who cannot steal a shape that means deceit?
Take heed, my lord; the welfare of us all
Hangs on the cutting short that fraudful man.

Enter SOMERSET.

Som. All health unto my gracious sovereign!
King. Welcome, Lord Somerset. What news from France?
Som. That all your interest in those territories
Is utterly bereft you; all is lost.
King. Cold news, Lord Somerset: but God's will be done!
York. [*Aside*] Cold news for me; for I had hope of France
As firmly as I hope for fertile England.
Thus are my blossoms blasted in the bud
And caterpillars eat my leaves away;
But I will remedy this gear ere long,
Or sell my title for a glorious grave.

Enter GLOUCESTER.

habit. 9. **since,** when. 12. **admir'd,** wondered at; see glossary. 18. **grin,** bare their teeth. 23. **Me seemeth,** it seems to me. 24. **Respecting,** considering; see glossary. 28. **By . . . hearts.** Holinshed records that Gloucester was "verie louing to the poore commons, and so beloued of them again." The queen's words here underline Suffolk's contempt for the Commons, expressed at several points in the play. 33. **husbandry,** care of the soil. 35. **collect,** gather, infer. 36. **fond,** foolish; see glossary. 40. **Reprove,** correct, prove, (me) wrong. 46. **practices,** intrigues; see glossary. 59. **Devise . . . done.** Cf. I, iii, 135-136, note. 66. **at once,** all of you, or, without more ado (Tucker Brooke); possibly, once for all. 74. **affiance,** trust. 79. **steal . . . deceit,** deceitfully assume an attitude. 83. **news from France.** Somerset presumably is just returned from exercising his office as regent of France, to which he was appointed in I, iii.

Glou. All happiness unto my lord the king!
Pardon, my liege, that I have stay'd so long.
Suf. Nay, Gloucester, know that thou art come too soon,
Unless thou wert more loyal than thou art:
I do arrest thee of high treason here.
Glou. Well, Suffolk, thou shalt not see me blush
Nor change my countenance for this arrest:
A heart unspotted is not easily daunted.
The purest spring is not so free from mud
As I am clear from treason to my sovereign:
Who can accuse me? wherein am I guilty?
York. 'Tis thought, my lord, that you took bribes of France,
And, being protector, stay'd the soldiers' pay;
By means whereof his highness hath lost France.
Glou. Is it but thought so? what are they that think it?
I never robb'd the soldiers of their pay,
Nor ever had one penny bribe from France.
So help me God, as I have watch'd the night,
Ay, night by night, in studying good for England,
That doit that e'er I wrested from the king,
Or any groat I hoarded to my use,
Be brought against me at my trial-day!
No; many a pound of mine own proper store,
Because I would not tax the needy commons,
Have I dispursed to the garrisons,
And never ask'd for restitution.
Car. It serves you well, my lord, to say so much.
Glou. I say no more than truth, so help me God!
York. In your protectorship you did devise
Strange tortures for offenders never heard of,
That England was defam'd by tyranny.
Glou. Why, 'tis well known that, whiles I was protector,
Pity was all the fault that was in me;
For I should melt at an offender's tears,
And lowly words were ransom for their fault.
Unless it were a bloody murderer,
Or foul felonious thief that fleec'd poor passengers,
I never gave them condign punishment:
Murder indeed, that bloody sin, I tortur'd
Above the felon or what trespass else.
Suf. My lord, these faults are easy, quickly answer'd:
But mightier crimes are laid unto your charge,
Whereof you cannot easily purge yourself.
I do arrest you in his highness' name;
And here commit you to my lord cardinal
To keep, until your further time of trial.
King. My Lord of Gloucester, 'tis my special hope
That you will clear yourself from all suspect:
My conscience tells me you are innocent.
Glou. Ah, gracious lord, these days are dangerous:
Virtue is chok'd with foul ambition
And charity chas'd hence by rancour's hand;
Foul subornation is predominant
And equity exil'd your highness' land.
I know their complot is to have my life,
And if my death might make this island happy
And prove the period of their tyranny,
I would expend it with all willingness:
But mine is made the prologue to their play;
For thousands more, that yet suspect no peril,
Will not conclude their plotted tragedy.
Beaufort's red sparkling eyes blab his heart's malice,
And Suffolk's cloudy brow his stormy hate;
Sharp Buckingham unburthens with his tongue
The envious load that lies upon his heart;
And dogged York, that reaches at the moon,
Whose overweening arm I have pluck'd back,
By false accuse doth level at my life:
And you, my sovereign lady, with the rest,
Causeless have laid disgraces on my head
And with your best endeavour have stirr'd up
My liefest liege to be mine enemy:
Ay, all of you have laid your heads together—
Myself had notice of your conventicles—
And all to make away my guiltless life.
I shall not want false witness to condemn me,
Nor store of treasons to augment my guilt;
The ancient proverb will be well effected:
'A staff is quickly found to beat a dog.'
Car. My liege, his railing is intolerable:
If those that care to keep your royal person
From treason's secret knife and traitors' rage
Be thus upbraided, chid and rated at,
And the offender granted scope of speech,
'Twill make them cool in zeal unto your grace.
Suf. Hath he not twit our sovereign lady here
With ignominious words, though clerkly couch'd,
As if she had suborned some to swear
False allegations to o'erthrow his state?
Queen. But I can give the loser leave to chide.
Glou. Far truer spoke than meant: I lose, indeed;
Beshrew the winners, for they play'd me false!
And well such losers may have leave to speak.
Buck. He'll wrest the sense and hold us here all day:
Lord cardinal, he is your prisoner.
Car. Sirs, take away the duke, and guard him sure.
Glou. Ah! thus King Henry throws away his crutch
Before his legs be firm to bear his body.
Thus is the shepherd beaten from thy side
And wolves are gnarling who shall gnaw thee first.
Ah, that my fear were false! ah, that it were!
For, good King Henry, thy decay I fear.
Exit Gloucester [*guarded*].
King. My lords, what to your wisdoms seemeth best,
Do or undo, as if ourself were here.
Queen. What, will your highness leave the parliament?
King. Ay, Margaret; my heart is drown'd with grief,
Whose flood begins to flow within mine eyes,
My body round engirt with misery,
For what 's more miserable than discontent?
Ah, uncle Humphrey! in thy face I see
The map of honour, truth and loyalty:
And yet, good Humphrey, is the hour to come
That e'er I prov'd thee false or fear'd thy faith.
What louring star now envies thy estate,
That these great lords and Margaret our queen
Do seek subversion of thy harmless life?
Thou never didst them wrong nor no man wrong;

112. **doit,** small Dutch coin, one-half an English farthing; see glossary. 113. **groat,** coin equal to four pence; see glossary. 130. **condign,** worthily deserved. 132. **Above . . . else,** beyond any other kind of felony or misdemeanor (Tucker Brooke). 145. **predominant,** in the ascendant, ruling; an astronomical metaphor. 146. **exil'd,** exiled from. 147. **complot,** plot, conspiracy. 160. **accuse,** accusation. **level,** aim; see glossary. 164. **liefest,** dearest. 166. **notice,** pronounced as one syllable, like "notes." **conventicles,** private or secret meetings. 168. **want,** lack; see glossary. 175. **rated,** scolded; see glossary. 176. **scope,** freedom; see glossary. 179. **clerkly,** learnedly. 184. **Beshrew,** curse; see glossary. 194. **decay,** downfall; see glossary. 206. **louring,** frowning, looking sullen or ominous. 229. **slough,** skin. 236. **colour,**

And as the butcher takes away the calf
And binds the wretch and beats it when it strays,
Bearing it to the bloody slaughter-house,
Even so remorseless have they borne him hence;
And as the dam runs lowing up and down,
Looking the way her harmless young one went,
And can do nought but wail her darling's loss,
Even so myself bewails good Gloucester's case
With sad unhelpful tears, and with dimm'd eyes
Look after him and cannot do him good,
So mighty are his vowed enemies.
His fortunes I will weep and 'twixt each groan
Say 'Who 's a traitor? Gloucester he is none.'

Exeunt [all but Queen, Cardinal Beaufort, Suffolk, and York; Somerset remains apart].

Queen. Free lords, cold snow melts with the sun's hot beams.
Henry my lord is cold in great affairs,
Too full of foolish pity, and Gloucester's show
Beguiles him as the mournful crocodile
With sorrow snares relenting passengers,
Or as the snake roll'd in a flow'ring bank,
With shining checker'd slough, doth sting a child
That for the beauty thinks it excellent.
Believe me, lords, were none more wise than I—
And yet herein I judge mine own wit good—
This Gloucester should be quickly rid the world,
To rid us from the fear we have of him.

Car. That he should die is worthy policy;
But yet we want a colour for his death:
'Tis meet he be condemn'd by course of law.

Suf. But, in my mind, that were no policy:
The king will labour still to save his life,
The commons haply rise, to save his life;
And yet we have but trivial argument,
More than mistrust, that shows him worthy death.

York. So that, by this, you would not have him die.

Suf. Ah, York, no man alive so fain as I!

York. 'Tis York that hath more reason for his death.
But, my lord cardinal, and you, my Lord of Suffolk,
Say as you think, and speak it from your souls,
Were 't not all one, an empty eagle were set
To guard the chicken from a hungry kite,
As place Duke Humphrey for the king's protector?

Queen. So the poor chicken should be sure of death.

Suf. Madam, 'tis true; and were 't not madness, then,
To make the fox surveyor of the fold?
Who being accus'd a crafty murderer,
His guilt should be but idly posted over,
Because his purpose is not executed.
No; let him die, in that he is a fox,
By nature prov'd an enemy to the flock,
Before his chaps be stain'd with crimson blood,
As Humphrey, prov'd by reasons, to my liege.
And do not stand on quillets how to slay him:
Be it by gins, by snares, by subtlety,
Sleeping or waking, 'tis no matter how,
So he be dead; for that is good deceit
Which mates him first that first intends deceit.

Queen. Thrice-noble Suffolk, 'tis resolutely spoke.

Suf. Not resolute, except so much were done;
For things are often spoke and seldom meant:
But that my heart accordeth with my tongue,
Seeing the deed is meritorious,
And to preserve my sovereign from his foe,
Say but the word, and I will be his priest.

Car. But I would have him dead, my Lord of Suffolk,
Ere you can take due orders for a priest:
Say you consent and censure well the deed,
And I'll provide his executioner,
I tender so the safety of my liege.

Suf. Here is my hand, the deed is worthy doing.

Queen. And so say I.

York. And I: and now we three have spoke it,
It skills not greatly who impugns our doom.

Enter a Post.

Post. Great lords, from Ireland am I come amain,
To signify that rebels there are up
And put the Englishmen unto the sword:
Send succours, lords, and stop the rage betime,
Before the wound do grow uncurable;
For, being green, there is great hope of help.

Car. A breach that craves a quick expedient stop!
What counsel give you in this weighty cause?

York. That Somerset be sent as regent thither:
'Tis meet that lucky ruler be employ'd;
Witness the fortune he hath had in France.

Som. If York, with all his far-fet policy,
Had been the regent there instead of me,
He never would have stay'd in France so long.

York. No, not to lose it all, as thou hast done:
I rather would have lost my life betimes
Than bring a burthen of dishonour home
By staying there so long till all were lost.
Show me one scar character'd on thy skin:
Men's flesh preserv'd so whole do seldom win.

Queen. Nay, then, this spark will prove a raging fire,
If wind and fuel be brought to feed it with:
No more, good York; sweet Somerset, be still:
Thy fortune, York, hadst thou been regent there,
Might happily have prov'd far worse than his.

York. What, worse than nought? nay, then, a shame take all!

Som. And, in the number, thee that wishest shame!

Car. My Lord of York, try what your fortune is.
Th' uncivil kerns of Ireland are in arms
And temper clay with blood of Englishmen:
To Ireland will you lead a band of men,
Collected choicely, from each county some,
And try your hap against the Irishmen?

York. I will, my lord, so please his majesty.

Suf. Why, our authority is his consent,
And what we do establish he confirms:
Then, noble York, take thou this task in hand.

York. I am content: provide me soldiers, lords,
Whiles I take order for mine own affairs.

Suf. A charge, Lord York, that I will see perform'd.
But now return we to the false Duke Humphrey.

Car. No more of him; for I will deal with him

pretext; see glossary. 244. **fain,** glad, pleased. 248. **empty,** hungry. 249. **kite,** bird of prey, hawk. 255. **posted over,** ignored, hastened over. 258. **prov'd,** shown by experience to be; see glossary. 261. **quillets,** subtle distinctions; see glossary. 262. **gins,** traps, devices for catching game. 265. **mates,** stupefies, confounds. 272. **be his priest,** i.e., perform the last rites for him. 275. **censure well,** pass a favorable judgment on; see *censure* in glossary. 277. **tender,** am concerned for, care for. 281. **skills not,** makes no (great) difference. **doom,** decision. 282. **amain,** with full speed. 285. **betime,** early. 293. **far-fet,** far-fetched. 300. **character'd,** written; see glossary. 306. **happily,** perhaps; see glossary. 310. **uncivil,** disorderly. **kerns,** light-armed Irish soldiers. 311. **temper clay,** moisten the soil.

That henceforth he shall trouble us no more.
And so break off; the day is almost spent:
Lord Suffolk, you and I must talk of that event.
York. My Lord of Suffolk, within fourteen days
At Bristow I expect my soldiers;
For there I'll ship them all for Ireland.
Suf. I'll see it truly done, my Lord of York.
Exeunt. Manet York.
York. Now, York, or never, steel thy fearful thoughts,
And change misdoubt to resolution:
Be that thou hop'st to be, or what thou art
Resign to death; it is not worth th' enjoying:
Let pale-fac'd fear keep with the mean-born man,
And find no harbour in a royal heart.
Faster than spring-time show'rs comes thought on thought,
And not a thought but thinks on dignity.
My brain more busy than the labouring spider
Weaves tedious snares to trap mine enemies.
Well, nobles, well, 'tis politicly done,
To send me packing with an host of men:
I fear me you but warm the starved snake,
Who, cherish'd in your breasts, will sting your hearts.
'Twas men I lack'd and you will give them me:
I take it kindly; yet be well assur'd
You put sharp weapons in a madman's hands.
Whiles I in Ireland nourish a mighty band,
I will stir up in England some black storm
Shall blow ten thousand souls to heaven or hell;
And this fell tempest shall not cease to rage
Until the golden circuit on my head,
Like to the glorious sun's transparent beams,
Do calm the fury of this mad-bred flaw.
And, for a minister of my intent,
I have seduc'd a headstrong Kentishman,
John Cade of Ashford,
To make commotion, as full well he can,
Under the title of John Mortimer.
In Ireland have I seen this stubborn Cade
Oppose himself against a troop of kerns,
And fought so long, till that his thighs with darts
Were almost like a sharp-quill'd porpentine;
And, in the end being rescued, I have seen
Him caper upright like a wild Morisco,
Shaking the bloody darts as he his bells.
Full often, like a shag-hair'd crafty kern,
Hath he conversed with the enemy,
And undiscover'd come to me again
And given me notice of their villanies.
This devil here shall be my substitute;
For that John Mortimer, which now is dead,
In face, in gait, in speech, he doth resemble:
By this I shall perceive the commons' mind,
How they affect the house and claim of York.
Say he be taken, rack'd and tortured,
I know no pain they can inflict upon him
Will make him say I mov'd him to those arms.
Say that he thrive, as 'tis great like he will,
Why, then from Ireland come I with my strength
And reap the harvest which that rascal sow'd;
For Humphrey being dead, as he shall be,
And Henry put apart, the next for me. *Exit.*

[SCENE II. *Bury St. Edmund's. A room of state.*]

Enter two or three running over the stage, from the murder of Duke Humphrey.

First Mur. Run to my Lord of Suffolk; let him know
We have dispatch'd the duke, as he commanded.
Sec. Mur. O that it were to do! What have we done?
Didst ever hear a man so penitent?

Enter SUFFOLK.

First Mur. Here comes my lord.
Suf. Now, sirs, have you dispatch'd this thing?
First Mur. Ay, my good lord, he 's dead.
Suf. Why, that 's well said. Go, get you to my house;
I will reward you for this venturous deed.
The king and all the peers are here at hand.
Have you laid fair the bed? Is all things well,
According as I gave directions?
First Mur. 'Tis, my good lord.
Suf. Away! be gone. *Exeunt [Murderers].*

Sound trumpets. Enter the KING, *the* QUEEN, CARDINAL [BEAUFORT], SOMERSET, *with Attendants.*

King. Go, call our uncle to our presence straight;
Say we intend to try his grace to-day,
If he be guilty, as 'tis published.
Suf. I'll call him presently, my noble lord. *Exit.*
King. Lords, take your places; and, I pray you all,
Proceed no straiter 'gainst our uncle Gloucester
Than from true evidence of good esteem
He be approv'd in practice culpable.
Queen. God forbid any malice should prevail,
That faultless may condemn a nobleman!
Pray God he may acquit him of suspicion!
King. I thank thee, Meg; these words content me much.

Enter SUFFOLK.

How now! why look'st thou pale? why tremblest thou?
Where is our uncle? what 's the matter, Suffolk?
Suf. Dead in his bed, my lord; Gloucester is dead.
Queen. Marry, God forfend!
Car. God's secret judgement: I did dream to-night
The duke was dumb and could not speak a word.
King swoons.
Queen. How fares my lord? Help, lords! the king is dead.
Som. Rear up his body; wring him by the nose.
Queen. Run, go, help, help! O Henry, ope thine eyes!
Suf. He doth revive again: madam, be patient.
King. O heavenly God!
Queen. How fares my gracious lord?
Suf. Comfort, my sovereign! gracious Henry, comfort!
King. What, doth my Lord of Suffolk comfort me?
Came he right now to sing a raven's note,
Whose dismal tune bereft my vital pow'rs;
And thinks he that the chirping of a wren,
By crying comfort from a hollow breast,

326. **event,** affair, business; see glossary. 328. **Bristow,** Bristol. 332. **misdoubt,** suspicion; see glossary. 338. **dignity,** i.e., the dignity of high office—kingship. 343. **starved,** frozen; see glossary. 354. **mad-bred,** produced by madness. **flaw,** tempest; see glossary. 365. **Morisco,** morris dancer, always fancily or grotesquely dressed. 372. **that John . . . dead.** Cf. *1 Henry VI*, II, v, 1. 375. **affect,** incline toward; see glossary. 378. **mov'd,** incited, prompted; see glossary.

SCENE II. 3. **that . . . do,** i.e., that it were not done. 17. **published,** publicly proclaimed. 20. **straiter,** more severely. 21. **of good esteem,** worthy of belief. 22. **approv'd,** proved. 24. **faultless,** modifies *nobleman*. 30. **forfend,** forbid; see glossary. 31. **to-night,** last night. 34. **wring . . . nose,** evidently a common first-aid remedy for restoring a person to consciousness; cf. *Venus and Adonis*, 475. 40. **raven's note.** It was a common folk superstition that the raven's croak

Can chase away the first-conceived sound?
Hide not thy poison with such sug'red words;
Lay not thy hands on me; forbear, I say;
Their touch affrights me as a serpent's sting.
Thou baleful messenger, out of my sight!
Upon thy eye-balls murderous tyranny
Sits in grim majesty, to fright the world.
Look not upon me, for thine eyes are wounding:
Yet do not go away: come, basilisk,
And kill the innocent gazer with thy sight;
For in the shade of death I shall find joy;
In life but double death, now Gloucester 's dead.
Queen. Why do you rate my Lord of Suffolk thus?
Although the duke was enemy to him,
Yet he most Christian-like laments his death:
And for myself, foe as he was to me,
Might liquid tears or heart-offending groans
Or blood-consuming sighs recall his life,
I would be blind with weeping, sick with groans,
Look pale as primrose with blood-drinking sighs,
And all to have the noble duke alive.
What know I how the world may deem of me?
For it is known we were but hollow friends:
It may be judg'd I made the duke away;
So shall my name with slander's tongue be wounded,
And princes' courts be fill'd with my reproach.
This get I by his death: ay me, unhappy!
To be a queen, and crown'd with infamy!
King. Ah, woe is me for Gloucester, wretched man!
Queen. Be woe for me, more wretched than he is.
What, dost thou turn away and hide thy face?
I am no loathsome leper; look on me.
What! art thou, like the adder, waxen deaf?
Be poisonous too and kill thy forlorn queen.
Is all thy comfort shut in Gloucester's tomb?
Why, then, dame Margaret was ne'er thy joy.
Erect his statue and worship it,
And make my image but an alehouse sign.
Was I for this nigh wrack'd upon the sea
And twice by awkward wind from England's bank
Drove back again unto my native clime?
What boded this, but well forewarning wind
Did seem to say 'Seek not a scorpion's nest,
Nor set no footing on this unkind shore'?
What did I then, but curs'd the gentle gusts
And he that loos'd them forth their brazen caves;
And bid them blow towards England's blessed shore,
Or turn our stern upon a dreadful rock?
Yet Æolus would not be a murderer,
But left that hateful office unto thee:
The pretty-vaulting sea refus'd to drown me,
Knowing that thou wouldst have me drown'd on shore,
With tears as salt as sea, through thy unkindness:
The splitting rocks cower'd in the sinking sands
And would not dash me with their ragged sides,
Because thy flinty heart, more hard than they,
Might in thy palace perish Margaret.
As far as I could ken thy chalky cliffs,
When from thy shore the tempest beat us back,
I stood upon the hatches in the storm,
And when the dusky sky began to rob
My earnest-gaping sight of thy land's view,
I took a costly jewel from my neck,
A heart it was, bound in with diamonds,
And threw it towards thy land: the sea receiv'd it,
And so I wish'd thy body might my heart:
And even with this I lost fair England's view
And bid mine eyes be packing with my heart
And call'd them blind and dusky spectacles,
For losing ken of Albion's wished coast.
How often have I tempted Suffolk's tongue,
The agent of thy foul inconstancy,
To sit and witch me, as Ascanius did
When he to madding Dido would unfold
His father's acts commenc'd in burning Troy!
Am I not witch'd like her? or thou not false like him?
Ay me, I can no more! die, Margaret!
For Henry weeps that thou dost live so long.

Noise within. Enter WARWICK, [SALISBURY,] *and many* Commons.

War. It is reported, mighty sovereign,
That good Duke Humphrey traitorously is murd'red
By Suffolk and the Cardinal Beaufort's means.
The commons, like an angry hive of bees
That want their leader, scatter up and down
And care not who they sting in his revenge.
Myself have calm'd their spleenful mutiny,
Until they hear the order of his death.
King. That he is dead, good Warwick, 'tis too true;
But how he died God knows, not Henry:
Enter his chamber, view his breathless corpse,
And comment then upon his sudden death.
War. That shall I do, my liege. Stay, Salisbury,
With the rude multitude till I return. [*Exit.*]
[*Exit Salisbury with the Commons.*]
King. O Thou that judgest all things, stay my thoughts,
My thoughts, that labour to persuade my soul
Some violent hands were laid on Humphrey's life!
If my suspect be false, forgive me, God,
For judgement only doth belong to Thee.
Fain would I go to chafe his paly lips
With twenty thousand kisses and to drain
Upon his face an ocean of salt tears,
To tell my love unto his dumb deaf trunk
And with my fingers feel his hand unfeeling:
But all in vain are these mean obsequies;

Bed put forth [*bearing Gloucester's body. Enter* WARWICK].

And to survey his dead and earthy image,
What were it but to make my sorrow greater?
War. Come hither, gracious sovereign, view this body.
King. That is to see how deep my grave is made;
For with his soul fled all my worldly solace,
For seeing him I see my life in death.
War. As surely as my soul intends to live
With that dread King that took our state upon him
To free us from his Father's wrathful curse,
I do believe that violent hands were laid

presaged death. 52. **basilisk,** fabulous reptile, said to kill by its look; see glossary. 56. **rate,** berate. 61, 63. **blood-consuming, blood-drinking.** It was commonly believed that a sigh cost the heart a drop of blood. 76. **like the adder.** Cf. Psalms 58:4-5: ". . . the deaf adder that stoppeth her ear, which hearkeneth not to the voice of charmers." References to the deafness of the adder are common in Renaissance books. **waxen,** grown. 80. **statue** (trisyllabic). 89. **he,** for "him"; see Abbott, 206-207; the antecedent is *Æolus*, god of the winds (l, 92). 101. **ken,** discern. 112. **spectacles,** organs of sight. 116. **Ascanius,** young son of Aeneas. During Aeneas' narration of his adventures and misfortunes in the court of Queen Dido, Venus, Aeneas' mother, sent Cupid to assume Ascanius' form in order to inflict the queen with love for Aeneas. 129. **order,** manner. 141. **chafe,** warm.

Upon the life of this thrice-famed duke.
Suf. A dreadful oath, sworn with a solemn tongue!
What instance gives Lord Warwick for his vow?
War. See how the blood is settled in his face.
Oft have I seen a timely-parted ghost,
Of ashy semblance, meagre, pale and bloodless,
Being all descended to the labouring heart;
Who, in the conflict that it holds with death,
Attracts the same for aidance 'gainst the enemy;
Which with the heart there cools and ne'er returneth
To blush and beautify the cheek again.
But see, his face is black and full of blood,
His eye-balls further out than when he liv'd,
Staring full ghastly like a strangled man;
His hair uprear'd, his nostrils stretch'd with struggling;
His hands abroad display'd, as one that grasp'd
And tugg'd for life and was by strength subdu'd:
Look, on the sheets his hair, you see, is sticking;
His well-proportion'd beard made rough and rugged,
Like to the summer's corn by tempest lodg'd.
It cannot be but he was murd'red here;
The least of all these signs were probable.
Suf. Why, Warwick, who should do the duke to death?
Myself and Beaufort had him in protection;
And we, I hope, sir, are no murderers.
War. But both of you were vow'd Duke Humphrey's foes,
And you, forsooth, had the good duke to keep:
'Tis like you would not feast him like a friend;
And 'tis well seen he found an enemy.
Queen. Then you, belike, suspect these noblemen
As guilty of Duke Humphrey's timeless death.
War. Who finds the heifer dead and bleeding fresh
And sees fast by a butcher with an axe,
But will suspect 'twas he that made the slaughter?
Who finds the partridge in the puttock's nest,
But may imagine how the bird was dead,
Although the kite soar with unbloodied beak?
Even so suspicious is this tragedy.
Queen. Are you the butcher, Suffolk? Where 's your knife?
Is Beaufort term'd a kite? Where are his talons?
Suf. I wear no knife to slaughter sleeping men;
But here 's a vengeful sword, rusted with ease,
That shall be scoured in his rancorous heart
That slanders me with murder's crimson badge.
Say, if thou dar'st, proud Lord of Warwickshire,
That I am faulty in Duke Humphrey's death.
[*Exeunt Cardinal*, *Somerset*, *and others.*]
War. What dares not Warwick, if false Suffolk dare him?
Queen. He dares not calm his contumelious spirit
Nor cease to be an arrogant controller,
Though Suffolk dare him twenty thousand times.
War. Madam, be still; with reverence may I say;
For every word you speak in his behalf
Is slander to your royal dignity.
Suf. Blunt-witted lord, ignoble in demeanour!
If ever lady wrong'd her lord so much,
Thy mother took into her blameful bed
Some stern untutor'd churl, and noble stock
Was graft with crab-tree slip; whose fruit thou art
And never of the Nevils' noble race.
War. But that the guilt of murder bucklers thee
And I should rob the deathsman of his fee,
Quitting thee thereby of ten thousand shames,
And that my sovereign's presence makes me mild,
I would, false murd'rous coward, on thy knee
Make thee beg pardon for thy passed speech
And say it was thy mother that thou meant'st,
That thou thyself wast born in bastardy;
And after all this fearful homage done,
Give thee thy hire and send thy soul to hell,
Pernicious blood-sucker of sleeping men!
Suf. Thou shalt be waking while I shed thy blood,
If from this presence thou dar'st go with me.
War. Away even now, or I will drag thee hence:
Unworthy though thou art, I'll cope with thee
And do some service to Duke Humphrey's ghost.
Exeunt [*Suffolk and Warwick*].
King. What stronger breastplate than a heart untainted!
Thrice is he arm'd that hath his quarrel just,
And he but naked, though lock'd up in steel,
Whose conscience with injustice is corrupted.
A noise within.
Queen. What noise is this?

Enter SUFFOLK *and* WARWICK, *with their weapons drawn.*

King. Why, how now, lords! your wrathful weapons drawn
Here in our presence! dare you be so bold?
Why, what tumultuous clamour have we here?
Suf. The trait'rous Warwick with the men of Bury
Set all upon me, mighty sovereign.

Enter Salisbury.

Sal. [*To the Commons, within*] Sirs, stand apart; the king shall know your mind.
Dread lord, the commons send you word by me,
Unless Lord Suffolk straight be done to death,
Or banished fair England's territories,
They will by violence tear him from your palace
And torture him with grievous ling'ring death.
They say, by him the good Duke Humphrey died;
They say, in him they fear your highness' death;
And mere instinct of love and loyalty,
Free from a stubborn opposite intent,
As being thought to contradict your liking,
Makes them thus forward in his banishment.
They say, in care of your most royal person,
That if your highness should intend to sleep
And charge that no man should disturb your rest
In pain of your dislike or pain of death,
Yet, notwithstanding such a strait edict,
Were there a serpent seen, with forked tongue,
That slily glided towards your majesty,
It were but necessary you were wak'd,
Lest, being suffer'd in that harmful slumber,

157. **thrice-famed,** widely famed, very famous. 159. **instance,** confirmation, proof; see glossary. 161. **timely-parted,** having died in the natural course of time. 176. **lodg'd,** beaten down. 178. **probable,** worthy of belief. 187. **timeless,** untimely. 191. **puttock's,** hawk's. 198. **with ease,** i.e., with disuse; see *ease* in glossary. 205. **controller,** detractor. 216. **bucklers,** defends. 218. **Quitting,** ridding. 221. **passed,** just spoken. 224. **fearful homage,** homage inspired by fear; see *fearful* in glossary. 230. **cope,** have to do with; see glossary. 250. **mere instinct,** sincere impulse; see *mere* in glossary. 263. **mortal worm,** deadly snake. 266. **fell,** cruel. 271. **hinds,** boors, rustics; see glossary. 274. **quaint,** skilled, clever; see glossary. 277. **a sort of tinkers,** a lot of common workmen. 281. **cited,** urged. 310. **mandrake's groan.** It was a folk belief that when the mandrake was pulled from the ground it uttered a shriek which was fatal to the hearer; cf. *Romeo and*

The mortal worm might make the sleep eternal;
And therefore do they cry, though you forbid,
That they will guard you, whe'r you will or no,
From such fell serpents as false Suffolk is,
With whose envenomed and fatal sting,
Your loving uncle, twenty times his worth,
They say, is shamefully bereft of life.

Commons. (Within) An answer from the king, my Lord of Salisbury!

Suf. 'Tis like the commons, rude unpolish'd hinds,
Could send such message to their sovereign:
But you, my lord, were glad to be employ'd,
To show how quaint an orator you are:
But all the honour Salisbury hath won
Is, that he was the lord ambassador
Sent from a sort of tinkers to the king.

Commons. (Within) An answer from the king, or we will all break in!

King. Go, Salisbury, and tell them all from me,
I thank them for their tender loving care;
And had I not been cited so by them,
Yet did I purpose as they do entreat;
For, sure, my thoughts do hourly prophesy
Mischance unto my state by Suffolk's means:
And therefore, by His majesty I swear,
Whose far unworthy deputy I am,
He shall not breathe infection in this air
But three days longer, on the pain of death.
[*Exit Salisbury.*]

Queen. O Henry, let me plead for gentle Suffolk!

King. Ungentle queen, to call him gentle Suffolk!
No more, I say: if thou dost plead for him,
Thou wilt but add increase unto my wrath.
Had I but said, I would have kept my word,
But when I swear, it is irrevocable.
If, after three days' space, thou here be'st found
On any ground that I am ruler of,
The world shall not be ransom for thy life.
Come, Warwick, come, good Warwick, go with me;
I have great matters to impart to thee.
Exit [*with all but Queen and Suffolk*].

Queen. Mischance and sorrow go along with you!
Heart's discontent and sour affliction
Be playfellows to keep you company!
There 's two of you; the devil make a third!
And threefold vengeance tend upon your steps!

Suf. Cease, gentle queen, these execrations
And let thy Suffolk take his heavy leave.

Queen. Fie, coward woman and soft-hearted wretch!
Hast thou not spirit to curse thine enemy?

Suf. A plague upon them! wherefore should I curse them?
Would curses kill, as doth the mandrake's groan,
I would invent as bitter-searching terms,
As curst, as harsh and horrible to hear,
Deliver'd strongly through my fixed teeth,
With full as many signs of deadly hate,
As lean-fac'd Envy in her loathsome cave:
My tongue should stumble in mine earnest words;
Mine eyes should sparkle like the beaten flint;
Mine hair be fix'd on end, as one distract;
Ay, every joint should seem to curse and ban:
And even now my burthen'd heart would break,
Should I not curse them. Poison be their drink!
Gall, worse than gall, the daintiest that they taste!
Their sweetest shade a grove of cypress trees!
Their chiefest prospect murd'ring basilisks!
Their softest touch as smart as lizards' stings!
Their music frightful as the serpent's hiss,
And boding screech-owls make the consort full!
All the foul terrors in dark-seated hell—

Queen. Enough, sweet Suffolk; thou torment'st thyself;
And these dread curses, like the sun 'gainst glass,
Or like an overcharged gun, recoil,
And turn the force of them upon thyself.

Suf. You bade me ban, and will you bid me leave?
Now, by the ground that I am banish'd from,
Well could I curse away a winter's night,
Though standing naked on a mountain top,
Where biting cold would never let grass grow,
And think it but a minute spent in sport.

Queen. O, let me entreat thee cease. Give me thy hand,
That I may dew it with my mournful tears;
Nor let the rain of heaven wet this place,
To wash away my woful monuments.
O, could this kiss be printed in thy hand,
That thou mightst think upon these by the seal,
Through whom a thousand sighs are breath'd for thee!
So, get thee gone, that I may know my grief;
'Tis but surmis'd whiles thou art standing by,
As one that surfeits thinking on a want.
I will repeal thee, or, be well assur'd,
Adventure to be banished myself:
And banished I am, if but from thee.
Go; speak not to me; even now be gone.
O, go not yet! Even thus two friends condemn'd
Embrace and kiss and take ten thousand leaves,
Loather a hundred times to part than die.
Yet now farewell; and farewell life with thee!

Suf. Thus is poor Suffolk ten times banished;
Once by the king, and three times thrice by thee.
'Tis not the land I care for, wert thou thence;
A wilderness is populous enough,
So Suffolk had thy heavenly company:
For where thou art, there is the world itself,
With every several pleasure in the world,
And where thou art not, desolation.
I can no more: live thou to joy thy life;
Myself no joy in nought but that thou liv'st.

Enter VAUX.

Queen. Whither goes Vaux so fast? what news, I prithee?

Vaux. To signify unto his majesty
That Cardinal Beaufort is at point of death;
For suddenly a grievous sickness took him,
That makes him gasp and stare and catch the air,
Blaspheming God and cursing men on earth.
Sometime he talks as if Duke Humphrey's ghost

Juliet, IV, iii, 47-49. 312. **curst,** malignant. 315. **lean-fac'd Envy,** a conventional description of this one of the seven deadly sins. Spenser depicts Envy riding on a ravenous wolf. (*Faerie Queene*, I, iv.) Hart points out as the probable immediate source of this passage the following lines from Golding's Ovid:

> She goes me straight to Envies house, a foule and irksome cave,
> Replete with blacke and lothly filth. . . .
> There saw she Envie . . .
> Hir body leane as any Rake. . . .

319. **ban,** curse. 323. **cypress trees,** symbols of grief. 327. **consort,** company of musicians. 342. **monuments,** i.e., traces of her tears. 349. **repeal,** recall from banishment. 350. **Adventure,** risk. 373. **Sometime,** from time to time; see glossary.

Were by his side; sometime he calls the king
And whispers to his pillow as to him
The secrets of his overcharged soul:
And I am sent to tell his majesty
That even now he cries aloud for him.
Queen. Go tell this heavy message to the king.
Exit [*Vaux*].
Ay me! what is this world! what news are these!
But wherefore grieve I at an hour's poor loss,
Omitting Suffolk's exile, my soul's treasure?
Why only, Suffolk, mourn I not for thee,
And with the southern clouds contend in tears,
Theirs for the earth's increase, mine for my sorrows?
Now get thee hence: the king, thou know'st, is coming;
If thou be found by me, thou art but dead.
Suf. If I depart from thee, I cannot live;
And in thy sight to die, what were it else
But like a pleasant slumber in thy lap?
Here could I breathe my soul into the air,
As mild and gentle as the cradle-babe
Dying with mother's dug between its lips:
Where, from thy sight, I should be raging mad
And cry out for thee to close up mine eyes,
To have thee with thy lips to stop my mouth;
So shouldst thou either turn my flying soul,
Or I should breathe it so into thy body,
And then it liv'd in sweet Elysium.
To die by thee were but to die in jest;
From thee to die were torture more than death:
O, let me stay, befall what may befall!
Queen. Away! though parting be a fretful corrosive,
It is applied to a deathful wound.
To France, sweet Suffolk: let me hear from thee;
For wheresoe'er thou art in this world's globe,
I'll have an Iris that shall find thee out.
Suf. I go.
Queen. And take my heart with thee.
Suf. A jewel, lock'd into the wofull'st cask
That ever did contain a thing of worth.
Even as a splitted bark, so sunder we:
This way fall I to death.
Queen. This way for me.
Exeunt [*severally*].

[SCENE III. *A bedchamber.*]

Enter the KING, SALISBURY, *and* WARWICK, *to the* CARDINAL *in bed.*

King. How fares my lord? speak, Beaufort, to thy sovereign.
Car. If thou be'st Death, I'll give thee England's treasure,
Enough to purchase such another island,
So thou wilt let me live, and feel no pain.
King. Ah, what a sign it is of evil life,
Where death's approach is seen so terrible!
War. Beaufort, it is thy sovereign speaks to thee.
Car. Bring me unto my trial when you will.
Died he not in his bed? where should he die?
Can I make men live, whe'r they will or no?
O, torture me no more! I will confess.
Alive again? then show me where he is:
I'll give a thousand pound to look upon him.
He hath no eyes, the dust hath blinded them.
Comb down his hair; look, look! it stands upright,
Like lime-twigs set to catch my winged soul.
Give me some drink; and bid the apothecary
Bring the strong poison that I bought of him.
King. O thou eternal Mover of the heavens,
Look with a gentle eye upon this wretch!
O, beat away the busy meddling fiend
That lays strong siege unto this wretch's soul
And from his bosom purge this black despair!
War. See, how the pangs of death do make him grin!
Sal. Disturb him not; let him pass peaceably.
King. Peace to his soul, if God's good pleasure be!
Lord cardinal, if thou think'st on heaven's bliss,
Hold up thy hand, make signal of thy hope.
He dies, and makes no sign. O God, forgive him!
War. So bad a death argues a monstrous life.
King. Forbear to judge, for we are sinners all.
Close up his eyes and draw the curtain close;
And let us all to meditation. *Exeunt.*

[ACT IV.

SCENE I. *The coast of Kent.*]

Alarum. Fight at sea. Ordnance goes off. Enter Lieutenant, [*a* Master, *a* Master's-Mate, WALTER WHITMORE, *and others; with them*] SUFFOLK, *and others* [*, prisoners*].

Lieut. The gaudy, blabbing and remorseful day
Is crept into the bosom of the sea;
And now loud-howling wolves arouse the jades
That drag the tragic melancholy night;
Who, with their drowsy, slow and flagging wings,
Clip dead men's graves and from their misty jaws
Breathe foul contagious darkness in the air.
Therefore bring forth the soldiers of our prize;
For, whilst our pinnace anchors in the Downs,
Here shall they make their ransom on the sand,
Or with their blood stain this discoloured shore.
Master, this prisoner freely give I thee;
And thou that art his mate, make boot of this;
The other, Walter Whitmore, is thy share.
First Gent. What is my ransom, master? let me know.
Mast. A thousand crowns, or else lay down your head.
Mate. And so much shall you give, or off goes yours.
Lieut. What, think you much to pay two thousand crowns,
And bear the name and port of gentlemen?
Cut both the villains' throats; for die you shall:
The lives of those which we have lost in fight

394. **dug,** breast. 407. **Iris,** Juno's messenger.

SCENE III. 5-6. **a sign . . . terrible.** Cf. l. 30 below. This passage echoes the commonplace that a good man makes a good end. There is misrepresentation of history here. Authentic records indicate that the cardinal died quietly, surrounded by his household, and that his mind was clear to the last. The scene may have been suggested by a paragraph in Holinshed where Winchester's greed is emphasized: "His covetise insaciable, and hope of long lyfe, made hym both to forget God, his Prynce, and hymself, in his latter daies." 9-16. **Died . . . soul.** Cf. the description of Gloucester's corpse (III, ii, 168-176) and Warwick's insinuations regarding who the murderer was (III, ii, 177-194).

ACT IV. SCENE I. 1. **blabbing,** revealing. **remorseful,** compassionate. 6. **Clip,** embrace; see glossary. 9. **pinnace,** one-masted vessel. 12. **this prisoner,** i.e., the First Gentleman. 13. **boot,** profit; see glossary. **this,** i.e., the Second Gentleman. 14. **The other,** i.e., Suffolk. 19. **port,** demeanor; see glossary. 25. **laying . . . abroad,** making an attack on the ship. 26-138. **shalt thou die,** etc. Holinshed gives the following account of Suffolk's death: ". . . intending to transport himselfe ouer into France, he was incountered with a ship of warre, apperteining to the duke of Excester, Constable of the Tower of London, called the Nicholas of the Tower. The capteine of that barke with small fight entered into the dukes ship, and perceiuing his person present, brought him to Douer road, and there, on the one side of a cock bote, caused his head to be striken off, and left his bodie with the

Be counterpois'd with such a petty sum!
First Gent. I'll give it, sir; and therefore spare my life.
Sec. Gent. And so will I and write home for it straight.
Whit. I lost mine eye in laying the prize aboard,
And therefore to revenge it, shalt thou die; [*To Suf.*]
And so should these, if I might have my will.
Lieut. Be not so rash; take ransom, let him live.
Suf. Look on my George; I am a gentleman:
Rate me at what thou wilt, thou shalt be paid.
Whit. And so am I; my name is Walter Whitmore.
How now! why starts thou? what, doth death affright?
Suf. Thy name affrights me, in whose sound is death.
A cunning man did calculate my birth
And told me that by water I should die:
Yet let not this make thee be bloody-minded;
Thy name is Gualtier, being rightly sounded.
Whit. Gualtier or Walter, which it is, I care not:
Never did base dishonour blur our name,
But with our sword we wip'd away the blot;
Therefore, when merchant-like I sell revenge,
Broke be my sword, my arms torn and defac'd,
And I proclaim'd a coward through the world!
Suf. Stay, Whitmore; for thy prisoner is a prince,
The Duke of Suffolk, William de la Pole.
Whit. The Duke of Suffolk muffled up in rags!
Suf. Ay, but these rags are no part of the duke:
Jove sometime went disguis'd, and why not I?
Lieut. But Jove was never slain, as thou shalt be.
Suf. Obscure and lowly swain, King Henry's blood,
The honourable blood of Lancaster,
Must not be shed by such a jaded groom.
Hast thou not kiss'd thy hand and held my stirrup?
Bare-headed plodded by my foot-cloth mule
And thought thee happy when I shook my head?
How often hast thou waited at my cup,
Fed from my trencher, kneel'd down at the board,
When I have feasted with Queen Margaret?
Remember it and let it make thee crest-fall'n,
Ay, and allay this thy abortive pride;
How in our voiding lobby hast thou stood
And duly waited for my coming forth?
This hand of mine hath writ in thy behalf
And therefore shall it charm thy riotous tongue.
Whit. Speak, captain, shall I stab the forlorn swain?
Lieut. First let my words stab him, as he hath me.
Suf. Base slave, thy words are blunt and so art thou.
Lieut. Convey him hence and on our longboat's side
Strike off his head.
Suf. Thou dar'st not, for thy own.
Lieut. Yes, Pole.
Suf. Pole!
Lieut. Pool! Sir Pool! lord!
Ay, kennel, puddle, sink; whose filth and dirt
Troubles the silver spring where England drinks.
Now will I dam up this thy yawning mouth
For swallowing the treasure of the realm:
Thy lips that kiss'd the queen shall sweep the ground;
And thou that smil'dst at good Duke Humphrey's death
Against the senseless winds shalt grin in vain,
Who in contempt shall hiss at thee again:
And wedded be thou to the hags of hell,
For daring to affy a mighty lord
Unto the daughter of a worthless king,
Having neither subject, wealth, nor diadem.
By devilish policy art thou grown great
And, like ambitious Sylla, overgorg'd
With gobbets of thy mother's bleeding heart.
By thee Anjou and Maine were sold to France,
The false revolting Normans thorough thee
Disdain to call us lord, and Picardy
Hath slain their governors, surpris'd our forts
And sent the ragged soldiers wounded home.
The princely Warwick, and the Nevils all,
Whose dreadful swords were never drawn in vain,
As hating thee, are rising up in arms:
And now the house of York, thrust from the crown
By shameful murder of a guiltless king
And lofty proud encroaching tyranny,
Burns with revenging fire; whose hopeful colours
Advance our half-fac'd sun, striving to shine,
Under the which is writ 'Invitis nubibus.'
The commons here in Kent are up in arms:
And, to conclude, reproach and beggary
Is crept into the palace of our king,
And all by thee. Away! convey him hence.
Suf. O that I were a god, to shoot forth thunder
Upon these paltry, servile, abject drudges!
Small things make base men proud: this villain here,
Being captain of a pinnace, threatens more
Than Bargulus the strong Illyrian pirate.
Drones suck not eagles' blood but rob beehives:
It is impossible that I should die
By such a lowly vassal as thyself.
Thy words move rage and not remorse in me:
I go of message from the queen to France;
I charge thee waft me safely cross the Channel.
Lieut. Walter,—
Whit. Come, Suffolk, I must waft thee to thy death.
Suf. Paene gelidus timor occupat artus, it is thee I fear.
Whit. Thou shalt have cause to fear before I leave thee.
What, are ye daunted now? now will ye stoop?
First Gent. My gracious lord, entreat him, speak him fair.
Suf. Suffolk's imperial tongue is stern and rough,
Us'd to command, untaught to plead for favour.
Far be it we should honour such as these
With humble suit: no, rather let my head
Stoop to the block than these knees bow to any
Save to the God of heaven and to my king;

head lieng there on the sands. Which corps, being there found by a chapleine of his, was conueied to Wingfield college in Suffolke, and there buried." 29. **George,** the gold or jeweled figure of St. George, worn as the insignium of the Order of the Knights of the Garter. 33. **Thy name,** i.e., Walter, pronounced like "water"; cf. line 37 below, where Suffolk tries desperately to avert the prophecy referred to in lines 34-35 (cf. I, iv, 35-36) by urging the French form of the name—Gaultier. 54. **foot-cloth,** large, richly ornamented cloth laid over the back of a horse, hanging down to the ground on each side. 57. **trencher,** wooden dish or plate; see glossary. 61. **voiding lobby,** anteroom. 70. **Pole, Pool,** words pronounced somewhat alike in Elizabethan speech. 71. **kennel,** gutter, sink, cesspool. 80. **affy,** betroth. 84. **ambitious Sylla,** i.e., Sulla, Roman dictator of the first century B.C., who rose to power by waging civil war against Marius. 85. **gobbets,** pieces of raw flesh. 87. **thorough,** through. 95. **shameful . . . king,** i.e., Richard II. 98. **Advance,** raise. **half-fac'd sun.** This may possibly allude to the banner of Edward III, which according to Camden (*Remains*) was "the rays of the sun dispersing themselues out of a cloud." Cf. *3 Henry VI*, II, i, 39-40, where Edward IV adopted the sun as an emblem. 99. **'Invitus nubibus,'** in spite of the clouds. 108. **Bargulus,** an allusion to Cicero's *De officiis*, where this famous pirate is mentioned. 112. **remorse,** pity. 117. **Paene . . . artus,** cold fear takes hold of the limbs almost entirely. 120. **fair,** courteously.

And sooner dance upon a bloody pole
Than stand uncover'd to the vulgar groom.
True nobility is exempt from fear:
More can I bear than you dare execute.

Lieut. Hale him away, and let him talk no more.

Suf. Come, soldiers, show what cruelty ye can,
That this my death may never be forgot!
Great men oft die by vile bezonians:
A Roman sworder and banditto slave
Murder'd sweet Tully; Brutus' bastard hand
Stabb'd Julius Cæsar; savage islanders
Pompey the Great; and Suffolk dies by pirates.

Exit Walter [Whitmore and others] with Suffolk.

Lieut. And as for these whose ransom we have set,
It is our pleasure one of them depart:
Therefore come you with us and let him go.

Exeunt Lieutenant and the rest. Manet the First Gent.

Enter WALTER [WHITMORE] *with the body [of* SUFFOLK].

Whit. There let his head and lifeless body lie,
Until the queen his mistress bury it. *Exit Walter.*

First Gent. O barbarous and bloody spectacle!
His body will I bear unto the king:
If he revenge it not, yet will his friends;
So will the queen, that living held him dear.

[Exit with the body.]

[SCENE II. *Blackheath.*]

Enter [GEORGE] BEVIS *and* JOHN HOLLAND.

Bevis. Come, and get thee a sword, though made of a lath: they have been up these two days.

Holl. They have the more need to sleep now, then.

Bevis. I tell thee, Jack Cade the clothier means to dress the commonwealth, and turn it, and set a new nap upon it.

Holl. So he had need, for 'tis threadbare. Well, I say it was never merry world in England since gentlemen came up.

Bevis. O miserable age! virtue is not regarded in handicrafts-men.

Holl. The nobility think scorn to go in leather aprons.

Bevis. Nay, more, the king's council are no good workmen.

Holl. True; and yet it is said, labour in thy vocation; which is as much to say as, let the magistrates be labouring men; and therefore should we be magistrates.

Bevis. Thou hast hit it; for there 's no better sign of a brave mind than a hard hand.

Holl. I see them! I see them! There 's Best's son, the tanner of Wingham,—

Bevis. He shall have the skins of our enemies, to make dog's-leather of.

Holl. And Dick the Butcher,—

Bevis. Then is sin struck down like an ox, and iniquity's throat cut like a calf.

Holl. And Smith the weaver,—

Bevis. Argo, their thread of life is spun.

Holl. Come, come, let 's fall in with them.

Drum. Enter CADE, DICK *Butcher*, SMITH *the Weaver, and a Sawyer, with infinite numbers.*

Cade. We John Cade, so termed of our supposed father,—

Dick. [*Aside*] Or rather, of stealing a cade of herrings.

Cade. For our enemies shall fall before us, inspired with the spirit of putting down kings and princes,—Command silence.

Dick. Silence!

Cade. My father was a Mortimer,—

Dick. [*Aside*] He was an honest man, and a good bricklayer.

Cade. My mother a Plantagenet,—

Dick. [*Aside*] I knew her well; she was a midwife.

Cade. My wife descended of the Lacies,—

Dick. [*Aside*] She was, indeed, a pedler's daughter, and sold many laces.

Smith. [*Aside*] But now of late, not able to travel with her furred pack, she washes bucks here at home.

Cade. Therefore am I of an honourable house.

Dick. [*Aside*] Ay, by my faith, the field is honourable; and there was he born, under a hedge, for his father had never a house but the cage.

Cade. Valiant I am.

Smith. [*Aside*] 'A must needs; for beggary is valiant.

Cade. I am able to endure much.

Dick. [*Aside*] No question of that; for I have seen him whipped three market-days together.

Cade. I fear neither sword nor fire.

Smith. [*Aside*] He need not fear the sword; for his coat is of proof.

Dick. [*Aside*] But methinks he should stand in fear of fire, being burnt i' the hand for stealing of sheep.

Cade. Be brave, then; for your captain is brave, and vows reformation. There shall be in England seven halfpenny loaves sold for a penny: the three-hooped pot shall have ten hoops; and I will make it felony to drink small beer: all the realm shall be in common; and in Cheapside shall my palfry go to grass: and when I am king, as king I will be,—

All. God save your majesty!

Cade. I thank you, good people: there shall be no money; all shall eat and drink on my score; and I will apparel them all in one livery, that they may agree like brothers and worship me their lord.

Dick. The first thing we do, let 's kill all the lawyers.

Cade. Nay, that I mean to do. Is not this a lamentable thing, that of the skin of an innocent lamb should be made parchment? that parchment, being scribbled o'er, should undo a man? Some say the bee stings: but I say, 'tis the bee's wax; for I did but seal once to a thing, and I was never mine own man since. How now! who 's there?

Enter [some, bringing forward] a Clerk [of Chatham].

Smith. The clerk of Chatham: he can write and read

134. **bezonians,** needy beggars, rascals. 136. **Tully,** Cicero. **bastard.** According to an unreliable tradition, Brutus was Caesar's bastard son. 137-138. **savage . . . Great.** According to Plutarch, Pompey was stabbed by one of his former officers in Egypt after his defeat by Caesar at Pharsalus.

SCENE II. 2. **up,** i.e., up in arms. 7. **a new nap,** alluding to Jack Cade's trade as a shearman, whose business it was to trim off the superfluous nap in the manufacture of cloth. 10. **came up,** came into fashion. 31. **Argo,** blunder for Latin *ergo*, therefore. 35. **cade,** barrel. 51. **furred pack,** pack made of hides. **bucks,** quantities of clothes put through the *buck* or lye. 55. **born, under a hedge.** Cf. *hedge-born swain, 1 Henry VI*, IV, i, 43. 56. **cage,** prison for petty malefactors. 65. **of proof,** tried by experience; also, well-worn. 70. **reformation,** social and political changes. 73. **three-hooped pot,** wooden quart-pot made and cast accompt.

Cade. O monstrous!

Smith. We took him setting of boys' copies.

Cade. Here 's a villain!

Smith. Has a book in his pocket with red letters in 't.

Cade. Nay, then, he is a conjurer.

Dick. Nay, he can make obligations, and write court-hand.

Cade. I am sorry for 't: the man is a proper man, of mine honour; unless I find him guilty, he shall not die. Come hither, sirrah, I must examine thee: what is thy name?

Clerk. Emmanuel.

Dick. They use to write it on the top of letters: 'twill go hard with you.

Cade. Let me alone. Dost thou use to write thy name? or hast thou a mark to thyself, like an honest plain-dealing man?

Clerk. Sir, I thank God, I have been so well brought up that I can write my name.

All. He hath confessed: away with him! he 's a villain and a traitor.

Cade. Away with him, I say! hang him with his pen and ink-horn about his neck. *Exit one with the Clerk.*

Enter MICHAEL.

Mich. Where 's our general?

Cade. Here I am, thou particular fellow.

Mich. Fly, fly, fly! Sir Humphrey Stafford and his brother are hard by, with the king's forces.

Cade. Stand, villain, stand, or I'll fell thee down. He shall be encountered with a man as good as himself: he is but a knight, is 'a?

Mich. No.

Cade. To equal him, I will make myself a knight presently. [*Kneels*] Rise up Sir John Mortimer. [*Rises*] Now have at him!

Enter SIR HUMPHREY STAFFORD *and his* Brother, *with drum and soldiers.*

Staf. Rebellious hinds, the filth and scum of Kent,
Mark'd for the gallows, lay your weapons down;
Home to your cottages, forsake this groom:
The king is merciful, if you revolt.

Bro. But angry, wrathful, and inclin'd to blood,
If you go forward; therefore yield, or die.

Cade. As for these silken-coated slaves, I pass not:
It is to you, good people, that I speak,
Over whom, in time to come, I hope to reign;
For I am rightful heir unto the crown.

Staf. Villain, thy father was a plasterer;
And thou thyself a shearman, art thou not?

Cade. And Adam was a gardener.

Bro. And what of that?

Cade. Marry, this: Edmund Mortimer, Earl of March,
Married the Duke of Clarence' daughter, did he not?

Staf. Ay, sir.

Cade. By her he had two children at one birth.

Bro. That 's false.

Cade. Ay, there 's the question; but I say, 'tis true:
The elder of them, being put to nurse,
Was by a beggar-woman stol'n away;
And, ignorant of his birth and parentage,
Became a bricklayer when he came to age:
His son am I; deny it, if you can.

Dick. Nay, 'tis too true; therefore he shall be king.

Smith. Sir, he made a chimney in my father's house, and the bricks are alive at this day to testify it; therefore deny it not.

Staf. And will you credit this base drudge's words,
That speaks he knows not what?

All. Ay, marry, will we; therefore get ye gone.

Bro. Jack Cade, the Duke of York hath taught you this.

Cade [*Aside*] He lies, for I invented it myself.— Go to, sirrah, tell the king from me, that, for his father's sake, Henry the Fifth, in whose time boys went to span-counter for French crowns, I am content he shall reign; but I'll be protector over him.

Dick. And furthermore, we'll have the Lord Say's head for selling the dukedom of Maine.

Cade. And good reason; for thereby is England mained, and fain to go with a staff, but that my puissance holds it up. Fellow kings, I tell you that that Lord Say hath gelded the commonwealth, and made it an eunuch: and more than that, he can speak French; and therefore he is a traitor.

Staf. O gross and miserable ignorance!

Cade. Nay, answer, if you can: the Frenchmen are our enemies; go to, then, I ask but this: can he that speaks with the tongue of an enemy be a good counsellor, or no?

All. No, no; and therefore we'll have his head.

Bro. Well, seeing gentle words will not prevail,
Assail them with the army of the king.

Staf. Herald, away; and throughout every town
Proclaim them traitors that are up with Cade;
That those which fly before the battle ends
May, even in their wives' and children's sight,
Be hang'd up for example at their doors:
And you that be the king's friends, follow me.

Exeunt [*the two Staffords, and soldiers*].

Cade. And you that love the commons, follow me.
Now show yourselves men; 'tis for liberty.
We will not leave one lord, one gentleman:
Spare none but such as go in clouted shoon;
For they are thrifty honest men and such
As would, but that they dare not, take our parts.

Dick. They are all in order and march toward us.

Cade. But then are we in order when we are most out of order. Come, march forward. [*Exeunt.*]

[SCENE III. *Another part of Blackheath.*]

Alarums to the fight, wherein both the STAFFORDS *are slain. Enter* CADE *and the rest.*

Cade. Where 's Dick, the butcher of Ashford?

Dick. Here, sir.

Cade. They fell before thee like sheep and oxen, and

with three hoops. 74. **small beer,** weaker kind of beer. 80. **score,** account. 88. **undo,** ruin; see glossary. 95. **setting . . . copies,** writing out words, etc., as models to be reproduced by boys. 101. **court-hand,** professional hand, used in preparing legal documents. 106. **Emmanuel,** i.e., God with us, used frequently as heading for letters and documents. 119. **particular,** opposed to *general* (l. 118). 133. **revolt,** turn back. 136. **pass,** care. 166. **span-counter,** a boys' game in which one throws a counter or piece of money that the other wins if he can throw another that hits it or falls within a span of it. 169-170. **Lord Say,** etc. As treasurer of England, this peer was implicated in the dealings negotiated by Suffolk that resulted in the loss of Anjou and Maine. He, among others, was accused by the irate Commons as one of the agents of the negotiations. 172. **mained,** old form of "maimed." 195. **clouted,** hobnailed. **shoon,** shoes.

thou behavedst thyself as if thou hadst been in thine own slaughter-house: therefore thus will I reward thee, the Lent shall be as long again as it is; and thou shalt have a license to kill for a hundred lacking one.

Dick. I desire no more.

Cade. And, to speak truth, thou deservest no less. This monument of the victory will I bear [*putting on Sir Humphrey's armor*]; and the bodies shall be dragged at my horse heels till I do come to London, where we will have the mayor's sword borne before us.

Dick. If we mean to thrive and do good, break open the gaols and let out the prisoners.

Cade. Fear not that, I warrant thee. Come, let 's march towards London. *Exeunt.*

[SCENE IV. *London. The palace.*]

Enter the KING *with a supplication, and the* QUEEN *with Suffolk's head, the* DUKE OF BUCKINGHAM *and the* LORD SAY.

Queen. Oft have I heard that grief softens the mind
And makes it fearful and degenerate;
Think therefore on revenge and cease to weep.
But who can cease to weep and look on this?
Here may his head lie on my throbbing breast:
But where 's the body that I should embrace?
Buck. What answer makes your grace to the rebels' supplication?
King. I'll send some holy bishop to entreat;
For God forbid so many simple souls
Should perish by the sword! And I myself,
Rather than bloody war shall cut them short,
Will parley with Jack Cade their general:
But stay, I'll read it over once again.
Queen. Ah, barbarous villains! hath this lovely face
Rul'd, like a wandering planet, over me,
And could it not enforce them to relent,
That were unworthy to behold the same?
King. Lord Say, Jack Cade hath sworn to have thy head.
Say. Ay, but I hope your highness shall have his.
King. How now, madam!
Still lamenting and mourning for Suffolk's death?
I fear me, love, if that I had been dead,
Thou wouldest not have mourn'd so much for me.
Queen. No, my love, I should not mourn, but die for thee.

Enter a Messenger.

King. How now! what news? why com'st thou in such haste?
Mess. The rebels are in Southwark; fly, my lord!
Jack Cade proclaims himself Lord Mortimer,
Descended from the Duke of Clarence' house,
And calls your grace usurper openly
And vows to crown himself in Westminster.
His army is a ragged multitude
Of hinds and peasants, rude and merciless:
Sir Humphrey Stafford and his brother's death
Hath given them heart and courage to proceed:
All scholars, lawyers, courtiers, gentlemen,
They call false caterpillars and intend their death.
King. O graceless men! they know not what they do.
Buck. My gracious lord, retire to Killingworth,
Until a power be rais'd to put them down.
Queen. Ah, were the Duke of Suffolk now alive,
These Kentish rebels would be soon appeas'd!
King. Lord Say, the traitors hate thee;
Therefore away with us to Killingworth.
Say. So might your grace's person be in danger.
The sight of me is odious in their eyes;
And therefore in this city will I stay
And live alone as secret as I may.

Enter another Messenger.

Mess. Jack Cade hath gotten London bridge:
The citizens fly and forsake their houses:
The rascal people, thirsting after prey,
Join with the traitor, and they jointly swear
To spoil the city and your royal court.
Buck. Then linger not, my lord; away, take horse.
King. Come, Margaret; God, our hope, will succour us.
Queen. My hope is gone, now Suffolk is deceas'd.
King. Farewell, my lord: trust not the Kentish rebels.
Buck. Trust nobody, for fear you be betray'd.
Say. The trust I have is in mine innocence,
And therefore am I bold and resolute. *Exeunt.*

[SCENE V. *London. The Tower.*]

Enter LORD SCALES *upon the Tower, walking. Then enter two or three* Citizens *below.*

Scales. How now! is Jack Cade slain?

First Cit. No, my lord, nor likely to be slain; for they have won the bridge, killing all those that withstand them: the lord mayor craves aid of your honour from the Tower to defend the city from the rebels.

Scales. Such aid as I can spare you shall command;
But I am troubled here with them myself;
The rebels have assay'd to win the Tower.
But get you to Smithfield and gather head,
And thither I will send you Matthew Goffe;
Fight for your king, your country and your lives;
And so, farewell, for I must hence again. *Exeunt.*

[SCENE VI. *London. Cannon Street.*]

Enter JACK CADE *and the rest, and strikes his staff on London-stone.*

Cade. Now is Mortimer lord of this city. And here, sitting upon London-stone, I charge and command that, of the city's cost, the pissing-conduit run nothing but claret wine this first year of our reign. And now henceforward it shall be treason for any that calls me other than Lord Mortimer.

Enter a Soldier, *running.*

Sold. Jack Cade! Jack Cade!

SCENE III. 7-9. **the Lent . . . lacking one.** The eating of flesh during Lent was forbidden in Elizabeth's reign, and killing of beasts at that time was permitted only by special license to provide for invalids (supposedly) unable to dispense with flesh. A license to kill for ninety-nine a week during a doubled Lent would thus constitute a valuable monopoly. *For* in line 9 may mean "at the rate of," allowing Dick to slaughter ninety-nine beasts a week (Tucker Brooke).

SCENE V. 9. **assay'd,** attempted; see glossary. 10. **head,** an armed force; see glossary.

SCENE VI. 2. **London-stone,** according to Camden, the central milestone of the town. 4. **pissing-conduit,** popular name of a conduit near the Royal Exchange. 17. **Tower.** Unlike London Bridge, the Tower was made of stone.

SCENE VII. *Stage Direction: **all the rest,*** i.e., of the forces loyal to the

Cade. Knock him down there. *They kill him.*

Smith. If this fellow be wise, he'll never call ye Jack Cade more: I think he hath a very fair warning.

Dick. My lord, there 's an army gathered together in Smithfield.

Cade. Come, then, let 's go fight with them: but first, go and set London bridge on fire; and, if you can, burn down the Tower too. Come, let's away.

Exeunt omnes.

[SCENE VII. *London. Smithfield.*]

Alarums. MATTHEW GOFFE *is slain, and all the rest. Then enter* JACK CADE, *with his company.*

Cade. So, sirs: now go some and pull down the Savoy; others to the inns of court; down with them all.

Dick. I have a suit unto your lordship.

Cade. Be it a lordship, thou shalt have it for that word.

Dick. Only that the laws of England may come out of your mouth.

Holl. [*Aside*] Mass, 'twill be sore law, then; for he was thrust in the mouth with a spear, and 'tis not whole yet.

Smith. [*Aside*] Nay, John, it will be stinking law; for his breath stinks with eating toasted cheese.

Cade. I have thought upon it, it shall be so. Away, burn all the records of the realm: my mouth shall be the parliament of England.

Holl. [*Aside*] Then we are like to have biting statutes, unless his teeth be pulled out.

Cade. And henceforward all things shall be in common.

Enter a Messenger.

Mess. My lord, a prize, a prize! here 's the Lord Say, which sold the towns in France; he that made us pay one and twenty fifteens, and one shilling to the pound, the last subsidy.

Enter GEORGE [BEVIS], *with the* LORD SAY.

Cade. Well, he shall be beheaded for it ten times. Ah, thou say, thou serge, nay, thou buckram lord! now art thou within point-blank of our jurisdiction regal. What canst thou answer to my majesty for giving up of Normandy unto Mounsieur Basimecu, the dauphin of France? Be it known unto thee by these presence, even the presence of Lord Mortimer, that I am the besom that must sweep the court clean of such filth as thou art. Thou hast most traitorously corrupted the youth of the realm in erecting a grammar school: and whereas, before, our forefathers had no other books but the score and the tally, thou hast caused printing to be used, and, contrary to the king, his crown and dignity, thou hast built a paper-mill. It will be proved to thy face that thou hast men about thee that usually talk of a noun and a verb, and such abominable words as no Christian ear can endure to hear. Thou hast appointed justices of peace, to call poor men before them about matters they were not able to answer. Moreover, thou hast put them in prison; and because they could not read, thou hast hanged them; when, indeed, only for that cause they have been most worthy to live. Thou dost ride in a foot-cloth, dost thou not?

Say. What of that?

Cade. Marry, thou oughtest not to let thy horse wear a cloak, when honester men than thou go in their hose and doublets.

Dick. And work in their shirt too; as myself, for example, that am a butcher.

Say. You men of Kent,—

Dick. What say you of Kent?

Say. Nothing but this; 'tis 'bona terra, mala gens.'

Cade. Away with him, away with him! he speaks Latin.

Say. Hear me but speak, and bear me where you will.
Kent, in the Commentaries Cæsar writ,
Is term'd the civil'st place of all this isle:
Sweet is the country, because full of riches;
The people liberal, valiant, active, wealthy;
Which makes me hope you are not void of pity.
I sold not Maine, I lost not Normandy,
Yet, to recover them, would lose my life.
Justice with favour have I always done;
Prayers and tears have mov'd me, gifts could never.
When have I aught exacted at your hands,
But to maintain the king, the realm and you?
Large gifts have I bestow'd on learned clerks,
Because my book preferr'd me to the king,
And seeing ignorance is the curse of God,
Knowledge the wing wherewith we fly to heaven,
Unless you be possess'd with devilish spirits,
You cannot but forbear to murder me:
This tongue hath parley'd unto foreign kings
For your behoof,—

Cade. Tut, when struck'st thou one blow in the field?

Say. Great men have reaching hands: oft have I struck
Those that I never saw and struck them dead.

Geo. O monstrous coward! what, to come behind folks?

Say. These cheeks are pale for watching for your good.

Cade. Give him a box o' the ear and that will make 'em red again.

Say. Long sitting to determine poor men's causes
Hath made me full of sickness and diseases.

Cade. Ye shall have a hempen caudle then and the help of hatchet.

Dick. Why dost thou quiver, man?

Say. The palsy, and not fear, provokes me.

Cade. Nay, he nods at us, as who should say, I'll be even with you: I'll see if his head will stand steadier on a pole, or no. Take him away, and behead him.

Say. Tell me wherein have I offended most?
Have I affected wealth or honour? speak.
Are my chests fill'd up with extorted gold?
Is my apparel sumptuous to behold?
Whom have I injur'd, that ye seek my death?
These hands are free from guiltless blood-shedding,

crown. 2. **the Savoy.** This palace, residence of the duke of Lancaster, was destroyed during Wat Tyler's rebellion in 1381. 23. **Lord Say.** Cf. IV, ii, 169-170, note. 24. **one . . . fifteens,** probably a reference to the matter that had been discussed more conservatively by the courtiers; cf. I, i, 131-134. 27, 28. **say, serge, buckram,** kinds of cloth. 31. **Mounsieur Basimecu,** "baiser-mon-cul," kiss my arse. 34. **besom,** broom. 39. **printing,** an anachronism; the first printing press was set up in England twenty-seven years after Cade's rebellion. 51. **foot-cloth.** See IV, i, 54. 61. **'bona . . . gens,'** good land, bad people. 68. **liberal,** refined, having the characteristics of gentlemen; see glossary. 77. **book,** learning. 95. **caudle,** warm gruel mixed with wine or ale, sweetened and spiced, given to sick people. The implication of the word *hempen* is that his remedy will be hanging.

This breast from harbouring foul deceitful thoughts.
O, let me live!

Cade. [*Aside*] I feel remorse in myself with his words; but I'll bridle it: he shall die, an it be for pleading so well for his life. Away with him! he has a familiar under his tongue; he speaks not a God's name. Go, take him away, I say, and strike off his head presently; and then break into his son-in-law's house, Sir James Cromer, and strike off his head, and bring them both upon two poles hither.

All. It shall be done.

Say. Ah, countrymen! if when you make your pray'rs,
God should be so obdurate as yourselves,
How would it fare with your departed souls?
And therefore yet relent, and save my life.

Cade. Away with him! and do as I command ye.
[*Exeunt some with Lord Say.*]
The proudest peer in the realm shall not wear a head on his shoulders, unless he pay me tribute; there shall not a maid be married, but she shall pay to me her maidenhead ere they have it: men shall hold of me in capite; and we charge and command that their wives be as free as heart can wish or tongue can tell.

Dick. My lord, when shall we go to Cheapside and take up commodities upon our bills?

Cade. Marry, presently.

All. O, brave!

Enter one with the heads.

Cade. But is not this braver? Let them kiss one another, for they loved well when they were alive. Now part them again, lest they consult about the giving up of some more towns in France. Soldiers, defer the spoil of the city until night: for with these borne before us, instead of maces, will we ride through the streets; and at every corner have them kiss. Away!
Exeunt.

[SCENE VIII. *Southwark.*]

Alarum and retreat. Enter again CADE *and all his rabblement.*

Cade. Up Fish Street! down Saint Magnus' Corner! kill and knock down! throw them into Thames! *(Sound a parley.)* What noise is this I hear? Dare any be so bold to sound retreat or parley, when I command them kill?

Enter BUCKINGHAM *and old* CLIFFORD [*attended*].

Buck. Ay, here they be that dare and will disturb thee:
Know, Cade, we come ambassadors from the king
Unto the commons whom thou hast misled;
And here pronounce free pardon to them all
That will forsake thee and go home in peace.

Clif. What say ye, countrymen? will ye relent,
And yield to mercy whilst 'tis offered you;
Or let a rebel lead you to your deaths?
Who loves the king and will embrace his pardon,
Fling up his cap, and say 'God save his majesty!'
Who hateth him and honours not his father,
Henry the Fifth, that made all France to quake,
Shake he his weapon at us and pass by.

All. God save the king! God save the king!

Cade. What, Buckingham and Clifford, are ye so brave? And you, base peasants, do ye believe him? will you needs be hanged with your pardons about your necks? Hath my sword therefore broke through London gates, that you should leave me at the White Hart in Southwark? I thought ye would never have given out these arms till you had recovered your ancient freedom: but you are all recreants and dastards, and delight to live in slavery to the nobility. Let them break your backs with burthens, take your houses over your heads, ravish your wives and daughters before your faces: for me, I will make shift for one; and so, God's curse light upon you all!

All. We'll follow Cade, we'll follow Cade!

Clif. Is Cade the son of Henry the Fifth,
That thus you do exclaim you'll go with him?
Will he conduct you through the heart of France,
And make the meanest of you earls and dukes?
Alas, he hath no home, no place to fly to;
Nor knows he how to live but by the spoil,
Unless by robbing of your friends and us.
Were 't not a shame, that whilst you live at jar,
The fearful French, whom you late vanquished,
Should make a start o'er seas and vanquish you?
Methinks already in this civil broil
I see them lording it in London streets,
Crying 'Villiago!' unto all they meet.
Better ten thousand base-born Cades miscarry
Than you should stoop unto a Frenchman's mercy.
To France, to France, and get what you have lost;
Spare England, for it is your native coast:
Henry hath money, you are strong and manly;
God on our side, doubt not of victory.

All. A Clifford! a Clifford! we'll follow the king and Clifford.

Cade. Was ever feather so lightly blown to and fro as this multitude? The name of Henry the Fifth hales them to an hundred mischiefs and makes them leave me desolate. I see them lay their heads together to surprise me. My sword make way for me, for here is no staying. In despite of the devils and hell, have through the very middest of you! and heavens and honour be witness that no want of resolution in me, but only my followers' base and ignominious treasons, makes me betake me to my heels. *Exit.*

Buck. What, is he fled? Go some, and follow him;
And he that brings his head unto the king
Shall have a thousand crowns for his reward.
Exeunt some of them.
Follow me, soldiers: we'll devise a mean
To reconcile you all unto the king. *Exeunt omnes.*

[SCENE IX. *Kenilworth Castle.*]

Sound trumpets. Enter KING, QUEEN, *and* SOMERSET, *on the terrace* [*aloft*].

King. Was ever king that joy'd an earthly throne,
And could command no more content than I?

114. **familiar,** familiar spirit; see glossary; cf. *1 Henry VI*, V, iii, 10. 131. **in capite,** legal term: as a tenant in chief, directly from the crown. 135. **bills,** military weapons having wooden handles and a blade or ax-shaped head, with quibble here on the meaning "credit." 137. **brave,** fine; see glossary. 142. **spoil,** plundering; see glossary. 144. **maces,** staves of office carried by sergeants.

SCENE VIII. 9. **free,** generous; see glossary. 28. **recreants,** cowardly wretches; see glossary. 32-33. **make shift,** manage; see *shift* in glossary. 43. **jar,** discord. 48. **'Villiago,'** villain. 55. **A Clifford,** a battle cry. 61. **surprise,** capture. 63-64. **have through . . . you,** may I go through

No sooner was I crept out of my cradle
But I was made a king, at nine months old.
Was never subject long'd to be a king
As I do long and wish to be a subject.

Enter BUCKINGHAM *and* [*old*] CLIFFORD.

Buck. Health and glad tidings to your majesty!
King. Why, Buckingham, is the traitor Cade
surpris'd?
Or is he but retir'd to make him strong?

Enter [*below*] *multitudes, with halters about their necks.*

Clif. He is fled, my lord, and all his powers do yield;
And humbly thus, with halters on their necks,
Expect your highness' doom, of life or death.
King. Then, heaven, set ope thy everlasting gates,
To entertain my vows of thanks and praise!
Soldiers, this day have you redeem'd your lives
And show'd how well you love your prince and
country:
Continue still in this so good a mind,
And Henry, though he be infortunate,
Assure yourselves, will never be unkind:
And so, with thanks and pardon to you all,
I do dismiss you to your several countries.
All. God save the king! God save the king!

Enter a Messenger.

Mess. Please it your grace to be advertised
The Duke of York is newly come from Ireland,
And with a puissant and a mighty power
Of gallowglasses and stout kerns
Is marching hitherward in proud array,
And still proclaimeth, as he comes along,
His arms are only to remove from thee
The Duke of Somerset, whom he terms a traitor.
King. Thus stands my state, 'twixt Cade and York
distress'd;
Like to a ship that, having 'scap'd a tempest,
Is straightway calm'd and boarded with a pirate:
But now is Cade driven back, his men dispers'd;
And now is York in arms to second him.
I pray thee, Buckingham, go and meet him,
And ask him what 's the reason of these arms.
Tell him I'll send Duke Edmund to the Tower;
And, Somerset, we will commit thee thither,
Until his army be dismiss'd from him.
Som. My lord,
I'll yield myself to prison willingly,
Or unto death, to do my country good.
King. In any case, be not too rough in terms;
For he is fierce and cannot brook hard language.
Buck. I will, my lord; and doubt not so to deal
As all things shall redound unto your good.
King. Come, wife, let 's in, and learn to govern
better;
For yet may England curse my wretched reign.
Flourish. Exeunt.

[SCENE X. *Kent. Iden's garden.*]

Enter CADE.

Cade. Fie on ambition! fie on myself, that have a sword, and yet am ready to famish! These five days have I hid me in these woods and durst not peep out, for all the country is laid for me; but now am I so hungry that if I might have a lease of my life for a thousand years I could stay no longer. Wherefore, on a brick wall have I climbed into this garden, to see if I can eat grass, or pick a sallet another while, which is not amiss to cool a man's stomach this hot weather. And I think this word 'sallet' was born to do me good: for many a time, but for a sallet, my brain-pan had been cleft with a brown bill; and many a time, when I have been dry and bravely marching, it hath served me instead of a quart pot to drink in; and now the word 'sallet' must serve me to feed on.

Enter IDEN.

Iden. Lord, who would live turmoiled in the court,
And may enjoy such quiet walks as these?
This small inheritance my father left me
Contenteth me, and worth a monarchy.
I seek not to wax great by others' waning,
Or gather wealth, I care not, with what envy:
Sufficeth that I have maintains my state
And sends the poor well pleased from my gate.

Cade. Here 's the lord of the soil come to seize me for a stray, for entering his fee-simple without leave. Ah, villain, thou wilt betray me, and get a thousand crowns of the king by carrying my head to him: but I'll make thee eat iron like an ostrich, and swallow my sword like a great pin, ere thou and I part.

Iden. Why, rude companion, whatsoe'er thou be,
I know thee not; why, then, should I betray thee?
Is 't not enough to break into my garden,
And, like a thief, to come to rob my grounds,
Climbing my walls in spite of me the owner,
But thou wilt brave me with these saucy terms?

Cade. Brave thee! ay, by the best blood that ever was broached, and beard thee too. Look on me well: I have eat no meat these five days; yet, come thou and thy five men, and if I do not leave you all as dead as a doornail, I pray God I may never eat grass more.

Iden. Nay, it shall ne'er be said, while England
stands,
That Alexander Iden, an esquire of Kent,
Took odds to combat a poor famish'd man.
Oppose thy steadfast-gazing eyes to mine,
See if thou canst outface me with thy looks:
Set limb to limb, and thou art far the lesser;
Thy hand is but a finger to my fist,
Thy leg a stick compared with this truncheon;
My foot shall fight with all the strength thou hast;
And if mine arm be heaved in the air,
Thy grave is digg'd already in the earth.
As for words, whose greatness answers words,
Let this my sword report what speech forbears.

Cade. By my valour, the most complete champion that ever I heard! Steel, if thou turn the edge, or cut not out the burly-boned clown in chines of beef ere thou sleep in thy sheath, I beseech God on my knees thou mayst be turned to hobnails.

Here they fight. [*Cade falls.*]

the very midst of you. 71. **mean,** means, method; see glossary.
SCENE IX. 14. **entertain,** receive; see glossary. 26. **gallowglasses,** soldiers or retainers formerly maintained by Irish chieftains.
SCENE X. 9. **sallet,** a light helmet; a "salad" (used quibblingly). 24. **that,** that which. 27. **fee-simple,** estate belonging to an owner and his heirs forever. 33. **companion,** fellow (used contemptuously); see glossary. 38. **brave,** defy; see glossary. 40. **broached,** tapped, as a cask (used figuratively). 52. **truncheon,** heavy staff; i.e., Iden's leg. 58. **complete,** accomplished; see glossary.

O, I am slain! famine and no other hath slain me: let ten thousand devils come against me, and give me but the ten meals I have lost, and I 'ld defy them all. Wither, garden; and be henceforth a burying-place to all that do dwell in this house, because the unconquered soul of Cade is fled.

Iden. Is 't Cade that I have slain, that monstrous traitor?
Sword, I will hallow thee for this thy deed,
And hang thee o'er my tomb when I am dead:
Ne'er shall this blood be wiped from thy point;
But thou shalt wear it as a herald's coat,
To emblaze the honour that thy master got.

Cade. Iden, farewell, and be proud of thy victory. Tell Kent from me, she hath lost her best man, and exhort all the world to be cowards; for I, that never feared any, am vanquished by famine, not by valour. *Dies.*

Iden. How much thou wrong'st me, heaven be my judge.
Die, damned wretch, the curse of her that bare thee;
And as I thrust thy body in with my sword,
So wish I, I might thrust thy soul to hell.
Hence will I drag thee headlong by the heels
Unto a dunghill which shall be thy grave,
And there cut off thy most ungracious head;
Which I will bear in triumph to the king,
Leaving thy trunk for crows to feed upon. *Exit.*

[ACT V.

SCENE I. *Fields between Dartford and Blackheath.*]

Enter YORK, *and his army of Irish, with drum and colours.*

York. From Ireland thus comes York to claim his right,
And pluck the crown from feeble Henry's head:
Ring, bells, aloud; burn, bonfires, clear and bright,
To entertain great England's lawful king.
Ah! sancta majestas, who would not buy thee dear?
Let them obey that know not how to rule;
This hand was made to handle nought but gold.
I cannot give due action to my words,
Except a sword or sceptre balance it:
A sceptre shall it have, have I a soul,
On which I'll toss the flower-de-luce of France.

Enter BUCKINGHAM.

Whom have we here? Buckingham, to disturb me?
The king hath sent him, sure: I must dissemble.

Buck. York, if thou meanest well, I greet thee well.

York. Humphrey of Buckingham, I accept thy greeting.
Art thou a messenger, or come of pleasure?

Buck. A messenger from Henry, our dread liege,
To know the reason of these arms in peace;
Or why thou, being a subject as I am,
Against thy oath and true allegiance sworn,
Should raise so great a power without his leave,
Or dare to bring thy force so near the court.

York. [*Aside*] Scarce can I speak, my choler is so great:
O, I could hew up rocks and fight with flint,
I am so angry at these abject terms;
And now, like Ajax Telamonius,
On sheep or oxen could I spend my fury.
I am far better born than is the king,
More like a king, more kingly in my thoughts:
But I must make fair weather yet a while,
Till Henry be more weak and I more strong.—
Buckingham, I prithee, pardon me,
That I have given no answer all this while;
My mind was troubled with deep melancholy.
The cause why I have brought this army hither
Is to remove proud Somerset from the king,
Seditious to his grace and to the state.

Buck. That is too much presumption on thy part:
But if thy arms be to no other end,
The king hath yielded unto thy demand:
The Duke of Somerset is in the Tower.

York. Upon thine honour, is he prisoner?

Buck. Upon mine honour, he is prisoner.

York. Then, Buckingham, I do dismiss my pow'rs.
Soldiers, I thank you all; disperse yourselves;
Meet me to-morrow in Saint George's field,
You shall have pay and every thing you wish.
And let my sovereign, virtuous Henry,
Command my eldest son, nay, all my sons,
As pledges of my fealty and love;
I'll send them all as willing as I live:
Lands, goods, horse, armour, any thing I have,
Is his to use, so Somerset may die.

Buck. York, I commend this kind submission:
We twain will go into his highness' tent.

Enter KING *and* Attendants.

King. Buckingham, doth York intend no harm to us,
That thus he marcheth with thee arm in arm?

York. In all submission and humility
York doth present himself unto your highness.

King. Then what intends these forces thou dost bring?

York. To heave the traitor Somerset from hence,
And fight against that monstrous rebel Cade,
Who since I heard to be discomfited.

Enter IDEN, *with* CADE'S *head.*

Iden. If one so rude and of so mean condition
May pass into the presence of a king,
Lo, I present your grace a traitor's head,
The head of Cade, whom I in combat slew.

King. The head of Cade! Great God, how just art Thou!
O, let me view his visage, being dead,
That living wrought me such exceeding trouble.
Tell me, my friend, art thou the man that slew him?

Iden. I was, an 't like your majesty.

King. How art thou call'd? and what is thy degree?

Iden. Alexander Iden, that 's my name;
A poor esquire of Kent, that loves his king.

ACT V. SCENE I. 4. **England's lawful king.** York's claims are rehearsed by the dying Mortimer in *1 Henry VI*, II, v, 63-97, and again by York himself in *2 Henry VI*, II, ii, 9-52. 5. **sancta majestas,** sacred majesty. 10. **have I a soul,** i.e., as I have a soul. 11. **toss,** carry aloft on the point of a pike. 13. **dissemble,** assume a false appearance. 25. **abject,** degrading. 26. **Ajax Telamonius,** Ajax, son of Telamon, one of the Greek heroes of the Trojan War. When the weapons of Achilles were allotted to Ulysses, Ajax in his fury slaughtered a flock of sheep. 64. **condition,** rank; see glossary. 98. **awful,** awe-inspiring. 100. **Achilles' spear.** Telephus, wounded by Achilles' spear, learned from an oracle that he could be cured only by the wounder. He was eventually cured by an application of rust from the point of the spear. 117.

Buck. So please it you, my lord, 'twere not amiss
He were created knight for his good service.
King. Iden, kneel down. [*He kneels.*] Rise up a knight.
We give thee for reward a thousand marks,
And will that thou henceforth attend on us.
Iden. May Iden live to merit such a bounty,
And never live but true unto his liege! [*Rises.*]

Enter QUEEN *and* SOMERSET.

King. See, Buckingham, Somerset comes with the queen:
Go, bid her hide him quickly from the duke.
Queen. For thousand Yorks he shall not hide his head,
But boldly stand and front him to his face.
York. How now! is Somerset at liberty?
Then, York, unloose thy long-imprisoned thoughts,
And let thy tongue be equal with thy heart.
Shall I endure the sight of Somerset?
False king! why hast thou broken faith with me,
Knowing how hardly I can brook abuse?
King did I call thee? no, thou art not king,
Not fit to govern and rule multitudes,
Which dar'st not, no, nor canst not rule a traitor.
That head of thine doth not become a crown;
Thy hand is made to grasp a palmer's staff,
And not to grace an awful princely sceptre.
That gold must round engirt these brows of mine,
Whose smile and frown, like to Achilles' spear,
Is able with the change to kill and cure.
Here is a hand to hold a sceptre up
And with the same to act controlling laws.
Give place: by heaven, thou shalt rule no more
O'er him whom heaven created for thy ruler.
Som. O monstrous traitor! I arrest thee, York,
Of capital treason 'gainst the king and crown:
Obey, audacious traitor; kneel for grace.
York. Wouldst have me kneel? first let me ask of these,
If they can brook I bow a knee to man.
Sirrah, call in my sons to be my bail: [*Exit Attendant.*]
I know, ere they will have me go to ward,
They'll pawn their swords for my enfranchisement.
Queen. Call hither Clifford; bid him come amain,
To say if that the bastard boys of York
Shall be the surety for their traitor father.
[*Exit Attendant.*]
York. O blood-bespotted Neapolitan,
Outcast of Naples, England's bloody scourge!
The sons of York, thy betters in their birth,
Shall be their father's bail; and bane to those
That for my surety will refuse the boys!

Enter EDWARD *and* RICHARD.

See where they come: I'll warrant they'll make it good.

Enter [*old*] CLIFFORD [*and his* Son].

Queen. And here comes Clifford to deny their bail.
Clif. Health and all happiness to my lord the king!
[*Kneels.*]
York. I thank thee, Clifford: say, what news with thee?
Nay, do not fright us with an angry look:
We are thy sovereign, Clifford, kneel again;
For thy mistaking so, we pardon thee.
Clif. This is my king, York, I do not mistake;
But thou mistakes me much to think I do:
To Bedlam with him! is the man grown mad?
King. Ay, Clifford; a bedlam and ambitious humour
Makes him oppose himself against his king.
Clif. He is a traitor; let him to the Tower,
And chop away that factious pate of his.
Queen. He is arrested, but will not obey;
His sons, he says, shall give their words for him.
York. Will you not, sons?
Edw. Ay, noble father, if our words will serve.
Rich. And if words will not, then our weapons shall.
Clif. Why, what a brood of traitors have we here!
York. Look in a glass, and call thy image so:
I am thy king, and thou a false-heart traitor.
Call hither to the stake my two brave bears,
That with the very shaking of their chains
They may astonish these fell-lurking curs:
Bid Salisbury and Warwick come to me.

Enter the EARLS OF WARWICK *and* SALISBURY.

Clif. Are these thy bears? we'll bait thy bears to death,
And manacle the bear 'ard in their chains,
If thou dar'st bring them to the baiting place.
Rich. Oft have I seen a hot o'erweening cur
Run back and bite, because he was withheld;
Who, being suffer'd with the bear's fell paw,
Hath clapp'd his tail between his legs and cried:
And such a piece of service will you do,
If you oppose yourselves to match Lord Warwick.
Clif. Hence, heap of wrath, foul indigested lump,
As crooked in thy manners as thy shape!
York. Nay, we shall heat you thoroughly anon.
Clif. Take heed, lest by your heat you burn yourselves.
King. Why, Warwick, hath thy knee forgot to bow?
Old Salisbury, shame to thy silver hair,
Thou mad misleader of thy brain-sick son!
What, wilt thou on thy death-bed play the ruffian,
And seek for sorrow with thy spectacles?
O, where is faith? O, where is loyalty?
If it be banish'd from the frosty head,
Where shall it find a harbour in the earth?
Wilt thou go dig a grave to find out war,
And shame thine honourable age with blood?
Why art thou old, and want'st experience?
Or wherefore dost abuse it, if thou hast it?
For shame! in duty bend thy knee to me
That bows unto the grave with mickle age.
Sal. My lord, I have considered with myself
The title of this most renowned duke;
And in my conscience do repute his grace

Neapolitan. The queen's father was titular king of Naples. 123. **deny,** refuse; see glossary. 131. **Bedlam,** hospital of St. Mary of Bethlehem in London, used as an asylum for the mentally deranged. The common noun in the next line means an inmate of Bedlam, or an insane person. 144. **brave bears.** Cf. lines 202-203 below, where Warwick describes the badge of his house. The passage here is a metaphor from the popular Elizabethan sport of bearbaiting. 146. **fell-lurking,** treacherous. 149. **bear 'ard,** bearkeeper. 153. **being suffer'd,** having been injured. 157. **indigested,** ill-formed. 158. **As . . . shape.** Young Richard, later King Richard III, was a hunchback. References to his deformity grow more and more pointed as this cycle of plays proceeds. 159. **anon,** soon; see glossary. 172. **abuse,** put to a bad use; see glossary.

The rightful heir to England's royal seat.
King. Hast thou not sworn allegiance unto me?
Sal. I have.
King. Canst thou dispense with heaven for such an oath?
Sal. It is great sin to swear unto a sin,
But greater sin to keep a sinful oath.
Who can be bound by any solemn vow
To do a murd'rous deed, to rob a man,
To force a spotless virgin's chastity,
To reave the orphan of his patrimony,
To wring the widow from her custom'd right,
And have no other reason for this wrong
But that he was bound by a solemn oath?
Queen. A subtle traitor needs no sophister.
King. Call Buckingham, and bid him arm himself.
York. Call Buckingham, and all the friends thou hast,
I am resolv'd for death or dignity.
Clif. The first I warrant thee, if dreams prove true.
War. You were best to go to bed and dream again,
To keep thee from the tempest of the field.
Clif. I am resolv'd to bear a greater storm
Than any thou canst conjure up to-day;
And that I'll write upon thy burgonet,
Might I but know thee by thy household badge.
War. Now, by my father's badge, old Nevil's crest,
The rampant bear chain'd to the ragged staff,
This day I'll wear aloft my burgonet,
As on a mountain top the cedar shows
That keeps his leaves in spite of any storm,
Even to affright thee with the view thereof.
Clif. And from thy burgonet I'll rend thy bear
And tread it under foot with all contempt,
Despite the bear 'ard that protects the bear.
Y. Clif. And so to arms, victorious father,
To quell the rebels and their complices.
Rich. Fie! charity, for shame! speak not in spite,
For you shall sup with Jesu Christ to-night.
Y. Clif. Foul stigmatic, that 's more than thou canst tell.
Rich. If not in heaven, you'll surely sup in hell.
Exeunt [*severally*].

[SCENE II. *Saint Alban's.*]

[*Alarums to the battle.*] *Enter* WARWICK.

War. Clifford of Cumberland, 'tis Warwick calls:
And if thou dost not hide thee from the bear,
Now, when the angry trumpet sounds alarum
And dead men's cries do fill the empty air,
Clifford, I say, come forth and fight with me:
Proud northern lord, Clifford of Cumberland,
Warwick is hoarse with calling thee to arms.

Enter YORK.

How now, my noble lord! what, all afoot?
York. The deadly-handed Clifford slew my steed,
But match to match I have encount'red him
And made a prey for carrion kites and crows
Even of the bonny beast he lov'd so well.

Enter [*old*] CLIFFORD.

War. Of one or both of us the time is come.
York. Hold, Warwick, seek thee out some other chase,
For I myself must hunt this deer to death.
War. Then, nobly, York; 'tis for a crown thou fight'st.
As I intend, Clifford, to thrive to-day,
It grieves my soul to leave thee unassail'd. *Exit War.*
Clif. What seest thou in me, York? why dost thou pause?
York. With thy brave bearing should I be in love,
But that thou art so fast mine enemy.
Clif. Nor should thy prowess want praise and esteem,
But that 'tis shown ignobly and in treason.
York. So let it help me now against thy sword
As I in justice and true right express it.
Clif. My soul and body on the action both!
York. A dreadful lay! Address thee instantly.
[*They fight, and Clifford falls.*]
Clif. La fin couronne les œuvres. [*Dies.*]
York. Thus war hath given thee peace, for thou art still.
Peace with his soul, heaven, if it be thy will! [*Exit.*]

Enter young CLIFFORD.

Y. Clif. Shame and confusion! all is on the rout;
Fear frames disorder, and disorder wounds
Where it should guard. O war, thou son of hell,
Whom angry heavens do make their minister,
Throw in the frozen bosoms of our part
Hot coals of vengeance! Let no soldier fly.
He that is truly dedicate to war
Hath no self-love, nor he that loves himself
Hath not essentially but by circumstance
The name of valour. [*Seeing his dead father*] O, let the vile world end,
And the premised flames of the last day
Knit earth and heaven together!
Now let the general trumpet blow his blast,
Particularities and petty sounds
To cease! Wast thou ordain'd, dear father,
To lose thy youth in peace, and to achieve
The silver livery of advised age,
And, in thy reverence and thy chair-days, thus
To die in ruffian battle? Even at this sight
My heart is turn'd to stone: and while 'tis mine,
It shall be stony. York not our old men spares;
No more will I their babes: tears virginal
Shall be to me even as the dew to fire,
And beauty that the tyrant oft reclaims
Shall to my flaming wrath be oil and flax.
Henceforth I will not have to do with pity:
Meet I an infant of the house of York,
Into as many gobbets will I cut it
As wild Medea young Absyrtus did:
In cruelty will I seek out my fame.
Come, thou new ruin of old Clifford's house:

182-190. **It is great sin,** etc. A parallel to this kind of casuistry occurs in *King John*, III, i, 268-273. 191. **sophister,** cunning or caviling disputer (Cotgrave). 200. **burgonet,** light casque or steel cap. 215. **stigmatic,** one branded with the mark of his crime.

SCENE II. 21. **fast,** completely. 26. **action,** outcome of action. 27. **lay,** wager, oath. **Address thee,** prepare yourself. 28. **La fin . . . œuvres,** the end crowns the work. 32. **frames,** causes. 35. **part,** party, faction; see *party* in glossary. 39. **not . . . circumstance,** not by any virtue of his own, but accidentally. 41. **premised,** foreordained. 44. **Particularities,** individual affairs. 48. **chair-days,** old age, days of inactivity. 54. **reclaims,** reduces to obedience. 59. **Medea,** daughter of Aeëtes, king of Colchis, who helped Jason recover the Golden Fleece. She fled with him and, to delay her father's pursuit, killed her brother Absyrtus and left his dismembered body in the father's path.

As did Æneas old Anchises bear,
So bear I thee upon my manly shoulders;
But then Æneas bare a living load,
Nothing so heavy as these woes of mine.
[*Exit, bearing off his father.*]

Enter RICHARD *and* SOMERSET *to fight.* [SOMERSET *is killed.*]

Rich. So, lie thou there;
For underneath an alehouse' paltry sign,
The Castle in Saint Alban's, Somerset
Hath made the wizard famous in his death.
Sword, hold thy temper; heart, be wrathful still:
Priests pray for enemies, but princes kill. [*Exit.*]

Fight: excursions. Enter KING, QUEEN, *and others.*

Queen. Away, my lord! you are slow; for shame, away!
King. Can we outrun the heavens? good Margaret, stay.
Queen. What are you made of? you'll nor fight nor fly:
Now is it manhood, wisdom and defence,
To give the enemy way, and to secure us
By what we can, which can no more but fly.
Alarum afar off.
If you be ta'en, we then should see the bottom
Of all our fortunes: but if we haply scape,
As well we may, if not through your neglect,
We shall to London get, where you are lov'd
And where this breach now in our fortunes made
May readily be stopp'd.

Enter [*young*] CLIFFORD.

Y. Clif. But that my heart 's on future mischief set,
I would speak blasphemy ere bid you fly:
But fly you must; uncurable discomfit
Reigns in the hearts of all our present parts.
Away, for your relief! and we will live
To see their day and them our fortune give:
Away, my lord, away! *Exeunt.*

[SCENE III. *Fields near St. Alban's.*]

Alarum. Retreat. Enter YORK, RICHARD, WARWICK, *and* Soldiers, *with drum and colours.*

York. Of Salisbury, who can report of him,
That winter lion, who in rage forgets
Aged contusions and all brush of time,
And, like a gallant in the brow of youth,
Repairs him with occasion? This happy day
Is not itself, nor have we won one foot,
If Salisbury be lost.
Rich. My noble father,
Three times to-day I holp him to his horse,
Three times bestrid him; thrice I led him off,
Persuaded him from any further act:
But still, where danger was, still there I met him;
And like rich hangings in a homely house,
So was his will in his old feeble body.
But, noble as he is, look where he comes.

Enter SALISBURY.

Sal. Now, by my sword, well hast thou fought to-day;
By th' mass, so did we all. I thank you, Richard:
God knows how long it is I have to live;
And it hath pleas'd him that three times to-day
You have defended me from imminent death.
Well, lords, we have not got that which we have:
'Tis not enough our foes are this time fled,
Being opposites of such repairing nature.
York. I know our safety is to follow them;
For, as I hear, the king is fled to London,
To call a present court of parliament.
Let us pursue him ere the writs go forth.
What says Lord Warwick? shall we after them?
War. After them! nay, before them, if we can.
Now, by my faith, lords, 'twas a glorious day:
Saint Alban's battle won by famous York
Shall be eterniz'd in all age to come.
Sound drum and trumpets, and to London all:
And more such days as these to us befall! *Exeunt.*

62. **Æneas, Anchises.** Aeneas, fleeing from Troy, carried his aged father on his shoulders; cf. *Julius Caesar*, I, ii, 112-114. 64. **bare,** bore; archaic past tense. 65. **Nothing,** not at all; see glossary. 67-69. **underneath . . . death.** Cf. I, iv, 38-40. 87. **our present parts,** those now adhering to our party.

SCENE III. 5. **Repairs . . . occasion,** i.e., opportunity stimulates him so that his strength is renewed. 8. **holp,** helped; see glossary. 22. **opposites,** adversaries. **repairing,** that recover easily. 25. **present,** instant; see glossary. 26. **the writs,** official summons issued by the king to members of Parliament.

THE THIRD PART OF KING HENRY THE SIXTH

[*Dramatis Personae*

KING HENRY the Sixth.
EDWARD, PRINCE OF WALES, *his son.*
LEWIS XI. KING OF FRANCE.
DUKE OF SOMERSET.
DUKE OF EXETER.
EARL OF OXFORD.
EARL OF NORTHUMBERLAND.
EARL OF WESTMORELAND.
LORD CLIFFORD.
RICHARD PLANTAGENET, *Duke of York.*
EDWARD, Earl of March, *afterwards* King Edward IV., } *his sons.*
EDMUND, Earl of Rutland, } *his sons.*
GEORGE, *afterwards* Duke of Clarence, } *his sons.*
RICHARD, *afterwards* Duke of Gloucester, } *his sons.*
DUKE OF NORFOLK.
MARQUESS OF MONTAGUE.
EARL OF WARWICK.
EARL OF PEMBROKE.
LORD HASTINGS.
LORD STAFFORD.
SIR JOHN MORTIMER, } *uncles to the Duke of York.*
SIR HUGH MORTIMER, } *uncles to the Duke of York.*
HENRY, Earl of Richmond, *a youth.*
LORD RIVERS, *brother to Lady Grey.*
SIR WILLIAM STANLEY.
SIR JOHN MONTGOMERY.
SIR JOHN SOMERVILLE.
Tutor to Rutland. Mayor of York.
Lieutenant of the Tower. A Nobleman.
Two Keepers. A Huntsman.
A Son that has killed his father.
A Father that has killed his son.

QUEEN MARGARET.
LADY GREY, *afterwards queen to Edward IV.*
BONA, *sister to the French queen.*

Soldiers, Attendants, Messengers, Watchmen, *&c.*

SCENE: *England and France.*]

ACT I.

SCENE I. [*London. The Parliament-house.*]

Alarum. Enter [RICHARD] PLANTAGENET [DUKE OF YORK], EDWARD, RICHARD, NORFOLK, MONTAGUE, WARWICK, *and soldiers.*

War. I wonder how the king escap'd our hands.
York. While we pursu'd the horsemen of the north,
He slily stole away and left his men:
Whereat the great Lord of Northumberland,
Whose warlike ears could never brook retreat,
Cheer'd up the drooping army; and himself,
Lord Clifford and Lord Stafford, all abreast,
Charg'd our main battle's front, and breaking in
Were by the swords of common soldiers slain.
Edw. Lord Stafford's father, Duke of Buckingham,
Is either slain or wounded dangerously;
I cleft his beaver with a downright blow:
That this is true, father, behold his blood.
Mont. And, brother, here 's the Earl of Wiltshire's blood,
Whom I encount'red as the battles join'd.
Rich. Speak thou for me and tell them what I did.
[*Throwing down the Duke of Somerset's head.*]
York. Richard hath best deserv'd of all my sons.
But is your grace dead, my Lord of Somerset?
Norf. Such hope have all the line of John of Gaunt!
Rich. Thus do I hope to shake King Henry's head.
War. And so do I. Victorious Prince of York,
Before I see thee seated in that throne
Which now the house of Lancaster usurps,
I vow by heaven these eyes shall never close.
This is the palace of the fearful king,
And this the regal seat: possess it, York;
For this is thine and not King Henry's heirs'.
York. Assist me, then, sweet Warwick, and I will;
For hither we have broken in by force.
Norf. We'll all assist you; he that flies shall die.
York. Thanks, gentle Norfolk: stay by me, my lords;
And, soldiers, stay and lodge by me this night.
They go up [*to the chair of state*].
War. And when the king comes, offer him no violence,
Unless he seek to thrust you out perforce.
York. The queen this day here holds her parliament,
But little thinks we shall be of her council:
By words or blows here let us win our right.
Rich. Arm'd as we are, let 's stay within this house.
War. The bloody parliament shall this be call'd,
Unless Plantagenet, Duke of York, be king,
And bashful Henry depos'd, whose cowardice
Hath made us by-words to our enemies.
York. Then leave me not, my lords; be resolute;
I mean to take possession of my right.
War. Neither the king, nor he that loves him best,
The proudest he that holds up Lancaster,
Dares stir a wing, if Warwick shake his bells.
I'll plant Plantagenet, root him up who dares:
Resolve thee, Richard; claim the English crown.

Flourish. Enter KING HENRY, CLIFFORD, NORTHUMBERLAND, WESTMORELAND, EXETER, *and the rest.*

K. Hen. My lords, look where the sturdy rebel sits,
Even in the chair of state: belike he means,
Back'd by the power of Warwick, that false peer,
To aspire unto the crown and reign as king.
Earl of Northumberland, he slew thy father,
And thine, Lord Clifford; and you both have vow'd revenge

ACT I. SCENE I. 4, 7. **Lord of Northumberland, Lord Clifford, Lord Stafford.** There are some historical discrepancies here. Northumberland, Stafford, and Clifford (i.e., the Young Clifford of *2 Henry VI*) were killed at the Battle of Towton on Palm Sunday, 1461; but that battle is presented dramatically below (II, iii-vi; Clifford dies in scene vi). York's account here appears to be of the Battle of St. Albans, where Old Clifford was killed. As to the two Staffords, the one mentioned here (l. 7) was Sir Harry, a Lancastrian sympathizer and son of the duke of Buckingham. The Lord Stafford of this play is Sir Humphrey, a York partisan who was raised to the peerage by Edward IV after the attainder of Sir Harry Stafford for opposition to the Yorkists.

On him, his sons, his favourites and his friends.
North. If I be not, heavens be reveng'd on me!
Clif. The hope thereof makes Clifford mourn in steel.
West. What, shall we suffer this? let 's pluck him down:
My heart for anger burns; I cannot brook it.
K. Hen. Be patient, gentle Earl of Westmoreland.
Clif. Patience is for poltroons, such as he:
He durst not sit there, had your father liv'd.
My gracious lord, here in the parliament
Let us assail the family of York.
North. Well hast thou spoken, cousin: be it so.
K. Hen. Ah, know you not the city favours them,
And they have troops of soldiers at their beck?
Exe. But when the duke is slain, they'll quickly fly.
K. Hen. Far be the thought of this from Henry's heart,
To make a shambles of the parliament-house!
Cousin of Exeter, frowns, words and threats
Shall be the war that Henry means to use.
Thou factious Duke of York, descend my throne,
And kneel for grace and mercy at my feet;
I am thy sovereign.
York. I am thine.
Exe. For shame, come down: he made thee Duke of York.
York. It was my inheritance, as the earldom was.
Exe. Thy father was a traitor to the crown.
War. Exeter, thou art a traitor to the crown
In following this usurping Henry.
Clif. Whom should he follow but his natural king?
War. True, Clifford; and that 's Richard Duke of York.
K. Hen. And shall I stand, and thou sit in my throne?
York. It must and shall be so: content thyself.
War. Be Duke of Lancaster; let him be king.
West. He is both king and Duke of Lancaster;
And that the Lord of Westmoreland shall maintain.
War. And Warwick shall disprove it. You forget
That we are those which chas'd you from the field
And slew your fathers, and with colours spread
March'd through the city to the palace gates.
North. Yes, Warwick, I remember it to my grief;
And, by his soul, thou and thy house shall rue it.
West. Plantagenet, of thee and these thy sons,
Thy kinsmen and thy friends, I'll have more lives
Than drops of blood were in my father's veins.
Clif. Urge it no more; lest that, instead of words,
I send thee, Warwick, such a messenger
As shall revenge his death before I stir.
War. Poor Clifford! how I scorn his worthless threats!
York. Will you we show our title to the crown?
If not, our swords shall plead it in the field.
K. Hen. What title hast thou, traitor, to the crown?
Thy father was, as thou art, Duke of York;
Thy grandfather, Roger Mortimer, Earl of March:
I am the son of Henry the Fifth,
Who made the Dauphin and the French to stoop
And seiz'd upon their towns and provinces.
War. Talk not of France, sith thou hast lost it all.
K. Hen. The lord protector lost it, and not I:
When I was crown'd I was but nine months old.
Rich. You are old enough now, and yet, methinks, you lose.
Father, tear the crown from the usurper's head.
Edw. Sweet father, do so; set it on your head.
Mont. Good brother, as thou lov'st and honourest arms,
Let 's fight it out and not stand cavilling thus.
Rich. Sound drums and trumpets, and the king will fly.
York. Sons, peace!
K. Hen. Peace, thou! and give King Henry leave to speak.
War. Plantagenet shall speak first: hear him, lords;
And be you silent and attentive too,
For he that interrupts him shall not live.
K. Hen. Think'st thou that I will leave my kingly throne,
Wherein my grandsire and my father sat?
No: first shall war unpeople this my realm;
Ay, and their colours, often borne in France,
And now in England to our heart's great sorrow,
Shall be my winding-sheet. Why faint you, lords?
My title 's good, and better far than his.
War. Prove it, Henry, and thou shalt be king.
K. Hen. Henry the Fourth by conquest got the crown.
York. 'Twas by rebellion against his king.
K. Hen. [*Aside*] I know not what to say; my title 's weak.—
Tell me, may not a king adopt an heir?
York. What then?
K. Hen. An if he may, then am I lawful king;
For Richard, in the view of many lords,
Resign'd the crown to Henry the Fourth,
Whose heir my father was, and I am his.
York. He rose against him, being his sovereign,
And made him to resign his crown perforce.
War. Suppose, my lords, he did it unconstrain'd,
Think you 'twere prejudicial to his crown?
Exe. No; for he could not so resign his crown
But that the next heir should succeed and reign.
K. Hen. Art thou against us, Duke of Exeter?
Exe. His is the right, and therefore pardon me.
York. Why whisper you, my lords, and answer not?
Exe. My conscience tells me he is lawful king.
K. Hen. [*Aside*] All will revolt from me, and turn to him.
North. Plantagenet, for all the claim thou lay'st,
Think not that Henry shall be so depos'd.
War. Depos'd he shall be, in despite of all.
North. Thou art deceiv'd: 'tis not thy southern power,

5. **brook,** endure; see glossary. **retreat,** i.e., the call sounding retreat. 8. **battle's,** army's; see glossary. 12. **beaver,** face guard of a helmet. 14. **And, brother.** Montague was brother to Warwick. His father (Salisbury of *2 Henry VI*) was brother-in-law of York; cf. I, i, 209, note. 18. **But . . . Somerset?** Is it really true that Somerset is dead? 19. **all . . . Gaunt.** Somerset was the grandson of John of Gaunt and Catherine Swynford. This malediction falls, of course, on King Henry VI, great-grandson of Gaunt. 34. **perforce,** forcibly; see glossary. 40. **be,** become. 41. **bashful,** easily cowed. 45-46. **he . . . Lancaster,** any of the Lancastrian party. 47. **shake his bells,** a metaphor from falconry; bells were sometimes fastened to the legs of the hawk. 49. **Resolve thee,** be resolved, resolute; see glossary. 62. **poltroons,** arrant cowards. 66. **cousin,** any relative not of one's immediate family; see glossary. 71. **shambles,** butcher-shop or slaughter-house. 77-78. **he . . . was.** Cf. *1 Henry VI*, III, i, 163-173, where the king restored to Richard the whole inheritance of the house of York, which included the earldom of March. 79. **Thy . . . traitor.** Cf. *Henry V*, II, ii; *1 Henry VI*, II, iv, 90-94; II, v, 84-91. 105. **Thy . . . York,** a historical inaccuracy; Richard's father was never Duke of York; cf. *1 Henry VI*, II, iv, 83, note. 110. **sith,** since; see glossary. 111. **lord protector,** i.e., Humphrey, Duke of Gloucester. 129. **winding-sheet,** sheet in which a corpse was wrapped.

Of Essex, Norfolk, Suffolk, nor of Kent,
Which makes thee thus presumptuous and proud,
Can set the duke up in despite of me.
Clif. King Henry, be thy title right or wrong,
Lord Clifford vows to fight in thy defence:
May that ground gape and swallow me alive,
Where I shall kneel to him that slew my father!
K. Hen. O Clifford, how thy words revive my heart!
York. Henry of Lancaster, resign thy crown.
What mutter you, or what conspire you, lords?
War. Do right unto this princely Duke of York,
Or I will fill the house with armed men,
And over the chair of state, where now he sits,
Write up his title with usurping blood.
He stamps with his foot, and the Soldiers show themselves.
K. Hen. My Lord of Warwick, hear me but one word:
Let me for this my life-time reign as king.
York. Confirm the crown to me and to mine heirs,
And thou shalt reign in quiet while thou liv'st.
K. Hen. I am content: Richard Plantagenet,
Enjoy the kingdom after my decease.
Clif. What wrong is this unto the prince your son!
War. What good is this to England and himself!
West. Base, fearful and despairing Henry!
Clif. How hast thou injur'd both thyself and us!
West. I cannot stay to hear these articles.
North. Nor I.
Clif. Come, cousin, let us tell the queen these news.
West. Farewell, faint-hearted and degenerate king,
In whose cold blood no spark of honour bides.
North. Be thou a prey unto the house of York,
And die in bands for this unmanly deed!
Clif. In dreadful war mayst thou be overcome,
Or live in peace abandon'd and despis'd!
[*Exeunt North., Clif., and West.*]
War. Turn this way, Henry, and regard them not.
Exe. They seek revenge and therefore will not yield.
K. Hen. Ah, Exeter!
War. Why should you sigh, my lord?
K. Hen. Not for myself, Lord Warwick, but my son,
Whom I unnaturally shall disinherit.
But be it as it may: [*To York.*] I here entail
The crown to thee and to thine heirs for ever;
Conditionally, that here thou take an oath
To cease this civil war, and, whilst I live,
To honour me as thy king and sovereign,
And neither by treason nor hostility
To seek to put me down and reign thyself.
York. This oath I willingly take and will perform.
War. Long live King Henry! Plantagenet, embrace him.
K. Hen. And long live thou and these thy forward sons!
York. Now York and Lancaster are reconcil'd.
Exe. Accurs'd be he that seeks to make them foes!
Sennet. Here they come down.
York. Farewell, my gracious lord; I'll to my castle.
War. And I'll keep London with my soldiers.
Norf. And I to Norfolk with my followers.
Mont. And I unto the sea from whence I came.
[*Exeunt York and his Sons, Warwick, Norfolk, Montague, their Soldiers, and Attendants.*]
K. Hen. And I, with grief and sorrow, to the court.

Enter the QUEEN [MARGARET *and the* PRINCE OF WALES].

Exe. Here comes the queen, whose looks bewray her anger:
I'll steal away.
K. Hen. Exeter, so will I.
Q. Mar. Nay, go not from me; I will follow thee.
K. Hen. Be patient, gentle queen, and I will stay.
Q. Mar. Who can be patient in such extremes?
Ah, wretched man! would I had died a maid,
And never seen thee, never borne thee son,
Seeing thou hast prov'd so unnatural a father!
Hath he deserv'd to lose his birthright thus?
Hadst thou but lov'd him half so well as I,
Or felt that pain which I did for him once,
Or nourish'd him as I did with my blood,
Thou wouldst have left thy dearest heart-blood there,
Rather than have made that savage duke thine heir
And disinherited thine only son.
Prince. Father, you cannot disinherit me:
If you be king, why should not I succeed?
K. Hen. Pardon me, Margaret; pardon me, sweet son:
The Earl of Warwick and the duke enforc'd me.
Q. Mar. Enforc'd thee! art thou king, and wilt be forc'd?
I shame to hear thee speak. Ah, timorous wretch!
Thou hast undone thyself, thy son and me;
And giv'n unto the house of York such head
As thou shalt reign but by their sufferance.
To entail him and his heirs unto the crown,
What is it, but to make thy sepulchre
And creep into it far before thy time?
Warwick is chancellor and the lord of Calais;
Stern Falconbridge commands the narrow seas;
The duke is made protector of the realm;
And yet shalt thou be safe? such safety finds
The trembling lamb environed with wolves.
Had I been there, which am a silly woman,
The soldiers should have toss'd me on their pikes
Before I would have granted to that act.
But thou preferr'st thy life before thine honour:
And seeing thou dost, I here divorce myself
Both from thy table, Henry, and thy bed,
Until that act of parliament be repeal'd
Whereby my son is disinherited.
The northern lords that have forsworn thy colours
Will follow mine, if once they see them spread;
And spread they shall be, to thy foul disgrace
And utter ruin of the house of York.
Thus do I leave thee. Come, son, let 's away;
Our army is ready; come, we'll after them.
K. Hen. Stay, gentle Margaret, and hear me speak.
Q. Mar. Thou hast spoke too much already: get thee gone.
K. Hen. Gentle son Edward, thou wilt stay with me?

186. **bands,** fetters, bonds; see glossary. 193. **unnaturally,** contrary to nature. 203. **forward,** ardent, zealous. 205. *Stage Direction:* ***Sennet,*** series of notes sounded on a trumpet to announce the approach of a procession; see glossary. 209. **unto the sea.** Cf. l. 239. Tucker Brooke points out a possible amalgamation of the roles of Montague and Faulconbridge. The latter was York's brother-in-law (cf. I, i, 14), who during this period controlled Calais and the Strait of Dover. Montague did not come from or return to the sea, as this speech represents him as doing. Mention of Faulconbridge, moreover, does not occur anywhere else in the play. 215. **patient,** pronounced as trisyllabic. 232. **undone,** ruined; see glossary. 233. **head,** headway. 243. **silly,** helpless. 245. **granted,** yielded. 269. **Tire,** prey upon.

Q. Mar. Ay, to be murder'd by his enemies.
Prince. When I return with victory from the field
I'll see your grace: till then I'll follow her.
Q. Mar. Come, son, away; we may not linger thus.
[*Exeunt Queen Margaret and the Prince.*]
K. Hen. Poor queen! how love to me and to her son
Hath made her break out into terms of rage!
Reveng'd may she be on that hateful duke,
Whose haughty spirit, winged with desire,
Will cost my crown, and like an empty eagle
Tire on the flesh of me and of my son!
The loss of those three lords torments my heart:
I'll write unto them and entreat them fair.
Come, cousin, you shall be the messenger.
Exe. And I, I hope, shall reconcile them all.
Exeunt. Flourish.

[SCENE II. *Sandal Castle.*]

Enter RICHARD, EDWARD, *and* MONTAGUE.

Rich. Brother, though I be youngest, give me leave.
Edw. No, I can better play the orator.
Mont. But I have reasons strong and forcible.

Enter the DUKE OF YORK.

York. Why, how now, sons and brother! at a strife?
What is your quarrel? how began it first?
Edw. No quarrel, but a slight contention.
York. About what?
Rich. About that which concerns your grace and us;
The crown of England, father, which is yours.
York. Mine, boy? not till King Henry be dead.
Rich. Your right depends not on his life or death.
Edw. Now you are heir, therefore enjoy it now:
By giving the house of Lancaster leave to breathe,
It will outrun you, father, in the end.
York. I took an oath that he should quietly reign.
Edw. But for a kingdom any oath may be broken:
I would break a thousand oaths to reign one year.
Rich. No; God forbid your grace should be forsworn.
York. I shall be, if I claim by open war.
Rich. I'll prove the contrary, if you'll hear me speak.
York. Thou canst not, son; it is impossible.
Rich. An oath is of no moment, being not took
Before a true and lawful magistrate,
That hath authority over him that swears:
Henry had none, but did usurp the place;
Then, seeing 'twas he that made you to depose,
Your oath, my lord, is vain and frivolous.
Therefore, to arms! And, father, do but think
How sweet a thing it is to wear a crown;
Within whose circuit is Elysium
And all that poets feign of bliss and joy.
Why do we linger thus? I cannot rest
Until the white rose that I wear be dy'd
Even in the lukewarm blood of Henry's heart.
York. Richard, enough; I will be king, or die.
Brother, thou shalt to London presently,
And whet on Warwick to this enterprise.
Thou, Richard, shalt to the Duke of Norfolk,
And tell him privily of our intent.
You, Edward, shall unto my Lord Cobham,
With whom the Kentishmen will willingly rise:
In them I trust; for they are soldiers,
Witty, courteous, liberal, full of spirit.
While you are thus employ'd, what resteth more,
But that I seek occasion how to rise,
And yet the king not privy to my drift,
Nor any of the house of Lancaster?

Enter a Messenger.

But, stay: what news? Why com'st thou in such post?
Mess. The queen with all the northern earls and lords
Intend here to besiege you in your castle:
She is hard by with twenty thousand men;
And therefore fortify your hold, my lord.
York. Ay, with my sword. What! think'st thou that we fear them?
Edward and Richard, you shall stay with me;
My brother Montague shall post to London:
Let noble Warwick, Cobham, and the rest,
Whom we have left protectors of the king,
With pow'rful policy strengthen themselves,
And trust not simple Henry nor his oaths.
Mont. Brother, I go; I'll win them, fear it not:
And thus most humbly I do take my leave. *Exit Mont.*

Enter [SIR JOHN] MORTIMER *and* [SIR HUGH,] *his Brother.*

York. Sir John and Sir Hugh Mortimer, mine uncles,
You are come to Sandal in a happy hour;
The army of the queen mean to besiege us.
Sir John. She shall not need; we'll meet her in the field.
York. What, with five thousand men?
Rich. Ay, with five hundred, father, for a need:
A woman 's general; what should we fear?
A march afar off.
Edw. I hear their drums: let 's set our men in order,
And issue forth and bid them battle straight.
York. Five men to twenty! though the odds be great,
I doubt not, uncle, of our victory.
Many a battle have I won in France,
When as the enemy hath been ten to one:
Why should I not now have the like success?
Alarum. Exeunt.

[SCENE III. *Field of battle betwixt Sandal Castle and Wakefield.*]

[*Alarums.*] *Enter* RUTLAND *and his* Tutor.

Rut. Ah, whither shall I fly to 'scape their hands?
Ah, tutor, look where bloody Clifford comes!

Enter CLIFFORD [*and* Soldiers].

Clif. Chaplain, away! thy priesthood saves thy life.
As for the brat of this accursed duke,
Whose father slew my father, he shall die.
Tut. And I, my lord, will bear him company.

271. **fair,** civilly, kindly; see glossary.
SCENE II. *Stage Direction: **Sandal Castle,*** near Wakefield, in Yorkshire. 4. **brother.** Cf. I, i, 14; I, i, 209, stage direction. 22. **moment,** significance. 26. **depose,** take an oath. 30. **Elysium,** according to Greek mythology, the abode of good souls, a realm of complete happiness. The passage suggests Marlowe's *Tamburlaine.* 36. **presently,** immediately; see glossary. 43. **liberal,** possessed of qualities of gentlemen; see glossary. 48. **stay,** stop, wait; see glossary. **post,** haste; see glossary. 52. **hold,** stronghold. 58. **pow'rful policy,** power gained by craft; see *policy* in glossary. 70. **straight,** immediately; see glossary.

Clif. Soldiers, away with him!
Tut. Ah, Clifford, murder not this innocent child,
Lest thou be hated both of God and man!
Exit [dragged off by Soldiers].
Clif. How now! is he dead already? or is it fear
That makes him close his eyes? I'll open them.
Rut. So looks the pent-up lion o'er the wretch
That trembles under his devouring paws;
And so he walks, insulting o'er his prey,
And so he comes, to rend his limbs asunder.
Ah, gentle Clifford, kill me with thy sword,
And not with such a cruel threat'ning look!
Sweet Clifford, hear me speak before I die!
I am too mean a subject for thy wrath:
Be thou reveng'd on men, and let me live.
Clif. In vain thou speak'st, poor boy; my father's blood
Hath stopp'd the passage where thy words should enter.
Rut. Then let my father's blood open it again:
He is a man, and, Clifford, cope with him.
Clif. Had I thy brethren here, their lives and thine
Were not revenge sufficient for me;
No, if I digg'd up thy forefathers' graves
And hung their rotten coffins up in chains,
It could not slake mine ire, nor ease my heart.
The sight of any of the house of York
Is as a fury to torment my soul;
And till I root out their accursed line
And leave not one alive, I live in hell.
Therefore— *[Lifting his hand.]*
Rut. O, let me pray before I take my death!
To thee I pray; sweet Clifford, pity me!
Clif. Such pity as my rapier's point affords.
Rut. I never did thee harm: why wilt thou slay me?
Clif. Thy father hath.
Rut. But 'twas ere I was born.
Thou hast one son; for his sake pity me,
Lest in revenge thereof, sith God is just,
He be as miserably slain as I.
Ah, let me live in prison all my days;
And when I give occasion of offence,
Then let me die, for now thou hast no cause.
Clif. No cause?
Thy father slew my father; therefore, die. *[Stabs him.]*
Rut. Di faciant laudis summa sit ista tuæ! *[Dies.]*
Clif. Plantagenet! I come, Plantagenet!
And this thy son's blood cleaving to my blade
Shall rust upon my weapon, till thy blood,
Congeal'd with this, do make me wipe off both. *Exit.*

[SCENE IV. *Another part of the field.*]

Alarum. Enter RICHARD, Duke of York.

York. The army of the queen hath got the field:
My uncles both are slain in rescuing me;
And all my followers to the eager foe
Turn back and fly, like ships before the wind
Or lambs pursu'd by hunger-starved wolves.
My sons, God knows what hath bechanced them:
But this I know, they have demean'd themselves
Like men born to renown by life or death.
Three times did Richard make a lane to me,
And thrice cried 'Courage, father! fight it out!'
And full as oft came Edward to my side,
With purple falchion, painted to the hilt
In blood of those that had encount'red him:
And when the hardiest warriors did retire,
Richard cried, 'Charge! and give no foot of ground!'
And cried 'A crown, or else a glorious tomb!
A sceptre, or an earthly sepulchre!'
With this, we charg'd again: but, out, alas!
We bodg'd again; as I have seen a swan
With bootless labour swim against the tide
And spend her strength with over-matching waves.
A short alarum within.
Ah, hark! the fatal followers do pursue;
And I am faint and cannot fly their fury:
And were I strong, I would not shun their fury:
The sands are numb'red that make up my life;
Here must I stay, and here my life must end.

Enter the QUEEN [MARGARET], CLIFFORD, NORTHUMBERLAND, *the* young Prince, *and* Soldiers.

Come, bloody Clifford, rough Northumberland,
I dare your quenchless fury to more rage:
I am your butt, and I abide your shot.
North. Yield to our mercy, proud Plantagenet.
Clif. Ay, to such mercy as his ruthless arm,
With downright payment, show'd unto my father.
Now Phaëthon hath tumbled from his car,
And made an evening at the noontide prick.
York. My ashes, as the phœnix, may bring forth
A bird that will revenge upon you all:
And in that hope I throw mine eyes to heaven,
Scorning whate'er you can afflict me with.
Why come you not? what! multitudes, and fear?
Clif. So cowards fight when they can fly no further;
So doves do peck the falcon's piercing talons;
So desperate thieves, all hopeless of their lives,
Breathe out invectives 'gainst the officers.
York. O Clifford, but bethink thee once again,
And in thy thought o'er-run my former time;
And, if thou canst for blushing, view this face,
And bite thy tongue, that slanders him with cowardice
Whose frown hath made thee faint and fly ere this!
Clif. I will not bandy with thee word for word,
But buckle with thee blows, twice two for one.
Q. Mar. Hold, valiant Clifford! for a thousand causes
I would prolong awhile the traitor's life.
Wrath makes him deaf: speak thou, Northumberland.
North. Hold, Clifford! do not honour him so much
To prick thy finger, though to wound his heart:
What valour were it, when a cur doth grin,
For one to thrust his hand between his teeth,
When he might spurn him with his foot away?
It is war's prize to take all vantages;

SCENE III. 14. **insulting,** gloating. 19. **mean,** of low degree; see glossary. 24. **cope with,** encounter; see glossary. 29. **slake,** relieve, assuage. 48. **Di . . . tuæ!** The gods grant that this may be the height of thy glory! (Ovid, *Heroides*, II, 66).

SCENE IV. 12. **falchion,** sword somewhat curved, with the edge on the convex side. 18. **out,** an expression of reproach; see glossary. 19. **bodg'd,** gave way. 29. **butt,** target; archery term. 33. **Phaëthon,** son of Helios the sun god (often equated with Phoebus Apollo). Prompted by pride, he begged his father to allow him to drive the chariot of the sun. Incapable of handling the fiery horses, he soon wandered from the proper course and came so near to the earth that it was threatened with destruction. Zeus hurled a thunderbolt at him to stop his disastrous course. 34. **noontide prick,** exact point of noon on a sundial. 35. **as the phœnix.** Cf. note to *1 Henry VI*, IV, vii, 93.

And ten to one is no impeach of valour.
[*They lay hands on York, who struggles.*]
Clif. Ay, ay, so strives the woodcock with the gin.
North. So doth the cony struggle in the net.
York. So triumph thieves upon their conquer'd booty;
So true men yield, with robbers so o'ermatch'd.
North. What would your grace have done unto him now?
Q. Mar. Brave warriors, Clifford and Northumberland,
Come, make him stand upon this molehill here,
That raught at mountains with outstretched arms,
Yet parted but the shadow with his hand.
What! was it you that would be England's king?
Was 't you that revell'd in our parliament,
And made a preachment of your high descent?
Where are your mess of sons to back you now?
The wanton Edward, and the lusty George?
And where 's that valiant crook-back prodigy,
Dicky your boy, that with his grumbling voice
Was wont to cheer his dad in mutinies?
Or, with the rest, where is your darling Rutland?
Look, York! I stain'd this napkin with the blood
That valiant Clifford, with his rapier's point,
Made issue from the bosom of the boy;
And if thine eyes can water for his death,
I give thee this to dry thy cheeks withal.
Alas, poor York! but that I hate thee deadly,
I should lament thy miserable state.
I prithee, grieve, to make me merry, York.
What, hath thy fiery heart so parch'd thine entrails
That not a tear can fall for Rutland's death?
Why art thou patient, man? thou shouldst be mad;
And I, to make thee mad, do mock thee thus.
Stamp, rave, and fret, that I may sing and dance.
Thou wouldst be fee'd, I see, to make me sport:
York cannot speak, unless he wear a crown.
A crown for York! and, lords, bow low to him:
Hold you his hands, whilst I do set it on.
[*Putting a paper crown on his head.*]
Ay, marry, sir, now looks he like a king!
Ay, this is he that took King Henry's chair,
And this is he was his adopted heir.
But how is it that great Plantagenet
Is crown'd so soon, and broke his solemn oath?
As I bethink me, you should not be king
Till our King Henry had shook hands with death.
And will you pale your head in Henry's glory,
And rob his temples of the diadem,
Now in his life, against your holy oath?
O, 'tis a fault too too unpardonable!
Off with the crown; and, with the crown, his head;
And, whilst we breathe, take time to do him dead.
Clif. That is my office, for my father's sake.
Q. Mar. Nay, stay; let 's hear the orisons he makes.
York. She-wolf of France, but worse than wolves of France,
Whose tongue more poisons than the adder's tooth!
How ill-beseeming is it in thy sex
To triumph, like an Amazonian trull,
Upon their woes whom fortune captivates!
But that thy face is, visard-like, unchanging,
Made impudent with use of evil deeds,
I would assay, proud queen, to make thee blush.
To tell thee whence thou cam'st, of whom deriv'd,
Were shame enough to shame thee, wert thou not shameless.
Thy father bears the type of King of Naples,
Of both the Sicils and Jerusalem,
Yet not so wealthy as an English yeoman.
Hath that poor monarch taught thee to insult?
It needs not, nor it boots thee not, proud queen,
Unless the adage must be verified,
That beggars mounted run their horse to death.
'Tis beauty that doth oft make women proud;
But, God he knows, thy share thereof is small:
'Tis virtue that doth make them most admir'd;
The contrary doth make thee wond'red at:
'Tis government that makes them seem divine;
The want thereof makes thee abominable:
Thou art as opposite to every good
As the Antipodes are unto us,
Or as the south to the septentrion.
O tiger's heart wrapt in a woman's hide!
How couldst thou drain the life-blood of the child,
To bid the father wipe his eyes withal,
And yet be seen to bear a woman's face?
Women are soft, mild, pitiful and flexible;
Thou stern, obdurate, flinty, rough, remorseless.
Bid'st thou me rage? why, now thou hast thy wish:
Wouldst have me weep? why, now thou hast thy will:
For raging wind blows up incessant showers,
And when the rage allays, the rain begins.
These tears are my sweet Rutland's obsequies:
And every drop cries vengeance for his death,
'Gainst thee, fell Clifford, and thee, false Frenchwoman.
North. Beshrew me, but his passion moves me so
That hardly can I check my eyes from tears.
York. That face of his the hungry cannibals
Would not have touch'd, would not have stain'd with blood:
But you are more inhuman, more inexorable,
O, ten times more, than tigers of Hyrcania.
See, ruthless queen, a hapless father's tears:
This cloth thou dip'dst in blood of my sweet boy,
And I with tears do wash the blood away.
Keep thou the napkin, and go boast of this:
And if thou tell'st the heavy story right,
Upon my soul, the hearers will shed tears;
Yea even my foes will shed fast-falling tears,
And say 'Alas, it was a piteous deed!'
There, take the crown, and, with the crown, my curse;
And in thy need such comfort come to thee
As now I reap at thy too cruel hand!
Hard-hearted Clifford, take me from the world:
My soul to heaven, my blood upon your heads!
North. Had he been slaughter-man to all my kin,
I should not for my life but weep with him,
To see how inly sorrow gripes his soul.

50. **buckle,** join in close combat. 60. **impeach,** act of calling in question. 61. **woodcock,** stupid bird; type of stupidity. **gin,** trap. 62. **cony,** rabbit. 68. **raught,** reached. 77. **cheer,** incite. 79. **napkin,** handkerchief; see glossary. 110. **orisons,** prayers. 114. **trull,** prostitute. 117. **with use of,** accustomed to; see *use* in glossary. 118. **assay,** attempt; see glossary. 125. **boots,** profits; see glossary. 135. **Antipodes,** parts of the globe diametrically opposite. 136. **septentrion,** north. 137. **O . . . hide.** This line has been made famous by Greene's application of it in the often-quoted allusion to Shakespeare—"the only Shake-scene in a country": "O Tyger's heart wrapt in a Players hide." 141. **pitiful,** capable of pity. 150. **passion,** grief; see glossary. 151. **check,** keep; see glossary. 155. **Hyrcania,** region of the ancient Persian empire, reputed to abound in wild beasts (see *Aeneid*, IV, 366-367). 171. **inly,** inwardly.

Q. Mar. What, weeping-ripe, my Lord Northumberland?
Think but upon the wrong he did us all,
And that will quickly dry thy melting tears.
Clif. Here 's for my oath, here 's for my father's death. [*Stabbing him.*]
Q. Mar. And here's to right our gentlehearted king. [*Stabbing him.*]
York. Open Thy gate of mercy, gracious God!
My soul flies through these wounds to seek out Thee. [*Dies.*]
Q. Mar. Off with his head, and set it on York gates;
So York may overlook the town of York.
Flourish. Exeunt.

[ACT II.

SCENE I. *A plain near Mortimer's Cross in Herefordshire.*]

A march. Enter EDWARD, RICHARD, *and their power.*

Edw. I wonder how our princely father 'scap'd,
Or whether he be 'scap'd away or no
From Clifford's and Northumberland's pursuit:
Had he been ta'en, we should have heard the news;
Had he been slain, we should have heard the news;
Or had he 'scap'd, methinks we should have heard
The happy tidings of his good escape.
How fares my brother? why is he so sad?
Rich. I cannot joy, until I be resolv'd
Where our right valiant father is become.
I saw him in the battle range about;
And watch'd him how he singled Clifford forth.
Methought he bore him in the thickest troop
As doth a lion in a herd of neat;
Or as a bear, encompass'd round with dogs,
Who having pinch'd a few and made them cry,
The rest stand all aloof, and bark at him.
So far'd our father with his enemies;
So fled his enemies my warlike father:
Methinks, 'tis prize enough to be his son.
See how the morning opes her golden gates,
And takes her farewell of the glorious sun!
How well resembles it the prime of youth,
Trimm'd like a younker prancing to his love!
Edw. Dazzle mine eyes, or do I see three suns?
Rich. Three glorious suns, each one a perfect sun;
Not separated with the racking clouds,
But sever'd in a pale clear-shining sky.
See, see! they join, embrace, and seem to kiss,
As if they vow'd some league inviolable:
Now are they but one lamp, one light, one sun.
In this the heaven figures some event.
Edw. 'Tis wondrous strange, the like yet never heard of.
I think it cites us, brother, to the field,
That we, the sons of brave Plantagenet,
Each one already blazing by our meeds,
Should notwithstanding join our lights together
And over-shine the earth as this the world.
Whate'er it bodes, henceforward will I bear
Upon my target three fair-shining suns.
Rich. Nay, bear three daughters: by your leave I speak it,
You love the breeder better than the male.

Enter one [a Messenger] *blowing* [*a horn*].

But what art thou, whose heavy looks foretell
Some dreadful story hanging on thy tongue?
Mess. Ah, one that was a wofui looker-on
When as the noble Duke of York was slain,
Your princely father and my loving lord!
Edw. O, speak no more, for I have heard too much.
Rich. Say how he died, for I will hear it all.
Mess. Environed he was with many foes,
And stood against them, as the hope of Troy
Against the Greeks that would have ent'red Troy.
But Hercules himself must yield to odds;
And many strokes, though with a little axe,
Hew down and fell the hardest-timber'd oak.
By many hands your father was subdu'd;
But only slaught'red by the ireful arm
Of unrelenting Clifford and the queen,
Who crown'd the gracious duke in high despite,
Laugh'd in his face; and when with grief he wept,
The ruthless queen gave him to dry his cheeks
A napkin steeped in the harmless blood
Of sweet young Rutland, by rough Clifford slain:
And after many scorns, many foul taunts,
They took his head, and on the gates of York
They set the same; and there it doth remain,
The saddest spectacle that e'er I view'd.
Edw. Sweet Duke of York, our prop to lean upon,
Now thou art gone, we have no staff, no stay.
O Clifford, boist'rous Clifford! thou hast slain
The flow'r of Europe for his chivalry;
And treacherously hast thou vanquish'd him,
For hand to hand he would have vanquish'd thee.
Now my soul's palace is become a prison:
Ah, would she break from hence, that this my body
Might in the ground be closed up in rest!
For never henceforth shall I joy again,
Never, O never, shall I see more joy!
Rich. I cannot weep; for all my body's moisture
Scarce serves to quench my furnace-burning heart:
Nor can my tongue unload my heart's great burthen;
For selfsame wind that I should speak withal
Is kindling coals that fires all my breast,
And burns me up with flames that tears would quench.
To weep is to make less the depth of grief:
Tears then for babes; blows and revenge for me!
Richard, I bear thy name; I'll venge thy death,

178. **My . . . wounds.** The soul was believed to issue from the body through an aperture, as the mouth (with the last breath) or a wound (with the outflow of blood).

ACT II. SCENE I. 9. **resolv'd,** informed; see glossary. 10. **Where . . . become,** what is become of. 14. **neat,** cattle. 16. **pinch'd,** bit. 19. **fled his enemies,** his enemies fled from. 24. **younker,** youngling. 25. **three suns.** Holinshed records that Edward "met with his enemies in a faire plaine neere to Mortimers crosse, not far from Hereford east, on Candlemasse daie in the morning. At which time the sun (as some write) appeared to the earle of March like three sunnes, and suddenlie joined altogither in one. Upon which sight he took such courage, that he, fiercelie setting on his enemies, put them to flight: and for this cause men imagined that he gaue the sunne in his full brightness for his badge or cognisance." 27. **racking,** driving. 32. **figures,** prefigures. 34. **cites,** impels, incites. 36. **meeds,** worth, deserts. 40. **target,** shield; see glossary. 49. **I will hear it all.** The character of Richard begins to reveal itself as a hard, relentless personality as his position in the play becomes more prominent. He is later (III, ii, 124-195) to emerge as a thoroughgoing Machiavel, a character which he maintains throughout this play and its sequel, *Richard III.* 51. **hope of Troy,** Hector. 59. **despite,** scorn. 68-69. **Sweet . . . stay.** Tucker Brooke calls attention to the similarity of these lines to a passage in Marlowe's

Or die renowned by attempting it.
Edw. His name that valiant duke hath left with thee;
His dukedom and his chair with me is left.
Rich. Nay, if thou be that princely eagle's bird,
Show thy descent by gazing 'gainst the sun:
For chair and dukedom, throne and kingdom say;
Either that is thine, or else thou wert not his.

March. Enter WARWICK, MARQUESS [OF] MONTAGUE, *and their army.*

War. How now, fair lords! What fare? what news abroad?
Rich. Great Lord of Warwick, if we should recount
Our baleful news, and at each word's deliverance
Stab poniards in our flesh till all were told,
The words would add more anguish than the wounds.
O valiant lord, the Duke of York is slain!
Edw. O Warwick, Warwick! that Plantagenet,
Which held thee dearly as his soul's redemption,
Is by the stern Lord Clifford done to death.
War. Ten days ago I drown'd these news in tears;
And now, to add more measure to your woes,
I come to tell you things sith then befall'n.
After the bloody fray at Wakefield fought,
Where your brave father breath'd his latest gasp,
Tidings, as swiftly as the posts could run,
Were brought me of your loss and his depart.
I, then in London, keeper of the king,
Muster'd my soldiers, gathered flocks of friends,
And very well appointed, as I thought,
March'd toward Saint Alban's to intercept the queen,
Bearing the king in my behalf along;
For by my scouts I was advertised
That she was coming with a full intent
To dash our late decree in parliament
Touching King Henry's oath and your succession.
Short tale to make, we at Saint Alban's met,
Our battles join'd, and both sides fiercely fought:
But whether 'twas the coldness of the king,
Who look'd full gently on his warlike queen,
That robb'd my soldiers of their heated spleen;
Or whether 'twas report of her success;
Or more than common fear of Clifford's rigour,
Who thunders to his captives blood and death,
I cannot judge: but, to conclude with truth,
Their weapons like to lightning came and went;
Our soldiers', like the night-owl's lazy flight,
Or like an idle thresher with a flail,
Fell gently down, as if they struck their friends.
I cheer'd them up with justice of our cause,
With promise of high pay and great rewards:
But all in vain; they had no heart to fight,
And we in them no hope to win the day;
So that we fled; the king unto the queen;
Lord George your brother, Norfolk and myself,
In haste, post-haste, are come to join with you;
For in the marches here we heard you were,
Making another head to fight again.
Edw. Where is the Duke of Norfolk, gentle Warwick?
And when came George from Burgundy to England?
War. Some six miles off the duke is with the soldiers;
And for your brother, he was lately sent
From your kind aunt, Duchess of Burgundy,
With aid of soldiers to this needful war.
Rich. 'Twas odds, belike, when valiant Warwick fled:
Oft have I heard his praises in pursuit,
But ne'er till now his scandal of retire.
War. Nor now my scandal, Richard, dost thou hear;
For thou shalt know this strong right hand of mine
Can pluck the diadem from faint Henry's head,
And wring the awful sceptre from his fist,
Were he as famous and as bold in war
As he is fam'd for mildness, peace, and prayer.
Rich. I know it well, Lord Warwick; blame me not:
'Tis love I bear thy glories makes me speak.
But in this troublous time what 's to be done?
Shall we go throw away our coats of steel,
And wrap our bodies in black mourning gowns,
Numb'ring our Ave-Maries with our beads?
Or shall we on the helmets of our foes
Tell our devotion with revengeful arms?
If for the last, say ay, and to it, lords.
War. Why, therefore Warwick came to seek you out;
And therefore comes my brother Montague.
Attend me, lords. The proud insulting queen,
With Clifford and the haught Northumberland,
And of their feather many moe proud birds,
Have wrought the easy-melting king like wax.
He swore consent to your succession,
His oath enrolled in the parliament;
And now to London all the crew are gone,
To frustrate both his oath and what beside
May make against the house of Lancaster.
Their power, I think, is thirty thousand strong:
Now, if the help of Norfolk and myself,
With all the friends that thou, brave Earl of March,
Amongst the loving Welshmen canst procure,
Will but amount to five and twenty thousand,
Why, Via! to London will we march amain,
And once again bestride our foaming steeds,
And once again cry 'Charge upon our foes!'
But never once again turn back and fly.
Rich. Ay, now methinks I hear great Warwick speak:
Ne'er may he live to see a sunshine day,
That cries 'Retire,' if Warwick bid him stay.
Edw. Lord Warwick, on thy shoulder will I lean;
And when thou fail'st—as God forbid the hour!—

Massacre at Paris: "Sweet Duke of Guise, our prop to leane vpon, Now thou art dead, heere is no stay for vs." 72. **treacherously,** sometimes the equivalent of "cowardly," which it seems to be here. 79-84. **I . . . quench.** This passage is not a conceit but a literal description of the effects of anger, which, according to Elizabethan psychologists, "maketh the blood to boil in our hearts" and "puts the whole body into a fire and fever." (Charron, *Of Wisdom*, Bk. I, Ch. XXV.) 90. **his chair,** the throne. 92. **gazing . . . sun.** Hart quotes from Holland's Pliny: ". . . the Aegle . . . to prove and trie her yong birds, useth to force them for to look directly upon the sunne. . . ." 95. **What fare?** How do our fortunes fare? 98. **poniards,** daggers. 110. **depart,** departure, i.e., death; see glossary. 115. **in my behalf,** for my advantage. 116. **advertised,** informed. 124. **heated spleen,** courage roused to a high pitch; see *spleen* in glossary. 138. **Lord George,** third son of York, next younger than Edmund Earl of Rutland; subsequently Duke of Clarence. 140. **the marches,** the borders of Wales. 141. **head,** armed force; see glossary. 148. **'Twas odds,** i.e., the odds were against you. 164. **Tell,** count, continuing the figure from line 162; see glossary. 167. **my brother Montague.** Cf. I, i, 209, note. 169. **haught,** haughty. 170. **moe,** more; see glossary. 176. **make,** be effective; see glossary. 179. **brave Earl of March,** addressed to Edward, who at his father's death inherited this with other titles. 182. **amain,** with full force or speed.

Must Edward fall, which peril heaven forfend!
War. No longer Earl of March, but Duke of York:
The next degree is England's royal throne;
For King of England shalt thou be proclaim'd
In every borough as we pass along;
And he that throws not up his cap for joy
Shall for the fault make forfeit of his head.
King Edward, valiant Richard, Montague,
Stay we no longer, dreaming of renown,
But sound the trumpets, and about our task.
Rich. Then, Clifford, were thy heart as hard as steel,
As thou hast shown it flinty by thy deeds,
I come to pierce it, or to give thee mine.
Edw. Then strike up drums: God and Saint George for us!

Enter a Messenger.

War. How now! what news?
Mess. The Duke of Norfolk sends you word by me,
The queen is coming with a puissant host;
And craves your company for speedy counsel.
War. Why then it sorts, brave warriors, let 's away.
Exeunt omnes.

[SCENE II. *Before York.*]

Flourish. Enter the KING [HENRY], *the* QUEEN [MARGARET], CLIFFORD, NORTHUMBERLAND, *and young* PRINCE, *with drum and trumpets.*

Q. Mar. Welcome, my lord, to this brave town of York.
Yonder 's the head of that arch-enemy
That sought to be encompass'd with your crown:
Doth not the object cheer your heart, my lord?
K. Hen. Ay, as the rocks cheer them that fear their wrack:
To see this sight, it irks my very soul.
Withhold revenge, dear God! 'tis not my fault,
Nor wittingly have I infring'd my vow.
Clif. My gracious liege, this too much lenity
And harmful pity must be laid aside.
To whom do lions cast their gentle looks?
Not to the beast that would usurp their den.
Whose hand is that the forest bear doth lick?
Not his that spoils her young before her face.
Who 'scapes the lurking serpent's mortal sting?
Not he that sets his foot upon her back.
The smallest worm will turn being trodden on,
And doves will peck in safeguard of their brood.
Ambitious York did level at thy crown,
Thou smiling while he knit his angry brows:
He, but a duke, would have his son a king,
And raise his issue, like a loving sire;
Thou, being a king, blest with a goodly son,
Didst yield consent to disinherit him,
Which argued thee a most unloving father.
Unreasonable creatures feed their young;
And though man's face be fearful to their eyes,
Yet, in protection of their tender ones,
Who hath not seen them, even with those wings
Which sometime they have us'd with fearful flight,
Make war with him that climb'd unto their nest,
Offering their own lives in their young's defence?
For shame, my liege, make them your precedent!
Were it not pity that this goodly boy
Should lose his birthright by his father's fault,
And long hereafter say unto his child,
'What my great-grandfather and grandsire got
My careless father fondly gave away'?
Ah, what a shame were this! Look on the boy;
And let his manly face, which promiseth
Successful fortune, steel thy melting heart
To hold thine own and leave thine own with him.
K. Hen. Full well hath Clifford play'd the orator,
Inferring arguments of mighty force.
But, Clifford, tell me, didst thou never hear
That things ill-got had ever bad success?
And happy always was it for that son
Whose father for his hoarding went to hell?
I'll leave my son my virtuous deeds behind;
And would my father had left me no more!
For all the rest is held at such a rate
As brings a thousand-fold more care to keep
Than in possession any jot of pleasure.
Ah, cousin York! would thy best friends did know
How it doth grieve me that thy head is here!
Q. Mar. My lord, cheer up your spirits: our foes are nigh,
And this soft courage makes your followers faint.
You promis'd knighthood to our forward son:
Unsheathe your sword, and dub him presently.
Edward, kneel down.
K. Hen. Edward Plantagenet, arise a knight;
And learn this lesson, draw thy sword in right.
Prince. My gracious father, by your kingly leave,
I'll draw it as apparent to the crown,
And in that quarrel use it to the death.
Clif. Why, that is spoken like a toward prince.

Enter a Messenger.

Mess. Royal commanders, be in readiness:
For with a band of thirty thousand men
Comes Warwick, backing of the Duke of York;
And in the towns, as they do march along,
Proclaims him king, and many fly to him:
Darraign your battle, for they are at hand.
Clif. I would your highness would depart the field:
The queen hath best success when you are absent.
Q. Mar. Ay, good my lord, and leave us to our fortune.
K. Hen. Why, that 's my fortune too; therefore I'll stay.
North. Be it with resolution then to fight.
Prince. My royal father, cheer these noble lords
And hearten those that fight in your defence:
Unsheathe your sword, good father; cry 'Saint George!'

March. Enter EDWARD, WARWICK, RICHARD, CLARENCE, NORFOLK, MONTAGUE, *and* Soldiers.

191. **forfend,** forbid; see glossary. 209. **sorts,** is fitting.
SCENE II. 1. **brave,** fine; see glossary. 19. **level,** aim; see glossary. 22. **raise,** raise in dignity; i.e., advance his son to the crown. 26. **Unreasonable,** not endowed with reason. 30. **sometime,** from time to time; see glossary. 38. **fondly,** foolishly. 44. **Inferring,** alleging, adducing. 46-48. **things . . . hell.** Hart finds several parallels to the two proverbs given here. The first appears in several forms, one of which is in Spenser's *Mother Hubbard's Tale:* "Ill might it prosper that ill gotten was." The second is found in one of Latimer's sermons: "Happy is the child whose father goeth to the devil." The king states the first here declaratively and the second he poses as a question. 46. **success,** outcome; see glossary. 51. **rate,** estimate; see glossary. 66. **toward,** ready, bold; see glossary. 72. **Darraign,** set in battle array. 81. **grace,** mercy, pardon; see glossary. 83. **bide,** wait for.

Edw. Now, perjur'd Henry! wilt thou kneel for grace,
And set thy diadem upon my head;
Or bide the mortal fortune of the field?
Q. Mar. Go, rate thy minions, proud insulting boy!
Becomes it thee to be thus bold in terms
Before thy sovereign and thy lawful king?
Edw. I am his king, and he should bow his knee;
I was adopted heir by his consent:
Since when, his oath is broke; for, as I hear,
You, that are king, though he do wear the crown,
Have caus'd him, by new act of parliament,
To blot out me, and put his own son in.
Clif. And reason too:
Who should succeed the father but the son?
Rich. Are you there, butcher? O, I cannot speak!
Clif. Ay, crook-back, here I stand to answer thee,
Or any he the proudest of thy sort.
Rich. 'Twas you that kill'd young Rutland, was it not?
Clif. Ay, and old York, and yet not satisfied.
Rich. For God's sake, lords, give signal to the fight.
War. What say'st thou, Henry, wilt thou yield the crown?
Q. Mar. Why, how now, long-tongu'd Warwick! dare you speak?
When you and I met at Saint Alban's last,
Your legs did better service than your hands.
War. Then 'twas my turn to fly, and now 'tis thine.
Clif. You said so much before, and yet you fled.
War. 'Twas not your valour, Clifford, drove me thence.
North. No, nor your manhood that durst make you stay.
Rich. Northumberland, I hold thee reverently.
Break off the parley; for scarce I can refrain
The execution of my big-swoln heart
Upon that Clifford, that cruel child-killer.
Clif. I slew thy father, call'st thou him a child?
Rich. Ay, like a dastard and a treacherous coward,
As thou didst kill our tender brother Rutland;
But ere sunset I'll make thee curse the deed.
K. Hen. Have done with words, my lords, and hear me speak.
Q. Mar. Defy them then, or else hold close thy lips.
K. Hen. I prithee, give no limits to my tongue:
I am a king, and privileg'd to speak.
Clif. My liege, the wound that bred this meeting here
Cannot be cur'd by words; therefore be still.
Rich. Then, executioner, unsheathe thy sword:
By him that made us all, I am resolv'd
That Clifford's manhood lies upon his tongue.
Edw. Say, Henry, shall I have my right, or no?
A thousand men have broke their fasts to-day,
That ne'er shall dine unless thou yield the crown.
War. If thou deny, their blood upon thy head;
For York in justice puts his armour on.
Prince. If that be right which Warwick says is right,
There is no wrong, but every thing is right.
Rich. Whoever got thee, there thy mother stands;
For, well I wot, thou hast thy mother's tongue.
Q. Mar. But thou art neither like thy sire nor dam;
But like a foul mis-shapen stigmatic,
Mark'd by the destinies to be avoided,
As venom toads, or lizards' dreadful stings.
Rich. Iron of Naples hid with English gilt,
Whose father bears the title of a king,—
As if a channel should be call'd the sea,—
Sham'st thou not, knowing whence thou art extraught,
To let thy tongue detect thy base-born heart?
Edw. A wisp of straw were worth a thousand crowns,
To make this shameless callet know herself.
Helen of Greece was fairer far than thou,
Although thy husband may be Menelaus;
And ne'er was Agamemnon's brother wrong'd
By that false woman, as this king by thee.
His father revell'd in the heart of France,
And tam'd the king, and made the dauphin stoop;
And had he match'd according to his state,
He might have kept that glory to this day;
But when he took a beggar to his bed,
And grac'd thy poor sire with his bridal-day,
Even then that sunshine brew'd a shower for him,
That wash'd his father's fortunes forth of France,
And heap'd sedition on his crown at home.
For what hath broach'd this tumult but thy pride?
Hadst thou been meek, our title still had slept;
And we, in pity of the gentle king,
Had slipp'd our claim until another age.
Geo. But when we saw our sunshine made thy spring,
And that thy summer bred us no increase,
We set the axe to thy usurping root;
And though the edge hath something hit ourselves,
Yet, know thou, since we have begun to strike,
We'll never leave till we have hewn thee down,
Or bath'd thy growing with our heated bloods.
Edw. And, in this resolution, I defy thee;
Not willing any longer conference,
Since thou deniest the gentle king to speak.
Sound trumpets! let our bloody colours wave!
And either victory, or else a grave.
Q. Mar. Stay, Edward.
Edw. No, wrangling woman, we'll no longer stay:
These words will cost ten thousand lives this day.
Exeunt omnes.

[SCENE III. *A field of battle between Towton and Saxton, in Yorkshire.*]

Alarum. Excursions. Enter WARWICK.

War. Forspent with toil, as runners with a race,
I lay me down a little while to breathe;
For strokes receiv'd, and many blows repaid,
Have robb'd my strong-knit sinews of their strength,
And spite of spite needs must I rest awhile.

Enter EDWARD, *running.*

mortal, fatal; see glossary. 84. **rate,** chide, berate; see glossary. **minions,** followers; see glossary. 97. **any he,** any man. 111. **execution,** i.e., giving practical effect to his passion. **big-swoln,** i.e., overcharged with anger. 127. **A . . . to-day,** i.e., have had breakfast. 129. **deny,** refuse; see glossary. 133. **got,** begot; see *get* in glossary. 134. **wot,** know; see glossary. 136. **stigmatic.** Cf. *2 Henry VI*, V, i, 215. 139. **of Naples.** The queen's father was titular king of Naples. 142. **extraught,** descended. 143. **detect,** expose. 145. **callet,** lewd woman. 147. **Menelaus,** Helen of Troy's husband and brother of Agamemnon; Edward implies that Margaret has cuckolded Henry. 152. **match'd . . . state,** married someone equal to him in social position; see *state* in glossary. 155. **grac'd,** honored. 159. **broach'd,** introduced.

SCENE III. 5. **spite of spite,** in spite of vexation.

Edw. Smile, gentle heaven! or strike, ungentle death!
For this world frowns, and Edward's sun is clouded.
War. How now, my lord! what hap? what hope of good?

Enter [GEORGE, DUKE OF] CLARENCE.

Geo. Our hap is loss, our hope but sad despair;
Our ranks are broke, and ruin follows us:
What counsel give you? whither shall we fly?
Edw. Bootless is flight, they follow us with wings;
And weak we are and cannot shun pursuit.

Enter RICHARD.

Rich. Ah, Warwick, why hast thou withdrawn thyself?
Thy brother's blood the thirsty earth hath drunk,
Broach'd with the steely point of Clifford's lance;
And in the very pangs of death he cried,
Like to a dismal clangor heard from far,
'Warwick, revenge! brother, revenge my death!'
So, underneath the belly of their steeds,
That stain'd their fetlocks in his smoking blood,
The noble gentleman gave up the ghost.
War. Then let the earth be drunken with our blood:
I'll kill my horse, because I will not fly.
Why stand we like soft-hearted women here,
Wailing our losses, whiles the foe doth rage;
And look upon, as if the tragedy
Were play'd in jest by counterfeiting actors?
Here on my knee I vow to God above,
I'll never pause again, never stand still,
Till either death hath clos'd these eyes of mine
Or fortune given me measure of revenge.
Edw. O Warwick, I do bend my knee with thine;
And in this vow do chain my soul to thine!
And, ere my knee rise from the earth's cold face,
I throw my hands, mine eyes, my heart to thee,
Thou setter up and plucker down of kings,
Beseeching thee, if with thy will it stands
That to my foes this body must be prey,
Yet that thy brazen gates of heaven may ope,
And give sweet passage to my sinful soul!
Now, lords, take leave until we meet again,
Where'er it be, in heaven or in earth.
Rich. Brother, give me thy hand; and, gentle Warwick,
Let me embrace thee in my weary arms:
I, that did never weep, now melt with woe
That winter should cut off our spring-time so.
War. Away, away! Once more, sweet lords, farewell.
Geo. Yet let us all together to our troops,
And give them leave to fly that will not stay;
And call them pillars that will stand to us;
And, if we thrive, promise them such rewards
As victors wear at the Olympian games:
This may plant courage in their quailing breasts;
For yet is hope of life and victory.
Forslow no longer, make we hence amain. *Exeunt.*

[SCENE IV. *Another part of the field.*]

Excursions. Enter RICHARD *and* CLIFFORD [*meeting*].

Rich. Now, Clifford, I have singled thee alone:
Suppose this arm is for the Duke of York,
And this for Rutland; both bound to revenge,
Wert thou environ'd with a brazen wall.
Clif. Now, Richard, I am with thee here alone:
This is the hand that stabb'd thy father York;
And this the hand that slew thy brother Rutland;
And here 's the heart that triumphs in their death
And cheers these hands that slew thy sire and brother
To execute the like upon thyself;
And so, have at thee!
They fight. Warwick comes; Clifford flies.
Rich. Nay, Warwick, single out some other chase;
For I myself will hunt this wolf to death. *Exeunt.*

[SCENE V. *Another part of the field.*]

Alarum. Enter KING HENRY *alone.*

King. This battle fares like to the morning's war,
When dying clouds contend with growing light,
What time the shepherd, blowing of his nails,
Can neither call it perfect day nor night.
Now sways it this way, like a mighty sea
Forc'd by the tide to combat with the wind;
Now sways it that way, like the selfsame sea
Forc'd to retire by fury of the wind:
Sometime the flood prevails, and then the wind;
Now one the better, then another best;
Both tugging to be victors, breast to breast,
Yet neither conqueror nor conquered:
So is the equal poise of this fell war.
Here on this molehill will I sit me down.
To whom God will, there be the victory!
For Margaret my queen, and Clifford too,
Have chid me from the battle; swearing both
They prosper best of all when I am thence.
Would I were dead! if God's good will were so;
For what is in this world but grief and woe?
O God! methinks it were a happy life,
To be no better than a homely swain;
To sit upon a hill, as I do now,
To carve out dials quaintly, point by point,
Thereby to see the minutes how they run,
How many make the hour full complete;
How many hours bring about the day;
How many days will finish up the year;
How many years a mortal man may live.
When this is known, then to divide the times:
So many hours must I tend my flock;
So many hours must I take my rest;
So many hours must I contemplate;
So many hours must I sport myself;

7. **Edward's sun.** The metaphor contains a reference to Edward's emblem; cf. II, i, 25, 40. 15-32. **Thy . . . revenge.** Warwick's brother, the Bastard of Salisbury, is not among the *Dramatis Personae*. Holinshed gives a graphic account of Warwick's conduct on hearing of his death: "When the earle of Warwike was informed hereof, like a man desperat, he mounted on his hacknie, and hasted puffing and blowing to king Edward, saieng; 'Sir, I praie God haue mercie of their soules, which in the beginning of your enterprise haue lost their liues! And bicause I see no succors of the world but in God, I remit the vengeance to him our creator and redeemer.' With that he alighted downe, and slue his horse with his sword, saieng: 'Let him flee that will, for suerlie I will tarrie with him that will tarrie with me': and kissed the crosse of his sword as it were for a vow to the promise." 37. **Thou . . . kings.** Its position—and Warwick's nickname of "kingmaker"—tempt one to think that this line might be addressed to Warwick, although the lines immediately following indicate that it is addressed to heaven. Margaret

So many days my ewes have been with young;
So many weeks ere the poor fools will ean;
So many years ere I shall shear the fleece:
So minutes, hours, days, months, and years,
Pass'd over to the end they were created,
Would bring white hairs unto a quiet grave.
Ah, what a life were this! how sweet! how lovely!
Gives not the hawthorn-bush a sweeter shade
To shepherds looking on their silly sheep,
Than doth a rich embroider'd canopy
To kings that fear their subjects' treachery?
O, yes, it doth; a thousand-fold it doth.
And to conclude, the shepherd's homely curds,
His cold thin drink out of his leather bottle,
His wonted sleep under a fresh tree's shade,
All which secure and sweetly he enjoys,
Is far beyond a prince's delicates,
His viands sparkling in a golden cup,
His body couched in a curious bed,
When care, mistrust, and treason waits on him.

Alarum. Enter a Son *that hath killed his father, at one door [dragging in the dead body].*

Son. Ill blows the wind that profits nobody.
This man, whom hand to hand I slew in fight,
May be possessed with some store of crowns;
And I, that haply take them from him now,
May yet ere night yield both my life and them
To some man else, as this dead man doth me.
Who 's this? O God! it is my father's face,
Whom in this conflict I unwares have kill'd.
O heavy times, begetting such events!
From London by the king was I press'd forth;
My father, being the Earl of Warwick's man,
Came on the part of York, press'd by his master;
And I, who at his hands receiv'd my life,
Have by my hands of life bereaved him.
Pardon me, God, I knew not what I did!
And pardon, father, for I knew not thee!
My tears shall wipe away these bloody marks;
And no more words till they have flow'd their fill.
K. Hen. O piteous spectacle! O bloody times!
Whiles lions war and battle for their dens,
Poor harmless lambs abide their enmity.
Weep, wretched man, I'll aid thee tear for tear;
And let our hearts and eyes, like civil war,
Be blind with tears, and break o'ercharg'd with grief.

Enter at another door, a Father *that hath killed his son, bearing of his son.*

Fath. Thou that so stoutly hast resisted me,
Give me thy gold, if thou hast any gold;
For I have bought it with an hundred blows.
But let me see: is this our foeman's face?
Ah, no, no, no, it is mine only son!
Ah, boy, if any life be left in thee,
Throw up thine eye! see, see what show'rs arise,
Blown with the windy tempest of my heart,
Upon thy wounds, that kill mine eye and heart!
O, pity, God, this miserable age!
What stratagems, how fell, how butcherly,
Erroneous, mutinous and unnatural,
This deadly quarrel daily doth beget!
O boy, thy father gave thee life too soon,
And hath bereft thee of thy life too late!
K. Hen. Woe above woe! grief more than common grief!
O that my death would stay these ruthful deeds!
O, pity, pity, gentle heaven, pity!
The red rose and the white are on his face,
The fatal colours of our striving houses:
The one his purple blood right well resembles;
The other his pale cheeks, methinks, presenteth:
Wither one rose, and let the other flourish;
If you contend, a thousand lives must wither.
Son. How will my mother for a father's death
Take on with me and ne'er be satisfied!
Fath. How will my wife for slaughter of my son
Shed seas of tears and ne'er be satisfied!
K. Hen. How will the country for these woful chances
Misthink the king and not be satisfied!
Son. Was ever son so ru'd a father's death?
Fath. Was ever father so bemoan'd his son?
K. Hen. Was ever king so griev'd for subjects' woe?
Much is your sorrow; mine ten times so much.
Son. I'll bear thee hence, where I may weep my fill.
[*Exit with the body.*]
Fath. These arms of mine shall be thy winding-sheet;
My heart, sweet boy, shall be thy sepulchre,
For from my heart thine image ne'er shall go;
My sighing breast shall be thy funeral bell;
And so obsequious will thy father be,
†Even for the loss of thee, having no more,
As Priam was for all his valiant sons.
I'll bear thee hence; and let them fight that will,
For I have murdered where I should not kill.
Exit [with the body].
K. Hen. Sad-hearted men, much overgone with care,
Here sits a king more woful than you are.

Alarums: excursions. Enter the Queen [Margaret], *the* Prince, *and* Exeter.

Prince. Fly, father, fly! for all your friends are fled,
And Warwick rages like a chafed bull:
Away! for death doth hold us in pursuit.
Q. Mar. Mount you, my lord; towards Berwick post amain:
Edward and Richard, like a brace of greyhounds
Having the fearful flying hare in sight,
With fiery eyes sparkling for very wrath,
And bloody steel grasp'd in their ireful hands,
Are at our backs; and therefore hence amain.
Exe. Away! for vengeance comes along with them:
Nay, stay not to expostulate, make speed;
Or else come after: I'll away before.
K. Hen. Nay, take me with thee, good sweet Exeter:
Not that I fear to stay, but love to go

speaks a similar line to Warwick, III, iii, 157. 56. **Forslow,** delay.
Scene iv. 11. **have at,** let me at; see glossary. 12. **chase,** hunting ground.
Scene v. 3. **blowing . . . nails,** i.e., his hands are cold; cf. *Love's Labour's Lost,* V, ii, 923. 13. **poise,** weight. **fell,** cruel. 14. **molehill.** Hart finds in this an allusion to the old saw "king of a molehill." The saying has application to the Duke of York's death scene (I, iv). 26-34. **hour, hours,** pronounced throughout this passage as dissyllabic. 36. **ean,** bring forth (lambs). 53. **curious,** skillfully and daintily made; see glossary. 57. **possessed,** in possession of; see glossary. 64. **press'd forth,** impressed into military service. 89. **stratagems,** deeds of violence. 90. **Erroneous,** criminal. 100. **presenteth,** representeth; see glossary. 108. **Misthink,** think ill of. 118. **obsequious,** dutiful in manifesting regard for the dead. 123. **overgone,** overcome. 126. **chafed,** enraged. 135. **expostulate,** discuss.

Whither the queen intends. Forward; away! *Exeunt.*

[SCENE VI. *Another part of the field.*]

A loud alarum. Enter CLIFFORD, *wounded.*

Clif. Here burns my candle out; ay, here it dies,
Which, whiles it lasted, gave King Henry light.
O Lancaster, I fear thy overthrow
More than my body's parting with my soul!
My love and fear glu'd many friends to thee;
And, now I fall, thy tough commixture melts.
Impairing Henry, strength'ning misproud York,
The common people swarm like summer flies;
And whither fly the gnats but to the sun?
And who shines now but Henry's enemies?
O Phœbus, hadst thou never given consent
That Phaëthon should check thy fiery steeds,
Thy burning car never had scorch'd the earth!
And, Henry, hadst thou sway'd as kings should do,
Or as thy father and his father did,
Giving no ground unto the house of York,
They never then had sprung like summer flies;
I and ten thousand in this luckless realm
Had left no mourning widows for our death;
And thou this day hadst kept thy chair in peace.
For what doth cherish weeds but gentle air?
And what makes robbers bold but too much lenity?
Bootless are plaints, and cureless are my wounds;
No way to fly, nor strength to hold out flight:
The foe is merciless, and will not pity;
For at their hands I have deserv'd no pity.
The air hath got into my deadly wounds,
And much effuse of blood doth make me faint.
Come, York and Richard, Warwick and the rest;
I stabb'd your fathers' bosoms, split my breast.
[*He faints.*]

Alarum and retreat. Enter EDWARD, WARWICK, RICHARD, *and* Soldiers, MONTAGUE, *and* CLARENCE.

Edw. Now breathe we, lords: good fortune bids us pause,
And smooth the frowns of war with peaceful looks.
Some troops pursue the bloody-minded queen,
That led calm Henry, though he were a king,
As doth a sail, fill'd with a fretting gust,
Command an argosy to stem the waves.
But think you, lords, that Clifford fled with them?
War. No, 'tis impossible he should escape;
For, though before his face I speak the words,
Your brother Richard mark'd him for the grave:
And wheresoe'er he is, he 's surely dead.
Clifford groans [*and dies*].
Edw. Whose soul is that which takes her heavy leave?
Rich. A deadly groan, like life and death's departing.
Edw. See who it is: and, now the battle 's ended,
If friend or foe, let him be gently used.
Rich. Revoke that doom of mercy, for 'tis Clifford;
Who not contented that he lopp'd the branch
In hewing Rutland when his leaves put forth,
But set his murd'ring knife unto the root
From whence that tender spray did sweetly spring,
I mean our princely father, Duke of York.
War. From off the gates of York fetch down the head,
Your father's head, which Clifford placed there;
Instead whereof let this supply the room:
Measure for measure must be answered.
Edw. Bring forth that fatal screech-owl to our house,
That nothing sung but death to us and ours:
Now death shall stop his dismal threat'ning sound,
And his ill-boding tongue no more shall speak.
War. I think his understanding is bereft.
Speak, Clifford, dost thou know who speaks to thee?
Dark cloudy death o'ershades his beams of life,
And he nor sees nor hears us what we say.
Rich. O, would he did! and so perhaps he doth:
'Tis but his policy to counterfeit,
Because he would avoid such bitter taunts
Which in the time of death he gave our father.
Geo. If so thou think'st, vex him with eager words.
Rich. Clifford, ask mercy and obtain no grace.
Edw. Clifford, repent in bootless penitence.
War. Clifford, devise excuses for thy faults.
Geo. While we devise fell tortures for thy faults.
Rich. Thou didst love York, and I am son to York.
Edw. Thou pitied'st Rutland; I will pity thee.
Geo. Where 's Captain Margaret, to fence you now?
War. They mock thee, Clifford: swear as thou wast wont.
Rich. What, not an oath? nay, then the world goes hard
When Clifford cannot spare his friends an oath.
I know by that he 's dead; and, by my soul,
If this right hand would buy two hours' life,
That I in all despite might rail at him,
This hand should chop it off, and with the issuing blood
Stifle the villain whose unstanched thirst
York and young Rutland could not satisfy.
War. Ay, but he 's dead: off with the traitor's head,
And rear it in the place your father's stands.
And now to London with triumphant march,
There to be crowned England's royal king:
From whence shall Warwick cut the sea to France,
And ask the Lady Bona for thy queen:
So shalt thou sinew both these lands together;
And, having France thy friend, thou shalt not dread
The scatt'red foe that hopes to rise again;
For though they cannot greatly sting to hurt,
Yet look to have them buzz to offend thine ears.
First will I see the coronation;
And then to Brittany I'll cross the sea,
To effect this marriage, so it please my lord.
Edw. Even as thou wilt, sweet Warwick, let it be;
For in thy shoulder do I build my seat,
And never will I undertake the thing
Wherein thy counsel and consent is wanting.
Richard, I will create thee Duke of Gloucester,
And George, of Clarence: Warwick, as ourself,
Shall do and undo as him pleaseth best.

SCENE VI. 5. **My love and fear,** fear and love of me. 6. **commixture,** compound. 9. **the sun,** probable quibble on Edward's emblem. 11, 12. **Phoebus, Phaëthon.** Cf. I, iv, 33, note. 14. **sway'd,** reigned. 24. **hold out,** sustain. 28. **effuse,** effusion. 34. **though he were,** a contrary-to-fact subjunctive. 36. **argosy,** merchant vessel of the largest size. 39. **his,** i.e., Richard's. 55. **answered,** accounted for; see glossary. 56. **fatal screech-owl.** The owl was superstitiously regarded as a prognosticator of death; cf. *Macbeth,* II, ii, 3. 75. **fence,** defend. 90. **Lady Bona,** sister to the queen of France. 107. **Gloucester's . . . ominous.** Two dukes of Gloucester had met with violent deaths. Thomas, youngest son of Edward III, was murdered at Calais in 1397; and Humphrey (as dramatized in *2 Henry VI*) was murdered in

Rich. Let me be Duke of Clarence, George of Gloucester;
For Gloucester's dukedom is too ominous.
War. Tut, that 's a foolish observation:
Richard, be Duke of Gloucester. Now to London,
To see these honours in possession. *Exeunt.*

[ACT III.

SCENE I. *A forest in the north of England.*]

Enter [*two* Keepers] *with cross-bows in their hands.*

First Keep. Under this thick-grown brake we'll shroud ourselves;
For through this laund anon the deer will come;
And in this covert will we make our stand,
Culling the principal of all the deer.
Sec. Keep. I'll stay above the hill, so both may shoot.
First Keep. That cannot be; the noise of thy cross-bow
Will scare the herd, and so my shoot is lost.
Here stand we both, and aim we at the best:
And, for the time shall not seem tedious,
I'll tell thee what befel me on a day
In this self-place where now we mean to stand.
Sec. Keep. Here comes a man; let 's stay till he be past.

Enter the KING [HENRY, *disguised,*] *with a prayer-book.*

K. Hen. From Scotland am I stol'n, even of pure love,
To greet mine own land with my wishful sight.
No, Harry, Harry, 'tis no land of thine!
Thy place is fill'd, thy sceptre wrung from thee,
Thy balm wash'd off wherewith thou wast anointed:
No bending knee will call thee Cæsar now,
No humble suitors press to speak for right,
No, not a man comes for redress of thee;
For how can I help them, and not myself?
First Keep. Ay, here 's a deer whose skin 's a keeper's fee:
This is the quondam king; let 's seize upon him.
K. Hen. Let me embrace thee, sour adversity,
For wise men say it is the wisest course.
Sec. Keep. Why linger we? let us lay hands upon him.
First Keep. Forbear awhile; we'll hear a little more.
K. Hen. My queen and son are gone to France for aid;
And, as I hear, the great commanding Warwick
Is thither gone, to crave the French king's sister
To wife for Edward: if this news be true,
Poor queen and son, your labour is but lost;
For Warwick is a subtle orator,
And Lewis a prince soon won with moving words.
By this account then Margaret may win him;
For she 's a woman to be pitied much:
Her sighs will make a batt'ry in his breast;
Her tears will pierce into a marble heart;
The tiger will be mild whiles she doth mourn;
And Nero will be tainted with remorse,
To hear and see her plaints, her brinish tears.
Ay, but she 's come to beg, Warwick, to give;
She, on his left side, craving aid for Henry,
He, on his right, asking a wife for Edward.
She weeps, and says her Henry is depos'd;
He smiles, and says his Edward is install'd;
That she, poor wretch, for grief can speak no more;
Whiles Warwick tells his title, smooths the wrong,
Inferreth arguments of mighty strength,
And in conclusion wins the king from her,
With promise of his sister, and what else,
To strengthen and support King Edward's place.
O Margaret, thus 'twill be; and thou, poor soul,
Art then forsaken, as thou went'st forlorn!
Sec. Keep. Say, what art thou that talk'st of kings and queens?
K. Hen. More than I seem, and less than I was born to:
A man at least, for less I should not be;
And men may talk of kings, and why not I?
Sec. Keep. Ay, but thou talk'st as if thou wert a king.
K. Hen. Why, so I am, in mind; and that 's enough.
Sec. Keep. But, if thou be a king, where is thy crown?
K. Hen. My crown is in my heart, not on my head;
Not deck'd with diamonds and Indian stones,
Nor to be seen: my crown is called content:
A crown it is that seldom kings enjoy.
Sec. Keep. Well, if you be a king crown'd with content,
Your crown content and you must be contented
To go along with us; for, as we think,
You are the king King Edward hath depos'd;
And we his subjects sworn in all allegiance
Will apprehend you as his enemy.
K. Hen. But did you never swear, and break an oath?
Sec. Keep. No, never such an oath; nor will not now.
K. Hen. Where did you dwell when I was King of England?
Sec. Keep. Here in this country, where we now remain.
K. Hen. I was anointed king at nine months old;
My father and my grandfather were kings,
And you were sworn true subjects unto me:
And tell me, then, have you not broke your oaths?
First Keep. No;
For we were subjects but while you were king.
K. Hen. Why, am I dead? do I not breathe a man?
Ah, simple men, you know not what you swear!
Look, as I blow this feather from my face,
And as the air blows it to me again,
Obeying with my wind when I do blow,
And yielding to another when it blows,
Commanded always by the greater gust;
Such is the lightness of you common men.
But do not break your oaths; for of that sin
My mild entreaty shall not make you guilty.
Go where you will, the king shall be commanded;

the Tower in 1447. The former's death figures as a motive in the political intrigues depicted in *Richard II*; cf. *Richard II*, I, i, 100, note. 110. **To . . . possession,** to possess ourselves of these honors.

ACT III. SCENE I. 1. **brake,** thicket. 2. **laund,** glade. **anon,** soon; see glossary. 9. **for,** so that. 11. **self-place,** selfsame place. 23. **quondam,** one-time. 37. **batt'ry,** wound, bruise. 40. **tainted,** used metaphorically to imply something entirely contrary to one's nature; i.e., remorse is a foreign quality in a tyrant and corresponds to a corruption in an otherwise good nature; it is like "some stain of soldier" in Parolles (*All's Well that Ends Well*, I, i, 122). **remorse,** pity; see glossary. 71. **apprehend,** arrest.

And be you kings, command, and I'll obey.
First Keep. We are true subjects to the king, King Edward.
K. Hen. So would you be again to Henry,
If he were seated as King Edward is.
First Keep. We charge you, in God's name, and the king's,
To go with us unto the officers.
K. Hen. In God's name, lead; your king's name be obey'd:
And what God will, that let your king perform;
And what he will, I humbly yield unto. *Exeunt.*

[SCENE II. *London. The palace.*]

Enter KING EDWARD, GLOUCESTER, CLARENCE, [*and*] LADY GREY.

K. Edw. Brother of Gloucester, at Saint Alban's field.
This lady's husband, Sir Richard Grey, was slain,
His lands then seiz'd on by the conqueror:
Her suit is now to repossess those lands;
Which we in justice cannot well deny,
Because in quarrel of the house of York
The worthy gentleman did lose his life.
Glou. Your highness shall do well to grant her suit;
It were dishonour to deny it her.
K. Edw. It were no less; but yet I'll make a pause.
Glou. [*Aside to Clar.*] Yea, is it so?
I see the lady hath a thing to grant,
Before the king will grant her humble suit.
Clar. [*Aside to Glou.*] He knows the game: how true he keeps the wind!
Glou. [*Aside to Clar.*] Silence!
K. Edw. Widow, we will consider of your suit;
And come some other time to know our mind.
L. Grey. Right gracious lord, I cannot brook delay:
May it please your highness to resolve me now;
And what your pleasure is, shall satisfy me.
Glou. [*Aside to Clar.*] Ay, widow? then I'll warrant you all your lands,
An if what pleases him shall pleasure you.
Fight closer, or, good faith, you'll catch a blow.
Clar. [*Aside to Glou.*] I fear her not, unless she chance to fall.
Glou. [*Aside to Clar.*] God forbid that! for he'll take vantages.
K. Edw. How many children hast thou, widow? tell me.
Clar. [*Aside to Glou.*] I think he means to beg a child of her.
Glou. [*Aside to Clar.*] Nay, whip me then: he'll rather give her two.
L. Grey. Three, my most gracious lord.
Glou. [*Aside to Clar.*] You shall have four, if you'll be rul'd by him.
K. Edw. 'Twere pity they should lose their father's lands.
L. Grey. Be pitiful, dread lord, and grant it then.
K. Edw. Lords, give us leave: I'll try this widow's wit.
Glou. [*Aside to Clar.*] Ay, good leave have you; for you will have leave,
Till youth take leave and leave you to the crutch.
[*Glou. and Clar. retire.*]
K. Edw. Now tell me, madam, do you love your children?
L. Grey. Ay, full as dearly as I love myself.
K. Edw. And would you not do much to do them good?
L. Grey. To do them good, I would sustain some harm.
K. Edw. Then get your husband's lands, to do them good.
L. Grey. Therefore I came unto your majesty.
K. Edw. I'll tell you how these lands are to be got.
L. Grey. So shall you bind me to your highness' service.
K. Edw. What service wilt thou do me, if I give them?
L. Grey. What you command, that rests in me to do.
K. Edw. But you will take exceptions to my boon.
L. Grey. No, gracious lord, except I cannot do it.
K. Edw. Ay, but thou canst do what I mean to ask.
L. Grey. Why, then I will do what your grace commands.
Glou. [*Aside to Clar.*] He plies her hard; and much rain wears the marble.
Clar. [*Aside to Glou.*] As red as fire! nay, then her wax must melt.
L. Grey. Why stops my lord? shall I not hear my task?
K. Edw. An easy task; 'tis but to love a king.
L. Grey. That 's soon perform'd, because I am a subject.
K. Edw. Why, then, thy husband's lands I freely give thee.
L. Grey. I take my leave with many thousand thanks.
Glou. [*Aside to Clar.*] The match is made; she seals it with a curtsy.
K. Edw. But stay thee, 'tis the fruits of love I mean.
L. Grey. The fruits of love I mean, my loving liege.
K. Edw. Ay, but, I fear me, in another sense.
What love, think'st thou, I sue so much to get?
L. Grey. My love till death, my humble thanks, my prayers;
That love which virtue begs and virtue grants.
K. Edw. No, by my troth, I did not mean such love.
L. Grey. Why, then you mean not as I thought you did.
K. Edw. But now you partly may perceive my mind.
L. Grey. My mind will never grant what I perceive
Your highness aims at, if I aim aright.
K. Edw. To tell thee plain, I aim to lie with thee.
L. Grey. To tell you plain, I had rather lie in prison.
K. Edw. Why, then thou shalt not have thy husband's lands.
L. Grey. Why, then mine honesty shall be my dower;
For by that loss I will not purchase them.
K. Edw. Therein thou wrong'st thy children mightily.

SCENE II. 14. **keeps the wind,** hunts downwind. 22. **pleasure,** give pleasure to. 23. **catch a blow.** The dueling terms here are used with sexual double meaning: *fall, vantages,* etc. See also *beg a child,* l. 27; *crutch* (crotch), l. 35; *service,* l. 44; *shift* (woman's smock), l. 108. 46. **my boon,** i.e., the boon I ask. 57. **seals,** ratifies, confirms; see glossary. 68. **aim,** conjecture, guess. 70. **lie,** be confined. 77. **sadness,** seriousness. 108. **for shift,** to serve a purpose. 109. **muse,** wonder; see glossary. 110. **sad,** serious; see glossary. 114. **a day longer,** a reference to the proverbial expression "nine days' wonder." 124-195. **Ay, Edward,** etc. This soliloquy shows Richard declaring himself as a conventional

L. Grey. Herein your highness wrongs both them and me.
But, mighty lord, this merry inclination
Accords not with the sadness of my suit:
Please you dismiss me, either with 'ay' or 'no.'
K. Edw. Ay, if thou wilt say 'ay' to my request;
No, if thou dost say 'no' to my demand.
L. Grey. Then, no, my lord. My suit is at an end.
Glou. [*Aside to Clar.*] The widow likes him not, she knits her brows.
Clar. [*Aside to Glou.*] He is the bluntest wooer in Christendom.
K. Edw. [*Aside*] Her looks do argue her replete with modesty;
Her words do show her wit incomparable;
All her perfections challenge sovereignty:
One way or other, she is for a king;
And she shall be my love, or else my queen.—
Say that King Edward take thee for his queen?
L. Grey. 'Tis better said than done, my gracious lord:
I am a subject fit to jest withal,
But far unfit to be a sovereign.
K. Edw. Sweet widow, by my state I swear to thee
I speak no more than what my soul intends;
And that is, to enjoy thee for my love.
L. Grey. And that is more than I will yield unto:
I know I am too mean to be your queen,
And yet too good to be your concubine.
K. Edw. You cavil, widow: I did mean, my queen.
L. Grey. 'Twill grieve your grace my sons should call you father.
K. Edw. No more than when my daughters call thee mother.
Thou art a widow, and thou hast some children;
And, by God's mother, I, being but a bachelor,
Have other some: why, 'tis a happy thing
To be the father unto many sons.
Answer no more, for thou shalt be my queen.
Glou. [*Aside to Clar.*] The ghostly father now hath done his shrift.
Clar. [*Aside to Glou.*] When he was made a shriver, 'twas for shift.
K. Edw. Brothers, you muse what chat we two have had.
Glou. The widow likes it not, for she looks very sad.
K. Edw. You 'ld think it strange if I should marry her.
Clar. To who, my lord?
K. Edw. Why, Clarence, to myself.
Glou. That would be ten days' wonder at the least.
Clar. That 's a day longer than a wonder lasts.
Glou. By so much is the wonder in extremes.
K. Edw. Well, jest on, brothers: I can tell you both
Her suit is granted for her husband's lands.

Enter a Nobleman.

Nob. My gracious lord, Henry your foe is taken,
And brought your prisoner to your palace gate.
K. Edw. See that he be convey'd unto the Tower:
And go we, brothers, to the man that took him,
To question of his apprehension.
Widow, go you along. Lords, use her honourably.
Exeunt. Manet Richard [*of Gloucester*].
Glou. Ay, Edward will use women honourably.
Would he were wasted, marrow, bones and all,
That from his loins no hopeful branch may spring,
To cross me from the golden time I look for!
And yet, between my soul's desire and me—
The lustful Edward's title buried—
Is Clarence, Henry, and his son young Edward,
And all the unlook'd for issue of their bodies,
To take their rooms, ere I can place myself:
A cold premeditation for my purpose!
Why, then, I do but dream on sovereignty;
Like one that stands upon a promontory,
And spies a far-off shore where he would tread,
Wishing his foot were equal with his eye,
And chides the sea that sunders him from thence,
Saying, he'll lade it dry to have his way:
So do I wish the crown, being so far off;
And so I chide the means that keeps me from it;
And so I say, I'll cut the causes off,
Flattering me with impossibilities.
My eye 's too quick, my heart o'erweens too much,
Unless my hand and strength could equal them.
Well, say there is no kingdom then for Richard;
What other pleasure can the world afford?
I'll make my heaven in a lady's lap,
And deck my body in gay ornaments,
And witch sweet ladies with my words and looks.
O miserable thought! and more unlikely
Than to accomplish twenty golden crowns!
Why, love forswore me in my mother's womb:
And, for I should not deal in her soft laws,
She did corrupt frail nature with some bribe,
To shrink mine arm up like a wither'd shrub;
To make an envious mountain on my back,
Where sits deformity to mock my body;
To shape my legs of an unequal size;
To disproportion me in every part,
Like to a chaos, or an unlick'd bear-whelp
That carries no impression like the dam.
And am I then a man to be belov'd?
O monstrous fault, to harbour such a thought!
Then, since this earth affords no joy to me,
But to command, to check, to o'erbear such
As are of better person than myself,
I'll make my heaven to dream upon the crown,
And, whiles I live, t' account this world but hell,
Until my mis-shap'd trunk that bears this head
Be round impaled with a glorious crown.
And yet I know not how to get the crown,
For many lives stand between me and home:
And I,—like one lost in a thorny wood,
That rends the thorns and is rent with the thorns,
Seeking a way and straying from the way;
Not knowing how to find the open air,
But toiling desperately to find it out,—
Torment myself to catch the English crown:
And from that torment I will free myself,
Or hew my way out with a bloody axe.
Why, I can smile, and murder whiles I smile,
And cry 'Content' to that which grieves my heart,

Machiavellian villain. Up to this point his character has been that of a ruthless, impetuous warrior after the manner of Tamburlaine. The change here anticipates the Machiavellian king in *Richard III*. Cf. II, i, 49, note. 132. **rooms,** places. 133. **cold premeditation,** hopeless outlook. 139. **lade,** empty (by bailing). 143. **me,** myself. 144. **o'erweens too much,** is overambitious. 157. **envious,** spiteful; see glossary. 161. **unlick'd bear-whelp.** It was a popular notion that bears licked their newly born cubs into a proper shape. 171. **impaled,** enclosed; specifically, encircled with a crown; cf. III, iii, 189.

And wet my cheeks with artificial tears,
And frame my face to all occasions.
I'll drown more sailors than the mermaid shall;
I'll slay more gazers than the basilisk;
I'll play the orator as well as Nestor,
Deceive more slily than Ulysses could,
And, like a Sinon, take another Troy.
I can add colours to the chameleon,
Change shapes with Proteus for advantages,
And set the murderous Machiavel to school.
Can I do this, and cannot get a crown?
Tut, were it farther off, I'll pluck it down. *Exit.*

[SCENE III. *France. The* KING'S *palace.*]

Flourish. Enter LEWIS *the French King, his sister* BONA, *his Admiral, called* BOURBON: PRINCE EDWARD, QUEEN MARGARET, *and the* EARL OF OXFORD. LEWIS *sits, and riseth up again.*

K. Lew. Fair Queen of England, worthy Margaret,
Sit down with us: it ill befits thy state
And birth, that thou shouldst stand while Lewis doth sit.
Q. Mar. No, mighty King of France: now Margaret
Must strike her sail and learn awhile to serve
Where kings command. I was, I must confess,
Great Albion's queen in former golden days:
But now mischance hath trod my title down,
And with dishonour laid me on the ground;
Where I must take like seat unto my fortune,
And to my humble seat conform myself.
K. Lew. Why, say, fair queen, whence springs this deep despair?
Q. Mar. From such a cause as fills mine eyes with tears
And stops my tongue, while heart is drown'd in cares.
K. Lew. Whate'er it be, be thou still like thyself,
And sit thee by our side: *(Seats her by him)* yield not thy neck
To fortune's yoke, but let thy dauntless mind
Still ride in triumph over all mischance.
Be plain, Queen Margaret, and tell thy grief;
It shall be eas'd, if France can yield relief.
Q. Mar. Those gracious words revive my drooping thoughts
And give my tongue-tied sorrows leave to speak.
Now, therefore, be it known to noble Lewis,
That Henry, sole possessor of my love,
Is of a king become a banish'd man,
And forc'd to live in Scotland a forlorn;
While proud ambitious Edward Duke of York
Usurps the regal title and the seat
Of England's true-anointed lawful king.
This is the cause that I, poor Margaret,
With this my son, Prince Edward, Henry's heir,
Am come to crave thy just and lawful aid;
And if thou fail us, all our hope is done:
Scotland hath will to help, but cannot help;
Our people and our peers are both misled,
Our treasure seiz'd, our soldiers put to flight,
And, as thou seest, ourselves in heavy plight.
K. Lew. Renowned queen, with patience calm the storm,
While we bethink a means to break it off.
Q. Mar. The more we stay, the stronger grows our foe.
K. Lew. The more I stay, the more I'll succour thee.
Q. Mar. O, but impatience waiteth on true sorrow.
And see where comes the breeder of my sorrow!

Enter WARWICK.

K. Lew. What 's he approacheth boldly to our presence?
Q. Mar. Our Earl of Warwick, Edward's greatest friend.
K. Lew. Welcome, brave Warwick! What brings thee to France? *He descends. She ariseth.*
Q. Mar. Ay, now begins a second storm to rise;
For this is he that moves both wind and tide.
War. From worthy Edward, King of Albion,
My lord and sovereign, and thy vowed friend,
I come, in kindness and unfeigned love,
First, to do greetings to thy royal person;
And then to crave a league of amity;
And lastly, to confirm that amity
With nuptial knot, if thou vouchsafe to grant
That virtuous Lady Bona, thy fair sister,
To England's king in lawful marriage.
Q. Mar. [*Aside*] If that go forward, Henry's hope is done.
War. (Speaking to Bona) And, gracious madam, in our king's behalf,
I am commanded, with your leave and favour,
Humbly to kiss your hand and with my tongue
To tell the passion of my sovereign's heart;
Where fame, late ent'ring at his heedful ears,
Hath plac'd thy beauty's image and thy virtue.
Q. Mar. King Lewis and Lady Bona, hear me speak,
Before you answer Warwick. His demand
Springs not from Edward's well-meant honest love,
But from deceit bred by necessity;
For how can tyrants safely govern home,
Unless abroad they purchase great alliance?
To prove him tyrant this reason may suffice,
That Henry liveth still; but were he dead,
Yet here Prince Edward stands, King Henry's son.
Look, therefore, Lewis, that by this league and marriage
Thou draw not on thy danger and dishonour;
For though usurpers sway the rule awhile,
Yet heav'ns are just, and time suppresseth wrongs.
War. Injurious Margaret!
Prince. And why not queen?
War. Because thy father Henry did usurp;
And thou no more art prince than she is queen.
Oxf. Then Warwick disannuls great John of Gaunt,
Which did subdue the greatest part of Spain;
And, after John of Gaunt, Henry the Fourth,
Whose wisdom was a mirror to the wisest;

186. **drown . . . shall.** Mermaids allegedly had the power to lure sailors to destruction by their singing or weeping. 187. **basilisk,** fabulous reptile said to kill by its look; see glossary. 188. **Nestor,** one of the Greek leaders in the siege of Troy, famous among other things for his eloquence. 189. **Ulysses.** The epithet "crafty" is frequently applied to Ulysses in the Homeric poems. 190. **Sinon,** Greek soldier who allowed himself to be taken prisoner by the Trojans, pretending that the Greeks had misused him. He persuaded Priam to bring the wooden horse within the city walls and at night released the soldiers hidden within it. 192. **Proteus,** old man of the sea, able to assume different shapes. **for advantages,** as it suits my convenience; see *advantage* in glossary. 193. **set the . . . school,** teach Machiavelli how to be ruthless; cf. *1 Henry VI*, V, iv, 74, note.

SCENE III. 7. **Albion's,** England's. 25. **of,** instead of; see glossary.

And, after that wise prince, Henry the Fifth,
Who by his prowess conquered all France:
From these our Henry lineally descends.
War. Oxford, how haps it, in this smooth discourse,
You told not how Henry the Sixth hath lost
All that which Henry the Fifth had gotten?
Methinks these peers of France should smile at that.
But for the rest, you tell a pedigree
Of threescore and two years; a silly time
To make prescription for a kingdom's worth.
Oxf. Why, Warwick, canst thou speak against thy liege,
Whom thou obeyed'st thirty and six years,
And not bewray thy treason with a blush?
War. Can Oxford, that did ever fence the right,
Now buckler falsehood with a pedigree?
For shame! leave Henry, and call Edward king.
Oxf. Call him my king by whose injurious doom
My elder brother, the Lord Aubrey Vere,
Was done to death? and more than so, my father,
Even in the downfall of his mellow'd years,
When nature brought him to the door of death?
No, Warwick, no; while life upholds this arm,
This arm upholds the house of Lancaster.
War. And I the house of York.
K. Lew. Queen Margaret, Prince Edward, and Oxford,
Vouchsafe, at our request, to stand aside,
While I use further conference with Warwick.
They stand aloof.
Q. Mar. Heavens grant that Warwick's words bewitch him not!
K. Lew. Now, Warwick, tell me, even upon thy conscience,
Is Edward your true king? for I were loath
To link with him that were not lawful chosen.
War. Thereon I pawn my credit and mine honour.
K. Lew. But is he gracious in the people's eye?
War. The more that Henry was unfortunate.
K. Lew. Then further, all dissembling set aside,
Tell me for truth the measure of his love
Unto our sister Bona.
War. Such it seems
As may beseem a monarch like himself.
Myself have often heard him say and swear
That this his love was an eternal plant,
Whereof the root was fix'd in virtue's ground,
The leaves and fruit maintain'd with beauty's sun,
Exempt from envy, but not from disdain,
Unless the Lady Bona quit his pain.
K. Lew. Now, sister, let us hear your firm resolve.
Bona. Your grant, or your denial, shall be mine:
(Speaks to War.) Yet I confess that often ere this day,
When I have heard your king's desert recounted,
Mine ear hath tempted judgement to desire.
K. Lew. Then, Warwick, thus: our sister shall be Edward's;
And now forthwith shall articles be drawn
Touching the jointure that your king must make,
Which with her dowry shall be counterpois'd.
Draw near, Queen Margaret, and be a witness
That Bona shall be wife to the English king.
Prince. To Edward, but not to the English king.
Q. Mar. Deceitful Warwick! it was thy device
By this alliance to make void my suit:
Before thy coming Lewis was Henry's friend.
K. Lew. And still is friend to him and Margaret:
But if your title to the crown be weak,
As may appear by Edward's good success,
Then 'tis but reason that I be releas'd
From giving aid which late I promised.
Yet shall you have all kindness at my hand
That your estate requires and mine can yield.
War. Henry now lives in Scotland at his ease,
Where having nothing, nothing can he lose.
And as for you yourself, our quondam queen,
You have a father able to maintain you;
And better 'twere you troubled him than France.
Q. Mar. Peace, impudent and shameless Warwick, peace,
Proud setter up and puller down of kings!
I will not hence, till, with my talk and tears,
Both full of truth, I make King Lewis behold
Thy sly conveyance and thy lord's false love;
For both of you are birds of selfsame feather.
Post blowing a horn within.
K. Lew. Warwick, this is some post to us or thee.

Enter the Post.

Post. (Speaks to Warwick) My lord ambassador, these letters are for you,
Sent from your brother, Marquess Montague:
(To Lewis) These from our king unto your majesty:
(To Margaret) And, madam, these for you; from whom I know not. *They all read their letters.*
Oxf. I like it well that our fair queen and mistress
Smiles at her news, while Warwick frowns at his.
Prince. Nay, mark how Lewis stamps, as he were nettled:
I hope all 's for the best.
K. Lew. Warwick, what are thy news? and yours, fair queen?
Q. Mar. Mine, such as fill my heart with unhop'd joys.
War. Mine, full of sorrow and heart's discontent.
K. Lew. What! has your king married the Lady Grey?
And now, to soothe your forgery and his,
Sends me a paper to persuade me patience?
Is this th' alliance that he seeks with France?
Dare he presume to scorn us in this manner?
Q. Mar. I told your majesty as much before:
This proveth Edward's love and Warwick's honesty.
War. King Lewis, I here protest, in sight of heaven,
And by the hope I have of heavenly bliss,
That I am clear from this misdeed of Edward's,
No more my king, for he dishonours me,
But most himself, if he could see his shame.
Did I forget that by the house of York
My father came untimely to his death?
Did I let pass th' abuse done to my niece?

26. **forlorn,** outcast. 41. **The . . . thee,** the longer preparation I make, the greater help I can give. 44. **he,** he who. 63. **fame,** report; see glossary. 81. **disannuls,** takes no account of. 93. **threescore and two,** i.e., from 1399, the date of Henry IV's accession, to 1461, that of Edward's. 94. **prescription,** claim founded upon long use. 97. **bewray,** reveal, betray. 127. **envy,** ill will, malice; see glossary. 128. **quit,** requite; see glossary. 133. **tempted . . . desire,** indulged in wishful thinking. 157. **Proud . . . kings.** Cf. II, iii, 37. 160. **conveyance,** underhand dealing. 175. **forgery,** deceit. 188. **abuse . . . niece.** Cf. a passage in Holinshed relating "that king Edward did attempt a thing once in the earles house, which was much against the earles honestie; (whether he would haue defloured his daughter or his neece, the certeintie was not for both their honours openlie reuealed;) for suerlie, such a thing was attempted by king Edward. . . ."

Did I impale him with the regal crown?
Did I put Henry from his native right?
And am I guerdon'd at the last with shame?
Shame on himself! for my desert is honour:
And to repair my honour lost for him,
I here renounce him and return to Henry.
My noble queen, let former grudges pass,
And henceforth I am thy true servitor:
I will revenge his wrong to Lady Bona
And replant Henry in his former state.
Q. Mar. Warwick, these words have turn'd my hate to love;
And I forgive and quite forget old faults,
And joy that thou becom'st King Henry's friend.
War. So much his friend, ay, his unfeigned friend,
That, if King Lewis vouchsafe to furnish us
With some few bands of chosen soldiers,
I'll undertake to land them on our coast
And force the tyrant from his seat by war.
'Tis not his new-made bride shall succour him:
And as for Clarence, as my letters tell me,
He 's very likely now to fall from him,
For matching more for wanton lust than honour,
Or than for strength and safety of our country.
Bona. Dear brother, how shall Bona be reveng'd
But by thy help to this distressed queen?
Q. Mar. Renowned prince, how shall poor Henry live,
Unless thou rescue him from foul despair?
Bona. My quarrel and this English queen's are one.
War. And mine, fair lady Bona, joins with yours.
K. Lew. And mine with hers, and thine, and Margaret's.
Therefore at last I firmly am resolv'd
You shall have aid.
Q. Mar. Let me give humble thanks for all at once.
K. Lew. Then, England's messenger, return in post,
And tell false Edward, thy supposed king,
That Lewis of France is sending over masquers
To revel it with him and his new bride:
Thou seest what 's past, go fear thy king withal.
Bona. Tell him, in hope he'll prove a widower shortly,
I'll wear the willow garland for his sake.
Q. Mar. Tell him, my mourning weeds are laid aside,
And I am ready to put armour on.
War. Tell him from me that he hath done me wrong,
And therefore I'll uncrown him ere 't be long.
There 's thy reward: be gone. *Exit Post.*
K. Lew. But, Warwick,
Thou and Oxford, with five thousand men,
Shall cross the seas, and bid false Edward battle;
And, as occasion serves, this noble queen
And prince shall follow with a fresh supply.
Yet, ere thou go, but answer me one doubt,
What pledge have we of thy firm loyalty?
War. This shall assure my constant loyalty,
That if our queen and this young prince agree,
I'll join mine eldest daughter and my joy
To him forthwith in holy wedlock bands.
Q. Mar. Yes, I agree, and thank you for your motion.
Son Edward, she is fair and virtuous,
Therefore delay not, give thy hand to Warwick;
And, with thy hand, thy faith irrevocable,
That only Warwick's daughter shall be thine.
Prince. Yes, I accept her, for she well deserves it;
And here, to pledge my vow, I give my hand.
He gives his hand to Warwick.
K. Lew. Why stay we now? These soldiers shall be levied,
And thou, Lord Bourbon, our high admiral,
Shalt waft them over with our royal fleet.
I long till Edward fall by war's mischance,
For mocking marriage with a dame of France.
Exeunt. Manet Warwick.
War. I came from Edward as ambassador,
But I return his sworn and mortal foe:
Matter of marriage was the charge he gave me,
But dreadful war shall answer his demand.
Had he none else to make a stale but me?
Then none but I shall turn his jest to sorrow.
I was the chief that rais'd him to the crown,
And I'll be chief to bring him down again:
Not that I pity Henry's misery,
But seek revenge on Edward's mockery. *Exit.*

[ACT IV.

SCENE I. *London. The palace.*]

Enter RICHARD [DUKE OF GLOUCESTER], CLARENCE, SOMERSET, *and* MONTAGUE.

Glou. Now tell me, brother Clarence, what think you
Of this new marriage with the Lady Grey?
Hath not our brother made a worthy choice?
Clar. Alas, you know, 'tis far from hence to France;
How could he stay till Warwick made return?
Som. My lords, forbear this talk; here comes the king.

Flourish. Enter KING EDWARD, LADY GREY [*as* QUEEN ELIZABETH], PEMBROKE, STAFFORD, HASTINGS. *Four stand on one side and four on the other.*

Glou. And his well-chosen bride.
Clar. I mind to tell him plainly what I think.
K. Edw. Now, brother of Clarence, how like you our choice,
That you stand pensive, as half malcontent?
Clar. As well as Lewis of France, or the Earl of Warwick,
Which are so weak of courage and in judgement
That they'll take no offence at our abuse.
K. Edw. Suppose they take offence without a cause,
They are but Lewis and Warwick: I am Edward,
Your king and Warwick's, and must have my will.
Glou. And shall have your will, because our king:
Yet hasty marriage seldom proveth well.
K. Edw. Yea, brother Richard, are you offended too?
Glou. Not I:
No, God forbid that I should wish them sever'd
Whom God hath join'd together; ay, and 'twere pity
To sunder them that yoke so well together.

191. **guerdon'd,** rewarded. 226. **fear,** frighten; see glossary. 228. **willow garland,** contemptuous reference to the willow as the symbol of a forsaken lover. 229. **weeds,** garments; see glossary. 242. **eldest daughter,** a historical inaccuracy. Prince Edward married a younger daughter of Warwick; the eldest was already the wife of the duke of Clarence. 244. **motion,** proposal; see glossary. 260. **stale,** tool, laughingstock. 262. **chief,** principal person.

ACT IV. SCENE I. 8. **I mind,** I have it in mind. 10. **malcontent,**

K. Edw. Setting your scorns and your mislike aside,
Tell me some reason why the Lady Grey
Should not become my wife and England's queen.
And you too, Somerset and Montague,
Speak freely what you think.
Clar. Then this is mine opinion: that King Lewis
Becomes your enemy, for mocking him
About the marriage of the Lady Bona.
Glou. And Warwick, doing what you gave in charge,
Is now dishonoured by this new marriage.
K. Edw. What if both Lewis and Warwick be appeas'd
By such invention as I can devise?
Mont. Yet, to have join'd with France in such alliance
Would more have strength'ned this our commonwealth
'Gainst foreign storms than any home-bred marriage.
Hast. Why, knows not Montague that of itself
England is safe, if true within itself?
Mont. But the safer when 'tis back'd with France.
Hast. 'Tis better using France than trusting France:
Let us be back'd with God and with the seas
Which He hath giv'n for fence impregnable,
And with their helps only defend ourselves;
In them and in ourselves our safety lies.
Clar. For this one speech Lord Hastings well deserves
To have the heir of the Lord Hungerford.
K. Edw. Ay, what of that? it was my will and grant;
And for this once my will shall stand for law.
Glou. And yet methinks your grace hath not done well,
To give the heir and daughter of Lord Scales
Unto the brother of your loving bride;
She better would have fitted me or Clarence:
But in your bride you bury brotherhood.
Clar. Or else you would not have bestow'd the heir
Of the Lord Bonville on your new wife's son,
And leave your brothers to go speed elsewhere.
K. Edw. Alas, poor Clarence! is it for a wife
That thou art malcontent? I will provide thee.
Clar. In choosing for yourself, you show'd your judgement,
Which being shallow, you shall give me leave
To play the broker in mine own behalf;
And to that end I shortly mind to leave you.
K. Edw. Leave me, or tarry, Edward will be king,
And not be tied unto his brother's will.
Q. Eliz. My lords, before it pleas'd his majesty
To raise my state to title of a queen,
Do me but right, and you must all confess
That I was not ignoble of descent;
And meaner than myself have had like fortune.
But as this title honours me and mine,
So your dislike, to whom I would be pleasing,
Doth cloud my joys with danger and with sorrow.
K. Edw. My love, forbear to fawn upon their frowns:
What danger or what sorrow can befall thee,
So long as Edward is thy constant friend,
And their true sovereign, whom they must obey?
Nay, whom they shall obey, and love thee too,
Unless they seek for hatred at my hands;
Which if they do, yet will I keep thee safe,
And they shall feel the vengeance of my wrath.
Glou. I hear, yet say not much, but think the more. [*Aside.*]

Enter a Post.

K. Edw. Now, messenger, what letters or what news
From France?
Post. My sovereign liege, no letters; and few words,
But such as I, without your special pardon,
Dare not relate.
K. Edw. Go to, we pardon thee: therefore, in brief,
Tell me their words as near as thou canst guess them.
What answer makes King Lewis unto our letters?
Post. At my depart, these were his very words:
'Go tell false Edward, thy supposed king,
That Lewis of France is sending over masquers
To revel it with him and his new bride.'
K. Edw. Is Lewis so brave? belike he thinks me Henry.
But what said Lady Bona to my marriage?
Post. These were her words, utt'red with mild disdain:
'Tell him, I hope he'll prove a widower shortly,
I'll wear the willow garland for his sake.'
K. Edw. I blame not her, she could say little less;
She had the wrong. But what said Henry's queen?
For I have heard that she was there in place.
Post. 'Tell him,' quoth she, 'my mourning weeds are done,
And I am ready to put armour on.'
K. Edw. Belike she minds to play the Amazon.
But what said Warwick to these injuries?
Post. He, more incens'd against your majesty
Than all the rest, discharg'd me with these words:
'Tell him from me that he hath done me wrong,
And therefore I'll uncrown him ere 't be long.'
K. Edw. Ha! durst the traitor breathe out so proud words?
Well, I will arm me, being thus forewarn'd:
They shall have wars and pay for their presumption.
But say, is Warwick friends with Margaret?
Post. Ay, gracious sovereign; they are so link'd in friendship,
That young Prince Edward marries Warwick's daughter.
Clar. Belike the elder; Clarence will have the younger.
Now, brother king, farewell, and sit you fast,
For I will hence to Warwick's other daughter;
That, though I want a kingdom, yet in marriage
I may not prove inferior to yourself.
You that love me and Warwick, follow me.
Exit Clarence, and Somerset follows.
Glou. [*Aside*] Not I:
My thoughts aim at a further matter; I
Stay not for the love of Edward, but the crown.
K. Edw. Clarence and Somerset both gone to Warwick!
Yet am I arm'd against the worst can happen;
And haste is needful in this desp'rate case.
Pembroke and Stafford, you in our behalf
Go levy men, and make prepare for war;
They are already, or quickly will be landed:

discontented; a cant term of the age suggesting a melancholy affection. 35. **invention,** scheme, plan; see glossary. 48. **To . . . Hungerford.** The reference is to the marriage of Lord Hastings to the daughter of Lord Hungerford. 58. **speed,** be successful; see glossary. 70. **not ignoble.** Elizabeth's mother was a sister-in-law of Henry V. 73. **dislike,** displeasure. 90. **guess,** remember, i.e., reproduce from memory. 118. **the elder.** Cf. III, iii, 242, note. 128. **worst can,** worst that can. 131. **prepare,** preparation.

Myself in person will straight follow you.
Exeunt Pembroke and Stafford.
But, ere I go, Hastings and Montague,
Resolve my doubt. You twain, of all the rest,
Are near to Warwick by blood and by alliance:
Tell me if you love Warwick more than me?
If it be so, then both depart to him;
I rather wish you foes than hollow friends:
But if you mind to hold your true obedience,
Give me assurance with some friendly vow,
That I may never have you in suspect.
Mont. So God help Montague as he proves true!
Hast. And Hastings as he favours Edward's cause!
K. Edw. Now, brother Richard, will you stand by us?
Glou. Ay, in despite of all that shall withstand you.
K. Edw. Why, so! then am I sure of victory.
Now therefore let us hence; and lose no hour,
Till we meet Warwick with his foreign pow'r. *Exeunt.*

[SCENE II. *A plain in Warwickshire.*]

Enter WARWICK *and* OXFORD *in England, with French soldiers.*

War. Trust me, my lord, all hitherto goes well;
The common people by numbers swarm to us.

Enter CLARENCE *and* SOMERSET.

But see where Somerset and Clarence comes!
Speak suddenly, my lords, are we all friends?
Clar. Fear not that, my lord.
War. Then, gentle Clarence, welcome unto Warwick;
And welcome, Somerset: I hold it cowardice
To rest mistrustful where a noble heart
Hath pawn'd an open hand in sign of love;
Else might I think that Clarence, Edward's brother,
Were but a feigned friend to our proceedings:
But welcome, sweet Clarence; my daughter shall be thine.
And now what rests but, in night's coverture,
Thy brother being carelessly encamp'd,
His soldiers lurking in the towns about,
And but attended by a simple guard,
We may surprise and take him at our pleasure?
Our scouts have found the adventure very easy:
That as Ulysses and stout Diomede
With sleight and manhood stole to Rhesus' tents,
And brought from thence the Thracian fatal steeds,
So we, well cover'd with the night's black mantle,
At unawares may beat down Edward's guard
And seize himself; I say not, slaughter him,
For I intend but only to surprise him.
You that will follow me to this attempt,
Applaud the name of Henry with your leader.
They all cry, 'Henry!'
Why, then, let 's on our way in silent sort:
For Warwick and his friends, God and Saint George!
Exeunt.

[SCENE III. *Edward's camp, near Warwick.*]

Enter three Watchmen, *to guard the* KING'S *tent.*

First Watch. Come on, my masters, each man take his stand:
The king by this is set him down to sleep.
Second Watch. What, will he not to bed?
First Watch. Why, no; for he hath made a solemn vow
Never to lie and take his natural rest
Till Warwick or himself be quite suppress'd.
Second Watch. To-morrow then belike shall be the day,
If Warwick be so near as men report.
Third Watch. But say, I pray, what nobleman is that
That with the king here resteth in his tent?
First Watch. 'Tis the Lord Hastings, the king's chiefest friend.
Third Watch. O, is it so? But why commands the king
That his chief followers lodge in towns about him,
While he himself keeps in the cold field?
Second Watch. 'Tis the more honour, because more dangerous.
Third Watch. Ay, but give me worship and quietness;
I like it better than a dangerous honour.
If Warwick knew in what estate he stands,
'Tis to be doubted he would waken him.
First Watch. Unless our halberds did shut up his passage.
Second Watch. Ay, wherefore else guard we his royal tent,
But to defend his person from night-foes?

Enter WARWICK, CLARENCE, OXFORD, SOMERSET, *and French soldiers, silent all.*

War. This is his tent; and see where stand his guard.
Courage, my masters! honour now or never!
But follow me, and Edward shall be ours.
First Watch. Who goes there?
Second Watch. Stay, or thou diest!
Warwick and the rest cry all, 'Warwick! Warwick!' *and set upon the Guard, who fly, crying,* 'Arm! arm!' *Warwick and the rest following them.*

The drum playing and trumpet sounding, enter WARWICK, SOMERSET, *and the rest, bringing the* KING *out in his gown, sitting in a chair.* RICHARD *and* HASTINGS *fly over the stage.*

Som. What are they that fly there?
War. Richard and Hastings: let them go; here is
The duke.
K. Edw. The duke! Why, Warwick, when we parted,
Thou call'dst me king.
War. Ay, but the case is alter'd:
When you disgrac'd me in my embassade,
Then I degraded you from being king,
And come now to create you Duke of York.
Alas! how should you govern any kingdom,
That know not how to use ambassadors,
Nor how to be contented with one wife,
Nor how to use your brothers brotherly,
Nor how to study for the people's welfare,
Nor how to shroud yourself from enemies?
K. Edw. Yea, brother of Clarence, art thou here too?
Nay, then I see that Edward needs must down.

SCENE II. 3. **comes,** a common plural form; see Abbott, 333. 9. **pawn'd,** pledged. 13. **rests,** remains. 19-21. **Ulysses . . . steeds,** an allusion to an incident in the tenth book of the *Iliad*. Ulysses and Diomedes under cover of night stealthily entered the camp of the Thracian leader Rhesus, slew him and twelve of his men, and led away his horses. They are called *fatal steeds* because a prophecy foretold that if they ever drank from the Xanthus River, the Greeks would lose the war.
SCENE III. 14. **keeps,** lodges; see glossary. 16. **worship,** a place of dignity. 18. **estate,** situation. 19. **doubted,** feared; see glossary. 20. **halberds,** weapons consisting of blades or spearheads mounted on

Yet, Warwick, in despite of all mischance,
Of thee thyself and all thy complices,
Edward will always bear himself as king:
Though fortune's malice overthrow my state,
My mind exceeds the compass of her wheel.
War. Then, for his mind, be Edward England's king: *Takes off his crown.*
But Henry now shall wear the English crown,
And be true king indeed, thou but the shadow.
My lord of Somerset, at my request,
See that forthwith Duke Edward be convey'd
Unto my brother, Archbishop of York.
When I have fought with Pembroke and his fellows,
I'll follow you, and tell what answer
Lewis and the Lady Bona send to him.
Now, for a while farewell, good Duke of York.
They lead him out forcibly.
K. Edw. What fates impose, that men must needs abide;
It boots not to resist both wind and tide. *Exit [guarded].*
Oxf. What now remains, my lords, for us to do
But march to London with our soldiers?
War. Ay, that 's the first thing that we have to do;
To free King Henry from imprisonment
And see him seated in the regal throne. *Exeunt.*

[SCENE IV. *London. The palace.*]

Enter RIVERS *and* LADY GREY [QUEEN ELIZABETH].

Riv. Madam, what makes you in this sudden change?
Q. Eliz. Why, brother Rivers, are you yet to learn
What late misfortune is befall'n King Edward?
Riv. What! loss of some pitch'd battle against Warwick?
Q. Eliz. No, but the loss of his own royal person.
Riv. Then is my sovereign slain?
Q. Eliz. Ay, almost slain, for he is taken prisoner,
Either betray'd by falsehood of his guard
Or by his foe surpris'd at unawares:
And, as I further have to understand,
Is new committed to the Bishop of York,
Fell Warwick's brother and by that our foe.
Riv. These news I must confess are full of grief;
Yet, gracious madam, bear it as you may:
Warwick may lose, that now hath won the day.
Q. Eliz. Till then fair hope must hinder life's decay.
And I the rather wean me from despair
For love of Edward's offspring in my womb:
This is it that makes me bridle passion
And bear with mildness my misfortune's cross;
Ay, ay, for this I draw in many a tear
And stop the rising of blood-sucking sighs,
Lest with my sighs or tears I blast or drown
King Edward's fruit, true heir to th' English crown.
Riv. But, madam, where is Warwick then become?
Q. Eliz. I am inform'd that he comes towards London,
To set the crown once more on Henry's head:
Guess thou the rest; King Edward's friends must down,
But, to prevent the tyrant's violence,—
For trust not him that hath once broken faith,—
I'll hence forthwith unto the sanctuary,
To save at least the heir of Edward's right:
There shall I rest secure from force and fraud.
Come, therefore, let us fly while we may fly:
If Warwick take us we are sure to die. *Exeunt.*

[SCENE V. *A park near Middleham Castle in Yorkshire.*]

Enter RICHARD [DUKE OF GLOUCESTER], LORD HASTINGS, *and* SIR WILLIAM STANLEY.

Glou. Now, my Lord Hastings and Sir William Stanley,
Leave off to wonder why I drew you hither,
Into this chiefest thicket of the park.
Thus stands the case: you know our king, my brother,
Is prisoner to the bishop here, at whose hands
He hath good usage and great liberty,
And, often but attended with weak guard,
Comes hunting this way to disport himself.
I have advertis'd him by secret means
That if about this hour he make this way
Under the colour of his usual game,
He shall here find his friends with horse and men
To set him free from his captivity.

Enter KING EDWARD *and a* Huntsman *with him.*

Hunt. This way, my lord; for this way lies the game.
K. Edw. Nay, this way, man: see where the huntsmen stand.
Now, brother of Gloucester, Lord Hastings, and the rest,
Stand you thus close, to steal the bishop's deer?
Glou. Brother, the time and case requireth haste:
Your horse stands ready at the park-corner.
K. Edw. But whither shall we then?
Hast. To Lynn, my lord,
And ship from thence to Flanders.
Glou. Well guess'd, believe me; for that was my meaning.
K. Edw. Stanley, I will requite thy forwardness.
Glou. But wherefore stay we? 'tis no time to talk.
K. Edw. Huntsman, what say'st thou? wilt thou go along?
Hunt. Better do so than tarry and be hang'd.
Glou. Come then, away; let 's ha' no more ado.
K. Edw. Bishop, farewell: shield thee from Warwick's frown;
And pray that I may repossess the crown. *Exeunt.*

[SCENE VI. *London. The Tower.*]

Flourish. Enter KING HENRY THE SIXTH, CLARENCE, WARWICK, SOMERSET, *young* HENRY [EARL OF RICHMOND], OXFORD, MONTAGUE, *and* Lieutenant [of the Tower].

K. Hen. Master lieutenant, now that God and friends
Have shaken Edward from the regal seat,
And turn'd my captive state to liberty,

long handles. 32. **embassade,** mission as an ambassador. 48. **for his mind,** i.e., in his own thoughts. 54. **fellows,** companions; see glossary.
SCENE IV. 22. **blood-sucking sighs.** Cf. *2 Henry VI*, III, ii, 61, 63, note. 28. **must down,** will inevitably be put down. 29. **prevent,** forestall; see glossary.

SCENE V. *Stage Direction:* ***park,*** enclosed hunting preserve. 2. **Leave off,** cease. 9. **advertis'd,** notified. 11. **colour,** pretext; see glossary. 17. **close,** concealed; see glossary. 23. **forwardness,** zeal.

My fear to hope, my sorrows unto joys,
At our enlargement what are thy due fees?
Lieu. Subjects may challenge nothing of their sovereigns;
But if an humble prayer may prevail,
I then crave pardon of your majesty.
K. Hen. For what, lieutenant? for well using me?
Nay, be thou sure I'll well requite thy kindness,
For that it made my imprisonment a pleasure;
Ay, such a pleasure as incaged birds
Conceive when after many moody thoughts
At last by notes of household harmony
They quite forget their loss of liberty.
But, Warwick, after God, thou set'st me free,
And chiefly therefore I thank God and thee;
He was the author, thou the instrument.
Therefore, that I may conquer fortune's spite
By living low, where fortune cannot hurt me,
And that the people of this blessed land
May not be punish'd with my thwarting stars,
Warwick, although my head still wear the crown,
I here resign my government to thee,
For thou art fortunate in all thy deeds.
War. Your grace hath still been fam'd for virtuous;
And now may seem as wise as virtuous,
By spying and avoiding fortune's malice,
For few men rightly temper with the stars:
Yet in this one thing let me blame your grace,
For choosing me when Clarence is in place.
Clar. No, Warwick, thou art worthy of the sway,
To whom the heav'ns in thy nativity
Adjudg'd an olive branch and laurel crown,
As likely to be blest in peace and war;
And therefore I yield thee my free consent.
War. And I choose Clarence only for protector.
K. Hen. Warwick and Clarence, give me both your hands:
Now join your hands, and with your hands your hearts,
That no dissension hinder government:
I make you both protectors of this land,
While I myself will lead a private life
And in devotion spend my latter days,
To sin's rebuke and my Creator's praise.
War. What answers Clarence to his sovereign's will?
Clar. That he consents, if Warwick yield consent;
For on thy fortune I repose myself.
War. Why, then, though loath, yet must I be content:
We'll yoke together, like a double shadow
To Henry's body, and supply his place;
I mean, in bearing weight of government,
While he enjoys the honour and his ease.
And, Clarence, now then it is more than needful
Forthwith that Edward be pronounc'd a traitor,
And all his lands and goods be confiscate.
Clar. What else? and that succession be determined.
War. Ay, therein Clarence shall not want his part.
K. Hen. But, with the first of all your chief affairs,
Let me entreat, for I command no more,
That Margaret your queen and my son Edward
Be sent for, to return from France with speed;
For, till I see them here, by doubtful fear
My joy of liberty is half eclips'd.
Clar. It shall be done, my sovereign, with all speed.
K. Hen. My Lord of Somerset, what youth is that,
Of whom you seem to have so tender care?
Som. My liege, it is young Henry, earl of Richmond.
K. Hen. Come hither, England's hope. *(Lays his hand on his head)* If secret powers
Suggest but truth to my divining thoughts,
This pretty lad will prove our country's bliss.
His looks are full of peaceful majesty,
His head by nature fram'd to wear a crown,
His hand to wield a sceptre, and himself
Likely in time to bless a regal throne.
Make much of him, my lords, for this is he
Must help you more than you are hurt by me.

Enter a Post.

War. What news, my friend?
Post. That Edward is escaped from your brother,
And fled, as he hears since, to Burgundy.
War. Unsavoury news! but how made he escape?
Post. He was convey'd by Richard Duke of Gloucester
And the Lord Hastings, who attended him
In secret ambush on the forest side
And from the bishop's huntsmen rescu'd him;
For hunting was his daily exercise.
War. My brother was too careless of his charge.
But let us hence, my sovereign, to provide
A salve for any sore that may betide.
Exeunt. Mane[n]t Somerset, Richmond, and Oxford.
Som. My lord, I like not of this flight of Edward's;
For doubtless Burgundy will yield him help,
And we shall have more wars before 't be long.
As Henry's late presaging prophecy
Did glad my heart with hope of this young Richmond,
So doth my heart misgive me, in these conflicts
What may befall him, to his harm and ours:
Therefore, Lord Oxford, to prevent the worst,
Forthwith we'll send him hence to Brittany,
Till storms be past of civil enmity.
Oxf. Ay, for if Edward repossess the crown,
'Tis like that Richmond with the rest shall down.
Som. It shall be so; he shall to Brittany.
Come, therefore, let 's about it speedily. *Exeunt.*

[SCENE VII. *Before York.*]

Flourish. Enter [KING] EDWARD, RICHARD [DUKE OF GLOUCESTER], HASTINGS, *and* Soldiers.

K. Edw. Now, brother Richard, Lord Hastings, and the rest,
Yet thus far fortune maketh us amends,
And says that once more I shall interchange
My waned state for Henry's regal crown.
Well have we pass'd and now repass'd the seas
And brought desired help from Burgundy:

SCENE VI. 5. **enlargement,** freedom from captivity or imprisonment. 6. **challenge,** claim as a right. 22. **thwarting,** crossing; cf. *Romeo and Juliet,* Prologue, 6. 29. **temper with,** blend or accord with. 34. **olive branch,** symbol of peace. **laurel crown,** symbol of honor. 36. **free,** generous; see glossary. 57. **Clarence . . . part.** Holinshed makes explicit this veiled reference to Clarence's nearness to the crown. If Edward and his heirs were set aside—as an attainder for treason would entail—and if Henry's line should die out, Clarence would be in a position to claim the kingship. This possibility was glanced at by Gloucester earlier in the play (III, ii, 130). **want,** lack; see glossary. 67. **Henry, earl of Richmond,** Henry Tudor, great-great-grandson of John of Gaunt and Catherine Swynford through his mother, Margaret

What then remains, we being thus arriv'd
From Ravenspurgh haven before the gates of York,
But that we enter, as into our dukedom?
Glou. The gates made fast! Brother, I like not this;
For many men that stumble at the threshold
Are well foretold that danger lurks within.
K. Edw. Tush, man, abodements must not now affright us:
By fair or foul means we must enter in,
For hither will our friends repair to us.
Hast. My liege, I'll knock once more to summon them.

Enter, on the walls, the Mayor of York, *and his Brethren.*

May. My lords, we were forewarned of your coming,
And shut the gates for safety of ourselves;
For now we owe allegiance unto Henry.
K. Edw. But, master mayor, if Henry be your king,
Yet Edward at the least is Duke of York.
May. True, my good lord; I know you for no less.
K. Edw. Why, and I challenge nothing but my dukedom,
As being well content with that alone.
Glou. [*Aside*] But when the fox hath once got in his nose,
He'll soon find means to make the body follow.
Hast. Why, master mayor, why stand you in a doubt?
Open the gates; we are King Henry's friends.
May. Ay, say you so? the gates shall then be opened.
He descends [*with the aldermen*].
Glou. A wise stout captain, and soon persuaded!
Hast. The good old man would fain that all were well,
So 'twere not 'long of him; but being ent'red,
I doubt not, I, but we shall soon persuade
Both him and all his brothers unto reason.

Enter [*below*] *the* Mayor *and two* Aldermen.

K. Edw. So, master mayor: these gates must not be shut
But in the night or in the time of war.
What! fear not, man, but yield me up the keys;
Takes his keys.
For Edward will defend the town and thee,
And all those friends that deign to follow me.

March. Enter MONTGOMERY, *with drum and soldiers.*

Glou. Brother, this is Sir John Montgomery,
Our trusty friend, unless I be deceiv'd.
K. Edw. Welcome, Sir John! But why come you in arms?
Mont. To help King Edward in his time of storm,
As every loyal subject ought to do.
K. Edw. Thanks, good Montgomery; but we now forget
Our title to the crown and only claim
Our dukedom till God please to send the rest.
Mont. Then fare you well, for I will hence again:
I came to serve a king and not a duke.
Drummer, strike up, and let us march away.
The drum begins to march.
K. Edw. Nay, stay, Sir John, awhile, and we'll debate
By what safe means the crown may be recover'd.
Mont. What talk you of debating? in few words,
If you'll not here proclaim yourself our king,
I'll leave you to your fortune and be gone
To keep them back that come to succour you:
Why shall we fight, if you pretend no title?
Glou. Why, brother, wherefore stand you on nice points?
K. Edw. When we grow stronger, then we'll make our claim:
Till then, 'tis wisdom to conceal our meaning.
Hast. Away with scrupulous wit! now arms must rule.
Glou. And fearless minds climb soonest unto crowns.
Brother, we will proclaim you out of hand;
The bruit thereof will bring you many friends.
K. Edw. Then be it as you will; for 'tis my right,
And Henry but usurps the diadem.
Mont. Ay, now my sovereign speaketh like himself;
And now will I be Edward's champion.
Hast. Sound trumpet; Edward shall be here proclaim'd:
Come, fellow-soldier, make thou proclamation.
Flourish. Sound.
Sold. Edward the Fourth, by the grace of God, king of England and France, and lord of Ireland, &c.
Mont. And whosoe'er gainsays King Edward's right,
By this I challenge him to single fight.
Throws down his gauntlet.
All. Long live Edward the Fourth!
K. Edw. Thanks, brave Montgomery; and thanks unto you all:
If fortune serve me, I'll requite this kindness.
Now, for this night, let's harbour here in York;
And when the morning sun shall raise his car
Above the border of this horizon,
We'll forward towards Warwick and his mates;
For well I wot that Henry is no soldier.
Ah, froward Clarence! how evil it beseems thee,
To flatter Henry and forsake thy brother!
Yet, as we may, we'll meet both thee and Warwick
Come on, brave soldiers: doubt not of the day,
And, that once gotten, doubt not of large pay. *Exeunt.*

[SCENE VIII. *London. The palace.*]

Flourish. Enter the KING [HENRY], WARWICK, MONTAGUE, CLARENCE, OXFORD, *and* EXETER.

War. What counsel, lords? Edward from Belgia,
With hasty Germans and blunt Hollanders,
Hath pass'd in safety through the narrow seas,
And with his troops doth march amain to London;
And many giddy people flock to him.
K. Hen. Let's levy men, and beat him back again.

Beaufort. He became King Henry VII in 1485. This intruded allusion is a direct compliment to Queen Elizabeth, granddaughter of King Henry VII; it is adapted from a similar compliment in Holinshed. Somerset is Henry Tudor's cousin. 79. **he.** The antecedent is *brother*.

SCENE VII. 9. **as,** as if; see glossary. 13. **abodements,** omens. 40. **Sir John Montgomery.** Holinshed calls him Thomas Montgomery. 51. **debate,** discuss; see glossary. 58. **stand . . . points?** Are you over-scrupulous? 61. **scrupulous,** cautious, crafty. 63. **out of hand,** at once. 64. **bruit,** rumor. 78. **serve,** be favorable; see glossary. 80. **his car,** i.e., Phoebus' chariot. 87. **the day,** the day's outcome.

SCENE VIII. 1. **Belgia,** Flanders; cf. IV, v, 21.

Clar. A little fire is quickly trodden out;
Which, being suffer'd, rivers cannot quench.
War. In Warwickshire I have true-hearted friends,
Not mutinous in peace, yet bold in war;
Those will I muster up: and thou, son Clarence,
Shalt stir up in Suffolk, Norfolk and in Kent,
The knights and gentlemen to come with thee:
Thou, brother Montague, in Buckingham,
Northampton and in Leicestershire, shalt find
Men well inclin'd to hear what thou command'st:
And thou, brave Oxford, wondrous well belov'd,
In Oxfordshire shalt muster up thy friends.
My sovereign, with the loving citizens,
Like to his island girt in with the ocean,
Or modest Dian circled with her nymphs,
Shall rest in London till we come to him.
Fair lords, take leave and stand not to reply.
Farewell, my sovereign.
K. Hen. Farewell, my Hector, and my Troy's true hope.
Clar. In sign of truth, I kiss your highness' hand.
K. Hen. Well-minded Clarence, be thou fortunate!
Mont. Comfort, my lord; and so I take my leave.
Oxf. And thus I seal my truth, and bid adieu.
K. Hen. Sweet Oxford, and my loving Montague,
And all at once, once more a happy farewell.
War. Farewell, sweet lords: let 's meet at Coventry.
Exeunt [all but King Henry and Exeter].
K. Hen. Here at the palace will I rest awhile.
Cousin of Exeter, what thinks your lordship?
Methinks the power that Edward hath in field
Should not be able to encounter mine.
Exe. The doubt is that he will seduce the rest.
K. Hen. That 's not my fear; my meed hath got me fame:
I have not stopp'd mine ears to their demands,
Nor posted off their suits with slow delays;
My pity hath been balm to heal their wounds,
My mildness hath allay'd their swelling griefs,
My mercy dried their water-flowing tears;
I have not been desirous of their wealth,
Nor much oppress'd them with great subsidies,
Nor forward of revenge, though they much err'd:
Then why should they love Edward more than me?
No, Exeter, these graces challenge grace:
And when the lion fawns upon the lamb,
The lamb will never cease to follow him.
Shout within, 'A Lancaster! A Lancaster!'
Exe. Hark, hark, my lord! what shouts are these?

Enter [KING] EDWARD *and his soldiers [with* GLOUCESTER].

K. Edw. Seize on the shame-fac'd Henry, bear him hence;
And once again proclaim us king of England.
You are the fount that makes small brooks to flow:
Now stops thy spring; my sea shall suck them dry,
And swell so much the higher by their ebb.
Hence with him to the Tower; let him not speak.
Exit [Guard] with King Henry.
And, lords, towards Coventry bend we our course,
Where peremptory Warwick now remains:
The sun shines hot; and, if we use delay,
Cold biting winter mars our hop'd-for hay.
Glou. Away betimes, before his forces join,
And take the great-grown traitor unawares:
Brave warriors, march amain towards Coventry.
Exeunt.

[ACT V.

SCENE I. *Coventry.*]

Enter WARWICK, *the* Mayor of Coventry, *two* Messengers, *and others upon the walls.*

War. Where is the post that came from valiant Oxford?
How far hence is thy lord, mine honest fellow?
First Mess. By this at Dunsmore, marching hitherward.
War. How far off is our brother Montague?
Where is the post that came from Montague?
Second Mess. By this at Daintry, with a puissant troop.

Enter [SIR JOHN] SOMERVILLE [*aloft*].

War. Say, Somerville, what says my loving son?
And, by thy guess, how nigh is Clarence now?
Som. At Southam I did leave him with his forces,
And do expect him here some two hours hence.
[*Drum heard.*]
War. Then Clarence is at hand; I hear his drum.
Som. It is not his, my lord; here Southam lies:
The drum your honour hears marcheth from Warwick.
War. Who should that be? belike, unlook'd-for friends.
Som. They are at hand, and you shall quickly know.

March: flourish. Enter [KING] EDWARD, RICHARD [DUKE OF GLOUCESTER], *and soldiers.*

K. Edw. Go, trumpet, to the walls, and sound a parle.
Glou. See how the surly Warwick mans the wall!
War. O unbid spite! is sportful Edward come?
Where slept our scouts, or how are they seduc'd,
That we could hear no news of his repair?
K. Edw. Now, Warwick, wilt thou ope the city gates,
Speak gentle words and humbly bend thy knee,
Call Edward king and at his hands beg mercy?
And he shall pardon thee these outrages.
War. Nay, rather, wilt thou draw thy forces hence,
Confess who set thee up and pluck'd thee down,
Call Warwick patron and be penitent?
And thou shalt still remain the Duke of York.
Glou. I thought, at least, he would have said 'the king';
Or did he make the jest against his will?
War. Is not a dukedom, sir, a goodly gift?
Glou. Ay, by my faith, for a poor earl to give:

21. **modest Dian,** chaste Diana; a possible allusion to Queen Elizabeth; see *modest* in glossary. 23. **stand,** wait. 37. **doubt,** danger, risk; see glossary. 38. **meed,** merits. 40. **posted off,** put off. 45. **subsidies,** taxes. 59. **peremptory,** overbearing.

ACT V. SCENE I. 16. **parle,** bugle call for a parley; see glossary. 18. **unbid,** unwelcome. **spite,** vexatious circumstance. 20. **repair,** approach. 26. **set . . . down.** Cf. II, iii, 37; III, iii, 157. 36. **Atlas,** an allusion to the mythological character who carried the world on his shoulders. 42. **forecast,** forethought. 49. **strike,** yield. 52. **bear . . . sail,** be so humble, abject. 65. **rouse,** cause (an animal) to rise

I'll do thee service for so good a gift.
War. 'Twas I that gave the kingdom to thy brother.
K. Edw. Why then 'tis mine, if but by Warwick's gift.
War. Thou art no Atlas for so great a weight:
And, weakling, Warwick takes his gift again;
And Henry is my king, Warwick his subject.
K. Edw. But Warwick's king is Edward's prisoner:
And, gallant Warwick, do but answer this:
What is the body when the head is off?
Glou. Alas, that Warwick had no more forecast,
But, whiles he thought to steal the single ten,
The king was slily finger'd from the deck!
You left poor Henry at the Bishop's palace,
And, ten to one, you'll meet him in the Tower.
K. Edw. 'Tis even so; yet you are Warwick still.
Glou. Come, Warwick, take the time; kneel down, kneel down:
Nay, when? strike now, or else the iron cools.
War. I had rather chop this hand off at a blow,
And with the other fling it at thy face,
Than bear so low a sail, to strike to thee.
K. Edw. Sail how thou canst, have wind and tide thy friend,
This hand, fast wound about thy coal-black hair,
Shall, whiles thy head is warm and new cut off,
Write in the dust this sentence with thy blood,
'Wind-changing Warwick now can change no more.'

Enter OXFORD, *with drum and colours.*

War. O cheerful colours! see where Oxford comes!
Oxf. Oxford, Oxford, for Lancaster!
[*He and his forces enter the city.*]
Glou. The gates are open, let us enter too.
K. Edw. So other foes may set upon our backs.
Stand we in good array; for they no doubt
Will issue out again and bid us battle:
If not, the city being but of small defence,
We'll quickly rouse the traitors in the same.
War. O, welcome, Oxford! for we want thy help.

Enter MONTAGUE, *with drum and colours.*

Mont. Montague, Montague, for Lancaster!
[*He and his forces enter the city.*]
Glou. Thou and thy brother both shall buy this treason
Even with the dearest blood your bodies bear.
K. Edw. The harder match'd, the greater victory:
My mind presageth happy gain and conquest.

Enter SOMERSET, *with drum and colours.*

Som. Somerset, Somerset, for Lancaster!
[*He and his forces enter the city.*]
Glou. Two of thy name, both Dukes of Somerset,
Have sold their lives unto the house of York;
And thou shalt be the third, if this sword hold.

Enter CLARENCE, *with drum and colours.*

War. And lo, where George of Clarence sweeps along,
Of force enough to bid his brother battle;
With whom an upright zeal to right prevails
More than the nature of a brother's love!
Come, Clarence, come; thou wilt, if Warwick call.
Clar. Father of Warwick, know you what this means? [*Taking his red rose out of his hat.*]
Look here, I throw my infamy at thee:
I will not ruinate my father's house,
Who gave his blood to lime the stones together,
And set up Lancaster. Why, trowest thou, Warwick,
That Clarence is so harsh, so blunt, unnatural,
To bend the fatal instruments of war
Against his brother and his lawful king?
Perhaps thou wilt object my holy oath:
To keep that oath were more impiety
Than Jephthah's, when he sacrific'd his daughter.
I am so sorry for my trespass made
That, to deserve well at my brother's hands,
I here proclaim myself thy mortal foe,
With resolution, wheresoe'er I meet thee—
As I will meet thee, if thou stir abroad—
To plague thee for thy foul misleading me.
And so, proud-hearted Warwick, I defy thee,
And to my brother turn my blushing cheeks.
Pardon me, Edward, I will make amends:
And, Richard, do not frown upon my faults,
For I will henceforth be no more unconstant.
K. Edw. Now welcome more, and ten times more belov'd,
Than if thou never hadst deserv'd our hate.
Glou. Welcome, good Clarence; this is brother-like.
War. O passing traitor, perjur'd and unjust!
K. Edw. What, Warwick, wilt thou leave the town and fight?
Or shall we beat the stones about thine ears?
War. Alas, I am not coop'd here for defence!
I will away towards Barnet presently,
And bid thee battle, Edward, if thou dar'st.
K. Edw. Yes, Warwick, Edward dares, and leads the way.
Lords, to the field; Saint George and victory!
Exeunt [*King Edward and his company*]. *March. Warwick and his company follows* [*out of the city*].

[SCENE II. *A field of battle near Barnet.*]

Alarum and excursions. Enter [KING] EDWARD, *bringing forth* WARWICK *wounded.*

K. Edw. So, lie thou there: die thou, and die our fear;
For Warwick was a bug that fear'd us all.
Now, Montague, sit fast; I seek for thee,
That Warwick's bones may keep thine company. *Exit.*
War. Ah, who is nigh? come to me, friend or foe,
And tell me who is victor, York or Warwick?
Why ask I that? my mangled body shows,
My blood, my want of strength, my sick heart shows,
That I must yield my body to the earth
And, by my fall, the conquest to my foe.
Thus yields the cedar to the axe's edge,
Whose arms gave shelter to the princely eagle,

from his lair. 73. **Two of thy name,** Edmund, killed at St. Albans in 1455, and his son Henry (not a character in this play), beheaded in 1464 for his Lancastrian sympathies. The duke addressed here is Henry's brother Edmund. They were Beauforts, descendants of John of Gaunt (see Genealogical Table). 84. **lime,** cement. 85. **trowest,** believest.

89. **object,** urge (i.e., in the sense "remind me of"). 91. **Jephthah's.** Cf. Judges 11:30ff. for the account of Jephthah's vow to sacrifice, if victorious, the first living creature that came to meet him on his return. His daughter was the victim. 106. **unjust,** unfaithful, false.
SCENE II. 2. **bug,** bogey. **fear'd,** frightened.

Under whose shade the ramping lion slept,
Whose top-branch overpeer'd Jove's spreading tree
And kept low shrubs from winter's pow'rful wind.
These eyes, that now are dimm'd with death's black veil,
Have been as piercing as the mid-day sun,
To search the secret treasons of the world:
The wrinkles in my brows, now fill'd with blood,
Were lik'ned oft to kingly sepulchres;
For who liv'd king, but I could dig his grave?
And who durst smile when Warwick bent his brow?
Lo, now my glory smear'd in dust and blood!
My parks, my walks, my manors that I had,
Even now forsake me, and of all my lands
Is nothing left me but my body's length.
Why, what is pomp, rule, reign, but earth and dust?
And, live we how we can, yet die we must.

Enter OXFORD *and* SOMERSET.

Som. Ah, Warwick, Warwick! wert thou as we are,
We might recover all our loss again:
The queen from France hath brought a puissant power:
Even now we heard the news: ah, couldst thou fly!

War. Why, then I would not fly. Ah, Montague,
If thou be there, sweet brother, take my hand,
And with thy lips keep in my soul awhile!
Thou lov'st me not; for, brother, if thou didst,
Thy tears would wash this cold congealed blood
That glues my lips and will not let me speak.
Come quickly, Montague, or I am dead.

Som. Ah, Warwick! Montague hath breath'd his last;
And to the latest gasp cried out for Warwick
And said 'Commend me to my valiant brother.'
And more he would have said, and more he spoke,
Which sounded like a clamour in a vault,
That mought not be distinguish'd; but at last
I well might hear, delivered with a groan,
'O, farewell, Warwick!'

War. Sweet rest his soul! Fly, lords, and save yourselves;
For Warwick bids you all farewell, to meet in heaven. [*Dies.*]

Oxf. Away, away, to meet the queen's great power!
Here they bear away his body. Exeunt.

[SCENE III. *Another part of the field.*]

Flourish. Enter KING EDWARD *in triumph; with* RICHARD [DUKE OF GLOUCESTER], CLARENCE, *and the rest.*

K. Edw. Thus far our fortune keeps an upward course,
And we are grac'd with wreaths of victory.
But, in the midst of this bright-shining day,
I spy a black, suspicious, threat'ning cloud,
That will encounter with our glorious sun,
Ere he attain his easeful western bed:
I mean, my lords, those powers that the queen
Hath rais'd in Gallia have arriv'd our coast
And, as we hear, march on to fight with us.

Clar. A little gale will soon disperse that cloud
And blow it to the source from whence it came:
The very beams will dry those vapours up,
For every cloud engenders not a storm.

Glou. The queen is valued thirty thousand strong,
And Somerset, with Oxford, fled to her:
If she have time to breathe, be well assur'd
Her faction will be full as strong as ours.

K. Edw. We are advertis'd by our loving friends
That they do hold their course toward Tewksbury:
We, having now the best at Barnet field,
Will thither straight, for willingness rids way;
And, as we march, our strength will be augmented
In every county as we go along.
Strike up the drum; cry 'Courage!' and away. *Exeunt.*

[SCENE IV. *Plains near Tewksbury.*]

Flourish. March. Enter the QUEEN [MARGARET], *young* [PRINCE] EDWARD, SOMERSET, OXFORD, *and soldiers.*

Q. Mar. Great lords, wise men ne'er sit and wail their loss,
But cheerly seek how to redress their harms.
What though the mast be now blown overboard,
The cable broke, the holding-anchor lost,
And half our sailors swallow'd in the flood?
Yet lives our pilot still. Is 't meet that he
Should leave the helm and like a fearful lad
With tearful eyes add water to the sea
And give more strength to that which hath too much,
Whiles, in his moan, the ship splits on the rock,
Which industry and courage might have sav'd?
Ah, what a shame! ah, what a fault were this!
Say Warwick was our anchor; what of that?
And Montague our topmast; what of him?
Our slaught'red friends the tackles; what of these?
Why, is not Oxford here another anchor?
And Somerset another goodly mast?
The friends of France our shrouds and tacklings?
And, though unskilful, why not Ned and I
For once allow'd the skilful pilot's charge?
We will not from the helm to sit and weep,
But keep our course, though the rough wind say no,
From shelves and rocks that threaten us with wrack.
As good to chide the waves as speak them fair.
And what is Edward but a ruthless sea?
What Clarence but a quicksand of deceit?
And Richard but a ragged fatal rock?
All these the enemies to our poor bark.
Say you can swim; alas, 'tis but a while!
Tread on the sand; why, there you quickly sink:
Bestride the rock; the tide will wash you off,
Or else you famish; that 's a threefold death.
This speak I, lords, to let you understand,
If case some one of you would fly from us,
That there 's no hop'd-for mercy with the brothers
More than with ruthless waves, with sands and rocks.
Why, courage then! what cannot be avoided
'Twere childish weakness to lament or fear.

Prince. Methinks a woman of this valiant spirit
Should, if a coward heard her speak these words,

14-15. **Whose . . . wind.** Two independent references are merged here: the oak, sacred to Jove, and the fable of the oak and the briar, related in Spenser's *Shepheardes Calender*. 25-26. **of all . . . length,** a variant of the "earth upon earth" motif; cf. *Richard II*, III, iii, 153-154; *1 Henry IV*, V, iv, 89-92. 35. **with thy lips,** with a kiss; a reference to the belief that the soul left the body through the open mouth.

SCENE. III. 8. **arriv'd,** reached; used transitively. 16. **time to breathe,** opportunity to muster her strength. 18. **advertis'd,** notified. 21. **rids way,** annihilates distance.

SCENE IV. 1-2. **Great . . . harms.** Cf. *Richard II*, III, ii, 178-179.

Infuse his breast with magnanimity
And make him, naked, foil a man at arms.
I speak not this as doubting any here;
For did I but suspect a fearful man,
He should have leave to go away betimes,
Lest in our need he might infect another
And make him of like spirit to himself.
If any such be here—as God forbid!—
Let him depart before we need his help.
Oxf. Women and children of so high a courage,
And warriors faint! why, 'twere perpetual shame.
O brave young prince! thy famous grandfather
Doth live again in thee: long mayst thou live
To bear his image and renew his glories!
Som. And he that will not fight for such a hope,
Go home to bed, and like the owl by day,
If he arise, be mock'd and wond'red at.
Q. Mar. Thanks, gentle Somerset; sweet Oxford, thanks.
Prince. And take his thanks that yet hath nothing else.

Enter a Messenger.

Mess. Prepare you, lords, for Edward is at hand,
Ready to fight; therefore be resolute.
Oxf. I thought no less: it is his policy
To haste thus fast, to find us unprovided.
Som. But he 's deceiv'd; we are in readiness.
Q. Mar. This cheers my heart, to see your forwardness.
Oxf. Here pitch our battle; hence we will not budge.

Flourish and march. Enter [KING] EDWARD, RICHARD [DUKE OF GLOUCESTER], CLARENCE, *and soldiers.*

K. Edw. Brave followers, yonder stands the thorny wood,
Which, by the heavens' assistance and your strength,
Must by the roots be hewn up yet ere night.
I need not add more fuel to your fire,
For well I wot ye blaze to burn them out:
Give signal to the fight, and to it, lords!
Q. Mar. Lords, knights, and gentlemen, what I should say
My tears gainsay; for every word I speak,
Ye see, I drink the water of mine eyes.
Therefore, no more but this: Henry, your sovereign,
Is prisoner to the foe; his state usurp'd,
His realm a slaughter-house, his subjects slain,
His statutes cancell'd and his treasure spent;
And yonder is the wolf that makes this spoil.
You fight in justice: then, in God's name, lords,
Be valiant and give signal to the fight.
Alarum: Retreat: Excursions. Exeunt.

[SCENE V. *Another part of the field.*]

Flourish. Enter [KING] EDWARD, RICHARD [DUKE OF GLOUCESTER], QUEEN [MARGARET, *as prisoner*], CLARENCE; OXFORD, SOMERSET [*as prisoners*].

K. Edw. Now here a period of tumultuous broils.
Away with Oxford to Hames Castle straight:
For Somerset, off with his guilty head.
Go, bear them hence; I will not hear them speak.
Oxf. For my part, I'll not trouble thee with words.
Som. Nor I, but stoop with patience to my fortune.
Exeunt [*Oxford and Somerset, guarded*].
Q. Mar. So part we sadly in this troublous world,
To meet with joy in sweet Jerusalem.
K. Edw. Is proclamation made, that who finds Edward
Shall have a high reward, and he his life?
Glou. It is: and lo, where youthful Edward comes!

Enter [*soldiers, with*] *the* PRINCE.

K. Edw. Bring forth the gallant, let us hear him speak.
What! can so young a thorn begin to prick?
Edward, what satisfaction canst thou make
For bearing arms, for stirring up my subjects,
And all the trouble thou hast turn'd me to?
Prince. Speak like a subject, proud ambitious York!
Suppose that I am now my father's mouth;
Resign thy chair, and where I stand kneel thou,
Whilst I propose the selfsame words to thee,
Which, traitor, thou wouldst have me answer to.
Q. Mar. Ah, that thy father had been so resolv'd!
Glou. That you might still have worn the petticoat,
And ne'er have stol'n the breech from Lancaster.
Prince. Let Æsop fable in a winter's night;
His currish riddles sort not with this place.
Glou. By heaven, brat, I'll plague ye for that word.
Q. Mar. Ay, thou wast born to be a plague to men.
Glou. For God's sake, take away this captive scold.
Prince. Nay, take away this scolding crook-back rather.
K. Edw. Peace, wilful boy, or I will charm your tongue.
Clar. Untutor'd lad, thou art too malapert.
Prince. I know my duty; you are all undutiful:
Lascivious Edward, and thou perjur'd George,
And thou mis-shapen Dick, I tell ye all
I am your better, traitors as ye are:
And thou usurp'st my father's right and mine.
K. Edw. Take that, thou likeness of this railer here!
Stabs him.
Glou. Sprawl'st thou? take that, to end thy agony.
Richard stabs him.
Clar. And there 's for twitting me with perjury.
Clarence stabs him.
Q. Mar. O, kill me too!
Glou. Marry, and shall. *Offers to kill her.*
K. Edw. Hold, Richard, hold; for we have done too much.
Glou. Why should she live, to fill the world with words?
K. Edw. What, doth she swoon? use means for her recovery.
Glou. Clarence, excuse me to the king my brother;
I'll hence to London on a serious matter:
Ere ye come there, be sure to hear some news.
Clar. What? what?
Glou. The Tower, the Tower. *Exit.*

9. **give . . . much.** Cf. *As You Like It*, II, i, 48-49. 23. **shelves,** sand-banks. 42. **foil,** defeat. 63. **unprovided,** unprepared. 80. **spoil,** destruction; see glossary.
SCENE V. 1. **period,** termination. 2. **Hames Castle,** in Picardy. 19. **chair,** throne. 24. **breech,** breeches, symbol of male authority.

25. **Æsop,** an allusion to Gloucester's deformity. Aesop was reputed to have been similarly deformed. 26. **sort not,** are not appropriate to. 32. **malapert,** saucy. 38. **this railer here,** i.e., Queen Margaret.

Q. Mar. O Ned, sweet Ned! speak to thy mother, boy!
Canst thou not speak? O traitors! murderers!
They that stabb'd Cæsar shed no blood at all,
Did not offend, nor were not worthy blame,
If this foul deed were by to equal it:
He was a man; this, in respect, a child:
And men ne'er spend their fury on a child.
What 's worse than murderer, that I may name it?
No, no, my heart will burst, an if I speak:
And I will speak, that so my heart may burst.
Butchers and villains! bloody cannibals!
How sweet a plant have you untimely cropp'd!
You have no children, butchers! if you had,
The thought of them would have stirr'd up remorse:
But if you ever chance to have a child,
Look in his youth to have him so cut off
As, deathsmen, you have rid this sweet young prince!
K. Edw. Away with her; go, bear her hence perforce.
Q. Mar. Nay, never bear me hence, dispatch me here;
Here sheathe thy sword, I'll pardon thee my death:
What, wilt thou not? then, Clarence, do it thou.
Clar. By heaven, I will not do thee so much ease.
Q. Mar. Good Clarence, do; sweet Clarence, do thou do it.
Clar. Didst thou not hear me swear I would not do it?
Q. Mar. Ay, but thou usest to forswear thyself:
'Twas sin before, but now 'tis charity.
What, wilt thou not? Where is that devil's butcher,
Hard-favour'd Richard? Richard, where art thou?
Thou art not here: murder is thy alms-deed;
Petitioners for blood thou ne'er put'st back.
K. Edw. Away, I say; I charge ye, bear her hence.
Q. Mar. So come to you and yours, as to this prince!
Exit Queen [led out forcibly].
K. Edw. Where 's Richard gone?
Clar. To London, all in post; and, as I guess,
To make a bloody supper in the Tower.
K. Edw. He 's sudden, if a thing comes in his head.
Now march we hence: discharge the common sort
With pay and thanks, and let 's away to London
And see our gentle queen how well she fares:
By this, I hope, she hath a son for me. *Exeunt.*

[SCENE VI. *London. The Tower.*]

Enter HENRY THE SIXTH *and* RICHARD [DUKE OF GLOUCESTER], *with the* Lieutenant, *on the walls.*

Glou. Good day, my lord. What, at your book so hard?
K. Hen. Ay, my good lord:—my lord, I should say rather;
'Tis sin to flatter; 'good' was little better:
'Good Gloucester' and 'good devil' were alike,
And both preposterous; therefore, not 'good lord.'
Glou. Sirrah, leave us to ourselves: we must confer.
[Exit Lieutenant.]
K. Hen. So flies the reckless shepherd from the wolf;
So first the harmless sheep doth yield his fleece
And next his throat unto the butcher's knife.
What scene of death hath Roscius now to act?
Glou. Suspicion always haunts the guilty mind;
The thief doth fear each bush an officer.
K. Hen. The bird that hath been limed in a bush,
With trembling wings misdoubteth every bush;
And I, the hapless male to one sweet bird,
Have now the fatal object in my eye
Where my poor young was lim'd, was caught and kill'd.
Glou. Why, what a peevish fool was that of Crete,
That taught his son the office of a fowl!
And yet, for all his wings, the fool was drown'd.
K. Hen. I, Dædalus; my poor boy, Icarus;
Thy father, Minos, that denied our course;
The sun that sear'd the wings of my sweet boy
Thy brother Edward, and thyself the sea
Whose envious gulf did swallow up his life.
Ah, kill me with thy weapon, not with words!
My breast can better brook thy dagger's point
Than can my ears that tragic history.
But wherefore dost thou come? is 't for my life?
Glou. Think'st thou I am an executioner?
K. Hen. A persecutor, I am sure, thou art:
If murdering innocents be executing,
Why, then thou art an executioner.
Glou. Thy son I kill'd for his presumption.
K. Hen. Hadst thou been kill'd when first thou didst presume,
Thou hadst not liv'd to kill a son of mine.
And thus I prophesy, that many a thousand,
Which now mistrust no parcel of my fear,
And many an old man's sigh and many a widow's,
And many an orphan's water-standing eye—
Men for their sons, wives for their husbands,
And orphans for their parents' timeless death—
Shall rue the hour that ever thou wast born.
The owl shriek'd at thy birth,—an evil sign;
The night-crow cried, aboding luckless time;
Dogs howl'd, and hideous tempest shook down trees;
The raven rook'd her on the chimney's top,
And chatt'ring pies in dismal discords sung.
Thy mother felt more than a mother's pain,
And yet brought forth less than a mother's hope,
To wit, an indigested and deformed lump,
Not like the fruit of such a goodly tree.
Teeth hadst thou in thy head when thou wast born,
To signify thou cam'st to bite the world:
And, if the rest be true which I have heard,
Thou cam'st—
Glou. I'll hear no more: die, prophet, in thy speech:
Stabs him.
For this, amongst the rest, was I ordain'd.
K. Hen. Ay, and for much more slaughter after this.
O, God forgive my sins, and pardon thee! *Dies.*
Glou. What, will the aspiring blood of Lancaster
Sink in the ground? I thought it would have mounted.
See how my sword weeps for the poor king's death!
O, may such purple tears be alway shed
From those that wish the downfall of our house!

56. **respect,** comparison. 63. **You . . . butchers.** This is not historically true; both Edward and Clarence were fathers of families.

SCENE VI. 1. **book,** i.e., the Bible, or possibly a book of devotions. 5. **preposterous,** contrary to the natural order of things. 6. **Sirrah,** customary form of address to inferiors; see glossary. 10. **Roscius,** celebrated Roman actor. 14. **misdoubteth,** is mistrustful of; see glossary. 15. **male,** father, begetter. 18. **peevish,** silly; see glossary. 21. **Dædalus, Icarus.** Cf. *1 Henry VI,* IV, vi, 55, note. 38. **mistrust no parcel,** suspect no item or detail. 42. **timeless,** untimely. 45. **aboding,** foreboding. 47. **rook'd her,** alighted, roosted. 48. **pies,** magpies.

If any spark of life be yet remaining,
Down, down to hell; and say I sent thee thither!
Stabs him again.
I, that have neither pity, love, nor fear.
Indeed, 'tis true that Henry told me of;
For I have often heard my mother say
I came into the world with my legs forward:
Had I not reason, think ye, to make haste,
And seek their ruin that usurp'd our right?
The midwife wonder'd and the women cried
'O, Jesus bless us, he is born with teeth!'
And so I was; which plainly signified
That I should snarl and bite and play the dog.
Then, since the heavens have shap'd my body so,
Let hell make crook'd my mind to answer it.
I have no brother, I am like no brother;
And this word 'love,' which greybeards call divine,
Be resident in men like one another
And not in me: I am myself alone.
Clarence, beware; thou keep'st me from the light:
But I will sort a pitchy day for thee;
For I will buz abroad such prophecies
That Edward shall be fearful of his life,
And then, to purge his fear, I'll be thy death.
King Henry and the prince his son are gone:
Clarence, thy turn is next, and then the rest,
Counting myself but bad till I be best.
I'll throw thy body in another room
And triumph, Henry, in thy day of doom.
Exit [with the body].

[SCENE VII. *London. The palace.*]

Flourish, Enter KING [EDWARD], QUEEN [ELIZABETH], CLARENCE, RICHARD [DUKE OF GLOUCESTER], HASTINGS, Nurse [*with the young Prince*], *and* Attendants.

K. Edw. Once more we sit in England's royal throne,
Re-purchas'd with the blood of enemies.
What valiant foemen, like to autumn's corn,
Have we mow'd down in tops of all their pride!
Three Dukes of Somerset, threefold renown'd
For hardy and undoubted champions;
Two Cliffords, as the father and the son,
And two Northumberlands; two braver men
Ne'er spurr'd their coursers at the trumpet's sound;
With them, the two brave bears, Warwick and Montague,
That in their chains fetter'd the kingly lion
And made the forest tremble when they roar'd.
Thus have we swept suspicion from our seat
And made our footstool of security.
Come hither, Bess, and let me kiss my boy.
Young Ned, for thee, thine uncles and myself
Have in our armours watch'd the winter's night,
Went all afoot in summer's scalding heat,
That thou mightst repossess the crown in peace;
And of our labours thou shalt reap the gain.

Glou. [*Aside*] I'll blast his harvest, if your head were laid;
For yet I am not look'd on in the world.
This shoulder was ordain'd so thick to heave;
And heave it shall some weight, or break my back:
Work thou the way,—and thou shalt execute.

K. Edw. Clarence and Gloucester, love my lovely queen;
And kiss your princely nephew, brothers both.

Clar. The duty that I owe unto your majesty
I seal upon the lips of this sweet babe.

Q. Eliz. Thanks, noble Clarence; worthy brother, thanks.

Glou. And, that I love the tree from whence thou sprang'st,
Witness the loving kiss I give the fruit.
[*Aside*] To say the truth, so Judas kiss'd his master,
And cried 'all hail!' when as he meant all harm.

K. Edw. Now am I seated as my soul delights,
Having my country's peace and brothers' loves.

Clar. What will your grace have done with Margaret?
Reignier, her father, to the king of France
Hath pawn'd the Sicils and Jerusalem,
And hither have they sent it for her ransom.

K. Edw. Away with her, and waft her hence to France,
And now what rests but that we spend the time
With stately triumphs, mirthful comic shows,
Such as befits the pleasure of the court?
Sound drums and trumpets! farewell sour annoy!
For here, I hope, begins our lasting joy. *Exeunt omnes.*

64. **purple,** blood-red. 68-83. **I . . . alone.** These lines of Gloucester's soliloquy anticipate the opening speech of *Richard III*. 85. **sort,** select. **pitchy,** black.
SCENE VII. 17. **in our armours,** i.e., in warlike dress. 25. **Work thou,** addressed to himself. **thou shalt,** addressed to his shoulder. 28. **duty,** obedience, reverence. 39. **the Sicils,** the Kingdom of the two Sicilies: Naples and Sicily. 40. **it,** the money raised by "pawn" (l. 39).

THE TRAGEDY OF KING RICHARD THE THIRD

Richard III begins where *3 Henry VI* left off, and completes the action of the four-play series. On the basis of its Senecan style, the play appears to have been written soon after its predecessors, some time between 1591 and 1594. Richard's evil character, which had already begun to emerge in the last of the *Henry VI* plays, now stands fully revealed. His opening soliloquy depends for its ironically mocking effect on our familiarity with recent events. An end to the Yorkist-Lancastrian hostilities has come at last, but we know Richard too well to expect that a "peace" dominated by this genius of evil can bring any lasting reconciliation yet. England must still pay the full price of her disobedience to God's will.

Richard dominates this play to an extraordinary extent. He is the central character that the earlier plays, especially *3 Henry VI*, lacked. He is on stage almost continually and, until the end, completely manipulates the actions of others. As chief actor and stage manager in his own drama, Richard chortlingly takes the audience into his confidence. His revelation of his plotting serves as a structuring device for the play; we know in advance that Clarence's turn is next, that Richard will then attempt to woo the Lady Anne, and so forth. The dramatic excitement we experience in watching the action is not that of wondering what will happen next, but in seeing how cleverly the preannounced plans will be executed.

Richard's ability as an actor is seemingly limitless. He has already boasted, in *3 Henry VI*, that he can deceive more slyly than Ulysses, Sinon, or Machiavelli, and put on more false shapes than Proteus. To us as audience he is cynically candid and boastful, setting us up in advance to watch his unbelievable performances. In an instant, before our eyes, he is the concerned younger brother of Clarence, sharing a hatred of Queen Elizabeth and her kindred; or he is the jocular uncle of the little princes; or he is the pious recluse studying divinity with his clerical teachers, reluctant to accept the responsibilities of state that are thrust upon him by his importunate subjects (that is to say, by Catesby and Buckingham, who are also actors in this staged scene). Yet none of these bravura performances can match the wooing of the Lady Anne.

Is the wooing of the Lady Anne credible? One key to credibility must lie in superb acting. The actor of Richard must transform himself from the gloating villain we know in soliloquy to the grief-stricken lover. Richard's argument is, after all, speciously plausible: that he has killed Anne's husband and his father out of desperate love for her. The argument appeals to vanity, that most fatal of human weaknesses. What power Anne suddenly appears to have over Richard! She can spare his life, or kill him. Richard shrewdly judges her as one not able to kill, and so risks offering her his sword. As stage manager, he has altered her role from that of sincere mourner to the stereotype of the proud woman worshiped by her groveling servant in love. With superb irony, Richard has inverted totally the appearance and reality of control in this struggle between man and woman. He wins absolute mastery by flattering her that only she can spare his miserable life. The very impossibility of what Richard has achieved merely illustrates his thesis that ordinary men and women can be made to believe anything, and betray their own best instincts, by "the plain devil and dissembling looks." Richard is of course devillike; his role as actor stems from that of the Vice in the morality play, brilliantly comic and sinister. Yet even the devil can prevail over his victims only when they acquiesce in evil. The devil can deceive the senses, but acceptance of evil is still an act of the perverted will. Anne is guilty, however much we can fearfully appreciate the mesmerizing power of Richard's personality. By the end of the scene she violates everything she had held sacred.

The image of Richard as devil or Vice raises the question of motivation and of symbolic meaning. Is Richard a human character propelled toward the throne by his insatiable ambition, like Macbeth? Is there a clue to his behavior in his ugliness and misanthropy? Modern psychological criticism might well be tempted to examine Richard's childhood: by his own admission, he was born feet forward, hunchbacked, withered in one arm, and already toothed ("which plainly signified That I should snarl and bite and play the dog," *3 Henry VI*, V,vi). Accordingly, one might argue, he compensates for his ugliness and unlovability by resolving to domineer. Feeling unwanted, he despises all men and undertakes to prove them weak and corrupt. This reading is not without merit; indeed, no matter how extraordinary Richard's behavior, he does seem plausible. He expresses a universal human penchant for cruelty and senseless domination. Yet the proposition that Richard is evil *because* he was born ugly can be logically reversed as well: he was born ugly *because* he is evil.

This concept axiomatically presupposes a struggle between the forces of absolute good and absolute evil in the cosmos, in which every smallest event in human life has divine meaning and cause. Richard's birth is a physical manifestation of that divine meaning. Providential destiny, having determined the need for a genius of evil at this point in English history, decrees that Richard shall be born. The teeth and hunched back merely give evidence of what is already predetermined. In the apt words of the choric Queen Margaret, Richard was "seal'd in thy nativity The slave of nature and the son of hell" (I,iii). Although Richard is also plausible as a man, he is in part an emissary of the devil. Such a symbolic reading clarifies our impression that Richard is fundamentally unlike many of Shakespeare's human villains such as Macbeth or King Claudius. Richard belongs instead to a special group of villains including Iago in *Othello* and Edmund in *King Lear*. Like them, Richard is driven less by human motivation than by his preexistent evil genius; he displays the "motiveless malignity" ascribed by Coleridge to Iago.

Such a reading helps explain not only Richard's delight in evil, but explains also the necessity for so much evil and suffering in England's civil wars. As with the *Henry VI* plays, this theory of history owes much to Edward Hall's *Union of the Two Noble and Illustre Famelies of Lancastre and Yorke*. In addition, *Richard III* is particularly indebted to Polydore Vergil's *Anglica Historia* (1534) and to *The History of King Richard the Third* attributed to Sir Thomas More (published 1557). This latter work, adopted in turn by Hall, Grafton, and Holinshed, purposefully blackens Richard's character. He becomes a study in the nature of tyranny, an object lesson to future rulers and their subjects. He is, moreover, a result of the curse placed by God on the English people for their sinful disobedience. Richard III functions as the scourge of God, destroying God's enemies until he too is ultimately destroyed for his own colossal evil. This final overthrow will take place once God's vengeance on the English nation has been satisfied. Only passive obedience to God's will, such as the common people in *Richard III* generally display, can soften God's anger and prepare for that deliverance.

Henry VII, in this Tudor explanation, becomes God's minister chosen to destroy the scourge and thereafter to fulfill a new and happy covenant between God and man. Although modern historians more impartially regard the defeat of Richard III at Bosworth Field in 1485 as a political overthrow not unlike Henry IV's overthrow of Richard II, and stress that Richard III was a talented administrator guilty of no worse political crimes than his more fortunate successor, Tudor Englishmen could not find meaning in such a neutral interpretation. History had to reveal God's intention. If Henry IV's rebellion against Richard II had aroused God's wrath, then Henry VII's accession could in no way be viewed as parallel. Otherwise Elizabeth I's claim to the throne would be suspect and vulnerable. Accordingly, the Tudor myth stressed the tyrannical nature of Richard III's seizure of power and conversely minimized the political element in Henry VII's takeover. Bosworth Field was an act of God, a rising up of some irresistible force, and under no circumstances a precedent for future rebellion.

This providential scheme imposes a double irony on *Richard III*. In the short run, Richard appears to be complete master over his victims. "Your imprisonment shall not be long," Richard assures his brother Clarence. "I will deliver you, or else lie for you." The audience, already let in on the secret, can shiver at the grisly humor of these double entendres. Clarence will indeed soon be delivered—to his death. Richard's henchmen are fond of such jokes too. When Lord Hastings is on his way to the tower, from which he will never return, and announces his intention of staying for dinner in the tower, Buckingham observes aside, "And supper too, although thou know'st it not." Shortly before, Catesby has assured Hastings of Richard's and Buckingham's favor toward him: "The princes both make high account of you—[*Aside*] For they account his head upon the Bridge" (III,ii). Richard has a phrase for such wit: "Thus, like the formal Vice, Iniquity, I moralize two meanings in one word" (III,i). The point of such ironies is always the same: the devil is cleverer than his victims, deceiving them through equivocation, triumphing in their spiritual blindness.

The delayed irony of the play, however, ultimately repudiates the seemingly nihilistic conclusions of the early scenes. The ultimate cosmic joke is on Richard: he is God's scourge, fulfilling a divine plan even in the process of what he chortlingly assumes to be his own self-aggrandizement. Divine plans are always complex, inscrutable to the minds of mortals, understood least by those who unwittingly execute them. In attempting to prove his own contention that human nature is bestial and that a Machiavellian man of utter self-confidence can force his way to the top, flouting all conventions of morality, Richard has succeeded in demonstrating exactly the opposite. He is the proverbial beguiler beguiled.

This pattern, finding divine causality in all the suffering of the civil wars, argues that virtually all of Richard's victims deserve their fate because they have offended God. Prophecies and dreams give structure to the sequence of retributive actions, and keep grim score. As the choric Margaret observes, a York must pay for a Lancaster, eye for an eye: Edward IV for Henry VI, young Edward V for Henry VI's son Edward. Thus the Yorkist princes, thought guiltless, die for their family's sins. The Yorkist queen Elizabeth, like the Lancastrian Margaret, must outlive her husband into impotent old age, bewailing her children's cruel deaths. Clarence sees that his death merely atones for his complicity in the murder of Henry VI's son, Edward. The queen's kindred have been guilty of ambition, and Lord Hastings in turn is vulnerable because he has been willing to plot with Richard against the queen's kindred. Margaret's curses serve both to warn the characters of their fates (a warning they blindly ignore) and to invite each person to curse himself unwittingly but with ironic appropriateness. The Lady Anne wishes unquietness on any woman so insane as to marry Richard. Buckingham protests in a most sacred oath that whenever he turns again on the queen's kindred, he will deserve to be punished by the treachery of his dearest friend (i.e., of Richard). Dreams serve the same purpose of divine warning, giving Clarence a grotesque intimation of his death by drowning (in a butt of malmsey wine), and warning Hastings (through Stanley's dream) that the boar, Richard, will raze off his helm. Thus the English court punishes itself through Richard. He is the essence of the courtiers' factionalism, able to succeed as he does only because they forswear their most holy vows and conspire to destroy one another. They deserve to be outwitted at their own dismal game.

As in *3 Henry VI*, the people have little to do with the action of the play. They are choric spokesmen and bystanders, virtuous in their attitude (except for the two suborned murderers of Clarence). In their plain folk wisdom they see the folly and evil their betters ignore: "O, full of danger is the Duke of Gloucester, And the queen's sons and brothers haught and proud" (II,iii). And although they accept Richard as ruler, they do so most reluctantly; Buckingham's first attempt to persuade the people to this course meets with apathy and silence. Their wisdom is to be patient and "leave it all to God." In the fullness of time, this passive obedience brings its just reward.

THE TRAGEDY OF KING RICHARD THE THIRD

[*Dramatis Personae*

KING EDWARD the Fourth.
EDWARD, Prince of Wales, *afterwards* King Edward v, } *sons to the King.*
RICHARD, Duke of York, } *sons to the King.*
GEORGE, Duke of Clarence, } *brothers to the King.*
RICHARD, Duke of Gloucester, *afterwards* King Richard III, } *brothers to the King.*
A young son of Clarence.
HENRY, Earl of Richmond, *afterwards* King Henry VII.
CARDINAL BOURCHIER, Archbishop of Canterbury.
THOMAS ROTHERHAM, Archbishop of York.
JOHN MORTON, Bishop of Ely.
DUKE OF BUCKINGHAM.
DUKE OF NORFOLK.
EARL OF SURREY, *his son.*
EARL RIVERS, *brother to Elizabeth.*
MARQUIS OF DORSET *and* LORD GREY, *sons to Elizabeth.*
EARL OF OXFORD.
LORD HASTINGS.
LORD STANLEY, *called also* Earl of Derby.
LORD LOVEL.
SIR THOMAS VAUGHAN.
SIR RICHARD RATCLIFFE.
SIR WILLIAM CATESBY.
SIR JAMES TYRREL.
SIR JAMES BLOUNT.
SIR WALTER HERBERT.
SIR ROBERT BRAKENBURY, *Lieutenant of the Tower.*
CHRISTOPHER URSWICK, *a priest.* Another Priest.
TRESSEL and BERKELEY, *gentlemen attending on the Lady Anne.*
Lord Mayor of London. Sheriff of Wiltshire.

ELIZABETH, *queen to King Edward IV.*
MARGARET, *widow of King Henry VI.*
DUCHESS OF YORK, *mother to King Edward IV.*
LADY ANNE, *widow of Edward Prince of Wales, son to King Henry VI; afterwards married to Richard.*
A young daughter of Clarence (MARGARET PLANTAGENET).

Ghosts of those murdered by Richard III, Lords *and* other Attendants; a Pursuivant, Scrivener, Citizens, Murderers, Messengers, Soldiers, *&c.*

SCENE: *England.*]

ACT I.

SCENE I. [*London. A street.*]

Enter RICHARD, DUKE OF GLOUCESTER, *solus.*

Glou. Now is the winter of our discontent
Made glorious summer by this sun of York;
And all the clouds that lour'd upon our house
In the deep bosom of the ocean buried.
Now are our brows bound with victorious wreaths;
Our bruised arms hung up for monuments;
Our stern alarums chang'd to merry meetings,
Our dreadful marches to delightful measures.
Grim-visag'd war hath smooth'd his wrinkled front;
And now, instead of mounting barbed steeds
To fright the souls of fearful adversaries,
He capers nimbly in a lady's chamber
To the lascivious pleasing of a lute.
But I, that am not shap'd for sportive tricks,
Nor made to court an amorous looking-glass;
I, that am rudely stamp'd, and want love's majesty
To strut before a wanton ambling nymph;
I, that am curtail'd of this fair proportion,
Cheated of feature by dissembling nature,
Deform'd, unfinish'd, sent before my time
Into this breathing world, scarce half made up,
And that so lamely and unfashionable
That dogs bark at me as I halt by them;
Why, I, in this weak piping time of peace,
Have no delight to pass away the time,
Unless to spy my shadow in the sun
And descant on mine own deformity:
And therefore, since I cannot prove a lover,
To entertain these fair well-spoken days,
I am determined to prove a villain
And hate the idle pleasures of these days.
Plots have I laid, inductions dangerous,
By drunken prophecies, libels and dreams,
To set my brother Clarence and the king
In deadly hate the one against the other:
And if King Edward be as true and just
As I am subtle, false and treacherous,
This day should Clarence closely be mew'd up,
About a prophecy, which says that G
Of Edward's heirs the murderer shall be.
Dive, thoughts, down to my soul: here Clarence comes.

Enter CLARENCE, *guarded, and* BRAKENBURY.

Brother, good day: what means this armed guard
That waits upon your grace?

ACT I. SCENE I. 2. **sun of York.** Edward IV assumed a sun as his badge in memory of the three suns which appeared to him before the Battle of Mortimer's Cross in 1461 (*3 Henry VI*, II, i, 26-40). As used here there is a play on the words "son" and "sun," probably reflected in the readings of Ff: *son*, and Qq: *sonne*. 3. **lour'd,** frowned, looked sullen or ominous. 6. **monuments,** probably memorial trophies. 8. **measures,** stately dances; see glossary. 9. **front,** forehead; see glossary. 10. **barbed,** properly, "barded," i.e., armored. 14. **sportive,** amorous. 16. **want,** lack; see glossary. 17. **ambling,** walking affectedly, i.e., wantonly. 18-23. **I . . . them.** From Sir Thomas More's life of Richard III comes the information that Richard was small of stature, ill-shapen in limbs, crookbacked, left shoulder higher than the right, ugly in visage. According to the theory of Plato, beauty of person should go with beauty of soul, an idea which is reflected in this passage and elsewhere in the play. 18. **proportion,** shape; see glossary. 19. **feature,** shapeliness; see glossary. **dissembling,** fraudulent, false. 22. **unfashionable,** without comeliness. 24. **piping time,** i.e., a time when

Clar. His majesty,
Tend'ring my person's safety, hath appointed
This conduct to convey me to the Tower.
Glou. Upon what cause?
Clar. Because my name is George.
Glou. Alack, my lord, that fault is none of yours;
He should, for that, commit your godfathers:
O, belike his majesty hath some intent
That you should be new-christ'ned in the Tower.
But what 's the matter, Clarence? may I know?
Clar. Yea, Richard, when I know; for I protest
As yet I do not: but, as I can learn,
He hearkens after prophecies and dreams;
And from the cross-row plucks the letter G,
And says a wizard told him that by G
His issue disinherited should be;
And, for my name of George begins with G,
It follows in his thought that I am he.
These, as I learn, and such like toys as these
Hath mov'd his highness to commit me now.
Glou. Why, this it is, when men are rul'd by women:
'Tis not the king that sends you to the Tower;
My Lady Grey his wife, Clarence, 'tis she
That tempers him to this extremity.
Was it not she and that good man of worship,
Anthony Woodville, her brother there,
That made him send Lord Hastings to the Tower,
From whence this present day he is delivered?
We are not safe, Clarence; we are not safe.
Clar. By heaven, I think there is no man secure
But the queen's kindred and night-walking heralds
That trudge betwixt the king and Mistress Shore.
Heard you not what an humble suppliant
Lord Hastings was to her for his delivery?
Glou. Humbly complaining to her deity
Got my lord chamberlain his liberty.
I'll tell you what; I think it is our way,
If we will keep in favour with the king,
To be her men and wear her livery:
The jealous o'erworn widow and herself,
Since that our brother dubb'd them gentlewomen,
Are mighty gossips in our monarchy.
Brak. I beseech your graces both to pardon me;
His majesty hath straitly given in charge
That no man shall have private conference,
Of what degree soever, with your brother.
Glou. Even so; an 't please your worship, Brakenbury,
You may partake of any thing we say:
We speak no treason, man: we say the king
Is wise and virtuous, and his noble queen
Well struck in years, fair, and not jealous;
We say that Shore's wife hath a pretty foot,
A cherry lip, a bonny eye, a passing pleasing tongue;
And that the queen's kindred are made gentlefolks:
How say you, sir? can you deny all this?
Brak. With this, my lord, myself have nought to do.
Glou. Naught to do with Mistress Shore! I tell thee, fellow,
He that doth naught with her, excepting one,
Were best to do it secretly, alone.
Brak. What one, my lord?
Glou. Her husband, knave: wouldst thou betray me?
Brak. I beseech your grace to pardon me, and withal
Forbear your conference with the noble duke.
Clar. We know thy charge, Brakenbury, and will obey.
Glou. We are the queen's abjects, and must obey.
Brother, farewell: I will unto the king;
And whatsoe'er you will employ me in,
Were it to call King Edward's widow sister,
I will perform it to enfranchise you.
Meantime, this deep disgrace in brotherhood
Touches me deeper than you can imagine.
Clar. I know it pleaseth neither of us well.
Glou. Well, your imprisonment shall not be long;
I will deliver you, or else lie for you:
Meantime, have patience.
Clar. I must perforce. Farewell.
Exit Clarence [with Brakenbury and Guard].
Glou. Go, tread the path that thou shalt ne'er return,
Simple, plain Clarence! I do love thee so,
That I will shortly send thy soul to heaven,
If heaven will take the present at our hands.
But who comes here? the new-delivered Hastings?

Enter LORD HASTINGS.

Hast. Good time of day unto my gracious lord!
Glou. As much unto my good lord chamberlain!
Well are you welcome to the open air.
How hath your lordship brook'd imprisonment?
Hast. With patience, noble lord, as prisoners must:
But I shall live, my lord, to give them thanks
That were the cause of my imprisonment.
Glou. No doubt, no doubt; and so shall Clarence too;
For they that were your enemies are his,
And have prevail'd as much on him as you.
Hast. More pity that the eagles should be mew'd,
Whiles kites and buzzards prey at liberty.
Glou. What news abroad?
Hast. No news so bad abroad as this at home;
The king is sickly, weak and melancholy,
And his physicians fear him mightily.

the music heard is that of pipes and not fifes and drums. 27. **descant,** warble, comment on. 29. **entertain,** pass away pleasurably; see glossary. 30. **I . . . villain.** This frank announcement is characteristic of the Machiavellian villain of Marlowe and other early dramatists and is to be connected with the idea that Richard is born outside the pale of normal humanity, so that his trend is toward evil as that of normal men is toward good. 32. **inductions,** preparations, beginnings. 33. **libels,** defamatory bills or pamphlets. 38. **mew'd up,** confined; see glossary. 39. **prophecy . . . G.** The prophecy is mentioned in the chronicles; the quibble is that *G* stands for Gloucester and not George, given name of the Duke of Clarence. 44. **Tend'ring,** having care for. 48. **commit your godfathers,** an example of Richard's cynical humor. 54. **hearkens,** inquires. 55. **cross-row,** Christ-cross-row, or alphabet, so called from the cross printed before the alphabet in the hornbook. 60. **toys,** trifles; see glossary. 61. **mov'd,** prompted; see glossary. **commit,** arrest. 64. **My Lady Grey,** a disrespectful reference to the queen, whose maiden name was Elizabeth Woodville and who, when the king married her, was the widow of Sir John Grey. 65. **tempers,** molds, persuades. 67. **Woodville,** (trisyllabic). Earl Rivers. 73. **Mistress Shore.** Jane Shore, the king's mistress, was the daughter of a Cheapside merchant and the wife of a goldsmith in Lombard Street. 77. **chamberlain,** i.e., Hastings. 81. **jealous o'erworn widow,** i.e., the queen. **herself,** i.e., Jane Shore. 82. **gentlewomen,** a sneer at the queen's family, which was gentle but not noble until after her marriage with the king; Jane Shore was, of course, neither gentle nor noble. 83. **gossips,** companions (conveying the idea of vulgar familiarity). 98. **Naught.** Richard quibbles on the meanings "nothing" and "the sexual act." 106. **abjects,** abjectly servile subjects. 109. **King Edward's widow,** i.e., the widow whom he has made queen. 115. **lie,** quibble on "lying in prison" and "telling lies"; see glossary. 116. **perforce,** necessarily; see glossary. 125. **brook'd,** endured; see glossary. 127. **give them thanks,** ironical for "pay them off." 133. **kites,** birds of prey, hawks. **buzzards,** common species of hawk.

Glou. Now, by Saint John, that news is bad indeed.
O, he hath kept an evil diet long,
And overmuch consum'd his royal person:
'Tis very grievous to be thought upon.
What, is he in his bed?
Hast. He is.
Glou. Go you before, and I will follow you.
Exit Hastings.
He cannot live, I hope; and must not die
Till George be pack'd with post-horse up to heaven.
I'll in, to urge his hatred more to Clarence,
With lies well steel'd with weighty arguments;
And, if I fail not in my deep intent,
Clarence hath not another day to live:
Which done, God take King Edward to his mercy,
And leave the world for me to bustle in!
For then I'll marry Warwick's youngest daughter.
What though I kill'd her husband and her father?
The readiest way to make the wench amends
Is to become her husband and her father:
The which will I; not all so much for love
As for another secret close intent,
By marrying her which I must reach unto.
But yet I run before my horse to market:
Clarence still breathes; Edward still lives and reigns:
When they are gone, then must I count my gains.
Exit.

SCENE II. [*The same. Another street.*]

Enter the corse of [KING] HENRY the Sixth, *with* Halberds *to guard it;* LADY ANNE *being the mourner* [*attended by* TRESSEL *and* BERKELEY].

Anne. Set down, set down your honourable load,
If honour may be shrouded in a hearse,
Whilst I awhile obsequiously lament
Th' untimely fall of virtuous Lancaster.
Poor key-cold figure of a holy king!
Pale ashes of the house of Lancaster!
Thou bloodless remnant of that royal blood!
Be it lawful that I invocate thy ghost,
To hear the lamentations of poor Anne,
Wife to thy Edward, to thy slaught'red son,
Stabb'd by the selfsame hand that made these wounds!
Lo, in these windows that let forth thy life,
I pour the helpless balm of my poor eyes.
O, cursed be the hand that made these holes!
Cursed the heart that had the heart to do it!
Cursed the blood that let this blood from hence!
More direful hap betide that hated wretch,
That makes us wretched by the death of thee,
Than I can wish to wolves, to spiders, toads,
Or any creeping venom'd thing that lives!
If ever he have child, abortive be it,
Prodigious, and untimely brought to light,
Whose ugly and unnatural aspect
May fright the hopeful mother at the view;
And that be heir to his unhappiness!
If ever he have wife, let her be made
More miserable by the life of him
Than I am made by my young lord and thee!
Come, now towards Chertsey with your holy load,
Taken from Paul's to be interred there;
And still, as you are weary of this weight,
Rest you, whiles I lament King Henry's corse.

Enter RICHARD, DUKE OF GLOUCESTER.

Glou. Stay, you that bear the corse, and set it down.
Anne. What black magician conjures up this fiend,
To stop devoted charitable deeds?
Glou. Villains, set down the corse; or, by Saint Paul,
I'll make a corse of him that disobeys.
Gent. My lord, stand back, and let the coffin pass.
Glou. Unmanner'd dog! stand thou, when I command:
Advance thy halberd higher than my breast,
Or, by Saint Paul, I'll strike thee to my foot,
And spurn upon thee, beggar, for thy boldness.
Anne. What, do you tremble? are you all afraid?
Alas, I blame you not; for you are mortal,
And mortal eyes cannot endure the devil.
Avaunt, thou dreadful minister of hell!
Thou hadst but power over his mortal body,
His soul thou canst not have; therefore, be gone.
Glou. Sweet saint, for charity, be not so curst.
Anne. Foul devil, for God's sake, hence, and trouble us not!
For thou hast made the happy earth thy hell,
Fill'd it with cursing cries and deep exclaims.
If thou delight to view thy heinous deeds,
Behold this pattern of thy butcheries.
O, gentlemen, see, see! dead Henry's wounds
Open their congeal'd mouths and bleed afresh!
Blush, blush, thou lump of foul deformity;
For 'tis thy presence that exhales this blood
From cold and empty veins, where no blood dwells;
Thy deed, inhuman and unnatural,
Provokes this deluge most unnatural.
O God, which this blood mad'st, revenge his death!
O earth, which this blood drink'st, revenge his death!
Either heav'n with lightning strike the murd'rer dead,
Or earth, gape open wide and eat him quick,
As thou dost swallow up this good king's blood,
Which his hell-govern'd arm hath butchered!
Glou. Lady, you know no rules of charity,
Which renders good for bad, blessings for curses.
Anne. Villain, thou know'st nor law of God nor man:
No beast so fierce but knows some touch of pity.
Glou. But I know none, and therefore am no beast.
Anne. O wonderful, when devils tell the truth!
Glou. More wonderful, when angels are so angry.
Vouchsafe, divine perfection of a woman,
Of these supposed crimes, to give me leave,
By circumstance, but to acquit myself.
Anne. Vouchsafe, diffus'd infection of a man,

146. **with post-horse,** by post horses, i.e., by swiftest possible means. 148. **steel'd,** reinforced. 153. **Warwick's youngest daughter.** Lady Anne, regarded by Shakespeare (following the chronicle) as widow of Edward Prince of Wales, son of King Henry VI, was, in fact, only his bethrothed.

SCENE II. *Stage Direction:* ***corse,*** corpse. **Halberds,** guards with long poleaxes. 3. **obsequiously,** as befits the funeral, mournfully. 5. **key-cold,** extremely cold; used proverbially. 8. **invocate,** invoke. 13. **helpless,** useless, unavailing. 17. **hap,** fortune. 22. **Prodigious,** monstrous, unnatural. 25. **that,** i.e., that creature. **unhappiness,** evil fortune. 29. **Chertsey,** a town in Surrey, where King Henry's body was buried. 30. **Paul's,** St. Paul's Church in London. 31. **still,** as often as; see glossary. 33. **Stay,** stop; see glossary. 34. **black magician,** one leagued with the devil. 35. **devoted,** pious, holy.

Of these known evils, but to give me leave,
By circumstance, to curse thy cursed self.
Glou. Fairer than tongue can name thee, let me have
Some patient leisure to excuse myself.
Anne. Fouler than heart can think thee, thou canst make
No excuse current, but to hang thyself.
Glou. By such despair, I should accuse myself.
Anne. And, by despairing, shalt thou stand excused;
For doing worthy vengeance on thyself,
That didst unworthy slaughter upon others.
Glou. Say that I slew them not?
Anne. Then say they were not slain:
But dead they are, and, devilish slave, by thee.
Glou. I did not kill your husband.
Anne. Why, then he is alive.
Glou. Nay, he is dead; and slain by Edward's hands.
Anne. In thy foul throat thou liest! Queen Margaret saw
Thy murd'rous falchion smoking in his blood;
The which thou once didst bend against her breast,
But that thy brothers beat aside the point.
Glou. I was provoked by her sland'rous tongue,
That laid their guilt upon my guiltless shoulders.
Anne. Thou wast provoked by thy bloody mind,
That never dream'st on aught but butcheries:
Didst thou not kill this king?
Glou. I grant ye.
Anne. Dost grant me, hedgehog? then, God grant me too
Thou mayst be damned for that wicked deed!
O, he was gentle, mild, and virtuous!
Glou. The better for the King of heaven, that hath him.
Anne. He is in heaven, where thou shalt never come.
Glou. Let him thank me, that holp to send him thither;
For he was fitter for that place than earth.
Anne. And thou unfit for any place but hell.
Glou. Yes, one place else, if you will hear me name it.
Anne. Some dungeon.
Glou. Your bed-chamber.
Anne. Ill rest betide the chamber where thou liest!
Glou. So will it, madam, till I lie with you.
Anne. I hope so.
Glou. I know so. But, gentle Lady Anne,
To leave this keen encounter of our wits,
And fall something into a slower method,
Is not the causer of the timeless deaths
Of these Plantagenets, Henry and Edward,
As blameful as the executioner?
Anne. Thou wast the cause, and most accurs'd effect.
Glou. Your beauty was the cause of that effect;
Your beauty, that did haunt me in my sleep
To undertake the death of all the world,
So I might live one hour in your sweet bosom.
Anne. If I thought that, I tell thee, homicide,
These nails should rend that beauty from my cheeks.
Glou. These eyes could not endure that beauty's wrack;
You should not blemish it, if I stood by:
As all the world is cheered by the sun,
So I by that; it is my day, my life.
Anne. Black night o'ershade thy day, and death thy life!
Glou. Curse not thyself, fair creature; thou art both.
Anne. I would I were, to be reveng'd on thee.
Glou. It is a quarrel most unnatural,
To be reveng'd on him that loveth thee.
Anne. It is a quarrel just and reasonable,
To be reveng'd on him that kill'd my husband.
Glou. He that bereft thee, lady, of thy husband,
Did it to help thee to a better husband.
Anne. His better doth not breathe upon the earth.
Glou. He lives that loves thee better than he could.
Anne. Name him.
Glou. Plantagenet.
Anne. Why, that was he.
Glou. The selfsame name, but one of better nature.
Anne. Where is he?
Glou. Here. [*She*] *spits at him.* Why dost thou spit at me?
Anne. Would it were mortal poison, for thy sake!
Glou. Never came poison from so sweet a place.
Anne. Never hung poison on a fouler toad.
Out of my sight! thou dost infect mine eyes.
Glou. Thine eyes, sweet lady, have infected mine.
Anne. Would they were basilisks, to strike thee dead!
Glou. I would they were, that I might die at once;
For now they kill me with a living death.
Those eyes of thine from mine have drawn salt tears,
Sham'd their aspect with store of childish drops:
These eyes, which never shed remorseful tear,
No, when my father York and Edward wept,
To hear the piteous moan that Rutland made
When black-fac'd Clifford shook his sword at him;
Nor when thy warlike father, like a child,
Told the sad story of my father's death,
And twenty times made pause to sob and weep,
That all the standers-by had wet their cheeks,
Like trees bedash'd with rain: in that sad time
My manly eyes did scorn an humble tear;
And what these sorrows could not thence exhale,
Thy beauty hath, and made them blind with weeping.
I never sued to friend nor enemy;
My tongue could never learn sweet smoothing words;
But, now thy beauty is propos'd my fee,
My proud heart sues and prompts my tongue to speak.
She looks scornfully at him.
Teach not thy lip such scorn, for it was made
For kissing, lady, not for such contempt.
If thy revengeful heart cannot forgive,
Lo, here I lend thee this sharp-pointed sword;
Which if thou please to hide in this true breast,
And let the soul forth that adoreth thee,
I lay it naked to the deadly stroke,

49. **curst,** spiteful, shrewish; see glossary. 52. **exclaims,** exclamations. 54. **pattern,** example. 58. **thy presence,** an allusion to the legend that dead bodies bleed in the presence of their murderers. 65. **quick,** alive; see glossary. 77. **circumstance,** detailed argument; see glossary. 78. **diffus'd,** disordered, shapeless. 82. **patient,** tranquil. **excuse myself,** maintain my innocence; see *excuse* in glossary. 84. **current,** genuine. 94. **falchion,** a curved sword. 95. **bend,** direct, aim. 102. **hedgehog,** a double allusion to Richard's hump and to his heraldic emblem, at boar. 107. **holp,** helped; see glossary. 117. **timeless,** untimely. 120. **effect,** agent. 151. **basilisks,** fabulous reptiles said to kill by their looks; see glossary. 158. **Rutland,** second son of Richard Duke of York. 163. **That,** so that. 169. **smoothing,** flattering.

And humbly beg the death upon my knee.
He lays his breast open: she offers at [it] with his sword.
Nay, do not pause; for I did kill King Henry,
But 'twas thy beauty that provoked me.
Nay, now dispatch; 'twas I that stabb'd young Edward,
But 'twas thy heavenly face that set me on.
She falls the sword.
Take up the sword again, or take up me.
Anne. Arise, dissembler: though I wish thy death,
I will not be thy executioner.
Glou. Then bid me kill myself, and I will do it.
Anne. I have already.
Glou. That was in thy rage:
Speak it again, and, even with the word,
That hand, which, for thy love, did kill thy love,
Shall, for thy love, kill a far truer love;
To both their deaths shalt thou be accessary.
Anne. I would I knew thy heart.
Glou. 'Tis figur'd in my tongue.
Anne. I fear me both are false.
Glou. Then never man was true.
Anne. Well, well, put up your sword.
Glou. Say, then, my peace is made.
Anne. That shalt thou know hereafter.
Glou. But shall I live in hope?
Anne. All men, I hope, live so.
Glou. Vouchsafe to wear this ring.
Anne. To take is not to give.
Glou. Look, how my ring encompasseth thy finger,
Even so thy breast encloseth my poor heart;
Wear both of them, for both of them are thine.
And if thy poor devoted suppliant may
But beg one favour at thy gracious hand,
Thou dost confirm his happiness for ever.
Anne. What is it?
Glou. That it may please you leave these sad designs
To him that hath most cause to be a mourner,
And presently repair to Crosby House;
Where, after I have solemnly interr'd
At Chertsey monast'ry this noble king,
And wet his grave with my repentant tears,
I will with all expedient duty see you:
For divers unknown reasons, I beseech you,
Grant me this boon.
Anne. With all my heart; and much it joys me too,
To see you are become so penitent.
Tressel and Berkeley, go along with me.
Glou. Bid me farewell.
Anne. 'Tis more than you deserve;
But since you teach me how to flatter you,
Imagine I have said farewell already.
Exeunt two [Tressel and Berkeley] with Anne.
Glou. Sirs, take up the corse.
Gent. Towards Chertsey, noble lord?
Glou. No, to White-Friars; there attend my coming.
Exeunt [bearers with] corse.
Was ever woman in this humour woo'd?
Was ever woman in this humour won?
I'll have her; but I will not keep her long.
What! I, that kill'd her husband and his father,
To take her in her heart's extremest hate,
With curses in her mouth, tears in her eyes,
The bleeding witness of my hatred by;
Having God, her conscience, and these bars against me,
And I no friends to back my suit withal,
But the plain devil and dissembling looks,
And yet to win her, all the world to nothing!
Ha!
Hath she forgot already that brave prince,
Edward, her lord, whom I, some three months since,
Stabb'd in my angry mood at Tewksbury?
A sweeter and a lovelier gentleman,
Fram'd in the prodigality of nature,
Young, valiant, wise, and, no doubt, right royal,
The spacious world cannot again afford:
And will she yet abase her eyes on me,
That cropp'd the golden prime of this sweet prince,
And made her widow to a woful bed?
On me, whose all not equals Edward's moiety?
On me, that halts and am misshapen thus?
My dukedom to a beggarly denier,
I do mistake my person all this while:
Upon my life, she finds, although I cannot,
Myself to be a marv'llous proper man.
I'll be at charges for a looking-glass,
And entertain a score or two of tailors,
To study fashions to adorn my body:
Since I am crept in favour with myself,
I will maintain it with some little cost.
But first I'll turn yon fellow in his grave;
And then return lamenting to my love.
Shine out, fair sun, till I have bought a glass,
That I may see my shadow as I pass. *Exit.*

SCENE III. [*The palace.*]

Enter the QUEEN MOTHER [ELIZABETH], LORD RIVERS, [DORSET,] *and* LORD GREY.

Riv. Have patience, madam: there 's no doubt his majesty
Will soon recover his accustom'd health.
Grey. In that you brook it ill, it makes him worse:
Therefore, for God's sake, entertain good comfort,
And cheer his grace with quick and merry eyes.
Q. Eliz. If he were dead, what would betide on me?
Grey. No other harm but loss of such a lord.
Q. Eliz. The loss of such a lord includes all harms.
Grey. The heavens have bless'd you with a goodly son,
To be your comforter when he is gone.
Q. Eliz. Ah, he is young, and his minority
Is put unto the trust of Richard Gloucester,
A man that loves not me, nor none of you.
Riv. Is it concluded he shall be protector?
Q. Eliz. It is determin'd, not concluded yet:

179. **the death,** i.e., death after judicial sentence. 194. **figur'd,** portrayed. 213. **presently,** at once; see glossary. **Crosby House,** built by Sir John Crosby in 1456 and fronted on Bishop's-gate Street Within. Richard, when Lord Protector, was lodged in this house. 217. **expedient,** expeditious. 227. **White-Friars,** the Carmelite priory in ancient London; the chronicles, however, state that the body was taken to Blackfriars. 228-229. **Was . . . won.** Similar passages are found in *Titus Andronicus*, II, i, 82-83, and *1 Henry VI*, V, iii, 77-78. 234. **her hatred,** i.e., Henry's wounds are a witness to the justice of Anne's hatred. 244. **the . . . nature,** i.e., nature's most lavish mood. 250. **moiety,** half of (Edward's virtues); see glossary. 252. **denier,** small copper coin, the twelfth part of a sou. 255. **proper,** handsome; see glossary. 261. **in,** into.

SCENE III. 3. **brook,** endure. 6. **betide on,** become of. 15. **determin'd . . . concluded,** i.e., decided though not performed. 16. **miscarry,** perish. 20. **Countess Richmond,** Margaret Beaufort (1443-

But so it must be, if the king miscarry.

Enter BUCKINGHAM *and* DERBY.

Grey. Here come the lords of Buckingham and Derby.
Buck. Good time of day unto your royal grace!
Der. God make your majesty joyful as you have been!
Q. Eliz. The Countess Richmond, good my Lord of Derby,
To your good prayer will scarcely say amen.
Yet, Derby, notwithstanding she 's your wife,
And loves not me, be you, good lord, assur'd
I hate not you for her proud arrogance.
Der. I do beseech you, either not believe
The envious slanders of her false accusers;
Or, if she be accus'd on true report,
Bear with her weakness, which, I think, proceeds
From wayward sickness, and no grounded malice.
Q. Eliz. Saw you the king to-day, my Lord of Derby?
Der. But now the Duke of Buckingham and I
Are come from visiting his majesty.
Q. Eliz. What likelihood of his amendment, lords?
Buck. Madam, good hope; his grace speaks cheerfully.
Q. Eliz. God grant him health! Did you confer with him?
Buck. Ay, madam: he desires to make atonement
Between the Duke of Gloucester and your brothers,
And between them and my lord chamberlain;
And sent to warn them to his royal presence.
Q. Eliz. Would all were well! but that will never be:
I fear our happiness is at the height.

Enter RICHARD [DUKE *of* GLOUCESTER, *and* HASTINGS].

Glou. They do me wrong, and I will not endure it!
Who is it that complains unto the king,
That I, forsooth, am stern and love them not?
By holy Paul, they love his grace but lightly
That fill his ears with such dissentious rumours.
Because I cannot flatter and look fair,
Smile in men's faces, smooth, deceive and cog,
Duck with French nods and apish courtesy,
I must be held a rancorous enemy.
Cannot a plain man live and think no harm,
But thus his simple truth must be abus'd
By silken, sly, insinuating Jacks?
Grey. To who in all this presence speaks your grace?
Glou. To thee, that hast nor honesty nor grace.
When have I injur'd thee? when done thee wrong?
Or thee? or thee? or any of your faction?
A plague upon you all! His royal grace—
Whom God preserve better than you would wish!—
Cannot be quiet scarce a breathing-while,
But you must trouble him with lewd complaints.
Q. Eliz. Brother of Gloucester, you mistake the matter.
The king, on his own royal disposition,
And not provok'd by any suitor else
Aiming, belike, at your interior hatred,
That in your outward action show itself
Against my children, brothers, and myself,
Makes him to send, that thereby he may gather
The ground of your ill-will, and so remove it.
Glou. I cannot tell: the world is grown so bad,
That wrens make prey where eagles dare not perch:
Since every Jack became a gentleman,
There 's many a gentle person made a Jack.
Q. Eliz. Come, come, we know your meaning, brother Gloucester;
You envy my advancement and my friends':
God grant we never may have need of you!
Glou. Meantime, God grants that I have need of you:
Our brother is imprison'd by your means,
Myself disgrac'd, and the nobility
Held in contempt; while great promotions
Are daily given to ennoble those
That scarce, some two days since, were worth a noble.
Q. Eliz. By Him that rais'd me to this careful height
From that contented hap which I enjoy'd,
I never did incense his majesty
Against the Duke of Clarence, but have been
An earnest advocate to plead for him.
My lord, you do me shameful injury,
Falsely to draw me in these vile suspects.
Glou. You may deny that you were not the mean
Of my Lord Hastings' late imprisonment.
Riv. She may, my lord, for—
Glou. She may, Lord Rivers! why, who knows not so?
She may do more, sir, than denying that:
She may help you to many fair preferments;
And then deny her aiding hand therein,
And lay those honours on your high desert.
What may she not? She may, ay, marry, may she,—
Riv. What, marry, may she?
Glou. What, marry, may she! marry with a king,
A bachelor, and a handsome stripling too:
I wis your grandam had a worser match.
Q. Eliz. My Lord of Gloucester, I have too long borne
Your blunt upbraidings and your bitter scoffs:
By heaven, I will acquaint his majesty
Of those gross taunts that oft I have endur'd.
I had rather be a country servant-maid
Than a great queen, with this condition,
To be so baited, scorn'd, and stormed at:

Enter old QUEEN MARGARET [*behind*].

Small joy have I in being England's queen.
Q. Mar. [*Aside*] And less'ned be that small, God, I beseech him!
Thy honour, state and seat is due to me.
Glou. What! threat you me with telling of the king?
Tell him, and spare not: look, what I have said
I will avouch 't in presence of the king:
I dare adventure to be sent to th' Tower.

1509), who married successively Edmund Tudor Earl of Richmond, Lord Henry Stafford, and Thomas Lord Stanley (here called also Earl of Derby). She was not friendly to Queen Elizabeth's faction. 26. **envious,** malicious. 37. **brothers.** Actually, Elizabeth had only one brother, Earl Rivers; Shakespeare may have thought that Lord Grey, her son, was her brother. 47. **fair,** courteously; see glossary. 48. **cog,** cheat; see glossary. 53. **Jacks,** lowbred persons. 57. **faction,** party; see glossary. 60. **breathing-while,** moment of rest. 61. **lewd,** vile, base. 63. **disposition,** inclination. 72. **Jack,** peasant, with play on the meaning "base fellow" in the next line. 82. **noble,** a coin, with quibble on the sense of "ennoblement." 89. **Falsely,** treacherously. **in,** into. **suspects,** suspicions. 100. **marry with.** In all preceding cases the word *marry* has been used as an oath meaning "by the Virgin Mary"; see glossary. 102. **I wis,** certainly. 112. **state,** degree; see glossary. **seat,** throne.

'Tis time to speak; my pains are quite forgot.
Q. Mar. [*Aside*] Out, devil! I do remember them too well:
Thou kill'dst my husband Henry in the Tower,
And Edward, my poor son, at Tewksbury.
Glou. Ere you were queen, ay, or your husband king,
I was a pack-horse in his great affairs;
A weeder-out of his proud adversaries,
A liberal rewarder of his friends:
To royalise his blood I spent mine own.
Q. Mar. [*Aside*] Ay, and much better blood than his or thine.
Glou. In all which time you and your husband Grey
Were factious for the house of Lancaster;
And, Rivers, so were you. Was not your husband
In Margaret's battle at Saint Alban's slain?
Let me put in your minds, if you forget,
What you have been ere this, and what you are;
Withal, what I have been, and what I am.
Q. Mar. [*Aside*] A murd'rous villain, and so still thou art.
Glou. Poor Clarence did forsake his father, Warwick;
Ay, and forswore himself,—which Jesu pardon!—
Q. Mar. [*Aside*] Which God revenge!
Glou. To fight on Edward's party for the crown;
And for his meed, poor lord, he is mewed up.
I would to God my heart were flint, like Edward's;
Or Edward's soft and pitiful, like mine:
I am too childish-foolish for this world.
Q. Mar. [*Aside*] Hie thee to hell for shame, and leave this world,
Thou cacodemon! there thy kingdom is.
Riv. My Lord of Gloucester, in those busy days
Which here you urge to prove us enemies,
We follow'd then our lord, our sovereign king:
So should we you, if you should be our king.
Glou. If I should be! I had rather be a pedlar:
Far be it from my heart, the thought thereof!
Q. Eliz. As little joy, my lord, as you suppose
You should enjoy, were you this country's king,
As little joy may you suppose in me,
That I enjoy, being the queen thereof.
Q. Mar. [*Aside*] A little joy enjoys the queen thereof;
For I am she, and altogether joyless.
I can no longer hold me patient. [*Advancing.*]
Hear me, you wrangling pirates, that fall out
In sharing that which you have pill'd from me!
Which of you trembles not that looks on me?
If not, that I am queen, you bow like subjects,
Yet that, by you depos'd, you quake like rebels?
Ah, gentle villain, do not turn away!
Glou. Foul wrinkled witch, what mak'st thou in my sight?
Q. Mar. But repetition of what thou hast marr'd;
That will I make before I let thee go.
Glou. Wert thou not banished on pain of death?
Q. Mar. I was; but I do find more pain in banishment
Than death can yield me here by my abode.
A husband and a son thou ow'st to me;
And thou a kingdom; all of you allegiance:
This sorrow that I have, by right is yours,
And all the pleasures you usurp are mine.
Glou. The curse my noble father laid on thee,
When thou didst crown his warlike brows with paper
And with thy scorns drew'st rivers from his eyes,
And then, to dry them, gav'st the duke a clout
Steep'd in the faultless blood of pretty Rutland,—
His curses, then from bitterness of soul
Denounc'd against thee, are all fall'n upon thee;
And God, not we, hath plagu'd thy bloody deed.
Q. Eliz. So just is God, to right the innocent.
Hast. O, 'twas the foulest deed to slay that babe,
And the most merciless that e'er was heard of!
Riv. Tyrants themselves wept when it was reported.
Dor. No man but prophesied revenge for it.
Buck. Northumberland, then present, wept to see it.
Q. Mar. What! were you snarling all before I came,
Ready to catch each other by the throat,
And turn you all your hatred now on me?
Did York's dread curse prevail so much with heaven
That Henry's death, my lovely Edward's death,
Their kingdom's loss, my woful banishment,
Should all but answer for that peevish brat?
Can curses pierce the clouds and enter heaven?
Why, then, give way, dull clouds, to my quick curses!
Though not by war, by surfeit die your king,
As ours by murder, to make him a king!
Edward thy son, that now is Prince of Wales,
For Edward our son, that was Prince of Wales,
Die in his youth by like untimely violence!
Thyself a queen, for me that was a queen,
Outlive thy glory, like my wretched self!
Long mayst thou live to wail thy children's death;
And see another, as I see thee now,
Deck'd in thy rights, as thou art stall'd in mine!
Long die thy happy days before thy death;
And, after many length'ned hours of grief,
Die neither mother, wife, nor England's queen!
Rivers and Dorset, you were standers by,
And so wast thou, Lord Hastings, when my son
Was stabb'd with bloody daggers: God, I pray him,
That none of you may live his natural age,
But by some unlook'd accident cut off!
Glou. Have done thy charm, thou hateful wither'd hag!
Q. Mar. And leave out thee? stay, dog, for thou shalt hear me.
If heaven have any grievous plague in store
Exceeding those that I can wish upon thee,
O, let them keep it till thy sins be ripe,
And then hurl down their indignation
On thee, the troubler of the poor world's peace!
The worm of conscience still begnaw thy soul!

116. **adventure to be,** risk being. 118. **Out,** exclamation of anger; see glossary. 121-122. **Ere . . . affairs.** Edward IV became king in 1460 when Richard was eight years old. 130. **Margaret's battle,** probably, the Battle of Bernard's Heath fought at St. Alban's in 1461. 138. **party,** side. 139. **meed,** reward. **mewed,** caged. (A "mew" is a cage for hawks.) 144. **cacodemon,** evil spirit. 159. **pill'd,** robbed, pillaged. 160-162. **Which . . . rebels?** If you do not tremble before me, bowing in awe because I am your queen, you quake as rebels who have deposed me? 164. **mak'st,** dost; see glossary. 165. **But . . . marr'd.** I merely rehearse your crimes. 167. **banished.** Margaret was banished in 1464, returned to England in 1471, and after the Battle of Tewkesbury was confined in the Tower until 1476 when she returned to France, dying there in 1482, one year before the historical time of this scene. 170. **thou,** Richard. 171. **thou,** i.e., Elizabeth. 174. **curse.** Cf. *3 Henry VI*, I, iv, 164-166. 177. **clout,** cloth. 187. **Northumberland,** Sir Henry Percy, third Earl of Northumberland, killed at Towton in 1461. Cf. *3 Henry VI*, I, iv, 150-151, 169-174. 194. **answer,** atone for; see glossary. **peevish,** silly; see glossary. 196. **quick,** sharp, piercing; see glossary. 197. **surfeit,** luxurious living. 206. **stall'd,** installed. 214. **cut off,** elliptic, but coordinate with the preceding line, i.e., live until you are cut off. 219. **them,** heaven, in the sense of "the heavens." 222. **begnaw,** gnaw, corrode (intensive). 228. **elvish-mark'd,** marked by elves at

Thy friends suspect for traitors while thou liv'st,
And take deep traitors for thy dearest friends!
No sleep close up that deadly eye of thine,
Unless it be while some tormenting dream
Affrights thee with a hell of ugly devils!
Thou elvish-mark'd, abortive, rooting hog!
Thou that wast seal'd in thy nativity
The slave of nature and the son of hell!
Thou slander of thy heavy mother's womb!
Thou loathed issue of thy father's loins!
Thou rag of honour! thou detested—
Glou. Margaret.
Q. Mar. Richard!
Glou. Ha!
Q. Mar. I call thee not.
Glou. I cry thee mercy then, for I did think
That thou hadst call'd me all these bitter names.
Q. Mar. Why, so I did; but look'd for no reply.
O, let me make the period to my curse!
Glou. 'Tis done by me, and ends in 'Margaret.'
Q. Eliz. Thus have you breath'd your curse against yourself.
Q. Mar. Poor painted queen, vain flourish of my fortune!
Why strew'st thou sugar on that bottled spider,
Whose deadly web ensnareth thee about?
Fool, fool! thou whet'st a knife to kill thyself.
The day will come that thou shalt wish for me
To help thee curse that poisonous bunch-back'd toad.
Hast. False-boding woman, end thy frantic curse,
Lest to thy harm thou move our patience.
Q. Mar. Foul shame upon you! you have all mov'd mine.
Riv. Were you well serv'd, you would be taught your duty.
Q. Mar. To serve me well, you all should do me duty,
Teach me to be your queen, and you my subjects:
O, serve me well, and teach yourselves that duty!
Dor. Dispute not with her; she is lunatic.
Q. Mar. Peace, master marquess, you are malapert:
Your fire-new stamp of honour is scarce current.
O, that your young nobility could judge
What 'twere to lose it, and be miserable!
They that stand high have many blasts to shake them;
And if they fall, they dash themselves to pieces.
Glou. Good counsel, marry: learn it, learn it, marquess.
Dor. It touches you, my lord, as much as me.
Glou. Ay, and much more: but I was born so high:
Our aery buildeth in the cedar's top,
And dallies with the wind and scorns the sun.
Q. Mar. And turns the sun to shade; alas! alas!
Witness my son, now in the shade of death;
Whose bright out-shining beams thy cloudy wrath
Hath in eternal darkness folded up.
Your aery buildeth in our aery's nest.
O God, that seest it, do not suffer it;
As it is won with blood, lost be it so!
Buck. Peace, peace! for shame, if not for charity.
Q. Mar. Urge neither charity nor shame to me:
Uncharitably with me have you dealt,
And shamefully my hopes by you are butcher'd.
My charity is outrage, life my shame;
And in that shame still live my sorrow's rage!
Buck. Have done, have done.
Q. Mar. O princely Buckingham, I'll kiss thy hand,
In sign of league and amity with thee:
Now fair befal thee and thy noble house!
Thy garments are not spotted with our blood,
Nor thou within the compass of my curse.
Buck. Nor no one here; for curses never pass
The lips of those that breathe them in the air.
Q. Mar. I will not think but they ascend the sky,
And there awake God's gentle-sleeping peace.
O Buckingham, take heed of yonder dog!
Look, when he fawns, he bites; and when he bites,
His venom tooth will rankle to the death:
Have not to do with him, beware of him;
Sin, death, and hell have set their marks on him,
And all their ministers attend on him.
Glou. What doth she say, my Lord of Buckingham?
Buck. Nothing that I respect, my gracious lord.
Q. Mar. What, dost thou scorn me for my gentle counsel?
And soothe the devil that I warn thee from?
O, but remember this another day,
When he shall split thy very heart with sorrow,
And say poor Margaret was a prophetess!
Live each of you the subjects to his hate,
And he to yours, and all of you to God's! *Exit.*
Buck. My hair doth stand on end to hear her curses.
Riv. And so doth mine: I muse why she 's at liberty.
Glou. I cannot blame her: by God's holy mother,
She hath had too much wrong; and I repent
My part thereof that I have done to her.
Q. Eliz. I never did her any, to my knowledge.
Glou. Yet you have all the vantage of her wrong.
I was too hot to do somebody good,
That is too cold in thinking of it now.
Marry, as for Clarence, he is well repaid;
He is frank'd up to fatting for his pains:
God pardon them that are the cause thereof!
Riv. A virtuous and a Christian-like conclusion,
To pray for them that have done scathe to us.
Glou. So do I ever: (*Speaks to himself*) being well advis'd.
For had I curs'd now, I had curs'd myself.

Enter CATESBY.

Cates. Madam, his majesty doth call for you;
And for your grace; and yours, my gracious lord.
Q. Eliz. Catesby, I come. Lords, will you go with me?
Riv. We wait upon your grace.
Exeunt all but Gloucester.

birth. **rooting hog,** an allusion to Richard's badge, the wild boar. In 1484 William Colyngborne, a Wiltshire gentleman, was executed for publishing the lines: "The Cat, the Rat, and Louell our dog | Rull all England vnder an hog." 229. **seal'd,** stamped; see glossary. 230. **slave of nature,** i.e., by the malignancy of nature. 235. **cry thee mercy,** beg thy pardon; see glossary. 238. **period,** conclusion. 239. **by me,** i.e., in line 234 where he completes Margaret's sentence. 241. **painted,** counterfeit; see glossary. **vain . . . fortune,** i.e., mere ornament of a position which is mine by right. 242. **bottled,** bottle-shaped, swollen. 250. **well serv'd,** i.e., if you had what you have deserved. Margaret takes the word in its other sense in line 253. **duty,** i.e., submission to authority; see glossary. 255. **malapert,** impudent. 256. **fire-new,** newly coined. **current,** put into circulation. 264. **aery,** brood of an eagle. 277. **My . . . outrage,** i.e., instead of charity I receive outrage. 285-286. **curses . . . air.** Probably, curses have no effect except on those who utter them. 291. **venom,** envenomed. **rankle,** cause a festering wound. 296. **respect,** heed; see glossary. 298. **soothe,** flatter. 310. **vantage,** advantage; see glossary. 311. **hot,** eager. 312. **cold,** ungrateful. 314. **frank'd up,** shut up in a frank, or sty. **to fatting,** to be fattened. 317. **scathe,** harm. 319. **curs'd myself,** i.e., Richard himself is the *cause* mentioned in line 315.

Glou. I do the wrong, and first begin to brawl.
The secret mischiefs that I set abroach
I lay unto the grievous charge of others.
Clarence, who I, indeed, have cast in darkness,
I do beweep to many simple gulls;
Namely, to Derby, Hastings, Buckingham;
And tell them 'tis the queen and her allies
That stir the king against the duke my brother.
Now, they believe it; and withal whet me
To be reveng'd on Rivers, Dorset, Grey:
But then I sigh; and, with a piece of scripture,
Tell them that God bids us do good for evil:
And thus I clothe my naked villainy
With odd old ends stol'n forth of holy writ;
And seem a saint, when most I play the devil.

Enter two Murderers.

But, soft! here come my executioners.
How now, my hardy, stout resolved mates!
Are you now going to dispatch this thing?
First Murd. We are, my lord; and come to have the warrant,
That we may be admitted where he is.
Glou. Well thought upon; I have it here about me. [*Gives the warrant.*]
When you have done, repair to Crosby Place.
But sirs, be sudden in the execution,
Withal obdurate, do not hear him plead;
For Clarence is well-spoken, and perhaps
May move your hearts to pity, if you mark him.
First Murd. Tut, tut, my lord, we will not stand to prate;
Talkers are no good doers: be assur'd
We go to use our hands and not our tongues.
Glou. Your eyes drop millstones, when fools' eyes fall tears:
I like you, lads; about your business straight;
Go, go, dispatch.
First Murd. We will, my noble lord. [*Exeunt.*]

SCENE IV. [*London. The Tower.*]

Enter CLARENCE *and* Keeper.

Keep. Why looks your grace so heavily to-day?
Clar. O, I have pass'd a miserable night,
So full of fearful dreams, of ugly sights,
That, as I am a Christian faithful man,
I would not spend another such a night,
Though 'twere to buy a world of happy days,
So full of dismal terror was the time!
Keep. What was your dream, my lord? I pray you tell me.
Clar. Methoughts that I had broken from the Tower,
And was embark'd to cross to Burgundy;
And, in my company, my brother Gloucester;
Who from my cabin tempted me to walk
Upon the hatches: thence we look'd toward England,
And cited up a thousand heavy times,
During the wars of York and Lancaster
That had befall'n us. As we pac'd along
Upon the giddy footing of the hatches,
Methought that Gloucester stumbled; and, in falling,
Struck me, that thought to stay him, overboard,
Into the tumbling billows of the main.
O Lord! methought, what pain it was to drown!
What dreadful noise of water in mine ears!
What sights of ugly death within mine eyes!
Methoughts I saw a thousand fearful wracks;
A thousand men that fishes gnaw'd upon;
Wedges of gold, great anchors, heaps of pearl,
Inestimable stones, unvalued jewels,
All scatt'red in the bottom of the sea:
Some lay in dead men's skulls; and, in the holes
Where eyes did once inhabit, there were crept,
As 'twere in scorn of eyes, reflecting gems,
That woo'd the slimy bottom of the deep,
And mock'd the dead bones that lay scatt'red by.
Keep. Had you such leisure in the time of death
To gaze upon these secrets of the deep?
Clar. Methought I had; and often did I strive
To yield the ghost: but still the envious flood
Stopp'd in my soul, and would not let it forth
To find the empty, vast and wand'ring air;
But smother'd it within my panting bulk,
Who almost burst to belch it in the sea.
Keep. Awak'd you not in this sore agony?
Clar. No, no, my dream was lengthen'd after life;
O, then began the tempest to my soul!
I pass'd, methought, the melancholy flood,
With that sour ferryman which poets write of,
Unto the kingdom of perpetual night.
The first that there did greet my stranger soul,
Was my great father-in-law, renowned Warwick;
Who spake aloud, 'What scourge for perjury
Can this dark monarchy afford false Clarence?'
And so he vanish'd: then came wand'ring by
A shadow like an angel, with bright hair
Dabbled in blood; and he shriek'd out aloud,
'Clarence is come; false, fleeting, perjur'd Clarence,
That stabb'd me in the field by Tewksbury;
Seize on him, Furies, take him unto torment!'
With that, methought, a legion of foul fiends
Environ'd me, and howled in mine ears
Such hideous cries, that with the very noise
I trembling wak'd, and for a season after
Could not believe but that I was in hell,
Such terrible impression made my dream.
Keep. No marvel, lord, though it affrighted you;
I am afraid, methinks to hear you tell it.
Clar. Ah, keeper, keeper, I have done these things,
That now give evidence against my soul,
For Edward's sake; and see how he requites me!
O God! if my deep pray'rs cannot appease thee,
But thou wilt be aveng'd on my misdeeds,
Yet execute thy wrath in me alone,
O, spare my guiltless wife and my poor children!
Keeper, I prithee sit by me awhile;
My soul is heavy, and I fain would sleep.
Keep. I will, my lord: God give your grace good rest! [*Clarence sleeps.*]

325. **set abroach,** begin, set on foot. 353. **fall,** drop. 354. **straight,** immediately; see glossary.
SCENE IV. 10. **Burgundy,** i.e., the Netherlands. Clarence when a child had been under the Burgundian protection at Utrecht. 14. **heavy,** gloomy. 39. **vast.** Malone suggests that this word is a substantive. 40. **bulk,** body. 45. **melancholy flood,** i.e., the river Styx. 46. **ferryman,** i.e., Charon, who ferried souls to Hades, *the kingdom of perpetual night* (l. 47). 49. **father-in-law.** Clarence's wife, Isabel Neville, was the elder daughter of the Earl of Warwick. 50. **scourge for perjury.** Cf. *3 Henry VI,* V, i, 106. 53. **shadow,** i.e., ghost of Edward

Enter BRACKENBURY, *the Lieutenant.*

Brak. Sorrow breaks seasons and reposing hours,
Makes the night morning, and the noon-tide night.
Princes have but their titles for their glories,
An outward honour for an inward toil;
And, for unfelt imaginations,
They often feel a world of restless cares:
So that, between their titles and low name,
There 's nothing differs but the outward fame.

Enter two Murderers.

First Murd. Ho! who 's here?

Brak. What would'st thou, fellow, and how cam'st thou hither?

First Murd. I would speak with Clarence, and I came hither on my legs.

Brak. What, so brief?

Sec. Murd. 'Tis better, sir, than to be tedious.
Let him see our commission, and talk no more.

[*Brackenbury*] *reads* [*it*].

Brak. I am, in this, commanded to deliver
The noble Duke of Clarence to your hands:
I will not reason what is meant hereby,
Because I will be guiltless from the meaning.
There lies the duke asleep, and there the keys:
I'll to the king; and signify to him
That thus I have resign'd to you my charge.

First Murd. You may, sir, 'tis a point of wisdom: fare you well. *Exit* [*Brackenbury with Keeper*].

Sec. Murd. What, shall we stab him as he sleeps?

First Murd. No; he'll say 'twas done cowardly, when he wakes.

Sec. Murd. Why, he shall never wake until the great judgement-day.

First Murd. Why, then he'll say we stabbed him sleeping.

Sec. Murd. The urging of that word 'judgement' hath bred a kind of remorse in me.

First Murd. What, art thou afraid?

Sec. Murd. Not to kill him, having a warrant; but to be damned for killing him, from the which no warrant can defend me.

First Murd. I thought thou hadst been resolute.

Sec. Murd. So I am, to let him live.

First Murd. I'll back to the Duke of Gloucester, and tell him so.

Sec. Murd. Nay, I prithee, stay a little: I hope this passionate humour of mine will change; it was wont to hold me but while one tells twenty.

First Murd. How dost thou feel thyself now?

Sec. Murd. Some certain dregs of conscience are yet within me.

First Murd. Remember our reward, when the deed 's done.

Sec. Murd. 'Zounds, he dies: I had forgot the reward.

First Murd. Where 's thy conscience now?

Sec. Murd. O, in the Duke of Gloucester's purse.

First Murd. When he opens his purse to give us our reward, thy conscience flies out.

Sec. Murd. 'Tis no matter, let it go; there 's few or none will entertain it.

First Murd. What if it come to thee again?

Sec. Murd. I'll not meddle with it: it is a dangerous thing: it makes a man a coward: a man cannot steal, but it accuseth him; a man cannot swear, but it checks him; a man cannot lie with his neighbour's wife, but it detects him: 'tis a blushing shamefac'd spirit that mutinies in a man's bosom; it fills a man full of obstacles: it made me once restore a purse of gold that by chance I found; it beggars any man that keeps it: it is turned out of towns and cities for a dangerous thing; and every man that means to live well endeavours to trust to himself and live without it.

First Murd. 'Zounds, 'tis even now at my elbow, persuading me not to kill the duke.

Sec. Murd. Take the devil in thy mind, and believe him not: he would insinuate with thee but to make thee sigh.

First Murd. I am strong-framed, he cannot prevail with me.

Sec. Murd. Spoke like a tall man that respects thy reputation. Come, shall we fall to work?

First Murd. Take him on the costard with the hilts of thy sword, and then throw him into the malmsey-butt in the next room.

Sec. Murd. O excellent device! and make a sop of him.

First Murd. Soft, he wakes.

Sec. Murd. Strike!

First Murd. No, we'll reason with him.

Clar. Where art thou, keeper? give me a cup of wine.

Sec. Murd. You shall have wine enough, my lord, anon.

Clar. In God's name, what art thou?

First Murd. A man, as you are.

Clar. But not, as I am, royal.

First Murd. Nor you, as we are, loyal.

Clar. Thy voice is thunder, but thy looks are humble.

First Murd. My voice is now the king's, my looks mine own.

Clar. How darkly and how deadly dost thou speak!
Your eyes do menace me: why look you pale?
Who sent you hither? Wherefore do you come?

Both. To, to, to—

Clar. To murder me?

Both. Ay, ay.

Clar. You scarcely have the hearts to tell me so,
And therefore cannot have the hearts to do it.
Wherein, my friends, have I offended you?

First Murd. Offended us you have not, but the king.

Clar. I shall be reconcil'd to him again.

Sec. Murd. Never, my lord; therefore prepare to die.

Clar. Are you drawn forth among a world of men
To slay the innocent? What is my offence?
Where is the evidence that doth accuse me?
What lawful quest have given their verdict up
Unto the frowning judge? or who pronounc'd
The bitter sentence of poor Clarence' death?
Before I be convict by course of law,
To threaten me with death is most unlawful.
I charge you, as you hope to have redemption
By Christ's dear blood shed for our grievous sins,
That you depart and lay no hands on me:

Prince of Wales, son of Henry VI; see glossary. 55. **fleeting,** fickle, deceitful. 56. **stabb'd me.** Cf. *3 Henry VI*, V, v, 40. 80. **unfelt,** unrealized. 83. **fame,** reputation; see glossary. 122. **tells,** counts; see glossary. 135. **entertain it,** follow the dictates of conscience. 140. **checks,** reproves; see glossary. 142. **shamefac'd,** bashful. 152. **him,** conscience, which he identifies with the devil. 156. **tall,** brave. 159. **costard,** head; literally, a kind of large apple. 161. **malmsey-butt,** wine barrel. 162. **sop,** bread dipped in wine. 168. **anon,** soon; see glossary. 175. **darkly,** frowningly. 189. **quest,** inquest; possibly, jury. 192. **convict,** convicted.

The deed you undertake is damnable.
First Murd. What we will do, we do upon command.
Sec. Murd. And he that hath commanded is our king.
Clar. Erroneous vassals! the great King of kings
Hath in the table of his law commanded
That thou shalt do no murder: will you, then,
Spurn at his edict and fulfil a man's?
Take heed; for he holds vengeance in his hand,
To hurl upon their heads that break his law.
Sec. Murd. And that same vengeance doth he hurl on thee,
For false forswearing and for murder too:
Thou didst receive the sacrament, to fight
In quarrel of the house of Lancaster.
First Murd. And, like a traitor to the name of God,
Didst break that vow; and with thy treacherous blade
Unrip'dst the bowels of thy sov'reign's son.
Sec. Murd. Whom thou wast sworn to cherish and defend.
First Murd. How canst thou urge God's dreadful law to us,
When thou hast broke it in such dear degree?
Clar. Alas! for whose sake did I that ill deed?
For Edward, for my brother, for his sake:
Why, sirs,
He sends you not to murder me for this;
For in that sin he is as deep as I.
If God will be avenged for the deed,
O, know you yet, he doth it publicly:
Take not the quarrel from his pow'rful arm;
He needs no indirect or lawless course
To cut off those that have offended him.
First Murd. Who made thee, then, a bloody minister,
When gallant-springing brave Plantagenet,
That princely novice, was struck dead by thee?
Clar. My brother's love, the devil, and my rage.
First Murd. Thy brother's love, our duty, and thy faults,
Provoke us hither now to slaughter thee.
Clar. If you do love my brother, hate not me;
I am his brother, and I love him well.
If you are hir'd for meed, go back again,
And I will send you to my brother Gloucester,
Who shall reward you better for my life
Than Edward will for tidings of my death.
Sec. Murd. You are deceiv'd, your brother Gloucester hates you.
Clar. O, no, he loves me, and he holds me dear:
Go you to him from me.
First Murd. Ay, so we will.
Clar. Tell him, when that our princely father York
Bless'd his three sons with his victorious arm,
And charg'd us from his soul to love each other,
He little thought of this divided friendship:
Bid Gloucester think on this, and he will weep.
First Murd. Ay, millstones; as he lessoned us to weep.
Clar. O, do not slander him, for he is kind.
First Murd. Right,
As snow in harvest. Come, you deceive yourself:
'Tis he that sends us to destroy you here.
Clar. It cannot be; for he bewept my fortune,
And hugg'd me in his arms, and swore, with sobs,
That he would labour my delivery.
First Murd. Why, so he doth, when he delivers you
From this earth's thraldom to the joys of heaven.
Sec. Murd. Make peace with God, for you must die, my lord.
Clar. Have you that holy feeling in your souls,
To counsel me to make my peace with God,
And are you yet to your own souls so blind,
That you will war with God by murd'ring me?
O, sirs, consider, they that set you on
To do this deed will hate you for the deed.
Sec. Murd. What shall we do?
Clar. Relent, and save your souls.
Which of you, if you were a prince's son,
Being pent from liberty, as I am now,
If two such murderers as yourselves came to you,
Would not entreat for life?
First Murd. Relent! No: 'tis cowardly and womanish.
Clar. Not to relent is beastly, savage, devilish.
My friend, I spy some pity in thy looks;
O, if thine eye be not a flatterer,
Come thou on my side, and entreat for me,
As you would beg, were you in my distress:
A begging prince what beggar pities not?
Sec. Murd. Look behind you, my lord.
First Murd. Take that! and that! If all this will not do, *Stabs him.*
I'll drown you in the malmsey-butt within.
Exit [with the body].
Sec. Murd. A bloody deed, and desperately dispatch'd!
How fain, like Pilate, would I wash my hands
Of this most grievous murder!

Enter First Murderer.

First Murd. How now! what mean'st thou, that thou help'st me not?
By heaven, the duke shall know how slack you have been!
Sec. Murd. I would he knew that I had sav'd his brother!
Take thou the fee, and tell him what I say;
For I repent me that the duke is slain. *Exit.*
First Murd. So do not I: go, coward as thou art.
Well, I'll go hide his body in some hole,
Till that the duke give order for his burial:
And when I have my meed, I will away;
For this will out, and then I must not stay. *Exit.*

ACT II.

SCENE I. [*London. The palace.*]

Flourish. Enter the KING [EDWARD], *sick, the* QUEEN [ELIZABETH], LORD MARQUESS DORSET, [GREY,] RIVERS, HASTINGS, CATESBY, BUCKINGHAM [, *and others*].

K. Edw. Why, so: now have I done a good day's work:
You peers, continue this united league:

200. **Erroneous,** mistaken. 201. **tables,** tablets; see glossary. 215. **dear,** grievous. 227. **gallant-springing,** blooming, in the springtime of life. 228. **novice,** youth. 247. **kind,** affectionate; see glossary. 249. **snow in harvest.** Cf. Proverbs 26:1. 253. **labour my delivery,** i.e., work to procure my freedom. 265. **pent from,** shut up from. 277. **malmsey-butt.** Shakespeare here follows Holinshed. Up to this point, the scene has no historical basis. 290. **this,** murder.

ACT II. SCENE I. 5. **part,** depart; see glossary. 8. **Dissemble . . . hatred,** i.e., do not conceal it merely. 12. **dally,** trifle. 14. **Confound,** undo, i.e., by exposing; see glossary. 15. **Either . . . end,** i.e., each of you to die at the hands of the other. 20. **factious,** i.e., guilty of factious conduct. 33. **but,** nor. 37. **most,** am most. 50. **of,** out of.

I every day expect an embassage
From my Redeemer to redeem me hence;
And more in peace my soul shall part to heaven,
Since I have made my friends at peace on earth.
Rivers and Hastings, take each other's hand;
Dissemble not your hatred, swear your love.
Riv. By heaven, my soul is purg'd from grudging hate;
And with my hand I seal my true heart's love.
Hast. So thrive I, as I truly swear the like!
K. Edw. Take heed you dally not before your king;
Lest he that is the supreme King of kings
Confound your hidden falsehood, and award
Either of you to be the other's end.
Hast. So prosper I, as I swear perfect love!
Riv. And I, as I love Hastings with my heart!
K. Edw. Madam, yourself is not exempt from this,
Nor you, son Dorset, Buckingham, nor you;
You have been factious one against the other.
Wife, love Lord Hastings, let him kiss your hand;
And what you do, do it unfeignedly.
Q. Eliz. There, Hastings; I will never more remember
Our former hatred, so thrive I and mine!
K. Edw. Dorset, embrace him; Hastings, love lord marquess.
Dor. This interchange of love, I here protest,
Upon my part shall be inviolable.
Hast. And so swear I. [*They embrace*.]
K. Edw. Now, princely Buckingham, seal thou this league
With thy embracements to my wife's allies,
And make me happy in your unity.
Buck. Whenever Buckingham doth turn his hate
Upon your grace [*to the Queen*], but with all duteous love
Doth cherish you and yours, God punish me
With hate in those where I expect most love!
When I have most need to employ a friend,
And most assured that he is a friend,
Deep, hollow, treacherous, and full of guile,
Be he unto me! this do I beg of God,
When I am cold in love to you or yours. [*They*] *embrace*.
K. Edw. A pleasing cordial, princely Buckingham,
Is this thy vow unto my sickly heart.
There wanteth now our brother Gloucester here,
To make the blessed period of this peace.
Buck. And, in good time, here comes Sir Richard Ratcliffe and the duke.

Enter RATCLIFFE *and* GLOUCESTER.

Glou. Good morrow to my sovereign king and queen;
And, princely peers, a happy time of day!
K. Edw. Happy, indeed, as we have spent the day.
Gloucester, we have done deeds of charity;
Made peace of enmity, fair love of hate,
Between these swelling wrong-incensed peers.
Glou. A blessed labour, my most sovereign lord:
Among this princely heap, if any here,
By false intelligence, or wrong surmise,
Hold me a foe;
If I unwittingly, or in my rage,
Have aught committed that is hardly borne
By any in this presence, I desire
To reconcile me to his friendly peace:
'Tis death to me to be at enmity;
I hate it, and desire all good men's love.
First, madam, I entreat true peace of you,
Which I will purchase with my duteous service;
Of you, my noble cousin Buckingham,
If ever any grudge were lodg'd between us;
Of you and you, Lord Rivers and of Dorset,
That all without desert have frown'd on me;
Dukes, earls, lords, gentlemen; indeed, of all.
I do not know that Englishman alive
With whom my soul is any jot at odds
More than the infant that is born to-night:
I thank my God for my humility.
Q. Eliz. A holy day shall this be kept hereafter:
I would to God all strifes were well compounded.
My sovereign lord, I do beseech your highness
To take our brother Clarence to your grace.
Glou. Why, madam, have I off'red love for this,
To be so flouted in this royal presence?
Who knows not that the gentle duke is dead?
They all start.
You do him injury to scorn his corse.
K. Edw. Who knows not he is dead! who knows he is?
Q. Eliz. All-seeing heaven, what a world is this!
Buck. Look I so pale, Lord Dorset, as the rest?
Dor. Ay, my good lord; and no man in this presence
But his red colour hath forsook his cheeks.
K. Edw. Is Clarence dead? the order was revers'd.
Glou. But he, poor man, by your first order died,
And that a winged Mercury did bear;
Some tardy cripple bore the countermand,
That came too lag to see him buried.
God grant that some, less noble and less loyal,
Nearer in bloody thoughts, but not in blood,
Deserve not worse than wretched Clarence did,
And yet go current from suspicion!

Enter EARL OF DERBY.

Der. A boon, my sovereign, for my service done!
K. Edw. I pray thee, peace: my soul is full of sorrow.
Der. I will not rise, unless your highness hear me.
K. Edw. Then say at once what is it thou requests.
Der. The forfeit, sovereign, of my servant's life;
Who slew to-day a riotous gentleman
Lately attendant on the Duke of Norfolk.
K. Edw. Have I a tongue to doom my brother's death,
And shall that tongue give pardon to a slave?
My brother kill'd no man; his fault was thought,
And yet his punishment was bitter death.
Who sued to me for him? who, in my wrath,
Kneel'd at my feet, and bid me be advis'd?
Who spoke of brotherhood? who spoke of love?
Who told me how the poor soul did forsake
The mighty Warwick, and did fight for me?
Who told me, in the field at Tewksbury,
When Oxford had me down, he rescued me,

51. **swelling,** i.e., with anger or rivalry. 53. **heap,** assembly. 54. **false intelligence,** being misinformed. 57. **hardly borne,** taken amiss; see *hardly* in glossary. 63. **purchase,** obtain; see glossary. 66. **Lord Rivers.** There is a difficult crux in this passage. After line 67 F adds *Of you Lord Wooduill and Lord Scales of you.* Woodville was Lord Rivers and, also, Lord Scales by right of his wife. Thus in F one person is given three names. 67. **without desert,** i.e., on my part. 74. **compounded,** settled; see glossary. 90. **lag,** late. 94. **current . . . suspicion,** free and not attacked by suspicion. 99. **forfeit,** i.e., the remission of the forfeit. 107. **advis'd,** cautious. 112. **Oxford.** Cf. *3 Henry VI*, V, v, 2.

And said, 'Dear brother, live, and be a king'?
Who told me, when we both lay in the field
Frozen almost to death, how he did lap me
Even in his garments, and did give himself,
All thin and naked, to the numb cold night?
All this from my remembrance brutish wrath
Sinfully pluck'd, and not a man of you
Had so much grace to put it in my mind.
But when your carters or your waiting-vassals
Have done a drunken slaughter, and defac'd
The precious image of our dear Redeemer,
You straight are on your knees for pardon, pardon;
And I, unjustly too, must grant it you:
But for my brother not a man would speak,
Nor I, ungracious, speak unto myself
For him, poor soul. The proudest of you all
Have been beholding to him in his life;
Yet none of you would once beg for his life.
O God, I fear thy justice will take hold
On me, and you, and mine, and yours for this!
Come, Hastings, help me to my closet. Ah, poor Clarence! *Exeunt some with King and Queen.*
Glou. This is the fruits of rashness! Mark'd you not
How that the guilty kindred of the queen
Look'd pale when they did hear of Clarence' death?
O, they did urge it still unto the king!
God will revenge it. Come, lords, will you go
To comfort Edward with our company?
Buck. We wait upon your grace. *Exeunt.*

SCENE II. [*The palace.*]

Enter the old DUCHESS OF YORK, *with the two children of* CLARENCE.

Boy. Good grandam, tell us, is our father dead?
Duch. No, boy.
Girl. Why do you weep so oft, and beat your breast,
And cry 'O Clarence, my unhappy son!'
Boy. Why do you look on us, and shake your head,
And call us orphans, wretches, castaways,
If that our noble father were alive?
Duch. My pretty cousins, you mistake me both;
I do lament the sickness of the king,
As loath to lose him, not your father's death;
It were lost sorrow to wail one that 's lost.
Boy. Then, you conclude, my grandam, he is dead.
The king mine uncle is to blame for it:
God will revenge it; whom I will importune
With earnest prayers all to that effect.
Girl. And so will I.
Duch. Peace, children, peace! the king doth love you well:
Incapable and shallow innocents,
You cannot guess who caus'd your father's death.
Boy. Grandam, we can; for my good uncle Gloucester
Told me, the king, provok'd to it by the queen,
Devis'd impeachments to imprison him:
And when my uncle told me so, he wept,
And pitied me, and kindly kiss'd my cheek;
Bade me rely on him as on my father,
And he would love me dearly as a child.
Duch. Ah, that deceit should steal such gentle shape,
And with a virtuous visor hide deep vice!
He is my son; ay, and therein my shame;
Yet from my dugs he drew not this deceit.
Boy. Think you my uncle did dissemble, grandam?
Duch. Ay, boy.
Boy. I cannot think it. Hark! what noise is this?

Enter the QUEEN [ELIZABETH], *with her hair about her ears;* RIVERS *and* DORSET *after her.*

Q. Eliz. Ah, who shall hinder me to wail and weep,
To chide my fortune, and torment myself?
I'll join with black despair against my soul,
And to myself become an enemy.
Duch. What means this scene of rude impatience?
Q. Eliz. To make an act of tragic violence:
Edward, my lord, thy son, our king, is dead.
Why grow the branches when the root is gone?
Why wither not the leaves that want their sap?
If you will live, lament; if die, be brief,
That our swift-winged souls may catch the king's;
Or, like obedient subjects, follow him
To his new kingdom of ne'er-changing night.
Duch. Ah, so much interest have I in thy sorrow
As I had title in thy noble husband!
I have bewept a worthy husband's death,
And liv'd with looking on his images:
But now two mirrors of his princely semblance
Are crack'd in pieces by malignant death,
And I for comfort have but one false glass,
That grieves me when I see my shame in him.
Thou art a widow; yet thou art a mother,
And hast the comfort of thy children left:
But death hath snatch'd my husband from mine arms,
And pluck'd two crutches from my feeble hands,
Clarence and Edward. O, what cause have I,
Thine being but a moiety of my moan,
To overgo thy woes and drown thy cries!
Boy. Ah, aunt, you wept not for our father's death;
How can we aid you with our kindred tears?
Girl. Our fatherless distress was left unmoan'd;
Your widow-dolour likewise be unwept!
Q. Eliz. Give me no help in lamentation;
I am not barren to bring forth complaints:
All springs reduce their currents to mine eyes,
That I, being govern'd by the watery moon,
May send forth plenteous tears to drown the world!
Ah for my husband, for my dear lord Edward!
Chil. Ah for our father, for our dear lord Clarence!
Duch. Alas for both, both mine, Edward and Clarence!
Q. Eliz. What stay had I but Edward? and he 's gone.
Chil. What stay had we but Clarence? and he 's gone.

SCENE II. 8. **cousins,** relations; here, grandchildren; see glossary. 18. **Incapable,** unable to understand. 22. **impeachments,** accusations. 28. **visor,** mask. 38. **rude,** violent. 39. **make,** perform, compose (picking up the theatrical metaphor in the previous line). **tragic violence,** i.e., suicide. 40. **Edward . . . dead.** Clarence's death (February 1478) and Edward IV's death (April 1483) are treated as if they had occurred near together. 50. **images,** likenesses; here, children; see glossary. 53. **false glass,** i.e., Richard. 65. **widow-dolour,** widow's grief. 67. **barren to,** unable to. 68. **reduce,** bring back. 94. **opposite with,** in opposition to. 112. **cloudy,** clouded with grief. 117-119. **The . . . kept,** i.e., the differences caused by the inveterate bitterness of the rancor in your hearts toward each other have recently been healed, and

Duch. What stays had I but they? and they are gone.
Q. Eliz. Was never widow had so dear a loss!
Chil. Were never orphans had so dear a loss!
Duch. Was never mother had so dear a loss!
Alas, I am the mother of these griefs!
Their woes are parcell'd, mine is general.
She for an Edward weeps, and so do I;
I for a Clarence weep, so doth not she:
These babes for Clarence weep, and so do I;
I for an Edward weep, so do not they:
Alas, you three, on me, threefold distress'd,
Pour all your tears! I am your sorrow's nurse,
And I will pamper it with lamentation.
Dor. Comfort, dear mother; God is much displeas'd
That you take with unthankfulness his doing:
In common worldly things, 'tis call'd ungrateful,
With dull unwillingness to repay a debt
Which with a bounteous hand was kindly lent;
Much more to be thus opposite with heaven,
For it requires the royal debt it lent you.
Riv. Madam, bethink you, like a careful mother,
Of the young prince your son: send straight for him;
Let him be crown'd; in him your comfort lives:
Drown desperate sorrow in dead Edward's grave,
And plant your joys in living Edward's throne.

Enter RICHARD [DUKE OF GLOUCESTER], BUCKINGHAM, DERBY, HASTINGS, *and* RATCLIFFE.

Glou. Sister, have comfort: all of us have cause
To wail the dimming of our shining star;
But none can help our harms by wailing them.
Madam, my mother, I do cry you mercy;
I did not see your grace: humbly on my knee
I crave your blessing.
Duch. God bless thee; and put meekness in thy breast,
Love, charity, obedience, and true duty!
Glou. Amen! [*Aside*] and make me die a good old man!
That is the butt-end of a mother's blessing:
I marvel that her grace did leave it out.
Buck. You cloudy princes and heart-sorrowing peers,
That bear this heavy mutual load of moan,
Now cheer each other in each other's love:
Though we have spent our harvest of this king,
We are to reap the harvest of his son.
The broken rancour of your high-swoln hates,
But lately splinter'd, knit, and join'd together,
Must gently be preserv'd, cherish'd, and kept:
Me seemeth good, that, with some little train,
Forthwith from Ludlow the young prince be fet
Hither to London, to be crown'd our king.
Riv. Why with some little train, my Lord of Buckingham?
Buck. Marry, my lord, lest, by a multitude,
The new-heal'd wound of malice should break out;
Which would be so much the more dangerous,
By how much the estate is green and yet ungovern'd:
Where every horse bears his commanding rein,
And may direct his course as please himself,
As well the fear of harm, as harm apparent,
In my opinion, ought to be prevented.
Glou. I hope the king made peace with all of us;
And the compact is firm and true in me.
Riv. And so in me; and so, I think, in all:
Yet, since it is but green, it should be put
To no apparent likelihood of breach,
Which haply by much company might be urg'd:
Therefore I say with noble Buckingham,
That it is meet so few should fetch the prince.
Hast. And so say I.
Glou. Then be it so; and go we to determine
Who they shall be that straight shall post to Ludlow.
Madam, and you, my sister, will you go
To give your censures in this business?
Q. Eliz. }
Duch. } With all our hearts.

Exeunt. Mane[n]t Buckingham and Richard.

Buck. My lord, whoever journeys to the prince,
For God's sake, let not us two stay at home;
For, by the way, I'll sort occasion,
As index to the story we late talk'd of,
To part the queen's proud kindred from the prince.
Glou. My other self, my counsel's consistory,
My oracle, my prophet! My dear cousin,
I, as a child, will go by thy direction.
Toward Ludlow then, for we'll not stay behind.

Exeunt.

SCENE III. [*London. A street.*]

Enter one Citizen *at one door, and another at the other.*

First Cit. Good morrow, neighbour: whither away so fast?
Sec. Cit. I promise you, I scarcely know myself:
Hear you the news abroad?
First Cit. Yes, that the king is dead.
Sec. Cit. Ill news, by 'r lady; seldom comes the better:
I fear, I fear 'twill prove a giddy world.

Enter another Citizen.

Third Cit. Neighbours, God speed!
First Cit. Give you good morrow, sir.
Third Cit. Doth the news hold of good King Edward's death?
Sec. Cit. Ay, sir, it is too true; God help the while!
Third Cit. Then, masters, look to see a troublous world.
First Cit. No, no; by God's good grace his son shall reign.
Third Cit. Woe to that land that 's govern'd by a child!
Sec. Cit. In him there is a hope of government,
Which in his nonage council under him,
And in his full and ripened years himself,
No doubt, shall then and till then govern well.
First Cit. So stood the state when Henry the Sixth
Was crown'd in Paris but at nine months old.

this peace between you must be preserved. 118. **splinter'd,** splinted, bound up with splints. 121. **Ludlow,** the royal castle at Ludlow in Shropshire, near the Welsh border. **fet,** fetched. 127. **estate,** state, government. **green,** i.e., newly established. 130. **apparent,** evident; see glossary. 137. **urg'd,** encouraged. 144. **censures,** judgments; see glossary. 148. **sort occasion,** contrive opportunity. 149. **index,** prologue. 151. **consistory,** council chamber.

SCENE III. 4. **by 'r lady,** by our Lady (oath by the Virgin Mary), 11. **Woe . . . child.** Cf. Ecclesiastes 10:16. 13. **nonage,** minority 17. **nine months.** Henry VI, proclaimed king of France, October 1422, was then about a year old. He was not crowned in Paris until December 1430.

Third Cit. Stood the state so? No, no, good friends, God wot;
For then this land was famously enrich'd
With politic grave counsel; then the king
Had virtuous uncles to protect his grace.
First Cit. Why, so hath this, both by his father and mother.
Third Cit. Better it were they all came by his father,
Or by his father there were none at all;
For emulation who shall now be nearest
Will touch us all too near, if God prevent not.
O, full of danger is the Duke of Gloucester!
And the queen's sons and brothers haught and proud:
And were they to be rul'd, and not to rule,
This sickly land might solace as before.
First Cit. Come, come, we fear the worst; all will be well.
Third Cit. When clouds are seen, wise men put on their cloaks;
When great leaves fall, then winter is at hand;
When the sun sets, who doth not look for night?
Untimely storms makes men expect a dearth.
All may be well; but, if God sort it so,
'Tis more than we deserve, or I expect.
Sec. Cit. Truly, the hearts of men are full of fear:
You cannot reason almost with a man
That looks not heavily and full of dread.
Third Cit. Before the days of change, still is it so:
By a divine instinct men's minds mistrust
Ensuing danger; as, by proof, we see
The water swell before a boist'rous storm.
But leave it all to God. Whither away?
Sec. Cit. Marry, we were sent for to the justices.
Third Cit. And so was I: I'll bear you company.
Exeunt.

SCENE IV. [*London. The palace.*]

Enter [*the*] ARCHBISHOP [OF YORK], [*the*] *young* [DUKE OF] YORK, *the* QUEEN [ELIZABETH], *and the* DUCHESS [OF YORK].

Arch. Last night, I hear, they lay at Stony-Stratford;
And at Northampton they do rest to-night:
To-morrow, or next day, they will be here.
Duch. I long with all my heart to see the prince:
I hope he is much grown since last I saw him.
Q. Eliz. But I hear, no; they say my son of York
Has almost overta'en him in his growth.
York. Ay, mother; but I would not have it so.
Duch. Why, my young cousin, it is good to grow.
York. Grandam, one night, as we did sit at supper,
My uncle Rivers talk'd how I did grow
More than my brother: 'Ay,' quoth my uncle Gloucester,
'Small herbs have grace, great weeds do grow apace:'
And since, methinks, I would not grow so fast,
Because sweet flow'rs are slow and weeds make haste.
Duch. Good faith, good faith, the saying did not hold
In him that did object the same to thee:
He was the wretched'st thing when he was young,
So long a-growing and so leisurely,
That, if this rule were true, he should be gracious.
Arch. And so no doubt he is, my gracious madam.
Duch. I hope he is; but yet let mothers doubt.
York. Now, by my troth, if I had been remember'd,
I could have given my uncle's grace a flout,
To touch his growth nearer than he touch'd mine.
Duch. How, my young York? I prithee, let me hear it.
York. Marry, they say my uncle grew so fast
That he could gnaw a crust at two hours old:
'Twas full two years ere I could get a tooth.
Grandam, this would have been a biting jest.
Duch. I prithee, pretty York, who told thee this?
York. Grandam, his nurse.
Duch. His nurse! why, she was dead ere thou wast born.
York. If 'twere not she, I cannot tell who told me.
Q. Eliz. A parlous boy: go to, you are too shrewd.
Arch. Good madam, be not angry with the child.
Q. Eliz. Pitchers have ears.

Enter a Messenger.

Arch. Here comes a messenger. What news?
Mess. Such news, my lord, as grieves me to report.
Q. Eliz. How doth the prince?
Mess. Well, madam, and in health.
Duch. What is thy news?
Mess. Lord Rivers and Lord Grey are sent to Pomfret,
And with them Sir Thomas Vaughan, prisoners.
Duch. Who hath committed them?
Mess. The mighty dukes
Gloucester and Buckingham.
Arch. For what offence?
Mess. The sum of all I can, I have disclos'd;
Why or for what these nobles were committed
Is all unknown to me, my gracious lord.
Q. Eliz. Ay me, I see the ruin of my house!
The tiger now hath seiz'd the gentle hind;
Insulting tyranny begins to jut
Upon the innocent and aweless throne:
Welcome, destruction, death, and massacre!
I see, as in a map, the end of all.
Duch. Accursed and unquiet wrangling days,
How many of you have mine eyes beheld!
My husband lost his life to get the crown;
And often up and down my sons were toss'd,
For me to joy and weep their gain and loss:
And being seated, and domestic broils
Clean over-blown, themselves, the conquerors,
Make war upon themselves; brother to brother,
Blood to blood, self against self: O, preposterous
And frantic outrage, end thy damned spleen;
Or let me die, to look on death no more!

18. **wot,** knows; see glossary. 30. **solace,** be happy, have comfort. 40. **heavily,** sad. 43. **proof,** experience; see glossary.

SCENE IV. *Stage Direction:* ***Enter the*** **Archbishop of York.** The archbishop of York was Thomas Rotherham; the Cardinal of III, i, was Thomas Bourchier, made archbishop of Canterbury in 1454. The Qq stage direction, *Enter Cardinal*, indicates perhaps that one actor took both parts. 1-3. **Last . . . here.** Stony-Stratford is nearer London; the prince was taken back to Northampton after the arrest of Rivers, Grey, and Vaughan. The F reading (which interchanges these two place names) is in accordance with the facts, but it is dramatically impossible, for if the archbishop is to have news of Richard's movements he must know also of his actions. That he does not know is clear from his conduct in this scene. 24. **flout,** dig, insult. 28. **That . . . old.** The legend is mentioned by More; cf. also *3 Henry VI*, V, vi, 53-54. 35. **parlous,** cunning, precocious. **go to,** expression of impatience; see glossary. **shrewd,** sharp-tongued; see glossary. 37. **Pitchers have ears.** Proverb: "Little pitchers have large ears." 39. **report,** reveal. 45 ***Arch.,*** so F; Globe: *Q. Eliz.* 50. **hind,** doe. 51. **jut,** encroach. 52. **aweless,** i.e.,

Q. Eliz. Come, come, my boy; we will to sanctuary.
Madam, farewell.
Duch. Stay, I will go with you.
Q. Eliz. You have no cause.
Arch. My gracious lady, go;
And thither bear your treasure and your goods.
For my part, I'll resign unto your grace
The seal I keep: and so betide to me
As well I tender you and all of yours!
Go, I'll conduct you to the sanctuary. *Exeunt.*

ACT III.

SCENE I. [*London. A street.*]

The trumpets sound. Enter [*the*] *young* PRINCE, *the Dukes of* GLOUCESTER *and* BUCKINGHAM, LORD CARDINAL [BOURCHIER, CATESBY], *with others.*

Buck. Welcome, sweet prince, to London, to your chamber.
Glou. Welcome, dear cousin, my thoughts' sovereign:
The weary way hath made you melancholy.
Prince. No, uncle; but our crosses on the way
Have made it tedious, wearisome, and heavy:
I want more uncles here to welcome me.
Glou. Sweet prince, the untainted virtue of your years
Hath not yet div'd into the world's deceit:
Nor more can you distinguish of a man
Than of his outward show; which, God he knows,
Seldom or never jumpeth with the heart.
Those uncles which you want were dangerous;
Your grace attended to their sug'red words,
But look'd not on the poison of their hearts:
God keep you from them, and from such false friends!
Prince. God keep me from false friends! but they were none.
Glou. My lord, the mayor of London comes to greet you.

Enter [*the*] Lord Mayor [*and his train*].

May. God bless your grace with health and happy days!
Prince. I thank you, good my lord; and thank you all.
I thought my mother, and my brother York,
Would long ere this have met us on the way:
Fie, what a slug is Hastings, that he comes not
To tell us whether they will come or no!

Enter LORD HASTINGS.

Buck. And, in good time, here comes the sweating lord.
Prince. Welcome, my lord: what, will our mother come?
Hast. On what occasion, God he knows, not I,
The queen your mother, and your brother York,
Have taken sanctuary: the tender prince
Would fain have come with me to meet your grace,
But by his mother was perforce withheld.
Buck. Fie, what an indirect and peevish course
Is this of hers! Lord cardinal, will your grace
Persuade the queen to send the Duke of York
Unto his princely brother presently?
If she deny, Lord Hastings, go with him,
And from her jealous arms pluck him perforce.
Card. My Lord of Buckingham, if my weak oratory
Can from his mother win the Duke of York,
Anon expect him here; but if she be obdurate
To mild entreaties, God in heaven forbid
We should infringe the holy privilege
Of blessed sanctuary! not for all this land
Would I be guilty of so deep a sin.
Buck. You are too senseless-obstinate, my lord,
Too ceremonious and traditional:
Weigh it but with the grossness of this age,
You break not sanctuary in seizing him.
The benefit thereof is always granted
To those whose dealings have deserv'd the place,
And those who have the wit to claim the place:
This prince hath neither claim'd it nor deserv'd it;
And therefore, in mine opinion, cannot have it:
Then, taking him from thence that is not there,
You break no privilege nor charter there.
Oft have I heard of sanctuary men;
But sanctuary children ne'er till now.
Card. My lord, you shall o'er-rule my mind for once.
Come on, Lord Hastings, will you go with me?
Hast. I go, my lord.
Prince. Good lords, make all the speedy haste you may. *Exeunt Cardinal and Hastings.*
Say, uncle Gloucester, if our brother come,
Where shall we sojourn till our coronation?
Glou. Where it seems best unto your royal self.
If I may counsel you, some day or two
Your highness shall repose you at the Tower:
Then where you please, and shall be thought most fit
For your best health and recreation.
Prince. I do not like the Tower, of any place.
Did Julius Cæsar build that place, my lord?
Buck. He did, my gracious lord, begin that place;
Which, since, succeeding ages have re-edified.
Prince. Is it upon record, or else reported
Successively from age to age, he built it?
Buck. Upon record, my gracious lord.
Prince. But say, my lord, it were not regist'red,
Methinks the truth should live from age to age,
As 'twere retail'd to all posterity,
Even to the general all-ending day.
Glou. [*Aside*] So wise so young, they say, do never live long.
Prince. What say you, uncle?
Glou. I say, without characters, fame lives long.
[*Aside*] Thus, like the formal vice, Iniquity,
I moralize two meanings in one word.

because of the youth of the king. 64. **spleen,** malice, hatred. 66. **sanctuary.** Queen Elizabeth lodged in the precincts of Westminster Abbey which served as a legal refuge for criminals and persons in danger of their lives. 71. **seal,** i.e., the Great Seal. 71-72. **so . . . you,** may my fortunes be measured by the care I take of yours.

ACT III. SCENE I. 1. **chamber,** i.e., London, anciently called the *camera regis*, or king's chamber. 11. **jumpeth,** agrees; see glossary. 22. **slug,** sluggard; it also means "impediment to progress." 26. **On what occasion,** for what reason. 35. **deny,** refuse; see glossary. 44. **senseless-obstinate,** unreasonably obstinate. 46. **Weigh . . . age,** i.e., take into consideration the laxness with which this age regards the right of sanctuary. 65. **Tower.** In the fifteenth century the Tower of London was a royal palace. 68. **of any place,** I dislike it most of all places. 71. **re-edified,** rebuilt. 77. **retail'd,** handed down from one to another. 81. **without characters,** lack of written records, with quibble on the sense, "having no moral character"; these are the *two meanings* referred to in line 83. 82. **vice,** conventional comic villain of the morality plays.

Prince. That Julius Cæsar was a famous man;
With what his valour did enrich his wit,
His wit set down to make his valour live:
Death makes no conquest of this conqueror;
For now he lives in fame, though not in life.
I'll tell you what, my cousin Buckingham,—
Buck. What, my gracious lord?
Prince. An if I live until I be a man,
I'll win our ancient right in France again,
Or die a soldier, as I liv'd a king.
Glou. [*Aside*] Short summers lightly have a forward spring.

Enter young York, Hastings, *and* [*the*] Cardinal.

Buck. Now, in good time, here comes the Duke of York.
Prince. Richard of York! how fares our loving brother?
York. Well, my dread lord; so must I call you now.
Prince. Ay, brother, to our grief, as it is yours:
Too late he died that might have kept that title,
Which by his death hath lost much majesty.
Glou. How fares our cousin, noble Lord of York?
York. I thank you, gentle uncle. O, my lord,
You said that idle weeds are fast in growth:
The prince my brother hath outgrown me far.
Glou. He hath, my lord.
York. And therefore is he idle?
Glou. O, my fair cousin, I must not say so.
York. Then he is more beholding to you than I.
Glou. He may command me as my sovereign;
But you have power in me as in a kinsman.
York. I pray you, uncle, give me this dagger.
Glou. My dagger, little cousin? with all my heart.
Prince. A beggar, brother?
York. Of my kind uncle, that I know will give;
And being but a toy, which is no grief to give.
Glou. A greater gift than that I'll give my cousin.
York. A greater gift! O, that 's the sword to it.
Glou. Ay, gentle cousin, were it light enough.
York. O, then, I see, you will part but with light gifts;
In weightier things you'll say a beggar nay.
Glou. It is too heavy for your grace to wear.
York. I weigh it lightly, were it heavier.
Glou. What, would you have my weapon, little lord?
York. I would, that I might thank you as you call me.
Glou. How?
York. Little.
Prince. My Lord of York will still be cross in talk:
Uncle, your grace knows how to bear with him.
York. You mean, to bear me, not to bear with me:
Uncle, my brother mocks both you and me;
Because that I am little, like an ape,
He thinks that you should bear me on your shoulders.
Buck. With what a sharp-provided wit he reasons!
To mitigate the scorn he gives his uncle,
He prettily and aptly taunts himself:
So cunning and so young is wonderful.
Glou. My lord, will 't please you pass along?
Myself and my good cousin Buckingham
Will to your mother, to entreat of her
To meet you at the Tower and welcome you.
York. What, will you go unto the Tower, my lord?
Prince. My lord protector needs will have it so.
York. I shall not sleep in quiet at the Tower.
Glou. Why, what should you fear?
York. Marry, my uncle Clarence' angry ghost:
My grandam told me he was murder'd there.
Prince. I fear no uncles dead.
Glou. Nor none that live, I hope.
Prince. An if they live, I hope I need not fear.
But come, my lord; and with a heavy heart,
Thinking on them, go I unto the Tower.
A sennet. Exeunt Prince, York, Hastings [*, Cardinal, and others*]. *Mane*[*n*]*t Richard, Buckingham, and Catesby.*
Buck. Think you, my lord, this little prating York
Was not incensed by his subtle mother
To taunt and scorn you thus opprobriously?
Glou. No doubt, no doubt: O, 'tis a parlous boy;
Bold, quick, ingenious, forward, capable:
He is all the mother's, from the top to toe.
Buck. Well, let them rest. Come hither, Catesby.
Thou art sworn as deeply to effect what we intend
As closely to conceal what we impart:
Thou know'st our reasons urg'd upon the way;
What think'st thou? is it not an easy matter
To make William Lord Hastings of our mind,
For the instalment of this noble duke
In the seat royal of this famous isle?
Cate. He for his father's sake so loves the prince,
That he will not be won to aught against him.
Buck. What think'st thou, then, of Stanley? what will he?
Cate. He will do all in all as Hastings doth.
Buck. Well, then, no more but this: go, gentle Catesby,
And, as it were far off, sound thou Lord Hastings,
How he doth stand affected to our purpose;
And summon him to-morrow to the Tower,
To sit about the coronation.
If thou dost find him tractable to us,
Encourage him, and tell him all our reasons:
If he be leaden, icy-cold, unwilling,
Be thou so too; and so break off the talk,
And give us notice of his inclination:
For we to-morrow hold divided councils,
Wherein thyself shalt highly be employ'd.
Glou. Commend me to Lord William: tell him, Catesby,
His ancient knot of dangerous adversaries
To-morrow are let blood at Pomfret-castle;
And bid my lord, for joy of this good news,
Give Mistress Shore one gentle kiss the more.
Buck. Good Catesby, go, effect this business soundly.
Cate. My good lords both, with all the heed I can.
Glou. Shall we hear from you, Catesby, ere we sleep?

85. **what,** that with which. 94. **lightly,** commonly, often. 99. **Too . . . died,** i.e., the loss is fresh in our memories. 109. **in me,** with me; 121. **were it heavier,** i.e., I should still consider it a trifling gift. 128-131. **bear . . . shoulders.** At fairs the bear commonly carried an ape on his back. The speech is doubtless an allusion to Richard's hump. 133. **scorn,** taunt, insult. 148. **fear,** i.e., fear for the uncles Richard has had arrested. 150. *Stage Direction:* ***sennet,*** series of notes played on a trumpet to announce the approach or departure of processions; see glossary. 152. **incensed,** instigated. 155. **capable,** intelligent; see glossary. 160. **the way,** the journey to London. 162. **mind,** opinion; see glossary. 165. **his father's sake.** Hastings was particularly intimate with Edward IV. 170. **far off,** i.e., with great tact. 171. **affected,** disposed; see glossary. 173. **sit,** sit in council. 179. **divided councils.** While the regular council meets, Richard plans also to have his own private consultation at Crosby House. 180. **highly,** i.e., on important errands. 183. **let blood,** i.e., will be executed. 185. **Mistress Shore.**

Cate. You shall, my lord.
Glou. At Crosby House, there shall you find us both. *Exit Catesby*.
Buck. Now, my lord, what shall we do, if we perceive
Lord Hastings will not yield to our complots?
Glou. Chop off his head. Something we will determine.
And look when I am king, claim thou of me
The earldom of Hereford, and all the moveables
Whereof the king my brother was possess'd.
Buck. I'll claim that promise at your grace's hand.
Glou. And look to have it yielded with all kindness.
Come, let us sup betimes, that afterwards
We may digest our complots in some form. *Exeunt*.

SCENE II. [*Before Lord Hastings' house*.]

Enter a Messenger *to the door of Hastings*.

Mess. My lord! my lord!
Hast. [*Within*] Who knocks?
Mess. One from the Lord Stanley.
Hast. What is 't o'clock?
Mess. Upon the stroke of four.

Enter LORD HASTINGS.

Hast. Cannot my Lord Stanley sleep these tedious nights?
Mess. So it appears by that I have to say.
First, he commends him to your noble self.
Hast. What then?
Mess. Then certifies your lordship that this night
He dreamt the boar had razed off his helm:
Besides, he says there are two councils kept;
And that may be determin'd at the one
Which may make you and him to rue at th' other.
Therefore he sends to know your lordship's pleasure,
If you will presently take horse with him,
And with all speed post with him toward the north,
To shun the danger that his soul divines.
Hast. Go, fellow, go, return unto thy lord;
Bid him not fear the separated council:
His honour and myself are at the one,
And at the other is my good friend Catesby;
Where nothing can proceed that toucheth us
Whereof I shall not have intelligence.
Tell him his fears are shallow, without instance:
And for his dreams, I wonder he 's so simple
To trust the mock'ry of unquiet slumbers:
To fly the boar before the boar pursues,
Were to incense the boar to follow us
And make pursuit where he did mean no chase.
Go, bid thy master rise and come to me;
And we will both together to the Tower,
Where, he shall see, the boar will use us kindly.
Mess. I'll go, my lord, and tell him what you say. *Exit*.

Enter CATESBY.

Cate. Many good morrows to my noble lord!
Hast. Good morrow, Catesby; you are early stirring:
What news, what news, in this our tott'ring state?
Cate. It is a reeling world, indeed, my lord;
And I believe will never stand upright
Till Richard wear the garland of the realm.
Hast. How! wear the garland! dost thou mean the crown?
Cate. Ay, my good lord.
Hast. I'll have this crown of mine cut from my shoulders
Before I'll see the crown so foul misplac'd.
But canst thou guess that he doth aim at it?
Cate. Ay, on my life; and hopes to find you forward
Upon his party for the gain thereof:
And thereupon he sends you this good news,
That this same very day your enemies,
The kindred of the queen, must die at Pomfret.
Hast. Indeed, I am no mourner for that news,
Because they have been still my adversaries:
But, that I'll give my voice on Richard's side,
To bar my master's heirs in true descent,
God knows I will not do it, to the death.
Cate. God keep your lordship in that gracious mind!
Hast. But I shall laugh at this a twelve-month hence,
That they which brought me in my master's hate,
I live to look upon their tragedy.
I tell thee, Catesby,—
Cate. What, my lord?
Hast. Ere a fortnight make me elder,
I'll send some packing that yet think not on 't.
Cate. 'Tis a vile thing to die, my gracious lord,
When men are unprepar'd and look not for it.
Hast. O monstrous, monstrous! and so falls it out
With Rivers, Vaughan, Grey: and so 'twill do
With some men else, that think themselves as safe
As thou and I; who, as thou know'st, are dear
To princely Richard and to Buckingham.
Cate. The princes both make high account of you;
[*Aside*] For they account his head upon the bridge.
Hast. I know they do; and I have well deserv'd it.

Enter LORD STANLEY.

Come on, come on; where is your boar-spear, man?
Fear you the boar, and go so unprovided?
Stan. My lord, good morrow; good morrow, Catesby:
You may jest on, but, by the holy rood,
I do not like these several councils, I.
Hast. My lord,
I hold my life as dear as you do yours;
And never in my days, I do protest,
Was it so precious to me as 'tis now:
Think you, but that I know our state secure,
I would be so triumphant as I am?
Stan. The lords at Pomfret, when they rode from London,

Jane Shore had become the mistress of Hastings after the death of Edward IV. 192. **complots,** conspiracies. 195. **earldom of Hereford.** This is an important promise. Buckingham claimed this earldom by right of his descent from Thomas of Woodstock. The offer is therefore peculiarly tempting to Buckingham. 200. **digest,** arrange, perfect; see glossary.

SCENE II. 11. **boar,** Richard. **razed,** cut, slashed. 19. **fellow,** form of address to inferiors; see glossary. 25. **instance,** proof, evidence; see glossary. 33. **kindly,** gently, courteously; see glossary. The sense "according to his nature" is not intended by Hastings, but is present as dramatic irony. 47. **Upon his party,** on his side. 55. **to the death,** though I lose my life. 71. **high account,** great estimation; the quibble on *high* appears in the next line. 72. **the bridge,** London Bridge, on a tower of which the heads of traitors were exposed. 77. **holy rood,** the cross of Christ. 78. **several,** separate; see glossary. 85. **London.** Ludlow seems to have been intended.

Were jocund, and suppos'd their states were sure,
And they indeed had no cause to mistrust;
But yet, you see, how soon the day o'ercast.
This sudden stab of rancour I misdoubt:
Pray God, I say, I prove a needless coward!
What, shall we toward the Tower? the day is spent.
Hast. Come, come, have with you. Wot you what, my lord?
To-day the lords you talk of are beheaded.
Stan. They, for their truth, might better wear their heads
Than some that have accus'd them wear their hats.
But come, my lord, let 's away.

Enter a Pursuivant.

Hast. Go on before; I'll talk with this good fellow.
Exit Lord Stanley and Catesby.
How now, sirrah! how goes the world with thee?
Purs. The better that your lordship please to ask.
Hast. I tell thee, man, 'tis better with me now
Than when thou met'st me last where now we meet:
Then was I going prisoner to the Tower,
By the suggestion of the queen's allies;
But now, I tell thee—keep it to thyself—
This day those enemies are put to death,
And I in better state than e'er I was.
Purs. God hold it, to your honour's good content!
Hast. Gramercy, fellow: there, drink that for me.
Throws him his purse.
Purs. I thank your honour. *Exit Purs.*

Enter a Priest.

Priest. Well met, my lord; I am glad to see your honour.
Hast. I thank thee, good Sir John, with all my heart.
I am in your debt for your last exercise;
Come the next Sabbath, and I will content you.
[*He whispers in his ear.*]

Enter Buckingham.

Buck. What, talking with a priest, lord chamberlain?
Your friends at Pomfret, they do need the priest;
Your honour hath no shriving work in hand.
Hast. Good faith, and when I met this holy man,
The men you talk of came into my mind.
What, go you toward the Tower?
Buck. I do, my lord; but long I cannot stay there.
I shall return before your lordship thence.
Hast. Nay, like enough, for I stay dinner there.
Buck. [*Aside*] And supper too, although thou know'st it not.
Come, will you go?
Hast. I'll wait upon your lordship. *Exeunt.*

SCENE III. [*Pomfret Castle.*]

Enter Sir Richard Ratcliffe, *with* Halberds, *carrying the nobles* [Rivers, Grey, *and* Vaughan] *to death at Pomfret.*

Rat. Come, bring forth the prisoners.
Riv. Sir Richard Ratcliffe, let me tell thee this:
To-day shalt thou behold a subject die
For truth, for duty, and for loyalty.
Grey. God bless the prince from all the pack of you!
A knot you are of damned blood-suckers.
Vaug. You live that shall cry woe for this hereafter.
Rat. Dispatch; the limit of your lives is out.
Riv. O Pomfret, Pomfret! O thou bloody prison,
Fatal and ominous to noble peers!
Within the guilty closure of thy walls
Richard the second here was hack'd to death;
And, for more slander to thy dismal seat,
We give to thee our guiltless blood to drink.
Grey. Now Margaret's curse is fall'n upon our heads,
When she exclaim'd on Hastings, you, and I,
For standing by when Richard stabb'd her son.
Riv. Then curs'd she Richard, then curs'd she Buckingham,
Then curs'd she Hastings. O, remember, God,
To hear her pray'r for them, as now for us!
And for my sister and her princely sons,
Be satisfied, dear God, with our true blood,
Which, as thou know'st, unjustly must be spilt.
Rat. Make haste; the hour of death is expiate.
Riv. Come, Grey, come, Vaughan, let us here embrace:
Farewell, until we meet again in heaven. *Exeunt.*

SCENE IV. [*The Tower of London.*]

Enter Buckingham, Derby, Hastings, Bishop of Ely, Norfolk, Ratcliffe, Lovel, *with others, at a table.*

Hast. Now, noble peers, the cause why we are met
Is, to determine of the coronation.
In God's name, speak: when is the royal day?
Buck. Is all things ready for that royal time?
Der. It is, and wants but nomination.
Ely. To-morrow, then, I judge a happy day.
Buck. Who knows the lord protector's mind herein?
Who is most inward with the noble duke?
Ely. Your grace, we think, should soonest know his mind.
Buck. Who, I, my lord! we know each other's faces,
But for our hearts, he knows no more of mine,
Than I of yours;
Or I of his, my lord, than you of mine.
Lord Hastings, you and he are near in love.
Hast. I thank his grace, I know he loves me well;
But, for his purpose in the coronation,
I have not sounded him, nor he deliver'd
His gracious pleasure any way therein:
But you, my honourable lords, may name the time;
And in the duke's behalf I'll give my voice,
Which, I presume, he'll take in gentle part.

Enter Gloucester.

Ely. In happy time, here comes the duke himself.
Glou. My noble lords and cousins all, good morrow.
I have been long a sleeper; but, I trust,
My absence doth neglect no great design,
Which by my presence might have been concluded.

92. **have with you,** come along; see glossary. 95. **wear their hats,** i.e., hold their offices. 96. *Stage Direction:* **Pursuivant.** According to More the pursuivant's name was also Hastings. A *pursuivant* is an attendant upon a herald. 98. **sirrah,** form of address to servants; see glossary. 103. **suggestion,** instigation. 107. **hold it,** continue it. 111. **Sir John,** common nickname for any priest. 112. **exercise,** sermon or religious service. 116. **shriving work,** confession and absolution. 122. **stay,** stay for.

Scene iii. 8. **out,** at an end; see glossary. 13. **seat,** place, habitation. 24. **expiate,** fully come.

Scene iv. 2. **determine of,** decide upon. 5. **nomination,** fixing of a date. 8. **inward with,** i.e., acquainted with the mind of, intimate.

Buck. Had you not come upon your cue, my lord,
William Lord Hastings had pronounc'd your part,—
I mean, your voice,—for crowning of the king.
Glou. Than my Lord Hastings no man might be bolder;
His lordship knows me well, and loves me well.
Hast. I thank your grace.
Glou. My lord of Ely!
Ely. My lord?
Glou. When I was last in Holborn,
I saw good strawberries in your garden there:
I do beseech you send for some of them.
Ely. Marry, and will, my lord, with all my heart.
Exit Bishop.
Glou. Cousin of Buckingham, a word with you.
[*Drawing him aside.*]
Catesby hath sounded Hastings in our business,
And finds the testy gentleman so hot,
That he will lose his head ere give consent
His master's child, as worshipfully he terms it,
Shall lose the royalty of England's throne.
Buck. Withdraw yourself a while, I'll go with you.
Exeunt [Gloucester and Buckingham].
Der. We have not yet set down this day of triumph.
To-morrow, in my judgement, is too sudden;
For I myself am not so well provided
As else I would be, were the day prolong'd.

Enter the BISHOP OF ELY.

Ely. Where is my lord the Duke of Gloucester?
I have sent for these strawberries.
Hast. His grace looks cheerfully and smooth this morning;
There 's some conceit or other likes him well,
When that he bids good morrow with such spirit.
I think there 's never a man in Christendom
Can lesser hide his love or hate than he;
For by his face straight shall you know his heart.
Der. What of his heart perceive you in his face
By any livelihood he show'd to-day?
Hast. Marry, that with no man here he is offended;
For, were he, he had shown it in his looks.
Der. I pray God he be not, I say.

Enter RICHARD *and* BUCKINGHAM.

Glou. I pray you all, tell me what they deserve
That do conspire my death with devilish plots
Of damned witchcraft, and that have prevail'd
Upon my body with their hellish charms?
Hast. The tender love I bear your grace, my lord,
Makes me most forward in this princely presence
To doom th' offenders, whosoe'er they be:
I say, my lord, they have deserved death.
Glou. Then be your eyes the witness of their evil!
Look how I am bewitch'd; behold mine arm
Is, like a blasted sapling, wither'd up:
And this is Edward's wife, that monstrous witch,
Consorted with that harlot strumpet Shore,
That by their witchcraft thus have marked me.
Hast. If they have done this deed, my noble lord,—
Glou. If! thou protector of this damned strumpet,
Talk'st thou to me of 'ifs'? Thou art a traitor:
Off with his head! Now, by Saint Paul I swear,
I will not dine until I see the same.
Lovel and Ratcliffe, look that it be done:
The rest, that love me, rise and follow me.
Exeunt. Mane[n]t Lovel and Ratcliffe, with the Lord Hastings.
Hast. Woe, woe for England! not a whit for me;
For I, too fond, might have prevented this.
Stanley did dream the boar did raze our helms;
But I did scorn it and disdain to fly:
Three times to-day my foot-cloth horse did stumble,
And started, when he look'd upon the Tower,
As loath to bear me to the slaughter-house.
O, now I need the priest that spake to me:
I now repent I told the pursuivant,
As too triumphing, how mine enemies,
Today at Pomfret bloodily were butcher'd,
And I myself secure in grace and favour.
O Margaret, Margaret, now thy heavy curse
Is lighted on poor Hastings' wretched head!
Rat. Come, come, dispatch; the duke would be at dinner:
Make a short shrift; he longs to see your head.
Hast. O momentary grace of mortal men,
Which we more hunt for than the grace of God!
Who builds his hope in air of your good looks,
Lives like a drunken sailor on a mast,
Ready, with every nod, to tumble down
Into the fatal bowels of the deep.
Lov. Come, come, dispatch; 'tis bootless to exclaim.
Hast. O bloody Richard! miserable England!
I prophesy the fearfull'st time to thee
That ever wretched age hath look'd upon.
Come, lead me to the block; bear him my head:
They smile at me who shortly shall be dead. *Exeunt.*

[SCENE V. *The Tower-walls.*]

Enter RICHARD *and* BUCKINGHAM, *in rotten armour, marvellous ill-favoured.*

Glou. Come, cousin, canst thou quake, and change thy colour,
Murder thy breath in middle of a word,
And then again begin, and stop again,
As if thou wert distraught and mad with terror?
Buck. Tut, I can counterfeit the deep tragedian;
Speak and look back, and pry on every side,
Tremble and start at wagging of a straw,
Intending deep suspicion: ghastly looks
Are at my service, like enforced smiles;
And both are ready in their offices,
At any time, to grace my stratagems.
But what, is Catesby gone?
Glou. He is; and, see, he brings the mayor along.

Enter the Mayor *and* CATESBY.

Buck. Lord mayor,—
Glou. Look to the drawbridge there!
Buck. Hark! a drum.

25. **design,** project, enterprise. 34. **strawberries,** apparently intended for the dinner after the meeting of the council. Richard is engaged in disarming suspicion. 47. **prolong'd,** postponed. 50. **smooth,** mild, bland. 51. **conceit,** idea, fancy; see glossary. **likes,** pleases; see glossary. 80. **look,** see to it; see glossary. 83. **prevented,** anticipated; see glossary. 86. **foot-cloth,** a large, richly ornamented cloth laid over the back of a horse, and hanging down to the ground on each side. **stumble.** The stumbling of one's horse was an omen of misfortune. 98. **grace,** fortune. 100. **air,** outward appearance, manner. 104. **exclaim,** protest; see glossary.
SCENE V. *Stage Direction:* ***rotten*** rusty. 8. **Intending,** pretending. 10. **offices,** uses, functions.

Glou. Catesby, o'erlook the walls.
Buck. Lord mayor, the reason we have sent—
Glou. Look back, defend thee, here are enemies.
Buck. God and our innocency defend and guard us!

Enter LOVEL *and* RATCLIFFE, *with* HASTINGS' *head.*

Glou. Be patient, they are friends, Ratcliffe and Lovel.
Lov. Here is the head of that ignoble traitor,
The dangerous and unsuspected Hastings.
Glou. So dear I lov'd the man, that I must weep.
I took him for the plainest harmless creature
That breath'd upon the earth a Christian;
Made him my book, wherein my soul recorded
The history of all her secret thoughts:
So smooth he daub'd his vice with show of virtue,
That, his apparent open guilt omitted,
I mean, his conversation with Shore's wife,
He liv'd from all attainder of suspects.
Buck. Well, well, he was the covert'st shelt'red traitor
That ever liv'd.
Would you imagine, or almost believe,
Were 't not that, by great preservation,
We live to tell it, that the subtle traitor
This day had plotted, in the council-house
To murder me and my good Lord of Gloucester?
May. Had he done so?
Glou. What, think you we are Turks or infidels?
Or that we would, against the form of law,
Proceed thus rashly in the villain's death,
But that the extreme peril of the case,
The peace of England and our persons' safety,
Enforc'd us to this execution?
May. Now, fair befall you! he deserv'd his death;
And your good graces both have well proceeded,
To warn false traitors from the like attempts.
Buck. I never look'd for better at his hands,
After he once fell in with Mistress Shore.
Yet had we not determin'd he should die,
Until your lordship came to see his end;
Which now the loving haste of these our friends,
Something against our meanings, have prevented:
Because, my lord, I would have had you heard
The traitor speak, and timorously confess
The manner and the purpose of his treasons;
That you might well have signified the same
Unto the citizens, who haply may
Misconster us in him and wail his death.
May. But, my good lord, your grace's words shall serve,
As well as I had seen and heard him speak:
And do not doubt, right noble princes both,
But I'll acquaint our duteous citizens
With all your just proceedings in this case.
Glou. And to that end we wish'd your lordship here,
T' avoid the censures of the carping world.
Buck. But since you come too late of our intent,
Yet witness what you hear we did intend:
And so, my good lord mayor, we bid farewell.
Exit Mayor.
Glou. Go, after, after, cousin Buckingham.
The mayor towards Guildhall hies him in all post:
There, at your meet'st advantage of the time,
Infer the bastardy of Edward's children:
Tell them how Edward put to death a citizen,
Only for saying he would make his son
Heir to the crown; meaning indeed his house,
Which, by the sign thereof, was termed so.
Moreover, urge his hateful luxury,
And bestial appetite in change of lust;
Which stretch'd unto their servants, daughters, wives,
Even where his raging eye or savage heart,
Without control, lusted to make a prey.
Nay, for a need, thus far come near my person:
Tell them, when that my mother went with child
Of that insatiate Edward, noble York
My princely father then had wars in France;
And, by true computation of the time,
Found that the issue was not his begot;
Which well appeared in his lineaments,
Being nothing like the noble duke my father:
Yet touch this sparingly, as 'twere far off;
Because, my lord, you know my mother lives.
Buck. Doubt not, my lord, I'll play the orator
As if the golden fee for which I plead
Were for myself: and so, my lord, adieu.
Glou. If you thrive well, bring them to Baynard's Castle;
Where you shall find me well accompanied
With reverend fathers and well-learned bishops.
Buck. I go; and towards three or four o'clock
Look for the news that the Guildhall affords. *Exit Buck.*
Glou. Go, Lovel, with all speed to Doctor Shaw;
[*To Cate.*] Go thou to Friar Penker; bid them both
Meet me within this hour at Baynard's Castle.
Exeunt [*all but Gloucester*].
Now will I go, to take some privy order,
To draw the brats of Clarence out of sight;
And to give order, that no manner person
Have any time recourse unto the princes. *Exit.*

[SCENE VI. *The same. A street.*]

Enter a Scrivener [*with a paper in his hand*].

Scriv. Here is the indictment of the good Lord Hastings;
Which in a set hand fairly is engross'd,
That it may be today read o'er in Paul's.
And mark how well the sequel hangs together:
Eleven hours I have spent to write it over,
For yesternight by Catesby was it sent me;
The precedent was full as long a-doing:
And yet within these five hours Hastings liv'd,
Untainted, unexamin'd, free, at liberty.
Here 's a good world the while! Who is so gross,
That cannot see this palpable device?

30. **omitted,** i.e., aside from that. 31. **conversation,** sexual intimacy. 32. **attainder of suspects,** stain of suspicion. 35. **almost,** even. 55. **have,** has. 73. **post,** haste. 74. **meet'st advantage,** most suitable opportunity. 75. **Infer,** allege, adduce. **bastardy.** It was said that Edward was contracted to one Elizabeth Lucy before his marriage to Lady Grey, the mother of his legitimate children. 76. **a citizen,** a grocer of Cheapside named Walker (or, according to Hall, Burdet). 80. **luxury,** lechery. 81. **in change of,** i.e., constantly desiring new mistresses. 98. **Baynard's Castle,** on the north bank of the Thames, between Paul's-wharf and Blackfriars. It was founded by Baynard, a nobleman of the time of the Conquest, and belonged to Richard's father, Duke of York. 103, 104. **Doctor Shaw, Friar Penker.** These men delivered sermons in Richard's favor. More describes them as "John Shaa clerke brother to the Maier, and freer Penker prouincial of the Augustine freers, both doctors of diuinite, both gret prechars, both of more learning then vertue, of more fame then learning."

Yet who 's so bold, but says he sees it not?
Bad is the world; and all will come to nought,
When such bad dealing must be seen in thought. *Exit.*

[SCENE VII. *Baynard's Castle.*]

Enter RICHARD *and* BUCKINGHAM, *at several doors.*

Glou. How now, how now, what say the citizens?
Buck. Now, by the holy mother of our Lord,
The citizens are mum, say not a word.
Glou. Touch'd you the bastardy of Edward's children?
Buck. I did; with his contract with Lady Lucy,
And his contract by deputy in France;
Th' unsatiate greediness of his desire,
And his enforcement of the city wives;
His tyranny for trifles; his own bastardy,
As being got, your father then in France,
And his resemblance, being not like the duke:
Withal I did infer your lineaments,
Being the right idea of your father,
Both in your form and nobleness of mind:
Laid open all your victories in Scotland,
Your discipline in war, wisdom in peace,
Your bounty, virtue, fair humility;
Indeed, left nothing fitting for your purpose
Untouch'd, or slightly handled, in discourse:
And when my oratory drew toward end,
I bid them that did love their country's good
Cry 'God save Richard, England's royal king!'
Glou. And did they so?
Buck. No, so God help me, they spake not a word;
But, like dumb statues or breathing stones,
Star'd each on other, and look'd deadly pale.
Which when I saw, I reprehended them;
And ask'd the mayor what meant this wilful silence:
His answer was, the people were not us'd
To be spoke to but by the recorder.
Then he was urg'd to tell my tale again,
'Thus saith the duke, thus hath the duke inferr'd;'
But nothing spoke in warrant from himself.
When he had done, some followers of mine own,
At lower end of the hall, hurl'd up their caps,
And some ten voices cried 'God save King Richard!'
And thus I took the vantage of those few,
'Thanks, gentle citizens and friends,' quoth I;
'This general applause and cheerful shout
Argues your wisdom and your love to Richard:'
And even here brake off, and came away.
Glou. What tongueless blocks were they! would they not speak?
Buck. No, by my troth, my lord.
Glou. Will not the mayor then and his brethren come?
Buck. The mayor is here at hand: intend some fear;
Be not you spoke with, but by mighty suit:
And look you get a prayer-book in your hand,
And stand between two churchmen, good my lord;
For on that ground I'll make a holy descant:
And be not easily won to our requests:
Play the maid's part, still answer nay, and take it.
Glou. I go; and if you plead as well for them
As I can say nay to thee for myself,
No doubt we'll bring it to a happy issue.
Buck. Go, go, up to the leads; the lord mayor knocks.
[*Exit Gloucester.*]

Enter the Mayor *and* Citizens.

Welcome, my lord: I dance attendance here;
I think the duke will not be spoke withal.

Enter CATESBY.

Here comes his servant: how now, Catesby,
What says your lord to my request?
Cate. He doth entreat your grace, my noble lord,
To visit him to-morrow or next day:
He is within, with two right reverend fathers,
Divinely bent to meditation;
And in no worldly suits would he be mov'd,
To draw him from his holy exercise.
Buck. Return, good Catesby, to the gracious duke;
Tell him, myself, the mayor and aldermen,
In deep designs, in matter of great moment,
No less importing than our general good,
Are come to have some conference with his grace.
Cate. I'll signify so much unto him straight. *Exit.*
Buck. Ah, ha, my lord, this prince is not an Edward!
He is not lolling on a lewd love-bed,
But on his knees at meditation;
Not dallying with a brace of courtezans,
But meditating with two deep divines;
Not sleeping, to engross his idle body,
But praying, to enrich his watchful soul:
Happy were England, would this virtuous prince
Take on his grace the sovereignty thereof:
But, sure, I fear, we shall not win him to it.
May. Marry, God defend his grace should say us nay!
Buck. I fear he will. Here Catesby comes again.

Enter CATESBY.

Now, Catesby, what says his grace?
Cate. My lord,
He wonders to what end you have assembled
Such troops of citizens to come to him,
His grace not being warn'd thereof before:
He fears, my lord, you mean no good to him.
Buck. Sorry I am my noble cousin should
Suspect me, that I mean no good to him:
By heaven, we come to him in perfect love;
And so once more return and tell his grace.
Exit [*Catesby*].
When holy and devout religious men
Are at their beads, 'tis much to draw them thence,
So sweet is zealous contemplation.

Enter RICHARD *aloft, between two* Bishops. [CATESBY *returns.*]

SCENE VI. 2. **set,** formal. **fairly,** handsomely. 4. **sequel,** what follows. 9. **Untainted,** unaccused. 10. **gross,** dull.

SCENE VII. 6. **deputy.** Cf. *3 Henry VI,* III, iii, 49 ff., where Warwick, as deputy, contracts with Louis VI of France for the marriage of King Edward to Lady Bona, sister of the French queen. 9. **tyranny for trifles,** harsh punishment of minor offenses. 10. **got,** begot. 13. **right idea,** exact image. 15. **victories in Scotland.** Richard had commanded the English forces in the Scottish expedition of 1482. 19. **discourse,** relating, i.e., by speech. 30. **recorder,** keeper of the city rolls; at this time Thomas Fitzwilliam. 33. **in . . . himself,** on his own responsibility. 45. **intend,** pretend. 49. **descant,** improvised melody. 53. **thee,** i.e., Buckingham, as spokesman for the citizens. 54. **it,** i.e., the plan to make Richard king. 55. **leads,** flat lead-covered roof. 72. **lolling,** so Pope; QqF: *lulling.* 76. **engross,** fatten. 94. *Stage Direction:* ***aloft,*** i.e., on the gallery above the stage.

May. See, where his grace stands, 'tween two clergymen!
Buck. Two props of virtue for a Christian prince,
To stay him from the fall of vanity:
And, see, a book of prayer in his hand,
True ornaments to know a holy man.
Famous Plantagenet, most gracious prince,
Lend favourable ear to our requests;
And pardon us the interruption
Of thy devotion and right Christian zeal.
Glou. My lord, there needs no such apology:
I do beseech your grace to pardon me,
Who, earnest in the service of my God,
Deferr'd the visitation of my friends.
But, leaving this, what is your grace's pleasure?
Buck. Even that, I hope, which pleaseth God above,
And all good men of this ungovern'd isle.
Glou. I do suspect I have done some offence
That seems disgracious in the city's eye,
And that you come to reprehend my ignorance.
Buck. You have, my lord: would it might please your grace,
On our entreaties, to amend your fault!
Glou. Else wherefore breathe I in a Christian land?
Buck. Know then, it is your fault that you resign
The supreme seat, the throne majestical,
The scept'red office of your ancestors,
Your state of fortune and your due of birth,
The lineal glory of your royal house,
To the corruption of a blemish'd stock:
Whiles, in the mildness of your sleepy thoughts,
Which here we waken to our country's good,
This noble isle doth want her proper limbs;
Her face defac'd with scars of infamy,
Her royal stock graft with ignoble plants,
And almost should'red in the swallowing gulf
Of dark forgetfulness and deep oblivion.
Which to recure, we heartily solicit
Your gracious self to take on you the charge
And kingly government of this your land,
Not as protector, steward, substitute,
Or lowly factor for another's gain;
But as successively from blood to blood,
Your right of birth, your empery, your own.
For this, consorted with the citizens,
Your very worshipful and loving friends,
And by their vehement instigation,
In this just cause come I to move your grace.
Glou. I cannot tell if to depart in silence,
Or bitterly to speak in your reproof,
Best fitteth my degree or your condition:
If not to answer, you might haply think
Tongue-tied ambition, not replying, yielded
To bear the golden yoke of sovereignty,
Which fondly you would here impose on me;
If to reprove you for this suit of yours,
So season'd with your faithful love to me,
Then, on the other side, I check'd my friends.
Therefore, to speak, and to avoid the first,
And then, in speaking, not to incur the last,
Definitively thus I answer you.
Your love deserves my thanks; but my desert
Unmeritable shuns your high request.
First, if all obstacles were cut away,
And that my path were even to the crown,
As the ripe revenue and due by birth;
Yet so much is my poverty of spirit,
So mighty and so many my defects,
That I would rather hide me from my greatness,
Being a bark to brook no mighty sea,
Than in my greatness covet to be hid,
And in the vapour of my glory smother'd.
But, God be thank'd, there is no need of me,
And much I need to help you, were there need;
The royal tree hath left us royal fruit,
Which, mellow'd by the stealing hours of time,
Will well become the seat of majesty,
And make, no doubt, us happy by his reign.
On him I lay that you would lay on me,
The right and fortune of his happy stars;
Which God defend that I should wring from him!
Buck. My lord, this argues conscience in your grace;
But the respects thereof are nice and trivial,
All circumstances well considered.
You say that Edward is your brother's son:
So say we too, but not by Edward's wife;
For first was he contract to Lady Lucy—
Your mother lives a witness to his vow—
And afterward by substitute betroth'd
To Bona, sister to the King of France.
These both put off, a poor petitioner,
A care-craz'd mother to a many sons,
A beauty-waning and distressed widow,
Even in the afternoon of her best days,
Made prize and purchase of his wanton eye,
Seduc'd the pitch and height of his degree
To base declension and loath'd bigamy:
By her, in his unlawful bed, he got
This Edward, whom our manners call the prince.
More bitterly could I expostulate,
Save that, for reverence to some alive,
I give a sparing limit to my tongue.
Then, good my lord, take to your royal self
This proffer'd benefit of dignity;
If not to bless us and the land withal,
Yet to draw forth your noble ancestry
From the corruption of abusing times,
Unto a lineal true-derived course.
May. Do, good my lord, your citizens entreat you.
Buck. Refuse not, mighty lord, this proffer'd love.
Cate. O, make them joyful, grant their lawful suit!
Glou. Alas, why would you heap this care on me?
I am unfit for state and majesty:
I do beseech you, take it not amiss;
I cannot nor I will not yield to you.
Buck. If you refuse it,—as, in love and zeal,

97. **stay,** sustain; see glossary. **the . . . vanity,** i.e., falling into the sin of vanity. 99. **ornaments,** i.e., the bishops as well as the prayer book. 112. **disgracious,** unbecoming. 116. **Else,** if not, otherwise. 128. **should'red,** jostled; or it may mean "immersed up to the shoulders." Johnson conjectured *smouldered*, smothered; anonymous conjecture: *foundered*. 130. **recure,** restore, make whole. 134. **factor,** agent. 136. **empery,** empire. 137. **consorted,** associated, leagued. 143. **degree,** rank. **condition,** social status. 147. **fondly,** foolishly. 155. **Unmeritable,** undeserving. 157. **even,** smooth. 158. **ripe revenue,** a possession ready to be inherited. 161. **my greatness,** my claim to the throne. 163. **in my greatness,** i.e., as king. **covet,** desire. 164. **vapour of my glory,** effluence of my kingship. 166. **need,** ought; perhaps, as Johnson suggested, lack the ability requisite. 175. **respects thereof,** considerations by which you support your argument. **nice,** insignificant; see glossary. 179-182. **For . . . France.** In the petition of 1484, ratified by Parliament at Richard's accession, it was stated that before his marriage to Elizabeth, Edward IV was engaged by trothplight to Lady Eleanor Butler, daughter of the Earl of Shrewsbury. A later tradition which Shakespeare followed held that Richard's mother, in her opposition to Edward's intention of marrying Lady Grey, which

Loath to depose the child, your brother's son;
As well we know your tenderness of heart
And gentle, kind, effeminate remorse,
Which we have noted in you to your kindred,
And egally indeed to all estates,—
Yet know, whe'r you accept our suit or no,
Your brother's son shall never reign our king;
But we will plant some other in the throne,
To the disgrace and downfall of your house:
And in this resolution here we leave you.—
Come, citizens: 'zounds! I'll entreat no more.

Glou. O, do not swear, my lord of Buckingham.

Exeunt [Buckingham and the citizens].

Cate. Call them again, sweet prince, accept their suit.
If you deny them, all the land will rue it.

Glou. Will you enforce me to a world of cares?
Call them again. I am not made of stones,
But penetrable to your kind entreaties,
Albeit against my conscience and my soul.

Enter BUCKINGHAM *and the rest.*

Cousin of Buckingham, and sage, grave men,
Since you will buckle fortune on my back,
To bear her burthen, whe'r I will or no,
I must have patience to endure the load:
But if black scandal or foul-fac'd reproach
Attend the sequel of your imposition,
Your mere enforcement shall acquittance me
From all the impure blots and stains thereof;
For God doth know, and you may partly see,
How far I am from the desire of this.

May. God bless your grace! we see it, and will say it.

Glou. In saying so, you shall but say the truth.

Buck. Then I salute you with this royal title:
Long live King Richard, England's worthy king!

May. and Cit. Amen.

Buck. To-morrow may it please you to be crown'd?

Glou. Even when you please, for you will have it so.

Buck. To-morrow, then, we will attend your grace:
And so most joyfully we take our leave.

Glou. Come, let us to our holy work again.
Farewell, my cousin; farewell, gentle friends. *Exeunt.*

ACT IV.

SCENE I. [*Before the Tower.*]

Enter [at one door] the QUEEN [ELIZABETH,] *the* DUCHESS OF YORK, *and* MARQUESS [OF] DORSET; *[at another door]* ANNE DUCHESS OF GLOUCESTER *[leading* LADY MARGARET PLANTAGENET, CLARENCE'S *young daughter].*

Duch. Who meets us here? my niece Plantagenet
Led in the hand of her kind aunt of Gloucester?
Now, for my life, she 's wand'ring to the Tower,
On pure heart's love to greet the tender prince.
Daughter, well met.

Anne. God give your graces both
A happy and a joyful time of day!

Q. Eliz. As much to you, good sister! Whither away?

Anne. No farther than the Tower; and, as I guess,
Upon the like devotion as yourselves,
To gratulate the gentle princes there.

Q. Eliz. Kind sister, thanks: we'll enter all together.

Enter [BRAKENBURY] *the Lieutenant.*

And, in good time, here the lieutenant comes.
Master lieutenant, pray you, by your leave,
How doth the prince, and my young son of York?

Brak. Right well, dear madam. By your patience,
I may not suffer you to visit them;
The king hath strictly charg'd the contrary.

Q. Eliz. The king! who's that?

Brak. I mean the lord protector.

Q. Eliz. The Lord protect him from that kingly title!
Hath he set bounds between their love and me?
I am their mother; who shall bar me from them?

Duch. I am their father's mother; I will see them.

Anne. Their aunt I am in law, in love their mother:
Then bring me to their sights; I'll bear thy blame
And take thy office from thee, on my peril.

Brak. No, madam, no; I may not leave it so:
I am bound by oath, and therefore pardon me.

Exit Lieut.

Enter [LORD] STANLEY.

Stan. Let me but meet you, ladies, one hour hence,
And I'll salute your grace of York as mother,
And reverend looker on, of two fair queens.
[*To Anne*] Come, madam, you must straight to Westminster,
There to be crowned Richard's royal queen.

Q. Eliz. Ah, cut my lace asunder, that my pent heart
May have some scope to beat, or else I swoon
With this dead-killing news!

Anne. Despiteful tidings! O unpleasing news!

Dor. Be of good cheer: mother, how fares your grace?

Q. Eliz. O Dorset, speak not to me, get thee gone!
Death and destruction dogs thee at thy heels;
Thy mother's name is ominous to children.
If thou wilt outstrip death, go cross the seas,
And live with Richmond, from the reach of hell:
Go, hie thee, hie thee from this slaughter-house,
Lest thou increase the number of the dead;
And make me die the thrall of Margaret's curse,
Nor mother, wife, nor England's counted queen.

Stan. Full of wise care is this your counsel, madam.
Take all the swift advantage of the hours;
You shall have letters from me to my son
In your behalf, to meet you on the way.

was interfering with the negotiations for his marriage to Bona of Savoy, asserted that Lady Elizabeth Lucy was already Edward's trothplight wife. Cf. III, v, 75, and vii, 6. 187. **purchase,** booty. 188. **pitch,** height. 189. **declension,** falling away from a high standard. 192. **expostulate,** discourse, argue. 193-194. **reverence . . . tongue.** The allusion is to the pretended illegitimacy of Edward and Clarence. By *some alive* he means their mother, the Duchess of York; cf. III, v, 93-94, where Richard says *my mother lives.* 213. **egally,** equally, evenly. 232. **your imposition,** the duty which you lay upon me. 233. **mere,** absolute. **acquittance,** acquit.

ACT IV. SCENE I. 1. **niece,** here, granddaughter. 9. **like devotion,** same devout errand. 10. **gratulate,** greet, salute. 20. **bounds,** barriers. 30. **reverend looker on,** beholder. **two fair queens,** Elizabeth and Anne (since Anne's husband, Richard, is about to be crowned). 33. **pent heart.** According to Elizabethan psychology, the passion of sorrow would cause a rush of spirits to the heart, thus making it swell. 42. **with Richmond,** i.e., Henry Tudor, Earl of Richmond, at this time in Brittany. 46. **counted,** accepted. 49. **son,** Richmond, whose mother Stanley had married. 50. **to meet,** i.e., instructing him to meet.

Be not ta'en tardy by unwise delay.

Duch. O ill-dispersing wind of misery!
O my accursed womb, the bed of death!
A cockatrice hast thou hatch'd to the world,
Whose unavoided eye is murderous.

Stan. Come, madam, come; I in all haste was sent.

Anne. And I with all unwillingness will go.
O, would to God that the inclusive verge
Of golden metal that must round my brow
Were red-hot steel, to sear me to the brains!
Anointed let me be with deadly venom,
And die, ere men can say, God save the queen!

Q. Eliz. Go, go, poor soul, I envy not thy glory;
To feed my humour, wish thyself no harm.

Anne. No! why? When he that is my husband now
Came to me, as I follow'd Henry's corse,
When scarce the blood was well wash'd from his hands
Which issued from my other angel husband
And that dear saint which then I weeping follow'd;
O, when, I say, I look'd on Richard's face,
This was my wish: 'Be thou,' quoth I, 'accurs'd,
For making me, so young, so old a widow!
And, when thou wed'st, let sorrow haunt thy bed;
And be thy wife—if any be so mad—
More miserable by the life of thee
Than thou hast made me by my dear lord's death!'
Lo, ere I can repeat this curse again,
Within so small a time my woman's heart
Grossly grew captive to his honey words
And prov'd the subject of mine own soul's curse,
Which hitherto hath held mine eyes from rest;
For never yet one hour in his bed
Did I enjoy the golden dew of sleep,
But with his timorous dreams was still awak'd.
Besides, he hates me for my father Warwick;
And will, no doubt, shortly be rid of me.

Q. Eliz. Poor heart, adieu! I pity thy complaining.

Anne. No more than with my soul I mourn for yours.

Dor. Farewell, thou woful welcomer of glory!

Anne. Adieu, poor soul, that tak'st thy leave of it!

Duch. [*To Dorset*] Go thou to Richmond, and good fortune guide thee!
[*To Anne*] Go thou to Richard, and good angels tend thee!
[*To Queen Eliz.*] Go thou to sanctuary, and good thoughts possess thee!
I to my grave, where peace and rest lie with me!
Eighty odd years of sorrow have I seen,
And each hour's joy wrack'd with a week of teen.

Q. Eliz. Stay, yet look back with me unto the Tower.
Pity, you ancient stones, those tender babes
Whom envy hath immur'd within your walls!
Rough cradle for such little pretty ones!
Rude ragged nurse, old sullen playfellow
For tender princes, use my babies well!
So foolish sorrows bids your stones farewell. *Exeunt.*

SCENE II. [*London. The palace.*]

Sound a sennet. Enter RICHARD, *in pomp;* BUCKINGHAM, CATESBY, RATCLIFFE, LOVEL [, *a* Page, *and others*].

K. Rich. Stand all apart. Cousin of Buckingham!

Buck. My gracious sovereign?

K. Rich. Give me thy hand. *Sound.* [*Here he ascendeth the throne.*] Thus high, by thy advice
And thy assistance, is King Richard seated:
But shall we wear these glories for a day?
Or shall they last, and we rejoice in them?

Buck. Still live they and for ever let them last!

K. Rich. Ah, Buckingham, now do I play the touch,
To try if thou be current gold indeed:
Young Edward lives: think now what I would speak.

Buck. Say on, my loving lord.

K. Rich. Why, Buckingham, I say, I would be king.

Buck. Why, so you are, my thrice renowned lord.

K. Rich. Ha! am I king? 'tis so: but Edward lives.

Buck. True, noble prince.

K. Rich. O bitter consequence,
That Edward still should live! 'True, noble prince!'
Cousin, thou wast not wont to be so dull:
Shall I be plain? I wish the bastards dead;
And I would have it suddenly perform'd.
What say'st thou now? speak suddenly; be brief.

Buck. Your grace may do your pleasure.

K. Rich. Tut, tut, thou art all ice, thy kindness freezes:
Say, have I thy consent that they shall die?

Buck. Give me some little breath, some pause, dear lord,
Before I positively speak in this:
I will resolve you herein presently. *Exit Buck.*

Cate. [*Aside to a stander by*] The king is angry: see, he gnaws his lip.

K. Rich. I will converse with iron-witted fools
And unrespective boys: none are for me
That look into me with considerate eyes:
High-reaching Buckingham grows circumspect.
Boy!

Page. My lord?

K. Rich. Know'st thou not any whom corrupting gold
Will tempt unto a close exploit of death?

Page. My lord, I know a discontented gentleman,
Whose humble means match not his haughty spirit:
Gold were as good as twenty orators,
And will, no doubt, tempt him to any thing.

K. Rich. What is his name?

Page. His name, my lord, is Tyrrel.

K. Rich. I partly know the man: go, call him hither, boy. *Exit* [*Page*].
The deep-revolving witty Buckingham
No more shall be the neighbour to my counsels:
Hath he so long held out with me untir'd,
And stops he now for breath? Well, be it so.

Enter STANLEY.

How now, Lord Stanley? What 's the news?

---

54. **cockatrice,** basilisk; see I, ii, 151, note. 60. **brains.** Anne is alluding to an ancient method of punishing regicides, or other criminals. 64. **To . . . humour,** to make me feel better. 69. **which,** whom. 72. **old,** i.e., old in sorrow. 79. **Grossly,** stupidly. 85. **Warwick,** Richard Neville, Earl of Warwick. 96. **teen,** woe. 99. **envy,** malice.

SCENE II. 8. **play the touch,** play the part of a touchstone. 9. **current,** sterling, genuine. 10. **Edward,** i.e., Edward V. 15. **O bitter consequence,** an intolerable answer to his words and an intolerable fact (Churchill). 26. **resolve,** answer; see glossary. 28. **converse,** associate; see glossary. **iron-witted,** dull-witted, unfeeling. 29. **unrespective,** unobservant, heedless. 30. **considerate,** considering, reflecting. 42. **deep-revolving,** deeply scheming. **witty,** cunning, clever. 53. **close,** imprisoned, confined. 54. **mean poor,** of low degree. 59. **stands . . . upon,** is a matter of the utmost importance to

Stan. Know, my loving lord, the Marquis Dorset, as I hear, is fled
To Richmond, in those parts beyond the sea
Where he abides. [*Stands apart.*]
K. Rich. Catesby!
Cate. My lord?
K. Rich. Rumour it abroad
That Anne, my wife, is very grievous sick;
I will take order for her keeping close.
Inquire me out some mean poor gentleman,
Whom I will marry straight to Clarence' daughter:
The boy is foolish, and I fear not him.
Look how thou dream'st! I say again, give out
That Anne my queen is sick and like to die:
About it; for it stands me much upon,
To stop all hopes whose growth may damage me.
[*Exit Catesby.*]
I must be married to my brother's daughter,
Or else my kingdom stands on brittle glass.
Murder her brothers, and then marry her!
Uncertain way of gain! But I am in
So far in blood that sin will pluck on sin:
Tear-falling pity dwells not in this eye.

Enter TYRREL.

Is thy name Tyrrel?
Tyr. James Tyrrel, and your most obedient subject.
K. Rich. Art thou, indeed?
Tyr. Prove me, my gracious lord.
K. Rich. Dar'st thou resolve to kill a friend of mine?
Tyr. Please you;
But I had rather kill two enemies.
K. Rich. Why, there thou hast it: two deep enemies,
Foes to my rest and my sweet sleep's disturbers
Are they that I would have thee deal upon:
Tyrrel, I mean those bastards in the Tower.
Tyr. Let me have open means to come to them,
And soon I'll rid you from the fear of them.
K. Rich. Thou sing'st sweet music. Hark, come hither, Tyrrel:
Go, by this token: rise, and lend thine ear: *Whispers.*
There is no more but so: say it is done,
And I will love thee, and prefer thee for it.
Tyr. I will dispatch it straight.
K. Rich. Shall we hear from thee, Tyrrel, ere we sleep?
Tyr. Ye shall, my lord. *Exit.*

Enter BUCKINGHAM.

Buck. My lord, I have consider'd in my mind
The late request that you did sound me in.
K. Rich. Well, let that rest. Dorset is fled to Richmond.
Buck. I hear that news, my lord.
K. Rich. Stanley, he is your wife's son: well, look unto it.
Buck. My lord, I claim the gift, my due by promise,
For which your honour and your faith is pawn'd;
Th' earldom of Hereford and the moveables
Which you have promised I shall possess.
K. Rich. Stanley, look to your wife: if she convey
Letters to Richmond, you shall answer it.
Buck. What says your highness to my just request?
K. Rich. I do remember me, Henry the Sixth
Did prophesy that Richmond should be king,
When Richmond was a little peevish boy.
A king, perhaps, perhaps,—
Buck. My lord!
K. Rich. How chance the prophet could not at that time
Have told me, I being by, that I should kill him?
Buck. My lord, your promise for the earldom,—
K. Rich. Richmond! When last I was at Exeter,
The mayor in courtesy show'd me the castle,
And call'd it Rougemont: at which name I started,
Because a bard of Ireland told me once,
I should not live long after I saw Richmond.
Buck. My lord!
K. Rich. Ay, what 's o'clock?
Buck. I am thus bold to put your grace in mind
Of what you promis'd me.
K. Rich. Well, but what 's o'clock?
Buck. Upon the stroke of ten.
K. Rich. Well, let it strike.
Buck. Why let it strike?
K. Rich. Because that, like a Jack, thou keep'st the stroke
Betwixt thy begging and my meditation.
I am not in the giving vein to-day.
Buck. May it please you to resolve me in my suit.
K. Rich. Tut, tut,
Thou troublest me; I am not in the vein.
Exit [*with all but Buckingham*].
Buck. And is it thus? repays he my deep service
With such contempt? made I him king for this?
O, let me think on Hastings, and be gone
To Brecknock, while my fearful head is on! *Exit.*

[SCENE III. *The same.*]

Enter TYRREL.

Tyr. The tyrannous and bloody act is done,
The most arch deed of piteous massacre
That ever yet this land was guilty of.
Dighton and Forrest, who I did suborn
To do this piece of ruthfull butchery,
Albeit they were flesh'd villains, bloody dogs,
Melted with tenderness and mild compassion,
Wept like to children in their deaths' sad story.
'O, thus,' quoth Dighton, 'lay the gentle babes:'
'Thus, thus,' quoth Forrest, 'girdling one another
Within their alabaster innocent arms:
Their lips were four red roses on a stalk,
Which in their summer beauty kiss'd each other.
A book of prayers on their pillow lay;
Which once,' quoth Forrest, 'almost chang'd my mind;
But O! the devil'—there the villain stopp'd;
When Dighton thus told on: 'We smothered
The most replenished sweet work of nature,

me. 61. **brother's daughter,** i.e., Elizabeth of York, daughter to Edward IV, who became the queen of Henry VII. 64-66. **But . . . eye.** Cf. *Macbeth*, III, iv, 136-138. 65. **pluck on,** draw on. 69. **Prove,** test; see glossary. 75. **deal upon,** set to work upon. 82. **prefer,** promote, advance. 90. **he,** i.e., Richmond. 96. **it,** i.e., for it. 117. **Jack,** the figure of a man which strikes the bell on the outside of a clock. 117-118. **thou . . . meditation,** i.e., regularly or mechanically as the striking of a clock you interrupt my meditation with your begging. 126. **Brecknock,** Brecknock Castle in Wales on Buckingham's estate.

SCENE III. 2. **arch deed,** i.e., chief or notorious act. 4. **Dighton and Forrest.** John Dighton, Tyrrel's horsekeeper, and Miles Forrest, one of the four appointed by Tyrrel to take charge of the princes. 6. **flesh'd,** experienced in bloodshed. 18. **replenished,** complete, perfect.

That from the prime creation e'er she framed.'
Hence both are gone with conscience and remorse;
They could not speak; and so I left them both,
To bring this tidings to the bloody king.

Enter [KING] RICHARD.

And here he comes. All health, my sovereign lord!
K. Rich. Kind Tyrrel, am I happy in thy news?
Tyr. If to have done the thing you gave in charge
Beget your happiness, be happy then,
For it is done.
K. Rich. But didst thou see them dead?
Tyr. I did, my lord.
K. Rich. And buried, gentle Tyrrel?
Tyr. The chaplain of the Tower hath buried them;
But where, to say the truth, I do not know.
K. Rich. Come to me, Tyrrel, soon at after supper,
When thou shalt tell the process of their death.
Meantime, but think how I may do thee good,
And be inheritor of thy desire.
Farewell till then.
Tyr. I humbly take my leave. [*Exit.*]
K. Rich. The son of Clarence have I pent up close;
His daughter meanly have I match'd in marriage;
The sons of Edward sleep in Abraham's bosom,
And Anne my wife hath bid this world good night.
Now, for I know the Breton Richmond aims
At young Elizabeth, my brother's daughter,
And, by that knot, looks proudly on the crown,
To her go I, a jolly thriving wooer.

Enter RATCLIFFE.

Rat. My lord!
K. Rich. Good or bad news, that thou com'st in so bluntly?
Rat. Bad news, my lord: Morton is fled to Richmond;
And Buckingham, back'd with the hardy Welshmen,
Is in the field, and still his power increaseth.
K. Rich. Ely with Richmond troubles me more near
Than Buckingham and his rash-levied strength.
Come, I have learn'd that fearful commenting
Is leaden servitor to dull delay;
Delay leads impotent and snail-pac'd beggary:
Then fiery expedition be my wing,
Jove's Mercury, and herald for a king!
Go, muster men: my counsel is my shield;
We must be brief when traitors brave the field. *Exeunt.*

SCENE [IV. *Before the palace.*]

Enter old QUEEN MARGARET.

Q. Mar. So, now prosperity begins to mellow
And drop into the rotten mouth of death.
Here in these confines slily have I lurk'd,
To watch the waning of mine enemies.
A dire induction am I witness to,
And will to France, hoping the consequence
Will prove as bitter, black, and tragical.
Withdraw thee, wretched Margaret: who comes here?

Enter DUCHESS [OF YORK] *and* QUEEN [ELIZABETH].

Q. Eliz. Ah, my poor princes! ah, my tender babes!
My unblown flowers, new-appearing sweets!
If yet your gentle souls fly in the air
And be not fix'd in doom perpetual,
Hover about me with your airy wings
And hear your mother's lamentation!
Q. Mar. Hover about her; say, that right for right
Hath dimm'd your infant morn to aged night.
Duch. So many miseries have craz'd my voice,
That my woe-wearied tongue is still and mute;
Edward Plantagenet, why art thou dead?
Q. Mar. Plantagenet doth quit Plantagenet.
Edward for Edward pays a dying debt.
Q. Eliz. Wilt thou, O God, fly from such gentle lambs,
And throw them in the entrails of the wolf?
When didst thou sleep when such a deed was done?
Q. Mar. When holy Harry died, and my sweet son.
Duch. Dead life, blind sight, poor mortal living ghost,
Woe's scene, world's shame, grave's due by life usurp'd,
Brief abstract and record of tedious days,
Rest thy unrest on England's lawful earth, [*Sitting down.*]
Unlawfully made drunk with innocent blood!
Q. Eliz. Ah, that thou wouldst as soon afford a grave
As thou canst yield a melancholy seat!
Then would I hide my bones, not rest them here.
Ah, who hath any cause to mourn but we? [*Sitting down by her.*]
Q. Mar. If ancient sorrow be most reverend,
Give mine the benefit of seniory,
And let my griefs frown on the upper hand.
If sorrow can admit society, [*Sitting down with them.*]
Tell o'er your woes again by viewing mine:
I had an Edward, till a Richard kill'd him;
I had a Harry, till a Richard kill'd him:
Thou hadst an Edward, till a Richard kill'd him;
Thou hadst a Richard, till a Richard kill'd him.
Duch. I had a Richard too, and thou didst kill him;
I had a Rutland too, thou holp'st to kill him.
Q. Mar. Thou hadst a Clarence too, and Richard kill'd him.
From forth the kennel of thy womb hath crept
A hell-hound that doth hunt us all to death:
That dog, that had his teeth before his eyes,
To worry lambs and lap their gentle blood,
That foul defacer of God's handiwork,
That excellent grand tyrant of the earth,

19. **prime,** first. 20. **gone with,** completely overcome by. 25. **gave in charge,** ordered, commanded. 30. **I . . . know.** More records that Tyrrel ordered the murderers to bury the bodies "at the staire foot, meetlie deepe in the ground vnder a great heape of stone." In 1674, during some repairs at the White Tower, there was unearthed a wooden chest containing bones which were pronounced those of two boys of 13 and 11 years. By the order of Charles II they were removed to Westminster Abbey. 31. **soon,** toward evening. **at after supper,** i.e., dessert after supper. 32. **process,** story; see glossary. 36. **The . . . close.** Richard kept Clarence's son prisoner at Sheriff Hutton Castle in Yorkshire. 37. **His . . . marriage.** Margaret Plantagenet was about twelve years old when Richard died. Shakespeare has apparently confused her with Lady Cicely, her first cousin, whom Richard, according to Holinshed, intended to marry to "a man found in a cloud, and of an unknown linage and familie." 38. **Abraham's bosom.** See Luke 16:22. 41. **my brother's,** Edward's. 42. **by that knot,** by virtue of that alliance. 46. **Morton,** John Morton, Bishop of Ely, who had been kept prisoner at Brecknock Castle. 51-52. **fearful . . . delay,** timorous thought and cautious disquisition are dull attendants on delay (Johnson). 54-55. **fiery . . . king.** Fiery expedition is to be Richard's herald, as Mercury was Jove's herald. 57. **brave,** challenge; see glossary.

SCENE IV. 5. **induction,** first step. 6. **the consequence,** what follows, the sequel. 10. **unblown,** unopened. 15. **right for right,** a just punishment for an offense against justice (Wright). 16. **dimm'd . . . night,** i.e., brought your recently acquired glory to eternal ruin. 17. **craz'd,** cracked. 20. **Plantagenet, Plantagenet,** Edward IV; Edward, son of Henry VI and Margaret, former Prince of Wales, killed by the Yorkists at Tewkesbury. **quit,** require, pay for. 25. **Harry,** i.e., Henry

That reigns in galled eyes of weeping souls,
Thy womb let loose, to chase us to our graves.
O upright, just, and true-disposing God,
How do I thank thee, that this carnal cur
Preys on the issue of his mother's body,
And makes her pew-fellow with others' moan!

Duch. O Harry's wife, triumph not in my woes!
God witness with me, I have wept for thine.

Q. Mar. Bear with me; I am hungry for revenge,
And now I cloy me with beholding it.
Thy Edward he is dead, that kill'd my Edward;
Thy other Edward dead, to quit my Edward;
Young York he is but boot, because both they
Match'd not the high perfection of my loss:
Thy Clarence he is dead that stabb'd my Edward;
And the beholders of this frantic play,
Th' adulterate Hastings, Rivers, Vaughan, Grey,
Untimely smother'd in their dusky graves.
Richard yet lives, hell's black intelligencer,
Only reserv'd their factor, to buy souls
And send them thither: but at hand, at hand,
Ensues his piteous and unpitied end:
Earth gapes, hell burns, fiends roar, saints pray,
To have him suddenly convey'd from hence.
Cancel his bond of life, dear God, I pray,
That I may live and say, The dog is dead!

Q. Eliz. O, thou didst prophesy the time would come
That I should wish for thee to help me curse
That bottled spider, that foul bunch-back'd toad!

Q. Mar. I call'd thee then vain flourish of my fortune;
I call'd thee then poor shadow, painted queen;
The presentation of but what I was;
The flattering index of a direful pageant;
One heav'd a-high, to be hurl'd down below;
A mother only mock'd with two fair babes;
A dream of what thou wast, a garish flag,
To be the aim of every dangerous shot;
A sign of dignity, a breath, a bubble,
A queen in jest, only to fill the scene.
Where is thy husband now? where be thy brothers?
Where be thy two sons? wherein dost thou joy?
Who sues and kneels and says 'God save the queen'?
Where be the bending peers that flattered thee?
Where be the thronging troops that followed thee?
Decline all this, and see what now thou art:
For happy wife, a most distressed widow;
For joyful mother, one that wails the name;
For one being sued to, one that humbly sues;
For queen, a very caitiff crown'd with care;
For she that scorn'd at me, now scorn'd of me;
For she being fear'd of all, now fearing one;
For she commanding all, obey'd of none.
Thus hath the course of justice whirl'd about,
And left thee but a very prey to time;
Having no more but thought of what thou wast,
To torture thee the more, being what thou art.
Thou didst usurp my place, and dost thou not
Usurp the just proportion of my sorrow?
Now thy proud neck bears half my burthen'd yoke;
From which even here I slip my wearied head,
And leave the burthen of it all on thee.
Farewell, York's wife, and queen of sad mischance:
These English woes shall make me smile in France.

Q. Eliz. O thou well skill'd in curses, stay awhile,
And teach me how to curse mine enemies!

Q. Mar. Forbear to sleep the nights, and fast the days;
Compare dead happiness with living woe;
Think that thy babes were sweeter than they were,
And he that slew them fouler than he is:
Bett'ring thy loss makes the bad causer worse:
Revolving this will teach thee how to curse.

Q. Eliz. My words are dull; O, quicken them with thine!

Q. Mar. Thy woes will make them sharp, and pierce like mine. *Exit Margaret.*

Duch. Why should calamity be full of words?

Q. Eliz. Windy attorneys to their client woes,
Airy succeeders of intestate joys,
Poor breathing orators of miseries!
Let them have scope: though what they will impart
Help nothing else, yet do they ease the heart.

Duch. If so, then be not tongue-tied: go with me,
And in the breath of bitter words let 's smother
My damned son, that thy two sweet sons smother'd.
The trumpet sounds: be copious in exclaims.

Enter KING RICHARD *and his train* [*marching, with drums and trumpets*].

K. Rich. Who intercepts me in my expedition?

Duch. O, she that might have intercepted thee,
By strangling thee in her accursed womb,
From all the slaughters, wretch, that thou hast done!

Q. Eliz. Hid'st thou that forehead with a golden crown,
Where should be branded, if that right were right,
The slaughter of the prince that ow'd that crown,
And the dire death of my poor sons and brothers?
Tell me, thou villain slave, where are my children?

Duch. Thou toad, thou toad, where is thy brother Clarence?
And little Ned Plantagenet, his son?

Q. Eliz. Where is the gentle Rivers, Vaughan, Grey?

Duch. Where is kind Hastings?

K. Rich. A flourish, trumpets! strike alarum, drums!
Let not the heavens hear these tell-tale women
Rail on the Lord's anointed: strike, I say!
Flourish. Alarums.
Either be patient, and entreat me fair,
Or with the clamorous report of war

VI. 26-27. **Dead . . . usurp'd.** By these paradoxes the mother of Edward IV describes herself and expresses her sense of the disordered state of the land. 28. **abstract,** epitome. 36. **seniory,** superiority of claim, priority. 37. **on . . . hand,** i.e., from a place of precedence. 40. **Edward,** her son, former Prince of Wales; cf. I. 20, note. 41. **Harry,** her husband. 42. **Edward,** i.e., Edward V. 43. **Richard,** the young Duke of York, son of Edward IV and Elizabeth Woodville. 44. **Richard,** Duke of York, her husband and father of Richard III, killed by Margaret's army at the Battle of Wakefield in 1460. 45. **Rutland,** Edmund, son of the Duke of York, also killed at Wakefield. 49. **teeth,** an allusion to the legend that Richard was born with teeth. 53. **galled,** sore with weeping. 56. **carnal,** flesh-eating. 58. **pew-fellow,** intimate associate. 63. **Thy Edward,** Edward IV. **my Edward,** son of Henry VI. 64. **other Edward,** Edward V. 65. **Young York,** Richard, Duke of York, the younger of the princes murdered in the Tower. **but boot,** merely that which is "thrown in"; see *boot* in glossary. 69. **adulterate,** adulterous. 71. **intelligencer,** agent, go-between. 72. **factor,** agent (of the powers of hell). 85. **index,** argument, preface, prologue. **pageant,** spectacular entertainment; see glossary. 90. **sign,** mere sign. 97. **Decline,** go through from beginning to end. 101. **caitiff,** wretch, slave (term of reproach). 102. **scorn'd at,** taunted. **scorn'd of,** taunted by. 122. **Bett'ring,** exaggerating. 127. **their client,** so Hanmer; F: *their Clients.* 128. **intestate,** apparently used in the sense "bequeathing nothing," the general notion being that words are of no consequence. 129. **breathing,** speaking. 135. **exclaims,** exclamations. 141. **right were right,** justice were done. 142. **ow'd,** owned; see glossary. 146. **Ned Plantagenet.** Cf. note, IV, iii, 36. 148. **alarum,** the cry or signal "allarme" (to arms). 149. **tell-tale,** tattling, gabbling.

Thus will I drown your exclamations.
Duch. Art thou my son?
K. Rich. Ay, I thank God, my father, and yourself.
Duch. Then patiently hear my impatience.
K. Rich. Madam, I have a touch of your condition,
That cannot brook the accent of reproof.
Duch. O, let me speak!
K. Rich. Do then; but I'll not hear.
Duch. I will be mild and gentle in my words.
K. Rich. And brief, good mother; for I am in haste.
Duch. Art thou so hasty? I have stay'd for thee,
God knows, in torment and in agony.
K. Rich. And came I not at last to comfort you?
Duch. No, by the holy rood, thou know'st it well,
Thou cam'st on earth to make the earth my hell.
A grievous burthen was thy birth to me;
Tetchy and wayward was thy infancy;
Thy school-days frightful, desp'rate, wild, and furious,
Thy prime of manhood daring, bold, and venturous,
Thy age confirm'd, proud, subtle, sly, and bloody,
More mild, but yet more harmful, kind in hatred:
What comfortable hour canst thou name,
That ever grac'd me with thy company?
K. Rich. Faith, none, but Humphrey Hour, that call'd your grace
To breakfast once forth of my company.
If I be so disgracious in your eye,
Let me march on, and not offend you, madam.
Strike up the drum.
Duch. I prithee, hear me speak.
K. Rich. You speak too bitterly.
Duch. Hear me a word;
For I shall never speak to thee again.
K. Rich. So.
Duch. Either thou wilt die, by God's just ordinance,
Ere from this war thou turn a conqueror,
Or I with grief and extreme age shall perish
And never more behold thy face again.
Therefore take with thee my most grievous curse;
Which, in the day of battle, tire thee more
Than all the complete armour that thou wear'st!
My prayers on the adverse party fight;
And there the little souls of Edward's children
Whisper the spirits of thine enemies
And promise them success and victory.
Bloody thou art, bloody will be thy end;
Shame serves thy life and doth thy death attend. *Exit.*
Q. Eliz. Though far more cause, yet much less spirit to curse
Abides in me; I say amen to her.
K. Rich. Stay, madam; I must talk a word with you.
Q. Eliz. I have no more sons of the royal blood
For thee to slaughter: for my daughters, Richard,
They shall be praying nuns, not weeping queens;
And therefore level not to hit their lives.
K. Rich. You have a daughter call'd Elizabeth,
Virtuous and fair, royal and gracious.
Q. Eliz. And must she die for this? O, let her live,
And I'll corrupt her manners, stain her beauty;
Slander myself as false to Edward's bed;
Throw over her the veil of infamy:
So she may live unscarr'd of bleeding slaughter,
I will confess she was not Edward's daughter.
K. Rich. Wrong not her birth, she is a royal princess.
Q. Eliz. To save her life, I'll say she is not so.
K. Rich. Her life is safest only in her birth.
Q. Eliz. And only in that safety died her brothers.
K. Rich. Lo, at their birth good stars were opposite.
Q. Eliz. No, to their lives ill friends were contrary.
K. Rich. All unavoided is the doom of destiny.
Q. Eliz. True, when avoided grace makes destiny:
My babes were destin'd to a fairer death,
If grace had bless'd thee with a fairer life.
K. Rich. You speak as if that I had slain my cousins.
Q. Eliz. Cousins, indeed; and by their uncle cozen'd
Of comfort, kingdom, kindred, freedom, life.
Whose hand soever lanc'd their tender hearts,
Thy head, all indirectly, gave direction:
No doubt the murd'rous knife was dull and blunt
Till it was whetted on thy stone-hard heart,
To revel in the entrails of my lambs.
But that still use of grief makes wild grief tame,
My tongue should to thy ears not name my boys
Till that my nails were anchor'd in thine eyes;
And I, in such a desp'rate bay of death,
Like a poor bark, of sails and tackling reft,
Rush all to pieces on thy rocky bosom.
K. Rich. Madam, so thrive I in my enterprise
And dangerous success of bloody wars,
As I intend more good to you and yours
Than ever you or yours by me were harm'd!
Q. Eliz. What good is cover'd with the face of heaven,
To be discovered, that can do me good?
K. Rich. Th' advancement of your children, gentle lady.
Q. Eliz. Up to some scaffold, there to lose their heads?
K. Rich. Unto the dignity and height of fortune,
The high imperial type of this earth's glory.
Q. Eliz. Flatter my sorrow with report of it;
Tell me what state, what dignity, what honour,
Canst thou demise to any child of mine?
K. Rich. Even all I have; ay, and myself and all,
Will I withal endow a child of thine;
So in the Lethe of thy angry soul
Thou drown the sad remembrance of those wrongs
Which thou supposest I have done to thee.
Q. Eliz. Be brief, lest that the process of thy kindness
Last longer telling than thy kindness' date.
K. Rich. Then know, that from my soul I love thy daughter.
Q. Eliz. My daughter's mother thinks it with her soul.
K. Rich. What do you think?
Q. Eliz. That thou dost love my daughter from thy soul:
So from thy soul's love didst thou love her brothers;
And from my heart's love I do thank thee for it.

157. **touch . . . condition,** a dash of your disposition. 162. **stay'd for,** waited the birth of; see *stay* in glossary. 168. **Tetchy,** fretful, peevish. 170. **prime of,** first. 171. **age confirm'd,** riper manhood. 172. **kind in hatred,** concealing hatred under pretense of kindness. 174. **grac'd,** honored, favored; see glossary. 175. **Humphrey Hour.** To "dine with Duke Humphrey" was to go hungry. The passage is obscure but seems to mean that Richard's comfortable hour came when his mother did not appear for breakfast. 188. **tire.** This and the coordinate verbs *fight* (l. 190), *Whisper* (l. 192), and *promise* (l. 193) are optative subjunctives. 195. **serves,** accompanies. 202. **level,** aim; see glossary. 206. **manners,** morals. 214. **only in,** by reason of. 215. **opposite,** hostile, antagonistic. 216. **contrary,** opposed. 217. **unavoided,** unavoidable. 218. **avoided grace,** i.e., Richard, in whom grace is void or lacking. 222. **cozen'd,** cheated; obvious pun. 229. **still,** constant; see glossary. **use,** habit; see glossary. 232. **bay,** a body of water in which the *poor bark* is floundering, and also a reference to the position of

K. Rich. Be not so hasty to confound my meaning:
I mean, that with my soul I love thy daughter,
And do intend to make her queen of England.
Q. Eliz. Well then, who dost thou mean shall be her king?
K. Rich. Even he that makes her queen: who else should be?
Q. Eliz. What, thou?
K. Rich. Even so. How think you of it?
Q. Eliz. How canst thou woo her?
K. Rich. That would I learn of you,
As one being best acquainted with her humour.
Q. Eliz. And wilt thou learn of me?
K. Rich. Madam, with all my heart.
Q. Eliz. Send to her, by the man that slew her brothers,
A pair of bleeding hearts; thereon engrave
Edward and York; then haply will she weep:
Therefore present to her,—as sometime Margaret
Did to thy father, steep'd in Rutland's blood,—
A handkerchief; which, say to her, did drain
The purple sap from her sweet brother's body.
And bid her wipe her weeping eyes withal.
If this inducement move her not to love,
Send her a letter of thy noble deeds;
Tell her thou mad'st away her uncle Clarence,
Her uncle Rivers; ay, and, for her sake,
Mad'st quick conveyance with her good aunt Anne.
K. Rich. You mock me, madam; this is not the way
To win your daughter.
Q. Eliz. There is no other way;
Unless thou couldst put on some other shape,
And not be Richard that hath done all this.
K. Rich. Say that I did all this for love of her.
Q. Eliz. Nay, then indeed she cannot choose but hate thee,
Having bought love with such a bloody spoil.
K. Rich. Look what is done cannot be now amended:
Men shall deal unadvisedly sometimes,
Which after hours gives leisure to repent.
If I did take the kingdom from your sons,
To make amends, I'll give it to your daughter.
If I have kill'd the issue of your womb,
To quicken your increase, I will beget
Mine issue of your blood upon your daughter:
A grandam's name is little less in love
Than is the doting title of a mother;
They are as children but one step below,
Even of your metal, of your very blood;
Of all one pain, save for a night of groans
Endur'd of her, for whom you bid like sorrow.
Your children were vexation to your youth,
But mine shall be a comfort to your age.
The loss you have is but a son being king,
And by that loss your daughter is made queen.
I cannot make you what amends I would,
Therefore accept such kindness as I can.
Dorset your son, that with a fearful soul
Leads discontented steps in foreign soil,
This fair alliance quickly shall call home
To high promotions and great dignity:
The king, that calls your beauteous daughter wife,
Familiarly shall call thy Dorset brother;
Again shall you be mother to a king,
And all the ruins of distressful times
Repair'd with double riches of content.
What! we have many goodly days to see:
The liquid drops of tears that you have shed
Shall come again, transform'd to orient pearl,
Advantaging their loan with interest
Of ten times double gain of happiness.
Go, then, my mother, to thy daughter go;
Make bold her bashful years with your experience;
Prepare her ears to hear a wooer's tale;
Put in her tender heart th' aspiring flame
Of golden sovereignty; acquaint the princess
With the sweet silent hours of marriage joys:
And when this arm of mine hath chastised
The petty rebel, dull-brain'd Buckingham,
Bound with triumphant garlands will I come
And lead thy daughter to a conqueror's bed;
To whom I will retail my conquest won,
And she shall be sole victoress, Cæsar's Cæsar.
Q. Eliz. What were I best to say? her father's brother
Would be her lord? or shall I say, her uncle?
Or, he that slew her brothers and her uncles?
Under what title shall I woo for thee,
That God, the law, my honour and her love,
Can make seem pleasing to her tender years?
K. Rich. Infer fair England's peace by this alliance.
Q. Eliz. Which she shall purchase with still lasting war.
K. Rich. Tell her the king, that may command, entreats.
Q. Eliz. That at her hands which the king's King forbids.
K. Rich. Say, she shall be a high and mighty queen.
Q. Eliz. To wail the title, as her mother doth.
K. Rich. Say, I will love her everlastingly.
Q. Eliz. But how long shall that title 'ever' last?
K. Rich. Sweetly in force unto her fair life's end.
Q. Eliz. But how long fairly shall her sweet life last?
K. Rich. As long as heaven and nature lengthens it.
Q. Eliz. As long as hell and Richard likes of it.
K. Rich. Say, I, her sovereign, am her subject low.
Q. Eliz. But she, your subject, loathes such sovereignty.
K. Rich. Be eloquent in my behalf to her.
Q. Eliz. An honest tale speeds best being plainly told.
K. Rich. Then plainly to her tell my loving tale.
Q. Eliz. Plain and not honest is too harsh a style.
K. Rich. Your reasons are too shallow and too quick.
Q. Eliz. O no, my reasons are too deep and dead;
Too deep and dead, poor infants, in their graves.
K. Rich. Harp not on that string, madam; that is past.

a hunted animal who has turned to face the hounds. 236. **success,** sequel, result; see glossary. 247. **demise,** convey, transmit, lease. 249. **withal,** with this. 250. **Lethe,** the river Lethe, the waters of which produce forgetfulness. 254. **date,** term of existence; see glossary. 259. **from,** used sarcastically in the sense "apart from." 270. **wilt thou,** i.e., do you really wish to. 274. **Therefore,** for that reason. **sometime,** once; see glossary. 283. **conveyance,** removal. 293. **Which,** i.e., from which dealing. 297. **quicken,** give new life to. 302. **metal,** substance. 304. **bid,** endured. 307. **son being king,** Edward, who was Edward v. 311-312. **Dorset . . . soil.** Dorset did not join Richmond abroad until after the failure of Buckingham's revolt. 322. **orient,** bright, shining. 323. **Advantaging,** augmenting; see glossary. 343. **Infer,** possibly, bring about; or adduce (as a reason). 351. **in force,** i.e., my love will continue. 358. **speeds,** succeeds; see glossary. 360. **too . . . style,** i.e., a discordant combination. 361. **reasons,** observations, remarks.

Q. Eliz. Harp on it still shall I till heartstrings break.
K. Rich. Now, by my George, my garter, and my crown,—
Q. Eliz. Profan'd, dishonour'd, and the third usurp'd.
K. Rich. I swear—
Q. Eliz. By nothing; for this is no oath:
Thy George, profan'd, hath lost his lordly honour;
Thy garter, blemish'd, pawn'd his knightly virtue;
Thy crown, usurp'd, disgrac'd his kingly glory.
If something thou wouldst swear to be believ'd,
Swear then by something that thou hast not wrong'd.
K. Rich. Then, by myself—
Q. Eliz. Thyself is self-misus'd.
K. Rich. Now, by the world—
Q. Eliz. 'Tis full of thy foul wrongs.
K. Rich. My father's death—
Q. Eliz. Thy life hath it dishonour'd.
K. Rich. Why then, by God—
Q. Eliz. God's wrong is most of all.
If thou didst fear to break an oath with Him,
The unity the king my husband made
Thou hadst not broken, nor my brothers died:
If thou hadst fear'd to break an oath by Him,
Th' imperial metal, circling now thy head,
Had grac'd the tender temples of my child,
And both the princes had been breathing here,
Which now, two tender bedfellows for dust,
Thy broken faith hath made the prey for worms.
What canst thou swear by now?
K. Rich. The time to come.
Q. Eliz. That thou hast wronged in the time o'erpast;
For I myself have many tears to wash
Hereafter time, for time past wrong'd by thee.
The children live, whose fathers thou hast slaughter'd,
Ungovern'd youth, to wail it in their age;
The parents live, whose children thou hast butcher'd,
Old barren plants, to wail it with their age.
Swear not by time to come; for that thou hast
Misus'd ere us'd, by times ill-us'd o'erpast.
K. Rich. As I intend to prosper and repent,
So thrive I in my dangerous affairs
Of hostile arms! myself myself confound!
Heaven and fortune bar me happy hours!
Day, yield me not thy light; nor, night, thy rest!
Be opposite all planets of good luck
To my proceeding, if, with dear heart's love,
Immaculate devotion, holy thoughts,
I tender not thy beauteous princely daughter!
In her consists my happiness and thine;
Without her, follows to myself and thee,
Herself, the land, and many a Christian soul,
Death, desolation, ruin and decay:
It cannot be avoided but by this;
It will not be avoided but by this.
Therefore, dear mother,—I must call you so—
Be the attorney of my love to her:
Plead what I will be, not what I have been;
Not my deserts, but what I will deserve:
Urge the necessity and state of times,
And be not peevish-fond in great designs.
Q. Eliz. Shall I be tempted of the devil thus?
K. Rich. Ay, if the devil tempt you to do good.
Q. Eliz. Shall I forget myself to be myself?
K. Rich. Ay, if yourself's remembrance wrong yourself.
Q. Eliz. Yet thou didst kill my children.
K. Rich. But in your daughter's womb I bury them:
Where in that nest of spicery they will breed
Selves of themselves, to your recomforture.
Q. Eliz. Shall I go win my daughter to thy will?
K. Rich. And be a happy mother by the deed.
Q. Eliz. I go. Write to me very shortly,
And you shall understand from me her mind.
K. Rich. Bear her my true love's kiss; and so, farewell. *Exit Queen [Elizabeth].*
Relenting fool, and shallow, changing woman!

Enter RATCLIFFE [; CATESBY *following*].

How now! what news?
Rat. Most mighty sovereign, on the western coast
Rideth a puissant navy; to our shores
Throng many doubtful hollow-hearted friends,
Unarm'd, and unresolv'd to beat them back:
'Tis thought that Richmond is their admiral;
And there they hull, expecting but the aid
Of Buckingham to welcome them ashore.
K. Rich. Some light-foot friend post to the Duke of Norfolk:
Ratcliffe, thyself, or Catesby; where is he?
Cate. Here, my good lord.
K. Rich. Catesby, fly to the duke.
Cate. I will, my lord, with all convenient haste.
K. Rich. Ratcliffe, come hither. Post to Salisbury.
When thou com'st thither,—[*To Catesby*] Dull, unmindful villain,
Why stay'st thou here, and go'st not to the duke?
Cate. First, mighty liege, tell me your highness' pleasure,
What from your grace I shall deliver to him.
K. Rich. O, true, good Catesby: bid him levy straight
The greatest strength and power that he can make,
And meet me suddenly at Salisbury.
Cate. I go. *Exit.*
Rat. What, may it please you, shall I do
At Salisbury?
K. Rich. Why, what wouldst thou do there before I go?
Rat. Your highness told me I should post before.
K. Rich. My mind is chang'd.

Enter LORD STANLEY.

Stanley, what news with you?

366. **George . . . garter.** The George, a badge showing St. George slaying the dragon, was not added to the insignia of the Order of the Garter until the reign of Henry VII or Henry VIII. 390. **Hereafter,** after this. 392. **Ungovern'd,** i.e., without a father's guidance or rule. 397-398. **As . . . I,** i.e., I swear that as I hope to thrive and intend to repent. 399. **myself . . . confound,** may I destroy myself. 405. **tender,** have a tender regard for. 406. **consists,** resides, inheres. 417. **peevish-fond,** childishly foolish; see *peevish* and *fond* in glossary. 420. **myself . . . myself,** i.e., that person wronged by Richard. 421. **wrong yourself,** i.e., interfere with what is to your advantage. 424. **nest of spicery,** a reference to the fabled phoenix which rose anew from the nest of spices, its funeral pyre. 425. **recomforture,** comfort, consolation. 438. **hull,** drift with the sails furled. 440. **light-foot,** swift-footed. 447-448. **First . . . him.** Note this first evidence of confusion in Richard's mind. 451. **at Salisbury,** where Richard would be in a position to prevent the junction of Buckingham and Richmond. 456. **post,** hasten. 465. **White-liver'd,** cowardly. **runagate,** renegade. 473. **great York's,** i.e., Richard, Duke of York, father of Edward IV.

Stan. None good, my liege, to please you with the hearing;
Nor none so bad, but well may be reported.
K. Rich. Hoyday, a riddle! neither good nor bad!
What need'st thou run so many mile about,
When thou mayest tell thy tale the nearest way?
Once more, what news?
Stan. Richmond is on the seas.
K. Rich. There let him sink, and be the seas on him!
White-liver'd runagate, what doth he there?
Stan. I know not, mighty sovereign, but by guess.
K. Rich. Well, as you guess?
Stan. Stirr'd up by Dorset, Buckingham, and Morton,
He makes for England, here to claim the crown.
K. Rich. Is the chair empty? is the sword unsway'd?
Is the king dead? the empire unpossess'd?
What heir of York is there alive but we?
And who is England's king but great York's heir?
Then, tell me, what makes he upon the seas?
Stan. Unless for that, my liege, I cannot guess.
K. Rich. Unless for that he comes to be your liege,
You cannot guess wherefore the Welshman comes.
Thou wilt revolt, and fly to him, I fear.
Stan. No, my good lord; therefore mistrust me not.
K. Rich. Where is thy power, then, to beat him back?
Where be thy tenants and thy followers?
Are they not now upon the western shore,
Safe-conducting the rebels from their ships?
Stan. No, my good lord, my friends are in the north.
K. Rich. Cold friends to me: what do they in the north,
When they should serve their sovereign in the west?
Stan. They have not been commanded, mighty king:
Pleaseth your majesty to give me leave,
I'll muster up my friends, and meet your grace
Where and what time your majesty shall please.
K. Rich. Ay, thou wouldst be gone to join with Richmond:
But I'll not trust thee.
Stan. Most mighty sovereign,
You have no cause to hold my friendship doubtful:
I never was nor never will be false.
K. Rich. Well,
Go then and muster men; but leave behind
Your son, George Stanley: look your heart be firm,
Or else his head's assurance is but frail.
Stan. So deal with him as I prove true to you.
Exit Stan.

Enter a Messenger.

Mess. My gracious sovereign, now in Devonshire,
As I by friends am well advertised,
Sir Edward Courtney, and the haughty prelate
Bishop of Exeter, his elder brother,
With many moe confederates, are in arms.

Enter another Messenger.

Sec. Mess. In Kent, my liege, the Guildfords are in arms;
And every hour more competitors
Flock to the rebels, and their power grows strong.

Enter another Messenger.

Third Mess. My lord, the army of great Buckingham—
K. Rich. Out on ye, owls! nothing but songs of death? *He striketh him.*
There, take thou that, till thou bring better news.
Third Mess. The news I have to tell your majesty
Is, that by sudden floods and fall of waters,
Buckingham's army is dispers'd and scatter'd;
And he himself wand'red away alone,
No man knows whither.
K. Rich. I cry thee mercy:
There is my purse to cure that blow of thine.
Hath any well-advised friend proclaim'd
Reward to him that brings the traitor in?
Third Mess. Such proclamation hath been made, my lord.

Enter another Messenger.

Fourth Mess. Sir Thomas Lovel and Lord Marquis Dorset,
'Tis said, my liege, in Yorkshire are in arms.
But this good comfort bring I to your highness,
The Breton navy is dispers'd by tempest:
Richmond, in Dorsetshire, sent out a boat
Unto the shore, to ask those on the banks
If they were his assistants, yea or no;
Who answer'd him, they came from Buckingham
Upon his party: he, mistrusting them,
Hois'd sail and made his course again for Brittaine.
K. Rich. March on, march on, since we are up in arms;
If not to fight with foreign enemies,
Yet to beat down these rebels here at home.

Enter CATESBY.

Cate. My liege, the Duke of Buckingham is taken;
That is the best news: that the Earl of Richmond
Is with a mighty power landed at Milford,
Is colder news, but yet they must be told.
K. Rich. Away towards Salisbury! while we reason here,
A royal battle might be won and lost:
Some one take order Buckingham be brought
To Salisbury; the rest march on with me.
Flourish. Exeunt.

SCENE [V. *Lord Derby's house.*]

Enter DERBY *and* SIR CHRISTOPHER [URSWICK].

Der. Sir Christopher, tell Richmond this from me:
That in the sty of the most deadly boar
My son George Stanley is frank'd up in hold:

475. **that,** i.e., to claim the crown. 477. **Welshman.** Richmond was the grandson of Owen Tudor, a Welshman of Anglesea, who had married Catharine of France, widow of Henry v. Richmond's claim was descent through the Beauforts from John of Gaunt and Catherine Swynford. 479. **therefore,** on that account. 501. **advertised,** informed. 502. **Sir Edward Courtney,** i.e., of Haccombe, created Earl of Devon on the accession of Henry VII. He was only distantly related to Peter Courtenay, Bishop of Exeter. 505. **Guildfords,** a family led by Sir Richard Guildford of Hempstead in Kent. 506. **competitors.** confederates. 509. **owls.** It was thought that the cry of the owl portended death. 529. **Hois'd,** hoisted. 535. **Milford,** Milford Haven on the coast of Wales in the county of Pembroke. A gap of two years is bridged here. Richmond's first fruitless expedition was in October 1483; his landing at Milford was in August 1485. 536. **colder,** more chilling, dampening. 538. **royal battle,** battle on which a kingdom depends.
SCENE V. *Stage Direction:* **Sir Christopher Urswick,** a priest, confessor to the Countess of Richmond, Henry VII's mother. 3. **frank'd up,** shut up in a pig-pen. **hold,** custody.

If I revolt, off goes young George's head;
The fear of that holds off my present aid.
So get thee gone; commend me to thy lord.
Withal say that the queen hath heartily consented
He should espouse Elizabeth her daughter.
But, tell me, where is princely Richmond now?
Chris. At Pembroke, or at Ha'rford-west, in Wales.
Der. What men of name resort to him?
Chris. Sir Walter Herbert, a renowned soldier;
Sir Gilbert Talbot, Sir William Stanley;
Oxford, redoubted Pembroke, Sir James Blunt,
And Rice ap Thomas, with a valiant crew;
And many other of great name and worth:
And towards London do they bend their power,
If by the way they be not fought withal.
Der. Well, hie thee to thy lord; I kiss his hand.
My letter will resolve him of my mind.
Farewell. *Exeunt.*

ACT V.

SCENE I. [*Salisbury. An open place.*]

Enter BUCKINGHAM, *with* [Sheriff *and*] Halberds, *led to execution.*

Buck. Will not King Richard let me speak with him?
Sher. No, my good lord; therefore be patient.
Buck. Hastings, and Edward's children, Grey, and Rivers,
Holy King Henry, and thy fair son Edward,
Vaughan, and all that have miscarried
By underhand corrupted foul injustice,
If that your moody discontented souls
Do through the clouds behold this present hour,
Even for revenge mock my destruction!
This is All-Souls' day, fellow, is it not?
Sher. It is, my lord.
Buck. Why, then All-Souls' day is my body's doomsday.
This is the day which, in King Edward's time,
I wish'd might fall on me, when I was found
False to his children and his wife's allies;
This is the day wherein I wish'd to fall
By the false faith of him whom most I trusted;
This, this All-Souls' day to my fearful soul
Is the determin'd respite of my wrongs:
That high All-Seer which I dallied with
Hath turn'd my feigned prayer on my head
And given in earnest what I begg'd in jest.
Thus doth he force the swords of wicked men
To turn their own points in their masters' bosoms:
Now Margaret's curse falls heavy on my neck;
'When he,' quoth she, 'shall split thy heart with sorrow,
Remember Margaret was a prophetess.'
Come, lead me, officers, to the block of shame;
Wrong hath but wrong, and blame the due of blame.
Exeunt Buckingham with officers.

SCENE II. [*The camp near Tamworth.*]

Enter RICHMOND, OXFORD, BLUNT, HERBERT, *and others, with drum and colours.*

Richm. Fellows in arms, and my most loving friends,
Bruis'd underneath the yoke of tyranny,
Thus far into the bowels of the land
Have we march'd on without impediment;
And here receive we from our father Stanley
Lines of fair comfort and encouragement.
The wretched, bloody, and usurping boar,
That spoil'd your summer fields and fruitful vines,
Swills your warm blood like wash, and makes his trough
In your embowell'd bosoms, this foul swine
Is now even in the centre of this isle,
Near to the town of Leicester, as we learn:
From Tamworth thither is but one day's march.
In God's name, cheerly on, courageous friends,
To reap the harvest of perpetual peace
By this one bloody trial of sharp war.
Oxf. Every man's conscience is a thousand men,
To fight against this guilty homicide.
Herb. I doubt not but his friends will turn to us.
Blunt. He hath no friends but what are friends for fear,
Which in his dearest need will fly from him.
Richm. All for our vantage. Then, in God's name, march:
True hope is swift, and flies with swallow's wings;
Kings it makes gods, and meaner creatures kings.
Exeunt omnes.

[SCENE III. *Bosworth Field.*]

Enter KING RICHARD *in arms, with* NORFOLK, RATCLIFFE, *and the* EARL OF SURREY [*and others*].

K. Rich. Here pitch our tent, even here in Bosworth field.
My Lord of Surrey, why look you so sad?
Sur. My heart is ten times lighter than my looks.
K. Rich. My Lord of Norfolk,—
Nor. Here, most gracious liege.
K. Rich. Norfolk, we must have knocks; ha! must we not?
Nor. We must both give and take, my loving lord.
K. Rich. Up with my tent! here will I lie to-night;
But where to-morrow? Well, all 's one for that.
Who hath descried the number of the traitors?
Nor. Six or seven thousand is their utmost power.
K. Rich. Why, our battalia trebles that account:
Besides, the king's name is a tower of strength,
Which they upon the adverse faction want.
Up with the tent! Come, noble gentlemen,
Let us survey the vantage of the ground;
Call for some men of sound direction:
Let 's lack no discipline, make no delay;

5. **present,** prompt; see glossary. 10. **Ha'rford-west,** Haverfordwest, near Milford Haven. 11. **name,** honorable repute. 12. **Sir Walter Herbert,** a Welshman of old family and considerable influence. 13. **Sir Gilbert Talbot,** uncle to the young Earl of Shrewsbury. **Sir William Stanley,** brother to Thomas, Lord Stanley. 14. **Oxford,** John de Vere, Earl of Oxford. **redoubted,** valiant, formidable. **Pembroke,** Jasper Tudor, Earl of Pembroke, uncle to Richmond. **Sir James Blunt,** son of Sir Walter Blunt, Baron Mountjoy; he was lieutenant of Hammes Castle, 1476, where he was custodian of the Earl of Oxford. 15. **Rice ap Thomas,** an influential Welsh knight. 20. **resolve him of,** inform him concerning.

ACT V. SCENE I. 4. **thy,** i.e., Henry's. 5. **miscarried,** perished. 10. **All-Souls' day,** *Festa Animarum*, November 2, in commemoration of the dead, who on this day may communicate with the living. 13. **day.** Cf. II, i, 32 ff. 19. **determin'd . . . wrongs,** the time to which the punishment of my evil practices was respited (Johnson following Hanmer). 20. **which I dallied with,** with whom I played the fool. 26. **'When he' . . . sorrow.** Cf. I, iii, 300-301.

SCENE II. 5. **father,** stepfather. 9. **wash,** hog's wash, swill. 10. **embowell'd,** disemboweled. 20. **for fear,** i.e., because they fear him.

For, lords, to-morrow is a busy day. *Exeunt.*

Enter [on the other side of the stage] RICHMOND, SIR WILLIAM BRANDON, OXFORD, *and* DORSET *[with others. Some of the* Soldiers *pitch Richmond's tent.]*

Richm. The weary sun hath made a golden set,
And, by the bright tract of his fiery car,
Gives token of a goodly day to-morrow.
Sir William Brandon, you shall bear my standard.
Give me some ink and paper in my tent:
I'll draw the form and model of our battle,
Limit each leader to his several charge,
And part in just proportion our small power.
My Lord of Oxford, you, Sir William Brandon,
And you, Sir Walter Herbert, stay with me.
The Earl of Pembroke keeps his regiment:
Good Captain Blunt, bear my good-night to him,
And by the second hour in the morning
Desire the earl to see me in my tent:
Yet one thing more, good captain, do for me:
Where is Lord Stanley quarter'd, do you know?

Blunt. Unless I have mista'en his colours much,
Which well I am assur'd I have not done,
His regiment lies half a mile at least
South from the mighty power of the king.

Richm. If without peril it be possible,
Sweet Blunt, make some good means to speak with him,
And give him from me this most needful note.

Blunt. Upon my life, my lord, I'll undertake it;
And so, God give you quiet rest to-night!

Richm. Good night, good Captain Blunt. Come, gentlemen,
Let us consult upon to-morrow's business:
Into my tent; the dew is raw and cold.
They withdraw into the tent.

Enter [to his tent, KING*]* RICHARD, RATCLIFFE, NORFOLK, *and* CATESBY *[with others].*

K. Rich. What is 't o'clock?

Cate. It 's supper-time, my lord;
It 's nine o'clock.

K. Rich. I will not sup to-night.
Give me some ink and paper.
What, is my beaver easier than it was?
And all my armour laid into my tent?

Cate. It is, my liege; and all things are in readiness.

K. Rich. Good Norfolk, hie thee to thy charge;
Use careful watch, choose trusty sentinels.

Nor. I go, my lord.

K. Rich. Stir with the lark to-morrow, gentle Norfolk.

Nor. I warrant you, my lord. *Exit.*

K. Rich. Catesby!

Cate. My lord?

K. Rich. Send out a pursuivant at arms
To Stanley's regiment; bid him bring his power
Before sunrising, lest his son George fall
Into the blind cave of eternal night. *[Exit Catesby.]*
Fill me a bowl of wine. Give me a watch.
Saddle white Surrey for the field to-morrow.
Look that my staves be sound, and not too heavy.
Ratcliffe!

Rat. My lord?

K. Rich. Saw'st thou the melancholy Lord Northumberland?

Rat. Thomas the Earl of Surrey, and himself,
Much about cock-shut time, from troop to troop
Went through the army, cheering up the soldiers.

K. Rich. So, I am satisfied. Give me a bowl of wine:
I have not that alacrity of spirit,
Nor cheer of mind, that I was wont to have.
Set it down. Is ink and paper ready?

Rat. It is, my lord.

K. Rich. Bid my guard watch; leave me.
Ratcliffe, about the mid of night come to my tent
And help to arm me. Leave me, I say.
Exit Ratcliffe. [Richard sleeps.]

Enter DERBY *to* RICHMOND *in his tent [, Lords and others attending].*

Der. Fortune and victory sit on thy helm!

Richm. All comfort that the dark night can afford
Be to thy person, noble father-in-law!
Tell me, how fares our loving mother?

Der. I, by attorney, bless thee from thy mother,
Who prays continually for Richmond's good:
So much for that. The silent hours steal on,
And flaky darkness breaks within the east.
In brief,—for so the season bids us be,—
Prepare thy battle early in the morning,
And put thy fortune to th' arbitrement
Of bloody strokes and mortal-staring war.
I, as I may—that which I would I cannot,—
With best advantage will deceive the time,
And aid thee in this doubtful shock of arms:
But on thy side I may not be too forward,
Lest, being seen, thy brother, tender George,
Be executed in his father's sight.
Farewell: the leisure and the fearful time
Cuts off the ceremonious vows of love
And ample interchange of sweet discourse,
Which so long sund'red friends should dwell upon:
God give us leisure for these rites of love!
Once more, adieu: be valiant, and speed well!

Richm. Good lords, conduct him to his regiment:
I'll strive, with troubled thoughts, to take a nap,
Lest leaden slumber peise me down to-morrow,
When I should mount with wings of victory:
Once more, good night, kind lords and gentlemen.
Exeunt. Manet Richmond.
O Thou, whose captain I account myself,
Look on my forces with a gracious eye;
Put in their hands thy bruising irons of wrath,
That they may crush down with a heavy fall

24. **meaner,** of lower degree; see glossary.
SCENE III. 8. **all 's . . . that,** be that as it may. 11. **battalia,** army. 16. **sound direction,** true judgment, sound military skill. 20. **tract,** track. **fiery car,** a reference to the car of Phoebus. 24. **model,** pattern; see glossary. 29. **keeps,** i.e., is with; see glossary. 50. **beaver,** helmet. **easier,** more loosely fitting. 57. **warrant,** promise. 59. **pursuivant at arms,** one of the junior officers attendant on the heralds. 63. **watch,** watch light, a candle marked into equal divisions to show time; or perhaps, sentinel. 64. **white Surrey.** The name seems to be Shakespeare's invention. Hall says that Richard was mounted on a "great white courser." 65. **staves,** the staves or handles of his lances. 70. **cock-shut time,** evening twilight; possibly, the time at which poultry are shut up. 81. **father-in-law.** Stanley was stepfather to Richmond. 86. **flaky,** streaked with light. 87. **season,** time of day. 90. **mortal-staring,** fatal-visaged. 91. **that . . . cannot,** i.e., fight openly for Richmond. 92. **With best advantage,** to the best purpose. 94. **be too forward,** appear too openly. 95. **tender,** young, of tender years. Historically, George Stanley was a mature man. 97. **leisure,** i.e., brief time allowed. 105. **peise,** weigh. 110. **bruising irons,** maces, weapons.

Th' usurping helmets of our adversaries!
Make us thy ministers of chastisement,
That we may praise thee in the victory!
To thee I do commend my watchful soul,
Ere I let fall the windows of mine eyes:
Sleeping and waking, O, defend me still! *Sleeps.*

Enter the Ghost of PRINCE EDWARD, *son to* HENRY the Sixth.

Ghost. (To Richard) Let me sit heavy on thy soul to-morrow!
Think, how thou stab'dst me in my prime of youth
At Tewksbury: despair, therefore, and die!
(To Richmond) Be cheerful, Richmond; for the wronged souls
Of butcher'd princes fight in thy behalf:
King Henry's issue, Richmond, comforts thee.

Enter the Ghost of HENRY the Sixth.

Ghost. [To Richard] When I was mortal, my anointed body
By thee was punched full of deadly holes:
Think on the Tower and me: despair, and die!
Harry the Sixth bids thee despair and die!
(To Richmond) Virtuous and holy, be thou conqueror!
Harry, that prophesied thou shouldst be king,
Doth comfort thee in thy sleep: live, and flourish!

Enter the Ghost of CLARENCE.

Ghost. [To Richard] Let me sit heavy on thy soul to-morrow!
I, that was wash'd to death with fulsome wine,
Poor Clarence, by thy guile betray'd to death!
To-morrow in the battle think on me,
And fall thy edgeless sword: despair, and die!—
(To Richmond) Thou offspring of the house of Lancaster,
The wronged heirs of York do pray for thee:
Good angels guard thy battle! live, and flourish!

Enter the Ghosts of RIVERS, GREY, *and* VAUGHAN.

Ghost of R. [To Richard] Let me sit heavy on thy soul to-morrow,
Rivers, that died at Pomfret! despair, and die!
Ghost of G. [To Richard] Think upon Grey, and let thy soul despair!
Ghost of V. [To Richard] Think upon Vaughan, and, with guilty fear,
Let fall thy lance: despair, and die!
All. (To Richmond) Awake, and think our wrongs in Richard's bosom
Will conquer him! awake, and win the day!

Enter the Ghost of Lord HASTINGS.

Ghost. [To Richard] Bloody and guilty, guiltily awake,
And in a bloody battle end thy days!
Think on Lord Hastings: despair, and die!
(To Richmond) Quiet untroubled soul, awake, awake!
Arm, fight, and conquer, for fair England's sake!

Enter the Ghosts of the two young Princes.

Ghosts. [To Richard] Dream on thy cousins smothered in the Tower:
Let us be lead within thy bosom, Richard,
And weigh thee down to ruin, shame, and death!
Thy nephews' souls bid thee despair and die!
(To Richmond) Sleep, Richmond, sleep in peace, and wake in joy;
Good angels guard thee from the boar's annoy!
Live, and beget a happy race of kings!
Edward's unhappy sons do bid thee flourish.

Enter the Ghost of ANNE, *his Wife.*

Ghost. (To Richard) Richard, thy wife, that wretched Anne thy wife,
That never slept a quiet hour with thee,
Now fills thy sleep with perturbations:
To-morrow in the battle think on me,
And fall thy edgeless sword: despair, and die!
(To Richmond) Thou quiet soul, sleep thou a quiet sleep;
Dream of success and happy victory!
Thy adversary's wife doth pray for thee.

Enter the Ghost of BUCKINGHAM.

Ghost. (To Richard) The first was I that help'd thee to the crown;
The last was I that felt thy tyranny:
O, in the battle think on Buckingham,
And die in terror of thy guiltiness!
Dream on, dream on, of bloody deeds and death:
Fainting, despair; despairing, yield thy breath!
(To Richmond) I died for hope ere I could lend thee aid:
But cheer thy heart, and be thou not dismay'd:
God and good angels fight on Richmond's side;
And Richard falls in height of all his pride.

[The Ghosts vanish.] Richard starts out of his dream.

K. Rich. Give me another horse: bind up my wounds.
Have mercy, Jesu!—Soft! I did but dream.
O coward conscience, how dost thou afflict me!
The lights burn blue. It is now dead midnight.
Cold fearful drops stand on my trembling flesh.
What do I fear? myself? there 's none else by:
Richard loves Richard; that is, I am I.
Is there a murderer here? No. Yes, I am:
Then fly. What, from myself? Great reason why:
Lest I revenge. What, myself upon myself?
Alack, I love myself. Wherefore? for any good
That I myself have done unto myself?
O, no! alas, I rather hate myself
For hateful deeds committed by myself!
I am a villain: yet I lie, I am not.
Fool, of thyself speak well: fool, do not flatter.
My conscience hath a thousand several tongues,
And every tongue brings in a several tale,
And every tale condemns me for a villain.
Perjury, perjury, in the high'st degree;
Murder, stern murder, in the dir'st degree;
All several sins, all us'd in each degree,
Throng to the bar, crying all, Guilty! guilty!
I shall despair. There is no creature loves me;
And if I die, no soul shall pity me:
Nay, wherefore should they, since that I myself

119. **prime,** early time. 123. **issue,** son. 126. **Tower,** where Henry VI was supposed to have been murdered. 132. **wash'd to death,** i.e., drowned in the butt of malmsey. **fulsome,** cloying. 135. **fall,** may it fall. **edgeless,** futile. 156. **the boar's annoy,** i.e., Richard's attack. 173. **for hope,** i.e., for want of hope; Steevens conjectured *for holpe,* deserted, unhelped. 180. **lights burn blue,** superstitiously regarded as evidence of the presence of ghosts. 193. **several,** different; see glossary. 198. **us'd,** committed; see glossary. 199. **bar,** i.e., bar of justice. 218. **substance,** bodies; used in contrast to *shadows* (l. 216). 219. **in proof,** in armor which is proof against weapons. 231. **cried**

Find in myself no pity to myself?
Methought the souls of all that I had murder'd
Came to my tent; and every one did threat
To-morrow's vengeance on the head of Richard.

Enter RATCLIFFE.

Rat. My lord!
K. Rich. 'Zounds! who is there?
Rat. Ratcliffe, my lord; 'tis I. The early village-cock
Hath twice done salutation to the morn;
Your friends are up, and buckle on their armour.
K. Rich. O Ratcliffe, I have dream'd a fearful dream!
What think'st thou, will our friends prove all true?
Rat. No doubt, my lord.
K. Rich. O Ratcliffe, I fear, I fear,—
Rat. Nay, good my lord, be not afraid of shadows.
K. Rich. By the apostle Paul, shadows to-night
Have struck more terror to the soul of Richard
Than can the substance of ten thousand soldiers
Armed in proof, and led by shallow Richmond.
'Tis not yet near day. Come, go with me;
Under our tents I'll play the eaves-dropper,
To see if any mean to shrink from me.
Exeunt Richard and Ratcliffe.

Enter the Lords *to* RICHMOND, *sitting in his tent.*

Lords. Good morrow, Richmond!
Richm. Cry mercy, lords and watchful gentlemen,
That you have ta'en a tardy sluggard here.
Lords. How have you slept, my lord?
Richm. The sweetest sleep, and fairest-boding dreams
That ever ent'red in a drowsy head,
Have I since your departure had, my lords.
Methought their souls, whose bodies Richard murder'd,
Came to my tent, and cried on victory:
I promise you, my heart is very jocund
In the remembrance of so fair a dream.
How far into the morning is it, lords?
Lords. Upon the stroke of four.
Richm. Why, then 'tis time to arm and give direction.

His oration to his soldiers.

More than I have said, loving countrymen,
The leisure and enforcement of the time
Forbids to dwell upon: yet remember this,
God and our good cause fight upon our side;
The prayers of holy saints and wronged souls,
Like high-rear'd bulwarks, stand before our faces;
Richard except, those whom we fight against
Had rather have us win than him they follow:
For what is he they follow? truly, gentlemen,
A bloody tyrant and a homicide;
One rais'd in blood, and one in blood establish'd;
One that made means to come by what he hath,
And slaughter'd those that were the means to help him;
A base foul stone, made precious by the foil
Of England's chair, where he is falsely set;
One that hath ever been God's enemy:
Then, if you fight against God's enemy,
God will in justice ward you as his soldiers;
If you do sweat to put a tyrant down,
You sleep in peace, the tyrant being slain;
If you do fight against your country's foes,
Your country's fat shall pay your pains the hire;
If you do fight in safeguard of your wives,
Your wives shall welcome home the conquerors;
If you do free your children from the sword,
Your children's children quits it in your age.
Then, in the name of God and all these rights,
Advance your standards, draw your willing swords.
For me, the ransom of my bold attempt
Shall be this cold corpse on the earth's cold face;
But if I thrive, the gain of my attempt
The least of you shall share his part thereof.
Sound drums and trumpets boldly and cheerfully;
God and Saint George! Richmond and victory!
[*Exeunt.*]

Enter KING RICHARD, RATCLIFFE [, *Attendants and Forces*].

K. Rich. What said Northumberland as touching Richmond?
Rat. That he was never trained up in arms.
K. Rich. He said the truth: and what said Surrey then?
Rat. He smil'd and said 'The better for our purpose.'
K. Rich. He was in the right; and so indeed it is.
Clock strikes.
Tell the clock there. Give me a calendar.
Who saw the sun to-day?
Rat. Not I, my lord.
K. Rich. Then he disdains to shine; for by the book
He should have brav'd the east an hour ago:
A black day will it be to somebody.
Ratcliffe!
Rat. My lord?
K. Rich. The sun will not be seen to-day;
The sky doth frown and lour upon our army.
I would these dewy tears were from the ground.
Not shine to-day! Why, what is that to me
More than to Richmond? for the selfsame heaven
That frowns on me looks sadly upon him.

Enter NORFOLK.

Nor. Arm, arm, my lord; the foe vaunts in the field.
K. Rich. Come, bustle, bustle; caparison my horse.
Call up Lord Stanley, bid him bring his power:
I will lead forth my soldiers to the plain,
And thus my battle shall be ordered:
My foreward shall be drawn out all in length,
Consisting equally of horse and foot;
Our archers shall be placed in the midst:
John Duke of Norfolk, Thomas Earl of Surrey,
Shall have the leading of this foot and horse.
They thus directed, we will follow
In the main battle, whose puissance on either side
Shall be well winged with our chiefest horse.
This, and Saint George to boot! What think'st thou, Norfolk?
Nor. A good direction, warlike sovereign.

on, uttered the cry of. 236. **direction,** orders. 238. **leisure,** i.e., brief time allowed. **enforcement,** exigency. 247. **in blood,** by bloodshed. 250. **foil,** a thin leaf of metal placed under a gem to set it off to advantage. 254. **ward,** protect. 258. **fat,** prosperity, wealth. 265. **ransom,** etc. If he fails, there will be no question of ransom, but of death.

272. **up in,** i.e., to. 278. **book,** i.e., the almanac. 279. **brav'd,** made splendid; see glossary. 288. **vaunts,** boasts his strength. 289. **caparison,** put on the battle trappings. 293. **foreward,** vanguard. 299. **main battle,** main body of troops. 301. **to boot,** i.e., to give us aid in addition.

This found I on my tent this morning.
[*He sheweth him a paper.*]
K. Rich. [*Reads*] 'Jockey of Norfolk, be not so bold,
For Dickon thy master is bought and sold.'
A thing devised by the enemy.
Go, gentlemen, every man unto his charge:
Let not our babbling dreams affright our souls:
Conscience is but a word that cowards use,
Devis'd at first to keep the strong in awe:
Our strong arms be our conscience, swords our law.
March on, join bravely, let us to 't pell-mell;
If not to heaven, then hand in hand to hell.

[*His oration to his Army.*]

What shall I say more than I have inferr'd?
Remember whom you are to cope withal;
A sort of vagabonds, rascals, and runaways,
A scum of Bretons, and base lackey peasants,
Whom their o'er-cloyed country vomits forth
To desperate ventures and assur'd destruction.
You sleeping safe, they bring to you unrest;
You having lands, and blest with beauteous wives,
They would restrain the one, distain the other.
And who doth lead them but a paltry fellow,
Long kept in Brittaine at our mother's cost?
A milk-sop, one that never in his life
Felt so much cold as over shoes in snow?
Let 's whip these stragglers o'er the seas again;
Lash hence these overweening rags of France,
These famish'd beggars, weary of their lives;
Who, but for dreaming on this fond exploit,
For want of means, poor rats, had hang'd themselves:
If we be conquer'd, let men conquer us,
And not these bastard Bretons; whom our fathers
Have in their own land beaten, bobb'd, and thump'd,
And in record, left them the heirs of shame.
Shall these enjoy our lands? lie with our wives?
Ravish our daughters? (*Drum afar off.*) Hark! I hear their drum.
Fight, gentlemen of England! fight, bold yeomen!
Draw, archers, draw your arrows to the head!
Spur your proud horses hard, and ride in blood;
Amaze the welkin with your broken staves!

Enter a Messenger.

What says Lord Stanley? will he bring his power?
Mess. My lord, he doth deny to come.
K. Rich. Off with his son George's head!
Nor. My lord, the enemy is past the marsh:
After the battle let George Stanley die.
K. Rich. A thousand hearts are great within my bosom:
Advance our standards, set upon our foes;
Our ancient word of courage, fair Saint George,
Inspire us with the spleen of fiery dragons!
Upon them! Victory sits on our helms. [*Exeunt.*]

[SCENE IV: *Another part of the field.*]

Alarum: excursions. Enter [NORFOLK *and forces fighting; to him*] CATESBY.

Cate. Rescue, my Lord of Norfolk, rescue, rescue!
The king enacts more wonders than a man,
Daring an opposite to every danger:
His horse is slain, and all on foot he fights,
Seeking for Richmond in the throat of death.
Rescue, fair lord, or else the day is lost!

Alarums. Enter [KING] RICHARD.

K. Rich. A horse! a horse! my kingdom for a horse!
Cate. Withdraw, my lord; I'll help you to a horse.
K. Rich. Slave, I have set my life upon a cast,
And I will stand the hazard of the die:
I think there be six Richmonds in the field;
Five have I slain to-day instead of him.
A horse! a horse! my kingdom for a horse! [*Exeunt.*]

[SCENE V. *Another part of the field.*]

Alarum. Enter RICHARD *and* RICHMOND; *they fight.* RICHARD *is slain. Retreat and flourish. Enter* RICHMOND, DERBY *bearing the crown, with divers other Lords.*

Richm. God and your arms be prais'd, victorious friends;
The day is ours, the bloody dog is dead.
Der. Courageous Richmond, well hast thou acquit thee.
Lo, here, this long-usurped royalty
From the dead temples of this bloody wretch
Have I pluck'd off, to grace thy brows withal:
Wear it, enjoy it, and make much of it.
Richm. Great God of heaven, say Amen to all!
But, tell me, is young George Stanley living?
Der. He is, my lord, and safe in Leicester town;
Whither, if it please you, we may now withdraw us.
Richm. What men of name are slain on either side?
Der. John Duke of Norfolk, Walter Lord Ferrers,
Sir Robert Brakenbury, and Sir William Brandon.
Richm. Inter their bodies as becomes their births:
Proclaim a pardon to the soldiers fled
That in submission will return to us:
And then, as we have ta'en the sacrament,
We will unite the white rose and the red:
Smile heaven upon this fair conjunction,
That long have frown'd upon their enmity!
What traitor hears me, and says not amen?
England hath long been mad, and scarr'd herself;
The brother blindly shed the brother's blood,
The father rashly slaughtered his own son,
The son, compell'd, been butcher to the sire:
All this divided York and Lancaster,
Divided in their dire division,
O, now, let Richmond and Elizabeth,
The true succeeders of each royal house,

304-305. **'Jockey . . . sold.'** The rhyme occurs in the chronicles. 304. **Jockey,** familiar form of "Jack." 305. **Dickon,** i.e., Dick, Richard. **bought and sold,** betrayed for a bribe. 308. **babbling,** foolish. 314. **inferr'd,** stated. 317. **lackey,** a running footman; here, servile. 322. **restrain,** keep back, withhold. **distain,** defile, sully. 324. **our mother's.** Richmond's mother was not Richard's. This error occurs in the second edition of Holinshed's *Chronicles*. The first edition reads "brothers," the reference being to the fact that Richmond had been supported at the court of the Duke of Bretagne at the cost of the Duke of Burgundy, Richard's brother-in-law. 326. **as over shoes,** i.e., as one being over his shoe-tops. 331. **want of means,** poverty. 334. **bobb'd,** struck. 335. **record,** history. 341. **Amaze . . . staves,** i.e., fright the skies with the shining of your lances (Johnson); see *welkin* in glossary.

SCENE IV. 2. **than a man,** than seems possible for a human being. 3. **Daring . . . danger,** boldly facing every danger of battle. 10. **hazard . . . die,** i.e., the turn of the die.

SCENE V. 18. **as . . . sacrament,** as I am sworn to do. 19. **white . . . red,** house of York and house of Lancaster, i.e., by his marriage to Elizabeth, daughter of Edward IV. 28. **division,** estrangement.

By God's fair ordinance conjoin together!
And let their heirs, God, if thy will be so,
Enrich the time to come with smooth-fac'd peace,
With smiling plenty and fair prosperous days!
Abate the edge of traitors, gracious Lord,
That would reduce these bloody days again,
And make poor England weep in streams of blood!
Let them not live to taste this land's increase
That would with treason wound this fair land's
peace!
Now civil wounds are stopp'd, peace lives again:
That she may long live here, God say amen! *Exeunt.*

33. **smooth-fac'd,** calm-visaged. 35. **Abate the edge,** i.e., render their opposition ineffective. 36. **reduce,** lead back. 38. **increase,** i.e., new prosperity.

THE LIFE AND DEATH OF KING JOHN

King John is usually dated on grounds of style between Shakespeare's two historical tetralogies, perhaps shortly before *Richard II* in 1594 or 1595. In structure and characterization it is also transitional from the episodic and morally straightforward first series (*Henry VI* through *Richard III*) to the more tightly organized and sophisticated second (*Richard II* through *Henry V*). It stands alone among Shakespeare's history plays of the 1590's in choosing the early thirteenth century for its subject rather than the fifteenth. Yet the political problems are familiar.

Foremost is the uncertainty of John's claim to the English throne. He occupies that throne by "strong possession" and also seemingly by the last will and testament of his deceased eldest brother, King Richard I. But could such a will disinherit Arthur, the son of John's older brother Geoffrey? English primogeniture specified that property must descend to the eldest son; after Richard's death without direct heirs, his next brother Geoffrey would inherit, and then Geoffrey's son Arthur. Significantly, even John's mother, Queen Elinor, who publicly supports John's claim, privately admits that "strong possession" is much more on their side than "right" (I,i). All parties concede, then, that young Arthur's claim is legally superior.

Yet such a claim raises serious practical questions, because it challenges the status quo. John is *de facto* king, and Arthur a child. To make the dilemma complete, Arthur has no ambitions to rule and seemingly no talent for leadership. Without the unremitting zeal of his widowed mother, Constance, Arthur would retire into the private world of kindness and love where his virtues shine. Moreover, Constance's uncompromising defense of her son's true claim requires her to seek alliance with the French for an invasion of England. Such an appalling prospect of invasion and civil war inevitably poses the question: is the replacement of John by Arthur worth the price? Which is better, an ongoing regime flawed by uncertain claim and political compromises, or restitution of the "right" by violent and potentially self-destructive means?

Shakespeare refuses to simplify the issues. John is neither a monstrous tyrant nor a martyred hero, although both interpretations were available to Shakespeare in sixteenth-century historical writings. Catholic historians of the late Middle Ages such as Polydore Vergil had uniformly condemned John, partly at least because of his interference with the church. The English Reformation brought about a conscious rewriting of history, and in John Bale's play of *King Johan* (1538, with later revisions) the protagonist is unassailably virtuous. Centuries ahead of his time, John comprehends the true interests of the state in fending off the encroachments of the international church. He fails only because his people are superstitious and his aristocrats are the dupes of Catholic meddling. The play is transparently a warning to Tudor England. This portrait of martyrdom continues unabated in John Foxe's *Actes and Monuments*, and in the chronicles of Grafton and Holinshed that were based on Foxe. Most virulent of all is the play called *The Troublesome Raigne of King John* (c. 1587–1591), once thought to be by Shakespeare and analyzed by one recent editor as a bad quarto of Shakespeare's text, but now almost universally regarded as the work of some more chauvinistic playwright such as Peele. Although generally close to Shakespeare's play in its narrative of events, it also contains scenes of the most degraded anti-Catholic humor, featuring gross abbots who conceal nuns in their private rooms, and the like. Against such a corrupt institution, the Bastard's economic raids are wholly justifiable. John and the Bastard would be invincible, were it not for the base Catholic loyalties of the nobility.

Shakespeare consciously declines to endorse either the Catholic or the Protestant interpretation of King John. (Interestingly, neither side showed any interest in Magna Carta; not until the seventeenth century was that event interpreted as a famous precedent for constitutional restraints imposed on the monarchy.) To be sure, some anticlericalism remains still in the play. John grandly proclaims that "no Italian priest Shall tithe or toll in our dominions." John is "supreme head" of the church and state (the actual title claimed by Henry VIII), defending his people against "this meddling priest" with his "juggling witchcraft" (III,i). Yet Shakespeare's King John is not vindictive against the church. He seizes some of its wealth not as a reprisal but to support his costly military campaigns; and, when he is poisoned by a monk, neither John nor anyone assumes that a Catholic conspiracy is responsible—as it is in *Troublesome Raigne*. Similarly, the baronial opposition to John is motivated not by secret Catholic leanings but by understandable revulsion at the apparent murder of Arthur.

Shakespeare's balanced treatment need not merely reflect his own political allegiances, whatever they were. Artistically, *King John* is a study of impasse, of tortured political dilemmas to which there can be no clear answer. How do men behave under such trying circumstances? Shakespeare's play is remarkable for its sensitivity and compassion toward all sides. His most completely sympathetic characters are those innocently caught in the middle, like Arthur and the Lady Blanch. Among the major contenders for power, all except for the ruthless Dauphin Lewis are guided by worthy intentions, and yet are forced to make unfortunate and self-contradictory compromises. Constance, for all her virtuous singleness of mind, must seek a French invasion of England. King Philip of France, bound to Constance's cause by all the holy vows of heaven, changes his purpose when England offers a profitable marriage-alliance, and then shifts quickly back again when the papacy demands in the name of the church that Philip punish King John for heresy. Philip's conscience is troubled about both decisions, but what is a king to do when faced with practical choices affecting his people's welfare and his own political safety?

Even Pandulph, the papal legate, can be viewed as a well-intentioned statesman caught in the web of political compromise. Presumably he is sincere in his belief that King John's heresy—in particular, his refusal to accept the pope's choice, Stephen Langton, as Archbishop of Canterbury—represents a grave threat to Western Catholicism. Yet Pandulph reveals an unprincipled cunning when he teaches King Philip how to "equivocate" a sacred vow, or instructs the apt young Lewis in Machiavellian intrigue. As Pandulph explains, the French can exploit King John's capture of Arthur by invading England in Arthur's name, thereby forcing John to murder his nephew in order to terminate the rival claim to the throne. Arthur's death will in turn drive the English nobility over to the French side. By this stratagem, the seemingly bad luck of Arthur's capture can neatly be turned to the advantage of France and the Catholic church (III,iv). Lewis learns his lesson only too well. What Pandulph has failed to take into account is the utter insincerity of Lewis' alliance with Catholic power. When the legate has achieved through the invasion what he wants—the submission of John—and then tries to call off Lewis' army, Pandulph discovers too late that the young Frenchman cares only for war on his own terms. Pandulph's cunning becomes a weapon turned against himself.

John is, like his enemies, a talented man justly punished by his own perjuries. Yet his failings are entirely understandable as they occur. Given the fact that he is king, his desire to maintain rule serves both his own interests and those of political order generally. The deal by which John bargains away his French territories of Angiers, Touraine, Maine, Poitiers, and the rest, in order to win peace with France, is prudent under the circumstances but a blow to those English dreams of greatness which John professes to uphold. When France immediately repudiates this treaty, John merely gets what he deserves for entering such a deal. His surrender of the crown to the papacy is again the canny result of yielding to the least dangerous of the alternatives available but diminishes John's already shaky authority nonetheless. Most heinous is John's determination to be rid of Arthur. He has compelling reasons, to be sure. As Pandulph predicts, the French invasion of England using Arthur's claim as its pretext forces John to consider Arthur as an immediate threat to himself. (Queen Elizabeth had long agonized over a similar problem with her captive, Mary, Queen of Scots; so long as Mary lived, a Catholic and claimant to the throne, English Catholics had a perennial rallying cry.) What is a ruling king to do with a rival claimant in his captivity? As Henry IV also discovers once he has captured Richard II, the logic demanding death is inexorable. Yet such a deed is not only murder, but murder of one's close kinsman and murder of the Lord's anointed in the eyes of those believing Arthur to be rightful king. Furthermore, it is a deed calculated to backfire and punish itself by arousing national resentment and rebellion. John quickly regrets his deed, but we suspect that the regret is in part motivated by fear of the consequences. The same unseen power that protects John against his own worst instincts, momentarily saving the boy from Hubert's instruments of torture, also justly prevents John from obtaining any political benefit from this brief reprieve; Hubert is too late, Arthur dies in a fall, the lords are convinced of John's guilt. With fitting irony, John is punished for his deed after he has decided not to do it and after the murder itself has failed to take place.

The word used to sum up the universal political scheming and oath-breaking in this play is "commodity," or self-interest. The word is introduced by the Bastard, the fascinating choric figure of *King John* whose reactions to the events of the play are so important in shaping our own. The Bastard is an outsider from the start, unconventionally born and so not beholden to society for its usual tawdry benefits. As the natural son of the great king Richard Coeur de Lion, the Bastard is a kind of folk hero: he is instinctively royal and yet a commoner, a projection of the audience's sentimental fondness for monarchy and at the same time a hero of the people. His quarrel with his effete brother Robert over the inheritance of their father's property comically underscores the futility of the dynastic quarrel between King John and Arthur. In both contentions a will left by the deceased confuses the issue of genealogical priority. Thus John, who defends the Bastard's unconventional claim to his inheritance, discovers a natural ally.

The Bastard is strangely drawn to "commodity" at first. He finds it exhilarating to trust his fortune to war and the king's favor, rather than to the easy comfort of a landed estate. The wars enable him to pursue a quest for self-identity. After learning from his reluctant mother who his real father was, the Bastard must venge himself upon the Duke of Austria, who killed his father. When first confronted with the moral ambiguity of the war, the Bastard's response is mischievous, almost Vicelike. He makes the cunning suggestion, for example, that France and England join against the city of Angiers until it surrenders, after which they may resume fighting one another. Clearly this Machiavellian proposal embodies, even satirizes, the spirit of "commodity." Yet the Bastard is not motivated by self-interest or a cynical delight in duping men, like the bastard Edmund in *King Lear*. This Bastard's illegitimacy has no such ominous cosmic import. Instead he is at first the detached witty observer, wrily amused at the seemingly inherent absurdity of politics. Although he does protest also that he will worship commodity for his own gain, we never see him doing so. Despite his philosophic detachment, he remains loyal to England and to John. In fact he is the play's greatest patriot.

The supreme test for the Bastard, as for all well-meaning characters and for the audience as well, is the death of Arthur. The Bastard must experience disaffection and even revulsion if he is to retain our sympathy as choric interpreter. Yet his chief function is to triumph over that revulsion, and in so doing to act as counterpart to the more rash English lords. They have jumped to the conclusion that John is guilty of Arthur's death. This is of course true in the main, but they do not know all the circumstances, and truth as always is more complicated than they suppose. Only the Bastard consistently phrases his condemnation in qualified terms: "It is a damned and a bloody work . . . *If* that it be the work of any hand" (IV,iii). Moreover, the lords have concluded that John's guilt justifies their rebellion. Yet they stoop to "commodity" of the very sort they condemn. They fight for the supposed good of England by allying themselves with Lewis of France. Once again, the ironies of cosmic justice demand that such "commodity" be repaid by treachery. The lords are luckily saved just in time by Lord Melun's revelation of Lewis' plan, just as John had been saved from his own headstrong folly by the kindness of Hubert. The Bastard's decision to remain loyal to John thus proves not only prudent but virtuous. He has led our sympathies through disaffection to acceptance. Rebellion only worsens matters by playing into the hands of opportunists. Loyalty to John is still, in a sense, a kind of "commodity," for it involves compromise and acceptance of politics as morally a world unto itself. Nevertheless, loyalty is a conscientious choice, and is rewarded finally by the accession of young Henry III who at last combines political legitimacy and the will to act.

THE LIFE AND DEATH OF KING JOHN

[*Dramatis Personae*

KING JOHN.
PRINCE HENRY, *son to the king.*
ARTHUR, Duke of Brittaine, *nephew to the king.*
The Earl of PEMBROKE.
The Earl of ESSEX.
The Earl of SALISBURY.
The Lord BIGOT.
HUBERT DE BURGH.
ROBERT FAULCONBRIDGE, *son to Sir Robert Faulconbridge.*
PHILIP the BASTARD, *his half-brother.*
JAMES GURNEY, *servant to Lady Faulconbridge.*
PETER of Pomfret, *a prophet.*

PHILIP, King of France.
LEWIS, *the* Dauphin.
LYMOGES, Duke of Austria.
CARDINAL PANDULPH, *the Pope's legate.*
MELUN, *a French Lord.*
CHATILLON, *ambassador from France to King John.*

QUEEN ELINOR, *mother to King John.*
CONSTANCE, *mother to Arthur.*
BLANCH of Spain, *niece to King John.*
LADY FAULCONBRIDGE.

Lords, Citizens of Angiers, Sheriff, Heralds, Officers, Soldiers, Messengers, *and* other Attendants.

SCENE: *Partly in England, and partly in France.*]

ACT I.

SCENE I. [KING JOHN'S *palace.*]

Enter KING JOHN, QUEEN ELINOR, PEMBROKE, ESSEX, *and* SALISBURY, *with* CHATILLON *of France.*

K. John. Now, say, Chatillon, what would France with us?
Chat. Thus, after greeting, speaks the King of France
In my behaviour to the majesty,
The borrowed majesty, of England here.
Eli. A strange beginning: 'borrowed majesty!'
K. John. Silence, good mother; hear the embassy.
Chat. Philip of France, in right and true behalf
Of thy deceased brother Geffrey's son,
Arthur Plantagenet, lays most lawful claim
To this fair island and the territories,
To Ireland, Poictiers, Anjou, Touraine, Maine,
Desiring thee to lay aside the sword
Which sways usurpingly these several titles,
And put the same into young Arthur's hand,
Thy nephew and right royal sovereign.

K. John. What follows if we disallow of this?
Chat. The proud control of fierce and bloody war,
To enforce these rights so forcibly withheld.
K. John. Here have we war for war and blood for blood,
Controlment for controlment: so answer France.
Chat. Then take my king's defiance from my mouth,
The farthest limit of my embassy.
K. John. Bear mine to him, and so depart in peace:
Be thou as lightning in the eyes of France;
For ere thou canst report I will be there,
The thunder of my cannon shall be heard:
So hence! Be thou the trumpet of our wrath
And sullen presage of your own decay.
An honourable conduct let him have:
Pembroke, look to 't. Farewell, Chatillon.
Exeunt Chatillon and Pembroke.
Eli. What now, my son! have I not ever said
How that ambitious Constance would not cease
Till she had kindled France and all the world,
Upon the right and party of her son?
This might have been prevented and made whole
With very easy arguments of love,
Which now the manage of two kingdoms must
With fearful bloody issue arbitrate.
K. John. Our strong possession and our right for us.
Eli. Your strong possession much more than your right,
Or else it must go wrong with you and me:
So much my conscience whispers in your ear,
Which none but heaven and you and I shall hear.

Enter a Sheriff.

Essex. My liege, here is the strangest controversy
Come from the country to be judg'd by you
That e'er I heard: shall I produce the men?
K. John. Let them approach.
Our abbeys and our priories shall pay
This expedition's charge.

Enter Robert Faulconbridge, *and* Philip [*his bastard brother*].

What men are you?
Bast. Your faithful subject I, a gentleman
Born in Northamptonshire and eldest son,
As I suppose, to Robert Faulconbridge,
A soldier, by the honour-giving hand
Of Cœur-de-lion knighted in the field.
K. John. What art thou?
Rob. The son and heir to that same Faulconbridge.
K. John. Is that the elder, and art thou the heir?
You came not of one mother then, it seems.
Bast. Most certain of one mother, mighty king;
That is well known; and, as I think, one father:
But for the certain knowledge of that truth
I put you o'er to heaven and to my mother:
Of that I doubt, as all men's children may.
Eli. Out on thee, rude man! thou dost shame thy mother
And wound her honour with this diffidence.
Bast. I, madam? no, I have no reason for it;
That is my brother's plea and none of mine;
The which if he can prove, 'a pops me out
At least from fair five hundred pound a year:
Heaven guard my mother's honour and my land!
K. John. A good blunt fellow. Why, being younger born,
Doth he lay claim to thine inheritance?
Bast. I know not why, except to get the land.
But once he slander'd me with bastardy:
But whe'r I be as true begot or no,
That still I lay upon my mother's head;
But that I am as well begot, my liege,—
Fair fall the bones that took the pains for me!—
Compare our faces and be judge yourself.
If old sir Robert did beget us both
And were our father and this son like him,
O old sir Robert, father, on my knee
I give heaven thanks I was not like to thee!
K. John. Why, what a madcap hath heaven lent us here!
Eli. He hath a trick of Cœur-de-lion's face;
The accent of his tongue affecteth him.
Do you not read some tokens of my son
In the large composition of this man?
K. John. Mine eye hath well examined his parts
And finds them perfect Richard. Sirrah, speak,
What doth move you to claim your brother's land?
Bast. Because he hath a half-face, like my father.
With half that face would he have all my land:
A half-fac'd groat five hundred pound a year!
Rob. My gracious liege, when that my father liv'd,
Your brother did employ my father much,—
Bast. Well, sir, by this you cannot get my land:
Your tale must be how he employ'd my mother.
Rob. And once dispatch'd him in an embassy
To Germany, there with the emperor
To treat of high affairs touching that time.
Th' advantage of his absence took the king
And in the mean time sojourn'd at my father's;
Where how he did prevail I shame to speak,
But truth is truth: large lengths of seas and shores
Between my father and my mother lay,
As I have heard my father speak himself,
When this same lusty gentleman was got.
Upon his death-bed he by will bequeath'd

Act i. scene i. 3. **In my behaviour,** in my person and conduct. 6. **embassy,** message. 10. **the territories,** possibly territories belonging to the English crown. The old play *The Troublesome Raigne,* on which this play is based (see Introduction), represents Arthur as demanding the English crown. According to Holinshed, Arthur's claim pressed by the French king was only to those French territories which had belonged to his father, Geoffrey, son next older than John of King Henry ii of England. Henry ii (reigned 1154-1189) had four sons who grew to manhood: Henry (1155-1183), who had no children; Richard Coeur-de-Lion (1157-1199), who had no children; Geoffrey (1158-1186), father of Arthur; and John (1166-1216), father of Henry iii. By right of primogeniture, therefore, Arthur's claim to the crown was prior to John's. 13. **sways,** manages, directs. 16. **disallow of,** reject. 20. **Controlment for controlment,** i.e., a check to your compulsion (New Cambridge). 28. **sullen,** dismal. **presage,** portent, omen. **decay,** ruin; see glossary. 29. **conduct,** escort, guard. 34. **Upon,** in behalf of. **party,** cause; see glossary. 35. **prevented,** foreseen; see glossary. **whole,** healthy (used figuratively). 37. **manage,** management; i.e., those who manage; see glossary. 38. **fearful,** terrible; see glossary. **issue,** outcome. 39. **strong possession.** Implied here is the idea expressed in the proverb, "Possession is nine-tenths of the law." 42. **conscience,** knowledge, conviction. 49. **This expedition,** the war in France. 65. **diffidence,** distrust, suspicion. 68. **'a,** he; see glossary. **pops me out.** Cf. *Hamlet,* V, ii, 65. 78. **fall,** befall; see glossary. 86. **affecteth,** resembles. 88. **composition,** constitution; see glossary. 90. **Sirrah,** customary form of address to inferiors; see glossary. 94. **half-fac'd groat,** i.e., the profile on the coin. The groat, worth four pence, is a figure for Robert's insignificance, in antithesis to his fortune, five hundred pounds a year; see *groat* in glossary. 95. **when that,** when. 96. **Your brother,** Richard Coeur-de-Lion. 108. **got,** begot; see glossary. 110. **took . . . death,** i.e., swore solemnly at his death; cf. the modern expression, "strike me dead." Cf. *1 Henry IV,* V, iv, 154 and Hubert's asseveration, III, iii, 57 below. 119. **lies on the hazards,** i.e., is the risk that all husbands must take. 137. **Lord . . . presence,**

His lands to me, and took it on his death
That this my mother's son was none of his;
And if he were, he came into the world
Full fourteen weeks before the course of time.
Then, good my liege, let me have what is mine,
My father's land, as was my father's will.
K. John. Sirrah, your brother is legitimate;
Your father's wife did after wedlock bear him,
And if she did play false, the fault was hers;
Which fault lies on the hazards of all husbands
That marry wives. Tell me, how if my brother,
Who, as you say, took pains to get this son,
Had of your father claim'd this son for his?
In sooth, good friend, your father might have kept
This calf bred from his cow from all the world;
In sooth he might; then, if he were my brother's,
My brother might not claim him; nor your father,
Being none of his, refuse him: this concludes;
My mother's son did get your father's heir;
Your father's heir must have your father's land.
Rob. Shall then my father's will be of no force
To dispossess that child which is not his?
Bast. Of no more force to dispossess me, sir,
Than was his will to get me, as I think.
Eli. Whether hadst thou rather be a Faulconbridge
And like thy brother, to enjoy thy land,
Or the reputed son of Cœur-de-lion,
Lord of thy presence and no land beside?
Bast. Madam, an if my brother had my shape,
And I had his, sir Robert's his, like him;
And if my legs were two such riding-rods,
My arms such eel-skins stuff'd, my face so thin
That in mine ear I durst not stick a rose
Lest men should say 'Look, where three-farthings goes!'
And, to his shape, were heir to all this land,
Would I might never stir from off this place,
I would give it every foot to have this face;
I would not be sir Nob in any case.
Eli. I like thee well: wilt thou forsake thy fortune,
Bequeath thy land to him and follow me?
I am a soldier and now bound to France.
Bast. Brother, take you my land, I'll take my chance.
Your face hath got five hundred pound a year,
Yet sell your face for five pence and 'tis dear.
Madam, I'll follow you unto the death.
Eli. Nay, I would have you go before me thither.
Bast. Our country manners give our betters way.
K. John. What is thy name?
Bast. Philip, my liege, so is my name begun;
Philip, good old sir Robert's wife's eldest son.
K. John. From henceforth bear his name whose form thou bearest:
Kneel thou down Philip, but rise more great,
Arise sir Richard and Plantagenet.
Bast. Brother by th' mother's side, give me your hand:
My father gave me honour, yours gave land.
Now blessed be the hour, by night or day,
When I was got, sir Robert was away!
Eli. The very spirit of Plantagenet!
I am thy grandam, Richard; call me so.
Bast. Madam, by chance but not by truth; what though?
Something about, a little from the right,
In at the window, or else o'er the hatch:
Who dares not stir by day must walk by night,
And have is have, however men do catch:
Near or far off, well won is still well shot,
And I am I, howe'er I was begot.
K. John. Go, Faulconbridge: now hast thou thy desire;
A landless knight makes thee a landed squire.
Come, madam, and come, Richard, we must speed
For France, for France, for it is more than need.
Bast. Brother, adieu: good fortune come to thee!
For thou wast got i' th' way of honesty.
Exeunt all but Bastard.
A foot of honour better than I was;
But many a many foot of land the worse.
Well, now can I make any Joan a lady.
'Good den, sir Richard!'—'God-a-mercy, fellow!'—
And if his name be George, I'll call him Peter;
For new-made honour doth forget men's names;
'Tis too respective and too sociable
For your conversion. Now your traveller,
He and his toothpick at my worship's mess,
And when my knightly stomach is suffic'd,
Why then I suck my teeth and catechize
My picked man of countries: 'My dear sir,'
Thus, leaning on mine elbow, I begin,
'I shall beseech you'—that is question now;
And then comes answer like an Absey book:
'O sir,' says answer, 'at your best command;
At your employment; at your service, sir:'
'No, sir,' says question, 'I, sweet sir, at yours:'
And so, ere answer knows what question would,
Saving in dialogue of compliment,
And talking of the Alps and Apennines,
The Pyrenean and the river Po,
It draws toward supper in conclusion so.
But this is worshipful society
And fits the mounting spirit like myself,
For he is but a bastard to the time
That doth not smack of observation;
And so am I, whether I smack or no;

i.e., of your identity as the son of Coeur-de-Lion, implying that such noble origin gives dignity which compensates for loss of lands. 138. **an if;** see glossary. 140. **riding-rods,** switches. 142. **stick a rose.** The queen's likeness on the three-farthing coin was distinguished from that on the three half-pence by a rose behind her head. The Bastard's taunt is based on the thinness of the coin. 147. **Nob.** Two explanations have been offered: diminutive of *Robert*, which might imply a taunt at his brother's size or at his juniority; and head, particularly the head of a stick, with reference again to Faulconbridge's slenderness. 169. **not by truth,** not honorably. 170. **Something about,** somewhat roundabout, clandestinely; see *something* in glossary. **a little . . . right,** away from the right. The New Cambridge editors see a suggestion of the "bar sinister," a term of heraldry. A bar is a set of horizontal stripes crossing the shield. It is sometimes said that illegitimacy was designated by a bar on the left (the sinister) field of the escutcheon. 171. **hatch,** lower half door. 184. **Joan,** frequently used to designate any girl, usually of the lower class; cf. *Love's Labour's Lost,* III, i, 207. 185-199. **'Good den . . . at yours.'** The Bastard amuses himself with an imaginary dialogue in *worshipful society*, where he represents himself with his *new-made honour* as a parvenu. Throughout he ridicules the artificial refinements of courtly circles. 185. **Good den,** good-even. **'God-a-mercy,** God have mercy. **fellow,** a condescending form of address; see glossary. 188. **respective,** considerate, careful, with reference to good breeding. 189. **conversion,** change of status, referring to his *new-made honour*. **traveller,** a man of the world. 190. **toothpick,** affectation associated with foreign travel. 192. **I suck my teeth,** i.e., in contrast to the toothpick of the *traveller*. 193. **picked,** refined. 196. **Absey,** A B C. 201. **dialogue of compliment,** polite but inane conversation. 204. **toward . . . conclusion.** The after-dinner conversation lasts until supper time. 207-208. **a bastard . . . observation,** i.e., not a true son of the times unless he observes and practices the obsequious mannerisms of polite society.

And not alone in habit and device,
Exterior form, outward accoutrement,
But from the inward motion to deliver
Sweet, sweet, sweet poison for the age's tooth:
Which, though I will not practise to deceive,
Yet, to avoid deceit, I mean to learn;
For it shall strew the footsteps of my rising.
But who comes in such haste in riding-robes?
What woman-post is this? hath she no husband
That will take pains to blow a horn before her?

Enter LADY FAULCONBRIDGE *and* JAMES GURNEY.

O me! 'tis my mother. How now, good lady!
What brings you here to court so hastily?
Lady F. Where is that slave, thy brother? where is he,
That holds in chase mine honour up and down?
Bast. My brother Robert? old sir Robert's son?
Colbrand the giant, that same mighty man?
Is it sir Robert's son that you seek so?
Lady F. Sir Robert's son! Ay, thou unreverend boy,
Sir Robert's son: why scorn'st thou at sir Robert?
He is sir Robert's son, and so art thou.
Bast. James Gurney, wilt thou give us leave awhile?
Gur. Good leave, good Philip.
Bast. Philip! sparrow: James,
There 's toys abroad: anon I'll tell thee more.
Exit James.
Madam, I was not old sir Robert's son:
Sir Robert might have eat his part in me
Upon Good-Friday and ne'er broke his fast:
Sir Robert could do well: marry, to confess,
Could he get me? Sir Robert could not do it:
We know his handiwork: therefore, good mother,
To whom am I beholding for these limbs?
Sir Robert never holp to make this leg.
Lady F. Hast thou conspired with thy brother too,
That for thine own gain shouldst defend mine honour?
What means this scorn, thou most untoward knave?
Bast. Knight, knight, good mother, Basilisco-like.
What! I am dubb'd! I have it on my shoulder.
But, mother, I am not sir Robert's son;
I have disclaim'd sir Robert and my land;
Legitimation, name and all is gone:
Then, good my mother, let me know my father;
Some proper man, I hope: who was it, mother?
Lady F. Hast thou denied thyself a Faulconbridge?
Bast. As faithfully as I deny the devil.
Lady F. King Richard Cœur-de-lion was thy father:
By long and vehement suit I was seduc'd
To make room for him in my husband's bed:
Heaven lay not my transgression to my charge!
Thou art the issue of my dear offence,
Which was so strongly urg'd past my defence.
Bast. Now, by this light, were I to get again,
Madam, I would not wish a better father.
Some sins do bear their privilege on earth,
And so doth yours; your fault was not your folly:
Needs must you lay your heart at his dispose,
Subjected tribute to commanding love,
Against whose fury and unmatched force
The aweless lion could not wage the fight,
Nor keep his princely heart from Richard's hand.
He that perforce robs lions of their hearts
May easily win a woman's. Ay, my mother,
With all my heart I thank thee for my father!
Who lives and dares but say thou didst not well
When I was got, I'll send his soul to hell.
Come, lady, I will show thee to my kin;
And they shall say, when Richard me begot,
If thou hadst said him nay, it had been sin:
Who says it was, he lies; I say 'twas not. *Exeunt.*

[ACT II.]

SCENE [I. *France. Before Angiers.*]

Enter, before Angiers, PHILIP KING of France, LEWIS [*the*] DAUPHIN, AUSTRIA, CONSTANCE, ARTHUR [*and Attendants*].

K. Phi. Before Angiers well met, brave Austria.
Arthur, that great forerunner of thy blood,
Richard, that robb'd the lion of his heart
And fought the holy wars in Palestine,
By this brave duke came early to his grave:
And for amends to his posterity,
At our importance hither is he come,
To spread his colours, boy, in thy behalf,
And to rebuke the usurpation
Of thy unnatural uncle, English John:
Embrace him, love him, give him welcome hither.
Arth. God shall forgive you Cœur-de-lion's death
The rather that you give his offspring life,
Shadowing their right under your wings of war:
I give you welcome with a powerless hand,
But with a heart full of unstained love:
Welcome before the gates of Angiers, duke.
Lew. A noble boy! Who would not do thee right?
Aust. Upon thy cheek lay I this zealous kiss,
As seal to this indenture of my love,
That to my home I will no more return,
Till Angiers and the right thou hast in France,
Together with that pale, that white-fac'd shore,
Whose foot spurns back the ocean's roaring tides
And coops from other lands her islanders,
Even till that England, hedg'd in with the main,
That water-walled bulwark, still secure
And confident from foreign purposes,
Even till that utmost corner of the west

210. **device,** coat of arms. 212. **motion,** impulse, intention, incitement. The same antithesis is in *Hamlet*, I, ii, 77-86. 214. **practise,** use craft; see glossary. 215. **deceit,** being deceived. 219. **blow . . . her.** Blowing a horn was the ordinary signal of approach. 225. **Colbrand the giant,** legendary Danish giant slain by Guy of Warwick. 231. **Philip! sparrow: James.** The Bastard, erstwhile Philip Faulconbridge, is now Richard Plantagenet. He is entitled to be called Sir Richard. "Philip" or "Phip" was frequently applied to the sparrow because of its chirp. The New Cambridge editors punctuate: *Philip Sparrow, James,* with reference understood to Skelton's mock elegy *Phylip Sparrow,* taking the line to mean "the late Philip, James," i.e., Philip is no more. 232. **toys,** follies (Schmidt); entertainment (New Cambridge); see glossary. 240. **holp,** helped; see glossary. 243. **untoward,** unmannerly. 244. **Basilisco-like.** Theobald was the first to note this as an allusion to the character Basilisco in the play *Solyman and Perseda* (presumably by Kyd), who, braggart-like, insisted on his knighthood but who, nevertheless, was called Knave by his servant. 250. **proper,** fine; see glossary. 257. **dear,** precious, costly (used quibblingly); see glossary. 261. **privilege,** immunity. 263. **dispose,** disposal; see glossary. 266. **aweless lion.** During his imprisonment by the Duke of Austria, according to legend, Coeur-de-Lion slew the duke's son and as punishment was given to a hungry lion. When the lion attacked him, he slew it by thrusting his hand down its throat and tearing out its heart, which he is supposed to have eaten. The story is preserved in several collections of popular tales. 268. **perforce,** forcibly; see glossary. 276. **it.** The antecedent is unexpressed. Hart suggests that the pronoun refers to Lady Faulconbridge's surrender to Richard.

ACT II. SCENE I. *Stage Direction:* **Austria.** After this name the New Cambridge editors add in parenthesis *clad in a lion-skin,* i.e., the skin he took from Coeur-de-Lion. 1. ***K. Phi.*** Globe, following F: *Lew.*

Salute thee for her king: till then, fair boy,
Will I not think of home, but follow arms.
Const. O, take his mother's thanks, a widow's thanks,
Till your strong hand shall help to give him strength
To make a more requital to your love!
Aust. The peace of heaven is theirs that lift their swords
In such a just and charitable war.
K. Phi. Well then, to work: our cannon shall be bent
Against the brows of this resisting town.
Call for our chiefest men of discipline,
To cull the plots of best advantages:
We'll lay before this town our royal bones,
Wade to the market-place in Frenchmen's blood,
But we will make it subject to this boy.
Const. Stay for an answer to your embassy,
Lest unadvis'd you stain your swords with blood:
My Lord Chatillon may from England bring
That right in peace which here we urge in war,
And then we shall repent each drop of blood
That hot rash haste so indirectly shed.

Enter CHATILLON.

K. Phi. A wonder, lady! lo, upon thy wish,
Our messenger Chatillon is arriv'd!
What England says, say briefly, gentle lord;
We coldly pause for thee; Chatillon, speak.
Chat. Then turn your forces from this paltry siege
And stir them up against a mightier task.
England, impatient of your just demands,
Hath put himself in arms: the adverse winds,
Whose leisure I have stay'd, have given him time
To land his legions all as soon as I;
His marches are expedient to this town,
His forces strong, his soldiers confident.
With him along is come the mother-queen,
An Ate, stirring him to blood and strife;
With her her niece, the Lady Blanch of Spain;
With them a bastard of the king's deceas'd;
And all th' unsettled humours of the land,
Rash, inconsiderate, fiery voluntaries,
With ladies' faces and fierce dragons' spleens,
Have sold their fortunes at their native homes,
Bearing their birthrights proudly on their backs,
To make a hazard of new fortunes here:
In brief, a braver choice of dauntless spirits
Than now the English bottoms have waft o'er
Did never float upon the swelling tide,
To do offence and scath in Christendom. *Drum beats.*
The interruption of their churlish drums
Cuts off more circumstance: they are at hand,
To parley or to fight; therefore prepare.
K. Phi. How much unlook'd for is this expedition!
Aust. By how much unexpected, by so much
We must awake endeavour for defence;
For courage mounteth with occasion:
Let them be welcome then; we are prepar'd.

Enter KING [JOHN] of England, BASTARD, QUEEN [ELINOR], BLANCHE, PEMBROKE, *and others.*

K. John. Peace be to France, if France in peace permit
Our just and lineal entrance to our own;
If not, bleed France, and peace ascend to heaven,
Whiles we, God's wrathful agent, do correct
Their proud contempt that beats His peace to heaven.
K. Phi. Peace be to England, if that war return
From France to England, there to live in peace.
England we love; and for that England's sake
With burden of our armour here we sweat.
This toil of ours should be a work of thine;
But thou from loving England art so far,
That thou hast under-wrought his lawful king,
Cut off the sequence of posterity,
Out-faced infant state and done a rape
Upon the maiden virtue of the crown.
Look here upon thy brother Geffrey's face;
These eyes, these brows, were moulded out of his:
This little abstract doth contain that large
Which died in Geffrey, and the hand of time
Shall draw this brief into as huge a volume.
That Geffrey was thy elder brother born,
And this his son; England was Geffrey's right
And this is Geffrey's: in the name of God
How comes it then that thou art call'd a king,
When living blood doth in these temples beat,
Which owe the crown that thou o'ermasterest?
K. John. From whom hast thou this great commission, France,
To draw my answer from thy articles?
K. Phi. From that supernal judge, that stirs good thoughts
In any breast of strong authority,
To look into the blots and stains of right:
That judge hath made me guardian to this boy:
Under whose warrant I impeach thy wrong
And by whose help I mean to chastise it.
K. John. Alack, thou dost usurp authority.
K. Phi. Excuse; it is to beat usurping down.
Eli. Who is it thou dost call usurper, France?
Const. Let me make answer; thy usurping son.
Eli. Out, insolent! thy bastard shall be king,
That thou mayst be a queen, and check the world!
Const. My bed was ever to thy son as true
As thine was to thy husband; and this boy
Liker in feature to his father Geffrey
Than thou and John in manners; being as like
As rain to water, or devil to his dam.
My boy a bastard! By my soul, I think

2. **forerunner.** Richard was not a direct ancestor of Arthur, but his uncle. 5. **By . . . duke,** a confusion of the Duke of Austria with Viscount Limoges, before whose castle Richard was mortally wounded. The roles of the two were combined in *The Troublesome Raigne* as they are in this play. 7. **importance,** importunity. 23. **pale . . . shore,** the chalk cliffs at Dover. 39. **men of discipline,** men trained in military strategy. 40. **To . . . advantages,** to select positions which are most favorable for attack (Wright). 44. **Stay,** wait; see glossary. 45. **unadvis'd,** rashly. 49. **indirectly,** wrongfully. 53. **coldly,** calmly. 60. **expedient,** speedy. 63. **Ate,** goddess of discord. 65. **of . . . deceas'd,** of the deceased king's. 66. **unsettled humours,** i.e., disgruntled individuals; see *humour* in glossary. 67. **voluntaries,** volunteers. 68. **ladies' faces,** beardless young men. **fierce dragons' spleens,** i.e., utmost fierceness; see *spleen* in glossary. 72. **choice,** picked company. 73. **bottoms,** keels or hulls of ships. 77. **circumstance,** detailed reporting. 85. **lineal,** by right of birth. 89. **if that,** if. 95. **under-wrought,** undermined. 96. **sequence of posterity,** lawful succession. 97. **Out-faced,** browbeat, intimidated. **infant state,** majesty of a boy-king (New Cambridge). 101. **little abstract,** abridgement or epitome; cf. *Hamlet*, II, ii, 548. 109. **owe,** own; see glossary. 111. **articles,** clauses or stipulations of a legal accusation. John challenges Philip's presumption in thus chiding him. 114. **of right,** on justice. 116. **impeach,** accuse. 122. **Out,** exclamation of anger; see glossary. 123. **check,** control; see glossary. 124-128. **My . . . dam.** I am every bit as true as you were, and my Arthur far less likely to be a bastard than your son John (although he is as like you as the devil is to his dam) or for the matter of that than your son Geoffrey himself (New Cambridge). 126. **feature,** form or shape of body; see glossary.

His father never was so true begot:
It cannot be, an if thou wert his mother.
Eli. There 's a good mother, boy, that blots thy father.
Const. There 's a good grandam, boy, that would blot thee.
Aust. Peace!
Bast. Hear the crier.
Aust. What the devil art thou?
Bast. One that will play the devil, sir, with you,
An 'a may catch your hide and you alone:
You are the hare of whom the proverb goes,
Whose valour plucks dead lions by the beard:
I'll smoke your skin-coat, an I catch you right;
Sirrah, look to 't; i' faith, I will, i' faith.
Blanch. O, well did he become that lion's robe
That did disrobe the lion of that robe!
Bast. It lies as sightly on the back of him
As great Alcides' shows upon an ass:
But, ass, I'll take that burthen from your back,
Or lay on that shall make your shoulders crack.
Aust. What cracker is this same that deafs our ears
With this abundance of superfluous breath?
K. Phi. Lewis, determine what we shall do straight.
Lew. Women and fools, break off your conference.
King John, this is the very sum of all;
England and Ireland, Anjou, Touraine, Maine,
In right of Arthur do I claim of thee:
Wilt thou resign them and lay down thy arms?
K. John. My life as soon: I do defy thee, France.
Arthur of Brittaine, yield thee to my hand;
And out of my dear love I'll give thee more
Than e'er the coward hand of France can win:
Submit thee, boy.
Eli. Come to thy grandam, child.
Const. Do, child, go to it grandam, child;
Give grandam kingdom, and it grandam will
Give it a plum, a cherry, and a fig:
There 's a good grandam.
Arth. Good my mother, peace!
I would that I were low laid in my grave:
I am not worth this coil that 's made for me.
Eli. His mother shames him so, poor boy, he weeps.
Const. Now shame upon you, whe'r she does or no!
His grandam's wrongs, and not his mother's shames,
Draws those heaven-moving pearls from his poor eyes,
Which heaven shall take in nature of a fee;
Ay, with these crystal beads heaven shall be brib'd
To do him justice and revenge on you.
Eli. Thou monstrous slanderer of heaven and earth!
Const. Thou monstrous injurer of heaven and earth!
Call not me slanderer; thou and thine usurp
The dominations, royalties and rights
Of this oppressed boy: this is thy eldest son's son,
Infortunate in nothing but in thee:
Thy sins are visited in this poor child;
The canon of the law is laid on him,
Being but the second generation
Removed from thy sin-conceiving womb.
K. John. Bedlam, have done.
Const. I have but this to say,
That he is not only plagued for her sin,
But God hath made her sin and her the plague
On this removed issue, plagu'd for her
And with her plague; her sin his injury,
Her injury the beadle to her sin,
All punish'd in the person of this child,
And all for her; a plague upon her!
Eli. Thou unadvised scold, I can produce
A will that bars the title of thy son.
Const. Ay, who doubts that? a will! a wicked will;
A woman's will; a cank'red grandam's will!
K. Phi. Peace, lady! pause, or be more temperate:
It ill beseems this presence to cry aim
To these ill-tuned repetitions.
Some trumpet summon hither to the walls
These men of Angiers: let us hear them speak
Whose title they admit, Arthur's or John's.

Trumpet sounds. Enter a Citizen *upon the walls.*

First Cit. Who is it that hath warn'd us to the walls?
K. Phi. 'Tis France, for England.
K. John. England, for itself.
You men of Angiers, and my loving subjects,—
K. Phi. You loving men of Angiers, Arthur's subjects,
Our trumpet call'd you to this gentle parle—
K. John. For our advantage; therefore hear us first.
These flags of France, that are advanced here
Before the eye and prospect of your town,
Have hither march'd to your endamagement:
The cannons have their bowels full of wrath,
And ready mounted are they to spit forth
Their iron indignation 'gainst your walls:
All preparation for a bloody siege
And merciless proceeding by these French
Confronts your city's eyes, your winking gates;
And but for our approach those sleeping stones,
That as a waist doth girdle you about,
By the compulsion of their ordinance
By this time from their fixed beds of lime
Had been dishabited, and wide havoc made
For bloody power to rush upon your peace.
But on the sight of us your lawful king,
Who painfully with much expedient march
Have brought a countercheck before your gates,
To save unscratch'd your city's threat'ned cheeks,
Behold, the French amaz'd vouchsafe a parle;
And now, instead of bullets wrapp'd in fire,
To make a shaking fever in your walls,
They shoot but calm words folded up in smoke,
To make a faithless error in your ears:
Which trust accordingly, kind citizens,
And let us in, your king, whose labour'd spirits,
Forwearied in this action of swift speed,
Crave harbourage within your city walls.
K. Phi. When I have said, make answer to us both.
Lo, in this right hand, whose protection
Is most divinely vow'd upon the right
Of him it holds, stands young Plantagenet,

137. **the proverb,** i.e., from Erasmus' *Adages: Mortuo leoni et lepores insultant,* even hares may insult the dead lion. 143. **him,** the Duke of Austria. 144. **Alcides,** Hercules, who slew the Nemean lion as one of his twelve labors and thereafter wore its pelt. 146. **that,** that which. 147. **cracker,** boaster. 160-163. **Do . . . grandam,** baby talk. 165. **coil,** disturbance, fuss; see glossary. 176. **dominations,** dominions, sovereignties. 180. **canon . . . law,** i.e., the sins of parents shall be visited upon their children to the third and fourth generations. 182. **sin-conceiving.** Constance once more implies that John is illegitimate. 183. **Bedlam,** lunatic. 184-190. **That . . . upon her.** The passage has caused perplexity. *Her sin* (l. 184) is her adultery; the same phrase in lines 185 and 187 means "the issue of her sin," i.e., King John. There is a play on *injury* (l. 187) meaning the wrong done Arthur, and (l. 188) Elinor's wrong deeds, which act as the officer (*beadle*) to punish her sin. 196. **ill . . . presence,** is not proper in the presence of royalty. 196-197. **cry aim To,** encourage. 205. **gentle parle,** peaceful parley; see *parle* in

Son to the elder brother of this man,
And king o'er him and all that he enjoys:
For this down-trodden equity, we tread
In warlike march these greens before your town,
Being no further enemy to you
Than the constraint of hospitable zeal
In the relief of this oppressed child
Religiously provokes. Be pleased then
To pay that duty which you truly owe
To him that owes it, namely this young prince:
And then our arms, like to a muzzled bear,
Save in aspect, hath all offence seal'd up;
Our cannons' malice vainly shall be spent
Against th' invulnerable clouds of heaven;
And with a blessed and unvex'd retire,
With unhack'd swords and helmets all unbruis'd,
We will bear home that lusty blood again
Which here we came to spout against your town,
And leave your children, wives and you in peace.
But if you fondly pass our proffer'd offer,
'Tis not the roundure of your old-fac'd walls
Can hide you from our messengers of war,
Though all these English and their discipline
Were harbour'd in their rude circumference.
Then tell us, shall your city call us lord,
In that behalf which we have challeng'd it?
Or shall we give the signal to our rage
And stalk in blood to our possession?
First Cit. In brief, we are the king of England's subjects:
For him, and in his right, we hold this town.
K. John. Acknowledge then the king, and let me in.
First Cit. That can we not; but he that proves the king,
To him will we prove loyal: till that time
Have we ramm'd up our gates against the world.
K. John. Doth not the crown of England prove the king?
And if not that, I bring you witnesses,
Twice fifteen thousand hearts of England's breed,—
Bast. Bastards, and else.
K. John. To verify our title with their lives.
K. Phi. As many and as well-born bloods as those,—
Bast. Some bastards too.
K. Phi. Stand in his face to contradict his claim.
First Cit. Till you compound whose right is worthiest,
We for the worthiest hold the right from both.
K. John. Then God forgive the sin of all those souls
That to their everlasting residence,
Before the dew of evening fall, shall fleet,
In dreadful trial of our kingdom's king!
K. Phi. Amen, amen! Mount, chevaliers to arms!
Bast. Saint George, that swing'd the dragon, and e'er since
Sits on 's horse back at mine hostess' door,
Teach us some fence! [*To Aust.*] Sirrah, were I at home,
At your den, sirrah, with your lioness,
I would set an ox-head to your lion's hide,
And make a monster of you.
Aust. Peace! no more.
Bast. O, tremble, for you hear the lion roar.
K. John. Up higher to the plain; where we'll set forth
In best appointment all our regiments.
Bast. Speed then, to take advantage of the field.
K. Phi. It shall be so; and at the other hill
Command the rest to stand. God and our right!
Exeunt.

Here after excursions, enter the Herald of France, *with trumpets, to the gates.*

F. Her. You men of Angiers, open wide your gates,
And let young Arthur, Duke of Brittaine, in,
Who by the hand of France this day hath made
Much work for tears in many an English mother,
Whose sons lie scattered on the bleeding ground;
Many a widow's husband grovelling lies,
Coldly embracing the discoloured earth;
And victory, with little loss, doth play
Upon the dancing banners of the French,
Who are at hand, triumphantly display'd,
To enter conquerors and to proclaim
Arthur of Brittaine England's king and yours.

Enter English Herald, *with trumpet.*

E. Her. Rejoice, you men of Angiers, ring your bells;
King John, your king and England's, doth approach,
Commander of this hot malicious day:
Their armours, that march'd hence so silver-bright,
Hither return all gilt with Frenchmen's blood;
There stuck no plume in any English crest
That is removed by a staff of France;
Our colours do return in those same hands
That did display them when we first march'd forth;
And, like a jolly troop of huntsmen, come
Our lusty English, all with purpled hands,
Dy'd in the dying slaughter of their foes:
Open your gates and give the victors way.
First Cit. Heralds, from off our tow'rs we might behold,
From first to last, the onset and retire
Of both your armies; whose equality
By our best eyes cannot be censured:
Blood hath bought blood and blows have answer'd blows;
Strength match'd with strength, and power confronted power:
Both are alike; and both alike we like.
One must prove greatest: while they weigh so even,
We hold our town for neither, yet for both.

Enter the two KINGS, *with their powers, at several doors.*

K. John. France, hast thou yet more blood to cast away?
Say, shall the current of our right run on?
Whose passage, vex'd with thy impediment,
Shall leave his native channel and o'erswell
With course disturb'd even thy confining shores,

glossary. 215. **winking,** closed; see glossary. 218. **their,** i.e., *these French* (l. 214). 220. **dishabited,** dislodged. 232. **labour'd,** oppressed with labor. 241. **equity,** justice. 242. **these greens,** the turf before the town gates. 247. **duty,** reverence; see glossary. 253. **retire,** withdrawal. 258. **fondly,** foolishly; see *fond* in glossary. 259. **roundure,** enclosure. 264. **which,** in which; an instance of ellipsis where the preposition is not repeated; see Abbott, 394. 270. **proves,** i.e., proves himself; see *prove* in glossary. 281. **compound,** settle, agree; see glossary. 286. **trial,** i.e., by combat to decide who is rightful king. 288. **swing'd,** whipped. 289. **Sits . . . door.** One of the most common signs at tavern doors was that of St. George and the Dragon. 290. **fence,** skill in fencing. 299. *Stage Direction:* ***excursions,*** stage battles or skirmishes; see glossary. 314. **Commander,** victor. **hot malicious day,** i.e., hotly and violently contested. 325. **might,** could; see glossary. 328. **censured,** estimated; see glossary. 332. **even,** equal. 333. *Stage Direction:* ***several,*** different.

Unless thou let his silver water keep
A peaceful progress to the ocean.

K. Phi. England, thou hast not sav'd one drop of blood,
In this hot trial, more than we of France;
Rather, lost more. And by this hand I swear,
That sways the earth this climate overlooks,
Before we will lay down our just-borne arms,
We'll put thee down, 'gainst whom these arms we bear,
Or add a royal number to the dead,
Gracing the scroll that tells of this war's loss
With slaughter coupled to the name of kings.

Bast. Ha, majesty! how high thy glory tow'rs,
When the rich blood of kings is set on fire!
O, now doth Death line his dead chaps with steel;
The swords of soldiers are his teeth, his fangs;
And now he feasts, mousing the flesh of men,
In undetermin'd differences of kings.
Why stand these royal fronts amazed thus?
Cry, 'havoc!' kings; back to the stained field,
You equal potents, fiery kindled spirits!
Then let confusion of one part confirm
The other's peace; till then, blows, blood and death!

K. John. Whose party do the townsmen yet admit?

K. Phi. Speak, citizens, for England; who 's your king?

First Cit. The king of England, when we know the king.

K. Phi. Know him in us, that here hold up his right.

K. John. In us, that are our own great deputy,
And bear possession of our person here,
Lord of our presence, Angiers, and of you.

First Cit. A greater pow'r than we denies all this;
And till it be undoubted, we do lock
Our former scruple in our strong-barr'd gates;
King'd of our fears, until our fears, resolv'd,
Be by some certain king purg'd and depos'd.

Bast. By heaven, these scroyles of Angiers flout you, kings,
And stand securely on their battlements,
As in a theatre, whence they gape and point
At your industrious scenes and acts of death.
Your royal presences be rul'd by me:
Do like the mutines of Jerusalem,
Be friends awhile and both conjointly bend
Your sharpest deeds of malice on this town:
By east and west let France and England mount
Their battering cannon charged to the mouths,
Till their soul-fearing clamours have brawl'd down
The flinty ribs of this contemptuous city:
I 'ld play incessantly upon these jades,
Even till unfenced desolation
Leave them as naked as the vulgar air.
That done, dissever your united strengths,
And part your mingled colours once again;
Turn face to face and bloody point to point;
Then, in a moment, Fortune shall cull forth
Out of one side her happy minion,
To whom in favour she shall give the day,
And kiss him with a glorious victory.
How like you this wild counsel, mighty states?
Smacks it not something of the policy?

K. John. Now, by the sky that hangs above our heads,
I like it well. France, shall we knit our pow'rs
And lay this Angiers even with the ground;
Then after fight who shall be king of it?

Bast. An if thou hast the mettle of a king,
Being wrong'd as we are by this peevish town,
Turn thou the mouth of thy artillery,
As we will ours, against these saucy walls;
And when that we have dash'd them to the ground,
Why then defy each other, and pell-mell
Make work upon ourselves, for heaven or hell.

K. Phi. Let it be so. Say, where will you assault?

K. John. We from the west will send destruction
Into this city's bosom.

Aust. I from the north.

K. Phi. Our thunder from the south
Shall rain their drift of bullets on this town.

Bast. O prudent discipline! From north to south:
Austria and France shoot in each other's mouth:
I'll stir them to it. Come, away, away!

First Cit. Hear us, great kings: vouchsafe awhile to stay,
And I shall show you peace and fair-fac'd league;
Win you this city without stroke or wound;
Rescue those breathing lives to die in beds,
That here come sacrifices for the field:
Persever not, but hear me, mighty kings.

K. John. Speak on with favour; we are bent to hear.

First Cit. That daughter there of Spain, the Lady Blanch,
Is niece to England: look upon the years
Of Lewis the Dauphin and that lovely maid:
If lusty love should go in quest of beauty,
Where should he find it fairer than in Blanch?
If zealous love should go in search of virtue,
Where should he find it purer than in Blanch?
If love ambitious sought a match of birth,
Whose veins bound richer blood than Lady Blanch?
Such as she is, in beauty, virtue, birth,
Is the young Dauphin every way complete:
If not complete of, say he is not she;
And she again wants nothing, to name want,
If want it be not that she is not he:
He is the half part of a blessed man,
Left to be finished by such as she;
And she a fair divided excellence,
Whose fulness of perfection lies in him.
O, two such silver currents, when they join,
Do glorify the banks that bound them in;
And two such shores to two such streams made one,
Two such controlling bounds shall you be, kings,
To these two princes, if you marry them.

344. **climate,** portion of the sky. 347. **a royal number,** i.e., a king's name. 352. **chaps,** jaws. 354. **mousing,** tearing. 355. **undetermin'd . . . kings,** i.e., making no difference between the flesh of kings and that of common men (New Cambridge). More probably, the phrase means unsettled quarrels between kings. 356. **royal fronts,** faces of kings; see *front* in glossary. 358. **potents,** potentates. 359. **confusion,** destruction, overthrow; see glossary. **part,** faction, party. 369. **it.** The antecedent is the idea expressed in line 359, the *confusion of one part.* **undoubted,** unquestioned. 371. **King'd of,** ruled by. **resolv'd,** dissolved, dissipated; see glossary. 373. **scroyles,** scoundrels. 378. **mutines,** mutineers. **Jerusalem.** During the siege of Jerusalem by Titus, two rival Jewish factions united to resist the Romans. 383. **soul-fearing,** inspiring fear in the soul. 385. **jades,** ill-conditioned horses (used contemptuously). 392. **minion,** favorite; see glossary. 395. **mighty states,** kings, i.e., persons of state. 396. **the policy,** the art of politics (Moore-Smith, who cites *The Taming of the Shrew,* I, i, 37: *the mathematics, the metaphysics*). 402. **peevish,** stubborn; see glossary. 406. **defy,** challenge to combat; see glossary. 421. **Persever,** accented on the second syllable. 422. **favour,** permission; see glossary. 433. **complete,** accomplished; see glossary. 434-440. **If . . . him.** The

This union shall do more than battery can
To our fast-closed gates; for at this match,
With swifter spleen than powder can enforce,
The mouth of passage shall we fling wide ope,
And give you entrance: but without this match,
The sea enraged is not half so deaf,
Lions more confident, mountains and rocks
More free from motion, no, not Death himself
In mortal fury half so peremptory,
As we to keep this city.

Bast. Here 's a stay
That shakes the rotten carcass of old Death
Out of his rags! Here 's a large mouth, indeed,
That spits forth death and mountains, rocks and seas,
Talks as familiarly of roaring lions
As maids of thirteen do of puppy-dogs!
What cannoneer begot this lusty blood?
He speaks plain cannon fire, and smoke and bounce;
He gives the bastinado with his tongue:
Our ears are cudgell'd; not a word of his
But buffets better than a fist of France:
Zounds! I was never so bethump'd with words
Since I first call'd my brother's father dad.

Eli. Son, list to this conjunction, make this match;
Give with our niece a dowry large enough:
For by this knot thou shalt so surely tie
Thy now unsur'd assurance to the crown,
That yon green boy shall have no sun to ripe
The bloom that promiseth a mighty fruit.
I see a yielding in the looks of France;
Mark, how they whisper: urge them while their souls
Are capable of this ambition,
Lest zeal, now melted by the windy breath
Of soft petitions, pity and remorse,
Cool and congeal again to what it was.

First Cit. Why answer not the double majesties
This friendly treaty of our threat'ned town?

K. Phi. Speak England first, that hath been forward first
To speak unto this city: what say you?

K. John. If that the Dauphin there, thy princely son,
Can in this book of beauty read 'I love,'
Her dowry shall weigh equal with a queen:
For Anjou and fair Touraine, Maine, Poictiers,
And all that we upon this side the sea,
Except this city now by us besieg'd,
Find liable to our crown and dignity,
Shall gild her bridal bed and make her rich
In titles, honours and promotions,
As she in beauty, education, blood,
Holds hand with any princess of the world.

K. Phi. What say'st thou, boy? look in the lady's face.

Lew. I do, my lord; and in her eye I find
A wonder, or a wondrous miracle,
The shadow of myself form'd in her eye;
Which, being but the shadow of your son,
Becomes a sun and makes your son a shadow:
I do protest I never lov'd myself
Till now infixed I beheld myself
Drawn in the flattering table of her eye.
Whispers with Blanch.

Bast. Drawn in the flattering table of her eye!
Hang'd in the frowning wrinkle of her brow!
And quarter'd in her heart! he doth espy
Himself love's traitor: this is pity now,
That, hang'd and drawn and quarter'd, there should be
In such a love so vile a lout as he.

Blanch. My uncle's will in this respect is mine:
If he see aught in you that makes him like,
That any thing he sees, which moves his liking,
I can with ease translate it to my will;
Or if you will, to speak more properly,
I will enforce it eas'ly to my love.
Further I will not flatter you, my lord,
That all I see in you is worthy love,
Than this; that nothing do I see in you,
Though churlish thoughts themselves should be your judge,
That I can find should merit any hate.

K. John. What say these young ones? What say you, my niece?

Blanch. That she is bound in honour still to do
What you in wisdom still vouchsafe to say.

K. John. Speak then, prince Dauphin; can you love this lady?

Lew. Nay, ask me if I can refrain from love;
For I do love her most unfeignedly.

K. John. Then do I give Volquessen, Touraine, Maine,
Poictiers and Anjou, these five provinces,
With her to thee; and this addition more,
Full thirty thousand marks of English coin.
Philip of France, if thou be pleas'd withal,
Command thy son and daughter to join hands.

K. Phi. It likes us well; young princes, close your hands.

Aust. And your lips too; for I am well assur'd
That I did so when I was first assur'd.

K. Phi. Now, citizens of Angiers, ope your gates,
Let in that amity which you have made;
For at Saint Mary's chapel presently
The rites of marriage shall be solemniz'd.
Is not the Lady Constance in this troop?
I know she is not, for this match made up
Her presence would have interrupted much:
Where is she and her son? tell me, who knows.

Lew. She is sad and passionate at your highness' tent.

K. Phi. And, by my faith, this league that we have made
Will give her sadness very little cure.
Brother of England, how may we content
This widow lady? In her right we came;
Which we, God knows, have turn'd another way,

idea here appears to be that the two young people lack only each other to be perfect in themselves. 434. **complete of,** generally regarded as corrupt; *complete, oh,* and *complete so* have been offered as emendations. The New Cambridge editors suggest *complete all* (spelled *al*) which would mean "complete in every way"; but see Abbott, 171. 435. **wants,** lacks; see glossary. 455. **stay,** hindrance, obstacle. 462. **bounce,** i.e., the noise of the cannon. 463. **bastinado,** beating with a stick. 476. **capable of,** susceptible to; see glossary. 477. **zeal,** i.e., the French king's zeal in Arthur's behalf. The metaphor is one of melting and hardening wax (New Cambridge). 478. **remorse,** compassion; see glossary. 490. **liable,** subject or subservient to. 498. **shadow,** image, reflection; see glossary. 503. **table,** tablet; see glossary. 519. **churlish,** sparing of praise. 527-528. **Then . . . provinces.** The lines are identical with a corresponding passage in *The Troublesome Raigne.* 527. **Volquessen,** the ancient country of the Velocasses, whose capital was Rouen (Wright). 531. **withal,** with these; see glossary. 533. **likes,** pleases; see glossary. 535. **assur'd,** betrothed. 538. **presently,** at once; see glossary.

To our own vantage.
K. John. We will heal up all;
For we'll create young Arthur Duke of Brittaine
And Earl of Richmond; and this rich fair town
We make him lord of. Call the Lady Constance;
Some speedy messenger bid her repair
To our solemnity: I trust we shall,
If not fill up the measure of her will,
Yet in some measure satisfy her so
That we shall stop her exclamation.
Go we, as well as haste will suffer us,
To this unlook'd for, unprepared pomp.
Exeunt [*all but the Bastard*].
Bast. Mad world! mad kings! mad composition!
John, to stop Arthur's title in the whole,
Hath willingly departed with a part,
And France, whose armour conscience buckled on,
Whom zeal and charity brought to the field
As God's own soldier, rounded in the ear
With that same purpose-changer, that sly devil,
That broker, that still breaks the pate of faith,
That daily break-vow, he that wins of all,
Of kings, of beggars, old men, young men, maids,
Who, having no external thing to lose
But the word 'maid,' cheats the poor maid of that,
That smooth-fac'd gentleman, tickling Commodity,
Commodity, the bias of the world,
The world, who of itself is peised well,
Made to run even upon even ground,
Till this advantage, this vile-drawing bias,
This sway of motion, this Commodity,
Makes it take head from all indifferency,
From all direction, purpose, course, intent:
And this same bias, this Commodity,
This bawd, this broker, this all-changing word,
Clapp'd on the outward eye of fickle France,
Hath drawn him from his own determin'd aid,
From a resolv'd and honourable war,
To a most base and vile-concluded peace.
And why rail I on this Commodity?
But for because he hath not woo'd me yet:
Not that I have the power to clutch my hand,
When his fair angels would salute my palm;
But for my hand, as unattempted yet,
Like a poor beggar, raileth on the rich.
Well, whiles I am a beggar, I will rail
And say there is no sin but to be rich;
And being rich, my virtue then shall be
To say there is no vice but beggary.
Since kings break faith upon commodity,
Gain, be my lord, for I will worship thee. *Exit.*

ACT [III.]

[SCENE I. *The French* KING'S *pavilion.*]

Enter CONSTANCE, ARTHUR, *and* SALISBURY.

Const. Gone to be married! gone to swear a peace!
False blood to false blood join'd! gone to be friends!
Shall Lewis have Blanch, and Blanch those provinces?
It is not so; thou hast misspoke, misheard;
Be well advis'd, tell o'er thy tale again:
It cannot be; thou dost but say 'tis so:
I trust I may not trust thee; for thy word
Is but the vain breath of a common man:
Believe me, I do not believe thee, man;
I have a king's oath to the contrary.
Thou shalt be punish'd for thus frighting me,
For I am sick and capable of fears,
Oppress'd with wrongs and therefore full of fears,
A widow, husbandless, subject to fears,
A woman, naturally born to fears;
And though thou now confess thou didst but jest,
With my vex'd spirits I cannot take a truce,
But they will quake and tremble all this day.
What dost thou mean by shaking of thy head?
Why dost thou look so sadly on my son?
What means that hand upon that breast of thine?
Why holds thine eye that lamentable rheum,
Like a proud river peering o'er his bounds?
Be these sad signs confirmers of thy words?
Then speak again; not all thy former tale,
But this one word, whether thy tale be true.
Sal. As true as I believe you think them false
That give you cause to prove my saying true.
Const. O, if thou teach me to believe this sorrow,
Teach thou this sorrow how to make me die,
And let belief and life encounter so
As doth the fury of two desperate men
Which in the very meeting fall and die.
Lewis marry Blanch! O boy, then where art thou?
France friend with England, what becomes of me?
Fellow, be gone: I cannot brook thy sight:
This news hath made thee a most ugly man.
Sal. What other harm have I, good lady, done,
But spoke the harm that is by others done?
Const. Which harm within itself so heinous is
As it makes harmful all that speak of it.
Arth. I do beseech you, madam, be content.
Const. If thou, that bid'st me be content, wert grim,
Ugly and sland'rous to thy mother's womb,
Full of unpleasing blots and sightless stains,
Lame, foolish, crooked, swart, prodigious,
Patch'd with foul moles and eye-offending marks,
I would not care, I then would be content,
For then I should not love thee, no, nor thou
Become thy great birth nor deserve a crown.
But thou art fair, and at thy birth, dear boy,
Nature and Fortune join'd to make thee great:
Of Nature's gifts thou mayst with lilies boast
And with the half-blown rose. But Fortune, O,
She is corrupted, chang'd and won from thee;
Sh' adulterates hourly with thine uncle John,
And with her golden hand hath pluck'd on France
To tread down fair respect of sovereignty,
And made his majesty the bawd to theirs.
France is a bawd to Fortune and King John,

550. **vantage,** advantage; see glossary. 563. **departed with,** given up; see glossary. 566. **rounded,** whispered. 567. **purpose-changer,** turncoat, timeserver. 574. **bias,** swaying influence; see glossary. 575. **peised,** poised, in equilibrium.

ACT III. SCENE I. 22. **lamentable rheum,** tears. 28. **prove,** find out by experience; see glossary. 36. **brook,** endure; see glossary. 45. **sightless,** unsightly. 65. **under-bear,** endure. 69-74. **For . . . it.** Several conjectures and explanations have been offered to elucidate this passage; most favored is Hanmer's *stout* for *stoop* (l. 69). Malone finds the difficulty in a too sudden "bounding" from one idea to another. The New Cambridge editors suggest the image of grief as a crown too heavy to be borne. The obscurity is due less to the inconsistency of the image than to the order of its presentation. The metaphor has two aspects: Constance conceives of her grief as a master before whom she must stoop in acknowledgment of his power; at the same time she identifies herself as the supporter or medium of that grief. The two images are not consecutive but parallel. In the second aspect of the figure she conceives of her grief—and of herself as the embodiment of that grief—as a person of state to whom kings must come; and only the earth itself is firm enough to serve as a throne to sustain her. 82, 83.

That strumpet Fortune, that usurping John!
Tell me, thou fellow, is not France forsworn?
Envenom him with words, or get thee gone
And leave those woes alone which I alone
Am bound to under-bear.
Sal. Pardon me, madam,
I may not go without you to the kings.
Const. Thou mayst, thou shalt; I will not go with thee:
I will instruct my sorrows to be proud;
For grief is proud and makes his owner stoop.
To me and to the state of my great grief
Let kings assemble; for my grief 's so great
That no supporter but the huge firm earth
Can hold it up: here I and sorrows sit;
Here is my throne, bid kings come bow to it.
[*Seats herself on the ground.*]

Enter KING JOHN, [KING PHILIP of] France, [LEWIS *the*] DAUPHIN, BLANCH, ELINOR, PHILIP [*the Bastard*], AUSTRIA, CONSTANCE [*and* Attendants].

K. Phi. 'Tis true, fair daughter; and this blessed day
Ever in France shall be kept festival:
To solemnize this day the glorious sun
Stays in his course and plays the alchemist,
Turning with splendour of his precious eye
The meagre cloddy earth to glittering gold:
The yearly course that brings this day about
Shall never see it but a holiday.
Const. A wicked day, and not a holy day! [*Rising.*]
What hath this day deserv'd? what hath it done,
That it in golden letters should be set
Among the high tides in the calendar?
Nay, rather turn this day out of the week,
This day of shame, oppression, perjury.
Or, if it must stand still, let wives with child
Pray that their burthens may not fall this day,
Lest that their hopes prodigiously be cross'd:
But on this day let seamen fear no wrack;
No bargains break that are not this day made:
This day, all things begun come to ill end,
Yea, faith itself to hollow falsehood change!
K. Phi. By heaven, lady, you shall have no cause
To curse the fair proceedings of this day:
Have I not pawn'd to you my majesty?
Const. You have beguil'd me with a counterfeit
Resembling majesty, which, being touch'd and tried,
Proves valueless: you are forsworn, forsworn;
You came in arms to spill mine enemies' blood,
But now in arms you strengthen it with yours:
The grappling vigour and rough frown of war
Is cold in amity and painted peace,
And our oppression hath made up this league.
Arm, arm, you heavens, against these perjur'd kings!
A widow cries; be husband to me, heavens!
Let not the hours of this ungodly day
Wear out the day in peace; but, ere sunset,
Set armed discord 'twixt these perjur'd kings!
Hear me, O, hear me!
Aust. Lady Constance, peace!
Const. War! war! no peace! peace is to me a war.
O Lymoges! O Austria! thou dost shame
That bloody spoil: thou slave, thou wretch, thou coward!
Thou little valiant, great in villany!
Thou ever strong upon the stronger side!
Thou Fortune's champion that dost never fight
But when her humorous ladyship is by
To teach thee safety! thou art perjur'd too,
And sooth'st up greatness. What a fool art thou,
A ramping fool, to brag and stamp and swear
Upon my party! Thou cold-blooded slave,
Hast thou not spoke like thunder on my side,
Been sworn my soldier, bidding me depend
Upon thy stars, thy fortune and thy strength,
And dost thou now fall over to my foes?
Thou wear a lion's hide! doff it for shame,
And hang a calf's-skin on those recreant limbs.
Aust. O, that a man should speak those words to me!
Bast. And hang a calf's-skin on those recreant limbs.
Aust. Thou dar'st not say so, villain, for thy life.
Bast. And hang a calf's-skin on those recreant limbs.
K. John. We like not this; thou dost forget thyself.

Enter PANDULPH.

K. Phi. Here comes the holy legate of the pope.
Pand. Hail, you anointed deputies of heaven!
To thee, King John, my holy errand is.
I Pandulph, of fair Milan cardinal,
And from Pope Innocent the legate here,
Do in his name religiously demand
Why thou against the church, our holy mother,
So wilfully dost spurn; and force perforce
Keep Stephen Langton, chosen archbishop
Of Canterbury, from that holy see?
This, in our foresaid holy father's name,
Pope Innocent, I do demand of thee.
K. John. What earthy name to interrogatories
Can task the free breath of a sacred king?
Thou canst not, cardinal, devise a name
So slight, unworthy and ridiculous,
To charge me to an answer, as the pope.
Tell him this tale; and from the mouth of England
Add thus much more, that no Italian priest
Shall tithe or toll in our dominions;
But as we, under heaven, are supreme head,
So under Him that great supremacy,
Where we do reign, we will alone uphold,
Without th' assistance of a mortal hand:
So tell the pope, all reverence set apart
To him and his usurp'd authority.
K. Phi. Brother of England, you blaspheme in this.
K. John. Though you and all the kings of Christendom
Are led so grossly by this meddling priest,
Dreading the curse that money may buy out;

holiday, holy day. The Elizabethan pronunciation was probably identical; in F both are printed *holy day*. 86. **high tides,** festivals. 92. **But,** except; i.e., this is the most evil of days. 105. **painted,** specious; see glossary. 114. **Lymoges.** Cf. II, i, 5, note. 115. **spoil,** booty, i.e., the lion's pelt. 121. **sooth'st up,** flatters. 127. **fall over,** go over. 129. **calf's-skin.** The New Cambridge editors quote Sir John Hawkins: "When fools were kept for diversion in great families, they were distinguished by a calf's-skin coat, which has buttons down the back." **recreant,** cowardly; see glossary. 136. **anointed . . . heaven,** the kings, Philip and John. 142. **spurn [against],** oppose contemptuously.

147. **earthy.** Pope's emendation *earthly* is accepted by the New Cambridge editors; *earthy* is used elsewhere by Shakespeare to connote grossness or some aspect of death. Here it is opposed to the divinity of kingship and suggests a repudiation of the pope as God's vicegerent. **interrogatories,** questions formally put, or drawn up in writing to be put, to an accused person or a witness to be answered as upon oath (Onions). 164. **curse . . . out,** an allusion to the alleged practice of buying indulgences.

And by the merit of vile gold, dross, dust,
Purchase corrupted pardon of a man,
Who in that sale sells pardon from himself,
Though you and all the rest so grossly led
This juggling witchcraft with revenue cherish,
Yet I alone, alone do me oppose
Against the pope and count his friends my foes.
Pand. Then, by the lawful power that I have,
Thou shalt stand curs'd and excommunicate:
And blessed shall he be that doth revolt
From his allegiance to an heretic;
And meritorious shall that hand be call'd,
Canonized and worshipp'd as a saint,
That takes away by any secret course
Thy hateful life.
Const. O, lawful let it be
That I have room with Rome to curse awhile!
Good father cardinal, cry thou amen
To my keen curses; for without my wrong
There is no tongue hath power to curse him right.
Pand. There 's law and warrant, lady, for my curse.
Const. And for mine too: when law can do no right,
Let it be lawful that law bar no wrong:
Law cannot give my child his kingdom here,
For he that holds his kingdom holds the law;
Therefore, since law itself is perfect wrong,
How can the law forbid my tongue to curse?
Pand. Philip of France, on peril of a curse,
Let go the hand of that arch-heretic;
And raise the power of France upon his head,
Unless he do submit himself to Rome.
Eli. Look'st thou pale, France? do not let go thy hand.
Const. Look to that, devil; lest that France repent,
And by disjoining hands, hell lose a soul.
Aust. King Philip, listen to the cardinal.
Bast. And hang a calf's-skin on his recreant limbs.
Aust. Well, ruffian, I must pocket up these wrongs,
Because—
Bast. Your breeches best may carry them.
K. John. Philip, what say'st thou to the cardinal?
Const. What should he say, but as the cardinal?
Lew. Bethink you, father; for the difference
Is purchase of a heavy curse from Rome,
Or the light loss of England for a friend:
Forego the easier.
Blanch. That 's the curse of Rome.
Const. O Lewis, stand fast! the devil tempts thee here
In likeness of a new untrimmed bride.
Blanch. The Lady Constance speaks not from her faith,
But from her need.
Const. O, if thou grant my need,
Which only lives but by the death of faith,
That need must needs infer this principle,
That faith would live again by death of need.
O then, tread down my need, and faith mounts up;
Keep my need up, and faith is trodden down!
K. John. The king is mov'd, and answers not to this.
Const. O, be remov'd from him, and answer well!
Aust. Do so, King Philip; hang no more in doubt.
Bast. Hang nothing but a calf's-skin, most sweet lout.
K. Phi. I am perplex'd, and know not what to say.
Pand. What canst thou say but will perplex thee more,
If thou stand excommunicate and curs'd?
K. Phi. Good reverend father, make my person yours,
And tell me how you would bestow yourself.
This royal hand and mine are newly knit,
And the conjunction of our inward souls
Married in league, coupl'd and link'd together
With all religious strength of sacred vows;
The latest breath that gave the sound of words
Was deep-sworn faith, peace, amity, true love
Between our kingdoms and our royal selves,
And even before this truce, but new before,
No longer than we well could wash our hands
To clap this royal bargain up of peace,
Heaven knows, they were besmear'd and overstain'd
With slaughter's pencil, where revenge did paint
The fearful difference of incensed kings:
And shall these hands, so lately purg'd of blood,
So newly join'd in love, so strong in both,
Unyoke this seizure and this kind regreet?
Play fast and loose with faith? so jest with heaven,
Make such unconstant children of ourselves,
As now again to snatch our palm from palm,
Unswear faith sworn, and on the marriage-bed
Of smiling peace to march a bloody host,
And make a riot on the gentle brow
Of true sincerity? O, holy sir,
My reverend father, let it not be so!
Out of your grace, devise, ordain, impose
Some gentle order; and then we shall be blest
To do your pleasure and continue friends.
Pand. All form is formless, order orderless,
Save what is opposite to England's love.
Therefore to arms! be champion of our church,
Or let the church, our mother, breathe her curse,
A mother's curse, on her revolting son.
France, thou mayst hold a serpent by the tongue,
A chafed lion by the mortal paw,
A fasting tiger safer by the tooth,
Than keep in peace that hand which thou dost hold.
K. Phi. I may disjoin my hand, but not my faith.
Pand. So mak'st thou faith an enemy to faith;
And like a civil war set'st oath to oath,
Thy tongue against thy tongue. O, let thy vow
First made to heaven, first be to heaven perform'd,
That is, to be the champion of our church!
What since thou swor'st is sworn against thyself
And may not be performed by thyself,
For that which thou hast sworn to do amiss
Is not amiss when it is truly done,

167. **from himself,** i.e., not from God (New Cambridge); also, incurring his own damnation. 180. **room, Rome,** an obvious pun; cf. *Julius Caesar*, I, ii, 156. 200. **pocket up,** submit to. 205. **purchase,** acquisition; see glossary. 209. **new untrimmed,** a phrase variously explained: newly divested of her bridal trimmings (John); with her hair hanging loose after the fashion of brides (Onions); *new and trimmed, new untamed, new betrimmed, new uptrimmed, new-intervened* are some of the suggested corrections. Constance may mean that the marriage has been celebrated so recently that the bride has not yet lost her maidenhood. 224. **make . . . yours,** put yourself in my place. 228. **Married, coupl'd, link'd.** The auxiliary verb *are* (l. 226) is understood with these verbs. 233. **new before,** recently. 235. **clap . . . up,** conclude with a handshake. 237. **pencil,** brush. 238. **difference,** dissension; see glossary. 240. **in both,** i.e., blood and love. 241. **Unyoke this seizure,** disjoin this handclasp. **regreet,** counterclasp. 242. **Play . . . loose.** Cf. *Love's Labour's Lost*, I, ii, 162, note. 265-266. **thy vow . . . heaven,** i.e., his coronation vow to defend the church. 268-273. **What . . . it.** What you have sworn since then is sworn against yourself and cannot be performed by

And being not done, where doing tends to ill,
The truth is then most done not doing it:
The better act of purposes mistook
Is to mistake again; though indirect,
Yet indirection thereby grows direct,
And falsehood falsehood cures, as fire cools fire
Within the scorched veins of one new-burn'd.
It is religion that doth make vows kept;
But thou hast sworn against religion,
By what thou swear'st against the thing thou swear'st,
And mak'st an oath the surety for thy truth
Against an oath: †the truth thou art unsure
To swear, swears only not to be forsworn;
Else what a mockery should it be to swear!
But thou dost swear only to be forsworn;
And most forsworn, to keep what thou dost swear.
Therefore thy later vows against thy first
Is in thyself rebellion to thyself;
And better conquest never canst thou make
Than arm thy constant and thy nobler parts
Against these giddy loose suggestions:
Upon which better part our pray'rs come in,
If thou vouchsafe them. But if not, then know
The peril of our curses light on thee
So heavy as thou shalt not shake them off,
But in despair die under their black weight.
Aust. Rebellion, flat rebellion!
Bast. Will 't not be?
Will not a calf's-skin stop that mouth of thine?
Lew. Father, to arms!
Blanch. Upon thy wedding-day?
Against the blood that thou hast married?
What, shall our feast be kept with slaughtered men?
Shall braying trumpets and loud churlish drums,
Clamours of hell, be measures to our pomp?
O husband, hear me! ay, alack, how new
Is husband in my mouth! even for that name,
Which till this time my tongue did ne'er pronounce,
Upon my knee I beg, go not to arms
Against mine uncle.
Const. O, upon my knee,
Made hard with kneeling, I do pray to thee,
Thou virtuous Dauphin, alter not the doom
Forethought by heaven!
Blanch. Now shall I see thy love: what motive may
Be stronger with thee than the name of wife?
Const. That which upholdeth him that thee upholds,
His honour: O, thine honour, Lewis, thine honour!
Lew. I muse your majesty doth seem so cold,
When such profound respects do pull you on.
Pand. I will denounce a curse upon his head.
K. Phi. Thou shalt not need. England, I will fall from thee.
Const. O fair return of banish'd majesty!
Eli. O foul revolt of French inconstancy!
K. John. France, thou shalt rue this hour within this hour.
Bast. Old Time the clock-setter, that bald sexton Time,
Is it as he will? well then, France shall rue.
Blanch. The sun 's o'ercast with blood: fair day, adieu!
Which is the side that I must go withal?
I am with both: each army hath a hand;
And in their rage, I having hold of both,
They whirl asunder and dismember me.
Husband, I cannot pray that thou mayst win;
Uncle, I needs must pray that thou mayst lose;
Father, I may not wish the fortune thine;
Grandam, I will not wish thy wishes thrive:
Whoever wins, on that side shall I lose;
Assured loss before the match be play'd.
Lew. Lady, with me, with me thy fortune lies.
Blanch. There where my fortune lives, there my life dies.
K. John. Cousin, go draw our puissance together.
[*Exit Bastard.*]
France, I am burn'd up with inflaming wrath;
A rage whose heat hath this condition,
That nothing can allay, nothing but blood,
The blood, and dearest-valued blood, of France.
K. Phi. Thy rage shall burn thee up, and thou shalt turn
To ashes, ere our blood shall quench that fire:
Look to thyself, thou art in jeopardy.
K. John. No more than he that threats. To arms let 's hie! *Exeunt.*

SCENE II. [*The same. Plains near Angiers.*]

Alarums, excursions. Enter [the] BASTARD, *with* AUSTRIA'S *head.*

Bast. Now, by my life, this day grows wondrous hot;
Some airy devil hovers in the sky
And pours down mischief. Austria's head lie there,
While Philip breathes.

Enter [KING] JOHN, ARTHUR, [*and*] HUBERT.

K. John. Hubert, keep this boy. Philip, make up:
My mother is assailed in our tent,
And ta'en, I fear.
Bast. My lord, I rescued her;
Her highness is in safety, fear you not:
But on, my liege; for very little pains
Will bring this labour to an happy end. *Exeunt.*

[SCENE III. *The same.*]

Alarums, excursions, retreat. Enter [KING] JOHN, ELINOR, ARTHUR, [*the*] BASTARD, HUBERT, [*and*] Lords.

K. John. [*To Elinor*] So shall it be; your grace shall stay behind
So strongly guarded. [*To Arthur*] Cousin, look not sad:
Thy grandam loves thee; and thy uncle will
As dear be to thee as thy father was.

you, for what wrong you have sworn to do is not wrong if truly performed, and if you do it not, because the doing of it would be wrong, then you are most truly performing it by not doing it (John). 283. **unsure,** unsafe. 292. **suggestions,** temptations; see glossary. 304. **measures,** musical accompaniment; see glossary. 317. **muse,** wonder, marvel; see glossary. 318. **respects,** considerations; see glossary. 319. **denounce,** proclaim, declare. 339. **Cousin,** any relative not a member of one's immediate family; see glossary. **puissance,** armed force. 341. **condition,** property, quality; see glossary.

SCENE II. 2. **Some airy devil.** "Aerial spirits or devils, are such as keep quarter most part in the air, cause many tempests, thunder, and lightnings, tear oaks, fire steeples, houses, strike men and beasts, make it rain stones . . . wool, frogs, &c." (Burton, *Anatomy of Melancholy*, I, 2, i, 2). 4. **breathes,** i.e., gets his breath. 5. **make up,** advance, press on.

Arth. O, this will make my mother die with grief!
K. John. [*To the Bastard*] Cousin, away for England! haste before:
And, ere our coming, see thou shake the bags
Of hoarding abbots; imprisoned angels
Set at liberty: the fat ribs of peace
Must by the hungry now be fed upon:
Use our commission in his utmost force.
Bast. Bell, book, and candle shall not drive me back,
When gold and silver becks me to come on.
I leave your highness. Grandam, I will pray,
If ever I remember to be holy,
For your fair safety; so, I kiss your hand.
Eli. Farewell, gentle cousin.
K. John. Coz, farewell. [*Exit Bastard.*]
Eli. Come hither, little kinsman; hark, a word.
K. John. Come hither, Hubert. O my gentle Hubert,
We owe thee much! within this wall of flesh
There is a soul counts thee her creditor
And with advantage means to pay thy love:
And, my good friend, thy voluntary oath
Lives in this bosom, dearly cherished.
Give me thy hand. I had a thing to say,
But I will fit it with some better tune.
By heaven, Hubert, I am almost asham'd
To say what good respect I have of thee.
Hub. I am much bounden to your majesty.
K. John. Good friend, thou hast no cause to say so yet,
But thou shalt have; and creep time ne'er so slow,
Yet it shall come for me to do thee good.
I had a thing to say, but let it go:
The sun is in the heaven, and the proud day,
Attended with the pleasures of the world,
Is all too wanton and too full of gawds
To give me audience: if the midnight bell
Did, with his iron tongue and brazen mouth,
Sound on into the drowsy race of night;
If this same were a churchyard where we stand,
And thou possessed with a thousand wrongs,
Or if that surly spirit, melancholy,
Had bak'd thy blood and made it heavy-thick,
Which else runs tickling up and down the veins,
Making that idiot, laughter, keep men's eyes
And strain their cheeks to idle merriment—
A passion hateful to my purposes;
Or if that thou couldst see me without eyes,
Hear me without thine ears, and make reply
Without a tongue, using conceit alone,
Without eyes, ears and harmful sound of words;
Then, in despite of brooded watchful day,
I would into thy bosom pour my thoughts:
But, ah, I will not! yet I love thee well;
And, by my troth, I think thou lov'st me well.
Hub. So well, that what you bid me undertake,
Though that my death were adjunct to my act,
By heaven, I would do it.
K. John. Do not I know thou wouldst?
Good Hubert, Hubert, Hubert, throw thine eye
On yon young boy: I'll tell thee what, my friend,
He is a very serpent in my way;
And wheresoe'er this foot of mine doth tread,
He lies before me: dost thou understand me?
Thou art his keeper.
Hub. And I'll keep him so,
That he shall not offend your majesty.
K. John. Death.
Hub. My lord?
K. John. A grave.
Hub. He shall not live.
K. John. Enough.
I could be merry now. Hubert, I love thee;
Well, I'll not say what I intend for thee:
Remember. Madam, fare you well:
I'll send those powers o'er to your majesty.
Eli. My blessing go with thee!
K. John. For England, cousin, go:
Hubert shall be your man, attend on you
With all true duty. On toward Calais, ho! *Exeunt.*

SCENE [IV. *The same. The French* KING'S *tent.*]

Enter [KING PHILIP of] France, [LEWIS *the*] DAUPHIN, PANDULPH, Attendants.

K. Phi. So, by a roaring tempest on the flood,
A whole armado of convicted sail
Is scattered and disjoin'd from fellowship.
Pand. Courage and comfort! all shall yet go well.
K. Phi. What can go well, when we have run so ill?
Are we not beaten? Is not Angiers lost?
Arthur ta'en prisoner? divers dear friends slain?
And bloody England into England gone,
O'erbearing interruption, spite of France?
Lew. What he hath won, that hath he fortified:
So hot a speed with such advice dispos'd,
Such temperate order in so fierce a cause,
Doth want example: who hath read or heard
Of any kindred action like to this?
K. Phi. Well could I bear that England had this praise,
So we could find some pattern of our shame.

Enter CONSTANCE.

Look, who comes here! a grave unto a soul;
Holding th' eternal spirit, against her will,
In the vile prison of afflicted breath.
I prithee, lady, go away with me.
Const. Lo, now! now see the issue of your peace.
K. Phi. Patience, good lady! comfort, gentle Constance!
Const. No, I defy all counsel, all redress,
But that which ends all counsel, true redress,
Death, death; O amiable lovely death!
Thou odoriferous stench! sound rottenness!
Arise forth from the couch of lasting night,
Thou hate and terror to prosperity,
And I will kiss thy detestable bones
And put my eyeballs in thy vaulty brows

SCENE III. 8. **angels,** gold coins; the pun is very common. 9. **fat ribs of peace,** i.e., in contrast to the skeleton of war—the *bare-ribb'd death* of V, ii, 177. 12. **Bell, book, candle,** articles used in the office of excommunication. 22. **advantage,** pecuniary profit; interest. 39. **race,** running, course; Collier and S. Walker conjecture *ear.* 50. **conceit,** wit, the mental faculty; imagination. 52. **brooded,** brooding. 71. **cousin,** i.e., Arthur.

SCENE IV. 2. **whole armado,** fleet of ships. **convicted,** doomed. 9. **O'erbearing interruption,** overthrowing resistance. 11. **So hot a speed,** so quick a success; see *speed* in glossary. **with . . . dispos'd,** i.e., carried out with such determination and judgment. 12. **temperate,** well regulated. 13. **example,** parallel instance. 16. **pattern,** precedent. 19. **prison . . . breath,** an allusion to the belief that the soul left the body from the mouth with the last expiring breath. 35. **buss,** kiss. 40. **anatomy,** i.e., the skeleton, which was the usual figure of death in pictorial representations. 42. **modern,** everyday, common-

And ring these fingers with thy household worms
And stop this gap of breath with fulsome dust
And be a carrion monster like thyself:
Come, grin on me, and I will think thou smil'st
And buss thee as thy wife. Misery's love,
O, come to me!
K. Phi. O fair affliction, peace!
Const. No, no, I will not, having breath to cry:
O, that my tongue were in the thunder's mouth!
Then with a passion would I shake the world;
And rouse from sleep that fell anatomy
Which cannot hear a lady's feeble voice,
Which scorns a modern invocation.
Pand. Lady, you utter madness, and not sorrow.
Const. Thou art not holy to belie me so;
I am not mad: this hair I tear is mine;
My name is Constance; I was Geffrey's wife;
Young Arthur is my son, and he is lost:
I am not mad: I would to heaven I were!
For then, 'tis like I should forget myself:
O, if I could, what grief should I forget!
Preach some philosophy to make me mad,
And thou shalt be canoniz'd, cardinal;
For being not mad but sensible of grief,
My reasonable part produces reason
How I may be deliver'd of these woes,
And teaches me to kill or hang myself:
If I were mad, I should forget my son,
Or madly think a babe of clouts were he:
I am not mad; too well, too well I feel
The different plague of each calamity.
K. Phi. Bind up those tresses. O, what love I note
In the fair multitude of those her hairs!
Where but by chance a silver drop hath fall'n,
Even to that drop ten thousand wiry friends
Do glue themselves in sociable grief,
Like true, inseparable, faithful loves,
Sticking together in calamity.
Const. To England, if you will.
K. Phi. Bind up your hairs.
Const. Yes, that I will; and wherefore will I do it?
I tore them from their bonds and cried aloud
'O that these hands could so redeem my son,
As they have given these hairs their liberty!'
But now I envy at their liberty,
And will again commit them to their bonds,
Because my poor child is a prisoner.
And, father cardinal, I have heard you say
That we shall see and know our friends in heaven:
If that be true, I shall see my boy again;
For since the birth of Cain, the first male child,
To him that did but yesterday suspire,
There was not such a gracious creature born.
But now will canker sorrow eat my bud
And chase the native beauty from his cheek
And he will look as hollow as a ghost,
As dim and meagre as an ague's fit,
And so he'll die; and, rising so again,
When I shall meet him in the court of heaven
I shall not know him: therefore never, never
Must I behold my pretty Arthur more.
Pand. You hold too heinous a respect of grief.
Const. He talks to me that never had a son.
K. Phi. You are as fond of grief as of your child.
Const. Grief fills the room up of my absent child,
Lies in his bed, walks up and down with me,
Puts on his pretty looks, repeats his words,
Remembers me of all his gracious parts,
Stuffs out his vacant garments with his form;
Then, have I reason to be fond of grief?
Fare you well: had you such a loss as I,
I could give better comfort than you do.
I will not keep this form upon my head,
When there is such disorder in my wit.
O Lord! my boy, my Arthur, my fair son!
My life, my joy, my food, my all the world!
My widow-comfort, and my sorrows' cure! *Exit.*
K. Phi. I fear some outrage, and I'll follow her. *Exit.*
Lew. There 's nothing in this world can make me joy:
Life is as tedious as a twice-told tale
Vexing the dull ear of a drowsy man;
And bitter shame hath spoil'd the sweet world's taste,
That it yields nought but shame and bitterness.
Pand. Before the curing of a strong disease,
Even in the instant of repair and health,
The fit is strongest; evils that take leave,
On their departure most of all show evil:
What have you lost by losing of this day?
Lew. All days of glory, joy and happiness.
Pand. If you had won it, certainly you had.
No, no; when Fortune means to men most good,
She looks upon them with a threat'ning eye.
'Tis strange to think how much King John hath lost
In this which he accounts so clearly won:
Are not you griev'd that Arthur is his prisoner?
Lew. As heartily as he is glad he hath him.
Pand. Your mind is all as youthful as your blood.
Now hear me speak with a prophetic spirit;
For even the breath of what I mean to speak
Shall blow each dust, each straw, each little rub,
Out of the path which shall directly lead
Thy foot to England's throne; and therefore mark.
John hath seiz'd Arthur; and it cannot be
That, whiles warm life plays in that infant's veins,
The misplac'd John should entertain an hour,
One minute, nay, one quiet breath of rest.
A sceptre snatch'd with an unruly hand
Must be as boisterously maintain'd as gain'd;
And he that stands upon a slipp'ry place
Makes nice of no vile hold to stay him up:
That John may stand, then Arthur needs must fall;
So be it, for it cannot be but so.
Lew. But what shall I gain by young Arthur's fall?
Pand. You, in the right of Lady Blanch your wife,
May then make all the claim that Arthur did.
Lew. And lose it, life and all, as Arthur did.
Pand. How green you are and fresh in this old world!
John lays you plots; the times conspire with you;
For he that steeps his safety in true blood
Shall find but bloody safety and untrue.

place; see glossary. 53. **sensible of,** capable of feeling; see glossary. 58. **babe of clouts,** rag doll. 68. **To England.** Many ingenious attempts have been made to explain the connection of this speech with the context, to which it has no apparent relation; the most generally accepted is that it is Constance's answer to Philip's invitation at line 20. The New Cambridge editors regard the difficulty as evidence of text revision (cf. their Introduction, xlix-l). 96. **Remembers,** reminds. 101. **keep . . . head.** Some stage business accompanies the line. Most editors introduce a stage direction here, indicating that she tears off her headdress or loosens her hair. 128. **rub,** obstacle; see glossary. 138. **Makes nice of,** is scrupulous about; see *makes* and *nice* in glossary. 146. **lays you plots,** i.e., plots by which you will profit. 147. **true blood,** blood of a true prince.

This act so evilly born shall cool the hearts
Of all his people and freeze up their zeal,
That none so small advantage shall step forth
To check his reign, but they will cherish it;
No natural exhalation in the sky,
No scope of nature, no distemper'd day,
No common wind, no customed event,
But they will pluck away his natural cause
And call them meteors, prodigies and signs,
Abortives, presages and tongues of heaven,
Plainly denouncing vengeance upon John.
Lew. May be he will not touch young Arthur's life,
But hold himself safe in his prisonment.
Pand. O, sir, when he shall hear of your approach,
If that young Arthur be not gone already,
Even at that news he dies; and then the hearts
Of all his people shall revolt from him
And kiss the lips of unacquainted change
And pick strong matter of revolt and wrath
Out of the bloody fingers' ends of John.
Methinks I see this hurly all on foot:
And, O, what better matter breeds for you
Than I have nam'd! The bastard Faulconbridge
Is now in England, ransacking the church,
Offending charity: if but a dozen French
Were there in arms, they would be as a call
To train ten thousand English to their side,
Or as a little snow, tumbled about,
Anon becomes a mountain. O noble Dauphin,
Go with me to the king: 'tis wonderful
What may be wrought out of their discontent,
Now that their souls are topfull of offence.
For England go: I will whet on the king.
Lew. Strong reasons make strong actions: let us go:
If you say ay, the king will not say no. *Exeunt.*

ACT IV.

SCENE I. [*A room in a castle.*]

Enter HUBERT *and* Executioners.

Hub. Heat me these irons hot; and look thou stand
Within the arras: when I strike my foot
Upon the bosom of the ground, rush forth,
And bind the boy which you shall find with me
Fast to the chair: be heedful: hence, and watch.
First Exec. I hope your warrant will bear out the deed.
Hub. Uncleanly scruples! fear not you: look to 't.
[*Exeunt Executioners.*]
Young lad, come forth; I have to say with you.

Enter ARTHUR.

Arth. Good morrow, Hubert.
Hub. Good morrow, little prince.
Arth. As little prince, having so great a title
To be more prince, as may be. You are sad.
Hub. Indeed, I have been merrier.
Arth. Mercy on me!
Methinks no body should be sad but I:
Yet, I remember, when I was in France,
Young gentlemen would be as sad as night,
Only for wantonness. By my christendom,
So I were out of prison and kept sheep,
I should be as merry as the day is long;
And so I would be here, but that I doubt
My uncle practises more harm to me:
He is afraid of me and I of him:
Is it my fault that I was Geffrey's son?
No, indeed, is 't not; and I would to heaven
I were your son, so you would love me, Hubert.
Hub. [*Aside*] If I talk to him, with his innocent prate
He will awake my mercy which lies dead:
Therefore I will be sudden and dispatch.
Arth. Are you sick, Hubert? you look pale to-day:
In sooth, I would you were a little sick,
That I might sit all night and watch with you:
I warrant I love you more than you do me.
Hub. [*Aside*] His words do take possession of my bosom.—
Read here, young Arthur. [*Showing a paper.*]
[*Aside*] How now, foolish rheum!
Turning dispiteous torture out of door!
I must be brief, lest resolution drop
Out at mine eyes in tender womanish tears.—
Can you not read it? is it not fair writ?
Arth. Too fairly, Hubert, for so foul effect:
Must you with hot irons burn out both mine eyes?
Hub. Young boy, I must.
Arth. And will you?
Hub. And I will.
Arth. Have you the heart? When your head did but ache,
I knit my handkercher about your brows,
The best I had, a princess wrought it me,
And I did never ask it you again;
And with my hand at midnight held your head,
And like the watchful minutes to the hour,
Still and anon cheer'd up the heavy time,
Saying, 'What lack you?' and 'Where lies your grief?'
Or 'What good love may I perform for you?'
Many a poor man's son would have lien still
And ne'er have spoke a loving word to you;
But you at your sick service had a prince.
Nay, you may think my love was crafty love
And call it cunning: do, an if you will:
If heaven be pleas'd that you must use me ill,
Why then you must. Will you put out mine eyes?
These eyes that never did nor never shall
So much as frown on you?
Hub. I have sworn to do it;
And with hot irons must I burn them out.
Arth. Ah, none but in this iron age would do it!
The iron of itself, though heat red-hot,
Approaching near these eyes, would drink my tears
And quench his fiery indignation
Even in the matter of mine innocence;
Nay, after that, consume away in rust,
But for containing fire to harm mine eye.
Are you more stubborn-hard than hammer'd iron?
An if an angel should have come to me

151. **none . . . advantage,** no opportunity, however small. 153-157. **exhalation . . . meteors.** Such phenomena were regarded as omens of disaster to princes and states; cf. *Julius Caesar*, II, ii, 30-31; *1 Henry VI*, I, i, 2. 158. **Abortives,** untimely or monstrous births. 166. **kiss . . . change,** i.e., welcome any change. 169. **hurly,** commotion. 173. **charity,** good will; also, the instruments of charity. 174. **call,** decoy. 175. **train,** attract; see glossary.

ACT IV. SCENE I. 1. **look,** take care; see glossary. 7. **Uncleanly,** improper. 10-11. **having . . . prince,** i.e., entitled to be greater. 16. **for wantonness,** out of affected behavior. **By my christendom,** as I am a Christian. 19. **doubt,** fear; see glossary. 20. **practises,** plots; see glossary. 34. **dispiteous,** pitiless. 37. **fair,** handsomely; see glossary. 52. **your sick service,** service when you were sick. 64. **matter . . . innocence,** substance which betokens my innocence—the

And told me Hubert should put out mine eyes,
I would not have believ'd him,—no tongue but
  Hubert's.
  Hub. Come forth. [*Stamps.*]

[*Enter* Executioners, *with a cord, irons, &c.*]

Do as I bid you do.
  Arth. O, save me, Hubert, save me! my eyes are out
Even with the fierce looks of these bloody men.
  Hub. Give me the iron, I say, and bind him here.
  Arth. Alas, what need you be so boist'rous-rough?
I will not struggle, I will stand stone-still.
For heaven sake, Hubert, let me not be bound!
Nay, hear me, Hubert, drive these men away,
And I will sit as quiet as a lamb;
I will not stir, nor wince, nor speak a word,
Nor look upon the iron angerly:
Thrust but these men away, and I'll forgive you,
Whatever torment you do put me to.
  Hub. Go, stand within; let me alone with him.
  First Exec. I am best pleas'd to be from such a deed.
[*Exeunt Executioners.*]
  Arth. Alas, I then have chid away my friend!
He hath a stern look, but a gentle heart:
Let him come back, that his compassion may
Give life to yours.
  Hub. Come, boy, prepare yourself.
  Arth. Is there no remedy?
  Hub. None, but to lose your eyes.
  Arth. O heaven, that there were but a mote in yours,
A grain, a dust, a gnat, a wandering hair,
Any annoyance in that precious sense!
Then feeling what small things are boisterous there,
Your vile intent must needs seem horrible.
  Hub. Is this your promise? go to, hold your tongue.
  Arth. Hubert, the utterance of a brace of tongues
Must needs want pleading for a pair of eyes:
Let me not hold my tongue, let me not, Hubert;
Or, Hubert, if you will, cut out my tongue,
So I may keep mine eyes: O, spare mine eyes,
Though to no use but still to look on you!
Lo, by my troth, the instrument is cold
And would not harm me.
  Hub. I can heat it, boy.
  Arth. No, in good sooth; the fire is dead with grief,
Being create for comfort, to be us'd
In undeserv'd extremes: see else yourself;
There is no malice in this burning coal;
The breath of heaven hath blown his spirit out
And strew'd repentant ashes on his head.
  Hub. But with my breath I can revive it, boy.
  Arth. An if you do, you will but make it blush
And glow with shame of your proceedings, Hubert:
Nay, it perchance will sparkle in your eyes;
And like a dog that is compell'd to fight,
Snatch at his master that doth tarre him on.
All things that you should use to do me wrong
Deny their office: only you do lack
That mercy which fierce fire and iron extends,
Creatures of note for mercy-lacking uses.
  Hub. Well, see to live; I will not touch thine eye
For all the treasure that thine uncle owes:
Yet am I sworn and I did purpose, boy,
With this same very iron to burn them out.
  Arth. O, now you look like Hubert! all this while
You were disguised.
  Hub. Peace; no more. Adieu.
Your uncle must not know but you are dead;
I'll fill these dogged spies with false reports:
And, pretty child, sleep doubtless and secure,
That Hubert, for the wealth of all the world,
Will not offend thee.
  Arth. O heaven! I thank you, Hubert.
  Hub. Silence; no more: go closely in with me:
Much danger do I undergo for thee. *Exeunt.*

SCENE II. [KING JOHN'S *palace.*]

Enter [KING] JOHN, PEMBROKE, SALISBURY, *and other* Lords.

  K. John. Here once again we sit, once again
  crown'd,
And look'd upon, I hope, with cheerful eyes.
  Pem. This 'once again,' but that your highness
  pleas'd,
Was once superfluous: you were crown'd before,
And that high royalty was ne'er pluck'd off,
The faiths of men ne'er stained with revolt;
Fresh expectation troubled not the land
With any long'd-for change or better state.
  Sal. Therefore, to be possess'd with double pomp,
To guard a title that was rich before,
To gild refined gold, to paint the lily,
To throw a perfume on the violet,
To smooth the ice, or add another hue
Unto the rainbow, or with taper-light
To seek the beauteous eye of heaven to garnish,
Is wasteful and ridiculous excess.
  Pem. But that your royal pleasure must be done,
This act is as an ancient tale new told,
And in the last repeating troublesome,
Being urged at a time unseasonable.
  Sal. In this the antique and well noted face
Of plain old form is much disfigured;
And, like a shifted wind unto a sail,
It makes the course of thoughts to fetch about,
Startles and frights consideration,
Makes sound opinion sick and truth suspected,
For putting on so new a fashion'd robe.
  Pem. When workmen strive to do better than well,
They do confound their skill in covetousness;
And oftentimes excusing of a fault
Doth make the fault the worse by the excuse,
As patches set upon a little breach
Discredit more in hiding of the fault
Than did the fault before it was so patch'd.
  Sal. To this effect, before you were new crown'd,
We breath'd our counsel: but it pleas'd your highness
To overbear it, and we are all well pleas'd,
Since all and every part of what we would
Doth make a stand at what your highness will.

water of my tears (Moore-Smith). 92. **mote,** minute particle of anything. 99. **want pleading,** be inadequate to plead sufficiently. 107. **create,** created. 108. **extremes,** i.e., extreme cruelties. 117. **tarre,** provoke, incite. 119. **Deny,** refuse to do; see glossary. 121. **Creatures . . . uses,** things (i.e., fire and iron) noted as instruments of torture. 130. **doubtless,** fearless. 133. **closely,** secretly.

SCENE II. 9. **be possess'd,** have possession of; see *possess* in glossary. 10. **guard,** trim, ornament; also, protect. 24. **fetch about,** change direction, tack. 25. **consideration,** reflection, i.e., on matters of state. 26. **opinion,** reputation, credit. 29. **confound,** destroy, disrupt. **in covetousness,** i.e., by their greedy desire to do better. 36. **breath'd,** spoke. 37. **overbear,** overrule. 39. **Doth . . . will,** may go no further than what your highness desires.

K. John. Some reasons of this double coronation
I have possess'd you with and think them strong;
And more, more strong, then lesser is my fear,
I shall indue you with: meantime but ask
What you would have reform'd that is not well,
And well shall you perceive how willingly
I will both hear and grant you your requests.
Pem. Then I, as one that am the tongue of these
To sound the purposes of all their hearts,
Both for myself and them, but, chief of all,
Your safety, for the which myself and them
Bend their best studies, heartily request
Th' enfranchisement of Arthur; whose restraint
Doth move the murmuring lips of discontent
To break into this dangerous argument,—
If what in rest you have in right you hold,
Why then your fears, which, as they say, attend
The steps of wrong, should move you to mew up
Your tender kinsman and to choke his days
With barbarous ignorance and deny his youth
The rich advantage of good exercise?
That the time's enemies may not have this
To grace occasions, let it be our suit
That you have bid us ask his liberty;
Which for our goods we do no further ask
Than whereupon our weal, on you depending,
Counts it your weal he have his liberty.

Enter HUBERT.

K. John. Let it be so: I do commit his youth
To your direction. Hubert, what news with you?
[*Taking him apart.*]
Pem. This is the man should do the bloody deed;
He show'd his warrant to a friend of mine:
The image of a wicked heinous fault
Lives in his eye; that close aspect of his
Does show the mood of a much troubled breast;
And I do fearfully believe 'tis done,
What we so fear'd he had a charge to do.
Sal. The colour of the king doth come and go
Between his purpose and his conscience,
Like heralds 'twixt two dreadful battles set:
His passion is so ripe, it needs must break.
Pem. And when it breaks, I fear will issue thence
The foul corruption of a sweet child's death.
K. John. We cannot hold mortality's strong hand:
Good lords, although my will to give is living,
The suit which you demand is gone and dead:
He tells us Arthur is deceas'd to-night.
Sal. Indeed we fear'd his sickness was past cure.
Pem. Indeed we heard how near his death he was
Before the child himself felt he was sick:
This must be answer'd either here or hence.
K. John. Why do you bend such solemn brows on
me?
Think you I bear the shears of destiny?
Have I commandment on the pulse of life?
Sal. It is apparent foul play; and 'tis shame
That greatness should so grossly offer it:
So thrive it in your game! and so, farewell.
Pem. Stay yet, Lord Salisbury; I'll go with thee,
And find th' inheritance of this poor child,
His little kingdom of a forced grave.
That blood which ow'd the breadth of all this isle,
Three foot of it doth hold: bad world the while!
This must not be thus borne: this will break out
To all our sorrows, and ere long I doubt. *Exeunt* [*Lords*].
K. John. They burn in indignation. I repent:
There is no sure foundation set on blood,
No certain life achiev'd by others' death.—

Enter Messenger.

A fearful eye thou hast: where is that blood
That I have seen inhabit in those cheeks?
So foul a sky clears not without a storm:
Pour down thy weather: how goes all in France?
Mess. From France to England. Never such a
pow'r
For any foreign preparation
Was levied in the body of a land.
The copy of your speed is learn'd by them;
For when you should be told they do prepare,
The tidings comes that they are all arriv'd.
K. John. O, where hath our intelligence been drunk?
Where hath it slept? Where is my mother's care,
That such an army could be drawn in France,
And she not hear of it?
Mess. My liege, her ear
Is stopp'd with dust; the first of April died
Your noble mother: and, as I hear, my lord,
The Lady Constance in a frenzy died
Three days before: but this from rumour's tongue
I idly heard; if true or false I know not.
K. John. Withhold thy speed, dreadful occasion!
O, make a league with me, till I have pleas'd
My discontented peers! What! mother dead!
How wildly then walks my estate in France!
Under whose conduct came those pow'rs of France
That thou for truth giv'st out are landed here?
Mess. Under the Dauphin.
K. John. Thou hast made me giddy
With these ill tidings.

Enter [*the*] BASTARD *and* PETER *of Pomfret.*

Now, what says the world
To your proceedings? do not seek to stuff
My head with more ill news, for it is full.
Bast. But if you be afeard to hear the worst,
Then let the worst unheard fall on your head.
K. John. Bear with me, cousin; for I was amaz'd
Under the tide: but now I breathe again
Aloft the flood, and can give audience
To any tongue, speak it of what it will.
Bast. How I have sped among the clergymen,
The sums I have collected shall express.
But as I travell'd hither through the land,
I find the people strangely fantasied;
Possess'd with rumours, full of idle dreams,
Not knowing what they fear, but full of fear:
And here 's a prophet, that I brought with me
From forth the streets of Pomfret, whom I found
With many hundreds treading on his heels;

42. **And more,** i.e., more reasons. 43. **indue,** furnish. 55. **in rest,** in security. 57. **mew up,** imprison; see glossary. 61. **the time's enemies,** enemies of the present state of affairs. 64. **goods,** i.e., our good, equivalent to *weal* in the next line. 72. **close,** uncommunicative, secret; see glossary. 78. **battles,** armies; see glossary. 84. **demand,** request; see glossary. 89. **answer'd,** atoned for; see glossary. 93. **apparent,** evident; see glossary. 94. **That . . . it,** i.e., that a king should flaunt foul play so flagrantly. 95. **So . . . game,** may your schemes lead to the same (bad) end. 97-100. **inheritance . . . hold.** The contrast between the greatness of kingdoms and the smallness of the graves of kings was a Renaissance commonplace; cf. *Richard II*, III, iii, 153-154. 109. **weather,** storm, tempest. 113. **copy,** example; see glossary. 116. **our intelligence,** our spies. 125. **occasion,** course of events (Onions); hour of trial (John). 137. **amaz'd,** bewildered.

To whom he sung, in rude harsh-sounding rhymes,
That, ere the next Ascension-day at noon,
Your highness should deliver up your crown.
K. John. Thou idle dreamer, wherefore didst thou so?
Peter. Foreknowing that the truth will fall out so.
K. John. Hubert, away with him; imprison him;
And on that day at noon, whereon he says
I shall yield up my crown, let him be hang'd.
Deliver him to safety; and return,
For I must use thee. [*Exit Hubert with Peter.*]
O my gentle cousin,
Hear'st thou the news abroad, who are arriv'd?
Bast. The French, my lord; men's mouths are full of it:
Besides, I met Lord Bigot and Lord Salisbury,
With eyes as red as new-enkindled fire,
And others more, going to seek the grave
Of Arthur, whom they say is kill'd to-night
On your suggestion.
K. John. Gentle kinsman, go,
And thrust thyself into their companies:
I have a way to win their loves again;
Bring them before me.
Bast. I will seek them out.
K. John. Nay, but make haste; the better foot before.
O, let me have no subject enemies,
When adverse foreigners affright my towns
With dreadful pomp of stout invasion!
Be Mercury, set feathers to thy heels,
And fly like thought from them to me again.
Bast. The spirit of the time shall teach me speed. *Exit.*
K. John. Spoke like a sprightful noble gentleman.
Go after him; for he perhaps shall need
Some messenger betwixt me and the peers;
And be thou he.
Mess. With all my heart, my liege. [*Exit.*]
K. John. My mother dead!

Enter HUBERT.

Hub. My lord, they say five moons were seen to-night;
Four fixed, and the fifth did whirl about
The other four in wondrous motion.
K. John. Five moons!
Hub. Old men and beldams in the streets
Do prophesy upon it dangerously:
Young Arthur's death is common in their mouths:
And when they talk of him, they shake their heads
And whisper one another in the ear;
And he that speaks doth gripe the hearer's wrist,
Whilst he that hears makes fearful action,
With wrinkled brows, with nods, with rolling eyes.
I saw a smith stand with his hammer, thus,
The whilst his iron did on the anvil cool,
With open mouth swallowing a tailor's news;
Who, with his shears and measure in his hand,
Standing on slippers, which his nimble haste
Had falsely thrust upon contrary feet,
Told of a many thousand warlike French
That were embattailed and rank'd in Kent:
Another lean unwash'd artificer
Cuts off his tale and talks of Arthur's death.
K. John. Why seek'st thou to possess me with these fears?
Why urgest thou so oft young Arthur's death?
Thy hand hath murd'red him: I had a mighty cause
To wish him dead, but thou hadst none to kill him.
Hub. No had, my lord! why, did you not provoke me?
K. John. It is the curse of kings to be attended
By slaves that take their humours for a warrant
To break within the bloody house of life,
And on the winking of authority
To understand a law, to know the meaning
Of dangerous majesty, when perchance it frowns
More upon humour than advis'd respect.
Hub. Here is your hand and seal for what I did.
K. John. O, when the last account 'twixt heaven and earth
Is to be made, then shall this hand and seal
Witness against us to damnation!
How oft the sight of means to do ill deeds
Make deeds ill done! Hadst not thou been by,
A fellow by the hand of nature mark'd,
Quoted and sign'd to do a deed of shame,
This murder had not come into my mind:
But taking note of thy abhorr'd aspect,
Finding thee fit for bloody villany,
Apt, liable to be employ'd in danger,
I faintly broke with thee of Arthur's death;
And thou, to be endeared to a king,
Made it no conscience to destroy a prince.
Hub. My lord,—
K. John. Hadst thou but shook thy head or made a pause
When I spake darkly what I purposed,
Or turn'd an eye of doubt upon my face,
As bid me tell my tale in express words,
Deep shame had struck me dumb, made me break off,
And those thy fears might have wrought fears in me:
But thou didst understand me by my signs
And didst in signs again parley with sin;
Yea, without stop, didst let thy heart consent,
And consequently thy rude hand to act
The deed, which both our tongues held vile to name.
Out of my sight, and never see me more!
My nobles leave me; and my state is brav'd,
Even at my gates, with ranks of foreign pow'rs:
Nay, in the body of this fleshly land,
This kingdom, this confine of blood and breath,
Hostility and civil tumult reigns
Between my conscience and my cousin's death.
Hub. Arm you against your other enemies,
I'll make a peace between your soul and you.
Young Arthur is alive: this hand of mine
Is yet a maiden and an innocent hand,

144. **fantasied,** full of strange fancies; see glossary. 158. **safety,** safe keeping. 174. **set feathers,** an allusion to Mercury's winged sandals. 177. **sprightful,** spirited. 185. **beldams,** old women. 198. **falsely,** improperly, wrongly; see glossary. 200. **embattailed,** drawn up in battle array. 207. **No had,** had I not. 210. **bloody . . . life,** the body animated by life blood; possibly, the body become bloody. 211. **winking of authority,** the merest hint (or perhaps the oversight) of the person in authority, the king. 215. **your hand and seal,** the *warrant* referred to in line 70. 227. **broke with,** i.e., broached the subject. 243. **my state is brav'd,** my power is challenged. 245-246. **body . . . breath.** The figure is the common one of the microcosm, in which man is conceived as the epitome of the universe. 246. **confine,** territorial limit; also, prison.

Not painted with the crimson spots of blood.
Within this bosom never ent'red yet
The dreadful motion of a murderous thought;
And you have slander'd nature in my form,
Which, howsoever rude exteriorly,
Is yet the cover of a fairer mind
Than to be butcher of an innocent child.
K. John. Doth Arthur live? O, haste thee to the peers,
Throw this report on their incensed rage,
And make them tame to their obedience!
Forgive the comment that my passion made
Upon thy feature; for my rage was blind,
And foul imaginary eyes of blood
Presented thee more hideous than thou art.
O, answer not, but to my closet bring
The angry lords with all expedient haste.
I conjure thee but slowly; run more fast. *Exeunt.*

SCENE III. [*Before the castle.*]

Enter ARTHUR, *on the walls.*

Arth. The wall is high, and yet will I leap down:
Good ground, be pitiful and hurt me not!
There 's few or none do know me: if they did,
This ship-boy's semblance hath disguis'd me quite.
I am afraid; and yet I'll venture it.
If I get down, and do not break my limbs,
I'll find a thousand shifts to get away:
As good to die and go, as die and stay. [*Leaps down.*]
O me! my uncle's spirit is in these stones:
Heaven take my soul, and England keep my bones! *Dies.*

Enter PEMBROKE, SALISBURY, *and* BIGOT.

Sal. Lords, I will meet him at Saint Edmundsbury:
It is our safety, and we must embrace
This gentle offer of the perilous time.
Pem. Who brought that letter from the cardinal?
Sal. The Count Melun, a noble lord of France;
Whose private with me of the Dauphin's love
Is much more general than these lines import.
Big. To-morrow morning let us meet him then.
Sal. Or rather then set forward; for 'twill be
Two long days' journey, lords, or ere we meet.

Enter [*the*] BASTARD.

Bast. Once more to-day well met, distemper'd lords!
The king by me requests your presence straight.
Sal. The king hath dispossess'd himself of us:
We will not line his thin bestained cloak
With our pure honours, nor attend the foot
That leaves the print of blood where'er it walks.
Return and tell him so: we know the worst.
Bast. Whate'er you think, good words, I think, were best.
Sal. Our griefs, and not our manners, reason now.
Bast. But there is little reason in your grief;
Therefore 'twere reason you had manners now.
Pem. Sir, sir, impatience hath his privilege.
Bast. 'Tis true, to hurt his master, no man else.
Sal. This is the prison. What is he lies here? [*Seeing Arthur.*]
Pem. O death, made proud with pure and princely beauty!
The earth had not a hole to hide this deed.
Sal. Murder, as hating what himself hath done,
Doth lay it open to urge on revenge.
Big. Or, when he doom'd this beauty to a grave,
Found it too precious-princely for a grave.
Sal. Sir Richard, what think you? have you beheld,
Or have you read or heard? or could you think?
Or do you almost think, although you see,
That you do see? could thought, without this object,
Form such another? This is the very top,
The height, the crest, or crest unto the crest,
Of murder's arms: this is the bloodiest shame,
The wildest savagery, the vilest stroke,
That ever wall-ey'd wrath or staring rage
Presented to the tears of soft remorse.
Pem. All murders past do stand excus'd in this;
And this, so sole and so unmatchable,
Shall give a holiness, a purity,
To the yet unbegotten sin of times;
And prove a deadly bloodshed but a jest,
Exampled by this heinous spectacle.
Bast. It is a damned and a bloody work;
The graceless action of a heavy hand,
If that it be the work of any hand.
Sal. If that it be the work of any hand!
We had a kind of light what would ensue:
It is the shameful work of Hubert's hand;
The practice and the purpose of the king:
From whose obedience I forbid my soul,
Kneeling before this ruin of sweet life,
And breathing to his breathless excellence
The incense of a vow, a holy vow,
Never to taste the pleasures of the world,
Never to be infected with delight,
Nor conversant with ease and idleness,
Till I have set a glory to this hand,
By giving it the worship of revenge.
Pem. } *Big.* } Our souls religiously confirm thy words.

Enter HUBERT.

Hub. Lords, I am hot with haste in seeking you:
Arthur doth live; the king hath sent for you.
Sal. O, he is bold and blushes not at death.
Avaunt, thou hateful villain, get thee gone!
Hub. I am no villain.
Sal. Must I rob the law? [*Drawing his sword.*]
Bast. Your sword is bright, sir; put it up again.
Sal. Not till I sheathe it in a murderer's skin.
Hub. Stand back, Lord Salisbury, stand back, I say;
By heaven, I think my sword 's as sharp as yours:
I would not have you, lord, forget yourself,

255. **motion,** impulse, prompting; see glossary. 269. **conjure,** beseech, influence (used quibblingly perhaps).
SCENE III. 7. **shifts,** stratagems; see glossary. 16. **private with me,** private communication to me (generally accepted); the New Cambridge editors suggest as emendation *private warrant.* 20. **or ere,** before; see *or* in glossary. 38. **lay . . . open,** display, expose. 49. **wall-ey'd,** having defective eyes which appear to glare fiercely. 54. **times,** i.e., future times. 63. **practice,** plot, treachery; see glossary. 70. **ease,** inactivity, leisure; see glossary. 71. **glory,** i.e., halo around Arthur's hand; or, splendor. **this hand,** either Arthur's hand, or Salisbury's own hand, which he raises in taking an oath. 79. **bright,** unused (said contemptuously); cf. *Othello,* I, ii, 59. 84. **tempt,** risk. 90. **prove me so,** i.e., make me a murderer by tempting me to kill you. 94. **gall,** wound. 98. **betime,** promptly. 99. **toasting-iron,** sword (used contemptuously). 101. **renowned Faulconbridge.** Salisbury in this scornful belittlement of the Bastard taunts him with illegitimacy and refuses to

Nor tempt the danger of my true defence;
Lest I, by marking of your rage, forget
Your worth, your greatness and nobility.
Big. Out, dunghill! dar'st thou brave a nobleman?
Hub. Not for my life: but yet I dare defend
My innocent life against an emperor.
Sal. Thou art a murderer.
Hub. Do not prove me so;
Yet I am none: whose tongue soe'er speaks false,
Not truly speaks; who speaks not truly, lies.
Pem. Cut him to pieces.
Bast. Keep the peace, I say.
Sal. Stand by, or I shall gall you, Faulconbridge.
Bast. Thou wert better gall the devil, Salisbury:
If thou but frown on me, or stir thy foot,
Or teach thy hasty spleen to do me shame,
I'll strike thee dead. Put up thy sword betime;
Or I'll so maul you and your toasting-iron,
That you shall think the devil is come from hell.
Big. What wilt thou do, renowned Faulconbridge?
Second a villain and a murderer?
Hub. Lord Bigot, I am none.
Big. Who kill'd this prince?
Hub. 'Tis not an hour since I left him well:
I honour'd him, I lov'd him, and will weep
My date of life out for his sweet life's loss.
Sal. Trust not those cunning waters of his eyes,
For villany is not without such rheum;
And he, long traded in it, makes it seem
Like rivers of remorse and innocency.
Away with me, all you whose souls abhor
Th' uncleanly savours of a slaughter-house;
For I am stifled with this smell of sin.
Big. Away toward Bury, to the Dauphin there!
Pem. There tell the king he may inquire us out.
Exeunt Lords.
Bast. Here 's a good world! Knew you of this fair work?
Beyond the infinite and boundless reach
Of mercy, if thou didst this deed of death,
Art thou damn'd, Hubert.
Hub. Do but hear me, sir.
Bast. Ha! I'll tell thee what;
Thou 'rt damn'd as black—nay, nothing is so black;
Thou art more deep damn'd than Prince Lucifer:
There is not yet so ugly a fiend of hell
As thou shalt be, if thou didst kill this child.
Hub. Upon my soul—
Bast. If thou didst but consent
To this most cruel act, do but despair;
And if thou want'st a cord, the smallest thread
That ever spider twisted from her womb
Will serve to strangle thee; a rush will be a beam
To hang thee on; or wouldst thou drown thyself,
Put but a little water in a spoon,
And it shall be as all the ocean,
Enough to stifle such a villain up.
I do suspect thee very grievously.
Hub. If I in act, consent, or sin of thought,
Be guilty of the stealing that sweet breath
Which was embounded in this beauteous clay,
Let hell want pains enough to torture me.
I left him well.
Bast. Go, bear him in thine arms.
I am amaz'd, methinks, and lose my way
Among the thorns and dangers of this world.
How easy dost thou take all England up!
From forth this morsel of dead royalty,
The life, the right and truth of all this realm
Is fled to heaven; and England now is left
To tug and scamble and to part by th' teeth
The unowed interest of proud-swelling state.
Now for the bare-pick'd bone of majesty
Doth dogged war bristle his angry crest
And snarleth in the gentle eyes of peace:
Now powers from home and discontents at home
Meet in one line; and vast confusion waits,
As doth a raven on a sick-fall'n beast,
The imminent decay of wrested pomp.
Now happy he whose cloak and cincture can
Hold out this tempest. Bear away that child
And follow me with speed: I'll to the king:
A thousand businesses are brief in hand,
And heaven itself doth frown upon the land. *Exeunt.*

ACT [V.]

SCENE I. [KING JOHN'S *palace.*]

Enter KING JOHN *and* PANDULPH, [*with*] Attendants.

K. John. Thus have I yielded up into your hand
The circle of my glory. [*Giving the crown.*]
Pand. Take again
From this my hand, as holding of the pope
Your sovereign greatness and authority.
K. John. Now keep your holy word: go meet the French,
And from his holiness use all your power
To stop their marches 'fore we are inflam'd.
Our discontented counties do revolt;
Our people quarrel with obedience,
Swearing allegiance and the love of soul
To stranger blood, to foreign royalty.
This inundation of mistemp'red humour
Rests by you only to be qualified:
Then pause not; for the present time 's so sick,
That present med'cine must be minist'red,
Or overthrow incurable ensues.
Pand. It was my breath that blew this tempest up,
Upon your stubborn usage of the pope;
But since you are a gentle convertite,
My tongue shall hush again this storm of war
And make fair weather in your blust'ring land.
On this Ascension-day, remember well,
Upon your oath of service to the pope,
Go I to make the French lay down their arms. *Exit.*
K. John. Is this Ascension-day? Did not the prophet
Say that before Ascension-day at noon
My crown I should get off? Even so I have:

recognize his newly received knighthood. 106. **date,** duration; see glossary. 122. **Prince Lucifer,** Satan, prince of the rebel angels who were expelled from heaven. 146. **scamble,** scramble, acquire by undignified means. 151. **from home,** i.e., foreign. 152. **waits,** waits for. 154. **wrested pomp,** usurped majesty. Ivor John notes that *Usurpyd Power* was one of the characters in Bale's *Kyng Johan.* 155. **cincture,** belt. 158. **are brief in hand,** demand immediate action.

ACT V. SCENE I. 3. **as . . . pope.** John, in receiving his crown back, acknowledges the supremacy of the pope as the highest prince in Christendom. **holding,** property held by lease. 8. **counties,** shires; possibly nobles. 10. **love of soul,** most sincere love. 12-13. **inundation . . . qualified,** excess of one humor is to be reduced to its right proportion (*qualified*). 15. **present,** prompt; see glossary. 19. **convertite,** convert.

I did suppose it should be on constraint;
But, heav'n be thank'd, it is but voluntary.

Enter [*the*] BASTARD.

Bast. All Kent hath yielded; nothing there holds out
But Dover castle: London hath receiv'd,
Like a kind host, the Dauphin and his powers:
Your nobles will not hear you, but are gone
To offer service to your enemy,
And wild amazement hurries up and down
The little number of your doubtful friends.

K. John. Would not my lords return to me again,
After they heard young Arthur was alive?

Bast. They found him dead and cast into the streets,
An empty casket, where the jewel of life
By some damn'd hand was robb'd and ta'en away.

K. John. That villain Hubert told me he did live.

Bast. So, on my soul, he did, for aught he knew.
But wherefore do you droop? why look you sad?
Be great in act, as you have been in thought;
Let not the world see fear and sad distrust
Govern the motion of a kingly eye:
Be stirring as the time; be fire with fire;
Threaten the threat'ner and outface the brow
Of bragging horror: so shall inferior eyes,
That borrow their behaviours from the great,
Grow great by your example and put on
The dauntless spirit of resolution.
Away, and glister like the god of war,
When he intendeth to become the field:
Show boldness and aspiring confidence.
What, shall they seek the lion in his den,
And fright him there? and make him tremble there?
O, let it not be said: forage, and run
To meet displeasure farther from the doors,
And grapple with him ere he come so nigh.

K. John. The legate of the pope hath been with me,
And I have made a happy peace with him;
And he hath promis'd to dismiss the powers
Led by the Dauphin.

Bast. O inglorious league!
Shall we, upon the footing of our land,
Send fair-play orders and make compromise,
Insinuation, parley and base truce
To arms invasive? shall a beardless boy,
A cock'red silken wanton, brave our fields,
And flesh his spirit in a warlike soil,
Mocking the air with colours idly spread,
And find no check? Let us, my liege, to arms:
Perchance the cardinal cannot make your peace;
Or if he do, let it at least be said
They saw we had a purpose of defence.

K. John. Have thou the ordering of this present time.

Bast. Away, then, with good courage! yet, I know,
Our party may well meet a prouder foe. *Exeunt.*

SCENE II. [*The* DAUPHIN'S *camp at St. Edmundsbury.*]

Enter, in arms, [LEWIS *the*] DAUPHIN, SALISBURY, MELUN, PEMBROKE, BIGOT, Soldiers.

Lew. My Lord Melun, let this be copied out,
And keep it safe for our remembrance:
Return the precedent to these lords again;
That, having our fair order written down,
Both they and we, perusing o'er these notes,
May know wherefore we took the sacrament
And keep our faiths firm and inviolable.

Sal. Upon our sides it never shall be broken.
And, noble Dauphin, albeit we swear
A voluntary zeal and an unurg'd faith
To your proceedings; yet believe me, prince,
I am not glad that such a sore of time
Should seek a plaster by contemn'd revolt,
And heal the inveterate canker of one wound
By making many. O, it grieves my soul,
That I must draw this metal from my side
To be a widow-maker! O, and there
Where honourable rescue and defence
Cries out upon the name of Salisbury!
But such is the infection of the time,
That, for the health and physic of our right,
We cannot deal but with the very hand
Of stern injustice and confused wrong.
And is 't not pity, O my grieved friends,
That we, the sons and children of this isle,
Were born to see so sad an hour as this;
Wherein we step after a stranger march
Upon her gentle bosom, and fill up
Her enemies' ranks,—I must withdraw and weep
Upon the spot of this enforced cause,—
To grace the gentry of a land remote,
And follow unacquainted colours here?
What, here? O nation, that thou couldst remove!
That Neptune's arms, who clippeth thee about,
Would bear thee from the knowledge of thyself,
And cripple thee unto a pagan shore;
Where these two Christian armies might combine
The blood of malice in a vein of league,
And not to spend it so unneighbourly!

Lew. A noble temper dost thou show in this;
And great affections wrestling in thy bosom
Doth make an earthquake of nobility.
O, what a noble combat hast thou fought
Between compulsion and a brave respect!
Let me wipe off this honourable dew,
That silverly doth progress on thy cheeks:
My heart hath melted at a lady's tears,
Being an ordinary inundation;
But this effusion of such manly drops,
This show'r, blown up by tempest of the soul,
Startles mine eyes, and makes me more amaz'd
Than had I seen the vaulty top of heaven
Figur'd quite o'er with burning meteors.
Lift up thy brow, renowned Salisbury,
And with a great heart heave away this storm:
Commend these waters to those baby eyes
That never saw the giant world enrag'd;

36. **doubtful,** not to be relied on; fearful. 55. **become,** grace, adorn. 68. **Insinuation,** act of currying favor, self-ingratiation. 70. **cock'red . . . wanton,** spoiled child. 71. **flesh,** initiate in or inure to bloodshed (Onions); make savage by a foretaste of flesh (John); see glossary. 73. **check,** restraint; see glossary.

SCENE II. 1. **this,** the agreement with the English lords; cf. lines 30-34 of the preceding scene. 3. **precedent,** original document. 19. **Cries out upon,** appeals to. 21. **physic,** medical cure. 30. **spot,** stain, blot. **enforced cause,** i.e., cause into which I am forced. 31. **grace,** honor; see glossary. 32. **unacquainted colours,** i.e., the banners of a foreign power. 34. **clippeth,** embraces; see glossary. 36. **cripple,** disable. (Often emended to *grapple*, as in Globe.) 44. **compulsion,** what you are compelled to do. 52. **had I seen,** if I had seen; an instance of the subjunctive used conditionally; see Abbott, 361. 64. **an angel spake.** There are several explanations: that the remark is prompted by the entrance of the papal legate with the *warrant from the*

Nor met with fortune other than at feasts,
Full of warm blood, of mirth, of gossiping.
Come, come; for thou shalt thrust thy hand as deep
Into the purse of rich prosperity
As Lewis himself: so, nobles, shall you all,
That knit your sinews to the strength of mine.

Enter PANDULPH.

And even there, methinks, an angel spake:
Look, where the holy legate comes apace,
To give us warrant from the hand of heaven,
And on our actions set the name of right
With holy breath.
Pand. Hail, noble prince of France!
The next is this, King John hath reconcil'd
Himself to Rome; his spirit is come in,
That so stood out against the holy church,
The great metropolis and see of Rome:
Therefore thy threat'ning colours now wind up;
And tame the savage spirit of wild war,
That, like a lion fostered up at hand,
It may lie gently at the foot of peace,
And be no further harmful than in show.
Lew. Your grace shall pardon me, I will not back:
I am too high-born to be propertied,
To be a secondary at control,
Or useful serving-man and instrument,
To any sovereign state throughout the world.
Your breath first kindled the dead coal of wars
Between this chastis'd kingdom and myself,
And brought in matter that should feed this fire;
And now 'tis far too huge to be blown out
With that same weak wind which enkindled it.
You taught me how to know the face of right,
Acquainted me with interest to this land,
Yea, thrust this enterprise into my heart;
And come ye now to tell me John hath made
His peace with Rome? What is that peace to me?
I, by the honour of my marriage-bed,
After young Arthur, claim this land for mine;
And, now it is half-conquer'd, must I back
Because that John hath made his peace with Rome?
Am I Rome's slave? What penny hath Rome borne,
What men provided, what munition sent,
To underprop this action? Is 't not I
That undergo this charge? who else but I,
And such as to my claim are liable,
Sweat in this business and maintain this war?
Have I not heard these islanders shout out
'Vive le roi!' as I have bank'd their towns?
Have I not here the best cards for the game,
To win this easy match play'd for a crown?
And shall I now give o'er the yielded set?
No, no, on my soul, it never shall be said.
Pand. You look but on the outside of this work.
Lew. Outside or inside, I will not return
Till my attempt so much be glorified
As to my ample hope was promised
Before I drew this gallant head of war,
And cull'd these fiery spirits from the world,
To outlook conquest and to win renown
Even in the jaws of danger and of death.
[*Trumpet sounds.*]
What lusty trumpet thus doth summon us?

Enter [*the*] BASTARD.

Bast. According to the fair play of the world,
Let me have audience; I am sent to speak:
My holy lord of Milan, from the king
I come, to learn how you have dealt for him;
And, as you answer, I do know the scope
And warrant limited unto my tongue.
Pand. The Dauphin is too wilful-opposite,
And will not temporize with my entreaties;
He flatly says he'll not lay down his arms.
Bast. By all the blood that ever fury breath'd,
The youth says well. Now hear our English king;
For thus his royalty doth speak in me.
He is prepar'd, and reason too he should:
This apish and unmannerly approach,
This harness'd masque and unadvised revel,
This unhair'd sauciness and boyish troops,
The king doth smile at; and is well prepar'd
To whip this dwarfish war, these pigmy arms,
From out the circle of his territories.
That hand which had the strength, even at your door,
To cudgel you and make you take the hatch,
To dive like buckets in concealed wells,
To crouch in litter of your stable planks,
To lie like pawns lock'd up in chests and trunks,
To hug with swine, to seek sweet safety out
In vaults and prisons, and to thrill and shake
Even at the crying of your nation's crow,
Thinking his voice an armed Englishman;
Shall that victorious hand be feebled here,
That in your chambers gave you chastisement?
No: know the gallant monarch is in arms
And like an eagle o'er his aery towers,
To souse annoyance that comes near his nest.
And you degenerate, you ingrate revolts,
You bloody Neroes, ripping up the womb
Of your dear mother England, blush for shame;
For your own ladies and pale-visag'd maids
Like Amazons come tripping after drums,
Their thimbles into armed gauntlets change,
Their needles to lances, and their gentle hearts
To fierce and bloody inclination.
Lew. There end thy brave, and turn thy face in peace;
We grant thou canst outscold us: fare thee well;
We hold our time too precious to be spent
With such a brabbler.
Pand. Give me leave to speak.
Bast. No, I will speak.
Lew. We will attend to neither.
Strike up the drums; and let the tongue of war
Plead for our interest and our being here.
Bast. Indeed, your drums, being beaten, will cry out;

hand of heaven (Malone); that it refers to a trumpet fanfare announcing the legate's arrival (Cowden Clarke, adopted by the New Cambridge editors, who introduce the stage direction, *a trumpet sounds*). The pun on *angel*, a coin (cf. III, iii, 8), is suggested by the words *purse* and *nobles* (gold coins) above. The Cambridge editors regarded the line as an "aside" contemptuously alluding to the dauphin's mercenary allies. 79. **propertied,** made a tool of. 89. **interest,** title, right. 101. **liable,** subject. 104. **bank'd,** coasted, skirted. 107. **give o'er,** abandon. **the yielded set,** the game already won; a figure from tennis or cards. 115. **outlook,** stare down. 125. **temporize,** come to an agreement. 132. **harness'd,** i.e., in armor. 133. **unhair'd,** beardless. 138. **take the hatch,** leap over the lower half door; i.e., make a hasty and undignified retreat. 141. **pawns,** things in pawn. 150. **souse,** to swoop down upon (as a bird of prey). 151. **revolts,** rebels. 159. **thy brave,** defiant boast.

And so shall you, being beaten: do but start
An echo with the clamour of thy drum,
And even at hand a drum is ready brac'd
That shall reverberate all as loud as thine;
Sound but another, and another shall
As loud as thine rattle the welkin's ear
And mock the deep-mouth'd thunder: for at hand,
Not trusting to this halting legate here,
Whom he hath us'd rather for sport than need,
Is warlike John; and in his forehead sits
A bare-ribb'd death, whose office is this day
To feast upon whole thousands of the French.
Lew. Strike up your drums, to find this danger out.
Bast. And thou shalt find it, Dauphin, do not doubt.
Exeunt.

SCENE III. [*The field of battle.*]

Alarums. Enter [KING] JOHN *and* HUBERT.

K. John. How goes the day with us? O, tell me, Hubert.
Hub. Badly, I fear. How fares your majesty?
K. John. This fever, that hath troubled me so long,
Lies heavy on me; O, my heart is sick!

Enter a Messenger.

Mess. My lord, your valiant kinsman, Faulconbridge,
Desires your majesty to leave the field
And send him word by me which way you go.
K. John. Tell him, toward Swinstead, to the abbey there.
Mess. Be of good comfort; for the great supply
That was expected by the Dauphin here,
Are wrack'd three nights ago on Goodwin Sands.
This news was brought to Richard but even now:
The French fight coldly, and retire themselves.
K. John. Ay me! this tyrant fever burns me up,
And will not let me welcome this good news.
Set on toward Swinstead: to my litter straight;
Weakness possesseth me, and I am faint. *Exeunt.*

SCENE IV. [*Another part of the field.*]

Enter SALISBURY, PEMBROKE, *and* BIGOT.

Sal. I did not think the king so stor'd with friends.
Pem. Up once again; put spirit in the French:
If they miscarry, we miscarry too.
Sal. That misbegotten devil, Faulconbridge,
In spite of spite, alone upholds the day.
Pem. They say King John sore sick hath left the field.

Enter MELUN, *wounded.*

Mel. Lead me to the revolts of England here.
Sal. When we were happy we had other names.
Pem. It is the Count Melun.
Sal. Wounded to death.
Mel. Fly, noble English, you are bought and sold;
Unthread the rude eye of rebellion
And welcome home again discarded faith.
Seek out King John and fall before his feet;
For if the French be lords of this loud day,
He means to recompense the pains you take
By cutting off your heads: thus hath he sworn
And I with him, and many moe with me,
Upon the altar at Saint Edmundsbury;
Even on that altar where we swore to you
Dear amity and everlasting love.
Sal. May this be possible? may this be true?
Mel. Have I not hideous death within my view,
Retaining but a quantity of life,
Which bleeds away, even as a form of wax
Resolveth from his figure 'gainst the fire?
What in the world should make me now deceive,
Since I must lose the use of all deceit?
Why should I then be false, since it is true
That I must die here and live hence by truth?
I say again, if Lewis do win the day,
He is forsworn, if e'er those eyes of yours
Behold another day break in the east:
But even this night, whose black contagious breath
Already smokes about the burning crest
Of the old, feeble and day-wearied sun,
Even this ill night, your breathing shall expire,
Paying the fine of rated treachery
Even with a treacherous fine of all your lives,
If Lewis by your assistance win the day.
Commend me to one Hubert with your king:
The love of him, and this respect besides,
For that my grandsire was an Englishman,
Awakes my conscience to confess all this.
In lieu whereof, I pray you, bear me hence
From forth the noise and rumour of the field,
Where I may think the remnant of my thoughts
In peace, and part this body and my soul
With contemplation and devout desires.
Sal. We do believe thee: and beshrew my soul
But I do love the favour and the form
Of this most fair occasion, by the which
We will untread the steps of damned flight,
And like a bated and retired flood,
Leaving our rankness and irregular course,
Stoop low within those bounds we have o'erlook'd
And calmly run on in obedience
Even to our ocean, to our great King John.
My arm shall give thee help to bear thee hence;
For I do see the cruel pangs of death
Right in thine eye. Away, my friends! New flight;
And happy newness, that intends old right.
Exeunt [*leading off Melun*].

SCENE V. [*The French camp.*]

Enter [LEWIS *the*] DAUPHIN *and his train.*

Lew. The sun of heaven methought was loath to set,
But stay'd and made the western welkin blush,

169. **ready brac'd,** i.e., tightened, ready to be struck. 172. **welkin's,** heaven's, sky's; see glossary.
SCENE IV. 11. **Unthread the rude eye,** i.e., withdraw from the hazardous undertaking in which they were engaged. 15. **He,** the French Dauphin. 17. **moe,** more; see glossary. 24-25. **as . . .fire.** An alleged practice of necromancers was to make and then abuse a waxen effigy of an enemy, who was believed to suffer in accordance with the treatment given the wax representation. As the waxen figure melted away before a fire, the enemy, it was believed, would die. The passage is a metaphor; Melun does not necessarily mean that he is a victim of witchcraft. 37. **rated,** assessed, evaluated; with quibble on *rebuked, chided.* 38. **fine,** end; see glossary. 54. **rankness,** overgrowth; stench.
SCENE V. 3. **measure,** traverse; see glossary. 7. **clearly,** completely. 14. **shrewd,** of evil import; see glossary. 20. **quarter,** watch.
SCENE VI. 12. **Unkind remembrance.** Hubert chides his own faulty memory; see *unkind* in glossary. 16. **sans,** without; see glossary. 28.

When English measure backward their own ground
In faint retire. O, bravely came we off,
When with a volley of our needless shot,
After such bloody toil, we bid good night;
And wound our tott'ring colours clearly up,
Last in the field, and almost lords of it!

Enter a Messenger.

Mess. Where is my prince, the Dauphin?
Lew. Here: what news?
Mess. The Count Melun is slain; the English lords
By his persuasion are again fall'n off,
And your supply, which you have wish'd so long,
Are cast away and sunk on Goodwin Sands.
Lew. Ah, foul shrewd news! beshrew thy very heart!
I did not think to be so sad to-night
As this hath made me. Who was he that said
King John did fly an hour or two before
The stumbling night did part our weary pow'rs?
Mess. Whoever spoke it, it is true, my lord.
Lew. Well; keep good quarter and good care to-night:
The day shall not be up so soon as I,
To try the fair adventure of to-morrow. *Exeunt.*

SCENE VI. [*An open place in the neighbourhood of Swinstead Abbey.*]

Enter [the] BASTARD *and* HUBERT, *severally.*

Hub. Who 's there? speak, ho! speak quickly, or I shoot.
Bast. A friend. What art thou?
Hub. Of the part of England.
Bast. Whither dost thou go?
Hub. What 's that to thee? why may not I demand
Of thine affairs, as well as thou of mine?
Bast. Hubert, I think?
Hub. Thou hast a perfect thought:
I will upon all hazards well believe
Thou art my friend, that know'st my tongue so well.
Who art thou?
Bast. Who thou wilt: and if thou please,
Thou mayst befriend me so much as to think
I come one way of the Plantagenets.
Hub. Unkind remembrance! thou and eyeless night
Have done me shame: brave soldier, pardon me,
That any accent breaking from thy tongue
Should 'scape the true acquaintance of mine ear.
Bast. Come, come; sans compliment, what news abroad?
Hub. Why, here walk I in the black brow of night,
To find you out.
Bast. Brief, then; and what 's the news?
Hub. O, my sweet sir, news fitting to the night,
Black, fearful, comfortless and horrible.
Bast. Show me the very wound of this ill news:
I am no woman, I'll not swoon at it.
Hub. The king, I fear, is poison'd by a monk:
I left him almost speechless; and broke out
To acquaint you with this evil, that you might
The better arm you to the sudden time,
Than if you had at leisure known of this.
Bast. How did he take it? who did taste to him?
Hub. A monk, I tell you; a resolved villain,
Whose bowels suddenly burst out: the king
Yet speaks and peradventure may recover.
Bast. Who didst thou leave to tend his majesty?
Hub. Why, know you not? the lords are all come back,
And brought Prince Henry in their company;
At whose request the king hath pardon'd them,
And they are all about his majesty.
Bast. Withhold thine indignation, mighty heaven,
And tempt us not to bear above our power!
I'll tell thee, Hubert, half my power this night,
Passing these flats, are taken by the tide;
These Lincoln Washes have devoured them;
Myself, well mounted, hardly have escap'd.
Away before: conduct me to the king;
I doubt he will be dead or ere I come. *Exeunt.*

SCENE VII. [*The orchard in Swinstead Abbey.*]

Enter Prince HENRY, SALISBURY, *and* BIGOT.

P. Hen. It is too late: the life of all his blood
Is touch'd corruptibly, and his pure brain,
Which some suppose the soul's frail dwelling-house,
Doth by the idle comments that it makes
Foretell the ending of mortality.

Enter PEMBROKE.

Pem. His highness yet doth speak, and holds belief
That, being brought into the open air,
It would allay the burning quality
Of that fell poison which assaileth him.
P. Hen. Let him be brought into the orchard here.
Doth he still rage? [*Exit Bigot.*]
Pem. He is more patient
Than when you left him; even now he sung.
P. Hen. O vanity of sickness! fierce extremes
In their continuance will not feel themselves.
Death, having prey'd upon the outward parts,
Leaves them invisible, and his siege is now
Against the mind, the which he pricks and wounds
With many legions of strange fantasies,
Which, in their throng and press to that last hold,
Confound themselves. 'Tis strange that death should sing.
I am the cygnet to this pale faint swan,
Who chants a doleful hymn to his own death,
And from the organ-pipe of frailty sings
His soul and body to their lasting rest.
Sal. Be of good comfort, prince; for you are born
To set a form upon that indigest
Which he hath left so shapeless and so rude.

who did taste to him, a reference to the practice of having a "taster" eat a portion of everything the king was to eat in order to protect him from poisoning (cf. *Richard II*, V, v, 99). The monk who did so here, took the poison knowingly—as a *resolved villain*—to insure the king's death. 38. **tempt . . . power,** don't try us beyond our power of endurance. 39. **power,** army. 40. **Passing,** traversing; see glossary. **flats,** tidal flatlands. 44. **doubt,** fear.

SCENE VII. 16. **invisible.** *Insensible, invincible, ill-visited* have been offered as emendations. The New Cambridge editors suggest *invasible* (modifying *outward parts*), i.e., easy of access. Most editors concur in Malone's explanation of *invisible* as an adverb. 18. **fantasies,** fancies, creatures of the imagination; cf. IV, ii, 144; see glossary. 21. **cygnet,** the young swan. It was a popular belief that the swan sang just before it died. 26. **indigest,** shapeless mass.

[KING] JOHN *brought in* [*in a chair*].

K. John. Ay, marry, now my soul hath elbow-room;
It would not out at windows nor at doors.
There is so hot a summer in my bosom,
That all my bowels crumble up to dust:
I am a scribbled form, drawn with a pen
Upon a parchment, and against this fire
Do I shrink up.
P. Hen. How fares your majesty?
K. John. Poison'd,—ill fare—dead, forsook, cast off:
And none of you will bid the winter come
To thrust his icy fingers in my maw,
Nor let my kingdom's rivers take their course
Through my burn'd bosom, nor entreat the north
To make his bleak winds kiss my parched lips
And comfort me with cold. I do not ask you much,
I beg cold comfort; and you are so strait
And so ingrateful, you deny me that.
P. Hen. O that there were some virtue in my tears,
That might relieve you!
K. John. The salt in them is hot.
Within me is a hell; and there the poison
Is as a fiend confin'd to tyrannize
On unreprievable condemned blood.

Enter [*the*] BASTARD.

Bast. O, I am scalded with my violent motion,
And spleen of speed to see your majesty!
K. John. O cousin, thou art come to set mine eye:
The tackle of my heart is crack'd and burn'd,
And all the shrouds wherewith my life should sail
Are turned to one thread, one little hair:
My heart hath one poor string to stay it by,
Which holds but till thy news be uttered;
And then all this thou seest is but a clod
And module of confounded royalty.
Bast. The Dauphin is preparing hitherward,
Where heaven He knows how we shall answer him;
For in a night the best part of my pow'r,
As I upon advantage did remove,
Were in the Washes all unwarily
Devoured by the unexpected flood. [*The king dies.*]
Sal. You breathe these dead news in as dead an ear.
My liege! my lord! but now a king, now thus.
P. Hen. Even so must I run on, and even so stop.
What surety of the world, what hope, what stay,
When this was now a king, and now is clay?
Bast. Art thou gone so? I do but stay behind
To do the office for thee of revenge,
And then my soul shall wait on thee to heaven,
As it on earth hath been thy servant still.
Now, now, you stars that move in your right spheres,
Where be your pow'rs? show now your mended
faiths,
And instantly return with me again,
To push destruction and perpetual shame
Out of the weak door of our fainting land.
Straight let us seek, or straight we shall be sought;
The Dauphin rages at our very heels.
Sal. It seems you know not, then, so much as we:
The Cardinal Pandulph is within at rest,
Who half an hour since came from the Dauphin,
And brings from him such offers of our peace
As we with honour and respect may take,
With purpose presently to leave this war.
Bast. He will the rather do it when he sees
Ourselves well sinewed to our defence.
Sal. Nay, it is in a manner done already;
For many carriages he hath dispatch'd
To the sea-side, and put his cause and quarrel
To the disposing of the cardinal:
With whom yourself, myself and other lords,
If you think meet, this afternoon will post
To consummate this business happily.
Bast. Let it be so: and you, my noble prince,
With other princes that may best be spar'd,
Shall wait upon your father's funeral.
P. Hen. At Worcester must his body be interr'd;
For so he will'd it.
Bast. Thither shall it then:
And happily may your sweet self put on
The lineal state and glory of the land!
To whom, with all submission, on my knee
I do bequeath my faithful services
And true subjection everlastingly.
Sal. And the like tender of our love we make,
To rest without a spot for evermore.
P. Hen. I have a kind soul that would give you
thanks
And knows not how to do it but with tears.
Bast. O, let us pay the time but needful woe,
Since it hath been beforehand with our griefs.
This England never did, nor never shall,
Lie at the proud foot of a conqueror,
But when it first did help to wound itself.
Now these her princes are come home again,
Come the three corners of the world in arms,
And we shall shock them. Nought shall make us rue,
If England to itself do rest but true. *Exeunt.*

32. **scribbled form,** badly drawn portrait. 42. **strait,** niggardly. 51. **set mine eye,** close my eyes in death. 58. **module,** counterfeit, mere image. 80. **rages,** pursues furiously; see glossary. 94. **post,** hasten; see glossary. 102. **lineal state,** the crown by right of succession. 116. **three . . . world,** England being the fourth (New Cambridge).

TITUS ANDRONICUS

Titus Andronicus has drawn some unusually harsh criticism. Ben Jonson singled it out, in his Induction to *Bartholomew Fair* (1614), as a horrid example of bombast rhetoric in a tragedy. T. S. Eliot called it "one of the stupidest and most uninspired plays ever written." Others have argued that it was not Shakespeare's at all, or his perfunctory revision of an old play by Marlowe, Kyd, Greene, or Peele, or a very early and experimental work, or even a burlesque of the revenge play then in vogue. Early it surely was; it appeared in quarto in 1594 as played by Derby's, Pembroke's, and Sussex' men, and could well have been written in 1590 or even before. The allusion in Henslowe's *Diary* for January 24, 1594, to a new production by Sussex' men of "Titus & Ondronicus" could refer to a new play or one newly revised or newly acquired by the company. Shakespeare's *Titus Andronicus* was widely separated in time from the great tragedies; *Romeo and Juliet* is the only other tragedy (excluding the English history plays) of the decade preceding 1599, and it probably followed *Titus* by five years or so. Unquestionably *Titus* is the least successful of Shakespeare's tragedies, the most deficient in cosmic significance or in affirmation of man's tragic dignity. This judgment compares the play, however, with the greatest dramas of the English language. Probably its greatest critical liability is that it continually reminds us of the later Roman plays and of *Hamlet* and *King Lear*. By any other playwright the play would not seem so imperfect as it seems when assigned to Shakespeare. *Titus* was an early stage success, and has shown its timeless theatrical appeal in a 1957 brilliant production at Stratford-upon-Avon by Sir Laurence Olivier.

Titus Andronicus is studded with bookish references to classical authors—another likely indication of early date. No other tragedy, perhaps no other Shakespearean play, reveals such signs of incompletely digested learning. Some of its numerous untranslated Latin phrases are old schoolboys' favorites, like the "Integer vitae" of Horace that is immediately recognized by Chiron. "I read it in the grammar long ago," he says (IV,ii). Numerous classical allusions compare the chief characters of the play with Aeneas and Dido Queen of Carthage, Hector, King Priam, and Queen Hecuba of Troy, Ajax and Odysseus among the Greeks, Hercules, Prometheus, Orpheus, Coriolanus, Semiramis the siren queen of Assyria, Pyramis, Cornelia the mother of the Gracchi, Actæon, and others. Especially significant for their thematic relevance are the classical victims of rape and vengeance: Virginia the Roman, killed by her father Virginius to save her from rape; the chaste Lucrece, ravished by Tarquin; Philomel, raped and deprived of her tongue by Tereus, whose name she then reveals by weaving the information into a tapestry; and Procne, her sister and the wife of Tereus, who avenges Philomel by serving Tereus' son Itys to him in a meal.

Ovid's *Metamorphoses* gave Shakespeare his ultimate source for many of the legends, especially that of Tereus, Philomel, and Procne. Seneca's *Thyestes* offered him in dramatic form a similar tale of vengeance, in which two sons are slain and served to their parent in a grisly banquet. Shakespeare appears to have used a chapbook called *The History of Titus Andronicus;* the only extant printed copy is from the eighteenth century, but it may give a reliable version of the original. Some scholars believe that one or even two plays about Titus may have existed prior to Shakespeare's, and that we can deduce their contributions to his work by examining two later continental plays derived from them: *Tito Andronico* (German, 1620) and *Aran en Titus* (Dutch, 1641). Possibly one of these earlier plays was the "Titus & Vespacia" entered in Henslowe's *Diary* for April 11, 1592, as acted by Lord Strange's men. Even if Shakespeare used such prose and dramatic sources, however, he also knew well the Ovidian and Senecan originals that had inspired them. Elizabethan revenge tragedy in Senecan style too was a strongly formative influence, especially Kyd's *The Spanish Tragedy* (c. 1587). The phenomenal recent stage success of Marlowe left its mark: Titus' killing of his son Alarbus recalls *Tamburlaine Part II*, and Aaron's Vicelike boasting of wanton villainy recalls *The Jew of Malta*.

As this welter of influences may suggest, *Titus* has a quality of derivativeness not found in Shakespeare's later tragedies. Although the play usefully anticipates several motifs in those later tragedies—the ingratitude of Rome toward its honored general as in *Coriolanus*, Roman political factionalism as in *Julius Caesar*, infirm old age confronted by human bestiality as in *King Lear*—*Titus* does not attempt to rise above the ethical level of its various models. It is best understood and judged as a revenge play in the sensational vein of Seneca, Kyd, and Marlowe, with generous additions of Ovidian pathos. It is almost untouched by that humane and generous spirit we associate with the mature Shakespeare. The style too is derivative, employing a decorative and florid mannerism more suited to the Ovidian poems, *Venus and Adonis* and *The Rape of Lucrece*, than to the nightmarish vision of evil through which Titus and Lavinia must pass. The play's most theatrically effective scenes, like the abduction of Lavinia to be ravished by the chortling Demetrius and Chiron, appeal to violence and gothic horror as ends in themselves. Kyd and Marlowe do this sort of thing often and brilliantly, but in Shakespeare we find deliberate shock effect unnerving. Even Shakespeare appears to have been troubled, for he strives belatedly to give the play a moral perspective. Aaron the Moor is caught and sentenced to execution, Titus' brother Marcus appeals to Roman justice for vindication on the grounds that his family had no alternative, and Titus' last remaining son Lucius vows as the new emperor to "heal Rome's harms and wipe away her woe" (V,iii). Yet this framework of morality does little more than confuse the play's orientation, which remains essentially that of a revenge play.

The first part of *Titus* functions to give the title figure, the avenger, a motive for his bloody course of action. Ironically, however, Titus is himself responsible for setting in motion the train of events that will overwhelm him. His family, the Andronici, are the first to practice vengeance, a fact which diminishes the moral sympathy they might later have been able to enjoy as victims and exiles. In fact it is Lucius, ultimately to become the great restorer of political stability, who first demands the ritual slaying of a captive Goth, Tamora's son Alarbus, to appease the spirits of the Andronici slain in battle. Such a demand is self-evidently vengeful and pagan. Despite Marcus' injunction to Titus that "Thou art a Roman, be not barbarous," the Roman Andronici do act like barbarian Goths. This irony is complete when the Gothic Queen Tamora and her sons become the spokesmen for godlike mercy. As Tamora's son Chiron bitterly observes, "Was never Scythia half so barbarous."

Equally violent and unnatural is Titus' slaying of his own son, Mutius, for assisting in the abduction of Titus' daughter Lavinia. This tragic error stems, like the first, from Titus' warped sense of family honor. Titus has unwisely refused the imperial crown, bestowing it instead on the treacherous Saturninus, and has promised Lavinia as bride to the new emperor despite her prior betrothal to Saturninus' virtuous rival, Bassianus. When Titus' sons and Bassianus are accordingly driven to the desperate expedient of abducting the lady, Titus cannot endure the shame of his violated promise and so kills Mutius in the ensuing melee. Yet for this sacrifice on behalf of the emperor, Titus receives ironically only ingratitude and hostility. Moreover, he has taught Tamora and her sons to seek vengeance.

Once the Andronici become the victims of the Goths, to be sure, they gain in sympathy. They suffer unspeakable atrocities. Hunted down by jeering sadists who amuse themselves through rape and mutilation, the Andronici band together in mutual tribulation and selflessly attempt to ease one another's agony. They discover Rome to be a "wilderness of tigers" in which the law blindly condemns Titus' innocent sons for the murder of Bassianus. Still, Titus has committed the first barbarism, and turns increasingly to barbarism in his desire for vengeance. Because the Andronici are too much like their enemies, the prevailing mood as in most revenge plays is more ironic than tragic. There is no cathartic vision, no real sense (despite the capture of Aaron) that moral order is restored along with political order. The Andronici are vindicated, but only as avengers who gave the first offense.

Titus displays many conventions of the revenge play, especially as set forth in *The Spanish Tragedy*. The avenger, Titus, is a man of high position conscientiously serving the state, like Kyd's Hieronimo, who discovers that the state itself is too corrupt to give him justice in his own private family wrong. The evildoers are members of the emperor's family, protected by their royal connection. Private and public interests clash, and public welfare is the loser. The avenger has difficulty proving the identity of the villains, but finds an ingenious way at last (through Lavinia's writing in the sand). Once he becomes the avenger, like Hieronimo, Titus grows as remorseless and canny as his enemies. He becomes a menace to public order, uttering enigmatic threats and blazoning forth the injustices of the state. Wavering on the brink of true madness, he also employs madness as a cloak for his Machiavellian intrigues. In this plotting he is successful, for he thereby dupes Queen Tamora into allowing him to arrange his gruesome banquet. The drama ends, like *The Spanish Tragedy*, in a kind of play-within-the-play, as Tamora's two sons take the roles of Rape and Murder, Tamora Revenge, and Titus the cook. Playacting turns deadly earnest with a rapid succession of slaughters. Titus and Lavinia, like Hieronimo and Bel-Imperia, do not outlive their act of vengeance.

This conventional pattern embraces revenge as self-justifying. As in *The Spanish Tragedy*, where the Ghost of Revenge controls the action for his own sinister purposes and welcomes the suffering of innocents or the collapse of governments as grist to his mill, *Titus* seems to accept the deeds of its avengers as necessary and defensible. Even Lavinia and Titus' young grandson endorse plotting and violence. Titus practices cunning toward his enemies, vowing to "o'erreach them in their own devices." Our attention is increasingly drawn to the method and artistry of the "devices" on both sides. The complex machinations of Aaron and Tamora demand ingeniousness in return. An eye must pay for an eye; the punishment must fit the crime. Titus and Lavinia accordingly lack the moral breadth of vision of Shakespeare's later tragic heroes and heroines. They are more suited to a play in which revenge is the ultimate ethical standard, brutality the dominant fact of life, and violence the only apparent means of self-justification.

As a tragedy of evil, then, *Titus Andronicus* illuminates the nature of that evil but makes no real attempt to transcend evil through human nobility, as in the later tragedies. This distinctive quality is made especially manifest by the play's outward resemblance to *King Lear*. Titus is old, infirm of judgment, and victimized by his own decision to relinquish power to a person whose villainy he does not comprehend. He is certainly more sinned against than sinning. He approaches madness, and generalizes in his grief about the omnipresence of murder and ingratitude in nature (III,ii). His reflections on human injustice suggest the inversion of appearance and reality ("Grief has so wrought on him He takes false shadows for true substances"), a motif of illusion that reappears in the allegorical play-within-the-play. Queen Tamora reveals an innate viciousness and sexual depravity like that of Goneril and Regan. Aaron the Moor, perhaps the first of Shakespeare's gloating Vicelike villains, resembles Edmund in *King Lear* as well as Richard III, Don John (in *Much Ado about Nothing*), and Iago (in *Othello*).

Like the Vice of the morality play or Marlowe's stage Machiavel, Aaron takes delight in pure evil and displays his cunning for the admiration of the audience. Evil to him is "sport," "wit," "stratagem," and above all "policy" (II,i). His malice encompasses all humanity, and proceeds from no motive other than the sinister pleasure he takes in devising his plots. Even when he is finally captured, Aaron boasts triumphantly of the extent and variety of his cruel accomplishments:

Even now I curse the day—and yet, I think,
Few come within the compass of my curse—
Wherein I did not some notorious ill,
As kill a man, or else devise his death,
Ravish a maid, or plot the way to do it,
Accuse some innocent and forswear myself,
Set deadly enmity between two friends,
Make poor men's cattle break their necks;
Set fire on barns and hay-stacks in the night,
And bid the owners quench them with their tears.
Oft have I digg'd up dead men from their graves,
And set them upright at their dear friends' door,
Even when their sorrows almost was forgot.

Through its stark depiction of evil as both comic and diabolical, this portrait gives us a valuable insight into the origins of one type of Shakespearean villain.

The only seemingly attractive side to Aaron, his fiercely protective instincts toward his bastard son born of Tamora, is part of the central evil of this play: pride of family turning to revengeful violence. His Negroid features, and those of his son—woolly hair, wall eyes, thick lips, black skin—are equated with barbarism, pagan atheism (Aaron scoffs at those who believe in God), and diabolism. This resourceful and single-minded villain is the most vital character in the play. Through him, and to an extent through Tamora and her kindred, naked evil is rendered with a terrifying brilliance. As a revenge play *Titus* has a stunning crude effectiveness. To be appreciated properly, *Titus* should be read in these terms rather than with the expectations we bring to *King Lear*. Shakespeare here presents barbarism and civilization as polar opposites, but allows Titus no escape from that barbarism which the protagonist himself sets in motion. No tragic self-awareness grows out of Titus' humiliation, as it does in *King Lear*, no regret other than for having relinquished power to Saturninus. Instead of tragic self-awareness we are left with an overpowering impression of man's potential for brutality. This vision is unameliorated. The constant reminder of a better world of justice and compassion merely serves to heighten the play's ironic and futile sense of wasted goodness.

TITUS ANDRONICUS

[*Dramatis Personae*

SATURNINUS, *son to the late Emperor of Rome, and afterwards declared Emperor.*
BASSIANUS, *brother to Saturninus; in love with Lavinia.*
TITUS ANDRONICUS, *a noble Roman, general against the Goths.*
MARCUS ANDRONICUS, *tribune of the people, and brother to Titus.*
LUCIUS, QUINTUS, MARTIUS, MUTIUS, } *sons to Titus Andronicus.*
YOUNG LUCIUS, *a boy, son to Lucius.*
PUBLIUS, *son to Marcus the Tribune.*
SEMPRONIUS, CAIUS, VALENTINE, } *kinsmen to Titus.*
ÆMILIUS, *a noble Roman.*
ALARBUS, DEMETRIUS, CHIRON, } *sons to Tamora.*
AARON, *a Moor, beloved by Tamora.*
A Captain, Tribune, Messenger, *and* Clown; Romans.
Goths *and* Romans.

TAMORA, *Queen of the Goths.*
LAVINIA, *daughter to Titus Andronicus.*
A Nurse.

Senators, Tribunes, Officers, Soldiers, *and* Attendants.

SCENE: *Rome, and the country near it.*]

[ACT I.

SCENE I. *Rome. Before the Capitol.*]

[*Flourish.*] *Enter the* Tribunes *and* Senators *aloft; and then enter* [*below*] SATURNINUS *and his* Followers *at one door, and* BASSIANUS *and his* Followers [*at the other,*] *with drums and trumpets.*

Sat. Noble patricians, patrons of my right,
Defend the justice of my cause with arms,
And, countrymen, my loving followers,
Plead my successive title with your swords:
I am his first-born son, that was the last
That ware the imperial diadem of Rome;
Then let my father's honours live in me,
Nor wrong mine age with this indignity.
Bas. Romans, friends, followers, favourers of my right,
If ever Bassianus, Cæsar's son,
Were gracious in the eyes of royal Rome,

Keep then this passage to the Capitol
And suffer not dishonour to approach
The imperial seat, to virtue consecrate,
To justice, continence and nobility;
But let desert in pure election shine,
And, Romans, fight for freedom in your choice.

[*Enter*] MARCUS ANDRONICUS, [*aloft,*] *with the crown.*

Marc. Princes, that strive by factions and by friends
Ambitiously for rule and empery,
Know that the people of Rome, for whom we stand
A special party, have, by common voice,
In election for the Roman empery,
Chosen Andronicus, surnamed Pius
For many good and great deserts to Rome:
A nobler man, a braver warrior,
Lives not this day within the city walls:
He by the senate is accited home
From weary wars against the barbarous Goths;
That, with his sons, a terror to our foes,
Hath yok'd a nation strong, train'd up in arms.
Ten years are spent since first he undertook
This cause of Rome and chastised with arms
Our enemies' pride: five times he hath return'd
Bleeding to Rome, bearing his valiant sons
In coffins from the field; and at this day
To the monument of the Andronici,
Done sacrifice of expiation,
And slain the noblest prisoner of the Goths.
And now at last, laden with honour's spoils,
Returns the good Andronicus to Rome,
Renowned Titus, flourishing in arms.
Let us entreat, by honour of his name,
Whom worthily you would have now succeed,
And in the Capitol and senate's right,
Whom you pretend to honour and adore,
That you withdraw you and abate your strength;
Dismiss your followers and, as suitors should,
Plead your deserts in peace and humbleness.

Sat. How fair the tribune speaks to calm my thoughts!

Bas. Marcus Andronicus, so I do affy
In thy uprightness and integrity,
And so I love and honour thee and thine,
Thy noble brother Titus and his sons,
And her to whom my thoughts are humbled all,
Gracious Lavinia, Rome's rich ornament,
That I will here dismiss my loving friends,
And to my fortunes and the people's favour
Commit my cause in balance to be weigh'd.

Exeunt Soldiers [*of Bassianus*].

Sat. Friends, that have been thus forward in my right,
I thank you all and here dismiss you all,
And to the love and favour of my country
Commit myself, my person and the cause.

[*Exeunt the Soldiers of Saturninus.*]

Rome, be as just and gracious unto me
As I am confident and kind to thee.
Open the gates, and let me in.

Bas. Tribunes, and me, a poor competitor.

[*Flourish.*] *They* [*Saturninus and Bassianus*] *go up into the Senate House.*

Enter a Captain.

Cap. Romans, make way: the good Andronicus,
Patron of virtue, Rome's best champion,
Successful in the battles that he fights,
With honour and with fortune is return'd
From where he circumscribed with his sword,
And brought to yoke, the enemies of Rome.

Sound drums and trumpets, and then enter two of Titus' Sons [, MARTIUS *and* MUTIUS]; *and then two men bearing a coffin covered with black; then two other Sons* [LUCIUS *and* QUINTUS]; *then* TITUS ANDRONICUS; *and then* TAMORA, *the Queen of Goths, and her three Sons* [ALARBUS,] CHIRON, *and* DEMETRIUS, *with* AARON *the Moor, and others as many as can be. Then set down the coffin, and* TITUS *speaks.*

Tit. Hail, Rome, victorious in thy mourning weeds!
Lo, as the bark, that hath discharg'd her fraught,
Returns with precious lading to the bay
From whence at first she weigh'd her anchorage,
Cometh Andronicus, bound with laurel boughs,
To re-salute his country with his tears,
Tears of true joy for his return to Rome.
Thou great defender of this Capitol,
Stand gracious to the rites that we intend!
Romans, of five and twenty valiant sons,
Half of the number that King Priam had,
Behold the poor remains, alive and dead!
These that survive let Rome reward with love;
These that I bring unto their latest home,
With burial amongst their ancestors:
Here Goths have given me leave to sheathe my sword.
Titus, unkind and careless of thine own,
Why suffer'st thou thy sons, unburied yet,
To hover on the dreadful shore of Styx?
Make way to lay them by their brethren.

They open the tomb.

There greet in silence, as the dead are wont,
And sleep in peace, slain in your country's wars!
O sacred receptacle of my joys,
Sweet cell of virtue and nobility,
How many sons hast thou of mine in store,
That thou wilt never render to me more!

Luc. Give us the proudest prisoner of the Goths,
That we may hew his limbs, and on a pile
Ad manes fratrum sacrifice his flesh,
Before this earthy prison of their bones;
That so the shadows be not unappeas'd,
Nor we disturb'd with prodigies on earth.

Tit. I give him you, the noblest that survives,
The eldest son of this distressed queen.

Tam. Stay, Roman brethren! Gracious conqueror,
Victorious Titus, rue the tears I shed,
A mother's tears in passion for her son:
And if thy sons were ever dear to thee,
O, think my son to be as dear to me!

ACT I. SCENE I. 4. **successive title,** title to the succession. 6. **ware,** so Q_1; Globe (orig. ed.), *wore*. 8. **age,** seniority. 12. **Keep,** defend. 14. **consecrate,** consecrated. 15. **continence,** restraint. 16. **pure election,** free choice; i.e., of the Roman citizens. 18. **factions,** parties, groups. 20-23. **for . . . Andronicus,** i.e., we are a faction that has chosen Andronicus as our candidate. 27. **accited,** summoned. 30. **yok'd,** subdued. 35 ff. **and at . . . the Goths.** These lines, not in Q_{2-3}F and consequently not in Globe, are introduced from the quarto of 1594, hereafter referred to as Q_1. **the Andronici,** Q_1: *that Andronicy.*

42. **pretend,** assert, profess. 43. **abate,** diminish, reduce. 46. **fair,** courteously, gently; see glossary. 47. **affy,** trust. 61. **confident,** without suspicion. 68. **circumscribed,** restrained, put limits on. 70. **weeds,** garments; see glossary. 71. **fraught,** freight, cargo. 77. **Thou,** i.e., Jupiter. 80. **King Priam,** king of Troy at the time of its fall; he had fifty sons. 83. **latest,** final. 86. **unkind,** unnatural; see glossary. 94. **sons . . . mine,** so Q_1; Globe, following Q_3F: *sons of mine hast thou.* 98. **Ad manes fratrum,** to the departed spirits of the brothers. 122, 123, 124. **These, their, their, they.** The reference in each case is to

Sufficeth not that we are brought to Rome,
To beautify thy triumphs and return,
Captive to thee and to thy Roman yoke,
But must my sons be slaughtered in the streets,
For valiant doings in their country's cause?
O, if to fight for king and commonweal
Were piety in thine, it is in these.
Andronicus, stain not thy tomb with blood:
Wilt thou draw near the nature of the gods?
Draw near them then in being merciful:
Sweet mercy is nobility's true badge:
Thrice noble Titus, spare my first-born son.
Tit. Patient yourself, madam, and pardon me.
These are their brethren, whom your Goths beheld
Alive and dead, and for their brethren slain
Religiously they ask a sacrifice:
To this your son is mark'd, and die he must,
T' appease their groaning shadows that are gone.
Luc. Away with him! and make a fire straight;
And with our swords, upon a pile of wood,
Let 's hew his limbs till they be clean consum'd.
Exeunt Titus' Sons, with Alarbus.
Tam. O cruel, irreligious piety!
Chi. Was never Scythia half so barbarous.
Dem. Oppose not Scythia to ambitious Rome.
Alarbus goes to rest; and we survive
To tremble under Titus' threat'ning look.
Then, madam, stand resolv'd, but hope withal
The self-same gods that arm'd the Queen of Troy
With opportunity of sharp revenge
Upon the Thracian tyrant in his tent,
May favour Tamora, the Queen of Goths—
When Goths were Goths and Tamora was queen—
To quit the bloody wrongs upon her foes.

Enter the Sons *of Andronicus again [with their swords bloody].*

Luc. See, lord and father, how we have perform'd
Our Roman rites: Alarbus' limbs are lopp'd,
And entrails feed the sacrificing fire,
Whose smoke, like incense, doth perfume the sky.
Remaineth nought, but to inter our brethren,
And with loud 'larums welcome them to Rome.
Tit. Let it be so; and let Andronicus
Make this his latest farewell to their souls.
Sound trumpets, and lay the coffin in the tomb.
In peace and honour rest you here, my sons;
Rome's readiest champions, repose you here in rest,
Secure from worldly chances and mishaps!
Here lurks no treason, here no envy swells,
Here grow no damned drugs; here are no storms,
No noise, but silence and eternal sleep:
In peace and honour rest you here, my sons!

Enter LAVINIA.

Lav. In peace and honour live Lord Titus long;
My noble lord and father, live in fame!
Lo, at this tomb my tributary tears
I render, for my brethren's obsequies;
And at thy feet I kneel, with tears of joy,
Shed on this earth, for thy return to Rome:
O, bless me here with thy victorious hand,
Whose fortunes Rome's best citizens applaud!
Tit. Kind Rome, that hast thus lovingly reserv'd
The cordial of mine age to glad my heart!
Lavinia, live; outlive thy father's days,
And fame's eternal date, for virtue's praise!

[*Enter, above,* MARCUS ANDRONICUS, SATURNINUS, *and* BASSIANUS, *attended.*]

Mar. Long live Lord Titus, my beloved brother,
Gracious triumpher in the eyes of Rome!
Tit. Thanks, gentle tribune, noble brother Marcus.
Marc. And welcome, nephews, from successful wars,
You that survive, and you that sleep in fame!
Fair lords, your fortunes are alike in all,
That in your country's service drew your swords:
But safer triumph is this funeral pomp,
That hath aspir'd to Solon's happiness
And triumphs over chance in honour's bed.
Titus Andronicus, the people of Rome,
Whose friend in justice thou hast ever been,
Send thee by me, their tribune and their trust,
This palliament of white and spotless hue;
And name thee in election for the empire,
With these our late-deceased emperor's sons:
Be candidatus then, and put it on,
And help to set a head on headless Rome.
Tit. A better head her glorious body fits
Than his that shakes for age and feebleness:
What should I don this robe, and trouble you?
Be chosen with proclamations to-day,
To-morrow yield up rule, resign my life,
And set abroad new business for you all?
Rome, I have been thy soldier forty years,
And led my country's strength successfully,
And buried one and twenty valiant sons,
Knighted in field, slain manfully in arms,
In right and service of their noble country:
Give me a staff of honour for mine age,
But not a sceptre to control the world:
Upright he held it, lords, that held it last.
Marc. Titus, thou shalt obtain and ask the empery.
Sat. Proud and ambitious tribune, canst thou tell?
Tit. Patience, Prince Saturninus.
Sat. Romans, do me right:
Patricians, draw your swords, and sheathe them not
Till Saturninus be Rome's emperor.
Andronicus, would thou were shipp'd to hell,
Rather than rob me of the people's hearts!
Luc. Proud Saturnine, interrupter of the good
That noble-minded Titus means to thee!
Tit. Content thee, prince; I will restore to thee
The people's hearts, and wean them from themselves.
Bas. Andronicus, I do not flatter thee,
But honour thee, and will do till I die:
My faction if thou strengthen with thy friends,
I will most thankful be; and thanks to men
Of noble minds is honourable meed.

the sons of Titus. 131. **never,** so Q_1; Globe, following Q_3F: *ever,* making the line a question. **Scythia,** the district north of the Black Sea; its people were notorious for their savagery. 132. **Oppose,** compare. 134. **look,** so Qq; Globe, following F: *looks.* 135. **withal,** together with this, at the same time. 136. **Queen of Troy,** Hecuba, wife of Priam, who after the fall of Troy was carried to Greece as a slave; here she found occasion to avenge the deaths of her children by killing the two sons of the king of Thrace, Polymnestor. 154. **drugs,** poisonous plants. 160. **obsequies,** acts performed in honor of the dead.

162. **this earth,** so Q_1; Globe, following Q_3F *the earth.* 166. **cordial,** restorative; or perhaps merely comfort, pleasure. 168. **date,** duration. 177. **Solon's happiness,** the happiness defined by Solon (a Greek sage and lawgiver): that no man may be called happy until after his death. 182. **palliament,** white gown of a candidate. 185. **candidatus,** candidate; properly, one clothed in white. 189. **What,** why. 211. **wean . . . themselves,** i.e., wean them over from their predisposition to favor me. 216. **meed,** recompense, reward.

Tit. People of Rome, and people's tribunes here,
I ask your voices and your suffrages:
Will you bestow them friendly on Andronicus?
Tribunes. To gratify the good Andronicus,
And gratulate his safe return to Rome,
The people will accept whom he admits.
Tit. Tribunes, I thank you: and this suit I make,
That you create your emperor's eldest son,
Lord Saturnine; whose virtues will, I hope,
Reflect on Rome as Titan's rays on earth,
And ripen justice in this commonweal:
Then, if you will elect by my advice,
Crown him, and say 'Long live our emperor!'
Marc. With voices and applause of every sort,
Patricians and plebeians, we create
Lord Saturninus Rome's great emperor,
And say 'Long live our Emperor Saturnine!'
[*A long flourish till they come down.*]
Sat. Titus Andronicus, for thy favours done
To us in our election this day,
I give thee thanks in part of thy deserts,
And will with deeds requite thy gentleness:
And, for an onset, Titus, to advance
Thy name and honourable family,
Lavinia will I make my empress,
Rome's royal mistress, mistress of my heart,
And in the sacred Pantheon her espouse:
Tell me, Andronicus, doth this motion please thee?
Tit. It doth, my worthy lord; and in this match
I hold me highly honoured of your grace:
And here in sight of Rome to Saturnine,
King and commander of our commonweal,
The wide world's emperor, do I consecrate
My sword, my chariot and my prisoners;
Presents well worthy Rome's imperious lord:
Receive them then, the tribute that I owe,
Mine honour's ensigns humbled at thy feet.
Sat. Thanks, noble Titus, father of my life!
How proud I am of thee and of thy gifts
Rome shall record, and when I do forget
The least of these unspeakable deserts,
Romans, forget your fealty to me.
Tit. [*To Tamora*] Now, madam, are you prisoner to an emperor;
To him that, for your honour and your state,
Will use you nobly and your followers.
Sat. [*Aside*] A goodly lady, trust me; of the hue
That I would choose, were I to choose anew.—
Clear up, fair queen, that cloudy countenance:
Though change of war hath wrought this change of cheer,
Thou com'st not to be made a scorn in Rome:
Princely shall be thy usage every way.
Rest on my word, and let not discontent
Daunt all your hopes: madam, he comforts you
Can make you greater than the Queen of Goths.
Lavinia, you are not displeas'd with this?
Lav. Not I, my lord; sith true nobility
Warrants these words in princely courtesy.
Sat. Thanks, sweet Lavinia. Romans, let us go:
Ransomless here we set our prisoners free:
Proclaim our honours, lords, with trump and drum.
[*Flourish. Saturninus courts Tamora in dumb show.*]
Bas. Lord Titus, by your leave, this maid is mine.
[*Seizing Lavinia.*]
Tit. How, sir! are you in earnest then, my lord?
Bas. Ay, noble Titus; and resolv'd withal
To do myself this reason and this right.
Marc. 'Suum cuique' is our Roman justice:
This prince in justice seizeth but his own.
Luc. And that he will, and shall, if Lucius live.
Tit. Traitors, avaunt! Where is the emperor's guard?
Treason, my lord! Lavinia is surpris'd!
Sat. Surpris'd! by whom?
Bas. By him that justly may
Bear his betroth'd from all the world away.
[*Exeunt Bassianus and Marcus with Lavinia.*]
Mut. Brothers, help to convey her hence away,
And with my sword I'll keep this door safe.
[*Exeunt Lucius, Quintus, and Martius.*]
Tit. Follow, my lord, and I'll soon bring her back.
Mut. My lord, you pass not here.
Tit. What, villain boy!
Barr'st me my way in Rome? [*Stabbing Mutius.*]
Mut. Help, Lucius, help! [*Dies.*]
[*During the fray, Saturninus, Tamora, Demetrius, Chiron and Aaron go out and re-enter, above.*]

[*Enter* LUCIUS.]

Luc. My lord, you are unjust, and, more than so,
In wrongful quarrel you have slain your son.
Tit. Nor thou, nor he, are any sons of mine;
My sons would never so dishonour me:
Traitor, restore Lavinia to the emperor.
Luc. Dead, if you will; but not to be his wife,
That is another's lawful promis'd love. [*Exit.*]

Enter aloft the emperor [SATURNINUS] *with* TAMORA *and her two Sons and* AARON *the Moor.*

Sat. No, Titus, no; the emperor needs her not,
Nor her, nor thee, nor any of thy stock:
I'll trust, by leisure, him that mocks me once;
Thee never, nor thy traitorous haughty sons,
Confederates all thus to dishonour me.
Was none in Rome to make a stale,
But Saturnine? Full well, Andronicus,
Agree these deeds with that proud brag of thine,
That said'st I begg'd the empire at thy hands.
Tit. O monstrous! what reproachful words are these?
Sat. But go thy ways; go, give that changing piece
To him that flourish'd for her with his sword:
A valiant son-in-law thou shalt enjoy;
One fit to bandy with thy lawless sons,
To ruffle in the commonwealth of Rome.
Tit. These words are razors to my wounded heart.
Sat. And therefore, lovely Tamora, queen of Goths,
That like the stately Phœbe 'mongst her nymphs
Dost overshine the gallant'st dames of Rome,
If thou be pleas'd with this my sudden choice,
Behold, I choose thee, Tamora, for my bride,
And will create thee empress of Rome.
Speak, Queen of Goths, dost thou applaud my choice?
And here I swear by all the Roman gods,
Sith priest and holy water are so near
And tapers burn so bright and every thing
In readiness for Hymenæus stand,

221. **gratulate,** salute. 238. **onset,** beginning. 243. **motion,** proposal. 245. **of,** by. 250. **imperious,** so Q_1; Globe, following Q_3F: *imperial.* 264. **change,** so Q_1; Globe, following $Q_{2-3}F_1$: *chance.* **cheer,** countenance. 268-269. **he . . . Goths,** i.e., he who can. 280. **'Suum cuique,'** to every man his own. 284. **surpris'd,** assaulted, or perhaps taken. 301. **by leisure,** barely. 304. **Was none,** so QqF_1; Globe, following F_{2-4}: *Was there none else.* **stale,** tool, laughing-stock. 309. **piece,** applied to a woman or girl; here contemptuously.

I will not re-salute the streets of Rome,
Or climb my palace, till from forth this place
I lead espous'd my bride along with me.
Tam. And here, in sight of heaven, to Rome I swear,
If Saturnine advance the Queen of Goths,
She will a handmaid be to his desires,
A loving nurse, a mother to his youth.
Sat. Ascend, fair queen, Pantheon. Lords, accompany
Your noble emperor and his lovely bride,
Sent by the heavens for Prince Saturnine,
Whose wisdom hath her fortune conquered:
There shall we consummate our spousal rites.
Exeunt omnes [except Titus].
Tit. I am not bid to wait upon this bride.
Titus, when wert thou wont to walk alone,
Dishonoured thus, and challenged of wrongs?

Enter MARCUS *and Titus' Sons* [LUCIUS, QUINTUS, *and* MARTIUS].

Marc. O Titus, see, O, see what thou hast done!
In a bad quarrel slain a virtuous son.
Tit. No, foolish tribune, no; no son of mine,
Nor thou, nor these, confederates in the deed
That hath dishonoured all our family;
Unworthy brother, and unworthy sons!
Luc. But let us give him burial, as becomes;
Give Mutius burial with our brethren.
Tit. Traitors, away! he rests not in this tomb:
This monument five hundred years hath stood,
Which I have sumptuously re-edified:
Here none but soldiers and Rome's servitors
Repose in fame; none basely slain in brawls:
Bury him where you can; he comes not here.
Marc. My lord, this is impiety in you:
My nephew Mutius' deeds do plead for him;
He must be buried with his brethren.
Quin.
Mart. } And shall, or him we will accompany.
Tit. 'And shall!' what villain was it spake that word?
Quin. He that would vouch it in any place but here.
Tit. What, would you bury him in my despite?
Marc. No, noble Titus, but entreat of thee
To pardon Mutius and to bury him.
Tit. Marcus, even thou hast struck upon my crest,
And, with these boys, mine honour thou hast wounded:
My foes I do repute you every one;
So, trouble me no more, but get you gone.
Mart. He is not with himself; let us withdraw.
Quin. Not I, till Mutius' bones be buried.
The Brother [Marcus] and the Sons kneel.
Marc. Brother, for in that name doth nature plead,—
Quin. Father, and in that name doth nature speak,—
Tit. Speak thou no more, if all the rest will speed.
Marc. Renowned Titus, more than half my soul,—
Luc. Dear father, soul and substance of us all,—
Marc. Suffer thy brother Marcus to inter
His noble nephew here in virtue's nest,
That died in honour and Lavinia's cause.
Thou art a Roman; be not barbarous:
The Greeks upon advice did bury Ajax
That slew himself; and wise Laertes' son
Did graciously plead for his funerals:
Let not young Mutius, then, that was thy joy,
Be barr'd his entrance here.
Tit. Rise, Marcus, rise.
The dismall'st day is this that e'er I saw,
To be dishonoured by my sons in Rome!
Well, bury him, and bury me the next.
They put him in the tomb.
Luc. There lie thy bones, sweet Mutius, with thy friends,
Till we with trophies do adorn thy tomb. *They all kneel.*
All. No man shed tears for noble Mutius;
He lives in fame that died in virtue's cause.
Marc. My lord, to step out of these dreary dumps,
How comes it that the subtle Queen of Goths
Is of a sudden thus advanc'd in Rome?
Tit. I know not, Marcus; but I know it is:
Whether by device or no, the heavens can tell:
Is she not then beholding to the man
That brought her for this high good turn so far?
Yes, and will nobly him remunerate.

Enter the emperor [SATURNINUS], TAMORA, *and her two Sons, with* [AARON] *the Moor, at one door. Enter at the other door* BASSIANUS *and* LAVINIA, *with others.*

Sat. So, Bassianus, you have play'd your prize:
God give you joy, sir, of your gallant bride!
Bas. And you of yours, my lord! I say no more,
Nor wish no less; and so, I take my leave.
Sat. Traitor, if Rome have law or we have power,
Thou and thy faction shall repent this rape.
Bas. Rape, call you it, my lord, to seize my own,
My true-betrothed love and now my wife?
But let the laws of Rome determine all;
Meanwhile I am possess'd of that is mine.
Sat. 'Tis good, sir: you are very short with us;
But, if we live, we'll be as sharp with you.
Bas. My lord, what I have done, as best I may,
Answer I must and shall do with my life.
Only thus much I give your grace to know:
By all the duties that I owe to Rome,
This noble gentleman, Lord Titus here,
Is in opinion and in honour wrong'd;
That in the rescue of Lavinia
With his own hand did slay his youngest son,
In zeal to you and highly mov'd to wrath
To be controll'd in that he frankly gave:
Receive him, then, to favour, Saturnine,
That hath express'd himself in all his deeds
A father and a friend to thee and Rome.
Tit. Prince Bassianus, leave to plead my deeds:
'Tis thou and those that have dishonoured me.
Rome and the righteous heavens be my judge,
How I have lov'd and honour'd Saturnine!
Tam. My worthy lord, if ever Tamora
Were gracious in those princely eyes of thine,
Then hear me speak indifferently for all;
And at my suit, sweet, pardon what is past.
Sat. What, madam! be dishonoured openly,
And basely put it up without revenge?
Tam. Not so, my lord; the gods of Rome forfend

313. **ruffle,** cause disturbance. 316. **Phœbe,** one of the names of the moon goddess. 325. **Hymenæus,** god of marriage. 340. **challenged,** accused. 347. **becomes,** is fitting. 366. **repute,** think of. 372. **speed,** succeed. 375. **Suffer,** permit. 379. **Ajax,** a hero of the Trojan War. 380. **Laertes' son,** Ulysses. 391. **dreary dumps,** mournful songs. 399. **play'd your prize,** won as in a contest. 408. **that,** that which. 416. **opinion,** reputation. 420. **controll'd,** opposed. 424. **leave to plead,** cease pleading. 433. **put it up,** put up with it. 434. **forfend,** avert.

I should be author to dishonour you!
But on mine honour dare I undertake
For good Lord Titus' innocence in all;
Whose fury not dissembled speaks his griefs:
Then, at my suit, look graciously on him;
Lose not so noble a friend on vain suppose,
Nor with sour looks afflict his gentle heart.
[*Aside to Sat.*] My lord, be rul'd by me, be won at last;
Dissemble all your griefs and discontents:
You are but newly planted in your throne;
Lest, then, the people, and patricians too,
Upon a just survey, take Titus' part,
And so supplant you for ingratitude,
Which Rome reputes to be a heinous sin,
Yield at entreats; and then let me alone:
I'll find a day to massacre them all
And raze their faction and their family,
The cruel father and his traitorous sons,
To whom I sued for my dear son's life,
And make them know what 'tis to let a queen
Kneel in the streets and beg for grace in vain.
[*Aloud.*]
Come, come, sweet emperor; come, Andronicus;
Take up this good old man, and cheer the heart
That dies in tempest of thy angry frown.
Sat. Rise, Titus, rise; my empress hath prevail'd.
Tit. I thank your majesty, and her, my lord:
These words, these looks, infuse new life in me.
Tam. Titus, I am incorporate in Rome,
A Roman now adopted happily,
And must advise the emperor for his good.
This day all quarrels die, Andronicus;
And let it be mine honour, good my lord,
That I have reconcil'd your friends and you.
For you, Prince Bassianus, I have pass'd
My word and promise to the emperor,
That you will be more mild and tractable.
And fear not, lords, and you, Lavinia;
By my advice, all humbled on your knees,
You shall ask pardon of his majesty. [*They kneel.*]
Luc. We do, and vow to heaven and to his highness,
That what we did was mildly as we might,
Tend'ring our sister's honour and our own.
Marc. That, on mine honour, here I do protest.
Sat. Away, and talk not; trouble us no more.
Tam. Nay, nay, sweet emperor, we must all be friends:
The tribune and his nephews kneel for grace;
I will not be denied: sweet heart, look back.
Sat. Marcus, for thy sake and thy brother's here,
And at my lovely Tamora's entreats,
I do remit these young men's heinous faults:
Stand up. [*They rise.*]
Lavinia, though you left me like a churl,
I found a friend, and sure as death I swore
I would not part a bachelor from the priest.
Come, if the emperor's court can feast two brides,
You are my guest, Lavinia, and your friends.
This day shall be a love-day, Tamora.
Tit. To-morrow, an it please your majesty
To hunt the panther and the hart with me,
With horn and hound we'll give your grace bonjour.
Sat. Be it so, Titus, and gramercy too.
Exeunt. Sound trumpets. Manet [*Aaron the*] *Moor.*

[ACT II.

SCENE I. *Rome. Before the palace.*]

[AARON *alone.*]

Aar. Now climbeth Tamora Olympus' top,
Safe out of fortune's shot; and sits aloft,
Secure of thunder's crack or lightning flash;
Advanc'd above pale envy's threat'ning reach.
As when the golden sun salutes the morn,
And, having gilt the ocean with his beams,
Gallops the zodiac in his glistering coach,
And overlooks the highest-peering hills;
So Tamora:
Upon her wit doth earthly honour wait,
And virtue stoops and trembles at her frown.
Then, Aaron, arm thy heart, and fit thy thoughts,
To mount aloft with thy imperial mistress,
And mount her pitch, whom thou in triumph long
Hast prisoner held, fett'red in amorous chains
And faster bound to Aaron's charming eyes
Than is Prometheus tied to Caucasus.
Away with slavish weeds and servile thoughts!
I will be bright, and shine in pearl and gold,
To wait upon this new-made empress.
To wait, said I? to wanton with this queen,
This goddess, this Semiramis, this nymph,
This siren, that will charm Rome's Saturnine,
And see his shipwrack and his commonweal's.
Holloa! what storm is this?

Enter CHIRON *and* DEMETRIUS, *braving.*

Dem. Chiron, thy years wants wit, thy wits wants edge,
And manners, to intrude where I am grac'd;
And may, for aught thou knowest, affected be.
Chi. Demetrius, thou dost over-ween in all;
And so in this, to bear me down with braves.
'Tis not the difference of a year or two
Makes me less gracious or thee more fortunate:
I am as able and as fit as thou
To serve, and to deserve my mistress' grace;
And that my sword upon thee shall approve,
And plead my passions for Lavinia's love.
Aar. [*Aside*] Clubs, clubs! these lovers will not keep the peace.
Dem. Why, boy, although our mother, unadvis'd,
Gave you a dancing-rapier by your side,
Are you so desperate grown, to threat your friends?
Go to; have your lath glued within your sheath
Till you know better how to handle it.
Chi. Meanwhile, sir, with the little skill I have,

436. **undertake,** assert. 440. **suppose,** supposition. 449. **entreats,** entreaties. 475. **mildly,** gently done. **might,** could. 488. **part,** depart. 491. **love-day,** day appointed to settle disputes. 492. **an,** if. 494. **bonjour,** good morning. 495. **gramercy,** thanks.

ACT II. SCENE I. 4. **envy's,** hate's, malice's. 7. **Gallops,** i.e., gallops over. 14. **pitch,** height to which a falcon soars before descending on its prey; see glossary. Aaron means that he will soar to a higher pitch than Tamora. 17. **Prometheus . . . Caucasus,** allusion to the myth of Prometheus, who stole fire from the chariot of the sun and gave it to man. As punishment, Zeus fastened him to a mountain in the Caucasus and sent a vulture to feast on his liver. 22. **Semiramis,** mythical queen of Assyria, famous for her cruelty and lust. 25. *Stage Direction:* ***braving,*** defying (each other). 26. **wants wit,** so QqF; Globe, following F_{2-4}: *want wit.* **wits wants,** so Q_1; Globe, following $Q_{2-3}F$: *wit wants.* 27. **intrude,** enter forcibly. **grace'd,** honored, favored. 28. **affected,** loved; see glossary. 29. **over-ween,** be arrogant. 32. **gracious,** acceptable, popular. 35. **approve,** prove. 38. **boy,** term of contempt. **unadvis'd,** ill-advisedly. 39. **dancing-rapier,** an ornamental weapon. 41. **lath,** counterfeit weapon. 46-47. **So . . . openly,** a reference to the law of arms; cf. *1 Henry VI*, I, iii, 46; II, iv, 86; and III, iv, 38-39. 48. **wot,** know. 62. **brabble,** quarrel, brawl. 64. **jet upon,** encroach upon. 67. **broach'd,** begun. 68. **controlment,** restraint. 70. **discord's ground,**

Full well shalt thou perceive how much I dare.
Dem. Ay, boy, grow ye so brave? *They draw.*
Aar. [*Coming forward*] Why, how now, lords!
So near the emperor's palace dare you draw,
And maintain such a quarrel openly?
Full well I wot the ground of all this grudge:
I would not for a million of gold
The cause were known to them it most concerns;
Nor would your noble mother for much more
Be so dishonoured in the court of Rome.
For shame, put up.
Dem. Not I, till I have sheath'd
My rapier in his bosom and withal
Thrust these reproachful speeches down his throat
That he hath breath'd in my dishonour here.
Chi. For that I am prepar'd and full resolv'd.
Foul-spoken coward, that thund'rest with thy tongue,
And with thy weapon nothing dar'st perform!
Aar. Away, I say!
Now, by the gods that warlike Goths adore,
This petty brabble will undo us all.
Why, lords, and think you not how dangerous
It is to jet upon a prince's right?
What, is Lavinia then become so loose,
Or Bassianus so degenerate,
That for her love such quarrels may be broach'd
Without controlment, justice, or revenge?
Young lords, beware! an should the empress know
This discord's ground, the music would not please.
Chi. I care not, I, knew she and all the world:
I love Lavinia more than all the world.
Dem. Youngling, learn thou to make some meaner choice:
Lavinia is thine elder brother's hope.
Aar. Why, are ye mad? or know ye not, in Rome
How furious and impatient they be,
And cannot brook competitors in love?
I tell you, lords, you do but plot your deaths
By this device.
Chi. Aaron, a thousand deaths
Would I propose to achieve her whom I love.
Aar. To achieve her! how?
Dem. Why makes thou it so strange?
She is a woman, therefore may be woo'd;
She is a woman, therefore may be won;
She is Lavinia, therefore must be lov'd.
What, man! more water glideth by the mill
Than wots the miller of; and easy it is
Of a cut loaf to steal a shive, we know:
Though Bassianus be the emperor's brother,
Better than he have worn Vulcan's badge.
Aar. [*Aside*] Ay, and as good as Saturninus may.
Dem. Then why should he despair that knows to court it
With words, fair looks and liberality?
What, hast not thou full often struck a doe,
And borne her cleanly by the keeper's nose?
Aar. Why, then, it seems, some certain snatch or so
Would serve your turns.
Chi. Ay, so the turn were serv'd.
Dem. Aaron, thou hast hit it.
Aar. Would you had hit it too!
Then should not we be tir'd with this ado.
Why, hark ye, hark ye! and are you such fools
To square for this? would it offend you, then,
That both should speed?
Chi. Faith, not me.
Dem. Nor me, so I were one.
Aar. For shame, be friends, and join for that you jar:
'Tis policy and stratagem must do
That you affect; and so must you resolve,
That what you cannot as you would achieve,
You must perforce accomplish as you may.
Take this of me: Lucrece was not more chaste
Than this Lavinia, Bassianus' love.
A speedier course than ling'ring languishment
Must we pursue, and I have found the path.
My lords, a solemn hunting is in hand;
There will the lovely Roman ladies troop:
The forest walks are wide and spacious;
And many unfrequented plots there are
Fitted by kind for rape and villany:
Single you thither then this dainty doe,
And strike her home by force, if not by words:
This way, or not at all, stand you in hope.
Come, come, our empress, with her sacred wit
To villany and vengeance consecrate,
Will we acquaint with all that we intend;
And she shall file our engines with advice,
That will not suffer you to square yourselves,
But to your wishes' height advance you both.
The emperor's court is like the house of Fame,
The palace full of tongues, of eyes, and ears:
The woods are ruthless, dreadful, deaf, and dull;
There speak, and strike, brave boys, and take your turns;
There serve your lust, shadow'd from heaven's eye,
And revel in Lavinia's treasury.
Chi. Thy counsel, lad, smells of no cowardice.
Dem. Sit fas aut nefas, till I find the stream
To cool this heat, a charm to calm these fits,
Per Stygia, per manes vehor. *Exeunt.*

[SCENE II. *A forest near Rome.*]

Enter TITUS ANDRONICUS *and his three* Sons [*and* MARCUS], *making a noise with hounds and horns.*

Tit. The hunt is up, the morn is bright and grey,
The fields are fragrant and the woods are green:
Uncouple here and let us make a bay
And wake the emperor and his lovely bride
And rouse the prince and ring a hunter's peal,
That all the court may echo with the noise.
Sons, let it be your charge, as it is ours,
To attend the emperor's person carefully:

cause for discord. 73. **meaner,** of lower degree. 77. **brook,** endure; see glossary. 80. **propose,** look forward to, be ready to meet. 81. **strange,** surprised. 87. **shive,** slice. 89. **Vulcan's badge,** cuckold's horns, alluding to the public shame to which he was exposed by his wife Venus' intrigue with Mars. 95. **snatch,** sudden or swift catch (with a probable bawdy pun). 96. **serve your turns,** answer your purposes; see glossary. 100. **square,** quarrel. 101. **speed,** succeed. 103. **join,** conspire. **jar,** quarrel. 104. **policy,** contrivance, craft; see glossary. 107. **perforce,** necessarily. 108. **Lucrece,** a chaste Roman lady ravished by Tarquin. 110. **languishment,** long courtship. 113. **troop,** march. 116. **by kind,** by nature; see *kind* in glossary. 118. **home,** effectually, thoroughly. 123. **file,** rub smooth, polish; here perhaps, perfect. **engines,** devices, plots; see glossary. 126. **house of Fame,** residence of rumor, described also in Chaucer's *Hous of Fame* and in Ovid. 130. **lust,** so Qq; Globe, following F: *lusts*. 133. **Sit fas aut nefas,** be it right or wrong. 135. **Per Stygia, per manes vehor,** I am carried across the Styx through the realm of the shades.

SCENE II. 1. **grey,** cold, sunless light of early morning; the phrase is equivalent to "bright and early." 3. **Uncouple,** unleash the hounds. **make a bay,** keep up a deep, prolonged barking.

I have been troubled in my sleep this night,
But dawning day new comfort hath inspir'd.

Here a cry of hounds, and wind horns in a peal. Then enter SATURNINUS, TAMORA, BASSIANUS, LAVINIA, CHIRON, DEMETRIUS, *and their* Attendants.

Many good morrows to your majesty;
Madam, to you as many and as good:
I promised your grace a hunter's peal.
Sat. And you have rung it lustily, my lords;
Somewhat too early for new-married ladies.
Bas. Lavinia, how say you?
Lav. I say, no;
I have been broad awake two hours and more.
Sat. Come on, then; horse and chariots let us have,
And to our sport. [*To Tamora*] Madam, now shall ye see
Our Roman hunting.
Marc. I have dogs, my lord,
Will rouse the proudest panther in the chase,
And climb the highest promontory top.
Tit. And I have horse will follow where the game
Makes way, and run like swallows o'er the plain.
Dem. Chiron, we hunt not, we, with horse nor hound,
But hope to pluck a dainty doe to ground. *Exeunt.*

[SCENE III. *A lonely part of the forest.*]

Enter AARON *alone* [*with a bag of gold*].

Aar. He that had wit would think that I had none,
To bury so much gold under a tree,
And never after to inherit it.
Let him that thinks of me so abjectly
Know that this gold must coin a stratagem,
Which, cunningly effected, will beget
A very excellent piece of villany:
And so repose, sweet gold, for their unrest [*Hides the gold.*]
That have their alms out of the empress' chest.

Enter TAMORA *alone to the Moor.*

Tam. My lovely Aaron, wherefore look'st thou sad,
When every thing doth make a gleeful boast?
The birds chant melody on every bush,
The snake lies rolled in the cheerful sun,
The green leaves quiver with the cooling wind
And make a chequer'd shadow on the ground:
Under their sweet shade, Aaron, let us sit,
And, whilst the babbling echo mocks the hounds,
Replying shrilly to the well-tun'd horns,
As if a double hunt were heard at once,
Let us sit down and mark their yellowing noise;
And, after conflict such as was suppos'd
The wand'ring prince and Dido once enjoy'd,
When with a happy storm they were surpris'd
And curtain'd with a counsel-keeping cave,
We may, each wreathed in the other's arms,
Our pastimes done, possess a golden slumber;
Whiles hounds and horns and sweet melodious birds
Be unto us as is a nurse's song
Of lullaby to bring her babe asleep.
Aar. Madam, though Venus govern your desires,
Saturn is dominator over mine:
What signifies my deadly-standing eye,
My silence and my cloudy melancholy,
My fleece of woolly hair that now uncurls
Even as an adder when she doth unroll
To do some fatal execution?
No, madam, these are no venereal signs:
Vengeance is in my heart, death in my hand,
Blood and revenge are hammering in my head.
Hark, Tamora, the empress of my soul,
Which never hopes more heaven than rests in thee,
This is the day of doom for Bassianus:
His Philomel must lose her tongue to-day,
Thy sons make pillage of her chastity
And wash their hands in Bassianus' blood.
Seest thou this letter? take it up, I pray thee,
And give the king this fatal-plotted scroll.
Now question me no more; we are espied;
Here comes a parcel of our hopeful booty,
Which dreads not yet their lives' destruction.

Enter BASSIANUS *and* LAVINIA.

Tam. Ah, my sweet Moor, sweeter to me than life!
Aar. No more, great empress; Bassianus comes:
Be cross with him; and I'll go fetch thy sons
To back thy quarrels, whatsoe'er they be. [*Exit.*]
Bas. Who have we here? Rome's royal empress,
Unfurnish'd of her well-beseeming troop?
Or is it Dian, habited like her,
Who hath abandoned her holy groves
To see the general hunting in this forest?
Tam. Saucy controller of our private steps!
Had I the power that some say Dian had,
Thy temples should be planted presently
With horns, as was Actæon's; and the hounds
Should drive upon thy new-transformed limbs,
Unmannerly intruder as thou art!
Lav. Under your patience, gentle empress,
'Tis thought you have a goodly gift in horning;
And to be doubted that your Moor and you
Are singled forth to try experiments:
Jove shield your husband from his hounds to-day!
'Tis pity they should take him for a stag.
Bas. Believe me, queen, your swarthy Cimmerian
Doth make your honour of his body's hue,
Spotted, detested, and abominable.
Why are you sequest'red from all your train,
Dismounted from your snow-white goodly steed,
And wand'red hither to an obscure plot,
Accompanied but with a barbarous Moor,
If foul desire had not conducted you?
Lav. And, being intercepted in your sport,
Great reason that my noble lord be rated
For sauciness. I pray you, let us hence,
And let her joy her raven-coloured love;
This valley fits the purpose passing well.

9. **troubled . . . sleep.** The ominousness of bad dreams is a commonplace in Elizabethan tragedy. 14. **lords,** so QqFf; Globe, following Dyce: *lord.*

SCENE III. 4. **abjectly,** basely. 5. **coin,** fabricate; here, to further Aaron's plot. 13. **rolled,** coiled. 20. **yellowing,** (so Qq), baying; Globe, following F: *yelping.* 22. **prince,** i.e., Aeneas (see *Aeneid*, IV). 24. **counsel-keeping,** secret-keeping. 31. **Saturn . . . mine.** Aaron describes himself in terms of current astrology, according to which the planet Saturn exercised a malign influence over those whom it dominated. 32. **deadly-standing,** fixed with a deathly stare. 37. **venereal,** erotic. 43. **Philomel,** an illusion to the story in Ovid's *Metamorphoses* of Philomela, raped by her brother-in-law, Tereus (cf. II, iv, 26 below); he cut out her tongue so that she could not disclose his villainy. She succeeded in weaving the account of her misfortune in a tapestry. 47. **fatal-plotted,** designed to prove fatal. 49. **parcel,** small party or company. 57. **Dian,** Diana, huntress and goddess of chastity; here used sarcastically. **habited,** dressed. 62. **presently,** immediately. 63. **Actæon's,** an allusion to the story of Actaeon, who was changed into a

Bas. The king my brother shall have notice of this.
Lav. Ay, for these slips have made him noted long:
Good king, to be so mightily abus'd!
Tam. Why have I patience to endure all this?

Enter CHIRON *and* DEMETRIUS.

Dem. How now, dear sovereign, and our gracious mother!
Why doth your highness look so pale and wan?
Tam. Have I not reason, think you, to look pale?
These two have 'tic'd me hither to this place:
A barren detested vale, you see it is;
The trees, though summer, yet forlorn and lean,
Overcome with moss and baleful mistletoe:
Here never shines the sun; here nothing breeds,
Unless the nightly owl or fatal raven:
And when they show'd me this abhorred pit,
They told me, here, at dead time of the night,
A thousand fiends, a thousand hissing snakes,
Ten thousand swelling toads, as many urchins,
Would make such fearful and confused cries
As any mortal body hearing it
Should straight fall mad, or else die suddenly.
No sooner had they told this hellish tale,
But straight they told me they would bind me here
Unto the body of a dismal yew,
And leave me to this miserable death:
And then they call'd me foul adulteress,
Lascivious Goth, and all the bitterest terms
That ever ear did hear to such effect:
And, had you not by wondrous fortune come,
This vengeance on me had they executed.
Revenge it, as you love your mother's life,
Or be ye not henceforth call'd my children.
Dem. This is a witness that I am thy son.
Stab him [Bassianus].
Chi. And this for me, struck home to show my strength. [*Also stabs Bassianus, who dies.*]
Lav. Ay, come, Semiramis, nay, barbarous Tamora,
For no name fits thy nature but thy own!
Tam. Give me thy poniard; you shall know, my boys,
Your mother's hand shall right your mother's wrong.
Dem. Stay, madam; here is more belongs to her;
First thrash the corn, then after burn the straw:
This minion stood upon her chastity,
Upon her nuptial vow, her loyalty,
†And with that painted hope braves your mightiness:
And shall she carry this unto her grave?
Chi. An if she do, I would I were an eunuch.
Drag hence her husband to some secret hole,
And make his dead trunk pillow to our lust.
Tam. But when ye have the honey ye desire,
Let not this wasp outlive, us both to sting.
Chi. I warrant you, madam, we will make that sure.
Come, mistress, now perforce we will enjoy
That nice-preserved honesty of yours.
Lav. O Tamora! thou bearest a woman's face,—
Tam. I will not hear her speak; away with her!
Lav. Sweet lords, entreat her hear me but a word.
Dem. Listen, fair madam: let it be your glory
To see her tears; but be your heart to them
As unrelenting flint to drops of rain.
Lav. When did the tiger's young ones teach the dam?
O, do not learn her wrath; she taught it thee;
The milk thou suck'dst from her did turn to marble;
Even at thy teat thou hadst thy tyranny.
Yet every mother breeds not sons alike:
[*To Chiron*] Do thou entreat her show a woman's pity.
Chi. What, wouldst thou have me prove myself a bastard?
Lav. 'Tis true; the raven doth not hatch a lark:
Yet have I heard,—O, could I find it now!—
The lion mov'd with pity did endure
To have his princely paws par'd all away:
Some say that ravens foster forlorn children,
The whilst their own birds famish in their nests:
O, be to me, though thy hard heart say no,
Nothing so kind, but something pitiful!
Tam. I know not what it means; away with her!
Lav. O, let me teach thee! for my father's sake,
That gave thee life, when well he might have slain thee,
Be not obdurate, open thy deaf ears.
Tam. Hadst thou in person ne'er offended me,
Even for his sake am I pitiless.
Remember, boys, I pour'd forth tears in vain,
To save your brother from the sacrifice;
But fierce Andronicus would not relent:
Therefore, away with her, and use her as you will,
The worse to her, the better lov'd of me.
Lav. O Tamora, be call'd a gentle queen,
And with thine own hands kill me in this place!
For 'tis not life that I have begg'd so long;
Poor I was slain when Bassianus died.
Tam. What begg'st thou, then? fond woman, let me go.
Lav. 'Tis present death I beg; and one thing more
That womanhood denies my tongue to tell:
O, keep me from their worse than killing lust,
And tumble me into some loathsome pit,
Where never man's eye may behold my body:
Do this, and be a charitable murderer.
Tam. So should I rob my sweet sons of their fee:
No, let them satisfy their lust on thee.
Dem. Away! for thou hast stay'd us here too long.
Lav. No grace? no womanhood? Ah, beastly creature!
The blot and enemy to our general name!
Confusion fall—
Chi. Nay, then I'll stop your mouth. Bring thou her husband:
This is the hole where Aaron bid us hide him.
[*Demetrius throws the body of Bassianus into the pit; then exeunt Demetrius and Chiron, dragging off Lavinia.*]
Tam. Farewell, my sons: see that you make her sure.
Ne'er let my heart know merry cheer indeed,
Till all the Andronici be made away.
Now will I hence to seek my lovely Moor,
And let my spleenful sons this trull deflour. [*Exit.*]

stag by Diana as punishment for watching her and her nymphs at their bath. 67. **horning,** cuckolding. 68. **doubted,** suspected, feared; see glossary. 72. **swarthy,** Qq: *swartie;* Globe, following F: *swarth.* **Cimmerian,** an allusion to the Cimmerii in the *Odyssey,* a race who lived in perpetual darkness; the reference is to Aaron's black complexion. 81. **rated,** chidden; see glossary. 83. **joy,** enjoy. 85. **notice,** so QqFf; Globe, following Pope: *note;* the pronunciation is "notes." 86. **noted,** stigmatized. 87. **abus'd,** deceived; see glossary. 92. **'tic'd,** enticed. 101. **urchins,** hedgehogs. 103. **mortal,** human. 110. **Goth,** a quibble; the word was pronounced somewhat like "goat," which is the allegorical symbol of lechery. 124. **minion,** hussy. 126. **painted,** specious, unreal; see glossary. 135. **nice,** fastidiously. **honesty,** chastity. 143. **learn,** teach; see glossary. 147. **woman's,** so Q_1; Globe, following Q_2-$_3$F: *woman.* 153. **forlorn,** abandoned. 156. **Nothing . . . pitiful,** i.e., not so kind as the raven, but still showing some pity. 172. **fond,** foolish; see glossary. 173. **present,** immediate; see glossary. 174. **denies,** refuses permission.

Enter AARON, *with two of Titus' Sons* [QUINTUS *and* MARTIUS].

Aar. Come on, my lords, the better foot before:
Straight will I bring you to the loathsome pit
Where I espied the panther fast asleep.
Quin. My sight is very dull, whate'er it bodes.
Mart. And mine, I promise you; were it not for shame,
Well could I leave our sport to sleep awhile.
[*Falls into the pit.*]
Quin. What, art thou fallen? What subtle hole is this,
Whose mouth is covered with rude-growing briers,
Upon whose leaves are drops of new-shed blood
As fresh as morning dew distill'd on flowers?
A very fatal place it seems to me.
Speak, brother, hast thou hurt thee with the fall?
Mart. O brother, with the dismall'st object hurt
That ever eye with sight made heart lament!
Aar. [*Aside*] Now will I fetch the king to find them here,
That he thereby may give a likely guess
How these were they that made away his brother. *Exit.*
Mart. Why dost not comfort me, and help me out
From this unhallowed and blood-stain'd hole?
Quin. I am surprised with an uncouth fear:
A chilling sweat o'er-runs my trembling joints:
My heart suspects more than mine eye can see.
Mart. To prove thou hast a true-divining heart,
Aaron and thou look down into this den,
And see a fearful sight of blood and death.
Quin. Aaron is gone; and my compassionate heart
Will not permit mine eyes once to behold
The thing whereat it trembles by surmise:
O, tell me who it is; for ne'er till now
Was I a child to fear I know not what.
Mart. Lord Bassianus lies beray'd in blood,
All on a heap, like to a slaughtered lamb,
In this detested, dark, blood-drinking pit.
Quin. If it be dark, how dost thou know 'tis he?
Mart. Upon his bloody finger he doth wear
A precious ring, that lightens all this hole,
Which, like a taper in some monument,
Doth shine upon the dead man's earthy cheeks,
And shows the ragged entrails of this pit:
So pale did shine the moon on Pyramus
When he by night lay bath'd in maiden blood.
O brother, help me with thy fainting hand—
If fear hath made thee faint, as me it hath—
Out of this fell devouring receptacle,
As hateful as Cocytus' misty mouth.
Quin. Reach me thy hand, that I may help thee out;
Or, wanting strength to do thee so much good,
I may be pluck'd into the swallowing womb
Of this deep pit, poor Bassianus' grave.
I have no strength to pluck thee to the brink.
Mart. Nor I no strength to climb without thy help.
Quin. Thy hand once more; I will not loose again,
Till thou art here aloft, or I below:
Thou canst not come to me: I come to thee. [*Falls in.*]

Enter the emperor [SATURNINUS] *and* AARON *the Moor.*

Sat. Along with me: I'll see what hole is here,
And what he is that now is leap'd into it.
Say, who art thou that lately didst descend
Into this gaping hollow of the earth?
Mart. The unhappy sons of old Andronicus;
Brought hither in a most unlucky hour,
To find thy brother Bassianus dead.
Sat. My brother dead! I know thou dost but jest:
He and his lady both are at the lodge
Upon the north side of this pleasant chase;
'Tis not an hour since I left him there.
Mart. We know not where you left them all alive;
But, out, alas! here have we found him dead.

Enter TAMORA, [TITUS] ANDRONICUS, *and* LUCIUS.

Tam. Where is my lord the king?
Sat. Here, Tamora, though griev'd with killing grief.
Tam. Where is thy brother Bassianus?
Sat. Now to the bottom dost thou search my wound:
Poor Bassianus here lies murdered.
Tam. Then all too late I bring this fatal writ,
The complot of this timeless tragedy;
And wonder greatly that man's face can fold
In pleasing smiles such murderous tyranny.
She giveth Saturnine a letter.
Sat. (*Reads the letter*) 'An if we miss to meet him handsomely—
Sweet huntsman, Bassianus 'tis we mean—
Do thou so much as dig the grave for him:
Thou know'st our meaning. Look for thy reward
Among the nettles at the elder-tree
Which overshades the mouth of that same pit
Where we decreed to bury Bassianus.
Do this, and purchase us thy lasting friends.'
O Tamora! was ever heard the like?
This is the pit, and this the elder-tree.
Look, sirs, if you can find the huntsman out
That should have murdered Bassianus here.
Aar. My gracious lord, here is the bag of gold.
Sat. [*To Titus*] Two of thy whelps, fell curs of bloody kind,
Have here bereft my brother of his life.
Sirs, drag them from the pit unto the prison:
There let them bide until we have devis'd
Some never-heard-of torturing pain for them.
Tam. What, are they in this pit? O wondrous thing!
How easily murder is discovered!
Tit. High emperor, upon my feeble knee
I beg this boon, with tears not lightly shed,
That this fell fault of my accursed sons,
Accursed, if the fault be prov'd in them,—
Sat. If it be prov'd! you see it is apparent.
Who found this letter? Tamora, was it you?
Tam. Andronicus himself did take it up.
Tit. I did, my lord: yet let me be their bail:
For, by my father's reverend tomb, I vow
They shall be ready at your highness' will
To answer their suspicion with their lives.
Sat. Thou shalt not bail them: see thou follow me.
Some bring the murdered body, some the murderers:
Let them not speak a word; the guilt is plain;
For, by my soul, were there worse end than death,

193. **Straight,** immediately. 211. **uncouth,** strange. 217. **compassionate,** piteous, lamenting. 220. **who,** so Q_{1-2}; Globe, following Q_3F_1: *how.* 222. **beray'd,** defiled. 227. **A precious ring,** presumably the carbuncle, which was believed to emit light. **this,** so Q_{1-2}; Globe, following Q_3F_1: *the.* 230. **this,** so Qq; Globe, following F_1: *the.* 231. **Pyramus.** Cf. the story of Pyramus and Thisbe dramatized by the "rude mechanicals" in *A Midsummer Night's Dream,* I, ii; III, i; and V, i, 127-369. 235. **fell,** savage. 236. **Cocytus,** one of the rivers of Hades—the river of lamentations. 250. **sons,** so Q_1; Globe, following $Q_{2-3}F_1$: *son.* 257. **them,** so Qq; Globe, following F_1: *him.* 265. **timeless,** untimely. 266. **fold,** hide. 279. **should,** was to. 292. **apparent,** evident. 298. **their suspicion,** i.e., suspicion they are under. 305. **Fear**

That end upon them should be executed.
Tam. Andronicus, I will entreat the king:
Fear not thy sons; they shall do well enough.
Tit. Come, Lucius, come; stay not to talk with them. [*Exeunt.*]

[SCENE IV. *Another part of the forest.*]

Enter the empress' Sons *with* LAVINIA, *her hands cut off, and her tongue cut out, and ravished.*

Dem. So, now go tell, an if thy tongue can speak,
Who 'twas that cut thy tongue and ravish'd thee.
Chi. Write down thy mind, bewray thy meaning so,
An if thy stumps will let thee play the scribe.
Dem. See, how with signs and tokens she can scrowl.
Chi. Go home, call for sweet water, wash thy hands.
Dem. She hath no tongue to call, nor hands to wash;
And so let 's leave her to her silent walks.
Chi. An 'twere my cause, I should go hang myself.
Dem. If thou hadst hands to help thee knit the cord.
Exeunt [*Chiron and Demetrius*].

Enter MARCUS *from hunting.*

Mar. Who is this? my niece, that flies away so fast!
Cousin, a word; where is your husband?
If I do dream, would all my wealth would wake me!
If I do wake, some planet strike me down,
That I may slumber in eternal sleep!
Speak, gentle niece, what stern ungentle hands
Hath lopp'd and hew'd and made thy body bare
Of her two branches, those sweet ornaments,
Whose circling shadows kings have sought to sleep in,
And might not gain so great a happiness
As have thy love? Why dost not speak to me?
Alas, a crimson river of warm blood,
Like to a bubbling fountain stirr'd with wind,
Doth rise and fall between thy rosed lips,
Coming and going with thy honey breath.
But, sure, some Tereus hath deflow'red thee,
And, lest thou shouldst detect him, cut thy tongue.
Ah, now thou turn'st away thy face for shame!
And, notwithstanding all this loss of blood,
As from a conduit with three issuing spouts,
Yet do thy cheeks look red as Titan's face
Blushing to be encount'red with a cloud.
Shall I speak for thee? shall I say 'tis so?
O, that I knew thy heart; and knew the beast,
That I might rail at him, to ease my mind!
Sorrow concealed, like an oven stopp'd,
Doth burn the heart to cinders where it is.
Fair Philomela, why she but lost her tongue,
And in a tedious sampler sew'd her mind:
But, lovely niece, that mean is cut from thee;
A craftier Tereus, cousin, hast thou met,
And he hath cut those pretty fingers off,
That could have better sew'd than Philomel.
O, had the monster seen those lily hands
Tremble, like aspen-leaves, upon a lute,
And make the silken strings delight to kiss them,
He would not then have touch'd them for his life!
Or, had he heard the heavenly harmony
Which that sweet tongue hath made,
He would have dropp'd his knife, and fell asleep
As Cerberus at the Thracian poet's feet.
Come, let us go, and make thy father blind;
For such a sight will blind a father's eye:
One hour's storm will drown the fragrant meads;
What will whole months of tears thy father's eyes?
Do not draw back, for we will mourn with thee:
O, could our mourning ease thy misery! *Exeunt.*

[ACT III.

SCENE I. *Rome. A street.*]

Enter the Judges *and* Senators *with Titus' two* Sons *bound, passing on the stage to the place of execution, and* TITUS *going before, pleading.*

Tit. Hear me, grave fathers! noble tribunes, stay!
For pity of mine age, whose youth was spent
In dangerous wars, whilst you securely slept;
For all my blood in Rome's great quarrel shed;
For all the frosty nights that I have watch'd;
And for these bitter tears, which now you see
Filling the aged wrinkles in my cheeks;
Be pitiful to my condemned sons,
Whose souls is not corrupted as 'tis thought.
For two and twenty sons I never wept,
Because they died in honour's lofty bed.
[*Titus*] *Andronicus lieth down and the Judges pass by him.*
For these, tribunes, in the dust I write
My heart's deep languor and my soul's sad tears:
Let my tears stanch the earth's dry appetite;
My sons' sweet blood will make it shame and blush.
O earth, I will befriend thee more with rain,
That shall distil from these two ancient urns,
Than youthful April shall with all his show'rs:
In summer's drought I'll drop upon thee still;
In winter with warm tears I'll melt the snow,
And keep eternal spring-time on thy face,
So thou refuse to drink my dear sons' blood.

Enter LUCIUS, *with his weapon drawn.*

O reverend tribunes! O gentle, aged men!
Unbind my sons, reverse the doom of death;
And let me say, that never wept before,
My tears are now prevailing orators.
Luc. O noble father, you lament in vain:
The tribunes hear you not; no man is by;
And you recount your sorrows to a stone.
Tit. Ah, Lucius, for thy brothers let me plead.
Grave tribunes, once more I entreat of you,—
Luc. My gracious lord, no tribune hears you speak.
Tit. Why, 'tis no matter, man: if they did hear,
They would not mark me, or if they did mark,
They would not pity me, yet plead I must;
†And bootless unto them . . . .
Therefore I tell my sorrows to the stones;
Who, though they cannot answer my distress,
Yet in some sort they are better than the tribunes,
For that they will not intercept my tale:
When I do weep, they humbly at my feet

not, fear not for.
SCENE IV. 3. **bewray,** reveal. 5. **scrowl,** scrawl, with play on "scroll." 9. **cause,** so QqF_1; Globe, following Pope: *case.* 12. **Cousin,** kinswoman. 17. **Hath,** so QqF_1; Globe, following $F_{2\text{-}4}$: *Have.* 26. **Tereus.** Cf. II, iii, 43, note. 27. **detect,** expose. 36. **stopp'd,** closed too long. 40. **mean,** means, agency; see glossary. 51. **Thracian poet's.** According to legend, Orpheus' sweet singing charmed even Cerberus, three-headed dog guarding the entrance to Hades.
ACT III. SCENE I. 4. **my blood,** i.e., blood of my sons. 9. **is,** so QqF_1; Globe, following $F_{2\text{-}4}$: *are.* 10. **two and twenty.** Cf. I, i, 79, 195. 12. **these,** so QqF; Globe, following $F_{2\text{-}4}$: *these, these.* 17. **urns,** eyes. 40. **For that,** because.

Receive my tears and seem to weep with me;
And, were they but attired in grave weeds,
Rome could afford no tribunes like to these.
A stone is soft as wax,—tribunes more hard than stones;
A stone is silent, and offendeth not,
And tribunes with their tongues doom men to death. [*Rises.*]
But wherefore stand'st thou with thy weapon drawn?

Luc. To rescue my two brothers from their death:
For which attempt the judges have pronounc'd
My everlasting doom of banishment.

Tit. O happy man! they have befriended thee.
Why, foolish Lucius, dost thou not perceive
That Rome is but a wilderness of tigers?
Tigers must prey, and Rome affords no prey
But me and mine: how happy art thou, then,
From these devourers to be banished!
But who comes with our brother Marcus here?

Enter MARCUS *with* LAVINIA.

Marc. Titus, prepare thy aged eyes to weep;
Or, if not so, thy noble heart to break:
I bring consuming sorrow to thine age.

Tit. Will it consume me? let me see it, then.

Marc. This was thy daughter.

Tit. Why, Marcus, so she is.

Luc. Ay me, this object kills me!

Tit. Faint-hearted boy, arise, and look upon her.
Speak, Lavinia, what accursed hand
Hath made thee handless in thy father's sight?
What fool hath added water to the sea,
Or brought a faggot to bright-burning Troy?
My grief was at the height before thou cam'st,
And now, like Nilus, it disdaineth bounds.
Give me a sword, I'll chop off my hands too;
For they have fought for Rome, and all in vain;
And they have nurs'd this woe, in feeding life;
In bootless prayer have they been held up,
And they have serv'd me to effectless use:
Now all the service I require of them
Is that the one will help to cut the other.
'Tis well, Lavinia, that thou hast no hands;
For hands, to do Rome service, is but vain.

Luc. Speak, gentle sister, who hath martyr'd thee?

Marc. O, that delightful engine of her thoughts,
That blabb'd them with such pleasing eloquence,
Is torn from forth that pretty hollow cage,
Where, like a sweet melodious bird, it sung
Sweet varied notes, enchanting every ear!

Luc. O, say thou for her, who hath done this deed?

Marc. O, thus I found her, straying in the park,
Seeking to hide herself, as doth the deer
That hath receiv'd some unrecuring wound.

Tit. It was my deer; and he that wounded her
Hath hurt me more than had he kill'd me dead:
For now I stand as one upon a rock
Environ'd with a wilderness of sea,
Who marks the waxing tide grow wave by wave,
Expecting ever when some envious surge
Will in his brinish bowels swallow him.
This way to death my wretched sons are gone;
Here stands my other son, a banish'd man,
And here my brother, weeping at my woes:
But that which gives my soul the greatest spurn,
Is dear Lavinia, dearer than my soul.
Had I but seen thy picture in this plight,
It would have madded me: what shall I do
Now I behold thy lively body so?
Thou hast no hands, to wipe away thy tears,
Nor tongue, to tell me who hath martyr'd thee:
Thy husband he is dead; and for his death
Thy brothers are condemn'd, and dead by this.
Look, Marcus! ah, son Lucius, look on her!
When I did name her brothers, then fresh tears
Stood on her cheeks, as doth the honey-dew
Upon a gath'red lily almost withered.

Marc. Perchance she weeps because they kill'd her husband;
Perchance because she knows them innocent.

Tit. If they did kill thy husband, then be joyful,
Because the law hath ta'en revenge on them.
No, no, they would not do so foul a deed;
Witness the sorrow that their sister makes.
Gentle Lavinia, let me kiss thy lips;
Or make some sign how I may do thee ease:
Shall thy good uncle, and thy brother Lucius,
And thou, and I, sit round about some fountain,
Looking all downwards, to behold our cheeks
How they are stain'd, as meadows, yet not dry,
With miry slime left on them by a flood?
And in the fountain shall we gaze so long
Till the fresh taste be taken from that clearness,
And made a brine-pit with our bitter tears?
Or shall we cut away our hands, like thine?
Or shall we bite our tongues, and in dumb shows
Pass the remainder of our hateful days?
What shall we do? let us, that have our tongues,
Plot some device of further misery,
To make us wonder'd at in time to come.

Luc. Sweet father, cease your tears; for, at your grief,
See how my wretched sister sobs and weeps.

Marc. Patience, dear niece. Good Titus, dry thine eyes.

Tit. Ah, Marcus, Marcus! brother, well I wot
Thy napkin cannot drink a tear of mine,
For thou, poor man, hast drown'd it with thine own.

Luc. Ah, my Lavinia, I will wipe thy cheeks.

Tit. Mark, Marcus, mark! I understand her signs:
Had she a tongue to speak, now would she say
That to her brother which I said to thee:
His napkin, with his true tears all bewet,
Can do no service on her sorrowful cheeks.
O, what a sympathy of woe is this,
As far from help as Limbo is from bliss!

Enter AARON *the Moor.*

Aar. Titus Andronicus, my lord the emperor
Sends thee this word,—that, if thou love thy sons,
Let Marcus, Lucius, or thyself, old Titus,
Or any one of you, chop off your hand,
And send it to the king: he for the same
Will send thee hither both thy sons alive;
And that shall be the ransom for their fault.

44. **tribunes,** so Q_1; Globe, following $Q_{2\text{-}3}F_1$: *tribune.* 64. **object,** sight. 71. **Nilus,** Nile. 80. **is,** so QqF_1; Globe, following Rowe: *are.* 90. **unrecuring,** incurable. 96. **envious,** spiteful; see glossary. 101. **spurn,** stroke. 104. **madded,** maddened. 109. **by this,** by now. 121. **ease,** comfort; see glossary. 140. **napkin,** handkerchief; see glossary. 148. **sympathy,** agreement, conformity. 149. **Limbo,** region bordering Hell, where were confined the souls of those barred from heaven through no fault of their own, such as good men who lived before the Christian era. 179. **meet,** fit, ready. 203-206. **O . . . face.** An early example in Shakespeare of the Machiavellian villain, a stage convention made popular by Marlowe's Barabas in *The Jew of Malta* and employed elsewhere in Shakespeare in Richard III, Edmund in *King Lear*, and Iago

Tit. O gracious emperor! O gentle Aaron!
Did ever raven sing so like a lark,
That gives sweet tidings of the sun's uprise?
With all my heart, I'll send the emperor
My hand:
Good Aaron, wilt thou help to chop it off?
Luc. Stay, father! for that noble hand of thine,
That hath thrown down so many enemies,
Shall not be sent: my hand will serve the turn:
My youth can better spare my blood than you;
And therefore mine shall save my brothers' lives.
Marc. Which of your hands hath not defended Rome,
And rear'd aloft the bloody battle-axe,
Writing destruction on the enemy's castle?
O, none of both but are of high desert:
My hand hath been but idle; let it serve
To ransom my two nephews from their death;
Then have I kept it to a worthy end.
Aar. Nay, come, agree whose hand shall go along,
For fear they die before their pardon come.
Marc. My hand shall go.
Luc. By heaven, it shall not go!
Tit. Sirs, strive no more: such with'red herbs as these
Are meet for plucking up, and therefore mine.
Luc. Sweet father, if I shall be thought thy son,
Let me redeem my brothers both from death.
Marc. And, for our father's sake and mother's care,
Now let me show a brother's love to thee.
Tit. Agree between you; I will spare my hand.
Luc. Then I'll go fetch an axe.
Marc. But I will use the axe.
Exeunt [*Lucius and Marcus*].
Tit. Come hither, Aaron; I'll deceive them both:
Lend me thy hand, and I will give thee mine.
Aar. [*Aside*] If that be call'd deceit, I will be honest,
And never, whilst I live, deceive men so:
But I'll deceive you in another sort,
And that you'll say, ere half an hour pass.
He cuts off Titus's hand.

Enter LUCIUS *and* MARCUS *again.*

Tit. Now stay your strife: what shall be is dispatch'd.
Good Aaron, give his majesty my hand:
Tell him it was a hand that warded him
From thousand dangers; bid him bury it;
More hath it merited; that let it have.
As for my sons, say I account of them
As jewels purchas'd at an easy price;
And yet dear too, because I bought mine own.
Aar. I go, Andronicus: and for thy hand
Look by and by to have thy sons with thee.
[*Aside*] Their heads, I mean. O, how this villany
Doth fat me with the very thoughts of it!
Let fools do good, and fair men call for grace,
Aaron will have his soul black like his face. *Exit.*
Tit. O, here I lift this one hand up to heaven,
And bow this feeble ruin to the earth:
If any power pities wretched tears,
To that I call! [*To Lav.*] What, wouldst thou kneel with me?
Do, then, dear heart; for heaven shall hear our prayers;
Or with our sighs we'll breathe the welkin dim,
And stain the sun with fog, as sometime clouds
When they do hug him in their melting bosoms.
Marc. O brother, speak with possibility,
And do not break into these deep extremes.
Tit. Is not my sorrow deep, having no bottom?
Then be my passions bottomless with them.
Marc. But yet let reason govern thy lament.
Tit. If there were reason for these miseries,
Then into limits could I bind my woes:
When heaven doth weep, doth not the earth o'erflow?
If the winds rage, doth not the sea wax mad,
Threat'ning the welkin with his big-swoln face?
And wilt thou have a reason for this coil?
I am the sea; hark, how her sighs doth flow!
She is the weeping welkin, I the earth:
Then must my sea be moved with her sighs;
Then must my earth with her continual tears
Become a deluge, overflow'd and drown'd;
For why my bowels cannot hide her woes,
But like a drunkard must I vomit them.
Then give me leave, for losers will have leave
To ease their stomachs with their bitter tongues.

Enter a Messenger, *with two heads and a hand.*

Mess. Worthy Andronicus, ill art thou repaid
For that good hand thou sent'st the emperor.
Here are the heads of thy two noble sons;
And here 's thy hand, in scorn to thee sent back;
Thy griefs their sports, thy resolution mock'd;
That woe is me to think upon thy woes
More than remembrance of my father's death. [*Exit.*]
Marc. Now let hot Ætna cool in Sicily,
And be my heart an ever-burning hell!
These miseries are more than may be borne.
To weep with them that weep doth ease some deal;
But sorrow flouted at is double death.
Luc. Ah, that this sight should make so deep a wound,
And yet detested life not shrink thereat!
That ever death should let life bear his name,
Where life hath no more interest but to breathe!
[*Lavinia kisses Titus.*]
Marc. Alas, poor heart, that kiss is comfortless
As frozen water to a starved snake.
Tit. When will this fearful slumber have an end?
Marc. Now, farewell, flatt'ry: die, Andronicus;
Thou dost not slumber: see, thy two sons' heads,
Thy warlike hand, thy mangled daughter here;
Thy other banish'd son, with this dear sight
Struck pale and bloodless; and thy brother, I,
Even like a stony image, cold and numb.
Ah, now no more will I control thy griefs:
Rend off thy silver hair, thy other hand
Gnawing with thy teeth; and be this dismal sight
The closing up of our most wretched eyes:
Now is a time to storm; why art thou still?
Tit. Ha, ha, ha!
Marc. Why dost thou laugh? it fits not with this hour.

in *Othello*. 204. **fat,** fatten, i.e., delight. 210. **wouldst,** so Q_1; Globe, following Ff: *wilt*. 212. **welkin,** sky, heavens; see glossary. 213. **sometime,** from time to time; see glossary. 215. **speak with possibility,** speak of things possible. 225. **coil,** noise, fuss; see glossary. 231. **For why,** because. **bowels,** seat of compassion. 234. **stomachs,** resentful feelings; see glossary. 239. **resolution,** resolute conduct. 240. **That,** so that. 242. **Ætna,** volcanic Mountain on the island of Sicily. 245. **some deal,** somewhat, a little. 252. **starved,** benumbed with cold; see glossary. 253. **fearful,** fear-inspiring, dreadful; see glossary. **slumber,** i.e., nightmare. 254. **flatt'ry,** gratifying deception. 257. **dear,** grievous; see glossary.

Tit. Why, I have not another tear to shed:
Besides, this sorrow is an enemy,
And would usurp upon my wat'ry eyes,
And make them blind with tributary tears:
Then which way shall I find Revenge's cave?
For these two heads do seem to speak to me,
And threat me I shall never come to bliss
Till all these mischiefs be return'd again
Even in their throats that hath committed them.
Come, let me see what task I have to do.
You heavy people, circle me about,
That I may turn me to each one of you,
And swear unto my soul to right your wrongs.
The vow is made. Come, brother, take a head;
And in this hand the other will I bear.
And, Lavinia, thou shalt be employ'd in these arms:
Bear thou my hand, sweet wench, between thy teeth.
As for thee, boy, go get thee from my sight;
Thou art an exile, and thou must not stay:
Hie to the Goths, and raise an army there:
And, if ye love me, as I think you do,
Let 's kiss and part, for we have much to do.
Exeunt [*Titus, Marcus, and Lavinia*].

Luc. Farewell, Andronicus, my noble father,
The wofull'st man that ever liv'd in Rome:
Farewell, proud Rome; till Lucius come again,
He leaves his pledges dearer than his life:
Farewell, Lavinia, my noble sister;
O, would thou wert as thou tofore hast been!
But now nor Lucius nor Lavinia lives
But in oblivion and hateful griefs.
If Lucius live, he will requite your wrongs;
And make proud Saturnine and his empress
Beg at the gates, like Tarquin and his queen.
Now will I to the Goths, and raise a pow'r,
To be reveng'd on Rome and Saturnine. *Exit Luc.*

[SCENE II. *A room in Titus's house.*]

A banquet. Enter [TITUS] ANDRONICUS, MARCUS, LAVINIA, *and the* BOY [LUCIUS].

Tit. So, so; now sit: and look you eat no more
Than will preserve just so much strength in us
As will revenge these bitter woes of ours.
Marcus, unknit that sorrow-wreathen knot:
Thy niece and I, poor creatures, want our hands,
And cannot passionate our tenfold grief
With folded arms. This poor right hand of mine
Is left to tyrannize upon my breast;
Who, when my heart, all mad with misery,
Beats in this hollow prison of my flesh,
Then thus I thump it down.
[*To Lavinia*] Thou map of woe, that thus dost talk in signs!
When thy poor heart beats with outrageous beating,
Thou canst not strike it thus to make it still.
Wound it with sighing, girl, kill it with groans;
Or get some little knife between thy teeth,
And just against thy heart make thou a hole;
That all the tears that thy poor eyes let fall
May run into that sink, and soaking in
Drown the lamenting fool in sea-salt tears.

Marc. Fie, brother, fie! teach her not thus to lay
Such violent hands upon her tender life.

Tit. How now! has sorrow made thee dote already?
Why, Marcus, no man should be mad but I.
What violent hands can she lay on her life?
Ah, wherefore dost thou urge the name of hands;
To bid Æneas tell the tale twice o'er,
How Troy was burnt and he made miserable?
O, handle not the theme, to talk of hands,
Lest we remember still that we have none.
Fie, fie, how franticly I square my talk,
As if we should forget we had no hands,
If Marcus did not name the word of hands!
Come, let 's fall to; and, gentle girl, eat this:
Here is no drink! Hark, Marcus, what she says;
I can interpret all her martyr'd signs;
She says she drinks no other drink but tears,
Brew'd with her sorrow, mesh'd upon her cheeks:
Speechless complainer, I will learn thy thought;
In thy dumb action will I be as perfect
As begging hermits in their holy prayers:
Thou shalt not sigh, nor hold thy stumps to heaven,
Nor wink, nor nod, nor kneel, nor make a sign,
But I of these will wrest an alphabet
And by still practice learn to know thy meaning.

Boy. Good grandsire, leave these bitter deep laments:
Make my aunt merry with some pleasing tale.

Marc. Alas, the tender boy, in passion mov'd,
Doth weep to see his grandsire's heaviness.

Tit. Peace, tender sapling; thou art made of tears,
And tears will quickly melt thy life away.
Marcus strikes the dish with a knife.
What dost thou strike at, Marcus, with thy knife?

Marc. At that that I have kill'd, my lord; a fly.

Tit. Out on thee, murderer! thou kill'st my heart;
Mine eyes are cloy'd with view of tyranny:
A deed of death done on the innocent
Becomes not Titus' brother: get thee gone;
I see thou art not for my company.

Marc. Alas, my lord, I have but kill'd a fly.

Tit. 'But'! How if that fly had a father and mother?
How would he hang his slender gilded wings,
And buzz lamenting doings in the air!
Poor harmless fly,
That, with his pretty buzzing melody,
Came here to make us merry! and thou hast kill'd him.

Marc. Pardon me, sir; it was a black ill-favour'd fly,
Like to the empress' Moor; therefore I kill'd him.

Tit. O, O, O,
Then pardon me for reprehending thee,
For thou hast done a charitable deed.
Give me thy knife, I will insult on him;
Flattering myself, as if it were the Moor
Come hither purposely to poison me.—
There 's for thyself, and that 's for Tamora. [*Strikes.*]
Ah, sirrah!
Yet, I think, we are not brought so low,

270. **tributary tears,** tears exacted as tribute. 275. **hath,** so Q_1; Globe, following $Q_{2\text{-}3}F_1$: *have*. 294. **tofore,** formerly. 299. **Tarquin,** Tarquinius Superbus, seventh king of Rome, who, because his son had raped a Roman lady, Lucretia, was banished and his kingdom overthrown; a republic was then established.

SCENE II. 4. **sorrow-wreathen,** arms folded in grief. 6. **passionate,** express passionately. 15. **Wound it with sighing,** an allusion to the belief that each sigh cost the heart the loss of a drop of blood. 20. **fool,** a term of pity or endearment. 27. **Æneas.** See *Æneid*, II, ii. 31. **square,** shape. 38. **mesh'd,** mashed, mixed. 45. **still,** continual. 71. **insult on,** exult over. 75. **sirrah,** ordinary form of address to inferiors. 80. **shadows,** pictures of the imagination. 82. **closet,** private room. 85. **dazzle,** become dazzled.

ACT IV. SCENE I. 12. **Cornelia,** the mother of the Gracchi, the two most famous tribunes in Roman history. Her success in educating her sons was highly regarded. 14. **Tully's Orator,** Cicero's treatise on

But that between us we can kill a fly
That comes in likeness of a coal-black Moor.
Marc. Alas, poor man! grief has so wrought on him,
He takes false shadows for true substances.
Tit. Come, take away. Lavinia, go with me:
I'll to thy closet; and go read with thee
Sad stories chanced in the times of old.
Come, boy, and go with me: thy sight is young,
And thou shalt read when mine begin to dazzle.
Exeunt.

[ACT IV.

SCENE I. *Rome. Titus's garden.*]

Enter LUCIUS' Son, *and* LAVINIA *running after him, and the boy flies from her, with his books under his arm. Enter* TITUS *and* MARCUS.

Young Luc. Help, grandsire, help! my aunt Lavinia
Follows me every where, I know not why:
Good uncle Marcus, see how swift she comes.
Alas, sweet aunt, I know not what you mean.
Marc. Stand by me, Lucius; do not fear thine aunt.
Tit. She loves thee, boy, too well to do thee harm.
Young Luc. Ay, when my father was in Rome she did.
Marc. What means my niece Lavinia by these signs?
Tit. Fear her not, Lucius: somewhat doth she mean:
See, Lucius, see how much she makes of thee:
Somewhither would she have thee go with her.
Ah, boy, Cornelia never with more care
Read to her sons than she hath read to thee
Sweet poetry and Tully's Orator.
Marc. Canst thou not guess wherefore she plies thee thus?
Young Luc. My lord, I know not, I, nor can I guess,
Unless some fit or frenzy do possess her:
For I have heard my grandsire say full oft,
Extremity of griefs would make men mad;
And I have read that Hecuba of Troy
Ran mad for sorrow: that made me to fear;
Although, my lord, I know my noble aunt
Loves me as dear as e'er my mother did,
And would not, but in fury, fright my youth:
Which made me down to throw my books, and fly,—
Causeless, perhaps. But pardon me, sweet aunt:
And, madam, if my uncle Marcus go,
I will most willingly attend your ladyship.
Marc. Lucius, I will.
[*Lavinia turns over with her stumps the books which Lucius has let fall.*]
Tit. How now, Lavinia! Marcus, what means this?
Some book there is that she desires to see.
Which is it, girl, of these? Open them, boy.
But thou art deeper read, and better skill'd:
Come, and take choice of all my library,
And so beguile thy sorrow, till the heavens
Reveal the damn'd contriver of this deed.
Why lifts she up her arms in sequence thus?
Marc. I think she means that there was more than one
Confederate in the fact: ay, more there was;
Or else to heaven she heaves them for revenge.
Tit. Lucius, what book is that she tosseth so?
Young Luc. Grandsire, 'tis Ovid's Metamorphoses;
My mother gave it me.
Marc. For love of her that 's gone,
Perhaps she cull'd it from among the rest.
Tit. Soft! so busily she turns the leaves!
Help her. What would she find? Lavinia, shall I read?
This is the tragic tale of Philomel,
And treats of Tereus' treason and his rape;
And rape, I fear, was root of thine annoy.
Marc. See, brother, see; note how she quotes the leaves.
Tit. Lavinia, wert thou thus surpris'd, sweet girl,
Ravish'd and wrong'd, as Philomela was,
Forc'd in the ruthless, vast, and gloomy woods?
See, see!
Ay, such a place there is, where we did hunt—
O, had we never, never hunted there!—
Pattern'd by that the poet here describes,
By nature made for murders and for rapes.
Marc. O, why should nature build so foul a den,
Unless the gods delight in tragedies?
Tit. Give signs, sweet girl, for here are none but friends,
What Roman lord it was durst do the deed:
Or slunk not Saturnine, as Tarquin erst,
That left the camp to sin in Lucrece' bed?
Marc. Sit down, sweet niece: brother, sit down by me.
Apollo, Pallas, Jove, or Mercury,
Inspire me, that I may this treason find!
My lord, look here: look here, Lavinia:
He writes his name with his staff, and guides it with feet and mouth.
This sandy plot is plain; guide, if thou canst,
This after me. I have writ my name
Without the help of any hand at all.
Curs'd be that heart that forc'd us to this shift!
Write thou, good niece; and here display, at last,
What God will have discovered for revenge:
Heaven guide thy pen to print thy sorrows plain,
That we may know the traitors and the truth!
She takes the staff in her mouth, and guides it with her stumps, and writes.
Tit. O, do ye read, my lord, what she hath writ?
'Stuprum. Chiron. Demetrius.'
Marc. What, what! the lustful sons of Tamora
Performers of this heinous, bloody deed?
Tit. Magni Dominator poli,
Tam lentus audis scelera? tam lentus vides?
Marc. O, calm thee, gentle lord; although I know
There is enough written upon this earth
To stir a mutiny in the mildest thoughts
And arm the minds of infants to exclaims.
My lord, kneel down with me; Lavinia, kneel;
And kneel, sweet boy, the Roman Hector's hope;
And swear with me, as, with the woful fere
And father of that chaste dishonoured dame,
Lord Junius Brutus sware for Lucrece' rape,

rhetoric, *De Oratore*. 20. **Hecuba.** See I, i, 136. 24. **fury,** insane madness. 37. **in sequence,** one after the other. 39. **fact,** deed. 40. **heaves,** lifts. 41. **tosseth,** turns the pages of. 45. **so,** so QqFf; Globe, following Rowe: *see how*. 46. **Help her,** so QqFf; Globe, following a conjecture of Dyce: *Helping her*, printed as a stage direction. 47, 48. **Philomel, Tereus'.** Cf. II, iii, 43, note. 50. **quotes,** examines, observes. 63. **erst,** once. 74. **discovered,** revealed, uncovered. 78. **Stuprum,** violation, rape. 81-82. **Magni . . . vides?** Ruler of the mighty heavens, art thou so slow to see and hear the crimes that are committed? (Derived from Seneca, *Hippolytus*, 668-669.) 86. **exclaims,** exclamations. 88. **the Roman Hector's,** i.e., Andronicus', whose warlike deeds are held comparable to the Trojan hero's. 89. **fere,** spouse. 91. **Brutus.** After Sextus Tarquinius had raped Lucretia (see II, i, 108 and Shakespeare's *Rape of Lucrece*), Junius Brutus led the Romans to expel the Tarquin dynasty; see also III, ii, 299 and *Julius Caesar*, II, i, 53-54.

That we will prosecute by good advice
Mortal revenge upon these traitorous Goths,
And see their blood, or die with this reproach.
Tit. 'Tis sure enough, an you knew how.
But if you hunt these bear-whelps, then beware:
The dam will wake; and, if she wind ye once,
She 's with the lion deeply still in league,
And lulls him whilst she playeth on her back,
And when he sleeps will she do what she list.
You are a young huntsman, Marcus; let alone;
And, come, I will go get a leaf of brass,
And with a gad of steel will write these words,
And lay it by: the angry northern wind
Will blow these sands, like Sibyl's leaves, abroad,
And where 's our lesson, then? Boy, what say you?
Young Luc. I say, my lord, that if I were a man,
Their mother's bed-chamber should not be safe
For these base bondmen to the yoke of Rome.
Marc. Ay, that 's my boy! thy father hath full oft
For his ungrateful country done the like.
Young Luc. And, uncle, so will I, an if I live.
Tit. Come, go with me into mine armoury;
Lucius, I'll fit thee; and withal, my boy,
Shalt carry from me to the empress' sons
Presents that I intend to send them both:
Come, come; thou 'lt do thy message, wilt thou not?
Young Luc. Ay, with my dagger in their bosoms, grandsire.
Tit. No, boy, not so; I'll teach thee another course.
Lavinia, come. Marcus, look to my house:
Lucius and I'll go brave it at the court;
Ay, marry, will we, sir; and we'll be waited on.
Exeunt [Titus, Lavinia, and Young Lucius].
Marc. O heavens, can you hear a good man groan,
And not relent, or not compassion him?
Marcus, attend him in his ecstasy,
That hath more scars of sorrow in his heart
Than foemen's marks upon his batt'red shield;
But yet so just that he will not revenge.
Revenge the heavens, for old Andronicus! *Exit.*

[SCENE II. *The same. A room in the palace.*]

Enter AARON, CHIRON, *and* DEMETRIUS, *at one door, and at the other door young* LUCIUS *and another, with a bundle of weapons and verses writ upon them.*

Chi. Demetrius, here 's the son of Lucius;
He hath some message to deliver us.
Aar. Ay, some mad message from his mad grandfather.
Young Luc. My lords, with all the humbleness I may,
I greet your honours from Andronicus.
[*Aside*] And pray the Roman gods confound you both!
Dem. Gramercy, lovely Lucius: what 's the news?
Young Luc. [*Aside*] That you are both decipher'd, that 's the news,
For villains mark'd with rape.—May it please you,
My grandsire, well advis'd, hath sent by me
The goodliest weapons of his armoury
To gratify your honourable youth,
The hope of Rome; for so he bid me say;
And so I do, and with his gifts present
Your lordships, that, whenever you have need,
You may be armed and appointed well:
And so I leave you both: [*Aside*] like bloody villains.
Exit [with Attendant].
Dem. What 's here? A scroll; and written round about?
Let 's see:
[*Reads*] 'Integer vitæ, scelerisque purus,
Non eget Mauri jaculis, nec arcu.'
Chi. O, 'tis a verse in Horace; I know it well:
I read it in the grammar long ago.
Aar. Ay, just; a verse in Horace; right, you have it.
[*Aside*] Now, what a thing it is to be an ass!
Here 's no sound jest! the old man hath found their guilt;
And sends them weapons wrapp'd about with lines,
That wound, beyond their feeling, to the quick.
But were our witty empress well afoot,
She would applaud Andronicus' conceit:
But let her rest in her unrest awhile.
[*Aloud.*]
And now, young lords, was 't not a happy star
Led us to Rome, strangers, and more than so,
Captives, to be advanced to this height?
It did me good, before the palace gate
To brave the tribune in his brother's hearing.
Dem. But me more good, to see so great a lord
Basely insinuate and send us gifts.
Aar. Had he not reason, Lord Demetrius?
Did you not use his daughter very friendly?
Dem. I would we had a thousand Roman dames
At such a bay, by turn to serve our lust.
Chi. A charitable wish and full of love.
Aar. Here lacks but your mother for to say amen.
Chi. And that would she for twenty thousand more.
Dem. Come, let us go; and pray to all the gods
For our beloved mother in her pains.
Aar. [*Aside*] Pray to the devils; the gods have given us over. *Trumpets sound [within].*
Dem. Why do the emperor's trumpets flourish thus?
Chi. Belike, for joy the emperor hath a son.
Dem. Soft! who comes here?

Enter Nurse, *with a blackamoor* Child [*in her arms*].

Nur. Good morrow, lords:
O, tell me, did you see Aaron the Moor?
Aar. Well, more or less, or ne'er a whit at all,
Here Aaron is; and what with Aaron now?
Nur. O gentle Aaron, we are all undone!
Now help, or woe betide thee evermore!
Aar. Why, what a caterwauling dost thou keep!
What dost thou wrap and fumble in thine arms?
Nur. O, that which I would hide from heaven's eye,
Our empress' shame, and stately Rome's disgrace!
She is delivered, lords; she is delivered.
Aar. To whom?
Nur. I mean, she is brought a-bed.

92. **advice,** deliberation; see glossary. 94. **reproach,** disgrace, infamy. 97. **wind,** scent. 100. **list,** choose; see glossary. 103. **gad,** stylus. 105. **Sibyl's leaves.** The Cumaean Sibyl, an inspired woman, wrote her prophecies on leaves which she placed at the entrance to her cave. Those wishing to consult them had to do so before they were scattered by the wind. 106. **our,** so Q_1; Globe, following Q_3F: *your*. 121. **brave it,** put on a bold front. 122. **marry,** mild interjection equivalent to "Indeed!" **we'll . . . on,** i.e., demand attention. 125. **ecstasy,** state of being beside oneself. 129. **Revenge the heavens,** may the heavens take revenge.

SCENE II. 4. **may,** can; see glossary. 6. **confound,** destroy; see glossary. 7. **Gramercy,** thanks. 20-21. **'Integer . . . arcu.'** The opening lines of perhaps the best known of the Odes of Horace (I, 22): "He who is spotless in life and free of crime needs not the Moorish bow and arrow." 28. **the quick,** the life. 30. **conceit,** design. 38. **insinuate,** i.e., to ingratiate himself with us by sending gifts. 64. **devil.** The devil was thought to be black. 68. **breeders,** used of female animals. 72.

Aar. Well, God give her good rest! What hath he sent her?
Nur. A devil.
Aar. Why, then she is the devil's dam; a joyful issue.
Nur. A joyless, dismal, black, and sorrowful issue:
Here is the babe, as loathsome as a toad
Amongst the fairest breeders of our clime:
The empress sends it thee, thy stamp, thy seal,
And bids thee christen it with thy dagger's point.
Aar. 'Zounds, ye whore! is black so base a hue?
Sweet blowse, you are a beauteous blossom, sure.
Dem. Villain, what hast thou done?
Aar. That which thou canst not undo.
Chi. Thou hast undone our mother.
Aar. Villain, I have done thy mother.
Dem. And therein, hellish dog, thou hast undone her.
Woe to her chance, and damn'd her loathed choice!
Accurs'd the offspring of so foul a fiend!
Chi. It shall not live.
Aar. It shall not die.
Nur. Aaron, it must; the mother wills it so.
Aar. What, must it, nurse? then let no man but I
Do execution on my flesh and blood.
Dem. I'll broach the tadpole on my rapier's point:
Nurse, give it me; my sword shall soon dispatch it.
Aar. Sooner this sword shall plough thy bowels up.
[*Takes the Child from the Nurse, and draws.*]
Stay, murderous villains! will you kill your brother?
Now, by the burning tapers of the sky,
That shone so brightly when this boy was got,
He dies upon my scimitar's sharp point
That touches this my first-born son and heir!
I tell you, younglings, not Enceladus,
With all his threat'ning band of Typhon's brood,
Nor great Alcides, nor the god of war,
Shall seize this prey out of his father's hands.
What, what, ye sanguine, shallow-hearted boys!
Ye white-lim'd walls! ye alehouse painted signs!
Coal-black is better than another hue,
In that it scorns to bear another hue;
For all the water in the ocean
Can never turn the swan's black legs to white,
Although she lave them hourly in the flood.
Tell the empress from me, I am of age
To keep mine own, excuse it how she can.
Dem. Wilt thou betray thy noble mistress thus?
Aar. My mistress is my mistress; this myself,
The vigour and the picture of my youth:
This before all the world do I prefer;
This maugre all the world will I keep safe,
Or some of you shall smoke for it in Rome.
Dem. By this our mother is for ever sham'd.
Chi. Rome will despise her for this foul escape.
Nur. The emperor, in his rage, will doom her death.
Chi. I blush to think upon this ignomy.
Aar. Why, there 's the privilege your beauty bears:
Fie, treacherous hue, that will betray with blushing
The close enacts and counsels of the heart!
Here 's a young lad fram'd of another leer:
Look, how the black slave smiles upon the father,
As who should say 'Old lad, I am thine own.'
He is your brother, lords, sensibly fed
Of that self-blood that first gave life to you,
And from that womb where you imprisoned were
He is enfranchised and come to light:
Nay, he is your brother by the surer side,
Although my seal be stamped in his face.
Nur. Aaron, what shall I say unto the empress?
Dem. Advise thee, Aaron, what is to be done,
And we will all subscribe to thy advice:
Save thou the child, so we may all be safe.
Aar. Then sit we down, and let us all consult.
My son and I will have the wind of you:
Keep there: now talk at pleasure of your safety.
[*They sit.*]
Dem. How many women saw this child of his?
Aar. Why, so, brave lords! when we join in league,
I am a lamb: but if you brave the Moor,
The chafed boar, the mountain lioness,
The ocean swells not so as Aaron storms.
But say, again, how many saw the child?
Nur. Cornelia the midwife and myself;
And no one else but the delivered empress.
Aar. The empress, the midwife, and yourself:
Two may keep counsel when the third 's away:
Go to the empress, tell her this I said. [*He kills her.*]
Weke, weke! so cries a pig prepared to the spit.
Dem. What mean'st thou, Aaron? wherefore didst thou this?
Aar. O Lord, sir, 'tis a deed of policy:
Shall she live to betray this guilt of ours,
A long-tongu'd babbling gossip? no, lords, no:
And now be it known to you my full intent.
Not far, one Muliteus my countryman
His wife but yesternight was brought to bed;
His child is like to her, fair as you are:
Go pack with him, and give the mother gold,
And tell them both the circumstance of all,
And how by this their child shall be advanc'd,
And be received for the emperor's heir,
And substituted in the place of mine,
To calm this tempest whirling in the court;
And let the emperor dandle him for his own.
Hark ye, lords; you see I have given her physic,
[*Pointing to the nurse.*]
And you must needs bestow her funeral;
The fields are near, and you are gallant grooms:
This done, see that you take no longer days,
But send the midwife presently to me.
The midwife and the nurse well made away,
Then let the ladies tattle what they please.
Chi. Aaron, I see thou wilt not trust the air
With secrets.
Dem. For this care of Tamora,
Herself and hers are highly bound to thee.
Exeunt [*Dem. and Chi. bearing off the Nurse's body*].
Aar. Now to the Goths, as swift as swallow flies;
There to dispose this treasure in mine arms,
And secretly to greet the empress' friends.
Come on, you thick-lipp'd slave, I'll bear you hence;
For it is you that puts us to our shifts:

blowse, wench. 76. **done,** i.e., made love to. 77. **undone her,** so Q_{1-2}; Globe, following Q_3F: *undone*. 78. **chance,** luck. 90. **got,** begotten; see *get* in glossary. 93. **Enceladus,** one of the Titans, sons of the giant Typhon (cf. l. 94, *Typhon's brood*), all of whom waged war against the gods on Olympus. 95. **Alcides,** i.e., Hercules. 97. **sanguine,** pink-cheeked. 103. **lave,** wash. 110. **maugre,** in spite of. 111. **smoke,** suffer, have a "warm" time. 113. **escape,** outrageous transgression. 115. **ignomy,** ignominy. 118. **close,** secret. **enacts,** purposes. 119. **leer,** countenance, complexion. 126. **surer,** i.e., mother's. 131. **so,** so long as. 152-153. **countryman His,** countryman's. 155. **pack,** make a deal. 156. **circumstance of all,** all the particulars; see *circumstance* in glossary. 162. **you,** so Q_{1-2}; Globe, following Q_3F: *ye*. **physic,** medicine. 176. **shifts,** stratagems, tricks.

I'll make you feed on berries and on roots,
And †feed on curds and whey, and suck the goat,
And cabin in a cave, and bring you up
To be a warrior, and command a camp. *Exit.*

[SCENE III. *The same. A public place.*]

Enter TITUS, *old* MARCUS, [*his Son* PUBLIUS,] *young* LUCIUS, *and other* Gentlemen, *with bows; and* TITUS *bears the arrows with letters on the ends of them.*

Tit. Come, Marcus; come, kinsmen; this is the way.
Sir boy, let me see your archery;
Look ye draw home enough, and 'tis there straight.
Terras Astræa reliquit:
Be you remember'd, Marcus, she 's gone, she 's fled.
Sirs, take you to your tools. You, cousins, shall
Go sound the ocean, and cast your nets;
Happily you may catch her in the sea;
Yet there 's as little justice as at land:
No; Publius and Sempronius, you must do it;
'Tis you must dig with mattock and with spade,
And pierce the inmost centre of the earth:
Then, when you come to Pluto's region,
I pray you, deliver him this petition;
Tell him, it is for justice and for aid,
And that it comes from old Andronicus,
Shaken with sorrows in ungrateful Rome.
Ah, Rome! Well, well; I made thee miserable
What time I threw the people's suffrages
On him that thus doth tyrannize o'er me.
Go, get you gone; and pray be careful all,
And leave you not a man-of-war unsearch'd:
This wicked emperor may have shipp'd her hence;
And, kinsmen, then we may go pipe for justice.

Marc. O Publius, is not this a heavy case,
To see thy noble uncle thus distract?

Pub. Therefore, my lord, it highly us concerns
By day and night t' attend him carefully,
And feed his humour kindly as we may,
Till time beget some careful remedy.

Marc. Kinsmen, his sorrows are past remedy.
Join with the Goths; and with revengeful war
Take wreak on Rome for this ingratitude,
And vengeance on the traitor Saturnine.

Tit. Publius, how now! how now, my masters!
What, have you met with her?

Pub. No, my good lord; but Pluto sends you word,
If you will have Revenge from hell, you shall:
Marry, for Justice, she is so employ'd,
He thinks, with Jove in heaven, or somewhere else,
So that perforce you must needs stay a time.

Tit. He doth me wrong to feed me with delays.
I'll dive into the burning lake below,
And pull her out of Acheron by the heels.
Marcus, we are but shrubs, no cedars we,
No big-bon'd men fram'd of the Cyclops' size;
But metal, Marcus, steel to the very back,
Yet wrung with wrongs more than our backs can bear:
And, sith there 's no justice in earth nor hell,
We will solicit heaven and move the gods
To send down Justice for to wreak our wrongs.
Come, to this gear. You are a good archer, Marcus;
He gives them the arrows.
'Ad Jovem,' that 's for you: here, 'Ad Apollinem:'
'Ad Martem,' that 's for myself:
Here, boy, to Pallas: here, to Mercury:
To Saturn, Caius, not to Saturnine;
You were as good to shoot against the wind.
To it, boy! Marcus, loose when I bid.
Of my word, I have written to effect;
There 's not a god left unsolicited.

Marc. Kinsmen, shoot all your shafts into the court:
We will afflict the emperor in his pride.

Tit. Now, masters, draw. [*They shoot.*] O, well said, Lucius!
Good boy, in Virgo's lap; give it Pallas.

Marc. My lord, I aim a mile beyond the moon;
Your letter is with Jupiter by this.

Tit. Ha, ha!
Publius, Publius, what hast thou done?
See, see, thou hast shot off one of Taurus' horns.

Marc. This was the sport, my lord: when Publius shot,
The Bull, being gall'd, gave Aries such a knock
That down fell both the Ram's horns in the court;
And who should find them but the empress' villain?
She laugh'd, and told the Moor he should not choose
But give them to his master for a present.

Tit. Why, there it goes: God give his lordship joy!

Enter a Clown, *with a basket, and two pigeons in it.*

News, news from heaven! Marcus, the post is come.
Sirrah, what tidings? have you any letters?
Shall I have justice? what says Jupiter?

Clo. O, the gibbet-maker! he says that he hath taken them down again, for the man must not be hanged till the next week.

Tit. But what says Jupiter, I ask thee?

Clo. Alas, sir, I know not Jupiter, I never drank with him in all my life.

Tit. Why, villain, art not thou the carrier?

Clo. Ay, of my pigeons, sir; nothing else.

Tit. Why, didst thou not come from heaven?

Clo. From heaven! alas, sir, I never came there: God forbid I should be so bold to press to heaven in my young days. Why, I am going with my pigeons to the tribunal plebs, to take up a matter of brawl betwixt my uncle and one of the emperial's men.

Marc. Why, sir, that is as fit as can be to serve for your oration; and let him deliver the pigeons to the emperor from you.

Tit. Tell me, can you deliver an oration to the emperor with a grace?

Clo. Nay, truly, sir, I could never say grace in all my life.

Tit. Sirrah, come hither: make no more ado,
But give your pigeons to the emperor:
By me thou shalt have justice at his hands.
Hold, hold; meanwhile here 's money for thy charges.
Give me pen and ink. Sirrah, can you with a grace deliver up a supplication?

Clo. Ay, sir.

Tit. Then here is a supplication for you. And when you come to him, at the first approach you must kneel,

SCENE III. 2. **boy, let,** so QqF; Globe, following F_{2-4}: *boy, now let.* 3. **home,** to the full extent of the bow. 4. **Terras Astræa reliquit,** Astrea has abandoned the earth; a passage from Ovid's *Metamorphoses;* she was goddess of Justice. 8. **Happily,** perhaps. 19. **What time,** when. 24. **pipe,** look in vain. 26. **distract,** crazed, desperate. 29. **humour,** mood, whim. 44. **Acheron,** river in Hades. 52. **gear,** business. 53, 54. **'Ad Jovem,' 'Ad Apollinem:,' 'Ad Martem,'** to Jove, to Apollo, to Mars. 58. **loose,** let fly, discharge. 64. **in Virgo's lap,** the constellation, the Virgin. 69, 71. **Taurus, Aries,** the Bull, the Ram; signs of the zodiac. 77. **post,** messenger. 80. **gibbet-maker,** comically sounding like "Jupiter." 92. **tribunal plebs,** tribune of the plebs. 107. **deliver up, so** Q_1; Globe, following Q_{2-3}Ff: *deliver.*

then kiss his foot, then deliver up your pigeons, and then look for your reward. I'll be at hand, sir; see you do it bravely.

Clo. I warrant you, sir, let me alone.

Tit. Sirrah, hast thou a knife? come, let me see it.
Here, Marcus, fold it in the oration;
For thou hast made it like an humble suppliant.
And when thou hast given it to the emperor,
Knock at my door, and tell me what he says.

Clo. God be with you, sir; I will. *Exit.*

Tit. Come, Marcus, let us go. Publius, follow me. *Exeunt.*

[SCENE IV. *The same. Before the palace.*]

Enter emperor [SATURNINUS] *and empress* [TAMORA] *and her two* Sons. *The emperor brings the arrows in his hand that Titus shot at him.*

Sat. Why, lords, what wrongs are these! was ever seen
An emperor in Rome thus overborne,
Troubled, confronted thus; and, for the extent
Of egal justice, us'd in such contempt?
My lords, you know, as know the mightful gods,
However these disturbers of our peace
Buz in the people's ears, there nought hath pass'd,
But even with law, against the wilful sons
Of old Andronicus. And what an if
His sorrows have so overwhelm'd his wits,
Shall we be thus afflicted in his wreaks,
His fits, his frenzy, and his bitterness?
And now he writes to heaven for his redress:
See, here 's to Jove, and this to Mercury;
This to Apollo; this to the god of war;
Sweet scrolls to fly about the streets of Rome!
What 's this but libelling against the senate,
And blazoning our injustice every where?
A goodly humour, is it not, my lords?
As who would say, in Rome no justice were.
But if I live, his feigned ecstasies
Shall be no shelter to these outrages:
But he and his shall know that justice lives
In Saturninus' health, whom, if he sleep,
He'll so awake as he in fury shall
Cut off the proud'st conspirator that lives.

Tam. My gracious lord, my lovely Saturnine,
Lord of my life, commander of my thoughts,
Calm thee, and bear the faults of Titus' age,
Th' effects of sorrow for his valiant sons,
Whose loss hath pierc'd him deep and scarr'd his heart;
And rather comfort his distressed plight
Than prosecute the meanest or the best
For these contempts. [*Aside*] Why, thus it shall become
High-witted Tamora to gloze with all:
But, Titus, I have touch'd thee to the quick,
Thy life-blood out; if Aaron now be wise,
Then is all safe, the anchor in the port.

Enter Clown.

How now, good fellow! wouldst thou speak with us?

Clo. Yea, forsooth, an your mistresship be emperial.

Tam. Empress I am, but yonder sits the emperor.

Clo. 'Tis he. God and Saint Stephen give you good den: I have brought you a letter and a couple of pigeons here. *He* [*Saturninus*] *reads the letter.*

Sat. Go, take him away, and hang him presently.

Clo. How much money must I have?

Tam. Come, sirrah, you must be hang'd.

Clo. Hanged! by 'r lady, then I have brought up a neck to a fair end. *Exit* [*guarded*].

Sat. Despiteful and intolerable wrongs!
Shall I endure this monstrous villany?
I know from whence this same device proceeds:
May this be borne?—as if his traitorous sons,
That died by law for murder of our brother,
Have by my means been butchered wrongfully!
Go, drag the villain hither by the hair;
Nor age nor honour shall shape privilege:
For this proud mock I'll be thy slaughter-man;
Sly frantic wretch, that holp'st to make me great,
In hope thyself should govern Rome and me.

Enter nuntius, ÆMILIUS.

What news with thee, Æmilius?

Æmil. Arm, my lords! Rome never had more cause.
The Goths have gathered head; and with a power
Of high-resolved men, bent to the spoil,
They hither march amain, under conduct
Of Lucius, son to old Andronicus;
Who threats, in course of this revenge, to do
As much as ever Coriolanus did.

Sat. Is warlike Lucius general of the Goths?
These tidings nip me, and I hang the head
As flowers with frost or grass beat down with storms:
Ay, now begins our sorrows to approach:
'Tis he the common people love so much;
Myself hath often over-heard them say,
When I have walked like a private man,
That Lucius' banishment was wrongfully,
And they have wish'd that Lucius were their emperor.

Tam. Why should you fear? is not your city strong?

Sat. Ay, but the citizens favour Lucius,
And will revolt from me to succour him.

Tam. King, be thy thoughts imperious, like thy name.
Is the sun dimm'd, that gnats do fly in it?
The eagle suffers little birds to sing,
And is not careful what they mean thereby,
Knowing that with the shadow of his wings
He can at pleasure stint their melody:
Even so mayst thou the giddy men of Rome.
Then cheer thy spirit: for know, thou emperor,
I will enchant the old Andronicus
With words more sweet, and yet more dangerous,
Than baits to fish, or honey-stalks to sheep,
When as the one is wounded with the bait,
The other rotted with delicious feed.

Sat. But he will not entreat his son for us.

Tam. If Tamora entreat him, then he will:
For I can smooth and fill his aged ears
With golden promises; that, were his heart
Almost impregnable, his old ears deaf,

SCENE IV. 4. **egal,** equal. 8. **even,** conformable. 11. **wreaks,** revenges. 18. **blazoning,** making public. 21. **feigned ecstasies,** pretended madness. 35. **gloze,** deceive. 38. **anchor,** so Q_{1-2}; Globe, following Q_3F: *anchor's*. 40. **mistresship,** so Q_1; Globe, following $Q_{2-3}F_1$: *mistership*. 42. **good den,** good evening. 57. **shape privilege,** make for exemption. 60. *Stage Direction:* **nuntius,** messenger. 62. **lords,** so QqFf; Globe, taking Capell's conjecture: *lord*. 63. **head,** an armed force. 68. **Coriolanus,** an early Roman hero, turned enemy of Rome, about whom Shakespeare wrote one of his later tragedies. 72. **begins,** so QqF; Globe, following Rowe: *begin*. 86. **stint,** stop. 91. **honey-stalks,** clovers. 96. **ears,** so Q_{1-2}; Globe, following Q_3F_1: *ear*.

Yet should both ear and heart obey my tongue.
[*To Æmilius*] Go thou before, to be our ambassador:
Say that the emperor requests a parley
Of warlike Lucius, and appoint the meeting
Even at his father's house, the old Andronicus.
Sat. Æmilius, do this message honourably:
And if he stand in hostage for his safety,
Bid him demand what pledge will please him best.
Æmil. Your bidding shall I do effectually. *Exit.*
Tam. Now will I to that old Andronicus,
And temper him with all the art I have,
To pluck proud Lucius from the warlike Goths.
And now, sweet emperor, be blithe again,
And bury all thy fear in my devices.
Sat. Then go successantly, and plead to him. *Exeunt.*

[ACT V.

SCENE I. *Plains near Rome.*]

Enter Lucius *with an army of* Goths, *with drums and* Soldiers.

Luc. Approved warriors, and my faithful friends,
I have received letters from great Rome,
Which signifies what hate they bear their emperor
And how desirous of our sight they are.
Therefore, great lords, be, as your titles witness,
Imperious and impatient of your wrongs,
And wherein Rome hath done you any scath,
Let him make treble satisfaction.
First Goth. Brave slip, sprung from the great Andronicus,
Whose name was once our terror, now our comfort;
Whose high exploits and honourable deeds
Ingrateful Rome requites with foul contempt,
Be bold in us: we'll follow where thou lead'st,
Like stinging bees in hottest summer's day
Led by their master to the flow'red fields,
And be aveng'd on cursed Tamora.
All the Goths. And as he saith, so say we all with him.
Luc. I humbly thank him, and I thank you all.
But who comes here, led by a lusty Goth?

Enter a Goth, *leading of* Aaron *with his Child in his arms.*

Sec. Goth. Renowned Lucius, from our troops I stray'd
To gaze upon a ruinous monastery;
And, as I earnestly did fix mine eye
Upon the wasted building, suddenly
I heard a child cry underneath a wall.
I made unto the noise; when soon I heard
The crying babe controll'd with this discourse:
'Peace, tawny slave, half me and half thy dam!
Did not thy hue bewray whose brat thou art,
Had nature lent thee but thy mother's look,
Villain, thou mightst have been an emperor:
But where the bull and cow are both milk-white,
They never do beget a coal-black calf.
Peace, villain, peace!'—even thus he rates the babe,—
'For I must bear thee to a trusty Goth;
Who, when he knows thou art the empress' babe,
Will hold thee dearly for thy mother's sake.'
With this, my weapon drawn, I rush'd upon him,
Surpris'd him suddenly, and brought him hither,
To use as you think needful of the man.
Luc. O worthy Goth, this is the incarnate devil
That robb'd Andronicus of his good hand;
This is the pearl that pleas'd your empress' eye,
And here 's the base fruit of his burning lust.
Say, wall-ey'd slave, whither wouldst thou convey
This growing image of thy fiend-like face?
Why dost not speak? what, deaf? not a word?
A halter, soldiers! hang him on this tree,
And by his side his fruit of bastardy.
Aar. Touch not the boy; he is of royal blood.
Luc. Too like the sire for ever being good.
First hang the child, that he may see it sprawl;
A sight to vex the father's soul withal.
Get me a ladder.
[*A ladder brought, which Aaron is made to ascend.*]
Aar. Lucius, save the child,
And bear it from me to the empress.
If thou do this, I'll show thee wondrous things,
That highly may advantage thee to hear:
If thou wilt not, befall what may befall,
I'll speak no more but 'Vengeance rot you all!'
Luc. Say on: an if it please me which thou speak'st,
Thy child shall live, and I will see it nourish'd.
Aar. An if it please thee! why, assure thee, Lucius,
'Twill vex thy soul to hear what I shall speak;
For I must talk of murders, rapes and massacres,
Acts of black night, abominable deeds,
Complots of mischief, treason, villanies
Ruthful to hear, yet piteously perform'd:
And this shall all be buried by my death,
Unless thou swear to me my child shall live.
Luc. Tell on thy mind; I say thy child shall live.
Aar. Swear that he shall, and then I will begin.
Luc. Who should I swear by? thou believest no god:
That granted, how canst thou believe an oath?
Aar. What if I do not? as, indeed, I do not;
Yet, for I know thou art religious
And hast a thing within thee called conscience,
With twenty popish tricks and ceremonies,
Which I have seen thee careful to observe,
Therefore I urge thy oath; for that I know
An idiot holds his bauble for a god
And keeps the oath which by that god he swears,
To that I'll urge him: therefore thou shalt vow
By that same god, what god soe'er it be,
That thou adorest and hast in reverence,
To save my boy, to nourish and bring him up;
Or else I will discover nought to thee.
Luc. Even by my god I swear to thee I will.
Aar. First know thou, I begot him on the empress.
Luc. O most insatiate and luxurious woman!
Aar. Tut, Lucius, this was but a deed of charity
To that which thou shalt hear of me anon.
'Twas her two sons that murdered Bassianus;
They cut thy sister's tongue and ravish'd her
And cut her hands and trimm'd her as thou sawest.
Luc. O detestable villain! call'st thou that trimming?
Aar. Why, she was wash'd and cut and trimm'd, and 'twas
Trim sport for them which had the doing of it.
Luc. O barbarous, beastly villains, like thyself!
Aar. Indeed, I was their tutor to instruct them:

100. **to be,** so Qq; Globe, following Capell: *be.* 105. **in,** so QqF_{1-3}; Globe, following F_4: *on.* 106. **demand,** request; see glossary. 113. **successantly,** successfully (?), in succession (?).
Act v. scene i. 1. **Approved,** put to proof, tried. 7. **scath,** injury. 9. **slip,** offspring. 13. **in us,** i.e., because we support you. 21. **ruinous,** decayed. 33. **rates,** chides. 44. **wall-ey'd,** glaring. 45. **image,** likeness. 56. **advantage,** be of benefit to. 65. **Complots,** conspiracies. 66. **piteously,** in a way to excite pity. 79. **bauble,** fool's stick. 88.

That codding spirit had they from their mother,
As sure a card as ever won the set;
That bloody mind, I think, they learn'd of me,
As true a dog as ever fought at head.
Well, let my deeds be witness of my worth.
I train'd thy brethren to that guileful hole
Where the dead corpse of Bassianus lay:
I wrote the letter that thy father found
And hid the gold within that letter mention'd,
Confederate with the queen and her two sons:
And what not done, that thou hast cause to rue,
Wherein I had no stroke of mischief in it?
I play'd the cheater for thy father's hand,
And, when I had it, drew myself apart
And almost broke my heart with extreme laughter:
I pry'd me through the crevice of a wall
When, for his hand, he had his two sons' heads;
Beheld his tears, and laugh'd so heartily,
That both mine eyes were rainy like to his:
And when I told the empress of this sport,
She sounded almost at my pleasing tale,
And for my tidings gave me twenty kisses.
First Goth. What, canst thou say all this, and never blush?
Aar. Ay, like a black dog, as the saying is.
Luc. Art thou not sorry for these heinous deeds?
Aar. Ay, that I had not done a thousand more.
Even now I curse the day—and yet, I think,
Few come within the compass of my curse—
Wherein I did not some notorious ill,
As kill a man, or else devise his death,
Ravish a maid, or plot the way to do it,
Accuse some innocent and forswear myself,
Set deadly enmity between two friends,
†Make poor men's cattle break their necks;
Set fire on barns and hay-stacks in the night,
And bid the owners quench them with their tears.
Oft have I digg'd up dead men from their graves,
And set them upright at their dear friends' door,
Even when their sorrows almost was forgot;
And on their skins, as on the bark of trees,
Have with my knife carved in Roman letters,
'Let not your sorrow die, though I am dead.'
Tut, I have done a thousand dreadful things
As willingly as one would kill a fly,
And nothing grieves me heartily indeed
But that I cannot do ten thousand more.
Luc. Bring down the devil; for he must not die
So sweet a death as hanging presently.
Aar. If there be devils, would I were a devil,
To live and burn in everlasting fire,
So I might have your company in hell,
But to torment you with my bitter tongue!
Luc. Sirs, stop his mouth, and let him speak no more.

Enter ÆMILIUS.

Third Goth. My lord, there is a messenger from Rome
Desires to be admitted to your presence.
Luc. Let him come near.
Welcome, Æmilius: what 's the news from Rome?
Æmil. Lord Lucius, and you princes of the Goths,
The Roman emperor greets you all by me;
And, for he understands you are in arms,
He craves a parley at your father's house,
Willing you to demand your hostages,
And they shall be immediately deliver'd.
First Goth. What says our general?
Luc. Æmilius, let the emperor give his pledges
Unto my father and my uncle Marcus,
And we will come. March away. [*Exeunt.*]

[SCENE II. *Rome. Before Titus's house.*]

Enter TAMORA *and her two* Sons, *disguised.*

Tam. Thus, in this strange and sad habiliment,
I will encounter with Andronicus,
And say I am Revenge, sent from below
To join with him and right his heinous wrongs.
Knock at his study, where, they say, he keeps,
To ruminate strange plots of dire revenge;
Tell him Revenge is come to join with him,
And work confusion on his enemies.

They knock, and TITUS [*above*] *opens his study door.*

Tit. Who doth molest my contemplation?
Is it your trick to make me ope the door,
That so my sad decrees may fly away,
And all my study be to no effect?
You are deceiv'd: for what I mean to do
See here in bloody lines I have set down;
And what is written shall be executed.
Tam. Titus, I am come to talk with thee.
Tit. No, not a word; how can I grace my talk,
Wanting a hand to give that accord?
Thou hast the odds of me; therefore no more.
Tam. If thou didst know me, thou wouldst talk with me.
Tit. I am not mad; I know thee well enough:
Witness this wretched stump, witness these crimson lines;
Witness these trenches made by grief and care;
Witness the tiring day and heavy night;
Witness all sorrow, that I know thee well
For our proud empress, mighty Tamora:
Is not thy coming for my other hand?
Tam. Know, thou sad man, I am not Tamora;
She is thy enemy, and I thy friend:
I am Revenge: sent from th' infernal kingdom,
To ease the gnawing vulture of thy mind,
By working wreakful vengeance on thy foes.
Come down, and welcome me to this world's light;
Confer with me of murder and of death:
There 's not a hollow cave or lurking-place,
No vast obscurity or misty vale,
Where bloody murder or detested rape
Can couch for fear, but I will find them out;
And in their ears tell them my dreadful name,
Revenge, which makes the foul offender quake.
Tit. Art thou Revenge? and art thou sent to me,
To be a torment to mine enemies?
Tam. I am; therefore come down, and welcome me.
Tit. Do me some service, ere I come to thee.
Lo, by thy side where Rape and Murder stands;
Now give some surance that thou art Revenge,

luxurious, lecherous. 90. **To,** compared to. 99. **codding,** lustful. 102. **as . . . head,** as ever went for the bear's head (in bearbaiting). 104. **train'd,** lured. 111. **cheater,** (1) deceiver, (2) escheater, one designated to take care of property forfeited to the crown. 119. **sounded,** swooned. 136. **door,** so Q_1; Globe, following Q_2F_1: *doors.* 137. **was,** so QqFf; Globe, following Malone: *were.*

SCENE II. 18. **give that accord,** provide suitable gestures. 23. **trenches,** wrinkles.

Stab them, or tear them on thy chariot-wheels;
And then I'll come and be thy waggoner,
And whirl along with thee about the globe.
Provide thee two proper palfreys, black as jet,
To hale thy vengeful waggon swift away,
And find out murd'rers in their guilty caves:
And when thy car is loaden with their heads,
I will dismount, and by the waggon-wheel
Trot, like a servile footman, all day long,
Even from Hyperion's rising in the east
Until his very downfall in the sea:
And day by day I'll do this heavy task,
So thou destroy Rapine and Murder there.
Tam. These are my ministers, and come with me.
Tit. Are these thy ministers? what are they call'd?
Tam. Rapine and Murder; therefore called so,
Cause they take vengeance of such kind of men.
Tit. Good Lord, how like the empress' sons they are!
And you, the empress! but we worldly men
Have miserable, mad, mistaking eyes.
O sweet Revenge, now do I come to thee;
And, if one arm's embracement will content thee,
I will embrace thee in it by and by. [*Exit above.*]
Tam. This closing with him fits his lunacy:
Whate'er I forge to feed his brain-sick humours,
Do you uphold and maintain in your speeches,
For now he firmly takes me for Revenge;
And, being credulous in this mad thought,
I'll make him send for Lucius his son;
And, whilst I at a banquet hold him sure,
I'll find some cunning practice out of hand,
To scatter and disperse the giddy Goths,
Or, at the least, make them his enemies.
See, here he comes, and I must ply my theme.

[*Enter* TITUS *below.*]

Tit. Long have I been forlorn, and all for thee:
Welcome, dread Fury, to my woful house:
Rapine and Murder, you are welcome too.
How like the empress and her sons you are!
Well are you fitted, had you but a Moor:
Could not all hell afford you such a devil?
For well I wot the empress never wags
But in her company there is a Moor;
And, would you represent our queen aright,
It were convenient you had such a devil:
But welcome, as you are. What shall we do?
Tam. What wouldst thou have us do, Andronicus?
Dem. Show me a murderer, I'll deal with him.
Chi. Show me a villain that hath done a rape,
And I am sent to be reveng'd on him.
Tam. Show me a thousand that hath done thee wrong,
And I will be revenged on them all.
Tit. Look round about the wicked streets of Rome;
And when thou find'st a man that 's like thyself,
Good Murder, stab him; he 's a murderer.
Go thou with him; and when it is thy hap
To find another that is like to thee,
Good Rapine, stab him; he is a ravisher.
Go thou with them; and in the emperor's court
There is a queen, attended by a Moor;
Well shalt thou know her by thy own proportion,
For up and down she doth resemble thee:
I pray thee, do on them some violent death;
They have been violent to me and mine.
Tam. Well hast thou lesson'd us; this shall we do.
But would it please thee, good Andronicus,
To send for Lucius, thy thrice-valiant son,
Who leads towards Rome a band of warlike Goths,
And bid him come and banquet at thy house;
When he is here, even at thy solemn feast,
I will bring in the empress and her sons,
The emperor himself and all thy foes;
And at thy mercy shall they stoop and kneel,
And on them shalt thou ease thy angry heart.
What says Andronicus to this device?
Tit. Marcus, my brother! 'tis sad Titus calls.

Enter MARCUS.

Go, gentle Marcus, to thy nephew Lucius;
Thou shalt inquire him out among the Goths:
Bid him repair to me, and bring with him
Some of the chiefest princes of the Goths;
Bid him encamp his soldiers where they are:
Tell him the emperor and the empress too
Feast at my house, and he shall feast with them.
This do thou for my love; and so let him,
As he regards his aged father's life.
Marc. This will I do, and soon return again. [*Exit.*]
Tam. Now will I hence about thy business,
And take my ministers along with me.
Tit. Nay, nay, let Rape and Murder stay with me;
Or else I'll call my brother back again,
And cleave to no revenge but Lucius.
Tam. [*Aside to her sons*] What say you, boys? will you abide with him,
Whiles I go tell my lord the emperor
How I have govern'd our determin'd jest?
Yield to his humour, smooth and speak him fair,
And tarry with him till I turn again.
Tit. [*Aside*] I know them all, though they suppose me mad,
And will o'erreach them in their own devices:
A pair of cursed hell-hounds and their dam!
Dem. Madam, depart at pleasure; leave us here.
Tam. Farewell, Andronicus: Revenge now goes
To lay a complot to betray thy foes.
Tit. I know thou dost; and, sweet Revenge, farewell. [*Exit Tamora.*]
Chi. Tell us, old man, how shall we be employ'd?
Tit. Tut, I have work enough for you to do.
Publius, come hither, Caius, and Valentine!

[*Enter* PUBLIUS *and others.*]

Pub. What is your will?
Tit. Know you these two?
Pub. The empress' sons, I take them, Chiron and Demetrius.
Tit. Fie, Publius, fie! thou art too much deceiv'd;
The one is Murder, and Rape is the other's name;
And therefore bind them, gentle Publius.
Caius and Valentine, lay hands on them.
Oft have you heard me wish for such an hour,
And now I find it; therefore bind them sure,
And stop their mouths, if they begin to cry. [*Exit.*]
[*Publius, &c. lay hold on Chiron and Demetrius.*]

50. **proper,** excellent. 56. **Hyperion,** one of the Titans; father of the sun; frequently used for the sun itself. 70. **closing,** agreeing. 71. **humours,** so Q_1; Globe, following $Q_{2\text{-}3}$F: *fits.* 76. **hold him sure,** keep him harmless. 77. **practice,** conspiracy. 87. **wags,** moves. 96. **hath,** so Q_1; Globe, following $Q_{2\text{-}3}$F: *have.* 106. **proportion,** form, appearance. 124. **repair,** come. 137. **abide,** so Q_1; Globe, following $Q_{2\text{-}3}$F: *bide.* 189. **coffin,** pie crust. 192. **increase,** produce. 196. **worse than Progne,** an allusion to Progne's revenge on Tereus for raping her sister

Chi. Villains, forbear! we are the empress' sons.
Pub. And therefore do we what we are commanded.
Stop close their mouths, let them not speak a word.
Is he sure bound? look that you bind them fast.

Enter TITUS ANDRONICUS *with a knife, and* LAVINIA *with a basin.*

Tit. Come, come, Lavinia; look, thy foes are bound.
Sirs, stop their mouths, let them not speak to me;
But let them hear what fearful words I utter.
O villains, Chiron and Demetrius!
Here stands the spring whom you have stain'd with mud,
This goodly summer with your winter mix'd.
You kill'd her husband, and for that vile fault
Two of her brothers were condemn'd to death,
My hand cut off and made a merry jest;
Both her sweet hands, her tongue, and that more dear
Than hands or tongue, her spotless chastity,
Inhuman traitors, you constrain'd and forc'd.
What would you say, if I should let you speak?
Villains, for shame you could not beg for grace.
Hark, wretches! how I mean to martyr you.
This one hand yet is left to cut your throats,
Whilst that Lavinia 'tween her stumps doth hold
The basin that receives your guilty blood.
You know your mother means to feast with me,
And calls herself Revenge, and thinks me mad:
Hark, villains! I will grind your bones to dust
And with your blood and it I'll make a paste,
And of the paste a coffin I will rear
And make two pasties of your shameful heads,
And bid that strumpet, your unhallowed dam,
Like to the earth swallow her own increase.
This is the feast that I have bid her to,
And this the banquet she shall surfeit on;
For worse than Philomel you us'd my daughter,
And worse than Progne I will be reveng'd:
And now prepare your throats. Lavinia, come,
He cuts their throats.
Receive the blood: and when that they are dead,
Let me go grind their bones to powder small
And with this hateful liquor temper it;
And in that paste let their vile heads be bak'd.
Come, come, be every one officious
To make this banquet; which I wish may prove
More stern and bloody than the Centaurs' feast.
So, now bring them in, for I'll play the cook,
And see them ready against their mother comes.
Exeunt [*bearing the dead bodies*].

[SCENE III. *Court of Titus's house. A banquet set out.*]

Enter LUCIUS, MARCUS, *and the* Goths [*with* AARON *prisoner, and an* Attendant *bearing his* Child].

Luc. Uncle Marcus, since it is my father's mind
That I repair to Rome, I am content.
First Goth. And ours with thine, befall what fortune will.
Luc. Good uncle, take you in this barbarous Moor,
This ravenous tiger, this accursed devil;
Let him receive no sust'nance, fetter him,
Till he be brought unto the empress' face,
For testimony of her foul proceedings:
And see the ambush of our friends be strong;
I fear the emperor means no good to us.
Aar. Some devil whisper curses in mine ear,
And prompt me, that my tongue may utter forth
The venomous malice of my swelling heart!
Luc. Away, inhuman dog! unhallowed slave!
Sirs, help our uncle to convey him in.
[*Exeunt Goths, with Aaron. Flourish within.*]
The trumpets show the emperor is at hand.

Sound trumpets. Enter emperor [SATURNINUS] *and empress* [TAMORA], *with* [ÆMILIUS,] Tribunes, *and others.*

Sat. What, hath the firmament mo suns than one?
Luc. What boots it thee to call thyself a sun?
Marc. Rome's emperor, and nephew, break the parle;
These quarrels must be quietly debated.
The feast is ready, which the careful Titus
Hath ordain'd to an honourable end,
For peace, for love, for league, and good to Rome:
Please you, therefore, draw nigh, and take your places.
Sat. Marcus, we will.
[*Hautboys sound. The Company sit down at table.*

Trumpets sounding, enter TITUS *like a cook, placing the dishes, and* LAVINIA *with a veil over her face* [*, young* LUCIUS, *and others*].

Tit. Welcome, my gracious lord; welcome, dread queen;
Welcome, ye warlike Goths; welcome, Lucius;
And welcome, all: although the cheer be poor,
'Twill fill your stomachs; please you eat of it.
Sat. Why art thou thus attir'd, Andronicus?
Tit. Because I would be sure to have all well,
To entertain your highness and your empress.
Tam. We are beholding to you, good Andronicus.
Tit. An if your highness knew my heart, you were.
My lord the emperor, resolve me this:
Was it well done of rash Virginius
To slay his daughter with his own right hand,
Because she was enforc'd, stain'd, and deflow'r'd?
Sat. It was, Andronicus.
Tit. Your reason, mighty lord?
Sat. Because the girl should not survive her shame,
And by her presence still renew his sorrows.
Tit. A reason mighty, strong, and effectual;
A pattern, precedent, and lively warrant,
For me, most wretched, to perform the like.
Die, die, Lavinia, and thy shame with thee;
[*Kills Lavinia.*]
And, with thy shame, thy father's sorrow die!
Sat. What hast thou done, unnatural and unkind?
Tit. Kill'd her, for whom my tears have made me blind.
I am as woful as Virginius was,
And have a thousand times more cause than he
To do this outrage: and it now is done.
Sat. What, was she ravish'd? tell who did the deed.
Tit. Will 't please you eat? will 't please your highness feed?
Tam. Why hast thou slain thine only daughter thus?

(cf. II, iii, 43, note); she killed her son Itys and served his flesh to Tereus, his father. 204. **Centaurs' feast,** refers to a wedding feast at which the Centaurs (fabulous creatures, half men and half horses), were slaughtered by their hosts.

SCENE III. 9. **ambush,** concealed escort. 17. **mo suns than one.** Lucius has assumed an imperial manner, which offends Saturninus. 18. **boots,** avails. 19. **break the parle,** cease quarreling. 25. *Stage Direction:* ***Hautboys,*** oboes. 35. **resolve,** answer. 48. **unkind,** unnatural.

Tit. Not I; 'twas Chiron and Demetrius:
They ravish'd her, and cut away her tongue;
And they, 'twas they, that did her all this wrong.
Sat. Go fetch them hither to us presently.
Tit. Why, there they are both, baked in this pie;
Whereof their mother daintily hath fed,
Eating the flesh that she herself hath bred.
'Tis true, 'tis true; witness my knife's sharp point.
He stabs the empress.
Sat. Die, frantic wretch, for this accursed deed!
[*Kills Titus.*]
Luc. Can the son's eye behold his father bleed?
There 's meed for meed, death for a deadly deed!
[*Kills Saturninus. A great tumult. Lucius, Marcus, and others go up into the balcony.*]
Marc. You sad-fac'd men, people and sons of Rome,
By uproars sever'd, as a flight of fowl
Scatter'd by winds and high tempestuous gusts,
O, let me teach you how to knit again
This scattered corn into one mutual sheaf,
These broken limbs again into one body;
Lest Rome herself be bane unto herself,
And she whom mighty kingdoms court'sy to,
Like a forlorn and desperate castaway,
Do shameful execution on herself.
But if my frosty signs and chaps of age,
Grave witnesses of true experience,
Cannot induce you to attend my words,
[*To Lucius*] Speak, Rome's dear friend, as erst our ancestor,
When with his solemn tongue he did discourse
To love-sick Dido's sad attending ear
The story of that baleful burning night
When subtle Greeks surpris'd King Priam's Troy,
Tell us what Sinon hath bewitch'd our ears,
Or who hath brought the fatal engine in
That gives our Troy, our Rome, the civil wound.
My heart is not compact of flint nor steel;
Nor can I utter all our bitter grief,
But floods of tears will drown my oratory,
And break my utt'rance, even in the time
When it should move ye to attend me most,
And force you to commiseration.
Here 's Rome's young captain, let him tell the tale;
While I stand by and weep to hear him speak.
Luc. Then, gracious auditory, be it known to you,
That Chiron and the damn'd Demetrius
Were they that murd'red our emperor's brother;
And they it were that ravished our sister:
For their fell faults our brothers were beheaded;
Our father's tears despis'd, and basely cozen'd
Of that true hand that fought Rome's quarrel out,
And sent her enemies unto the grave.
Lastly, myself unkindly banished,
The gates shut on me, and turn'd weeping out,
To beg relief among Rome's enemies;
Who drown'd their enmity in my true tears,
And op'd their arms to embrace me as a friend.
I am the turned forth, be it known to you,
That have preserv'd her welfare in my blood;
And from her bosom took the enemy's point,
Sheathing the steel in my advent'rous body.
Alas, you know I am no vaunter, I;
My scars can witness, dumb although they are,
That my report is just and full of truth.
But, soft! methinks I do digress too much,
Citing my worthless praise: O, pardon me;
For when no friends are by, men praise themselves.
Marc. Now is my turn to speak. Behold the child:
[*Pointing to the Child in the arms of an Attendant.*]
Of this was Tamora delivered;
The issue of an irreligious Moor,
Chief architect and plotter of these woes:
The villain is alive in Titus' house,
†And as he is to witness, this is true.
Now judge what cause had Titus to revenge
These wrongs, unspeakable, past patience,
Or more than any living man could bear.
Now you have heard the truth, what say you, Romans?
Have we done aught amiss,—show us wherein,
And, from the place where you behold us pleading,
The poor remainder of Andronici
Will, hand in hand, all headlong hurl ourselves,
And on the ragged stones beat forth our souls,
And make a mutual closure of our house.
Speak, Romans, speak; and if you say we shall,
Lo, hand in hand, Lucius and I will fall.
Æmil. Come, come, thou reverend man of Rome,
And bring our emperor gently in thy hand,
Lucius our emperor; for well I know
The common voice do cry it shall be so.
All. Lucius, all hail, Rome's royal emperor!
Marc. Go, go into old Titus' sorrowful house,
[*To Attendants.*]
And hither hale that misbelieving Moor,
To be adjudg'd some direful slaught'ring death,
As punishment for his most wicked life.
[*Exeunt Attendants.*]

[LUCIUS, MARCUS, *and the others descend.*]

All. Lucius, all hail, Rome's gracious governor!
Luc. Thanks, gentle Romans: may I govern so,
To heal Rome's harms, and wipe away her woe!
But, gentle people, give me aim awhile,
For nature puts me to a heavy task:
Stand all aloof: but, uncle, draw you near,
To shed obsequious tears upon this trunk.
O, take this warm kiss on thy pale cold lips,
[*Kissing Titus.*]
These sorrowful drops upon thy blood-stain'd face,
The last true duties of thy noble son!
Marc. Tear for tear, and loving kiss for kiss,
Thy brother Marcus tenders on thy lips:
O, were the sum of these that I should pay
Countless and infinite, yet would I pay them!
Luc. Come hither, boy; come, come, and learn of us
To melt in showers: thy grandsire lov'd thee well:
Many a time he danc'd thee on his knee,

60. **this,** so Q_1; Globe, following Q_{2-3}F: *that.* 68. **uproars,** so QqF_1; Globe, following F_{2-4}: *uproar.* **as,** so Q_{1-2}; Globe, following Q_3F: *like.* 71. **corn,** small grain. 77. **chaps,** wrinkles. 88. **compact,** composed of. 92. **ye,** so Q_1; Globe, following Q_{2-3}F: *you.* 93. **And force you to,** so Q_1; Globe, following Q_2: *Lending your kind.* 94. **Here 's Rome's young,** so Q_1; Globe, following Q_2: *Here is a.* 95. **While I stand by,** so Q_1; Globe, following Q_2; *Your hearts will throb.* 96. **gracious,** so Q_1; Globe, following Q_2: *noble.* 97. **Chiron and the damn'd,** so Q_1; Globe, following Q_2: *cursed Chiron and.* 101. **cozen'd,** cheated. 130. **pleading,** so Q_1; Globe, following Q_2: *now.* 132. **hurl ourselves,** so Q_1; Globe, following Q_2: *cast us down.* 133. **souls,** so Q_1; Globe, following Q_2: *brains.* 134. **closure,** conclusion, death. 164. **story,** so Q_1; Globe, following $Q_{2-3}F_1$: *matter.* 165-171. **And bid . . . of them.** These lines are found only in Q_1; Q_2 and all subsequent texts based on it, including the Globe, have the following:

Meet and agreeing with thine infancy;
In that respect, then, like a loving child,
Shed yet some small drops from thy tender spring,
Because kind nature doth require it so:
Friends should associate friends in grief and woe:

Sung thee asleep, his loving breast thy pillow;
Many a story hath he told to thee,
And bid thee bear his pretty tales in mind,
And talk of them when he was dead and gone.
Marc. How many thousand times hath these poor lips,
When they were living, warm'd themselves on thine?
Oh now, sweet boy, give them their latest kiss.
Bid him farewell; commit him to the grave;
Do them that kindness and take leave of them.
Young Luc. O grandsire, grandsire! ev'n with all my heart
Would I were dead, so you did live again!
O Lord, I cannot speak to him for weeping;
My tears will choke me, if I ope my mouth.

[*Enter* Attendants *with* AARON.]

Roman. You sad Andronici, have done with woes:
Give sentence on this execrable wretch,
That hath been breeder of these dire events.
Luc. Set him breast-deep in earth, and famish him;
There let him stand, and rave, and cry for food:
If any one relieves or pities him,
For the offence he dies. This is our doom:
Some stay to see him fast'ned in the earth.
Aar. Ah, why should wrath be mute, and fury dumb?
I am no baby, I, that with base prayers
I should repent the evils I have done:
Ten thousand worse than ever yet I did
Would I perform, if I might have my will:
If one good deed in all my life I did,
I do repent it from my very soul.
Luc. Some loving friends convey the emperor hence,
And give him burial in his father's grave:
My father and Lavinia shall forthwith
Be closed in our household's monument.
As for that heinous tiger, Tamora,
No funeral rite, nor man in mourning weeds,
No mournful bell shall ring her burial;
But throw her forth to beasts and birds of prey:
Her life was beastly and devoid of pity;
And, being dead, let birds on her take pity. *Exeunt.*

Bid him farewell; commit him to the grave;
Do him that kindness, and take leave of him.
182. **doom,** decision, judgment. 199. **beastly,** so Qq; Globe, following F_1: *beast-like.* 200. The Q_1 text closes the play with this line. Q_2 and all subsequent texts, including the Globe, add the following four lines:

See justice done on Aaron, that damn'd Moor,
By whom our heavy haps had their beginning:
Then, afterwards, to order well the state,
That like events may ne'er it ruinate.

ROMEO AND JULIET

Though a tragedy, *Romeo and Juliet* is more closely comparable to Shakespeare's romantic comedies than to his other tragedies. Stylistically belonging to the years 1594–1596, it is in the lyric vein of the sonnets, *A Midsummer Night's Dream,* and *The Merchant of Venice,* all from the mid-1590's. Like them, it uses a variety of rhyme schemes (couplets, quatrains, octets, even sonnets) and revels in punning, flowery Petrarchan metaphor, and wit combat. It is separated in tone and in time from the earliest of the great tragedies, *Julius Caesar* and *Hamlet,* by almost half a decade, and, except for the experimental *Titus Andronicus,* it is Shakespeare's only tragedy (that is not also a "History") in the first decade of his productivity—a period devoted otherwise to exuberant comedy and patriotic English history.

Like many comedies, *Romeo and Juliet* is a love story, celebrating the exquisite brief joy of youthful passion. Even its tragic ending stresses the poignancy of that brief beauty, not the bitter futility of love as in *Troilus and Cressida* or *Othello.* The tragic ending of *Romeo and Juliet* underscores the observation made by a vexed lover in *A Midsummer Night's Dream* that "The course of true love never did run smooth" (I,i). True love in *Romeo and Juliet,* as in *A Midsummer,* is destined to be crossed by differences in "blood" or family background, differences in age, the arbitrary choice of family or friends, or other uncontrollable catastrophes such as war, death, and sickness. Love is thus, as in *A Midsummer,* "momentary as a sound, Swift as a shadow, short as any dream," swallowed up by darkness; "So quick bright things come to confusion." A dominant image pattern in *Romeo and Juliet* evokes a corresponding sense of suddenness and violence: fire, gunpowder, hot blood, lightning, the inconstant wind, the storm-tossed or shipwrecked vessel. Love so threatened and fragile is beautiful because it is brief. Tragic outcome therefore affirms the uniqueness and pristine youthful ecstasy of the experience. The flowering and fading of a joy "too rich for use, for earth too dear" (I,v), does not condemn the unfeeling world so much as it welcomes the martyrdom of literally dying for love.

As protagonists, Romeo and Juliet lack tragic stature by any classical definition or by the medieval convention of the Fall of Princes. The lovers are not extraordinary except in their passionate attachment to one another. By birth they are respectable citizens rather than nobility. Their dilemma of parental opposition is of the domestic sort often found in comedy. Accordingly, several characters in the play partly resemble the conventional character types of Plautus or Italian neoclassical comedy: the domineering father who insists that his daughter marry according to his choice, the unwelcome rival wooer, the garrulous and bawdy nurse, and of course the lovers. The Italian *novella*, from which Shakespeare ultimately derived his plot, made use of these same types and paid little attention to classical precepts whereby the protagonists in a tragic story ought to be persons of lofty station who are humbled through some inner flaw or *hamartia*. Luigi da Porto told (c. 1530) of a feud between the two Veronese families of Montecchi and Cappelletti and of two young lovers, Romeo and Giulietta, who with a friar's help resorted to the dire expedient of a soporific drug. Luigi based his account on an older *novella* of Masuccio of Salerno (1476) and on the still older tradition of a sleeping potion as found in the Greek romance of *Ephesiaca* (by the fifth century A.D.). Luigi's version was followed in turn by Bandello in his famous *Novelle* of 1554, whence the story was translated into the French of Pierre Boaistuau (1559) and thus into English in the long narrative poem of Arthur Brooke called *The Tragicall Historye of Romeus and Juliet* (1562). Brooke mentions having seen a play on the subject, but we must doubt that Shakespeare made much use of this old play even if he knew it. Brooke's poem was his chief and probably only source. Shakespeare has condensed Brooke's action from nine months to less than a week, greatly expanded the role of Mercutio, and given to the Nurse a warmth and humorous richness not found in the usual Italian duenna or *balia*. He has also tidied up the friar's immorality and deleted the antipapal tone. Still, Shakespeare retains the basically romantic (rather than classically tragic) conception of love overwhelmed by external obstacles.

Like the romantic comedies, *Romeo and Juliet* is often funny and erotic. Samson and Gregory in the first scene are slapstick cowards, hiding behind the law and daring to quarrel only when reinforcements arrive. The Nurse delights us with her earthy recollection of the day she weaned Juliet: the child tasting "the wormwood on the nipple Of my dug," the hot Italian sun, an earthquake, the Nurse's husband telling his lame but often-repeated bawdy joke. Mercutio employs his inventive and sardonic humor to twit Romeo for lovesickness and the Nurse for her pomposity. She in turn scolds Peter, and plagues Juliet (who is breathlessly awaiting news from Romeo) with a history of her back ailments. Mercutio and the Nurse are among Shakespeare's bawdiest characters. Their wry and salacious view of love contrasts with the nobly innocent and yet physically passionate love of Romeo and Juliet. Mercutio and the Nurse cannot take part in the play's denouement; one dies, misinterpreting Romeo's appeasement of Tybalt, while the other proves insensitive to Juliet's spiritual needs. Yet the play loses much of its funniness and vitality with the disappearance of these engaging companions.

The lovers too are at first well suited to Shakespearean romantic comedy. When we meet Romeo he is not in love with Juliet at all, despite the play's title, but is mooning over a "hard-hearted wench" named Rosaline. This "goddess" appropriately never appears in the play; she is almost a disembodied idea in Romeo's mind, a typically Petrarchan scornful beauty like Phebe in *As You Like It*. Romeo's love for her is tedious and self-pitying, like that of the conventional Petrarchan wooer in a sonnet sequence. Juliet, although not yet fourteen years of age, must change all this by teaching him the nature of true love. She will have none of his shopworn clichés learned in the service of Rosaline, his flowery protestations and swearing by the moon, lest they prove to be love's perjuries. With her innocent candor she instead insists (like many heroines of the romantic comedies) on dispelling the mask of pretense that lovers too often show one another. "Capulet" and "Montague" are mere labels, not the inner self. Although Juliet would have been more coy, she confesses, had she known that Romeo was overhearing her, she will now "prove more true Than those that have more cunning to be strange." She is more practical than he in assessing danger and making plans. Later she also proves herself remarkably able to bear misfortune.

This comic mood of the play's first half is, of course, overshadowed by the certainty of disaster. The opening chorus plainly warns us that the lovers will die. They are "star-cross'd," and speak of themselves as such. Romeo fears "Some consequence yet hanging in the stars" when he reluctantly goes to the Capulets' feast (I,iv); after he has slain Tybalt, he cries "O, I am fortune's fool!" (III,i); and at the news of Juliet's supposed death he proclaims "Then I defy you, stars!" (V,i). Yet in what sense are Romeo and Juliet "star-cross'd"? The concept is deliberately broad in this play, encompassing many factors such as hatred, bumbling, bad luck, and simple lack of awareness.

The first scene presents feuding as a major cause in the tragedy. The quarrel between the two families is so ancient that the original motives are no longer even discussed. Inspired by the "fiery" Tybalt, factionalism pursues its mindless course despite the efforts of the Prince to end the slaughter. Although the elders of both families talk of peace, they draw their swords quickly enough when a fray begins. Still, this senseless hatred does not in itself lead to tragedy until its effects are fatally complicated through misunderstanding. With poignant irony, good intentions are repeatedly undermined by lack of knowledge. We can see why Juliet does not tell her family of her elopement with a presumably hated Montague, but in fact Capulet has accepted Romeo as a guest in his house, praising him as a "virtuous and well govern'd youth." For all his dictatorial ways, Capulet would never force his daughter into bigamy if he knew the truth. Not knowing, he and his wife can only interpret her refusal to marry Paris as exasperating caprice. Count Paris himself is perhaps the greatest victim of this tragedy of unawareness. He is an eminently suitable wooer for Juliet, rich and nobly born yet considerate, peace-loving, and deeply fond of Juliet (as he demonstrates by his private and sincere grief at her tomb). Certainly he would never force his attentions on a married young woman if he knew the truth. Not knowing, he must play the unattractive role of the rival wooer and must even die for it. Similarly, Mercutio cannot understand Romeo's seemingly craven behavior toward Tybalt, and so begins the duel that leads to Romeo's banishment. The final scene, with Friar Laurence's retelling of the tragic story, allows us to see the survivors confronted with what they have all unknowingly done.

Chance or "accident" plays a role of equal importance to that of hatred and unawareness. An outbreak of the plague prevents Friar John from conveying Friar Laurence's letter to Romeo at Mantua. Friar Laurence, dashing off at this news to the Capulets' tomb, arrives only minutes after Romeo has taken poison. Juliet awakens only moments later. As Friar Laurence laments, "what an unkind hour Is guilty of this lamentable chance!" (V,iii). Earlier, Capulet's decision to move the wedding date up one day has crucially affected the timing. Human miscalculation makes its contribution also to the catastrophe: Mercutio is killed under Romeo's arm, and Friar Laurence wonders unhappily if any of his complicated plans "Miscarried by my fault." Even character and human decision play a part in this tragedy, for Romeo should not have dueled with Tybalt no matter what the provocation. To blame the tragedy in Aristotelean fashion on his and Juliet's impulsiveness is, however, a desperate argument.

Instead, the ending of the play brings together a pattern out of the seeming welter of mistakes and animosities. "A greater power than we can contradict Hath thwarted our intents," says Friar Laurence, thus implying piously that the seeming bad luck of the delayed letter was in fact the intent of a mysterious higher intelligence. Prince Escalus identifies this "greater power" as divine providence. "See, what a scourge is laid upon your hate," he admonishes the Montagues and Capulets, "That heaven finds means to kill your joys with love." Romeo and Juliet are "Poor sacrifices of our enmity." As the Prologue had foretold, their deaths will "bury their parents' strife." The families' feud is a stubborn evil force "which, but their children's end, nought could remove." Order is preciously restored; the price is great, but the sacrifice nonetheless confirms a sense of meaning in a divinely ordained universe. Throughout the play, love and hate are interrelated opposites, yoked through the rhetorical device of oxymoron or inherent contradiction. Romeo apostrophizes "O brawling love, O loving hate," and Juliet later echoes his words: "My only love sprung from my only hate." This paradox expresses a conflict in man as in the universe itself. "Two such opposed kings encamp them still In man as well as herbs," says Friar Laurence, "grace and rude will." Through hatred and misunderstanding, man kills the things most dear to him, but he can at least learn from his wanton destructiveness to strive to be worthy of the sacrifice.

ROMEO AND JULIET

[*Dramatis Personae*

ESCALUS, *Prince of Verona.*
PARIS, *a young nobleman, kinsman to the prince.*
MONTAGUE, } *heads of two houses at variance*
CAPULET, } *with each other.*
An old man, *cousin to Capulet.*
ROMEO, *son to Montague.*
MERCUTIO, *kinsman to the prince, and friend to Romeo.*
BENVOLIO, *nephew to Montague, and friend to Romeo.*
TYBALT, *nephew to Lady Capulet.*
FRIAR LAURENCE, } *Franciscans.*
FRIAR JOHN, }
BALTHASAR, *servant to Romeo.*
SAMPSON, } *servants to Capulet.*
GREGORY, }
PETER, *servant to Juliet's nurse.*
ABRAHAM, *servant to Montague.*
An Apothecary.
Three Musicians.
Page to Paris; another Page; an Officer.

LADY MONTAGUE, *wife to Montague.*
LADY CAPULET, *wife to Capulet.*
JULIET, *daughter to Capulet.*
Nurse to Juliet.

Citizens of Verona; several Men *and* Women, relations to both houses; Maskers, Guards, Watchmen, *and* Attendants.

Chorus.

SCENE: *Verona: Mantua.*]

THE PROLOGUE.

[*Enter* CHORUS.]

Chorus. Two households, both alike in dignity,
In fair Verona, where we lay our scene,
From ancient grudge break to new mutiny,
Where civil blood makes civil hands unclean.
From forth the fatal loins of these two foes
A pair of star-cross'd lovers take their life;
Whose misadventur'd piteous overthrows
Doth with their death bury their parents' strife.
The fearful passage of their death-mark'd love,
And the continuance of their parents' rage
Which, but their children's end, nought could remove,
Is now the two hours' traffic of our stage;
The which if you with patient ears attend,
What here shall miss, our toil shall strive to mend. [*Exit.*]

[ACT I.

SCENE I. *Verona. A public place.*]

Enter SAMPSON *and* GREGORY, *with swords and bucklers, of the house of Capulet.*

Sam. Gregory, on my word, we'll not carry coals.

Gre. No, for then we should be colliers.

Sam. I mean, an we be in choler, we'll draw.

Gre. Ay, while you live, draw your neck out of collar.

Sam. I strike quickly, being moved.

Gre. But thou art not quickly moved to strike.

Sam. A dog of the house of Montague moves me.

Gre. To move is to stir; and to be valiant is to stand: therefore, if thou art moved, thou runn'st away.

Sam. A dog of that house shall move me to stand: I will take the wall of any man or maid of Montague's.

Gre. That shows thee a weak slave; for the weakest goes to the wall.

Sam. 'Tis true; and therefore women, being the weaker vessels, are ever thrust to the wall: therefore I will push Montague's men from the wall, and thrust his maids to the wall.

Gre. The quarrel is between our masters and us their men.

Sam. 'Tis all one, I will show myself a tyrant: when I have fought with the men, I will be civil with the maids—I will cut off their heads.

Gre. The heads of the maids?

Sam. Ay, the heads of the maids, or their maidenheads; take it in what sense thou wilt.

Gre. They must take it in sense that feel it.

Sam. Me they shall feel while I am able to stand: and 'tis known I am a pretty piece of flesh.

Gre. 'Tis well thou art not fish; if thou hadst, thou hadst been poor John. Draw thy tool; here comes two of the house of the Montagues.

Enter two other Servingmen [ABRAHAM *and* BALTHASAR].

Sam. My naked weapon is out: quarrel, I will back thee.

Gre. How! turn thy back and run?

Sam. Fear me not.

Gre. No, marry; I fear thee!

Sam. Let us take the law of our sides; let them begin.

Gre. I will frown as I pass by, and let them take it as they list.

Sam. Nay, as they dare. I will bite my thumb at them; which is disgrace to them, if they bear it.

Abr. Do you bite your thumb at us, sir?

Sam. I do bite my thumb, sir.

Abr. Do you bite your thumb at us, sir?

Sam. [*Aside to Gre.*] Is the law of our side, if I say ay?

Gre. No.

Sam. No, sir, I do not bite my thumb at you, sir, but I bite my thumb, sir.

Gre. Do you quarrel, sir?

Abr. Quarrel, sir! no, sir.

Sam. But if you do, sir, I am for you: I serve as good a man as you.

Abr. No better.

Sam. Well, sir.

Enter BENVOLIO.

Gre. Say 'better:' here comes one of my master's kinsmen.

Sam. Yes, better, sir.

Abr. You lie.

Sam. Draw, if you be men. Gregory, remember thy swashing blow. *They fight.*

Ben. Part, fools!
Put up your swords; you know not what you do.
[*Beats down their swords.*]

Enter TYBALT.

Tyb. What, art thou drawn among these heartless hinds?
Turn thee, Benvolio, look upon thy death.

Ben. I do but keep the peace: put up thy sword,
Or manage it to part these men with me.

Tyb. What, drawn, and talk of peace! I hate the word,
As I hate hell, all Montagues, and thee:
Have at thee, coward! [*They fight.*]

Enter [*an* Officer, *and*] *three or four* Citizens *with clubs or partisans.*

Officer. Clubs, bills, and partisans! strike! beat them down!
Down with the Capulets! down with the Montagues!

Enter old CAPULET *in his gown, and his* Wife.

Cap. What noise is this? Give me my long sword, ho!

La. Cap. A crutch, a crutch! why call you for a sword?

Cap. My sword, I say! Old Montague is come,
And flourishes his blade in spite of me.

Enter old MONTAGUE *and his* Wife.

Mon. Thou villain Capulet,—Hold me not, let me go.

La. Mon. Thou shalt not stir one foot to seek a foe.

Enter PRINCE ESCALUS, *with his train.*

Prin. Rebellious subjects, enemies to peace,
Profaners of this neighbour-stained steel,—
Will they not hear? What, ho! you men, you beasts,
That quench the fire of your pernicious rage
With purple fountains issuing from your veins,
On pain of torture, from those bloody hands
Throw your mistempered weapons to the ground,
And hear the sentence of your moved prince.
Three civil brawls, bred of an airy word,
By thee, old Capulet, and Montague,
Have thrice disturb'd the quiet of our streets,
And made Verona's ancient citizens
Cast by their grave beseeming ornaments,
To wield old partisans, in hands as old,

PROLOGUE. 3. **mutiny,** state of discord. 6. **star-cross'd,** thwarted by destiny. Shakespeare shows in this play particularly, and throughout his plays generally, the current belief in the influence of the stars. The idea blends with that of divine providence. 9. **fearful,** full of fear; see glossary. **passage,** progress. 12. **two hours' traffic of our stage.** This line is one of a small number of references which enable us to tell the length of time occupied by a Shakespearean play. If the time was nearer two hours than three, the play must have been rapidly recited, with little loss of time between scenes. The bareness of the stage and the lack of a curtain would have contributed to the speed of presentation.

ACT I. SCENE I. This scene serves to give us the atmosphere of the whole play, an atmosphere of feud. Sampson is a stupid bully, Gregory a merry one. 1. **carry coals,** endure insults. 4. **choler,** one of the four humors, productive of anger. 10. **moves,** incites; see glossary. 15. **take the wall,** take the side of the walk nearest the wall, an act of discourtesy. 37. **poor John,** hake salted and dried—a poor kind of food. 42. **Fear,** mistrust; see glossary. 43. **marry,** mild oath; see glossary. 47. **list,** please; see glossary. 48. **bite my thumb,** an insulting gesture. 70. **swashing,** crushing. 73. **drawn,** with drawn sword. **heartless hinds,** cowardly menials; see *hind* in glossary. 79. **Have at thee,** I shall attack thee, defend thyself; see glossary. 80.

Cank'red with peace, to part your cank'red hate:
If ever you disturb our streets again,
Your lives shall pay the forfeit of the peace.
For this time, all the rest depart away:
You, Capulet, shall go along with me:
And, Montague, come you this afternoon,
To know our further pleasure in this case,
To old Free-town, our common judgement-place.
Once more, on pain of death, all men depart.
Exeunt [all but Montague, Lady Montague, and Benvolio].
Mon. Who set this ancient quarrel new abroach?
Speak, nephew, were you by when it began?
Ben. Here were the servants of your adversary,
And yours, close fighting ere I did approach:
I drew to part them: in the instant came
The fiery Tybalt, with his sword prepar'd,
Which, as he breath'd defiance to my ears,
He swung about his head and cut the winds,
Who nothing hurt withal hiss'd him in scorn:
While we were interchanging thrusts and blows,
Came more and more and fought on part and part,
Till the prince came, who parted either part.
La. Mon. O, where is Romeo? saw you him to-day?
Right glad I am he was not at this fray.
Ben. Madam, an hour before the worshipp'd sun
Peer'd forth the golden window of the east,
A troubled mind drave me to walk abroad;
Where, underneath the grove of sycamore
That westward rooteth from the city's side,
So early walking did I see your son:
Towards him I made, but he was ware of me
And stole into the covert of the wood:
I, measuring his affections by my own,
Which then most sought where most might not be found,
[Being one too many by my weary self,]
Pursu'd my humour not pursuing his,
And gladly shunn'd who gladly fled from me.
Mon. Many a morning hath he there been seen,
With tears augmenting the fresh morning's dew,
Adding to clouds more clouds with his deep sighs;
But all so soon as the all-cheering sun
Should in the farthest east begin to draw
The shady curtains from Aurora's bed,
Away from light steals home my heavy son,
And private in his chamber pens himself,
Shuts up his windows, locks fair daylight out
And makes himself an artificial night:
Black and portentous must this humour prove,
Unless good counsel may the cause remove.
Ben. My noble uncle, do you know the cause?
Mon. I neither know it nor can learn of him.
Ben. Have you importun'd him by any means?
Mon. Both by myself and many other friends:
But he, his own affections' counsellor,
Is to himself—I will not say how true—
But to himself so secret and so close,
So far from sounding and discovery,
As is the bud bit with an envious worm,
Ere he can spread his sweet leaves to the air,
Or dedicate his beauty to the sun.
Could we but learn from whence his sorrows grow,
We would as willingly give cure as know.

Enter ROMEO.

Ben. See, where he comes: so please you, step aside;
I'll know his grievance, or be much denied.
Mon. I would thou wert so happy by thy stay,
To hear true shrift. Come, madam, let 's away.
Exeunt [Montague and Lady].
Ben. Good morrow, cousin.
Rom. Is the day so young?
Ben. But new struck nine.
Rom. Ay me! sad hours seem long.
Was that my father that went hence so fast?
Ben. It was. What sadness lengthens Romeo's hours?
Rom. Not having that, which, having, makes them short.
Ben. In love?
Rom. Out—
Ben. Of love?
Rom. Out of her favour, where I am in love.
Ben. Alas, that love, so gentle in his view,
Should be so tyrannous and rough in proof!
Rom. Alas, that love, whose view is muffled still,
Should, without eyes, see pathways to his will!
Where shall we dine? O me! What fray was here?
Yet tell me not, for I have heard it all.
Here 's much to do with hate, but more with love.
Why, then, O brawling love! O loving hate!
O any thing, of nothing first create!
O heavy lightness! serious vanity!
Mis-shapen chaos of well-seeming forms!
Feather of lead, bright smoke, cold fire, sick health!
Still-waking sleep, that is not what it is!
This love feel I, that feel no love in this.
Dost thou not laugh?
Ben. No, coz, I rather weep.
Rom. Good heart, at what?
Ben. At thy good heart's oppression.
Rom. Why, such is love's transgression.
Griefs of mine own lie heavy in my breast,
Which thou wilt propagate, to have it prest
With more of thine: this love that thou hast shown
Doth add more grief to too much of mine own.
Love is a smoke rais'd with the fume of sighs;
Being purg'd, a fire sparkling in lovers' eyes;
Being vex'd, a sea nourish'd with lovers' tears:
What is it else? a madness most discreet,
A choking gall and a preserving sweet.
Farewell, my coz.
Ben. Soft! I will go along;
An if you leave me so, you do me wrong.
Rom. Tut, I have lost myself; I am not here;
This is not Romeo, he 's some other where.
Ben. Tell me in sadness, who is that you love.
Rom. What, shall I groan and tell thee?

Clubs, bills, and partisans, a rallying cry of London apprentices. *Bills* and *partisans* were long-handled spears with cutting blades. 83. **crutch,** i.e., a crutch would befit him better than a sword. 102. **Cank'red . . . cank'red,** corroded . . . malignant. 109. **Free-town,** Villa Franca in Brooke's poem *Romeus and Juliet.* 111. **set . . . abroach,** reopened. 119. **nothing,** not at all; see glossary. **withal,** with this; see glossary. 121. **on part and part,** on one side and the other. 133. **affections,** wishes, inclination; see glossary. 134. **Which then . . . self],** so Q; Globe follows F, which has only one line in place of two lines here. 135. **humour,** mood, whim; see glossary. 143. **heavy,** sad. 151. **means,** agency; see *mean* in glossary. 155. **close,** secret, private; see glossary. 157. **envious,** malicious; see glossary. 159. **sun,** so Theobald; Qq: *same.* 163. **denied,** refused; see *deny* in glossary. 165. **shrift,** confession. 166. **morrow,** morning. **cousin,** any relative not belonging to one's immediate family; see glossary. 174. **favour,** good will, liking; see glossary. 176. **proof,** experience; see glossary. 181-188. **Here 's . . . this.** These lines, abounding in paradoxical phrases called oxymoron, such as *loving hate, cold fire,* are characteristic of artificial love poetry. 183. **create,** created. 193. **propagate,** increase. 206. **sadness,** seriousness.

Ben. Groan! why, no:
But sadly tell me who.
Rom. Bid a sick man in sadness make his will:
Ah, word ill urg'd to one that is so ill!
In sadness, cousin, I do love a woman.
Ben. I aim'd so near, when I suppos'd you lov'd.
Rom. A right good mark-man! And she 's fair I love.
Ben. A right fair mark, fair coz, is soonest hit.
Rom. Well, in that hit you miss: she'll not be hit
With Cupid's arrow; she hath Dian's wit;
And, in strong proof of chastity well arm'd,
From love's weak childish bow she lives unharm'd.
She will not stay the siege of loving terms,
Nor bide th' encounter of assailing eyes,
Nor ope her lap to saint-seducing gold:
O, she is rich in beauty, only poor,
That when she dies with beauty dies her store.
Ben. Then she hath sworn that she will still live chaste?
Rom. She hath, and in that sparing makes huge waste,
For beauty starv'd with her severity
Cuts beauty off from all posterity.
She is too fair, too wise, wisely too fair,
To merit bliss by making me despair:
She hath forsworn to love, and in that vow
Do I live dead that live to tell it now.
Ben. Be rul'd by me, forget to think of her.
Rom. O, teach me how I should forget to think!
Ben. By giving liberty unto thine eyes;
Examine other beauties.
Rom. 'Tis the way
To call hers exquisite, in question more:
These happy masks that kiss fair ladies' brows
Being black put us in mind they hide the fair;
He that is strucken blind cannot forget
The precious treasure of his eyesight lost:
Show me a mistress that is passing fair,
What doth her beauty serve, but as a note
Where I may read who pass'd that passing fair?
Farewell: thou canst not teach me to forget.
Ben. I'll pay that doctrine, or else die in debt.
Exeunt.

[SCENE II. *A street.*]

Enter CAPULET, COUNTY PARIS, *and the Clown* [*a* Servant].

Cap. But Montague is bound as well as I,
In penalty alike; and 'tis not hard, I think,
For men so old as we to keep the peace.
Par. Of honourable reckoning are you both;
And pity 'tis you liv'd at odds so long.
But now, my lord, what say you to my suit?
Cap. But saying o'er what I have said before:
My child is yet a stranger in the world;
She hath not seen the change of fourteen years;
Let two more summers wither in their pride,
Ere we may think her ripe to be a bride.
Par. Younger than she are happy mothers made.
Cap. And too soon marr'd are those so early made.
The earth hath swallowed all my hopes but she,
She is the hopeful lady of my earth:
But woo her, gentle Paris, get her heart,
My will to her consent is but a part;
An she agree, within her scope of choice
Lies my consent and fair according voice.
This night I hold an old accustom'd feast,
Whereto I have invited many a guest,
Such as I love; and you, among the store,
One more, most welcome, makes my number more.
At my poor house look to behold this night
Earth-treading stars that make dark heaven light:
Such comfort as do lusty young men feel
When well-apparell'd April on the heel
Of limping winter treads, even such delight
Among fresh fennel buds shall you this night
Inherit at my house; hear all, all see,
And like her most whose merit most shall be:
†Which on more view, of many mine being one
May stand in number, though in reck'ning none.
Come, go with me. [*To Serv., giving a paper.*] Go, sirrah, trudge about
Through fair Verona; find those persons out
Whose names are written there, and to them say,
My house and welcome on their pleasure stay.
Exit [*with Paris*].

Serv. Find them out whose names are written here! It is written, that the shoemaker should meddle with his yard, and the tailor with his last, the fisher with his pencil, and the painter with his nets; but I am sent to find those persons whose names are here writ, and can never find what names the writing person hath here writ. I must to the learned.—In good time.

Enter BENVOLIO *and* ROMEO.

Ben. Tut, man, one fire burns out another's burning,
One pain is less'ned by another's anguish;
Turn giddy, and be holp by backward turning;
One desperate grief cures with another's languish:
Take thou some new infection to thy eye,
And the rank poison of the old will die.
Rom. Your plaintain-leaf is excellent for that.
Ben. For what, I pray thee?
Rom. For your broken shin.
Ben. Why, Romeo, art thou mad?
Rom. Not mad, but bound more than a madman is;
Shut up in prison, kept without my food,
Whipp'd and tormented and—God-den, good fellow.
Serv. God gi' god-den. I pray, sir, can you read?
Rom. Ay, mine own fortune in my misery.
Serv. Perhaps you have learned it without book: but, I pray, can you read any thing you see?
Rom. Ay, if I know the letters and the language.
Serv. Ye say honestly: rest you merry!
Rom. Stay, fellow; I can read. *He reads the letter.*
'Signior Martino and his wife and daughters; County Anselme and his beauteous sisters; the lady

212. **fair,** beautiful; see glossary. 213. **fair,** clear, distinct; see glossary. 218. **stay,** submit to. 222. **store.** She will die without children and therefore her beauty will die with her. 223. **still,** always. 225. **starv'd,** allowed to die; see glossary. 235. **in question more,** even more strongly to my mind. 240. **passing,** surpassingly; see glossary. 244. **pay that doctrine,** give that instruction.

SCENE II. 4. **reckoning,** estimation, repute. 9. **fourteen years.** Juliet is younger than in Shakespeare's source, Brooke's *Romeus and Juliet*, where she is sixteen. 15. **hopeful . . . earth,** my heir and hope for posterity. 18. **An,** if; see glossary. **scope,** limit; see glossary. 29. **fennel,** flowering herb thought to have the power of awakening passion. Often emended to *female* (as in Globe). 32-33. **Which . . . none.** Capulet may mean that his daughter will lose her identity by being swallowed up in a number of others. He is punning on the saying, "one is no number." Dowden places a comma after *of* and dashes after *many* and *one*. He explains *reckoning* to mean "estimation" (as in line 4, above), with word play, i.e., "counting heads." 34. **sirrah,** customary form of address to servants; see glossary. 48. **holp,** helped; see glossary. 51.

widow of Vitruvio; Signior Placentio and his lovely nieces; Mercutio and his brother Valentine; mine uncle Capulet, his wife, and daughters; my fair niece Rosaline; Livia; Signior Valentio and his cousin Tybalt; Lucio and the lively Helena.'
A fair assembly: whither should they come?
Serv. Up.
Rom. Whither? to supper?
Serv. To our house.
Rom. Whose house?
Serv. My master's.
Rom. Indeed, I should have ask'd you that before.
Serv. Now I'll tell you without asking: my master is the great rich Capulet; and if you be not of the house of Montagues, I pray, come and crush a cup of wine. Rest you merry! [*Exit.*]
Ben. At this same ancient feast of Capulet's
Sups the fair Rosaline whom thou so loves,
With all the admired beauties of Verona:
Go thither; and, with unattainted eye,
Compare her face with some that I shall show,
And I will make thee think thy swan a crow.
Rom. When the devout religion of mine eye
Maintains such falsehood, then turn tears to fires;
And these, who often drown'd could never die,
Transparent heretics, be burnt for liars!
One fairer than my love! the all-seeing sun
Ne'er saw her match since first the world begun.
Ben. Tut, you saw her fair, none else being by,
Herself pois'd with herself in either eye:
But in that crystal scales let there be weigh'd
Your lady's love against some other maid
That I will show you shining at this feast,
And she shall scant show well that now seems best.
Rom. I'll go along, no such sight to be shown,
But to rejoice in splendour of mine own. [*Exeunt.*]

[SCENE III. *A room in Capulet's house.*]

Enter CAPULET'S WIFE *and* Nurse.

La. Cap. Nurse, where 's my daughter? call her forth to me.
Nurse. Now, by my maidenhead, at twelve year old,
I bade her come. What, lamb! what, ladybird!
God forbid! Where 's this girl? What, Juliet!

Enter JULIET.

Jul. How now! who calls?
Nurse. Your mother.
Jul. Madam, I am here.
What is your will?
La. Cap. This is the matter:—Nurse, give leave awhile,
We must talk in secret:—nurse, come back again;
I have remember'd me, thou 's hear our counsel.
Thou knowest my daughter 's of a pretty age.
Nurse. Faith, I can tell her age unto an hour.
La. Cap. She 's not fourteen.
Nurse. I'll lay fourteen of my teeth,—
And yet, to my teen be it spoken, I have but four,—
She is not fourteen. How long is it now
To Lammas-tide?
La. Cap. A fortnight and odd days.
Nurse. Even or odd, of all days in the year,
Come Lammas-eve at night shall she be fourteen.
Susan and she—God rest all Christian souls!—
Were of an age: well, Susan is with God;
She was too good for me: but, as I said,
On Lammas-eve at night shall she be fourteen;
That shall she, marry; I remember it well.
'Tis since the earthquake now eleven years;
And she was wean'd,—I never shall forget it,—
Of all the days of the year, upon that day:
For I had then laid wormwood to my dug,
Sitting in the sun under the dove-house wall;
My lord and you were then at Mantua:—
Nay, I do bear a brain:—but, as I said,
When it did taste the wormwood on the nipple
Of my dug and felt it bitter, pretty fool,
To see it tetchy and fall out with the dug!
'Shake' quoth the dove-house: 'twas no need, I trow,
To bid me trudge:
And since that time it is eleven years;
For then she could stand high lone; nay, by th' rood,
She could have run and waddled all about;
For even the day before, she broke her brow:
And then my husband—God be with his soul!
'A was a merry man—took up the child:
'Yea,' quoth he, 'dost thou fall upon thy face?
Thou wilt fall backward when thou hast more wit;
Wilt thou not, Jule?' and, by my holidame,
The pretty wretch left crying and said 'Ay.'
To see, now, how a jest shall come about!
I warrant, an I should live a thousand years,
I never should forget it: 'Wilt thou not, Jule?' quoth he;
And, pretty fool, it stinted and said 'Ay.'
La. Cap. Enough of this; I pray thee, hold thy peace.
Nurse. Yes, madam: yet I cannot choose but laugh,
To think it should leave crying and say 'Ay.'
And yet, I warrant, it had upon it brow
A bump as big as a young cock'rel's stone;
A perilous knock; and it cried bitterly:
'Yea,' quoth my husband, 'fall'st upon thy face?
Thou wilt fall backward when thou comest to age;
Wilt thou not, Jule?' it stinted and said 'Ay.'
Jul. And stint thou too, I pray thee, nurse, say I.
Nurse. Peace, I have done. God mark thee to his grace!
Thou wast the prettiest babe that e'er I nurs'd:
An I might live to see thee married once,
I have my wish.
La. Cap. Marry, that 'marry' is the very theme
I came to talk of. Tell me, daughter Juliet,
How stands your disposition to be married?
Jul. It is an honour that I dream not of.

rank, corrupt; see glossary. 57. **God-den,** good evening. **fellow,** usual term for a servant; see glossary. 66-74. **Signior . . . Helena,** actually, a verse passage. 86. **crush a cup of wine,** drink a cup of wine. Cf. "crack a bottle." 87. **ancient,** customary. 89. **admired,** wondered at; see glossary. 90. **unattainted,** impartial. 95. **these,** i.e., these eyes.
SCENE III. 3. **ladybird,** sweetheart; also, loose woman (used endearingly). 7. **give leave,** leave us. 9. **thou 's,** thou shalt. 13. **teen,** sorrow. 15. **Lammas-tide,** the time around Lammas, August 1. 18. **Susan,** the Nurse's own child who has evidently died. 29. **bear a brain.** The nurse prides herself on her memory. 31. **fool,** term of endearment; see glossary. 32. **tetchy,** fretful. 33. **trow,** believe; see glossary. 36. **high lone,** on her feet, without help. **rood,** cross. 38. **broke her brow,** banged her head (by falling). 40. **'A,** he. 43. **holidame,** same as "halidom," a relic or holy thing. 48. **stinted,** ceased. 52. **it,** so QqF; Globe: *its*. 53. **cock'rel's stone,** young rooster's testicle.

Nurse. An honour! were not I thine only nurse,
I would say thou hadst suck'd wisdom from thy teat.
La. Cap. Well, think of marriage now; younger than you,
Here in Verona, ladies of esteem,
Are made already mothers: by my count,
I was your mother much upon these years
That you are now a maid. Thus then in brief:
The valiant Paris seeks you for his love.
Nurse. A man, young lady! lady, such a man
As all the world—why, he 's a man of wax.
La. Cap. Verona's summer hath not such a flower.
Nurse. Nay, he 's a flower; in faith, a very flower.
La. Cap. What say you? can you love the gentleman?
This night you shall behold him at our feast;
Read o'er the volume of young Paris' face
And find delight writ there with beauty's pen;
Examine every married lineament
And see how one another lends content,
And what obscur'd in this fair volume lies
Find written in the margent of his eyes.
This precious book of love, this unbound lover,
To beautify him, only lacks a cover:
The fish lives in the sea, and 'tis much pride
For fair without the fair within to hide:
That book in many's eyes doth share the glory,
That in gold clasps locks in the golden story;
So shall you share all that he doth possess,
By having him, making yourself no less.
Nurse. No less! nay, bigger; women grow by men.
La. Cap. Speak briefly, can you like of Paris' love?
Jul. I'll look to like, if looking liking move:
But no more deep will I endart mine eye
Than your consent gives strength to make it fly.

Enter Servingman.

Serv. Madam, the guests are come, supper served up, you called, my young lady asked for, the nurse cursed in the pantry, and every thing in extremity. I must hence to wait; I beseech you, follow straight.

La. Cap. We follow thee. [*Exit Servingman*.] Juliet, the county stays.
Nurse. Go, girl, seek happy nights to happy days.
Exeunt.

[SCENE IV. *A street*.]

Enter ROMEO, MERCUTIO, BENVOLIO, *with five or six other* Maskers; Torch-bearers.

Rom. What, shall this speech be spoke for our excuse?
Or shall we on without apology?
Ben. The date is out of such prolixity:
We'll have no Cupid hoodwink'd with a scarf,
Bearing a Tartar's painted bow of lath,
Scaring the ladies like a crow-keeper;
Nor no without-book prologue, faintly spoke
After the prompter, for our entrance:
But let them measure us by what they will;
We'll measure them a measure, and be gone.
Rom. Give me a torch: I am not for this ambling;
Being but heavy, I will bear the light.
Mer. Nay, gentle Romeo, we must have you dance.
Rom. Not I, believe me: you have dancing shoes
With nimble soles: I have a soul of lead
So stakes me to the ground I cannot move.
Mer. You are a lover; borrow Cupid's wings,
And soar with them above a common bound.
Rom. I am too sore enpierced with his shaft
To soar with his light feathers, and so bound,
I cannot bound a pitch above dull woe:
Under love's heavy burden do I sink.
Mer. And, to sink in it, should you burden love;
Too great oppression for a tender thing.
Rom. Is love a tender thing? it is too rough,
Too rude, too boist'rous, and it pricks like thorn.
Mer. If love be rough with you, be rough with love;
Prick love for pricking, and you beat love down.
Give me a case to put my visage in:
A visor for a visor! what care I
What curious eye doth quote deformities?
Here are the beetle brows shall blush for me.
Ben. Come, knock and enter; and no sooner in,
But every man betake him to his legs.
Rom. A torch for me: let wantons light of heart
Tickle the senseless rushes with their heels,
For I am proverb'd with a grandsire phrase;
I'll be a candle-holder, and look on.
The game was ne'er so fair, and I am done.
Mer. Tut, dun 's the mouse, the constable's own word:
If thou art dun, we'll draw thee from the mire
Of this sir-reverence love, wherein thou stickest
Up to the ears. Come, we burn daylight, ho!
Rom. Nay, that 's not so.
Mer. I mean, sir, in delay
We waste our lights in vain, like lamps by day.
Take our good meaning, for our judgement sits
Five times in that ere once in our five wits.
Rom. And we mean well in going to this mask;
But 'tis no wit to go.
Mer. Why, may one ask?
Rom. I dream'd a dream to-night.
Mer. And so did I.
Rom. Well, what was yours?
Mer. That dreamers often lie.
Rom. In bed asleep, while they do dream things true.
Mer. O, then, I see Queen Mab hath been with you.
She is the fairies' midwife, and she comes
In shape no bigger than an agate-stone
On the fore-finger of an alderman,

76. **a man of wax,** such as one would picture in wax, i.e., handsome. 83. **married,** harmonized into mutual helpfulness (Hudson). 86. **margent,** commentary or marginal gloss. 89. **fish lives in the sea.** Shakespeare may mean that, just as the sea enfolds the fish, being thereby both handsome in appearance and rich in inner value, so Juliet is to enclose Paris in her arms and add beauty to his worth. 105. **county,** count.

SCENE IV. 1. **speech.** The older fashion was for maskers to be preceded by a messenger with a set speech, but *the date is out* for *such prolixity;* see *date* and *out* in glossary. 4. **hoodwink'd,** blindfolded. 5. **Tartar's painted bow.** Tartar's bows are said to have resembled the old Roman bow with which Cupid was pictured. 6. **crow-keeper,** scarecrow. 10. **measure . . . measure,** perform a dance; see glossary. 11. **ambling,** walking affectedly; used contemptuously of dancing. 21. **pitch,** height; see glossary. 30. **visor,** a mask, for an ugly masklike face. 31. **quote,** take notice of. 36. **rushes.** Rushes were used for floor coverings. 38. **candle-holder,** an allusion to the proverb "A good candle-holder (i.e., a mere onlooker) is a good gamester." 40. **dun 's the mouse,** a common phrase usually taken to mean "keep still." *Dun* (l. 41) alludes to a Christmas game, "Dun is in the mire," in which a heavy log was lifted by the players. 42. **sir-reverence,** corruption of "save-reverence" (*salve-reverentia*), an apology for something improper.

Drawn with a team of little atomies
Over men's noses as they lie asleep;
Her waggon-spokes made of long spinners' legs,
The cover of the wings of grasshoppers,
Her traces of the smallest spider web,
Her collars of the moonshine's wat'ry beams,
Her whip of cricket's bone, the lash of film,
Her waggoner a small grey-coated gnat,
Not half so big as a round little worm
Prick'd from the lazy finger of a maid;
Her chariot is an empty hazel-nut
Made by the joiner squirrel or old grub,
Time out o' mind the fairies' coachmakers.
And in this state she gallops night by night
Through lovers' brains, and then they dream of love;
O'er courtiers' knees, that dream on court'sies straight,
O'er lawyers' fingers, who straight dream on fees,
O'er ladies' lips, who straight on kisses dream,
Which oft the angry Mab with blisters plagues,
Because their breaths with sweetmeats tainted are:
Sometime she gallops o'er a courtier's nose,
And then dreams he of smelling out a suit;
And sometime comes she with a tithe-pig's tail
Tickling a parson's nose as 'a lies asleep,
Then dreams he of another benefice:
Sometime she driveth o'er a soldier's neck,
And then dreams he of cutting foreign throats,
Of breaches, ambuscadoes, Spanish blades,
Of healths five-fathom deep; and then anon
Drums in his ear, at which he starts and wakes,
And being thus frighted swears a prayer or two
And sleeps again. This is that very Mab
That plats the manes of horses in the night,
And bakes the elf-locks in foul sluttish hairs,
Which once untangled much misfortune bodes:
This is the hag, when maids lie on their backs,
That presses them and learns them first to bear,
Making them women of good carriage:
This is she—

Rom. Peace, peace, Mercutio, peace!
Thou talk'st of nothing.

Mer. True, I talk of dreams,
Which are the children of an idle brain,
Begot of nothing but vain fantasy,
Which is as thin of substance as the air
And more inconstant than the wind, who wooes
Even now the frozen bosom of the north,
And, being anger'd, puffs away from thence,
Turning his side to the dew-dropping south.

Ben. This wind, you talk of, blows us from ourselves;
Supper is done, and we shall come too late.

Rom. I fear, too early: for my mind misgives
Some consequence yet hanging in the stars
Shall bitterly begin his fearful date
With this night's revels and expire the term
Of a despised life clos'd in my breast
By some vile forfeit of untimely death.
But He, that hath the steerage of my course,
Direct my sail! On, lusty gentlemen.

Ben. Strike, drum.

They march about the stage, and [retire to one side].

[SCENE V. *A hall in Capulet's house.*]

Servingmen *come forth with napkins.*

First Serv. Where 's Potpan, that he helps not to take away? He shift a trencher? he scrape a trencher!

Sec. Serv. When good manners shall lie all in one or two men's hands and they unwashed too, 'tis a foul thing.

First Serv. Away with the joint-stools, remove the court-cupboard, look to the plate. Good thou, save me a piece of marchpane; and, as thou loves me, let the porter let in Susan Grindstone and Nell. Antony, and Potpan!

Sec. Serv. Ay, boy, ready.

First Serv. You are looked for and called for, asked for and sought for, in the great chamber.

Third Serv. We cannot be here and there too. Cheerly, boys; be brisk awhile, and the longer liver take all.

Exeunt.

Enter [CAPULET *and family and*] *all the* Guests *and* Gentlewomen *to the* Maskers.

Cap. Welcome, gentlemen! ladies that have their toes
Unplagu'd with corns will walk about with you.
Ah ha, my mistresses! which of you all
Will now deny to dance? she that makes dainty,
She, I'll swear, hath corns; am I come near ye now?
Welcome, gentlemen! I have seen the day
That I have worn a visor and could tell
A whispering tale in a fair lady's ear,
Such as would please: 'tis gone, 'tis gone, 'tis gone:
You are welcome, gentlemen! Come, musicians, play. *Music plays, and they dance.*
A hall, a hall! give room! and foot it, girls.
More light, you knaves; and turn the tables up,
And quench the fire, the room is grown too hot.
Ah, sirrah, this unlook'd-for sport comes well.
Nay, sit, nay, sit, good cousin Capulet;
For you and I are past our dancing days:
How long is 't now since last yourself and I
Were in a mask?

Sec. Cap. By 'r lady, thirty years.

Cap. What, man! 'tis not so much, 'tis not so much:
'Tis since the nuptial of Lucentio,
Come Pentecost as quickly as it will,
Some five and twenty years; and then we mask'd.

Sec. Cap. 'Tis more, 'tis more: his son is elder, sir;
His son is thirty.

Cap. Will you tell me that?

46-47. **Take . . . wits,** i.e., try to understand what I intend to say, relying on common sense rather than on one single mental faculty. (The five faculties were common sense, imagination, fantasy, judgment, and reason.) 53. **Queen Mab,** a name of Celtic origin for the fairy queen. 57. **atomies,** tiny creatures. 63. **film,** gossamer thread. 65. **worm.** This alludes to an ancient superstition that "worms breed in the fingers of the idle." 70. **state,** pomp, dignity; see glossary. 73. **straight,** immediately; see glossary. 77. **Sometime,** from time to time, sometimes; see glossary. 78. **suit,** a request or plea at court. 79. **tithe-pig's tail.** This alludes to the tenth pig given the parson as a church tax. 85. **anon,** by an by. 89. **plats the manes of horses,** an allusion to the familiar superstition of "witches stirrups," tangles in the manes of horses. 90. **elf-locks,** tangles. 93. **learns,** teaches; see glossary. 98. **vain,** empty, foolish. **fantasy,** imagination. 108. **date,** time. 109. **expire,** (transitive), bring to an end.

SCENE V. The action is continuous from the previous scene. 2. **trencher,** wooden dish or plate; see glossary. 7. **joint-stools,** stools, properly those made by a joiner. 8. **court-cupboard,** sideboard. 9. **marchpane,** cake made from sugar and almonds. 21. **makes dainty,** seems coyly reluctant (to dance). 29. **turn the tables up.** Tables were probably made of hinged leaves and placed on trestles. They were put aside for dancing.

His son was but a ward two years ago.
Rom. [*To a Servingman*] What lady 's that, which doth enrich the hand
Of yonder knight?
Serv. I know not, sir.
Rom. O, she doth teach the torches to burn bright!
It seems she hangs upon the cheek of night
As a rich jewel in an Ethiope's ear;
Beauty too rich for use, for earth too dear!
So shows a snowy dove trooping with crows,
As yonder lady o'er her fellows shows.
The measure done, I'll watch her place of stand,
And, touching hers, make blessed my rude hand.
Did my heart love till now? forswear it, sight!
For I ne'er saw true beauty till this night.
Tyb. This, by his voice, should be a Montague.
Fetch me my rapier, boy. What dares the slave
Come hither, cover'd with an antic face,
To fleer and scorn at our solemnity?
Now, by the stock and honour of my kin,
To strike him dead I hold it not a sin.
Cap. Why, how now, kinsman! wherefore storm you so?
Tyb. Uncle, this is a Montague, our foe,
A villain that is hither come in spite,
To scorn at our solemnity this night.
Cap. Young Romeo is it?
Tyb. 'Tis he, that villain Romeo.
Cap. Content thee, gentle coz, let him alone;
'A bears him like a portly gentleman;
And, to say truth, Verona brags of him
To be a virtuous and well govern'd youth:
I would not for the wealth of all this town
Here in my house do him disparagement:
Therefore be patient, take no note of him:
It is my will, the which if thou respect,
Show a fair presence and put off these frowns,
An ill-beseeming semblance for a feast.
Tyb. It fits, when such a villain is a guest:
I'll not endure him.
Cap. He shall be endur'd:
What, goodman boy! I say, he shall: go to;
Am I the master here, or you? go to.
You'll not endure him! God shall mend my soul!
You'll make a mutiny among my guests!
You will set cock-a-hoop! you'll be the man!
Tyb. Why, uncle, 'tis a shame.
Cap. Go to, go to;
You are a saucy boy: is 't so, indeed?
This trick may chance to scathe you, I know what:
You must contrary me! marry, 'tis time.
Well said, my hearts! You are a princox; go:
Be quiet, or—More light, more light! For shame!
I'll make you quiet. What, cheerly, my hearts!
Tyb. Patience perforce with wilful choler meeting
Makes my flesh tremble in their different greeting.
I will withdraw: but this intrusion shall
Now seeming sweet convert to bitt'rest gall. *Exit.*

Rom. [*To Juliet*] If I profane with my unworthiest hand
This holy shrine, the gentle sin is this:
My lips, two blushing pilgrims, ready stand
To smooth that rough touch with a tender kiss.
Jul. Good pilgrim, you do wrong your hand too much,
Which mannerly devotion shows in this;
For saints have hands that pilgrims' hands do touch,
And palm to palm is holy palmers' kiss.
Rom. Have not saints lips, and holy palmers too?
Jul. Ay, pilgrim, lips that they must use in pray'r.
Rom. O, then, dear saint, let lips do what hands do;
They pray, grant thou, lest faith turn to despair.
Jul. Saints do not move, though grant for prayers' sake.
Rom. Then move not, while my prayer's effect I take. [*Kiss.*]
Thus from my lips, by yours, my sin is purg'd.
Jul. Then have my lips the sin that they have took.
Rom. Sin from my lips? O trespass sweetly urg'd!
Give me my sin again. [*Kiss again.*]
Jul. You kiss by th' book.
Nurse. Madam, your mother craves a word with you.
Rom. What is her mother?
Nurse. Marry, bachelor,
Her mother is the lady of the house,
And a good lady, and a wise and virtuous:
I nurs'd her daughter, that you talk'd withal;
I tell you, he that can lay hold of her
Shall have the chinks.
Rom. Is she a Capulet?
O dear account! my life is my foe's debt.
Ben. Away, be gone; the sport is at the best.
Rom. Ay, so I fear; the more is my unrest.
Cap. Nay, gentlemen, prepare not to be gone;
We have a trifling foolish banquet towards.
Is it e'en so? why, then, I thank you all;
I thank you, honest gentlemen; good night.
More torches here! Come on then, let 's to bed.
Ah, sirrah, by my fay, it waxes late:
I'll to my rest. [*Exeunt all but Juliet and Nurse.*]
Jul. Come hither, nurse. What is yond gentleman?
Nurse. The son and heir of old Tiberio.
Jul. What 's he that now is going out of door?
Nurse. Marry, that, I think, be young Petrucio.
Jul. What 's he that follows there, that would not dance?
Nurse. I know not.
Jul. Go, ask his name: if he be married,
My grave is like to be my wedding bed.
Nurse. His name is Romeo, and a Montague;
The only son of your great enemy.
Jul. My only love sprung from my only hate!
Too early seen unknown, and known too late!
Prodigious birth of love it is to me,
That I must love a loathed enemy.

42. **ward,** a minor under guardianship. 49. **dear,** precious; see glossary. 50. **shows,** appears. 52. **The measure done,** when this dance is over. 58. **antic face,** fantastic mask. 59. **fleer,** to look mockingly. 68. **portly,** of good deportment. 79. **goodman boy.** "Goodman" applied to one below the rank of gentleman, but still of some substance, like a wealthy farmer. **go to,** an expression of impatience. 83. **You . . . cock-a-hoop,** i.e., you want to be cock of the walk. 86. **scathe,** harm. 91. **Patience perforce,** patience upon compulsion; see *perforce* in glossary; *patience* is a general word for self-control. 94. **convert,** change (to). 95-108. **If . . . take.** These lines are in the form of a sonnet. They afford an example of Shakespeare's early exuberance in poetic style. 96. **shrine,** i.e., Juliet's hand. 112. **book,** book of etiquette. 119. **chinks,** plenty of money. 120. **my foe's debt,** due to my foe, at his mercy. 124. **foolish,** insignificant. **banquet,** light refreshment. **towards,** in preparation; see glossary. 128. **fay,** faith.

ACT II. PROLOGUE. This may be an addition to the original text. It provides no needed information, and interrupts a continuous scene. 10. **use to swear,** are in the habit of swearing; see *use* in glossary. 13. **passion,** feeling of love; see glossary.

SCENE I. 2. **dull earth,** Romeo himself. **thy centre,** Juliet. The figure of speech is that of man as a microcosm or little world. 6. **conjure,** utter incantation. 12. **purblind,** completely blind. 13. **Abraham.**

Nurse. What 's this? what 's this?
Jul. A rhyme I learn'd even now
Of one I danc'd withal. *One calls within* 'Juliet.'
Nurse. Anon, anon!
Come, let 's away; the strangers all are gone. *Exeunt.*

[ACT II.

PROLOGUE.]

[*Enter*] Chorus.

Chor. Now old desire doth in his death-bed lie,
And young affection gapes to be his heir;
That fair for which love groan'd for and would die,
With tender Juliet match'd, is now not fair.
Now Romeo is belov'd and loves again,
Alike bewitched by the charm of looks,
But to his foe suppos'd he must complain,
And she steal love's sweet bait from fearful hooks:
Being held a foe, he may not have access
To breathe such vows as lovers use to swear;
And she as much in love, her means much less
To meet her new-beloved any where:
But passion lends them power, time means, to meet,
Temp'ring extremities with extreme sweet. [*Exit.*]

[SCENE I. *Near Capulet's orchard.*]

Enter ROMEO *alone.*

Rom. Can I go forward when my heart is here?
Turn back, dull earth, and find thy centre out.

Enter BENVOLIO *with* MERCUTIO. [ROMEO *retires.*]

Ben. Romeo! my cousin Romeo! Romeo!
Mer. He is wise;
And, on my life, hath stol'n him home to bed.
Ben. He ran this way, and leap'd this orchard wall:
Call, good Mercutio.
Mer. Nay, I'll conjure too.
Romeo! humours! madman! passion! lover!
Appear thou in the likeness of a sigh:
Speak but one rhyme, and I am satisfied;
Cry but 'Ay me!' pronounce but 'love' and 'dove;'
Speak to my gossip Venus one fair word,
One nick-name for her purblind son and heir,
Young Abraham Cupid, he that shot so true,
When King Cophetua lov'd the beggar-maid!
He heareth not, he stirreth not, he moveth not;
The ape is dead, and I must conjure him.
I conjure thee by Rosaline's bright eyes,
By her high forehead and her scarlet lip,
By her fine foot, straight leg and quivering thigh
And the demesnes that there adjacent lie,
That in thy likeness thou appear to us!
Ben. An if he hear thee, thou wilt anger him.
Mer. This cannot anger him: 'twould anger him
To raise a spirit in his mistress' circle
Of some strange nature, letting it there stand
Till she had laid it and conjur'd it down;
That were some spite: my invocation
Is fair and honest; in his mistress' name
I conjure only but to raise up him.
Ben. Come, he hath hid himself among these trees,
To be consorted with the humorous night:
Blind is his love and best befits the dark.
Mer. If love be blind, love cannot hit the mark.
Now will he sit under a medlar tree,
And wish his mistress were that kind of fruit
As maids call medlars, when they laugh alone.
O, Romeo, that she were, O, that she were
An open et cætera, thou a pop'rin pear!
Romeo, good night: I'll to my truckle-bed;
This field-bed is too cold for me to sleep:
Come, shall we go?
Ben. Go, then; for 'tis in vain
To seek him here that means not to be found.
Exit [*with Mercutio*].

[SCENE II. *Capulet's orchard.*]

[ROMEO *comes forward.*]

Rom. He jests at scars that never felt a wound.
[*Juliet appears above, as at a window.*]
But, soft! what light through yonder window breaks?
It is the east, and Juliet is the sun.
Arise, fair sun, and kill the envious moon,
Who is already sick and pale with grief,
That thou her maid art far more fair than she:
Be not her maid, since she is envious;
Her vestal livery is but sick and green
And none but fools do wear it; cast it off.
It is my lady, O, it is my love!
O, that she knew she were!
She speaks, yet she says nothing: what of that?
Her eye discourses; I will answer it.
I am too bold, 'tis not to me she speaks:
Two of the fairest stars in all the heaven,
Having some business, do entreat her eyes
To twinkle in their spheres till they return.
What if her eyes were there, they in her head?
The brightness of her cheek would shame those stars,
As daylight doth a lamp; her eyes in heaven
Would through the airy region stream so bright
That birds would sing and think it were not night.
See, how she leans her cheek upon her hand!
O, that I were a glove upon that hand,
That I might touch that cheek!
Jul. Ay me!
Rom. She speaks:
O, speak again, bright angel! for thou art
As glorious to this night, being o'er my head,
As is a winged messenger of heaven
Unto the white-upturned wond'ring eyes

Globe: *Adam*, supposing that Shakespeare was referring to Adam Bell, a famous archer in old ballads. "Abraham" may suggest that young Cupid is also very old. 14. **King Cophetua,** who in an old ballad falls in love with a beggar-maid and makes her his queen. 16. **ape,** used as a term of endearment. 20. **desmesnes,** regions, with bawdy suggestion that is continued in *raise, circle, stand, laid it, raise up*. 22. **An if,** if; see glossary. 25. **strange,** belonging to another person; see glossary. 27. **spite,** injury. 31. **consorted,** associated. **humorous,** moist; also, influenced by humor or mood. 34, 38. **medlar, pop'rin,** fruits used as slang terms for the sexual organs. The medlar was edible only when partly decayed; poperin, derived from *Poperinghe* in Flanders, has a bawdily suggestive sound. 39. **truckle-bed,** a bed on casters to be shoved under a standing bed.

SCENE II. There is no break in the action. A rhymed couplet links the two scenes. Romeo has been hiding from his friends as though concealed by the orchard wall. He speaks at once, then turns to observe Juliet. 13. **discourses,** speaks; see glossary. 17. **spheres,** transparent concentric shells supposed to carry the heavenly bodies with them in their revolution around the earth.

Of mortals that fall back to gaze on him
When he bestrides the lazy-pacing clouds
And sails upon the bosom of the air.
Jul. O Romeo, Romeo! wherefore art thou Romeo?
Deny thy father and refuse thy name;
Or, if thou wilt not, be but sworn my love,
And I'll no longer be a Capulet.
Rom. [*Aside*] Shall I hear more, or shall I speak at this?
Jul. 'Tis but thy name that is my enemy;
Thou art thyself, though not a Montague.
What 's Montague? it is nor hand, nor foot,
Nor arm, nor face, nor any other part
Belonging to a man. O, be some other name!
What 's in a name? that which we call a rose
By any other name would smell as sweet;
So Romeo would, were he not Romeo call'd,
Retain that dear perfection which he owes
Without that title. Romeo, doff thy name,
And for that name which is no part of thee
Take all myself.
Rom. I take thee at thy word:
Call me but love, and I'll be new baptiz'd;
Henceforth I never will be Romeo.
Jul. What man art thou that thus bescreen'd in night
So stumblest on my counsel?
Rom. By a name
I know not how to tell thee who I am:
My name, dear saint, is hateful to myself,
Because it is an enemy to thee;
Had I it written, I would tear the word.
Jul. My ears have not yet drunk a hundred words
Of thy tongue's uttering, yet I know the sound:
Art thou not Romeo and a Montague?
Rom. Neither, fair maid, if either thee dislike.
Jul. How camest thou hither, tell me, and wherefore?
The orchard walls are high and hard to climb,
And the place death, considering who thou art,
If any of my kinsmen find thee here.
Rom. With love's light wings did I o'erperch these walls;
For stony limits cannot hold love out,
And what love can do that dares love attempt;
Therefore thy kinsmen are no stop to me.
Jul. If they do see thee, they will murder thee.
Rom. Alack, there lies more peril in thine eye
Than twenty of their swords: look thou but sweet,
And I am proof against their enmity.
Jul. I would not for the world they saw thee here.
Rom. I have night's cloak to hide me from their eyes;
And but thou love me, let them find me here:
My life were better ended by their hate,
Than death prorogued, wanting of thy love.
Jul. By whose direction found'st thou out this place?
Rom. By love that first did prompt me to inquire;
He lent me counsel and I lent him eyes.
I am no pilot; yet, wert thou as far
As that vast shore wash'd with the farthest sea,
I should adventure for such merchandise.
Jul. Thou knowest the mask of night is on my face,
Else would a maiden blush bepaint my cheek
For that which thou hast heard me speak tonight.
Fain would I dwell on form, fain, fain deny
What I have spoke: but farewell compliment!
Dost thou love me? I know thou wilt say 'Ay,'
And I will take thy word: yet, if thou swear'st,
Thou mayst prove false; at lovers' perjuries,
They say, Jove laughs. O gentle Romeo,
If thou dost love, pronounce it faithfully:
Or if thou thinkest I am too quickly won,
I'll frown and be perverse and say thee nay,
So thou wilt woo; but else, not for the world.
In truth, fair Montague, I am too fond,
And therefore thou mayst think my 'haviour light:
But trust me, gentleman, I'll prove more true
Than those that have more cunning to be strange.
I should have been more strange, I must confess,
But that thou overheard'st, ere I was ware,
My true-love passion; therefore pardon me,
And not impute this yielding to light love,
Which the dark night hath so discovered.
Rom. Lady, by yonder blessed moon I vow
That tips with silver all these fruit-tree tops—
Jul. O, swear not by the moon, th' inconstant moon,
That monthly changes in her circled orb,
Lest that thy love prove likewise variable.
Rom. What shall I swear by?
Jul. Do not swear at all;
Or, if thou wilt, swear by thy gracious self,
Which is the god of my idolatry,
And I'll believe thee.
Rom. If my heart's dear love—
Jul. Well, do not swear: although I joy in thee,
I have no joy of this contract to-night:
It is too rash, too unadvis'd, too sudden;
Too like the lightning, which doth cease to be
Ere one can say 'It lightens.' Sweet, good night!
This bud of love, by summer's ripening breath,
May prove a beauteous flow'r when next we meet.
Good night, good night! as sweet repose and rest
Come to thy heart as that within my breast!
Rom. O, wilt thou leave me so unsatisfied?
Jul. What satisfaction canst thou have to-night?
Rom. Th' exchange of thy love's faithful vow for mine.
Jul. I gave thee mine before thou didst request it:
And yet I would it were to give again.
Rom. Wouldst thou withdraw it? for what purpose, love?
Jul. But to be frank, and give it thee again.
And yet I wish but for the thing I have:
My bounty is as boundless as the sea,
My love as deep; the more I give to thee,
The more I have, for both are infinite.
[*Nurse calls within.*]
I hear some noise within; dear love, adieu!
Anon, good nurse! Sweet Montague, be true.
Stay but a little, I will come again. [*Exit, above.*]
Rom. O blessed, blessed night! I am afeard,

30. **mortals,** human beings. 46. **owes,** owns; see glossary. 53. **counsel,** secret thought. 61. **dislike,** displease. 66. **o'er-perch,** fly over and perch beyond. 69. **stop,** hindrance. 73. **proof,** protected. 78. **prorogued,** postponed. **wanting,** lacking. 89. **compliment,** punctiliousness, ceremony. 98. **fond,** foolish; see glossary. 101. **strange,** reserved; see glossary. 106. **discovered,** revealed; see *discover* in glossary. 110. **orb,** equivalent to *sphere;* see above, line 17. 131. **frank,** liberal, bounteous. 143. **bent,** purpose; from the idea of the tension of a bow. 145. **procure,** provide for. 151. **By and by,** immediately. 160. **tassel-gentle,** tercel-gentle, the male of the goshawk. 173. **still,** always; see

Being in night, all this is but a dream,
Too flattering-sweet to be substantial.

[*Enter* JULIET, *above.*]

Jul. Three words, dear Romeo, and good night indeed.
If that thy bent of love be honourable,
Thy purpose marriage, send me word to-morrow,
By one that I'll procure to come to thee,
Where and what time thou wilt perform the rite;
And all my fortunes at thy foot I'll lay
And follow thee my lord throughout the world.

Nurse. [*Within*] Madam!

Jul. I come, anon.—But if thou meanest not well,
I do beseech thee—

Nurse. [*Within*] Madam!

Jul. By and by, I come:—
To cease thy suit, and leave me to my grief:
To-morrow will I send.

Rom. So thrive my soul—

Jul. A thousand times good night! [*Exit, above.*]

Rom. A thousand times the worse, to want thy light.
Love goes toward love, as schoolboys from their books,
But love from love, toward school with heavy looks. [*Retiring.*]

Enter JULIET, [*above*] *again.*

Jul. Hist! Romeo, hist! O, for a falc'ner's voice,
To lure this tassel-gentle back again!
Bondage is hoarse, and may not speak aloud;
Else would I tear the cave where Echo lies,
And make her airy tongue more hoarse than mine,
With repetition of 'my Romeo!'

Rom. It is my soul that calls upon my name:
How silver-sweet sound lovers' tongues by night,
Like softest music to attending ears!

Jul. Romeo!

Rom. My dear?

Jul. What o'clock to-morrow
Shall I send to thee?

Rom. By the hour of nine.

Jul. I will not fail: 'tis twenty years till then.
I have forgot why I did call thee back.

Rom. Let me stand here till thou remember it.

Jul. I shall forget, to have thee still stand there,
Rememb'ring how I love thy company.

Rom. And I'll still stay, to have thee still forget,
Forgetting any other home but this.

Jul. 'Tis almost morning; I would have thee gone:
And yet no farther than a wanton's bird;
That lets it hop a little from her hand,
Like a poor prisoner in his twisted gyves,
And with a silken thread plucks it back again,
So loving-jealous of his liberty.

Rom. I would I were thy bird.

Jul. Sweet, so would I:
Yet I should kill thee with much cherishing.
Good night, good night! parting is such sweet sorrow,
That I shall say good night till it be morrow. [*Exit, above.*]

Rom. Sleep dwell upon thine eyes, peace in thy breast!
Would I were sleep and peace, so sweet to rest!
Hence will I to my ghostly father's cell,
His help to crave, and my dear hap to tell. *Exit.*

[SCENE III. *Friar Laurence's cell.*]

Enter FRIAR [LAURENCE] *alone, with a basket.*

Fri. L. The grey-ey'd morn smiles on the frowning night,
Chequ'ring the eastern clouds with streaks of light,
And flecked darkness like a drunkard reels
From forth day's path and Titan's fiery wheels:
Now, ere the sun advance his burning eye,
The day to cheer and night's dank dew to dry,
I must up-fill this osier cage of ours
With baleful weeds and precious-juiced flowers.
The earth that 's nature's mother is her tomb;
What is her burying grave that is her womb,
And from her womb children of divers kind
We sucking on her natural bosom find,
Many for many virtues excellent,
None but for some and yet all different.
O, mickle is the powerful grace that lies
In plants, herbs, stones, and their true qualities:
For nought so vile that on the earth doth live
But to the earth some special good doth give,
Nor aught so good but strain'd from that fair use
Revolts from true birth, stumbling on abuse:
Virtue itself turns vice, being misapplied;
And vice sometime by action dignified.
Within the infant rind of this weak flower
Poison hath residence and medicine power:
For this, being smelt, with that part cheers each part;
Being tasted, slays all senses with the heart.
Two such opposed kings encamp them still
In man as well as herbs, grace and rude will;
And where the worser is predominant,
Full soon the canker death eats up that plant.

Enter ROMEO.

Rom. Good morrow, father.

Fri. L. Benedicite!
What early tongue so sweet saluteth me?
Young son, it argues a distempered head
So soon to bid good morrow to thy bed:
Care keeps his watch in every old man's eye,
And where care lodges, sleep will never lie;
But where unbruised youth with unstuff'd brain
Doth couch his limbs, there golden sleep doth reign:
Therefore thy earliness doth me assure
Thou art up-rous'd with some distemp'rature;
Or if not so, then here I hit it right,
Our Romeo hath not been in bed to-night.

Rom. That last is true; the sweeter rest was mine.

Fri. L. God pardon sin! wast thou with Rosaline?

Rom. With Rosaline, my ghostly father? no;
I have forgot that name, and that name's woe.

Fri. L. That 's my good son: but where hast thou been, then?

Rom. I'll tell thee, ere thou ask it me again.
I have been feasting with mine enemy,

glossary. 180. **gyves,** fetters. 189. **ghostly,** spiritual. 190. **dear hap,** good fortune.

SCENE III. 3. **flecked,** dappled. 4. **Titan's.** Helios, the sun god, was a descendant of the race of Titans. 7. **osier cage,** willow basket. 15. **mickle,** great. **grace,** beneficent virtue; see glossary. 16. **qualities,** properties; see glossary. 30. **canker,** cankerworm. 33. **distempered,** out of temper or balance, ill. 34. **good morrow,** good morning, i.e., farewell. 37. **unstuff'd,** not overcharged; another reference to the state of the humors.

Where on a sudden one hath wounded me,
That 's by me wounded: both our remedies
Within thy help and holy physic lies:
I bear no hatred, blessed man, for, lo,
My intercession likewise steads my foe.

Fri. L. Be plain, good son, and homely in thy drift;
Riddling confession finds but riddling shrift.

Rom. Then plainly know my heart's dear love is set
On the fair daughter of rich Capulet:
As mine on hers, so hers is set on mine;
And all combin'd, save what thou must combine
By holy marriage: when and where and how
We met, we woo'd and made exchange of vow,
I'll tell thee as we pass; but this I pray,
That thou consent to marry us to-day.

Fri. L. Holy Saint Francis, what a change is here!
Is Rosaline, that thou didst love so dear,
So soon forsaken? young men's love then lies
Not truly in their hearts, but in their eyes.
Jesu Maria, what a deal of brine
Hath wash'd thy sallow cheeks for Rosaline!
How much salt water thrown away in waste,
To season love, that of it doth not taste!
The sun not yet thy sighs from heaven clears,
Thy old groans ring yet in mine ancient ears;
Lo, here upon thy cheek the stain doth sit
Of an old tear that is not wash'd off yet:
If e'er thou wast thyself and these woes thine,
Thou and these woes were all for Rosaline:
And art thou chang'd? pronounce this sentence then,
Women may fall, when there 's no strength in men.

Rom. Thou chid'st me oft for loving Rosaline.

Fri. L. For doting, not for loving, pupil mine.

Rom. And bad'st me bury love.

Fri. L. Not in a grave,
To lay one in, another out to have.

Rom. I pray thee, chide not: she whom I love now
Doth grace for grace and love for love allow;
The other did not so.

Fri. L. O, she knew well
Thy love did read by rote, that could not spell.
But come, young waverer, come, go with me,
In one respect I'll thy assistant be;
For this alliance may so happy prove,
To turn your households' rancour to pure love.

Rom. O, let us hence; I stand on sudden haste.

Fri. L. Wisely and slow; they stumble that run fast.
Exeunt.

[SCENE IV. *A street.*]

Enter BENVOLIO *and* MERCUTIO.

Mer. Where the devil should this Romeo be?
Came he not home to-night?

Ben. Not to his father's; I spoke with his man.

Mer. Why, that same pale hard-hearted wench, that Rosaline,
Torments him so, that he will sure run mad.

Ben. Tybalt, the kinsman to old Capulet,
Hath sent a letter to his father's house.

Mer. A challenge, on my life.

Ben. Romeo will answer it.

Mer. Any man that can write may answer a letter.

Ben. Nay, he will answer the letter's master, how he dares, being dared.

Mer. Alas poor Romeo! he is already dead; stabbed with a white wench's black eye; run thorough the ear with a love-song; the very pin of his heart cleft with the blind bow-boy's butt-shaft: and is he a man to encounter Tybalt?

Ben. Why, what is Tybalt?

Mer. More than prince of cats, I can tell you. O, he's the courageous captain of complements. He fights as you sing prick-song, keeps time, distance, and proportion; he rests his minim rests, one, two, and the third in your bosom: the very butcher of a silk button, a duellist, a duellist; a gentleman of the very first house, of the first and second cause: ah, the immortal passado! the punto reverso! the hai!

Ben. The what?

Mer. The pox of such antic, lisping, affecting fantasticoes; these new tuners of accents! 'By Jesu, a very good blade! a very tall man! a very good whore!' Why, is not this a lamentable thing, grandsire, that we should be thus afflicted with these strange flies, these fashion-mongers, these perdona-mi's, who stand so much on the new form, that they cannot sit at ease on the old bench? O, their bones, their bones!

Enter ROMEO.

Ben. Here comes Romeo, here comes Romeo.

Mer. Without his roe, like a dried herring: O flesh, flesh, how art thou fishified! Now is he for the numbers that Petrarch flowed in: Laura to his lady was but a kitchen-wench; marry, she had a better love to be-rhyme her; Dido a dowdy; Cleopatra a gipsy; Helen and Hero hildings and harlots; Thisbe a grey eye or so, but not to the purpose. Signior Romeo, bon jour! there 's a French salutation to your French slop. You gave us the counterfeit fairly last night.

Rom. Good morrow to you both. What counterfeit did I give you?

Mer. The slip, sir, the slip; can you not conceive?

Rom. Pardon, good Mercutio, my business was great; and in such a case as mine a man may strain courtesy.

Mer. That 's as much as to say, such a case as yours constrains a man to bow in the hams.

Rom. Meaning, to court'sy.

Mer. Thou hast most kindly hit it.

Rom. A most courteous exposition.

Mer. Nay, I am the very pink of courtesy.

Rom. Pink for flower.

52. **physic,** medicine, healing property; see glossary. 54 **steads,** helps; see glossary. 88. **did read by rote,** was merely a matter of repeating conventional expressions of love. 93. **stand on,** am in need of.

SCENE IV. 15. **pin,** peg in the center of a target. 16. **butt-shaft,** an unbarbed arrow. 19. **prince of cats.** The name of the king of cats in *Reynard the Fox* was Tybalt or Tybert. 20. **captain of complements,** master of ceremony and outward show. 21. **prick-song,** music written out. 22. **proportion,** rhythm. 23. **minim,** short note in music. 24. **butcher of a silk button,** one able to strike a button on his adversary's person. 26. **first house,** possibly of the best school of fencing. **first and second cause,** ready to quarrel for a trifle; probably an allusion to the supposed code of quarreling. 27. **passado,** forward thrust. **punto reverso,** backhanded stroke. **hai,** home thrust. 30. **fantasticoes,** coxcombs. 31. **accents,** language. **tall,** valiant. 35. **flies,** parasites. **perdona-mi's,** Italian for "pardon me's"; a reference to the affectation of using foreign phrases. 36-37. **form . . . bench.** *Form* means both "fashion" and "bench." 37. **bones,** French *bon* with play on English "bone." 39. **Without his roe,** sometimes explained as a pun on first syllable of Romeo's name, in which case the last syllables might be taken as an expression of woe. 41. **Petrarch,** Italian poet of the Renaissance who addressed his sonnets to Laura. 45. **hildings,** good-for-nothings. 48. **slop,** loose trousers of French fashion. **fairly,** handsomely; see glossary. 51. **slip.** Counterfeit coins

Mer. Right.

Rom. Why, then is my pump well flowered.

Mer. Sure wit, follow me this jest now till thou hast worn out thy pump, that when the single sole of it is worn, the jest may remain after the wearing solely singular.

Rom. O single-soled jest, solely singular for the singleness!

Mer. Come between us, good Benvolio; my wits faint.

Rom. Swits and spurs, swits and spurs; or I'll cry a match.

Mer. Nay, if our wits run the wild-goose chase, I am done, for thou hast more of the wild-goose in one of thy wits than, I am sure, I have in my whole five: was I with you there for the goose?

Rom. Thou wast never with me for any thing when thou wast not there for the goose.

Mer. I will bite thee by the ear for that jest.

Rom. Nay, good goose, bite not.

Mer. Thy wit is a very bitter sweeting; it is a most sharp sauce.

Rom. And is it not, then, well served in to a sweet goose?

Mer. O, here 's a wit of cheveril, that stretches from an inch narrow to an ell broad!

Rom. I stretch it out for that word 'broad;' which added to the goose, proves thee far and wide a broad goose.

Mer. Why, is not this better now than groaning for love? now art thou sociable, now art thou Romeo; now art thou what thou art, by art as well as by nature: for this drivelling love is like a great natural, that runs lolling up and down to hide his bauble in a hole.

Ben. Stop there, stop there.

Mer. Thou desirest me to stop in my tale against the hair.

Ben. Thou wouldst else have made thy tale large.

Mer. O, thou art deceived; I would have made it short: for I was come to the whole depth of my tale; and meant, indeed, to occupy the argument no longer.

Rom. Here 's goodly gear!

Enter Nurse *and her Man* [PETER].

A sail, a sail!

Mer. Two, two; a shirt and a smock.

Nurse. Peter!

Peter. Anon!

Nurse. My fan, Peter.

Mer. Good Peter, to hide her face; for her fan 's the fairer face.

Nurse. God ye good morrow, gentlemen.

Mer. God ye good den, fair gentlewoman.

Nurse. Is it good den?

Mer. 'Tis no less, I tell ye, for the bawdy hand of the dial is now upon the prick of noon.

Nurse. Out upon you! what a man are you!

Rom. One, gentlewoman, that God hath made for himself to mar.

Nurse. By my troth, it is well said; 'for himself to mar,' quoth 'a? Gentlemen, can any of you tell me where I may find the young Romeo?

Rom. I can tell you; but young Romeo will be older when you have found him than he was when you sought him: I am the youngest of that name, for fault of a worse.

Nurse. You say well.

Mer. Yea, is the worst well? very well took, i' faith; wisely, wisely.

Nurse. If you be he, sir, I desire some confidence with you.

Ben. She will indite him to some supper.

Mer. A bawd, a bawd, a bawd! So ho!

Rom. What hast thou found?

Mer. No hare, sir; unless a hare, sir, in a lenten pie, that is something stale and hoar ere it be spent. [*Sings.*]

An old hare hoar,
And an old hare hoar,
Is very good meat in lent:
But a hare that is hoar
Is too much for a score,
When it hoars ere it be spent.

Romeo, will you come to your father's? we'll to dinner, thither.

Rom. I will follow you.

Mer. Farewell, ancient lady; farewell, [*singing*] 'lady, lady, lady.' *Exeunt* [*Mercutio and Benvolio*].

Nurse. Marry, farewell! I pray you, sir, what saucy merchant was this, that was so full of his ropery?

Rom. A gentleman, nurse, that loves to hear himself talk, and will speak more in a minute than he will stand to in a month.

Nurse. An 'a speak any thing against me, I'll take him down, an 'a were lustier than he is, and twenty such Jacks; and if I cannot, I'll find those that shall. Scurvy knave! I am none of his flirt-gills; I am none of his skains-mates. And thou must stand by too, and suffer every knave to use me at his pleasure?

Peter. I saw no man use you at his pleasure; if I had, my weapon should quickly have been out, I warrant you: I dare draw as soon as another man, if I see occasion in a good quarrel, and the law on my side.

Nurse. Now, afore God, I am so vexed, that every part about me quivers. Scurvy knave! Pray you, sir, a word: and as I told you, my young lady bid me inquire you out; what she bid me say, I will keep to myself: but first let me tell ye, if ye should lead her into a fool's paradise, as they say, it were a very gross kind of behaviour, as they say: for the gentlewoman is young; and, therefore, if you should deal double with her, truly it were an ill thing to be offered to any gentlewoman, and very weak dealing.

were called "slips." 56. **case,** situation; also, physical condition. 59. **kindly,** naturally; politely. 64. **is my pump well flowered.** The shoe is pinked or perforated in ornamental figures. 69. **single-soled,** thin; contemptible, with pun on "soul." 70. **singleness,** feebleness. 73. **Swits,** switches. 74. **cry a match,** claim a victory. 75. **wild-goose chase,** a horse race in which the leading rider might force his competitors to follow him wherever he went. 80. **goose,** prostitute. 83. **sweeting,** probably a pun on a tart-tasting apple called the "sweeting." 87. **cheveril,** kid leather. 96. **natural,** idiot. 97. **bauble,** a jester's wand; here with bawdy suggestion. 100. **against the hair,** against the grain (with a bawdy play on *tale, tail;* continued with *large, short, depth, occupy,* etc.). 107. **gear,** general word meaning "substance" or "stuff"; see glossary. 109. **a shirt . . . smock,** a man and a woman; see *smock* in glossary. 119. **prick,** point on the dial of a clock (with bawdy suggestion). 120. **Out upon you,** expression of indignation; see *out* in glossary. 134. **confidence,** the nurse's mistake for "conference." 135. **indite,** Benvolio's deliberate malapropism for "invite." 138. **hare,** used as a slang word for "courtesan." 144. **hoar,** moldy (with pun). 151. **'lady, lady, lady,'** refrain from the ballad *Chaste Susanna.* 153. **merchant,** fellow. 154. **ropery,** the nurse's mistake for "roguery." 160. **Jacks,** used as a term of disparagement. 162. **flirt-gills,** loose women. 163. **skains-mates,** perhaps dagger-mates, outlaws, or gangster molls.

Rom. Nurse, commend me to thy lady and mistress. I protest unto thee—

Nurse. Good heart, and, i' faith, I will tell her as much: Lord, Lord, she will be a joyful woman.

Rom. What wilt thou tell her, nurse? thou dost not mark me.

Nurse. I will tell her, sir, that you do protest; which, as I take it, is a gentlemanlike offer.

Rom. Bid her devise
Some means to come to shrift this afternoon;
And there she shall at Friar Laurence' cell
Be shriv'd and married. Here is for thy pains.

Nurse. No, truly, sir; not a penny.

Rom. Go to; I say you shall.

Nurse. This afternoon, sir? well, she shall be there.

Rom. And stay, good nurse, behind the abbey wall:
Within this hour my man shall be with thee,
And bring thee cords made like a tackled stair;
Which to the high top-gallant of my joy
Must be my convoy in the secret night.
Farewell; be trusty, and I'll quit thy pains:
Farewell; commend me to thy mistress.

Nurse. Now God in heaven bless thee! Hark you, sir.

Rom. What say'st thou, my dear nurse?

Nurse. Is your man secret? Did you ne'er hear say,
Two may keep counsel, putting one away?

Rom. I warrant thee, my man 's as true as steel.

Nurse. Well, sir; my mistress is the sweetest lady—Lord, Lord! when 'twas a little prating thing:—O, there is a nobleman in town, one Paris, that would fain lay knife aboard; but she, good soul, had as lief see a toad, a very toad, as see him. I anger her sometimes and tell her that Paris is the properer man; but, I'll warrant you, when I say so, she looks as pale as any clout in the versal world. Doth not rosemary and Romeo begin both with a letter?

Rom. Ay, nurse; what of that? both with an R.

Nurse. Ah, mocker! that 's the dog's name; R is for the—No; I know it begins with some other letter:—and she hath the prettiest sententious of it, of you and rosemary, that it would do you good to hear it.

Rom. Commend me to thy lady.

Nurse. Ay, a thousand times. [*Exit Romeo.*] Peter!

Pet. Anon!

Nurse. Peter, take my fan, and go before, and apace.
Exeunt.

[SCENE V. *Capulet's orchard.*]

Enter JULIET.

Jul. The clock struck nine when I did send the nurse;
In half an hour she promised to return.
Perchance she cannot meet him: that 's not so.
O, she is lame! love's heralds should be thoughts,
Which ten times faster glide than the sun's beams,
Driving back shadows over louring hills:
Therefore do nimble-pinion'd doves draw love,
And therefore hath the wind-swift Cupid wings.
Now is the sun upon the highmost hill
Of this day's journey, and from nine till twelve
Is three long hours, yet she is not come.
Had she affections and warm youthful blood,
She would be as swift in motion as a ball;
My words would bandy her to my sweet love,
And his to me:
†But old folks, many feign as they were dead;
Unwieldy, slow, heavy and pale as lead.
O God, she comes!

Enter Nurse [*and* PETER].

O honey nurse, what news?
Hast thou met with him? Send thy man away.

Nurse. Peter, stay at the gate. [*Exit Peter.*]

Jul. Now, good sweet nurse,—O Lord, why lookest thou sad?
Though news be sad, yet tell them merrily;
If good, thou shamest the music of sweet news
By playing it to me with so sour a face.

Nurse. I am a-weary, give me leave awhile:
Fie, how my bones ache! what a jaunce have I had!

Jul. I would thou hadst my bones, and I thy news.
Nay, come, I pray thee, speak; good, good nurse, speak.

Nurse. Jesu, what haste! can you not stay awhile?
Do you not see that I am out of breath?

Jul. How art thou out of breath, when thou hast breath
To say to me that thou art out of breath?
The excuse that thou dost make in this delay
Is longer than the tale thou dost excuse.
Is thy news good, or bad? answer to that;
Say either, and I'll stay the circumstance:
Let me be satisfied, is 't good or bad?

Nurse. Well, you have made a simple choice; you know not how to choose a man: Romeo! no, not he; though his face be better than any man's, yet his leg excels all men's; and for a hand, and a foot, and a body, though they be not to be talked on, yet they are past compare: he is not the flower of courtesy, but, I'll warrant him, as gentle as a lamb. Go thy ways, wench; serve God. What, have you dined at home?

Jul. No, no: but all this did I know before.
What says he of our marriage? what of that?

Nurse. Lord, how my head aches! what a head have I!
It beats as it would fall in twenty pieces.
My back a t' other side,—ah, my back, my back!
Beshrew your heart for sending me about,
To catch my death with jauncing up and down!

Jul. I' faith, I am sorry that thou art not well.
Sweet, sweet, sweet nurse, tell me, what says my love?

Nurse. Your love says, like an honest gentleman, and a courteous, and a kind, and a handsome, and, I warrant, a virtuous,—Where is your mother?

Jul. Where is my mother! why, she is within;
Where should she be? How oddly thou repliest!
'Your love says, like an honest gentleman,
Where is your mother?'

Nurse. O God's lady dear!
Are you so hot? marry, come up, I trow;

183. **protest,** vow. 188. **mark,** attend to. 201. **tackled stair,** rope ladder. 202. **top-gallant,** summit. 203. **convoy,** a thing that conducts. 204. **quit,** reward, requite; see glossary. 208. **secret,** trustworthy. 217. **properer,** handsomer; see glossary. 219. **clout,** rag; a proverbial expression. **versal,** universal. 220. **a,** the same. 223. **the dog's name.** The letter *R* was thought to resemble the dog's growl. 226. **sententious.** The nurse probably means "sentences," pithy sayings.

SCENE V. 7. **love,** Venus, whose chariot was drawn by doves. 14. **bandy,** toss to and fro. 16. **many,** Johnson: *marry*. 25. **give me leave,** let me alone. 26. **jaunce,** so Q_2; Globe: *jaunt*. 36. **stay the circumstance,** await details; see *circumstance* in glossary. 52. **Beshrew,** common objurgation meaning "ill-luck"; see glossary. 64. **come up,**

Is this the poultice for my aching bones?
Henceforward do your messages yourself.
Jul. Here 's such a coil! come, what says Romeo?
Nurse. Have you got leave to go to shrift to-day?
Jul. I have.
Nurse. Then hie you hence to Friar Laurence' cell;
There stays a husband to make you a wife:
Now comes the wanton blood up in your cheeks,
They'll be in scarlet straight at any news.
Hie you to church; I must another way,
To fetch a ladder, by the which your love
Must climb a bird's nest soon when it is dark:
I am the drudge and toil in your delight,
But you shall bear the burden soon at night.
Go; I'll to dinner; hie you to the cell.
Jul. Hie to high fortune! Honest nurse, farewell.
Exeunt.

[SCENE VI. *Friar Laurence's cell.*]

Enter FRIAR [LAURENCE] *and* ROMEO.

Fri. L. So smile the heavens upon this holy act,
That after hours with sorrow chide us not!
Rom. Amen, amen! but come what sorrow can,
It cannot countervail the exchange of joy
That one short minute gives me in her sight:
Do thou but close our hands with holy words,
Then love-devouring death do what he dare;
It is enough I may but call her mine.
Fri. L. These violent delights have violent ends
And in their triumph die, like fire and powder,
Which as they kiss consume: the sweetest honey
Is loathsome in his own deliciousness
And in the taste confounds the appetite:
Therefore love moderately; long love doth so;
Too swift arrives as tardy as too slow.

Enter JULIET.

Here comes the lady: O, so light a foot
Will ne'er wear out the everlasting flint:
A lover may bestride the gossamer
That idles in the wanton summer air,
And yet not fall; so light is vanity.
Jul. Good even to my ghostly confessor.
Fri. L. Romeo shall thank thee, daughter, for us both.
Jul. As much to him, else is his thanks too much.
Rom. Ah, Juliet, if the measure of thy joy
Be heap'd like mine and that thy skill be more
To blazon it, then sweeten with thy breath
This neighbour air, and let rich music's tongue
Unfold the imagin'd happiness that both
Receive in either by this dear encounter.
Jul. Conceit, more rich in matter than in words,
Brags of his substance, not of ornament:
They are but beggars that can count their worth;
But my true love is grown to such excess
I cannot sum up sum of half my wealth.
Fri. L. Come, come with me, and we will make short work;
For, by your leaves, you shall not stay alone
Till holy church incorporate two in one. [*Exeunt.*]

[ACT III.

SCENE I. *A public place.*]

Enter MERCUTIO, BENVOLIO, *and* Men.

Ben. I pray thee, good Mercutio, let 's retire:
The day is hot, the Capulets abroad,
And, if we meet, we shall not scape a brawl;
For now, these hot days, is the mad blood stirring.

Mer. Thou art like one of those fellows that when he enters the confines of a tavern claps me his sword upon the table and says 'God send me no need of thee!' and by the operation of the second cup draws him on the drawer, when indeed there is no need.

Ben. Am I like such a fellow?

Mer. Come, come, thou art as hot a Jack in thy mood as any in Italy, and as soon moved to be moody, and as soon moody to be moved.

Ben. And what to?

Mer. Nay, an there were two such, we should have none shortly, for one would kill the other. Thou! why, thou wilt quarrel with a man that hath a hair more, or a hair less, in his beard, than thou hast: thou wilt quarrel with a man for cracking nuts, having no other reason but because thou hast hazel eyes: what eye but such an eye would spy out such a quarrel? Thy head is as full of quarrels as an egg is full of meat, and yet thy head hath been beaten as addle as an egg for quarrelling: thou hast quarrelled with a man for coughing in the street, because he hath wakened thy dog that hath lain asleep in the sun: didst thou not fall out with a tailor for wearing his new doublet before Easter? with another, for tying his new shoes with old riband? and yet thou wilt tutor me from quarrelling!

Ben. An I were so apt to quarrel as thou art, any man should buy the fee-simple of my life for an hour and a quarter.

Mer. The fee simple! O simple!

Enter TYBALT *and others.*

Ben. By my head, here come the Capulets.
Mer. By my heel, I care not.
Tyb. Follow me close, for I will speak to them.
Gentlemen, good den: a word with one of you.

Mer. And but one word with one of us? couple it with something; make it a word and a blow.

Tyb. You shall find me apt enough to that, sir, an you will give me occasion.

Mer. Could you not take some occasion without giving?

Tyb. Mercutio, thou consortest with Romeo,—

Mer. Consort! what, dost thou make us minstrels? an thou make minstrels of us, look to hear nothing but discords: here 's my fiddlestick; here 's that shall make you dance. 'Zounds, consort!

Ben. We talk here in the public haunt of men:
Either withdraw unto some private place,

expressive of impatience like "go to." 67. **coil,** turmoil, bustle; see glossary.
SCENE VI. 4. **countervail,** equal. 9. **These violent delights,** etc., expresses a premonition of evil. 13. **confounds,** destroys; see glossary. 18. **gossamer,** spider's thread. 26. **blazon,** heraldic term meaning "to describe" or "to set forth." 28. **Unfold,** make known; see glossary. 30. **Conceit,** imagination, thought; see glossary.
ACT III. SCENE I. 9. **draws . . . drawer,** draws his sword against the waiter. 14. **moody,** angry. 47. **consortest.** *To consort* meant "to accompany" in a musical sense and also "to attend or wait upon." 52. **'Zounds,** a modified form of the oath, "by God's wounds."

Or reason coldly of your grievances,
Or else depart; here all eyes gaze on us.
Mer. Men's eyes were made to look, and let them gaze;
I will not budge for no man's pleasure, I.

Enter ROMEO.

Tyb. Well, peace be with you, sir: here comes my man.
Mer. But I'll be hang'd, sir, if he wear your livery:
Marry, go before to field, he'll be your follower;
Your worship in that sense may call him 'man.'
Tyb. Romeo, the love I bear thee can afford
No better term than this,—thou art a villain.
Rom. Tybalt, the reason that I have to love thee
Doth much excuse the appertaining rage
To such a greeting: villain am I none;
Therefore farewell; I see thou knowest me not.
Tyb. Boy, this shall not excuse the injuries
That thou hast done me; therefore turn and draw.
Rom. I do protest, I never injur'd thee,
But love thee better than thou canst devise,
Till thou shalt know the reason of my love:
And so, good Capulet,—which name I tender
As dearly as my own,—be satisfied.
Mer. O calm, dishonourable, vile submission!
Alla stoccata carries it away. [*Draws.*]
Tybalt, you rat-catcher, will you walk?
Tyb. What wouldst thou have with me?
Mer. Good king of cats, nothing but one of your nine lives; that I mean to make bold withal, and, as you shall use me hereafter, dry-beat the rest of the eight. Will you pluck your sword out of his pilcher by the ears? make haste, lest mine be about your ears ere it be out.
Tyb. I am for you. [*Drawing.*]
Rom. Gentle Mercutio, put thy rapier up.
Mer. Come, sir, your passado. [*They fight.*]
Rom. Draw, Benvolio; beat down their weapons.
Gentlemen, for shame, forbear this outrage!
Tybalt, Mercutio, the prince expressly hath
Forbid this bandying in Verona streets:
Hold, Tybalt! good Mercutio!
[*Tybalt under Romeo's arm stabs Mercutio, and flies with his followers.*]
Mer. I am hurt.
A plague o' both your houses! I am sped.
Is he gone, and hath nothing?
Ben. What, art thou hurt?
Mer. Ay, ay, a scratch, a scratch; marry, 'tis enough.
Where is my page? Go, villain, fetch a surgeon.
[*Exit Page.*]
Rom. Courage, man; the hurt cannot be much.
Mer. No, 'tis not so deep as a well, nor so wide as a church-door; but 'tis enough, 'twill serve: ask for me to-morrow, and you shall find me a grave man. I am peppered, I warrant, for this world. A plague o' both your houses! 'Zounds, a dog, a rat, a mouse, a cat, to scratch a man to death! a braggart, a rogue, a villain, that fights by the book of arithmetic! Why the devil came you between us? I was hurt under your arm.
Rom. I thought all for the best.
Mer. Help me into some house, Benvolio,
Or I shall faint. A plague o' both your houses!
They have made worms' meat of me: I have it,
And soundly too: your houses!
Exit [*supported by Benvolio*].
Rom. This gentleman, the prince's near ally,
My very friend, hath got his mortal hurt
In my behalf; my reputation stain'd
With Tybalt's slander,—Tybalt, that an hour
Hath been my cousin! O sweet Juliet,
Thy beauty hath made me effeminate
And in my temper soft'ned valour's steel!

Enter BENVOLIO.

Ben. O Romeo, Romeo, brave Mercutio is dead!
That gallant spirit hath aspir'd the clouds,
Which too untimely here did scorn the earth.
Rom. This day's black fate on moe days doth depend;
This but begins the woe others must end.

[*Enter* TYBALT.]

Ben. Here comes the furious Tybalt back again.
Rom. Alive, in triumph! and Mercutio slain!
Away to heaven, respective lenity,
And fire-ey'd fury be my conduct now!
Now, Tybalt, take the 'villain' back again,
That late thou gavest me; for Mercutio's soul
Is but a little way above our heads,
Staying for thine to keep him company:
Either thou, or I, or both, must go with him.
Tyb. Thou, wretched boy, that didst consort him here,
Shalt with him hence.
Rom. This shall determine that.
They fight; Tybalt falls.
Ben. Romeo, away, be gone!
The citizens are up, and Tybalt slain.
Stand not amaz'd: the prince will doom thee death,
If thou art taken: hence, be gone, away!
Rom. O, I am fortune's fool!
Ben. Why dost thou stay? *Exit Romeo.*

Enter Citizens.

First Cit. Which way ran he that kill'd Mercutio?
Tybalt, that murderer, which way ran he?
Ben. There lies that Tybalt.
First Cit. Up, sir, go with me;
I charge thee in the prince's name, obey.

Enter PRINCE [*attended*], *old* MONTAGUE, CAPULET, *their* Wives, *and all.*

Prin. Where are the vile beginners of this fray?
Ben. O noble prince, I can discover all
The unlucky manage of this fatal brawl:
There lies the man, slain by young Romeo,
That slew thy kinsman, brave Mercutio.
La. Cap. Tybalt, my cousin! O my brother's child!
O prince! O cousin! husband! O, the blood is spilt

61. **field,** field of encounter. 77. **Alla stoccata,** Italian, "with the thrust"; i.e., the fencing master wins the victory. 78. **rat-catcher,** an allusion to Tybalt as king of cats (see II, iv, 19). 81. **make bold,** make free with. 83. **dry-beat,** beat soundly. 84. **pilcher,** scabbard. 88. **passado,** forward thrust; used derisively. 94. **sped,** done for. 102. **grave man.** Mercutio thus makes puns with his last breath. 106. **by the book of arithmetic,** merely by theory. Back of the whole scene lies a current controversy between the old broadsword style of fencing and the new French style of rapier fencing. 114. **ally,** kinsman. 115. **very,** true. 124. **moe,** more; so Q_2F; Globe: *more.* 128. **respective lenity,** considerate gentleness. 129. **conduct,** guide. 139. **doom,** adjudge. 141. **fortune's fool.** At this crucial moment in the play Romeo again alludes to destiny. 148. **manage,** management; see glossary. 158. **fair,** civilly; see glossary. 159. **nice,** trivial; see glossary. 162. **take truce,** make peace. **unruly spleen,** ungovernable rage; see *spleen* in glossary. 163. **tilts,** strikes. 169. **Retorts,** throws back upon his

Of my dear kinsman! Prince, as thou art true,
For blood of ours, shed blood of Montague.
O cousin, cousin!
Prin. Benvolio, who began this bloody fray?
Ben. Tybalt, here slain, whom Romeo's hand did slay;
Romeo that spoke him fair, bade him bethink
How nice the quarrel was, and urg'd withal
Your high displeasure: all this uttered
With gentle breath, calm look, knees humbly bow'd,
Could not take truce with the unruly spleen
Of Tybalt deaf to peace, but that he tilts
With piercing steel at bold Mercutio's breast,
Who, all as hot, turns deadly point to point,
And, with a martial scorn, with one hand beats
Cold death aside, and with the other sends
It back to Tybalt, whose dexterity
Retorts it: Romeo he cries aloud,
'Hold, friends! friends, part!' and, swifter than his tongue,
His agile arm beats down their fatal points,
And 'twixt them rushes; underneath whose arm
An envious thrust from Tybalt hit the life
Of stout Mercutio, and then Tybalt fled;
But by and by comes back to Romeo,
Who had but newly entertain'd revenge,
And to 't they go like lightning, for, ere I
Could draw to part them, was stout Tybalt slain,
And, as he fell, did Romeo turn and fly.
This is the truth, or let Benvolio die.
La. Cap. He is a kinsman to the Montague;
Affection makes him false; he speaks not true:
Some twenty of them fought in this black strife,
And all those twenty could but kill one life.
I beg for justice, which thou, prince, must give;
Romeo slew Tybalt, Romeo must not live.
Prin. Romeo slew him, he slew Mercutio;
Who now the price of his dear blood doth owe?
Mon. Not Romeo, prince, he was Mercutio's friend;
His fault concludes but what the law should end,
The life of Tybalt.
Prin. And for that offence
Immediately we do exile him hence:
I have an interest in your hate's proceeding,
My blood for your rude brawls doth lie a-bleeding;
But I'll amerce you with so strong a fine
That you shall all repent the loss of mine:
I will be deaf to pleading and excuses;
Nor tears nor prayers shall purchase out abuses:
Therefore use none: let Romeo hence in haste,
Else, when he is found, that hour is his last.
Bear hence this body and attend our will:
Mercy but murders, pardoning those that kill. *Exeunt.*

[SCENE II. *Capulet's orchard.*]

Enter JULIET *alone.*

Jul. Gallop apace, you fiery-footed steeds,
Towards Phœbus' lodging: such a waggoner
As Phæthon would whip you to the west,
And bring in cloudy night immediately.
Spread thy close curtain, love-performing night,
That runaways' eyes may wink, and Romeo
Leap to these arms, untalk'd of and unseen.
Lovers can see to do their amorous rites
By their own beauties; or, if love be blind,
It best agrees with night. Come, civil night,
Thou sober-suited matron, all in black,
And learn me how to lose a winning match,
Play'd for a pair of stainless maidenhoods:
Hood my unmann'd blood, bating in my cheeks,
With thy black mantle; till strange love, grown bold,
Think true love acted simple modesty.
Come, night; come, Romeo; come, thou day in night;
For thou wilt lie upon the wings of night
Whiter than new snow upon a raven's back.
Come, gentle night, come, loving, black-brow'd night,
Give me my Romeo; and, when he shall die,
Take him and cut him out in little stars,
And he will make the face of heaven so fine
That all the world will be in love with night
And pay no worship to the garish sun.
O, I have bought the mansion of a love,
But not possess'd it, and, though I am sold,
Not yet enjoy'd: so tedious is this day
As is the night before some festival
To an impatient child that hath new robes
And may not wear them. O, here comes my nurse,

Enter Nurse, *with cords.*

And she brings news; and every tongue that speaks
But Romeo's name speaks heavenly eloquence.
Now, nurse, what news? What hast thou there? the cords
That Romeo bid thee fetch?
Nurse. Ay, ay, the cords.
[*Throws them down.*]
Jul. Ay me! what news? why dost thou wring thy hands?
Nurse. An, weraday! he 's dead, he 's dead, he 's dead!
We are undone, lady, we are undone!
Alack the day! he 's gone, he 's kill'd, he 's dead!
Jul. Can heaven be so envious?
Nurse. Romeo can,
Though heaven cannot: O Romeo, Romeo!
Who ever would have thought it? Romeo!
Jul. What devil art thou, that dost torment me thus?
This torture should be roar'd in dismal hell.
Hath Romeo slain himself? say thou but 'I,'
And that bare vowel 'I' shall poison more
Than the death-darting eye of cockatrice:
I am not I, if there be such an I;
Or those eyes shut, that make thee answer 'I.'
If he be slain, say 'I'; or if not, no:
Brief sounds determine of my weal or woe.
Nurse. I saw the wound, I saw it with mine eyes,—
God save the mark!—here on his manly breast:
A piteous corse, a bloody piteous corse;

adversary. 176. **entertain'd,** harbored thoughts of; see glossary. 195. **amerce,** punish by fine. 198. **purchase out,** redeem, exempt from penalty. **abuses,** misdeeds; see glossary.

SCENE II. 2-3. **such . . . Phæthon,** i.e., a young man like Phæthon would understand our haste. Phæthon was son of the sun god, Helios, and was allowed to assume the reins of the sun for a day; not being able to restrain the steeds, he had to be slain by the thunderbolt of Jupiter. 6. **runaways.** Perhaps refers to the horses of the sun chariot which ran away with Phæthon. **wink,** shut; see glossary. 10. **civil,** well-ordered. 14. **Hood,** cover; term in falconry. The hawk's eyes were covered so that it would not bate or beat the wings. **unmann'd,** another term in falconry meaning "untamed." 37. **weraday,** Globe: *well-a-day.* 45. **'I,'** ay, yes. 47. **cockatrice,** basilisk, a fabulous serpent which could kill by its look. 53. **God save the mark,** God forbid; a familiar oath originally intended to avert ill omen.

Pale, pale as ashes, all bedaub'd in blood,
All in gore-blood; I swounded at the sight.
Jul. O, break, my heart! poor bankrout, break at once!
To prison, eyes, ne'er look on liberty!
Vile earth, to earth resign; end motion here;
And thou and Romeo press one heavy bier!
Nurse. O Tybalt, Tybalt, the best friend I had!
O courteous Tybalt! honest gentleman!
That ever I should live to see thee dead!
Jul. What storm is this that blows so contrary?
Is Romeo slaught'red, and is Tybalt dead?
My dearest cousin, and my dearer lord?
Then, dreadful trumpet, sound the general doom!
For who is living, if those two are gone?
Nurse. Tybalt is gone, and Romeo banished;
Romeo that kill'd him, he is banished.
Jul. O God! did Romeo's hand shed Tybalt's blood?
Nurse. It did, it did; alas the day, it did!
Jul. O serpent heart, hid with a flow'ring face!
Did ever dragon keep so fair a cave?
Beautiful tyrant! fiend angelical!
Dove-feather'd raven! wolvish-ravening lamb!
Despised substance of divinest show!
Just opposite to what thou justly seem'st,
A damned saint, an honourable villain!
O nature, what hadst thou to do in hell,
When thou didst bower the spirit of a fiend
In mortal paradise of such sweet flesh?
Was ever book containing such vile matter
So fairly bound? O, that deceit should dwell
In such a gorgeous palace!
Nurse. There 's no trust,
No faith, no honesty in men; all perjur'd,
All forsworn, all naught, all dissemblers.
Ah, where 's my man? give me some aqua vitæ:
These griefs, these woes, these sorrows make me old.
Shame come to Romeo!
Jul. Blister'd be thy tongue
For such a wish! he was not born to shame:
Upon his brow shame is asham'd to sit;
For 'tis a throne where honour may be crown'd
Sole monarch of the universal earth.
O, what a beast was I to chide at him!
Nurse. Will you speak well of him that kill'd your cousin?
Jul. Shall I speak ill of him that is my husband?
Ah, poor my lord, what tongue shall smooth thy name,
When I, thy three-hours wife, have mangled it?
But, wherefore, villain, didst thou kill my cousin?
That villain cousin would have kill'd my husband:
Back, foolish tears, back to your native spring;
Your tributary drops belong to woe,
Which you, mistaking, offer up to joy.
My husband lives, that Tybalt would have slain;
And Tybalt 's dead, that would have slain my husband:
All this is comfort; wherefore weep I then?
Some word there was, worser than Tybalt's death,
That murd'red me: I would forget it fain;
But, O, it presses to my memory,
Like damned guilty deeds to sinners' minds:
'Tybalt is dead, and Romeo—banished;'
That 'banished,' that one word 'banished,'
Hath slain ten thousand Tybalts. Tybalt's death
Was woe enough, if it had ended there:
Or, if sour woe delights in fellowship
And needly will be rank'd with other griefs,
Why followed not, when she said 'Tybalt 's dead,'
Thy father, or thy mother, nay, or both,
Which modern lamentation might have mov'd?
But with a rearward following Tybalt's death,
'Romeo is banished,' to speak that word,
Is father, mother, Tybalt, Romeo, Juliet,
All slain, all dead. 'Romeo is banished!'
There is no end, no limit, measure, bound,
In that word's death; no words can that woe sound.
Where is my father, and my mother, nurse?
Nurse. Weeping and wailing over Tybalt's corse:
Will you go to them? I will bring you thither.
Jul. Wash they his wounds with tears: mine shall be spent,
When theirs are dry, for Romeo's banishment.
Take up those cords: poor ropes, you are beguil'd,
Both you and I; for Romeo is exil'd:
He made you for a highway to my bed;
But I, a maid, die maiden-widowed.
Come, cords, come, nurse; I'll to my wedding-bed;
And death, not Romeo, take my maidenhead!
Nurse. Hie to your chamber: I'll find Romeo
To comfort you: I wot well where he is.
Hark ye, your Romeo will be here at night:
I'll to him; he is hid at Laurence' cell.
Jul. O, find him! give this ring to my true knight,
And bid him come to take his last farewell. *Exeunt.*

[SCENE III. *Friar Laurence's cell.*]

Enter FRIAR [LAURENCE.]

Fri. L. Romeo, come forth; come forth, thou fearful man:
Affliction is enamour'd of thy parts,
And thou art wedded to calamity.

[*Enter*] ROMEO.

Rom. Father, what news? what is the prince's doom?
What sorrow craves acquaintance at my hand,
That I yet know not?
Fri. L. Too familiar
Is my dear son with such sour company:
I bring thee tidings of the prince's doom.
Rom. What less than dooms-day is the prince's doom?
Fri. L. A gentler judgement vanish'd from his lips,
Not body's death, but body's banishment.
Rom. Ha, banishment! be merciful, say 'death;'
For exile hath more terror in his look,
Much more than death: do not say 'banishment.'
Fri. L. Hence from Verona art thou banished:
Be patient, for the world is broad and wide.
Rom. There is no world without Verona walls,
But purgatory, torture, hell itself.
Hence-banished is banish'd from the world,
And world's exile is death: then 'banished'
Is death mis-term'd; calling death 'banished,'

56. **gore-blood,** clotted blood. 59. **motion,** power of movement, life. 81. **bower,** give lodging to. 87. **naught,** worthless; see glossary. 117. **needly,** of necessity. 120. **modern,** ordinary; see glossary. 121. **rearward,** rear guard. 139. **wot,** know; see glossary.
SCENE III. 10. **vanish'd,** issued. 26. **rush'd,** thrust (aside). 33.

Thou cutt'st my head off with a golden axe,
And smilest upon the stroke that murders me.
Fri. L. O deadly sin! O rude unthankfulness!
Thy fault our law calls death; but the kind prince,
Taking thy part, hath rush'd aside the law,
And turn'd that black word death to banishment:
This is dear mercy, and thou seest it not.
Rom. 'Tis torture, and not mercy: heaven is here,
Where Juliet lives; and every cat and dog
And little mouse, every unworthy thing,
Live here in heaven and may look on her;
But Romeo may not: more validity,
More honourable state, more courtship lives
In carrion-flies than Romeo: they may seize
On the white wonder of dear Juliet's hand
And steal immortal blessing from her lips,
Who, even in pure and vestal modesty,
Still blush, as thinking their own kisses sin;
But Romeo may not; he is banished:
Flies may do this, but I from this must fly:
They are free men, but I am banished.
And sayest thou yet that exile is not death?
Hadst thou no poison mix'd, no sharp-ground knife,
No sudden mean of death, though ne'er so mean,
But 'banished' to kill me?—'banished'?
O friar, the damned use that word in hell;
Howlings attend it: how hast thou the heart,
Being a divine, a ghostly confessor,
A sin-absolver, and my friend profess'd,
To mangle me with that word 'banished'?
Fri. L. Thou fond mad man, hear me a little speak.
Rom. O, thou wilt speak again of banishment.
Fri. L. I'll give thee armour to keep off that word;
Adversity's sweet milk, philosophy,
To comfort thee, though thou art banished.
Rom. Yet 'banished'? Hang up philosophy!
Unless philosophy can make a Juliet,
Displant a town, reverse a prince's doom,
It helps not, it prevails not: talk no more.
Fri. L. O, then I see that madmen have no ears.
Rom. How should they, when that wise men have no eyes?
Fri. L. Let me dispute with thee of thy estate.
Rom. Thou canst not speak of that thou dost not feel:
Wert thou as young as I, Juliet thy love,
An hour but married, Tybalt murdered,
Doting like me and like me banished,
Then mightst thou speak, then mightst thou tear thy hair,
And fall upon the ground, as I do now,
Taking the measure of an unmade grave.
Knock.
Fri. L. Arise; one knocks; good Romeo, hide thyself.
Rom. Not I; unless the breath of heart-sick groans,
Mist-like, infold me from the search of eyes. *Knock.*
Fri. L. Hark, how they knock! Who 's there? Romeo, arise;
Thou wilt be taken. Stay awhile! Stand up; *Knock.*
Run to my study. By and by! God's will,
What simpleness is this! I come, I come! *Knock.*
Who knocks so hard? whence come you? what 's your will?
Nurse. [*Within*] Let me come in, and you shall know my errand;
I come from Lady Juliet.
Fri. L. Welcome, then.

Enter Nurse.

Nurse. O holy friar, O, tell me, holy friar,
Where is my lady's lord, where 's Romeo?
Fri. L. There on the ground, with his own tears made drunk.
Nurse. O, he is even in my mistress' case,
Just in her case! O woful sympathy!
Piteous predicament! Even so lies she,
Blubb'ring and weeping, weeping and blubb'ring.
Stand up, stand up; stand, an you be a man:
For Juliet's sake, for her sake, rise and stand;
Why should you fall into so deep an O?
Rom. Nurse!
Nurse. Ah sir! ah sir! Well, death 's the end of all.
Rom. Spakest thou of Juliet? how is it with her?
Doth not she think me an old murderer,
Now I have stain'd the childhood of our joy
With blood remov'd but little from her own?
Where is she? and how doth she? and what says
My conceal'd lady to our cancell'd love?
Nurse. O, she says nothing, sir, but weeps and weeps;
And now falls on her bed; and then starts up,
And Tybalt calls; and then on Romeo cries,
And then down falls again.
Rom. As if that name,
Shot from the deadly level of a gun,
Did murder her; as that name's cursed hand
Murder'd her kinsman. O, tell me, friar, tell me,
In what vile part of this anatomy
Doth my name lodge? tell me that I may sack
The hateful mansion. [*Drawing his sword.*]
Fri. L. Hold thy desperate hand:
Art thou a man? thy form cries out thou art:
Thy tears are womanish; thy wild acts denote
The unreasonable fury of a beast:
Unseemly woman in a seeming man!
And ill-beseeming beast in seeming both!
Thou hast amaz'd me: by my holy order,
I thought thy disposition better temper'd.
Hast thou slain Tybalt? wilt thou slay thyself?
And slay thy lady that in thy life lives,
By doing damned hate upon thyself?
Why railest thou on thy birth, the heaven, and earth?
Since birth, and heaven, and earth, all three do meet
In thee at once; which thou at once wouldst lose.
Fie, fie, thou shamest thy shape, thy love, thy wit;
Which, like a usurer, abound'st in all,
And usest none in that true use indeed
Which should bedeck thy shape, thy love, thy wit:
Thy noble shape is but a form of wax,
Digressing from the valour of a man;
Thy dear love sworn but hollow perjury,
Killing that love which thou hast vow'd to cherish;
Thy wit, that ornament to shape and love,
Mis-shapen in the conduct of them both,
Like powder in a skilless soldier's flask,
Is set a-fire by thine own ignorance,
And thou dismemb'red with thine own defence.

validity, value. 34. **courtship,** both courtliness and wooing. 45. **mean . . . mean,** means . . . base; see glossary. 63. **dispute,** reason; see glossary. **estate,** situation. 94. **old,** (colloquial), real, actual. 103. **level,** aim. 107. **sack,** destroy. 123. **Which,** (you) who.

What, rouse thee, man! thy Juliet is alive,
For whose dear sake thou wast but lately dead;
There art thou happy: Tybalt would kill thee,
But thou slewest Tybalt; there art thou happy.
The law that threat'ned death becomes thy friend
And turns it to exile; there art thou happy:
A pack of blessings lights upon thy back;
Happiness courts thee in her best array;
But, like a misbehav'd and sullen wench,
Thou pout'st upon thy fortune and thy love:
Take heed, take heed, for such die miserable.
Go, get thee to thy love, as was decreed,
Ascend her chamber, hence and comfort her:
But look thou stay not till the watch be set,
For then thou canst not pass to Mantua;
Where thou shalt live, till we can find a time
To blaze your marriage, reconcile your friends,
Beg pardon of the prince, and call thee back
With twenty hundred thousand times more joy
Than thou went'st forth in lamentation.
Go before, nurse: commend me to thy lady;
And bid her hasten all the house to bed,
Which heavy sorrow makes them apt unto:
Romeo is coming.

Nurse. O Lord, I could have stay'd here all the night
To hear good counsel: O, what learning is!
My lord, I'll tell my lady you will come.

Rom. Do so, and bid my sweet prepare to chide.

Nurse. Here, sir, a ring she bid me give you, sir:
Hie you, make haste, for it grows very late. [*Exit.*]

Rom. How well my comfort is reviv'd by this!

Fri. L. Go hence; good night; and here stands all your state:
Either be gone before the watch be set,
Or by the break of day disguis'd from hence:
Sojourn in Mantua; I'll find out your man,
And he shall signify from time to time
Every good hap to you that chances here:
Give me thy hand; 'tis late: farewell; good night.

Rom. But that a joy past joy calls out on me,
It were a grief, so brief to part with thee:
Farewell. *Exeunt.*

[SCENE IV. *A room in Capulet's house.*]

Enter old CAPULET, *his* Wife, *and* PARIS.

Cap. Things have fall'n out, sir, so unluckily,
That we have had no time to move our daughter:
Look you, she lov'd her kinsman Tybalt dearly,
And so did I:—Well, we were born to die.
'Tis very late, she'll not come down to-night:
I promise you, but for your company,
I would have been a-bed an hour ago.

Par. These times of woe afford no times to woo.
Madam, good night: commend me to your daughter.

La. Cap. I will, and know her mind early to-morrow;
To-night she 's mew'd up to her heaviness.

Cap. Sir Paris, I will make a desperate tender
Of my child's love: I think she will be rul'd
In all respects by me; nay, more, I doubt it not.
Wife, go you to her ere you go to bed;
Acquaint her here of my son Paris' love;
And bid her, mark you me, on Wednesday next—
But, soft! what day is this?

Par. Monday, my lord.

Cap. Monday! ha, ha! Well, Wednesday is too soon,
A Thursday let it be: a Thursday, tell her,
She shall be married to this noble earl.
Will you be ready? do you like this haste?
We'll keep no great ado,—a friend or two;
For, hark you, Tybalt being slain so late,
It may be thought we held him carelessly,
Being our kinsman, if we revel much:
Therefore we'll have some half a dozen friends,
And there an end. But what say you to Thursday?

Par. My lord, I would that Thursday were to-morrow.

Cap. Well, get you gone: a Thursday be it, then.
Go you to Juliet ere you go to bed,
Prepare her, wife, against this wedding-day.
Farewell, my lord. Light to my chamber, ho!
Afore me! it is so very very late,
That we may call it early by and by.
Goodnight. *Exeunt.*

[SCENE V. *Capulet's orchard.*]

Enter ROMEO *and* JULIET *aloft* [*at the window*].

Jul. Wilt thou be gone? it is not yet near day:
It was the nightingale, and not the lark,
That pierc'd the fearful hollow of thine ear;
Nightly she sings on yond pomegranate-tree:
Believe me, love, it was the nightingale.

Rom. It was the lark, the herald of the morn,
No nightingale: look, love, what envious streaks
Do lace the severing clouds in yonder east:
Night's candles are burnt out, and jocund day
Stands tiptoe on the misty mountain tops.
I must be gone and live, or stay and die.

Jul. Yond light is not day-light, I know it, I:
It is some meteor that the sun exhales,
To be to thee this night a torch-bearer,
And light thee on thy way to Mantua:
Therefore stay yet; thou need'st not to be gone.

Rom. Let me be ta'en, let me be put to death;
I am content, so thou wilt have it so.
I'll say yon grey is not the morning's eye,
'Tis but the pale reflex of Cynthia's brow;
Nor that is not the lark, whose notes do beat
The vaulty heaven so high above our heads:
I have more care to stay than will to go:
Come, death, and welcome! Juliet wills it so.
How is 't, my soul? let 's talk; it is not day.

Jul. It is, it is: hie hence, be gone, away!
It is the lark that sings so out of tune,
Straining harsh discords and unpleasing sharps.
Some say the lark makes sweet division;
This doth not so, for she divideth us:
Some say the lark and loathed toad change eyes;
O, now I would they had chang'd voices too!
Since arm from arm that voice doth us affray,

151. **blaze,** publish, divulge. 157. **apt,** ready, inclined. 166. **here stands all your state,** your fortune depends on what follows.
SCENE IV. 11. **mew'd,** cooped; see glossary. 12. **desperate tender,** rash offer. 25. **held,** regarded. 34. **Afore me,** by my life.
SCENE V. 8. **lace,** stripe. 20. **Cynthia's,** the moon's. 28. **sharps,** high notes. 29. **division,** variations on a melody, made by dividing each note into notes of briefer duration. 31. **change eyes,** an allusion to a popular saying that the toad and the lark had changed eyes, since the lark has ugly eyes and the toad beautiful ones. 34. **hunt's-up,** a song or tune to awaken huntsmen. 57. **fails,** errs. 59. **Dry sorrow.**

Hunting thee hence with hunt's-up to the day.
O, now be gone; more light and light it grows.
Rom. More light and light; more dark and dark our woes!

Enter Nurse [*hastily*].

Nurse. Madam!
Jul. Nurse?
Nurse. Your lady mother is coming to your chamber:
The day is broke; be wary, look about. [*Exit.*]
Jul. Then, window, let day in, and let life out.
Rom. Farewell, farewell! one kiss, and I'll descend. [*He goeth down.*]
Jul. Art thou gone so? love, lord, ay, husband, friend!
I must hear from thee every day in the hour,
For in a minute there are many days:
O, by this count I shall be much in years
Ere I again behold my Romeo!
Rom. Farewell!
I will omit no opportunity
That may convey my greetings, love, to thee.
Jul. O, think'st thou we shall ever meet again?
Rom. I doubt it not; and all these woes shall serve
For sweet discourses in our times to come.
Jul. O God, I have an ill-divining soul!
Methinks I see thee, now thou art so low,
As one dead in the bottom of a tomb:
Either my eyesight fails, or thou look'st pale.
Rom. And trust me, love, in my eye so do you:
Dry sorrow drinks our blood. Adieu, adieu! *Exit.*
Jul. O Fortune, Fortune! all men call thee fickle:
If thou art fickle, what dost thou with him
That is renown'd for faith? Be fickle, fortune;
For then, I hope, thou wilt not keep him long,
But send him back.

Enter Mother [LADY CAPULET].

La. Cap. Ho, daughter! are you up?
Jul. Who is 't that calls? It is my lady mother.
Is she not down so late, or up so early?
What unaccustom'd cause procures her hither?
La. Cap. Why, how now, Juliet!
Jul. Madam, I am not well.
La. Cap. Evermore weeping for your cousin's death?
What, wilt thou wash him from his grave with tears?
An if thou couldst, thou couldst not make him live;
Therefore, have done: some grief shows much of love;
But much of grief shows still some want of wit.
Jul. Yet let me weep for such a feeling loss.
La. Cap. So shall you feel the loss, but not the friend
Which you weep for.
Jul. Feeling so the loss,
I cannot choose but ever weep the friend.
La. Cap. Well, girl, thou weep'st not so much for his death,
As that the villain lives which slaughter'd him.
Jul. What villain, madam?
La. Cap. That same villain, Romeo.
Jul. [*Aside*] Villain and he be many miles asunder.—
God pardon him! I do, with all my heart;
And yet no man like he doth grieve my heart.
La. Cap. That is, because the traitor murderer lives.
Jul. Ay, madam, from the reach of these my hands:
Would none but I might venge my cousin's death!
La. Cap. We will have vengeance for it, fear thou not:
Then weep no more. I'll send to one in Mantua,
Where that same banish'd runagate doth live,
Shall give him such an unaccustom'd dram,
That he shall soon keep Tybalt company:
And then, I hope, thou wilt be satisfied.
Jul. Indeed, I never shall be satisfied
With Romeo, till I behold him—dead—
Is my poor heart so for a kinsman vex'd:
Madam, if you could find out but a man
To bear a poison, I would temper it;
That Romeo should, upon receipt thereof,
Soon sleep in quiet. O, how my heart abhors
To hear him nam'd, and cannot come to him,
To wreak the love I bore my cousin
Upon his body that hath slaughter'd him!
La. Cap. Find thou the means, and I'll find such a man.
But now I'll tell thee joyful tidings, girl.
Jul. And joy comes well in such a needy time:
What are they, beseech your ladyship?
La. Cap. Well, well, thou hast a careful father, child;
One who, to put thee from thy heaviness,
Hath sorted out a sudden day of joy,
That thou expects not nor I look'd not for.
Jul. Madam, in happy time, what day is that?
La. Cap. Marry, my child, early next Thursday morn,
The gallant, young and noble gentleman,
The County Paris, at Saint Peter's Church,
Shall happily make thee there a joyful bride.
Jul. Now, by Saint Peter's Church and Peter too,
He shall not make me there a joyful bride!
I wonder at this haste; that I must wed
Ere he, that should be husband, comes to woo.
I pray you, tell my lord and father, madam,
I will not marry yet; and, when I do, I swear,
It shall be Romeo, whom you know I hate,
Rather than Paris. These are news indeed!
La. Cap. Here comes your father; tell him so yourself,
And see how he will take it at your hands.

Enter CAPULET *and* Nurse.

Cap. When the sun sets, the earth doth drizzle dew;
But for the sunset of my brother's son
It rains downright.
How now! a conduit, girl? what, still in tears?
Evermore show'ring? In one little body
Thou counterfeits a bark, a sea, a wind;
For still thy eyes, which I may call the sea,
Do ebb and flow with tears; the bark thy body is,
Sailing in this salt flood; the winds, thy sighs;
Who, raging with thy tears, and they with them,
Without a sudden calm, will overset
Thy tempest-tossed body. How now, wife!
Have you delivered to her our decree?

The heat of the body in sorrow and despair was thought to descend into the bowels and dry up the blood. 67. **down,** in bed. 68. **procures,** induces to come. At this point Juliet, who has appeared until now at her "window" above the stage, probably descends to the main stage for the remainder of the scene. 84. **like,** so much as. 95. **dead** This word is placed between the clauses so that it can be understood with either what precedes or what follows it. 98. **temper,** used equivocally, meaning "to mix" or "to alloy." 108. **careful,** provident. 112. **in happy time,** a vague expression like "by the way." 130. **conduit,** water pipe.

La. Cap. Ay, sir; but she will none, she gives you thanks.
I would the fool were married to her grave!
Cap. Soft! take me with you, take me with you, wife.
How! will she none? doth she not give us thanks?
Is she not proud? doth she not count her blest,
Unworthy as she is, that we have wrought
So worthy a gentleman to be her bridegroom?
Jul. Not proud, you have; but thankful, that you have:
Proud can I never be of what I hate;
But thankful even for hate, that is meant love.
Cap. How, how, how, how, chop-logic! What is this?
'Proud,' and 'I thank you,' and 'I thank you not;'
And yet 'not proud:' mistress minion, you,
Thank me no thankings, nor proud me no prouds,
But fettle your fine joints 'gainst Thursday next,
To go with Paris to Saint Peter's Church,
Or I will drag thee on a hurdle thither.
Out, you green-sickness carrion! out, you baggage!
You tallow-face!
La. Cap. Fie, fie! what, are you mad?
Jul. Good father, I beseech you on my knees,
Hear me with patience but to speak a word.
Cap. Hang thee, young baggage! disobedient wretch!
I tell thee what: get thee to church a Thursday,
Or never after look me in the face:
Speak not, reply not, do not answer me;
My fingers itch. Wife, we scarce thought us blest
That God had lent us but this only child;
But now I see this one is one too much,
And that we have a curse in having her:
Out on her, hilding!
Nurse. God in heaven bless her!
You are to blame, my lord, to rate her so.
Cap. And why, my lady wisdom? hold your tongue,
Good prudence; smatter with your gossips, go.
Nurse. I speak no treason.
Cap. O, God ye god-den!
Nurse. May not one speak?
Cap. Peace, you mumbling fool!
Utter your gravity o'er a gossip's bowl;
For here we need it not.
La. Cap. You are too hot.
Cap. † God's bread! it makes me mad:
†Day, night, hour, tide, time, work, play,
Alone, in company, still my care hath been
To have her match'd: and having now provided
A gentleman of noble parentage,
Of fair demesnes, youthful, and nobly train'd,
Stuff'd, as they say, with honourable parts,
Proportion'd as one's thought would wish a man;
And then to have a wretched puling fool,
A whining mammet, in her fortune's tender,
To answer 'I'll not wed; I cannot love,
I am too young; I pray you, pardon me.'
But, an you will not wed, I'll pardon you:
Graze where you will, you shall not house with me:
Look to 't, think on 't, I do not use to jest.
Thursday is near; lay hand on heart, advise:
An you be mine, I'll give you to my friend;
An you be not, hang, beg, starve, die in the streets,
For, by my soul, I'll ne'er acknowledge thee,
Nor what is mine shall never do thee good:
Trust to 't, bethink you; I'll not be forsworn. *Exit.*
Jul. Is there no pity sitting in the clouds,
That sees into the bottom of my grief?
O, sweet my mother, cast me not away!
Delay this marriage for a month, a week;
Or, if you do not, make the bridal bed
In that dim monument where Tybalt lies.
La. Cap. Talk not to me, for I'll not speak a word:
Do as thou wilt, for I have done with thee. *Exit.*
Jul. O God!—O nurse, how shall this be prevented?
My husband is on earth, my faith in heaven;
How shall that faith return again to earth,
Unless that husband send it me from heaven
By leaving earth? comfort me, counsel me.
Alack, alack, that heaven should practise stratagems
Upon so soft a subject as myself!
What say'st thou? hast thou not a word of joy?
Some comfort, nurse.
Nurse. Faith, here it is.
Romeo is banish'd; and all the world to nothing,
That he dares ne'er come back to challenge you;
Or, if he do, it needs must be by stealth.
Then, since the case so stands as now it doth,
I think it best you married with the county.
O, he 's a lovely gentleman!
Romeo 's a dishclout to him: an eagle, madam,
Hath not so green, so quick, so fair an eye
As Paris hath. Beshrew my very heart,
I think you are happy in this second match,
For it excels your first: or if it did not,
Your first is dead; or 'twere as good he were,
As living here and you no use of him.
Jul. Speak'st thou from thy heart?
Nurse. And from my soul too;
Else beshrew them both.
Jul. Amen!
Nurse. What?
Jul. Well, thou hast comforted me marvellous much.
Go in; and tell my lady I am gone,
Having displeas'd my father, to Laurence' cell,
To make confession and to be absolv'd.
Nurse. Marry, I will; and this is wisely done. [*Exit.*]
Jul. Ancient damnation! O most wicked fiend!
Is it more sin to wish me thus forsworn,
Or to dispraise my lord with that same tongue
Which she hath prais'd him with above compare
So many thousand times? Go, counsellor;
Thou and my bosom henceforth shall be twain.
I'll to the friar, to know his remedy:
If all else fail, myself have power to die. *Exit.*

[ACT IV.

SCENE I. *Friar Laurence's cell.*]

Enter FRIAR [LAURENCE] *and* COUNTY PARIS.

Fri. L. On Thursday, sir? the time is very short.

140. **will none,** refuses it. 142. **take me with you,** let me understand you. 145. **wrought,** procured. 150. **chop-logic,** a shallow and sophistical arguer. 152. **minion,** spoiled darling, minx. 154. **fettle,** make ready. 156. **hurdle,** a conveyance for criminals. 157. **green-sickness,** an anemic ailment of young women; it suggests Juliet's paleness. 170. **rate,** berate, scold; see glossary. 172. **smatter,** chatter. 175. **gravity,** wisdom; used contemptuously. 177. **God's bread,** an oath by the sacrament. 186. **mammet,** doll. **fortune's tender,** offer of good fortune. 207. **my faith in heaven.** Juliet refers to her marriage vows. 211. **practise,** scheme, contrive; see glossary. **stratagems,**

Par. My father Capulet will have it so;
And I am nothing slow to slack his haste.
Fri. L. You say you do not know the lady's mind:
Uneven is the course, I like it not.
Par. Immoderately she weeps for Tybalt's death,
And therefore have I little talk'd of love;
For Venus smiles not in a house of tears.
Now, sir, her father counts it dangerous
That she do give her sorrow so much sway,
And in his wisdom hastes our marriage,
To stop the inundation of her tears;
Which, too much minded by herself alone,
May be put from her by society:
Now do you know the reason of this haste.
Fri. L. [*Aside*] I would I knew not why it should be slow'd.—
Look, sir, here comes the lady toward my cell.

Enter JULIET.

Par. Happily met, my lady and my wife!
Jul. That may be, sir, when I may be a wife.
Par. That may be must be, love, on Thursday next.
Jul. What must be shall be.
Fri. L. That 's a certain text.
Par. Come you to make confession to this father?
Jul. To answer that, I should confess to you.
Par. Do not deny to him that you love me.
Jul. I will confess to you that I love him.
Par. So will ye, I am sure, that you love me.
Jul. If I do so, it will be of more price,
Being spoke behind your back, than to your face.
Par. Poor soul, thy face is much abus'd with tears.
Jul. The tears have got small victory by that;
For it was bad enough before their spite.
Par. Thou wrong'st it, more than tears, with that report.
Jul. That is no slander, sir, which is a truth;
And what I spake, I spake it to my face.
Par. Thy face is mine, and thou hast sland'red it.
Jul. It may be so, for it is not mine own.
Are you at leisure, holy father, now;
Or shall I come to you at evening mass?
Fri. L. My leisure serves me, pensive daughter, now.
My lord, we must entreat the time alone.
Par. God shield I should disturb devotion!
Juliet, on Thursday early will I rouse ye:
Till then, adieu; and keep this holy kiss. *Exit.*
Jul. O, shut the door! and when thou hast done so,
Come weep with me; past hope, past cure, past help!
Fri. L. Ah, Juliet, I already know thy grief;
It strains me past the compass of my wits:
I hear thou must, and nothing may prorogue it,
On Thursday next be married to this county.
Jul. Tell me not, friar, that thou hearest of this,
Unless thou tell me how I may prevent it:
If, in thy wisdom, thou canst give no help,
Do thou but call my resolution wise,
And with this knife I'll help it presently.
God join'd my heart and Romeo's, thou our hands;
And ere this hand, by thee to Romeo seal'd,
Shall be the label to another deed,
Or my true heart with treacherous revolt
Turn to another, this shall slay them both:
Therefore, out of thy long-experienc'd time,
Give me some present counsel, or, behold,
'Twixt my extremes and me this bloody knife
Shall play the umpire, arbitrating that
Which the commission of thy years and art
Could to no issue of true honour bring.
Be not so long to speak; I long to die,
If what thou speak'st speak not of remedy.
Fri. L. Hold, daughter: I do spy a kind of hope,
Which craves as desperate an execution
As that is desperate which we would prevent.
If, rather than to marry County Paris,
Thou hast the strength of will to slay thyself,
Then is it likely thou wilt undertake
A thing like death to chide away this shame,
That cop'st with death himself to scape from it;
And, if thou darest, I'll give thee remedy.
Jul. O, bid me leap, rather than marry Paris,
From off the battlements of any tower;
Or walk in thievish ways; or bid me lurk
Where serpents are; chain me with roaring bears;
Or hide me nightly in a charnel-house,
O'er-cover'd quite with dead men's rattling bones,
With reeky shanks and yellow chapless skulls;
Or bid me go into a new-made grave
And hide me with a dead man in his shroud;
Things that, to hear them told, have made me tremble;
And I will do it without fear or doubt,
To live an unstain'd wife to my sweet love.
Fri. L. Hold, then; go home, be merry, give consent
To marry Paris: Wednesday is to-morrow:
To-morrow night look that thou lie alone;
Let not thy nurse lie with thee in thy chamber:
Take thou this vial, being then in bed,
And this distilling liquor drink thou off;
When presently through all thy veins shall run
A cold and drowsy humour, for no pulse
Shall keep his native progress, but surcease:
No warmth, no breath, shall testify thou livest;
The roses in thy lips and cheeks shall fade
To paly ashes, thy eyes' windows fall,
Like death, when he shuts up the day of life;
Each part, depriv'd of supple government,
Shall, stiff and stark and cold, appear like death:
And in this borrowed likeness of shrunk death
Thou shalt continue two and forty hours,
And then awake as from a pleasant sleep.
Now, when the bridegroom in the morning comes
To rouse thee from thy bed, there art thou dead:
Then, as the manner of our country is,
In thy best robes uncovered on the bier
Thou shalt be borne to that same ancient vault
Where all the kindred of the Capulets lie.
In the mean time, against thou shalt awake,
Shall Romeo by my letters know our drift,
And hither shall he come: and he and I
Will watch thy waking, and that very night
Shall Romeo bear thee hence to Mantua.
And this shall free thee from this present shame;
If no inconstant toy, nor womanish fear,

dreadful deeds. 215. **all . . . nothing,** the odds are overwhelming.
ACT IV. SCENE I. 5. **Uneven,** not straightforward. 13. **minded,** thought about. 40. **entreat,** ask to have. 41. **shield,** prevent (that). 54. **presently,** at once; see glossary. 57. **label,** a strip attached to a deed to carry the seal. 61. **present,** instant; see glossary. 62. **extremes,** extreme difficulties. 64. **commission,** authority. 75. **cop'st,** encounters, negotiates. 81. **charnel house,** vault for old bones. 83. **reeky,** malodorous. **chapless,** without the lower jaw. 94. **distilling,** infusing. 97. **surcease,** cease. 119. **toy,** idle fancy; see glossary.

Abate thy valour in the acting it.
Jul. Give me, give me! O, tell not me of fear!
Fri. L. Hold; get you gone, be strong and prosperous
In this resolve: I'll send a friar with speed
To Mantua, with my letters to thy lord.
Jul. Love give me strength! and strength shall help afford.
Farewell, dear father! *Exeunt.*

[SCENE II. *Hall in Capulet's house.*]

Enter Father CAPULET, *Mother* [LADY CAPULET], Nurse, *and* Servingmen, *two or three.*

Cap. So many guests invite as here are writ. [*Exit First Servant.*]
Sirrah, go hire me twenty cunning cooks.

Sec. Serv. You shall have none ill, sir; for I'll try if they can lick their fingers.

Cap. How canst thou try them so?

Sec. Serv. Marry, sir, 'tis an ill cook that cannot lick his own fingers: therefore he that cannot lick his fingers goes not with me.

Cap. Go, be gone. [*Exit Sec. Servant.*]
We shall be much unfurnish'd for this time.
What, is my daughter gone to Friar Laurence?
Nurse. Ay, forsooth.
Cap. Well, he may chance to do some good on her:
A peevish self-will'd harlotry it is.

Enter JULIET.

Nurse. See where she comes from shrift with merry look.
Cap. How now, my headstrong! where have you been gadding?
Jul. Where I have learn'd me to repent the sin
Of disobedient opposition
To you and your behests, and am enjoin'd
By holy Laurence to fall prostrate here,
To beg your pardon: pardon, I beseech you!
Henceforward I am ever rul'd by you.
Cap. Send for the county; go tell him of this:
I'll have this knot knit up to-morrow morning.
Jul. I met the youthful lord at Laurence' cell;
And gave him what becomed love I might,
Not stepping o'er the bounds of modesty.
Cap. Why, I am glad on 't; this is well: stand up:
This is as 't should be. Let me see the county;
Ay, marry, go, I say, and fetch him hither.
Now, afore God! this reverend holy friar,
All our whole city is much bound to him.
Jul. Nurse, will you go with me into my closet,
To help me sort such needful ornaments
As you think fit to furnish me to-morrow?
La. Cap. No, not till Thursday; there is time enough.
Cap. Go, nurse, go with her: we'll to church to-morrow. *Exeunt* [*Juliet and Nurse*].
La. Cap. We shall be short in our provision:
'Tis now near night.
Cap. Tush, I will stir about,
And all things shall be well, I warrant thee, wife:
Go thou to Juliet, help to deck up her;
I'll not to bed to-night; let me alone;
I'll play the housewife for this once. What, ho!
They are all forth. Well, I will walk myself
To County Paris, to prepare him up
Against to-morrow: my heart is wondrous light,
Since this same wayward girl is so reclaim'd. *Exeunt.*

[SCENE III. *Juliet's chamber.*]

Enter JULIET *and* Nurse.

Jul. Ay, those attires are best: but, gentle nurse,
I pray thee, leave me to myself to-night;
For I have need of many orisons
To move the heavens to smile upon my state,
Which, well thou knowest, is cross and full of sin.

Enter Mother [LADY CAPULET].

La. Cap. What, are you busy, ho? need you my help?
Jul. No, madam; we have cull'd such necessaries
As are behoveful for our state to-morrow:
So please you, let me now be left alone,
And let the nurse this night sit up with you;
For, I am sure, you have your hands full all,
In this so sudden business.
La. Cap. Good night:
Get thee to bed, and rest; for thou hast need.
Exeunt [*Lady Capulet and Nurse*].
Jul. Farewell! God knows when we shall meet again.
I have a faint cold fear thrills through my veins,
That almost freezes up the heat of life:
I'll call them back again to comfort me:
Nurse!—What should she do here?
My dismal scene I needs must act alone.
Come, vial.
What if this mixture do not work at all?
Shall I be married then to-morrow morning?
No, no: this shall forbid it: lie thou there.
[*Laying down her dagger.*]
What if it be a poison, which the friar
Subtly hath minist'red to have me dead,
Lest in this marriage he should be dishonour'd,
Because he married me before to Romeo?
I fear it is: and yet, methinks, it should not,
For he hath still been tried a holy man.
How if, when I am laid into the tomb,
I wake before the time that Romeo
Come to redeem me? there 's a fearful point!
Shall I not, then, be stifled in the vault,
To whose foul mouth no healthsome air breathes in,
And there die strangled ere my Romeo comes?
Or, if I live, is it not very like,
The horrible conceit of death and night,
Together with the terror of the place,—
As in a vault, an ancient receptacle,
Where, for this many hundred years, the bones
Of all my buried ancestors are pack'd:
Where bloody Tybalt, yet but green in earth,

120. **Abate,** diminish; see glossary.

SCENE II. 14. **A . . . is,** i.e., she's a silly good-for-nothing. 26. **becomed,** befitting. 33. **closet,** private room. 35. **furnish,** fit out; see glossary.

SCENE III. 3. **orisons,** prayers. 5. **cross,** contrary. 8. **behoveful,** needful. 25. **minist'red,** administered (something healing or the reverse). 29. **tried,** proved. After this line, Q_1: ***I will not entertain so bad a thought.*** 39. **As,** namely; see glossary. 47. **mandrakes'.** Mandragora or mandrake was a narcotic plant, the root of which resembled the human form; it was fabled to utter a shriek when torn from the ground. 50. **fears,** objects of fear; see glossary. 53. **rage,** madness; see glossary.

Lies fest'ring in his shroud; where, as they say,
At some hours in the night spirits resort;—
Alack, alack, is it not like that I,
So early waking, what with loathsome smells,
And shrieks like mandrakes' torn out of the earth,
That living mortals, hearing them, run mad:—
O, if I wake, shall I not be distraught,
Environed with all these hideous fears?
And madly play with my forefathers' joints?
And pluck the mangled Tybalt from his shroud?
And, in this rage, with some great kinsman's bone,
As with a club, dash out my desp'rate brains?
O, look! methinks I see my cousin's ghost
Seeking out Romeo, that did spit his body
Upon a rapier's point: stay, Tybalt, stay!
Romeo, I come! this do I drink to thee.
[*She falls upon her bed, within the curtains.*]

[SCENE IV. *Hall in Capulet's house.*]

Enter Lady of the House [LADY CAPULET] *and* Nurse.

La. Cap. Hold, take these keys, and fetch more spices, nurse.
Nurse. They call for dates and quinces in the pastry.

Enter old CAPULET.

Cap. Come, stir, stir, stir! the second cock hath crow'd,
The curfew-bell hath rung, 'tis three o'clock:
Look to the bak'd meats, good Angelica:
Spare not for cost.
Nurse. Go, you cot-quean, go,
Get you to bed; faith, you'll be sick to-morrow
For this night's watching.
Cap. No, not a whit: what! I have watch'd ere now
All night for lesser cause, and ne'er been sick.
La. Cap. Ay, you have been a mouse-hunt in your time;
But I will watch you from such watching now.
Exeunt Lady and Nurse.
Cap. A jealous-hood, a jealous-hood!

Enter three or four [Fellows] *with spits and logs, and baskets.*

Now, fellow,
What is there?
First Fellow. Things for the cook, sir; but I know not what.
Cap. Make haste, make haste. [*Exit First Fellow.*]
Sirrah, fetch drier logs:
Call Peter, he will show thee where they are.
Sec. Fellow. I have a head, sir, that will find out logs,
And never trouble Peter for the matter. [*Exit.*]
Cap. Mass, and well said; a merry whoreson, ha!
Thou shalt be logger-head. Good faith, 'tis day:
The county will be here with music straight,
For so he said he would: I hear him near.
Play music.
Nurse! Wife! What, ho! What, nurse, I say!

Enter Nurse.

Go waken Juliet, go and trim her up;
I'll go and chat with Paris: hie, make haste,
Make haste; the bridegroom he is come already:
Make haste, I say. [*Exit Capulet.*]

[SCENE V. *Juliet's chamber.*]

[*The* NURSE *goes to the curtains.*]

Nurse. Mistress! what, mistress! Juliet! fast, I warrant her, she:
Why, lamb! why, lady! fie, you slug-a-bed!
Why, love, I say! madam! sweet-heart! why, bride!
What, not a word? you take your pennyworths now;
Sleep for a week; for the next night, I warrant,
The County Paris hath set up his rest,
That you shall rest but little. God forgive me,
Marry, and amen, how sound is she asleep!
I must needs wake her. Madam, madam, madam!
Ay, let the county take you in your bed;
He'll fright you up, i' faith. Will it not be?
[*Undraws the curtains.*]
What, dress'd! and in your clothes! and down again!
I must needs wake you: Lady! lady! lady!
Alas, alas! Help, help! my lady 's dead!
O, weraday, that ever I was born!
Some aqua vitæ, ho! My lord! my lady!

[*Enter* LADY CAPULET.]

La. Cap. What noise is here?
Nurse. O lamentable day!
La. Cap. What is the matter?
Nurse. Look, look! O heavy day!
La. Cap. O me, O me! My child, my only life,
Revive, look up, or I will die with thee!
Help, help! Call help.

Enter Father [CAPULET].

Cap. For shame, bring Juliet forth; her lord is come.
Nurse. She 's dead, deceas'd, she 's dead; alack the day!
La. Cap. Alack the day, she 's dead, she 's dead, she 's dead!
Cap. Ha! let me see her: out, alas! she 's cold;
Her blood is settled, and her joints are stiff;
Life and these lips have long been separated:
Death lies on her like an untimely frost
Upon the sweetest flower of all the field.
Nurse. O lamentable day!
La. Cap. O woful time!
Cap. Death, that hath ta'en her hence to make me wail,
Ties up my tongue, and will not let me speak.

Enter FRIAR [LAURENCE] *and the* COUNTY [PARIS, *with* Musicians].

Fri. L. Come, is the bride ready to go to church?
Cap. Ready to go, but never to return.
O son! the night before thy wedding-day
Hath Death lain with thy wife. There she lies,
Flower as she was, deflowered by him.
Death is my son-in-law, Death is my heir;

SCENE IV. 2. **pastry,** room in which pastry was made. 4. **curfew-bell,** apparently rung at other times than at curfew. 5. **bak'd meats,** pies, pastry. 6. **cot-quean,** a man who acts the housewife. 8. **watching,** waking; see glossary. 11. **mouse-hunt,** hunter of women. 13. **jealous-hood,** (you wear) the cap of jealousy. 19. **Mass,** by the Mass. 20. **logger-head,** blockhead.

SCENE V. The action here is uninterrupted from the previous scene. The Nurse opens the curtains rear-stage where Juliet has lain since IV, ii. 1. **fast,** fast asleep. 4. **pennyworths,** small portions. 6. **set up his rest,** firmly resolved (with bawdy suggestion of readying a lance for the charge). 15. **weraday,** Globe: *well-a-day*. 26. **settled,** congealed.

My daughter he hath wedded: I will die,
And leave him all; life, living, all is Death's.

Par. Have I thought long to see this morning's face,
And doth it give me such a sight as this?

La. Cap. Accurs'd, unhappy, wretched, hateful day!
Most miserable hour that e'er time saw
In lasting labour of his pilgrimage!
But one, poor one, one poor and loving child,
But one thing to rejoice and solace in,
And cruel death hath catch'd it from my sight!

Nurse. O woe! O woful, woful, woful day!
Most lamentable day, most woful day,
That ever, ever, I did yet behold!
O day! O day! O day! O hateful day!
Never was seen so black a day as this:
O woful day, O woful day!

Par. Beguil'd, divorced, wronged, spited, slain!
Most detestable death, by thee beguil'd,
By cruel cruel thee quite overthrown!
O love! O life! not life, but love in death!

Cap. Despis'd, distressed, hated, martyr'd, kill'd!
Uncomfortable time, why cam'st thou now
To murder, murder our solemnity?
O child! O child! my soul, and not my child!
Dead art thou! Alack! my child is dead;
And with my child my joys are buried.

Fri. L. Peace, ho, for shame! confusion's cure lives not
In these confusions. Heaven and yourself
Had part in this fair maid; now heaven hath all,
And all the better is it for the maid:
Your part in her you could not keep from death,
But heaven keeps his part in eternal life.
The most you sought was her promotion;
For 'twas your heaven she should be advanc'd:
And weep ye now, seeing she is advanc'd
Above the clouds, as high as heaven itself?
O, in this love, you love your child so ill,
That you run mad, seeing that she is well:
She 's not well married that lives married long;
But she 's best married that dies married young.
Dry up your tears, and stick your rosemary
On this fair corse; and, as the custom is,
In all her best array bear her to church:
For though fond nature bids us all lament,
Yet nature's tears are reason's merriment.

Cap. All things that we ordained festival,
Turn from their office to black funeral;
Our instruments to melancholy bells,
Our wedding cheer to a sad burial feast,
Our solemn hymns to sullen dirges change,
Our bridal flowers serve for a buried corse,
And all things change them to the contrary.

Fri. L. Sir, go you in; and, madam, go with him;
And go, Sir Paris; every one prepare
To follow this fair corse unto her grave:
The heavens do lour upon you for some ill;
Move them no more by crossing their high will.

Exeunt. Mane[n]t [Musicians and Nurse].

First Mus. Faith, we may put up our pipes, and be gone.

Nurse. Honest good fellows, ah, put up, put up;
For, well you know, this is a pitiful case. [*Exit.*]

First Mus. Ay, by my troth, the case may be amended.

Enter PETER.

Pet. Musicians, O, musicians, 'Heart's ease, Heart's ease:' O, an you will have me live, play 'Heart's ease.'

First Mus. Why 'Heart's ease'?

Pet. O, musicians, because my heart itself plays 'My heart is full of woe:' O, play me some merry dump, to comfort me.

First Mus. Not a dump we; 'tis no time to play now.

Pet. You will not, then?

First Mus. No.

Pet. I will then give it you soundly.

First Mus. What will you give us?

Pet. No money, on my faith, but the gleek; I will give you the minstrel.

First Mus. Then will I give you the serving-creature.

Pet. Then will I lay the serving-creature's dagger on your pate. I will carry no crotchets: I'll re you, I'll fa you; do you note me?

First Mus. An you re us and fa us, you note us.

Sec. Mus. Pray you, put up your dagger, and put out your wit.

Pet. Then have at you with my wit! I will dry-beat you with an iron wit, and put up my iron dagger. Answer me like men:

'When griping grief the heart doth wound,
And doleful dumps the mind oppress,
Then music with her silver sound'—

why 'silver sound'? why 'music with her silver sound'? What say you, Simon Catling?

First Mus. Marry, sir, because silver hath a sweet sound.

Pet. Pretty! What say you, Hugh Rebeck?

Sec. Mus. I say 'silver sound,' because musicians sound for silver.

Pet. Pretty too! What say you, James Soundpost?

Third Mus. Faith, I know not what to say.

Pet. O, I cry you mercy; you are the singer: I will say for you. It is 'music with her silver sound,' because musicians have no gold for sounding:

'Then music with her silver sound
With speedy help doth lend redress.' *Exit.*

First Mus. What a pestilent knave is this same!

Sec. Mus. Hang him, Jack! Come, we'll in here; tarry for the mourners, and stay dinner. *Exeunt.*

[ACT V.

SCENE I. *Mantua. A street.*]

Enter ROMEO.

Rom. If I may trust the flattering truth of sleep,

41. **thought long,** looked forward to. 43. **unhappy,** fatal; see glossary. 61. **solemnity,** festivity. 65. **confusion's,** calamity's. 79. **rosemary,** symbol of immortality and enduring love; therefore used at both funerals and weddings. 83. **Yet . . . merriment.** Nature is here used as the opposite of reason. 101. **amended,** bettered. *Stage Direction:* ***Enter*** **Peter.** Q2 has *Enter Will Kemp.* This well-known comic actor was a member of Shakespeare's company. Shakespeare evidently had Kemp (or Kempe) in mind when he wrote this part, and named him in the manuscript. 102. **'Heart's ease,'** popular tune, as also '*My heart is full of woe,*' line 107. 108. **dump,** mournful tune. 115. **gleek,** jest, gibe. 120. **carry,** endure; see glossary. **crotchets,** meaning both "quarter notes" and "whims." 122. **note,** set to music; used punningly. 124. **put out,** display. 128-130. **'When . . . sound.'** This is a part of a song by Richard Edwards preserved in the *Paradise of Daintie Devices* (1576). 132. **Catling.** A catling was a small lutestring made of catgut. 135. **Rebeck.** A rebeck was a fiddle with three strings. 139. **Soundpost.** A

My dreams presage some joyful news at hand:
My bosom's lord sits lightly in his throne;
And all this day an unaccustom'd spirit
Lifts me above the ground with cheerful thoughts.
I dreamt my lady came and found me dead—
Strange dream, that gives a dead man leave to think!—
And breath'd such life with kisses in my lips,
That I reviv'd, and was an emperor.
Ah me! how sweet is love itself possess'd,
When but love's shadows are so rich in joy!

Enter ROMEO'*s Man* [BALTHASAR, *booted*].

News from Verona!—How now, Balthasar!
Dost thou not bring me letters from the friar?
How doth my lady? Is my father well?
How fares my Juliet? that I ask again;
For nothing can be ill, if she be well.
Bal. Then she is well, and nothing can be ill:
Her body sleeps in Capels' monument,
And her immortal part with angels lives.
I saw her laid low in her kindred's vault,
And presently took post to tell it you:
O, pardon me for bringing these ill news,
Since you did leave it for my office, sir.
Rom. Is it e'en so? then I defy you, stars!
Thou knowest my lodging: get me ink and paper,
And hire post-horses; I will hence to-night.
Bal. I do beseech you, sir, have patience:
Your looks are pale and wild, and do import
Some misadventure.
Rom. Tush, thou art deceiv'd:
Leave me, and do the thing I bid thee do.
Hast thou no letters to me from the friar?
Bal. No, my good lord.
Rom. No matter: get thee gone,
And hire those horses; I'll be with thee straight.
Exit [*Balthasar*].
Well, Juliet, I will lie with thee to-night.
Let 's see for means: O mischief, thou art swift
To enter in the thoughts of desperate men!
I do remember an apothecary,—
And hereabouts 'a dwells,—which late I noted
In tatt'red weeds, with overwhelming brows,
Culling of simples; meagre were his looks,
Sharp misery had worn him to the bones:
And in his needy shop a tortoise hung,
An alligator stuff'd, and other skins
Of ill-shap'd fishes; and about his shelves
A beggarly account of empty boxes,
Green earthen pots, bladders and musty seeds,
Remnants of packthread and old cakes of roses,
Were thinly scattered, to make up a show.
Noting this penury, to myself I said
'An if a man did need a poison now,
Whose sale is present death in Mantua,
Here lives a caitiff wretch would sell it him.'
O, this same thought did but forerun my need;
And this same needy man must sell it me.
As I remember, this should be the house.
Being holiday, the beggar's shop is shut.
What, ho! apothecary!

[*Enter* Apothecary.]

Ap. Who calls so loud?
Rom. Come hither, man. I see that thou art poor:
Hold, there is forty ducats: let me have
A dram of poison, such soon-speeding gear
As will disperse itself through all the veins
That the life-weary taker may fall dead
And that the trunk may be discharg'd of breath
As violently as hasty powder fir'd
Doth hurry from the fatal cannon's womb.
Ap. Such mortal drugs I have; but Mantua's law
Is death to any he that utters them.
Rom. Art thou so bare and full of wretchedness,
And fearest to die? famine is in thy cheeks,
Need and oppression starveth in thy eyes,
Contempt and beggary hangs upon thy back;
The world is not thy friend nor the world's law;
The world affords no law to make thee rich;
Then be not poor, but break it, and take this.
Ap. My poverty, but not my will, consents.
Rom. I pay thy poverty, and not thy will.
Ap. Put this in any liquid thing you will,
And drink it off; and, if you had the strength
Of twenty men, it would dispatch you straight.
Rom. There is thy gold, worse poison to men's souls,
Doing more murder in this loathsome world,
Than these poor compounds that thou mayst not sell.
I sell thee poison; thou hast sold me none.
Farewell: buy food, and get thyself in flesh.
Come, cordial and not poison, go with me
To Juliet's grave; for there must I use thee. *Exeunt.*

[SCENE II. *Friar Laurence's cell.*]

Enter FRIAR JOHN *to* FRIAR LAURENCE.

Fri. J. Holy Franciscan friar! brother, ho!

Enter FRIAR LAURENCE.

Fri. L. This same should be the voice of Friar John.
Welcome from Mantua: what says Romeo?
Or, if his mind be writ, give me his letter.
Fri. J. Going to find a bare-foot brother out,
One of our order, to associate me,
Here in this city visiting the sick,
And finding him, the searchers of the town,
Suspecting that we both were in a house
Where the infectious pestilence did reign,
Seal'd up the doors, and would not let us forth;
So that my speed to Mantua there was stay'd.
Fri. L. Who bare my letter, then, to Romeo?
Fri. J. I could not send it,—here it is again,—
Nor get a messenger to bring it thee,
So fearful were they of infection.
Fri. L. Unhappy fortune! by my brotherhood,

soundpost is the pillar or peg which supports the body of a stringed instrument. 141. **cry you mercy,** beg your pardon; see glossary. 143. **sounding,** playing music.

ACT V. SCENE I. 1. **flattering,** illusive. 2. **presage some joyful news.** The premonition here is ironical. 3. **bosom's lord,** heart. 11. **shadows,** phantoms; see glossary. 21. **took post,** started with post horses. 33. **straight,** immediately. 39. **weeds,** clothes. **overwhelming brows,** eyebrows jutting out over his eyes. 40. **simples,** medicinal herbs. 45. **beggarly account,** poor array. 47. **cakes of roses,** rose petals caked to be used as perfume. 51. **present,** immediate. 52. **caitiff,** miserable. 59. **ducats,** coins, usually gold, of varying value. 63. **trunk,** body. 67. **utters,** issues, gives out. 85. **cordial,** restorative.

SCENE II. 4. **mind,** thoughts, message; see glossary. 6. **associate,** accompany. 8. **searchers of the town,** town officials charged with public health (and especially concerned about the plague).

The letter was not nice but full of charge
Of dear import, and the neglecting it
May do much danger. Friar John, go hence;
Get me an iron crow, and bring it straight
Unto my cell.
Fri. J. Brother, I'll go and bring it thee. *Exit.*
Fri. L. Now must I to the monument alone;
Within this three hours will fair Juliet wake:
She will beshrew me much that Romeo
Hath had no notice of these accidents;
But I will write again to Mantua,
And keep her at my cell till Romeo come;
Poor living corse, clos'd in a dead man's tomb! *Exit.*

[SCENE III. *A Churchyard; in it a tomb belonging to the Capulets.*]

Enter PARIS, *and his* Page [*bearing flowers and a torch*].

Par. Give me thy torch, boy: hence, and stand aloof:
Yet put it out, for I would not be seen.
Under yond yew-trees lay thee all along,
Holding thine ear close to the hollow ground;
So shall no foot upon the churchyard tread,
Being loose, unfirm, with digging up of graves,
But thou shalt hear it: whistle then to me,
As signal that thou hearest something approach.
Give me those flowers. Do as I bid thee, go.
Page. [*Aside*] I am almost afraid to stand alone
Here in the churchyard; yet I will adventure. [*Retires.*]
Par. Sweet flower, with flowers thy bridal bed I strew,—
O woe! thy canopy is dust and stones;—
Which with sweet water nightly I will dew,
Or, wanting that, with tears distill'd by moans:
The obsequies that I for thee will keep
Nightly shall be to strew thy grave and weep.
Whistle Boy.
The boy gives warning something doth approach.
What cursed foot wanders this way to-night,
To cross my obsequies and true love's rite?
What, with a torch! muffle me, night, awhile. [*Retires.*]

Enter ROMEO *and* [BALTHASAR, *with a torch, mattock, &c.*].

Rom. Give me that mattock and the wrenching iron.
Hold, take this letter; early in the morning
See thou deliver it to my lord and father.
Give me the light: upon thy life, I charge thee,
Whate'er thou hearest or seest, stand all aloof,
And do not interrupt me in my course.
Why I descend into this bed of death,
Is partly to behold my lady's face;
But chiefly to take thence from her dead finger
A precious ring, a ring that I must use
In dear employment: therefore hence, be gone:
But if thou, jealous, dost return to pry
In what I further shall intend to do,
By heaven, I will tear thee joint by joint
And strew this hungry churchyard with thy limbs:
The time and my intents are savage-wild,
More fierce and more inexorable far
Than empty tigers or the roaring sea.
Bal. I will be gone, sir, and not trouble you.
Rom. So shalt thou show me friendship. Take thou that:
Live, and be prosperous: and farewell, good fellow.
Bal. [*Aside*] For all this same, I'll hide me hereabout:
His looks I fear, and his intents I doubt. [*Retires.*]
Rom. Thou detestable maw, thou womb of death,
Gorg'd with the dearest morsel of the earth,
Thus I enforce thy rotten jaws to open,
And, in despite, I'll cram thee with more food!
[*Opens the tomb.*]
Par. This is that banish'd haughty Montague,
That murd'red my love's cousin, with which grief,
It is supposed, the fair creature died;
And here is come to do some villanous shame
To the dead bodies: I will apprehend him.
[*Comes forward.*]
Stop thy unhallowed toil, vile Montague!
Can vengeance be pursued further than death?
Condemned villain, I do apprehend thee:
Obey, and go with me; for thou must die.
Rom. I must indeed; and therefore came I hither.
Good gentle youth, tempt not a desp'rate man;
Fly hence, and leave me: think upon these gone;
Let them affright thee. I beseech thee, youth,
Put not another sin upon my head,
By urging me to fury: O, be gone!
By heaven, I love thee better than myself;
For I come hither arm'd against myself:
Stay not, be gone; live, and hereafter say,
A madman's mercy bid thee run away.
Par. I do defy thy conjurations,
And apprehend thee for a felon here.
Rom. Wilt thou provoke me? then have at thee, boy!
[*They fight.*]
Page. O Lord, they fight! I will go call the watch.
[*Exit.*]
Par. O, I am slain! [*Falls.*] If thou be merciful,
Open the tomb, lay me with Juliet. [*Dies.*]
Rom. In faith, I will. Let me peruse this face.
Mercutio's kinsman, noble County Paris!
What said my man, when my betossed soul
Did not attend him as we rode? I think
He told me Paris should have married Juliet:
Said he not so? or did I dream it so?
Or am I mad, hearing him talk of Juliet,
To think it was so? O, give me thy hand,
One writ with me in sour misfortune's book!
I'll bury thee in a triumphant grave;
A grave? O, no! a lantern, slaught'red youth,
For here lies Juliet, and her beauty makes
This vault a feasting presence full of light.
Death, lie thou there, by a dead man interr'd.
[*Laying Paris in the tomb.*]
How oft when men are at the point of death
Have they been merry! which their keepers call
A lightning before death: O, how may I
Call this a lightning? O my love! my wife!
Death, that hath suck'd the honey of thy breath,
Hath had no power yet upon thy beauty:
Thou art not conquer'd; beauty's ensign yet
Is crimson in thy lips and in thy cheeks,

18. **nice,** trivial. **charge,** importance. 21. **iron crow,** crowbar.
SCENE III. 3. **all along,** at full length. 16. **obsequies,** dutiful acts performed in memory of the dead. 21. **muffle,** hide. 33. **jealous,** suspicious. 44. **doubt,** suspect; see glossary. 45. **womb,** belly. 68. **conjurations,** solemn appeals, which seem perhaps like incantations. 74. **peruse,** scrutinize. 84. **lantern,** a turret full of windows. 86. **presence,** presence chamber. 90. **lightning,** a shedding of light; also, a revival of the spirits. 110. **set up my everlasting rest.** See IV, v, 6.

And death's pale flag is not advanced there.
Tybalt, liest thou there in thy bloody sheet?
O, what more favour can I do to thee,
Than with that hand that cut thy youth in twain
To sunder his that was thine enemy?
Forgive me, cousin! Ah, dear Juliet,
Why art thou yet so fair? shall I believe
That unsubstantial Death is amorous,
And that the lean abhorred monster keeps
Thee here in dark to be his paramour?
For fear of that, I still will stay with thee;
And never from this pallet of dim night
Depart again: here, here will I remain
With worms that are thy chamber-maids; O, here
Will I set up my everlasting rest,
And shake the yoke of inauspicious stars
From this world-wearied flesh. Eyes, look your last!
Arms, take your last embrace! and, lips, O you
The doors of breath, seal with a righteous kiss
A dateless bargain to engrossing death!
Come, bitter conduct, come, unsavoury guide!
Thou desperate pilot, now at once run on
The dashing rocks thy sea-sick weary bark!
Here 's to my love! [*Drinks.*] O true apothecary!
Thy drugs are quick. Thus with a kiss I die. [*Dies.*]

Enter [at the other end of the churchyard] FRIAR [LAURENCE] *with lantern, crow, and spade.*

Fri. L. Saint Francis be my speed! how oft to-night
Have my old feet stumbled at graves! Who 's there?
Bal. Here 's one, a friend, and one that knows you well.
Fri. L. Bliss be upon you! Tell me, good my friend,
What torch is yond, that vainly lends his light
To grubs and eyeless skulls? as I discern,
It burneth in the Capels' monument.
Bal. It doth so, holy sir; and there 's my master,
One that you love.
Fri. L. Who is it?
Bal. Romeo.
Fri. L. How long hath he been there?
Bal. Full half an hour.
Fri. L. Go with me to the vault.
Bal. I dare not, sir:
My master knows not but I am gone hence;
And fearfully did menace me with death,
If I did stay to look on his intents.
Fri. L. Stay, then; I'll go alone. Fear comes upon me:
O, much I fear some ill unthrifty thing.
Bal. As I did sleep under this yew-tree here,
I dreamt my master and another fought,
And that my master slew him.
Fri. L. Romeo! [*Advances.*]
Alack, alack, what blood is this, which stains
The stony entrance of this sepulchre?
What mean these masterless and gory swords
To lie discolour'd by this place of peace? [*Enters the tomb.*]
Romeo! O, pale! Who else? what, Paris too?
And steep'd in blood? Ah, what an unkind hour
Is guilty of this lamentable chance!
The lady stirs. [*Juliet wakes.*]

Jul. O comfortable friar! where is my lord?
I do remember well where I should be,
And there I am. Where is my Romeo? [*Noise within.*]
Fri. L. I hear some noise. Lady, come from that nest
Of death, contagion, and unnatural sleep:
A greater power than we can contradict
Hath thwarted our intents. Come, come away.
Thy husband in thy bosom there lies dead;
And Paris too. Come, I'll dispose of thee
Among a sisterhood of holy nuns:
Stay not to question, for the watch is coming;
Come, go, good Juliet [*Noise again*], I dare no longer stay.
Jul. Go, get thee hence, for I will not away.
Exit [*Fri. L.*].
What 's here? a cup, clos'd in my true love's hand?
Poison, I see, hath been his timeless end:
O churl! drunk all, and left no friendly drop
To help me after? I will kiss thy lips;
Haply some poison yet doth hang on them,
To make me die with a restorative. [*Kisses him.*]
Thy lips are warm.
First Watch. [*Within*] Lead, boy: which way?
Jul. Yea, noise? then I'll be brief. O happy dagger!
[*Snatching Romeo's dagger.*]
This is thy sheath [*Stabs herself*]; there rust, and let me die. [*Falls on Romeo's body, and dies.*]

Enter [PARIS'] Boy *and* Watch.

Page. This is the place; there, where the torch doth burn.
First Watch. The ground is bloody; search about the churchyard:
Go, some of you, whoe'er you find attach.
Pitiful sight! here lies the county slain;
And Juliet bleeding, warm, and newly dead,
Who here hath lain these two days buried.
Go, tell the prince: run to the Capulets:
Raise up the Montagues: some others search:
We see the ground whereon these woes do lie;
But the true ground of all these piteous woes
We cannot without circumstance descry.

Enter [some of the Watch, *with*]ROMEO'S *Man* [BALTHASAR].

Sec. Watch. Here 's Romeo's man; we found him in the churchyard.
First Watch. Hold him in safety, till the prince come hither.

Enter FRIAR [LAURENCE], *and another* Watchman.

Third Watch. Here is a friar, that trembles, sighs, and weeps:
We took this mattock and this spade from him,
As he was coming from this churchyard side.
First Watch. A great suspicion: stay the friar too.

Enter the PRINCE [*and* Attendants].

Prince. What misadventure is so early up,
That calls our person from our morning's rest?

Enter CAPULET *and his* Wife [*with others*].

Cap. What should it be, that is so shriek'd abroad?
La. Cap. O, the people in the street cry Romeo,

The meaning is, "make my final determination," with allusion also to the idea of repose. 115. **dateless,** everlasting. **engrossing,** monopolizing. 121. **speed,** protector and assistant; see glossary. 122. **stumbled at graves,** a bad omen. 137. **yew-,** so Pope; Q_2F: *yong.*

162. **timeless,** everlasting, or untimely. 165. **Haply,** perhaps. 173. **attach,** arrest; see glossary.

Some Juliet, and some Paris; and all run,
With open outcry, toward our monument.
Prince. What fear is this which startles in our ears?
First Watch. Sovereign, here lies the County Paris slain;
And Romeo dead; and Juliet, dead before,
Warm and new kill'd.
Prince. Search, seek, and know how this foul murder comes.
First Watch. Here is a friar, and slaughter'd Romeo's man;
With instruments upon them, fit to open
These dead men's tombs.
Cap. O heavens! O wife, look how our daughter bleeds!
This dagger hath mista'en,—for, lo, his house
Is empty on the back of Montague,—
And it mis-sheathed in my daughter's bosom!
La. Cap. O me! this sight of death is as a bell,
That warns my old age to a sepulchre.

Enter MONTAGUE [*and others*].

Prince. Come, Montague; for thou art early up,
To see thy son and heir more early down.
Mon. Alas, my liege, my wife is dead tonight;
Grief of my son's exile hath stopp'd her breath:
What further woe conspires against mine age?
Prince. Look, and thou shalt see.
Mon. O thou untaught! what manners is in this,
To press before thy father to a grave?
Prince. Seal up the mouth of outrage for a while,
Till we can clear these ambiguities,
And know their spring, their head, their true descent;
And then will I be general of your woes,
And lead you even to death: meantime forbear,
And let mischance be slave to patience.
Bring forth the parties of suspicion.
Fri. L. I am the greatest, able to do least,
Yet most suspected, as the time and place
Doth make against me, of this direful murder:
And here I stand, both to impeach and purge
Myself condemned and myself excus'd.
Prince. Then say at once what thou dost know in this.
Fri. L. I will be brief, for my short date of breath
Is not so long as is a tedious tale.
Romeo, there dead, was husband to that Juliet;
And she, there dead, that Romeo's faithful wife:
I married them; and their stol'n marriage-day
Was Tybalt's dooms-day, whose untimely death
Banish'd the new-made bridegroom from this city,
For whom, and not for Tybalt, Juliet pin'd.
You, to remove that siege of grief from her,
Betroth'd and would have married her perforce
To County Paris: then comes she to me,
And, with wild looks, bid me devise some mean
To rid her from this second marriage,
Or in my cell there would she kill herself.
Then gave I her, so tutor'd by my art,
A sleeping potion; which so took effect
As I intended, for it wrought on her
The form of death: meantime I writ to Romeo,
That he should hither come as this dire night,
To help to take her from her borrowed grave,
Being the time the potion's force should cease.
But he which bore my letter, Friar John,
Was stay'd by accident, and yesternight
Return'd my letter back. Then all alone
At the prefixed hour of her waking,
Came I to take her from her kindred's vault;
Meaning to keep her closely at my cell,
Till I conveniently could send to Romeo:
But when I came, some minute ere the time
Of her awakening, here untimely lay
The noble Paris and true Romeo dead.
She wakes; and I entreated her come forth,
And bear this work of heaven with patience:
But then a noise did scare me from the tomb;
And she, too desperate, would not go with me,
But, as it seems, did violence on herself.
All this I know; and to the marriage
Her nurse is privy: and, if aught in this
Miscarried by my fault, let my old life
Be sacrific'd, some hour before his time,
Unto the rigour of severest law.
Prince. We still have known thee for a holy man.
Where 's Romeo's man? what can he say in this?
Bal. I brought my master news of Juliet's death;
And then in post he came from Mantua
To this same place, to this same monument.
This letter he early bid me give his father,
And threat'ned me with death, going in the vault,
If I departed not and left him there.
Prince. Give me the letter; I will look on it.
Where is the county's page, that rais'd the watch?
Sirrah, what made your master in this place?
Page. He came with flowers to strew his lady's grave;
And bid me stand aloof, and so I did:
Anon comes one with light to ope the tomb;
And by and by my master drew on him;
And then I ran away to call the watch.
Prince. This letter doth make good the friar's words,
Their course of love, the tidings of her death:
And here he writes that he did buy a poison
Of a poor 'pothecary, and therewithal
Came to this vault to die, and lie with Juliet.
Where be these enemies? Capulet! Montague!
See, what a scourge is laid upon your hate,
That heaven finds means to kill your joys with love.
And I for winking at your discords too
Have lost a brace of kinsmen: all are punish'd.
Cap. O brother Montague, give me thy hand:
This is my daughter's jointure, for no more
Can I demand.
Mon. But I can give thee more:
For I will raise her statue in pure gold;
That whiles Verona by that name is known,
There shall no figure at such rate be set
As that of true and faithful Juliet.
Cap. As rich shall Romeo's by his lady's lie;
Poor sacrifices of our enmity!
Prince. A glooming peace this morning with it brings;
The sun, for sorrow, will not show his head:
Go hence, to have more talk of these sad things;
Some shall be pardon'd, and some punished:
For never was a story of more woe
Than this of Juliet and her Romeo. [*Exeunt.*]

203. **house,** scabbard. 216. **outrage,** outcry. 226. **purge,** purify, cleanse. 247. **as this,** this very. 253. **prefixed,** agreed upon previously. 255. **closely,** secretly. 273. **post,** haste; see glossary. 297. **jointure,** marriage portion. 301. **rate,** value; see glossary.

VENUS AND ADONIS

Like most of his contemporaries, Shakespeare apparently did not regard the writing of plays as an elegant literary pursuit. He must have known that he was good at it, and he certainly became famous in his day as a playwright, but he took no pains over the publication of his plays. We have no literary prefaces for them, no indication that Shakespeare saw them through the press. Writing for the theatre was rather like writing for the movies today, a profitable and even glamorous venture but subliterary. When Ben Jonson brought out his collected *Works* (mostly plays) during his lifetime, he was jeered at for pretentiousness.

The writing of sonnets and other "serious" poetry, on the other hand, was conventionally a bid for true literary fame. Shakespeare's prefatory epistle to his *Venus and Adonis* betrays an eagerness for recognition. Deferentially he seeks the sponsorship of the Earl of Southampton, in hopes of cachet as well as financial support. He speaks of *Venus and Adonis* as "the first heir of my invention," as though he had written no plays earlier, and promises Southampton a "graver labour" to appear shortly. *Venus and Adonis* in 1593 and *The Rape of Lucrece* in 1594 were in fact Shakespeare's first publications. Both were carefully and correctly printed. They were probably composed between June of 1592 and May of 1594, a period when the theatres were closed because of the plague. Shakespeare's belief in their importance to his literary career is confirmed by the reports of his contemporaries. Richard Barnfield singled them out as the works most likely to assure a place for Shakespeare in "fames immortall Booke." Francis Meres exclaimed in 1598 that "the sweete wittie soule of *Ouid* liues in mellifluous & hony-tongued *Shakespeare*, witnes his *Venus* and *Adonis*, his *Lucrece*, his sugred Sonnets among his priuate friends, &c." Gabriel Harvey, although preferring *Lucrece* and *Hamlet* as more pleasing to "the wiser sort," conceded that "the younger sort takes much delight in Shakespeares Venus, & Adonis." John Weever and still others add further testimonials to the extraordinary reputation of Shakespeare's nondramatic poems.

As Gabriel Harvey's puritanical comment on *Venus and Adonis* suggests, this poem was regarded as amatory and even risqué. It mirrored a current vogue for Ovidian erotic poetry, as exemplified by Thomas Lodge's *Scilla's Metamorphosis*, 1589 (in which an amorous nymph courts a reluctant young man), and by Christopher Marlowe's *Hero and Leander*. This latter poem, left unfinished at Marlowe's death in 1593 and published in 1598 with a continuation by George Chapman, was evidently circulated in manuscript as were so many poems of this sophisticated sort (including Shakespeare's sonnets). Shakespeare may well have been influenced by Marlowe's tone of wryly comic detachment and sensuous grace. He may also have read Michael Drayton's *Endimion and Phoebe* (published 1595 but written earlier), in which the erotic tradition is somewhat idealized into moral allegory. Most importantly, however, Shakespeare knew his Ovid, both firsthand and in Golding's English translation (1567). He appears to have combined three mythical tales from the *Metamorphoses*. The narrative outline is to be found in Venus' pursuit of Adonis (Book X), but the bashful reluctance of the young man is more reminiscent of Hermaphroditus (Book IV) and Narcissus (Book III). Hermaphroditus pleads youth as his reason for wishing to escape the clutches of the water-nymph Salmacis, and so is transformed with her into a single body containing both sexes; Narcissus evades the nymph Echo out of self-infatuation. Shakespeare has thus drawn a composite portrait of male coyness, a subject he was to explore further in the sonnets. Such a theme was suited to a nobleman of Southampton's youth and prospects. In tone it was also well suited to the aristocratic and intellectual set who read such poetry. Shakespeare here aimed at a more elegant clientele than that for which he wrote plays. The ornate qualities of *Venus and Adonis* should be judged in the fashionable context of a sophisticated audience.

Essentially, the poem is a tour de force of stylized poetic techniques. The story itself is relatively insignificant, and the characters are static. For two-thirds of the poem, very little happens other than a series of amorous claspings from which Adonis feebly attempts to extricate himself. Even his subsequent fight with the boar and his violent death are occasions for rhetorical pathos rather than for vivid narrative description. The story is merely a frame. Similarly, we must not expect psychological insight or meaningful self-discovery. The conventions of this sort of erotic love poetry do not encourage a serious interest in character. Venus and Adonis are mouthpieces for two contrasting attitudes toward love. They debate a favorite courtly topic in the style of John Lyly. Both parties appeal to conventional wisdom and speak in *sententiae*, or aphoristic pronouncements. Venus, for example, warning Adonis of the need for caution in pursuing the boar, opines that "Danger deviseth shifts, wit waits on fear" (690). Adonis, pleading his unreadiness for love, cites commonplace analogies: "No fisher but the ungrown fry forbears. The mellow plum doth fall, the green sticks fast" (526–527). In substance, their arguments are equally stereotyped. Venus urges a *carpe diem* philosophy of seizing the moment of pleasure. "Make use of time, let not advantage slip; Beauty within itself should not be wasted" (129–130). She bolsters her claim with an appeal to the "law of nature," according to which all living things are obliged to reproduce themselves; only by such begetting can man conquer time and death. Yet however close this position may be to a major theme of the sonnets, it does not go unchallenged. Adonis can plausibly charge that Venus is only rationalizing her lustful desires: "O strange excuse, When reason is the bawd to lust's abuse!" (791–792). His plea for more time in which to mature and prove his manliness is commendable, however much we may smile at his inability to be aroused by Venus' blandishments. Thus, neither contestant wins the argument. Venus is proved right in her fear that Adonis will be killed by the boar he hunts, but Adonis' rejection of idle lust for manly activity affirms a conventional truth. The debate is really an ingeniously elaborate literary exercise, not a moral object lesson.

The author's persona does little to remove the ambivalence in the debate. He too speaks in *sententiae*, but his aphorisms appear to sympathize with both contestants. At times, he affirms the irresistible force of love: "What though the rose have prickles, yet 'tis plucked" (574). At other times he laughs at Venus for her vacillation of mood: "Thy weal and woe are both of them extremes; Despair and hope makes thee ridiculous" (987–988). Like Ovid's usual persona, the speaker here is both intrigued and amused by love, compelled to heed its power and yet aware of the absurdities. The result is a characteristic Ovidian blend of irony and pathos. The irony is especially evident in the delightful comic touches which consistently undermine the potential seriousness of the action: Venus like an Amazon pulling Adonis off his mount and tucking him under one arm, pouting and blushing; Adonis' horse chasing away after a mare in heat, leaving Adonis to fend for himself; Venus fainting at the thought of the boar and pulling Adonis right on top of her, "in the very lists of love, Her champion mounted for the hot encounter" (595–596). These devices "distance" us from the action and create an atmosphere of elegant entertainment. Yet the poem is also suffused with a rich pathos that invites us to revel in sensuous emotion. The sensuousness would cloy without the ironic humor, whereas the humor would seem frivolous without the pathos.

The poem often hints at moral allegory, in the manner of Ovidian mythologizing. Venus represents herself as the goddess not only of erotic passion but of eternal love conquering time and death. Because Adonis perversely spurns this ideal, Venus concludes that human beauty must perish and that man's happiness must be subject to mischance. Yet this reading emerges only fitfully, and is contradicted by an entirely opposite suggestion that Adonis is the rational principle attempting unsuccessfully to govern man's libidinal impulses (the boar, and Adonis' unbridled horse). These contradictions, which derive from the debate structure of the poem, confirm our impression that the allegory is merely decorative. It elevates the tone, adding poetic dignity to what might otherwise appear to be an unabashedly erotic poem. We should not minimize the sexual teasing, or fail to acknowledge our own erotic pleasure in it. Venus' repeated encounters with Adonis take the form of ingeniously varied love positions, ending in coital embrace although without consummation. Adonis' passive role invites the male reader to fantasize himself in Adonis' place, being seduced by the goddess of beauty. The famous passage comparing Venus' body to a deer park with "pleasant fountains," "sweet bottom-grass," and "round rising hillocks" (229–240) is, through the use of double entendre, genitally explicit without being pornographic. The poem is equally explicit in its appeal to a "banquet" of the five senses (433–450). This is the "naughty" Ovid of the *Ars Amatoria*.

Most of all, however, Shakespeare's poem is an embroidery of poetic flourishes, of "conceits" or ingeniously wrought similes, of artfully constructed digressions such as the narrative of Adonis' horse and of color symbolism. Images are usually drawn from nature (eagles, birds caught in nets, wolves, berries) or connote burning, blazing, and shining (torches, jewels). The dominant colors are red and white, usually paired antithetically: the red of the rising sun or Adonis' blushing face or Mars' ensign, the white of an alabaster hand or fresh bed linen or "ashy-pale" anger. Ironically, too, the boar's frothy-white mouth is stained with red, and Adonis' red blood blemishes his "wonted lily white." Adonis' flower, the anemone, is reddish-purple and white. A similarly balanced antithesis pervades virtually all the play's rhetorical figures, as in the symmetrical repetition of words in grammatically parallel phrases (*parison*), or in phrases of equal length (*isocolon*), or in inverted order (*antimetabole*), or at the beginning and ending of a line (*epanalepsis*), and so on. These pyrotechnics seem mechanical to us today, but one can still appreciate the uninhibited zeal of Shakespeare's first bid for poetic fame.

VENUS AND ADONIS

'Vilia miretur vulgus; mihi flavus Apollo
Pocula Castalia plena ministret aqua.'

TO THE

RIGHT HONOURABLE
HENRY WRIOTHESLEY,

EARL OF SOUTHAMPTON,
AND BARON OF TICHFIELD.

RIGHT HONOURABLE

I KNOW not how I shall offend in dedicating my unpolished lines to your lordship, nor how the world will censure me for choosing so strong a prop to support so weak a burden: only if your honour seem but pleased, I account myself highly praised, and vow to take advantage of all idle hours, till I have honoured you with some graver labour. But if the first heir of my invention prove deformed, I shall be sorry it had so noble a godfather, and never after ear so barren a land, for fear it yield me still so bad a harvest. I leave it to your honourable survey, and your honour to your heart's content; which I wish may always answer your own wish and the world's hopeful expectation.

Your honour's in all duty,

WILLIAM SHAKESPEARE.

Even as the sun with purple-colour'd face
Had ta'en his last leave of the weeping morn,
Rose-cheek'd Adonis hied him to the chase;
Hunting he lov'd, but love he laugh'd to scorn;
  Sick-thoughted Venus makes amain unto him,
  And like a bold-fac'd suitor 'gins to woo him.

'Thrice-fairer than myself,' thus she began,
'The field's chief flower, sweet above compare,
Stain to all nymphs, more lovely than a man,
More white and red than doves or roses are;
  Nature that made thee, with herself at strife,
  Saith that the world hath ending with thy life.

'Vouchsafe, thou wonder, to alight thy steed,
And rein his proud head to the saddle-bow;
If thou wilt deign this favour, for thy meed
A thousand honey secrets shalt thou know:
  Here come and sit, where never serpent hisses,
  And being set, I'll smother thee with kisses;

'And yet not cloy thy lips with loath'd satiety,
But rather famish them amid their plenty,
Making them red and pale with fresh variety,
Ten kisses short as one, one long as twenty:
  A summer's day will seem an hour but short,
  Being wasted in such time-beguiling sport.'

With this she seizeth on his sweating palm,
The precedent of pith and livelihood,
And trembling in her passion, calls it balm,
Earth's sovereign salve to do a goddess good:
  Being so enrag'd, desire doth lend her force
  Courageously to pluck him from his horse.

Over one arm the lusty courser's rein,
Under her other was the tender boy,
Who blush'd and pouted in a dull disdain,
With leaden appetite, unapt to toy;
  She red and hot as coals of glowing fire,
  He red for shame, but frosty in desire.

The studded bridle on a ragged bough
Nimbly she fastens:—O, how quick is love!—
The steed is stalled up, and even now
To tie the rider she begins to prove:
  Backward she push'd him, as she would be thrust,
  And govern'd him in strength, though not in lust.

So soon was she along as he was down,
Each leaning on their elbows and their hips:
Now doth she stroke his cheek, now doth he frown,
And 'gins to chide, but soon she stops his lips;
  And kissing speaks, with lustful language broken,
  'If thou wilt chide, thy lips shall never open.'

He burns with bashful shame: she with her tears
Doth quench the maiden burning of his cheeks:
Then with her windy sighs and golden hairs
To fan and blow them dry again she seeks:
  He saith she is immodest, blames her 'miss;
  What follows more she murders with a kiss.

Even as an empty eagle, sharp by fast,
Tires with her beak on feathers, flesh and bone,
Shaking her wings, devouring all in haste,
Till either gorge be stuff'd or prey be gone;
  Even so she kiss'd his brow, his cheek, his chin,
  And where she ends she doth anew begin.

Forc'd to content, but never to obey,
Panting he lies and breatheth in her face;
She feedeth on the steam as on a prey,
And calls it heavenly moisture, air of grace;
  Wishing her cheeks were gardens full of flowers,
  So they were dew'd with such distilling showers.

MOTTO: **Vilia miretur,** etc. Let the base vulgar admire trash; may golden-haired Apollo serve me goblets filled from the Castalian spring (Ovid, *Amores*, I, xv, 35-36).

DEDICATION: **Henry Wriothesley, Earl of Southampton,** a popular and brilliant young gentleman of nineteen years, already prominent at court. Subsequent dedications by Shakespeare and others indicate that he was a genuinely devoted patron of literature throughout his life. 10. **the first . . . invention.** This phrase has been variously interpreted to mean Shakespeare's first written work, his first printed work, his first "invented" work (recognizing that the plots of his plays were unoriginal), his first work independent of collaborators, his first "literary" work (recognizing plays to be uniliterary in the Elizabethan sense). The second and last are the most probable interpretations. 12. **ear,** plough, till.

THE POEM. 1. **purple-colour'd,** i.e., red. 5. **Sick-thoughted,** oppressed with desire. **makes amain,** hastens. 9. **Stain to,** eclipsing. 11-12. **Nature . . . life,** nature strove to surpass herself in making her masterpiece, Adonis, and if he dies will cease to work (Pooler). 15. **meed,** reward. 25-26. **sweating . . . livelihood.** Cf. *Othello*, III, iv, 36-43. 29. **enrag'd,** ardent. 34. **toy,** dally amorously. 39. **stalled,** fastened, secured. 40. **prove,** try. 53. **'miss,** amiss, offense. 55. **by fast,** as a result of fasting. 56. **Tires,** tears, feeds upon ravenously. 61. **content,** acquiesce.

Look how a bird lies tangled in a net,
So fast'ned in her arms Adonis lies;
Pure shame and aw'd resistance made him fret,
Which bred more beauty in his angry eyes:
Rain added to a river that is rank
Perforce will force it overflow the bank.

Still she entreats, and prettily entreats,
For to a pretty ear she tunes her tale;
Still is he sullen, still he lours and frets,
'Twixt crimson shame and anger ashy-pale:
Being red, she loves him best; and being white,
Her best is better'd with a more delight.

Look how he can, she cannot choose but love;
And by her fair immortal hand she swears,
From his soft bosom never to remove,
Till he take truce with her contending tears,
Which long have rain'd, making her cheeks all wet;
And one sweet kiss shall pay this comptless debt.

Upon this promise did he raise his chin,
Like a dive-dapper peering through a wave,
Who, being look'd on, ducks as quickly in;
So offers he to give what she did crave;
But when her lips were ready for his pay,
He winks, and turns his lips another way.

Never did passenger in summer's heat
More thirst for drink than she for this good turn.
Her help she sees, but help she cannot get;
She bathes in water, yet her fire must burn:
'O, pity,' 'gan she cry, 'flint-hearted boy!
'Tis but a kiss I beg; why art thou coy?

'I have been woo'd, as I entreat thee now,
Even by the stern and direful god of war,
Whose sinewy neck in battle ne'er did bow,
Who conquers where he comes in every jar;
Yet hath he been my captive and my slave,
And begg'd for that which thou unask'd shalt have.

'Over my altars hath he hung his lance,
His batt'red shield, his uncontrolled crest,
And for my sake hath learn'd to sport and dance,
To toy, to wanton, dally, smile and jest,
Scorning his churlish drum and ensign red,
Making my arms his field, his tent my bed.

'Thus he that overrul'd I overswayed,
Leading him prisoner in a red-rose chain:
Strong-temper'd steel his stronger strength obeyed,
Yet was he servile to my coy disdain.
O, be not proud, nor brag not of thy might,
For mast'ring her that foil'd the god of fight!

'Touch but my lips with those fair lips of thine,—
Though mine be not so fair, yet are they red—
The kiss shall be thine own as well as mine.
What seest thou in the ground? hold up thy head:
Look in mine eye-balls, there thy beauty lies;
Then why not lips on lips, since eyes in eyes?

'Art thou asham'd to kiss? then wink again,
And I will wink; so shall the day seem night;
Love keeps his revels where there are but twain;
Be bold to play, our sport is not in sight:
These blue-vein'd violets whereon we lean
Never can blab, nor know not what we mean.

'The tender spring upon thy tempting lip
Shows thee unripe; yet mayst thou well be tasted:
Make use of time, let not advantage slip;
Beauty within itself should not be wasted:
Fair flowers that are not gath'red in their prime
Rot and consume themselves in little time.

'Were I hard-favour'd, foul, or wrinkled-old,
Ill-nurtur'd, crooked, churlish, harsh in voice,
O'erworn, despised, rheumatic and cold,
Thick-sighted, barren, lean and lacking juice,
Then mightst thou pause, for then I were not for thee;
But having no defects, why dost abhor me?

'Thou canst not see one wrinkle in my brow;
Mine eyes are gray and bright and quick in turning;
My beauty as the spring doth yearly grow,
My flesh is soft and plump, my marrow burning;
My smooth moist hand, were it with thy hand felt,
Would in thy palm dissolve, or seem to melt.

'Bid me discourse, I will enchant thine ear,
Or, like a fairy, trip upon the green,
Or, like a nymph, with long dishevelled hair,
Dance on the sands, and yet no footing seen:
Love is a spirit all compact of fire,
Not gross to sink, but light, and will aspire.

'Witness this primrose bank whereon I lie;
These forceless flowers like sturdy trees support me;
Two strengthless doves will draw me through the sky,
From morn till night, even where I list to sport me:
Is love so light, sweet boy, and may it be
That thou shouldst think it heavy unto thee?

'Is thine own heart to thine own face affected?
Can thy right hand seize love upon thy left?
Then woo thyself, be of thyself rejected,
Steal thine own freedom and complain on theft.
Narcissus so himself himself forsook,
And died to kiss his shadow in the brook.

'Torches are made to light, jewels to wear,
Dainties to taste, fresh beauty for the use,
Herbs for their smell, and sappy plants to bear;
Things growing to themselves are growth's abuse:
Seeds spring from seeds and beauty breedeth beauty;
Thou wast begot; to get it is thy duty.

'Upon the earth's increase why shouldst thou feed,
Unless the earth with thy increase be fed?
By law of nature thou art bound to breed,

69. **aw'd resistance,** resistance which arises from modest timidity (Delius). 71. **rank,** full. 84. **comptless,** countless. 86. **dive-dapper,** the dabchick, a common English water bird. 90. **winks,** to shut the eyes or to have them closed (most editors); Lee and W. J. Craig thought the word akin etymologically to "wince"; see glossary. 91. **passenger,** wayfarer. 100. **jar,** fight. 104. **uncontrolled,** unconquered, i.e., never bowed in acknowledgment to a superior. 127. **spring,** growth (i.e., a coming beard). 131-132. **Fair . . . time,** a conventional idea in the love poetry of the Renaissance. 136. **Thick-sighted,** dim-eyed. 148. **footing,** footprints. 150. **aspire,** rise. 152. **forceless,** frail. 157. **affected,** drawn by affection. 161. **Narcissus . . . forsook,** allusion to the story of the beautiful youth who fell in love with his reflection and,

That thine may live when thou thyself art dead;
And so, in spite of death, thou dost survive,
In that thy likeness still is left alive.'

By this the love-sick queen began to sweat,
For where they lay the shadow had forsook them,
And Titan, tired in the mid-day heat,
With burning eye did hotly overlook them;
Wishing Adonis had his team to guide,
So he were like him and by Venus' side.

And now Adonis, with a lazy spright,
And with a heavy, dark, disliking eye,
His louring brows o'erwhelming his fair sight,
Like misty vapours when they blot the sky,
Souring his cheeks cries 'Fie, no more of love!
The sun doth burn my face; I must remove.'

'Ay me,' quoth Venus, 'young, and so unkind?
What bare excuses mak'st thou to be gone!
I'll sigh celestial breath, whose gentle wind
Shall cool the heat of this descending sun:
I'll make a shadow for thee of my hairs;
If they burn too, I'll quench them with my tears.

'The sun that shines from heaven shines but warm,
And, lo, I lie between that sun and thee:
The heat I have from thence doth little harm,
Thine eye darts forth the fire that burneth me;
And were I not immortal, life were done
Between this heavenly and earthly sun.

'Art thou obdurate, flinty, hard as steel,
Nay, more than flint, for stone at rain relenteth?
Art thou a woman's son, and canst not feel
What 'tis to love? how want of love tormenteth?
O, had thy mother borne so hard a mind,
She had not brought forth thee, but died unkind.

'What am I, that thou shouldst contemn me this?
Or what great danger dwells upon my suit?
What were thy lips the worse for one poor kiss?
Speak, fair; but speak fair words, or else be mute:
Give me one kiss, I'll give it thee again,
And one for int'rest, if thou wilt have twain.

'Fie, lifeless picture, cold and senseless stone,
Well-painted idol, image dull and dead,
Statue contenting but the eye alone,
Thing like a man, but of no woman bred!
Thou art no man, though of a man's complexion,
For men will kiss even by their own direction.'

This said, impatience chokes her pleading tongue,
And swelling passion doth provoke a pause;
Red cheeks and fiery eyes blaze forth her wrong;
Being judge in love, she cannot right her cause:
And now she weeps, and now she fain would speak,
And now her sobs do her intendments break.

Sometime she shakes her head and then his hand,
Now gazeth she on him, now on the ground;
Sometime her arms infold him like a band:
She would, he will not in her arms be bound;
And when from thence he struggles to be gone,
She locks her lily fingers one in one.

'Fondling,' she saith, 'since I have hemm'd thee here
Within the circuit of this ivory pale,
I'll be a park, and thou shalt be my deer;
Feed where thou wilt, on mountain or in dale:
Graze on my lips; and if those hills be dry,
Stray lower, where the pleasant fountains lie.

'Within this limit is relief enough,
Sweet bottom-grass and high delightful plain,
Round rising hillocks, brakes obscure and rough,
To shelter thee from tempest and from rain:
Then be my deer, since I am such a park;
No dog shall rouse thee, though a thousand bark.'

At this Adonis smiles as in disdain,
That in each cheek appears a pretty dimple:
Love made those hollows, if himself were slain,
He might be buried in a tomb so simple;
Foreknowing well, if there he came to lie,
Why, there Love liv'd and there he could not die.

These lovely caves, these round enchanting pits,
Open'd their mouths to swallow Venus' liking.
Being mad before, how doth she now for wits?
Struck dead at first, what needs a second striking?
Poor queen of love, in thine own law forlorn,
To love a cheek that smiles at thee in scorn!

Now which way shall she turn? what shall she say?
Her words are done, her woes the more increasing;
The time is spent, her object will away,
And from her twining arms doth urge releasing.
'Pity,' she cries, 'some favour, some remorse!'
Away he springs and hasteth to his horse.

But, lo, from forth a copse that neighbours by,
A breeding jennet, lusty, young and proud,
Adonis' trampling courser doth espy,
And forth she rushes, snorts and neighs aloud:
The strong-neck'd steed, being tied unto a tree,
Breaketh his rein, and to her straight goes he.

Imperiously he leaps, he neighs, he bounds,
And now his woven girths he breaks asunder;
The bearing earth with his hard hoof he wounds,
Whose hollow womb resounds like heaven's thunder;
The iron bit he crusheth 'tween his teeth,
Controlling what he was controlled with.

His ears up-prick'd; his braided hanging mane
Upon his compass'd crest now stand on end;
His nostrils drink the air, and forth again,
As from a furnace, vapours doth he send:
His eye, which scornfully glisters like fire,
Shows his hot courage and his high desire.

for standing over a pool admiring himself, was punished by being changed into a flower. 177. **Titan,** the sun god. **tired,** attired. 183. **o'erwhelming,** overhanging, so as to cover. **sight,** eyes. 185. **Souring,** looking sullen. 188. **bare,** shamelessly inadequate (Pooler). 205. **contemn,** refuse scornfully. 219. **blaze,** metaphorical, her eyes appear to burn. 222. **intendments,** intention to speak. 230. **pale,** fence (i.e., her arms; the sexual topography is continued in *fountains, bottom-grass, hillocks, brakes,* etc.). 236. **bottom-grass,** grass growing in low valleys. 240. **rouse,** to cause to stir from his lair. 243. **if,** so that if. 248. **liking,** desire. 260. **jennet,** small Spanish horse. 272. **compass'd,** arched by clipping (Pooler).

Sometime he trots, as if he told the steps,
With gentle majesty and modest pride;
Anon he rears upright, curvets and leaps,
As who should say 'Lo, thus my strength is tried,
  And this I do to captivate the eye
  Of the fair breeder that is standing by.'

What recketh he his rider's angry stir,
His flattering 'Holla,' or his 'Stand, I say'?
What cares he now for curb or pricking spur?
For rich caparisons or trapping gay?
  He sees his love, and nothing else he sees,
  For nothing else with his proud sight agrees.

Look when a painter would surpass the life,
In limning out a well-proportioned steed,
His art with nature's workmanship at strife,
As if the dead the living should exceed;
  So did this horse excel a common one
  In shape, in courage, colour, pace and bone.

Round-hoof'd, short-jointed, fetlocks shag and long,
Broad breast, full eye, small head and nostril wide,
High crest, short ears, straight legs and passing strong,
Thin mane, thick tail, broad buttock, tender hide:
  Look what a horse should have he did not lack,
  Save a proud rider on so proud a back.

Sometime he scuds far off and there he stares;
Anon he starts at stirring of a feather;
To bid the wind a base he now prepares,
And whe'r he run or fly they know not whether;
  For through his mane and tail the high wind sings,
  Fanning the hairs, who wave like feath'red wings.

He looks upon his love and neighs unto her;
She answers him as if she knew his mind:
Being proud, as females are, to see him woo her,
She puts on outward strangeness, seems unkind,
  Spurns at his love and scorns the heat he feels,
  Beating his kind embracements with her heels.

Then, like a melancholy malcontent,
He vails his tail that, like a falling plume,
Cool shadow to his melting buttock lent:
He stamps and bites the poor flies in his fume.
  His love, perceiving how he is enrag'd,
  Grew kinder, and his fury was assuag'd.

His testy master goeth about to take him;
When, lo, the unback'd breeder, full of fear,
Jealous of catching, swiftly doth forsake him,
With her the horse, and left Adonis there:
  As they were mad, unto the wood they hie them,
  Out-stripping crows that strive to over-fly them.

All swoln with chafing, down Adonis sits,
Banning his boist'rous and unruly beast:
And now the happy season once more fits,
That love-sick Love by pleading may be blest;
  For lovers say, the heart hath treble wrong
  When it is barr'd the aidance of the tongue.

An oven that is stopp'd, or river stay'd,
Burneth more hotly, swelleth with more rage:
So of concealed sorrow may be said;
Free vent of words love's fire doth assuage;
  But when the heart's attorney once is mute,
  The client breaks, as desperate in his suit.

He sees her coming, and begins to glow,
Even as a dying coal revives with wind,
And with his bonnet hides his angry brow;
Looks on the dull earth with disturbed mind,
  Taking no notice that she is so nigh,
  For all askance he holds her in his eye.

O, what a sight it was, wistly to view
How she came stealing to the wayward boy!
To note the fighting conflict of her hue,
How white and red each other did destroy!
  But now her cheek was pale, and by and by
  It flash'd forth fire, as lightning from the sky.

Now was she just before him as he sat,
And like a lowly lover down she kneels;
With one fair hand she heaveth up his hat,
Her other tender hand his fair cheek feels:
  His tend'rer cheek receives her soft hand's print,
  As apt as new-fall'n snow takes any dint.

O, what a war of looks was then between them!
Her eyes petitioners to his eyes suing;
His eyes saw her eyes as they had not seen them;
Her eyes woo'd still, his eyes disdain'd the wooing:
  And all this dumb play had his acts made plain
  With tears, which, chorus-like, her eyes did rain.

Full gently now she takes him by the hand,
A lily prison'd in a gaol of snow,
Or ivory in an alabaster band;
So white a friend engirts so white a foe:
  This beauteous combat, wilful and unwilling,
  Show'd like two silver doves that sit a-billing.

Once more the engine of her thoughts began:
'O fairest mover on this mortal round,
Would thou wert as I am, and I a man,
My heart all whole as thine, thy heart my wound;
  For one sweet look thy help I would assure thee,
  Though nothing but my body's bane would cure
      thee.'

'Give me my hand,' saith he, 'why dost thou feel it?'
'Give me my heart,' saith she, 'and thou shalt have it;
O, give it me, lest thy hard heart do steel it,
And being steel'd, soft sighs can never grave it:
  Then love's deep groans I never shall regard,
  Because Adonis' heart hath made mine hard.'

'For shame,' he cries, 'let go, and let me go;
My day's delight is past, my horse is gone,
And 'tis your fault I am bereft him so:
I pray you hence, and leave me here alone;
  For all my mind, my thought, my busy care,
  Is how to get my palfrey from the mare.'

277. **told,** numbered. 289. **Look when,** just as. 303. **bid the wind a base,** challenge the wind, metaphor from the boys' game of prisoner's base. 304. **whe'r,** whether. 310. **strangeness,** seeming coyness. 314. **vails,** lowers. 319. **goeth about,** makes an effort. 326. **Banning,** cursing. 335. **heart's attorney,** i.e., the tongue. 343. **wistly,** earnestly, attentively. 357. **as,** as if. 367. **engine of her thoughts,** i.e., her tongue. 368. **mortal round,** earth. 370. **thy heart my wound,** thy heart wounded as mine is. 372. **bane,** ruin. 376. **grave,** engrave.

Thus she replies: 'Thy palfrey, as he should,
Welcomes the warm approach of sweet desire:
Affection is a coal that must be cool'd;
Else, suffer'd, it will set the heart on fire:
  The sea hath bounds, but deep desire hath none;
  Therefore no marvel though thy horse be gone.

'How like a jade he stood, tied to the tree,
Servilely master'd with a leathern rein!
But when he saw his love, his youth's fair fee,
He held such petty bondage in disdain;
  Throwing the base thong from his bending crest,
  Enfranchising his mouth, his back, his breast.

'Who sees his true-love in her naked bed,
Teaching the sheets a whiter hue than white,
But, when his glutton eye so full hath fed,
His other agents aim at like delight?
  Who is so faint, that dares not be so bold
  To touch the fire, the weather being cold?

'Let me excuse thy courser, gentle boy;
And learn of him, I heartily beseech thee,
To take advantage on presented joy;
Though I were dumb, yet his proceedings teach thee:
  O, learn to love; the lesson is but plain,
  And once made perfect, never lost again.'

'I know not love,' quoth he, 'nor will not know it,
Unless it be a boar, and then I chase it;
'Tis much to borrow, and I will not owe it;
My love to love is love but to disgrace it;
  For I have heard it is a life in death,
  That laughs and weeps, and all but with a breath.

'Who wears a garment shapeless and unfinish'd?
Who plucks the bud before one leaf put forth?
If springing things be any jot diminish'd,
They wither in their prime, prove nothing worth:
  The colt that 's back'd and burden'd being young
  Loseth his pride and never waxeth strong.

'You hurt my hand with wringing; let us part,
And leave this idle theme, this bootless chat:
Remove your siege from my unyielding heart;
To love's alarms it will not ope the gate:
  Dismiss your vows, your feigned tears, your flatt'ry;
  For where a heart is hard they make no batt'ry.'

'What! canst thou talk?' quoth she, 'hast thou a tongue?
O, would thou hadst not, or I had no hearing!
Thy mermaid's voice hath done me double wrong;
I had my load before, now press'd with bearing:
  Melodious discord, heavenly tune harsh-sounding,
  Ear's deep-sweet music, and heart's deep-sore wounding.

'Had I no eyes but ears, my ears would love
That inward beauty and invisible;
Or were I deaf, thy outward parts would move
Each part in me that were but sensible:
  Though neither eyes nor ears, to hear nor see,
  Yet should I be in love by touching thee.

'Say, that the sense of feeling were bereft me,
And that I could not see, nor hear, nor touch,
And nothing but the very smell were left me,
Yet would my love to thee be still as much;
  For from the stillitory of thy face excelling
  Comes breath perfum'd that breedeth love by smelling.

'But, O, what banquet wert thou to the taste,
Being nurse and feeder of the other four!
Would they not wish the feast might ever last,
And bid Suspicion double-lock the door,
  Lest Jealousy, that sour unwelcome guest,
  Should, by his stealing in, disturb the feast?'

Once more the ruby-colour'd portal open'd,
Which to his speech did honey passage yield;
Like a red morn, that ever yet betoken'd
Wrack to the seaman, tempest to the field,
  Sorrow to shepherds, woe unto the birds,
  Gusts and foul flaws to herdmen and to herds.

This ill presage advisedly she marketh:
Even as the wind is hush'd before it raineth,
Or as the wolf doth grin before he barketh,
Or as the berry breaks before it staineth,
  Or like the deadly bullet of a gun,
  His meaning struck her ere his words begun.

And at his look she flatly falleth down,
For looks kill love and love by looks reviveth;
A smile recures the wounding of a frown;
But blessed bankrout, that by love so thriveth!
  The silly boy, believing she is dead,
  Claps her pale cheek, till clapping makes it red;

And all amaz'd brake off his late intent,
For sharply he did think to reprehend her,
Which cunning love did wittily prevent:
Fair fall the wit that can so well defend her!
  For on the grass she lies as she were slain,
  Till his breath breatheth life in her again.

He wrings her nose, he strikes her on the cheeks,
He bends her fingers, holds her pulses hard,
He chafes her lips; a thousand ways he seeks
To mend the hurt that his unkindness marr'd:
  He kisses her; and she, by her good will,
  Will never rise, so he will kiss her still.

The night of sorrow now is turn'd to day:
Her two blue windows faintly she up-heaveth,
Like the fair sun, when in his fresh array
He cheers the morn and all the earth relieveth;
  And as the bright sun glorifies the sky,
  So is her face illumin'd with her eye;

Whose beams upon his hairless face are fix'd,
As if from thence they borrow'd all their shine.
Were never four such lamps together mix'd,
Had not his clouded with his brow's repine;
  But hers, which through the crystal tears gave light,
  Shone like the moon in water seen by night.

387. **coal . . . cool'd.** The pronunciation was sufficiently alike to make the word play obvious. 393. **fair fee,** due reward (Rollins). 400. **agents,** organs. 411. **owe,** own. 412. **My . . . it,** my inclination toward love is only a desire to render it contemptible (Malone). 419. **back'd,** broken in. 430. **press'd,** oppressed; the load was his indifference, the last straw of his refusal (Pooler). 443. **stillitory,** alembic, still. 456. **flaws,** gusts of wind. 465. **recures,** restores. 472. **fall,** befall. 490. **repine,** dissatisfaction.

'O, where am I?' quoth she, 'in earth or heaven,
Or in the ocean drench'd, or in the fire?
What hour is this? or morn or weary even?
Do I delight to die, or life desire?
  But now I liv'd, and life was death's annoy;
  But now I died, and death was lively joy.

'O, thou didst kill me: kill me once again:
Thy eyes' shrewd tutor, that hard heart of thine,
Hath taught them scornful tricks and such disdain
That they have murd'red this poor heart of mine;
  And these mine eyes, true leaders to their queen,
  But for thy piteous lips no more had seen.

'Long may they kiss each other, for this cure!
O, never let their crimson liveries wear!
And as they last, their verdure still endure,
To drive infection from the dangerous year!
  That the star-gazers, having writ on death,
  May say, the plague is banish'd by thy breath.

'Pure lips, sweet seals in my soft lips imprinted,
What bargains may I make, still to be sealing?
To sell myself I can be well contented,
So thou wilt buy and pay and use good dealing;
  Which purchase if thou make, for fear of slips
  Set thy seal-manual on my wax-red lips.

'A thousand kisses buys my heart from me;
And pay them at thy leisure, one by one.
What is ten hundred touches unto thee?
Are they not quickly told and quickly gone?
  Say, for non-payment that the debt should double,
  Is twenty hundred kisses such a trouble?'

'Fair queen,' quoth he, 'if any love you owe me,
Measure my strangeness with my unripe years:
Before I know myself, seek not to know me;
No fisher but the ungrown fry forbears:
  The mellow plum doth fall, the green sticks fast,
  Or being early pluck'd is sour to taste.

'Look, the world's comforter, with weary gait,
His day's hot task hath ended in the west;
The owl, night's herald, shrieks, " 'Tis very late;"
The sheep are gone to fold, birds to their nest,
  And coal-black clouds that shadow heaven's light
  Do summon us to part and bid good night.

'Now let me say "Good night," and so say you;
If you will say so, you shall have a kiss.'
'Good night,' quoth she, and, ere he says 'Adieu,'
The honey fee of parting tend'red is:
  Her arms do lend his neck a sweet embrace;
  Incorporate then they seem; face grows to face.

Till, breathless, he disjoin'd, and backward drew
The heavenly moisture, that sweet coral mouth,
Whose precious taste her thirsty lips well knew,
Whereon they surfeit, yet complain on drouth:
  He with her plenty press'd, she faint with dearth,
  Their lips together glued, fall to the earth.

Now quick desire hath caught the yielding prey,
And glutton-like she feeds, yet never filleth;
Her lips are conquerors, his lips obey,
Paying what ransom the insulter willeth;
  Whose vulture thought doth pitch the price so high,
  That she will draw his lips' rich treasure dry:

And having felt the sweetness of the spoil,
With blindfold fury she begins to forage;
Her face doth reek and smoke, her blood doth boil,
And careless lust stirs up a desperate courage;
  Planting oblivion, beating reason back,
  Forgetting shame's pure blush and honour's wrack.

Hot, faint, and weary, with her hard embracing,
Like a wild bird being tam'd with too much handling,
Or as the fleet-foot roe that 's tir'd with chasing,
Or like the froward infant still'd with dandling,
  He now obeys, and now no more resisteth,
  While she takes all she can, not all she listeth.

What wax so frozen but dissolves with temp'ring,
And yields at last to very light impression?
Things out of hope are compass'd oft with vent'ring,
Chiefly in love, whose leave exceeds commission:
  Affection faints not like a pale-fac'd coward,
  But then woos best when most his choice is froward.

When he did frown, O, had she then gave over,
Such nectar from his lips she had not suck'd.
Foul words and frowns must not repel a lover;
What though the rose have prickles, yet 'tis pluck'd:
  Were beauty under twenty locks kept fast,
  Yet love breaks through and picks them all at last.

For pity now she can no more detain him;
The poor fool prays her that he may depart:
She is resolv'd no longer to restrain him;
Bids him farewell, and look well to her heart,
  The which, by Cupid's bow she doth protest,
  He carries thence incaged in his breast.

'Sweet boy,' she says, 'this night I'll waste in sorrow,
For my sick heart commands mine eyes to watch.
Tell me, Love's master, shall we meet to-morrow?
Say, shall we? shall we? wilt thou make the match?'
  He tells her, no; to-morrow he intends
  To hunt the boar with certain of his friends.

'The boar!' quoth she; whereat a sudden pale,
Like lawn being spread upon the blushing rose,
Usurps her cheek; she trembles at his tale,
And on his neck her yoking arms she throws:
  She sinketh down, still hanging by his neck,
  He on her belly falls, she on her back.

Now is she in the very lists of love,
Her champion mounted for the hot encounter:
All is imaginary she doth prove,
He will not manage her, although he mount her;
  That worse than Tantalus' is her annoy,
  To clip Elysium and to lack her joy.

506. **wear,** wear out. 507-508. **verdure . . . year,** may allude to the belief in the wholesome effects of plants in the presence of the sick. 508-510. **infection . . . plague,** a probable allusion to the epidemic of bubonic plague raging in London during 1592-1593. 512. **still to be sealing,** i.e., to continue kissing. 515. **slips,** counterfeit money (Steevens); errors (Feuillerat); probably a quibble on these two meanings. 520. **told,** counted. 526. **No . . . forbears,** every fisherman spares the ungrown fry. 540. **Incorporate,** united in one body. 557. **Planting oblivion,** causing forgetfulness of all that she ought to remember (Pooler). 562. **froward,** fretful. 568. **exceeds commission,** goes beyond due warrant (Lee). 590. **lawn,** fine linen. 595. **lists,** tournament field (with erotic suggestion). 597. **she doth prove,** that she

Even as poor birds, deceiv'd with painted grapes,
Do surfeit by the eye and pine the maw,
Even so she languisheth in her mishaps,
As those poor birds that helpless berries saw.
The warm effects which she in him finds missing
She seeks to kindle with continual kissing.

But all in vain; good queen, it will not be:
She hath assay'd as much as may be prov'd;
Her pleading hath deserv'd a greater fee;
She 's Love, she loves, and yet she is not lov'd.
'Fie, fie,' he says, 'you crush me; let me go;
You have no reason to withhold me so.'

'Thou hadst been gone,' quoth she, 'sweet boy, ere this,
But that thou told'st me thou wouldst hunt the boar.
O, be advis'd! thou know'st not what it is
With javelin's point a churlish swine to gore,
Whose tushes never sheath'd he whetteth still,
Like to a mortal butcher bent to kill.

'On his bow-back he hath a battle set
Of bristly pikes, that ever threat his foes;
His eyes, like glow-worms, shine when he doth fret;
His snout digs sepulchres where'er he goes;
Being mov'd, he strikes whate'er is in his way,
And whom he strikes his crooked tushes slay.

'His brawny sides, with hairy bristles armed,
Are better proof than thy spear's point can enter;
His short thick neck cannot be easily harmed;
Being ireful, on the lion he will venter:
The thorny brambles and embracing bushes,
As fearful of him, part, through whom he rushes.

'Alas, he nought esteems that face of thine,
To which Love's eyes pay tributary gazes;
Nor thy soft hands, sweet lips and crystal eyne,
Whose full perfection all the world amazes;
But having thee at vantage,—wondrous dread!—
Would root these beauties as he roots the mead.

'O, let him keep his loathsome cabin still;
Beauty hath nought to do with such foul fiends:
Come not within his danger by thy will;
They that thrive well take counsel of their friends.
When thou didst name the boar, not to dissemble,
I fear'd thy fortune, and my joints did tremble.

'Didst thou not mark my face? was it not white?
Saw'st thou not signs of fear lurk in mine eye?
Grew I not faint? and fell I not downright?
Within my bosom, whereon thou dost lie,
My boding heart pants, beats, and takes no rest,
But, like an earthquake, shakes thee on my breast.

'For where Love reigns, disturbing Jealousy
Doth call himself Affection's sentinel;
Gives false alarms, suggesteth mutiny,
And in a peaceful hour doth cry "Kill, kill!"
Distemp'ring gentle Love in his desire,
As air and water do abate the fire.

'This sour informer, this bate-breeding spy,
This canker that eats up Love's tender spring,
This carry-tale, dissentious Jealousy,
That sometime true news, sometime false doth bring,
Knocks at my heart and whispers in mine ear
That if I love thee, I thy death should fear:

'And more than so, presenteth to mine eye
The picture of an angry-chafing boar,
Under whose sharp fangs on his back doth lie
An image like thyself, all stain'd with gore;
Whose blood upon the fresh flowers being shed
Doth make them droop with grief and hang the head.

'What should I do, seeing thee so indeed,
That tremble at th' imagination?
The thought of it doth make my faint heart bleed,
And fear doth teach it divination:
I prophesy thy death, my living sorrow,
If thou encounter with the boar to-morrow.

'But if thou needs wilt hunt, be rul'd by me;
Uncouple at the timorous flying hare,
Or at the fox which lives by subtlety,
Or at the roe which no encounter dare:
Pursue these fearful creatures o'er the downs,
And on thy well-breath'd horse keep with thy hounds.

'And when thou hast on foot the purblind hare,
Mark the poor wretch, to overshoot his troubles
How he outruns the wind and with what care
He cranks and crosses with a thousand doubles:
The many musets through the which he goes
Are like a labyrinth to amaze his foes.

'Sometime he runs among a flock of sheep,
To make the cunning hounds mistake their smell,
And sometime where earth-delving conies keep,
To stop the loud pursuers in their yell,
And sometime sorteth with a herd of deer:
Danger deviseth shifts; wit waits on fear:

'For there his smell with others being mingled,
The hot scent-snuffing hounds are driven to doubt,
Ceasing their clamorous cry till they have singled
With much ado the cold fault cleanly out;
Then do they spend their mouths: Echo replies,
As if another chase were in the skies.

'By this, poor Wat, far off upon a hill,
Stands on his hinder legs with list'ning ear,
To hearken if his foes pursue him still:
Anon their loud alarums he doth hear;
And now his grief may be compared well
To one sore sick that hears the passing-bell.

experiences. 599. **Tantalus,** a son of Zeus who was punished by perpetual hunger and thirst with food and drink always in sight. 601. **birds . . . grapes,** allusion to Zeuxis, a Greek painter of the fifth century B.C., so skillful an artist that birds were said to peck at his picture of a bunch of grapes. 602. **pine the maw,** starve the stomach. 617. **tushes,** tusks. 628. **venter,** venture. 639. **Come . . . will,** don't willfully expose yourself to the danger it can inflict. 655. **bate-breeding,** breeding strife. 656. **spring,** young shoot of a plant. 678. **well-breath'd,** sound in wind. 682. **cranks,** turns. 683. **musets,** gaps in hedge or fence. 687. **conies,** rabbits. 689. **sorteth,** mingles. 690. **shifts,** tricks. **waits on,** attends. 694. **cold fault,** cold or lost scent. 697. **Wat,** a common name applied to the hare. 702. **passing-bell,** funeral bell.

'Then shalt thou see the dew-bedabbled wretch
Turn, and return, indenting with the way;
Each envious brier his weary legs doth scratch,
Each shadow makes him stop, each murmur stay:
For misery is trodden on by many,
And being low never reliev'd by any.

'Lie quietly, and hear a little more;
Nay, do not struggle, for thou shalt not rise:
To make thee hate the hunting of the boar,
Unlike myself thou hear'st me moralize,
Applying this to that, and so to so;
For love can comment upon every woe.

'Where did I leave?' 'No matter where;' quoth he,
'Leave me, and then the story aptly ends:
The night is spent.' 'Why, what of that?' quoth she.
'I am,' quoth he, 'expected of my friends;
And now 'tis dark, and going I shall fall.'
'In night,' quoth she, 'desire sees best of all.

'But if thou fall, O, then imagine this,
The earth, in love with thee, thy footing trips,
And all is but to rob thee of a kiss.
Rich preys make true men thieves; so do thy lips
Make modest Dian cloudy and forlorn,
Lest she should steal a kiss and die forsworn.

'Now of this dark night I perceive the reason:
Cynthia for shame obscures her silver shine,
Till forging Nature be condemn'd of treason,
For stealing moulds from heaven that were divine;
Wherein she fram'd thee in high heaven's despite,
To shame the sun by day and her by night.

'And therefore hath she brib'd the Destinies
To cross the curious workmanship of nature,
To mingle beauty with infirmities,
And pure perfection with impure defeature,
Making it subject to the tyranny
Of mad mischances and much misery;

'As burning fevers, agues pale and faint,
Life-poisoning pestilence and frenzies wood,
The marrow-eating sickness, whose attaint
Disorder breeds by heating of the blood:
Surfeits, imposthumes, grief, and damn'd despair,
Swear Nature's death for framing thee so fair.

'And not the least of all these maladies
But in one minute's fight brings beauty under:
Both favour, savour, hue and qualities,
Whereat th' impartial gazer late did wonder,
Are on the sudden wasted, thaw'd and done,
As mountain-snow melts with the midday sun.

'Therefore, despite of fruitless chastity,
Love-lacking vestals and self-loving nuns,
That on the earth would breed a scarcity
And barren dearth of daughters and of sons,
Be prodigal: the lamp that burns by night
Dries up his oil to lend the world his light.

'What is thy body but a swallowing grave,
Seeming to bury that posterity
Which by the rights of time thou needs must have,
If thou destroy them not in dark obscurity?
If so, the world will hold thee in disdain,
Sith in thy pride so fair a hope is slain.

'So in thyself thyself art made away;
A mischief worse than civil home-bred strife,
Or theirs whose desperate hands themselves do slay,
Or butcher-sire that reaves his son of life.
Foul-cank'ring rust the hidden treasure frets,
But gold that 's put to use more gold begets.'

'Nay, then,' quoth Adon, 'you will fall again
Into your idle over-handled theme:
The kiss I gave you is bestow'd in vain,
And all in vain you strive against the stream;
For, by this black-fac'd night, desire's foul nurse,
Your treatise makes me like you worse and worse.

'If love have lent you twenty thousand tongues,
And every tongue more moving than your own,
Bewitching like the wanton mermaid's songs,
Yet from mine ear the tempting tune is blown;
For know, my heart stands armed in mine ear,
And will not let a false sound enter there;

'Lest the deceiving harmony should run
Into the quiet closure of my breast;
And then my little heart were quite undone,
In his bedchamber to be barr'd of rest.
No, lady, no; my heart longs not to groan,
But soundly sleeps, while now it sleeps alone.

'What have you urg'd that I cannot reprove?
The path is smooth that leadeth on to danger:
I hate not love, but your device in love,
That lends embracements unto every stranger.
You do it for increase: O strange excuse,
When reason is the bawd to lust's abuse!

'Call it not love, for Love to heaven is fled,
Since sweating Lust on earth usurp'd his name;
Under whose simple semblance he hath fed
Upon fresh beauty, blotting it with blame;
Which the hot tyrant stains and soon bereaves,
As caterpillars do the tender leaves.

'Love comforteth like sunshine after rain,
But Lust's effect is tempest after sun;
Love's gentle spring doth always fresh remain,
Lust's winter comes ere summer half be done;
Love surfeits not, Lust like a glutton dies;
Love is all truth, Lust full of forged lies.

'More I could tell, but more I dare not say;
The text is old, the orator too green.
Therefore, in sadness, now I will away;
My face is full of shame, my heart of teen:
Mine ears, that to your wanton talk attended,
Do burn themselves for having so offended.'

704. **indenting,** moving in a zigzag line. 725. **Dian,** Diana, goddess of chastity and the hunt. 728. **Cynthia,** i.e., Diana, the moon. 729. **forging,** counterfeiting. 732. **her,** the moon. 734. **cross,** thwart. **curious,** ingenious. 736. **defeature,** disfigurement. 740. **wood,** mad. 743. **imposthumes,** abscesses. 748. **impartial,** indifferent. 762. **Sith,** since. 766. **reaves,** bereaves. 769. **you will fall,** not an expression of futurity but of volition; i.e., you are determined to fall (Brown). 774. **treatise,** discourse. 779-784. **my . . . rest,** an application of the psychological notion of the Elizabethans that the senses were the doors through which the soul was assailed by the several passions. 787. **reprove,**

With this, he breaketh from the sweet embrace
Of those fair arms which bound him to her breast,
And homeward through the dark laund runs apace;
Leaves Love upon her back deeply distress'd.
  Look how a bright star shooteth from the sky,
  So glides he in the night from Venus' eye;

Which after him she darts, as one on shore
Gazing upon a late-embarked friend,
Till the wild waves will have him seen no more,
Whose ridges with the meeting clouds contend:
  So did the merciless and pitchy night
  Fold in the object that did feed her sight.

Whereat amaz'd, as one that unaware
Hath dropp'd a precious jewel in the flood,
Or stonish'd as night-wand'rers often are,
Their light blown out in some mistrustful wood,
  Even so confounded in the dark she lay,
  Having lost the fair discovery of her way.

And now she beats her heart, whereat it groans,
That all the neighbour caves, as seeming troubled,
Make verbal repetition of her moans;
Passion on passion deeply is redoubled:
  'Ay me!' she cries, and twenty times 'Woe, woe!'
  And twenty echoes twenty times cry so.

She marking them begins a wailing note
And sings extemporally a woeful ditty;
How love makes young men thrall and old men dote;
How love is wise in folly, foolish-witty:
  Her heavy anthem still concludes in woe,
  And still the choir of echoes answer so.

Her song was tedious and outwore the night,
For lovers' hours are long, though seeming short:
If pleas'd themselves, others, they think, delight
In such-like circumstance, with such-like sport:
  Their copious stories oftentimes begun
  End without audience and are never done.

For who hath she to spend the night withal
But idle sounds resembling parasites,
Like shrill-tongu'd tapsters answering every call,
Soothing the humour of fantastic wits?
  She says ''Tis so:' they answer all ''Tis so;'
  And would say after her, if she said 'No.'

Lo, here the gentle lark, weary of rest,
From his moist cabinet mounts up on high,
And wakes the morning, from whose silver breast
The sun ariseth in his majesty;
  Who doth the world so gloriously behold
  That cedar-tops and hills seem burnish'd gold.

Venus salutes him with this fair good-morrow:
'O thou clear god, and patron of all light,
From whom each lamp and shining star doth borrow
The beauteous influence that makes him bright,
  There lives a son that suck'd an earthly mother,
  May lend thee light, as thou dost lend to other.'

This said, she hasteth to a myrtle grove,
Musing the morning is so much o'erworn,
And yet she hears no tidings of her love:
She hearkens for his hounds and for his horn:
  Anon she hears them chant it lustily,
  And all in haste she coasteth to the cry.

And as she runs, the bushes in the way
Some catch her by the neck, some kiss her face,
Some twine about her thigh to make her stay:
She wildly breaketh from their strict embrace,
  Like a milch doe, whose swelling dugs do ache,
  Hasting to feed her fawn hid in some brake.

By this, she hears the hounds are at a bay;
Whereat she starts, like one that spies an adder
Wreath'd up in fatal folds just in his way,
The fear whereof doth make him shake and shudder;
  Even so the timorous yelping of the hounds
  Appals her senses and her spirit confounds.

For now she knows it is no gentle chase,
But the blunt boar, rough bear, or lion proud,
Because the cry remaineth in one place,
Where fearfully the dogs exclaim aloud:
  Finding their enemy to be so curst,
  They all strain court'sy who shall cope him first.

This dismal cry rings sadly in her ear,
Through which it enters to surprise her heart;
Who, overcome by doubt and bloodless fear,
With cold-pale weakness numbs each feeling part:
  Like soldiers, when their captain once doth yield,
  They basely fly and dare not stay the field.

Thus stands she in a trembling ecstasy;
Till, cheering up her senses all dismay'd,
She tells them 'tis a causeless fantasy,
And childish error, that they are afraid;
  Bids them leave quaking, bids them fear no more:—
  And with that word she spied the hunted boar,

Whose frothy mouth, bepainted all with red,
Like milk and blood being mingled both together,
A second fear through all her sinews spread,
Which madly hurries her she knows not whither:
  This way she runs, and now she will no further,
  But back retires to rate the boar for murther.

A thousand spleens bear her a thousand ways;
She treads the path that she untreads again;
Her more than haste is mated with delays,
Like the proceedings of a drunken brain,
  Full of respects, yet nought at all respecting;
  In hand with all things, nought at all effecting.

Here kennell'd in a brake she finds a hound,
And asks the weary caitiff for his master,
And there another licking of his wound,
'Gainst venom'd sores the only sovereign plaster;
  And here she meets another sadly scowling,
  To whom she speaks, and he replies with howling.

refute. 789. **device,** cunning, deceitful conduct. 797. **bereaves,** spoils. 808. **teen,** affliction, grief. 813. **laund,** glade. 837. **thrall,** captive. 838. **wise . . . witty,** probably a quibbling phrase: love applies its wit to doing foolish things and is foolish in doing sensible things. 854. **cabinet,** dwelling. 870. **coasteth,** makes progress against obstacles (Onions). 887. **curst,** savage. 888. **strain court'sy,** be punctiliously polite, stand upon ceremony. The phrase was not infrequently applied to hounds in the chase (see Rollins, Variorum). 907. **spleens,** impulses. 909. **mated,** confounded, checked (Malone). 911. **nought at all respecting,** i.e., heedless.

When he hath ceas'd his ill-resounding noise,
Another flap-mouth'd mourner, black and grim,
Against the welkin volleys out his voice;
Another and another answer him,
  Clapping their proud tails to the ground below,
  Shaking their scratch'd ears, bleeding as they go.

Look how the world's poor people are amazed
At apparitions, signs and prodigies,
Whereon with fearful eyes they long have gazed,
Infusing them with dreadful prophecies;
  So she at these sad signs draws up her breath
  And sighing it again, exclaims on Death.

'Hard-favour'd tyrant, ugly, meagre, lean,
Hateful divorce of love,'—thus chides she Death,—
'Grim-grinning ghost, earth's worm, what dost thou mean
To stifle beauty and to steal his breath,
  Who when he liv'd, his breath and beauty set
  Gloss on the rose, smell to the violet?

'If he be dead,—O no, it cannot be,
Seeing his beauty, thou shouldst strike at it:—
O yes, it may; thou hast no eyes to see,
But hatefully at randon dost thou hit.
  Thy mark is feeble age, but thy false dart
  Mistakes that aim and cleaves an infant's heart.

'Hadst thou but bid beware, then he had spoke,
And, hearing him, thy power had lost his power.
The Destinies will curse thee for this stroke;
They bid thee crop a weed, thou pluck'st a flower:
  Love's golden arrow at him should have fled,
  And not Death's ebon dart, to strike him dead.

'Dost thou drink tears, that thou provok'st such weeping?
What may a heavy groan advantage thee?
Why hast thou cast into eternal sleeping
Those eyes that taught all other eyes to see?
  Now Nature cares not for thy mortal vigour,
  Since her best work is ruin'd with thy rigour.'

Here overcome, as one full of despair,
She vail'd her eyelids, who, like sluices, stopt
The crystal tide that from her two cheeks fair
In the sweet channel of her bosom dropt;
  But through the flood-gates breaks the silver rain,
  And with his strong course opens them again.

O, how her eyes and tears did lend and borrow!
Her eyes seen in the tears, tears in her eye;
Both crystals, where they view'd each other's sorrow,
Sorrow that friendly sighs sought still to dry;
  But like a stormy day, now wind, now rain,
  Sighs dry her cheeks, tears make them wet again.

Variable passions throng her constant woe,
As striving who should best become her grief;
All entertain'd, each passion labours so,
That every present sorrow seemeth chief,
  But none is best: then join they all together,
  Like many clouds consulting for foul weather.

By this, far off she hears some huntsman hollo;
A nurse's song ne'er pleas'd her babe so well:
The dire imagination she did follow
This sound of hope doth labour to expel;
  For now reviving joy bids her rejoice,
  And flatters her it is Adonis' voice.

Whereat her tears began to turn their tide,
Being prison'd in her eye like pearls in glass;
Yet sometimes falls an orient drop beside,
Which her cheek melts, as scorning it should pass,
  To wash the foul face of the sluttish ground,
  Who is but drunken when she seemeth drown'd.

O hard-believing love, how strange it seems
Not to believe, and yet too credulous!
Thy weal and woe are both of them extremes;
Despair and hope makes thee ridiculous:
  The one doth flatter thee in thoughts unlikely,
  In likely thoughts the other kills thee quickly.

Now she unweaves the web that she hath wrought;
Adonis lives, and Death is not to blame;
It was not she that call'd him all-to naught:
Now she adds honours to his hateful name;
  She clepes him king of graves and grave for kings,
  Imperious supreme of all mortal things.

'No, no,' quoth she, 'sweet Death, I did but jest;
Yet pardon me I felt a kind of fear
When as I met the boar, that bloody beast,
Which knows no pity, but is still severe;
  Then, gentle shadow,—truth I must confess,—
  I rail'd on thee, fearing my love's decease.

''Tis not my fault: the boar provok'd my tongue;
Be wreak'd on him, invisible commander;
'Tis he, foul creature, that hath done thee wrong;
I did but act, he 's author of thy slander:
  Grief hath two tongues, and never woman yet
  Could rule them both without ten women's wit.'

Thus hoping that Adonis is alive,
Her rash suspect she doth extenuate;
And that his beauty may the better thrive,
With Death she humbly doth insinuate;
  Tells him of trophies, statues, tombs, and stories
  His victories, his triumphs and his glories.

'O Jove,' quoth she, 'how much a fool was I
To be of such a weak and silly mind
To wail his death who lives and must not die
Till mutual overthrow of mortal kind!
  For he being dead, with him is beauty slain,
  And, beauty dead, black chaos comes again.

'Fie, fie, fond love, thou art so full of fear
As one with treasure laden, hemm'd with thieves;
Trifles, unwitnessed with eye or ear,
Thy coward heart with false bethinking grieves.'
  Even at this word she hears a merry horn,
  Whereat she leaps that was but late forlorn.

920. **flap-mouth'd,** having broad, hanging lips. 930. **exclaims on,** denounces. 933. **earth's worm.** Death was always associated with the idea of worms. 940. **randon,** random. 944. **his,** its. 953. **mortal vigour,** death-dealing power. 967. **throng,** oppress. 968. **who,** which. 993. **all-to,** entirely; so explained by Dyce, who introduced the hyphen; Q: *all to naught;* Kittredge explains *all* as adverbial and defines the idiom

As falcon to the lure, away she flies;
The grass stoops not, she treads on it so light;
And in her haste unfortunately spies
The foul boar's conquest on her fair delight;
  Which seen, her eyes, as murd'red with the view,
  Like stars asham'd of day, themselves withdrew;

Or, as the snail, whose tender horns being hit,
Shrinks backward in his shelly cave with pain,
And there, all smoth'red up, in shade doth sit,
Long after fearing to creep forth again;
  So, at his bloody view, her eyes are fled
  Into the deep dark cabins of her head.

Where they resign their office and their light
To the disposing of her troubled brain;
Who bids them still consort with ugly night,
And never wound the heart with looks again;
  Who, like a king perplexed in his throne,
  By their suggestion gives a deadly groan,

Whereat each tributary subject quakes;
As when the wind, imprison'd in the ground,
Struggling for passage, earth's foundation shakes,
Which with cold terror doth men's minds confound.
  This mutiny each part doth so surprise
  That from their dark beds once more leap her eyes;

And, being open'd, threw unwilling light
Upon the wide wound that the boar had trench'd
In his soft flank; whose wonted lily white
With purple tears, that his wound wept, was drench'd:
  No flow'r was nigh, no grass, herb, leaf, or weed,
  But stole his blood and seem'd with him to bleed.

This solemn sympathy poor Venus noteth;
Over one shoulder doth she hang her head;
Dumbly she passions, franticly she doteth;
She thinks he could not die, he is not dead:
  Her voice is stopt, her joints forget to bow;
  Her eyes are mad that they have wept till now.

Upon his hurt she looks so steadfastly,
That her sight dazzling makes the wound seem three;
And then she reprehends her mangling eye,
That makes more gashes where no breach should be:
  His face seems twain, each several limb is doubled;
  For oft the eye mistakes, the brain being troubled.

'My tongue cannot express my grief for one,
And yet,' quoth she, 'behold two Adons dead!
My sighs are blown away, my salt tears gone,
Mine eyes are turn'd to fire, my heart to lead:
  Heavy heart's lead, melt at mine eyes' red fire!
  So shall I die by drops of hot desire.

'Alas, poor world, what treasure hast thou lost!
What face remains alive that 's worth the viewing?
Whose tongue is music now? what canst thou boast
Of things long since, or any thing ensuing?
  The flowers are sweet, their colours fresh and trim;
  But true-sweet beauty liv'd and died with him.

'Bonnet nor veil henceforth no creature wear!
Nor sun nor wind will ever strive to kiss you:
Having no fair to lose, you need not fear;
The sun doth scorn you and the wind doth hiss you:
  But when Adonis liv'd, sun and sharp air
  Lurk'd like two thieves, to rob him of his fair:

'And therefore would he put his bonnet on,
Under whose brim the gaudy sun would peep;
The wind would blow it off and, being gone,
Play with his locks: then would Adonis weep;
  And straight, in pity of his tender years,
  They both would strive who first should dry his tears.

'To see his face the lion walk'd along
Behind some hedge, because he would not fear him;
To recreate himself when he hath sung,
The tiger would be tame and gently hear him;
  If he had spoke, the wolf would leave his prey
  And never fright the silly lamb that day.

'When he beheld his shadow in the brook,
The fishes spread on it their golden gills;
When he was by, the birds such pleasure took,
That some would sing, some other in their bills
  Would bring him mulberries and ripe-red cherries;
  He fed them with his sight, they him with berries.

'But this foul, grim, and urchin-snouted boar,
Whose downward eye still looketh for a grave,
Ne'er saw the beauteous livery that he wore;
Witness the entertainment that he gave:
  If he did see his face, why then I know
  He thought to kiss him, and hath kill'd him so.

''Tis true, 'tis true; thus was Adonis slain:
He ran upon the boar with his sharp spear,
Who did not whet his teeth at him again,
But by a kiss thought to persuade him there;
  And nuzzling in his flank, the loving swine
  Sheath'd unaware the tusk in his soft groin.

'Had I been tooth'd like him, I must confess,
With kissing him I should have kill'd him first;
But he is dead, and never did he bless
My youth with his; the more am I accurst.'
  With this, she falleth in the place she stood,
  And stains her face with his congealed blood.

She looks upon his lips, and they are pale;
She takes him by the hand, and that is cold;
She whispers in his ears a heavy tale,
As if they heard the woeful words she told;
  She lifts the coffer-lids that close his eyes,
  Where, lo, two lamps, burnt out, in darkness lies;

Two glasses, where herself herself beheld
A thousand times, and now no more reflect;
Their virtue lost, wherein they late excell'd,
And every beauty robb'd of his effect:
  'Wonder of time,' quoth she, 'this is my spite,
  That, thou being dead, the day should yet be light.

call to naught as "upbraid as villainous." 995. **clepes,** names. 1010. **suspect,** suspicion. 1012. **insinuate,** ingratiate herself. 1046. **wind . . . ground,** the common explanation of earthquakes; cf. *1 Henry IV*, III, i, 30. 1054. **purple tears,** drops of blood; cf. l. 1. 1094. **fear,** frighten. 1105. **urchin-snouted,** having a snout like a hedgehog.

'Since thou art dead, lo, here I prophesy:
Sorrow on love hereafter shall attend:
It shall be waited on with jealousy,
Find sweet beginning, but unsavoury end,
  Ne'er settled equally, but high or low,
  That all love's pleasure shall not match his woe.

'It shall be fickle, false and full of fraud,
Bud and be blasted in a breathing-while;
The bottom poison, and the top o'erstraw'd
With sweets that shall the truest sight beguile:
  The strongest body shall it make most weak,
  Strike the wise dumb and teach the fool to speak.

'It shall be sparing and too full of riot,
Teaching decrepit age to tread the measures;
The staring ruffian shall it keep in quiet,
Pluck down the rich, enrich the poor with treasures;
  It shall be raging-mad and silly-mild,
  Make the young old, the old become a child.

'It shall suspect where is no cause of fear;
It shall not fear where it should most mistrust;
It shall be merciful and too severe,
And most deceiving when it seems most just;
  Perverse it shall be where it shows most toward,
  Put fear to valour, courage to the coward.

'It shall be cause of war and dire events,
And set dissension 'twixt the son and sire;
Subject and servile to all discontents,
As dry combustious matter is to fire:
  Sith in his prime Death doth my love destroy,
  They that love best their loves shall not enjoy.'

By this, the boy that by her side lay kill'd
Was melted like a vapour from her sight,
And in his blood that on the ground lay spill'd,
A purple flower sprung up, chek'red with white,
  Resembling well his pale cheeks and the blood
  Which in round drops upon their whiteness stood.

She bows her head, the new-sprung flower to smell,
Comparing it to her Adonis' breath,
And says, within her bosom it shall dwell,
Since he himself is reft from her by death:
  She crops the stalk, and in the breach appears
  Green dropping sap, which she compares to tears.

'Poor flow'r,' quoth she, 'this was thy father's guise—
Sweet issue of a more sweet-smelling sire—
For every little grief to wet his eyes:
To grow unto himself was his desire,
  And so 'tis thine; but know, it is as good
  To wither in my breast as in his blood.

'Here was thy father's bed, here in my breast;
Thou art the next of blood, and 'tis thy right:
Lo, in this hollow cradle take thy rest,
My throbbing heart shall rock thee day and night:
  There shall not be one minute in an hour
  Wherein I will not kiss my sweet love's flow'r.'

Thus weary of the world, away she hies,
And yokes her silver doves; by whose swift aid
Their mistress mounted through the empty skies
In her light chariot quickly is convey'd;
  Holding their course to Paphos, where their queen
  Means to immure herself and not be seen.

1142. **breathing-while,** short time. 1143. **o'erstraw'd,** strewn over. 1149. **staring,** looking savage. 1157. **toward,** tractable. 1193. **Paphos,** a city in Cypress where stood a temple to Venus.

THE RAPE OF LUCRECE

The Rape of Lucrece is a companion poem to *Venus and Adonis*. The two were published about a year apart, in 1593 and 1594, both printed by Richard Field. Both are dedicated to the young Earl of Southampton, Henry Wriothesley, whose confidence and friendship Shakespeare appears to have gained during the interim between the two poems; the dedicatory preface to *The Rape of Lucrece* sounds vastly more assured and grateful for acceptance. Stylistically the two poems are of a piece, excessively reliant on Petrarchan ornament and rhetorical showmanship, steeped in Ovidian pathos. Yet they are complementary rather than similar in attitude and subject. *The Rape of Lucrece* appears to be the "graver labour" promised to Southampton in the dedication of the earlier poem, a planned sequel in which love would be subjected to a darker treatment. *Venus and Adonis* is chiefly about sensual pleasure whereas *The Rape of Lucrece* is about heroic chastity. The first poem is amatory, erotic, and amusing despite its sad end; the second is moral, declamatory, and lugubrious. As Gabriel Harvey observed (c. 1598–1601), "The younger sort takes much delight in Shakespeares Venus, & Adonis: but his Lucrece, & his tragedie of Hamlet, Prince of Denmarke, haue it in them, to please the wiser sort."

As the pairing with *Hamlet* suggests, Shakespeare aspires to sublime effects in *Lucrece*. For his verse pattern he chooses the seven-line rhyme royal stanza, traditionally used for tragic expression as in Chaucer's *Troilus and Criseyde* and several of the more didactic *Canterbury Tales*, in Lydgate's *The Fall of Princes* and its continuation in *A Myrroure for Magistrates*, in Samuel Daniel's *The Complaint of Rosamond*, and others. Although Shakespeare turns to Ovid once again as his chief source, he chooses a tale of ravishment, suicide, and vengeance rather than of titillating amatory pursuit. The story of Lucrece had gained wide currency in the ancient and medieval worlds as an *exemplum* of chaste conduct in women. Shakespeare seems to have known Livy's *History of Rome* (Book I, chaps. 57–59), though he relied most on Ovid's *Fasti* (II, 721–852). Among later versions he may have known Chaucer's *The Legend of Good Women* and a translation of Livy in Painter's *Palace of Pleasure* (1566). He encountered other "complaints" in *A Myrroure for Magistrates* and in Daniel's *The Complaint of Rosamond*, and it is to this well-established genre that *Lucrece* belongs. The poem had the desired effect of enhancing Shakespeare's reputation for elegant poetry; it was reprinted five times during his lifetime and was frequently admired by his contemporaries. *Venus and Adonis* was, to be sure, more popular still (it was reprinted nine times during Shakespeare's lifetime), but no one in Shakespeare's day seems to have regarded *Lucrece* as anything other than a noble work.

To recapture today some of that earlier enthusiasm for the poem, we must recognize its conventions and not expect it to be other than what it professes to be. As in *Venus and Adonis*, plot and character are secondary. Although the story outlined in "The Argument" is potentially sensational and swift-moving, Shakespeare deliberately cuts away most of the action. We do not see Lucius Tarquinius' murder of his father-in-law and tyrannical seizure of Rome, or Collatinus' rash boasting of his wife Lucrece's virtue in the presence of the king's lustful son Sextus Tarquinius. Nor, at the conclusion of the story, do we learn much about the revenging of Lucrece's rape. Shakespeare's focus is on the attitudes of the two protagonists immediately before and after the ravishment. Even here, despite obvious opportunities for psychological probing, Shakespeare is not really interested in a consistent portrayal of motive. Instead, he gives us a series of rhetorical disputations, each a set piece cast as a debate or as a formal declamation. The debates are built around familiar antitheses: honor versus lust, rude will versus conscience, "affection" versus reason, nobility versus baseness, and so on. Many of the image patterns are similarly arranged in contrasting pairs: dove and owl, daylight and darkness, clear and cloudy weather, white and red. Tarquin debates with himself the reasons for and against rape; Lucrece tries to persuade him of the evilness of his course; Lucrece ponders suicide. These debates generate in turn a number of rhetorical apostrophes to marital fidelity (22–28), to the ideal of kingship as a moral example to others (610–637), to Night (764–812), to Opportunity (876–924), and to Time (925–1022).

Another rhetorical formula, perhaps the most successful in the poem, is the use of structural digression. The most notable describes a painting of Troy with obvious relevance to Lucrece's sad fate: Troy is a city destroyed by a rape, Paris achieves his selfish pleasure at the expense of the public good, Sinon wins his sinister victory through deceitful appearance. Not all the poem's ornament is equally appealing, however. Sometimes the forced ingeniousness of the comparison overwhelms the seriousness of the occasion. One such is the Petrarchan catalogue of Lucrece's charms, comparing her breasts to round turrets subjected to military siege (440–441). Again, at her death Lucrece is likened to a "late-sack'd island" as she is surrounded by rivers of her own blood (1740). The rhetorical devices of antithesis are displayed with the same pyrotechnic versatility as in *Venus and Adonis*, but the campy playfulness of that jeu d'esprit is missing and so the effect is at times incongruous and excessive.

THE RAPE OF LUCRECE

TO THE

RIGHT HONOURABLE
HENRY WRIOTHESLEY,

EARL OF SOUTHAMPTON,
AND BARON OF TICHFIELD.

THE love I dedicate to your lordship is without end; whereof this pamphlet, without beginning, is but a superfluous moiety. The warrant I have of your honourable disposition, not the worth of my untutored lines, makes it assured of acceptance. What I have done is yours; what I have to do is yours; being part in all I have, devoted yours. Were my worth greater, my duty would show greater; meantime, as it is, it is bound to your lordship, to whom I wish long life, still lengthened with all happiness.

Your lordship's in all duty,

WILLIAM SHAKESPEARE.

THE ARGUMENT

LUCIUS TARQUINIUS, for his excessive pride surnamed Superbus, after he had caused his own father-in-law Servius Tullius to be cruelly murdered, and, contrary to the Roman laws and customs, not requiring or staying for the people's suffrages, had possessed himself of the kingdom, went, accompanied with his sons and other noblemen of Rome, to besiege Ardea. During which siege the principal men of the army meeting one evening at the tent of Sextus Tarquinius, the king's son, in their discourses after supper every one commended the virtues of his own wife; among whom Collatinus extolled the incomparable chastity of his wife Lucretia. In that pleasant humour they all posted to Rome; and intending, by their secret and sudden arrival, to make trial of that which every one had before avouched, only Collatinus finds his wife, though it were late in the night, spinning amongst her maids: the other ladies were all found dancing and revelling, or in several disports. Whereupon the noblemen yielded Collatinus the victory, and his wife the fame. At that time Sextus Tarquinius being inflamed with Lucrece' beauty, yet smothering his passions for the present, departed with the rest back to the camp; from whence he shortly after privily withdrew himself, and was, according to his estate, royally entertained and lodged by Lucrece at Collatium. The same night he treacherously stealeth into her chamber, violently ravished her, and early in the morning speedeth away. Lucrece, in this lamentable plight, hastily dispatcheth messengers, one to Rome for her father, another to the camp for Collatine. They came, the one accompanied with Junius Brutus, the other with Publius Valerius; and finding Lucrece attired in mourning habit, demanded the cause of her sorrow. She, first taking an oath of them for her revenge, revealed the actor, and whole manner of his dealing, and withal suddenly stabbed herself. Which done, with one consent they all vowed to root out the whole hated family of the Tarquins; and bearing the dead body to Rome, Brutus acquainted the people with the doer and manner of the vile deed, with a bitter invective against the tyranny of the king: wherewith the people were so moved, that with one consent and a general acclamation the Tarquins were all exiled, and the state government changed from kings to consuls.

FROM the besieged Ardea all in post,
Borne by the trustless wings of false desire,
Lust-breathed Tarquin leaves the Roman host,
And to Collatium bears the lightless fire
Which, in pale embers hid, lurks to aspire
  And girdle with embracing flames the waist
  Of Collatine's fair love, Lucrece the chaste.

Haply that name of 'chaste' unhapp'ly set
This bateless edge on his keen appetite;
When Collatine unwisely did not let
To praise the clear unmatched red and white
Which triumph'd in that sky of his delight,
  Where mortal stars, as bright as heaven's beauties,
  With pure aspects did him peculiar duties.

For he the night before, in Tarquin's tent,
Unlock'd the treasure of his happy state;
What priceless wealth the heavens had him lent
In the possession of his beauteous mate;
Reck'ning his fortune at such high-proud rate,
  That kings might be espoused to more fame,
  But king nor peer to such a peerless dame.

O happiness enjoy'd but of a few!
And, if possess'd, as soon decay'd and done
As is the morning's silver melting dew
Against the golden splendour of the sun!
An expir'd date, cancell'd ere well begun:
  Honour and beauty, in the owner's arms,
  Are weakly fortress'd from a world of harms.

Beauty itself doth of itself persuade
The eyes of men without an orator;
What needeth then apologies be made,

DEDICATION. 2. **pamphlet,** used by Shakespeare, probably in a self-derogatory sense, as something too slight to be called a book. *Pamphlet* was used in the sixteenth century to designate a work of small bulk. **without beginning,** taken by most commentators to mean that Shakespeare takes the reader *in medias res*. 3 **The warrant I have.** Nicholas Rowe in 1709 recorded on William Davenant's authority that Southampton at one time gave Shakespeare "a thousand Pounds to enable him to go through with a Purchase which he heard he had a mind to." Most commentators are inclined to regard the amount as an exaggeration; most of them acknowledge that this dedication expresses gratitude for favors already received.

THE ARGUMENT. 5. **requiring,** requesting. 22. **disports,** pastimes. 23. **fame,** honorable title. 37. **Junius Brutus.** This is the Brutus

To set forth that which is so singular?
Or why is Collatine the publisher
Of that rich jewel he should keep unknown
From thievish ears, because it is his own?

Perchance his boast of Lucrece' sov'reignty
Suggested this proud issue of a king;
For by our ears our hearts oft tainted be:
Perchance that envy of so rich a thing,
Braving compare, disdainfully did sting
His high-pitch'd thoughts, that meaner men should vaunt
That golden hap which their superiors want.

But some untimely thought did instigate
His all too timeless speed, if none of those:
His honour, his affairs, his friends, his state,
Neglected all, with swift intent he goes
To quench the coal which in his liver glows.
O rash false heat, wrapp'd in repentant cold,
Thy hasty spring still blasts, and ne'er grows old!

When at Collatium this false lord arrived,
Well was he welcom'd by the Roman dame,
Within whose face beauty and virtue strived
Which of them both should underprop her fame:
When virtue bragg'd, beauty would blush for shame;
When beauty boasted blushes, in despite
Virtue would stain that o'er with silver white.

But beauty, in that white intituled,
From Venus' doves doth challenge that fair field:
Then virtue claims from beauty beauty's red,
Which virtue gave the golden age to gild
Their silver cheeks, and call'd it then their shield;
Teaching them thus to use it in the fight,
When shame assail'd, the red should fence the white.

This heraldry in Lucrece' face was seen,
Argued by beauty's red and virtue's white:
Of either's colour was the other queen,
Proving from world's minority their right:
Yet their ambition makes them still to fight;
The sovereignty of either being so great,
That oft they interchange each other's seat.

Their silent war of lilies and of roses,
Which Tarquin view'd in her fair face's field,
In their pure ranks his traitor eye encloses;
Where, lest between them both it should be kill'd,
The coward captive vanquished doth yield
To those two armies that would let him go,
Rather than triumph in so false a foe.

Now thinks he that her husband's shallow tongue,—
The niggard prodigal that prais'd her so,—
In that high task hath done her beauty wrong,
Which far exceeds his barren skill to show:
Therefore that praise which Collatine doth owe
Enchanted Tarquin answers with surmise,
In silent wonder of still-gazing eyes.

This earthly saint, adored by this devil,
Little suspecteth the false worshipper;
For unstain'd thoughts do seldom dream on evil;
Birds never lim'd no secret bushes fear:
So guiltless she securely gives good cheer
And reverend welcome to her princely guest,
Whose inward ill no outward harm express'd:

For that he colour'd with his high estate,
Hiding base sin in plaits of majesty;
That nothing in him seem'd inordinate,
Save sometime too much wonder of his eye,
Which, having all, all could not satisfy;
But, poorly rich, so wanteth in his store,
That, cloy'd with much, he pineth still for more.

But she, that never cop'd with stranger eyes,
Could pick no meaning from their parling looks,
Nor read the subtle-shining secrecies
Writ in the glassy margents of such books:
She touch'd no unknown baits, nor fear'd no hooks;
Nor could she moralize his wanton sight,
More than his eyes were open'd to the light.

He stories to her ears her husband's fame,
Won in the fields of fruitful Italy;
And decks with praises Collatine's high name,
Made glorious by his manly chivalry
With bruised arms and wreaths of victory:
Her joy with heav'd-up hand she doth express,
And, wordless, so greets heaven for his success.

Far from the purpose of his coming hither,
He makes excuses for his being there:
No cloudy show of stormy blust'ring weather
Doth yet in his fair welkin once appear;
Till sable Night, mother of Dread and Fear,
Upon the world dim darkness doth display,
And in her vaulty prison stows the Day.

For then is Tarquin brought unto his bed,
Intending weariness with heavy spright;
For, after supper, long he questioned
With modest Lucrece, and wore out the night:
Now leaden slumber with life's strength doth fight;
And every one to rest themselves betake,
Save thieves, and cares, and troubled minds, that wake.

As one of which doth Tarquin lie revolving

referred to by Cassius in *Julius Caesar*, I, ii, 159-160.

THE POEM. 1. **Ardea,** a city twenty-four miles south of Rome. 3. **Lust-breathed,** excited by lust. 4. **Collatium,** a city about ten miles east of Rome. **lightless,** smouldering. 5. **aspire,** rise; i.e., break into flames. 8. **Haply,** perchance. **unhapp'ly,** unfavorably. Q$_{1-4}$ print these words as *Hap'ly* and *vnhap'ly,* which makes the word play more obvious. 9. **bateless,** not to be blunted. 10. **let,** forbear. 13. **mortal,** human; i.e., her eyes. 24. **silver melting,** so Q; Globe hyphenates, following Malone. 37. **Suggested,** tempted. **issue,** son. 38. **For . . . be.** The relation between the five senses—particularly sight and hearing—and the passions is stressed several times in this poem; cf. ll. 369, 558-559, 1324-1325; and cf. *Venus and Adonis,* 779-784, note. 40. **Braving compare,** challenging comparison. 42. **hap,** fortune. 44. **all too timeless,** so Q; Globe hyphenates, following Malone. **timeless,** unseemly, unseasonable. 47. **liver,** regarded as the seat of the passions. 57. **intituled,** designated, blazoned; the metaphor is derived from heraldry. 58. **challenge,** claim. **field,** the surface of the shield, where the armorial device is displayed. 63. **fence,** defend. 67. **world's minority,** the golden age; i.e., their right is as old as the doves of Venus and the first blush (Pooler). 83. **surmise,** thought, reflection. 88. **lim'd,** caught with bird lime. 90. **reverend,** i.e., because he is the king's son. 93. **plaits of majesty,** the cunning folds or concealments of dignified demeanor (Lee). 100. **parling,** speaking, conferring. 102. **glassy . . . books,** refers to the custom of printing comments in book margins. 104. **moralize,** interpret. 121. **Intending,** pretending.

The sundry dangers of his will's obtaining;
Yet ever to obtain his will resolving,
Though weak-built hopes persuade him to abstaining:
Despair to gain doth traffic oft for gaining;
And when great treasure is the meed proposed,
Though death be adjunct, there 's no death supposed.

Those that much covet are with gain so fond,
For what they have not, that which they possess
They scatter and unloose it from their bond,
And so, by hoping more, they have but less;
Or, gaining more, the profit of excess
Is but to surfeit, and such griefs sustain,
That they prove bankrout in this poor-rich gain.

The aim of all is but to nurse the life
With honour, wealth, and ease, in waning age;
And in this aim there is such thwarting strife,
That one for all, or all for one we gage;
As life for honour in fell battle's rage;
Honour for wealth; and oft that wealth doth cost
The death of all, and all together lost.

So that in vent'ring ill we leave to be
The things we are for that which we expect;
And this ambitious foul infirmity,
In having much, torments us with defect
Of that we have: so then we do neglect
The thing we have; and, all for want of wit,
Make something nothing by augmenting it.

Such hazard now must doting Tarquin make,
Pawning his honour to obtain his lust;
And for himself himself he must forsake:
Then where is truth, if there be no self-trust?
When shall he think to find a stranger just,
When he himself himself confounds, betrays
To sland'rous tongues and wretched hateful days?

Now stole upon the time the dead of night,
When heavy sleep had clos'd up mortal eyes:
No comfortable star did lend his light,
No noise but owls' and wolves' death-boding cries;
Now serves the season that they may surprise
The silly lambs: pure thoughts are dead and still,
While lust and murder wake to stain and kill.

And now this lustful lord leap'd from his bed,
Throwing his mantle rudely o'er his arm;
Is madly toss'd between desire and dread;
Th' one sweetly flatters, th' other feareth harm;
But honest fear, bewitch'd with lust's foul charm
Doth too too oft betake him to retire,
Beaten away by brain-sick rude desire.

His falchion on a flint he softly smiteth,
That from the cold stone sparks of fire do fly;
Whereat a waxen torch forthwith he lighteth,
Which must be lode-star to his lustful eye;
And to the flame thus speaks advisedly,
'As from this cold flint I enforc'd this fire,
So Lucrece must I force to my desire.'

Here pale with fear he doth premeditate
The dangers of his loathsome enterprise,
And in his inward mind he doth debate
What following sorrow may on this arise:
Then looking scornfully, he doth despise
His naked armour of still-slaughtered lust,
And justly thus controls his thoughts unjust:

'Fair torch, burn out thy light, and lend it not
To darken her whose light excelleth thine:
And die, unhallowed thoughts, before you blot
With your uncleanness that which is divine;
Offer pure incense to so pure a shrine:
Let fair humanity abhor the deed
That spots and stains love's modest snow-white weed.

'O shame to knighthood and to shining arms!
O foul dishonour to my household's grave!
O impious act, including all foul harms!
A martial man to be soft fancy's slave!
True valour still a true respect should have;
Then my digression is so vile, so base,
That it will live engraven in my face.

'Yea, though I die, the scandal will survive,
And be an eye-sore in my golden coat;
Some loathsome dash the herald will contrive,
To cipher me how fondly I did dote;
That my posterity, sham'd with the note,
Shall curse my bones, and hold it for no sin
To wish that I their father had not been.

'What win I, if I gain the thing I seek?
A dream, a breath, a froth of fleeting joy.
Who buys a minute's mirth to wail a week?
Or sells eternity to get a toy?
For one sweet grape who will the vine destroy?
Or what fond beggar, but to touch the crown,
Would with the sceptre straight be strucken down?

'If Collatinus dream of my intent,
Will he not wake, and in a desp'rate rage
Post hither, this vile purpose to prevent?
This siege that hath engirt his marriage,
This blur to youth, this sorrow to the sage,
This dying virtue, this surviving shame,
Whose crime will bear an ever-during blame?

'O, what excuse can my invention make,
When thou shalt charge me with so black a deed?
Will not my tongue be mute, my frail joints shake,
Mine eyes forego their light, my false heart bleed?
The guilt being great, the fear doth still exceed;
And extreme fear can neither fight nor fly,
But coward-like with trembling terror die.

131. **Despair to gain,** hopelessness of gain. **traffic,** engage in commerce. 134. **fond,** infatuated. 136. **bond,** possession. 138. **profit of excess,** advantage of having more than enough. 139. **such griefs sustain,** i.e., to sustain such griefs as accompany surfeit. 140. **bankrout,** bankrupt. 144. **gage,** pledge. Pooler suggests "risk." 148. **leave to be,** cease being. 150. **infirmity,** i.e., covetousness. 151. **defect,** deficiency. 155. **doting.** The word suggests the complete overthrow of the understanding by the passions; it carries also the metaphor of the covetous man completely foolish in his ventures. 164. **comfortable,** cheering, benevolent. 167. **silly,** helpless, defenseless. 188. **naked . . . lust,** i.e., his lust is no armor because it is always killed when satisfied. 196. **weed,** garment (of chastity). 205. **golden coat,** i.e., coat of arms. 206. **loathsome dash,** a glance at the bar sinister. 207. **cipher,** disclose, decipher. 221. **marriage,** state of union (Schmidt); abstract for concrete: his wife (Brown). 224. **ever-during,** everlasting. 236. **quittal,** requital. 244. **saw,** saying, proverb. 245. **painted cloth,** wall hanging

'Had Collatinus kill'd my son or sire,
Or lain in ambush to betray my life,
Or were he not my dear friend, this desire
Might have excuse to work upon his wife,
As in revenge or quittal of such strife:
But as he is my kinsman, my dear friend,
The shame and fault finds no excuse nor end.

'Shameful it is; ay, if the fact be known:
Hateful it is; there is no hate in loving:
I'll beg her love; but she is not her own:
The worst is but denial and reproving:
My will is strong, past reason's weak removing.
Who fears a sentence or an old man's saw
Shall by a painted cloth be kept in awe.'

Thus, graceless, holds he disputation
'Tween frozen conscience and hot-burning will,
And with good thoughts makes dispensation,
Urging the worser sense for vantage still;
Which in a moment doth confound and kill
All pure effects, and doth so far proceed,
That what is vile shows like a virtuous deed.

Quoth he, 'She took me kindly by the hand,
And gaz'd for tidings in my eager eyes,
Fearing some hard news from the warlike band,
Where her beloved Collatinus lies.
O, how her fear did make her colour rise!
First red as roses that on lawn we lay,
Then white as lawn, the roses took away.

'And how her hand, in my hand being lock'd,
Forc'd it to tremble with her loyal fear!
Which struck her sad, and then it faster rock'd,
Until her husband's welfare she did hear;
Whereat she smiled with so sweet a cheer,
That had Narcissus seen her as she stood,
Self-love had never drown'd him in the flood.

'Why hunt I then for colour or excuses?
All orators are dumb when beauty pleadeth;
Poor wretches have remorse in poor abuses;
Love thrives not in the heart that shadows dreadeth:
Affection is my captain, and he leadeth;
And when his gaudy banner is display'd,
The coward fights and will not be dismay'd.

'Then, childish fear, avaunt! debating, die!
Respect and reason, wait on wrinkled age!
My heart shall never countermand mine eye:
Sad pause and deep regard beseem the sage;
My part is youth, and beats these from the stage:
Desire my pilot is, beauty my prize;
Then who fears sinking where such treasure lies?'

As corn o'ergrown by weeds, so heedful fear
Is almost chok'd by unresisted lust.
Away he steals with open list'ning ear,
Full of foul hope and full of fond mistrust;
Both which, as servitors to the unjust,
So cross him with their opposite persuasion,
That now he vows a league, and now invasion.

Within his thought her heavenly image sits,
And in the self-same seat sits Collatine:
That eye which looks on her confounds his wits;
That eye which him beholds, as more divine,
Unto a view so false will not incline;
But with a pure appeal seeks to the heart,
Which once corrupted takes the worser part;

And therein heartens up his servile powers,
Who, flatt'red by their leader's jocund show,
Stuff up his lust, as minutes fill up hours;
And as their captain, so their pride doth grow,
Paying more slavish tribute than they owe.
By reprobate desire thus madly led,
The Roman lord marcheth to Lucrece' bed.

The locks between her chamber and his will,
Each one by him enforc'd retires his ward;
But, as they open, they all rate his ill,
Which drives the creeping thief to some regard:
The threshold grates the door to have him heard;
Night-wand'ring weasels shriek to see him there;
They fright him, yet he still pursues his fear.

As each unwilling portal yields him way,
Through little vents and crannies of the place
The wind wars with his torch to make him stay,
And blows the smoke of it into his face,
Extinguishing his conduct in this case;
But his hot heart, which fond desire doth scorch,
Puffs forth another wind that fires the torch:

And being lighted, by the light he spies
Lucretia's glove, wherein her needle sticks:
He takes it from the rushes where it lies,
And griping it, the needle his finger pricks;
As who should say 'This glove to wanton tricks
Is not inur'd; return again in haste;
Thou see'st our mistress' ornaments are chaste.'

But all these poor forbiddings could not stay him;
He in the worst sense consters their denial:
The doors, the wind, the glove, that did delay him,
He takes for accidental things of trial;
Or as those bars which stop the hourly dial,
Who with a ling'ring stay his course doth let,
Till every minute pays the hour his debt.

'So, so,' quoth he, 'these lets attend the time,
Like little frosts that sometime threat the spring,
To add a more rejoicing to the prime,
And give the sneaped birds more cause to sing.
Pain pays the income of each precious thing;
Huge rocks, high winds, strong pirates, shelves and sands,
The merchant fears, ere rich at home he lands.'

in which moral tales and maxims were sometimes depicted; cf. ll. 1366-1456, below, where such a painted cloth is described. 248. **makes dispensation** [*with*], sets aside. 265. **Narcissus,** youth who fell in love with his own reflection. 269. **have . . . abuses,** feel remorse for paltry sins. 286. **cross,** thwart. 292. **a view so false.** The eye which beholds Collatine (in imagination) has a degree of loyalty and will not be so false as to look toward Lucrece, as the other eye has done; i.e., he cannot think of Collatine and Lucrece at the same time. 295. **servile powers,** base passions. The image is the common one of the faculties as an army: the heart as captain of the sensible soul commands all the affections to serve his lust; cf. l. 426, below. 303. **retires,** draws back. **ward,** lock, bolt. 304. **rate his ill,** chide his evil deed (by creaking). 305. **regard,** caution. 308. **fear,** i.e., his peril. 313. **conduct,** conductor, i.e., his torch. 318. **rushes,** floor covering. 324. **consters,** construes. 330. **lets,** hindrances, obstacles. **attend the time,** are incidental to the occasion. 333. **sneaped,** nipped, or pinched with cold.

Now is he come unto the chamber door,
That shuts him from the heaven of his thought,
Which with a yielding latch, and with no more,
Hath barr'd him from the blessed thing he sought.
So from himself impiety hath wrought,
  That for his prey to pray he doth begin,
  As if the heavens should countenance his sin.

But in the midst of his unfruitful prayer,
Having solicited th' eternal power
That his foul thoughts might compass his fair fair,
And they would stand auspicious to the hour,
Even there he starts: quoth he, 'I must deflow'r:
  The powers to whom I pray abhor this fact,
  How can they then assist me in the act?

'Then Love and Fortune be my gods, my guide!
My will is back'd with resolution:
Thoughts are but dreams till their effects be tried;
The blackest sin is clear'd with absolution;
Against love's fire fear's frost hath dissolution.
  The eye of heaven is out, and misty night
  Covers the shame that follows sweet delight.'

This said, his guilty hand pluck'd up the latch,
And with his knee the door he opens wide.
The dove sleeps fast that this night-owl will catch:
Thus treason works ere traitors be espied.
Who sees the lurking serpent steps aside;
  But she, sound sleeping, fearing no such thing,
  Lies at the mercy of his mortal sting.

Into the chamber wickedly he stalks,
And gazeth on her yet unstained bed.
The curtains being close, about he walks,
Rolling his greedy eyeballs in his head:
By their high treason is his heart misled;
  Which gives the watch-word to his hand full soon
  To draw the cloud that hides the silver moon.

Look as the fair and fiery-pointed sun,
Rushing from forth a cloud, bereaves our sight;
Even so, the curtain drawn, his eyes begun
To wink, being blinded with a greater light:
Whether it is that she reflects so bright,
  That dazzleth them, or else some shame supposed;
  But blind they are, and keep themselves enclosed.

O, had they in that darksome prison died!
Then had they seen the period of their ill;
Then Collatine again, by Lucrece' side,
In his clear bed might have reposed still:
But they must ope, this blessed league to kill;
  And holy-thoughted Lucrece to their sight
  Must sell her joy, her life, her world's delight.

Her lily hand her rosy cheek lies under,
Coz'ning the pillow of a lawful kiss;
Who, therefore angry, seems to part in sunder,
Swelling on either side to want his bliss;
Between whose hills her head entombed is:
  Where, like a virtuous monument, she lies,
  To be admir'd of lewd unhallowed eyes.

Without the bed her other fair hand was,
On the green coverlet; whose perfect white
Show'd like an April daisy on the grass,
With pearly sweat, resembling dew of night.
Her eyes, like marigolds, had sheath'd their light,
  And canopied in darkness sweetly lay,
  Till they might open to adorn the day.

Her hair, like golden threads, play'd with her breath;
O modest wantons! wanton modesty!
Showing life's triumph in the map of death,
And death's dim look in life's mortality:
Each in her sleep themselves so beautify,
  As if between them twain there were no strife,
  But that life liv'd in death, and death in life.

Her breasts, like ivory globes circled with blue,
A pair of maiden worlds unconquered,
Save of their lord no bearing yoke they knew,
And him by oath they truly honoured.
These worlds in Tarquin new ambition bred;
  Who, like a foul usurper, went about
  From this fair throne to heave the owner out.

What could he see but mightily he noted?
What did he note but strongly he desired?
What he beheld, on that he firmly doted,
And in his will his wilful eye he tired.
With more than admiration he admired
  Her azure veins, her alabaster skin,
  Her coral lips, her snow-white dimpled chin.

As the grim lion fawneth o'er his prey,
Sharp hunger by the conquest satisfied,
So o'er this sleeping soul doth Tarquin stay,
His rage of lust by gazing qualified;
Slack'd, not suppress'd; for standing by her side,
  His eye, which late this mutiny restrains,
  Unto a greater uproar tempts his veins:

And they, like straggling slaves for pillage fighting,
Obdurate vassals fell exploits effecting,
In bloody death and ravishment delighting,
Nor children's tears nor mothers' groans respecting,
Swell in their pride, the onset still expecting:
  Anon his beating heart, alarum striking,
  Gives the hot charge and bids them do their liking.

His drumming heart cheers up his burning eye,
His eye commends the leading to his hand;
His hand, as proud of such a dignity,
Smoking with pride, march'd on to make his stand
On her bare breast, the heart of all her land;
  Whose ranks of blue veins, as his hand did scale,
  Left their round turrets destitute and pale.

They, must'ring to the quiet cabinet
Where their dear governess and lady lies,
Do tell her she is dreadfully beset,
And fright her with confusion of their cries:
She, much amaz'd, breaks ope her lock'd-up eyes,
  Who, peeping forth this tumult to behold,
  Are by his flaming torch dimm'd and controll'd.

341. **wrought,** i.e., wrought him. 346. **compass,** possess. 364. **sting,** lust (with phallic suggestion). 380. **period,** end. 387. **Coz'ning,** cheating. 402. **map of death,** i.e., sleep. 417. **tired,** a falconry term: glutted, fed upon ravenously. 418. **more than admiration,** lustful anticipation. 424. **qualified,** softened, abated. 453. **taking,** agitation. 459. **antics,** phantoms (Herford); odd and fantastic appearances (Schmidt). 471. **heartless,** wanting courage. 476. **colour,** pretext; flag, ensign. 507. **Coucheth,** causes (one) to couch, 523. **obloquy,**

Imagine her as one in dead of night
From forth dull sleep by dreadful fancy waking,
That thinks she hath beheld some ghastly sprite,
Whose grim aspect sets every joint a-shaking:
What terror 'tis! but she, in worser taking,
From sleep disturbed, heedfully doth view
The sight which makes supposed terror true.

Wrapp'd and confounded in a thousand fears,
Like to a new-kill'd bird she trembling lies;
She dares not look; yet, winking, there appears
Quick-shifting antics, ugly in her eyes:
Such shadows are the weak brain's forgeries;
Who, angry that the eyes fly from their lights,
In darkness daunts them with more dreadful sights.

His hand, that yet remains upon her breast,—
Rude ram, to batter such an ivory wall!—
May feel her heart—poor citizen!—distress'd,
Wounding itself to death, rise up and fall,
Beating her bulk, that his hand shakes withal.
This moves in him more rage and lesser pity,
To make the breach and enter this sweet city.

First, like a trumpet, doth his tongue begin
To sound a parley to his heartless foe;
Who o'er the white sheet peers her whiter chin,
The reason of this rash alarm to know,
Which he by dumb demeanour seeks to show;
But she with vehement prayers urgeth still
Under what colour he commits this ill.

Thus he replies: 'The colour in thy face,
That even for anger makes the lily pale,
And the red rose blush at her own disgrace,
Shall plead for me and tell my loving tale:
Under that colour am I come to scale
Thy never-conquered fort: the fault is thine,
For those thine eyes betray thee unto mine.

'Thus I forestall thee, if thou mean to chide:
Thy beauty hath ensnar'd thee to this night,
Where thou with patience must my will abide;
My will that marks thee for my earth's delight,
Which I to conquer sought with all my might;
But as reproof and reason beat it dead,
By thy bright beauty was it newly bred.

'I see what crosses my attempt will bring;
I know what thorns the growing rose defends;
I think the honey guarded with a sting;
All this beforehand counsel comprehends:
But will is deaf and hears no heedful friends;
Only he hath an eye to gaze on beauty,
And dotes on what he looks, 'gainst law or duty.

'I have debated, even in my soul,
What wrong, what shame, what sorrow I shall breed;
But nothing can affection's course control,
Or stop the headlong fury of his speed.
I know repentant tears ensue the deed,
Reproach, disdain, and deadly enmity;
Yet strive I to embrace mine infamy.'

This said, he shakes aloft his Roman blade,
Which, like a falcon tow'ring in the skies,
Coucheth the fowl below with his wings' shade,
Whose crooked beak threats if he mount he dies:
So under his insulting falchion lies
Harmless Lucretia, marking what he tells
With trembling fear, as fowl hear falcon's bells.

'Lucrece,' quoth he, 'this night I must enjoy thee:
If thou deny, then force must work my way,
For in thy bed I purpose to destroy thee:
That done, some worthless slave of thine I'll slay,
To kill thine honour with thy life's decay;
And in thy dead arms do I mean to place him,
Swearing I slew him, seeing thee embrace him.

'So thy surviving husband shall remain
The scornful mark of every open eye;
Thy kinsmen hang their heads at this disdain,
Thy issue blurr'd with nameless bastardy:
And thou, the author of their obloquy,
Shalt have thy trespass cited up in rhymes,
And sung by children in succeeding times.

'But if thou yield, I rest thy secret friend:
The fault unknown is as a thought unacted;
A little harm done to a great good end
For lawful policy remains enacted.
The poisonous simple sometime is compacted
In a pure compound; being so applied,
His venom in effect is purified.

'Then, for thy husband and thy children's sake,
Tender my suit: bequeath not to their lot
The shame that from them no device can take,
The blemish that will never be forgot;
Worse than a slavish wipe or birth-hour's blot:
For marks descried in men's nativity
Are nature's faults, not their own infamy.'

Here with a cockatrice' dead-killing eye
He rouseth up himself and makes a pause;
While she, the picture of pure piety,
Like a white hind under the gripe's sharp claws,
Pleads, in a wilderness where are no laws,
To the rough beast that knows no gentle right,
Nor aught obeys but his foul appetite.

But when a black-fac'd cloud the world doth threat,
In his dim mist th' aspiring mountains hiding,
From earth's dark womb some gentle gust doth get,
Which blows these pitchy vapours from their biding,
Hind'ring their present fall by this dividing;
So his unhallowed haste her words delays,
And moody Pluto winks while Orpheus plays.

Yet, foul night-waking cat, he doth but dally,
While in his hold-fast foot the weak mouse panteth:
Her sad behaviour feeds his vulture folly,
A swallowing gulf that even in plenty wanteth:
His ear her prayers admits, but his heart granteth
No penetrable entrance to her plaining:
Tears harden lust, though marble wear with raining.

reproach, disgrace. 529. **For lawful policy,** modifies *done* (l. 528). 530. **simple,** ingredient. 531. **compound,** compounded drug. 537. **slavish wipe,** brand with which slaves were marked. **birth-hour's blot,** birthmark. 540. **cockatrice,** the basilisk, said to be hatched by a serpent from a cock's egg and said to kill by its breath and look. 543. **hind,** doe. **gripe's,** vulture's. 553. **Orpheus,** singer whose music charmed Pluto into allowing Orpheus' wife Eurydice to return to earth. 556. **folly,** lewdness, depravity. 559. **plaining,** complaining.

Her pity-pleading eyes are sadly fixed
In the remorseless wrinkles of his face;
Her modest eloquence with sighs is mixed,
Which to her oratory adds more grace.
She puts the period often from his place;
And midst the sentence so her accent breaks,
That twice she doth begin ere once she speaks.

She conjures him by high almighty Jove,
By knighthood, gentry, and sweet friendship's oath,
By her untimely tears, her husband's love,
By holy human law, and common troth,
By heaven and earth, and all the power of both,
That to his borrowed bed he make retire,
And stoop to honour, not to foul desire.

Quoth she, 'Reward not hospitality
With such black payment as thou hast pretended;
Mud not the fountain that gave drink to thee;
Mar not the thing that cannot be amended;
End thy ill aim before thy shoot be ended;
He is no woodman that doth bend his bow
To strike a poor unseasonable doe.

'My husband is thy friend; for his sake spare me:
Thyself art mighty; for thine own sake leave me:
Myself a weakling; do not then ensnare me:
Thou look'st not like deceit; do not deceive me.
My sighs, like whirlwinds, labour hence to heave thee:
If ever man were mov'd with woman's moans,
Be moved with my tears, my sighs, my groans:

'All which together, like a troubled ocean,
Beat at thy rocky and wrack-threat'ning heart,
To soften it with their continual motion;
For stones dissolv'd to water do convert.
O, if no harder than a stone thou art,
Melt at my tears, and be compassionate!
Soft pity enters at an iron gate.

'In Tarquin's likeness I did entertain thee:
Hast thou put on his shape to do him shame?
To all the host of heaven I complain me,
Thou wrong'st his honour, wound'st his princely name.
Thou art not what thou seem'st; and if the same,
Thou seem'st not what thou art, a god, a king;
For kings like gods should govern every thing.

'How will thy shame be seeded in thine age,
When thus thy vices bud before thy spring!
If in thy hope thou dar'st do such outrage,
What dar'st thou not when once thou art a king?
O, be remember'd, no outrageous thing
From vassal actors can be wip'd away;
Then kings' misdeeds cannot be hid in clay.

'This deed will make thee only lov'd for fear;
But happy monarchs still are fear'd for love:
With foul offenders thou perforce must bear,
When they in thee the like offences prove:
If but for fear of this, thy will remove;
For princes are the glass, the school, the book,
Where subjects' eyes do learn, do read, do look.

'And wilt thou be the school where Lust shall learn?
Must he in thee read lectures of such shame?
Wilt thou be glass wherein it shall discern
Authority for sin, warrant for blame,
To privilege dishonour in thy name?
Thou back'st reproach against long-living laud,
And mak'st fair reputation but a bawd.

'Hast thou command? by him that gave it thee,
From a pure heart command thy rebel will:
Draw not thy sword to guard iniquity,
For it was lent thee all that brood to kill.
Thy princely office how canst thou fulfil,
When, pattern'd by thy fault, foul Sin may say,
He learn'd to sin, and thou didst teach the way?

'Think but how vile a spectacle it were,
To view thy present trespass in another.
Men's faults do seldom to themselves appear;
Their own transgressions partially they smother:
This guilt would seem death-worthy in thy brother.
O, how are they wrapp'd in with infamies
That from their own misdeeds askance their eyes!

'To thee, to thee, my heav'd-up hands appeal,
Not to seducing lust, thy rash relier:
I sue for exil'd majesty's repeal;
Let him return, and flatt'ring thoughts retire:
His true respect will prison false desire,
And wipe the dim mist from thy doting eyne,
That thou shalt see thy state and pity mine.'

'Have done,' quoth he: 'my uncontrolled tide
Turns not, but swells the higher by this let.
Small lights are soon blown out, huge fires abide,
And with the wind in greater fury fret:
The petty streams that pay a daily debt
To their salt sovereign, with their fresh falls' haste
Add to his flow, but alter not his taste.'

'Thou art,' quoth she, 'a sea, a sovereign king;
And, lo, there falls into thy boundless flood
Black lust, dishonour, shame, misgoverning,
Who seek to stain the ocean of thy blood.
If all these petty ills shall change thy good,
Thy sea within a puddle's womb is hearsed,
And not the puddle in thy sea dispersed.

'So shall these slaves be king, and thou their slave;
Thou nobly base, they basely dignified;
Thou their fair life, and they thy fouler grave:
Thou loathed in their shame, they in thy pride:
The lesser thing should not the greater hide;
The cedar stoops not to the base shrub's foot,
But low shrubs wither at the cedar's root.

'So let thy thoughts, low vassals to thy state'—
'No more,' quoth he; 'by heaven, I will not hear thee:
Yield to my love; if not, enforced hate,
Instead of love's coy touch, shall rudely tear thee;
That done, despitefully I mean to bear thee

562. **wrinkles,** frowns. 571. **holy human law,** i.e., laws governing matrimony. 574. **stoop,** a play here on the meanings "subjecting oneself to" and "debasing oneself." 576. **pretended,** intended. 603. **seeded,** matured. 604. **thy spring,** i.e., he is not yet king; he is in the period of his life when he gives promise. 607. **be rememb'red,** be reminded, bear in mind. 608. **vassal actors,** i.e., vassals who commit

Unto the base bed of some rascal groom,
To be thy partner in this shameful doom.'

This said, he sets his foot upon the light,
For light and lust are deadly enemies:
Shame folded up in blind concealing night,
When most unseen, then most doth tyrannize.
The wolf hath seiz'd his prey, the poor lamb cries;
Till with her own white fleece her voice controll'd
Entombs her outcry in her lips' sweet fold:

For with the nightly linen that she wears
He pens her piteous clamours in her head;
Cooling his hot face in the chastest tears
That ever modest eyes with sorrow shed.
O, that prone lust should stain so pure a bed!
The spots whereof could weeping purify,
Her tears should drop on them perpetually.

But she hath lost a dearer thing than life,
And he hath won what he would lose again:
This forced league doth force a further strife;
This momentary joy breeds months of pain;
This hot desire converts to cold disdain:
Pure Chastity is rifled of her store,
And Lust, the thief, far poorer than before.

Look as the full-fed hound or gorged hawk,
Unapt for tender smell or speedy flight,
Make slow pursuit, or altogether balk
The prey wherein by nature they delight;
So surfeit-taking Tarquin fares this night:
His taste delicious, in digestion souring,
Devours his will, that liv'd by foul devouring.

O, deeper sin than bottomless conceit
Can comprehend in still imagination!
Drunken Desire must vomit his receipt,
Ere he can see his own abomination.
While Lust is in his pride, no exclamation
Can curb his heat or rein his rash desire,
Till like a jade Self-will himself doth tire.

And then with lank and lean discolour'd cheek,
With heavy eye, knit brow, and strengthless pace,
Feebly Desire, all recreant, poor, and meek,
Like to a bankrout beggar wails his case:
The flesh being proud, Desire doth fight with Grace,
For there it revels; and when that decays,
The guilty rebel for remission prays.

So fares it with this faultful lord of Rome,
Who this accomplishment so hotly chased;
For now against himself he sounds this doom,
That through the length of times he stands disgraced:
Besides, his soul's fair temple is defaced;
To whose weak ruins muster troops of cares,
To ask the spotted princess how she fares.

She says, her subjects with foul insurrection
Have batter'd down her consecrated wall,
And by their mortal fault brought in subjection
Her immortality, and made her thrall
To living death and pain perpetual:
Which in her prescience she controlled still,
But her foresight could not forestall their will.

Ev'n in this thought through the dark night he stealeth,
A captive victor that hath lost in gain;
Bearing away the wound that nothing healeth,
The scar that will, despite of cure, remain;
Leaving his spoil perplex'd in greater pain.
She bears the load of lust he left behind,
And he the burthen of a guilty mind.

He like a thievish dog creeps sadly thence;
She like a wearied lamb lies panting there;
He scowls and hates himself for his offence;
She, desperate, with her nails her flesh doth tear;
He faintly flies, sweating with guilty fear;
She stays, exclaiming on the direful night;
He runs, and chides his vanish'd, loath'd delight.

He thence departs a heavy convertite;
She there remains a hopeless castaway;
He in his speed looks for the morning light;
She prays she never may behold the day,
'For day,' quoth she, 'night's scapes doth open lay,
And my true eyes have never practis'd how
To cloak offences with a cunning brow.

'They think not but that every eye can see
The same disgrace which they themselves behold;
And therefore would they still in darkness be,
To have their unseen sin remain untold;
For they their guilt with weeping will unfold,
And grave, like water that doth eat in steel,
Upon my cheeks what helpless shame I feel.'

Here she exclaims against repose and rest,
And bids her eyes hereafter still be blind.
She wakes her heart by beating on her breast,
And bids it leap from thence, where it may find
Some purer chest to close so pure a mind.
Frantic with grief thus breathes she forth her spite
Against the unseen secrecy of night:

'O comfort-killing Night, image of hell!
Dim register and notary of shame!
Black stage for tragedies and murders fell!
Vast sin-concealing chaos! nurse of blame!
Blind muffled bawd! dark harbour for defame!
Grim cave of death! whisp'ring conspirator
With close-tongu'd treason and the ravisher!

'O hateful, vaporous, and foggy Night!
Since thou art guilty of my cureless crime,
Muster thy mists to meet the eastern light,
Make war against proportion'd course of time;
Or if thou wilt permit the sun to climb
His wonted height, yet ere he go to bed,
Knit poisonous clouds about his golden head.

'With rotten damps ravish the morning air;
Let their exhal'd unwholesome breaths make sick

crimes. 609. **hid in clay,** i.e., even in death. 614. **thy will remove,** cease your lust. 621. **privilege,** license, authorize. 622. **laud,** praise. 640. **repeal,** restoration; i.e., your *majesty* is exiled. 646. **let,** hindrance.

657. **hearsed,** buried, coffined. 743. **heavy,** sad. **convertite,** penitent. 755. **grave,** engrave. 768. **defame,** infamy. 774. **proportion'd,** i.e., regulated interchange of day and night.

The life of purity, the supreme fair,
Ere he arrive his weary noon-tide prick;
And let thy musty vapours march so thick,
  That in their smoky ranks his smoth'red light
  May set at noon and make perpetual night.

'Were Tarquin Night, as he is but Night's child,
The silver-shining queen he would distain;
Her twinkling handmaids too, by him defil'd,
Through Night's black bosom should not peep again:
So should I have co-partners in my pain;
  And fellowship in woe doth woe assuage,
  As palmers' chat makes short their pilgrimage.

'Where now I have no one to blush with me,
To cross their arms and hang their heads with mine,
To mask their brows and hide their infamy;
But I alone alone must sit and pine,
Seasoning the earth with show'rs of silver brine,
  Mingling my talk with tears, my grief with groans,
  Poor wasting monuments of lasting moans.

'O Night, thou furnace of foul-reeking smoke,
Let not the jealous Day behold that face
Which underneath thy black all-hiding cloak
Immodestly lies martyr'd with disgrace!
Keep still possession of thy gloomy place,
  That all the faults which in thy reign are made
  May likewise be sepulchr'd in thy shade!

'Make me not object to the tell-tale Day!
The light will show, character'd in my brow,
The story of sweet chastity's decay,
The impious breach of holy wedlock vow:
Yea, the illiterate, that know not how
  To cipher what is writ in learned books,
  Will quote my loathsome trespass in my looks.

'The nurse, to still her child, will tell my story,
And fright her crying babe with Tarquin's name;
The orator, to deck his oratory,
Will couple my reproach to Tarquin's shame;
Feast-finding minstrels, tuning my defame,
  Will tie the hearers to attend each line,
  How Tarquin wronged me, I Collatine.

'Let my good name, that senseless reputation,
For Collatine's dear love be kept unspotted:
If that be made a theme for disputation,
The branches of another root are rotted,
And undeserv'd reproach to him allotted
  That is as clear from this attaint of mine
  As I, ere this, was pure to Collatine.

'O unseen shame! invisible disgrace!
O unfelt sore! crest-wounding, private scar!
Reproach is stamp'd in Collatinus' face,
And Tarquin's eye may read the mot afar,
How he in peace is wounded, not in war.
  Alas, how many bear such shameful blows,
  Which not themselves, but he that gives them
    knows!

'If, Collatine, thine honour lay in me,
From me by strong assault it is bereft.
My honey lost, and I, a drone-like bee,
Have no perfection of my summer left,
But robb'd and ransack'd by injurious theft:
  In thy weak hive a wand'ring wasp hath crept,
  And suck'd the honey which thy chaste bee kept.

'Yet am I guilty of thy honour's wrack;
Yet for thy honour did I entertain him;
Coming from thee, I could not put him back,
For it had been dishonour to disdain him:
Besides, of weariness he did complain him,
  And talk'd of virtue: O unlook'd-for evil,
  When virtue is profan'd in such a devil!

'Why should the worm intrude the maiden bud?
Or hateful cuckoos hatch in sparrows' nests?
Or toads infect fair founts with venom mud?
Or tyrant folly lurk in gentle breasts?
Or kings be breakers of their own behests?
  But no perfection is so absolute,
  That some impurity doth not pollute.

'The aged man that coffers-up his gold
Is plagu'd with cramps and gouts and painful fits;
And scarce hath eyes his treasure to behold,
But like still-pining Tantalus he sits,
And useless barns the harvest of his wits;
  Having no other pleasure of his gain
  But torment that it cannot cure his pain.

'So then he hath it when he cannot use it,
And leaves it to be mast'red by his young;
Who in their pride do presently abuse it:
Their father was too weak, and they too strong,
To hold their cursed-blessed fortune long.
  The sweets we wish for turn to loathed sours
  Even in the moment that we call them ours.

'Unruly blasts wait on the tender spring;
Unwholesome weeds take root with precious flow'rs;
The adder hisses where the sweet birds sing;
What virtue breeds iniquity devours:
We have no good that we can say is ours,
  But ill-annexed Opportunity
  Or kills his life or else his quality.

'O Opportunity, thy guilt is great!
'Tis thou that execut'st the traitor's treason:
Thou set'st the wolf where he the lamb may get;
Whoever plots the sin, thou 'point'st the season;
'Tis thou that spurn'st at right, at law, at reason;
  And in thy shady cell, where none may spy him,
  Sits Sin, to seize the souls that wander by him.

'Thou makest the vestal violate her oath;
Thou blowest the fire when temperance is thaw'd;
Thou smother'st honesty, thou murd'rest troth;
Thou foul abettor! thou notorious bawd!
Thou plantest scandal and displacest laud:

780. **supreme fair,** the sun. 781. **prick,** point (on a sundial). 786. **distain,** defile. 792. **Where now,** whereas. 806. **Make . . . object,** i.e., she prays that her face may never be seen. 807. **character'd,** lettered. 811. **cipher,** decipher. 812. **quote,** note. 820. **senseless,** impalpable and pure. 828. **crest-wounding,** disgraceful to the crest or cognizance. 830. **mot,** motto. 850. **toads . . . venom.** Seagar (*Shakespeare's Natural History*, pp. 306-308) quotes from several documents attesting to the belief in the venomous quality of toads; cf. *As You Like It*, II, i, 13. 858. **Tantalus,** one who was punished in Hades by being unable to reach food and drink placed just beyond his grasp. 859. **barns,** stores, as in a barn. 864. **presently,** immediately. 869. **tender spring,** young shoot. 892. **smoothing,** flattering. 899. **sort,** choose. 907. **Advice**

Thou ravisher, thou traitor, thou false thief,
Thy honey turns to gall, thy joy to grief!

'Thy secret pleasure turns to open shame,
Thy private feasting to a public fast,
Thy smoothing titles to a ragged name,
Thy sug'red tongue to bitter wormwood taste:
Thy violent vanities can never last.
How comes it then, vile Opportunity,
Being so bad, such numbers seek for thee?

'When wilt thou be the humble suppliant's friend,
And bring him where his suit may be obtained?
When wilt thou sort an hour great strifes to end?
Or free that soul which wretchedness hath chained?
Give physic to the sick, ease to the pained?
The poor, lame, blind, halt, creep, cry out for thee;
But they ne'er meet with Opportunity.

'The patient dies while the physician sleeps;
The orphan pines while the oppressor feeds;
Justice is feasting while the widow weeps;
Advice is sporting while infection breeds:
Thou grant'st no time for charitable deeds:
Wrath, envy, treason, rape, and murder's rages,
Thy heinous hours wait on them as their pages.

'When Truth and Virtue have to do with thee,
A thousand crosses keep them from thy aid:
They buy thy help; but Sin ne'er gives a fee,
He gratis comes; and thou art well appaid
As well to hear as grant what he hath said.
My Collatine would else have come to me
When Tarquin did, but he was stay'd by thee.

'Guilty thou art of murder and of theft,
Guilty of perjury and subornation,
Guilty of treason, forgery, and shift,
Guilty of incest, that abomination;
An accessary by thine inclination
To all sins past, and all that are to come,
From the creation to the general doom.

'Mis-shapen Time, copesmate of ugly Night,
Swift subtle post, carrier of grisly care,
Eater of youth, false slave to false delight,
Base watch of woes, sin's pack-horse, virtue's snare;
Thou nursest all and murd'rest all that are:
O, hear me then, injurious, shifting Time!
Be guilty of my death, since of my crime.

'Why hath thy servant, Opportunity,
Betray'd the hours thou gav'st me to repose,
Cancell'd my fortunes, and enchained me
To endless date of never-ending woes?
Time's office is to fine the hate of foes;
To eat up errors by opinion bred,
Not spend the dowry of a lawful bed.

'Time's glory is to calm contending kings,
To unmask falsehood and bring truth to light,
To stamp the seal of time in aged things,
To wake the morn and sentinel the night,
To wrong the wronger till he render right,
To ruinate proud buildings with thy hours,
And smear with dust their glitt'ring golden tow'rs;

'To fill with worm-holes stately monuments,
To feed oblivion with decay of things,
To blot old books and alter their contents,
To pluck the quills from ancient ravens' wings,
To dry the old oak's sap and cherish springs,
To spoil antiquities of hammer'd steel,
And turn the giddy round of Fortune's wheel;

'To show the beldam daughters of her daughter,
To make the child a man, the man a child,
To slay the tiger that doth live by slaughter,
To tame the unicorn and lion wild,
To mock the subtle in themselves beguil'd,
To cheer the ploughman with increaseful crops,
And waste huge stones with little water-drops.

'Why work'st thou mischief in thy pilgrimage,
Unless thou couldst return to make amends?
One poor retiring minute in an age
Would purchase thee a thousand thousand friends,
Lending him wit that to bad debtors lends:
O, this dread night, wouldst thou one hour come
back,
I could prevent this storm and shun thy wrack!

'Thou ceaseless lackey to Eternity,
With some mischance cross Tarquin in his flight:
Devise extremes beyond extremity,
To make him curse this cursed crimeful night:
Let ghastly shadows his lewd eyes affright;
And the dire thought of his committed evil
Shape every bush a hideous shapeless devil.

'Disturb his hours of rest with restless trances,
Afflict him in his bed with bedrid groans;
Let there bechance him pitiful mischances,
To make him moan; but pity not his moans:
Stone him with hard'ned hearts, harder than stones;
And let mild women to him lose their mildness,
Wilder to him than tigers in their wildness.

'Let him have time to tear his curled hair,
Let him have time against himself to rave,
Let him have time of Time's help to despair,
Let him have time to live a loathed slave,
Let him have time a beggar's orts to crave,
And time to see one that by alms doth live
Disdain to him disdained scraps to give.

'Let him have time to see his friends his foes,
And merry fools to mock at him resort;
Let him have time to mark how slow time goes
In time of sorrow, and how swift and short
His time of folly and his time of sport;
And ever let his unrecalling crime
Have time to wail th' abusing of his time.

. . . **breeds.** While infection is spreading, the grave rulers of the state, who ought to guard against its further progress, are careless and inattentive (Malone). Steevens thought the line alluded to the plague epidemic in London. 925. **copesmate,** companion. 928. **watch,** picket, sentinel. 936. **fine,** put an end to (Steevens); cf. *Troilus and Cressida*, IV, iv, 3. 950. **To . . . springs,** to dry up the old and foster the young. 953. **beldam,** old woman. 958. **increaseful,** fruitful. 959. **waste,** wear away. 962. **retiring,** returning. 974. **trances,** visions. 981. **curled hair,** suggests the exquisite toilet of a prince. 985. **orts,** refuse, fragments. 993. **unrecalling crime,** crime that may not be undone.

'O Time, thou tutor both to good and bad,
Teach me to curse him that thou taught'st this ill!
At his own shadow let the thief run mad,
Himself himself seek every hour to kill!
Such wretched hands such wretched blood should spill;
For who so base would such an office have
As sland'rous deathsman to so base a slave?

'The baser is he, coming from a king,
To shame his hope with deeds degenerate:
The mightier man, the mightier is the thing
That makes him honour'd, or begets him hate;
For greatest scandal waits on greatest state.
The moon being clouded presently is miss'd,
But little stars may hide them when they list.

'The crow may bathe his coal-black wings in mire,
And unperceiv'd fly with the filth away;
But if the like the snow-white swan desire,
The stain upon his silver down will stay.
Poor grooms are sightless night, kings glorious day:
Gnats are unnoted wheresoe'er they fly,
But eagles gaz'd upon with every eye.

'Out, idle words, servants to shallow fools!
Unprofitable sounds, weak arbitrators!
Busy yourselves in skill-contending schools;
Debate where leisure serves with dull debaters;
To trembling clients be you mediators:
For me, I force not argument a straw,
Since that my case is past the help of law.

'In vain I rail at Opportunity,
At Time, at Tarquin, and uncheerful Night;
In vain I cavil with mine infamy,
In vain I spurn at my confirm'd despite:
This helpless smoke of words doth me no right.
The remedy indeed to do me good
Is to let forth my foul-defiled blood.

'Poor hand, why quiver'st thou at this decree?
Honour thyself to rid me of this shame;
For if I die, my honour lives in thee;
But if I live, thou liv'st in my defame:
Since thou couldst not defend thy loyal dame,
And wast afeard to scratch her wicked foe,
Kill both thyself and her for yielding so.'

This said, from her be-tumbled couch she starteth,
To find some desp'rate instrument of death:
But this no slaughterhouse no tool imparteth
To make more vent for passage of her breath;
Which, thronging through her lips, so vanisheth
As smoke from Ætna, that in air consumes,
Or that which from discharged cannon fumes.

'In vain,' quoth she, 'I live, and seek in vain
Some happy mean to end a hapless life.
I fear'd by Tarquin's falchion to be slain,
Yet for the self-same purpose seek a knife:
But when I fear'd I was a loyal wife:
So am I now: O no, that cannot be;
Of that true type hath Tarquin rifled me.

'O, that is gone for which I sought to live,
And therefore now I need not fear to die.
To clear this spot by death, at least I give
A badge of fame to slander's livery;
A dying life to living infamy:
Poor helpless help, the treasure stol'n away,
To burn the guiltless casket where it lay!

'Well, well, dear Collatine, thou shalt not know
The stained taste of violated troth;
I will not wrong thy true affection so,
To flatter thee with an infringed oath;
This bastard graff shall never come to growth:
He shall not boast who did thy stock pollute
That thou art doting father of his fruit.

'Nor shall he smile at thee in secret thought,
Nor laugh with his companions at thy state;
But thou shalt know thy int'rest was not bought
Basely with gold, but stol'n from forth thy gate.
For me, I am the mistress of my fate,
And with my trespass never will dispense,
Till life to death acquit my forc'd offence.

'I will not poison thee with my attaint,
Nor fold my fault in cleanly-coin'd excuses;
My sable ground of sin I will not paint,
To hide the truth of this false night's abuses:
My tongue shall utter all; mine eyes, like sluices,
As from a mountain-spring that feeds a dale,
Shall gush pure streams to purge my impure tale.'

By this, lamenting Philomel had ended
The well-tun'd warble of her nightly sorrow,
And solemn night with slow sad gait descended
To ugly hell; when, lo, the blushing morrow
Lends light to all fair eyes that light will borrow:
But cloudy Lucrece shames herself to see,
And therefore still in night would cloist'red be.

Revealing day through every cranny spies,
And seems to point her out where she sits weeping;
To whom she sobbing speaks: 'O eye of eyes,
Why pry'st thou through my window? leave thy peeping:
Mock with thy tickling beams eyes that are sleeping:
Brand not my forehead with thy piercing light,
For day hath nought to do what 's done by night.'

Thus cavils she with every thing she sees:
True grief is fond and testy as a child,
Who wayward once, his mood with nought agrees:
Old woes, not infant sorrows, bear them mild;
Continuance tames the one; the other wild,
Like an unpractis'd swimmer plunging still,
With too much labour drowns for want of skill.

1013. **sightless,** invisible. 1021. **force,** attach importance to. 1054. **badge of fame,** good reputation; the metaphor is from the custom of servants wearing on their liveries badges that bore their masters' coats of arms (Malone). 1061. **flatter,** deceive. 1062. **graff,** graft, scion. 1070. **dispense** [*with*], condone by dispensation. 1071. **acquit,** atone for. 1073. **cleanly,** cleverly. 1079. **Philomel.** Cf. *Titus Andronicus*, II, iii, 43, note. 1096. **them,** themselves. **mild,** mildly, calmly. 1109. **search,** probe. **annoy,** grief, injury. 1112. **suffic'd,** contented. 1114. **ken,** sight; a nautical term to signify the distance that bounds the range of ordinary vision at sea. 1127. **dumps,** mournful melodies. 1132. **diapason,** bass notes an octave or more below the melody. 1133. **burden-wise,** in the manner of an undersong or bass. 1134. **Tereus.** Cf. *Titus Andronicus*, II, iii, 43, note. **better skill.** Malone thought the sense incomplete and suggested *with better skill;* many editors define it so.

So she, deep-drenched in a sea of care,
Holds disputation with each thing she views,
And to herself all sorrow doth compare;
No object but her passion's strength renews;
And as one shifts, another straight ensues:
Sometime her grief is dumb and hath no words;
Sometime 'tis mad and too much talk affords.

The little birds that tune their morning's joy
Make her moans mad with their sweet melody:
For mirth doth search the bottom of annoy;
Sad souls are slain in merry company;
Grief best is pleas'd with grief's society:
True sorrow then is feelingly suffic'd
When with like semblance it is sympathiz'd.

'Tis double death to drown in ken of shore;
He ten times pines that pines beholding food;
To see the salve doth make the wound ache more;
Great grief grieves most at that would do it good;
Deep woes roll forward like a gentle flood,
Who, being stopp'd, the bounding banks o'erflows;
Grief dallied with nor law nor limit knows.

'You mocking birds,' quoth she, 'your tunes entomb
Within your hollow-swelling feathered breasts,
And in my hearing be you mute and dumb:
My restless discord loves no stops nor rests;
A woeful hostess brooks not merry guests:
Relish your nimble notes to pleasing ears;
Distress likes dumps when time is kept with tears.

'Come, Philomel, that sing'st of ravishment,
Make thy sad grove in my dishevell'd hair:
As the dank earth weeps at thy languishment,
So I at each sad strain will strain a tear,
And with deep groans the diapason bear;
For burden-wise I'll hum on Tarquin still,
While thou on Tereus descants better skill.

'And whiles against a thorn thou bear'st thy part,
To keep thy sharp woes waking, wretched I,
To imitate thee well, against my heart
Will fix a sharp knife to affright mine eye;
Who, if it wink, shall thereon fall and die.
These means, as frets upon an instrument,
Shall tune our heart-strings to true languishment.

'And for, poor bird, thou sing'st not in the day,
As shaming any eye should thee behold,
Some dark deep desert, seated from the way,
That knows not parching heat nor freezing cold,
Will we find out; and there we will unfold
To creatures stern sad tunes, to change their kinds:
Since men prove beasts, let beasts bear gentle minds.'

As the poor frighted deer, that stands at gaze,
Wildly determining which way to fly,
Or one encompass'd with a winding maze,
That cannot tread the way out readily;
So with herself is she in mutiny,
To live or die which of the twain were better,
When life is sham'd, and death reproach's debtor.

'To kill myself,' quoth she, 'alack, what were it,
But with my body my poor soul's pollution?
They that lose half with greater patience bear it
Than they whose whole is swallowed in confusion.
That mother tries a merciless conclusion
Who, having two sweet babes, when death takes one,
Will slay the other and be nurse to none.

'My body or my soul, which was the dearer,
When the one pure, the other made divine?
Whose love of either to myself was nearer,
When both were kept for heaven and Collatine?
Ay me! the bark peel'd from the lofty pine,
His leaves will wither and his sap decay;
So must my soul, her bark being peel'd away.

'Her house is sack'd, her quiet interrupted,
Her mansion batter'd by the enemy;
Her sacred temple spotted, spoil'd, corrupted,
Grossly engirt with daring infamy:
Then let it not be call'd impiety,
If in this blemish'd fort I make some hole
Through which I may convey this troubled soul.

'Yet die I will not till my Collatine
Have heard the cause of my untimely death;
That he may vow, in that sad hour of mine,
Revenge on him that made me stop my breath.
My stained blood to Tarquin I'll bequeath,
Which by him tainted shall for him be spent,
And as his due writ in my testament.

'My honour I'll bequeath unto the knife
That wounds my body so dishonoured.
'Tis honour to deprive dishonour'd life;
The one will live, the other being dead:
So of shame's ashes shall my fame be bred;
For in my death I murder shameful scorn:
My shame so dead, mine honour is new-born.

'Dear lord of that dear jewel I have lost,
What legacy shall I bequeath to thee?
My resolution, love, shall be thy boast,
By whose example thou reveng'd mayst be.
How Tarquin must be us'd, read it in me:
Myself, thy friend, will kill myself, thy foe,
And for my sake serve thou false Tarquin so.

'This brief abridgement of my will I make:
My soul and body to the skies and ground;
My resolution, husband, do thou take;
Mine honour be the knife's that makes my wound;

Wyndham takes *descants* as a transitive verb and *skill* as its object. Lucrece contrasts her *deep groans* uttered *burden-wise* with the *better skill* of the nightingale's treble melody. 1135. **against a thorn,** alludes to a commonplace of natural history, that the nightingale perched deliberately with a thorn against her breast to keep her awake. The wakefulness of the nightingale is a common detail of medieval romances. 1139. **Who,** which, i.e., her heart. **if it wink,** if her eye close. 1140. **frets,** bars placed on finger boards of stringed instruments to regulate the fingering. 1142. **for,** because. **sing'st not in the day,** one of the vulgar errors of the time; nightingales sing both by day and by night. 1144. **seated from,** situated away from. 1149. **at gaze,** transfixed. 1155. **death reproach's debtor,** i.e., she can die only by killing herself shamefully. 1160. **tries . . . conclusion,** finds out if by a cruel experiment she can regain her peace of mind (Pooler). 1176. **convey,** let out.

My shame be his that did my fame confound;
And all my fame that lives disbursed be
To those that live, and think no shame of me.

'Thou, Collatine, shalt oversee this will;
How was I overseen that thou shalt see it!
My blood shall wash the slander of mine ill;
My life's foul deed, my life's fair end shall free it.
Faint not, faint heart, but stoutly say "So be it:"
Yield to my hand; my hand shall conquer thee:
Thou dead, both die, and both shall victors be.'

This plot of death when sadly she had laid,
And wip'd the brinish pearl from her bright eyes,
With untun'd tongue she hoarsely calls her maid,
Whose swift obedience to her mistress hies;
For fleet-wing'd duty with thought's feathers flies.
Poor Lucrece' cheeks unto her maid seem so
As winter meads when sun doth melt their snow.

Her mistress she doth give demure good-morrow,
With soft-slow tongue, true mark of modesty,
And sorts a sad look to her lady's sorrow,
For why her face wore sorrow's livery;
But durst not ask of her audaciously
Why her two suns were cloud-eclipsed so,
Nor why her fair cheeks over-wash'd with woe.

But as the earth doth weep, the sun being set,
Each flower moist'ned like a melting eye;
Even so the maid with swelling drops gan wet
Her circled eyne, enforc'd by sympathy
Of those fair suns set in her mistress' sky,
Who in a salt-wav'd ocean quench their light,
Which makes the maid weep like the dewy night.

A pretty while these pretty creatures stand,
Like ivory conduits coral cisterns filling:
One justly weeps; the other takes in hand
No cause, but company, of her drops spilling:
Their gentle sex to weep are often willing;
Grieving themselves to guess at others' smarts,
And then they drown their eyes or break their hearts.

For men have marble, women waxen, minds,
And therefore are they form'd as marble will;
The weak oppress'd, th' impression of strange kinds
Is form'd in them by force, by fraud, or skill:
Then call them not the authors of their ill,
No more than wax shall be accounted evil
Wherein is stamp'd the semblance of a devil.

Their smoothness, like a goodly champaign plain,
Lays open all the little worms that creep;
In men, as in a rough-grown grove, remain
Cave-keeping evils that obscurely sleep:
Through crystal walls each little mote will peep:
Though men can cover crimes with bold stern looks,
Poor women's faces are their own faults' books.

No man inveigh against the withered flow'r,
But chide rough winter that the flow'r hath kill'd:
Not that devour'd, but that which doth devour,
Is worthy blame. O, let it not be hild
Poor women's faults, that they are so fulfill'd
With men's abuses: those proud lords, to blame,
Make weak-made women tenants to their shame.

The precedent whereof in Lucrece view,
Assail'd by night with circumstances strong
Of present death, and shame that might ensue
By that her death, to do her husband wrong:
Such danger to resistance did belong,
That dying fear through all her body spread;
And who cannot abuse a body dead?

By this, mild patience bid fair Lucrece speak
To the poor counterfeit of her complaining:
'My girl,' quoth she, 'on what occasion break
Those tears from thee, that down thy cheeks are raining?
If thou dost weep for grief of my sustaining,
Know, gentle wench, it small avails my mood:
If tears could help, mine own would do me good.

'But tell me, girl, when went'—and there she stay'd
Till after a deep groan—'Tarquin from hence?'
'Madam, ere I was up,' replied the maid,
'The more to blame my sluggard negligence:
Yet with the fault I thus far can dispense;
Myself was stirring ere the break of day,
And, ere I rose, was Tarquin gone away.

'But, lady, if your maid may be so bold,
She would request to know your heaviness.'
'O, peace!' quoth Lucrece: 'if it should be told,
The repetition cannot make it less;
For more it is than I can well express:
And that deep torture may be call'd a hell
When more is felt than one hath power to tell.

'Go, get me hither paper, ink, and pen:
Yet save that labour, for I have them here.
What should I say? One of my husband's men
Bid thou be ready, by and by, to bear
A letter to my lord, my love, my dear:
Bid him with speed prepare to carry it;
The cause craves haste, and it will soon be writ.'

Her maid is gone, and she prepares to write,
First hovering o'er the paper with her quill:
Conceit and grief an eager combat fight;
What wit sets down is blotted straight with will;
This is too curious-good, this blunt and ill:
Much like a press of people at a door,
Throng her inventions, which shall go before.

At last she thus begins: 'Thou worthy lord
Of that unworthy wife that greeteth thee,
Health to thy person! next vouchsafe t' afford—
If ever, love, thy Lucrece thou wilt see—
Some present speed to come and visit me.

1206. **overseen,** deluded, taken advantage of; quibblingly used with *oversee* (l. 1205), i.e., attend to as an executor of an estate. 1214. **untun'd,** discordant. 1221. **sorts,** adapts, 1222. **For why,** because. 1234. **conduits,** alludes to the conduit spouts and fountains shaped in the form of human figures. 1235. **takes in hand,** acknowledges. 1257. **hild,** variant form of "held." 1258. **fulfill'd,** filled. 1261. **precedent,** proof, example. 1269. **counterfeit,** likeness, imitation. 1300. **curious,** fastidiously. 1309. **tedious,** painful. 1316. **her stain'd excuse,** i.e., explanation of her shame. 1329. **Deep sounds,** depths of the sea which may be sounded. 1338. **villain,** servant. 1345. **seely,**

So, I commend me from our house in grief:
My woes are tedious, though my words are brief.'

Here folds she up the tenour of her woe,
Her certain sorrow writ uncertainly.
By this short schedule Collatine may know
Her grief, but not her grief's true quality:
She dares not thereof make discovery,
Lest he should hold it her own gross abuse,
Ere she with blood had stain'd her stain'd excuse.

Besides, the life and feeling of her passion
She hoards, to spend when he is by to hear her:
When sighs and groans and tears may grace the fashion
Of her disgrace, the better so to clear her
From that suspicion which the world might bear her.
To shun this blot, she would not blot the letter
With words, till action might become them better.

To see sad sights moves more than hear them told:
For then the eye interprets to the ear
The heavy motion that it doth behold,
When every part a part of woe doth bear.
'Tis but a part of sorrow that we hear:
Deep sounds make lesser noise than shallow fords,
And sorrow ebbs, being blown with wind of words.

Her letter now is seal'd, and on it writ
'At Ardea to my lord with more than haste.'
The post attends, and she delivers it,
Charging the sour-fac'd groom to hie as fast
As lagging fowls before the northern blast:
Speed more than speed but dull and slow she deems:
Extremity still urgeth such extremes.

The homely villain court'sies to her low;
And, blushing on her, with a steadfast eye
Receives the scroll without or yea or no,
And forth with bashful innocence doth hie.
But they whose guilt within their bosoms lie
Imagine every eye beholds their blame;
For Lucrece thought he blush'd to see her shame:

When, seely groom! God wot, it was defect
Of spirit, life, and bold audacity.
Such harmless creatures have a true respect
To talk in deeds, while others saucily
Promise more speed, but do it leisurely:
Even so this pattern of the worn-out age
Pawn'd honest looks, but laid no words to gage.

His kindled duty kindled her mistrust,
That two red fires in both their faces blazed;
She thought he blush'd, as knowing Tarquin's lust,
And, blushing with him, wistly on him gazed;
Her earnest eye did make him more amazed:
The more she saw the blood his cheeks replenish,
The more she thought he spied in her some blemish.

But long she thinks till he return again,
And yet the duteous vassal scarce is gone.
The weary time she cannot entertain,
For now 'tis stale to sigh, to weep, and groan:
So woe hath wearied woe, moan tired moan,
That she her plaints a little while doth stay,
Pausing for means to mourn some newer way.

At last she calls to mind where hangs a piece
Of skilful painting, made for Priam's Troy;
Before the which is drawn the power of Greece,
For Helen's rape the city to destroy,
Threat'ning cloud-kissing Ilion with annoy;
Which the conceited painter drew so proud,
As heaven, it seem'd, to kiss the turrets bow'd.

A thousand lamentable objects there,
In scorn of nature, art gave lifeless life:
Many a dry drop seem'd a weeping tear,
Shed for the slaught'red husband by the wife:
The red blood reek'd, to show the painter's strife;
And dying eyes gleam'd forth their ashy lights,
Like dying coals burnt out in tedious nights.

There might you see the labouring pioner
Begrim'd with sweat, and smeared all with dust;
And from the tow'rs of Troy there would appear
The very eyes of men through loop-holes thrust,
Gazing upon the Greeks with little lust:
Such sweet observance in this work was had,
That one might see those far-off eyes look sad.

In great commanders grace and majesty
You might behold, triumphing in their faces;
In youth, quick bearing and dexterity;
And here and there the painter interlaces
Pale cowards, marching on with trembling paces;
Which heartless peasants did so well resemble,
That one would swear he saw them quake and tremble.

In Ajax and Ulysses, O, what art
Of physiognomy might one behold!
The face of either cipher'd either's heart;
Their face their manners most expressly told:
In Ajax' eyes blunt rage and rigour roll'd;
But the mild glance that sly Ulysses lent
Show'd deep regard and smiling government.

There pleading might you see grave Nestor stand,
As 'twere encouraging the Greeks to fight;
Making such sober action with his hand,
That it beguil'd attention, charm'd the sight:
In speech, it seem'd, his beard, all silver white,
Wagg'd up and down, and from his lips did fly
Thin winding breath, which purl'd up to the sky.

About him were a press of gaping faces,
Which seem'd to swallow up his sound advice;
All jointly list'ning, but with several graces,
As if some mermaid did their ears entice,
Some high, some low, the painter was so nice;
The scalps of many, almost hid behind,
To jump up higher seem'd, to mock the mind.

simple. 1350. **pattern,** one who resembles dwellers in the good early times (Craig). **worn-out,** departed, i.e., golden age. 1351. **Pawn'd,** offered as security. **to gage,** as guarantee. 1355. **wistly,** attentively. 1362. **stale,** wearisome repetition. 1371. **conceited,** ingenious. 1377. **strife,** rivalry, i.e., with Nature. 1380. **pioner,** digger, miner. 1384. **lust,** pleasure, delight. 1390. **interlaces,** interweaves. 1396. **cipher'd,** showed, expressed. 1400. **deep . . . government,** profound wisdom and the complacency arising from passions being under the command of reason (Malone). 1406. **Wagg'd,** moved. 1407. **purl'd,** flowed with a whirling motion. 1413. **scalps,** skulls, crowns of heads.

Here one man's hand lean'd on another's head,
His nose being shadowed by his neighbour's ear;
Here one being throng'd bears back, all boll'n and red;
Another smother'd seems to pelt and swear;
And in their rage such signs of rage they bear,
As, but for loss of Nestor's golden words,
It seem'd they would debate with angry swords.

For much imaginary work was there;
Conceit deceitful, so compact, so kind,
That for Achilles' image stood his spear,
Grip'd in an armed hand; himself, behind,
Was left unseen, save to the eye of mind:
A hand, a foot, a face, a leg, a head,
Stood for the whole to be imagined.

And from the walls of strong-besieged Troy
When their brave hope, bold Hector, march'd to field,
Stood many Troyan mothers, sharing joy
To see their youthful sons bright weapons wield;
And to their hope they such odd action yield,
That through their light joy seemed to appear,
Like bright things stain'd, a kind of heavy fear.

And from the strond of Dardan, where they fought,
To Simois' reedy banks the red blood ran,
Whose waves to imitate the battle sought
With swelling ridges; and their ranks began
To break upon the galled shore, and than
Retire again, till, meeting greater ranks,
They join and shoot their foam at Simois' banks.

To this well-painted piece is Lucrece come,
To find a face where all distress is stell'd.
Many she sees where cares have carved some,
But none where all distress and dolour dwell'd,
Till she despairing Hecuba beheld,
Staring on Priam's wounds with her old eyes,
Which bleeding under Pyrrhus' proud foot lies.

In her the painter had anatomiz'd
Time's ruin, beauty's wrack, and grim care's reign:
Her cheeks with chops and wrinkles were disguis'd;
Of what she was no semblance did remain:
Her blue blood chang'd to black in every vein,
Wanting the spring that those shrunk pipes had fed,
Show'd life imprison'd in a body dead.

On this sad shadow Lucrece spends her eyes,
And shapes her sorrow to the beldam's woes,
Who nothing wants to answer her but cries,
And bitter words to ban her cruel foes:
The painter was no god to lend her those;
And therefore Lucrece swears he did her wrong,
To give her so much grief and not a tongue.

'Poor instrument,' quoth she, 'without a sound,
I'll tune thy woes with my lamenting tongue;
And drop sweet balm in Priam's painted wound,
And rail on Pyrrhus that hath done him wrong;
And with my tears quench Troy that burns so long;
And with my knife scratch out the angry eyes
Of all the Greeks that are thine enemies.

'Show me the strumpet that began this stir,
That with my nails her beauty I may tear.
Thy heat of lust, fond Paris, did incur
This load of wrath that burning Troy doth bear:
Thy eye kindled the fire that burneth here;
And here in Troy, for trespass of thine eye,
The sire, the son, the dame, and daughter die.

'Why should the private pleasure of some one
Become the public plague of many moe?
Let sin, alone committed, light alone
Upon his head that hath transgressed so;
Let guiltless souls be freed from guilty woe:
For one's offence why should so many fall,
To plague a private sin in general?

'Lo, here weeps Hecuba, here Priam dies,
Here manly Hector faints, here Troilus swounds,
Here friend by friend in bloody channel lies,
And friend to friend gives unadvised wounds,
And one man's lust these many lives confounds:
Had doting Priam check'd his son's desire,
Troy had been bright with fame and not with fire.'

Here feelingly she weeps Troy's painted woes:
For sorrow, like a heavy-hanging bell,
Once set on ringing, with his own weight goes;
Then little strength rings out the doleful knell:
So Lucrece, set a-work, sad tales doth tell
To pencill'd pensiveness and colour'd sorrow;
She lends them words, and she their looks doth borrow.

She throws her eyes about the painting round,
And who she finds forlorn she doth lament.
At last she sees a wretched image bound,
That piteous looks to Phrygian shepherds lent:
His face, though full of cares, yet show'd content;
Onward to Troy with the blunt swains he goes,
So mild, that Patience seem'd to scorn his woes.

In him the painter labour'd with his skill
To hide deceit, and give the harmless show
An humble gait, calm looks, eyes wailing still,
A brow unbent, that seem'd to welcome woe;
Cheeks neither red nor pale, but mingled so
That blushing red no guilty instance gave,
Nor ashy pale the fear that false hearts have.

But, like a constant and confirmed devil,
He entertain'd a show so seeming just,
And therein so ensconc'd his secret evil,
That jealousy itself could not mistrust
False-creeping craft and perjury should thrust
Into so bright a day such black-fac'd storms,
Or blot with hell-born sin such saint-like forms.

The well-skill'd workman this mild image drew
For perjur'd Sinon, whose enchanting story
The credulous old Priam after slew;
Whose words like wildfire burnt the shining glory

1417. **boll'n,** swollen. 1418. **pelt,** scold. 1444. **stell'd,** portrayed. 1450. **anatomiz'd,** dissected. 1452. **chops,** chaps, cracks and lines in the skin. 1460. **ban,** curse. 1484. **in general,** publicly; i.e., to punish the general public for an individual's sin. 1488. **unadvised,** inadvertent. 1497. **pencill'd,** painted. 1501. **image,** i.e., Sinon, betrayer of Troy. 1502. **lent,** drew from. 1511. **guilty instance,** symptom of guilt (Malone). 1514. **entertain'd . . . just,** kept up an appearance of justice. 1516. **mistrust,** suspect. 1521. **enchanting,** bewitching.

Of rich-built Ilion, that the skies were sorry,
And little stars shot from their fixed places,
When their glass fell wherein they view'd their faces.

This picture she advisedly perus'd,
And chid the painter for his wondrous skill,
Saying, some shape in Sinon's was abus'd;
So fair a form lodg'd not a mind so ill:
And still on him she gaz'd; and gazing still,
Such signs of truth in his plain face she spied,
That she concludes the picture was belied.

'It cannot be,' quoth she, 'that so much guile'—
She would have said 'can lurk in such a look;'
But Tarquin's shape came in her mind the while,
And from her tongue 'can lurk' from 'cannot' took:
'It cannot be' she in that sense forsook,
And turn'd it thus, 'It cannot be, I find,
But such a face should bear a wicked mind:

'For even as subtle Sinon here is painted,
So sober-sad, so weary, and so mild,
As if with grief or travail he had fainted,
To me came Tarquin armed; so beguil'd
With outward honesty, but yet defil'd
With inward vice: as Priam him did cherish,
So did I Tarquin; so my Troy did perish.

'Look, look, how list'ning Priam wets his eyes,
To see those borrowed tears that Sinon sheeds!
Priam, why art thou old and yet not wise?
For every tear he falls a Troyan bleeds:
His eye drops fire, no water thence proceeds;
Those round clear pearls of his, that move thy pity,
Are balls of quenchless fire to burn thy city.

'Such devils steal effects from lightless hell;
For Sinon in his fire doth quake with cold,
And in that cold hot-burning fire doth dwell;
These contraries such unity do hold,
Only to flatter fools and make them bold:
So Priam's trust false Sinon's tears doth flatter,
That he finds means to burn his Troy with water.'

Here, all enrag'd, such passion her assails,
That patience is quite beaten from her breast.
She tears the senseless Sinon with her nails,
Comparing him to that unhappy guest
Whose deed hath made herself herself detest:
At last she smilingly with this gives o'er;
'Fool, fool!' quoth she, 'his wounds will not be sore.'

Thus ebbs and flows the current of her sorrow,
And time doth weary time with her complaining.
She looks for night, and then she longs for morrow,
And both she thinks too long with her remaining:
Short time seems long in sorrow's sharp sustaining:
Though woe be heavy, yet it seldom sleeps;
And they that watch see time how slow it creeps.

Which all this time hath overslipp'd her thought,
That she with painted images hath spent;
Being from the feeling of her own grief brought
By deep surmise of others' detriment;
Losing her woes in shows of discontent.
It easeth some, though none it ever cured,
To think their dolour others have endured.

But now the mindful messenger, come back,
Brings home his lord and other company;
Who finds his Lucrece clad in mourning black:
And round about her tear-distained eye
Blue circles stream'd, like rainbows in the sky:
These water-galls in her dim element
Foretell new storms to those already spent.

Which when her sad-beholding husband saw,
Amazedly in her sad face he stares:
Her eyes, though sod in tears, look'd red and raw,
Her lively colour kill'd with deadly cares.
He hath no power to ask her how she fares:
Both stood, like old acquaintance in a trance,
Met far from home, wond'ring each other's chance.

At last he takes her by the bloodless hand,
And thus begins: 'What uncouth ill event
Hath thee befall'n, that thou dost trembling stand?
Sweet love, what spite hath thy fair colour spent?
Why art thou thus attir'd in discontent?
Unmask, dear dear, this moody heaviness,
And tell thy grief, that we may give redress.'

Three times with sighs she gives her sorrow fire,
Ere once she can discharge one word of woe:
At length address'd to answer his desire,
She modestly prepares to let them know
Her honour is ta'en prisoner by the foe;
While Collatine and his consorted lords
With sad attention long to hear her words.

And now this pale swan in her wat'ry nest
Begins the sad dirge of her certain ending;
'Few words,' quoth she, 'shall fit the trespass best,
Where no excuse can give the fault amending:
In me moe woes than words are now depending;
And my laments would be drawn out too long,
To tell them all with one poor tired tongue.

'Then be this all the task it hath to say:
Dear husband, in the interest of thy bed
A stranger came, and on that pillow lay
Where thou wast wont to rest thy weary head;
And what wrong else may be imagined
By foul enforcement might be done to me,
From that, alas, thy Lucrece is not free.

'For in the dreadful dead of dark midnight,
With shining falchion in my chamber came
A creeping creature, with a flaming light,
And softly cried "Awake, thou Roman dame,
And entertain my love; else lasting shame
On thee and thine this night I will inflict,
If thou my love's desire do contradict.

' "For some hard-favour'd groom of thine," quoth he,

1523. **wildfire,** gunpowder rolled up wet and set on fire. 1544. **beguil'd,** disguised. 1549. **borrowed,** counterfeited. **sheeds,** sheds. 1584. **other company.** Cf. *The Argument*, l. 18, and ll. 1731, 1734, below. 1586. **tear-distained,** tear-stained. 1588. **water-galls,** secondary rainbows. 1592. **sod,** scalded. 1604-1605. **Three . . . woe,** metaphor based on the discharging of ancient firearms by means of a match (Staunton). 1611-1612. **pale . . . ending,** alludes to the belief that the swan sang at his death.

"Unless thou yoke thy liking to my will,
I'll murder straight, and then I'll slaughter thee
And swear I found you where you did fulfil
The loathsome act of lust, and so did kill
The lechers in their deed: this act will be
My fame and thy perpetual infamy."

'With this, I did begin to start and cry;
And then against my heart he sets his sword,
Swearing, unless I took all patiently,
I should not live to speak another word;
So should my shame still rest upon record,
And never be forgot in mighty Rome
Th' adulterate death of Lucrece and her groom.

'Mine enemy was strong, my poor self weak,
And far the weaker with so strong a fear:
My bloody judge forbod my tongue to speak;
No rightful plea might plead for justice there:
His scarlet lust came evidence to swear
That my poor beauty had purloin'd his eyes;
And when the judge is robb'd the prisoner dies.

'O, teach me how to make mine own excuse!
Or at the least this refuge let me find;
Though my gross blood be stain'd with this abuse,
Immaculate and spotless is my mind;
That was not forc'd; that never was inclin'd
To accessary yieldings, but still pure
Doth in her poison'd closet yet endure.'

Lo, here, the hopeless merchant of this loss,
With head declin'd, and voice damm'd up with woe,
With sad set eyes, and wreathed arms across,
From lips new-waxen pale begins to blow
The grief away that stops his answer so:
But, wretched as he is, he strives in vain;
What he breathes out his breath drinks up again.

As through an arch the violent roaring tide
Outruns the eye that doth behold his haste,
Yet in the eddy boundeth in his pride
Back to the strait that forc'd him on so fast;
In rage sent out, recall'd in rage, being past:
Even so his sighs, his sorrows, make a saw,
To push grief on, and back the same grief draw.

Which speechless woe of his poor she attendeth,
And his untimely frenzy thus awaketh:
'Dear lord, thy sorrow to my sorrow lendeth
Another power; no flood by raining slaketh.
My woe too sensible thy passion maketh
More feeling-painful: let it then suffice
To drown one woe, one pair of weeping eyes.

'And for my sake, when I might charm thee so
For she that was thy Lucrece, now attend me:
Be suddenly revenged on my foe,
Thine, mine, his own: suppose thou dost defend me
From what is past: the help that thou shalt lend me
Comes all too late, yet let the traitor die;
For sparing justice feeds iniquity.

'But ere I name him, you fair lords,' quoth she,
Speaking to those that came with Collatine,
'Shall plight your honourable faiths to me,
With swift pursuit to venge this wrong of mine;
For 'tis a meritorious fair design
To chase injustice with revengeful arms:
Knights, by their oaths, should right poor ladies' harms.'

At this request, with noble disposition
Each present lord began to promise aid,
As bound in knighthood to her imposition,
Longing to hear the hateful foe bewray'd.
But she, that yet her sad task hath not said,
The protestation stops. 'O, speak,' quoth she,
'How may this forced stain be wip'd from me?

'What is the quality of mine offence,
Being constrain'd with dreadful circumstance?
May my pure mind with the foul act dispense,
My low-declined honour to advance?
May any terms acquit me from this chance?
The poisoned fountain clears itself again;
And why not I from this compelled stain?'

With this, they all at once began to say,
Her body's stain her mind untainted clears;
While with a joyless smile she turns away
The face, that map which deep impression bears
Of hard misfortune, carv'd in it with tears.
'No, no,' quoth she, 'no dame, hereafter living,
By my excuse shall claim excuse's giving.'

Here with a sigh, as if her heart would break,
She throws forth Tarquin's name: 'He, he,' she says,
But more than 'he' her poor tongue could not speak;
Till after many accents and delays,
Untimely breathings, sick and short assays,
She utters this, 'He, he, fair lords, 'tis he,
That guides this hand to give this wound to me.'

Even here she sheathed in her harmless breast
A harmful knife, that thence her soul unsheathed:
That blow did bail it from the deep unrest
Of that polluted prison where it breathed:
Her contrite sighs unto the clouds bequeathed
Her winged sprite, and through her wounds doth fly
Life's lasting date from cancell'd destiny.

Stone-still, astonish'd with this deadly deed,
Stood Collatine and all his lordly crew;
Till Lucrece' father, that beholds her bleed,
Himself on her self-slaught'red body threw;
And from the purple fountain Brutus drew
The murd'rous knife, and, as it left the place,
Her blood, in poor revenge, held it in chase;

And bubbling from her breast, it doth divide
In two slow rivers, that the crimson blood
Circles her body in on every side,
Who, like a late-sack'd island, vastly stood
Bare and unpeopled in this fearful flood.
Some of her blood still pure and red remain'd,
And some look'd black, and that false Tarquin stain'd.

1648. **forbod,** forbade. 1658. **accessary yieldings,** i.e., as an accessory to crime. 1671. **In . . . past,** alludes to the motion of the tide under old London Bridge. 1682. **she,** her. 1693. **chase,** punish. 1697. **imposition,** injunction. 1740. **vastly,** far and wide. 1745. **rigol,** rim of serum.

About the mourning and congealed face
Of that black blood a wat'ry rigol goes,
Which seems to weep upon the tainted place:
And ever since, as pitying Lucrece' woes,
Corrupted blood some watery token shows;
And blood untainted still doth red abide,
Blushing at that which is so putrified.

'Daughter, dear daughter,' old Lucretius cries,
'That life was mine which thou hast here deprived.
If in the child the father's image lies,
Where shall I live now Lucrece is unlived?
Thou wast not to this end from me derived.
If children pre-decease progenitors,
We are their offspring, and they none of ours.

'Poor broken glass, I often did behold
In thy sweet semblance my old age new born;
But now that fair fresh mirror, dim and old,
Shows me a bare-bon'd death by time outworn:
O, from thy cheeks my image thou hast torn,
And shiver'd all the beauty of my glass,
That I no more can see what once I was!

'O time, cease thou thy course and last no longer,
If they surcease to be that should survive.
Shall rotten death make conquest of the stronger
And leave the falt'ring feeble souls alive?
The old bees die, the young possess their hive:
Then live, sweet Lucrece, live again and see
Thy father die, and not thy father thee!'

By this, starts Collatine as from a dream,
And bids Lucretius give his sorrow place;
And then in key-cold Lucrece' bleeding stream
He falls, and bathes the pale fear in his face,
And counterfeits to die with her a space;
Till manly shame bids him possess his breath
And live to be revenged on her death.

The deep vexation of his inward soul
Hath serv'd a dumb arrest upon his tongue;
Who, mad that sorrow should his use control,
Or keep him from heart-easing words so long,
Begins to talk; but through his lips do throng
Weak words, so thick come in his poor heart's aid,
That no man could distinguish what he said.

Yet sometime 'Tarquin' was pronounced plain,
But through his teeth, as if the name he tore.
This windy tempest, till it blow up rain,
Held back his sorrow's tide, to make it more;
At last it rains, and busy winds give o'er:
Then son and father weep with equal strife
Who should weep most, for daughter or for wife.

The one doth call her his, the other his,
Yet neither may possess the claim they lay.
The father says 'She 's mine.' 'O, mine she is,'
Replies her husband: 'do not take away
My sorrow's interest; let no mourner say
He weeps for her, for she was only mine,
And only must be wail'd by Collatine.'

'O,' quoth Lucretius, 'I did give that life
Which she too early and too late hath spill'd.'
'Woe, woe,' quoth Collatine, 'she was my wife,
I owed her, and 'tis mine that she hath kill'd.'
'My daughter' and 'my wife' with clamours fill'd
The dispers'd air, who, holding Lucrece' life,
Answer'd their cries, 'my daughter' and 'my wife.'

Brutus, who pluck'd the knife from Lucrece' side,
Seeing such emulation in their woe,
Began to clothe his wit in state and pride,
Burying in Lucrece' wound his folly's show.
He with the Romans was esteemed so
As seely-jeering idiots are with kings,
For sportive words and utt'ring foolish things:

But now he throws that shallow habit by,
Wherein deep policy did him disguise;
And arm'd his long-hid wits advisedly,
To check the tears in Collatinus' eyes.
'Thou wronged lord of Rome,' quoth he, 'arise:
Let my unsounded self, suppos'd a fool,
Now set thy long-experienc'd wit to school.

'Why, Collatine, is woe the cure for woe?
Do wounds help wounds, or grief help grievous deeds?
Is it revenge to give thyself a blow
For his foul act by whom thy fair wife bleeds?
Such childish humour from weak minds proceeds:
Thy wretched wife mistook the matter so,
To slay herself, that should have slain her foe.

'Courageous Roman, do not steep thy heart
In such relenting dew of lamentations;
But kneel with me and help to bear thy part,
To rouse our Roman gods with invocations,
That they will suffer these abominations,
Since Rome herself in them doth stand disgraced,
By our strong arms from forth her fair streets
chased.

'Now, by the Capitol that we adore,
And by this chaste blood so unjustly stained,
By heaven's fair sun that breeds the fat earth's store,
By all our country rights in Rome maintained,
And by chaste Lucrece' soul that late complained
Her wrongs to us, and by this bloody knife,
We will revenge the death of this true wife.'

This said, he struck his hand upon his breast,
And kiss'd the fatal knife, to end his vow;
And to his protestation urg'd the rest,
Who, wond'ring at him, did his words allow:
Then jointly to the ground their knees they bow;
And that deep vow, which Brutus made before,
He doth again repeat, and that they swore.

When they had sworn to this advised doom,
They did conclude to bear dead Lucrece thence;
To show her bleeding body thorough Rome,
And so to publish Tarquin's foul offence:
Which being done with speedy diligence,
The Romans plausibly did give consent
To Tarquin's everlasting banishment.

1766. **surcease,** cease. 1774. **key-cold,** i.e., cold as steel. 1776. **a space,** for a period of time. 1791. **strife,** striving. 1803. **owed,** owned. 1819. **unsounded,** unexplored. 1845. **allow,** approve. 1854. **plausibly,** with applause.

THE PASSIONATE PILGRIM

Shakespeare became so famous in his own day that his name was inevitably used by publishers to sell books. Most of the poems in *The Passionate Pilgrim*, offered to the public in 1599 as entirely by Shakespeare, are either careless versions of his earlier work or efforts of other Elizabethan writers passed off as his. Although the printer, William Jaggard, was later to be instrumental in publishing the First Folio, his work on this octavo collection seems to have been unauthorized and unscrupulous. He brought out what appears to be a second edition in 1599, setting up his text from an earlier edition of which two leaves (containing two poems) still exist in a Folger Library copy. When Jaggard printed another edition in 1612, adding materials from Thomas Heywood's *Troia Britanica* (1609), Heywood complained that both he and Shakespeare had been annoyed by the piracy.

The contents of the volume itself hardly inspire confidence in its integrity. Of the twenty or twenty-one poems (numbers 14 and 15 appear as one poem in the original text but are sometimes divided by modern editors), five are indisputably Shakespeare's but are not newly composed for the volume. Poems 1 and 2 are sonnets 138 and 144, whereas 3, 5, and 17 are from Act IV of *Love's Labour's Lost* (published 1598). Poem 11 is a sonnet from Bartholomew Griffin's *Fidessa More Chaste than Kind* (1596), and 4, 6, and 9 are so closely related to it in subject and style that they seem part of a sequence. The obvious resemblance in all four to Shakespeare's *Venus and Adonis* is probably a tribute to that poem's popularity rather than an indication of Shakespeare's authorship of these sonnets. Poems 8 and 21 first appeared in *Poems in Divers Humors*, 1598, by Richard Barnfield. The second of these was reprinted in another popular anthology, *England's Helicon* (1600), in which poem 18 also appears and is attributed to the author of 21, that is, to Barnfield. (Poem 18 was first published in Thomas Weelkes' *Madrigals*, 1597.) *England's Helicon* also printed a version of poem 20, attributing this famous lyric to "Chr. Marlowe," although its Reply (signed "Ignoto") was later said to be by Sir Walter Ralegh.

These attributions, most of them fairly reliable, leave only 7, 10, 12, 13, 14, 15, 16, and 19 as possible new works by Shakespeare. Because of the volume's unreliability, and because most of these unattributed verses are mediocre, no good reason exists to credit any of them to Shakespeare. If one poem is to be singled out for praise, the usual choice is 12. Even here we find no unequivocal sign of Shakespeare's genius.

THE PHOENIX AND THE TURTLE

"The Phoenix and the Turtle" first appeared in a collection of poems called *Loves Martyr: Or, Rosalins Complaint* by Robert Chester (1601). This quarto volume offered various poetic exercises about the Phoenix and the Turtle "by the best and chiefest of our moderne writers." The poem assigned to Shakespeare has been universally accepted as his, and is one of his most remarkable productions. With a deceptively simple diction, in gracefully pure tetrameter quatrains and triplets, the poem effortlessly evokes the transcendental ideal of a love existing eternally beyond death. The occasion is an assembly of birds to observe the funeral rites of the Phoenix and the Turtle. The Phoenix, legendary bird of resurrection from her own ashes, once more finds life through death in the company of the Turtledove, emblem of pure constancy in affection. Their spiritual union becomes a mystical oneness in whose presence Reason stands virtually speechless. Baffled human discourse must resort to paradox in order to explain how two beings become one essence, "Hearts remote yet not asunder." Mathematics and logic are "confounded" by this joining of two spirits into a "concordant one." The poignant brevity of this vision is rendered all the more mysterious by our not knowing what human tragedy may have prompted this metaphysical affirmation.

A LOVER'S COMPLAINT

Thomas Thorpe published "A Lover's Complaint" in his 1609 quarto of Shakespeare's *Sonnets*, ascribing the poem to "William Shake-speare" in its title heading (sig. K^v). The ascription must not be given too much weight, for Thorpe evidently did not have Shakespeare's authorization to publish the sonnets and may possibly have added the last two sonnets from some other source. Yet Thorpe's edition remains the only objective evidence we have, and its authority has never been convincingly refuted. The modern tendency to dismiss "A Lover's Complaint" as unworthy of Shakespeare's genius rests on subjective judgment and on stylistic "tests" that are too often proved unreliable. The poem was never ascribed to anyone else during Shakespeare's lifetime. On balance, the evidence is in favor of his authorship, though the issue will continue to remain in doubt.

The poem's genre, the "complaint" of a forsaken maiden, is conventional, along with the pastoral setting, the catalogue of the fickle lover's features, and the sententious warnings against blind passion. The poem did not add to Shakespeare's contemporary reputation. Still, it cannot safely be assigned to any other Elizabethan poet. Nor does it read like a mere effusion of Shakespeare's youth. Though written in *Lucrece*'s seven-line rhyme royal stanza, the poem eschews Ovidian and Petrarchan conceit for an occasional richness and complexity of metaphor.

THE PASSIONATE PILGRIM

I.

When my love swears that she is made of truth,
I do believe her, though I know she lies,
That she might think me some untutor'd youth,
Unskilful in the world's false forgeries.
Thus vainly thinking that she thinks me young,
Although I know my years be past the best,
I smiling credit her false-speaking tongue,
Outfacing faults in love with love's ill rest.
But wherefore says my love that she is young?
And wherefore say not I that I am old?
O, love's best habit is a soothing tongue,
And age, in love, loves not to have years told.
Therefore I'll lie with love, and love with me,
Since that our faults in love thus smother'd be.

II.

Two loves I have, of comfort and despair,
That like two spirits do suggest me still;
My better angel is a man right fair,
My worser spirit a woman colour'd ill.
To win me soon to hell, my female evil
Tempteth my better angel from my side,
And would corrupt my saint to be a devil,
Wooing his purity with her fair pride.
And whether that my angel be turn'd fiend,
Suspect I may, yet not directly tell:
For being both to me, both to each friend,
I guess one angel in another's hell:
The truth I shall not know, but live in doubt,
Till my bad angel fire my good one out.

III.

Did not the heavenly rhetoric of thine eye,
'Gainst whom the world could not hold argument,
Persuade my heart to this false perjury?
Vows for thee broke deserve not punishment.
A woman I forswore; but I will prove,
Thou being a goddess, I forswore not thee:
My vow was earthly, thou a heavenly love;
Thy grace being gain'd cures all disgrace in me.
My vow was breath, and breath a vapour is;
Then, thou fair sun, that on this earth doth shine,
Exhale this vapour vow; in thee it is:
If broken, then it is no fault of mine.
If by me broke, what fool is not so wise
To break an oath, to win a paradise?

IV.

Sweet Cytherea, sitting by a brook
With young Adonis, lovely, fresh, and green,
Did court the lad with many a lovely look,
Such looks as none could look but beauty's queen.
She told him stories to delight his ear;
She show'd him favours to allure his eye;
To win his heart, she touch'd him here and there,—
Touches so soft still conquer chastity.
But whether unripe years did want conceit,
Or he refus'd to take her figur'd proffer,
The tender nibbler would not touch the bait,
But smile and jest at every gentle offer:
Then fell she on her back, fair queen, and toward:
He rose and ran away; ah, fool too froward!

V.

If love make me forsworn, how shall I swear to love?
O never faith could hold, if not to beauty vow'd:
Though to myself forsworn, to thee I'll constant
prove;
Those thoughts, to me like oaks, to thee like osiers
bow'd.
Study his bias leaves, and makes his book thine eyes,
Where all those pleasures live that art can
comprehend.
If knowledge be the mark, to know thee shall suffice;
Well learned is that tongue that well can thee
commend;
All ignorant that soul that sees thee without wonder;
Which is to me some praise, that I thy parts admire:
Thine eye Jove's lightning seems, thy voice his
dreadful thunder,
Which, not to anger bent, is music and sweet fire.
Celestial as thou art, O do not love that wrong,
To sing heaven's praise with such an earthly tongue.

VI.

Scarce had the sun dried up the dewy morn,
And scarce the herd gone to the hedge for shade,
When Cytherea, all in love forlorn,
A longing tarriance for Adonis made
Under an osier growing by a brook,
A brook where Adon us'd to cool his spleen:
Hot was the day; she hotter that did look
For his approach, that often there had been.
Anon he comes, and throws his mantle by,
And stood stark naked on the brook's green brim:
The sun look'd on the world with glorious eye,
Yet not so wistly as this queen on him.
He, spying her, bounc'd in, whereas he stood:
'O Jove,' quoth she, 'why was not I a flood!'

VII.

Fair is my love, but not so fair as fickle;

I. A slightly varying version of Sonnet CXXXVIII. 6. **Although . . . best,** although I know she knows my years are past the best (Dowden). 8. **Outfacing,** modifies *I.* **ill rest,** inconsistency, lack of stability. 11. **habit,** demeanor, with, however, a suggestion of garb, i.e., something put on; see glossary. **soothing,** flattering.

II. A variant of Sonnet CXLIV. 15-22. **Two . . . pride,** a variation of the myth of man's good and evil angels, as presented in Marlowe's *Dr. Faustus* (Brooke). 18. **a woman colour'd ill.** This phrase is the basis of extensive conjecture as to who the "dark lady" of the Sonnets was. 25. **For . . . friend,** being both friends to me and also to each other (Feuillerat). 26. **I . . . hell,** I suspect that she (the evil angel) has him in her power. 28. **fire . . . out,** drive out fire with fire; Rollins suggests the meaning, "communicate a venereal disease."

III. From *Love's Labour's Lost*, IV, iii, 60-73. 39. **Exhale,** draw up, as the sun draws vapor from the earth (Herford). 41. **so,** so . . . as. 42. **break,** *Love's Labour's Lost: lose.*

IV. 43. **Cytherea,** Venus. 44. **green,** young. 45. **lovely,** amorous. 52. **take,** accept, or possibly understand (Pooler). 55. **toward,** willing. 56. **froward,** not willing to yield, perverse.

V. From *Love's Labour's Lost*, IV, ii, 109-122. 61. **Study,** the student. **bias,** particular or habitual inclination. 70. **To sing,** *Love's Labour's Lost: That sings*, which gives a clearer sense.

VI. This sonnet, following Ovid, deals with Adonis bathing in a brook; cf. *The Taming of the Shrew*, Induction, ii, 51-53. 74. **tarriance,** tarrying. 76. **spleen,** hot temper. 82. **wistly,** eagerly, intently. 83. **whereas,** where.

VII. The theme of this poem is a faithless woman's profession of love (Dowden).

Mild as a dove, but neither true nor trusty;
Brighter than glass, and yet, as glass is, brittle;
Softer than wax, and yet, as iron, rusty:
  A lily pale, with damask dye to grace her,
  None fairer, nor none falser to deface her.

Her lips to mine how often hath she joined,
Between each kiss her oaths of true love swearing!
How many tales to please me hath she coined,
Dreading my love, the loss thereof still fearing!
  Yet in the midst of all her pure protestings,
  Her faith, her oaths, her tears, and all were jestings.

She burn'd with love, as straw with fire flameth;
She burn'd out love, as soon as straw outburneth;
She fram'd the love, and yet she foil'd the framing;
She bade love last, and yet she fell a-turning.
  Was this a lover, or a lecher whether?
  Bad in the best, though excellent in neither.

VIII.

If music and sweet poetry agree,
As they must needs, the sister and the brother,
Then must the love be great 'twixt thee and me,
Because thou lov'st the one, and I the other.
Dowland to thee is dear, whose heavenly touch
Upon the lute doth ravish human sense;
Spenser to me, whose deep conceit is such
As, passing all conceit, needs no defence.
Thou lov'st to hear the sweet melodious sound
That Phœbus' lute, the queen of music, makes;
And I in deep delight am chiefly drown'd
Whenas himself to singing he betakes.
  One god is god of both, as poets feign;
  One knight loves both, and both in thee remain.

IX.

Fair was the morn when the fair queen of love,
*   *   *   *   *
Paler for sorrow than her milk-white dove,
For Adon's sake, a youngster proud and wild;
Her stand she takes upon a steep-up hill:
Anon Adonis comes with horn and hounds;
She, silly queen, with more than love's good will,
Forbade the boy he should not pass those grounds:
'Once,' quoth she, 'did I see a fair sweet youth
Here in these brakes deep-wounded with a boar,
Deep in the thigh, a spectacle of ruth!
See, in my thigh,' quoth she, 'here was the sore.'
  She showed hers: he saw more wounds than one,
  And blushing fled, and left her all alone.

X.

Sweet rose, fair flower, untimely pluck'd, soon vaded,
Pluck'd in the bud, and vaded in the spring!
Bright orient pearl, alack, too timely shaded!
Fair creature, kill'd too soon by death's sharp sting!
  Like a green plum that hangs upon a tree,
  And falls, through wind, before the fall should be.

I weep for thee, and yet no cause I have;
For why thou left'st me nothing in thy will:
And yet thou left'st me more than I did crave;
For why I craved nothing of thee still:
  O yes, dear friend, I pardon crave of thee,
  Thy discontent thou didst bequeath to me.

XI.

Venus, with young Adonis sitting by her
Under a myrtle shade, began to woo him:
She told the youngling how god Mars did try her,
And as he fell to her, so fell she to him.
'Even thus,' quoth she, 'the warlike god embrac'd me,'
And then she clipp'd Adonis in her arms;
'Even thus,' quoth she, 'the warlike god unlac'd me,'
As if the boy should use like loving charms;
'Even thus,' quoth she, 'he seized on my lips,'
And with her lips on his did act the seizure:
And as she fetched breath, away he skips,
And would not take her meaning nor her pleasure.
  Ah, that I had my lady at this bay,
  To kiss and clip me till I run away!

XII.

Crabbed age and youth cannot live together:
Youth is full of pleasance, age is full of care;
Youth like summer morn, age like winter weather;
Youth like summer brave, age like winter bare.
Youth is full of sport, age's breath is short;
  Youth is nimble, age is lame;
Youth is hot and bold, age is weak and cold;
  Youth is wild, and age is tame.
Age, I do abhor thee; youth, I do adore thee;
  O, my love, my love is young!
Age, I do defy thee: O, sweet shepherd, hie thee,
  For methinks thou stay'st too long.

XIII.

Beauty is but a vain and doubtful good;
A shining gloss that vadeth suddenly;
A flower that dies when first it gins to bud;
A brittle glass that 's broken presently:
  A doubtful good, a gloss, a glass, a flower,
  Lost, vaded, broken, dead within an hour.

And as goods lost are seld or never found,
As vaded gloss no rubbing will refresh,
As flowers dead lie withered on the ground,
As broken glass no cement can redress,
  So beauty blemish'd once 's for ever lost,
  In spite of physic, painting, pain and cost.

87. **brittle.** Perhaps for the rhyme we should read *brickle*, which was a common form of "brittle" (White). 89. **damask,** pale red (Schmidt). 101. **whether,** which of the two.

VIII. A sonnet by Barnfield. 105. **'twixt thee and me,** i.e., between Barnfield and R.L., to whom he addressed the poem. 107. **Dowland,** John Dowland (1563?-1626?), lutanist and composer. 109, 110. **conceit, conceit,** imaginative conception, play of fancy. 116. **One knight.** It has been suggested that the knight is Sir George Carey, K.G., to whom Dowland dedicated his first book of airs (Rollins).

IX. There is apparently a line missing in this sonnet. The rhyme is with *wild* (l. 120); for the many conjectures see the Variorum. 121. **steep-up.** Cf. Sonnet VII, 5. 129. **wounds,** a double entendre. **one,** in Shakespeare's English a possible rhyme with *alone*.

X. 131, 132. **vaded.** The forms "fade" and "vade" are distinct, not only in spelling but in origin. The latter (from Lat. *vadere*) means "to depart, to disappear," and is therefore a stronger word than *fade*, "to lose color" (Carleton Brown).

XI. This sonnet is believed to be the work of Bartholomew Griffin and closely resembles a sonnet (No. III) in the collection entitled *Fidessa* (1596). 153. **And,** regarded by Dyce as an error for *But*. 155. **at this bay,** in my power (Herford).

XII. A popular song several times alluded to in the seventeenth century. 158. **pleasance,** gaiety, merriment.

XIII. 176. **vaded.** Cf. x, 131, 132. **gloss,** variously interpreted as "polish," "faded silk," "gilding." 178. **cement,** accented on the first syllable.

XIV. This and the following are printed as one poem in *The Passionate Pilgrim*. Malone divided them as in the text; Dowden objected

XIV.

Good night, good rest. Ah, neither be my share:
She bade good night that kept my rest away;
And daff'd me to a cabin hang'd with care,
To descant on the doubts of my decay.
  'Farewell,' quoth she, 'and come again to-morrow:'
  Fare well I could not, for I supp'd with sorrow.

Yet at my parting sweetly did she smile,
In scorn or friendship, nill I conster whether:
'T may be, she joy'd to jest at my exile,
'T may be, again to make me wander thither:
  'Wander,' a word for shadows like myself,
  As take the pain, but cannot pluck the pelf.

XV.

Lord, how mine eyes throw gazes to the east!
My heart doth charge the watch; the morning rise
Doth cite each moving sense from idle rest.
Not daring trust the office of mine eyes,
  While Philomela sits and sings, I sit and mark,
  And wish her lays were tuned like the lark;

For she doth welcome daylight with her ditty,
And drives away dark dismal-dreaming night:
The night so pack'd, I post unto my pretty;
Heart hath his hope, and eyes their wished sight;
  Sorrow chang'd to solace, and solace mix'd with sorrow;
  For why, she sigh'd and bade me come to-morrow.

Were I with her, the night would post too soon;
But now are minutes added to the hours;
To spite me now, each minute seems a moon;
Yet not for me, shine sun to succour flowers!
  Pack night, peep day; good day, of night now borrow:
  Short, night, to-night, and length thyself to-morrow.

SONNETS TO SUNDRY NOTES OF MUSIC

[XVI.]

It was a lording's daughter, the fairest one of three,
That liked of her master as well as well might be,
Till looking on an Englishman, the fair'st that eye could see,
  Her fancy fell a-turning.
Long was the combat doubtful that love with love did fight,
To leave the master loveless, or kill the gallant knight:
To put in practice either, alas, it was a spite
  Unto the silly damsel!
But one must be refused; more mickle was the pain
That nothing could be used to turn them both to gain,
For of the two the trusty knight was wounded with disdain:
  Alas, she could not help it!
Thus art with arms contending was victor of the day,
Which by a gift of learning did bear the maid away:
Then, lullaby, the learned man hath got the lady gay;
  For now my song is ended.

XVII.

On a day, alack the day!
Love, whose month was ever May,
Spied a blossom passing fair,
Playing in the wanton air:
Through the velvet leaves the wind,
All unseen, gan passage find;
That the lover, sick to death,
Wish'd himself the heaven's breath,
'Air,' quoth he, 'thy cheeks may blow;
Air, would I might triumph so!
But, alas! my hand hath sworn
Ne'er to pluck thee from thy thorn:
Vow, alack! for youth unmeet:
Youth, so apt to pluck a sweet.
Thou for whom Jove would swear
Juno but an Ethiope were;
And deny himself for Jove,
Turning mortal for thy love.'

[XVIII.]

My flocks feed not,
My ewes breed not,
My rams speed not,
  All is amiss:
Love's denying,
Faith's defying,
Heart's renying,
  Causer of this.
All my merry jigs are quite forgot,
All my lady's love is lost, God wot:
Where her faith was firmly fix'd in love,
There a nay is plac'd without remove.
One silly cross
Wrought all my loss;
  O frowning Fortune, cursed, fickle dame!
For now I see
Inconstancy
  More in women than in men remain.

In black mourn I,
All fears scorn I,
Love hath forlorn me,
  Living in thrall:
Heart is bleeding,
All help needing,
O cruel speeding,
  Fraughted with gall.
My shepherd's pipe can sound no deal;
My wether's bell rings doleful knell;

to this division. 181. **be,** is (Schmidt); are (Pooler); let neither be (Kittredge). 183. **daff'd,** put aside, turned away. **cabin,** small room, bedroom. 184. **descant,** compose variations, make musical variations (Rollins). 192. **As,** rather *who* than *which* (Kittredge).

XV. 194. **My . . . watch,** variously interpreted: my heart doth charge my eyes to watch the morning rise (Pooler); accuse the watch for marking the time so slowly (Rolfe); give notice to the watchman to proclaim the dawn (Kittredge). 205-207. **Were . . . moon.** Malone cites *Romeo and Juliet*, III, v, 44 ff.

XVI. A popular song in which a maiden hesitates in her choice between a learned man and a knight and takes the learned man. Brown connects the song with the medieval ballad theme *Disputatio inter militem et clericum*. 211. **lording's,** lord's. 212. **master,** teacher, tutor.

XVII. From *Love's Labour's Lost*, IV, iii, 101-120. 230. **wanton,** frolicsome, sportive. 240. Brown suggests the introduction after this line of two verses from *Love's Labour's Lost* which are necessary to the sense:

Do not call it sin in me
That I am forsworn for thee.

XVIII. First published in a collection of madrigals by Thomas Weelkes; reprinted in *England's Helicon* (1600) as "The Unknown Shepherd's Complaint." There is an excellent contemporary manuscript of the poem, Harl. 6910, fol. 156b. 249. **Love's denying,** so Malone *et al.; The Passionate Pilgrim: Love is dying; England's Helicon: Loue is denying*. 251. **renying,** forswearing (Malone); disowning (Schmidt). 253. **jigs,** ballads and songs or dance tunes (Rollins). 270. **Fraughted,** loaded, burdened. 271. **no deal,** nothing.

My curtail dog, that wont to have play'd,
Plays not at all, but seems afraid;
With sighs so deep
Procures to weep,
In howling wise, to see my doleful plight.
How sighs resound
Through heartless ground,
Like a thousand vanquish'd men in bloody fight!

Clear wells spring not,
Sweet birds sing not,
Green plants bring not
Forth their dye;
Herds stand weeping,
Flocks all sleeping,
Nymphs back peeping
Fearfully:
All our pleasure known to us poor swains,
All our merry meetings on the plains,
All our evening sport from us is fled,
All our love is lost, for Love is dead.
Farewell, sweet lass,
Thy like ne'er was
For a sweet content, the cause of all my moan:
Poor Corydon
Must live alone;
Other help for him I see that there is none.

XIX.

When as thine eye hath chose the dame,
And stall'd the deer that thou shouldst strike,
Let reason rule things worthy blame,
† As well as fancy partial might:
Take counsel of some wiser head,
Neither too young nor yet unwed.

And when thou com'st thy tale to tell,
Smooth not thy tongue with filed talk,
Lest she some subtle practice smell,—
A cripple soon can find a halt;—
But plainly say thou lov'st her well,
And set thy person forth to sell.

What though her frowning brows be bent,
Her cloudy looks will calm ere night:
And then too late she will repent
That thus dissembled her delight;
And twice desire, ere it be day,
That which with scorn she put away.

What though she strive to try her strength,
And ban and brawl, and say thee nay,
Her feeble force will yield at length,
When craft hath taught her thus to say,
'Had women been so strong as men,
In faith, you had not had it then.'

And to her will frame all thy ways;
Spare not to spend, and chiefly there
Where thy desert may merit praise,
By ringing in thy lady's ear:
The strongest castle, tower, and town,
The golden bullet beats it down.

Serve always with assured trust,
And in thy suit be humble true;
Unless thy lady prove unjust,
Press never thou to choose anew:
When time shall serve, be thou not slack
To proffer, though she put thee back.

The wiles and guiles that women work,
Dissembled with an outward show,
The tricks and toys that in them lurk,
The cock that treads them shall not know.
Have you not heard it said full oft,
A woman's nay doth stand for nought?

† Think women still to strive with men,
To sin and never for to saint:
There is no heaven, by holy then,
When time with age doth them attaint.
Were kisses all the joys in bed,
One woman would another wed.

But, soft! enough, too much, I fear;
Lest that my mistress hear my song,
She will not stick to round me on th' ear,
To teach my tongue to be so long:
Yet will she blush, here be it said,
To hear her secrets so bewray'd.

[XX.]

Live with me, and be my love,
And we will all the pleasures prove
That hills and valleys, dales and fields,
And all the craggy mountains yields.

There will we sit upon the rocks,
And see the shepherds feed their flocks,
By shallow rivers, by whose falls
Melodious birds sing madrigals.

There will I make thee a bed of roses,
With a thousand fragrant posies,
A cap of flowers, and a kirtle
Embroider'd all with leaves of myrtle.

A belt of straw and ivy buds,
With coral clasps and amber studs;
And if these pleasures may thee move,
Then live with me and be my love.

Love's Answer.

If that the world and love were young,
And truth in every shepherd's tongue,
These pretty pleasures might me move
To live with thee and be thy love.

276. **Procures,** so *The Passionate Pilgrim;* Globe *et al.: Procure*. The dog *procures* (i.e., manages matters) so as to weep (Steevens). 279. **heartless,** possibly exhausted (Steevens).

XIX. The text of *The Passionate Pilgrim* is poor. There exists a much better version in a contemporary manuscript now in the Folger Library. 300. **stall'd,** enclosed, got within range of. 302. **As . . . might,** a difficult crux. Some editors follow Lyson's manuscript, reading *like* for *might;* Furnivall suggested: *as fancy's partial might*. 306. **filed talk,** studied or polished language (Malone). 340. **A . . . nought.** Cf. *The Two Gentlemen of Verona*, I, ii, 55-56. 341. **Think,** expect. 342. **To . . . saint,** Folger MS.: *and not to live so like a saint*. 343. **by holy then,** possibly, by all that's sacred (Steevens); Folger MS.: *be holy then*. 349. **to round . . . ear,** to whisper or to tell secretly (Johnson); some editors explain "strike me on the ear"; some follow Boswell's conjecture: *wring mine ear*.

XX. The first publication of Marlowe's lyric, which appeared also in *England's Helicon* (1600), with the accompanying poem, "The Nymph's Reply to the Shepherd," attributed to Sir Walter Raleigh;

[XXI.]

As it fell upon a day
In the merry month of May,
Sitting in a pleasant shade
Which a grove of myrtles made,
Beasts did leap, and birds did sing,
Trees did grow, and plants did spring;
Every thing did banish moan,
Save the nightingale alone:
She, poor bird, as all forlorn,
Lean'd her breast up-till a thorn,
And there sung the dolefull'st ditty,
That to hear it was great pity:
'Fie, fie, fie,' now would she cry;
'Tereu, tereu!' by and by;
That to hear her so complain,
Scarce I could from tears refrain;
For her griefs, so lively shown,
Made me think upon mine own.
Ah, thought I, thou mourn'st in vain!
None takes pity on thy pain:
Senseless trees they cannot hear thee;
Ruthless beasts they will not cheer thee:
King Pandion he is dead;
All thy friends are lapp'd in lead;
All thy fellow birds do sing,
Careless of thy sorrowing.
Even so, poor bird, like thee,
None alive will pity me.
Whilst as fickle Fortune smil'd,
Thou and I were both beguil'd.
  Every one that flatters thee
Is no friend in misery.
Words are easy, like the wind;
Faithful friends are hard to find:
Every man will be thy friend
Whilst thou hast wherewith to spend;
But if store of crowns be scant,
No man will supply thy want.
If that one be prodigal,
Bountiful they will him call,
And with such-like flattering,
'Pity but he were a king;'
If he be addict to vice,
Quickly him they will entice;
If to women he be bent,
They have at commandement:
But if Fortune once do frown,
Then farewell his great renown;
They that fawn'd on him before
Use his company no more.
He that is thy friend indeed,
He will help thee in thy need:
If thou sorrow, he will weep;
If thou wake, he cannot sleep;
Thus of every grief in heart
He with thee doth bear a part.
These are certain signs to know
Faithful friend from flatt'ring foe.

many publications and manuscripts. 360. **madrigals,** pastoral songs or love songs. 360-362. Cf. *The Merry Wives of Windsor*, III, i, 17-20.

XXI. From Richard Barnfield's *Poems in Divers Humors* (1598). 382. **up-till,** up against. 386. **Tereu.** Pooler suggests allusion to Tereus in Ovid's *Metamorphoses*, VI, 424-676. 395. **King Pandion,** the king of Athens, father of Philomela and Progne in Ovid's story. 396. **lapp'd in lead,** placed in a leaden coffin. 415. **addict,** inclined, addicted. 418. **They have.** One should understand "them," i.e., women, after *have*.

THE PHOENIX AND THE TURTLE

Let the bird of loudest lay,
On the sole Arabian tree,
Herald sad and trumpet be,
To whose sound chaste wings obey.

But thou shrieking harbinger,
Foul precurrer of the fiend,
Augur of the fever's end,
To this troop come thou not near!

From this session interdict
Every fowl of tyrant wing,
Save the eagle, feath'red king:
Keep the obsequy so strict.

Let the priest in surplice white,
That defunctive music can,
Be the death-divining swan,
Lest the requiem lack his right.

And thou treble-dated crow,
That thy sable gender mak'st
With the breath thou giv'st and tak'st,
'Mongst our mourners shalt thou go.

Here the anthem doth commence:
Love and constancy is dead;
Phœnix and the turtle fled
In a mutual flame from hence.

So they lov'd, as love in twain
Had the essence but in one;
Two distincts, division none:
Number there in love was slain.

1. **the bird.** Rollins suggests the nightingale. It may be no special bird but merely the bird of loudest song. 2. **Arabian tree.** Malone cites *The Tempest*, III, iii, 22-24, and Lyly's *Euphues and his England:* "As there is but one *Phenix* in the world, so is there but one tree in Arabia where-in she buyldeth." 3. **trumpet,** trumpeter; cf. *King John*, I, i, 27-28. 4. **chaste wings,** refers not to the bird of line 1 but to the other birds summoned to the obsequies by the trumpeter bird of loudest lay (Rollins, following Fairchild). **obey,** are obedient. 5. **harbinger.** Malone defines as the "scritch-owl" and cites *A Midsummer Night's Dream*, V, i, 383-385. 6. **precurrer,** forerunner. 14. **That . . . can,** that understands funeral music (Malone). 15. **death-divining swan,** alludes to the belief that the swan sings when it is about to die. 16. **his right,** its right (of music) (Fairchild quoted by Rollins). 17. **treble-dated crow.** The word *treble-dated* means "a comparatively large number." Pooler quotes Holland's Pliny (VII, xlviii, 180): "*Hesiodus* . . . saith forsooth, That a crow liveth 9 times as long as we; and the harts or stags 4 times as long as the crow; but the ravens thrice as long as they." 18-19. **That . . . tak'st.** These lines seem best explained by a quotation from *Hortus Sanitatis*, bk. iii, sec. 34, in Seager's *Natural History in Shakespeare's Time:* "They [ravens] are said to conceive and to lay eggs at the bill. The young become black on the seventh day." 27. **distincts,** separate or individual persons or things (*NED*). 28. **Number . . . slain,** refers to the mathematical dictum "one is no number." That is, by the "two" being "one" they "slay" the number (Rollins, following Adams). They are distinct and yet are made one by the power of love.

Hearts remote, yet not asunder;
Distance, and no space was seen
'Twixt this turtle and his queen:
But in them it were a wonder.

So between them love did shine,
That the turtle saw his right
Flaming in the phœnix' sight;
Either was the other's mine.

Property was thus appalled,
That the self was not the same;
Single nature's double name
Neither two nor one was called.

Reason, in itself confounded,
Saw division grow together,
To themselves yet either neither,
Simple were so well compounded,

That it cried, How true a twain
Seemeth this concordant one!
Love hath reason, reason none,
If what parts can so remain.

Whereupon it made this threne
To the phœnix and the dove,
Co-supremes and stars of love,
As chorus to their tragic scene.

THRENOS.

Beauty, truth, and rarity,
Grace in all simplicity,
Here enclos'd in cinders lie.

Death is now the phœnix' nest;
And the turtle's loyal breast
To eternity doth rest,

Leaving no posterity:
'Twas not their infirmity,
It was married chastity.

Truth may seem, but cannot be:
Beauty brag, but 'tis not she;
Truth and beauty buried be.

To this urn let those repair
That are either true or fair;
For these dead birds sigh a prayer.

31. **this,** Globe: *the*, a reading due to Malone's error. 32. **But . . . wonder,** this phenomenon, had it been seen anywhere but in them, would have seemed wonderful. 36. **mine,** may mean "mine own" or "rich treasure." The latter is the more probable. 37-38. **Property . . . same.** Property is a Latinism, *proprietas*, peculiar or essential quality; cf. *Richard II*, III, ii, 135. "Property" was appalled to find out that personality had been destroyed, since each lover's identity was merged into the other's and was no longer itself (Feuillerat). 41-44. **Reason . . . compounded,** pure reason had seen those unlike and, according to its insight quite incompatible, unite together. In the union neither had an entirely separate identity, *simple*, that is, simples or elementary elements, were so perfectly compounded or united (Fairchild, quoted by Rollins). 47-48. **Love . . . remain,** love, which ordinarily lacks reason, is reasonable, and reason itself lacks reason if two that are disunited nevertheless remain in union. 49. **threne,** (and THRENOS below), lamentation, funeral song. 55. **cinders,** ashes.

A LOVER'S COMPLAINT

From off a hill whose concave womb re-worded
A plaintful story from a sist'ring vale,
My spirits t' attend this double voice accorded,
And down I laid to list the sad-tun'd tale;
Ere long espied a fickle maid full pale,
Tearing of papers, breaking rings a-twain,
Storming her world with sorrow's wind and rain.

Upon her head a platted hive of straw,
Which fortified her visage from the sun,
Whereon the thought might think sometime it saw
The carcass of a beauty spent and done:
Time had not scythed all that youth begun,
Nor youth all quit; but, spite of heaven's fell rage,
Some beauty peep'd through lattice of sear'd age.

Oft did she heave her napkin to her eyne,
Which on it had conceited characters,
Laund'ring the silken figures in the brine
That season'd woe had pelleted in tears,
And often reading what contents it bears;
As often shrieking undistinguish'd woe,
In clamours of all size, both high and low.

Sometimes her levell'd eyes their carriage ride,
As they did batt'ry to the spheres intend;
Sometime diverted their poor balls are tied
To th' orbed earth; sometimes they do extend
Their view right on; anon their gazes lend
To every place at once, and, nowhere fix'd,
The mind and sight distractedly commix'd.

Her hair, nor loose nor tied in formal plat,
Proclaim'd in her a careless hand of pride;
For some, untuck'd, descended her sheav'd hat,
Hanging her pale and pined cheek beside;
Some in her threaden fillet still did bide,
And true to bondage would not break from thence,
Though slackly braided in loose negligence.

A thousand favours from a maund she drew
Of amber, crystal, and of beaded jet,
Which one by one she in a river threw,
Upon whose weeping margent she was set;
Like usury, applying wet to wet,
Or monarch's hands that let not bounty fall
Where want cries some, but where excess begs all.

Of folded schedules had she many a one,

1. **re-worded,** re-echoed. 2. **sist'ring,** neighboring. 3. **spirits,** pronounced as one syllable, probably "spirts." 10. **the thought,** the mind; that which thinks. 14. **lattice,** i.e., wrinkles. 16. **conceited characters,** fanciful or emblematic devices. 18. **pelleted,** formed into small globules. 22. **levell'd . . . carriage,** metaphor from the aiming and firing of a gun. 24. **diverted,** turned away. 28. **commix'd,** confused. 29. **in formal plat,** neatly braided. 30. **careless hand of pride,** studied carelessness. 31. **sheav'd hat.** Cf. l. 8, *platted hive of straw*. 33. **threaden,** made of woven threads. 36. **maund,** woven basket with handles. 43. **schedules,** papers containing writing. 45. **posied,** inscribed with a motto. 48. **sleided silk,** floss silk. **feat,** featly, adroitly. **affectedly,** lovingly. 50. **fluxive,** flowing. 52. **register,** recorder. 55. **top of,** extreme. 57. **reverend,** i.e., suggesting old

Which she perus'd, sigh'd, tore, and gave the flood;
Crack'd many a ring of posied gold and bone,
Bidding them find their sepulchres in mud;
Found yet moe letters sadly penn'd in blood,
With sleided silk feat and affectedly
Enswath'd, and seal'd to curious secrecy.

These often bath'd she in her fluxive eyes,
And often kiss'd, and often 'gan to tear;
Cried 'O false blood, thou register of lies,
What unapproved witness dost thou bear!
Ink would have seem'd more black and damned here!'
This said, in top of rage the lines she rents,
Big discontent so breaking their contents.

A reverend man that graz'd his cattle nigh—
Sometime a blusterer, that the ruffle knew
Of court, of city, and had let go by
The swiftest hours, observed as they flew—
Towards this afflicted fancy fastly drew,
And, privileg'd by age, desires to know
In brief the grounds and motives of her woe.

So slides he down upon his grained bat,
And comely-distant sits he by her side;
When he again desires her, being sat,
Her grievance with his hearing to divide:
If that from him there may be aught applied
Which may her suffering ecstasy assuage,
'Tis promis'd in the charity of age.

'Father,' she says, 'though in me you behold
The injury of many a blasting hour,
Let it not tell your judgement I am old;
Not age, but sorrow, over me hath power:
I might as yet have been a spreading flower,
Fresh to myself, if I had self-applied
Love to myself and to no love beside.

'But, woe is me! too early I attended
A youthful suit—it was to gain my grace—
Of one by nature's outwards so commended,
That maidens' eyes stuck over all his face:
Love lack'd a dwelling, and made him her place;
And when in his fair parts she did abide,
She was new lodg'd and newly deified.

'His browny locks did hang in crooked curls;
And every light occasion of the wind
Upon his lips their silken parcels hurls.
What 's sweet to do, to do will aptly find:
Each eye that saw him did enchant the mind,
For on his visage was in little drawn
What largeness thinks in Paradise was sawn.

'Small show of man was yet upon his chin;
His phœnix down began but to appear
Like unshorn velvet on that termless skin
Whose bare out-bragg'd the web it seem'd to wear:
Yet show'd his visage by that cost more dear;
And nice affections wavering stood in doubt
If best were as it was, or best without.

'His qualities were beauteous as his form,
For maiden-tongu'd he was, and thereof free;
Yet, if men mov'd him, was he such a storm
As oft 'twixt May and April is to see,
When winds breathe sweet, unruly though they be.
His rudeness so with his authoriz'd youth
Did livery falseness in a pride of truth.

'Well could he ride, and often men would say
"That horse his mettle from his rider takes:
Proud of subjection, noble by the sway,
What rounds, what bounds, what course, what stop he makes!"
And controversy hence a question takes,
Whether the horse by him became his deed,
Or he his manage by th' well-doing steed.

'But quickly on this side the verdict went:
His real habitude gave life and grace
To appertainings and to ornament,
Accomplish'd in himself, not in his case:
All aids, themselves made fairer by their place,
Came for additions; yet their purpos'd trim
Piec'd not his grace, but were all grac'd by him.

'So on the tip of his subduing tongue
All kind of arguments and question deep,
All replication prompt, and reason strong,
For his advantage still did wake and sleep:
To make the weeper laugh, the laugher weep,
He had the dialect and different skill,
Catching all passions in his craft of will:

'That he did in the general bosom reign
Of young, of old; and sexes both enchanted,
To dwell with him in thoughts, or to remain
In personal duty, following where he haunted:
Consents bewitch'd, ere he desire, have granted;
And dialogu'd for him what he would say,
Ask'd their own wills, and made their wills obey.

'Many there were that did his picture get,
To serve their eyes, and in it put their mind;
Like fools that in th' imagination set
The goodly objects which abroad they find
Of lands and mansions, theirs in thought assign'd;
And labouring in moe pleasures to bestow them
Than the true gouty landlord which doth owe them:

'So many have, that never touch'd his hand,
Sweetly suppos'd them mistress of his heart.

age. 58. **blusterer,** boisterous fellow. **ruffle,** commotion. 61. **fancy,** person in love. **fastly,** rapidly. 64. **grained,** worn and showing the grain. **bat,** club. 69. **ecstasy,** temporary madness. 88. **to do . . . find,** i.e., will find a doer. 89. **the mind,** i.e., of the beholder. 91. **sawn,** to be seen; an archaism. 93. **phœnix,** suggesting his unique perfection. 94. **termless,** youthful (Pooler). 95. **bare,** bareness. 96. **cost,** perhaps a double pun: cost, "expense" and French *coste* (*côte*), "refuse silk." The meaning may be, his face seemed lovelier from its rich (or silken) covering (Pooler). 102. **to see,** to be seen. 105. **livery,** dress. **pride,** magnificent costume. 109. **stop,** sudden check in a horse's "career" or trial gallop at full speed. 111-112. **Whether . . . steed,** whether it was owing to his horsemanship that his horse acted so becomingly or whether he seemed such a good rider because he had so good a horse (Pooler). 114. **real,** two syllables. **habitude,** constitution, temperament. 115. **appertainings,** belongings, appurtenances. 116. **case,** the body, as enclosing the soul (Onions); conditions and circumstances, e.g., the possession of so good a horse (Pooler). 118. **for,** equivalent to "as." 119. **Piec'd,** added to. 122. **replication,** reply. 125. **dialect,** manner of expression. **different,** varied, readily adaptable. 126. **craft of will,** skill in achieving his desires. 127. **general bosom,** hearts of all. 128-130. **sexes . . . haunted,** by his fascination he caused both men and women to think of him continually or even to live as his attendants, going where he went (Pooler). 131. **Consents,** consenting persons (Pooler); it is the subject of the verbs *have granted* and (*have*) *dialogued*. 135. **in it put their mind,** let their minds become engrossed. 140. **owe,** own.

My woeful self, that did in freedom stand,
And was my own fee-simple, not in part,
What with his art in youth, and youth in art,
Threw my affection in his charmed power,
Reserv'd the stalk and gave him all my flower.

'Yet did I not, as some my equals did,
Demand of him, nor being desired yielded;
Finding myself in honour so forbid,
With safest distance I mine honour shielded:
Experience for me many bulwarks builded
Of proofs new-bleeding, which remain'd the foil
Of this false jewel, and his amorous spoil.

'But, ah, who ever shunn'd by precedent
The destin'd ill she must herself assay?
Or forc'd examples, 'gainst her own content,
To put the by-past perils in her way?
Counsel may stop awhile what will not stay;
For when we rage, advice is often seen
By blunting us to make our wits more keen.

'Nor gives it satisfaction to our blood,
That we must curb it upon others' proof;
To be forbod the sweets that seem so good,
For fear of harms that preach in our behoof.
O appetite, from judgement stand aloof!
The one a palate hath that needs will taste,
Though Reason weep, and cry "It is thy last."

'For further I could say "This man 's untrue,"
And knew the patterns of his foul beguiling;
Heard where his plants in others' orchards grew,
Saw how deceits were gilded in his smiling;
Knew vows were ever brokers to defiling;
Thought characters and words merely but art,
And bastards of his foul adulterate heart.

'And long upon these terms I held my city,
Till thus he gan besiege me: "Gentle maid,
Have of my suffering youth some feeling pity,
And be not of my holy vows afraid:
That 's to ye sworn to none was ever said;
For feasts of love I have been call'd unto,
Till now did ne'er invite, nor never woo.

'"All my offences that abroad you see
Are errors of the blood, none of the mind;
Love made them not: with acture they may be,
Where neither party is nor true nor kind:
They sought their shame that so their shame did find;
And so much less of shame in me remains,
By how much of me their reproach contains.

'"Among the many that mine eyes have seen,
Not one whose flame my heart so much as warmed,
Or my affection put to th' smallest teen,
Or any of my leisures ever charmed:
Harm have I done to them, but ne'er was harmed;
Kept hearts in liveries, but mine own was free,
And reign'd, commanding in his monarchy.

'"Look here what tributes wounded fancies sent me,
Of pallid pearls and rubies red as blood;
Figuring that they their passions likewise lent me
Of grief and blushes, aptly understood
In bloodless white and the encrimson'd mood;
Effects of terror and dear modesty,
Encamp'd in hearts, but fighting outwardly.

'"And, lo, behold these talents of their hair,
With twisted metal amorously impleach'd,
I have receiv'd from many a several fair,
Their kind acceptance weepingly beseech'd,
With the annexions of fair gems enrich'd,
And deep-brain'd sonnets that did amplify
Each stone's dear nature, worth, and quality.

'"The diamond,—why, 'twas beautiful and hard,
Whereto his invis'd properties did tend;
The deep-green em'rald, in whose fresh regard
Weak sights their sickly radiance do amend;
The heaven-hu'd sapphire and the opal blend
With objects manifold: each several stone,
With wit well blazon'd, smil'd or made some moan.

'"Lo, all these trophies of affections hot,
Of pensiv'd and subdu'd desires the tender,
Nature hath charg'd me that I hoard them not,
But yield them up where I myself must render,
That is, to you, my origin and ender;
For these, of force, must your oblations be,
Since I their altar, you enpatron me.

'"O, then, advance of yours that phraseless hand,
Whose white weighs down the airy scale of praise;
Take all these similes to your own command,
Hallow'd with sighs that burning lungs did raise;
What me your minister, for you obeys,
Works under you; and to your audit comes
Their distract parcels in combined sums.

'"Lo, this device was sent me from a nun,
Or sister sanctified, of holiest note;
Which late her noble suit in court did shun,
Whose rarest havings made the blossoms dote;
For she was sought by spirits of richest coat,
But kept cold distance, and did thence remove,
To spend her living in eternal love.

'"But, O my sweet, what labour is 't to leave
The thing we have not, mast'ring what not strives,
†Playing the place which did no form receive,
Playing patient sports in unconstrained gyves?
She that her fame so to herself contrives,
The scars of battle 'scapeth by the flight,
And makes her absence valiant, not her might.

'"O, pardon me, in that my boast is true:
The accident which brought me to her eye

144. **my own fee-simple,** absolute power over myself (Malone). **in part,** a part-owner. 146. **charmed power,** i.e., he has the power to charm. 155. **precedent,** advice. 156. **assay,** learn by experience (Onions). 163. **proof,** experience. 164. **forbod,** forbidden. 173. **brokers,** panders. 174. **characters and words,** i.e., the written and spoken word. 180. **That 's,** that which is. 185. **acture,** action, performance. 195. **in liveries,** i.e., the uniform of a person in service. 198. **pallid,** Globe, following Malone: *paled;* Q: *palyd.* 204. **talents,** treasures, riches. 205. **impleach'd,** intertwined. 206. **several fair,** different ladies. 209. **deep-brain'd,** full of profound thought (Onions). 212. **invis'd,** invisible (Onions); perhaps, inspected, investigated, tried (Schmidt); possibly related to "vise." 213. **regard,** sight, view; i.e., in viewing which. 215. **blend,** usually explained as blended; perhaps "blending with" or "that blends with" in the sense of matching or resembling (Pooler). 219. **pensiv'd,** saddened. 224. **Since . . . me,** since I am the altar, you are my patron saint. 225. **phraseless,** which

Upon the moment did her force subdue,
And now she would the caged cloister fly:
Religious love put out Religion's eye:
Not to be tempted, would she be immur'd,
And now, to tempt, all liberty procur'd.

'"How mighty then you are, O, hear me tell!
The broken bosoms that to me belong
Have emptied all their fountains in my well,
And mine I pour your ocean all among:
I strong o'er them, and you o'er me being strong,
Must for your victory us all congest,
As compound love to physic your cold breast.

'"My parts had pow'r to charm a sacred nun,
Who, disciplin'd, ay, dieted in grace,
Believ'd her eyes when they t' assail begun,
All vows and consecrations giving place:
O most potential love! vow, bond, nor space,
In thee hath neither sting, knot, nor confine,
For thou art all, and all things else are thine.

'"When thou impressest, what are precepts worth
Of stale example? When thou wilt inflame,
How coldly those impediments stand forth
Of wealth, of filial fear, law, kindred, fame!
†Love's arms are peace, 'gainst rule, 'gainst sense,
  'gainst shame,
And sweetens, in the suff'ring pangs it bears,
The aloes of all forces, shocks, and fears.

'"Now all these hearts that do on mine depend,
Feeling it break, with bleeding groans they pine;
And supplicant their sighs to you extend,
To leave the batt'ry that you make 'gainst mine,
Lending soft audience to my sweet design,
And credent soul to that strong-bonded oath
That shall prefer and undertake my troth."

'This said, his wat'ry eyes he did dismount,
Whose sights till then were levell'd on my face;
Each cheek a river running from a fount
With brinish current downward flow'd apace:
O, how the channel to the stream gave grace!
Who glaz'd with crystal gate the glowing roses
That flame through water which their hue
  encloses.

'O father, what a hell of witchcraft lies
In the small orb of one particular tear!
But with the inundation of the eyes
What rocky heart to water will not wear?
What breast so cold that is not warmed here?
O cleft effect! cold modesty, hot wrath,
Both fire from hence and chill extincture hath.

'For, lo, his passion, but an art of craft,
Even there resolv'd my reason into tears;
There my white stole of chastity I daff'd,
Shook off my sober guards and civil fears;
Appear to him, as he to me appears,
All melting; though our drops this diff'rence bore,
His poison'd me, and mine did him restore.

'In him a plenitude of subtle matter,
Applied to cautels, all strange forms receives,
Of burning blushes, or of weeping water,
Or sounding paleness; and he takes and leaves,
In either's aptness, as it best deceives,
To blush at speeches rank, to weep at woes,
Or to turn white and swoon at tragic shows:

'That not a heart which in his level came
Could 'scape the hail of his all-hurting aim,
Showing fair nature is both kind and tame;
And, veil'd in them, did win whom he would maim:
Against the thing he sought he would exclaim;
When he most burn'd in heart-wish'd luxury,
He preach'd pure maid, and prais'd cold chastity.

'Thus merely with the garment of a Grace
The naked and concealed fiend he cover'd;
That th' unexperient gave the tempter place,
Which like a cherubin above them hover'd.
Who, young and simple, would not be so lover'd?
Ay me! I fell; and yet do question make
What I should do again for such a sake.

'O, that infected moisture of his eye,
O, that false fire which in his cheek so glow'd,
O, that forc'd thunder from his heart did fly,
O, that sad breath his spongy lungs bestow'd,
O, all that borrowed motion seeming ow'd,
Would yet again betray the fore-betray'd,
And new pervert a reconciled maid!'

there is no word to describe (Onions). 227. **similes,** love tokens accompanied by sonnets. 229. **What . . . obeys,** whatever obeys me, your minister, acting on your authority. 235. **blossoms,** the flower of the young nobility (Malone). 236. **coat,** coat of arms. 241. **Playing,** so Q; many emendations; Malone's *Paling*, i.e., enclosing, makes a sort of sense. 242. **unconstrained gyves,** fetters imposing no restraint (Schmidt); fetters one is not obliged to wear (Pooler). 250. **Religious,** dutiful. 258. **congest,** gather together. 264. **potential,** potent. 267. **impressest,** compellest. 273. **aloes,** bitterness. 280. **prefer,** advance. 281. **dismount,** lower. 293. **cleft,** twofold. 294. **extincture,** extinction. 297. **daff'd,** doffed; i.e., put off. 303. **cautels,** crafty devices. 305. **sounding,** swooning. 312. **them.** The antecedent is *strange forms* (l. 303) or *kindness*, *tameness*. 314. **luxury,** lechery. 318. **unexperient,** unexperienced. 322. **sake,** inducement. 323. **infected,** i.e., not natural, insincere. 327. **seeming ow'd,** seemingly owned; i.e., emotion which he seemed to have or feel.

SONNETS

Shakespeare seems to have cared more about his reputation as a lyric poet than as a dramatist. He contributed to the major nondramatic genres of his day: to amatory Ovidian narrative in *Venus and Adonis*, to the "Complaint" in *The Rape of Lucrece*, to philosophical poetry in "The Phoenix and the Turtle." He cooperated in the publication of his first two important poems, dedicating them to the young Earl of Southampton with a plea for sponsorship. To write poetry in this vein was more elegantly fashionable than to write plays, which one did mainly for money.

A poet with ambitions of this sort simply had to write a sonnet sequence. Sonneteering was the rage in the early and mid 1590's. It began in 1591, with the publication of Sir Philip Sidney's *Astrophel and Stella*, and ended almost as suddenly as it began in 1596 or 1597. The sonnet-sequences of this brief period bear the names of most well-known and minor poets of the day: *Amoretti* by Edmund Spenser (1595), *Delia* by Samuel Daniel (1591 and 1592), *Caelica* by Fulke Greville (not published until 1633), *Idea's Mirror* by Michael Drayton (1594), *Diana* by Henry Constable (1592), *Phyllis* by Thomas Lodge (1593), and the more imitative sequences of Barnabe Barnes, Giles Fletcher, William Percy, Bartholomew Griffin, William Smith, and Robert Tofte.

Shakespeare wrote sonnets during this heyday of the genre, for in 1598 Francis Meres praised Shakespeare's "sugred Sonnets among his priuate friends." Even though they were not printed at the time, we know from Meres' remark that they were circulated in manuscript among the cognoscenti and commanded great respect. Shakespeare may actually have preferred to delay publication of his sonnets, not through indifference to their literary worth but through a desire not to seem too professional. The "courtly makers" of the English Renaissance, those gentlemen whose chivalric accomplishments were supposed to include versifying, looked on the writing of poetry as a dilettantish avocation designed to amuse one's peers or court a lady. Publication was not quite genteel, and many such authors affected dismay when their verses were pirated into print. The young wits about London of the 1590's, whether aristocratically born or not, sometimes imitated this fashion. Like that gay blade, young John Donne, they sought the favorable verdict of their fellow-wits at the Inns of Court, and professed not to care about wider recognition. Whether Shakespeare was motivated in this way we do not know, but in any event his much-sought-after sonnet sequence was not published until 1609, long after the vogue had passed. The publisher, Thomas Thorpe, seems not to have obtained Shakespeare's authorization. Two sonnets, numbers 138 and 144, had been pirated ten years earlier by William Jaggard in *The Passionate Pilgrim*, 1599. The sonnets were not reprinted until 1640, either because the sonnet vogue had passed or because Thorpe's edition had been suppressed.

The unexplained circumstances of publication have given rise to a host of vexing and apparently unanswerable questions. Probably no puzzle in all English literature has provoked so much speculation and produced so little agreement. To whom are the sonnets addressed? Do they tell a consistent story that can be unraveled, and if so do they tell us anything about Shakespeare's life? The basic difficulty is that we cannot trust the order in which Thorpe published the sonnets, nor can we assume that Thorpe spoke for Shakespeare when he dedicated the sonnets to "Mr. W. H." As they stand, most of the first 126 sonnets appear to be addressed in warm friendship to a handsome young aristocrat, whereas sonnets 127–152 speak of the poet's dark-haired mistress. Yet the last two sonnets, 153–154, seem unrelated to anything previous, and cast some doubt on the authenticity of the collection. Within each large grouping of the sonnets, moreover, we find manifest inconsistencies: jealousies disappear and suddenly reappear, the poet bewails his absolute rejection by the friend and then speaks a few sonnets later of harmonious affection as though nothing had happened, and so on. Some sonnets are closely linked to their predecessors, some are entirely disconnected. We cannot be sure if the friend of sonnets 1–126 is really one person or several. By the same token, we can only speculate that the unhappy love triangle described in 40–42, in which the friend has usurped the poet's mistress, can be identified with the love triangle of the "Dark Lady" sonnets, 127–152. Most readers sense a narrative continuity of the whole, yet find blocks of sonnets stubbornly out of place. The temptation to rearrange the order has proved irresistible, but no alternative order has ever won acceptance. The consensus is that Thorpe's order is defective and non-Shakespearean, but is the only authoritative order we have.

No less frustrating is Thorpe's dedication "To the onlie begetter of these insuing sonnets, Mr. W. H." Given the late and unauthorized publication, we cannot assume that Thorpe speaks for Shakespeare. Quite possibly he is only thanking the person who obtained the sonnets for him, making publication possible. Mundanely enough, Mr. W. H. could be William Hall, an associate of Thorpe's in the publishing business. Yet Elizabethan usage affords few instances of "begetter" in this sense of "obtainer." Besides, Thorpe does offer to Mr. W. H. "that eternitie promised by our ever-living poet," as though Mr. W. H. were the very subject of those sonnets whom Shakespeare vows to immortalize. At any rate, this interpretation of "begetter" as "inspirer" has prompted many enthusiasts to search for a Mr. W. H. in Shakespeare's life, a nobleman who befriended him. The chief candidates are two. First is the young Earl of Southampton, to whom Shakespeare had dedicated *Venus and Adonis* and *The Rape of Lucrece.* The dedication to the second of these poems bespeaks a real warmth and gratitude that had been lacking in the first. The earl's name, Henry Wriothesley, yields initials that are the reverse of W. H.; or, if this lack of correspondence seems unconvincing, W. H. could stand for Sir William Harvey, third husband of Mary, Lady Southampton, the young earl's mother. Some researchers would have us believe that Shakespeare wrote the sonnets for Lady Southampton, especially those urging a young man (her son) to marry and procreate. This entire case is based, however, on pure speculation, and we have no evidence that Shakespeare had any dealings whatever with Southampton after *The Rape of Lucrece.* The plain ascription "Mr. W. H." seems an oddly uncivil way for Thorpe to have addressed an earl. If meant for Southampton, the sonnets must have been written fairly early in the 1590's, for they give no hint of Southampton's later career: his courtship of Elizabeth Vernon, her pregnancy and their secret marriage in 1598, his later involvement in Essex' Irish campaign and abortive uprising against Queen Elizabeth. Those literary sleuths who stress similarities to the Southampton relationship are too willing to overlook dissimilarities.

The second chief candidate for Mr. W. H. is William Herbert, third Earl of Pembroke, to whom, along with his brother, Shakespeare's colleagues dedicated the First Folio of 1623. In 1595 Pembroke's parents were attempting to arrange his marriage with Lady Elizabeth Carey, granddaughter of the first Lord Hunsdon who was Lord Chamberlain and patron of Shakespeare's company. In 1597 another alliance was attempted with Bridget Vere, granddaughter of Lord Burghley. In both negotiations, young Pembroke objected to the girl in question. This hypothesis requires, however, an uncomfortably late date for the sonnets, and postulates a gap in age between Shakespeare and Pembroke that would have afforded little opportunity for genuine friendship. Pembroke was only fifteen in 1595, Shakespeare thirty-one. Besides, no evidence whatever supports the claim other than historical coincidence. The common initials W. H. can be made to produce other candidates as well, such as the Lincolnshire lawyer named William Hatcliffe proposed (to no one's satisfaction) by Leslie Hotson. Hotson wants to date most of the sonnets before 1589, since Hatcliffe came to London in 1587–1588. When such speculations are constructed on the single enigmatic testimonial of Thomas Thorpe, who may well have had no connection with Shakespeare, we are left with a case that would not be worth describing had it not captured the imagination of so many researchers. The whole effort is a dismal tribute to idolatry, to a fervid but empty religiosity that too often takes the place of a genuine critical interest in Shakespeare as a poet.

Other biographical identifications have been proposed for the various personages in the sonnet sequence, predictably with no better success. The rival poet, with "the proud full sail of his great verse" (86), has been linked to Marlowe (who died in 1593), Chapman, and others. The sequence gives us little to go on, other than that the rival poet possesses a considerable enough talent to intimidate the author of the sonnets and ingratiate himself with the author's aristocratic friend. No biographical circumstances even distantly resembling this rivalry have come to light. Similarly, various candidates have been found for the "Dark Lady." One is Mary Fitton, a lady-in-waiting at court who bore a child by Pembroke in 1601. Again, however, no external evidence links Shakespeare with her, nor is he likely to have carried on an affair with one of such high rank. We are left finally without knowing who any of these people were, or if indeed Shakespeare was attempting to be biographical at all.

The same irresolution afflicts dating of the sonnets. Do they give hints of a personal chronicle extending over some years, following Thorpe's arrangement of the sonnets or some alternative order? Sonnet 104 speaks of three years having elapsed since the poet met his friend. Are there other signposts that relate to contemporary events? A line in Sonnet 107 ("The mortal moon hath her eclipse endur'd") is usually linked to the death of Queen Elizabeth (Cynthia) in 1603, though Leslie Hotson prefers to see in it an allusion to the Spanish Armada, shaped for sea battle in a moonlike crescent when it met defeat in 1588. The newly built pyramids in Sonnet 123 remind Hotson of the obelisks built by Pope Sixtus V in Rome, 1586–1589; other researchers have discovered pyramids erected on London's streets in 1603 to celebrate the coronation of James I. As these illustrations suggest, speculative dating can be used to support a hypothesis of early or late composition. Probably the wary consensus of most scholars is that the sonnets were written over a number of years, a large number certainly before 1598 but some perhaps later and even up to the date of publication in 1609.

However fruitless this quest for nonexistent certainties, it does at least direct us to a meaningful critical question: should we expect sonnets of this "personal" nature to be at least partly autobiographical? Shakespeare's sonnets have struck many readers as cries from the heart, voicing fears of rejection, self-hatred, humiliation, and at other times a serene gratitude for reciprocated affection. This power of expression may, however, be a tribute to Shakespeare's unparalleled dramatic gift rather than evidence of personal involvement. Earlier sonnet sequences, both Elizabethan and pre-Elizabethan, had established a variety of artistic conventions that tended to displace biography. Petrarch's famous *Rime*, though addressed to Laura in two sequences (during her life and after her death), idealized her into the unapproachable lady worshiped by the self-abasing and miserable lover. Petrarch's imitators—Aquilano, Bembo, Ariosto, and Tasso among the Italians, Marot, Du Bellay, Ronsard, and Desportes among the French

Plèiade—reworked this configuration in countless minor variations. In England the fashion was taken up by Wyatt, Surrey, Gascoigne, Thomas Watson, and others. Spenser's *Amoretti* and Sidney's *Astrophel and Stella*, though inspired at least in part by real women in the poets' lives, are also deeply concerned with theories of writing poetry. The rejection of stereotyped attitudes and relationships that had come to dominate the typical Petrarchan sonnet sequence is evidence not of biographical literalism in art but of a new insistence on lifelike emotion in art; as Sidney's muse urges him, "look in thy heart and write." Thus, both the Petrarchan and the anti-Petrarchan schools avoid biographical writing for its own sake. This is essentially true of all Elizabethan sonneteering, from Drayton's serious pursuit of Platonic abstraction in his *Idea* to the facile chorusing of lesser sonnet-writers about Diana, Phyllis, Zepheria, or Fidessa.

Moreover, the "story" connecting the individual poems of an Elizabethan sonnet sequence is never very important or consistent, even when we can be sure of the order in which the sonnets were written. Dante had used prose links in his *Vita Nuova* to stress narrative continuity, and so had Petrarch, but this sturdy framework had been abandoned by the late sixteenth century. Rather than telling a cohesive story, the typical Elizabethan sonnet sequence offers a loosely connected series of lyrical meditations, chiefly on love but also on poetic theory, the adversities of fortune, death, or what have you. The narrative events mentioned from time to time are not the substance of the sequence but the mere occasion for meditative reflection. Attitudes need not be consistent throughout, and the characters need not be consistently motivated like *dramatis personae* in a play.

Shakespeare's sonnet sequence retains these conventions of Elizabethan sonneteering and employs many archetypal situations and themes that had been explored by his predecessors and contemporaries. His emphasis on friendship seems new, for no other sequence addressed a majority of its sonnets to a friend rather than to a mistress, but even here the anti-Petrarchan quest for spontaneity and candor is paradoxically in the best Elizabethan tradition of Sidney and Spenser. Besides, the exaltation of friendship over love was itself a widespread neo-Platonic commonplace recently popularized in the writings of John Lyly. Structurally, Shakespeare's sonnet sequence follows the pattern of its contemporaries. Even though we cannot reconstruct a rigorously consistent chronological narrative of the sonnets in their present order, and even though the identity of the person being addressed is sometimes in doubt, we can still discern an overall pattern out of which the poet's emotional crises arise and upon which he constructs his meditative lyrics. We can account for most of the poet's dilemmas by postulating four figures: the poet-speaker himself, his friend, his mistress, and a rival poet. The order of events in this tangled relationship is not what the poet wishes to describe; instead, he touches upon this situation from time to time as he introspectively explores his own reaction to love in all its various aspects.

The poet's relationship to his friend is a vulnerable one. This friend to whom he writes is aristocratic, handsome, younger than he is. The poet is beholden to this friend as a sponsor, and must consider himself as subservient no matter how deep their mutual affection. Even at its happiest, their relationship is hierarchical. The poet abases himself in order to extol his friend's beauty and virtues (52–54, 105–106). He confesses that his love would be idolatry, except that the friend's goodness excels all poetic hyperbole. As the older of the two, the poet sententiously urges his young friend to marry and eternize his beauty through the engendering of children (1–17). Such a course, he argues, is the surest way to conquer devouring Time, the enemy of all earthly beauty and love. Yet elsewhere the poet exalts his own art as the surest defense against Time (55, 60, 63–65, etc.). These conclusions are nominally contradictory, offering procreation in one instance and poetry in another as the best hope for immortality, but thematically the two are obviously interrelated. In even the happiest of the sonnets, such as those giving thanks for "the marriage of true minds" (116, 123), Time is always present with his scythe. If love and celebratory poetry can sometimes triumph over Time, the victory is all the more precious because it is achieved in the face of such terrible odds.

Indeed, love and perfect friendship are a refuge for the poet faced with hostile fortune and an indifferent world. He is too often "in disgrace with Fortune and men's eyes" (29), oppressed by his own failings, saddened by the facile success of opportunists (66–68), ashamed of having sold himself cheap in his own profession (110–111). If biographically interpreted, this could mean that Shakespeare was not happy about his career as actor and playwright, but the motif makes complete sense in the sonnet sequence without resort to biography. The poet is pathetically dependent on his friend. Occasional absences torture him with the physical separation, even though he realizes that pure love of the spirit ought not to be hampered by distance or time (43–51). The absence is especially painful when the poet must confess his own disloyalty (117–118). The chronology of these absences cannot be worked out satisfactorily, but the haunting theme of separation is incessant, overwhelming. By extension it includes the fear of separation through death (71–73, 126). Thus the theme of absence is closely related to the poet's obsession with devouring Time.

All the poet's misfortunes would be bearable if love were constant, but his status of dependency on the aristocratic friend leaves him at the mercy of that friend's changeable mood. The poet must not complain when his well-born friend entertains a rival poet (78–86) or forms other emotional attachments, even with the poet's own mistress (40–42). These disloyalties evoke paranoid outbursts. The poet vacillates between forgiveness and angry recrimination. Sometimes even his forgiveness is a form of self-loathing, in which the poet confesses he would take back the friend on any terms (93–95). At times the poet grovels, conceding that he deserves no better treatment (57–58), but at other times his stored-up resentment bursts forth (93–95). The poet's fears, though presented in no clear chronological order, run the gamut from a fatalistic sense that rejection will come one day (49) to an abject and bitter final farewell (87). Sometimes he is tormented by jealousy (61), sometimes by self-hate (88–89).

The sonnets addressed to the poet's mistress, the "Dark Lady," similarly convey fear, self-abasement, and a panicky awareness of loss of self-control. In rare moments of happiness, the poet praises her dark features as proof of her being a real woman, not a Petrarchan goddess (130). Too often, however, her lack of beauty merely reminds the poet of his irrational enchantment (148–150). She is tyrannous, disdainful, spiteful, disloyal, a "female evil" (144) who has tempted away from the poet his better self, his friend. The poet is obsessed not so much with her perfidy as with his own compulsive self-betrayal; he sees with bitter clarity that he is offending his nobler reason by his attachment to the rebellious flesh. He worships what others abhor, and perjures himself by swearing to what he knows to be false (150–152). His only hope for escape is to punish his flesh and renounce the vanity of all worldly striving (146), but this solution evades him as he plunges helplessly back into the perverse enslavement of a sickened appetite.

This inadequate survey of only some themes of the sequence may suggest the range and yet the interconnectedness of Shakespeare's meditations on love, friendship, and poetry. The overall pattern of a sonnet sequence is visible, even if the exact chronology (never important in the Elizabethan sonnet sequence) cannot be determined. This pattern is equally evident in matters of versification and imagery. The sonnets are written throughout in the "Shakespearean" or English form, *abab cdcd efef gg*. (Number 126, written entirely in couplets, is an exception, perhaps because it was intended as the envoy to the series addressed to the poet's friend.) This familiar sonnet form, introduced by Wyatt and developed by Sidney, differs markedly from the octave-sestet division of the Petrarchan, or Italian, sonnet. The English form of three quatrains and a concluding couplet lends itself to a step-by-step development of idea and image, culminating in an epigrammatic two-line conclusion that may summarize the thought of the preceding twelve lines or give a sententious interpretation of the images developed up to this point. Thus, Sonnet 7 pursues the image of the sun at morning, noon, and evening through three quatrains, one for each phase of the day, and then in the couplet "applies" the image to the friend's unwillingness to beget children. Sonnet 29 moves from resentment of misfortune to a rejoicing in the friend's love, and rhetorically mirrors this sudden elevation of mood in the image of the lark "at break of day arising From sullen earth." Shakespeare's rhetorical and imagistic devices cleverly exploit the sonnet structure he inherited and perfected, and remind us again of the strong element of convention and artifice in these supremely "personal" sonnets. The recurring images—the canker on the rose, the pleading of a case at law, the seasonal rhythms of summer and winter or day and night, the harmonies and dissonances of music—also testify to the artistic unity of the whole and to the artist's extraordinary discipline in evoking a sense of helpless loss of self-control.

SONNETS

TO THE ONLIE BEGETTER OF
THESE INSUING SONNETS
MR. W. H. ALL HAPPINESSE
AND THAT ETERNITIE
PROMISED BY
OUR EVER-LIVING POET
WISHETH
THE WELL-WISHING
ADVENTURER IN
SETTING
FORTH

T. T.

I.

FROM fairest creatures we desire increase,
That thereby beauty's rose might never die,
But as the riper should by time decease,
His tender heir might bear his memory:
But thou, contracted to thine own bright eyes,
Feed'st thy light's flame with self-substantial fuel,
Making a famine where abundance lies,
Thyself thy foe, to thy sweet self too cruel.
Thou that art now the world's fresh ornament
And only herald to the gaudy spring,
Within thine own bud buriest thy content
And, tender churl, mak'st waste in niggarding.
  Pity the world, or else this glutton be,
  To eat the world's due, by the grave and thee.

II.

When forty winters shall besiege thy brow,
And dig deep trenches in thy beauty's field,
Thy youth's proud livery, so gaz'd on now,
Will be a totter'd weed, of small worth held:
Then being ask'd where all thy beauty lies,
Where all the treasure of thy lusty days,
To say, within thine own deep-sunken eyes,
Were an all-eating shame and thriftless praise.
How much more praise deserv'd thy beauty's use,
If thou couldst answer 'This fair child of mine
Shall sum my count and make my old excuse,'
Proving his beauty by succession thine!
  This were to be new made when thou art old,
  And see thy blood warm when thou feel'st it cold.

III.

Look in thy glass, and tell the face thou viewest
Now is the time that face should form another;
Whose fresh repair if now thou not renewest,
Thou dost beguile the world, unbless some mother.
For where is she so fair whose unear'd womb
Disdains the tillage of thy husbandry?
Or who is he so fond will be the tomb
Of his self-love, to stop posterity?
Thou art thy mother's glass, and she in thee
Calls back the lovely April of her prime:
So thou through windows of thine age shalt see
Despite of wrinkles this thy golden time.
  But if thou live, rememb'red not to be,
  Die single, and thine image dies with thee.

IV.

Unthrifty loveliness, why dost thou spend
Upon thyself thy beauty's legacy?
Nature's bequest gives nothing but doth lend,
And being frank she lends to those are free.
Then, beauteous niggard, why dost thou abuse
The bounteous largess given thee to give?
Profitless usurer, why dost thou use
So great a sum of sums, yet canst not live?
For having traffic with thyself alone,
Thou of thyself thy sweet self dost deceive.
Then how, when nature calls thee to be gone,
What acceptable audit canst thou leave?
  Thy unus'd beauty must be tomb'd with thee,
  Which, used, lives th' executor to be.

V.

Those hours, that with gentle work did frame
The lovely gaze where every eye doth dwell,
Will play the tyrants to the very same
And that unfair which fairly doth excel;
For never-resting time leads summer on
To hideous winter and confounds him there;
Sap check'd with frost and lusty leaves quite gone,
Beauty o'ersnow'd and bareness every where:
Then, were not summer's distillation left,
A liquid prisoner pent in walls of glass,
Beauty's effect with beauty were bereft,
Nor it nor no remembrance what it was:
  But flowers distill'd, though they with winter meet,
  Leese but their show; their substance still lives
    sweet.

VI.

Then let not winter's ragged hand deface
In thee thy summer, ere thou be distill'd:
Make sweet some vial; treasure thou some place
With beauty's treasure, ere it be self-kill'd.
That use is not forbidden usury
Which happies those that pay the willing loan;
That 's for thyself to breed another thee,
Or ten times happier, be it ten for one;

Sonnets I-XVII are addressed to a young friend of the poet's. In them the young man is urged to marry so that his beauty may be perpetuated in his children.

I. 5. **contracted,** engaged, espoused; Pooler sees a possible allusion to the fable of Narcissus; cf. *Venus and Adonis*, 161, note. 6. **self-substantial,** fuel of the substance of the flame itself (Dowden). 11. **thy content,** that which is contained in you; potential fatherhood (Pooler). 12. **mak'st . . . niggarding,** squander your substance by being miserly. The *Sonnets* are replete with such instances of oxymoron. 14. **by . . . thee,** by death and by your wilfully remaining childless.

II. 4. **totter'd weed,** worn-out garment. 8. **an all-eating . . . praise.** The phrases may be parallel: the shame of gluttony and the praise of extravagance, since you devour the world's due and are an unthrift of your beauty (Pooler). 9. **deserv'd,** would deserve (subjunctive). **use,** investment. Note with what variety this image of usury recurs in the next few sonnets (IV, 7, 13, 14; VI, 5; IX, 12), accompanied often with subtle word play.

III. 3. **fresh repair,** healthful state. 4. **beguile,** cheat. **unbless,** withhold happiness from. 5. **unear'd,** untilled, uncultivated. 7. **fond,** foolish. **will be,** i.e., that he will be (an ellipsis). 9. **thy mother's glass.** Dowden takes this line (comparing XIII, 14) as an indication that the young man's father was not living—a view in which Tucker Brooke concurs. It has been urged, however, that the lines imply only that the boy resembles his mother more than his father. The same image is used in *The Rape of Lucrece*, 1758-1759 (as Malone noted) to indicate parental resemblance. 13. **rememb'red not to be,** in such a way as not to be remembered. Only for the sake of being forgotten (Beeching). 14. **thine image,** any likeness of you.

Ten times thyself were happier than thou art,
If ten of thine ten times refigur'd thee:
Then what could death do, if thou shouldst depart,
Leaving thee living in posterity?
  Be not self-will'd, for thou art much too fair
  To be death's conquest and make worms thine heir.

VII.

Lo! in the orient when the gracious light
Lifts up his burning head, each under eye
Doth homage to his new-appearing sight,
Serving with looks his sacred majesty;
And having climb'd the steep-up heavenly hill,
Resembling strong youth in his middle age,
Yet mortal looks adore his beauty still,
Attending on his golden pilgrimage;
But when from highmost pitch, with weary car,
Like feeble age, he reeleth from the day,
The eyes, 'fore duteous, now converted are
From his low tract and look another way:
  So thou, thyself out-going in thy noon,
  Unlook'd on diest, unless thou get a son.

VIII.

Music to hear, why hear'st thou music sadly?
Sweets with sweets war not, joy delights in joy.
Why lov'st thou that which thou receiv'st not gladly,
Or else receiv'st with pleasure thine annoy?
If the true concord of well-tuned sounds,
By unions married, do offend thine ear,
They do but sweetly chide thee, who confounds
In singleness the parts that thou shouldst bear.
Mark how one string, sweet husband to another,
Strikes each in each by mutual ordering,
Resembling sire and child and happy mother
Who all in one, one pleasing note do sing:
  Whose speechless song, being many, seeming one,
  Sings this to thee: 'thou single wilt prove none.'

IX.

Is it for fear to wet a widow's eye
That thou consum'st thyself in single life?
Ah! if thou issueless shalt hap to die,
The world will wail thee, like a makeless wife;
The world will be thy widow and still weep
That thou no form of thee hast left behind,
When every private widow well may keep
By children's eyes her husband's shape in mind.
Look what an unthrift in the world doth spend
Shifts but his place, for still the world enjoys it;
But beauty's waste hath in the world an end,
And kept unus'd, the user so destroys it.
  No love toward others in that bosom sits
  That on himself such murd'rous shame commits.

X.

For shame! deny that thou bear'st love to any,
Who for thyself art so unprovident.
Grant, if thou wilt, thou art belov'd of many,
But that thou none lov'st is most evident;
For thou art so possess'd with murd'rous hate
That 'gainst thyself thou stick'st not to conspire,
Seeking that beauteous roof to ruinate
Which to repair should be thy chief desire.
O, change thy thought, that I may change my mind!
Shall hate be fairer lodg'd than gentle love?
Be, as thy presence is, gracious and kind,
Or to thyself at least kind-hearted prove:
  Make thee another self, for love of me,
  That beauty still may live in thine or thee.

XI.

As fast as thou shalt wane, so fast thou grow'st
In one of thine, from that which thou departest;
And that fresh blood which youngly thou bestow'st
Thou mayst call thine when thou from youth
    convertest.
Herein lives wisdom, beauty and increase;
Without this, folly, age and cold decay:
If all were minded so, the times should cease
And threescore year would make the world away.
Let those whom Nature hath not made for store,
Harsh, featureless and rude, barrenly perish:
Look whom she best endow'd she gave the more;
Which bounteous gift thou shouldst in bounty
    cherish:
  She carv'd thee for her seal, and meant thereby
  Thou shouldst print more, not let that copy die.

XII.

When I do count the clock that tells the time,
And see the brave day sunk in hideous night;
When I behold the violet past prime,
And sable curls all silver'd o'er with white;
When lofty trees I see barren of leaves
Which erst from heat did canopy the herd,
And summer's green all girded up in sheaves
Borne on the bier with white and bristly beard,
Then of thy beauty do I question make,
That thou among the wastes of time must go,
Since sweets and beauties do themselves forsake
And die as fast as they see others grow;
  And nothing 'gainst Time's scythe can make
      defence
  Save breed, to brave him when he takes thee hence.

XIII.

O, that you were yourself! but, love, you are
No longer yours than you yourself here live:
Against this coming end you should prepare,
And your sweet semblance to some other give.
So should that beauty which you hold in lease
Find no determination; then you were

IV. 4. **frank,** liberal, bounteous. 8. **live,** quibble on the two meanings, "having a livelihood" and "living in your posterity."
V. 1-3. **Those . . . same,** an application of the Renaissance commonplace of Time as both constructive and destructive; frequent in the *Sonnets*. 2. **gaze,** object of gazes. 4. **unfair,** make unlovely; cf. *unbless*, iii, 4. **fairly,** i.e., in beauty. 9. **summer's distillation,** distilled perfume of flowers. 14. **Leese,** lose.
VI. 2. **distill'd,** i.e., dissolved in death, quibbling on the uses in the preceding sonnet. 3. **vial,** i.e., continuing the metaphor of distilling perfume from the preceding sonnet; cf. v, 10, *walls of glass*. **treasure,** enrich. 8. **ten for one,** continues the usury metaphor.
VII. 1. **light,** sun. 2. **under,** earthly.
VIII. 1. **Music to hear,** an absolute construction, a verbal noun introducing the subject of hearing music. **sadly.** Cf. *Measure for Measure*, IV, i, 13-15, note. 8. **In singleness,** i.e., by being unmarried.
IX. 4. **makeless wife,** a widow. 9. **Look what,** whatever.
X. 6. **stick'st,** scruple. 7. **beauteous roof,** i.e., your person. 9. **change . . . mind,** give up your aversion from marriage that I may no longer believe that you hate mankind (Pooler). 11. **presence,** appearance, bearing; a repetition of the idea in the words *fairer lodg'd*.
XI. 1-2. **As . . . departest.** Cf. v, 1-3. 6. **Without this,** the antithesis of *Herein* (l. 5). 9. **for store,** as a source of supply (Pooler).
XII. 6. **erst,** formerly. 11. **sweets . . . forsake,** sweetness and beauty forsake sweet and beautiful things. 14. **Save . . . him,** except children whose youth may set the scythe of Time at defiance.
XIII. 3. **Against,** in anticipation of. 6. **determination,** end.

Yourself again after yourself's decease,
When your sweet issue your sweet form should bear.
Who lets so fair a house fall to decay,
Which husbandry in honour might uphold
Against the stormy gusts of winter's day
And barren rage of death's eternal cold?
  O, none but unthrifts! Dear my love, you know
  You had a father: let your son say so.

XIV.

Not from the stars do I my judgement pluck;
And yet methinks I have astronomy,
But not to tell of good or evil luck,
Of plagues, of dearths, or seasons' quality;
Nor can I fortune to brief minutes tell,
Pointing to each his thunder, rain and wind,
Or say with princes if it shall go well,
By oft predict that I in heaven find:
But from thine eyes my knowledge I derive,
And, constant stars, in them I read such art
As truth and beauty shall together thrive,
If from thyself to store thou wouldst convert;
  Or else of thee this I prognosticate:
  Thy end is truth's and beauty's doom and date.

XV.

When I consider every thing that grows
Holds in perfection but a little moment,
That this huge stage presenteth nought but shows
Whereon the stars in secret influence comment;
When I perceive that men as plants increase,
Cheered and check'd even by the self-same sky,
Vaunt in their youthful sap, at height decrease,
And wear their brave state out of memory;
Then the conceit of this inconstant stay
Sets you most rich in youth before my sight,
Where wasteful Time debateth with Decay,
To change your day of youth to sullied night;
  And all in war with Time for love of you,
  As he takes from you, I engraft you new.

XVI.

But wherefore do not you a mightier way
Make war upon this bloody tyrant, Time?
And fortify yourself in your decay
With means more blessed than my barren rhyme?
Now stand you on the top of happy hours,
And many maiden gardens yet unset
With virtuous wish would bear your living flowers,
Much liker than your painted counterfeit:
So should the lines of life that life repair,
Which this time's pencil, or my pupil pen,
Neither in inward worth nor outward fair,
Can make you live yourself in eyes of men.
  To give away yourself keeps yourself still,
  And you must live, drawn by your own sweet skill.

XVII.

Who will believe my verse in time to come,
If it were fill'd with your most high deserts?
Though yet, heaven knows, it is but as a tomb
Which hides your life and shows not half your parts.
If I could write the beauty of your eyes
And in fresh numbers number all your graces,
The age to come would say 'This poet lies;
Such heavenly touches ne'er touch'd earthly faces.'
So should my papers yellowed with their age
Be scorn'd like old men of less truth than tongue,
And your true rights be term'd a poet's rage
And stretched metre of an antique song:
  But were some child of yours alive that time,
  You should live twice; in it and in my rhyme.

XVIII.

Shall I compare thee to a summer's day?
Thou art more lovely and more temperate:
Rough winds do shake the darling buds of May,
And summer's lease hath all too short a date:
Sometime too hot the eye of heaven shines,
And often is his gold complexion dimm'd;
And every fair from fair sometime declines,
By chance or nature's changing course untrimm'd;
But thy eternal summer shall not fade
Nor lose possession of that fair thou ow'st;
Nor shall Death brag thou wand'rest in his shade,
When in eternal lines to time thou grow'st:
  So long as men can breathe or eyes can see,
  So long lives this and this gives life to thee.

XIX.

Devouring Time, blunt thou the lion's paws,
And make the earth devour her own sweet brood;
Pluck the keen teeth from the fierce tiger's jaws,
And burn the long-liv'd phœnix in her blood;
Make glad and sorry seasons as thou fleets,
And do whate'er thou wilt, swift-footed Time,
To the wide world and all her fading sweets;
But I forbid thee one most heinous crime:
O, carve not with thy hours my love's fair brow,
Nor draw no lines there with thine antique pen;

XIV. 1. **pluck,** derive. 5. **to brief minutes,** i.e., foretell events to the precise minute. 6. **Pointing,** appointing. **his,** its. 8. **oft predict,** frequent predictions. 11-12, 14. **truth . . . convert; Thy end . . . date.** Dowden set off these examples of *such art* with quotation marks, a form which makes the structure more immediately clear. 12. **store,** replenishment. **convert,** turn.

XV. 2. **Holds in perfection,** maintains its prime. 3. **this huge stage.** Pooler notes that the metaphor of the stage and the audience is sustained through the next three lines in *comment* (l. 4) and *Cheered* and *check'd* (l. 6). 9. **inconstant stay,** constant or continual change. 11. **debateth with,** combines in battle with; *with* here implies association, not opposition, as is frequently its meaning in this idiom.

XVI. 6. **unset,** unplanted. 8. **Much liker,** i.e., much more like you. 9. **lines of life,** usually explained as lineage, i.e., children. Dowden sees a play in *lines* on the meanings "lines of a picture or portrait," and "lines of verse"; living poems and pictures are children. 10. **this time's pencil,** a portraiture done in this present age. **pupil,** apprenticed, inexpert. 13. **give away yourself,** i.e., beget children. **keeps,** preserves.

XVII. 11. **rage,** exaggerated inspiration. 12. **stretched metre,** overstrained poetry (Dowden); poetic license (Tucker Brooke).

XVIII. This and the following sonnet develop the theme of the immortalizing power of poetry. 7. **fair from fair,** beautiful thing from beauty. 8. **untrimm'd,** stripped of ornaments. 10. **ow'st,** own. 12. **to . . . grow'st.** To grow to time is to be incorporated or become one with it and so to live while time lasts (Pooler).

XIX. 1. **Devouring Time.** Cf. the apostrophe to Time in *The Rape of Lucrece*, 925 ff. 5. **fleets,** fleetest. 11. **untainted,** a metaphor from tilting; a taint was a hit (Pooler).

Sonnets xx and xxi are in praise of the friend's beauty.

XX. 1. **with . . . painted,** i.e., without cosmetics. 5. **rolling,** i.e., roving. 7. **A man . . . controlling,** one who has a manly appearance, and embodies all handsomeness (?). 11. **defeated,** defrauded. 12. **to my purpose nothing,** out of line with my wishes. 13. **prick'd,** designated (with bawdy suggestion; the "thing" in l. 12 is a phallus).

XXI. 1. **Muse,** poet. 4. **every fair,** every lovely thing. **rehearse,** mention. 5. **Making . . . compare,** joining in proud comparison (Dowden); uniting his *fair* to heaven by extravagant comparisons (Pooler). 8. **rondure,** sphere. 12. **gold candles,** stars. 13. **like . . . well,** like to deal in second-hand ideas (Tucker Brooke); like rumors

Him in thy course untainted do allow
For beauty's pattern to succeeding men.
Yet, do thy worst, old Time: despite thy wrong,
My love shall in my verse ever live young.

XX.

A woman's face with Nature's own hand painted
Hast thou, the master-mistress of my passion;
A woman's gentle heart, but not acquainted
With shifting change, as is false women's fashion;
An eye more bright than theirs, less false in rolling,
Gilding the object whereupon it gazeth;
A man in hue, all hues in his controlling,
Which steals men's eyes and women's souls amazeth.
And for a woman wert thou first created;
Till Nature, as she wrought thee, fell a-doting,
And by addition me of thee defeated,
By adding one thing to my purpose nothing.
But since she prick'd thee out for women's pleasure,
Mine be thy love and thy love's use their treasure.

XXI.

So is it not with me as with that Muse
Stirr'd by a painted beauty to his verse,
Who heaven itself for ornament doth use
And every fair with his fair doth rehearse;
Making a couplement of proud compare,
With sun and moon, with earth and sea's rich gems,
With April's first-born flowers, and all things rare
That heaven's air in this huge rondure hems.
O, let me, true in love, but truly write,
And then believe me, my love is as fair
As any mother's child, though not so bright
As those gold candles fix'd in heaven's air:
Let them say more that like of hearsay well;
I will not praise that purpose not to sell.

XXII.

My glass shall not persuade me I am old,
So long as youth and thou are of one date;
But when in thee time's furrows I behold,
Then look I death my days should expiate.
For all that beauty that doth cover thee
Is but the seemly raiment of my heart,
Which in thy breast doth live, as thine in me:
How can I then be elder than thou art?
O, therefore, love, be of thyself so wary
As I, not for myself, but for thee will;
Bearing thy heart, which I will keep so chary
As tender nurse her babe from faring ill.
Presume not on thy heart when mine is slain;
Thou gav'st me thine, not to give back again.

XXIII.

As an unperfect actor on the stage
Who with his fear is put besides his part,
Or some fierce thing replete with too much rage,
Whose strength's abundance weakens his own heart,
So I, for fear of trust, forget to say
The perfect ceremony of love's rite,
And in mine own love's strength seem to decay,
O'ercharg'd with burden of mine own love's might.
O, let my books be then the eloquence
And dumb presagers of my speaking breast,
Who plead for love and look for recompense
More than that tongue that more hath more express'd.
O, learn to read what silent love hath writ:
To hear with eyes belongs to love's fine wit.

XXIV.

Mine eye hath play'd the painter and hath stell'd
Thy beauty's form in table of my heart;
My body is the frame wherein 'tis held,
And perspective it is best painter's art.
For through the painter must you see his skill,
To find where your true image pictur'd lies;
Which in my bosom's shop is hanging still,
That hath his windows glazed with thine eyes.
Now see what good turns eyes for eyes have done:
Mine eyes have drawn thy shape, and thine for me
Are windows to my breast, where-through the sun
Delights to peep, to gaze therein on thee;
Yet eyes this cunning want to grace their art;
They draw but what they see, know not the heart.

XXV.

Let those who are in favour with their stars
Of public honour and proud titles boast,
Whilst I, whom fortune of such triumph bars,
Unlook'd for joy in that I honour most.
Great princes' favourites their fair leaves spread
But as the marigold at the sun's eye,
And in themselves their pride lies buried,
For at a frown they in their glory die.
The painful warrior famoused for fight,
After a thousand victories once foil'd,
Is from the book of honour razed quite,
And all the rest forgot for which he toil'd:
Then happy I, that love and am beloved
Where I may not remove nor be removed.

rather than facts (Pooler). 14. **that . . . sell.** Pooler sees this line as the converse of Proverbs 20:14: "It is naught, it is naught, saith the buyer." Malone notes parallels in *Love's Labour's Lost*, IV, iii, 240, and in *Troilus and Cressida*, IV, i, 78.

Sonnets XXII-XXV are four separate expressions of the poet's joy in his friend's love, introducing themes later elaborated (Tucker Brooke).

XXII. 4. **look I,** I foresee. **expiate,** end. 13. **Presume not on,** do not expect to receive back (Beeching).

XXIII. 5. **for fear of trust,** doubting of being trusted (Schmidt). Dowden thought the comparison was to the *unperfect actor* who dare not trust himself. He observed that in the first eight lines 5 and 6 refer to 1 and 2, 7 and 8 refer to 3 and 4. 9. **books,** the manuscript books in which he writes his *Sonnets* (Dowden); the *Sonnets* themselves (Massey); the most natural interpretation is that the poet refers to *Venus and Adonis* and *The Rape of Lucrece,* which he describes as *dumb presagers* of the love he cannot directly express, an interpretation which favors the Southampton theory (Tucker Brooke). Those who favor Sewell's emendation *looks* justify it on the ground that *books* are not *dumb presagers;* that the love which expresses itself in love poems is not silent. 10. **presagers,** those which indicate. 12. **More, more, more,** to a greater degree; more ardors of love; more fully.

XXIV. 1. **stell'd,** fixed, installed; or possibly *steel'd,* i.e., engraved; Q: *steeld.* 4. **perspective,** optical device for producing fantastic images (Onions); a painter's highest art is to produce the illusion of distance, one thing seeming to lie behind another. You must look through the painter (my eye or myself) to see your picture, the product of his skill, which lies within him, i.e., in my heart (Dowden); the word *perspective* is used quibblingly. 7. **my bosom's shop.** The imagery is here changed; in 1-4 Shakespeare's eye is the brush, his heart the canvas, his body the frame, of his friend's picture. The second quatrain, 5-8, is connected with the first by the punning explanation of *perspective;* but by a turn of this strange kaleidoscope, the body ceases to be the frame, for part of it, viz., the bosom, has become a shop or studio in which the picture hangs. The windows of this shop are the friend's eyes looking in (Pooler). 13-14. **Yet . . . heart.** Cf. *The Merchant of Venice,* III, ii, 63-69.

XXV. 4. **Unlook'd for,** unexpectedly. 9. **painful,** enduring much. **fight,** Theobald's emendation of Q: *worth,* to rhyme with *quite;* he suggested as an alternative the emendation of *forth* for *quite.*

XXVI.

Lord of my love, to whom in vassalage
Thy merit hath my duty strongly knit,
To thee I send this written embassage,
To witness duty, not to show my wit:
Duty so great, which wit so poor as mine
May make seem bare, in wanting words to show it,
But that I hope some good conceit of thine
In thy soul's thought, all naked, will bestow it;
Till whatsoever star that guides my moving
Points on me graciously with fair aspect
And puts apparel on my tottered loving,
To show me worthy of thy sweet respect:
  Then may I dare to boast how I do love thee;
  Till then not show my head where thou mayst prove me.

XXVII.

Weary with toil, I haste me to my bed,
The dear repose for limbs with travel tired;
But then begins a journey in my head,
To work my mind, when body's work's expired:
For then my thoughts, from far where I abide,
Intend a zealous pilgrimage to thee,
And keep my drooping eyelids open wide,
Looking on darkness which the blind do see:
Save that my soul's imaginary sight
Presents thy shadow to my sightless view,
Which, like a jewel hung in ghastly night,
Makes black night beauteous and her old face new.
  Lo! thus, by day my limbs, by night my mind,
  For thee and for myself no quiet find.

XXVIII.

How can I then return in happy plight,
That am debarr'd the benefit of rest?
When day's oppression is not eas'd by night,
But day by night, and night by day, oppress'd?
And each, though enemies to either's reign,
Do in consent shake hands to torture me;
The one by toil, the other to complain
How far I toil, still farther off from thee.
I tell the day, to please him thou art bright
And dost him grace when clouds do blot the heaven:
So flatter I the swart-complexion'd night,
When sparkling stars twire not thou gild'st the even.
  But day doth daily draw my sorrows longer
  And night doth nightly make grief's strength seem stronger.

XXIX.

When, in disgrace with fortune and men's eyes,
I all alone beweep my outcast state
And trouble deaf heaven with my bootless cries
And look upon myself and curse my fate,
Wishing me like to one more rich in hope,
Featur'd like him, like him with friends possess'd,
Desiring this man's art and that man's scope,
With what I most enjoy contented least;
Yet in these thoughts myself almost despising,
Haply I think on thee, and then my state,
Like to the lark at break of day arising
From sullen earth, sings hymns at heaven's gate;
  For thy sweet love rememb'red such wealth brings
  That then I scorn to change my state with kings.

XXX.

When to the sessions of sweet silent thought
I summon up remembrance of things past,
I sigh the lack of many a thing I sought,
And with old woes new wail my dear time's waste:
Then can I drown an eye, unus'd to flow,
For precious friends hid in death's dateless night,
And weep afresh love's long since cancell'd woe,
And moan th' expense of many a vanish'd sight:
Then can I grieve at grievances foregone,
And heavily from woe to woe tell o'er
The sad account of fore-bemoaned moan,
Which I new pay as if not paid before.
  But if the while I think on thee, dear friend,
  All losses are restor'd and sorrows end.

XXXI.

Thy bosom is endeared with all hearts,
Which I by lacking have supposed dead,
And there reigns love and all love's loving parts,
And all those friends which I thought buried.
How many a holy and obsequious tear
Hath dear religious love stol'n from mine eye
As interest of the dead, which now appear
But things remov'd that hidden in thee lie!
Thou art the grave where buried love doth live,
Hung with the trophies of my lovers gone,
Who all their parts of me to thee did give;

XXVI. This is regarded variously as an "envoy" to the twenty-five preceding sonnets and as a dedication to the next sequence (XXVI-XXXII). Its similarity in tone and phrasing to the dedication of *The Rape of Lucrece* has been frequently noted. 8. **all naked,** modifies *Duty* (l. 5). **bestow,** equip, clothe (Tyler). 9. **moving,** life. 11. **tottered,** tattered. 12. **thy,** so Malone; Q: *their*, regarded generally as a misprint; retained by some editors and explained variously as referring to (1) the stars, (2) thy soul's thought, (3) the sweet respect of the star. 14. **prove,** test.

Beginning with XXVII and continuing through the next five, the poet writes as one on a journey which takes him far from his friend.

XXVII. 6. **Intend,** direct. 11. **ghastly,** fearful. 13-14. **by day . . . find,** by day my limbs find no quiet for myself, i.e., on account of business of my own; by night my mind finds no quiet for thee, i.e., on your account, thinking of you (Dowden); this type of construction is called "chiastic," i.e., interlaced. It is not infrequent in Renaissance poetry.

XXVIII. 1. **plight,** state, condition. 6. **consent,** i.e., mutual agreement. 7. **to complain,** by causing me to complain. 9. **to please him.** There is some argument as to whether this phrase modifies *tell* or *bright;* the absence of any punctuation in Q leaves the line ambiguous. 10. **dost . . . heaven,** i.e., that you shine in place of the sun when the sun is overclouded. 12. **twire,** twinkle, peek. **thou gild'st the even,** you make bright the evening.

XXIX. 6. **Featur'd,** situated (Onions); more likely, formed; i.e., envying their good looks, their beauty of face. **like him, like him,** not a repetition but, as Pooler points out, "like a second man, like a third." 7. **scope,** probably implies both "range of powers" and "opportunity."

XXX. 1-2. **sessions . . . summon.** The metaphor is that of a court of law. Malone cites *Othello*, III, iii, 138-141. Unlike many of the sonnets this one does not sustain the figure. 4. **new wail,** lament anew. **dear time's waste,** i.e., the wasting of precious time, or time's erosion of those things held precious (?). 6. **dateless,** endless. 8. **expense,** that which is spent. 9. **foregone,** past. 10. **tell,** count.

XXXI. 1. **endeared,** enhanced in value, made more precious. You have become dearer to me as representing all I have loved (Pooler). 6. **religious,** i.e., as fulfilling a duty. 7. **As interest of the dead.** The phrase carries out the idea of mourning as a duty owed to the dead. 8. **remov'd,** separated by time or space; i.e., absent. 12. **due of many,** i.e., the duty or obligation to many.

XXXII. 1. **my . . . day,** i.e., the day which will content me well. 5. **bett'ring,** i.e., improvement in the writing of poetry. 7. **Reserve,** preserve. 8. **happier,** more gifted. 11. **dearer birth,** i.e., better poem, better artistic creation. 12. **To . . . equipage.** Sir Sidney Lee points

That due of many now is thine alone:
Their images I lov'd I view in thee,
And thou, all they, hast all the all of me.

XXXII.

If thou survive my well-contented day,
When that churl Death my bones with dust shall cover,
And shalt by fortune once more re-survey
These poor rude lines of thy deceased lover,
Compare them with the bett'ring of the time,
And though they be outstripp'd by every pen,
Reserve them for my love, not for their rhyme,
Exceeded by the height of happier men.
O, then vouchsafe me but this loving thought:
'Had my friend's Muse grown with this growing age,
A dearer birth than this his love had brought,
To march in ranks of better equipage:
But since he died and poets better prove,
Theirs for their style I'll read, his for his love.'

XXXIII.

Full many a glorious morning have I seen
Flatter the mountain-tops with sovereign eye,
Kissing with golden face the meadows green,
Gilding pale streams with heavenly alchemy;
Anon permit the basest clouds to ride
With ugly rack on his celestial face,
And from the forlorn world his visage hide,
Stealing unseen to west with this disgrace:
Even so my sun one early morn did shine
With all-triumphant splendour on my brow;
But out, alack! he was but one hour mine;
The region cloud hath mask'd him from me now.
Yet him for this my love no whit disdaineth;
Suns of the world may stain when heaven's sun staineth.

XXXIV.

Why didst thou promise such a beauteous day
And make me travel forth without my cloak,
To let base clouds o'ertake me in my way,
Hiding thy brav'ry in their rotten smoke?
'Tis not enough that through the cloud thou break,
To dry the rain on my storm-beaten face,
For no man well of such a salve can speak
That heals the wound and cures not the disgrace:
Nor can thy shame give physic to my grief;
Though thou repent, yet I have still the loss:
Th' offender's sorrow lends but weak relief
To him that bears the strong offence's cross.
Ah! but those tears are pearl which thy love sheeds,
And they are rich and ransom all ill deeds.

XXXV.

No more be griev'd at that which thou hast done:
Roses have thorns, and silver fountains mud;
Clouds and eclipses stain both moon and sun,
And loathsome canker lives in sweetest bud.
All men make faults, and even I in this,
Authorizing thy trespass with compare,
Myself corrupting, salving thy amiss,
Excusing thy sins more than thy sins are;
For to thy sensual fault I bring in sense—
Thy adverse party is thy advocate—
And 'gainst myself a lawful plea commence:
Such civil war is in my love and hate
That I an accessary needs must be
To that sweet thief which sourly robs from me.

XXXVI.

Let me confess that we two must be twain,
Although our undivided loves are one:
So shall those blots that do with me remain
Without thy help by me be borne alone.
In our two loves there is but one respect,
Though in our lives a separable spite,
Which though it alter not love's sole effect,
Yet doth it steal sweet hours from love's delight.
I may not evermore acknowledge thee,
Lest my bewailed guilt should do thee shame,
Nor thou with public kindness honour me,
Unless thou take that honour from thy name:
But do not so; I love thee in such sort
As, thou being mine, mine is thy good report.

XXXVII.

As a decrepit father takes delight
To see his active child do deeds of youth,
So I, made lame by Fortune's dearest spite,
Take all my comfort of thy worth and truth.
For whether beauty, birth, or wealth, or wit,
Or any of these all, or all, or more,
Entitled in thy parts do crowned sit,
I make my love engrafted to this store:
So then I am not lame, poor, nor despis'd,
Whilst that this shadow doth such substance give

out the frequency of this metaphor in Elizabethan literature. Tyler traced the line to a similar treatment of the figure in Marston's *Pygmalion* (1598); Marston was probably the borrower. **of better equipage,** more finely equipped.

XXXIII. This sonnet begins a new theme. The poet has endured some indignity at the friend's hands and the friend has repented. 2. **Flatter,** explained by *sovereign;* the glance of a king is a compliment to a courtier (Pooler). The *NED* definition, "to encourage with hopeful or pleasing representations," is applicable here. 5. **permit,** to be construed as parallel with *Flatter.* 6. **rack,** mass of cloud driven before the wind in the upper air. 7. **forlorn,** accent on the first syllable. 8. **to west,** westward. 12. **region,** pertaining to the upper air. 14. **stain,** grow dim, be obscured, soiled (Pooler); cf. XXXV, 3.

XXXIV. 4. **brav'ry,** finery, fine clothes. 8. **disgrace,** i.e., the scar, the disfigurement caused by his friend's harsh treatment. Pooler points out that this is the *loss* of line 10. 9. **shame,** repentance for the wrong done. **physic,** remedy. 13. **sheeds,** sheds.

XXXV. 3. **stain.** Cf. XXXIII, 14, note. 4. **canker,** canker worm. 6. **Authorizing,** sanctioning, justifying. **with compare,** by comparison. 7. **salving,** parallel in construction with *Authorizing, corrupting,* and *Excusing.* **amiss,** misdeed. 8. **Excusing . . . are,** making the excuse more than proportioned to the offense (Steevens). 9. **sensual,** pertaining to the flesh. **sense,** pertaining to the rational faculty; i.e., I reason away your offenses. 14. **sourly,** cruelly.

XXXVI. Another series on the theme of separation begins here, interrupting the group that dwells on the wrongs suffered by the poet. Here it is the friend who has gone on a journey. 1. **twain,** parted. 3. **those blots,** several possible explanations: not moral turpitude but the professional occupation and lower social standing of the poet (Tyler); perhaps his *disgrace with fortune and men's eyes,* XXIX, whatever that may have been (Pooler); may be the darkening of soul expressed in sonnets CXLVII and CLII (Tucker Brooke). 5. **respect,** i.e., a mutual regard. 6. **separable spite,** spiteful separation (Schmidt); separating spite (Malone). The latter is warranted by Abbott's observation that adjectives in *-able* are active as well as passive. 7. **sole,** unique. 14. **report,** reputation.

XXXVII. 3. **made lame,** i.e., handicapped in life. For other figurative occurrences of the word in Shakespeare, cf. *As You Like It,* I, iii, 6, and *Coriolanus,* IV, vii, 7. **dearest,** most bitter. 4. **of,** in, from. 5-7. **beauty, birth,** etc. These lines are usually accepted as evidence that the *Sonnets* were addressed to a person of high rank. 7. **Entitled,** ennobled (Malone); as rightful owner by a just title (Pooler). 10. **shadow,** reflection, i.e., in the Platonic sense (Wyndham).

That I in thy abundance am suffic'd
And by a part of all thy glory live.
  Look, what is best, that best I wish in thee:
  This wish I have; then ten times happy me!

XXXVIII.

How can my Muse want subject to invent,
While thou dost breathe, that pour'st into my verse
Thine own sweet argument, too excellent
For every vulgar paper to rehearse?
O, give thyself the thanks, if aught in me
Worthy perusal stand against thy sight;
For who 's so dumb that cannot write to thee,
When thou thyself dost give invention light?
Be thou the tenth Muse, ten times more in worth
Than those old nine which rhymers invocate;
And he that calls on thee, let him bring forth
Eternal numbers to outlive long date.
  If my slight Muse do please these curious days,
  The pain be mine, but thine shall be the praise.

XXXIX.

O, how thy worth with manners may I sing,
When thou art all the better part of me?
What can mine own praise to mine own self bring?
And what is 't but mine own when I praise thee?
Even for this let us divided live,
And our dear love lose name of single one,
That by this separation I may give
That due to thee which thou deserv'st alone.
O absence, what a torment wouldst thou prove,
Were it not thy sour leisure gave sweet leave
To entertain the time with thoughts of love,
Which time and thoughts so sweetly doth deceive,
  And that thou teachest how to make one twain,
  By praising him here who doth hence remain!

XL.

Take all my loves, my love, yea, take them all;
What hast thou then more than thou hadst before?
No love, my love, that thou mayst true love call;
All mine was thine before thou hadst this more.
Then if for my love thou my love receivest,
I cannot blame thee for my love thou usest;
But yet be blam'd, if thou this self deceivest
By wilful taste of what thyself refusest.
I do forgive thy robb'ry, gentle thief,
Although thou steal thee all my poverty;
And yet, love knows, it is a greater grief
To bear love's wrong than hate's known injury.
  Lascivious grace, in whom all ill well shows,
  Kill me with spites; yet we must not be foes.

XLI.

Those pretty wrongs that liberty commits,
When I am sometime absent from thy heart,
Thy beauty and thy years full well befits,
For still temptation follows where thou art.
Gentle thou art and therefore to be won,
Beauteous thou art, therefore to be assailed;
And when a woman woos, what woman's son
Will sourly leave her till she have prevailed?
Ay me! but yet thou mightst my seat forbear,
And chide thy beauty and thy straying youth,
Who lead thee in their riot even there
Where thou art forc'd to break a twofold truth,
  Hers, by thy beauty tempting her to thee,
  Thine, by thy beauty being false to me.

XLII.

That thou hast her, it is not all my grief,
And yet it may be said I lov'd her dearly;
That she hath thee, is of my wailing chief,
A loss in love that touches me more nearly.
Loving offenders, thus I will excuse ye:
Thou dost love her, because thou know'st I love her;
And for my sake even so doth she abuse me,
Suff'ring my friend for my sake to approve her.
If I lose thee, my loss is my love's gain,
And losing her, my friend hath found that loss;
Both find each other, and I lose both twain,
And both for my sake lay on me this cross:
  But here 's the joy; my friend and I are one;
  Sweet flattery! then she loves but me alone.

XLIII.

When most I wink, then do mine eyes best see,
For all the day they view things unrespected;
But when I sleep, in dreams they look on thee,
And darkly bright are bright in dark directed.
Then thou, whose shadow shadows doth make bright,
How would thy shadow's form form happy show
To the clear day with thy much clearer light,
When to unseeing eyes thy shade shines so!
How would, I say, mine eyes be blessed made
By looking on thee in the living day,
When in dead night thy fair imperfect shade
Through heavy sleep on sightless eyes doth stay!

XXXVIII. Sir Sidney Lee points out the frequency in dedicatory lines of the conceit developed in this sonnet; viz., that the patron may claim as his own handiwork the protégé's accomplishment because he inspires it. 1. **want . . . invent,** lack something to write about. 2. **that,** who. 3. **argument,** subject. 4. **vulgar,** common. 12. **numbers,** verses. 13. **curious,** critical.

XXXIX. 1. **with manners,** decently, becomingly. 10. **sour,** bitter, harsh; cf. *sourly*, XXXV, 14.

The three following sonnets revert to the theme of XXXIII-XXXV. Tucker Brooke rearranges the six in a continuous series, placing XXXVI-XXXIX after XLII. The commentators are inclined to interpret XL (considering it with five others—XLI, XLII, CXXXIII, CXXXIV, CLXIV) as biographically significant. Sir Sidney Lee finds here "strands of wholly original sentiment" distinguishing these six from the rest of the *Sonnets*, which for the most part are vigorous and original treatments of stereotyped themes (see his chapter, "The Supposed Story of Intrigue in the Sonnets," *Life*, pp. 151-160).

XL. 5. **my love . . . my love,** love of me . . . her whom I love (Dowden). 6. **for,** because. **thou usest,** you enjoy. 7. **this self,** i.e., this other self of yours, the poet. (Often emended to *thyself*, as in Globe.) 10. **steal thee,** take for your own. **all my poverty,** the poor little that I have (Rolfe). 13. **Lascivious grace,** i.e., you who are gracious even in your lasciviousness.

XLI. Dowden points out that this sonnet develops the idea of line 13 of the preceding one. 1. **pretty,** minor. **liberty,** licentiousness. 2. **absent,** probably to be taken in a literal and local as well as figurative sense (Tucker Brooke). 3. **befits.** The subject is *wrongs* (l. 1); Abbott (333) points out the frequency in Shakespeare of the third person plural in *-s*. 5-6. **Gentle . . . assailed.** The phrasing and the sentiment recall *1 Henry VI*, V, iii, 78-79. 9. **seat,** place. 11. **Who,** which. 12. **twofold truth,** her plighted love and your plighted friendship (Pooler).

XLII. 3. **is . . . chief,** is chief cause of my lamentation. 8. **approve,** try, test. 9. **my love's,** hers whom I love (as in LX, 5, 6). 14. **flattery,** gratifying deception (Onions), as in *Othello*, IV, i, 133.

XLIII. This picks up the theme of XXXVI-XXXIX, i.e., the friend's absence, and continues it through XLVII. 2. **unrespected,** unnoticed. 4. **And . . . directed,** and illumined although closed are clearly directed in the darkness (Dowden); is it possible that the phrase *darkly bright* may mean that the eyes are bright most of all in the dark, because of what they see in dreams? (Alden). 5. **whose . . . bright,** whose image makes darkness bright (Pooler). 6. **thy shadow's form,** probably, the substance of the shadow; i.e., your presence. 8. **unseeing eyes,** i.e.,

All days are nights to see till I see thee,
And nights bright days when dreams do show thee me.

XLIV.

If the dull substance of my flesh were thought,
Injurious distance should not stop my way;
For then despite of space I would be brought,
From limits far remote, where thou dost stay.
No matter then although my foot did stand
Upon the farthest earth remov'd from thee;
For nimble thought can jump both sea and land
As soon as think the place where he would be.
But, ah! thought kills me that I am not thought,
To leap large lengths of miles when thou art gone,
But that so much of earth and water wrought
I must attend time's leisure with my moan,
Receiving nought by elements so slow
But heavy tears, badges of either's woe.

XLV.

The other two, slight air and purging fire,
Are both with thee, wherever I abide;
The first my thought, the other my desire,
These present-absent with swift motion slide.
For when these quicker elements are gone
In tender embassy of love to thee,
My life, being made of four, with two alone
Sinks down to death, oppress'd with melancholy;
Until life's composition be recured
By those swift messengers return'd from thee,
Who even but now come back again, assured
Of thy fair health, recounting it to me:
This told, I joy; but then no longer glad,
I send them back again and straight grow sad.

XLVI.

Mine eye and heart are at a mortal war
How to divide the conquest of thy sight;
Mine eye my heart thy picture's sight would bar,
My heart mine eye the freedom of that right.
My heart doth plead that thou in him dost lie,—
A closet never pierc'd with crystal eyes—
But the defendant doth that plea deny
And says in him thy fair appearance lies.
To 'cide this title is impanneled
A quest of thoughts, all tenants to the heart,
And by their verdict is determined
The clear eye's moiety and the dear heart's part:
As thus; mine eye's due is thy outward part,
And my heart's right thy inward love of heart.

XLVII.

Betwixt mine eye and heart a league is took,
And each doth good turns now unto the other:
When that mine eye is famish'd for a look,
Or heart in love with sighs himself doth smother,
With my love's picture then my eye doth feast
And to the painted banquet bids my heart;
Another time mine eye is my heart's guest
And in his thoughts of love doth share a part:
So, either by thy picture or my love,
Thyself away art present still with me;
For thou not farther than my thoughts canst move,
And I am still with them and they with thee;
Or, if they sleep, thy picture in my sight
Awakes my heart to heart's and eye's delight.

XLVIII.

How careful was I, when I took my way,
Each trifle under truest bars to thrust,
That to my use it might unused stay
From hands of falsehood, in sure wards of trust!
But thou, to whom my jewels trifles are,
Most worthy comfort, now my greatest grief,
Thou, best of dearest and mine only care,
Art left the prey of every vulgar thief.
Thee have I not lock'd up in any chest,
Save where thou art not, though I feel thou art,
Within the gentle closure of my breast,
From whence at pleasure thou mayst come and part;
And even thence thou wilt be stol'n, I fear,
For truth proves thievish for a prize so dear.

XLIX.

Against that time, if ever that time come,
When I shall see thee frown on my defects,
When as thy love hath cast his utmost sum,
Call'd to that audit by advis'd respects;
Against that time when thou shalt strangely pass
And scarcely greet me with that sun, thine eye,
When love, converted from the thing it was,
Shall reasons find of settled gravity,—
Against that time do I ensconce me here
Within the knowledge of mine own desart,
And this my hand against myself uprear,
To guard the lawful reasons on thy part:

closed eyes of the dreamer. 11. **imperfect,** unsubstantial (Tyler); perhaps indistinct as in a dream. 13. **All . . . to see,** all days are gloomy to behold (Steevens).

XLIV. 4. **where,** i.e., to the place where. 6. **farthest earth remov'd,** that part of earth farthest removed. 8. **he,** it. 11. **earth and water,** the baser elements; cf. *Antony and Cleopatra,* V, ii, 292-293; *Henry V,* III, vii, 22-23. 14. **either's,** i.e., because the earth is heavy and the sea is salt and wet, both like tears.

XLV. 1. **other two,** i.e., of the four elements discussed in Sonnet XLIV. 4. **present-absent,** now here and immediately gone (Tucker Brooke). 7. **two alone,** i.e., earth and water. 8. **melancholy,** may have been pronounced *melanch'ly;* so printed by some editors. 9. **recured,** restored. 10. **swift messengers,** i.e., fire and air, thought and desire.

The following two sonnets treat a theme that Lee points out is a favorite one with the Elizabethan sonneteers; i.e., the war between the eye and the heart. Pooler and others think it might be a continuation of XXIV, which develops the conceit of a portrait of the poet's beloved painted on his heart.

XLVI. 2. **thy sight,** the sight of you. 6. **crystal,** i.e., because of their clarity. 9. **'cide,** decide; so Malone and most editors; Q: *side* retained by some who explain "to assign to one side or another." 10. **quest,** inquest, jury. 12. **moiety,** portion.

XLVII. 1. **a league is took,** an agreement is reached. 6. **painted banquet,** i.e., a visual feast, or, a picture of the friend. 8. **his,** its, the heart's.

Sonnets XLVIII-LV form another series on the poet's absence from his friend, occasioned by the poet's having gone on a second journey.

XLVIII. 1. **took my way,** set out on my journey. 2. **truest,** most trusty. 4. **hands of falsehood,** thieves. 5. **to whom,** in comparison to whom. 6. **now . . . grief,** i.e., because of his absence. 12. **part,** depart.

XLIX. 3. **cast . . . sum,** added up the sum total. A metaphor from closing accounts on a dissolution of partnership (Pooler). 4. **advis'd respects,** considerations. 5. **strangely,** as a stranger. 8. **reasons . . . gravity,** find reasons for a dignified reserve (Schmidt); *settled gravity* is taken by many editors to mean "weight"; i.e., find reasons of considerable weight. 10. **desart,** (slight) merit. 11-14. **And . . . cause,** I take your part against myself by admitting that you have a legal right to disown me, since I can show no cause why you should love me (Pooler). 11. **against myself,** i.e., to take an oath, not as if with a weapon.

To leave poor me thou hast the strength of laws,
Since why to love I can allege no cause.

L.

How heavy do I journey on the way,
When what I seek, my weary travel's end,
Doth teach that ease and that repose to say
'Thus far the miles are measur'd from thy friend!'
The beast that bears me, tired with my woe,
Plods dully on, to bear that weight in me,
As if by some instinct the wretch did know
His rider lov'd not speed, being made from thee:
The bloody spur cannot provoke him on
That sometimes anger thrusts into his hide;
Which heavily he answers with a groan,
More sharp to me than spurring to his side;
For that same groan doth put this in my mind;
My grief lies onward and my joy behind.

LI.

Thus can my love excuse the slow offence
Of my dull bearer when from thee I speed:
From where thou art why should I haste me thence?
Till I return, of posting is no need.
O, what excuse will my poor beast then find,
When swift extremity can seem but slow?
Then should I spur, though mounted on the wind;
In winged speed no motion shall I know:
Then can no horse with my desire keep pace;
Therefore desire, of perfect'st love being made,
Shall neigh—no dull flesh—in his fiery race;
But love, for love, thus shall excuse my jade;
Since from thee going he went wilful-slow,
Towards thee I'll run, and give him leave to go.

LII.

So am I as the rich, whose blessed key
Can bring him to his sweet up-locked treasure,
The which he will not ev'ry hour survey,
For blunting the fine point of seldom pleasure.
Therefore are feasts so solemn and so rare,
Since, seldom coming, in the long year set,
Like stones of worth they thinly placed are,
Or captain jewels in the carcanet.
So is the time that keeps you as my chest,
Or as the wardrobe which the robe doth hide,
To make some special instant special blest,
By new unfolding his imprison'd pride.
Blessed are you, whose worthiness gives scope,
Being had, to triumph, being lack'd, to hope.

LIII.

What is your substance, whereof are you made,
That millions of strange shadows on you tend?
Since every one hath, every one, one shade,
And you, but one, can every shadow lend.
Describe Adonis, and the counterfeit
Is poorly imitated after you;
On Helen's cheek all art of beauty set,
And you in Grecian tires are painted new:
Speak of the spring and foison of the year;
The one doth shadow of your beauty show,
The other as your bounty doth appear;
And you in every blessed shape we know.
In all external grace you have some part,
But you like none, none you, for constant heart.

LIV.

O, how much more doth beauty beauteous seem
By that sweet ornament which truth doth give!
The rose looks fair, but fairer we it deem
For that sweet odour which doth in it live.
The canker-blooms have full as deep a dye
As the perfumed tincture of the roses,
Hang on such thorns and play as wantonly
When summer's breath their masked buds discloses:
But, for their virtue only is their show,
They live unwoo'd and unrespected fade,
Die to themselves. Sweet roses do not so;
Of their sweet deaths are sweetest odours made:
And so of you, beauteous and lovely youth,
When that shall vade, by verse distills your truth.

LV.

Not marble, nor the gilded monuments
Of princes, shall outlive this pow'rful rhyme;
But you shall shine more bright in these contents
Than unswept stone besmear'd with sluttish time.
When wasteful war shall statues overturn,
And broils root out the work of masonry,
Nor Mars his sword nor war's quick fire shall burn
The living record of your memory.
'Gainst death and all-oblivious enmity
Shall you pace forth; your praise shall still find room
Even in the eyes of all posterity
That wear this world out to the ending doom.

L. 6. **to bear,** at bearing.

LI. 1. **slow offence,** offense which consists in slowness (Beeching). 4. **posting,** hastening. 6. **swift extremity,** extreme swiftness. 10-11. **desire . . . race,** a recurrence with metaphorical application of the concept developed in XLV. 11. **dull.** Cf. *dully*, l. 6. 12. **jade,** nag. 14. **go,** walk, as contrasted with running.

LII. This sonnet is a complement to XLVIII, where the image is that of a man locking up his treasure. 4. **For blunting,** lest it blunt. 5. **feasts,** i.e., chief festivals of the church year—e.g., Christmas, Easter, Corpus Christi, Michaelmas. 5-8. **so solemn,** etc. Malone cites *1 Henry IV*, I, ii, 229-230; and III, ii, 57-59. 8. **captain,** principal. **carcanet,** necklace of jewels. 11. **special instant,** particular moment. **special blest,** particularly blest. The image has a parallel in *1 Henry IV*, III, ii, 56-57. 12. **his,** its.

LIII. 1. **substance.** Pooler finds a touch of Platonism here in the implication that the substance is divine—the idea of which the shadows are the *idola*, or representation. 2, 3, 4. **shadows, shade,** used quibblingly with the meanings "silhouette" and "picture, reflection, symbol." 2. **tend,** attend, wait upon. 4. **And . . . lend,** i.e., and yet you, being only one person, are endowed with the virtues of numerous types of beauty (*you* is the object of *lend*). 5. **counterfeit,** likeness (of beauty). 8. **tires,** clothes, attire. 9. **foison,** abundance; i.e., autumn.

LIV. 2. **truth,** constancy. 5. **canker-blooms,** dog roses (outwardly attractive, but not as sweetly scented as the damask rose). 8. **discloses,** causes to open. 9. **for,** because; i.e., because their appearance is their only virtue. 10. **unrespected,** unnoticed. 11. **to themselves,** i.e., without profit to others (Pooler). 14. **vade,** perish, depart. **by . . . truth,** i.e., by means of (my) verse, your essence will be distilled and so preserved.

LV. 3. **these contents,** i.e., the contents of my poems written in praise of you. 4. **unswept stone,** parallel with *contents;* i.e., *in* is to be supplied from the preceding line (Pooler). 6. **broils,** battles. 9. **all-oblivious,** causing to be forgotten. 12. **wear . . . out,** i.e., outlast (Pooler). 13. **till . . . arise,** till the decree of the judgment day when you will arise from the dead; cf. Abbott, 284.

LVI. This, like the sonnets immediately preceding, is written in absence (Dowden). Perhaps a plea for the renewal of intimacy (Pooler). 1. **Sweet love.** The address is to the spirit of love. The friend is not directly mentioned in this sonnet (Tucker Brooke). 2. **edge,** keenness. 6. **wink,** shut. 9. **sad int'rim,** i.e., the period of love's abatement or absence. 9-12. **like the ocean,** etc. The image is variously explained. Some editors see a reference to the story of Hero and Leander; others regard *the ocean* figuratively as some kind of barrier which separates lovers (even Death has been suggested); still others take *the ocean* more literally as a separating body of water—a bay or estuary which parts the shore. Alden, although he favors the last interpretation, records a

So, till the judgement that yourself arise,
You live in this, and dwell in lovers' eyes.

LVI.

Sweet love, renew thy force; be it not said
Thy edge should blunter be than appetite,
Which but to-day by feeding is allay'd,
To-morrow sharp'ned in his former might:
So, love, be thou; although to-day thou fill
Thy hungry eyes even till they wink with fullness,
To-morrow see again, and do not kill
The spirit of love with a perpetual dullness.
Let this sad int'rim like the ocean be
Which parts the shore, where two contracted new
Come daily to the banks, that, when they see
Return of love, more blest may be the view;
Else call it winter, which being full of care
Makes summer's welcome thrice more wish'd,
more rare.

LVII.

Being your slave, what should I do but tend
Upon the hours and times of your desire?
I have no precious time at all to spend,
Nor services to do, till you require.
Nor dare I chide the world-without-end hour
Whilst I, my sovereign, watch the clock for you,
Nor think the bitterness of absence sour
When you have bid your servant once adieu;
Nor dare I question with my jealous thought
Where you may be, or your affairs suppose,
But, like a sad slave, stay and think of nought
Save, where you are how happy you make those.
So true a fool is love that in your will,
Though you do any thing, he thinks no ill.

LVIII.

That god forbid that made me first your slave,
I should in thought control your times of pleasure,
Or at your hand th' account of hours to crave,
Being your vassal, bound to stay your leisure!
O, let me suffer, being at your beck,
Th' imprison'd absence of your liberty;
And patience, tame to sufferance, bide each check,
Without accusing you of injury.
Be where you list, your charter is so strong
That you yourself may privilege your time
To what you will; to you it doth belong
Yourself to pardon of self-doing crime.
I am to wait, though waiting so be hell;
Not blame your pleasure, be it ill or well.

LIX.

If there be nothing new, but that which is
Hath been before, how are our brains beguil'd,
Which, labouring for invention, bear amiss
The second burthen of a former child!
O, that record could with a backward look,
Even of five hundred courses of the sun,
Show me your image in some antique book,
Since mind at first in character was done!
That I might see what the old world could say
To this composed wonder of your frame;
Whether we are mended, or whe'r better they,
Or whether revolution be the same.
O, sure I am, the wits of former days
To subjects worse have given admiring praise.

LX.

Like as the waves make towards the pebbled shore,
So do our minutes hasten to their end;
Each changing place with that which goes before,
In sequent toil all forwards do contend.
Nativity, once in the main of light,
Crawls to maturity, wherewith being crown'd,
Crooked eclipses 'gainst his glory fight,
And Time that gave doth now his gift confound.
Time doth transfix the flourish set on youth
And delves the parallels in beauty's brow,
Feeds on the rarities of nature's truth,
And nothing stands but for his scythe to mow:
†And yet to times in hope my verse shall stand,
Praising thy worth, despite his cruel hand.

LXI.

Is it thy will thy image should keep open
My heavy eyelids to the weary night?
Dost thou desire my slumbers should be broken,
While shadows like to thee do mock my sight?
Is it thy spirit that thou send'st from thee
So far from home into my deeds to pry,
To find out shames and idle hours in me,
The scope and tenour of thy jealousy?
O, no! thy love, though much, is not so great:
It is my love that keeps mine eye awake;
Mine own true love that doth my rest defeat,

suggestion of A. G. Newcomer, who thought *part* might mean "recede" or "depart from." He paraphrased as follows: Let this sad interim be only like waters that recede from their shore where, viz., by this ocean of love (dropping the image of the ocean at this point), two, *contracted new*, come daily to the banks, so that when they see the tide of love come in again, more blest may be the sight. 10. **contracted new,** lately betrothed.

LVII. 1. **tend,** wait. 5. **world-without-end,** interminable. 7. **think,** i.e., dare to think. 10. **suppose,** make conjectures about. 13. **will.** This word, capitalized in the 1609 quarto, is regarded by some as a pun on Shakespeare's name. Dowden explains as possibly: "Love in your Will (i.e., in me) can think no ill of anything you do," and "love can discover no evil in your will." Sir Sidney Lee thinks the Elizabethan practice of capitalizing nouns too common for this instance to have any significance.

LVIII. 3. **to crave,** parallel with *control* (l. 2); *to* might be omitted or *should* (from l. 2) might be inserted instead, but the omission would create ambiguity, and the insertion would be a tedious repetition (Abbott, 416). 4. **to stay,** to await. 6. **Th' . . . liberty,** i.e., your absence from me, due to your independence of me, makes me as one imprisoned, dependent on (or vassal to) you. 7. **tame to,** subdued by; cf. *King Lear*, IV, vi, 225. **bide each check,** endure each rebuke. 9. **charter,** privilege or right recorded in writing. Pooler notes the loose employment of the word to denote any freedom of action. 10. **privilege,** authorize. 12. **self-doing crime,** crime committed by oneself. 14. **blame,** parallel with *wait* (l. 13).

LIX. Most editors discern a break in the sequence here. 3. **labouring for invention,** striving to give birth to a new creation. 4. **The . . . child,** i.e., a mere repetition of something created before. 5. **record,** memory, especially memory preserved by history (Schmidt); accented on the second syllable. 8. **Since . . . done,** since thought was first expressed in writing. 10. **composed wonder,** wonderful composition (Rolfe). 11. **whe'r,** whether. 12. **revolution,** i.e., of the ages.

LX. 4. **sequent,** one after another. 5. **main,** main body. The entrance of a child into the world at birth is an entrance into the main or ocean of light (Dowden). 6. **Crawls.** Cf. *Hamlet*, III, i, 130; the word denotes the abject condition of mankind (Tyler). 7. **Crooked,** perverse, malignant. 9. **transfix,** destroy. **flourish,** decoration, embellishment; the figure is possibly from penmanship, but the general meaning is older than the scribal flourish. 10. **parallels,** wrinkles. 11. **rarities . . . truth,** rare things created by the fidelity of nature (Alden). 13. **times in hope,** times to come.

LXI. The jealous feeling of LVII reappears (Dowden). 7. **shames and idle hours,** a hendiadys, the meaning being "to see how badly I spend my spare time" (Pooler). 8. **scope . . . jealousy,** aim and purport of your suspicion (Pooler).

To play the watchman ever for thy sake:
  For thee watch I whilst thou dost wake elsewhere,
  From me far off, with others all too near.

LXII.

Sin of self-love possesseth all mine eye
And all my soul and all my every part;
And for this sin there is no remedy,
It is so grounded inward in my heart.
Methinks no face so gracious is as mine,
No shape so true, no truth of such account;
And for myself mine own worth do define,
As I all other in all worths surmount.
But when my glass shows me myself indeed,
Beated and chopp'd with tann'd antiquity,
Mine own self-love quite contrary I read;
Self so self-loving were iniquity.
  'Tis thee, myself, that for myself I praise,
  Painting my age with beauty of thy days.

LXIII.

Against my love shall be, as I am now,
With Time's injurious hand crush'd and o'erworn;
When hours have drain'd his blood and fill'd his brow
With lines and wrinkles; when his youthful morn
Hath travell'd on to Age's steepy night,
And all those beauties whereof now he 's king
Are vanishing or vanish'd out of sight,
Stealing away the treasure of his spring;
For such a time do I now fortify
Against confounding Age's cruel knife,
That he shall never cut from memory
My sweet love's beauty, though my lover's life:
  His beauty shall in these black lines be seen,
  And they shall live, and he in them still green.

LXIV.

When I have seen by Time's fell hand defaced
The rich proud cost of outworn buried age;
When sometime lofty towers I see down-razed
And brass eternal slave to mortal rage;
When I have seen the hungry ocean gain
Advantage on the kingdom of the shore,
And the firm soil win of the wat'ry main,
Increasing store with loss and loss with store;
When I have seen such interchange of state,
Or state itself confounded to decay;
Ruin hath taught me thus to ruminate,
That Time will come and take my love away.
  This thought is as a death, which cannot choose
  But weep to have that which it fears to lose.

LXV.

Since brass, nor stone, nor earth, nor boundless sea,
But sad mortality o'er-sways their power,
How with this rage shall beauty hold a plea,
Whose action is no stronger than a flower?
O, how shall summer's honey breath hold out
Against the wrackful siege of batt'ring days,
When rocks impregnable are not so stout,
Nor gates of steel so strong, but Time decays?
O fearful meditation! where, alack,
Shall Time's best jewel from Time's chest lie hid?
Or what strong hand can hold his swift foot back?
Or who his spoil of beauty can forbid?
  O, none, unless this miracle have might,
  That in black ink my love may still shine bright.

LXVI.

Tir'd with all these, for restful death I cry,
As, to behold desert a beggar born,
And needy nothing trimm'd in jollity,
And purest faith unhappily forsworn,
And gilded honour shamefully misplac'd,
And maiden virtue rudely strumpeted,
And right perfection wrongfully disgrac'd,
And strength by limping sway disabled,
And art made tongue-tied by authority,
And folly doctor-like controlling skill,
And simple truth miscall'd simplicity,
And captive good attending captain ill:
  Tir'd with all these, from these would I be gone,
  Save that, to die, I leave my love alone.

LXVII.

Ah! wherefore with infection should he live,
And with his presence grace impiety,
That sin by him advantage should achieve
And lace itself with his society?
Why should false painting imitate his cheek
And steal dead seeing of his living hue?
Why should poor beauty indirectly seek

12. **watchman,** one who stays awake. 13. **watch, wake.** The words were originally identical in meaning; i.e., to be awake.

LXII. 1. **Sin of self-love.** Cf. *All's Well that Ends Well*, I, i, 157. 4. **grounded . . . heart,** fixed or established inwardly. 8. **As,** as if. **other,** a sixteenth-century plural; see Abbott, 12. 9. **indeed,** i.e., as I actually am. 10. **Beated,** battered; Malone conjectured *Bated*, i.e., laid low. **chopp'd,** chapped, roughened. 12. **so self-loving,** i.e., to love oneself as the glass *indeed* shows him. 13. **thee, myself,** i.e., my other self. 14. **days,** i.e., youth.

LXIII. 1. **Against,** i.e., anticipating the time when. 5. **steepy,** having a precipitous declivity (Schmidt); difficult to ascend (Onions); Dowden cites VII, 5, 6, and 9, 10, where the sun, likened to youth, climbs the *steep-up heavenly hill*, and like old age, *reeleth from the day*. 9. **For such a time,** etc., parallel in construction with the phrase (l. 1) *Against my love*, etc. **fortify,** raise works of defense; possibly, fortify myself, gird my strength. 10. **confounding,** destroying.

LXIV. 1. **fell,** cruel. 2. **rich proud,** proud on account of its wealth. 4. **brass . . . rage.** *Mortal* may be contrasted with *eternal* in the sense of destroying as opposed to indestructible (Pooler); brass, i.e., bronze, was the enduring material for sculpture. 5-8. **When . . . store.** Lee points out the similarity of these lines to a passage in Ovid's *Metamorphoses*, XV, 288-290. Shakespeare has used similar imagery in *The Rape of Lucrece*, 944 ff.; *1 Henry IV*, III, i. 108-111; *2 Henry IV*, III, i, 46-52. The notion is expressed also in *Timon of Athens*, the opening dialogue between Poet and Painter. 8. **Increasing . . . store,** i.e., one gaining as the other loses, and losing as the other gains. 9, 10. **state, state,** condition . . . pomp or greatness (Schmidt, Beeching, Tyler); Wyndham glosses both as "condition," the first used particularly, the second in the abstract. 13. **which cannot choose,** modifies *thought*. 14. **to have,** i.e., because it now has.

LXV. 1-2. **Since . . . power,** an elliptical clause: Since there is neither brass, etc., but that sad mortality o'ersways, etc. The ellipsis shows the closeness of the idea to the preceding sonnet. 4. **action,** case (for permanence); legal figure. 10. **Time's chest.** The chest of Time is the repository into which he is poetically supposed to throw those things which he designs to be forgotten (Steevens); cf. *time's wallet*, *Troilus and Cressida*, III, iii, 145-146, wherein he puts *alms for oblivion*. 12. **spoil,** act of spoiling; possibly, spoils, booty.

LXVI. The thoughts of death developed in the preceding series bring the poet to thoughts of his own death and his willingness to part from the world. The theme of the world's infection continues from this sonnet through LXX. 1. **all these.** The antecedent is what follows; many commentators point out the similarity to Hamlet's famous soliloquy, especially *Hamlet*, III, i, 70-75. 2. **As,** for instance. **desert,** i.e., those who have merit, as contrasted with *needy nothing* in the next line. 3. **needy nothing,** moral and mental emptiness (Tucker Brooke). **jollity,** finery. 8. **limping sway,** inept leadership. **disabled,** four syllables. 10. **doctor-like,** like a learned person. 11. **simplicity,** silliness,

Roses of shadow, since his rose is true?
Why should he live, now Nature bankrout is,
Beggar'd of blood to blush through lively veins?
For she hath no exchequer now but his,
And, proud of many, lives upon his gains.
  O, him she stores, to show what wealth she had
  In days long since, before these last so bad.

LXVIII.

Thus is his cheek the map of days outworn,
When beauty liv'd and died as flowers do now,
Before these bastard signs of fair were born,
Or durst inhabit on a living brow;
Before the golden tresses of the dead,
The right of sepulchres, were shorn away,
To live a second life on second head;
Ere beauty's dead fleece made another gay:
In him those holy antique hours are seen,
Without all ornament, itself and true,
Making no summer of another's green,
Robbing no old to dress his beauty new;
  And him as for a map doth Nature store,
  To show false Art what beauty was of yore.

LXIX.

Those parts of thee that the world's eye doth view
Want nothing that the thought of hearts can mend;
All tongues, the voice of souls, give thee that due,
Utt'ring bare truth, even so as foes commend.
Thy outward thus with outward praise is crown'd;
But those same tongues that give thee so thine own
In other accents do this praise confound
By seeing farther than the eye hath shown.
They look into the beauty of thy mind,
And that, in guess, they measure by thy deeds;
Then, churls, their thoughts, although their eyes were kind,
To thy fair flower add the rank smell of weeds:
  But why thy odour matcheth not thy show,
  The soil is this, that thou dost common grow.

LXX.

That thou art blam'd shall not be thy defect,
For slander's mark was ever yet the fair;
The ornament of beauty is suspect,
A crow that flies in heaven's sweetest air.
So thou be good, slander doth but approve
Thy worth the greater, being woo'd of time;
For canker vice the sweetest buds doth love,
And thou present'st a pure unstained prime.
Thou hast pass'd by the ambush of young days,
Either not assail'd or victor being charg'd;
Yet this thy praise cannot be so thy praise,
To tie up envy evermore enlarg'd:
  If some suspect of ill mask'd not thy show,
  Then thou alone kingdoms of hearts shouldst owe.

LXXI.

No longer mourn for me when I am dead
Than you shall hear the surly sullen bell
Give warning to the world that I am fled
From this vile world, with vilest worms to dwell:
Nay, if you read this line, remember not
The hand that writ it; for I love you so
That I in your sweet thoughts would be forgot
If thinking on me then should make you woe.
O, if, I say, you look upon this verse
When I perhaps compounded am with clay,
Do not so much as my poor name rehearse,
But let your love even with my life decay,
  Lest the wise world should look into your moan
  And mock you with me after I am gone.

LXXII.

O, lest the world should task you to recite
What merit liv'd in me, that you should love
After my death, dear love, forget me quite,
For you in me can nothing worthy prove;
Unless you would devise some virtuous lie,
To do more for me than mine own desert,
And hang more praise upon deceased I
Than niggard truth would willingly impart:
O, lest your true love may seem false in this,
That you for love speak well of me untrue,
My name be buried where my body is,
And live no more to shame nor me nor you.
  For I am sham'd by that which I bring forth,
  And so should you, to love things nothing worth.

LXXIII.

That time of year thou mayst in me behold
When yellow leaves, or none, or few, do hang

folly. 12. **attending,** waiting on, subordinated to.

LXVII. 1. **with infection,** i.e., the world's ills enumerated in the preceding sonnet. **he,** i.e., *my love* of LXVI, 14. 4. **lace,** trim with ornament. 6. **dead seeing.** Dowden's gloss, "lifeless appearance," would better define Farmer's emendation, *dead seeming*, a reading adopted by some editors. 7. **poor,** inferior. **indirectly,** imitatively. 8. **Roses of shadow,** i.e., color of roses placed on his cheeks. 9. **bankrout,** bankrupt. 10. **Beggar'd,** modifies *Nature.* **to blush,** which blushes. 11. **exchequer,** i.e., treasury of natural beauty. 13. **stores,** keeps in store.

LXVIII. This sonnet contrasts the real beauty of youth with artificial beauty. The subject of the sonnet is the epitome of natural beauty. 1. **map,** picture, image. 3. **bastard . . . fair,** i.e., cosmetics. 9. **antique hours,** ancient times. 10. **itself.** Malone conjectured *himself*, thinking the antecedent to be *him* (l. 9). Pooler refers the pronoun to *holy antique hours*, singular in idea, since the phrase means "the beauty of the past"; *itself* is equivalent to "unadulterated."

LXIX. 2. **Want . . . mend,** lack nothing which the imagination can and customarily does supply. 3. **voice of souls.** This is a Renaissance commonplace, that the tongue (power of speech) is the voice of the soul. 4. **even . . . commend,** as even ill-disposed persons are forced to admit. 6. **thine own,** i.e., *that due* of line 3. 14. **soil.** Globe, following Malone, has *solve* defined as solution; Q: *solye*; the 1640 Q: soyle; most editors, *soil*, but explain it variously: solution (*NED*); blemish, fault (Verity, citing *Hamlet*, I, iii, 15); ground, i.e., origin, source (Tucker Brooke, who explains it as continuing the figure of the garden). **common,** stale, vulgar.

LXX. 2. **slander's mark,** object of slander. 3. **suspect,** suspicion (as also in l. 13). 5. **So,** provided that. The implied reasoning is: Slandered goodness is more than ordinarily good, for slander is evidence of beauty, and beauty of temptation (Pooler). 6. **woo'd of time,** i.e., by fashion, tempted by the world. 8. **thou . . . prime,** i.e., you have a reputation for an unspotted youth. 12. **enlarg'd,** at liberty. Dowden quotes a letter from J. W. Hales, who saw here a reference to Spenser's *Faerie Queene*, Bk. VI, where Calidore bound the Blatant Beast, now broken loose again and always set free; note also in Bk. II that Occasion is always being set free; so is Maleger. 14. **owe,** own.

LXXI. With this sonnet the theme of death as a release from the world's ills gives place to a more contemplative mood, wherein once more the immortalizing power of poetry is the theme; not its immortalizing of the poet, but of his friend. This theme is continued through LXXIV. 14. **with me,** i.e., as they mock me.

LXXII. 1. **task you to recite,** place upon you the task of reciting. 5. **virtuous lie,** lie about my virtue. 7. **I.** The rhyme is accountable for the pronoun. Abbott (205, 209) remarks the tendency to use *I* for *me* after the sounds *d* and *t*. 10. **untrue,** untruly. 11. **My name be,** let my name be.

Upon those boughs which shake against the cold,
Bare ruin'd choirs, where late the sweet birds sang.
In me thou see'st the twilight of such day
As after sunset fadeth in the west,
Which by and by black night doth take away,
Death's second self, that seals up all in rest.
In me thou see'st the glowing of such fire
That on the ashes of his youth doth lie,
As the death-bed whereon it must expire
Consum'd with that which it was nourish'd by.
  This thou perceiv'st, which makes thy love more
    strong,
  To love that well which thou must leave ere long.

LXXIV.

But be contented: when that fell arrest
Without all bail shall carry me away,
My life hath in this line some interest,
Which for memorial still with thee shall stay.
When thou reviewest this, thou dost review
The very part was consecrate to thee:
The earth can have but earth, which is his due;
My spirit is thine, the better part of me:
So then thou hast but lost the dregs of life,
The prey of worms, my body being dead,
The coward conquest of a wretch's knife,
Too base of thee to be remembered.
  The worth of that is that which it contains,
  And that is this, and this with thee remains.

LXXV.

So are you to my thoughts as food to life,
Or as sweet-season'd showers are to the ground;
And for the peace of you I hold such strife
As 'twixt a miser and his wealth is found;
Now proud as an enjoyer and anon
Doubting the filching age will steal his treasure,
Now counting best to be with you alone,
Then better'd that the world may see my pleasure;
Sometime all full with feasting on your sight
And by and by clean starved for a look;
Possessing or pursuing no delight,
Save what is had or must from you be took.
  Thus do I pine and surfeit day by day,
  Or gluttoning on all, or all away.

LXXVI.

Why is my verse so barren of new pride,
So far from variation or quick change?
Why with the time do I not glance aside
To new-found methods and to compounds strange?
Why write I still all one, ever the same,
And deep invention in a noted weed,
That every word doth almost tell my name,
Showing their birth and where they did proceed?
O, know, sweet love, I always write of you,
And you and love are still my argument;
So all my best is dressing old words new,
Spending again what is already spent:
  For as the sun is daily new and old,
  So is my love still telling what is told.

LXXVII.

Thy glass will show thee how thy beauties wear,
Thy dial how thy precious minutes waste;
The vacant leaves thy mind's imprint will bear,
And of this book this learning mayst thou taste.
The wrinkles which thy glass will truly show
Of mouthed graves will give thee memory;
Thou by thy dial's shady stealth mayst know
Time's thievish progress to eternity.
Look, what thy memory can not contain
Commit to these waste blanks, and thou shalt find
Those children nurs'd, deliver'd from thy brain,
To take a new acquaintance of thy mind.
  These offices, so oft as thou wilt look,
  Shall profit thee and much enrich thy book.

LXXVIII.

So oft have I invok'd thee for my Muse
And found such fair assistance in my verse
As every alien pen hath got my use
And under thee their poesy disperse.
Thine eyes that taught the dumb on high to sing
And heavy ignorance aloft to fly,
Have added feathers to the learned's wing
And given grace a double majesty.
Yet be most proud of that which I compile,
Whose influence is thine and born of thee:
In others' works thou dost but mend the style,
And arts with thy sweet graces graced be;
  But thou art all my art and dost advance
  As high as learning my rude ignorance.

LXXIX.

Whilst I alone did call upon thy aid,
My verse alone had all thy gentle grace,
But now my gracious numbers are decay'd
And my sick Muse doth give another place.
I grant, sweet love, thy lovely argument
Deserves the travail of a worthier pen,
Yet what of thee thy poet doth invent

LXXIII. 4. **choirs,** that part of cathedrals where the service is said; in apposition with *boughs* (l. 3). This image was probably suggested to Shakespeare by our desolated monasteries. The resemblance between the vaulting of a Gothic aisle and an avenue of trees whose upper branches meet and form an arch overhead is too striking not to be acknowledged. When the roof of the one is shattered, and the boughs of the other leafless, the comparison becomes yet more solemn and picturesque (Steevens). 12. **that,** i.e., the ashes of what was formerly the fuel.

LXXIV. 1. **that fell arrest,** i.e., death; Capell cites *Hamlet*, V, ii, 347-348. 3. **line,** verse. **interest,** legal concern, right, or title. 7. **The . . . earth,** an echo, probably, of the medieval earth-upon-earth rhymes; also of the "earth to earth" phrase in the burial service of the prayer book. 11. **coward . . . knife,** i.e., the conquest that even a poor cowardly wretch like Death can make with his scythe (?). Dowden cites LXIII, 10. The line also suggests some of the pictorial representations of death in the Dance of Death motifs. 12. **of thee,** by thee; modifies *remembered*. 13-14. **The worth . . . remains,** the only worth of my body is the spirit it contains—i.e., this verse, which will remain with you.

LXXV. 2. **sweet-season'd,** (of rain) soft (Onions). 3. **of you,** to be found in you (Dowden). 6. **Doubting,** suspecting, fearing. 8. **better'd,** made happier. 10. **clean,** completely, absolutely. 12. **from you,** modifies both verbs, *had* and *must be took*. 14. **Or . . . or,** either . . . or. **all away,** i.e., all food being taken away.

LXXVI. This sonnet implies on the friend's part a not unnatural restiveness at Shakespeare's plain-spokenness and abstention from the fashionable devices of eulogy (Tucker Brooke). 3. **time,** way of the world, fashion. 4. **compounds,** compound words (Onions); Lee refers the phrase to the extravagances of Shakespeare's contemporaries in inventing new words. 6. **noted weed,** dress by which it is recognizable, well-known garment. 8. **where,** from whence.

LXXVII. Apparently these lines accompanied the gift of a book of blank pages, a memorandum book. 3. **vacant leaves,** blank pages. 4. **learning,** mental profit; what it is is explained in line 9 ff. (Tucker Brooke). 6. **mouthed,** all-devouring (Malone); gaping (Schmidt). 7. **shady stealth,** slow progress of the shadow on the dial (Onions).

LXXVIII. With this sonnet the poet begins his complaint that his friend's patronage is being sought by other poets. The theme continues

He robs thee of and pays it thee again.
He lends thee virtue and he stole that word
From thy behaviour; beauty doth he give
And found it in thy cheek; he can afford
No praise to thee but what in thee doth live.
Then thank him not for that which he doth say,
Since what he owes thee thou thyself dost pay.

LXXX.

O, how I faint when I of you do write,
Knowing a better spirit doth use your name,
And in the praise thereof spends all his might,
To make me tongue-tied, speaking of your fame!
But since your worth, wide as the ocean is,
The humble as the proudest sail doth bear,
My saucy bark inferior far to his
On your broad main doth wilfully appear.
Your shallowest help will hold me up afloat,
Whilst he upon your soundless deep doth ride;
Or, being wrack'd, I am a worthless boat,
He of tall building and of goodly pride:
Then if he thrive and I be cast away,
The worst was this; my love was my decay.

LXXXI.

Or I shall live your epitaph to make,
Or you survive when I in earth am rotten;
From hence your memory death cannot take,
Although in me each part will be forgotten.
Your name from hence immortal life shall have,
Though I, once gone, to all the world must die:
The earth can yield me but a common grave,
When you entombed in men's eyes shall lie.
Your monument shall be my gentle verse,
Which eyes not yet created shall o'er-read,
And tongues to be your being shall rehearse
When all the breathers of this world are dead;
You still shall live—such virtue hath my pen—
Where breath most breathes, even in the mouths of men.

LXXXII.

I grant thou wert not married to my Muse
And therefore mayst without attaint o'erlook
The dedicated words which writers use
Of their fair subject, blessing every book.
Thou art as fair in knowledge as in hue,
Finding thy worth a limit past my praise,
And therefore art enforc'd to seek anew
Some fresher stamp of the time-bettering days.
And do so, love; yet when they have devis'd
What strained touches rhetoric can lend,
Thou truly fair wert truly sympathiz'd
In true plain words by thy true-telling friend;
And their gross painting might be better us'd
Where cheeks need blood; in thee it is abus'd.

LXXXIII.

I never saw that you did painting need
And therefore to your fair no painting set;
I found, or thought I found, you did exceed
The barren tender of a poet's debt;
And therefore have I slept in your report,
That you yourself being extant well might show
How far a modern quill doth come too short,
Speaking of worth, what worth in you doth grow.
This silence for my sin you did impute,
Which shall be most my glory, being dumb;
For I impair not beauty being mute,
When others would give life and bring a tomb.
There lives more life in one of your fair eyes
Than both your poets can in praise devise.

LXXXIV.

Who is it that says most? which can say more
Than this rich praise, that you alone are you?
In whose confine immured is the store
Which should example where your equal grew.
Lean penury within that pen doth dwell
That to his subject lends not some small glory;
But he that writes of you, if he can tell
That you are you, so dignifies his story,
Let him but copy what in you is writ,
Not making worse what nature made so clear,
And such a counterpart shall fame his wit,
Making his style admired every where.
You to your beauteous blessings add a curse,
Being fond on praise, which makes your praises worse.

LXXXV.

My tongue-tied Muse in manners holds her still,
While comments of your praise, richly compil'd,
Reserve their character with golden quill
And precious phrase by all the Muses fil'd.
I think good thoughts whilst other write good words,
And like unlettered clerk still cry 'Amen'
To every hymn that able spirit affords
In polish'd form of well-refined pen.
Hearing you prais'd, I say ''Tis so, 'tis true,'
And to the most of praise add something more;
But that is in my thought, whose love to you,

to the close of LXXXVI. 3. **use,** habit; i.e., of writing in celebration of his friend. 4. **under thee,** with you as their muse. 5. **on high,** loftily, exultingly. 5-6. **Thine . . . fly.** Cf. *my rude ignorance* (l. 14). 7-8. **Have . . . majesty,** a complaint of the rival poet. 9. **compile,** write, compose. 10. **influence,** inspiration; suggestion of astrological meaning. 12. **arts,** literary culture, scholarship. 13. **advance,** lift up.

LXXIX. 3. **numbers,** verse. 5. **thy lovely argument,** the celebration of thy loveliness. 11. **afford,** offer.

LXXX: 2. **a better spirit,** i.e., the rival poet, whom Shakespeare admires. 4. **tongue-tied.** Hearing his friend's virtues praised has stricken the poet with awe. 6. **as,** as well as. 10. **soundless,** unfathomable. 13. **cast away,** shipwrecked. 14. **my love . . . decay,** i.e., because it prompted me to write.

LXXXI. After belittling his own verse, the poet here takes courage and asserts his power. 1. **Or,** either. 4. **in . . . part,** every quality of mine. 5. **Your . . . have.** The theme of the perpetuation of the object's name is common throughout the *Sonnets* and is found in practically all sonnet cycles. 12. **breathers,** living people; cf. *As You Like It*, III, ii, 297.

LXXXII. 2. **attaint,** blame, discredit. 3. **dedicated,** devoted (with a punning reference to dedicatory prefaces addressed to patrons). 8. **time-bettering days.** For this theme of progress in the age see XXXII, 5. 11. **truly sympathiz'd,** faithfully described. 13. **gross painting,** extravagant compliment.

LXXXIII. 1-2. **painting . . . painting,** a continuation of the theme of *gross painting* in the preceding sonnet. 2. **fair,** beauty. 5. **slept in your report,** made no poem about you. 7. **modern,** commonplace. 14. **both your poets,** i.e., Shakespeare and the rival poet.

LXXXIV. 3-4. **In . . . grew,** in whom is contained all the qualities needed to serve as a model for any equal. 5-6. **Lean . . . glory,** i.e., it is a poor book that does not confer some honor on the person to whom it is dedicated. 11. **fame,** endow with fame. 13-14. **You . . . worse.** Probably the intended meaning is that the friend's excellence puts to shame those poets who try to praise him.

LXXXV. 2. **While . . . compil'd,** eulogies composed in fine language. 3. **Reserve their character,** preserve their features. 4. **fil'd,** polished. 11. **But that,** i.e., that which I add.

Though words come hindmost, holds his rank before.
Then others for the breath of words respect,
Me for my dumb thoughts, speaking in effect.

LXXXVI.

Was it the proud full sail of his great verse,
Bound for the prize of all too precious you,
That did my ripe thoughts in my brain inhearse,
Making their tomb the womb wherein they grew?
Was it his spirit, by spirits taught to write
Above a mortal pitch, that struck me dead?
No, neither he, nor his compeers by night
Giving him aid, my verse astonished.
He, nor that affable familiar ghost
Which nightly gulls him with intelligence,
As victors of my silence cannot boast;
I was not sick of any fear from thence:
But when your countenance fill'd up his line,
Then lack'd I matter; that enfeebled mine.

LXXXVII.

Farewell! thou art too dear for my possessing,
And like enough thou know'st thy estimate:
The charter of thy worth gives thee releasing;
My bonds in thee are all determinate.
For how do I hold thee but by thy granting?
And for that riches where is my deserving?
The cause of this fair gift in me is wanting,
And so my patent back again is swerving.
Thyself thou gav'st, thy own worth then not knowing,
Or me, to whom thou gav'st it, else mistaking;
So thy great gift, upon misprision growing,
Comes home again, on better judgement making.
Thus have I had thee, as a dream doth flatter,
In sleep a king, but waking no such matter.

LXXXVIII.

When thou shalt be dispos'd to set me light
And place my merit in the eye of scorn,
Upon thy side against myself I'll fight
And prove thee virtuous, though thou art forsworn.
With mine own weakness being best acquainted,
Upon thy part I can set down a story
Of faults conceal'd, wherein I am attainted,
That thou in losing me shalt win much glory:
And I by this will be a gainer too;
For bending all my loving thoughts on thee,
The injuries that to myself I do,
Doing thee vantage, double-vantage me.
Such is my love, to thee I so belong,
That for thy right myself will bear all wrong.

LXXXIX.

Say that thou didst forsake me for some fault,
And I will comment upon that offence;
Speak of my lameness, and I straight will halt,
Against thy reasons making no defence.
Thou canst not, love, disgrace me half so ill,
To set a form upon desired change,
As I'll myself disgrace: knowing thy will,
I will acquaintance strangle and look strange,
Be absent from thy walks, and in my tongue
Thy sweet beloved name no more shall dwell,
Lest I, too much profane, should do it wrong
And haply of our old acquaintance tell.
For thee against myself I'll vow debate,
For I must ne'er love him whom thou dost hate.

XC.

Then hate me when thou wilt; if ever, now;
Now, while the world is bent my deeds to cross,
Join with the spite of fortune, make me bow,
And do not drop in for an after-loss:
Ah, do not, when my heart hath 'scap'd this sorrow,
Come in the rearward of a conquer'd woe;
Give not a windy night a rainy morrow,
To linger out a purpos'd overthrow.
If thou wilt leave me, do not leave me last,
When other petty griefs have done their spite,
But in the onset come; so shall I taste
At first the very worst of fortune's might,
And other strains of woe, which now seem woe,
Compar'd with loss of thee will not seem so.

XCI.

Some glory in their birth, some in their skill,
Some in their wealth, some in their bodies' force,
Some in their garments, though new-fangled ill,
Some in their hawks and hounds, some in their horse;
And every humour hath his adjunct pleasure,
Wherein it finds a joy above the rest:
But these particulars are not my measure;
All these I better in one general best.
Thy love is better than high birth to me,
Richer than wealth, prouder than garments' cost,
Of more delight than hawks or horses be;
And having thee, of all men's pride I boast:
Wretched in this alone, that thou mayst take
All this away and me most wretched make.

XCII.

But do thy worst to steal thyself away,
For term of life thou art assured mine,
And life no longer than thy love will stay,
For it depends upon that love of thine.
Then need I not to fear the worst of wrongs,
When in the least of them my life hath end.
I see a better state to me belongs
Than that which on thy humour doth depend;
Thou canst not vex me with inconstant mind,
Since that my life on thy revolt doth lie.
O, what a happy title do I find,

14. **speaking in effect,** i.e., which have the quality of speech.

LXXXVI. This sonnet is devoted to generous praise of his rival. 3. **inhearse,** coffin up. 4. **Making . . . grew.** Cf. *Romeo and Juliet*, II, iii, 9-10. 7. **compeers by night,** spirits visiting and aiding the poet in his dreams. (See also the *familiar ghost* in line 9.) 8. **astonished,** struck dumb. 10. **gulls . . . intelligence,** deceives him with rumors or secret information (?). 13. **countenance fill'd up,** approval repaired any defect in; also, beauty served as subject for.

LXXXVII. 4. **determinate,** ended, expired (a legal term). 6. **riches,** wealth; a singular noun. 8. **patent,** charter granting rights of monopoly; hence, privilege. 11. **upon misprision growing,** arising out of error or mistake. 13. **as . . . flatter.** Cf. *Romeo and Juliet*, V, i, 1-5. 14. **no such matter,** nothing of the sort.

LXXXVIII. 1. **set me light,** despise me, make light of me. 6. **Upon thy part,** in support of your opinions.

LXXXIX. 3. **halt,** limp. 6. **To . . . change,** to provide a pretext for (in the interest of justifying) your change of affection. 7. **disgrace,** disfigure. 8. **acquaintance,** familiarity (with the friend). **strangle,** put an end to. 9. **walks,** haunts. 12. **haply,** perchance. 13. **vow debate,** entertain hostility, quarrel.

XC. 2. **cross,** thwart. 4. **do . . . after-loss,** i.e., do not casually add to my sorrow at some future time. 6. **in the rearward of,** at the end of. 8. **purpos'd,** intended. 13. **strains,** kinds.

XCI. 4. **horse,** horses. 5. **his,** its.

XCII. 5-6. **Then . . . end,** i.e., my very least misfortune would be my worst—that is, the loss of your friendship. 10. **Since . . . lie,** since

Happy to have thy love, happy to die!
But what 's so blessed-fair that fears no blot?
Thou mayst be false, and yet I know it not.

XCIII.

So shall I live, supposing thou art true,
Like a deceived husband; so love's face
May still seem love to me, though alter'd new;
Thy looks with me, thy heart in other place:
For there can live no hatred in thine eye,
Therefore in that I cannot know thy change.
In many's looks the false heart's history
Is writ in moods and frowns and wrinkles strange,
But heaven in thy creation did decree
That in thy face sweet love should ever dwell;
Whate'er thy thoughts or thy heart's workings be,
Thy looks should nothing thence but sweetness tell.
How like Eve's apple doth thy beauty grow,
If thy sweet virtue answer not thy show!

XCIV.

They that have pow'r to hurt and will do none,
That do not do the thing they most do show,
Who, moving others, are themselves as stone,
Unmoved, cold, and to temptation slow,
They rightly do inherit heaven's graces
And husband nature's riches from expense;
They are the lords and owners of their faces,
Others but stewards of their excellence.
The summer's flow'r is to the summer sweet,
Though to itself it only live and die,
But if that flow'r with base infection meet,
The basest weed outbraves his dignity:
For sweetest things turn sourest by their deeds;
Lilies that fester smell far worse than weeds.

XCV.

How sweet and lovely dost thou make the shame
Which, like a canker in the fragrant rose,
Doth spot the beauty of thy budding name!
O, in what sweets dost thou thy sins enclose!
That tongue that tells the story of thy days,
Making lascivious comments on thy sport,
Cannot dispraise but in a kind of praise;
Naming thy name blesses an ill report.
O, what a mansion have those vices got
Which for their habitation chose out thee,
Where beauty's veil doth cover every blot,
And all things turn to fair that eyes can see!
Take heed, dear heart, of this large privilege;
The hardest knife ill-us'd doth lose his edge.

XCVI.

Some say thy fault is youth, some wantonness;
Some say thy grace is youth and gentle sport;
Both grace and faults are lov'd of more and less;
Thou mak'st faults graces that to thee resort.
As on the finger of a throned queen
The basest jewel will be well esteem'd,
So are those errors that in thee are seen
To truths translated and for true things deem'd.
How many lambs might the stern wolf betray,
If like a lamb he could his looks translate!
How many gazers mightst thou lead away,
If thou wouldst use the strength of all thy state!
But do not so; I love thee in such sort
As, thou being mine, mine is thy good report.

XCVII.

How like a winter hath my absence been
From thee, the pleasure of the fleeting year!
What freezings have I felt, what dark days seen!
What old December's bareness every where!
And yet this time remov'd was summer's time,
The teeming autumn, big with rich increase,
Bearing the wanton burthen of the prime,
Like widow'd wombs after their lords' decease:
Yet this abundant issue seem'd to me
But hope of orphans and unfathered fruit;
For summer and his pleasures wait on thee,
And, thou away, the very birds are mute;
Or, if they sing, 'tis with so dull a cheer
That leaves look pale, dreading the winter's near.

XCVIII.

From you have I been absent in the spring,
When proud-pied April dress'd in all his trim
Hath put a spirit of youth in every thing,
That heavy Saturn laugh'd and leap'd with him.
Yet nor the lays of birds nor the sweet smell
Of different flowers in odour and in hue
Could make me any summer's story tell,
Or from their proud lap pluck them where they grew;
Nor did I wonder at the lily's white,
Nor praise the deep vermilion in the rose;
They were but sweet, but figures of delight,
Drawn after you, you pattern of all those.
Yet seem'd it winter still, and, you away,
As with your shadow I with these did play:

XCIX.

The forward violet thus did I chide:
Sweet thief, whence didst thou steal thy sweet that smells,
If not from my love's breath? The purple pride
Which on thy soft cheek for complexion dwells
In my love's veins thou hast too grossly dy'd.
The lily I condemned for thy hand,
And buds of marjoram had stol'n thy hair:
The roses fearfully on thorns did stand,
One blushing shame, another white despair;
A third, nor red nor white, had stol'n of both

if you desert me it will cost me my life.

XCIII. 14. **show,** appearance, looks.

XCIV. 1. **and will do none,** i.e., hurt without intending to do so. 2. **show,** i.e., show themselves capable of; or, seem to do. 6. **expense,** waste, expenditure. 7. **They . . . faces,** they are completely masters of themselves. 12. **his,** its. 14. **Lilies . . . weeds.** This line appears in the anonymous tragedy *Edward III*, usually dated before 1595.

XCV. 2. **canker,** worm that destroys buds and leaves. The figure is frequent in the early works of Shakespeare; cf. xxxv, 4 and lxx, 7. 6. **sport,** amours. 14. **his,** its.

XCVI. 3. **more and less,** great and small. 8. **translated,** transformed. 9. **stern,** cruel. 12. **the strength . . . state,** the full glory of thy eminent position. 13-14. **But . . . report.** Cf. xxxvi, 13-14.

XCVII. A new group of three sonnets begins here. They deal with the theme of absence. 5. **time remov'd,** absence. 7. **prime,** spring.

XCVIII. 4. **That,** so that. 5. **nor the lays,** neither the songs. 7. **any summer's story,** any pleasant story. 11. **but sweet . . . delight,** only sweetness, only delightful forms.

XCIX. This sonnet has fifteen lines, the first being merely introductory. It is devoted to the figure, general among sonneteers, of the flowers stealing their beauty from the beloved. 1. **forward,** early. 6. **for thy hand,** i.e., because it has stolen its whiteness from thy hand. 7. **buds of marjoram.** These are dark purple red, and it may be that the reference is to color, although marjoram is noted for its sweet scent.

And to his robb'ry had annex'd thy breath;
But, for his theft, in pride of all his growth
A vengeful canker eat him up to death.
  More flowers I noted, yet I none could see
  But sweet or colour it had stol'n from thee.

C.

Where art thou, Muse, that thou forget'st so long
To speak of that which gives thee all thy might?
Spend'st thou thy fury on some worthless song,
Dark'ning thy pow'r to lend base subjects light?
Return, forgetful Muse, and straight redeem
In gentle numbers time so idly spent;
Sing to the ear that doth thy lays esteem
And gives thy pen both skill and argument.
Rise, resty Muse, my love's sweet face survey,
If Time have any wrinkle graven there;
If any, be a satire to decay,
And make Time's spoils despised every where.
  Give my love fame faster than Time wastes life;
  So thou prevent'st his scythe and crooked knife.

CI.

O truant Muse, what shall be thy amends
For thy neglect of truth in beauty dy'd?
Both truth and beauty on my love depends;
So dost thou too, and therein dignified.
Make answer, Muse: wilt thou not haply say
'Truth needs no colour, with his colour fix'd;
Beauty no pencil, beauty's truth to lay;
But best is best, if never intermix'd'?
Because he needs no praise, wilt thou be dumb?
Excuse not silence so; for 't lies in thee
To make him much outlive a gilded tomb,
And to be prais'd of ages yet to be.
  Then do thy office, Muse; I teach thee how
  To make him seem long hence as he shows now.

CII.

My love is strength'ned, though more weak in seeming;
I love not less, though less the show appear:
That love is merchandiz'd whose rich esteeming
The owner's tongue doth publish every where.
Our love was new and then but in the spring
When I was wont to greet it with my lays,
As Philomel in summer's front doth sing
And stops her pipe in growth of riper days:
Not that the summer is less pleasant now
Than when her mournful hymns did hush the night,
But that wild music burthens every bough
And sweets grown common lose their dear delight.
  Therefore like her I sometime hold my tongue,
  Because I would not dull you with my song.

CIII.

Alack, what poverty my Muse brings forth,
That having such a scope to show her pride,
The argument all bare is of more worth
Than when it hath my added praise beside!
O, blame me not, if I no more can write!
Look in your glass, and there appears a face
That over-goes my blunt invention quite,
Dulling my lines and doing me disgrace.
Were it not sinful then, striving to mend,
To mar the subject that before was well?
For to no other pass my verses tend
Than of your graces and your gifts to tell;
  And more, much more, than in my verse can sit
  Your own glass shows you when you look in it.

CIV.

To me, fair friend, you never can be old,
For as you were when first your eye I ey'd,
Such seems your beauty still. Three winters cold
Have from the forests shook three summers' pride,
Three beauteous springs to yellow autumn turn'd
In process of the seasons have I seen,
Three April perfumes in three hot Junes burn'd,
Since first I saw you fresh, which yet are green.
Ah! yet doth beauty, like a dial-hand,
Steal from his figure and no pace perceiv'd;
So your sweet hue, which methinks still doth stand,
Hath motion and mine eye may be deceiv'd:
  For fear of which, hear this, thou age unbred;
  Ere you were born was beauty's summer dead.

CV.

Let not my love be call'd idolatry,
Nor my beloved as an idol show,
Since all alike my songs and praises be
To one, of one, still such, and ever so.
Kind is my love to-day, to-morrow kind,
Still constant in a wondrous excellence;
Therefore my verse to constancy confin'd,
One thing expressing, leaves out difference.
'Fair, kind, and true' is all my argument,
'Fair, kind, and true' varying to other words;
And in this change is my invention spent,
Three themes in one, which wondrous scope affords.
  'Fair, kind, and true,' have often liv'd alone,
  Which three till now never kept seat in one.

12. **in pride . . . growth,** in his prime.

C. This sonnet marks another break. The implication is that the poet has been using his pen in unworthy themes—possibly plays. 3. **fury,** poetic inspiration. 6. **numbers,** verse. 8. **argument,** subject. 9. **resty,** inactive, inert. 10. **If,** to see if. 11. **satire,** satirist; rebuke (Alden). 14. **prevent'st,** anticipatest, forestallest.

CI. This sonnet has to do, like LXXXII-LXXXIV, with writing in praise of the friend; the main purpose is to preserve his virtues for the future. 5. **haply,** perhaps. 6. **colour . . . colour,** pretense . . . hue; cf. *1 Henry VI*, II, iv, 34-36. 7. **lay,** lay in, as with a brush.

CII. 3. **merchandiz'd,** degraded by being treated as "a thing of sale." 7. **Philomel,** the nightingale; regarded as feminine. **front,** forehead, beginning. 10. **mournful hymns,** reference to the tragic tale of Philomela.

CIII. 2. **her pride,** power of which she is proud. 3. **argument . . . bare,** subject unadorned. 7. **blunt invention,** unpolished style. 8. **Dulling,** making uninteresting. 11. **pass,** result.

CIV. 4. **pride,** splendor. 9-10. **Ah . . . perceiv'd,** beauty slips away like the shadow of the hand on the dial. 11. **hue,** appearance, complexion. 13. **this,** i.e., the poet's message to posterity.

CV. 4. **still,** always. 8. **difference.** Difference in logic divides genus from species; there has been no division in the completeness of the poet's theme. 11. **this change,** variations on this theme. **spent,** expended. 14. **Which . . . one,** the friend alone possesses all three of the virtues.

CVI. 1. **wasted,** past. 2. **wights,** persons. 5. **blazon,** heraldic metaphor, meaning here "glorification." 7. **antique,** accented on the first syllable. 8. **master,** possess, control. 11. **And, for,** and because. **divining,** guessing. 13. **For,** for even.

CVII. 1-2. **soul . . . world.** "Soul of the world" is a conception in the mystical philosophy of Giordano Bruno. 3. **lease,** term, allotted time. 4. **Suppos'd . . . doom.** The fears supposed his love would have an end. But it is not so (Stopes). 5. **mortal moon,** usually taken as a reference to Queen Elizabeth, ill or deceased. She was known as Diana,

CVI.

When in the chronicle of wasted time
I see descriptions of the fairest wights,
And beauty making beautiful old rhyme
In praise of ladies dead and lovely knights,
Then, in the blazon of sweet beauty's best,
Of hand, of foot, of lip, of eye, of brow,
I see their antique pen would have express'd
Even such a beauty as you master now.
So all their praises are but prophecies
Of this our time, all you prefiguring;
And, for they look'd but with divining eyes,
They had not skill enough your worth to sing:
  For we, which now behold these present days,
  Have eyes to wonder, but lack tongues to praise.

CVII.

Not mine own fears, nor the prophetic soul
Of the wide world dreaming on things to come,
Can yet the lease of my true love control,
Suppos'd as forfeit to a confin'd doom.
The mortal moon hath her eclipse endur'd
And the sad augurs mock their own presage;
Incertainties now crown themselves assur'd
And peace proclaims olives of endless age.
Now with the drops of this most balmy time
My love looks fresh, and Death to me subscribes,
Since, spite of him, I'll live in this poor rhyme,
While he insults o'er dull and speechless tribes:
  And thou in this shalt find thy monument,
  When tyrants' crests and tombs of brass are spent.

CVIII.

What 's in the brain that ink may character
Which hath not figur'd to thee my true spirit?
What 's new to speak, what new to register,
That may express my love or thy dear merit?
Nothing, sweet boy; but yet, like prayers divine,
I must each day say o'er the very same,
Counting no old thing old, thou mine, I thine,
Even as when first I hallowed thy fair name.
So that eternal love in love's fresh case
Weighs not the dust and injury of age,
Nor gives to necessary wrinkles place,
But makes antiquity for aye his page,
  Finding the first conceit of love there bred
  Where time and outward form would show it dead.

CIX.

O, never say that I was false of heart,
Though absence seem'd my flame to qualify.
As easy might I from myself depart
As from my soul, which in thy breast doth lie:
That is my home of love: if I have rang'd,
Like him that travels I return again,
Just to the time, not with the time exchang'd,
So that myself bring water for my stain.
Never believe, though in my nature reign'd
All frailties that besiege all kinds of blood,
That it could so preposterously be stain'd,
To leave for nothing all thy sum of good;
  For nothing this wide universe I call,
  Save thou, my rose; in it thou art my all.

CX.

Alas, 'tis true I have gone here and there
And made myself a motley to the view,
Gor'd mine own thoughts, sold cheap what is most
  dear,
Made old offences of affections new;
Most true it is that I have look'd on truth
Askance and strangely: but, by all above,
These blenches gave my heart another youth,
And worse essays prov'd thee my best of love.
Now all is done, have what shall have no end:
Mine appetite I never more will grind
On newer proof, to try an older friend,
A god in love, to whom I am confin'd.
  Then give me welcome, next my heaven the best,
  Even to thy pure and most most loving breast.

CXI.

O, for my sake do you with Fortune chide,
The guilty goddess of my harmful deeds,
That did not better for my life provide
Than public means which public manners breeds.
Thence comes it that my name receives a brand,
And almost thence my nature is subdu'd
To what it works in, like the dyer's hand:
Pity me then and wish I were renew'd;
Whilst, like a willing patient, I will drink
Potions of eisel 'gainst my strong infection;
No bitterness that I will bitter think,
Nor double penance, to correct correction.
  Pity me then, dear friend, and I assure ye
  Even that your pity is enough to cure me.

CXII.

Your love and pity doth th' impression fill
Which vulgar scandal stamp'd upon my brow;
For what care I who calls me well or ill,

Cynthia, and other epithets of the moon goddess. Hotson explains as a reference to the Armada. 6. **And . . . presage,** and the solemn prophets of disaster are mocked by their own predictions. 7. **Incertainties . . . assur'd,** uncertainties have triumphantly given way to certainties. 8. **endless age,** i.e., without foreseen end. 10. **subscribes,** yields. 12. **insults,** triumphs. 14. **crests,** trophies in a tomb.

CVIII. 1. **character,** write. 2. **figur'd,** revealed. 7. **Counting . . . thine,** a summation of themes of praise—perpetuity and unity. 9. **fresh case,** youthful body. 10. **Weighs not,** is unconcerned about. 12. **page,** servant. 13. **conceit,** conception.

CIX. 2. **qualify,** temper, moderate. 5. **rang'd,** traveled, wandered. 7. **Just,** punctual. **exchang'd,** changed. 8. **So . . . stain,** i.e., so that I myself provide the means of excusing my absence. 12. **To . . . good,** to abandon all thy virtues for a mere nothing.

CX. Sometimes taken as an indictment by Shakespeare of the actor's trade. It means, however, only that he has traveled and made new acquaintances, but has now returned to his only permanent attachment. 2. **motley,** parti-colored dress of the professional fool. 4. **offences,** trespasses. **affections,** passions. 5. **truth,** constancy. 6. **Askance,** sidewise. **strangely,** mistrustfully. 7. **blenches,** swervings. 8. **essays,** experiments (in friendship). 9. **have . . . end,** take what is eternal (my friendship). 10. **grind,** whet. 11. **newer proof,** further experiment. 12. **god in love,** i.e., his friend.

CXI. 1. **chide,** argue. 4. **Than . . . breeds,** i.e., than providing me a means of livelihood which depends on catering to the public (a probable reference to Shakespeare's career as an actor). 5. **receives a brand,** is disgraced (through prejudice against his occupation). 8. **renew'd,** restored to what he was by nature. 10. **eisel,** vinegar, used as an antiseptic against the plague. 12. **Nor . . . correction,** i.e., no bitter cure will seem worse to me than the disease it corrects.

CXII. 1. **impression,** scar. Cf. *brand,* CXI, 5. **fill,** efface.

So you o'er-green my bad, my good allow?
You are my all the world, and I must strive
To know my shames and praises from your tongue;
None else to me, nor I to none alive,
That my steel'd sense or changes right or wrong.
In so profound abysm I throw all care
Of others' voices, that my adder's sense
To critic and to flatterer stopped are.
Mark how with my neglect I do dispense:
  You are so strongly in my purpose bred
  That all the world besides methinks are dead.

CXIII.

Since I left you, mine eye is in my mind;
And that which governs me to go about
Doth part his function and is partly blind,
Seems seeing, but effectually is out;
For it no form delivers to the heart
Of bird, of flow'r, or shape, which it doth latch:
Of his quick objects hath the mind no part,
Nor his own vision holds what it doth catch;
For if it see the rud'st or gentlest sight,
The most sweet favour or deformed'st creature,
The mountain or the sea, the day or night,
The crow or dove, it shapes them to your feature:
  Incapable of more, replete with you,
  My most true mind thus mak'th mine eye untrue.

CXIV.

Or whether doth my mind, being crown'd with you,
Drink up the monarch's plague, this flattery?
Or whether shall I say, mine eye saith true,
And that your love taught it this alchemy,
To make of monsters and things indigest
Such cherubins as your sweet self resemble,
Creating every bad a perfect best,
As fast as objects to his beams assemble?
O, 'tis the first; 'tis flatt'ry in my seeing,
And my great mind most kingly drinks it up:
Mine eye well knows what with his gust is 'greeing,
And to his palate doth prepare the cup:
  If it be poison'd, 'tis the lesser sin
  That mine eye loves it and doth first begin.

CXV.

Those lines that I before have writ do lie,
Even those that said I could not love you dearer:
Yet then my judgement knew no reason why
My most full flame should afterwards burn clearer.
But reckoning time, whose million'd accidents
Creep in 'twixt vows and change decrees of kings,
Tan sacred beauty, blunt the sharp'st intents,
Divert strong minds to th' course of alt'ring things;
Alas, why, fearing of time's tyranny,
Might I not then say 'Now I love you best,'
When I was certain o'er incertainty,
Crowning the present, doubting of the rest?
  Love is a babe; then might I not say so,
  To give full growth to that which still doth grow.

CXVI.

Let me not to the marriage of true minds
Admit impediments. Love is not love
Which alters when it alteration finds,
Or bends with the remover to remove:
O, no! it is an ever-fixed mark
That looks on tempests and is never shaken;
It is the star to every wand'ring bark,
Whose worth 's unknown, although his height be
    taken.
Love 's not Time's fool, though rosy lips and cheeks
Within his bending sickle's compass come;
Love alters not with his brief hours and weeks,
But bears it out even to the edge of doom.
  If this be error and upon me prov'd,
  I never writ, nor no man ever lov'd.

CXVII.

Accuse me thus: that I have scanted all
Wherein I should your great deserts repay,
Forgot upon your dearest love to call,
Whereto all bonds do tie me day by day;
That I have frequent been with unknown minds
And given to time your own dear-purchas'd right;
That I have hoisted sail to all the winds
Which should transport me farthest from your sight.
Book both my wilfulness and errors down
And on just proof surmise accumulate;
Bring me within the level of your frown,
But shoot not at me in your wakened hate;
  Since my appeal says I did strive to prove
  The constancy and virtue of your love.

CXVIII.

Like as, to make our appetites more keen,
With eager compounds we our palate urge,
As, to prevent our maladies unseen,
We sicken to shun sickness when we purge,
Even so, being full of your ne'er-cloying sweetness,
To bitter sauces did I frame my feeding
And, sick of welfare, found a kind of meetness
To be diseas'd ere that there was true needing.
Thus policy in love, t' anticipate
The ills that were not, grew to faults assured

4. **o'er-green my bad,** cover my evil with green leaves. **allow,** approve. 7-8. **None . . . wrong,** i.e., no one else but you affects my fixed sense of what is right and wrong (?). 8. **steel'd sense,** what is engraven on my sense. 10. **adder's sense.** Adders were supposed to be deaf. 12. **Mark . . . dispense,** i.e., see how I disregard the opinion of others. 13. **You . . . bred,** i.e., you are such a powerful influence over my intentions.

CXIII. 2. **governs,** guides. 3. **part his,** divide its. 4. **effectually,** in reality. 5. **For . . . heart,** I have no knowledge of what passes. 6. **latch,** catch or receive (the sight or sound). 12. **shapes . . . feature,** makes them resemble you.

CXIV. 1, 3. **Or whether,** indicates alternative possibilities. 1. **crown'd with you,** elevated by possession of you. 4. **alchemy,** science of transmuting base metals. 5. **indigest,** chaotic, formless. 6. **cherubins,** another suggestion of the youth and beauty of the friend. 10. **it,** i.e., he accepts the cup of flattery. 11. **what . . . 'greeing,** what suits the eye's taste. Steevens sees in this and the following lines an allusion to tasters for the food of kings.

CXV. 5. **But reckoning time,** merely considering the power of Time as a destroyer. 7. **Tan,** darken, i.e., coarsen. 9. **fearing of,** fearing. 13. **then,** therefore. **so,** i.e., "Now I love you best" (l. 10).

CXVI. 4. **Or . . . remove,** or inclines to inconstancy at the demand of the inconstant. 8. **Whose . . . taken.** The star has an influence over and above the determination of its altitude (for purposes of navigation). 9. **fool,** plaything. 11. **his,** i.e., Time's. 12. **But . . . doom,** endures or holds out to the very day of judgment.

CXVII. 4. **bonds,** a pun on the legal sense of the word. 5. **unknown minds,** persons not worth knowing. 6. **And . . . right,** squandered your rights in me on temporary matters and alliances.

CXVIII. 2. **eager,** pungent, bitter. 3. **prevent,** anticipate. 9-12. **Thus . . . cured,** thus the attempt of love to forestall the evils of satiety had brought in sickness, when in health I had taken medicine for disease. 12. **rank of goodness,** sick with good health.

CXIX. 1. **Siren tears,** deceitful tears of seductive women. 2. **lim-**

And brought to medicine a healthful state
Which, rank of goodness, would by ill be cured:
But thence I learn, and find the lesson true,
Drugs poison him that so fell sick of you.

CXIX.

What potions have I drunk of Siren tears,
Distill'd from limbecks foul as hell within,
Applying fears to hopes and hopes to fears,
Still losing when I saw myself to win!
What wretched errors hath my heart committed,
Whilst it hath thought itself so blessed never!
How have mine eyes out of their spheres been fitted
In the distraction of this madding fever!
O benefit of ill! now I find true
That better is by evil still made better;
And ruin'd love, when it is built anew,
Grows fairer than at first, more strong, far greater.
So I return rebuk'd to my content
And gain by ill thrice more than I have spent.

CXX.

That you were once unkind befriends me now,
And for that sorrow which I then did feel
Needs must I under my transgression bow,
Unless my nerves were brass or hammered steel.
For if you were by my unkindness shaken
As I by yours, y' have pass'd a hell of time,
And I, a tyrant, have no leisure taken
To weigh how once I suffered in your crime.
O, that our night of woe might have rememb'red
My deepest sense, how hard true sorrow hits,
And soon to you, as you to me then, tend'red
The humble salve which wounded bosoms fits!
But that your trespass now becomes a fee;
Mine ransoms yours, and yours must ransom me.

CXXI.

'Tis better to be vile than vile esteemed,
When not to be receives reproach of being,
And the just pleasure lost which is so deemed
Not by our feeling but by others' seeing:
For why should others' false adulterate eyes
Give salutation to my sportive blood?
Or on my frailties why are frailer spies,
Which in their wills count bad what I think good?
No, I am that I am, and they that level
At my abuses reckon up their own:
I may be straight, though they themselves be bevel;
By their rank thoughts my deeds must not be shown;
Unless this general evil they maintain,
All men are bad, and in their badness reign.

CXXII.

Thy gift, thy tables, are within my brain
Full character'd with lasting memory,
Which shall above that idle rank remain
Beyond all date, even to eternity;
Or at the least, so long as brain and heart
Have faculty by nature to subsist;
Till each to raz'd oblivion yield his part
Of thee, thy record never can be miss'd.
That poor retention could not so much hold,
Nor need I tallies thy dear love to score;
Therefore to give them from me was I bold,
To trust those tables that receive thee more:
To keep an adjunct to remember thee
Were to import forgetfulness in me.

CXXIII.

No, Time, thou shalt not boast that I do change:
Thy pyramids built up with newer might
To me are nothing novel, nothing strange;
They are but dressings of a former sight.
Our dates are brief, and therefore we admire
What thou dost foist upon us that is old,
And rather make them born to our desire
Than think that we before have heard them told.
Thy registers and thee I both defy,
Not wond'ring at the present nor the past,
For thy records and what we see doth lie,
Made more or less by thy continual haste.
This I do vow and this shall ever be;
I will be true, despite thy scythe and thee.

CXXIV.

If my dear love were but the child of state,
It might for Fortune's bastard be unfather'd,
As subject to Time's love or to Time's hate,
Weeds among weeds, or flowers with flowers gather'd.
No, it was builded far from accident;
It suffers not in smiling pomp, nor falls
Under the blow of thralled discontent,
Whereto th' inviting time our fashion calls:
It fears not Policy, that heretic,
Which works on leases of short-numb'red hours,
But all alone stands hugely politic,
That it nor grows with heat nor drowns with show'rs.
To this I witness call the fools of time,
Which die for goodness, who have liv'd for crime.

CXXV.

Were 't aught to me I bore the canopy,
With my extern the outward honouring,

becks, vessels used in distillation. 7. **How . . . fitted,** how my eyes have popped out in convulsive fit.

CXX. 4. **nerves,** sinews. 9. **our night of woe,** the dark and woeful time of our estrangement. **rememb'red,** reminded. 11. **soon,** as soon. **tend'red,** offered. 13. **fee,** compensation.

CXXI. 2. **When . . . being,** when not to be vile receives the reproach of vileness. 3-4. **which . . . seeing,** which is measured by the opinions of others, not by our own conscience. 5-6. **For . . . blood,** why should others who are really wicked greet as an equal me, who am only mirthful. 8. **in their wills,** at their pleasure. 9. **that,** what. 11. **bevel,** out of square, crooked. 13. **this general evil,** this general principle of evil.

CXXII. 1. **tables,** writing tablets. 2. **Full . . . memory,** written all over in my lasting memory. 3. **above . . . rank,** i.e., the rank or importance of that memorandum book. 7. **raz'd oblivion,** obliterating forgetfulness. 9. **retention,** i.e., the book, an instrument for retaining memoranda. 10. **tallies,** sticks notched to serve for reckoning. 14. **import,** impute.

CXXIII. 2. **Thy . . . might.** Taken by Hotson to refer to the erection by Pope Sixtus v of four obelisks (known as *pyramids*) in Rome in 1586 and succeeding years; see Introduction. 4. **They . . . sight,** they but repeat all objects in new forms; apparent assertion of the indestructibility of matter. 7-8. **And . . . told,** and rather hold the impression that they are our new structures than remember that we have seen them before.

CXXIV. 1. **child of state,** child of rank or power; possibly circumstance, which is always changing (Lee). 10. **leases . . . hours,** possible allusion to short-term leases granted by heretics to their friends to avoid confiscation of property. 11. **politic,** wise, prudent. 13-14. **To . . . crime,** I call to witness the transitory unworthy loves (sports of time; see CVI), whose death was a virtue since their life was a crime (Dowden).

CXXV. 1. **bore the canopy,** i.e., honor you (or another) as those are honored over whose heads a cloth of state is carried (Pooler). 2. **With . . . honouring,** i.e., to honor the outward by the outward (Alden).

Or laid great bases for eternity,
Which prove more short than waste or ruining?
Have I not seen dwellers on form and favour
Lose all, and more, by paying too much rent,
For compound sweet forgoing simple savour,
Pitiful thrivers, in their gazing spent?
No, let me be obsequious in thy heart,
And take thou my oblation, poor but free,
Which is not mix'd with seconds, knows no art,
But mutual render, only me for thee.
Hence, thou suborn'd informer! a true soul
When most impeach'd stands least in thy control.

CXXVI.

O thou, my lovely boy, who in thy power
Dost hold Time's fickle glass, his sickle, hour;
Who hast by waning grown, and therein show'st
Thy lovers withering as thy sweet self grow'st;
If Nature, sovereign mistress over wrack,
As thou goest onwards, still will pluck thee back,
She keeps thee to this purpose, that her skill
May time disgrace and wretched minutes kill.
Yet fear her, O thou minion of her pleasure!
She may detain, but not still keep, her treasure:
Her audit, though delay'd, answer'd must be,
And her quietus is to render thee.

CXXVII.

In the old age black was not counted fair,
Or if it were, it bore not beauty's name;
But now is black beauty's successive heir,
And beauty slander'd with a bastard shame:
For since each hand hath put on nature's power,
Fairing the foul with art's false borrow'd face,
Sweet beauty hath no name, no holy bower,
But is profan'd, if not lives in disgrace.
Therefore my mistress' eyes are raven black,
Her eyes so suited, and they mourners seem
At such who, not born fair, no beauty lack,
Sland'ring creation with a false esteem:
Yet so they mourn, becoming of their woe,
That every tongue says beauty should look so.

CXXVIII.

How oft, when thou, my music, music play'st,
Upon that blessed wood whose motion sounds
With thy sweet fingers, when thou gently sway'st
The wiry concord that mine ear confounds,
Do I envy those jacks that nimble leap
To kiss the tender inward of thy hand,
Whilst my poor lips, which should that harvest reap,
At the wood's boldness by thee blushing stand!
To be so tickled, they would change their state
And situation with those dancing chips,
O'er whom thy fingers walk with gentle gait,
Making dead wood more blest than living lips.
Since saucy jacks so happy are in this,
Give them thy fingers, me thy lips to kiss.

CXXIX.

Th' expense of spirit in a waste of shame
Is lust in action; and till action, lust
Is perjur'd, murd'rous, bloody, full of blame,
Savage, extreme, rude, cruel, not to trust,
Enjoy'd no sooner but despised straight,
Past reason hunted, and no sooner had
Past reason hated, as a swallowed bait
On purpose laid to make the taker mad;
Mad in pursuit and in possession so;
Had, having, and in quest to have, extreme;
A bliss in proof, and prov'd, a very woe;
Before, a joy propos'd; behind, a dream.
All this the world well knows; yet none knows well
To shun the heaven that leads men to this hell.

CXXX.

My mistress' eyes are nothing like the sun;
Coral is far more red than her lips' red;
If snow be white, why then her breasts are dun;
If hairs be wires, black wires grow on her head.
I have seen roses damask'd, red and white,
But no such roses see I in her cheeks;
And in some perfumes is there more delight
Than in the breath that from my mistress reeks.
I love to hear her speak, yet well I know
That music hath a far more pleasing sound;
I grant I never saw a goddess go;
My mistress, when she walks, treads on the ground:
And yet, by heaven, I think my love as rare
As any she belied with false compare.

CXXXI.

Thou art as tyrannous, so as thou art,
As those whose beauties proudly make them cruel;
For well thou know'st to my dear doting heart
Thou art the fairest and most precious jewel.
Yet, in good faith, some say that thee behold
Thy face hath not the power to make love groan:
To say they err I dare not be so bold,
Although I swear it to myself alone.
And, to be sure that is not false I swear,
A thousand groans, but thinking on thy face,
One on another's neck, do witness bear
Thy black is fairest in my judgement's place.

3. **Or . . . eternity,** laid foundations for lasting fame. 6. **by paying too much rent,** by overdoing their obligations. 7. **For . . . savour,** fore-going actual love for the sake of obsequious flattery. 8. **spent,** wasted (by merely looking at outward honor). 9. **obsequious,** devoted. 10. **oblation,** offering. 11. **seconds,** inferior parts, as of grain. 12. **mutual render,** fair exchange. 13. **suborn'd informer,** perjured witness. 14. **impeach'd,** charged with treason.

CXXVI. With this sonnet (which is made up of six couplets) the first great cycle, that addressed to the friend, comes to an end. 2. **fickle glass,** ever-changing hourglass. Some editors prefer the reading: *fickle hour*. 3. **by waning grown,** grown more youthful as your age increases. 5. **wrack,** ruin. Nature is mistress of decay because of her power of restoration. 10. **She . . . treasure.** The poet warns his friend that, although nature will keep and restore him for a time, Time will ultimately triumph over him. 11. **audit,** i.e., Nature's account to Time. 12. **quietus,** discharge, quittance.

Here begins a separate series of sonnets, apparently belonging to the same period of time as XXXIII-XLII. They are addressed to, or refer to, a dark woman who passes from loving the poet to loving the friend.

CXXVII. 1. **In . . . fair.** Black was traditionally associated with ugliness; cf. *Love's Labour's Lost*, IV, iii, 247, 261 ff. 3. **successive heir,** lawful successor. 6. **borrow'd face,** i.e., cosmetics. 9. **eyes,** i.e., eyebrows. 10. **so suited,** i.e., similarly black. 11. **At,** for. **no beauty lack,** i.e., nonetheless seem attractive. 12. **Sland'ring . . . esteem,** dishonoring nature by a false reputation for beauty. 13. **becoming of,** gracing.

CXXVIII. 5. **jacks,** upright pieces of wood fixed to the key-lever and fitted with a quill which plucked the strings of the virginal (Onions). 6. **tender inward,** delicate inside.

CXXIX. 1. **expense,** expenditure, waste. 5. **Enjoy'd . . . straight.** Cf. *The Rape of Lucrece*, 211-212, 742. 11. **in proof,** while experienced. **prov'd,** i.e., afterwards.

In nothing art thou black save in thy deeds,
And thence this slander, as I think, proceeds.

CXXXII.

Thine eyes I love, and they, as pitying me,
Knowing thy heart torments me with disdain,
Have put on black and loving mourners be,
Looking with pretty ruth upon my pain.
And truly not the morning sun of heaven
Better becomes the grey cheeks of the east,
Nor that full star that ushers in the even
Doth half that glory to the sober west,
As those two mourning eyes become thy face:
O, let it then as well beseem thy heart
To mourn for me, since mourning doth thee grace,
And suit thy pity like in every part.
Then will I swear beauty herself is black
And all they foul that thy complexion lack.

CXXXIII.

Beshrew that heart that makes my heart to groan
For that deep wound it gives my friend and me!
Is 't not enough to torture me alone,
But slave to slavery my sweet'st friend must be?
Me from myself thy cruel eye hath taken,
And my next self thou harder hast engrossed:
Of him, myself, and thee, I am forsaken;
A torment thrice threefold thus to be crossed.
Prison my heart in thy steel bosom's ward,
But then my friend's heart let my poor heart bail;
Whoe'er keeps me, let my heart be his guard;
Thou canst not then use rigour in my gaol:
And yet thou wilt; for I, being pent in thee,
Perforce am thine, and all that is in me.

CXXXIV.

So, now I have confess'd that he is thine,
And I myself am mortgag'd to thy will,
Myself I'll forfeit, so that other mine
Thou wilt restore, to be my comfort still:
But thou wilt not, nor he will not be free,
For thou art covetous and he is kind;
He learn'd but surety-like to write for me
Under that bond that him as fast doth bind.
The statute of thy beauty thou wilt take,
Thou usurer, that put'st forth all to use,
And sue a friend came debtor for my sake;
So him I lose through my unkind abuse.
Him have I lost; thou hast both him and me:
He pays the whole, and yet am I not free.

CXXXV.

Whoever hath her wish, thou hast thy 'Will,'
And 'Will' to boot, and 'Will' in overplus;
More than enough am I that vex thee still,
To thy sweet will making addition thus.
Wilt thou, whose will is large and spacious,
Not once vouchsafe to hide my will in thine?
Shall will in others seem right gracious,
And in my will no fair acceptance shine?
The sea, all water, yet receives rain still
And in abundance addeth to his store;
So thou, being rich in 'Will,' add to thy 'Will'
One will of mine, to make thy large 'Will' more.
Let no unkind, no fair beseechers kill;
Think all but one, and me in that one 'Will.'

CXXXVI.

If thy soul check thee that I come so near,
Swear to thy blind soul that I was thy 'Will,'
And will, thy soul knows, is admitted there;
Thus far for love my love-suit, sweet, fulfil.
'Will' will fulfil the treasure of thy love,
Ay, fill it full with wills, and my will one.
In things of great receipt with ease we prove
Among a number one is reckon'd none:
Then in the number let me pass untold,
Though in thy stores' account I one must be;
For nothing hold me, so it please thee hold
That nothing me, a something, sweet, to thee:
Make but my name thy love, and love that still,
And then thou lovest me, for my name is 'Will.'

CXXXVII.

Thou blind fool, Love, what dost thou to mine eyes,
That they behold, and see not what they see?
They know what beauty is, see where it lies,
Yet what the best is take the worst to be.
If eyes corrupt by over-partial looks
Be anchor'd in the bay where all men ride,
Why of eyes' falsehood hast thou forged hooks,
Whereto the judgement of my heart is tied?
Why should my heart think that a several plot
Which my heart knows the wide world's common place?
Or mine eyes seeing this, say this is not,
To put fair truth upon so foul a face?
In things right true my heart and eyes have err'd,
And to this false plague are they now transferr'd.

CXXXVIII.

When my love swears that she is made of truth
I do believe her, though I know she lies,
That she might think me some untutor'd youth,
Unlearned in the world's false subtleties.
Thus vainly thinking that she thinks me young,
Although she knows my days are past the best,

CXXX. 5. **damask'd,** mingled red and white. 8. **reeks,** issues as smell. 11. **go,** walk. 14. **she,** woman. **compare,** comparison.
CXXXI. 1. **so as thou art,** even as you are (dark, not considered handsome). 11. **One on another's neck,** one after another. 12. **my judgement's place,** my critical opinion.
CXXXII. 4. **ruth,** pity. 12. **suit thy pity like,** clothe your pity in the same way.
CXXXIII. 6. **my next self,** my dearest friend. 8. **crossed,** tried. 9. **steel bosom's ward,** the prison cell of thy hard heart.
CXXXIV. 3. **that other mine,** my other self, my friend. 9. **statute,** security; e.g., of a usurer. 11. **came,** i.e., who became. 12. **unkind abuse,** unnatural ill-usage (of me).
CXXXV. This and the following sonnet ring the changes on the word *will*—desire, temper, passion, and the poet's name; possibly also the friend's name. 13. **Let . . . kill,** a puzzling line, in which *unkind* is usually taken as a noun, i.e., unkind one. Several editors favor Tyler's suggestion, "Let no unkind 'no' your beseechers kill."
CXXXVI. 5. **fulfil,** fill full. 7. **receipt,** capacity. 8. **one is reckon'd none,** variant of the common saying "one is no number." 9. **untold,** uncounted. 13-14. **Make . . . Will,** love only my name (something less than loving myself), and then thou lovest me, for my name is Will, and I myself am all will, that is, all desire (Dowden). The lines may also be taken as a surrender of his mistress to his friend, also named Will.
CXXXVII. A vituperative sonnet, in which the poet blames love for blinding his eyes, so that he has chosen the worst for the best; cf. CXIII. 6. **ride,** with an implication of sexual promiscuity. 9. **several plot,** private field. 10. **common,** open, promiscuous.
CXXXVIII. This sonnet is I in *The Passionate Pilgrim.* 2. **believe her,** i.e., pretend to believe her. 3. **That,** let that.

Simply I credit her false-speaking tongue:
On both sides thus is simple truth suppress'd.
But wherefore says she not she is unjust?
And wherefore say not I that I am old?
O, love's best habit is in seeming trust,
And age in love loves not to have years told:
  Therefore I lie with her and she with me,
  And in our faults by lies we flattered be.

CXXXIX.

O, call not me to justify the wrong
That thy unkindness lays upon my heart;
Wound me not with thine eye but with thy tongue;
Use power with power and slay me not by art.
Tell me thou lov'st elsewhere, but in my sight,
Dear heart, forbear to glance thine eye aside:
What need'st thou wound with cunning when thy might
Is more than my o'er-press'd defence can bide?
Let me excuse thee: ah! my love well knows
Her pretty looks have been mine enemies,
And therefore from my face she turns my foes,
That they elsewhere might dart their injuries:
  Yet do not so; but since I am near slain,
  Kill me outright with looks and rid my pain.

CXL.

Be wise as thou art cruel; do not press
My tongue-tied patience with too much disdain;
Lest sorrow lend me words and words express
The manner of my pity-wanting pain.
If I might teach thee wit, better it were,
Though not to love, yet, love, to tell me so;
As testy sick men, when their deaths be near,
No news but health from their physicians know;
For if I should despair, I should grow mad,
And in my madness might speak ill of thee:
Now this ill-wresting world is grown so bad,
Mad slanderers by mad ears believed be.
  That I may not be so, nor thou belied,
  Bear thine eyes straight, though thy proud heart go wide.

CXLI.

In faith, I do not love thee with mine eyes,
For they in thee a thousand errors note;
But 'tis my heart that loves what they despise,
Who in despite of view is pleas'd to dote;
Nor are mine ears with thy tongue's tune delighted,
Nor tender feeling, to base touches prone,
Nor taste, nor smell, desire to be invited
To any sensual feast with thee alone:
But my five wits nor my five senses can
Dissuade one foolish heart from serving thee,
Who leaves unsway'd the likeness of a man,
Thy proud heart's slave and vassal wretch to be:
  Only my plague thus far I count my gain,
  That she that makes me sin awards me pain.

CXLII.

Love is my sin and thy dear virtue hate,
Hate of my sin, grounded on sinful loving:
O, but with mine compare thou thine own state,
And thou shalt find it merits not reproving;
Or, if it do, not from those lips of thine,
That have profan'd their scarlet ornaments
And seal'd false bonds of love as oft as mine,
Robb'd others' beds' revenues of their rents.
Be it lawful I love thee, as thou lov'st those
Whom thine eyes woo as mine importune thee:
Root pity in thy heart, that when it grows
Thy pity may deserve to pitied be.
  If thou dost seek to have what thou dost hide,
  By self-example mayst thou be denied!

CXLIII.

Lo! as a careful housewife runs to catch
One of her feathered creatures broke away,
Sets down her babe and makes all swift dispatch
In pursuit of the thing she would have stay,
Whilst her neglected child holds her in chase,
Cries to catch her whose busy care is bent
To follow that which flies before her face,
Not prizing her poor infant's discontent;
So runn'st thou after that which flies from thee,
Whilst I thy babe chase thee afar behind;
But if thou catch thy hope, turn back to me,
And play the mother's part, kiss me, be kind:
  So will I pray that thou mayst have thy 'Will,'
  If thou turn back, and my loud crying still.

CXLIV.

Two loves I have of comfort and despair,
Which like two spirits do suggest me still:
The better angel is a man right fair,
The worser spirit a woman colour'd ill.
To win me soon to hell, my female evil
Tempteth my better angel from my side,
And would corrupt my saint to be a devil,
Wooing his purity with her foul pride.
And whether that my angel be turn'd fiend
Suspect I may, yet not directly tell;
But being both from me, both to each friend,
I guess one angel in another's hell:
  Yet this shall I ne'er know, but live in doubt,
  Till my bad angel fire my good one out.

7. **Simply,** pretending to be foolish. **credit,** believe. 9. **unjust,** unfaithful. 11. **habit,** deportment, with play on the idea of habiliment, that which is put on. 12. **told,** counted. 13. **lie with,** deceive (with sexual pun).

CXXXIX. 3. **Wound . . . tongue.** Cf. *Romeo and Juliet*, II, iv, 14, and *3 Henry VI*, V, vi, 26. 4. **with power,** i.e., directly. **art,** artifice. 11. **foes,** i.e., the "pretty looks" of l. 10.

CXL. 4. **The . . . pain,** the nature of my pain, on which you bestow no pity. 5. **wit,** wisdom, prudence. 6. **to tell me so,** to tell me thou dost love me. 11. **ill-wresting,** misinterpreting. 13-14. **That . . . wide,** that I may not be mad and you may not be exposed, control your eyes, whatever course your heart may take.

CXLI. 6. **base touches,** sensual indulgence. 9. **five wits,** intellectual, the same in number as the five senses—the common sense, imagination, fancy, judgment, and memory. 11. **Who . . . man,** i.e., in my foolish heart, which abandons the government of my personality. 14. **pain,** punishment.

CXLII. 2. **Hate . . . loving,** i.e., hatred of the adulterous character of my love. 6. **profan'd,** desecrated, as a temple. **scarlet ornaments,** lips (here likened to the red wax used to seal documents). 7. **seal'd . . . love,** i.e., with kisses; cf. *The Merchant of Venice*, II, vi, 6. 8. **Robb'd . . . rents,** implication of adultery. 13-14. **If . . . denied,** if thou dost seek to have the pity thou hidst from me, thou mayst by thy own example be denied it.

CXLIII. 4. **pursuit,** accented on first syllable. 13. **will . . . Will,** pun on will, desire, and the Christian name. Whether the *Will* refers to the poet or the rival friend is a matter of doubt.

CXLIV. The second sonnet in *The Passionate Pilgrim*. It depicts the conflict in the poet's mind between his affection for his friend and his mistress. 2. **suggest,** tempt (Malone); prompt (to good or evil). 6. **Tempteth . . . side.** Cf. *Othello*, V, ii, 208. 8. **foul,** wicked. 11. **from me,** away from me. The poet suspects they are together. 12. **I . . . hell,** i.e., I suspect the friend lies in the embraces of the woman (referring to her sexual organs as the gates of hell). 14. **fire**

CXLV.

Those lips that Love's own hand did make
Breath'd forth the sound that said 'I hate'
To me that languish'd for her sake;
But when she saw my woeful state,
Straight in her heart did mercy come,
Chiding that tongue that ever sweet
Was us'd in giving gentle doom,
And taught it thus anew to greet;
'I hate' she alter'd with an end,
That follow'd it as gentle day
Doth follow night, who like a fiend
From heaven to hell is flown away;
'I hate' from hate away she threw,
And sav'd my life, saying 'not you.'

CXLVI.

Poor soul, the centre of my sinful earth,
[Thrall to] these rebel pow'rs that thee array,
Why dost thou pine within and suffer dearth,
Painting thy outward walls so costly gay?
Why so large cost, having so short a lease,
Dost thou upon thy fading mansion spend?
Shall worms, inheritors of this excess,
Eat up thy charge? is this thy body's end?
Then, soul, live thou upon thy servant's loss,
And let that pine to aggravate thy store;
Buy terms divine in selling hours of dross;
Within be fed, without be rich no more:
So shalt thou feed on Death, that feeds on men,
And Death once dead, there 's no more dying then.

CXLVII.

My love is as a fever, longing still
For that which longer nurseth the disease,
Feeding on that which doth preserve the ill,
Th' uncertain sickly appetite to please.
My reason, the physician to my love,
Angry that his prescriptions are not kept,
Hath left me, and I desperate now approve
Desire is death, which physic did except.
Past cure I am, now reason is past care,
And frantic-mad with evermore unrest;
My thoughts and my discourse as madmen's are,
At random from the truth vainly express'd;
For I have sworn thee fair and thought thee bright,
Who art as black as hell, as dark as night.

CXLVIII.

O me, what eyes hath Love put in my head,
Which have no correspondence with true sight!
Or, if they have, where is my judgement fled,
That censures falsely what they see aright?
If that be fair whereon my false eyes dote,
What means the world to say it is not so?
If it be not, then love doth well denote
Love's eye is not so true as all men's 'No.'
How can it? O, how can Love's eye be true,
That is so vex'd with watching and with tears?
No marvel then, though I mistake my view;
The sun itself sees not till heaven clears.
O cunning Love! with tears thou keep'st me blind,
Lest eyes well-seeing thy foul faults should find.

CXLIX.

Canst thou, O cruel! say I love thee not,
When I against myself with thee partake?
Do I not think on thee, when I forgot
Am of myself, all tyrant, for thy sake?
Who hateth thee that I do call my friend?
On whom frown'st thou that I do fawn upon?
Nay, if thou lour'st on me, do I not spend
Revenge upon myself with present moan?
What merit do I in myself respect,
That is so proud thy service to despise,
When all my best doth worship thy defect,
Commanded by the motion of thine eyes?
But, love, hate on, for now I know thy mind;
Those that can see thou lov'st and I am blind.

CL.

O, from what pow'r hast thou this pow'rful might
With insufficiency my heart to sway?
To make me give the lie to my true sight,
And swear that brightness doth not grace the day?
Whence hast thou this becoming of things ill,
That in the very refuse of thy deeds
There is such strength and warrantise of skill
That, in my mind, thy worst all best exceeds?
Who taught thee how to make me love thee more
The more I hear and see just cause of hate?
O, though I love what others do abhor,
With others thou shouldst not abhor my state:
If thy unworthiness rais'd love in me,
More worthy I to be belov'd of thee.

CLI.

Love is too young to know what conscience is;
Yet who knows not conscience is born of love?
Then, gentle cheater, urge not my amiss,
Lest guilty of my faults thy sweet self prove:
For, thou betraying me, I do betray
My nobler part to my gross body's treason;
My soul doth tell my body that he may
Triumph in love; flesh stays no farther reason;

. . . **out,** drive him out with fire (with suggestion of venereal disease).

CXLV. A sonnet in eight-syllable meter. Critics have regarded it as out of place, or have rejected it. It has been compared to Lyly's "Cupid and my Campaspe played." 6-7. **Chiding . . . doom.** Her tongue was accustomed to dismiss her lover's guilt. 13. **'I . . . threw,'** i.e., she took away the pain and danger by saying, "I do not hate you."

CXLVI. 1. **sinful earth,** the body. 2. **[Thrall to],** anonymous conjecture; Q repeats "My sinfull earth" from l. 1; Globe, *et al.*, leave blank. 8. **thy charge,** that on which thou hast expended so much. 10. **aggravate,** increase. 11. **Buy terms divine,** purchase long periods of divine salvation.

CXLVII. This sonnet is associated in theme with CXLI and CXLIV—his hopeless love for an unworthy mistress. 1. **still,** always. 5. **My . . . love.** Cf. *The Merry Wives of Windsor,* II, i, 5. 7-8. **I . . . except,** I, being in despair, now recognize that desire to be fatal, which took exception to the teaching of physic (Stopes). 9. **cure . . . care,** an adaptation of the proverb, things past cure are past care.

CXLVIII. 4. **censures,** judges. 6. **What . . . so.** The opinion of the world refutes the warped judgment of the poet. 11. **mistake my view,** err in what I see. 13. **O cunning Love,** perhaps refers to the mistress as well as to the god of love.

CXLIX. 2. **partake,** take part (against myself). 3-4. **Do . . . sake,** it is for your sake that I neglect and tyrannize over myself. 7. **lour'st,** frown'st.

CL. 2. **insufficiency,** lack of every virtue and charm. 5. **becoming . . . ill,** ability to render evil things attractive. 7. **warrantise of skill,** warrant or pledge of mental ability. 13. **rais'd,** with bawdy suggestion.

CLI. The vein of the preceding sonnet continues; cf. CXLVI. 1. **Love . . . is,** cf. CXV. 2. **Yet . . . love?** Who knows not that the power of love awakens conscience? 3. **cheater,** rogue; with possible reference to "escheater," a king's officer charged with reversions of land. **amiss,** sin. 6. **My . . . treason.** She was the cause of his betraying his nobler part to the lusts of his body. 8. **stays,** awaits. **reason,** reasoning.

But, rising at thy name, doth point out thee
As his triumphant prize. Proud of this pride,
He is contented thy poor drudge to be,
To stand in thy affairs, fall by thy side.
  No want of conscience hold it that I call
  Her 'love' for whose dear love I rise and fall.

CLII.

In loving thee thou know'st I am forsworn,
But thou art twice forsworn, to me love swearing,
In act thy bed-vow broke and new faith torn
In vowing new hate after new love bearing.
But why of two oaths' breach do I accuse thee,
When I break twenty? I am perjur'd most;
For all my vows are oaths but to misuse thee
And all my honest faith in thee is lost,
For I have sworn deep oaths of thy deep kindness,
Oaths of thy love, thy truth, thy constancy,
And, to enlighten thee, gave eyes to blindness,
Or made them swear against the thing they see;
  For I have sworn thee fair; more perjur'd I,
  To swear against the truth so foul a lie!

CLIII.

Cupid laid by his brand, and fell asleep:
A maid of Dian's this advantage found,
And his love-kindling fire did quickly steep
In a cold valley-fountain of that ground;
Which borrow'd from this holy fire of Love
A dateless lively heat, still to endure,
And grew a seething bath, which yet men prove
Against strange maladies a sovereign cure.
But at my mistress' eye Love's brand new-fired,
The boy for trial needs would touch my breast;
I, sick withal, the help of bath desired,
And thither hied, a sad distemper'd guest,
  But found no cure: the bath for my help lies
  Where Cupid got new fire—my mistress' eyes.

CLIV.

The little Love-god lying once asleep
Laid by his side his heart-inflaming brand,
Whilst many nymphs that vow'd chaste life to keep
Came tripping by; but in her maiden hand
The fairest votary took up that fire
Which many legions of true hearts had warm'd;
And so the general of hot desire
Was sleeping by a virgin hand disarm'd.
This brand she quenched in a cool well by,
Which from Love's fire took heat perpetual,
Growing a bath and healthful remedy
For men diseas'd; but I, my mistress' thrall,
  Came there for cure, and this by that I prove,
  Love's fire heats water, water cools not love.

9. **rising,** with bawdy suggestion (continued in *point, stand, fall*). 10. **Proud of,** swelling with.

CLII. 9. **kindness,** affection, tenderness. 11. **to enlighten thee,** in order to invest thee with brightness; she was a dark lady.

The following two sonnets have no direct connection with those preceding. They are adaptations of epigrams in the Palatine Anthology, Greek poems of the fifth century (translated into Latin in the sixteenth century). The discovery was made by Hertzbert, *Shakespeare Jahrbuch*, XIII (1878), 158-162. Malone suggested that they were early exercises of the poet.

CLIII. 1. **brand,** firebrand, torch. 2. **Dian,** Diana, goddess of chastity. 6. **dateless,** endless, eternal. 7. **seething bath,** spring of hot medicinal waters. 9. **But . . . new-fired,** love has kindled his torch at my mistress' eyes.

CLIV. 7. **general,** cause and commander, i.e., Cupid. 12. **thrall,** slave, bondman. 13. **this by that,** i.e., *this* is what follows in l. 14, *by that* is by my coming which failed to cure me (Pooler).

the period of comedies and histories

By the year 1594, Shakespeare had already achieved a considerable reputation as a poet. Throughout his lifetime, in fact, his contemporary fame rested to a remarkable degree on his nondramatic poems, *Venus and Adonis*, *The Rape of Lucrece*, and the *Sonnets* (which were circulated in manuscript prior to their unauthorized publication in 1609). One of the earliest tributes suggesting the importance of the poems is to be found in an anonymous commendatory verse prefixed to Henry Willobie's *Willobie His Avisa* (1594):

> Though *Collatine* haue deerely bought,
> To high renowne, a lasting life,
> And found, that most in vaine haue sought,
> To haue a *Faire*, and *Constant* wife,
> Yet *Tarquyne* pluckt his glistering grape,
> And *Shake-speare*, paints poore Lucrece rape.

Richard Barnfield, in his *Poems in Divers Humors* (1598), praised the "hony-flowing Vaine" of Shakespeare's *Venus and Adonis* and *The Rape of Lucrece*. The poet Edmund Spenser may also have had Shakespeare's nondramatic poetry in mind when, in *Colin Clout's Come Home Again* (in a passage probably composed in 1594–1595) he listed twelve contemporary poets, most of them by fictional names, and included that of Aetion, "though last not least." Aetion has been identified by many scholars as Shakespeare, though other candidates have been proposed as well. Spenser wrote of Aetion:

> A gentler shepheard may no where be found:
> Whose *Muse* full of high thoughts inuention,
> Doth like himselfe Heroically sound.

Despite the common assumption that the writing of narrative and lyrical poems was more of a true literary achievement than the writing of dramas for the popular stage, however, Shakespeare's plays were highly regarded by his contemporaries. Francis Meres insisted, in 1598, that Shakespeare deserved to be compared not only with Ovid for his verse, but with Plautus and Seneca for his comedies and tragedies:

> As the soule of *Euphorbus* was thought to liue in *Pythagoras:* so the sweete wittie soule of *Ouid* liues in mellifluous & hony-tongued *Shakespeare*, witnes his *Venus* and *Adonis*, his *Lucrece*, his sugred Sonnets among his priuate friends, &c.
>
> As *Plautus* and *Seneca* are accounted the best for Comedy and Tragedy among the Latines: so *Shakespeare* among the English is the most excellent in both kinds for the stage; for Comedy, witnes his *Gentlemen of Verona*, his *Errors*, his *Loue labors lost*, his *Loue labours wonne*, his *Midsummers night dreame*, & his *Merchant of Venice:* for Tragedy his *Richard the* 2. *Richard the 3. Henry the* 4. *King Iohn*, *Titus Andronicus* and his *Romeo* and *Juliet*.

Comedy and tragedy were, after all, literary forms sanctioned by classical precept. By calling Shakespeare's English history plays "tragedies," Meres endowed them with the respectability of an ancient literary tradition.

John Weever too, in his epigram *Ad Gulielmum Shakespeare* in *Epigrammes in the oldest Cut, and newest Fashion* (1599), mentioned not only the ever-popular narrative poems but also *Romeo and Juliet* and a history play about one of the Richards:

> Honie-tong'd *Shakespeare* when I saw thine issue
> I swore *Apollo* got them and none other,
> Their rosie-tainted features cloth'd in tissue,
> Some heauen born goddesse said to be their mother:
> Rose-checkt *Adonis* with his amber tresses,
> Faire fire-hot *Venus* charming him to loue her,
> Chaste *Lucretia* virgine-like her dresses,
> Prowd lust-stung *Tarquine* seeking still to proue her:
> *Romea Richard;* more whose names I know not,
> Their sugred tongues, and power attractiue beuty
> Say they are Saints, althogh that Sts they shew not
> For thousands vowes to them subiectiue dutie:
> They burn in loue thy children *Shakespear* het them,
> Go, wo thy Muse more Nymphish brood beget them.

Even Gabriel Harvey, an esteemed classical scholar and friend of Edmund Spenser, considered Shakespeare's play of *Hamlet* to be worthy of no less praise than the best of the Ovidian poems. Harvey's comments are to be found in a marginal note to a copy of Speght's *Chaucer*, written down some time between 1598 and 1601:

> The younger sort takes much delight in Shakespeares Venus, & Adonis: but his Lucrece, & his tragedie of

Hamlet, Prince of Denmarke, haue it in them, to please the wiser sort.

Not surprisingly, the name of Falstaff became a by-word almost as soon as he made his appearance on the English stage. The references were not always friendly. A play written to be performed by the rival Admiral's company in answer to *1 Henry IV*, called *Sir John Oldcastle* (1599), took Falstaff to task for being a "pamper'd glutton" and an "aged Counsellor to youthfull sinne." Evidently the authors of this attack were offended by the fact that Falstaff had been named "Oldcastle" in an early version of *1 Henry IV*, thereby dishonoring the name of one whom many Puritans regarded as a martyr to their cause (see Play Introduction). Generally, however, the references during this period to Falstaff and his cronies were fond. In a letter to a friend in London, for example, Sir Charles Percy fretted jocosely that his prolonged stay in the country among his rustic neighbors might cause him to "be taken for Justice Silence or Justice Shallow" (1600). In another letter, from the Countess of Southampton to her husband (written seemingly in 1599), Falstaff's name has become so familiar that it is used apparently as a privately understood substitute for the name of some real person in an item of court gossip:

Al the nues I can send you that I thinke wil make you mery is that I reade in a letter from London that Sir John Falstaf is by his M[rs] Dame Pintpot made father of a godly milers [miller's] thum, a boye thats all heade and veri litel body; but this is a secrit.

The Parnassus Trilogy

Shakespeare's immense popularity as a dramatist did not please everyone. One interesting example of a hostile reaction comes from the so-called *Parnassus* trilogy (1598–1603). The three plays in this series consist of *The Pilgrimage to Parnassus* and *The Return from Parnassus* in two parts, all acted by the students of St. John's College, Cambridge. The third play was published in 1606, the other two not until recently.

These *Parnassus* plays take a mordantly satirical view of English life around 1600, from the point of view of university graduates attempting to find gainful employment. The graduates discover to their vocal dismay that they must seek the patronage of fashion-mongering courtiers, complacent justices of the peace, professional acting companies who offer them pitifully small wages, and the like. One especially foolish patron, to whom the witty Ingenioso applies for a position, is a poetaster named Gullio. This courtly fop aspires to be a fashionable poet himself, and agrees to hire Ingenioso if the latter will help him with his verse-writing. In fact, however, as Ingenioso scornfully observes in a series of asides, Gullio's verses are "nothinge but pure Shakespeare and shreds of poetrie that he hath gathered at the theators." Most of all, Gullio loves to plagiarize from *Venus and Adonis* and *Romeo and Juliet*. With unparalleled presumption, he actually requests Ingenioso to compose poems "in two or three divers vayns, in Chaucer's, Gower's and Spencer's and Mr. Shakespeare's," which Gullio will then pass off as his own inspiration. When Ingenioso does so extempore, producing among other things a fine parody of *Venus and Adonis*, Gullio is as delighted as a child. Although he admires Spenser, Chaucer, and Gower, Gullio confesses that Shakespeare is his favorite; he longs to hang Shakespeare's portrait "in my study at the courte," and vows he will sleep with *Venus and Adonis* under his pillow (*The Return from Parnassus*, Part I, 1009–1217).

Elsewhere in the same play (ll. 1875–1880), some university graduates trying out as actors in Shakespeare's company are requested to recite a few famous lines from the beginning of *Richard III*—lines that in the satirical context of this play sound both stereotyped and bombastic. From such passages in the *Parnassus* plays, we can see that Shakespeare had become not only famous but notorious among some Cambridge intellectuals. The dramatist of the *Parnassus* series treats Shakespeare satirically, and regards those who worship him as lowbrows. Still, Shakespeare's immense popularity is undeniable.

Shakespeare's Career and Private Life

During the years from 1594 to 1601, Shakespeare seems to have prospered as an actor and writer for the Lord Chamberlain's men. Whether he had previously belonged to Lord Strange's company or to the Earl of Pembroke's company, or possibly to some other group, is uncertain; but we know that he took part in 1594 in the general reorganization of the companies out of which emerged the Lord Chamberlain's company. In 1595 his name appeared for the first time in the accounts of the Treasurer of the Royal Chamber, as a member of the Chamberlain's company of players who had presented two comedies before Queen Elizabeth at Greenwich in the Christmas season of 1594. This company usually performed at the Theatre, northeast of London, from 1594 until 1599, when they moved to the Globe theatre south of the Thames. They seem to have been the victors in the intense economic rivalry between themselves and the Lord Admiral's company at the Rose theatre under Philip Henslowe's management. Fortunately for all the adult companies, the boys' private theatrical companies were shut down during most of the 1590's. Shakespeare's company enjoyed a phenomenal success, and in short time became the most successful theatrical organization in England.

The nucleus of the Chamberlain's company in 1594 was the family of Burbage. James Burbage, the father, was owner of the Theatre, Cuthbert Burbage was a manager, and Richard Burbage became the principal actor of the troupe. Together the Burbages owned five "shares" in the company, entitling them to half the profits. Shakespeare and four other principal actors—John Heminges, Thomas Pope, Augustine Phillips, and Will Kempe—owned one share each. Not only was Shakespeare a full sharing actor, but he was also the principal playwright of the company. He was named as a chief actor in the 1616 edition of Ben Jonson's *Every Man in His Humour*, performed by the Chamberlain's company in 1598. Later tradition reports, with questionable reliability, that Shakespeare specialized in "kingly parts" or in the roles of older men, such as Adam in *As You Like It* and the Ghost in *Hamlet*. Shakespeare was more celebrated as a playwright than as an actor, and his acting responsibilities may well have diminished as his writing reputation grew. The last occasion on which he is known to have acted was in Jonson's *Sejanus* in 1603.

His prosperity appears in the first record of his residence in London. The tax returns, or Subsidy Rolls, of a parliamentary subsidy granted to Queen Elizabeth for the year 1596, show Shakespeare resident in the parish of St. Helen's, Bishopsgate, near the Theatre, and assessed at the respectable sum of £5. By the next year Shakespeare had evidently moved to Southwark near the Bear Garden, for the returns from Bishopsgate show his taxes delinquent. He was later located and the taxes paid.

In 1596 Shakespeare suffered a serious personal loss: the death of his only son Hamnet, at the age of eleven. Hamnet was buried at Stratford in August. Except for this misfortune, however, Shakespeare continued to prosper. In the following year he purchased New Place in Stratford, a house of importance and one of the two largest in the town. Shakespeare's family entered the house as residents shortly after the purchase and continued there until long after Shakespeare's death. The last of his family, his granddaughter, Lady Bernard, died in 1670, and New Place was sold.

Shakespeare was also interested in the purchase of land at Shottery in 1598. He was listed among the chief holders of corn and malt in Stratford that same year, and sold a load of stone to the Stratford corporation in 1599.

No less suggestive of Shakespeare's rapid rise in the world is his acquisition of the right to bear arms, or, in other words, his establishment in the rank and title of gentleman. The Herald's College in London preserves two drafts of a grant of arms to Shakespeare's father devised by one William Dethick and dated October 20, 1596. Although we may certainly believe that the application was put forward by William Shakespeare, John Shakespeare was still living, and the grant was drawn up in the father's name. The device for Shakespeare's coat-of-arms makes a somewhat easy use of the meaning of his name:

> Gould, on a Bend Sables, a Speare of the first steeled argent. And for his creast or cognizaunce a falcon his winges displayed Argent standing on a wrethe of his coullers: supporting a Speare Gould steeled as aforesaid sett vppon a helmett with mantelles & tasselles as hath ben accustomed and doth more playnely appeare depicted on this margent.

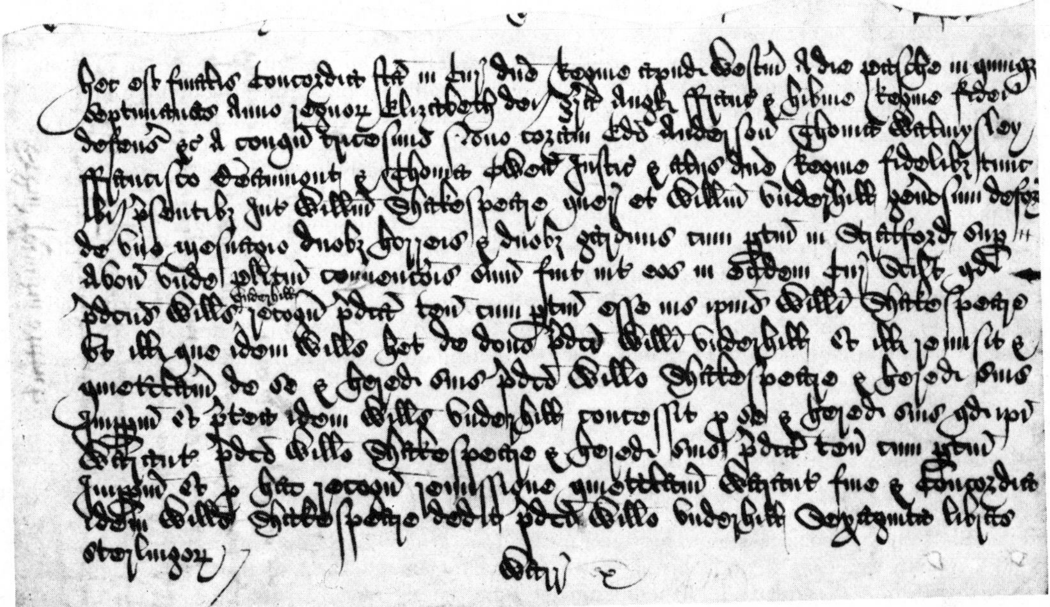

The lower part of the record of Shakespeare's purchase of New Place in 1597 for sixty pounds—a very reasonable sum for a dwelling with a sixty-foot frontage and ten fireplaces.

THE FOLGER SHAKESPEARE LIBRARY

A rough sketch (c. 1602) of the coat of arms granted to "Shakespeare the player" in 1596 by William Dethick, Garter King of Arms.

According to one of the documents in the grant, John Shakespeare, at the height of his prosperity as a Stratford burgher, had applied twenty years before to the Herald's College for authority to bear arms. The family may not have been able to meet the expense of seeing the application through, however, until William Shakespeare had made his fortune. The grant of heraldic honors to John Shakespeare was confirmed in 1599.

A lawsuit during this period gives us a rather baffling glimpse into Shakespeare's life in the theatre. From a writ discovered by Leslie Hotson (*Shakespeare Versus Shallow*, 1931) in the records of the Court of the Queen's Bench, Michaelmas term 1596, we learn that a person named William Wayte sought "for fear of death" to have William Shakespeare, Francis Langley, and two unknown women bound over to keep the peace. Earlier in the same term, moreover, Francis Langley had sworn out a similar writ against this same William Wayte and his stepfather William Gardiner, a justice of the peace in Surrey. Langley was owner of the Swan theatre on the bankside, near the later-built Globe. His quarrel with Gardiner and Wayte appears to have jeopardized all the acting companies who performed plays south of the Thames, for William Gardiner's jurisdiction included the Bankside theatre district. Gardiner and Wayte vengefully tried to drive the theatres out of the area.

We do not know why Shakespeare is named in Wayte's writ; conceivably his company was acting at the Swan in 1596. At any rate, Leslie Hotson has argued that Shakespeare took occasion to punish Gardiner and Wayte by satirizing them in his plays. According to this theory, the greedy and meddlesome Justice Shallow of *2 Henry IV* and *The Merry Wives of Windsor* represents Gardiner, whereas Shallow's dim-witted cousin Slender in *The Merry Wives* represents Wayte. The joke about the "white luces" in Shallow's coat of arms (*Merry Wives*, I,i) is a dig not at Sir Thomas Lucy of Stratford, argues Hotson, but at Justice Gardiner who did in fact wear three white luces in his coat of arms by right of his wife (*née* Lucy). This theory has not won universal acceptance, however, in part because it requires such an early date for *The Merry Wives*.

During this period Shakespeare's plays began to appear occasionally in print, attesting to his popularity as a dramatist. His name was becoming such a drawing card that it appeared on the title pages of the second and third quartos of *Richard II* (1598), the second quarto of *Richard III* (1598), *Love's Labour's Lost* (1598), and the second quarto of *1 Henry IV* (1599).

In 1599 the printer William Jaggard sought to capitalize unscrupulously on Shakespeare's growing reputation by bringing out a slender volume of twenty or twenty-one poems called *The Passionate Pilgrim*, attributed to Shakespeare. In fact, only five of the poems were assuredly his, and none of them was newly composed for the occasion. Three came from *Love's Labour's Lost* (published 1598) and two from Shakespeare's as yet unpublished sonnet sequence. (See Introduction to "The Minor Poems" for further details.)

Contemporary Drama

Shakespeare was without doubt the leading dramatist of the period from 1595 to 1601, not only in our view but in that of his contemporaries. The earlier group of dramatists from whom he had learned so much—Lyly, Greene, Marlowe, Peele, Kyd, Nashe—were either dead or no longer writing plays. The group of dramatists who were to rival him in the 1600's, and eventually surpass him in contemporary popularity, had not yet become well known.

Ben Jonson's early career is obscure. He may have written an early version of his *A Tale of a Tub* in 1596 and *The Case Is Altered* in 1597, though both were later revised. Unquestionably his first major play was *Every Man in His Humour* (1598), in which Shakespeare acted. This comedy did much to establish the new vogue of comedy of humours, a realistic and satirical kind of drama featuring "humours" characters whose personalities are dominated by some exaggerated trait. We are invited to laugh at the country simpleton, the jealous husband, the overly careful father, the cowardly braggart soldier, the poetaster, and the like. Shakespeare responded to the vogue of humours comedy in his *Henry IV* plays and *The Merry Wives*. Jonson followed his great success with *Every Man Out of His Humour* (1599), an even more biting vision of human folly. George Chapman also deserves important credit for the establishment of humours comedy, with his *The Blind Beggar of Alexandria* (1596) and *An Humorous Day's Mirth* (1597).

Despite the emergence of humours comedy, however, with its important anticipations of Jacobean and even Restoration comedy of manners, the prevailing comedy to be seen on the London stage between 1595 and 1601 was romantic comedy. William Haughton wrote *Englishmen for My Money* in 1598. Thomas Dekker's *Old Fortunatus*, the dramatization of a German folk tale, appeared in 1599. Dekker's *Shoemakers' Holiday* (1599), despite its seemingly realistic touches of life among the apprentices of London, is a thoroughly romanticized saga of rags to riches. A young aristocrat disguises himself as a shoemaker to woo a mayor's daughter; love conquers social rank, and the king himself sentimentally blesses the union. Thomas Heywood wrote heroical romances and comedies perhaps including *Godfrey of Boulogne*, 1594), although most of his early works have disappeared. The boys' private theatres were closed during most of the 1590's, until 1598–1599, and thus could not perform the satirical comedies at which they were so adept.

Patriotic history drama also continued to flourish on the public stage during these years when Shakespeare wrote his best history plays. Heywood wrote the two parts of *Edward IV* between 1592 and 1599. The anonymous *Edward III* appeared in 1595 or earlier, written with such poetic force that it still is a serious contender to join the Shakespeare canon. *Sir Thomas More*, by Munday, Dekker, Chettle, and perhaps Heywood, was written some time in the later 1590's and very probably revised by Shakespeare himself. Chettle and Munday wrote a trilogy of plays about *Robert, Earl of Huntingdon*, or Robin Hood (1598–1599), on themes that remind us of Shakespeare's *As You Like It*. These plays were performed by the Admiral's men, who also produced the two parts of *Sir John Oldcastle* (1599–1600) by Drayton, Hathway, Munday and others, in rivalry with Shakespeare's *Henry IV* plays.

Shakespeare's Work

Shakespeare thus wrote his greatest history plays for an audience that knew the genre well. Through a fortunate historical coincidence, the history play had first become popular just at the start of Shakespeare's career, during the patriotic aftermath of the defeat of the Spanish Armada (1588). Shakespeare himself did much to establish the genre. He wrote first his tetralogy or four-play series dealing with the Lancastrian wars of the fifteenth century, and then went backwards in historical time to King John's reign and to the famous reigns of Henry IV and V. In this way he was able to end his second four-play series on a positive note, with the triumphant completion of the education of Prince Hal.

His romantic comedies were also written for audiences that knew what to expect from the genre. From the comedies of Greene, Peele, Munday, and the rest, as well as Shakespeare himself, Elizabethan audiences were thoroughly familiar with such conventions as fairy charms, improbable adventures in forests, heroines disguised as young men, shipwrecks, love overcoming differences in social rank, and the like. Yet the convention also demanded more than mere horseplay or foolish antics. Plays of this sort customarily affirmed "wholesome" moral values and appealed to generosity and decency. They were written, like the history plays, for a socially diversified and genuinely popular audience.

Several critical terms have been used to suggest the special quality of Shakespeare's comedies during this period of the later 1590's. "Romantic comedy" implies first of all a story in which the main action is about love, but it can also imply elements of the improbable and the miraculous. (The difference between the "romantic comedies" of the later 1590's and the "romances" of Shakespeare's last period, 1606–1613, is more one of degree than of kind.) "Philosophical comedy" emphasizes the moral and sometimes Christian idealism underlying many of these comedies of the 1590's: the quest for deep and honest understanding between men and women in *Much Ado about Nothing*, the awareness of an eternal and spiritual dimension to love in *The Merchant of Venice*, the theme of love as a mysterious force able to regenerate a corrupted social world from which it has been banished in *As You Like It*. "Love-game comedy" pays particular attention to the witty battle of the sexes we find in several of these plays. "Festive comedy" urges the celebratory nature of comedy, especially in *Twelfth Night* and the *Henry IV* plays, in which Saturnalian revelry must contend against grim and disapproving forces of sobriety. "Comedy of forgiveness," although applicable to only a limited number of plays of this period (especially *Much Ado*), stresses the unexpected second chance that the world of comedy extends to even the most undeserving of heroes.

COURTESY OF THE TRUSTEES, THE BRITISH MUSEUM

This recreation of what New Place purportedly looked like during Shakespeare's ownership suggests that it must have indeed been an imposing structure, even for prosperous Stratford.

THE MERCHANT OF VENICE

Although Shylock is the most prominent character in *The Merchant of Venice*, he takes part in neither the beginning nor the ending of the play. Nor is he the "merchant" of the title, but a moneylender whose usury is portrayed as the very opposite of true commerce. His revengeful struggle to obtain a pound of flesh from Antonio contrasts with the various romantic episodes woven together in this play: Bassanio's choosing of Portia by means of the caskets, Gratiano's wooing of Nerissa, Jessica's elopement with Lorenzo, Launcelot Gobbo's changing of masters, and the episode of the rings. In all these stories, friendship and love triumph over faithlessness and hatred. However much we may come to sympathize with Shylock's own misfortunes and question the motives of his enemies, Shylock remains essentially as the villain of a love-comedy. Structurally he is the "blocking" character or "heavy" character. His remorseless pursuit of Antonio darkens the mood of the play, so that it becomes tragicomic. His overthrow signals the providential triumph of love and friendship. Before we examine the undoubted ironies of his situation more closely, we need to establish the philosophical context of the love-comedy as a whole.

Like many of Shakespeare's philosophical and festive comedies, *The Merchant of Venice* presents two contrasting worlds, one idealized and the other more recognizably worldly. To an extent, these contrasting worlds can be identified with the locations of Belmont and Venice. Belmont, to which the various happy lovers and their friends eventually retire, is a place of magic and love. As its name implies it is on a mountain, reached by a journey across water. It is pure, serene, ethereal. As often happens in fairy stories, a princess dwells on this mountain who must be won by means of a riddling contest. We usually see Belmont at night. Music surrounds it, and women preside over it. Even its caskets, houses, and rings are essentially feminine symbols. Venice, on the other hand, is a place of bustle and economic competition, seen most characteristically in the heat of the day. It lies low and flat, at a point where rivers reach the sea. Men preside over its contentious marketplace and its haggling law courts. Actually, the apparent opposition of Venice and Belmont is not quite so clear-cut: Venice contains much compassionate friendship, whereas Belmont is subject to the arbitrary command of Portia's dead father. (Portia somewhat resembles Jessica in being "imprisoned" by her father's will.) Even though Portia descends to Venice in the angelic role of mercy-giver, she also remains very human: sharp-tongued and even venomous in caricaturing her unwelcome wooers, crafty in her legal maneuvering, saucily prankish in her torturing of Bassanio about the rings. Nevertheless the polarity of two contrasting localities and two groups of characters is vividly real in this play.

The play's opening scene, from which Shylock is excluded, sets forth the interrelated themes of friendship, romantic love, and risk or "hazard." The actual merchant of the title, Antonio, is the victim of a mysterious melancholy. He is wealthy enough and surrounded by friends, but something is missing from his life. He assures his solicitous companions that he has no financial worries, for he has been too careful to trust all his cargoes to one sea vessel. Antonio in fact has no idea why he is so sad. The question is haunting: what is the matter? Perhaps the answer is to be found in a paradox: those who strive to prosper in the world's terms are doomed to frustration, not because prosperity will necessarily elude them but because it will not satisfy the spirit. "You have too much respect upon the world," argues the carefree Gratiano. "They lose it that do buy it with much care." Portia and Jessica too are at first afflicted by a melancholy that stems from the incompleteness of living isolated lives, with insufficient opportunities for love and sacrifice. They must learn, as Antonio learns with the help of his dear friend Bassanio, to seek happiness by daring to risk everything for friendship. Antonio's risk is most extreme: only when he has thrown away concern for his very life can he discover what there is to live for.

At first, Bassanio's request for assistance seems just as materialistic as the worldliness from which Antonio suffers. Bassanio proposes to marry a rich young lady, Portia, in order to recoup his fortune lost through prodigality, and he needs money from Antonio so that he may woo Portia in proper fashion. She is "richly left," the heiress of a dead father, a golden fleece for whom this new Jason will make a "quest." Bassanio's adventure is partly commercial. Yet his "pilgrimage" for Portia is magnanimous as well. The modern tendency to play Bassanio and Portia as cynical antiheroes of a "black" comedy is one-sided, and it inevitably distorts the play. Bassanio has lost his previous fortune through the amiable faults of reckless generosity and a lack of concern for financial prudence. The money he must now borrow, and the fortune he hopes to acquire, are to him no more than a means to carefree happiness. Although Portia's rich dowry is a strong consideration, he describes her also as "fair, and fairer than that word, Of wondrous virtues." Moreover, he enjoys the element of risk in wooing her. It is like shooting a second arrow in order to recover one that has been lost—double or nothing. This gamble, or "hazard," involves risk for Antonio as well as for Bassanio, and ultimately brings a double reward to them both, spiritual as well as financial. Unless one recognizes these aspects of Bassanio's quest, as well as the clear "fairy-tale" quality with which Shakespeare deliberately invests this part of the plot, one cannot properly assess Bassanio's role in this romantic comedy.

Bassanio's quest for Portia can in fact never succeed until he disavows the very financial considerations which brought him to Belmont in the first place. This is the lesson of the riddle of the three caskets, an ancient parable stressing the need for choosing by true substance rather than by outward show. To choose "what many men desire," as the Prince of Morocco does, is to pin one's hopes on worldly wealth; to believe that one "deserves" good fortune, as the Prince of Arragon does, is to reveal a fatal pride in one's own merit. Bassanio knows that in order to win true love he must "give and hazard all he hath." He is not "deceiv'd with ornament." Just as Antonio must risk all for friendship, and just as Bassanio himself must later be willing to risk losing Portia for the higher cause of true friendship (in the episode of the rings), Bassanio must now renounce worldly ambition and beauty before he can be rewarded with success. Paradoxically, only those who learn to subdue such worldly desires may then legitimately enjoy the world's pleasure. Only they have acknowledged the hierarchical subservience of the flesh to the spirit. These are the philosophical truisms of Renaissance neo-Platonism, depicting love as a chain or ladder from the basest carnality to the supreme love of God for man. On this ladder, perfect friendship and spiritual union are more sublimely Godlike than sexual fulfillment. This idealism may seem a strange doctrine for Bassanio the fortune-hunter, but actually its conventional wisdom simply confirms his role as romantic hero. He and Portia are not denied worldly happiness or erotic pleasure; they are merely asked to give first thought to their Christian duty in marriage. The essentially Christian paradox of losing the world in order to gain the world lies at the center of their love relationship. This paradox illuminates not only the casket episode but the struggle for the pound of flesh, the elopement of Jessica, the ring episode, and even the comic foolery of Launcelot Gobbo.

Shylock, in his quest for the pound of flesh, represents a denial of all the paradoxical Christian truths just described. As a usurer he refuses to lend money interest free in the name of friendship. Instead of taking risks, he insists on his bond. He spurns mercy and demands strict justice. By calculating all his chances too craftily, he appears to win at first but must eventually lose all. He has "too much respect upon the world." His God is the Old-Testament God of Moses, the God of wrath, the God of the Ten Commandments with their forbidding emphasis on "Thou shalt not." (This oversimplified contrast between Judaism and Christianity was commonplace in Shakespeare's time.) Shylock abhors stealing but admires equivocation as a means of outmaneuvering a competitor; he cites approvingly Jacob's ruse to deprive Laban of his sheep (I,iii). Any tactic is permissible so long as it falls within the realm of legality and contract.

Shylock's ethical outlook, then, justifies both usury and the old dispensation of the Jewish law. The two are philosophically combined, just as usury and Judaism had become equated in the popular imagination of Renaissance Europe. Even though lending at interest was becoming increasingly necessary and common, old phobias against it still persisted. Angry moralists pointed out that the New Testament had condemned usury and that Aristotle had described money as barren. To breed money was therefore regarded as unnatural. Usury was sinful because, unlike commerce, it involved no risk; the usurer seemed to be getting something for nothing. Partly because usury was at times illegal, its practitioners were often corrupt and grasping, hated as misers. In some European countries, Jews were permitted to practice this un-Christian living (and permitted to do very little else) and then were hypocritically detested for performing un-Christian deeds. Ironically, however, very few Jewish moneylenders were to be found in England. Nominally excluded since Edward I's reign, the Jews had returned in small numbers to London but did not practice their Judaism openly. They attended Anglican services as required by law and then worshiped in private, relatively undisturbed by the authorities. They followed ordinary trades and professions rather than usury. Shylock is not based on observation from London life. He is derived from continental tradition, and reflects a widespread conviction that Jews and usurers were alike in being non-Christian and sinister.

Shylock is unquestionably sinister. On the Elizabethan stage he apparently wore a red beard like Judas, and a hooked nose. He bears an "ancient grudge" against Antonio simply because Antonio is "a Christian." We recognize in Shylock the archetype of the Jew who wishes to kill a Christian and obtain his flesh. In early medieval anti-Semitic legends of this sort, the flesh thus obtained was imagined to be eaten ritually during Passover. The Jews who had once persecuted Christ were presumed to be implacable enemies of all Christians. These anti-Semitic superstitions were likely to erupt into hysteria at any time, as in 1594 when Dr. Roderigo Lopez, a Portuguese Jewish physician, was accused of having plotted against the life of Queen Elizabeth and of Don Antonio, pretender to the Portuguese throne. Marlowe's *The Jew of Malta* was revived for this occasion, enjoying an unusually successful run of fifteen performances, and scholars have often wondered if Shakespeare's play was not written under the same impetus. On this score the evidence is inconclusive, and the play might have been written any time between 1594 and 1598 (when it is mentioned by Francis Meres), but in any case Shakespeare has made no attempt to avoid the anti-Semitic nature of his story.

To offset the portrayal of Jewish villainy, however, the play also dramatizes the possibility of conversion to Christianity, suggesting that Judaism is more a matter of benighted faith than of ethnic origin. Converted Jews were not new on the stage: they had appeared in medieval cycle drama, in the Croxton *Play of the Sacrament* (late fifteenth century), and more recently in *The Jew of Malta*, in which Barabas' daughter Abigail falls in love with a Christian and eventually becomes a nun. Shylock's daughter Jessica similarly embraces Christianity as Lorenzo's wife and is received into the happy comradeship of Belmont. Shylock is forced to accept Christianity, presumably for the benefit of his eternal soul. Earlier in the play, Antonio repeatedly indicates his willingness to befriend Shylock if the latter will only give up usury, and is even cautiously hopeful when Shylock offers him an interest-free loan: "The Hebrew will turn Christian; he grows kind" (I,iii). True Christianity is a state of faith, not an accident of birth. By the same token, the Prince of Morocco is condemned to failure in his quest for Portia not so much because he is black as because he is an infidel, one who worships "blind fortune" and therefore chooses a worldly rather than a spiritual reward. Although Portia pertly dismisses him with "Let all of his complexion choose me so" (II,vii), she professes earlier to find him handsome and agrees that he should not be judged by his complexion (II,i). Unless she is merely being hypocritical, she means by her later remark that black-skinned men are generally infidels, just as Jews are as a group non-Christian. She rejects the Prince of Arragon because he too lacks proper faith, though nominally a Christian. All men, therefore, may aspire to truly virtuous conduct, and those who choose virtue are equally blessed; but the terms of defining that ideal are essentially Christian. Jews and blacks may rise spiritually only by abandoning their pagan creeds for the new dispensation of charity and forgiveness.

The superiority of Christian teaching to the older Jewish dispensation is a basic assumption in this play, reflecting a universally accepted notion of Shakespeare's time. After all, these were the years when men fought and died to maintain their religious beliefs. Today we find the notion of a single true church intolerant, and we have difficulty understanding why anyone would wish to force conversion on Shylock. Modern productions find it tempting to portray Shylock as a victim of bigotry, and to put great stress on his heartrending assertions of his humanity: "Hath not a Jew eyes? . . . If you prick us, do we not bleed?" Shylock does indeed suffer from his enemies, and his sufferings add a tortured complexity to this play—even, one suspects, for an Elizabethan audience. Those who profess Christianity must surely examine their own motives and conduct. Is it fair to steal treasure from Shylock's house along with his eloped daughter? Is it thoughtful of Jessica and Lorenzo to squander Shylock's turquoise ring, the gift of his wife Leah, on a monkey? Does Shylock's vengeful insistence on law justify the quibbling countermeasures devised by Portia even as she piously declaims about mercy? Do Shylock's misfortunes deserve the mirthful parodies of Solanio ("My daughter! O my ducats!") or the hostile jeering of Gratiano at the conclusion of the trial? Because he stands outside Christian faith, Shylock can serve as a perspective whereby we see the hypocrisies of those who profess a higher ethical code. Nevertheless, Shylock's compulsive desire for vengeance according to an Old Testament code of an eye for an eye cannot be justified by the wrongdoings of any particular Christian. Such deeds condemn the doer rather than undermine the Christian standards of true virtue upon which the play is based. Shakespeare humanizes Shylock by portraying him as a believable and sensitive man, but still puts Shylock fatally in the wrong by his refusal to forgive his enemies.

Shylock thus loses everything through his effort to win everything on his own terms. His daughter Jessica, by her elopement, follows an opposite course. She characterizes her father's home as "hell," and she resents being locked up behind closed windows. Shylock detests music and the sounds of merriment; Jessica's new life in Belmont is immersed in music. He is old, suspicious, miserly; she is young, loving, adventurous. Most important, she seems to be at least part Christian when we first see her. As Launcelot jests half in earnest, "if a Christian did not play the knave and get thee, I am much deceived." Her removal from Shylock's house is avowedly a theft, and her running from Venice is, she confesses, an "unthrift love." Paradoxically, however, this recklessness is of more blessed effect than her father's legalistic caution. As she says, "I shall be saved by my husband. He hath made me a Christian."

Launcelot Gobbo's clowning offers a similarly paradoxical comment on the tragedy of Shylock. Launcelot debates whether or not to leave Shylock's service in terms of a soul-struggle between his conscience and the devil (II,ii). Conscience bids him stay, for service is a debt, a bond, an obligation, whereas abandonment of one's indenture is a kind of rebellion or stealing away. Yet Shylock's house is "hell" to Launcelot as to Jessica. Comparing his new master with his old, Launcelot observes to Bassanio, "You have the grace of God, sir, and he hath enough." Service with Bassanio involves imprudent risks, since Bassanio is a spendthrift. The miserly Shylock rejoices to see the ever hungry Launcelot, this "huge feeder," wasting the substance of a hated Christian. Once again, however, Shylock will lose everything in his grasping quest for security. Another spiritual renewal occurs when Launcelot encounters his old and nearly blind father (II,ii). In a scene echoing the biblical stories of the Prodigal Son and of Jacob and Esau, Launcelot teases the old man with false rumors of Launcelot's own death in order to make their reunion seem all the more unexpected and precious. The illusion of tragedy gives way to joy: Launcelot is, in language adapted from the liturgy, "your boy that was, your son that is, your child that shall be."

In the episode of the rings we encounter a final playful variation on the paradox of winning through losing. Portia and Nerissa cleverly present their new husbands with a cruel choice: disguised as a doctor of law and his clerk, who have just saved the life of

Antonio from Shylock's wrath, the two wives ask nothing more for their services than the rings they see on the fingers of Bassanio and Gratiano. The two husbands, who have vowed never to part with these wedding rings, must therefore choose between love and friendship. The superior claim of friendship is clear, no matter what the cost, and Portia knows well enough that Bassanio's obedience to this neo-Platonic ideal is an essential part of his virtue. Just as he previously renounced beauty and riches before he could deserve Portia, he must now risk losing her for friendship's sake. The testing of the husbands' constancy poses no real threat to romantic happiness, for we know that the wives' little joke is farcically based on mistaken identity. The young men have accordingly been tricked into bestowing their rings on their wives for a second time in the name of perfect friendship, thereby confirming a relationship that is both Platonic and fleshly. As Gratiano bawdily points out in the play's last line, the ring is both a spiritual and a sexual symbol of marriage. The resolution of this illusory quarrel also brings to an end the merry battle of the sexes between wives and husbands. Having hinted at the sorts of misunderstandings that afflict even the best of human relationships, and having proved themselves wittily able to torture and deceive their husbands, Portia and Nerissa happily submit themselves to the authority of Bassanio and Gratiano.

All is harmony in Belmont. The disorders of Venice have been left far behind, however imperfectly they may have been resolved. Jessica and Lorenzo contrast their present happiness with the sufferings of less fortunate lovers of long ago: Troilus and Cressida, Pyramus and Thisbe, Aeneas and Dido, Jason and Medea. The tranquil joy found in Belmont is attuned to the music of the spheres, the singing of the "young-ey'd cherubin," although with a proper Christian humility the lovers also realize that the harmony of immortal souls is infinitely beyond their comprehension. Bound in by the grossness of the flesh, "this muddy vesture of decay," they can only reach toward the bliss of eternity through music and the perfect friendship of true love. Even in their final joy, accordingly, the lovers find an incompleteness that lends a wistful and slightly melancholy reflective tone to the play's ending; but this Christian sense of the unavoidable incompleteness of all human life is of a very different order from that earlier melancholy of isolation and lack of commitment experienced by Portia, Jessica, Antonio, and others.

The thematic linking of the numerous episodes of this play is perhaps Shakespeare's most important contribution to his sources. To be sure, in Ser Giovanni Fiorentino's *Il Pecorone* (written c. 1378, published in Italian in 1558), Shakespeare did find three plot lines already combined: Gianotto's wooing of the lady of Belmonte, the pawning of a pound of flesh to a Jewish moneylender by a Venetian merchant who is subsequently rescued by the lady disguised as a lawyer, and the exchanging of the rings. Nevertheless, Shakespeare's changes are extensive. In Fiorentino's *novella* the Jew is an underdeveloped character who makes no attempt to pass off his "merry bond" as a jest. The ring story is a comic afterthought. Most significantly, the casket-choosing story is missing. The mercenary lady of Belmonte has devised her own scheme for confiscating the fortunes of her hapless suitors: after setting them the task of staying awake all night to win her, she drugs them asleep and then confiscates all their worldly wealth as the penalty for failure. Shakespeare retains the folk-tale element of a contest, but substitutes a choice among three caskets. (See Appendix II on sources for numerous earlier instances of this ancient and widespread motif.) The plot of Jessica's elopement recalls not only Marlowe's *The Jew of Malta* but also Massucio of Salerno's *Novellino* and Anthony Munday's *Zelauto*. No source has been found for Launcelot Gobbo, but he contributes to a central thematic purpose as does every element of this masterfully constructed play.

THE MERCHANT OF VENICE

[*Dramatis Personae*

THE DUKE OF VENICE.
THE PRINCE OF MOROCCO, } *suitors to Portia.*
THE PRINCE OF ARRAGON, }
ANTONIO, *a merchant of Venice.*
BASSANIO, *his friend, suitor likewise to Portia.*
SOLANIO, }
SALERIO, } *friends to Antonio and Bassanio.*
GRATIANO, }
LORENZO, *in love with Jessica.*
SHYLOCK, *a rich Jew.*
TUBAL, *a Jew, his friend.*
LAUNCELOT GOBBO, *the clown, servant to Shylock.*
OLD GOBBO, *father to Launcelot.*
LEONARDO, *servant to Bassanio.*
BALTHASAR, } *servants to Portia.*
STEPHANO, }

PORTIA, *a rich heiress.*
NERISSA, *her waiting-maid.*
JESSICA, *daughter to Shylock.*

Magnificoes of Venice, Officers of the Court of Justice, Gaoler, Servants to Portia, *and* other Attendants.

SCENE: *Partly at Venice, and partly at Belmont, the seat of Portia.*]

[ACT I.

SCENE I. *Venice. A street.*]

Enter ANTONIO, SALERIO, *and* SOLANIO.

Ant. In sooth, I know not why I am so sad:
It wearies me; you say it wearies you;
But how I caught it, found it, or came by it,
What stuff 'tis made of, whereof it is born,
I am to learn;
And such a want-wit sadness makes of me,
That I have much ado to know myself.
Saler. Your mind is tossing on the ocean;
There, where your argosies with portly sail,
Like signiors and rich burghers on the flood,
Or, as it were, the pageants of the sea,
Do overpeer the petty traffickers,
That curtsy to them, do them reverence,
As they fly by them with their woven wings.
Solan. Believe me, sir, had I such venture forth,
The better part of my affections would
Be with my hopes abroad. I should be still
Plucking the grass, to know where sits the wind,
Peering in maps for ports and piers and roads;
And every object that might make me fear
Misfortune to my ventures, out of doubt
Would make me sad.
Saler. My wind cooling my broth
Would blow me to an ague, when I thought
What harm a wind too great might do at sea.
I should not see the sandy hour-glass run,
But I should think of shallows and of flats,
And see my wealthy Andrew dock'd in sand,
Vailing her high-top lower than her ribs
To kiss her burial. Should I go to church
And see the holy edifice of stone,
And not bethink me straight of dangerous rocks,
Which touching but my gentle vessel's side,
Would scatter all her spices on the stream,
Enrobe the roaring waters with my silks,
And, in a word, but even now worth this,
And now worth nothing? Shall I have the thought
To think on this, and shall I lack the thought
That such a thing bechanc'd would make me sad?
But tell not me; I know, Antonio
Is sad to think upon his merchandise.
Ant. Believe me, no: I thank my fortune for it,
My ventures are not in one bottom trusted,
Nor to one place; nor is my whole estate
Upon the fortune of this present year:
Therefore my merchandise makes me not sad.
Solan. Why, then you are in love.
Ant. Fie, fie!
Solan. Not in love neither? Then let us say you are sad,
Because you are not merry: and 'twere as easy
For you to laugh and leap and say you are merry,
Because you are not sad. Now, by two-headed Janus,
Nature hath fram'd strange fellows in her time:
Some that will evermore peep through their eyes
And laugh like parrots at a bag-piper,
And other of such vinegar aspect
That they'll not show their teeth in way of smile,
Though Nestor swear the jest be laughable.

Enter BASSANIO, LORENZO, *and* GRATIANO.

Here comes Bassanio, your most noble kinsman,
Gratiano and Lorenzo. Fare ye well:
We leave you now with better company.
Saler. I would have stay'd till I had made you merry,
If worthier friends had not prevented me.
Ant. Your worth is very dear in my regard.
I take it, your own business calls on you
And you embrace th' occasion to depart.
Saler. Good morrow, my good lords.
Bass. Good signiors both, when shall we laugh? say, when?
You grow exceeding strange: must it be so?
Saler. We'll make our leisures to attend on yours.
Exeunt Salerio and Solanio.
Lor. My Lord Bassanio, since you have found Antonio,

ACT I. SCENE I. 5. **am to learn,** have yet to learn. 9. **argosies,** large merchant ships; word derived from Ragusa, an Italian seaport. **portly,** large and full. 12. **overpeer,** look down upon. 15. **venture forth,** investment risked. 26. **flats,** sandbanks. 27. **Andrew,** name of a ship. 28. **Vailing,** lowering. **high-top,** probably topsail. 35. **this,** probably expressed by a gesture. 42. **bottom,** ship. 50. **two-headed Janus.** Janus, Roman god of all beginnings, was represented by a figure with two faces, one smiling and one sad. 54. **aspect,** look; accented on second syllable. 56. **Nestor,** a character in the *Iliad,* noted for gravity. 61. **prevented,** forestalled. 64. **occasion,** opportunity. 67.

We two will leave you: but at dinner-time,
I pray you, have in mind where we must meet.
Bass. I will not fail you.
Gra. You look not well, Signior Antonio;
You have too much respect upon the world:
They lose it that do buy it with much care:
Believe me, you are marvellously chang'd.
Ant. I hold the world but as the world, Gratiano;
A stage where every man must play a part,
And mine a sad one.
Gra. Let me play the fool:
With mirth and laughter let old wrinkles come,
And let my liver rather heat with wine
Than my heart cool with mortifying groans.
Why should a man, whose blood is warm within,
Sit like his grandsire cut in alabaster?
Sleep when he wakes and creep into the jaundice
By being peevish? I tell thee what, Antonio—
I love thee, and 'tis my love that speaks—
There are a sort of men whose visages
Do cream and mantle like a standing pond,
And do a wilful stillness entertain,
With purpose to be dress'd in an opinion
Of wisdom, gravity, profound conceit,
As who should say 'I am Sir Oracle,
And when I ope my lips let no dog bark!'
O my Antonio, I do know of these
That therefore only are reputed wise
For saying nothing, when, I am very sure,
If they should speak, would almost damn those ears
Which, hearing them, would call their brothers fools.
I'll tell thee more of this another time:
But fish not, with this melancholy bait,
For this fool gudgeon, this opinion.
Come, good Lorenzo. Fare ye well awhile:
I'll end my exhortation after dinner.
Lor. Well, we will leave you then till dinner-time:
I must be one of these same dumb wise men,
For Gratiano never lets me speak.
Gra. Well, keep me company but two years moe,
Thou shalt not know the sound of thine own tongue.
Ant. Farewell: I'll grow a talker for this gear.
Gra. Thanks, i' faith, for silence is only commendable
In a neat's tongue dried and a maid not vendible.
Exeunt [Gratiano and Lorenzo].
Ant. Is that any thing now?
Bass. Gratiano speaks an infinite deal of nothing, more than any man in all Venice. His reasons are as two grains of wheat hid in two bushels of chaff: you shall seek all day ere you find them, and when you have them, they are not worth the search.
Ant. Well, tell me now what lady is the same
To whom you swore a secret pilgrimage,
That you to-day promis'd to tell me of?
Bass. 'Tis not unknown to you, Antonio,
How much I have disabled mine estate,
By something showing a more swelling port
Than my faint means would grant continuance:
Nor do I now make moan to be abridg'd
From such a noble rate; but my chief care
Is to come fairly off from the great debts
Wherein my time something too prodigal
Hath left me gag'd. To you, Antonio,
I owe the most, in money and in love,
And from your love I have a warranty
To unburden all my plots and purposes
How to get clear of all the debts I owe.
Ant. I pray you, good Bassanio, let me know it;
And if it stand, as you yourself still do,
Within the eye of honour, be assur'd,
My purse, my person, my extremest means,
Lie all unlock'd to your occasions.
Bass. In my school-days, when I had lost one shaft,
I shot his fellow of the self-same flight
The self-same way with more advised watch,
To find the other forth, and by adventuring both
I oft found both: I urge this childhood proof,
Because what follows is pure innocence.
I owe you much, and, like a wilful youth,
That which I owe is lost; but if you please
To shoot another arrow that self way
Which you did shoot the first, I do not doubt,
As I will watch the aim, or to find both
Or bring your latter hazard back again
And thankfully rest debtor for the first.
Ant. You know me well, and herein spend but time
To wind about my love with circumstance;
And out of doubt you do me now more wrong
In making question of my uttermost
Than if you had made waste of all I have:
Then do but say to me what I should do
That in your knowledge may by me be done,
And I am prest unto it: therefore, speak.
Bass. In Belmont is a lady richly left;
And she is fair and, fairer than that word,
Of wondrous virtues: sometimes from her eyes
I did receive fair speechless messages:
Her name is Portia, nothing undervalu'd
To Cato's daughter, Brutus' Portia:
Nor is the wide world ignorant of her worth,
For the four winds blow in from every coast
Renowned suitors, and her sunny locks
Hang on her temples like a golden fleece;
Which makes her seat of Belmont Colchos' strond,
And many Jasons come in quest of her.
O my Antonio, had I but the means
To hold a rival place with one of them,
I have a mind presages me such thrift,
That I should questionless be fortunate!
Ant. Thou know'st that all my fortunes are at sea;
Neither have I money nor commodity
To raise a present sum: therefore go forth;
Try what my credit can in Venice do:
That shall be rack'd, even to the uttermost,
To furnish thee to Belmont, to fair Portia.
Go, presently inquire, and so will I,
Where money is, and I no question make

strange, distant. **must it be so?** Must you go? or, must you show unfriendliness? 74. **have . . . upon,** pay too much attention to. 81. **heat with wine.** The liver was regarded as the seat of the passions and wine as an agency for inflaming them. 82. **mortifying,** deadly. 85. **jaundice,** regarded as arising from the effects of violent passions. 89. **mantle,** become covered with scum. 90. **wilful stillness,** obstinate silence. 92. **profound conceit,** deep thought. 99. **fools.** Cf. Matthew 5:22. 102. **gudgeon,** a fish used for bait. 112. **neat's.** *Neat* is defined as "cattle of the ox kind." 124. **port,** style of living; see glossary. 127. **rate,** style of living. 130. **gag'd,** pledged. 142. **advised,** considered. 143. **forth,** out. 145. **innocence,** ingenuousness, sincerity. 148. **self,** same. 150. **or,** either. 154. **wind about,** approach circuitously. 160. **prest,** ready. 161. **richly left,** left a large fortune (by her father's will). 165-166. **nothing undervalu'd To,** of no less worth than. 166. **Brutus' Portia,** a woman famous in ancient times for constancy and courage; she is a character in *Julius Caesar*. 168. **coast,** country. 172. **Jasons.** Jason adventured for the golden fleece in the land of Colchos, on the Black Sea. 175. **presages,** i.e., which presages; relative pronoun omitted. **thrift,** profit and good fortune.

To have it of my trust or for my sake. *Exeunt.*

[SCENE II. *Belmont. A room in* PORTIA'S *house.*]

Enter PORTIA *with her waiting woman,* NERISSA.

Por. By my troth, Nerissa, my little body is aweary of this great world.

Ner. You would be, sweet madam, if your miseries were in the same abundance as your good fortunes are: and yet, for aught I see, they are as sick that surfeit with too much as they that starve with nothing. It is no mean happiness therefore, to be seated in the mean: superfluity comes sooner by white hairs, but competency lives longer.

Por. Good sentences and well pronounced.

Ner. They would be better, if well followed.

Por. If to do were as easy as to know what were good to do, chapels had been churches and poor men's cottages princes' palaces. It is a good divine that follows his own instructions: I can easier teach twenty what were good to be done, than to be one of the twenty to follow mine own teaching. The brain may devise laws for the blood, but a hot temper leaps o'er a cold decree: such a hare is madness the youth, to skip o'er the meshes of good counsel the cripple. But this reasoning is not in the fashion to choose me a husband. O me, the word 'choose!' I may neither choose who I would nor refuse who I dislike; so is the will of a living daughter curbed by the will of a dead father. Is it not hard, Nerissa, that I cannot choose one nor refuse none?

Ner. Your father was ever virtuous; and holy men at their death have good inspirations: therefore the lottery, that he hath devised in these three chests of gold, silver and lead, whereof who chooses his meaning chooses you, will, no doubt, never be chosen by any rightly but one who you shall rightly love. But what warmth is there in your affection towards any of these princely suitors that are already come?

Por. I pray thee, over-name them; and as thou namest them, I will describe them; and, according to my description, level at my affection.

Ner. First, there is the Neapolitan prince.

Por. Ay, that 's a colt indeed, for he doth nothing but talk of his horse; and he makes it a great appropriation to his own good parts, that he can shoe him himself. I am much afeard my lady his mother played false with a smith.

Ner. Then there is the County Palatine.

Por. He doth nothing but frown, as who should say 'An you will not have me, choose:' he hears merry tales and smiles not: I fear he will prove the weeping philosopher when he grows old, being so full of unmannerly sadness in his youth. I had rather be married to a death's-head with a bone in his mouth than to either of these. God defend me from these two!

Ner. How say you by the French lord, Monsieur Le Bon?

Por. God made him, and therefore let him pass for a man. In truth, I know it is a sin to be a mocker: but, he! why, he hath a horse better than the Neapolitan's, a better bad habit of frowning than the Count Palatine; he is every man in no man; if a throstle sing, he falls straight a capering: he will fence with his own shadow: if I should marry him, I should marry twenty husbands. If he would despise me, I would forgive him, for if he love me to madness, I shall never requite him.

Ner. What say you, then, to Falconbridge, the young baron of England?

Por. You know I say nothing to him, for he understands not me, nor I him: he hath neither Latin, French, nor Italian, and you will come into the court and swear that I have a poor pennyworth in the English. He is a proper man's picture, but, alas, who can converse with a dumb-show? How oddly he is suited! I think he bought his doublet in Italy, his round hose in France, his bonnet in Germany and his behaviour every where.

Ner. What think you of the Scottish lord, his neighbour?

Por. That he hath a neighbourly charity in him, for he borrowed a box of the ear of the Englishman and swore he would pay him again when he was able: I think the Frenchman became his surety and sealed under for another.

Ner. How like you the young German, the Duke of Saxony's nephew?

Por. Very vilely in the morning, when he is sober, and most vilely in the afternoon, when he is drunk: when he is best, he is a little worse than a man, and when he is worst, he is little better than a beast: an the worst fall that ever fell, I hope I shall make shift to go without him.

Ner. If he should offer to choose, and choose the right casket, you should refuse to perform your father's will, if you should refuse to accept him.

Por. Therefore, for fear of the worst, I pray thee, set a deep glass of rhenish wine on the contrary casket, for if the devil be within and that temptation without, I know he will choose it. I will do any thing, Nerissa, ere I will be married to a sponge.

Ner. You need not fear, lady, the having any of these lords: they have acquainted me with their determinations; which is, indeed, to return to their home and to trouble you with no more suit, unless you may be won by some other sort than your father's imposition depending on the caskets.

Por. If I live to be as old as Sibylla, I will die as chaste as Diana, unless I be obtained by the manner of my father's will. I am glad this parcel of wooers are so reasonable, for there is not one among them but I dote on his very absence, and I pray God grant them a fair departure.

Ner. Do you not remember, lady, in your father's

SCENE II. 9. **comes sooner by,** acquires sooner. 11. **sentences,** maxims. 20. **blood,** thought of as a chief agent of the passions, which in turn were regarded as the enemies of reason; see glossary. 22. **meshes,** nets; allusion to hare hunting with nets. A *cripple* could not follow the hare if it skipped over the net. 23. **reasoning,** discourse, talk. 27, 28. **will, will,** volition, testament. 32. **lottery,** subject of *will*, line 35. 34. **his,** i.e., the father's. 44-48. **Ay . . . smith.** In Shakespeare's chief source, the lady of Belmont is even more unsentimental toward her wooers than is Portia. 49. **County,** count. 51. **An,** if. **choose,** possibly, "do as you please." 53. **weeping philosopher,** Heraclitus of Ephesus, who wept at everything. 65. **throstle,** thrush. 80. **suited,** dressed. **doublet,** an upper garment corresponding to a jacket. 81. **hose,** tight-fitting breeches. **bonnet,** hat. It was a common subject of censure in Elizabethan days that Englishmen rigged themselves out in foreign clothes. 83. **Scottish.** F has *other*, apparently substituted for *Scottish* to avoid offense to King James. 89. **became . . . another,** an allusion to the age-old alliance of the French and the Scots against the English. The Frenchman put his seal under the Scotsman's as his surety, promising to give the Englishman another box on the ear. 96. **fall,** befall. 114. **sort,** way, manner. **imposition,** time, a Venetian, a scholar and a soldier, that came hither in company of the Marquis of Montferrat?

Por. Yes, yes, it was Bassanio; as I think, so was he called.

Ner. True, madam: he, of all the men that ever my foolish eyes looked upon, was the best deserving a fair lady.

Por. I remember him well, and I remember him worthy of thy praise.

Enter a Servingman.

How now! what news?

Serv. The four strangers seek for you, madam, to take their leave: and there is a forerunner come from a fifth, the Prince of Morocco, who brings word the prince his master will be here to-night.

Por. If I could bid the fifth welcome with so good a heart as I can bid the other four farewell, I should be glad of his approach: if he have the condition of a saint and the complexion of a devil, I had rather he should shrive me than wive me.
Come, Nerissa. Sirrah, go before.
Whiles we shut the gates upon one wooer, another
knocks at the door. *Exeunt.*

[SCENE III. *Venice. A public place.*]

Enter BASSANIO *with* SHYLOCK *the Jew.*

Shy. Three thousand ducats; well.

Bass. Ay, sir, for three months.

Shy. For three months; well.

Bass. For the which, as I told you, Antonio shall be bound.

Shy. Antonio shall become bound; well.

Bass. May you stead me? will you pleasure me? shall I know your answer?

Shy. Three thousand ducats for three months and Antonio bound.

Bass. Your answer to that.

Shy. Antonio is a good man.

Bass. Have you heard any imputation to the contrary?

Shy. Oh, no, no, no, no: my meaning in saying he is a good man is to have you understand me that he is sufficient. Yet his means are in supposition: he hath an argosy bound to Tripolis, another to the Indies; I understand, moreover, upon the Rialto, he hath a third at Mexico, a fourth for England, and other ventures he hath, squandered abroad. But ships are but boards, sailors but men: there be land-rats and water-rats, water-thieves and land-thieves, I mean pirates, and then there is the peril of waters, winds and rocks. The man is, notwithstanding, sufficient. Three thousand ducats; I think I may take his bond.

Bass. Be assured you may.

Shy. I will be assured I may; and, that I may be assured, I will bethink me. May I speak with Antonio?

Bass. If it please you to dine with us.

Shy. Yes, to smell pork; to eat of the habitation which your prophet the Nazarite conjured the devil into. I will buy with you, sell with you, talk with you, walk with you, and so following, but I will not eat with you, drink with you, nor pray with you. What news on the Rialto? Who is he comes here?

Enter ANTONIO.

Bass. This is Signior Antonio.

Shy. [*Aside*] How like a fawning publican he looks!
I hate him for he is a Christian,
But more for that in low simplicity
He lends out money gratis and brings down
The rate of usance here with us in Venice.
If I can catch him once upon the hip,
I will feed fat the ancient grudge I bear him.
He hates our sacred nation, and he rails,
Even there where merchants most do congregate,
On me, my bargains and my well-won thrift,
Which he calls interest. Cursed be my tribe,
If I forgive him!

Bass. Shylock, do you hear?

Shy. I am debating of my present store,
And, by the near guess of my memory,
I cannot instantly raise up the gross
Of full three thousand ducats. What of that?
Tubal, a wealthy Hebrew of my tribe,
Will furnish me. But soft! how many months
Do you desire? [*To Ant.*] Rest you fair, good signior;
Your worship was the last man in our mouths.

Ant. Shylock, although I neither lend nor borrow
By taking nor by giving of excess,
Yet, to supply the ripe wants of my friend,
I'll break a custom. [To Bass.] Is he yet possess'd
How much ye would?

Shy. Ay, ay, three thousand ducats.

Ant. And for three months.

Shy. I had forgot; three months; you told me so.
Well then, your bond; and let me see; but hear you;
Methoughts you said you neither lend nor borrow
Upon advantage.

Ant. I do never use it.

Shy. When Jacob graz'd his uncle Laban's sheep—
This Jacob from our holy Abram was,
As his wise mother wrought in his behalf,
The third possessor; ay, he was the third—

Ant. And what of him? did he take interest?

Shy. No, not take interest, not, as you would say,
Directly int'rest: mark what Jacob did.
When Laban and himself were compromis'd
That all the eanlings which were streak'd and pied
Should fall as Jacob's hire, the ewes, being rank,
In end of autumn turned to the rams,
And, when the work of generation was
Between these woolly breeders in the act,
The skilful shepherd pill'd me certain wands
And, in the doing of the deed of kind,
He stuck them up before the fulsome ewes,

conditions imposed. 116. **Sibylla,** the Cumaean Sibyl, to whom Apollo gave as many years as there were grains in her handful of sand. 119. **parcel,** party. 135. **four.** Nerissa actually names six suitors. This may be a sign of revision; Shakespeare may have added two suitors and neglected to change "four" to "six." 145. **shrive me,** act as my confessor. 146. **Sirrah,** addressed to the servingman.

SCENE III. 1. **ducats,** gold coins. The total is worth about $2000. **well,** possibly interrogative. 7. **stead,** help, supply a need. 12. **good.** Shylock means "solvent," a good credit risk; Bassanio interprets in the moral sense. 17. **in supposition,** doubtful, uncertain. 19. **Rialto,** the merchants' exchange in Venice and center of commercial activity. 29, 30. **assured, assured.** Bassanio means that Shylock may trust Antonio, whereas Shylock means that he will provide legal assurances. 35. **Nazarite,** Nazarene; cf. Luke 7:32-33. 42. **publican,** Roman tax-gatherer, a term of opprobrium; or, innkeeper. 46. **usance,** usury, interest. 47. **catch . . . hip,** figure of speech from wrestling. 65. **possess'd,** informed. 75. **possessor,** i.e., of God's promise. 79. **compromis'd,** agreed; cf. Genesis 30:35. 80. **eanlings,** young lambs or kids. **pied,** spotted. 81. **rank,** in heat; see glossary. 85. **pill'd,** stripped, peeled.

Who then conceiving did in eaning time
Fall parti-colour'd lambs, and those were Jacob's.
This was a way to thrive, and he was blest:
And thrift is blessing, if men steal it not.
Ant. This was a venture, sir, that Jacob serv'd for;
A thing not in his power to bring to pass,
But sway'd and fashion'd by the hand of heaven.
Was this inserted to make interest good?
Or is your gold and silver ewes and rams?
Shy. I cannot tell; I make it breed as fast:
But note me, signior.
Ant. Mark you this, Bassanio,
The devil can cite Scripture for his purpose.
An evil soul producing holy witness
Is like a villain with a smiling cheek,
A goodly apple rotten at the heart:
O, what a goodly outside falsehood hath!
Shy. Three thousand ducats; 'tis a good round sum.
Three months from twelve; then, let me see; the rate—
Ant. Well, Shylock, shall we be beholding to you?
Shy. Signior Antonio, many a time and oft
In the Rialto you have rated me
About my moneys and my usances:
Still have I borne it with a patient shrug,
For suff'rance is the badge of all our tribe.
You call me misbeliever, cut-throat dog,
And spit upon my Jewish gaberdine,
And all for use of that which is mine own.
Well then, it now appears you need my help:
Go to, then; you come to me, and you say
'Shylock, we would have moneys:' you say so;
You, that did void your rheum upon my beard
And foot me as you spurn a stranger cur
Over your threshold: moneys is your suit.
What should I say to you? Should I not say
'Hath a dog money? is it possible
A cur can lend three thousand ducats?' Or
Shall I bend low and in a bondman's key,
With bated breath and whisp'ring humbleness,
Say this;
'Fair sir, you spet on me on Wednesday last;
You spurn'd me such a day; another time
You call'd me dog; and for these courtesies
I'll lend you thus much moneys'?
Ant. I am as like to call thee so again,
To spit on thee again, to spurn thee too.
If thou wilt lend this money, lend it not
As to thy friends; for when did friendship take
A breed for barren metal of his friend?
But lend it rather to thine enemy,
Who, if he break, thou mayst with better face
Exact the penalty.
Shy. Why, look you, how you storm!
I would be friends with you and have your love,
Forget the shames that you have stain'd me with,
Supply your present wants and take no doit
Of usance for my moneys, and you'll not hear me:
This is kind I offer.
Bass. This were kindness.
Shy. This kindness will I show.
Go with me to a notary, seal me there
Your single bond; and, in a merry sport,
If you repay me not on such a day,
In such a place, such sum or sums as are
Express'd in the condition, let the forfeit
Be nominated for an equal pound
Of your fair flesh, to be cut off and taken
In what part of your body pleaseth me.
Ant. Content, in faith: I'll seal to such a bond
And say there is much kindness in the Jew.
Bass. You shall not seal to such a bond for me:
I'll rather dwell in my necessity.
Ant. Why, fear not, man; I will not forfeit it:
Within these two months, that 's a month before
This bond expires, I do expect return
Of thrice three times the value of this bond.
Shy. O father Abram, what these Christians are,
Whose own hard dealings teaches them suspect
The thoughts of others! Pray you, tell me this;
If he should break his day, what should I gain
By the exaction of the forfeiture?
A pound of man's flesh taken from a man
Is not so estimable, profitable neither,
As flesh of muttons, beefs, or goats. I say,
To buy his favour, I extend this friendship:
If he will take it, so; if not, adieu;
And, for my love, I pray you wrong me not.
Ant. Yes, Shylock, I will seal unto this bond.
Shy. Then meet me forthwith at the notary's;
Give him direction for this merry bond,
And I will go and purse the ducats straight,
See to my house, left in the fearful guard
Of an unthrifty knave, and presently
I'll be with you. *Exit.*
Ant. Hie thee, gentle Jew.
The Hebrew will turn Christian: he grows kind.
Bass. I like not fair terms and a villain's mind.
Ant. Come on: in this there can be no dismay;
My ships come home a month before the day. *Exeunt.*

[ACT II.

SCENE I. *Belmont. A room in* PORTIA'S *house.*]

[Flourish of cornets.] Enter [the PRINCE OF] MOROCCO, *a tawny Moor all in white, and three or four followers accordingly, with* PORTIA, NERISSA, *and their train.*

Mor. Mislike me not for my complexion,
The shadowed livery of the burnish'd sun,
To whom I am a neighbour and near bred.
Bring me the fairest creature northward born,
Where Phœbus' fire scarce thaws the icicles,
And let us make incision for your love,
To prove whose blood is reddest, his or mine.
I tell thee, lady, this aspect of mine
Hath fear'd the valiant: by my love, I swear
The best-regarded virgins of our clime
Have lov'd it too: I would not change this hue,
Except to steal your thoughts, my gentle queen.

89. **Fall,** give birth to. 108. **rated,** rebuked. 113. **gaberdine,** cape or mantle. 116. **Go to, then,** an exclamation of impatience or annoyance. 118. **rheum,** spittle. 127. **spet,** spit. 135. **breed for barren metal,** an ancient argument against interest (see Introduction). F has *of* instead of *for*. 137. **Who,** from whom. **break,** fail to pay on time. 141. **doit,** a Dutch coin of very small value. 146. **single bond,** bond without other security. 162. **suspect,** i.e., to suspect.

ACT II. SCENE I. 7. **reddest.** Red blood was regarded as a sign of courage. 9. **fear'd,** frightened. 14. **nice direction,** dainty guidance. 17. **scanted,** limited. 24. **scimitar,** a sword with curved blade. 25. **Sophy,** shah of Persia. 26. **Solyman,** a Turkish sultan ruling 1520-1566. 27. **o'erstare,** outstare. 32. **Lichas,** a page of Hercules. 35. **Alcides,** Hercules. 44. **temple,** probably church, in order to take the oaths.

Por. In terms of choice I am not solely led
By nice direction of a maiden's eyes;
Besides, the lott'ry of my destiny
Bars me the right of voluntary choosing:
But if my father had not scanted me
And hedg'd me by his wit, to yield myself
His wife who wins me by that means I told you,
Yourself, renowned prince, then stood as fair
As any comer I have look'd on yet
For my affection.

Mor. Even for that I thank you:
Therefore, I pray you, lead me to the caskets
To try my fortune. By this scimitar
That slew the Sophy and a Persian prince,
That won three fields of Sultan Solyman,
I would o'erstare the sternest eyes that look,
Outbrave the heart most daring on the earth,
Pluck the young sucking cubs from the she-bear,
Yea, mock the lion when he roars for prey,
To win thee, lady. But, alas the while!
If Hercules and Lichas play at dice
Which is the better man, the greater throw
May turn by fortune from the weaker hand:
So is Alcides beaten by his page;
And so may I, blind fortune leading me,
Miss that which one unworthier may attain,
And die with grieving.

Por. You must take your chance,
And either not attempt to choose at all
Or swear before you choose, if you choose wrong
Never to speak to lady afterward
In way of marriage: therefore be advis'd.

Mor. Nor will not. Come, bring me unto my chance.

Por. First, forward to the temple: after dinner
Your hazard shall be made.

Mor. Good fortune then!
To make me blest or cursed'st among men.

[*Cornets, and*] *exeunt.*

[SCENE II. *Venice. A street.*]

Enter [LAUNCELOT] *the Clown, alone.*

Laun. Certainly my conscience will serve me to run from this Jew my master. The fiend is at mine elbow and tempts me saying to me 'Gobbo, Launcelot Gobbo, good Launcelot,' or 'good Gobbo,' or 'good Launcelot Gobbo, use your legs, take the start, run away.' My conscience says 'No; take heed, honest Launcelot; take heed, honest Gobbo,' or, as aforesaid, 'honest Launcelot Gobbo; do not run; scorn running with thy heels.' Well, the most courageous fiend bids me pack: 'Via!' says the fiend; 'away!' says the fiend; 'for the heavens, rouse up a brave mind,' says the fiend, 'and run.' Well, my conscience, hanging about the neck of my heart, says very wisely to me 'My honest friend Launcelot, being an honest man's son,' or rather an honest woman's son; for, indeed, my father did something smack, something grow to, he had a kind of taste; well, my conscience says 'Launcelot, budge not.' 'Budge,' says the fiend. 'Budge not,' says my conscience. 'Conscience,' say I, 'you counsel well;' 'Fiend,' say I, 'you counsel well:' to be ruled by my conscience, I should stay with the Jew my master, who, God bless the mark, is a kind of devil; and, to run away from the Jew, I should be ruled by the fiend, who, saving your reverence, is the devil himself. Certainly the Jew is the very devil incarnation; and, in my conscience, my conscience is but a kind of hard conscience, to offer to counsel me to stay with the Jew. The fiend gives the more friendly counsel: I will run, fiend; my heels are at your commandment; I will run.

Enter Old GOBBO, *with a basket.*

Gob. Master young man, you, I pray you, which is the way to master Jew's?

Laun. [*Aside*] O heavens, this is my true-begotten father! who, being more than sand-blind, high-gravel blind, knows me not: I will try confusions with him.

Gob. Master young gentleman, I pray you, which is the way to master Jew's?

Laun. Turn up on your right hand at the next turning, but, at the next turning of all, on your left; marry, at the very next turning, turn of no hand, but turn down indirectly to the Jew's house.

Gob. By God's sonties, 'twill be a hard way to hit. Can you tell me whether one Launcelot, that dwells with him, dwell with him or no?

Laun. Talk you of young Master Launcelot? [*Aside*] Mark me now; now will I raise the waters.—Talk you of young Master Launcelot?

Gob. No master, sir, but a poor man's son: his father, though I say it, is an honest exceeding poor man and, God be thanked, well to live.

Laun. Well, let his father be what 'a will, we talk of young Master Launcelot.

Gob. Your worship's friend and Launcelot, sir.

Laun. But I pray you, ergo, old man, ergo, I beseech you, talk you of young Master Launcelot?

Gob. Of Launcelot, an 't please your mastership.

Laun. Ergo, Master Launcelot. Talk not of Master Launcelot, father; for the young gentleman, according to Fates and Destinies and such odd sayings, the Sisters Three and such branches of learning, is indeed deceased, or, as you would say in plain terms, gone to heaven.

Gob. Marry, God forbid! the boy was the very staff of my age, my very prop.

Laun. Do I look like a cudgel or a hovel-post, a staff or a prop? Do you know me, father?

Gob. Alack the day, I know you not, young gentleman: but, I pray you, tell me, is my boy, God rest his soul, alive or dead?

Laun. Do you not know me, father?

Gob. Alack, sir, I am sand-blind; I know you not.

Laun. Nay, indeed, if you had your eyes, you might fail of the knowing me: it is a wise father that knows

SCENE II. 3. **tempts.** The situation of the tempting fiend is a familiar one in all medieval and Renaissance literature, perhaps commonest in morality plays. 11. **'Via!'** Italian, "begone!" 18. **some thing smack,** i.e., of a tendency to vice. 25. **God . . . mark,** an exclamation by way of apology for introducing something; origin of expression not understood. 27. **incarnation.** Launcelot means "incarnate." 37. **sand-blind,** dim-sighted. 38. **high-gravel blind,** more than sand-blind as gravel is greater than sand. 47. **sonties,** probably a corruption of "saints" or "sanctities." 50. **Master.** The title was applied to gentlefolk only. 55. **well to live,** possibly Gobbo's corruption of "well-to-do." 59. **ergo,** therefore (if it means anything). 66. **Sisters Three,** the three Fates. 71. **hovel-post,** support for a hovel or open shed.

his own child. Well, old man, I will tell you news of your son: give me your blessing: truth will come to light; murder cannot be hid long; a man's son may, but in the end truth will out.

Gob. Pray you, sir, stand up: I am sure you are not Launcelot, my boy.

Laun. Pray you, let 's have no more fooling about it, but give me your blessing: I am Launcelot, your boy that was, your son that is, your child that shall be.

Gob. I cannot think you are my son.

Laun. I know not what I shall think of that: but I am Launcelot, the Jew's man, and I am sure Margery your wife is my mother.

Gob. Her name is Margery, indeed: I'll be sworn, if thou be Launcelot, thou art mine own flesh and blood. Lord worshipped might he be! what a beard hast thou got! thou hast got more hair on thy chin than Dobbin my fill-horse has on his tail.

Laun. It should seem, then, that Dobbin's tail grows backward: I am sure he had more hair of his tail than I have of my face when I last saw him.

Gob. Lord, how art thou changed! How dost thou and thy master agree? I have brought him a present. How 'gree you now?

Laun. Well, well: but, for mine own part, as I have set up my rest to run away, so I will not rest till I have run some ground. My master 's a very Jew: give him a present! give him a halter: I am famished in his service; you may tell every finger I have with my ribs. Father, I am glad you are come: give me your present to one Master Bassanio, who, indeed, gives rare new liveries: if I serve not him, I will run as far as God has any ground. O rare fortune! here comes the man: to him, father; for I am a Jew, if I serve the Jew any longer.

Enter BASSANIO, *with* [LEONARDO *and*] *a follower or two*.

Bass. You may do so; but let it be so hasted that supper be ready at the farthest by five of the clock. See these letters delivered; put the liveries to making, and desire Gratiano to come anon to my lodging.

[*Exit a Servant*.]

Laun. To him, father.

Gob. God bless your worship!

Bass. Gramercy! wouldst thou aught with me?

Gob. Here 's my son, sir, a poor boy,—

Laun. Not a poor boy, sir, but the rich Jew's man; that would, sir, as my father shall specify—

Gob. He hath a great infection, sir, as one would say, to serve,—

Laun. Indeed, the short and the long is, I serve the Jew, and have a desire, as my father shall specify—

Gob. His master and he, saving your worship's reverence, are scarce cater-cousins—

Laun. To be brief, the very truth is that the Jew, having done me wrong, doth cause me, as my father, being, I hope, an old man, shall frutify unto you—

Gob. I have here a dish of doves that I would bestow upon your worship, and my suit is—

Laun. In very brief, the suit is impertinent to myself, as your worship shall know by this honest old man; and, though I say it, though old man, yet poor man, my father.

Bass. One speak for both. What would you?

Laun. Serve you, sir.

Gob. That is the very defect of the matter, sir.

Bass. I know thee well; thou hast obtain'd thy suit:
Shylock thy master spoke with me this day,
And hath preferr'd thee, if it be preferment
To leave a rich Jew's service, to become
The follower of so poor a gentleman.

Laun. The old proverb is very well parted between my master Shylock and you, sir: you have the grace of God, sir, and he hath enough.

Bass. Thou speak'st it well. Go, father, with thy son.
Take leave of thy old master and inquire
My lodging out. [*To a Serv*.] Give him a livery
More guarded than his fellows': see it done.

Laun. Father, in. I cannot get a service, no; I have ne'er a tongue in my head! Well, if any man in Italy have a fairer table which doth offer to swear upon a book, I shall have good fortune. Go to, here 's a simple line of life: here 's a small trifle of wives: alas, fifteen wives is nothing! eleven widows and nine maids is a simple coming-in for one man: and then to 'scape drowning thrice, and to be in peril of my life with the edge of a feather-bed! Here are simple scapes. Well, if Fortune be a woman, she 's a good wench for this gear. Father, come; I'll take my leave of the Jew in the twinkling. *Exit Clown* [*with Old Gobbo*].

Bass. I pray thee, good Leonardo, think on this:
These things being bought and orderly bestow'd,
Return in haste, for I do feast to-night
My best-esteem'd acquaintance: hie thee, go.

Leon. My best endeavours shall be done herein.

Enter GRATIANO.

Gra. Where 's your master?

Leon. Yonder, sir, he walks. *Exit Leon*.

Gra. Signior Bassanio!

Bass. Gratiano!

Gra. I have a suit to you.

Bass. You have obtain'd it.

Gra. You must not deny me: I must go with you to Belmont.

Bass. Why, then you must. But hear thee, Gratiano;
Thou art too wild, too rude and bold of voice;
Parts that become thee happily enough
And in such eyes as ours appear not faults;
But where thou art not known, why, there they show
Something too liberal. Pray thee, take pain
To allay with some cold drops of modesty
Thy skipping spirit, lest through thy wild behaviour
I be misconst'red in the place I go to
And lose my hopes.

Gra. Signior Bassanio, hear me:
If I do not put on a sober habit,
Talk with respect and swear but now and then,
Wear prayer-books in my pocket, look demurely,
Nay more, while grace is saying, hood mine eyes
Thus with my hat, and sigh and say 'amen,'
Use all the observance of civility,

99. **beard.** Stage tradition has old Gobbo mistake Launcelot's long hair for a beard. 101. **fill-horse,** cart-horse. 104. **of,** in. 110. **set . . . rest,** determined; metaphor from the card game *primero*, in which a final wager is made. 112. **very,** veritable. 113. **halter,** hangman's noose. 114. **tell,** count. 128. **Gramercy,** thanks. 132. **infection,** for "affection" or "inclination." 139. **cater-cousins,** good friends; sometimes thought to have meant originally fourth cousins. 143. **frutify.** Launcelot may be trying to say "fructify," but he means "certify" or "notify." 146. **impertinent,** for "pertinent." 152. **defect,** for "purport." 155. **preferr'd,** recommended. 158. **old proverb.** The grace of God is better than riches; or the Scottish form: God's grace is gear enough. 164. **guarded,** trimmed with braided ornaments. 167. **table,**

Like one well studied in a sad ostent
To please his grandam, never trust me more.
Bass. Well, we shall see your bearing.
Gra. Nay, but I bar to-night: you shall not gauge me
By what we do to-night.
Bass. No, that were pity:
I would entreat you rather to put on
Your boldest suit of mirth, for we have friends
That purpose merriment. But fare you well:
I have some business.
Gra. And I must to Lorenzo and the rest:
But we will visit you at supper-time. *Exeunt.*

[SCENE III. *The same. A room in* SHYLOCK'S *house.*]

Enter JESSICA *and* [LAUNCELOT] *the Clown.*

Jes. I am sorry thou wilt leave my father so:
Our house is hell, and thou, a merry devil,
Didst rob it of some taste of tediousness.
But fare thee well, there is a ducat for thee:
And, Launcelot, soon at supper shalt thou see
Lorenzo, who is thy new master's guest:
Give him this letter; do it secretly;
And so farewell: I would not have my father
See me in talk with thee.

Laun. Adieu! tears exhibit my tongue. Most beautiful pagan, most sweet Jew! if a Christian did not play the knave and get thee, I am much deceived. But, adieu: these foolish drops do something drown my manly spirit: adieu.

Jes. Farewell, good Launcelot. [*Exit Launcelot.*]
Alack, what heinous sin is it in me
To be asham'd to be my father's child!
But though I am a daughter to his blood,
I am not to his manners. O Lorenzo,
If thou keep promise, I shall end this strife,
Become a Christian and thy loving wife. *Exit.*

[SCENE IV. *The same. A street.*]

Enter GRATIANO, LORENZO, SALERIO, *and* SOLANIO.

Lor. Nay, we will slink away in supper-time,
Disguise us at my lodging and return,
All in an hour.
Gra. We have not made good preparation.
Saler. We have not spoke us yet of torch-bearers.
Solan. 'Tis vile, unless it may be quaintly ordered,
And better in my mind not undertook.
Lor. 'Tis now but four o'clock: we have two hours
To furnish us.

Enter LAUNCELOT [*with a letter*].

Friend Launcelot, what 's the news?

Laun. An it shall please you to break up this, it shall seem to signify.

Lor. I know the hand: in faith, 'tis a fair hand;
And whiter than the paper it writ on
Is the fair hand that writ.
Gra. Love-news, in faith.
Laun. By your leave, sir.
Lor. Whither goest thou?

Laun. Marry, sir, to bid my old master the Jew to sup to-night with my new master the Christian.

Lor. Hold here, take this: tell gentle Jessica
I will not fail her; speak it privately.
Go. Gentlemen, *Exit Clown* [*Launcelot*].
Will you prepare you for this masque to-night?
I am provided of a torch-bearer.
Saler. Ay, marry, I'll be gone about it straight.
Solan. And so will I.
Lor. Meet me and Gratiano
At Gratiano's lodging some hour hence.
Saler. 'Tis good we do so. *Exit* [*with Solan*].
Gra. Was not that letter from fair Jessica?
Lor. I must needs tell thee all. She hath directed
How I shall take her from her father's house,
What gold and jewels she is furnish'd with,
What page's suit she hath in readiness.
If e'er the Jew her father come to heaven,
It will be for his gentle daughter's sake:
And never dare misfortune cross her foot,
Unless she do it under this excuse,
That she is issue to a faithless Jew.
Come, go with me; peruse this as thou goest:
Fair Jessica shall be my torch-bearer. *Exeunt.*

[SCENE V. *The same. Before* SHYLOCK'S *house.*]

Enter [SHYLOCK *the*] *Jew and* [LAUNCELOT,] *his man that was, the Clown.*

Shy. Well, thou shalt see, thy eyes shall be thy judge,
The difference of old Shylock and Bassanio:—
What, Jessica!—thou shalt not gormandise,
As thou hast done with me:—What, Jessica!—
And sleep and snore, and rend apparel out;—
Why, Jessica, I say!
Laun. Why, Jessica!
Shy. Who bids thee call? I do not bid thee call.

Laun. Your worship was wont to tell me I could do nothing without bidding.

Enter JESSICA.

Jes. Call you? what is your will?
Shy. I am bid forth to supper, Jessica:
There are my keys. But wherefore should I go?
I am not bid for love; they flatter me:
But yet I'll go in hate, to feed upon
The prodigal Christian. Jessica, my girl,
Look to my house. I am right loath to go:
There is some ill a-brewing towards my rest,
For I did dream of money-bags to-night.

Laun. I beseech you, sir, go: my young master doth expect your reproach.

Shy. So do I his.

Laun. And they have conspired together, I will not say you shall see a masque; but if you do, then it was

palm of his hand. (Launcelot now reads the lines of his palm.) 170. **trifle of wives.** "Long and deep lines from the Mount of Venus toward the line of life signifieth so many wives."—Saunders, *Chiromancie* (Furness). 205. **sad ostent,** grave appearance.

SCENE III. 10. **exhibit,** for "inhibit." 12. **get,** beget, sire.

SCENE IV. 5. **us,** ethical dative. 6. **'Tis vile,** it is a vulgar and useless thing to do. **quaintly,** elegantly, tastefully. 10. **break up,** break open.

SCENE V. 3. **gormandise,** eat greedily. 18. **to-night,** last night. 20. **reproach,** Launcelot's blunder for "approach." Shylock takes it in grim humor.

not for nothing that my nose fell a-bleeding on Black-Monday last at six o'clock i' the morning, falling out that year on Ash-Wednesday was four year, in the afternoon.

Shy. What, are there masques? Hear you me, Jessica:
Lock up my doors; and when you hear the drum
And the vile squealing of the wry-neck'd fife,
Clamber not you up to the casements then,
Nor thrust your head into the public street
To gaze on Christian fools with varnish'd faces,
But stop my house's ears, I mean my casements:
Let not the sound of shallow fopp'ry enter
My sober house. By Jacob's staff, I swear,
I have no mind of feasting forth to-night:
But I will go. Go you before me, sirrah;
Say I will come.

Laun. I will go before, sir. Mistress, look out at window, for all this; 41

There will come a Christian by,
Will be worth a Jewess' eye. [*Exit.*]

Shy. What says that fool of Hagar's offspring, ha?

Jes. His words were 'Farewell, mistress;' nothing else.

Shy. The patch is kind enough, but a huge feeder;
Snail-slow in profit, and he sleeps by day
More than the wild-cat: drones hive not with me;
Therefore I part with him, and part with him
To one that I would have him help to waste
His borrowed purse. Well, Jessica, go in:
Perhaps I will return immediately:
Do as I bid you; shut doors after you:
Fast bind, fast find;
A proverb never stale in thrifty mind. *Exit.*

Jes. Farewell; and if my fortune be not crost,
I have a father, you a daughter, lost. *Exit.*

[SCENE VI. *The same.*]

Enter the masquers, GRATIANO *and* SALERIO.

Gra. This is the pent-house under which Lorenzo
Desir'd us to make stand.

Saler. His hour is almost past.

Gra. And it is marvel he out-dwells his hour,
For lovers ever run before the clock.

Saler. O, ten times faster Venus' pigeons fly
To seal love's bonds new-made, than they are wont
To keep obliged faith unforfeited!

Gra. That ever holds: who riseth from a feast
With that keen appetite that he sits down?
Where is the horse that doth untread again
His tedious measures with the unbated fire
That he did pace them first? All things that are,
Are with more spirit chased than enjoy'd.
How like a younker or a prodigal
The scarfed bark puts from her native bay,
Hugg'd and embraced by the strumpet wind!
How like the prodigal doth she return,
With over-weather'd ribs and ragged sails,
Lean, rent and beggar'd by the strumpet wind!

Enter LORENZO.

Saler. Here comes Lorenzo: more of this hereafter.

Lor. Sweet friends, your patience for my long abode;
Not I, but my affairs, have made you wait:
When you shall please to play the thieves for wives,
I'll watch as long for you then. Approach;
Here dwells my father Jew. Ho! who 's within?

[*Enter*] JESSICA, *above* [*in boy's clothes*].

Jes. Who are you? Tell me, for more certainty,
Albeit I'll swear that I do know your tongue.

Lor. Lorenzo, and thy love.

Jes. Lorenzo, certain, and my love indeed,
For who love I so much? And now who knows
But you, Lorenzo, whether I am yours?

Lor. Heaven and thy thoughts are witness that thou art.

Jes. Here, catch this casket; it is worth the pains.
I am glad 'tis night, you do not look on me,
For I am much asham'd of my exchange:
But love is blind and lovers cannot see
The pretty follies that themselves commit;
For if they could, Cupid himself would blush
To see me thus transformed to a boy.

Lor. Descend, for you must be my torch-bearer.

Jes. What, must I hold a candle to my shames?
They in themselves, good sooth, are too too light.
Why, 'tis an office of discovery, love;
And I should be obscur'd.

Lor. So are you, sweet,
Even in the lovely garnish of a boy.
But come at once;
For the close night doth play the runaway,
And we are stay'd for at Bassanio's feast.

Jes. I will make fast the doors, and gild myself
With some moe ducats, and be with you straight.
[*Exit above.*]

Gra. Now, by my hood, a Gentile and no Jew.

Lor. Beshrew me but I love her heartily;
For she is wise, if I can judge of her,
And fair she is, if that mine eyes be true,
And true she is, as she hath prov'd herself,
And therefore, like herself, wise, fair and true,
Shall she be placed in my constant soul.

Enter JESSICA [*below*].

What, art thou come? On, gentlemen; away!
Our masquing mates by this time for us stay.
Exit [*with Jessica and Salerio*].

Enter ANTONIO.

Ant. Who 's there?

Gra. Signior Antonio!

Ant. Fie, fie, Gratiano! where are all the rest?
'Tis nine o'clock: our friends all stay for you.
No masque to-night: the wind is come about;
Bassanio presently will go aboard:
I have sent twenty out to seek for you.

Gra. I am glad on 't: I desire no more delight
Than to be under sail and gone to-night. *Exeunt.*

25. **Black-Monday,** Easter Monday, so called, according to Stow, because of a cold and stormy Easter Monday when Edward III was besieging Paris. Launcelot's talk of omens is perhaps intentional gibberish, a parody of Shylock's fears. 30. **wry-neck'd,** played with the musician's head awry (?). 44. **Hagar's offspring.** Hagar, Abraham's servant, gave birth to Ishmael; both mother and son were cast out after the birth of Isaac. 46. **patch,** fool, fellow.

SCENE VI. 1. **pent-house,** projecting roof from a house. 5. **Venus' pigeons.** Venus' chariot was drawn by doves. 14. **younker,** youth ("younger" in QF). 15. **scarfed,** decorated with flags. 16. **strumpet,** referring metaphorically to the harlots with whom the Prodigal Son wasted his fortune. 42. **light,** immodest (with pun). 43. **office of**

[SCENE VII. *Belmont. A room in* PORTIA'S *house.*]

[*Flourish of cornets.*] *Enter* PORTIA, *with* [*the* PRINCE OF] MOROCCO, *and both their trains.*

Por. Go draw aside the curtains and discover
The several caskets to this noble prince.
Now make your choice. [*Curtains are drawn.*]
Mor. The first, of gold, who this inscription bears,
'Who chooseth me shall gain what many men desire;
The second, silver, which this promise carries,
'Who chooseth me shall get as much as he deserves;
This third, dull lead, with warning all as blunt,
'Who chooseth me must give and hazard all he hath.'
How shall I know if I do choose the right?
Por. The one of them contains my picture, prince:
If you choose that, then I am yours withal.
Mor. Some god direct my judgement! Let me see;
I will survey th' inscriptions back again.
What says this leaden casket?
'Who chooseth me must give and hazard all he hath.'
Must give: for what? for lead? hazard for lead?
This casket threatens. Men that hazard all
Do it in hope of fair advantages:
A golden mind stoops not to shows of dross;
I'll then nor give nor hazard aught for lead.
What says the silver with her virgin hue?
'Who chooseth me shall get as much as he deserves.'
As much as he deserves! Pause there, Morocco,
And weigh thy value with an even hand:
If thou be'st rated by thy estimation,
Thou dost deserve enough; and yet enough
May not extend so far as to the lady:
And yet to be afeard of my deserving
Were but a weak disabling of myself.
As much as I deserve! Why, that 's the lady:
I do in birth deserve her, and in fortunes,
In graces and in qualities of breeding;
But more than these, in love I do deserve.
What if I stray'd no further, but chose here?
Let 's see once more this saying grav'd in gold;
'Who chooseth me shall gain what many men desire.'
Why, that 's the lady; all the world desires her;
From the four corners of the earth they come,
To kiss this shrine, this mortal-breathing saint:
The Hyrcanian deserts and the vasty wilds
Of wide Arabia are as throughfares now
For princes to come view fair Portia:
The watery kingdom, whose ambitious head
Spits in the face of heaven, is no bar
To stop the foreign spirits, but they come,
As o'er a brook, to see fair Portia.
One of these three contains her heavenly picture.
Is 't like that lead contains her? 'Twere damnation
To think so base a thought: it were too gross
To rib her cerecloth in the obscure grave.
Or shall I think in silver she 's immur'd,
Being ten times undervalued to tried gold?
O sinful thought! Never so rich a gem
Was set in worse than gold. They have in England
A coin that bears the figure of an angel
Stamped in gold, but that 's insculp'd upon;
But here an angel in a golden bed
Lies all within. Deliver me the key:
Here do I choose, and thrive I as I may!
Por. There, take it, prince; and if my form lie there,
Then I am yours. [*He unlocks the golden casket.*]
Mor. O hell! what have we here?
A carrion Death, within whose empty eye
There is a written scroll! I'll read the writing.
[*Reads*] All that glisters is not gold;
Often have you heard that told:
Many a man his life hath sold
But my outside to behold:
Gilded tombs do worms infold.
Had you been as wise as bold,
Young in limbs, in judgement old,
Your answer had not been inscroll'd:
Fare you well; your suit is cold.

Cold, indeed; and labour lost:
Then, farewell, heat, and welcome, frost!
Portia, adieu. I have too griev'd a heart
To take a tedious leave: thus losers part.
Exit [*with his train. Flourish of cornets*].
Por. A gentle riddance. Draw the curtains, go.
Let all of his complexion choose me so. *Exeunt.*

[SCENE VIII. *Venice. A street.*]

Enter SALERIO *and* SOLANIO.

Saler. Why, man, I saw Bassanio under sail:
With him is Gratiano gone along;
And in their ship I am sure Lorenzo is not.
Solan. The villain Jew with outcries rais'd the duke,
Who went with him to search Bassanio's ship.
Saler. He came too late, the ship was under sail:
But there the duke was given to understand
That in a gondola were seen together
Lorenzo and his amorous Jessica:
Besides, Antonio certified the duke
They were not with Bassanio in his ship.
Solan. I never heard a passion so confus'd,
So strange, outrageous, and so variable,
As the dog Jew did utter in the streets:
'My daughter! O my ducats! O my daughter!
Fled with a Christian! O my Christian ducats!
Justice! the law! my ducats, and my daughter!
A sealed bag, two sealed bags of ducats,
Of double ducats, stol'n from me by my daughter!
And jewels, two stones, two rich and precious stones,
Stol'n by my daughter! Justice! find the girl;
She hath the stones upon her, and the ducats.'
Saler. Why, all the boys in Venice follow him,
Crying, his stones, his daughter, and his ducats.
Solan. Let good Antonio look he keep his day,
Or he shall pay for this.
Saler. Marry, well remember'd.
I reason'd with a Frenchman yesterday,
Who told me, in the narrow seas that part
The French and English, there miscarried
A vessel of our country richly fraught:

discovery, occupation in which my disguise will be revealed. 45. **garnish,** outfit.

SCENE VII. 41. **Hyrcanian.** Hyrcania was the country south of the Caspian Sea. 51. **cerecloth,** wax cloth used in embalming. 63. **carrion Death,** death's-head. 65. **glisters,** glitters. 72. **inscroll'd,** i.e., written on this scroll. 79. **complexion,** temperament (not merely skin color).

SCENE VIII. 15-17. **daughter . . . ducats.** Barabas in Marlowe's *The Jew of Malta* shows the same confused passion in Act I: "O girl! O gold! O beauty! O my bliss!" 25. **look . . . day,** see to it that he repays his loan on time. 27. **reason'd,** talked with. 28. **narrow seas,** the English Channel.

I thought upon Antonio when he told me;
And wish'd in silence that it were not his.
Solan. You were best to tell Antonio what you hear;
Yet do not suddenly, for it may grieve him.
Saler. A kinder gentleman treads not the earth.
I saw Bassanio and Antonio part:
Bassanio told him he would make some speed
Of his return: he answered, 'Do not so;
Slubber not business for my sake, Bassanio,
But stay the very riping of the time;
And for the Jew's bond which he hath of me,
Let it not enter in your mind of love:
Be merry, and employ your chiefest thoughts
To courtship and such fair ostents of love
As shall conveniently become you there:'
And even there, his eye being big with tears,
Turning his face, he put his hand behind him,
And with affection wondrous sensible
He wrung Bassanio's hand; and so they parted.
Solan. I think he only loves the world for him.
I pray thee, let us go and find him out
And quicken his embraced heaviness
With some delight or other.
Saler. Do we so. *Exeunt.*

[SCENE IX. *Belmont. A room in* PORTIA's *house.*]

Enter NERISSA *and a* Servitor.

Ner. Quick, quick, I pray thee; draw the curtain straight:
The Prince of Arragon hath ta'en his oath,
And comes to his election presently.

[*Flourish of cornets.*] *Enter* [*the* PRINCE OF] ARRAGON, *his train, and* PORTIA.

Por. Behold, there stand the caskets, noble prince:
If you choose that wherein I am contain'd,
Straight shall our nuptial rites be solemniz'd:
But if you fail, without more speech, my lord,
You must be gone from hence immediately.
Ar. I am enjoin'd by oath to observe three things:
First, never to unfold to any one
Which casket 'twas I chose; next, if I fail
Of the right casket, never in my life
To woo a maid in way of marriage:
Lastly,
If I do fail in fortune of my choice,
Immediately to leave you and be gone.
Por. To these injunctions every one doth swear
That comes to hazard for my worthless self.
Ar. And so have I address'd me. Fortune now
To my heart's hope! Gold; silver; and base lead.
'Who chooseth me must give and hazard all he hath.'
You shall look fairer, ere I give or hazard.
What says the golden chest? ha! let me see:
'Who chooseth me shall gain what many men desire.'
What many men desire! that 'many' may be meant
By the fool multitude, that choose by show,
Not learning more than the fond eye doth teach;
Which pries not to th' interior, but, like the martlet,
Builds in the weather on the outward wall,
Even in the force and road of casualty.
I will not choose what many men desire,
Because I will not jump with common spirits
And rank me with the barbarous multitudes.
Why, then to thee, thou silver treasure-house;
Tell me once more what title thou dost bear:
'Who chooseth me shall get as much as he deserves:'
And well said too; for who shall go about
To cozen fortune and be honourable
Without the stamp of merit? Let none presume
To wear an undeserved dignity.
O, that estates, degrees and offices
Were not deriv'd corruptly, and that clear honour
Were purchas'd by the merit of the wearer!
How many then should cover that stand bare!
How many be commanded that command!
How much low peasantry would then be gleaned
From the true seed of honour! and how much honour
Pick'd from the chaff and ruin of the times
To be new-varnish'd! Well, but to my choice:
'Who chooseth me shall get as much as he deserves.'
I will assume desert. Give me a key for this,
And instantly unlock my fortunes here.
[*He opens the silver casket.*]
Por. Too long a pause for that which you find there.
Ar. What 's here? the portrait of a blinking idiot,
Presenting me a schedule! I will read it.
How much unlike art thou to Portia!
How much unlike my hopes and my deservings!
'Who chooseth me shall have as much as he deserves.'
Did I deserve no more than a fool's head?
Is that my prize? are my deserts no better?
Por. To offend, and judge, are distinct offices
And of opposed natures.
Ar. What is here?
[*Reads*] The fire seven times tried this:
Seven times tried that judgement is,
That did never choose amiss.
Some there be that shadows kiss;
Such have but a shadow's bliss:
There be fools alive, I wis,
Silver'd o'er; and so was this.
Take what wife you will to bed,
I will ever be your head:
So be gone: you are sped.

Still more fool I shall appear
By the time I linger here:
With one fool's head I came to woo,
But I go away with two.
Sweet, adieu. I'll keep my oath,
Patiently to bear my wroth.
[*Exeunt Arragon and train.*]
Por. Thus hath the candle sing'd the moth.
O, these deliberate fools! when they do choose,
They have the wisdom by their wit to lose.
Ner. The ancient saying is no heresy,
Hanging and wiving goes by destiny.

30. **fraught,** freighted. 39. **Slubber,** to do hastily and badly. 40. **But . . . time,** i.e., pursue your business at Belmont until it is brought to completion. 44. **ostents,** expressions, shows. 52. **quicken . . . heaviness,** lighten the sorrow he has embraced.

SCENE IX. 3. **election,** choice. **presently,** immediately. 6. **Straight,** immediately. 18. **hazard,** may be either a verb or a noun. 19. **so,** in these terms. **address'd me,** prepared myself (by thus swearing). 28. **martlet,** martin. 30. **casualty,** mischance. 32. **jump,** agree; see glossary. 38. **cozen,** cheat. 41. **degrees,** ranks. **offices,** official positions. 44. **cover . . . bare,** i.e., wear hats (of authority) who now stand bareheaded. 45. **How . . . command,** how many then should be servants that are now masters. 46. **glean'd,** culled out. 47. **seed of honour,** persons of noble descent. 49. **new-varnish'd,** i.e., having the luster of their true nobility restored to them. 55. **schedule,** written paper. 61. **To . . . offices.** You have no right, having submitted your case to judgment, to object to the tribunal. 68. **I wis,** either "I know"

Por. Come, draw the curtain, Nerissa.

Enter Messenger.

Mess. Where is my lady?
Por. Here: what would my lord?
Mess. Madam, there is alighted at your gate
A young Venetian, one that comes before
To signify th' approaching of his lord;
From whom he bringeth sensible regreets,
To wit, besides commends and courteous breath,
Gifts of rich value. Yet I have not seen
So likely an ambassador of love:
A day in April never came so sweet,
To show how costly summer was at hand,
As this fore-spurrer comes before his lord.
Por. No more, I pray thee: I am half afeard
Thou wilt say anon he is some kin to thee,
Thou spend'st such high-day wit in praising him.
Come, come, Nerissa; for I long to see
Quick Cupid's post that comes so mannerly.
Ner. Bassanio, lord Love, if thy will it be! *Exeunt.*

[ACT III.

SCENE I. *Venice. A street.*]

[*Enter*] SOLANIO *and* SALERIO.

Solan. Now, what news on the Rialto?

Saler. Why, yet it lives there unchecked that Antonio hath a ship of rich lading wracked on the narrow seas; the Goodwins, I think they call the place; a very dangerous flat and fatal, where the carcases of many a tall ship lie buried, as they say, if my gossip Report be an honest woman of her word.

Solan. I would she were as lying a gossip in that as ever knapped ginger or made her neighbours believe she wept for the death of a third husband. But it is true, without any slips of prolixity or crossing the plain highway of talk, that the good Antonio, the honest Antonio,——O that I had a title good enough to keep his name company!—

Saler. Come, the full stop.

Solan. Ha! what sayest thou? Why, the end is, he hath lost a ship.

Saler. I would it might prove the end of his losses.

Solan. Let me say 'amen' betimes, lest the devil cross my prayer, for here he comes in the likeness of a Jew.

Enter SHYLOCK.

How now, Shylock! what news among the merchants?

Shy. You knew, none so well, none so well as you, of my daughter's flight.

Saler. That 's certain: I, for my part, knew the tailor that made the wings she flew withal.

Solan. And Shylock, for his own part, knew the bird was fledge; and then it is the complexion of them all to leave the dam.

Shy. She is damned for it.

Saler. That 's certain, if the devil may be her judge.

Shy. My own flesh and blood to rebel!

Solan. Out upon it, old carrion! rebels it at these years?

Shy. I say, my daughter is my flesh and my blood.

Saler. There is more difference between thy flesh and hers than between jet and ivory; more between your bloods than there is between red wine and rhenish. But tell us, do you hear whether Antonio have had any loss at sea or no?

Shy. There I have another bad match: a bankrout, a prodigal, who dare scarce show his head on the Rialto; a beggar, that was used to come so smug upon the mart; let him look to his bond: he was wont to call me usurer; let him look to his bond: he was wont to lend money for a Christian cursy; let him look to his bond.

Saler. Why, I am sure, if he forfeit, thou wilt not take his flesh: what 's that good for?

Shy. To bait fish withal: if it will feed nothing else, it will feed my revenge. He hath disgraced me, and hindered me half a million; laughed at my losses, mocked at my gains, scorned my nation, thwarted my bargains, cooled my friends, heated mine enemies; and what 's his reason? I am a Jew. Hath not a Jew eyes? hath not a Jew hands, organs, dimensions, senses, affections, passions? fed with the same food, hurt with the same weapons, subject to the same diseases, healed by the same means, warmed and cooled by the same winter and summer, as a Christian is? If you prick us, do we not bleed? if you tickle us, do we not laugh? if you poison us, do we not die? and if you wrong us, shall we not revenge? If we are like you in the rest, we will resemble you in that. If a Jew wrong a Christian, what is his humility? Revenge. If a Christian wrong a Jew, what should his sufferance be by Christian example? Why, revenge. The villany you teach me, I will execute, and it shall go hard but I will better the instruction.

Enter Man *from Antonio.*

[*Man.*] Gentlemen, my master Antonio is at his house and desires to speak with you both.

Saler. We have been up and down to seek him.

Enter TUBAL.

Solan. Here comes another of the tribe: a third cannot be matched, unless the devil himself turn Jew.

Exeunt gentlemen [*Solan., Saler., and Man*].

Shy. How now, Tubal! what news from Genoa? hast thou found my daughter?

Tub. I often came where I did hear of her, but cannot find her.

Shy. Why, there, there, there, there! a diamond gone, cost me two thousand ducats in Frankfort! The curse never fell upon our nation till now; I never felt it till now: two thousand ducats in that; and other precious, precious jewels. I would my daughter were dead at my foot, and the jewels in her ear! would she were hearsed at my foot, and the ducats in her coffin! No news of them? Why, so: and I know not what 's spent in the search: why, thou loss upon loss! the thief

or "certainly." It is derived from the old adverb *ywis*, often spelled as in the text. 72. **sped,** done for. 78. **wroth,** sorrow; probably an error for "roth" (ruth). 85. **my lord,** a jesting response to "my lady." 89. **sensible regreets,** heartfelt greeting; also, tangible greetings, gifts. 90. **commends,** greetings. 92. **likely,** promising. 94. **costly,** lavish, rich.

ACT III, SCENE I. 4. **Goodwins,** Goodwin Sands off the Kentish coast. 10. **knapped,** chewed. 13. **slips of prolixity,** any long-winded lies. 18. **Come . . . stop,** finish your story. 23. **cross,** thwart. 32. **fledge,** able to fly. **complexion,** natural disposition. 33. **dam,** mother bird. 46. **match,** bargain. **bankrout,** bankrupt. 51. **cursy,** courtesy. 72. **what . . . humility,** what does his Christian humility amount to. 74. **sufferance,** patience, endurance. 81. **matched,** i.e., to them. 89. **Frankfort.** There was a fair at Frankfort famous for goldsmiths' wares. 94. **hearsed,** coffined.

gone with so much, and so much to find the thief; and no satisfaction, no revenge: nor no ill luck stirring but what lights o' my shoulders; no sighs but o' my breathing; no tears but o' my shedding.

Tub. Yes, other men have ill luck too: Antonio, as I heard in Genoa,—

Shy. What, what, what? ill luck, ill luck?

Tub. Hath an argosy cast away, coming from Tripolis.

Shy. I thank God, I thank God. Is it true, is it true?

Tub. I spoke with some of the sailors that escaped the wrack.

Shy. I thank thee, good Tubal: good news, good news! ha, ha! heard in Genoa?

Tub. Your daughter spent in Genoa, as I heard, one night fourscore ducats.

Shy. Thou stickest a dagger in me: I shall never see my gold again: fourscore ducats at a sitting! fourscore ducats!

Tub. There came divers of Antonio's creditors in my company to Venice, that swear he cannot choose but break.

Shy. I am very glad of it: I'll plague him; I'll torture him: I am glad of it.

Tub. One of them showed me a ring that he had of your daughter for a monkey.

Shy. Out upon her! Thou torturest me, Tubal: it was my turquoise; I had it of Leah when I was a bachelor: I would not have given it for a wilderness of monkeys.

Tub. But Antonio is certainly undone.

Shy. Nay, that 's true, that 's very true. Go, Tubal, fee me an officer; bespeak him a fortnight before. I will have the heart of him, if he forfeit; for, were he out of Venice, I can make what merchandise I will. Go, Tubal, and meet me at our synagogue; go, good Tubal; at our synagogue, Tubal. *Exeunt.*

[SCENE II. *Belmont. A room in* PORTIA'S *house.*]

Enter BASSANIO, PORTIA, GRATIANO, [NERISSA,] *and all their trains.*

Por. I pray you, tarry: pause a day or two
Before you hazard; for, in choosing wrong,
I lose your company: therefore forbear awhile.
There 's something tells me, but it is not love,
I would not lose you; and you know yourself,
Hate counsels not in such a quality.
But lest you should not understand me well,—
And yet a maiden hath no tongue but thought,—
I would detain you here some month or two
Before you venture for me. I could teach you
How to choose right, but I am then forsworn;
So will I never be: so may you miss me;
But if you do, you'll make me wish a sin,
That I had been forsworn. Beshrew your eyes,
They have o'erlook'd me and divided me;
One half of me is yours, the other half yours,
Mine own, I would say; but if mine, then yours,
And so all yours. O, these naughty times
Put bars between the owners and their rights!
And so, though yours, not yours. Prove it so,
Let fortune go to hell for it, not I.
I speak too long; but 'tis to peize the time,
To eke it and to draw it out in length,
To stay you from election.

Bass. Let me choose;
For as I am, I live upon the rack.

Por. Upon the rack, Bassanio! then confess
What treason there is mingled with your love.

Bass. None but that ugly treason of mistrust,
Which makes me fear th' enjoying of my love:
There may as well be amity and life
'Tween snow and fire, as treason and my love.

Por. Ay, but I fear you speak upon the rack,
Where men enforced do speak anything.

Bass. Promise me life, and I'll confess the truth.

Por. Well then, confess and live.

Bass. 'Confess' and 'love'
Had been the very sum of my confession:
O happy torment, when my torturer
Doth teach me answers for deliverance!
But let me to my fortune and the caskets.

Por. Away, then! I am lock'd in one of them:
If you do love me, you will find me out.
Nerissa and the rest, stand all aloof.
Let music sound while he doth make his choice;
Then, if he lose, he makes a swan-like end,
Fading in music: that the comparison
May stand more proper, my eye shall be the stream
And wat'ry death-bed for him. He may win;
And what is music then? Then music is
Even as the flourish when true subjects bow
To a new-crowned monarch: such it is
As are those dulcet sounds in break of day
That creep into the dreaming bridegroom's ear
And summon him to marriage. Now he goes,
With no less presence, but with much more love,
Than young Alcides, when he did redeem
The virgin tribute paid by howling Troy
To the sea-monster: I stand for sacrifice;
The rest aloof are the Dardanian wives,
With bleared visages, come forth to view
The issue of th' exploit. Go, Hercules!
Live thou, I live: with much much more dismay
I view the fight than thou that mak'st the fray.

A song, the whilst BASSANIO *comments on the caskets to himself.*

[SONG.]

Tell me where is fancy bred,
Or in the heart or in the head?
How begot, how nourished?
Reply, reply.
It is engend'red in the eyes,
With gazing fed; and fancy dies
In the cradle where it lies.
Let us all ring fancy's knell:
I'll begin it,—Ding, dong, bell.

120. **break,** go bankrupt. 126. **Leah,** Shylock's wife. 131. **fee,** hire. **officer,** bailiff. **bespeak,** engage. 133. **make . . . I will,** drive whatever bargains I please.

SCENE II. 6. **quality,** way, manner (of speaking). 15. **o'erlook'd,** bewitched. 18. **naughty,** good for nothing, worthless; see glossary. 22. **peize,** retard (by hanging on of weights). 44. **swan-like,** an allusion to the belief that swans sing when they come to die. 55. **Alcides.** Hercules rescued Hesione, daughter of the Trojan king, Laomedon, from a monster to which, by command of Neptune, she was about to be sacrificed. Hercules was rewarded, however, not with the lady's love, but with a famous pair of horses. 56. **howling,** lamenting. 57. **stand for sacrifice,** represent the sacrificial victim. 58. **Dardanian,** Trojan. 63. **fancy,** sensuous love. 64. **Or,** either. 67. **eyes.** Love entered the heart especially through the eyes. 79.

All. Ding, dong, bell.
Bass. So may the outward shows be least themselves:
The world is still deceiv'd with ornament.
In law, what plea so tainted and corrupt
But, being season'd with a gracious voice,
Obscures the show of evil? In religion,
What damned error, but some sober brow
Will bless it and approve it with a text,
Hiding the grossness with fair ornament?
There is no vice so simple but assumes
Some mark of virtue on his outward parts:
How many cowards, whose hearts are all as false
As stairs of sand, wear yet upon their chins
The beards of Hercules and frowning Mars,
Who, inward search'd, have livers white as milk;
And these assume but valour's excrement
To render them redoubted! Look on beauty,
And you shall see 'tis purchas'd by the weight;
Which therein works a miracle in nature,
Making them lightest that wear most of it:
So are those crisped snaky golden locks
Which make such wanton gambols with the wind,
Upon supposed fairness, often known
To be the dowry of a second head,
The skull that bred them in the sepulchre.
Thus ornament is but the guiled shore
To a most dangerous sea; the beauteous scarf
†Veiling an Indian beauty; in a word,
The seeming truth which cunning times put on
To entrap the wisest. Therefore, thou gaudy gold,
Hard food for Midas, I will none of thee;
Nor none of thee, thou pale and common drudge
'Tween man and man: but thou, thou meagre lead,
Which rather threaten'st than dost promise aught,
Thy paleness moves me more than eloquence;
And here choose I: joy be the consequence!
Por. [*Aside*] How all the other passions fleet to air,
As doubtful thoughts, and rash-embrac'd despair,
And shudd'ring fear, and green-ey'd jealousy!
O love,
Be moderate; allay thy ecstasy;
In measure rein thy joy; scant this excess.
I feel too much thy blessing: make it less,
For fear I surfeit.
Bass. What find I here?
[*Opening the leaden casket.*]
Fair Portia's counterfeit! What demi-god
Hath come so near creation? Move these eyes?
Or whether, riding on the balls of mine,
Seem they in motion? Here are sever'd lips,
Parted with sugar breath: so sweet a bar
Should sunder such sweet friends. Here in her hairs
The painter plays the spider and hath woven
A golden mesh t' entrap the hearts of men
Faster than gnats in cobwebs: but her eyes,—
How could he see to do them? having made one,
Methinks it should have power to steal both his
And leave itself unfurnish'd. Yet look, how far
The substance of my praise doth wrong this shadow
In underprizing it, so far this shadow
Doth limp behind the substance. Here 's the scroll,
The continent and summary of my fortune.
[*Reads*] You that choose not by the view,
Chance as fair and choose as true!
Since this fortune falls to you,
Be content and seek no new.
If you be well pleas'd with this
And hold your fortune for your bliss,
Turn you where your lady is
And claim her with a loving kiss.
A gentle scroll. Fair lady, by your leave; [*Kiss.*]
I come by note, to give and to receive.
Like one of two contending in a prize,
That thinks he hath done well in people's eyes,
Hearing applause and universal shout,
Giddy in spirit, still gazing in a doubt
Whether those peals of praise be his or no;
So, thrice-fair lady, stand I, even so;
As doubtful whether what I see be true,
Until confirm'd, sign'd, ratified by you.
Por. You see me, Lord Bassanio, where I stand,
Such as I am: though for myself alone
I would not be ambitious in my wish,
To wish myself much better; yet, for you
I would be trebled twenty times myself;
A thousand times more fair, ten thousand times
More rich;
That only to stand high in your account,
I might in virtues, beauties, livings, friends,
Exceed account; but the full sum of me
†Is sum of something, which, to term in gross,
Is an unlesson'd girl, unschool'd, unpractised;
Happy in this, she is not yet so old
†But she may learn; happier than this,
She is not bred so dull but she can learn;
Happiest of all is that her gentle spirit
Commits itself to yours to be directed,
As from her lord, her governor, her king.
Myself and what is mine to you and yours
Is now converted: but now I was the lord
Of this fair mansion, master of my servants,
Queen o'er myself; and even now, but now,
This house, these servants and this same myself
Are yours, my lord's: I give them with this ring;
Which when you part from, lose, or give away,
Let it presage the ruin of your love
And be my vantage to exclaim on you.
Bass. Madam, you have bereft me of all words,
Only my blood speaks to you in my veins;
And there is such confusion in my powers,
As, after some oration fairly spoke
By a beloved prince, there doth appear
Among the buzzing pleased multitude;
Where every something, being blent together,
Turns to a wild of nothing, save of joy,
Express'd and not express'd. But when this ring
Parts from this finger, then parts life from hence:
O, then be bold to say Bassanio 's dead!
Ner. My lord and lady, it is now our time,
That have stood by and seen our wishes prosper,

approve, confirm. 81. **simple,** unadulterated. 84. **stairs,** steps. 86. **livers.** The liver was thought to be the seat of courage; for it to be deserted by the blood would be the condition of cowardice. 87. **valour's excrement,** the outward appearance of bravery. 92. **crisped,** curly. 97. **guiled,** treacherous. 102. **Midas,** the Phrygian king whose touch turned everything to gold. 113. **scant,** lessen. 116. **counterfeit,** portrait. 118. **balls of mine,** my eyeballs. 120. **so sweet a bar,** i.e., Portia's breath. 121. **sweet friends,** i.e., her lips. 127. **unfurnish'd,** i.e., with a companion. 141. **by note,** i.e., as directed. 142. **prize,** contest. 157. **account,** estimation. 169. **but now,** only a short while ago. 173. **ring.** The ring, which is to serve as a test in the love-friendship contest, is thus bestowed at the very acme of the love plot. 176. **exclaim on,** reproach; see glossary.

To cry, good joy: good joy, my lord and lady!
Gra. My lord Bassanio and my gentle lady,
I wish you all the joy that you can wish;
For I am sure you can wish none from me:
And when your honours mean to solemnize
The bargain of your faith, I do beseech you,
Even at that time I may be married too.
Bass. With all my heart, so thou canst get a wife.
Gra. I thank your lordship, you have got me one.
My eyes, my lord, can look as swift as yours:
You saw the mistress, I beheld the maid;
You lov'd, I lov'd; for intermission
No more pertains to me, my lord, than you.
Your fortune stood upon the casket there,
And so did mine too, as the matter falls;
For wooing here until I sweat again,
And swearing till my very roof was dry
With oaths of love, at last, if promise last,
I got a promise of this fair one here
To have her love, provided that your fortune
Achiev'd her mistress.
Por. Is this true, Nerissa?
Ner. Madam, it is, so you stand pleas'd withal.
Bass. And do you, Gratiano, mean good faith?
Gra. Yes, faith, my lord.
Bass. Our feast shall be much honoured in your marriage.
Gra. We'll play with them the first boy for a thousand ducats.
Ner. What, and stake down?
Gra. No; we shall ne'er win at that sport, and stake down.
But who comes here? Lorenzo and his infidel?
What, and my old Venetian friend Salerio?

Enter LORENZO, JESSICA, *and* SALERIO, *a Messenger from Venice.*

Bass. Lorenzo and Salerio, welcome hither;
If that the youth of my new int'rest here
Have power to bid you welcome. By your leave,
I bid my very friends and countrymen,
Sweet Portia, welcome.
Por. So do I, my lord:
They are entirely welcome.
Lor. I thank your honour. For my part, my lord,
My purpose was not to have seen you here;
But meeting with Salerio by the way,
He did intreat me, past all saying nay,
To come with him along.
Saler. I did, my lord;
And I have reason for it. Signor Antonio
Commends him to you. [*Gives Bassanio a letter.*]
Bass. Ere I ope his letter,
I pray you, tell me how my good friend doth.
Saler. Not sick, my lord, unless it be in mind;
Nor well, unless in mind: his letter there
Will show you his estate. *Open the letter.*
Gra. Nerissa, cheer yond stranger; bid her welcome.
Your hand, Salerio: what 's the news from Venice?
How doth that royal merchant, good Antonio?
I know he will be glad of our success;
We are the Jasons, we have won the fleece.
Saler. I would you had won the fleece that he hath lost.
Por. There are some shrewd contents in yond same paper,
That steals the colour from Bassanio's cheek:
Some dear friend dead; else nothing in the world
Could turn so much the constitution
Of any constant man. What, worse and worse!
With leave, Bassanio; I am half yourself,
And I must freely have the half of anything
That this same paper brings you.
Bass. O sweet Portia,
Here are a few of the unpleasant'st words
That ever blotted paper! Gentle lady,
When I did first impart my love to you,
I freely told you, all the wealth I had
Ran in my veins, I was a gentleman;
And then I told you true: and yet, dear lady,
Rating myself at nothing, you shall see
How much I was a braggart. When I told you
My state was nothing, I should then have told you
That I was worse than nothing; for, indeed,
I have engag'd myself to a dear friend,
Engag'd my friend to his mere enemy,
To feed my means. Here is a letter, lady;
The paper as the body of my friend,
And every word in it a gaping wound,
Issuing life-blood. But is it true, Salerio?
Hath all his ventures fail'd? What, not one hit?
From Tripolis, from Mexico and England,
From Lisbon, Barbary and India?
And not one vessel 'scape the dreadful touch
Of merchant-marring rocks?
Saler. Not one, my lord.
Besides, it should appear, that if he had
The present money to discharge the Jew,
He would not take it. Never did I know
A creature, that did bear the shape of man,
So keen and greedy to confound a man:
He plies the duke at morning and at night,
And doth impeach the freedom of the state,
If they deny him justice: twenty merchants,
The duke himself, and the magnificoes
Of greatest port, have all persuaded with him;
But none can drive him from the envious plea
Of forfeiture, of justice and his bond.
Jes. When I was with him I have heard him swear
To Tubal and to Chus, his countrymen,
That he would rather have Antonio's flesh
Than twenty times the value of the sum
That he did owe him: and I know, my lord,
If law, authority and power deny not,
It will go hard with poor Antonio.
Por. Is it your dear friend that is thus in trouble?
Bass. The dearest friend to me, the kindest man,
The best-condition'd and unwearied spirit
In doing courtesies, and one in whom
The ancient Roman honour more appears
Than any that draws breath in Italy.
Por. What sum owes he the Jew?
Bass. For me three thousand ducats.
Por. What, no more?
Pay him six thousand, and deface the bond;
Double six thousand, and then treble that,
Before a friend of this description
Shall lose a hair through Bassanio's fault.

206. **roof,** roof of my mouth. 228. **entirely,** cordially. 235. **Commends him,** desires to be remembered. 239. **estate,** condition. 242. **royal merchant,** merchant prince. 246. **shrewd,** evil. 250. **constant,** settled, not swayed by passion. 265. **mere,** absolute. 281. **impeach,** call in question. 283. **magnificoes,** chief men of Venice. 315. **cheer,** face. 324-325. **Notwithstanding . . . letter.** Complete self-abnegation is

First go with me to church and call me wife,
And then away to Venice to your friend;
For never shall you lie by Portia's side
With an unquiet soul. You shall have gold
To pay the petty debt twenty times over:
When it is paid, bring your true friend along.
My maid Nerissa and myself meantime
Will live as maids and widows. Come, away!
For you shall hence upon your wedding-day:
Bid your friends welcome, show a merry cheer:
Since you are dear bought, I will love you dear.
But let me hear the letter of your friend.

Bass. [*Reads*] Sweet Bassanio, my ships have all miscarried, my creditors grow cruel, my estate is very low, my bond to the Jew is forfeit; and since in paying it, it is impossible I should live, all debts are cleared between you and I, if I might but see you at my death. Notwithstanding, use your pleasure: if your love do not persuade you to come, let not my letter.

Por. O love, dispatch all business, and be gone!
Bass. Since I have your good leave to go away,
I will make haste: but, till I come again,
No bed shall e'er be guilty of my stay,
Nor rest be interposer 'twixt us twain. *Exeunt.*

[SCENE III. *Venice. A street.*]

Enter [SHYLOCK] *the Jew and* SOLANIO *and* ANTONIO *and the* GAOLER.

Shy. Gaoler, look to him: tell not me of mercy;
This is the fool that lent out money gratis:
Gaoler, look to him.
Ant. Hear me yet, good Shylock.
Shy. I'll have my bond; speak not against my bond:
I have sworn an oath that I will have my bond.
Thou call'dst me dog before thou hadst a cause;
But, since I am a dog, beware my fangs:
The duke shall grant me justice. I do wonder,
Thou naughty gaoler, that thou art so fond
To come abroad with him at his request.
Ant. I pray thee, hear me speak.
Shy. I'll have my bond; I will not hear thee speak:
I'll have my bond; and therefore speak no more.
I'll not be made a soft and dull-ey'd fool,
To shake the head, relent, and sigh, and yield
To Christian intercessors. Follow not;
I'll have no speaking: I will have my bond. *Exit Jew.*
Solan. It is the most impenetrable cur
That ever kept with men.
Ant. Let him alone:
I'll follow him no more with bootless prayers.
He seeks my life; his reason well I know:
I oft deliver'd from his forfeitures
Many that have at times made moan to me;
Therefore he hates me.
Solan. I am sure the duke
Will never grant this forfeiture to hold.
Ant. The duke cannot deny the course of law:
For the commodity that strangers have
With us in Venice, if it be denied,
Will much impeach the justice of his state;
Since that the trade and profit of the city
Consisteth of all nations. Therefore, go:
These griefs and losses have so bated me,
That I shall hardly spare a pound of flesh
To-morrow to my bloody creditor.
Well, gaoler, on. Pray God, Bassanio come
To see me pay his debt, and then I care not! *Exeunt.*

[SCENE IV. *Belmont. A room in* PORTIA'S *house.*]

Enter PORTIA, NERISSA, LORENZO, JESSICA, *and* [BALTHASAR,] *a Man of Portia's.*

Lor. Madam, although I speak it in your presence,
You have a noble and a true conceit
Of god-like amity; which appears most strongly
In bearing thus the absence of your lord.
But if you knew to whom you show this honour,
How true a gentleman you send relief,
How dear a lover of my lord your husband,
I know you would be prouder of the work
Than customary bounty can enforce you.
Por. I never did repent for doing good,
Nor shall not now: for in companions
That do converse and waste the time together,
Whose souls do bear an equal yoke of love,
There must be needs a like proportion
Of lineaments, of manners and of spirit;
Which makes me think that this Antonio,
Being the bosom lover of my lord,
Must needs be like my lord. If it be so,
How little is the cost I have bestow'd
In purchasing the semblance of my soul
From out the state of hellish cruelty!
This comes too near the praising of myself;
Therefore no more of it: hear other things.
Lorenzo, I commit into your hands
The husbandry and manage of my house
Until my lord's return: for mine own part,
I have toward heaven breath'd a secret vow
To live in prayer and contemplation,
Only attended by Nerissa here,
Until her husband and my lord's return:
There is a monastery two miles off;
And there will we abide. I do desire you
Not to deny this imposition;
The which my love and some necessity
Now lays upon you.
Lor. Madam, with all my heart;
I shall obey you in all fair commands.
Por. My people do already know my mind,
And will acknowledge you and Jessica
In place of Lord Bassanio and myself.
So fare you well, till we shall meet again.
Lor. Fair thoughts and happy hours attend on you!
Jes. I wish your ladyship all heart's content.
Por. I thank you for your wish, and am well pleas'd
To wish it back on you: fare you well, Jessica.
Exeunt [*Jessica and Lorenzo*].
Now, Balthasar,
As I have ever found thee honest-true,
So let me find thee still. Take this same letter,
And use thou all th' endeavour of a man
In speed to Padua: see thou render this
Into my cousin's hand, Doctor Bellario;

here thought of as a condition of ideal friendship as well as of ideal love.
SCENE III. 19. **kept,** associated. 20. **bootless,** unavailing. 27. **commodity,** facilities or privileges for trading. 32. **bated,** dejected.

SCENE IV. 9. **customary bounty,** ordinary kindness. 20. **my soul,** Bassanio. 25. **husbandry,** care of the household. **manage,** administration; see glossary. 33. **imposition,** charge imposed. 49. **render,** deliver.

And, look what notes and garments he doth give thee,
Bring them, I pray thee, with imagin'd speed
Unto the tranect, to the common ferry
Which trades to Venice. Waste no time in words,
But get thee gone: I shall be there before thee.

Balth. Madam, I go with all convenient speed. [*Exit.*]

Por. Come on, Nerissa; I have work in hand
That you yet know not of: we'll see our husbands
Before they think of us.

Ner. Shall they see us?

Por. They shall, Nerissa; but in such a habit,
That they shall think we are accomplished
With that we lack. I'll hold thee any wager,
When we are both accoutred like young men,
I'll prove the prettier fellow of the two,
And wear my dagger with the braver grace,
And speak between the change of man and boy
With a reed voice, and turn two mincing steps
Into a manly stride, and speak of frays
Like a fine bragging youth, and tell quaint lies,
How honourable ladies sought my love,
Which I denying, they fell sick and died;
I could not do withal; then I'll repent,
And wish, for all that, that I had not kill'd them;
And twenty of these puny lies I'll tell,
That men shall swear I have discontinued school
Above a twelvemonth. I have within my mind
A thousand raw tricks of these bragging Jacks,
Which I will practise.

Ner. Why, shall we turn to men?

Por. Fie, what a question 's that,
If thou wert near a lewd interpreter!
But come, I'll tell thee all my whole device
When I am in my coach, which stays for us
At the park gate; and therefore haste away,
For we must measure twenty miles to-day. *Exeunt.*

[SCENE V. *The same. A garden.*]

Enter [LAUNCELOT *the*] *Clown and* JESSICA.

Laun. Yes, truly; for, look you, the sins of the father are to be laid upon the children: therefore, I promise you, I fear you. I was always plain with you, and so now I speak my agitation of the matter: therefore be o' good cheer, for truly I think you are damned. There is but one hope in it that can do you any good; and that is but a kind of bastard hope neither.

Jes. And what hope is that, I pray thee?

Laun. Marry, you may partly hope that your father got you not, that you are not the Jew's daughter.

Jes. That were a kind of bastard hope, indeed: so the sins of my mother should be visited upon me.

Laun. Truly then I fear you are damned both by father and mother: thus when I shun Scylla, your father, I fall into Charybdis, your mother: well, you are gone both ways.

Jes. I shall be saved by my husband; he hath made me a Christian.

Laun. Truly, the more to blame he: we were Christians enow before; e'en as many as could well live, one by another. This making of Christians will raise the price of hogs: if we grow all to be pork-eaters, we shall not shortly have a rasher on the coals for money.

Enter LORENZO.

Jes. I'll tell my husband, Launcelot, what you say: here he comes.

Lor. I shall grow jealous of you shortly, Launcelot, if you thus get my wife into corners.

Jes. Nay, you need not fear us, Lorenzo: Launcelot and I are out. He tells me flatly, there 's no mercy for me in heaven, because I am a Jew's daughter: and he says, you are no good member of the commonwealth, for in converting Jews to Christians, you raise the price of pork.

Lor. I shall answer that better to the commonwealth than you can the getting up of the negro's belly: the Moor is with child by you, Launcelot.

Laun. It is much that the Moor should be more than reason: but if she be less than an honest woman, she is indeed more than I took her for.

Lor. How every fool can play upon the word! I think the best grace of wit will shortly turn into silence, and discourse grow commendable in none only but parrots. Go in, sirrah; bid them prepare for dinner.

Laun. That is done, sir; they have all stomachs.

Lor. Goodly Lord, what a wit-snapper are you! then bid them prepare dinner.

Laun. That is done too, sir; only 'cover' is the word.

Lor. Will you cover then, sir?

Laun. Not so, sir, neither; I know my duty.

Lor. Yet more quarrelling with occasion! Wilt thou show the whole wealth of thy wit in an instant? I pray thee, understand a plain man in his plain meaning: go to thy fellows; bid them cover the table, serve in the meat, and we will come in to dinner.

Laun. For the table, sir, it shall be served in; for the meat, sir, it shall be covered; for your coming in to dinner, sir, why, let it be as humours and conceits shall govern. *Exit Clown.*

Lor. O dear discretion, how his words are suited!
The fool hath planted in his memory
An army of good words; and I do know
A many fools, that stand in better place,
Garnish'd like him, that for a tricksy word
Defy the matter. How cheer'st thou, Jessica?
And now, good sweet, say thy opinion,
How dost thou like the Lord Bassanio's wife?

Jes. Past all expressing. It is very meet
The Lord Bassanio live an upright life;
For, having such a blessing in his lady,
He finds the joys of heaven here on earth;
†And if on earth he do not merit it,
In reason he should never come to heaven.
Why, if two gods should play some heavenly match
And on the wager lay two earthly women,
And Portia one, there must be something else
Pawn'd with the other, for the poor rude world
Hath not her fellow.

52. **imagined speed,** speed of imagination, as quick as thought. 53. **tranect.** Rowe conjectured *traject* (Italian *traghetto*, ferry). 61. **accomplished,** supplied. 72. **do withal,** help it. 77. **Jacks,** fellows.
SCENE V. 3. **fear you,** i.e., for you. 5. **agitation,** for "cogitation." 19. **Scylla, Charybdis,** twin dangers of *Odyssey*, xii, 235, a rock and a whirlpool guarding the straits between Italy and Sicily. 25. **one by another,** together. 57. **'cover,'** two meanings: "spread the table for the meal" and "put on your hat." 60. **quarrelling with occasion,** answering perversely. 70. **suited,** fitted to special uses. 74. **Garnish'd,** i.e., with words. 74-75. **that . . . matter,** who for the sake of ingenious word-play do violence to common sense. **How cheer'st thou,** i.e., what cheer? 82. **merit it,** i.e., lead an upright life.

Lor. Even such a husband
Hast thou of me as she is for a wife.
Jes. Nay, but ask my opinion too of that!
Lor. I will anon: first, let us go to dinner.
Jes. Nay, let me praise you while I have a stomach.
Lor. No, pray thee, let it serve for table-talk;
Then, howsoe'er thou speak'st, 'mong other things
I shall digest it.
Jes. Well, I'll set you forth. *Exeunt.*

[ACT IV.

SCENE I. *Venice. A court of justice.*]

Enter the DUKE, *the* Magnificoes, ANTONIO, BASSANIO, [SALERIO,] *and* GRATIANO [*with others*].

Duke. What, is Antonio here?
Ant. Ready, so please your grace.
Duke. I am sorry for thee: thou art come to answer
A stony adversary, an inhuman wretch
Uncapable of pity, void and empty
From any dram of mercy.
Ant. I have heard
Your grace hath ta'en great pains to qualify
His rigorous course; but since he stands obdurate
And that no lawful means can carry me
Out of his envy's reach, I do oppose
My patience to his fury, and am arm'd
To suffer, with a quietness of spirit,
The very tyranny and rage of his.
Duke. Go one, and call the Jew into the court.
Saler. He is ready at the door: he comes, my lord.

Enter SHYLOCK.

Duke. Make room, and let him stand before our face.
Shylock, the world thinks, and I think so too,
That thou but leadest this fashion of thy malice
To the last hour of act; and then 'tis thought
Thou 'lt show thy mercy and remorse more strange
Than is thy strange apparent cruelty;
And where thou now exacts the penalty,
Which is a pound of this poor merchant's flesh,
Thou wilt not only loose the forfeiture,
But, touch'd with human gentleness and love,
Forgive a moiety of the principal;
Glancing an eye of pity on his losses,
That have of late so huddled on his back,
Enow to press a royal merchant down
And pluck commiseration of his state
From brassy bosoms and rough hearts of flint,
From stubborn Turks and Tartars, never train'd
To offices of tender courtesy.
We all expect a gentle answer, Jew.
Shy. I have possess'd your grace of what I purpose;
And by our holy Sabbath have I sworn
To have the due and forfeit of my bond:
If you deny it, let the danger light
Upon your charter and your city's freedom.
You'll ask me, why I rather choose to have
A weight of carrion flesh than to receive
Three thousand ducats: I'll not answer that:
But, say, it is my humour: is it answer'd?
What if my house be troubled with a rat
And I be pleas'd to give ten thousand ducats
To have it ban'd? What, are you answer'd yet?
Some men there are love not a gaping pig;
Some, that are mad if they behold a cat;
And others, when the bagpipe sings i' th' nose,
Cannot contain their urine: for affection,
Mistress of passion, sways it to the mood
Of what it likes or loathes. Now, for your answer:
As there is no firm reason to be rend'red,
Why he cannot abide a gaping pig;
Why he, a harmless necessary cat;
†Why he, a woollen bag-pipe; but of force
Must yield to such inevitable shame
As to offend, himself being offended;
So can I give no reason, nor I will not,
More than a lodg'd hate and a certain loathing
I bear Antonio, that I follow thus
A losing suit against him. Are you answered?
Bass. This is no answer, thou unfeeling man,
To excuse the current of thy cruelty.
Shy. I am not bound to please thee with my answers.
Bass. Do all men kill the things they do not love?
Shy. Hates any man the thing he would not kill?
Bass. Every offence is not a hate at first.
Shy. What, wouldst thou have a serpent sting thee twice?
Ant. I pray you, think you question with the Jew:
You may as well go stand upon the beach
And bid the main flood bate his usual height;
You may as well use question with the wolf
Why he hath made the ewe bleat for the lamb;
You may as well forbid the mountain pines
To wag their high tops and to make no noise,
When they are fretten with the gusts of heaven;
You may as well do any thing most hard,
As seek to soften that—than which what's harder?—
His Jewish heart: therefore, I do beseech you,
Make no more offers, use no farther means,
But with all brief and plain conveniency
Let me have judgement and the Jew his will.
Bass. For thy three thousand ducats here is six.
Shy. If every ducat in six thousand ducats
Were in six parts and every part a ducat,
I would not draw them; I would have my bond.
Duke. How shalt thou hope for mercy, rend'ring none?
Shy. What judgement shall I dread, doing no wrong?
You have among you many a purchas'd slave,
Which, like your asses and your dogs and mules,
You use in abject and in slavish parts,
Because you bought them: shall I say to you,
Let them be free, marry them to your heirs?
Why sweat they under burthens? let their beds
Be made as soft as yours and let their palates
Be season'd with such viands? You will answer
'The slaves are ours:' so do I answer you:

ACT IV. SCENE I. 7. **qualify,** moderate. 13. **tyranny,** cruelty. 18. **fashion,** mere form. 19. **act,** action. 26. **moiety,** part, portion; see glossary. 29. **Enow,** enough. 35. **possess'd,** informed. 38. **danger,** injury. 39. **Upon . . . freedom.** The Venetians were celebrated for their strict adherence to law. 46. **ban'd,** killed, especially by poison. 47. **gaping pig,** explained as "pig roasted whole with its mouth open"; also as "bawling" or "shouting," i.e., squealing. 50. **affection,** mental state or inclination; see glossary. Shylock means to say that the mental state from which passion arises may originate from mere likes and dislikes. 60. **lodg'd,** settled, steadfast. **certain,** definite. 72. **bate,** abate. 77. **fretten,** fretted. 87. **draw,** receive. 92. **parts,** duties, capacities.

The pound of flesh, which I demand of him,
Is dearly bought; 'tis mine and I will have it.
If you deny me, fie upon your law!
There is no force in the decrees of Venice.
I stand for judgement: answer; shall I have it?
Duke. Upon my power I may dismiss this court,
Unless Bellario, a learned doctor,
Whom I have sent for to determine this,
Come here to-day.
Saler. My lord, here stays without
A messenger with letters from the doctor,
New come from Padua.
Duke. Bring us the letters; call the messenger.
Bass. Good cheer, Antonio! What, man, courage yet!
The Jew shall have my flesh, blood, bones and all,
Ere thou shalt lose for me one drop of blood.
Ant. I am a tainted wether of the flock,
Meetest for death: the weakest kind of fruit
Drops earliest to the ground; and so let me:
You cannot better be employ'd, Bassanio,
Than to live still and write mine epitaph.

Enter NERISSA [*dressed like a lawyer's clerk*].

Duke. Came you from Padua, from Bellario?
Ner. From both, my lord. Bellario greets your grace. [*Presenting a letter.*]
Bass. Why dost thou whet thy knife so earnestly?
Shy. To cut the forfeiture from that bankrout there.
Gra. Not on thy sole, but on thy soul, harsh Jew,
Thou mak'st thy knife keen; but no metal can,
No, not the hangman's axe, bear half the keenness
Of thy sharp envy. Can no prayers pierce thee?
Shy. No, none that thou hast wit enough to make.
Gra. O, be thou damn'd, inexecrable dog!
And for thy life let justice be accus'd.
Thou almost mak'st me waver in my faith
To hold opinion with Pythagoras,
That souls of animals infuse themselves
Into the trunks of men: thy currish spirit
Govern'd a wolf, who, hang'd for human slaughter,
Even from the gallows did his fell soul fleet,
And, whilst thou layest in thy unhallowed dam,
Infus'd itself in thee; for thy desires
Are wolvish, bloody, starv'd and ravenous.
Shy. Till thou canst rail the seal from off my bond,
Thou but offend'st thy lungs to speak so loud:
Repair thy wit, good youth, or it will fall
To cureless ruin. I stand here for law.
Duke. This letter from Bellario doth commend
A young and learned doctor to our court.
Where is he?
Ner. He attendeth here hard by,
To know your answer, whether you'll admit him.
Duke. With all my heart. Some three or four of you
Go give him courteous conduct to this place.
Meantime the court shall hear Bellario's letter.

Clerk. [*Reads*] Your grace shall understand that at the receipt of your letter I am very sick: but in the instant that your messenger came, in loving visitation was with me a young doctor of Rome; his name is Balthasar. I acquainted him with the cause in controversy between the Jew and Antonio the merchant: we turned o'er many books together: he is furnished with my opinion; which, bettered with his own learning, the greatness whereof I cannot enough commend, comes with him, at my importunity, to fill up your grace's request in my stead. I beseech you, let his lack of years be no impediment to let him lack a reverend estimation; for I never knew so young a body with so old a head. I leave him to your gracious acceptance, whose trial shall better publish his commendation.

Duke. You hear the learn'd Bellario, what he writes:
And here, I take it, is the doctor come.

Enter PORTIA *for Balthasar* [*dressed like a doctor of laws*].

Give me your hand. Come you from old Bellario?
Por. I did, my lord.
Duke. You are welcome: take your place.
Are you acquainted with the difference
That holds this present question in the court?
Por. I am informed throughly of the cause.
Which is the merchant here, and which the Jew?
Duke. Antonio and old Shylock, both stand forth.
Por. Is your name Shylock?
Shy. Shylock is my name.
Por. Of a strange nature is the suit you follow;
Yet in such rule that the Venetian law
Cannot impugn you as you do proceed.—
You stand within his danger, do you not?
Ant. Ay, so he says.
Por. Do you confess the bond?
Ant. I do.
Por. Then must the Jew be merciful.
Shy. On what compulsion must I? tell me that.
Por. The quality of mercy is not strain'd,
It droppeth as the gentle rain from heaven
Upon the place beneath: it is twice blest;
It blesseth him that gives and him that takes:
'Tis mightiest in the mightiest: it becomes
The throned monarch better than his crown;
His sceptre shows the force of temporal power,
The attribute to awe and majesty,
Wherein doth sit the dread and fear of kings;
But mercy is above this sceptred sway;
It is enthroned in the hearts of kings,
It is an attribute to God himself;
And earthly power doth then show likest God's
When mercy seasons justice. Therefore, Jew,
Though justice be thy plea, consider this,
That, in the course of justice, none of us
Should see salvation: we do pray for mercy;
And that same prayer doth teach us all to render
The deeds of mercy. I have spoke thus much
To mitigate the justice of thy plea;
Which if thou follow, this strict court of Venice
Must needs give sentence 'gainst the merchant there.
Shy. My deeds upon my head! I crave the law,
The penalty and forfeit of my bond.
Por. Is he not able to discharge the money?
Bass. Yes, here I tender it for him in the court;
Yea, twice the sum: if that will not suffice,
I will be bound to pay it ten times o'er,
On forfeit of my hands, my head, my heart:
If this will not suffice, it must appear
That malice bears down truth. And I beseech you,

114. **tainted wether,** old and diseased ram. 115. **Meetest,** fittest. 121. **Why . . . earnestly.** The traditional stage business at this point is for the actor who plays the part of Shylock to be discovered whetting his knife on the sole of his shoe. 128. **inexecrable,** most execrable. 134. **hang'd for human slaughter,** a possible allusion to the ancient practice of trying and punishing animals for various crimes. 135. **fell,** fierce. **fleet,** flit. 140. **offend'st,** injurest. 173. **throughly,** thoroughly; see glossary. 179. **impugn,** find fault with. 180. **danger,** power to

Wrest once the law to your authority:
To do a great right, do a little wrong,
And curb this cruel devil of his will.
Por. It must not be; there is no power in Venice
Can alter a decree established:
'Twill be recorded for a precedent,
And many an error by the same example
Will rush into the state: it cannot be.
Shy. A Daniel come to judgement! yea, a Daniel!
O wise young judge, how I do honour thee!
Por. I pray you, let me look upon the bond.
Shy. Here 'tis, most reverend doctor, here it is.
Por. Shylock, there 's thrice thy money off'red thee.
Shy. An oath, an oath, I have an oath in heaven:
Shall I lay perjury upon my soul?
No, not for Venice.
Por. Why, this bond is forfeit;
And lawfully by this the Jew may claim
A pound of flesh, to be by him cut off
Nearest the merchant's heart. Be merciful:
Take thrice thy money; bid me tear the bond.
Shy. When it is paid according to the tenure.
It doth appear you are a worthy judge;
You know the law, your exposition
Hath been most sound: I charge you by the law,
Whereof you are a well-deserving pillar,
Proceed to judgement: by my soul I swear
There is no power in the tongue of man
To alter me: I stay here on my bond.
Ant. Most heartily I do beseech the court
To give the judgement.
Por. Why then, thus it is:
You must prepare your bosom for his knife.
Shy. O noble judge! O excellent young man!
Por. For the intent and purpose of the law
Hath full relation to the penalty,
Which here appeareth due upon the bond.
Shy. 'Tis very true: O wise and upright judge!
How much more elder art thou than thy looks!
Por. Therefore lay bare your bosom.
Shy. Ay, his breast:
So says the bond: doth it not, noble judge?
'Nearest his heart:' those are the very words.
Por. It is so. Are there balance here to weigh
The flesh?
Shy. I have them ready.
Por. Have by some surgeon, Shylock, on your charge,
To stop his wounds, lest he do bleed to death.
Shy. Is it so nominated in the bond?
Por. It is not so express'd: but what of that?
'Twere good you do so much for charity.
Shy. I cannot find it; 'tis not in the bond.
Por. You, merchant, have you any thing to say?
Ant. But little: I am arm'd and well prepar'd.
Give me your hand, Bassanio: fare you well!
Grieve not that I am fall'n to this for you;
For herein Fortune shows herself more kind
Than is her custom: it is still her use
To let the wretched man outlive his wealth,
To view with hollow eye and wrinkled brow
An age of poverty; from which ling'ring penance
Of such misery doth she cut me off.
Commend me to your honourable wife:
Tell her the process of Antonio's end;
Say how I lov'd you, speak me fair in death;
And, when the tale is told, bid her be judge
Whether Bassanio had not once a love.
Repent but you that you shall lose your friend,
And he repents not that he pays your debt;
For if the Jew do cut but deep enough,
I'll pay it presently with all my heart.
Bass. Antonio, I am married to a wife
Which is as dear to me as life itself;
But life itself, my wife, and all the world,
Are not with me esteem'd above thy life:
I would lose all, ay, sacrifice them all
Here to this devil, to deliver you.
Por. Your wife would give you little thanks for that,
If she were by, to hear you make the offer.
Gra. I have a wife, whom, I protest, I love:
I would she were in heaven, so she could
Entreat some power to change this currish Jew.
Ner. 'Tis well you offer it behind her back;
The wish would make else an unquiet house.
Shy. These be the Christian husbands. I have a daughter;
Would any of the stock of Barrabas
Had been her husband rather than a Christian! [*Aside.*]
We trifle time: I pray thee, pursue sentence.
Por. A pound of that same merchant's flesh is thine:
The court awards it, and the law doth give it.
Shy. Most rightful judge!
Por. And you must cut this flesh from off his breast:
The law allows it, and the court awards it.
Shy. Most learned judge! A sentence! Come, prepare!
Por. Tarry a little; there is something else.
This bond doth give thee here no jot of blood;
The words expressly are 'a pound of flesh:'
Take then thy bond, take thou thy pound of flesh;
But, in the cutting it, if thou dost shed
One drop of Christian blood, thy lands and goods
Are, by the laws of Venice, confiscate
Unto the state of Venice.
Gra. O upright judge! Mark, Jew: O learned judge!
Shy. Is that the law?
Por. Thyself shalt see the act:
For, as thou urgest justice, be assur'd
Thou shalt have justice, more than thou desir'st.
Gra. O learned judge! Mark, Jew: a learned judge!
Shy. I take this offer, then; pay the bond thrice
And let the Christian go.
Bass. Here is the money.
Por. Soft!
The Jew shall have all justice; soft! no haste:
He shall have nothing but the penalty.
Gra. O Jew! an upright judge, a learned judge!
Por. Therefore prepare thee to cut off the flesh.
Shed thou no blood, nor cut thou less nor more
But just a pound of flesh: if thou tak'st more
Or less than a just pound, be it but so much
As makes it light or heavy in the substance,
Or the division of the twentieth part
Of one poor scruple, nay, if the scale do turn
But in the estimation of a hair,

harm; possibly a legal term. 184. **strain'd,** forced, constrained; in reply to Shylock's reference to compulsion. 214. **truth,** honesty (Johnson). 223. **Daniel.** In the Apocryphal book of *Susannah*, Daniel is the judge who rescues Susannah from her false accusers. 235. **tenure,** conditions. 242. **stay . . . on,** take stand upon. 274. **process,** story; see glossary. 328. **substance,** mass or gross weight. 329-330. **division . . . scruple,** fraction of the twentieth of a scruple (20 grains apothecaries' weight).

Thou diest and all thy goods are confiscate.
Gra. A second Daniel, a Daniel, Jew!
Now, infidel, I have you on the hip.
Por. Why doth the Jew pause? take thy forfeiture.
Shy. Give me my principal, and let me go.
Bass. I have it ready for thee; here it is.
Por. He hath refus'd it in the open court:
He shall have merely justice and his bond.
Gra. A Daniel, still say I, a second Daniel!
I thank thee, Jew, for teaching me that word.
Shy. Shall I not have barely my principal?
Por. Thou shalt have nothing but the forfeiture,
To be so taken at thy peril, Jew.
Shy. Why, then the devil give him good of it!
I'll stay no longer question.
Por. Tarry, Jew:
The law hath yet another hold on you.
It is enacted in the laws of Venice,
If it be prov'd against an alien
That by direct or indirect attempts
He seek the life of any citizen,
The party 'gainst the which he doth contrive
Shall seize one half his goods; the other half
Comes to the privy coffer of the state;
And the offender's life lies in the mercy
Of the duke only, 'gainst all other voice.
In which predicament, I say, thou stand'st;
For it appears, by manifest proceeding,
That indirectly and directly too
Thou hast contriv'd against the very life
Of the defendant; and thou hast incurr'd
The danger formerly by me rehears'd.
Down therefore and beg mercy of the duke.
Gra. Beg that thou mayst have leave to hang thyself:
And yet, thy wealth being forfeit to the state,
Thou hast not left the value of a cord;
Therefore thou must be hang'd at the state's charge.
Duke. That thou shalt see the difference of our spirit,
I pardon thee thy life before thou ask it:
For half thy wealth, it is Antonio's;
The other half comes to the general state,
Which humbleness may drive unto a fine.
Por. Ay, for the state, not for Antonio.
Shy. Nay, take my life and all! Pardon not that!
You take my house when you do take the prop
That doth sustain my house; you take my life
When you do take the means whereby I live.
Por. What mercy can you render him, Antonio?
Gra. A halter gratis; nothing else, for God's sake.
Ant. So please my lord the duke and all the court
To quit the fine for one half of his goods,
I am content; so he will let me have
The other half in use, to render it,
Upon his death, unto the gentleman
That lately stole his daughter:
Two things provided more, that, for this favour,
He presently become a Christian;
The other, that he do record a gift,
Here in the court, of all he dies possess'd,
Unto his son Lorenzo and his daughter.
Duke. He shall do this, or else I do recant
The pardon that I late pronounced here.
Por. Art thou contented, Jew? what dost thou say?
Shy. I am content.
Por. Clerk, draw a deed of gift.
Shy. I pray you, give me leave to go from hence;
I am not well: send the deed after me,
And I will sign it.
Duke. Get thee gone, but do it.
Gra. In christ'ning shalt thou have two godfathers:
Had I been judge, thou shouldst have had ten more,
To bring thee to the gallows, not the font. *Exit* [*Shylock*].
Duke. Sir, I entreat you home with me to dinner.
Por. I humbly do desire your grace of pardon:
I must away this night toward Padua,
And it is meet I presently set forth.
Duke. I am sorry that your leisure serves you not.
Antonio, gratify this gentleman,
For, in my mind, you are much bound to him.
Exeunt Duke and his train.
Bass. Most worthy gentleman, I and my friend
Have by your wisdom been this day acquitted
Of grievous penalties; in lieu whereof,
Three thousand ducats, due unto the Jew,
We freely cope your courteous pains withal.
Ant. And stand indebted, over and above,
In love and service to you evermore.
Por. He is well paid that is well satisfied;
And I, delivering you, am satisfied
And therein do account myself well paid:
My mind was never yet more mercenary.
I pray you, know me when we meet again:
I wish you well, and so I take my leave.
Bass. Dear sir, of force I must attempt you further:
Take some remembrance of us, as a tribute,
Not as a fee: grant me two things, I pray you,
Not to deny me, and to pardon me.
Por. You press me far, and therefore I will yield.
[*To Ant.*] Give me your gloves, I'll wear them for your sake;
[*To Bass.*] And, for your love, I'll take this ring from you:
Do not draw back your hand; I'll take no more;
And you in love shall not deny me this.
Bass. This ring, good sir, alas, it is a trifle!
I will not shame myself to give you this.
Por. I will have nothing else but only this;
And now methinks I have a mind to it.
Bass. There 's more depends on this than on the value.
The dearest ring in Venice will I give you,
And find it out by proclamation:
Only for this, I pray you, pardon me.
Por. I see, sir, you are liberal in offers:
You taught me first to beg; and now methinks
You teach me how a beggar should be answer'd.
Bass. Good sir, this ring was given me by my wife;
And when she put it on, she made me vow
That I should neither sell nor give nor lose it.
Por. That 'scuse serves many men to save their gifts.
An if your wife be not a mad-woman,
And know how well I have deserv'd the ring,

346. **I'll . . . question,** I'll stay for no further questioning. 367. **charge,** expense. 372. **Which . . . fine,** i.e., penitence on your part may persuade me to reduce the sentence to a fine. 381-385. **To quit . . . daughter,** i.e., I am content to have even the fine in lieu of a heavier penalty forgiven, on the condition that Shylock will let me have the other half in trust (in use) to be administered by me till his death, and then bequeathed to Lorenzo as his heir. 406. **gratify,** reward. 426. **gloves,** a customary and relatively valuable gift in Elizabethan times.

SCENE II. 6. **advice,** consideration. 15. **old,** plenty of.

ACT V. SCENE I. 4. **Troilus.** Cf. Chaucer, *Troilus and Criseyde,* lines

She would not hold out enemy for ever,
For giving it to me. Well, peace be with you!
Exeunt [*Portia and Nerissa*].

Ant. My Lord Bassanio, let him have the ring:
Let his deservings and my love withal
Be valued 'gainst your wife's commandement.

Bass. Go, Gratiano, run and overtake him;
Give him the ring, and bring him, if thou canst,
Unto Antonio's house: away! make haste.
Exit Gratiano.
Come, you and I will thither presently;
And in the morning early will we both
Fly toward Belmont: come, Antonio. *Exeunt.*

[SCENE II. *The same. A street.*]

Enter [PORTIA *and*] NERISSA [*still disguised*].

Por. Inquire the Jew's house out, give him this deed
And let him sign it: we'll away to-night
And be a day before our husbands home:
This deed will be well welcome to Lorenzo.

Enter GRATIANO.

Gra. Fair sir, you are well o'erta'en:
My Lord Bassanio upon more advice
Hath sent you here this ring, and doth entreat
Your company at dinner.

Por. That cannot be:
His ring I do accept most thankfully:
And so, I pray you, tell him: furthermore,
I pray you, show my youth old Shylock's house.

Gra. That will I do.

Ner. Sir, I would speak with you.
[*Aside to Por.*] I'll see if I can get my husband's ring,
Which I did make him swear to keep for ever.

Por. [*Aside to Ner.*] Thou mayst, I warrant. We shall have old swearing
That they did give the rings away to men;
But we'll outface them, and outswear them too.
[*Aloud*] Away! make haste: thou know'st where I will tarry.

Ner. Come, good sir, will you show me to this house? [*Exeunt.*]

[ACT V.

SCENE I. *Belmont. Avenue to* PORTIA'*s house.*]

Enter LORENZO *and* JESSICA.

Lor. The moon shines bright: in such a night as this,
When the sweet wind did gently kiss the trees
And they did make no noise, in such a night
Troilus methinks mounted the Troyan walls
And sigh'd his soul toward the Grecian tents,
Where Cressid lay that night.

Jes. In such a night
Did Thisbe fearfully o'ertrip the dew
And saw the lion's shadow ere himself
And ran dismay'd away.

Lor. In such a night
Stood Dido with a willow in her hand
Upon the wild sea banks and waft her love
To come again to Carthage.

Jes. In such a night
Medea gathered the enchanted herbs
That did renew old Æson.

Lor. In such a night
Did Jessica steal from the wealthy Jew
And with an unthrift love did run from Venice
As far as Belmont.

Jes. In such a night
Did young Lorenzo swear he lov'd her well,
Stealing her soul with many vows of faith
And ne'er a true one.

Lor. In such a night
Did pretty Jessica, like a little shrew,
Slander her love, and he forgave it her.

Jes. I would out-night you, did no body come;
But, hark, I hear the footing of a man.

Enter [STEPHANO,] *a Messenger*.

Lor. Who comes so fast in silence of the night?

Steph. A friend.

Lor. A friend! what friend? your name, I pray you, friend?

Steph. Stephano is my name; and I bring word
My mistress will before the break of day
Be here at Belmont: she doth stray about
By holy crosses, where she kneels and prays
For happy wedlock hours.

Lor. Who comes with her?

Steph. None but a holy hermit and her maid.
I pray you, is my master yet return'd?

Lor. He is not, nor we have not heard from him.
But go we in, I pray thee, Jessica,
And ceremoniously let us prepare
Some welcome for the mistress of the house.

Enter [LAUNCELOT, *the*] *Clown*.

Laun. Sola, sola! wo ha, ho! sola, sola!

Lor. Who calls?

Laun. Sola! did you see Master Lorenzo? Master Lorenzo, sola, sola!

Lor. Leave hollaing, man: here.

Laun. Sola! where? where?

Lor. Here.

Laun. Tell him there 's a post come from my master, with his horn full of good news: my master will be here ere morning. [*Exit.*]

Lor. Sweet soul, let 's in, and there expect their coming.
And yet no matter: why should we go in?
My friend Stephano, signify, I pray you,
Within the house, your mistress is at hand;
And bring your music forth into the air. [*Exit Stephano.*]
How sweet the moonlight sleeps upon this bank!
Here will we sit and let the sounds of music
Creep in our ears: soft stillness and the night
Become the touches of sweet harmony.
Sit, Jessica. Look how the floor of heaven

647-679. 7. **Thisbe.** The story of Pyramus and Thisbe was the subject of the play presented by Bottom and his companions in *A Midsummer Night's Dream*. 10. **willow,** symbol of forsaken love. 11. **waft,** beckoned. 13. **Medea,** allusion to the famous sorceress of Colchis, who pretended to restore youth to Æson, father of Jason, as told by Ovid.

24. **footing,** footsteps. 39. **Sola,** imitation of a postman's horn. 51. **signify,** make known. 49. **expect,** await.

Is thick inlaid with patens of bright gold:
There's not the smallest orb which thou behold'st
But in his motion like an angel sings,
Still quiring to the young-ey'd cherubins;
Such harmony is in immortal souls;
But whilst this muddy vesture of decay
Doth grossly close it in, we cannot hear it.

[*Enter* Musicians.]

Come, ho! and wake Diana with a hymn:
With sweetest touches pierce your mistress' ear
And draw her home with music. *Play music.*
Jes. I am never merry when I hear sweet music.
Lor. The reason is, your spirits are attentive:
For do but note a wild and wanton herd,
Or race of youthful and unhandled colts,
Fetching mad bounds, bellowing and neighing loud,
Which is the hot condition of their blood;
If they but hear perchance a trumpet sound,
Or any air of music touch their ears,
You shall perceive them make a mutual stand,
Their savage eyes turn'd to a modest gaze
By the sweet power of music: therefore the poet
Did feign that Orpheus drew trees, stones and floods;
Since nought so stockish, hard and full of rage,
But music for the time doth change his nature.
The man that hath no music in himself,
Nor is not mov'd with concord of sweet sounds,
Is fit for treasons, stratagems and spoils;
The motions of his spirit are dull as night
And his affections dark as Erebus:
Let no such man be trusted. Mark the music.

Enter PORTIA *and* NERISSA.

Por. That light we see is burning in my hall.
How far that little candle throws his beams!
So shines a good deed in a naughty world.
Ner. When the moon shone, we did not see the candle.
Por. So doth the greater glory dim the less:
A substitute shines brightly as a king
Until a king be by, and then his state
Empties itself, as doth an inland brook
Into the main of waters. Music! hark!
Ner. It is your music, madam, of the house.
Por. Nothing is good, I see, without respect:
Methinks it sounds much sweeter than by day.
Ner. Silence bestows that virtue on it, madam.
Por. The crow doth sing as sweetly as the lark
When neither is attended, and I think
The nightingale, if she should sing by day,
When every goose is cackling, would be thought
No better a musician than the wren.
How many things by season season'd are
To their right praise and true perfection!
Peace, ho! the moon sleeps with Endymion
And would not be awak'd. [*Music ceases.*]
Lor. That is the voice,
Or I am much deceiv'd, of Portia.
Por. He knows me as the blind man knows the cuckoo,
By the bad voice.
Lor. Dear lady, welcome home.
Por. We have been praying for our husbands' healths,
Which speed, we hope, the better for our words.
Are they return'd?
Lor. Madam, they are not yet;
But there is come a messenger before,
To signify their coming.
Por. Go in, Nerissa;
Give order to my servants that they take
No note at all of our being absent hence;
Nor you, Lorenzo; Jessica, nor you. [*A tucket sounds.*]
Lor. Your husband is at hand; I hear his trumpet:
We are no tell-tales, madam; fear you not.
Por. This night methinks is but the daylight sick;
It looks a little paler: 'tis a day,
Such as the day is when the sun is hid.

Enter BASSANIO, ANTONIO, GRATIANO, *and their followers.*

Bass. We should hold day with the Antipodes,
If you would walk in absence of the sun.
Por. Let me give light, but let me not be light;
For a light wife doth make a heavy husband,
And never be Bassanio so for me:
But God sort all! You are welcome home, my lord.
Bass. I thank you, madam. Give welcome to my friend.
This is the man, this is Antonio,
To whom I am so infinitely bound.
Por. You should in all sense be much bound to him,
For, as I hear, he was much bound for you.
Ant. No more than I am well acquitted of.
Por. Sir, you are very welcome to our house:
It must appear in other ways than words,
Therefore I scant this breathing courtesy.
Gra. [*To Ner.*] By yonder moon I swear you do me wrong;
In faith, I gave it to the judge's clerk:
Would he were gelt that had it, for my part,
Since you do take it, love, so much at heart.
Por. A quarrel, ho, already! what 's the matter?
Gra. About a hoop of gold, a paltry ring
That she did give me, whose posy was
For all the world like cutler's poetry
Upon a knife, 'Love me, and leave me not.'
Ner. What talk you of the posy or the value?
You swore to me, when I did give it you,
That you would wear it till your hour of death
And that it should lie with you in your grave:
Though not for me, yet for your vehement oaths,
You should have been respective and have kept it.
Gave it a judge's clerk! no, God 's my judge,
The clerk will ne'er wear hair on 's face that had it.
Gra. He will, an if he live to be a man.
Ner. Ay, if a woman live to be a man.
Gra. Now, by this hand, I gave it to a youth,
A kind of boy, a little scrubbed boy,
No higher than thyself, the judge's clerk,
A prating boy, that begg'd it as a fee:

59. **patens,** thin, circular plates of metal. 60-65. **There's . . . hear it.** The universe was thought to be made up of revolving concentric spheres, each incorporating heavenly bodies and growing larger as the distance from the earth increased. Beyond the most distant planet was the sphere of the fixed stars, and beyond that the *primum mobile.* The spheres produced, as they moved, a harmony which the soul, itself by nature harmonious, might perceive were it not rendered dull by its covering of flesh. 70. **spirits are attentive.** The spirits would be in motion within the body in merriment, whereas in sadness they would be drawn to the heart, and, as it were, busy listening. 72. **race,** herd. 77. **mutual,** common or simultaneous. 79. **poet,** possibly Ovid, with whom the story of Orpheus was a favorite theme. 81. **stockish,** un-

I could not for my heart deny it him.
Por. You were to blame, I must be plain with you,
To part so slightly with your wife's first gift;
A thing stuck on with oaths upon your finger
And so riveted with faith unto your flesh.
I gave my love a ring and made him swear
Never to part with it; and here he stands;
I dare be sworn for him he would not leave it
Nor pluck it from his finger, for the wealth
That the world masters. Now, in faith, Gratiano,
You give your wife too unkind a cause of grief:
An 'twere to me, I should be mad at it.
Bass. [*Aside*] Why, I were best to cut my left hand off
And swear I lost the ring defending it.
Gra. My Lord Bassanio gave his ring away
Unto the judge that begg'd it and indeed
Deserv'd it too; and then the boy, his clerk,
That took some pains in writing, he begg'd mine;
And neither man nor master would take aught
But the two rings.
Por. What ring gave you, my lord?
Not that, I hope, which you receiv'd of me.
Bass. If I could add a lie unto a fault,
I would deny it; but you see my finger
Hath not the ring upon it; it is gone.
Por. Even so void is your false heart of truth.
By heaven, I will ne'er come in your bed
Until I see the ring.
Ner. Nor I in yours
Till I again see mine.
Bass. Sweet Portia,
If you did know to whom I gave the ring,
If you did know for whom I gave the ring
And would conceive for what I gave the ring
And how unwillingly I left the ring,
When nought would be accepted but the ring,
You would abate the strength of your displeasure.
Por. If you had known the virtue of the ring,
Or half her worthiness that gave the ring,
Or your own honour to contain the ring,
You would not then have parted with the ring.
What man is there so much unreasonable,
If you had pleas'd to have defended it
With any terms of zeal, wanted the modesty
To urge the thing held as a ceremony?
Nerissa teaches me what to believe:
I'll die for 't but some woman had the ring.
Bass. No, by my honour, madam, by my soul,
No woman had it, but a civil doctor,
Which did refuse three thousand ducats of me
And begg'd the ring; the which I did deny him
And suffer'd him to go displeas'd away;
Even he that did uphold the very life
Of my dear friend. What should I say, sweet lady?
I was enforc'd to send it after him;
I was beset with shame and courtesy;
My honour would not let ingratitude
So much besmear it. Pardon me, good lady;
For, by these blessed candles of the night,
Had you been there, I think you would have begg'd
The ring of me to give the worthy doctor.
Por. Let not that doctor e'er come near my house:
Since he hath got the jewel that I lov'd,
And that which you did swear to keep for me,
I will become as liberal as you;
I'll not deny him any thing I have,
No, not my body nor my husband's bed:
Know him I shall, I am well sure of it:
Lie not a night from home; watch me like Argus:
If you do not, if I be left alone,
Now, by mine honour, which is yet mine own,
I'll have that doctor for my bedfellow.
Ner. And I his clerk; therefore be well advis'd
How you do leave me to mine own protection.
Gra. Well, do you so: let not me take him, then;
For if I do, I'll mar the young clerk's pen.
Ant. I am th' unhappy subject of these quarrels.
Por. Sir, grieve not you; you are welcome notwithstanding.
Bass. Portia, forgive me this enforced wrong;
And, in the hearing of these many friends,
I swear to thee, even by thine own fair eyes,
Wherein I see myself—
Por. Mark you but that!
In both my eyes he doubly sees himself;
In each eye, one: swear by your double self,
And there 's an oath of credit.
Bass. Nay, but hear me:
Pardon this fault, and by my soul I swear
I never more will break an oath with thee.
Ant. I once did lend my body for his wealth;
Which, but for him that had your husband's ring,
Had quite miscarried: I dare be bound again,
My soul upon the forfeit, that your lord
Will never more break faith advisedly.
Por. Then you shall be his surety. Give him this
And bid him keep it better than the other.
Ant. Here, Lord Bassanio; swear to keep this ring.
Bass. By heaven, it is the same I gave the doctor!
Por. I had it of him: pardon me, Bassanio;
For, by this ring, the doctor lay with me.
Ner. And pardon me, my gentle Gratiano;
For that same scrubbed boy, the doctor's clerk,
In lieu of this last night did lie with me.
Gra. Why, this is like the mending of highways
In summer, where the ways are fair enough:
What, are we cuckolds ere we have deserv'd it?
Por. Speak not so grossly. You are all amaz'd:
Here is a letter; read it at your leisure;
It comes from Padua, from Bellario:
There you shall find that Portia was the doctor,
Nerissa there her clerk: Lorenzo here
Shall witness I set forth as soon as you
And even but now return'd; I have not yet
Enter'd my house. Antonio, you are welcome;
And I have better news in store for you
Than you expect: unseal this letter soon;
There you shall find three of your argosies
Are richly come to harbour suddenly:
You shall not know by what strange accident
I chanced on this letter.

feeling. 85. **spoils,** acts of pillage. 87. **Erebus,** classical abode of darkness. 99. **respect,** comparison. 109. **Endymion,** shepherd of Elis who, as he slept in a cave on Mount Latmos, was visited by Diana, the moon goddess; cf. line 66, above. 121. *Stage Direction:* ***tucket,*** flourish on a trumpet. 127. **Antipodes,** those who dwell on the opposite side of the globe. 132. **sort,** decide. 141. **breathing courtesy,** courteous speaking. 148. **posy,** a motto on a ring. 156. **respective,** mindful. 162. **scrubbed,** stunted. 164. **prating,** prattling. 176. **mad,** beside oneself with wrath. 201. **contain,** retain. 206. **ceremony,** something sacred. 210. **civil doctor,** i.e., doctor of civil law. 230. **Argus,** i.e., with a hundred eyes. 245. **double,** deceitful. 249. **wealth,** welfare. 265. **cuckolds,** husbands whose wives are unfaithful; see glossary.

Ant. I am dumb.

Bass. Were you the doctor and I knew you not?

Gra. Were you the clerk that is to make me cuckold?

Ner. Ay, but the clerk that never means to do it,
Unless he live until he be a man.

Bass. Sweet doctor, you shall be my bedfellow:
When I am absent, then lie with my wife.

Ant. Sweet lady, you have given me life and living;
For here I read for certain that my ships
Are safely come to road.

Por. How now, Lorenzo!
My clerk hath some good comforts too for you.

Ner. Ay, and I'll give them him without a fee.
There do I give to you and Jessica,
From the rich Jew, a special deed of gift,
After his death, of all he dies possess'd of.

Lor. Fair ladies, you drop manna in the way
Of starved people.

Por. It is almost morning,
And yet I am sure you are not satisfied
Of these events at full. Let us go in;
And charge us there upon inter'gatories,
And we will answer all things faithfully.

Gra. Let it be so: the first inter'gatory
That my Nerissa shall be sworn on is,
Whether till the next night she had rather stay
Or go to bed now, being two hours to day:
But were the day come, I should wish it dark,
That I were couching with the doctor's clerk.
Well, while I live I'll fear no other thing
So sore as keeping safe Nerissa's ring. *Exeunt.*

288. **road,** anchorage. 298. **charge . . . inter'gatories,** take oath to answer all things truly, like persons charged with contempt in the court of the Queen's Bench.

MUCH ADO ABOUT NOTHING

Much Ado about Nothing belongs to a group of Shakespeare's most mature romantic comedies, linked by similar titles, that also includes *As You Like It* and *Twelfth Night.* All date from the period 1598 (the year of Francis Meres' *Palladis Tamia,* which mentions none of them) to 1600 (when *Much Ado* and *As You Like It* were entered in the Stationers' Register but briefly stayed from publication). These plays are the culmination of Shakespeare's exuberant, philosophical, and "festive" vein in comedy, with only an occasional anticipation of the darker "problem" comedies of the early 1600's. They also parallel the culmination of Shakespeare's writing of history plays, in *Henry IV* and *V.*

Much Ado excels in combative wit and in swift, colloquial prose. It differs too from several other comedies (including *A Midsummer Night's Dream* and *The Merchant of Venice*) in that it features no journey of the lovers, no heroine disguised as a man, no envious court or city contrasted with an idealized landscape of the artist's imagination. Instead, the prevailing motif is that of the mask. Prominent scenes include a masked ball (II,i), a charade offstage in which the villainous Borachio misrepresents himself as the lover of Hero (actually Margaret in disguise), and a marriage ceremony with the supposedly dead bride masking as her own cousin (V,iii). Overhearings are constant, and are essential to the process of both misunderstanding (as in the false rumor of Don Pedro's wooing Hero for himself) and eventual clarification (as in the discovery by the night watch of the slander done to Hero's reputation, or in the revelation to Beatrice and Benedick of each other's true state of mind). The masks, or roles, that the characters are incessantly playing toward one another are for the most part defensive and inimical to mutual understanding. How can they be dispelled? It is the search for candor and self-awareness in relationships with others, the quest for a transforming inner reality beneath conventional outward appearances, that provides the "journey" in this play.

Structurally the play contrasts two pairs of lovers. The young ladies, Beatrice and Hero, are cousins and close friends. The gentlemen, Benedick and Claudio, Italian gentlemen and fellow-officers under the command of Don Pedro, have returned from the war in which they have fought bravely. These similarities only serve, however, to accentuate the differences between the two couples. Hero is modest, retiring, usually silent, and obedient to her father's will. Claudio appears ideally suited to her, since he is also respectful and decorous. They are conventional Petrarchan lovers in the roles of ingenue hero and heroine. Beatrice and Benedick, on the other hand, are renowned for "a kind of merry war" between them. Although obviously destined to come together, they are seemingly too independent and skeptical of convention to be tolerant and accepting in love. They scoff so at romantic sentimentality that they cannot permit themselves to drop their satirical masks. Yet paradoxically their relationship is the more surefooted because it is relentlessly probing and candid.

As in some of his other comic double plots (*The Taming of the Shrew*, for example), Shakespeare has linked together two stories of diverse origins and contrasting tones in order to set off one against the other. The Hero-Claudio plot is Italianate in flavor and origin, sensational, melodramatic, potentially tragic. In fact the often-told story of the maiden falsely slandered did frequently end in disaster—as, for example, in Spenser's *Faerie Queene*, II,iv (1590). Spenser was apparently indebted to Ariosto's *Orlando Furioso* (translated into English by Sir John Harington, 1591), as were Peter Beverly in *The Historie of Ariodanto and Ieneura* (1566) and Richard Mulcaster in his play *Ariodante and Genevora* (1583). Shakespeare seems to have relied more on the Italian version by Matteo Bandello (Lucca, 1554) and its French translation by Belleforest, *Histoires Tragiques* (1569). Still other versions have been discovered, both nondramatic and dramatic, although it cannot be established that Shakespeare was reworking an old play. Various factual inconsistencies in Shakespeare's text (such as Leonato's wife Imogen and a "kinsman" who are named briefly in both quarto and Folio but have no roles in the play) can perhaps be explained by Shakespeare's having worked quickly from more than one source.

Shakespeare's other plot, of Benedick and Beatrice, is much more English and his own. The battle of the sexes is a staple of English medieval humor (Chaucer's Wife of Bath, the Wakefield *Noah*) and of Shakespeare's own early comedy: Berowne and Rosaline in *Love's Labour's Lost*, Petruchio and Katharine in *The Taming of the Shrew*. The merry war of Benedick and Beatrice is Shakespeare's finest achievement in this vein, and was to become a rich legacy in the later English comedy of Congreve, Wilde, and Shaw. The tone is lighthearted, bantering, and reassuring, in contrast with the Italianate mood of vengeance and duplicity. No less English are the clownish antics of Dogberry and his crew, representing still another group of characters although not a separate plot. Like Constable Dull in *Love's Labour's Lost* or the tradesmen of *A Midsummer Night's Dream*, the buffoons of *Much Ado* function in a nominally Mediterranean setting but are nonetheless recognizable London types. Their preposterous antics not only puncture the ominous mood threatening our enjoyment of the main plot, but absurdly enough even help to abort a potential crime. When Dogberry comes, laughter cannot be far behind.

The two plots provide contrasting perspectives on the nature of love. Because it is sensational and melodramatic, the Claudio-Hero plot stresses situation at the expense of character. The conspiracy that nearly overwhelms the lovers is an engrossing story, but they themselves remain one dimensional. They interest us more as Petrarchan types, and hence as "foils" to Benedick and Beatrice, than as lovers in their own right. Benedick and Beatrice, on the other hand, are psychologically complex. Clearly they are fascinated with one another. Beatrice's questions in the first scene, although abusive in tone, betray her concern for Benedick's welfare. Has he safely returned from the wars? How did he bear himself in battle? Who are his companions? She tests his moral character by high standards, suspecting that he will fail because she demands so much. We are not surprised when she lectures her docile cousin, Hero, on the folly of submitting to parental choice in marriage: "It is my cousin's duty to make curtsy and say 'Father, as it please you.' But yet for all that, cousin, let him be a handsome fellow, or else make another curtsy and say 'Father, as it please me' " (II,i). Beatrice remains single not from love of spinsterhood but from insistence on a nearly perfect mate. Paradoxically, she who is the inveterate scoffer is the true idealist. And we know from her unceasing fascination with Benedick that he, of all the men in her acquaintance, comes closest to her mark. The only fear preventing the revelation of her love—a not unnatural fear, in view of the insults she and Benedick exchange—is that he will prove faithless and jest at her weakness.

Benedick is similarly hemmed in by his posturing as "a professed tyrant to their sex." Despite his reputation as a perennial bachelor, and his wry amusement at Claudio's new-found passion, Benedick confesses in soliloquy (II,iii) that he could be won to affection by the ideal woman. Again his criteria are chiefly those of temperament and moral character, although he by no means spurns wealth, beauty, and social position; the happiest couples are those well-matched in fortune's gifts. "Rich she shall be, that's certain; wise, or I'll none; virtuous, or I'll never cheapen her; fair, or I'll never look on her; mild, or come not near me; noble, or not I for an angel; of good discourse, an excellent musician, and her hair shall be of what colour it please God." This last self-amused concession indicates that Benedick is aware how impossibly much he is asking. Still, there is one woman, Beatrice, possessing most of these qualities except mildness. Even her sharp wit is part of her admirable intelligence. She is a match for Benedick, and he is a man who would never tolerate the submissive conventionality of someone like Hero. All that appears to be lacking, in fact, is any sign of fondness on Beatrice's part. For him to make overtures would be to invite her withering scorn—not to mention the I-told-you-so mockery of his friends.

Benedick and Beatrice have been playing the game

of verbal abuse so long they scarcely remember how it started—perhaps as a squaring-off between the only two intelligences worthy of contending with one another, perhaps as a more profoundly defensive reaction of two sensitive persons not willing to part lightly with their independence. They know that true involvement with others is a complex matter, one that can cause heartache. Yet the masks they wear to one another are scarcely satisfactory. At the masked ball (II,i), we see how hurtful the "merry war" has become. Benedick, attempting to pass himself off as a stranger in a mask, abuses Beatrice by telling her of her reputation for disdain; but she, perceiving who he is, retaliates by telling him as a purported stranger what she "really" thinks of Benedick. These devices cut deeply, and confirm the worst fears of each partner. Ironically, these fears can be dispelled only by the virtuous deceptions practiced on them by their friends. For, once Benedick is assured that Beatrice secretly loves him, masking her affection with scorn, he acquires the confidence he needs to make a commitment, and vice versa. The beauty of the virtuous deceptions, moreover, is that they are so plausible—because, indeed, they are essentially true. Benedick overhears himself described as a person so satirical that Beatrice dare not reveal her affection, for fear of being repulsed (II,iii). Beatrice learns that she is indeed called disdainful by her friends (III,i). Both lovers respond nobly to these revelations, accepting the accusations as richly deserved and placing no blame on the other. As Beatrice proclaims to herself, "Contempt, farewell! and maiden pride, adieu!" The relief afforded by this honesty is genuine and lasting.

Because Claudio knows so little about Hero, and is content with superficial expectations, he is vulnerable to a far more ugly sort of deception. Claudio's first questions about Hero betray his romantically stereotyped attitudes and his willingness to let Don Pedro and Hero's father, Leonato, arrange a financially advantageous match. Claudio treasures Hero's outward reputation for modesty, an appearance easily besmirched. When a false rumor suggests that Don Pedro is wooing the lady for himself, Claudio's response is predictably cliché-ridden: all's fair in love and war, you can't trust friends in an affair of the heart, and so farewell Hero. The rumor has a superficial plausibility about it, especially when the villainous Don John steps into the situation. Motivated in part by pure malice and the sport of ruining others' happiness, John speaks to the masked Claudio at the ball (II,i) as though he were speaking to Benedick, and in this guise pretends to reveal the secret "fact" of Don Pedro's duplicity in love. (The device is precisely that used by Beatrice to put down Benedick in the same scene.) With this specious confirmation, Claudio leaps to a wrong conclusion, thereby judging both his friend and mistress to be false. He gives them no chance to speak in their own defense. To be sure, Hero's father and uncle have also believed in the false report, and have welcomed the prospect of the wealthy Don Pedro as Hero's husband. The lady herself raises no objection to marriage with the older man. Still, Claudio has revealed a lack of faith resulting from his slender knowledge of Hero and of himself.

The nearly tragic "demonstration" of Hero's infidelity follows the same course, because Claudio has not learned from his first experience. Once again the diabolical Don John first implants the insidious suggestion in Claudio's mind, then creates an illusion entirely plausible to the senses, and finally confirms it with Borachio's testimony. What Claudio and Don Pedro have actually seen is Margaret wooed at Hero's window, shrouded in the dark of night and seen from "afar off in the orchard." The power of suggestion is enough to do the rest. John's method, and his pleasure in evil, are much like those of his later counterparts, Iago in *Othello* and Edmund in *King Lear*. Indeed, John is compared with the devil, who has power over men's frail senses but must rely on their complicity and acquiescence in evil. Claudio is once again led to denounce faithlessly the virtuous woman whose loyalty he no longer deserves. Yet his fault is very typically human, and is shared by Don Pedro. Providence gives him a second chance, through the ludicrous and bumbling intervention of Dogberry's night watch. These men overhear the plot of Don John as soon as it is announced to us, so that we know justice will eventually prevail even though it will also be farcically delayed. Once again, misunderstanding has become "much ado about nothing," an escalating of recriminations based on a purely chimerical assumption that must eventually be deflated. The painful experience is not without value, for it tests men's spiritual worth in a crisis. Beatrice, like Friar Francis, shows herself to be a person of unshakable faith in goodness. Benedick, though puzzled and torn in his loyalties, also passes the test and proves himself worthy of Beatrice. Claudio is found wanting, but Hero forgives and accepts him anyway. In her role as the granter of a merciful second chance, she foreshadows the beatifically symbolic nature of many of Shakespeare's later heroines.

Much Ado about Nothing comes perhaps closer to potentially tragic action than Shakespeare's other festive comedies. Virtually all the characters are affected by misunderstanding, resort to deception, or take refuge in protective masks. Candor and straightforwardness are ideals more easily praised than achieved. Even Benedick and Beatrice, marvelous though they may be, are far from perfect. Beatrice almost provokes Benedick into a vindictive and unnecessary murder. Despite their self-awareness, these lovers must be rescued from their isolation by a trick that ironically resembles the villainous practices of Don John. In this important sense, Benedick and Beatrice are not wholly unlike Claudio and Hero after all. Both pairs of lovers are saved from their own worst selves by a harmonizing force that works its will through strange and improbable means—even through Constable Dogberry and his watch.

MUCH ADO ABOUT NOTHING

[*Dramatis Personae*

DON PEDRO, *Prince of Arragon.*
DON JOHN, *his bastard brother.*
CLAUDIO, *a young lord of Florence.*
BENEDICK, *a young lord of Padua.*
LEONATO, *governor of Messina.*
ANTONIO, *his brother.*
BALTHASAR, *attendant on Don Pedro.*
CONRADE, BORACHIO, } *followers of Don John.*
FRIAR FRANCIS.
DOGBERRY, *a constable.*
VERGES, *a headborough.*
A Sexton.
A Boy.

HERO, *daughter to Leonato.*
BEATRICE, *niece to Leonato.*
MARGARET, URSULA, } *gentlewomen attending on Hero.*

Messengers, Watch, Attendants, *&c.*

SCENE: *Messina.*]

[ACT I.

SCENE I. *Before* LEONATO's *house.*]

Enter LEONATO, *Governor of Messina,* HERO *his Daughter, and* BEATRICE *his Niece, with a* Messenger.

Leon. I learn in this letter that Don Peter of Arragon comes this night to Messina.

Mess. He is very near by this: he was not three leagues off when I left him.

Leon. How many gentlemen have you lost in this action?

Mess. But few of any sort, and none of name.

Leon. A victory is twice itself when the achiever brings home full numbers. I find here that Don Peter hath bestowed much honour on a young Florentine called Claudio.

Mess. Much deserved on his part and equally remembered by Don Pedro: he hath borne himself beyond the promise of his age, doing, in the figure of a lamb, the feats of a lion: he hath indeed better bettered expectation than you must expect of me to tell you how.

Leon. He hath an uncle here in Messina will be very much glad of it.

Mess. I have already delivered him letters, and there appears much joy in him; even so much that joy could not show itself modest enough without a badge of bitterness.

Leon. Did he break out into tears?

Mess. In great measure.

Leon. A kind overflow of kindness: there are no faces truer than those that are so washed. How much better is it to weep at joy than to joy at weeping!

Beat. I pray you, is Signior Mountanto returned from the wars or no?

Mess. I know none of that name, lady: there was none such in the army of any sort.

Leon. What is he that you ask for, niece?

Hero. My cousin means Signior Benedick of Padua.

Mess. O, he 's returned; and as pleasant as ever he was.

Beat. He set up his bills here in Messina and challenged Cupid at the flight; and my uncle's fool, reading the challenge, subscribed for Cupid, and challenged him at the bird-bolt. I pray you, how many hath he killed and eaten in these wars? But how many hath he killed? for indeed I promised to eat all of his killing.

Leon. Faith, niece, you tax Signior Benedick too much; but he'll be meet with you, I doubt it not.

Mess. He hath done good service, lady, in these wars.

Beat. You had musty victual, and he hath holp to eat it: he is a very valiant trencher-man; he hath an excellent stomach.

Mess. And a good soldier too, lady.

Beat. And a good soldier to a lady: but what is he to a lord?

Mess. A lord to a lord, a man to a man; stuffed with all honourable virtues.

Beat. It is so, indeed; he is no less than a stuffed man: but for the stuffing,—well, we are all mortal.

Leon. You must not, sir, mistake my niece. There is a kind of merry war betwixt Signior Benedick and her: they never meet but there 's a skirmish of wit between them.

Beat. Alas! he gets nothing by that. In our last conflict four of his five wits went halting off, and now is the whole man governed with one: so that if he have wit enough to keep himself warm, let him bear it for a difference between himself and his horse; for it is all the wealth that he hath left, to be known a reasonable creature. Who is his companion now? He hath every month a new sworn brother.

Mess. Is 't possible?

Beat. Very easily possible: he wears his faith but as the fashion of his hat; it ever changes with the next block.

Mess. I see, lady, the gentleman is not in your books.

Beat. No; an he were, I would burn my study. But, I pray you, who is his companion? Is there no young

ACT I. SCENE I. 7. **sort,** rank, or kind. **name,** reputation, or noble name. 16. **bettered,** surpassed. 23. **badge,** mark of service; here, the livery of sorrow. 30. **Mountanto.** *Montant* is an upright blow in fencing; the implication is that Benedick is a bravo. Beatrice's inquiry about him betrays a certain interest. 37. **pleasant,** jocular. 39. **bills,** placards, advertisements. 40. **challenged . . . flight,** undertook to rival Cupid as an archer. **my uncle's fool,** usually explained as a professional fool in her uncle's service; it has also been suggested that, since Beatrice herself is a jester, and *fool* is often a pet name, Beatrice is referring to herself and thus recalling an earlier flirtation with Benedick. 42. **bird-bolt,** blunt-headed arrow used for fowling. 46. **tax,** blame; see glossary. 47. **meet,** even, quits. 51. **valiant trencher-man,** great eater. 59. **stuffed,** stuffed with food or anything, with play on preceding sense of "filled with." 66. **five wits,** not the five senses, but the five faculties; memory, imagination, judgment, fantasy, common wit. 70. **difference,** heraldic term, used with a play on the usual sense; see glossary. 71. **to be known,** i.e., in order that he may be known as. 73. **sworn brother,** brother in arms (*frater juratus*), an allusion to the ancient practice of swearing brotherhood. 76. **faith,** allegiance, or fidelity. 77. **block,** mold for shaping hats. 78-79. **in your books,** i.e., in favor with you, in your account books for credit.

squarer now that will make a voyage with him to the devil?

Mess. He is most in the company of the right noble Claudio.

Beat. O Lord, he will hang upon him like a disease: he is sooner caught than the pestilence, and the taker runs presently mad. God help the noble Claudio! if he have caught the Benedick, it will cost him a thousand pound ere 'a be cured.

Mess. I will hold friends with you, lady.

Beat. Do, good friend.

Leon. You will never run mad, niece.

Beat. No, not till a hot January.

Mess. Don Pedro is approached.

Enter DON PEDRO, CLAUDIO, BENEDICK, BALTHASAR, *and* [DON] JOHN *the Bastard.*

D. Pedro. Good Signior Leonato, are you come to meet your trouble? The fashion of the world is to avoid cost, and you encounter it.

Leon. Never came trouble to my house in the likeness of your grace: for trouble being gone, comfort should remain; but when you depart from me, sorrow abides and happiness takes his leave.

D. Pedro. You embrace your charge too willingly. I think this is your daughter.

Leon. Her mother hath many times told me so.

Bene. Were you in doubt, sir, that you asked her?

Leon. Signior Benedick, no; for then were you a child.

D. Pedro. You have it full, Benedick: we may guess by this what you are, being a man. Truly, the lady fathers herself. Be happy, lady; for you are like an honourable father.

Bene. If Signior Leonato be her father, she would not have his head on her shoulders for all Messina, as like him as she is.

Beat. I wonder that you will still be talking, Signior Benedick: nobody marks you.

Bene. What, my dear Lady Disdain! are you yet living?

Beat. Is it possible disdain should die while she hath such meet food to feed it as Signior Benedick? Courtesy itself must convert to disdain, if you come in her presence.

Bene. Then is courtesy a turncoat. But it is certain I am loved of all ladies, only you excepted: and I would I could find in my heart that I had not a hard heart; for, truly, I love none.

Beat. A dear happiness to women: they would else have been troubled with a pernicious suitor. I thank God and my cold blood, I am of your humour for that: I had rather hear my dog bark at a crow than a man swear he loves me.

Bene. God keep your ladyship still in that mind! so some gentleman or other shall 'scape a predestinate scratched face.

Beat. Scratching could not make it worse, an 'twere such a face as yours were.

Bene. Well, you are a rare parrot-teacher.

Beat. A bird of my tongue is better than a beast of yours.

Bene. I would my horse had the speed of your tongue, and so good a continuer. But keep your way, a God's name; I have done.

Beat. You always end with a jade's trick: I know you of old.

D. Pedro. That is the sum of all, Leonato. Signior Claudio and Signior Benedick, my dear friend Leonato hath invited you all. I tell him we shall stay here at the least a month; and he heartily prays some occasion may detain us longer. I dare swear he is no hypocrite, but prays from his heart.

Leon. If you swear, my lord, you shall not be forsworn. [*To Don John*] Let me bid you welcome, my lord: being reconciled to the prince your brother, I owe you all duty.

D. John. I thank you: I am not of many words, but I thank you.

Leon. Please it your grace lead on?

D. Pedro. Your hand, Leonato; we will go together.

Exeunt. Manent Benedick and Claudio.

Claud. Benedick, didst thou note the daughter of Signior Leonato?

Bene. I noted her not; but I looked on her.

Claud. Is she not a modest young lady?

Bene. Do you question me, as an honest man should do, for my simple true judgement; or would you have me speak after my custom, as being a professed tyrant to their sex?

Claud. No; I pray thee speak in sober judgement.

Bene. Why, i' faith, methinks she 's too low for a high praise, too brown for a fair praise and too little for a great praise: only this commendation I can afford her, that were she other than she is, she were unhandsome; and being no other but as she is, I do not like her.

Claud. Thou thinkest I am in sport: I pray thee tell me truly how thou likest her.

Bene. Would you buy her, that you inquire after her?

Claud. Can the world buy such a jewel?

Bene. Yea, and a case to put it into. But speak you this with a sad brow? or do you play the flouting Jack, to tell us Cupid is a good hare-finder and Vulcan a rare carpenter? Come, in what key shall a man take you, to go in the song?

Claud. In mine eye she is the sweetest lady that ever I looked on.

Bene. I can see yet without spectacles and I see no such matter: there 's her cousin, an she were not possessed with a fury, exceeds her as much in beauty as the first of May doth the last of December. But I hope you have no intent to turn husband, have you?

Claud. I would scarce trust myself, though I had sworn the contrary, if Hero would be my wife.

82. **squarer,** quarreler. 89. **caught the Benedick,** i.e., as if he were a disease. It seems rather too meticulous to see an allusion to a disease of that name. 91. **hold friends,** keep on friendly terms. 98. **encounter,** go to meet. 103. **embrace your charge,** accept your burden. 110. **full,** i.e., full in the face, completely. 112. **fathers herself,** shows by appearance who her father is. 115. **his head.** Benedick suggests that Leonato's white beard would look odd on Hero. 123. **convert,** change itself into. 129. **dear happiness,** precious good luck. 131. **I am . . . that,** I am of the same disposition in that matter. Beatrice counters with a similar boast as to her spinsterhood. 136. **predestinate,** i.e., which he would have if she married him. 140. **of my tongue,** taught to speak like me. 141. **of yours,** taught to speak like you (since such a beast would be dumb). 143. **continuer,** i.e., in staying power. 145. **jade's trick,** ill-conditioned horse's trick of balking or of stopping suddenly, thus throwing the rider. 156. **being,** since you are. 165. **noted,** a possible pun on the meaning, "set to music." 170. **tyrant,** cruel or pitiless in attitude. 186. **flouting Jack,** mocking rascal. 186-187. **to tell . . . carpenter,** i.e., are you mocking us with nonsense? (Cupid was blind and Vulcan a blacksmith.) 188. **go in,** join in. 200-201. **wear . . . suspicion,** i.e., be suspected of wearing his cap to hide his cuckold's horns. 204. **sigh away Sundays,** i.e., when, owing to the domesticity of the day, you cannot escape from your yoke-fellow (Furness). 217. **If this . . . uttered,** i.e., if I really were in love with Hero, and told Benedick, he would blab the secret this way. 218. **old tale,** an allusion

Bene. Is 't come to this? In faith, hath not the world one man but he will wear his cap with suspicion? Shall I never see a bachelor of threescore again? Go to, i' faith; an thou wilt needs thrust thy neck into a yoke, wear the print of it and sigh away Sundays. Look; Don Pedro is returned to seek you.

Enter DON PEDRO.

D. Pedro. What secret hath held you here, that you followed not to Leonato's?

Bene. I would your grace would constrain me to tell.

D. Pedro. I charge thee on thy allegiance.

Bene. You hear, Count Claudio: I can be secret as a dumb man; I would have you think so; but, on my allegiance, mark you this, on my allegiance. He is in love. With who? now that is your grace's part. Mark how short his answer is;—With Hero, Leonato's short daughter.

Claud. If this were so, so were it uttered.

Bene. Like the old tale, my lord: 'it is not so, nor 'twas not so, but, indeed, God forbid it should be so.'

Claud. If my passion change not shortly, God forbid it should be otherwise.

D. Pedro. Amen, if you love her; for the lady is very well worthy.

Claud. You speak this to fetch me in, my lord.

D. Pedro. By my troth, I speak my thought.

Claud. And, in faith, my lord, I spoke mine.

Bene. And, by my two faiths and troths, my lord, I spoke mine.

Claud. That I love her, I feel.

D. Pedro. That she is worthy, I know.

Bene. That I neither feel how she should be loved nor know how she should be worthy, is the opinion that fire cannot melt out of me: I will die in it at the stake.

D. Pedro. Thou wast ever an obstinate heretic in the despite of beauty.

Claud. And never could maintain his part but in the force of his will.

Bene. That a woman conceived me, I thank her; that she brought me up, I likewise give her most humble thanks: but that I will have a recheat winded in my forehead, or hang my bugle in an invisible baldrick, all women shall pardon me. Because I will not do them the wrong to mistrust any, I will do myself the right to trust none; and the fine is, for the which I may go the finer, I will live a bachelor.

D. Pedro. I shall see thee, ere I die, look pale with love.

Bene. With anger, with sickness, or with hunger, my lord, not with love: prove that ever I lose more blood with love than I will get again with drinking, pick out mine eyes with a ballad-maker's pen and hang me up at the door of a brothel-house for the sign of blind Cupid.

D. Pedro. Well, if ever thou dost fall from this faith, thou wilt prove a notable argument.

Bene. If I do, hang me in a bottle like a cat and shoot at me; and he that hits me, let him be clapped on the shoulder, and called Adam.

D. Pedro. Well, as time shall try:
'In time the savage bull doth bear the yoke.'

Bene. The savage bull may; but if ever the sensible Benedick bear it, pluck off the bull's horns and set them in my forehead: and let me be vilely painted, and in such great letters as they write 'Here is good horse to hire,' let them signify under my sign 'Here you may see Benedick the married man.'

Claud. If this should ever happen, thou wouldst be horn-mad.

D. Pedro. Nay, if Cupid have not spent all his quiver in Venice, thou wilt quake for this shortly.

Bene. I look for an earthquake too, then.

D. Pedro. Well, you will temporize with the hours. In the meantime, good Signior Benedick, repair to Leonato's: commend me to him and tell him I will not fail him at supper; for indeed he hath made great preparation.

Bene. I have almost matter enough in me for such an embassage; and so I commit you—

Claud. To the tuition of God: From my house, if I had it,—

D. Pedro. The sixth of July: Your loving friend, Benedick.

Bene. Nay, mock not, mock not. The body of your discourse is sometime guarded with fragments, and the guards are but slightly basted on neither: ere you flout old ends any further, examine your conscience: and so I leave you. *Exit.*

Claud. My liege, your highness now may do me
good.

D. Pedro. My love is thine to teach: teach it but how,
And thou shalt see how apt it is to learn
Any hard lesson that may do thee good.

Claud. Hath Leonato any son, my lord?

D. Pedro. No child but Hero; she 's his only heir.
Dost thou affect her, Claudio?

Claud. O, my lord,
When you went onward on this ended action,
I look'd upon her with a soldier's eye,
That lik'd, but had a rougher task in hand
Than to drive liking to the name of love:
But now I am return'd and that war-thoughts
Have left their places vacant, in their rooms
Come thronging soft and delicate desires,
All prompting me how fair young Hero is,
Saying, I lik'd her ere I went to wars.

D. Pedro. Thou wilt be like a lover presently
And tire the hearer with a book of words.
If thou dost love fair Hero, cherish it,
And I will break with her and with her father
And thou shalt have her. Was 't not to this end
That thou began'st to twist so fine a story?

to a children's tale in which the quotation following occurred. 222. **otherwise,** i.e., than so. 225. **fetch me in,** get me to confess. 237. **despite,** contempt. 239. **force of his will,** will, refusing to be guided by reason, which was the state of the heretic, as defined by the Schoolmen. 242-245. **but that . . . me,** women must pardon me for refusing to have my horn placed on my head (like a cuckold). 243. **recheat,** blast blown to recall the hounds. 244. **baldrick,** strap that supports the horn. 247. **fine,** end; see glossary. 248. **go the finer,** have more to spend on fine clothes. 252. **prove that,** if you discover. 253-254. **lose . . . drinking.** According to current theory, each sigh cost the heart a drop of blood, whereas blood was replenished by wine. 258. **argument,** subject for conversation, example. 259. **bottle,** wicker basket to hold the cat used as target in shooting matches in archery. 261. **Adam,** Adam Bell, archer outlaw of the ballads. 263. **'In time . . . yoke,'** proverbial. 272. **horn-mad,** stark mad (from the fury of horned beasts), with allusion to cuckoldry. 274. **Venice,** noted for licentiousness. 276. **temporize . . . hours,** come to terms, or become milder, in time. 281. **matter,** wit, intelligence. 283. **tuition,** protection. 288. **guarded,** ornamented. 289. **guards,** border or trimming on a garment. 290. **old ends,** old tags, quotations. 311. **break,** open the subject. 313. **twist,** draw out the thread of.

Claud. How sweetly you do minister to love,
That know love's grief by his complexion!
But lest my liking might too sudden seem,
I would have salv'd it with a longer treatise.

D. Pedro. What need the bridge much broader than the flood?
The fairest grant is the necessity.
Look, what will serve is fit: 'tis once, thou lovest,
And I will fit thee with the remedy.
I know we shall have revelling to-night:
I will assume thy part in some disguise
And tell fair Hero I am Claudio,
And in her bosom I'll unclasp my heart
And take her hearing prisoner with the force
And strong encounter of my amorous tale;
Then after to her father will I break;
And the conclusion is, she shall be thine.
In practice let us put it presently. *Exeunt.*

[SCENE II. *A room in* LEONATO'*s house.*]

Enter LEONATO *and an Old Man* [ANTONIO], *Brother to Leonato.*

Leon. How now, brother! Where is my cousin, your son? hath he provided this music?

Ant. He is very busy about it. But, brother, I can tell you strange news that you yet dreamt not of.

Leon. Are they good?

Ant. As the event stamps them: but they have a good cover; they show well outward. The prince and Count Claudio, walking in a thick-pleached alley in mine orchard, were thus much overheard by a man of mine: the prince discovered to Claudio that he loved my niece your daughter and meant to acknowledge it this night in a dance; and if he found her accordant, he meant to take the present time by the top and instantly break with you of it.

Leon. Hath the fellow any wit that told you this?

Ant. A good sharp fellow: I will send for him; and question him yourself.

Leon. No, no; we will hold it as a dream till it appear itself: but I will acquaint my daughter withal, that she may be the better prepared for an answer, if peradventure this be true. Go you and tell her of it. [*Enter Antonio's son with a Musician.*] Cousin, you know what you have to do.—O, I cry you mercy, friend; go you with me, and I will use your skill.—Good cousin, have a care this busy time. *Exeunt.*

[SCENE III. *The same.*]

Enter Sir [DON] JOHN *the Bastard and* CONRADE, *his companion.*

Con. What the good-year, my lord! why are you thus out of measure sad?

D. John. There is no measure in the occasion that breeds; therefore the sadness is without limit.

Con. You should hear reason.

D. John. And when I have heard it, what blessing brings it?

Con. If not a present remedy, at least a patient sufferance.

D. John. I wonder that thou, being, as thou sayest thou art, born under Saturn, goest about to apply a moral medicine to a mortifying mischief. I cannot hide what I am: I must be sad when I have cause and smile at no man's jests, eat when I have stomach and wait for no man's leisure, sleep when I am drowsy and tend on no man's business, laugh when I am merry and claw no man in his humour.

Con. Yea, but you must not make the full show of this till you may do it without controlment. You have of late stood out against your brother, and he hath ta'en you newly into his grace; where it is impossible you should take true root but by the fair weather that you make yourself: it is needful that you frame the season for your own harvest.

D. John. I had rather be a canker in a hedge than a rose in his grace, and it better fits my blood to be disdained of all than to fashion a carriage to rob love from any: in this, though I cannot be said to be a flattering honest man, it must not be denied but I am a plain-dealing villain. I am trusted with a muzzle and enfranchised with a clog; therefore I have decreed not to sing in my cage. If I had my mouth, I would bite; if I had my liberty, I would do my liking: in the meantime let me be that I am and seek not to alter me.

Con. Can you make no use of your discontent?

D. John. I make all use of it, for I use it only. Who comes here?

Enter BORACHIO.

What news, Borachio?

Bora. I came yonder from a great supper· the prince your brother is royally entertained by Leonato; and I can give you intelligence of an intended marriage.

D. John. Will it serve for any model to build mischief on? What is he for a fool that betroths himself to unquietness?

Bora. Marry, it is your brother's right hand.

D. John. Who? the most exquisite Claudio?

Bora. Even he.

D. John. A proper squire! And who and who? which way looks he?

Bora. Marry, one Hero, the daughter and heir of Leonato.

D. John. A very forward March-chick! How came you to this?

Bora. Being entertained for a perfumer, as I was smoking a musty room, comes me the prince and Claudio, hand in hand, in sad conference: I whipt me behind the arras; and there heard it agreed upon that the prince should woo Hero for himself, and

---

317. **salv'd,** softened. 319. **fairest . . . necessity,** the best gifts are those that are really needed. 320. **'tis once,** in short.

SCENE II. 10. **thick-pleached,** made with dense hedges of intertwined shrubs. **in mine orchard.** Boas would read *the* for *mine*, which would enable us to understand that the conversation overheard and misunderstood by the servant had been held in Leonato's orchard; otherwise one cannot reconcile the first and second scenes as to time relation. 12. **discovered,** disclosed. 15. **accordant,** agreeing, consenting. 16. **top,** forelock, as we say. 17. **wit,** sense, intelligence. 22. **till . . . itself,** till it manifest itself.

SCENE III. 1. **What the good-year,** undefined expletive. 2. **out of measure,** immeasurably. 10. **sufferance,** endurance. 12. **under Saturn.** To be born under Saturn produces a morose disposition. **goest about** endeavorest. 13. **mortifying mischief,** deadly disease. 17. **tend on,** attend to. 19. **claw,** flatter. 26. **frame,** produce. 28. **canker,** dog rose. 30. **blood,** mood, disposition; probable reference also to Don John's illegitimacy, on which his villainy rests. 31. **fashion a carriage,** counterfeit a behavior. **rob love,** gain undeserved affection. 58. **March-chick,** overprecocious youth (like a chick hatched prematurely). 61. **smoking,** fumigating. 63. **arras,** tapestry, hanging. 69.

having obtained her, give her to Count Claudio.

D. John. Come, come, let us thither: this may prove food to my displeasure. That young start-up hath all the glory of my overthrow: if I can cross him any way, I bless myself every way. You are both sure, and will assist me?

Con. To the death, my lord.

D. John. Let us to the great supper: their cheer is the greater that I am subdued. Would the cook were o' my mind! Shall we go prove what 's to be done?

Bora. We'll wait upon your lordship. *Exeunt.*

[ACT II.

SCENE I. *A hall in* LEONATO's *house.*]

Enter LEONATO, *his Brother* [ANTONIO], HERO *his Daughter, and* BEATRICE *his Niece* [*with* MARGARET *and* URSULA].

Leon. Was not Count John here at supper?

Ant. I saw him not.

Beat. How tartly that gentleman looks! I never can see him but I am heart-burned an hour after.

Hero. He is of a very melancholy disposition.

Beat. He were an excellent man that were made just in the midway between him and Benedick: the one is too like an image and says nothing, and the other too like my lady's eldest son, evermore tattling.

Leon. Then half Signior Benedick's tongue in Count John's mouth, and half Count John's melancholy in Signior Benedick's face,—

Beat. With a good leg and a good foot, uncle, and money enough in his purse, such a man would win any woman in the world, if 'a could get her good-will.

Leon. By my troth, niece, thou wilt never get thee a husband, if thou be so shrewd of thy tongue.

Ant. In faith, she 's too curst.

Beat. Too curst is more than curst: I shall lessen God's sending that way; for it is said, 'God sends a curst cow short horns;' but to a cow too curst he sends none.

Leon. So, by being too curst, God will send you no horns.

Beat. Just, if he send me no husband; for the which blessing I am at him upon my knees every morning and evening. Lord, I could not endure a husband with a beard on his face: I had rather lie in the woollen.

Leon. You may light on a husband that hath no beard.

Beat. What should I do with him? dress him in my apparel and make him my waiting-gentlewoman? He that hath a beard is more than a youth, and he that hath no beard is less than a man: and he that is more than a youth is not for me, and he that is less than a man, I am not for him: therefore I will even take sixpence in earnest of the bear-ward, and lead his apes into hell.

Leon. Well, then, go you into hell?

Beat. No, but to the gate; and there will the devil meet me, like an old cuckold, with horns on his head, and say 'Get you to heaven, Beatrice, get you to heaven; here 's no place for you maids:' so deliver I up my apes, and away to Saint Peter for the heavens; he shows me where the bachelors sit, and there live we as merry as the day is long.

Ant. [*To Hero*] Well, niece, I trust you will be ruled by your father.

Beat. Yes, faith; it is my cousin's duty to make curtsy and say 'Father, as it please you.' But yet for all that, cousin, let him be a handsome fellow, or else make another curtsy and say 'Father, as it please me.'

Leon. Well, niece, I hope to see you one day fitted with a husband.

Beat. Not till God make men of some other metal than earth. Would it not grieve a woman to be overmastered with a piece of valiant dust? to make an account of her life to a clod of wayward marl? No, uncle, I'll none: Adam's sons are my brethren; and, truly, I hold it a sin to match in my kindred.

Leon. Daughter, remember what I told you: if the prince do solicit you in that kind, you know your answer.

Beat. The fault will be in the music, cousin, if you be not wooed in good time: if the prince be too important, tell him there is measure in every thing and so dance out the answer. For, hear me, Hero: wooing, wedding, and repenting, is as a Scotch jig, a measure, and a cinque pace: the first suit is hot and hasty, like a Scotch jig, and full as fantastical; the wedding, mannerly-modest, as a measure, full of state and ancientry; and then comes Repentance and, with his bad legs, falls into the cinque pace faster and faster, till he sink into his grave.

Leon. Cousin, you apprehend passing shrewdly.

Beat. I have a good eye, uncle; I can see a church by daylight.

Leon. The revellers are entering, brother: make good room. [*All put on their masks.*]

Enter [*masked*] PRINCE [DON] PEDRO, CLAUDIO, *and* BENEDICK, *and* BALTHASAR; [*unmasked*, BORACHIO *and*] DON JOHN.

D. Pedro. Lady, will you walk about with your friend?

Hero. So you walk softly and look sweetly and say nothing, I am yours for the walk; and especially when I walk away.

D. Pedro. With me in your company?

Hero. I may say so, when I please.

D. Pedro. And when please you to say so?

Hero. When I like your favour; for God defend the lute should be like the case!

D. Pedro. My visor is Philemon's roof; within the house is Jove.

Hero. Why, then, your visor should be thatched.

start-up, upstart. 70. **cross,** thwart, with allusion to making the sign of the cross. 71. **sure,** trustworthy. 75. **Would . . . mind,** i.e., apparently that he might poison the food.

ACT II. SCENE I. 4. **heart-burned,** suffering from heartburn, affected with indigestion. 10. **my . . . son,** spoiled child. 21. **shrewd,** sharp. 22. **curst,** shrewish. 25. **curst,** savage, vicious. 29. **Just,** right, exactly so. 33. **lie in the woollen,** sleep between blankets. 42. **in earnest,** in advance payment for. 43. **bear-ward,** one who keeps and exhibits a bear. **lead . . . hell,** ancient proverb: "Such as die maids do all lead apes in hell." 50. **for the heavens,** on my way to heaven. 51. **bachelors,** unmarried persons, or possibly, unmarried women. 63. **metal,** substance. 66. **clod . . . marl,** lump of wayward earth, i.e., a man. 74. **important,** urgent, importunate. 78. **cinque pace,** lively dance, the steps of which are supposed to be based on the number five; the first five steps of the galliard. 81. **ancientry,** old-fashioned style. 84. **apprehend,** understand. 90. **friend,** lover of both sexes. 99. **visor,** mask. **Philemon's roof,** an allusion to Ovid, *Metamorphoses*, viii. Philemon and Baucis, his wife, entertained Jupiter in their peasant cottage unawares (see *thatched*, line 102).

D. Pedro. Speak low, if you speak love. [*They step aside.*]

Balth. Well, I would you did like me.

Marg. So would not I, for your own sake; for I have many ill qualities.

Balth. Which is one?

Marg. I say my prayers aloud.

Balth. I love you the better: the hearers may cry, Amen.

Marg. God match me with a good dancer!

Balth. Amen.

Marg. And God keep him out of my sight when the dance is done! Answer, clerk.

Balth. No more words: the clerk is answered. [*They step aside.*]

Urs. I know you well enough; you are Signior Antonio.

Ant. At a word, I am not.

Urs. I know you by the waggling of your head.

Ant. To tell you true, I counterfeit him.

Urs. You could never do him so ill-well, unless you were the very man. Here 's his dry hand up and down: you are he, you are he.

Ant. At a word, I am not.

Urs. Come, come, do you think I do not know you by your excellent wit? can virtue hide itself? Go to, mum, you are he: graces will appear, and there 's an end. [*They step aside.*]

Beat. Will you not tell me who told you so?

Bene. No, you shall pardon me.

Beat. Nor will you not tell me who you are?

Bene. Not now.

Beat. That I was disdainful, and that I had my good wit out of the 'Hundred Merry Tales:'—well, this was Signior Benedick that said so.

Bene. What 's he?

Beat. I am sure you know him well enough.

Bene. Not I, believe me.

Beat. Did he never make you laugh?

Bene. I pray you, what is he?

Beat. Why, he is the prince's jester: a very dull fool; only his gift is in devising impossible slanders: none but libertines delight in him; and the commendation is not in his wit, but in his villany; for he both pleases men and angers them, and then they laugh at him and beat him. I am sure he is in the fleet: I would he had boarded me.

Bene. When I know the gentleman, I'll tell him what you say.

Beat. Do, do: he'll but break a comparison or two on me; which, peradventure not marked or not laughed at, strikes him into melancholy; and then there 's a partridge wing saved, for the fool will eat no supper that night. [*Music.*] We must follow the leaders.

Bene. In every good thing.

Beat. Nay, if they lead to any ill, I will leave them at the next turning.

Dance. Exeunt [*all except Don John, Borachio, and Claudio*].

D. John. Sure my brother is amorous on Hero and hath withdrawn her father to break with him about it. The ladies follow her and but one visor remains.

Bora. And that is Claudio: I know him by his bearing.

D. John. Are not you Signior Benedick?

Claud. You know me well; I am he.

D. John. Signior, you are very near my brother in his love: he is enamoured on Hero; I pray you, dissuade him from her: she is no equal for his birth: you may do the part of an honest man in it.

Claud. How know you he loves her?

D. John. I heard him swear his affection.

Bora. So did I too; and he swore he would marry her to-night.

D. John. Come, let us to the banquet.

Exeunt. Manet Claudio.

Claud. Thus answer I in name of Benedick,
But hear these ill news with the ears of Claudio.
'Tis certain so; the prince wooes for himself.
Friendship is constant in all other things
Save in the office and affairs of love:
Therefore all hearts in love use their own tongues;
Let every eye negotiate for itself
And trust no agent; for beauty is a witch
Against whose charms faith melteth into blood.
This is an accident of hourly proof,
Which I mistrusted not. Farewell, therefore, Hero!

Enter BENEDICK.

Bene. Count Claudio?

Claud. Yea, the same.

Bene. Come, will you go with me?

Claud. Whither?

Bene. Even to the next willow, about your own business, county. What fashion will you wear the garland of? about your neck, like an usurer's chain? or under your arm, like a lieutenant's scarf? You must wear it one way, for the prince hath got your Hero.

Claud. I wish him joy of her.

Bene. Why, that 's spoken like an honest drovier: so they sell bullocks. But did you think the prince would have served you thus?

Claud. I pray you, leave me.

Bene. Ho! now you strike like the blind man: 'twas the boy that stole your meat, and you'll beat the post.

Claud. If it will not be, I'll leave you. *Exit.*

Bene. Alas, poor hurt fowl! now will he creep into sedges. But that my Lady Beatrice should know me,

104, 107, 109. ***Balth.,*** so Theobald; QF: *Bene.* 114. **clerk,** so addressed because of Balthasar's *Amen* in preceding speeches. He is giving responses like the parish clerk. 118. **At a word,** in short. 122. **do . . . ill-well,** imitate his imperfections so perfectly. 124. **dry hand,** a sign of age. **up and down,** all over, exactly. 128. **mum,** be silent. 135. **'Hundred Merry Tales,'** a popular collection of anecdotes published by Rastell in 1526; his point is that Beatrice borrows her wit from a book of stale jests. 143. **only his gift,** his only talent. **impossible,** incredible. 148. **fleet,** crowd, company (with pun on ships that are boarded). 149. **boarded,** accosted, with a play on the usual meaning. 152. **break a comparison,** make a scornful simile, innuendo. 155-157. **there's . . . night,** sarcastic thrust at Benedick, whose appetite she has before referred to. 157. **leaders,** i.e., of the dance. 169. **near,** intimate with. 178. **banquet,** light repast of fruit, wine, and dessert.

181. **certain,** certainly. 187. **faith . . . blood,** honor gives way to passion. 188. **accident,** occurrence. 194. **willow,** emblem of disappointed love. 197. **usurer's chain.** Costly chains were worn by persons of the moneyed class. 202. **drovier,** cattle dealer. 205. **like the blind man,** an allusion to the romance of Lazarillo de Tormes, in which the hero steals his master's meat and revenges himself for the beating he receives by causing the blind man to jump against a stone pillar. 210. **creep into sedges,** i.e., as wounded ducks into rushes along the river. 215-217. **it is . . . out,** it is Beatrice's low and harsh disposition that causes her to attribute to the world her own attitudes and to represent me accordingly. 216. **puts . . . person,** identifies the world with herself. 217. **gives me out,** represents me. 220. **Troth,** by my faith. 221. **Lady Fame,** Dame Rumor. 222. **lodge in a warren,** hutch in a rabbit warren. (Rabbits symbolized melancholy.) 227.

and not know me! The prince's fool! Ha? It may be I go under that title because I am merry. Yea, but so I am apt to do myself wrong; I am not so reputed: it is the base, though bitter, disposition of Beatrice that puts the world into her person, and so gives me out. Well, I'll be revenged as I may.

Enter the Prince [DON PEDRO], HERO, LEONATO.

D. Pedro. Now, signior, where 's the count? did you see him?

Bene. Troth, my lord, I have played the part of Lady Fame. I found him here as melancholy as a lodge in a warren: I told him, and I think I told him true, that your grace had got the good will of this young lady; and I offered him my company to a willow-tree, either to make him a garland, as being forsaken, or to bind him up a rod, as being worthy to be whipped.

D. Pedro. To be whipped! What 's his fault?

Bene. The flat transgression of a school-boy, who, being overjoyed with finding a birds' nest, shows it his companion, and he steals it.

D. Pedro. Wilt thou make a trust a transgression? The transgression is in the stealer.

Bene. Yet it had not been amiss the rod had been made, and the garland too; for the garland he might have worn himself, and the rod he might have bestowed on you, who, as I take it, have stolen his birds' nest.

D. Pedro. I will but teach them to sing, and restore them to the owner.

Bene. If their singing answer your saying, by my faith, you say honestly.

D. Pedro. The Lady Beatrice hath a quarrel to you: the gentleman that danced with her told her she is much wronged by you.

Bene. O, she misused me past the endurance of a block! an oak but with one green leaf on it would have answered her; my very visor began to assume life and scold with her. She told me, not thinking I had been myself, that I was the prince's jester, that I was duller than a great thaw; huddling jest upon jest with such impossible conveyance upon me that I stood like a man at a mark, with a whole army shooting at me. She speaks poniards, and every word stabs: if her breath were as terrible as her terminations, there were no living near her; she would infect to the north star. I would not marry her, though she were endowed with all that Adam had left him before he transgressed: she would have made Hercules have turned spit, yea, and have cleft his club to make the fire too. Come, talk not of her: you shall find her the infernal Ate in good apparel. I would to God some scholar would conjure her; for certainly, while she is here, a man may live as quiet in hell as in a sanctuary; and people sin upon purpose, because they would go thither; so, indeed, all disquiet, horror and perturbation follows her.

Enter CLAUDIO *and* BEATRICE.

D. Pedro. Look, here she comes.

Bene. Will your grace command me any service to the world's end? I will go on the slightest errand now to the Antipodes that you can devise to send me on; I will fetch you a toothpicker now from the furthest inch of Asia, bring you the length of Prester John's foot, fetch you a hair off the great Cham's beard, do you any embassage to the Pigmies, rather than hold three words' conference with this harpy. You have no employment for me?

D. Pedro. None, but to desire your good company.

Bene. O God, sir, here 's a dish I love not: I cannot endure my Lady Tongue. *Exit.*

D. Pedro. Come, lady, come; you have lost the heart of Signior Benedick.

Beat. Indeed, my lord, he lent it me awhile; and I gave him use for it, a double heart for his single one: marry, once before he won it of me with false dice, therefore your grace may well say I have lost it.

D. Pedro. You have put him down, lady, you have put him down.

Beat. So I would not he should do me, my lord, lest I should prove the mother of fools. I have brought Count Claudio, whom you sent me to seek.

D. Pedro. Why, how now, count! wherefore are you sad?

Claud. Not sad, my lord.

D. Pedro. How then? sick?

Claud. Neither, my lord.

Beat. The count is neither sad, nor sick, nor merry, nor well; but civil count, civil as an orange, and something of that jealous complexion.

D. Pedro. I' faith, lady, I think your blazon to be true; though, I'll be sworn, if he be so, his conceit is false. Here, Claudio, I have wooed in thy name, and fair Hero is won: I have broke with her father, and his good will obtained: name the day of marriage, and God give thee joy!

Leon. Count, take of me my daughter, and with her my fortunes: his grace hath made the match, and all grace say Amen to it.

Beat. Speak, count, 'tis your cue.

Claud. Silence is the perfectest herald of joy: I were but little happy, if I could say how much. Lady, as you are mine, I am yours: I give away myself for you and dote upon the exchange.

Beat. Speak, cousin; or, if you cannot, stop his mouth with a kiss, and let not him speak neither.

D. Pedro. In faith, lady, you have a merry heart.

Beat. Yea, my lord; I thank it, poor fool, it keeps

bind . . . rod, tie several willow switches into a scourge. 229. **flat,** absolute, downright. 241. **answer . . . saying,** correspond to what you say. 244. **to,** with. 246. **misused,** abused. 252. **great thaw,** i.e., when roads are muddy and impassable, obliging one to stay dully at home. **huddling,** piling, heaping up. 253. **impossible,** incredible. **conveyance,** dexterity. 254. **man at a mark,** man who stood by the target in archery to check off the arrows. 256. **terminations,** terms, expressions. 258. **north star,** supposed the most remote of stars. 261. **Hercules . . . spit.** Omphale put Hercules to menial tasks about the house; turning the spit was the most menial of kitchen duties. 264. **Ate,** goddess of discord. 265. **scholar . . . conjure.** Scholars were supposed to have the power to control evil spirits, which had to be addressed in Latin. 275. **toothpicker,** toothpick. 276. **Prester John's.** Prester John was a legendary Christian king of the Far East. 277. **great Cham's,** of the khan of Tartary. 279. **Pigmies,** legendary small race which beset Hercules in his sleep (*Iliad,* Bk. iii); frequently mentioned during the Renaissance. 287-291. **Indeed . . . lost it.** This seems an unquestionable allusion to an earlier flirtation between Benedick and Beatrice. 288, 289. **double, single.** The former word seems to imply that he had her heart as well as his own, with a possible pun on the meaning of "deceitful." (It was a deceitful heart that she gave him.) The latter word seems to pun on the meanings "sincere" and "unmarried." 292. **put him down,** got the better of him. 304. **civil count.** Some editors place a comma between these words. **civil,** serious, grave. **civil,** pun on Seville, whence oranges came. 305. **jealous complexion.** Yellow, associated with melancholy, was the accepted symbol of jealousy. 307. **blazon,** description. 315. **all grace,** the source of grace, God.

on the windy side of care. My cousin tells him in his ear that he is in her heart.

Claud. And so she doth, cousin.

Beat. Good Lord, for alliance! Thus goes every one to the world but I, and I am sunburnt; I may sit in a corner and cry heigh-ho for a husband!

D. Pedro. Lady Beatrice, I will get you one.

Beat. I would rather have one of your father's getting. Hath your grace ne'er a brother like you? Your father got excellent husbands, if a maid could come by them.

D. Pedro. Will you have me, lady?

Beat. No, my lord, unless I might have another for working-days: your grace is too costly to wear every day. But, I beseech your grace, pardon me: I was born to speak all mirth and no matter.

D. Pedro. Your silence most offends me, and to be merry best becomes you; for, out of question, you were born in a merry hour.

Beat. No, sure, my lord, my mother cried; but then there was a star danced, and under that was I born. Cousins, God give you joy!

Leon. Niece, will you look to those things I told you of?

Beat. I cry you mercy, uncle. By your grace's pardon. *Exit Beatrice.*

D. Pedro. By my troth, a pleasant-spirited lady.

Leon. There 's little of the melancholy element in her, my lord: she is never sad but when she sleeps, and not ever sad then; for I have heard my daughter say, she hath often dreamed of unhappiness and waked herself with laughing.

D. Pedro. She cannot endure to hear tell of a husband.

Leon. O, by no means: she mocks all her wooers out of suit.

D. Pedro. She were an excellent wife for Benedick.

Leon. O Lord, my lord, if they were but a week married, they would talk themselves mad.

D. Pedro. County Claudio, when mean you to go to church?

Claud. To-morrow, my lord: time goes on crutches till love have all his rites.

Leon. Not till Monday, my dear son, which is hence a just seven-night; and a time too brief, too, to have all things answer my mind.

D. Pedro. Come, you shake the head at so long a breathing: but, I warrant thee, Claudio, the time shall not go dully by us. I will in the interim undertake one of Hercules' labours; which is, to bring Signior Benedick and the Lady Beatrice into a mountain of affection the one with the other. I would fain have it a match, and I doubt not but to fashion it, if you three will but minister such assistance as I shall give you direction.

Leon. My lord, I am for you, though it cost me ten nights' watchings.

Claud. And I, my lord.

D. Pedro. And you too, gentle Hero?

Hero. I will do any modest office, my lord, to help my cousin to a good husband.

D. Pedro. And Benedick is not the unhopefullest husband that I know. Thus far can I praise him; he is of a noble strain, of approved valour and confirmed honesty. I will teach you how to humour your cousin, that she shall fall in love with Benedick; and I, with your two helps, will so practise on Benedick that, in despite of his quick wit and his queasy stomach, he shall fall in love with Beatrice. If we can do this, Cupid is no longer an archer: his glory shall be ours, for we are the only love-gods. Go in with me, and I will tell you my drift. *Exeunt.*

[SCENE II. *The same.*]

Enter [DON] JOHN *and* BORACHIO.

D. John. It is so; the Count Claudio shall marry the daughter of Leonato.

Bora. Yea, my lord; but I can cross it.

D. John. Any bar, any cross, any impediment will be medicinable to me: I am sick in displeasure to him, and whatsoever comes athwart his affection ranges evenly with mine. How canst thou cross this marriage?

Bora. Not honestly, my lord; but so covertly that no dishonesty shall appear in me.

D. John. Show me briefly how.

Bora. I think I told your lordship a year since, how much I am in the favour of Margaret, the waiting gentlewoman to Hero.

D. John. I remember.

Bora. I can, at any unseasonable instant of the night, appoint her to look out at her lady's chamber-window.

D. John. What life is in that, to be the death of this marriage?

Bora. The poison of that lies in you to temper. Go you to the prince your brother; spare not to tell him that he hath wronged his honour in marrying the renowned Claudio—whose estimation do you mightily hold up—to a contaminated stale, such a one as Hero.

D. John. What proof shall I make of that?

Bora. Proof enough to misuse the prince, to vex Claudio, to undo Hero and kill Leonato. Look you for any other issue?

D. John. Only to despite them, I will endeavour any thing.

327. **windy,** windward, safe. 331. **goes . . . world** i.e., gets married. 332. **sunburnt.** The Renaissance considered dark complexions unattractive. 333. **heigh-ho . . . husband,** title of a ballad. 357. **melancholy element,** i.e., earth, associated with the humor of melancholy in the old physiology; see *element* in glossary. 359. **ever,** always. Some editors prefer the anonymous conjecture *even.* 361. **unhappiness,** misfortune. 365. **out of suit,** out of love, with play on the legal sense of "nonsuiting." 375. **a just seven-night,** exactly a week. 378. **breathing,** pause, rest. 385. **minister,** furnish, supply. 387. **am for you,** accept your proposal. **watchings,** staying awake. 395. **approved,** tested. **honesty,** honor. 400. **queasy stomach,** squeamish taste. 403. **drift,** purpose.

SCENE II. 1. **shall,** is going to. 5. **medicinable,** medicinal. 6. **displeasure,** dislike. 7. **whatsoever . . . mine,** whatever crosses his inclination runs parallel with mine. **ranges,** lies in the same plane; see glossary. 21. **lies in,** rests with. **temper,** mix, compound. 25. **estimation,** worth. 26. **contaminated stale,** impure harlot. 28. **misuse,** abuse; deceive. 29. **vex,** afflict. 32. **meet,** suitable. 36. **intend,** pretend. 37. **as,** i.e., saying as follows. The words between the dashes are to be understood as instructions to Don John as to what he is to say. 39. **like,** likely. **cozened,** deceived, cheated. **semblance,** semblance only, outward appearance. 40. **discovered,** revealed. 44-45. **hear . . . Claudio.** Many editors follow Theobald and read *Borachio* for *Claudio.* The present reading may be defended if one imagines that, by arrangement with Margaret, Borachio is playing the part of Claudio. D. J. Gordon points out a similar confusion in Della Porta's *Gli Duoi Fratelli Rivalli.* 50. **jealousy,** suspicion. 51. **preparation,** i.e., for the marriage. 55. **ducats,** Italian coins worth about one dollar each.

Bora. Go, then; find me a meet hour to draw Don Pedro and the Count Claudio alone: tell them that you know that Hero loves me; intend a kind of zeal both to the prince and Claudio, as,—in love of your brother's honour, who hath made this match, and his friend's reputation, who is thus like to be cozened with the semblance of a maid,—that you have discovered thus. They will scarcely believe this without trial: offer them instances; which shall bear no less likelihood than to see me at her chamber-window, hear me †call Margaret Hero, hear Margaret term me Claudio; and bring them to see this the very night before the intended wedding,—for in the meantime I will so fashion the matter that Hero shall be absent,—and there shall appear such seeming truth of Hero's disloyalty that jealousy shall be called assurance and all the preparation overthrown.

D. John. Grow this to what adverse issue it can, I will put it in practice. Be cunning in the working this, and thy fee is a thousand ducats.

Bora. Be you constant in the accusation, and my cunning shall not shame me.

D. John. I will presently go learn their day of marriage. *Exit [with Borachio].*

[SCENE III. LEONATO'S *orchard.*]

Enter BENEDICK *alone.*

Bene. Boy!

[*Enter* Boy.]

Boy. Signior?

Bene. In my chamber-window lies a book: bring it hither to me in the orchard.

Boy. I am here already, sir.

Bene. I know that; but I would have thee hence, and here again. *Exit [Boy].* I do much wonder that one man, seeing how much another man is a fool when he dedicates his behaviours to love, will, after he hath laughed at such shallow follies in others, become the argument of his own scorn by falling in love: and such a man is Claudio. I have known when there was no music with him but the drum and the fife; and now had he rather hear the tabor and the pipe: I have known when he would have walked ten mile a-foot to see a good armour; and now will he lie ten nights awake, carving the fashion of a new doublet. He was wont to speak plain and to the purpose, like an honest man and a soldier; and now is he turned orthography; his words are a very fantastical banquet, just so many strange dishes. May I be so converted and see with these eyes? I cannot tell; I think not: I will not be sworn but love may transform me to an oyster; but I'll take my oath on it, till he have made an oyster of me, he shall never make me such a fool. One woman is fair, yet I am well; another is wise, yet I am well; another virtuous, yet I am well; but till all graces be in one woman, one woman shall not come in my grace. Rich she shall be, that 's certain; wise, or I'll none; virtuous, or I'll never cheapen her; fair, or I'll never look on her; mild, or come not near me; noble, or not I for an angel; of good discourse, an excellent musician, and her hair shall be of what colour it please God. Ha! the prince and Monsieur Love! I will hide me in the arbour. [*Withdraws.*]

Enter Prince [DON PEDRO], LEONATO, CLAUDIO.

D. Pedro. Come, shall we hear this music?
Claud. Yea, my good lord. How still the evening is,
As hush'd on purpose to grace harmony!
D. Pedro. See you where Benedick hath hid himself?
Claud. O, very well, my lord: the music ended,
We'll fit the kid-fox with a pennyworth.

Enter BALTHASAR *with Music.*

D. Pedro. Come, Balthasar, we'll hear that song again.
Balth. O, good my lord, tax not so bad a voice
To slander music any more than once.
D. Pedro. It is the witness still of excellency
To put a strange face on his own perfection.
I pray thee, sing, and let me woo no more.
Balth. Because you talk of wooing, I will sing;
Since many a wooer doth commence his suit
To her he thinks not worthy, yet he wooes,
Yet will he swear he loves.
D. Pedro. Nay, pray thee, come;
Or, if thou wilt hold longer argument,
Do it in notes.
Balth. Note this before my notes;
There 's not a note of mine that 's worth the noting.
D. Pedro. Why, these are very crotchets that he speaks;
Note, notes, forsooth, and nothing. [*Air.*]

Bene. Now, divine air! now is his soul ravished! Is it not strange that sheeps' guts should hale souls out of men's bodies? Well, a horn for my money, when all 's done.

The Song.

[*Balth.*] Sigh no more, ladies, sigh no more,
Men were deceivers ever,
One foot in sea and one on shore,
To one thing constant never:
Then sigh not so, but let them go,
And be you blithe and bonny,
Converting all your sounds of woe
Into Hey nonny, nonny.

SCENE III. 5. **here already,** i.e., he will be so quick as to use no time at all. 9. **behaviours,** details of behavior. 15. **tabor . . . pipe,** symbols of peaceful merriment. 17. **armour,** suit of armor. 18. **carving,** planning. 21. **orthography,** either abstract for concrete, or, as Rowe and many editors have it, an error for "orthographer." 33. **I'll none,** I'll have none. 34. **cheapen,** ask the price of, bid for. 35, 36. **noble, angel.** Each of these words involves a pun on the meaning "a coin," a *noble* being worth 6s. 8d. and an *angel*, 10s. 37-38. **of . . . God,** i.e., of any color whatever. Some editors see an allusion to the practice of dyeing the hair. 38. *Stage Direction:* F: *Enter Prince, Leonato, Claudio,* and *Jacke Wilson;* Q has *Musicke* for *and Jacke Wilson.* Wilson was evidently the actor who played Balthasar. 41. **grace harmony,** do honor to music. 43. **the music ended,** when the music is over. 44. **kid-fox.** Cass suggests an allusion to Spenser's *Shepheardes Calender* (*Eclogue* v), to the story of the kid captured by the wily fox, seeing in Benedick's situation something both of the wily fox and the innocent kid; Warburton: *hid-fox;* Onions: *cub-fox.* **pennyworth,** i.e., his money's worth. 48-49. **It . . . perfection.** It is always a proof of excellence that, in demeanor, it is unconscious, or unknowing, of its own perfection (Furness). 50. **woo,** entreat. 56. **notes,** music. 58. **crotchets,** used with play on the meanings "whim" or "fancy," and "musical notes." 59. **Note,** knows not, pretends not to know. **nothing,** with play on "noting." It has been suggested that this same pun is concealed in the title of the play, where *Nothing* would suggest "noting," or eavesdropping. 61. **sheeps' guts,** fiddle-strings. **hale,** draw. 62. **horn,** a hunting horn, a more masculine interest than a fiddle.

Sing no more ditties, sing no moe,
 Of dumps so dull and heavy;
The fraud of men was ever so,
 Since summer first was leavy:
  Then sigh not so, &c.

D. Pedro. By my troth, a good song.

Balth. And an ill singer, my lord.

D. Pedro. Ha, no, no, faith; thou singest well enough for a shift.

Bene. [*Aside*] An he had been a dog that should have howled thus, they would have hanged him: and I pray God his bad voice bode no mischief. I had as lief have heard the night-raven, come what plague could have come after it.

D. Pedro. Yea, marry, dost thou hear, Balthasar? I pray thee, get us some excellent music; for to-morrow night we would have it at the Lady Hero's chamber-window.

Balth. The best I can, my lord.

D. Pedro. Do so: farewell. *(Exit Balthasar.)* Come hither, Leonato. What was it you told me of to-day, that your niece Beatrice was in love with Signior Benedick?

Claud. O, ay! [*Aside to Pedro*] Stalk on, stalk on; the fowl sits.—I did never think that lady would have loved any man.

Leon. No, nor I neither; but most wonderful that she should so dote on Signior Benedick, whom she hath in all outward behaviours seemed ever to abhor.

Bene. [*Aside*] Is 't possible? Sits the wind in that corner?

Leon. By my troth, my lord, I cannot tell what to think of it but that she loves him with an enraged affection; it is past the infinite of thought.

D. Pedro. May be she doth but counterfeit.

Claud. Faith, like enough.

Leon. O God, counterfeit! There was never counterfeit of passion came so near the life of passion as she discovers it.

D. Pedro. Why, what effects of passion shows she?

Claud. [*Aside*] Bait the hook well; this fish will bite.

Leon. What effects, my lord? She will sit you, you heard my daughter tell you how.

Claud. She did, indeed.

D. Pedro. How, how, I pray you? You amaze me: I would have thought her spirit had been invincible against all assaults of affection.

Leon. I would have sworn it had, my lord; especially against Benedick.

Bene. [*Aside*] I should think this a gull, but that the white-bearded fellow speaks it: knavery cannot, sure, hide himself in such reverence.

Claud. [*Aside*] He hath ta'en the infection: hold it up.

D. Pedro. Hath she made her affection known to Benedick?

Leon. No; and swears she never will: that 's her torment.

Claud. 'Tis true, indeed; so your daughter says: 'Shall I,' says she, 'that have so oft encountered him with scorn, write to him that I love him?'

Leon. This says she now when she is beginning to write to him; for she'll be up twenty times a night, and there will she sit in her smock till she have writ a sheet of paper: my daughter tells us all.

Claud. Now you talk of a sheet of paper, I remember a pretty jest your daughter told us of.

Leon. O, when she had writ it and was reading it over, she found Benedick and Beatrice between the sheet?

Claud. That.

Leon. O, she tore the letter into a thousand halfpence; railed at herself, that she should be so immodest to write to one that she knew would flout her; 'I measure him,' says she, 'by my own spirit; for I should flout him, if he writ to me; yea, though I love him, I should.'

Claud. Then down upon her knees she falls, weeps, sobs, beats her heart, tears her hair, prays, curses; 'O sweet Benedick! God give me patience!'

Leon. She doth indeed; my daughter says so: and the ecstasy hath so much overborne her that my daughter is sometime afeard she will do a desperate outrage to herself: it is very true.

D. Pedro. It were good that Benedick knew of it by some other, if she will not discover it.

Claud. To what end? He would make but a sport of it and torment the poor lady worse.

D. Pedro. An he should, it were an alms to hang him. She 's an excellent sweet lady; and, out of all suspicion, she is virtuous.

Claud. And she is exceeding wise.

D. Pedro. In every thing but in loving Benedick.

Leon. O, my lord, wisdom and blood combatting in so tender a body, we have ten proofs to one that blood hath the victory. I am sorry for her, as I have just cause, being her uncle and her guardian.

D. Pedro. I would she had bestowed this dotage on me: I would have daffed all other respects and made her half myself. I pray you, tell Benedick of it, and hear what 'a will say.

Leon. Were it good, think you?

Claud. Hero thinks surely she will die; for she says she will die, if he love her not, and she will die, ere she make her love known, and she will die, if he woo her, rather than she will bate one breath of her accustomed crossness.

D. Pedro. She doth well: if she should make tender of her love, 'tis very possible he'll scorn it; for the man, as you know all, hath a contemptible spirit.

Claud. He is a very proper man.

D. Pedro. He hath indeed a good outward happiness.

Claud. Before God! and, in my mind, very wise.

D. Pedro. He doth indeed show some sparks that are like wit.

Claud. And I take him to be valiant.

D. Pedro. As Hector, I assure you: and in the managing of quarrels you may say he is wise; for either he avoids them with great discretion, or undertakes them with a most Christian-like fear.

Leon. If he do fear God, 'a must necessarily keep peace: if he break the peace, he ought to enter into a quarrel with fear and trembling.

D. Pedro. And so will he do; for the man doth fear

84. **night-raven,** variously identified as the owl, the night-heron, and the bittern. 86. **Yea, marry,** a continuation of Don Pedro's speech preceding Benedick's aside. 95. **stalk . . . sits,** an allusion to the practice of hunting birds by means of a stalking-horse, i.e., a horse trained to the business, or an artificial structure resembling a horse. 123. **gull,** trick, deception. 126. **hold it up,** keep up the jest. 145. **That,** that was it. 147. **halfpence,** very tiny, silver coins; i.e., small pieces. 164. **alms,** good deed. 166. **out of,** beyond. 176. **daffed,** put or thrust aside. 177. **half myself,** i.e., my wife. 188. **contemptible,** contemptuous. 190. **outward happiness,** fortunate in his good looks. 194. **wit,** sense. 206. **large,** indelicate. 210. **counsel,** reflection, deliberation. 225. **no such matter,** the reality is quite otherwise. 229. **sadly borne,**

God, howsoever it seems not in him by some large jests he will make. Well, I am sorry for your niece. Shall we go seek Benedick, and tell him of her love?

Claud. Never tell him, my lord: let her wear it out with good counsel.

Leon. Nay, that 's impossible: she may wear her heart out first.

D. Pedro. Well, we will hear further of it by your daughter: let it cool the while. I love Benedick well; and I could wish he would modestly examine himself, to see how much he is unworthy so good a lady.

Leon. My lord, will you walk? dinner is ready.
[*They walk aside.*]

Claud. If he do not dote on her upon this, I will never trust my expectation.

D. Pedro. Let there be the same net spread for her; and that must your daughter and her gentlewomen carry. The sport will be, when they hold one an opinion of another's dotage, and no such matter: that 's the scene that I would see, which will be merely a dumb-show. Let us send her to call him in to dinner.
[*Exeunt Don Pedro, Claudio, and Leonato.*]

Bene. [*Coming forward*] This can be no trick: the conference was sadly borne. They have the truth of this from Hero. They seem to pity the lady: it seems her affections have their full bent. Love me! why, it must be requited. I hear how I am censured: they say I will bear myself proudly, if I perceive the love come from her; they say too that she will rather die than give any sign of affection. I did never think to marry: I must not seem proud: happy are they that hear their detractions and can put them to mending. They say the lady is fair; 'tis a truth, I can bear them witness; and virtuous; 'tis so, I cannot reprove it; and wise, but for loving me; by my troth, it is no addition to her wit, nor no great argument of her folly, for I will be horribly in love with her. I may chance have some odd quirks and remnants of wit broken on me, because I have railed so long against marriage: but doth not the appetite alter? a man loves the meat in his youth that he cannot endure in his age. Shall quips and sentences and these paper bullets of the brain awe a man from the career of his humour? No, the world must be peopled. When I said I would die a bachelor, I did not think I should live till I were married. Here comes Beatrice. By this day! she 's a fair lady: I do spy some marks of love in her.

Enter BEATRICE.

Beat. Against my will I am sent to bid you come in to dinner.

Bene. Fair Beatrice, I thank you for your pains.

Beat. I took no more pains for those thanks than you take pains to thank me: if it had been painful, I would not have come.

Bene. You take pleasure then in the message?

Beat. Yea, just so much as you may take upon a knife's point and choke a daw withal. You have no stomach, signior: fare you well. *Exit.*

Bene. Ha! 'Against my will I am sent to bid you come in to dinner;' there 's a double meaning in that. 'I took no more pains for those thanks than you took pains to thank me;' that 's as much as to say, Any pains that I take for you is as easy as thanks. If I do not take pity of her, I am a villain; if I do not love her, I am a Jew. I will go get her picture. *Exit.*

[ACT III.

SCENE I. LEONATO'S *garden.*]

Enter HERO *and two gentlewomen,* MARGARET, *and* URSULA.

Hero. Good Margaret, run thee to the parlour;
There shalt thou find my cousin Beatrice
Proposing with the prince and Claudio:
Whisper her ear and tell her, I and Ursula
Walk in the orchard and our whole discourse
Is all of her; say that thou overheard'st us;
And bid her steal into the pleached bower,
Where honeysuckles, ripened by the sun,
Forbid the sun to enter, like favourites,
Made proud by princes, that advance their pride
Against that power that bred it: there will she hide her,
To listen our propose. This is thy office.
Bear thee well in it and leave us alone.

Marg. I'll make her come, I warrant you, presently.
[*Exit.*]

Hero. Now, Ursula, when Beatrice doth come,
As we do trace this alley up and down,
Our talk must only be of Benedick.
When I do name him, let it be thy part
To praise him more than ever man did merit:
My talk to thee must be how Benedick
Is sick in love with Beatrice. Of this matter
Is little Cupid's crafty arrow made,
That only wounds by hearsay.

Enter BEATRICE [*behind*].

Now begin;
For look where Beatrice, like a lapwing, runs
Close by the ground, to hear our conference.

Urs. The pleasant'st angling is to see the fish
Cut with her golden oars the silver stream,
And greedily devour the treacherous bait:
So angle we for Beatrice; who even now
Is couched in the woodbine coverture.
Fear you not my part of the dialogue.

Hero. Then go we near her, that her ear lose nothing
Of the false sweet bait that we lay for it.
[*Approaching the bower.*]
No, truly, Ursula, she is too disdainful;
I know her spirits are as coy and wild
As haggards of the rock.

Urs. But are you sure
That Benedick loves Beatrice so entirely?

Hero. So says the prince and my new-trothed lord.

Urs. And did they bid you tell her of it, madam?

Hero. They did entreat me to acquaint her of it;
But I persuaded them, if they lov'd Benedick,
To wish him wrestle with affection,

gravely conducted. 232. **have . . . bent,** are tightly stretched. 238. **put . . . mending,** undertake to remedy the defect. 241. **reprove,** refute. 245. **quirks,** witty conceits or jokes. 249. **quips,** sharp or sarcastic remarks. **sentences,** saws, maxims. **paper bullets,** i.e., taken from books. 250. **career of his humour,** pursuit of his inclination. 264. **choke . . . withal,** i.e., make a mouthful for a jackdaw.

ACT III. SCENE I. 3. **Proposing,** conversing. 8. **honeysuckles,** identified with the woodbine. 12. **propose,** conversation. 16. **trace,** walk. 23. **only . . . hearsay,** wounds by mere report. 30. **woodbine coverture,** bower, or arbor, of honeysuckle. 36. **haggards,** untrained female hawks.

And never to let Beatrice know of it.
Urs. Why did you so? Doth not the gentleman
Deserve as full as fortunate a bed
As ever Beatrice shall couch upon?
Hero. O god of love! I know he doth deserve
As much as may be yielded to a man:
But Nature never fram'd a woman's heart
Of prouder stuff than that of Beatrice;
Disdain and scorn ride sparkling in her eyes,
Misprising what they look on, and her wit
Values itself so highly that to her
All matter else seems weak: she cannot love,
Nor take no shape nor project of affection,
She is so self-endeared.
Urs. Sure, I think so;
And therefore certainly it were not good
She knew his love, lest she'll make sport at it.
Hero. Why, you speak truth. I never yet saw man,
How wise, how noble, young, how rarely featur'd,
But she would spell him backward: if fair-fac'd,
She would swear the gentleman should be her sister;
If black, why, Nature, drawing of an antique,
Made a foul blot; if tall, a lance ill-headed;
If low, an agate very vilely cut;
If speaking, why, a vane blown with all winds;
If silent, why, a block moved with none.
So turns she every man the wrong side out
And never gives to truth and virtue that
Which simpleness and merit purchaseth.
Urs. Sure, sure, such carping is not commendable.
Hero. No, not to be so odd and from all fashions
As Beatrice is, cannot be commendable:
But who dare tell her so? If I should speak,
She would mock me into air; O, she would laugh me
Out of myself, press me to death with wit.
Therefore let Benedick, like cover'd fire,
Consume away in sighs, waste inwardly:
It were a better death than die with mocks,
Which is as bad as die with tickling.
Urs. Yet tell her of it: hear what she will say.
Hero. No; rather I will go to Benedick
And counsel him to fight against his passion.
And, truly, I'll devise some honest slanders
To stain my cousin with: one doth not know
How much an ill word may empoison liking.
Urs. O, do not do your cousin such a wrong.
She cannot be so much without true judgement—
Having so swift and excellent a wit
As she is priz'd to have—as to refuse
So rare a gentleman as Signior Benedick.
Hero. He is the only man of Italy,
Always excepted my dear Claudio.
Urs. I pray you, be not angry with me, madam,
Speaking my fancy: Signior Benedick,
For shape, for bearing, argument and valour,
Goes foremost in report through Italy.
Hero. Indeed, he hath an excellent good name.
Urs. His excellence did earn it, ere he had it.
When are you married, madam?
Hero. Why, every day, to-morrow. Come, go in:
I'll show thee some attires, and have thy counsel
Which is the best to furnish me to-morrow.
[*They walk away.*]
Urs. She 's lim'd, I warrant you: we have caught her, madam.
Hero. If it proves so, then loving goes by haps:
Some Cupid kills with arrows, some with traps.
[*Exeunt Hero and Ursula.*]
Beat. [*Coming forward*] What fire is in mine ears? Can this be true?
Stand I condemn'd for pride and scorn so much?
Contempt, farewell! and maiden pride, adieu!
No glory lives behind the back of such.
And, Benedick, love on; I will requite thee,
Taming my wild heart to thy loving hand:
If thou dost love, my kindness shall incite thee
To bind our loves up in a holy band;
For others say thou dost deserve, and I
Believe it better than reportingly. *Exit.*

[SCENE II. *A room in* LEONATO'S *house.*]

Enter Prince [DON PEDRO], CLAUDIO, BENEDICK, *and* LEONATO.

D. Pedro. I do but stay till your marriage be consummate, and then go I toward Arragon.

Claud. I'll bring you thither, my lord, if you'll vouchsafe me.

D. Pedro. Nay, that would be as great a soil in the new gloss of your marriage as to show a child his new coat and forbid him to wear it. I will only be bold with Benedick for his company; for, from the crown of his head to the sole of his foot, he is all mirth: he hath twice or thrice cut Cupid's bow-string and the little hangman dare not shoot at him; he hath a heart as sound as a bell and his tongue is the clapper, for what his heart thinks his tongue speaks.

Bene. Gallants, I am not as I have been.

Leon. So say I: methinks you are sadder.

Claud. I hope he be in love.

D. Pedro. Hang him, truant! there 's no true drop of blood in him, to be truly touched with love: if he be sad, he wants money.

Bene. I have the toothache.

D. Pedro. Draw it.

Bene. Hang it!

Claud. You must hang it first, and draw it afterwards.

D. Pedro. What! sigh for the toothache?

Leon. Where is but a humour or a worm.

Bene. Well, every one can master a grief but he that has it.

Claud. Yet say I, he is in love.

D. Pedro. There is no appearance of fancy in him, unless it be a fancy that he hath to strange disguises; as, to be a Dutchman to-day, a Frenchman to-mor-

45. **as full as,** fully as; New Cambridge (following Boas): *at full.* 52. **Misprising,** undervaluing. 55. **project,** conception, idea. 56. **self-endeared,** full of self-love. 61. **spell him backward,** say the exactly contrary thing; a possible allusion to witches' prayers, which were said backward. 63. **black,** dark. **antique** (*antic*), buffoon. 65. **agate,** diminutive person; an allusion to the small figures cut in agate for rings. 70. **simpleness,** integrity, plainness. 72. **from,** different from. 78. **Consume . . . sighs,** an allusion to the belief that each sigh costs the heart a drop of blood. 84. **some honest slanders,** slanders which do not involve her virtue. 90. **priz'd,** estimated. 101. **every day, to-morrow,** every day after tomorrow. 104. **lim'd,** caught, as a bird in birdlime. 105. **by haps,** by chance. 107. **What . . . ears,** an allusion to the old saying that a person's ears burn when he is being discussed in his absence. 110. **No . . . such.** No good is spoken of such persons when their backs are turned. 112. **Taming . . . hand,** figure derived from the taming of the hawk by the hand of the falconer. 116. **better than reportingly,** on better evidence than mere report.

SCENE II. 3. **bring,** escort. 11. **little hangman,** playfully applied to Cupid. 27. **Where . . . worm.** Toothache was ascribed to "humors" or unhealthy secretions and to actual worms in the teeth. 36. **slops,** row, or in the shape of two countries at once, as, a German from the waist downward, all slops, and a Spaniard from the hip upward, no doublet. Unless he have a fancy to this foolery, as it appears he hath, he is no fool for fancy, as you would have it appear he is.

Claud. If he be not in love with some woman, there is no believing old signs: 'a brushes his hat o' mornings; what should that bode?

D. Pedro. Hath any man seen him at the barber's?

Claud. No, but the barber's man hath been seen with him, and the old ornament of his cheek hath already stuffed tennis-balls.

Leon. Indeed, he looks younger than he did, by the loss of a beard.

D. Pedro. Nay, 'a rubs himself with civet: can you smell him out by that?

Claud. That 's as much as to say, the sweet youth 's in love.

D. Pedro. The greatest note of it is his melancholy.

Claud. And when was he wont to wash his face?

D. Pedro. Yea, or to paint himself? for the which, I hear what they say of him.

Claud. Nay, but his jesting spirit; which is now crept into a lute-string and now governed by stops.

D. Pedro. Indeed, that tells a heavy tale for him: conclude, conclude he is in love.

Claud. Nay, but I know who loves him.

D. Pedro. That would I know too: I warrant, one that knows him not.

Claud. Yes, and his ill conditions; and, in despite of all, dies for him.

D. Pedro. She shall be buried with her face upwards.

Bene. Yet is this no charm for the toothache. Old signior, walk aside with me: I have studied eight or nine wise words to speak to you, which these hobby-horses must not hear. [*Exeunt Benedick and Leonato.*]

D. Pedro. For my life, to break with him about Beatrice.

Claud. 'Tis even so. Hero and Margaret have by this played their parts with Beatrice; and then the two bears will not bite one another when they meet.

Enter [DON] JOHN *the Bastard.*

D. John. My lord and brother, God save you!

D. Pedro. Good den, brother.

D. John. If your leisure served, I would speak with you.

D. Pedro. In private?

D. John. If it please you: yet Count Claudio may hear; for what I would speak of concerns him.

D. Pedro. What 's the matter?

D. John. [*To Claudio*] Means your lordship to be married to-morrow?

D. Pedro. You know he does.

D. John. I know not that, when he knows what I know.

Claud. If there be any impediment, I pray you discover it.

D. John. You may think I love you not: let that appear hereafter, and aim better at me by that I now will manifest. For my brother, I think he holds you well, and in dearness of heart hath holp to effect your ensuing marriage;—surely suit ill spent and labour ill bestowed.

D. Pedro. Why, what 's the matter?

D. John. I came hither to tell you; and, circumstances shortened, for she has been too long a talking of, the lady is disloyal.

Claud. Who, Hero?

D. John. Even she; Leonato's Hero, your Hero, every man's Hero.

Claud. Disloyal?

D. John. The word is too good to paint out her wickedness; I could say she were worse: think you of a worse title, and I will fit her to it. Wonder not till further warrant: go but with me to-night, you shall see her chamber-window entered, even the night before her wedding-day: if you love her then, to-morrow wed her; but it would better fit your honour to change your mind.

Claud. May this be so?

D. Pedro. I will not think it.

D. John. If you dare not trust that you see, confess not that you know: if you will follow me, I will show you enough; and when you have seen more and heard more, proceed accordingly.

Claud. If I see any thing to-night why I should not marry her to-morrow, in the congregation, where I should wed, there will I shame her.

D. Pedro. And, as I wooed for thee to obtain her, I will join with thee to disgrace her.

D. John. I will disparage her no farther till you are my witnesses: bear it coldly but till midnight, and let the issue show itself.

D. Pedro. O day untowardly turned!

Claud. O mischief strangely thwarting!

D. John. O plague right well prevented! so will you say when you have seen the sequel. [*Exeunt.*]

[SCENE III. *A street.*]

Enter DOGBERRY *and his compartner* [VERGES] *with the* Watch.

Dog. Are you good men and true?

Verg. Yea, or else it were pity but they should suffer salvation, body and soul.

Dog. Nay, that were a punishment too good for them, if they should have any allegiance in them, being chosen for the prince's watch.

Verg. Well, give them their charge, neighbour Dogberry.

Dog. First, who think you the most desartless man to be constable?

First Watch. Hugh Otecake, sir, or George Seacole; for they can write and read.

Dog. Come hither, neighbour Seacole. God hath

loose breeches. 37. **no doublet,** i.e., with a Spanish cloak instead. 46-47. **old . . . tennis-balls.** Benedick's beard has gone to stuff tennis balls. 50. **civet,** perfume derived from the civet cat. 56. **wash,** i.e., with cosmetics. 61. **now crept.** Boas: *new crept*, followed by New Cambridge. 62. **stops,** frets on the finger board. 68. **ill conditions,** bad qualities. 70-71. **buried . . . upwards.** Suicides were sometimes buried with their faces downwards. Beatrice will not be responsible for her own death. (Probably there is also a ribald suggestion, continuing the joke on "dies for him" meaning to perform the act of love.) 75. **hobby-horses,** buffoons. 78. **Margaret.** Ursula joined Hero in playing the trick on Beatrice, but Margaret has been in on it. 83. **Good den,** good evening. 99. **aim better at,** judge better of. 101. **holds you well,** i.e., thinks well of you. 106. **circumstances shortened,** without unnecessary details. 107. **a talking of,** under discussion. 112. **paint out,** portray in full. 115. **till further warrant,** till further proof appears. 122-123. **If . . . know,** i.e., when you have seen what I'll show you, either admit that what you know is true or admit that you're denying a certainty. 134. **untowardly turned,** perversely altered.

SCENE III. 3. **salvation,** blunder for "damnation." 7. **charge,** instructions. 9. **desartless,** for "deserving."

blessed you with a good name: to be a well-favoured man is the gift of fortune; but to write and read comes by nature.

Sec. Watch. Both which, master constable,—

Dog. You have: I knew it would be your answer. Well, for your favour, sir, why, give God thanks, and make no boast of it; and for your writing and reading, let that appear when there is no need of such vanity. You are thought here to be the most senseless and fit man for the constable of the watch; therefore bear you the lantern. This is your charge: you shall comprehend all vagrom men; you are to bid any man stand, in the prince's name.

Sec. Watch. How if 'a will not stand?

Dog. Why, then, take no note of him, but let him go; and presently call the rest of the watch together and thank God you are rid of a knave.

Verg. If he will not stand when he is bidden, he is none of the prince's subjects.

Dog. True, and they are to meddle with none but the prince's subjects. You shall also make no noise in the streets; for for the watch to babble and to talk is most tolerable and not to be endured.

Watch. We will rather sleep than talk: we know what belongs to a watch.

Dog. Why, you speak like an ancient and most quiet watchman; for I cannot see how sleeping should offend: only, have a care that your bills be not stolen. Well, you are to call at all the ale-houses, and bid those that are drunk get them to bed.

Watch. How if they will not?

Dog. Why, then, let them alone till they are sober: if they make you not then the better answer, you may say they are not the men you took them for.

Watch. Well, sir.

Dog. If you meet a thief, you may suspect him, by virtue of your office, to be no true man; and, for such kind of men, the less you meddle or make with them, why, the more is for your honesty.

Watch. If we know him to be a thief, shall we not lay hands on him?

Dog. Truly, by your office, you may; but I think they that touch pitch will be defiled: the most peaceable way for you, if you do take a thief, is to let him show himself what he is and steal out of your company.

Verg. You have been always called a merciful man, partner.

Dog. Truly, I would not hang a dog by my will, much more a man who hath any honesty in him.

Verg. If you hear a child cry in the night, you must call to the nurse and bid her still it.

Watch. How if the nurse be asleep and will not hear us?

Dog. Why, then, depart in peace, and let the child wake her with crying; for the ewe that will not hear her lamb when it baes will never answer a calf when he bleats.

Verg. 'Tis very true.

Dog. This is the end of the charge:—you, constable, are to present the prince's own person: if you meet the prince in the night, you may stay him.

Verg. Nay, by 'r lady, that I think 'a cannot.

Dog. Five shillings to one on 't, with any man that knows the statutes, he may stay him: marry, not without the prince be willing; for, indeed, the watch ought to offend no man; and it is an offence to stay a man against his will.

Verg. By 'r lady, I think it be so.

Dog. Ha, ah, ha! Well, masters, good night: an there be any matter of weight chances, call up me: keep your fellows' counsels and your own; and good night. Come, neighbour.

Watch. Well, masters, we hear our charge: let us go sit here upon the church-bench till two, and then all to bed.

Dog. One word more, honest neighbours. I pray you, watch about Signior Leonato's door; for the wedding being there to-morrow, there is a great coil to-night. Adieu: be vigitant, I beseech you.

Exeunt [Dogberry and Verges].

Enter BORACHIO *and* CONRADE.

Bora. What, Conrade!

Watch. [*Aside*] Peace! stir not.

Bora. Conrade, I say!

Con. Here, man; I am at thy elbow.

Bora. Mass, and my elbow itched; I thought there would a scab follow.

Con. I will owe thee an answer for that: and now forward with thy tale.

Bora. Stand thee close, then, under this pent-house, for it drizzles rain; and I will, like a true drunkard, utter all to thee.

Watch. [*Aside*] Some treason, masters: yet stand close.

Bora. Therefore know I have earned of Don John a thousand ducats.

Con. Is it possible that any villany should be so dear?

Bora. Thou shouldst rather ask if it were possible any villany should be so rich; for when rich villains have need of poor ones, poor ones may make what price they will.

Con. I wonder at it.

Bora. That shows thou art unconfirmed. Thou knowest that the fashion of a doublet, or a hat, or a cloak, is nothing to a man.

Con. Yes, it is apparel.

Bora. I mean, the fashion.

Con. Yes, the fashion is the fashion.

Bora. Tush! I may as well say the fool 's the fool. But seest thou not what a deformed thief this fashion is?

Watch. [*Aside*] I know that Deformed; 'a has been a vile thief this seven year; 'a goes up and down like a gentleman: I remember his name.

Bora. Didst thou not hear somebody?

23. **senseless,** for "sensible." 25. **comprehend,** for "apprehend." **vagrom,** vagrant. 38. **tolerable,** for "intolerable." 40. **belongs to,** are the duties of. 44. **bills,** kind of pike, an ax fixed to a long pole. 54. **true,** honest. 56. **meddle or make,** have to do. **is,** it is. 101. **vigitant,** for "vigilant." 106. **Mass,** by the Mass. 107. **scab,** scurvy fellow. 111. **pent-house,** overhanging roof. 124. **unconfirmed,** inexperienced. 126. **nothing to a man,** does not make the man. 131. **deformed,** deforming. 143. **Pharaoh's soldiers,** possible allusion to some picture of the Israelites passing through the Red Sea. **reechy,** dirty, filthy. 144. **god Bel's priests,** with probable allusion to the story of Bel and the Dragon, from the Apocryphal book of *Daniel*, depicted in a stained-glass window. 145. **shaven Hercules.** A reference either to Hercules disguised as a maiden in the service of Omphale, or (confusedly) to the story of Samson. 147. **codpiece,** decorative pouch at the fly of a man's breeches, indelicately conspicuous in this tapestry. 178. **right master constable,** comic title on the pattern of "right worshipful," etc. 179. **recovered,** for "discovered." 180. **lechery,** for "treachery." 183. **lock,** lock of hair hanging down on the left shoulder; the lovelock. 189. **let . . . to,** for "obey us and." 190. **commodity,** goods acquired. 191. **taken up,** obtained on credit; also, arrested. **bills,** bonds given as security; also, pikes. 192. **in question,** subject to judicial examination; also, of doubtful value.

Con. No; 'twas the vane on the house.

Bora. Seest thou not, I say, what a deformed thief this fashion is? how giddily 'a turns about all the hot bloods between fourteen and five-and-thirty? sometimes fashioning them like Pharaoh's soldiers in the reechy painting, sometime like god Bel's priests in the old church-window, sometime like the shaven Hercules in the smirched worm-eaten tapestry, where his codpiece seems as massy as his club?

Con. All this I see; and I see that the fashion wears out more apparel than the man. But art not thou thyself giddy with the fashion too, that thou hast shifted out of thy tale into telling me of the fashion?

Bora. Not so, neither: but know that I have to-night wooed Margaret, the Lady Hero's gentlewoman, by the name of Hero: she leans me out at her mistress' chamber-window, bids me a thousand times good night,—I tell this tale vilely:—I should first tell thee how the prince, Claudio and my master, planted and placed and possessed by my master Don John, saw afar off in the orchard this amiable encounter.

Con. And thought they Margaret was Hero?

Bora. Two of them did, the prince and Claudio; but the devil my master knew she was Margaret; and partly by his oaths, which first possessed them, partly by the dark night, which did deceive them, but chiefly by my villany, which did confirm any slander that Don John had made, away went Claudio enraged; swore he would meet her, as he was appointed, next morning at the temple, and there, before the whole congregation, shame her with what he saw o'er night and send her home again without a husband.

First Watch. We charge you, in the prince's name, stand!

Sec. Watch. Call up the right master constable. We have here recovered the most dangerous piece of lechery that ever was known in the commonwealth.

First Watch. And one Deformed is one of them: I know him; 'a wears a lock.

Con. Masters, masters,—

Sec. Watch. You'll be made bring Deformed forth, I warrant you.

Con. Masters,—

First Watch. Never speak: we charge you let us obey you to go with us.

Bora. We are like to prove a goodly commodity, being taken up of these men's bills.

Con. A commodity in question, I warrant you. Come, we'll obey you. *Exeunt.*

[SCENE IV. HERO's *apartment*.]

Enter HERO, *and* MARGARET *and* URSULA.

Hero. Good Ursula, wake my cousin Beatrice, and desire her to rise.

Urs. I will, lady.

Hero. And bid her come hither.

Urs. Well. [*Exit.*]

Marg. Troth, I think your other rabato were better.

Hero. No, pray thee, good Meg, I'll wear this.

Marg. By my troth, 's not so good; and I warrant your cousin will say so.

Hero. My cousin 's a fool, and thou art another: I'll wear none but this.

Marg. I like the new tire within excellently, if the hair were a thought browner; and your gown 's a most rare fashion, i' faith. I saw the Duchess of Milan's gown that they praise so.

Hero. O, that exceeds, they say.

Marg. By my troth, 's but a night-gown in respect of yours: cloth o' gold, and cuts, and laced with silver, set with pearls, down sleeves, side sleeves, and skirts, round underborne with a bluish tinsel: but for a fine, quaint, graceful and excellent fashion, yours is worth ten on 't.

Hero. God give me joy to wear it! for my heart is exceeding heavy.

Marg. 'Twill be heavier soon by the weight of a man.

Hero. Fie upon thee! art not ashamed?

Marg. Of what, lady? of speaking honourably? Is not marriage honourable in a beggar? Is not your lord honourable without marriage? I think you would have me say, 'saving your reverence, a husband:' an bad thinking do not wrest true speaking, I'll offend nobody: is there any harm in 'the heavier for a husband'? None, I think, an it be the right husband and the right wife; otherwise 'tis light, and not heavy: ask my Lady Beatrice else; here she comes.

Enter BEATRICE.

Hero. Good morrow, coz.

Beat. Good morrow, sweet Hero.

Hero. Why, how now? do you speak in the sick tune?

Beat. I am out of all other tune, methinks.

Marg. Clap 's into 'Light o' love;' that goes without a burden: do you sing it, and I'll dance it.

Beat. Ye light o' love, with your heels! then, if your husband have stables enough, you'll see he shall lack no barns.

Marg. O illegitimate construction! I scorn that with my heels.

Beat. 'Tis almost five o'clock, cousin; 'tis time you were ready. By my troth, I am exceeding ill: heigh-ho!

Marg. For a hawk, a horse, or a husband?

Beat. For the letter that begins them all, H.

Marg. Well, an you be not turned Turk, there 's no more sailing by the star.

Beat. What means the fool, trow?

Marg. Nothing I; but God send every one their heart's desire!

SCENE IV. 6. **rabato,** a ruff or tall collar, stiffened with wire. 9. **troth, 's,** faith, it is. 13. **tire within,** headdress in the inner room, or inner trimming of hair upon the headdress. 17. **exceeds,** excels. 18. **night-gown,** dressing gown. 19. **in respect of,** compared to. **cuts,** slashes in a garment. 20. **laced,** trimmed. 20-22. **set . . . tinsel.** R. G. White explained *down sleeves* as tight-fitting sleeves to the wrist, and *side sleeves* as secondary ornamental sleeves hanging from the shoulder. Other editors, following Capell, explain that the pearls were set down the sleeves and the skirt, and were stitched on to strips of blue tinsel to set them off, *round* implying that the pearls encircled the sleeves and skirts in a series of rings. By the other interpretation *underborne* would mean "with a lining or undergarment of tinsel." 33. **'saving . . . husband.'** By this apologetic formula, Margaret suggests that Hero is too prudish even to hear the word "husband" mentioned. 34. **wrest,** misinterpret. 37. **light,** a pun on the meaning "wanton." 42. **sick tune,** melancholy tone. 44. **'Light o' love,'** a popular song. 45. **burden,** bass accompaniment. 47. **with your heels,** i.e., with your legs upraised and spread (a bawdy suggestion). 49. **barns,** with pun on "bairns," children. 56. **H,** pun on "ache," pronounced "aitch." 57. **turned Turk,** proverbial for "changed completely." 58. **star,** polestar.

Hero. These gloves the count sent me; they are an excellent perfume.

Beat. I am stuffed, cousin; I cannot smell.

Marg. A maid, and stuffed! there 's goodly catching of cold.

Beat. O, God help me! God help me! how long have you professed apprehension?

Marg. Ever since you left it. Doth not my wit become me rarely?

Beat. It is not seen enough, you should wear it in your cap. By my troth, I am sick.

Marg. Get you some of this distilled Carduus Benedictus, and lay it to your heart: it is the only thing for a qualm.

Hero. There thou prickest her with a thistle.

Beat. Benedictus! why Benedictus? you have some moral in this Benedictus.

Marg. Moral! no, by my troth, I have no moral meaning; I meant, plain holy-thistle. You may think perchance that I think you are in love: nay, by 'r lady, I am not such a fool to think what I list, nor I list not to think what I can, nor indeed I cannot think, if I would think my heart out of thinking, that you are in love or that you will be in love or that you can be in love. Yet Benedick was such another, and now is he become a man: he swore he would never marry, and yet now, in despite of his heart, he eats his meat without grudging: and how you may be converted I know not, but methinks you look with your eyes as other women do.

Beat. What pace is this that thy tongue keeps?

Marg. Not a false gallop.

Enter URSULA.

Urs. Madam, withdraw: the prince, the count, Signior Benedick, Don John, and all the gallants of the town, are come to fetch you to church.

Hero. Help to dress me, good coz, good Meg, good Ursula. [*Exeunt.*]

[SCENE V. *Another room in* LEONATO's *house.*]

Enter LEONATO *and the Constable* [DOGBERRY] *and the Headborough* [VERGES].

Leon. What would you with me, honest neighbour?

Dog. Marry, sir, I would have some confidence with you that decerns you nearly.

Leon. Brief, I pray you; for you see it is a busy time with me.

Dog. Marry, this it is, sir.

Verg. Yes, in truth it is, sir.

Leon. What is it, my good friends?

Dog. Goodman Verges, sir, speaks a little off the matter: an old man, sir, and his wits are not so blunt as, God help, I would desire they were; but, in faith, honest as the skin between his brows.

Verg. Yes, I thank God I am as honest as any man living that is an old man and no honester than I.

Dog. Comparisons are odorous: palabras, neighbour Verges.

Leon. Neighbours, you are tedious.

Dog. It pleases your worship to say so, but we are the poor duke's officers; but truly, for mine own part, if I were as tedious as a king, I could find it in my heart to bestow it all of your worship.

Leon. All thy tediousness on me, ah?

Dog. Yea, an 'twere a thousand pound more than 'tis; for I hear as good exclamation on your worship as of any man in the city; and though I be but a poor man, I am glad to hear it.

Verg. And so am I.

Leon. I would fain know what you have to say.

Verg. Marry, sir, our watch to-night, excepting your worship's presence, ha' ta'en a couple of as arrant knaves as any in Messina.

Dog. A good old man, sir; he will be talking: as they say, When the age is in, the wit is out: God help us! it is a world to see. Well said, i' faith, neighbour Verges: well, God 's a good man; an two men ride of a horse, one must ride behind. An honest soul, i' faith, sir; by my troth he is, as ever broke bread; but God is to be worshipped; all men are not alike; alas, good neighbour!

Leon. Indeed, neighbour, he comes too short of you.

Dog. Gifts that God gives.

Leon. I must leave you.

Dog. One word, sir: our watch, sir, have indeed comprehended two aspicious persons, and we would have them this morning examined before your worship.

Leon. Take their examination yourself and bring it me: I am now in great haste, as it may appear unto you.

Dog. It shall be suffigance.

Leon. Drink some wine ere you go: fare you well.

[*Enter a* Messenger.]

Mess. My lord, they stay for you to give your daughter to her husband.

Leon. I'll wait upon them: I am ready. [*Exeunt Leonato and Messenger.*]

Dog. Go, good partner, go, get you to Francis Seacole; bid him bring his pen and inkhorn to the gaol: we are now to examination these men.

Verg. And we must do it wisely.

Dog. We will spare for no wit, I warrant you; here 's that shall drive some of them to a noncome: only get the learned writer to set down our excommunication and meet me at the gaol. [*Exeunt.*]

[ACT IV.

SCENE I. *A church.*]

Enter Prince [DON PEDRO], [DON JOHN *the*] *Bastard,* LEONATO, FRIAR [FRANCIS], CLAUDIO, BENEDICK, HERO, *and* BEATRICE [*with* Attendants].

64. **stuffed,** afflicted with a cold. 68. **apprehension,** wit. 72. **wear . . . cap,** i.e., as a fool does his coxcomb. 73. **Carduus Benedictus,** the blessed thistle, noted for medicinal properties. 78. **moral,** hidden meaning. 90. **eats . . . grudging,** has a normal appetite, like other men's (in love). 94. **false gallop,** canter.

SCENE V. 3. **confidence,** possibly misused for "conference." 4. **decerns,** for "concerns." 10. **Goodman,** title of persons under the social rank of gentleman. 13-14. **honest . . . brows,** proverbial expression of honesty, the brow being regarded as an open book. 18. **odorous,** for "odious." **palabras,** for *pocas palabras,* few words. 22. **poor duke's officers,** for "the duke's poor officers." 28. **exclamation,** possibly for "acclamation." 34. **to-night,** last night. 38. **When . . . out,** adaptation of the proverb: "When ale is in, wit is out." 39. **a world,** wonderful. 40-41. **God 's . . . man,** a proverbial saying. 50. **aspicious,** for "suspicious." 56. **suffigance,** for "sufficient." 61. **wait upon,** attend. 68. **noncome,** usually taken as contraction for *non compos mentis* (not of

Leon. Come, Friar Francis, be brief; only to the plain form of marriage, and you shall recount their particular duties afterwards.
Friar. You come hither, my lord, to marry this lady.
Claud. No.
Leon. To be married to her: friar, you come to marry her.
Friar. Lady, you come hither to be married to this count.
Hero. I do.
Friar. If either of you know any inward impediment why you should not be conjoined, I charge you, on your souls, to utter it.
Claud. Know you any, Hero?
Hero. None, my lord.
Friar. Know you any, count?
Leon. I dare make his answer, none.
Claud. O, what men dare do! what men may do! what men daily do, not knowing what they do!
Bene. How now! interjections? Why, then, some be of laughing, as, ah, ha, he!
Claud. Stand thee by, friar. Father, by your leave:
Will you with free and unconstrained soul
Give me this maid, your daughter?
Leon. As freely, son, as God did give her me.
Claud. And what have I to give you back, whose worth
May counterpoise this rich and precious gift?
D. Pedro. Nothing, unless you render her again.
Claud. Sweet prince, you learn me noble thankfulness.
There, Leonato, take her back again:
Give not this rotten orange to your friend;
She 's but the sign and semblance of her honour.
Behold how like a maid she blushes here!
O, what authority and show of truth
Can cunning sin cover itself withal!
Comes not that blood as modest evidence
To witness simple virtue? Would you not swear,
All you that see her, that she were a maid,
By these exterior shows? But she is none:
She knows the heat of a luxurious bed;
Her blush is guiltiness, not modesty.
Leon. What do you mean, my lord?
Claud. Not to be married,
Not to knit my soul to an approved wanton.
Leon. Dear my lord, if you, in your own proof,
Have vanquish'd the resistance of her youth,
And made defeat of her virginity,—
Claud. I know what you would say: if I have known her,
You will say she did embrace me as a husband,
And so extenuate the 'forehand sin:
No, Leonato,
I never tempted her with word too large;
But, as a brother to his sister, show'd
Bashful sincerity and comely love.
Hero. And seem'd I ever otherwise to you?
Claud. Out on thee! Seeming! I will write against it:
You seem to me as Dian in her orb,
As chaste as is the bud ere it be blown;
But you are more intemperate in your blood
Than Venus, or those pamp'red animals
That rage in savage sensuality.
Hero. Is my lord well, that he doth speak so wide?
Leon. Sweet prince, why speak not you?
D. Pedro. What should I speak?
I stand dishonour'd, that have gone about
To link my dear friend to a common stale.
Leon. Are these things spoken, or do I but dream?
D. John. Sir, they are spoken, and these things are true.
Bene. This looks not like a nuptial.
Hero. True! O God!
Claud. Leonato, stand I here?
Is this the prince? is this the prince's brother?
Is this face Hero's? are our eyes our own?
Leon. All this is so: but what of this, my lord?
Claud. Let me but move one question to your daughter;
And, by that fatherly and kindly power
That you have in her, bid her answer truly.
Leon. I charge thee do so, as thou art my child.
Hero. O, God defend me! how am I beset!
What kind of catechising call you this?
Claud. To make you answer truly to your name.
Hero. Is it not Hero? Who can blot that name
With any just reproach?
Claud. Marry, that can Hero;
Hero itself can blot out Hero's virtue.
What man was he talk'd with you yesternight
Out at your window betwixt twelve and one?
Now, if you are a maid, answer to this.
Hero. I talk'd with no man at that hour, my lord.
D. Pedro. Why, then are you no maiden. Leonato,
I am sorry you must hear: upon mine honour,
Myself, my brother and this grieved count
Did see her, hear her, at that hour last night
Talk with a ruffian at her chamber-window;
Who hath indeed, most like a liberal villain,
Confess'd the vile encounters they have had
A thousand times in secret.
D. John. Fie, fie! they are not to be nam'd, my lord,
Not to be spoke of;
There is not chastity enough in language
Without offence to utter them. Thus, pretty lady,
I am sorry for thy much misgovernment.
Claud. O Hero, what a Hero hadst thou been,
If half thy outward graces had been plac'd
About thy thoughts and counsels of thy heart!
But fare thee well, most foul, most fair! farewell,
Thou pure impiety and impious purity!
For thee I'll lock up all the gates of love,
And on my eyelids shall conjecture hang,
To turn all beauty into thoughts of harm,
And never shall it more be gracious.
Leon. Hath no man's dagger here a point for me?
[*Hero swoons.*]

sound mind), but perhaps intended as a substitute for "nonplus." 69. **excommunication,** for "examination" or "communication."

ACT IV. SCENE I. 22. **interjections.** Benedick seems to be reminded, by Claudio's strained manner of utterance, of interjections, and proceeds to recite a tag from the current Latin grammars, *some . . . he*. 29. **counterpoise,** balance, be equivalent to. 31. **learn,** teach. 36. **authority,** assurance. 38. **modest evidence,** evidence of modesty. 42. **luxurious,** lascivious, lustful. 45. **approved,** convicted. 46. **in . . . proof,** in making trial of her yourself (Wright). 51. **extenuate,** excuse, lessen. **'forehand sin,** sin of anticipating (marriage). 58. **Dian . . . orb,** Diana, goddess of chastity, enthroned in the moon. 63. **wide,** wide of the mark. 69. **True,** a reply to Don John's speech. 83. **Hero itself,** the name Hero. 100. **misgovernment,** evil conduct. 105. **pure . . . purity.** Note the oxymoron, i.e., association of words of contradictory senses. 107. **conjecture,** evil suspicion. 109. **gracious,** attractive, graceful.

Beat. Why, how now, cousin! wherefore sink you down?
D. John. Come, let us go. These things, come thus to light,
Smother her spirits up.
[*Exeunt Don Pedro, Don John, and Claudio.*]
Bene. How doth the lady?
Beat. Dead, I think. Help, uncle!
Hero! why, Hero! Uncle! Signior Benedick! Friar!
Leon. O Fate! take not away thy heavy hand.
Death is the fairest cover for her shame
That may be wish'd for.
Beat. How now, cousin Hero!
Friar. Have comfort, lady.
Leon. Dost thou look up?
Friar. Yea, wherefore should she not?
Leon. Wherefore! Why, doth not every earthly thing
Cry shame upon her? Could she here deny
The story that is printed in her blood?
Do not live, Hero; do not ope thine eyes:
For, did I think thou wouldst not quickly die,
Thought I thy spirits were stronger than thy shames,
Myself would, on the rearward of reproaches,
Strike at thy life. Griev'd I, I had but one?
Chid I for that at frugal nature's frame?
O, one too much by thee! Why had I one?
Why ever wast thou lovely in my eyes?
Why had I not with charitable hand
Took up a beggar's issue at my gates,
Who smirched thus and mir'd with infamy,
I might have said 'No part of it is mine;
This shame derives itself from unknown loins'?
But mine and mine I lov'd and mine I prais'd
And mine that I was proud on, mine so much
That I myself was to myself not mine,
Valuing of her,—why, she, O, she is fall'n
Into a pit of ink, that the wide sea
Hath drops too few to wash her clean again
And salt too little which may season give
To her foul-tainted flesh!
Bene. Sir, sir, be patient.
For my part, I am so attir'd in wonder,
I know not what to say.
Beat. O, on my soul, my cousin is belied!
Bene. Lady, were you her bedfellow last night?
Beat. No, truly not; although, until last night,
I have this twelvemonth been her bedfellow.
Leon. Confirm'd, confirm'd! O, that is stronger made
Which was before barr'd up with ribs of iron!
Would the two princes lie, and Claudio lie,
Who lov'd her so, that, speaking of her foulness,
Wash'd it with tears? Hence from her! let her die.
Friar. Hear me a little; for I have only been
Silent so long and given way unto
†This course of fortune . . .
By noting of the lady I have mark'd
A thousand blushing apparitions
To start into her face, a thousand innocent shames
In angel whiteness beat away those blushes;
And in her eye there hath appear'd a fire,
To burn the errors that these princes hold
Against her maiden truth. Call me a fool;
Trust not my reading nor my observations,
Which with experimental seal doth warrant
The tenour of my book; trust not my age,
My reverence, calling, nor divinity,
If this sweet lady lie not guiltless here
Under some biting error.
Leon. Friar, it cannot be.
Thou seest that all the grace that she hath left
Is that she will not add to her damnation
A sin of perjury; she not denies it:
Why seek'st thou then to cover with excuse
That which appears in proper nakedness?
Friar. Lady, what man is he you are accus'd of?
Hero. They know that do accuse me; I know none:
If I know more of any man alive
Than that which maiden modesty doth warrant,
Let all my sins lack mercy! O my father,
Prove you that any man with me convers'd
At hours unmeet, or that I yesternight
Maintain'd the change of words with any creature,
Refuse me, hate me, torture me to death!
Friar. There is some strange misprision in the princes.
Bene. Two of them have the very bent of honour;
And if their wisdoms be misled in this,
The practice of it lives in John the bastard,
Whose spirits toil in frame of villanies.
Leon. I know not. If they speak but truth of her,
These hands shall tear her; if they wrong her honour
The proudest of them shall well hear of it.
Time hath not yet so dried this blood of mine,
Nor age so eat up my invention,
Nor fortune made such havoc of my means,
Nor my bad life reft me so much of friends,
But they shall find, awak'd in such a kind,
Both strength of limb and policy of mind,
Ability in means and choice of friends,
To quit me of them throughly.
Friar. Pause awhile,
And let my counsel sway you in this case.
Your daughter here the princes left for dead:
Let her awhile be secretly kept in,
And publish it that she is dead indeed;
Maintain a mourning ostentation
And on your family's old monument
Hang mournful epitaphs and do all rites
That appertain unto a burial.
Leon. What shall become of this? what will this do?
Friar. Marry, this well carried shall on her behalf
Change slander to remorse; that is some good:
But not for that dream I on this strange course,
But on this travail look for greater birth.
She dying, as it must be so maintain'd,
Upon the instant that she was accus'd,

124. **blood,** blushes. 130. **frame,** plan, order. 140. **That . . . mine,** she was so much a part of me that by comparison I was not myself (Yale). 141. **Valuing,** when establishing the value. 144. **season,** preservative. 157-159. Text possibly corrupt; New Cambridge omits *for . . . fortune.* 164-165. **a fire . . . burn,** an allusion to the burning of heretics. 168. **experimental seal,** stamp of experience. 169. **tenour . . . book,** what he has learned from reading. **tenour,** purport. 185. **Maintain'd the change,** held exchange. 187. **misprision,** mistake, misunderstanding. 188. **bent,** inclination of the mind. 190. **practice,** scheming. 191. **frame,** contriving. 202. **quit,** revenge. 207. **Maintain . . . ostentation,** perform all the resemblances of mourning. 225. **upon,** in consequence of. 227. **study of imagination,** musing, imaginative contemplation. 228. **every . . . life,** every feature of her lovely life. 229. **habit,** dress. 231. **prospect,** range of vision. 233. **liver,** sup-

Shall be lamented, pitied and excus'd
Of every hearer: for it so falls out
That what we have we prize not to the worth
Whiles we enjoy it, but being lack'd and lost,
Why, then we rack the value, then we find
The virtue that possession would not show us
Whiles it was ours. So will it fare with Claudio:
When he shall hear she died upon his words,
Th' idea of her life shall sweetly creep
Into his study of imagination,
And every lovely organ of her life
Shall come apparell'd in more precious habit,
More moving-delicate and full of life,
Into the eye and prospect of his soul,
Than when she liv'd indeed; then shall he mourn,
If ever love had interest in his liver,
And wish he had not so accused her,
No, though he thought his accusation true.
Let this be so, and doubt not but success
Will fashion the event in better shape
Than I can lay it down in likelihood.
But if all aim but this be levell'd false,
The supposition of the lady's death
Will quench the wonder of her infamy:
And if it sort not well, you may conceal her,
As best befits her wounded reputation,
In some reclusive and religious life,
Out of all eyes, tongues, minds and injuries.

Bene. Signior Leonato, let the friar advise you:
And though you know my inwardness and love
Is very much unto the prince and Claudio,
Yet, by mine honour, I will deal in this
As secretly and justly as your soul
Should with your body.

Leon. Being that I flow in grief,
The smallest twine may lead me.

Friar. 'Tis well consented: presently away;
For to strange sores strangely they strain the cure.
Come, lady, die to live: this wedding-day
Perhaps is but prolong'd: have patience and
endure. *Exeunt* [*all but Benedick and Beatrice*].

Bene. Lady Beatrice, have you wept all this while?

Beat. Yea, and I will weep a while longer.

Bene. I will not desire that.

Beat. You have no reason; I do it freely.

Bene. Surely I do believe your fair cousin is wronged.

Beat. Ah, how much might the man deserve of me that would right her!

Bene. Is there any way to show such friendship?

Beat. A very even way, but no such friend.

Bene. May a man do it?

Beat. It is a man's office, but not yours.

Bene. I do love nothing in the world so well as you: is not that strange?

Beat. As strange as the thing I know not. It were as possible for me to say I loved nothing so well as you: but believe me not; and yet I lie not; I confess nothing, nor I deny nothing. I am sorry for my cousin.

Bene. By my sword, Beatrice, thou lovest me.

Beat. Do not swear, and eat it.

Bene. I will swear by it that you love me; and I will make him eat it that says I love not you.

Beat. Will you not eat your word?

Bene. With no sauce that can be devised to it. I protest I love thee.

Beat. Why, then, God forgive me!

Bene. What offence, sweet Beatrice?

Beat. You have stayed me in a happy hour: I was about to protest I loved you.

Bene. And do it with all thy heart.

Beat. I love you with so much of my heart that none is left to protest.

Bene. Come, bid me do any thing for thee.

Beat. Kill Claudio.

Bene. Ha! not for the wide world.

Beat. You kill me to deny it. Farewell.

Bene. Tarry, sweet Beatrice.

Beat. I am gone, though I am here: there is no love in you: nay, I pray you, let me go.

Bene. Beatrice,—

Beat. In faith, I will go.

Bene. We'll be friends first.

Beat. You dare easier be friends with me than fight with mine enemy.

Bene. Is Claudio thine enemy?

Beat. Is 'a not approved in the height a villain, that hath slandered, scorned, dishonoured my kinswoman? O that I were a man! What, bear her in hand until they come to take hands; and then, with public accusation, uncovered slander, unmitigated rancour,—O God, that I were a man! I would eat his heart in the market-place.

Bene. Hear me, Beatrice,—

Beat. Talk with a man out at a window! A proper saying!

Bene. Nay, but, Beatrice,—

Beat. Sweet Hero! She is wronged, she is slandered, she is undone.

Bene. Beat—

Beat. Princes and counties! Surely, a princely testimony, a goodly count, Count Comfect; a sweet gallant, surely! O that I were a man for his sake! or that I had any friend would be a man for my sake! But manhood is melted into courtesies, valour into compliment, and men are only turned into tongue, and trim ones too: he is now as valiant as Hercules that only tells a lie and swears it. I cannot be a man with wishing, therefore I will die a woman with grieving.

Bene. Tarry, good Beatrice. By this hand, I love thee.

Beat. Use it for my love some other way than swearing by it.

Bene. Think you in your soul the Count Claudio hath wronged Hero?

Beat. Yea, as sure as I have a thought or a soul.

Bene. Enough, I am engaged; I will challenge him. I will kiss your hand, and so I leave you. By this hand, Claudio shall render me a dear account. As you hear of me, so think of me. Go, comfort your cousin: I must say she is dead: and so, farewell. [*Exeunt.*]

---

posed seat of the passion of love. 239. **But . . . false,** if every other aim miscarry. 242. **sort,** turn out. 245. **injuries,** insults. 247. **inwardness,** close friendship. 251. **Being that,** seeing that, since. **flow in,** overflow with. 254. **For . . . cure,** strange diseases require strange and desperate cures. 256. **prolong'd,** deferred, put off. 265. **even,** without obstacles. 285. **in a happy hour,** at an appropriate moment. 295. **gone,** i.e., in spirit. 303. **in the height,** in the extreme. 306. **bear her in hand,** delude with false hopes. 308. **uncovered,** open, unconcealed. 317. **counties,** counts. 318. **count,** play on the title and the meaning, "declaration of complaint in an indictment." **Comfect,** comfit, sweetmeat. 323. **trim,** nice (used ironically). 334. **I am engaged,** I pledge myself. 335. **dear,** expensive.

[SCENE II. *A prison.*]

Enter the Constables [DOGBERRY *and* VERGES] *and the Town Clerk* [SEXTON] *in gowns*, BORACHIO [, CONRADE, *and* Watch].

Dog. Is our whole dissembly appeared?

Verg. O, a stool and a cushion for the sexton.

Sex. Which be the malefactors?

Dog. Marry, that am I and my partner.

Verg. Nay, that's certain; we have the exhibition to examine.

Sex. But which are the offenders that are to be examined? let them come before master constable.

Dog. Yea, marry, let them come before me. What is your name, friend?

Bora. Borachio.

Dog. Pray, write down, Borachio. Yours, sirrah?

Con. I am a gentleman, sir, and my name is Conrade.

Dog. Write down, master gentleman Conrade. Masters, do you serve God?

Con. } *Bora.* } Yea, sir, we hope.

Dog. Write down, that they hope they serve God: and write God first; for God defend but God should go before such villains! Masters, it is proved already that you are little better than false knaves; and it will go near to be thought so shortly. How answer you for yourselves?

Con. Marry, sir, we say we are none.

Dog. A marvellous witty fellow, I assure you; but I will go about with him. Come you hither, sirrah; a word in your ear: sir, I say to you, it is thought you are false knaves.

Bora. Sir, I say to you we are none.

Dog. Well, stand aside. 'Fore God, they are both in a tale. Have you writ down, that they are none?

Sex. Master constable, you go not the way to examine: you must call forth the watch that are their accusers.

Dog. Yea, marry, that's the eftest way. Let the watch come forth. Masters, I charge you, in the prince's name, accuse these men.

First Watch. This man said, sir, that Don John, the prince's brother, was a villain.

Dog. Write down Prince John a villain. Why, this is flat perjury, to call a prince's brother villain.

Bora. Master constable,—

Dog. Pray thee, fellow, peace: I do not like thy look, I promise thee.

Sex. What heard you him say else?

Sec. Watch. Marry, that he had received a thousand ducats of Don John for accusing the Lady Hero wrongfully.

Dog. Flat burglary as ever was committed.

Verg. Yea, by mass, that it is.

Sex. What else, fellow?

First Watch. And that Count Claudio did mean, upon his words, to disgrace Hero before the whole assembly, and not marry her.

Dog. O villain! thou wilt be condemned into everlasting redemption for this.

Sex. What else?

Watch. This is all.

Sex. And this is more, masters, than you can deny. Prince John is this morning secretly stolen away; Hero was in this manner accused, in this very manner refused, and upon the grief of this suddenly died. Master constable, let these men be bound, and brought to Leonato's: I will go before and show him their examination. [*Exit.*]

Dog. Come, let them be opinioned.

Verg. †Let them be in the hands—

Con. Off, coxcomb!

Dog. God's my life, where's the sexton? let him write down the prince's officer coxcomb. Come, bind them. Thou naughty varlet!

Con. Away! you are an ass, you are an ass.

Dog. Dost thou not suspect my place? dost thou not suspect my years? O that he were here to write me down an ass! But, masters, remember that I am an ass; though it be not written down, yet forget not that I am an ass. No, thou villain, thou art full of piety, as shall be proved upon thee by good witness. I am a wise fellow, and, which is more, an officer, and, which is more, a householder, and, which is more, as pretty a piece of flesh as any is in Messina, and one that knows the law, go to; and a rich fellow enough, go to; and a fellow that hath had losses, and one that hath two gowns and every thing handsome about him. Bring him away. O that I had been writ down an ass! *Exeunt.*

[ACT V.

SCENE I. *Before* LEONATO'S *house.*]

Enter LEONATO *and his Brother* [ANTONIO].

Ant. If you go on thus, you will kill yourself;
And 'tis not wisdom thus to second grief
Against yourself.

Leon. I pray thee, cease thy counsel,
Which falls into mine ears as profitless
As water in a sieve: give not me counsel;
Nor let no comforter delight mine ear
But such a one whose wrongs do suit with mine.
Bring me a father that so lov'd his child,
Whose joy of her is overwhelm'd like mine,
And bid him speak of patience;
Measure his woe the length and breadth of mine
And let it answer every strain for strain,
As thus for thus and such a grief for such,
In every lineament, branch, shape, and form:
If such a one will smile and stroke his beard,
†Bid sorrow wag, cry 'hem!' when he should groan,
Patch grief with proverbs, make misfortune drunk
With candle-wasters; bring him yet to me,

SCENE II. Throughout the scene in Q, Dogberry's lines are given to *Kemp* (spelled variously) except that the speech beginning in line 4 is given to *Andrew*, and the one beginning in line 69 to *Const.* Verges' speeches are headed *Cowley* or *Couley* except in line 53, where he is *Const.* Will Kempe and Richard Cowley were actors in Shakespeare's company. 1. **dissembly,** blunder for "assembly." 5. **exhibition,** possibly for "commission" or "examination" (to exhibit). 13. **sirrah.** Used to address inferiors; Conrade objects. 21. **defend,** forbid. 24. **go near to,** almost. 27. **witty,** clever, cunning. 28. **go about with,** get the better of. 33. **in a tale,** in agreement. 38. **eftest,** an unexplained blunder of Dogberry's; Theobald: *deftest;* Rowe: *easiest.* 59. **redemption,** for "damnation." 69. **opinioned,** for "pinioned." 70-71. Text possibly corrupt; reading due to Malone; New Cambridge: *Let them be —in the hands.* 76. **suspect,** for "respect." 81. **piety,** for "impiety." 85. **piece of flesh,** sample of humanity.

ACT V. SCENE I. 2-3. **second . . . yourself,** encourage grief which will destroy you. 12. **strain,** strong impulse of the mind. 16. **Bid . . . 'hem!',** so Capell; QF: *And, sorrow, wagge, crie hem;* Steevens: *And sorry wag, cry 'hem!'* 18. **candle-wasters,** those who waste candles by late study; bookworms; also explained as revelers. **yet,** why then, or, yet

And I of him will gather patience.
But there is no such man: for, brother, men
Can counsel and speak comfort to that grief
Which they themselves not feel; but, tasting it,
Their counsel turns to passion, which before
Would give preceptial medicine to rage,
Fetter strong madness in a silken thread,
Charm ache with air and agony with words:
No, no; 'tis all men's office to speak patience
To those that wring under the load of sorrow,
But no man's virtue nor sufficiency
To be so moral when he shall endure
The like himself. Therefore give me no counsel:
My griefs cry louder than advertisement.
Ant. Therein do men from children nothing differ.
Leon. I pray thee, peace. I will be flesh and blood;
For there was never yet philosopher
That could endure the toothache patiently,
However they have writ the style of gods
And made a push at chance and sufferance.
Ant. Yet bend not all the harm upon yourself;
Make those that do offend you suffer too.
Leon. There thou speak'st reason: nay, I will do so.
My soul doth tell me Hero is belied;
And that shall Claudio know; so shall the prince
And all of them that thus dishonour her.
Ant. Here comes the prince and Claudio hastily.

Enter Prince [DON PEDRO] *and* CLAUDIO.

D. Pedro. Good den, good den.
Claud. Good day to both of you.
Leon. Hear you, my lords,—
D. Pedro. We have some haste, Leonato.
Leon. Some haste, my lord! well, fare you well, my lord:
Are you so hasty now? well, all is one.
D. Pedro. Nay, do not quarrel with us, good old man.
Ant. If he could right himself with quarrelling,
Some of us would lie low.
Claud. Who wrongs him?
Leon. Marry, thou dost wrong me; thou dissembler, thou:—
Nay, never lay thy hand upon thy sword;
I fear thee not.
Claud. Marry, beshrew my hand,
If it should give your age such cause of fear:
In faith, my hand meant nothing to my sword.
Leon. Tush, tush, man; never fleer and jest at me:
I speak not like a dotard nor a fool,
As under privilege of age to brag
What I have done being young, or what would do
Were I not old. Know, Claudio, to thy head,
Thou hast so wrong'd mine innocent child and me
That I am forc'd to lay my reverence by
And, with grey hairs and bruise of many days,
Do challenge thee to trial of a man.
I say thou hast belied mine innocent child;
Thy slander hath gone through and through her heart,
And she lies buried with her ancestors;
O, in a tomb where never scandal slept,
Save this of hers, fram'd by thy villany!
Claud. My villany?
Leon. Thine, Claudio; thine, I say.
D. Pedro. You say not right, old man.
Leon. My lord, my lord,
I'll prove it on his body, if he dare,
Despite his nice fence and his active practice,
His May of youth and bloom of lustihood.
Claud. Away! I will not have to do with you.
Leon. Canst thou so daff me? Thou hast kill'd my child:
If thou kill'st me, boy, thou shalt kill a man.
Ant. He shall kill two of us, and men indeed:
But that 's no matter; let him kill one first;
Win me and wear me; let him answer me.
Come, follow me, boy; come, sir boy, come, follow me:
Sir boy, I'll whip you from your foining fence;
Nay, as I am a gentleman, I will.
Leon. Brother,—
Ant. Content yourself. God knows I lov'd my niece;
And she is dead, slander'd to death by villains,
That dare as well answer a man indeed
As I dare take a serpent by the tongue:
Boys, apes, braggarts, Jacks, milksops!
Leon. Brother Antony,—
Ant. Hold you content. What, man! I know them, yea,
And what they weigh, even to the utmost scruple,—
Scambling, out-facing, fashion-monging boys,
That lie and cog and flout, deprave and slander,
Go anticly, show outward hideousness,
And speak off half a dozen dang'rous words,
How they might hurt their enemies, if they durst;
And this is all.
Leon. But, brother Antony,—
Ant. Come, 'tis no matter:
Do not you meddle; let me deal in this.
D. Pedro. Gentlemen both, we will not wake your patience.
My heart is sorry for your daughter's death:
But, on my honour, she was charg'd with nothing
But what was true and very full of proof.
Leon. My lord, my lord,—
D. Pedro. I will not hear you.
Leon. No? Come, brother; away! I will be heard.
Ant. And shall, or some of us will smart for it.
Exeunt ambo [*Leonatus and Antonio*].

Enter BENEDICK.

D. Pedro. See, see; here comes the man we went to seek.
Claud. Now, signior, what news?
Bene. Good day, my lord.
D. Pedro. Welcome, signior: you are almost come to part almost a fray.

if you do (find such a man, bring him to me). 24. **preceptial medicine,** medicine consisting of precepts. 26. **air,** mere breath. 28. **wring,** writhe. 29. **sufficiency,** ability, power. 30. **moral,** prone to moralizing. 32. **advertisement,** advice, counsel. 37. **style of,** language worthy of. 38. **push at,** defiance of. **sufferance,** suffering. 49. **now,** possibly expletive, meaning "after all that has happened," or "after my daughter is dead." It has been thought to refer to Don Pedro's promise to stay a month. **all is one,** it makes no difference. 53. **thou,** used contemptuously instead of the more polite "you." 57. **my hand . . . sword,** I had no intention of using my sword. 58. **fleer,** sneer (with pretended humility). 62. **to thy head,** to thy face. 75. **nice fence,** dexterous swordsmanship. 76. **lustihood,** bodily vigor. 78. **daff,** put off. 82. **Win . . . me,** proverbial expression. **answer me,** i.e., in a duel. 84. **foining,** thrusting. 94. **Scambling,** contentious. **out-facing,** swaggering. **fashion-monging,** dandified. 95. **deprave,** detract, traduce. 96. **anticly,** fantastically. 97. **dang'rous,** threatening, haughty. 102. **wake your patience,** put your patience to any test.

Claud. We had liked to have had our two noses snapped off with two old men without teeth.

D. Pedro. Leonato and his brother. What thinkest thou? Had we fought, I doubt we should have been too young for them.

Bene. In a false quarrel there is no true valour. I came to seek you both.

Claud. We have been up and down to seek thee; for we are high-proof melancholy and would fain have it beaten away. Wilt thou use thy wit?

Bene. It is in my scabbard: shall I draw it?

D. Pedro. Dost thou wear thy wit by thy side?

Claud. Never any did so, though very many have been beside their wit. I will bid thee draw, as we do the minstrels; draw, to pleasure us.

D. Pedro. As I am an honest man, he looks pale. Art thou sick, or angry?

Claud. What, courage, man! What though care killed a cat, thou hast mettle enough in thee to kill care.

Bene. Sir, I shall meet your wit in the career, an you charge it against me. I pray you choose another subject.

Claud. Nay, then, give him another staff: this last was broke cross.

D. Pedro. By this light, he changes more and more: I think he be angry indeed.

Claud. If he be, he knows how to turn his girdle.

Bene. Shall I speak a word in your ear?

Claud. God bless me from a challenge!

Bene. [*Aside to Claudio*] You are a villain; I jest not: I will make it good how you dare, with what you dare, and when you dare. Do me right, or I will protest your cowardice. You have killed a sweet lady, and her death shall fall heavy on you. Let me hear from you.

Claud. Well, I will meet you, so I may have good cheer.

D. Pedro. What, a feast, a feast?

Claud. I' faith, I thank him; he hath bid me to a calf's head and a capon; the which if I do not carve most curiously, say my knife 's naught. Shall I not find a woodcock too?

Bene. Sir, your wit ambles well; it goes easily.

D. Pedro. I'll tell thee how Beatrice praised thy wit the other day. I said, thou hadst a fine wit: 'True,' said she, 'a fine little one.' 'No,' said I, 'a great wit:' 'Right,' says she, 'a great gross one.' 'Nay,' said I, 'a good wit:' 'Just,' said she, 'it hurts nobody.' 'Nay,' said I, 'the gentleman is wise:' 'Certain,' said she, 'a wise gentleman.' 'Nay,' said I, 'he hath the tongues:' 'That I believe,' said she, 'for he swore a thing to me on Monday night, which he forswore on Tuesday morning; there 's a double tongue; there 's two tongues.' Thus did she, an hour together, trans-shape thy particular virtues: yet at last she concluded with a sigh, thou wast the properest man in Italy.

Claud. For the which she wept heartily and said she cared not.

D. Pedro. Yea, that she did; but yet, for all that, an if she did not hate him deadly, she would love him dearly: the old man's daughter told us all.

Claud. All, all; and, moreover, God saw him when he was hid in the garden.

D. Pedro. But when shall we set the savage bull's horns on the sensible Benedick's head?

Claud. Yea, and text underneath, 'Here dwells Benedick the married man'?

Bene. Fare you well, boy: you know my mind. I will leave you now to your gossip-like humour: you break jests as braggarts do their blades, which, God be thanked, hurt not. My lord, for your many courtesies I thank you: I must discontinue your company: your brother the bastard is fled from Messina: you have among you killed a sweet and innocent lady. For my Lord Lackbeard there, he and I shall meet: and, till then, peace be with him. [*Exit.*]

D. Pedro. He is in earnest.

Claud. In most profound earnest; and, I'll warrant you, for the love of Beatrice.

D. Pedro. And hath challenged thee.

Claud. Most sincerely.

D. Pedro. What a pretty thing man is when he goes in his doublet and hose and leaves off his wit!

Claud. He is then a giant to an ape; but then is an ape a doctor to such a man.

D. Pedro. But, soft you, let me be: pluck up, my heart, and be sad. Did he not say, my brother was fled?

Enter Constables, [DOGBERRY *and* VERGES, *and the* Watch, *with*] CONRADE *and* BORACHIO.

Dog. Come you, sir: if justice cannot tame you, she shall ne'er weigh more reasons in her balance: nay, an you be a cursing hypocrite once, you must be looked to.

D. Pedro. How now? two of my brother's men bound! Borachio one!

Claud. Hearken after their offence, my lord.

D. Pedro. Officers, what offence have these men done?

Dog. Marry, sir, they have committed false report; moreover, they have spoken untruths; secondarily, they are slanders; sixth and lastly, they have belied a lady; thirdly, they have verified unjust things; and, to conclude, they are lying knaves.

D. Pedro. First, I ask thee what they have done; thirdly, I ask thee what 's their offence; sixth and lastly, why they are committed; and, to conclude, what you lay to their charge.

Claud. Rightly reasoned, and in his own division; and, by my troth, there 's one meaning well suited.

D. Pedro. Who have you offended, masters, that you are thus bound to your answer? this learned constable is too cunning to be understood: what 's your offence?

Bora. Sweet prince, let me go no farther to mine answer: do you hear me, and let this count kill me.

115. **We had . . . had,** we almost had. 123. **high-proof,** to the highest degree. **fain,** gladly. 128. **beside their wit,** out of their wits. 129. **draw,** draw as a bow across a fiddle. 136. **career,** short gallop at full speed (as in tourney). **charge,** level (as a weapon). 138. **staff,** spear shaft. 139. **broke cross,** i.e., by clumsily allowing the spear to break crosswise against his opponent's shield. (In other words, Claudio accuses Benedick of having failed in his sally of wit.) 142. **turn his girdle,** explained as shifting his girdle about so that he can reach his dagger; also as a reference to wrestling, since wrestlers turned the buckles of their girdles to the back before beginning. 147-148. **Do me right,** give me satisfaction. 148. **protest,** proclaim before witnesses. 156, 158. **calf's head, capon, woodcock,** used as types of dullness. 157. **curiously,** daintily. 167. **hath the tongues,** is a linguist. 172. **trans-shape,** distort, turn the wrong side out. 189-190. **as . . . blades,** possibly, getting their blades broken without harming themselves. 202-204. **What . . . wit.** Doublet and hose formed the Elizabethan undercostume, a cloak being worn over them on formal occasions. The prince possibly means to suggest that man's wit is like a cloak

I have deceived even your very eyes: what your wisdoms could not discover, these shallow fools have brought to light; who in the night overheard me confessing to this man how Don John your brother incensed me to slander the Lady Hero, how you were brought into the orchard and saw me court Margaret in Hero's garments, how you disgraced her, when you should marry her: my villany they have upon record; which I had rather seal with my death than repeat over to my shame. The lady is dead upon mine and my master's false accusation; and, briefly, I desire nothing but the reward of a villain.

D. Pedro. Runs not this speech like iron through your blood?

Claud. I have drunk poison whiles he utter'd it.

D. Pedro. But did my brother set thee on to this?

Bora. Yea, and paid me richly for the practice of it.

D. Pedro. He is compos'd and fram'd of treachery:
And fled he is upon this villany.

Claud. Sweet Hero! now thy image doth appear
In the rare semblance that I lov'd it first.

Dog. Come, bring away the plaintiffs: by this time our sexton hath reformed Signior Leonato of the matter: and, masters, do not forget to specify, when time and place shall serve, that I am an ass.

Verg. Here, here comes master Signior Leonato, and the sexton too.

Enter LEONATO, *his Brother* [ANTONIO], *and the* Sexton.

Leon. Which is the villain? let me see his eyes,
That, when I note another man like him,
I may avoid him: which of these is he?

Bora. If you would know your wronger, look on me.

Leon. Art thou the slave that with thy breath hast kill'd
Mine innocent child?

Bora. Yea, even I alone.

Leon. No, not so, villain; thou beliest thyself:
Here stand a pair of honourable men;
A third is fled, that had a hand in it.
I thank you, princes, for my daughter's death:
Record it with your high and worthy deeds:
'Twas bravely done, if you bethink you of it.

Claud. I know not how to pray your patience;
Yet I must speak. Choose your revenge yourself;
Impose me to what penance your invention
Can lay upon my sin: yet sinn'd I not
But in mistaking.

D. Pedro. By my soul, nor I:
And yet, to satisfy this good old man,
I would bend under any heavy weight
That he'll enjoin me to.

Leon. I cannot bid you bid my daughter live;
That were impossible: but, I pray you both,
Possess the people in Messina here
How innocent she died; and if your love
Can labour aught in sad invention,
Hang her an epitaph upon her tomb
And sing it to her bones, sing it to-night:
To-morrow morning come you to my house,
And since you could not be my son-in-law,
Be yet my nephew: my brother hath a daughter,
Almost the copy of my child that 's dead,
And she alone is heir to both of us:
Give her the right you should have giv'n her cousin,
And so dies my revenge.

Claud. O noble sir,
Your over-kindness doth wring tears from me!
I do embrace your offer; and dispose
For henceforth of poor Claudio.

Leon. To-morrow then I will expect your coming;
To-night I take my leave. This naughty man
Shall face to face be brought to Margaret,
Who I believe was pack'd in all this wrong,
Hir'd to it by your brother.

Bora. No, by my soul, she was not,
Nor knew not what she did when she spoke to me,
But always hath been just and virtuous
In any thing that I do know by her.

Dog. Moreover, sir, which indeed is not under white and black, this plaintiff here, the offender, did call me ass: I beseech you, let it be remembered in his punishment. And also, the watch heard them talk of one Deformed: they say he wears a key in his ear and a lock hanging by it, and borrows money in God's name, the which he hath used so long and never paid that now men grow hard-hearted and will lend nothing for God's sake: pray you, examine him upon that point.

Leon. I thank thee for thy care and honest pains.

Dog. Your worship speaks like a most thankful and reverend youth; and I praise God for you.

Leon. There 's for thy pains. [*Gives money.*]

Dog. God save the foundation!

Leon. Go, I discharge thee of thy prisoner, and I thank thee.

Dog. I leave an arrant knave with your worship; which I beseech your worship to correct yourself, for the example of others. God keep your worship! I wish your worship well; God restore you to health! I humbly give you leave to depart; and if a merry meeting may be wished, God prohibit it! Come, neighbour. [*Exeunt Dogberry and Verges.*]

Leon. Until to-morrow morning, lords, farewell.

Ant. Farewell, my lords: we look for you to-morrow.

D. Pedro. We will not fail.

Claud. To-night I'll mourn with Hero.

Leon. [*To the Watch*] Bring you these fellows on.
We'll talk with Margaret,
How her acquaintance grew with this lewd fellow.
Exeunt [*severally*].

[SCENE II. LEONATO'S *garden.*]

Enter BENEDICK *and* MARGARET [*meeting*].

Bene. Pray thee, sweet Mistress Margaret, deserve

which he can leave off, and go about in his natural stupidity. 205-206. **He . . . man.** He is superior to an ape in stature, but an ape is superior to him in wit. 206. **doctor,** learned man. 207. **soft you,** gently. **pluck up,** rouse thyself. 216. **Hearken after,** inquire into. 221. **slanders,** for "slanderers." 223. **verified,** for "testified to." 231. **well suited,** put into many different dresses (Johnson). 233. **bound,** play on the meanings "pinioned" and "headed for a destination." **answer,** trial, account. 242. **incensed,** instigated. 249. **upon,** in consequence of. 256. **practice of it,** bringing it to pass by deceitful contrivance. 261. **plaintiffs,** for "defendants." 262. **reformed,** for "informed." 264. **specify,** for "testify" (?) 283. **me to,** on me. 300. **heir to both.** He overlooks Antonio's son mentioned in I, ii, 2. 313. **by,** concerning. 314-315. **under white and black,** written down in black and white. 320. **in God's name,** a phrase of the professional beggar. 328. **God . . . foundation,** formula of those who received alms at religious houses. 336. **prohibit,** for "permit." 342. **lewd,** wicked, worthless.

well at my hands by helping me to the speech of Beatrice.

Marg. Will you then write me a sonnet in praise of my beauty?

Bene. In so high a style, Margaret, that no man living shall come over it; for, in most comely truth, thou deservest it.

Marg. To have no man come over me! why, shall I always keep below stairs?

Bene. Thy wit is as quick as the greyhound's mouth; it catches.

Marg. And yours as blunt as the fencer's foils, which hit, but hurt not.

Bene. A most manly wit, Margaret; it will not hurt a woman: and so, I pray thee, call Beatrice: I give thee the bucklers.

Marg. Give us the swords; we have bucklers of our own.

Bene. If you use them, Margaret, you must put in the pikes with a vice; and they are dangerous weapons for maids.

Marg. Well, I will call Beatrice to you, who I think hath legs.

Bene. And therefore will come. *Exit Margaret.*

[*Sings*] The god of love,
That sits above,
And knows me, and knows me,
How pitiful I deserve,—

I mean in singing; but in loving, Leander the good swimmer, Troilus the first employer of pandars, and a whole bookful of these quondam carpet-mongers, whose names yet run smoothly in the even road of a blank verse, why, they were never so truly turned over and over as my poor self in love. Marry, I cannot show it in rhyme; I have tried: I can find out no rhyme to 'lady' but 'baby,' an innocent rhyme; for 'scorn,' 'horn,' a hard rhyme; for 'school,' 'fool,' a babbling rhyme; very ominous endings: no, I was not born under a rhyming planet, nor I cannot woo in festival terms.

Enter BEATRICE.

Sweet Beatrice, wouldst thou come when I called thee?

Beat. Yea, signior, and depart when you bid me.

Bene. O, stay but till then!

Beat. 'Then' is spoken; fare you well now: and yet, ere I go, let me go with that I came; which is, with knowing what hath passed between you and Claudio.

Bene. Only foul words; and thereupon I will kiss thee.

Beat. Foul words is but foul wind, and foul wind is but foul breath, and foul breath is noisome; therefore I will depart unkissed.

Bene. Thou hast frighted the word out of his right sense, so forcible is thy wit. But I must tell thee plainly, Claudio undergoes my challenge; and either I must shortly hear from him, or I will subscribe him a coward. And, I pray thee now, tell me for which of my bad parts didst thou first fall in love with me?

Beat. For them all together; which maintained so politic a state of evil that they will not admit any good part to intermingle with them. But for which of my good parts did you first suffer love for me?

Bene. Suffer love! a good epithet! I do suffer love indeed, for I love thee against my will.

Beat. In spite of your heart, I think; alas, poor heart! If you spite it for my sake, I will spite it for yours; for I will never love that which my friend hates.

Bene. Thou and I are too wise to woo peaceably.

Beat. It appears not in this confession: there 's not one wise man among twenty that will praise himself.

Bene. An old, an old instance, Beatrice, that lived in the time of good neighbours. If a man do not erect in this age his own tomb ere he dies, he shall live no longer in monument than the bell rings and the widow weeps.

Beat. And how long is that, think you?

Bene. Question: why, an hour in clamour and a quarter in rheum: therefore is it most expedient for the wise, if Don Worm, his conscience, find no impediment to the contrary, to be the trumpet of his own virtues, as I am to myself. So much for praising myself, who, I myself will bear witness, is praiseworthy: and now tell me, how doth your cousin?

Beat. Very ill.

Bene. And how do you?

Beat. Very ill too.

Bene. Serve God, love me and mend. There will I leave you too, for here comes one in haste.

Enter URSULA.

Urs. Madam, you must come to your uncle. Yonder 's old coil at home: it is proved my Lady Hero hath been falsely accused, the prince and Claudio mightily abused; and Don John is the author of all, who is fled and gone. Will you come presently?

Beat. Will you go hear this news, signior?

Bene. I will live in thy heart, die in thy lap and be buried in thy eyes; and moreover I will go with thee to thy uncle's. *Exeunt.*

[SCENE III. *A church.*]

Enter CLAUDIO, *Prince* [DON PEDRO, *Lord*], *and three or four with tapers.*

Claud. Is this the monument of Leonato?

A Lord. It is, my lord.

Claud. [*Reading out of a scroll*]

EPITAPH

Done to death by slanderous tongues
Was the Hero that here lies:
Death, in guerdon of her wrongs,
Gives her fame which never dies.
So the life that died with shame
Lives in death with glorious fame.

Hang thou there upon the tomb,

SCENE II. 6. **style,** play on the critical phrase for epic grandeur, "a high style," and the word "stile." 8. **comely,** good, with allusion to Margaret's beauty. 17. **I . . . bucklers.** I acknowledge myself beaten (in repartee). 21. **pikes,** spikes in the center of a shield. **vice,** screw. 26-29. **The god . . . deserve,** beginning of an old song by William Elderton (Ritson). 30. **Leander.** The tale of Hero and Leander (from the Greek of Musaeus?) had been written in part by Marlowe and completed and published by Chapman shortly before the date of this play (1598). 31. **Troilus,** hero of the tale of Troilus and Cressida. Both he and Leander are stock examples of faithful lovers. 32-33. **quondam carpet-mongers,** ancient carpet-knights. 38. **innocent,** silly. 41. **festival terms,** fanciful language (suitable for festivals). 59. **subscribe,** formally proclaim. 63. **politic,** prudently governed. 67. **epithet,** expression. 79. **time . . . neighbours,** good old times (when one's neighbors spoke well of one). 84. **Question,** that is the question. **clamour,** noise (of the bell). 85. **rheum,** tears

Praising her when I am dumb.
Now, music, sound, and sing your solemn hymn.

SONG.

Pardon, goddess of the night,
Those that slew thy virgin knight;
For the which, with songs of woe,
Round about her tomb they go.
Midnight, assist our moan;
Help us to sigh and groan,
Heavily, heavily:
Graves, yawn and yield your dead,
Till death be uttered,
Heavily, heavily.

Claud. Now, unto thy bones good night!
Yearly will I do this rite.

D. Pedro. Good morrow, masters; put your torches out:
The wolves have prey'd; and look, the gentle day,
Before the wheels of Phœbus, round about
Dapples the drowsy east with spots of grey.
Thanks to you all, and leave us: fare you well.

Claud. Good morrow, masters: each his several way.

D. Pedro. Come, let us hence, and put on other weeds;
And then to Leonato's we will go.

Claud. And Hymen now with luckier issue speed 's
Than this for whom we rend'red up this woe. *Exeunt.*

[SCENE IV. *A room in* LEONATO'S *house.*]

Enter LEONATO, BENEDICK, [BEATRICE,] MARGARET, URSULA, *Old Man* [ANTONIO], FRIAR [FRANCIS], HERO.

Friar. Did I not tell you she was innocent?

Leon. So are the prince and Claudio, who accus'd her
Upon the error that you heard debated:
But Margaret was in some fault for this,
Although against her will, as it appears
In the true course of all the question.

Ant. Well, I am glad that all things sort so well.

Bene. And so am I, being else by faith enforc'd
To call young Claudio to a reckoning for it.

Leon. Well, daughter, and you gentlewomen all,
Withdraw into a chamber by yourselves,
And when I send for you, come hither mask'd.
The prince and Claudio promis'd by this hour
To visit me. You know your office, brother:
You must be father to your brother's daughter,
And give her to young Claudio. *Exeunt Ladies.*

Ant. Which I will do with confirm'd countenance.

Bene. Friar, I must entreat your pains, I think.

Friar. To do what, signior?

Bene. To bind me, or undo me; one of them.
Signior Leonato, truth it is, good signior,
Your niece regards me with an eye of favour.

Leon. That eye my daughter lent her: 'tis most true.

Bene. And I do with an eye of love requite her.

Leon. The sight whereof I think you had from me,
From Claudio and the prince: but what 's your will?

Bene. Your answer, sir, is enigmatical:
But, for my will, my will is your good will
May stand with ours, this day to be conjoin'd
In the state of honourable marriage:
In which, good friar, I shall desire your help.

Leon. My heart is with your liking.

Friar. And my help.
Here comes the prince and Claudio.

Enter Prince [DON PEDRO] *and* CLAUDIO, *and two or three other.*

D. Pedro. Good morrow to this fair assembly.

Leon. Good morrow, prince; good morrow, Claudio:
We here attend you. Are you yet determin'd
To-day to marry with my brother's daughter?

Claud. I'll hold my mind, were she an Ethiope.

Leon. Call her forth, brother; here 's the friar ready. [*Exit Antonio.*]

D. Pedro. Good morrow, Benedick. Why, what 's the matter,
That you have such a February face,
So full of frost, of storm and cloudiness?

Claud. I think he thinks upon the savage bull.
Tush, fear not, man; we'll tip thy horns with gold
And all Europa shall rejoice at thee,
As once Europa did at lusty Jove,
When he would play the noble beast in love.

Bene. Bull Jove, sir, had an amiable low;
And some such strange bull leap'd your father's cow,
And got a calf in that same noble feat
Much like to you, for you have just his bleat.

Claud. For this I owe you: here comes other reck'nings.

Enter [*Leonato's*] *Brother* [ANTONIO], HERO, BEATRICE, MARGARET, URSULA [*the ladies masked*].

Which is the lady I must seize upon?

Ant. This same is she, and I do give you her.

Claud. Why, then she 's mine. Sweet, let me see your face.

Leon. No, that you shall not, till you take her hand
Before this friar and swear to marry her.

Claud. Give me your hand: before this holy friar,
I am your husband, if you like of me.

Hero. And when I liv'd, I was your other wife: [*Unmasking.*]
And when you lov'd, you were my other husband.

Claud. Another Hero!

Hero. Nothing certainer:
One Hero died defil'd, but I do live,
And surely as I live, I am a maid.

D. Pedro. The former Hero! Hero that is dead!

Leon. She died, my lord, but whiles her slander liv'd.

Friar. All this amazement can I qualify;
When after that the holy rites are ended,
I'll tell you largely of fair Hero's death:
Meantime let wonder seem familiar,

(of the widow). 86-87. **Don . . . conscience.** The action of the conscience was traditionally described (in the morality plays, etc.) as the gnawing of a worm; Mark 9:48. 100. **abused,** deceived.

SCENE III. 5. **guerdon,** recompense. 20. **uttered,** fully expressed. 25. **have prey'd,** have ceased preying. 32. **speed 's,** favor or speed us; so Thirlby; QF: *speeds.*

SCENE IV. 6. **question,** investigation. 7. **sort,** turn out, eventuate. 8. **by faith,** i.e., by his promise to Beatrice. 17. **confirm'd,** grave, unmoved. 20. **undo,** ruin, with play on the meaning "untie" or "unbind." 43. **I . . . bull,** a jocular reminiscence of the conversation in I, i, 263 ff. (See also V, i, 83-84.) 45. **Europa,** Europe. 46. **Europa,** a reference to the story of Jove's infatuation for Europa, whom he approached in the form of a white bull and bore on his back through the sea to the island of Crete. 52. **owe you,** i.e., an answer. 59. **like of,** care for. 69. **largely,** at large, in full. 70. **let . . . familiar,** treat these marvels as ordinary matters.

And to the chapel let us presently.
Bene. Soft and fair, friar. Which is Beatrice?
Beat. [*Unmasking*] I answer to that name. What is your will?
Bene. Do not you love me?
Beat. Why, no; no more than reason.
Bene. Why, then your uncle and the prince and Claudio
Have been deceiv'd; they swore you did.
Beat. Do not you love me?
Bene. Troth, no; no more than reason.
Beat. Why, then my cousin Margaret and Ursula
Are much deceiv'd; for they did swear you did.
Bene. They swore that you were almost sick for me.
Beat. They swore that you were well-nigh dead for me.
Bene. 'Tis no such matter. Then you do not love me?
Beat. No, truly, but in friendly recompense.
Leon. Come, cousin, I am sure you love the gentleman.
Claud. And I'll be sworn upon 't that he loves her;
For here 's a paper written in his hand,
A halting sonnet of his own pure brain,
Fashion'd to Beatrice.
Hero. And here 's another
Writ in my cousin's hand, stol'n from her pocket,
Containing her affection unto Benedick.

Bene. A miracle! here 's our own hands against our hearts. Come, I will have thee; but, by this light, I take thee for pity.

Beat. I would not deny you; but, by this good day, I yield upon great persuasion; and partly to save your life, for I was told you were in a consumption.

Bene. Peace! I will stop your mouth. [*Kissing her.*]

D. Pedro. How dost thou, Benedick, the married man?

Bene. I'll tell thee what, prince; a college of wit-crackers cannot flout me out of my humour. Dost thou think I care for a satire or an epigram? No: if a man will be beaten with brains, 'a shall wear nothing handsome about him. In brief, since I do purpose to marry, I will think nothing to any purpose that the world can say against it; and therefore never flout at me for what I have said against it; for man is a giddy thing, and this is my conclusion. For thy part, Claudio, I did think to have beaten thee; but in that thou art like to be my kinsman, live unbruised and love my cousin.

Claud. I had well hoped thou wouldst have denied Beatrice, that I might have cudgelled thee out of thy single life, to make thee a double-dealer; which, out of question, thou wilt be, if my cousin do not look exceeding narrowly to thee.

Bene. Come, come, we are friends: let 's have a dance ere we are married, that we may lighten our own hearts and our wives' heels.

Leon. We'll have dancing afterward.

Bene. First, of my word; therefore play, music. Prince, thou art sad; get thee a wife, get thee a wife: there is no staff more reverend than one tipped with horn.

Enter Messenger.

Mess. My lord, your brother John is ta'en in flight,
And brought with armed men back to Messina.

Bene. Think not on him till to-morrow: I'll devise thee brave punishments for him. Strike up, pipers.
Dance. [*Exeunt.*]

87. **his own pure,** purely his own. 104-105. **beaten with brains,** subjected to ridicule. 105-106. **'a shall . . . him,** i.e., so as not to attract attention. 117. **double-dealer,** a married man and also a deceiver.

THE MERRY WIVES OF WINDSOR

According to an early eighteenth-century tradition, Shakespeare composed *The Merry Wives of Windsor* at the behest of Queen Elizabeth. John Dennis asserted in 1702 that the queen "was so eager to see it acted, that she commanded it to be finished in fourteen days." Nicholas Rowe added in 1709 that the queen, having been so pleased with Falstaff in the *Henry IV* plays, wished to see him in love. Such legends, emerging more than a century after the event, must be regarded with extreme caution. Whether true or not, however, they do point to a passage of courtly flattery unlike anything we find elsewhere in Shakespeare. The fairy blessing bestowed on Windsor Castle in Act V is unquestionably intended to celebrate the famous Order of the Garter. Mistress Quickly, disguised as leader of the fairies, orders her charges to sing nightly "Like to the Garter's compass, in a ring," to write "Honi soit qui mal y pense," the motto of the Garter, and to tend carefully the "several chairs of order"—those decorated stalls in the Chapel of St. George belonging to the illustrious lords who made up the Order of the Garter. Every such "instalment" receives her blessing, along with each knight's "coat," "crest," and "blazon." The topical nature of this passage is stressed by its apparent lack of relevance to the plot.

Other extraneous bits of action may allude to courtly matters or to Windsor gossip. The business about the three German horse thieves and their Duke (IV,iii–v), which makes little sense in the play as it stands, can perhaps be explained as an in-group joke on Frederick of Würtemburg, Count Mompelgard, a German nobleman obsessively intent on joining the Garter. He was the object of much anti-German scorn. His name, Mompelgard, is possibly scrambled into "garmombles" in the corrupt 1602 quarto text (IV,v,80). Also, the geography of Windsor is rendered with loving and accurate attention to detail, as though for an audience familiar with its environs.

Such topical flourishes do not rob the drama of its general appeal; it has had great success, both as a stage play and in Verdi's and Nicolai's operatic versions, and was no doubt popular with Shakespeare's London audience. Shakespeare never composed exclusively for special audiences, and indeed the blessing of Windsor Castle could easily have been added to a commercial play for royal performance. The allusion to "the fat woman of Brainford," a notorious tavern keeper of Brentford (halfway between London and Windsor) would have been as meaningful to Shakespeare's London audience as to the court. The same may be true of the "luces" in the coat of arms of Justice Shallow (I,i), sometimes thought to ridicule Shakespeare's Stratford neighbor Sir Thomas Lucy, but believed by Leslie Hotson to be a dig at William Gardiner, a Justice of the Peace in Surrey near London. Nevertheless, *The Merry Wives* could have been originally planned as entertainment to please Queen Elizabeth. A Feast of St. George in honor of the Garter was held at Westminster on April 23, 1597, in the queen's presence. Among those elected to the Order was George Carey, Lord Hunsdon, the patron of Shakespeare's company and the new Lord Chamberlain. He was actually installed in the Order at Windsor in May. This date is troublesomely early for a play that must follow the *Henry IV* plays and makes best sense after *Henry V* as well (usually dated 1599). Accordingly, many scholars have rejected the special occasion in 1597. Recently, however, the connection with the Garter has been urged anew, so that dating must remain uncertain from 1597 to 1601.

Responding in any event to popular request as well as to royal command, Shakespeare resurrected his best-known comic types from the history plays and boldly translated them into a ludicrously different kind of situation. Their new roles, especially that of buffoonish scapegoat for the once resourceful and self-aware Falstaff, have given rise to much critical dissatisfaction. Yet Shakespeare knew what he was doing. The comic types in *The Merry Wives* should not be judged against their counterparts in the history plays, even though an awareness of their prior existence is an essential part of the jest. To see Falstaff in love! This tour de force required that Shakespeare devise a multiple plot as unlike that of the history plays as possible, in order to stress the comic discrepancy.

The result is hard to describe generically, for *The Merry Wives* is unlike any other comedy Shakespeare wrote. At its nominal center is a familiar plot of romantic intrigue, featuring a young heroine (Anne Page) whose parents object to her attachment to young Fenton. They pester her with unwelcome rival wooers (Slender and Dr. Caius), obliging her finally to dupe her parents by a cleverly engineered elopement. This plot of "a trick to catch the old one" has an ancestry in Plautine and neoclassical comedy, though Shakespeare uses no particular recognizable source. To this plot he adds a second and parallel story of a lover (Falstaff) caught in the act of making love to two women. Italian *novelle* provide many situations of this sort, including that in which the husband is deceived by concealment of the lover in a clothes-basket; see especially "Of Two Brethren and Their Wives" from *Riche his Farewell to Militarie profession*, 1581, "Two Lovers of Pisa" from *Tarltons Newes Out of Purgatorie*, 1590, and the second story of the first day from Ser Giovanni Fiorentino's *Il Pecorone*, 1558. The effect of the combined plots is often farcelike, especially in the emphasis on swift, hilarious action and comic physical abuse at the expense of consistency in character. For example, we must accept as a "given" the preference of wise Master Page for Slender as his son-in-law, and the inexplicable preference of Mistress Page for the suit of Dr. Caius. Reasons are stated, but symmetry of the design is paramount.

In addition, Shakespeare enriches these two plot situations with minor characters, such as the rival wooers, go-betweens, and informers who inevitably come in conflict with one another and thereby reveal their "humours." Only tangentially connected with the plot, these characters are prized for their eccentricity. The Welsh Parson Evans and the French Dr. Caius nearly come to blows over Caius' courtship of Anne Page. They are safely kept apart by the genial Host of the Garter Inn, and are reconciled to the extent of plotting against the Host for having deceived them both. (Perhaps they carry out their threat as the mysterious Germans who steal the Host's horses, though the text is murky on this point.) Justice Shallow is brought in from *2 Henry IV* and is given nominal justification as cousin of Anne's second unwanted suitor, Slender; but Shallow's essential function is to quarrel with Falstaff about the latter's poaching and riotous behavior. This "plot" goes nowhere, and indeed is little more than a means for the revelation of humorous characters. Shallow's is a "cameo" role, like many others, enabling him to assume once more the fatuous postures we learned to love in an earlier play. Pistol and Nym, similarly needing some pretext for being on hand, revenge their dismissal from Falstaff's service by informing the two husbands of Falstaff's designs on the two merry wives. Bardolph finds suitable employment as a bartender. Mistress Quickly's transformation is perhaps the most gloriously improbable of all: she becomes confidante of all three wooers of Anne Page (offering equal encouragement to each, and receiving payment from each), as well as go-between for Falstaff and the two wives. She triumphs over Falstaff in a way not possible in the earlier history plays, joining the entire cast as they jeer at the discomfited horn-browed knight.

By providing occasion for the exhibition of idiosyncratic character for its own sake, side by side with his fast-moving farcical action, Shakespeare seems to have been responding to the newest dramatic genre of the late 1590's: the "humours" comedy. Chapman's *The Blind Beggar of Alexandria* (1596) had done much to establish the new fashion. Ben Jonson's *Every Man in His Humour* (1598) either influenced Shakespeare or was influenced by him, depending upon the dates. Jonson's plot, like Shakespeare's, is chiefly a vehicle for displaying various "humours" or comically obsessed types: the overly watchful father, the jealous husband, the braggart soldier, the country simpleton intent on learning to quarrel like a gentleman, the waspishly impatient man. Similar types appear in *The Merry Wives*, although Shakespeare characteristically does not satirize affectation so much as cherish it.

Shakespeare's comic types endear themselves chiefly through their verbal traits: Nym with his use of the word "humour"; Pistol with his anachronistic terms, recondite allusions, stilted poetic inversions, and hyperboles ("O base Hungarian wight! Wilt thou the spigot wield?"); Mistress Quickly with her pungent homely metaphors (comparing a beard to "a glover's paring knife") and her pat phrases ("But let that pass"); Shallow with his legal jargon; and the French Caius and the Welsh Evans with their ability to "keep their limbs whole and hack our English." Shakespeare also caricatures these humorous types by distinctive physical traits, such as Bardolph's "tinder-box" nose, or Slender's wee face and his little yellow beard that so aptly suit his passion for bearbaiting and his idiotic deference to his superiors. We laugh at these deformities, and yet see that no one is incorrigible. The characters amiably poke fun at one another, and every discomfiture leads ultimately to a reconciliation. Few escape laughter, even those we might regard as "normative" characters if this were a satire; the Host, for example, loses his horses, and Mistress Page is tricked at last by her daughter's elopement.

Nevertheless, the merry wives of the play's title come as close as any to representing the normative vision of the play, functioning as witty manipulators in a plot to expose hypocrisy and lechery. The devices they invent for Falstaff are rather like Maria's schemes for Malvolio in *Twelfth Night*, since all depend upon the complicity of the self-blinded victim. Falstaff is the dominant "humours" character of the play, obsessed both with lust and greed, amusing to us because the greed is predominant. His hypocritical reasons for lovemaking deserve comic reprisal, or "vengeance." His greed and his fatuous belief in his own charm overwhelm his natural sagacity and leave him vulnerable. He credulously accepts the bribes of the jealous Ford, disguised as Brook, and is deceived by the wives on no less than three occasions. For their part, the wives are delighted with their "sport," for they must devise increasingly clever schemes to offset Falstaff's growing suspicions. The more unlikely he is to return for more punishment, the greater must be their ingenuity in order to fool him once again. Mistress Ford enjoys the added pleasure of teaching her husband a lesson about jealousy. The cleverness of their sport is justified by its moral intent, and conversely the moral point is deprived of any tedious didacticism by the good humor of the jest. In his final humiliation, plagued by virtually all the play's characters, reduced to an absurd belief in fairies, Falstaff becomes a "scapegoat" in the truest sense of that term: a horned figure who embodies the faults of an entire society, and whose chastisement brings about purification. Yet as Mistress Quickly observes, "nobody but has his fault," and this comic rejection of Falstaff leads not to banishment but to a reconciling feast at the Pages' house. Without intending it, Falstaff has cured Ford's jealousy and has helped show that "Wives may be merry, and yet honest too."

THE MERRY WIVES OF WINDSOR

[*Dramatis Personae*

SIR JOHN FALSTAFF.
FENTON, *a gentleman.*
SHALLOW, *a country justice.*
SLENDER, *cousin to Shallow.*
FORD, PAGE, *two gentlemen dwelling at Windsor.*
WILLIAM PAGE, *a boy, son to Page.*
SIR HUGH EVANS, *a Welsh parson.*
DOCTOR CAIUS, *a French physician.*
Host of the Garter Inn.
BARDOLPH, PISTOL, NYM, *followers of Falstaff.*
ROBIN, *page to Falstaff.*
SIMPLE, *servant to Slender.*
RUGBY, *servant to Doctor Caius.*

MISTRESS FORD.
MISTRESS PAGE.
ANNE PAGE, *her daughter.*
MISTRESS QUICKLY, *servant to Doctor Caius.*

Servants to Page, Ford, *&c.*

SCENE: *Windsor, and the neighbourhood.*]

ACT I.

SCENE I. [*Windsor. Before* PAGE'S *house.*]

Enter JUSTICE SHALLOW, SLENDER, [*and*] SIR HUGH EVANS.

Shal. Sir Hugh, persuade me not; I will make a Star-chamber matter of it: if he were twenty Sir John Falstaffs, he shall not abuse Robert Shallow, esquire.

Slen. In the county of Gloucester, justice of peace and 'Coram.'

Shal. Ay, cousin Slender, and 'Custalorum.'

Slen. Ay, and 'Rato-lorum' too; and a gentleman born, master parson; who writes himself 'Armigero,' in any bill, warrant, quittance, or obligation, 'Armigero.'

Shal. Ay, that I do; and have done any time these three hundred years.

Slen. All his successors gone before him hath done 't; and all his ancestors that come after him may: they may give the dozen white luces in their coat.

Shal. It is an old coat.

Evans. The dozen white louses do become an old coat well; it agrees well, passant; it is a familiar beast to man, and signifies love.

Shal. The luce is the fresh fish; the salt fish is an old coat.

Slen. I may quarter, coz.

Shal. You may, by marrying.

Evans. It is marring indeed, if he quarter it.

Shal. Not a whit.

Evans. Yes, py 'r lady: if he has a quarter of your coat, there is but three skirts for yourself, in my simple conjectures: but that is all one. If Sir John Falstaff have committed disparagements unto you, I am of the church, and will be glad to do my benevolence to make atonements and compremises between you.

Shal. The council shall hear it; it is a riot.

Evans. It is not meet the council hear a riot; there is no fear of Got in a riot: the council, look you, shall desire to hear the fear of Got, and not to hear a riot; take your vizaments in that.

Shal. Ha! o' my life, if I were young again, the sword should end it.

Evans. It is petter that friends is the sword, and end it: and there is also another device in my prain, which peradventure prings goot discretions with it: there is Anne Page, which is daughter to Master George Page, which is pretty virginity.

Slen. Mistress Anne Page? She has brown hair, and speaks small like a woman?

Evans. It is that fery person for all the orld, as just as you will desire; and seven hundred pounds of moneys, and gold and silver, is her grandsire upon his death's-bed—Got deliver to a joyful resurrections!—give, when she is able to overtake seventeen years old: it were a goot motion if we leave our pribbles and prabbles, and desire a marriage between Master Abraham and Mistress Anne Page.

Shal. Did her grandsire leave her seven hundred pound?

Evans. Ay, and her father is make her a petter penny.

Shal. I know the young gentlewoman; she has good gifts.

Evans. Seven hundred pounds and possibilities is goot gifts.

Shal. Well, let us see honest Master Page. Is Falstaff there?

Evans. Shall I tell you a lie? I do despise a liar as I do despise one that is false, or as I despise one that is not true. The knight, Sir John, is there; and, I beseech you, be ruled by your well-willers. I will peat the door for Master Page. [*Knocks*] What, hoa! Got pless your house here!

Page. [*Within*] Who 's there?

[*Enter*] Master Page.

Evans. Here is Got's plessing, and your friend, and Justice Shallow; and here young Master Slender, that peradventures shall tell you another tale, if matters grow to your likings.

Page. I am glad to see your worships well. I thank you for my venison, Master Shallow.

Shal. Master Page, I am glad to see you: much good do it your good heart! I wished your venison better; it was ill killed. How doth good Mistress Page?—and I thank you always with my heart, la! with my heart.

Page. Sir, I thank you.

Shal. Sir, I thank you; by yea and no, I do.

Page. I am glad to see you, good Master Slender.

Slen. How does your fallow greyhound, sir? I heard say he was outrun on Cotsall.

Page. It could not be judged, sir.

Slen. You'll not confess, you'll not confess.

Shal. That he will not. 'Tis your fault, 'tis your fault; 'tis a good dog.

Page. A cur, sir.

Shal. Sir, he 's a good dog, and a fair dog: can there be more said? he is good and fair. Is Sir John Falstaff here?

Page. Sir, he is within; and I would I could do a good office between you.

Evans. It is spoke as a Christians ought to speak.

Shal. He hath wronged me, Master Page.

Page. Sir, he doth in some sort confess it.

Shal. If it be confessed, it is not redressed: is not that so, Master Page? He hath wronged me; indeed he hath; at a word, he hath, believe me: Robert Shallow, esquire, saith, he is wronged.

Page. Here comes Sir John.

[*Enter* Sir John] Falstaff, Bardolph, Nym, [*and*] Pistol.

Fal. Now, Master Shallow, you'll complain of me to the king?

Shal. Knight, you have beaten my men, killed my deer, and broke open my lodge.

Fal. But not kissed your keeper's daughter?

Shal. Tut, a pin! this shall be answered.

Fal. I will answer it straight; I have done all this. That is now answered.

Shal. The council shall know this.

Fal. 'Twere better for you if it were known in counsel: you'll be laughed at.

Evans. Pauca verba, Sir John; goot worts.

Fal. Good worts! good cabbage. Slender, I broke your head: what matter have you against me?

Slen. Marry, sir, I have matter in my head against you; and against your cony-catching rascals, Bardolph, Nym, and Pistol.

Bard. You Banbury cheese!

Slen. Ay, it is no matter.

Pist. How now, Mephostophilus!

Slen. Ay, it is no matter.

Nym. Slice, I say! pauca, pauca: slice! that 's my humour.

Slen. Where 's Simple, my man? Can you tell, cousin?

Act I. Scene I. 2. **a Star-chamber matter.** The court of Star Chamber, composed chiefly of the king's council, was the highest and most powerful civil court in the realm. 6. **'Coram,'** i.e., quorum, a title of certain justices whose presence was necessary to constitute a bench. 7. **'Custalorum,'** a corruption of Latin *custos rotulorum*, keeper of the rolls. 8. **'Rato-lorum,'** for *rotulorum*. 10. **'Armigero,'** esquire. 16-17. **luces in their coat.** The luce, a fresh-water fish, was displayed in the coat of arms of Sir Thomas Lucy of Charlcote, an estate near Stratford. This passage provides a basis for the deer-stalking legend considered in the biographical section of the General Introduction. Cf. Leslie Hotson, *Shakespeare Versus Shallow*, for other possible topical allusions in this passage. 19. **louses.** The pronunciations of *luce* and *louse* were sufficiently close to give the quibble point. 24. **quarter,** i.e., to arrange or display different coats of arms on one escutcheon; also, to add a coat of arms to another, or others, in this way. 33. **compremises,** a corruption of "compromises"; i.e., settlement by arbitration. 35. **The council . . . riot.** The king's council, sitting in Star Chamber, frequently concerned itself with riots. 39. **vizaments,** for "advisements," deliberations. 42. **that friends . . . sword,** i.e., that the quarrel be ended by friendly motions. 65. **possibilities,** pecuniary prospects. 72. **well-willers,** well wishers, friends. 73. **peat,** beat, knock. 84. **ill,** i.e., illegally. 92. **Cotsall,** Cotswold. 122. **in counsel,** secretly. 123. **Pauca verba,** few words. 124. **worts,** vegetables; a quibble on Sir Hugh's mispronunciation of "words." 128. **cony-catching,** cheating. 130. **Banbury cheese.** Banbury cheeses were noted for their thinness; a reference to Slender's name. 134. **Slice,** a reference to Bardolph's calling Slender a cheese.

Evans. Peace, I pray you. Now let us understand. There is three umpires in this matter, as I understand; that is, Master Page, fidelicet Master Page; and there is myself, fidelicet myself; and the three party is, lastly and finally, mine host of the Garter.

Page. We three, to hear it and end it between them.

Evans. Fery goot: I will make a prief of it in my note-book; and we will afterwards ork upon the cause with as great discreetly as we can.

Fal. Pistol!

Pist. He hears with ears.

Evans. The tevil and his tam! what phrase is this, 'He hears with ear'? why, it is affectations.

Fal. Pistol, did you pick Master Slender's purse?

Slen. Ay, by these gloves, did he, or I would I might never come in mine own great chamber again else, of seven groats in mill-sixpences, and two Edward shovel-boards, that cost me two shilling and two pence a-piece of Yead Miller, by these gloves.

Fal. Is this true, Pistol?

Evans. No; it is false, if it is a pick-purse.

Pist. Ha, thou mountain-foreigner! Sir John and master mine,
I combat challenge of this latten bilbo.
Word of denial in thy labras here!
Word of denial: froth and scum, thou liest!

Slen. By these gloves, then, 'twas he.

Nym. Be avised, sir, and pass good humours: I will say 'marry trap' with you, if you run the nuthook's humour on me; that is the very note of it.

Slen. By this hat, then, he in the red face had it; for though I cannot remember what I did when you made me drunk, yet I am not altogether an ass.

Fal. What say you, Scarlet and John?

Bard. Why, sir, for my part, I say the gentleman had drunk himself out of his five sentences.

Evans. It is his five senses: fie, what the ignorance is!

Bard. And being fap, sir, was, as they say, cashiered; and so conclusions passed the careires.

Slen. Ay, you spake in Latin then too; but 'tis no matter: I'll ne'er be drunk whilst I live again, but in honest, civil, godly company, for this trick: if I be drunk, I'll be drunk with those that have the fear of God, and not with drunken knaves.

Evans. So Got udge me, that is a virtuous mind.

Fal. You hear all these matters denied, gentlemen; you hear it.

[*Enter*] Anne Page [*with wine*]; Mistress Ford [*and*] Mistress Page [*following*].

Page. Nay, daughter, carry the wine in; we'll drink within. [*Exit Anne Page*.]

Slen. O heaven! this is Mistress Anne Page.

Page. How now, Mistress Ford!

Fal. Mistress Ford, by my troth, you are very well met: by your leave, good mistress. [*Kisses her*.]

Page. Wife, bid these gentlemen welcome. Come, we have a hot venison pasty to dinner: come, gentlemen, I hope we shall drink down all unkindness.

[*Exeunt all except Shal., Slen., and Evans*.]

Slen. I had rather than forty shillings I had my Book of Songs and Sonnets here.

[*Enter*] Simple.

How now, Simple! where have you been? I must wait on myself, must I? You have not the Book of Riddles about you, have you?

Sim. Book of Riddles! why, did you not lend it to Alice Shortcake upon All-hallowmas last, a fortnight afore Michaelmas?

Shal. Come, coz; come, coz; we stay for you. A word with you, coz; marry, this, coz: there is, as 'twere, a tender, a kind of tender, made afar off by Sir Hugh here. Do you understand me?

Slen. Ay, sir, you shall find me reasonable; if it be so, I shall do that that is reason.

Shal. Nay, but understand me.

Slen. So I do, sir.

Evans. Give ear to his motions, Master Slender: I will description the matter to you, if you be capacity of it.

Slen. Nay, I will do as my cousin Shallow says: I pray you, pardon me; he 's a justice of peace in his country, simple though I stand here.

Evans. But that is not the question: the question is concerning your marriage.

Shal. Ay, there 's the point, sir.

Evans. Marry, is it; the very point of it; to Mistress Anne Page.

Slen. Why, if it be so, I will marry her upon any reasonable demands.

Evans. But can you affection the 'oman? Let us command to know that of your mouth or of your lips; for divers philosophers hold that the lips is parcel of the mouth. Therefore, precisely, can you carry your good will to the maid?

Shal. Cousin Abraham Slender, can you love her?

Slen. I hope, sir, I will do as it shall become one that would do reason.

Evans. Nay, Got's lords and his ladies! you must speak possitable, if you can carry her your desires towards her.

Shal. That you must. Will you, upon good dowry, marry her?

Slen. I will do a greater thing than that, upon your request, cousin, in any reason.

Shal. Nay, conceive me, conceive me, sweet coz: what I do is to pleasure you, coz. Can you love the maid?

Slen. I will marry her, sir, at your request: but if there be no great love in the beginning, yet heaven may decrease it upon better acquaintance, when we are married and have more occasion to know one another; I hope, upon familiarity will grow more contempt: but if you say, 'Marry her,' I will marry her; that I am freely dissolved, and dissolutely.

140. **fidelicet,** *videlicet*, namely. 143. **Garter,** the name of an inn. 158. **groats,** coins equal to four pence; see glossary. **mill-sixpences,** coins stamped by means of the mill and press. 159. **Edward shovel-boards,** shillings coined in the reign of Edward VI, so called from their use in the gambling game of shovelboard. 160. **Yead,** dialect form of "Edward." 164. **mountain-foreigner,** Welshman. 165. **latten,** mixed metal of yellow color, resembling brass. **bilbo,** finely tempered sword of Bilbao in Spain. Pistol refers to Evans as a "brass sword." 166. **labras,** the lips; blunder for the neuter plural, *labra*. 169. **avised,** advised. **pass good humours,** do nothing ill-natured. 170. **'marry trap,'** an insulting phrase meaning "run off," "beat it." **nuthook's,** beadle's, constable's. 177. **Scarlet and John,** names of Robin Hood's companions, Will Scarlet and Little John; *Scarlet* is humorously applied to Bardolph's color. 183. **fap,** drunk. 184. **careires,** careers, short gallop at full speed; a feat in horsemanship. Bardolph probably means that Slender got what he deserved. 191. **udge,** judge. 206. **Book of Songs and Sonnets.** Probably refers to Tottel's *Miscellany*, published 1557 and quite old-fashioned by the late 1590's. 209. **Book of Riddles.** Such a book is mentioned as in the library of Captain Cox in *Laneham's Letter*, 1575. No copy is extant of an earlier date than 1629. 211. **All-hallowmas . . . Michaelmas,** Simple's blunder. Michaelmas occurs in September, All-hallowmas on November 1. 244. **possitable,** the

Evans. It is a fery discretion answer; save the fall is in the ort 'dissolutely:' the ort is, according to our meaning, 'resolutely:' his meaning is good.

Shal. Ay, I think my cousin meant well.

Slen. Ay, or else I would I might be hanged, la!

Shal. Here comes fair Mistress Anne.

[*Enter* ANNE PAGE.]

Would I were young for your sake, Mistress Anne!

Anne. The dinner is on the table; my father desires your worships' company.

Shal. I will wait on him, fair Mistress Anne.

Evans. Od's plessed will! I will not be absence at the grace. [*Exeunt Shallow and Evans.*]

Anne. Will 't please your worship to come in, sir?

Slen. No, I thank you, forsooth, heartily; I am very well.

Anne. The dinner attends you, sir.

Slen. I am not a-hungry, I thank you, forsooth.—Go, sirrah, for all you are my man, go wait upon my cousin Shallow. [*Exit Simple.*] A justice of peace sometime may be beholding to his friend for a man. I keep but three men and a boy yet, till my mother be dead: but what though? yet I live like a poor gentleman born.

Anne. I may not go in without your worship: they will not sit till you come.

Slen. I' faith, I'll eat nothing; I thank you as much as though I did.

Anne. I pray you, sir, walk in.

Slen. I had rather walk here, I thank you. I bruised my shin th' other day with playing at sword and dagger with a master of fence; three veneys for a dish of stewed prunes; and, by my troth, I cannot abide the smell of hot meat since. Why do your dogs bark so? be there bears i' the town?

Anne. I think there are, sir; I heard them talked of.

Slen. I love the sport well; but I shall as soon quarrel at it as any man in England. You are afraid, if you see the bear loose, are you not?

Anne. Ay, indeed, sir.

Slen. That 's meat and drink to me, now. I have seen Sackerson loose twenty times, and have taken him by the chain; but, I warrant you, the women have so cried and shrieked at it, that it passed: but women, indeed, cannot abide 'em; they are very ill-favoured rough things.

[*Enter* PAGE.]

Page. Come, gentle Master Slender, come; we stay for you.

Slen. I'll eat nothing, I thank you, sir.

Page. By cock and pie, you shall not choose, sir! come, come.

Slen. Nay, pray you, lead the way.

Page. Come on, sir.

Slen. Mistress Anne, yourself shall go first.

Anne. Not I, sir; pray you, keep on.

Slen. Truly, I will not go first; truly, la! I will not do you that wrong.

Anne. I pray you, sir.

Slen. I'll rather be unmannerly than troublesome. You do yourself wrong, indeed, la! *Exeunt.*

SCENE II. [*The same.*]

Enter [SIR HUGH] EVANS *and* SIMPLE.

Evans. Go your ways, and ask of Doctor Caius' house which is the way: and there dwells one Mistress Quickly, which is in the manner of his nurse, or his dry nurse, or his cook, or his laundry, his washer, and his wringer.

Sim. Well, sir.

Evans. Nay, it is petter yet. Give her this letter; for it is a 'oman that altogether 's acquaintance with Mistress Anne Page: and the letter is, to desire and require her to solicit your master's desires to Mistress Anne Page. I pray you, be gone: I will make an end of my dinner; there 's pippins and cheese to come. *Exeunt.*

SCENE III. [*A room in the Garter Inn.*]

Enter FALSTAFF, HOST, BARDOLPH, NYM, PISTOL, [*and* ROBIN, *Falstaff's*] *Page.*

Fal. Mine host of the Garter!

Host. What says my bully-rook? speak scholarly and wisely.

Fal. Truly, mine host, I must turn away some of my followers.

Host. Discard, bully Hercules; cashier: let them wag; trot, trot.

Fal. I sit at ten pounds a week.

Host. Thou 'rt an emperor, Cæsar, Keisar, and Pheezar. I will entertain Bardolph; he shall draw, he shall tap: said I well, bully Hector?

Fal. Do so, good mine host.

Host. I have spoke; let him follow. [*To Bard.*] Let me see thee froth and lime: I am at a word; follow. [*Exit.*]

Fal. Bardolph, follow him. A tapster is a good trade: an old cloak makes a new jerkin; a withered serving-man a fresh tapster. Go; adieu.

Bard. It is a life that I have desired: I will thrive.

Pist. O base Hungarian wight! wilt thou the spigot wield? [*Exit Bardolph.*]

Nym. He was gotten in drink: is not the humour conceited?

Fal. I am glad I am so acquit of this tinderbox: his thefts were too open; his filching was like an unskilful singer; he kept not time.

Nym. The good humour is to steal at a minute's rest.

Pist. 'Convey,' the wise it call. 'Steal!' foh! a fico for the phrase!

Welshman's error for "positively" (Hart). 257-258. **upon . . . contempt,** an allusion to the proverb "Familiarity breeds contempt." 279. **attends,** waits for. 296. **veneys,** thrusts in fencing. **stewed prunes,** an indelicate remark to address to a lady. Stewed prunes were associated with the "stews," or brothel houses. 307. **Sackerson,** a famous bear at the Paris Garden near the theaters on the Bankside. 316. **cock,** perversion of "God." **pie,** service book of the pre-Reformation church.

SCENE II. 1. **ask of,** inquire at. 13. **pippins and cheese.** Fruit and cheese were commonly used as desserts.

SCENE III. 2. **bully-rook,** not hyphenated in F; *bully,* gallant, fine; *rook,* a probable quibble on the meanings "the castle at chess" and "a sharper." 7. **wag,** move on. 8. **sit at,** live on. 10. **Pheezar,** i.e., Vizier (Hart). 11. **tap,** serve as tapster. 15. **froth,** to draw liquor in such a way as to make it frothy. **lime,** adulterate wine by putting lime into it to make it sparkle. **at a word,** a man of few words (Hart). 23. **Hungarian,** a reference to discarded and cashiered soldiers from Hungary, and to the war (1593-1606) between the empire and the Turks. 31. **minute's.** Hart suggests a play on the phrase "steal a minute's rest"; Langton conjectured *minim's,* the shortest note in music; New Cambridge emends to *minim-rest.* 33. **fico,** Italian for "fig."

Fal. Well, sirs, I am almost out at heels.

Pist. Why, then, let kibes ensue.

Fal. There is no remedy; I must cony-catch; I must shift.

Pist. Young ravens must have food.

Fal. Which of you know Ford of this town?

Pist. I ken the wight: he is of substance good.

Fal. My honest lads, I will tell you what I am about.

Pist. Two yards, and more.

Fal. No quips now, Pistol! Indeed, I am in the waist two yards about; but I am now about no waste; I am about thrift. Briefly, I do mean to make love to Ford's wife: I spy entertainment in her; she discourses, she carves, she gives the leer of invitation: I can construe the action of her familiar style; and the hardest voice of her behaviour, to be Englished rightly, is, 'I am Sir John Falstaff's.'

Pist. He hath studied her will, and translated her will, out of honesty into English.

Nym. The anchor is deep: will that humour pass?

Fal. Now, the report goes she has all the rule of her husband's purse: he hath a legion of angels.

Pist. As many devils entertain; and 'To her, boy,' say I.

Nym. The humour rises; it is good: humour me the angels.

Fal. I have writ me here a letter to her: and here another to Page's wife, who even now gave me good eyes too, examined my parts with most judicious œillades; sometimes the beam of her view gilded my foot, sometimes my portly belly.

Pist. [*Aside*] Then did the sun on dunghill shine.

Nym. [*Aside*] I thank thee for that humour.

Fal. O, she did so course o'er my exteriors with such a greedy intention, that the appetite of her eye did seem to scorch me up like a burning-glass! Here 's another letter to her: she bears the purse too; she is a region in Guiana, all gold and bounty. I will be cheater to them both, and they shall be exchequers to me; they shall be my East and West Indies, and I will trade to them both. [*To Pist.*] Go bear thou this letter to Mistress Page; [*To Nym*] and thou this to Mistress Ford: we will thrive, lads, we will thrive.

Pist. Shall I Sir Pandarus of Troy become,
And by my side wear steel? then, Lucifer take all!

Nym. I will run no base humour: here, take the humour-letter: I will keep the haviour of reputation.

Fal. [*To Robin*] Hold, sirrah, bear you these letters tightly;
Sail like my pinnace to these golden shores.
Rogues, hence, avaunt! vanish like hailstones, go;
Trudge, plod away o' the hoof; seek shelter, pack!
Falstaff will learn the humour of the age,
French thrift, you rogues; myself and skirted page.
[*Exeunt Falstaff and Robin.*]

Pist. Let vultures gripe thy guts! for gourd and fullam holds,
And high and low beguiles the rich and poor:
Tester I'll have in pouch when thou shalt lack,
Base Phrygian Turk!

Nym. I have operations which be humours of revenge.

Pist. Wilt thou revenge?

Nym. By welkin and her star!

Pist. With wit or steel?

Nym. With both the humours, I:
I will discuss the humour of this love to Page.

Pist. And I to Ford shall eke unfold
How Falstaff, varlet vile,
His dove will prove, his gold will hold,
And his soft couch defile.

Nym. My humour shall not cool: I will incense Page to deal with poison; I will possess him with yellowness, for the †revolt of mine is dangerous: that is my true humour.

Pist. Thou art the Mars of malecontents: I second thee; troop on. *Exeunt.*

SCENE IV. [*A room in* DOCTOR CAIUS's *house.*]

Enter MISTRESS QUICKLY, SIMPLE, [*and*] JOHN RUGBY.

Quick. What, John Rugby! I pray thee, go to the casement, and see if you can see my master, Master Doctor Caius, coming. If he do, i' faith, and find any body in the house, here will be an old abusing of God's patience and the king's English.

Rug. I'll go watch.

Quick. Go; and we'll have a posset for 't soon at night, in faith, at the latter end of a sea-coal fire. [*Exit Rugby.*] An honest, willing, kind fellow, as ever servant shall come in house withal, and, I warrant you, no tell-tale nor no breed-bate: his worst fault is, that he is given to prayer; he is something peevish that way: but nobody but has his fault; but let that pass. Peter Simple, you say your name is?

Sim. Ay, for fault of a better.

Quick. And Master Slender 's your master?

Sim. Ay, forsooth.

Quick. Does he not wear a great round beard, like a glover's paring-knife?

Sim. No, forsooth: he hath but a little wee face, with a little yellow beard, a Cain-coloured beard.

Quick. A softly-sprighted man, is he not?

Sim. Ay, forsooth: but he is as tall a man of his hands as any is between this and his head; he hath fought with a warrener.

Quick. How say you? O, I should remember him: does he not hold up his head, as it were, and strut in his gait?

Sim. Yes, indeed, does he.

Quick. Well, heaven send Anne Page no worse fortune! Tell Master Parson Evans I will do what I can for your master: Anne is a good girl, and I wish—

[*Enter* RUGBY.]

35. **kibes,** chilblains. 40. **wight,** person. 49. **carves,** shows courtesy and affability. 52. **Englished,** expressed in English. 56. **The anchor is deep.** This phrase baffles most of the commentators. Steevens thought it might mean "his hopes are well founded"; Johnson thought *anchor* should be read *author*, taking his cue from *translated* in the preceding speech. Hart sees in the phrase Nym's acceptance of Falstaff's scheme, making the words equivalent to "the plan is fixed firmly." New Cambridge editors favor Kinnear's conjecture: *angle*, in view of *English* in the preceding speech and *angels* in the following. 60. **angels,** coins stamped with the figure of the archangel Michael. 64. **me,** the ethical dative. 68. **œillades,** amorous glances. 76. **region in Guiana.** Theobald thought this a possible compliment to Raleigh. Raleigh's *Discoverie of the Large, Rich, and Beautiful Empyre of Guiana* was published in 1596. 77. **cheater,** officer appointed to look after the king's escheats, i.e., land reverted to the crown; a quibble on the ordinary sense of "one who cheats." 83. **Sir Pandarus,** uncle of Cressida in the story of Troilus and Cressida; from his name originated the word "pander." 84. **Lucifer,** used synonymously for Satan. 86. **keep . . . reputation,** keep up good appearances. 88. **tightly,** soundly. 93. **French thrift,** alludes to the fashion of hiring French pages and of dismissing excess serving men (Hart). 94. **fullam,** a kind of false dice loaded at the corner. 96. **Tester,** sixpence. 97. **Phrygian Turk,** a term of opprobrium; cf. note to line 23 above. 98. **operations,** plans. 104. **discuss,** declare. 111. **yellowness,** jealousy. **is dangerous.** Nym means that

Rug. Out, alas! here comes my master.

Quick. We shall all be shent. Run in here, good young man; go into this closet: he will not stay long. [*Shuts Simple in the closet.*] What, John Rugby! John! what, John, I say! Go, John, go inquire for my master; I doubt he be not well, that he comes not home.

[*Exit Rugby.*]

[*Singing*] And down, down, adown-a, &c.

[*Enter*] Doctor Caius.

Caius. Vat is you sing? I do not like des toys. Pray you, go and vetch me in my closet un boitier vert, a box, a green-a box: do intend vat I speak? a green-a box.

Quick. Ay, forsooth; I'll fetch it you. [*Aside*] I am glad he went not in himself: if he had found the young man, he would have been horn-mad.

Caius. Fe, fe, fe, fe! ma foi, il fait fort chaud. Je m'en vais a la cour—la grande affaire.

Quick. Is it this, sir?

Caius. Oui; mette le au mon pocket: depeche, quickly. Vere is dat knave Rugby?

Quick. What, John Rugby! John! [*Enter Rugby.*]

Rug. Here, sir!

Caius. You are John Rugby, and you are Jack Rugby. Come, take-a your rapier, and come after my heel to the court.

Rug. 'Tis ready, sir, here in the porch.

Caius. By my trot, I tarry too long. Od's me! Qu'ai-j'oublie! dere is some simples in my closet, dat I vill not for the varld I shall leave behind.

Quick. [*Aside*] Ay me, he'll find the young man there, and be mad!

Caius. O diable, diable! vat is in my closet? Villain! larron! [*Pulling Simple out.*] Rugby, my rapier!

Quick. Good master, be content.

Caius. Wherefore shall I be content-a?

Quick. The young man is an honest man.

Caius. What shall de honest man do in my closet? dere is no honest man dat shall come in my closet.

Quick. I beseech you, be not so phlegmatic. Hear the truth of it: he came of an errand to me from Parson Hugh.

Caius. Vell.

Sim. Ay, forsooth; to desire her to—

Quick. Peace, I pray you.

Caius. Peace-a your tongue. Speak-a your tale.

Sim. To desire this honest gentlewoman, your maid, to speak a good word to Mistress Anne Page for my master in the way of marriage.

Quick. This is all, indeed, la! but I'll ne'er put my finger in the fire, and need not.

Caius. Sir Hugh send-a you? Rugby, baille me some paper. Tarry you a little-a while. [*Writes.*]

Quick. [*Aside to Simple*] I am glad he is so quiet: if he had been throughly moved, you should have heard him so loud and so melancholy. But notwithstanding, man, I'll do you your master what good I can: and the very yea and the no is, the French doctor, my master,—I may call him my master, look you, for I keep his house; and I wash, wring, brew, bake, scour, dress meat and drink, make the beds, and do all myself,—

Sim. [*Aside to Quickly*] 'Tis a great charge to come under one body's hand.

Quick. [*Aside to Simple*] Are you avised o' that? you shall find it a great charge: and to be up early and down late; but notwithstanding,—to tell you in your ear; I would have no words of it,—my master himself is in love with Mistress Anne Page: but notwithstanding that, I know Anne's mind,—that 's neither here nor there.

Caius. You jack'nape, give-a this letter to Sir Hugh; by gar, it is a shallenge: I will cut his troat in de park; and I will teach a scurvy jack-a-nape priest to meddle or make. You may be gone; it is not good you tarry here. By gar, I will cut all his two stones; by gar, he shall not have a stone to throw at his dog.

[*Exit Simple.*]

Quick. Alas, he speaks but for his friend.

Caius. It is no matter-a ver dat: do not you tell-a me dat I shall have Anne Page for myself? By gar, I vill kill de Jack priest; and I have appointed mine host of de Jarteer to measure our weapon. By gar, I will myself have Anne Page.

Quick. Sir, the maid loves you, and all shall be well. We must give folks leave to prate: what, the good-jer!

Caius. Rugby, come to the court with me. By gar, if I have not Anne Page, I shall turn your head out of my door. Follow my heels, Rugby.

[*Exeunt Caius and Rugby.*]

Quick. You shall have An fool's-head of your own. No, I know Anne's mind for that: never a woman in Windsor knows more of Anne's mind than I do; nor can do more than I do with her, I thank heaven.

Fent. [*Within*] Who 's within there? ho!

Quick. Who 's there, I trow! Come near the house, I pray you.

[*Enter*] Fenton.

Fent. How now, good woman! how dost thou?

Quick. The better that it pleases your good worship to ask.

Fent. What news? how does pretty Mistress Anne?

Quick. In truth, sir, and she is pretty, and honest, and gentle; and one that is your friend, I can tell you that by the way; I praise heaven for it.

Fent. Shall I do any good, thinkest thou? shall I not lose my suit?

Quick. Troth, sir, all is in his hands above: but notwithstanding, Master Fenton, I'll be sworn on a book, she loves you. Have not your worship a wart above your eye?

Fent. Yes, marry, have I; what of that?

his reaction against Falstaff for his dismissal will lead to disaster for the fat knight. 113. **Mars of malecontents,** i.e., a malcontent with respect to warlike matters, as contrasted with the melancholy of lovers, *et al.*

Scene iv. 8. **posset,** a drink of hot milk curdled with ale or wine. 9. **sea-coal,** mineral coal as distinguished from charcoal. 12. **breed-bate,** mischiefmaker. 22. **wee.** New Cambridge editors emend to *whey-face,* taking a cue from an error in Q_1 at line 20, *whey-colored beard.* 23. **Cain-coloured,** Ff: *Caine;* Q: *Kane;* most editors read *cane-coloured.* Theobald thought it referred to the pictures of Cain in old tapestries where he is given a yellow beard. 25. **softly-sprighted,** gentle. 26-27. **as tall . . . hands.** *New English Dictionary* defines *tall of one's hands* as dexterous, handy; also as stout of arms, formidable with weapons. 28. **warrener,** keeper of a warren, a place privileged by grant from the king for keeping certain animals. 38. **shent,** blamed, disgraced. 39. **closet,** private room. 47. **un boitier vert,** a green box. 52. **horn-mad,** originally of horned beasts enraged so as to horn anyone; hence, of persons stark mad; quibblingly, mad with rage at being made a cuckold. 53-54. **ma foi . . . affaire.** By my faith, it is very hot; I am going to court—the great affair. 56. **Oui . . . depeche.** Yes, put it in my pocket; be quick. 61. **your rapier,** your master's rapier. 65. **Qu'ai-j'oublie!** What have I forgotten! **simples,** medicinal herbs. 71. **larron,** robber. 92. **baille,** fetch. 129. **good-jer,** good year; an expletive of doubtful meaning; see *NED* under "goodyear."

Quick. Well, thereby hangs a tale: good faith, it is such another Nan; but, I detest, an honest maid as ever broke bread: we had an hour's talk of that wart. I shall never laugh but in that maid's company! But indeed she is given too much to allicholy and musing: but for you—well, go to.

Fent. Well, I shall see her to-day. Hold, there 's money for thee; let me have thy voice in my behalf: if thou seest her before me, commend me.

Quick. Will I? i' faith, that we will; and I will tell your worship more of the wart the next time we have confidence; and of other wooers.

Fent. Well, farewell; I am in great haste now.

Quick. Farewell to your worship. [*Exit Fenton.*] Truly, an honest gentleman: but Anne loves him not; for I know Anne's mind as well as another does. Out upon 't! what have I forgot? *Exit.*

ACT II.

SCENE I. [*Before* PAGE'S *house.*]

Enter MISTRESS PAGE [*with a letter*].

Mrs Page. What, have I scaped love-letters in the holiday-time of my beauty, and am I now a subject for them? Let me see. [*Reads.*]

'Ask me no reason why I love you; for though Love use Reason for his precisian, he admits him not for his counsellor. You are not young, no more am I; go to then, there 's sympathy: you are merry, so am I; ha, ha! then there 's more sympathy: you love sack, and so do I; would you desire better sympathy? Let it suffice thee, Mistress Page,—at the least, if the love of soldier can suffice,—that I love thee. I will not say, pity me; 'tis not a soldier-like phrase: but I say, love me. By me,

Thine own true knight,
By day or night,
Or any kind of light,
With all his might
For thee to fight,
JOHN FALSTAFF.'

What a Herod of Jewry is this! O wicked, wicked world! One that is well-nigh worn to pieces with age to show himself a young gallant! What an unweighed behaviour hath this Flemish drunkard picked—with the devil's name!—out of my conversation, that he dares in this manner assay me? Why, he hath not been thrice in my company! What should I say to him? I was then frugal of my mirth: Heaven forgive me! Why, I'll exhibit a bill in the parliament for the putting down of men. How shall I be revenged on him? for revenged I will be, as sure as his guts are made of puddings.

[*Enter*] MISTRESS FORD.

Mrs Ford. Mistress Page! trust me, I was going to your house.

Mrs Page. And, trust me, I was coming to you. You look very ill.

Mrs Ford. Nay, I'll ne'er believe that; I have to show to the contrary.

Mrs Page. Faith, but you do, in my mind.

Mrs Ford. Well, I do then; yet I say I could show you to the contrary. O Mistress Page, give me some counsel!

Mrs Page. What 's the matter, woman?

Mrs Ford. O woman, if it were not for one trifling respect, I could come to such honour!

Mrs Page. Hang the trifle, woman! take the honour. What is it? dispense with trifles; what is it?

Mrs Ford. If I would but go to hell for an eternal moment or so, I could be knighted.

Mrs Page. What? thou liest! Sir Alice Ford! These knights will hack; and so thou shouldst not alter the article of thy gentry.

Mrs Ford. We burn daylight: here, read, read; perceive how I might be knighted. I shall think the worse of fat men, as long as I have an eye to make difference of men's liking: and yet he would not swear; praised women's modesty; and gave such orderly and well-behaved reproof to all uncomeliness, that I would have sworn his disposition would have gone to the truth of his words; but they do no more adhere and keep place together than the Hundredth Psalm to the tune of 'Green Sleeves.' What tempest, I trow, threw this whale, with so many tuns of oil in his belly, ashore at Windsor? How shall I be revenged on him? I think the best way were to entertain him with hope, till the wicked fire of lust have melted him in his own grease. Did you ever hear the like?

Mrs Page. Letter for letter, but that the name of Page and Ford differs! To thy great comfort in this mystery of ill opinions, here 's the twin-brother of thy letter: but let thine inherit first; for, I protest, mine never shall. I warrant he hath a thousand of these letters, writ with blank space for different names,—sure, more,—and these are of the second edition: he will print them, out of doubt; for he cares not what he puts into the press, when he would put us two. I had rather be a giantess, and lie under Mount Pelion. Well, I will find you twenty lascivious turtles ere one chaste man.

Mrs Ford. Why, this is the very same; the very hand, the very words. What doth he think of us?

Mrs Page. Nay, I know not: it makes me almost ready to wrangle with mine own honesty. I'll entertain myself like one that I am not acquainted withal; for, sure, unless he know some strain in me, that I know not myself, he would never have boarded me in this fury.

Mrs Ford. 'Boarding,' call you it? I'll be sure to keep him above deck.

Mrs Page. So will I: if he come under my hatches, I'll never to sea again. Let 's be revenged on him: let 's appoint him a meeting; give him a show of comfort in his suit and lead him on with a fine-baited delay, till he hath pawned his horses to mine host of the Garter.

Mrs Ford. Nay, I will consent to act any villany against him, that may not sully the chariness of our honesty. O, that my husband saw this letter! it would give eternal food to his jealousy.

160. **detest,** a malapropism for "protest." 164. **allicholy,** melancholy. ACT II. SCENE I. 5. **precisian,** rigid spiritual adviser; antithetical to *counselor*, i.e., worldly adviser (Hart); Globe, following Johnson: *physician.* 23. **unweighed,** inconsiderate. 26. **assay,** accost, address with proposals of love; see glossary. 29. **exhibit,** submit. 32. **puddings,** mixture of meat, herbs, etc., stuffed into intestines of animals, as sausage. 50. **moment,** period of time. 52. **hack,** of uncertain meaning; the context suggests some indelicate reference (Onions). 53. **article of thy gentry,** character of your rank. 57. **make difference,** discriminate. **men's liking,** what men are like. 64. **'Green Sleeves,'** a popular tune to which many sets of words have been sung; cf. V, v, 22. 80. **press,** a quibble on the meanings "squeeze" and "print." 82. **lascivious turtles.** The turtle dove was proverbially chaste, i.e., faithful to its mate. 92. **boarded,** accosted, made advances to. 99. **fine-**

Mrs Page. Why, look where he comes; and my good man too: he 's as far from jealousy as I am from giving him cause; and that I hope is an unmeasurable distance.

Mrs Ford. You are the happier woman.

Mrs Page. Let 's consult together against this greasy knight. Come hither. [*They retire.*]

[*Enter*] MASTER PAGE [*with*] NYM, MASTER FORD [*with*] PISTOL.

Ford. Well, I hope it be not so.

Pist. Hope is a curtal dog in some affairs:
Sir John affects thy wife.

Ford. Why, sir, my wife is not young.

Pist. He wooes both high and low, both rich and poor,
Both young and old, one with another, Ford;
He loves the gallimaufry: Ford, perpend.

Ford. Love my wife!

Pist. With liver burning hot. Prevent, or go thou,
Like Sir Actæon he, with Ringwood at thy heels:
O, odious is the name!

Ford. What name, sir?

Pist. The horn, I say. Farewell.
Take heed, have open eye, for thieves do foot by night:
Take heed, ere summer comes or cuckoo-birds do sing.
Away, Sir Corporal Nym!
Believe it, Page; he speaks sense. [*Exit.*]

Ford. [*Aside*] I will be patient; I will find out this.

Nym. [*To Page*] And this is true; I like not the humour of lying. He hath wronged me in some humours: I should have borne the humoured letter to her; but I have a sword and it shall bite upon my necessity. He loves your wife; there 's the short and the long. My name is Corporal Nym; I speak and I avouch; 'tis true: my name is Nym and Falstaff loves your wife. Adieu. I love not the humour of bread and cheese, and there 's the humour of it. Adieu. [*Exit.*]

Page. 'The humour of it,' quoth 'a! here 's a fellow frights English out of his wits.

Ford [*Aside*] I will seek out Falstaff.

Page. [*Aside*] I never heard such a drawling, affecting rogue.

Ford. [*Aside*] If I do find it: well.

Page. [*Aside*] I will not believe such a Cataian, though the priest o' the town commended him for a true man.

Ford. [*Aside*] 'Twas a good sensible fellow: well.

Page. How now, Meg!

[*Mrs Page and Mrs Ford come forward.*]

Mrs Page. Whither go you, George? Hark you.

Mrs Ford. How now, sweet Frank! why art thou melancholy?

Ford. I melancholy! I am not melancholy. Get you home, go.

Mrs Ford. Faith, thou hast some crotchets in thy head. Now, will you go, Mistress Page?

Mrs Page. Have with you. You'll come to dinner, George. [*Aside to Mrs Ford*] Look who comes yonder: she shall be our messenger to this paltry knight.

Mrs Ford. [*Aside to Mrs Page*] Trust me, I thought on her: she'll fit it.

[*Enter* MISTRESS] QUICKLY.

Mrs Page. You are come to see my daughter Anne?

Quick. Ay, forsooth; and, I pray, how does good Mistress Anne?

Mrs Page. Go in with us and see: we have an hour's talk with you.

[*Exeunt Mrs Page, Mrs Ford, and Mrs Quickly.*]

Page. How now, Master Ford!

Ford. You heard what this knave told me, did you not?

Page. Yes: and you heard what the other told me?

Ford. Do you think there is truth in them?

Page. Hang 'em, slaves! I do not think the knight would offer it: but these that accuse him in his intent towards our wives are a yoke of his discarded men; very rogues, now they be out of service.

Ford. Were they his men?

Page. Marry, were they.

Ford. I like it never the better for that. Does he lie at the Garter?

Page. Ay, marry, does he. If he should intend this voyage toward my wife, I would turn her loose to him; and what he gets more of her than sharp words, let it lie on my head.

Ford. I do not misdoubt my wife; but I would be loath to turn them together. A man may be too confident: I would have nothing lie on my head: I cannot be thus satisfied.

Page. Look where my ranting host of the Garter comes: there is either liquor in his pate or money in his purse when he looks so merrily.

[*Enter*] HOST.

How now, mine host!

Host. How now, bully-rook! thou 'rt a gentleman. Cavaleiro-justice, I say!

[*Enter*] SHALLOW.

Shal. I follow, mine host, I follow. Good even and twenty, good Master Page! Master Page, will you go with us? we have sport in hand.

Host. Tell him, cavaleiro-justice; tell him, bully-rook.

Shal. Sir, there is a fray to be fought between Sir Hugh the Welsh priest and Caius the French doctor.

Ford. Good mine host o' the Garter, a word with you. [*Drawing him aside.*]

Host. What sayest thou, my bully-rook?

Shal. [*To Page*] Will you go with us to behold it? My merry host hath had the measuring of their weapons; and, I think, hath appointed them contrary places; for, believe me, I hear the parson is no jester. Hark, I will tell you what our sport shall be. [*They converse apart.*]

Host. Hast thou no suit against my knight, my guest-cavaleiro?

Ford. None, I protest: but I'll give you a pottle of burnt sack to give me recourse to him and tell him my

baited, subtly alluring. 114. **curtal,** having the tail docked. 119. **gallimaufry,** all types indiscriminately. **perpend,** consider. 121. **burning hot,** an allusion to the liver as the seat of the passions. 122. **Actæon.** Cf. *Titus Andronicus,* II, iii, 63, note. **Ringwood,** one of Actaeon's dogs, mentioned in Golding's translation of Ovid. 127. **cuckoo-birds,** superstitiously regarded as birds presaging ill luck in love; cf. *Love's Labour's Lost,* V, ii, 910-911. 136. **upon my necessity,** when I have need. 140. **humour . . . cheese.** Nym alludes to the scant rations he received as Falstaff's retainer. 148. **Cataian,** Cathaian, man or woman of Cathay, i.e., China; a pejorative word meaning sharper, scoundrel. 161. **Have with,** I shall go along with; see glossary. 201. **Cavaleiro,** gentleman trained in arms, a gay military man. 202-203. **Good . . . twenty,** good evening, twenty times. 223. **pottle,** two-quart measure. **burnt,** heated.

name is Brook; only for a jest.

Host. My hand, bully; thou shalt have egress and regress;—said I well?—and thy name shall be Brook. It is a merry knight. Will you go, mynheers?

Shal. Have with you, mine host.

Page. I have heard the Frenchman hath good skill in his rapier.

Shal. Tut, sir, I could have told you more. In these times you stand on distance, your passes, stoccadoes, and I know not what: 'tis the heart, Master Page; 'tis here, 'tis here. I have seen the time, with my long sword I would have made you four tall fellows skip like rats.

Host. Here, boys, here, here! shall we wag?

Page. Have with you. I had rather hear them scold than fight. *Exeunt* [*Host, Shal., and Page*].

Ford. Though Page be a secure fool, and stands so firmly on his wife's frailty, yet I cannot put off my opinion so easily: she was in his company at Page's house; and what they made there, I know not. Well, I will look further into 't: and I have a disguise to sound Falstaff. If I find her honest, I lose not my labour; if she be otherwise, 'tis labour well bestowed. [*Exit.*]

SCENE II. [*A room in the Garter Inn.*]

Enter FALSTAFF [*and*] PISTOL.

Fal. I will not lend thee a penny.

Pist. Why, then the world 's mine oyster,
Which I with sword will open.

Fal. Not a penny. I have been content, sir, you should lay my countenance to pawn: I have grated upon my good friends for three reprieves for you and your coach-fellow Nym; or else you had looked through the grate, like a geminy of baboons. I am damned in hell for swearing to gentlemen my friends, you were good soldiers and tall fellows; and when Mistress Bridget lost the handle of her fan, I took 't upon mine honour thou hadst it not.

Pist. Didst not thou share? hadst thou not fifteen pence?

Fal. Reason, you rogue, reason: thinkest thou I'll endanger my soul gratis? At a word, hang no more about me, I am no gibbet for you. Go. A short knife and a throng! To your manor of Pickt-hatch! Go. You'll not bear a letter for me, you rogue! you stand upon your honour! Why, thou unconfinable baseness, it is as much as I can do to keep the terms of my honour precise: I, I, I myself sometimes, leaving the fear of God on the left hand and hiding mine honour in my necessity, am fain to shuffle, to hedge and to lurch; and yet you, rogue, will ensconce your rags, your cat-a-mountain looks, your red-lattice phrases, and your bold-beating oaths, under the shelter of your honour! You will not do it, you!

Pist. I do relent: what would thou more of man?

[*Enter*] ROBIN.

Rob. Sir, here 's a woman would speak with you.

Fal. Let her approach.

[*Enter* MISTRESS] QUICKLY.

Quick. Give your worship good morrow.

Fal. Good morrow, good wife.

Quick. Not so, an 't please your worship.

Fal. Good maid, then.

Quick. I'll be sworn,
As my mother was, the first hour I was born.

Fal. I do believe the swearer. What with me?

Quick. Shall I vouchsafe your worship a word or two?

Fal. Two thousand, fair woman: and I'll vouchsafe thee the hearing.

Quick. There is one Mistress Ford, sir:—I pray, come a little nearer this ways:—I myself dwell with Master Doctor Caius,—

Fal. Well, on: Mistress Ford, you say,—

Quick. Your worship says very true: I pray your worship, come a little nearer this ways.

Fal. I warrant thee, nobody hears; mine own people, mine own people.

Quick. Are they so? God bless them and make them his servants!

Fal. Well, Mistress Ford; what of her?

Quick. Why, sir, she 's a good creature. Lord, Lord! your worship 's a wanton! Well, heaven forgive you and all of us, I pray!

Fal. Mistress Ford; come, Mistress Ford,—

Quick. Marry, this is the short and the long of it; you have brought her into such a canaries as 'tis wonderful. The best courtier of them all, when the court lay at Windsor, could never have brought her to such a canary. Yet there has been knights, and lords, and gentlemen, with their coaches, I warrant you, coach after coach, letter after letter, gift after gift; smelling so sweetly, all musk, and so rushling, I warrant you, in silk and gold; and in such alligant terms; and in such wine and sugar of the best and the fairest, that would have won any woman's heart; and, I warrant you, they could never get an eye-wink of her: I had myself twenty angels given me this morning; but I defy all angels, in any such sort, as they say, but in the way of honesty: and, I warrant you, they could never get her so much as sip on a cup with the proudest of them all: and yet there has been earls, nay, which is more, pensioners; but, I warrant you, all is one with her.

Fal. But what says she to me? be brief, my good she-Mercury.

Quick. Marry, she hath received your letter, for the which she thanks you a thousand times; and she gives you to notify that her husband will be absence from his house between ten and eleven.

Fal. Ten and eleven?

Quick. Ay, forsooth; and then you may come and see the picture, she says, that you wot of: Master Ford, her husband, will be from home. Alas! the sweet woman leads an ill life with him: he 's a very jealousy man: she leads a very frampold life with him, good heart.

228. **mynheers,** gentlemen. Globe: *An-heires*, following F. 233-237. **In these . . . like rats,** an allusion to the new styles in dueling; see *Shakespeare's England*, II, 392. 233. **passes,** lunges. **stoccadoes,** thrusts. 238. **wag,** go.

SCENE II. 2. **mine oyster.** To open an oyster was a metaphorical phrase for laying bare any difficult matter (Hart). 5. **countenance,** patronage. 8. **geminy,** pair. 18. **A short . . . throng,** i.e., with a short knife one might cut purses in a crowd. 19. **Pickt-hatch,** quarter in London famous in Elizabethan times for houses of ill fame, the houses having hatches, or half doors, guarded with spikes. 21. **unconfinable,** infinite. 27. **cat-a-mountain,** leopard or panther. 28. **red-lattice phrases,** alehouse talk, from lattice painted red as the sign of an alehouse. **bold-beating,** a confusion of "bold-faced" and "brow-beating." 41. **vouchsafe,** deign to grant; Quickly's error. 61.

Fal. Ten and eleven. Woman, commend me to her; I will not fail her.

Quick. Why, you say well. But I have another messenger to your worship. Mistress Page hath her hearty commendations to you too: and let me tell you in your ear, she 's as fartuous a civil modest wife, and one, I tell you, that will not miss you morning nor evening prayer, as any is in Windsor, whoe'er be the other: and she bade me tell your worship that her husband is seldom from home; but she hopes there will come a time. I never knew a woman so dote upon a man: surely I think you have charms, la; yes, in truth.

Fal. Not I, I assure thee: setting the attraction of my good parts aside I have no other charms.

Quick. Blessing on your heart for 't!

Fal. But, I pray thee, tell me this: has Ford's wife and Page's wife acquainted each other how they love me?

Quick. That were a jest indeed! they have not so little grace, I hope: that were a trick indeed! But Mistress Page would desire you to send her your little page, of all loves: her husband has a marvellous infection to the little page; and truly Master Page is an honest man. Never a wife in Windsor leads a better life than she does: do what she will, say what she will, take all, pay all, go to bed when she list, rise when she list, all is as she will: and truly she deserves it; for if there be a kind woman in Windsor, she is one. You must send her your page; no remedy.

Fal. Why, I will.

Quick. Nay, but do so, then: and, look you, he may come and go between you both; and in any case have a nay-word, that you may know one another's mind, and the boy never need to understand any thing; for 'tis not good that children should know any wickedness: old folks, you know, have discretion, as they say, and know the world.

Fal. Fare thee well: commend me to them both: there 's my purse; I am yet thy debtor. Boy, go along with this woman. [*Exeunt Mistress Quickly and Robin.*] This news distracts me!

Pist. [*Aside*] This punk is one of Cupid's carriers:
Clap on more sails; pursue; up with your fights:
Give fire: she is my prize, or ocean whelm them all!
[*Exit.*]

Fal. Sayest thou so, old Jack? go thy ways; I'll make more of thy old body than I have done. Will they yet look after thee? Wilt thou, after the expense of so much money, be now a gainer? Good body, I thank thee. Let them say 'tis grossly done; so it be fairly done, no matter.

[*Enter*] BARDOLPH.

Bard. Sir John, there 's one Master Brook below would fain speak with you, and be acquainted with you; and hath sent your worship a morning's draught of sack.

Fal. Brook is his name?

Bard. Ay, sir.

Fal. Call him in. [*Exit Bardolph.*] Such Brooks are welcome to me, that o'erflow such liquor. Ah, ha! Mistress Ford and Mistress Page, have I encompassed you? go to; via!

[*Enter* BARDOLPH, *with*] FORD [*disguised*].

Ford. Bless you, sir!

Fal. And you, sir! Would you speak with me?

Ford. I make bold to press with so little preparation upon you.

Fal. You 're welcome. What 's your will? Give us leave, drawer. [*Exit Bardolph.*]

Ford. Sir, I am a gentleman that have spent much; my name is Brook.

Fal. Good Master Brook, I desire more acquaintance of you.

Ford. Good Sir John, I sue for yours: not to charge you; for I must let you understand I think myself in better plight for a lender than you are: the which hath something emboldened me to this unseasoned intrusion; for they say, if money go before, all ways do lie open.

Fal. Money is a good soldier, sir, and will on.

Ford. Troth, and I have a bag of money here troubles me: if you will help to bear it, Sir John, take all, or half, for easing me of the carriage.

Fal. Sir, I know not how I may deserve to be your porter.

Ford. I will tell you, sir, if you will give me the hearing.

Fal. Speak, good Master Brook: I shall be glad to be your servant.

Ford. Sir, I hear you are a scholar,—I will be brief with you,—and you have been a man long known to me, though I had never so good means, as desire, to make myself acquainted with you. I shall discover a thing to you, wherein I must very much lay open mine own imperfection: but, good Sir John, as you have one eye upon my follies, as you hear them unfolded, turn another into the register of your own; that I may pass with a reproof the easier, sith you yourself know how easy it is to be such an offender.

Fal. Very well, sir; proceed.

Ford. There is a gentlewoman in this town; her husband's name is Ford.

Fal. Well, sir.

Ford. I have long loved her, and, I protest to you, bestowed much on her; followed her with a doting observance; engrossed opportunities to meet her: fee'd every slight occasion that could but niggardly give me sight of her; not only bought many presents to give her, but have given largely to many to know what she would have given; briefly, I have pursued her as love hath pursued me; which hath been on the wing of all occasions. But whatsoever I have merited, either in my mind or in my means, meed, I am sure, I have received none; unless experience be a jewel. That I have purchased at an infinite rate, and that hath taught me to say this:
'Love like a shadow flies when substance love pursues;
Pursuing that that flies, and flying what pursues.'

Fal. Have you received no promise of satisfaction at her hands?

canaries, a malapropism for "quandaries" (Steevens); a quibble on "canary," suggesting that she was drunk. 68. **rushling,** i.e., rustling. 69. **alligant,** elegant. 79. **pensioners,** bodyguard to a sovereign in the royal palace. 82. **she-Mercury,** woman messenger. 94. **frampold,** disagreeable. 100. **fartuous,** mistake for "virtuous." **modest,** characterized by decency and propriety; see glossary. 102. **you,** ethical dative. 120. **infection to,** affection for. 131. **nay-word,** watchword.

140. **distracts,** perplexes, bewilders. 141. **punk,** harlot. 142. **fights,** fighting sails, i.e., screens raised during naval engagements to conceal and protect the crew. 159. **encompassed,** outwitted. **via,** go on. 203. **engrossed,** monopolized. 204. **fee'd,** employed.

Ford. Never.

Fal. Have you importuned her to such a purpose?

Ford. Never.

Fal. Of what quality was your love, then?

Ford. Like a fair house built on another man's ground; so that I have lost my edifice by mistaking the place where I erected it.

Fal. To what purpose have you unfolded this to me?

Ford. When I have told you that, I have told you all. Some say, that though she appear honest to me, yet in other places she enlargeth her mirth so far that there is shrewd construction made of her. Now, Sir John, here is the heart of my purpose: you are a gentleman of excellent breeding, admirable discourse, of great admittance, authentic in your place and person, generally allowed for your many war-like, court-like, and learned preparations.

Fal. O, sir!

Ford. Believe it, for you know it. There is money; spend it, spend it; spend more; spend all I have; only give me so much of your time in exchange of it, as to lay an amiable siege to the honesty of this Ford's wife: use your art of wooing; win her to consent to you: if any man may, you may as soon as any.

Fal. Would it apply well to the vehemency of your affection, that I should win what you would enjoy? Methinks you prescribe to yourself very preposterously.

Ford. O, understand my drift. She dwells so securely on the excellency of her honour, that the folly of my soul dares not present itself: she is too bright to be looked against. Now, could I come to her with any detection in my hand, my desires had instance and argument to commend themselves: I could drive her then from the ward of her purity, her reputation, her marriage-vow, and a thousand other her defences, which now are too too strongly embattled against me. What say you to 't, Sir John?

Fal. Master Brook, I will first make bold with your money; next, give me your hand; and last, as I am a gentleman, you shall, if you will, enjoy Ford's wife.

Ford. O good sir!

Fal. I say you shall.

Ford. Want no money, Sir John; you shall want none.

Fal. Want no Mistress Ford, Master Brook; you shall want none. I shall be with her, I may tell you, by her own appointment; even as you came in to me, her assistant or go-between parted from me: I say I shall be with her between ten and eleven; for at that time the jealous rascally knave her husband will be forth. Come you to me at night; you shall know how I speed.

Ford. I am blest in your acquaintance. Do you know Ford, sir?

Fal. Hang him, poor cuckoldly knave! I know him not: yet I wrong him to call him poor; they say the jealous wittolly knave hath masses of money; for the which his wife seems to me well-favoured. I will use her as the key of the cuckoldly rogue's coffer; and there 's my harvest-home.

Ford. I would you knew Ford, sir, that you might avoid him if you saw him.

Fal. Hang him, mechanical salt-butter rogue! I will stare him out of his wits; I will awe him with my cudgel: it shall hang like a meteor o'er the cuckold's horns. Master Brook, thou shalt know I will predominate over the peasant, and thou shalt lie with his wife. Come to me soon at night. Ford 's a knave, and I will aggravate his style; thou, Master Brook, shalt know him for knave and cuckold. Come to me soon at night. [*Exit.*]

Ford. What a damned Epicurean rascal is this! My heart is ready to crack with impatience. Who says this is improvident jealousy? my wife hath sent to him; the hour is fixed; the match is made. Would any man have thought this? See the hell of having a false woman! My bed shall be abused, my coffers ransacked, my reputation gnawn at; and I shall not only receive this villanous wrong, but stand under the adoption of abominable terms, and by him that does me this wrong. Terms! names! Amaimon sounds well; Lucifer, well; Barbason, well; yet they are devils' additions, the names of fiends: but Cuckold! Wittol!—Cuckold! the devil himself hath not such a name. Page is an ass, a secure ass: he will trust his wife; he will not be jealous. I will rather trust a Fleming with my butter, Parson Hugh the Welshman with my cheese, an Irishman with my aqua-vitæ bottle, or a thief to walk my ambling gelding, than my wife with herself: then she plots, then she ruminates, then she devises; and what they think in their hearts they may effect, they will break their hearts but they will effect. God be praised for my jealousy! Eleven o'clock the hour. I will prevent this, detect my wife, be revenged on Falstaff, and laugh at Page. I will about it; better three hours too soon than a minute too late. Fie, fie, fie! cuckold! cuckold! cuckold! *Exit.*

SCENE III. [*A field near Windsor.*]

Enter CAIUS [*and*] RUGBY.

Caius. Jack Rugby!

Rug. Sir?

Caius. Vat is de clock, Jack?

Rug. 'Tis past the hour, sir, that Sir Hugh promised to meet.

Caius. By gar, he has save his soul, dat he is no come; he has pray his Pible well, dat he is no come: by gar, Jack Rugby, he is dead already, if he be come.

Rug. He is wise, sir; he knew your worship would kill him, if he came.

Caius. By gar, de herring is no dead so as I vill kill him. Take your rapier, Jack; I vill tell you how I vill kill him.

Rug. Alas, sir, I cannot fence.

Caius. Villany, take your rapier.

Rug. Forbear; here 's company.

[*Enter*] PAGE, SHALLOW, SLENDER, [*and*] HOST.

Host. Bless thee, bully doctor!

231. **enlargeth,** gives free scope to; see glossary. 235. **admittance,** fashion, vogue. 238. **preparations,** accomplishments. 250. **preposterously,** with the natural order of things inverted. 283. **wittolly,** cuckoldly. 290. **mechanical,** engaged in manual occupation. 296. **aggravate his style,** increase or add to his title. 311. **Amaimon, Lucifer, Barbason,** names of devils; they occur in Scot's *Discoverie of Witchcraft* (1584).

SCENE III. 24. **foin,** thrust (in fencing). 25. **traverse,** march, especially backward and forward. 26. **punto,** stroke or thrust with the point of the sword. **stock,** stoccado, thrust. **reverse,** backward stroke. 27. **montant,** upright thrust. 29. **Æsculapius,** god of medicine. **Galen,** famous Greek physician. 30. **heart of elder,** opposite of "heart of oak"; the elder has no heart (Steevens). Hence, the phrase suggests

Shal. Save you, Master Doctor Caius!

Page. Now, good master doctor!

Slen. Give you good morrow, sir.

Caius. Vat be all you, one, two, tree, four, come for?

Host. To see thee fight, to see thee foin, to see thee traverse; to see thee here, to see thee there; to see thee pass thy punto, thy stock, thy reverse, thy distance, thy montant. Is he dead, my Ethiopian? is he dead, my Francisco? ha, bully! What says my Æsculapius? my Galen? my heart of elder? ha! is he dead, bully stale? is he dead?

Caius. By gar, he is de coward Jack priest of de vorld; he is not show his face.

Host. Thou art a Castalion-King-Urinal. Hector of Greece, my boy!

Caius. I pray you, bear vitness that me have stay six or seven, two, tree hours for him, and he is no come.

Shal. He is the wiser man, master doctor: he is a curer of souls, and you a curer of bodies; if you should fight, you go against the hair of your professions. Is it not true, Master Page?

Page. Master Shallow, you have yourself been a great fighter, though now a man of peace.

Shal. Bodykins, Master Page, though I now be old and of the peace, if I see a sword out, my finger itches to make one. Though we are justices and doctors and churchmen, Master Page, we have some salt of our youth in us; we are the sons of women, Master Page.

Page. 'Tis true, Master Shallow.

Shal. It will be found so, Master Page. Master Doctor Caius, I am come to fetch you home. I am sworn of the peace: you have showed yourself a wise physician, and Sir Hugh hath shown himself a wise and patient churchman. You must go with me, master doctor.

Host. Pardon, guest-justice. A word, Mounseur Mockwater.

Caius. Mock-vater! vat is dat?

Host. Mock-water, in our English tongue, is valour, bully.

Caius. By gar, den, I have as mush mock-vater as de Englishman. Scurvy jack-dog priest! by gar, me vill cut his ears.

Host. He will clapper-claw thee tightly, bully.

Caius. Clapper-de-claw! vat is dat?

Host. That is, he will make thee amends.

Caius. By gar, me do look he shall clapper-de-claw me; for, by gar, me vill have it.

Host. And I will provoke him to 't, or let him wag.

Caius. Me tank you for dat.

Host. And, moreover, bully,—but first, master guest, and Master Page, and eke Cavaleiro Slender, go you through the town to Frogmore. [*Aside to them.*]

Page. Sir Hugh is there, is he?

Host. He is there: see what humour he is in; and I will bring the doctor about by the fields. Will it do well?

Shal. We will do it.

Page, Shal., and Slen. Adieu, good master doctor.

[*Exeunt Page, Shal., and Slen.*]

Caius. By gar, me vill kill de priest; for he speak for a jack-an-ape to Anne Page.

Host. Let him die: sheathe thy impatience, throw cold water on thy choler: go about the fields with me through Frogmore: I will bring thee where Mistress Anne Page is, at a farmhouse a-feasting; and thou shalt woo her. Cried game; said I well?

Caius. By gar, me dank you vor dat: by gar, I love you; and I shall procure-a you de good guest, de earl, de knight, de lords, de gentlemen, my patients.

Host. For the which I will be thy adversary toward Anne Page. Said I well?

Caius. By gar, 'tis good; vell said.

Host. Let us wag, then.

Caius. Come at my heels, Jack Rugby. *Exeunt.*

ACT III.

SCENE I. [*A field near Frogmore.*]

Enter [SIR HUGH] EVANS, [*and*] SIMPLE.

Evans. I pray you now, good Master Slender's serving-man, and friend Simple by your name, which way have you looked for Master Caius, that calls himself doctor of physic?

Sim. Marry, sir, the pittie-ward, the park-ward, every way; old Windsor way, and every way but the town way.

Evans. I most fehemently desire you you will also look that way.

Sim. I will, sir. [*Exit.*]

Evans. 'Pless my soul, how full of chollors I am, and trempling of mind! I shall be glad if he have deceived me. How melancholies I am! I will knog his urinals about his knave's costard when I have good opportunities for the ork. 'Pless my soul! [*Sings.*]

To shallow rivers, to whose falls
Melodious birds sings madrigals;
There will we make our peds of roses,
And a thousand fragrant posies.
To shallow—

Mercy on me! I have a great dispositions to cry. [*Sings.*]

Melodious birds sing madrigals—
When as I sat in Pabylon—
And a thousand vagram posies.
To shallow &c.

[*Enter* SIMPLE.]

Sim. Yonder he is coming, this way, Sir Hugh.

Evans. He 's welcome. [*Sings.*]

To shallow rivers, to whose falls—

Heaven prosper the right! What weapons is he?

Sim. No weapons, sir. There comes my master, Master Shallow, and another gentleman, from Frogmore, over the stile, this way.

Evans. Pray you, give me my gown; or else keep it in your arms. [*Reads in a book.*]

[*Enter*] PAGE, SHALLOW, [*and*] SLENDER.

cowardice. 50. **salt,** wantonness. 60. **Mounseur Mockwater.** Dr. Johnson says, "The Host means to reflect on the inspection of urine, which made a considerable part of practical physic in that time; yet I do not see the meaning of mock-water." Farmer suggested *muck-water*, the drain of a dunghill. 92. **Cried game,** the game is announced and under way (from bearbaiting).

ACT III. SCENE I. 5. **pittie-ward,** toward Windsor Petty (or Little) Park. **park-ward,** toward Windsor Great Park. 14. **knog,** knock. **costard,** apple; humorously applied to the head. 17-20. **To shallow rivers,** etc., lines from Marlowe's *Come live with me and be my love.* 24. **When . . . Pabylon.** Evans interpolates the opening lines of Psalm 137. 25. **vagram,** vagrant.

Shal. How now, master Parson! Good morrow, good Sir Hugh. Keep a gamester from the dice, and a good student from his book, and it is wonderful.

Slen. [*Aside*] Ah, sweet Anne Page!

Page. 'Save you, good Sir Hugh!

Evans. 'Pless you from his mercy sake, all of you!

Shal. What, the sword and the word! do you study them both, master parson?

Page. And youthful still! in your doublet and hose this raw rheumatic day!

Evans. There is reasons and causes for it.

Page. We are come to you to do a good office, master parson.

Evans. Fery well: what is it?

Page. Yonder is a most reverend gentleman, who, belike having received wrong by some person, is at most odds with his own gravity and patience that ever you saw.

Shal. I have lived fourscore years and upward; I never heard a man of his place, gravity and learning, so wide of his own respect.

Evans. What is he?

Page. I think you know him; Master Doctor Caius, the renowned French physician.

Evans. Got's will, and his passion of my heart! I had as lief you would tell me of a mess of porridge.

Page. Why?

Evans. He has no more knowledge in Hibocrates and Galen,—and he is a knave besides; a cowardly knave as you would desires to be acquainted withal.

Page. I warrant you, he 's the man should fight with him.

Slen. [*Aside*] O sweet Anne Page!

Shal. It appears so by his weapons. Keep them asunder: here comes Doctor Caius.

[*Enter*] Host, Caius, [*and*] Rugby.

Page. Nay, good master parson, keep in your weapon.

Shal. So do you, good master doctor.

Host. Disarm them, and let them question: let them keep their limbs whole and hack our English.

Caius. I pray you, let-a me speak a word with your ear. Vherefore vill you not meet-a me?

Evans. [*Aside to Caius*] Pray you, use your patience: in good time.

Caius. By gar, you are de coward, de Jack dog, John ape.

Evans. [*Aside to Caius*] Pray you, let us not be laughing-stocks to other men's humours; I desire you in friendship, and I will one way or other make you amends. [*Aloud*] I will knog your urinals about your knave's cogscomb for missing your meetings and appointments.

Caius. Diable! Jack Rugby,—mine host de Jarteer,—have I not stay for him to kill him? have I not, at de place I did appoint?

Evans. As I am a Christians soul now, look you, this is the place appointed: I'll be judgement by mine host of the Garter.

Host. Peace, I say, Gallia and Gaul, French and Welsh, soul-curer and body-curer!

Caius. Ay, dat is very good; excellent.

Host. Peace, I say! hear mine host of the Garter. Am I politic? am I subtle? am I a Machiavel? Shall I lose my doctor? no; he gives me the potions and the motions. Shall I lose my parson, my priest, my Sir Hugh? no: he gives me the proverbs and the no-verbs. Give me thy hand, terrestrial; so. Give me thy hand, celestial; so. Boys of art, I have deceived you both; I have directed you to wrong places: your hearts are mighty, your skins are whole, and let burnt sack be the issue. Come, lay their swords to pawn. Follow me, lads of peace; follow, follow, follow.

Shal. Trust me, a mad host. Follow, gentlemen, follow.

Slen. [*Aside*] O sweet Anne Page!

[*Exeunt Shal., Slen., Page, and Host.*]

Caius. Ha, do I perceive dat? have you make-a de sot of us, ha, ha?

Evans. This is well; he has made us his vlouting-stog. I desire you that we may be friends; and let us knog our prains together to be revenge on this same scall, scurvy, cogging companion, the host of the Garter.

Caius. By gar, with all my heart. He promise to bring me where is Anne Page; by gar, he deceive me too.

Evans. Well, I will smite his noddles. Pray you, follow. [*Exeunt.*]

Scene II. [*A street.*]

[*Enter*] Mistress Page, [*and*] Robin.

Mrs Page. Nay, keep your way, little gallant; you were wont to be a follower, but now you are a leader. Whether had you rather lead mine eyes, or eye your master's heels?

Rob. I had rather, forsooth, go before you like a man than follow him like a dwarf.

Mrs Page. O, you are a flattering boy: now I see you'll be a courtier.

[*Enter*] Ford.

Ford. Well met, Mistress Page. Whither go you?

Mrs Page. Truly, sir, to see your wife. Is she at home?

Ford. Ay; and as idle as she may hang together, for want of company. I think, if your husbands were dead, you two would marry.

Mrs Page. Be sure of that,—two other husbands.

Ford. Where had you this pretty weathercock?

Mrs Page. I cannot tell what the dickens his name is my husband had him of. What do you call your knight's name, sirrah?

Rob. Sir John Falstaff.

Ford. Sir John Falstaff!

Mrs Page. He, he; I can never hit on 's name. There is such a league between my good man and he! Is your wife at home indeed?

Ford. Indeed she is.

44. **the word,** the Bible; it may possibly have an association with the phrase "the sword of the Spirit," meaning the Bible. 58. **respect,** modest deportment; see glossary. 99. **Gallia and Gaul,** Wales and France. 104. **Machiavel.** Cf. *1 Henry VI*, V, iv, 74, note. 119. **sot,** fool. 120. **vlouting-stog,** flouting-stock, i.e., laughingstock. 123. **scall,** scald, i.e., scurvy. **cogging,** cheating; see glossary.

Scene ii. 13. **hang together,** i.e., as idle as she can be without going to pieces. 18. **pretty weathercock,** a reference to the page's gaudy clothes; cf. *Love's Labour's Lost*, IV, i, 97. 19. **dickens,** epithet for the devil (devilkins?). 34. **twelve score,** i.e., twelvescore paces. 35. **folly,** wantonness. **motion,** instigation. 43. **divulge,** proclaim (a person) to be. 52. **knot,** group, company. 69. **speaks holiday,** uses choice language. 70. **carry 't,** win the day; see *carry* in glossary. 73. **having,** estate; see glossary. 74. **Poins,** a character in *1* and *2*

Mrs Page. By your leave, sir: I am sick till I see her. [*Exeunt Mrs Page and Robin.*]

Ford. Has Page any brains? hath he any eyes? hath he any thinking? Sure, they sleep; he hath no use of them. Why, this boy will carry a letter twenty mile, as easy as a cannon will shoot point-blank twelve score. He pieces out his wife's inclination; he gives her folly motion and advantage: and now she 's going to my wife, and Falstaff's boy with her. A man may hear this shower sing in the wind. And Falstaff's boy with her! Good plots, they are laid; and our revolted wives share damnation together. Well; I will take him, then torture my wife, pluck the borrowed veil of modesty from the so seeming Mistress Page, divulge Page himself for a secure and wilful Actæon; and to these violent proceedings all my neighbours shall cry aim. [*Clock heard.*] The clock gives me my cue, and my assurance bids me search: there I shall find Falstaff: I shall be rather praised for this than mocked; for it is as positive as the earth is firm that Falstaff is there: I will go.

[*Enter*] PAGE, SHALLOW, SLENDER, HOST, [SIR HUGH] EVANS, CAIUS [, *and* RUGBY].

Shal., *Page*, *&c.* Well met, Master Ford.

Ford. Trust me, a good knot: I have good cheer at home; and I pray you all go with me.

Shal. I must excuse myself, Master Ford.

Slen. And so must I, sir: we have appointed to dine with Mistress Anne, and I would not break with her for more money than I'll speak of.

Shal. We have lingered about a match between Anne Page and my cousin Slender, and this day we shall have our answer.

Slen. I hope I have your good will, father Page.

Page. You have, Master Slender; I stand wholly for you: but my wife, master doctor, is for you altogether.

Caius. Ay, be-gar; and de maid is love-a me: my nursh-a Quickly tell me so mush.

Host. What say you to young Master Fenton? he capers, he dances, he has eyes of youth, he writes verses, he speaks holiday, he smells April and May: he will carry 't, he will carry 't; 'tis in his buttons; he will carry 't.

Page. Not by my consent, I promise you. The gentleman is of no having: he kept company with the wild prince and Poins; he is of too high a region; he knows too much. No, he shall not knit a knot in his fortunes with the finger of my substance: if he take her, let him take her simply; the wealth I have waits on my consent, and my consent goes not that way.

Ford. I beseech you heartily, some of you go home with me to dinner: besides your cheer, you shall have sport; I will show you a monster. Master doctor, you shall go; so shall you, Master Page; and you, Sir Hugh.

Shal. Well, fare you well: we shall have the freer wooing at Master Page's. [*Exeunt Shal. and Slen.*]

Caius. Go home, John Rugby; I come anon. [*Exit Rugby.*]

Host. Farewell, my hearts: I will to my honest knight Falstaff, and drink canary with him. [*Exit.*]

Ford. [*Aside*] I think I shall drink in pipe-wine first with him; I'll make him dance.—Will you go, gentles?

All. Have with you to see this monster. *Exeunt.*

SCENE III. [*A room in* FORD'S *house.*]

Enter MISTRESS FORD, [*and*] MISTRESS PAGE.

Mrs Ford. What, John! What, Robert!

Mrs Page. Quickly, quickly! Is the buck-basket—

Mrs Ford. I warrant. What, Robin, I say!

[*Enter*] Servants [*with a basket*].

Mrs Page. Come, come, come.

Mrs Ford. Here, set it down.

Mrs Page. Give your men the charge; we must be brief.

Mrs Ford. Marry, as I told you before, John and Robert, be ready here hard by in the brew-house: and when I suddenly call you, come forth, and without any pause or staggering take this basket on your shoulders: that done, trudge with it in all haste, and carry it among the whitsters in Datchet-mead, and there empty it in the muddy ditch close by the Thames side.

Mrs Page. You will do it?

Mrs Ford. I ha' told them over and over; they lack no direction. Be gone, and come when you are called. [*Exeunt Servants.*]

Mrs Page. Here comes little Robin.

[*Enter*] ROBIN.

Mrs Ford. How now, my eyas-musket! what news with you?

Rob. My master, Sir John, is come in at your back-door, Mistress Ford, and requests your company.

Mrs Page. You little Jack-a-Lent, have you been true to us?

Rob. Ay, I'll be sworn. My master knows not of your being here and hath threatened to put me into everlasting liberty if I tell you of it; for he swears he'll turn me away.

Mrs Page. Thou 'rt a good boy: this secrecy of thine shall be a tailor to thee and shall make thee a new doublet and hose. I'll go hide me.

Mrs Ford. Do so. Go tell thy master I am alone. [*Exit Robin.*] Mistress Page, remember you your cue.

Mrs Page. I warrant thee; if I do not act it, hiss me. [*Exit.*]

Mrs Ford. Go to, then: we'll use this unwholesome humidity, this gross watery pumpion; we'll teach him to know turtles from jays.

[*Enter*] FALSTAFF.

Fal. Have I caught thee, my heavenly jewel? Why, now let me die, for I have lived long enough: this is the period of my ambition: O this blessed hour!

Mrs Ford. O sweet Sir John!

Fal. Mistress Ford, I cannot cog, I cannot prate,

Henry IV. New Cambridge editors think this an indication that Shakespeare intended to connect this play with others of the Prince Hal cycle and argue from the presence of the mention of Poins here, that the *Merry Wives* was hastily composed. 76. **knit a knot in,** mend. 89. **canary,** sweet wine from the Canaries. 90. **pipe-wine,** wine from the cask, or wood.

SCENE III. 2. **buck-basket,** basket for soiled linen. 14. **whitsters,** bleachers of linen. **Datchet-mead,** a meadow along the Thames, near Windsor Park. 22. **eyas-musket,** young sparrow hawk; used jocularly of a sprightly child. 27. **Jack-a-Lent,** figure of a man set up to be pelted; hence a contemptible person. 31. **liberty,** unemployment. 43. **pumpion,** pumpkin. 44. **turtles,** turtle doves, a type of constancy in love. **jays,** used to designate flashy or light women.

Mistress Ford. Now shall I sin in my wish: I would thy husband were dead: I'll speak it before the best lord; I would make thee my lady.

Mrs Ford. I your lady, Sir John! alas, I should be a pitiful lady!

Fal. Let the court of France show me such another. I see how thine eye would emulate the diamond: thou hast the right arched beauty of the brow that becomes the ship-tire, the tire-valiant, or any tire of Venetian admittance.

Mrs Ford. A plain kerchief, Sir John: my brows become nothing else; nor that well neither.

Fal. By the Lord, thou art a tyrant to say so: thou wouldst make an absolute courtier; and the firm fixture of thy foot would give an excellent motion to thy gait in a semi-circled farthingale. I see what thou wert, if Fortune thy foe were not, Nature thy friend. Come, thou canst not hide it.

Mrs Ford. Believe me, there 's no such thing in me.

Fal. What made me love thee? let that persuade thee there 's something extraordinary in thee. Come, I cannot cog and say thou art this and that, like a many of these lisping hawthornbuds, that come like women in men's apparel, and smell like Bucklersbury in simple time; I cannot: but I love thee; none but thee; and thou deservest it.

Mrs Ford. Do not betray me, sir. I fear you love Mistress Page.

Fal. Thou mightst as well say I love to walk by the Counter-gate, which is as hateful to me as the reek of a lime-kiln.

Mrs Ford. Well, heaven knows how I love you; and you shall one day find it.

Fal. Keep in that mind; I'll deserve it.

Mrs Ford. Nay, I must tell you, so you do; or else I could not be in that mind.

[*Enter* Robin.]

Rob. Mistress Ford, Mistress Ford! here 's Mistress Page at the door, sweating and blowing and looking wildly, and would needs speak with you presently.

Fal. She shall not see me: I will ensconce me behind the arras.

Mrs Ford. Pray you, do so: she 's a very tattling woman. [*Falstaff hides himself.*]

[*Enter* Mistress Page.]

What 's the matter? how now!

Mrs Page. O Mistress Ford, what have you done? You 're shamed, y' are overthrown, y' are undone for ever!

Mrs Ford. What 's the matter, good Mistress Page?

Mrs Page. O well-a-day, Mistress Ford! having an honest man to your husband, to give him such cause of suspicion!

Mrs Ford. What cause of suspicion?

Mrs Page. What cause of suspicion! Out upon you! how am I mistook in you!

Mrs Ford. Why, alas, what 's the matter?

Mrs Page. Your husband 's coming hither, woman, with all the officers in Windsor, to search for a gentleman that he says is here now in the house by your consent, to take an ill advantage of his absence: you are undone.

Mrs Ford. 'Tis not so, I hope.

Mrs Page. Pray heaven it be not so, that you have such a man here! but 'tis most certain your husband 's coming, with half Windsor at his heels, to search for such a one. I come before to tell you. If you know yourself clear, why, I am glad of it; but if you have a friend here, convey, convey him out. Be not amazed; call all your senses to you; defend your reputation, or bid farewell to your good life for ever.

Mrs Ford. What shall I do? There is a gentleman my dear friend; and I fear not mine own shame so much as his peril: I had rather than a thousand pound he were out of the house.

Mrs Page. For shame! never stand 'you had rather' and 'you had rather:' your husband 's here at hand; bethink you of some conveyance: in the house you cannot hide him. O, how have you deceived me! Look, here is a basket: if he be of any reasonable stature, he may creep in here; and throw foul linen upon him, as if it were going to bucking: or—it is whiting-time—send him by your two men to Datchet-mead.

Mrs Ford. He 's too big to go in there. What shall I do?

Fal. [*Coming forward*] Let me see 't, let me see 't, O, let me see 't! I'll in, I'll in. Follow your friend's counsel. I'll in.

Mrs Page. What, Sir John Falstaff! Are these your letters, knight?

Fal. I love thee. Help me away. Let me creep in here. I'll never—

[*Gets into the basket; they cover him with foul linen.*]

Mrs Page. Help to cover your master, boy. Call your men, Mistress Ford. You dissembling knight!

Mrs Ford. What, John! Robert! John! [*Exit Robin.*]

[*Enter* Servants.]

Go take up these clothes here quickly. Where 's the cowl-staff? look, how you drumble! Carry them to the laundress in Datchet-mead; quickly, come.

[*Enter*] Ford, Page, Caius, [*and* Sir Hugh] Evans.

Ford. Pray you, come near: if I suspect without cause, why then make sport at me; then let me be your jest; I deserve it. How now! whither bear you this?

Serv. To the laundress, forsooth.

Mrs Ford. Why, what have you to do whither they bear it? You were best meddle with buck-washing.

Ford. Buck! I would I could wash myself of the buck! Buck, buck, buck! Ay, buck; I warrant you, buck; and of the season too, it shall appear. [*Exeunt Servants with the basket.*] Gentlemen, I have dreamed to-night; I'll tell you my dream. Here, here, here be my keys: ascend my chambers; search, seek, find out: I'll warrant we'll unkennel the fox. Let me stop this way first. [*Locking the door.*] So, now uncape.

Page. Good Master Ford, be contented: you wrong yourself too much.

Ford. True, Master Page. Up, gentlemen; you shall see sport anon: follow me, gentlemen. [*Exit.*]

60. **ship-tire,** woman's headdress resembling a ship. **tire-valiant,** fanciful headdress. 69. **farthingale,** hooped petticoat. 69-70. **if Fortune . . . friend,** so punctuated in F_{2-4}; F_1Q_3: . . . *foe, were not,* etc.; Capell: *foe were not; nature is,* etc. (*is* was introduced by Pope). New Cambridge editors suggest: *if fortune, thy foe, were but as nature, thy friend. Fortune thy Foe* is the name of a popular ballad. Capell says the tune was one to which lamentations of criminals were sung. 79. **simple time,** midsummer, the time when apothecaries were supplied with simples. 85. **Counter-gate,** gate of the Counter, name for two debtors prisons in London. 127. **your good life,** your respect-

Evans. This is fery fantastical humours and jealousies.

Caius. By gar, 'tis no the fashion of France; it is not jealous in France.

Page. Nay, follow him, gentlemen; see the issue of his search. [*Exeunt Page, Caius, and Evans.*]

Mrs Page. Is there not a double excellency in this?

Mrs Ford. I know not which pleases me better, that my husband is deceived, or Sir John.

Mrs Page. What a taking was he in when your husband asked who was in the basket!

Mrs Ford. I am half afraid he will have need of washing; so throwing him into the water will do him a benefit.

Mrs Page. Hang him, dishonest rascal! I would all of the same strain were in the same distress.

Mrs Ford. I think my husband hath some special suspicion of Falstaff's being here; for I never saw him so gross in his jealousy till now.

Mrs Page. I will lay a plot to try that; and we will yet have more tricks with Falstaff: his dissolute disease will scarce obey this medicine.

Mrs Ford. Shall we send that foolish carrion, Mistress Quickly, to him, and excuse his throwing into the water; and give him another hope, to betray him to another punishment?

Mrs Page. We will do it: let him be sent for to-morrow, eight o'clock, to have amends.

[*Enter* FORD, PAGE, CAIUS, *and* SIR HUGH EVANS.]

Ford. I cannot find him: may be the knave bragged of that he could not compass.

Mrs Page. [*Aside to Mrs Ford*] Heard you that?

Mrs Ford. You use me well, Master Ford, do you?

Ford. Ay, I do so.

Mrs Ford. Heaven make you better than your thoughts!

Ford. Amen!

Mrs Page. You do yourself mighty wrong, Master Ford.

Ford. Ay, ay; I must bear it.

Evans. If there be any pody in the house, and in the chambers, and in the coffers, and in the presses, heaven forgive my sins at the day of judgement!

Caius. By gar, nor I too: there is no bodies.

Page. Fie, fie, Master Ford! are you not ashamed? What spirit, what devil suggests this imagination? I would not ha' your distemper in this kind for the wealth of Windsor Castle.

Ford. 'Tis my fault, Master Page: I suffer for it.

Evans. You suffer for a pad conscience: your wife is as honest a 'omans as I will desires among five thousand, and five hundred too.

Caius. By gar, I see 'tis an honest woman.

Ford. Well, I promised you a dinner. Come, come, walk in the Park: I pray you, pardon me; I will hereafter make known to you why I have done this. Come, wife; come, Mistress Page. I pray you, pardon me; pray heartily, pardon me.

Page. Let 's go in, gentlemen; but, trust me, we'll mock him. I do invite you to-morrow morning to my house to breakfast: after, we'll a-birding together; I have a fine hawk for the bush. Shall it be so?

Ford. Any thing.

Evans. If there is one, I shall make two in the company.

Caius. If dere be one or two, I shall make-a the turd.

Ford. Pray you, go, Master Page.

Evans. I pray you now, remembrance to-morrow on the lousy knave, mine host.

Caius. Dat is good; by gar, with all my heart!

Evans. A lousy knave, to have his gibes and his mockeries! *Exeunt.*

SCENE IV. [*A room in* PAGE'S *house.*]

Enter FENTON, [*and*] ANNE PAGE.

Fent. I see I cannot get thy father's love;
Therefore no more turn me to him, sweet Nan.
Anne. Alas, how then?
Fent. Why, thou must be thyself.
He doth object I am too great of birth;
And that, my state being gall'd with my expense,
I seek to heal it only by his wealth:
Besides these, other bars he lays before me,
My riots past, my wild societies;
And tells me 'tis a thing impossible
I should love thee but as a property.
Anne. May be he tells you true.
Fent. No, heaven so speed me in my time to come!
Albeit I will confess thy father's wealth
Was the first motive that I woo'd thee, Anne:
Yet, wooing thee, I found thee of more value
Than stamps in gold or sums in sealed bags;
And 'tis the very riches of thyself
That now I aim at.
Anne. Gentle Master Fenton,
Yet seek my father's love; still seek it, sir:
If opportunity and humblest suit
Cannot attain it, why, then,—hark you hither!
[*They converse apart.*]

[*Enter*] SHALLOW, SLENDER, [*and* MISTRESS] QUICKLY.

Shal. Break their talk, Mistress Quickly: my kinsman shall speak for himself.

Slen. I'll make a shaft or a bolt on 't: 'slid, 'tis but venturing.

Shal. Be not dismayed.

Slen. No, she shall not dismay me: I care not for that, but that I am afeard.

Quick. Hark ye; Master Slender would speak a word with you.

Anne. I come to him. [*Aside*] This is my father's choice.
O, what a world of vile ill-favour'd faults
Looks handsome in three hundred pounds a-year!

Quick. And how does good Master Fenton? Pray you, a word with you.

Shal. She 's coming; to her, coz. O boy, thou hadst a father!

Slen. I had a father, Mistress Anne; my uncle can tell you good jests of him. Pray you, uncle, tell Mis-

ability. 140. **bucking,** washing. 156. **cowl-staff,** pole on which a "cowl" or basket is carried between two persons. **drumble,** be sluggish. 174. **unkennel,** reveal, unearth. 176. **uncape,** unearth (as of a fox?). 177. **be contented,** be calm; do not worry. 197. **strain,** character, kind. 255-256. **remembrance . . . host,** a seeming allusion to the plot carried out in IV, v.

SCENE IV. 16. **stamps in gold,** gold coins. 24. **make . . . on 't,** make a good or bad job of it; a reference to the difference in the degree of skill required for making a shaft or a bolt (Hart). **'slid,** an oath, by God's lid.

tress Anne the jest, how my father stole two geese out of a pen, good uncle.

Shal. Mistress Anne, my cousin loves you.

Slen. Ay, that I do; as well as I love any woman in Gloucestershire.

Shal. He will maintain you like a gentlewoman.

Slen. Ay, that I will, come cut and long-tail, under the degree of a squire.

Shal. He will make you a hundred and fifty pounds jointure.

Anne. Good Master Shallow, let him woo for himself.

Shal. Marry, I thank you for it; I thank you for that good comfort. She calls you, coz: I'll leave you.

Anne. Now, Master Slender,—

Slen. Now, good Mistress Anne,—

Anne. What is your will?

Slen. My will! 'od's heartlings, that 's a pretty jest indeed! I ne'er made my will yet, I thank God; I am not such a sickly creature, I give heaven praise.

Anne. I mean, Master Slender, what would you with me?

Slen. Truly, for mine own part, I would little or nothing with you. Your father and my uncle hath made motions: if it be my luck, so; if not, happy man be his dole! They can tell you how things go better than I can: you may ask your father; here he comes.

[*Enter*] PAGE, [*and*] MISTRESS PAGE.

Page. Now, Master Slender: love him, daughter Anne.
Why, how now! what does Master Fenton here?
You wrong me, sir, thus still to haunt my house:
I told you, sir, my daughter is dispos'd of.

Fent. Nay, Master Page, be not impatient.

Mrs Page. Good Master Fenton, come not to my child.

Page. She is no match for you.

Fent. Sir, will you hear me?

Page. No, good Master Fenton.
Come, Master Shallow; come, son Slender, in.
Knowing my mind, you wrong me, Master Fenton.
[*Exeunt Page, Shal., and Slen.*]

Quick. Speak to Mistress Page.

Fent. Good Mistress Page, for that I love your daughter
In such a righteous fashion as I do,
Perforce, against all checks, rebukes and manners,
I must advance the colours of my love
And not retire: let me have your good will.

Anne. Good mother, do not marry me to yond fool.

Mrs Page. I mean it not; I seek you a better husband.

Quick. That 's my master, master doctor.

Anne. Alas, I had rather be set quick i' th' earth
And bowl'd to death with turnips!

Mrs Page. Come, trouble not yourself. Good Master Fenton,
I will not be your friend nor enemy:
My daughter will I question how she loves you,
And as I find her, so am I affected.
Till then farewell, sir: she must needs go in;
Her father will be angry.

Fent. Farewell, gentle mistress: farewell, Nan.
[*Exeunt Mrs Page and Anne.*]

Quick. This is my doing, now: 'Nay,' said I, 'will you cast away your child on a fool, and a physician? Look on Master Fenton:' this is my doing.

Fent. I thank thee; and I pray thee, once to-night
Give my sweet Nan this ring: there 's for thy pains.

Quick. Now heaven send thee good fortune! [*Exit Fenton.*] A kind heart he hath: a woman would run through fire and water for such a kind heart. But yet I would my master had Mistress Anne; or I would Master Slender had her; or, in sooth, I would Master Fenton had her: I will do what I can for them all three; for so I have promised, and I'll be as good as my word; but speciously for Master Fenton. Well, I must of another errand to Sir John Falstaff from my two mistresses: what a beast am I to slack it! *Exit.*

SCENE V. [*A room in the Garter Inn.*]

Enter FALSTAFF, [*and*] BARDOLPH.

Fal. Bardolph, I say,—

Bard. Here, sir.

Fal. Go fetch me a quart of sack; put a toast in 't. [*Exit Bard.*] Have I lived to be carried in a basket, like a barrow of butcher's offal, and to be thrown in the Thames? Well, if I be served such another trick, I'll have my brains ta'en out and buttered, and give them to a dog for a new-year's gift. The rogues slighted me into the river with as little remorse as they would have drowned a blind bitch's puppies, fifteen i' the litter: and you may know by my size that I have a kind of alacrity in sinking; if the bottom were as deep as hell, I should down. I had been drowned, but that the shore was shelvy and shallow,—a death that I abhor; for the water swells a man; and what a thing should I have been when I had been swelled! I should have been a mountain of mummy.

[*Enter* BARDOLPH *with sack.*]

Bard. Here 's Mistress Quickly, sir, to speak with you.

Fal. Come, let me pour in some sack to the Thames water; for my belly 's as cold as if I had swallowed snowballs for pills to cool the reins. Call her in.

Bard. Come in, woman!

[*Enter* MISTRESS] QUICKLY.

Quick. By your leave; I cry you mercy: give your worship good morrow.

Fal. Take away these chalices. Go brew me a pottle of sack finely.

Bard. With eggs, sir?

Fal. Simple of itself; I'll no pullet-sperm in my brewage. [*Exit Bardolph.*] How now!

Quick. Marry, sir, I come to your worship from Mistress Ford.

Fal. Mistress Ford! I have had ford enough; I was thrown into the ford; I have my belly full of ford.

Quick. Alas the day! good heart, that was not her fault: she does so take on with her men; they mistook their erection.

47. **cut and long-tail,** horses or dogs with docked and long tails; i.e., all sorts of people. 59. **'od's,** minced form of "God's" used in oaths. **heartlings,** little hearts. 68. **happy . . . dole,** may it be (his) portion to be a happy man. 84. **checks,** reproofs; see glossary. 113. **speciously,** a malapropism for "specially."
SCENE V. 3. **toast,** piece of toast put into a drink. 9. **slighted,**

Fal. So did I mine, to build upon a foolish woman's promise.

Quick. Well, she laments, sir, for it, that it would yearn your heart to see it. Her husband goes this morning a-birding; she desires you once more to come to her between eight and nine: I must carry her word quickly: she'll make you amends, I warrant you.

Fal. Well, I will visit her: tell her so; and bid her think what a man is: let her consider his frailty, and then judge of my merit.

Quick. I will tell her.

Fal. Do so. Between nine and ten, sayest thou?

Quick. Eight and nine, sir.

Fal. Well, be gone: I will not miss her.

Quick. Peace be with you, sir. [*Exit.*]

Fal. I marvel I hear not of Master Brook; he sent me word to stay within: I like his money well. O, here he comes.

[*Enter*] FORD.

Ford. Bless you, sir!

Fal. Now, Master Brook, you come to know what hath passed between me and Ford's wife?

Ford. That, indeed, Sir John, is my business.

Fal. Master Brook, I will not lie to you: I was at her house the hour she appointed me.

Ford. And sped you, sir?

Fal. Very ill-favouredly, Master Brook.

Ford. How so, sir? Did she change her determination?

Fal. No, Master Brook; but the peaking Cornuto her husband, Master Brook, dwelling in a continual 'larum of jealousy, comes me in the instant of our encounter, after we had embraced, kissed, protested, and, as it were, spoke the prologue of our comedy; and at his heels a rabble of his companions, thither provoked and instigated by his distemper, and, forsooth, to search his house for his wife's love.

Ford. What, while you were there?

Fal. While I was there.

Ford. And did he search for you, and could not find you?

Fal. You shall hear. As good luck would have it, comes in one Mistress Page; gives intelligence of Ford's approach; and, in her invention and Ford's wife's distraction, they conveyed me into a buck-basket.

Ford. A buck-basket!

Fal. By the Lord, a buck-basket! rammed me in with foul shirts and smocks, socks, foul stockings, greasy napkins; that, Master Brook, there was the rankest compound of villanous smell that ever offended nostril.

Ford. And how long lay you there?

Fal. Nay, you shall hear, Master Brook, what I have suffered to bring this woman to evil for your good. Being thus crammed in the basket, a couple of Ford's knaves, his hinds, were called forth by their mistress to carry me in the name of foul clothes to Datchet-lane: they took me on their shoulders; met the jealous knave their master in the door, who asked them once or twice what they had in their basket: I quaked for fear, lest the lunatic knave would have searched it; but fate, ordaining he should be a cuckold, held his hand. Well: on went he for a search, and away went I for foul clothes. But mark the sequel, Master Brook: I suffered the pangs of three several deaths; first, an intolerable fright, to be detected with a jealous rotten bell-wether; next, to be compassed, like a good bilbo, in the circumference of a peck, hilt to point, heel to head; and then, to be stopped in, like a strong distillation, with stinking clothes that fretted in their own grease: think of that,—a man of my kidney,—think of that,—that am as subject to heat as butter; a man of continual dissolution and thaw: it was a miracle to 'scape suffocation. And in the height of this bath, when I was more than half stewed in grease, like a Dutch dish, to be thrown into the Thames, and cooled, glowing hot, in that surge, like a horse-shoe; think of that,—hissing hot,—think of that, Master Brook.

Ford. In good sadness, sir, I am sorry that for my sake you have suffered all this. My suit then is desperate; you'll undertake her no more?

Fal. Master Brook, I will be thrown into Etna, as I have been into Thames, ere I will leave her thus. Her husband is this morning gone a-birding: I have received from her another embassy of meeting; 'twixt eight and nine is the hour, Master Brook.

Ford. 'Tis past eight already, sir.

Fal. Is it? I will then address me to my appointment. Come to me at your convenient leisure, and you shall know how I speed; and the conclusion shall be crowned with your enjoying her. Adieu. You shall have her, Master Brook; Master Brook, you shall cuckold Ford. [*Exit.*]

Ford. Hum! ha! is this a vision? is this a dream? do I sleep? Master Ford, awake! awake, Master Ford! there 's a hole made in your best coat, Master Ford. This 'tis to be married! this 'tis to have linen and buck-baskets! Well, I will proclaim myself what I am: I will now take the lecher; he is at my house; he cannot 'scape me; 'tis impossible he should; he cannot creep into a halfpenny purse, nor into a pepper-box: but, lest the devil that guides him should aid him, I will search impossible places. Though what I am I cannot avoid, yet to be what I would not shall not make me tame: if I have horns to make one mad, let the proverb go with me: I'll be horn-mad. *Exit.*

ACT IV.

SCENE I. [*A street.*]

Enter MISTRESS PAGE, [MISTRESS] QUICKLY, [*and*] WILLIAM.

Mrs Page. Is he at Master Ford's already, think'st thou?

Quick. Sure he is by this, or will be presently: but, truly, he is very courageous mad about his throwing into the water. Mistress Ford desires you to come suddenly.

Mrs Page. I'll be with her by and by; I'll but bring my young man here to school. Look, where his master comes; 'tis a playing-day, I see.

tossed heedlessly. 10. **remorse,** pity, compassion; see glossary. 24. **reins,** kidneys. 29. **chalices,** wine cups. 41. **erection,** a malapropism for "direction." 71. **Cornuto,** cuckold. 112. **bilbo.** Cf. I, i, 165, note. 116. **kidney,** temperament.

ACT IV. SCENE I. 4. **courageous,** Quickly's error for "outrageous." 9. **playing-day,** holiday.

[*Enter* Sir Hugh] Evans.

How now, Sir Hugh! no school to-day?

Evans. No; Master Slender is let the boys leave to play.

Quick. Blessing of his heart!

Mrs Page. Sir Hugh, my husband says my son profits nothing in the world at his book. I pray you, ask him some questions in his accidence.

Evans. Come hither, William; hold up your head; come.

Mrs Page. Come on, sirrah; hold up your head; answer your master, be not afraid.

Evans. William, how many numbers is in nouns?

Will. Two.

Quick. Truly, I thought there had been one number more, because they say, ''Od's nouns.'

Evans. Peace your tattlings! What is 'fair,' William?

Will. Pulcher.

Quick. Polecats! there are fairer things than polecats, sure.

Evans. You are a very simplicity 'oman: I pray you, peace. What is 'lapis,' William?

Will. A stone.

Evans. And what is 'a stone,' William?

Will. A pebble.

Evans. No, it is 'lapis:' I pray you, remember in your prain.

Will. Lapis.

Evans. That is a good William. What is he, William, that does lend articles?

Will. Articles are borrowed of the pronoun, and be thus declined, Singulariter, nominativo, hic, hæc, hoc.

Evans. Nominativo, hig, hag, hog; pray you, mark: genitivo, hujus. Well, what is your accusative case?

Will. Accusativo, hinc.

Evans. I pray you, have your remembrance, child; accusativo, hung, hang, hog.

Quick. 'Hang-hog' is Latin for bacon, I warrant you.

Evans. Leave your prabbles, 'oman. What is the focative case, William?

Will. O,—vocativo, O.

Evans. Remember, William; focative is caret.

Quick. And that 's a good root.

Evans. 'Oman, forbear.

Mrs Page. Peace!

Evans. What is your genitive case plural, William?

Will. Genitive case!

Evans. Ay.

Will. Genitive,—horum, harum, horum.

Quick. Vengeance of Jenny's case! fie on her! never name her, child, if she be a whore.

Evans. For shame, 'oman.

Quick. You do ill to teach the child such words: he teaches him to hick and to hack, which they'll do fast enough of themselves, and to call 'horum:' fie upon you!

Evans. 'Oman, art thou lunatics? hast thou no understandings for thy cases and the numbers of the genders? Thou art as foolish Christian creatures as I would desires.

Mrs Page. Prithee, hold thy peace.

Evans. Show me now, William, some declensions of your pronouns.

Will. Forsooth, I have forgot.

Evans. It is qui, quæ, quod: if you forget your 'quies,' your 'quæs,' and your 'quods,' you must be preeches. Go your ways, and play; go.

Mrs Page. He is a better scholar than I thought he was.

Evans. He is a good sprag memory. Farewell, Mistress Page.

Mrs Page. Adieu, good Sir Hugh. [*Exit Sir Hugh.*] Get you home, boy. Come, we stay too long. *Exeunt.*

Scene II. [*A room in* Ford's *house.*]

Enter Falstaff, [*and*] Mistress Ford.

Fal. Mistress Ford, your sorrow hath eaten up my sufferance. I see you are obsequious in your love, and I profess requital to a hair's breadth; not only, Mistress Ford, in the simple office of love, but in all the accoutrement, complement and ceremony of it. But are you sure of your husband now?

Mrs Ford. He 's a-birding, sweet Sir John.

Mrs Page. [*Within*] What, ho, gossip Ford! what, ho!

Mrs Ford. Step into the chamber, Sir John. [*Exit Falstaff.*]

[*Enter*] Mistress Page.

Mrs Page. How now, sweetheart! who 's at home besides yourself?

Mrs Ford. Why, none but mine own people.

Mrs Page. Indeed!

Mrs Ford. No, certainly. [*Aside to her*] Speak louder.

Mrs Page. Truly, I am so glad you have nobody here.

Mrs Ford. Why?

Mrs Page. Why, woman, your husband is in his old lunes again: he so takes on yonder with my husband; so rails against all married mankind; so curses all Eve's daughters, of what complexion soever; and so buffets himself on the forehead, crying, 'Peer out, peer out!' that any madness I ever yet beheld seemed but tameness, civility and patience, to this his distemper he is in now: I am glad the fat knight is not here.

Mrs Ford. Why, does he talk of him?

Mrs Page. Of none but him; and swears he was carried out, the last time he searched for him, in a basket; protests to my husband he is now here, and hath drawn him and the rest of their company from their sport, to make another experiment of his suspicion: but I am glad the knight is not here; now he shall see his own foolery.

Mrs Ford. How near is he, Mistress Page?

Mrs Page. Hard by; at street end; he will be here anon.

Mrs Ford. I am undone! The knight is here.

Mrs Page. Why then you are utterly shamed, and he 's but a dead man. What a woman are you!—Away with him, away with him! better shame than murder.

Mrs Ford. Which way should he go? how should I

16. **accidence,** rudiments of Latin grammar. 25. **nouns,** wounds; Quickly's error. 29. **polecats.** Many of Quickly's misconstruings are bawdy: polecats (prostitutes), horum (whores), harum (hare, prostitute), Jenny's case (a whore's pudendum), etc.
81. **preeches,** breeched, i.e., whipped. 84. **sprag,** sprack, lively, alert.
Scene II. 2. **sufferance,** suffering, pain. 3. **obsequious,** devoted

bestow him? Shall I put him into the basket again?

[*Enter* FALSTAFF.]

Fal. No, I'll come no more i' the basket. May I not go out ere he come?

Mrs Page. Alas, three of Master Ford's brothers watch the door with pistols, that none shall issue out; otherwise you might slip away ere he came. But what make you here?

Fal. What shall I do? I'll creep up into the chimney.

Mrs Ford. There they always use to discharge their birding-pieces.

Mrs Page. Creep into the kiln-hole.

Fal. Where is it?

Mrs Ford. He will seek there, on my word. Neither press, coffer, chest, trunk, well, vault, but he hath an abstract for the remembrance of such places, and goes to them by his note: there is no hiding you in the house.

Fal. I'll go out then.

Mrs Page. If you go out in your own semblance, you die, Sir John. Unless you go out disguised—

Mrs Ford. How might we disguise him?

Mrs Page. Alas the day, I know not! There is no woman's gown big enough for him; otherwise he might put on a hat, a muffler and a kerchief, and so escape.

Fal. Good hearts, devise something; any extremity rather than a mischief.

Mrs Ford. My maid's aunt, the fat woman of Brainford, has a gown above.

Mrs Page. On my word, it will serve him; she 's as big as he is: and there 's her thrummed hat and her muffler too. Run up, Sir John.

Mrs Ford. Go, go, sweet Sir John: Mistress Page and I will look some linen for your head.

Mrs Page. Quick, quick! we'll come dress you straight: put on the gown the while. [*Exit Falstaff.*]

Mrs. Ford. I would my husband would meet him in this shape: he cannot abide the old woman of Brainford; he swears she 's a witch; forbade her my house and hath threatened to beat her.

Mrs Page. Heaven guide him to thy husband's cudgel, and the devil guide his cudgel afterwards!

Mrs Ford. But is my husband coming?

Mrs Page. Ay, in good sadness, is he; and talks of the basket too, howsoever he hath had intelligence.

Mrs Ford. We'll try that; for I'll appoint my men to carry the basket again, to meet him at the door with it, as they did last time.

Mrs Page. Nay, but he'll be here presently: let 's go dress him like the witch of Brainford.

Mrs Ford. I'll first direct my men what they shall do with the basket. Go up; I'll bring linen for him straight. [*Exit.*]

Mrs Page. Hang him, dishonest varlet! we cannot misuse him enough.

We'll leave a proof, by that which we will do,
Wives may be merry, and yet honest too:
We do not act that often jest and laugh;
'Tis old, but true, Still swine eats all the draff. [*Exit.*]

[*Enter* MISTRESS FORD *with two*] Servants.

Mrs Ford. Go, sirs, take the basket again on your shoulders: your master is hard at door; if he bid you set it down, obey him: quickly, dispatch. [*Exit.*]

First Serv. Come, come, take it up.

Sec. Serv. Pray heaven it be not full of knight again.

First Serv. I hope not; I had as lief bear so much lead.

[*Enter*] FORD, PAGE, CAIUS, [SIR HUGH] EVANS, [*and*] SHALLOW.

Ford. Ay, but if it prove true, Master Page, have you any way then to unfool me again? Set down the basket, villain! Somebody call my wife. Youth in a basket! O you pandarly rascals! there 's a knot, a ging, a pack, a conspiracy against me: now shall the devil be shamed. What, wife, I say! Come, come forth! Behold what honest clothes you send forth to bleaching!

Page. Why, this passes, Master Ford; you are not to go loose any longer; you must be pinioned.

Evans. Why, this is lunatics! this is mad as a mad dog!

Shal. Indeed, Master Ford, this is not well, indeed.

Ford. So say I too, sir.

[*Enter* MISTRESS FORD.]

Come hither, Mistress Ford; Mistress Ford, the honest woman, the modest wife, the virtuous creature, that hath the jealous fool to her husband! I suspect without cause, mistress, do I?

Mrs Ford. Heaven be my witness you do, if you suspect me in any dishonesty.

Ford. Well said, brazen-face! hold it out. Come forth, sirrah! [*Pulling clothes out of the basket.*]

Page. This passes!

Mrs Ford. Are you not ashamed? let the clothes alone.

Ford. I shall find you anon.

Evans. 'Tis unreasonable! Will you take up your wife's clothes? Come away.

Ford. Empty the basket, I say!

Mrs Ford. Why, man, why?

Ford. Master Page, as I am a man, there was one conveyed out of my house yesterday in this basket: why may not he be there again? In my house I am sure he is: my intelligence is true; my jealousy is reasonable. Pluck me out all the linen.

Mrs Ford. If you find a man there, he shall die a flea's death.

Page. Here 's no man.

Shal. By my fidelity, this is not well, Master Ford; this wrongs you.

Evans. Master Ford, you must pray, and not follow the imaginations of your own heart: this is jealousies.

Ford. Well, he 's not here I seek for.

Page. No, nor nowhere else but in your brain.

Ford. Help to search my house this one time. If I find not what I seek, show no colour for my extremity; let me for ever be your table-sport; let them say of me, 'As jealous as Ford, that searched a hollow walnut for his wife's leman.' Satisfy me once more; once more search with me.

Mrs Ford. What, ho, Mistress Page! come you and

zealously. 22. **lunes,** lunacies. 63. **abstract,** inventory. 77. **Brainford,** Brentford. 80. **thrummed,** made of coarse yarn. 109. **draff,** pig-wash. 122. **Youth . . . basket.** A contemporary phrase meaning "fortunate lover." 123. **ging,** gang, set. 128. **passes,** surpasses, goes beyond all bounds. 169. **your table-sport,** butt or laughingstock of the company. 172. **leman,** paramour.

the old woman down; my husband will come into the chamber.

Ford. Old woman! what old woman 's that?

Mrs Ford. Why, it is my maid's aunt of Brainford.

Ford. A witch, a quean, an old cozening quean! Have I not forbid her my house? She comes of errands, does she? We are simple men; we do not know what 's brought to pass under the profession of fortune-telling. She works by charms, by spells, by the figure, and such daubery as this is, beyond our element: we know nothing. Come down, you witch, you hag, you; come down, I say!

Mrs Ford. Nay, good, sweet husband! Good gentlemen, let him not strike the old woman.

[*Enter* FALSTAFF *in woman's clothes, and* MISTRESS PAGE.]

Mrs Page. Come, Mother Prat; come, give me your hand.

Ford. I'll prat her. [*Beating him*] Out of my door, you witch, you hag, you baggage, you polecat, you ronyon! out, out! I'll conjure you, I'll fortune-tell you. [*Exit Falstaff.*]

Mrs Page. Are you not ashamed? I think you have killed the poor woman.

Mrs Ford. Nay, he will do it. 'Tis a goodly credit for you.

Ford. Hang her, witch!

Evans. By Jeshu, I think the 'oman is a witch indeed: I like not when a 'oman has a great peard; I spy a great peard under his muffler.

Ford. Will you follow, gentlemen? I beseech you, follow; see but the issue of my jealousy: if I cry out thus upon no trail, never trust me when I open again.

Page. Let 's obey his humour a little further: come, gentlemen. [*Exeunt Ford, Page, Shal., Caius, and Evans.*]

Mrs Page. Trust me, he beat him most pitifully.

Mrs Ford. Nay, by the mass, that he did not; he beat him most unpitifully, methought.

Mrs Page. I'll have the cudgel hallowed and hung o'er the altar; it hath done meritorious service.

Mrs Ford. What think you? may we, with the warrant of womanhood and the witness of a good conscience, pursue him with any further revenge?

Mrs Page. The spirit of wantonness is, sure, scared out of him: if the devil have him not in fee-simple, with fine and recovery, he will never, I think, in the way of waste, attempt us again.

Mrs Ford. Shall we tell our husbands how we have served him?

Mrs Page. Yes, by all means; if it be but to scrape the figures out of your husband's brains. If they can find in their hearts the poor unvirtuous fat knight shall be any further afflicted, we two will still be the ministers.

Mrs Ford. I'll warrant they'll have him publicly shamed: and methinks there would be no period to the jest, should he not be publicly shamed.

Mrs Page. Come, to the forge with it then; shape it: I would not have things cool. *Exeunt.*

SCENE III. [*A room in the Garter Inn.*]

Enter HOST *and* BARDOLPH.

Bard. Sir, the Germans desire to have three of your horses: the duke himself will be to-morrow at court, and they are going to meet him.

Host. What duke should that be comes so secretly? I hear not of him in the court. Let me speak with the gentlemen: they speak English?

Bard. Ay, sir; I'll call them to you.

Host. They shall have my horses; but I'll make them pay; I'll sauce them: they have had my house a week at command; I have turned away my other guests: they must come off; I'll sauce them. Come. *Exeunt.*

SCENE IV. [*A room in* FORD'S *house.*]

Enter PAGE, FORD, MISTRESS PAGE, MISTRESS FORD, *and* [SIR HUGH] EVANS.

Evans. 'Tis one of the best discretions of a 'oman as ever I did look upon.

Page. And did he send you both these letters at an instant?

Mrs Page. Within a quarter of an hour.

Ford. Pardon me, wife. Henceforth do what thou wilt;
I rather will suspect the sun with cold
Than thee with wantonness: now doth thy honour stand,
In him that was of late an heretic,
As firm as faith.

Page. 'Tis well, 'tis well; no more:
Be not as extreme in submission
As in offence.
But let our plot go forward: let our wives
Yet once again, to make us public sport,
Appoint a meeting with this old fat fellow,
Where we may take him and disgrace him for it.

Ford. There is no better way than that they spoke of.

Page. How? to send him word they'll meet him in the park at midnight? Fie, fie! he'll never come.

Evans. You say he has been thrown in the rivers and has been grievously peaten as an old 'oman: methinks there should be terrors in him that he should not come; methinks his flesh is punished, he shall have no desires.

Page. So think I too.

Mrs Ford. Devise but how you'll use him when he comes,
And let us two devise to bring him thither.

Mrs Page. There is an old tale goes that Herne the hunter,
Sometime a keeper here in Windsor forest,
Doth all the winter-time, at still midnight,
Walk round about an oak, with great ragg'd horns;
And there he blasts the tree and takes the cattle
And makes milch-kine yield blood and shakes a chain
In a most hideous and dreadful manner:
You have heard of such a spirit, and well you know
The superstitious idle-headed eld
Receiv'd and did deliver to our age
This tale of Herne the hunter for a truth.

Page. Why, yet there want not many that do fear
In deep of night to walk by this Herne's oak:
But what of this?

180. **quean,** jade, hussy. 186. **daubery,** false show. 195. **ronyon,** abusive term for a woman. 208. **upon no trail,** i.e., when there is no scent. 225. **fee-simple,** estate belonging to an owner and his heirs forever; hence, absolute possession. 226. **waste,** spoliation. 231. **figures,** fantasies, conceits.

SCENE III. 11. **sauce,** to make (a person) pay dearly. 12. **at command,** retained for their use upon their expected arrival (Hart). 13. **come off,** pay, disburse handsomely.

Mrs Ford. Marry, this is our device;
That Falstaff at that oak shall meet with us,
[Disguis'd like Herne, with huge horns on his head.]
Page. Well, let it not be doubted but he'll come:
And in this shape when you have brought him thither,
What shall be done with him? what is your plot?
Mrs Page. That likewise have we thought upon, and thus:
Nan Page my daughter and my little son
And three or four more of their growth we'll dress
Like urchins, ouphes and fairies, green and white,
With rounds of waxen tapers on their heads,
And rattles in their hands: upon a sudden,
As Falstaff, she and I, are newly met,
Let them from forth a sawpit rush at once
With some diffused song: upon their sight,
We two in great amazedness will fly:
Then let them all encircle him about
And, fairy-like, to pinch the unclean knight,
And ask him why, that hour of fairy revel,
In their so sacred paths he dares to tread
In shape profane.
Mrs Ford. And till he tell the truth,
Let the supposed fairies pinch him sound
And burn him with their tapers.
Mrs Page. The truth being known,
We'll all present ourselves, dis-horn the spirit,
And mock him home to Windsor.
Ford. The children must
Be practis'd well to this, or they'll nev'r do 't.

Evans. I will teach the children their behaviours; and I will be like a jack-an-apes also, to burn the knight with my taber.

Ford. That will be excellent. I'll go buy them vizards.

Mrs Page. My Nan shall be the queen of all the fairies,
Finely attired in a robe of white.
Page. That silk will I go buy. [*Aside*] And in that tire
Shall Master Slender steal my Nan away
And marry her at Eton.—Go send to Falstaff straight.
Ford. Nay, I'll to him again in name of Brook:
He'll tell me all his purpose: sure, he'll come.
Mrs Page. Fear not you that. Go get us properties
And tricking for our fairies.

Evans. Let us about it: it is admirable pleasures and fery honest knaveries. [*Exeunt Page, Ford, and Evans.*]

Mrs Page. Go, Mistress Ford,
Send quickly to Sir John, to know his mind.
[*Exit Mrs Ford.*]
I'll to the doctor: he hath my good will,
And none but he, to marry with Nan Page.
That Slender, though well landed, is an idiot;
And he my husband best of all affects.
The doctor is well money'd, and his friends
Potent at court: he, none but he, shall have her,
Though twenty thousand worthier come to crave her.
[*Exit.*]

SCENE V. [*A room in the Garter Inn.*]

Enter HOST, [*and*] SIMPLE.

Host. What wouldst thou have, boor? what, thick-skin? speak, breathe, discuss; brief, short, quick, snap.

Sim. Marry, sir, I come to speak with Sir John Falstaff from Master Slender.

Host. There 's his chamber, his house, his castle, his standing-bed and truckle-bed; 'tis painted about with the story of the Prodigal, fresh and new. Go knock and call; he'll speak like an Anthropophaginian unto thee: knock, I say.

Sim. There 's an old woman, a fat woman, gone up into his chamber: I'll be so bold as stay, sir, till she come down; I come to speak with her, indeed.

Host. Ha! a fat woman! the knight may be robbed: I'll call. Bully knight! bully Sir John! speak from thy lungs military: art thou there? it is thine host, thine Ephesian, calls.

Fal. [*Within*] How now, mine host!

Host. Here 's a Bohemian-Tartar tarries the coming down of thy fat woman. Let her descend, bully, let her descend; my chambers are honourable: fie! privacy? fie!

[*Enter*] FALSTAFF.

Fal. There was, mine host, an old fat woman even now with me; but she 's gone.

Sim. Pray you, sir, was 't not the wise woman of Brainford?

Fal. Ay, marry, was it, mussel-shell: what would you with her?

Sim. My master, sir, Master Slender, sent to her, seeing her go thorough the streets, to know, sir, whether one Nym, sir, that beguiled him of a chain, had the chain or no.

Fal. I spake with the old woman about it.

Sim. And what says she, I pray, sir?

Fal. Marry, she says that the very same man that beguiled Master Slender of his chain cozened him of it.

Sim. I would I could have spoken with the woman herself; I had other things to have spoken with her too from him.

Fal. What are they? let us know.

Host. Ay, come; quick.

Sim. I may not conceal them, sir.

Host. Conceal them, or thou diest.

Sim. Why, sir, they were nothing but about Mistress Anne Page; to know if it were my master's fortune to have her or no.

Fal. 'Tis, 'tis his fortune.

Sim. What, sir?

Fal. To have her, or no. Go; say the woman told me so.

Sim. May I be bold to say so, sir?

Fal. Ay, sir; like who more bold.

Sim. I thank your worship: I shall make my master glad with these tidings. [*Exit.*]

Host. Thou art clerkly, thou art clerkly, Sir John. Was there a wise woman with thee?

Fal. Ay, that there was, mine host; one that hath taught me more wit than ever I learned before in my life; and I paid nothing for it neither, but was paid for my learning.

[*Enter*] BARDOLPH.

SCENE IV. 1-2. **best . . . 'oman,** most discreet woman. 36. **eld,** old age. 49. **urchins, ouphes,** terms for goblins. 54. **diffused,** confused, disorderly. 70. **vizards,** visors. 73. **tire,** attire.

SCENE V. 8. **the Prodigal.** Cf. *2 Henry IV*, II, i, 157, where this story is again associated with Falstaff. 10. **Anthropophaginian,** cannibal. 19. **Ephesian,** boon companion (Onions). 21. **Bohemian-Tartar.** Cf. *Hungarian* (I, iii, 23) and *Phrygian Turk* (I, iii, 97). 29. **mussel-shell,** one who gapes (Onions).

Bard. Out, alas, sir! cozenage, mere cozenage!

Host. Where be my horses? speak well of them, varletto.

Bard. Run away with the cozeners; for so soon as I came beyond Eton, they threw me off from behind one of them, in a slough of mire; and set spurs and away, like three German devils, three Doctor Faustuses.

Host. They are gone but to meet the duke, villain: do not say they be fled; Germans are honest men.

[*Enter* SIR HUGH] EVANS.

Evans. Where is mine host?

Host. What is the matter, sir?

Evans. Have a care of your entertainments: there is a friend of mine come to town, tells me there is three cozen-germans that has cozened all the hosts of Readins, of Maidenhead, of Colebrook, of horses and money. I tell you for good will, look you: you are wise and full of gibes and vlouting-stocks, and 'tis not convenient you should be cozened. Fare you well. [*Exit.*]

[*Enter* DOCTOR] CAIUS.

Caius. Vere is mine host de Jarteer?

Host. Here, master doctor, in perplexity and doubtful dilemma.

Caius. I cannot tell vat is dat: but it is tell-a me dat you make grand preparation for a duke de Jamany: by my trot, dere is no duke dat the court is know to come. I tell you for good vill: adieu. [*Exit.*]

Host. Hue and cry, villain, go! Assist me, knight. I am undone! Fly, run, hue and cry, villain! I am undone! [*Exeunt Host and Bard.*]

Fal. I would all the world might be cozened; for I have been cozened and beaten too. If it should come to the ear of the court, how I have been transformed and how my transformation hath been washed and cudgelled, they would melt me out of my fat drop by drop and liquor fishermen's boots with me: I warrant they would whip me with their fine wits till I were as crest-fallen as a dried pear. I never prospered since I forswore myself at primero. Well, if my wind were but long enough to say my prayers, I would repent.

[*Enter* MISTRESS] QUICKLY.

Now, whence come you?

Quick. From the two parties, forsooth.

Fal. The devil take one party and his dam the other! and so they shall be both bestowed. I have suffered more for their sakes, more than the villanous inconstancy of man's disposition is able to bear.

Quick. And have not they suffered? Yes, I warrant; speciously one of them; Mistress Ford, good heart, is beaten black and blue, that you cannot see a white spot about her.

Fal. What tellest thou me of black and blue? I was beaten myself into all the colours of the rainbow; and I was like to be apprehended for the witch of Brainford: but that my admirable dexterity of wit, my counterfeiting the action of an old woman, delivered me, the knave constable had set me i' the stocks, i' the common stocks, for a witch.

Quick. Sir, let me speak with you in your chamber: you shall hear how things go; and, I warrant, to your content. Here is a letter will say somewhat. Good hearts, what ado here is to bring you together! Sure, one of you does not serve heaven well, that you are so crossed.

Fal. Come up into my chamber. *Exeunt.*

SCENE VI. [*Another room in the Garter Inn.*]

Enter FENTON, [*and*] HOST.

Host. Master Fenton, talk not to me; my mind is heavy: I will give over all.

Fent. Yet hear me speak. Assist me in my purpose,
And, as I am a gentleman, I'll give thee
A hundred pound in gold more than your loss.

Host. I will hear you, Master Fenton; and I will at the least keep your counsel.

Fent. From time to time I have acquainted you
With the dear love I bear to fair Anne Page;
Who mutually hath answer'd my affection,
So far forth as herself might be her chooser,
Even to my wish: I have a letter from her
Of such contents as you will wonder at;
The mirth whereof so larded with my matter,
That neither singly can be manifested,
Without the show of both; fat Falstaff
Hath a great scene: the image of the jest
I'll show you here at large. Hark, good mine host.
To-night at Herne's oak, just 'twixt twelve and one,
Must my sweet Nan present the Fairy Queen;
The purpose why, is here: in which disguise,
While other jests are something rank on foot,
Her father hath commanded her to slip
Away with Slender and with him at Eton
Immediately to marry: she hath consented:
Now, sir,
Her mother, ever strong against that match
And firm for Doctor Caius, hath appointed
That he shall likewise shuffle her away,
While other sports are tasking of their minds,
And at the dean'ry, where a priest attends,
Straight marry her: to this her mother's plot
She seemingly obedient likewise hath
Made promise to the doctor. Now, thus it rests:
Her father means she shall be all in white,
And in that habit, when Slender sees his time
To take her by the hand and bid her go,
She shall go with him: her mother hath intended,
The better to denote her to the doctor,
For they must all be mask'd and vizarded,
That quaint in green she shall be loose enrob'd,
With ribands pendent, flaring 'bout her head;
And when the doctor spies his vantage ripe,
To pinch her by the hand, and, on that token,
The maid hath given consent to go with him.

Host. Which means she to deceive, father or mother?

Fent. Both, my good host, to go along with me:
And here it rests, that you'll procure the vicar
To stay for me at church 'twixt twelve and one,
And, in the lawful name of marrying,
To give our hearts united ceremony.

100-101. **liquor fishermen's boots,** i.e., saturate them with oil to make them waterproof. 104. **primero,** gambling card game.
SCENE VI. 20. **present,** represent. 22. **rank,** abundantly.

ACT V. SCENE I. 4. **divinity,** divination. 9. **mince,** trip off. 23. **Goliath . . . beam.** See I Samuel 17:7: "the staff of his [Goliath's] spear was like a weaver's beam." See also II Samuel 21:19. 24. **life**

Host. Well, husband your device; I'll to the vicar:
Bring you the maid, you shall not lack a priest.
Fent. So shall I evermore be bound to thee;
Besides, I'll make a present recompense. *Exeunt.*

ACT V.

SCENE I. [*A room in the Garter Inn.*]

Enter FALSTAFF, [*and* MISTRESS] *Quickly.*

Fal. Prithee, no more prattling; go. I'll hold. This is the third time; I hope good luck lies in odd numbers. Away! go. They say there is divinity in odd numbers, either in nativity, chance, or death. Away!

Quick. I'll provide you a chain; and I'll do what I can to get you a pair of horns.

Fal. Away, I say; time wears: hold up your head, and mince. [*Exit Mrs Quickly.*]

[*Enter*] FORD.

How now, Master Brook! Master Brook, the matter will be known to-night, or never. Be you in the Park about midnight, at Herne's oak, and you shall see wonders.

Ford. Went you not to her yesterday, sir, as you told me you had appointed?

Fal. I went to her, Master Brook, as you see, like a poor old man: but I came from her, Master Brook, like a poor old woman. That same knave Ford, her husband, hath the finest mad devil of jealousy in him, Master Brook, that ever governed frenzy. I will tell you: he beat me grievously, in the shape of a woman; for in the shape of man, Master Brook, I fear not Goliath with a weaver's beam; because I know also life is a shuttle. I am in haste; go along with me: I'll tell you all, Master Brook. Since I plucked geese, played truant and whipped top, I knew not what 'twas to be beaten till lately. Follow me: I'll tell you strange things of this knave Ford, on whom to-night I will be revenged, and I will deliver his wife into your hand. Follow. Strange things in hand, Master Brook! Follow. *Exeunt.*

SCENE II. [*Windsor Park.*]

Enter PAGE, SHALLOW, [*and*] SLENDER.

Page. Come, come; we'll couch i' the castle-ditch till we see the light of our fairies. Remember, son Slender, my daughter.

Slen. Ay, forsooth; I have spoke with her and we have a nay-word how to know one another: I come to her in white, and cry 'mum;' she cries 'budget;' and by that we know one another.

Shal. That 's good too: but what needs either your 'mum' or her 'budget?' the white will decipher her well enough. It hath struck ten o'clock.

Page. The night is dark; light and spirits will become it well. Heaven prosper our sport! No man means evil but the devil, and we shall know him by his horns. Let 's away; follow me. *Exeunt.*

SCENE III. [*A street leading to the Park.*]

Enter MISTRESS PAGE, MISTRESS FORD, [*and* DOCTOR] CAIUS.

Mrs Page. Master doctor, my daughter is in green: when you see your time, take her by the hand, away with her to the deanery, and dispatch it quickly. Go before into the Park: we two must go together.

Caius. I know vat I have to do. Adieu.

Mrs Page. Fare you well, sir. [*Exit Caius.*] My husband will not rejoice so much at the abuse of Falstaff as he will chafe at the doctor's marrying my daughter: but 'tis no matter; better a little chiding than a great deal of heart-break.

Mrs Ford. Where is Nan now and her troop of fairies, and the Welsh devil Hugh?

Mrs Page. They are all couched in a pit hard by Herne's oak, with obscured lights; which, at the very instant of Falstaff's and our meeting, they will at once display to the night.

Mrs Ford. That cannot choose but amaze him.

Mrs Page. If he be not amazed, he will be mocked; if he be amazed, he will every way be mocked.

Mrs Ford. We'll betray him finely.

Mrs Page. Against such lewdsters and their lechery
Those that betray them do no treachery.

Mrs Ford. The hour draws on. To the oak, to the oak! *Exeunt.*

SCENE IV. [*Windsor Park*].

Enter [SIR HUGH] EVANS *and* [*others disguised as*] *Fairies.*

Evans. Trib, trib, fairies; come; and remember your parts: be pold, I pray you; follow me into the pit; and when I give the watch-'ords, do as I pid you: come, come; trib, trib. *Exeunt.*

SCENE V. [*Another part of the Park.*]

Enter FALSTAFF [*disguised as Herne*].

Fal. The Windsor bell hath struck twelve; the minute draws on. Now, the hot-blooded gods assist me! Remember, Jove, thou wast a bull for thy Europa; love set on thy horns. O powerful love! that, in some respects, makes a beast a man, in some other, a man a beast. You were also, Jupiter, a swan for the love of Leda. O omnipotent Love! how near the god drew to the complexion of a goose! A fault done first in the form of a beast. O Jove, a beastly fault! And then another fault in the semblance of a fowl; think on 't, Jove; a foul fault! When gods have hot backs, what shall poor men do? For me, I am here a Windsor stag; and the fattest, I think, i' the forest. Send me a cool rut-time, Jove, or who can blame me to piss my tallow? Who comes here? my doe?

[*Enter*] MISTRESS PAGE [*and*] MISTRESS FORD.

Mrs Ford. Sir John! art thou there, my deer? my male deer?

. . . **shuttle.** See Job 7:6: "My days are swifter than a weaver's shuttle." 26. **plucked geese . . . whipped top,** types of boyish pranks.
SCENE II. 1. **couch,** hide.

SCENE III. 18. **amaze,** perplex. 23. **lewdsters,** lascivious persons.
SCENE V. 3, 7. **bull . . . Europa, swan . . . Leda,** references to legends of Jupiter's disguises when engaged in various amours.

Fal. My doe with the black scut! Let the sky rain potatoes; let it thunder to the tune of Green Sleeves, hail kissing-comfits and snow eringoes; let there come a tempest of provocation, I will shelter me here.

Mrs Ford. Mistress Page is come with me, sweetheart.

Fal. Divide me like a bribed buck, each a haunch: I will keep my sides to myself, my shoulders for the fellow of this walk, and my horns I bequeath your husbands. Am I a woodman, ha? Speak I like Herne the hunter? Why, now is Cupid a child of conscience; he makes restitution. As I am a true spirit, welcome! [*Noise within.*]

Mrs Page. Alas, what noise?
Mrs Ford. Heaven forgive our sins!
Fal. What should this be?
Mrs Ford., *Mrs Page.* Away, away! [*They run off.*]

Fal. I think the devil will not have me damned, lest the oil that 's in me should set hell on fire; he would never else cross me thus.

[*Enter* SIR HUGH] EVANS, [*disguised as before,* MISTRESS] QUICKLY, ANNE PAGE, [*and others as*] *Fairies,* [*with tapers, and*] PISTOL [*as Hobgoblin*].

Quick. Fairies, black, grey, green, and white,
You moonshine revellers, and shades of night,
You orphan heirs of fixed destiny,
Attend your office and your quality.
Crier Hobgoblin, make the fairy oyes.
Pist. Elves, list your names; silence, you airy toys.
Cricket, to Windsor chimneys shalt thou leap:
Where fires thou find'st unrak'd and hearths unswept,
There pinch the maids as blue as bilberry:
Our radiant queen hates sluts and sluttery.
Fal. They are fairies; he that speaks to them shall die:
I'll wink and couch: no man their works must eye.
[*Lies down upon his face.*]
Evans. Where 's Bede? Go you, and where you find a maid
That, ere she sleep, has thrice her prayers said,
Raise up the organs of her fantasy;
Sleep she as sound as careless infancy:
But those as sleep and think not on their sins,
Pinch them, arms, legs, backs, shoulders, sides and shins.
Quick. About, about;
Search Windsor Castle, elves, within and out:
Strew good luck, ouphes, on every sacred room:
That it may stand till the perpetual doom,
In state as wholesome as in state 'tis fit,
Worthy the owner, and the owner it.
The several chairs of order look you scour
With juice of balm and every precious flow'r:
Each fair instalment, coat, and sev'ral crest,
With loyal blazon, evermore be blest!
And nightly, meadow-fairies, look you sing,
Like to the Garter's compass, in a ring:
Th' expressure that it bears, green let it be,
More fertile-fresh than all the field to see;
And 'Honi soit qui mal y pense' write
In em'rald tufts, flow'rs purple, blue, and white;
Like sapphire, pearl and rich embroidery,
Buckled below fair knighthood's bending knee:
Fairies use flow'rs for their charactery.
Away; disperse: but till 'tis one o'clock,
Our dance of custom round about the oak
Of Herne the hunter, let us not forget.
Evans. Pray you, lock hand in hand; yourselves in order set;
And twenty glow-worms shall our lanterns be,
To guide our measure round about the tree.
But, stay; I smell a man of middle-earth.

Fal. Heavens defend me from that Welsh fairy, lest he transform me to a piece of cheese!

Pist. Vile worm, thou wast o'erlook'd even in thy birth.
Quick. With trial-fire touch me his finger-end:
If he be chaste, the flame will back descend
And turn him to no pain; but if he start,
It is the flesh of a corrupted heart.
Pist. A trial, come.
Evans. Come, will this wood take fire?
[*They burn him with their tapers.*]
Fal. Oh, Oh, Oh!
Quick. Corrupt, corrupt, and tainted in desire!
About him, fairies; sing a scornful rhyme;
And, as you trip, still pinch him to your time.

THE SONG.

Fie on sinful fantasy!
Fie on lust and luxury!
Lust is but a bloody fire,
Kindled with unchaste desire,
Fed in heart, whose flames aspire
As thoughts do blow them, higher and higher.
Pinch him, fairies, mutually;
Pinch him for his villany;
Pinch him, and burn him, and turn him about,
Till candles and starlight and moonshine be out.

[*During this song they pinch* FALSTAFF. DOCTOR] CAIUS [*comes one way, and steals away a boy in green*]; SLENDER, [*another way, and takes off a boy in white; and*] FENTON [*comes, and steals away Mrs* ANNE PAGE. *A noise of hunting is heard within. All the Fairies run away.* FALSTAFF *pulls off his buck's head, and rises.*]

[*Enter*] PAGE, FORD [, MISTRESS PAGE *and* MISTRESS FORD].

Page. Nay, do not fly; I think we have watch'd you now:
Will none but Herne the hunter serve your turn?
Mrs Page. I pray you, come, hold up the jest no higher.
Now, good Sir John, how like you Windsor wives?

20. **scut,** tail of a deer. 21, 23. **potatoes, eringoes,** formerly regarded as excitements to lust. 22. **Green Sleeves.** Cf. II, i, 64, note. The term came to be applied to wanton women. **kissing-comfits,** perfumed sweetmeats for sweetening the breath. 27. **bribed,** stolen. 43. **You orphan . . . destiny.** There have been many attempts to emend and explain. Theobald and Warburton: *ouphen;* New Cambridge editors find this paleographically possible. The older critics objected to *heirs of Destiny,* since Destiny was still existing. Hart notes that *orphan* may mean merely "bereft, unprotected," and that *heirs* does not necessarily imply parentage (citing *Hamlet:* "that flesh is heir to"); he paraphrases: "You bereft creatures whose lot is an unchanging fate." 45. **oyes,** call of the public crier: hear ye? 48. **unrak'd,** uncovered. 49. **bilberry,** whortleberry, a European species of blueberry. 55. **Raise up . . . fantasy,** give her elevating and pleasant dreams (Hart). 56. **Sleep she,** let her sleep. 65. **several . . . order,** i.e., the places or seats of varying degrees of public authority. 66. **juice of balm,** i.e., aromatic herbs. 67. **instalment,** place or seat in which a person is installed. 68. **blazon,** coat of arms. 71. **expressure,** image, picture. 73. **'Honi . . . pense,'** Evil to him who evil thinks. This is the motto of the Order of the Garter. 84. **middle-earth,** the earth, the center

See you these, husband? do not these fair yokes
Become the forest better than the town?

Ford. Now, sir, who 's a cuckold now? Master Brook, Falstaff 's a knave, a cuckoldly knave; here are his horns, Master Brook: and, Master Brook, he hath enjoyed nothing of Ford's but his buck-basket, his cudgel, and twenty pounds of money, which must be paid to Master Brook; his horses are arrested for it, Master Brook.

Mrs Ford. Sir John, we have had ill luck; we could never meet. I will never take you for my love again; but I will always count you my deer.

Fal. I do begin to perceive that I am made an ass.

Ford. Ay, and an ox too: both the proofs are extant.

Fal. And these are not fairies? I was three or four times in the thought they were not fairies: and yet the guiltiness of my mind, the sudden surprise of my powers, drove the grossness of the foppery into a received belief, in despite of the teeth of all rhyme and reason, that they were fairies. See now how wit may be made a Jack-a-Lent, when 'tis upon ill employment!

Evans. Sir John Falstaff, serve Got, and leave your desires, and fairies will not pinse you.

Ford. Well said, fairy Hugh.

Evans. And leave your jealousies too, I pray you.

Ford. I will never mistrust my wife again, till thou art able to woo her in good English.

Fal. Have I laid my brain in the sun and dried it, that it wants matter to prevent so gross o'erreaching as this? Am I ridden with a Welsh goat too? shall I have a coxcomb of frize? 'Tis time I were choked with a piece of toasted cheese.

Evans. Seese is not good to give putter; your belly is all putter.

Fal. 'Seese' and 'putter'! have I lived to stand at the taunt of one that makes fritters of English? This is enough to be the decay of lust and late-walking through the realm.

Mrs Page. Why, Sir John, do you think, though we would have thrust virtue out of our hearts by the head and shoulders and have given ourselves without scruple to hell, that ever the devil could have made you our delight?

Ford. What, a hodge-pudding? a bag of flax?

Mrs Page. A puffed man?

Page. Old, cold, withered and of intolerable entrails?

Ford. And one that is as slanderous as Satan?

Page. And as poor as Job?

Ford. And as wicked as his wife?

Evans. And given to fornications, and to taverns and sack and wine and metheglins, and to drinkings and swearings and starings, pribbles and prabbles?

Fal. Well, I am your theme: you have the start of me; I am dejected; I am not able to answer the Welsh flannel; ignorance itself is a plummet o'er me: use me as you will.

Ford. Marry, sir, we'll bring you to Windsor, to one Master Brook, that you have cozened of money, to whom you should have been a pandar: over and above that you have suffered, I think to repay that money will be a biting affliction.

Page. Yet be cheerful, knight: thou shalt eat a posset to-night at my house; where I will desire thee to laugh at my wife, that now laughs at thee: tell her Master Slender hath married her daughter.

Mrs Page. [*Aside*] Doctors doubt that: if Anne Page be my daughter, she is, by this, Doctor Caius' wife.

[*Enter* SLENDER.]

Slen. Whoa, ho! ho, father Page!

Page. Son, how now! how now, son! have you dispatched?

Slen. Dispatched! I'll make the best in Gloucestershire know on 't; would I were hanged, la, else!

Page. Of what, son?

Slen. I came yonder at Eton to marry Mistress Anne Page, and she 's a great lubberly boy. If it had not been i' the church, I would have swinged him, or he should have swinged me. If I did not think it had been Anne Page, would I might never stir!—and 'tis a postmaster's boy.

Page. Upon my life, then, you took the wrong.

Slen. What need you tell me that? I think so, when I took a boy for a girl. If I had been married to him, for all he was in woman's apparel, I would not have had him.

Page. Why, this is your own folly. Did not I tell you how you should know my daughter by her garments?

Slen. I went to her in white, and cried 'mum,' and she cried 'budget,' as Anne and I had appointed; and yet it was not Anne, but a postmaster's boy.

Mrs Page. Good George, be not angry: I knew of your purpose; turned my daughter into green; and, indeed, she is now with the doctor at the deanery, and there married.

[*Enter* CAIUS.]

Caius. Vere is Mistress Page? By gar, I am cozened: I ha' married un garçon, a boy; un paysan, by gar, a boy; it is not Anne Page: by gar, I am cozened.

Mrs Page. Why, did you take her in green?

Caius. Ay, by gar, and 'tis a boy: by gar, I'll raise all Windsor. [*Exit.*]

Ford. This is strange. Who hath got the right Anne?

Page. My heart misgives me: here comes Master Fenton.

[*Enter* FENTON *and* ANNE PAGE.]

How now, Master Fenton!

Anne. Pardon, good father! good my mother, pardon!

Page. Now, mistress, how chance you went not with Master Slender?

of the universe, conceived of as between heaven and hell. 87. **o'erlook'd,** bewitched, looked on with an evil eye. 103. **mutually,** jointly, in common. 106. *Stage Direction:* ***Mrs.*** "Mistress" as a title of courtesy originally referred to both married and unmarried women; now superseded by two contracted forms, "Mrs." and "Miss," differently pronounced. 109. **hold . . . higher,** maintain the jest no longer. 111. **these fair yokes,** alluding to the horns; Hart suggests that they may have been of oak branches, making an obvious pun. 126. **an ox.** New Cambridge editors apply the idiom "to make an ox of someone," i.e., to make a fool of, with an obvious reference to the ox's horns. 132. **foppery,** deceit. 145-146. **Welsh goat.** New Cambridge editors think it alludes to Evans' costume of a satyr. Hart quotes Scot's *Discoverie of Witchcraft:* "First as touching the divell (Bodin saith) that he dooth most properlie and commonlie transforme himselfe into a gote." 146. **frize,** kind of coarse woolen cloth. 153. **late-walking,** keeping late hours. 159. **hodge-pudding,** pudding made of a medley of ingredients. 167. **metheglins,** spiced drink made from wort and honey, Welsh in origin. 173. **plummet,** a quibble on "plumbet," a woolen fabric, and "plummet," a line for fathoming (New Cambridge). 197. **swinged,** thrashed. 218. **garçon,** boy. 219. **paysan,** peasant.

Mrs Page. Why went you not with master doctor,
maid?
Fent. You do amaze her: hear the truth of it.
You would have married her most shamefully,
Where there was no proportion held in love.
The truth is, she and I, long since contracted,
Are now so sure that nothing can dissolve us.
Th' offence is holy that she hath committed;
And this deceit loses the name of craft,
Of disobedience, or unduteous title,
Since therein she doth evitate and shun
A thousand irreligious cursed hours,
Which forced marriage would have brought upon her.
Ford. Stand not amaz'd; here is no remedy:
In love the heavens themselves do guide the state;
Money buys lands, and wives are sold by fate.
Fal. I am glad, though you have ta'en a special stand to strike at me, that your arrow hath glanced.
Page. Well, what remedy? Fenton, heaven give thee
joy!
What cannot be eschew'd must be embrac'd.
Fal. When night-dogs run, all sorts of deer are
chas'd.
Mrs Page. Well, I will muse no further. Master
Fenton,
Heaven give you many, many merry days!
Good husband, let us every one go home,
And laugh this sport o'er by a country fire;
Sir John and all.
Ford. Let it be so. Sir John,
To Master Brook you yet shall hold your word;
For he to-night shall lie with Mistress Ford. *Exeunt.*

241. **evitate,** avoid. 253. **muse,** grumble, complain.

AS YOU LIKE IT

As *You Like It* represents, together with *Much Ado about Nothing* and *Twelfth Night*, the summation of Shakespeare's achievement in festive, happy comedy during the years 1598–1600. (This play, not appearing in Francis Meres' list of 1598, was entered in the Stationers' Register in 1600 although not actually published until the Folio of 1623.) *As You Like It* contains several motifs found in other Shakespearean comedies: the journey from a jaded court into a transforming silvan environment and back to a revitalized court (as in *A Midsummer Night's Dream*); hence, a contrasting of two "worlds" in the play, presided over by a virtuous but exiled older brother and a usurping younger brother (as in *The Tempest*); the heroine disguised as a man (as in *The Merchant of Venice* and *Twelfth Night*); and a structure of multiple plotting in which numerous groups of characters are thematically played off against one another (as in several of Shakespeare's comedies). What chiefly distinguishes this play from the others, however, is the nature and function of its pastoral setting—the Forest of Arden.

The Forest of Arden is seen in many perspectives. As a natural wilderness, it is probably most like the real forest Shakespeare knew near Stratford-upon-Avon in Warwickshire—a place capable of producing the vulgarity of an Audrey or the gentle simplicity of a Corin. As the abode of Robin Hood, it is a mythic folk world compensating for social injustice, offering an alternative way of life to those persons in retreat from a society seemingly beyond repair. As the "golden world," the forest evokes an even deeper longing for a mythological past age of innocence and plenty, when men shared some attributes of the giants and the gods. This myth has its parallel in the biblical Garden of Eden, before men learned to feel "the penalty of Adam" (II,i). Finally, in another of its aspects, the forest is Arcadia, a pastoral landscape embodied in an ancient and sophisticated literary tradition.

All but the first of these Ardens, compared and contrasted with one another, involve some idealization not only of "nature" and the natural landscape, but also of the human condition. These various Ardens place our real life in a complex perspective, and force us to a fresh appraisal of our own ordinary existence. Duke Senior, for example, describes the forest environment as a corrective for the evils of society. He addresses his followers in the forest as "my co-mates and brothers in exile" (II,i), suggesting a kind of social equality that he could never know in the cramped formality of his previous official existence. The banished duke and his followers have perforce left behind their lands and revenues in the grip of the usurping Frederick. No longer rich though adequately provided with all of life's necessities, the duke and his "merry men" live "like the old Robin Hood of England," and "fleet the time carelessly as they did in the golden world" (I,i). In this friendly society, a strong communal sense replaces the necessity for individual proprietorship. All comers are welcome, with food for all.

There are no luxuries in the forest, to be sure, but even this spare existence affords relief from the decadence of courtly life. "Sweet are the uses of adversity," insists the duke. He welcomes the cold of winter because, instead of flattering him as courtiers do, it teaches him the true condition of mankind and of himself. The forest is serenely impartial, neither malicious nor compassionate. Death, and even killing for food, are an inevitable part of forest existence. The duke concedes that his presence in the forest means the slaughter of deer, who were the original inhabitants; Orlando and Adam find that death through starvation in the forest is all too real a possibility. The forest never stoops to the degrading perversity of man at his worst, but it is equally incapable of charity and forgiveness.

Shakespeare's sources reflect the complexity of his vision of Arden. The original of the Orlando story, which Shakespeare may not have used directly, is *The Cokes Tale of Gamelyn*, found in a number of manuscripts of *The Canterbury Tales* and wrongly attributed to Chaucer. This hearty English romance glorifies the rebellious and even violent spirit of its Robin Hood hero, the neglected youngest son Gamelyn, who, aided by faithful old Adam the Spencer, evades his wicked eldest brother in a cunning and bloody escape. As king of the outlaws in Sherwood Forest, Gamelyn eventually triumphs over his eldest brother (now the sheriff) and sees him hanged. Here then originates the motif of refuge from social injustice in Arden, even though most of the actual violence has been omitted from Shakespeare's version. (A series of Robin Hood plays on a similar theme, beginning in 1598 with Anthony Munday's *The Downfall of Robert Earl of Huntingdon after called Robin Hood*, were being performed with great success by the Admiral's company, chief rivals of the Lord Chamberlain's company to which Shakespeare belonged.)

As You Like It is clearly indebted to Thomas Lodge's version of the Gamelyn story entitled *Rosalynde: Euphues Golden Legacie* (published 1590), a prose narrative romance in the ornate Euphuistic style of the 1580's. (Lodge's Epistle to the Gentleman Readers, casually inviting them to be pleased with this story if they are so inclined—"*If you like it*, so"—probably gave Shakespeare a hint for the name of his own play.) Lodge accentuated the love story with its courtship in masquerade, provided some charming songs, and introduced the pastoral love motif involving Corin, Silvius, Phebe, and Ganymede. Shakespeare's ordering of episode is generally close to that of Lodge. "Pastoral" literature, which had become a literary rage in the 1580's and early 1590's owing particularly to Spenser's *Shepherd's Calendar* (1579) and Sidney's *Arcadia* (1590), traced its ancestry through such Renaissance continental writers as Montemayor, Sannazaro, and Guarini to the so-called Greek romances, and finally back to the *Eclogues* of Virgil, Theocritus, and Bion. A literary mode that had begun originally as a realistic evocation of difficult country life had become, in the Renaissance, an elegant vehicle for the loftiest and most patrician sentiments in love, for philosophic debate, and even for extensive political analysis.

Shakespeare's alterations and additions give us insight into his method of construction and his thematic focus. Whereas Lodge cheerfully accepts the pastoral conventions of his day, Shakespeare exposes those conventions to some criticism and considerable irony. Alongside of the mannered and literary Silvius and Phebe, he places William and Audrey, as peasantlike a couple as ever drew milk from a cow's teat. They are Shakespeare's own creation, based on observation and also on the dramatic convention of the rustic clown and wench as exemplified earlier in his Costard and Jaquenetta (*Love's Labour's Lost*). Equally original, and essential to the many-sided debate concerning the virtues of the court versus those of the country, are Touchstone and Jaques. Touchstone is a professional court fool, dressed in motley, a new comic type in Shakespeare, created apparently in response to the recent addition to the Lord Chamberlain's company of the brilliant actor Robert Armin. Jaques is also a new type, the malcontent satirist, reflecting the very latest literary vogue in the nondramatic poetry and drama for the private theatre of Chapman, Marston, and Jonson. (The private theatres, featuring boy actors, reopened in 1598–1599 after nearly a decade of enforced silence, and proceeded at once to specialize in satirical drama.) Once we have been exposed to this assortment of newly created characters, we can no longer view either pastoral life or pastoral love as simply as Lodge and other writers of the period portray them.

When *As You Like It* is compared with its chief source, Shakespeare can also be seen to have altered and softened considerably the characters of the wicked brothers Oliver and Frederick. Whereas Lodge's Saladyne is motivated by a greedy desire to seize his younger brother Rosader's property, Shakespeare's Oliver is envious of Orlando's natural goodness and popularity. As he confesses in soliloquy, Orlando is "so much in the heart of the world, and especially of my own people . . . that I am altogether misprised" (I,i). In his warped way Oliver desires to be more like Orlando, and in the enchanted forest of Arden he eventually becomes so. Duke Frederick too is plainly envious of goodness. Trying to persuade his daughter Celia of the need for banishing Rosalind, he argues, "thou wilt show more bright and seem more virtuous When she is gone" (I,iii). In a sense Frederick is ripe for conversion. Penitence and conciliation replace the vengeful conclusion of Lodge's novel, in which the nobles of France finally overthrow and execute the usurping king. Although Shakespeare's resolutions are sudden and inadequately explained, like all miracles they attest to the inexplicable power of goodness.

The court of Duke Frederick is "the envious court," identified by this fixed epithet. In it, brothers turn unnaturally against brothers: the younger Frederick usurps his older brother's throne, whereas the older Oliver denies the younger Orlando his birthright of education. In still another parallel, both Rosalind and Orlando find themselves mistrusted as the children of Frederick's political enemies, Duke

Senior and Sir Rowland de Boys. A daughter and a son are held to be guilty by association. "Thou art thy father's daughter, there's enough" (I,iii), Frederick curtly retorts in explaining Rosalind's exile. And to Orlando, triumphant in wrestling with Charles, Frederick asserts, "I would thou hadst been son to some man else" (I,ii). Here again, Frederick plaintively reveals his attraction to goodness, even if at present this attraction is thwarted by tyrannous whim. Many of Frederick's entourage might also be better persons, if they only knew how to escape the insincerities of their courtly life. Charles the wrestler, for example, places himself at Oliver's service, and yet he would happily avoid breaking Orlando's neck if to do so were consistent with self-interest. Even Le Beau, the giddy fop so delighted at first with the cruel sport of wrestling, takes Orlando aside at some personal risk to warn him of Duke Frederick's foul humor. Ideally, Le Beau would prefer to be a companion of Orlando's "in a better world than this" (I,ii). The vision of a regenerative Utopia secretly abides in the heart of this courtly creature.

It is easier to anatomize the defects of a social order than to propound solutions. As have other Utopian visionaries (including Thomas More), Shakespeare uses playful debate to elicit complicated responses on the part of his audience. Which is preferable, the court or the country? Jaques and Touchstone are adept gadflies, incessantly pointing out contradictions and ironies. Jaques, the malcontent railer derived from literary satire, takes delight in being out of step with everyone. Seemingly his chief reason for having joined the others in the forest is to jibe at their motives for being there. To their song about the rejection of courtly ambition he mockingly supplies another verse, charging them with having left their wealth and ease out of mere willfulness (II,v). With ironic appropriateness, Jaques eventually decides to remain in the forest in the company of Frederick; Jaques cannot thrive on resolution and harmony. His humor is "melancholy," from which, as he observes, he draws consolation as a weasel sucks eggs. The others treat him as a sort of profane jester whose soured conceits add relish to their enjoyment of the forest life.

Despite his affectation, however, Jaques is serious and even excited in his defense of satire as a curative form of laughter (II,vii). The appearance of Touchstone in the forest has reaffirmed in Jaques his profound commitment to a view of life as a meaningless process of decay governed by inexorable time. His function in such a life is to be mordant, unsparing. As literary satirist he must be free to awaken men's minds to their own folly. To the duke's protestation that the satirist is merely self-indulgent and licentious, Jaques counters with a thoughtful and classically Horatian defense of satire as an art form devoted not to libelous attacks on individuals but to exposing "types" of folly. Any observer who feels himself individually portrayed merely condemns himself by confessing his resemblance to the type. This particular debate between the duke and Jaques ends, appropriately, in a draw. The duke's point is well taken, for Jaques' famous "Seven Ages of Man" speech, so often read out of context, occurs in a scene that also witnesses the rescue of Orlando and Adam from the forest. As though in answer to Jaques' acid depiction of covetous old age, we see the self-sacrifice and trust in Providence of old Adam. Instead of "mere oblivion," we see charitable compassion prompting the duke to aid Orlando and Orlando to aid Adam. Perhaps this vision seems of a higher spiritual order than that of Jaques. Nonetheless, without him the forest would be a dull and humorless place.

Touchstone's name suggests that he similarly offers a multiplicity of viewpoints. He shares with Jaques a skeptical view of life, but for Touchstone the inconsistency and absurdity of life are occasions for wit and humor rather than melancholy and cynicism. As a professional fool he observes that sane men are more foolish than he—as, for example, in their elaborate dueling code of the Retort Courteous and the Reply Churlish, leading finally to the Lie Circumstantial and the Lie Direct. He is fascinated by the games people make of their lives, and amused by their inability to be content with what they already have. Of the shepherd's life, he comments, "In respect that it is solitary, I like it very well; but in respect that it is private, it is a very vile life" (III,ii). This paradox, though nonsensical, captures the restlessness of human striving for a life that can somehow combine the peaceful solitude of nature with the convenience and excitement of city life. Although Touchstone marries, even his marriage is a spoof of the institution rather than a serious attempt at commitment. Like all fools, who in Renaissance times were regarded as a breed apart, Touchstone exists outside the realm of ordinary human responses. There he can comment disinterestedly on human folly. He is prevented, however, from sharing fully in the human love and conciliation with which the play ends. He and Jaques are not touched by the play's regenerative magic; Jaques will remain in the forest, Touchstone will remain forever a childlike entertainer.

The regenerative power of Arden, as we have seen, is not the forest's alone. What saves Orlando is the human charity practiced by himself and by the duke who, for all his love of the forest, longs to rejoin that human society where he has "with holy bell been knoll'd to church" (II,vii). Civilization at its best is no less necessary to man's spirit than is the "natural" order of the forest. In love, also, perception and wisdom must be combined with nature's gifts. Orlando, when we first see him, is a young man of the finest natural qualities, but admittedly lacking experience in the nuances of complex human relationships. Nowhere does his lack of "breeding" betray him more unhappily than in his first encounter with Rosalind, following the wrestling match. In response to her unmistakable hints of favor he stands oxlike, tongue-tied. Later, however, in the forest, his first attempts at self-education in love lead him into an opposite danger: an excess of platitudinous "manners" parading in the guise of Petrarchism. Orlando's newfound self-abasement and idealization of his absent mistress are as unsatisfactory as his former naiveté. He must learn from Rosalind that a quest for true understanding in love avoids the extreme of pretentious mannerism as well as that of mere artlessness. Orlando as Petrarchan lover too much resembles Silvius, the greensick young man, cowering before the imperious will of his coy mistress Phebe. This stereotyped relationship, taken from the pages of fashionable pastoral romance, represents a posturing which Rosalind hopes to cure in Silvius and Phebe even as she will also cure Orlando.

Rosalind is above all the realistic one, the plucky Shakespearean heroine showing her mettle in the world of men, emotionally more mature than her lover. Her concern is with a working and clear-sighted relationship in love, and to that end she daringly insists that Orlando learn something of woman's changeable mood. Above all, she must disabuse him of the dangerously misleading clichés of the Petrarchan love myth. When he protests he would die for love of Rosalind, she lectures him mockingly: "No, faith, die by attorney. The poor world is almost six thousand years old, and in all this time there was not any man died in his own person, videlicet, in a love-cause." She debunks the legends of Troilus and Leander, youths supposed to have died for love who in fact met with more prosaic ends. "But these are all lies: men have died from time to time and worms have eaten them, but not for love" (IV,i). When Orlando has been sufficiently tested as to patience, loyalty, and understanding, she unmasks herself to him and simultaneously unravels the plot of Silvius and Phebe.

Rosalind's disguise name, Ganymede, taken from Jove's amorous cupbearer, has faintly homosexual connotations. Shakespeare delicately exploits these overtones, both in Phebe's pursuit of a young lady (but really a boy actor) in male attire, and in Orlando's courtship of Ganymede as though addressed to Rosalind. In this innocent titillation, found also in Shakespeare's source, there is no suggestion of deviate sexual practice. On the contrary, the point is that Orlando can speak frankly and personally to "Ganymede" as to a perfect friend, one to whom he can relate in Platonically spiritual terms without the potentially distracting note of sexual attraction. Once this disinterested love has grown strong between them, the unmasking of Rosalind's sexual identity makes possible a physical union between them to confirm and express the spiritual. In these terms, the play's happy ending affirms marriage as an institution, not simply as the expected denouement. The procession to the altar is synchronous with the return to civilization's other institutions, made whole again not solely by the forest but by the power of goodness embodied in Rosalind, Orlando, Duke Senior, and the others who persevere.

AS YOU LIKE IT

[*Dramatis Personae*

DUKE, *living in banishment.*
FREDERICK, *his brother, and usurper of his dominions.*
AMIENS, JAQUES, } *lords attending on the banished duke.*
LE BEAU, *a courtier attending upon Frederick.*
CHARLES, *wrestler to Frederick.*
OLIVER, JAQUES, ORLANDO, } *sons of Sir Rowland de Boys.*
ADAM, DENNIS, } *servants to Oliver.*
TOUCHSTONE, *a clown.*
SIR OLIVER MARTEXT, *a vicar.*
CORIN, SILVIUS, } *shepherds.*
WILLIAM, *a country fellow, in love with Audrey.*
HYMEN, *god of marriage.*

ROSALIND, *daughter to the banished duke.*
CELIA, *daughter to Frederick.*
PHEBE, *a shepherdess.*
AUDREY, *a country wench.*

Lords, pages, *and* attendants, *&c.*

SCENE: *Oliver's house; Duke Frederick's court; and the Forest of Arden.*]

ACT I.

SCENE I. [*Orchard of* OLIVER'S *house.*]

Enter ORLANDO *and* ADAM.

Orl. As I remember, Adam, it was upon this fashion bequeathed me by will but poor a thousand crowns, and, as thou sayest, charged my brother, on his blessing, to breed me well: and there begins my sadness. My brother Jaques he keeps at school, and report speaks goldenly of his profit: for my part, he keeps me rustically at home, or, to speak more properly, stays me here at home unkept; for call you that keeping for a gentleman of my birth, that differs not from the stalling of an ox? His horses are bred better; for, besides that they are fair with their feeding, they are taught their manage, and to that end riders dearly hired: but I, his brother, gain nothing under him but growth; for the which his animals on his dunghills are as much bound to him as I. Besides this nothing that he so plentifully gives me, the something that nature gave me his countenance seems to take from me: he lets me feed with his hinds, bars me the place of a brother, and, as much as in him lies, mines my gentility with my education. This is it, Adam, that grieves me; and the spirit of my father, which I think is within me, begins to mutiny against this servitude: I will no longer endure it, though yet I know no wise remedy how to avoid it.

Enter OLIVER.

Adam. Yonder comes my master, your brother.

Orl. Go apart, Adam, and thou shalt hear how he will shake me up.

Oli. Now, sir! what make you here?

Orl. Nothing: I am not taught to make any thing.

Oli. What mar you then, sir?

Orl. Marry, sir, I am helping you to mar that which God made, a poor unworthy brother of yours, with idleness.

Oli. Marry, sir, be better employed, and be naught awhile.

Orl. Shall I keep your hogs and eat husks with them? What prodigal portion have I spent, that I should come to such penury?

Oli. Know you where you are, sir?

Orl. O, sir, very well: here in your orchard.

Oli. Know you before whom, sir?

Orl. Ay, better than him I am before knows me. I know you are my eldest brother; and, in the gentle condition of blood, you should so know me. The courtesy of nations allows you my better, in that you are the first-born; but the same tradition takes not away my blood, were there twenty brothers betwixt us: I have as much of my father in me as you; albeit, I confess, your coming before me is nearer to his reverence.

Oli. What, boy! [*Strikes him.*]

Orl. Come, come, elder brother, you are too young in this. [*Seizes him.*]

Oli. Wilt thou lay hands on me, villain?

Orl. I am no villain; I am the youngest son of Sir Rowland de Boys; he was my father, and he is thrice a villain that says such a father begot villains. Wert thou not my brother, I would not take this hand from thy throat till this other had pulled out thy tongue for saying so: thou hast railed on thyself.

Adam. Sweet masters, be patient: for your father's remembrance, be at accord.

Oli. Let me go, I say.

Orl. I will not, till I please: you shall hear me. My father charged you in his will to give me good education: you have trained me like a peasant, obscuring and hiding from me all gentleman-like qualities. The spirit of my father grows strong in me, and I will no longer endure it: therefore allow me such exercises as may become a gentleman, or give me the poor allottery my father left me by testament; with that I will go buy my fortunes.

Oli. And what wilt thou do? beg, when that is spent? Well, sir, get you in: I will not long be troubled with you; you shall have some part of your will: I pray you, leave me.

Orl. I will no further offend you than becomes me for my good.

Oli. Get you with him, you old dog.

Adam. Is 'old dog' my reward? Most true, I have lost my teeth in your service. God be with my old master! he would not have spoke such a word.

Exeunt Orlando [*and*] *Adam.*

Oli. Is it even so? begin you to grow upon me? I will physic your rankness, and yet give no thousand crowns neither. Holla, Dennis!

Enter DENNIS.

Den. Calls your worship?

Oli. Was not Charles, the duke's wrestler, here to speak with me?

Den. So please you, he is here at the door and importunes access to you.

Oli. Call him in. [*Exit Dennis.*] 'Twill be a good way; and to-morrow the wrestling is.

Enter CHARLES.

Cha. Good morrow to your worship.

Oli. Good Monsieur Charles, what 's the new news at the new court?

Cha. There 's no news at the court, sir, but the old news: that is, the old duke is banished by his younger brother the new duke; and three or four loving lords have put themselves into voluntary exile with him, whose lands and revenues enrich the new duke; therefore he gives them good leave to wander.

Oli. Can you tell if Rosalind, the duke's daughter, be banished with her father?

Cha. O, no; for the duke's daughter, her cousin, so loves her, being ever from their cradles bred together, that she would have followed her exile, or have died to stay behind her. She is at the court, and no less beloved of her uncle than his own daughter; and never two ladies loved as they do.

Oli. Where will the old duke live?

Cha. They say he is already in the forest of Arden, and a many merry men with him; and there they live like the old Robin Hood of England: they say many young gentlemen flock to him every day, and fleet the time carelessly, as they did in the golden world.

Oli. What, you wrestle to-morrow before the new duke?

Cha. Marry, do I, sir; and I came to acquaint you with a matter. I am given, sir, secretly to understand that your younger brother Orlando hath a disposition to come in disguised against me to try a fall. To-morrow, sir, I wrestle for my credit; and he that escapes me without some broken limb shall acquit him well. Your brother is but young and tender; and, for your love, I would be loath to foil him, as I must, for my own honour, if he come in: therefore, out of my love to you, I came hither to acquaint you withal, that either you might stay him from his intendment or brook such disgrace well as he shall run into, in that it is a thing of his own search and altogether against my will.

ACT I. SCENE I. 2. **but poor,** merely. 4. **on his blessing,** on pain of losing his blessing. 6. **school,** university. 7. **profit,** progress. 20. **countenance,** attitude; patronage. 22. **bars me,** excludes me from. 23. **mines,** undermines. 39. **be naught awhile,** a slight malediction; possibly, efface yourself, withdraw. 41. **prodigal portion,** i.e., portion prodigally. 46. **him,** he whom. 48. **gentle condition of blood,** i.e., the bond of our kinship. 49. **courtesy of nations,** recognized custom of primogeniture. 54. **nearer to his reverence,** more worthy of the respect due him; Warburton suggested *revenue*, a reading which would account for Oliver's offense. 57. **young,** raw, inexperienced; here, indicative of Orlando's superiority at wrestling. Oliver has apparently struck him. 58. **villain,** bondman, servant. 67. **your father's remembrance,** memory of your father. 72. **obscuring and hiding,** obscuring in me, and hiding. 77. **allottery,** share, portion. 79. **thou,** used contemptuously instead of the more polite "you." 90. **grow upon me,** encroach on my place. 91. **rankness,** insolence, suggesting also the figure of *grow upon*. 115. **died to stay,** died from staying. 121. **a many,** many (as in "a dozen"); explained also as "a menie," company. 124. **fleet,** pass. 125. **golden world,** golden age, i.e., the traditional age of innocence from which man was thought to have degenerated. 134. **shall,** will inevitably. 141. **intendment,** purpose, intent. 147. **underhand means,** indirect or quiet methods. 151.

Oli. Charles, I thank thee for thy love to me, which thou shalt find I will most kindly requite. I had myself notice of my brother's purpose herein and have by underhand means laboured to dissuade him from it, but he is resolute. I'll tell thee, Charles: it is the stubbornest young fellow of France, full of ambition, an envious emulator of every man's good parts, a secret and villanous contriver against me his natural brother: therefore use thy discretion; I had as lief thou didst break his neck as his finger. And thou wert best look to 't; for if thou dost him any slight disgrace or if he do not mightily grace himself on thee, he will practise against thee by poison, entrap thee by some treacherous device and never leave thee till he hath ta'en thy life by some indirect means or other; for, I assure thee, and almost with tears I speak it, there is not one so young and so villanous this day living. I speak but brotherly of him; but should I anatomize him to thee as he is, I must blush and weep and thou must look pale and wonder.

Cha. I am heartily glad I came hither to you. If he come to-morrow, I'll give him his payment: if ever he go alone again, I'll never wrestle for prize more: and so God keep your worship!

Oli. Farewell, good Charles. *Exit* [*Charles*]. Now will I stir this gamester: I hope I shall see an end of him; for my soul, yet I know not why, hates nothing more than he. Yet he 's gentle, never schooled and yet learned, full of noble device, of all sorts enchantingly beloved, and indeed so much in the heart of the world, and especially of my own people, who best know him, that I am altogether misprised: but it shall not be so long; this wrestler shall clear all: nothing remains but that I kindle the boy thither; which now I'll go about. *Exit.*

SCENE II. [*Lawn before the* DUKE'S *palace.*]

Enter ROSALIND *and* CELIA.

Cel. I pray thee, Rosalind, sweet my coz, be merry.

Ros. Dear Celia, I show more mirth than I am mistress of; and would you yet I were merrier? Unless you could teach me to forget a banished father, you must not learn me how to remember any extraordinary pleasure.

Cel. Herein I see thou lovest me not with the full weight that I love thee. If my uncle, thy banished father, had banished thy uncle, the duke my father, so thou hadst been still with me, I could have taught my love to take thy father for mine: so wouldst thou, if the truth of thy love to me were so righteously tempered as mine is to thee.

Ros. Well, I will forget the condition of my estate, to rejoice in yours.

Cel. You know my father hath no child but I, nor none is like to have: and, truly, when he dies, thou shalt be his heir, for what he hath taken away from thy father perforce, I will render thee again in affection; by mine honour, I will; and when I break that oath, let me turn monster: therefore, my sweet Rose, my dear Rose, be merry.

Ros. From henceforth I will, coz, and devise sports. Let me see; what think you of falling in love?

Cel. Marry, I prithee, do, to make sport withal: but love no man in good earnest; nor no further in sport neither than with safety of a pure blush thou mayst in honour come off again.

Ros. What shall be our sport, then?

Cel. Let us sit and mock the good housewife Fortune from her wheel, that her gifts may henceforth be bestowed equally.

Ros. I would we could do so, for her benefits are mightily misplaced, and the bountiful blind woman doth most mistake in her gifts to women.

Cel. 'Tis true; for those that she makes fair she scarce makes honest, and those that she makes honest she makes very ill-favouredly.

Ros. Nay, now thou goest from Fortune's office to Nature's: Fortune reigns in gifts of the world, not in the lineaments of Nature.

Enter [TOUCHSTONE *the*] *Clown.*

Cel. No? when Nature hath made a fair creature, may she not by Fortune fall into the fire? Though Nature hath given us wit to flout at Fortune, hath not Fortune sent in this fool to cut off the argument?

Ros. Indeed, there is Fortune too hard for Nature, when Fortune makes Nature's natural the cutter-off of Nature's wit.

Cel. Peradventure this is not Fortune's work neither, but Nature's; who perceiveth our natural wits too dull to reason of such goddesses and hath sent this natural for our whetstone; for always the dulness of the fool is the whetstone of the wits. How now, wit! whither wander you?

Touch. Mistress, you must come away to your father.

Cel. Were you made the messenger?

Touch. No, by mine honour, but I was bid to come for you.

Ros. Where learned you that oath, fool?

Touch. Of a certain knight that swore by his honour they were good pancakes and swore by his honour the mustard was naught: now I'll stand to it, the pancakes were naught and the mustard was good, and yet was not the knight forsworn.

Cel. How prove you that, in the great heap of your knowledge?

Ros. Ay, marry, now unmuzzle your wisdom.

Touch. Stand you both forth now: stroke your chins, and swear by your beards that I am a knave.

Cel. By our beards, if we had them, thou art.

Touch. By my knavery, if I had it, then I were; but if you swear by that that is not, you are not forsworn: no more was this knight, swearing by his honour, for he never had any; or if he had, he had sworn it away

emulator, rival. 152. **contriver,** plotter. 153. **natural brother,** brother by blood, legitimate brother. 157. **grace himself on thee,** distinguish himself at your expense. 164. **brotherly,** with a reserve proper to a brother. 165. **anatomize,** lay open in detail, analyze; F: *anathomize.* 170. **payment,** punishment. 174. **gamester,** frolicsome person. 178. **noble device,** lofty aspiration. **sorts,** classes of people. **enchantingly,** as if by the effect of enchantment. 182. **misprised,** despised. 184. **kindle,** incite (to go). **thither,** i.e., to the wrestling match.

SCENE II. 1. **sweet my coz,** my sweet cousin. 10. **so,** provided that. 12-14. **if the . . . thee,** if the composition of your love were really as perfect as mine. 30-31. **safety . . . blush,** a degree of safety costing no more than an innocent blush. 31. **come off,** escape. 34. **housewife,** hussy; an epithet of slight contempt. Also, one who spins at her spinning wheel. 42. **ill-favouredly,** ugly, ill-favored. 49. **flout,** mock, scoff at. 53. **natural,** idiot, half-wit. 59. **whither wander you,** an allusion to the expression "wandering wits." 60. **Mistress,** not a polite title to address to a princess. 62. **messenger,** possibly, police officer. Celia says in effect, "Were you sent to arrest me?" (New Cambridge). 67. **pancakes,** fritters (which might be made of meat and so require mustard).

before ever he saw those pancakes or that mustard.

Cel. Prithee, who is 't that thou meanest?

Touch. One that old Frederick, your father, loves.

Cel. My father's love is enough to honour him: enough! speak no more of him; you'll be whipped for taxation one of these days.

Touch. The more pity, that fools may not speak wisely what wise men do foolishly.

Cel. By my troth, thou sayest true; for since the little wit that fools have was silenced, the little foolery that wise men have makes a great show. Here comes Monsieur Le Beau.

Enter LE BEAU.

Ros. With his mouth full of news.

Cel. Which he will put on us, as pigeons feed their young.

Ros. Then shall we be news-crammed.

Cel. All the better; we shall be the more marketable.—
Bon jour, Monsieur Le Beau: what 's the news?

Le Beau. Fair princess, you have lost much good sport.

Cel. Sport! of what colour?

Le Beau. What colour, madam! how shall I answer you?

Ros. As wit and fortune will.

Touch. Or as the Destinies decree.

Cel. Well said: that was laid on with a trowel.

Touch. Nay, if I keep not my rank,—

Ros. Thou losest thy old smell.

Le Beau. You amaze me, ladies: I would have told you of good wrestling, which you have lost the sight of.

Ros. Yet tell us the manner of the wrestling.

Le Beau. I will tell you the beginning; and, if it please your ladyships, you may see the end; for the best is yet to do; and here, where you are, they are coming to perform it.

Cel. Well, the beginning, that is dead and buried.

Le Beau. There comes an old man and his three sons,—

Cel. I could match this beginning with an old tale.

Le Beau. Three proper young men, of excellent growth and presence.

Ros. With bills on their necks, 'Be it known unto all men by these presents.'

Le Beau. The eldest of the three wrestled with Charles, the duke's wrestler; which Charles in a moment threw him and broke three of his ribs, that there is little hope of life in him: so he served the second, and so the third. Yonder they lie; the poor old man, their father, making such pitiful dole over them that all the beholders take his part with weeping.

Ros. Alas!

Touch. But what is the sport, monsieur, that the ladies have lost?

Le Beau. Why, this that I speak of.

Touch. Thus men may grow wiser every day: it is the first time that ever I heard breaking of ribs was sport for ladies.

Cel. Or I, I promise thee.

Ros. But is there any else longs to see this broken music in his sides? is there yet another dotes upon rib-breaking? Shall we see this wrestling, cousin?

Le Beau. You must, if you stay here; for here is the place appointed for the wrestling, and they are ready to perform it.

Cel. Yonder, sure, they are coming: let us now stay and see it.

Flourish. Enter DUKE [FREDERICK], LORDS, ORLANDO, CHARLES, *and* Attendants.

Duke F. Come on: since the youth will not be entreated, his own peril on his forwardness.

Ros. Is yonder the man?

Le Beau. Even he, madam.

Cel. Alas, he is too young! yet he looks successfully.

Duke F. How now, daughter and cousin! are you crept hither to see the wrestling?

Ros. Ay, my liege, so please you give us leave.

Duke F. You will take little delight in it, I can tell you; there is such odds in the man. In pity of the challenger's youth I would fain dissuade him, but he will not be entreated. Speak to him, ladies; see if you can move him.

Cel. Call him hither, good Monsieur Le Beau.

Duke F. Do so: I'll not be by.

Le Beau. Monsieur the challenger, the princess calls for you.

Orl. I attend them with all respect and duty.

Ros. Young man, have you challenged Charles the wrestler?

Orl. No, fair princess; he is the general challenger: I come but in, as others do, to try with him the strength of my youth.

Cel. Young gentleman, your spirits are too bold for your years. You have seen cruel proof of this man's strength: if you saw yourself with your eyes or knew yourself with your judgement, the fear of your adventure would counsel you to a more equal enterprise. We pray you, for your own sake, to embrace your own safety and give over this attempt.

Ros. Do, young sir; your reputation shall not therefore be misprised: we will make it our suit to the duke that the wrestling might not go forward.

Orl. I beseech you, punish me not with your hard thoughts; wherein I confess me much guilty, to deny so fair and excellent ladies any thing. But let your fair eyes and gentle wishes go with me to my trial: wherein if I be foiled, there is but one shamed that was never gracious; if killed, but one dead that is willing to be so: I shall do my friends no wrong, for I have none to lament me, the world no injury, for in it I have nothing; only in the world I fill up a place, which may be better supplied when I have made it empty.

Ros. The little strength that I have, I would it were with you.

Cel. And mine, to eke out hers.

Ros. Fare you well: pray heaven I be deceived in you!

91. **taxation,** satire, censure; in this case directed at the reigning duke. 99. **put on,** force upon, communicate to. 107. **colour,** kind. 112. **laid . . . trowel,** i.e., clumsily, bluntly. 131. **bills,** advertisements, proclamations. 132. **presents,** document presented, with pun on *presence.* 139. **dole,** grief, lamentation. 149. **any,** anyone. 150. **broken music,** music arranged in parts for different instruments (with a pun on broken ribs). 159. **peril on,** i.e., be upon. 163. **successfully,** i.e., as if he would be successful. 169. **such odds in the man,** such advantage on the side of the man (i.e., the wrestler, Charles, as contrasted with the youth, Orlando). 176. **princess calls.** So F. New Cambridge editors defend the F reading on the ground that Le Beau, as an adherent of the usurping duke, would recognize only one princess. 185-187. **if . . . judgement,** if you saw yourself as you really are in relation to your opponent and used your judgment. Some older editors

Cel. Your heart's desires be with you!

Cha. Come, where is this young gallant that is so desirous to lie with his mother earth?

Orl. Ready, sir; but his will hath in it a more modest working.

Duke F. You shall try but one fall.

Cha. No, I warrant your grace, you shall not entreat him to a second, that have so mightily persuaded him from a first.

Orl. An you mean to mock me after, you should not have mocked me before: but come your ways.

Ros. Now Hercules be thy speed, young man!

Cel. I would I were invisible, to catch the strong fellow by the leg. [*They*] *wrestle.*

Ros. O excellent young man!

Cel. If I had a thunderbolt in mine eye, I can tell who should down. *Shout.* [*Charles is thrown.*]

Duke F. No more, no more.

Orl. Yes, I beseech your grace: I am not yet well breathed.

Duke F. How dost thou, Charles?

Le Beau. He cannot speak, my lord.

Duke F. Bear him away. What is thy name, young man? [*Charles is borne out.*]

Orl. Orlando, my liege; the youngest son of Sir Rowland de Boys.

Duke F. I would thou hadst been son to some man else:
The world esteem'd thy father honourable,
But I did find him still mine enemy:
Thou shouldst have better pleas'd me with this deed,
Hadst thou descended from another house.
But fare thee well; thou art a gallant youth:
I would thou hadst told me of another father.
Exit Duke [*with train*].

Cel. Were I my father, coz, would I do this?

Orl. I am more proud to be Sir Rowland's son,
His youngest son; and would not change that calling,
To be adopted heir to Frederick.

Ros. My father lov'd Sir Rowland as his soul,
And all the world was of my father's mind:
Had I before known this young man his son,
I should have given him tears unto entreaties,
Ere he should thus have ventur'd.

Cel. Gentle cousin,
Let us go thank him and encourage him:
My father's rough and envious disposition
Sticks me at heart. Sir, you have well deserv'd:
If you do keep your promises in love
But justly, as you have exceeded all promise,
Your mistress shall be happy.

Ros. Gentleman,
[*Giving him a chain from her neck.*]
Wear this for me, one out of suits with fortune,
That could give more, but that her hand lacks means.
Shall we go, coz?

Cel. Ay. Fare you well, fair gentleman.

Orl. Can I not say, I thank you? My better parts
Are all thrown down, and that which here stands up
Is but a quintain, a mere lifeless block.

Ros. He calls us back: my pride fell with my fortunes;
I'll ask him what he would. Did you call, sir?
Sir, you have wrestled well and overthrown
More than your enemies.

Cel. Will you go, coz?

Ros. Have with you. Fare you well.
Exit [*with Celia*].

Orl. What passion hangs these weights upon my tongue?
I cannot speak to her, yet she urg'd conference.
O poor Orlando, thou art overthrown!
Or Charles or something weaker masters thee.

Enter LE BEAU.

Le Beau. Good sir, I do in friendship counsel you
To leave this place. Albeit you have deserv'd
High commendation, true applause and love,
Yet such is now the duke's condition
That he misconsters all that you have done.
The duke is humorous: what he is indeed,
More suits you to conceive than I to speak of.

Orl. I thank you, sir: and, pray you, tell me this;
Which of the two was daughter of the duke
That here was at the wrestling?

Le Beau. Neither his daughter, if we judge by manners;
But yet indeed the taller is his daughter:
The other is daughter to the banish'd duke,
And here detain'd by her usurping uncle,
To keep his daughter company; whose loves
Are dearer than the natural bond of sisters.
But I can tell you that of late this duke
Hath ta'en displeasure 'gainst his gentle niece,
Grounded upon no other argument
But that the people praise her for her virtues
And pity her for her good father's sake;
And, on my life, his malice 'gainst the lady
Will suddenly break forth. Sir, fare you well:
Hereafter, in a better world than this,
I shall desire more love and knowledge of you.

Orl. I rest much bounden to you: fare you well.
[*Exit Le Beau.*]
Thus must I from the smoke into the smother;
From tyrant duke unto a tyrant brother:
But heavenly Rosalind! *Exit.*

SCENE III. [*A room in the palace.*]

Enter CELIA *and* ROSALIND.

Cel. Why, cousin! why, Rosalind! Cupid have mercy! not a word?

Ros. Not one to throw at a dog.

Cel. No, thy words are too precious to be cast away

read *our* for *your* in line 186. 192. **therefore,** on that account. **misprised,** despised. 200. **gracious,** looked upon with favor. 215. **working,** endeavor. 222. **come your ways,** come on. 223. **Hercules . . . speed,** may Hercules favor you. 230. **well breathed,** warmed up. 245. **calling,** appellation, name. 249. **known,** i.e., known to be. 250. **unto,** in addition to. 254. **Sticks me at heart,** stabs me to the heart. 258. **out . . . fortune,** not wearing the livery of fortune; not in her service; or one whose suits to fortune are rejected. 263. **quintain,** wooden figure at which to tilt. 272. **Or,** either. 276. **condition,** state of mind, disposition. 277. **misconsters,** misconstrues. 278. **humorous,** given to whims, capricious, self-willed. 284. **taller,** possibly an error for "smaller" or "lesser," or else an inconsistency on Shakespeare's part; later on, Rosalind is shown to be the taller. 299. **smoke into the smother,** frying-pan into the fire.

upon curs; throw some of them at me; come, lame me with reasons.

Ros. Then there were two cousins laid up; when the one should be lamed with reasons and the other mad without any.

Cel. But is all this for your father?

Ros. No, some of it is for my child's father. O, how full of briers is this working-day world!

Cel. They are but burs, cousin, thrown upon thee in holiday foolery: if we walk not in the trodden paths, our very petticoats will catch them.

Ros. I could shake them off my coat: these burs are in my heart.

Cel. Hem them away.

Ros. I would try, if I could cry 'hem' and have him.

Cel. Come, come, wrestle with thy affections.

Ros. O, they take the part of a better wrestler than myself!

Cel. O, a good wish upon you! you will try in time, in despite of a fall. But, turning these jests out of service, let us talk in good earnest: is it possible, on such a sudden, you should fall into so strong a liking with old Sir Rowland's youngest son?

Ros. The duke my father loved his father dearly.

Cel. Doth it therefore ensue that you should love his son dearly? By this kind of chase, I should hate him, for my father hated his father dearly; yet I hate not Orlando.

Ros. No, faith, hate him not, for my sake.

Cel. Why should I not? doth he not deserve well?

Enter DUKE [FREDERICK], *with* Lords.

Ros. Let me love him for that, and do you love him because I do. Look, here comes the duke.

Cel. With his eyes full of anger.

Duke F. Mistress, dispatch you with your safest haste
And get you from our court.
Ros. Me, uncle?
Duke F. You, cousin:
Within these ten days if that thou be'st found
So near our public court as twenty miles,
Thou diest for it.
Ros. I do beseech your grace,
Let me the knowledge of my fault bear with me:
If with myself I hold intelligence
Or have acquaintance with mine own desires,
If that I do not dream or be not frantic,—
As I do trust I am not—then, dear uncle,
Never so much as in a thought unborn
Did I offend your highness.
Duke F. Thus do all traitors:
If their purgation did consist in words,
They are as innocent as grace itself:
Let it suffice thee that I trust thee not.
Ros. Yet your mistrust cannot make me a traitor:
Tell me whereon the likelihood depends.
Duke F. Thou art thy father's daughter; there 's enough.
Ros. So was I when your highness took his dukedom;
So was I when your highness banish'd him:
Treason is not inherited, my lord;
Or, if we did derive it from our friends,
What 's that to me? my father was no traitor:
Then, good my liege, mistake me not so much
To think my poverty is treacherous.
Cel. Dear sovereign, hear me speak.
Duke F. Ay, Celia; we stay'd her for your sake,
Else had she with her father rang'd along.
Cel. I did not then entreat to have her stay;
It was your pleasure and your own remorse:
I was too young that time to value her;
But now I know her: if she be a traitor,
Why so am I; we still have slept together,
Rose at an instant, learn'd, play'd, eat together,
And wheresoe'er we went, like Juno's swans,
Still we went coupled and inseparable.
Duke F. She is too subtle for thee; and her smoothness,
Her very silence and her patience
Speak to the people, and they pity her.
Thou art a fool: she robs thee of thy name;
And thou wilt show more bright and seem more virtuous
When she is gone. Then open not thy lips:
Firm and irrevocable is my doom
Which I have pass'd upon her; she is banish'd.
Cel. Pronounce that sentence then on me, my liege:
I cannot live out of her company.
Duke F. You are a fool. You, niece, provide yourself:
If you outstay the time, upon mine honour,
And in the greatness of my word, you die.
Exit Duke, &c.
Cel. O my poor Rosalind, whither wilt thou go?
Wilt thou change fathers? I will give thee mine.
I charge thee, be not thou more griev'd than I am.
Ros. I have more cause.
Cel. Thou hast not, cousin;
Prithee, be cheerful: know'st thou not, the duke
Hath banish'd me, his daughter?
Ros. That he hath not.
Cel. No, hath not? Rosalind lacks then the love
Which teacheth thee that thou and I am one:
Shall we be sund'red? shall we part, sweet girl?
No: let my father seek another heir.
Therefore devise with me how we may fly,
Whither to go and what to bear with us;
And do not seek to take your change upon you,
To bear your griefs yourself and leave me out;
For, by this heaven, now at our sorrows pale,
Say what thou canst, I'll go along with thee.
Ros. Why, whither shall we go?
Cel. To seek my uncle in the forest of Arden.
Ros. Alas, what danger will it be to us,
Maids as we are, to travel forth so far!
Beauty provoketh thieves sooner than gold.
Cel. I'll put myself in poor and mean attire
And with a kind of umber smirch my face;
The like do you: so shall we pass along
And never stir assailants.

SCENE III. 6. **lame . . . reasons.** Rosalind has talked about throwing words at a dog and thus perhaps laming him. Celia says, "Lame me by throwing reasons at me." 12. **working-day,** trivial. 20. **cry 'hem,'** clear away with a "hem" or a cough, with a play on *him*. 27. **on such a sudden,** so suddenly. 37. **deserve well,** i.e., to be hated. 43. **safest haste,** speed, which is your best security. 45. **ten,** anonymous conjecture: *two*. 55. **purgation,** exculpation. 64. **friends,** relatives, kinsfolk. 70. **rang'd,** roamed; see glossary. 73. **that time,** then. 77. **Juno's swans.** It has been pointed out that it was Venus and not Juno who possessed swans. 104. **change,** change of fortune. 114. **umber,** brown pigment used to disguise the face. 118. **suit,** dress. 119. **curtle-axe,** broad cutting sword. 122. **swashing,** swaggering. 127. **Ganymede,** the name of Jupiter's cupbearer; used also in Lodge's *Rosalynde*. 139. **content,** contentment.

Ros. Were it not better,
Because that I am more than common tall,
That I did suit me all points like a man?
A gallant curtle-axe upon my thigh,
A boar-spear in my hand; and—in my heart
Lie there what hidden woman's fear there will—
We'll have a swashing and a martial outside,
As many other mannish cowards have
That do outface it with their semblances.
Cel. What shall I call thee when thou art a man?
Ros. I'll have no worse a name than Jove's own page;
And therefore look you call me Ganymede.
But what will you be call'd?
Cel. Something that hath a reference to my state;
No longer Celia, but Aliena.
Ros. But, cousin, what if we assay'd to steal
The clownish fool out of your father's court?
Would he not be a comfort to our travel?
Cel. He'll go along o'er the wide world with me;
Leave me alone to woo him. Let 's away,
And get our jewels and our wealth together,
Devise the fittest time and safest way
To hide us from pursuit that will be made
After my flight. Now go we in content
To liberty and not to banishment. *Exeunt.*

ACT II.

SCENE I. [*The Forest of Arden.*]

Enter DUKE Senior, AMIENS, *and two or three* Lords, *like foresters.*

Duke S. Now, my co-mates and brothers in exile,
Hath not old custom made this life more sweet
Than that of painted pomp? Are not these woods
More free from peril than the envious court?
Here feel we not the penalty of Adam,
The seasons' difference, as the icy fang
And churlish chiding of the winter's wind,
Which, when it bites and blows upon my body,
Even till I shrink with cold, I smile and say
'This is no flattery: these are counsellors
That feelingly persuade me what I am.'
Sweet are the uses of adversity,
Which, like the toad, ugly and venomous,
Wears yet a precious jewel in his head;
And this our life exempt from public haunt
Finds tongues in trees, books in the running brooks,
Sermons in stones and good in every thing.
Ami. I would not change it. Happy is your grace,
That can translate the stubbornness of fortune
Into so quiet and so sweet a style.
Duke S. Come, shall we go and kill us venison?
And yet it irks me the poor dappled fools,
Being native burghers of this desert city,
Should in their own confines with forked heads
Have their round haunches gor'd.
First Lord. Indeed, my lord,
The melancholy Jaques grieves at that,
And, in that kind, swears you do more usurp
Than doth your brother that hath banish'd you.
To-day my Lord of Amiens and myself
Did steal behind him as he lay along
Under an oak whose antique root peeps out
Upon the brook that brawls along this wood:
To the which place a poor sequest'red stag,
That from the hunter's aim had ta'en a hurt,
Did come to languish, and indeed, my lord,
The wretched animal heav'd forth such groans
That their discharge did stretch his leathern coat
Almost to bursting, and the big round tears
Cours'd one another down his innocent nose
In piteous chase; and thus the hairy fool,
Much marked of the melancholy Jaques,
Stood on th' extremest verge of the swift brook,
Augmenting it with tears.
Duke S. But what said Jaques?
Did he not moralize this spectacle?
First Lord. O, yes, into a thousand similes.
First, for his weeping into the needless stream;
'Poor deer,' quoth he, 'thou mak'st a testament
As worldings do, giving thy sum of more
To that which had too much:' then, being there alone,
Left and abandoned of his velvet friends,
''Tis right,' quoth he; 'thus misery doth part
The flux of company:' anon a careless herd,
Full of the pasture, jumps along by him
And never stays to greet him; 'Ay,' quoth Jaques,
'Sweep on, you fat and greasy citizens;
'Tis just the fashion: wherefore do you look
Upon that poor and broken bankrupt there?'
Thus most invectively he pierceth through
The body of the country, city, court,
Yea, and of this our life, swearing that we
Are mere usurpers, tyrants and what 's worse,
To fright the animals and to kill them up
In their assign'd and native dwelling-place.
Duke S. And did you leave him in this contemplation?
Sec. Lord. We did, my lord, weeping and commenting
Upon the sobbing deer.
Duke S. Show me the place:
I love to cope him in these sullen fits,
For then he 's full of matter.
First Lord. I'll bring you to him straight. *Exeunt.*

SCENE II. [*A room in the palace.*]

Enter DUKE [FREDERICK], *with* Lords.

Duke F. Can it be possible that no man saw them?
It cannot be: some villains of my court
Are of consent and sufferance in this.
First Lord. I cannot hear of any that did see her.
The ladies, her attendants of her chamber,
Saw her a-bed, and in the morning early
They found the bed untreasur'd of their mistress.

ACT II. SCENE I. 5. **feel we not,** we do not feel. Globe emends *not* to *but*. **penalty of Adam,** expulsion from Eden, loss of innocence. 6. **as,** such as. 13-14. **like . . . head.** The idea that the toad was venomous comes from Pliny's *Natural History*. The jewel referred to is the toadstone, which was thought to be in the head of the toad. 15. **exempt,** cut off. 22. **irks,** grieves, vexes. 23. **burghers,** citizens. 31. **antique,** ancient. 44. **moralize,** draw out the hidden meaning of. 50. **velvet,** courtierlike. Velvet was the typical dress of the courtier; a probable allusion also to the velvet of the deer's horn. 58. **invectively,** with denunciation. 68. **matter,** sense, substance.

SCENE II. 3. **consent and sufferance,** agreement as to course of action and permission for events to take place without opposition; metaphor from law.

Sec. Lord. My lord, the roynish clown, at whom so oft
Your grace was wont to laugh, is also missing.
Hisperia, the princess' gentlewoman,
Confesses that she secretly o'erheard
Your daughter and her cousin much commend
The parts and graces of the wrestler
That did but lately foil the sinewy Charles;
And she believes, wherever they are gone,
That youth is surely in their company.
Duke F. Send to his brother; fetch that gallant hither;
If he be absent, bring his brother to me;
I'll make him find him: do this suddenly,
And let not search and inquisition quail
To bring again these foolish runaways. *Exeunt.*

SCENE III. [*Before* OLIVER's *house.*]

Enter ORLANDO *and* ADAM [, *meeting*].

Orl. Who 's there?
Adam. What, my young master? O my gentle master!
O my sweet master! O you memory
Of old Sir Rowland! why, what make you here?
Why are you virtuous? why do people love you?
And wherefore are you gentle, strong and valiant?
Why would you be so fond to overcome
The bonny priser of the humorous duke?
Your praise is come too swiftly home before you.
Know you not, master, to some kind of men
Their graces serve them but as enemies?
No more do yours: your virtues, gentle master,
Are sanctified and holy traitors to you.
O, what a world is this, when what is comely
Envenoms him that bears it!
Orl. Why, what 's the matter?
Adam. O unhappy youth!
Come not within these doors; within this roof
The enemy of all your graces lives:
Your brother—no, no brother; yet the son—
Yet not the son, I will not call him son
Of him I was about to call his father—
Hath heard your praises, and this night he means
To burn the lodging where you use to lie
And you within it: if he fail of that,
He will have other means to cut you off.
I overheard him and his practices.
This is no place; this house is but a butchery:
Abhor it, fear it, do not enter it.
Orl. Why, whither, Adam, wouldst thou have me go?
Adam. No matter whither, so you come not here.
Orl. What, wouldst thou have me go and beg my food?
Or with a base and boist'rous sword enforce
A thievish living on the common road?
This I must do, or know not what to do:
Yet this I will not do, do how I can;
I rather will subject me to the malice
Of a diverted blood and bloody brother.
Adam. But do not so. I have five hundred crowns,
The thrifty hire I saved under your father,
Which I did store to be my foster-nurse
When service should in my old limbs lie lame
And unregarded age in corners thrown:
Take that, and He that doth the ravens feed,
Yea, providently caters for the sparrow,
Be comfort to my age! Here is the gold;
All this I give you. Let me be your servant:
Though I look old, yet I am strong and lusty;
For in my youth I never did apply
Hot and rebellious liquors in my blood,
Nor did not with unbashful forehead woo
The means of weakness and debility;
Therefore my age is as a lusty winter,
Frosty, but kindly: let me go with you;
I'll do the service of a younger man
In all your business and necessities.
Orl. O good old man, how well in thee appears
The constant service of the antique world,
When service sweat for duty, not for meed!
Thou art not for the fashion of these times,
Where none will sweat but for promotion,
And having that, do choke their service up
Even with the having: it is not so with thee.
But, poor old man, thou prunest a rotten tree,
That cannot so much as a blossom yield
In lieu of all thy pains and husbandry.
But come thy ways; we'll go along together,
And ere we have thy youthful wages spent,
We'll light upon some settled low content.
Adam. Master, go on, and I will follow thee,
To the last gasp, with truth and loyalty.
From seventeen years till now almost fourscore
Here lived I, but now live here no more.
At seventeen years many their fortunes seek;
But at fourscore it is too late a week:
Yet fortune cannot recompense me better
Than to die well and not my master's debtor. *Exeunt.*

SCENE IV. [*The Forest of Arden.*]

Enter ROSALIND *for* GANYMEDE, CELIA *for* ALIENA, *and Clown, alias* TOUCHSTONE.

Ros. O Jupiter, how weary are my spirits!

Touch. I care not for my spirits, if my legs were not weary.

Ros. I could find in my heart to disgrace my man's apparel and to cry like a woman; but I must comfort the weaker vessel, as doublet and hose ought to show itself courageous to petticoat: therefore courage, good Aliena!

Cel. I pray you, bear with me; I cannot go no further.

Touch. For my part, I had rather bear with you than bear you; yet I should bear no cross if I did bear you, for I think you have no money in your purse.

8. **roynish,** scurvy, coarse. 17. **that gallant,** i.e., Orlando. 19. **suddenly,** speedily. 20. **inquisition,** inquiry. **quail,** fail, slacken. 21. **again,** back.

SCENE III. 3. **memory,** memorial, memento. 7. **to,** as to. 8. **bonny priser,** big champion or prize fighter. 14-15. **when . . . it,** i.e., as did the shirt of Nessus, or the poisoned garment sent by Medea to Creusa. 23. **use,** are wont. 27. **place,** residence, dwelling. **butchery,** slaughter house. 37. **diverted blood,** kinship diverted from the natural course. 39. **thrifty,** obtained by economy. 43-44. **He . . . sparrow.** See Luke 12:22-24. 57. **service,** probably, body of servants collectively. 58. **meed,** reward. 65. **lieu of,** return for. 68. **low content,** lowly contented state. 74. **too late a week,** too late by a good deal.

SCENE IV. 1. **weary,** so Theobald; F: *merry.* 6. **weaker vessel,** woman. See I Peter 3:7. 7. **doublet and hose,** typical male attire. 13.

Ros. Well, this is the forest of Arden.

Touch. Ay, now am I in Arden; the more fool I; when I was at home, I was in a better place: but travellers must be content.

Ros. Ay, be so, good Touchstone.

Enter CORIN *and* SILVIUS.

Look you, who comes here; a young man and an old in solemn talk.

Cor. That is the way to make her scorn you still.

Sil. O Corin, that thou knew'st how I do love her!

Cor. I partly guess; for I have lov'd ere now.

Sil. No, Corin, being old, thou canst not guess,
Though in thy youth thou wast as true a lover
As ever sigh'd upon a midnight pillow:
But if thy love were ever like to mine—
As sure I think did never man love so—
How many actions most ridiculous
Hast thou been drawn to by thy fantasy?

Cor. Into a thousand that I have forgotten.

Sil. O, thou didst then ne'er love so heartily!
If thou rememb'rest not the slightest folly
That ever love did make thee run into,
Thou hast not lov'd:
Or if thou hast not sat as I do now,
Wearing thy hearer in thy mistress' praise,
Thou hast not lov'd:
Or if thou hast not broke from company
Abruptly, as my passion now makes me,
Thou hast not lov'd.
O Phebe, Phebe, Phebe! *Exit.*

Ros. Alas, poor shepherd! searching of thy wound,
I have by hard adventure found mine own.

Touch. And I mine. I remember, when I was in love I broke my sword upon a stone and bid him take that for coming a-night to Jane Smile; and I remember the kissing of her batler and the cow's dugs that her pretty chopt hands had milked; and I remember the wooing of a peascod instead of her, from whom I took two cods and, giving her them again, said with weeping tears 'Wear these for my sake.' We that are true lovers run into strange capers; but as all is mortal in nature, so is all nature in love mortal in folly.

Ros. Thou speakest wiser than thou art ware of.

Touch. Nay, I shall ne'er be ware of mine own wit till I break my shins against it.

Ros. Jove, Jove! this shepherd's passion
Is much upon my fashion.

Touch. And mine; but it grows something stale with me.

Cel. I pray you, one of you question yond man
If he for gold will give us any food:
I faint almost to death.

Touch. Holla, you clown!

Ros. Peace, fool: he 's not thy kinsman.

Cor. Who calls?

Touch. Your betters, sir.

Cor. Else are they very wretched.

Ros. Peace, I say.—Good even to you, friend.

Cor. And to you, gentle sir, and to you all.

Ros. I prithee, shepherd, if that love or gold
Can in this desert place buy entertainment,
Bring us where we may rest ourselves and feed:
Here 's a young maid with travel much oppress'd
And faints for succour.

Cor. Fair sir, I pity her
And wish, for her sake more than for mine own,
My fortunes were more able to relieve her;
But I am shepherd to another man
And do not shear the fleeces that I graze:
My master is of churlish disposition
And little recks to find the way to heaven
By doing deeds of hospitality:
Besides, his cote, his flocks and bounds of feed
Are now on sale, and at our sheepcote now,
By reason of his absence, there is nothing
That you will feed on; but what is, come see,
And in my voice most welcome shall you be.

Ros. What is he that shall buy his flock and pasture?

Cor. That young swain that you saw here but erewhile,
That little cares for buying any thing.

Ros. I pray thee, if it stand with honesty,
Buy thou the cottage, pasture and the flock,
And thou shalt have to pay for it of us.

Cel. And we will mend thy wages. I like this place,
And willingly could waste my time in it.

Cor. Assuredly the thing is to be sold:
Go with me: if you like upon report
The soil, the profit and this kind of life,
I will your very faithful feeder be
And buy it with your gold right suddenly. *Exeunt.*

SCENE V. [*The forest.*]

Enter AMIENS, JAQUES, *and others.*

SONG.

[*Ami.*] Under the greenwood tree
Who loves to lie with me,
And turn his merry note
Unto the sweet bird's throat,
Come hither, come hither, come hither:
Here shall he see
No enemy
But winter and rough weather.

Jaq. More, more, I prithee, more.

Ami. It will make you melancholy, Monsieur Jaques.

Jaq. I thank it. More, I prithee, more. I can suck melancholy out of a song, as a weasel sucks eggs. More, I prithee, more.

Ami. My voice is ragged: I know I cannot please you.

Jaq. I do not desire you to please me; I do desire you to sing. Come, more; another stanzo: call you 'em stanzos?

Ami. What you will, Monsieur Jaques.

Jaq. Nay, I care not for their names; they owe me nothing. Will you sing?

cross, coin having on it a figure of a cross. 38. **Wearing,** wearying. 44. **searching,** probing. 48. **a-night,** by night. 50. **batler,** club or bat for beating clothes in process of washing. 51. **chopt,** chapped. 52. **peascod,** pea pod; regarded as a lucky gift by rustic lovers. 56. **mortal,** subject to death. 58. **ware,** aware. 62. **upon,** after, according to. 75. **for succour,** for want of succor. 79. **fleeces,** flock. 80. **churlish,** niggardly, miserly. 81. **recks,** heeds, cares. 83. **cote,** shepherd's cottage. **bounds of feed,** limits within which he has the right of pasturage. 87. **in my voice,** insofar as I have authority to speak. 89. **erewhile,** a short time since. 91. **stand,** be consistent. 99. **feeder,** servant.

SCENE V. 3. **turn,** attune, adopt. 21. **names,** i.e., of debts owed, signatures (to a bond).

Ami. More at your request than to please myself.

Jaq. Well then, if ever I thank any man, I'll thank you; but that they call compliment is like the encounter of two dog-apes, and when a man thanks me heartily, methinks I have given him a penny and he renders me the beggarly thanks. Come, sing; and you that will not, hold your tongues.

Ami. Well, I'll end the song. Sirs, cover the while; the duke will drink under this tree. He hath been all this day to look you.

Jaq. And I have been all this day to avoid him. He is too disputable for my company: I think of as many matters as he, but I give heaven thanks and make no boast of them. Come, warble, come.

SONG.

Who doth ambition shun *All together here.*
And loves to live i' th' sun,
Seeking the food he eats
And pleas'd with what he gets,
Come hither, come hither, come hither:
Here shall he see
No enemy
But winter and rough weather.

Jaq. I'll give you a verse to this note that I made yesterday in despite of my invention.

Ami. And I'll sing it.

Jaq. Thus it goes:—

If it do come to pass
That any man turn ass,
Leaving his wealth and ease,
A stubborn will to please,
Ducdame, ducdame, ducdame:
Here shall he see
Gross fools as he,
An if he will come to me.

Ami. What 's that 'ducdame'?

Jaq. 'Tis a Greek invocation, to call fools into a circle. I'll go sleep, if I can; if I cannot, I'll rail against all the first-born of Egypt.

Ami. And I'll go seek the duke: his banquet is prepared. *Exeunt [severally].*

SCENE VI. [*The forest.*]

Enter ORLANDO *and* ADAM.

Adam. Dear master, I can go no further: O, I die for food! Here lie I down, and measure out my grave. Farewell, kind master.

Orl. Why, how now, Adam! no greater heart in thee? Live a little; comfort a little; cheer thyself a little. If this uncouth forest yield any thing savage, I will either be food for it or bring it for food to thee. Thy conceit is nearer death than thy powers. For my sake be comfortable; hold death awhile at the arm's end: I will here be with thee presently; and if I bring thee not something to eat, I will give thee leave to die: but if thou diest before I come, thou art a mocker of my labour. Well said! thou lookest cheerly, and I'll be with thee quickly. Yet thou liest in the bleak air: come, I will bear thee to some shelter; and thou shalt not die for lack of a dinner, if there live any thing in this desert. Cheerly, good Adam! *Exeunt.*

SCENE VII. [*The forest.*]

Enter DUKE *Senior, and* Lords, *like* outlaws.

Duke S. I think he be transform'd into a beast;
For I can no where find him like a man.

First Lord. My lord, he is but even now gone hence:
Here was he merry, hearing of a song.

Duke S. If he, compact of jars, grow musical,
We shall have shortly discord in the spheres.
Go, seek him: tell him I would speak with him.

Enter JAQUES.

First Lord. He saves my labour by his own approach.

Duke S. Why, how now, monsieur! what a life is this,
That your poor friends must woo your company?
What, you look merrily!

Jaq. A fool, a fool! I met a fool i' th' forest,
A motley fool; a miserable world!
As I do live by food, I met a fool;
Who laid him down and bask'd him in the sun,
And rail'd on Lady Fortune in good terms,
In good set terms and yet a motley fool.
'Good morrow, fool,' quoth I. 'No, sir,' quoth he,
'Call me not fool till heaven hath sent me fortune:'
And then he drew a dial from his poke,
And, looking on it with lack-lustre eye,
Says very wisely, 'It is ten o'clock:
Thus we may see,' quoth he, 'how the world wags:
'Tis but an hour ago since it was nine,
And after one hour more 'twill be eleven;
And so, from hour to hour, we ripe and ripe,
And then, from hour to hour, we rot and rot;
And thereby hangs a tale.' When I did hear
The motley fool thus moral on the time,
My lungs began to crow like chanticleer,
That fools should be so deep-contemplative,
And I did laugh sans intermission
An hour by his dial. O noble fool!
A worthy fool! Motley 's the only wear.

Duke S. What fool is this?

Jaq. O worthy fool! One that hath been a courtier,
And says, if ladies be but young and fair,
They have the gift to know it: and in his brain,
Which is as dry as the remainder biscuit
After a voyage, he hath strange places cramm'd

27. **dog-apes,** dog-faced baboons. 32. **cover,** spread the cloth for a meal. 33. **the while,** in the meantime. 34. **to look,** looking for. 36. **disputable,** inclined to dispute. 49. **in . . . invention,** although I lack imagination; or, without even using my imagination. 56. **Ducdame,** unexplained. New Cambridge editors, following Charles Strachey and John Sampson, explain *ducdame* as a corruption of the gypsy words *dukrā mē*, meaning "I foretell," "I tell fortunes or prophesy"; therefore as the call of a gypsy fortuneteller at fairs, it is a "Greek" (or sharper's) invocation. This also renders the allusion to *the first-born of Egypt* intelligible, since the first-born duke is banished and in the condition of a gypsy. 64. **banquet,** wine and dessert after dinner.

SCENE VI. 5. **comfort,** anonymous conjecture: *comfort thee.* 6. **uncouth,** strange, wild. 10. **comfortable,** cheerful. 19. **Cheerly,** blithely.

SCENE VII. 5. **compact of jars,** composed of discords. 6. **spheres,** reference to the music supposed to be produced by the revolving concentric spheres of the Ptolemaic solar system. 13. **motley,** the particolored dress of the clown. 19. **'Call . . . fortune,'** an allusion to the proverb, "Fortune favors fools." 20. **dial,** watch, or portable sundial. **poke,** pocket. 29. **moral,** moralize. 30. **crow,** laugh merrily. 34. **only wear,** only thing worth wearing. 40. **places,** topics, subjects for

With observation, the which he vents
In mangled forms. O that I were a fool!
I am ambitious for a motley coat.

Duke S. Thou shalt have one.

Jaq. It is my only suit;
Provided that you weed your better judgements
Of all opinion that grows rank in them
That I am wise. I must have liberty
Withal, as large a charter as the wind,
To blow on whom I please; for so fools have;
And they that are most galled with my folly,
They most must laugh. And why, sir, must they so?
The 'why' is plain as way to parish church:
He that a fool doth very wisely hit
Doth very foolishly, although he smart,
Not to seem senseless of the bob: if not,
The wise man's folly is anatomiz'd
Even by the squand'ring glances of the fool.
Invest me in my motley; give me leave
To speak my mind, and I will through and through
Cleanse the foul body of th' infected world,
If they will patiently receive my medicine.

Duke S. Fie on thee! I can tell what thou wouldst do.

Jaq. What, for a counter, would I do but good?

Duke S. Most mischievous foul sin, in chiding sin:
For thou thyself hast been a libertine,
As sensual as the brutish sting itself;
And all th' embossed sores and headed evils,
That thou with license of free foot hast caught,
Wouldst thou disgorge into the general world.

Jaq. Why, who cries out on pride,
That can therein tax any private party?
Doth it not flow as hugely as the sea,
†Till that the weary very means do ebb?
What woman in the city do I name,
When that I say the city-woman bears
The cost of princes on unworthy shoulders?
Who can come in and say that I mean her,
When such a one as she such is her neighbour?
Or what is he of basest function
That says his bravery is not on my cost,
Thinking that I mean him, but therein suits
His folly to the mettle of my speech?
There then; how then? what then? Let me see wherein
My tongue hath wrong'd him: if it do him right,
Then he hath wrong'd himself; if he be free,
Why then my taxing like a wild-goose flies,
Unclaim'd of any man. But who comes here?

Enter Orlando [*with his sword drawn*].

Orl. Forbear, and eat no more.

Jaq. Why, I have eat none yet.

Orl. Nor shalt not, till necessity be serv'd.

Jaq. Of what kind should this cock come of?

Duke S. Art thou thus bolden'd, man, by thy distress,
Or else a rude despiser of good manners,
That in civility thou seem'st so empty?

Orl. You touch'd my vein at first: the thorny point
Of bare distress hath ta'en from me the show
Of smooth civility: yet am I inland bred
And know some nurture. But forbear, I say:
He dies that touches any of this fruit
Till I and my affairs are answered.

Jaq. An you will not be answer'd with reason, I must die.

Duke S. What would you have? Your gentleness shall force
More than your force move us to gentleness.

Orl. I almost die for food; and let me have it.

Duke S. Sit down and feed, and welcome to our table.

Orl. Speak you so gently? Pardon me, I pray you:
I thought that all things had been savage here;
And therefore put I on the countenance
Of stern commandment. But whate'er you are
That in this desert inaccessible,
Under the shade of melancholy boughs,
Lose and neglect the creeping hours of time;
If ever you have look'd on better days,
If ever been where bells have knoll'd to church,
If ever sat at any good man's feast,
If ever from your eyelids wip'd a tear
And know what 'tis to pity and be pitied,
Let gentleness my strong enforcement be:
In the which hope I blush, and hide my sword.

Duke S. True is it that we have seen better days,
And have with holy bell been knoll'd to church
And sat at good men's feasts and wip'd our eyes
Of drops that sacred pity hath engend'red:
And therefore sit you down in gentleness
And take upon command what help we have
That to your wanting may be minist'red.

Orl. Then but forbear your food a little while,
Whiles, like a doe, I go to find my fawn
And give it food. There is an old poor man,
Who after me hath many a weary step
Limp'd in pure love: till he be first suffic'd,
Oppress'd with two weak evils, age and hunger,
I will not touch a bit.

Duke S. Go find him out,
And we will nothing waste till you return.

Orl. I thank ye; and be blest for your good comfort! [*Exit.*]

Duke S. Thou seest we are not all alone unhappy:
This wide and universal theatre
Presents more woeful pageants than the scene
Wherein we play in.

Jaq. All the world 's a stage,
And all the men and women merely players:
They have their exits and their entrances;
And one man in his time plays many parts,
His acts being seven ages. At first the infant,
Mewling and puking in the nurse's arms.
And then the whining school-boy, with his satchel
And shining morning face, creeping like snail

discourse; or possibly, texts, wise bits. 48. **large . . . wind,** i.e., to blow where it listeth. 55. **Not to seem,** so Theobald; F: *Seeme.* **bob,** jibe, taunt. 57. **squand'ring glances,** random shots. 63. **counter,** type of a thing of no intrinsic value, as a metal disk used in counting. 66. **sting,** carnal impulse. 67. **embossed,** swollen, tumid. **evils,** diseases, maladies. 71. **tax,** blame, accuse; see glossary. 73. **Till . . . ebb,** until the ostentation finally subsides, having exhausted what fed it (?). There are many conjectures—Singer: *wearer's very means;* Lloyd: *tributary stream;* New Cambridge: *weary very mints*, i.e., in coining money fast enough. 75. **city-woman,** citizen's wife. 79. **function,** position in society. 80. **bravery,** splendor, finery. 84. **right,** justice. 93. **civility,** politeness, code of good manners. 94. **vein,** disposition, situation. 96. **inland bred,** i.e., civilized. 97. **nurture,** education, training. 109. **commandment,** command. 118. **my strong enforcement,** that which strongly supports my request. 125. **upon command,** at pleasure. 132. **weak,** causing weakness. 143. **At,** Capell: *As;* anonymous conjecture: *Act.* 144. **Mewling,** crying feebly.

Unwillingly to school. And then the lover,
Sighing like furnace, with a woeful ballad
Made to his mistress' eyebrow. Then a soldier,
Full of strange oaths and bearded like the pard,
Jealous in honour, sudden and quick in quarrel,
Seeking the bubble reputation
Even in the cannon's mouth. And then the justice,
In fair round belly with good capon lin'd,
With eyes severe and beard of formal cut,
Full of wise saws and modern instances;
And so he plays his part. The sixth age shifts
Into the lean and slipper'd pantaloon,
With spectacles on nose and pouch on side,
His youthful hose, well sav'd, a world too wide
For his shrunk shank; and his big manly voice,
Turning again toward childish treble, pipes
And whistles in his sound. Last scene of all,
That ends this strange eventful history,
Is second childishness and mere oblivion,
Sans teeth, sans eyes, sans taste, sans every thing.

Enter ORLANDO, *with* ADAM.

Duke S. Welcome. Set down your venerable burden
And let him feed.
Orl. I thank you most for him.
Adam. So had you need:
I scarce can speak to thank you for myself.
Duke S. Welcome; fall to: I will not trouble you
As yet, to question you about your fortunes.
Give us some music; and, good cousin, sing.

SONG.

[*Ami.*] Blow, blow, thou winter wind,
Thou art not so unkind
As man's ingratitude;
Thy tooth is not so keen,
Because thou art not seen,
Although thy breath be rude.
Heigh-ho! sing, heigh-ho! unto the green holly:
Most friendship is feigning, most loving mere folly:
Then, heigh-ho, the holly!
This life is most jolly.

Freeze, freeze, thou bitter sky,
That dost not bite so nigh
As benefits forgot:
Though thou the waters warp,
Thy sting is not so sharp
As friend remembr'red not.
Heigh-ho! sing, &c.

Duke S. If that you were the good Sir Rowland's son,
As you have whisper'd faithfully you were,
And as mine eye doth his effigies witness
Most truly limn'd and living in your face,
Be truly welcome hither: I am the duke
That lov'd your father: the residue of your fortune,
Go to my cave and tell me. Good old man,
Thou art right welcome as thy master is.
Support him by the arm. Give me your hand,
And let me all your fortunes understand. *Exeunt.*

ACT III.

SCENE I. [*A room in the palace.*]

Enter DUKE [FREDERICK], LORDS, *and* OLIVER.

Duke F. Not see him since? Sir, sir, that cannot be:
But were I not the better part made mercy,
I should not seek an absent argument
Of my revenge, thou present. But look to it:
Find out thy brother, wheresoe'er he is;
Seek him with candle; bring him dead or living
Within this twelvemonth, or turn thou no more
To seek a living in our territory.
Thy lands and all things that thou dost call thine
Worth seizure do we seize into our hands,
Till thou canst quit thee by thy brother's mouth
Of what we think against thee.
Oli. O that your highness knew my heart in this!
I never lov'd my brother in my life.
Duke F. More villain thou. Well, push him out of doors;
And let my officers of such a nature
Make an extent upon his house and lands:
Do this expediently and turn him going. *Exeunt.*

SCENE II. [*The forest.*]

Enter ORLANDO [*with a paper*].

Orl. Hang there, my verse, in witness of my love:
And thou, thrice-crowned queen of night, survey
With thy chaste eye, from thy pale sphere above,
Thy huntress' name that my full life doth sway.
O Rosalind! these trees shall be my books
And in their barks my thoughts I'll character;
That every eye which in this forest looks
Shall see thy virtue witness'd every where.
Run, run, Orlando; carve on every tree
The fair, the chaste and unexpressive she. *Exit.*

Enter CORIN *and* [TOUCHSTONE *the*] *Clown.*

Cor. And how like you this shepherd's life, Master Touchstone?

Touch. Truly, shepherd, in respect of itself, it is a good life; but in respect that it is a shepherd's life, it is naught. In respect that it is solitary, I like it very well; but in respect that it is private, it is a very vile life. Now, in respect it is in the fields, it pleaseth me well; but in respect it is not in the court, it is tedious. As it is a spare life, look you, it fits my humour well; but as there is no more plenty in it, it goes much against my stomach. Hast any philosophy in thee, shepherd?

Cor. No more but that I know the more one sickens the worse at ease he is; and that he that wants money, means and content is without three good friends; that

150. **bearded . . . pard,** having bristling mustaches like the panther's or leopard's whiskers. 156. **modern,** ordinary, commonplace; see glossary. 158. **pantaloon,** ridiculous, enfeebled old man. 178. **Because . . . seen,** i.e., because thou art an enemy that doth not brave us with thy presence (Johnson). 180. **holly,** emblem of mirth. 187. **warp,** apparently, freeze or ruffle (Onions). 193. **effigies,** likenesses, portraits. 194. **limn'd,** painted, portrayed.

ACT III. SCENE I. 2. **better,** greater. 6. **Seek . . . candle.** See Luke 15:8. 11. **quit,** acquit. **mouth,** i.e., evidence. 16. **of such a nature,** i.e., who attend to such duties. 17. **extent,** seizure of land in execution of a writ. 18. **expediently,** expeditiously. **turn him going,** send him packing.

SCENE II. 2. **thrice-crowned queen,** Diana in the three aspects of her divinity: as Luna or Cynthia, goddess of the moon; as Diana, goddess on earth; and as Hecate or Proserpina, goddess in the lower world. 10. **unexpressive,** inexpressible. **she,** mistress, love. 31. **complain . . .**

the property of rain is to wet and fire to burn; that good pasture makes fat sheep, and that a great cause of the night is lack of the sun; that he that hath learned no wit by nature nor art may complain of good breeding or comes of a very dull kindred.

Touch. Such a one is a natural philosopher. Wast ever in court, shepherd?

Cor. No, truly.

Touch. Then thou art damned.

Cor. Nay, I hope.

Touch. Truly, thou art damned, like an ill-roasted egg all on one side.

Cor. For not being at court? Your reason.

Touch. Why, if thou never wast at court, thou never sawest good manners; if thou never sawest good manners, then thy manners must be wicked; and wickedness is sin, and sin is damnation. Thou art in a parlous state, shepherd.

Cor. Not a whit, Touchstone: those that are good manners at the court are as ridiculous in the country as the behaviour of the country is most mockable at the court. You told me you salute not at the court, but you kiss your hands: that courtesy would be uncleanly, if courtiers were shepherds.

Touch. Instance, briefly; come, instance.

Cor. Why, we are still handling our ewes, and their fells, you know, are greasy.

Touch. Why, do not your courtier's hands sweat? and is not the grease of a mutton as wholesome as the sweat of a man? Shallow, shallow. A better instance, I say; come.

Cor. Besides, our hands are hard.

Touch. Your lips will feel them the sooner. Shallow again. A more sounder instance, come.

Cor. And they are often tarred over with the surgery of our sheep; and would you have us kiss tar? The courtier's hands are perfumed with civet.

Touch. Most shallow man! thou worms-meat, in respect of a good piece of flesh indeed! Learn of the wise, and perpend: civet is of a baser birth than tar, the very uncleanly flux of a cat. Mend the instance, shepherd.

Cor. You have too courtly a wit for me: I'll rest.

Touch. Wilt thou rest damned? God help thee, shallow man! God make incision in thee! thou art raw.

Cor. Sir, I am a true labourer: I earn that I eat, get that I wear, owe no man hate, envy no man's happiness, glad of other men's good, content with my harm, and the greatest of my pride is to see my ewes graze and my lambs suck.

Touch. That is another simple sin in you, to bring the ewes and the rams together and to offer to get your living by the copulation of cattle; to be bawd to a bell-wether, and to betray a she-lamb of a twelvemonth to a crooked-pated, old, cuckoldly ram, out of all reasonable match. If thou beest not damned for this, the devil himself will have no shepherds; I cannot see else how thou shouldst 'scape.

Cor. Here comes young Master Ganymede, my new mistress's brother.

Enter Rosalind [*with a paper, reading*].

Ros. From the east to western Ind,
No jewel is like Rosalind.
Her worth, being mounted on the wind,
Through all the world bears Rosalind.
All the pictures fairest lin'd
Are but black to Rosalind.
Let no face be kept in mind
But the fair of Rosalind.

Touch. I'll rhyme you so eight years together, dinners and suppers and sleeping-hours excepted: it is the right butter-women's rank to market.

Ros. Out, fool!

Touch. For a taste:

If a hart do lack a hind,
Let him seek out Rosalind.
If the cat will after kind,
So be sure will Rosalind.
Wint'red garments must be lin'd,
So must slender Rosalind.
They that reap must sheaf and bind;
Then to cart with Rosalind.
Sweetest nut hath sourest rind,
Such a nut is Rosalind.
He that sweetest rose will find
Must find love's prick and Rosalind.

This is the very false gallop of verses: why do you infect yourself with them?

Ros. Peace, you dull fool! I found them on a tree.

Touch. Truly, the tree yields bad fruit.

Ros. I'll graff it with you, and then I shall graff it with a medlar: then it will be the earliest fruit i' the country; for you'll be rotten ere you be half ripe, and that 's the right virtue of the medlar.

Touch. You have said; but whether wisely or no, let the forest judge.

Enter Celia, *with a writing.*

Ros. Peace!
Here comes my sister, reading: stand aside.

Cel. [*Reads*]

Why should this a desert be?
For it is unpeopled? No;
Tongues I'll hang on every tree,
That shall civil sayings show:
Some, how brief the life of man
Runs his erring pilgrimage,
That the stretching of a span
Buckles in his sum of age;
Some, of violated vows
'Twixt the souls of friend and friend:
But upon the fairest boughs,
Or at every sentence end,
Will I Rosalinda write,
Teaching all that read to know

breeding, i.e., of want of good breeding. 45. **parlous,** perilous, dangerous. 50. **but you kiss,** without kissing. 53. **Instance,** i.e., cite an example. 54. **still,** always. 55. **fells,** skin with the wool, or fleece. 66. **worms-meat,** food for worms. **respect of,** comparison with. 69. **perpend,** reflect, consider. 75. **incision,** cutting for the purpose of letting blood. 76. **raw,** inexperienced; also, sore. 77. **that,** what. 80. **harm,** ill fortune. 85. **cattle,** livestock. 97. **lin'd,** drawn. 103. **butter-women's rank.** The rhymes, all alike, follow each other like a line of butter-women jogging along to market. 113. **sheaf,** make into sheaves. 118. **prick,** thorn (with bawdy suggestion). 119. **false gallop,** canter. 120. **infect,** pollute (either morally or physically). 125. **graff,** insert a graft. **medlar,** a fruit like a small brown-skinned apple which is eaten when decayed; a pun on "meddler." 127. **right,** true. 136. **civil sayings,** maxims of civilized life. 138. **erring,** wandering. 139. **That,** so that. 140. **Buckles,** encompasses.

The quintessence of every sprite
Heaven would in little show.
Therefore Heaven Nature charg'd
That one body should be fill'd
With all graces wide-enlarg'd:
Nature presently distill'd
Helen's cheek, but not her heart,
Cleopatra's majesty,
Atalanta's better part,
Sad Lucretia's modesty.
Thus Rosalind of many parts
By heavenly synod was devis'd,
Of many faces, eyes and hearts,
To have the touches dearest priz'd.

Heaven would that she these gifts should have,
And I to live and die her slave.

Ros. O most gentle pulpiter! what tedious homily of love have you wearied your parishioners withal, and never cried 'Have patience, good people'!

Cel. How now! back, friends! Shepherd, go off a little. Go with him, sirrah.

Touch. Come, shepherd, let us make an honourable retreat; though not with bag and baggage, yet with scrip and scrippage. *Exit* [*with Corin*].

Cel. Didst thou hear these verses?

Ros. O, yes, I heard them all, and more too; for some of them had in them more feet than the verses would bear.

Cel. That's no matter: the feet might bear the verses.

Ros. Ay, but the feet were lame and could not bear themselves without the verse and therefore stood lamely in the verse.

Cel. But didst thou hear without wondering how thy name should be hanged and carved upon these trees?

Ros. I was seven of the nine days out of the wonder before you came; for look here what I found on a palm-tree. I was never so berhymed since Pythagoras' time, that I was an Irish rat, which I can hardly remember.

Cel. Trow you who hath done this?

Ros. Is it a man?

Cel. And a chain, that you once wore, about his neck. Change you colour?

Ros. I prithee, who?

Cel. O Lord, Lord! it is a hard matter for friends to meet; but mountains may be removed with earthquakes and so encounter.

Ros. Nay, but who is it?

Cel. Is it possible?

Ros. Nay, I prithee now with most petitionary vehemence, tell me who it is.

Cel. O wonderful, wonderful, and most wonderful wonderful! and yet again wonderful, and after that, out of all hooping!

Ros. Good my complexion! dost thou think, though I am caparisoned like a man, I have a doublet and hose in my disposition? One inch of delay more is a South-sea of discovery; I prithee, tell me who is it quickly, and speak apace. I would thou couldst stammer, that thou mightst pour this concealed man out of thy mouth, as wine comes out of a narrow-mouthed bottle, either too much at once, or none at all. I prithee, take the cork out of thy mouth that I may drink thy tidings.

Cel. So you may put a man in your belly.

Ros. Is he of God's making? What manner of man? Is his head worth a hat, or his chin worth a beard?

Cel. Nay, he hath but a little beard.

Ros. Why, God will send more, if the man will be thankful: let me stay the growth of his beard, if thou delay me not the knowledge of his chin.

Cel. It is young Orlando, that tripped up the wrestler's heels and your heart both in an instant.

Ros. Nay, but the devil take mocking: speak, sad brow and true maid.

Cel. I' faith, coz, 'tis he.

Ros. Orlando?

Cel. Orlando.

Ros. Alas the day! what shall I do with my doublet and hose? What did he when thou sawest him? What said he? How looked he? Wherein went he? What makes he here? Did he ask for me? Where remains he? How parted he with thee? and when shalt thou see him again? Answer me in one word.

Cel. You must borrow me Gargantua's mouth first: 'tis a word too great for any mouth of this age's size. To say ay and no to these particulars is more than to answer in a catechism.

Ros. But doth he know that I am in this forest and in man's apparel? Looks he as freshly as he did the day he wrestled?

Cel. It is as easy to count atomies as to resolve the propositions of a lover; but take a taste of my finding him, and relish it with good observance. I found him under a tree, like a dropped acorn.

Ros. It may well be called Jove's tree, when it drops forth such fruit.

Cel. Give me audience, good madam.

Ros. Proceed.

Cel. There lay he, stretched along, like a wounded knight.

Ros. Though it be pity to see such a sight, it well becomes the ground.

Cel. Cry 'holla' to thy tongue, I prithee; it curvets unseasonably. He was furnished like a hunter.

Ros. O, ominous! he comes to kill my heart.

Cel. I would sing my song without a burden: thou bringest me out of tune.

Ros. Do you not know I am a woman? when I think, I must speak. Sweet, say on.

Cel. You bring me out. Soft! comes he not here?

147. **quintessence,** the fifth essence or element of the medieval alchemists, purer even than fire. 148. **in little.** In this Furness sees an allusion to the microcosm (man); the heavenly bodies would be composed of quintessence, which is here thought of as the supreme quality of a person. 151. **wide-enlarg'd,** spread through the world until they are concentrated in Rosalind (J. C. Smith). 155. **Atalanta's better part,** i.e., her fleetness of foot. 156. **Lucretia's.** Lucretia was the Roman lady dishonored by Tarquin, whose story Shakespeare tells in *The Rape of Lucrece.* 160. **touches,** traits. 163. **pulpiter,** so Spedding; F: *Iupiter.* 167. **back, friends.** Celia, reading, becomes aware of the others; her words are addressed to Corin and Touchstone. 170. **bag and baggage.** Note the pun on *baggage,* meaning "women." 171. **scrip and scrippage,** shepherd's pouch and its contents. 184. **seven . . . wonder,** a reference to the common phrase, "a nine days' wonder." 187. **Pythagoras'.** Pythagoras was a Greek philosopher credited with the doctrine of the transmigration of souls. 188. **Irish rat,** reference to a current belief that Irish enchanters could rhyme rats to death. 189. **Trow you,** have you any idea. 191. **And a chain,** i.e., and with a chain. 195-196. **friends . . . encounter,** reference to the proverb, "Friends may meet, but mountains never greet." **removed with,** moved by. 203. **out . . . hooping,** beyond exclamations of surprise. 204. **Good my complexion,** O, my (feminine) temperament. 205. **caparisoned,** equipped (as of a horse). 207. **South-sea of discovery,** probable reference to the long delays of voyages to the South Seas;

Enter ORLANDO *and* JAQUES.

Ros. 'Tis he: slink by, and note him.

Jaq. I thank you for your company; but, good faith, I had as lief have been myself alone.

Orl. And so had I; but yet, for fashion sake, I thank you too for your society.

Jaq. God be wi' you: let 's meet as little as we can.

Orl. I do desire we may be better strangers.

Jaq. I pray you, mar no more trees with writing love-songs in their barks.

Orl. I pray you, mar no moe of my verses with reading them ill-favouredly.

Jaq. Rosalind is your love's name?

Orl. Yes, just.

Jaq. I do not like her name.

Orl. There was no thought of pleasing you when she was christened.

Jaq. What stature is she of?

Orl. Just as high as my heart.

Jaq. You are full of pretty answers. Have you not been acquainted with goldsmiths' wives, and conned them out of rings?

Orl. Not so; but I answer you right painted cloth, from whence you have studied your questions.

Jaq. You have a nimble wit: I think 'twas made of Atalanta's heels. Will you sit down with me? and we two will rail against our mistress the world and all our misery.

Orl. I will chide no breather in the world but myself, against whom I know most faults.

Jaq. The worst fault you have is to be in love.

Orl. 'Tis a fault I will not change for your best virtue. I am weary of you.

Jaq. By my troth, I was seeking for a fool when I found you.

Orl. He is drowned in the brook: look but in, and you shall see him.

Jaq. There I shall see mine own figure.

Orl. Which I take to be either a fool or a cipher.

Jaq. I'll tarry no longer with you: farewell, good Signior Love.

Orl. I am glad of your departure: adieu, good Monsieur Melancholy. [*Exit Jaques.*]

Ros. [*Aside to Celia*] I will speak to him like a saucy lackey and under that habit play the knave with him.—Do you hear, forester?

Orl. Very well: what would you?

Ros. I pray you, what is 't o'clock?

Orl. You should ask me what time o' day: there 's no clock in the forest.

Ros. Then there is no true lover in the forest; else sighing every minute and groaning every hour would detect the lazy foot of Time as well as a clock.

Orl. And why not the swift foot of Time? had not that been as proper?

Ros. By no means, sir: Time travels in divers paces with divers persons. I'll tell you who Time ambles withal, who Time trots withal, who Time gallops withal and who he stands still withal.

Orl. I prithee, who doth he trot withal?

Ros. Marry, he trots hard with a young maid between the contract of her marriage and the day it is solemnized: if the interim be but a se'nnight, Time's pace is so hard that it seems the length of seven year.

Orl. Who ambles Time withal?

Ros. With a priest that lacks Latin and a rich man that hath not the gout, for the one sleeps easily because he cannot study and the other lives merrily because he feels no pain, the one lacking the burden of lean and wasteful learning, the other knowing no burden of heavy tedious penury; these Time ambles withal.

Orl. Who doth he gallop withal?

Ros. With a thief to the gallows, for though he go as softly as foot can fall, he thinks himself too soon there.

Orl. Who stays it still withal?

Ros. With lawyers in the vacation; for they sleep between term and term and then they perceive not how Time moves.

Orl. Where dwell you, pretty youth?

Ros. With this shepherdess, my sister; here in the skirts of the forest, like fringe upon a petticoat.

Orl. Are you native of this place?

Ros. As the cony that you see dwell where she is kindled.

Orl. Your accent is something finer than you could purchase in so removed a dwelling.

Ros. I have been told so of many: but indeed an old religious uncle of mine taught me to speak, who was in his youth an inland man; one that knew courtship too well, for there he fell in love. I have heard him read many lectures against it, and I thank God I am not a woman, to be touched with so many giddy offences as he hath generally taxed their whole sex withal.

Orl. Can you remember any of the principal evils that he laid to the charge of women?

Ros. There were none principal; they were all like one another as half-pence are, every one fault seeming monstrous till his fellow-fault came to match it.

Orl. I prithee, recount some of them.

Ros. No, I will not cast away my physic but on those that are sick. There is a man haunts the forest, that abuses our young plants with carving 'Rosalind' on their barks; hangs odes upon hawthorns and elegies on brambles, all, forsooth, deifying the name of Rosalind: if I could meet that fancy-monger, I would give him some good counsel, for he seems to have the quotidian of love upon him.

Orl. I am he that is so love-shaked: I pray you, tell me your remedy.

Ros. There is none of my uncle's marks upon you: he taught me how to know a man in love; in which

many emendations; *discovery* may mean "disclosure." 216. **of God's making,** i.e., or his tailor's. 234. **Wherein went he,** in what clothes. 238. **Gargantua's mouth.** Gargantua is the giant in Rabelais who swallowed five pilgrims in a salad. 241. **catechism,** catechizing. 245. **atomies,** motes. 247. **relish,** taste, or make pleasant to the palate. 248. **observance,** attention, observation. 249. **Jove's tree,** the oak. 256. **becomes,** adorns. 257. **'holla,'** stop. **curvets,** prances. 258. **furnished,** equipped, dressed. 261. **burden,** undersong, bass part. 262. **bringest,** puttest. 265. **bring me out,** put me out (of my part). 270. **myself alone,** alone, by myself. 281. **just,** just so. 289. **rings,** reference to the verses inscribed in rings, posies. 290. **right,** true, perfect. **painted cloth,** canvas painted with pictures (frequently scriptural) used for hangings; here, suggestive of commonplace. 297. **breather,** living being. 331. **hard,** slowly, with uneven pace. 333. **se'nnight,** week. 346. **go as softly,** walk as slowly. 357. **cony,** rabbit. 358. **kindled,** littered, brought forth young. 360. **removed,** remote. 362. **religious,** i.e., member of a religious order. 364. **courtship,** play on the meaning, "knowledge of courtly manners." 372. **half-pence.** Halfpence were almost the only uniform coins in circulation. 382. **fancy-monger,** love-monger, devotee of love. 383. **quotidian,** fever recurring daily (a symptom of love); hence, *love-shaked* below.

cage of rushes I am sure you are not prisoner.

Orl. What were his marks?

Ros. A lean cheek, which you have not, a blue eye and sunken, which you have not, an unquestionable spirit, which you have not, a beard neglected, which you have not; but I pardon you for that, for simply your having in beard is a younger brother's revenue: then your hose should be ungartered, your bonnet unbanded, your sleeve unbuttoned, your shoe untied and every thing about you demonstrating a careless desolation; but you are no such man; you are rather point-device in your accoutrements as loving yourself than seeming the lover of any other.

Orl. Fair youth, I would I could make thee believe I love.

Ros. Me believe it! you may as soon make her that you love believe it; which, I warrant, she is apter to do than to confess she does: that is one of the points in the which women still give the lie to their consciences. But, in good sooth, are you he that hangs the verses on the trees, wherein Rosalind is so admired?

Orl. I swear to thee, youth, by the white hand of Rosalind, I am that he, that unfortunate he.

Ros. But are you so much in love as your rhymes speak?

Orl. Neither rhyme nor reason can express how much.

Ros. Love is merely a madness, and, I tell you, deserves as well a dark house and a whip as madmen do: and the reason why they are not so punished and cured is, that the lunacy is so ordinary that the whippers are in love too. Yet I profess curing it by counsel.

Orl. Did you ever cure any so?

Ros. Yes, one, and in this manner. He was to imagine me his love, his mistress; and I set him every day to woo me: at which time would I, being but a moonish youth, grieve, be effeminate, changeable, longing and liking, proud, fantastical, apish, shallow, inconstant, full of tears, full of smiles, for every passion something and for no passion truly any thing, as boys and women are for the most part cattle of this colour; would now like him, now loathe him; then entertain him, then forswear him; now weep for him, then spit at him; that I drave my suitor from his mad humour of love to a living humour of madness; which was, to forswear the full stream of the world and to live in a nook merely monastic. And thus I cured him; and this way will I take upon me to wash your liver as clean as a sound sheep's heart, that there shall not be one spot of love in 't.

Orl. I would not be cured, youth.

Ros. I would cure you, if you would but call me Rosalind and come every day to my cote and woo me.

Orl. Now, by the faith of my love, I will: tell me where it is.

Ros. Go with me to it and I'll show it you: and by the way you shall tell me where in the forest you live. Will you go?

Orl. With all my heart, good youth.

Ros. Nay, you must call me Rosalind. Come, sister, will you go? *Exeunt.*

SCENE III. [*The forest.*]

Enter [TOUCHSTONE *the*] *Clown*, AUDREY; *and* JAQUES [*apart*].

Touch. Come apace, good Audrey: I will fetch up your goats, Audrey. And how, Audrey? am I the man yet? doth my simple feature content you?

Aud. Your features! Lord warrant us! what features?

Touch. I am here with thee and thy goats, as the most capricious poet, honest Ovid, was among the Goths.

Jaq. [*Aside*] O knowledge ill-inhabited, worse than Jove in a thatched house!

Touch. When a man's verses cannot be understood, nor a man's good wit seconded with the forward child Understanding, it strikes a man more dead than a great reckoning in a little room. Truly, I would the gods had made thee poetical.

Aud. I do not know what 'poetical' is: is it honest in deed and word? is it a true thing?

Touch. No, truly; for the truest poetry is the most feigning; and lovers are given to poetry, and what they swear in poetry may be said as lovers they do feign.

Aud. Do you wish then that the gods had made me poetical?

Touch. I do, truly; for thou swearest to me thou art honest: now, if thou wert a poet, I might have some hope thou didst feign.

Aud. Would you not have me honest?

Touch. No, truly, unless thou wert hard-favoured; for honesty coupled to beauty is to have honey a sauce to sugar.

Jaq. [*Aside*] A material fool!

Aud. Well, I am not fair; and therefore I pray the gods make me honest.

Touch. Truly, and to cast away honesty upon a foul slut were to put good meat into an unclean dish.

Aud. I am not a slut, though I thank the gods I am foul.

Touch. Well, praised be the gods for thy foulness! sluttishness may come hereafter. But be it as it may be, I will marry thee, and to that end I have been with Sir Oliver Martext, the vicar of the next village, who hath promised to meet me in this place of the forest and to couple us.

Jaq. [*Aside*] I would fain see this meeting.

Aud. Well, the gods give us joy!

Touch. Amen. A man may, if he were of a fearful heart, stagger in this attempt; for here we have no

393. **blue eye,** eye having dark circles. 394. **unquestionable,** unwilling. 396-397. **simply . . . revenue,** i.e., truly what you have by way of a beard is small. (Younger brothers traditionally received small inheritances.) 398. **bonnet,** hat. 402. **point-device,** faultless, precise. 409. **still,** always. 410. **good sooth,** honest truth. 421. **dark . . . whip,** an allusion to the common treatment of lunatics. 430. **moonish,** changeable. 439-440. **mad . . . madness,** pass from a madness of love to a real madness; Johnson read *loving* for *living* (real, not affected). 444. **liver,** seat of the emotion of love. 447. **cote,** cottage. 447-449. **I would . . . woo me.** This introduces the central comic theme in the play, which is so slight that it might not be realized. It presents a lover making love to his mistress, she being aware of the fact, he not.

5. **warrant,** assure, protect. 7, 8, 9. **goats, capricious, Goths.** Ovid (a pastoral poet; hence *goats*) was banished by Augustus to the country of the *Goths* (pun on *goats*); *capricious* is derived from Latin *capra*, she-goat. 10. **ill-inhabited,** ill-lodged. 11. **Jove in a thatched house,** an allusion to Ovid's *Metamorphoses*, viii, the story of Jupiter and Mercury lodging in the house of Baucis and Philemon. 15. **great . . . room,** great charge for lodging in a small room. Recent scholars see in this passage an allusion to the death of Marlowe, who was stabbed by Ingram Frysar at an inn at Deptford in a quarrel over a tavern reckoning, May 30, 1593. New Cambridge editors use the reference as a means of dating the original version of the play. 20. **feigning,** inventive, imaginative. 21. **may be said,** i.e., it may be said. 27. **feign,**

temple but the wood, no assembly but horn-beasts. But what though? Courage! As horns are odious, they are necessary. It is said, 'many a man knows no end of his goods:' right; many a man has good horns, and knows no end of them. Well, that is the dowry of his wife; 'tis none of his own getting. Horns? Even so. Poor men alone? No, no; the noblest deer hath them as huge as the rascal. Is the single man therefore blessed? No: as a walled town is more worthier than a village, so is the forehead of a married man more honourable than the bare brow of a bachelor; and by how much defence is better than no skill, by so much is a horn more precious than to want.

Enter Sir Oliver Martext.

Here comes Sir Oliver. Sir Oliver Martext, you are well met: will you dispatch us here under this tree, or shall we go with you to your chapel?

Sir Oli. Is there none here to give the woman?

Touch. I will not take her on gift of any man.

Sir Oli. Truly, she must be given, or the marriage is not lawful.

Jaq. [*Advancing*] Proceed, proceed: I'll give her.

Touch. Good even, good Master What-ye-call 't: how do you, sir? You are very well met: God 'ild you for your last company: I am very glad to see you: even a toy in hand here, sir: nay, pray be covered.

Jaq. Will you be married, motley?

Touch. As the ox hath his bow, sir, the horse his curb and the falcon her bells, so man hath his desires; and as pigeons bill, so wedlock would be nibbling.

Jaq. And will you, being a man of your breeding, be married under a bush like a beggar? Get you to church, and have a good priest that can tell you what marriage is: this fellow will but join you together as they join wainscot; then one of you will prove a shrunk panel and, like green timber, warp, warp.

Touch. [*Aside*] I am not in the mind but I were better to be married of him than of another: for he is not like to marry me well; and not being well married, it will be a good excuse for me hereafter to leave my wife.

Jaq. Go thou with me, and let me counsel thee.

Touch. Come, sweet Audrey:
We must be married, or we must live in bawdry.
Farewell, good Master Oliver: not,—
O sweet Oliver,
O brave Oliver,
Leave me not behind thee:
but,—
Wind away,
Begone, I say,
I will not to wedding with thee.

Exeunt [*Jaques, Touchstone and Audrey*].

Sir Oli. 'Tis no matter: ne'er a fantastical knave of them all shall flout me out of my calling. [*Exit.*]

SCENE IV. [*The forest.*]

Enter Rosalind *and* Celia.

Ros. Never talk to me; I will weep.

Cel. Do, I prithee; but yet have the grace to consider that tears do not become a man.

Ros. But have I not cause to weep?

Cel. As good cause as one would desire; therefore weep.

Ros. His very hair is of the dissembling colour.

Cel. Something browner than Judas's: marry, his kisses are Judas's own children.

Ros. I' faith, his hair is of a good colour.

Cel. An excellent colour: your chestnut was ever the only colour.

Ros. And his kissing is as full of sanctity as the touch of holy bread.

Cel. He hath bought a pair of cast lips of Diana: a nun of winter's sisterhood kisses not more religiously; the very ice of chastity is in them.

Ros. But why did he swear he would come this morning, and comes not?

Cel. Nay, certainly, there is no truth in him.

Ros. Do you think so?

Cel. Yes; I think he is not a pick-purse nor a horse-stealer, but for his verity in love, I do think him as concave as a covered goblet or a worm-eaten nut.

Ros. Not true in love?

Cel. Yes, when he is in; but I think he is not in.

Ros. You have heard him swear downright he was.

Cel. 'Was' is not 'is:' besides, the oath of a lover is no stronger than the word of a tapster; they are both the confirmer of false reckonings. He attends here in the forest on the duke your father.

Ros. I met the duke yesterday and had much question with him: he asked me of what parentage I was; I told him, of as good as he; so he laughed and let me go. But what talk we of fathers, when there is such a man as Orlando?

Cel. O, that 's a brave man! he writes brave verses, speaks brave words, swears brave oaths and breaks them bravely, quite traverse, athwart the heart of his lover; as a puisny tilter, that spurs his horse but on one side, breaks his staff like a noble goose: but all 's brave that youth mounts and folly guides. Who comes here?

Enter Corin.

Cor. Mistress and master, you have oft inquir'd
After the shepherd that complain'd of love,
Who you saw sitting by me on the turf,
Praising the proud disdainful shepherdess
That was his mistress.

Cel. Well, and what of him?

Cor. If you will see a pageant truly play'd,
Between the pale complexion of true love
And the red glow of scorn and proud disdain,
Go hence a little and I shall conduct you,

pretend (with pun on *fain*, desire). 30. **honesty,** chastity. 32. **material,** full of sense, or possibly, gross or carnal. 36. **foul,** ugly. 41. **foulness,** dirtiness. 43. **Sir,** usual title for a priest. 49. **stagger,** hesitate. 51. **what though?** What though it be so? 52. **necessary,** unavoidable. 58. **rascal,** deer lean and out of season. 62. **defence,** art of self-defense. 64. **than to want,** i.e., than to be without a horn. 76. **God 'ild you,** God yield you, reward you. 78. **pray be covered,** pray put on your hat. 80. **bow,** yoke. 90. **warp,** pun on the sense "go astray from the straight path" (New Cambridge). 91. **I am . . . but,** I do not know but. 108. **fantastical knave.** Capell suggests that Touchstone dances round the priest like a harlequin while he sings the ballad about Oliver.

Scene iv. 9. **browner than Judas's,** an allusion to the traditional representation of Judas as having a red beard. 15. **holy bread,** ordinary leavened bread which was blessed after the Eucharist and distributed to those who had not communed. 16. **cast,** cast off, discarded also, cast, molded. 17. **Diana,** goddess of chastity. 26. **covered goblet,** i.e., a goblet having a convex top and therefore more hollow because the cover is on only when the goblet is empty. 39. **question,** conversation. 41. **what,** why. 45. **traverse,** a term from tilting, meaning to strike an opponent sideways, awkwardly, rather than head-on. 46. **puisny,** petty, paltry (literally, junior). 56. **pale complexion.** Sighing was believed to draw the blood from the heart.

If you will mark it.
Ros. O, come, let us remove:
The sight of lovers feedeth those in love.
Bring us to this sight, and you shall say
I'll prove a busy actor in their play. *Exeunt.*

SCENE V. [*Another part of the forest.*]

Enter SILVIUS *and* PHEBE.

Sil. Sweet Phebe, do not scorn me; do not, Phebe;
Say that you love me not, but say not so
In bitterness. The common executioner,
Whose heart th' accustom'd sight of death makes hard,
Falls not the axe upon the humbled neck
But first begs pardon: will you sterner be
†Than he that dies and lives by bloody drops?

Enter ROSALIND, CELIA, *and* CORIN [*behind*].

Phe. I would not be thy executioner:
I fly thee, for I would not injure thee.
Thou tell'st me there is murder in mine eye:
'Tis pretty, sure, and very probable,
That eyes, that are the frail'st and softest things,
Who shut their coward gates on atomies,
Should be call'd tyrants, butchers, murderers!
Now I do frown on thee with all my heart;
And if mine eyes can wound, now let them kill thee:
Now counterfeit to swoon; why now fall down;
Or if thou canst not, O, for shame, for shame,
Lie not, to say mine eyes are murderers!
Now show the wound mine eye hath made in thee:
Scratch thee but with a pin, and there remains
Some scar of it; lean but upon a rush,
The cicatrice and capable impressure
Thy palm some moment keeps; but now mine eyes,
Which I have darted at thee, hurt thee not,
Nor, I am sure, there is no force in eyes
That can do hurt.
Sil. O dear Phebe,
If ever,—as that ever may be near,—
You meet in some fresh cheek the power of fancy,
Then shall you know the wounds invisible
That love's keen arrows make.
Phe. But till that time
Come not thou near me: and when that time comes,
Afflict me with thy mocks, pity me not;
As till that time I shall not pity thee.
Ros. And why, I pray you? Who might be your mother,
That you insult, exult, and all at once,
Over the wretched? What though you have no beauty,—
As, by my faith, I see no more in you
Than without candle may go dark to bed—
Must you be therefore proud and pitiless?
Why, what means this? Why do you look on me?
I see no more in you than in the ordinary
Of nature's sale-work. 'Od 's my little life,
I think she means to tangle my eyes too!
No, faith, proud mistress, hope not after it:
'Tis not your inky brows, your black silk hair,
Your bugle eyeballs, nor your cheek of cream,
That can entame my spirits to your worship.
You foolish shepherd, wherefore do you follow her,
Like foggy south puffing with wind and rain?
You are a thousand times a properer man
Than she a woman: 'tis such fools as you
That makes the world full of ill-favour'd children:
'Tis not her glass, but you, that flatters her;
And out of you she sees herself more proper
Than any of her lineaments can show her.
But, mistress, know yourself: down on your knees,
And thank heaven, fasting, for a good man's love:
For I must tell you friendly in your ear,
Sell when you can: you are not for all markets:
Cry the man mercy; love him; take his offer:
Foul is most foul, being foul to be a scoffer.
So take her to thee, shepherd: fare you well.
Phe. Sweet youth, I pray you, chide a year together:
I had rather hear you chide than this man woo.

Ros. [*Aside*] He 's fallen in love with your foulness and she'll fall in love with my anger. If it be so, as fast as she answers thee with frowning looks, I'll sauce her with bitter words.—Why look you so upon me?

Phe. For no ill will I bear you.
Ros. I pray you, do not fall in love with me,
For I am falser than vows made in wine:
Besides, I like you not. If you will know my house,
'Tis at the tuft of olives here hard by.
Will you go, sister? Shepherd, ply her hard.
Come, sister. Shepherdess, look on him better,
And be not proud: though all the world could see,
None could be so abus'd in sight as he.
Come, to our flock. *Exit* [*with Celia and Corin*].
Phe. Dead shepherd, now I find thy saw of might,
'Who ever lov'd that lov'd not at first sight?'
Sil. Sweet Phebe,—
Phe. Ha, what say'st thou, Silvius?
Sil. Sweet Phebe, pity me.
Phe. Why, I am sorry for thee, gentle Silvius.
Sil. Wherever sorrow is, relief would be:
If you do sorrow at my grief in love,
By giving love your sorrow and my grief
Were both extermin'd.
Phe. Thou hast my love: is not that neighbourly?
Sil. I would have you.
Phe. Why, that were covetousness.
Silvius, the time was that I hated thee,
And yet it is not that I bear thee love;
But since that thou canst talk of love so well,
Thy company, which erst was irksome to me,
I will endure, and I'll employ thee too:
But do not look for further recompense
Than thine own gladness that thou art employ'd.
Sil. So holy and so perfect is my love,
And I in such a poverty of grace,

SCENE V. 6. **But first begs,** without first begging. 7. **Than . . . drops,** obscure line; probable meaning: "Will you be sterner than he (the executioner) who makes his living (lives and dies) by shedding blood?" 11. **sure,** surely. 23. **cicatrice,** mark, impression. **impressure,** impression. 33. **mocks,** mockeries, taunts. 36. **all at once,** i.e., all in a breath. 39. **without candle,** i.e., your beauty is not so brilliant that it will suffice to light you to bed. 43. **sale-work,** ready-made work, i.e., not of the best quality, not distinctive. **'Od 's,** minced form of "God's," used in petty oaths. 47. **bugle,** black and glassy. 48. **entame,** subdue. **to your worship,** to worship you. 50. **foggy south.** South was the direction from which came fog and rain. 51. **properer,** handsomer. 55. **out of you,** i.e., as her mirror. 62. **Foul,** two meanings of the word played upon: Ugliness is most ugly when it is rough and abusive. 81-82. **Dead . . . sight.** Line 82 is quoted from Marlowe's *Hero and Leander*, Sestiad I, 176. Marlowe died on May 30, 1593; the poem was not printed until 1598. The publication of the poem may have occasioned the quotation. 89. **extermin'd,** banished, ended. 90. **neighbourly.** This serves to take back Phebe's preceding

That I shall think it a most plenteous crop
To glean the broken ears after the man
That the main harvest reaps: loose now and then
A scatt'red smile, and that I'll live upon.

Phe. Know'st thou the youth that spoke to me erewhile?

Sil. Not very well, but I have met him oft;
And he hath bought the cottage and the bounds
That the old carlot once was master of.

Phe. Think not I love him, though I ask for him;
'Tis but a peevish boy; yet he talks well;
But what care I for words? yet words do well
When he that speaks them pleases those that hear.
It is a pretty youth: not very pretty:
But, sure, he 's proud, and yet his pride becomes him:
He'll make a proper man: the best thing in him
Is his complexion; and faster than his tongue
Did make offence his eye did heal it up.
He is not very tall; yet for his years he 's tall:
His leg is but so so; and yet 'tis well:
There was a pretty redness in his lip,
A little riper and more lusty red
Than that mix'd in his cheek; 'twas just the difference
Betwixt the constant red and mingled damask.
There be some women, Silvius, had they mark'd him
In parcels as I did, would have gone near
To fall in love with him; but, for my part,
I love him not nor hate him not; and yet
I have more cause to hate him than to love him:
For what had he to do to chide at me?
He said mine eyes were black and my hair black;
And, now I am rememb'red, scorn'd at me:
I marvel why I answer'd not again:
But that 's all one; omittance is no quittance.
I'll write to him a very taunting letter,
And thou shalt bear it: wilt thou, Silvius?

Sil. Phebe, with all my heart.

Phe. I'll write it straight;
The matter 's in my head and in my heart:
I will be bitter with him and passing short.
Go with me, Silvius. *Exeunt.*

ACT IV.

SCENE I. [*The forest.*]

Enter ROSALIND *and* CELIA, *and* JAQUES.

Jaq. I prithee, pretty youth, let me be better acquainted with thee.

Ros. They say you are a melancholy fellow.

Jaq. I am so; I do love it better than laughing.

Ros. Those that are in extremity of either are abominable fellows and betray themselves to every modern censure worse than drunkards.

Jaq. Why, 'tis good to be sad and say nothing.

Ros. Why then, 'tis good to be a post.

Jaq. I have neither the scholar's melancholy, which is emulation, nor the musician's, which is fantastical, nor the courtier's, which is proud, nor the soldier's, which is ambitious, nor the lawyer's, which is politic, nor the lady's, which is nice, nor the lover's, which is all these: but it is a melancholy of mine own, compounded of many simples, extracted from many objects, and indeed the sundry contemplation of my travels, in which my often rumination wraps me in a most humorous sadness.

Ros. A traveller! By my faith, you have great reason to be sad: I fear you have sold your own lands to see other men's; then, to have seen much and to have nothing, is to have rich eyes and poor hands.

Jaq. Yes, I have gained my experience.

Enter ORLANDO.

Ros. And your experience makes you sad: I had rather have a fool to make me merry than experience to make me sad; and to travel for it too!

Orl. Good day and happiness, dear Rosalind!

Jaq. Nay, then, God be wi' you, an you talk in blank verse. [*Exit.*]

Ros. Farewell, Monsieur Traveller: look you lisp and wear strange suits, disable all the benefits of your own country, be out of love with your nativity and almost chide God for making you that countenance you are, or I will scarce think you have swam in a gundello. Why, how now, Orlando! where have you been all this while? You a lover! An you serve me such another trick, never come in my sight more.

Orl. My fair Rosalind, I come within an hour of my promise.

Ros. Break an hour's promise in love! He that will divide a minute into a thousand parts and break but a part of the thousandth part of a minute in the affairs of love, it may be said of him that Cupid hath clapped him o' the shoulder, but I'll warrant him heart-whole.

Orl. Pardon me, dear Rosalind.

Ros. Nay, an you be so tardy, come no more in my sight: I had as lief be wooed of a snail.

Orl. Of a snail?

Ros. Ay, of a snail; for though he comes slowly, he carries his house on his head; a better jointure, I think, than you make a woman: besides, he brings his destiny with him.

Orl. What 's that?

Ros. Why, horns, which such as you are fain to be beholding to your wives for: but he comes armed in his fortune and prevents the slander of his wife.

Orl. Virtue is no horn-maker; and my Rosalind is virtuous.

Ros. And I am your Rosalind.

Cel. It pleases him to call you so; but he hath a Rosalind of a better leer than you.

Ros. Come, woo me, woo me, for now I am in a holiday humour and like enough to consent. What would you say to me now, an I were your very very Rosalind?

Orl. I would kiss before I spoke.

Ros. Nay, you were better speak first, and when you

statement, since love was divided into conjugal love and neighborly love. 100. **poverty of grace.** Love is his divinity, and love has been ungracious to him. 107. **bounds,** i.e., bounds within which he can feed stock. 108. **carlot,** churl, countryman. 123. **constant,** uniform. **mingled damask,** striped red and white damask, i.e., the color of the damask rose (pink or rose color). 125. **In parcels,** piecemeal, in detail. 129. **what . . . do,** what business had he. 131. **am rememb'red,** remember, recollect. 133. **But . . . quittance,** i.e., but just the same, my failure to answer him doesn't mean I won't do so later. 136. **straight,** immediately.

ACT IV. SCENE I. 14. **politic,** pretended, calculated, in an attempt to appear grave and profoundly learned. 15. **nice,** fastidious. 17. **simples,** ingredients (usually herbs) of a drug. 34. **disable,** depreciate, disparage. 38. **swam in a gundello,** i.e., been in Venice. 48. **clapped . . . shoulder,** accosted him. 56. **jointure,** marriage settlement. 60. **beholding,** beholden, indebted. 61. **armed . . . fortune,** i.e., with the horns of a cuckold, which it was his fate to earn. 67. **leer,** complexion, countenance.

were gravelled for lack of matter, you might take occasion to kiss. Very good orators, when they are out, they will spit; and for lovers lacking—God warn us!—matter, the cleanliest shift is to kiss.

Orl. How if the kiss be denied?

Ros. Then she puts you to entreaty, and there begins new matter.

Orl. Who could be out, being before his beloved mistress?

Ros. Marry, that should you, if I were your mistress, or I should think my honesty ranker than my wit.

Orl. What, of my suit?

Ros. Not out of your apparel, and yet out of your suit. Am not I your Rosalind?

Orl. I take some joy to say you are, because I would be talking of her.

Ros. Well, in her person I say I will not have you.

Orl. Then in mine own person I die.

Ros. No, faith, die by attorney. The poor world is almost six thousand years old, and in all this time there was not any man died in his own person, videlicet, in a love-cause. Troilus had his brains dashed out with a Grecian club; yet he did what he could to die before, and he is one of the patterns of love. Leander, he would have lived many a fair year, though Hero had turned nun, if it had not been for a hot midsummer night; for, good youth, he went but forth to wash him in the Hellespont and being taken with the cramp was drowned: and the foolish chroniclers of that age found it was 'Hero of Sestos.' But these are all lies: men have died from time to time and worms have eaten them, but not for love.

Orl. I would not have my right Rosalind of this mind, for, I protest, her frown might kill me.

Ros. By this hand, it will not kill a fly. But come, now I will be your Rosalind in a more coming-on disposition, and ask me what you will, I will grant it.

Orl. Then love me, Rosalind.

Ros. Yes, faith, will I, Fridays and Saturdays and all.

Orl. And wilt thou have me?

Ros. Ay, and twenty such.

Orl. What sayest thou?

Ros. Are you not good?

Orl. I hope so.

Ros. Why then, can one desire too much of a good thing? Come, sister, you shall be the priest and marry us. Give me your hand, Orlando. What do you say, sister?

Orl. Pray thee, marry us.

Cel. I cannot say the words.

Ros. You must begin, 'Will you, Orlando—'

Cel. Go to. Will you, Orlando, have to wife this Rosalind?

Orl. I will.

Ros. Ay, but when?

Orl. Why now; as fast as she can marry us.

Ros. Then you must say, 'I take thee, Rosalind, for wife.'

Orl. I take thee, Rosalind, for wife.

Ros. I might ask you for your commission; but I do take thee, Orlando, for my husband: there 's a girl goes before the priest; and certainly a woman's thought runs before her actions.

Orl. So do all thoughts; they are winged.

Ros. Now tell me how long you would have her after you have possessed her.

Orl. For ever and a day.

Ros. Say 'a day,' without the 'ever.' No, no, Orlando; men are April when they woo, December when they wed: maids are May when they are maids, but the sky changes when they are wives. I will be more jealous of thee than a Barbary cock-pigeon over his hen, more clamorous than a parrot against rain, more new-fangled than an ape, more giddy in my desires than a monkey: I will weep for nothing, like Diana in the fountain, and I will do that when you are disposed to be merry; I will laugh like a hyen, and that when thou art inclined to sleep.

Orl. But will my Rosalind do so?

Ros. By my life, she will do as I do.

Orl. O, but she is wise.

Ros. Or else she could not have the wit to do this: the wiser, the waywarder: make the doors upon a woman's wit and it will out at the casement; shut that and 'twill out at the key-hole; stop that, 'twill fly with the smoke out at the chimney.

Orl. A man that had a wife with such a wit, he might say 'Wit, whither wilt?'

Ros. Nay, you might keep that check for it till you met your wife's wit going to your neighbour's bed.

Orl. And what wit could wit have to excuse that?

Ros. Marry, to say she came to seek you there. You shall never take her without her answer, unless you take her without her tongue. O, that woman that cannot make her fault her husband's occasion, let her never nurse her child herself, for she will breed it like a fool!

Orl. For these two hours, Rosalind, I will leave thee.

Ros. Alas! dear love, I cannot lack thee two hours.

Orl. I must attend the duke at dinner: by two o'clock I will be with thee again.

Ros. Ay, go your ways, go your ways; I knew what you would prove: my friends told me as much, and I thought no less: that flattering tongue of yours won me: 'tis but one cast away, and so, come, death! Two o'clock is your hour?

Orl. Ay, sweet Rosalind.

Ros. By my troth, and in good earnest, and so God mend me, and by all pretty oaths that are not dangerous, if you break one jot of your promise or come one minute behind your hour, I will think you the most pathetical break-promise and the most hollow lover and the most unworthy of her you call Rosalind that may be chosen out of the gross band of the unfaithful: therefore beware my censure and keep your promise.

Orl. With no less religion than if thou wert indeed my Rosalind: so adieu.

74. **gravelled,** stuck, at a standstill. 77. **warn,** for "warrant" (defend). 78. **cleanliest shift,** best way out of it. 94. **attorney,** proxy. 97. **videlicet,** namely. **Troilus,** hero of the story of Troilus and Cressida, pattern of faithful love. 100. **Leander,** hero of the story of Hero and Leander, who lost his life swimming the Hellespont to visit his sweetheart; also a pattern of faithful love. Both the *club* and the *cramp* are Shakespeare's inventions. 138. **ask . . . commission,** ask you what authority you have for taking her (since no one is there to give the bride away). 140. **goes before,** anticipates. 151. **Barbary cock-pigeon.** The epithet suggests oriental jealousy (Furness). 152. **against,** before, in expectation of. 155. **Diana in the fountain.** Diana, of course, frequently appeared as the centerpiece of fountains. Stow's *Survey of London* describes the setting up of a fountain with a Diana in green marble in the year 1596. 157. **hyen,** hyena. 162. **make,** shut. 168. **'Wit, whither wilt,'** a common Elizabethan expression implying that one is talking fantastically, with a wildly wandering wit. 177-178. **make . . . occasion,** i.e., turn a defense of her own conduct into an accusation against her husband. 196. **pathetical,** pitiable, miserable,

Ros. Well, Time is the old justice that examines all such offenders, and let Time try: adieu. *Exit* [*Orlando*].

Cel. You have simply misused our sex in your love-prate: we must have your doublet and hose plucked over your head, and show the world what the bird hath done to her own nest.

Ros. O coz, coz, coz, my pretty little coz, that thou didst know how many fathom deep I am in love! But it cannot be sounded: my affection hath an unknown bottom, like the bay of Portugal.

Cel. Or rather, bottomless, that as fast as you pour affection in, it runs out.

Ros. No, that same wicked bastard of Venus that was begot of thought, conceived of spleen and born of madness, that blind rascally boy that abuses every one's eyes because his own are out, let him be judge how deep I am in love. I'll tell thee, Aliena, I cannot be out of the sight of Orlando: I'll go find a shadow and sigh till he come.

Cel. And I'll sleep. *Exeunt.*

SCENE II. [*The forest.*]

Enter JAQUES, *and* Lords [*as*] Foresters.

Jaq. Which is he that killed the deer?

A Lord. Sir, it was I.

Jaq. Let 's present him to the duke, like a Roman conqueror; and it would do well to set the deer's horns upon his head, for a branch of victory. Have you no song, forester, for this purpose?

For. Yes, sir.

Jaq. Sing it: 'tis no matter how it be in tune, so it make noise enough. *Music.*

SONG.

[*For.*] What shall he have that kill'd the deer?
His leather skin and horns to wear.
Then sing him home;
(*The rest shall bear this burden.*)
Take thou no scorn to wear the horn;
It was a crest ere thou wast born:
Thy father's father wore it,
And thy father bore it:
The horn, the horn, the lusty horn
Is not a thing to laugh to scorn. *Exeunt.*

SCENE III. [*The forest.*]

Enter ROSALIND *and* CELIA.

Ros. How say you now? Is it not past two o'clock? and here much Orlando!

Cel. I warrant you, with pure love and troubled brain, he hath ta'en his bow and arrows and is gone forth to sleep. Look, who comes here.

Enter SILVIUS.

Sil. My errand is to you, fair youth;
My gentle Phebe bid me give you this:
I know not the contents; but, as I guess
By the stern brow and waspish action
Which she did use as she was writing of it,
It bears an angry tenour: pardon me;
I am but as a guiltless messenger.

Ros. Patience herself would startle at this letter
And play the swaggerer; bear this, bear all:
She says I am not fair, that I lack manners;
She calls me proud, and that she could not love me,
Were man as rare as phœnix, 'Od 's my will!
Her love is not the hare that I do hunt:
Why writes she so to me? Well, shepherd, well,
This is a letter of your own device.

Sil. No, I protest, I know not the contents:
Phebe did write it.

Ros. Come, come, you are a fool
And turn'd into the extremity of love.
I saw her hand: she has a leathern hand,
A freestone-coloured hand: I verily did think
That her old gloves were on, but 'twas her hands:
She has a huswife's hand; but that 's no matter:
I say she never did invent this letter;
This is a man's invention and his hand.

Sil. Sure, it is hers.

Ros. Why, 'tis a boisterous and a cruel style,
A style for challengers; why, she defies me,
Like Turk to Christian: women's gentle brain
Could not drop forth such giant-rude invention,
Such Ethiope words, blacker in their effect
Than in their countenance. Will you hear the letter?

Sil. So please you, for I never heard it yet;
Yet heard too much of Phebe's cruelty.

Ros. She Phebes me: mark how the tyrant writes. *Read.*

Art thou god to shepherd turn'd,
That a maiden's heart hath burn'd?

Can a woman rail thus?

Sil. Call you this railing?

Ros. *Read.*

Why, thy godhead laid apart,
Warr'st thou with a woman's heart?

Did you ever hear such railing?

Whiles the eye of man did woo me,
That could do no vengeance to me.

Meaning me a beast.

If the scorn of your bright eyne
Have power to raise such love in mine,
Alack, in me what strange effect
Would they work in mild aspect!
Whiles you chid me, I did love;
How then might your prayers move!
He that brings this love to thee
Little knows this love in me:
And by him seal up thy mind;
Whether that thy youth and kind
Will the faithful offer take
Of me and all that I can make;

or passion-moving. 201. **religion,** strict fidelity. 206. **simply misused,** absolutely slandered. 218. **bastard of Venus,** i.e., Cupid. 219. **thought,** fancy. **spleen,** impulse.

SCENE II. The scene presents a procession of huntsmen with their kill and is full of the customs of the chase, reflecting also the heathen background of the ceremony in the decking of the chief huntsman with the hide and horns of the slain deer as a fetish. 14. **Take . . . scorn,** be not ashamed.

SCENE III. 2. **and . . . Orlando,** ironical; Steevens: *here's much Orlando.* 5. **sleep,** unexpected turn; one would have expected her to say "hunt." 17. **phœnix,** a fabulous bird of Arabia, the only one of its kind, which lived five hundred years and was reborn of its own ashes. 23. **turn'd,** brought. 25. **freestone-coloured,** color of freestone, brown. 29. **hand,** handwriting, with play on the ordinary meaning. 35. **Ethiope,** blackamoor; here, black. 39. **Phebes,** i.e., treats cruelly. 48. **vengeance,** mischief, harm. 53. **aspect,** appearance of a planet; astrological term. 59. **youth and kind,** youthful nature.

Or else by him my love deny,
And then I'll study how to die.

Sil. Call you this chiding?

Cel. Alas, poor shepherd!

Ros. Do you pity him? no, he deserves no pity. Wilt thou love such a woman? What, to make thee an instrument and play false strains upon thee! not to be endured! Well, go your way to her, for I see love hath made thee a tame snake, and say this to her: that if she love me, I charge her to love thee; if she will not, I will never have her unless thou entreat for her. If you be a true lover, hence, and not a word; for here comes more company. *Exit Silvius.*

Enter OLIVER.

Oli. Good morrow, fair ones: pray you, if you know,
Where in the purlieus of this forest stands
A sheep-cote fenc'd about with olive trees?

Cel. West of this place, down in the neighbour bottom:
The rank of osiers by the murmuring stream
Left on your right hand brings you to the place.
But at this hour the house doth keep itself;
There 's none within.

Oli. If that an eye may profit by a tongue,
Then should I know you by description;
Such garments and such years: 'The boy is fair,
Of female favour, and bestows himself
Like a ripe sister: the woman low
And browner than her brother.' Are not you
The owner of the house I did enquire for?

Cel. It is no boast, being ask'd, to say we are.

Oli. Orlando doth commend him to you both,
And to that youth he calls his Rosalind
He sends this bloody napkin. Are you he?

Ros. I am: what must we understand by this?

Oli. Some of my shame; if you will know of me
What man I am, and how, and why, and where
This handkercher was stain'd.

Cel. I pray you, tell it.

Oli. When last the young Orlando parted from you
He left a promise to return again
Within an hour, and pacing through the forest,
Chewing the food of sweet and bitter fancy,
Lo, what befel! he threw his eye aside,
And mark what object did present itself:
Under an old oak, whose boughs were moss'd with age
And high top bald with dry antiquity,
A wretched ragged man, o'ergrown with hair,
Lay sleeping on his back: about his neck
A green and gilded snake had wreath'd itself,
Who with her head nimble in threats approach'd
The opening of his mouth; but suddenly,
Seeing Orlando, it unlink'd itself,
And with indented glides did slip away
Into a bush: under which bush's shade
A lioness, with udders all drawn dry,
Lay couching, head on ground, with catlike watch,
When that the sleeping man should stir; for 'tis
The royal disposition of that beast
To prey on nothing that doth seem as dead:
This seen, Orlando did approach the man
And found it was his brother, his elder brother.

Cel. O, I have heard him speak of that same brother;
And he did render him the most unnatural
That liv'd amongst men.

Oli. And well he might so do,
For well I know he was unnatural.

Ros. But, to Orlando: did he leave him there,
Food to the suck'd and hungry lioness?

Oli. Twice did he turn his back and purpos'd so;
But kindness, nobler ever than revenge,
And nature, stronger than his just occasion,
Made him give battle to the lioness,
Who quickly fell before him: in which hurtling
From miserable slumber I awak'd.

Cel. Are you his brother?

Ros. Was 't you he rescu'd?

Cel. Was 't you that did so oft contrive to kill him?

Oli. 'Twas I; but 'tis not I: I do not shame
To tell you what I was, since my conversion
So sweetly tastes, being the thing I am.

Ros. But, for the bloody napkin?

Oli. By and by.
When from the first to last betwixt us two
Tears our recountments had most kindly bath'd,
As how I came into that desert place:—
In brief, he led me to the gentle duke,
Who gave me fresh array and entertainment,
Committing me unto my brother's love;
Who led me instantly unto his cave,
There stripp'd himself, and here upon his arm
The lioness had torn some flesh away,
Which all this while had bled; and now he fainted
And cried, in fainting, upon Rosalind.
Brief, I recover'd him, bound up his wound;
And, after some small space, being strong at heart,
He sent me hither, stranger as I am,
To tell this story, that you might excuse
His broken promise, and to give this napkin
Dyed in his blood unto the shepherd youth
That he in sport doth call his Rosalind.
[*Rosalind swoons.*]

Cel. Why, how now, Ganymede! sweet Ganymede!

Oli. Many will swoon when they do look on blood.

Cel. There is more in it. Cousin Ganymede!

Oli. Look, he recovers.

Ros. I would I were at home.

Cel. We'll lead you thither.
I pray you, will you take him by the arm?

Oli. Be of good cheer, youth: you a man! you lack a man's heart.

Ros. I do so, I confess it. Ah, sirrah, a body would think this was well counterfeited! I pray you, tell your brother how well I counterfeited. Heigh-ho!

Oli. This was not counterfeit: there is too great testimony in your complexion that it was a passion of earnest.

Ros. Counterfeit, I assure you.

Oli. Well then, take a good heart and counterfeit to be a man.

68. **instrument,** tool and musical instrument. 76. **fair ones,** sometimes thought inappropriate as addressed to a boy as well as a girl, but there is nothing against such a greeting. 77. **purlieus,** tracts of land on the border of a forest. 79. **neighbour bottom,** neighboring dell. 80. **rank of osiers,** row of willows. 87. **bestows,** behaves. 88. **ripe sister,** mature or elder sister; Lettsom and New Cambridge: *forester.* 113. **indented,** zigzag. 115. **udders . . . dry,** therefore fierce with hunger.

126. **to,** with regard to. 130. **just occasion,** fair chance (of revenge). 132. **hurtling,** clattering, clashing. 136. **do not shame,** am not ashamed. 139. **for,** as regards. 141. **recountments,** relation, recital. 142. **As,** as for instance. 151. **Brief,** in brief. **recover'd,** brought back to consciousness or health. 166. **sirrah.** Onions suggests that this is addressed by Rosalind to herself, since the word is frequently so used in soliloquies. 172. **passion of earnest,** real attack.

Ros. So I do: but, i' faith, I should have been a woman by right.

Cel. Come, you look paler and paler: pray you, draw homewards. Good sir, go with us.

Oli. That will I, for I must bear answer back
How you excuse my brother, Rosalind.

Ros. I shall devise something: but, I pray you, commend my counterfeiting to him. Will you go? *Exeunt.*

ACT V.

SCENE I. [*The forest.*]

Enter [TOUCHSTONE *the*] *Clown and* AUDREY.

Touch. We shall find a time, Audrey; patience, gentle Audrey.

Aud. Faith, the priest was good enough, for all the old gentleman's saying.

Touch. A most wicked Sir Oliver, Audrey, a most vile Martext. But, Audrey, there is a youth here in the forest lays claim to you.

Aud. Ay, I know who 'tis; he hath no interest in me in the world: here comes the man you mean.

Enter WILLIAM.

Touch. It is meat and drink to me to see a clown: by my troth, we that have good wits have much to answer for; we shall be flouting; we cannot hold.

Will. Good even, Audrey.

Aud. God ye good even, William.

Will. And good even to you, sir.

Touch. Good even, gentle friend. Cover thy head, cover thy head; nay, prithee, be covered. How old are you, friend?

Will. Five and twenty, sir.

Touch. A ripe age. Is thy name William?

Will. William, sir.

Touch. A fair name. Wast born i' the forest here?

Will. Ay, sir, I thank God.

Touch. 'Thank God;' a good answer. Art rich?

Will. Faith, sir, so so.

Touch. 'So so' is good, very good, very excellent good; and yet it is not; it is but so so. Art thou wise?

Will. Ay, sir, I have a pretty wit.

Touch. Why, thou sayest well. I do now remember a saying, 'The fool doth think he is wise, but the wise man knows himself to be a fool.' The heathen philosopher, when he had a desire to eat a grape, would open his lips when he put it into his mouth; meaning thereby that grapes were made to eat and lips to open. You do love this maid?

Will. I do, sir.

Touch. Give me your hand. Art thou learned?

Will. No, sir.

Touch. Then learn this of me: to have, is to have; for it is a figure in rhetoric that drink, being poured out of a cup into a glass, by filling the one doth empty the other; for all your writers do consent that ipse is he: now, you are not ipse, for I am he.

Will. Which he, sir?

Touch. He, sir, that must marry this woman. Therefore, you clown, abandon,—which is in the vulgar leave,—the society,—which in the boorish is company,—of this female,—which in the common is woman; which together is, abandon the society of this female, or, clown, thou perishest; or, to thy better understanding, diest; or, to wit, I kill thee, make thee away, translate thy life into death, thy liberty into bondage: I will deal in poison with thee, or in bastinado, or in steel; I will bandy with thee in faction; I will o'errun thee with policy; I will kill thee a hundred and fifty ways: therefore tremble, and depart.

Aud. Do, good William.

Will. God rest you merry, sir. *Exit.*

Enter CORIN.

Cor. Our master and mistress seeks you; come, away, away!

Touch. Trip, Audrey! trip, Audrey! I attend, I attend. *Exeunt.*

SCENE II. [*The forest.*]

Enter ORLANDO *and* OLIVER.

Orl. Is 't possible that on so little acquaintance you should like her? that but seeing you should love her? and loving woo? and, wooing, she should grant? and will you persever to enjoy her?

Oli. Neither call the giddiness of it in question, the poverty of her, the small acquaintance, my sudden wooing, nor her sudden consenting; but say with me, I love Aliena; say with her that she loves me; consent with both that we may enjoy each other: it shall be to your good; for my father's house and all the revenue that was old Sir Rowland's will I estate upon you, and here live and die a shepherd.

Enter ROSALIND.

Orl. You have my consent. Let your wedding be tomorrow: thither will I invite the duke and all 's contented followers. Go you and prepare Aliena; for look you, here comes my Rosalind.

Ros. God save you, brother.

Oli. And you, fair sister. [*Exit.*]

Ros. O, my dear Orlando, how it grieves me to see thee wear thy heart in a scarf!

Orl. It is my arm.

Ros. I thought thy heart had been wounded with the claws of a lion.

Orl. Wounded it is, but with the eyes of a lady.

Ros. Did your brother tell you how I counterfeited to swoon when he showed me your handkercher?

Orl. Ay, and greater wonders than that.

Ros. O, I know where you are: nay, 'tis true: there was never any thing so sudden but the fight of two rams and Cæsar's thrasonical brag of 'I came, saw, and overcame:' for your brother and my sister no sooner met but they looked, no sooner looked but they loved, no sooner loved but they sighed, no sooner sighed but they asked one another the reason, no

ACT V. SCENE I. 4. **old gentleman's,** interesting comment on the age of Jaques. 12. **clown,** countryman. 13. **shall,** must. **flouting,** scoffing, expressing contempt. 16. **God ye good even,** God give you good evening. 36-40. **The heathen . . . open.** New Cambridge editors elucidate this as a way of telling William (whose mouth is probably gaping like a rustic's) that the grape (Audrey) is not for his lips. 46-47. **drink . . . other,** i.e., both Touchstone and William cannot possess Audrey. 48. **ipse,** Latin, he himself. 60. **bastinado,** duel with cudgels. 61. **bandy,** contend. 65. **God . . . merry,** common salutation at parting.

SCENE II. 4. **persever.** Accent is on second syllable. 13. **estate,** settle as an estate, bestow. 21. **sister,** i.e., future sister-in-law. 23. **wear . . . scarf,** possible allusion to Orlando's wearing his heart on his sleeve. 32. **where you are,** what you mean. 34. **thrasonical,** boastful; from Thraso, the boaster in Terence's *Eunuchus.*

sooner knew the reason but they sought the remedy; and in these degrees have they made a pair of stairs to marriage which they will climb incontinent, or else be incontinent before marriage: they are in the very wrath of love and they will together; clubs cannot part them.

Orl. They shall be married to-morrow, and I will bid the duke to the nuptial. But, O, how bitter a thing it is to look into happiness through another man's eyes! By so much the more shall I to-morrow be at the height of heart-heaviness, by how much I shall think my brother happy in having what he wishes for.

Ros. Why then, to-morrow I cannot serve your turn for Rosalind?

Orl. I can live no longer by thinking.

Ros. I will weary you then no longer with idle talking. Know of me then, for now I speak to some purpose, that I know you are a gentleman of good conceit: I speak not this that you should bear a good opinion of my knowledge, insomuch I say I know you are; neither do I labour for a greater esteem than may in some little measure draw a belief from you, to do yourself good and not to grace me. Believe then, if you please, that I can do strange things: I have, since I was three years old, conversed with a magician, most profound in his art and yet not damnable. If you do love Rosalind so near the heart as your gesture cries it out, when your brother marries Aliena, shall you marry her: I know into what straits of fortune she is driven; and it is not impossible to me, if it appear not inconvenient to you, to set her before your eyes to-morrow human as she is and without any danger.

Orl. Speakest thou in sober meanings?

Ros. By my life, I do; which I tender dearly, though I say I am a magician. Therefore, put you in your best array; bid your friends; for if you will be married to-morrow, you shall, and to Rosalind, if you will.

Enter SILVIUS *and* PHEBE.

Look, here comes a lover of mine and a lover of hers.

Phe. Youth, you have done me much ungentleness,
To show the letter that I writ to you.

Ros. I care not if I have: it is my study
To seem despiteful and ungentle to you:
You are there followed by a faithful shepherd;
Look upon him, love him; he worships you.

Phe. Good shepherd, tell this youth what 'tis to love.

Sil. It is to be all made of sighs and tears;
And so am I for Phebe.

Phe. And I for Ganymede.

Orl. And I for Rosalind.

Ros. And I for no woman.

Sil. It is to be all made of faith and service;
And so am I for Phebe.

Phe. And I for Ganymede.

Orl. And I for Rosalind.

Ros. And I for no woman.

Sil. It is to be all made of fantasy,
All made of passion and all made of wishes,
All adoration, duty, and observance,
All humbleness, all patience and impatience,
†All purity, all trial, all observance;
And so am I for Phebe.

Phe. And so am I for Ganymede.

Orl. And so am I for Rosalind.

Ros. And so am I for no woman.

Phe. If this be so, why blame you me to love you?

Sil. If this be so, why blame you me to love you?

Orl. If this be so, why blame you me to love you?

Ros. Who do you speak to, 'Why blame you me to love you?'

Orl. To her that is not here, nor doth not hear.

Ros. Pray you, no more of this; 'tis like the howling of Irish wolves against the moon. [*To Sil.*] I will help you, if I can: [*To Phe.*] I would love you, if I could. To-morrow meet me all together. [*To Phe.*] I will marry you, if ever I marry woman, and I'll be married to-morrow: [*To Orl.*] I will satisfy you, if ever I satisfied man, and you shall be married to-morrow: [*To Sil.*] I will content you, if what pleases you contents you, and you shall be married to-morrow. [*To Orl.*] As you love Rosalind, meet: [*To Sil.*] as you love Phebe, meet: and as I love no woman, I'll meet. So fare you well: I have left you commands.

Sil. I'll not fail, if I live.

Phe. Nor I.

Orl. Nor I. *Exeunt.*

SCENE III. [*The forest.*]

Enter [TOUCHSTONE *the*] *Clown and* AUDREY.

Touch. To-morrow is the joyful day, Audrey; to-morrow will we be married.

Aud. I do desire it with all my heart; and I hope it is no dishonest desire to desire to be a woman of the world. Here come two of the banished duke's pages.

Enter two Pages.

First Page. Well met, honest gentleman.

Touch. By my troth, well met. Come, sit, sit, and a song.

Sec. Page. We are for you: sit i' the middle.

First Page. Shall we clap into 't roundly, without hawking or spitting or saying we are hoarse, which are the only prologues to a bad voice?

Sec. Page. I' faith, i' faith; and both in a tune, like two gipsies on a horse.

SONG.

It was a lover and his lass,
With a hey, and a ho, and a hey nonino,

41. **degrees,** play on the original meaning, "steps." 42. **incontinent,** immediately. 44. **wrath,** impetuosity, ardor. 59. **conceit,** intelligence. 61. **insomuch,** inasmuch as. 63. **belief,** i.e., confidence in my ability. 64. **grace me,** bring favor on myself. 66. **conversed,** associated. 67. **damnable,** worthy of condemnation, i.e., he was not a practicer of forbidden magic. 69. **gesture,** bearing. **cries it out,** proclaims. 74-75. **human . . . danger,** i.e., not a phantom but the real Rosalind without any of the danger generally conceived to attend the rites of incantation (Johnson). 77. **tender dearly,** value highly, a possible reference to the anti-witchcraft statutes of Elizabeth, by which witchcraft causing death was punishable by death. 85. **study,** conscious endeavor. 102. **observance,** respect. 104. **observance.** Since the word appears on line 102, it may have been repeated in error by the compositor; many editors emend to "obedience." 110. **If . . . you,** addressed to Rosalind. **to love,** for loving. 111. **If . . . you,** addressed to Phebe. 119. **howling . . . moon,** a possible allusion to the rebellion of the Irish rebels against Elizabeth, the Virgin Queen.

SCENE III. 4. **dishonest,** immodest. 5. **woman of the world,** married woman; also, one who advances herself socially. 10. **sit i' the middle,** sit between us (in order to enter into the song). 11. **clap . . . roundly,** begin at once and with spirit. 13. **the only prologues,** only the prologues. 15. **both in a tune,** both in unison, or both keep in time.

That o'er the green corn-field did pass
In the spring time, the only pretty ring time,
When birds do sing, hey ding a ding, ding:
Sweet lovers love the spring.

Between the acres of the rye,
With a hey, and a ho, and a hey nonino,
These pretty country folks would lie,
In spring time, &c.

This carol they began that hour,
With a hey, and a ho, and a hey nonino,
How that a life was but a flower
In spring time, &c.

And therefore take the present time,
With a hey, and a ho, and a hey nonino;
For love is crowned with the prime
In spring time, &c.

Touch. Truly, young gentlemen, though there was no great matter in the ditty, yet the note was very untuneable.

First Page. You are deceived, sir: we kept time, we lost not our time.

Touch. By my troth, yes; I count it but time lost to hear such a foolish song. God be wi' you; and God mend your voices! Come, Audrey. *Exeunt.*

SCENE IV. [*The forest.*]

Enter DUKE Senior, AMIENS, JAQUES, ORLANDO, OLIVER, [*and*] CELIA.

Duke S. Dost thou believe, Orlando, that the boy
Can do all this that he hath promised?

Orl. I sometimes do believe, and sometimes do not;
†As those that fear they hope, and know they fear.

Enter ROSALIND, SILVIUS, *and* PHEBE.

Ros. Patience once more, whiles our compact is urg'd:
You say, if I bring in your Rosalind,
You will bestow her on Orlando here?

Duke S. That would I, had I kingdoms to give with her.

Ros. And you say, you will have her, when I bring her?

Orl. That would I, were I of all kingdoms king.

Ros. You say, you'll marry me, if I be willing?

Phe. That will I, should I die the hour after.

Ros. But if you do refuse to marry me,
You'll give yourself to this most faithful shepherd?

Phe. So is the bargain.

Ros. You say, that you'll have Phebe, if she will?

Sil. Though to have her and death were both one thing.

Ros. I have promis'd to make all this matter even.
Keep you your word, O duke, to give your daughter;
You yours, Orlando, to receive his daughter:
Keep you your word, Phebe, that you'll marry me,
Or else refusing me, to wed this shepherd:
Keep your word, Silvius, that you'll marry her,
If she refuse me: and from hence I go,
To make these doubts all even.
Exeunt Rosalind and Celia.

Duke S. I do remember in this shepherd boy
Some lively touches of my daughter's favour.

Orl. My lord, the first time that I ever saw him
Methought he was a brother to your daughter:
But, my good lord, this boy is forest-born,
And hath been tutor'd in the rudiments
Of many desperate studies by his uncle,
Whom he reports to be a great magician,
Obscured in the circle of this forest.

Enter [TOUCHSTONE *the*] *Clown and* AUDREY.

Jaq. There is, sure, another flood toward, and these couples are coming to the ark. Here comes a pair of very strange beasts, which in all tongues are called fools.

Touch. Salutation and greeting to you all!

Jaq. Good my lord, bid him welcome: this is the motley-minded gentleman that I have so often met in the forest: he hath been a courtier, he swears.

Touch. If any man doubt that, let him put me to my purgation. I have trod a measure; I have flattered a lady; I have been politic with my friend, smooth with mine enemy; I have undone three tailors; I have had four quarrels, and like to have fought one.

Jaq. And how was that ta'en up?

Touch. Faith, we met, and found the quarrel was upon the seventh cause.

Jaq. How seventh cause? Good my lord, like this fellow.

Duke S. I like him very well.

Touch. God 'ild you, sir; I desire you of the like. I press in here, sir, amongst the rest of the country copulatives, to swear and to forswear; according as marriage binds and blood breaks: a poor virgin, sir, an ill-favoured thing, sir, but mine own; a poor humour of mine, sir, to take that that no man else will: rich honesty dwells like a miser, sir, in a poor house; as your pearl in your foul oyster.

Duke S. By my faith, he is very swift and sententious.

Touch. According to the fool's bolt, sir, and such dulcet diseases.

Jaq. But, for the seventh cause; how did you find the quarrel on the seventh cause?

Touch. Upon a lie seven times removed:—bear your body more seeming, Audrey:—as thus, sir. I did dislike the cut of a certain courtier's beard: he sent me word, if I said his beard was not cut well, he was in the mind it was: this is called the Retort Courteous. If I

20. **ring time,** time most apt for marriage. 23. **acres,** fields, or according to Ridgeway, grass balks dividing grainfields into strips. 27. **carol,** originally a ring-dance; hence, any kind of song at a festival. 31. **And . . . time.** This stanza stands second in F; MS. discovered by Chappell (*Popular Music of the Olden Time*, p. 204) places it at the end, where it properly belongs. 33. **prime,** spring; also, choicest quality. 36. **matter,** sense, meaning. 37. **untuneable,** discordant.

SCENE IV. 4. **they hope,** that they merely hope; many conjectures on this difficult line. 25. **doubts all even,** seemingly impossible things all come true. 27. **lively,** lifelike. 32. **desperate,** dangerous (as tampering with forbidden arts). 34. **Obscured,** hidden; a possible allusion to the magic circle which protected the magician from the devil during incantation. 35. **toward,** coming on. 45. **purgation,** proof. 49. **like,** been likely. 50. **ta'en up,** settled, made up. 56. **desire . . . like,** I wish the same to you; a polite phrase used to reply to a compliment. 58. **copulatives,** people about to be joined in marriage. 60. **blood,** passion. 63. **your,** expletive used colloquially; not translatable. 65. **swift,** quick-witted. 66. **sententious,** pithy. 67. **fool's bolt,** proverb: "A fool's bolt is soon shot." 68. **dulcet diseases,** pleasant afflictions, idle and aimless but entertaining. 71. **seven times removed,** i.e., reckoning backward from the Lie Direct. 72. **seeming,** seemly, becomingly. 73. **dislike,** express dislike of.

sent him word again 'it was not well cut,' he would send me word, he cut it to please himself: this is called the Quip Modest. If again 'it was not well cut,' he disabled my judgement: this is called the Reply Churlish. If again, 'it was not well cut,' he would answer, I spake not true: this is called the Reproof Valiant. If again 'it was not well cut,' he would say, I lie: this is called the Countercheck Quarrelsome: and so to the Lie Circumstantial and the Lie Direct.

Jaq. And how oft did you say his beard was not well cut?

Touch. I durst go no further than the Lie Circumstantial, nor he durst not give me the Lie Direct; and so we measured swords and parted.

Jaq. Can you nominate in order now the degrees of the lie?

Touch. O sir, we quarrel in print, by the book; as you have books for good manners: I will name you the degrees. The first, the Retort Courteous; the second, the Quip Modest; the third, the Reply Churlish; the fourth, the Reproof Valiant; the fifth, the Countercheck Quarrelsome; the sixth, the Lie with Circumstance; the seventh, the Lie Direct. All these you may avoid but the Lie Direct; and you may avoid that too, with an If. I knew when seven justices could not take up a quarrel, but when the parties were met themselves, one of them thought but of an If, as, 'If you said so, then I said so;' and they shook hands and swore brothers. Your If is the only peace-maker; much virtue in If.

Jaq. Is not this a rare fellow, my lord? he 's as good at any thing and yet a fool.

Duke S. He uses his folly like a stalking-horse and under the presentation of that he shoots his wit.

Enter HYMEN, ROSALIND, *and* CELIA.

Still Music.

Hym. Then is there mirth in heaven,
When earthly things made even
Atone together.
Good duke, receive thy daughter:
Hymen from heaven brought her,
Yea, brought her hither,
That thou mightst join her hand with his
Whose heart within his bosom is.

Ros. [*To Duke*] To you I give myself, for I am yours.
[*To Orl.*] To you I give myself, for I am yours.

Duke S. If there be truth in sight, you are my daughter.

Orl. If there be truth in sight, you are my Rosalind.

Phe. If sight and shape be true,
Why then, my love adieu!

Ros. [*To Duke*] I'll have no father, if you be not he:
To Orl.] I'll have no husband, if you be not he:
[*To Phe.*] Nor ne'er wed woman, if you be not she.

Hym. Peace, ho! I bar confusion:
'Tis I must make conclusion
Of these most strange events:
Here 's eight that must take hands
To join in Hymen's bands,
If truth holds true contents.
You and you no cross shall part:
You and you are heart in heart:
You to his love must accord,
Or have a woman to your lord:
You and you are sure together,
As the winter to foul weather.
Whiles a wedlock-hymn we sing,
Feed yourselves with questioning;
That reason wonder may diminish,
How thus we met, and these things finish.

SONG.

Wedding is great Juno's crown:
O blessed bond of board and bed!
'Tis Hymen peoples every town;
High wedlock then be honoured:
Honour, high honour and renown,
To Hymen, god of every town!

Duke S. O my dear niece, welcome thou art to me!
Even daughter, welcome, in no less degree.

Phe. I will not eat my word, now thou art mine;
Thy faith my fancy to thee doth combine.

Enter Second Brother [JAQUES DE BOYS].

Jaq. de B. Let me have audience for a word or two:
I am the second son of old Sir Rowland,
That bring these tidings to this fair assembly.
Duke Frederick, hearing how that every day
Men of great worth resorted to this forest,
Address'd a mighty power; which were on foot,
In his own conduct, purposely to take
His brother here and put him to the sword:
And to the skirts of this wild wood he came;
Where meeting with an old religious man,
After some question with him, was converted
Both from his enterprise and from the world,
His crown bequeathing to his banish'd brother,
And all their lands restor'd to them again
That were with him exil'd. This to be true,
I do engage my life.

Duke S. Welcome, young man;
Thou offer'st fairly to thy brothers' wedding:
To one his lands withheld, and to the other
A land itself at large, a potent dukedom.
First, in this forest let us do those ends
That here were well begun and well begot:
And after, every of this happy number

79. **Quip,** smart jest. 80. **disabled,** disparaged. 85. **Countercheck,** rebuff; metaphor from chess. 91. **measured swords,** i.e., as preliminary to a duel. 94-95. **quarrel . . . book.** Touchstone is travestying books on the general subject of honor and arms, which dealt with occasions and circumstances of the duel. 95. **in print,** in type, and with precision (New Cambridge). **books . . . manners,** books of etiquette. 107. **swore brothers,** allusion to the practice of swearing brotherhood, becoming *fratres jurati.* 111. **stalking-horse,** a real or artificial horse under cover of which the hunter approaches his game. 112. **presentation,** semblance. 113. *Stage Direction:* **Hymen,** god of marriage. ***Still Music,*** soft music. 116. **Atone,** are at one. 125. **sight.** Johnson wished to read *shape* to be in accord with Phebe's *sight and shape.* 136. **If . . . contents,** if truth be true. This offers a rhyme for *events* above. 137. **You and you,** i.e., Orlando and Rosalind. 138. **You and you,** i.e., Oliver and Celia. 139. **You,** Phebe. **his,** Silvius'. **accord,** agree, consent. 140. **to,** for. 141. **You and you,** i.e., Touchstone and Audrey. **sure,** closely united. 147. **Juno's.** Juno was queen of gods, presiding over wedlock. 150. **High,** solemn. 154. **Even daughter,** i.e., my daughter equally with Rosalind. 155. **thou,** i.e., Silvius. 162. **Address'd,** prepared. 163. **In . . . conduct,** under his own command. 166. **religious man,** hermit. 167. **question,** conversation. 173. **offer'st fairly,** contributest handsomely. 174. **the other,** i.e., Orlando. 176. **do those ends,** accomplish those purposes. 181. **states,** status. 186. **by your patience,** by your leave, i.e., let the music

That have endur'd shrewd days and nights with us
Shall share the good of our returned fortune,
According to the measure of their states.
Meantime, forget this new-fall'n dignity
And fall into our rustic revelry.
Play, music! And you, brides and bridegrooms all,
With measure heap'd in joy, to th' measures fall.
Jaq. Sir, by your patience. If I heard you rightly,
The duke hath put on a religious life
And thrown into neglect the pompous court?
Jaq. de B. He hath.
Jaq. To him will I: out of these convertites
There is much matter to be heard and learn'd.
[*To Duke*] You to your former honour I bequeath;
Your patience and your virtue well deserves it:
[*To Orl.*] You to a love that your true faith doth merit:
[*To Oli.*] You to your land and love and great allies:
[*To Sil.*] You to a long and well-deserved bed:
[*To Touch.*] And you to wrangling; for thy loving voyage
Is but for two months victuall'd. So, to your pleasures:
I am for other than for dancing measures.
Duke S. Stay, Jaques, stay.
Jaq. To see no pastime I: what you would have
I'll stay to know at your abandon'd cave. *Exit.*
Duke S. Proceed, proceed: we'll begin these rites,
As we do trust they'll end, in true delights.
Exit [*in a dance*].

[EPILOGUE.]

Ros. It is not the fashion to see the lady the epilogue; but it is no more unhandsome than to see the lord the prologue. If it be true that good wine needs no bush, 'tis true that a good play needs no epilogue; yet to good wine they do use good bushes, and good plays prove the better by the help of good epilogues. What a case am I in then, that am neither a good epilogue nor cannot insinuate with you in the behalf of a good play! I am not furnished like a beggar, therefore to beg will not become me: my way is to conjure you; and I'll begin with the women. I charge you, O women, for the love you bear to men, to like as much of this play as please you: and I charge you, O men, for the love you bear to women—as I perceive by your simpering, none of you hates them—that between you and the women the play may please. If I were a woman I would kiss as many of you as had beards that pleased me, complexions that liked me and breaths that I defied not: and, I am sure, as many as have good beards or good faces or sweet breaths will, for my kind offer, when I make curtsy, bid me farewell. *Exit.*

wait a moment. 188. **pompous,** ceremonious. 190. **convertites,** converts. 191. **matter,** sound sense, good stuff.

EPILOGUE. 2. **unhandsome,** in bad taste. 4. **good . . . bush,** a proverb derived from the custom of displaying a piece of ivy or holly at the tavern door to denote that wine was for sale there. 9. **insinuate,** ingratiate myself. 15. **as please,** as may please. 19. **If I were a woman.** Women's parts on the Elizabethan stage were played by boys in feminine costume. 22. **defied,** disliked. 25. **bid me farewell,** i.e., applaud me.

TWELFTH NIGHT; OR, WHAT YOU WILL

Twelfth Night is possibly the latest in the festive group of comedies, including *Much Ado about Nothing* and *As You Like It*, with which Shakespeare climaxed his distinctively philosophical and joyous vein of comic writing. Performed on February 2, 1602, at the Middle Temple and written possibly as early as 1599, *Twelfth Night* is usually dated 1600 or 1601. This play is indeed the most festive of the lot. Its keynote is Saturnalian release and the innocently carnival pursuit of youth, love, and mirth. Along with such familiar motifs (found, for example, in *As You Like It* and *The Merchant of Venice*) as the plucky heroine disguised as a man, *Twelfth Night* also returns to the more hilariously farcical routines of mistaken identity found in Shakespeare's early comedy. As a witness of the 1602 performance, John Manningham, observes, the play is "much like the Commedy of Errores, or Menechmi in Plautus, but most like and neere to that in Italian called *Inganni*." Manningham might have added Shakespeare's *Two Gentlemen of Verona* as another early instance, since it too employs the device of the heroine Julia disguised in the service of her unresponsive lover Proteus.

The carnival atmosphere is appropriate to the season designated in the play's title: the twelfth night of Christmas, January 6, the Feast of Epiphany. (The prologue to *Gl'Ingannati*, perhaps the Italian play referred to by Manningham, speaks of "La Notte di Beffania," Epiphany night.) Although Epiphany has of course a primary Christian significance as the Feast of the Magi, it was also in Renaissance times the last day of the Christmas revels. Over a twelve-day period, from Christmas until January 6, noble households sponsored numerous performances of plays, masks, banquets, and every kind of festivity. (Leslie Hotson argues, in fact, that *Twelfth Night* was first performed on twelfth night in early 1601, in the presence of Queen Elizabeth.) Students left schools for vacations, celebrating release from study with plays and revels of their own. The stern rigors of a rule-bound society gave way temporarily to playful inversions of authority. The reign of the Boy Bishop and the Feast of Fools, for example, gave choristers and minor church functionaries the cherished opportunity to boss the hierarchy around, mock the liturgy with outrageous lampooning, and generally let off steam. Although such customs occasionally got out of hand, the idea was to channel potentially destructive insubordination into playacting and thereby promote harmony. Behind these Elizabethan midwinter customs lies the Roman Saturnalia, with its pagan spirit of gift-giving, sensual indulgence, and satirical hostility to those who would curb merriment.

Shakespeare's choice of sources for *Twelfth Night* underscores his commitment to mirth. Renaissance literature offered numerous instances of mistaken identity among twins, and of the disguised heroine serving as page to her beloved. Among those in English were the anonymous play *Sir Clyomon and Sir Clamydes* (c. 1570–1583), Sidney's *Arcadia* (1590), and the prose romance *Parismus* by Emanuel Forde (1598), featuring both a shipwreck and two characters with the names of Olivia and Violetta. Of particular significance, but largely for negative reasons, is Barnabe Riche's tale of "Apolonius and Silla" in *Riche his Farewell to Militarie profession*, 1581, based on Belleforest's 1571 French version of Bandello's *Novelle*, 1554. Here we find most of the requisite plot elements: the shipwreck, Silla's disguise as a page in Duke Apolonius' court, her office as ambassador of love from Apolonius to the Lady Julina who thereupon falls in love with Silla, the arrival of Silla's twin brother Silvio and his consequent success in winning Julina's affection. To Riche, however, this tale is merely a long testimonial to the enervating power of infatuation. Silvio gets Julina with child and disappears forthwith, making his belated reappearance almost too late to save the wrongly accused Silla (who is, of course, sexually incapable of fatherhood). Riche's moralizing, in the cautionary vein of Geoffrey Fenton's 1567 translation of Belleforest, puts the blame on the gross and drunken appetite of carnal love. The total mismatching of affection with which the story begins, and the sudden realignments of desire based on mere outward resemblances, are seen as proofs of love's unreasonableness. Shakespeare of course retains and capitalizes on the irrational quality of love, as in *A Midsummer Night's Dream*, but in doing so he minimizes the harm done (Olivia is not made pregnant) and repudiates any negative moral judgments. The added subplot, with its rebuking of Malvolio's censoriousness, may have been conceived as a further answer to Riche, Fenton, and their sober school.

Shakespeare's festive spirit owes much, as Manningham observed, to Plautus and the neoclassical Italian comic writers. At least three Italian comedies called *Gl'Inganni* ("The Frauds") employ the motif of mistaken identity, and one of them, by Curzio Gonzaga, 1592, supplies Viola's assumed name of "Cesare" or Cesario. Another play with the same title appeared in 1562. More useful is *Gl'Ingannati* ("The Deceived"), acted 1531, translated into French in 1543. Besides a plot line generally similar to *Twelfth Night*, and the reference to La Notte di Beffania (Epiphany), this play offers the suggestive name *Malevolti*, evil-faced, and *Fabio* (resembling "Fabian"). It also contains possible hints for Malvolio, Toby, and company, although the plot of the counterfeit letter is original with Shakespeare. Essentially, Shakespeare superimposes his own subplot on an Italianate novelle plot, as he did in *The Taming of the Shrew* and *Much Ado*. And it is in the Malvolio story that Shakespeare most pointedly defends merriment. Feste the professional fool, an original stage type for Shakespeare in *Twelfth Night* and in *As You Like It*, also reinforces the theme of seizing the moment of mirth.

This great lesson, of savoring life's pleasures while one is still young, is something that Duke Orsino and the Countess Olivia have not yet learned when the play commences. Although suited to one another in rank, wealth, and attractiveness, they are unable to overcome their own willful posturing in the elaborate charade of courtship. Like Silvius in *As You Like It*, Orsino is the conventional Petrarchan wooer trapped in the courtly artifice of love's rules. He opens the play on a cloying note of self-pity. He is fascinated with his own degradation as a rejected suitor, and bores his listeners with his changeable moods and fondness for poetical "conceits." He sees himself as a hart pursued by his desires "like fell and cruel hounds," reminding us that enervating lovesickness has in fact robbed him of his manly occupation, hunting. He sends ornately contrived messages to Olivia but has not seen her in so long that his passion has become unreal and fantastical, feeding on itself.

Olivia plays the predictably opposite role of chaste,

denying womanhood. She explains her retirement from the world as mourning for a dead brother, but this brother (whose name we never learn) is another unreal vision. Olivia's practice of mourning, whereby she will "water once a day her chamber round With eye-offending brine" (I,i), is ritually lifeless. As others view the matter, she is senselessly wasting her beauty and affection on the dead. "What a plague means my niece, to take the death of her brother thus?" Sir Toby expostulates (I,iii). Viola, though she too has seemingly lost a brother, is an important foil in this regard, for she continues to hope for her brother's safety, trusts his soul is in heaven if he is dead, and refuses to give up her commitment to life in any case. We suspect that Olivia takes a willful pleasure in self-denial not unlike Orsino's self-congratulatory suffering. She appears to derive satisfaction from the power she holds over Orsino, a power of refusal. And she must know that she looks stunning in black.

Olivia's household reflects in part her mood of self-denial. She keeps Malvolio as steward because he too dresses somberly, insists on quiet as befits a house in mourning, and maintains order. Yet Olivia also retains the fool, Feste, who is Malvolio's opposite in every way. Hard-pressed to defend his mirthful function in a household so given over to melancholy, Feste must find some way of persuading his mistress that her very gravity is itself the essence of folly. This is a paradox, because sobriety and order appeal to the conventional wisdom of the world. Malvolio, sensing that his devotion to propriety is being challenged by the fool's prating, chides Olivia for taking "delight in such a barren rascal" (I,v).

Feste must argue for an inversion of appearance and reality whereby many of the world's ordinary pursuits can be seen to be ridiculous. As he observes, in his habitually elliptical manner of speech, "*cucullus non facit monachum* [the cowl doesn't make the monk]; that's as much to say as I wear not motley in my brain." Feste wins his case by making Olivia laugh at her own illogic in grieving for a brother whose soul she assumes to be in heaven. By extension, Olivia has indeed been a fool for allowing herself to be deprived of happiness in love by her brother's death ("there is no true cuckold but calamity"), and for failing to consider the brevity of youth ("beauty's a flower"). Yet paradoxically only one who professes to be a fool can point this out, enabled by his detachment and innocence to perceive simple but profound truths denied to supposedly rational persons. This vision of the fool as naturally wise, and of society as self-indulgently insane, fascinated Renaissance writers, as in Erasmus' *In Praise of Folly* to Cervantes' *Don Quixote* to Shakespeare's *King Lear*.

Viola, although not dressed in motley, aligns herself with Feste's rejection of self-denial. Refreshingly, even comically, she challenges the staid artifice of Orsino's and Olivia's lives. She is an ocean traveler, like many of Shakespeare's later heroines (Marina in *Pericles*, Perdita in *The Winter's Tale*), arriving on Illyria's shore plucky and determined. On her first embassy to Olivia from Orsino, she exposes with disarming candor the willfully ritualistic quality of Olivia's existence. Viola discards the flowery set speech she had prepared and memorized at Orsino's behest; despite her charmingly conceited assertion that the speech has been "excellently well penned," she senses that its elegant but empty rhetoric is all too familiar to the disdainful Olivia. Instead, Viola departs from her text to urge seizing the moment of happiness. "You do usurp yourself," she lectures Olivia, "for what is yours to bestow is not yours to reserve" (I,v). Beauty is a gift of nature, and failure to use it is a sin against nature. Or, again, "Lady, you are the cruell'st she alive If you will lead these graces [Olivia's beauty] to the grave And leave the world no copy." An essential argument in favor of love, as in Shakespeare's sonnets, is the necessity of marriage and childbearing in order to perpetuate beauty. Needless to say this line is new to Olivia, and sweeps her off her feet. In part she reacts, like Phebe in *As You Like It*, with perversely feminine logic, rejecting a too-willing wooer for one who is hard to get. Yet Olivia is also attracted by a new note of sincerity, prompting her to reenter life and accept maturely both the risks and rewards of romantic involvement. Her longing for "Cesario" is of course sexually misdirected, but the appearance of Viola's identical twin Sebastian soon puts all to rights.

The motifs of Olivia's attraction for another woman (both are really boy actors), and of Orsino's deep fondness for "Cesario" that matures into sexual love, evoke delicately homosexual titillations as in *As You Like It*. Once again, however, we must approach the notion circumspectly, remembering that these elements are also found in Shakespeare's sources and reflect a convention wholly different from a modern psychological analysis of sexual aberration. Like Rosalind, Viola uses her male attire to win Orsino's pure affection, in a friendship devoid of sexual interest since both are seemingly men. Viola as Cesario can teach Orsino about the conventions of love, in relaxed and frank conversations that would not be possible if she were known to be a woman. She teaches him to avoid the beguiling but misleading myths of Petrarchan love, and so prepares him for the realities of marriage. Comparing men and women in love, she confides, "We men may say more, swear more: but indeed Our shows are more than will; for still we prove Much in our vows, but little in our love" (II,iv). Once she and Orsino are friends on a properly spiritual basis, Viola's unmasking can make possible a physical communion as well. The friendship of Sebastian and Antonio, sorely tested by the mix-ups of the mistaken identity plot, presents further insight into the debate of love and friendship.

The below-stairs characters of the subplot, Sir Toby and the rest, share with Feste and Viola a commitment to joy. As Sir Toby proclaims in his first speech, "care's an enemy to life" (I,iii). Even the simpleton

Sir Andrew, although gulled by Sir Toby into spending his money on a hopeless pursuit of Olivia, seems none the worse for his treatment; he loves to drink in Sir Toby's company, and can afford to pay for his entertainment. Sir Toby gives us some of the richly inventive humor of Falstaff, another lovable fat roguish knight. In this subplot, however, the confrontations between merriment and sobriety are more harshly drawn than in the main plot. Whereas the gracious Olivia is won away from her folly, the obdurate Malvolio can only be exposed to ridicule. He is chiefly to blame for the polarization of attitudes, for he insists on rebuking the mirth of others. His name, Mal-Volio, the ill-wisher, implies a self-satisfied determination to impose his rigid moral code on others. As Sir Toby taunts him, "Dost thou think, because thou art virtuous, there shall be no more cakes and ale?" (II,iii). Malvolio's inflexible hostility provokes a desire for comic vengeance. The method is satiric: the clever manipulators, Maria and Toby, invent a scheme to entrap Malvolio in his own self-deceit. The punishment fits the crime, for he has long dreamed of himself as Count Malvolio, rich, powerful, in a position to demolish Toby and the rest. Without Malvolio's infatuated predisposition to believe that Olivia could actually love him and write such a letter as he finds, Maria's scheme would have no hope of success. He tortures the text to make it yield a suitable meaning, much in the style of Puritan theologizing.

Indeed, Malvolio does in some ways resemble a Puritan, as Maria observes (II,iii), even though she qualifies the assertion by saying that he is not a religious fanatic but a "time-pleaser." She directs her observation not at a religious group but at all who would be killjoys; if the Puritans are like that, she intimates, so much the worse for them. This uncustomary lack of charity gives a sharp tone to the vengeance practiced on Malvolio, evoking from Olivia a protestation that "he hath been most notoriously abus'd" (V,i). The belated attempt to make a reconciliation with him seems, however, doomed to failure, in light of his grim resolve to "be reveng'd on the whole pack of you." At the height of his discomfiture he has been tricked into doing the one thing he hates most: smiling affably, and wearing sportive attire. The appearance of merriment is so grossly unsuited to him that he is declared mad and put into safekeeping. The apostle of sobriety in this play thus comes before us as a declared madman, while the fool Feste offers him sage comment in the guise of a priest. Wisdom and folly have changed places. The upside-down character of the play is epitomized in Malvolio's plaintive remark to Feste (no longer posing as the priest): "I am as well in my wits, fool, as thou art" (IV,ii). Malvolio's comeuppance is richly deserved, but the severity of vengeance and countervengeance suggests that the triumph of festival will not last long. This brevity is, of course, inherent in the nature of such holiday release from responsibility. As Feste sings, "What's to come is still unsure. In delay there lies no plenty."

TWELFTH NIGHT; OR, WHAT YOU WILL

[*Dramatis Personae*

ORSINO, Duke of Illyria.
SEBASTIAN, *brother to Viola.*
ANTONIO, *a sea captain, friend to Sebastian.*
A Sea Captain, *friend to Viola.*
VALENTINE, } *gentlemen attending on the Duke.*
CURIO, }
SIR TOBY BELCH, *uncle to Olivia.*
SIR ANDREW AGUECHEEK.
MALVOLIO, *steward to Olivia.*
FABIAN, } *servants to Olivia.*
FESTE, a Clown, }

OLIVIA.
VIOLA.
MARIA, *Olivia's woman.*

Lords, Priests, Sailors, Officers, Musicians, *and other* Attendants.

SCENE: *A city in Illyria, and the sea-coast near it.*]

ACT I.

SCENE I. [*The* DUKE'S *palace.*]

Enter ORSINO DUKE of Illyria, CURIO, *and other* Lords [*with* Musicians].

Duke. If music be the food of love, play on;
Give me excess of it, that, surfeiting,
The appetite may sicken, and so die.
That strain again! it had a dying fall:
O, it came o'er my ear like the sweet sound,
That breathes upon a bank of violets,
Stealing and giving odour! Enough; no more:
'Tis not so sweet now as it was before.
O spirit of love! how quick and fresh art thou,
That, notwithstanding thy capacity
Receiveth as the sea, nought enters there,
Of what validity and pitch soe'er,
But falls into abatement and low price,
Even in a minute: so full of shapes is fancy
That it alone is high fantastical.
Cur. Will you go hunt, my lord?
Duke. What, Curio?
Cur. The hart.
Duke. Why, so I do, the noblest that I have:
O, when mine eyes did see Olivia first,
Methought she purg'd the air of pestilence!
That instant was I turn'd into a hart;
And my desires, like fell and cruel hounds,
E'er since pursue me.

Enter VALENTINE.

How now! what news from her?
Val. So please my lord, I might not be admitted;
But from her handmaid do return this answer:
The element itself, till seven years' heat,
Shall not behold her face at ample view;
But, like a cloistress, she will veiled walk
And water once a day her chamber round
With eye-offending brine: all this to season
A brother's dead love, which she would keep fresh
And lasting in her sad remembrance.
Duke. O, she that hath a heart of that fine frame
To pay this debt of love but to a brother,
How will she love, when the rich golden shaft
Hath kill'd the flock of all affections else
That live in her; when liver, brain and heart,
These sovereign thrones, are all supplied, and fill'd
Her sweet perfections with one self king!
Away before me to sweet beds of flow'rs:
Love-thoughts lie rich when canopied with bow'rs.
Exeunt.

SCENE II. [*The sea-coast.*]

Enter VIOLA, *a* Captain, *and* Sailors.

Vio. What country, friends, is this?
Cap. This is Illyria, lady.
Vio. And what should I do in Illyria?
My brother he is in Elysium.
Perchance he is not drown'd: what think you, sailors?
Cap. It is perchance that you yourself were sav'd.
Vio. O my poor brother! and so perchance may he be.
Cap. True, madam: and, to comfort you with chance,
Assure yourself, after our ship did split,
When you and those poor number sav'd with you
Hung on our driving boat, I saw your brother,
Most provident in peril, bind himself,
Courage and hope both teaching him the practice,
To a strong mast that liv'd upon the sea;
Where, like Arion on the dolphin's back,
I saw him hold acquaintance with the waves
So long as I could see.
Vio. For saying so, there 's gold:
Mine own escape unfoldeth to my hope,
Whereto thy speech serves for authority,
The like of him. Know'st thou this country?
Cap. Ay, madam, well; for I was bred and born
Not three hours' travel from this very place.
Vio. Who governs here?
Cap. A noble duke, in nature as in name.
Vio. What is his name?
Cap. Orsino.
Vio. Orsino! I have heard my father name him:
He was a bachelor then.
Cap. And so is now, or was so very late;
For but a month ago I went from hence,
And then 'twas fresh in murmur,—as, you know,
What great ones do the less will prattle of,—
That he did seek the love of fair Olivia.
Vio. What 's she?
Cap. A virtuous maid, the daughter of a count
That died some twelvemonth since, then leaving her
In the protection of his son, her brother,
Who shortly also died: for whose dear love,
They say, she hath abjur'd the sight
And company of men.
Vio. O that I serv'd that lady
And might not be delivered to the world,
Till I had made mine own occasion mellow,
What my estate is!
Cap. That were hard to compass;
Because she will admit no kind of suit,
No, not the duke's.
Vio. There is a fair behaviour in thee, captain;
And though that nature with a beauteous wall
Doth oft close in pollution, yet of thee
I will believe thou hast a mind that suits
With this thy fair and outward character.
I prithee, and I'll pay thee bounteously,
Conceal me what I am, and be my aid
For such disguise as haply shall become
The form of my intent. I'll serve this duke:
Thou shalt present me as an eunuch to him:
It may be worth thy pains; for I can sing
And speak to him in many sorts of music
That will allow me very worth his service.
What else may hap to time I will commit;
Only shape thou thy silence to my wit.
Cap. Be you his eunuch, and your mute I'll be:
When my tongue blabs, then let mine eyes not see.
Vio. I thank thee: lead me on. *Exeunt.*

SCENE III. [OLIVIA'S *house.*]

Enter SIR TOBY [BELCH] *and* MARIA.

Sir To. What a plague means my niece, to take the death of her brother thus? I am sure care 's an enemy to life.

Mar. By my troth, Sir Toby, you must come in earlier o' nights: your cousin, my lady, takes great exceptions to your ill hours.

Sir To. Why, let her except, before excepted.

TITLE. **Twelfth Night,** the feast of the Epiphany, or the visit of the Magi. It occurred on the twelfth night after Christmas. The association of this name with "What You Will" lends some plausibility to the suggestion that the title came from the Prologue to *Gl' Ingannati,* an Italian comedy on a similar theme, which states that the story came from the brains of its authors "just as you draw your lots on Twelfth Night."

ACT I. SCENE I. 1. **food of love.** See *Antony and Cleopatra,* II, v, 1-2. 4. **fall,** cadence. 12. **validity,** value. **pitch,** superiority (literally, the highest point of a falcon's flight). 14. **fancy,** love. 18. **noblest . . . have,** i.e., his noblest part, his heart. 22. **fell,** fierce. 23. **pursue me,** reference to the story in Ovid of Actaeon, who was transformed into a hart and killed by his own hounds. 30. **season,** keep fresh. 35. **golden shaft,** i.e., of Cupid. 37. **liver, brain and heart.** In medieval and Elizabethan psychology these organs were the seats of the passions. 39. **self,** single.

SCENE II. 2. **Illyria,** a country along the eastern shore of the Adriatic. 4. **Elysium,** abode of the blessed dead. 8. **chance,** i.e., what chance may bring about. 11. **driving,** drifting. 14. **liv'd,** kept afloat. 15. **Arion,** a Greek poet who, leaping into the sea to escape murderous sailors, so charmed the dolphins with his lyre that they saved him. This was a favorite subject for pageants and paintings. 19. **unfoldeth . . . hope,** i.e., reinforces my hope for my brother. 21. **like of him,** i.e., he, too, may be saved. 32. **murmur,** gossip. 42. **delivered,** discovered, made known. 43. **mellow,** ready or convenient (to be made known). 47. **behaviour.** The word means "appearance" as well as "behavior." 51. **character,** face or features as indicating moral qualities; see glossary. 55. **form of my intent,** nature of my purpose, with suggestion of outward appearance in *form.* 59. **allow me,** cause me to be acknowledged. 61. **wit,** plan, invention.

SCENE III. 7. **except, before excepted,** legal phrase, *exceptis excipiendis,* "with the exceptions before named." Sir Toby means that enough exceptions to his behavior have already been taken.

Mar. Ay, but you must confine yourself within the modest limits of order.

Sir To. Confine! I'll confine myself no finer than I am: these clothes are good enough to drink in; and so be these boots too: an they be not, let them hang themselves in their own straps.

Mar. That quaffing and drinking will undo you: I heard my lady talk of it yesterday; and of a foolish knight that you brought in one night here to be her wooer.

Sir To. Who, Sir Andrew Aguecheek?

Mar. Ay, he.

Sir To. He 's as tall a man as any 's in Illyria.

Mar. What 's that to the purpose?

Sir To. Why, he has three thousand ducats a year.

Mar. Ay, but he'll have but a year in all these ducats: he 's a very fool and a prodigal.

Sir To. Fie, that you'll say so! he plays o' the viol-de-gamboys, and speaks three or four languages word for word without book, and hath all the good gifts of nature.

Mar. He hath indeed, almost natural: for besides that he 's a fool, he 's a great quarreller; and but that he hath the gift of a coward to allay the gust he hath in quarrelling, 'tis thought among the prudent he would quickly have the gift of a grave.

Sir To. By this hand, they are scoundrels and substractors that say so of him. Who are they?

Mar. They that add, moreover, he 's drunk nightly in your company.

Sir To. With drinking healths to my niece: I'll drink to her as long as there is a passage in my throat and drink in Illyria: he 's a coward and a coystrill that will not drink to my niece till his brains turn o' the toe like a parish-top. What, wench! Castiliano vulgo! for here comes Sir Andrew Agueface.

Enter SIR ANDREW [AGUECHEEK].

Sir And. Sir Toby Belch! how now, Sir Toby Belch!

Sir To. Sweet Sir Andrew!

Sir And. Bless you, fair shrew.

Mar. And you too, sir.

Sir To. Accost, Sir Andrew, accost.

Sir And. What 's that?

Sir To. My niece's chambermaid.

Sir And. Good Mistress Accost, I desire better acquaintance.

Mar. My name is Mary, sir.

Sir And. Good Mistress Mary Accost,—

Sir To. You mistake, knight: 'accost' is front her, board her, woo her, assail her.

Sir And. By my troth, I would not undertake her in this company. Is that the meaning of 'accost'?

Mar. Fare you well, gentlemen.

Sir To. An thou let part so, Sir Andrew, would thou mightst never draw sword again.

Sir And. An you part so, mistress, I would I might never draw sword again. Fair lady, do you think you have fools in hand?

Mar. Sir, I have not you by the hand.

Sir And. Marry, but you shall have; and here 's my hand.

Mar. Now, sir, 'thought is free:' I pray you, bring your hand to the buttery-bar and let it drink.

Sir And. Wherefore, sweet-heart? what 's your metaphor?

Mar. It 's dry, sir.

Sir And. Why, I think so: I am not such an ass but I can keep my hand dry. But what 's your jest?

Mar. A dry jest, sir.

Sir And. Are you full of them?

Mar. Ay, sir, I have them at my fingers' ends: marry, now I let go your hand, I am barren. *Exit Mar.*

Sir To. O knight, thou lackest a cup of canary: when did I see thee so put down?

Sir And. Never in your life, I think; unless you see canary put me down. Methinks sometimes I have no more wit than a Christian or an ordinary man has: but I am a great eater of beef and I believe that does harm to my wit.

Sir To. No question.

Sir And. An I thought that, I 'ld forswear it. I'll ride home to-morrow, Sir Toby.

Sir To. Pourquoi, my dear knight?

Sir And. What is 'pourquoi'? do or not do? I would I had bestowed that time in the tongues that I have in fencing, dancing and bear-baiting: O, had I but followed the arts!

Sir To. Then hadst thou had an excellent head of hair.

Sir And. Why, would that have mended my hair?

Sir To. Past question; for thou seest it will not curl by nature.

Sir And. But it becomes me well enough, does 't not?

Sir To. Excellent; it hangs like flax on a distaff; and I hope to see a housewife take thee between her legs and spin it off.

Sir And. Faith, I'll home to-morrow, Sir Toby: your niece will not be seen; or if she be, it 's four to one she'll none of me: the count himself here hard by woos her.

Sir To. She'll none o' the count: she'll not match above her degree, neither in estate, years, nor wit; I have heard her swear 't. Tut, there 's life in 't, man.

Sir And. I'll stay a month longer. I am a fellow o' the strangest mind i' the world; I delight in masques and revels sometimes altogether.

Sir To. Art thou good at these kickshawses, knight?

Sir And. As any man in Illyria, whatsoever he be, under the degree of my betters; and yet I will not compare with an old man.

Sir To. What is thy excellence in a galliard, knight?

10. **confine myself,** dress myself. 27. **viol-de-gamboys,** bass viol. 28. **without book,** by heart. Sir Andrew's complete ignorance of languages and lack of all accomplishments is one of the sources of Sir Toby's fun at his expense. 30. **natural,** with pun on the sense "born idiot." 33. **allay the gust,** moderate the taste. 37. **substractors,** for "detractors." 43. **coystrill,** horse-groom, base fellow. 45. **parish-top,** a large top provided by the parish to be spun by whipping, apparently for exercise in cold weather. **Castiliano vulgo,** literally, vulgar Spaniard; possibly a slang phrase, or nonsense. 52. **Accost,** make up to. 54. **chambermaid,** lady's maid. 73. **'thought is free,'** reply to *do you think,* above. 74-75. **bring . . . drink,** said to be a proverbial phrase meaning to ask at once for a kiss and a present (Kenrick, quoted by Luce). The buttery-bar was the hatch or half door of the ale-cellar (buttery) where drinks were served. 77. **dry,** i.e., a sign of age and debility. 81. **dry,** dull. 83. **fingers' ends.** Sir Andrew is holding her by the hand. 86. **canary,** sack, a wine from the Canary Islands. 90. **beef,** traditional cause of dull wits. The English were frequently twitted on account of the coarseness and quantity of their food and the dullness of their wit. 95. **Pourquoi,** why. 98. **tongues,** languages and "tongs" (used for curling hair). 99. **arts.** Cf. *nature,* below. 122. **kickshawses,** corruption of the French words *quelque chose;* delicacies, fancy dishes. 126. **old man,** a puzzling reference. Furness suggests that Sir Andrew wishes to express deference to age. 128. **galliard,** lively dance in triple time. 129. **cut a caper.** Sir Andrew uses the phrase in the ordinary sense. Sir

Sir And. Faith, I can cut a caper.

Sir To. And I can cut the mutton to 't.

Sir And. And I think I have the back-trick simply as strong as any man in Illyria.

Sir To. Wherefore are these things hid? wherefore have these gifts a curtain before 'em? are they like to take dust, like Mistress Mall's picture? why dost thou not go to church in a galliard and come home in a coranto? My very walk should be a jig; I would not so much as make water but in a sink-a-pace. What dost thou mean? Is it a world to hide virtues in? I did think, by the excellent constitution of thy leg, it was formed under the star of a galliard.

Sir And. Ay, 'tis strong, and it does indifferent well in a flame-coloured stock. Shall we set about some revels?

Sir To. What shall we do else? were we not born under Taurus?

Sir And. Taurus! That 's sides and heart.

Sir To. No, sir; it is legs and thighs. Let me see thee caper: ha! higher: ha, ha! excellent! *Exeunt.*

SCENE IV. [*The* DUKE'S *palace.*]

Enter VALENTINE, *and* VIOLA *in man's attire.*

Val. If the duke continue these favours towards you, Cesario, you are like to be much advanced: he hath known you but three days, and already you are no stranger.

Vio. You either fear his humour or my negligence, that you call in question the continuance of his love: is he inconstant, sir, in his favours?

Val. No, believe me.

Enter DUKE, CURIO, *and* Attendants.

Vio. I thank you. Here comes the count.
Duke. Who saw Cesario, ho?
Vio. On your attendance, my lord; here.
Duke. Stand you a while aloof. Cesario,
Thou know'st no less but all; I have unclasp'd
To thee the book even of my secret soul:
Therefore, good youth, address thy gait unto her;
Be not denied access, stand at her doors,
And tell them, there thy fixed foot shall grow
Till thou have audience.
Vio. Sure, my noble lord,
If she be so abandon'd to her sorrow
As it is spoke, she never will admit me.
Duke. Be clamorous and leap all civil bounds
Rather than make unprofited return.
Vio. Say I do speak with her, my lord, what then?
Duke. O, then unfold the passion of my love,
Surprise her with discourse of my dear faith:
It shall become thee well to act my woes;
She will attend it better in thy youth
Than in a nuncio's of more grave aspect.
Vio. I think not so, my lord.
Duke. Dear lad, believe it;
For they shall yet belie thy happy years,
That say thou art a man: Diana's lip
Is not more smooth and rubious; thy small pipe
Is as the maiden's organ, shrill and sound,
And all is semblative a woman's part.
I know thy constellation is right apt
For this affair. Some four or five attend him;
All, if you will; for I myself am best
When least in company. Prosper well in this,
And thou shalt live as freely as thy lord,
To call his fortunes thine.
Vio. I'll do my best
To woo your lady: [*Aside*] yet, a barful strife!
Whoe'er I woo, myself would be his wife. *Exeunt.*

SCENE V. [OLIVIA'S *house.*]

Enter MARIA *and* CLOWN.

Mar. Nay, either tell me where thou hast been, or I will not open my lips so wide as a bristle may enter in way of thy excuse: my lady will hang thee for thy absence.

Clo. Let her hang me: he that is well hanged in this world needs to fear no colours.

Mar. Make that good.

Clo. He shall see none to fear.

Mar. A good lenten answer: I can tell thee where that saying was born, of 'I fear no colours.'

Clo. Where, good Mistress Mary?

Mar. In the wars; and that may you be bold to say in your foolery.

Clo. Well, God give them wisdom that have it; and those that are fools, let them use their talents.

Mar. Yet you will be hanged for being so long absent; or to be turned away, is not that as good as a hanging to you?

Clo. Many a good hanging prevents a bad marriage; and, for turning away, let summer bear it out.

Mar. You are resolute, then?

Clo. Not so, neither; but I am resolved on two points.

Mar. That if one break, the other will hold; or, if both break, your gaskins fall.

Clo. Apt, in good faith; very apt. Well, go thy way; if Sir Toby would leave drinking, thou wert as witty a piece of Eve's flesh as any in Illyria.

Mar. Peace, you rogue, no more o' that. Here comes my lady: make your excuse wisely, you were best. [*Exit.*]

Enter Lady OLIVIA *with* MALVOLIO.

Toby makes a pun referring to *caper* sauce. 131. **back-trick,** some figure in the galliard; apparently, dancing backward. 135. **Mistress Mall's picture.** It has been suggested (1) that this refers to Moll Cutpurse or some other notorious female criminal; (2) that it is Maria's picture; (3) that it is a picture of no particular person. 138. **coranto,** lively dance. 140. **sink-a-pace,** French, *cinque-pace*, a dance. 143. **under the star,** i.e., a dancing star. Men's destinies and characters were thought to be influenced by the stars. 145. **flame-coloured,** so Rowe; F: *dam'd colour'd;* Collier: *dun-coloured.* **stock,** stocking. 147, 148. **Taurus,** zodiacal sign. Sir Andrew is mistaken, since Leo governed *sides and hearts* in medical astrology.

SCENE IV. 12. **you,** addressed to the attendants. 15. **address thy gait,** go. 21. **civil bounds,** bounds of civility. 28. **nuncio's,** messenger's. 30. **yet,** i.e., for a long time to come. 32. **rubious,** ruby red. **pipe,** voice. 33. **sound,** clear. 34. **semblative,** resembling, like. 41. **barful,** full of impediments.

SCENE V. *Stage Direction:* **Clown,** the technical word for those who played comic parts in the theatre. *Fool* is more commonly used in the text to denote the jester or domestic fool. 6. **fear no colours,** fear no enemies, with pun on "colors" and "collars" (halters). 9. **lenten,** meager, scanty (like lenten fare). 27. **gaskins,** hose, breeches, held up by laces or *points;* hence Maria's quibble. 29. **Sir Toby.** The Clown hints at a match between Maria and Sir Toby.

Clo. Wit, an 't be thy will, put me into good fooling! Those wits, that think they have thee, do very oft prove fools; and I, that am sure I lack thee, may pass for a wise man: for what says Quinapalus? 'Better a witty fool than a foolish wit.'—God bless thee, lady!

Oli. Take the fool away.

Clo. Do you not hear, fellows? Take away the lady.

Oli. Go to, y' are a dry fool; I'll no more of you: besides, you grow dishonest.

Clo. Two faults, madonna, that drink and good counsel will amend: for give the dry fool drink, then is the fool not dry: bid the dishonest man mend himself; if he mend, he is no longer dishonest; if he cannot let the botcher mend him. Any thing that 's mended is but patched: virtue that transgresses is but patched with sin; and sin that amends is but patched with virtue. If that this simple syllogism will serve, so; if it will not, what remedy? As there is no true cuckold but calamity, so beauty 's a flower. The lady bade take away the fool; therefore, I say again, take her away.

Oli. Sir, I bade them take away you.

Clo. Misprision in the highest degree! Lady, cucullus non facit monachum; that 's as much to say as I wear not motley in my brain. Good madonna, give me leave to prove you a fool.

Oli. Can you do it?

Clo. Dexteriously, good madonna.

Oli. Make your proof.

Clo. I must catechize you for it, madonna: good my mouse of virtue, answer me.

Oli. Well, sir, for want of other idleness, I'll bide your proof.

Clo. Good madonna, why mournest thou?

Oli. Good fool, for my brother's death.

Clo. I think his soul is in hell, madonna.

Oli. I know his soul is in heaven, fool.

Clo. The more fool, madonna, to mourn for your brother's soul being in heaven. Take away the fool, gentlemen.

Oli. What think you of this fool, Malvolio? doth he not mend?

Mal. Yes, and shall do till the pangs of death shake him: infirmity, that decays the wise, doth ever make the better fool.

Clo. God send you, sir, a speedy infirmity, for the better increasing your folly! Sir Toby will be sworn that I am no fox; but he will not pass his word for two pence that you are no fool.

Oli. How say you to that, Malvolio?

Mal. I marvel your ladyship takes delight in such a barren rascal: I saw him put down the other day with an ordinary fool that has no more brain than a stone. Look you now, he 's out of his guard already; unless you laugh and minister occasion to him, he is gagged. I protest, I take these wise men, that crow so at these set kind of fools, no better than the fools' zanies.

Oli. O, you are sick of self-love, Malvolio, and taste with a distempered appetite. To be generous, guiltless and of free disposition, is to take those things for bird-bolts that you deem cannon-bullets: there is no slander in an allowed fool, though he do nothing but rail; nor no railing in a known discreet man, though he do nothing but reprove.

Clo. Now Mercury endue thee with leasing, for thou speakest well of fools!

Enter MARIA.

Mar. Madam, there is at the gate a young gentleman much desires to speak with you.

Oli. From the Count Orsino, is it?

Mar. I know not, madam: 'tis a fair young man, and well attended.

Oli. Who of my people hold him in delay?

Mar. Sir Toby, madam, your kinsman.

Oli. Fetch him off, I pray you; he speaks nothing but madman: fie on him! [*Exit Maria.*] Go you, Malvolio: if it be a suit from the count, I am sick, or not at home; what you will, to dismiss it. *(Exit Malvolio.)* Now you see, sir, how your fooling grows old, and people dislike it.

Clo. Thou hast spoke for us, madonna, as if thy eldest son should be a fool; whose skull Jove cram with brains! for,—here he comes,—one of thy kin has a most weak pia mater.

Enter SIR TOBY.

Oli. By mine honour, half drunk. What is he at the gate, cousin?

Sir To. A gentleman.

Oli. A gentleman! what gentleman?

Sir To. 'Tis a gentleman here—a plague o' these pickle-herring! How now, sot!

Clo. Good Sir Toby.

Oli. Cousin, cousin, how have you come so early by this lethargy?

Sir To. Lechery! I defy lechery. There 's one at the gate.

Oli. Ay, marry, what is he?

Sir To. Let him be the devil, an he will, I care not: give me faith, say I. Well, it 's all one. *Exit.*

Oli. What 's a drunken man like, fool?

Clo. Like a drowned man, a fool and a mad man: one draught above heat makes him a fool; the second mads him; and a third drowns him.

Oli. Go thou and seek the crowner, and let him sit o' my coz; for he 's in the third degree of drink, he 's drowned: go, look after him.

Clo. He is but mad yet, madonna; and the fool shall look to the madman. [*Exit.*]

Enter MALVOLIO.

Mal. Madam, yond young fellow swears he will speak with you. I told him you were sick; he takes on him to understand so much, and therefore comes to

39. **Quinapalus,** apparently an invented authority. 45. **dry,** dull. 46. **dishonest,** unreliable. 52. **botcher,** mender of old clothes and shoes. 56-57. **As . . . flower,** i.e., since Fortune, to which every man is wedded, is notoriously unfaithful, our best course is to seize the moment of youth and beauty before we lose it. 61. **Misprision,** mistake, misunderstanding, with suggestion of the legal use meaning "contempt," the arrest or imprisonment of the wrong person. 62. **cucullus . . . monachum,** the cowl does not make the monk. 63. **motley,** the many-colored garment of jesters. 69. **mouse of virtue,** term of endearment. 70. **idleness,** pastime. 91. **ordinary fool,** probably a fool from the street not regularly attached to a household. 92-93. **out of his guard,** defenseless. 93-94. **minister occasion,** provide opportunity (for his fooling). 96. **zanies,** fools' subordinates or imitators. 100. **bird-bolts,** blunt arrows for shooting small birds. 102. **allowed,** licensed. 105. **Mercury,** god of guile and trickery. **leasing,** lying. 115. **madman,** i.e., the words of madness. 119. **old,** stale. 123. **pia mater,** soft inner lining of the brain. 128. **here.** Sir Toby hiccoughs at this point and tries to conceal his condition. 137. **give me faith,** i.e., to resist the devil. 140. **above heat,** above the point needed to make him normally warm. 142. **crowner,** coroner. 157.

speak with you. I told him you were asleep; he seems to have a foreknowledge of that too, and therefore comes to speak with you. What is to be said to him, lady? he 's fortified against any denial.

Oli. Tell him he shall not speak with me.

Mal. Has been told so; and he says, he'll stand at your door like a sheriff's post, and be the supporter to a bench, but he'll speak with you.

Oli. What kind o' man is he?

Mal. Why, of mankind.

Oli. What manner of man?

Mal. Of very ill manner; he'll speak with you, will you or no.

Oli. Of what personage and years is he?

Mal. Not yet old enough for a man, nor young enough for a boy; as a squash is before 'tis a peascod, or a codling when 'tis almost an apple: 'tis with him in standing water, between boy and man. He is very well-favoured and he speaks very shrewishly; one would think his mother's milk were scarce out of him.

Oli. Let him approach: call in my gentlewoman.

Mal. Gentlewoman, my lady calls. *Exit.*

Enter MARIA.

Oli. Give me my veil: come, throw it o'er my face.
We'll once more hear Orsino's embassy.

Enter VIOLA.

Vio. The honourable lady of the house, which is she?

Oli. Speak to me; I shall answer for her. Your will?

Vio. Most radiant, exquisite and unmatchable beauty,—I pray you, tell me if this be the lady of the house, for I never saw her: I would be loath to cast away my speech, for besides that it is excellently well penned, I have taken great pains to con it. Good beauties, let me sustain no scorn; I am very comptible, even to the least sinister usage.

Oli. Whence came you, sir?

Vio. I can say little more than I have studied, and that question 's out of my part. Good gentle one, give me modest assurance if you be the lady of the house, that I may proceed in my speech.

Oli. Are you a comedian?

Vio. No, my profound heart: and yet, by the very fangs of malice I swear, I am not that I play. Are you the lady of the house?

Oli. If I do not usurp myself, I am.

Vio. Most certain, if you are she, you do usurp yourself; for what is yours to bestow is not yours to reserve. But this is from my commission: I will on with my speech in your praise, and then show you the heart of my message.

Oli. Come to what is important in 't: I forgive you the praise.

Vio. Alas, I took great pains to study it, and 'tis poetical.

Oli. It is the more like to be feigned: I pray you, keep it in. I heard you were saucy at my gates, and allowed your approach rather to wonder at you than to hear you. If you be not mad, be gone; if you have reason, be brief: 'tis not that time of moon with me to make one in so skipping a dialogue.

Mar. Will you hoist sail, sir? here lies your way.

Vio. No, good swabber; I am to hull here a little longer. Some mollification for your giant, sweet lady. Tell me your mind: I am a messenger.

Oli. Sure, you have some hideous matter to deliver, when the courtesy of it is so fearful. Speak your office.

Vio. It alone concerns your ear. I bring no overture of war, no taxation of homage: I hold the olive in my hand; my words are as full of peace as matter.

Oli. Yet you began rudely. What are you? what would you?

Vio. The rudeness that hath appeared in me have I learned from my entertainment. What I am, and what I would, are as secret as maidenhead; to your ears, divinity, to any other's, profanation.

Oli. Give us the place alone; we will hear this divinity. [*Exeunt Maria and Attendants.*]
Now, sir, what is your text?

Vio. Most sweet lady,—

Oli. A comfortable doctrine, and much may be said of it. Where lies your text?

Vio. In Orsino's bosom.

Oli. In his bosom! In what chapter of his bosom?

Vio. To answer by the method, in the first of his heart.

Oli. O, I have read it: it is heresy. Have you no more to say?

Vio. Good madam, let me see your face.

Oli. Have you any commission from your lord to negotiate with my face? You are now out of your text: but we will draw the curtain and show you the picture. Look you, sir, such a one I was this present: is 't not well done? [*Unveiling.*]

Vio. Excellently done, if God did all.

Oli. 'Tis in grain, sir; 'twill endure wind and weather.

Vio. 'Tis beauty truly blent, whose red and white
Nature's own sweet and cunning hand laid on:
Lady, you are the cruell'st she alive,
If you will lead these graces to the grave
And leave the world no copy.

Oli. O, sir, I will not be so hard-hearted; I will give out divers schedules of my beauty: it shall be inventoried, and every particle and utensil labelled to my will: as, item, two lips, indifferent red; item, two grey eyes, with lids to them; item, one neck, one chin, and so forth. Were you sent hither to praise me?

Vio. I see you what you are, you are too proud;
But, if you were the devil, you are fair.
My lord and master loves you: O, such love
Could be but recompens'd, though you were crown'd
The nonpareil of beauty!

Oli. How does he love me?

Vio. With adorations, fertile tears,

sheriff's post, post before the sheriff's door on which proclamations and notices were fixed. 165-171. **Not yet . . . him.** Nowhere else does Malvolio speak in this vein. 166. **squash,** unripe pea pod. 167. **peascod,** pea pod. **codling,** unripe apple. 170. **shrewishly,** sharply; possibly, like a woman. 181. **Most . . . beauty.** This line is a part of Viola's prepared speech. 186. **con,** learn by heart. 188. **comptible,** susceptible, sensitive. **sinister,** discourteous. 196. **that,** that which. 201. **from,** outside of. 204-205. **forgive you,** excuse you from repeating. 213. **moon,** as affecting lunatics. 214. **skipping,** flighty, frivolous. 217. **swabber,** one who washes the decks; a nautical retort to *hoist sail* (l. 215). 218-219. **Some . . . giant,** pray pacify your giant; alluding ironically to Maria's small size. 222. **courtesy,** ceremonious introduction. 223. **office,** commission. 225. **taxation,** demand for the payment of. 239. **comfortable,** comforting. 244. **method,** i.e., your method, your metaphor. 253. **this present,** just now, presently. Since it was customary to hang curtains in front of pictures, Olivia in unveiling speaks as if she were displaying a picture of herself. 255. **in grain,** fast dyed. 263. **schedules,** inventories. 265. **labelled,** added as a codicil. 274. **fertile,** copious.

With groans that thunder love, with sighs of fire.
Oli. Your lord does know my mind; I cannot love him:
Yet I suppose him virtuous, know him noble,
Of great estate, of fresh and stainless youth;
In voices well divulg'd, free, learn'd and valiant;
And in dimension and the shape of nature
A gracious person: but yet I cannot love him;
He might have took his answer long ago.
Vio. If I did love you in my master's flame,
With such a suff'ring, such a deadly life,
In your denial I would find no sense;
I would not understand it.
Oli. Why, what would you?
Vio. Make me a willow cabin at your gate,
And call upon my soul within the house;
Write loyal cantons of contemned love
And sing them loud even in the dead of night;
Halloo your name to the reverberate hills
And make the babbling gossip of the air
Cry out 'Olivia!' O, you should not rest
Between the elements of air and earth,
But you should pity me!
Oli. You might do much.
What is your parentage?
Vio. Above my fortunes, yet my state is well:
I am a gentleman.
Oli. Get you to your lord;
I cannot love him: let him send no more;
Unless, perchance, you come to me again,
To tell me how he takes it. Fare you well:
I thank you for your pains: spend this for me.
Vio. I am no fee'd post, lady; keep your purse:
My master, not myself, lacks recompense.
Love make his heart of flint that you shall love;
And let your fervour, like my master's, be
Plac'd in contempt! Farewell, fair cruelty. *Exit.*
Oli. 'What is your parentage?'
'Above my fortunes, yet my state is well:
I am a gentleman.' I'll be sworn thou art;
Thy tongue, thy face, thy limbs, actions and spirit,
Do give thee five-fold blazon: not too fast: soft, soft!
Unless the master were the man. How now!
Even so quickly may one catch the plague?
Methinks I feel this youth's perfections
With an invisible and subtle stealth
To creep in at mine eyes. Well, let it be.
What ho, Malvolio!

Enter MALVOLIO.

Mal. Here, madam, at your service.
Oli. Run after that same peevish messenger,
The county's man: he left this ring behind him,
Would I or not: tell him I'll none of it.
Desire him not to flatter with his lord,
Nor hold him up with hopes; I am not for him:
If that the youth will come this way to-morrow,
I'll give him reasons for 't: hie thee, Malvolio.
Mal. Madam, I will. *Exit.*
Oli. I do I know not what, and fear to find
Mine eye too great a flatterer for my mind.
Fate, show thy force: ourselves we do not owe;
What is decreed must be, and be this so. [*Exit.*]

ACT II.

SCENE I. [*The sea-coast.*]

Enter ANTONIO *and* SEBASTIAN.

Ant. Will you stay no longer? nor will you not that I go with you?

Seb. By your patience, no. My stars shine darkly over me: the malignancy of my fate might perhaps distemper yours; therefore I shall crave of you your leave that I may bear my evils alone: it were a bad recompense for your love, to lay any of them on you.

Ant. Let me yet know of you whither you are bound.

Seb. No, sooth, sir: my determinate voyage is mere extravagancy. But I perceive in you so excellent a touch of modesty, that you will not extort from me what I am willing to keep in; therefore it charges me in manners the rather to express myself. You must know of me then, Antonio, my name is Sebastian, which I called Roderigo. My father was that Sebastian of Messaline, whom I know you have heard of. He left behind him myself and a sister, both born in an hour: if the heavens had been pleased, would we had so ended! but you, sir, altered that; for some hour before you took me from the breach of the sea was my sister drowned.

Ant. Alas the day!

Seb. A lady, sir, though it was said she much resembled me, was yet of many accounted beautiful: but, though I could not with such estimable wonder overfar believe that, yet thus far I will boldly publish her; she bore a mind that envy could not but call fair. She is drowned already, sir, with salt water, though I seem to drown her remembrance again with more.

Ant. Pardon me, sir, your bad entertainment.

Seb. O good Antonio, forgive me your trouble.

Ant. If you will not murder me for my love, let me be your servant.

Seb. If you will not undo what you have done, that is, kill him whom you have recovered, desire it not. Fare ye well at once: my bosom is full of kindness, and I am yet so near the manners of my mother, that upon the least occasion more mine eyes will tell tales of me. I am bound to the Count Orsino's court: farewell. *Exit.*

Ant. The gentleness of all the gods go with thee!
I have many enemies in Orsino's court,
Else would I very shortly see thee there.
But, come what may, I do adore thee so,
That danger shall seem sport, and I will go. *Exit.*

283. **flame,** passion. 284. **deadly,** death-doomed. 287. **willow cabin,** arbor. Willow is a symbol of unrequited love. 288. **my soul,** i.e., Olivia. 289. **cantons,** songs. **contemned,** rejected. 292. **babbling . . . air,** echo. 303. **fee'd post,** messenger to be tipped. 305. **Love . . . love,** may Love make the heart of the man you love as hard as flint. 310. **thou,** suggestive of tenderness. She has used *your* before (l. 308). 312. **blazon,** heraldic description. 317. **eyes.** Love was thought to enter through the eye.

ACT II. SCENE I. 4. **malignancy,** malevolence (of the stars). 12. **extravagancy,** aimless wandering. 15. **it charges me,** I am bound. 16. **express,** reveal. 19. **Messaline,** possibly, Mytilene or Messina in Sicily. 21. **an,** one. 29. **estimable wonder,** admiring judgment. 34. **entertainment,** reception. 41. **kindness,** tenderness. 42. **manners . . . mother,** womanish qualities.

SCENE II. *Stage Direction: several,* different. 8. **desperate,** without hope. 10. **hardy,** audacious. 13. **She . . . it.** Viola tells a quick and friendly lie to shield Olivia. 21. **lost,** caused her to lose. 29. **pregnant,** quick, resourceful; possibly alluding to Satan. 30. **proper-false,** handsome and deceitful. 31. **set their forms,** stamp their images. 34. **fadge,** turn out. 35. **monster,** i.e., being both man and woman.

SCENE III. 3. **'diluculo surgere'** (*saluberrimum est*), to rise early is most healthful; a sentence from Lilly's *Latin Grammar.* 13. **Th' art**

SCENE II. [*A street.*]

Enter VIOLA *and* MALVOLIO *at several doors.*

Mal. Were not you even now with the Countess Olivia?

Vio. Even now, sir; on a moderate pace I have since arrived but hither.

Mal. She returns this ring to you, sir: you might have saved me my pains, to have taken it away yourself. She adds, moreover, that you should put your lord into a desperate assurance she will none of him: and one thing more, that you be never so hardy to come again in his affairs, unless it be to report your lord's taking of this. Receive it so.

Vio. She took the ring of me: I'll none of it.

Mal. Come, sir, you peevishly threw it to her; and her will is, it should be so returned: if it be worth stooping for, there it lies in your eye; if not, be it his that finds it. *Exit.*

Vio. I left no ring with her: what means this lady?
Fortune forbid my outside have not charm'd her!
She made good view of me; indeed, so much,
That sure methought her eyes had lost her tongue,
For she did speak in starts distractedly.
She loves me, sure; the cunning of her passion
Invites me in this churlish messenger.
None of my lord's ring! why, he sent her none.
I am the man: if it be so, as 'tis,
Poor lady, she were better love a dream.
Disguise, I see, thou art a wickedness,
Wherein the pregnant enemy does much.
How easy is it for the proper-false
In women's waxen hearts to set their forms!
Alas, our frailty is the cause, not we!
For such as we are made of, such we be.
How will this fadge? my master loves her dearly;
And I, poor monster, fond as much on him;
And she, mistaken, seems to dote on me.
What will become of this? As I am man,
My state is desperate for my master's love;
As I am woman,—now alas the day!—
What thriftless sighs shall poor Olivia breathe!
O time! thou must untangle this, not I;
It is too hard a knot for me t' untie! [*Exit.*]

SCENE III. [OLIVIA'S *house.*]

Enter SIR TOBY *and* SIR ANDREW.

Sir To. Approach, Sir Andrew: not to be abed after midnight is to be up betimes; and 'diluculo surgere,' thou know'st,—

Sir And. Nay, by my troth, I know not: but I know, to be up late is to be up late.

Sir To. A false conclusion: I hate it as an unfilled can. To be up after midnight and to go to bed then, is early: so that to go to bed after midnight is to go to bed betimes. Does not our lives consist of the four elements?

Sir And. Faith, so they say; but I think it rather consists of eating and drinking.

Sir To. Th' art a scholar; let us therefore eat and drink. Marian, I say! a stoup of wine!

Enter CLOWN.

Sir And. Here comes the fool, i' faith.

Clo. How now, my hearts! did you never see the picture of 'we three'?

Sir To. Welcome, ass. Now let 's have a catch.

Sir And. By my troth, the fool has an excellent breast. I had rather than forty shillings I had such a leg, and so sweet a breath to sing, as the fool has. In sooth, thou wast in very gracious fooling last night, when thou spokest of Pigrogromitus, of the Vapians passing the equinoctial of Queubus: 'twas very good, i' faith. I sent thee sixpence for thy leman: hadst it?

Clo. I did impeticos thy gratillity; for Malvolio's nose is no whipstock: my lady has a white hand, and the Myrmidons are no bottle-ale houses.

Sir And. Excellent! why, this is the best fooling, when all is done. Now, a song.

Sir To. Come on; there is sixpence for you: let 's have a song.

Sir And. There 's a testril of me too: if one knight give a—

Clo. Would you have a love-song, or a song of good life?

Sir To. A love-song, a love-song.

Sir And. Ay, ay: I care not for good life.

Clo. (*Sings*)
O mistress mine, where are you roaming?
O, stay and hear; your true love 's coming,
That can sing both high and low:
Trip no further, pretty sweeting;
Journeys end in lovers meeting,
Every wise man's son doth know.

Sir And. Excellent good, i' faith.

Sir To. Good, good.

Clo. [*Sings*]
What is love? 'tis not hereafter;
Present mirth hath present laughter;
What 's to come is still unsure:
In delay there lies no plenty;
Then come kiss me, sweet and twenty,
Youth 's a stuff will not endure.

Sir And. A mellifluous voice, as I am true knight.

Sir To. A contagious breath.

Sir And. Very sweet and contagious, i' faith.

Sir To. To hear by the nose, it is dulcet in contagion. But shall we make the welkin dance indeed? shall we rouse the night-owl in a catch that will draw three souls out of one weaver? shall we do that?

Sir And. An you love me, let 's do 't: I am dog at a catch.

Clo. By 'r lady, sir, and some dogs will catch well.

a scholar. Sir Toby is making fun of him. 14. **stoup,** drinking vessel. 17. **picture of 'we three,'** picture of two asses inscribed "we three," the spectator being the third. 18. **catch,** a song so arranged that the second singer takes up the first line just as the first singer is beginning the second line, and so on. 20. **breast,** voice. 21. **leg,** probably, obeisance made by drawing back one leg and bending the other. 24-25. **Pigrogromitus . . . Queubus,** mock erudition. 26. **leman,** sweetheart. 27. **impeticos thy gratillity,** suggests "impetticoat (or pocket up) thy gratuity." 28. **whipstock,** whip handle. 29. **Myrmidons,** followers of Achilles; here, perhaps, taverns of high grade. **bottle-ale,** used contemptuously of taverns because they sold low-class drink. 34. **testril,** a coin worth sixpence. 37. **good life,** respectability. 40. **O mistress mine.** This song is found in several Elizabethan songbooks, but is nevertheless thought by some authorities to be Shakespeare's. 43. **sweeting,** sweet one. 52. **sweet and twenty,** possibly meant originally "twenty times as sweet," *twenty* being used as an intensive; or, kiss me twenty times again. 59. **welkin dance,** drink till the sky seems to turn round (Johnson). 61-62. **draw . . . weaver,** usually explained as a reference to psalm-singing weavers, Protestant refugees from Belgium. There is a reference also to the Renaissance conception of the soul which was held to be threefold, the vegetal, the sensible, and the intellectual soul. 64. **dog at,** clever at.

Sir And. Most certain. Let our catch be, 'Thou knave.'

Clo. 'Hold thy peace, thou knave,' knight? I shall be constrained in 't to call thee knave, knight.

Sir And. 'Tis not the first time I have constrained one to call me knave. Begin, fool: it begins 'Hold thy peace.'

Clo. I shall never begin if I hold my peace.

Sir And. Good, i' faith. Come, begin. *Catch sung.*

Enter MARIA.

Mar. What a caterwauling do you keep here! If my lady have not called up her steward Malvolio and bid him turn you out of doors, never trust me.

Sir To. My lady 's a Cataian, we are politicians, Malvolio 's a Peg-a-Ramsey, and 'Three merry men be we.' Am not I consanguineous? am I not of her blood? Tillyvally. Lady! [*Sings*] 'There dwelt a man in Babylon, lady, lady!'

Clo. Beshrew me, the knight 's in admirable fooling.

Sir And. Ay, he does well enough if he be disposed, and so do I too: he does it with a better grace, but I do it more natural.

Sir To. [*Sings*] 'O, the twelfth day of December,'—

Mar. For the love o' God, peace!

Enter MALVOLIO.

Mal. My masters, are you mad? or what are you? Have you no wit, manners, nor honesty, but to gabble like tinkers at this time of night? Do ye make an alehouse of my lady's house, that ye squeak out your coziers' catches without any mitigation or remorse of voice? Is there no respect of place, persons, nor time in you?

Sir To. We did keep time, sir, in our catches. Sneck up!

Mal. Sir Toby, I must be round with you. My lady bade me tell you, that, though she harbours you as her kinsman, she 's nothing allied to your disorders. If you can separate yourself and your misdemeanours, you are welcome to the house; if not, an it would please you to take leave of her, she is very willing to bid you farewell.

Sir To. [*Sings.*] 'Farewell, dear heart, since I must needs be gone.'

Mar. Nay, good Sir Toby.

Clo. 'His eyes do show his days are almost done.'

Mal. Is 't even so?

Sir To. 'But I will never die.'

Clo. Sir Toby, there you lie.

Mal. This is much credit to you.

Sir To. 'Shall I bid him go?'

Clo. 'What an if you do?'

Sir To. 'Shall I bid him go, and spare not?'

Clo. 'O no, no, no, no, you dare not.'

Sir To. Out o' tune, sir: ye lie. Art any more than a steward? Dost thou think, because thou art virtuous, there shall be no more cakes and ale?

Clo. Yes, by Saint Anne, and ginger shall be hot i' the mouth too.

Sir To. Th' art i' the right. Go, sir, rub your chain with crums. A stoup of wine, Maria!

Mal. Mistress Mary, if you prized my lady's favour at any thing more than contempt, you would not give means for this uncivil rule: she shall know of it, by this hand. *Exit.*

Mar. Go shake your ears.

Sir And. 'Twere as good a deed as to drink when a man 's a-hungry, to challenge him the field, and then to break promise with him and make a fool of him.

Sir To. Do 't, knight: I'll write thee a challenge; or I'll deliver thy indignation to him by word of mouth.

Mar. Sweet Sir Toby, be patient for to-night: since the youth of the count's was to-day with my lady, she is much out of quiet. For Monsieur Malvolio, let me alone with him: if I do not gull him into a nayword, and make him a common recreation, do not think I have wit enough to lie straight in my bed: I know I can do it.

Sir To. Possess us, possess us; tell us something of him.

Mar. Marry, sir, sometimes he is a kind of puritan.

Sir And. O, if I thought that, I 'ld beat him like a dog!

Sir To. What, for being a puritan? thy exquisite reason, dear knight?

Sir And. I have no exquisite reason for 't, but I have reason good enough.

Mar. The devil a puritan that he is, or any thing constantly, but a time-pleaser; an affectioned ass, that cons state without book and utters it by great swarths: the best persuaded of himself, so crammed, as he thinks, with excellencies, that it is his grounds of faith that all that look on him love him; and on that vice in him will my revenge find notable cause to work.

Sir To. What wilt thou do?

Mar. I will drop in his way some obscure epistles of love; wherein, by the colour of his beard, the shape of his leg, the manner of his gait, the expressure of his eye, forehead, and complexion, he shall find himself most feelingly personated. I can write very like my lady your niece: on a forgotten matter we can hardly make distinction of our hands.

Sir To. Excellent! I smell a device.

Sir And. I have 't in my nose too.

Sir To. He shall think, by the letters that thou wilt drop, that they come from my niece, and that she 's in love with him.

Mar. My purpose is, indeed, a horse of that colour.

Sir And. And your horse now would make him an ass.

Mar. Ass, I doubt not.

Sir And. O, 'twill be admirable!

Mar. Sport royal, I warrant you: I know my physic will work with him. I will plant you two, and

80. **Cataian,** explained as Chinese, i.e., from Cathay, suggested by *caterwauling.* **politicians,** schemers, intriguers. 81. **Peg-a-Ramsey,** common name of a tune, evidently of low character. 83. **Tillyvally,** a term of contempt, possibly from a song. 84. **'There . . . lady,'** first line of a ballad having the refrain "Lady, lady." Sir Toby's use of the word, above, suggested the song. 89. **natural,** unconsciously suggesting idiocy. 90-91. **'O . . . December.'** Kittredge suggests that this is the ballad of "Musselburgh Field" in Child's *English and Scottish Popular Ballads,* IV, 507. 97. **coziers',** cobblers'. 98. **mitigation or remorse,** considerate lowering. 101. **Sneck up!** Go hang! 102. **round,** plain. 109-110. **'Farewell . . . gone,'** from the ballad, "Corydon's Farewell to Phyllis." 125. **cakes and ale,** reveling (proverbial). 126. **Saint Anne,** invoked because of her care for material welfare. 128-129. **Go . . . crums,** i.e., scour your steward's chain with crumbs; attend to your own business. 132. **give means,** i.e., by supplying drink. 133. **rule,** conduct. 146. **nayword,** byword. 147. **recreation,** laughingstock. 152. **puritan.** Note that Maria is careful in her distinctions; she raises the prospect of regarding Malvolio as a kind of puritan, but then refuses to regard him simply as a satirical type of the Puritan sect. The extent of the resemblance is left unstated. 160. **time-pleaser,**

let the fool make a third, where he shall find the letter: observe his construction of it. For this night, to bed, and dream on the event. Farewell. *Exit.*

Sir To. Good night, Penthesilea.

Sir And. Before me, she 's a good wench.

Sir To. She 's a beagle, true-bred, and one that adores me: what o' that?

Sir And. I was adored once too.

Sir To. Let 's to bed, knight. Thou hadst need send for more money.

Sir And. If I cannot recover your niece, I am a foul way out.

Sir To. Send for money, knight: if thou hast her not i' the end, call me cut.

Sir And. If I do not, never trust me, take it how you will.

Sir To. Come, come, I'll go burn some sack; 'tis too late to go to bed now: come, knight; come, knight.
Exeunt.

SCENE IV. [*The* DUKE'S *Palace.*]

Enter DUKE, VIOLA, CURIO, *and others.*

Duke. Give me some music. Now, good morrow, friends.
Now, good Cesario, but that piece of song,
That old and antique song we heard last night:
Methought it did relieve my passion much,
More than light airs and recollected terms
Of these most brisk and giddy-paced times:
Come, but one verse.

Cur. He is not here, so please your lordship, that should sing it.

Duke. Who was it?

Cur. Feste, the jester, my lord; a fool that the lady Olivia's father took much delight in. He is about the house.

Duke. Seek him out, and play the tune the while.
[*Exit Curio.*] *Music plays.*
Come hither, boy: if ever thou shalt love,
In the sweet pangs of it remember me;
For such as I am all true lovers are,
Unstaid and skittish in all motions else,
Save in the constant image of the creature
That is belov'd. How dost thou like this tune?

Vio. It gives a very echo to the seat
Where Love is thron'd.

Duke. Thou dost speak masterly:
My life upon 't, young though thou art, thine eye
Hath stay'd upon some favour that it loves:
Hath it not, boy?

Vio. A little, by your favour.

Duke. What kind of woman is 't?

Vio. Of your complexion.

Duke. She is not worth thee, then. What years, i' faith?

Vio. About your years, my lord.

Duke. Too old, by heaven: let still the woman take
An elder than herself; so wears she to him,
So sways she level in her husband's heart:
For, boy, however we do praise ourselves,
Our fancies are more giddy and unfirm,
More longing, wavering, sooner lost and worn,
Than women's are.

Vio. I think it well, my lord.

Duke. Then let thy love be younger than thyself,
Or thy affection cannot hold the bent;
For women are as roses, whose fair flow'r
Being once display'd, doth fall that very hour.

Vio. And so they are: alas, that they are so;
To die, even when they to perfection grow!

Enter CURIO *and* CLOWN.

Duke. O, fellow, come, the song we had last night.
Mark it, Cesario, it is old and plain;
The spinsters and the knitters in the sun
And the free maids that weave their thread with bones
Do use to chant it: it is silly sooth,
And dallies with the innocence of love,
Like the old age.

Clo. Are you ready, sir?

Duke. Ay; prithee, sing. *Music.*

THE SONG.

[*Clo.*] Come away, come away, death,
And in sad cypress let me be laid;
Fly away, fly away, breath;
I am slain by a fair cruel maid.
My shroud of white, stuck all with yew,
O, prepare it!
My part of death, no one so true
Did share it.

Not a flower, not a flower sweet,
On my black coffin let there be strown;
Not a friend, not a friend greet
My poor corpse, where my bones shall be thrown:
A thousand thousand sighs to save,
Lay me, O, where
Sad true lover never find my grave,
To weep there!

Duke. There 's for thy pains.

Clo. No pains, sir; I take pleasure in singing, sir.

Duke. I'll pay thy pleasure then.

Clo. Truly, sir, and pleasure will be paid, one time or another.

Duke. Give me now leave to leave thee.

Clo. Now, the melancholy god protect thee; and the tailor make thy doublet of changeable taffeta, for thy mind is a very opal. I would have men of such constancy put to sea, that their business might be every

time-server, sycophant. 161. **cons . . . book,** learns the phrases of high society by heart. 162. **best persuaded,** has the best opinion. 171. **expressure,** expression. 173. **personated,** described. 193. **Penthesilea,** queen of the Amazons; another ironical allusion to Maria's stature. 195. **beagle,** small hound; possibly also alluding to Maria's size. 200. **recover,** win. 201. **foul way out,** explained as "out of pocket" and as "off the track." 203. **cut,** a horse with a docked tail.
SCENE IV. 3. **antique,** quaint. 5. **recollected terms,** studied and artificial expressions. 21. **seat,** i.e., the heart. 25. **stay'd . . . favour,** rested upon some face. 30. **still,** always. 31. **wears she,** adapts herself. 32. **sways she level,** keeps steady, constant. 33. **praise,** appraise. 35. **worn,** F: *worne;* Hanmer: *won* (for *wonne*), which is possibly correct. 38. **bent,** degree of tension (as in archery). 45. **spinsters,** spinners. 46. **bones,** bobbins with which bone-lace was made. 47. **silly sooth,** simple truth. 49. **old age,** good old times. 53. **cypress,** interpreted as meaning coffin of cypress wood, or bier strewn with sprigs of cypress. 58-59. **My . . . it,** no one died for love so true to love as I (Luce). 75. **melancholy god,** Saturn, if the Clown has any god in mind. 76. **doublet,** close-fitting body garment with or without sleeves. 77. **taffeta,** silk.

thing and their intent every where; for that 's it that always makes a good voyage of nothing. Farewell. *Exit.*

Duke. Let all the rest give place.
[*Curio and Attendants retire.*]
Once more, Cesario,
Get thee to yond same sovereign cruelty:
Tell her, my love, more noble than the world,
Prizes not quantity of dirty lands;
The parts that fortune hath bestow'd upon her,
Tell her, I hold as giddily as fortune;
But 'tis that miracle and queen of gems
That nature pranks her in attracts my soul.

Vio. But if she cannot love you, sir?

Duke. I cannot be so answer'd.

Vio. Sooth, but you must.
Say that some lady, as perhaps there is,
Hath for your love as great a pang of heart
As you have for Olivia: you cannot love her;
You tell her so; must she not then be answer'd?

Duke. There is no woman's sides
Can bide the beating of so strong a passion
As love doth give my heart; no woman's heart
So big, to hold so much; they lack retention.
Alas, their love may be call'd appetite,
No motion of the liver, but the palate,
That suffer surfeit, cloyment and revolt;
But mine is all as hungry as the sea,
And can digest as much: make no compare
Between that love a woman can bear me
And that I owe Olivia.

Vio. Ay, but I know—

Duke. What dost thou know?

Vio. Too well what love women to men may owe:
In faith, they are as true of heart as we.
My father had a daughter lov'd a man,
As it might be, perhaps, were I a woman,
I should your lordship.

Duke. And what's her history?

Vio. A blank, my lord. She never told her love,
But let concealment, like a worm i' th' bud,
Feed on her damask cheek: she pin'd in thought,
And with a green and yellow melancholy
She sat like Patience on a monument,
Smiling at grief. Was not this love indeed?
We men may say more, swear more: but indeed
Our shows are more than will; for still we prove
Much in our vows, but little in our love.

Duke. But died thy sister of her love, my boy?

Vio. I am all the daughters of my father's house,
And all the brothers too: and yet I know not.
Sir, shall I to this lady?

Duke. Ay, that 's the theme.
To her in haste; give her this jewel; say,
My love can give no place, bide no denay. *Exeunt.*

SCENE V. [OLIVIA's *garden.*]

Enter SIR TOBY, SIR ANDREW, *and* FABIAN.

Sir To. Come thy ways, Signior Fabian.

Fab. Nay, I'll come: if I lose a scruple of this sport, let me be boiled to death with melancholy.

Sir To. Wouldst thou not be glad to have the niggardly rascally sheep-biter come by some notable shame?

Fab. I would exult, man: you know, he brought me out o' favour with my lady about a bear-baiting here.

Sir To. To anger him we'll have the bear again; and we will fool him black and blue: shall we not, Sir Andrew?

Sir And. An we do not, it is pity of our lives.

Enter MARIA.

Sir To. Here comes the little villain. How now,
my metal of India!

Mar. Get ye all three into the box-tree: Malvolio 's coming down this walk: he has been yonder i' the sun practising behaviour to his own shadow this half hour: observe him, for the love of mockery; for I know this letter will make a contemplative idiot of him. Close, in the name of jesting! Lie thou there [*throws down a letter*]; for here comes the trout that must be caught with tickling. *Exit.*

Enter MALVOLIO.

Mal. 'Tis but fortune; all is fortune. Maria once told me she did affect me: and I have heard herself come thus near, that, should she fancy, it should be one of my complexion. Besides, she uses me with a more exalted respect than any one else that follows her. What should I think on 't?

Sir To. Here 's an overweening rogue!

Fab. O, peace! Contemplation makes a rare turkey-cock of him: how he jets under his advanced plumes!

Sir And. 'Slight, I could so beat the rogue!

Sir To. Peace, I say.

Mal. To be Count Malvolio!

Sir To. Ah, rogue!

Sir And. Pistol him, pistol him.

Sir To. Peace, peace!

Mal. There is example for 't; the lady of the Strachy married the yeoman of the wardrobe.

Sir And. Fie on him, Jezebel!

Fab. O, peace! now he 's deeply in: look how imagination blows him.

Mal. Having been three months married to her, sitting in my state,—

Sir To. O, for a stone-bow, to hit him in the eye!

Mal. Calling my officers about me, in my branched velvet gown; having come from a daybed, where I have left Olivia sleeping,—

80-81. **for . . . nothing,** possibly ironical, meaning that such changeable enterprise will make a good voyage come to nothing. 86. **parts,** gifts, as wealth or rank. 87. **giddily,** carelessly, indifferently. 89. **pranks,** adorns. 96-106. **There . . . Olivia.** The duke has just said in lines 33-36 that men are more inconstant than women. 99. **retention,** constancy, power of retaining. 101. **liver . . . palate.** The distinction seems to be that real love is a passion of the liver, whereas fancy (light love) is born in the eye and nourished in the palate. 102. **That suffer,** that suffers. *That* is sometimes thought to refer back to *their* (l. 100). **cloyment,** satiety to the point of losing appetite. **revolt,** sickness, revulsion. 113. **blank,** i.e., her history is a blank. 115. **damask,** pink like the damask rose. 116. **green and yellow.** Green denoted hopefulness and yellow jealousy; so that a green and yellow melancholy was a melancholy in which there was jealousy, yet hope. This accords exactly with the state of mind of Viola (Hunter). 127. **denay,** denial.

SCENE V. 3. **boiled to death.** Melancholy being a settled passion, the spirits descended to the intestines, carrying with them their boiling heat. 6. **sheep-biter,** i.e., a sneaky dog. 17. **metal,** gold, probably with pun on "mettle," spirit. 23. **contemplative,** i.e., from contemplating himself. 26. **tickling,** groping gently with the hands—a method of fishing. 28. **she,** i.e., Olivia. 30. **fancy,** fall in love. 36. **jets,** struts. 44. **lady of the Strachy,** apparently a lady who had married below her station; no satisfactory explanation. 46. **Jezebel,** a blunder of Sir Andrew, unless, as has been suggested, we should read *her* for *him* in this line. 48. **blows,** puffs up. 51. **stone-bow,** crossbow that shoots stones. 54. **branched,** adorned with a figured pattern suggesting

Sir To. Fire and brimstone!

Fab. O, peace, peace!

Mal. And then to have the humour of state; and after a demure travel of regard, telling them I know my place as I would they should do theirs, to ask for my kinsman Toby,—

Sir To. Bolts and shackles!

Fab. O peace, peace, peace! now, now.

Mal. Seven of my people, with an obedient start, make out for him: I frown the while; and perchance wind up my watch, or play with my—some rich jewel. Toby approaches; courtesies there to me,—

Sir To. Shall this fellow live?

Fab. Though our silence be drawn from us with cars, yet peace.

Mal. I extend my hand to him thus, quenching my familiar smile with an austere regard of control,—

Sir To. And does not Toby take you a blow o' the lips then?

Mal. Saying, 'Cousin Toby, my fortunes having cast me on your niece give me this prerogative of speech,'—

Sir To. What, what?

Mal. 'You must amend your drunkenness.'

Sir To. Out, scab!

Fab. Nay, patience, or we break the sinews of our plot.

Mal. 'Besides, you waste the treasure of your time with a foolish knight,'—

Sir And. That 's me, I warrant you.

Mal. 'One Sir Andrew,'—

Sir And. I knew 'twas I; for many do call me fool.

Mal. What employment have we here?

[*Taking up the letter.*]

Fab. Now is the woodcock near the gin.

Sir To. O, peace! and the spirit of humours intimate reading aloud to him!

Mal. By my life, this is my lady's hand: these be her very C's, her U's and her T's; and thus makes she her great P's. It is, in contempt of question, her hand.

Sir And. Her C's, her U's and her T's: why that?

Mal. [*Reads*] 'To the unknown beloved, this, and my good wishes:'—her very phrases! By your leave, wax. Soft! and the impressure her Lucrece, with which she uses to seal: 'tis my lady. To whom should this be?

Fab. This wins him, liver and all.

Mal. [*Reads*]

Jove knows I love:
But who?
Lips, do not move;
No man must know.

'No man must know.' What follows? the numbers altered! 'No man must know:' if this should be thee, Malvolio?

Sir To. Marry, hang thee, brock!

Mal. [*Reads*]

I may command where I adore;
But silence, like a Lucrece knife,
With bloodless stroke my heart doth gore:
M, O, A, I, doth sway my life.

Fab. A fustian riddle!

Sir To. Excellent wench, say I.

Mal. 'M, O, A, I, doth sway my life.' Nay, but first, let me see, let me see, let me see.

Fab. What dish o' poison has she dressed him!

Sir To. And with what wing the staniel checks at it!

Mal. 'I may command where I adore.' Why, she may command me: I serve her; she is my lady. Why, this is evident to any formal capacity; there is no obstruction in this: and the end,—what should that alphabetical position portend? If I could make that resemble something in me,—Softly! M, O, A, I,—

Sir To. O, ay, make up that: he is now at a cold scent.

Fab. Sowter will cry upon 't for all this, though it be as rank as a fox.

Mal. M,—Malvolio; M,—why, that begins my name.

Fab. Did not I say he would work it out? the cur is excellent at faults.

Mal. M,—but then there is no consonancy in the sequel; that suffers under probation: A should follow, but O does.

Fab. And O shall end, I hope.

Sir To. Ay, or I'll cudgel him, and make him cry O!

Mal. And then I comes behind.

Fab. Ay, an you had any eye behind you, you might see more detraction at your heels than fortunes before you.

Mal. M, O, A, I; this simulation is not as the former: and yet, to crush this a little, it would bow to me, for every one of these letters are in my name. Soft! here follows prose.

[*Reads*] 'If this fall into thy hand, revolve. In my stars I am above thee; but be not afraid of greatness: some are born great, some achieve greatness and some have greatness thrust upon 'em. Thy Fates open their hands; let thy blood and spirit embrace them; and, to inure thyself to what thou art like to be, cast thy humble slough and appear fresh. Be opposite with a kinsman, surly with servants; let thy tongue tang arguments of state; put thyself into the trick of singularity: she thus advises thee that sighs for thee. Remember who commended thy yellow stockings, and wished to see thee ever cross-gartered: I say, remember. Go to, thou art made, if thou desirest to be so; if not, let me see thee a steward still, the fellow of servants, and not worthy to touch Fortune's fingers. Farewell. She that would alter services with thee,

THE FORTUNATE-UNHAPPY.'

branches. 55. **daybed,** sofa, couch. 58. **humour of state,** imperious manner of authority. 59. **demure . . . regard,** grave survey of the company. 61. **Toby,** i.e., not *Sir* Toby. 66. **wind up my watch,** an impressive act in those days. 71. **cars,** used like "team of horses." 74. **regard of control,** look of authority. 82. **scab,** scurvy fellow. 92. **woodcock,** proverbial for its stupidity. **gin,** snare. 94. **intimate,** suggest. 98. **in contempt of question,** i.e., it is absurd to question it. 103. **By . . . wax,** addressed to the seal on the letter. **impressure,** impression. 104. **Lucrece,** a seal engraved with the picture of Lucrece. 114. **brock,** badger; used contemptuously. 119. **fustian,** bombastic, ridiculously pompous. 123. **dressed,** prepared for. 124. **staniel,** an inferior kind of hawk; F: *stallion,* which may be a dialectal form of the same word. 125. **checks.** A hawk "checked" when it left its quarry and flew at a chance bird. 128. **formal capacity,** normal mind. 134. **cold scent,** cold trail. 135. **Sowter,** cobbler; probably, the name for a hound. 136. **rank as a fox,** i.e., Malvolio is so crude a hunter that he will leave the trail of a hare and follow the rank scent of a fox. 140. **faults,** breaks in the line of scent. 141. **consonancy,** consistency. 142. **probation,** when put to trial. 144. **O,** interpreted as a hempen collar (Johnson), or as a sigh (Steevens), or as an outcry of pain. 151. **simulation,** disguised meaning. 152. **crush,** force. 155. **revolve,** consider. 156. **stars,** fortunes. 159. **blood and spirit,** i.e., as the agents of passion. 161. **slough,** skin of a snake. 162. **opposite,** contradictory. 163. **tang,** sound loud with. 164. **trick of singularity,** eccentricity of manner. 167. **cross-gartered,** wearing garters above and below the knee so as to cross behind it (Onions).

Daylight and champain discovers not more: this is open. I will be proud, I will read politic authors, I will baffle Sir Toby, I will wash off gross acquaintance, I will be point-devise the very man. I do not now fool myself, to let imagination jade me; for every reason excites to this, that my lady loves me. She did commend my yellow stockings of late, she did praise my leg being cross-gartered; and in this she manifests herself to my love, and with a kind of injunction drives me to these habits of her liking. I thank my stars I am happy. I will be strange, stout, in yellow stockings, and cross-gartered, even with the swiftness of putting on. Jove and my stars be praised! Here is yet a postscript. [*Reads*] 'Thou canst not choose but know who I am. If thou entertainest my love, let it appear in thy smiling; thy smiles become thee well; therefore in my presence still smile, dear my sweet, I prithee.'

Jove, I thank thee: I will smile; I will do everything that thou wilt have me. *Exit.*

Fab. I will not give my part of this sport for a pension of thousands to be paid from the Sophy.

Sir To. I could marry this wench for this device.

Sir And. So could I too.

Sir To. And ask no other dowry with her but such another jest.

Enter MARIA.

Sir And. Nor I neither.

Fab. Here comes my noble gull-catcher.

Sir To. Wilt thou set thy foot o' my neck?

Sir And. Or o' mine either?

Sir To. Shall I play my freedom at tray-trip, and become thy bond-slave?

Sir And. I' faith, or I either?

Sir To. Why, thou hast put him in such a dream, that when the image of it leaves him he must run mad.

Mar. Nay, but say true; does it work upon him?

Sir To. Like aqua-vitæ with a midwife.

Mar. If you will then see the fruits of the sport, mark his first approach before my lady: he will come to her in yellow stockings, and 'tis a colour she abhors, and cross-gartered, a fashion she detests; and he will smile upon her, which will now be so unsuitable to her disposition, being addicted to a melancholy as she is, that it cannot but turn him into a notable contempt. If you will see it, follow me.

Sir To. To the gates of Tartar, thou most excellent devil of wit!

Sir And. I'll make one too. *Exeunt.*

ACT III.

SCENE I. [OLIVIA'S *garden.*]

Enter VIOLA, *and* CLOWN [*with a tabor*].

Vio. Save thee, friend, and thy music: dost thou live by thy tabor?

Clo. No, sir, I live by the church.

Vio. Art thou a churchman?

Clo. No such matter, sir: I do live by the church; for I do live at my house, and my house doth stand by the church.

Vio. So thou mayst say, the king lies by a beggar, if a beggar dwell near him; or, the church stands by thy tabor, if thy tabor stand by the church.

Clo. You have said, sir. To see this age! A sentence is but a cheveril glove to a good wit: how quickly the wrong side may be turned outward!

Vio. Nay, that 's certain; they that dally nicely with words may quickly make them wanton.

Clo. I would, therefore, my sister had had no name, sir.

Vio. Why, man?

Clo. Why, sir, her name 's a word; and to dally with that word might make my sister wanton. But indeed words are very rascals since bonds disgraced them.

Vio. Thy reason, man?

Clo. Troth, sir, I can yield you none without words; and words are grown so false, I am loath to prove reason with them.

Vio. I warrant thou art a merry fellow and carest for nothing.

Clo. Not so, sir, I do care for something; but in my conscience, sir, I do not care for you: if that be to care for nothing, sir, I would it would make you invisible.

Vio. Art not thou the Lady Olivia's fool?

Clo. No, indeed, sir; the Lady Olivia has no folly: she will keep no fool, sir, till she be married; and fools are as like husbands as pilchers are to herrings; the husband 's the bigger: I am indeed not her fool, but her corrupter of words.

Vio. I saw thee late at the Count Orsino's.

Clo. Foolery, sir, does walk about the orb like the sun, it shines every where. I would be sorry, sir, but the fool should be as oft with your master as with my mistress: I think I saw your wisdom there.

Vio. Nay, an thou pass upon me, I'll no more with thee. Hold, there 's expenses for thee.

Clo. Now Jove, in his next commodity of hair, send thee a beard!

Vio. By my troth, I'll tell thee, I am almost sick for one; [*Aside*] though I would not have it grow on my chin. Is thy lady within?

Clo. Would not a pair of these have bred, sir?

Vio. Yes, being kept together and put to use.

Clo. I would play Lord Pandarus of Phrygia, sir, to bring a Cressida to this Troilus.

Vio. I understand you, sir; 'tis well begged.

Clo. The matter, I hope, is not great, sir, begging but a beggar: Cressida was a beggar. My lady is within, sir. I will conster to them whence you come; who you are and what you would are out of my welkin, I might say 'element,' but the word is over-worn. *Exit.*

Vio. This fellow is wise enough to play the fool;
And to do that well craves a kind of wit:
He must observe their mood on whom he jests,
The quality of persons, and the time,

174. **champain,** open country. 175. **open,** obvious. 176. **politic,** dealing with state affairs. 177. **point-devise,** extremely precise (in following the letter). 179. **jade,** trick. 185. **stout,** haughty. 198. **Sophy,** Shah of Persia. 208. **tray-trip,** a game with dice, success in which depended on throwing a three. 216. **aqua-vitæ,** distilled liquors.

ACT III. SCENE I. 2. **tabor,** drum used by clowns and jesters. 13. **cheveril,** kidskin. 25. **bonds disgraced them,** i.e., were needed to make them good. 40. **pilchers,** fish resembling herring. 43. **orb,** earth. 44. **but,** but that. 48. **pass upon me,** make jokes at my expense. 50. **commodity,** supply. 55. **pair of these,** two coins like the one he had just received. 58. **Pandarus,** the go-between in the story of Troilus and Cressida; uncle to Cressida. 62. **begging . . . Cressida,** a reference to Henryson's *Testament of Cresseid* in which the heroine becomes a leper and a beggar. The Clown desires another coin to be the mate of the one he has, as Cressida, the beggar, was mate to Troilus. 64. **conster,** construe. 65. **welkin,** sky; here used with play upon *element,* one of whose meanings was "sky." 71. **haggard,** untrained hawk. **check,** forsake quarry for another game. 75. **folly-fall'n,** having fallen into

And, like the haggard, check at every feather
That comes before his eye. This is a practice
As full of labour as a wise man's art:
For folly that he wisely shows is fit;
But wise men, folly-fall'n, quite taint their wit.

Enter SIR TOBY *and* [SIR] ANDREW.

Sir To. Save you, gentleman.

Vio. And you, sir.

Sir And. Dieu vous garde, monsieur.

Vio. Et vous aussi; votre serviteur.

Sir And. I hope, sir, you are; and I am yours.

Sir To. Will you encounter the house? my niece is desirous you should enter, if your trade be to her.

Vio. I am bound to your niece, sir; I mean, she is the list of my voyage.

Sir To. Taste your legs, sir; put them to motion.

Vio. My legs do better understand me, sir, than I understand what you mean by bidding me taste my legs.

Sir To. I mean, to go, sir, to enter.

Vio. I will answer you with gait and entrance. But we are prevented.

Enter OLIVIA *and Gentlewoman* [MARIA].

Most excellent accomplished lady, the heavens rain odours on you!

Sir And. That youth 's a rare courtier: 'Rain odours;' well.

Vio. My matter hath no voice, lady, but to your own most pregnant and vouchsafed ear.

Sir And. 'Odours,' 'pregnant' and 'vouchsafed;' I'll get 'em all three all ready.

Oli. Let the garden door be shut, and leave me to my hearing. [*Exeunt Sir Toby, Sir Andrew, and Maria.*]
Give me your hand, sir.

Vio. My duty, madam, and most humble service.

Oli. What is your name?

Vio. Cesario is your servant's name, fair princess.

Oli. My servant, sir! 'Twas never merry world
Since lowly feigning was call'd compliment:
Y' are servant to the Count Orsino, youth.

Vio. And he is yours, and his must needs be yours:
Your servant's servant is your servant, madam.

Oli. For him, I think not on him: for his thoughts,
Would they were blanks, rather than fill'd with me!

Vio. Madam, I come to whet your gentle thoughts
On his behalf.

Oli. O, by your leave, I pray you,
I bade you never speak again of him:
But, would you undertake another suit,
I had rather hear you to solicit that
Than music from the spheres.

Vio. Dear lady,—

Oli. Give me leave, beseech you. I did send,
After the last enchantment you did here,
A ring in chase of you: so did I abuse
Myself, my servant and, I fear me, you:
Under your hard construction must I sit,
To force that on you, in a shameful cunning,
Which you knew none of yours: what might you think?
Have you not set mine honour at the stake
And baited it with all th' unmuzzled thoughts
That tyrannous heart can think? To one of your receiving
Enough is shown: a cypress, not a bosom,
Hides my heart. So, let me hear you speak.

Vio. I pity you.

Oli. That 's a degree to love.

Vio. No, not a grize; for 'tis a vulgar proof,
That very oft we pity enemies.

Oli. Why, then, methinks 'tis time to smile again.
O world, how apt the poor are to be proud!
If one should be a prey, how much the better
To fall before the lion than the wolf! *Clock strikes.*
The clock upbraids me with the waste of time.
Be not afraid, good youth, I will not have you:
And yet, when wit and youth is come to harvest,
Your wife is like to reap a proper man:
There lies your way, due west.

Vio. Then westward-ho! Grace and good disposition
Attend your ladyship!
You'll nothing, madam, to my lord by me?

Oli. Stay:
I prithee, tell me what thou think'st of me.

Vio. That you do think you are not what you are.

Oli. If I think so, I think the same of you.

Vio. Then think you right: I am not what I am.

Oli. I would you were as I would have you be!

Vio. Would it be better, madam, than I am?
I wish it might, for now I am your fool.

Oli. O, what a deal of scorn looks beautiful
In the contempt and anger of his lip!
A murd'rous guilt shows not itself more soon
Than love that would seem hid: love's night is noon.
Cesario, by the roses of the spring,
By maidhood, honour, truth and every thing,
I love thee so, that, maugre all thy pride,
Nor wit nor reason can my passion hide.
Do not extort thy reasons from this clause,
For that I woo, thou therefore hast no cause;
But rather reason thus with reason fetter,
Love sought is good, but given unsought is better.

Vio. By innocence I swear, and by my youth,
I have one heart, one bosom and one truth,
And that no woman has; nor never none
Shall mistress be of it, save I alone.
And so adieu, good madam: never more
Will I my master's tears to you deplore.

Oli. Yet come again; for thou perhaps mayst move
That heart, which now abhors, to like his love. *Exeunt.*

SCENE II. [OLIVIA'S *house.*]

Enter SIR TOBY, SIR ANDREW, *and* FABIAN.

Sir And. No, faith, I'll not stay a jot longer.

folly. **taint their wit,** lose their reputation for wisdom. 78. **Dieu . . . monsieur,** God keep you, sir. 79. **Et . . . serviteur.** And you, too; I am your servant. 82. **encounter,** high-sounding word to express "enter." 86. **list,** destination. 87. **Taste,** try. 110. **lowly feigning,** affected humility. 121. **music from the spheres,** reference to the belief that the heavenly bodies were fixed in hollow concentric spheres which revolved one about the other, producing a harmony too exquisite to be heard by human ears. 126. **hard construction,** harsh interpretation. 127. **To force,** for forcing. 129. **stake.** The figure of speech is from bearbaiting.

131. **receiving,** capacity, intelligence. 132. **cypress,** described as a thin, gauzelike material, mostly black in color. 135. **grize,** step corresponding to *degree* in the preceding line. 146. **westward-ho,** the cry of Thames watermen to attract westward-bound passengers. 151. **That . . . are,** that you think you are in love with a man, and you are mistaken (Luce). 152. **If . . . you.** If I think I lower myself, I think the same of you, i.e., that you are a nobleman in disguise. 156. **now . . . fool.** You are making a fool of me, but implying, also, I am making a fool of you. 163. **maugre,** in spite of.

Sir To. Thy reason, dear venom, give thy reason.

Fab. You must needs yield your reason, Sir Andrew.

Sir And. Marry, I saw your niece do more favours to the count's serving-man than ever she bestowed upon me; I saw 't i' the orchard.

Sir To. Did she see thee the while, old boy? tell me that.

Sir And. As plain as I see you now.

Fab. This was a great argument of love in her toward you.

Sir And. 'Slight, will you make an ass o' me?

Fab. I will prove it legitimate, sir, upon the oaths of judgement and reason.

Sir To. And they have been grand-jurymen since before Noah was a sailor.

Fab. She did show favour to the youth in your sight only to exasperate you, to awake your dormouse valour, to put fire in your heart, and brimstone in your liver. You should then have accosted her; and with some excellent jests, fire-new from the mint, you should have banged the youth into dumbness. This was looked for at your hand, and this was balked: the double gilt of this opportunity you let time wash off, and you are now sailed into the north of my lady's opinion; where you will hang like an icicle on a Dutchman's beard, unless you do redeem it by some laudable attempt either of valour or policy.

Sir And. An 't be any way, it must be with valour; for policy I hate: I had as lief be a Brownist as a politician.

Sir To. Why, then, build me thy fortunes upon the basis of valour. Challenge me the count's youth to fight with him; hurt him in eleven places: my niece shall take note of it; and assure thyself, there is no love-broker in the world can more prevail in man's commendation with woman than report of valour.

Fab. There is no way but this, Sir Andrew.

Sir And. Will either of you bear me a challenge to him?

Sir To. Go, write it in a martial hand; be curst and brief; it is no matter how witty, so it be eloquent and full of invention: taunt him with the license of ink: if thou thou'st him some thrice, it shall not be amiss; and as many lies as will lie in thy sheet of paper, although the sheet were big enough for the bed of Ware in England, set 'em down: go, about it. Let there be gall enough in thy ink, though thou write with a goose-pen, no matter: about it.

Sir And. Where shall I find you?

Sir To. We'll call thee at the cubiculo: go.

Exit Sir Andrew.

Fab. This is a dear manakin to you, Sir Toby.

Sir To. I have been dear to him, lad, some two thousand strong, or so.

Fab. We shall have a rare letter from him: but you'll not deliver 't?

Sir To. Never trust me, then; and by all means stir on the youth to an answer. I think oxen and wainropes cannot hale them together. For Andrew, if he were opened, and you find so much blood in his liver as will clog the foot of a flea, I'll eat the rest of the anatomy.

Fab. And his opposite, the youth, bears in his visage no great presage of cruelty.

Enter MARIA.

Sir To. Look, where the youngest wren of nine comes.

Mar. If you desire the spleen, and will laugh yourselves into stitches, follow me. Yond gull Malvolio is turned heathen, a very renegado; for there is no Christian, that means to be saved by believing rightly, can ever believe such impossible passages of grossness. He 's in yellow stockings.

Sir To. And cross-gartered?

Mar. Most villanously; like a pedant that keeps a school i' the church. I have dogged him, like his murderer. He does obey every point of the letter that I dropped to betray him: he does smile his face into more lines than is in the new map with the augmentation of the Indies: you have not seen such a thing as 'tis. I can hardly forbear hurling things at him. I know my lady will strike him: if she do, he'll smile and take 't for a great favour.

Sir To. Come, bring us, bring us where he is.

Exeunt omnes.

SCENE III. [*A street.*]

Enter SEBASTIAN *and* ANTONIO.

Seb. I would not by my will have troubled you;
But, since you make your pleasure of your pains,
I will no further chide you.

Ant. I could not stay behind you: my desire,
More sharp than filed steel, did spur me forth;
And not all love to see you, though so much
As might have drawn one to a longer voyage,
But jealousy what might befall your travel,
Being skilless in these parts; which to a stranger,
Unguided and unfriended, often prove
Rough and unhospitable: my willing love,
The rather by these arguments of fear,
Set forth in your pursuit.

Seb. My kind Antonio,
I can no other answer make but thanks,
†And thanks; and ever . . . . . . oft good turns
Are shuffled off with such uncurrent pay:
But, were my worth as is my conscience firm,
You should find better dealing. What 's to do?
Shall we go see the reliques of this town?

Ant. To-morrow, sir: best first go see your lodging.

Seb. I am not weary, and 'tis long to night:
I pray you, let us satisfy our eyes
With the memorials and the things of fame
That do renown this city.

Ant. Would you 'ld pardon me;
I do not without danger walk these streets:
Once, in a sea-fight, 'gainst the count his galleys

SCENE II. 8. **orchard,** garden. 14. **'Slight,** oath, by God's light. 21. **dormouse valour.** The dormouse was proverbially sleepy. 27. **double gilt,** twice plated; quibble on "guilt." 28. **north,** i.e., out of the warmth and sunshine of her favor. 31. **valour or policy,** frequently associated as the qualities of a nobleman; *policy* means "discretion." 34. **Brownist,** early name of the Congregationalists, from the name of the founder, Robert Brown (1582). **politician,** intriguer. 39. **love-broker,** one who acts as an agent between lovers. 48. **thou'st.** "Thou" was used only between friends or to inferiors. 51. **bed of Ware,** a famous bedstead capable of holding twelve persons, said to have been at the Stag Inn in Ware, Hertfordshire. 56. **cubiculo,** Italian or Latin for "lodging." 64. **wainropes,** cart ropes. 71. **nine.** Wrens have many young birds all of which are small; presumably the last hatched would be smallest. 75. **renegado,** Spanish, *renegado*, "deserter." 77. **passages of grossness,** grossly foolish tricks. 80. **pedant,** schoolmaster. 85. **new map.** This is regarded as a reference to a map published in the 1599 edition of Hakluyt's *Voyages*, which showed more of the East Indies than had ever been mapped before. The reference is used in dating the play.

I did some service; of such note indeed,
That were I ta'en here it would scarce be answer'd.
Seb. Belike you slew great number of his people.
Ant. Th' offence is not of such a bloody nature;
Albeit the quality of the time and quarrel
Might well have given us bloody argument.
It might have since been answer'd in repaying
What we took from them; which, for traffic's sake,
Most of our city did: only myself stood out;
For which, if I be lapsed in this place,
I shall pay dear.
Seb. Do not then walk too open.
Ant. It doth not fit me. Hold, sir, here 's my purse.
In the south suburbs, at the Elephant,
Is best to lodge: I will bespeak our diet,
Whiles you beguile the time and feed your knowledge
With viewing of the town: there shall you have me.
Seb. Why I your purse?
Ant. Haply your eye shall light upon some toy
You have desire to purchase; and your store,
I think, is not for idle markets, sir.
Seb. I'll be your purse-bearer and leave you
For an hour.
Ant. To th' Elephant.
Seb. I do remember. *Exeunt.*

SCENE IV. [OLIVIA'S *garden.*]

Enter OLIVIA *and* MARIA.

Oli. I have sent after him: he says he'll come;
How shall I feast him? what bestow of him?
For youth is bought more oft than begg'd or borrow'd.
I speak too loud.
Where's Malvolio? he is sad and civil,
And suits well for a servant with my fortunes:
Where is Malvolio?

Mar. He 's coming, madam; but in very strange manner. He is, sure, possessed, madam.

Oli. Why, what 's the matter? does he rave?

Mar. No, madam, he does nothing but smile: your ladyship were best to have some guard about you, if he come; for, sure, the man is tainted in 's wits.

Oli. Go call him hither. [*Exit Maria.*] I am as mad as he,
If sad and merry madness equal be.

Enter [MARIA, *with*] MALVOLIO.

How now, Malvolio!

Mal. Sweet lady, ho, ho.

Oli. Smilest thou?
I sent for thee upon a sad occasion.

Mal. Sad, lady! I could be sad: this does make some obstruction in the blood, this cross-gartering; but what of that? if it please the eye of one, it is with me as the very true sonnet is, 'Please one, and please all.'

Oli. Why, how dost thou, man? what is the matter with thee?

Mal. Not black in my mind, though yellow in my legs. It did come to his hands, and commands shall be executed: I think we do know the sweet Roman hand.

Oli. Wilt thou go to bed, Malvolio?

Mal. To bed! ay, sweet-heart, and I'll come to thee.

Oli. God comfort thee! Why dost thou smile so and kiss thy hand so oft?

Mar. How do you, Malvolio?

Mal. At your request! yes; nightingales answer daws.

Mar. Why appear you with this ridiculous boldness before my lady?

Mal. 'Be not afraid of greatness:' 'twas well writ.

Oli. What meanest thou by that, Malvolio?

Mal. 'Some are born great,'—

Oli. Ha?

Mal. 'Some achieve greatness,'—

Oli. What sayest thou?

Mal. 'And some have greatness thrust upon them.'

Oli. Heaven restore thee!

Mal. 'Remember who commended thy yellow stockings,'—

Oli. Thy yellow stockings!

Mal. 'And wished to see thee cross-gartered.'

Oli. Cross-gartered!

Mal. 'Go to, thou art made, if thou desirest to be so;'—

Oli. Am I made?

Mal. 'If not, let me see thee a servant still.'

Oli. Why, this is very midsummer madness.

Enter Servant.

Ser. Madam, the young gentleman of the Count Orsino's is returned: I could hardly entreat him back: he attends your ladyship's pleasure.

Oli. I'll come to him. [*Exit Servant.*] Good Maria, let this fellow be looked to. Where 's my cousin Toby? Let some of my people have a special care of him: I would not have him miscarry for the half of my dowry. *Exit* [*with Maria*].

Mal. O, ho! do you come near me now? no worse man than Sir Toby to look to me! This concurs directly with the letter: she sends him on purpose, that I may appear stubborn to him; for she incites me to that in the letter. 'Cast thy humble slough,' says she; 'be opposite with a kinsman, surly with servants; let thy tongue tang with arguments of state; put thyself into the trick of singularity;' and consequently sets down the manner how; as, a sad face, a reverend carriage, a slow tongue, in the habit of some sir of note, and so forth. I have limed her; but it is Jove's doing, and Jove make me thankful! And when she went away now, 'Let this fellow be looked to:' fellow! not Malvolio, nor after my degree, but fellow. Why, every thing adheres together, that no dram of a scruple, no scruple of a scruple, no obstacle, no incredulous or unsafe circumstance—What can be said? Nothing that can be can come between me and the full prospect of my hopes. Well, Jove, not I, is the doer of this, and he is to be thanked.

Enter [SIR] TOBY, FABIAN, *and* MARIA.

SCENE III. 6. **not all love,** not altogether love. 8. **jealousy,** anxiety. 9. **skilless,** ignorant, unacquainted with. 15. **And thanks,** etc. This corrupt line is usually made to read, *And thanks and ever thanks. Too oft*, etc. 17. **worth,** wealth. 19. **reliques,** antiquities. 26. **count his,** count's. 32. **argument,** cause. 33. **answer'd,** compensated. 34. **traffic's,** trade's. 36. **lapsed,** caught. 39. **Elephant,** name of an inn. 40. **diet,** dinner, food. 46. **idle markets,** unnecessary purchases.

SCENE IV. 1. **he . . . come,** i.e., suppose he says, etc. 9. **possessed,** i.e., with an evil spirit. 25. **sonnet,** song, ballad. **'Please . . . all,'** the refrain of a ballad. 31. **Roman hand,** fashionable Italian cursive style of handwriting. 38. **nightingales answer daws,** i.e. (to Maria), do you suppose a fine fellow like me would answer a lowly creature like you? 61. **midsummer madness,** a proverbial phrase; the midsummer moon was supposed to cause madness. 69. **miscarry,** come to harm. 71. **come near,** understand. 79. **consequently,** thereafter. 82. **limed,** caught like a bird with birdlime. 86. **fellow.** Malvolio takes the original meaning, companion; Olivia had used it in its degenerated sense. 88. **incredulous,** incredible.

Sir To. Which way is he, in the name of sanctity? If all the devils of hell be drawn in little, and Legion himself possessed him, yet I'll speak to him.

Fab. Here he is, here he is. How is 't with you, sir? how is 't with you, man?

Mal. Go off; I discard you: let me enjoy my private: go off.

Mar. Lo, how hollow the fiend speaks within him! did not I tell you? Sir Toby, my lady prays you to have a care of him.

Mal. Ah, ha! does she so?

Sir To. Go to, go to; peace, peace; we must deal gently with him: let me alone. How do you, Malvolio? how is 't with you? What, man! defy the devil: consider, he 's an enemy to mankind.

Mal. Do you know what you say?

Mar. La you, an you speak ill of the devil, how he takes it at heart! Pray God, he be not bewitched!

Fab. Carry his water to the wise woman.

Mar. Marry, and it shall be done to-morrow morning, if I live. My lady would not lose him for more than I'll say.

Mal. How now, mistress!

Mar. O Lord!

Sir To. Prithee, hold thy peace; this is not the way: do you not see you move him? let me alone with him.

Fab. No way but gentleness; gently, gently: the fiend is rough, and will not be roughly used.

Sir To. Why, how now, my bawcock! how dost thou, chuck?

Mal. Sir!

Sir To. Ay, Biddy, come with me. What, man! 'tis not for gravity to play at cherry-pit with Satan: hang him, foul collier!

Mar. Get him to say his prayers, good Sir Toby, get him to pray.

Mal. My prayers, minx!

Mar. No, I warrant you, he will not hear of godliness.

Mal. Go, hang yourselves all! you are idle shallow things: I am not of your element: you shall know more hereafter. *Exit.*

Sir To. Is 't possible?

Fab. If this were played upon a stage now, I could condemn it as an improbable fiction.

Sir To. His very genius hath taken the infection of the device, man.

Mar. Nay, pursue him now, lest the device take air and taint.

Fab. Why, we shall make him mad indeed.

Mar. The house will be the quieter.

Sir To. Come, we'll have him in a dark room and bound. My niece is already in the belief that he 's mad: we may carry it thus, for our pleasure and his penance, till our very pastime, tired out of breath, prompt us to have mercy on him: at which time we will bring the device to the bar and crown thee for a finder of madmen. But see, but see.

Enter SIR ANDREW.

Fab. More matter for a May morning.

Sir And. Here 's the challenge, read it: I warrant there 's vinegar and pepper in 't.

Fab. Is 't so saucy?

Sir And. Ay, is 't, I warrant him: do but read.

Sir To. Give me. [*Reads*] 'Youth, whatsoever thou art, thou art but a scurvy fellow.'

Fab. Good, and valiant.

Sir To. [*Reads*] 'Wonder not, nor admire not in thy mind, why I do call thee so, for I will show thee no reason for 't.'

Fab. A good note; that keeps you from the blow of the law.

Sir To. [*Reads*] 'Thou comest to the lady Olivia, and in my sight she uses thee kindly: but thou liest in thy throat; that is not the matter I challenge thee for.'

Fab. Very brief, and to exceeding good sense—less.

Sir To. [*Reads*] 'I will waylay thee going home; where if it be thy chance to kill me,'—

Fab. Good.

Sir To. [*Reads*] 'Thou killest me like a rogue and a villain.'

Fab. Still you keep o' the windy side of the law: good.

Sir To. [*Reads*] 'Fare thee well; and God have mercy upon one of our souls! He may have mercy upon mine; but my hope is better, and so look to thyself. Thy friend, as thou usest him, and thy sworn enemy,
ANDREW AGUECHEEK.'
If this letter move him not, his legs cannot: I'll give 't him.

Mar. You may have very fit occasion for 't: he is now in some commerce with my lady, and will by and by depart.

Sir To. Go, Sir Andrew; scout me for him at the corner of the orchard like a bum-baily: so soon as ever thou seest him, draw; and, as thou drawest, swear horrible; for it comes to pass oft that a terrible oath, with a swaggering accent sharply twanged off, gives manhood more approbation than ever proof itself would have earned him. Away!

Sir And. Nay, let me alone for swearing. *Exit.*

Sir To. Now will not I deliver his letter: for the behaviour of the young gentleman gives him out to be of good capacity and breeding; his employment between his lord and my niece confirms no less: therefore this letter, being so excellently ignorant, will breed no terror in the youth: he will find it comes from a clodpole. But, sir, I will deliver his challenge by word of mouth; set upon Aguecheek a notable report of valour; and drive the gentleman, as I know his youth will aptly receive it, into a most hideous opinion of his rage, skill, fury and impetuosity. This will so fright them both that they will kill one another by the look, like cockatrices.

Enter OLIVIA *and* VIOLA.

Fab. Here he comes with your niece: give them way till he take leave, and presently after him.

Sir To. I will meditate the while upon some horrid message for a challenge.

[*Exeunt Sir Toby, Fabian, and Maria.*]

94-95. **in little,** in miniature. 95. **Legion,** evil spirits mentioned in the Scriptures; Mark 5:9. 100. **private,** privacy. 114. **water,** urine (for medical analysis). 125. **bawcock,** French, *beau-coq,* fine fellow. 126. **chuck,** a form of "chick," term of endearment. 129. **for gravity,** suitable to your dignity. **cherry-pit,** a children's game consisting of throwing cherry stones into a hole. 130. **collier,** Satan. 142. **genius,** soul, spirit. 145. **take air,** become exposed. **taint,** spoil. 154. **bar,** court (in order to be judged). 156. **May,** reference to the many Mayings and holidays in May. 168. **note,** observation, remark. 181. **windy,** to windward; so that the law may get no scent of you. 191. **commerce,** conversation. 194. **bum-baily,** minor sheriff's officer. 199. **approbation,** reputation (for courage). 209. **clodpole,** blockhead. 215. **cockatrices,** basilisks, fabulous serpents reputed to be able to kill by a mere look. 218. **presently,** immediately. 228. **jewel,** used of

Oli. I have said too much unto a heart of stone
And laid mine honour too unchary on 't.
There 's something in me that reproves my fault;
But such a headstrong potent fault it is,
That it but mocks reproof.

Vio. With the same 'haviour that your passion bears
Goes on my master's griefs.

Oli. Here, wear this jewel for me, 'tis my picture;
Refuse it not; it hath no tongue to vex you;
And I beseech you come again to-morrow.
What shall you ask of me that I'll deny,
That honour sav'd may upon asking give?

Vio. Nothing but this; your true love for my master.

Oli. How with mine honour may I give him that
Which I have given to you?

Vio. I will acquit you.

Oli. Well, come again to-morrow: fare thee well:
A fiend like thee might bear my soul to hell. [*Exit.*]

Enter [SIR] TOBY *and* FABIAN.

Sir To. Gentleman, God save thee.

Vio. And you, sir.

Sir To. That defence thou hast, betake thee to 't: of what nature the wrongs are thou hast done him, I know not; but thy intercepter, full of despite, bloody as the hunter, attends thee at the orchard-end: dismount thy tuck, be yare in thy preparation, for thy assailant is quick, skilful and deadly.

Vio. You mistake, sir; I am sure no man hath any quarrel to me: my remembrance is very free and clear from any image of offence done to any man.

Sir To. You'll find it otherwise, I assure you: therefore, if you hold your life at any price, betake you to your guard; for your opposite hath in him what youth, strength, skill and wrath can furnish man withal.

Vio. I pray you, sir, what is he?

Sir To. He is knight, dubbed with unhatched rapier and on carpet consideration; but he is a devil in private brawl: souls and bodies hath he divorced three; and his incensement at this moment is so implacable, that satisfaction can be none but by pangs of death and sepulchre. Hob, nob, is his word; give 't or take 't.

Vio. I will return again into the house and desire some conduct of the lady. I am no fighter. I have heard of some kind of men that put quarrels purposely on others, to taste their valour: belike this is a man of that quirk.

Sir To. Sir, no, his indignation derives itself out of a very competent injury: therefore, get you on and give him his desire. Back you shall not to the house, unless you undertake that with me which with as much safety you might answer him: therefore, on, or strip your sword stark naked; for meddle you must, that 's certain, or forswear to wear iron about you.

Vio. This is as uncivil as strange. I beseech you, do me this courteous office, as to know of the knight what my offence to him is: it is something of my negligence, nothing of my purpose.

Sir To. I will do so. Signior Fabian, stay you by this gentleman till my return. *Exit Toby.*

Vio. Pray you, sir, do you know of this matter?

Fab. I know the knight is incensed against you, even to a mortal arbitrement; but nothing of the circumstance more.

Vio. I beseech you, what manner of man is he?

Fab. Nothing of that wonderful promise, to read him by his form, as you are like to find him in the proof of his valour. He is, indeed, sir, the most skilful, bloody and fatal opposite that you could possibly have found in any part of Illyria. Will you walk towards him? I will make your peace with him if I can.

Vio. I shall be much bound to you for 't: I am one that had rather go with sir priest than sir knight: I care not who knows so much of my mettle. *Exeunt.*

Enter [SIR] TOBY *and* [SIR] ANDREW.

Sir To. Why, man, he 's a very devil; I have not seen such a firago. I had a pass with him, rapier, scabbard and all, and he gives me the stuck in with such a mortal motion, that it is inevitable; and on the answer, he pays you as surely as your feet hit the ground they step on. They say he has been fencer to the Sophy.

Sir And. Pox on 't, I'll not meddle with him.

Sir To. Ay, but he will not now be pacified: Fabian can scarce hold him yonder.

Sir And. Plague on 't, an I thought he had been valiant and so cunning in fence, I 'ld have seen him damned ere I 'ld have challenged him. Let him let the matter slip, and I'll give him my horse, grey Capilet.

Sir To. I'll make the motion: stand here, make a good show on 't: this shall end without the perdition of souls. [*Aside*] Marry, I'll ride your horse as well as I ride you.

Enter FABIAN *and* VIOLA.

[*To Fab.*] I have his horse to take up the quarrel: I have persuaded him the youth 's a devil.

Fab. He is as horribly conceited of him; and pants and looks pale, as if a bear were at his heels.

Sir To. [*To Vio.*] There 's no remedy, sir; he will fight with you for 's oath sake: marry, he hath better bethought him of his quarrel, and he finds that now scarce to be worth talking of: therefore draw, for the supportance of his vow; he protests he will not hurt you.

Vio. [*Aside*] Pray God defend me! A little thing would make me tell them how much I lack of a man.

Fab. Give ground, if you see him furious.

Sir To. Come, Sir Andrew, there 's no remedy; the gentleman will, for his honour's sake, have one bout with you; he cannot by the duello avoid it: but he has promised me, as he is a gentleman and a soldier, he will not hurt you. Come on; to 't.

Sir And. Pray God, he keep his oath!

Vio. I do assure you, 'tis against my will. [*They draw.*]

Enter ANTONIO.

Ant. Put up your sword. If this young gentleman
Have done offence, I take the fault on me:

any piece of jewelry. 235. **acquit you,** release you of your promise. 242. **intercepter,** i.e., he who lies in wait. 243. **despite,** spite, malice. 244-245. **dismount thy tuck,** draw thy sword. 245. **yare,** ready, nimble. 257. **unhatched,** for "unhacked." 258. **carpet consideration,** i.e., he is a carpet knight, not a warrior. A carpet knight was one whose title was obtained only through connections at court. 263. **Hob, nob,** originally, have or have not; here, hit or miss. 265. **conduct,** escort. 268. **quirk,** peculiar humor. 273. **that,** i.e., to give satisfaction. 275. **meddle,** engage in conflict. 286. **mortal arbitrement,** trial to the death. 294. **opposite,** antagonist. 299. **sir,** commonly used as the title of priests as well as knights. 302. **firago,** virago. 304. **stuck in,** stoccado, a thrust in fencing. 315. **Capilet,** from "capel," a nag. 320. **take up,** make up. 322. **is as horribly conceited,** has as horrible a conception. 338. **duello,** duelling code.

If you offend him, I for him defy you.
Sir To. You, sir! why, what are you?
Ant. One, sir, that for his love dares yet do more
Than you have heard him brag to you he will.
Sir To. Nay, if you be an undertaker, I am for you. [*They draw.*]

Enter Officers.

Fab. O good Sir Toby, hold! here come the officers.
Sir To. I'll be with you anon.
Vio. Pray, sir, put your sword up, if you please.

Sir And. Marry, will I, sir; and, for that I promised you, I'll be as good as my word: he will bear you easily and reins well.

First Off. This is the man; do thy office.

Sec. Off. Antonio, I arrest thee at the suit of Count Orsino.

Ant. You do mistake me, sir.
First Off. No, sir, no jot; I know your favour well,
Though now you have no sea-cap on your head.
Take him away: he knows I know him well.
Ant. I must obey. [*To Vio.*] This comes with seeking you:
But there 's no remedy; I shall answer it.
What will you do, now my necessity
Makes me to ask you for my purse? It grieves me
Much more for what I cannot do for you
Than what befalls myself. You stand amaz'd;
But be of comfort.
Sec. Off. Come, sir, away.
Ant. I must entreat of you some of that money.
Vio. What money, sir?
For the fair kindness you have show'd me here,
And, part, being prompted by your present trouble,
Out of my lean and low ability
I'll lend you something: my having is not much;
I'll make division of my present with you:
Hold, there 's half my coffer.
Ant. Will you deny me now?
Is 't possible that my deserts to you
Can lack persuasion? Do not tempt my misery,
Lest that it make me so unsound a man
As to upbraid you with those kindnesses
That I have done for you.
Vio. I know of none;
Nor know I you by voice or any feature:
I hate ingratitude more in a man
Than lying, vainness, babbling, drunkenness,
Or any taint of vice whose strong corruption
Inhabits our frail blood.
Ant. O heavens themselves!
Sec. Off. Come, sir, I pray you, go.
Ant. Let me speak a little. This youth that you see here
I snatch'd one half out of the jaws of death,
Reliev'd him with such sanctity of love,
And to his image, which methought did promise
Most venerable worth, did I devotion.
First Off. What 's that to us? The time goes by: away!
Ant. But O how vile an idol proves this god!
Thou hast, Sebastian, done good feature shame.
In nature there 's no blemish but the mind;
None can be call'd deform'd but the unkind:
Virtue is beauty, but the beauteous evil
Are empty trunks o'erflourish'd by the devil.
First Off. The man grows mad: away with him! Come, come, sir.
Ant. Lead me on. *Exit* [*with Officers*].
Vio. Methinks his words do from such passion fly,
That he believes himself: so do not I.
Prove true, imagination, O, prove true,
That I, dear brother, be now ta'en for you!

Sir To. Come hither, knight; come hither, Fabian: we'll whisper o'er a couplet or two of most sage saws.

Vio. He nam'd Sebastian: I my brother know
Yet living in my glass; even such and so
In favour was my brother, and he went
Still in this fashion, colour, ornament,
For him I imitate: O, if it prove,
Tempests are kind and salt waves fresh in love. [*Exit.*]

Sir To. A very dishonest paltry boy, and more a coward than a hare: his dishonesty appears in leaving his friend here in necessity and denying him; and for his cowardship, ask Fabian.

Fab. A coward, a most devout coward, religious in it.

Sir And. 'Slid, I'll after him again and beat him.

Sir To. Do; cuff him soundly, but never draw thy sword.

Sir And. An I do not,— [*Exit.*]

Fab. Come, let 's see the event.

Sir To. I dare lay any money 'twill be nothing yet. *Exeunt.*

ACT IV.

SCENE I. [*Before* OLIVIA'S *house.*]

Enter SEBASTIAN *and* CLOWN.

Clo. Will you make me believe that I am not sent for you?

Seb. Go to, go to, thou art a foolish fellow:
Let me be clear of thee.

Clo. Well held out, i' faith! No, I do not know you; nor I am not sent to you by my lady, to bid you come speak with her; nor your name is not Master Cesario; nor this is not my nose neither. Nothing that is so is so.

Seb. I prithee, vent thy folly somewhere else:
Thou know'st not me.

Clo. Vent my folly! he has heard that word of some great man and now applies it to a fool. Vent my folly! I am afraid this great lubber, the world, will prove a cockney. I prithee now, ungird thy strangeness and tell me what I shall vent to my lady: shall I vent to her that thou art coming?

Seb. I prithee, foolish Greek, depart from me:

349. **undertaker,** one who takes upon himself a task or business; here, suggests meddling. 377. **part,** partly. 379. **having,** wealth; see glossary. 380. **present,** present store. 381. **coffer,** purse. 382-383. **deserts . . . persuasion,** claims on you can fail to persuade you to help me. 389. **vainness,** boastfulness. 396. **image,** what he appeared to be. 397. **venerable,** worthy of honor (no reference to age). 400-404. **Thou . . . devil.** It was a widespread belief in the Renaissance that the outward and inward parts of man correspond in quality. 404. **o'erflourish'd,** covered with ornamental carvings. 408. **so do not I,** may mean "I do not believe him" or "I do not believe myself" (in the hope that has arisen in me). 418. **prove,** prove true. 421. **dishonesty,** dishonorable character. 427. **'Slid,** oath, "by God's (eye-) lid."

ACT IV. SCENE I. 15. **cockney,** effeminate or foppish fellow. 19. **Greek,** jester. 24. **fourteen years' purchase,** reference to the valuation

There 's money for thee: if you tarry longer,
I shall give worse payment.

Clo. By my troth, thou hast an open hand. These wise men that give fools money get themselves a good report—after fourteen years' purchase.

Enter [SIR] ANDREW, [SIR] TOBY, *and* FABIAN.

Sir And. Now, sir, have I met you again? there 's for you. [*Strikes Seb.*]

Seb. Why, there 's for thee, and there, and there.
Are all the people mad? [*Strikes Sir And.*]

Sir To. Hold, sir, or I'll throw your dagger o'er the house.

Clo. This will I tell my lady straight: I would not be in some of your coats for two pence. [*Exit.*]

Sir To. Come on, sir; hold.

Sir And. Nay, let him alone: I'll go another way to work with him; I'll have an action of battery against him, if there be any law in Illyria: though I struck him first, yet it 's no matter for that.

Seb. Let go thy hand.

Sir To. Come, sir, I will not let you go. Come, my young soldier, put up your iron: you are well fleshed; come on.

Seb. I will be free from thee. What wouldst thou now?
If thou dar'st tempt me further, draw thy sword.

Sir To. What, what? Nay, then I must have an ounce or two of this malapert blood from you.

Enter OLIVIA.

Oli. Hold, Toby; on thy life I charge thee, hold!

Sir To. Madam!

Oli. Will it be ever thus? Ungracious wretch,
Fit for the mountains and the barbarous caves,
Where manners ne'er were preach'd! out of my sight!
Be not offended, dear Cesario.
Rudesby, be gone!

[*Exeunt Sir Toby, Sir Andrew, and Fabian.*]

I prithee, gentle friend,
Let thy fair wisdom, not thy passion, sway
In this uncivil and unjust extent
Against thy peace. Go with me to my house,
And hear thou there how many fruitless pranks
This ruffian hath botch'd up, that thou thereby
Mayst smile at this: thou shalt not choose but go:
Do not deny. Beshrew his soul for me,
He started one poor heart of mine in thee.

Seb. What relish is in this? how runs the stream?
Or I am mad, or else this is a dream:
Let fancy still my sense in Lethe steep;
If it be thus to dream, still let me sleep!

Oli. Nay, come, I prithee; would thou 'ldst be rul'd by me!

Seb. Madam, I will.

Oli. O, say so, and so be! *Exeunt.*

SCENE II. [OLIVIA'S *house.*]

Enter MARIA *and* CLOWN.

Mar. Nay, I prithee, put on this gown and this beard; make him believe thou art Sir Topas the curate: do it quickly; I'll call Sir Toby the whilst. [*Exit.*]

Clo. Well, I'll put it on, and I will dissemble myself in 't; and I would I were the first that ever dissembled in such a gown. I am not tall enough to become the function well, nor lean enough to be thought a good student; but to be said an honest man and a good housekeeper goes as fairly as to say a careful man and a great scholar. The competitors enter.

Enter [SIR] TOBY [*and* MARIA].

Sir To. Jove bless thee, master Parson.

Clo. Bonos dies, Sir Toby: for, as the old hermit of Prague, that never saw pen and ink, very wittily said to a niece of King Gorboduc, 'That that is is;' so I, being master Parson, am master Parson; for, what is 'that' but 'that,' and 'is' but 'is'?

Sir To. To him, Sir Topas.

Clo. What, ho, I say! peace in this prison!

Sir To. The knave counterfeits well; a good knave.

Mal. (*Within*) Who calls there?

Clo. Sir Topas the curate, who comes to visit Malvolio the lunatic.

Mal. Sir Topas, Sir Topas, good Sir Topas, go to my lady.

Clo. Out, hyperbolical fiend! how vexest thou this man! talkest thou nothing but of ladies?

Sir To. Well said, master Parson.

Mal. Sir Topas, never was man thus wronged: good Sir Topas, do not think I am mad: they have laid me here in hideous darkness.

Clo. Fie, thou dishonest Satan! I call thee by the most modest terms; for I am one of those gentle ones that will use the devil himself with courtesy: sayest thou that house is dark?

Mal. As hell, Sir Topas.

Clo. Why, it hath bay windows transparent as barricadoes, and the clerestories toward the south north are as lustrous as ebony; and yet complainest thou of obstruction?

Mal. I am not mad, Sir Topas: I say to you, this house is dark.

Clo. Madman, thou errest: I say, there is no darkness but ignorance; in which thou art more puzzled than the Egyptians in their fog.

Mal. I say, this house is as dark as ignorance, though ignorance were as dark as hell; and I say, there was never man thus abused. I am no more mad than you are: make the trial of it in any constant question.

Clo. What is the opinion of Pythagoras concerning wild fowl?

Mal. That the soul of our grandam might haply inhabit a bird.

Clo. What thinkest thou of his opinion?

Mal. I think nobly of the soul, and no way approve his opinion.

Clo. Fare thee well. Remain thou still in darkness:

of land at the price of twelve years' rental. The fool adds two years; see *purchase* in glossary. 47. **malapert,** saucy, impudent. 55. **Rudesby,** ruffian. 57. **extent,** attack. 60. **botch'd up,** clumsily contrived. 63. **heart,** with play on "hart." 66. **Lethe,** forgetfulness.

SCENE II. 4. **the whilst,** in the meantime. 5. **dissemble,** disguise. 9. **said,** called. 10. **housekeeper,** good liver, hospitable person. 15. **hermit of Prague,** usually thought to refer to Jerome of Prague, but the allusion is obscure. 16. **niece of King Gorboduc.** Gorboduc was an ancient British king; his niece is apparently an invention of the Clown's. 29. **hyperbolical,** boisterous. 41. **clerestories,** upper walls of a building containing windows by which it is lighted. 48. **Egyptians . . . fog.** See Exodus 10:21, 22. 53. **constant question,** consistent discussion. 54-55. **Pythagoras . . . wild fowl,** an opening for the discussion of transmigration of souls, a doctrine held by Pythagoras.

thou shalt hold the opinion of Pythagoras ere I will allow of thy wits, and fear to kill a woodcock, lest thou dispossess the soul of thy grandam. Fare thee well.

Mal. Sir Topas, Sir Topas!

Sir To. My most exquisite Sir Topas!

Clo. Nay, I am for all waters.

Mar. Thou mightst have done this without thy beard and gown: he sees thee not.

Sir To. To him in thine own voice, and bring me word how thou findest him: I would we were well rid of this knavery. If he may be conveniently delivered, I would he were, for I am now so far in offence with my niece that I cannot pursue with any safety this sport to the upshot. Come by and by to my chamber.
Exit [*with Maria*].

Clo. [*Singing*] 'Hey, Robin, jolly Robin,
Tell me how thy lady does.'

Mal. Fool!

Clo. 'My lady is unkind, perdy.'

Mal. Fool!

Clo. 'Alas, why is she so?'

Mal. Fool, I say!

Clo. 'She loves another'—Who calls, ha?

Mal. Good fool, as ever thou wilt deserve well at my hand, help me to a candle, and pen, ink and paper: as I am a gentleman, I will live to be thankful to thee for 't.

Clo. Master Malvolio?

Mal. Ay, good fool.

Clo. Alas, sir, how fell you besides your five wits?

Mal. Fool, there was never man so notoriously abused: I am as well in my wits, fool, as thou art.

Clo. But as well? then you are mad indeed, if you be no better in your wits than a fool.

Mal. They have here propertied me; keep me in darkness, send ministers to me, asses, and do all they can to face me out of my wits.

Clo. Advise you what you say; the minister is here. —Malvolio, Malvolio, thy wits the heavens restore! endeavour thyself to sleep, and leave thy vain bibble babble.

Mal. Sir Topas!

Clo. Maintain no words with him, good fellow. —Who, I, sir? not I, sir. God be wi' you, good Sir Topas.—Marry, amen.—I will, sir, I will.

Mal. Fool, fool, fool, I say!

Clo. Alas, sir, be patient. What say you, sir? I am shent for speaking to you.

Mal. Good fool, help me to some light and some paper: I tell thee, I am as well in my wits as any man in Illyria.

Clo. Well-a-day that you were, sir!

Mal. By this hand, I am. Good fool, some ink, paper and light; and convey what I will set down to my lady: it shall advantage thee more than ever the bearing of letter did.

Clo. I will help you to 't. But tell me true, are you not mad indeed? or do you but counterfeit?

Mal. Believe me, I am not; I tell thee true.

Clo. Nay, I'll ne'er believe a madman till I see his brains. I will fetch you light and paper and ink.

Mal. Fool, I'll requite it in the highest degree: I prithee, be gone.

Clo. [*Singing*] I am gone, sir,
And anon, sir,
I'll be with you again,
In a trice,
Like to the old Vice,
Your need to sustain;

Who, with dagger of lath,
In his rage and his wrath,
Cries, ah, ha! to the devil:
Like a mad lad,
Pare thy nails, dad;
†Adieu, good man devil. *Exit.*

SCENE III. [OLIVIA'S *garden.*]

Enter SEBASTIAN.

Seb. This is the air; that is the glorious sun;
This pearl she gave me, I do feel 't and see 't;
And though 'tis wonder that enwraps me thus,
Yet 'tis not madness. Where 's Antonio, then?
I could not find him at the Elephant:
Yet there he was; and there I found this credit,
That he did range the town to seek me out.
His counsel now might do me golden service;
For though my soul disputes well with my sense,
That this may be some error, but no madness,
Yet doth this accident and flood of fortune
So far exceed all instance, all discourse,
That I am ready to distrust mine eyes
And wrangle with my reason that persuades me
To any other trust but that I am mad
Or else the lady 's mad; yet, if 'twere so,
She could not sway her house, command her followers,
Take and give back affairs and their dispatch
With such a smooth, discreet and stable bearing
As I perceive she does: there 's something in 't.
That is deceiveable. But here the lady comes.

Enter OLIVIA *and* Priest.

Oli. Blame not this haste of mine. If you mean well,
Now go with me and with this holy man
Into the chantry by: there, before him,
And underneath that consecrated roof,
Plight me the full assurance of your faith;
That my most jealous and too doubtful soul
May live at peace. He shall conceal it
Whiles you are willing it shall come to note,
What time we will our celebration keep
According to my birth. What do you say?

64. **woodcock.** The woodcock was a type of stupidity because it was easily caught. 68. **for all waters,** i.e., able to sail in all waters. 73. **knavery,** practical joke. 78-85. **'Hey, Robin . . . another,'** fragments of an old song. 92. **besides,** out of. 92-93. **five wits,** intellectual faculties given as common wit, imagination, fantasy, judgment, and memory. 94-95. **notoriously abused,** shamefully mistreated. 99. **propertied,** explained as "treated me as property and thrown me into the lumber-room"; may mean "have chosen to endow me with madness." 102. **Advise you,** take care. 103. **Malvolio.** The Clown here again impersonates Sir Topas. 112. **shent,** scolded, rebuked. 116. **Well-a-day,** alas, would that. 134. **Vice,** the buffoon of moralities and interludes. 136. **dagger of lath,** symbol of the Vice, who was apparently notorious for using it for paring his nails; cf. *Henry V*, IV, iv, 75-77. 141. **good man,** title for a person of substance but not of gentle birth.

SCENE III. 6. **credit,** belief. 15. **trust,** belief. 17. **sway,** rule. 18. **Take and give back,** undertake and discharge. 21. **deceiveable,** deceptive. 24. **chantry,** chapel privately endowed. 27. **jealous,**

Seb. I'll follow this good man, and go with you;
And, having sworn truth, ever will be true.
Oli. Then lead the way, good father; and heavens so shine,
That they may fairly note this act of mine! *Exeunt.*

ACT V.

SCENE I. [*Before* OLIVIA's *house.*]

Enter CLOWN *and* FABIAN.

Fab. Now, as thou lovest me, let me see his letter.

Clo. Good Master Fabian, grant me another request.

Fab. Any thing.

Clo. Do not desire to see this letter.

Fab. This is, to give a dog, and in recompense desire my dog again.

Enter DUKE, VIOLA, CURIO, *and* Lords.

Duke. Belong you to the Lady Olivia, friends?

Clo. Ay, sir; we are some of her trappings.

Duke. I know thee well: how dost thou, my good fellow?

Clo. Truly, sir, the better for my foes and the worse for my friends.

Duke. Just the contrary; the better for thy friends.

Clo. No, sir, the worse.

Duke. How can that be?

Clo. Marry, sir, they praise me and make an ass of me; now my foes tell me plainly I am an ass: so that by my foes, sir, I profit in the knowledge of myself, and by my friends I am abused: so that, conclusions to be as kisses, if your four negatives make your two affirmatives, why then, the worse for my friends and the better for my foes.

Duke. Why, this is excellent.

Clo. By my troth, sir, no; though it please you to be one of my friends.

Duke. Thou shalt not be the worse for me: there 's gold.

Clo. But that it would be double-dealing, sir, I would you could make it another.

Duke. O, you give me ill counsel.

Clo. Put your grace in your pocket, sir, for this once, and let your flesh and blood obey it.

Duke. Well, I will be so much a sinner, to be a double-dealer: there 's another.

Clo. Primo, secundo, tertio, is a good play; and the old saying is, the third pays for all: the triplex, sir, is a good tripping measure; or the bells of Saint Bennet, sir, may put you in mind; one, two, three.

Duke. You can fool no more money out of me at this throw: if you will let your lady know I am here to speak with her, and bring her along with you, it may awake my bounty further.

Clo. Marry, sir, lullaby to your bounty till I come again. I go, sir; but I would not have you to think that my desire of having is the sin of covetousness: but, as you say, sir, let your bounty take a nap, I will awake it anon. *Exit.*

Enter ANTONIO *and* Officers.

Vio. Here comes the man, sir, that did rescue me.
Duke. That face of his I do remember well;
Yet, when I saw it last, it was besmear'd
As black as Vulcan in the smoke of war:
A bawbling vessel was he captain of,
For shallow draught and bulk unprizable;
With which such scathful grapple did he make
With the most noble bottom of our fleet,
That very envy and the tongue of loss
Cried fame and honour on him. What 's the matter?
First Off. Orsino, this is that Antonio
That took the Phœnix and her fraught from Candy;
And this is he that did the Tiger board,
When your young nephew Titus lost his leg:
Here in the streets, desperate of shame and state,
In private brabble did we apprehend him.
Vio. He did me kindness, sir, drew on my side;
But in conclusion put strange speech upon me:
I know not what 'twas but distraction.
Duke. Notable pirate! thou salt-water thief!
What foolish boldness brought thee to their mercies,
Whom thou, in terms so bloody and so dear,
Hast made thine enemies?
Ant. Orsino, noble sir,
Be pleas'd that I shake off these names you give me:
Antonio never yet was thief or pirate,
Though I confess, on base and ground enough,
Orsino's enemy. A witchcraft drew me hither:
That most ingrateful boy there by your side,
From the rude sea's enrag'd and foamy mouth
Did I redeem; a wrack past hope he was:
His life I gave him and did thereto add
My love, without retention or restraint,
All his in dedication; for his sake
Did I expose myself, pure for his love,
Into the danger of this adverse town;
Drew to defend him when he was beset:
Where being apprehended, his false cunning,
Not meaning to partake with me in danger,
Taught him to face me out of his acquaintance,
And grew a twenty years removed thing
While one would wink; denied me mine own purse,
Which I had recommended to his use
Not half an hour before.
Viol. How can this be?
Duke. When came he to this town?
Ant. To-day, my lord; and for three months before,
No int'rim, not a minute's vacancy,
Both day and night did we keep company.

Enter OLIVIA *and* Attendants.

Duke. Here comes the countess: now heaven walks on earth.

anxious. 29. **Whiles,** until. **come to note,** become known.
ACT V. SCENE I. 1. **his,** i.e., Malvolio's. 23-24. **conclusions . . . kisses,** i.e., as when a young lady, asked for a kiss, says "no" really meaning "yes," showing that things are the opposite of what they seem. 29. **friends,** probably, flatterers. The duke gives a coin to show that he is sincere. The Clown would ask for two except for seeming to be a *double-dealer,* i.e., insincere in his turn. 35. **grace,** apparently a play on *grace* meaning "favor of God," and the title, "Your *Grace.*" 39-40. **Primo, secundo, tertio . . . all,** probably dicing terms. 41. **triplex,** triple time in music. 42. **Saint Bennet,** church of St. Benedict; reference to the sound of the church bell, which may have been embodied in a rhyme. 45. **throw,** i.e., of dice. 48. **lullaby,** suggested by *awake,* above. 57. **bawbling,** insignificant. 58. **unprizable,** of value too slight to be estimated. 59. **scathful,** destructive. 64. **fraught,** cargo. **Candy,** Candia, Crete. 67. **desperate . . . state,** reckless of disgrace and position. 68. **brabble,** brawl. 71. **distraction,** madness. 86. **pure,** entirely. 87. **Into,** unto. **adverse,** hostile. 91. **face . . . acquaintance,** deny he knew me. 94. **recommended,** consigned.

But for thee, fellow; fellow, thy words are madness:
Three months this youth hath tended upon me;
But more of that anon. Take him aside.
Oli. What would my lord, but that he may not have,
Wherein Olivia may seem serviceable?
Cesario, you do not keep promise with me.
Vio. Madam!
Duke. Gracious Olivia,—
Oli. What do you say, Cesario? Good my lord,—
Vio. My lord would speak; my duty hushes me.
Oli. If it be aught to the old tune, my lord,
It is as fat and fulsome to mine ear
As howling after music.
Duke. Still so cruel?
Oli. Still so constant, lord.
Duke. What, to perverseness? you uncivil lady,
To whose ingrate and unauspicious altars
My soul the faithfull'st off'rings have breath'd out
That e'er devotion tender'd! What shall I do?
Oli. Even what it please my lord, that shall become him.
Duke. Why should I not, had I the heart to do it,
Like to th' Egyptian thief at point of death,
Kill what I love?—a savage jealousy
That sometime savours nobly. But hear me this:
Since you to non-regardance cast my faith,
And that I partly know the instrument
That screws me from my true place in your favour,
Live you the marble-breasted tyrant still;
But this your minion, whom I know you love,
And whom, by heaven I swear, I tender dearly,
Him will I tear out of that cruel eye,
Where he sits crowned in his master's spite.
Come, boy, with me; my thoughts are ripe in mischief:
I'll sacrifice the lamb that I do love,
To spite a raven's heart within a dove. [*Going.*]
Vio. And I, most jocund, apt and willingly,
To do you rest, a thousand deaths would die. [*Going.*]
Oli. Where goes Cesario?
Vio. After him I love
More than I love these eyes, more than my life,
More, by all mores, than e'er I shall love wife.
If I do feign, you witnesses above
Punish my life for tainting of my love!
Oli. Ay me, detested! how am I beguil'd!
Vio. Who does beguile you? who does do you wrong?
Oli. Hast thou forgot thyself? is it so long?
Call forth the holy father. [*Exit an Attendant.*]
Duke. [*To Vio.*] Come, away!
Oli. Whither, my lord? Cesario, husband, stay.
Duke. Husband!
Oli. Ay, husband: can he that deny?
Duke. Her husband, sirrah!
Vio. No, my lord, not I.
Oli. Alas, it is the baseness of thy fear
That makes thee strangle thy propriety:
Fear not, Cesario; take thy fortunes up;
Be that thou know'st thou art, and then thou art
As great as that thou fear'st.

Enter Priest.

O, welcome, father!
Father, I charge thee, by thy reverence,
Here to unfold, though lately we intended
To keep in darkness what occasion now
Reveals before 'tis ripe, what thou dost know
Hath newly pass'd between this youth and me.
Priest. A contract of eternal bond of love,
Confirm'd by mutual joinder of your hands,
Attested by the holy close of lips,
Strength'ned by interchangement of your rings;
And all the ceremony of this compact
Seal'd in my function, by my testimony:
Since when, my watch hath told me, toward my grave
I have travell'd but two hours.
Duke. O thou dissembling cub! what wilt thou be
When time hath sow'd a grizzle on thy case?
Or will not else thy craft so quickly grow,
That thine own trip shall be thine overthrow?
Farewell, and take her; but direct thy feet
Where thou and I henceforth may never meet.
Vio. My Lord, I do protest—
Oli. O, do not swear!
Hold little faith, though thou hast too much fear.

Enter SIR ANDREW.

Sir And. For the love of God, a surgeon! Send one presently to Sir Toby.

Oli. What 's the matter?

Sir And. H' as broke my head across and has given Sir Toby a bloody coxcomb too: for the love of God, your help! I had rather than forty pound I were at home.

Oli. Who has done this, Sir Andrew?

Sir And. The count's gentleman, one Cesario: we took him for a coward, but he 's the very devil incardinate.

Duke. My gentleman, Cesario?

Sir And. 'Od's lifelings, here he is! You broke my head for nothing; and that that I did, I was set on to do 't by Sir Toby.

Vio. Why do you speak to me? I never hurt you:
You drew your sword upon me without cause;
But I bespake you fair, and hurt you not.

Sir And. If a bloody coxcomb be a hurt, you have hurt me: I think you set nothing by a bloody coxcomb.

Enter [SIR] TOBY *and* CLOWN.

Here comes Sir Toby halting: you shall hear more: but if he had not been in drink, he would have tickled you othergates than he did.

Duke. How now, gentleman! how is 't with you?

Sir To. That 's all one: has hurt me, and there 's the end on 't. Sot, didst see Dick surgeon, sot?

102. **Three months.** This statement is seemingly inconsistent with the hint found in I, iv, 3; it seems reasonable, however, in this connection. 112. **fat and fulsome,** nauseating. 121. **Egyptian thief,** allusion to the story of Theagenes and Chariclea in the *Ethiopica*, a Greek romance by Heliodorus. The robber chief, Thyamis of Memphis, having captured Chariclea and fallen in love with her, was attacked by a larger band of robbers; threatened with death, he attempted to slay her first. 123. **savours nobly,** is not without nobility. 124. **non-regardance,** neglect. 136. **do you rest,** give you ease. 150. **strangle thy propriety,** disavow thyself. 160. **joinder,** joining. 168. **grizzle,** gray hair. **case,** skin, or possibly, body as containing the soul. 170. **trip,** probably from the trip in wrestling; here, dissembling. 174. **little,** i.e., a little. 179. **coxcomb,** fool's cap with the crest of a cock; here, head. 185. **incardinate,** blunder for "incarnate." 187. **'Od's lifelings,** from the oath "By God's life." 196. **halting,** limping. 198. **othergates,** otherwise. 205. **set,** fixed, closed with drink. 206-207. **passy measures pavin,** so Malone; F reads *panyn*. Explained as connected with Italian, *passo e mezzo* (slow moving) and *pavana* (a

Clo. O, he 's drunk, Sir Toby, an hour agone; his eyes were set at eight i' the morning.

Sir To. Then he 's a rogue, †and a passy measures pavin: I hate a drunken rogue.

Oli. Away with him! Who hath made this havoc with them?

Sir And. I'll help you, Sir Toby, because we'll be dressed together.

Sir To. Will you help? an ass-head and a coxcomb and a knave, a thin-faced knave, a gull!

Oli. Get him to bed, and let his hurt be look'd to.
[*Exeunt Clown, Fabian, Sir Toby, and Sir Andrew.*]

Enter SEBASTIAN.

Seb. I am sorry, madam, I have hurt your kinsman;
But, had it been the brother of my blood,
I must have done no less with wit and safety.
You throw a strange regard upon me, and by that
I do perceive it hath offended you:
Pardon me, sweet one, even for the vows
We made each other but so late ago.

Duke. One face, one voice, one habit, and two persons,
A natural perspective, that is and is not!

Seb. Antonio, O my dear Antonio!
How have the hours rack'd and tortur'd me,
Since I have lost thee!

Ant. Sebastian are you?

Seb. Fear'st thou that, Antonio?

Ant. How have you made division of yourself?
An apple, cleft in two, is not more twin
Than these two creatures. Which is Sebastian?

Oli. Most wonderful!

Seb. Do I stand there? I never had a brother;
Nor can there be that deity in my nature,
Of here and every where. I had a sister,
Whom the blind waves and surges have devour'd.
Of charity, what kin are you to me?
What countryman? what name? what parentage?

Vio. Of Messaline: Sebastian was my father;
Such a Sebastian was my brother too,
So went he suited to his watery tomb:
If spirits can assume both form and suit
You come to fright us.

Seb. A spirit I am indeed;
But am in that dimension grossly clad
Which from the womb I did participate.
Were you a woman, as the rest goes even,
I should my tears let fall upon your cheek,
And say 'Thrice-welcome, drowned Viola!'

Vio. My father had a mole upon his brow.

Seb. And so had mine.

Vio. And died that day when Viola from her birth
Had numb'red thirteen years.

Seb. O, that record is lively in my soul!
He finished indeed his mortal act
That day that made my sister thirteen years.

Vio. If nothing lets to make us happy both
But this my masculine usurp'd attire,
Do not embrace me till each circumstance
Of place, time, fortune, do cohere and jump
That I am Viola: which to confirm,
I'll bring you to a captain in this town,
Where lie my maiden weeds; by whose gentle help
I was preserv'd to serve this noble count.
All the occurrence of my fortune since
Hath been between this lady and this lord.

Seb. [*To Olivia*] So comes it, lady, you have been mistook:
But nature to her bias drew in that.
You would have been contracted to a maid;
Nor are you therein, by my life, deceiv'd,
You are betroth'd both to a maid and man.

Duke. Be not amaz'd; right noble is his blood.
If this be so, as yet the glass seems true,
I shall have share in this most happy wrack.
[*To Viola*] Boy, thou hast said to me a thousand times
Thou never shouldst love woman like to me.

Vio. And all those sayings will I over-swear;
And all those swearings keep as true in soul
As doth that orbed continent the fire
That severs day from night.

Duke. Give me thy hand;
And let me see thee in thy woman's weeds.

Vio. The captain that did bring me first on shore
Hath my maid's garments: he upon some action
Is now in durance, at Malvolio's suit,
A gentleman, and follower of my lady's.

Oli. He shall enlarge him: fetch Malvolio hither:
And yet, alas, now I remember me,
They say, poor gentleman, he 's much distract.

Enter CLOWN *with a letter, and* FABIAN.

A most extracting frenzy of mine own
From my remembrance clearly banish'd his.
How does he, sirrah?

Clo. Truly, madam, he holds Belzebub at the stave's end as well as a man in his case may do: has here writ a letter to you; I should have given 't you to-day morning, but as a madman's epistles are no gospels, so it skills not much when they are delivered.

Oli. Open 't, and read it.

Clo. Look then to be well edified when the fool delivers the madman. [*Reads loudly*] 'By the Lord, madam,'—

Oli. How now! art thou mad?

Clo. No, madam, I do but read madness: an your ladyship will have it as it ought to be, you must allow vox.

Oli. Prithee, read i' thy right wits.

Clo. So I do, madonna; but to read his right wits is to read thus: therefore perpend, my princess, and give ear.

Oli. Read it you, sirrah. [*To Fabian.*]

Fab. (Reads) 'By the Lord, madam, you wrong me, and the world shall know it: though you have put me into darkness and given your drunken cousin rule over me, yet have I the benefit of my senses as well as

grave and stately dance). It may thus be connected with Sir Toby's impatience to have his wounds dressed. 218. **with wit and safety,** my wits looking out for my safety. 219. **strange regard,** offended look. 224. **perspective,** any optical device or illusion. 235. **here and every where,** omnipresence. 237. **Of charity,** in kindness. 241. **suited,** dressed. 244. **dimension,** body or bodily shape. **grossly clad,** i.e., in flesh. 245. **participate,** share in common with others. 246. **as . . . even,** since everything else agrees. 253. **record,** recollection. 256. **lets,** hinders. 259. **jump,** coincide, fit exactly; see glossary. 267. **nature . . . that,** nature was true to her bent in that. 272. **glass,** i.e., the *natural perspective* of line 224. 276. **over-swear,** swear again. 278. **orbed continent,** in Ptolemaic astronomy, the sphere of the sun, which divides day from night. 283. **durance,** prison, captivity. 285. **enlarge,** release; see glossary. 288. **extracting,** i.e., that obsessed me and drew me away from all other thoughts. 295. **epistles . . . gospels,** an allusion to readings in the church service. 296. **skills,** matters. 304. **vox,** an appropriately loud voice. 307. **perpend,** consider, attend.

your ladyship. I have your own letter that induced me to the semblance I put on; with the which I doubt not but to do myself much right, or you much shame. Think of me as you please. I leave my duty a little unthought of and speak out of my injury.

THE MADLY-USED MALVOLIO.'

Oli. Did he write this?
Clo. Ay, madam.
Duke. This savours not much of distraction.
Oli. See him deliver'd, Fabian; bring him hither.
[*Exit Fabian.*]
My lord, so please you, these things further thought on,
To think me as well a sister as a wife,
One day shall crown th' alliance on 't, so please you,
Here at my house and at my proper cost.
Duke. Madam, I am most apt t' embrace your offer.
[*To Viola*] Your master quits you; and for your service done him,
So much against the mettle of your sex,
So far beneath your soft and tender breeding,
And since you call'd me master for so long,
Here is my hand: you shall from this time be
Your master's mistress.
Oli. A sister! you are she.

Enter [FABIAN, *with*] MALVOLIO.

Duke. Is this the madman?
Oli. Ay, my lord, this same.
How now, Malvolio!
Mal. Madam, you have done me wrong,
Notorious wrong.
Oli. Have I, Malvolio? no.
Mal. Lady, you have. Pray you, peruse that letter.
You must not now deny it is your hand:
Write from it, if you can, in hand or phrase;
Or say 'tis not your seal, not your invention:
You can say none of this: well, grant it then
And tell me, in the modesty of honour,
Why you have given me such clear lights of favour,
Bade me come smiling and cross-garter'd to you,
To put on yellow stockings and to frown
Upon Sir Toby and the lighter people;
And, acting this in an obedient hope,
Why have you suffer'd me to be imprison'd,
Kept in a dark house, visited by the priest,
And made the most notorious geck and gull
That e'er invention play'd on? tell me why.
Oli. Alas, Malvolio, this is not my writing,
Though, I confess, much like the character:
But out of question 'tis Maria's hand.
And now I do bethink me, it was she
First told me thou wast mad; then cam'st in smiling,
And in such forms which here were presuppos'd
Upon thee in the letter. Prithee, be content:
This practice hath most shrewdly pass'd upon thee;
But when we know the grounds and authors of it,
Thou shalt be both the plaintiff and the judge
Of thine own cause.
Fab. Good madam, hear me speak,
And let no quarrel nor no brawl to come
Taint the condition of this present hour,
Which I have wond'red at. In hope it shall not,
Most freely I confess, myself and Toby
Set this device against Malvolio here,
Upon some stubborn and uncourteous parts
We had conceiv'd against him: Maria writ
The letter at Sir Toby's great importance;
In recompense whereof he hath married her.
How with a sportful malice it was follow'd,
May rather pluck on laughter than revenge;
If that the injuries be justly weigh'd
That have on both sides pass'd.
Oli. Alas, poor fool, how have they baffled thee!

Clo. Why, 'some are born great, some achieve greatness, and some have greatness thrown upon them.' I was one, sir, in this interlude; one Sir Topas, sir; but that 's all one. 'By the Lord, fool, I am not mad.' But do you remember? 'Madam, why laugh you at such a barren rascal? an you smile not, he 's gagged:' and thus the whirligig of time brings in his revenges.

Mal. I'll be reveng'd on the whole pack of you! [*Exit.*]
Oli. He hath been most notoriously abus'd.
Duke. Pursue him, and entreat him to a peace:
He hath not told us of the captain yet:
When that is known and golden time convents,
A solemn combination shall be made
Of our dear souls. Meantime, sweet sister,
We will not part from hence. Cesario, come;
For so you shall be, while you are a man;
But when in other habits you are seen,
Orsino's mistress and his fancy's queen.
Exeunt [*all, except Clown*].

Clo. (Sings)
When that I was and a little tiny boy,
With hey, ho, the wind and the rain,
A foolish thing was but a toy,
For the rain it raineth every day.

But when I came to man's estate,
With hey, ho, &c.
'Gainst knaves and thieves men shut their gate,
For the rain, &c.

But when I came, alas! to wive,
With hey, ho, &c.
By swaggering could I never thrive,
For the rain, &c.

But when I came unto my beds,
With hey, ho, &c.
With toss-pots still had drunken heads,
For the rain, &c.

A great while ago the world begun,
With hey, ho, &c.
But that 's all one, our play is done,
And we'll strive to please you every day. [*Exit.*]

324. **these . . . on,** i.e., when they have been considered. 327. **proper,** own. 330. **mettle,** natural disposition. 340. **from it,** differently. 343. **modesty of honour,** sense of propriety belonging to honorable persons. 347. **lighter,** less important. 351. **geck,** dupe. 355. **out of,** beyond. 358. **presuppos'd,** offered beforehand for adoption. 360. **shrewdly,** cruelly. 364. **to come,** i.e., future brawl. 369. **Upon,** on account of. **parts,** qualities. 370. **conceiv'd against,** observed in and charged against. 371. **importance,** importunity. 377. **baffled,** treated ignominiously. 391. **convents,** suits; the word elsewhere means "summons." 412. **toss-pots,** drunkards.

THE TRAGEDY OF KING RICHARD THE SECOND

Richard II (c. 1595–1596) is the first in Shakespeare's great four-play historical saga, or tetralogy, that continues with the two parts of *Henry IV* (c. 1596–1598) and concludes with *Henry V* (1599). This second tetralogy completes the action of Shakespeare's great cycle on the Wars of the Roses, begun in the earlier tetralogy on Henry VI and Richard III (c. 1589–1594). Both sequences move from an outbreak of civil faction to the eventual triumph of political stability. Together, they comprise the story of England's long century of political turmoil from the 1390's until Henry Tudor's victory over Richard III in 1485. Yet Shakespeare chose to relate the two halves of this chronicle in reverse order. His crowning statement about kingship in *Henry V* focuses on the education and kingly success of Prince Hal.

With *Richard II*, then, Shakespeare returns to the events which had launched England's century of crisis. These events were still fresh and relevant to Elizabethan minds. Richard and Bolingbroke's contest for the English crown provided a "mirror for magistrates": a sobering example of political wrongdoing and, at least by implication, a rule for political right conduct. One prominent reason for studying history, to an Elizabethan, was to avoid errors of the past. What are the rights and wrongs of Richard's deposition, and to what extent can political lessons be drawn from Shakespeare's presentation?

To begin with, we should not underestimate Richard's attractive qualities, as a man and even as a king. Throughout the play, Richard is consistently more impressive and majestic in appearance than his rival Bolingbroke. Richard fascinates us with his verbal sensitivity, his poetic insight, and his dramatic self-consciousness. He eloquently expounds a sacramental view of kingship, according to which "Not all the water in the rough rude sea Can wash the balm off from an anointed king" (III,ii). Bolingbroke can depose Richard but can never capture the aura of majesty Richard possesses; Bolingbroke may succeed politically, but only at the expense of desecrating an idea. Richard is much more interesting to us as a man than Bolingbroke, more capable of grief, more tender in his personal relationships, more in need of being understood. Indeed, a major factor in Richard's tragedy is the conflict between his public role (wherein he sees himself as divinely appointed, almost superhuman) and his private role (wherein he is emotionally dependent and easily hurt). Although Richard sometimes indulges in childish sentimentality, at his best he is superbly refined, perceptive, and poetic.

These qualities notwithstanding, Richard is an incompetent ruler compared with the man who supplants him. Richard himself confesses to the prodigal expense of "too great a court." In order to raise funds, he has been obliged to "farm our royal realm": that is, sell for ready cash the right of collecting taxes to individual courtiers, who are then free to extort what the market will bear (I,iv). Similarly, Richard proposes to issue "blank charters" to his minions, who will then be authorized to fill in the amount of tax to be paid by any hapless subject. These abuses were infamous to Elizabethan audiences as symbols of autocratic misgovernment. No less heinous is Richard's seizure of the dukedom of Lancaster from his cousin Bolingbroke. Although Richard does receive the consent of his council to banish Bolingbroke, he violates the very idea of inheritance of property when he takes away Bolingbroke's title and lands. And, as his uncle the Duke of York remonstrates, Richard's own right to the throne depends on that idea of due inheritance. By offending against the most sacred concepts of order and degree, he teaches others to rebel.

Richard's behavior even prior to the commencement of the play arouses suspicion. The nature of his complicity in the death of his uncle Thomas of Woodstock, Duke of Gloucester, is perhaps never entirely clear, and Gloucester may have given provocation. Indeed, one can sympathize with the predicament of a very young ruler prematurely thrust into the center of power by the untimely death of his father, the crown prince, now having to cope with an array of worldly-wise, advice-giving uncles. Nevertheless, Richard is unambiguously guilty of murder in the eyes of Gloucester's widow and of her brother-in-law John of Gaunt, Duke of Lancaster. Apparently, too, Gaunt's son Bolingbroke believes Richard to be a murderer, and brings accusation against Thomas Mowbray, Duke of Norfolk, partly as a means of embarrassing the king whom he cannot accuse directly. Mowbray's lot is an unenviable one: he was in command at Calais when Gloucester was executed there, and he hints that Richard ordered the execution (even though Mowbray alleges that he himself did not carry out the order). For his part, Richard is only too glad to banish the man suspected of having been his agent in murder. Mowbray is a convenient scapegoat.

The polished, ceremonial tone of the play's opening is vitiated, then, by our growing awareness of some very dirty politics going on beneath the surface. Our first impression of Richard is of a king devoted to the public display of conciliatory evenhandedness. He listens to the claims and counterclaims of Bolingbroke and Mowbray, and, when he cannot manage to reconcile them peacefully, he allows a trial by combat. This trial (I,iii) is replete with ceremonial repetition and ritual. The combatants are duly sworn in the justice of their cause, and God is to decide the merits of the quarrel by awarding victory to the champion who speaks the truth. Richard, the presiding officer, is God's anointed deputy on earth. Yet it becomes evident in due course that Richard is a major perpetrator of injustice rather than an impartial judge, that Bolingbroke is after greater stakes than he acknowledges even to himself, and that the banishment of the two contenders is Richard's desperate way of sweeping his problems under the carpet. His uncles reluctantly consent to the banishment only because they too see that disaffection has reached alarming proportions.

Bolingbroke's motivation in these opening scenes is perhaps even more obscure than that of Richard. Our first impression of Bolingbroke is of forthrightness, moral indignation, and patriotic zeal. In fact we never really question the earnestness of his outrage at Richard's misgovernance, his longing to avenge a family murder (for Gloucester was his uncle, too), or his bitter disappointment at being banished from his fatherland. Yet we are prompted to ask further: what is the essential cause of the enmity between Bolingbroke and Richard? If Mowbray is only a stalking-horse, is not Gloucester's death also the excuse for pursuing a preexistent animosity? Richard, for one, appears to think so. His portrayal of Bolingbroke as a scheming politician, one who curries favor with the populace in order to build a power base against the king himself, is telling and prophetic. Bolingbroke, says Richard, acts "As were our England in reversion his, And he our subjects' next degree in hope" (I,iv). This unflattering appraisal might be ascribed to malicious envy on Richard's part, were it not proved by subsequent events to be wholly accurate.

Paradoxically, Richard is far the more prescient of the two contenders for the English throne. It is he, in fact, who perceives from the start that the conflict between them is irreconcilable. He banishes Bolingbroke as his chief rival, and does not doubt what motives will call Bolingbroke home again. Meanwhile, Bolingbroke disclaims any motive for his deed other than love of country and hatred of injustice. Although born with a political sixth sense that Richard lacks, Bolingbroke does not theorize about the consequences of his acts. As a man of action, he lives in the present. Richard, conversely, a person of exquisite contemplative powers and poetic imagination, does not deign to cope with the practical. He both envies and despises Bolingbroke's easy way with the commoners. Richard cherishes kingship for the majesty and the royal prerogative it confers, not for the power to govern wisely. Thus it is that, despite his perception of what will follow, Richard habitually indulges his worst instincts, buying a moment of giddy pleasure at the expense of long-term disaster.

We cannot doubt Richard's incompetence as a ruler. Does this incompetence condone Bolingbroke's armed rebellion? According to John of Gaunt, to York (despite his later shift of allegiance), and to the Bishop of Carlisle, it does not. The attitude of these men can be summed up by the phrase "passive obedience." As Gaunt expresses the concept, "God's is the quarrel." Because Richard is God's anointed deputy on earth, only God may punish the king's wrongdoing. Gaunt does not question Richard's guilt, but he does not question God's ability to avenge, either. Gaunt sees human intervention in God's affair as blasphemous: "for I may never lift An angry arm against His minister" (I,ii). To be sure, Gaunt does acknowledge a solemn duty to offer frank advice to extremists of both sides, and he does so unsparingly. He consents to the banishment of his son, and he rebukes Richard savagely with his dying breath.

This doctrine of passive obedience was familiar to Elizabethans, for they heard it in church periodically in official homilies against rebellion. It was the Tudor state's answer to those who asserted a right to overthrow reputedly evil kings. The argument was logically ingenious. Why are evil rulers permitted to govern from time to time? Presumably because God wishes to test a people or punish them for waywardness. Any king performing such chastisement is a divine "scourge." Accordingly, the worst thing a people can do is to rebel against God's scourge, thereby manifesting more waywardness. Instead, they must attempt to remedy the insolence in their hearts, advise the king to mend his ways, and patiently await God's pardon. If they do so they will not long be disappointed. The doctrine is essentially conservative, defending the Establishment. Nevertheless, in *Richard II* it is a moderate position between the extremes of tyranny and rebellion, and is expressed by thoughtful, selfless men. We might be tempted to label it the authorial viewpoint, if we did not also perceive that the doctrine is continually placed in ironic conflict with harsh political realities. The character who most reflects the ironies and even ludicrous incongruities of the situation is the Duke of York.

York is to an extent a choric character—that is, one who helps direct our viewpoint—because his transfer of loyalties from Richard to Bolingbroke structurally delineates the decline of Richard's fortunes and the concurrent rise of Bolingbroke's. At first York shares with his brother Gaunt a dismay at Richard's willfulness, together with a reluctance to act. It is only when Richard seizes the dukedom of Lancaster that York can no longer hold his tongue. His condemnation is as bitter as that of Gaunt, hinting even at loss of allegiance (II,i). Still, he accepts the responsibility, so cavalierly bestowed by Richard, of governing England in the king's absence. He musters what force he can to oppose Bolingbroke's advance, and lectures against this rebellion with the same vehemence he had used against Richard's despotism. Yet when faced with Bolingbroke's overwhelming military superiority, he accedes rather than fight in behalf of a lost cause. However much this may resemble cowardice or mere expediency, it also displays a pragmatic logic. Once Bolingbroke has become *de facto* king, in York's view he must be acknowledged and obeyed. By a kind of analogy to the doctrine of passive obedience (which more rigorous theorists would never allow), York accepts the status quo as inevitable. He is vigorously ready to defend the new regime, just as he earlier defended Richard's rule.

When, however, this conclusion brings York to the point of turning in his own son Aumerle for a traitor, and quarreling with his wife as to whether their son shall live, the ironic absurdity is apparent. King Henry himself is amused, in one of the play's rare lighthearted moments (V,iii). When a family and a kingdom are divided against one another, there can be no really satisfactory resolution.

We are never entirely convinced that all the fine old medieval theories surrounding kingship—divine right, passive obedience, trial by combat, and the like—can ever wholly explain or remedy the complex and nasty political situation afflicting England. The one man capable of decisive action, in fact, is he who never theorizes at all: Bolingbroke. As we have seen, his avowed motive for opposing Mowbray—simple patriotic indignation—is uttered with such earnestness that we wonder if indeed Bolingbroke has examined in himself those political ambitions so plainly visible to Richard and others. This same discrepancy between surface and depth applies to Bolingbroke's motives in returning to England. With seemingly passionate sincerity he protests to York that he comes only for his dukedom of Lancaster (II,iii). But does he seriously think he can reclaim that dukedom by force, and then yield to Richard without either maintaining Richard as a puppet king or placing himself in intolerable jeopardy? And can he suppose that his allies, Northumberland and the rest, who have now openly defied the king, will countenance the return to power of one who would never trust them again? It is in this context that York protests, "Well, well, I see the issue of these arms." Not only the deposition of Richard, but Richard's death, are foregone conclusions once Bolingbroke has succeeded in an armed rebellion. There can be no turning back. Yet Bolingbroke simply will not theorize in these terms. He repeatedly admonishes Northumberland for treating Richard harshly, even though Northumberland is only taking upon himself the unpleasant but unavoidable duty of arresting and impeaching a king. When the new King Henry discovers—to his surprise, evidently—that Richard's life is now a burden to the state, he ponders aloud, "Have I no friend will rid me of this living fear?" and then rebukes Exton for proceeding on cue.

The phrase for Bolingbroke's pragmatic spirit, and for his new government, is "*de facto.*" Ultimately, the justification for his rule is the very fact of its existence, its functioning. Bolingbroke is the man of the hour. In Yeats' fine maxim, Bolingbroke is the vessel of clay, Richard the vessel of porcelain. One is durable and utilitarian, yet unattractive; the other is exquisite, fragile, impractical. The comparison does not force us to prefer one to the other, even though Yeats himself characteristically sided with beauty against politics. Rather, Shakespeare gives us our choice, allowing us to see in ourselves an inclination toward political and social stability or toward artistic temperament.

The paradox may suggest that the qualities of a good administrator are not those of a sensitive, thoughtful man. However hopeless as a king, Richard stands before us increasingly as an introspective and fascinating person. When his power crumbles, his spirit is enhanced, as though loss of power and royal identity were necessary for the discovery of true values.

In this there is a faint anticipation of King Lear's self-learning, fearfully and preciously bought. The trace is only slight here, because in good part *Richard II* is a political history play rather than a tragedy, and because Richard's self-realization is imperfect. Nevertheless, when Richard faces deposition and separation from his queen, and especially when he is alone in prison expecting to die, he strives to understand his life and through it the general condition of humanity. He perceives a contradiction in heaven's assurances about salvation: on the one hand Christ promises to receive all God's children, whereas He also warns that it is as hard for a rich man to enter heaven as for a camel to thread a needle's eye (V,v). The paradox echoes the Beatitudes: the last shall be first, the meek shall inherit the earth. Richard, now one of the downtrodden, gropes for an understanding of the vanity of human achievement whereby he can aspire to the victory Christ promised. At his death, that victory seems to him assured: his soul will mount to its seat on high "Whilst my gross flesh sinks downward, here to die."

In this triumph of spirit over flesh, the long downward motion of Richard's worldly fortune is crucially reversed. By the same token, the worldly success of Bolingbroke is shown to be no more than that:

THE FOLGER SHAKESPEARE LIBRARY

Holbein's "Dance of Death" (1538)—the king, despite power and wealth, is stalked by Death; see III,ii,155 ff.

worldly success. His archetype is Cain, the primal murderer of a brother. To the extent that the play is a history, Bolingbroke's *de facto* success is still a matter of political relevance; but in the belated movement toward Richard's personal tragedy, we experience a profound countermovement that partly achieves a purgative sense of atonement and reassurance. Whatever Richard may have lost, his gain is also great.

The image patterns of *Richard II* reinforce structure and meaning. The play is unusual for its extensive use of blank verse and rhyme, and for its interwoven sets of recurring images. England is a garden mismanaged by her royal gardener, so that weeds and caterpillars (e.g., Bushy, Bagot, and Green) flourish. She is also a sick body ill-tended by her royal physician, and a family divided against itself yielding abortive and sterile progeny. Her political ills are attested to by disorders in the cosmos: comets, shooting stars, withered bay trees, weeping rains. Night owls, associated with death, prevail over the larks of morning. The sun, royally associated at first with Richard, deserts him for Bolingbroke and leaves Richard as the Phaëthon who has mishandled the sun-god's chariot and so scorched the earth. Linked to the sun image is the prevalent *leit-motif* of ascent and descent. And, touching upon all these, a cluster of Biblical images sees England as a despoiled garden of Eden witnessing a second fall of man. Richard repeatedly brands his enemies and deserters as Judases and Pilates, not always fairly; nonetheless, in his last agony he finds genuine consolation in Christ's example. This poetic method is intensely suitable for a man so self-absorbed in the drama of his existence.

The poetry also confirms the date of *Richard II* as of the so-called lyric period, c. 1594–1596, that also produced *Romeo and Juliet* and *A Midsummer Night's Dream*. The play, registered and carefully published in quarto form in 1597, appears to have drawn on Samuel Daniel's *Civill Wars* (1595) as well as Holinshed's *Chronicles*. For its structure it surely owed something to Marlowe's *Edward II* (c. 1592), and it may have relied on the anonymous *Thomas of Woodstock* (c. 1591–1595) for an understanding of the occasionally obscure events surrounding the death of Richard's uncle. Shakespeare must have known he was dealing with a politically explosive topic often used as a libelous analogy against Queen Elizabeth. The deposition scene is missing from the earlier quartos, as though it had been excised by the censor. And in 1601 the Earl of Essex commissioned Shakespeare's company to perform a revived play about Richard II on the eve of an abortive rebellion, presumably as a means of inciting to riot. Whether the play was Shakespeare's is not certain, but seems likely. The acting company was ultimately exonerated, but not before Elizabeth believed that she was being compared to Richard. However little Shakespeare may have intended the analogy when he wrote, he chose a subject of intense political relevance to Elizabethans, for which the greatest tact was needed.

THE TRAGEDY OF KING RICHARD THE SECOND

[*Dramatis Personae*

KING RICHARD the Second.
JOHN OF GAUNT, Duke of Lancaster, } *uncles to the King.*
EDMUND OF LANGLEY, Duke of York, }
HENRY, *surnamed* BOLINGBROKE, Duke of Hereford, *son to John of Gaunt; afterwards* KING HENRY IV.
DUKE OF AUMERLE, *son to the Duke of York.*
THOMAS MOWBRAY, Duke of Norfolk.
DUKE OF SURREY.
EARL OF SALISBURY.
LORD BERKELEY.
BUSHY, }
BAGOT, } *servants to King Richard.*
GREEN, }
EARL OF NORTHUMBERLAND.
HENRY PERCY, *surnamed* Hotspur, *his son.*
LORD ROSS.
LORD WILLOUGHBY.
LORD FITZWATER.
Bishop of Carlisle.
Abbot of Westminster.
Lord Marshal.
SIR STEPHEN SCROOP.
SIR PIERCE of Exton.
Captain of a band of Welshmen.

QUEEN to King Richard.
DUCHESS OF YORK.
DUCHESS OF GLOUCESTER.
Ladies attending on the Queen.

Lords, Heralds, Officers, Soldiers, Gardeners, Keeper, Messenger, Groom, *and other* Attendants.

SCENE: *England and Wales.*]

[ACT I.

SCENE I. *London.* KING RICHARD'S *palace.*]

Enter KING RICHARD, JOHN OF GAUNT, *with other* Nobles *and* Attendants.

K. Rich. Old John of Gaunt, time-honoured Lancaster,
Hast thou, according to thy oath and band,
Brought hither Henry Hereford thy bold son,
Here to make good the boist'rous late appeal,
Which then our leisure would not let us hear,
Against the Duke of Norfolk, Thomas Mowbray?
Gaunt. I have, my liege.
K. Rich. Tell me, moreover, hast thou sounded him,
If he appeal the duke on ancient malice;

Or worthily, as a good subject should,
On some known ground of treachery in him?
Gaunt. As near as I could sift him on that argument,
On some apparent danger seen in him
Aim'd at your highness, no inveterate malice.
K. Rich. Then call them to our presence; face to face,
And frowning brow to brow, ourselves will hear
The accuser and the accused freely speak:
High-stomach'd are they both, and full of ire,
In rage deaf as the sea, hasty as fire.

Enter BOLINGBROKE *and* MOWBRAY.

Boling. Many years of happy days befal
My gracious sovereign, my most loving liege!
Mow. Each day still better other's happiness;
Until the heavens, envying earth's good hap,
Add an immortal title to your crown!
K. Rich. We thank you both: yet one but flatters us,
As well appeareth by the cause you come;
Namely, to appeal each other of high treason.
Cousin of Hereford, what dost thou object
Against the Duke of Norfolk, Thomas Mowbray?
Boling. First, heaven be the record to my speech!
In the devotion of a subject's love,
Tend'ring the precious safety of my prince,
And free from other misbegotten hate,
Come I appellant to this princely presence.
Now, Thomas Mowbray, do I turn to thee,
And mark my greeting well; for what I speak
My body shall make good upon this earth,
Or my divine soul answer it in heaven.
Thou art a traitor and a miscreant,
Too good to be so and too bad to live,
Since the more fair and crystal is the sky,
The uglier seem the clouds that in it fly.
Once more, the more to aggravate the note,
With a foul traitor's name stuff I thy throat;
And wish, so please my sovereign, ere I move,
What my tongue speaks my right drawn sword may prove.
Mow. Let not my cold words here accuse my zeal:
'Tis not the trial of a woman's war,
The bitter clamour of two eager tongues,
Can arbitrate this cause betwixt us twain;
The blood is hot that must be cool'd for this:
Yet can I not of such tame patience boast
As to be hush'd and nought at all to say:
First, the fair reverence of your highness curbs me
From giving reins and spurs to my free speech;
Which else would post until it had return'd
These terms of treason doubled down his throat.
Setting aside his high blood's royalty,
And let him be no kinsman to my liege,
I do defy him, and I spit at him;
Call him a slanderous coward and a villain:
Which to maintain I would allow him odds,
And meet him, were I tied to run afoot
Even to the frozen ridges of the Alps,
Or any other ground inhabitable,
Where ever Englishman durst set his foot.
Mean time let this defend my loyalty,
By all my hopes, most falsely doth he lie.
Boling. Pale trembling coward, there I throw my gage,
Disclaiming here the kindred of the king,
And lay aside my high blood's royalty,
Which fear, not reverence, makes thee to except.
If guilty dread have left thee so much strength
As to take up mine honour's pawn, then stoop:
By that and all the rites of knighthood else,
Will I make good against thee, arm to arm,
What I have spoke, or thou canst worse devise.
Mow. I take it up; and by that sword I swear,
Which gently laid my knighthood on my shoulder,
I'll answer thee in any fair degree,
Or chivalrous design of knightly trial:
And when I mount, alive may I not light,
If I be traitor or unjustly fight!
K. Rich. What doth our cousin lay to Mowbray's charge?
It must be great that can inherit us
So much as of a thought of ill in him.
Boling. Look what I speak, my life shall prove it true;
That Mowbray hath receiv'd eight thousand nobles
In name of lendings for your highness' soldiers,
The which he hath detain'd for lewd employments,
Like a false traitor and injurious villain.
Besides I say and will in battle prove,
Or here or elsewhere to the furthest verge
That ever was survey'd by English eye,
That all the treasons for these eighteen years
Complotted and contrived in this land
Fetch from false Mowbray their first head and spring.
Further I say and further will maintain
Upon his bad life to make all this good,
That he did plot the Duke of Gloucester's death,
Suggest his soon-believing adversaries,
And consequently, like a traitor coward,
Sluic'd out his innocent soul through streams of blood:
Which blood, like sacrificing Abel's, cries,
Even from the tongueless caverns of the earth,
To me for justice and rough chastisement;
And, by the glorious worth of my descent,
This arm shall do it, or this life be spent.
K. Rich. How high a pitch his resolution soars!
Thomas of Norfolk, what say'st thou to this?
Mow. O, let my sovereign turn away his face

ACT I. SCENE I. *Stage Direction:* **London.** Holinshed places this scene at Windsor; he is followed by many editors. 1. **Old John of Gaunt,** born in 1340 at Ghent; hence the surname *Gaunt*. At this time, April 29, 1398, he was only fifty-eight, although Shakespeare represents him as being very old. 2. **band,** bond. 4. **appeal,** accusation, formal challenge or impeachment which the accuser was obliged to maintain in combat. 9. **appeal,** accuse. 12. **sift,** discover true motives by questioning. **argument,** subject. 13. **apparent,** obvious. 18. **High-stomach'd,** haughty, having an appetite for combat. 23. **hap,** fortune. 32. **Tend'ring,** holding dear. 34. **appellant,** in accusation, as the accuser. 43. **note,** reproach. 46. **right drawn,** justly or rightly drawn. 47. **accuse my zeal,** accuse me of wanting zeal. 49. **eager,** sharp, biting. 58. **Setting . . . royalty,** disregarding Bolingbroke's royal blood. 59. **let him be,** suppose him to be. 63. **tied,** obliged. 65. **inhabitable,** uninhabitable. 67. **this,** i.e., his sword, or his assertion of Bolingbroke's guilt. 69. **gage,** a gauntlet as a sign of the pledge to combat. 72. **except,** use as an excuse. 74. **pawn,** i.e., his gage. 82. **light,** dismount. 85. **inherit,** put in possession of. 88. **nobles,** gold coins worth twenty groats or 6s. 8d. 89. **lendings,** money advanced to soldiers when the regular pay cannot be given (Onions). 90. **lewd,** vile, base. 97. **head and spring,** synonymous words meaning "origin." 100. **Duke of Gloucester's death.** Thomas of Woodstock, Duke of Gloucester, sixth (or seventh) son of Edward III and brother of John of Gaunt, was murdered at Calais in September 1397. 101. **Suggest,** prompt, incite. 102. **consequently,** afterwards. 104. **Abel's.** See Genesis 4:3-12. 105. **tongueless,** resonant but without articulate speech.

And bid his ears a little while be deaf,
Till I have told this slander of his blood,
How God and good men hate so foul a liar.
K. Rich. Mowbray, impartial are our eyes and ears:
Were he my brother, nay, my kingdom's heir,
As he is but my father's brother's son,
Now, by my sceptre's awe, I make a vow,
Such neighbour nearness to our sacred blood
Should nothing privilege him, nor partialize
The unstooping firmness of my upright soul:
He is our subject, Mowbray; so art thou:
Free speech and fearless I to thee allow.
Mow. Then, Bolingbroke, as low as to thy heart,
Through the false passage of thy throat, thou liest!
Three parts of that receipt I had for Calais
Disburs'd I duly to his highness' soldiers;
The other part reserv'd I by consent,
For that my sovereign liege was in my debt
Upon remainder of a dear account,
Since last I went to France to fetch his queen:
Now swallow down that lie. For Gloucester's death,
I slew him not; but to my own disgrace
Neglected my sworn duty in that case.
For you, my noble Lord of Lancaster,
The honourable father to my foe,
Once did I lay an ambush for your life,
A trespass that doth vex my grieved soul;
But ere I last receiv'd the sacrament
I did confess it, and exactly begg'd
Your grace's pardon, and I hope I had it.
This is my fault: as for the rest appeal'd,
It issues from the rancour of a villain,
A recreant and most degenerate traitor:
Which in myself I boldly will defend;
And interchangeably hurl down my gage
Upon this overweening traitor's foot,
To prove myself a loyal gentleman
Even in the best blood chamber'd in his bosom.
In haste whereof, most heartily I pray
Your highness to assign our trial day.
K. Rich. Wrath-kindled gentlemen, be rul'd by me;
Let's purge this choler without letting blood:
This we prescribe, though no physician;
Deep malice makes too deep incision;
Forget, forgive; conclude and be agreed;
Our doctors say this is no month to bleed.
Good uncle, let this end where it begun;
We'll calm the Duke of Norfolk, you your son.
Gaunt. To be a make-peace shall become my age:
Throw down, my son, the Duke of Norfolk's gage.
K. Rich. And, Norfolk, throw down his.
Gaunt. When, Harry, when?
Obedience bids I should not bid again.
K. Rich. Norfolk, throw down, we bid; there is no boot.
Mow. Myself I throw, dread sovereign, at thy foot.
My life thou shalt command, but not my shame:
The one my duty owes; but my fair name,
Despite of death that lives upon my grave,
To dark dishonour's use thou shalt not have.
I am disgrac'd, impeach'd and baffled here,
Pierc'd to the soul with slander's venom'd spear,
The which no balm can cure but his heart-blood
Which breath'd this poison.
K. Rich. Rage must be withstood:
Give me his gage: lions make leopards tame.
Mow. Yea, but not change his spots: take but my shame,
And I resign my gage. My dear dear lord,
The purest treasure mortal times afford
Is spotless reputation: that away,
Men are but gilded loam or painted clay.
A jewel in a ten-times-barr'd-up chest
Is a bold spirit in a loyal breast.
Mine honour is my life; both grow in one;
Take honour from me, and my life is done:
Then, dear my liege, mine honour let me try;
In that I live and for that will I die.
K. Rich. Cousin, throw up your gage; do you begin.
Boling. O, God defend my soul from such deep sin!
Shall I seem crest-fallen in my father's sight?
Or with pale beggar-fear impeach my height
Before this out-dar'd dastard? Ere my tongue
Shall wound my honour with such feeble wrong,
Or sound so base a parle, my teeth shall tear
The slavish motive of recanting fear,
And spit it bleeding in his high disgrace,
Where shame doth harbour, even in Mowbray's face.
[*Exit Gaunt.*]
K. Rich. We were not born to sue, but to command;
Which since we cannot do to make you friends,
Be ready, as your lives shall answer it,
At Coventry, upon Saint Lambert's day:
There shall your swords and lances arbitrate
The swelling difference of your settled hate:
Since we can not atone you, we shall see
Justice design the victor's chivalry.
Lord marshal, command our officers at arms
Be ready to direct these home alarms. *Exit* [*with others*].

[SCENE II. *The* DUKE OF LANCASTER'S *palace.*]

Enter JOHN OF GAUNT *with the* DUCHESS OF GLOUCESTER.

Gaunt. Alas, the part I had in Woodstock's blood
Doth more solicit me than your exclaims,
To stir against the butchers of his life!
But since correction lieth in those hands
Which made the fault that we cannot correct,
Put we our quarrel to the will of heaven;
Who, when they see the hours ripe on earth,
Will rain hot vengeance on offenders' heads.
Duch. Finds brotherhood in thee no sharper spur?
Hath love in thy old blood no living fire?
Edward's seven sons, whereof thyself art one,
Were as seven vials of his sacred blood,

113. **slander of,** disgrace or reproach to. 126. **receipt,** thing received. 132-134. **For . . . case.** Mowbray's excuse is at the king's expense; he vaguely hints at the king's connivance. In Holinshed Mowbray ignores the charge. 140. **exactly,** explicitly, formally. 144. **recreant,** cowardly. 146. **interchangeably,** in exchange. 153. **choler,** excess of the humor choler, anger. **letting blood,** used with a quibble on the sense of "mortal combat." 156. **conclude,** come to a final agreement. 157. **no month to bleed.** Spring and autumn were regarded as the proper times to bleed patients. Ff: *time;* Q_1: *month.* 160. **make-peace,** peacemaker. 164. **boot,** alternative, remedy. 170. **impeach'd,** called into question, discredited. **baffled,** disgraced, as of a recreant knight. A part of the punishment of coward knights was hanging by the heels, which is the original meaning of the word. 174. **lions, leopards.** The royal arms showed a rampant lion; the Norfolk arms may have shown a leopard. 184. **try,** put to the test. 189. **beggar-fear,** a beggar's fear. **height,** high position. 190. **out-dar'd,** dared down, cowed. 192. **parle,** parley, overture to peace. 193. **motive,** instrument. 199. **Saint Lambert's day,** September 17. 203. **design,** point out.

Or seven fair branches springing from one root:
Some of those seven are dried by nature's course,
Some of those branches by the Destinies cut;
But Thomas, my dear lord, my life, my Gloucester,
One vial full of Edward's sacred blood,
One flourishing branch of his most royal root,
Is crack'd, and all the precious liquor spilt,
Is hack'd down, and his summer leaves all faded,
By envy's hand and murder's bloody axe.
Ah, Gaunt, his blood was thine! that bed, that womb,
That metal, that self mould, that fashioned thee
Made him a man; and though thou livest and
breathest,
Yet art thou slain in him: thou dost consent
In some large measure to thy father's death,
In that thou seest thy wretched brother die,
Who was the model of thy father's life.
Call it not patience, Gaunt; it is despair:
In suff'ring thus thy brother to be slaught'red,
Thou showest the naked pathway to thy life,
Teaching stern murder how to butcher thee:
That which in mean men we intitle patience
Is pale cold cowardice in noble breasts.
What shall I say? to safeguard thine own life,
The best way is to venge my Gloucester's death.

Gaunt. God's is the quarrel; for God's substitute,
His deputy anointed in His sight,
Hath caus'd his death: the which if wrongfully,
Let heaven revenge; for I may never lift
An angry arm against His minister.

Duch. Where then, alas, may I complain myself?

Gaunt. To God, the widow's champion and defence.

Duch. Why, then, I will. Farewell, old Gaunt.
Thou goest to Coventry, there to behold
Our cousin Hereford and fell Mowbray fight:
O, sit my husband's wrongs on Hereford's spear,
That it may enter butcher Mowbray's breast!
Or, if misfortune miss the first career,
Be Mowbray's sins so heavy in his bosom,
That they may break his foaming courser's back,
And throw the rider headlong in the lists,
A caitiff recreant to my cousin Hereford!
Farewell, old Gaunt: thy sometimes brother's wife
With her companion Grief must end her life.

Gaunt. Sister, farewell; I must to Coventry:
As much good stay with thee as go with me!

Duch. Yet one word more: grief boundeth where it
falls,
Not with the empty hollowness, but weight:
I take my leave before I have begun,
For sorrow ends not when it seemeth done.
Commend me to thy brother, Edmund York.
Lo, this is all:—nay, yet depart not so;
Though this be all, do not so quickly go;
I shall remember more. Bid him—ah, what?—
With all good speed at Plashy visit me.
Alack, and what shall good old York there see
But empty lodgings and unfurnish'd walls,
Unpeopled offices, untrodden stones?
And what hear there for welcome but my groans?
Therefore commend me; let him not come there,
To seek out sorrow that dwells every where.
Desolate, desolate, will I hence and die:
The last leave of thee takes my weeping eye. *Exeunt*.

[SCENE III. *The lists at Coventry*.]

Enter Lord Marshal *and the* DUKE [OF] AUMERLE.

Mar. My Lord Aumerle, is Harry Hereford arm'd?

Aum. Yea, at all points; and longs to enter in.

Mar. The Duke of Norfolk, sprightfully and bold,
Stays but the summons of the appellant's trumpet.

Aum. Why, then, the champions are prepar'd, and
stay
For nothing but his majesty's approach.

The trumpets sound, and the KING *enters with his nobles* [GAUNT, BUSHY, BAGOT, GREEN, *and others*]. *When they are set, enter* [MOWBRAY] *the* DUKE OF NORFOLK *in arms, defendant* [*with a* Herald].

K. Rich. Marshal, demand of yonder champion
The cause of his arrival here in arms:
Ask him his name and orderly proceed
To swear him in the justice of his cause.

Mar. In God's name and the king's, say who thou
art
And why thou comest thus knightly clad in arms,
Against what man thou com'st, and what thy quarrel:
Speak truly, on thy knighthood and thy oath;
As so defend thee heaven and thy valour!

Mow. My name is Thomas Mowbray, Duke of
Norfolk;
Who hither come engaged by my oath—
Which God defend a knight should violate!—
Both to defend my loyalty and truth
To God, my king and my succeeding issue,
Against the Duke of Hereford that appeals me;
And, by the grace of God and this mine arm,
To prove him, in defending of myself,
A traitor to my God, my king, and me:
And as I truly fight, defend me heaven!

The trumpets sound. Enter [BOLINGBROKE,] DUKE OF HEREFORD, *appellant, in armour* [*with a* Herald].

K. Rich. Marshal, ask yonder knight in arms,
Both who he is and why he cometh hither
Thus plated in habiliments of war,
And formally, according to our law,
Depose him in the justice of his cause.

Mar. What is thy name? and wherefore com'st thou
hither,
Before King Richard in his royal lists?
Against whom comest thou? and what 's thy quarrel?
Speak like a true knight, so defend thee heaven!

Boling. Harry of Hereford, Lancaster and Derby
Am I; who ready here do stand in arms,
To prove, by God's grace and my body's valour,

SCENE II. 1. **part . . . blood,** my kinship with Woodstock (the Duke of Gloucester; see I, i, 100, note). 2. **exclaims,** exclamations. 4. **those hands,** i.e., Richard's, whom he charges with responsibility for Gloucester's death. Gaunt is more explicit in lines 37-41. 23. **self mould,** selfsame mold. 28. **model,** likeness. 36. **venge,** avenge. 47. **O . . . spear.** The duchess regards Bolingbroke as the family champion, as he seems to regard himself (I, i, 104-108). 49. **career,** the charge of the horse in the tourney or combat. 53. **caitiff,** cowardly. 58. **boundeth,** bounces. 62. **Edmund York,** Edmund of Langley, fifth son of Edward III. 66. **Plashy,** Gloucester's seat in Essex. 68. **unfurnish'd,** bare. 69. **offices,** servants' quarters. 73. **will I hence.** The adverb of place is used here, as frequently in Shakespeare, without the verb of motion.

SCENE III. The events of this scene took place historically on September 16, 1398. 3. **sprightfully,** with high spirit. 7-10. **Marshal . . . cause.** One finds here, as elsewhere in Richard's public behavior, an illustration of what Coleridge calls his "attention to decorum and high feeling of kingly dignity." 28. **plated,** clothed in armor. 30. **Depose,** put under oath.

In lists, on Thomas Mowbray, Duke of Norfolk,
That he is a traitor, foul and dangerous,
To God of heaven, King Richard and to me;
And as I truly fight, defend me heaven!
Mar. On pain of death, no person be so bold
Or daring-hardy as to touch the lists,
Except the marshal and such officers
Appointed to direct these fair designs.
Boling. Lord marshal, let me kiss my sovereign's hand,
And bow my knee before his majesty:
For Mowbray and myself are like two men
That vow a long and weary pilgrimage;
Then let us take a ceremonious leave
And loving farewell of our several friends.
Mar. The appellant in all duty greets your highness,
And craves to kiss your hand and take his leave.
K. Rich. We will descend and fold him in our arms.
Cousin of Hereford, as thy cause is right,
So be thy fortune in this royal fight!
Farewell, my blood; which if to-day thou shed,
Lament we may, but not revenge thee dead.
Boling. O, let no noble eye profane a tear
For me, if I be gor'd with Mowbray's spear:
As confident as is the falcon's flight
Against a bird, do I with Mowbray fight.
My loving lord, I take my leave of you;
Of you, my noble cousin, Lord Aumerle;
Not sick, although I have to do with death,
But lusty, young, and cheerly drawing breath.
Lo, as at English feasts, so I regreet
The daintiest last, to make the end most sweet:
O thou, the earthly author of my blood,
Whose youthful spirit, in me regenerate,
Doth with a twofold vigour lift me up
To reach at victory above my head,
Add proof unto mine armour with thy prayers;
And with thy blessings steel my lance's point,
That it may enter Mowbray's waxen coat,
And furbish new the name of John a Gaunt,
Even in the lusty haviour of his son.
Gaunt. God in thy good cause make thee prosperous!
Be swift like lightning in the execution;
And let thy blows, doubly redoubled,
Fall like amazing thunder on the casque
Of thy adverse pernicious enemy:
Rouse up thy youthful blood, be valiant and live.
Boling. Mine innocency and Saint George to thrive!
Mow. However God or fortune cast my lot,
There lives or dies, true to King Richard's throne,
A loyal, just and upright gentleman:
Never did captive with a freer heart
Cast off his chains of bondage and embrace
His golden uncontroll'd enfranchisement,
More than my dancing soul doth celebrate
This feast of battle with mine adversary.
Most mighty liege, and my companion peers,
Take from my mouth the wish of happy years:
As gentle and as jocund as to jest
Go I to fight: truth hath a quiet breast.
K. Rich. Farewell, my lord: securely I espy
Virtue with valour couched in thine eye.
Order the trial, marshal, and begin.
Mar. Harry of Hereford, Lancaster and Derby,
Receive thy lance; and God defend the right!
Boling. Strong as a tower in hope, I cry amen.
Mar. Go bear this lance to Thomas, Duke of Norfolk.
First Her. Harry of Hereford, Lancaster and Derby,
Stands here for God, his sovereign and himself,
On pain to be found false and recreant,
To prove the Duke of Norfolk, Thomas Mowbray,
A traitor to his God, his king and him;
And dares him to set forward to the fight.
Sec. Her. Here standeth Thomas Mowbray, Duke of Norfolk,
On pain to be found false and recreant,
Both to defend himself and to approve
Henry of Hereford, Lancaster, and Derby,
To God, his sovereign and to him disloyal;
Courageously and with a free desire
Attending but the signal to begin.
Mar. Sound, trumpets; and set forward, combatants. [*A charge sounded*.]
Stay, the king hath thrown his warder down.
K. Rich. Let them lay by their helmets and their spears,
And both return back to their chairs again:
Withdraw with us: and let the trumpets sound
While we return these dukes what we decree.
[*A long flourish*.]
Draw near,
And list what with our council we have done.
For that our kingdom's earth should not be soil'd
With that dear blood which it hath fostered;
And for our eyes do hate the dire aspect
Of civil wounds plough'd up with neighbours' sword;
And for we think the eagle-winged pride
Of sky-aspiring and ambitious thoughts,
With rival-hating envy, set on you
To wake our peace, which in our country's cradle
Draws the sweet infant breath of gentle sleep;
Which so rous'd up with boist'rous untun'd drums,
With harsh-resounding trumpets' dreadful bray,
And grating shock of wrathful iron arms,
Might from our quiet confines fright fair peace
And make us wade even in our kindred's blood;
Therefore, we banish you our territories:
You, cousin Hereford, upon pain of life,
Till twice five summers have enrich'd our fields
Shall not regreet our fair dominions,
But tread the stranger paths of banishment.
Boling. Your will be done: this must my comfort be,
That sun that warms you here shall shine on me;
And those his golden beams to you here lent
Shall point on me and gild my banishment.

43. **daring-hardy,** daringly bold, reckless. 59. **profane,** be profaned by. 66. **cheerly,** cheerfully. 67. **regreet,** greet, salute. 70. **regenerate,** born anew. 73. **proof,** invulnerability. 75. **waxen,** penetrable, soft. 77. **haviour,** behavior, deportment. 81. **amazing,** confusing, bewildering. **casque,** helmet. 95. **jest,** take part in a play or pastime. 97. **securely,** confidently. 102. **Strong . . . hope,** an allusion to Psalms 61:3. 106. **On pain to be,** at the risk of being. 112. **approve,** prove. 118. **Stay . . . down.** Shakespeare fails to disclose Richard's motive here. According to Froissart, several noblemen of the king's party warned him not to let the combat proceed because the people were aroused on Bolingbroke's behalf. The victory of either knight would be perilous to the king's own safety. **warder,** staff or truncheon borne by the king when presiding over a trial by combat. 122. **While,** until. 124. **list,** hear. 134-137. **Which . . . peace.** Syntactically the antecedent of *which* is *peace*, line 132. Both the syntax and the metaphor have gone astray. Note the figurative representation of *peace*, lines 132-133. 139. **we . . . territories.** Richard shows what Gardiner calls the "unwise cunning of a madman" and takes the one course which would be sure

K. Rich. Norfolk, for thee remains a heavier doom,
Which I with some unwillingness pronounce:
The sly slow hours shall not determinate
The dateless limit of thy dear exile;
The hopeless word of 'never to return'
Breathe I against thee, upon pain of life.
Mow. A heavy sentence, my most sovereign liege,
And all unlook'd for from your highness' mouth:
A dearer merit, not so deep a maim
As to be cast forth in the common air,
Have I deserved at your highness' hands.
The language I have learn'd these forty years,
My native English, now I must forego:
And now my tongue's use is to me no more
Than an unstringed viol or a harp,
Or like a cunning instrument cas'd up,
Or, being open, put into his hands
That knows no touch to tune the harmony:
Within my mouth you have engaol'd my tongue,
Doubly portcullis'd with my teeth and lips;
And dull unfeeling barren ignorance
Is made my gaoler to attend on me.
I am too old to fawn upon a nurse,
Too far in years to be a pupil now:
What is thy sentence then but speechless death,
Which robs my tongue from breathing native breath?
K. Rich. It boots thee not to be compassionate:
After our sentence plaining comes too late.
Mow. Then thus I turn me from my country's light,
To dwell in solemn shades of endless night.
K. Rich. Return again, and take an oath with thee.
Lay on our royal sword your banish'd hands;
Swear by the duty that you owe to God—
Our part therein we banish with yourselves—
To keep the oath that we administer:
You never shall, so help you truth and God!
Embrace each other's love in banishment;
Nor never look upon each other's face;
Nor never write, regreet, nor reconcile
This louring tempest of your home-bred hate;
Nor never by advised purpose meet
To plot, contrive, or complot any ill
'Gainst us, our state, our subjects, or our land.
Boling. I swear.
Mow. And I, to keep all this.
Boling. Norfolk, so far as to mine enemy:—
By this time, had the king permitted us,
One of our souls had wand'red in the air,
Banish'd this frail sepulchre of our flesh,
As now our flesh is banish'd from this land:
Confess thy treasons ere thou fly the realm;
Since thou hast far to go, bear not along
The clogging burthen of a guilty soul.
Mow. No, Bolingbroke: if ever I were traitor,
My name be blotted from the book of life,
And I from heaven banish'd as from hence!
But what thou art, God, thou, and I do know;
And all too soon, I fear, the king shall rue.
Farewell, my liege. Now no way can I stray;
Save back to England, all the world 's my way. *Exit.*
K. Rich. Uncle, even in the glasses of thine eyes
I see thy grieved heart: thy sad aspect
Hath from the number of his banish'd years
Pluck'd four away. [*To Boling.*] Six frozen winters spent,
Return with welcome home from banishment.
Boling. How long a time lies in one little word!
Four lagging winters and four wanton springs
End in a word: such is the breath of kings.
Gaunt. I thank my liege, that in regard of me
He shortens four years of my son's exile:
But little vantage shall I reap thereby;
For, ere the six years that he hath to spend
Can change their moons and bring their times about,
My oil-dried lamp and time-bewasted light
Shall be extinct with age and endless night;
My inch of taper will be burnt and done,
And blindfold death not let me see my son.
K. Rich. Why, uncle, thou hast many years to live.
Gaunt. But not a minute, king, that thou canst give:
Shorten my days thou canst with sullen sorrow,
And pluck nights from me, but not lend a morrow;
Thou canst help time to furrow me with age,
But stop no wrinkle in his pilgrimage;
Thy word is current with him for my death,
But dead, thy kingdom cannot buy my breath.
K. Rich. Thy son is banish'd upon good advice,
Whereto thy tongue a party-verdict gave:
Why at our justice seem'st thou then to lour?
Gaunt. Things sweet to taste prove in digestion sour.
You urg'd me as a judge; but I had rather
You would have bid me argue like a father.
O, had it been a stranger, not my child,
To smooth his fault I should have been more mild:
A partial slander sought I to avoid,
And in the sentence my own life destroy'd.
Alas, I look'd when some of you should say,
I was too strict to make mine own away;
But you gave leave to my unwilling tongue
Against my will to do myself this wrong.
K. Rich. Cousin, farewell; and, uncle, bid him so:
Six years we banish him, and he shall go.
[*Flourish.*] Exit [*King Richard with his train*].
Aum. Cousin, farewell: what presence must not know,
From where you do remain let paper show.
Mar. My lord, no leave take I; for I will ride,
As far as land will let me, by your side.
Gaunt. O, to what purpose dost thou hoard thy words,
That thou returnest no greeting to thy friends?
Boling. I have too few to take my leave of you,
When the tongue's office should be prodigal
To breathe the abundant dolour of the heart.
Gaunt. Thy grief is but thy absence for a time.
Boling. Joy absent, grief is present for that time.

to work injustice to both men. 150. **determinate,** put an end to. 151. **dear,** costly, severe. 174. **boots,** avails. 175. **plaining,** complaining. 202. **book of life.** See Revelation 3:5. 204-205. **But . . . rue.** The historical Richard probably meant to recall Mowbray and make Bolingbroke's exile permanent; but such an intention is not implied in this play. 208. **glasses,** mirrors. 210. **banish'd years,** years of banishment. *Banish'd* is not a past participle, but an adjective. 211. **Pluck'd four away.** According to Holinshed the amelioration of Bolingbroke's sentence took place later, at Eltham, when the king was taking leave of Bolingbroke. 214. **wanton,** luxuriant. 230. **But . . . pilgrimage,** efface no wrinkle that comes with time. 231. **current,** i.e., as good as current coin. 234. **a party-verdict,** one person's share in a joint verdict. 241. **partial slander,** accusation of partiality. Cf. line 210. 244. **too strict to make,** i.e., in making; a gerundive use of the infinitive, common in Shakespeare. 249. **what . . . know,** what I cannot learn from you in person.

Gaunt. What is six winters? they are quickly gone.
Boling. To men in joy; but grief makes one hour ten.
Gaunt. Call it a travel that thou tak'st for pleasure.
Boling. My heart will sigh when I miscall it so,
Which finds it an inforced pilgrimage.
Gaunt. The sullen passage of thy weary steps
Esteem as foil wherein thou art to set
The precious jewel of thy home return.
Boling. Nay, rather, every tedious stride I make
Will but remember me what a deal of world
I wander from the jewels that I love.
Must I not serve a long apprenticehood
To foreign passages, and in the end,
Having my freedom, boast of nothing else
But that I was a journeyman to grief?
Gaunt. All places that the eye of heaven visits
Are to a wise man ports and happy havens.
Teach thy necessity to reason thus;
There is no virtue like necessity.
Think not the king did banish thee,
But thou the king. Woe doth the heavier sit,
Where it perceives it is but faintly borne.
Go, say I sent thee forth to purchase honour
And not the king exil'd thee; or suppose
Devouring pestilence hangs in our air
And thou art flying to a fresher clime:
Look what thy soul holds dear, imagine it
To lie that way thou goest, not whence thou com'st:
Suppose the singing birds musicians,
The grass whereon thou tread'st the presence strew'd,
The flowers fair ladies, and thy steps no more
Than a delightful measure or a dance;
For gnarling sorrow hath less power to bite
The man that mocks at it and sets it light.
Boling. O, who can hold a fire in his hand
By thinking on the frosty Caucasus?
Or cloy the hungry edge of appetite
By bare imagination of a feast?
Or wallow naked in December snow
By thinking on fantastic summer's heat?
O, no! the apprehension of the good
Gives but the greater feeling to the worse:
Fell sorrow's tooth doth never rankle more
Than when he bites, but lanceth not the sore.
Gaunt. Come, come, my son, I'll bring thee on thy way:
Had I thy youth and cause, I would not stay.
Boling. Then, England's ground, farewell; sweet soil, adieu;
My mother, and my nurse, that bears me yet!
Where'er I wander, boast of this I can,
Though banish'd, yet a trueborn Englishman. *Exeunt.*

[SCENE IV. *The court.*]

Enter the KING, *with* BAGOT, [GREEN,] *&c. at one door; and the* LORD AUMERLE *at another.*

K. Rich. We did observe. Cousin Aumerle,
How far brought you high Hereford on his way?
Aum. I brought high Hereford, if you call him so,
But to the next highway, and there I left him.
K. Rich. And say, what store of parting tears were shed?
Aum. Faith, none for me; except the northeast wind,
Which then blew bitterly against our faces,
Awak'd the sleeping rheum, and so by chance
Did grace our hollow parting with a tear.
K. Rich. What said our cousin when you parted with him?
Aum. 'Farewell:'
And, for my heart disdained that my tongue
Should so profane the word, that taught me craft
To counterfeit oppression of such grief
That words seem'd buried in my sorrow's grave.
Marry, would the word 'farewell' have length'ned hours
And added years to his short banishment,
He should have had a volume of farewells;
But since it would not, he had none of me.
K. Rich. He is our cousin, cousin; but 'tis doubt,
When time shall call him home from banishment,
Whether our kinsman come to see his friends.
Ourself and Bushy, Bagot here and Green
Observ'd his courtship to the common people;
How he did seem to dive into their hearts
With humble and familiar courtesy,
What reverence he did throw away on slaves,
Wooing poor craftsmen with the craft of smiles
And patient underbearing of his fortune,
As 'twere to banish their affects with him.
Off goes his bonnet to an oyster-wench;
A brace of draymen bid God speed him well
And had the tribute of his supple knee,
With 'Thanks, my countrymen, my loving friends;'
As were our England in reversion his,
And he our subjects' next degree in hope.
Green. Well, he is gone; and with him go these thoughts.
Now for the rebels which stand out in Ireland,
Expedient manage must be made, my liege,
Ere further leisure yield them further means
For their advantage and your highness' loss.
K. Rich. We will ourself in person to this war:
And, for our coffers, with too great a court
And liberal largess, are grown somewhat light,
We are inforc'd to farm our royal realm;
The revenue whereof shall furnish us
For our affairs in hand: if that come short,
Our substitutes at home shall have blank charters;
Whereto, when they shall know what men are rich,
They shall subscribe them for large sums of gold
And send them after to supply our wants;
For we will make for Ireland presently.

266. **foil,** metal surface used in setting gems to show off their luster; hence, that which sets something off to advantage. 272. **passages,** wanderings, experiences. 274. **journeyman,** laborer hired by the day; at the end of such service would come the settlement in his trade. 289. **presence strew'd,** i.e., the royal presence chamber strewn with rushes. 292. **gnarling,** snarling, growling. 299. **fantastic,** imaginary. 300. **apprehension,** idea, product of mere imagination. 302-303. **Fell . . . sore,** i.e., never poisons more than when it irritates the sore instead of lancing to cure it. 302. **rankle,** cause to fester, i.e., produce irritation by poison.

SCENE IV. 8. **rheum,** tears. 12-13. **for . . . word.** This clause is the antecedent of *that.* Aumerle says he pretended to be overcome by grief in order to avoid saying "Farewell" to Bolingbroke. 23. **Ourself . . . Green:** so Q_5; QF: *Our selfe, and Bushy: heere. Bagot and Greene,* which may be construed by omitting punctuation except comma after *heere.* 24. **his courtship to the common people.** Compare Bolingbroke's own account, *1 Henry IV,* III, ii, 46 ff. 29. **underbearing,** bearing, enduring. 30. **affects,** affections. 35. **reversion,** right of future possession. 37. **go,** let go. 38. **rebels . . . Ireland.** Many of the colonies planted by Henry II in the "English Pale" had thrown off their allegiance and were in rebellion. 39. **Expedient manage,** expeditious management. 43. **too great a court.** Holinshed says that Richard "kept the greatest court, and mainteined the most plentiful house that euer any king in England did either before his time or since." 45. **farm,**

Enter BUSHY.

Bushy, what news?
Bushy. Old John of Gaunt is grievous sick, my lord,
Suddenly taken; and hath sent post haste
To entreat your majesty to visit him.
K. Rich. Where lies he?
Bushy. At Ely House.
K. Rich. Now put it, God, in the physician's mind
To help him to his grave immediately!
The lining of his coffers shall make coats
To deck our soldiers for these Irish wars.
Come, gentlemen, let 's all go visit him:
Pray God we may make haste, and come too late!
[*All.*] Amen. *Exeunt.*

[ACT II.

SCENE I. *Ely House.*]

Enter JOHN OF GAUNT *sick, with the* DUKE OF YORK, *&c.*

Gaunt. Will the king come, that I may breathe my last
In wholesome counsel to his unstaid youth?
York. Vex not yourself, nor strive not with your breath;
For all in vain comes counsel to his ear.
Gaunt. O, but they say the tongues of dying men
Enforce attention like deep harmony:
Where words are scarce, they are seldom spent in vain,
For they breathe truth that breathe their words in pain.
He that no more must say is listened more
Than they whom youth and ease have taught to glose;
More are men's ends mark'd than their lives before:
The setting sun, and music at the close,
As the last taste of sweets, is sweetest last,
Writ in remembrance more than things long past:
Though Richard my life's counsel would not hear,
My death's sad tale may yet undeaf his ear.
York. No; it is stopp'd with other flattering sounds,
As praises, of whose taste the wise are fond,
Lascivious metres, to whose venom sound
The open ear of youth doth always listen;
Report of fashions in proud Italy,
Whose manners still our tardy apish nation
Limps after in base imitation.
Where doth the world thrust forth a vanity—
So it be new, there 's no respect how vile—
That is not quickly buzz'd into his ears?
Then all too late comes counsel to be heard,
Where will doth mutiny with wit's regard.
Direct not him whose way himself will choose:
'Tis breath thou lack'st, and that breath wilt thou lose.
Gaunt. Methinks I am a prophet new inspir'd
And thus expiring do foretell of him:
His rash fierce blaze of riot cannot last,
For violent fires soon burn out themselves;
Small show'rs last long, but sudden storms are short;
He tires betimes that spurs too fast betimes;
With eager feeding food doth choke the feeder:
Light vanity, insatiate cormorant,
Consuming means, soon preys upon itself.
This royal throne of kings, this scept'red isle,
This earth of majesty, this seat of Mars,
This other Eden, demi-paradise,
This fortress built by Nature for herself
Against infection and the hand of war,
This happy breed of men, this little world,
This precious stone set in the silver sea,
Which serves it in the office of a wall
Or as a moat defensive to a house,
Against the envy of less happier lands,
This blessed plot, this earth, this realm, this England,
This nurse, this teeming womb of royal kings,
Fear'd by their breed and famous by their birth,
Renowned for their deeds as far from home,
For Christian service and true chivalry,
As is the sepulchre in stubborn Jewry
Of the world's ransom, blessed Mary's Son,
This land of such dear souls, this dear dear land,
Dear for her reputation through the world,
Is now leas'd out, I die pronouncing it,
Like to a tenement or pelting farm:
England, bound in with the triumphant sea,
Whose rocky shore beats back the envious siege
Of wat'ry Neptune, is now bound in with shame,
With inky blots and rotten parchment bonds:
That England, that was wont to conquer others,
Hath made a shameful conquest of itself.
Ah, would the scandal vanish with my life,
How happy then were my ensuing death!

Enter KING [RICHARD] *and* QUEEN, [AUMERLE, BUSHY, GREEN, BAGOT, ROSS, *and* WILLOUGHBY,] *&c.*

York. The king is come: deal mildly with his youth;
For young hot colts being †rag'd do rage the more.
Queen. How fares our noble uncle, Lancaster?
K. Rich. What comfort, man? how is 't with aged Gaunt?
Gaunt. O, how that name befits my composition!
Old Gaunt indeed, and gaunt in being old:
Within me grief hath kept a tedious fast;
And who abstains from meat that is not gaunt?
For sleeping England long time have I watch'd;
Watching breeds leanness, leanness is all gaunt:
The pleasure that some fathers feed upon,
Is my strict fast; I mean, my children's looks;
And therein fasting, hast thou made me gaunt:

to let the right of collecting taxes, for a present cash payment, to the highest bidder. 48. **blank charters,** ready-drawn obligations, blank spaces being left for the names of the parties and the sums they were to provide. 50. **subscribe them,** make them write their names under. 58. **Ely House,** palace of the bishop of Ely in Holborn. 61. **lining,** contents (with pun on lining for coats).

ACT II. SCENE I. 2. **unstaid,** thoughtless, rash. 9. **listened,** listened to. 10. **glose,** flatter, deceive in speech. 12. **close,** harmonious chords at the end of a piece of music. 16. **undeaf,** make capable of hearing. 19. **venom,** pernicious, poisonous. 21. **proud Italy.** Ascham, Lyly, and other sixteenth-century writers complain of the growing influence of Italian luxury. 22. **still,** always. **tardy apish,** imitative but behind the times. 26. **buzz'd,** whispered; used contemptuously. 28. **with wit's regard,** against the consideration due to reason. 33. **riot,** profligacy. 36. **betimes,** soon, early. 38. **cormorant,** glutton. 40-55. **This . . . Jewry.** These lines, except line 50, were published in *England's Parnassus* (1600) and attributed to M. Dr. (Michael Drayton). 44. **infection,** pollution; possibly, plague. 52. **breed,** ancestral reputation for warlike prowess. 55. **stubborn Jewry,** Judea, called stubborn because it resisted Christianity. 60. **tenement,** land held by a tenant. **pelting,** paltry. 70. **rag'd,** enraged. 73. **composition,** constitution. 77. **watch'd,** stayed awake at night.

Gaunt am I for the grave, gaunt as a grave,
Whose hollow womb inherits nought but bones.
K. Rich. Can sick men play so nicely with their names?
Gaunt. No, misery makes sport to mock itself:
Since thou dost seek to kill my name in me,
I mock my name, great king, to flatter thee.
K. Rich. Should dying men flatter with those that live?
Gaunt. No, no, men living flatter those that die.
K. Rich. Thou, now a-dying, sayest thou flatterest me.
Gaunt. O, no! thou diest, though I the sicker be.
K. Rich. I am in health, I breathe, and see thee ill.
Gaunt. Now He that made me knows I see thee ill;
Ill in myself to see, and in thee seeing ill.
Thy death-bed is no lesser than thy land
Wherein thou liest in reputation sick;
And thou, too careless patient as thou art,
Commit'st thy anointed body to the cure
Of those physicians that first wounded thee:
A thousand flatterers sit within thy crown,
Whose compass is no bigger than thy head;
And yet, incaged in so small a verge,
The waste is no whit lesser than thy land.
O, had thy grandsire with a prophet's eye
Seen how his son's son should destroy his sons,
From forth thy reach he would have laid thy shame,
Deposing thee before thou wert possess'd,
Which art possess'd now to depose thyself.
Why, cousin, wert thou regent of the world,
It were a shame to let this land by lease;
But for thy world enjoying but this land,
Is it not more than shame to shame it so?
Landlord of England art thou now, not king:
Thy state of law is bondslave to the law;
And thou—
K. Rich. A lunatic lean-witted fool,
Presuming on an ague's privilege,
Darest with thy frozen admonition
Make pale our cheek, chasing the royal blood
With fury from his native residence.
Now, by my seat's right royal majesty,
Wert thou not brother to great Edward's son,
This tongue that runs so roundly in thy head
Should run thy head from thy unreverent shoulders.
Gaunt. O, spare me not, my brother Edward's son,
For that I was his father Edward's son;
That blood already, like the pelican,
Hast thou tapp'd out and drunkenly carous'd:
My brother Gloucester, plain well-meaning soul,
Whom fair befal in heaven 'mongst happy souls!
May be a precedent and witness good
That thou respect'st not spilling Edward's blood:
Join with the present sickness that I have;
And thy unkindness be like crooked age,
To crop at once a too long withered flower.
Live in thy shame, but die not shame with thee!
These words hereafter thy tormentors be!
Convey me to my bed, then to my grave:
Love they to live that love and honour have.
Exit [*borne off by his Attendants*].
K. Rich. And let them die that age and sullens have;
For both hast thou, and both become the grave.
York. I do beseech your majesty, impute his words
To wayward sickliness and age in him:
He loves you, on my life, and holds you dear
As Harry Duke of Hereford, were he here.
K. Rich. Right, you say true: as Hereford's love, so his;
As theirs, so mine; and all be as it is.

[*Enter* NORTHUMBERLAND.]

North. My liege, old Gaunt commends him to your majesty.
K. Rich. What says he?
North. Nay, nothing; all is said:
His tongue is now a stringless instrument;
Words, life and all, old Lancaster hath spent.
York. Be York the next that must be bankrout so!
Though death be poor, it ends a mortal woe.
K. Rich. The ripest fruit first falls, and so doth he;
His time is spent, our pilgrimage must be.
So much for that. Now for our Irish wars:
We must supplant those rough rug-headed kerns,
Which live like venom where no venom else
But only they have privilege to live.
And for these great affairs do ask some charge,
Towards our assistance we do seize to us
The plate, coin, revenues and moveables,
Whereof our uncle Gaunt did stand possess'd.
York. How long shall I be patient? ah, how long
Shall tender duty make me suffer wrong?
Not Gloucester's death, nor Hereford's banishment,
Not Gaunt's rebukes, nor England's private wrongs,
Nor the prevention of poor Bolingbroke
About his marriage, nor my own disgrace,
Have ever made me sour my patient cheek,
Or bend one wrinkle on my sovereign's face.
I am the last of noble Edward's sons,
Of whom thy father, Prince of Wales, was first:
In war was never lion rag'd more fierce,
In peace was never gentle lamb more mild,
Than was that young and princely gentleman.
His face thou hast, for even so look'd he,
Accomplish'd with the number of thy hours;
But when he frown'd, it was against the French
And not against his friends; his noble hand
Did win what he did spend and spent not that
Which his triumphant father's hand had won;
His hands were guilty of no kindred blood,
But bloody with the enemies of his kin.
O Richard! York is too far gone with grief,
Or else he never would compare between.

83. **inherits,** possesses. 84. **nicely,** delicately, fantastically. 86. **kill my name in me,** i.e., by banishing my son. 102. **verge,** circle, ring; technically, "the compass about the king's court which extended for twelve miles." 103. **waste,** a legal use meaning "destruction of houses, woods, lands, etc., done by a tenant to the prejudice of the heir" (Onions). 109. **cousin,** any kinsman not of the immediate family. 114. **Thy state . . . law,** i.e., your legal status as king is now subservient to and at the mercy of the law governing contracts, such as blank charters. 118. **Make pale our cheek.** Richard's physical sensitiveness, which caused him to turn pale readily (see III, ii, 75; III, iii, 67), is recorded by Froissart and other chroniclers. 122. **roundly,** unceremoniously; see glossary. 126. **pelican,** allusion to the belief that the pelican fed its young on its own blood; accordingly, the bird was seen as an emblem of Christian sacrifice. 133. **unkindness,** unnaturalness. 139. **sullens,** moroseness, sullenness. 144. **As Harry Duke of Hereford,** i.e., as he holds Harry, etc. Richard purposely misinterprets the ambiguous speech of York. 156. **rug-headed,** rough-haired. **kerns,** Irish foot soldiers. 157. **no venom else,** allusion to the freedom of Ireland from reptiles, traditionally ascribed to St. Patrick. 159. **charge,** expense. 166. **Gaunt's rebukes,** i.e., the rebuke given to Gaunt. 173. **rag'd,** may equal *enraged*, as in line 70, or we may understand a relative pronoun *that* omitted after lion. 177. **Accomplish'd . . . hours,** i.e., when

K. Rich. Why, uncle, what 's the matter?
York. O my liege,
Pardon me, if you please; if not, I, pleas'd
Not to be pardoned, am content withal.
Seek you to seize and gripe into your hands
The royalties and rights of banish'd Hereford?
Is not Gaunt dead, and doth not Hereford live?
Was not Gaunt just, and is not Harry true?
Did not the one deserve to have an heir?
Is not his heir a well-deserving son?
Take Hereford's rights away, and take from Time
His charters and his customary rights;
Let not to-morrow then ensue to-day;
Be not thyself; for how art thou a king
But by fair sequence and succession?
Now, afore God—God forbid I say true!—
If you do wrongfully seize Hereford's rights,
Call in the letters patents that he hath
By his attorneys-general to sue
His livery, and deny his off'red homage,
You pluck a thousand dangers on your head,
You lose a thousand well-disposed hearts
And prick my tender patience to those thoughts
Which honour and allegiance cannot think.
K. Rich. Think what you will, we seize into our hands
His plate, his goods, his money and his lands.
York. I'll not be by the while: my liege, farewell:
What will ensue hereof, there 's none can tell;
But by bad courses may be understood
That their events can never fall out good. *Exit.*
K. Rich. Go, Bushy, to the Earl of Wiltshire straight:
Bid him repair to us to Ely House
To see this business. To-morrow next
We will for Ireland; and 'tis time, I trow:
And we create, in absence of ourself,
Our uncle York lord governor of England;
For he is just and always lov'd us well.
Come on, our queen: to-morrow must we part;
Be merry, for our time of stay is short.
[*Flourish.*] *Exeunt King and Queen. Manet Northumberland* [*with Willoughby and Ross*].
North. Well, lords, the Duke of Lancaster is dead.
Ross. And living too; for now his son is duke.
Willo. Barely in title, not in revenues.
North. Richly in both, if justice had her right.
Ross. My heart is great; but it must break with silence,
Ere 't be disburdened with a liberal tongue.
North. Nay, speak thy mind; and let him ne'er speak more
That speaks thy words again to do thee harm!
Willo. Tends that thou wouldst speak to the Duke of Hereford?
If it be so, out with it boldly, man;
Quick is mine ear to hear of good towards him.
Ross. No good at all that I can do for him;
Unless you call it good to pity him,
Bereft and gelded of his patrimony.
North. Now, afore God, 'tis shame such wrongs are borne
In him, a royal prince, and many moe
Of noble blood in this declining land.
The king is not himself, but basely led
By flatterers; and what they will inform,
Merely in hate, 'gainst any of us all,
That will the king severely prosecute
'Gainst us, our lives, our children, and our heirs.
Ross. The commons hath he pill'd with grievous taxes,
†And quite lost their hearts: the nobles hath he fin'd
For ancient quarrels, and quite lost their hearts.
Willo. And daily new exactions are devis'd,
As blanks, benevolences, and I wot not what:
But what, o' God's name, doth become of this?
North. Wars hath not wasted it, for warr'd he hath not,
But basely yielded upon compromise
That which his noble ancestors achiev'd with blows:
More hath he spent in peace than they in wars.
Ross. The Earl of Wiltshire hath the realm in farm.
Willo. The king 's grown bankrout, like a broken man.
North. Reproach and dissolution hangeth over him.
Ross. He hath not money for these Irish wars,
His burthenous taxations notwithstanding,
But by the robbing of the banish'd duke.
North. His noble kinsman: most degenerate king!
But, lords, we hear this fearful tempest sing,
Yet seek no shelter to avoid the storm;
We see the wind sit sore upon our sails,
And yet we strike not, but securely perish.
Ross. We see the very wrack that we must suffer;
And unavoided is the danger now,
For suffering so the causes of our wrack.
North. Not so; even through the hollow eyes of death
I spy life peering; but I dare not say
How near the tidings of our comfort is.
Willo. Nay, let us share thy thoughts, as thou dost ours.
Ross. Be confident to speak, Northumberland:
We three are but thyself; and, speaking so,
Thy words are but as thoughts; therefore, be bold.
North. Then thus: I have from Le Port Blanc, a bay
In Brittaine receiv'd intelligence
That Harry Duke of Hereford, Rainold Lord Cobham,
†. . . . .
That late broke from the Duke of Exeter,
His brother, Archbishop late of Canterbury,
Sir Thomas Erpingham, Sir John Ramston,
Sir John Norbery, Sir Robert Waterton and Francis Quoint,
All these well furnish'd by the Duke of Brittaine

he was your age. 185. **compare between,** draw comparisons. 190. **royalties,** privileges belonging to a member of the royal house. 197. **ensue,** follow upon. 202. **Call . . . patents.** This occurred some six weeks after Gaunt's death. **letters patents,** letters addressed by a sovereign to the patentee granting him some dignity, office, or privilege. 203. **attorneys-general,** deputies, legal substitutes. 227. **if . . . right.** This conversation marks the beginning of the counterplot. 242. **inform,** charge against (used technically); see glossary. 246. **pill'd,** plundered, robbed. 247. **And . . . fin'd.** This line is defective in meter, and is probably corrupt; Pope omitted *quite*. 250. **blanks,** *cartes blanches*, referred to in I, iv, 48. **wot,** know. 253. **basely yielded,** allusion to Richard's unpopular foreign policy of peace with France. 266. **strike,** furl (of sails) (with pun on striking blows). **securely,** heedlessly, overconfidently. 268. **unavoided,** unavoidable. 280. The break indicated here may be due to an omission of a line by the printer. Holinshed records that "the earle of Arundels sonne, named Thomas, which was kept in the duke of Exeters house, escaped out of the realme . . . and went to his vncle Thomas Arundell late archbishop of Canturburie." Malone supplying this detail from Holinshed inserts here the line, "The son of Richard Earle of Arundel." This puts the text into accord with Holinshed, since it is this Thomas and not Lord Cobham who escaped from the Duke of Exeter.

With eight tall ships, three thousand men of war,
Are making hither with all due expedience
And shortly mean to touch our northern shore:
Perhaps they had ere this, but that they stay
The first departing of the king for Ireland.
If then we shall shake off our slavish yoke,
Imp out our drooping country's broken wing,
Redeem from broking pawn the blemish'd crown,
Wipe off the dust that hides our sceptre's gilt
And make high majesty look like itself,
Away with me in post to Ravenspurgh;
But if you faint, as fearing to do so,
Stay and be secret, and myself will go.

Ross. To horse, to horse! urge doubts to them that fear.

Willo. Hold out my horse, and I will first be there.

Exeunt.

[SCENE II. *Windsor Castle.*]

Enter the QUEEN, BUSHY, [*and*] BAGOT.

Bushy. Madam, your majesty is too much sad:
You promis'd, when you parted with the king,
To lay aside life-harming heaviness
And entertain a cheerful disposition.

Queen. To please the king I did; to please myself
I cannot do it; yet I know no cause
Why I should welcome such a guest as grief,
Save bidding farewell to so sweet a guest
As my sweet Richard: yet again, methinks,
Some unborn sorrow, ripe in fortune's womb,
Is coming towards me, and my inward soul
With nothing trembles: at some thing it grieves,
More than with parting from my lord the king.

Bushy. Each substance of a grief hath twenty shadows,
Which shows like grief itself, but is not so;
For sorrow's eye, glazed with blinding tears,
Divides one thing entire to many objects;
Like perspectives, which rightly gaz'd upon
Show nothing but confusion, ey'd awry
Distinguish form: so your sweet majesty,
Looking awry upon your lord's departure,
Find shapes of grief, more than himself, to wail;
Which, look'd on as it is, is nought but shadows
Of what it is not. Then, thrice-gracious queen,
More than your lord's departure weep not: more 's not seen;
Or if it be, 'tis with false sorrow's eye,
Which for things true weeps things imaginary.

Queen. It may be so; but yet my inward soul
Persuades me it is otherwise: howe'er it be,
I cannot but be sad; so heavy sad
As, though on thinking on no thought I think,
Makes me with heavy nothing faint and shrink.

Bushy. 'Tis nothing but conceit, my gracious lady.

Queen. 'Tis nothing less: conceit is still deriv'd
From some forefather grief; mine is not so,
For nothing hath begot my something grief;
Or something hath the nothing that I grieve:
'Tis in reversion that I do possess;
But what it is, that is not yet known; what
I cannot name; 'tis nameless woe, I wot.

[*Enter* GREEN.]

Green. God save your majesty! and well met, gentlemen:
I hope the king is not yet shipp'd for Ireland.

Queen. Why hopest thou so? 'tis better hope he is;
For his designs crave haste, his haste good hope:
Then wherefore dost thou hope he is not shipp'd?

Green. That he, our hope, might have retir'd his power,
And driven into despair an enemy's hope,
Who strongly hath set footing in this land:
The banish'd Bolingbroke repeals himself,
And with uplifted arms is safe arriv'd
At Ravenspurgh.

Queen. Now God in heaven forbid!

Green. Ah, madam, 'tis too true: and that is worse,
The Lord Northumberland, his son young Henry Percy,
The Lords of Ross, Beaumond, and Willoughby,
With all their powerful friends, are fled to him.

Bushy. Why have you not proclaim'd Northumberland
And all the rest revolted faction traitors?

Green. We have: whereupon the Earl of Worcester
Hath broken his staff, resign'd his stewardship,
And all the household servants fled with him
To Bolingbroke.

Queen. So, Green, thou art the midwife to my woe,
And Bolingbroke my sorrow's dismal heir:
Now hath my soul brought forth her prodigy,
And I, a gasping new-deliver'd mother,
Have woe to woe, sorrow to sorrow join'd.

Bushy. Despair not, madam.

Queen. Who shall hinder me?
I will despair, and be at enmity
With cozening hope: he is a flatterer,
A parasite, a keeper back of death,
Who gently would dissolve the bands of life,
Which false hope lingers in extremity.

[*Enter* YORK.]

Green. Here comes the Duke of York.

Queen. With signs of war about his aged neck:
O, full of careful business are his looks!
Uncle, for God's sake, speak comfortable words.

York. Should I do so, I should belie my thoughts:
Comfort 's in heaven; and we are on the earth,
Where nothing lives but crosses, cares and grief.
Your husband, he is gone to save far off,
Whilst others come to make him lose at home:
Here am I left to underprop his land,
Who, weak with age, cannot support myself:
Now comes the sick hour that his surfeit made;

287. **expedience,** expedition, swiftness. 292. **Imp out,** piece out; a term from falconry meaning to attach new feathers to a disabled wing of a bird. 293. **broking pawn,** the security held by a broker; used scornfully. 294. **gilt,** gold (with pun on *guilt*). 296. **Away . . . Ravenspurgh.** The Earl of Northumberland, head of the powerful family of the Percys, is the leader among the nobles in the rebellion against Richard; see V, i, 55 ff. *Ravenspurgh* was a busy seaport in Yorkshire on the Humber, destroyed since by the sea. 300. **Hold out my horse,** if my horse holds out.

SCENE II. 18. **perspectives,** pictures of figures made to appear distorted or confused except when seen from a special point of view. **rightly,** directly, straight. 20. **Distinguish form,** make the form distinct. 31. **As . . . think,** as though in thinking, I fix my thoughts on nothing. 33. **conceit,** fancy. 34. **'Tis nothing less,** i.e., it is anything but that. 36-38. **For . . . possess.** As in line 12, the queen's play on the antithesis between *something* and *nothing* is confusing. She says: Either *nothing* caused her real grief, or else there is *something* in this unknown subject of her grief. The cause of the grief can only be revealed in the future

Now shall he try his friends that flatter'd him.

[*Enter a* Servingman.]

Serv. My lord, your son was gone before I came.
York. He was? Why, so! go all which way it will!
The nobles they are fled, the commons they are cold,
And will, I fear, revolt on Hereford's side.
Sirrah, get thee to Plashy, to my sister Gloucester;
Bid her send me presently a thousand pound:
Hold, take my ring.
Serv. My lord, I had forgot to tell your lordship,
To-day, as I came by, I called there;
But I shall grieve you to report the rest.
York. What is 't, knave?
Serv. An hour before I came, the duchess died.
York. God for his mercy! what a tide of woes
Comes rushing on this woeful land at once!
I know not what to do: I would to God,
So my untruth had not provok'd him to it,
The king had cut off my head with my brother's.
What, are there no posts dispatch'd for Ireland?
How shall we do for money for these wars?
Come, sister,—cousin, I would say,—pray, pardon me.
Go, fellow, get thee home, provide some carts
And bring away the armour that is there.
[*Exit Servingman.*]
Gentlemen, will you go muster men?
If I know how or which way to order these affairs
Thus disorderly thrust into my hands,
Never believe me. Both are my kinsmen:
Th' one is my sovereign, whom both my oath
And duty bids defend; t' other again
Is my kinsman, whom the king hath wrong'd,
Whom conscience and my kindred bids to right.
Well, somewhat we must do. Come, cousin, I'll
Dispose of you.
Gentlemen, go, muster up your men,
And meet me presently at Berkeley.
I should to Plashy too;
But time will not permit: all is uneven,
And every thing is left at six and seven.
Exeunt Duke [*of York*], *Queen. Manent Bushy,* [*Bagot,*] *Green.*

Bushy. The wind sits fair for news to go to Ireland,
But none returns. For us to levy power
Proportionable to the enemy
Is all unpossible.
Green. Besides, our nearness to the king in love
Is near the hate of those love not the king.
Bagot. And that 's the wavering commons: for their love
Lies in their purses, and whoso empties them
By so much fills their hearts with deadly hate.
Bushy. Wherein the king stands generally condemn'd.
Bagot. If judgement lie in them, then so do we,
Because we ever have been near the king.
Green. Well, I will for refuge straight to Bristol castle:
The Earl of Wiltshire is already there.
Bushy. Thither will I with you; for little office
The hateful commons will perform for us,
Except like curs to tear us all to pieces.
Will you go along with us?
Bagot. No; I will to Ireland to his majesty.
Farewell: if heart's presages be not vain,
We three here part that ne'er shall meet again.
Bushy. That 's as York thrives to beat back Bolingbroke.
Green. Alas, poor duke! the task he undertakes
Is numb'ring sands and drinking oceans dry:
Where one on his side fights, thousands will fly.
Farewell at once, for once, for all, and ever.
Bushy. Well, we may meet again.
Bagot. I fear me, never. [*Exeunt.*]

[SCENE III. *Wilds in Gloucestershire.*]

Enter [BOLINGBROKE, DUKE OF] HEREFORD, [*and*] NORTHUMBERLAND [*with Forces*].

Boling. How far is it, my lord, to Berkeley now?
North. Believe me, noble lord,
I am a stranger here in Gloucestershire:
These high wild hills and rough uneven ways
Draws out our miles, and makes them wearisome;
And yet your fair discourse hath been as sugar,
Making the hard way sweet and delectable.
But I bethink me what a weary way
From Ravenspurgh to Cotshall will be found
In Ross and Willoughby, wanting your company,
Which, I protest, hath very much beguil'd
The tediousness and process of my travel:
But theirs is sweet'ned with the hope to have
The present benefit which I possess;
And hope to joy is little less in joy
Than hope enjoy'd: by this the weary lords
Shall make their way seem short, as mine hath done
By sight of what I have, your noble company.
Boling. Of much less value is my company
Than your good words. But who comes here?

Enter HARRY PERCY.

North. It is my son, young Harry Percy,
Sent from my brother Worcester, whencesoever.
Harry, how fares your uncle?
Percy. I had thought, my lord, to have learn'd his health of you.
North. Why, is he not with the queen?
Percy. No, my good lord; he hath forsook the court,
Broken his staff of office and dispers'd
The household of the king.
North. What was his reason?
He was not so resolv'd when last we spake together.
Percy. Because your lordship was proclaimed traitor.
But he, my lord, is gone to Ravenspurgh,
To offer service to the Duke of Hereford,
And sent me over by Berkeley, to discover

(*in reversion*). 46. **retir'd,** drawn back. 59. **broken his staff,** i.e., in token of the resignation of his office of Lord High Steward. Thomas Percy, Earl of Worcester, brother of the Earl of Northumberland, provokes the rebellion of the Percys in *1* and *2 Henry IV*. 64. **prodigy,** monstrous birth. 69. **cozening,** cheating. 72. **lingers,** causes to linger. 74. **signs of war.** York is in armor. 76. **comfortable,** affording comfort. 86. **your son,** the Duke of Aumerle, who had accompanied Richard to Ireland. 90. **sister,** sister-in-law. 96. **knave,** familiar term in addressing servants (without evil significance). 97. **the duchess died.** The death of the Duchess of Gloucester is anticipated by several months (in order to add to York's consternation). 101. **untruth,** disloyalty. 122. **at six and seven,** at sixes and sevens, in confusion. 125. **Proportionable,** proportionate.

SCENE III. 9. **Cotshall,** Cotswold, hilly district in Gloucestershire. 12. **tediousness and process,** tedious process. 15. **joy,** enjoy. 22. **whencesoever,** from wherever he is.

What power the Duke of York had levied there;
Then with directions to repair to Ravenspurgh.
North. Have you forgot the Duke of Hereford, boy?
Percy. No, my good lord, for that is not forgot
Which ne'er I did remember: to my knowledge,
I never in my life did look on him.
North. Then learn to know him now; this is the duke.
Percy. My gracious lord, I tender you my service,
Such as it is, being tender, raw and young;
Which elder days shall ripen and confirm
To more approved service and desert.
Boling. I thank thee, gentle Percy; and be sure
I count myself in nothing else so happy
As in a soul rememb'ring my good friends;
And, as my fortune ripens with thy love,
It shall be still thy true love's recompense:
My heart this covenant makes, my hand thus seals it.
North. How far is it to Berkeley? and what stir
Keeps good old York there with his men of war?
Percy. There stands the castle, by yon tuft of trees,
Mann'd with three hundred men, as I have heard;
And in it are the Lords of York, Berkeley, and Seymour;
None else of name and noble estimate.

[*Enter* ROSS *and* WILLOUGHBY.]

North. Here come the Lords of Ross and Willoughby,
Bloody with spurring, fiery-red with haste.
Boling. Welcome, my lords. I wot your love pursues
A banish'd traitor: all my treasury
Is yet but unfelt thanks, which more enrich'd
Shall be your love and labour's recompense.
Ross. Your presence makes us rich, most noble lord.
Willo. And far surmounts our labour to attain it.
Boling. Evermore thanks, the exchequer of the poor;
Which, till my infant fortune comes to years,
Stands for my bounty. But who comes here?

[*Enter* BERKELEY.]

North. It is my Lord of Berkeley, as I guess.
Berk. My Lord of Hereford, my message is to you.
Boling. My lord, my answer is—to Lancaster;
And I am come to seek that name in England;
And I must find that title in your tongue,
Before I make reply to aught you say.
Berk. Mistake me not, my lord; 'tis not my meaning
To rase one title of your honour out:
To you, my lord, I come, what lord you will,
From the most gracious regent of this land,
The Duke of York, to know what pricks you on
To take advantage of the absent time
And fright our native peace with self-born arms.

[*Enter* YORK *attended.*]

Boling. I shall not need transport my words by you;
Here comes his grace in person.
My noble uncle! [*Kneels.*]
York. Show me thy humble heart, and not thy knee,
Whose duty is deceivable and false.
Boling. My gracious uncle—
York. Tut, tut!
Grace me no grace, nor uncle me no uncle:
I am no traitor's uncle; and that word 'grace'
In an ungracious mouth is but profane.
Why have those banish'd and forbidden legs
Dar'd once to touch a dust of England's ground?
But then more 'why?' why have they dar'd to march
So many miles upon her peaceful bosom,
Frighting her pale-fac'd villages with war
And ostentation of despised arms?
Com'st thou because the anointed king is hence?
Why, foolish boy, the king is left behind,
And in my loyal bosom lies his power.
Were I but now the lord of such hot youth
As when brave Gaunt, thy father, and myself
Rescued the Black Prince, that young Mars of men,
From forth the ranks of many thousand French,
O, then how quickly should this arm of mine,
Now prisoner to the palsy, chastise thee
And minister correction to thy fault!
Boling. My gracious uncle, let me know my fault:
On what condition stands it and wherein?
York. Even in condition of the worst degree,
In gross rebellion and detested treason:
Thou art a banish'd man, and here art come
Before the expiration of thy time,
In braving arms against thy sovereign.
Boling. As I was banish'd, I was banish'd Hereford;
But as I come, I come for Lancaster.
And, noble uncle, I beseech your grace
Look on my wrongs with an indifferent eye:
You are my father, for methinks in you
I see old Gaunt alive; O, then, my father,
Will you permit that I shall stand condemn'd
A wandering vagabond; my rights and royalties
Pluck'd from my arms perforce and given away
To upstart unthrifts? Wherefore was I born?
If that my cousin king be King of England,
It must be granted I am Duke of Lancaster.
You have a son, Aumerle, my noble cousin;
Had you first died, and he been thus trod down,
He should have found his uncle Gaunt a father,
To rouse his wrongs and chase them to the bay.
I am denied to sue my livery here,
And yet my letters-patents give me leave:
My father's goods are all distrain'd and sold,
And these and all are all amiss employ'd.
What would you have me do? I am a subject,
And I challenge law: attorneys are denied me;
And therefore personally I lay my claim
To my inheritance of free descent.
North. The noble duke hath been too much abus'd.
Ross. It stands your grace upon to do him right.
Willo. Base men by his endowments are made great.

42. **raw and young.** Henry Percy, called "Hotspur," was born in 1364; Prince Hal in 1387. Shakespeare represents them as of the same age. 45-49. **I thank . . . recompense.** Cf. *1 Henry IV*, I, iii, 251 ff., where Hotspur bitterly recalls this speech. 56. **name,** rank, title. 61. **unfelt,** impalpable, not perceived. 70. **Lancaster.** Bolingbroke will enter into no negotiations unless his proper title is given him. 75. **rase,** erase. 79. **the absent time,** the time of the king's absence. 80. **native,** entitled (i.e., to peace) by birth, rightful. **self-born,** indigenous, home-sprung (Clark and Wright); some editors read *self-borne*, i.e., borne for himself, not for the king. 84. **deceivable,** deceptive. 91. **dust,** a particle of dust. 92. **more 'why?'** more questions to ask. 114. **I come for Lancaster,** i.e., in the character of Lancaster. Compare *2 Henry IV*, IV, v, 184-186. 116. **indifferent,** impartial. 122. **unthrifts,** spendthrifts, prodigals. 128. **to the bay,** to the extremity where the hunted animal turns on its pursuers. 129. **sue my livery,** sue for legal delivery of my freehold as heir. 131. **distrain'd,** seized by legal process. 134. **challenge,** claim. 138. **stands . . . upon,** is incumbent upon. 139. **his endowments,** i.e., his properties which they have seized. 154. **ill left,** left with inadequate means. 159. **neuter,** neutral. 164. **Bristow,** Bristol. 165. **Bagot.** He had gone to Ireland, not to Bristol; see II, ii, 141.

York. My lords of England, let me tell you this:
I have had feeling of my cousin's wrongs
And labour'd all I could to do him right;
But in this kind to come, in braving arms,
Be his own carver and cut out his way,
To find out right with wrong, it may not be;
And you that do abet him in this kind
Cherish rebellion and are rebels all.
North. The noble duke hath sworn his coming is
But for his own; and for the right of that
We all have strongly sworn to give him aid;
And let him never see joy that breaks that oath!
York. Well, well, I see the issue of these arms:
I cannot mend it, I must needs confess,
Because my power is weak and all ill left:
But if I could, by Him that gave me life,
I would attach you all and make you stoop
Unto the sovereign mercy of the king;
But since I cannot, be it known to you
I do remain as neuter. So, fare you well;
Unless you please to enter in the castle
And there repose you for this night.
Boling. An offer, uncle, that we will accept:
But we must win your grace to go with us
To Bristow castle, which they say is held
By Bushy, Bagot and their complices,
The caterpillars of the commonwealth,
Which I have sworn to weed and pluck away.
York. It may be I will go with you: but yet I'll pause;
For I am loath to break our country's laws.
Nor friends nor foes, to me welcome you are:
Things past redress are now with me past care. *Exeunt.*

[SCENE IV. *A camp in Wales.*]

Enter EARL OF SALISBURY *and a* Welsh Captain.

Cap. My Lord of Salisbury, we have stay'd ten days,
And hardly kept our countrymen together,
And yet we hear no tidings from the king;
Therefore we will disperse ourselves: farewell.
Sal. Stay yet another day, thou trusty Welshman:
The king reposeth all his confidence in thee.
Cap. 'Tis thought the king is dead; we will not stay.
The bay-trees in our country are all wither'd
And meteors fright the fixed stars of heaven;
The pale-fac'd moon looks bloody on the earth
And lean-look'd prophets whisper fearful change;
Rich men look sad and ruffians dance and leap,
The one in fear to lose what they enjoy,
The other to enjoy by rage and war:
These signs forerun the death or fall of kings.
Farewell: our countrymen are gone and fled,
As well assur'd Richard their king is dead. [*Exit.*]
Sal. Ah, Richard, with the eyes of heavy mind
I see thy glory like a shooting star
Fall to the base earth from the firmament.
Thy sun sets weeping in the lowly west,
Witnessing storms to come, woe and unrest:
Thy friends are fled to wait upon thy foes,
And crossly to thy good all fortune goes. [*Exit.*]

[ACT III.

SCENE I. *Bristol. Before the castle.*]

Enter [BOLINGBROKE,] DUKE OF HEREFORD, YORK, NORTHUMBERLAND, [ROSS, PERCY, WILLOUGHBY, *with*] BUSHY *and* GREEN, *prisoners.*

Boling. Bring forth these men.
Bushy and Green, I will not vex your souls—
Since presently your souls must part your bodies—
With too much urging your pernicious lives,
For 'twere no charity; yet, to wash your blood
From off my hands, here in the view of men
I will unfold some causes of your deaths.
You have misled a prince, a royal king,
A happy gentleman in blood and lineaments,
By you unhappied and disfigured clean:
You have in manner with your sinful hours
Made a divorce betwixt his queen and him,
Broke the possession of a royal bed
And stain'd the beauty of a fair queen's cheeks
With tears drawn from her eyes by your foul wrongs.
Myself, a prince by fortune of my birth,
Near to the king in blood, and near in love
Till you did make him misinterpret me,
Have stoop'd my neck under your injuries,
And sigh'd my English breath in foreign clouds,
Eating the bitter bread of banishment;
Whilst you have fed upon my signories,
Dispark'd my parks and fell'd my forest woods,
From my own windows torn my household coat,
Ras'd out my imprese, leaving me no sign,
Save men's opinions and my living blood,
To show the world I am a gentleman.
This and much more, much more than twice all this,
Condemns you to the death. See them delivered over
To execution and the hand of death.
Bushy. More welcome is the stroke of death to me
Than Bolingbroke to England. Lords, farewell.
Green. My comfort is that heaven will take our souls
And plague injustice with the pains of hell.
Boling. My Lord Northumberland, see them dispatch'd.
[*Exeunt Northumberland and others, with the prisoners.*]
Uncle, you say the queen is at your house;
For God's sake, fairly let her be entreated:
Tell her I send to her my kind commends;
Take special care my greetings be delivered.
York. A gentleman of mine I have dispatch'd
With letters of your love to her at large.
Boling. Thanks, gentle uncle. Come, lords, away,
To fight with Glendower and his complices:

complices, accomplices.

SCENE IV. 8. **bay-trees.** In this yeare . . . old baie trees withered, and afterwards . . . grew greene againe; a strange sight, and supposed to import some vnknowne euent (Holinshed; in second edition, 1587, only). 11. **lean-look'd,** lean-looking. 24. **crossly,** adversely.

ACT III. SCENE I. 3. **presently,** immediately. 4. **urging,** emphasizing as reasons (for your executions). 9. **happy,** fortunate. 10. **unhappied,** made wretched, ruined. **clean,** completely. 12. **Made a divorce.** There is no basis for this charge; but see V, i, 71 ff. It may have been suggested by the situation in Marlowe's *Edward II.* 14. **fair queen's.** Queen Isabella, daughter of Charles VI of France and consort of Richard II, was historically only eleven years old at this time. 22. **signories,** lordships, estates. 23. **Dispark'd,** destroyed the enclosures and thrown the parks open. 24. **my household coat,** coat of arms, frequently emblazoned on stained or painted windows. 25. **Ras'd,** erased. **imprese,** device, emblematic design. 37. **entreated,** treated. 43. **Glendower.** Owen Glendower was not at this time in arms against Bolingbroke; perhaps Bolingbroke thinks he is the Welsh commander (see preceding scene).

Awhile to work, and after holiday. *Exeunt.*

[SCENE II. *The coast of Wales, near Barkloughly castle.*]

[*Drum: flourish and colours.*] *Enter the* KING, AUMERLE, [*the* BISHOP OF] CARLISLE, *&c.* [*with* Soldiers].

K. Rich. Barkloughly castle call they this at hand?
Aum. Yea, my lord. How brooks your grace the air,
After your late tossing on the breaking seas?
K. Rich. Needs must I like it well: I weep for joy
To stand upon my kingdom once again.
Dear earth, I do salute thee with my hand,
Though rebels wound thee with their horses' hoofs:
As a long-parted mother with her child
Plays fondly with her tears and smiles in meeting,
So, weeping, smiling, greet I thee, my earth,
And do thee favours with my royal hands.
Feed not thy sovereign's foe, my gentle earth,
Nor with thy sweets comfort his ravenous sense;
But let thy spiders, that suck up thy venom,
And heavy-gaited toads lie in their way,
Doing annoyance to the treacherous feet
Which with usurping steps do trample thee:
Yield stinging nettles to mine enemies;
And when they from thy bosom pluck a flower,
Guard it, I pray thee, with a lurking adder
Whose double tongue may with a mortal touch
Throw death upon thy sovereign's enemies.
Mock not my senseless conjuration, lords:
This earth shall have a feeling and these stones
Prove armed soldiers, ere her native king
Shall falter under foul rebellion's arms.
Car. Fear not, my lord: that Power that made you king
Hath power to keep you king in spite of all.
The means that heaven yields must be embrac'd,
And not neglected; else, if heaven would,
And we will not, heaven's offer we refuse,
The proffered means of succour and redress.
Aum. He means, my lord, that we are too remiss;
Whilst Bolingbroke, through our security,
Grows strong and great in substance and in power.
K. Rich. Discomfortable cousin! know'st thou not
That when the searching eye of heaven is hid,
Behind the globe, that lights the lower world,
Then thieves and robbers range abroad unseen
In murders and in outrage, boldly here;
But when from under this terrestrial ball
He fires the proud tops of the eastern pines
And darts his light through every guilty hole,
Then murders, treasons and detested sins,
The cloak of night being pluck'd from off their backs,
Stand bare and naked, trembling at themselves?
So when this thief, this traitor, Bolingbroke,
Who all this while hath revell'd in the night
Whilst we were wand'ring with the antipodes,
Shall see us rising in our throne, the east,
His treasons will sit blushing in his face,
Not able to endure the sight of day,
But self-affrighted tremble at his sin.
Not all the water in the rough rude sea
Can wash the balm off from an anointed king;
The breath of worldly men cannot depose
The deputy elected by the Lord:
For every man that Bolingbroke hath press'd
To lift shrewd steel against our golden crown,
God for his Richard hath in heavenly pay
A glorious angel: then, if angels fight,
Weak men must fall, for heaven still guards the right.

Enter SALISBURY.

Welcome, my lord: how far off lies your power?
Sal. Nor near nor farther off, my gracious lord,
Than this weak arm: discomfort guides my tongue
And bids me speak of nothing but despair.
One day too late, I fear me, noble lord,
Hath clouded all thy happy days on earth:
O, call back yesterday, bid time return,
And thou shalt have twelve thousand fighting men!
To-day, to-day, unhappy day, too late,
O'erthrows thy joys, friends, fortune and thy state:
For all the Welshmen, hearing thou wert dead,
Are gone to Bolingbroke, dispers'd and fled.
Aum. Comfort, my liege: why looks your grace so pale?
K. Rich. But now the blood of twenty thousand men
Did triumph in my face, and they are fled;
And, till so much blood thither come again,
Have I not reason to look pale and dead?
All souls that will be safe fly from my side,
For time hath set a blot upon my pride.
Aum. Comfort, my liege; remember who you are.
K. Rich. I had forgot myself: am I not king?
Awake, thou coward majesty! thou sleepest.
Is not the king's name twenty thousand names?
Arm, arm, my name! a puny subject strikes
At thy great glory. Look not to the ground,
Ye favourites of a king: are we not high?
High be our thoughts: I know my uncle York
Hath power enough to serve our turn. But who comes here?

Enter SCROOP.

Scroop. More health and happiness betide my liege
Than can my care-tun'd tongue deliver him!
K. Rich. Mine ear is open and my heart prepar'd:
The worst is worldly loss thou canst unfold.
Say, is my kingdom lost? why, 'twas my care;
And what loss is it to be rid of care?
Strives Bolingbroke to be as great as we?
Greater he shall not be; if he serve God,
We'll serve Him too and be his fellow so:
Revolt our subjects? that we cannot mend;
They break their faith to God as well as us:
Cry woe, destruction, ruin and decay;
The worst is death, and death will have his day.
Scroop. Glad am I that your highness is so arm'd

SCENE II. 1. **Barkloughly,** probably Harlech, a castle in Wales between Caernarvon and Aberystwyth. 2. **brooks,** enjoys. 3. **late,** recent. 21. **double,** forked. **mortal,** deadly. 23. **senseless conjuration.** adjuration of senseless things. 25. **native,** entitled (to the crown) by birth, rightful. 33. **He . . . remiss.** The stern, practical bishop has attempted to bring Richard back to reality; Richard hardly understands; Aumerle interprets in this line. 34. **security,** confidence, heedlessness. 36. **Discomfortable,** uncomforting. 38. **that lights the lower world.** This clause modifies *eye of heaven.* 55. **balm,** consecrated oil used in anointing a king. 58. **press'd,** impressed, forced into the ranks. 64. **near,** nearer. 65. **discomfort,** discouragement. 76. **twenty thousand men.** Holinshed puts Salisbury's force at forty thousand. 76-81. **But . . . pride.** Note that Richard's highly emotional speech is in the form of a sestet. 112. **thin,** thin-haired (Schmidt); possibly, shrunken to thinness. 114. **clap,** thrust. **female,** weak and delicate like a woman, implying their youth. 116. **beadsmen,** almsmen whose duty it was to pray for the king. 117. **double-fatal,** doubly fatal (since the wood of the yew was used for bows and the berry as poison). 118. **manage,** wield. **bills,** weapons used by infantry; a *bill* was a long-handled ax with hook-shaped blade and spearhead. 122. **Bagot.** Bagot's name seems in-

To bear the tidings of calamity.
Like an unseasonable stormy day,
Which makes the silver rivers drown their shores,
As if the world were all dissolv'd to tears,
So high above his limits swells the rage
Of Bolingbroke, covering your fearful land
With hard bright steel and hearts harder than steel.
White-beards have arm'd their thin and hairless scalps
Against thy majesty; boys, with women's voices,
Strive to speak big and clap their female joints
In stiff unwieldy arms against thy crown:
Thy very beadsmen learn to bend their bows
Of double-fatal yew against thy state;
Yea, distaff-women manage rusty bills
Against thy seat: both young and old rebel,
And all goes worse than I have power to tell.
K. Rich. Too well, too well thou tell'st a tale so ill.
Where is the Earl of Wiltshire? where is Bagot?
What is become of Bushy? where is Green?
That they have let the dangerous enemy
Measure our confines with such peaceful steps?
If we prevail, their heads shall pay for it:
I warrant they have made peace with Bolingbroke.
Scroop. Peace have they made with him indeed, my lord.
K. Rich. O villains, vipers, damn'd without redemption!
Dogs, easily won to fawn on any man!
Snakes, in my heart-blood warm'd, that sting my heart!
Three Judases, each one thrice worse than Judas!
Would they make peace? terrible hell make war
Upon their spotted souls for this offence!
Scroop. Sweet love, I see, changing his property,
Turns to the sourest and most deadly hate:
Again uncurse their souls; their peace is made
With heads, and not with hands: those whom you curse
Have felt the worst of death's destroying wound
And lie full low, grav'd in the hollow ground.
Aum. Is Bushy, Green, and the Earl of Wiltshire dead?
Scroop. Ay, all of them at Bristow lost their heads.
Aum. Where is the duke my father with his power?
K. Rich. No matter where; of comfort no man speak:
Let 's talk of graves, of worms and epitaphs;
Make dust our paper and with rainy eyes
Write sorrow on the bosom of the earth,
Let 's choose executors and talk of wills:
And yet not so, for what can we bequeath
Save our deposed bodies to the ground?
Our lands, our lives and all are Bolingbroke's,
And nothing can we call our own but death
And that small model of the barren earth
Which serves as paste and cover to our bones.
For God's sake, let us sit upon the ground
And tell sad stories of the death of kings:
How some have been depos'd; some slain in war;
Some haunted by the ghosts they have depos'd;
Some poisoned by their wives; some sleeping kill'd;
All murdered: for within the hollow crown
That rounds the mortal temples of a king
Keeps Death his court and there the antic sits,
Scoffing his state and grinning at his pomp,
Allowing him a breath, a little scene,
To monarchize, be fear'd and kill with looks,
Infusing him with self and vain conceit,
As if this flesh which walls about our life
Were brass impregnable, and humour'd thus
Comes at the last and with a little pin
Bores through his castle wall, and farewell king!
Cover your heads and mock not flesh and blood
With solemn reverence: throw away respect,
Tradition, form and ceremonious duty,
For you have but mistook me all this while:
†I live with bread like you, feel want,
Taste grief, need friends: subjected thus,
How can you say to me, I am a king?
Car. My lord, wise men ne'er sit and wail their woes,
But presently prevent the ways to wail.
To fear the foe, since fear oppresseth strength,
Gives in your weakness strength unto your foe,
And so your follies fight against yourself.
Fear, and be slain; no worse can come to fight:
And fight and die is death destroying death;
Where fearing dying pays death servile breath.
Aum. My father hath a power; inquire of him,
And learn to make a body of a limb.
K. Rich. Thou chid'st me well: proud Bolingbroke, I come
To change blows with thee for our day of doom.
This ague fit of fear is over-blown;
An easy task it is to win our own.
Say, Scroop, where lies our uncle with his power?
Speak sweetly, man, although thy looks be sour.
Scroop. Men judge by the complexion of the sky
The state and inclination of the day:
So may you by my dull and heavy eye,
My tongue hath but a heavier tale to say.
I play the torturer, by small and small
To lengthen out the worst that must be spoken:
Your uncle York is join'd with Bolingbroke,
And all your northern castles yielded up,
And all your southern gentlemen in arms
Upon his party.
K. Rich. Thou hast said enough.
Beshrew thee, cousin, which didst lead me forth [*To Aumerle.*]
Of that sweet way I was in to despair!
What say you now? what comfort have we now?
By heaven, I'll hate him everlastingly
That bids me be of comfort any more.
Go to Flint castle: there I'll pine away;
A king, woe's slave, shall kingly woe obey.
That power I have, discharge; and let them go
To ear the land that hath some hope to grow,

advertently mentioned here. The king speaks, line 132, of *three Judases;* Aumerle does not ask about Bagot in line 141. 125. **peaceful,** unopposed. 135. **property,** distinctive quality. 153. **model,** may refer to Richard's own mortal body, or to the grave mound. 162. **Death.** Douce called attention to a print in the *Imagines Mortis* of a king sitting on a throne, sword in hand, surrounded by courtiers, with a grinning skeleton arising from his crown. **antic,** grotesque figure. 163. **Scoffing,** scoffing at. 164. **breath,** breathing space, moment. 166. **self and vain conceit,** selfish and vain conceit. 168. **humour'd,** having satisfied his humor or whim (referring to Death); sometimes defined as "humored" or "indulged" (referring to the king). 176. **subjected,** made subject to grief, want, etc. (with pun on "being treated like a subject"). 183-185. **Fear . . . breath.** To die fighting is to triumph over death; to fear death is to become its slave. 189. **change,** exchange. 198. **by small and small,** little by little. 211. **That power . . . discharge,** discharge what army I have. 212. **ear,** plough. (Richard suggests bitterly that his followers pursue Bolingbroke's prospects for hope and growth.) **grow,** produce fruit.

For I have none: let no man speak again
To alter this, for counsel is but vain.

Aum. My liege, one word.

K. Rich. He does me double wrong
That wounds me with the flatteries of his tongue.
Discharge my followers: let them hence away,
From Richard's night to Bolingbroke's fair day.
[*Exeunt.*]

[SCENE III. *Wales. Before Flint castle.*]

Enter [*with drum and colours*] BOLINGBROKE, YORK, NORTHUMBERLAND[, Attendants, *and forces*].

Boling. So that by this intelligence we learn
The Welshmen are dispers'd, and Salisbury
Is gone to meet the king, who lately landed
With some few private friends upon this coast.

North. The news is very fair and good, my lord:
Richard not far from hence hath hid his head.

York. It would beseem the Lord Northumberland
To say 'King Richard:' alack the heavy day
When such a sacred king should hide his head.

North. Your grace mistakes; only to be brief,
Left I his title out.

York. The time hath been,
Would you have been so brief with him, he would
Have been so brief with you, to shorten you,
For taking so the head, your whole head's length.

Boling. Mistake not, uncle, further than you should.

York. Take not, good cousin, further than you should,
Lest you mistake the heavens are over our heads.

Boling. I know it, uncle, and oppose not myself
Against their will. But who comes here?

Enter PERCY.

Welcome, Harry: what, will not this castle yield?

Percy. The castle royally is mann'd, my lord,
Against thy entrance.

Boling. Royally!
Why, it contains no king?

Percy. Yes, my good lord,
It doth contain a king; King Richard lies
Within the limits of yon lime and stone:
And with him are the Lord Aumerle, Lord Salisbury,
Sir Stephen Scroop, besides a clergyman
Of holy reverence; who, I cannot learn.

North. O, belike it is the Bishop of Carlisle.

Boling. Noble lords,
Go to the rude ribs of that ancient castle;
Through brazen trumpet send the breath of parley
Into his ruin'd ears, and thus deliver:
Henry Bolingbroke
On both his knees doth kiss King Richard's hand
And sends allegiance and true faith of heart
To his most royal person, hither come
Even at his feet to lay my arms and power,
Provided that my banishment repeal'd
And lands restor'd again be freely granted:
If not, I'll use the advantage of my power
And lay the summer's dust with show'rs of blood
Rain'd from the wounds of slaughtered Englishmen:
The which, how far off from the mind of Bolingbroke
It is, such crimson tempest should bedrench
The fresh green lap of fair King Richard's land,
My stooping duty tenderly shall show.
Go, signify as much, while here we march
Upon the grassy carpet of this plain.
Let 's march without the noise of threat'ning drum,
That from this castle's tattered battlements
Our fair appointments may be well perus'd.
Methinks King Richard and myself should meet
With no less terror than the elements
Of fire and water, when their thund'ring shock
At meeting tears the cloudy cheeks of heaven.
Be he the fire, I'll be the yielding water:
The rage be his, whilst on the earth I rain
My waters; on the earth, and not on him.
March on, and mark King Richard how he looks.

The trumpets sound [*a parle without and within, then a flourish.* KING] RICHARD *appeareth on the walls* [*with the* BISHOP OF CARLISLE, AUMERLE, SCROOP, *and* SALISBURY].

See, see, King Richard doth himself appear,
As doth the blushing discontented sun
From out the fiery portal of the east,
When he perceives the envious clouds are bent
To dim his glory and to stain the track
Of his bright passage to the occident.

York. Yet looks he like a king: behold, his eye,
As bright as is the eagle's, lightens forth
Controlling majesty: alack, alack, for woe,
That any harm should stain so fair a show!

K. Rich. We are amaz'd; and thus long have we stood
To watch the fearful bending of thy knee, [*To North.*]
Because we thought ourself thy lawful king:
And if we be, how dare thy joints forget
To pay their awful duty to our presence?
If we be not, show us the hand of God
That hath dismiss'd us from our stewardship;
For well we know, no hand of blood and bone
Can gripe the sacred handle of our sceptre,
Unless he do profane, steal, or usurp.
And though you think that all, as you have done,
Have torn their souls by turning them from us,
And we are barren and bereft of friends;
Yet know, my master, God omnipotent,
Is mustering in his clouds on our behalf
Armies of pestilence; and they shall strike
Your children yet unborn and unbegot,
That lift your vassal hands against my head
And threat the glory of my precious crown.
Tell Bolingbroke—for yon methinks he stands—
That every stride he makes upon my land
Is dangerous treason: he is come to open
The purple testament of bleeding war;

SCENE III. 6. **Richard . . . head.** The plot here diverges from Holinshed. Richard fled to Conway Castle, where he found Salisbury. To this place, then, Bolingbroke dispatched Northumberland, who induced Richard to a conference, assuring him that Bolingbroke came merely to demand his rights and advising that a parliament should be called to restore order to the kingdom. On their riding forth from Conway, Northumberland led Richard into an ambush, by which means Richard was taken to Flint Castle as a prisoner. Later he was taken to Chester and to London. The divergence in plot may be accounted for by a marginal note in Holinshed which reads: "K. Richard stealeth awaie from his armie, and taketh the castell of Flint." 62-67. **See . . . occident,** assigned by Dyce to Percy, by Warburton and Hanmer to York; but Bolingbroke is everywhere sensitive to Richard's personal charm. See IV, i, 304; V, vi, 40. 69. **lightens forth,** flashes out, like lightning. 76. **awful,** reverential. 81. **profane,** commit sacrilege. 83. **torn their souls,** injured their souls by treason to the king. 93-94. **open The purple testament,** begin to carry out a bequest of blood to England. Blood was often said to be purple. 97. **flower of England's face,** the

But ere the crown he looks for live in peace,
Ten thousand bloody crowns of mothers' sons
Shall ill become the flower of England's face,
Change the complexion of her maid-pale peace
To scarlet indignation and bedew
Her pastures' grass with faithful English blood.
North. The king of heaven forbid our lord the king
Should so with civil and uncivil arms
Be rush'd upon! Thy thrice noble cousin
Harry Bolingbroke doth humbly kiss thy hand;
And by the honourable tomb he swears,
That stands upon your royal grandsire's bones,
And by the royalties of both your bloods,
Currents that spring from one most gracious head,
And by the buried hand of warlike Gaunt,
And by the worth and honour of himself,
Comprising all that may be sworn or said,
His coming hither hath no further scope
Than for his lineal royalties and to beg
Enfranchisement immediate on his knees:
Which on thy royal party granted once,
His glittering arms he will commend to rust,
His barbed steeds to stables, and his heart
To faithful service of your majesty.
This swears he, as he is a prince, is just;
And, as I am a gentleman, I credit him.
K. Rich. Northumberland, say thus the king returns:
His noble cousin is right welcome hither;
And all the number of his fair demands
Shall be accomplish'd without contradiction:
With all the gracious utterance thou hast
Speak to his gentle hearing kind commends.
We do debase ourselves, cousin, do we not, [*To Aumerle.*]
To look so poorly and to speak so fair?
Shall we call back Northumberland, and send
Defiance to the traitor, and so die?
Aum. No, good my lord; let 's fight with gentle words
Till time lend friends and friends their helpful swords.
K. Rich. O God, O God! that e'er this tongue of mine,
That laid the sentence of dread banishment
On yon proud man, should take it off again
With words of sooth! O that I were as great
As is my grief, or lesser than my name!
Or that I could forget what I have been,
Or not remember what I must be now!
Swell'st thou, proud heart? I'll give thee scope to beat,
Since foes have scope to beat both thee and me.
Aum. Northumberland comes back from Bolingbroke.
K. Rich. What must the king do now? must he submit?
The king shall do it: must he be depos'd?
The king shall be contented: must he lose
The name of king? a God's name, let it go:
I'll give my jewels for a set of beads,
My gorgeous palace for a hermitage,
My gay apparel for an almsman's gown,
My figur'd goblets for a dish of wood,
My sceptre for a palmer's walking-staff,
My subjects for a pair of carved saints
And my large kingdom for a little grave,
A little little grave, an obscure grave;
Or I'll be buried in the king's highway,
Some way of common trade, where subjects' feet
May hourly trample on their sovereign's head;
For on my heart they tread now whilst I live;
And buried once, why not upon my head?
Aumerle, thou weep'st, my tender-hearted cousin!
We'll make foul weather with despised tears;
Our sighs and they shall lodge the summer corn,
And make a dearth in this revolting land.
Or shall we play the wantons with our woes,
And make some pretty match with shedding tears?
As thus, to drop them still upon one place,
Till they have fretted us a pair of graves
Within the earth; and, therein laid,—there lies
Two kinsmen digg'd their graves with weeping eyes.
Would not this ill do well? Well, well, I see
I talk but idly, and you laugh at me.
Most mighty prince, my Lord Northumberland,
What says King Bolingbroke? will his majesty
Give Richard leave to live till Richard die?
You make a leg, and Bolingbroke says ay.
North. My lord, in the base court he doth attend
To speak with you; may it please you to come down.
K. Rich. Down, down I come; like glist'ring Phaethon,
Wanting the manage of unruly jades.
In the base court? Base court, where kings grow base,
To come at traitors' calls and do them grace.
In the base court? Come down? Down, court! down, king!
For night-owls shriek where mounting larks should sing. [*Exeunt from above.*]
Boling. What says his majesty?
North. Sorrow and grief of heart
Makes him speak fondly, like a frantic man:
Yet he is come.

[*Enter* King Richard *and his attendants below.*]

Boling. Stand all apart,
And show fair duty to his majesty. *He kneels down.*
My gracious lord,—
K. Rich. Fair cousin, you debase your princely knee
To make the base earth proud with kissing it:
Me rather had my heart might feel your love
Than my unpleas'd eye see your courtesy.
Up, cousin, up; your heart is up, I know,
Thus high at least, although your knee be low.
Boling. My gracious lord, I come but for mine own.
K. Rich. Your own is yours, and I am yours, and all.
Boling. So far be mine, my most redoubted lord,
As my true service shall deserve your love.
K. Rich. Well you deserve: they well deserve to have,

blooming face of England. Cf. Daniel, *Civil Wars*, I, 118: "Th' vngodly bloodshed that . . . did marre the flowre of thy chiefe pride . . ." The abundance of Richard's metaphors is startling. Blood, which disfigures war and also the heads of ten thousand Englishmen, stains purple the will or testament, makes the face of England scarlet with indignation, and bedews the grass of the pastures. 102. **civil,** used in civil strife. **uncivil,** barbarous, violent. 114. **Enfranchisement,** recall from banishment and restoration to his rights. 116. **commend,** give over. 117. **barbed,** armed. 121. **returns,** answers. 136. **sooth,** cajolery, flattery.

162. **lodge,** beat down. 167. **fretted,** eaten away, worn. 175. **make a leg,** assent by making an obeisance or curtsy. 176. **base court,** outer or lower court of a castle. 178. **glist'ring,** glistening. **Phaethon,** son of the sun-god Helios, who, unable to control the horses of the sun, was hurled from the chariot by Jupiter. 179. **Wanting,** lacking. **jades,** worthless horses. 192. **Me rather had,** a construction resulting from a combination of "me were liefer" and "I had rather." 195. **Thus high.** Richard touches his crown here.

That know the strong'st and surest way to get.
Uncle, give me your hands: nay, dry your eyes;
Tears show their love, but want their remedies.
Cousin, I am too young to be your father,
Though you are old enough to be my heir.
What you will have, I'll give, and willing too;
For do we must what force will have us do.
Set on towards London, cousin, is it so?
Boling. Yea, my good lord.
K. Rich. Then I must not say no.
[*Flourish. Exeunt.*]

[SCENE IV. *Langley. The* DUKE OF YORK'S *garden.*]

Enter the QUEEN *with* [*two* Ladies,] *her Attendants.*

Queen. What sport shall we devise here in this garden,
To drive away the heavy thought of care?
Lady. Madam, we'll play at bowls.
Queen. 'Twill make me think the world is full of rubs,
And that my fortune runs against the bias.
Lady. Madam, we'll dance.
Queen. My legs can keep no measure in delight,
When my poor heart no measure keeps in grief:
Therefore, no dancing, girl; some other sport.
Lady. Madam, we'll tell tales.
Queen. Of sorrow or of joy?
Lady. Of either, madam.
Queen. Of neither, girl:
For if of joy, being altogether wanting,
It doth remember me the more of sorrow;
Or if of grief, being altogether had,
It adds more sorrow to my want of joy:
For what I have I need not to repeat;
And what I want it boots not to complain.
Lady. Madam, I'll sing.
Queen. 'Tis well that thou hast cause;
But thou shouldst please me better, wouldst thou weep.
Lady. I could weep, madam, would it do you good.
Queen. And I could sing, would weeping do me good,
And never borrow any tear of thee.

Enter Gardeners [*a Master and two Men*].

But stay, here come the gardeners:
Let 's step into the shadow of these trees.
My wretchedness unto a row of pins,
They will talk of state; for every one doth so
Against a change; woe is forerun with woe.
[*Queen and Ladies retire.*]
Gard. Go, bind thou up yon dangling apricocks,
Which, like unruly children, make their sire
Stoop with oppression of their prodigal weight:
Give some supportance to the bending twigs.
Go thou, and like an executioner,
Cut off the heads of too fast growing sprays
That look too lofty in our commonwealth:
All must be even in our government.
You thus employ'd, I will go root away
The noisome weeds, which without profit suck
The soil's fertility from wholesome flowers.
Man. Why should we in the compass of a pale
Keep law and form and due proportion,
Showing, as in a model, our firm estate,
When our sea-walled garden, the whole land,
Is full of weeds, her fairest flowers chok'd up,
Her fruit-trees all unprun'd, her hedges ruin'd,
Her knots disordered and her wholesome herbs
Swarming with caterpillars?
Gard. Hold thy peace:
He that hath suffered this disordered spring
Hath now himself met with the fall of leaf:
The weeds which his broad-spreading leaves did shelter,
That seem'd in eating him to hold him up,
Are pluck'd up root and all by Bolingbroke,
I mean the Earl of Wiltshire, Bushy, Green.
Man. What, are they dead?
Gard. They are; and Bolingbroke
Hath seiz'd the wasteful king. O, what pity is it
That he had not so trimm'd and dress'd his land
As we this garden! We at time of year
Do wound the bark, the skin of our fruit-trees,
Lest, being over-proud in sap and blood,
With too much riches it confound itself:
Had he done so to great and growing men,
They might have liv'd to bear and he to taste
Their fruits of duty: superfluous branches
We lop away, that bearing boughs may live:
Had he done so, himself had borne the crown,
Which waste of idle hours hath quite thrown down.
Man. What, think you the king shall be depos'd?
Gard. Depress'd he is already, and depos'd
'Tis doubt he will be: letters came last night
To a dear friend of the good Duke of York's,
That tell black tidings.
Queen. O, I am press'd to death through want of speaking! [*Coming forward.*]
Thou, old Adam's likeness, set to dress this garden,
How dares thy harsh rude tongue sound this unpleasing news?
What Eve, what serpent, hath suggested thee
To make a second fall of cursed man?
Why dost thou say King Richard is depos'd?
Dar'st thou, thou little better thing than earth,
Divine his downfall? Say, where, when, and how,
Cam'st thou by this ill tidings? speak, thou wretch.
Gard. Pardon me, madam: little joy have I
To breathe this news; yet what I say is true.
King Richard, he is in the mighty hold
Of Bolingbroke: their fortunes both are weigh'd:
In your lord's scale is nothing but himself,
And some few vanities that make him light;
But in the balance of great Bolingbroke,
Besides himself, are all the English peers,
And with that odds he weighs King Richard down.
Post you to London, and you will find it so;
I speak no more than every one doth know.
Queen. Nimble mischance, that art so light of foot,
Doth not thy embassage belong to me,

203. **Tears . . . remedies,** tears show love, but offer no remedies. 204. **too . . . father.** Bolingbroke was born in 1367, and Richard a few months later in 1368.

SCENE IV. 13. **wanting,** lacking. 14. **remember,** remind. 18. **boots,** avails. 28. **Against,** anticipating. 29. **apricocks,** apricots. 40. **pale,** enclosure. 46. **knots,** laid-out garden plots. 69. **doubt,** feared likely. 72. **press'd to death,** allusion to the *peine forte et dure,* inflicted by pressure of heavy weights upon the chests of indicted persons who refused to plead. 75. **suggested,** tempted. 79. **Divine,** foretell prophetically. 93. **embassage,** message. 105. **rue,** "herb of grace," a plant symbolical of repentance, ruth, or sorrow for another's misery.

ACT IV. SCENE I. *Stage Direction:* ***Westminster Hall.*** It had just been rebuilt by King Richard's orders. 5. **timeless,** untimely; also, eternal. 10. **dead time,** past time (?) night time (?). 14. **that very**

And am I last that knows it? O, thou thinkest
To serve me last, that I may longest keep
Thy sorrow in my breast. Come, ladies, go,
To meet at London London's king in woe.
What, was I born to this, that my sad look
Should grace the triumph of great Bolingbroke?
Gard'ner, for telling me these news of woe,
Pray God the plants thou graft'st may never grow.
Exit [*with Ladies*].

Gard. Poor queen! so that thy state might be no worse,
I would my skill were subject to thy curse.
Here did she fall a tear; here in this place
I'll set a bank of rue, sour herb of grace:
Rue, even for ruth, here shortly shall be seen,
In the remembrance of a weeping queen. *Exeunt*.

[ACT IV.

SCENE I. *Westminster Hall*.]

Enter BOLINGBROKE *with the Lords* [AUMERLE, NORTHUMBERLAND, PERCY, FITZWATER, SURREY, *the* BISHOP OF CARLISLE, *the* ABBOT OF WESTMINSTER, *and another* Lord, Herald, Officers] *to Parliament*.

Boling. Call forth Bagot.

Enter [Officers *with*] BAGOT.

Now, Bagot, freely speak thy mind;
What thou dost know of noble Gloucester's death,
Who wrought it with the king, and who perform'd
The bloody office of his timeless end.
Bagot. Then set before my face the Lord Aumerle.
Boling. Cousin, stand forth, and look upon that man.
Bagot. My Lord Aumerle, I know your daring tongue
Scorns to unsay what once it hath deliver'd.
In that dead time when Gloucester's death was plotted,
I heard you say, 'Is not my arm of length,
That reacheth from the restful English court
As far as Calais, to mine uncle's head?'
Amongst much other talk, that very time,
I heard you say that you had rather refuse
The offer of an hundred thousand crowns
Than Bolingbroke's return to England;
Adding withal, how blest this land would be
In this your cousin's death.
Aum. Princes and noble lords,
What answer shall I make to this base man?
Shall I so much dishonour my fair stars,
On equal terms to give him chastisement?
Either I must, or have mine honour soil'd
With the attainder of his slanderous lips.
There is my gage, the manual seal of death,
That marks thee out for hell: I say, thou liest,
And will maintain what thou hast said is false
In thy heart-blood, though being all too base
To stain the temper of my knightly sword.
Boling. Bagot, forbear; thou shalt not take it up.
Aum. Excepting one, I would he were the best
In all this presence that hath mov'd me so.
Fitz. If that thy valour stand on sympathy,
There is my gage, Aumerle, in gage to thine:
By that fair sun which shows me where thou stand'st,
I heard thee say, and vauntingly thou spak'st it,
That thou wert cause of noble Gloucester's death.
If thou deniest it twenty times, thou liest;
And I will turn thy falsehood to thy heart,
Where it was forged, with my rapier's point.
Aum. Thou dar'st not, coward, live to see that day.
Fitz. Now, by my soul, I would it were this hour.
Aum. Fitzwater, thou art damn'd to hell for this.
Percy. Aumerle, thou liest; his honour is as true
In this appeal as thou art all unjust;
And that thou art so, there I throw my gage,
To prove it on thee to the extremest point
Of mortal breathing: seize it, if thou dar'st.
Aum. An if I do not, may my hands rot off
And never brandish more revengeful steel
Over the glittering helmet of my foe!
Another Lord. I task the earth to the like, forsworn Aumerle;
And spur thee on with full as many lies
As may be holloa'd in thy treacherous ear
From sun to sun: there is my honour's pawn;
Engage it to the trial, if thou darest.
Aum. Who sets me else? by heaven, I'll throw at all:
I have a thousand spirits in one breast,
To answer twenty thousand such as you.
Surrey. My Lord Fitzwater, I do remember well
The very time Aumerle and you did talk.
Fitz. 'Tis very true: you were in presence then;
And you can witness with me this is true.
Surrey. As false, by heaven, as heaven itself is true.
Fitz. Surrey, thou liest.
Surrey. Dishonourable boy!
That lie shall lie so heavy on my sword,
That it shall render vengeance and revenge
Till thou the lie-giver and that lie do lie
In earth as quiet as thy father's skull:
In proof whereof, there is my honour's pawn;
Engage it to the trial, if thou dar'st.
Fitz. How fondly dost thou spur a forward horse!
If I dare eat, or drink, or breathe, or live,
I dare meet Surrey in a wilderness,
And spit upon him, whilst I say he lies,
And lies, and lies: there is my bond of faith,
To tie thee to my strong correction.
As I intend to thrive in this new world,
Aumerle is guilty of my true appeal:
Besides, I heard the banish'd Norfolk say
That thou, Aumerle, didst send two of thy men
To execute the noble duke at Calais.
Aum. Some honest Christian trust me with a gage,
That Norfolk lies: here do I throw down this,
If he may be repeal'd, to try his honour.
Boling. These differences shall all rest under gage
Till Norfolk be repeal'd: repeal'd he shall be,
And, though mine enemy, restor'd again
To all his lands and signories: when he is return'd,

time. An inconsistency; Gloucester's death occurred before Bolingbroke left England. 21. **stars,** i.e., his sphere or fortune. 24. **attainder,** dishonoring accusation. 25. **manual seal of death,** death warrant. 33. **sympathy,** correspondence, or equality, of blood or rank. 52. **task the earth,** charge the earth with the task of bearing my gage. 53. **full as many lies,** giving the lie as many times. 56. **Engage,** take up (a pledge). 57. **sets,** challenges to a game (properly, by laying down stakes). 60. ***Surrey,*** Richard's nephew, who with Aumerle represents the Yorkist faction. 67. **vengeance and revenge,** possibly tautological, meaning "furious revenge." 72. **fondly,** foolishly. 80. **Besides, I heard,** etc. John Hall, a groom of Mowbray's at Calais, confessed on October 18, 1399, that he and two servants murdered Gloucester. They were sent, Mowbray told him, by Aumerle. 85. **repeal'd,** recalled from exile.

Against Aumerle we will enforce his trial.
Car. That honourable day shall ne'er be seen.
Many a time hath banish'd Norfolk fought
For Jesu Christ in glorious Christian field,
Streaming the ensign of the Christian cross
Against black pagans, Turks, and Saracens;
And toil'd with works of war, retir'd himself
To Italy; and there at Venice gave
His body to that pleasant country's earth,
And his pure soul unto his captain Christ,
Under whose colours he had fought so long.
Boling. Why, bishop, is Norfolk dead?
Car. As surely as I live, my lord.
Boling. Sweet peace conduct his sweet soul to the bosom
Of good old Abraham! Lords appellants,
Your differences shall all rest under gage
Till we assign you to your days of trial.

Enter York [*attended*].

York. Great Duke of Lancaster, I come to thee
From plume-pluck'd Richard; who with willing soul
Adopts thee heir, and his high sceptre yields
To the possession of thy royal hand:
Ascend his throne, descending now from him;
And long live Henry, fourth of that name!
Boling. In God's name, I'll ascend the regal throne.
Car. Marry, God forbid!
Worst in this royal presence may I speak,
Yet best beseeming me to speak the truth.
Would God that any in this noble presence
Were enough noble to be upright judge
Of noble Richard! then true noblesse would
Learn him forbearance from so foul a wrong.
What subject can give sentence on his king?
And who sits here that is not Richard's subject?
Thieves are not judg'd but they are by to hear,
Although apparent guilt be seen in them;
And shall the figure of God's majesty,
His captain, steward, deputy-elect,
Anointed, crowned, planted many years,
Be judg'd by subject and inferior breath,
And he himself not present? O, forfend it, God,
That in a Christian climate souls refin'd
Should show so heinous, black, obscene a deed!
I speak to subjects, and a subject speaks,
Stirr'd up by God, thus boldly for his king.
My Lord of Hereford here, whom you call king,
Is a foul traitor to proud Hereford's king:
And if you crown him, let me prophesy:
The blood of English shall manure the ground,
And future ages groan for this foul act;
Peace shall go sleep with Turks and infidels,
And in this seat of peace tumultuous wars
Shall kin with kin and kind with kind confound;
Disorder, horror, fear and mutiny
Shall here inhabit, and this land be call'd
The field of Golgotha and dead men's skulls.
O, if you raise this house against this house,
It will the woefullest division prove
That ever fell upon this cursed earth.
Prevent it, resist it, let it not be so,
Lest child, child's children, cry against you 'woe!'
North. Well have you argued, sir; and, for your pains,
Of capital treason we arrest you here.
My Lord of Westminster, be it your charge
To keep him safely till his day of trial.
May it please you, lords, to grant the commons' suit.
Boling. Fetch hither Richard, that in common view
He may surrender; so we shall proceed
Without suspicion.
York. I will be his conduct. *Exit.*
Boling. Lords, you that here are under our arrest,
Procure your sureties for your days of answer.
Little are we beholding to your love,
And little look'd for at your helping hands.

Enter Richard *and* York [*with* Officers *bearing the regalia*].

K. Rich. Alack, why am I sent for to a king,
Before I have shook off the regal thoughts
Wherewith I reign'd? I hardly yet have learn'd
To insinuate, flatter, bow, and bend my limbs:
Give sorrow leave awhile to tutor me
To this submission. Yet I well remember
The favours of these men: were they not mine?
Did they not sometime cry, 'all hail!' to me?
So Judas did to Christ: but he, in twelve,
Found truth in all but one; I, in twelve thousand, none.
God save the king! Will no man say amen?
Am I both priest and clerk? well then, amen.
God save the king! although I be not he;
And yet, amen, if heaven do think him me.
To do what service am I sent for hither?
York. To do that office of thine own good will
Which tired majesty did make thee offer,
The resignation of thy state and crown
To Henry Bolingbroke.
K. Rich. Give me the crown. Here, cousin, seize the crown;
Here, cousin;
On this side my hand, and on that side yours.
Now is this golden crown like a deep well
That owes two buckets, filling one another,
The emptier ever dancing in the air,
The other down, unseen and full of water:
That bucket down and full of tears am I,
Drinking my griefs, whilst you mount up on high.
Boling. I thought you had been willing to resign.
K. Rich. My crown I am; but still my griefs are mine:

91-100. **That . . . long.** This year (1399) Thomas Mowbraie, Duke of Norffolke, died in exile at Venice (Holinshed). Norffolk . . . died at Venice in his return from Jerusalem (Stow, *Annals*). 94. **Streaming,** flying. 96. **toil'd,** wearied. 104. **good old Abraham.** See Luke 16:22. **Lords appellants,** lords who appear as formal accusers. 108. **plume-pluck'd,** humbled. 113. **In . . . throne.** Shakespeare gives no ground for Henry's claim; in Holinshed he claims the throne as descended from Henry III according to a false tradition that his ancestor, Edward Crouchback, was older than his brother Edward I, but was set aside on account of physical deformity. 114. **Marry, God forbid,** etc. Carlisle's speech, according to Holinshed, from whom it is largely taken, was made on October 22, three weeks before the deposition. 115. **Worst,** least in rank. 119. **noblesse,** noble birth, nobleness. 120. **Learn,** teach. 123. **but,** unless. 124. **apparent,** manifest. 125. **figure,** image. 129. **forfend,** forbid. 131. **obscene,** odious, repulsive. 141. **kin,** relationship (of family). **kind,** relationship (of race and nation). 144. **Golgotha,** "the place of a skull," Calvary. See Mark 15:22. 145. **house . . . house.** See Mark 3:25. 152. **My . . . charge.** Carlisle was committed to the Abbey of St. Albans and some months later transferred to the Abbey of Westminster. 154-318. Omitted from Q_{1-2}. That they belonged originally to the play is clear from line 321. 154. **commons' suit,** i.e., request that the charges against Richard be publicly aired. 156-

You may my glories and my state depose,
But not my griefs; still am I king of those.
Boling. Part of your cares you give me with your crown.
K. Rich. Your cares set up do not pluck my cares down.
My care is loss of care, by old care done;
Your care is gain of care, by new care won:
The cares I give I have, though given away;
They tend the crown, yet still with me they stay.
Boling. Are you contented to resign the crown?
K. Rich. Ay, no; no, ay; for I must nothing be;
Therefore no no, for I resign to thee.
Now mark me, how I will undo myself:
I give this heavy weight from off my head
And this unwieldy sceptre from my hand,
The pride of kingly sway from out my heart;
With mine own tears I wash away my balm,
With mine own hands I give away my crown,
With mine own tongue deny my sacred state,
With mine own breath release all duteous oaths:
All pomp and majesty I do forswear;
My manors, rents, revenues I forego;
My acts, decrees, and statutes I deny:
God pardon all oaths that are broke to me!
God keep all vows unbroke are made to thee!
Make me, that nothing have, with nothing griev'd,
And thou with all pleas'd, that hast all achiev'd!
Long mayst thou live in Richard's seat to sit,
And soon lie Richard in an earthy pit!
God save King Henry, unking'd Richard says,
And send him many years of sunshine days!
What more remains?
North. No more, but that you read
These accusations and these grievous crimes
Committed by your person and your followers
Against the state and profit of this land;
That, by confessing them, the souls of men
May deem that you are worthily depos'd.
K. Rich. Must I do so? and must I ravel out
My weav'd-up folly? Gentle Northumberland,
If thy offences were upon record,
Would it not shame thee in so fair a troop
To read a lecture of them? If thou wouldst,
There shouldst thou find one heinous article,
Containing the deposing of a king
And cracking the strong warrant of an oath,
Mark'd with a blot, damn'd in the book of heaven:
Nay, all of you that stand and look upon,
Whilst that my wretchedness doth bait myself,
Though some of you with Pilate wash your hands
Showing an outward pity; yet you Pilates
Have here deliver'd me to my sour cross,
And water cannot wash away your sin.
North. My lord, dispatch; read o'er these articles.
K. Rich. Mine eyes are full of tears, I cannot see:
And yet salt water blinds them not so much
But they can see a sort of traitors here.
Nay, if I turn mine eyes upon myself,
I find myself a traitor with the rest;
For I have given here my soul's consent
To undeck the pompous body of a king;
Made glory base and sovereignty a slave,
Proud majesty a subject, state a peasant.
North. My lord,—
K. Rich. No lord of thine, thou haught insulting man,
Nor no man's lord; I have no name, no title,
No, not that name was given me at the font,
But 'tis usurp'd: alack the heavy day,
That I have worn so many winters out,
And know not now what name to call myself!
O that I were a mockery king of snow,
Standing before the sun of Bolingbroke,
To melt myself away in water-drops!
Good king, great king, and yet not greatly good,
An if my word be sterling yet in England,
Let it command a mirror hither straight,
That it may show me what a face I have,
Since it is bankrout of his majesty.
Boling. Go some of you and fetch a looking-glass.
[*Exit an attendant.*]
North. Read o'er this paper while the glass doth come.
K. Rich. Fiend, thou torments me ere I come to hell!
Boling. Urge it no more, my Lord Northumberland.
North. The commons will not then be satisfied.
K. Rich. They shall be satisfied: I'll read enough,
When I do see the very book indeed
Where all my sins are writ, and that 's myself.

Enter one with a glass.

Give me the glass, and therein will I read.
No deeper wrinkles yet? hath sorrow struck
So many blows upon this face of mine,
And made no deeper wounds? O flattering glass,
Like to my followers in prosperity,
Thou dost beguile me! Was this face the face
That every day under his household roof
Did keep ten thousand men? was this the face
That, like the sun, did make beholders wink?
Was this the face that fac'd so many follies,
And was at last out-fac'd by Bolingbroke?
A brittle glory shineth in this face:
As brittle as the glory is the face;
[*Dashes the glass against the ground.*]
For there it is, crack'd in a hundred shivers.
Mark, silent king, the moral of this sport,
How soon my sorrow hath destroy'd my face.
Boling. The shadow of your sorrow hath destroy'd
The shadow of your face.

157. **we . . . suspicion.** The deposition scene is without historical basis. Richard signed, perhaps under compulsion, an act of abdication, but before witnesses in the Tower. Daniel (*Civil Wars*) gives an elaborate description of the scene. 160. **beholding,** obliged, indebted. 165. **insinuate,** wheedle, ingratiate oneself. 168. **favours,** faces; also, benefits. 185. **owes,** owns, has. 195. **cares.** Three meanings of "care" are involved in the word play which follows: "care" in the sense of responsibility; in the sense of duty or task; in the sense of grief. 201-202. **Ay,** i.e., I. But *I*=nothing; therefore *Ay*=I=no. 204-221. **I give . . . days.** The speech follows with some faithfulness the formula of abdication, as recorded in the Rolls of Parliament. 210. **duteous oaths;** so F; Q_{3-4} and Globe: *duty's rites*. 215. **are made;** so F; Q_{3-4} and Globe: *that swear*. 220. **Henry,** so F; Q_{3-4} and Globe: *Harry*. 232-233. **wouldst . . . shouldst.** In modern usage these words would be reversed. 239. **wash your hands.** See Matthew 27:24. Richard persistently compares himself with Christ; see also III, ii, 24, 61; IV, i, 170. 254. **haught,** haughty, proud. 255. **I have no name.** Richard laments that his whole being and identity are dependent on his now-lost title. 260. **mockery,** counterfeit. 265. **straight,** at once. 267. **bankrout,** bankrupt. 281. **Was this . . . face.** An echo of Marlowe's *Doctor Faustus*. 285. **fac'd,** countenanced. 292. **shadow,** outward show. 293. **shadow,** reflection (in the mirror).

K. Rich. Say that again.
The shadow of my sorrow! ha! let 's see:
'Tis very true, my grief lies all within;
And these external manners of laments
Are merely shadows to the unseen grief
That swells with silence in the tortur'd soul;
There lies the substance: and I thank thee, king,
For thy great bounty, that not only giv'st
Me cause to wail but teachest me the way
How to lament the cause. I'll beg one boon,
And then be gone and trouble you no more.
Shall I obtain it?
Boling. Name it, fair cousin.
K. Rich. 'Fair cousin'? I am greater than a king:
For when I was a king, my flatterers
Were then but subjects; being now a subject,
I have a king here to my flatterer.
Being so great, I have no need to beg.
Boling. Yet ask.
K. Rich. And shall I have?
Boling. You shall.
K. Rich. Then give me leave to go.
Boling. Whither?
K. Rich. Whither you will, so I were from your sights.
Boling. Go, some of you convey him to the Tower.
K. Rich. O, good! convey? conveyers are you all,
That rise thus nimbly by a true king's fall.
[*Exeunt King Richard, some Lords, and a Guard.*]
Boling. On Wednesday next we solemnly set down
Our coronation: lords, prepare yourselves.
Exeunt. Manent [*the Abbot of*] *Westminster*, [*the Bishop of*] *Carlisle*, *Aumerle.*
Abbot. A woeful pageant have we here beheld.
Car. The woe 's to come; the children yet unborn
Shall feel this day as sharp to them as thorn.
Aum. You holy clergymen, is there no plot
To rid the realm of this pernicious blot?
Abbot. My lord,
Before I freely speak my mind herein,
You shall not only take the sacrament
To bury mine intents, but also to effect
Whatever I shall happen to devise.
I see your brows are full of discontent,
Your hearts of sorrow and your eyes of tears:
Come home with me to supper; and I'll lay
A plot shall show us all a merry day. *Exeunt.*

[ACT V.

SCENE I. *London. A street leading to the Tower.*]

Enter the QUEEN *with* [Ladies,] *her Attendants.*

Queen. This way the king will come; this is the way
To Julius Cæsar's ill-erected tower,
To whose flint bosom my condemned lord
Is doom'd a prisoner by proud Bolingbroke:
Here let us rest, if this rebellious earth
Have any resting for her true king's queen.

Enter RICHARD [*and* Guard].

But soft, but see, or rather do not see,
My fair rose wither: yet look up, behold,
That you in pity may dissolve to dew,
And wash him fresh again with true-love tears.
Ah, thou, the model where old Troy did stand,
Thou map of honour, thou King Richard's tomb,
And not King Richard; thou most beauteous inn,
Why should hard-favour'd grief be lodg'd in thee,
When triumph is become an alehouse guest?
K. Rich. Join not with grief, fair woman, do not so,
To make my end too sudden: learn, good soul,
To think our former state a happy dream;
From which awak'd, the truth of what we are
Shows us but this: I am sworn brother, sweet,
To grim Necessity, and he and I
Will keep a league till death. Hie thee to France
And cloister thee in some religious house:
Our holy lives must win a new world's crown,
Which our profane hours here have stricken down.
Queen. What, is my Richard both in shape and mind
Transform'd and weak'ned? hath Bolingbroke depos'd
Thine intellect? hath he been in thy heart?
The lion dying thrusteth forth his paw,
And wounds the earth, if nothing else, with rage
To be o'erpow'r'd; and wilt thou, pupil-like,
Take thy correction mildly, kiss the rod,
And fawn on rage with base humility,
Which art a lion and the king of beasts?
K. Rich. A king of beasts, indeed; if aught but beasts,
I had been still a happy king of men.
Good sometime queen, prepare thee hence for France:
Think I am dead and that even here thou takest,
As from my death-bed, thy last living leave.
In winter's tedious nights sit by the fire
With good old folks and let them tell thee tales
Of woeful ages long ago betid;
And ere thou bid good night, to quite their griefs,
Tell thou the lamentable tale of me
And send the hearers weeping to their beds:
For why, the senseless brands will sympathize
The heavy accent of thy moving tongue
And in compassion weep the fire out;
And some will mourn in ashes, some coal-black,
For the deposing of a rightful king.

Enter NORTHUMBERLAND [*and* others].

North. My lord, the mind of Bolingbroke is chang'd;
You must to Pomfret, not unto the Tower.
And, madam, there is order ta'en for you;
With all swift speed you must away to France.
K. Rich. Northumberland, thou ladder wherewithal
The mounting Bolingbroke ascends my throne,
The time shall not be many hours of age

308. **to my flatterer,** as, or in the capacity of, my flatterer. 316. **convey,** escort. 317. **convey,** steal, with a play upon the normal sense of the word.

ACT V. SCENE I. 1. **This . . . come.** There is no historical authority for this interview between Richard and the queen; they did not meet again after Richard left for Ireland. In Daniel, *Civil Wars*, II, 89-94, the queen visits him in prison, and there is a striking parallel to Daniel in the passage (II, 66 ff.) where she watches the king ride into the city. 2. **Julius Cæsar's.** The Tower, ascribed by tradition to Julius Caesar, was built by William the Conqueror to hold the city in subordination. **ill-erected,** erected for evil ends, or under evil auspices. 8. **My fair rose.** Hotspur calls Richard *that sweet lovely rose*, *1 Henry IV*, I, iii, 175. 11. **thou . . . stand,** thou ruined majesty that resemblest the desolate waste where Troy once stood (Malone). 12. **map of honour,** i.e., the mere outline. 13. **inn,** mansion, abode (with some sense, however, of its more common meaning). 20. **sworn brother,** allusion to the *fratres jurati* of chivalry. 24. **new world's,** heaven's. 42. **betid,** past; happened. 43. **quite their griefs,** make return for their tragic tales. 46. **For why,**

More than it is ere foul sin gathering head
Shall break into corruption: thou shalt think,
Though he divide the realm and give thee half,
It is too little, helping him to all;
And he shall think that thou, which knowest the way
To plant unrightful kings, wilt know again,
Being ne'er so little urg'd, another way
To pluck him headlong from the usurped throne.
The love of wicked men converts to fear;
That fear to hate, and hate turns one or both
To worthy danger and deserved death.
North. My guilt be on my head, and there an end.
Take leave and part; for you must part forthwith.
K. Rich. Doubly divorc'd! Bad men, you violate
A twofold marriage, 'twixt my crown and me,
And then betwixt me and my married wife.
Let me unkiss the oath 'twixt thee and me;
And yet not so, for with a kiss 'twas made.
Part us, Northumberland; I towards the north,
Where shivering cold and sickness pines the clime;
My wife to France: from whence, set forth in pomp,
She came adorned hither like sweet May,
Sent back like Hallowmas or short'st of day.
Queen. And must we be divided? must we part?
K. Rich. Ay, hand from hand, my love, and heart from heart.
Queen. Banish us both and send the king with me.
North. That were some love but little policy.
Queen. Then whither he goes, thither let me go.
K. Rich. So two, together weeping, make one woe.
Weep thou for me in France, I for thee here;
Better far off than near, be ne'er the near.
Go, count thy way with sighs; I mine with groans.
Queen. So longest way shall have the longest moans.
K. Rich. Twice for one step I'll groan, the way being short,
And piece the way out with a heavy heart.
Come, come, in wooing sorrow let 's be brief,
Since, wedding it, there is such length in grief:
One kiss shall stop our mouths, and dumbly part;
Thus give I mine, and thus take I thy heart.
Queen. Give me mine own again; 'twere no good part
To take on me to keep and kill thy heart.
So, now I have mine own again, be gone,
That I may strive to kill it with a groan.
K. Rich. We make woe wanton with this fond delay:
Once more, adieu; the rest let sorrow say. *Exeunt.*

[SCENE II. *The* DUKE OF YORK'S *palace.*]

Enter DUKE OF YORK *and the* DUCHESS.

Duch. My lord, you told me you would tell the rest,
When weeping made you break the story off,
Of our two cousins coming into London.
York. Where did I leave?
Duch. At that sad stop, my lord,
Where rude misgovern'd hands from windows' tops
Threw dust and rubbish on King Richard's head.
York. Then, as I said, the duke, great Bolingbroke,
Mounted upon a hot and fiery steed
Which his aspiring rider seem'd to know,
With slow but stately pace kept on his course,
Whilst all tongues cried 'God save thee, Bolingbroke!'
You would have thought the very windows spake,
So many greedy looks of young and old
Through casements darted their desiring eyes
Upon his visage, and that all the walls
With painted imagery had said at once
'Jesu preserve thee! welcome, Bolingbroke!'
Whilst he, from the one side to the other turning,
Bareheaded, lower than his proud steed's neck,
Bespake them thus: 'I thank you, countrymen:'
And thus still doing, thus he pass'd along.
Duch. Alack, poor Richard! where rode he the whilst?
York. As in a theatre, the eyes of men,
After a well-grac'd actor leaves the stage,
Are idly bent on him that enters next,
Thinking his prattle to be tedious;
Even so, or with much more contempt, men's eyes
Did scowl on gentle Richard; no man cried 'God save him!'
No joyful tongue gave him his welcome home:
But dust was thrown upon his sacred head;
Which with such gentle sorrow he shook off,
His face still combating with tears and smiles,
The badges of his grief and patience,
That had not God, for some strong purpose, steel'd
The hearts of men, they must perforce have melted
And barbarism itself have pitied him.
But heaven hath a hand in these events,
To whose high will we bound our calm contents.
To Bolingbroke are we sworn subjects now,
Whose state and honour I for aye allow.
Duch. Here comes my son Aumerle.
York. Aumerle that was;
But that is lost for being Richard's friend,
And, madam, you must call him Rutland now:
I am in parliament pledge for his truth
And lasting fealty to the new made king.

[*Enter* AUMERLE.]

Duch. Welcome, my son: who are the violets now
That strew the green lap of the new come spring?
Aum. Madam, I know not, nor I greatly care not:
God knows I had as lief be none as one.
York. Well, bear you well in this new spring of time,
Lest you be cropp'd before you come to prime.
What news from Oxford? Do those justs and triumphs hold?
Aum. For aught I know, my lord, they do.
York. You will be there, I know.
Aum. If God prevent not, I purpose so.
York. What seal is that, that hangs without thy bosom?

because. **brands,** firebrands. **sympathize,** respond to. 52. **Pomfret,** Pontefract in Yorkshire, twenty-two miles from York. 53. **order ta'en,** arrangements made. 55. **Northumberland, thou ladder,** etc. Henry recalls this speech, quoting lines 55 and 56 in altered form, in *2 Henry IV*, III, i, 70. 59. **corruption,** putrid matter, pus. 66. **converts,** changes to, turns to. 74. **unkiss,** annul with a kiss (regarded as the seal of a ceremonial bond). 77. **pines,** afflicts, distresses. 80. **Hallowmas,** All Saints' Day (November 1); regarded as the beginning of winter; ten days later in the old calendar than it is now. 88. **Better . . . near,** better be far off than near and yet be unable to meet. The second *near* is the old short comparative form for "nearer."

SCENE II. 4. **leave,** leave off. 20. **Bespake,** spoke to. 25. **idly,** indifferently. 40. **allow,** acknowledge. 41. **Aumerle that was.** Aumerle, with others of Richard's party, lost all titles and honors conferred upon him by King Richard. 44. **truth,** loyalty. 46-47. **who are . . . spring?** Who are the favorites of the new king?

Yea, look'st thou pale? let me see the writing.
Aum. My lord, 'tis nothing.
York. No matter, then, who see it:
I will be satisfied; let me see the writing.
Aum. I do beseech your grace to pardon me:
It is a matter of small consequence,
Which for some reasons I would not have seen.
York. Which for some reasons, sir, I mean to see.
I fear, I fear,—
Duch. What should you fear?
'Tis nothing but some bond, that he is ent'red into
For gay apparel 'gainst the triumph day.
York. Bound to himself! what doth he with a bond
That he is bound to? Wife, thou art a fool.
Boy, let me see the writing.
Aum. I do beseech you, pardon me; I may not show it.
York. I will be satisfied; let me see it, I say.
He plucks it out of his bosom and reads it.
Treason! foul treason! Villain! traitor! slave!
Duch. What is the matter, my lord?
York. Ho! who is within there?

[*Enter a* Servant.]

Saddle my horse.
God for his mercy, what treachery is here!
Duch. Why, what is it, my lord?
York. Give me my boots, I say; saddle my horse.
[*Exit Servant.*]
Now, by mine honour, by my life, by my troth,
I will appeach the villain.
Duch. What is the matter?
York. Peace, foolish woman.
Duch. I will not peace. What is the matter, Aumerle?
Aum. Good mother, be content; it is no more
Than my poor life must answer.
Duch. Thy life answer!
York. Bring me my boots: I will unto the king.

His Man *enters with his boots.*

Duch. Strike him, Aumerle. Poor boy, thou art amaz'd.— [*To York's Man.*]
Hence, villain! never more come in my sight.
York. Give me my boots, I say.
Duch. Why, York, what wilt thou do?
Wilt thou not hide the trespass of thine own?
Have we more sons? or are we like to have?
Is not my teeming date drunk up with time?
And wilt thou pluck my fair son from mine age,
And rob me of a happy mother's name?
Is he not like thee? is he not thine own?
York. Thou fond mad woman,
Wilt thou conceal this dark conspiracy?
A dozen of them here have ta'en the sacrament,
And interchangeably set down their hands,
To kill the king at Oxford.
Duch. He shall be none;
We'll keep him here: then what is that to him?
York. Away, fond woman! were he twenty times my son,
I would appeach him.
Duch. Hadst thou groan'd for him
As I have done, thou wouldst be more pitiful.
But now I know thy mind; thou dost suspect
That I have been disloyal to thy bed,
And that he is a bastard, not thy son:
Sweet York, sweet husband, be not of that mind:
He is as like thee as a man may be,
Not like to me, or any of my kin,
And yet I love him.
York. Make way, unruly woman! *Exit.*
Duch. After, Aumerle! mount thee upon his horse;
Spur post, and get before him to the king,
And beg thy pardon ere he do accuse thee.
I'll not be long behind; though I be old,
I doubt not but to ride as fast as York:
And never will I rise up from the ground
Till Bolingbroke have pardon'd thee. Away, be gone!
[*Exeunt.*]

[SCENE III. *A royal palace.*]

Enter [BOLINGBROKE, *now*] *the* KING, *with his* Nobles [PERCY *and others*].

Boling. Can no man tell me of my unthrifty son?
'Tis full three months since I did see him last:
If any plague hang over us, 'tis he.
I would to God, my lords, he might be found:
Inquire at London, 'mongst the taverns there,
For there, they say, he daily doth frequent,
With unrestrained loose companions,
Even such, they say, as stand in narrow lanes,
And beat our watch, and rob our passengers;
Which he, young wanton and effeminate boy,
Takes on the point of honour to support
So dissolute a crew.
Percy. My lord, some two days since I saw the prince,
And told him of those triumphs held at Oxford.
Boling. And what said the gallant?
Percy. His answer was, he would unto the stews,
And from the common'st creature pluck a glove,
And wear it as a favour; and with that
He would unhorse the lustiest challenger.
Boling. As dissolute as desperate; yet through both
I see some sparks of better hope, which elder years
May happily bring forth. But who comes here?

Enter AUMERLE, *amazed.*

Aum. Where is the king?
Boling. What means our cousin, that he stares and looks
So wildly?
Aum. God save your grace! I do beseech your majesty,
To have some conference with your grace alone.

78. **troth,** faith, allegiance. 79. **appeach,** inform against. 80. **Peace,** keep silent. 85. **Strike him,** i.e., strike the servant. **amaz'd,** confused, bewildered. 90. **Have we more sons.** Historically this Duchess of York was the duke's second wife and was not Aumerle's mother. 91. **teeming date,** period of childbearing. 97-99. **A . . . Oxford.** Hervpon was an indenture sextipartite made, sealed with their seales, and signed with their hands, in the which each stood bound to other, to do their whole indeuor for the accomplishing of their purposed exploit (Holinshed). 99. **none,** not one of them. 111. **his horse,** i.e., one of York's horses.

SCENE III. 1. **my unthrifty son.** Prince Henry was twelve years old at this time. Shakespeare has in mind the traditions of Prince Hal's wayward youth followed in the later plays of the series. 6. **frequent,** be there as a matter of habit. 9. **passengers,** passers-by, wayfarers. 10-12. **Which . . . crew.** This passage will not construe in strict syntax, *which* and *crew* both standing as objects of *support*. 10. **wanton,** spoiled or pampered person. **effeminate,** licentious (?) 13. **I saw the prince.** This is the first bringing together of Hotspur and Prince Hal.

Boling. Withdraw yourselves, and leave us here alone. [*Exeunt Percy and Lords.*]
What is the matter with our cousin now?
Aum. For ever may my knees grow to the earth,
My tongue cleave to my roof within my mouth,
Unless a pardon ere I rise or speak.
Boling. Intended or committed was this fault?
If on the first, how heinous e'er it be,
To win thy after-love I pardon thee.
Aum. Then give me leave that I may turn the key,
That no man enter till my tale be done.
Boling. Have thy desire.
[*Aumerle locks the door.*] *The Duke of York knocks at the door and crieth.*
York. [*Within*] My liege, beware; look to thyself;
Thou hast a traitor in thy presence there.
Boling. Villain, I'll make thee safe. [*Drawing.*]
Aum. Stay thy revengeful hand; thou hast no cause to fear.
York. [*Within*] Open the door, secure, foolhardy king:
Shall I for love speak treason to thy face?
Open the door, or I will break it open.

[*Enter* YORK.]

Boling. What is the matter, uncle? speak;
Recover breath; tell us how near is danger,
That we may arm us to encounter it.
York. Peruse this writing here, and thou shalt know
The treason that my haste forbids me show.
Aum. Remember, as thou read'st, thy promise pass'd:
I do repent me; read not my name there;
My heart is not confederate with my hand.
York. It was, villain, ere thy hand did set it down.
I tore it from the traitor's bosom, king;
Fear, and not love, begets his penitence:
Forget to pity him, lest thy pity prove
A serpent that will sting thee to the heart.
Boling. O heinous, strong and bold conspiracy!
O loyal father of a treacherous son!
Thou sheer, immaculate and silver fountain,
From whence this stream through muddy passages
Hath held his current and defil'd himself!
Thy overflow of good converts to bad,
And thy abundant goodness shall excuse
This deadly blot in thy digressing son.
York. So shall my virtue be his vice's bawd;
And he shall spend mine honour with his shame,
As thriftless sons their scraping fathers' gold.
Mine honour lives when his dishonour dies,
Or my sham'd life in his dishonour lies:
Thou kill'st me in his life; giving him breath,
The traitor lives, the true man 's put to death.
Duch. [*Within*] What ho, my liege! for God's sake, let me in.
Boling. What shrill-voic'd suppliant makes this eager cry?
Duch. A woman, and thy aunt, great king; 'tis I.
Speak with me, pity me, open the door:
A beggar begs that never begg'd before.
Boling. Our scene is alt'red from a serious thing,
And now chang'd to 'The Beggar and the King.'
My dangerous cousin, let your mother in:
I know she is come to pray for your foul sin.
York. If thou do pardon, whosoever pray,
More sins for this forgiveness prosper may.
This fest'red joint cut off, the rest rest sound;
This let alone will all the rest confound.

[*Enter* DUCHESS.]

Duch. O king, believe not this hard-hearted man!
Love loving not itself none other can.
York. Thou frantic woman, what dost thou make here?
Shall thy old dugs once more a traitor rear?
Duch. Sweet York, be patient. Hear me, gentle liege. [*Kneels.*]
Boling. Rise up, good aunt.
Duch. Not yet, I thee beseech:
For ever will I walk upon my knees,
And never see day that the happy sees,
Till thou give joy; until thou bid me joy,
By pardoning Rutland, my transgressing boy.
Aum. Unto my mother's prayers I bend my knee. [*Kneels.*]
York. Against them both my true joints bended be. [*Kneels.*]
Ill mayst thou thrive, if thou grant any grace!
Duch. Pleads he in earnest? look upon his face;
His eyes do drop no tears, his prayers are in jest;
His words come from his mouth, ours from our breast:
He prays but faintly and would be denied;
We pray with heart and soul and all beside:
His weary joints would gladly rise, I know;
Our knees shall kneel till to the ground they grow:
His prayers are full of false hypocrisy;
Ours of true zeal and deep integrity.
Our prayers do out-pray his; then let them have
That mercy which true prayer ought to have.
Boling. Good aunt, stand up.
Duch. Nay, do not say, 'stand up;'
Say 'pardon' first, and afterwards 'stand up.'
An if I were thy nurse, thy tongue to teach,
'Pardon' should be the first word of thy speech.
I never long'd to hear a word till now;
Say 'pardon,' king; let pity teach thee how:
The word is short, but not so short as sweet;
No word like 'pardon' for kings' mouths so meet.
York. Speak it in French, king; say 'pardonne moi.'
Duch. Dost thou teach pardon pardon to destroy?
Ah, my sour husband, my hard-hearted lord,
That sets the word itself against the word!
Speak 'pardon' as 'tis current in our land;
The chopping French we do not understand.
Thine eye begins to speak; set thy tongue there;

See Bolingbroke's reflection on Hal and Hotspur in *1 Henry IV*, I, i, 78-90; and the tavern view of the matter from the same play, II, iv, 114-121. 16. **stews,** houses of ill fame. 22. **happily,** haply; possibly, combining also the modern sense of the word. 31. **My . . . mouth.** See Psalms 137:6. 43. **secure,** unsuspecting, heedless. 44. **speak . . . face,** i.e., by calling him *secure* and *foolhardy*. 58. **serpent,** allusion to the fable of the *Countryman and the Viper*. See also III, ii, 131. 61-66. **Thou . . . son.** Chambers quotes a parallel passage from Lyly's *Euphues* (Arbor ed., page 191): "As the water that springeth from the fountain's head," etc. 61. **sheer,** clear, pure. 66. **digressing,** transgressing. 69. **scraping,** parsimonious. 80. **'The Beggar and the King,'** one of the many allusions in Shakespeare to the ballad of *King Cophetua and the Beggar Maid*; see *Love's Labour's Lost*, I, ii, 114 ff.; *Romeo and Juliet*, II, i, 14; *2 Henry IV*, V, iii, 106. 88. **Love . . . can.** He who does not love his own kin can love no one else, not even the king. 119. **'pardonne moi,'** excuse me (affectedly polite refusal). 124. **chopping,** jerky, shifting suddenly; also, changing (the sense of words).

Or in thy piteous heart plant thou thine ear;
That hearing how our plaints and prayers do pierce,
Pity may move thee 'pardon' to rehearse.
Boling. Good aunt, stand up.
Duch. I do not sue to stand;
Pardon is all the suit I have in hand.
Boling. I pardon him, as God shall pardon me.
Duch. O happy vantage of a kneeling knee!
Yet am I sick for fear: speak it again;
Twice saying 'pardon' doth not pardon twain,
But makes one pardon strong.
Boling. With all my heart
I pardon him.
Duch. A god on earth thou art. [*Rises.*]
Boling. But for our trusty brother-in-law and the abbot,
With all the rest of that consorted crew,
Destruction straight shall dog them at the heels.
Good uncle, help to order several powers
To Oxford, or where'er these traitors are:
They shall not live within this world, I swear,
But I will have them, if I once know where.
Uncle, farewell: and, cousin too, adieu:
Your mother well hath pray'd, and prove you true.
Duch. Come, my old son: I pray God make thee new. *Exeunt.*

[SCENE IV. *The same.*]

Enter SIR PIERCE EXTON *and* [Servant].

Exton. Didst thou not mark the king, what words he spake,
'Have I no friend will rid me of this living fear?'
Was it not so?
Ser. These were his very words.
Exton. 'Have I no friend?' quoth he: he spake it twice,
And urg'd it twice together, did he not?
Serv. He did.
Exton. And speaking it, he wishtly look'd on me,
As who should say, 'I would thou wert the man
That would divorce this terror from my heart;'
Meaning the king at Pomfret. Come, let 's go:
I am the king's friend, and will rid his foe. [*Exeunt.*]

[SCENE V. *Pomfret castle.*]

Enter RICHARD *alone.*

K. Rich. I have been studying how I may compare
This prison where I live unto the world:
And for because the world is populous
And here is not a creature but myself,
I cannot do it; yet I'll hammer it out.
My brain I'll prove the female to my soul,
My soul the father; and these two beget
A generation of still-breeding thoughts,
And these same thoughts people this little world,
In humours like the people of this world,
For no thought is contented. The better sort,
As thoughts of things divine, are intermix'd
With scruples and do set the word itself
Against the word:
As thus, 'Come, little ones,' and then again,
'It is as hard to come as for a camel
To thread the postern of a small needle's eye.'
Thoughts tending to ambition, they do plot
Unlikely wonders; how these vain weak nails
May tear a passage through the flinty ribs
Of this hard world, my ragged prison walls,
And, for they cannot, die in their own pride.
Thoughts tending to content flatter themselves
That they are not the first of fortune's slaves,
Nor shall not be the last; like seely beggars
Who sitting in the stocks refuge their shame,
That many have and others must sit there;
And in this thought they find a kind of ease,
Bearing their own misfortunes on the back
Of such as have before endur'd the like.
Thus play I in one person many people,
And none contented: sometimes am I king;
Then treasons make me wish myself a beggar,
And so I am: then crushing penury
Persuades me I was better when a king;
Then am I king'd again: and by and by
Think that I am unking'd by Bolingbroke,
And straight am nothing: but whate'er I be,
Nor I nor any man that but man is
With nothing shall be pleas'd, till he be eas'd
With being nothing. Music do I hear? *The music plays.*
Ha, ha! keep time: how sour sweet music is,
When time is broke and no proportion kept!
So is it in the music of men's lives.
And here have I the daintiness of ear
To check time broke in a disordered string;
But for the concord of my state and time
Had not an ear to hear my true time broke.
I wasted time, and now doth time waste me;
For now hath time made me his numb'ring clock:
My thoughts are minutes; and with sighs they jar
Their watches on unto mine eyes, the outward watch,
Whereto my finger, like a dial's point,
Is pointing still, in cleansing them from tears.
Now sir, the sound that tells what hour it is
Are clamorous groans, which strike upon my heart,
Which is the bell: so sighs and tears and groans
Show minutes, times, and hours: but my time
Runs posting on in Bolingbroke's proud joy,
While I stand fooling here, his Jack of the clock.
This music mads me; let it sound no more;
For though it have holp madmen to their wits,
In me it seems it will make wise men mad.
Yet blessing on his heart that gives it me!

---

130. **suit,** petition (with play upon the term as used at cards). 137. **our trusty brother-in-law,** the Duke of Exeter, who had married Bolingbroke's sister. 138. **consorted,** confederate. 145. **prove you true.** Aumerle, as Duke of York, died leading the van at Agincourt.

SCENE IV. 7. **And speaking it,** etc. Cf. Daniel's *Civil Wars*, II, 57:

"And wisht that some would so his life esteeme,
As *ridde* him of these feares wherein he stood:
And there-with eyes a knight, that then was by,
Who soone could learne his lesson by his eye."

wishtly, intently; also, wistfully.

SCENE V. 1. **I have been studying,** etc. Daniel (III, 64-69) presents Richard soliloquizing, "Conferring captiue-Crownes with freedome poore," somewhat in the spirit of this passage. 15-17. **Come, little . . . eye.** See Matthew 19:14, 24. 21. **ragged,** rugged. 25. **seely,** simpleminded. 26. **refuge,** protect themselves from. 50. **numb'ring clock.** Henley explains thus: " . . . his sighs correspond to the jarring of the pendulum, which, at the same time that it watches or numbers the seconds, marks also their progress in minutes on the dial or outward watch, to which the king compares his eyes; and their want of figures is supplied by a succession of tears, or, to use the expression of Milton, minute-drops; his finger, by as regularly wiping these tears

For 'tis a sign of love; and love to Richard
Is a strange brooch in this all-hating world.

Enter a Groom of the Stable.

Groom. Hail, royal prince!
K. Rich. Thanks, noble peer;
The cheapest of us is ten groats too dear.
What art thou? and how comest thou hither,
Where no man never comes but that sad dog
That brings me food to make misfortune live?
Groom. I was a poor groom of thy stable, king,
When thou wert king; who, travelling towards York,
With much ado at length have gotten leave
To look upon my sometimes royal master's face.
O, how it ern'd my heart when I beheld
In London streets, that coronation-day,
When Bolingbroke rode on roan Barbary,
That horse that thou so often hast bestrid,
That horse that I so carefully have dress'd!
K. Rich. Rode he on Barbary? Tell me, gentle friend,
How went he under him?
Groom. So proudly as if he disdain'd the ground.
K. Rich. So proud that Bolingbroke was on his back!
That jade hath eat bread from my royal hand;
This hand hath made him proud with clapping him.
Would he not stumble? would he not fall down,
Since pride must have a fall, and break the neck
Of that proud man that did usurp his back?
Forgiveness, horse! why do I rail on thee,
Since thou, created to be aw'd by man,
Wast born to bear? I was not made a horse;
And yet I bear a burthen like an ass,
Spurr'd, gall'd, and tir'd by jauncing Bolingbroke.

Enter one [*a* Keeper] *to* RICHARD *with meat.*

Keep. Fellow, give place; here is no longer stay.
K. Rich. If thou love me, 'tis time thou wert away.
Groom. What my tongue dares not, that my heart shall say. *Exit Groom.*
Keep. My lord, will 't please you to fall to?
K. Rich. Taste of it first, as thou art wont to do.
Keep. My lord, I dare not: Sir Pierce of Exton, who lately came from the king, commands the contrary.
K. Rich. The devil take Henry of Lancaster and thee!
Patience is stale, and I am weary of it. [*Beats the keeper.*]
Keep. Help, help, help!

The Murderers [EXTON *and* Servants] rush in.

K. Rich. How now! what means death in this rude assault?
Villain, thy own hand yields thy death's instrument.
[*Snatching an axe from a Servant and killing him.*]
Go thou, and fill another room in hell.
[*He kills another.*] *Here Exton strikes him down.*
That hand shall burn in never-quenching fire
That staggers thus my person. Exton, thy fierce hand
Hath with the king's blood stain'd the king's own land.
Mount, mount, my soul! thy seat is up on high;
Whilst my gross flesh sinks downward, here to die.
[*Dies.*]

Exton. As full of valour as of royal blood:
Both have I spill'd; O would the deed were good!
For now the devil, that told me I did well,
Says that this deed is chronicled in hell.
This dead king to the living king I'll bear:
Take hence the rest, and give them burial here.
[*Exeunt.*]

[SCENE VI. *Windsor castle.*]

[*Flourish.*] *Enter* BOLINGBROKE [*as King*], *with the* DUKE OF YORK [,*other* Lords, *and* Attendants].

Boling. Kind uncle York, the latest news we hear
Is that the rebels have consum'd with fire
Our town of Cicester in Gloucestershire;
But whether they be ta'en or slain we hear not.

Enter NORTHUMBERLAND.

Welcome, my lord: what is the news?
North. First, to thy sacred state wish I all happiness.
The next news is, I have to London sent
The heads of Oxford, Salisbury, Blunt, and Kent:
The manner of their taking may appear
At large discoursed in this paper here.
Boling. We thank thee, gentle Percy, for thy pains;
And to thy worth will add right worthy gains.

Enter LORD FITZWATER.

Fitz. My lord, I have from Oxford sent to London
The heads of Brocas and Sir Bennet Seely,
Two of the dangerous consorted traitors
That sought at Oxford thy dire overthrow.
Boling. Thy pains, Fitzwater, shall not be forgot;
Right noble is thy merit, well I wot.

Enter HENRY PERCY [*and the* BISHOP OF CARLISLE].

Percy. The grand conspirator, Abbot of Westminster,
With clog of conscience and sour melancholy
Hath yielded up his body to the grave;
But here is Carlisle living, to abide
Thy kingly doom and sentence of his pride.
Boling. Carlisle, this is your doom:
Choose out some secret place, some reverend room,
More than thou hast, and with it joy thy life;
So as thou liv'st in peace, die free from strife:
For though mine enemy thou hast ever been,
High sparks of honour in thee have I seen.

Enter EXTON, *with* [*persons bearing*] *the coffin.*

Exton. Great king, within this coffin I present
Thy buried fear: herein all breathless lies
The mightiest of thy greatest enemies,

away performs the office of the dial point; his clamorous groans are the sounds that tell the hour." 51. **jar,** tick. 60. **Jack of the clock,** a figure which struck the bell on a clock. 62. **holp madmen to their wits,** probable allusion to the story of the cure of Saul by David. 66. **brooch,** ornament (worn in a man's hat). 68. **ten groats too dear.** There is a pun on *royal* and *noble* in the preceding lines. Though a royal (10s.) is worth 10 groats (ten times 4d.) more than a noble (6s. 8d.) is, a noble itself is 10 groats too high a price for either Richard or the Groom. 76. **ern'd,** grieved. 78. **roan Barbary.** Boswell-Stone suggests that the story of "roan Barbary" may come from an account repeated in Froissart of a greyhound, Mathe, which forsook his old master, Richard, and followed Bolingbroke. 94. **gall'd,** annoyed; literally, made sore by rubbing. **jauncing,** making prance up and down (of a horse); here, hard-riding. 108. **room,** a particular place assigned to a person. 115. **O . . . good!** It is said, that sir Piers of Exton, after he had thus slaine him, wept right bitterlie, as one stricken with the pricke of a giltie conscience, for murthering him, whom he had so long time obeied as king (Holinshed).

SCENE VI. 8. **Oxford.** No such name occurs in Holinshed; F reads *Spencer*. Shakespeare antedates the death of Richard, since the conspiracy was put down before his death. 15. **consorted,** confederate.

Richard of Bordeaux, by me hither brought.
Boling. Exton, I thank thee not; for thou hast wrought
A deed of slander with thy fatal hand
Upon my head and all this famous land.
Exton. From your own mouth, my lord, did I this deed.
Boling. They love not poison that do poison need,
Nor do I thee: though I did wish him dead,
I hate the murderer, love him murdered.
The guilt of conscience take thou for thy labour,
But neither my good word nor princely favour:
With Cain go wander thorough shades of night,
And never show thy head by day nor light.
Lords, I protest, my soul is full of woe,
That blood should sprinkle me to make me grow:
Come, mourn with me for that I do lament,
And put on sullen black incontinent:
I'll make a voyage to the Holy Land,
To wash this blood off from my guilty hand:
March sadly after; grace my mournings here;
In weeping after this untimely bier. [*Exeunt*.]

48. **incontinent,** immediately. 49-50. **I'll . . . hand.** Henry never fulfilled his vow, though he had it always in mind; see *1 Henry IV*, I, i, 19 ff.; *2 Henry IV*, III, i, 108; IV, iv, 3; v, 210 ff. and 233 ff. 52. **In . . . bier.** Richard probably died in January 1400; he was buried at Pomfret. His body was then carried to London, displayed in Cheapside and St. Paul's on March 12, 1400, and buried in an obscure grave at Langley. Through the piety of Henry v, his body was placed in the tomb in Westminster Abbey that Richard himself had built for his first queen, Anne of Bohemia.

THE HENRY THE FOURTH PLAYS

The opening of *1 Henry IV* is taut and grave in tone. England is "shaken" and "wan with care." The troubles of *Richard II*, to which this play (1596–1597) is a close sequel, have not been left behind. However much King Henry would prefer to unite his countrymen against a common foreign enemy, in a crusade to the holy lands, he is prevented from doing so by uninterrupted war. The impassioned rhetoric of his opening speech proclaiming a new era of peace can only end in anticlimax, for the actual purpose of this meeting in council is to receive and assess reports of military action against the throne.

Henry's current troubles are in the far reaches of his kingdom: Scots in the north, Welsh in the west. Fighting for Henry on these two fronts are the nobles of the Percy family who helped him to power: Henry Percy ("Hotspur"), his father the Earl of Northumberland, his uncle the Earl of Worcester, and his brother-in-law Edmund Mortimer the Earl of March. Apparently they have fought bravely. Yet we soon sense that all is not well between the new king and those who rebelled with him against Richard. A quarrel breaks out because Hotspur refuses to deliver to Henry some prisoners as required by feudal obedience. The matter of the ransom money is only a technicality; what is really at issue? In part, it is Henry's insistence on being obeyed on principle. Admiring Hotspur inordinately, the king feels he must discipline affectionately this fine young warrior as a father would discipline his son. Even more deeply, however, the issue of the prisoners galls Henry because of the proviso that he ransom Mortimer, captured by the Welsh. Henry does not forget that Mortimer is his chief rival for the English crown, being descended from the Duke of Clarence (elder brother to Henry's father, Gaunt), and proclaimed by Richard heir to the throne. Mortimer is the last person Henry would wish ransomed. Moreover, the king suspects Mortimer of having fought with something less than total zeal against the Welsh Glendower. Mortimer's marriage to Glendower's daughter starkly confirms the king's worst fears. Henry knows Northumberland and Worcester to be expert in treasonous plotting, since they conspired with him to overthrow Richard. Now, Henry believes, these Percys are extending their alliance by a series of calculated marriages in order to seize power once again. This time their claimant is Mortimer.

Shakespeare's sympathies are many-sided. The Percy clan is in fact organizing against Henry, but not without cause. As they see it, the man they helped to the throne has done precious little for them since. His manner of disciplining them sounds too much like hostility and ingratitude. Other counselors attend the king constantly while Worcester is banished from court. In such an atmosphere of distrust, suspicion breeds still more suspicion. The situation has polarized, surely more than either party originally intended.

Hotspur is the most attractive of the rebels, to us as to King Henry. He is outspoken, courageous, witty, domineering in conversation. Above all, he is a disciple of manliness, loyalty, chivalry, bravery in battle—the attributes of an upstanding and somewhat old-fashioned sense of honor. Yet a fatal defect dwells even in these attractive qualities. Hotspur is impatient, proud, unwilling to tolerate a rival—be it Glendower or Prince Hal. In his very first speech, purporting to explain his refusal to deliver the prisoners, he brilliantly satirizes an effete courtier who had come to him from King Henry in the midst of a battle. The satire betrays many harsh qualities in Hotspur: the self-indulgent wrath which returns fully to him even in recollection of the encounter, the pride in his own stoical indifference to suffering, and especially the obsessive character (revealed in the repetitive pattern of the rhetoric) of his contempt for courtiers generally. Surely his scorn for stay-at-home politicians is directed in part at King Henry himself. All courtiers are to Hotspur effeminate, perfume-wearing, affected in mannerism and speech, scarcely masculine. This obsession of Hotspur makes him extraordinarily prone to one-sided judgments. Like most excessive devotees of chivalry, he divides mankind into sheep and goats: those who are gentlemen, like himself, and those who are beneath contempt. The "vile politician" Bolingbroke and his son the "sword-and-buckler Prince of Wales" fall into the latter category.

Prone as he is to such an overly simple view of political behavior, Hotspur can see no good in the king's cause and no evil in his own. He is a poor listener because of his obsession, and yet an easy prey to his uncle and father who desperately require his leadership for their cause. They need only implant the suggestion that King Henry is trying to pull a political maneuver in his refusal to ransom Mortimer, and Hotspur is ready to leap incautiously to the defense of their cause. The great irony is that Hotspur fails to read political motives in his own relatives' machinations. While he fights for bright honor, they jockey cautiously for position and prove uncertain allies when the hour of battle approaches. Most crucially, they betray Hotspur in the pre-battle negotiations, at which he is not present. As Worcester explains to Vernon during their return to rebel headquarters (V,ii), they cannot let Hotspur know of the king's offer to settle matters by a general pardon. Although, as they realize, the king could pardon Hotspur's youth, there can be no turning back for themselves. Thus the honor for which Hotspur fights is at bottom a lie, and the mutual esteem that might have grown between him and a much-reformed Prince of Wales is thwarted by the polarization of attitudes in the two camps. Hotspur's brand of honor is the victim of its own excess, and lends some credence to Falstaff's wry conclusion that honor "is a mere scutcheon."

The contrasting of Falstaff and Hotspur on the theme of honor suggests that they are dramatic "foils" to one another, representing extremes of life-styles between which Hal must choose. Shakespeare uses this "foil" device structurally and consciously; for example, he has considerably reduced the age of the Hotspur he found in Holinshed's *Chronicles* in order to accentuate the similarity of age between Hotspur and Hal. Conversely, to emphasize the contrast between Falstaff and Hotspur, Shakespeare envisages Falstaff as old (nearly sixty, by his own admission), fat, humorous, and without honor. Falstaff's vices are Hotspur's virtues, and vice versa. Whereas Hotspur offers to Hal a model of chivalric striving and attention to duty, Falstaff is a highwayman and liar. On the other hand, Hotspur is a fanatic, unbending and self-absorbed even in the company of his sprightly wife Kate, irritated by music and poetry; Falstaff is the epitome of merriment and *joi de vivre*. We excuse much in him because he lusts after life with such an appetite, and ingratiates himself to others by inviting them to laugh at his expense.

The two most pronounced motifs of the first scene between Hal and Falstaff (I,ii) are the hanging of thieves and temptation to sinfulness. Beneath the gay surface of their raillery, the two are already debating the need for the ultimate rejection of Falstaff. Can their relationship continue unchanged into the reign of Henry v? Will there be gallows standing, and justice for highwaymen? Will "Monsieur Remorse," as Poins calls Falstaff, ever sincerely repent? Will the prince, for that matter? It is to allay our fears in this regard that Hal comes before us in soliloquy at the scene's end, vowing his determination to use these scapegrace companions as mere "foils" to his triumphal reformation at the appropriate time. But this explanation raises an opposite danger in our sympathies: is he callously using his companions merely to create a public-relations myth of Prince Hal, the Politician with the Common Touch? Since the rejection of Falstaff is, by Hal's own words, a foregone conclusion, can we credit him with a serious friendship? Where do Shakespeare's sympathies lie, with the need for political order or with the hedonistic spirit of youth? Perhaps he recognizes the validity of both, and accordingly shows us a prince who is genuinely fond of Falstaff's exuberant company, but who also knows that he is a king's son and must sooner or later accept the consequences of that unsought role. Falstaff's gift to him is youthful irresponsibility, which must be cherished (by all of us) even though it cannot last.

In the Gadshill robbery episode, Falstaff reveals that his "cowardice" differs from the natural craven fear of Bardolph and Peto. He fights no longer than he sees "reason," that is, not against unfair odds such as two athletic young men in the dark (or later, at Shrewsbury, against the burly Scots giant, the Douglas). A man could get killed that way. Falstaff's cowardice, then, is philosophic, seen by himself in a humorous perspective. The same is true of his lying about the robbery. However much Hal exults in exposing Falstaff as a fraud, we cannot dismiss the possibility that Falstaff may see through the prince's scheme, and may then feed Hal the expectedly outlandish lie (two men in buckram green become eleven men) as a means of begging for affection. Falstaff's only way of pleading his cause is to tickle the prince's fancy, in his role as a kind of court fool. What Falstaff most wants is to be loved and retained for what he is; and that, poignantly enough, is the one thing the mature Henry v cannot grant.

Falstaff is a foil not only to Hotspur, but to Henry IV, and (in *2 Henry IV*) to the Lord Chief Justice; perhaps also to Prince John of Lancaster. Three of these are father-figures. All offer Hal varying models of conduct which he alone must adapt and transform. Just as he must achieve Hotspur's bright honor without the fanaticism, he must discover his father's sense of responsibility without yielding to the political expediency and drabness of the older man (balefully bequeathed to Hal's brother Prince John). Once again, the spirit of Falstaff is a corrective even though he himself must be rejected. In *2 Henry IV*, however, this dualism in which Falstaff makes a positive contribution begins to fade. The Lord Chief Justice now represents the correct path, Falstaff the wayward path already abandoned by Hal. To emphasize the contrast, we see Falstaff as a fugitive before the law, evading his promise of marriage to Mistress Quickly, falling into debt and illness, seeking the companionship of foul-mouthed swaggerers like Pistol and pathetic whores like Doll Tearsheet, and then trafficking corruptly with those mockeries of justice, Shallow and Silence. His outrages perpetrated at the expense of the military draft are not as clever and ebullient as in the first play. Hal scarcely knows of Falstaff's whereabouts anymore, and his one return to familiar haunts fills him with dismay and self-loathing.

All that keeps Falstaff out of prison are his illusory and self-deceiving hopes of favor from King Hal, and the equally illusory reputation for bravery he gained in the wars. False reputation, or Rumour, indeed plays a prominent role in this second play. It creates havoc with the rebels' hopes, and teaches Hal the bitter lesson that personal reform comes more easily than a reputation for virtue. Twice in these plays he must appear before his stricken and angry father; and the second such visit is necessary because Henry IV, like others at court, cannot put much stock in Hal's newfound show of obedience. Hal, because he youthfully never considered this problem of appearances, miscalculated the difficulty of throwing off his riotous past and has thereby deeply offended the stern, awesome father with whom he must come to terms. This lesson of respect for outward appearances is not lost on the now-wary prince standing on the threshold of his kingship.

2 Henry IV was probably written in 1597, closely following Part I and drawing similarly on material from Holinshed and *Famous Victories of Henry V*. However much Shakespeare may have improvised in Part II to capitalize on the favorable response to Part I, it seems certain that he planned from the start to depict the rejection of Falstaff. We can recognize the inevitability of that rejection, however, and still suppose that King Hal acts with an inner realization of the loss to himself. He must accept his new role as a public figure, and the inner man must dwindle.

THE FIRST PART OF KING HENRY THE FOURTH

[*Dramatis Personae*

KING HENRY the Fourth.
HENRY, Prince of Wales, } *sons to the King.*
JOHN of Lancaster, }
EARL OF WESTMORELAND.
SIR WALTER BLUNT.
THOMAS PERCY, Earl of Worcester.
HENRY PERCY, Earl of Northumberland.
HENRY PERCY, *surnamed* HOTSPUR, *his son.*
EDMUND MORTIMER, Earl of March.
RICHARD SCROOP, Archbishop of York.
ARCHIBALD, Earl of DOUGLAS.
OWEN GLENDOWER.
SIR RICHARD VERNON.
SIR JOHN FALSTAFF.
SIR MICHAEL, *a friend to the Archbishop of York.*
POINS.
GADSHILL.
PETO.
BARDOLPH.

LADY PERCY, *wife to Hotspur, and sister to Mortimer.*
LADY MORTIMER, *daughter to Glendower, and wife to Mortimer.*
MISTRESS QUICKLY, *hostess of a tavern in Eastcheap.*

Lords, Officers, Sheriff, Vintner, Chamberlain, Drawers, *two* Carriers, Travellers, *and* Attendants.

SCENE: *England and Wales.*]

[ACT I.

SCENE I. *London. The palace.*]

Enter the KING, LORD JOHN OF LANCASTER, [*the*] EARL OF WESTMORELAND, [SIR WALTER BLUNT,] *with others.*

King. So shaken as we are, so wan with care,
Find we a time for frighted peace to pant,
And breathe short-winded accents of new broils
To be commenc'd in stronds afar remote.
†No more the thirsty entrance of this soil
Shall daub her lips with her own children's blood;
No more shall trenching war channel her fields,
Nor bruise her flow'rets with the armed hoofs
Of hostile paces: those opposed eyes,
Which, like the meteors of a troubled heaven,
All of one nature, of one substance bred,
Did lately meet in the intestine shock

And furious close of civil butchery
Shall now, in mutual well-beseeming ranks,
March all one way and be no more oppos'd
Against acquaintance, kindred and allies:
The edge of war, like an ill-sheathed knife,
No more shall cut his master. Therefore, friends,
As far as to the sepulchre of Christ,
Whose soldier now, under whose blessed cross
We are impressed and engag'd to fight,
Forthwith a power of English shall we levy;
Whose arms were moulded in their mothers' womb
To chase these pagans in those holy fields
Over whose acres walk'd those blessed feet
Which fourteen hundred years ago were nail'd
For our advantage on the bitter cross.
But this our purpose now is twelve month old,
And bootless 'tis to tell you we will go:
Therefore we meet not now. Then let me hear
Of you, my gentle cousin Westmoreland,
What yesternight our council did decree
In forwarding this dear expedience.

West. My liege, this haste was hot in question,
And many limits of the charge set down
But yesternight: when all athwart there came
A post from Wales loaden with heavy news;
Whose worst was, that the noble Mortimer,
Leading the men of Herefordshire to fight
Against the irregular and wild Glendower,
Was by the rude hands of that Welshman taken,
A thousand of his people butchered;
Upon whose dead corpse there was such misuse,
Such beastly shameless transformation,
By those Welshwomen done as may not be
Without much shame retold or spoken of.

King. It seems then that the tidings of this broil
Brake off our business for the Holy Land.

West. This match'd with other did, my gracious lord;
For more uneven and unwelcome news
Came from the north and thus it did import:
On Holy-rood day, the gallant Hotspur there,
Young Harry Percy and brave Archibald,
That ever-valiant and approved Scot,
At Holmedon met,
Where they did spend a sad and bloody hour;
As by discharge of their artillery,
And shape of likelihood, the news was told;
For he that brought them, in the very heat
And pride of their contention did take horse,
Uncertain of the issue any way.

King. Here is a dear, a true industrious friend,
Sir Walter Blunt, new lighted from his horse,
Stain'd with the variation of each soil
Betwixt that Holmedon and this seat of ours;
And he hath brought us smooth and welcome news.
The Earl of Douglas is discomfited:
Ten thousand bold Scots, two and twenty knights,
Balk'd in their own blood did Sir Walter see
On Holmedon's plains. Of prisoners, Hotspur took
Mordake the Earl of Fife, and eldest son
To beaten Douglas; and the Earl of Athol,
Of Murray, Angus, and Menteith:
And is not this an honourable spoil?
A gallant prize? ha, cousin, is it not?

West. In faith,
It is a conquest for a prince to boast of.

King. Yea, there thou mak'st me sad and mak'st me sin
In envy that my Lord Northumberland
Should be the father to so blest a son,
A son who is the theme of honour's tongue;
Amongst a grove, the very straightest plant;
Who is sweet Fortune's minion and her pride:
Whilst I, by looking on the praise of him,
See riot and dishonour stain the brow
Of my young Harry. O that it could be prov'd
That some night-tripping fairy had exchang'd
In cradle-clothes our children where they lay,
And call'd mine Percy, his Plantagenet!
Then would I have his Harry, and he mine.
But let him from my thoughts. What think you, coz,
Of this young Percy's pride? the prisoners,
Which he in this adventure hath surpris'd,
To his own use he keeps; and sends me word,
I shall have none but Mordake Earl of Fife.

West. This is his uncle's teaching: this is Worcester,
Malevolent to you in all aspects;
Which makes him prune himself, and bristle up
The crest of youth against your dignity.

King. But I have sent for him to answer this;
And for this cause awhile we must neglect
Our holy purpose to Jerusalem.
Cousin, on Wednesday next our council we
Will hold at Windsor; so inform the lords:
But come yourself with speed to us again;
For more is to be said and to be done
Than out of anger can be uttered.

West. I will, my liege. *Exeunt.*

[SCENE II. *London. An apartment of the Prince's.*]

Enter PRINCE OF WALES *and* SIR JOHN FALSTAFF.

Fal. Now, Hal, what time of day is it, lad?

Prince. Thou art so fat-witted, with drinking of old sack and unbuttoning thee after supper and sleeping upon benches after noon, that thou hast forgotten to demand that truly which thou wouldst truly know. What a devil hast thou to do with the time of the day? Unless hours were cups of sack and minutes capons and clocks the tongues of bawds and dials the signs of leaping-houses and the blessed sun himself a fair hot wench in flame-coloured taffeta, I see no reason why thou shouldst be so superfluous to demand the time of the day.

ACT I. SCENE I. 4. **stronds,** shores. 9. **opposed,** hostile (of enemies). 12. **intestine,** internal. 13. **close,** encounter. 22. **power,** army. 28. **twelve month,** a year; used collectively. 29. **bootless,** useless. 33. **dear expedience,** urgent expedition. 34. **hot in question,** being hotly debated. 35. **limits of the charge,** military arrangements; possibly, estimates of expense. 36. **athwart,** frustrating, interrupting. 38. **worst,** i.e., worst news. 40. **irregular,** lawless. 43-46. **Upon . . . spoken of.** Holinshed also says that the outrages are unmentionable. 49. **This . . . other,** this piece of news matched with another. 50. **uneven,** embarrassing. 55. **Holmedon,** Humbleton, a town in Northumberland. 57. **by,** i.e., judging from. 64. **the variation of each,** every kind of. 66. **smooth,** flattering, pleasant. 69. **Balk'd,** heaped up in balks or ridges. 71. **Mordake,** i.e., Murdoch. 95. **none but Mordake.** Since the prisoner in question was of royal blood, being grandson to Robert II, Hotspur could not claim him as his prisoner. 97. **Malevolent, aspects,** astrological terms. 98. **prune,** preen (as a bird its feathers).

SCENE II. 8. **sack,** a Spanish white wine. 9. **dials,** sundials. 9-10. **leaping-houses,** houses of prostitution. 11. **taffeta,** commonly worn by prostitutes.

Fal. Indeed, you come near me now, Hal; for we that take purses go by the moon and the seven stars, and not by Phœbus, he, 'that wandering knight so fair.' And, I prithee, sweet wag, when thou art king, as, God save thy grace,—majesty I should say, for grace thou wilt have none,—

Prince. What, none?

Fal. No, by my troth, not so much as will serve to be prologue to an egg and butter.

Prince. Well, how then? come, roundly, roundly.

Fal. Marry, then, sweet wag, when thou art king, let not us that are squires of the night's body be called thieves of the day's beauty: let us be Diana's foresters, gentlemen of the shade, minions of the moon; and let men say we be men of good government, being governed, as the sea is, by our noble and chaste mistress the moon, under whose countenance we steal.

Prince. Thou sayest well, and it holds well too; for the fortune of us that are the moon's men doth ebb and flow like the sea, being governed, as the sea is, by the moon. As, for proof, now: a purse of gold most resolutely snatched on Monday night and most dissolutely spent on Tuesday morning; got with swearing 'Lay by' and spent with crying 'Bring in;' now in as low an ebb as the foot of the ladder and by and by in as high a flow as the ridge of the gallows.

Fal. By the Lord, thou sayest true, lad. And is not my hostess of the tavern a most sweet wench?

Prince. As the honey of Hybla, my old lad of the castle. And is not a buff jerkin a most sweet robe of durance?

Fal. How now, how now, mad wag! what, in thy quips and thy quiddities? what a plague have I to do with a buff jerkin?

Prince. Why, what a pox have I to do with my hostess of the tavern?

Fal. Well, thou hast called her to a reckoning many a time and oft.

Prince. Did I ever call for thee to pay thy part?

Fal. No; I'll give thee thy due, thou hast paid all there.

Prince. Yea, and elsewhere, so far as my coin would stretch; and where it would not, I have used my credit.

Fal. Yea, and so used it that, were it not here apparent that thou art heir apparent—But, I prithee, sweet wag, shall there be gallows standing in England when thou art king? and resolution thus fubbed as it is with the rusty curb of old father antic the law? Do not thou, when thou art king, hang a thief.

Prince. No; thou shalt.

Fal. Shall I? O rare! By the Lord, I'll be a brave judge.

Prince. Thou judgest false already: I mean, thou shalt have the hanging of the thieves and so become a rare hangman.

Fal. Well, Hal, well; and in some sort it jumps with my humour as well as waiting in the court, I can tell you.

Prince. For obtaining of suits?

Fal. Yea, for obtaining of suits, whereof the hangman hath no lean wardrobe. 'Sblood, I am as melancholy as a gib cat or a lugged bear.

Prince. Or an old lion, or a lover's lute.

Fal. Yea, or the drone of a Lincolnshire bagpipe.

Prince. What sayest thou to a hare, or the melancholy of Moor-ditch?

Fal. Thou hast the most unsavoury similes and art indeed the most comparative, rascalliest, sweet young prince. But, Hal, I prithee, trouble me no more with vanity. I would to God thou and I knew where a commodity of good names were to be bought. An old lord of the council rated me the other day in the street about you, sir, but I marked him not; and yet he talked very wisely, but I regarded him not; and yet he talked wisely, and in the street too.

Prince. Thou didst well; for wisdom cries out in the streets, and no man regards it.

Fal. O, thou hast damnable iteration and art indeed able to corrupt a saint. Thou hast done much harm upon me, Hal; God forgive thee for it! Before I knew thee, Hal, I knew nothing; and now am I, if a man should speak truly, little better than one of the wicked. I must give over this life, and I will give it over: by the Lord, an I do not, I am a villain: I'll be damned for never a king's son in Christendom.

Prince. Where shall we take a purse to-morrow, Jack?

Fal. 'Zounds, where thou wilt, lad; I'll make one; an I do not, call me villain and baffle me.

Prince. I see a good amendment of life in thee; from praying to purse-taking.

Fal. Why, Hal, 'tis my vocation, Hal; 'tis no sin for a man to labour in his vocation.

Enter POINS.

Poins! Now shall we know if Gadshill have set a match. O, if men were to be saved by merit, what hole in hell were hot enough for him? This is the most omnipotent villain that ever cried 'Stand' to a true man.

Prince. Good morrow, Ned.

Poins. Good morrow, sweet Hal. What says Monsieur Remorse? what says Sir John Sack and Sugar? Jack! how agrees the devil and thee about thy soul, that thou soldest him on Good-Friday last for a cup of Madeira and a cold capon's leg?

Prince. Sir John stands to his word, the devil shall have his bargain; for he was never yet a breaker of proverbs: he will give the devil his due.

Poins. Then art thou damned for keeping thy word with the devil.

Prince. Else he had been damned for cozening the devil.

SCENE II. 14. **you come near me now,** you've scored a point on me. Prince Hal's speech has been full of extravagant abuse; Falstaff parries by taking it in a sense of his own. 16. **the seven stars,** the Pleiades. **Phœbus,** the sun. 17-18. **'that . . . fair,'** a line from some ballad. 19. **grace,** royal highness, with pun on spiritual grace and also on "grace" or blessing before a meal. 23. **prologue,** punning allusion to grace before meat. 24. **roundly,** out with it. It is a wit combat. 29. **Diana's.** Diana was goddess of the moon, of chastity, and of the hunt. 30. **minions,** favorites. 33. **steal,** move quietly; also, take purses. 40. **'Lay by,'** a cry of highwaymen, like "Hands up!" 41. **'Bring in,'** i.e., the orders in the tavern. 47. **Hybla,** a mountain region in Sicily near Syracuse, famed for honey. 48. **old lad of the castle,** a pun on the name, Sir John Oldcastle, borne by Falstaff in the earlier versions of the Henry IV plays; also on The Castle, a famous brothel in Southwark. **buff jerkin,** a leather jacket worn by officers of the law; a *robe of durance* in two senses, since *durance* means "imprisonment" and "durability." 51. **quips,** jests. **quiddities,** subtleties of speech. 67-68. **resolution,** courage (of a highwayman). 68. **fubbed,** cheated. 69. **antic,** buffoon. 80. **suits,** suits at court and suits of clothes. 82. **'Sblood,** an oath. 83. **gib cat,** tomcat. **lugged bear,** bear tied to a stake and baited by

Poins. But, my lads, my lads, to-morrow morning, by four o'clock, early at Gadshill! there are pilgrims going to Canterbury with rich offerings, and traders riding to London with fat purses: I have vizards for you all; you have horses for yourselves: Gadshill lies to-night in Rochester: I have bespoke supper to-morrow night in Eastcheap: we may do it as secure as sleep. If you will go, I will stuff your purses full of crowns; if you will not, tarry at home and be hanged.

Fal. Hear ye, Yedward; if I tarry at home and go not, I'll hang you for going.

Poins. You will, chops?

Fal. Hal, wilt thou make one?

Prince. Who, I rob? I a thief? not I, by my faith.

Fal. There 's neither honesty, manhood, nor good fellowship in thee, nor thou camest not of the blood royal, if thou darest not stand for ten shillings.

Prince. Well then, once in my days I'll be a madcap.

Fal. Why, that 's well said.

Prince. Well, come what will, I'll tarry at home.

Fal. By the Lord, I'll be a traitor then, when thou art king.

Prince. I care not.

Poins. Sir John, I prithee, leave the prince and me alone: I will lay him down such reasons for this adventure that he shall go.

Fal. Well, God give thee the spirit of persuasion and him the ears of profiting, that what thou speakest may move and what he hears may be believed, that the true prince may, for recreation sake, prove a false thief; for the poor abuses of the time want countenance. Farewell: you shall find me in Eastcheap.

Prince. Farewell, thou latter spring! farewell, All-hallown summer! [*Exit Falstaff.*]

Poins. Now, my good sweet honey lord, ride with us to-morrow: I have a jest to execute that I cannot manage alone. Falstaff, Bardolph, Peto and Gadshill shall rob those men that we have already waylaid; yourself and I will not be there; and when they have the booty, if you and I do not rob them, cut this head off from my shoulders.

Prince. How shall we part with them in setting forth?

Poins. Why, we will set forth before or after them, and appoint them a place of meeting, wherein it is at our pleasure to fail, and then will they adventure upon the exploit themselves; which they shall have no sooner achieved, but we'll set upon them.

Prince. Yea, but 'tis like that they will know us by our horses, by our habits and by every other appointment, to be ourselves.

Poins. Tut! our horses they shall not see; I'll tie them in the wood; our vizards we will change after we leave them: and, sirrah, I have cases of buckram for the nonce, to immask our noted outward garments.

Prince. Yea, but I doubt they will be too hard for us.

Poins. Well, for two of them, I know them to be as true-bred cowards as ever turned back; and for the third, if he fight longer than he sees reason, I'll forswear arms. The virtue of this jest will be, the incomprehensible lies that this same fat rogue will tell us when we meet at supper: how thirty, at least, he fought with; what wards, what blows, what extremities he endured; and in the reproof of this lies the jest.

Prince. Well, I'll go with thee: provide us all things necessary and meet me to-morrow night in Eastcheap; there I'll sup. Farewell.

Poins. Farewell, my lord. *Exit Poins.*

Prince. I know you all, and will awhile uphold
The unyok'd humour of your idleness:
Yet herein will I imitate the sun,
Who doth permit the base contagious clouds
To smother up his beauty from the world,
That, when he please again to be himself,
Being wanted, he may be more wond'red at,
By breaking through the foul and ugly mists
Of vapours that did seem to strangle him.
If all the year were playing holidays,
To sport would be as tedious as to work;
But when they seldom come, they wish'd for come,
And nothing pleaseth but rare accidents.
So, when this loose behaviour I throw off
And pay the debt I never promised,
By how much better than my word I am,
By so much shall I falsify men's hopes;
And like bright metal on a sullen ground,
My reformation, glitt'ring o'er my fault,
Shall show more goodly and attract more eyes
Than that which hath no foil to set it off.
I'll so offend, to make offence a skill;
Redeeming time when men think least I will. *Exit.*

[SCENE III. *London. The palace.*]

Enter the KING, NORTHUMBERLAND, WORCESTER, HOTSPUR, SIR WALTER BLUNT, *with others.*

King. My blood hath been too cold and temperate,
Unapt to stir at these indignities,
And you have found me; for accordingly
You tread upon my patience: but be sure
I will from henceforth rather be myself,
Mighty and to be fear'd, than my condition;
Which hath been smooth as oil, soft as young down,
And therefore lost that title of respect
Which the proud soul ne'er pays but to the proud.

Wor. Our house, my sovereign liege, little deserves
The scourge of greatness to be us'd on it;
And that same greatness too which our own hands
Have holp to make so portly.

North. My lord,—

King. Worcester, get thee gone; for I do see

dogs. 88. **Moor-ditch,** a foul ditch draining Moorfields. 99. **wisdom cries out,** etc., an allusion to Proverbs 1:20-24. 103. **much harm upon me.** Oldcastle was traditionally a religious hypocrite and a Lollard, or follower of John Wycliffe; Falstaff retains his faculty for insincere repentance. 112. **'Zounds,** an oath, "God's wounds." 113. **baffle,** hang up by the heels as a recreant knight. 116. **vocation,** a cant term for religious conversion. 119. **set a match,** arranged a robbery. In the old play *The Famous Victories of Henry V* Gadshill is called a "setter." 136. **cozening,** cheating. 139. **Gadshill,** a town near Rochester on the road from London to Canterbury. (One of the highwaymen is also called Gadshill.) 142. **vizards,** masks. 149. **Yedward,** Edward; a colloquialism. 151. **chops,** apparently alluding to Falstaff's fat jaws. 170, 171. **spirit of persuasion, ears of profiting,** cant phrases of religious connotation. 175. **want countenance,** lack encouragement and protection from men of rank. 178. **All-hallown summer.** Falstaff's summer (his youth) has lasted to All Saints' Day, November 1st. 182. **Bardolph, Peto,** so Theobald; QF: *Harvey, Rossill.* 201. **cases,** suits. 202. **noted,** known. 208. **incomprehensible,** unlimited.

SCENE III. 3. **found me,** i.e., found me so. 13. **portly,** prosperous, with a suggestion of overprosperity.

Danger and disobedience in thine eye:
O, sir, your presence is too bold and peremptory,
And majesty might never yet endure
The moody frontier of a servant brow.
You have good leave to leave us: when we need
Your use and counsel, we shall send for you. *Exit Wor.*
You were about to speak. [*To North.*]
North. Yea, my good lord.
Those prisoners in your highness' name demanded,
Which Harry Percy here at Holmedon took,
Were, as he says, not with such strength denied
As is delivered to your majesty:
Either envy, therefore, or misprision
Is guilty of this fault and not my son.
Hot. My liege, I did deny no prisoners.
But I remember, when the fight was done,
When I was dry with rage and extreme toil,
Breathless and faint, leaning upon my sword,
Came there a certain lord, neat, and trimly dress'd,
Fresh as a bridegroom; and his chin new reap'd
Show'd like a stubble-land at harvest-home;
He was perfumed like a milliner;
And 'twixt his finger and his thumb he held
A pouncet-box, which ever and anon
He gave his nose and took 't away again;
Who therewith angry, when it next came there,
Took it in snuff; and still he smil'd and talk'd,
And as the soldiers bore dead bodies by,
He call'd them untaught knaves, unmannerly,
To bring a slovenly unhandsome corse
Betwixt the wind and his nobility.
With many holiday and lady terms
He questioned me; amongst the rest, demanded
My prisoners in your majesty's behalf.
I then, all smarting with my wounds being cold,
To be so pest'red with a popinjay,
Out of my grief and my impatience,
Answer'd neglectingly I know not what,
He should, or he should not; for he made me mad
To see him shine so brisk and smell so sweet
And talk so like a waiting-gentlewoman
Of guns and drums and wounds,—God save the mark!—
And telling me the sovereignest thing on earth
Was parmaceti for an inward bruise;
And that it was great pity, so it was,
This villanous salt-petre should be digg'd
Out of the bowels of the harmless earth,
Which many a good tall fellow had destroy'd
So cowardly; and but for these vile guns,
He would himself have been a soldier.
This bald unjointed chat of his, my lord,
I answer'd indirectly, as I said;
And I beseech you, let not his report
Come current for an accusation
Betwixt my love and your high majesty.
Blunt. The circumstance considered, good my lord,
Whate'er Lord Harry Percy then had said
To such a person and in such a place,
At such a time, with all the rest retold,
May reasonably die and never rise
To do him wrong or any way impeach
What then he said, so he unsay it now.
King. Why, yet he doth deny his prisoners,
But with proviso and exception,
That we at our own charge shall ransom straight
His brother-in-law, the foolish Mortimer;
Who, on my soul, hath wilfully betray'd
The lives of those that he did lead to fight
Against that great magician, damn'd Glendower,
Whose daughter, as we hear, that Earl of March
Hath lately married. Shall our coffers, then,
Be emptied to redeem a traitor home?
Shall we buy treason? and indent with fears,
When they have lost and forfeited themselves?
No, on the barren mountains let him starve;
For I shall never hold that man my friend
Whose tongue shall ask me for one penny cost
To ransom home revolted Mortimer.
Hot. Revolted Mortimer!
He never did fall off, my sovereign liege,
But by the chance of war: to prove that true
Needs no more but one tongue for all those wounds,
Those mouthed wounds, which valiantly he took,
When on the gentle Severn's sedgy bank,
In single opposition, hand to hand,
He did confound the best part of an hour
In changing hardiment with great Glendower:
Three times they breath'd and three times did they drink,
Upon agreement, of swift Severn's flood;
Who then, affrighted with their bloody looks,
Ran fearfully among the trembling reeds,
And hid his crisp head in the hollow bank
Bloodstained with these valiant combatants.
Never did base and rotten policy
Colour her working with such deadly wounds;
Nor never could the noble Mortimer
Receive so many, and all willingly:
Then let not him be slandered with revolt.
King. Thou dost belie him, Percy, thou dost belie him;
He never did encounter with Glendower:
I tell thee,
He durst as well have met the devil alone
As Owen Glendower for an enemy.
Art thou not asham'd? But, sirrah, henceforth
Let me not hear you speak of Mortimer:
Send me your prisoners with the speediest means
Or you shall hear in such a kind from me
As will displease you. My Lord Northumberland,
We license your departure with your son.
Send us your prisoners, or you will hear of it.
Exit King [*with Blunt, and train*].
Hot. An if the devil come and roar for them,
I will not send them: I will after straight
And tell him so; for I will ease my heart,
Albeit I make a hazard of my head.

19. **moody,** passionate, angry. **frontier,** outwork or fortification; here with play on the word *front* or *brow*. 27. **envy,** malice. **misprision,** misunderstanding. 34. **reap'd,** i.e., with beard newly trimmed according to the latest fashion, not like a soldier's beard. 35. **Show'd,** looked. **harvest-home,** end of harvest, fields being neat and bare. 36. **milliner,** man dealing in fancy articles. 38. **pouncet-box,** perfume box with perforated lid. 40. **Who,** i.e., his nose. 41. **Took it in snuff,** proverbially meaning to take offense, but here with literal meaning also; the nose sniffs in the perfume. (This snuff is not tobacco, but perfumed herbs.) 46. **lady,** ladylike. 50. **popinjay,** parrot. 51. **grief,** pain. 56. **God save the mark.** Probably originally a formula to avert evil omen; here, an expression of impatience. 57. **sovereignest,** most efficacious. 58. **parmaceti,** spermaceti, sperm from the whale. 80, 84. **Mortimer, Earl of March.** There were two Edmund Mortimers; Shakespeare confuses them and combines their stories. It was the uncle (1378-1409?) who was captured by Glendower and married Glen-

North. What, drunk with choler? stay and pause awhile:
Here comes your uncle.

Enter Worcester.

Hot. Speak of Mortimer!
'Zounds, I will speak of him; and let my soul
Want mercy, if I do not join with him:
Yea, on his part I'll empty all these veins,
And shed my dear blood drop by drop in the dust,
But I will lift the down-trod Mortimer
As high in the air as this unthankful king,
As this ingrate and cank'red Bolingbroke.
North. Brother, the king hath made your nephew mad.
Wor. Who struck this heat up after I was gone?
Hot. He will, forsooth, have all my prisoners;
And when I urg'd the ransom once again
Of my wife's brother, then his cheek look'd pale,
And on my face he turn'd an eye of death,
Trembling even at the name of Mortimer.
Wor. I cannot blame him: was not he proclaim'd
By Richard that dead is the next of blood?
North. He was; I heard the proclamation:
And then it was when the unhappy king,—
Whose wrongs in us God pardon!—did set forth
Upon his Irish expedition;
From whence he intercepted did return
To be depos'd and shortly murdered.
Wor. And for whose death we in the world's wide mouth
Live scandaliz'd and foully spoken of.
Hot. But, soft, I pray you; did King Richard then
Proclaim my brother Edmund Mortimer
Heir to the crown?
North. He did; myself did hear it.
Hot. Nay, then I cannot blame his cousin king,
That wish'd him on the barren mountains starve.
But shall it be, that you, that set the crown
Upon the head of this forgetful man
And for his sake wear the detested blot
Of murderous subornation, shall it be,
That you a world of curses undergo,
Being the agents, or base second means,
The cords, the ladder, or the hangman rather?
O, pardon me that I descend so low,
To show the line and the predicament
Wherein you range under this subtle king;
Shall it for shame be spoken in these days,
Or fill up chronicles in time to come,
That men of your nobility and power
Did gage them both in an unjust behalf,
As both of you—God pardon it!—have done,
To put down Richard, that sweet lovely rose,
And plant this thorn, this canker, Bolingbroke?
And shall it in more shame be further spoken,
That you are fool'd, discarded and shook off
By him for whom these shames ye underwent?
No; yet time serves wherein you may redeem
Your banish'd honours and restore yourselves
Into the good thoughts of the world again,
Revenge the jeering and disdain'd contempt
Of this proud king, who studies day and night
To answer all the debt he owes to you
Even with the bloody payment of your deaths:
Therefore, I say,—
Wor. Peace, cousin, say no more:
And now I will unclasp a secret book,
And to your quick-conceiving discontents
I'll read you matter deep and dangerous,
As full of peril and adventurous spirit
As to o'er-walk a current roaring loud
On the unsteadfast footing of a spear.
Hot. If he fall in, good night! or sink or swim:
Send danger from the east unto the west,
So honour cross it from the north to south,
And let them grapple: O, the blood more stirs
To rouse a lion than to start a hare!
North. Imagination of some great exploit
Drives him beyond the bounds of patience.
Hot. By heaven, methinks it were an easy leap,
To pluck bright honour from the pale-fac'd moon,
Or dive into the bottom of the deep,
Where fathom-line could never touch the ground,
And pluck up drowned honour by the locks;
So he that doth redeem her thence might wear
Without corrival all her dignities:
But out upon this half-fac'd fellowship!
Wor. He apprehends a world of figures here,
But not the form of what he should attend.
Good cousin, give me audience for a while.
Hot. I cry you mercy.
Wor. Those same noble Scots
That are your prisoners,—
Hot. I'll keep them all;
By God, he shall not have a Scot of them!
No, if a Scot would save his soul, he shall not:
I'll keep them, by this hand!
Wor. You start away
And lend no ear unto my purposes.
Those prisoners you shall keep.
Hot. Nay, I will; that 's flat:
He said he would not ransom Mortimer;
Forbad my tongue to speak of Mortimer;
But I will find him when he lies asleep,
And in his ear I'll holla 'Mortimer!'
Nay,
I'll have a starling shall be taught to speak
Nothing but 'Mortimer,' and give it him,
To keep his anger still in motion.
Wor. Hear you, cousin; a word.
Hot. All studies here I solemnly defy,
Save how to gall and pinch this Bolingbroke:
And that same sword-and-buckler Prince of Wales,
But that I think his father loves him not
And would be glad he met with some mischance,
I would have him poisoned with a pot of ale.
Wor. Farewell, kinsman: I'll talk to you

dower's daughter; it was the nephew (1391-1425), fourth Earl of March, who had been proclaimed heir to King Richard II. 87. **indent,** bargain, make an indenture. 101. **changing hardiment,** exchanging blows. 102. **breath'd,** paused for breath. 108. **policy,** cunning. 137. **cank'red,** spoiled, malignant. 149. **in us,** caused by our doings. 163. **murderous subornation,** the suborning of or inciting to murder. 168. **line,** rank; also, hangman's rope. **predicament,** dilemma, dangerous situation; also, category. 173. **gage,** pledge. 176. **canker,** canker rose, dog rose, wild and unfragrant; also, ulcer. 183. **disdain'd,** disdainful. 194. **or sink or swim,** i.e., such a man, walking over a roaring stream, is doomed if he fall in, whether he sink or swim. 207. **corrival,** rival, competitor. 208. **But . . . fellowship,** i.e., down with this business of sharing glory with others. 230. **sword-and-buckler,** arms improper for a prince, who should carry rapier and dagger.

When you are better temper'd to attend.
North. Why, what a wasp-stung and impatient fool
Art thou to break into this woman's mood,
Tying thine ear to no tongue but thine own!
Hot. Why, look you, I am whipp'd and scourg'd with rods,
Nettled and stung with pismires, when I hear
Of this vile politician, Bolingbroke.
In Richard's time,—what do you call the place?—
A plague upon it, it is in Gloucestershire;
'Twas where the madcap duke his uncle kept,
His uncle York; where I first bow'd my knee
Unto this king of smiles, this Bolingbroke,—
'Sblood!—
When you and he came back from Ravenspurgh.
North. At Berkeley castle.
Hot. You say true:
Why, what a candy deal of courtesy
This fawning greyhound then did proffer me!
'Look when his infant fortune came to age,'
And 'gentle Harry Percy,' and 'kind cousin;'
O, the devil take such cozeners! God forgive me!
Good uncle, tell your tale; I have done.
Wor. Nay, if you have not, to it again;
We will stay your leisure.
Hot. I have done, i' faith.
Wor. Then once more to your Scottish prisoners.
Deliver them up without their ransom straight,
And make the Douglas' son your only mean
For powers in Scotland; which, for divers reasons
Which I shall send you written, be assur'd,
Will easily be granted. You, my lord,
[*To Northumberland.*]
Your son in Scotland being thus employ'd,
Shall secretly into the bosom creep
Of that same noble prelate, well belov'd,
The archbishop.
Hot. Of York, is it not?
Wor. True; who bears hard
His brother's death at Bristow, the Lord Scroop.
I speak not this in estimation,
As what I think might be, but what I know
Is ruminated, plotted and set down,
And only stays but to behold the face
Of that occasion that shall bring it on.
Hot. I smell it: upon my life, it will do well.
North. Before the game is afoot, thou still let'st slip.
Hot. Why, it cannot choose but be a noble plot:
And then the power of Scotland and of York,
To join with Mortimer, ha?
Wor. And so they shall.
Hot. In faith, it is exceedingly well aim'd.
Wor. And 'tis no little reason bids us speed,
To save our heads by raising of a head;
For, bear ourselves as even as we can,
The king will always think him in our debt,
And think we think ourselves unsatisfied,
Till he hath found a time to pay us home:
And see already how he doth begin
To make us strangers to his looks of love.
Hot. He does, he does: we'll be reveng'd on him.
Wor. Cousin, farewell: no further go in this
Than I by letters shall direct your course.
When time is ripe, which will be suddenly,
I'll steal to Glendower and Lord Mortimer;
Where you and Douglas and our pow'rs at once,
As I will fashion it, shall happily meet,
To bear our fortunes in our own strong arms,
Which now we hold at much uncertainty.
North. Farewell, good brother: we shall thrive, I trust.
Hot. Uncle, adieu: O, let the hours be short
Till fields and blows and groans applaud our sport!
Exeunt.

[ACT II.

SCENE I. *Rochester. An inn yard.*]

Enter a Carrier *with a lantern in his hand.*

First Car. Heigh-ho! an it be not four by the day, I'll be hanged: Charles' wain is over the new chimney, and yet our horse not packed. What, ostler!

Ost. [*Within*] Anon, anon.

First Car. I prithee, Tom, beat Cut's saddle, put a few flocks in the point; poor jade, is wrung in the withers out of all cess.

Enter another Carrier.

Sec. Car. Peas and beans are as dank here as a dog, and that is the next way to give poor jades the bots: this house is turned upside down since Robin Ostler died.

First Car. Poor fellow, never joyed since the price of oats rose; it was the death of him.

Sec. Car. I think this be the most villanous house in all London road for fleas: I am stung like a tench.

First Car. Like a tench! by the mass, there is ne'er a king christen could be better bit than I have been since the first cock.

Sec. Car. Why, they will allow us ne'er a jordan, and then we leak in your chimney; and your chamber-lie breeds fleas like a loach.

First Car. What, ostler! come away and be hanged! come away.

Sec. Car. I have a gammon of bacon and two razes of ginger, to be delivered as far as Charing-cross.

First Car. God's body! the turkeys in my pannier are quite starved. What, ostler! A plague on thee! hast thou never an eye in thy head? canst not hear? An 'twere not as good deed as drink, to break the pate on thee, I am a very villain. Come, and be hanged! hast no faith in thee?

Enter GADSHILL.

240. **pismires,** ants. 241. **politician,** deceitful schemer. 244. **kept,** dwelled. 251. **candy,** sugared, flattering. 255. **cozeners,** cheats, with pun on "cousins." 261. **mean,** i.e., means of procuring. 272. **estimation,** guesswork. 278. **let'st slip,** i.e., let loose the dogs.

ACT II. SCENE I. *Stage Direction:* **Carrier,** one whose trade was conveying goods, usually by pack horses. 1-2. **by the day,** in the morning. 2. **Charles' wain,** the constellation of the Great Bear. 3. **horse,** horses. 6. **beat,** soften. **Cut's saddle,** packsaddle of the horse named *Cut*, meaning "bob-tailed." 7. **flocks,** locks of wool. **point,** pommel of the saddle. **wrung,** chafed. 8. **cess,** measure, estimate. 10. **next,** nearest, quickest. 11. **bots,** a disease of horses. 17. **tench,** a kind of fish; probably an allusion to an ancient belief that the spots on certain fishes were due to flea bites. 19. **christen,** in Christendom. 20. **first cock,** i.e., midnight. 22. **jordan,** chamberpot. 23. **chamber-lie,** urine. **loach,** a prolific fish. 26. **gammon,** side. 27. **razes,** roots. 30. **pannier,** basket. 43. **Ay, when? canst tell?** Don't you wish I would? 51, 64. **charge,** baggage. 53. **At hand, quoth pick-purse,** slang expression for "Coming immediately." Gadshill's reply shows the chamberlain's alliance with the robbers. 60. **holds current,** holds true. 61. **franklin,** a farmer owning his own land. **wild of Kent,**

Gads. Good morrow, carriers. What 's o'clock?

First Car. I think it be two o'clock.

Gads. I prithee, lend me thy lantern, to see my gelding in the stable.

First Car. Nay, by God, soft; I know a trick worth two of that, i' faith.

Gads. I pray thee, lend me thine.

Sec. Car. Ay, when? canst tell? Lend me thy lantern, quoth he? marry, I'll see thee hanged first.

Gads. Sirrah carrier, what time do you mean to come to London?

Sec. Car. Time enough to go to bed with a candle, I warrant thee. Come, neighbour Mugs, we'll call up the gentlemen: they will along with company, for they have great charge. *Exeunt* [*Carriers*].

Gads. What, ho! chamberlain!

Enter Chamberlain.

Cham. At hand, quoth pick-purse.

Gads. That 's even as fair as—at hand, quoth the chamberlain; for thou variest no more from picking of purses than giving direction doth from labouring; thou layest the plot how.

Cham. Good morrow, Master Gadshill. It holds current that I told you yesternight: there 's a franklin in the wild of Kent hath brought three hundred marks with him in gold: I heard him tell it to one of his company last night at supper; a kind of auditor; one that hath abundance of charge too, God knows what. They are up already, and call for eggs and butter: they will away presently.

Gads. Sirrah, if they meet not with Saint Nicholas' clerks, I'll give thee this neck.

Cham. No, I'll none of it: I pray thee, keep that for the hangman; for I know thou worshippest Saint Nicholas as truly as a man of falsehood may.

Gads. What talkest thou to me of the hangman? if I hang, I'll make a fat pair of gallows; for if I hang, old Sir John hangs with me, and thou knowest he is no starveling. Tut! there are other Troyans that thou dreamest not of, the which for sport sake are content to do the profession some grace; that would, if matters should be looked into, for their own credit sake, make all whole. I am joined with no foot land-rakers, no long-staff sixpenny strikers, none of these mad mustachio purple-hued malt-worms; but with nobility and tranquillity, burgomasters and great oneyers, such as can hold in, such as will strike sooner than speak, and speak sooner than drink, and drink sooner than pray: and yet, 'zounds, I lie; for they pray continually to their saint, the commonwealth; or rather, not pray to her, but prey on her, for they ride up and down on her and make her their boots.

Cham. What, the commonwealth their boots? will she hold out water in foul way?

Gads. She will, she will; justice hath liquored her. We steal as in a castle, cocksure; we have the receipt of fern-seed, we walk invisible.

Cham. Nay, by my faith, I think you are more beholding to the night than to fern-seed for your walking invisible.

Gads. Give me thy hand: thou shalt have a share in our purchase, as I am a true man.

Cham. Nay, rather let me have it, as you are a false thief.

Gads. Go to; 'homo' is a common name to all men. Bid the ostler bring my gelding out of the stable. Farewell, you muddy knave. [*Exeunt.*]

[SCENE II. *The highway, near Gadshill.*]

Enter PRINCE, POINS, *and* PETO, *&c.*

Poins. Come, shelter, shelter: I have removed Falstaff's horse, and he frets like a gummed velvet.

Prince. Stand close.

Enter FALSTAFF.

Fal. Poins! Poins, and be hanged! Poins!

Prince. Peace, ye fat-kidneyed rascal! what a brawling dost thou keep!

Fal. Where 's Poins, Hal?

Prince. He is walked up to the top of the hill: I'll go seek him. [*Steps aside.*]

Fal. I am accursed to rob in that thief's company: the rascal hath removed my horse, and tied him I know not where. If I travel but four foot by the squier further afoot, I shall break my wind. Well, I doubt not but to die a fair death for all this, if I 'scape hanging for killing that rogue. I have forsworn his company hourly any time this two and twenty years, and yet I am bewitched with the rogue's company. If the rascal have not given me medicines to make me love him, I'll be hanged; it could not be else; I have drunk medicines. Poins! Hal! a plague upon you both! Bardolph! Peto! I'll starve ere I'll rob a foot further. An 'twere not as good a deed as drink, to turn true man and to leave these rogues, I am the veriest varlet that ever chewed with a tooth. Eight yards of uneven ground is threescore and ten miles afoot with me; and the stony-hearted villains know it well enough: a plague upon it when thieves cannot be true one to another! (*They whistle.*) Whew! A plague upon you all! Give me my horse, you rogues; give me my horse, and be hanged!

Prince. [*Comes forward*] Peace, ye fat-guts! lie down; lay thine ear close to the ground and list if thou canst hear the tread of travellers.

Fal. Have you any levers to lift me up again, being down? 'Sblood, I'll not bear mine own flesh so far afoot again for all the coin in thy father's exchequer. What a plague mean ye to colt me thus?

Prince. Thou liest; thou art not colted, thou art uncolted.

Fal. I prithee, good Prince Hal, help me to my horse, good king's son.

weald (wooded region) of Kent. 62. **marks,** coins of the value in that day of 13s. 6d. 68. **Saint Nicholas' clerks,** highwaymen. St. Nicholas was vulgarly supposed the patron of thieves. 77. **Troyans,** slang for "thieves." 81. **foot land-rakers,** footpads. 82. **long-staff sixpenny strikers,** robbers with long staves who would knock down their victims for sixpence. 83. **mustachio purple-hued malt-worms,** common drunkards with mustaches stained with drink. 84. **tranquillity,** those who lead easy lives. 85. **oneyers,** many conjectures; possibly, a coinage from *ones* with pun on *owner* (White). **hold in,** keep confidence. 91. **boots,** booty, with pun on "boots." 95. **liquored,** made waterproof by oiling, and made drunk. 96. **of fern-seed,** i.e., of becoming invisible, since fern seed was popularly supposed to render its possessor invisible. 104. **'homo' . . . men,** i.e., the Latin name for man applies to all types.

SCENE II. 2. **frets,** chafes, with pun on another meaning of the word applying to velvet with the nap awry. 13. **squier,** square, measure. 20. **medicines,** love potions. 25. **turn true man,** turn honest man; also, turn informer. 40. **colt,** cheat.

Prince. Out, ye rogue! shall I be your ostler?

Fal. Go hang thyself in thine own heir-apparent garters! If I be ta'en, I'll peach for this. An I have not ballads made on you all and sung to filthy tunes, let a cup of sack be my poison: when a jest is so forward, and afoot too! I hate it.

Enter GADSHILL [*and* BARDOLPH].

Gads. Stand.

Fal. So I do, against my will.

Poins. O, 'tis our setter: I know his voice. Bardolph, what news?

Bard. Case ye, case ye; on with your vizards: there 's money of the king's coming down the hill; 'tis going to the king's exchequer.

Fal. You lie, ye rogue; 'tis going to the king's tavern.

Gads. There 's enough to make us all.

Fal. To be hanged.

Prince. Sirs, you four shall front them in the narrow lane; Ned Poins and I will walk lower: if they 'scape from your encounter, then they light on us.

Peto. How many be there of them?

Gads. Some eight or ten.

Fal. 'Zounds, will they not rob us?

Prince. What, a coward, Sir John Paunch?

Fal. Indeed, I am not John of Gaunt, your grandfather; but yet no coward, Hal.

Prince. Well, we leave that to the proof.

Poins. Sirrah Jack, thy horse stands behind the hedge: when thou needest him, there thou shalt find him. Farewell, and stand fast.

Fal. Now cannot I strike him, if I should be hanged.

Prince. [*To Poins*] Ned, where are our disguises?

Poins. [*To Prince*] Here, hard by: stand close.

[*Exeunt Prince and Poins.*]

Fal. Now, my masters, happy man be his dole, say I: every man to his business.

Enter the Travellers.

First Trav. Come, neighbour: the boy shall lead our horses down the hill; we'll walk afoot awhile, and ease our legs.

Thieves. Stand!

Travellers. Jesus bless us!

Fal. Strike; down with them; cut the villains' throats: ah! whoreson caterpillars! bacon-fed knaves! they hate us youth: down with them; fleece them.

Travellers. O, we are undone, both we and ours for ever!

Fal. Hang ye, gorbellied knaves, are ye undone? No, ye fat chuffs; I would your store were here! On, bacons, on! What, ye knaves! young men must live. You are grandjurors, are ye? we'll jure ye, 'faith.

Here they rob them and bind them. Exeunt.

Enter the PRINCE *and* POINS.

Prince. The thieves have bound the true men. Now could thou and I rob the thieves and go merrily to London, it would be argument for a week, laughter for a month and a good jest for ever.

Poins. Stand close; I hear them coming.

Enter the Thieves again.

Fal. Come, my masters, let us share, and then to horse before day. An the Prince and Poins be not two arrant cowards, there 's no equity stirring: there 's no more valour in that Poins than in a wild-duck.

Prince. Your money!

Poins. Villains!

As they are sharing, the Prince and Poins set upon them; they all run away; and Falstaff, after a blow or two, runs away too, leaving the booty behind them.

Prince. Got with much ease. Now merrily to horse:
The thieves are all scattered and possess'd with fear
So strongly that they dare not meet each other;
Each takes his fellow for an officer.
Away, good Ned. Falstaff sweats to death,
And lards the lean earth as he walks along:
Were 't not for laughing, I should pity him.

Poins. How the fat rogue roar'd! *Exeunt.*

[SCENE III. *Warkworth castle.*]

Enter HOTSPUR, *solus, reading a letter.*

Hot. 'But, for mine own part, my lord, I could be well contented to be there, in respect of the love I bear your house.' He could be contented: why is he not, then? In respect of the love he bears our house: he shows in this, he loves his own barn better than he loves our house. Let me see some more. 'The purpose you undertake is dangerous;'—why, that 's certain: 'tis dangerous to take a cold, to sleep, to drink; but I tell you, my lord fool, out of this nettle, danger, we pluck this flower, safety. 'The purpose you undertake is dangerous; the friends you have named uncertain; the time itself unsorted; and your whole plot too light for the counterpoise of so great an opposition.' Say you so, say you so? I say unto you again, you are a shallow cowardly hind, and you lie. What a lack-brain is this! By the Lord, our plot is a good plot as ever was laid; our friends true and constant: a good plot, good friends, and full of expectation; an excellent plot, very good friends. What a frosty-spirited rogue is this! Why, my lord of York commends the plot and the general course of the action. 'Zounds, an I were now by this rascal, I could brain him with his lady's fan. Is there not my father, my uncle and myself? lord Edmund Mortimer, my lord of York and Owen Glendower? is there not besides the Douglas? have I not all their letters to meet me in arms by the ninth of the next month? and are they not some of them set forward already? What a pagan rascal is this! an infidel! Ha! you shall see now in very sincerity of fear and cold heart, will he to the king and lay open all our proceedings. O, I could divide myself and go to buffets, for moving such a dish of skim milk with so honourable an action! Hang him! let him tell the king: we are prepared. I will set forward to-night.

47. **peach,** inform on you. 53. **setter,** arranger of the robbery. 55. **Case ye,** put on your disguises. 70. **Gaunt,** with pun on *gaunt,* thin. 80. **happy man be his dole,** may happiness be his portion. 88. **caterpillars,** those who thrive off the commonwealth. 93. **gorbellied,** big-bellied. 94. **chuffs,** churls, rich but miserly. **store,** total wealth. 95. **bacons,** swine. 96. **grandjurors,** i.e., men of wealth, able to serve on juries. 100. **argument,** a subject for conversation. 107. **equity,** justice; variously interpreted. 116. **lards the lean earth,** an allusion to the practice on the part of butchers of inserting fat into lean meat. 118. **fat,** introduced by Neilson from a fragmentary QO; not in Globe.

SCENE III. 13. **unsorted,** unsuitable. 16. **hind,** menial. 34-35. **divide . . . buffets,** i.e., fight with myself. 50. **watch'd,** lain awake. 55. **palisadoes,** stakes set in the ground for defense. 56. **basilisks,** large cannon. **culverin,** long cannon. 58. **currents,** occurrences.

Enter his LADY.

How now, Kate! I must leave you within these two hours.

Lady. O, my good lord, why are you thus alone?
For what offence have I this fortnight been
A banish'd woman from my Harry's bed?
Tell me, sweet lord, what is 't that takes from thee
Thy stomach, pleasure and thy golden sleep?
Why dost thou bend thine eyes upon the earth,
And start so often when thou sit'st alone?
Why hast thou lost the fresh blood in thy cheeks;
And given my treasures and my rights of thee
To thick-ey'd musing and curs'd melancholy?
In thy faint slumbers I by thee have watch'd,
And heard thee murmur tales of iron wars;
Speak terms of manage to thy bounding steed;
Cry 'Courage! to the field!' And thou hast talk'd
Of sallies and retires, of trenches, tents,
Of palisadoes, frontiers, parapets,
Of basilisks, of cannon, culverin,
Of prisoners' ransom and of soldiers slain,
And all the currents of a heady fight.
Thy spirit within thee hath been so at war
And thus hath so bestirr'd thee in thy sleep,
That beads of sweat have stood upon thy brow,
Like bubbles in a late-disturbed stream;
And in thy face strange motions have appear'd,
Such as we see when men restrain their breath
On some great sudden hest. O, what portents are these?
Some heavy business hath my lord in hand,
And I must know it, else he loves me not.

Hot. What, ho!

[*Enter* Servant.]

Is Gilliams with the packet gone?

Serv. He is, my lord, an hour ago.

Hot. Hath Butler brought those horses from the sheriff?

Serv. One horse, my lord, he brought even now.

Hot. What horse? a roan, a crop-ear, is it not?

Serv. It is, my lord.

Hot. That roan shall be my throne.
Well, I will back him straight: O esperance!
Bid Butler lead him forth into the park. [*Exit Servant.*]

Lady. But hear you, my lord.

Hot. What say'st thou, my lady?

Lady. What is it carries you away?

Hot. Why, my horse, my love, my horse.

Lady. Out, you mad-headed ape!
A weasel hath not such a deal of spleen
As you are toss'd with. In faith,
I'll know your business, Harry, that I will.
I fear my brother Mortimer doth stir
About his title, and hath sent for you
To line his enterprize: but if you go,—

Hot. So far afoot, I shall be weary, love.

Lady. Come, come, you paraquito, answer me
Directly unto this question that I ask:
In faith, I'll break thy little finger, Harry,
An if thou wilt not tell me all things true.

Hot. Away,
Away, you trifler! Love! I love thee not,
I care not for thee, Kate: this is no world
To play with mammets and to tilt with lips:
We must have bloody noses and crack'd crowns,
And pass them current too. God 's me, my horse!
What say'st thou, Kate? what would'st thou have with me?

Lady. Do you not love me? do you not, indeed?
Well, do not then; for since you love me not,
I will not love myself. Do you not love me?
Nay, tell me if you speak in jest or no.

Hot. Come, wilt thou see me ride?
And when I am a-horseback, I will swear
I love thee infinitely. But hark you, Kate:
I must not have you henceforth question me
Whither I go, nor reason whereabout:
Whither I must, I must; and, to conclude,
This evening must I leave you, gentle Kate.
I know you wise, but yet no farther wise
Than Harry Percy's wife: constant you are,
But yet a woman: and for secrecy,
No lady closer; for I well believe
Thou wilt not utter what thou dost not know;
And so far will I trust thee, gentle Kate.

Lady. How! so far?

Hot. Not an inch further. But hark you, Kate:
Whither I go, thither shall you go too;
To-day will I set forth, to-morrow you.
Will this content you, Kate?

Lady. It must of force. *Exeunt.*

[SCENE IV. *The Boar's-Head Tavern, Eastcheap.*]

Enter PRINCE *and* POINS.

Prince. Ned, prithee, come out of that fat room, and lend me thy hand to laugh a little.

Poins. Where hast been, Hal?

Prince. With three or four loggerheads amongst three or four score hogsheads. I have sounded the very base-string of humility. Sirrah, I am sworn brother to a leash of drawers; and can call them all by their christen names, as Tom, Dick, and Francis. They take it already upon their salvation, that though I be but Prince of Wales, yet I am the king of courtesy; and tell me flatly I am no proud Jack, like Falstaff, but a Corinthian, a lad of mettle, a good boy, by the Lord, so they call me, and when I am king of England, I shall command all the good lads in Eastcheap. They call drinking deep, dyeing scarlet; and when you breathe in your watering, they cry 'hem!' and bid you play it off. To conclude, I am so good a proficient in one quarter of an hour, that I can drink with any tinker in his own language during my life. I tell thee, Ned, thou hast lost much honour, that thou wert not with me in this action. But, sweet Ned,—to sweeten which name of Ned, I give thee this pennyworth of sugar, clapped even now into

65. **hest,** command. 74. **esperance,** hope; the motto of the Percy family. 86. **line,** strengthen. 88. **paraquito,** little parrot; term of endearment. 95. **mammets,** dolls; or else breasts. 96. **crowns,** obvious pun on the coin called a "crown." 120. **of force,** of necessity.

SCENE IV. *Stage Direction:* **The Boar's-Head.** Never named as such in this play, but see *2 Henry IV*, II, ii, 159. 1. **fat,** stuffy; or, a vat-room. 4. **loggerheads,** blockheads. 7. **sworn brother,** allusion to the practice of becoming *fratres jurati.* **leash of drawers,** i.e., three waiters (like three greyhounds). 13. **Corinthian,** gay fellow, with suggestion of profligacy. 17. **breathe,** pause. 18. **watering,** drinking. 20-21. **tinker . . . language.** Tinkers' language was cant or jargon, and tinkers were proverbial drinkers.

my hand by an under-skinker, one that never spake other English in his life than 'Eight shillings and sixpence,' and 'You are welcome,' with this shrill addition, 'Anon, anon, sir! Score a pint of bastard in the Half-moon,' or so. But, Ned, to drive away the time till Falstaff come, I prithee, do thou stand in some by-room, while I question my puny drawer to what end he gave me the sugar; and do thou never leave calling 'Francis,' that his tale to me may be nothing but 'Anon.' Step aside, and I'll show thee a precedent.

Poins. Francis!

Prince. Thou art perfect.

Poins. Francis! [*Exit Poins.*]

Enter [FRANCIS, *a*] *Drawer.*

Fran. Anon, anon, sir. Look down into the Pomgarnet, Ralph.

Prince. Come hither, Francis.

Fran. My lord?

Prince. How long hast thou to serve, Francis?

Fran. Forsooth, five years, and as much as to—

Poins. [*Within*] Francis!

Fran. Anon, anon, sir.

Prince. Five year! by 'r lady, a long lease for the clinking of pewter. But, Francis, darest thou be so valiant as to play the coward with thy indenture and show it a fair pair of heels and run from it?

Fran. O Lord, sir, I'll be sworn upon all the books in England, I could find in my heart—

Poins. [*Within*] Francis!

Fran. Anon, sir.

Prince. How old art thou, Francis?

Fran. Let me see—about Michaelmas next I shall be—

Poins. [*Within*] Francis!

Fran. Anon, sir. Pray stay a little, my lord.

Prince. Nay, but hark you, Francis: for the sugar thou gavest me, 'twas a pennyworth, was 't not?

Fran. O Lord, I would it had been two!

Prince. I will give thee for it a thousand pound: ask me when thou wilt, and thou shalt have it.

Poins. [*Within*] Francis!

Fran. Anon, anon.

Prince. Anon, Francis? No, Francis; but to-morrow, Francis; or Francis, a Thursday; or indeed, Francis, when thou wilt. But, Francis!

Fran. My lord?

Prince. Wilt thou rob this leathern jerkin, crystal-button, not-pated, agate-ring, puke-stocking, caddis-garter, smooth-tongue, Spanish-pouch,—

Fran. O Lord, sir, who do you mean?

Prince. Why, then, your brown bastard is your only drink; for look you, Francis, your white canvas doublet will sully: in Barbary, sir, it cannot come to so much.

Fran. What, sir?

Poins. [*Within*] Francis!

Prince. Away, you rogue! dost thou not hear them call?

Here they both call him; the drawer stands amazed, not knowing which way to go.

Enter Vintner.

Vint. What, standest thou still, and hearest such a calling? Look to the guests within. [*Exit Francis.*] My lord, old Sir John, with half-a-dozen more, are at the door: shall I let them in?

Prince. Let them alone awhile, and then open the door. [*Exit Vintner.*] Poins!

Enter POINS.

Poins. Anon, anon, sir.

Prince. Sirrah, Falstaff and the rest of the thieves are at the door: shall we be merry?

Poins. As merry as crickets, my lad. But hark ye; what cunning match have you made with this jest of the drawer? come, what 's the issue?

Prince. I am now of all humours that have showed themselves humours since the old days of goodman Adam to the pupil age of this present twelve o'clock at midnight.

[*Enter* FRANCIS.]

What 's o'clock, Francis?

Fran. Anon, anon, sir. [*Exit.*]

Prince. That ever this fellow should have fewer words than a parrot, and yet the son of a woman! His industry is up-stairs and down-stairs; his eloquence the parcel of a reckoning. I am not yet of Percy's mind, the Hotspur of the north; he that kills me some six or seven dozen of Scots at a breakfast, washes his hands, and says to his wife 'Fie upon this quiet life! I want work.' 'O my sweet Harry,' says she, 'how many hast thou killed to-day?' 'Give my roan horse a drench,' says he; and answers 'Some fourteen,' an hour after; 'a trifle, a trifle.' I prithee, call in Falstaff: I'll play Percy, and that damned brawn shall play Dame Mortimer his wife. 'Rivo!' says the drunkard. Call in ribs, call in tallow.

Enter FALSTÀFF [, GADSHILL, BARDOLPH, *and* PETO; FRANCIS *following with wine*].

Poins. Welcome, Jack: where hast thou been?

Fal. A plague of all cowards, I say, and a vengeance too! marry, and amen! Give me a cup of sack, boy. Ere I lead this life long, I'll sew nether stocks and mend them and foot them too. A plague of all cowards! Give me a cup of sack, rogue. Is there no virtue extant? *He drinketh.*

Prince. Didst thou never see Titan kiss a dish of butter? pitiful-hearted Titan, that melted at the sweet tale of the sun's! if thou didst, then behold that compound.

Fal. You rogue, here 's lime in this sack too: there is nothing but roguery to be found in villanous man: yet a coward is worse than a cup of sack with lime in

26. **under-skinker,** under-tapster. 31. **Score,** charge. **bastard,** sweet Spanish wine. **Half-moon,** name of a room in the inn. 42. **Pomgarnet,** pomegranate (another room in the inn). 78. **not-pated,** crop-haired. **puke-stocking,** woolen stocking. 79. **caddis-garter,** worsted garter. Since garters were worn in sight, they needed to be of better stuff than common worsted. The prince's epithets seem to apply to the vintner, the boy's master. 82-85. **Why . . . much.** The prince talks nonsense in order to bewilder Francis; but he also implies that Francis should endure his life as a drawer, not run away. 106. **goodman,** a sort of familiar title. **pupil age,** i.e., the day is young. 113. **parcel,** item. 123. **brawn,** fat boar. 124. **'Rivo!'** An interjection of doubtful meaning; certainly bacchanalian. 130. **nether stocks,** stockings. 134. **pitiful-hearted Titan.** Theobald suggested *butter* for *Titan,* which still seems the best way to explain this apparently contradictory passage. 137. **lime in this sack,** i.e., added to make it sparkle. 143. **shotten herring,** a herring that has cast its roe and is thin. 147. **weaver,** allusion to psalm-singing Protestants from Flanders, mainly weavers. 151. **dagger of lath.** The Vice in the interludes was

it. A villanous coward! Go thy ways, old Jack; die when thou wilt, if manhood, good manhood, be not forgot upon the face of the earth, then am I a shotten herring. There lives not three good men unhanged in England; and one of them is fat and grows old: God help the while! a bad world, I say. I would I were a weaver; I could sing psalms or any thing. A plague of all cowards, I say still.

Prince. How now, wool-sack! what mutter you?

Fal. A king's son! If I do not beat thee out of thy kingdom with a dagger of lath, and drive all thy subjects afore thee like a flock of wild-geese, I'll never wear hair on my face more. You Prince of Wales!

Prince. Why, you whoreson round man, what 's the matter?

Fal. Are not you a coward? answer me to that: and Poins there?

Poins. 'Zounds, ye fat paunch, and ye call me coward, by the Lord, I'll stab thee.

Fal. I call thee coward! I'll see thee damned ere I call thee coward: but I would give a thousand pound I could run as fast as thou canst. You are straight enough in the shoulders, you care not who sees your back: call you that backing of your friends? A plague upon such backing! give me them that will face me. Give me a cup of sack: I am a rogue, if I drunk to-day.

Prince. O villain! thy lips are scarce wiped since thou drunkest last.

Fal. All 's one for that. (*He drinketh.*) A plague of all cowards, still say I.

Prince. What 's the matter?

Fal. What 's the matter! there be four of us here have ta'en a thousand pound this day morning.

Prince. Where is it, Jack? where is it?

Fal. Where is it! taken from us it is: a hundred upon poor four of us.

Prince. What, a hundred, man?

Fal. I am a rogue, if I were not at half-sword with a dozen of them two hours together. I have 'scaped by miracle. I am eight times thrust through the doublet, four through the hose; my buckler cut through and through; my sword hacked like a hand-saw—ecce signum! I never dealt better since I was a man: all would not do. A plague of all cowards! Let them speak: if they speak more or less than truth, they are villains and the sons of darkness.

Prince. Speak, sirs; how was it?

Gads. We four set upon some dozen—

Fal. Sixteen at least, my lord.

Gads. And bound them.

Peto. No, no, they were not bound.

Fal. You rogue, they were bound, every man of them; or I am a Jew else, an Ebrew Jew.

Gads. As we were sharing, some six or seven fresh men set upon us—

Fal. And unbound the rest, and then come in the other.

Prince. What, fought you with them all?

Fal. All! I know not what you call all; but if I fought not with fifty of them, I am a bunch of radish: if there were not two or three and fifty upon poor old Jack, then am I no two-legged creature.

Prince. Pray God you have not murdered some of them.

Fal. Nay, that 's past praying for: I have peppered two of them; two I am sure I have paid, two rogues in buckram suits. I tell thee what, Hal, if I tell thee a lie, spit in my face, call me horse. Thou knowest my old ward; here I lay, and thus I bore my point. Four rogues in buckram let drive at me—

Prince. What, four? thou saidst but two even now.

Fal. Four, Hal; I told thee four.

Poins. Ay, ay, he said four.

Fal. These four came all a-front, and mainly thrust at me. I made me no more ado but took all their seven points in my target, thus.

Prince. Seven? why, there were but four even now.

Fal. In buckram?

Poins. Ay, four, in buckram suits.

Fal. Seven, by these hilts, or I am a villain else.

Prince. [*Aside to Poins*] Prithee, let him alone; we shall have more anon.

Fal. Dost thou hear me, Hal?

Prince. Ay, and mark thee too, Jack.

Fal. Do so, for it is worth the listening to. These nine in buckram that I told thee of—

Prince. So, two more already.

Fal. Their points being broken,—

Poins. Down fell their hose.

Fal. Began to give me ground: but I followed me close, came in foot and hand; and with a thought seven of the eleven I paid.

Prince. O monstrous! eleven buckram men grown out of two!

Fal. But, as the devil would have it, three misbegotten knaves in Kendal green came at my back and let drive at me; for it was so dark, Hal, that thou couldst not see thy hand.

Prince. These lies are like their father that begets them; gross as a mountain, open, palpable. Why, thou clay-brained guts, thou knotty-pated fool, thou whoreson, obscene, greasy tallow-catch,—

Fal. What, art thou mad? art thou mad? is not the truth the truth?

Prince. Why, how couldst thou know these men in Kendal green, when it was so dark thou couldst not see thy hand? come, tell us your reason: what sayest thou to this?

Poins. Come, your reason, Jack, your reason.

Fal. What, upon compulsion? 'Zounds, an I were at the strappado, or all the racks in the world, I would not tell you on compulsion. Give you a reason on compulsion! if reasons were as plentiful as blackberries, I would give no man a reason upon compulsion, I.

Prince. I'll be no longer guilty of this sin; this san-

so armed, as no doubt other clowns were. 182. **half-sword,** fighting at close quarters. 185. **doublet,** Elizabethan upper garment like a jacket. **hose,** close-fitting breeches. 187. **ecce signum,** behold the proof; familiar words from the Mass. 213. **buckram,** coarse linen cloth stiffened. 215. **ward,** guard in fencing. 223. **mainly,** powerfully. 224. **target,** shield; see glossary. 238. **points.** Falstaff uses *points* to mean "swords"; Poins' reply introduces a pun on the same word meaning the "laces" by which the hose were attached to the doublet and so supported. 240. **followed me,** a sort of reflexive or middle voice. 241-242. **with a thought,** quick as a thought. 246. **Kendal green,** green cloth worn by foresters. 251-252. **knotty-pated,** thickheaded. 253. **tallow-catch,** explained as "tallow-tub," and as "tallow-keech," a roll of fat delivered by the butcher to the tallow chandler. It has been pointed out that such breathless strings of epithets of abuse are characteristic of Latin comedy. 262. **strappado,** a kind of torture. 264. **reasons . . . blackberries.** Falstaff not only avoids the issue, but also turns it into a jest by punning on the word "raisins," which was pronounced nearly like *reasons*.

guine coward, this bed-presser, this horseback-breaker, this huge hill of flesh,—

Fal. 'Sblood, you starveling, you elf-skin, you dried neat's tongue, you bull's pizzle, you stock-fish! O for breath to utter what is like thee! you tailor's-yard, you sheath, you bow-case, you vile standing-tuck,—

Prince. Well, breathe awhile, and then to it again: and when thou hast tired thyself in base comparisons, hear me speak but this.

Poins. Mark, Jack.

Prince. We two saw you four set on four and bound them, and were masters of their wealth. Mark now, how a plain tale shall put you down. Then did we two set on you four; and, with a word, out-faced you from your prize, and have it; yea, and can show it you here in the house: and, Falstaff, you carried your guts away as nimbly, with as quick dexterity, and roared for mercy and still run and roared, as ever I heard bull-calf. What a slave art thou, to hack thy sword as thou hast done, and then say it was in fight! What trick, what device, what starting-hole, canst thou now find out to hide thee from this open and apparent shame?

Poins. Come, let 's hear, Jack; what trick hast thou now?

Fal. By the Lord, I knew ye as well as he that made ye. Why, hear you, my masters: was it for me to kill the heir-apparent? should I turn upon the true prince? why, thou knowest I am as valiant as Hercules: but beware instinct; the lion will not touch the true prince. Instinct is a great matter; I was now a coward on instinct. I shall think the better of myself and thee during my life; I for a valiant lion, and thou for a true prince. But, by the Lord, lads, I am glad you have the money. Hostess, clap to the doors: watch to-night, pray to-morrow. Gallants, lads, boys, hearts of gold, all the titles of good fellowship come to you! What, shall we be merry? shall we have a play extempore?

Prince. Content; and the argument shall be thy running away.

Fal. Ah, no more of that, Hal, an thou lovest me!

Enter Hostess.

Host. O Jesu, my lord the prince!

Prince. How now, my lady the hostess! what sayest thou to me?

Host. Marry, my lord, there is a nobleman of the court at door would speak with you: he says he comes from your father.

Prince. Give him as much as will make him a royal man, and send him back again to my mother.

Fal. What manner of man is he?

Host. An old man.

Fal. What doth gravity out of his bed at midnight? Shall I give him his answer?

Prince. Prithee, do, Jack.

Fal. 'Faith, and I'll send him packing. *Exit.*

Prince. Now, sirs: by 'r lady, you fought fair; so did you, Peto; so did you, Bardolph: you are lions too, you ran away upon instinct, you will not touch the true prince; no, fie!

Bard. 'Faith, I ran when I saw others run.

Prince. 'Faith, tell me now in earnest, how came Falstaff's sword so hacked?

Peto. Why, he hacked it with his dagger, and said he would swear truth out of England but he would make you believe it was done in fight, and persuaded us to do the like.

Bard. Yea, and to tickle our noses with spear-grass to make them bleed, and then to beslubber our garments with it and swear it was the blood of true men. I did that I did not this seven year before, I blushed to hear his monstrous devices.

Prince. O villain, thou stolest a cup of sack eighteen years ago, and wert taken with the manner, and ever since thou hast blushed extempore. Thou hadst fire and sword on thy side, and yet thou rannest away: what instinct hadst thou for it?

Bard. My lord, do you see these meteors? do you behold these exhalations?

Prince. I do.

Bard. What think you they portend?

Prince. Hot livers and cold purses.

Bard. Choler, my lord, if rightly taken.

Prince. No, if rightly taken, halter.

Enter FALSTAFF.

Here comes lean Jack, here comes bare-bone. How now, my sweet creature of bombast! How long is 't ago, Jack, since thou sawest thine own knee?

Fal. My own knee! when I was about thy years, Hal, I was not an eagle's talent in the waist; I could have crept into any alderman's thumb-ring: a plague of sighing and grief! it blows a man up like a bladder. There 's villanous news abroad: here was Sir John Bracy from your father; you must to the court in the morning. That same mad fellow of the north, Percy, and he of Wales, that gave Amamon the bastinado and made Lucifer cuckold and swore the devil his true liegeman upon the cross of a Welsh hook—what a plague call you him?

Poins. Owen Glendower.

Fal. Owen, Owen, the same; and his son-in-law Mortimer, and old Northumberland, and that sprightly Scot of Scots, Douglas, that runs a-horseback up a hill perpendicular,—

Prince. He that rides at high speed and with his pistol kills a sparrow flying.

Fal. You have hit it.

Prince. So did he never the sparrow.

Fal. Well, that rascal hath good mettle in him; he will not run.

Prince. Why, what a rascal art thou then, to praise him so for running!

Fal. A-horseback, ye cuckoo; but afoot he will not budge a foot.

Prince. Yes, Jack, upon instinct.

Fal. I grant ye, upon instinct. Well, he is there too, and one Mordake, and a thousand blue-caps more:

271. **neat's tongue,** ox tongue. 272. **stock-fish,** dried cod. 274. **standing-tuck,** rapier standing on end. 283. **out-faced,** frightened. 290. **starting-hole,** point of shelter (like a rabbit's hole). 306. **watch,** stay awake (see Matthew 26:41). 310. **argument,** subject. 321. **royal.** The man is a noble (6s. 8d); give him 3s. 4d. and he will be a *royal* (10s.) *man*. 348. **fire . . . side.** Bardolph is a drunkard, and his flaming face is continually harped upon. 351. **meteors,** i.e., the red blotches on Bardolph's face. 355. **Hot . . . purses,** livers made hot by drink, and purses made empty by spending. 356. **taken,** understood. 357. **halter.** The pun is on "collar" pronounced like *choler*, i.e., the hangman's noose. 359. **bombast,** cotton padding. 363. **talent,** talon. 370. **Amamon,** name of a demon. **bastinado,** beating with a cudgel. 372-373. **Welsh hook,** a weapon having no cross, such as a sword-hilt. 380. **pistol.** There were, of course, no pistols in the time of King Henry's reign. 392. **blue-caps,** Scottish soldiers. 414. **particulars,** details of a private nature; see glossary. 418. **joined-stool,**

Worcester is stolen away to-night; thy father's beard is turned white with the news: you may buy land now as cheap as stinking mackerel.

Prince. Why, then, it is like, if there come a hot June and this civil buffeting hold, we shall buy maidenheads as they buy hob-nails, by the hundreds.

Fal. By the mass, lad, thou sayest true; it is like we shall have good trading that way. But tell me, Hal, art not thou horrible afeard? thou being heir-apparent, could the world pick thee out three such enemies again as that fiend Douglas, that spirit Percy, and that devil Glendower? Art thou not horribly afraid? doth not thy blood thrill at it?

Prince. Not a whit, i' faith; I lack some of thy instinct. 409

Fal. Well, thou wilt be horribly chid to-morrow when thou comest to thy father: if thou love me, practise an answer.

Prince. Do thou stand for my father, and examine me upon the particulars of my life.

Fal. Shall I? content: this chair shall be my state, this dagger my sceptre, and this cushion my crown. 417

Prince. Thy state is taken for a joined-stool, thy golden sceptre for a leaden dagger, and thy precious rich crown for a pitiful bald crown!

Fal. Well, an the fire of grace be not quite out of thee, now shalt thou be moved. Give me a cup of sack to make my eyes look red, that it may be thought I have wept; for I must speak in passion, and I will do it in King Cambyses' vein. 426

Prince. Well, here is my leg.

Fal. And here is my speech. Stand aside, nobility.

Host. O Jesu, this is excellent sport, i' faith!

Fal. Weep not, sweet queen; for trickling tears are
vain.

Host. O, the father, how he holds his countenance!

Fal. For God's sake, lords, convey my tristful queen;
For tears do stop the flood-gates of her eyes.

Host. O Jesu, he doth it as like one of these harlotry players as ever I see! 437

Fal. Peace, good pint-pot; peace, good tickle-brain. Harry, I do not only marvel where thou spendest thy time, but also how thou art accompanied: for though the camomile, the more it is trodden on the faster it grows, yet youth, the more it is wasted the sooner it wears. That thou art my son, I have partly thy mother's word, partly my own opinion, but chiefly a villanous trick of thine eye and a foolish hanging of thy nether lip, that doth warrant me. If then thou be son to me, here lies the point; why, being son to me, art thou so pointed at? Shall the blessed sun of heaven prove a micher and eat blackberries? a question not to be asked. Shall the son of England prove a thief and take purses? a question to be asked. There is a thing, Harry, which thou hast often heard of and it is known to many in our land by the name of pitch: this pitch, as ancient writers do report, doth defile; so doth the company thou keepest: for, Harry, now I do not speak to thee in drink but in tears, not in pleasure but in passion, not in words only, but in woes also: and yet there is a virtuous man whom I have often noted in thy company, but I know not his name. 461

Prince. What manner of man, an it like your majesty?

Fal. A goodly portly man, i' faith, and a corpulent; of a cheerful look, a pleasing eye and a most noble carriage; and, as I think, his age some fifty, or, by 'r lady, inclining to three score; and now I remember me, his name is Falstaff: if that man should be lewdly given, he deceiveth me; for, Harry, I see virtue in his looks. If then the tree may be known by the fruit, as the fruit by the tree, then, peremptorily I speak it, there is virtue in that Falstaff: him keep with, the rest banish. And tell me now, thou naughty varlet, tell me, where hast thou been this month?

Prince. Dost thou speak like a king? Do thou stand for me, and I'll play my father. 478

Fal. Depose me? if thou dost it half so gravely, so majestically, both in word and matter, hang me up by the heels for a rabbit-sucker or a poulter's hare.

Prince. Well, here I am set.

Fal. And here I stand: judge, my masters.

Prince. Now, Harry, whence come you?

Fal. My noble lord, from Eastcheap.

Prince. The complaints I hear of thee are grievous.

Fal. 'Sblood, my lord, they are false: nay, I'll tickle ye for a young prince, i' faith. 489

Prince. Swearest thou, ungracious boy? henceforth ne'er look on me. Thou art violently carried away from grace: there is a devil haunts thee in the likeness of an old fat man; a tun of man is thy companion. Why dost thou converse with that trunk of humours, that bolting-hutch of beastliness, that swollen parcel of dropsies, that huge bombard of sack, that stuffed cloak-bag of guts, that roasted Manningtree ox with the pudding in his belly, that reverend vice, that grey iniquity, that father ruffian, that vanity in years? Wherein is he good, but to taste sack and drink it? wherein neat and cleanly, but to carve a capon and eat it? wherein cunning, but in craft? wherein crafty, but in villany? wherein villanous, but in all things? wherein worthy, but in nothing?

Fal. I would your grace would take me with you: whom means your grace?

Prince. That villanous abominable misleader of youth, Falstaff, that old white-bearded Satan.

Fal. My lord, the man I know. 510

Prince. I know thou dost.

Fal. But to say I know more harm in him than in myself, were to say more than I know. That he is old, the more the pity, his white hairs do witness it; but that he is, saving your reverence, a whoremaster, that I utterly deny. If sack and sugar be a fault, God help the wicked! if to be old and merry be a sin, then many an old host that I know is damned: if to be fat be to be hated, then Pharaoh's lean kine are to be loved. No, my good lord; banish Peto, banish Bardolph, banish Poins: but for sweet Jack Falstaff, kind Jack Falstaff, true Jack Falstaff, valiant Jack Falstaff,

a stool made by a joiner, hence, of rough workmanship. 426. **King Cambyses' vein,** allusion to Thomas Preston's bombastic tragedy *Cambises*, still preserved. 427. **leg,** bow. 434. **tristful,** sorrowing. 437. **harlotry,** vagabond. 439. **tickle-brain,** strong drink. 441. **camomile.** This parodies an actual passage in Lyly's *Euphues* and exaggerates the balance and alliteration of the style. 450. **micher,** truant. 456-457. **pitch . . . defile,** an allusion to the familiar proverb from Ecclesiasticus 13:1, about the defilement of touching pitch. This proverb appears also in Lyly's *Euphues*. 480. **rabbit-sucker,** sucking rabbit. 481. **poulter's,** poulterer's. 495. **bolting-hutch,** large flour bin. 497. **bombard,** leathern drinking vessel. 498. **Manningtree ox.** Manningtree, a town in Essex, had noted fairs where, no doubt, oxen were roasted whole. 499-500. **vice . . . iniquity.** These terms suggest another feature of Manningtree, which was the acting of morality plays; the word *vanity* also suggests a character in such plays. 521. **Pharaoh's lean kine.** See Genesis 41:3-4, 18-21.

and therefore more valiant, being, as he is, old Jack Falstaff, banish not him thy Harry's company, banish not him thy Harry's company: banish plump Jack, and banish all the world.

Prince. I do, I will. [*A knocking heard.*]

[*Exeunt Hostess, Francis, and Bardolph.*]

Enter BARDOLPH, *running.*

Bard. O, my lord, my lord! the sheriff with a most monstrous watch is at the door.

Fal. Out, ye rogue! Play out the play: I have much to say in the behalf of that Falstaff.

Enter the Hostess.

Host. O Jesu, my lord, my lord!

Prince. Heigh, heigh! the devil rides upon a fiddlestick: what 's the matter?

Host. The sheriff and all the watch are at the door: they are come to search the house. Shall I let them in?

Fal. Dost thou hear, Hal? never call a true piece of gold a counterfeit: thou art essentially mad, without seeming so.

Prince. And thou a natural coward, without instinct.

Fal. I deny your major: if you will deny the sheriff, so; if not, let him enter: if I become not a cart as well as another man, a plague on my bringing up! I hope I shall as soon be strangled with a halter as another.

Prince. Go, hide thee behind the arras: the rest walk up above. Now, my masters, for a true face and good conscience.

Fal. Both which I have had: but their date is out, and therefore I'll hide me.

Prince. Call in the sheriff.

[*Exeunt all except the Prince and Peto.*]

Enter Sheriff *and the* Carrier.

Now, master sheriff, what is your will with me?
Sher. First, pardon me, my lord. A hue and cry
Hath followed certain men unto this house.
Prince. What men?
Sher. One of them is well known, my gracious lord,
A gross fat man.
Car. As fat as butter.
Prince. The man, I do assure you, is not here;
For I myself at this time have employ'd him.
And, sheriff, I will engage my word to thee
That I will, by to-morrow dinner-time,
Send him to answer thee, or any man,
For any thing he shall be charg'd withal:
And so let me entreat you leave the house.
Sher. I will, my lord. There are two gentlemen
Have in this robbery lost three hundred marks.
Prince. It may be so: if he have robb'd these men,
He shall be answerable; and so farewell.
Sher. Good night, my noble lord.
Prince. I think it is good morrow, is it not?
Sher. Indeed, my lord, I think it be two o'clock.

Exit [*with Carrier*].

Prince. This oily rascal is known as well as Paul's. Go, call him forth.

Peto. Falstaff!—Fast asleep behind the arras, and snorting like a horse.

Prince. Hark, how hard he fetches breath. Search his pockets. (*He searcheth his pockets, and findeth certain papers.*) What hast thou found?

Peto. Nothing but papers, my lord.

Prince. Let 's see what they be: read them.

Peto. [*Reads*]

Item, A capon, ...	2s. 2d.
Item, Sauce, ...	4d.
Item, Sack, two gallons, . . .	5s. 8d.
Item, Anchovies and sack after supper, ...	2s. 6d.
Item, Bread, ...	ob.

Prince. O monstrous! but one half-pennyworth of bread to this intolerable deal of sack! What there is else, keep close; we'll read it at more advantage: there let him sleep till day. I'll to the court in the morning. We must all to the wars, and thy place shall be honourable. I'll procure this fat rogue a charge of foot; and I know his death will be a march of twelve-score. The money shall be paid back again with advantage. Be with me betimes in the morning; and so, good morrow, Peto.

Peto. Good morrow, good my lord. *Exeunt.*

[ACT III.

SCENE I. *Bangor. The Archdeacon's house.*]

Enter HOTSPUR, WORCESTER, LORD MORTIMER, *and* OWEN GLENDOWER.

Mort. These promises are fair, the parties sure,
And our induction full of prosperous hope.
Hot. Lord Mortimer, and cousin Glendower,
Will you sit down?
And uncle Worcester: a plague upon it!
I have forgot the map.
Glend. No, here it is.
Sit, cousin Percy; sit, good cousin Hotspur,
For by that name as oft as Lancaster
Doth speak of you, his cheek looks pale and with
A rising sigh he wisheth you in heaven.

Hot. And you in hell, as oft as he hears Owen Glendower spoke of.

Glend. I cannot blame him: at my nativity
The front of heaven was full of fiery shapes,
Of burning cressets; and at my birth
The frame and huge foundation of the earth
Shak'd like a coward.

Hot. Why, so it would have done at the same season, if your mother's cat had but kittened, though yourself had never been born.

Glend. I say the earth did shake when I was born.
Hot. And I say the earth was not of my mind,
If you suppose as fearing you it shook.
Glend. The heavens were all on fire, the earth did tremble.
Hot. O, then the earth shook to see the heavens on fire,

530. **watch,** a posse of constables. 534. **the devil . . . fiddlestick,** proverbial; suggesting, here's much ado about nothing. 539-541. **Dost . . . seeming so.** In this difficult passage, Falstaff seems to suggest that he is true gold, not counterfeit, and so should not be betrayed to the watch by the Prince who (he hopes) is not merely playacting at the tavern but is truly one of its madcap members. 544. **major,** major proposition. Falstaff denies that he is a natural coward; he does not deny that he is affected by instinct. 546. **cart,** hangman's cart, tumbril. 556. **hue and cry,** pursuit of criminals by horn and halloo; technical term. 575. **Paul's,** St. Paul's Cathedral, a familiar landmark. 577. **arras,** wall-hanging. 590. **ob.,** abbreviation for *obolus* (Greek coin) meaning "halfpenny." 592. **deal,** lot. 597. **charge of foot,** company of infantry. 598. **twelve-score,** i.e., yards; a distance familiar from its use in archery. 599-600. **advantage,** interest. **betimes,** early.

ACT III. SCENE I. 2. **induction,** beginning. 8. **Lancaster,** King

And not in fear of your nativity.
Diseased nature oftentimes breaks forth
In strange eruptions; oft the teeming earth
Is with a kind of colic pinch'd and vex'd
By the imprisoning of unruly wind
Within her womb; which, for enlargement striving,
Shakes the old beldam earth and topples down
Steeples and moss-grown towers. At your birth
Our grandam earth, having this distemp'rature,
In passion shook.
Glend. Cousin, of many men
I do not bear these crossings. Give me leave
To tell you once again that at my birth
The front of heaven was full of fiery shapes,
The goats ran from the mountains, and the herds
Were strangely clamorous to the frighted fields.
These signs have mark'd me extraordinary;
And all the courses of my life do show
I am not in the roll of common men.
Where is he living, clipp'd in with the sea
That chides the banks of England, Scotland, Wales,
Which calls me pupil, or hath read to me?
And bring him out that is but woman's son
Can trace me in the tedious ways of art
And hold me pace in deep experiments.
Hot. I think there 's no man speaks better Welsh.
I'll to dinner.
Mort. Peace, cousin Percy; you will make him mad.
Glend. I can call spirits from the vasty deep.
Hot. Why, so can I, or so can any man;
But will they come when you do call for them?
Glend. Why, I can teach you, cousin, to command
The devil.
Hot. And I can teach thee, coz, to shame the devil
By telling truth: tell truth and shame the devil.
If thou have power to raise him, bring him hither,
And I'll be sworn I have power to shame him hence.
O, while you live, tell truth and shame the devil!
Mort. Come, come, no more of this unprofitable chat.
Glend. Three times hath Henry Bolingbroke made head
Against my power; thrice from the banks of Wye
And sandy-bottom'd Severn have I sent him
Bootless home and weather-beaten back.
Hot. Home without boots, and in foul weather too!
How 'scapes he agues, in the devil's name?
Glend. Come, here is the map: shall we divide our right
According to our threefold order ta'en?
Mort. The archdeacon hath divided it
Into three limits very equally:
England, from Trent and Severn hitherto,
By south and east is to my part assign'd:
All westward, Wales beyond the Severn shore,
And all the fertile land within that bound,
To Owen Glendower: and, dear coz, to you
The remnant northward, lying off from Trent.
And our indentures tripartite are drawn;
Which being sealed interchangeably,
A business that this night may execute,
To-morrow, cousin Percy, you and I
And my good Lord of Worcester will set forth
To meet your father and the Scottish power,
As is appointed us, at Shrewsbury.
My father Glendower is not ready yet,
Nor shall we need his help these fourteen days.
Within that space you may have drawn together
Your tenants, friends and neighbouring gentlemen.
Glend. A shorter time shall send me to you, lords:
And in my conduct shall your ladies come;
From whom you now must steal and take no leave,
For there will be a world of water shed
Upon the parting of your wives and you.
Hot. Methinks my moiety, north from Burton here,
In quantity equals not one of yours:
See how this river comes me cranking in,
And cuts me from the best of all my land
A huge half-moon, a monstrous cantle out.
I'll have the current in this place damm'd up;
And here the smug and silver Trent shall run
In a new channel, fair and evenly;
It shall not wind with such a deep indent,
To rob me of so rich a bottom here.
Glend. Not wind? it shall, it must; you see it doth.
Mort. Yea, but
Mark how he bears his course, and runs me up
With like advantage on the other side;
Gelding the opposed continent as much
As on the other side it takes from you.
Wor. Yea, but a little charge will trench him here
And on this north side win this cape of land;
And then he runs straight and even.
Hot. I'll have it so: a little charge will do it.
Glend. I'll not have it alt'red.
Hot. Will not you?
Glend. No, nor you shall not.
Hot. Who shall say me nay?
Glend. Why, that will I.
Hot. Let me not understand you, then; speak it in Welsh.
Glend. I can speak English, lord, as well as you;
For I was train'd up in the English court;
Where, being but young, I framed to the harp
Many an English ditty lovely well
And gave the tongue a helpful ornament,
A virtue that was never seen in you.
Hot. Marry,
And I am glad of it with all my heart:
I had rather be a kitten and cry mew
Than one of these same metre ballad-mongers;
I had rather hear a brazen canstick turn'd,
Or a dry wheel grate on the axle-tree;
And that would set my teeth nothing on edge,
Nothing so much as mincing poetry:
'Tis like the forc'd gait of a shuffling nag.
Glend. Come, you shall have Trent turn'd.
Hot. I do not care: I'll give thrice so much land
To any well-deserving friend;
But in the way of bargain, mark ye me,

Henry IV, formerly Duke of Lancaster. 13. **at my nativity.** Holinshed recounts the happening of portents at Glendower's birth; Shakespeare has developed his vanity and strange rapt quality. 14. **front,** forehead. 15. **cressets,** beacons. 27-35. **Diseased . . . shook.** These lines give the currently accepted scientific explanation of earthquakes. 31. **enlargement,** release. 32. **beldam,** grandmother. 46. **read to,** instructed. 48. **trace,** follow. **tedious,** laborious. **art,** i.e., magic. 67. **Bootless,** without advantage. 72. **archdeacon,** an official of an Episcopal diocese. The divisions of the Kingdom are really very ancient; they appear in Geoffrey of Monmouth's *Chronicle*, and are those into which King Lear divided his kingdom. 87. **father,** father-in-law. 98. **comes me cranking in,** comes bending in on my share; *me* is an ethical dative. 100. **cantle,** piece. 115. **charge,** expenditure. 131. **canstick,** candlestick.

I'll cavil on the ninth part of a hair.
Are the indentures drawn? shall we be gone?
Glend. The moon shines fair; you may away by night:
I'll haste the writer and withal
Break with your wives of your departure hence:
I am afraid my daughter will run mad,
So much she doteth on her Mortimer. *Exit.*
Mort. Fie, cousin Percy! how you cross my father!
Hot. I cannot choose: sometime he angers me
With telling me of the moldwarp and the ant,
Of the dreamer Merlin and his prophecies,
And of a dragon and a finless fish,
A clip-wing'd griffin and a moulten raven,
A couching lion and a ramping cat,
And such a deal of skimble-skamble stuff
As puts me from my faith. I tell you what;
He held me last night at least nine hours
In reckoning up the several devils' names
That were his lackeys: I cried 'hum,' and 'well, go to,'
But mark'd him not a word. O, he is as tedious
As a tired horse, a railing wife;
Worse than a smoky house: I had rather live
With cheese and garlic in a windmill, far,
Than feed on cates and have him talk to me
In any summer-house in Christendom.
Mort. In faith, he is a worthy gentleman,
Exceedingly well read, and profited
In strange concealments, valiant as a lion
And wondrous affable and as bountiful
As mines of India. Shall I tell you, cousin?
He holds your temper in a high respect
And curbs himself even of his natural scope
When you come 'cross his humour; faith, he does:
I warrant you, that man is not alive
Might so have tempted him as you have done,
Without the taste of danger and reproof:
But do not use it oft, let me entreat you.
Wor. In faith, my lord, you are too wilful-blame;
And since your coming hither have done enough
To put him quite besides his patience.
You must needs learn, lord, to amend this fault:
Though sometimes it show greatness, courage, blood,—
And that 's the dearest grace it renders you,—
Yet oftentimes it doth present harsh rage,
Defect of manners, want of government,
Pride, haughtiness, opinion and disdain:
The least of which haunting a nobleman
Loseth men's hearts and leaves behind a stain
Upon the beauty of all parts besides,
Beguiling them of commendation.
Hot. Well, I am school'd: good manners be your speed!
Here come our wives, and let us take our leave.

Enter GLENDOWER *with the ladies.*

Mort. This is the deadly spite that angers me;
My wife can speak no English, I no Welsh.
Glend. My daughter weeps: she will not part with you;
She'll be a soldier too, she'll to the wars.
Mort. Good father, tell her that she and my aunt Percy
Shall follow in your conduct speedily.

Glendower speaks to her in Welsh, and she answers him in the same.

Glend. She is desperate here; a peevish self-will'd harlotry, one that no persuasion can do good upon.

The lady speaks in Welsh.

Mort. I understand thy looks: that pretty Welsh
Which thou pourest down from these swelling heavens
I am too perfect in; and, but for shame,
In such a parley should I answer thee.

The lady again in Welsh.

I understand thy kisses and thou mine,
And that 's a feeling disputation:
But I will never be a truant, love,
Till I have learn'd thy language; for thy tongue
Makes Welsh as sweet as ditties highly penn'd,
Sung by a fair queen in a summer's bower,
With ravishing division, to her lute.
Glend. Nay, if you melt, then will she run mad.

The lady speaks again in Welsh.

Mort. O, I am ignorance itself in this!
Glend. She bids you on the wanton rushes lay you down
And rest your gentle head upon her lap,
And she will sing the song that pleaseth you
And on your eyelids crown the god of sleep,
Charming your blood with pleasing heaviness,
Making such difference 'twixt wake and sleep
As is the difference betwixt day and night
The hour before the heavenly-harness'd team
Begins his golden progress in the east.
Mort. With all my heart I'll sit and hear her sing:
By that time will our book, I think, be drawn.
Glend. Do so;
And those musicians that shall play to you
Hang in the air a thousand leagues from hence,
And straight they shall be here: sit, and attend.

Hot. Come, Kate, thou art perfect in lying down: come, quick, quick, that I may lay my head in thy lap.

Lady P. Go, ye giddy goose. *The music plays.*

Hot. Now I perceive the devil understands Welsh;
And 'tis no marvel he is so humorous.
By 'r lady, he is a good musician.

Lady P. Then should you be nothing but musical, for you are altogether governed by humours. Lie still, ye thief, and hear the lady sing in Welsh.

Hot. I had rather hear Lady, my brach, howl in Irish.

Lady P. Wouldst thou have thy head broken?
Hot. No.
Lady P. Then be still.
Hot. Neither; 'tis a woman's fault.
Lady P. Now God help thee!
Hot. To the Welsh lady's bed.
Lady P. What 's that?

143. **writer,** the scrivener who would be drawing the indentures. 144. **Break with,** communicate with. 149. **moldwarp,** mole. Holinshed tells us that the division was arranged because of a prophecy which represented King Henry as the mole and the others as the dragon, the lion, and the wolf, who should divide the land among them. 150. **Merlin,** the traditional bard and prophet of the Welsh. 152. **griffin,** a fabulous beast. 153. **ramping,** rampant, advancing on its hind legs. (Hotspur is ridiculing the heraldic emblems which Glendower holds so dear.) 154. **skimble-skamble,** confused and foolish. 163. **cates,** delicacies. 177. **wilful-blame,** to blame for excessive willfulness. 179. **besides,** out of. 182. **dearest grace,** best credit. 183. **present,** represent. 190. **be your speed,** give you good fortune. 199. **harlotry,** silly wench. 202. **heavens,** i.e., eyes. 203. **perfect,** proficient. 204. **such a parley,** i.e., the same language. 206. **disputation,** conversation. 211. **division,** variation (in music). 214. **wanton,** soft, luxurious. 224. **book,** document, indentures. 234. **humorous,** capricious. 240.

Hot. Peace! she sings. *Here the lady sings a Welsh song.*
Hot. Come, Kate, I'll have your song too.
Lady P. Not mine, in good sooth.

Hot. Not yours, in good sooth! Heart! you swear like a comfit-maker's wife. 'Not you, in good sooth,' and 'as true as I live,' and 'as God shall mend me,' and 'as sure as day,'
And givest such sarcenet surety for thy oaths,
As if thou never walk'st further than Finsbury.
Swear me, Kate, like a lady as thou art,
A good mouth-filling oath, and leave 'in sooth,'
And such protest of pepper-gingerbread,
To velvet-guards and Sunday-citizens.
Come, sing.
Lady P. I will not sing.

Hot. 'Tis the next way to turn tailor, or be red-breast teacher. An the indentures be drawn, I'll away within these two hours; and so, come in when ye will. *Exit.*

Glend. Come, come, Lord Mortimer; you are as slow
As hot Lord Percy is on fire to go.
By this our book is drawn; we'll but seal,
And then to horse immediately.
Mort. With all my heart. *Exeunt.*

[SCENE II. *London. The palace.*]

Enter the KING, PRINCE OF WALES, *and others.*

King. Lords, give us leave; the Prince of Wales and I
Must have some private conference: but be near at hand,
For we shall presently have need of you. *Exeunt Lords.*
I know not whether God will have it so,
For some displeasing service I have done,
That, in his secret doom, out of my blood
He'll breed revengement and a scourge for me;
But thou dost in thy passages of life
Make me believe that thou art only mark'd
For the hot vengeance and the rod of heaven
To punish my mistreadings. Tell me else,
Could such inordinate and low desires,
Such poor, such bare, such lewd, such mean attempts,
Such barren pleasures, rude society,
As thou art match'd withal and grafted to,
Accompany the greatness of thy blood
And hold their level with thy princely heart?
Prince. So please your majesty, I would I could
Quit all offences with as clear excuse
As well as I am doubtless I can purge
Myself of many I am charg'd withal:
Yet such extenuation let me beg,
As, in reproof of many tales devis'd,
Which oft the ear of greatness needs must hear,
By smiling pick-thanks and base newsmongers,
I may, for some things true, wherein my youth
Hath faulty wand'red and irregular,
Find pardon on my true submission.
King. God pardon thee! yet let me wonder, Harry,
At thy affections, which do hold a wing
Quite from the flight of all thy ancestors.
Thy place in council thou hast rudely lost,
Which by thy younger brother is supplied,
And art almost an alien to the hearts
Of all the court and princes of my blood:
The hope and expectation of thy time
Is ruin'd, and the soul of every man
Prophetically do forethink thy fall.
Had I so lavish of my presence been,
So common-hackney'd in the eyes of men,
So stale and cheap to vulgar company,
Opinion, that did help me to the crown,
Had still kept loyal to possession
And left me in reputeless banishment,
A fellow of no mark nor likelihood.
By being seldom seen, I could not stir
But like a comet I was wond'red at;
That men would tell their children 'This is he;'
Others would say 'Where, which is Bolingbroke?'
And then I stole all courtesy from heaven,
And dress'd myself in such humility
That I did pluck allegiance from men's hearts,
Loud shouts and salutations from their mouths,
Even in the presence of the crowned king.
Thus did I keep my person fresh and new;
My presence, like a robe pontifical,
Ne'er seen but wond'red at: and so my state,
Seldom but sumptuous, show'd like a feast
And won by rareness such solemnity.
The skipping king, he ambled up and down
With shallow jesters and rash bavin wits,
Soon kindled and soon burnt; carded his state,
Mingled his royalty with cap'ring fools,
Had his great name profaned with their scorns
And gave his countenance, against his name,
To laugh at gibing boys and stand the push
Of every beardless vain comparative,
Grew a companion to the common streets,
Enfeoff'd himself to popularity;
That, being daily swallowed by men's eyes,
They surfeited with honey and began
To loathe the taste of sweetness, whereof a little
More than a little is by much too much.
So when he had occasion to be seen,
He was but as the cuckoo is in June,
Heard, not regarded; seen, but with such eyes
As, sick and blunted with community,
Afford no extraordinary gaze,
Such as is bent on sun-like majesty
When it shines seldom in admiring eyes;
But rather drows'd and hung their eyelids down,
Slept in his face and rend'red such aspect
As cloudy men use to their adversaries,
Being with his presence glutted, gorg'd and full.
And in that very line, Harry, standest thou;
For thou hast lost thy princely privilege
With vile participation: not an eye
But is a-weary of thy common sight,

brach, bitch hound. 253. **comfit-maker's,** confectioner's. 256. **sarcenet,** soft, from the silken material known as "sarcenet." 257. **Finsbury,** an archery ground outside Moorgate, resorted to by citizens. 261. **velvet-guards,** wearers of velvet trimmings. 264. **turn tailor.** Tailors were noted for singing.

SCENE II. 1. **give us leave,** leave us. 6. **doom,** judgment. 8. **passages,** course, conduct. 25. **pick-thanks,** flatterers. 43. **to possession,** i.e., to Richard II's sovereignty. 50. **stole . . . heaven.** He assumed a bearing of the utmost graciousness. 60. **skipping,** flighty. 61. **bavin,** brushwood, soon burnt out. 62. **carded,** debased; a term applied to the adulteration of wool. 65. **name,** i.e., dignity. 66. **stand the push,** put up with the impudence. 67. **comparative,** rival (in wit). 69. **Enfeoff'd,** gave himself up to. 77. **community,** commonness. 83. **cloudy,** sullen (also referring back to the image of the sun). 87. **vile participation,** base association or companionship.

Save mine, which hath desir'd to see thee more;
Which now doth that I would not have it do,
Make blind itself with foolish tenderness.

Prince. I shall hereafter, my thrice gracious lord,
Be more myself.

King. For all the world
As thou art to this hour was Richard then
When I from France set foot at Ravenspurgh,
And even as I was then is Percy now.
Now, by my sceptre and my soul to boot,
He hath more worthy interest to the state
Than thou the shadow of succession;
For of no right, nor colour like to right,
He doth fill fields with harness in the realm,
Turns head against the lion's armed jaws,
And, being no more in debt to years than thou,
Leads ancient lords and reverend bishops on
To bloody battles and to bruising arms.
What never-dying honour hath he got
Against renowned Douglas! whose high deeds,
Whose hot incursions and great name in arms
Holds from all soldiers chief majority
And military title capital
Through all the kingdoms that acknowledge Christ:
Thrice hath this Hotspur, Mars in swathling clothes,
This infant warrior, in his enterprizes
Discomfited great Douglas, ta'en him once,
Enlarged him and made a friend of him,
To fill the mouth of deep defiance up
And shake the peace and safety of our throne.
And what say you to this? Percy, Northumberland,
The Archbishop's grace of York, Douglas, Mortimer,
Capitulate against us and are up.
But wherefore do I tell these news to thee?
Why, Harry, do I tell thee of my foes,
Which art my nearest and dearest enemy?
Thou that art like enough, through vassal fear,
Base inclination and the start of spleen,
To fight against me under Percy's pay,
To dog his heels and curtsy at his frowns,
To show how much thou art degenerate.

Prince. Do not think so; you shall not find it so:
And God forgive them that so much have sway'd
Your majesty's good thoughts away from me!
I will redeem all this on Percy's head
And in the closing of some glorious day
Be bold to tell you that I am your son;
When I will wear a garment all of blood
And stain my favours in a bloody mask,
Which, wash'd away, shall scour my shame with it:
And that shall be the day, whene'er it lights,
That this same child of honour and renown,
This gallant Hotspur, this all-praised knight,
And your unthought-of Harry chance to meet.
For every honour sitting on his helm,
Would they were multitudes, and on my head
My shames redoubled! for the time will come,
That I shall make this northern youth exchange
His glorious deeds for my indignities.
Percy is but my factor, good my lord,
To engross up glorious deeds on my behalf;
And I will call him to so strict account,
That he shall render every glory up,
Yea, even the slightest worship of his time,
Or I will tear the reckoning from his heart.
This, in the name of God, I promise here:
The which if He be pleas'd I shall perform,
I do beseech your majesty may salve
The long-grown wounds of my intemperance:
If not, the end of life cancels all bands;
And I will die a hundred thousand deaths
Ere break the smallest parcel of this vow.

King. A hundred thousand rebels die in this!
Thou shalt have charge and sovereign thrust herein.

Enter BLUNT.

How now, good Blunt? thy looks are full of speed.

Blunt. So hath the business that I come to speak of.
Lord Mortimer of Scotland hath sent word
That Douglas and the English rebels met
The eleventh of this month at Shrewsbury:
A mighty and a fearful head they are,
If promises be kept on every hand,
As ever off'red foul play in a state.

King. The Earl of Westmoreland set forth to-day;
With him my son, Lord John of Lancaster;
For this advertisement is five days old:
On Wednesday next, Harry, you shall set forward;
On Thursday we ourselves will march: our meeting
Is Bridgenorth: and, Harry, you shall march
Through Gloucestershire; by which account,
Our business valued, some twelve days hence
Our general forces at Bridgenorth shall meet.
Our hands are full of business: let 's away;
Advantage feeds him fat, while men delay. *Exeunt.*

[SCENE III. *Eastcheap. The Boar's-Head Tavern.*]

Enter FALSTAFF *and* BARDOLPH.

Fal. Bardolph, am I not fallen away vilely since this last action? do I not bate? do I not dwindle? Why, my skin hangs about me like an old lady's loose gown; I am withered like an old apple-john. Well, I'll repent, and that suddenly, while I am in some liking; I shall be out of heart shortly, and then I shall have no strength to repent. An I have not forgotten what the inside of a church is made of, I am a peppercorn, a brewer's horse: the inside of a church! Company, villanous company, hath been the spoil of me.

Bard. Sir John, you are so fretful, you cannot live long.

Fal. Why, there is it: come sing me a bawdy song; make me merry. I was as virtuously given as a gentleman need to be; virtuous enough; swore little; diced not above seven times a week; went to a bawdy-house not above once in a quarter—of an hour; paid money that I borrowed, three or four times; lived well and in good compass: and now I live out of all order, out of all compass.

Bard. Why, you are so fat, Sir John, that you must needs be out of all compass, out of all reasonable compass, Sir John.

91. **tenderness,** i.e., tears. 98. **interest,** claim. 99. **shadow of succession.** Hal's claim is a shadow compared to the real services toward gaining the crown which Hotspur has rendered. 100. **colour,** pretense. 101. **harness,** armor. 109. **majority,** preëminence. 110. **capital,** chief. 112. **swathling,** swaddling. 120. **Capitulate,** form a league. 124. **vassal,** slavish. 125. **Base inclination,** inclination for baseness. **start of spleen,** perversity. 147. **factor,** agent. 172. **advertisement,** tidings, news. 180. **Advantage feeds him,** opportunity feeds itself.

SCENE III. 2. **bate,** lose weight. 5. **apple-john,** a kind of apple still in perfect condition even when shriveled and withered. 6. **liking,** (good) bodily condition. 10. **peppercorn,** grain of pepper. **brewer's horse,** one that is old, withered, and decrepit. 22. **good compass,** reasonable limits. 25. **compass,** girth, circumference. 28. **admiral,** flagship. 35. **memento mori,** reminder of death, such as skull and

Fal. Do thou amend thy face, and I'll amend my life: thou art our admiral, thou bearest the lantern in the poop, but 'tis in the nose of thee; thou art the Knight of the Burning Lamp.

Bard. Why, Sir John, my face does you no harm.

Fal. No, I'll be sworn; I make as good use of it as many a man doth of a Death's-head or a memento mori: I never see thy face but I think upon hell-fire and Dives that lived in purple; for there he is in his robes, burning, burning. If thou wert any way given to virtue, I would swear by thy face; my oath should be 'By this fire, that 's God's angel:' but thou art altogether given over; and wert indeed, but for the light in thy face, the son of utter darkness. When thou rannest up Gadshill in the night to catch my horse, if I did not think thou hadst been an ignis fatuus or a ball of wildfire, there 's no purchase in money. O, thou art a perpetual triumph, an ever-lasting bonfire-light! Thou hast saved me a thousand marks in links and torches, walking with thee in the night betwixt tavern and tavern: but the sack that thou hast drunk me would have bought me lights as good cheap at the dearest chandler's in Europe. I have maintained that salamander of yours with fire any time this two and thirty years; God reward me for it!

Bard. 'Sblood, I would my face were in your belly!

Fal. God-a-mercy! so should I be sure to be heart-burned.

Enter HOSTESS.

How now, Dame Partlet the hen! have you inquired yet who picked my pocket?

Host. Why, Sir John, what do you think, Sir John? do you think I keep thieves in my house? I have searched, I have inquired, so has my husband, man by man, boy by boy, servant by servant: the tithe of a hair was never lost in my house before.

Fal. Ye lie, hostess: Bardolph was shaved and lost many a hair; and I'll be sworn my pocket was picked. Go to, you are a woman, go.

Host. Who, I? no; I defy thee: God's light, I was never called so in mine own house before.

Fal. Go to, I know you well enough.

Host. No, Sir John; you do not know me, Sir John. I know you, Sir John: you owe me money, Sir John; and now you pick a quarrel to beguile me of it: I bought you a dozen of shirts to your back.

Fal. Dowlas, filthy dowlas: I have given them away to bakers' wives; they have made bolters of them.

Host. Now, as I am a true woman, holland of eight shillings an ell. You owe money here besides, Sir John, for your diet and by-drinkings, and money lent you, four and twenty pound.

Fal. He had his part of it; let him pay.

Host. He? alas, he is poor; he hath nothing.

Fal. How! poor? look upon his face; what call you rich? let them coin his nose, let them coin his cheeks: I'll not pay a denier. What, will you make a younker of me? shall I not take mine ease in mine inn but I shall have my pocket picked? I have lost a seal-ring of my grandfather's worth forty mark.

Host. O Jesu, I have heard the prince tell him, I know not how oft, that that ring was copper!

Fal. How! the prince is a Jack, a sneak-cup: 'sblood, an he were here, I would cudgel him like a dog, if he would say so.

Enter the PRINCE [*with* PETO], *marching, and* FALSTAFF *meets them playing on his truncheon like a fife.*

How now, lad! is the wind in that door, i' faith? must we all march?

Bard. Yea, two and two, Newgate fashion.

Host. My lord, I pray you, hear me.

Prince. What sayest thou, Mistress Quickly? How doth thy husband? I love him well; he is an honest man.

Host. Good my lord, hear me.

Fal. Prithee, let her alone, and list to me.

Prince. What sayest thou, Jack?

Fal. The other night I fell asleep here behind the arras and had my pocket picked: this house is turned bawdy-house; they pick pockets.

Prince. What didst thou lose, Jack?

Fal. Wilt thou believe me, Hal? three or four bonds of forty pound a-piece, and a seal-ring of my grand-father's.

Prince. A trifle, some eight-penny matter.

Host. So I told him, my lord; and I said I heard your grace say so: and, my lord, he speaks most vilely of you, like a foul-mouthed man as he is; and said he would cudgel you.

Prince. What! he did not?

Host. There 's neither faith, truth, nor womanhood in me else.

Fal. There 's no more faith in thee than in a stewed prune; nor no more truth in thee than in a drawn fox; and for womanhood, Maid Marian may be the deputy's wife of the ward to thee. Go, you thing, go.

Host. Say, what thing! what thing?

Fal. What thing? why, a thing to thank God on.

Host. I am no thing to thank God on, I would thou shouldst know it; I am an honest man's wife: and, setting thy knighthood aside, thou art a knave to call me so.

Fal. Setting thy womanhood aside, thou art a beast to say otherwise.

Host. Say, what beast, thou knave, thou?

Fal. What beast! why, an otter.

Prince. An otter, Sir John! why an otter?

Fal. Why, she 's neither fish nor flesh; a man knows not where to have her.

Host. Thou art an unjust man in saying so: thou or any man knows where to have me, thou knave, thou!

Prince. Thou sayest true, hostess; and he slanders thee most grossly.

Host. So he doth you, my lord; and said this other day you ought him a thousand pound.

Prince. Sirrah, do I owe you a thousand pound?

Fal. A thousand pound, Hal! a million: thy love is worth a million: thou owest me thy love.

crossbones. 36. **Dives,** the rich man referred to in Luke 16:19-31. 39. **'By . . . angel,'** allusion to Psalms 104:4 and Hebrews 1:7. 44-45. **ignis fatuus,** will-o'-the-wisp. 48. **links,** torches. 51. **good cheap,** cheap. 53. **salamander,** a fabled monster able to live in fire. 60. **Partlet,** traditional name of a hen. 66. **tithe,** tenth part. 79. **Dowlas,** a coarse kind of linen. 81. **bolters,** cloths for sifting meal. 82. **holland,** fine linen. 83. **ell,** a measure of a yard and a quarter. 91. **denier,** one twelfth of a sou; type of very small coin. 92. **younker,** youth, greenhorn. 99. **sneak-cup.** Nares defines this as "one who shirks his liquor"; Johnson modifies to *sneak-up,* meaning "a sneak." 104. **Newgate,** famous city prison in London. (Prisoners marched two by two.) 128. **stewed prune,** customarily served in bawdy houses. 129. **drawn fox,** fox driven from cover and wily in getting back. 147. **have,** understand (with suggestion of enjoying sexually). 152. **ought,** owed.

Host. Nay, my lord, he called you Jack, and said he would cudgel you.

Fal. Did I, Bardolph?

Bard. Indeed, Sir John, you said so.

Fal. Yea, if he said my ring was copper.

Prince. I say 'tis copper: darest thou be as good as thy word now?

Fal. Why, Hal, thou knowest, as thou art but man, I dare: but as thou art prince, I fear thee as I fear the roaring of the lion's whelp.

Prince. And why not as the lion?

Fal. The king himself is to be feared as the lion: dost thou think I'll fear thee as I fear thy father? nay, an I do, I pray God my girdle break.

Prince. O, if it should, how would thy guts fall about thy knees! But, sirrah, there 's no room for faith, truth, nor honesty in this bosom of thine; it is all filled up with guts and midriff. Charge an honest woman with picking thy pocket! why, thou whoreson, impudent, embossed rascal, if there were anything in thy pocket but tavern-reckonings, memorandums of bawdy-houses, and one poor penny-worth of sugar-candy to make thee long-winded, if thy pocket were enriched with any other injuries but these, I am a villain: and yet you will stand to it; you will not pocket up wrong: art thou not ashamed?

Fal. Dost thou hear, Hal? thou knowest in the state of innocency Adam fell; and what should poor Jack Falstaff do in the days of villany? Thou seest I have more flesh than another man, and therefore more frailty. You confess then, you picked my pocket?

Prince. It appears so by the story.

Fal. Hostess, I forgive thee: go, make ready breakfast; love thy husband, look to thy servants, cherish thy guests: thou shalt find me tractable to any honest reason: thou seest I am pacified still. Nay, prithee, be gone. (*Exit Hostess.*) Now, Hal, to the news at court: for the robbery, lad, how is that answered?

Prince. O, my sweet beef, I must still be good angel to thee: the money is paid back again.

Fal. O, I do not like that paying back; 'tis a double labour.

Prince. I am good friends with my father and may do any thing.

Fal. Rob me the exchequer the first thing thou doest, and do it with unwashed hands too.

Bard. Do, my lord.

Prince. I have procured thee, Jack, a charge of foot.

Fal. I would it had been of horse. Where shall I find one that can steal well? O for a fine thief, of the age of two and twenty or thereabouts! I am heinously unprovided. Well, God be thanked for these rebels, they offend none but the virtuous: I laud them, I praise them.

Prince. Bardolph!

Bard. My lord?

Prince. Go bear this letter to Lord John of Lancaster, to my brother John; this to my Lord of Westmoreland. [*Exit Bardolph.*] Go, Peto, to horse, to horse; for thou and I have thirty miles to ride yet ere dinner time. [*Exit Peto.*] Jack, meet me to-morrow in the Temple hall at two o'clock in the afternoon.
There shalt thou know thy charge; and there receive
Money and order for their furniture.
The land is burning; Percy stands on high;
And either we or they must lower lie. [*Exit.*]

Fal. Rare words! brave world! Hostess, my breakfast, come!
O, I could wish this tavern were my drum! [*Exit.*]

[ACT IV.

SCENE I. *The rebel camp near Shrewsbury.*]

[*Enter* HOTSPUR, WORCESTER, *and* DOUGLAS.]

Hot. Well said, my noble Scot: if speaking truth
In this fine age were not thought flattery,
Such attribution should the Douglas have,
As not a soldier of this season's stamp
Should go so general current through the world.
By God, I cannot flatter; I do defy
The tongues of soothers; but a braver place
In my heart's love hath no man than yourself:
Nay, task me to my word; approve me, lord.

Doug. Thou art the king of honour:
No man so potent breathes upon the ground
But I will beard him.

Enter one with letters.

Hot. Do so, and 'tis well.—
What letters hast thou there?—I can but thank you.

Mess. These letters come from your father.

Hot. Letters from him! why comes he not himself?

Mess. He cannot come, my lord; he is grievous sick.

Hot. 'Zounds! how has he the leisure to be sick
In such a justling time? Who leads his power?
Under whose government come they along?

Mess. His letters bear his mind, not I, my lord.

Wor. I prithee, tell me, doth he keep his bed?

Mess. He did, my lord, four days ere I set forth;
And at the time of my departure thence
He was much fear'd by his physicians.

Wor. I would the state of time had first been whole
Ere he by sickness had been visited:
His health was never better worth than now.

Hot. Sick now! droop now! this sickness doth infect
The very life-blood of our enterprise;
'Tis catching hither, even to our camp.
†He writes me here, that inward sickness—
And that his friends by deputation could not
So soon be drawn, nor did he think it meet
To lay so dangerous and dear a trust
On any soul remov'd but on his own.
Yet doth he give us bold advertisement,
That with our small conjunction we should on,
To see how fortune is dispos'd to us;
For, as he writes, there is no quailing now,
Because the king is certainly possess'd

177. **embossed,** swollen (with fat). 182. **injuries,** i.e., those things you claim to have lost, thereby suffering harm. 183. **stand to it,** make a stand, insist on your supposed rights. **pocket up,** endure silently. 206. **with unwashed hands,** at once. 212. **thief,** i.e., to steal a horse. 226. **furniture,** equipment, provision. 230. **drum.** Possibly Falstaff means to say that he could wish that he might recruit his soldiers by means of this tavern.

ACT IV. SCENE I. 3. **attribution,** praise. 4-5. **stamp . . . current,** a figure of speech derived from coining, meaning to be widely accepted. 7. **soothers,** flatterers. 9. **task . . . word,** challenge me to make good my word. **approve,** test. 18. **justling,** jostling, busy. 36. **advertisement,** counsel, advice. 37. **conjunction,** joint force, with allusion to the conjunction of planets. 44. **want,** i.e., the lack of him. 47. **cast,** throw of the dice. **main,** stake in gambling; also, an army. 48. **nice,** precarious. 51. **list,** limit; see glossary. 53. **reversion,** part of an estate yet to be inherited; hope of future profit. 58. **big,** threateningly.

Of all our purposes. What say you to it?
Wor. Your father's sickness is a maim to us.
Hot. A perilous gash, a very limb lopp'd off:
And yet, in faith, it is not; his present want
Seems more than we shall find it: were it good
To set the exact wealth of all our states
All at one cast? to set so rich a main
On the nice hazard of one doubtful hour?
It were not good; †for therein should we read
The very bottom and the soul of hope,
The very list, the very utmost bound
Of all our fortunes.
Doug. 'Faith, and so we should;
Where now remains a sweet reversion:
†We may boldly spend upon the hope of what
Is to come in:
A comfort of retirement lives in this.
Hot. A rendezvous, a home to fly unto,
If that the devil and mischance look big
Upon the maidenhead of our affairs.
Wor. But yet I would your father had been here.
The quality and hair of our attempt
Brooks no division: it will be thought
By some, that know not why he is away,
That wisdom, loyalty and mere dislike
Of our proceedings kept the earl from hence:
And think how such an apprehension
May turn the tide of fearful faction
And breed a kind of question in our cause;
For well you know we of the off'ring side
Must keep aloof from strict arbitrement,
And stop all sight-holes, every loop from whence
The eye of reason may pry in upon us:
This absence of your father's draws a curtain,
That shows the ignorant a kind of fear
Before not dreamt of.
Hot. You strain too far.
I rather of his absence make this use:
It lends a lustre and more great opinion,
A larger dare to our great enterprise,
Than if the earl were here; for men must think,
If we without his help can make a head
To push against a kingdom, with his help
We shall o'erturn it topsy-turvy down.
Yet all goes well, yet all our joints are whole.
Doug. As heart can think: there is not such a word
Spoke of in Scotland as this term of fear.

Enter SIR RICHARD VERNON.

Hot. My cousin Vernon! welcome, by my soul.
Ver. Pray God my news be worth a welcome, lord.
The Earl of Westmoreland, seven thousand strong,
Is marching hitherwards; with him Prince John.
Hot. No harm: what more?
Ver. And further, I have learn'd,
The king himself in person is set forth,
Or hitherwards intended speedily,
With strong and mighty preparation.
Hot. He shall be welcome too. Where is his son,
The nimble-footed madcap Prince of Wales,
And his comrades, that daff'd the world aside,
And bid it pass?
Ver. All furnish'd, all in arms;
†All plum'd like estridges that with the wind
Bated like eagles having lately bath'd;
Glittering in golden coats, like images;
As full of spirit as the month of May,
And gorgeous as the sun at midsummer;
Wanton as youthful goats, wild as young bulls.
I saw young Harry, with his beaver on,
His cuisses on his thighs, gallantly arm'd,
Rise from the ground like feathered Mercury,
And vaulted with such ease into his seat,
As if an angel dropp'd down from the clouds,
To turn and wind a fiery Pegasus
And witch the world with noble horsemanship.
Hot. No more, no more: worse than the sun in March,
This praise doth nourish agues. Let them come;
They come like sacrifices in their trim,
And to the fire-ey'd maid of smoky war
All hot and bleeding will we offer them:
The mailed Mars shall on his altar sit
Up to the ears in blood. I am on fire
To hear this rich reprisal is so nigh
And yet not ours. Come, let me taste my horse,
Who is to bear me like a thunderbolt
Against the bosom of the Prince of Wales:
Harry to Harry shall, hot horse to horse,
Meet and ne'er part till one drop down a corse.
O that Glendower were come!
Ver. There is more news:
I learn'd in Worcester, as I rode along,
He cannot draw his power this fourteen days.
Doug. That 's the worst tidings that I hear of yet.
Wor. Ay, by my faith, that bears a frosty sound.
Hot. What may the king's whole battle reach unto?
Ver. To thirty thousand.
Hot. Forty let it be:
My father and Glendower being both away,
The powers of us may serve so great a day.
Come, let us take a muster speedily:
Doomsday is near; die all, die merrily.
Doug. Talk not of dying: I am out of fear
Of death or death's hand for this one-half year.
Exeunt.

[SCENE II. *A public road near Coventry.*]

Enter FALSTAFF, [*and*] BARDOLPH.

Fal. Bardolph, get thee before to Coventry; fill me a bottle of sack: our soldiers shall march through; we'll to Sutton Co'fil' to-night.

Bard. Will you give me money, captain?

Fal. Lay out, lay out.

Bard. This bottle makes an angel.

Fal. An if it do, take it for thy labour; and if it make twenty, take them all; I'll answer the coinage. Bid my lieutenant Peto meet me at town's end.

61. **hair,** kind, nature. 69. **off'ring side,** side which attacks. 70. **arbitrement,** just inquiry or investigation. 96. **daff'd,** put aside with a gesture. 97. **furnish'd,** equipped. 98. **like estridges,** a reference to ostrich plumes on crests. 99. **Bated,** flapped their wings. 100. **images,** gilded statues. 104. **beaver,** visor (of helmet); also, the helmet itself. 105. **cuisses,** armor for the thighs. 109. **wind a fiery Pegasus,** turn or wheel like the winged horse of Greek mythology. 110. **witch,** bewitch. 111-112. **worse . . . agues.** The spring sun was believed to give impetus to chills and fevers, by drawing up vapors. 113. **trim,** fine apparel, trappings. 114. **maid,** Bellona, goddess of war. 118. **reprisal,** prize. 126. **power,** army.

SCENE II. 3. **Sutton Co'fil',** Sutton Coldfield in Warwickshire near Coventry. 5. **Lay out,** pay yourself. 6. **makes an angel,** i.e., that I have spent. **angel,** coin worth ten shillings.

Bard. I will, captain: farewell. *Exit.*

Fal. If I be not ashamed of my soldiers, I am a soused gurnet. I have misused the king's press damnably. I have got, in exchange of a hundred and fifty soldiers, three hundred and odd pounds. I press me none but good householders, yeomen's sons; inquire me out contracted bachelors, such as had been asked twice on the banns; such a commodity of warm slaves, as had as lieve hear the devil as a drum; such as fear the report of a caliver worse than a struck fowl or a hurt wild-duck. I pressed me none but such toasts-and-butter, with hearts in their bellies no bigger than pins' heads, and they have bought out their services; and now my whole charge consists of ancients, corporals, lieutenants, gentlemen of companies, slaves as ragged as Lazarus in the painted cloth, where the glutton's dogs licked his sores; and such as indeed were never soldiers, but discarded unjust serving-men, younger sons to younger brothers, revolted tapsters and ostlers trade-fallen, the cankers of a calm world and a long peace, ten times more dishonourable ragged than an old faced ancient: and such have I, to fill up the rooms of them that have bought out their services, that you would think that I had a hundred and fifty tattered prodigals lately come from swine-keeping, from eating draff and husks. A mad fellow met me on the way and told me I had unloaded all the gibbets and pressed the dead bodies. No eye hath seen such scarecrows. I'll not march through Coventry with them, that 's flat: nay, and the villains march wide betwixt the legs, as if they had gyves on; for indeed I had the most of them out of prison. There 's but a shirt and a half in all my company; and the half shirt is two napkins tacked together and thrown over the shoulders like a herald's coat without sleeves; and the shirt, to say the truth, stolen from my host at Saint Alban's, or the red-nose innkeeper of Daventry. But that 's all one; they'll find linen enough on every hedge.

Enter the PRINCE [*and the*] Lord *of* WESTMORELAND.

Prince. How now, blown Jack! how now, quilt!

Fal. What, Hal! how now, mad wag! what a devil dost thou in Warwickshire? My good Lord of Westmoreland, I cry you mercy: I thought your honour had already been at Shrewsbury.

West. Faith, Sir John, 'tis more than time that I were there, and you too; but my powers are there already. The king, I can tell you, looks for us all: we must away all night.

Fal. Tut, never fear me: I am as vigilant as a cat to steal cream.

Prince. I think, to steal cream indeed, for thy theft hath already made thee butter. But tell me, Jack, whose fellows are these that come after?

Fal. Mine, Hal, mine.

Prince. I did never see such pitiful rascals.

Fal. Tut, tut; good enough to toss; food for powder, food for powder; they'll fill a pit as well as better: tush, man, mortal men, mortal men.

West. Ay, but, Sir John, methinks they are exceeding poor and bare, too beggarly.

Fal. 'Faith, for their poverty, I know not where they had that; and for their bareness, I am sure they never learned that of me.

Prince. No, I'll be sworn; unless you call three fingers in the ribs bare. But, sirrah, make haste: Percy is already in the field. *Exit.*

Fal. What, is the king encamped?

West. He is, Sir John: I fear we shall stay too long. [*Exit.*]

Fal. Well,
To the latter end of a fray and the beginning of a feast
Fits a dull fighter and a keen guest. *Exit.*

[SCENE III. *The rebel camp near Shrewsbury.*]

Enter HOTSPUR, WORCESTER, DOUGLAS, [*and*] VERNON.

Hot. We'll fight with him to-night.
Wor. It may not be.
Doug. You give him then advantage.
Ver. Not a whit.
Hot. Why say you so? looks he not for supply?
Ver. So do we.
Hot. His is certain, ours is doubtful.
Wor. Good cousin, be advis'd; stir not to-night.
Ver. Do not, my lord.
Doug. You do not counsel well:
You speak it out of fear and cold heart.
Ver. Do me no slander, Douglas: by my life,
And I dare well maintain it with my life,
If well-respected honour bid me on,
I hold as little counsel with weak fear
As you, my lord, or any Scot that this day lives:
Let it be seen to-morrow in the battle
Which of us fears.
Doug. Yea, or to-night.
Ver. Content.
Hot. To-night, say I.
Ver. Come, come, it may not be. I wonder much,
Being men of such great leading as you are,
That you foresee not what impediments
Drag back our expedition: certain horse
Of my cousin Vernon's are not yet come up:
Your uncle Worcester's horse came but to-day;
And now their pride and mettle is asleep,
Their courage with hard labour tame and dull,
That not a horse is half the half of himself.
Hot. So are the horses of the enemy
In general, journey-bated and brought low:
The better part of ours are full of rest.
Wor. The number of the king exceedeth ours:
For God's sake, cousin, stay till all come in.
The trumpet sounds a parley.

Enter SIR WALTER BLUNT.

Blunt. I come with gracious offers from the king,
If you vouchsafe me hearing and respect.
Hot. Welcome, Sir Walter Blunt; and would to God
You were of our determination!
Some of us love you well; and even those some

13. **soused gurnet,** a kind of fish pickled; opprobrious. 14. **king's press,** royal warrant for the impressment of troops. 16. **yeomen's,** small freeholders'. 17. **contracted,** engaged to be married. 21. **caliver,** musket or harquebus. **struck,** wounded. 26. **ancients,** ensigns, standardbearers. 28. **painted cloth,** hangings for a room; in this case painted with the story of Lazarus, Luke 16:20. 32. **cankers,** worms which destroy leaves and buds; used figuratively. 34. **old faced ancient,** defined as an old standard mended with new cloth, or as a standard presenting an old aspect. Cambridge reads *old feaz'd,* meaning "frayed." 37. **prodigals.** See Luke 15:15-16. 39. **draff,** hogwash. 44. **gyves,** fetters. 50, 51. **Saint Alban's, Daventry,** towns on the road from London to Coventry. 53. **blown,** swollen, inflated; also, short

Envy your great deservings and good name,
Because you are not of our quality,
But stand against us like an enemy.
Blunt. And God defend but still I should stand so,
So long as out of limit and true rule
You stand against anointed majesty.
But to my charge. The king hath sent to know
The nature of your griefs, and whereupon
You conjure from the breast of civil peace
Such bold hostility, teaching his duteous land
Audacious cruelty. If that the king
Have any way your good deserts forgot,
Which he confesseth to be manifold,
He bids you name your griefs; and with all speed
You shall have your desires with interest
And pardon absolute for yourself and these
Herein misled by your suggestion.
Hot. The king is kind; and well we know the king
Knows at what time to promise, when to pay.
My father and my uncle and myself
Did give him that same royalty he wears;
And when he was not six and twenty strong,
Sick in the world's regard, wretched and low,
A poor unminded outlaw sneaking home,
My father gave him welcome to the shore;
And when he heard him swear and vow to God
He came but to be Duke of Lancaster,
To sue his livery and beg his peace,
With tears of innocency and terms of zeal,
My father, in kind heart and pity mov'd,
Swore him assistance and perform'd it too.
Now when the lords and barons of the realm
Perceiv'd Northumberland did lean to him,
The more and less came in with cap and knee;
Met him in boroughs, cities, villages,
Attended him on bridges, stood in lanes,
Laid gifts before him, proffer'd him their oaths,
Gave him their heirs, as pages followed him
Even at the heels in golden multitudes.
He presently, as greatness knows itself,
Steps me a little higher than his vow
Made to my father, while his blood was poor,
Upon the naked shore at Ravenspurgh;
And now, forsooth, takes on him to reform
Some certain edicts and some strait decrees
That lie too heavy on the commonwealth,
Cries out upon abuses, seems to weep
Over his country's wrongs; and by this face,
This seeming brow of justice, did he win
The hearts of all that he did angle for;
Proceeded further; cut me off the heads
Of all the favourites that the absent king
In deputation left behind him here,
When he was personal in the Irish war.
Blunt. Tut, I came not to hear this.
Hot. Then to the point.
In short time after, he depos'd the king;
Soon after that, depriv'd him of his life;
And in the neck of that, task'd the whole state;
To make that worse, suff'red his kinsman March,
Who is, if every owner were well plac'd,
Indeed his king, to be engag'd in Wales,
There without ransom to lie forfeited;
Disgrac'd me in my happy victories,
Sought to entrap me by intelligence;
Rated mine uncle from the council-board;
In rage dismiss'd my father from the court;
Broke oath on oath, committed wrong on wrong,
And in conclusion drove us to seek out
This head of safety; and withal to pry
Into his title, the which we find
Too indirect for long continuance.
Blunt. Shall I return this answer to the king?
Hot. Not so, Sir Walter: we'll withdraw awhile.
Go to the king; and let there be impawn'd
Some surety for a safe return again,
And in the morning early shall mine uncle
Bring him our purposes: and so farewell.
Blunt. I would you would accept of grace and love.
Hot. And may be so we shall.
Blunt. Pray God you do. [*Exeunt.*]

[SCENE IV. *York. The* ARCHBISHOP'S *palace.*]

Enter [*the*] ARCHBISHOP OF YORK, [*and*] SIR MICHAEL.

Arch. Hie, good Sir Michael; bear this sealed brief
With winged haste to the lord marshal;
This to my cousin Scroop, and all the rest
To whom they are directed. If you knew
How much they do import, you would make haste.
Sir M. My good lord,
I guess their tenour.
Arch. Like enough you do.
To-morrow, good Sir Michael, is a day
Wherein the fortune of ten thousand men
Must bide the touch; for, sir, at Shrewsbury,
As I am truly given to understand,
The king with mighty and quick-raised power
Meets with Lord Harry: and, I fear, Sir Michael,
What with the sickness of Northumberland,
Whose power was in the first proportion,
And what with Owen Glendower's absence thence,
Who with them was a rated sinew too
And comes not in, o'er-rul'd by prophecies,
I fear the power of Percy is too weak
To wage an instant trial with the king.
Sir M. Why, my good lord, you need not fear;
There is Douglas and Lord Mortimer.
Arch. No, Mortimer is not there.
Sir M. But there is Mordake, Vernon, Lord Harry Percy,
And there is my Lord of Worcester and a head
Of gallant warriors, noble gentlemen.
Arch. And so there is: but yet the king hath drawn
The special head of all the land together:
The Prince of Wales, Lord John of Lancaster,
The noble Westmoreland and warlike Blunt;
And many moe corrivals and dear men
Of estimation and command in arms.
Sir M. Doubt not, my lord, they shall be well oppos'd.

of wind. 71. **toss,** i.e., on a pike.

SCENE III. 10. **well-respected,** well weighed or considered. 26. **journey-bated,** tired from the journey. 51. **suggestion,** instigation. 62. **sue his livery,** sue as an heir come of age for the delivery of his lands held by the crown. 68. **more and less,** persons of all ranks. 88. **personal,** in person. 92. **in . . . that,** next. **task'd,** laid taxes upon. 98. **intelligence,** secret information, i.e., from spies. 103. **head of safety,** armed force for their protection.

SCENE IV. 1. **brief,** letter, dispatch. 10. **bide the touch,** be put to the test (like gold). 17. **rated sinew,** main strength or support reckoned upon. 31. **moe corrivals,** more partners in the enterprise. 32. **estimation,** reputation, importance.

Arch. I hope no less, yet needful 'tis to fear;
And, to prevent the worst, Sir Michael, speed:
For if Lord Percy thrive not, ere the king
Dismiss his power, he means to visit us,
For he hath heard of our confederacy,
And 'tis but wisdom to make strong against him:
Therefore make haste. I must go write again
To other friends; and so farewell, Sir Michael. *Exeunt.*

[ACT V.

SCENE I. *The* KING'S *camp near Shrewsbury.*]

Enter the KING, PRINCE OF WALES, LORD JOHN OF LANCASTER, EARL OF WESTMORELAND, SIR WALTER BLUNT, [*and*] FALSTAFF.

King. How bloodily the sun begins to peer
Above yon busky hill! the day looks pale
At his distemp'rature.
Prince. The southern wind
Doth play the trumpet to his purposes,
And by his hollow whistling in the leaves
Foretells a tempest and a blust'ring day.
King. Then with the losers let it sympathise,
For nothing can seem foul to those that win.
The trumpet sounds.

Enter WORCESTER [*and* VERNON].

How now, my Lord of Worcester! 'tis not well
That you and I should meet upon such terms
As now we meet. You have deceiv'd our trust,
And made us doff our easy robes of peace,
To crush our old limbs in ungentle steel:
This is not well, my lord, this is not well.
What say you to it? will you again unknit
This churlish knot of all-abhorred war?
And move in that obedient orb again
Where you did give a fair and natural light,
And be no more an exhal'd meteor,
A prodigy of fear and a portent
Of broached mischief to the unborn times?
Wor. Hear me, my liege:
For mine own part, I could be well content
To entertain the lag-end of my life
With quiet hours; for I do protest,
I have not sought the day of this dislike.
King. You have not sought it! how comes it, then?
Fal. Rebellion lay in his way, and he found it.
Prince. Peace, chewet, peace!
Wor. It pleas'd your majesty to turn your looks
Of favour from myself and all our house;
And yet I must remember you, my lord,
We were the first and dearest of your friends.
For you my staff of office did I break
In Richard's time; and posted day and night
To meet you on the way, and kiss your hand,
When yet you were in place and in account
Nothing so strong and fortunate as I.
It was myself, my brother and his son,
That brought you home and boldly did outdare
The dangers of the time. You swore to us,
And you did swear that oath at Doncaster,
That you did nothing purpose 'gainst the state;
Nor claim no further than your new-fall'n right,
The seat of Gaunt, dukedom of Lancaster:
To this we swore our aid. But in short space
It rain'd down fortune show'ring on your head;
And such a flood of greatness fell on you,
What with our help, what with the absent king,
What with the injuries of a wanton time,
The seeming sufferances that you had borne,
And the contrarious winds that held the king
So long in his unlucky Irish wars
That all in England did repute him dead:
And from this swarm of fair advantages
You took occasion to be quickly woo'd
To gripe the general sway into your hand;
Forgot your oath to us at Doncaster;
And being fed by us you us'd us so
As that ungentle gull, the cuckoo's bird,
Useth the sparrow; did oppress our nest;
Grew by our feeding to so great a bulk
That even our love durst not come near your sight
For fear of swallowing; but with nimble wing
We were enforc'd, for safety sake, to fly
Out of your sight and raise this present head;
Whereby we stand opposed by such means
As you yourself have forg'd against yourself
By unkind usage, dangerous countenance,
And violation of all faith and troth
Sworn to us in your younger enterprise.
King. These things indeed you have articulate,
Proclaim'd at market-crosses, read in churches,
To face the garment of rebellion
With some fine colour that may please the eye
Of fickle changelings and poor discontents,
Which gape and rub the elbow at the news
Of hurlyburly innovation:
And never yet did insurrection want
Such water-colours to impaint his cause;
Nor moody beggars, starving for a time
Of pellmell havoc and confusion.
Prince. In both your armies there is many a soul
Shall pay full dearly for this encounter,
If once they join in trial. Tell your nephew,
The Prince of Wales doth join with all the world
In praise of Henry Percy: by my hopes,
This present enterprise set off his head,
I do not think a braver gentleman,
More active-valiant or more valiant-young,
More daring or more bold, is now alive
To grace this latter age with noble deeds.
For my part, I may speak it to my shame,
I have a truant been to chivalry;
And so I hear he doth account me too;
Yet this before my father's majesty—
I am content that he shall take the odds
Of his great name and estimation,
And will, to save the blood on either side,
Try fortune with him in a single fight.
King. And, Prince of Wales, so dare we venture thee,

ACT V. SCENE I. 2. **busky,** bosky, bushy. 3. **distemp'rature,** ill-humor, or possibly, inclemency. 4. **his,** its, the sun's. 17. **orb,** orbit, sphere of action. 19. **exhal'd meteor,** a phenomenon created by vapor drawn up by the sun and visible as streaks of light; regarded as an ill omen. 21. **broached,** already begun. 29. **chewet,** chough, jackdaw; piece of fried pie; also, here, a chatterer. 32. **remember,** remind. 51. **sufferances,** suffering, distress. 60. **gull,** unfledged nestling. **cuckoo's bird,** allusion to the cuckoo's habit of laying its eggs in the sparrow's nest. 69. **dangerous,** menacing. 72. **articulate,** set forth, specified. 74. **face,** trim, adorn. 77. **rub the elbow,** i.e., hug themselves with delight. 78. **innovation,** revolution. 79. **want,** lack. 88. **set off his head,** taken from his account. 102. **Albeit,** on the other

Albeit considerations infinite
Do make against it. No, good Worcester, no,
We love our people well; even those we love
That are misled upon your cousin's part;
And, will they take the offer of our grace,
Both he and they and you, yea, every man
Shall be my friend again and I'll be his:
So tell your cousin, and bring me word
What he will do: but if he will not yield,
Rebuke and dread correction wait on us
And they shall do their office. So, be gone;
We will not now be troubled with reply:
We offer fair; take it advisedly.

Exeunt Worcester [and Vernon].

Prince. It will not be accepted, on my life:
The Douglas and the Hotspur both together
Are confident against the world in arms.

King. Hence, therefore, every leader to his charge;
For, on their answer, will we set on them:
And God befriend us, as our cause is just!

Exeunt. Manent Prince, Falstaff.

Fal. Hal, if thou see me down in the battle and bestride me, so; 'tis a point of friendship.

Prince. Nothing but a colossus can do thee that friendship. Say thy prayers, and farewell.

Fal. I would 'twere bed-time, Hal, and all well.

Prince. Why, thou owest God a death. [*Exit.*]

Fal. 'Tis not due yet; I would be loath to pay him before his day. What need I be so forward with him that calls not on me? Well, 'tis no matter; honour pricks me on. Yea, but how if honour prick me off when I come on? how then? Can honour set to a leg? no: or an arm? no: or take away the grief of a wound? no. Honour hath no skill in surgery, then? no. What is honour? a word. What is in that word honour? what is that honour? air. A trim reckoning! Who hath it? he that died a Wednesday. Doth he feel it? no. Doth he hear it? no. 'Tis insensible, then? Yea, to the dead. But will it not live with the living? no. Why? detraction will not suffer it. Therefore I'll none of it. Honour is a mere scutcheon: and so ends my catechism. *Exit.*

[SCENE II. *The rebel camp.*]

Enter WORCESTER, [*and*] SIR RICHARD VERNON.

Wor. O, no, my nephew must not know, Sir Richard,
The liberal and kind offer of the king.

Ver. 'Twere best he did.

Wor. Then are we all undone.
It is not possible, it cannot be,
The king should keep his word in loving us;
He will suspect us still and find a time
To punish this offence in other faults:
Supposition all our lives shall be stuck full of eyes;
For treason is but trusted like the fox,
Who, ne'er so tame, so cherish'd and lock'd up,
Will have a wild trick of his ancestors.
Look how we can, or sad or merrily,
Interpretation will misquote our looks,
And we shall feed like oxen at a stall,
The better cherish'd, still the nearer death.
My nephew's trespass may be well forgot;
It hath the excuse of youth and heat of blood,
And an adopted name of privilege,
A hare-brain'd Hotspur, govern'd by a spleen:
All his offences live upon my head
And on his father's; we did train him on,
And, his corruption being ta'en from us,
We, as the spring of all, shall pay for all.
Therefore, good cousin, let not Harry know,
In any case, the offer of the king.

Enter HOTSPUR [*and* DOUGLAS].

Ver. Deliver what you will; I'll say 'tis so.
Here comes your cousin.

Hot. My uncle is return'd:
Deliver up my Lord of Westmoreland.
Uncle, what news?

Wor. The king will bid you battle presently.

Doug. Defy him by the Lord of Westmoreland.

Hot. Lord Douglas, go you and tell him so.

Doug. Marry, and shall, and very willingly.

Exit Doug.

Wor. There is no seeming mercy in the king.

Hot. Did you beg any? God forbid!

Wor. I told him gently of our grievances,
Of his oath-breaking; which he mended thus,
By now forswearing that he is forsworn:
He calls us rebels, traitors; and will scourge
With haughty arms this hateful name in us.

Enter DOUGLAS.

Doug. Arm, gentlemen; to arms! for I have thrown
A brave defiance in King Henry's teeth,
And Westmoreland, that was engag'd, did bear it;
Which cannot choose but bring him quickly on.

Wor. The Prince of Wales stepp'd forth before the king,
And, nephew, challeng'd you to single fight.

Hot. O, would the quarrel lay upon our heads,
And that no man might draw short breath to-day
But I and Harry Monmouth! Tell me, tell me,
How show'd his tasking? seem'd it in contempt?

Ver. No, by my soul; I never in my life
Did hear a challenge urg'd more modestly,
Unless a brother should a brother dare
To gentle exercise and proof of arms.
He gave you all the duties of a man;
Trimm'd up your praises with a princely tongue,
Spoke your deservings like a chronicle,
Making you ever better than his praise
By still dispraising praise valued with you;
And, which became him like a prince indeed,
He made a blushing cital of himself;
And chid his truant youth with such a grace
As if he mast'red there a double spirit
Of teaching and of learning instantly.
There did he pause: but let me tell the world,
If he outlive the envy of this day,
England did never owe so sweet a hope,
So much misconstrued in his wantonness.

hand, were it not that. 111. **wait on us,** are in attendance upon us. 126. **thou . . . death,** proverbial, with a pun on "debt." 131. **prick me off,** mark me off as one dead. 142. **detraction,** slander. 143. **scutcheon,** emblem or hatchment carried in funerals. It was the lowest form of symbol, having no pennon or other insignia.

SCENE II. 8. **Supposition,** suspicious conjecture. 18. **adopted name of privilege.** Hotspur has taken a nickname, "hotspur," to justify his rashness. 21. **train,** incite, draw. 51. **tasking,** challenge. 62. **cital,** impeachment. 68. **owe,** own.

Hot. Cousin, I think thou art enamoured
On his follies: never did I hear
Of any prince so wild a libertine.
But be he as he will, yet once ere night
I will embrace him with a soldier's arm,
That he shall shrink under my courtesy.
Arm, arm with speed: and, fellows, soldiers, friends,
Better consider what you have to do
Than I, that have not well the gift of tongue,
Can lift your blood up with persuasion.

Enter a Messenger.

Mess. My lord, here are letters for you.
Hot. I cannot read them now.
O gentlemen, the time of life is short!
To spend that shortness basely were too long,
If life did ride upon a dial's point,
Still ending at the arrival of an hour.
An if we live, we live to tread on kings;
If die, brave death, when princes die with us!
Now, for our consciences, the arms are fair,
When the intent of bearing them is just.

Enter another [Messenger].

Mess. My lord, prepare; the king comes on apace.
Hot. I thank him, that he cuts me from my tale,
For I profess not talking; only this—
Let each man do his best: and here draw I
A sword, whose temper I intend to stain
With the best blood that I can meet withal
In the adventure of this perilous day.
Now, Esperance! Percy! and set on.
Sound all the lofty instruments of war,
And by that music let us all embrace;
For, heaven to earth, some of us never shall
A second time do such a courtesy.
Here they embrace. The trumpets sound. [*Exeunt.*]

[SCENE III. *Plain between the camps.*]

The KING *enters with his power. Alarum to the battle. Then enter* DOUGLAS *and* SIR WALTER BLUNT.

Blunt. What is thy name, that in the battle thus
Thou crossest me? what honour dost thou seek
Upon my head?
Doug. Know then, my name is Douglas;
And I do haunt thee in the battle thus
Because some tell me that thou art a king.
Blunt. They tell thee true.
Doug. The Lord of Stafford dear to-day hath bought
Thy likeness, for instead of thee, King Harry,
This sword hath ended him: so shall it thee,
Unless thou yield thee as my prisoner.
Blunt. I was not born a yielder, thou proud Scot;
And thou shalt find a king that will revenge
Lord Stafford's death. *They fight. Douglas kills Blunt.*

Then enter HOTSPUR.

Hot. O Douglas, hadst thou fought at Holmedon thus,
I never had triumph'd upon a Scot.
Doug. All 's done, all 's won; here breathless lies the king.
Hot. Where?
Doug. Here.
Hot. This, Douglas? no: I know this face full well:
A gallant knight he was, his name was Blunt;
Semblably furnish'd like the king himself.
Doug. A fool go with thy soul, whither it goes!
A borrowed title hast thou bought too dear:
Why didst thou tell me that thou wert a king?
Hot. The king hath many marching in his coats.
Doug. Now, by my sword, I will kill all his coats;
I'll murder all his wardrobe, piece by piece,
Until I meet the king.
Hot. Up, and away!
Our soldiers stand full fairly for the day. [*Exeunt.*]

Alarum. Enter FALSTAFF, *solus.*

Fal. Though I could 'scape shot-free at London, I fear the shot here; here 's no scoring but upon the pate. Soft! who are you? Sir Walter Blunt: there 's honour for you! here 's no vanity! I am as hot as molten lead, and as heavy too: God keep lead out of me! I need no more weight than mine own bowels. I have led my ragamuffins where they are peppered: there 's not three of my hundred and fifty left alive; and they are for the town's end, to beg during life. But who comes here?

Enter the PRINCE.

Prince. What, stand'st thou idle here? lend me thy sword:
Many a nobleman lies stark and stiff
Under the hoofs of vaunting enemies,
Whose deaths are yet unrevenged: I prithee, lend me thy sword.
Fal. O Hal, I prithee, give me leave to breathe awhile. Turk Gregory never did such deeds in arms as I have done this day. I have paid Percy, I have made him sure.
Prince. He is, indeed; and living to kill thee. I prithee, lend me thy sword.
Fal. Nay, before God, Hal, if Percy be alive, thou get'st not my sword; but take my pistol, if thou wilt.
Prince. Give it me: what, is it in the case?
Fal. Ay, Hal; 'tis hot, 'tis hot; there 's that will sack a city.
The Prince draws it out, and finds it to be a bottle of sack.
Prince. What, is it a time to jest and dally now?
He throws the bottle at him. Exit.
Fal. Well, if Percy be alive, I'll pierce him. If he do come in my way, so: if he do not, if I come in his willingly, let him make a carbonado of me. I like not such grinning honour as Sir Walter hath: give me life: which if I can save, so; if not, honour comes unlooked for, and there 's an end. [*Exit.*]

[SCENE IV. *Another part of the field.*]

Alarum. Excursions. Enter the KING, *the* PRINCE, LORD JOHN OF LANCASTER, [*and*] EARL OF WESTMORELAND.

King. I prithee,

84. **dial's point,** hand of watch or clock.
SCENE III. 21. **Semblably furnish'd,** similarly accoutered. 30. **shot-free,** without paying the bill. 31. **scoring,** marking up of charges (often on the inn door). 46. **Turk Gregory,** a sort of combined allusion to the famous pope Gregory the Great, and to the Grand Turk. 59. **Percy . . . pierce.** Current pronunciation probably rendered the pun more obvious than it is now. 62. **carbonado,** meat scored across for broiling.
SCENE IV. 5. **make up,** go forward. 6. **amaze,** alarm. 22. **mainte-**

Harry, withdraw thyself; thou bleedest too much.
Lord John of Lancaster, go you with him.
Lan. Not I, my lord, unless I did bleed too.
Prince. I beseech your majesty, make up,
Lest your retirement do amaze your friends.
King. I will do so.
My Lord of Westmoreland, lead him to his tent.
West. Come, my lord, I'll lead you to your tent.
Prince. Lead me, my lord? I do not need your help:
And God forbid a shallow scratch should drive
The Prince of Wales from such a field as this,
Where stain'd nobility lies trodden on,
And rebels' arms triumph in massacres!
Lan. We breathe too long: come, cousin Westmoreland,
Our duty this way lies; for God's sake, come.
[*Exeunt Prince John and Westmoreland.*]
Prince. By God, thou hast deceiv'd me, Lancaster;
I did not think thee lord of such a spirit:
Before, I lov'd thee as a brother, John;
But now, I do respect thee as my soul.
King. I saw him hold Lord Percy at the point
With lustier maintenance than I did look for
Of such an ungrown warrior.
Prince. O, this boy
Lends mettle to us all! *Exit.*

[*Enter* DOUGLAS.]

Doug. Another king! they grow like Hydra's heads:
I am the Douglas, fatal to all those
That wear those colours on them: what art thou,
That counterfeit'st the person of a king?
King. The king himself; who, Douglas, grieves at heart
So many of his shadows thou hast met
And not the very king. I have two boys
Seek Percy and thyself about the field:
But, seeing thou fall'st on me so luckily,
I will assay thee: so, defend thyself.
Doug. I fear thou art another counterfeit;
And yet, in faith, thou bearest thee like a king:
But mine I am sure thou art, whoe'er thou be,
And thus I win thee.
They fight; the King being in danger, enter Prince of Wales.
Prince. Hold up thy head, vile Scot, or thou art like
Never to hold it up again! the spirits
Of valiant Shirley, Stafford, Blunt, are in my arms:
It is the Prince of Wales that threatens thee;
Who never promiseth but he means to pay.
They fight: Douglas flieth.
Cheerly, my lord: how fares your grace?
Sir Nicholas Gawsey hath for succour sent,
And so hath Clifton: I'll to Clifton straight.
King. Stay, and breathe awhile:
Thou hast redeem'd thy lost opinion,
And show'd thou mak'st some tender of my life,
In this fair rescue thou hast brought to me.
Prince. O God! they did me too much injury
That ever said I heark'ned for your death.
If it were so, I might have let alone
The insulting hand of Douglas over you,
Which would have been as speedy in your end
As all the poisonous potions in the world
And sav'd the treacherous labour of your son.
King. Make up to Clifton: I'll to Sir Nicholas Gawsey. *Exit King.*

Enter HOTSPUR.

Hot. If I mistake not, thou art Harry Monmouth.
Prince. Thou speak'st as if I would deny my name.
Hot. My name is Harry Percy.
Prince. Why, then I see
A very valiant rebel of the name.
I am the Prince of Wales; and think not, Percy,
To share with me in glory any more:
Two stars keep not their motion in one sphere;
Nor can one England brook a double reign,
Of Harry Percy and the Prince of Wales.
Hot. Nor shall it, Harry; for the hour is come
To end the one of us; and would to God
Thy name in arms were now as great as mine!
Prince. I'll make it greater ere I part from thee;
And all the budding honours on thy crest
I'll crop, to make a garland for my head.
Hot. I can no longer brook thy vanities. *They fight.*

Enter FALSTAFF.

Fal. Well said, Hal! to it, Hal! Nay, you shall find no boy's play here, I can tell you.

Enter DOUGLAS. *He fighteth with* FALSTAFF, *who falls down as if he were dead.* [*Exit* DOUGLAS.] *The* PRINCE *killeth* PERCY.

Hot. O, Harry, thou hast robb'd me of my youth!
I better brook the loss of brittle life
Than those proud titles thou hast won of me;
They wound my thoughts worse than thy sword my flesh:
But thought 's the slave of life, and life time's fool;
And time, that takes survey of all the world,
Must have a stop. O, I could prophesy,
But that the earthy and cold hand of death
Lies on my tongue: no, Percy, thou art dust,
And food for— [*Dies.*]
Prince. For worms, brave Percy: fare thee well, great heart!
Ill-weav'd ambition, how much art thou shrunk!
When that this body did contain a spirit,
A kingdom for it was too small a bound;
But now two paces of the vilest earth
Is room enough: this earth that bears thee dead
Bears not alive so stout a gentleman.
If thou wert sensible of courtesy,
I should not make so dear a show of zeal:
But let my favours hide thy mangled face;
And, even in thy behalf, I'll thank myself
For doing these fair rites of tenderness.
Adieu, and take thy praise with thee to heaven!
Thy ignominy sleep with thee in the grave,
But not remember'd in thy epitaph!
He spieth Falstaff on the ground.
What, old acquaintance! could not all this flesh
Keep in a little life? Poor Jack, farewell!
I could have better spar'd a better man:
O, I should have a heavy miss of thee,
If I were much in love with vanity!

nance, bearing, demeanor. 25. **Hydra's heads,** allusion to the Lernean Hydra, whose heads grew again as fast as they were cut off. 49. **mak'st some tender,** hast some care for. 52. **heark'ned,** listened (as for welcome intelligence). 65. **Two . . . sphere,** proverbial allusion to the fact that each planet has its own orbit. 81-83. **But . . . stop.** Thought ends with life, and life is ended by time; and time, though it serve as the measure for the world, must itself come to an end. 93. **stout,** valiant. 96. **favours,** knots of ribbon, scarf, etc.

Death hath not struck so fat a deer to-day,
Though many dearer, in this bloody fray.
Embowell'd will I see thee by and by:
Till then in blood by noble Percy lie. *Exit.*

Falstaff riseth up.

Fal. Embowelled! if thou embowel me to-day, I'll give you leave to powder me and eat me too to-morrow. 'Sblood, 'twas time to counterfeit, or that hot termagant Scot had paid me scot and lot too. Counterfeit? I lie, I am no counterfeit: to die, is to be a counterfeit; for he is but the counterfeit of a man who hath not the life of a man: but to counterfeit dying, when a man thereby liveth, is to be no counterfeit, but the true and perfect image of life indeed. The better part of valour is discretion; in the which better part I have saved my life. 'Zounds, I am afraid of this gunpowder Percy, though he be dead: how, if he should counterfeit too and rise? by my faith, I am afraid he would prove the better counterfeit. Therefore I'll make him sure; yea, and I'll swear I killed him. Why may not he rise as well as I? Nothing confutes me but eyes, and nobody sees me. Therefore, sirrah [*stabbing him*], with a new wound in your thigh, come you along with me.

He takes up Hotspur on his back.

Enter PRINCE [*and*] JOHN OF LANCASTER.

Prince. Come, brother John; full bravely hast thou flesh'd
Thy maiden sword.
Lan. But, soft! whom have we here?
Did you not tell me this fat man was dead?
Prince. I did; I saw him dead,
Breathless and bleeding on the ground. Art thou alive?
Or is it fantasy that plays upon our eyesight?
I prithee, speak; we will not trust our eyes
Without our ears: thou art not what thou seem'st.

Fal. No, that 's certain; I am not a double man: but if I be not Jack Falstaff, then am I a Jack. There is Percy [*throwing the body down*]: if your father will do me any honour, so; if not, let him kill the next Percy himself. I look to be either earl or duke, I can assure you.

Prince. Why, Percy I killed myself and saw thee dead.

Fal. Didst thou? Lord, Lord, how this world is given to lying! I grant you I was down and out of breath; and so was he: but we rose both at an instant and fought a long hour by Shrewsbury clock. If I may be believed, so; if not, let them that should reward valour bear the sin upon their own heads. I'll take it upon my death, I gave him this wound in the thigh: if the man were alive and would deny it, 'zounds, I would make him eat a piece of my sword.

Lan. This is the strangest tale that ever I heard.
Prince. This is the strangest fellow, brother John.
Come, bring your luggage nobly on your back:
For my part, if a lie may do thee grace,
I'll gild it with the happiest terms I have.

A retreat is sounded.

The trumpet sounds retreat; the day is ours.
Come, brother, let us to the highest of the field,
To see what friends are living, who are dead.

Exeunt [*Prince of Wales and Lancaster*].

Fal. I'll follow, as they say, for reward. He that rewards me, God reward him! If I do grow great, I'll grow less; for I'll purge, and leave sack, and live cleanly as a nobleman should do. *Exit* [*with body*].

[SCENE V. *Another part of the field.*]

The trumpets sound. Enter the KING, PRINCE OF WALES, LORD JOHN OF LANCASTER, EARL OF WESTMORELAND, *with* WORCESTER *and* VERNON *prisoners.*

King. Thus ever did rebellion find rebuke.
Ill-spirited Worcester! did not we send grace,
Pardon and terms of love to all of you?
And wouldst thou turn our offers contrary?
Misuse the tenour of thy kinsman's trust?
Three knights upon our party slain to-day,
A noble earl and many a creature else
Had been alive this hour,
If like a Christian thou hadst truly borne
Betwixt our armies true intelligence.
Wor. What I have done my safety urg'd me to;
And I embrace this fortune patiently,
Since not to be avoided it falls on me.
King. Bear Worcester to the death and Vernon too:
Other offenders we will pause upon.

[*Exeunt Worcester and Vernon, guarded.*]

How goes the field?
Prince. The noble Scot, Lord Douglas, when he saw
The fortune of the day quite turn'd from him,
The noble Percy slain, and all his men
Upon the foot of fear, fled with the rest;
And falling from a hill, he was so bruis'd
That the pursuers took him. At my tent
The Douglas is; and I beseech your grace
I may dispose of him.
King. With all my heart.
Prince. Then, brother John of Lancaster, to you
This honourable bounty shall belong:
Go to the Douglas, and deliver him
Up to his pleasure, ransomless and free:
His valours shown upon our crests to-day
Have taught us how to cherish such high deeds
Even in the bosom of our adversaries.
Lan. I thank your grace for this high courtesy,
Which I shall give away immediately.
King. Then this remains, that we divide our power.
You, son John, and my cousin Westmoreland
Towards York shall bend you with your dearest speed,
To meet Northumberland and the prelate Scroop,
Who, as we hear, are busily in arms:
Myself and you, son Harry, will towards Wales,
To fight with Glendower and the Earl of March.
Rebellion in this land shall lose his sway,
Meeting the check of such another day:
And since this business so fair is done,
Let us not leave till all our own be won. *Exeunt.*

109. **Embowell'd,** disemboweled, i.e., for burial. 112. **powder,** salt. 114. **termagant,** violent; derived from the name of a heathen god of the Saracens in the miracle play of St. Nicholas. 115. **scot and lot,** used figuratively to denote complete payment. "Scot" and "lot" were parish taxes. 132. *Stage Direction:* ***He takes up,*** etc. Bodies of slain persons had to be removed from the stage in the Elizabethan theatre. This is a famous example of Shakespeare's skill in having the duty performed naturally. 138. **fantasy,** hallucination. 141. **double man,** spectre; also, two men. 143. **Jack,** knave.

SCENE V. 20. **Upon the foot of fear,** in flight.

THE SECOND PART OF KING HENRY THE FOURTH

The Actors' Names

RUMOUR, *the Presenter.*
KING HENRY THE FOURTH.
PRINCE HENRY, *afterwards crowned* KING HENRY THE FIFTH.

PRINCE JOHN OF LANCASTER,
HUMPHREY OF GLOUCESTER,
THOMAS OF CLARENCE,
} *sons to Henry IV and brethren to Henry V.*

[EARL OF] NORTHUMBERLAND,
[SCROOP,] THE ARCHBISHOP OF YORK,
[LORD] MOWBRAY,
[LORD] HASTING,
LORD BARDOLPH,
TRAVERS,
MORTON,
[SIR JOHN] COLEVILLE,
} *opposites against King Henry IV.*

[EARL OF] WARWICK,
[EARL OF] WESTMORLAND,
[EARL OF] SURREY,
GOWER,
HARCOURT,
[BLUNT,]
LORD CHIEF JUSTICE,
[His Servant,]
} *of the king's party.*

POINS,
[SIR JOHN] FALSTAFF,
BARDOLPH,
PISTOL,
PETO,
[FALSTAFF'S] PAGE,
} *irregular humourists.*

SHALLOW,
SILENCE,
} *both country justices.*

DAVY, *Servant to Shallow.*
FANG *and* SNARE, *two sergeants.*
MOULDY, SHADOW, WART, FEEBLE, [*and*] BULLCALF, *country soldiers.*

Northumberland's Wife.
Percy's Widow [LADY PERCY].
HOSTESS QUICKLY.
DOLL TEARSHEET.

[Lords *and* Attendants; Porter,] Drawers, Beadles, Grooms, [*&c.*]
[A Dancer, *speaker of the*] *epilogue.*

[SCENE: *England.*]

[INDUCTION.]

[*Warkworth. Before the castle.*]

Enter Rumour, *painted full of tongues.*

Rum. Open your ears; for which of you will stop
The vent of hearing when loud Rumour speaks?
I, from the orient to the drooping west,
Making the wind my post-horse, still unfold
The acts commenced on this ball of earth:
Upon my tongues continual slanders ride,
The which in every language I pronounce,
Stuffing the ears of men with false reports.
I speak of peace, while covert enmity
Under the smile of safety wounds the world:
And who but Rumour, who but only I,
Make fearful musters and prepar'd defence,
Whiles the big year, swoln with some other grief,
Is thought with child by the stern tyrant War,
And no such matter? Rumour is a pipe
Blown by surmises, jealousies, conjectures,
And of so easy and so plain a stop
That the blunt monster with uncounted heads,
The still-discordant wav'ring multitude,
Can play upon it. But what need I thus
My well-known body to anatomize
Among my household? Why is Rumour here?
I run before King Harry's victory;
Who in a bloody field by Shrewsbury
Hath beaten down young Hotspur and his troops,
Quenching the flame of bold rebellion
Even with the rebels' blood. But what mean I
To speak so true at first? my office is
To noise abroad that Harry Monmouth fell
Under the wrath of noble Hotspur's sword,
And that the king before the Douglas' rage
Stoop'd his anointed head as low as death.
This have I rumour'd through the peasant towns
Between that royal field of Shrewsbury
And this worm-eaten hold of ragged stone,
Where Hotspur's father, old Northumberland,
Lies crafty-sick: the posts come tiring on,
And not a man of them brings other news
Than they have learn'd of me: from Rumour's tongues
They bring smooth comforts false, worse than true wrongs. *Exit Rumour.*

[ACT I.

SCENE I. *The same.*]

Enter the LORD BARDOLPH *at one door.*

L. Bard. Who keeps the gate here, ho?

[*Enter the* Porter.]

Where is the earl?
Port. What shall I say you are?
L. Bard. Tell thou the earl
That the Lord Bardolph doth attend him here.
Port. His lordship is walk'd forth into the orchard:
Please it your honour, knock but at the gate,
And he himself will answer.

The Second Part of King Henry the Fourth. The play is supposed to open immediately after the Battle of Shrewsbury, in which Henry Percy, or Hotspur, and the Scottish Earl of Douglas have been overthrown. We are concerned first of all with the news of the battle.

INDUCTION. *Stage Direction:* **Rumour . . . *tongues.*** Rumor wears a symbolic costume. Virgil describes her as full of eyes, ears, and tongues (*Aeneid*, iv, 174). 17. **stop,** hole in wind instruments. 18. **blunt,** stupid, dull-witted. 21. **anatomize,** lay open minutely, explain. 22. **household,** i.e., the audience. 33. **peasant,** rural, or provincial. 35. **hold,** stronghold. 37. **crafty-sick,** feigning sickness.

ACT I. SCENE I. 2. **What,** etc., of what name and station.

Enter the EARL [OF] NORTHUMBERLAND.

L. Bard. Here comes the earl.
[*Exit Porter.*]
North. What news, Lord Bardolph? every minute now
Should be the father of some stratagem:
The times are wild; contention, like a horse
Full of high feeding, madly hath broke loose
And bears down all before him.
L. Bard. Noble earl,
I bring you certain news from Shrewsbury.
North. Good, an God will!
L. Bard. As good as heart can wish:
The king is almost wounded to the death;
And, in the fortune of my lord your son,
Prince Harry slain outright; and both the Blunts
Kill'd by the hand of Douglas; young Prince John
And Westmoreland and Stafford fled the field;
And Harry Monmouth's brawn, the hulk Sir John,
Is prisoner to your son: O, such a day,
So fought, so followed and so fairly won,
Came not till now to dignify the times,
Since Cæsar's fortunes!
North. How is this deriv'd?
Saw you the field? came you from Shrewsbury?
L. Bard. I spake with one, my lord, that came from thence,
A gentleman well bred and of good name,
That freely rend'red me these news for true.
North. Here comes my servant Travers, whom I sent
On Tuesday last to listen after news.

Enter TRAVERS.

L. Bard. My lord, I over-rode him on the way;
And he is furnish'd with no certainties
More than he haply may retail from me.
North. Now, Travers, what good tidings comes with you?
Tra. My lord, Sir John Umfrevile turn'd me back
With joyful tidings; and, being better hors'd,
Out-rode me. After him came spurring hard
A gentleman, almost forspent with speed,
That stopp'd by me to breathe his bloodied horse.
He ask'd the way to Chester; and of him
I did demand what news from Shrewsbury:
He told me that rebellion had bad luck
And that young Harry Percy's spur was cold.
With that, he gave his able horse the head,
And bending forward struck his armed heels
Against the panting sides of his poor jade
Up to the rowel-head, and starting so
He seem'd in running to devour the way,
Staying no longer question.
North. Ha! Again:
Said he young Harry Percy's spur was cold?
Of Hotspur Coldspur? that rebellion
Had met ill luck?
L. Bard. My lord, I'll tell you what;
If my young lord your son have not the day,
Upon mine honour, for a silken point
I'll give my barony: never talk of it.
North. Why should that gentleman that rode by Travers
Give then such instances of loss?
L. Bard. Who, he?
He was some hilding fellow that had stol'n
The horse he rode on, and, upon my life,
Spoke at a venture. Look, here comes more news.

Enter MORTON.

North. Yea, this man's brow, like to a title-leaf,
Foretells the nature of a tragic volume:
So looks the strond whereon the imperious flood
Hath left a witness'd usurpation.
Say, Morton, didst thou come from Shrewsbury?
Mor. I ran from Shrewsbury, my noble lord;
Where hateful death put on his ugliest mask
To fright our party.
North. How doth my son and brother?
Thou tremblest; and the whiteness in thy cheek
Is apter than thy tongue to tell thy errand.
Even such a man, so faint, so spiritless,
So dull, so dead in look, so woe-begone,
Drew Priam's curtain in the dead of night,
And would have told him half his Troy was burnt;
But Priam found the fire ere he his tongue,
And I my Percy's death ere thou report'st it.
This thou wouldst say, 'Your son did thus and thus;
Your brother thus: so fought the noble Douglas:'
Stopping my greedy ear with their bold deeds:
But in the end, to stop my ear indeed,
Thou hast a sigh to blow away this praise,
Ending with 'Brother, son, and all are dead.'
Mor. Douglas is living, and your brother, yet;
But, for my lord your son,—
North. Why, he is dead.
See what a ready tongue suspicion hath!
He that but fears the thing he would not know
Hath by instinct knowledge from others' eyes
That what he fear'd is chanced. Yet speak, Morton;
Tell thou an earl his divination lies,
And I will take it as a sweet disgrace
And make thee rich for doing me such wrong.
Mor. You are too great to be by me gainsaid:
Your spirit is too true, your fears too certain.
North. Yet, for all this, say not that Percy 's dead.
I see a strange confession in thine eye:
Thou shak'st thy head and hold'st it fear or sin
To speak a truth. If he be slain, say so;
The tongue offends not that reports his death:
And he doth sin that doth belie the dead,
Not he which says the dead is not alive.
Yet the first bringer of unwelcome news
Hath but a losing office, and his tongue
Sounds ever after as a sullen bell,
Rememb'red tolling a departing friend.
L. Bard. I cannot think, my lord, your son is dead.
Mor. I am sorry I should force you to believe
That which I would to God I had not seen;
But these mine eyes saw him in bloody state,
Rend'ring faint quittance, wearied and outbreath'd,
To Harry Monmouth; whose swift wrath beat down

8. **stratagem,** deed of violence. 15. **in the fortune of,** by the good fortune of. 19. **brawn,** fat boar. 21. **followed,** carried through. 37. **forspent,** exhausted. 38. **bloodied,** i.e., with spurring. 45. **jade,** tired horse. 46. **rowel-head,** the end of the spur, in which the barbed wheel turns. 53. **point,** lace for fastening hose to doublet. 57. **hilding,** good-for-nothing. 62. **strond,** shore. 63. **witness'd usurpation,** evidence of its ravages. 72. **Priam's.** Priam was the king of Troy. 91. **gainsaid,** contradicted. 103. **tolling,** ringing the passing bell for. 108. **quittance,** requital, i.e., resistance. 112. **In few,** in few words. 114. **bruited,** noised abroad, reported. 116. **metal,** courage, temperament. 120. **enforcement,** compulsion. 128. **appearance,** i.e., warriors dressed like the king. 129. **'Gan vail,** began to abate or lower (his courage). 137. **physic,** medicine. 141. **buckle,** bend (under stress). 144. **grief . . . grief,** sickness . . . sorrow. 145. **nice,** delicate. 147.

The never-daunted Percy to the earth,
From whence with life he never more sprung up.
In few, his death, whose spirit lent a fire
Even to the dullest peasant in his camp,
Being bruited once, took fire and heat away
From the best-temper'd courage in his troops;
For from his metal was his party steel'd;
Which once in him abated, all the rest
Turn'd on themselves, like dull and heavy lead:
And as the thing that's heavy in itself,
Upon enforcement flies with greatest speed,
So did our men, heavy in Hotspur's loss,
Lend to this weight such lightness with their fear
That arrows fled not swifter toward their aim
Than did our soldiers, aiming at their safety,
Fly from the field. Then was that noble Worcester
Too soon ta'en prisoner; and that furious Scot,
The bloody Douglas, whose well-labouring sword
Had three times slain th' appearance of the king,
'Gan vail his stomach and did grace the shame
Of those that turn'd their backs, and in his flight,
Stumbling in fear, was took. The sum of all
Is that the king hath won, and hath sent out
A speedy power to encounter you, my lord,
Under the conduct of young Lancaster
And Westmoreland. This is the news at full.
North. For this I shall have time enough to mourn.
In poison there is physic; and these news,
Having been well, that would have made me sick,
Being sick, have in some measure made me well:
And as the wretch, whose fever-weak'ned joints,
Like strengthless hinges, buckle under life,
Impatient of his fit, breaks like a fire
Out of his keeper's arms, even so my limbs,
Weaken'd with grief, being now enrag'd with grief,
Are thrice themselves. Hence, therefore, thou nice crutch!
A scaly gauntlet now with joints of steel
Must glove this hand: and hence, thou sickly quoif!
Thou art a guard too wanton for the head
Which princes, flesh'd with conquest, aim to hit.
Now bind my brows with iron; and approach
The ragged'st hour that time and spite dare bring
To frown upon th' enrag'd Northumberland!
Let heaven kiss earth! now let not Nature's hand
Keep the wild flood confin'd! let order die!
And let this world no longer be a stage
To feed contention in a ling'ring act;
But let one spirit of the first-born Cain
Reign in all bosoms, that, each heart being set
On bloody courses, the rude scene may end,
And darkness be the burier of the dead!
Tra. This strained passion doth you wrong, my lord.
L. Bard. Sweet earl, divorce not wisdom from your honour.
Mor. The lives of all your loving complices
Lean on your health; the which, if you give o'er
To stormy passion, must perforce decay.
You cast th' event of war, my noble lord,
And summ'd the account of chance, before you said
'Let us make head.' It was your presurmise,
That, in the dole of blows, your son might drop:
You knew he walk'd o'er perils, on an edge,
More likely to fall in than to get o'er;
You were advis'd his flesh was capable
Of wounds and scars and that his forward spirit
Would lift him where most trade of danger rang'd:
Yet did you say 'Go forth;' and none of this,
Though strongly apprehended, could restrain
The stiff-borne action: what hath then befall'n,
Or what hath this bold enterprise brought forth,
More than that being which was like to be?
L. Bard. We all that are engaged to this loss
Knew that we ventur'd on such dangerous seas
That if we wrought out life 'twas ten to one;
And yet we ventur'd, for the gain propos'd
Chok'd the respect of likely peril fear'd;
And since we are o'erset, venture again.
Come, we will all put forth, body and goods.
Mor. 'Tis more than time: and, my most noble lord,
I hear for certain, and do speak the truth,
The gentle Archbishop of York is up
With well-appointed pow'rs: he is a man
Who with a double surety binds his followers.
My lord your son had only but the corpse,
But shadows and the shows of men, to fight;
For that same word, rebellion, did divide
The action of their bodies from their souls;
And they did fight with queasiness, constrain'd,
As men drink potions, that their weapons only
Seem'd on our side; but, for their spirits and souls,
This word, rebellion, it had froze them up,
As fish are in a pond. But now the bishop
Turns insurrection to religion:
Suppos'd sincere and holy in his thoughts,
He 's follow'd both with body and with mind;
And doth enlarge his rising with the blood
Of fair King Richard, scrap'd from Pomfret stones;
Derives from heaven his quarrel and his cause;
Tells them he doth bestride a bleeding land,
Gasping for life under great Bolingbroke;
And more and less do flock to follow him.
North. I knew of this before; but, to speak truth,
This present grief had wip'd it from my mind.
Go in with me; and counsel every man
The aptest way for safety and revenge:
Get posts and letters, and make friends with speed:
Never so few, and never yet more need. *Exeunt.*

[SCENE II. *London. A street.*]

Enter SIR JOHN [FALSTAFF] *alone, with his* Page *bearing his sword and buckler.*

Fal. Sirrah, you giant, what says the doctor to my water?

Page. He said, sir, the water itself was a good healthy water; but, for the party that owed it, he might have moe diseases than he knew for.

Fal. Men of all sorts take a pride to gird at me: the brain of this foolish-compounded clay, man, is not

quoif, close-fitting cap. 148. **wanton,** effeminate. 149. **flesh'd,** inflamed by foretaste of success. 161. **strained,** excessive. 163. **complices,** allies, confederates. 166. **cast,** calculated. **event,** outcome. 168. **make head,** raise an army. 169. **dole,** dealing, or distribution. 172. **advis'd,** aware. 177. **stiff-borne,** obstinately carried out. 180. **engaged to,** involved in. 184. **respect,** consideration. 192. **corpse,** used as plural here, referring to living bodies. 193. **fight,** to use for fighting. 204. **enlarge,** enhance the merit of his insurrection (Hunter); widen the limits or scope (Onions). 205. **Pomfret.** Richard was murdered at Pomfret Castle. 208. **Bolingbroke,** King Henry IV. 209. **more and less,** all classes.

SCENE II. 2. **water,** urine. 5. **owed,** owned. 6. **moe,** more. 7. **gird,** banter, attack with words. 9. **foolish-compounded,** composed of folly.

able to invent any thing that intends to laughter, more than I invent or is invented on me: I am not only witty in myself, but the cause that wit is in other men. I do here walk before thee like a sow that hath overwhelmed all her litter but one. If the prince put thee into my service for any other reason than to set me off, why then I have no judgement. Thou whoreson mandrake, thou art fitter to be worn in my cap than to wait at my heels. I was never manned with an agate till now: but I will inset you neither in gold nor silver, but in vile apparel, and send you back again to your master, for a jewel,—the juvenal, the prince your master, whose chin is not yet fledge. I will sooner have a beard grow in the palm of my hand than he shall get one on his cheek; and yet he will not stick to say his face is a face-royal: God may finish it when he will, 'tis not a hair amiss yet: he may keep it still at a face-royal, for a barber shall never earn sixpence out of it; and yet he'll be crowing as if he had writ man ever since his father was a bachelor. He may keep his own grace, but he 's almost out of mine, I can assure him. What said Master Dombledon about the satin for my short cloak and my slops?

Page. He said, sir, you should procure him better assurance than Bardolph: he would not take his band and yours; he liked not the security.

Fal. Let him be damned, like the glutton! pray God his tongue be hotter! A whoreson Achitophel! a rascally yea-forsooth knave! to bear a gentleman in hand, and then stand upon security! The whoreson smooth-pates do now wear nothing but high shoes, and bunches of keys at their girdles; and if a man is through with them in honest taking up, then they must stand upon security. I had as lief they would put ratsbane in my mouth as offer to stop it with security. I looked 'a should have sent me two and twenty yards of satin, as I am a true knight, and he sends me security. Well, he may sleep in security; for he hath the horn of abundance, and the lightness of his wife shines through it: and yet cannot he see, though he have his own lanthorn to light him. Where 's Bardolph?

Page. He 's gone into Smithfield to buy your worship a horse.

Fal. I bought him in Paul's, and he'll buy me a horse in Smithfield: an I could get me but a wife in the stews, I were manned, horsed, and wived.

Enter [*the*] Lord Chief Justice [*and* Servant].

Page. Sir, here comes the nobleman that committed the prince for striking him about Bardolph.

Fal. Wait close; I will not see him.

Ch. Just. What 's he that goes there?

Serv. Falstaff, an 't please your lordship.

Ch. Just. He that was in question for the robbery?

Serv. He, my lord: but he hath since done good service at Shrewsbury; and, as I hear, is now going with some charge to the Lord John of Lancaster.

Ch. Just. What, to York? Call him back again.

Serv. Sir John Falstaff!

Fal. Boy, tell him I am deaf.

Page. You must speak louder; my master is deaf.

Ch. Just. I am sure he is, to the hearing of any thing good. Go, pluck him by the elbow; I must speak with him.

Serv. Sir John!

Fal. What! a young knave, and begging! Is there not wars? is there not employment? doth not the king lack subjects? do not the rebels need soldiers? Though it be a shame to be on any side but one, it is worse shame to beg than to be on the worst side, were it worse than the name of rebellion can tell how to make it.

Serv. You mistake me, sir.

Fal. Why, sir, did I say you were an honest man? setting my knighthood and my soldiership aside, I had lied in my throat, if I had said so.

Serv. I pray you, sir, then set your knighthood and your soldiership aside; and give me leave to tell you, you lie in your throat, if you say I am any other than an honest man.

Fal. I give thee leave to tell me so! I lay aside that which grows to me! If thou gettest any leave of me, hang me; if thou takest leave, thou wert better be hanged. You hunt counter: hence! avaunt!

Serv. Sir, my lord would speak with you.

Ch. Just. Sir John Falstaff, a word with you.

Fal. My good lord! God give your lordship good time of day. I am glad to see your lordship abroad: I heard say your lordship was sick: I hope your lordship goes abroad by advice. Your lordship, though not clean past your youth, hath yet some smack of age in you, some relish of the saltness of time; and I most humbly beseech your lordship to have a reverent care of your health.

Ch. Just. Sir John, I sent for you before your expedition to Shrewsbury.

Fal. An 't please your lordship, I hear his majesty is returned with some discomfort from Wales.

Ch. Just. I talk not of his majesty: you would not come when I sent for you.

Fal. And I hear, moreover, his highness is fallen into this same whoreson apoplexy.

Ch. Just. Well, God mend him! I pray you, let me speak with you.

Fal. This apoplexy, as I take it, is a kind of lethargy, an 't please your lordship; a kind of sleeping in the blood, a whoreson tingling.

Ch. Just. What tell you me of it? be it as it is.

Fal. It hath it original from much grief, from study and perturbation of the brain: I have read the cause of his effects in Galen: it is a kind of deafness.

Ch. Just. I think you are fallen into the disease; for you hear not what I say to you.

Fal. Very well, my lord, very well: rather, an 't

17. **mandrake,** man-shaped root. 20. **agate,** small figure cut in agate for jewelry. 21. **inset,** set. 22. **juvenal,** youth. 23. **fledge,** covered with down. 28. **face-royal,** face of the king on the *royal*, a coin, with pun (l. 30) on *royal face*. 34. **slops,** loose breeches. 39. **glutton,** a reference to the parable of Dives (Luke 16:19-31). 41. **Achitophel,** abettor of Absalom's treason against David (II Samuel, Chap. 15-17). 42. **bear . . . in hand,** delude with false hopes. 43. **smooth-pates,** allusion to the short hair of tradesmen. 45-47. **if a man . . . security,** if a man orders goods with them on credit, then they demand payment before making delivery. 52. **horn,** an allusion to the cuckold's horn, as also in *lanthorn* below. 56. **Smithfield,** famous then as now as a livestock market. 58. **Paul's,** St. Paul's Cathedral, resort of serving-men seeking employment. 60. **stews,** houses of ill fame. 63. **committed,** i.e., to prison. 68. **in question,** under judicial examination. 72. **charge,** commission for soldiers. 100. **grows to,** is an integral part of. 103. **hunt counter,** a hunting term meaning "run backward on the trail." 111. **smack of age,** the savor of age. 131. **it original,** its origin. 133. **Galen,** the famous Greek authority on medicine. 141. **punish . . . heels,** punish in the stocks or fetters. 148-149. **dram of a scruple,** small portion of doubt, with puns on *dram* and *scruple* as weights. 154-156. **As I . . . come.** Falstaff plays on "land-service"—military service—as a means whereby he has avoided the "service" of

please you, it is the disease of not listening, the malady of not marking, that I am troubled withal.

Ch. Just. To punish you by the heels would amend the attention of your ears; and I care not if I do become your physician.

Fal. I am as poor as Job, my lord, but not so patient: your lordship may minister the potion of imprisonment to me in respect of poverty; but how should I be your patient to follow your prescriptions, the wise may make some dram of a scruple, or indeed a scruple itself.

Ch. Just. I sent for you, when there were matters against you for your life, to come speak with me.

Fal. As I was then advised by my learned counsel in the laws of this land-service, I did not come.

Ch. Just. Well, the truth is, Sir John, you live in great infamy.

Fal. He that buckles him in my belt cannot live in less.

Ch. Just. Your means are very slender, and your waste is great.

Fal. I would it were otherwise; I would my means were greater, and my waist slenderer.

Ch. Just. You have misled the youthful prince.

Fal. The young prince hath misled me: I am the fellow with the great belly, and he my dog.

Ch. Just. Well, I am loath to gall a new-healed wound: your day's service at Shrewsbury hath a little gilded over your night's exploit on Gad's-hill: you may thank the unquiet time for your quiet o'er-posting that action.

Fal. My lord?

Ch. Just. But since all is well, keep it so: wake not a sleeping wolf.

Fal. To wake a wolf is as bad as smell a fox.

Ch. Just. What! you are as a candle, the better part burnt out.

Fal. A wassail candle, my lord, all tallow: if I did say of wax, my growth would approve the truth.

Ch. Just. There is not a white hair on your face but should have his effect of gravity.

Fal. His effect of gravy, gravy, gravy.

Ch. Just. You follow the young prince up and down, like his ill angel.

Fal. Not so, my lord; your ill angel is light; but I hope he that looks upon me will take me without weighing: and yet, in some respects, I grant, I cannot go: I cannot tell. Virtue is of so little regard in these costermongers' times that true valour is turned bear-herd: pregnancy is made a tapster, and hath his quick wit wasted in giving reckonings: all the other gifts appertinent to man, as the malice of this age shapes them, are not worth a gooseberry. You that are old consider not the capacities of us that are young; you do measure the heat of our livers with the bitterness of your galls: and we that are in the vaward of our youth, I must confess, are wags too.

Ch. Just. Do you set down your name in the scroll of youth, that are written down old with all the characters of age? Have you not a moist eye? a dry hand? a yellow cheek? a white beard? a decreasing leg? an increasing belly? is not your voice broken? your wind short? your chin double? your wit single? and every part about you blasted with antiquity? and will you yet call yourself young? Fie, fie, fie, Sir John!

Fal. My lord, I was born about three of the clock in the afternoon, with a white head and something a round belly. For my voice, I have lost it with halloing and singing of anthems. To approve my youth further, I will not: the truth is, I am only old in judgement and understanding; and he that will caper with me for a thousand marks, let him lend me the money, and have at him! For the box of the ear that the prince gave you, he gave it like a rude prince, and you took it like a sensible lord. I have checked him for it, and the young lion repents; marry, not in ashes and sackcloth, but in new silk and old sack.

Ch. Just. Well, God send the prince a better companion!

Fal. God send the companion a better prince! I cannot rid my hands of him.

Ch. Just. Well, the king hath severed you and Prince Harry: I hear you are going with Lord John of Lancaster against the Archbishop and the Earl of Northumberland.

Fal. Yea; I thank your pretty sweet wit for it. But look you pray, all you that kiss my lady Peace at home, that our armies join not in a hot day; for, by the Lord, I take but two shirts out with me, and I mean not to sweat extraordinarily: if it be a hot day, and I brandish any thing but a bottle, I would I might never spit white again. There is not a dangerous action can peep out his head but I am thrust upon it: well, I cannot last ever: but it was alway yet the trick of our English nation, if they have a good thing, to make it too common. If ye will needs say I am an old man, you should give me rest. I would to God my name were not so terrible to the enemy as it is: I were better to be eaten to death with a rust than to be scoured to nothing with perpetual motion.

Ch. Just. Well, be honest, be honest; and God bless your expedition!

Fal. Will your lordship lend me a thousand pound to furnish me forth?

Ch. Just. Not a penny, not a penny; you are too impatient to bear crosses. Fare you well: commend me to my cousin Westmoreland.

[*Exeunt Chief Justice and Servant.*]

Fal. If I do, fillip me with a three-man beetle. A man can no more separate age and covetousness than 'a can part young limbs and lechery: but the gout galls the one, and the pox pinches the other; and so both the degrees prevent my curses. Boy!

a legal summons. 169. **exploit,** the famous robbery in *1 Henry IV,* II, ii. 170. **o'er-posting,** escaping the consequences of. 175. **smell a fox,** suspect something, smell a mouse. 179. **wassail candle,** candle lighted up at a feast. 180. **wax,** beeswax, with a pun on "growth." 183. **his,** its. 184. **gravy,** mimicking the sound of *gravity* and alluding to Falstaff's own fattiness, as in a fatty gravy. 186. **ill angel,** an evil attendant spirit. Falstaff quibbles on the other sense of the word meaning "a clipped angel," a coin worth 6s. 8d., current at 10s. 190. **cannot go,** i.e., walk, with pun on the meaning "pass current." 191. **costermongers'** commercial; used contemptuously. 192. **bear-herd,** one who handles tame bears. **pregnancy,** quickness (of wit). 194. **appertinent,** belonging to, becoming to. 198-199. **heat . . . galls.** The liver was the source of vegetative spirits and active in youth; the gall was the seat of melancholy and prevalent in age. 200. **vaward,** vanguard, early part. 214. **approve,** prove. 217. **marks,** coins worth 13s. 4d. 219. **box of the ear.** This event of the striking of the Chief Justice by the young prince is important in *The Famous Victories;* Shakespeare does not depict the scene. 238. **spit white.** Spitting white is a sign of thirst. 253. **crosses,** quibble on bearing affliction and receiving money; money was often marked with a figure of the cross. 255. **fillip,** knock into the air. **beetle,** a huge pile-driving mallet requiring three men to wield it.

Page. Sir?
Fal. What money is in my purse?
Page. Seven groats and two pence.
Fal. I can get no remedy against this consumption of the purse: borrowing only lingers and lingers it out, but the disease is incurable. Go bear this letter to my Lord of Lancaster; this to the prince; this to the Earl of Westmoreland; and this to old Mistress Ursula, whom I have weekly sworn to marry since I perceived the first white hair on my chin. About it: you know where to find me. [*Exit Page.*] A pox of this gout! or, a gout of this pox! for the one or the other plays the rogue with my great toe. 'Tis no matter if I do halt; I have the wars for my colour, and my pension shall seem the more reasonable. A good wit will make use of any thing: I will turn diseases to commodity. [*Exit.*]

[SCENE III. *York. The* ARCHBISHOP'S *palace.*]

Enter the ARCHBISHOP, THOMAS MOWBRAY (*Earl Marshall*), *the* LORD HASTINGS, *and* [LORD] BARDOLPH.

Arch. Thus have you heard our cause and know our means;
And, my most noble friends, I pray you all,
Speak plainly your opinions of our hopes:
And first, lord marshal, what say you to it?
Mowb. I well allow the occasion of our arms;
But gladly would be better satisfied
How in our means we should advance ourselves
To look with forehead bold and big enough
Upon the power and puissance of the king.
Hast. Our present musters grow upon the file
To five and twenty thousand men of choice;
And our supplies live largely in the hope
Of great Northumberland, whose bosom burns
With an incensed fire of injuries.
L. Bard. The question then, Lord Hastings, standeth thus;
Whether our present five and twenty thousand
May hold up head without Northumberland?
Hast. With him, we may.
L. Bard. Yea, marry, there 's the point:
But if without him we be thought too feeble,
My judgement is, we should not step too far
Till we had his assistance by the hand;
For in a theme so bloody-fac'd as this
Conjecture, expectation, and surmise
Of aids incertain should not be admitted.
Arch. 'Tis very true, Lord Bardolph; for indeed
It was young Hotspur's case at Shrewsbury.
L. Bard. It was, my lord; who lin'd himself with hope,
Eating the air on promise of supply,
Flatt'ring himself in project of a power
Much smaller than the smallest of his thoughts:
And so, with great imagination
Proper to madmen, led his powers to death
And winking leap'd into destruction.
Hast. But, by your leave, it never yet did hurt
To lay down likelihoods and forms of hope.
L. Bard. †Yes, if this present quality of war,
Indeed the instant action: a cause on foot
Lives so in hope as in an early spring
We see th' appearing buds; which to prove fruit,
Hope gives not so much warrant as despair
That frosts will bite them. When we mean to build,
We first survey the plot, then draw the model;
And when we see the figure of the house,
Then must we rate the cost of the erection;
Which if we find outweighs ability,
What do we then but draw anew the model
In fewer offices, or at last desist
To build at all? Much more, in this great work,
Which is almost to pluck a kingdom down
And set another up, should we survey
The plot of situation and the model,
Consent upon a sure foundation,
Question surveyors, know our own estate,
How able such a work to undergo,
To weigh against his opposite; or else
We fortify in paper and in figures,
Using the names of men instead of men:
Like one that draws the model of a house
Beyond his power to build it; who, half through,
Gives o'er and leaves his part-created cost
A naked subject to the weeping clouds
And waste for churlish winter's tyranny.
Hast. Grant that our hopes, yet likely of fair birth,
Should be still-born, and that we now possess'd
The utmost man of expectation,
I think we are a body strong enough,
Even as we are, to equal with the king.
L. Bard. What, is the king but five and twenty thousand?
Hast. To us no more; nay, not so much, Lord Bardolph.
For his divisions, as the times do brawl,
Are in three heads: one power against the French,
And one against Glendower; perforce a third
Must take up us: so is the unfirm king
In three divided; and his coffers sound
With hollow poverty and emptiness.
Arch. That he should draw his several strengths together
And come against us in full puissance,
Need not be dreaded.
Hast. If he should do so,
He leaves his back unarm'd, the French and Welsh
Baying him at the heels: never fear that.
L. Bard. Who is it like should lead his forces hither?
Hast. The Duke of Lancaster and Westmoreland;
Against the Welsh, himself and Harry Monmouth:
But who is substituted 'gainst the French,
I have no certain notice.
Arch. Let us on,
And publish the occasion of our arms.

275. **halt,** limp. **colour,** excuse. 279. **commodity,** profit.
SCENE III. 7. **in,** with. 10. **file,** roll. 22. **theme,** business. 27. **lin'd,** strengthened. 29. **project . . . power,** anticipation of an armed force. 33. **winking,** shutting his eyes. 35. **forms of hope,** shapes that hope assumes. 36-41. **Yes . . . them.** Yale Shakespeare: Lord Hastings has just been remonstrating with Lord Bardolph for his pessimism, saying that hope never injured any cause. Lord Bardolph replies: "Yes, it does—if, for example, this present business of war (indeed this very action now contemplated, this cause that is now on foot), lives merely on such desperate hopes as buds which appear too early in the spring; for hope gives less warrant that these buds will become fruit than despair gives that the frosts will destroy them." If we read *Yes, if,* in line 36 as *Yet is,* and understand *which* as the subject of *Lives,* in line 38, we obtain a fair sense. 43. **figure,** design. 47. **offices,** apartments devoted to household business. 54. **undergo,** undertake; see glossary. 55. **opposite,** opponent. 60. **part-created cost,** partly finished splendor. 67. **equal with,** cope on equal terms with. 73. **take up,** encounter, oppose. 76. **several strengths,** various armies. 80. **Baying him,** driving him to

The commonwealth is sick of their own choice;
Their over-greedy love hath surfeited:
An habitation giddy and unsure
Hath he that buildeth on the vulgar heart.
O thou fond many, with what loud applause
Didst thou beat heaven with blessing Bolingbroke,
Before he was what thou wouldst have him be!
And being now trimm'd in thine own desires,
Thou, beastly feeder, art so full of him,
That thou provok'st thyself to cast him up.
So, so, thou common dog, didst thou disgorge
Thy glutton bosom of the royal Richard;
And now thou wouldst eat thy dead vomit up,
And howl'st to find it. What trust is in these times?
They that, when Richard liv'd, would have him die,
Are now become enamour'd on his grave:
Thou, that threw'st dust upon his goodly head
When through proud London he came sighing on
After th' admired heels of Bolingbroke,
Criest now 'O earth, yield us that king again,
And take thou this!' O thoughts of men accurs'd!
Past and to come seems best; things present worst.

Mowb. Shall we go draw our numbers and set on?

Hast. We are time's subjects, and time bids be gone.

Exeunt.

[ACT II.

SCENE I. *London. A street.*]

Enter HOSTESS *of the Tavern and an* Officer *or two* [FANG *and another, followed by* SNARE].

Host. Master Fang, have you entered the action?

Fang. It is entered.

Host. Where 's your yeoman? Is 't a lusty yeoman? will 'a stand to 't?

Fang. Sirrah, where 's Snare?

Host. O Lord, ay! good Master Snare.

Snare. Here, here.

Fang. Snare, we must arrest Sir John Falstaff.

Host. Yea, good Master Snare; I have entered him and all.

Snare. It may chance cost some of us our lives, for he will stab.

Host. Alas the day! take heed of him; he stabbed me in mine own house, and that most beastly: in good faith, 'a cares not what mischief he does, if his weapon be out: he will foin like any devil; he will spare neither man, woman, nor child.

Fang. If I can close with him, I care not for his thrust.

Host. No, nor I neither: I'll be at your elbow.

Fang. An I but fist him once; and 'a come but within my vice,—

Host. I am undone by his going; I warrant you, he 's an infinitive thing upon my score. Good Master Fang, hold him sure: good Master Snare, let him not 'scape. 'A comes continuantly to Pie-corner—saving your manhoods—to buy a saddle; and he is indited to dinner to the Lubber's-head in Lumbert street, to Master Smooth's the silkman: I pray you, since my exion is entered and my case so openly known to the world, let him be brought in to his answer. A hundred mark is a long one for a poor lone woman to bear: and I have borne, and borne, and borne, and have been fubbed off, and fubbed off, and fubbed off, from this day to that day, that it is a shame to be thought on. There is no honesty in such dealing; unless a woman should be made an ass and a beast, to bear every knave's wrong. Yonder he comes; and that arrant malmsey-nose knave, Bardolph, with him. Do your offices, do your offices: Master Fang and Master Snare, do me, do me, do me your offices.

Enter SIR JOHN [FALSTAFF], *and* BARDOLPH, *and the Boy* [Page].

Fal. How now! whose mare 's dead? what 's the matter?

Fang. Sir John, I arrest you at the suit of Mistress Quickly.

Fal. Away, varlets! Draw, Bardolph: cut me off the villain's head: throw the quean in the channel.

Host. Throw me in the channel! I'll throw thee in the channel. Wilt thou? wilt thou? thou bastardly rogue! Murder, murder! Ah, thou honey-suckle villain! wilt thou kill God's officers and the king's? Ah, thou honey-seed rogue! thou art a honey-seed, a man-queller, and a woman-queller.

Fal. Keep them off, Bardolph.

Fang. A rescue! a rescue!

Host. Good people, bring a rescue or two. Thou wo 't, wo 't thou? thou wo 't, wo 't ta? do, do, thou rogue! do, thou hemp-seed!

Fal. Away, you scullion! you rampallian! you fustilarian! I'll tickle your catastrophe.

Enter [*the*] LORD CHIEF JUSTICE, *and his men.*

Ch. Just. What is the matter? keep the peace here, ho!

Host. Good my lord, be good to me. I beseech you, stand to me.

Ch. Just. How now, Sir John! what are you brawling here?
Doth this become your place, your time and business?
You should have been well on your way to York.
Stand from him, fellow: wherefore hang'st thou upon him?

Host. O my most worshipful lord, an 't please your grace, I am a poor widow of Eastcheap, and he is arrested at my suit.

Ch. Just. For what sum?

Host. It is more than for some, my lord; it is for all, all I have. He hath eaten me out of house and home; he hath put all my substance into that fat belly of his: but I will have some of it out again, or I will ride thee o' nights like the mare.

Fal. I think I am as like to ride the mare, if I have

bay. 81. **like,** likely. 91. **fond many,** foolish multitude. 94. **trimm'd in,** furnished with. 109. **draw,** assemble, muster. **set on,** march.

ACT II. SCENE I. 4. **yeoman,** sheriff's officer. 11. **entered,** brought action against in court. 18. **foin,** thrust in fencing; with sexual double meaning, as also in stabbed, weapon, thrust, entered, case (female pudendum), open to the world, brought in, long one, borne, fubbed off (meaning also to be put off with excuses), stand to me, etc. 23. **fist,** i.e., seize. 24. **vice,** grip. 26. **infinitive,** for "infinite," endless. 29. **continuantly,** a mixup of "continually" and "incontinently," immediately. 31. **indited,** for "invited." **Lubber's-head,** blunder for "Libbard's-head" (Leopard's-head Inn). 32. **Lumbert,** for "Lombard." 33. **exion,** action, lawsuit. 42. **malmsey-nose,** red-nosed. 46. **whose mare 's dead,** i.e., what's all the fuss about? 51. **quean,** jade, hussy. 52. **channel,** street gutter. 56. **honey-suckle,** for "homicidal." 58. **honey-seed,** for "homicide." 59. **man-queller,** murderer. 63. **wo 't thou?** Wilt thou? 64. **hemp-seed,** a possible allusion to the hangman's rope. 65. **scullion,** kitchen wench. **rampallian,** scoundrel. 66. **fustilarian,** comic formation on "fustilugs," a fat, frowsy woman (Onions).

any vantage of ground to get up.

Ch. Just. How comes this, Sir John? Fie! what man of good temper would endure this tempest of exclamation? Are you not ashamed to enforce a poor widow to so rough a course to come by her own?

Fal. What is the gross sum that I owe thee?

Host. Marry, if thou wert an honest man, thyself and the money too. Thou didst swear to me upon a parcel-gilt goblet, sitting in my Dolphin-chamber, at the round table, by a sea-coal fire, upon Wednesday in Wheeson week, when the prince broke thy head for liking his father to a singing-man of Windsor, thou didst swear to me then, as I was washing thy wound, to marry me and make me my lady thy wife. Canst thou deny it? Did not goodwife Keech, the butcher's wife, come in then and call me gossip Quickly? coming in to borrow a mess of vinegar; telling us she had a good dish of prawns; whereby thou didst desire to eat some; whereby I told thee they were ill for a green wound? And didst thou not, when she was gone down stairs, desire me to be no more so familiarity with such poor people; saying that ere long they should call me madam? And didst thou not kiss me and bid me fetch thee thirty shillings? I put thee now to thy book-oath: deny it, if thou canst.

Fal. My lord, this is a poor mad soul; and she says up and down the town that her eldest son is like you: she hath been in good case, and the truth is, poverty hath distracted her. But for these foolish officers, I beseech you I may have redress against them.

Ch. Just. Sir John, Sir John, I am well acquainted with your manner of wrenching the true cause the false way. It is not a confident brow, nor the throng of words that come with such more than impudent sauciness from you, can thrust me from a level consideration: you have, as it appears to me, practised upon the easy-yielding spirit of this woman, and made her serve your uses both in purse and in person.

Host. Yea, in truth, my lord.

Ch. Just. Pray thee, peace. Pay her the debt you owe her, and unpay the villany you have done her: the one you may do with sterling money, and the other with current repentance.

Fal. My lord, I will not undergo this sneap without reply. You call honourable boldness impudent sauciness: if a man will make courtesy and say nothing, he is virtuous: no, my lord, my humble duty remembered, I will not be your suitor. I say to you, I do desire deliverance from these officers, being upon hasty employment in the king's affairs.

Ch. Just. You speak as having power to do wrong: but answer in the effect of your reputation, and satisfy the poor woman.

Fal. Come hither, hostess.

Enter a Messenger [Gower].

Ch. Just. Now, Master Gower, what news?

Gow. The king, my lord, and Harry Prince of Wales
Are near at hand: the rest the paper tells.

Fal. As I am a gentleman.

Host. Faith, you said so before.

Fal. As I am a gentleman. Come, no more words of it.

Host. By this heavenly ground I tread on, I must be fain to pawn both my plate and the tapestry of my dining-chambers.

Fal. Glasses, glasses, is the only drinking: and for thy walls, a pretty slight drollery, or the story of the Prodigal, or the German hunting in water-work, is worth a thousand of these bed-hangers and these fly-bitten tapestries. Let it be ten pound, if thou canst. Come, and 'twere not for thy humours, there 's not a better wench in England. Go, wash thy face, and draw the action. Come, thou must not be in this humour with me; dost not know me? come, come, I know thou wast set on to this.

Host. Pray thee, Sir John, let it be but twenty nobles: i' faith, I am loath to pawn my plate, so God save me, la!

Fal. Let it alone; I'll make other shift: you'll be a fool still.

Host. Well, you shall have it, though I pawn my gown. I hope you'll come to supper. You'll pay me all together?

Fal. Will I live? [*To Bardolph*] Go, with her, with her; hook on, hook on.

Host. Will you have Doll Tearsheet meet you at supper?

Fal. No more words; let 's have her.

Exeunt Hostess and Sergeant [*Fang, Bardolph, and others*].

Ch. Just. I have heard better news.

Fal. What 's the news, my lord?

Ch. Just. Where lay the king to-night?

Gow. At Basingstoke, my lord.

Fal. I hope, my lord, all 's well: what is the news, my lord?

Ch. Just. Come all his forces back?

Gow. No; fifteen hundred foot, five hundred horse,
Are march'd up to my lord of Lancaster,
Against Northumberland and the Archbishop.

Fal. Comes the king back from Wales, my noble lord?

Ch. Just. You shall have letters of me presently:
Come, go along with me, good Master Gower.

Fal. My lord!

Ch. Just. What 's the matter?

Fal. Master Gower, shall I entreat you with me to dinner?

Gow. I must wait upon my good lord here; I thank you, good Sir John.

Ch. Just. Sir John, you loiter here too long, being you are to take soldiers up in counties as you go.

Fal. Will you sup with me, Master Gower?

Ch. Just. What foolish master taught you these manners, Sir John?

Fal. Master Gower, if they become me not, he was a fool that taught them me. This is the right fencing grace, my lord; tap for tap, and so part fair.

Ch. Just. Now the Lord lighten thee! thou art a

84. **mare,** nightmare. 94. **parcel-gilt,** partly gilt. 95. **Dolphin-chamber,** one of the fanciful names for chambers in inns. 96. **sea-coal,** bituminous coal, brought in by sea. **Wheeson,** Whitsun. 97. **liking,** likening. 101. **goodwife,** title of married women; *Keech* means "a lump of tallow." 102. **gossip,** familiar term applied to a female friend. 104. **mess of vinegar,** enough vinegar for one meal. 105. **prawns,** crustaceans like large shrimp. 115. **in good case,** well-to-do. 132. **current repentance,** genuine repentance; allusion to current coin. 134. **sneap,** reproof, snub. 142. **effect of,** manner becoming. 153. **fain,** obliged. 155. **Glasses . . . drinking.** It is a question of selling her cups of silver and pewter and using glasses for serving drinks. 156. **drollery,** comic picture. 158. **water-work,** water color. 159. **bed-hangers,** bed curtains. 162. **draw,** withdraw. 167. **nobles,** coins current at 6s. 8d. 175. **hook on,** follow her. 181. **to-night,** last night. 182. **Basingstoke,** a town in Hampshire. 199. **being . . . up,** seeing that you are to levy soldiers. 207. **tap for tap,** tit for tat. 208. **lighten,**

great fool. [*Exeunt.*]

[SCENE II. *London. Another street.*]

Enter the PRINCE [HENRY], POINS, *with others.*

Prince. Before God, I am exceeding weary.

Poins. Is 't come to that? I had thought weariness durst not have attached one of so high blood.

Prince. Faith, it does me; though it discolours the complexion of my greatness to acknowledge it. Doth it not show vilely in me to desire small beer?

Poins. Why, a prince should not be so loosely studied as to remember so weak a composition.

Prince. Belike then my appetite was not princely got; for, by my troth, I do now remember the poor creature, small beer. But, indeed, these humble considerations make me out of love with my greatness. What a disgrace is it to me to remember thy name! or to know thy face to-morrow! or to take note how many pair of silk stockings thou hast, viz. these, and those that were thy peach-coloured ones! or to bear the inventory of thy shirts, as, one for superfluity, and another for use! But that the tennis-court-keeper knows better than I; for it is a low ebb of linen with thee when thou keepest not racket there; as thou hast not done a great while, because the rest of thy low countries have made a shift to eat up thy holland: and God knows, whether those that bawl out the ruins of thy linen shall inherit his kingdom: but the midwives say the children are not in the fault; whereupon the world increases, and kindreds are mightily strengthened.

Poins. How ill it follows, after you have laboured so hard, you should talk so idly! Tell me, how many good young princes would do so, their fathers being so sick as yours at this time is?

Prince. Shall I tell thee one thing, Poins?

Poins. Yes, faith; and let it be an excellent good thing.

Prince. It shall serve among wits of no higher breeding than thine.

Poins. Go to; I stand the push of your one thing that you will tell.

Prince. Marry, I tell thee, it is not meet that I should be sad, now my father is sick: albeit I could tell to thee, as to one it pleases me, for fault of a better, to call my friend, I could be sad, and sad indeed too.

Poins. Very hardly upon such a subject.

Prince. By this hand, thou thinkest me as far in the devil's book as thou and Falstaff for obduracy and persistency: let the end try the man. But I tell thee, my heart bleeds inwardly that my father is so sick: and keeping such vile company as thou art hath in reason taken from me all ostentation of sorrow.

Poins. The reason?

Prince. What wouldst thou think of me, if I should weep?

Poins. I would think thee a most princely hypocrite.

Prince. It would be every man's thought; and thou art a blessed fellow to think as every man thinks: never a man's thought in the world keeps the roadway better than thine: every man would think me an hypocrite indeed. And what accites your most worshipful thought to think so?

Poins. Why, because you have been so lewd and so much engraffed to Falstaff.

Prince. And to thee.

Poins. By this light, I am well spoke on; I can hear it with mine own ears: the worst that they can say of me is that I am a second brother and that I am a proper fellow of my hands; and those two things, I confess, I cannot help. By the mass, here comes Bardolph.

Enter BARDOLPH *and Boy* [Page].

Prince. And the boy that I gave Falstaff: 'a had him from me Christian; and look, if the fat villain have not transformed him ape.

Bard. God save your grace!

Prince. And yours, most noble Bardolph!

Poins. Come, you virtuous ass, you bashful fool, must you be blushing? wherefore blush you now? What a maidenly man-at-arms are you become! Is 't such a matter to get a pottle-pot's maidenhead?

Page. 'A calls me e'en now, my lord, through a red lattice, and I could discern no part of his face from the window: at last I spied his eyes, and methought he had made two holes in the ale-wife's new petticoat and so peeped through.

Prince. Has not the boy profited?

Bard. Away, you whoreson upright rabbit, away!

Page. Away, you rascally Althæa's dream, away!

Prince. Instruct us, boy; what dream, boy?

Page. Marry, my lord, Althæa dreamed she was delivered of a fire-brand; and therefore I call him her dream.

Prince. A crown's worth of good interpretation: there 'tis, boy.

Poins. O, that this good blossom could be kept from cankers! Well, there is sixpence to preserve thee.

Bard. An you do not make him hanged among you, the gallows shall have wrong.

Prince. And how doth thy master, Bardolph?

Bard. Well, my lord. He heard of your grace's coming to town: there 's a letter for you.

Poins. Delivered with good respect. And how doth the martlemas, your master?

Bard. In bodily health, sir.

Poins. Marry, the immortal part needs a physician; but that moves not him: though that be sick, it dies not.

Prince. I do allow this wen to be as familiar with me as my dog; and he holds his place; for look you how he writes.

Poins. [*Reads*] 'John Falstaff, knight,'— every man must know that, as oft as he has occasion to name himself: even like those that are kin to the king; for they never prick their finger but they say, 'There 's

enlighten: with side reference to Falstaff's weight.

SCENE II. 7. **small beer,** weak kind of beer. 9. **studied,** versed, inclined. 10. **Belike,** I suppose. 24. **low countries,** Netherlands; also, genital region. 25. **holland,** a kind of linen; pun on "Holland" as a low country. 26. **bawl out,** bawl in swaddling clothes made out of Poins' old shirts (Herford). 40. **push,** attack, onset. 65. **accites,** induces. 67. **engraffed,** closely attached to. 71. **a second brother,** as a second brother he would have no inheritance. 72-73. **proper . . . hands,** capital fellow in using my hands (for stealing?). 83. **pottle-pot's,** two-quart tankard's. 93. **Althæa's dream.** Althaea dreamed that her newborn son would live only so long as a brand on the fire lasted. The Page mistakenly relates Hecuba's dream. 99. **crown's worth,** five shillings. 102. **cankers,** worms which destroy buds and leaves. 103. **to preserve thee,** allusion to the cross on the sixpence. 110. **martlemas,** Martinmas (November 11); probably short for "Martinmas beef." 115. **wen,** swelling.

some of the king's blood spilt.' 'How comes that?' says he, that takes upon him not to conceive. The answer is as ready as a borrower's cap, 'I am the king's poor cousin, sir.'

Prince. Nay, they will be kin to us, or they will fetch it from Japhet. But to the letter: [*Reads*] 'Sir John Falstaff, knight, to the son of the king, nearest his father, Harry Prince of Wales, greeting.'

Poins. Why, this is a certificate.

Prince. Peace! [*Reads*] 'I will imitate the honourable Romans in brevity.'

Poins. He sure means brevity in breath, short-winded.

[*Prince reads.*] 'I commend me to thee, I commend thee, and I leave thee. Be not too familiar with Poins; for he misuses thy favours so much, that he swears thou art to marry his sister Nell. Repent at idle times as thou mayest; and so, farewell.

'Thine, by yea and no, which is as much as to say, as thou usest him, JACK FALSTAFF with my familiars, JOHN with my brothers and sisters, and SIR JOHN with all Europe.'

Poins. My lord, I'll steep this letter in sack and make him eat it.

Prince. That 's to make him eat twenty of his words. But do you use me thus, Ned? must I marry your sister?

Poins. God send the wench no worse fortune! But I never said so.

Prince. Well, thus we play the fools with the time, and the spirits of the wise sit in the clouds and mock us. Is your master here in London?

Bard. Yea, my lord.

Prince. Where sups he? doth the old boar feed in the old frank?

Bard. At the old place, my lord, in Eastcheap.

Prince. What company?

Page. Ephesians, my lord, of the old church.

Prince. Sup any women with him?

Page. None, my lord, but old Mistress Quickly and Mistress Doll Tearsheet.

Prince. What pagan may that be?

Page. A proper gentlewoman, sir, and a kinswoman of my master's.

Prince. Even such kin as the parish heifers are to the town bull. Shall we steal upon them, Ned, at supper?

Poins. I am your shadow, my lord; I'll follow you.

Prince. Sirrah, you boy, and Bardolph, no word to your master that I am yet come to town: there 's for your silence. [*Gives money.*]

Bard. I have no tongue, sir.

Page. And for mine, sir, I will govern it.

Prince. Fare you well; go. [*Exeunt Bardolph and Page.*] This Doll Tearsheet should be some road.

Poins. I warrant you, as common as the way between Saint Alban's and London.

Prince. How might we see Falstaff bestow himself to-night in his true colours, and not ourselves be seen?

Poins. Put on two leathern jerkins and aprons, and wait upon him at his table as drawers.

Prince. From a God to a bull? a heavy descension! it was Jove's case. From a prince to a prentice? a low transformation! that shall be mine; for in every thing the purpose must weigh with the folly. Follow me, Ned. *Exeunt.*

[SCENE III. *Warkworth. Before the castle.*]

Enter NORTHUMBERLAND, *his Wife* [LADY NORTHUMBERLAND], *and the Wife to Harry Percy* [LADY PERCY].

North. I pray thee, loving wife, and gentle daughter,
Give even way unto my rough affairs:
Put not you on the visage of the times
And be like them to Percy troublesome.
Lady N. I have given over, I will speak no more:
Do what you will; your wisdom be your guide.
North. Alas, sweet wife, my honour is at pawn;
And, but my going, nothing can redeem it.
Lady P. O yet, for God's sake, go not to these wars!
The time was, father, that you broke your word,
When you were more endear'd to it than now;
When your own Percy, when my heart's dear Harry,
Threw many a northward look to see his father
Bring up his powers; but he did long in vain.
Who then persuaded you to stay at home?
There were two honours lost, yours and your son's.
For yours, the God of heaven brighten it!
For his, it stuck upon him as the sun
In the grey vault of heaven, and by his light
Did all the chivalry of England move
To do brave acts: he was indeed the glass
Wherein the noble youth did dress themselves:
He had no legs that practis'd not his gait;
And speaking thick, which nature made his blemish,
Became the accents of the valiant;
For those that could speak low and tardily
Would turn their own perfection to abuse,
To seem like him: so that in speech, in gait,
In diet, in affections of delight,
In military rules, humours of blood,
He was the mark and glass, copy and book,
That fashion'd others. And him, O wondrous him!
O miracle of men! him did you leave,
Second to none, unseconded by you,
To look upon the hideous god of war
In disadvantage; to abide a field
Where nothing but the sound of Hotspur's name
Did seem defensible: so you left him.
Never, O never, do his ghost the wrong
To hold your honour more precise and nice
With others than with him! let them alone:
The marshal and the archbishop are strong:
Had my sweet Harry had but half their numbers,
To-day might I, hanging on Hotspur's neck,
Have talk'd of Monmouth's grave.
North. Beshrew your heart,
Fair daughter, you do draw my spirits from me
With new lamenting ancient oversights.

128. **Japhet,** one of the sons of Noah (Genesis 10:2-5). 135. **Romans.** Warburton suggested *Roman* as an allusion to Caesar's "I came, I saw, I conquered." 160. **frank,** sty, pen (presumably with reference to the Boar's Head Tavern). 164. **Ephesians,** cant term for good fellows. **old church,** i.e., pagan and licentious. 168. **pagan,** courtesan; a cant name. 183. **road,** i.e., common whore. 186. **bestow,** behave. 191. **drawers,** tavern waiters. 192. **heavy descension,** grievous descent. 193. **Jove's case,** an allusion to Jupiter, who for love of Europa transformed himself into a bull. 196. **weigh with,** match.

SCENE III. 1. **daughter,** daughter-in-law. 2. **even way,** free scope. 11. **endear'd,** pledged. 20. **chivalry,** men-at-arms. 21. **glass,** mirror. 23. **He,** any man. 24. **thick,** fast. 38. **defensible,** able to make defense. 40. **nice,** punctilious. 57. **came,** became. 61. **recordation,** remembrance. 64. **still-stand,** standstill.

SCENE IV. 2. **apple-johns,** a kind of apple said to keep two years and to be in perfect condition when shriveled and withered. 13.

But I must go and meet with danger there,
Or it will seek me in another place
And find me worse provided.

Lady N. O, fly to Scotland,
Till that the nobles and the armed commons
Have of their puissance made a little taste.

Lady P. If they get ground and vantage of the king,
Then join you with them, like a rib of steel,
To make strength stronger; but, for all our loves,
First let them try themselves. So did your son;
He was so suff'red: so came I a widow;
And never shall have length of life enough
To rain upon remembrance with mine eyes,
That it may grow and sprout as high as heaven,
For recordation to my noble husband.

North. Come, come, go in with me. 'Tis with my mind
As with the tide swell'd up unto his height,
That makes a still-stand, running neither way:
Fain would I go to meet the archbishop,
But many thousand reasons hold me back.
I will resolve for Scotland: there am I,
Till time and vantage crave my company. *Exeunt.*

[SCENE IV. *London. The Boar's-head Tavern in Eastcheap.*]

Enter a Drawer *or two* [FRANCIS *and another*].

Fran. What the devil hast thou brought there? apple-johns? thou knowest Sir John cannot endure an apple-john.

Sec. Draw. Mass, thou sayest true. The prince once set a dish of apple-johns before him, and told him there were five more Sir Johns, and, putting off his hat, said 'I will now take my leave of these six dry, round, old, withered knights.' It angered him to the heart: but he hath forgot that.

Fran. Why, then, cover, and set them down: and see if thou canst find out Sneak's noise; Mistress Tearsheet would fain hear some music.

Enter WILL [*a third Drawer*].

Third Draw. Dispatch! The room where they supped is too hot; they'll come in straight.

Fran. Sirrah, here will be the prince and Master Poins anon; and they will put on two of our jerkins and aprons; and Sir John must not know of it: Bardolph hath brought word.

Third Draw. By the mass, here will be old Utis: it will be an excellent stratagem.

Sec. Draw. I'll see if I can find out Sneak. *Exit.*

Enter MISTRESS QUICKLY [*the Hostess*] *and* DOLL TEARSHEET.

Host. I' faith, sweetheart, methinks now you are in an excellent good temperality: your pulsidge beats as extraordinarily as heart would desire; and your color, I warrant you, is as red as any rose, in good truth, la! But, i' faith, you have drunk too much canaries; and that 's a marvelous searching wine, and it perfumes the blood ere one can say 'What 's this?' How do you now?

Dol. Better than I was: hem!

Host. Why, that 's well said; a good heart 's worth gold. Lo, here comes Sir John.

Enter SIR JOHN [FALSTAFF].

Fal. [*Singing*] 'When Arthur first in court'—Empty the jordan. [*Exit a Drawer.*]—[*Singing*] 'And was a worthy king.' How now, Mistress Doll!

Host. Sick of a calm; yea, good faith.

Fal. So is all her sect; an they be once in a calm, they are sick.

Dol. A pox damn you, you muddy rascal, is that all the comfort you give me?

Fal. You make fat rascals, Mistress Doll.

Dol. I make them! gluttony and diseases make them; I make them not.

Fal. If the cook help to make the gluttony, you help to make the diseases, Doll: we catch of you, Doll, we catch of you; grant that, my poor virtue, grant that.

Dol. Yea, joy, our chains and our jewels.

Fal. 'Your brooches, pearls, and ouches:' for to serve bravely is to come halting off, you know: to come off the breach with his pike bent bravely, and to surgery bravely; to venture upon the charged chambers bravely,—

Dol. Hang yourself, you muddy conger, hang yourself!

Host. By my troth, this is the old fashion; you two never meet but you fall to some discord: you are both, i' good truth, as rheumatic as two dry toasts: you cannot one bear with another's confirmities. What the good-year! one must bear, and that must be you: you are the weaker vessel, as they say, the emptier vessel.

Dol. Can a weak empty vessel bear such a huge full hogshead? there 's a whole merchant's venture of Bourdeaux stuff in him; you have not seen a hulk better stuffed in the hold. Come, I'll be friends with thee, Jack: thou art going to the wars; and whether I shall ever see thee again or no, there is nobody cares.

Enter Drawer.

Draw. Sir, Ancient Pistol 's below, and would speak with you.

Dol. Hang him, swaggering rascal! let him not come hither: it is the foul-mouthed'st rogue in England.

Host. If he swagger, let him not come here: no, by my faith; I must live among my neighbours; I'll no swaggerers: I am in good name and fame with the very best: shut the door; there comes no swaggerers here: I have not lived all this while, to have swaggering now: shut the door, I pray you.

Fal. Dost thou hear, hostess?

Host. Pray ye, pacify yourself, Sir John: there comes no swaggerers here.

Fal. Dost thou hear? it is mine ancient.

Sneak's noise, band of musicians. 21. **old Utis,** rare fun. *Utas* or *utaves* was the eighth day or "octave" of a feast. 25. **temperality,** for "temper," or "temperature." 26. **pulsidge,** for "pulse." **extraordinarily,** for "ordinarily." 30. **canaries,** light, sweet wine from the Canary Islands. 37. **jordan,** chamberpot. 40. **calm,** probably pun on "qualm." 45. **fat rascals.** A *rascal* was a lean deer; used here with pun on "rascal" meaning "good-for-nothing." 53. **ouches,** gems, or jewels. The line is from a ballad. 57. **charged chambers,** small cannon; with bawdy double meaning, as also in breach, pike, surgery (venereal treatment), conger (eel, with sexual connotation), bear. 62. **rheumatic.** She probably meant to say "choleric." 64. **confirmities,** for "infirmities." **What . . . year,** expletive; no special meaning. 69. **Bordeaux stuff,** wine. 74. **Ancient,** ensign, standard-bearer; a common military title. 79. **swagger,** bluster.

Host. Tilly-fally, Sir John, ne'er tell me: your ancient swaggerer comes not in my doors. I was before Master Tisick, the debuty, t' other day; and, as he said to me, 'twas no longer ago than Wednesday last, 'I' good faith, neighbour Quickly,' says he; Master Dumbe, our minister was by then; 'neighbour Quickly,' says he, 'receive those that are civil; for,' said he, 'you are in an ill name:' now 'a said so, I can tell whereupon; 'for,' says he, 'you are an honest woman, and well thought on; therefore take heed what guests you receive: receive,' says he, 'no swaggering companions.' There comes none here: you would bless you to hear what he said: no, I'll no swaggerers.

Fal. He 's no swaggerer, hostess; a tame cheater, i' faith; you may stroke him as gently as a puppy greyhound: he'll not swagger with a Barbary hen, if her feathers turn back in any show of resistance. Call him up, drawer. [*Exit Drawer.*]

Host. Cheater, call you him? I will bar no honest man my house, nor no cheater: but I do not love swaggering, by my troth; I am the worse, when one says swagger: feel, masters, how I shake; look you, I warrant you.

Dol. So you do, hostess.

Host. Do I? yea, in very truth, do I, an 'twere an aspen leaf: I cannot abide swaggerers.

Enter ANCIENT PISTOL, [BARDOLPH,] *and Bardolph's Boy* [PAGE].

Pist. God save you, Sir John!

Fal. Welcome, Ancient Pistol. Here, Pistol, I charge you with a cup of sack: do you discharge upon mine hostess.

Pist. I will discharge upon her, Sir John, with two bullets.

Fal. She is pistol-proof, sir; you shall hardly offend her.

Host. Come, I'll drink no proofs nor no bullets: I'll drink no more than will do me good, for no man's pleasure, I.

Pist. Then to you, Mistress Dorothy; I will charge you.

Dol. Charge me! I scorn you, scurvy companion. What! you poor, base, rascally, cheating, lack-linen mate! Away, you mouldy rogue, away! I am meat for your master.

Pist. I know you, Mistress Dorothy.

Dol. Away, you cut-purse rascal! you filthy bung, away! by this wine, I'll thrust my knife in your mouldy chaps, an you play the saucy cuttle with me. Away, you bottle-ale rascal! you basket-hilt stale juggler, you! Since when, I pray you, sir? God's light, with two points on your shoulder? much!

Pist. God let me not live, but I will murder your ruff for this.

Fal. No more, Pistol; I would not have you go off here: discharge yourself of our company, Pistol.

Host. No, good Captain Pistol; not here, sweet captain.

Dol. Captain! thou abominable damned cheater, art thou not ashamed to be called captain? An captains were of my mind, they would truncheon you out, for taking their names upon you before you have earned them. You a captain! you slave, for what? for tearing a poor whore's ruff in a bawdy-house? He a captain! hang him, rogue! he lives upon mouldy stewed prunes and dried cakes. A captain! God's light, these villains will make the word as odious as the word 'occupy;' which was an excellent good word before it was ill sorted: therefore captains had need look to 't.

Bard. Pray thee, go down, good ancient.

Fal. Hark thee hither, Mistress Doll.

Pist. Not I: I tell thee what, Corporal Bardolph, I could tear her: I'll be revenged of her.

Page. Pray thee, go down.

Pist. I'll see her damned first; to Pluto's damned lake, by this hand, to the infernal deep, with Erebus and tortures vile also. Hold hook and line, say I. Down, down, dogs! down, faitors! Have we not Hiren here?

Host. Good Captain Peesel, be quiet; 'tis very late, i' faith: I beseek you now, aggravate your choler.

Pist. These be good humours, indeed! Shall pack-horses
And hollow pamper'd jades of Asia,
Which cannot go but thirty mile a-day,
Compare with Cæsars, and with Cannibals,
And Trojan Greeks? nay, rather damn them with
King Cerberus; and let the welkin roar.
Shall we fall foul for toys?

Host. By my troth, captain, these are very bitter words.

Bard. Be gone, good ancient: this will grow to a brawl anon.

Pist. Die men like dogs! give crowns like pins! Have we not Hiren here?

Host. O' my word, captain, there 's none such here. What the good-year! do you think I would deny her? For God's sake, be quiet.

Pist. Then feed, and be fat, my fair Calipolis.
Come, give 's some sack.
'Si fortune me tormente, sperato me contento.'
Fear we broadsides? no, let the fiend give fire:
Give me some sack: and, sweetheart, lie thou there.
[*Laying down his sword.*]
Come we to full points here; and are etceteras nothing?

Fal. Pistol, I would be quiet.

Pist. Sweet knight, I kiss thy neif: what! we have seen the seven stars.

90. **Tilly-fally,** expression of contempt. 92. **Tisick,** suggests an elderly citizen with a cough. 93. **debuty,** deputy of the ward; a grave citizen charged with the good conduct of his ward. 96. **Master Dumbe.** Ministers who were not permitted to preach were said to be dumb. 105. **tame cheater,** a decoy for a card-sharper. 108. **Barbary hen,** guinea hen; prostitute. 110. **Cheater.** Mistress Quickly understands the word as *escheator*, an officer of the king's exchequer. 121. **discharge,** with bawdy double meaning; see also Pistol, bullets (testicles), meat (slang for whore), etc. 131. **charge,** pledge, drink to. 138. **bung,** pickpocket. 140. **cuttle,** cutthroat or cutpurse. 141. **basket-hilt,** sword hilt with protector for the hand; evidently a term of contempt, possibly suggesting a sword trickster or a braggart swordsman. 142. **God's light,** by God's light. 143. **points,** tags for securing armor. **much,** ironical for "not much," or "no." 145. **ruff,** large frilled collar.

154. **truncheon,** staff carried by captains. 158. **stewed prunes,** served in brothels. 160. **occupy,** fornicate. 173. **faitors,** impostors, cheats; doubtful meaning here. **Hiren,** an allusion to a lost play by Peele, *Turkish Mahomet and the Fair Greek. Hiren* is Irene. 175. **beseek,** beseech. **aggravate,** blunder for "moderate." 177. **humours,** freaks of conduct; current slang. 177-179. **Shall . . . a-day,** misquotation from Marlowe's *Second Part of Tamburlaine*, IV, iv, 1-2. 180. **Cannibals,** for Hannibals. 193. **Then . . . Calipolis,** burlesque of a line in Peele's *Battle of Alcazar.* 195. **'Si . . . contento,'** if fortune torments me, hope contents me. It is not clear what language Pistol is speaking, Italian or Spanish. 197. **points,** stops. **etceteras,** with bawdy meaning. 200. **neif,** fist. 201. **seven stars,** Pleiades. 203. **fustian,** bombast. 205. **Galloway nags,** an inferior breed of horses (suggesting Doll is a nag to be ridden). 206. **Quoit,** throw. 207. **shove-groat shilling,** an Edward VI shilling

Dol. For God's sake, thrust him down stairs: I cannot endure such a fustian rascal.

Pist. Thrust him down stairs! know we not Galloway nags?

Fal. Quoit him down, Bardolph, like a shove-groat shilling: nay, an 'a do nothing but speak nothing, 'a shall be nothing here.

Bard. Come, get you down stairs.

Pist. What! shall we have incision? shall we imbrue?
[*Snatching up his sword.*]
Then death rock me asleep, abridge my doleful days!
Why, then, let grievous, ghastly, gaping wounds
Untwine the Sisters Three! Come, Atropos, I say!

Host. Here 's goodly stuff toward!

Fal. Give me my rapier, boy.

Dol. I pray thee, Jack, I pray thee, do not draw.

Fal. Get you down stairs.
[*Drawing, and driving Pistol out.*]

Host. Here 's a goodly tumult! I'll forswear keeping house, afore I'll be in these tirrits and frights. So; murder, I warrant now. Alas, alas! put up your naked weapons, put up your naked weapons.
[*Exeunt Pistol and Bardolph.*]

Dol. I pray thee, Jack, be quiet; the rascal 's gone. Ah, you whoreson little valiant villain, you!

Host. Are you not hurt i' the groin? methought 'a made a shrewd thrust at your belly.

[*Enter* BARDOLPH.]

Fal. Have you turned him out o' doors?

Bard. Yea, sir. The rascal 's drunk: you have hurt him, sir, i' the shoulder.

Fal. A rascal! to brave me!

Dol. Ah, you sweet little rogue, you! Alas, poor ape, how thou sweatest! come, let me wipe thy face; come on, you whoreson chops: ah, rogue! i' faith, I love thee: thou art as valorous as Hector of Troy, worth five of Agamemnon, and ten times better than the Nine Worthies: ah, villain!

Fal. A rascally slave! I will toss the rogue in a blanket.

Dol. Do, an thou darest for thy heart: an thou dost, I'll canvass thee between a pair of sheets.

Enter Music.

Page. The music is come, sir.

Fal. Let them play. Play, sirs. Sit on my knee, Doll. A rascal bragging slave! the rogue fled from me like quicksilver.

Dol. I' faith, and thou followedst him like a church. Thou whoreson little tidy Bartholomew boar-pig, when wilt thou leave fighting o' days and foining o' nights, and begin to patch up thine old body for heaven?

Enter [*behind*] PRINCE *and* POINS [*disguised*].

Fal. Peace, good Doll! do not speak like a death's-head; do not bid me remember mine end.

Dol. Sirrah, what humour 's the prince of?

Fal. A good shallow young fellow: 'a would have made a good pantler, 'a would ha' chipped bread well.

Dol. They say Poins has a good wit.

Fal. He a good wit? hang him, baboon! his wit 's as thick as Tewksbury mustard; there 's no more conceit in him than is in a mallet.

Dol. Why does the prince love him so, then?

Fal. Because their legs are both of a bigness, and 'a plays at quoits well, and eats conger and fennel, and drinks off candles' ends for flap-dragons, and rides the wild-mare with the boys, and jumps upon joined-stools, and swears with a good grace, and wears his boots very smooth, like unto the sign of the leg, and breeds no bate with telling of discreet stories; and such other gambol faculties 'a has, that show a weak mind and an able body, for the which the prince admits him: for the prince himself is such another; the weight of a hair will turn the scales between their avoirdupois.

Prince. Would not this nave of a wheel have his ears cut off?

Poins. Let 's beat him before his whore.

Prince. Look, whe'r the withered elder hath not his poll clawed like a parrot.

Poins. Is it not strange that desire should so many years outlive performance?

Fal. Kiss me, Doll.

Prince. Saturn and Venus this year in conjunction! what says the almanac to that?

Poins. And, look, whether the fiery Trigon, his man, be not lisping to his master's old tables, his note-book, his counsel-keeper.

Fal. Thou dost give me flattering busses.

Dol. By my troth, I kiss thee with a most constant heart.

Fal. I am old, I am old.

Dol. I love thee better than I love e'er a scurvy young boy of them all.

Fal. What stuff wilt have a kirtle of? I shall receive money o' Thursday: shalt have a cap to-morrow. A merry song, come: it grows late; we'll to bed. Thou 'lt forget me when I am gone.

Dol. By my troth, thou 'lt set me a-weeping, and thou sayest so: prove that ever I dress myself handsome till thy return: well, hearken a' the end.

Fal. Some sack, Francis.

Prince. }
Poins. } Anon, anon, sir. [*Coming forward.*]

Fal. Ha! a bastard son of the king's? And art not thou Poins his brother?

Prince. Why, thou globe of sinful continents, what a life dost thou lead!

used in shove-groat, a game in which the coins were shoved toward a mark. 208. **speak nothing,** talk nonsense. **be nothing here,** be gone from here. 210. **incision,** bloodshed. **imbrue,** shed blood. 211. **death . . . asleep,** quotation from a current poem about Anne Boleyn and her brother. 213. **Sisters Three,** allusion to the three Fates, Clotho, Lachesis, and Atropos. Atropos severed the thread of life. 221. **tirrits,** possibly "terrors." 236. **chops,** fat jaws. 237. **Hector of Troy,** leader of the Trojans; the type of valor. 238. **Agamemnon,** leader of the Greeks at Troy. 239. **Nine Worthies,** Arthur, Charlemagne, Godfrey of Boulogne; Hector, Alexander, Julius Caesar; Joshua, David, Judas Maccabaeus. 243. **canvass,** toss. 250. **Bartholomew boar-pig,** allusion to roast pig at Bartholomew fair. 252. **foining,** fornicating. 258. **pantler,** pantryworker. 262. **Tewksbury mustard.** Tewkesbury was famous for mustard. 267. **fennel,** yellow-flowered herb used in pickles and sauces. 268. **flap-dragons,** raisins snatched out of burning spirits and swallowed in the game of snapdragon. **wild-mare,** seesaw. 269. **joined-stools,** stools made by joiners. 271. **breeds no bate,** causes no strife. 272. **gambol,** sportive. 278. **nave,** hub; reference to Falstaff's rotundity (with a pun on *knave*). 282. **poll . . . parrot.** Doll is rumpling Falstaff's hair. 286. **conjunction,** two planets in the same direction as viewed from the earth. 288. **fiery Trigon,** the conjunction of three fiery constellations, Aries, Leo, and Sagittarius. Poins alludes to Bardolph's complexion. 289. **lisping . . . note-book,** making love to Falstaff's old confidante, i.e., Mistress Quickly. 291. **busses,** kisses. 297. **kirtle,** gown or petticoat. 304. **hearken a',** wait for.

Fal. A better than thou: I am a gentleman; thou art a drawer.

Prince. Very true, sir; and I come to draw you out by the ears.

Host. O, the Lord preserve thy good grace! by my troth, welcome to London. Now, the Lord bless that sweet face of thine! O Jesu, are you come from Wales?

Fal. Thou whoreson mad compound of majesty, by this light flesh and corrupt blood, thou art welcome.

Dol. How, you fat fool! I scorn you.

Poins. My lord, he will drive you out of your revenge and turn all to a merriment, if you take not the heat.

Prince. You whoreson candle-mine, you, how vilely did you speak of me even now before this honest, virtuous, civil gentlewoman!

Host. God's blessing of your good heart! and so she is, by my troth.

Fal. Didst thou hear me?

Prince. Yea, and you knew me, as you did when you ran away by Gad's-hill: you knew I was at your back, and spoke it on purpose to try my patience.

Fal. No, no, no; not so; I did not think thou wast within hearing.

Prince. I shall drive you then to confess the wilful abuse; and then I know how to handle you.

Fal. No abuse, Hal, o' mine honour; no abuse.

Prince. Not to dispraise me, and call me pantler and bread-chipper and I know not what?

Fal. No abuse, Hal.

Poins. No abuse?

Fal. No abuse, Ned, i' the world; honest Ned, none. I dispraised him before the wicked, that the wicked might not fall in love with him; in which doing, I have done the part of a careful friend and a true subject, and thy father is to give me thanks for it. No abuse, Hal: none, Ned, none: no, faith, boys, none.

Prince. See now, whether pure fear and entire cowardice doth not make thee wrong this virtuous gentlewoman to close with us. Is she of the wicked? is thine hostess here of the wicked? or is thy boy of the wicked? or honest Bardolph, whose zeal burns in his nose, of the wicked?

Poins. Answer, thou dead elm, answer.

Fal. The fiend hath pricked down Bardolph irrecoverable; and his face is Lucifer's privy-kitchen, where he doth nothing but roast malt-worms. For the boy, there is a good angel about him; but the devil blinds him too.

Prince. For the women?

Fal. For one of them, she is in hell already, and burns poor souls. For the other, I owe her money; and whether she be damned for that, I know not.

Host. No, I warrant you.

Fal. No, I think thou art not; I think thou art quit for that. Marry, there is another indictment upon thee, for suffering flesh to be eaten in thy house, contrary to the law; for the which I think thou wilt howl.

Host. All victuallers do so: what 's a joint of mutton or two in a whole Lent?

Prince. You, gentlewoman,—

Dol. What says your grace?

Fal. His grace says that which his flesh rebels against. *Peto knocks at door.*

Host. Who knocks so loud at door? Look to the door there, Francis.

[*Enter* PETO.]

Prince. Peto, how now! what news?

Peto. The king your father is at Westminster;
And there are twenty weak and wearied posts
Come from the north: and, as I came along,
I met and overtook a dozen captains,
Bare-headed, sweating, knocking at the taverns,
And asking every one for Sir John Falstaff.

Prince. By heaven, Poins, I feel me much to blame,
So idly to profane the precious time,
When tempest of commotion, like the south
Borne with black vapour, doth begin to melt
And drop upon our bare unarmed heads.
Give me my sword and cloak. Falstaff, good night.
Exeunt Prince and Poins [, *Peto, and Bardolph*].

Fal. Now comes in the sweetest morsel of the night, and we must hence and leave it unpicked. [*Knocking within.*] More knocking at the door!

[*Enter* BARDOLPH].

How now! what 's the matter?

Bard. You must away to court, sir, presently;
A dozen captains stay at door for you.

Fal. [*To the Page*] Pay the musicians, sirrah. Farewell, hostess; farewell, Doll. You see, my good wenches, how men of merit are sought after: the undeserver may sleep, when the man of action is called on. Farewell, good wenches: if I be not sent away post, I will see you again ere I go.

Dol. I cannot speak; if my heart be not ready to burst,—well, sweet Jack, have a care of thyself.

Fal. Farewell, farewell. *Exit* [*with Bardolph*].

Host. Well, fare thee well: I have known thee these twenty nine years, come peascod-time; but an honester and truer-hearted man,—well, fare thee well.

Bard. [*Within*] Mistress Tearsheet!

Host. What 's the matter?

Bard. [*Within*] Bid Mistress Tearsheet come to my master.

Host. O, run, Doll, run; run, good Doll: come. [*To Bard. within*] She comes blubbered. Yea, will you come, Doll? *Exeunt.*

[ACT III.

SCENE I. *Westminster. The palace.*]

Enter the KING *in his nightgown, alone* [*with a* Page].

King. Go call the Earls of Surrey and of Warwick;
But, ere they come, bid them o'er-read these letters,
And well consider of them: make good speed.
[*Exit Page.*]

325. **heat,** start. 326. **candle-mine,** magazine of tallow. 346-348. **I dispraised . . . him.** This is a bit of the cant of puritanism which Falstaff uses as a mock excuse. 354. **close,** come to terms, agree. 359. **elm,** a very thick tree. 360. **pricked down,** marked, or designated. 363. **malt-worms,** topers. 364. **good angel,** an allusion to the belief in spirits of good and evil which accompanied man. 372. **flesh to be eaten,** allusion to enactments to prevent the sale of meat in Lent (with sexual double entendre on *mutton,* whore). 379. **grace,** used quibblingly on the meanings "royal grace" and "heavenly grace." 392. **south,** south wind, regarded as a breeder of tempests. 393. **Borne with,** laden with. 409. **post,** immediately. 421. **blubbered,** disfigured with weeping.

ACT III. SCENE I. *Stage Direction:* **nightgown,** dressing gown.

How many thousand of my poorest subjects
Are at this hour asleep! O sleep, O gentle sleep,
Nature's soft nurse, how have I frighted thee,
That thou no more wilt weigh my eyelids down
And steep my senses in forgetfulness?
Why rather, sleep, liest thou in smoky cribs,
Upon uneasy pallets stretching thee
And hush'd with buzzing night-flies to thy slumber,
Than in the perfum'd chambers of the great,
Under the canopies of costly state,
And lull'd with sound of sweetest melody?
O thou dull god, why liest thou with the vile
In loathsome beds, and leavest the kingly couch
A watch-case or a common 'larum-bell?
Wilt thou upon the high and giddy mast
Seal up the ship-boy's eyes, and rock his brains
In cradle of the rude imperious surge
And in the visitation of the winds,
Who take the ruffian billows by the top,
Curling their monstrous heads and hanging them
With deafening clamour in the slippery clouds,
That, with the hurly, death itself awakes?
Canst thou, O partial sleep, give thy repose
To the wet sea-boy in an hour so rude,
And in the calmest and most stillest night,
With all appliances and means to boot,
Deny it to a king? Then happy low, lie down!
Uneasy lies the head that wears a crown.

Enter WARWICK, SURREY, *and* SIR JOHN BLUNT.

War. Many good morrows to your majesty!
King. Is it good morrow, lords?
War. 'Tis one o'clock, and past.
King. Why, then, good morrow to you all, my lords.
Have you read o'er the letters that I sent you?
War. We have, my liege.
King. Then you perceive the body of our kingdom
How foul it is; what rank diseases grow,
And with what danger, near the heart of it.
War. It is but as a body yet distempered;
Which to his former strength may be restor'd
With good advice and little medicine:
My Lord Northumberland will soon be cool'd.
King. O God! that one might read the book of fate,
And see the revolution of the times
Make mountains level, and the continent,
Weary of solid firmness, melt itself
Into the sea! and, other times, to see
The beachy girdle of the ocean
Too wide for Neptune's hips; how chances mock,
And changes fill the cup of alteration
With divers liquors! O, if this were seen,
The happiest youth, viewing his progress through,
What perils past, what crosses to ensue,
Would shut the book, and sit him down and die.
'Tis not ten years gone
Since Richard and Northumberland, great friends,
Did feast together, and in two years after
Were they at wars: it is but eight years since
This Percy was the man nearest my soul,
Who like a brother toil'd in my affairs
And laid his love and life under my foot,
Yea, for my sake, even to the eyes of Richard
Gave him defiance. But which of you was by—
You, cousin Nevil, as I may remember—[*To Warwick.*]
When Richard, with his eye brimful of tears,
Then check'd and rated by Northumberland,
Did speak these words, now prov'd a prophecy?
'Northumberland, thou ladder by the which
My cousin Bolingbroke ascends my throne;'
Though then, God knows, I had no such intent,
But that necessity so bow'd the state
That I and greatness were compell'd to kiss:
'The time shall come,' thus did he follow it,
'The time will come, that foul sin, gathering head,
Shall break into corruption:' so went on,
Foretelling this same time's condition
And the division of our amity.
War. There is a history in all men's lives,
Figuring the nature of the times deceas'd;
The which observ'd, a man may prophesy,
With a near aim, of the main chance of things
As yet not come to life, which in their seeds
And weak beginnings lie intreasured.
Such things become the hatch and brood of time;
And by the necessary form of this
King Richard might create a perfect guess
That great Northumberland, then false to him,
Would of that seed grow to a greater falseness;
Which should not find a ground to root upon,
Unless on you.
King. Are these things then necessities?
Then let us meet them like necessities:
And that same word even now cries out on us:
They say the bishop and Northumberland
Are fifty thousand strong.
War. It cannot be, my lord;
Rumour doth double, like the voice and echo,
The numbers of the fear'd. Please it your grace
To go to bed. Upon my soul, my lord,
The powers that you already have sent forth
Shall bring this prize in very easily.
To comfort you the more, I have receiv'd
A certain instance that Glendower is dead.
Your majesty hath been this fortnight ill,
And these unseason'd hours perforce must add
Unto your sickness.
King. I will take your counsel:
And were these inward wars out of hand,
We would, dear lords, unto the Holy Land. *Exeunt.*

[SCENE II. *Gloucestershire. Before* JUSTICE SHALLOW'S *house.*]

Enter JUSTICE SHALLOW *and* JUSTICE SILENCE [*with* MOULDY, SHADOW, WART, FEEBLE, BULLCALF].

Shal. Come on, come on, come on; give me your hand, sir, give me your hand, sir: an early stirrer, by the rood! And how doth my good cousin Silence?

9. **cribs,** hovels. 15. **dull,** drowsy. **vile,** i.e., in rank. 17. **watch-case,** sentry box. 25. **hurly,** tumult. 28. **most stillest,** double superlative, as often in Shakespeare. 30. **low,** humble. 39. **foul,** infected. 47. **continent,** dry land. 56. **shut the book,** expression of despair. He would shut the book of his future. 64. **to the eyes,** to the face. 67. **Richard.** See *Richard II*, V, i, 55 ff. 68. **check'd and rated,** rebuked.

81. **Figuring,** symbolizing. **deceas'd,** past. 85. **intreasured,** in store. 87. **necessary form,** logical necessity. 103. **instance,** proof. 105. **unseason'd,** unseasonable.

SCENE II. 1. **Come on.** In Shallow's repetitions there is a suggestion of fussiness and possibly old age. 3. **rood,** cross.

Sil. Good morrow, good cousin Shallow.

Shal. And how doth my cousin, your bedfellow? and your fairest daughter and mine, my god-daughter Ellen?

Sil. Alas, a black ousel, cousin Shallow!

Shal. By yea and no, sir, I dare say my cousin William is become a good scholar: he is at Oxford still, is he not?

Sil. Indeed, sir, to my cost.

Shal. 'A must, then, to the inns o' court shortly. I was once of Clement's Inn, where I think they will talk of mad Shallow yet.

Sil. You were called 'lusty Shallow' then, cousin.

Shal. By the mass, I was called any thing; and I would have done any thing indeed too, and roundly too. There was I, and Little John Doit of Staffordshire, and black George Barnes, and Francis Pickbone, and Will Squele, a Cotswold man; you had not four such swinge-bucklers in all the inns o' court again: and I may say to you, we knew where the bona-robas were and had the best of them all at commandment. Then was Jack Falstaff, now Sir John, a boy, and page to Thomas Mowbray, Duke of Norfolk.

Sil. This Sir John, cousin, that comes hither anon about soldiers?

Shal. The same Sir John, the very same. I see him break Skogan's head at the court-gate, when 'a was a crack not thus high: and the very same day did I fight with one Sampson Stockfish, a fruiterer, behind Gray's Inn. Jesu, Jesu, the mad days that I have spent! and to see how many of my old acquaintance are dead!

Sil. We shall all follow, cousin.

Shal. Certain, 'tis certain; very sure, very sure: death, as the Psalmist saith, is certain to all; all shall die. How a good yoke of bullocks at Stamford fair?

Sil. By my troth, I was not there.

Shal. Death is certain. Is old Double of your town living yet?

Sil. Dead, sir.

Shal. Jesu, Jesu, dead! 'a drew a good bow; and dead! 'a shot a fine shoot: John a Gaunt loved him well, and betted much money on his head. Dead! 'a would have clapped i' the clout at twelve score; and carried you a forehand shaft a fourteen and fourteen and a half, that it would have done a man's heart good to see. How a score of ewes now?

Sil. Thereafter as they be: a score of good ewes may be worth ten pounds.

Shal. And is old Double dead?

Sil. Here come two of Sir John Falstaff's men, as I think.

Enter BARDOLPH *and one with him.*

Shal. Good morrow, honest gentlemen.

Bard. I beseech you, which is Justice Shallow?

Shal. I am Robert Shallow, sir; a poor esquire of this county, and one of the king's justices of the peace: what is your good pleasure with me?

Bard. My captain, sir, commends him to you; my captain, Sir John Falstaff, a tall gentleman, by heaven, and a most gallant leader.

Shal. He greets me well, sir. I knew him a good backsword man. How doth the good knight? may I ask how my lady his wife doth?

Bard. Sir, pardon; a soldier is better accommodated than with a wife.

Shal. It is well said, in faith, sir; and it is well said indeed too. Better accommodated! it is good; yea, indeed, is it: good phrases are surely, and ever were, very commendable. Accommodated! it comes of 'accommodo:' very good; a good phrase.

Bard. Pardon, sir; I have heard the word. Phrase call you it? by this good day, I know not the phrase; but I will maintain the word with my sword to be a soldier-like word, and a word of exceeding good command, by heaven. Accommodated; that is, when a man is, as they say, accommodated; or when a man is, being, whereby 'a may be thought to be accommodated; which is an excellent thing.

Shal. It is very just.

Enter FALSTAFF.

Look, here comes good Sir John. Give me your good hand, give me your worship's good hand: by my troth, you like well and bear your years very well: welcome, good Sir John.

Fal. I am glad to see you well, good Master Robert Shallow: Master Surecard, as I think?

Shal. No, Sir John; it is my cousin Silence, in commission with me.

Fal. Good Master Silence, it well befits you should be of the peace.

Sil. Your good worship is welcome.

Fal. Fie! this is hot weather, gentlemen. Have you provided me here half a dozen sufficient men?

Shal. Marry, have we, sir. Will you sit?

Fal. Let me see them, I beseech you.

Shal. Where 's the roll? where 's the roll? where 's the roll? Let me see, let me see, let me see. So, so, so, so, so, so, so: yea, marry, sir: Ralph Mouldy! Let them appear as I call; let them do so, let them do so. Let me see; where is Mouldy?

Moul. Here, an 't please you.

Shal. What think you, Sir John? a good-limbed fellow; young, strong, and of good friends.

Fal. Is thy name Mouldy?

Moul. Yea, an 't please you.

Fal. 'Tis the more time thou wert used.

Shal. Ha, ha, ha! most excellent, i' faith! things that are mouldy lack use: very singular good! in faith, well said, Sir John, very well said.

Fal. Prick him.

Moul. I was pricked well enough before, an you could have let me alone: my old dame will be undone now for one to do her husbandry and her drudgery: you need not to have pricked me; there are other men fitter to go out than I.

Fal. Go to: peace, Mouldy; you shall go. Mouldy, it is time you were spent.

Moul. Spent!

9. **ousel,** blackbird. 15. **Clement's Inn,** one of the inns of chancery. 17. **lusty,** merry. 24. **Cotswold,** Cotswold Hills; a region famous for athletic sports. 25. **swinge-bucklers,** roisterers, swashbucklers. 27. **bona-robas,** showily dressed wantons. 29. **page to Thomas Mowbray.** Both Sir John Oldcastle (Falstaff's original) and Sir John Fastolfe (for whom Falstaff was renamed) were pages to the Duke of Norfolk, who figures in the play *Richard II.* 33. **Skogan.** There was a court jester to Edward IV whose name was John Skogan, and a jestbook known as "Skogan's Jests." 34. **crack,** pert little boy. 42. **How,** how much. 52. **clapped i' the clout,** hit the bull's-eye. **twelve score,** i.e., yards. 53. **forehand shaft,** arrow used for shooting straight before one. 70. **backsword man,** singlestick fencer. 72. **accommodated,** furnished,

Shal. Peace, fellow, peace; stand aside: know you where you are? For the other, Sir John: let me see: Simon Shadow!

Fal. Yea, marry, let me have him to sit under: he 's like to be a cold soldier.

Shal. Where 's Shadow?

Shad. Here, sir.

Fal. Shadow, whose son art thou?

Shad. My mother's son, sir.

Fal. Thy mother's son! like enough, and thy father's shadow: so the son of the female is the shadow of the male: it is often so, indeed; but much of the father's substance!

Shal. Do you like him, Sir John?

Fal. Shadow will serve for summer; prick him, for we have a number of shadows to fill up the muster-book.

Shal. Thomas Wart!

Fal. Where 's he?

Wart. Here, sir.

Fal. Is thy name Wart?

Wart. Yea, sir.

Fal. Thou art a very ragged wart.

Shal. Shall I prick him, Sir John?

Fal. It were superfluous; for his apparel is built upon his back and the whole frame stands upon pins: prick him no more.

Shal. Ha, ha, ha! you can do it, sir; you can do it: I commend you well. Francis Feeble!

Fee. Here, sir.

Fal. What trade art thou, Feeble?

Fee. A woman's tailor, sir.

Shal. Shall I prick him, sir?

Fal. You may: but if he had been a man's tailor, he 'ld ha' pricked you. Wilt thou make as many holes in an enemy's battle as thou hast done in a woman's petticoat?

Fee. I will do my good will, sir: you can have no more.

Fal. Well said, good woman's tailor! well said, courageous Feeble! thou wilt be as valiant as the wrathful dove or most magnanimous mouse. Prick the woman's tailor: well, Master Shallow; deep, Master Shallow.

Fee. I would Wart might have gone, sir.

Fal. I would thou wert a man's tailor, that thou mightst mend him and make him fit to go. I cannot put him to a private soldier that is the leader of so many thousands: let that suffice, most forcible Feeble.

Fee. It shall suffice, sir.

Fal. I am bound to thee, reverend Feeble. Who is next?

Shal. Peter Bullcalf o' the green!

Fal. Yea, marry, let 's see Bullcalf.

Bull. Here, sir.

Fal. 'Fore God, a likely fellow! Come, prick me Bullcalf till he roar again.

Bull. O Lord! good my lord captain,—

Fal. What, dost thou roar before thou art pricked?

Bull. O Lord, sir! I am a diseased man.

Fal. What disease hast thou?

Bull. A whoreson cold, sir, a cough, sir, which I caught with ringing in the king's affairs upon his coronation-day, sir.

Fal. Come, thou shalt go to the wars in a gown; we will have away thy cold; and I will take such order that thy friends shall ring for thee. Is here all?

Shal. Here is two more called than your number; you must have but four here, sir: and so, I pray you, go in with me to dinner.

Fal. Come, I will go drink with you, but I cannot tarry dinner. I am glad to see you, by my troth, Master Shallow.

Shal. O, Sir John, do you remember since we lay all night in the Windmill in Saint George's field?

Fal. No more of that, good Master Shallow, no more of that.

Shal. Ha! 'twas a merry night. And is Jane Nightwork alive?

Fal. She lives, Master Shallow.

Shal. She never could away with me.

Fal. Never, never; she would always say she could not abide Master Shallow.

Shal. By the mass, I could anger her to the heart. She was then a bona-roba. Doth she hold her own well?

Fal. Old, old, Master Shallow.

Shal. Nay, she must be old; she cannot choose but be old; certain she 's old; and had Robin Nightwork by old Nightwork before I came to Clement's Inn.

Sil. That 's fifty five years ago.

Shal. Ha, cousin Silence, that thou hadst seen that that this knight and I have seen! Ha, Sir John, said I well?

Fal. We have heard the chimes at midnight, Master Shallow.

Shal. That we have, that we have, that we have; in faith, Sir John, we have: our watchword was 'Hem boys!' Come, let 's to dinner; come, let 's to dinner: Jesus, the days that we have seen! Come, come. *Exeunt [Falstaff and the Justices].*

Bull. Good Master Corporate Bardolph, stand my friend; and here 's four Harry ten shillings in French crowns for you. In very truth, sir, I had as lief be hanged, sir, as go: and yet, for mine own part, sir, I do not care; but rather, because I am unwilling, and, for mine own part, have a desire to stay with my friends; else, sir, I did not care, for mine own part, so much.

Bard. Go to; stand aside.

Moul. And, good master corporal captain, for my dame's sake, stand my friend: she has nobody to do any thing about her when I am gone; and she is old, and cannot help herself: you shall have forty, sir.

Bard. Go to; stand aside.

Fee. By my troth, I care not; a man can die but once: we owe God a death: I'll ne'er bear a base mind: an 't be my destiny, so; an 't be not, so: no man 's too good to serve 's prince; and let it go which way it will, he that dies this year is quit for the next.

Bard. Well said; th' art a good fellow.

Fee. Faith, I'll bear no base mind.

equipped; a bit of fine language on Bardolph's part. 92. **like well,** are in good condition. 95. **Surecard,** boon companion. 99. **of the peace,** i.e., a magistrate; reference to the name *Silence*. 103. **sufficient,** fit for service. 122. **pricked,** dressed; marked, designated for service; also a bawdy quibble. 144-146. **Shadow . . . muster-book,** an allusion to the practice of employing false muster lists and drawing pay for imaginary soldiers. 177. **to,** in the character of. 178. **thousands,** i.e., of vermin. 207. **Windmill,** evidently a brothel, in a low district. 213. **away with,** get on with. 235. **Corporate,** for "corporal." 236. **Harry ten shillings,** i.e., coined in the reign of Henry VII; current at half the face value. The reference is anachronistic. 248. **forty,** i.e., shillings.

Enter FALSTAFF *and the* Justices.

Fal. Come, sir, which men shall I have?

Shal. Four of which you please.

Bard. Sir, a word with you: I have three pound to free Mouldy and Bullcalf.

Fal. Go to; well.

Shal. Come, Sir John, which four will you have?

Fal. Do you choose for me.

Shal. Marry, then, Mouldy, Bullcalf, Feeble and Shadow.

Fal. Mouldy and Bullcalf: for you, Mouldy, stay at home till you are past service: and for your part, Bullcalf, grow till you come unto it: I will none of you.

Shal. Sir John, Sir John, do not yourself wrong: they are your likeliest men, and I would have you served with the best.

Fal. Will you tell me, Master Shallow, how to choose a man? Care I for the limb, the thews, the stature, bulk, and big assemblance of a man! Give me the spirit, Master Shallow. Here 's Wart; you see what a ragged appearance it is: 'a shall charge you and discharge you with the motion of a pewterer's hammer, come off and on swifter than he that gibbets on the brewer's bucket. And this same half-faced fellow, Shadow; give me this man: he presents no mark to the enemy; the foeman may with as great aim level at the edge of a penknife. And for a retreat; how swiftly will this Feeble the woman's tailor run off! O, give me the spare men, and spare me the great ones. Put me a caliver into Wart's hand, Bardolph.

Bard. Hold, Wart, traverse; thus, thus, thus.

Fal. Come, manage me your caliver. So; very well: go to: very good, exceeding good. O, give me always a little, lean, old, chapt, bald shot. Well said, i' faith, Wart; th' art a good scab: hold, there 's a tester for thee.

Shal. He is not his craft's master; he doth not do it right. I remember at Mile-end Green, when I lay at Clement's Inn,—I was then Sir Dagonet in Arthur's show,—there was a little quiver fellow, and 'a would manage you his piece thus; and 'a would about and about, and come you in and come you in: 'rah, tah, tah,' would 'a say; 'bounce' would 'a say; and away again would 'a go, and again would 'a come: I shall ne'er see such a fellow.

Fal. These fellows will do well, Master Shallow. God keep you, Master Silence: I will not use many words with you. Fare you well, gentlemen both: I thank you: I must a dozen mile to-night. Bardolph, give the soldiers coats.

Shal. Sir John, the Lord bless you! God prosper your affairs! God send us peace! At your return visit our house; let our old acquaintance be renewed: peradventure I will with ye to the court.

Fal. 'Fore God, I would you would, Master Shallow.

Shal. Go to; I have spoke at a word. God keep you.

Fal. Fare you well, gentle gentlemen. *Exeunt [Justices.]* On, Bardolph; lead the men away. [*Exeunt Bardolph, Recruits, &c.*] As I return, I will fetch off these justices: I do see the bottom of Justice Shallow. Lord, Lord, how subject we old men are to this vice of lying! This same starved justice hath done nothing but prate to me of the wildness of his youth, and the feats he hath done about Turnbull Street; and every third word a lie, duer paid to the hearer than the Turk's tribute. I do remember him at Clement's Inn like a man made after supper of a cheese-paring: when 'a was naked, he was, for all the world, like a forked radish, with a head fantastically carved upon it with a knife: 'a was so forlorn, that his dimensions to any thick sight were invincible: 'a was the very genius of famine; yet lecherous as a monkey, and the whores called him mandrake: 'a came ever in the rearward of the fashion, and sung those tunes to the overscutched huswives that he heard the carmen whistle, and sware they were his fancies or his good-nights. And now is this Vice's dagger become a squire, and talks as familiarly of John a Gaunt as if he had been sworn brother to him; and I'll be sworn 'a ne'er saw him but once in the Tilt-yard; and then he burst his head for crowding among the marshal's men. I saw it, and told John a Gaunt he beat his own name; for you might have thrust him and all his apparel into an eel-skin; the case of a treble hautboy was a mansion for him, a court: and now has he land and beefs. Well, I'll be acquainted with him, if I return; and 't shall go hard but I'll make him a philosopher's two stones to me: if the young dace be a bait for the old pike, I see no reason in the law of nature but I may snap at him. Let time shape, and there an end. [*Exit.*]

[ACT IV.

SCENE I. *Yorkshire. Gaultree Forest.*]

Enter the ARCHBISHOP [OF YORK], MOWBRAY, HASTINGS [, *and others*], *within the Forest of Gaultree.*

Arch. What is this forest call'd?
Hast. 'Tis Gaultree Forest, an 't shall please your grace.
Arch. Here stand, my lords; and send discoverers forth
To know the numbers of our enemies.
Hast. We have sent forth already.
Arch. 'Tis well done.
My friends and brethren in these great affairs,
I must acquaint you that I have receiv'd
New-dated letters from Northumberland;
Their cold intent, tenour and substance, thus:
Here doth he wish his person, with such powers
As might hold sortance with his quality,

276. **thews,** strength, bodily forces. 277. **assemblance,** appearance. 280. **charge,** discharge, load, and fire. 281-283. **come . . . bucket,** raise and lower his musket quicker than a brewer's man raises and lowers the beam (bucket) of the brewer's crane across his shoulders. 286. **level,** aim. 290. **caliver,** light musket or harquebus. 291. **traverse,** march. 295. **shot,** marksman. 296. **scab,** scurvy fellow. **tester,** sixpence. 298-300. **I remember . . . show.** There was an exhibition of archery held annually at Mile-end Green called "Arthur's show"; in this show Shallow played the part of Sir Dagonet, King Arthur's fool. 301. **quiver,** nimble. 304. **'bounce,'** bang. 319. **at a word,** briefly and sincerely. 324. **fetch off,** get the better of. 329. **Turnbull Street,** a street in Clerkenwell, ill-reputed. 330. **Turk's tribute.** Much of Christendom was paying tribute to the sultan of Turkey. 336. **forlorn,** meager, thin. **thick,** imperfect. 339. **mandrake,** root of a plant, the white mandrake, said to resemble the body of a man; said also to be an emblem of incontinence. 340. **overscutched huswives,** outworn and often-whipped prostitutes. 342. **fancies . . . good-nights,** love songs, of which he claims authorship. 343. **Vice's dagger.** The Vice, or comic character of the morality plays, was armed with a wooden dagger. 347. **Tilt-yard,** arena for jousting.

The which he could not levy; whereupon
He is retir'd, to ripe his growing fortunes,
To Scotland: and concludes in hearty prayers
That your attempts may overlive the hazard
And fearful meeting of their opposite.

Mowb. Thus do the hopes we have in him touch ground
And dash themselves to pieces.

Enter Messenger.

Hast. Now, what news?

Mess. West of this forest, scarcely off a mile,
In goodly form comes on the enemy;
And, by the ground they hide, I judge their number
Upon or near the rate of thirty thousand.

Mowb. The just proportion that we gave them out.
Let us sway on and face them in the field.

Arch. What well-appointed leader fronts us here?

Enter WESTMORELAND.

Mowb. I think it is my Lord of Westmoreland.

West. Health and fair greeting from our general,
The prince, Lord John and Duke of Lancaster.

Arch. Say on, my Lord of Westmoreland, in peace:
What doth concern your coming?

West. Then, my lord,
Unto your grace do I in chief address
The substance of my speech. If that rebellion
Came like itself, in base and abject routs,
Led on by bloody youth, guarded with rags,
And countenanc'd by boys and beggary,
I say, if damn'd commotion so appear'd,
In his true, native and most proper shape,
You, reverend father, and these noble lords
Had not been here, to dress the ugly form
Of base and bloody insurrection
With your fair honours. You, lord archbishop,
Whose see is by a civil peace maintain'd,
Whose beard the silver hand of peace hath touch'd,
Whose learning and good letters peace hath tutor'd,
Whose white investments figure innocence,
The dove and very blessed spirit of peace,
Wherefore do you so ill translate yourself
Out of the speech of peace that bears such grace,
Into the harsh and boist'rous tongue of war;
Turning your books to †graves, your ink to blood,
Your pens to lances and your tongue divine
To a loud trumpet and a point of war?

Arch. Wherefore do I this? so the question stands.
Briefly to this end: we are all diseas'd,
And with our surfeiting and wanton hours
Have brought ourselves into a burning fever,
And we must bleed for it; of which disease
Our late king, Richard, being infected, died.
But, my most noble Lord of Westmoreland,
I take not on me here as a physician,
Nor do I as an enemy to peace
Troop in the throngs of military men;
But rather show awhile like fearful war,
To diet rank minds sick of happiness
And purge th' obstructions which begin to stop
Our very veins of life. Hear me more plainly.
I have in equal balance justly weigh'd
What wrongs our arms may do, what wrongs we suffer,
And find our griefs heavier than our offences.
We see which way the stream of time doth run,
And are enforc'd from our most quiet there
By the rough torrent of occasion;
And have the summary of all our griefs,
When time shall serve, to show in articles;
Which long ere this we offer'd to the king,
And might by no suit gain our audience:
When we are wrong'd and would unfold our griefs,
We are denied access unto his person
Even by those men that most have done us wrong.
The dangers of the days but newly gone,
Whose memory is written on the earth
With yet appearing blood, and the examples
Of every minute's instance, present now,
Hath put us in these ill-beseeming arms,
Not to break peace or any branch of it,
But to establish here a peace indeed,
Concurring both in name and quality.

West. When ever yet was your appeal denied?
Wherein have you been galled by the king?
What peer hath been suborn'd to grate on you,
That you should seal this lawless bloody book
Of forg'd rebellion with a seal divine
And consecrate commotion's bitter edge?

Arch. †My brother general, the commonwealth,
To brother born an household cruelty,
I make my quarrel in particular.

West. There is no need of any such redress;
Or if there were, it not belongs to you.

Mowb. Why not to him in part, and to us all
That feel the bruises of the days before,
And suffer the condition of these times
To lay a heavy and unequal hand
Upon our honours?

West. O, my good Lord Mowbray,
Construe the times to their necessities,
And you shall say indeed, it is the time,
And not the king, that doth you injuries.
Yet for your part, it not appears to me
Either from the king or in the present time
That you should have an inch of any ground
To build a grief on: were you not restor'd
To all the Duke of Norfolk's signories,
Your noble and right well rememb'red father's?

Mowb. What thing, in honour, had my father lost,
That need to be reviv'd and breath'd in me?
The king that lov'd him, as the state stood then,
Was force perforce compell'd to banish him:
And then that Henry Bolingbroke and he,
Being mounted and both roused in their seats,

he, i.e., John of Gaunt. **his,** i.e., Shallow's. 349. **beat his own name,** i.e., was more gaunt than John a Gaunt. 351. **hautboy,** oboe. 355. **philosopher's two stones,** i.e., yield twice as much as the philosopher's stone, which would produce boundless wealth. 356. **young dace . . . old pike.** The fish dace, or luce, was the pike's food; this passage has been thought to allude to Shakespeare's animosity for Sir Thomas Lucy of Charlecote. See Shakespeare's Life and Work 1564-1594.

ACT IV. SCENE I. 2. **Gaultree Forest,** ancient forest of Galtres north of York. 11. **hold sortance,** accord. 15. **overlive,** outlive. 24. **sway on,** move on. 34. **bloody,** passionate. **guarded,** adorned, trimmed. 36. **commotion,** tumult, sedition. 42. **civil,** orderly, law-abiding. 45. **investments,** clothes, vestments. 52. **point of war,** trumpet, signal of war. 55-79. **And . . . wrong.** Omitted from Q_1 probably because of censorship, since these lines plead the cause of rebellion; also ll. 103-139. 69. **griefs,** grievances. 89. **galled,** injured, made sore with chafing. 90. **suborn'd . . . on,** induced by secret plot to annoy. 94-96. **My . . . particular.** This is a textual crux of which the sense seems to be: I make this my quarrel on both public and private grounds, that is, because of the sufferings of the commonwealth and of my own family at the hands of the king (Yale); see *particular* in glossary.

Their neighing coursers daring of the spur,
Their armed staves in charge, their beavers down,
Their eyes of fire sparkling through sights of steel
And the loud trumpet blowing them together,
Then, then, when there was nothing could have stay'd
My father from the breast of Bolingbroke,
O, when the king did throw his warder down,
His own life hung upon the staff he threw;
Then threw he down himself and all their lives
That by indictment and by dint of sword
Have since miscarried under Bolingbroke.
West. You speak, Lord Mowbray, now you know not what.
The Earl of Hereford was reputed then
In England the most valiant gentleman:
Who knows on whom fortune would then have smil'd?
But if your father had been victor there,
He ne'er had borne it out of Coventry:
For all the country in a general voice
Cried hate upon him; and all their prayers and love
Were set on Hereford, whom they doted on
And bless'd and grac'd indeed, more than the king.
But this is mere digression from my purpose.
Here come I from our princely general
To know your griefs; to tell you from his grace
That he will give you audience; and wherein
It shall appear that your demands are just,
You shall enjoy them, every thing set off
That might so much as think you enemies.
Mowb. But he hath forc'd us to compel this offer;
And it proceeds from policy, not love.
West. Mowbray, you overween to take it so;
This offer comes from mercy, not from fear:
For, lo! within a ken our army lies,
Upon mine honour, all too confident
To give admittance to a thought of fear.
Our battle is more full of names than yours,
Our men more perfect in the use of arms,
Our armour all as strong, our cause the best;
Then reason will our hearts should be as good:
Say you not then our offer is compell'd.
Mowb. Well, by my will we shall admit no parley.
West. That argues but the shame of your offence:
A rotten case abides no handling.
Hast. Hath the Prince John a full commission,
In very ample virtue of his father,
To hear and absolutely to determine
Of what conditions we shall stand upon?
West. That is intended in the general's name:
I muse you make so slight a question.
Arch. Then take, my Lord of Westmoreland, this schedule,
For this contains our general grievances:
Each several article herein redress'd,
All members of our cause, both here and hence,
That are insinewed to this action,
Acquitted by a true substantial form
And present execution of our wills
To us and to our purposes confin'd,
We come within our awful banks again
And knit our powers to the arm of peace.
West. This will I show the general. Please you, lords,
In sight of both our battles we may meet;
And either end in peace, which God so frame!
Or to the place of diff'rence call the swords
Which must decide it.
Arch. My lord, we will do so.
Exit West.
Mowb. There is a thing within my bosom tells me
That no conditions of our peace can stand.
Hast. Fear you not that: if we can make our peace
Upon such large terms and so absolute
As our conditions shall consist upon,
Our peace shall stand as firm as rocky mountains.
Mowb. Yea, but our valuation shall be such
That every slight and false-derived cause,
Yea, every idle, nice and wanton reason
Shall to the king taste of this action;
That, were our royal faiths martyrs in love,
We shall be winnow'd with so rough a wind
That even our corn shall seem as light as chaff
And good from bad find no partition.
Arch. No, no, my lord. Note this; the king is weary
Of dainty and such picking grievances:
For he hath found to end one doubt by death
Revives two greater in the heirs of life,
And therefore will he wipe his tables clean
And keep no tell-tale to his memory
That may repeat and history his loss
To new remembrance; for full well he knows
He cannot so precisely weed this land
As his misdoubts present occasion:
His foes are so enrooted with his friends
That, plucking to unfix an enemy,
He doth unfasten so and shake a friend:
So that this land, like an offensive wife
That hath enrag'd him on to offer strokes,
As he is striking, holds his infant up
And hangs resolv'd correction in the arm
That was uprear'd to execution.
Hast. Besides, the king hath wasted all his rods
On late offenders, that he now doth lack
The very instruments of chastisement:
So that his power, like to a fangless lion,
May offer, but not hold.
Arch. 'Tis very true:
And therefore be assur'd, my good lord marshal,
If we do now make our atonement well,
Our peace will, like a broken limb united,
Grow stronger for the breaking.
Mowb. Be it so.
Here is return'd my Lord of Westmoreland.

Enter WESTMORELAND.

120. **armed staves,** lances. **in charge,** ready for the charge. **beavers,** movable fronts of helmets. 121. **sights of steel,** visors, eyeholes of the helmet. 125. **warder,** staff of command. 131. **Earl of Hereford,** title of King Henry IV in the earlier part of the play of *Richard II*. 145. **set off,** put out of consideration. 149. **overween,** are arrogant or presumptuous. 151. **ken,** seeing distance. 154. **names,** noble names. 163. **virtue,** authority. 166. **intended,** understood, implied. 167. **slight,** trivial. 172. **insinewed,** joined as by strong sinews. 176. **awful banks,** banks or bounds of respect. 189. **valuation,** what we are valued at. 193. **royal faiths,** allegiance to the king. He means: "were our integrity unimpeachable and our devotion to the throne that of martyrs." 198. **picking,** fastidious. 203. **history,** record, chronicle. 210-214. **like . . . execution.** The figure is mixed by being partly simile and partly metaphor; the meaning is, however, clear. 210. **offensive wife,** wife having provoked her husband to offer blows. 213. **hangs resolv'd correction,** stops the punishment which had been determined upon. 216. **late,** (other) recent. 219. **May . . . hold,** offer violence, but not hold out in the purpose of carrying it out. 225. **pleaseth,** may it

West. The prince is here at hand: pleaseth your lordship
To meet his grace just distance 'tween our armies.
Mowb. Your grace of York, in God's name, then, set forward.
Arch. Before, and greet his grace: my lord, we come.

[SCENE II. *The same.*]

Enter PRINCE JOHN [OF LANCASTER] *and his army.*

Lan. You are well encount'red here, my cousin Mowbray:
Good day to you, gentle lord archbishop;
And so to you, Lord Hastings, and to all.
My Lord of York, it better show'd with you
When that your flock, assembled by the bell,
Encircled you to hear with reverence
Your exposition on the holy text
Than now to see you here an iron man,
Cheering a rout of rebels with your drum,
Turning the word to sword and life to death.
That man that sits within a monarch's heart,
And ripens in the sunshine of his favour,
Would he abuse the countenance of the king,
Alack, what mischiefs might he set abroach
In shadow of such greatness! With you, lord bishop,
It is even so. Who hath not heard it spoken
How deep you were within the books of God?
To us the speaker in his parliament;
To us th' imagin'd voice of God himself;
The very opener and intelligencer
Between the grace, the sanctities of heaven
And our dull workings. O, who shall believe
But you misuse the reverence of your place,
Employ the countenance and grace of heav'n,
As a false favourite doth his prince's name,
In deeds dishonourable? You have ta'en up,
Under the counterfeited zeal of God,
The subjects of his substitute, my father,
And both against the peace of heaven and him
Have here up-swarm'd them.
Arch. Good my Lord of Lancaster,
I am not here against your father's peace;
But, as I told my Lord of Westmoreland,
The time misord'red doth, in common sense,
Crowd us and crush us to this monstrous form,
To hold our safety up. I sent your grace
The parcels and particulars of our grief,
The which hath been with scorn shov'd from the court,
Whereon this Hydra son of war is born;
Whose dangerous eyes may well be charm'd asleep
With grant of our most just and right desires,
And true obedience, of this madness cur'd,
Stoop tamely to the foot of majesty.
Mowb. If not, we ready are to try our fortunes
To the last man.
Hast. And though we here fall down,
We have supplies to second our attempt:
If they miscarry, theirs shall second them;
And so success of mischief shall be born
And heir from heir shall hold this quarrel up
Whiles England shall have generation.
Lan. You are too shallow, Hastings, much too shallow,
To sound the bottom of the after-times.
West. Pleaseth your grace to answer them directly
How far forth you do like their articles.
Lan. I like them all, and do allow them well,
And swear here, by the honour of my blood,
My father's purposes have been mistook,
And some about him have too lavishly
Wrested his meaning and authority.
My lord, these griefs shall be with speed redress'd;
Upon my soul, they shall. If this may please you,
Discharge your powers unto their several counties,
As we will ours: and here between the armies
Let 's drink together friendly and embrace,
That all their eyes may bear those tokens home
Of our restored love and amity.
Arch. I take your princely word for these redresses.
Lan. I give it you, and will maintain my word:
And thereupon I drink unto your grace.
Hast. Go, captain, and deliver to the army
This news of peace: let them have pay, and part:
I know it will well please them. Hie thee, captain.
[*Exit Officer.*]
Arch. To you, my noble Lord of Westmoreland.
West. I pledge your grace; and, if you knew what pains
I have bestow'd to breed this present peace,
You would drink freely: but my love to ye
Shall show itself more openly hereafter.
Arch. I do not doubt you.
West. I am glad of it.
Health to my lord and gentle cousin, Mowbray.
Mowb. You wish me health in very happy season;
For I am, on the sudden, something ill.
Arch. Against ill chances men are ever merry;
But heaviness foreruns the good event.
West. Therefore be merry, coz; since sudden sorrow
Serves to say thus, 'some good thing comes to-morrow.'
Arch. Believe me, I am passing light in spirit.
Mowb. So much the worse, if your own rule be true.
Shout [*within*].
Lan. The word of peace is rend'red: hark, how they shout!
Mowb. This had been cheerful after victory.
Arch. A peace is of the nature of a conquest;
For then both parties nobly are subdu'd,
And neither party loser.
Lan. Go, my lord,
And let our army be discharged too.
[*Exit Westmoreland.*]

please. 226. **just,** exact. 228. **Before,** i.e., go before.

SCENE II. This scene is apparently continuous with the previous scene. In Q, Prince John and his army enter before the last two lines of IV, 1. 8. **iron man,** warrior clad in armor. 14. **set abroach,** set on foot, begin. 18. **speaker,** allusion to the speaker of Parliament, who acted as the voice or interpreter for the monarch, just as, in the comparison, the archbishop speaks for God. 20. **opener,** revealer. **intelligencer,** interpreter, agent. 22. **dull workings,** imperfect mental processes. 27. **zeal.** Herford suggests a play on "seal." 28. **substitute,** deputy. Note the current theory of the position and function of the king. In this speech the prince gives a preliminary justification of the breach of faith with the rebels, whom he regarded as outside the pale of rectitude. 33. **time misord'red,** disorders of the time. 36. **parcels,** items, parts. 38. **Hydra.** The Lernaean Hydra was a fabulous monster with several heads; when one was cut off, others grew in its place. 42. **Stoop tamely,** yield, submit; a metaphor from falconry. 45. **supplies,** forces in reserve. 49. **generation,** issue, offspring. 54. **allow,** approve, sanction. 81. **Against,** when about to face.

And, good my lord, so please you, let our trains
March by us, that we may peruse the men
We should have cop'd withal.
Arch. Go, good Lord Hastings,
And, ere they be dismiss'd, let them march by.
[*Exit Hastings.*]
Lan. I trust, lords, we shall lie to-night together.

Enter WESTMORELAND.

Now cousin, wherefore stands our army still?
West. The leaders, having charge from you to stand,
Will not go off until they hear you speak.
Lan. They know their duties.

Enter HASTINGS.

Hast. My lord, our army is dispers'd already:
Like youthful steers unyok'd, they take their courses
East, west, north, south; or, like a school broke up,
Each hurries toward his home and sporting-place.
West. Good tidings, my Lord Hastings; for the which
I do arrest thee, traitor, of high treason:
And you, lord archbishop, and you, lord Mowbray,
Of capital treason I attach you both.
Mowb. Is this proceeding just and honourable?
West. Is your assembly so?
Arch. Will you thus break your faith?
Lan. I pawn'd thee none:
I promis'd you redress of these same grievances
Whereof you did complain; which, by mine honour,
I will perform with a most Christian care.
But for you, rebels, look to taste the due
Meet for rebellion and such acts as yours.
Most shallowly did you these arms commence,
Fondly brought here and foolishly sent hence.
Strike up our drums, pursue the scatt'red stray:
God, and not we, hath safely fought to-day.
Some guard these traitors to the block of death,
Treason's true bed and yielder up of breath. [*Exeunt.*]

[SCENE III. *The same.*]

Alarum. Excursions. Enter FALSTAFF [*and* COLEVILE, *meeting*].

Fal. What 's your name, sir? of what condition are you, and of what place, I pray?

Cole. I am a knight, sir; and my name is Colevile of the dale.

Fal. Well, then, Colevile is your name, a knight is your degree, and your place the dale: Colevile shall be still your name, a traitor your degree, and the dungeon your place, a place deep enough; so shall you be still Colevile of the dale.

Cole. Are not you Sir John Falstaff?

Fal. As good a man as he, sir, whoe'er I am. Do ye yield, sir? or shall I sweat for you? If I do sweat, they are the drops of thy lovers, and they weep for thy death: therefore rouse up fear and trembling, and do observance to my mercy.

Cole. I think you are Sir John Falstaff, and in that thought yield me.

Fal. I have a whole school of tongues in this belly of mine, and not a tongue of them all speaks any other word but my name. An I had but a belly of any indifferency, I were simply the most active fellow in Europe: my womb, my womb, my womb, undoes me. Here comes our general.

Enter [PRINCE] JOHN [OF LANCASTER], WESTMORELAND, [BLUNT,] *and the rest. Retreat* [*sounded*].

Lan. The heat is past; follow no further now:
Call in the powers, good cousin Westmoreland.
[*Exit Westmoreland.*]
Now, Falstaff, where have you been all this while?
When every thing is ended, then you come:
These tardy tricks of yours will, on my life,
One time or other break some gallows' back.

Fal. I would be sorry, my lord, but it should be thus: I never knew yet but rebuke and check was the reward of valour. Do you think me a swallow, an arrow, or a bullet? have I, in my poor and old motion, the expedition of thought? I have speeded hither with the very extremest inch of possibility; I have foundered nine score and odd posts: and here, travel-tainted as I am, have, in my pure and immaculate valour, taken Sir John Colevile of the dale, a most furious knight and valorous enemy. But what of that? he saw me, and yielded; that I may justly say, with the hook-nosed fellow of Rome, 'I came, saw, and overcame.'

Lan. It was more of his courtesy than your deserving.

Fal. I know not: here is he, and here I yield him: and I beseech your grace, let it be booked with the rest of this day's deeds; or, by the Lord, I will have it in a particular ballad else, with mine own picture on the top on 't, Colevile kissing my foot: to the which course if I be enforced, if you do not all show like gilt two-pences to me, and I in the clear sky of fame o'ershine you as much as the full moon doth the cinders of the element, which show like pins' heads to her, believe not the word of the noble: therefore let me have right, and let desert mount.

Lan. Thine 's too heavy to mount.

Fal. Let it shine, then.

Lan. Thine 's too thick to shine.

Fal. Let it do something, my good lord, that may do me good, and call it what you will.

Lan. Is thy name Colevile?

Cole. It is, my lord.

Lan. A famous rebel art thou, Colevile.

Fal. And a famous true subject took him.

Cole. I am, my lord, but as my betters are
That led me hither: had they been rul'd by me,
You should have won them dearer than you have.

Fal. I know how they sold themselves: but thou,

94. **peruse,** survey. 95. **cop'd withal,** encountered, fought with. 109. **capital,** punishable by death. **attach,** arrest. 111. **assembly,** unlawful assembly, in a rebellion. 112. **pawn'd,** pledged. 117. **Meet,** fit. 118. **shallowly,** without adequate cause. 119. **Fondly,** foolishly. 120. **stray,** stragglers.

SCENE III. 2. **condition,** rank. 14. **drops,** tears. **lovers,** friends. 17. **observance,** reverence, homage. 23. **indifferency,** moderate size. 25. **womb,** belly. 27. **heat,** pursuit, race. 37. **expedition,** speed. 39. **foundered,** made lame. 40. **posts,** post horses. 45. **hook-nosed fellow of Rome,** Julius Caesar. 49. **booked,** recorded by the chroniclers. 51. **particular ballad,** allusion to the practice of having broadside ballads written and published. 54. **show,** look. **gilt two-pences,** coins gilded to pass for half-crowns of the same size. 55. **to,** compared to. 58. **cinders of the element,** stars. 61. **desert mount,** merit be promoted. 64. **thick,** opaque. 78. **execution stay'd,** slaughter stopped. 80. **present,** immediate. 82. **dispatch we,** let us hasten. 89. **Stand my good lord,** act as my patron. 98. **come to any proof,** stand up well under testing. 100. **green-sickness,** kind of anemia affecting young women.

like a kind fellow, gavest thyself away gratis; and I thank thee for thee.

Enter WESTMORELAND.

Lan. Now, have you left pursuit?
West. Retreat is made and execution stay'd.
Lan. Send Colevile with his confederates
To York, to present execution:
Blunt, lead him hence; and see you guard him sure.
[*Exeunt Blunt and others with Colevile.*]
And now dispatch we toward the court, my lords:
I hear the king my father is sore sick:
Our news shall go before us to his majesty,
Which, cousin, you shall bear to comfort him,
And we with sober speed will follow you.
Fal. My lord, I beseech you, give me leave to go
Through Gloucestershire: and, when you come to court,
Stand my good lord, pray, in your good report.
Lan. Fare you well, Falstaff: I, in my condition,
Shall better speak of you than you deserve.
[*Exeunt all but Falstaff.*]

Fal. I would you had but the wit: 'twere better than your dukedom. Good faith, this same young sober-blooded boy doth not love me; nor a man cannot make him laugh; but that 's no marvel, he drinks no wine. There 's never none of these demure boys come to any proof; for thin drink doth so over-cool their blood, and making many fish-meals, that they fall into a kind of male green-sickness; and then when they marry, they get wenches: they are generally fools and cowards; which some of us should be too, but for inflammation. A good sherris-sack hath a two-fold operation in it. It ascends me into the brain; dries me there all the foolish and dull and crudy vapours which environ it; makes it apprehensive, quick, forgetive, full of nimble fiery and delectable shapes; which, delivered o'er to the voice, the tongue, which is the birth, becomes excellent wit. The second property of your excellent sherris is, the warming of the blood; which, before cold and settled, left the liver white and pale, which is the badge of pusillanimity and cowardice; but the sherris warms it and makes it course from the inwards to the parts extreme: it illumineth the face, which as a beacon gives warning to all the rest of this little kingdom, man, to arm; and then the vital commoners and inland petty spirits muster me all to their captain, the heart, who, great and puffed up with this retinue, doth any deed of courage; and this valour comes of sherris. So that skill in the weapon is nothing without sack, for that sets it a-work; and learning a mere hoard of gold kept by a devil, till sack commences it and sets it in act and use. Hereof comes it that Prince Harry is valiant; for the cold blood he did naturally inherit of his father, he hath, like lean, sterile and bare land, manured, husbanded and tilled with excellent endeavour of drinking good and good store of fertile sherris, that he is become very hot and valiant. If I had a thousand sons, the first humane principle I would teach them should be, to forswear thin potations and to addict themselves to sack.

Enter BARDOLPH.

How now, Bardolph?

Bard. The army is discharged all and gone.

Fal. Let them go. I'll through Gloucestershire; and there will I visit Master Robert Shallow, esquire: I have him already tempering between my finger and my thumb, and shortly will I seal with him. Come away. [*Exeunt.*]

[SCENE IV. *Westminster.*]

Enter the KING, WARWICK, THOMAS DUKE OF CLARENCE, HUMPHREY [DUKE] OF GLOUCESTER [*, and others*].

King. Now, lords, if God doth give successful end
To this debate that bleedeth at our doors,
We will our youth lead on to higher fields
And draw no swords but what are sanctified.
Our navy is address'd, our power collected,
Our substitutes in absence well invested,
And every thing lies level to our wish:
Only, we want a little personal strength;
And pause us, till these rebels, now afoot,
Come underneath the yoke of government.
War. Both which we doubt not but your majesty
Shall soon enjoy.
King. Humphrey, my son of Gloucester,
Where is the prince your brother?
Glou. I think he 's gone to hunt, my lord, at Windsor.
King. And how accompanied?
Glou. I do not know, my lord.
King. Is not his brother, Thomas of Clarence, with him?
Glou. No, my good lord; he is in presence here.
Clar. What would my lord and father?
King. Nothing but well to thee, Thomas of Clarence.
How chance thou art not with the prince thy brother?
He loves thee, and thou dost neglect him, Thomas;
Thou hast a better place in his affection
Than all thy brothers: cherish it, my boy,
And noble offices thou mayst effect
Of mediation, after I am dead,
Between his greatness and thy other brethren:
Therefore omit him not; blunt not his love,
Nor lose the good advantage of his grace
By seeming cold or careless of his will;
For he is gracious, if he be observ'd:
He hath a tear for pity and a hand
Open as day for melting charity:
Yet notwithstanding, being incens'd, he is flint,
As humorous as winter and as sudden
As flaws congealed in the spring of day.
His temper, therefore, must be well observ'd:
Chide him for faults, and do it reverently,
When you perceive his blood inclin'd to mirth;

101. **get,** beget. 103. **inflammation,** excitement with liquor. 106. **crudy,** defined as "thick"; wet and cold vapors were conducive to dullness. 107. **apprehensive,** quick to perceive. **forgetive,** seems to mean "inventive"; it has been connected with "forge." 118. **little kingdom,** microcosm. Man was thought of as a microcosm corresponding in parts and qualities to the universe, or macrocosm. 140. **tempering,** softening (like a piece of wax).

SCENE IV. 3. **higher fields.** He will lead them on a crusade. 5. **address'd,** ready, prepared. 6. **substitutes,** deputies. **invested,** i.e., with power. 7. **level,** conformable. 27. **omit,** neglect. 30. **observ'd,** paid proper respect. 32. **melting,** compassionate. 33. **flint,** i.e., in emitting fire. 34. **humorous,** unpredictable in action. 35. **flaws,** defined as "snow" (Onions), or as blades of ice seen at the edge of water on winter mornings (Yale); see glossary. **spring of day,** early morning. 36. **temper,** disposition, mood.

But, being moody, give him line and scope,
Till that his passions, like a whale on ground,
Confound themselves with working. Learn this, Thomas,
And thou shalt prove a shelter to thy friends,
A hoop of gold to bind thy brothers in,
That the united vessel of their blood,
Mingled with venom of suggestion—
As, force perforce, the age will pour it in—
Shall never leak, though it do work as strong
As aconitum or rash gunpowder.
Clar. I shall observe him with all care and love.
King. Why art thou not at Windsor with him, Thomas?
Clar. He is not there to-day; he dines in London.
King. And how accompanied? canst thou tell that?
Clar. With Poins, and other his continual followers.
King. Most subject is the fattest soil to weeds;
And he, the noble image of my youth,
Is overspread with them: therefore my grief
Stretches itself beyond the hour of death:
The blood weeps from my heart when I do shape
In forms imaginary th' unguided days
And rotten times that you shall look upon
When I am sleeping with my ancestors.
For when his headstrong riot hath no curb,
When rage and hot blood are his counsellors,
When means and lavish manners meet together,
O, with what wings shall his affections fly
Towards fronting peril and oppos'd decay!
War. My gracious lord, you look beyond him quite:
The prince but studies his companions
Like a strange tongue, wherein, to gain the language,
'Tis needful that the most immodest word
Be look'd upon and learn'd; which once attain'd,
Your highness knows, comes to no further use
But to be known and hated. So, like gross terms,
The prince will in the perfectness of time
Cast off his followers; and their memory
Shall as a pattern or a measure live,
By which his grace must mete the lives of others,
Turning past evils to advantages.
King. 'Tis seldom when the bee doth leave her comb
In the dead carrion.

Enter WESTMORELAND.

Who 's here? Westmoreland?
West. Health to my sovereign, and new happiness
Added to that that I am to deliver!
Prince John your son doth kiss your grace's hand:
Mowbray, the Bishop Scroop, Hastings and all
Are brought to the correction of your law;
There is not now a rebel's sword unsheath'd,
But Peace puts forth her olive every where.
The manner how this action hath been borne
Here at more leisure may your highness read,
With every course in his particular.
King. O Westmoreland, thou art a summer bird,
Which ever in the haunch of winter sings
The lifting up of day.

Enter HARCOURT.

Look, here 's more news.
Har. From enemies heaven keep your majesty;
And, when they stand against you, may they fall
As those that I am come to tell you of!
The Earl Northumberland and the Lord Bardolph,
With a great power of English and of Scots,
Are by the shrieve of Yorkshire overthrown:
The manner and true order of the fight
This packet, please it you, contains at large.
King. And wherefore should these good news make me sick?
Will Fortune never come with both hands full,
But write her fair words still in foulest letters?
She either gives a stomach and no food;
Such are the poor, in health; or else a feast
And takes away the stomach; such are the rich,
That have abundance and enjoy it not.
I should rejoice now at this happy news;
And now my sight fails, and my brain is giddy:
O me! come near me; now I am much ill.
Glou. Comfort, your majesty!
Clar. O my royal father!
West. My sovereign lord, cheer up yourself, look up.
War. Be patient, princes; you do know, these fits
Are with his highness very ordinary.
Stand from him, give him air; he'll straight be well.
Clar. No, no, he cannot long hold out these pangs:
Th' incessant care and labour of his mind
Hath wrought the mure that should confine it in
So thin that life looks through and will break out.
Glou. The people fear me; for they do observe
Unfather'd heirs and loathly births of nature:
The seasons change their manners, as the year
Had found some months asleep and leap'd them over.
Clar. The river hath thrice flow'd, no ebb between;
And the old folk, time's doting chronicles,
Say it did so a little time before
That our great-grandsire, Edward, sick'd and died.
War. Speak lower, princes, for the king recovers.
Glou. This apoplexy will certain be his end.
King. I pray you, take me up, and bear me hence
Into some other chamber: softly, pray.

[SCENE V. *The same.*]

[*The* KING *is borne to another part of the stage, to bed.*]

[*King*.] Let there be no noise made, my gentle friends;
Unless some dull and favourable hand
Will whisper music to my weary spirit.
War. Call for the music in the other room.
King. Set me the crown upon my pillow here.
Clar. His eye is hollow, and he changes much.
War. Less noise, less noise!

Enter [PRINCE] HARRY.

39. **moody,** angry. **line,** full play, scope. 40. **whale on ground.** Holinshed tells of a whale cast up on the coast of Kent in July 1573, which, beating itself about in the sand, perished. 45. **suggestion,** insinuation. 47. **never leak,** an allusion to the belief that aconitum, or wolfsbane, was so powerful in its action that it could make its way through the strongest vessel. 58. **weeps from my heart,** an allusion to the belief that each sigh cost the heart a drop of blood. 64. **lavish,** unrestrained, licentious. 66. **fronting . . . decay,** danger and ruin which confront him. 67. **look beyond,** misjudge. 77. **mete,** measure. 79-80. **leave . . . carrion,** an expression of the king's belief that the prince will not forsake his evil company. 90. **course,** event. 92. **haunch,** latter end. 93. **lifting up,** dawn. 95. **stand against,** oppose in arms. 99. **shrieve,** sheriff; identified as Thomas de Rokeby. 119. **mure,** wall. 121. **fear,** frighten. 122. **Unfather'd,** supernaturally generated. 125. **The . . . between.** This event is recorded by Holinshed as having happened on October 12, 1411. There are many cases in which

Prince. Who saw the Duke of Clarence?
Clar. I am here, brother, full of heaviness.
Prince. How now! rain within doors, and none abroad!
How doth the king?
Glou. Exceeding ill.
Prince. Heard he the good news yet!
Tell it him.
Glou. He alter'd much upon the hearing it.
Prince. If he be sick with joy, he'll recover without physic.
War. Not so much noise, my lords: sweet prince, speak low;
The king your father is dispos'd to sleep.
Clar. Let us withdraw into the other room.
War. Will 't please your grace to go along with us?
Prince. No; I will sit and watch here by the king.
[*Exeunt all but the Prince.*]
Why doth the crown lie there upon his pillow,
Being so troublesome a bedfellow?
O polish'd perturbation! golden care!
That keep'st the ports of slumber open wide
To many a watchful night! sleep with it now!
Yet not so sound and half so deeply sweet
As he whose brow with homely biggen bound
Snores out the watch of night. O majesty!
When thou dost pinch thy bearer, thou dost sit
Like a rich armour worn in heat of day,
That scald'st with safety. By his gates of breath
There lies a downy feather which stirs not:
Did he suspire, that light and weightless down
Perforce must move. My gracious lord! my father!
This sleep is sound indeed; this is a sleep
That from this golden rigol hath divorc'd
So many English kings. Thy due from me
Is tears and heavy sorrows of the blood,
Which nature, love, and filial tenderness,
Shall, O dear father, pay thee plenteously:
My due from thee is this imperial crown,
Which, as immediate from thy place and blood,
Derives itself to me. Lo, here it sits, [*Puts it on.*]
Which God shall guard: and put the world's whole strength
Into one giant arm, it shall not force
This lineal honour from me: this from thee
Will I to mine leave, as 'tis left to me. *Exit.*
King. Warwick! Gloucester! Clarence!

Enter WARWICK, GLOUCESTER, CLARENCE.

Clar. Doth the king call?
War. What would your majesty? How fares your grace?
King. Why did you leave me here alone, my lords?
Clar. We left the prince my brother here, my liege,
Who undertook to sit and watch by you.
King. The Prince of Wales! Where is he? let me see him:
He is not here.
War. This door is open; he is gone this way.
Glou. He came not through the chamber where we stay'd.
King. Where is the crown? who took it from my pillow?
War. When we withdrew, my liege, we left it here.
King. The prince hath ta'en it hence: go, seek him out.
Is he so hasty that he doth suppose
My sleep my death?
Find him, my Lord of Warwick; chide him hither.
[*Exit Warwick.*]
This part of his conjoins with my disease,
And helps to end me. See, sons, what things you are!
How quickly nature falls into revolt
When gold becomes her object!
For this the foolish over-careful fathers
Have broke their sleep with thoughts, their brains with care,
Their bones with industry;
For this they have engrossed and pil'd up
The cank'red heaps of strange-achieved gold;
For this they have been thoughtful to invest
Their sons with arts and martial exercises:
When, like the bee, tolling from every flower
The virtuous sweets,
Our thighs pack'd with wax, our mouths with honey,
We bring it to the hive, and, like the bees,
Are murd'red for our pains. This bitter taste
Yield his engrossments to the ending father.

Enter WARWICK.

Now, where is he that will not stay so long
Till his friend sickness hath determin'd me?
War. My lord, I found the prince in the next room,
Washing with kindly tears his gentle cheeks,
With such a deep demeanour in great sorrow
That tyranny, which never quaff'd but blood,
Would, by beholding him, have wash'd his knife
With gentle eye-drops. He is coming hither.
King. But wherefore did he take away the crown?

Enter [PRINCE] HARRY.

Lo, where he comes. Come hither to me, Harry.
Depart the chamber, leave us here alone.
Exeunt [*Warwick and the rest*].
Prince. I never thought to hear you speak again.
King. Thy wish was father, Harry, to that thought:
I stay too long by thee, I weary thee.
Dost thou so hunger for mine empty chair
That thou wilt needs invest thee with my honours
Before thy hour be ripe? O foolish youth!
Thou seek'st the greatness that will overwhelm thee.
Stay but a little; for my cloud of dignity
Is held from falling with so weak a wind
That it will quickly drop: my day is dim.
Thou hast stol'n that which after some few hours
Were thine without offence; and at my death
Thou hast seal'd up my expectation:
Thy life did manifest thou lov'dst me not,
And thou wilt have me die assur'd of it.

Shakespeare follows Holinshed in recording portents in nature.
SCENE V. The scene is continuous. 2. **dull,** soft, soothing. 3. **music.** The medical practice of the time attributed healing power to music. 6. **changes,** changes color, turns pale. 23. **perturbation,** agitation by the passions; here used to mean the cause of agitation. 25. **watchful,** wakeful. 27. **biggen,** nightcap. 28. **watch of night,** period of night. 31. **scald'st,** burns (while providing safety). 33. **suspire,** breathe. 36. **rigol,** circle, crown. 38. **blood,** usually taken a meaning the source of tears and sorrows; probably, parenthood, bloodkinship. 42. **immediate,** passing in direct succession. 64. **part,** act, action; or role (?). **conjoins,** unites, joins. 69. **thoughts,** cares. 71. **engrossed,** amassed. 72. **cank'red,** rusting and malignant. **strange-achieved,** hard-won. 75. **tolling,** taking as toll; so Q; F and Globe: *culling.* 79. **Are . . . pains.** It is the drones, not the worker bees, that are murdered. 80. **engrossments,** stored-up treasures. 82. **determin'd,** ended, put an end to.

Thou hid'st a thousand daggers in thy thoughts,
Which thou hast whetted on thy stony heart,
To stab at half an hour of my life.
What! canst thou not forbear me half an hour?
Then get thee gone and dig my grave thyself,
And bid the merry bells ring to thine ear
That thou art crowned, not that I am dead.
Let all the tears that should bedew my hearse
Be drops of balm to sanctify thy head:
Only compound me with forgotten dust;
Give that which gave thee life unto the worms.
Pluck down my officers, break my decrees;
For now a time is come to mock at form:
Harry the Fifth is crown'd: up, vanity!
Down, royal state! all you sage counsellors, hence!
And to the English court assemble now,
From every region, apes of idleness!
Now, neighbour confines, purge you of your scum:
Have you a ruffian that will swear, drink, dance,
Revel the night, rob, murder, and commit
The oldest sins the newest kind of ways?
Be happy, he will trouble you no more;
England shall double gild his treble guilt,
England shall give him office, honour, might;
For the fifth Harry from curb'd license plucks
The muzzle of restraint, and the wild dog
Shall flesh his tooth on every innocent.
O my poor kingdom, sick with civil blows!
When that my care could not withhold thy riots,
What wilt thou do when riot is thy care?
O, thou wilt be a wilderness again,
Peopled with wolves, thy old inhabitants!
Prince. O, pardon me, my liege! but for my tears,
The moist impediments unto my speech,
I had forestall'd this dear and deep rebuke
Ere you with grief had spoke and I had heard
The course of it so far. There is your crown;
And He that wears the crown immortally
Long guard it yours! If I affect it more [*Kneels.*]
Than as your honour and as your renown,
Let me no more from this obedience rise,
Which my most inward true and duteous spirit
Teacheth, this prostrate and exterior bending.
God witness with me, when I here came in,
And found no course of breath within your majesty,
How cold it struck my heart! If I do feign,
O, let me in my present wildness die
And never live to show th' incredulous world
The noble change that I have purposed!
Coming to look on you, thinking you dead,
And dead almost, my liege, to think you were,
I spake unto this crown as having sense,
And thus upbraided it: 'The care on thee depending
Hath fed upon the body of my father;
Therefore, thou best of gold art worst of gold:
Other, less fine in carat, is more precious,
Preserving life in med'cine potable;
But thou, most fine, most honour'd, most renown'd,
Hast eat thy bearer up.' Thus, my most royal liege,
Accusing it, I put it on my head,
To try with it, as with an enemy
That had before my face murder'd my father,
The quarrel of a true inheritor.
But if it did infect my blood with joy,
Or swell my thoughts to any strain of pride;
If any rebel or vain spirit of mine
Did with the least affection of a welcome
Give entertainment to the might of it,
Let God for ever keep it from my head
And make me as the poorest vassal is
That doth with awe and terror kneel to it!
King. O my son,
God put it in thy mind to take it hence,
That thou mightst win the more thy father's love,
Pleading so wisely in excuse of it!
Come hither, Harry, sit thou by my bed;
And hear, I think, the very latest counsel
That ever I shall breathe. God knows, my son,
By what by-paths and indirect crook'd ways
I met this crown; and I myself know well
How troublesome it sat upon my head.
To thee it shall descend with better quiet,
Better opinion, better confirmation;
For all the soil of the achievement goes
With me into the earth. It seem'd in me
But as an honour snatch'd with boist'rous hand,
And I had many living to upbraid
My gain of it by their assistances;
Which daily grew to quarrel and to bloodshed,
Wounding supposed peace: all these bold fears
Thou see'st with peril I have answered;
For all my reign hath been but as a scene
Acting that argument: and now my death
Changes the mood; for what in me was purchas'd,
Falls upon thee in a more fairer sort;
So thou the garland wear'st successively.
Yet, though thou stand'st more sure than I could do,
Thou art not firm enough, since griefs are green;
And all my friends, which thou must make thy friends,
Have but their stings and teeth newly ta'en out;
By whose fell working I was first advanc'd
And by whose power I well might lodge a fear
To be again displac'd: which to avoid,
I cut them off; and had a purpose now,
To lead out many to the Holy Land,
Lest rest and lying still might make them look
Too near unto my state. Therefore, my Harry,
Be it thy course to busy giddy minds
With foreign quarrels; that action, hence borne out,
May waste the memory of the former days.
More would I, but my lungs are wasted so
That strength of speech is utterly denied me.
How I came by the crown, O God forgive;
And grant it may with thee in true peace live!
Prince. My gracious liege,
You won it, wore it, kept it, gave it me;

110. **forbear,** spare. 115. **balm,** consecrated oil used in anointing the king at his coronation. 119. **form,** laws, orderly usages. 120. **vanity,** folly. 124. **neighbour confines,** territories of neighboring countries. 136. **care,** special study. 141. **dear and deep,** heartfelt and severe. 144. **immortally,** eternally. 147. **obedience,** obeisance. 148. **inward,** sincere. 162. **carat,** standard of fineness in gold with pun on "charact," character. **precious,** double meaning suggesting, besides the usual sense, the idea of curing. 163. **med'cine potable,** potable gold, an elixir, thought from Galen's time to possess magical power to cure. 169. **inheritor,** owner. 171. **strain,** height of emotion; also, musical theme. 172. **vain,** vainglorious. 183. **latest,** last. 188. **quiet,** by some defined as "conscience"; more probably, peace and acquiescence. 200. **mood,** state of mind; pun on "mode," musical key. 201. **sort,** manner, way. 202. **successively,** by right of succession. 204. **green,** fresh. 207. **fell working,** evil effort. 215. **hence,** in other lands. 216. **waste,** efface, obliterate. 231. **makes a period,** comes to an end, rounds out a whole (as a sentence ends). 234. **lodging,** apartment. 235. **Jerusalem,** a chamber adjoining the southwest tower

Then plain and right must my possession be:
Which I with more than with a common pain
'Gainst all the world will rightfully maintain.

Enter [Lord John of] Lancaster [*and* Warwick].

King. Look, look, here comes my John of Lancaster.
Lan. Health, peace, and happiness to my royal father!
King. Thou bring'st me happiness and peace, son John;
But health, alack, with youthful wings is flown
From this bare wither'd trunk: upon thy sight
My worldly business makes a period.
Where is my Lord of Warwick?
Prince. My Lord of Warwick!

[Warwick *comes forward.*]

King. Doth any name particular belong
Unto the lodging where I first did swoon?
War. 'Tis call'd Jerusalem, my noble lord.
King. Laud be to God! even there my life must end.
It hath been prophesied to me many years,
I should not die but in Jerusalem;
Which vainly I suppos'd the Holy Land:
But bear me to that chamber; there I'll lie;
In that Jerusalem shall Harry die. [*Exeunt.*]

[ACT V.

scene i. *Gloucestershire.* Shallow's *house.*]

Enter Shallow, Falstaff, *and* Bardolph [*and* Page].

Shal. By cock and pie, sir, you shall not away to-night. What, Davy, I say!

Fal. You must excuse me, Master Robert Shallow.

Shal. I will not excuse you; you shall not be excused; excuses shall not be admitted; there is no excuse shall serve; you shall not be excused. Why, Davy!

[*Enter* Davy.]

Davy. Here, sir.

Shal. Davy, Davy, Davy, Davy, let me see, Davy; let me see, Davy; let me see: yea, marry, William cook, bid him come hither. Sir John, you shall not be excused.

Davy. Marry, sir, thus; those precepts cannot be served: and, again, sir, shall we sow the headland with wheat?

Shal. With red wheat, Davy. But for William cook: are there no young pigeons?

Davy. Yes, sir. Here is now the smith's note for shoeing and plough-irons.

Shal. Let it be cast and paid. Sir John, you shall not be excused.

Davy. Now, sir, a new link to the bucket must needs be had: and, sir, do you mean to stop any of William's wages, about the sack he lost the other day at Hinckley fair?

Shal. 'A shall answer it. Some pigeons, Davy, a couple of short-legged hens, a joint of mutton, and any pretty little tiny kickshaws, tell William cook.

Davy. Doth the man of war stay all night, sir?

Shal. Yea, Davy. I will use him well: a friend i' the court is better than a penny in purse. Use his men well, Davy; for they are arrant knaves, and will back-bite.

Davy. No worse than they are backbitten, sir; for they have marvellous foul linen.

Shal. Well conceited, Davy: about thy business, Davy.

Davy. I beseech you, sir, to countenance William Visor of Woncot against Clement Perkes o' the hill.

Shal. There is many complaints, Davy, against that Visor: that Visor is an arrant knave, on my knowledge.

Davy. I grant your worship that he is a knave, sir; but yet, God forbid, sir, but a knave should have some countenance at his friend's request. An honest man, sir, is able to speak for himself, when a knave is not. I have served your worship truly, sir, this eight years; and if I cannot once or twice in a quarter bear out a knave against an honest man, I have but a very little credit with your worship. The knave is mine honest friend, sir; therefore, I beseech your worship, let him be countenanced.

Shal. Go to; I say he shall have no wrong. Look about, Davy. [*Exit Davy.*] Where are you, Sir John? Come, come, come, off with your boots. Give me your hand, Master Bardolph.

Bard. I am glad to see your worship.

Shal. I thank thee with all my heart, kind Master Bardolph: and welcome, my tall fellow [*to the Page*]. Come, Sir John.

Fal. I'll follow you, good Master Robert Shallow. [*Exit Shallow.*] Bardolph, look to our horses. [*Exeunt Bardolph and Page.*] If I were sawed into quantities, I should make four dozen of such bearded hermits' staves as Master Shallow. It is a wonderful thing to see the semblable coherence of his men's spirits and his: they, by observing of him, do bear themselves like foolish justices; he, by conversing with them, is turned into a justice-like serving-man: their spirits are so married in conjunction with the participation of society that they flock together in consent, like so many wild-geese. If I had a suit to Master Shallow, I would humour his men with the imputation of being near their master: if to his men, I would curry with Master Shallow that no man could better command his servants. It is certain that either wise bearing or ignorant carriage is caught, as men take diseases, one of another: therefore let men take heed of their company. I will devise matter enough out of this Shallow to keep Prince Harry in continual laughter the wearing out of six fashions, which is four terms,

of Westminster Abbey, so called perhaps from tapestries hung there which depicted matters connected with Jerusalem. This chamber was the traditional place of the king's death, and its occurrence there was regarded as the fulfillment of the prophecy referred to.

Act v. scene i. 1. **cock and pie,** a trivial oath. 2. **What,** an exclamation of impatience. 14. **precepts,** writs requiring something to be done. 16. **headland,** a strip of unploughed land between two ploughed fields. 19. **note,** bill. 21. **cast,** verified. 23. **link,** chain. **bucket,** yoke. 26. **Hinckley,** market town near Stratford. 29. **kick-shaws,** fancy dishes; from French *quelque chose*. 39. **Well conceited,** ingeniously punned. 41. **countenance,** favor. 42, 43. **Visor, Perkes.** Madden identified these names in Gloucestershire records. 53. **bear out,** support. 59. **Look about,** look sharp, be on the alert. 65. **tall fellow,** brave man; applied jocularly to the diminutive page. 70. **quantities,** fragments. 73. **semblable coherence,** similar or complete agreement. 75. **conversing,** associating. 79. **consent,** agreement. 82. **curry with,** employ flattery with. 85. **carriage,** demeanor, behavior. 90. **terms,** i.e., of court.

or two actions, and 'a shall laugh without intervallums. O, it is much that a lie with a slight oath and a jest with a sad brow will do with a fellow that never had the ache in his shoulders! O, you shall see him laugh till his face be like a wet cloak ill laid up!

Shal. [*Within*] Sir John!

Fal. I come, Master Shallow; I come, Master Shallow. [*Exit.*]

[SCENE II. *Westminster. The palace.*]

Enter WARWICK [*and the*] LORD CHIEF JUSTICE [*meeting*].

War. How now, my lord chief-justice! whither away?
Ch. Just. How doth the king?
War. Exceeding well; his cares are now all ended.
Ch. Just. I hope, not dead.
War. He 's walk'd the way of nature;
And to our purposes he lives no more.
Ch. Just. I would his majesty had call'd me with him:
The service that I truly did his life
Hath left me open to all injuries.
War. Indeed I think the young king loves you not.
Ch. Just. I know he doth not, and do arm myself
To welcome the condition of the time,
Which cannot look more hideously upon me
Than I have drawn it in my fantasy.

Enter [PRINCE] JOHN [OF LANCASTER], THOMAS [OF CLARENCE], *and* HUMPHREY [OF GLOUCESTER, *with* WESTMORELAND].

War. Here come the heavy issue of dead Harry:
O that the living Harry had the temper
Of him, the worst of these three gentlemen!
How many nobles then should hold their places,
That must strike sail to spirits of vile sort!
Ch. Just. O God, I fear all will be overturn'd!
Lan. Good morrow, cousin Warwick, good morrow.
Glou., *Clar.* Good morrow, cousin.
Lan. We meet like men that had forgot to speak.
War. We do remember; but our argument
Is all too heavy to admit much talk.
Lan. Well, peace be with him that hath made us heavy!
Ch. Just. Peace be with us, lest we be heavier!
Glou. O, good my lord, you have lost a friend indeed;
And I dare swear you borrow not that face
Of seeming sorrow, it is sure your own.
Lan. Though no man be assur'd what grace to find,
You stand in coldest expectation:
I am the sorrier; would 'twere otherwise.
Clar. Well, you must now speak Sir John Falstaff fair;
Which swims against your stream of quality.

Ch. Just. Sweet princes, what I did, I did in honour,
Led by th' impartial conduct of my soul;
And never shall you see that I will beg
A ragged and forestall'd remission.
If truth and upright innocency fail me,
I'll to the king my master that is dead,
And tell him who hath sent me after him.
War. Here comes the prince.

Enter the PRINCE [*as* HENRY THE FIFTH] *and* BLUNT.

Ch. Just. Good morrow; and God save your majesty!
King. This new and gorgeous garment, majesty,
Sits not so easy on me as you think.
Brothers, you mix your sadness with some fear:
This is the English, not the Turkish court;
Not Amurath an Amurath succeeds,
But Harry Harry. Yet be sad, good brothers,
For, by my faith, it very well becomes you:
Sorrow so royally in you appears
That I will deeply put the fashion on
And wear it in my heart: why then, be sad;
But entertain no more of it, good brothers,
Than a joint burden laid upon us all.
For me, by heaven, I bid you be assur'd,
I'll be your father and your brother too;
Let me but bear your love, I'll bear your cares:
Yet weep that Harry 's dead; and so will I;
But Harry lives, that shall convert those tears
By number into hours of happiness.
Princes. We hope no otherwise from your majesty.
King. You all look strangely on me: and you most;
You are, I think, assur'd I love you not.
Ch. Just. I am assur'd, if I be measur'd rightly,
Your majesty hath no just cause to hate me.
King. No?
How might a prince of my great hopes forget
So great indignities you laid upon me?
What! rate, rebuke, and roughly send to prison
Th' immediate heir of England! Was this easy?
May this be wash'd in Lethe, and forgotten?
Ch. Just. I then did use the person of your father;
The image of his power lay then in me:
And, in th' administration of his law,
Whiles I was busy for the commonwealth,
Your highness pleased to forget my place,
The majesty and power of law and justice,
The image of the king whom I presented,
And struck me in my very seat of judgement;
Whereon, as an offender to your father,
I gave bold way to my authority
And did commit you. If the deed were ill,
Be you contented, wearing now the garland,
To have a son set your decrees at nought,
To pluck down justice from your awful bench,
To trip the course of law and blunt the sword
That guards the peace and safety of your person;
Nay, more, to spurn at your most royal image
And mock your workings in a second body.

90. **actions,** lawsuits. 91. **intervallums,** intervals. 95. **ill laid up,** carelessly put away so that it wrinkles.

SCENE II. 14. **heavy issue,** grieving sons. 18. **strike sail,** salute as a token of submission. 31. **coldest expectation,** gloomiest prospects. 34. **swims . . . quality,** goes against the current of your honor. 38. **A . . . remission,** a half-hearted (beggarly) pardon, which is sure to be refused, or whose effect is gone before it is granted. 48. **Amurath,** one of the few contemporary allusions in the play. The Turkish sultan Amurath IV succeeded his father in 1596; he called his brothers to a feast and had them strangled. 62. **no otherwise,** nothing else. 71. **immediate heir,** next heir in succession. **easy,** of small importance. 72. **wash'd in Lethe,** forgotten; an allusion to the river of forgetfulness in Hades. 73-121. **I . . . directions.** This episode, derived from Sir Thomas Elyot's *Governour,* figured largely in all the accounts of the reformation of Prince Hal, including *The Famous Victories.* 73. **use the person,** make use of my prerogative as personal representative. 83. **commit,** i.e., to prison. 86. **awful,** inspiring awe. 90. **second body,** representative. 92. **propose,** imagine, suppose. 97. **soft,** gently. 98. **cold considerance,** calm reflection. 103. **balance, sword,** emblems of justice. 109. **proper,** own. 115. **remembrance,** reminder, admoni-

Question your royal thoughts, make the case yours;
Be now the father and propose a son,
Hear your own dignity so much profan'd,
See your most dreadful laws so loosely slighted,
Behold yourself so by a son disdain'd;
And then imagine me taking your part
And in your power soft silencing your son:
After this cold considerance, sentence me;
And, as you are a king, speak in your state
What I have done that misbecame my place,
My person, or my liege's sovereignty.

King. You are right, justice, and you weigh this well;
Therefore still bear the balance and the sword:
And I do wish your honours may increase,
Till you do live to see a son of mine
Offend you and obey you, as I did.
So shall I live to speak my father's words:
'Happy am I, that have a man so bold,
That dares do justice on my proper son;
And not less happy, having such a son,
That would deliver up his greatness so
Into the hands of justice.' You did commit me:
For which, I do commit into your hand
Th' unstained sword that you have us'd to bear;
With this remembrance, that you use the same
With the like bold, just and impartial spirit
As you have done 'gainst me. There is my hand.
You shall be as a father to my youth:
My voice shall sound as you do prompt mine ear,
And I will stoop and humble my intents
To your well-practis'd wise directions.
And, princes all, believe me, I beseech you;
My father is gone wild into his grave,
For in his tomb lie my affections;
And with his spirit sadly I survive,
To mock the expectation of the world,
To frustrate prophecies and to rase out
Rotten opinion, who hath writ me down
After my seeming. The tide of blood in me
Hath proudly flow'd in vanity till now:
Now doth it turn and ebb back to the sea,
Where it shall mingle with the state of floods
And flow henceforth in formal majesty.
Now call we our high court of parliament:
And let us choose such limbs of noble counsel,
That the great body of our state may go
In equal rank with the best govern'd nation;
That war, or peace, or both at once, may be
As things acquainted and familiar to us;
In which you, father, shall have foremost hand.
Our coronation done, we will accite,
As I before rememb'red, all our state:
And, God consigning to my good intents,
No prince nor peer shall have just cause to say,
God shorten Harry's happy life one day! *Exeunt.*

[SCENE III. *Gloucestershire.* SHALLOW'S *orchard.*]

Enter SIR JOHN [FALSTAFF], SHALLOW, SILENCE, DAVY, BARDOLPH, [*and the*] Page.

Shal. Nay, you shall see my orchard, where, in an arbour, we will eat a last year's pippin of mine own graffing, with a dish of caraways, and so forth: come, cousin Silence: and then to bed.

Fal. 'Fore God, you have here a goodly dwelling and a rich.

Shal. Barren, barren, barren; beggars all, beggars all, Sir John: marry, good air. Spread, Davy; spread, Davy: well said, Davy.

Fal. This Davy serves you for good uses; he is your serving-man and your husband.

Shal. A good varlet, a good varlet, a very good varlet, Sir John: by the mass, I have drunk too much sack at supper: a good varlet. Now sit down, now sit down: come, cousin.

Sil. Ah, sirrah! quoth-a, we shall
Do nothing but eat, and make good cheer, [*Singing.*]
And praise God for the merry year;
When flesh is cheap and females dear,
And lusty lads roam here and there
So merrily,
And ever among so merrily.

Fal. There 's a merry heart! Good Master Silence, I'll give you a health for that anon.

Shal. Give Master Bardolph some wine, Davy.

Davy. Sweet sir, sit; I'll be with you anon; most sweet sir, sit. Master page, good master page, sit. Proface! What you want in meat, we'll have in drink: but you must bear; the heart 's all. [*Exit.*]

Shal. Be merry, Master Bardolph; and, my little soldier there, be merry.

Sil. Be merry, be merry, my wife has all; [*Singing.*]
For women are shrews, both short and tall:
'Tis merry in hall when beards wag all,
And welcome merry Shrove-tide.
Be merry, be merry.

Fal. I did not think Master Silence had been a man of this mettle.

Sil. Who, I? I have been merry twice and once ere now.

Enter DAVY.

Davy. There 's a dish of leather-coats for you. [*To Bardolph.*]

Shal. Davy!

Davy. Your worship? I'll be with you straight [*to Bardolph*]. A cup of wine, sir?

Sil. A cup of wine that 's brisk and fine, [*Singing.*]
And drink unto the leman mine;
And a merry heart lives long-a.

Fal. Well said, Master Silence.

Sil. An we shall be merry, now comes in the sweet o' the night.

Fal. Health and long life to you, Master Silence.

Sil. Fill the cup, and let it come; [*Singing.*]
I'll pledge you a mile to th' bottom.

tion. 123-124. **My . . . affections.** He means that, since his own wildness has disappeared with his father's death, that wildness is buried along with his father. 127. **rase out,** erase. 129. **After my seeming,** according to what I seemed. 132. **state of floods,** majesty of ocean. 135. **limbs,** members. 137. **equal rank,** step by step. 141. **accite,** summon. 142. **rememb'red,** mentioned. 143. **consigning to,** sanctioning.

SCENE III. 3. **graffing,** grafting. 4. **caraways,** sweetmeats containing caraway seeds. 9. **Spread,** spread the cloth. **said,** done. 12. **husband,** manager of the household. 13. **varlet,** servant; normally used in a bad sense, but here affectionately. 17. **quoth-a,** said he (the singer). 20. **flesh,** meat (with sexual suggestion). 23. **ever among,** all the while. 30. **Proface,** formula of welcome to a meal, meaning "May it do you good." 30-31. **What . . . drink,** a proverbial saying. 31. **bear,** be forbearing, excuse the deficiencies of the entertainment. 37. **'Tis . . . all,** an old English proverb. 38. **Shrove-tide,** a season of merrymaking before Lent. 42. **twice and once,** adverbial expression denoting something like "now and again." 44. **leather-coats,** russet apples. 48. **brisk,** agreeably sharp to the taste. 49. **leman,** sweetheart. 57. **mile,** i.e., if it were a mile.

Shal. Honest Bardolph, welcome: if thou wantest any thing, and wilt not call, beshrew thy heart. Welcome, my little tiny thief [*to the Page*], and welcome indeed too. I'll drink to Master Bardolph, and to all the cabileros about London.

Davy. I hope to see London once ere I die.

Bard. An I might see you there, Davy,—

Shal. By the mass, you'll crack a quart together, ha! will you not, Master Bardolph?

Bard. Yea, sir, in a pottle-pot.

Shal. By God's liggens, I thank thee: the knave will stick by thee, I can assure thee that. 'A will not out, 'a; 'tis true bred.

Bard. And I'll stick by him, sir.

Shal. Why, there spoke a king. Lack nothing: be merry. (*One knocks at door.*) Look who 's at door there, ho! who knocks? [*Exit Davy.*]

Fal. Why, now you have done me right.
[*To Silence, seeing him take off a bumper.*]

Sil. Do me right, [*Singing.*]
And dub me knight:
Samingo.
Is 't not so?

Fal. 'Tis so.

Sil. Is 't so? Why then, say an old man can do somewhat.

[*Enter* DAVY.]

Davy. An 't please your worship, there 's one Pistol come from the court with news.

Fal. From the court! let him come in.

Enter PISTOL.

How now, Pistol!

Pist. Sir John, God save you!

Fal. What wind blew you hither, Pistol?

Pist. Not the ill wind which blows no man to good. Sweet knight, thou art now one of the greatest men in this realm.

Sil. By 'r lady, I think 'a be, but goodman Puff of Barson.

Pist. Puff!
Puff i' thy teeth, most recreant coward base!
Sir John, I am thy Pistol and thy friend,
And helter-skelter have I rode to thee,
And tidings do I bring and lucky joys
And golden times and happy news of price.

Fal. I pray thee now, deliver them like a man of this world.

Pist. A foutre for the world and worldlings base!
I speak of Africa and golden joys.

Fal. O base Assyrian knight, what is thy news?
Let King Cophetua know the truth thereof.

Sil. And Robin Hood, Scarlet, and John. [*Singing.*]

Pist. Shall dunghill curs confront the Helicons?
And shall good news be baffled?
Then, Pistol, lay thy head in Furies' lap.

Shal. Honest gentleman, I know not your breeding.

Pist. Why then, lament therefore.

Shal. Give me pardon, sir: if, sir, you come with news from the court, I take it there 's but two ways, either to utter them, or conceal them. I am, sir, under the king, in some authority.

Pist. Under which king, Besonian? speak, or die.

Shal. Under King Harry.

Pist. Harry the Fourth? or Fifth?

Shal. Harry the Fourth.

Pist. A foutre for thine office!
Sir John, thy tender lambkin now is king;
Harry the Fifth 's the man. I speak the truth:
When Pistol lies, do this; and fig me, like
The bragging Spaniard.

Fal. What, is the old king dead?

Pist. As nail in door: the things I speak are just.

Fal. Away, Bardolph! saddle my horse. Master Robert Shallow, choose what office thou wilt in the land, 'tis thine. Pistol, I will double-charge thee with dignities.

Bard. O joyful day!
I would not take a knighthood for my fortune.

Pist. What! I do bring good news.

Fal. Carry Master Silence to bed. Master Shallow, my Lord Shallow,—be what thou wilt; I am fortune's steward—get on thy boots: we'll ride all night. O sweet Pistol! Away, Bardolph! [*Exit Bard.*] Come, Pistol, utter more to me; and withal devise something to do thyself good. Boot, boot, Master Shallow: I know the young king is sick for me. Let us take any man's horses; the laws of England are at my commandment. Blessed are they that have been my friends; and woe to my lord chief justice!

Pist. Let vultures vile seize on his lungs also!
'Where is the life that late I led?' say they:
Why, here it is; welcome these pleasant days! *Exeunt.*

[SCENE IV. *London. A street.*]

Enter Beadle *and three or four* Officers [*with* HOSTESS QUICKLY *and* DOLL TEARSHEET].

Host. No, thou arrant knave; I would to God that I might die, that I might have thee hanged: thou hast drawn my shoulder out of joint.

First Bead. The constables have delivered her over to me; and she shall have whipping-cheer enough, I warrant her: there hath been a man or two lately killed about her.

Dol. Nut-hook, nut-hook, you lie. Come on; I'll tell thee what, thou damned tripe-visaged rascal, an the child I now go with do miscarry, thou wert better thou hadst struck thy mother, thou paper-faced villain.

Host. O the Lord, that Sir John were come! he would make this a bloody day to somebody. But I pray God the fruit of her womb miscarry!

63. **cabileros,** cavaliers. 69. **liggens,** an original oath of Shallow's. 71. **will not out,** will not fail you; or, pass out. 77. **Do me right,** pledge me. 78-79. **dub . . . Samingo,** fragment of a drinking song, with an allusion to the custom of drinking to one's mistress on one's knees, for which one was "dubbed a knight." *Samingo,* Sir Mingo, the hero of the song. 83. **somewhat,** something. 93. **but,** except. **goodman Puff of Barson,** an allusion to some fat man not known. 102. **man of this world,** ordinary man. 103. **foutre,** French *foutre,* fornicate. 104. **Africa,** fabled for wealth. 106. **Cophetua.** King Cophetua married a beggar maid according to the popular ballad, *King Cophetua and the Beggar-Maid.* 107. **And . . . John,** a scrap from the ballad, *Robin Hood and the Pinner of Wakefield.* 108. **Helicons.** Helicon was the abode of the Muses; Pistol resents the intrusion of Robin Hood. 109. **baffled,** treated with contumely. 112. **breeding,** parentage, rank. 119. **Besonian,** a low, beggarly, and unskillful soldier. Shallow is thus designated because of his assertion of authority. 124. **do this.** Pistol makes a vulgar gesture, said to consist in thrusting the thumb between the first and middle finger; in any case, to make such gesture was called *to fig.* 147. **'Where . . . led,'** fragment of a ballad.

SCENE IV. 3. **shoulder out of joint,** a reference to the rough methods

First Bead. If it do, you shall have a dozen of cushions again; you have but eleven now. Come, I charge you both go with me; for the man is dead that you and Pistol beat amongst you.

Dol. I'll tell you what, you thin man in a censer, I will have you as soundly swinged for this,—you blue-bottle rogue, you filthy famished correctioner, if you be not swinged, I'll forswear half-kirtles.

First Bead. Come, come, you she knight-errant, come.

Host. O God, that right should thus overcome might! Well, of sufferance comes ease.

Dol. Come, you rogue, come; bring me to a justice.

Host. Ay, come, you starved blood-hound.

Dol. Goodman death, goodman bones!

Host. Thou atomy, thou!

Dol. Come, you thin thing; come, you rascal.

First Bead. Very well. [*Exeunt.*]

[SCENE V. *A public place near Westminster Abbey.*]

Enter [Grooms *as*] *strewers of rushes.*

First Groom. More rushes, more rushes.

Sec. Groom. The trumpets have sounded twice.

Third Groom. 'Twill be two o'clock ere they come from the coronation: dispatch, dispatch. [*Exeunt.*]

Trumpets sound, and the KING *and his train pass over the stage. After them enter* FALSTAFF, SHALLOW, PISTOL, BARDOLPH, *and the Boy* [PAGE].

Fal. Stand here by me, Master Robert Shallow; I will make the king do you grace: I will leer upon him as 'a comes by; and do but mark the countenance that he will give me.

Pist. God bless thy lungs, good knight.

Fal. Come here, Pistol; stand behind me. O, if I had had time to have made new liveries, I would have bestowed the thousand pound I borrowed of you. But 'tis no matter; this poor show doth better: this doth infer the zeal I had to see him.

Shal. It doth so.

Fal. It shows my earnestness of affection,—

Shal. It doth so.

Fal. My devotion,—

Shal. It doth, it doth, it doth.

Fal. As it were, to ride day and night; and not to deliberate, not to remember, not to have patience to shift me,—

Shal. It is best, certain.

Fal. But to stand stained with travel, and sweating with desire to see him; thinking of nothing else, putting all affairs else in oblivion, as if there were nothing else to be done but to see him.

Pist. 'Tis 'semper idem,' for 'obsque hoc nihil est:' 'tis all in every part.

Shal. 'Tis so, indeed.

Pist. My knight, I will inflame thy noble liver,
And make thee rage.
Thy Doll, and Helen of thy noble thoughts,
Is in base durance and contagious prison;
Hal'd thither
By most mechanical and dirty hand:
Rouse up revenge from ebon den with fell Alecto's snake,
For Doll is in. Pistol speaks nought but truth.

Fal. I will deliver her.

[*Shouts within, and the trumpets sound.*]

Pist. There roar'd the sea, and trumpet-clangor sounds.

Enter the KING *and his train*[,*the* LORD CHIEF JUSTICE *among them*].

Fal. God save thy grace, King Hal! my royal Hal!

Pist. The heavens thee guard and keep, most royal imp of fame!

Fal. God save thee, my sweet boy!

King. My lord chief justice, speak to that vain man.

Ch. Just. Have you your wits? know you what 'tis you speak?

Fal. My king! my Jove! I speak to thee, my heart!

King. I know thee not, old man: fall to thy prayers;
How ill white hairs become a fool and jester!
I have long dream'd of such a kind of man,
So surfeit-swell'd, so old and so profane;
But, being awak'd, I do despise my dream.
Make less thy body hence, and more thy grace;
Leave gormandizing; know the grave doth gape
For thee thrice wider than for other men.
Reply not to me with a fool-born jest:
Presume not that I am the thing I was;
For God doth know, so shall the world perceive,
That I have turn'd away my former self;
So will I those that kept me company.
When thou dost hear I am as I have been,
Approach me, and thou shalt be as thou wast,
The tutor and the feeder of my riots:
Till then, I banish thee, on pain of death,
As I have done the rest of my misleaders,
Not to come near our person by ten mile.
For competence of life I will allow you,
That lack of means enforce you not to evils:
And, as we hear you do reform yourselves,
We will, according to your strengths and qualities,
Give you advancement. Be it your charge, my lord,
To see perform'd the tenour of our word.
Set on. [*Exeunt King, &c.*]

Fal. Master Shallow, I owe you a thousand pound.

Shal. Yea, marry, Sir John; which I beseech you to let me have home with me.

Fal. That can hardly be, Master Shallow. Do not you grieve at this; I shall be sent for in private to him: look you, he must seem thus to the world: fear not

of arrest in vogue. 5. **whipping-cheer,** banquet of lashes with a whip. 7. **about her,** in her company. 8. **Nut-hook,** hook for pulling down branches in nutting; here, a constable. 9, 12. **tripe-visaged, paper-faced,** allusions to the pock-marked and sallow complexion of the first Beadle. 20. **thin . . . censer,** probable allusion to the figure of a man on the lid of the censer, or perfume pan, embossed in low relief. 22. **blue-bottle,** an allusion to the beadle's blue coat. 23. **correctioner,** one who administered correction. 24. **half-kirtle,** probably, a short petticoat which was attached to a jacket, the two together forming a kirtle. 28. **sufference,** suffering. 33. **atomy,** skeleton.

SCENE V. 7. **leer,** smile. 12. **bestowed,** spent. 23. **shift me,** change my apparel. 30-31. **'semper . . . est,'** always the same, for without this there is nothing; common heraldic device. 36. **durance,** imprisonment. **contagious,** pestilential, pernicious. 38. **mechanical,** pertaining to a mechanical occupation, base. 39. **Rouse . . . snake.** This seems to be rant from the various plays which called for vengeance. Alecto was one of the Furies, who were depicted with snakes twined in their hair. 40 **in,** i.e., in Bridewell, a prison for prostitutes. 56. **hence,** henceforth.

your advancements; I will be the man yet that shall make you great.

Shal. I cannot well perceive how, unless you should give me your doublet and stuff me out with straw. I beseech you, good Sir John, let me have five hundred of my thousand.

Fal. Sir, I will be as good as my word: this that you heard was but a colour.

Shal. A colour that I fear you will die in, Sir John.

Fal. Fear no colours: go with me to dinner: come, Lieutenant Pistol; come, Bardolph: I shall be sent for soon at night.

Enter [*the* LORD CHIEF] JUSTICE *and* PRINCE JOHN [OF LANCASTER, *with* Officers].

Ch. Just. Go, carry Sir John Falstaff to the Fleet:
Take all his company along with him.

Fal. My lord, my lord,—

Ch. Just. I cannot now speak: I will hear you soon.
Take them away.

Pist. Si fortuna me tormenta, spero contenta.

Exeunt [*all but Prince John and the Chief Justice*].

Lan. I like this fair proceeding of the king's:
He hath intent his wonted followers
Shall all be very well provided for;
But all are banish'd till their conversations
Appear more wise and modest to the world.

Ch. Just. And so they are.

Lan. The king hath call'd his parliament, my lord.

Ch. Just. He hath.

Lan. I will lay odds that, ere this year expire,
We bear our civil swords and native fire
As far as France: I heard a bird so sing,
Whose music, to my thinking, pleas'd the king.
Come, will you hence? [*Exeunt.*]

EPILOGUE.

[*Spoken by a* Dancer.]

First my fear; then my courtesy; last my speech. My fear is, your displeasure; my courtesy, my duty; and my speech, to beg your pardons. If you look for a good speech now, you undo me: for what I have to say is of mine own making; and what indeed I should say will, I doubt, prove mine own marring. But to the purpose, and so to the venture. Be it known to you, as it is very well, I was lately here in the end of a displeasing play, to pray your patience for it and to promise you a better. I meant indeed to pay you with this; which, if like an ill venture it come unluckily home, I break, and you, my gentle creditors, lose. Here I promised you I would be and here I commit my body to your mercies: bate me some and I will pay you some and, as most debtors do, promise you infinitely.

If my tongue cannot entreat you to acquit me, will you command me to use my legs? and yet that were but light payment, to dance out of your debt. But a good conscience will make any possible satisfaction, and so would I. All the gentlewomen here have forgiven me: if the gentlemen will not, then the gentlemen do not agree with the gentlewomen, which was never seen before in such an assembly.

One word more, I beseech you. If you be not too much cloyed with fat meat, our humble author will continue the story, with Sir John in it, and make you merry with fair Katharine of France: where, for any thing I know, Falstaff shall die of a sweat, unless already a' be killed with your hard opinions; for Oldcastle died a martyr, and this is not the man. My tongue is weary; when my legs are too, I will bid you good night: and so kneel down before you; but, indeed, to pray for the queen.

94. **colours,** pretenses, with quibble on the meaning "standard" or "enemy." 96. **soon at night,** toward evening. 97. **Fleet,** a famous London prison standing beside Fleet ditch. 102. **Si . . . contenta.** See note on II, iv, 195, above.

EPILOGUE. 1. **courtesy,** curtsy. 10. **displeasing play.** No satisfactory explanation has ever been offered. W. J. Lawrence suggested Ben Jonson's *Every Man out of His Humour*. 13. **venture,** probable allusion to the ventures of merchant vessels. Any voyage might prove a losing venture. **break,** become bankrupt. 16. **bate me some,** let me off from some portion of the debt. 31. **Sir John in it.** Shakespeare evidently intended to introduce Falstaff into a play on Henry v and, subsequent to the writing of this Epilogue, gave up the intention. Coleridge suggested that Falstaff had no place in the new world of glorious enthusiasm and patriotic fervor which opened with the coronation of King Henry v. In any case, this promise in the Epilogue is very hard to reconcile with a theory of the very early composition of *Henry V*. It is not ordinarily thought that the revision from Oldcastle to Falstaff was made very long before the publication of the Q of *1 Henry IV* (1598), and yet a quarto version of *Henry V*, printed in 1600, depicts the death of Falstaff before the opening of the French campaign. 34. **Oldcastle died a martyr.** It is supposed with good reason, since there was an extensive controversy, that the Lord Cobham of the day resented the caricature of his ancestor, Sir John Oldcastle, Lollard martyr under Henry v (1417), and that this Epilogue, together with the change of the name to *Falstaff*, was intended to placate him. 38. **pray for the queen,** a customary way to end plays.

THE LIFE OF KING HENRY THE FIFTH

Henry V (1599) is Shakespeare's culminating statement in the genre of the English history play. Unlike the late and atypical *Henry VIII* (1613), separated from the rest of Shakespeare's history plays by some fourteen years and possibly written in collaboration with John Fletcher, *Henry V* sums up the historical themes with which Shakespeare had been fascinated for an entire decade. The play, first published in a "bad" quarto in 1600, must have been written not long after *2 Henry IV*. To be sure, the play does not entirely fulfill the promise made in *2 Henry IV* to "continue the story, with Sir John in it, and make you merry with fair Katharine of France." Falstaff is missing. As before, Shakespeare apparently saw a grand design to his four-play sequence, but improvised when he came to the writing of each part. Despite these minor alterations, however, *Henry V* is clearly intended to bring to fulfillment the education of a Christian prince, and to illustrate the arts of kingship which Prince Hal had derived from his various experiences and contacts in the earlier plays of the sequence. In a sense, too, *Henry V* sums up the achievement of the English history play not only for Shakespeare but for other popular playwrights as well. The patriotic history play, born in the excitement of the Armada era, had nearly run its course by 1599 and was soon to be supplanted by other dramatic genres such as satire and revenge tragedy.

Henry V has become a controversial play, chiefly because its heroic king can, from the viewpoint of modern history, be looked upon as a warmonger and imperialist. George Bernard Shaw is prominent among those who have recently deplored Henry as a priggish and complacent chauvinist. Historical scholars have argued, on the other hand, that Henry is a perfect model of conduct according to Renaissance notions of statecraft and military leadership. What is Shakespeare's attitude toward his war hero? Does he patriotically sympathize with Henry's condescending attitude toward the French, and his ordering every soldier to kill his French prisoners as an act of reprisal? Or is Shakespeare's admiration qualified by ironic reservations? As usual in Shakespeare, the perspective seems many-sided and delicately balanced. Although the chorus who "interprets" the play for us unabashedly approves of Henry's military posture, we can nevertheless perceive that the grandiose rhetoric of war is consistently undercut by a matter-of-fact revelation of men's self-interested motives. This contrast between rhetorical illusion and political reality extends from the justification of Henry's French campaign to his state marriage with Katharine of France. The irony never amounts to open disillusionment in this play; it is instead the acknowledgment of a special kind of morality pertaining to kingship.

Skill in rhetoric is the key to Henry's success—in defying the French dauphin, in preparing troops for battle, or in wooing the French princess for his queen. As the Archbishop of Canterbury notes approvingly, King Henry's versatility as a rhetorician applies to all the vital disciplines of kingship: Henry can "reason in divinity," "debate of commonwealth affairs," "discourse of war," handle "any cause of policy," and in all such matters speak in "sweet and honey'd sentences" (I,i). Through the arts of language Henry displays piety, learning, administrative sagacity, political cunning, and military intrepidity. Like the contemporary play *Julius Caesar* (1599), *Henry V* is concerned with techniques of persuasion. (The earlier *Richard III* is also a highly rhetorical play, though chiefly through the negative example of tyrannical behavior.) However much we may be swayed emotionally by the rhetoric, however, we also realize that the public figure of Henry v is a mask behind which we can perceive little of the inner man. Only rarely do we glimpse the affable young companion of the *Henry IV* plays. King Henry has accepted the responsibility of playing a political role. It denies him a private and separate identity, even—or especially—in choosing a wife. And it complicates our task of assessing his sincerity of utterance. Is he genuinely pious, or has he merely learned the usefulness of pious utterance in swaying men's hearts? What especially are his motives for going to war against France?

Shakespeare could have begun his play with the stirring scene (I,ii) in which Hal, urged on by his advisers, issues a defiant challenge to the French ambassadors. Instead, Shakespeare treats us to a prior glimpse beneath the patriotic surface. It seems that the Archbishop of Canterbury, threatened with a bill in parliament designed to take away the better half of the church's possessions, has resolved to parry with a counterproposal, whereby the church will "give" Henry a very substantial sum for his French campaign, provided the offensive tax bill can be conveniently forgotten. The archbishop has already been dickering with Henry, and surmises that the plan will work. This revelation is not shocking to us; it is simply politics-as-usual. The faint undercurrent of anticlericalism suggests that Henry is to be admired for putting pressure on his clergy with such success; they are rich enough and can well afford to support the war. In any case, the dramatic effect is to uncover men's real motives as distinguished from their rhetorical statements. When, in the subsequent scene, the archbishop delivers a public lecture on the English claim to France, we know that this learned prelate has a prior and self-interested commitment to the war. His intricate and even impenetrable dynastic argument, which he proclaims to be "as clear as is the summer's sun," gives to the war a veneer of public justification. Henry's questions indicate his political need for the church's endorsement of his cause; he has already sent into France claiming dukedoms, and must have the church's official approval of those claims before he can proceed. He similarly needs the backing of his nobles, who also have their own reasons for approving the campaign. Henry skillfully stage-manages the scene to produce the desired effect of unanimous and patriotic consent.

Although never directly stated, Henry's own motives for going to war must also combine sincere zeal with calculated self-interest. Patriotically, he longs for England to recover the territories in France which she actually governed in the great days of Poitiers and Crécy. Personally, he bristles at the contemptuous challenge of the Dauphin; Hal must still strive to overcome his reputation as a wastrel, and must prove himself worthy of honorable comparison with his great ancestors. Politically (and this motive remains most hidden), King Harry has absorbed his father's sage advice to "busy giddy minds With foreign quarrels" (*2 Henry IV*, IV,v), to blunt political opposition at home by uniting English resentment against a foreign scapegoat.

The exigencies of war do indeed provide Henry with an admirable opportunity for proceeding against his political enemies. He arrests the Earl of Cambridge, Scroop, and Grey at Southampton on charges of conspiring with France. The scene (II,iv) is, for Shakespeare, uncharacteristically one-sided. We are never even told that Cambridge is the chief pretender to the English throne, son of the Duke of York, married to Anne Mortimer, and founder of the Yorkist claim in the York-Lancastrian wars—the sort of rival whom Shakespeare elsewhere portrays with understanding. Instead, the rhetoric of the Chorus to Act II blatantly warns us to expect "hell and treason." These three conspirators, like Judases, have bargained away their king for love of gold. The playwright does not permit them to reveal motives of a more complex nature. Incredibly enough, they are so horrified by their own sins that they are actually grateful to be caught.

Comedy also contributes to the rhetorical image-making of the hero in *Henry V*. The Boarshead crew is on hand, but decorously more distant from Henry than in the earlier history plays. Only briefly and in disguise, on the night before the battle, does the king encounter Pistol. The name of Bardolph comes to Henry as though in recollection of a very distant past, when he hears that Bardolph is about to be executed for stealing from French churches. Henry confirms the sentence: "We would have all such offenders so cut off" (III,vi). Whatever momentary pang of memory Henry may feel, he unhesitatingly remains constant to his action in having banished Falstaff. And, although Shakespeare pleads for our sympathies in the exquisitely touching account of Falstaff's last moments, as seen through the childlike naiveté of Mistress Quickly, we realize that there is no hope of reconciliation between Henry and his old mates. Falstaff is better off where he is, wistfully remembered by those close to him. Pistol, despite his ornamental language, is little better than a boaster, pure coward, and thief. The old Boarshead revelers are now the opportunists of war, troublemakers such as are found in every army, engaging rascals deserving to be cudgeled by more honorable men.

Pistol gets his comeuppance from Captain Fluellen, who in a sense replaces Falstaff as the chief comic figure both in prominence (his role is second in length to that of Henry) and in proximity to the king. Fluellen is a Welshman, like Harry of Monmouth, and is proud of this kinship. Because Fluellen is loyal and valiant, he is a person worthy to be seen in Henry's company. Yet there is none of the brilliant duel of wits previously linking Hal and Falstaff. Fluellen is a "humorous" character, identified at once by such comically exaggerated features as his Welsh accent and mannerisms of speech, his old-fashioned and somewhat fanatical sense of military propriety, and his obsession with the rules of military discipline as derived from ancient writers. As a caricature he is mildly subject to satirical laughter, and there is unquestionably a note of condescension in Hal's habit of playing practical jokes on the captain. Unlike Falstaff, Fluellen utterly lacks a sense of perspective on his own pomposity. He is a zealot for duty, and one feels Hal is taking unfair advantage to pick on one who is such an easy mark for laughter. We suspect that Hal is "using" people again, bolstering his public image as the king with the common touch, borrowing a little Welsh color for myth-making purposes. At the same time, Fluellen is steadfast, upright, a credit to his fellow-countryman Hal. With his fellow-captains from Scotland, Ireland, and England, he demonstrates that Britishers can fight together even if they do antagonize one another with their proud regional customs. Those customs are to be cherished as part of the British character; because Pistol offers gratuitous insult to the Welsh tradition of wearing a leek in the cap on St. Davy's day, he must be thrashed.

As with the comic characters and Hal's political enemies, *Henry V* is rhetorically one-sided in its presentation of the French. Patriotism is a raw emotion, and Henry cannot appeal to it without awakening hostility toward the enemy. (Ironically enough, the great film version of *Henry V* by Laurence Oliver was created during World War II to arouse national feeling more against the Germans than against the French, and with complete success. Any enemy will do in such patriotic moods.) The French are haughty, vastly superior in numbers, envious of one another, contemptuous of their own leadership (especially the Dauphin), treacherous (attacking the boys with the luggage), and craven. The British—"we few, we happy few"—are tired and outnumbered, but invincible, ethically evenhanded in war, and protected by God. Only in Montjoy, Burgundy, and Katharine of France does Shakespeare offer redeeming portraits of the French character. Even here, of course, the terms of hierarchical ascendancy are clear: masculine English dominance, gentle French submissiveness. Katharine becomes "la belle France," depicted in Burgundy's eloquent peacemaking speech as being so much in need of competent management.

Henry woos Katharine with real flair, despite their mutual unstated recognition that their courtship is above all a matter of statecraft in which they must play predetermined roles. The individual within Henry V gives way to the public personality, but he never loses his style. And, if we are less attracted by this successful politician than by the carefree young man, we can still honor Henry's choice of responsible maturity and see that in a sense it is even compassionately self-denying. A king cannot be like other men, and Henry is willing to accept this price of leadership.

THE LIFE OF KING HENRY THE FIFTH

[*Dramatis Personae*

KING HENRY the Fifth.
DUKE OF GLOUCESTER, } *brothers to the King.*
DUKE OF BEDFORD, }
DUKE OF EXETER, *uncle to the King.*
DUKE OF YORK, *cousin to the King.*
EARLS OF SALISBURY, WESTMORELAND, *and* WARWICK.
ARCHBISHOP OF CANTERBURY.
BISHOP OF ELY.
EARL OF CAMBRIDGE.
LORD SCROOP.
SIR THOMAS GREY.
SIR THOMAS ERPINGHAM, GOWER, FLUELLEN, MACMORRIS, JAMY, *officers in King Henry's army.*
BATES, COURT, WILLIAMS, *soldiers in the same.*
PISTOL, NYM, BARDOLPH.
Boy.
A Herald.

CHARLES the Sixth, King of France.
LEWIS, the Dauphin.
DUKES OF BURGUNDY, ORLEANS, BERRI, *and* BRITTAINE.
The Constable of France.
RAMBURES *and* GRANDPRÉ, *French Lords.*
Governor of Harfleur.
MONTJOY, *a French Herald.*
Ambassadors to the King of England.

ISABEL, Queen of France.
KATHARINE, *daughter to Charles and Isabel.*
ALICE, *a lady attending on her.*
Hostess of a tavern in Eastcheap, *formerly* Mistress Quickly, *and now married to Pistol.*

Lords, Ladies, Officers, Soldiers, Citizens, Messengers, *and* Attendants.

Chorus.

SCENE: *England; afterwards France.*]

[PROLOGUE.]

Enter [Chorus *as*] *Prologue.*

[*Chor.*] O for a Muse of fire, that would ascend
The brightest heaven of invention,
A kingdom for a stage, princes to act
And monarchs to behold the swelling scene!
Then should the warlike Harry, like himself,
Assume the port of Mars; and at his heels,
Leash'd in like hounds, should famine, sword and fire
Crouch for employment. But pardon, gentles all,
The flat unraised spirits that hath dar'd
On this unworthy scaffold to bring forth
So great an object: can this cockpit hold
The vasty fields of France? or may we cram
Within this wooden O the very casques
That did affright the air at Agincourt?
O, pardon! since a crooked figure may
Attest in little place a million;
And let us, ciphers to this great accompt,
On your imaginary forces work.
Suppose within the girdle of these walls
Are now confin'd two mighty monarchies,
Whose high upreared and abutting fronts
The perilous narrow ocean parts asunder:
Piece out our imperfections with your thoughts;
Into a thousand parts divide one man,
And make imaginary puissance;
Think, when we talk of horses, that you see them
Printing their proud hoofs i' th' receiving earth;
For 'tis your thoughts that now must deck our kings,
Carry them here and there; jumping o'er times,
Turning th' accomplishment of many years
Into an hour-glass: for the which supply,
Admit me Chorus to this history;
Who prologue-like your humble patience pray,
Gently to hear, kindly to judge, our play. *Exit.*

ACT I.

SCENE I. [*London. An ante-chamber in the* KING'S *palace.*]

Enter the two bishops, [*the* ARCHBISHOP] OF CANTERBURY *and* [*the* BISHOP OF] ELY.

Cant. My lord, I'll tell you; that self bill is urg'd,
Which in th' eleventh year of the last king's reign
Was like, and had indeed against us pass'd,
But that the scambling and unquiet time
Did push it out of farther question.
Ely. But how, my lord, shall we resist it now?
Cant. It must be thought on. If it pass against us,
We lose the better half of our possession:
For all the temporal lands which men devout
By testament have given to the church
Would they strip from us; being valu'd thus:
As much as would maintain, to the king's honour,
Full fifteen earls and fifteen hundred knights,
Six thousand and two hundred good esquires;
And, to relief of lazars and weak age,
Of indigent faint souls past corporal toil,
A hundred almshouses right well supplied;
And to the coffers of the king beside,
A thousand pounds by th' year: thus runs the bill.
Ely. This would drink deep.
Cant. 'Twould drink the cup and all.

PROLOGUE. 1. **Muse of fire.** Of the four elements, earth, air, fire, and water, fire is the most sublime and mounting. 6. **port,** bearing. 7. **famine, sword and fire.** According to Holinshed, Henry told the people of Rouen that Bellona, the goddess of battle, had three handmaidens attendant upon her called "blood, fire, and famine." 10. **scaffold,** stage. 11. **cockpit.** Elizabethan theatres were shaped rather like arenas for cockfighting. 13. **O,** refers to a round theatre such as the Globe. **casques,** helmets. 16. **Attest,** stand for. 17. **accompt,** sum total; also, account. 18. **imaginary forces,** forces of imagination. 22. **narrow ocean,** the English Channel. 31. **supply,** service.
ACT I. SCENE I. 1. **self,** same. 3. **like,** likely. 4. **scambling,** unsettled. 15. **lazars,** lepers.

Ely. But what prevention?
Cant. The king is full of grace and fair regard.
Ely. And a true lover of the holy church.
Cant. The courses of his youth promis'd it not.
The breath no sooner left his father's body,
But that his wildness, mortified in him,
Seem'd to die too; yea, at that very moment
Consideration, like an angel, came
And whipp'd th' offending Adam out of him,
Leaving his body as a paradise,
T' envelope and contain celestial spirits.
Never was such a sudden scholar made;
Never came reformation in a flood,
With such a heady currance, scouring faults;
Nor never Hydra-headed wilfulness
So soon did lose his seat and all at once
As in this king.
Ely. We are blessed in the change.
Cant. Hear him but reason in divinity,
And all-admiring with an inward wish
You would desire the king were made a prelate:
Hear him debate of commonwealth affairs,
You would say it hath been all in all his study:
List his discourse of war, and you shall hear
A fearful battle rend'red you in music:
Turn him to any cause of policy,
The Gordian knot of it he will unloose,
Familiar as his garter: that, when he speaks,
The air, a charter'd libertine, is still,
And the mute wonder lurketh in men's ears,
To steal his sweet and honey'd sentences;
So that the art and practic part of life
Must be the mistress to this theoric:
Which is a wonder how his grace should glean it,
Since his addiction was to courses vain,
His companies unletter'd, rude and shallow,
His hours fill'd up with riots, banquets, sports,
And never noted in him any study,
Any retirement, any sequestration
From open haunts and popularity.
Ely. The strawberry grows underneath the nettle
And wholesome berries thrive and ripen best
Neighbour'd by fruit of baser quality:
And so the prince obscur'd his contemplation
Under the veil of wildness; which, no doubt,
Grew like the summer grass, fastest by night,
Unseen, yet crescive in his faculty.
Cant. It must be so; for miracles are ceas'd;
And therefore we must needs admit the means
How things are perfected.
Ely. But, my good lord,
How now for mitigation of this bill
Urg'd by the commons? Doth his majesty
Incline to it, or no?
Cant. He seems indifferent,
Or rather swaying more upon our part
Than cherishing th' exhibiters against us;
For I have made an offer to his majesty,
Upon our spiritual convocation
And in regard of causes now in hand,
Which I have open'd to his grace at large,
As touching France, to give a greater sum
Than ever at one time the clergy yet
Did to his predecessors part withal.
Ely. How did this offer seem receiv'd, my lord?
Cant. With good acceptance of his majesty;
Save that there was not time enough to hear,
As I perceiv'd his grace would fain have done,
The severals and unhidden passages
Of his true titles to some certain dukedoms
And generally to the crown and seat of France
Deriv'd from Edward, his great-grandfather.
Ely. What was th' impediment that broke this off?
Cant. The French ambassador upon that instant
Crav'd audience; and the hour, I think, is come
To give him hearing: is it four o'clock?
Ely. It is.
Cant. Then go we in, to know his embassy;
Which I could with a ready guess declare,
Before the Frenchman speak a word of it.
Ely. I'll wait upon you, and I long to hear it. *Exeunt*.

[SCENE II. *The same. The Presence chamber.*]

Enter the KING, HUMPHREY [DUKE OF GLOUCESTER], BEDFORD, CLARENCE, WARWICK, WESTMORELAND, *and* EXETER [*with* Attendants].

K. Hen. Where is my gracious Lord of Canterbury?
Exe. Not here in presence.
K. Hen. Send for him, good uncle.
West. Shall we call in th' ambassador, my liege?
K. Hen. Not yet, my cousin: we would be resolv'd,
Before we hear him, of some things of weight
That task our thoughts, concerning us and France.

Enter two bishops [*the* ARCHBISHOP OF CANTERBURY *and the* BISHOP OF ELY].

Cant. God and his angels guard your sacred throne
And make you long become it!
K. Hen. Sure, we thank you.
My learned lord, we pray you to proceed
And justly and religiously unfold
Why the law Salique that they have in France
Or should, or should not, bar us in our claim:
And God forbid, my dear and faithful lord,
That you should fashion, wrest, or bow your reading,
Or nicely charge your understanding soul
With opening titles miscreate, whose right
Suits not in native colours with the truth;
For God doth know how many now in health
Shall drop their blood in approbation
Of what your reverence shall incite us to.
Therefore take heed how you impawn our person,
How you awake our sleeping sword of war:
We charge you, in the name of God, take heed;
For never two such kingdoms did contend
Without much fall of blood; whose guiltless drops

28. **Consideration,** meditation. 29. **offending Adam,** original sin. Henry's offenses have been driven out of him as Adam was driven out of Paradise. 34. **heady currance,** headlong current. 35. **Hydra-headed,** an allusion to the Lernaean Hydra overcome by Hercules. 38-47. **Hear ... garter.** These lines enumerate the principal subjects of princely education. Note that policy (statecraft) as well as war held a recognized place. 46. **Gordian knot,** an allusion to the knot of Gordius, of which it was foretold that whoever should untie it would rule Asia. Alexander solved the problem by cutting the knot. 47. **Familiar,** familiarly. **that,** so that. 48. **charter'd libertine,** one privileged to lead a dissolute life. 49. **wonder,** wonderer. 50. **sentences,** sayings. 51. **practic,** practical. 52. **mistress,** teacher. **theoric,** theory. 55. **companies,** companions. 59. **popularity,** intercourse with low society. 63. **obscur'd,** concealed. 66. **crescive,** tending to grow. **his faculty,** its nature. 74. **exhibiters,** those who introduce bills in Parliament. 76. **Upon,** on behalf of. **convocation,** formal assembly of

Are every one a woe, a sore complaint
'Gainst him whose wrongs gives edge unto the swords
That makes such waste in brief mortality.
Under this conjuration speak, my lord;
For we will hear, note and believe in heart
That what you speak is in your conscience wash'd
As pure as sin with baptism.
Cant. Then hear me, gracious sovereign, and you peers,
That owe yourselves, your lives and services
To this imperial throne. There is no bar
To make against your highness' claim to France
But this, which they produce from Pharamond,
'In terram Salicam mulieres ne succedant:'
'No woman shall succeed in Salique land:'
Which Salique land the French unjustly glose
To be the realm of France, and Pharamond
The founder of this law and female bar.
Yet their own authors faithfully affirm
That the land Salique is in Germany,
Between the floods of Sala and of Elbe;
Where Charles the Great, having subdu'd the Saxons,
There left behind and settled certain French;
Who, holding in disdain the German women
For some dishonest manners of their life,
Establish'd then this law; to wit, no female
Should be inheritrix in Salique land:
Which Salique, as I said, 'twixt Elbe and Sala,
Is at this day in Germany call'd Meisen.
Then doth it well appear the Salique law
Was not devised for the realm of France;
Nor did the French possess the Salique land
Until four hundred one and twenty years
After defunction of King Pharamond,
Idly suppos'd the founder of this law;
Who died within the year of our redemption
Four hundred twenty-six; and Charles the Great
Subdu'd the Saxons, and did seat the French
Beyond the river Sala, in the year
Eight hundred five. Besides, their writers say,
King Pepin, which deposed Childeric,
Did, as heir general, being descended
Of Blithild, which was daughter to King Clothair,
Make claim and title to the crown of France.
Hugh Capet also, who usurp'd the crown
Of Charles the duke of Lorraine, sole heir male
Of the true line and stock of Charles the Great,
To find his title with some shows of truth,
Though, in pure truth, it was corrupt and naught,
Convey'd himself as heir to th' Lady Lingare,
Daughter to Charlemain, who was the son
To Lewis the emperor, and Lewis the son
Of Charles the Great. Also King Lewis the Tenth,
Who was sole heir to the usurper Capet,
Could not keep quiet in his conscience,
Wearing the crown of France, till satisfied
That fair Queen Isabel, his grandmother,
Was lineal of the Lady Ermengare,
Daughter to Charles the foresaid duke of Lorraine:
By the which marriage the line of Charles the Great
Was re-united to the crown of France.
So that, as clear as is the summer's sun,
King Pepin's title and Hugh Capet's claim,
King Lewis his satisfaction, all appear
To hold in right and title of the female:
So do the kings of France unto this day;
Howbeit they would hold up this Salique law
To bar your highness claiming from the female,
And rather choose to hide them in a net
Than amply to imbar their crooked titles
Usurp'd from you and your progenitors.
K. Hen. May I with right and conscience make this claim?
Cant. The sin upon my head, dread sovereign!
For in the book of Numbers is it writ,
When the man dies, let the inheritance
Descend unto the daughter. Gracious lord,
Stand for your own; unwind your bloody flag;
Look back into your mighty ancestors:
Go, my dread lord, to your great-grandsire's tomb,
From whom you claim; invoke his warlike spirit,
And your great-uncle's, Edward the Black Prince,
Who on the French ground play'd a tragedy,
Making defeat on the full power of France,
Whiles his most mighty father on a hill
Stood smiling to behold his lion's whelp
Forage in blood of French nobility.
O noble English, that could entertain
With half their forces the full pride of France
And let another half stand laughing by,
All out of work and cold for action!
Ely. Awake remembrance of these valiant dead
And with your puissant arm renew their feats:
You are their heir; you sit upon their throne;
The blood and courage that renowned them
Runs in your veins; and my thrice-puissant liege
Is in the very May-morn of his youth,
Ripe for exploits and mighty enterprises.
Exe. Your brother kings and monarchs of the earth
Do all expect that you should rouse yourself,
As did the former lions of your blood.
West. They know your grace hath cause and means and might;
So hath your highness; never king of England
Had nobles richer and more loyal subjects,
Whose hearts have left their bodies here in England
And lie pavilion'd in the fields of France.
Cant. O, let their bodies follow, my dear liege,
With blood and sword and fire to win your right;
In aid whereof we of the spiritualty
Will raise your highness such a mighty sum
As never did the clergy at one time
Bring in to any of your ancestors.
K. Hen. We must not only arm t' invade the French,
But lay down our proportions to defend
Against the Scot, who will make road upon us
With all advantages.

the clergy. 78. **open'd,** revealed. 79. **to give a greater sum.** An underlying motive of the churchmen in urging on the French war is here disclosed. 86. **unhidden passages,** obvious lines of descent.

Scene ii. 12. **Or,** either. 15. **nicely,** subtly. 16. **opening,** examining. **miscreate,** improperly framed. 21. **impawn,** pledge. 40. **glose,** explain. 58. **defunction,** death. 61. **Charles the Great,** Charlemagne. 66. **heir general,** heir through male or female line. 72. **find,** to provide or trace out. 75. **Charlemain,** Holinshed's and Hall's error for Charles the Bold. 82. **lineal of,** descended from. 88. **Lewis his,** Lewis'. 93. **net,** possibly expressive of something easily seen through; also explained as "a tangle of contradictions." 94. **imbar,** bar in, secure, or bar claim to. 98. **Numbers.** See Numbers 27:8. 107. **defeat,** ruin; see glossary. 108. **his most mighty father.** Holinshed gives the story of Edward iii's watching the Battle of Crécy (1346) as recounted in the text. 114. **cold for action,** cold for want of action. 137. **lay down our proportions,** set down the proper numbers.

Cant. They of those marches, gracious sovereign,
Shall be a wall sufficient to defend
Our inland from the pilfering borderers.
K. Hen. We do not mean the coursing snatchers only,
But fear the main intendment of the Scot,
Who hath been still a giddy neighbour to us;
For you shall read that my great-grandfather
Never went with his forces into France
But that the Scot on his unfurnish'd kingdom
Came pouring, like the tide into a breach,
With ample and brim fulness of his force,
Galling the gleaned land with hot assays,
Girding with grievous siege castles and towns;
That England, being empty of defence,
Hath shook and trembled at th' ill neighbourhood.
Cant. She hath been then more fear'd than harm'd, my liege;
For hear her but exampled by herself:
When all her chivalry hath been in France
And she a mourning widow of her nobles,
She hath herself not only well defended
But taken and impounded as a stray
The King of Scots; whom she did send to France,
To fill King Edward's fame with prisoner kings
And make her chronicle as rich with praise
As is the ooze and bottom of the sea
With sunken wrack and sumless treasuries.
Ely. But there 's a saying very old and true,
'If that you will France win,
Then with Scotland first begin:'
For once the eagle England being in prey,
To her unguarded nest the weasel Scot
Comes sneaking and so sucks her princely eggs,
Playing the mouse in absence of the cat,
To tame and havoc more than she can eat.
Exe. It follows then the cat must stay at home:
Yet that is but a crush'd necessity,
Since we have locks to safeguard necessaries,
And pretty traps to catch the petty thieves.
While that the armed hand doth fight abroad,
Th' advised head defends itself at home;
For government, though high and low and lower,
Put into parts, doth keep in one consent,
Congreeing in a full and natural close,
Like music.
Cant. Therefore doth heaven divide
The state of man in divers functions,
Setting endeavour in continual motion;
To which is fixed, as an aim or butt,
Obedience: for so work the honey-bees,
Creatures that by a rule in nature teach
The act of order to a peopled kingdom.
They have a king and officers of sorts;
Where some, like magistrates, correct at home,
Others, like merchants, venture trade abroad,
Others, like soldiers, armed in their stings,
Make boot upon the summer's velvet buds,
Which pillage they with merry march bring home
To the tent-royal of their emperor;
Who, busied in his majesty, surveys
The singing masons building roofs of gold,
The civil citizens kneading up the honey,
The poor mechanic porters crowding in
Their heavy burdens at his narrow gate,
The sad-ey'd justice, with his surly hum,
Delivering o'er to executors pale
The lazy yawning drone. I this infer,
That many things, having full reference
To one consent, may work contrariously:
As many arrows, loosed several ways,
Come to one mark; as many ways meet in one town;
As many fresh streams meet in one salt sea;
As many lines close in the dial's centre;
So may a thousand actions, once afoot,
End in one purpose, and be all well borne
Without defeat. Therefore to France, my liege.
Divide your happy England into four;
Whereof take you one quarter into France,
And you withal shall make all Gallia shake.
If we, with thrice such powers left at home,
Cannot defend our own doors from the dog,
Let us be worried and our nation lose
The name of hardiness and policy.
K. Hen. Call in the messengers sent from the Dauphin. [*Exeunt some Attendants.*]
Now are we well resolv'd; and, by God's help,
And yours, the noble sinews of our power,
France being ours, we'll bend it to our awe,
Or break it all to pieces: or there we'll sit,
Ruling in large and ample empery
O'er France and all her almost kingly dukedoms,
Or lay these bones in an unworthy urn,
Tombless, with no remembrance over them:
Either our history shall with full mouth
Speak freely of our acts, or else our grave,
Like Turkish mute, shall have a tongueless mouth,
Not worshipp'd with a waxen epitaph.

Enter Ambassadors *of France* [*attended*].

Now are we well prepar'd to know the pleasure
Of our fair cousin Dauphin; for we hear
Your greeting is from him, not from the king.
First Amb. May 't please your majesty to give us leave
Freely to render what we have in charge;
Or shall we sparingly show you far off
The Dauphin's meaning and our embassy?
K. Hen. We are no tyrant, but a Christian king;
Unto whose grace our passion is as subject
As is our wretches fett'red in our prisons:
Therefore with frank and with uncurbed plainness
Tell us the Dauphin's mind.
First Amb. Thus, then, in few.
Your highness, lately sending into France,
Did claim some certain dukedoms, in the right
Of your great predecessor, King Edward the Third.
In answer of which claim, the prince our master
Says that you savour too much of your youth,
And bids you be advis'd there 's nought in France

140. **marches,** here, northern borderlands. 143. **coursing snatchers,** mounted raiders. 144. **intendment,** plan. 151. **gleaned,** stripped (of defenders). **assays,** assaults. 160. **impounded as a stray.** David II was captured and imprisoned in 1346 while Edward III was in France. 173. **tame,** attame, broach, cut into. **havoc,** the signal for slaughter; here, destroy. 175. **crush'd,** forced. 182. **Congreeing,** agreeing together. **close,** musical cadence. 184-204. **The state . . . drone.** This elaborate comparison of human society to a hive of bees is a familiar Renaissance theme. It expresses the current political theory of the naturalness of rank and class and the necessity of order. 200. **mechanic,** engaged in manual labor. 202. **sad-ey'd,** grave-eyed. 203. **executors,** executioners. 216. **Gallia,** Latin name for France. 220. **hardiness and policy,** bravery and statesmanship, the two highest virtues of a king. 221. **Dauphin,** heir apparent to the French throne. 225. **or,** either. 226. **empery,** dominion. 233. **Not . . . epitaph,** i.e., with not even so much as a wax (as opposed to bronze) epitaph; one

That can be with a nimble galliard won;
You cannot revel into dukedoms there.
He therefore sends you, meeter for your spirit,
This tun of treasure; and, in lieu of this,
Desires you let the dukedoms that you claim
Hear no more of you. This the Dauphin speaks.

K. Hen. What treasure, uncle?

Exe. Tennis-balls, my liege.

K. Hen. We are glad the Dauphin is so pleasant with us;
His present and your pains we thank you for:
When we have match'd our rackets to these balls,
We will, in France, by God's grace, play a set
Shall strike his father's crown into the hazard.
Tell him he hath made a match with such a wrangler
That all the courts of France will be disturb'd
With chaces. And we understand him well,
How he comes o'er us with our wilder days,
Not measuring what use we made of them.
We never valu'd this poor seat of England;
And therefore, living hence, did give ourself
To barbarous license; as 'tis ever common
That men are merriest when they are from home.
But tell the Dauphin I will keep my state,
Be like a king and show my sail of greatness
When I do rouse me in my throne of France:
For that I have laid by my majesty
And plodded like a man for working-days,
But I will rise there with so full a glory
That I will dazzle all the eyes of France,
Yea, strike the Dauphin blind to look on us.
And tell the pleasant prince this mock of his
Hath turn'd his balls to gun-stones; and his soul
Shall stand sore charged for the wasteful vengeance
That shall fly with them: for many a thousand widows
Shall this his mock mock out of their dear husbands;
Mock mothers from their sons, mock castles down;
And some are yet ungotten and unborn
That shall have cause to curse the Dauphin's scorn.
But this lies all within the will of God,
To whom I do appeal; and in whose name
Tell you the Dauphin I am coming on,
To venge me as I may and to put forth
My rightful hand in a well-hallow'd cause.
So get you hence in peace; and tell the Dauphin
His jest will savour but of shallow wit,
When thousands weep more than did laugh at it.
Convey them with safe conduct. Fare you well.

Exeunt Ambassadors [and Attendants].

Exe. This was a merry message.

K. Hen. We hope to make the sender blush at it.
Therefore, my lords, omit no happy hour
That may give furth'rance to our expedition;
For we have now no thought in us but France,
Save those to God, that run before our business.
Therefore let our proportions for these wars
Be soon collected and all things thought upon
That may with reasonable swiftness add
More feathers to our wings; for, God before,
We'll chide this Dauphin at his father's door.
Therefore let every man now task his thought,
That this fair action may on foot be brought.

Exeunt.

[ACT II.

PROLOGUE.]

Flourish. Enter Chorus.

[*Chor.*] Now all the youth of England are on fire,
And silken dalliance in the wardrobe lies:
Now thrive the armourers, and honour's thought
Reigns solely in the breast of every man:
They sell the pasture now to buy the horse,
Following the mirror of all Christian kings,
With winged heels, as English Mercuries.
For now sits Expectation in the air,
And hides a sword from hilts unto the point
With crowns imperial, crowns and coronets,
Promis'd to Harry and his followers.
The French, advis'd by good intelligence
Of this most dreadful preparation,
Shake in their fear and with pale policy
Seek to divert the English purposes.
O England! model to thy inward greatness,
Like little body with a mighty heart,
What mightst thou do, that honour would thee do,
Were all thy children kind and natural!
But see thy fault! France hath in thee found out
A nest of hollow bosoms, which he fills
With treacherous crowns; and three corrupted men,
One, Richard Earl of Cambridge, and the second,
Henry Lord Scroop of Masham, and the third,
Sir Thomas Grey, knight, of Northumberland,
Have, for the gilt of France,—O guilt indeed!—
Confirm'd conspiracy with fearful France;
And by their hands this grace of kings must die,
If hell and treason hold their promises,
Ere he take ship for France, and in Southampton.
Linger your patience on; †and we'll digest
Th' abuse of distance; force a play.
The sum is paid; the traitors are agreed;
The king is set from London; and the scene
Is now transported, gentles, to Southampton;
There is the playhouse now, there must you sit:
And thence to France shall we convey you safe,
And bring you back, charming the narrow seas
To give you gentle pass; for, if we may,
We'll not offend one stomach with our play.
But, till the king come forth, and not till then,
Unto Southampton do we shift our scene. *Exit.*

[SCENE I. *London. A street.*]

Enter Corporal NYM *and* Lieutenant BARDOLPH.

Bard. Well met, Corporal Nym.

Nym. Good morrow, Lieutenant Bardolph.

Bard. What, are Ancient Pistol and you friends yet?

Nym. For my part, I care not: I say little; but when

easily effaced. 252. **galliard,** a lively dance. 255. **tun,** a cask. Holinshed speaks of "a barrel of Paris balls." 263. **hazard,** in tennis of that time, an opening in the wall; hitting the ball into it scored a point. 264. **wrangler,** stubborn adversary. 266. **chaces.** A *chace* is the second bound of a ball which the opponent fails to return; obvious pun on "chase." 267. **comes o'er,** taunts. 269. **seat,** throne. 270. **living hence,** not frequenting the royal court. 282. **gun-stones,** cannon balls.

ACT II. PROLOGUE. 18. **would,** would have. 22. **crowns,** crown pieces. 26. **gilt,** gold. 31-32. **digest Th' abuse of distance,** overcome the difficulties of representing distance. 32. **force a play,** fill out the actions of a play in spite of difficulties. 41-42. **But . . . scene,** i.e., the scene will be shifted to Southampton after a scene in London.

SCENE I. 3. **Ancient,** ensign.

time shall serve, there shall be smiles; but that shall be as it may. I dare not fight; but I will wink and hold out mine iron: it is a simple one; but what though? it will toast cheese, and it will endure cold as another man's sword will: and there 's an end.

Bard. I will bestow a breakfast to make you friends; and we'll be all three sworn brothers to France: let 't be so, good Corporal Nym.

Nym. Faith, I will live so long as I may, that 's the certain of it; and when I cannot live any longer, I will do as I may: that is my rest, that is the rendezvous of it.

Bard. It is certain, corporal, that he is married to Nell Quickly: and certainly she did you wrong; for you were troth-plight to her.

Nym. I cannot tell: things must be as they may: men may sleep, and they may have their throats about them at that time; and some say knives have edges. It must be as it may: though patience be a tired mare, yet she will plod. There must be conclusions. Well, I cannot tell.

Enter PISTOL *and* [Hostess] QUICKLY.

Bard. Here comes Ancient Pistol and his wife: good corporal, be patient here.

Nym. How now, mine host Pistol!

Pist. Base tike, call'st thou me host?
Now, by this hand, I swear, I scorn the term;
Nor shall my Nell keep lodgers.

Host. No, by my troth, not long; for we cannot lodge and board a dozen or fourteen gentlewomen that live honestly by the prick of their needles, but it will be thought we keep a bawdy house straight. [*Nym and Pistol draw.*] O well a day, Lady, if he be not drawn now! we shall see wilful adultery and murder committed.

Bard. Good lieutenant! good corporal! offer nothing here.

Nym. Pish!

Pist. Pish for thee, Iceland dog! thou prick-ear'd cur of Iceland!

Host. Good Corporal Nym, show thy valour, and put up your sword.

Nym. Will you shog off? I would have you solus.

Pist. 'Solus,' egregious dog? O viper vile!
The 'solus' in thy most mervailous face;
The 'solus' in thy teeth, and in thy throat,
And in thy hateful lungs, yea, in thy maw, perdy,
And, which is worse, within thy nasty mouth!
I do retort the 'solus' in thy bowels;
For I can take, and Pistol's cock is up,
And flashing fire will follow.

Nym. I am not Barbason; you cannot conjure me. I have an humour to knock you indifferently well. If you grow foul with me, Pistol, I will scour you with my rapier, as I may, in fair terms: if you would walk off, I would prick your guts a little, in good terms, as I may: and that 's the humour of it.

Pist. O braggart vile and damned furious wight!
The grave doth gape, and doting death is near;
Therefore exhale.

Bard. Hear me, hear me what I say: he that strikes the first stroke, I'll run him up to the hilts, as I am a soldier. [*Draws.*]

Pist. An oath of mickle might; and fury shall abate.
Give me thy fist, thy fore-foot to me give:
Thy spirits are most tall.

Nym. I will cut thy throat, one time or other, in fair terms: that is the humour of it.

Pist. 'Couple a gorge!'
That is the word. I thee defy again.
O hound of Crete, think'st thou my spouse to get?
No; to the spital go,
And from the powdering-tub of infamy
Fetch forth the lazar kite of Cressid's kind,
Doll Tearsheet she by name, and her espouse:
I have, and I will hold, the quondam Quickly
For the only she; and—pauca, there 's enough.
Go to.

Enter the Boy.

Boy. Mine host Pistol, you must come to my master, and you, hostess: he is very sick, and would to bed. Good Bardolph, put thy face between his sheets, and do the office of a warming-pan. Faith, he 's very ill.

Bard. Away, you rogue!

Host. By my troth, he'll yield the crow a pudding one of these days. The king has killed his heart. Good husband, come home presently.

Exit [*with Boy*].

Bard. Come, shall I make you two friends? We must to France together: why the devil should we keep knives to cut one another's throats?

Pist. Let floods o'erswell, and fiends for food howl on!

Nym. You'll pay me the eight shillings I won of you at betting?

Pist. Base is the slave that pays.

Nym. That now I will have: that 's the humour of it.

Pist. As manhood shall compound: push home.

[*They*] *draw.*

Bard. By this sword, he that makes the first thrust, I'll kill him; by this sword, I will. [*Draws.*]

Pist. Sword is an oath, and oaths must have their course. [*Sheathes his sword.*]

Bard. Corporal Nym, an thou wilt be friends, be friends: an thou wilt not, why, then, be enemies with me too. Prithee, put up.

Nym. I shall have my eight shillings I won of you at betting?

Pist. A noble shalt thou have, and present pay;
And liquor likewise will I give to thee,
And friendship shall combine, and brotherhood:
I'll live by Nym, and Nym shall live by me;
Is not this just? for I shall sutler be
Unto the camp, and profits will accrue.
Give me thy hand. [*Nym sheathes his sword.*]

Nym. I shall have my noble?

8. **wink,** shut the eyes; also, give a significant look. **iron,** sword. 10. **endure cold,** i.e., doesn't mind being drawn from its sheath. 11. **there's an end,** that's all there is to it. 18. **rendezvous,** last resort. 25-26. **though . . . plod,** i.e., patient persistence will ultimately achieve its goal. (Nym hints at violence toward Pistol.) 31. **tike,** cur. 36. **prick,** with a bawdy double meaning, as also in *Pistol's cock*, l. 55. 38. **Lady,** an oath by the Virgin Mary. 40. **adultery,** for "battery" (?). 44. **Iceland dog.** Pistol's humor is to use extravagant epithets (this being one), tags from current plays, and scraps of foreign languages. 47. **shog,** slang or cant for "move." 55. **take,** take fire; also, cause harm by my spell. 57. **Barbason,** the name of a fiend. Pistol's preceding speech is a parody of the service of exorcism. 66. **exhale,** draw (sword). 70. **mickle might,** great power. 75. **'Couple a gorge!'** *Coupe la gorge* Cut the throat! 77. **hound of Crete,** parallel to *Iceland dog* (l. 44). 78. **spital,** hospital. 79. **powdering-tub,** tub used for salting beef; here, alluding to a method of curing venereal disease. 80. **lazar kite,** i.e., leprous whore. (A kite is a bird of prey.) **Cressid's kind.** Cressida was proverbial as a courtesan. She is represented in

Pist. In cash most justly paid.
Nym. Well, then, that 's the humour of 't.

Enter Hostess.

Host. As ever you came of women, come in quickly to Sir John. Ah, poor heart! he is so shaked of a burning quotidian tertian, that it is most lamentable to behold. Sweet men, come to him.

Nym. The king hath run bad humours on the knight; that 's the even of it.

Pist. Nym, thou hast spoke the right;
His heart is fracted and corroborate.

Nym. The king is a good king: but it must be as it may; he passes some humours and careers.

Pist. Let us condole the knight; for, lambkins, we will live. [*Exeunt.*]

[SCENE II. *Southampton. A council-chamber.*]

Enter EXETER, BEDFORD, *and* WESTMORELAND.

Bed. 'Fore God, his grace is bold, to trust these traitors.
Exe. They shall be apprehended by and by.
West. How smooth and even they do bear themselves!
As if allegiance in their bosoms sat,
Crowned with faith and constant loyalty.
Bed. The king hath note of all that they intend,
By interception which they dream not of.
Exe. Nay, but the man that was his bedfellow,
Whom he hath dull'd and cloy'd with gracious favours,
That he should, for a foreign purse, so sell
His sovereign's life to death and treachery!

Sound trumpets. Enter the KING, SCROOP, CAMBRIDGE, *and* GREY [, Lords, *and* Attendants].

K. Hen. Now sits the wind fair, and we will aboard.
My Lord of Cambridge, and my kind Lord of Masham,
And you, my gentle knight, give me your thoughts:
Think you not that the pow'rs we bear with us
Will cut their passage through the force of France,
Doing the execution and the act
For which we have in head assembled them?
Scroop. No doubt, my liege, if each man do his best.
K. Hen. I doubt not that; since we are well persuaded
We carry not a heart with us from hence
That grows not in a fair consent with ours,
Nor leave not one behind that doth not wish
Success and conquest to attend on us.
Cam. Never was monarch better fear'd and lov'd
Than is your majesty: there 's not, I think, a subject
That sits in heart-grief and uneasiness
Under the sweet shade of your government.
Grey. True: those that were your father's enemies
Have steep'd their galls in honey and do serve you
With hearts create of duty and of zeal.
K. Hen. We therefore have great cause of thankfulness;
And shall forget the office of our hand,
Sooner than quittance of desert and merit
According to the weight and worthiness.
Scroop. So service shall with steeled sinews toil,
And labour shall refresh itself with hope,
To do your grace incessant services.
K. Hen. We judge no less. Uncle of Exeter,
Enlarge the man committed yesterday,
That rail'd against our person: we consider
It was excess of wine that set him on;
And on his more advice we pardon him.
Scroop. That 's mercy, but too much security:
Let him be punish'd, sovereign, lest example
Breed, by his sufferance, more of such a kind.
K. Hen. O, let us yet be merciful.
Cam. So may your highness, and yet punish too.
Grey. Sir,
You show great mercy, if you give him life,
After the taste of much correction.
K. Hen. Alas, your too much love and care of me
Are heavy orisons 'gainst this poor wretch!
If little faults, proceeding on distemper,
Shall not be wink'd at, how shall we stretch our eye
When capital crimes, chew'd, swallow'd and digested,
Appear before us? We'll yet enlarge that man,
Though Cambridge, Scroop and Grey, in their dear care
And tender preservation of our person,
Would have him punish'd. And now to our French causes:
Who are the late commissioners?
Cam. I one, my lord:
Your highness bade me ask for it to-day.
Scroop. So did you me, my liege.
Grey. And I, my royal sovereign.
K. Hen. Then, Richard Earl of Cambridge, there is yours;
There yours, Lord Scroop of Masham; and, sir knight,
Grey of Northumberland, this same is yours:
Read them; and know, I know your worthiness.
My Lord of Westmoreland, and uncle Exeter,
We will aboard to night. Why, how now, gentlemen!
What see you in those papers that you lose
So much complexion? Look ye, how they change!
Their cheeks are paper. Why, what read you there,
That hath so cowarded and chas'd your blood
Out of appearance?
Cam. I do confess my fault;
And do submit me to your highness' mercy.
Grey., *Scroop.* To which we all appeal.
K. Hen. The mercy that was quick in us but late,
By your own counsel is suppress'd and kill'd:
You must not dare, for shame, to talk of mercy;
For your own reasons turn into your bosoms,

Robert Henryson's *Testament of Cresseid* as being rejected by Diomede and infected with leprosy. 82. **quondam,** former. 83. **pauca,** in brief. 88. **face.** Bardolph's face was fiery with drinking. 91. **crow,** i.e., eater of carrion. 112. **noble,** a gold coin. 116. **sutler,** seller of liquor and provisions to the solders. 124. **quotidian tertian.** Mistress Quickly confuses terms; a *quotidian* fever was one that came daily; a *tertian* fever, one that came every three days. 130. **fracted and corroborate.** Like the others, Pistol believes Falstaff's heart is broken by the king's rejection of him. *Corroborate* may however mean repentant in a religious sense. 132-133. **he . . . careers,** he indulges in some humors and pranks. *Career* means the dashing back and forward of a horse at full speed.

SCENE II. 30. **galls,** resentment. 34. **quittance,** requital. 43. **more advice,** thinking better of it. 53. **orisons,** prayers. 55. **stretch our eye,** wink at, seem not to see. 61. **late,** newly appointed. 63. **it,** i.e., my commission.

As dogs upon their masters, worrying you.
See you, my princes and my noble peers,
These English monsters! My Lord of Cambridge here,
You know how apt our love was to accord
To furnish him with all appertinents
Belonging to his honour; and this man
Hath, for a few light crowns, lightly conspir'd,
And sworn unto the practices of France,
To kill us here in Hampton: to the which
This knight, no less for bounty bound to us
Than Cambridge is, hath likewise sworn. But, O,
What shall I say to thee, Lord Scroop? thou cruel,
Ingrateful, savage and inhuman creature!
Thou that didst bear the key of all my counsels,
That knew'st the very bottom of my soul,
That almost mightst have coin'd me into gold,
Wouldst thou have practis'd on me for thy use!
May it be possible, that foreign hire
Could out of thee extract one spark of evil
That might annoy my finger? 'tis so strange,
That, though the truth of it stands off as gross
As black and white, my eye will scarcely see it.
Treason and murder ever kept together,
As two yoke-devils sworn to either's purpose,
Working so grossly in a natural cause,
That admiration did not hoop at them:
But thou, 'gainst all proportion, didst bring in
Wonder to wait on treason and on murder:
And whatsoever cunning fiend it was
That wrought upon thee so preposterously
Hath got the voice in hell for excellence:
All other devils that suggest by treasons
Do botch and bungle up damnation
With patches, colours, and with forms being fetch'd
From glist'ring semblances of piety;
But he that temper'd thee bade thee stand up,
Gave thee no instance why thou shouldst do treason,
Unless to dub thee with the name of traitor.
If that same demon that hath gull'd thee thus
Should with his lion gait walk the whole world,
He might return to vasty Tartar back,
And tell the legions 'I can never win
A soul so easy as that Englishman's.'
O, how hast thou with jealousy infected
The sweetness of affiance! Show men dutiful?
Why, so didst thou: seem they grave and learned?
Why, so didst thou: come they of noble family?
Why, so didst thou: seem they religious?
Why, so didst thou: or are they spare in diet,
Free from gross passion or of mirth or anger,
Constant in spirit, not swerving with the blood,
Garnish'd and deck'd in modest complement,
Not working with the eye without the ear,
And but in purged judgement trusting neither?
Such and so finely bolted didst thou seem:
And thus thy fall hath left a kind of blot,
To mark the full-fraught man and best indu'd
With some suspicion. I will weep for thee;
For this revolt of thine, methinks, is like
Another fall of man. Their faults are open:
Arrest them to the answer of the law;
And God acquit them of their practices!

Exe. I arrest thee of high treason, by the name of Richard Earl of Cambridge.

I arrest thee of high treason, by the name of Henry Lord Scroop of Masham.

I arrest thee of high treason, by the name of Thomas Grey, knight, of Northumberland.

Scroop. Our purposes God justly hath discover'd;
And I repent my fault more than my death;
Which I beseech your highness to forgive,
Although my body pay the price of it.

Cam. For me, the gold of France did not seduce;
Although I did admit it as a motive
The sooner to effect what I intended:
But God be thanked for prevention;
Which I in sufferance heartily will rejoice,
Beseeching God and you to pardon me.

Grey. Never did faithful subject more rejoice
At the discovery of most dangerous treason
Than I do at this hour joy o'er myself,
Prevented from a damned enterprise:
My fault, but not my body, pardon, sovereign.

K. Hen. God quit you in his mercy! Hear your sentence.
You have conspir'd against our royal person,
Join'd with an enemy proclaim'd and from his coffers
Receiv'd the golden earnest of our death;
Wherein you would have sold your king to slaughter,
His princes and his peers to servitude,
His subjects to oppression and contempt
And his whole kingdom into desolation.
Touching our person seek we no revenge;
But we our kingdom's safety must so tender,
Whose ruin you have sought, that to her laws
We do deliver you. Get you therefore hence,
Poor miserable wretches, to your death:
The taste whereof, God of his mercy give
You patience to endure, and true repentance
Of all your dear offences! Bear them hence.

Exeunt [*Cambridge, Scroop and Grey, guarded*].

Now, lords, for France; the enterprise whereof
Shall be to you, as us, like glorious.
We doubt not of a fair and lucky war,
Since God so graciously hath brought to light
This dangerous treason lurking in our way
To hinder our beginnings. We doubt not now
But every rub is smoothed on our way.
Then forth, dear countrymen: let us deliver
Our puissance into the hand of God,
Putting it straight in expedition.
Cheerly to sea; the signs of war advance:
No king of England, if not king of France!

Flourish. [*Exeunt.*]

[SCENE III. *London. Before a tavern.*]

Enter PISTOL, NYM, BARDOLPH, BOY, *and* HOSTESS.

Host. Prithee, honey-sweet husband, let me bring thee to Staines.

---

87. **appertinents,** things appertaining (to). 102. **annoy,** injure. 106. **yoke-devils,** fellow-devils. 107-108. **Working . . . at them,** i.e., cooperating with such obvious fitness in a cause to which they were naturally inclined, that no one cried out in astonishment. 114. **suggest,** tempt. 117. **glist'ring semblances,** outwardly glittering manifestations. 118. **temper'd,** molded. **stand up,** volunteer. 123. **Tartar,** for *Tartarus*, hell. 133. **swerving with the blood,** sinning through passion. 134. **deck'd in modest complement,** wearing the look of modesty. 135. **Not working . . . ear,** i.e., trusting neither eye nor ear alone. 137. **bolted,** sifted (like flour). 166. **quit,** acquit. 169. **golden earnest,** advance payment.

SCENE III. 2. **Staines,** first stage on the road to Southampton. 3. **earn,** grieve. 11. **Arthur's bosom,** malapropism for Abraham's bosom. 13. **cristom child,** a child in its white robe of innocence used at christening. 18. **'a babbled of green fields.** This line contains Theobald's famous emendation. F has *and a Table of greene fields*. Falstaff would seem

Pist. No; for my manly heart doth earn.
Bardolph, be blithe: Nym, rouse thy vaunting veins:
Boy, bristle thy courage up; for Falstaff he is dead,
And we must earn therefore.

Bard. Would I were with him, wheresome'er he is, either in heaven or in hell!

Host. Nay, sure, he 's not in hell: he 's in Arthur's bosom, if ever man went to Arthur's bosom. 'A made a finer end and went away an it had been any christom child; 'a parted even just between twelve and one, even at the turning o' the tide: for after I saw him fumble with the sheets and play with flowers and smile upon his fingers' ends, I knew there was but one way; for his nose was as sharp as a pen, and 'a babbled of green fields. 'How now, Sir John!' quoth I: 'what, man! be o' good cheer.' So 'a cried out, 'God, God, God!' three or four times. Now I, to comfort him, bid him 'a should not think of God; I hoped there was no need to trouble himself with any such thoughts yet. So 'a bade me lay more clothes on his feet: I put my hand into the bed and felt them, and they were as cold as any stone; then I felt to his knees, and so upward and upward, and all was as cold as any stone.

Nym. They say he cried out of sack.

Host. Ay, that 'a did.

Bard. And of women.

Host. Nay, that 'a did not.

Boy. Yes, that 'a did; and said they were devils incarnate.

Host. 'A could never abide carnation; 'twas a colour he never liked.

Boy. 'A said once, the devil would have him about women.

Host. 'A did in some sort, indeed, handle women; but then he was rheumatic, and talked of the whore of Babylon.

Boy. Do you not remember, 'a saw a flea stick upon Bardolph's nose, and 'a said it was a black soul burning in hell-fire?

Bard. Well, the fuel is gone that maintained that fire: that 's all the riches I got in his service.

Nym. Shall we shog? the king will be gone from Southampton.

Pist. Come, let 's away. My love, give me thy lips.
Look to my chattels and my movables:
Let senses rule; the word is 'Pitch and Pay:'
Trust none;
For oaths are straws, men's faiths are wafer-cakes,
And hold-fast is the only dog, my duck:
Therefore, Caveto be thy counsellor.
Go, clear thy crystals. Yoke-fellows in arms,
Let us to France; like horse-leeches, my boys,
To suck, to suck, the very blood to suck!

Boy. And that 's but unwholesome food, they say.

Pist. Touch her soft mouth, and march.

Bard. Farewell, hostess. [*Kissing her.*]

Nym. I cannot kiss, that is the humour of it; but, adieu.

Pist. Let housewifery appear: keep close, I thee command.

Host. Farewell; adieu. *Exeunt.*

[SCENE IV. *France. The* KING'S *palace.*]

Flourish. Enter the FRENCH KING, *the* DAUPHIN, *the* DUKES OF BERRI *and* BRITTAINE [, *the* CONSTABLE, *and others*].

Fr. King. Thus comes the English with full power upon us;
And more than carefully it us concerns
To answer royally in our defences.
Therefore the Dukes of Berri and of Brittaine,
Of Brabant and of Orleans, shall make forth,
And you, Prince Dauphin, with all swift dispatch,
To line and new repair our towns of war
With men of courage and with means defendant;
For England his approaches makes as fierce
As waters to the sucking of a gulf.
It fits us then to be as provident
As fear may teach us out of late examples
Left by the fatal and neglected English
Upon our fields.

Dau. My most redoubted father,
It is most meet we arm us 'gainst the foe;
For peace itself should not so dull a kingdom,
Though war nor no known quarrel were in question,
But that defences, musters, preparations,
Should be maintain'd, assembled and collected,
As were a war in expectation.
Therefore, I say 'tis meet we all go forth
To view the sick and feeble parts of France:
And let us do it with no show of fear;
No, with no more than if we heard that England
Were busied with a Whitsun morris-dance:
For, my good liege, she is so idly king'd,
Her sceptre so fantastically borne
By a vain, giddy, shallow, humorous youth,
That fear attends her not.

Con. O peace, Prince Dauphin!
You are too much mistaken in this king:
Question your grace the late ambassadors,
With what great state he heard their embassy,
How well supplied with noble counsellors,
How modest in exception, and withal
How terrible in constant resolution,
And you shall find his vanities forespent
Were but the outside of the Roman Brutus,
Covering discretion with a coat of folly;
As gardeners do with ordure hide those roots
That shall first spring and be most delicate.

Dau. Well, 'tis not so, my lord high constable;
But though we think it so, it is no matter:
In cases of defence 'tis best to weigh
The enemy more mighty than he seems:
So the proportions of defence are fill'd;
Which of a weak and niggardly projection

to have been reciting the Twenty-third Psalm. 40. **rheumatic,** i.e., feverish, or perhaps for "lunatic." Pronounced "rome-atic," preparing for the allusion to the Whore of Babylon, i.e., the Church of Rome (see also Revelation 17:4-5). 51. **senses,** possibly, common sense. **'Pitch and Pay,'** proverbial for "cash payment"; supposed to be derived from a rule at Cloth-Hall in London that, when a bale of cloth was deposited (*pitched*), a penny must be paid. 54. **hold-fast.** Cf. the proverb, "Brag is a good dog, but hold-fast is a better." 55. **Caveto,** be cautious; Latin imperative of *caveo*. 56. **clear thy crystals,** wipe thine eyes.

SCENE IV. 25. **Whitsun morris-dance,** dance performed on spring holidays by persons in fancy costumes. 28. **humorous,** capricious. 34. **exception,** making objections. 37. **Brutus.** The elder Brutus pretended idiocy in order to overthrow the Tarquins. 46. **Which . . . projection,** i.e., defense is futile if calculated on a niggardly scale.

Doth, like a miser, spoil his coat with scanting
A little cloth.
Fr. King. Think we King Harry strong;
And, princes, look you strongly arm to meet him.
The kindred of him hath been flesh'd upon us;
And he is bred out of that bloody strain
That haunted us in our familiar paths:
Witness our too much memorable shame
When Cressy battle fatally was struck,
And all our princes captiv'd by the hand
Of that black name, Edward, Black Prince of Wales;
Whiles that his mountain sire, on mountain standing,
Up in the air, crown'd with the golden sun,
Saw his heroical seed, and smil'd to see him,
Mangle the work of nature and deface
The patterns that by God and by French fathers
Had twenty years been made. This is a stem
Of that victorious stock; and let us fear
The native mightiness and fate of him.

Enter a Messenger.

Mess. Ambassadors from Harry King of England
Do crave admittance to your majesty.
Fr. King. We'll give them present audience. Go, and bring them. [*Exeunt Messenger and certain Lords.*]
You see this chase is hotly followed, friends.
Dau. Turn head, and stop pursuit; for coward dogs
Most spend their mouths when what they seem to threaten
Runs far before them. Good my sovereign,
Take up the English short, and let them know
Of what a monarchy you are the head:
Self-love, my liege, is not so vile a sin
As self-neglecting.

Enter [Lords, *with*] EXETER [*and train*].

Fr. King. From our brother of England?
Exe. From him; and thus he greets your majesty.
He wills you, in the name of God Almighty,
That you divest yourself, and lay apart
The borrowed glories that by gift of heaven,
By law of nature and of nations, 'longs,
To him and to his heirs; namely, the crown
And all wide-stretched honours that pertain
By custom and the ordinance of times
Unto the crown of France. That you may know
'Tis no sinister nor no awkward claim,
Pick'd from the worm-holes of long-vanish'd days,
Nor from the dust of old oblivion rak'd,
He sends you this most memorable line,
In every branch truly demonstrative;
Willing you overlook this pedigree:
And when you find him evenly deriv'd
From his most fam'd of famous ancestors,
Edward the Third, he bids you then resign
Your crown and kingdom, indirectly held
From him the native and true challenger.
Fr. King. Or else what follows?
Exe. Bloody constraint; for if you hide the crown
Even in your hearts, there will he rake for it:
Therefore in fierce tempest is he coming,
In thunder and in earthquake, like a Jove,
That, if requiring fail, he will compel;
And bids you, in the bowels of the Lord,
Deliver up the crown, and to take mercy
On the poor souls for whom this hungry war
Opens his vasty jaws; and on your head
Turning the widows' tears, the orphans' cries,
The dead men's blood, the pining maidens' groans,
For husbands, fathers and betrothed lovers,
That shall be swallowed in this controversy.
This is his claim, his threat'ning, and my message;
Unless the Dauphin be in presence here,
To whom expressly I bring greeting too.
Fr. King. For us, we will consider of this further:
To-morrow shall you bear our full intent
Back to our brother of England.
Dau. For the Dauphin,
I stand here for him: what to him from England?
Exe. Scorn and defiance; slight regard, contempt,
And any thing that may not misbecome
The mighty sender, doth he prize you at.
Thus says my king; an if your father's highness
Do not, in grant of all demands at large,
Sweeten the bitter mock you sent his majesty,
He'll call you to so hot an answer of it,
That caves and womby vaultages of France
Shall chide your trespass and return your mock
In second accent of his ordnance.
Dau. Say, if my father render fair return,
It is against my will; for I desire
Nothing but odds with England: to that end,
As matching to his youth and vanity,
I did present him with the Paris balls.
Exe. He'll make your Paris Louvre shake for it,
Were it the mistress-court of mighty Europe:
And, be assur'd, you'll find a diff'rence,
As we his subjects have in wonder found,
Between the promise of his greener days
And these he masters now: now he weighs time
Even to the utmost grain: that you shall read
In your own losses, if he stay in France.
Fr. King. To-morrow shall you know our mind at full. *Flourish.*
Exe. Dispatch us with all speed, lest that our king
Come here himself to question our delay;
For he is footed in this land already.
Fr. King. You shall be soon dispatch'd with fair conditions:
A night is but small breath and little pause
To answer matters of this consequence.
Exeunt.

ACT [III.

PROLOGUE.]

Flourish. Enter Chorus.

[*Chor.*] Thus with imagin'd wing our swift scene flies

50. **flesh'd,** initiated in the shedding of blood, with foretaste of further success. 57. **mountain sire,** Edward III, born in mountainous Wales, and of sturdy proportions. 59. **seed,** son. 64. **fate,** what he is destined to do. 70. **spend their mouths,** bay. 80. **'longs,** belong. 83. **ordinance of times,** the decrees of tradition. 85. **sinister,** illegitimate. 88. **line,** pedigree. 90. **overlook,** look over. 91. **evenly,** directly. 102. **bowels,** mercy, or innermost being. Cf. Philippians 1:8. 124. **womby vaultages,** deep caverns. 126. **second accent,** echo. **ordnance,** cannon. 131. **Paris balls,** tennis balls. 132. **Louvre,** the French royal palace. 136. **greener,** younger, cruder.

ACT III. PROLOGUE. 1. **imagin'd wing,** wings of imagination. 10. **threaden,** woven of thread. 14. **rivage,** shore. 18. **to sternage,** astern. 33. **linstock,** staff holding a gunner's match. *Stage Direction:* ***chambers,*** small cannon.

In motion of no less celerity
Than that of thought. Suppose that you have seen
The well-appointed king at Hampton pier
Embark his royalty; and his brave fleet
With silken streamers the young Phœbus fanning:
Play with your fancies, and in them behold
Upon the hempen tackle ship-boys climbing;
Hear the shrill whistle which doth order give
To sounds confus'd; behold the threaden sails,
Borne with th' invisible and creeping wind,
Draw the huge bottoms through the furrowed sea,
Breasting the lofty surge: O, do but think
You stand upon the rivage and behold
A city on th' inconstant billows dancing;
For so appears this fleet majestical,
Holding due course to Harfleur. Follow, follow:
Grapple your minds to sternage of this navy,
And leave your England, as dead midnight still,
Guarded with grandsires, babies and old women,
Either past or not arriv'd to pith and puissance;
For who is he, whose chin is but enrich'd
With one appearing hair, that will not follow
These cull'd and choice-drawn cavaliers to France?
Work, work your thoughts, and therein see a siege;
Behold the ordnance on their carriages,
With fatal mouths gaping on girded Harfleur.
Suppose th' ambassador from the French comes back;
Tells Harry that the king doth offer him
Katharine his daughter, and with her, to dowry,
Some petty and unprofitable dukedoms.
The offer likes not: and the nimble gunner
With linstock now the devilish cannon touches,
Alarum, and chambers go off.
And down goes all before them. Still be kind,
And eke out our performance with your mind. *Exit.*

[SCENE I. *France. Before Harfleur.*]

Enter the KING, EXETER, BEDFORD, *and* GLOUCESTER. *Alarum,* [*with* Soldiers *carrying*] *scaling ladders at Harfleur.*

K. Hen. Once more unto the breach, dear friends, once more;
Or close the wall up with our English dead.
In peace there 's nothing so becomes a man
As modest stillness and humility:
But when the blast of war blows in our ears,
Then imitate the action of the tiger;
Stiffen the sinews, summon up the blood,
Disguise fair nature with hard-favour'd rage;
Then lend the eye a terrible aspect;
Let it pry through the portage of the head
Like the brass cannon; let the brow o'erwhelm it
As fearfully as doth a galled rock
O'erhang and jutty his confounded base,
Swill'd with the wild and wasteful ocean.
Now set the teeth and stretch the nostril wide,
Hold hard the breath and bend up every spirit
To his full height. On, on, you noblest English,
Whose blood is fet from fathers of war-proof!
Fathers that, like so many Alexanders,
Have in these parts from morn till even fought
And sheath'd their swords for lack of argument:
Dishonour not your mothers; now attest
That those whom you call'd fathers did beget you.
Be copy now to men of grosser blood,
And teach them how to war. And you, good yeomen,
Whose limbs were made in England, show us here
The mettle of your pasture; let us swear
That you are worth your breeding; which I doubt not;
For there is none of you so mean and base,
That hath not noble lustre in your eyes.
I see you stand like greyhounds in the slips,
Straining upon the start. The game 's afoot:
Follow your spirit, and upon this charge
Cry 'God for Harry, England, and Saint George!'
[*Exeunt.*] *Alarum, and chambers go off.*

[SCENE II. *The same.*]

Enter NYM, BARDOLPH, PISTOL, *and* BOY.

Bard. On, on, on, on, on! to the breach, to the breach!

Nym. Pray thee, corporal, stay: the knocks are too hot; and, for mine own part, I have not a case of lives: the humour of it is too hot, that is the very plain-song of it.

Pist. The plain-song is most just; for humours do abound:
Knocks go and come; God's vassals drop and die;
And sword and shield,
In bloody field,
Doth win immortal fame.

Boy. Would I were in an alehouse in London! I would give all my fame for a pot of ale and safety.

Pist. And I:
If wishes would prevail with me,
My purpose should not fail with me,
But thither would I hie.

Boy. As duly, but not as truly,
As bird doth sing on bough.

Enter FLUELLEN.

Flu. Up to the breach, you dogs! avaunt, you cullions! [*Driving them forward.*]

Pist. Be merciful, great duke, to men of mould.
Abate thy rage, abate thy manly rage,
Abate thy rage, great duke!
Good bawcock, bate thy rage; use lenity, sweet chuck!

Nym. These be good humours! your honour wins bad humours. *Exit* [*with all but Boy*].

Boy. As young as I am, I have observed these three swashers. I am boy to them all three: but all they three, though they would serve me, could not be man to me; for indeed three such antics do not amount to a man. For Bardolph, he is white-livered and red-faced; by the means whereof 'a faces it out, but fights not. For Pistol, he hath a killing tongue and a quiet sword;

SCENE I. 10. **portage,** porthole. 11. **o'erwhelm,** project over. 12. **galled,** washed away, undermined. 13. **jutty,** overhang. 14. **Swill'd,** washed. 18. **fet,** fetched. **war-proof,** proved in war. 27. **mettle of your pasture,** quality of your breeding (literally, "feeding"). 31. **slips,** leashes.

SCENE II. The action is continuous. 5. **case,** set. 6. **plain-song,** chant without harmony or counterpoint. Nym probably means "that is the truth of the matter." 22. **cullions,** rascals. 23. **men of mould,** mere mortals. 26. **bawcock,** French, *beau coq,* fine fellow. **chuck,** a term of endearment. 30. **swashers,** swashbucklers. 33. **antics,** grotesque figures. 34. **white-livered,** cowardly. In extreme fear the blood was thought to sink below the liver, leaving it bloodless.

by the means whereof 'a breaks words, and keeps whole weapons. For Nym, he hath heard that men of few words are the best men; and therefore he scorns to say his prayers. lest 'a should be thought a coward: but his few bad words are matched with as few good deeds; for 'a never broke any man's head but his own, and that was against a post when he was drunk. They will steal any thing, and call it purchase. Bardolph stole a lute-case, bore it twelve leagues, and sold it for three half-pence. Nym and Bardolph are sworn brothers in filching, and in Calais they stole a fire-shovel: I knew by that piece of service the men would carry coals. They would have me as familiar with men's pockets as their gloves or their handkerchers: which makes much against my manhood, if I should take from another's pocket to put into mine; for it is plain pocketing up of wrongs. I must leave them, and seek some better service: their villany goes against my weak stomach, and therefore I must cast it up. *Exit.*

Enter GOWER [*and* FLUELLEN].

Gow. Captain Fluellen, you must come presently to the mines; the Duke of Gloucester would speak with you.

Flu. To the mines! tell you the duke, it is not so good to come to the mines; for, look you, the mines is not according to the disciplines of the war: the concavities of it is not sufficient; for, look you, th' athversary, you may discuss unto the duke, look you, is digt himself four yard under the countermines: by Cheshu, I think 'a will plow up all, if there is not better directions.

Gow. The Duke of Gloucester, to whom the order of the siege is given, is altogether directed by an Irishman, a very valiant gentleman, i' faith.

Flu. It is Captain Macmorris, is it not?

Gow. I think it be.

Flu. By Cheshu, he is an ass, as in the world: I will verify as much in his beard: he has no more directions in the true disciplines of the wars, look you, of the Roman disciplines, than is a puppy-dog.

Enter MACMORRIS *and* Captain JAMY.

Gow. Here 'a comes; and the Scots captain, Captain Jamy, with him.

Flu. Captain Jamy is a marvellous falorous gentleman, that is certain; and of great expedition and knowledge in th' aunchient wars, upon my particular knowledge of his directions: by Cheshu, he will maintain his argument as well as any military man in the world, in the disciplines of the pristine wars of the Romans.

Jamy. I say gud-day, Captain Fluellen.

Flu. God-den to your worship, good Captain James.

Gow. How now, Captain Macmorris! have you quit the mines? have the pioners given o'er?

Mac. By Chrish, la! tish ill done: the work ish give over, the trompet sound the retreat. By my hand, I swear, and my father's soul, the work ish ill done; it ish give over: I would have blowed up the town, so Chrish save me, la! in an hour: O, tish ill done, tish ill done; by my hand, tish ill done!

Flu. Captain Macmorris, I beseech you now, will you voutsafe me, look you, a few disputations with you, as partly touching or concerning the disciplines of the war, the Roman wars, in the way of argument, look you, and friendly communication; partly to satisfy my opinion, and partly for the satisfaction, look you, of my mind, as touching the direction of the military discipline; that is the point.

Jamy. It sall be vary gud, gud feith, gud captains bath: and I sall quit you with gud leve, as I may pick occasion; that sall I, marry.

Mac. It is no time to discourse, so Chrish save me: the day is hot, and the weather, and the wars, and the king, and the dukes: it is no time to discourse. The town is beseeched, and the trumpet call us to the breach; and we talk, and, be Chrish, do nothing: 'tis shame for us all: so God sa' me, 'tis shame to stand still; it is shame, by my hand: and there is throats to be cut, and works to be done; and there ish nothing done, so Chrish sa' me, la!

Jamy. By the mess, ere theise eyes of mine take themselves to slomber, ay'll de gud service, or ay'll lig i' the grund for it; ay, or go to death; and ay'll pay 't as valorously as I may, that sall I suerly do, that is the breff and the long. Marry, I wad full fain hear some question 'tween you tway.

Flu. Captain Macmorris, I think, look you, under your correction, there is not many of your nation—

Mac. Of my nation! What ish my nation? Ish a villain, and a bastard, and a knave, and a rascal—What ish my nation? Who talks of my nation?

Flu. Look you, if you take the matter otherwise than is meant, Captain Macmorris, peradventure I shall think you do not use me with that affability as in discretion you ought to use me, look you; being as good a man as yourself, both in the disciplines of war, and in the derivation of my birth, and in other particularities.

Mac. I do not know you so good a man as myself: so Chrish save me, I will cut off your head.

Gow. Gentlemen both, you will mistake each other.

Jamy. A! that 's a foul fault. *A parley* [*sounded*].

Gow. The town sounds a parley.

Flu. Captain Macmorris, when there is more better opportunity to be required, look you, I will be so bold as to tell you I know the disciplines of war; and there is an end. *Exit* [*with others*].

---

45. **purchase,** thieves' cant for "stolen goods." 50. **carry coals,** proverbial expression for submitting to insult or degradation. 54. **pocketing up of,** putting up with; also, receiving stolen goods. 56-57. **goes . . . stomach,** goes against my inclination; also, makes me sick. 64. **disciplines of the war.** It is Fluellen's humor to discuss the science of warfare, about which there were many books from Greek and Roman times down to the Renaissance. 67. **Cheshu.** Fluellen's dialect is Welsh, Jamy's Scots, and Macmorris' Irish. 74. **as,** as great as is. 89. **God-den,** good evening. 92. **pioners,** sappers, engineering troops. 116. **beseeched,** for "besieged." 122. **mess,** Mass. 124. **lig, lie.** 127. **breff,** short.

SCENE III. 17. **fell,** savage. 26. **precepts,** summons. **leviathan,** whale. 31. **O'erblows,** blows away. Contagion was thought to reside in clouds and mists. 32. **heady,** headlong. 46. **Returns,** replies to. 50. **defensible,** able to defend ourselves. 58. **addrest,** prepared.

SCENE IV. Translation.

Kath. Alice, you have been in England and speak the language well.

Alice. A little, my lady.

Kath. I pray you, teach me; I have to learn to speak it. What do you call *la main* in English?

Alice. La main? it is called de hand.

Kath. De hand. And *les doigts?*

Alice. Les doigts? Dear me, I forget *les doigts*; but I shall remember. I think that they are called de fingres; yes, de fingres.

Kath. La main, de hand; *les doigts*, de fingres. I think that I am a clever scholar; I have learned two English words in no time. What do

[SCENE III. *The same. Before the gates.*]

[*Enter the* Governor *and some* Citizens *on the walls.*] *Enter the* KING [HENRY] *and all his train before the gates.*

K. Hen. How yet resolves the governor of the town?
This is the latest parle we will admit:
Therefore to our best mercy give yourselves;
Or like to men proud of destruction
Defy us to our worst: for, as I am a soldier,
A name that in my thoughts becomes me best,
If I begin the batt'ry once again,
I will not leave the half-achieved Harfleur
Till in her ashes she lie buried.
The gates of mercy shall be all shut up,
And the flesh'd soldier, rough and hard of heart,
In liberty of bloody hand shall range
With conscience wide as hell, mowing like grass
Your fresh-fair virgins and your flow'ring infants.
What is it then to me, if impious war,
Array'd in flames like to the prince of fiends,
Do, with his smirch'd complexion, all fell feats
Enlink'd to waste and desolation?
What is 't to me, when you yourselves are cause,
If your pure maidens fall into the hand
Of hot and forcing violation?
What rein can hold licentious wickedness
When down the hill he holds his fierce career?
We may as bootless spend our vain command
Upon th' enraged soldiers in their spoil
As send precepts to the leviathan
To come ashore. Therefore, you men of Harfleur,
Take pity of your town and of your people,
Whiles yet my soldiers are in my command;
Whiles yet the cool and temperate wind of grace
O'erblows the filthy and contagious clouds
Of heady murder, spoil and villany.
If not, why, in a moment look to see
The blind and bloody soldier with foul hand
Defile the locks of your shrill-shrieking daughters;
Your fathers taken by the silver beards,
And their most reverend heads dash'd to the walls,
Your naked infants spitted upon pikes,
Whiles the mad mothers with their howls confus'd
Do break the clouds, as did the wives of Jewry
At Herod's bloody-hunting slaughtermen.
What say you? will you yield, and this avoid,
Or, guilty in defence, be thus destroy'd?

Gov. Our expectation hath this day an end:
The Dauphin, whom of succours we entreated,
Returns us that his powers are yet not ready
To raise so great a siege. Therefore, great king,
We yield our town and lives to thy soft mercy.
Enter our gates; dispose of us and ours;
For we no longer are defensible.

K. Hen. Open your gates. Come, uncle Exeter,
Go you and enter Harfleur; there remain,
And fortify it strongly 'gainst the French:
Use mercy to them all. For us, dear uncle,
The winter coming on and sickness growing
Upon our soldiers, we will retire to Calais.
To-night in Harfleur will we be your guest;
To-morrow for the march are we addrest.

Flourish, and enter the town.

[SCENE IV. *The* FRENCH KING'S *palace.*]

Enter KATHARINE *and* [ALICE,] *an old Gentlewoman.*

Kath. Alice, tu as été en Angleterre, et tu parles bien le langage.

Alice. Un peu, madame.

Kath. Je te prie, m'enseignez; il faut que j'apprenne à parler. Comment appelez-vous la main en Anglois?

Alice. La main? elle est appelée de hand.

Kath. De hand. Et les doigts?

Alice. Les doigts? ma foi, j'oublie les doigts; mais je me souviendrai. Les doigts? je pense qu'ils sont appelés de fingres; oui, de fingres.

Kath. La main, de hand; les doigts, de fingres. Je pense que je suis le bon écolier; j'ai gagné deux mots d'Anglois vîtement. Comment appelez-vous les ongles?

Alice. Les ongles? nous les appelons de nails.

Kath. De nails. Écoutez; dites-moi, si je parle bien: de hand, de fingres, et de nails.

Alice. C'est bien dit, madame; il est fort bon Anglois.

Kath. Dites-moi l'Anglois pour le bras.

Alice. De arm, madame.

Kath. Et le coude?

Alice. De elbow.

Kath. De elbow. Je m'en fais la répétition de tous les mots que vous m'avez appris dès à présent.

Alice. Il est trop difficile, madame, comme je pense.

Kath. Excusez-moi, Alice; écoutez: de hand, de fingres, de nails, de arma, de bilbow.

Alice. De elbow, madame.

Kath. O Seigneur Dieu, je m'en oublie! de elbow. Comment appelez-vous le col?

Alice. De nick, madame.

Kath. De nick. Et le menton?

Alice. De chin.

Kath. De sin. Le col, de nick; le menton, de sin.

Alice. Oui. Sauf votre honneur, en vérite, vous prononcez les mots aussi droit que les natifs d'Angleterre.

Kath. Je ne doute point d'apprendre, par la grace de Dieu, et en peu de temps.

Alice. N'avez vous pas déjà oublié ce que je vous ai enseigné?

you call *les ongles?*
Alice. Les ongles? We call them de nails.
Kath. De nails. Listen; tell me whether or not I speak correctly: de hand, de fingres, and de nails.
Alice. That is correct, my lady; it is very good English.
Kath. Tell me the English for *le bras.*
Alice. De arm, my lady.
Kath. And *le coude?*
Alice. De elbow.
Kath. De elbow. I am going to repeat all the words you have taught me so far.
Alice. It is too hard, my lady, I fear.
Kath. Pardon me, Alice; listen: de hand, de fingres, de nails, de arma, de bilbow.
Alice. De elbow, my lady.
Kath. O Lord, I can't remember! de elbow. What do you call *le col?*
Alice. De nick, my lady.
Kath. De nick. And *le menton?*
Alice. De chin.
Kath. De sin. *Le col,* de nick; *le menton,* de sin.
Alice. Yes. On my word, really you pronounce the words just as English people themselves do.
Kath. I have no doubt that I shall learn, with God's help, in a very short time.
Alice. Have you not already forgotten what I have taught you?

Kath. Non, je reciterai à vous promptement: de hand, de fingres, de mails,—

Alice. De nails, madame.

Kath. De nails, de arm, de ilbow.

Alice. Sauf votre honneur, de elbow.

Kath. Ainsi dis-je; de elbow, de nick, et de sin. Comment appelez-vous le pied et la robe?

Alice. De foot, madame; et de coun.

Kath. De foot et de coun! O Seigneur Dieu! ce sont mots de son mauvais, corruptible, gros, et impudique, et non pour les dames d'honneur d'user: je ne voudrais prononcer ces mots devant les seigneurs de France pour tout le monde. Foh! le foot et le coun! Néanmoins, je réciterai une autre fois ma leçon ensemble: de hand, de fingres, de nails, de arm, de elbow, de nick, de sin, de foot, de coun.

Alice. Excellent, madame!

Kath. C'est assez pour une fois: allons-nous à dîner.
Exit [with Alice].

[SCENE V. *The same.*]

Enter the KING OF FRANCE, *the* DAUPHIN, [*the* DUKE OF BRITTAINE,] *the* CONSTABLE OF FRANCE, *and others.*

Fr. King. 'Tis certain he hath pass'd the river Somme.
Con. And if he be not fought withal, my lord,
Let us not live in France; let us quit all
And give our vineyards to a barbarous people.
Dau. O Dieu vivant! shall a few sprays of us,
The emptying of our fathers' luxury,
Our scions, put in wild and savage stock,
Spirt up so suddenly into the clouds,
And overlook their grafters?
Brit. Normans, but bastard Normans, Norman bastards!
Mort de ma vie! if they march along
Unfought withal, but I will sell my dukedom,
To buy a slobb'ry and a dirty farm
In that nook-shotten isle of Albion.
Con. Dieu de batailles! where have they this mettle?
Is not their climate foggy, raw and dull,
On whom, as in despite, the sun looks pale,
Killing their fruit with frowns? Can sodden water,
A drench for sur-rein'd jades, their barley-broth,
Decoct their cold blood to such valiant heat?
And shall our quick blood, spirited with wine,
Seem frosty? O, for honour of our land,
Let us not hang like roping icicles
Upon our houses' thatch, whiles a more frosty people
Sweat drops of gallant youth in our rich fields!
Poor we may call them in their native lords.
Dau. By faith and honour,
Our madams mock at us, and plainly say
Our mettle is bred out and they will give
Their bodies to the lust of English youth
To new-store France with bastard warriors.
Brit. They bid us to the English dancing-schools,
And teach lavoltas high and swift corantos;
Saying our grace is only in our heels,
And that we are most lofty runaways.
Fr. King. Where is Montjoy the herald? speed him hence:
Let him greet England with our sharp defiance.
Up, princes! and, with spirit of honour edged
More sharper than your swords, hie to the field:
Charles Delabreth, high constable of France;
You Dukes of Orleans, Bourbon, and of Berri,
Alençon, Brabant, Bar, and Burgundy;
Jaques Chatillon, Rambures, Vaudemont,
Beaumont, Grandpré, Roussi, and Faulconbridge,
Foix, Lestrale, Bouciqualt, and Charolois;
High dukes, great princes, barons, lords and knights,
For your great seats now quit you of great shames.
Bar Harry England, that sweeps through our land
With pennons painted in the blood of Harfleur:
Rush on his host, as doth the melted snow
Upon the valleys, whose low vassal seat
The Alps doth spit and void his rheum upon:
Go down upon him, you have power enough,
And in a captive chariot into Rouen
Bring him our prisoner.
Con. This becomes the great.
Sorry am I his numbers are so few,
His soldiers sick and famish'd in their march,
For I am sure, when he shall see our army,
He'll drop his heart into the sink of fear
And for achievement offer us his ransom.
Fr. King. Therefore, lord constable, haste on Montjoy,
And let him say to England that we send
To know what willing ransom he will give.
Prince Dauphin, you shall stay with us in Rouen.
Dau. Not so, I do beseech your majesty.
Fr. King. Be patient, for you shall remain with us.
Now forth, lord constable and princes all,
And quickly bring us word of England's fall. *Exeunt.*

[SCENE VI. *The English camp in Picardy.*]

Enter Captains, English and Welsh: GOWER *and* FLUELLEN.

Gow. How now, Captain Fluellen! come you from the bridge?

Flu. I assure you, there is very excellent services committed at the bridge.

Gow. Is the Duke of Exeter safe?

Flu. The Duke of Exeter is as magnanimous as Agamemnon; and a man that I love and honour with my soul, and my heart, and my duty, and my life, and my living, and my uttermost power: he is not—God be praised and blessed!—any hurt in the world; but keeps the bridge most valiantly, with excellent discipline. There is an aunchient lieutenant there at the pridge, I think in my very conscience he is as valiant

---

Kath. No, I shall recite to you at once: de hand, de fingres, de nails—

Alice. De nails, my lady.

Kath. De nails, de arm, de ilbow.

Alice. By your leave, de elbow.

Kath. That's what I said; de elbow, de nick, and de sin. What do you call *le pied* and *la robe?*

Alice. De foot, my lady; and de coun. [As she pronounces them, *foot* sounds to Katharine like *foutre*, fornicate, and *coun* sounds like French for the female sexual organ.]

Kath. De foot and de coun! O Lord! those are naughty words, wicked, coarse, and immodest, and are not fit to be used by nice ladies; I wouldn't say those words before French gentlemen for the whole world. Bah! le foot and le coun! Nevertheless, I shall recite my whole lesson once more: de hand, de fingres, de nails, de arm, de elbow, de nick, de sin, de foot, de coun.

Alice. Excellent, my lady.

Kath. That's enough for one time; let's go to dinner.

a man as Mark Antony; and he is a man of no estimation in the world; but I did see him do as gallant service.

Gow. What do you call him?

Flu. He is called Aunchient Pistol.

Gow. I know him not.

Enter Pistol.

Flu. Here is the man.

Pist. Captain, I thee beseech to do me favours:
The Duke of Exeter doth love thee well.

Flu. Ay, I praise God; and I have merited some love at his hands.

Pist. Bardolph, a soldier, firm and sound of heart,
And of buxom valour, hath, by cruel fate,
And giddy Fortune's furious fickle wheel,
That goddess blind,
That stands upon the rolling restless stone—

Flu. By your patience, Aunchient Pistol. Fortune is painted blind, with a muffler afore her eyes, to signify to you that Fortune is blind; and she is painted also with a wheel, to signify to you, which is the moral of it, that she is turning, and inconstant, and mutability, and variation: and her foot, look you, is fixed upon a spherical stone, which rolls, and rolls, and rolls: in good truth, the poet makes a most excellent description of it: Fortune is an excellent moral.

Pist. Fortune is Bardolph's foe, and frowns on him;
For he hath stol'n a pax, and hanged must 'a be:
A damned death!
Let gallows gape for dog; let man go free
And let not hemp his wind-pipe suffocate:
But Exeter hath given the doom of death
For pax of little price.
Therefore, go speak; the duke will hear thy voice;
And let not Bardolph's vital thread be cut
With edge of penny cord and vile reproach:
Speak, captain, for his life, and I will thee requite.

Flu. Aunchient Pistol, I do partly understand your meaning.

Pist. Why then, rejoice therefore.

Flu. Certainly, aunchient, it is not a thing to rejoice at: for if, look you, he were my brother, I would desire the duke to use his good pleasure, and put him to execution; for discipline ought to be used.

Pist. Die and be damn'd! and figo for thy
friendship!

Flu. It is well.

Pist. The fig of Spain! *Exit.*

Flu. Very good.

Gow. Why, this is an arrant counterfeit rascal; I remember him now; a bawd, a cutpurse.

Flu. I'll assure you, 'a uttered as prave words at the pridge as you shall see in a summer's day. But it is very well; what he has spoke to me, that is well, I warrant you, when time is serve.

Gow. Why, 'tis a gull, a fool, a rogue, that now and then goes to the wars, to grace himself at his return into London under the form of a soldier. And such fellows are perfect in the great commanders' names: and they will learn you by rote where services were done; at such and such a sconce, at such a breach, at such a convoy; who came off bravely, who was shot, who disgraced, what terms the enemy stood on; and this they con perfectly in the phrase of war, which they trick up with new-tuned oaths: and what a beard of the general's cut and a horrid suit of the camp will do among foaming bottles and ale-washed wits, is wonderful to be thought on. But you must learn to know such slanders of the age, or else you may be marvellously mistook.

Flu. I tell you what, Captain Gower; I do perceive he is not the man that he would gladly make show to the world he is: if I find a hole in his coat, I will tell him my mind. [*Drum heard.*] Hark you, the king is coming, and I must speak with him from the pridge.

Drum and colours. Enter the King *and his poor* Soldiers [*and* Gloucester].

God pless your majesty!

K. Hen. How now, Fluellen! camest thou from the
bridge?

Flu. Ay, so please your majesty. The Duke of Exeter has very gallantly maintained the pridge: the French is gone off, look you; and there is gallant and most prave passages; marry, th' athversary was have possession of the pridge; but he is enforced to retire, and the Duke of Exeter is master of the pridge: I can tell your majesty, the duke is a prave man.

K. Hen. What men have you lost, Fluellen?

Flu. The perdition of th' athversary hath been very great, reasonable great: marry, for my part, I think the duke hath lost never a man, but one that is like to be executed for robbing a church, one Bardolph, if your majesty know the man: his face is all bubukles, and whelks, and knobs, and flames o' fire: and his lips blows at his nose, and it is like a coal of fire, sometimes plue and sometimes red; but his nose is executed, and his fire 's out.

K. Hen. We would have all such offenders so cut off: and we give express charge, that in our marches through the country, there be nothing compelled from the villages, nothing taken but paid for, none of the French upbraided or abused in disdainful language; for when lenity and cruelty play for a kingdom, the gentler gamester is the soonest winner.

Tucket. Enter Montjoy.

Mont. You know me by my habit.

K. Hen. Well then I know thee: what shall I know
of thee?

Mont. My master's mind.

K. Hen. Unfold it.

Mont. Thus says my king: Say thou to Harry of England: Though we seemed dead, we did but sleep: advantage is a better soldier than rashness. Tell him we could have rebuked him at Harfleur, but that we thought not good to bruise an injury till it were full

Scene v. 5. **sprays,** branches. 6. **luxury,** lust. 9. **overlook,** rise above. **grafters,** trees from which scions are taken. 14. **nook-shotten,** full of nooks and angles. 18. **sodden,** boiled. 19. **sur-rein'd jades,** overridden horses. **barley-broth,** beer. 20. **Decoct,** warm up. 23. **roping,** hanging down like a rope. 33. **lavoltas, corantos,** fashionable dances. 36. **Montjoy,** title of the chief herald of France. Shakespeare apparently took it for a name. 52. **void his rheum,** spit.

Scene vi. 2. **bridge.** According to Holinshed, the French were beaten in their attempt to break down the bridge over the Ternois. 13. **aunchient lieutenant.** Pistol is elsewhere given the rank of ancient, or ensign. 27. **buxom,** lively. 42. **pax.** Holinshed describes the object stolen as a *pyx*, the vessel containing the consecrated host. Shakespeare may have changed this into *pax*, a metal disk engraved with the crucifix, kissed during Mass. 60. **figo,** fig. 70. **gull,** simpleton. 76. **sconce,** a fort. 103. **perdition,** losses. 108. **bubukles.** Fluellen confuses "bubo" and "carbuncle." 109. **whelks,** boils. 120. *Stage Direction:* ***Tucket,*** trumpet signal. 121. **habit,** tabard, herald's coat.

ripe: now we speak upon our cue, and our voice is imperial: England shall repent his folly, see his weakness, and admire our sufferance. Bid him therefore consider of his ransom; which must proportion the losses we have borne, the subjects we have lost, the disgrace we have digested; which in weight to re-answer, his pettiness would bow under. For our losses, his exchequer is too poor; for the effusion of our blood, the muster of his kingdom too faint a number; and for our disgrace, his own person, kneeling at our feet, but a weak and worthless satisfaction. To this add defiance: and tell him, for conclusion, he hath betrayed his followers, whose condemnation is pronounced. So far my king and master; so much my office.

K. Hen. What is thy name? I know thy quality.

Mont. Montjoy.

K. Hen. Thou dost thy office fairly. Turn thee back,
And tell thy king I do not seek him now;
But could be willing to march on to Calais
Without impeachment: for, to say the sooth,
Though 'tis no wisdom to confess so much
Unto an enemy of craft and vantage,
My people are with sickness much enfeebled,
My numbers lessen'd, and those few I have
Almost no better than so many French;
Who when they were in health, I tell thee, herald,
I thought upon one pair of English legs
Did march three Frenchmen. Yet, forgive me, God,
That I do brag thus! This your air of France
Hath blown that vice in me; I must repent.
Go therefore, tell thy master here I am;
My ransom is this frail and worthless trunk,
My army but a weak and sickly guard;
Yet, God before, tell him we will come on,
Though France himself and such another neighbour
Stand in our way. There 's for thy labour, Montjoy.
Go, bid thy master well advise himself:
If we may pass, we will; if we be hind'red,
We shall your tawny ground with your red blood
Discolour: and so, Montjoy, fare you well.
The sum of all our answer is but this:
We would not seek a battle, as we are;
Nor, as we are, we say we will not shun it:
So tell your master.

Mont. I shall deliver so. Thanks to your highness. [*Exit.*]

Glou. I hope they will not come upon us now.

K. Hen. We are in God's hand, brother, not in theirs.
March to the bridge; it now draws toward night:
Beyond the river we'll encamp ourselves,
And on to-morrow bid them march away. *Exeunt.*

[SCENE VII. *The French camp, near Agincourt.*]

Enter the CONSTABLE OF FRANCE, *the* LORD RAMBURES, ORLEANS, DAUPHIN, *with others.*

Con. Tut! I have the best armour of the world. Would it were day!

Orl. You have an excellent armour; but let my horse have his due.

Con. It is the best horse of Europe.

Orl. Will it never be morning?

Dau. My Lord of Orleans, and my lord high constable, you talk of horse and armour?

Orl. You are as well provided of both as any prince in the world.

Dau. What a long night is this! I will not change my horse with any that treads but on four pasterns. Ça, ha! he bounds from the earth, as if his entrails were hairs; le cheval volant, the Pegasus, chez les narines de feu! When I bestride him, I soar, I am a hawk: he trots the air; the earth sings when he touches it; the basest horn of his hoof is more musical than the pipe of Hermes.

Orl. He 's of the colour of the nutmeg.

Dau. And of the heat of the ginger. It is a beast for Perseus: he is pure air and fire; and the dull elements of earth and water never appear in him, but only in patient stillness while his rider mounts him: he is indeed a horse; and all other jades you may call beasts.

Con. Indeed, my lord, it is a most absolute and excellent horse.

Dau. It is the prince of palfreys; his neigh is like the bidding of a monarch and his countenance enforces homage.

Orl. No more, cousin.

Dau. Nay, the man hath no wit that cannot, from the rising of the lark to the lodging of the lamb, vary deserved praise on my palfrey: it is a theme as fluent as the sea: turn the sands into eloquent tongues, and my horse is argument for them all: 'tis a subject for a sovereign to reason on, and for a sovereign's sovereign to ride on; and for the world, familiar to us and unknown, to lay apart their particular functions and wonder at him. I once writ a sonnet in his praise and began thus: 'Wonder of nature,'—

Orl. I have heard a sonnet begin so to one's mistress.

Dau. Then did they imitate that which I composed to my courser, for my horse is my mistress.

Orl. Your mistress bears well.

Dau. Me well; which is the prescript praise and perfection of a good and particular mistress.

Con. Nay, for methought yesterday your mistress shrewdly shook your back.

Dau. So perhaps did yours.

Con. Mine was not bridled.

Dau. O then belike she was old and gentle; and you rode, like a kern of Ireland, your French hose off, and in your strait strossers.

Con. You have good judgement in horsemanship.

Dau. Be warned by me, then: they that ride so and ride not warily, fall into foul bogs. I had rather have my horse to my mistress.

Con. I had as lief have my mistress a jade.

Dau. I tell thee, constable, my mistress wears his own hair.

Con. I could make as true a boast as that, if I had a sow to my mistress.

SCENE VII. 14. **hairs,** used as stuffing for tennis balls. 15-16. **le cheval . . . feu,** the flying horse, Pegasus, with nostrils breathing fire. 19. **pipe of Hermes.** Hermes charmed Argus to sleep with playing on his pipe. 34. **lodging,** lying down. 46. **horse is my mistress.** Here begins a series of bawdy double entendres involving human and animal sexuality: bears, shook your back, rode, foul bogs, doing, etc. 49. **prescript,** prescribed. 52. **shrewdly,** viciously. 56. **kern,** foot soldier. 57. **strait strossers,** tight trousers, i.e., barelegged. 68-69. **'Le chien . . . bourbier.'** Cf. II Peter 2:22. 79. **want,** be lacking (in honor). 90. **faced . . . way,** put to shame. 93. **go to hazard,** bet. 121. **hooded valour.**

Dau. 'Le chien est retourné à son propre vomissement, et la truie lavée au bourbier:' thou makest use of any thing.

Con. Yet do I not use my horse for my mistress, or any such proverb so little kin to the purpose.

Ram. My lord constable, the armour that I saw in your tent to-night, are those stars or suns upon it?

Con. Stars, my lord.

Dau. Some of them will fall to-morrow, I hope.

Con. And yet my sky shall not want.

Dau. That may be, for you bear a many superfluously, and 'twere more honour some were away.

Con. Even as your horse bears your praises; who would trot as well, were some of your brags dismounted.

Dau. Would I were able to load him with his desert! Will it never be day? I will trot to-morrow a mile, and my way shall be paved with English faces.

Con. I will not say so, for fear I should be faced out of my way: but I would it were morning; for I would fain be about the ears of the English.

Ram. Who will go to hazard with me for twenty prisoners?

Con. You must first go yourself to hazard, ere you have them.

Dau. 'Tis midnight; I'll go arm myself. *Exit.*

Orl. The Dauphin longs for morning.

Ram. He longs to eat the English.

Con. I think he will eat all he kills.

Orl. By the white hand of my lady, he 's a gallant prince.

Con. Swear by her foot, that she may tread out the oath.

Orl. He is simply the most active gentleman of France.

Con. Doing is activity; and he will still be doing.

Orl. He never did harm, that I heard of.

Con. Nor will do none to-morrow: he will keep that good name still.

Orl. I know him to be valiant.

Con. I was told that by one that knows him better than you.

Orl. What 's he?

Con. Marry, he told me so himself; and he said he cared not who knew it.

Orl. He needs not; it is no hidden virtue in him.

Con. By my faith, sir, but it is; never any body saw it but his lackey: 'tis a hooded valour; and when it appears, it will bate.

Orl. Ill will never said well.

Con. I will cap that proverb with 'There is flattery in friendship.'

Orl. And I will take up that with 'Give the devil his due.'

Con. Well placed: there stands your friend for the devil: have at the very eye of that proverb with 'A pox of the devil.'

Orl. You are the better at proverbs, by how much 'A fool's bolt is soon shot.'

Con. You have shot over.

Orl. 'Tis not the first time you were overshot.

Enter a Messenger.

Mess. My lord high constable, the English lie within fifteen hundred paces of your tents.

Con. Who hath measured the ground?

Mess. The Lord Grandpré.

Con. A valiant and most expert gentleman. Would it were day! Alas, poor Harry of England! he longs not for the dawning as we do.

Orl. What a wretched and peevish fellow is this king of England, to mope with his fat-brained followers so far out of his knowledge!

Con. If the English had any apprehension, they would run away.

Orl. That they lack; for if their heads had any intellectual armour, they could never wear such heavy head-pieces.

Ram. That island of England breeds very valiant creatures; their mastiffs are of unmatchable courage.

Orl. Foolish curs, that run winking into the mouth of a Russian bear and have their heads crushed like rotten apples! You may as well say, that 's a valiant flea that dare eat his breakfast on the lip of a lion.

Con. Just, just; and the men do sympathize with the mastiffs in robustious and rough coming on, leaving their wits with their wives: and then give them great meals of beef and iron and steel, they will eat like wolves and fight like devils.

Orl. Ay, but these English are shrewdly out of beef.

Con. Then shall we find to-morrow they have only stomachs to eat and none to fight. Now is it time to arm: come, shall we about it?

Orl. It is now two o'clock: but, let me see, by ten
We shall have each a hundred Englishmen. *Exeunt.*

ACT [IV.

PROLOGUE.]

[*Enter*] Chorus.

[*Chor.*] Now entertain conjecture of a time
When creeping murmur and the poring dark
Fills the wide vessel of the universe.
From camp to camp through the foul womb of night
The hum of either army stilly sounds,
That the fix'd sentinels almost receive
The secret whispers of each other's watch:
Fire answers fire, and through their paly flames
Each battle sees the other's umber'd face;
Steed threatens steed, in high and boastful neighs
Piercing the night's dull ear; and from the tents
The armourers, accomplishing the knights,
With busy hammers closing rivets up,
Give dreadful note of preparation:
The country cocks do crow, the clocks do toll,
And the third hour of drowsy morning name.
Proud of their numbers and secure in soul,
The confident and over-lusty French
Do the low-rated English play at dice;
And chide the cripple tardy-gaited night

The hawk was kept hooded to prevent it from beating its wings (baiting). 122. **bate,** merely flutter its wings; also, diminish. 145. **apprehension,** as used by the constable it means "sense" and "sense of danger." Orleans takes it to mean "sense" or "perception" only. 153-155. **Foolish curs . . . apples,** a picturesque reference to the courage of the dogs in the cruel sport of bearbaiting.

ACT IV. PROLOGUE. 2. **poring,** straining the eyes to see. 9. **umber'd,** shadowed, possibly by firelight. 12. **accomplishing,** equipping. 13. **rivets.** Parts of the armor might be riveted together even after it had been donned. 18. **over-lusty,** merry.

Who, like a foul and ugly witch, doth limp
So tediously away. The poor condemned English,
Like sacrifices, by their watchful fires
Sit patiently and inly ruminate
The morning's danger, and their gesture sad
Investing lank-lean cheeks and war-worn coats
Presenteth them unto the gazing moon
So many horrid ghosts. O now, who will behold
The royal captain of this ruin'd band
Walking from watch to watch, from tent to tent,
Let him cry 'Praise and glory on his head!'
For forth he goes and visits all his host,
Bids them good morrow with a modest smile
And calls them brothers, friends and countrymen.
Upon his royal face there is no note
How dread an army hath enrounded him;
Nor doth he dedicate one jot of colour
Unto the weary and all-watched night,
But freshly looks and over-bears attaint
With cheerful semblance and sweet majesty;
That every wretch, pining and pale before,
Beholding him, plucks comfort from his looks:
A largess universal like the sun
His liberal eye doth give to every one,
Thawing cold fear, that mean and gentle all
Behold, as may unworthiness define,
A little touch of Harry in the night.
And so our scene must to the battle fly;
Where—O for pity!—we shall much disgrace
With four or five most vile and ragged foils,
Right ill-dispos'd in brawl ridiculous,
The name of Agincourt. Yet sit and see,
Minding true things by what their mock'ries be. *Exit.*

[SCENE I. *The English camp at Agincourt.*]

Enter the KING, BEDFORD, *and* GLOUCESTER.

K. Hen. Gloucester, 'tis true that we are in great danger;
The greater therefore should our courage be.
Good morrow, brother Bedford. God Almighty!
There is some soul of goodness in things evil,
Would men observingly distil it out.
For our bad neighbour makes us early stirrers,
Which is both healthful and good husbandry:
Besides, they are our outward consciences,
And preachers to us all, admonishing
That we should dress us fairly for our end.
Thus may we gather honey from the weed,
And make a moral of the devil himself.

Enter ERPINGHAM.

Good morrow, old Sir Thomas Erpingham:
A good soft pillow for that good white head
Were better than a churlish turf of France.
Erp. Not so, my liege: this lodging likes me better,
Since I may say 'Now lie I like a king.'
K. Hen. 'Tis good for men to love their present pains
Upon example; so the spirit is eased:
And when the mind is quick'ned, out of doubt,
The organs, though defunct and dead before,
Break up their drowsy grave and newly move,
With casted slough and fresh legerity.
Lend me thy cloak, Sir Thomas. Brothers both,
Commend me to the princes in our camp;
Do my good morrow to them, and anon
Desire them all to my pavilion.
Glou. We shall, my liege.
Erp. Shall I attend your grace?
K. Hen. No, my good knight,
Go with my brothers to my lords of England:
I and my bosom must debate a while,
And then I would no other company.
Erp. The Lord in heaven bless thee, noble Harry!
Exeunt [*all but King*].
K. Hen. God-a-mercy, old heart! thou speak'st cheerfully.

Enter PISTOL.

Pist. Qui va là?
K. Hen. A friend.
Pist. Discuss unto me; art thou officer?
Or art thou base, common and popular?
K. Hen. I am a gentleman of a company.
Pist. Trail'st thou the puissant pike?
K. Hen. Even so. What are you?
Pist. As good a gentleman as the emperor.
K. Hen. Then you are a better than the king.
Pist. The king 's a bawcock, and a heart of gold,
A lad of life, an imp of fame;
Of parents good, of fist most valiant:
I kiss his dirty shoe, and from heart-string
I love the lovely bully. What is thy name?
K. Hen. Harry le Roy.
Pist. Le Roy! a Cornish name: art thou of Cornish crew?
K. Hen. No, I am a Welshman.
Pist. Know'st thou Fluellen?
K. Hen. Yes.
Pist. Tell him, I'll knock his leek about his pate
Upon Saint Davy's day.
K. Hen. Do not you wear your dagger in your cap that day, lest he knock that about yours.
Pist. Art thou his friend?
K. Hen. And his kinsman too.
Pist. The figo for thee, then!
K. Hen. I thank you: God be with you!
Pist. My name is Pistol call'd. *Exit.*
K. Hen. It sorts well with your fierceness.
Manet King [*aside*].

Enter FLUELLEN *and* GOWER.

Gow. Captain Fluellen!
Flu. So! in the name of Jesu Christ, speak lower. It is the greatest admiration in the universal world, when the true and aunchient prerogatifes and laws of the wars is not kept: if you would take the pains but to examine the wars of Pompey the Great, you shall find, I warrant you, that there is no tiddle taddle nor pibble pabble in Pompey's camp; I warrant you, you shall find the ceremonies of the wars, and the cares of

22. **The poor condemned English.** Shakespeare has somewhat exaggerated the wretchedness of the English in order to exalt the courage of his hero. 25. **gesture,** bearing. 26. **Investing,** clothing, adorning. 36. **enrounded,** surrounded. 38. **all-watched,** spent entirely in wakefulness and waiting. 39. **over-bears attaint,** overcomes the effects of weariness and depression. 45. **mean and gentle,** those of low and those of high birth. 46. **as . . . define,** as we can express to you only imperfectly. 53. **Minding,** bearing in mind. **mock'ries,** inadequate imitations.

SCENE I. 8. **they,** may refer to *things evil,* above, or to the French. 10. **dress,** prepare. 19. **Upon example,** in exemplary fashion. 23. **slough,** skin of a snake. **legerity,** nimbleness. 35. **Qui va là?** Who goes there? 38. **popular,** of low birth. 40. **Trail'st . . . pike?** Are you in the infantry? The pike was a long weapon which, in the pike exercise, was it, and the forms of it, and the sobriety of it, and the modesty of it, to be otherwise.

Gow. Why, the enemy is loud; you hear him all night.

Flu. If the enemy is an ass and a fool and a prating coxcomb, is it meet, think you, that we should also, look you, be an ass and a fool and a prating coxcomb? in your own conscience, now?

Gow. I will speak lower.

Flu. I pray you and beseech you that you will.

Exit [*with Gower*].

K. Hen. Though it appear a little out of fashion,
There is much care and valour in this Welshman.

Enter three soldiers, John Bates, Alexander Court, *and* Michael Williams.

Court. Brother John Bates, is not that the morning which breaks yonder?

Bates. I think it be: but we have no great cause to desire the approach of day.

Will. We see yonder the beginning of the day, but I think we shall never see the end of it. Who goes there?

K. Hen. A friend.

Will. Under what captain serve you?

K. Hen. Under Sir Thomas Erpingham.

Will. A good old commander and a most kind gentleman: I pray you, what thinks he of our estate?

K. Hen. Even as men wracked upon a sand, that look to be washed off the next tide.

Bates. He hath not told his thought to the king?

K. Hen. No; nor it is not meet he should. For, though I speak to you, I think the king is but a man, as I am: the violet smells to him as it doth to me; the element shows to him as it doth to me; all his senses have but human conditions: his ceremonies laid by, in his nakedness he appears but a man; and though his affections are higher mounted than ours, yet, when they stoop, they stoop with the like wing. Therefore when he sees reason of fears, as we do, his fears, out of doubt, be of the same relish as ours are: yet, in reason, no man should possess him with any appearance of fear, lest he, by showing it, should dishearten his army.

Bates. He may show what outward courage he will; but I believe, as cold a night as 'tis, he could wish himself in Thames up to the neck; and so I would he were, and I by him, at all adventures, so we were quit here.

K. Hen. By my troth, I will speak my conscience of the king: I think he would not wish himself any where but where he is.

Bates. Then I would he were here alone; so should he be sure to be ransomed, and a many poor men's lives saved.

K. Hen. I dare say you love him not so ill, to wish him here alone, howsoever you speak this to feel other men's minds: methinks I could not die any where so contented as in the king's company; his cause being just and his quarrel honourable.

Will. That 's more than we know.

Bates. Ay, or more than we should seek after; for we know enough, if we know we are the king's subjects: if his cause be wrong, our obedience to the king wipes the crime of it out of us.

Will. But if the cause be not good, the king himself hath a heavy reckoning to make, when all those legs and arms and heads, chopped off in a battle, shall join together at the latter day and cry all 'We died at such a place;' some swearing, some crying for a surgeon, some upon their wives left poor behind them, some upon the debts they owe, some upon their children rawly left. I am afeard there are few die well that die in a battle; for how can they charitably dispose of any thing, when blood is their argument? Now, if these men do not die well, it will be a black matter for the king that led them to it; who to disobey were against all proportion of subjection.

K. Hen. So, if a son that is by his father sent about merchandise do sinfully miscarry upon the sea, the imputation of his wickedness, by your rule, should be imposed upon his father that sent him: or if a servant, under his master's command transporting a sum of money, be assailed by robbers and die in many irreconciled iniquities, you may call the business of the master the author of the servant's damnation: but this is not so: the king is not bound to answer the particular endings of his soldiers, the father of his son, nor the master of his servant; for they purpose not their death, when they purpose their services. Besides, there is no king, be his cause never so spotless, if it come to the arbitrement of swords, can try it out with all unspotted soldiers: some peradventure have on them the guilt of premeditated and contrived murder; some, of beguiling virgins with the broken seals of perjury; some, making the wars their bulwark, that have before gored the gentle bosom of peace with pillage and robbery. Now, if these men have defeated the law and outrun native punishment, though they can outstrip men, they have no wings to fly from God: war is his beadle, war is his vengeance; so that here men are punished for before-breach of the king's laws in now the king's quarrel: where they feared the death, they have borne life away; and where they would be safe, they perish: then if they die unprovided, no more is the king guilty of their damnation than he was before guilty of those impieties for the which they are now visited. Every subject's duty is the king's; but every subject's soul is his own. Therefore should every soldier in the wars do as every sick man in his bed, wash every mote out of his conscience: and dying so, death is to him advantage; or not dying, the time was blessedly lost wherein such preparation was gained: and in him that escapes, it were not sin to think that, making God so free an offer, He let him outlive that day to see His greatness and to teach others how they should prepare.

Will. 'Tis certain, every man that dies ill, the ill upon his own head, the king is not to answer it.

Bates. I do not desire he should answer for me; and yet I determine to fight lustily for him.

K. Hen. I myself heard the king say he would not be ransomed.

grasped below the head, the foot being allowed to trail on the ground. 45. **imp,** child. 51. **Welshman.** Henry was born at Monmouth, then considered part of Wales. 54-55. **leek . . . day.** On St. David's Day, March 1, the leek was worn in memory of a Welsh victory over the Saxons, since St. David, the Welsh leader, had commanded his followers to wear leeks in their caps on that occasion. The leek is therefore a patriotic emblem. 81. **conscience,** inmost thought. 107. **element shows,** sky appears. 108. **conditions,** qualities. 109. **ceremonies,** observances due royalty. 112. **stoop,** swoop down. 147. **rawly,** without provision. 153. **proportion of subjection,** proper duty of a subject. 155. **sinfully miscarry,** die in his sins. 173. **bulwark,** refuge. 176. **native,** at home. 177. **beadle,** a parish officer responsible for punishing petty offenders. 183. **unprovided,** unprepared. 188. **mote,** small impurity.

Will. Ay, he said so, to make us fight cheerfully: but when our throats are cut, he may be ransomed, and we ne'er the wiser.

K. Hen. If I live to see it, I will never trust his word after.

Will. You pay him then! That 's a perilous shot out of an elder-gun, that a poor and a private displeasure can do against a monarch! you may as well go about to turn the sun to ice with fanning in his face with a peacock's feather. You'll never trust his word after! come, 'tis a foolish saying.

K. Hen. Your reproof is something too round: I should be angry with you, if the time were convenient.

Will. Let it be a quarrel between us, if you live.

K. Hen. I embrace it.

Will. How shall I know thee again?

K. Hen. Give me any gage of thine, and I will wear it in my bonnet: then, if ever thou darest acknowledge it, I will make it my quarrel.

Will. Here 's my glove: give me another of thine.

K. Hen. There.

Will. This will I also wear in my cap: if ever thou come to me and say, after to-morrow, 'This is my glove,' by this hand, I will take thee a box on the ear.

K. Hen. If ever I live to see it, I will challenge it.

Will. Thou darest as well be hanged.

K. Hen. Well, I will do it, though I take thee in the king's company.

Will. Keep thy word: fare thee well.

Bates. Be friends, you English fools, be friends: we have French quarrels enow, if you could tell how to reckon.

K. Hen. Indeed, the French may lay twenty French crowns to one, they will beat us; for they bear them on their shoulders: but it is no English treason to cut French crowns, and to-morrow the king himself will be a clipper. *Exeunt Soldiers.*

Upon the king! let us our lives, our souls,
Our debts, our careful wives,
Our children and our sins lay on the king!
We must bear all. O hard condition,
Twin-born with greatness, subject to the breath
Of every fool, whose sense no more can feel
But his own wringing! What infinite heart's-ease
Must kings neglect, that private men enjoy!
And what have kings, that privates have not too,
Save ceremony, save general ceremony?
And what art thou, thou idol ceremony?
What kind of god art thou, that suffer'st more
Of mortal griefs than do thy worshippers?
What are thy rents? what are thy comings in?
O ceremony, show me but thy worth!
What is thy soul of adoration?
Art thou aught else but place, degree and form,
Creating awe and fear in other men?
Wherein thou art less happy being fear'd
Than they in fearing.
What drink'st thou oft, instead of homage sweet,
But poison'd flattery? O, be sick, great greatness,
And bid thy ceremony give thee cure!
Think'st thou the fiery fever will go out
With titles blown from adulation?
Will it give place to flexure and low bending?
Canst thou, when thou command'st the beggar's knee,
Command the health of it? No, thou proud dream,
That play'st so subtly with a king's repose;
I am a king that find thee, and I know
'Tis not the balm, the sceptre and the ball,
The sword, the mace, the crown imperial,
The intertissued robe of gold and pearl,
The farced title running 'fore the king,
The throne he sits on, nor the tide of pomp
That beats upon the high shore of this world,
No, not all these, thrice-gorgeous ceremony,
Not all these, laid in bed majestical,
Can sleep so soundly as the wretched slave,
Who with a body fill'd and vacant mind
Gets him to rest, cramm'd with distressful bread;
Never sees horrid night, the child of hell,
But, like a lackey, from the rise to set
Sweats in the eye of Phœbus and all night
Sleeps in Elysium; next day after dawn,
Doth rise and help Hyperion to his horse,
And follows so the ever-running year,
With profitable labour, to his grave:
And, but for ceremony, such a wretch,
Winding up days with toil and nights with sleep,
Had the fore-hand and vantage of a king.
The slave, a member of the country's peace,
Enjoys it; but in gross brain little wots
What watch the king keeps to maintain the peace,
Whose hours the peasant best advantages.

Enter ERPINGHAM.

Erp. My lord, your nobles, jealous of your absence,
Seek through your camp to find you.
K. Hen. Good old knight,
Collect them all together at my tent:
I'll be before thee.
Erp. I shall do 't, my lord. *Exit.*
K. Hen. O God of battles! steel my soldiers' hearts;
Possess them not with fear; take from them now
The sense of reck'ning, if th' opposed numbers
Pluck their hearts from them. Not to-day, O Lord,
O, not to-day, think not upon the fault
My father made in compassing the crown!
I Richard's body have interred new;
And on it have bestow'd more contrite tears
Than from it issued forced drops of blood:
Five hundred poor I have in yearly pay,
Who twice a-day their wither'd hands hold up
Toward heaven, to pardon blood; and I have built
Two chantries, where the sad and solemn priests
Sing still for Richard's soul. More will I do;
Though all that I can do is nothing worth,
Since that my penitence comes after all,
Imploring pardon.

Enter GLOUCESTER.

209. **pay him,** pay him out. 210. **elder-gun,** popgun made from a hollowed branch of elder. 217. **round,** direct, brusque; see glossary. 224. **gage,** pledge. 232. **take,** give, strike. 241. **enow,** enough. 245. **crowns,** double pun on *crown* meaning "coin" and *crown* meaning "head." 246. **clipper,** one who mutilates coins by clipping the edges. 253. **wringing,** suffering. 262. **soul of adoration,** essence of the adoration (paid thee). 271. **blown,** breathed; also, bloated. 276. **find,** find out. 280. **farced,** stuffed with pompous phrases. 287. **distressful,** earned by hard work. 291. **Elysium,** the abode of the blessed. 292. **Hyperion,** the sun god. The peasant is up before the sun. 297. **fore-hand,** upper hand. 298. **member,** sharer. 301. **peasant best advantages,** most benefit the peasant. 302. **jealous of,** apprehensive because of. 308. **sense of reck'ning,** ability to count (the enemy). 310. **fault,** i.e., the deposition and murder of Richard II.

SCENE II. 2. **Montez à cheval!** To horse! 4-6. **Via . . . Orleans.** The dauphin, admiring his horse, says, "Begone, water and earth." He

Glou. My liege!
K. Hen. My brother Gloucester's voice? Ay;
I know thy errand, I will go with thee:
The day, my friends and all things stay for me. *Exeunt.*

[SCENE II. *The French camp.*]

Enter the DAUPHIN, ORLEANS, RAMBURES, *and* BEAUMONT.

Orl. The sun doth gild our armour; up, my lords!
Dau. Montez à cheval! My horse! varlet! laquais! ha!
Orl. O brave spirit!
Dau. Via! les eaux et la terre.
Orl. Rien puis? l'air et le feu.
Dau. Ciel, cousin Orleans.

Enter CONSTABLE.

Now, my lord constable!
Con. Hark, how our steeds for present service neigh!
Dau. Mount them, and make incision in their hides,
That their hot blood may spin in English eyes,
And dout them with superfluous courage, ha!
Ram. What, will you have them weep our horses' blood?
How shall we, then, behold their natural tears?

Enter Messenger.

Mess. The English are embattail'd, you French peers.
Con. To horse, you gallant princes! straight to horse!
Do but behold yon poor and starved band,
And your fair show shall suck away their souls,
Leaving them but the shales and husks of men.
There is not work enough for all our hands;
Scarce blood enough in all their sickly veins
To give each naked curtle-axe a stain,
That our French gallants shall to-day draw out,
And sheathe for lack of sport: let us but blow on them,
The vapour of our valour will o'erturn them.
'Tis positive 'gainst all exceptions, lords,
That our superfluous lackeys and our peasants,
Who in unnecessary action swarm
About our squares of battle, were enow
To purge this field of such a hilding foe,
Though we upon this mountain's basis by
Took stand for idle speculation:
But that our honours must not. What 's to say?
A very little little let us do,
And all is done. Then let the trumpets sound
The tucket sonance and the note to mount;
For our approach shall so much dare the field
That England shall couch down in fear and yield.

Enter GRANDPRÉ.

Grand. Why do you stay so long, my lords of France?
Yon island carrions, desperate of their bones,
Ill-favouredly become the morning field:
Their ragged curtains poorly are let loose,
And our air shakes them passing scornfully:
Big Mars seems bankrout in their beggar'd host
And faintly through a rusty beaver peeps:
The horsemen sit like fixed candlesticks,
With torch-staves in their hand; and their poor jades
Lob down their heads, dropping the hides and hips,
The gum down-roping from their pale-dead eyes,
And in their pale dull mouths the gimmal'd bit
Lies foul with chew'd grass, still and motionless;
And their executors, the knavish crows,
Fly o'er them, all impatient for their hour.
Description cannot suit itself in words
To demonstrate the life of such a battle
In life so lifeless as it shows itself.
Con. They have said their prayers, and they stay for death.
Dau. Shall we go send them dinners and fresh suits
And give their fasting horses provender,
And after fight with them?
Con. I stay but for my guard. On to the field!
I will the banner from a trumpet take,
And use it for my haste. Come, come, away!
The sun is high, and we outwear the day. *Exeunt.*

[SCENE III. *The English camp.*]

Enter GLOUCESTER, BEDFORD, EXETER, ERPINGHAM, *with all his host:* SALISBURY *and* WESTMORELAND.

Glou. Where is the king?
Bed. The king himself is rode to view their battle.
West. Of fighting men they have full three score thousand.
Exe. There 's five to one; besides, they all are fresh.
Sal. God's arm strike with us! 'tis a fearful odds.
God be wi' you, princes all; I'll to my charge:
If we no more meet till we meet in heaven,
Then, joyfully, my noble Lord of Bedford,
My dear Lord Gloucester, and my good Lord Exeter,
And my kind kinsman, warriors all, adieu!
Bed. Farewell, good Salisbury; and good luck go with thee!
Exe. Farewell, kind lord; fight valiantly to-day:
And yet I do thee wrong to mind thee of it,
For thou art fram'd of the firm truth of valour.
[*Exit Salisbury.*]
Bed. He is as full of valour as of kindness;
Princely in both.

Enter the KING.

West. O that we now had here
But one ten thousand of those men in England
That do no work to-day!
K. Hen. What 's he that wishes so?
My cousin Westmoreland? No, my fair cousin:
If we are mark'd to die, we are enow
To do our country loss; and if to live,
The fewer men, the greater share of honour.
God's will! I pray thee, wish not one man more.
By Jove, I am not covetous for gold,
Nor care I who doth feed upon my cost;

apparently thinks of his horse as being made only of the elements of fire and air. Orleans, with the same thought in mind, says in effect, "There is nothing [in him] then but air and fire." The dauphin replies, "There is also heaven." 9. **incision,** i.e., with spurs. 10. **spin,** gush, spatter. 11. **And . . . courage,** i.e., and put out the English eyes with the horses' superfluous blood, the proof of their excessive courage. **dout,** put out. 18. **shales,** shells. 21. **curtle-axe,** cutlass, short sword. 25. **exceptions,** objections. 29. **hilding,** worthless, base. 35. **tucket sonance,** trumpet call. 36. **dare,** cause to stare, to be stupefied. 41. **curtains,** colors, banners. 44. **beaver,** visor. 46. **torch-staves,** staves to fix candles on. 47. **Lob,** hang down. 48. **down-roping,** hanging down rope-like. 49. **gimmal'd,** jointed. 61. **trumpet,** trumpeter; the action is sometimes explained as taking a banderole, or little fringed flag, from a trumpet.

SCENE III. 13. **mind,** remind.

It yearns me not if men my garments wear;
Such outward things dwell not in my desires:
But if it be a sin to covet honour,
I am the most offending soul alive.
No, faith, my coz, wish not a man from England:
God's peace! I would not lose so great an honour
As one man more, methinks, would share from me
For the best hope I have. O, do not wish one more!
Rather proclaim it, Westmoreland, through my host,
That he which hath no stomach to this fight,
Let him depart; his passport shall be made
And crowns for convoy put into his purse:
We would not die in that man's company
That fears his fellowship to die with us.
This day is call'd the feast of Crispian:
He that outlives this day, and comes safe home,
Will stand a tip-toe when this day is nam'd,
And rouse him at the name of Crispian.
He that shall see this day, and live old age,
Will yearly on the vigil feast his neighbours,
And say 'To-morrow is Saint Crispian:'
Then will he strip his sleeve and show his scars,
And say 'These wounds I had on Crispin's day.'
Old men forget; yet all shall be forgot,
But he'll remember with advantages
What feats he did that day: then shall our names,
Familiar in his mouth as household words,
Harry the king, Bedford and Exeter,
Warwick and Talbot, Salisbury and Gloucester,
Be in their flowing cups freshly remember'd.
This story shall the good man teach his son;
And Crispin Crispian shall ne'er go by,
From this day to the ending of the world,
But we in it shall be remembered;
We few, we happy few, we band of brothers;
For he to-day that sheds his blood with me
Shall be my brother; be he ne'er so vile,
This day shall gentle his condition:
And gentlemen in England now a-bed
Shall think themselves accurs'd they were not here,
And hold their manhoods cheap whiles any speaks
That fought with us upon Saint Crispin's day.

Enter SALISBURY.

Sal. My sovereign lord, bestow yourself with speed:
The French are bravely in their battles set,
And will with all expedience charge on us.
K. Hen. All things are ready, if our minds be so.
West. Perish the man whose mind is backward now!
K. Hen. Thou dost not wish more help from England, coz?
West. God's will! my liege, would you and I alone,
Without more help, could fight this royal battle!
K. Hen. Why, now thou hast unwish'd five thousand men;
Which likes me better than to wish us one.
You know your places: God be with you all!

Tucket. Enter MONTJOY.

Mont. Once more I come to know of thee, King Harry,
If for thy ransom thou wilt now compound,
Before thy most assured overthrow:
For certainly thou art so near the gulf,
Thou needs must be englutted. Besides, in mercy,
The constable desires thee thou wilt mind
Thy followers of repentance; that their souls
May make a peaceful and a sweet retire
From off these fields, where, wretches, their poor bodies
Must lie and fester.
K. Hen. Who hath sent thee now?
Mont. The Constable of France.
K. Hen. I pray thee, bear my former answer back:
Bid them achieve me and then sell my bones.
Good God! why should they mock poor fellows thus?
The man that once did sell the lion's skin
While the beast liv'd, was kill'd with hunting him.
A many of our bodies shall no doubt
Find native graves; upon the which, I trust,
Shall witness live in brass of this day's work:
And those that leave their valiant bones in France,
Dying like men, though buried in your dunghills,
They shall be fam'd; for there the sun shall greet them,
And draw their honours reeking up to heaven;
Leaving their earthly parts to choke your clime,
The smell whereof shall breed a plague in France.
Mark then abounding valour in our English,
That being dead, like to the bullet's grazing,
Break out into a second course of mischief,
Killing in relapse of mortality.
Let me speak proudly: tell the constable
We are but warriors for the working-day;
Our gayness and our gilt are all besmirch'd
With rainy marching in the painful field;
There 's not a piece of feather in our host—
Good argument, I hope, we will not fly—
And time hath worn us into slovenry:
But, by the mass, our hearts are in the trim;
And my poor soldiers tell me, yet ere night
They'll be in fresher robes, or they will pluck
The gay new coats o'er the French soldiers' heads
And turn them out of service. If they do this,—
As, if God please, they shall,—my ransom then
Will soon be levied. Herald, save thou thy labour;
Come thou no more for ransom, gentle herald:
They shall have none, I swear, but these my joints;
Which if they have as I will leave 'em them,
Shall yield them little, tell the constable.
Mont. I shall, King Harry. And so fare thee well:
Thou never shalt hear herald any more. *Exit.*
K. Hen. I fear thou wilt once more come again for a ransom.

Enter YORK.

York. My lord, most humbly on my knee I beg

26. **yearns,** grieves. 37. **crowns for convoy,** travel pay. 39. **That . . . us,** that is afraid to risk his life in our company. 40. **Crispian.** Crispinus and Crispianus were martyrs who fled from Rome in the third century; they disguised themselves as shoemakers, and afterward became the patron saints of that craft. 45. **vigil,** evening before a feast day. 50. **advantages,** additions of his own. 63. **gentle,** raise to the rank of gentleman. 69. **bravely,** finely arrayed. 70. **expedience,** speed. 83. **englutted,** swallowed up. 84. **mind,** remind. 96. **native,** in their own land (i.e., England). 105. **grazing,** glancing off. 107. **Killing . . . mortality,** killing (their foes) as they fall back (decompose) into their elements; also, like the bullet, with a deadly rebound. 130. **vaward,** vanguard.

SCENE IV. 2-3. **Je . . . qualité.** I think that you are a gentleman of high rank. Most of Pistol's replies are nonsense. 4. **calmie custure me.** These words are perhaps derived from the refrain of a popular song, supposed to be Irish, "Calen o custure me" (Young maiden, my treasure). 8. **Perpend,** attend to, consider. 9. **fox,** sword. 11. **Egregious,** huge. 12-13. **O . . . moi!** Oh, have mercy! have pity on me! 14. **Moy.** Pistol, not understanding the French, imagines that his captive is referring to a unit of measurement, roughly equal to a bushel. 15. **rim,** midriff, diaphragm. 17-18. **Est-il . . . bras?** Is there no way to escape the strength of your arm? 20. **luxurious,** lecherous. 26.

The leading of the vaward.

K. Hen. Take it, brave York. Now, soldiers, march away:
And how thou pleasest, God, dispose the day! *Exeunt.*

[SCENE IV. *The field of battle.*]

Alarum. Excursions. Enter PISTOL, French Soldier, [*and*] Boy.

Pist. Yield, cur!

Fr. Sol. Je pense que vous êtes gentilhomme de bonne qualité.

Pist. Qualtitie calmie custure me! Art thou a gentleman? what is thy name? discuss.

Fr. Sol. O Seigneur Dieu!

Pist. O, Signieur Dew should be a gentleman:
Perpend my words, O Signieur Dew, and mark;
O Signieur Dew, thou diest on point of fox,
Except, O signieur, thou do give to me
Egregious ransom.

Fr. Sol. O, prenez miséricorde! ayez pitié de moi!

Pist. Moy shall not serve; I will have forty moys;
Or I will fetch thy rim out at thy throat
In drops of crimson blood.

Fr. Sol. Est-il impossible d'échapper la force de ton bras?

Pist. Brass, cur!
Thou damned and luxurious mountain goat,
Offer'st me brass?

Fr. Sol. O pardonnez moi!

Pist. Say'st thou me so? is that a ton of moys?
Come hither, boy: ask me this slave in French
What is his name.

Boy. Écoutez: comment êtes-vous appelé?

Fr. Sol. Monsieur le Fer.

Boy. He says his name is Master Fer.

Pist. Master Fer! I'll fer him, and firk him, and ferret him: discuss the same in French unto him.

Boy. I do not know the French for fer, and ferret, and firk.

Pist. Bid him prepare; for I will cut his throat.

Fr. Sol. Que dit-il, monsieur?

Boy. Il me commande de vous dire que vous faites vous prêt; car ce soldat ici est disposé tout à cette heure de couper votre gorge.

Pist. Owy, cuppele gorge, permafoy.
Peasant, unless thou give me crowns, brave crowns;
Or mangled shalt thou be by this my sword.

Fr. Sol. O, je vous supplie, pour l'amour de Dieu, me pardonner! Je suis gentilhomme de bonne maison: gardez ma vie, et je vous donnerai deux cents écus.

Pist. What are his words?

Boy. He prays you to save his life: he is a gentleman of a good house; and for his ransom he will give you two hundred crowns.

Pist. Tell him my fury shall abate, and I
The crowns will take.

Fr. Sol. Petit monsieur, que dit-il?

Boy. Encore qu'il est contre son jurement de pardonner aucun prisonnier, néanmoins, pour les écus que vous l'avez promis, il est content de vous donner la liberté, le franchisement.

Fr. Sol. Sur mes genoux je vous donne mille remercîmens; et je m'estime heureux que je suis tombé entre les mains d'un chevalier, je pense, le plus brave, vaillant, et très distingué seigneur d'Angleterre.

Pist. Expound unto me, boy.

Boy. He gives you, upon his knees, a thousand thanks; and he esteems himself happy that he hath fallen into the hands of one, as he thinks, the most brave, valorous, and thrice-worthy signieur of England.

Pist. As I suck blood, I will some mercy show.
Follow me!

Boy. Suivez-vous le grand capitaine. [*Exeunt Pistol, and French Soldier.*] I did never know so full a voice issue from so empty a heart: but the saying is true, 'The empty vessel makes the greatest sound.' Bardolph and Nym had ten times more valour than this roaring devil i' the old play, that every one may pare his nails with a wooden dagger; and they are both hanged; and so would this be, if he durst steal any thing adventurously. I must stay with the lackeys, with the luggage of our camp: the French might have a good prey of us, if he knew of it; for there is none to guard it but boys. *Exit.*

[SCENE V. *Another part of the field.*]

Enter CONSTABLE, ORLEANS, BOURBON, DAUPHIN, *and* RAMBURES.

Con. O diable!

Orl. O seigneur! le jour est perdu, tout est perdu!

Dau. Mort de ma vie! all is confounded, all!
Reproach and everlasting shame
Sits mocking in our plumes. O méchante fortune!
Do not run away. *A short alarum.*

Con. Why, all our ranks are broke.

Dau. O perdurable shame! let 's stab ourselves.
Be these the wretches that we play'd at dice for?

Orl. Is this the king we sent to for his ransom?

Bour. Shame and eternal shame, nothing but shame!
Let us die in honour: once more back again;
And he that will not follow Bourbon now,
Let him go hence, and with his cap in hand,
Like a base pandar, hold the chamber-door
Whilst by a slave, no gentler than my dog,
His fairest daughter is contaminated.

Con. Disorder, that hath spoil'd us, friend us now!
Let us on heaps go offer up our lives.

Orl. We are enow yet living in the field
To smother up the English in our throngs,

Écoutez . . . appelé? Listen: what is your name? 29. **firk,** trounce, with obscene double meaning. 30. **ferret,** probably, worry like a ferret. 35-38. **Que . . . gorge.** What does he say, sir? *Boy:* He bids me tell you that you must prepare yourself, because this soldier intends to cut your throat immediately. 42-45. **O . . . écus.** Oh, I pray you, for the love of God, to pardon me. I am a gentleman of a good house; preserve my life, and I shall give you two hundred crowns. 52-56. **Petit . . . franchisement.** What does he say, little sir? *Boy:* I tell you again that it is against his oath to pardon any prisoner; nevertheless for the sake of the crowns you have promised, he is willing to give you your liberty, your freedom. 57-61. **Sur . . . d'Angleterre.** On my knees I give you a thousand thanks; and I consider myself happy that I have fallen into the hands of a knight, as I think, the bravest, most valiant and distinguished gentleman in England. 70. **Suivez-vous . . . capitaine.** Follow the great captain. 76. **old play,** an allusion probably to moralities rather than the cycle plays. The Vice is traditionally associated with the wooden dagger.

SCENE V. 2. **O . . . perdu!** O sir, the day is lost, all is lost! 7. **perdurable,** everlasting. 18. **on,** in.

If any order might be thought upon.

Bour. The devil take order now! I'll to the throng:
Let life be short; else shame will be too long. *Exeunt.*

[SCENE VI. *Another part of the field.*]

Alarum. Enter the KING *and his train,* [EXETER, *and others,*] *with prisoners.*

K. Hen. Well have we done, thrice valiant countrymen:
But all 's not done; yet keep the French the field.

Exe. The Duke of York commends him to your majesty.

K. Hen. Lives he, good uncle? thrice within this hour
I saw him down; thrice up again, and fighting;
From helmet to the spur all blood he was.

Exe. In which array, brave soldier, doth he lie,
Larding the plain; and by his bloody side,
Yoke-fellow to his honour-owing wounds,
The noble Earl of Suffolk also lies.
Suffolk first died: and York, all haggled over,
Comes to him, where in gore he lay insteep'd,
And takes him by the beard; kisses the gashes
That bloodily did yawn upon his face;
And cries aloud 'Tarry, dear cousin Suffolk!
My soul shall thine keep company to heaven;
Tarry, sweet soul, for mine, then fly abreast,
As in this glorious and well-foughten field
We kept together in our chivalry!'
Upon these words I came and cheer'd him up:
He smil'd me in the face, raught me his hand,
And, with a feeble gripe, says 'Dear my lord,
Commend my service to my sovereign.'
So did he turn and over Suffolk's neck
He threw his wounded arm and kiss'd his lips;
And so espous'd to death, with blood he seal'd
A testament of noble-ending love.
The pretty and sweet manner of it forc'd
Those waters from me which I would have stopp'd;
But I had not so much of man in me,
And all my mother came into mine eyes
And gave me up to tears.

K. Hen. I blame you not;
For, hearing this, I must perforce compound
With mistful eyes, or they will issue too. *Alarum.*
But, hark! what new alarum is this same?
The French have reinforc'd their scatter'd men:
Then every soldier kill his prisoners:
Give the word through. *Exit* [*with others*].

[SCENE VII. *Another part of the field.*]

Enter FLUELLEN *and* GOWER.

Flu. Kill the poys and the luggage! 'tis expressly against the law of arms: 'tis as arrant a piece of knavery, mark you now, as can be offer 't; in your conscience, now, is it not?

Gow. 'Tis certain there 's not a boy left alive; and the cowardly rascals that ran from the battle ha' done this slaughter: besides, they have burned and carried away all that was in the king's tent; wherefore the king, most worthily, hath caused every soldier to cut his prisoner's throat. O, 'tis a gallant king!

Flu. Ay, he was porn at Monmouth, Captain Gower. What call you the town's name where Alexander the Pig was born?

Gow. Alexander the Great.

Flu. Why, I pray you, is not pig great? the pig, or the great, or the mighty, or the huge, or the magnanimous, are all one reckonings, save the phrase is a little variations.

Gow. I think Alexander the Great was born in Macedon: his father was called Philip of Macedon, as I take it.

Flu. I think it is in Macedon where Alexander is porn. I tell you, captain, if you look in the maps of the 'orld, I warrant you sall find, in the comparisons between Macedon and Monmouth, that the situations, look you, is both alike. There is a river in Macedon; and there is also moreover a river at Monmouth: it is called Wye at Monmouth; but it is out of my prains what is the name of the other river; but 'tis all one, 'tis alike as my fingers is to my fingers, and there is salmons in both. If you mark Alexander's life well, Harry of Monmouth's life is come after it indifferent well; for there is figures in all things. Alexander, God knows, and you know, in his rages, and his furies, and his wraths, and his cholers, and his moods, and his displeasures, and his indignations, and also being a little intoxicates in his prains, did, in his ales and his angers, look you, kill his best friend, Cleitus.

Gow. Our king is not like him in that: he never killed any of his friends.

Flu. It is not well done, mark you now, to take the tales out of my mouth, ere it is made and finished. I speak but in the figures and comparisons of it: as Alexander killed his friend Cleitus, being in his ales and his cups; so also Harry Monmouth, being in his right wits and his good judgements, turned away the fat knight with the great-belly doublet: he was full of jests, and gipes, and knaveries, and mocks; I have forgot his name.

Gow. Sir John Falstaff.

Flu. That is he: I'll tell you there is good men porn at Monmouth.

Gow. Here comes his majesty.

Alarum. Enter KING HARRY *and* BOURBON, [WARWICK, GLOUCESTER, EXETER, *and others,*] *with prisoners. Flourish.*

K. Hen. I was not angry since I came to France
Until this instant. Take a trumpet, herald;
Ride thou unto the horsemen on yond hill:
If they will fight with us, bid them come down,
Or void the field; they do offend our sight:
If they'll do neither, we will come to them,
And make them skirr away, as swift as stones
Enforced from the old Assyrian slings:
Besides, we'll cut the throats of those we have,
And not a man of them that we shall take
Shall taste our mercy. Go and tell them so.

Enter MONTJOY.

SCENE VI. 9. **honour-owing,** honor-owning, honorable. 21. **raught,** past tense of *reach*. 29. **waters,** tears. 31. **mother,** the tenderer part of me. 33. **compound,** come to terms. 37. **kill his prisoners.** This follows Holinshed, who says that Henry, alarmed by the outcry of the lackeys and boys of the camp, feared a new attack and ordered the prisoners killed as a means of precaution. Gower, Scene VII, 9-10, attributes the king's action to revenge.

SCENE VII. 35. **figures,** analogies, points of comparison. 41. **Cleitus,** one of the generals of Alexander the Great. 51. **great-belly doublet,** a long waistcoat then in style. 59. **trumpet,** trumpeter. 62. **void,**

Exe. Here comes the herald of the French, my liege.
Glo. His eyes are humbler than they us'd to be.
K. Hen. How now! what means this, herald? know'st thou not
That I have fin'd these bones of mine for ransom?
Com'st thou again for ransom?
Mont. No, great king:
I come to thee for charitable license,
That we may wander o'er this bloody field
To book our dead, and then to bury them;
To sort our nobles from our common men.
For many of our princes—woe the while!—
Lie drown'd and soak'd in mercenary blood;
So do our vulgar drench their peasant limbs
In blood of princes; and their wounded steeds
Fret fetlock deep in gore and with wild rage
Yerk out their armed heels at their dead masters,
Killing them twice. O, give us leave, great king,
To view the field in safety and dispose
Of their dead bodies!
K. Hen. I tell thee truly, herald,
I know not if the day be ours or no;
For yet a many of your horsemen peer
And gallop o'er the field.
Mont. The day is yours.
K. Hen. Praised be God, and not our strength, for it!
What is this castle call'd that stands hard by?
Mont. They call it Agincourt.
K. Hen. Then call we this the field of Agincourt,
Fought on the day of Crispin Crispianus.

Flu. Your grandfather of famous memory, an 't please your majesty, and your great-uncle Edward the Plack Prince of Wales, as I have read in the chronicles, fought a most prave pattle here in France.

K. Hen. They did, Fluellen.

Flu. Your majesty says very true: if your majesties is remembered of it, the Welshmen did good service in a garden where leeks did grow, wearing leeks in their Monmouth caps; which, your majesty know, to this hour is an honourable badge of the service; and I do believe your majesty takes no scorn to wear the leek upon Saint Tavy's day.

K. Hen. I wear it for a memorable honour;
For I am Welsh, you know, good countryman.

Flu. All the water in Wye cannot wash your majesty's Welsh plood out of your pody, I can tell you that: God pless it and preserve it, as long as it pleases his grace, and his majesty too!

K. Hen. Thanks, good my countryman.

Flu. By Jeshu, I am your majesty's countryman, I care not who know it; I will confess it to all the 'orld: I need not to be ashamed of your majesty, praised be God, so long as your majesty is an honest man.

K. Hen. God keep me so! Our heralds go with him.

Enter WILLIAMS.

Bring me just notice of the numbers dead
On both our parts. Call yonder fellow hither.
[*Exeunt Heralds and Gower with Montjoy.*]

Exe. Soldier, you must come to the king.

K. Hen. Soldier, why wearest thou that glove in thy cap?

Will. An 't please your majesty, 'tis the gage of one that I should fight withal, if he be alive.

K. Hen. An Englishman?

Will. An 't please your majesty, a rascal that swaggered with me last night; who, if 'a live and ever dare to challenge this glove, I have sworn to take him a box o' th' ear: or if I can see my glove in his cap, which he swore, as he was a soldier, he would wear if alive, I will strike it out soundly.

K. Hen. What think you, Captain Fluellen? is it fit this soldier keep his oath?

Flu. He is a craven and a villain else, an't please your majesty, in my conscience.

K. Hen. It may be his enemy is a gentleman of great sort, quite from the answer of his degree.

Flu. Though he be as good a gentleman as the devil is, as Lucifer and Belzebub himself, it is necessary, look your grace, that he keep his vow and his oath: if he be perjured, see you now, his reputation is as arrant a villain and a Jacksauce, as ever his black shoe trod upon God's ground and his earth, in my conscience, la!

K. Hen. Then keep thy vow, sirrah, when thou meetest the fellow.

Will. So I will, my liege, as I live.

K. Hen. Who servest thou under?

Will. Under Captain Gower, my liege.

Flu. Gower is a good captain, and is good knowledge and literatured in the wars.

K. Hen. Call him hither to me, soldier.

Will. I will, my liege. *Exit.*

K. Hen. Here, Fluellen, wear thou this favour for me and stick it in thy cap: when Alençon and myself were down together, I plucked this glove from his helm: if any man challenge this, he is a friend to Alençon, and an enemy to our person; if thou encounter any such, apprehend him, an thou dost me love.

Flu. Your grace doo's me as great honours as can be desired in the hearts of his subjects: I would fain see the man, that has but two legs, that shall find himself aggriefed at this glove; that is all; but I would fain see it once, an please God of his grace that I might see.

K. Hen. Knowest thou Gower?

Flu. He is my dear friend, an please you.

K. Hen. Pray thee, go seek him, and bring him to my tent.

Flu. I will fetch him. *Exit.*

K. Hen. My Lord of Warwick, and my brother Gloucester,
Follow Fluellen closely at the heels:
The glove which I have given him for a favour
May haply purchase him a box o' th' ear;
It is the soldier's; I by bargain should
Wear it myself. Follow, good cousin Warwick:
If that the soldier strike him, as I judge
By his blunt bearing he will keep his word,
Some sudden mischief may arise of it;
For I do know Fluellen valiant
And, touch'd with choler, hot as gunpowder,
And quickly will return an injury:
Follow, and see there be no harm between them.

leave. 64. **skirr,** scurry. 65. **Enforced,** discharged. 72. **fin'd,** agreed to pay as a fine or ransom. Henry reiterates that he has offered no ransom but his bones. 76. **book,** record. Globe (following Collier): *look.* 79. **mercenary,** of mercenary soldiers. 83. **Yerk,** kick. 88. **peer,** appear. 142. **quite . . . degree,** i.e., too high in rank to answer the challenge of one so low. 148. **Jacksauce,** saucy knave. 188. **choler,** anger.

Go you with me, uncle of Exeter. *Exeunt.*

[SCENE VIII. *Before* KING HENRY'S *pavilion.*]

Enter GOWER *and* WILLIAMS.

Will. I warrant it is to knight you, captain.

Enter FLUELLEN.

Flu. God's will and his pleasure, captain, I beseech you now, come apace to the king: there is more good toward you peradventure than is in your knowledge to dream of.

Will. Sir, know you this glove?

Flu. Know the glove! I know the glove is a glove.

Will. I know this; and thus I challenge it. *Strikes him.*

Flu. 'Sblood! an arrant traitor as any 's in the universal world, or in France, or in England!

Gow. How now, sir! you villain!

Will. Do you think I'll be forsworn?

Flu. Stand away, Captain Gower; I will give treason his payment into plows, I warrant you.

Will. I am no traitor.

Flu. That 's a lie in thy throat. I charge you in his majesty's name, apprehend him: he 's a friend of the Duke Alençon's.

Enter WARWICK *and* GLOUCESTER.

War. How now, how now! what 's the matter?

Flu. My Lord of Warwick, here is—praised be God for it!—a most contagious treason come to light, look you, as you shall desire in a summer's day. Here is his majesty.

Enter KING [HENRY] *and* EXETER.

K. Hen. How now! what 's the matter?

Flu. My liege, here is a villain and a traitor, that, look your grace, has struck the glove which your majesty is take out of the helmet of Alençon.

Will. My liege, this was my glove; here is the fellow of it; and he that I gave it to in change promised to wear it in his cap: I promised to strike him, if he did: I met this man with my glove in his cap, and I have been as good as my word.

Flu. Your majesty hear now, saving your majesty's manhood, what an arrant, rascally, beggarly, lousy knave it is: I hope your majesty is pear me testimony and witness, and will avouchment, that this is the glove of Alençon, that your majesty is give me; in your conscience, now.

K. Hen. Give me thy glove, soldier: look, here is the fellow of it.
'Twas I, indeed, thou promised'st to strike;
And thou hast given me most bitter terms.

Flu. And please your majesty, let his neck answer for it, if there is any martial law in the world.

K. Hen. How canst thou make me satisfaction?

Will. All offences, my lord, come from the heart: never came any from mine that might offend your majesty.

K. Hen. It was ourself thou didst abuse.

Will. Your majesty came not like yourself: you appeared to me but as a common man; witness the night, your garments, your lowliness; and what your highness suffered under that shape, I beseech you take it for your own fault and not mine: for had you been as I took you for, I made no offence; therefore, I beseech your highness, pardon me.

K. Hen. Here, uncle Exeter, fill this glove with crowns,
And give it to this fellow. Keep it, fellow;
And wear it for an honour in thy cap
Till I do challenge it. Give him the crowns:
And, captain, you must needs be friends with him.

Flu. By this day and this light, the fellow has mettle enough in his belly. Hold, there is twelve pence for you; and I pray you to serve God, and keep you out of prawls, and prabbles, and quarrels, and dissensions, and, I warrant you, it is the better for you.

Will. I will none of your money.

Flu. It is with a good will; I can tell you, it will serve you to mend your shoes: come, wherefore should you be so pashful? your shoes is not so good: 'tis a good silling, I warrant you, or I will change it.

Enter [*an* English] Herald.

K. Hen. Now, herald, are the dead numb'red?

Her. Here is the number of the slaught'red French.

K. Hen. What prisoners of good sort are taken, uncle?

Exe. Charles Duke of Orleans, nephew to the king;
John Duke of Bourbon, and Lord Bouciqualt:
Of other lords and barons, knights and squires,
Full fifteen hundred, besides common men.

K. Hen. This note doth tell me of ten thousand French
That in the field lie slain: of princes, in this number,
And nobles bearing banners, there lie dead
One hundred twenty-six: added to these,
Of knights, esquires, and gallant gentlemen,
Eight thousand and four hundred; of the which,
Five hundred were but yesterday dubb'd knights:
So that, in these ten thousand they have lost,
There are but sixteen hundred mercenaries;
The rest are princes, barons, lords, knights, squires,
And gentlemen of blood and quality.
The names of those their nobles that lie dead:
Charles Delabreth, high constable of France;
Jacques of Chatillon, admiral of France;
The master of the cross-bows, Lord Rambures;
Great Master of France, the brave Sir Guichard Dolphin,
John Duke of Alençon, Anthony Duke of Brabant,
The brother to the Duke of Burgundy,
And Edward Duke of Bar: of lusty earls,
Grandpré and Roussi, Faulconbridge and Foix,
Beaumont and Marle, Vaudemont and Lestrale.
Here was a royal fellowship of death!
Where is the number of our English dead?
[*Herald shows him another paper.*]
Edward the Duke of York, the Earl of Suffolk,

SCENE VIII. 15. **his,** its. 22. **contagious,** noxious, outrageous (?). 80. **sort,** rank. 85-117. **This . . . thine.** The catalogue of the slain is from Holinshed. 110. **name,** rank, importance. 128. **Non nobis,** Psalm 115, beginning "Not unto us, O Lord, not unto us, but unto thy name give glory." **Te Deum,** a song of thanksgiving beginning, "We thank thee O God." 131. **happy,** fortunate.

ACT V. Between Acts IV and V there is historically an interval of about five years during which Henry made a second campaign in France and brought the French to terms in the Treaty of Troyes.
PROLOGUE. 10. **Pales,** hems in, surrounds. 12. **whiffler,** an usher heading the procession to clear the way. 21. **signal,** token (of victory). **ostent,** external show. 29-35. **As . . . him,** seemingly an allusion to the

Sir Richard Ketly, Davy Gam, esquire:
None else of name; and of all other men
But five and twenty. O God, thy arm was here;
And not to us, but to thy arm alone,
Ascribe we all! When, without stratagem,
But in plain shock and even play of battle,
Was ever known so great and little loss
On one part and on th' other? Take it, God,
For it is none but thine!

Exe. 'Tis wonderful!

K. Hen. Come, go we in procession to the village:
And be it death proclaimed through our host
To boast of this or take that praise from God
Which is his only.

Flu. Is it not lawful, an please your majesty, to tell how many is killed?

K. Hen. Yes, captain; but with this acknowledgement,
That God fought for us.

Flu. Yes, my conscience, he did us great good.

K. Hen. Do we all holy rites;
Let there be sung 'Non nobis' and 'Te Deum;'
The dead with charity enclos'd in clay:
And then to Calais; and to England then;
Where ne'er from France arriv'd more happy men.
Exeunt.

ACT V.

[PROLOGUE.]

Enter Chorus.

[*Chor.*] Vouchsafe to those that have not read the story,
That I may prompt them: and of such as have,
I humbly pray them to admit th' excuse
Of time, of numbers and due course of things,
Which cannot in their huge and proper life
Be here presented. Now we bear the king
Toward Calais: grant him there; there seen,
Heave him away upon your winged thoughts
Athwart the sea. Behold, the English beach
Pales in the flood with men, with wives and boys,
Whose shouts and claps out-voice the deep-mouth'd sea,
Which like a mighty whiffler 'fore the king
Seems to prepare his way: so let him land,
And solemnly see him set on to London.
So swift a pace hath thought that even now
You may imagine him upon Blackheath;
Where that his lords desire him to have borne
His bruised helmet and his bended sword
Before him through the city: he forbids it,
Being free from vainness and self-glorious pride;
Giving full trophy, signal and ostent
Quite from himself to God. But now behold,
In the quick forge and working-house of thought,
How London doth pour out her citizens!
The mayor and all his brethren in best sort,
Like to the senators of th' antique Rome,
With the plebeians swarming at their heels,
Go forth and fetch their conqu'ring Cæsar in:
As by a lower but loving likelihood,
Were now the general of our gracious empress,
As in good time he may, from Ireland coming,
Bringing rebellion broached on his sword,
How many would the peaceful city quit,
To welcome him! much more, and much more cause,
Did they this Harry. Now in London place him;
As yet the lamentation of the French
Invites the King of England's stay at home;
The emperor 's coming in behalf of France,
To order peace between them; and omit
All the occurrences, whatever chanc'd,
Till Harry 's back-return again to France:
There must we bring him; and myself have play'd
The interim, by rememb'ring you 'tis past.
Then brook abridgement, and your eyes advance,
After your thoughts, straight back again to France.
Exit.

[SCENE I. *France. The English camp.*]

Enter FLUELLEN *and* GOWER.

Gow. Nay, that 's right; but why wear you your leek to-day? Saint Davy's day is past.

Flu. There is occasions and causes why and wherefore in all things: I will tell you, asse my friend, Captain Gower: the rascally, scauld, beggarly, lousy, pragging knave, Pistol, which you and yourself and all the world know to be no petter than a fellow, look you now, of no merits, he is come to me and prings me pread and salt yesterday, look you, and bid me eat my leek: it was in a place where I could not breed no contention with him; but I will be so bold as to wear it in my cap till I see him once again, and then I will tell him a little piece of my desires.

Enter PISTOL.

Gow. Why, here he comes, swelling like a turkey-cock.

Flu. 'Tis no matter for his swellings nor his turkey-cocks. God pless you, Aunchient Pistol! you scurvy, lousy knave, God pless you!

Pist. Ha! art thou bedlam? dost thou thirst, base Troyan,
To have me fold up Parca's fatal web?
Hence! I am qualmish at the smell of leek.

Flu. I peseech you heartily, scurvy, lousy knave, at my desires, and my requests, and my petitions, to eat, look you, this leek: because, look you, you do not love it, nor your affections and your appetites and your disgestions doo's not agree with it, I would desire you to eat it.

Pist. Not for Cadwallader and all his goats.

Flu. There is one goat for you. (*Strikes him.*) Will you be so good, scauld knave, as eat it?

Pist. Base Troyan, thou shalt die.

Flu. You say very true, scauld knave, when God's will is: I will desire you to live in the mean time, and

Earl of Essex, who left London on his Irish expedition on March 27, 1599; he returned unsuccessful and under a cloud on September 28 of the same year. These lines, therefore, were probably written between the dates mentioned. 32. **broached,** transfixed, spitted. 38. **emperor 's.** The Holy Roman Emperor, Sigismund, came to England on behalf of France in May 1416. 43. **rememb'ring,** reminding. 44. **brook,** tolerate, excuse.

SCENE I. 6. **scauld,** scurvy. 20. **bedlam,** crazy. **Troyan,** dissolute fellow; a current term of contempt. 21. **Parca's.** The fates, or Parcae, spun the web of life. 29. **Cadwallader,** last king of the Welsh. Pistol makes the customary taunt that the Welsh were goatherds.

eat your victuals: come, there is sauce for it. [*Strikes him.*] You called me yesterday mountain-squire; but I will make you to-day a squire of low degree. I pray you, fall to: if you can mock a leek, you can eat a leek.

Gow. Enough, captain: you have astonished him.

Flu. I say, I will make him eat some part of my leek, or I will peat his pate four days. Bite, I pray you; it is good for your green wound and your ploody coxcomb.

Pist. Must I bite?

Flu. Yes, certainly, and out of doubt and out of question too, and ambiguities.

Pist. By this leek, I will most horribly revenge: I eat and eat, I swear—

Flu. Eat, I pray you: will you have some more sauce to your leek? there is not enough leek to swear by.

Pist. Quiet thy cudgel; thou dost see I eat.

Flu. Much good do you, scauld knave, heartily. Nay, pray you, throw none away; the skin is good for your broken coxcomb. When you take occasions to see leeks hereafter, I pray you, mock at 'em; that is all.

Pist. Good.

Flu. Ay, leeks is good: hold you, there is a groat to heal your pate.

Pist. Me a groat!

Flu. Yes, verily and in truth, you shall take it; or I have another leek in my pocket, which you shall eat.

Pist. I take thy groat in earnest of revenge.

Flu. If I owe you any thing, I will pay you in cudgels: you shall be a woodmonger, and buy nothing of me but cudgels. God b' wi' you, and keep you, and heal your pate. *Exit.*

Pist. All hell shall stir for this.

Gow. Go, go; you are a counterfeit cowardly knave. Will you mock at an ancient tradition, begun upon an honourable respect, and worn as a memorable trophy of predeceased valour and dare not avouch in your deeds any of your words? I have seen you gleeking and galling at this gentleman twice or thrice. You thought, because he could not speak English in the native garb, he could not therefore handle an English cudgel: you find it otherwise; and henceforth let a Welsh correction teach you a good English condition. Fare ye well. *Exit.*

Pist. Doth Fortune play the huswife with me now?
News have I, that my Nell is dead i' th' spital
Of malady of France;
And there my rendezvous is quite cut off.
Old I do wax; and from my weary limbs
Honour is cudgell'd. Well, bawd I'll turn,
And something lean to cutpurse of quick hand.
To England will I steal, and there I'll steal:
And patches will I get unto these cudgell'd scars,
And swear I got them in the Gallia wars. *Exit.*

[SCENE II. *France. A royal palace.*]

Enter, at one door, KING HENRY, EXETER, BEDFORD, [GLOUCESTER,] WARWICK, [WESTMORELAND,] *and other* Lords; *at another,* QUEEN ISABEL, *the* [FRENCH] KING, *the* DUKE OF BURGUNDY, [*the* PRINCESS KATHARINE, ALICE,] *and other French.*

K. Hen. Peace to this meeting, wherefore we are met!
Unto our brother France, and to our sister,
Health and fair time of day; joy and good wishes
To our most fair and princely cousin Katharine;
And, as a branch and member of this royalty,
By whom this great assembly is contriv'd,
We do salute you, Duke of Burgundy;
And, princes French, and peers, health to you all!

Fr. King. Right joyous are we to behold your face,
Most worthy brother England; fairly met:
So are you, princes English, every one.

Q. Isa. So happy be the issue, brother England,
Of this good day and of this gracious meeting,
As we are now glad to behold your eyes;
Your eyes, which hitherto have borne in them
Against the French, that met them in their bent,
The fatal balls of murdering basilisks:
The venom of such looks, we fairly hope,
Have lost their quality, and that this day
Shall change all griefs and quarrels into love.

K. Hen. To cry amen to that, thus we appear.

Q. Isa. You English princes all, I do salute you.

Bur. My duty to you both, on equal love,
Great Kings of France and England! That I have labour'd,
With all my wits, my pains and strong endeavours,
To bring your most imperial majesties
Unto this bar and royal interview,
Your mightiness on both parts best can witness.
Since then my office hath so far prevail'd
That, face to face and royal eye to eye,
You have congreeted, let it not disgrace me,
If I demand, before this royal view,
What rub or what impediment there is,
Why that the naked, poor and mangled Peace,
Dear nurse of arts, plenties and joyful births,
Should not in this best garden of the world,
Our fertile France, put up her lovely visage?
Alas, she hath from France too long been chas'd,
And all her husbandry doth lie on heaps,
Corrupting in it own fertility.
Her vine, the merry cheerer of the heart,
Unpruned dies; her hedges even-pleach'd,
Like prisoners wildly over-grown with hair,
Put forth disorder'd twigs; her fallow leas
The darnel, hemlock and rank fumitory
Doth root upon, while that the coulter rusts
That should deracinate such savagery;
The even mead, that erst brought sweetly forth
The freckled cowslip, burnet and green clover,
Wanting the scythe, all uncorrected, rank,
Conceives by idleness and nothing teems
But hateful docks, rough thistles, kecksies, burs,
Losing both beauty and utility.
And as our vineyards, fallows, meads and hedges,
Defective in their natures, grow to wildness,

---

37. **mountain-squire,** an allusion to the mountainous surface of Wales. 38. **squire of low degree,** allusion to a medieval romance, *The Squire of Low Degree*. 40. **astonished,** terrified. 45. **green,** raw. **coxcomb,** fool's cap; here, the scalp. 61. **groat,** fourpenny coin. 75. **respect,** consideration. 78. **gleeking and galling,** gibing and scoffing. 85. **huswife,** hussy. 86. **Nell,** F: *Doll;* text follows Capell on the ground that Mistress Quickly's name was Nell. **spital,** hospital. 87. **malady of France,** venereal disease. 91. **something lean to,** incline somewhat to.

SCENE II. 1. **wherefore,** on account of which (the peace). 16. **bent,** direction. 17. **basilisks,** large cannon; also, reptiles supposed to kill with their gaze. *Balls* probably offers a pun on "eyeballs." 27. **bar,** court. 31. **congreeted,** greeted each other. 40. **it,** its. 42. **even-pleach'd,** smoothly intertwined. 44. **fallow,** uncultivated. **leas,** meadows. 45. **darnel,** a weed. **fumitory,** a weed with a bitter taste.

Even so our houses and ourselves and children
Have lost, or do not learn for want of time,
The sciences that should become our country;
But grow like savages,—as soldiers will
That nothing do but meditate on blood,—
To swearing and stern looks, diffus'd attire
And every thing that seems unnatural.
Which to reduce into our former favour
You are assembled: and my speech entreats
That I may know the let, why gentle Peace
Should not expel these inconveniences
And bless us with her former qualities.

K. Hen. If, Duke of Burgundy, you would the peace,
Whose want gives growth to th' imperfections
Which you have cited, you must buy that peace
With full accord to all our just demands;
Whose tenours and particular effects
You have enschedul'd briefly in your hands.

Bur. The king hath heard them; to the which as yet
There is no answer made.

K. Hen. Well then the peace,
Which you before so urg'd, lies in his answer.

Fr. King. I have but with a cursitory eye
O'erglanc'd the articles: pleaseth your grace
To appoint some of your council presently
To sit with us once more, with better heed
To re-survey them, we will suddenly
Pass our accept and peremptory answer.

K. Hen. Brother, we shall. Go, uncle Exeter,
And brother Clarence, and you, brother Gloucester,
Warwick and Huntingdon, go with the king;
And take with you free power to ratify,
Augment, or alter, as your wisdoms best
Shall see advantageable for our dignity,
Any thing in or out of our demands,
And we'll consign thereto. Will you, fair sister,
Go with the princes, or stay here with us?

Q. Isa. Our gracious brother, I will go with them:
Haply a woman's voice may do some good,
When articles too nicely urg'd be stood on.

K. Hen. Yet leave our cousin Katharine here with us:
She is our capital demand, compris'd
Within the fore-rank of our articles.

Q. Isa. She hath good leave.

Exeunt omnes. Mane[n]t KING [HENRY] *and* KATHARINE [*with* ALICE].

K. Hen. Fair Katharine, and most fair,
Will you vouchsafe to teach a soldier terms
Such as will enter at a lady's ear
And plead his love-suit to her gentle heart?

Kath. Your majesty shall mock at me; I cannot speak your England.

K. Hen. O fair Katharine, if you will love me soundly with your French heart, I will be glad to hear you confess it brokenly with your English tongue. Do you like me, Kate?

Kath. Pardonnez-moi, I cannot tell vat is 'like me.'

K. Hen. An angel is like you, Kate, and you are like an angel.

Kath. Que dit-il? que je suis semblable à les anges?

Alice. Oui, vraiment, sauf votre grace, ainsi dit-il.

K. Hen. I said so, dear Katharine; and I must not blush to affirm it.

Kath. O bon Dieu! les langues des hommes sont pleines de tromperies.

K. Hen. What says she, fair one? that the tongues of men are full of deceits?

Alice. Oui, dat de tongues of de mans is be full of deceits: dat is de princess.

K. Hen. The princess is the better Englishwoman. I' faith, Kate, my wooing is fit for thy understanding: I am glad thou canst speak no better English; for, if thou couldst, thou wouldst find me such a plain king that thou wouldst think I had sold my farm to buy my crown. I know no ways to mince it in love, but directly to say 'I love you:' then if you urge me farther than to say 'do you in faith?' I wear out my suit. Give me your answer; i' faith, do: and so clap hands and a bargain: how say you, lady?

Kath. Sauf votre honneur, me understand vell.

K. Hen. Marry, if you would put me to verses or to dance for your sake, Kate, why you undid me: for the one, I have neither words nor measure, and for the other, I have no strength in measure, yet a reasonable measure in strength. If I could win a lady at leap-frog, or by vaulting into my saddle with my armour on my back, under the correction of bragging be it spoken, I should quickly leap into a wife. Or if I might buffet for my love, or bound my horse for her favours, I could lay on like a butcher and sit like a jack-an-apes, never off. But, before God, Kate, I cannot look greenly nor gasp out my eloquence, nor I have no cunning in protestation; only downright oaths, which I never use till urged, nor never break for urging. If thou canst love a fellow of this temper, Kate, whose face is not worth sunburning, that never looks in his glass for love of any thing he sees there, let thine eye be thy cook. I speak to thee plain soldier: if thou canst love me for this, take me; if not, to say to thee that I shall die, is true; but for thy love, by the Lord, no; yet I love thee too. And while thou livest, dear Kate, take a fellow of plain and uncoined constancy; for he perforce must do thee right, because he hath not the gift to woo in other places: for these fellows of infinite tongue, that can rhyme themselves into ladies' favours, they do always reason themselves out again. What! a speaker is but a prater; a rhyme is but a ballad. A good leg will fall; a straight back will stoop; a black beard will turn white; a curled pate will grow bald; a fair face will wither; a full eye will wax hollow: but a good heart, Kate, is the sun and the moon; or rather the sun and not the moon; for it shines bright and never changes, but keeps his course truly. If thou would have such a one, take me; and take me, take a soldier; take a soldier, take a king. And what sayest thou then to my love? speak, my fair, and fairly, I pray thee.

Kath. Is it possible dat I sould love de enemy of France?

46. **coulter,** cutting blade preceding the ploughshare. 47. **deracinate,** root out. 48. **erst,** formerly. 49. **burnet,** an herb. 51. **teems,** grows. 52. **kecksies,** dry-stemmed plants, possibly dried hemlock stalks. 54. **fallows,** land plowed and left lying. 61. **diffus'd,** disordered. 72. **Whose . . . effects,** whose general purport and specific details. 73. **enschedul'd,** drawn up in writing. 77. **cursitory,** cursory, hasty. 81. **suddenly,** speedily. 90. **consign,** agree, subscribe. 94. **nicely,** with insistence on detail. **stood on,** insisted on. 112-115. **Que . . . dit-il.** What does he say? That I am like the angels? *Alice:* Yes truly, save your grace, he says so. 133. **clap,** clasp. 145. **buffet,** box. 146. **bound,** make prance. 148. **jack-an-apes,** monkey. 156. **cook.** Probably the meaning is that she must dress him with fine qualities as a cook dresses meat. 161. **uncoined,** not coined for circulation; also, unalloyed; therefore, fixed, steady. 167. **fall,** shrink.

K. Hen. No; it is not possible you should love the enemy of France, Kate: but, in loving me, you should love the friend of France; for I love France so well that I will not part with a village of it; I will have it all mine; and, Kate, when France is mine and I am yours, then yours is France and you are mine.

Kath. I cannot tell vat is dat.

K. Hen. No, Kate? I will tell thee in French; which I am sure will hang upon my tongue like a new-married wife about her husband's neck, hardly to be shook off. Je quand sur le possession de France, et quand vous avez le possession de moi,—let me see, what then? Saint Denis be my speed!—donc votre est France et vous êtes mienne. It is as easy for me, Kate, to conquer the kingdom as to speak so much more French: I shall never move thee in French, unless it be to laugh at me.

Kath. Sauf votre honneur, le François que vous parlez, il est meilleur que l' Anglois lequel je parle.

K. Hen. No, faith, is't not, Kate: but thy speaking of my tongue, and I thine, most truly-falsely, must needs be granted to be much at one. But, Kate, dost thou understand thus much English, canst thou love me?

Kath. I cannot tell.

K. Hen. Can any of your neighbours tell, Kate? I'll ask them. Come, I know thou lovest me: and at night, when you come into your closet, you'll question this gentlewoman about me; and I know, Kate, you will to her dispraise those parts in me that you love with your heart: but, good Kate, mock me mercifully; the rather, gentle princess, because I love thee cruelly. If ever thou beest mine, Kate, as I have a saving faith within me tells me thou shalt, I get thee with scambling, and thou must therefore needs prove a good soldier-breeder: shall not thou and I, between Saint Denis and Saint George, compound a boy, half French, half English, that shall go to Constantinople and take the Turk by the beard? shall we not? what sayest thou, my fair flower-de-luce?

Kath. I do not know dat.

K. Hen. No; 'tis hereafter to know, but now to promise: do but now promise, Kate, you will endeavour for your French part of such a boy; and for my English moiety take the word of a king and a bachelor. How answer you, la plus belle Katharine du monde, mon très cher et devin déesse?

Kath. Your majestee ave fausse French enough to deceive de most sage demoiselle dat is en France.

K. Hen. Now, fie upon my false French! By mine honour, in true English, I love thee, Kate: by which honour I dare not swear thou lovest me; yet my blood begins to flatter me that thou dost, notwithstanding the poor and untempering effect of my visage. Now, beshrew my father's ambition! he was thinking of civil wars when he got me: therefore was I created with a stubborn outside, with an aspect of iron, that, when I come to woo ladies, I fright them. But, in faith, Kate, the elder I wax, the better I shall appear: my comfort is, that old age, that ill layer up of beauty, can do no more spoil upon my face: thou hast me, if thou hast me, at the worst; and thou shalt wear me, if thou wear me, better and better: and therefore tell me, most fair Katharine, will you have me? Put off your maiden blushes; avouch the thoughts of your heart with the looks of an empress; take me by the hand, and say 'Harry of England, I am thine:' which word thou shalt no sooner bless mine ear withal, but I will tell thee aloud 'England is thine, Ireland is thine, France is thine, and Henry Plantagenet is thine;' who, though I speak it before his face, if he be not fellow with the best king, thou shalt find the best king of good fellows. Come, your answer in broken music; for thy voice is music and thy English broken; therefore, queen of all, Katharine, break thy mind to me in broken English; wilt thou have me?

Kath. Dat is as it sall please de roi mon père.

K. Hen. Nay, it will please him well, Kate; it shall please him, Kate.

Kath. Den it sall also content me.

K. Hen. Upon that I kiss your hand, and I call you my queen.

Kath. Laissez, mon seigneur, laissez, laissez: ma foi, je ne veux point que vous abaissiez votre grandeur en baisant la main d'une de votre seigneurie indigne serviteur; excusez-moi, je vous supplie, mon très-puissant seigneur.

K. Hen. Then I will kiss your lips, Kate.

Kath. Les dames et demoiselles pour être baisées devant leur noces, il n'est pas la coutume de France.

K. Hen. Madam my interpreter, what says she?

Alice. Dat it is not be de fashion pour les ladies of France,—I cannot tell vat is baiser en Anglish.

K. Hen. To kiss.

Alice. Your majesty entendre bettre que moi.

K. Hen. It is not the fashion for the maids in France to kiss before they are married, would she say?

Alice. Oui, vraiment.

K. Hen. O Kate, nice customs curtsy to great kings. Dear Kate, you and I cannot be confined within the weak list of a country's fashion: we are the makers of manners, Kate; and the liberty that follows our places stops the mouth of all find-faults; as I will do yours, for upholding the nice fashion of your country in denying me a kiss: therefore, patiently and yielding. [*Kissing her.*] You have witchcraft in your lips, Kate: there is more eloquence in a sugar touch of them than in the tongues of the French council; and they should sooner persuade Harry of England than a general petition of monarchs. Here comes your father.

Enter the French Power *and the English* Lords.

Bur. God save your majesty! my royal cousin, teach you our princess English?

K. Hen. I would have her learn, my fair cousin, how perfectly I love her; and that is good English.

Bur. Is she not apt?

K. Hen. Our tongue is rough, coz, and my condition is not smooth; so that, having neither the voice nor the heart of flattery about me, I cannot so conjure up the spirit of love in her, that he will appear in his true likeness.

Bur. Pardon the frankness of my mirth, if I answer

192-195. **Je quand . . . mienne.** When I have possession of France, and you have possession of me . . . then France is yours and you are mine. 194. **Saint Denis,** patron saint of France. 199-201. **Sauf . . . parle.** Save your honor, the French that you speak is better than the English that I speak. 218. **scambling,** scrambling, struggling. 224. **flower-de-luce,** fleur-de-lis, the emblem of France. 231-232. **la plus . . . déesse,** the most beautiful Katharine in the world, my very dear and divine goddess. 241. **untempering,** unsoftening. 262. **broken music,** music in parts for different instruments. 273-277. **Laissez . . . seigneur.** Don't, my lord, don't, don't; by my faith, I do not wish you to lower your greatness by kissing the hand of your unworthy servant; excuse me, I beg you, my most powerful lord. 279-281. **Les dames . . . France.** It is not customary in France for ladies and young girls to be kissed before their marriage. 288. **Your . . . moi.** Your majesty you for that. If you would conjure in her, you must make a circle; if conjure up love in her in his true likeness, he must appear naked and blind. Can you blame her then, being a maid yet rosed over with the virgin crimson of modesty, if she deny the appearance of a naked blind boy in her naked seeing self? It were, my lord, a hard condition for a maid to consign to.

K. Hen. Yet they do wink and yield, as love is blind and enforces.

Bur. They are then excused, my lord, when they see not what they do.

K. Hen. Then, good my lord, teach your cousin to consent winking.

Bur. I will wink on her to consent, my lord, if you will teach her to know my meaning: for maids, well summered and warm kept, are like flies at Bartholomew-tide, blind, though they have their eyes; and then they will endure handling, which before would not abide looking on.

K. Hen. This moral ties me over to time and a hot summer; and so I shall catch the fly, your cousin, in the latter end and she must be blind too.

Bur. As love is, my lord, before it loves.

K. Hen. It is so: and you may, some of you, thank love for my blindness, who cannot see many a fair French city for one fair French maid that stands in my way.

Fr. King. Yes, my lord, you see them perspectively, the cities turned into a maid; for they are all girdled with maiden walls that war hath never entered.

K. Hen. Shall Kate be my wife?

Fr. King. So please you.

K. Hen. I am content; so the maiden cities you talk of may wait on her: so the maid that stood in the way for my wish shall show me the way to my will.

Fr. King. We have consented to all terms of reason.

K. Hen. Is 't so, my lords of England?

West. The king hath granted every article:
His daughter first, and then in sequel all,
According to their firm proposed natures.

Exe. Only he hath not yet subscribed this: Where your majesty demands, that the King of France, having any occasion to write for matter of grant, shall name your highness in this form and with this addition, in French, Notre très-cher fils Henri, Roi d'Angleterre, Héritier de France; and thus in Latin, Præclarissimus filius noster Henricus, Rex Angliæ, et Hæres Franciæ.

Fr. King. Nor this I have not, brother, so denied,
But your request shall make me let it pass.

K. Hen. I pray you then, in love and dear alliance,
Let that one article rank with the rest;
And thereupon give me your daughter.

Fr. King. Take her, fair son, and from her blood raise up
Issue to me; that the contending kingdoms
Of France and England, whose very shores look pale
With envy of each other's happiness,
May cease their hatred, and this dear conjunction
Plant neighbourhood and Christian-like accord
In their sweet bosoms, that never war advance
His bleeding sword 'twixt England and fair France.

All. Amen!

K. Hen. Now, welcome, Kate: and bear me witness all,
That here I kiss her as my sovereign queen. *Flourish.*

Q. Isa. God, the best maker of all marriages,
Combine your hearts in one, your realms in one!
As man and wife, being two, are one in love,
So be there 'twixt your kingdoms such a spousal,
That never may ill office, or fell jealousy,
Which troubles oft the bed of blessed marriage,
Thrust in between the paction of these kingdoms,
To make divorce of their incorporate league;
That English may as French, French Englishmen,
Receive each other. God speak this Amen!

All. Amen!

K. Hen. Prepare we for our marriage: on which day,
My Lord of Burgundy, we'll take your oath,
And all the peers', for surety of our leagues.
Then shall I swear to Kate, and you to me;
And may our oaths well kept and prosp'rous be!
Sennet. Exeunt.

[EPILOGUE.]

Enter Chorus.

[*Chor.*] Thus far, with rough and all-unable pen,
Our bending author hath pursu'd the story,
In little room confining mighty men,
Mangling by starts the full course of their glory.
Small time, but in that small most greatly liv'd
This star of England: Fortune made his sword;
By which the world's best garden he achiev'd,
And of it left his son imperial lord.
Henry the Sixth, in infant bands crown'd King
Of France and England, did this king succeed;
Whose state so many had the managing,
That they lost France and made his England bleed:
Which oft our stage hath shown; and, for their sake,
In your fair minds let this acceptance take. [*Exit.*]

understands better than I. 292. **Oui, vraiment.** Yes, truly. 293. **nice,** fastidious. 295. **list,** limit, barrier. 320. **conjure in her,** with bawdy double meaning, continued in *circle, hard,* etc. 326. **consign,** agree. 336. **Bartholomew-tide,** St. Bartholomew's Day, August 24. 347. **perspectively,** distorted by a perspective glass. 368. **fils,** son. 369. **Héritier,** heir. **Præclarissimus,** most renowned. Shakespeare repeats an error in Holinshed for *praecarissimus*, i.e., most dear. 393. **paction,** alliance, compact.

EPILOGUE. 2. **bending,** i.e., under the weight of his task. 13. **Which . . . shown,** a reference to the three parts of *King Henry VI*, which were written probably about 1591-1592 and may have been revived about the time that *Henry V* was on the stage.

JULIUS CAESAR

Julius Caesar stands midway in Shakespeare's dramatic career, at a critical juncture. In some ways it is an epilogue to his English history plays of the 1590's; in other ways it introduces the period of the great tragedies. The play was evidently first performed at the new Globe theatre in the fall of 1599, shortly after *Henry V* (the last of Shakespeare's history plays about medieval England) and around the time of *As You Like It* (one of the last of Shakespeare's happy romantic comedies). It may have shortly preceded *Hamlet*. It is placed among the tragedies in the Folio of 1623, where it was first published, and is entitled *The Tragedie of Julius Caesar*, but in the table of contents it is listed as *The Life and death of Julius Caesar* as though it were a history.

Julius Caesar shares with Shakespeare's history plays an absorption in the problems of civil war and popular unrest. Rome, like England, suffers an internal division reflecting the perturbed state of the heavens themselves. The commons, or plebeians, are easily swayed by demagogues. Opportunists prosper in this atmosphere of crisis, although fittingly even they are sometimes undone by their own scheming. Politics seems to require a morality quite apart from that of personal life, posing a tragic dilemma for Brutus as for Richard II or Henry VI. The blending of history and tragedy in *Julius Caesar*, then, is not unlike that found in several English history plays. Rome was a natural subject to which Shakespeare might turn in his continuing study of man's political behavior. Roman civilization had recently been elevated to new importance by the classical orientation of the Renaissance. As a model of political organization it perhaps loomed larger in Elizabethan consciousness than in ours because so few other models were available at that time, and because Greek civilization was less accessible in language and tradition. According to a widely accepted mythology, Elizabethans considered themselves descended from the Romans through another Brutus, the great-grandson of Aeneas.

Yet the differences between Roman and English history are as important as the similarities. Rome's choice during her civil wars lay between a senatorial republican form of government and strong single rule. Although the monarchical English might incline to be suspicious of republicanism, they had no experience to compare with it—certainly not their various revolutionary peasants' revolts such as Jack Cade's rebellion (in *2 Henry VI*). On the other hand, Roman one-man rule as it flourished under Octavius Caesar lacked the English sanctions of divine right and monarchical primogeniture. Rome was, after all, a pagan civilization, and Shakespeare carefully preserves this non-Christian frame of reference. The gods are frequently invoked, and appear to respond with prophetic dreams and auguries, but their ultimate intentions are baffling. Man strives blindly; the will of the gods is inscrutable. The outcome of *Julius Caesar* is far different from the restoration of providential order at the end of *Richard III* or *Henry V*. Calm is restored and political authority reestablished, but we are by no means sure that a divine morality has been served. Roman history for Shakespeare is history divested of its divine imperatives and located in a distant political setting, where dispassionate appraisal is less difficult. In Plutarch's *Lives* as translated by Sir Thomas North (which he consulted only briefly before, in writing *A Midsummer Night's Dream*), Shakespeare discovers a rich opportunity for pursuing the ironies of political life to which he has been increasingly drawn even in the English histories. Less restricted by the orthodoxies of the Elizabethan world view, he turns in the Roman or classical plays toward irony or outright satire (as in *Troilus and Cressida*) and toward the personal tragedy of political dilemma (as in *Coriolanus*). These are to be the dominant motifs of the Roman or classical plays, as distinguished from both the English histories and the great tragedies of evil in which politics plays a lesser part (*Hamlet*, *Othello*, *King Lear*, *Macbeth*).

Julius Caesar is a profoundly ambiguous study of civil conflict. As in *Richard II*, the play is structured around two antithetical protagonists rather than one. Caesar and Brutus, men of extraordinary abilities and debilitating weaknesses, are more like one another than either would care to admit. This antithetical balance reflects a dual tradition: the medieval view of Dante and Chaucer condemning Brutus and Cassius as conspirators, and the Renaissance view of Sir Philip Sidney and Ben Jonson condemning Caesar as a tyrant. These opposing views still live on in vari-

THE FOLGER SHAKESPEARE LIBRARY

The slaying of Caesar—a frieze by John Gregory at the Folger Shakespeare Library, Washington, D.C.

ous modern productions which seek to enlist the play on the side of conservatism or liberalism. In one famous production by Orson Welles, 1937, Caesar was made out to resemble Benito Mussolini, Italy's fascist dictator. This interpretation reflects what the conspirators themselves believe, as they cry "Liberty! Freedom! Tyranny is dead!" but the play itself will not sustain so one-sided a view.

Caesar himself is a study in paradox. He is unquestionably a great general, charismatic in politics, decisive in his judgments, and sharp in his evaluation of men—as, for example, in his distrust of Cassius with his "lean and hungry look." Yet this godlike giant, who in Cassius' phrase bestrides the narrow world "like a Colossus," is also deaf in one ear, prone to fevers and epilepsy, unable to compete with Cassius by swimming the Tiber fully armed, and afflicted with a sterile marriage. Physical limitations of this sort are common enough, but in Caesar they are constantly juxtaposed with his aspirations to be above mortal weakness. He dies boasting that he is like the "northern star," constant, unique, "Unshak'd of motion." He professes to fear nothing and yet is notoriously superstitious. On the subject of death he calmly reflects that "death, a necessary end, Will come when it will come," and then arrogantly boasts in the next moment that "danger knows full well That Caesar is more dangerous than he" (II,ii). As his wife eloquently puts it, Caesar's "wisdom is consum'd in confidence." He willfully betrays his own best instincts and ignores plain warnings through self-deception. He stops a procession to hear a soothsayer and then dismisses the man as "a dreamer." He commissions his augurers to determine whether he should stay at home on the ides of March, and then persuades himself that acting on their advice would be a sign of weakness. Most fatally, he thinks himself above flattery and so is especially vulnerable to it. The irony is that so wise and powerful a man cannot stop the process of his own fate, because his fate is inextricably woven with his character: he is the victim of his own *hubris*. His insatiable desire for the crown overbalances his judgment; no warnings of the gods can save him. Ironically, too, his complacent self-image of one who puts his own interests after those of the state leads him to ignore the letter of Artemidorus that would have told him of the conspiracy.

Brutus, for all his opposition to Caesar, is an equally paradoxical figure. His strengths are quite unlike those of Caesar, but his weaknesses are surprisingly similar. Brutus is a truly noble Roman from an ancient family whose glory it has been to defend the personal liberties of Rome, the republican tradition. Brutus' virtues are accordingly personal virtues. He enjoys an admirable rapport with his courageous and intelligent wife, and is genuinely kind to his servants. In friendship he is trustworthy. He deplores oaths in the conspiracy because his word is his bond. He finds Caesar's ambition for power distasteful and vulgar; his opposition to Caesar is both idealistic and patrician. Brutus' *hubris* is a pride of family, and on this score he is vulnerable to flattery. As Cassius reminds him, alluding to Brutus' ancestor Lucius Junius Brutus, who founded the Roman Republic in 509 B.C.: "There was a Brutus once that would have brook'd Th' eternal devil to keep his state in Rome As easily as a king" (I,ii). Should not Marcus Brutus be the second savior of his country from tyranny? Is not he a more fit leader for Rome than Caesar? " 'Brutus' and 'Caesar.' What should be in that 'Caesar'? Why should that name be sounded more than yours?" Cassius' strategy is to present to Brutus numerous testimonials "all tending to the great opinion That Rome holds of his name." Cassius plays the role of tempter here, but the notion he suggests is not new to Brutus.

Cassius works on Brutus' sense of pride much as, in a parallel and adjoining scene, Decius works on Caesar's ambition (II,i and II,ii). In these two scenes, the protagonists enter alone during the troubled night, call for a servant, receive the conspirators, and dispute the wise caution of their respective wives. Both men are prone to temptation because of their own predisposition toward what is suggested. Brutus has often thought of himself as the indispensable man for the preservation of Rome's liberties. Despite his good breeding and coolly rational manner, he is as dominating a personality as Caesar, as hard to move once his mind is made up. Indeed, the conspiracy founders on Brutus' repeated insistence on having his way. He allows no oaths among the conspirators and will not kill Antony along with Caesar. He permits Antony to speak after him in Caesar's funeral. He vetoes Cicero as a fellow-conspirator. In each instance the other conspirators are unanimously opposed to Brutus' choice but yield to him. Brutus cuts off Cassius' objections before hearing them fully, being accustomed to having his way without dispute. His motives are in part noble and idealistic: Brutus wishes to have the conspirators behave generously and openly, as heroes rather than as henchmen. Yet there is something loftily patrician in his desire to have the fruits of conspiracy without any of the dirty work. His willingness to have Antony speak after him betrays a vain confidence in his own oratory and an unjustifiable faith in the plebeian mob. Moreover, when Brutus overrides Cassius once more in the decision to fight at Philippi and is proved wrong by the event, no idealistic motive can excuse Brutus' insistence on being obeyed; Cassius is the more experienced soldier. Still, Brutus' fatal limitations as a conspirator are inseparable from his virtues as a private man. The tragic irony is that such a noble man is, by his very nature, unsuited for the stern exigencies of assassination and civil war. Brutus is strong-minded about his ideals, but he cannot be ruthless. The means and the end of revolution drift further and further apart. He cannot supply his troops at Philippi because he will not forage among the peasants of the countryside, and will not countenance among his allies the routine corruptions of an army in time of war. Even suicide is distasteful for Brutus, obliging him to embarrass his friends by asking their help. Brutus is too high-minded and genteel a man for the troubled times in which he lives.

The times indeed seem to demand ruthless action of the sort Antony and Octavius are all too ready to provide. The greatest irony of Brutus' fall is that the coup he undertakes for Roman liberty yields only further diminutions of that liberty. The plebeians are not ready for the commonwealth Brutus envisages. From the first they are portrayed as amiable but "saucy" (even in the opinion of their tribunes, Flavius and Marullus). They adulate Caesar at the expense of their previous idol, Pompey. When Brutus successfully appeals for a moment to their changeable loyalties, they cry "Let him be Caesar!" and "Caesar's better parts Shall be crown'd in Brutus" (III,ii). If Brutus were not swayed by this hero-worship, he would have good cause to be disillusioned. To his personal credit he is not the demagogue they take him for, and so cannot continue to bend them to his will. Cassius, too, for all his villain-like role as tempter to Brutus, his envious motive, and his "Epicurean" skepticism, reveals a finer nature as the play progresses. Inspired perhaps by Brutus' philosophic idealism, Cassius turns philosopher also and chooses defeat in a noble but ineffectual cause. Yet even this death is ironically futile; Cassius is misinformed about the fate of his friend Titinius and so stabs himself just when the battle is going well for the conspirators.

The ultimate victors are Antony and Octavius. Antony is the practiced Machiavel, the hypocritical bargainer with the conspirators, the masterful rhetorician who characterizes himself to the plebeians as a "plain blunt man." In cynical soliloquy at the end of his funeral oration he observes, "Now let it work. Mischief, thou art afoot, Take thou what course thou wilt" (III,ii). To be sure, he is stirred by loyalty to Caesar's memory, but he is above all one to whom the end justifies any means. He contemptuously regards Lepidus as a mere "creature" under his command. Antony is older than Octavius, and teaches the younger man about political realities, but an Elizabethan audience would probably savor the irony that Octavius will subsequently beat Antony at his own game. At Philippi, Octavius gives us a glimpse of the peremptory manner for which he is to become famous, like his predecessor. Antony and Octavius together are in any case a fearsome pair, matter-of-factly noting down the names of those who must die, including their own kinsmen. They cut off the bequests left to the populace in Caesar's will, by which Antony had won the hearts of the plebeians (IV,i). Many innocent lives must be sacrificed by the new reign of terror, including Cicero's and the unluckily named poet Cinna's. In such deaths, art and civilization must yield to expediency. Calm rationality gives way to frenzied rhetoric and to a power struggle in which Rome's republican tradition is buried forever. Such is the achievement of Brutus' noble revolution.

JULIUS CÆSAR

[*Dramatis Personae*

JULIUS CÆSAR.
OCTAVIUS CÆSAR, MARCUS ANTONIUS, M. ÆMILIUS LEPIDUS, } *triumvirs after the death of Julius Cæsar.*
CICERO, PUBLIUS, POPILIUS LENA, } *senators.*
MARCUS BRUTUS, CASSIUS, CASCA, TREBONIUS, LIGARIUS, DECIUS BRUTUS, METELLUS CIMBER, CINNA, } *conspirators against Julius Cæsar.*
FLAVIUS *and* MARULLUS, *tribunes.*
ARTEMIDORUS of Cnidos, *a teacher of Rhetoric.*
A Soothsayer.
CINNA, *a poet.* Another Poet.
LUCILIUS, TITINIUS, MESSALA, Young CATO, VOLUMNIUS, } *friends to Brutus and Cassius.*
VARRO, CLITUS, CLAUDIUS, STRATO, LUCIUS, DARDANIUS, } *servants to Brutus.*
PINDARUS, *servant to Cassius.*

CALPURNIA, *wife to Cæsar.*
PORTIA, *wife to Brutus.*

Senators, Citizens, Guards, Attendants, *&c.*

SCENE: *Rome: the neighbourhood of Sardis: the neighbourhood of Philippi.*]

ACT I.

SCENE I. [*Rome. A street.*]

Enter FLAVIUS, MARULLUS, *and certain* Commoners *over the stage.*

Flav. Hence! home, you idle creatures, get you home:
Is this a holiday? what! know you not,
Being mechanical, you ought not walk
Upon a labouring day without the sign
Of your profession? Speak, what trade art thou?
First Com. Why, sir, a carpenter.
Mar. Where is thy leather apron and thy rule?
What dost thou with thy best apparel on?
You, sir, what trade are you?
Sec. Com. Truly, sir, in respect of a fine workman,

I am but, as you would say, a cobbler.

Mar. But what trade art thou? answer me directly.

Sec. Com. A trade, sir, that, I hope, I may use with a safe conscience; which is, indeed, sir, a mender of bad soles.

Mar. What trade, thou knave? thou naughty knave, what trade?

Sec. Com. Nay, I beseech you, sir, be not out with me: yet, if you be out, sir, I can mend you.

Mar. What meanest thou by that? mend me, thou saucy fellow!

Sec. Com. Why, sir, cobble you.

Flav. Thou art a cobbler, art thou?

Sec. Com. Truly, sir, all that I live by is with the awl: I meddle with no tradesman's matters, nor women's matters; but withal I am, indeed, sir, a surgeon to old shoes; when they are in great danger, I recover them. As proper men as ever trod upon neat's leather have gone upon my handiwork.

Flav. But wherefore art not in thy shop to-day?
Why dost thou lead these men about the streets?

Sec. Com. Truly, sir, to wear out their shoes, to get myself into more work. But, indeed, sir, we make holiday, to see Cæsar and to rejoice in his triumph.

Mar. Wherefore rejoice? What conquest brings he home?
What tributaries follow him to Rome,
To grace in captive bonds his chariot-wheels?
You blocks, you stones, you worse than senseless things!
O you hard hearts, you cruel men of Rome,
Knew you not Pompey? Many a time and oft
Have you climb'd up to walls and battlements,
To tow'rs and windows, yea, to chimney-tops,
Your infants in your arms, and there have sat
The live-long day, with patient expectation,
To see great Pompey pass the streets of Rome:
And when you saw his chariot but appear,
Have you not made an universal shout,
That Tiber trembled underneath her banks,
To hear the replication of your sounds
Made in her concave shores?
And do you now put on your best attire?
And do you now cull out a holiday?
And do you now strew flowers in his way
That comes in triumph over Pompey's blood?
Be gone!
Run to your houses, fall upon your knees,
Pray to the gods to intermit the plague
That needs must light on this ingratitude.

Flav. Go, go, good countrymen, and, for this fault,
Assemble all the poor men of your sort;
Draw them to Tiber banks, and weep your tears
Into the channel, till the lowest stream
Do kiss the most exalted shores of all.

Exeunt all the Commoners.

See, whe'r their basest metal be not mov'd;
They vanish tongue-tied in their guiltiness.
Go you down that way towards the Capitol;
This way will I: disrobe the images,
If you do find them deck'd with ceremonies.

Mar. May we do so?
You know it is the feast of Lupercal.

Flav. It is no matter; let no images
Be hung with Cæsar's trophies. I'll about,
And drive away the vulgar from the streets:
So do you too, where you perceive them thick.
These growing feathers pluck'd from Cæsar's wing
Will make him fly an ordinary pitch,
Who else would soar above the view of men
And keep us all in servile fearfulness. *Exeunt.*

[SCENE II. *A public place.*]

[*Music.*] *Enter* CÆSAR; ANTONY, *for the course;* CALPURNIA, PORTIA, DECIUS, CICERO, BRUTUS, CASSIUS, CASCA, *a* Soothsayer; *after them,* MARULLUS *and* FLAVIUS.

Cæs. Calpurnia!

Casca. Peace, ho! Cæsar speaks.

Cæs. Calpurnia!

Cal. Here, my lord.

Cæs. Stand you directly in Antonius' way,
When he doth run his course. Antonius!

Ant. Cæsar, my lord?

Cæs. Forget not, in your speed, Antonius,
To touch Calpurnia; for our elders say,
The barren, touched in this holy chase,
Shake off their sterile curse.

Ant. I shall remember:
When Cæsar says 'do this,' it is perform'd.

Cæs. Set on; and leave no ceremony out. [*Music.*]

Sooth. Cæsar!

Cæs. Ha! who calls?

Casca. Bid every noise be still: peace yet again!

Cæs. Who is it in the press that calls on me?
I hear a tongue, shriller than all the music,
Cry 'Cæsar!' Speak; Cæsar is turn'd to hear.

Sooth. Beware the ides of March.

Cæs. What man is that?

Bru. A soothsayer bids you beware the ides of March.

Cæs. Set him before me; let me see his face.

Cas. Fellow, come from the throng; look upon Cæsar.

Cæs. What say'st thou to me now? speak once again.

Sooth. Beware the ides of March.

Cæs. He is a dreamer; let us leave him: pass.

Sennet. Exeunt. Mane[n]t Brutus and Cassius.

Cas. Will you go see the order of the course?

ACT I. SCENE I. 3. **mechanical,** of the class of mechanics or artisans. 4. **sign,** garb and implements. 18. **out,** i.e., of temper; also, having worn-out shoes. 26. **withal,** nevertheless; punning on "with awl." 28. **recover,** resole; cure. 29. **neat's.** *Neat* means "cattle of the ox kind." 36. **triumph.** Caesar had just overthrown the sons of Pompey in Spain at the Battle of Munda (March 17, 45 B.C.). Caesar's triumph historically took place in October of the year previous to the feast of the Lupercal or Lupercalia portrayed in this scene, but Shakespeare combines these events for compression of dramatic effect. 42. **Pompey.** Caesar had overthrown the great soldier, Pompey, at the Battle of Pharsalia in 48 B.C., and Pompey had been murdered in Egypt. This story was itself the subject of various tragedies. In the dramatic treatment of the whole theme the tragedy of Pompey had been a first part, and the tragedy of Caesar a second part. 50. **her.** The Roman custom was to speak of Father Tiber, but the English feeling for rivers as feminine here prevails. 51. **replication,** echo. 66. **whe'r,** whether. 70. **ceremonies,** ceremonial trappings. 72. **Lupercal,** a feast of purification in honor of Pan celebrated from ancient times in Rome on February 15 of each year. The celebrants, called *Luperci*, raced around the Palatine Hill and the Circus carrying thongs of goatskin called *februa* (whence *February*). With the thongs they struck those who came in their way. Women so lashed were cured of barrenness; hence Caesar's wish that Antony would strike Calpurnia (I, ii, 6-8).

SCENE II. 9. **sterile curse,** curse of sterility. 17. **Cæsar.** Caesar's referring to himself in the third person suggests a royal habit. It was, however, his custom in his *Commentaries*. 18. **ides of March,** March 15. 25. **order of the course,** performance of the race.

Bru. Not I.
Cas. I pray you, do.
Bru. I am not gamesome: I do lack some part
Of that quick spirit that is in Antony.
Let me not hinder, Cassius, your desires;
I'll leave you.
Cas. Brutus, I do observe you now of late:
I have not from your eyes that gentleness
And show of love as I was wont to have:
You bear too stubborn and too strange a hand
Over your friend that loves you.
Bru. Cassius,
Be not deceiv'd: if I have veil'd my look,
I turn the trouble of my countenance
Merely upon myself. Vexed I am
Of late with passions of some difference,
Conceptions only proper to myself,
Which give some soil perhaps to my behaviours;
But let not therefore my good friends be griev'd—
Among which number, Cassius, be you one—
Nor construe any further my neglect,
Than that poor Brutus, with himself at war,
Forgets the shows of love to other men.
Cas. Then, Brutus, I have much mistook your passion;
By means whereof this breast of mine hath buried
Thoughts of great value, worthy cogitations.
Tell me, good Brutus, can you see your face?
Bru. No, Cassius; for the eye sees not itself,
But by reflection, by some other things.
Cas. 'Tis just:
And it is very much lamented, Brutus,
That you have no such mirrors as will turn
Your hidden worthiness into your eye,
That you might see your shadow. I have heard,
Where many of the best respect in Rome,
Except immortal Cæsar, speaking of Brutus
And groaning underneath this age's yoke,
Have wish'd that noble Brutus had his eyes.
Bru. Into what dangers would you lead me, Cassius,
That you would have me seek into myself
For that which is not in me?
Cas. Therefore, good Brutus, be prepar'd to hear:
And since you know you cannot see yourself
So well as by reflection, I, your glass,
Will modestly discover to yourself
That of yourself which you yet know not of.
And be not jealous on me, gentle Brutus;
Were I a common laugher, or did use
To stale with ordinary oaths my love
To every new protester; if you know
That I do fawn on men and hug them hard
And after scandal them, or if you know
That I profess myself in banqueting
To all the rout, then hold me dangerous.
Flourish, and shout.
Bru. What means this shouting? I do fear, the people
Choose Cæsar for their king.
Cas. Ay, do you fear it?
Then must I think you would not have it so.
Bru. I would not, Cassius; yet I love him well.
But wherefore do you hold me here so long?
What is it that you would impart to me?
If it be aught toward the general good,
Set honour in one eye and death i' th' other,
And I will look on both indifferently:
For let the gods so speed me as I love
The name of honour more than I fear death.
Cas. I know that virtue to be in you, Brutus,
As well as I do know your outward favour.
Well, honour is the subject of my story.
I cannot tell what you and other men
Think of this life; but, for my single self,
I had as lief not be as live to be
In awe of such a thing as I myself.
I was born free as Cæsar; so were you:
We both have fed as well, and we can both
Endure the winter's cold as well as he:
For once, upon a raw and gusty day,
The troubled Tiber chafing with her shores,
Cæsar said to me 'Dar'st thou, Cassius, now
Leap in with me into this angry flood,
And swim to yonder point?' Upon the word,
Accoutred as I was, I plunged in
And bade him follow; so indeed he did.
The torrent roar'd, and we did buffet it
With lusty sinews, throwing it aside
And stemming it with hearts of controversy;
But ere we could arrive the point propos'd,
Cæsar cried 'Help me, Cassius, or I sink!'
I, as Æneas, our great ancestor,
Did from the flames of Troy upon his shoulder
The old Anchises bear, so from the waves of Tiber
Did I the tired Cæsar. And this man
Is now become a god, and Cassius is
A wretched creature and must bend his body,
If Cæsar carelessly but nod on him.
He had a fever when he was in Spain,
And when the fit was on him, I did mark
How he did shake: 'tis true, this god did shake:
His coward lips did from their colour fly,
And that same eye whose bend doth awe the world
Did lose his lustre: I did hear him groan:
Ay, and that tongue of his that bade the Romans
Mark him and write his speeches in their books,
Alas, it cried 'Give me some drink, Titinius,'
As a sick girl. Ye gods, it doth amaze me
A man of such a feeble temper should
So get the start of the majestic world
And bear the palm alone. *Shout. Flourish.*
Bru. Another general shout!
I do believe that these applauses are
For some new honours that are heap'd on Cæsar.
Cas. Why, man, he doth bestride the narrow world
Like a Colossus, and we petty men
Walk under his huge legs and peep about
To find ourselves dishonourable graves.
Men at some time are masters of their fates:
The fault, dear Brutus, is not in our stars,
But in ourselves, that we are underlings.
Brutus and Cæsar: what should be in that 'Cæsar'?

28. **gamesome,** fond of sports, merry. 29. **quick spirit,** liveliness, but also quick obedience. 33. **wont,** accustomed. 35. **stubborn,** rough. 40. **of some difference,** conflicting. 41. **only proper,** peculiar, relating merely. 42. **give . . . to,** sully. 49. **By means whereof,** i.e., by which mistake. 54. **just,** true. 59. **best respect,** highest repute. 71. **jealous on,** suspicious of. 73. **stale,** render stale. 74. **protester,** i.e., one who protests friendship. 76. **scandal,** slander. 77. **profess myself,** make declarations of friendship. 87. **indifferently,** impartially. 109. **hearts of controversy,** competing courage. 112. **Æneas,** son of Anchises and hero of Virgil's *Æneid;* the legendary founder of Rome (hence, "our great ancestor"). 123. **bend,** glance. 136. **Colossus,** the gigantic statue that stood astride the entrance to the harbor of Rhodes. 140.

Why should that name be sounded more than yours?
Write them together, yours is as fair a name;
Sound them, it doth become the mouth as well;
Weigh them, it is as heavy; conjure with 'em,
Brutus will start a spirit as soon as Cæsar.
Now, in the names of all the gods at once,
Upon what meat doth this our Cæsar feed,
That he is grown so great? Age, thou art sham'd!
Rome, thou hast lost the breed of noble bloods!
When went there by an age, since the great flood,
But it was fam'd with more than with one man?
When could they say till now, that talk'd of Rome,
That her wide walks encompass'd but one man?
Now is it Rome indeed and room enough,
When there is in it but one only man.
O, you and I have heard our fathers say,
There was a Brutus once that would have brook'd
Th' eternal devil to keep his state in Rome
As easily as a king.

Bru. That you do love me, I am nothing jealous;
What you would work me to, I have some aim:
How I have thought of this and of these times,
I shall recount hereafter; for this present,
I would not, so with love I might entreat you,
Be any further mov'd. What you have said
I will consider; what you have to say
I will with patience hear, and find a time
Both meet to hear and answer such high things.
Till then, my noble friend, chew upon this:
Brutus had rather be a villager
Than to repute himself a son of Rome
Under these hard conditions as this time
Is like to lay upon us.

Cas. I am glad that my weak words
Have struck but thus much show of fire from Brutus.

Enter Cæsar *and his train.*

Bru. The games are done and Cæsar is returning.

Cas. As they pass by, pluck Casca by the sleeve;
And he will, after his sour fashion, tell you
What hath proceeded worthy note to-day.

Bru. I will do so. But, look you, Cassius,
The angry spot doth glow on Cæsar's brow,
And all the rest look like a chidden train:
Calpurnia's cheek is pale; and Cicero
Looks with such ferret and such fiery eyes
As we have seen him in the Capitol,
Being cross'd in conference by some senators.

Cas. Casca will tell us what the matter is.

Cæs. Antonius!

Ant. Cæsar?

Cæs. Let me have men about me that are fat;
Sleek-headed men and such as sleep o' nights:
Yond Cassius has a lean and hungry look;
He thinks too much: such men are dangerous.

Ant. Fear him not, Cæsar; he 's not dangerous;
He is a noble Roman and well given.

Cæs. Would he were fatter! But I fear him not:
Yet if my name were liable to fear,
I do not know the man I should avoid
So soon as that spare Cassius. He reads much;
He is a great observer and he looks
Quite through the deeds of men; he loves no plays,
As thou dost, Antony; he hears no music;
Seldom he smiles, and smiles in such a sort
As if he mock'd himself and scorn'd his spirit
That could be mov'd to smile at any thing.
Such men as he be never at heart's ease
Whiles they behold a greater than themselves,
And therefore are they very dangerous.
I rather tell thee what is to be fear'd
Than what I fear; for always I am Cæsar.
Come on my right hand, for this ear is deaf,
And tell me truly what thou think'st of him.

Sennet. Exeunt Cæsar and his Train. [*Manet Casca.*]

Casca. You pull'd me by the cloak; would you speak with me?

Bru. Ay, Casca; tell us what hath chanc'd to-day,
That Cæsar looks so sad.

Casca. Why, you were with him, were you not?

Bru. I should not then ask Casca what had chanc'd.

Casca. Why, there was a crown offered him: and being offered him, he put it by with the back of his hand, thus; and then the people fell a-shouting.

Bru. What was the second noise for?

Casca. Why, for that too.

Cas. They shouted thrice: what was the last cry for?

Casca. Why, for that too.

Bru. Was the crown offered him thrice?

Casca. Ay, marry, was 't, and he put it by thrice, every time gentler than other, and at every putting-by mine honest neighbours shouted.

Cas. Who offered him the crown?

Casca. Why, Antony.

Bru. Tell us the manner of it, gentle Casca.

Casca. I can as well be hanged as tell the manner of it: it was mere foolery; I did not mark it. I saw Mark Antony offer him a crown;—yet 'twas not a crown neither, 'twas one of these coronets;—and, as I told you, he put it by once: but, for all that, to my thinking, he would fain have had it. Then he offered it to him again; then he put it by again: but, to my thinking, he was very loath to lay his fingers off it. And then he offered it the third time; he put it the third time by: and still as he refused it, the rabblement hooted and clapped their chopped hands and threw up their sweaty night-caps and uttered such a deal of stinking breath because Cæsar refused the crown that it had almost choked Cæsar; for he swounded and fell down at it: and for mine own part, I durst not laugh, for fear of opening my lips and receiving the bad air.

Cas. But, soft, I pray you: what, did Cæsar swound?

Casca. He fell down in the market-place, and foamed at mouth, and was speechless.

Bru. 'Tis very like: he hath the falling sickness.

Cas. No, Cæsar hath it not; but you and I
And honest Casca, we have the falling sickness.

Casca. I know not what you mean by that; but, I am sure, Cæsar fell down. If the tag-rag people did not clap him and hiss him, according as he pleased

stars. Cassius is defying an Elizabethan orthodoxy according to which a person's temperament was thought to be influenced by astrological factors. 159. **Brutus,** Lucius Junius Brutus, who expelled the Tarquins and founded the Roman Republic (509 B.C.). 163. **aim,** inkling. 186. **ferret,** ferretlike, i.e., small and red. 197. **given,** disposed. 204. **hears no music,** regarded as a sign of a morose and treacherous character.

238. **coronets,** chaplets, garlands. 246. **chopped,** chapped. 247. **night-caps,** scornful allusion to the *pileus*, a cap worn by the populace. Patricians went bareheaded. 249. **swounded,** fainted. 258. **falling sickness,** epilepsy. 261. **tag-rag,** literally rag; customarily applied to the rabble.

and displeased them, as they use to do the players in the theatre, I am no true man.

Bru. What said he when he came unto himself?

Casca. Marry, before he fell down, when he perceived the common herd was glad he refused the crown, he plucked me ope his doublet and offered them his throat to cut. An I had been a man of any occupation, if I would not have taken him at a word, I would I might go to hell among the rogues. And so he fell. When he came to himself again, he said, If he had done or said any thing amiss, he desired their worships to think it was his infirmity. Three or four wenches, where I stood, cried 'Alas, good soul!' and forgave him with all their hearts: but there 's no heed to be taken of them; if Cæsar had stabbed their mothers, they would have done no less.

Bru. And after that, he came, thus sad, away?

Casca. Ay.

Cas. Did Cicero say any thing?

Casca. Ay, he spoke Greek.

Cas. To what effect?

Casca. Nay, an I tell you that, I'll ne'er look you i' the face again: but those that understood him smiled at one another and shook their heads; but, for mine own part, it was Greek to me. I could tell you more news too: Marullus and Flavius, for pulling scarfs off Cæsar's images, are put to silence. Fare you well. There was more foolery yet, if I could remember it.

Cas. Will you sup with me to-night, Casca?

Casca. No, I am promised forth.

Cas. Will you dine with me to-morrow?

Casca. Ay, if I be alive and your mind hold and your dinner worth the eating.

Cas. Good: I will expect you.

Casca. Do so. Farewell, both. *Exit.*

Bru. What a blunt fellow is this grown to be!
He was quick mettle when he went to school.

Cas. So is he now in execution
Of any bold or noble enterprise,
However he puts on this tardy form.
This rudeness is a sauce to his good wit,
Which gives men stomach to digest his words
With better appetite.

Bru. And so it is. For this time I will leave you:
To-morrow, if you please to speak with me,
I will come home to you; or, if you will,
Come home to me, and I will wait for you.

Cas. I will do so: till then, think of the world.
Exit Brutus.
Well, Brutus, thou art noble; yet, I see,
Thy honourable metal may be wrought
From that it is dispos'd: therefore it is meet
That noble minds keep ever with their likes;
For who so firm that cannot be seduc'd?
Cæsar doth bear me hard; but he loves Brutus:
If I were Brutus now and he were Cassius,
He should not humour me. I will this night,
In several hands, in at his windows throw,
As if they came from several citizens,
Writings all tending to the great opinion
That Rome holds of his name; wherein obscurely
Cæsar's ambition shall be glanced at:
And after this let Cæsar seat him sure;
For we will shake him, or worse days endure. *Exit.*

[SCENE III. *The same. A street.*]

Thunder and lightning. Enter [from opposite sides] CASCA *[with his sword drawn] and* CICERO.

Cic. Good even, Casca: brought you Cæsar home?
Why are you breathless? and why stare you so?

Casca. Are not you mov'd, when all the sway of earth
Shakes like a thing unfirm? O Cicero,
I have seen tempests, when the scolding winds
Have riv'd the knotty oaks, and I have seen
Th' ambitious ocean swell and rage and foam,
To be exalted with the threat'ning clouds:
But never till to-night, never till now,
Did I go through a tempest dropping fire.
Either there is a civil strife in heaven,
Or else the world, too saucy with the gods,
Incenses them to send destruction.

Cic. Why, saw you any thing more wonderful?

Casca. A common slave—you know him well by sight—
Held up his left hand, which did flame and burn
Like twenty torches join'd, and yet his hand,
Not sensible of fire, remain'd unscorch'd.
Besides—I ha' not since put up my sword—
Against the Capitol I met a lion,
Who glaz'd upon me, and went surly by,
Without annoying me: and there were drawn
Upon a heap a hundred ghastly women,
Transformed with their fear; who swore they saw
Men all in fire walk up and down the streets.
And yesterday the bird of night did sit
Even at noon-day upon the market-place,
Hooting and shrieking. When these prodigies
Do so conjointly meet, let not men say
'These are their reasons; they are natural;'
For, I believe, they are portentous things
Unto the climate that they point upon.

Cic. Indeed, it is a strange-disposed time:
But men may construe things after their fashion,
Clean from the purpose of the things themselves.
Comes Cæsar to the Capitol to-morrow?

Casca. He doth; for he did bid Antonius
Send word to you he would be there to-morrow.

Cic. Good night then, Casca: this disturbed sky
Is not to walk in.

Casca. Farewell, Cicero. *Exit Cicero.*

Enter CASSIUS.

Cas. Who 's there?

Casca. A Roman.

Cas. Casca, by your voice.

Casca. Your ear is good. Cassius, what night is this!

Cas. A very pleasing night to honest men.

Casca. Who ever knew the heavens menace so?

262. **use,** are accustomed. 267. **ope,** open. 268. **doublet,** Elizabethan upper garment, like a jacket. 269. **occupation,** handicraft; also, with a play on "man of action." 279. **sad,** seriously. 288. **scarfs,** fillets. 290. **put to silence,** dismissed from office and banished, or executed. 293. **promised forth,** engaged to dine out. 300. **quick mettle,** of a lively temperament. 303. **However,** however much. **tardy form,** sluggishness. 317. **bear me hard,** dislike me.

SCENE III. 1. **brought,** escorted. 3. **sway,** established order. 6. **riv'd,** split. 18. **Not sensible of fire,** i.e., not feeling it. 20. **Against,** opposite or near. 21. **glaz'd,** stared. 22-23. **drawn Upon a heap,** huddled together. **ghastly,** pallid. 26. **bird of night,** owl, a bird of evil omen. 28. **prodigies,** portents. 32. **climate,** region. 35. **Clean . . . purpose,** contrary to the import or meaning. 42. **what night,** what a night. 48. **unbraced,** with doublet unfastened. 49. **thunder-stone,**

Cas. Those that have known the earth so full of faults.
For my part, I have walk'd about the streets,
Submitting me unto the perilous night,
And, thus unbraced, Casca, as you see,
Have bar'd my bosom to the thunder-stone;
And when the cross blue lightning seem'd to open
The breast of heaven, I did present myself
Even in the aim and very flash of it.
Casca. But wherefore did you so much tempt the heavens?
It is the part of men to fear and tremble,
When the most mighty gods by tokens send
Such dreadful heralds to astonish us.
Cas. You are dull, Casca, and those sparks of life
That should be in a Roman you do want,
Or else you use not. You look pale and gaze
And put on fear and cast yourself in wonder,
To see the strange impatience of the heavens:
But if you would consider the true cause
Why all these fires, why all these gliding ghosts,
Why birds and beasts from quality and kind,
Why old men, fools, and children calculate,
Why all these things change from their ordinance
Their natures and preformed faculties
To monstrous quality,—why, you shall find
That heaven hath infus'd them with these spirits,
To make them instruments of fear and warning
Unto some monstrous state.
Now could I, Casca, name to thee a man
Most like this dreadful night,
That thunders, lightens, opens graves, and roars
As doth the lion in the Capitol,
A man no mightier than thyself or me
In personal action, yet prodigious grown
And fearful, as these strange eruptions are.
Casca. 'Tis Cæsar that you mean; is it not, Cassius?
Cas. Let it be who it is: for Romans now
Have thews and limbs like to their ancestors;
But, woe the while! our fathers' minds are dead,
And we are govern'd with our mothers' spirits;
Our yoke and sufferance show us womanish.
Casca. Indeed, they say the senators to-morrow
Mean to establish Cæsar as a king;
And he shall wear his crown by sea and land,
In every place, save here in Italy.
Cas. I know where I will wear this dagger then;
Cassius from bondage will deliver Cassius:
Therein, ye gods, you make the weak most strong;
Therein, ye gods, you tyrants do defeat:
Nor stony tower, nor walls of beaten brass,
Nor airless dungeon, nor strong links of iron,
Can be retentive to the strength of spirit;
But life, being weary of these worldly bars,
Never lacks power to dismiss itself.
If I know this, know all the world besides,
That part of tyranny that I do bear
I can shake off at pleasure. *Thunder still.*
Casca. So can I:
So every bondman in his own hand bears
The power to cancel his captivity.
Cas. And why should Cæsar be a tyrant then?
Poor man! I know he would not be a wolf,
But that he sees the Romans are but sheep:
He were no lion, were not Romans hinds.
Those that with haste will make a mighty fire
Begin it with weak straws: what trash is Rome,
What rubbish and what offal, when it serves
For the base matter to illuminate
So vile a thing as Cæsar! But, O grief,
Where hast thou led me? I perhaps speak this
Before a willing bondman; then I know
My answer must be made. But I am arm'd,
And dangers are to me indifferent.
Casca. You speak to Casca, and to such a man
That is no fleering tell-tale. Hold, my hand:
Be factious for redress of all these griefs,
And I will set this foot of mine as far
As who goes farthest. [*They shake hands.*]
Cas. There 's a bargain made.
Now know you, Casca, I have mov'd already
Some certain of the noblest-minded Romans
To undergo with me an enterprise
Of honourable-dangerous consequence;
And I do know, by this, they stay for me
In Pompey's porch: for now, this fearful night,
There is no stir or walking in the streets;
And the complexion of the element
In favour's like the work we have in hand,
Most bloody, fiery, and most terrible.

Enter CINNA.

Casca. Stand close awhile, for here comes one in haste.
Cas. 'Tis Cinna; I do know him by his gait;
He is a friend.—Cinna, where haste you so?
Cin. To find out you. Who 's that? Metellus Cimber?
Cas. No, it is Casca; one incorporate
To our attempts. Am I not stay'd for, Cinna?
Cin. I am glad on 't. What a fearful night is this!
There 's two or three of us have seen strange sights.
Cas. Am I not stay'd for? tell me.
Cin. Yes, you are.
O Cassius, if you could
But win the noble Brutus to our party—
Cas. Be you content: good Cinna, take this paper,
And look you lay it in the prætor's chair,
Where Brutus may but find it; and throw this
In at his window; set this up with wax
Upon old Brutus' statue: all this done,
Repair to Pompey's porch, where you shall find us.
Is Decius Brutus and Trebonius there?
Cin. All but Metellus Cimber; and he 's gone
To seek you at your house. Well, I will hie,
And so bestow these papers as you bade me.
Cas. That done, repair to Pompey's theatre.
Exit Cinna.
Come, Casca, you and I will yet ere day
See Brutus at his house: three parts of him
Is ours already, and the man entire

thunderbolt. 50. **cross,** forked, jagged. 54. **part,** appropriate role. 58. **want,** lack. 60. **put on,** show signs of. 65. **old men,** dotards. **calculate,** prophesy. 66. **ordinance,** ordinary character and nature. 81. **thews,** sinews, muscles. 84. **yoke and sufferance,** patience under the yoke. 106. **hinds,** females of the red deer; also, servants, rustics. 114. **My answer . . . made,** I will have to answer for what I have said. 115. **indifferent,** unimportant. 117. **fleering,** mocking, flattering.

118. **factious,** active as a partisan. 126. **Pompey's porch,** a magnificent colonnade built by Pompey in 55 B.C., and attached to his great open theatre. The recesses along the sides were convenient for such meetings. 135. **incorporate,** admitted as a member. 143. **prætor's chair,** official seat of the praetor, a Roman magistrate ranking next below the consul. Brutus was praetor. 146. **old Brutus'.** Brutus was reputed to be a descendant of Lucius Junius Brutus.

Upon the next encounter yields him ours.
Casca. O, he sits high in all the people's hearts:
And that which would appear offence in us,
His countenance, like richest alchemy,
Will change to virtue and to worthiness.
Cas. Him and his worth and our great need of him
You have right well conceited. Let us go,
For it is after midnight; and ere day
We will awake him and be sure of him. *Exeunt.*

ACT II.

[SCENE I. *Rome. Brutus's orchard.*]

Enter BRUTUS *in his orchard.*

Bru. What, Lucius, ho!
I cannot, by the progress of the stars,
Give guess how near to day. Lucius, I say!
I would it were my fault to sleep so soundly.
When, Lucius, when? awake, I say! what, Lucius!

Enter LUCIUS.

Luc. Call'd you, my lord?
Bru. Give me a taper in my study, Lucius:
When it is lighted, come and call me here.
Luc. I will, my lord. *Exit.*
Bru. It must be by his death: and for my part,
I know no personal cause to spurn at him,
But for the general. He would be crown'd:
How that might change his nature, there 's the question.
It is the bright day that brings forth the adder;
And that craves wary walking. Crown him?—that;—
And then, I grant, we put a sting in him,
That at his will he may do danger with.
Th' abuse of greatness is, when it disjoins
Remorse from power: and, to speak truth of Cæsar,
I have not known when his affections sway'd
More than his reason. But 'tis a common proof,
That lowliness is young ambition's ladder,
Whereto the climber-upward turns his face;
But when he once attains the upmost round,
He then unto the ladder turns his back,
Looks in the clouds, scorning the base degrees
By which he did ascend. So Cæsar may.
Then, lest he may, prevent. And, since the quarrel
Will bear no colour for the thing he is,
Fashion it thus; that what he is, augmented,
Would run to these and these extremities:
And therefore think him as a serpent's egg
Which, hatch'd, would, as his kind, grow mischievous,
And kill him in the shell.

Enter LUCIUS.

Luc. The taper burneth in your closet, sir.
Searching the window for a flint, I found
This paper, thus seal'd up; and, I am sure,
It did not lie there when I went to bed.
Gives him the letter.
Bru. Get you to bed again; it is not day.
Is not to-morrow, boy, the ides of March?
Luc. I know not, sir.
Bru. Look in the calendar, and bring me word.
Luc. I will, sir. *Exit.*
Bru. The exhalations whizzing in the air
Give so much light that I may read by them.
Opens the letter and reads.
'Brutus, thou sleep'st: awake, and see thyself.
Shall Rome, &c. Speak, strike, redress!
Brutus, thou sleep'st: awake!'
Such instigations have been often dropp'd
Where I have took them up.
'Shall Rome, &c.' Thus must I piece it out:
Shall Rome stand under one man's awe? What, Rome?
My ancestors did from the streets of Rome
The Tarquin drive, when he was call'd a king.
'Speak, strike, redress!' Am I entreated
To speak and strike? O Rome, I make thee promise;
If the redress will follow, thou receivest
Thy full petition at the hand of Brutus!

Enter LUCIUS.

Luc. Sir, March is wasted fourteen days.
Knock within.
Bru. 'Tis good. Go to the gate; somebody knocks.
[*Exit Lucius.*]
Since Cassius first did whet me against Cæsar,
I have not slept.
Between the acting of a dreadful thing
And the first motion, all the interim is
Like a phantasma, or a hideous dream:
The Genius and the mortal instruments
Are then in council; and the state of man,
Like to a little kingdom, suffers then
The nature of an insurrection.

Enter LUCIUS.

Luc. Sir, 'tis your brother Cassius at the door,
Who doth desire to see you.
Bru. Is he alone?
Luc. No, sir, there are moe with him.
Bru. Do you know them?
Luc. No, sir; their hats are pluck'd about their ears,
And half their faces buried in their cloaks,
That by no means I may discover them
By any mark of favour.
Bru. Let 'em enter. [*Exit Lucius.*]
They are the faction. O conspiracy,
Sham'st thou to show thy dang'rous brow by night,
When evils are most free? O, then by day
Where wilt thou find a cavern dark enough
To mask thy monstrous visage? Seek none, conspiracy;
Hide it in smiles and affability:
For if thou path, thy native semblance on,
Not Erebus itself were dim enough
To hide thee from prevention.

159. **alchemy,** chemistry, the chief object of which was the transmutation of metals. 162. **conceited,** conceived, described.

ACT II. SCENE I. 12. **general,** i.e., for the sake of the general welfare. 15-27. **Crown . . . ascend.** This is a condensed statement of Brutus' motive. By *affections* (l. 20) he means "passions," but it need not be understood that he means to compliment Caesar; rather, he means to say that Caesar has those cold-blooded qualities which will make him disregard pity (*Remorse,* l. 19) when he is in power. 36. **flint,** i.e., with which to strike a light. 44. **exhalations,** meteors. 63-69. **Between . . . insurrection.** This is one of the most perfect expressions in Shakespeare of the psychology of warring emotions, hesitation, and inward conflict. The *Genius* is used to signify the soul; the *mortal instruments* are the spirits, which are the agents of reason and the will. 67. **state of man,** familiar designation of man as a microcosm. 70. **brother.** Cassius had

Enter the conspirators, CASSIUS, CASCA, DECIUS, CINNA, METELLUS [CIMBER], *and* TREBONIUS.

Cas. I think we are too bold upon your rest:
Good morrow, Brutus; do we trouble you?
Bru. I have been up this hour, awake all night.
Know I these men that come along with you?
Cas. Yes, every man of them, and no man here
But honours you; and every one doth wish
You had but that opinion of yourself
Which every noble Roman bears of you.
This is Trebonius.
Bru. He is welcome hither.
Cas. This, Decius Brutus.
Bru. He is welcome too.
Cas. This, Casca; this, Cinna; and this, Metellus Cimber.
Bru. They are all welcome.
What watchful cares do interpose themselves
Betwixt your eyes and night?
Cas. Shall I entreat a word?
They [*Brutus and Cassius*] *whisper.*
Dec. Here lies the east: doth not the day break here?
Casca. No.
Cin. O, pardon, sir, it doth; and yon gray lines
That fret the clouds are messengers of day.
Casca. You shall confess that you are both deceiv'd.
Here, as I point my sword, the sun arises,
Which is a great way growing on the south,
Weighing the youthful season of the year.
Some two months hence up higher toward the north
He first presents his fire; and the high east
Stands, as the Capitol, directly here.
Bru. Give me your hands all over, one by one.
Cas. And let us swear our resolution.
Bru. No, not an oath: if not the face of men,
The sufferance of our souls, the time's abuse,—
If these be motives weak, break off betimes,
And every man hence to his idle bed;
So let high-sighted tyranny range on,
Till each man drop by lottery. But if these,
As I am sure they do, bear fire enough
To kindle cowards and to steel with valour
The melting spirits of women, then, countrymen,
What need we any spur but our own cause,
To prick us to redress? what other bond
Than secret Romans, that have spoke the word,
And will not palter? and what other oath
Than honesty to honesty engag'd,
That this shall be, or we will fall for it?
Swear priests and cowards and men cautelous,
Old feeble carrions and such suffering souls
That welcome wrongs; unto bad causes swear
Such creatures as men doubt; but do not stain
The even virtue of our enterprise,
Nor th' insuppressive mettle of our spirits,
To think that or our cause or our performance
Did need an oath; when every drop of blood
That every Roman bears, and nobly bears,
Is guilty of a several bastardy,
If he do break the smallest particle
Of any promise that hath pass'd from him.
Cas. But what of Cicero? shall we sound him?
I think he will stand very strong with us.
Casca. Let us not leave him out.
Cin. No, by no means.
Met. O, let us have him, for his silver hairs
Will purchase us a good opinion
And buy men's voices to commend our deeds:
It shall be said, his judgement rul'd our hands;
Our youths and wildness shall no whit appear,
But all be buried in his gravity.
Bru. O, name him not: let us not break with him;
For he will never follow any thing
That other men begin.
Cas. Then leave him out.
Casca. Indeed he is not fit.
Dec. Shall no man else be touch'd but only Cæsar?
Cas. Decius, well urg'd: I think it is not meet,
Mark Antony, so well belov'd of Cæsar,
Should outlive Cæsar: we shall find of him
A shrewd contriver; and, you know, his means,
If he improve them, may well stretch so far
As to annoy us all: which to prevent,
Let Antony and Cæsar fall together.
Bru. Our course will seem too bloody, Caius Cassius,
To cut the head off and then hack the limbs,
Like wrath in death and envy afterwards;
For Antony is but a limb of Cæsar:
Let 's be sacrificers, but not butchers, Caius.
We all stand up against the spirit of Cæsar;
And in the spirit of men there is no blood:
O, that we then could come by Cæsar's spirit,
And not dismember Cæsar! But, alas,
Cæsar must bleed for it! And, gentle friends,
Let 's kill him boldly, but not wrathfully;
Let 's carve him as a dish fit for the gods,
Not hew him as a carcass fit for hounds:
And let our hearts, as subtle masters do,
Stir up their servants to an act of rage,
And after seem to chide 'em. This shall make
Our purpose necessary and not envious:
Which so appearing to the common eyes,
We shall be call'd purgers, not murderers.
And for Mark Antony, think not of him;
For he can do no more than Cæsar's arm
When Cæsar's head is off.
Cas. Yet I fear him;
For in the ingrafted love he bears to Cæsar—
Bru. Alas, good Cassius, do not think of him:
If he love Cæsar, all that he can do
Is to himself, take thought and die for Cæsar:
And that were much he should; for he is given
To sports, to wildness and much company.
Treb. There is no fear in him; let him not die;
For he will live, and laugh at this hereafter.
Clock strikes.
Bru. Peace! count the clock.
Cas. The clock hath stricken three.
Treb. 'Tis time to part.

married the sister of Brutus. 83. **path,** proceed. 84. **Erebus,** the region of darkness between earth and Hades. 104. **fret,** mark with interlacing lines. 107. **growing on,** toward. 114. **not an oath.** Brutus is thus refusing a genuine means of security in view of the importance of oaths to conspirators and the penalties which befell those who broke them. 115. **sufferance,** state of suffering. 118. **high-sighted,** haughty. 124. **prick,** spur. 125. **secret,** able to keep silence. 126. **palter,** use trickery. 129. **cautelous,** deceitful. 134. **insuppressive,** not to be suppressed. 138. **several bastardy,** individual act dishonoring its origin. 150. **break with,** tell to, confide in. 153. **fit.** Plutarch tells us that they feared Cicero lacked courage and that they thought him too old; he was sixty-three. 160. **annoy,** injure. 187. **take thought,** despond. 188. **much he should,** a good deal for him to do. 192. **clock.** Striking clocks were not invented until the Middle Ages.

Cas. But it is doubtful yet,
Whether Cæsar will come forth to-day, or no;
For he is superstitious grown of late,
Quite from the main opinion he held once
Of fantasy, of dreams and ceremonies:
It may be, these apparent prodigies,
The unaccustom'd terror of this night,
And the persuasion of his augurers,
May hold him from the Capitol to-day.
Dec. Never fear that: if he be so resolv'd,
I can o'ersway him; for he loves to hear
That unicorns may be betray'd with trees,
And bears with glasses, elephants with holes,
Lions with toils and men with flatterers;
But when I tell him he hates flatterers,
He says he does, being then most flattered.
Let me work;
For I can give his humour the true bent,
And I will bring him to the Capitol.
Cas. Nay, we will all of us be there to fetch him.
Bru. By the eighth hour: is that the uttermost?
Cin. Be that the uttermost, and fail not then.
Met. Caius Ligarius doth bear Cæsar hard,
Who rated him for speaking well of Pompey:
I wonder none of you have thought of him.
Bru. Now, good Metellus, go along by him:
He loves me well, and I have given him reasons;
Send him but hither, and I'll fashion him.
Cas. The morning comes upon 's: we'll leave you, Brutus.
And, friends, disperse yourselves; but all remember
What you have said, and show yourselves true Romans.
Bru. Good gentlemen, look fresh and merrily;
Let not our looks put on our purposes,
But bear it as our Roman actors do,
With untir'd spirits and formal constancy:
And so good morrow to you every one.
Exeunt. Manet Brutus.
Boy! Lucius! Fast asleep? It is no matter;
Enjoy the honey-heavy dew of slumber:
Thou hast no figures nor no fantasies,
Which busy care draws in the brains of men;
Therefore thou sleep'st so sound.

Enter PORTIA.

Por. Brutus, my lord!
Bru. Portia, what mean you? wherefore rise you now?
It is not for your health thus to commit
Your weak condition to the raw cold morning.
Por. Nor for yours neither. Y' have ungently, Brutus,
Stole from my bed: and yesternight, at supper,
You suddenly arose, and walk'd about,
Musing and sighing, with your arms across,
And when I ask'd you what the matter was,
You star'd upon me with ungentle looks;
I urg'd you further; then you scratch'd your head,
And too impatiently stamp'd with your foot;
Yet I insisted, yet you answer'd not,
But, with an angry wafture of your hand,
Gave sign for me to leave you: so I did;
Fearing to strengthen that impatience
Which seem'd too much enkindled, and withal
Hoping it was but an effect of humour,
Which sometime hath his hour with every man.
It will not let you eat, nor talk, nor sleep,
And could it work so much upon your shape
As it hath much prevail'd on your condition,
I should not know you, Brutus. Dear my lord,
Make me acquainted with your cause of grief.
Bru. I am not well in health, and that is all.
Por. Brutus is wise, and, were he not in health,
He would embrace the means to come by it.
Bru. Why, so I do. Good Portia, go to bed.
Por. Is Brutus sick? and is it physical
To walk unbraced and suck up the humours
Of the dank morning? What, is Brutus sick,
And will he steal out of his wholesome bed,
To dare the vile contagion of the night
And tempt the rheumy and unpurged air
To add unto his sickness? No, my Brutus;
You have some sick offence within your mind,
Which, by the right and virtue of my place,
I ought to know of: and, upon my knees,
I charm you, by my once-commended beauty,
By all your vows of love and that great vow
Which did incorporate and make us one,
That you unfold to me, yourself, your half,
Why you are heavy, and what men to-night
Have had resort to you: for here have been
Some six or seven, who did hide their faces
Even from darkness.
Bru. Kneel not, gentle Portia.
Por. I should not need, if you were gentle Brutus.
Within the bond of marriage, tell me, Brutus,
Is it excepted I should know no secrets
That appertain to you? Am I yourself
But, as it were, in sort or limitation,
To keep with you at meals, comfort your bed,
And talk to you sometimes? Dwell I but in the suburbs
Of your good pleasure? If it be no more,
Portia is Brutus' harlot, not his wife.
Bru. You are my true and honourable wife,
As dear to me as are the ruddy drops
That visit my sad heart.
Por. If this were true, then should I know this secret.
I grant I am a woman; but withal
A woman that Lord Brutus took to wife:
I grant I am a woman; but withal
A woman well-reputed, Cato's daughter.
Think you I am no stronger than my sex,
Being so father'd and so husbanded?
Tell me your counsels, I will not disclose 'em:
I have made strong proof of my constancy,
Giving myself a voluntary wound
Here, in the thigh: can I bear that with patience,
And not my husband's secrets?
Bru. O ye gods,
Render me worthy of this noble wife! *Knock [within].*
Hark, hark! one knocks: Portia, go in awhile;
And by and by thy bosom shall partake

196. **from the main,** contrary to the strong. 198. **apparent,** obvious. 204. **unicorns . . . betray'd,** i.e., by having the unicorn imprison himself by driving his horn into a tree as he charged at the hunter. 205. **glasses,** mirrors. **holes,** pitfalls. 206. **toils,** nets, snares. 210. **bent,** inclination of the mind. 213. **uttermost,** latest. 218. **by him,** by way of his house. 220. **fashion,** shape (to our purposes). 225. **put on,** display.

227. **formal constancy,** steadfast manner. 246. **wafture,** act of waving. 253-254. **shape . . . condition,** i.e., outward appearance . . . inner state of mind. 261. **physical,** healthful. 266. **rheumy,** damp. **unpurged,** not purified (by the sun). 271. **charm,** entreat. 281. **excepted,** made an exception that. 295. **Cato's daughter.** Cato of Utica was famous for his integrity; he fought with Pompey against Caesar in 46 B.C. and killed

The secrets of my heart.
All my engagements I will construe to thee,
All the charactery of my sad brows:
Leave me with haste. *Exit Portia.*
Lucius, who 's that knocks?

Enter Lucius *and* Ligarius.

Luc. Here is a sick man that would speak with you.
Bru. Caius Ligarius, that Metellus spake of.
Boy, stand aside. Caius Ligarius! how?
Lig. Vouchsafe good morrow from a feeble tongue.
Bru. O, what a time have you chose out, brave Caius,
To wear a kerchief! Would you were not sick!
Lig. I am not sick, if Brutus have in hand
Any exploit worthy the name of honour.
Bru. Such an exploit have I in hand, Ligarius,
Had you a healthful ear to hear of it.
Lig. By all the gods that Romans bow before,
I here discard my sickness! Soul of Rome!
Brave son, deriv'd from honourable loins!
Thou, like an exorcist, hast conjur'd up
My mortified spirit. Now bid me run,
And I will strive with things impossible;
Yea, get the better of them. What 's to do?
Bru. A piece of work that will make sick men whole.
Lig. But are not some whole that we must make sick?
Bru. That must we also. What it is, my Caius,
I shall unfold to thee, as we are going
To whom it must be done.
Lig. Set on your foot,
And with a heart new-fir'd I follow you,
To do I know not what: but it sufficeth
That Brutus leads me on. *Thunder.*
Bru. Follow me, then. *Exeunt.*

[Scene II. *Cæsar's house.*]

Thunder and lightning. Enter Julius Cæsar, *in his night-gown.*

Cæs. Nor heaven nor earth have been at peace to-night:
Thrice hath Calpurnia in her sleep cried out,
'Help, ho! they murder Cæsar!' Who 's within?

Enter a Servant.

Serv. My lord?
Cæs. Go bid the priests do present sacrifice
And bring me their opinions of success.
Serv. I will, my lord. *Exit.*

Enter Calpurnia.

Cal. What mean you, Cæsar? think you to walk forth?
You shall not stir out of your house to-day.
Cæs. Cæsar shall forth: the things that threaten'd me
Ne'er look'd but on my back; when they shall see
The face of Cæsar, they are vanished.
Cal. Cæsar, I never stood on ceremonies,
Yet now they fright me. There is one within,
Besides the things that we have heard and seen,
Recounts most horrid sights seen by the watch.
A lioness hath whelped in the streets;
And graves have yawn'd, and yielded up their dead;
Fierce fiery warriors fought upon the clouds,
In ranks and squadrons and right form of war,
Which drizzled blood upon the Capitol;
The noise of battle hurtled in the air,
Horses did neigh, and dying men did groan,
And ghosts did shriek and squeal about the streets.
O Cæsar! these things are beyond all use,
And I do fear them.
Cæs. What can be avoided
Whose end is purpos'd by the mighty gods?
Yet Cæsar shall go forth; for these predictions
Are to the world in general as to Cæsar.
Cal. When beggars die, there are no comets seen;
The heavens themselves blaze forth the death of princes.
Cæs. Cowards die many times before their deaths;
The valiant never taste of death but once.
Of all the wonders that I yet have heard,
It seems to me most strange that men should fear;
Seeing that death, a necessary end,
Will come when it will come.

Enter a Servant.

What say the augurers?
Serv. They would not have you to stir forth to-day.
Plucking the entrails of an offering forth,
They could not find a heart within the beast.
Cæs. The gods do this in shame of cowardice:
Cæsar should be a beast without a heart,
If he should stay at home to-day for fear.
No, Cæsar shall not: danger knows full well
That Cæsar is more dangerous than he:
We are two lions litter'd in one day,
And I the elder and more terrible:
And Cæsar shall go forth.
Cal. Alas, my lord,
Your wisdom is consum'd in confidence.
Do not go forth to-day: call it my fear
That keeps you in the house, and not your own.
We'll send Mark Antony to the senate-house;
And he shall say you are not well to-day:
Let me, upon my knee, prevail in this.
Cæs. Mark Antony shall say I am not well;
And, for thy humour, I will stay at home.

Enter Decius.

Here 's Decius Brutus, he shall tell them so.
Dec. Cæsar, all hail! good morrow, worthy Cæsar:
I come to fetch you to the senate-house.
Cæs. And you are come in very happy time,
To bear my greeting to the senators
And tell them that I will not come to-day:
Cannot, is false, and that I dare not, falser:
I will not come to-day: tell them so, Decius.
Cal. Say he is sick.
Cæs. Shall Cæsar send a lie?

himself to avoid capture. He was Brutus' uncle as well as father-in-law. 300. **voluntary wound.** Plutarch recounts of Portia that in order to give proof of her sincerity she gave herself a great gash in the thigh with a little razor. 309. **who 's,** who is it. 313. **Vouchsafe,** deign to accept. 315. **To wear a kerchief,** i.e., to be ill. 323. **exorcist,** conjurer. 324. **mortified,** deadened.

Scene II. *Stage Direction:* **night-gown,** dressing gown. 13. **stood on ceremonies,** attached importance to omens. 17-24. **A lioness . . . streets.** Similar enumerations of portents are made in I, iii, in *Hamlet,* I, i, and elsewhere in Shakespeare. Most of the omens here mentioned are from Plutarch. 22. **hurtled,** clashed (of weapons). 25. **use,** normal experience.

Have I in conquest stretch'd mine arm so far,
To be afeard to tell graybeards the truth?
Decius, go tell them Cæsar will not come.
Dec. Most mighty Cæsar, let me know some cause,
Lest I be laugh'd at when I tell them so.
Cæs. The cause is in my will: I will not come;
That is enough to satisfy the senate.
But for your private satisfaction,
Because I love you, I will let you know:
Calpurnia here, my wife, stays me at home:
She dreamt to-night she saw my statue,
Which, like a fountain with an hundred spouts,
Did run pure blood; and many lusty Romans
Came smiling, and did bathe their hands in it:
And these does she apply for warnings, and portents,
And evils imminent; and on her knee
Hath begg'd that I will stay at home to-day.
Dec. This dream is all amiss interpreted;
It was a vision fair and fortunate:
Your statue spouting blood in many pipes,
In which so many smiling Romans bath'd,
Signifies that from you great Rome shall suck
Reviving blood, and that great men shall press
For tinctures, stains, relics and cognizance.
This by Calpurnia's dream is signified.
Cæs. And this way have you well expounded it.
Dec. I have, when you have heard what I can say:
And know it now: the senate have concluded
To give this day a crown to mighty Cæsar.
If you shall send them word you will not come,
Their minds may change. Besides, it were a mock
Apt to be render'd, for some one to say
'Break up the senate till another time,
When Cæsar's wife shall meet with better dreams.'
If Cæsar hide himself, shall they not whisper
'Lo, Cæsar is afraid'?
Pardon me, Cæsar; for my dear dear love
To your proceeding bids me tell you this;
And reason to my love is liable.
Cæs. How foolish do your fears seem now, Calpurnia!
I am ashamed I did yield to them.
Give me my robe, for I will go.

Enter BRUTUS, LIGARIUS, METELLUS, CASCA, TREBONIUS, CINNA, *and* PUBLIUS.

And look where Publius is come to fetch me.
Pub. Good morrow, Cæsar.
Cæs. Welcome, Publius.
What, Brutus, are you stirr'd so early too?
Good morrow, Casca. Caius Ligarius,
Cæsar was ne'er so much your enemy
As that same ague which has made you lean.
What is 't o'clock?
Bru. Cæsar, 'tis strucken eight.
Cæs. I thank you for your pains and courtesy.

Enter ANTONY.

See! Antony, that revels long o' nights,
Is notwithstanding up. Good morrow, Antony.
Ant. So to most noble Cæsar.
Cæs. Bid them prepare within:
I am to blame to be thus waited for.
Now, Cinna: now, Metellus: what, Trebonius!
I have an hour's talk in store for you;
Remember that you call on me to-day:
Be near me, that I may remember you.
Treb. Cæsar, I will: [*Aside*] and so near will I be,
That your best friends shall wish I had been further.
Cæs. Good friends, go in, and taste some wine with me;
And we, like friends, will straightway go together.
Bru. [*Aside*] That every like is not the same, O Cæsar,
The heart of Brutus earns to think upon! *Exeunt.*

[SCENE III. *A street near the Capitol.*]

Enter ARTEMIDORUS [*reading a paper*].

Art. 'Cæsar, beware of Brutus; take heed of Cassius; come not near Casca; have an eye to Cinna; trust not Trebonius; mark well Metellus Cimber: Decius Brutus loves thee not: thou hast wronged Caius Ligarius. There is but one mind in all these men, and it is bent against Cæsar. If thou beest not immortal, look about you: security gives way to conspiracy. The mighty gods defend thee! Thy lover,
'ARTEMIDORUS.'
Here will I stand till Cæsar pass along,
And as a suitor will I give him this.
My heart laments that virtue cannot live
Out of the teeth of emulation.
If thou read this, O Cæsar, thou mayest live;
If not, the Fates with traitors do contrive. *Exit.*

[SCENE IV. *Another part of the same street, before the house of Brutus.*]

Enter PORTIA *and* LUCIUS.

Por. I prithee, boy, run to the senate-house;
Stay not to answer me, but get thee gone:
Why dost thou stay?
Luc. To know my errand, madam.
Por. I would have had thee there, and here again,
Ere I can tell thee what thou shouldst do there.
O constancy, be strong upon my side,
Set a huge mountain 'tween my heart and tongue!
I have a man's mind, but a woman's might.
How hard it is for women to keep counsel!
Art thou here yet?
Luc. Madam, what should I do?
Run to the Capitol, and nothing else?
And so return to you, and nothing else?
Por. Yes, bring me word, boy, if thy lord look well,
For he went sickly forth: and take good note
What Cæsar doth, what suitors press to him.
Hark, boy! what noise is that?

76. **to-night,** last night. **statue,** pronounced with three syllables here. 78. **lusty,** vigorous. 89. **tinctures,** handkerchiefs dipped in the blood of martyrs, with healing power, or colors in a coat of arms. **relics,** venerated properties of martyred saints. **cognizance,** heraldic emblems worn by a nobleman's followers. 96. **mock,** jibe. 103. **proceeding,** advancement. 104. **liable,** under the sway of. 129. **earns,** grieves.

SCENE III. 8. **security,** want of caution. 10. **lover,** friend. 14. **emulation,** grudge against the superiority of others.
SCENE IV. 37. **void,** empty.
ACT III. SCENE I. *Stage Direction: Capitol.* The scene is not located in F, but is indicated by the text. Shakespeare implies (l. 12) that Caesar was assassinated in the Capitol, but it is clear from Plutarch

Luc. I hear none, madam.
Por. Prithee, listen well;
I heard a bustling rumour, like a fray,
And the wind brings it from the Capitol.
Luc. Sooth, madam, I hear nothing.

Enter the Soothsayer.

Por. Come hither, fellow: which way hast thou been?
Sooth. At mine own house, good lady.
Por. What is 't o'clock?
Sooth. About the ninth hour, lady.
Por. Is Cæsar yet gone to the Capitol?
Sooth. Madam, not yet: I go to take my stand,
To see him pass on to the Capitol.
Por. Thou hast some suit to Cæsar, hast thou not?
Sooth. That I have, lady: if it will please Cæsar
To be so good to Cæsar as to hear me,
I shall beseech him to befriend himself.
Por. Why, know'st thou any harm 's intended towards him?
Sooth. None that I know will be, much that I fear may chance.
Good morrow to you. Here the street is narrow:
The throng that follows Cæsar at the heels,
Of senators, of prætors, common suitors,
Will crowd a feeble man almost to death:
I'll get me to a place more void, and there
Speak to great Cæsar as he comes along. *Exit.*
Por. I must go in. Ay me, how weak a thing
The heart of woman is! O Brutus,
The heavens speed thee in thine enterprise!
Sure, the boy heard me: Brutus hath a suit
That Cæsar will not grant. O, I grow faint.
Run, Lucius, and commend me to my lord;
Say I am merry: come to me again,
And bring me word what he doth say to thee.
Exeunt [severally].

ACT III.

[SCENE I. *Rome. Before the Capitol.*]

Flourish. Enter CÆSAR, BRUTUS, CASSIUS, CASCA, DECIUS, METELLUS [CIMBER], TREBONIUS, CINNA, ANTONY, LEPIDUS, ARTEMIDORUS, PUBLIUS, [POPILIUS,] *and the* Soothsayer.

Cæs. [*To the Soothsayer*] The ides of March are come.
Sooth. Ay, Cæsar; but not gone.
Art. Hail, Cæsar! read this schedule.
Dec. Trebonius doth desire you to o'er-read,
At your best leisure, this his humble suit.
Art. O Cæsar, read mine first; for mine 's a suit
That touches Cæsar nearer: read it, great Cæsar.
Cæs. What touches us ourself shall be last serv'd.
Art. Delay not, Cæsar; read it instantly.
Cæs. What, is the fellow mad?
Pub. Sirrah, give place.
Cas. What, urge you your petitions in the street?
Come to the Capitol.

[CÆSAR *goes to the Senate-House, the rest following.*]

Pop. I wish your enterprise to-day may thrive.
Cas. What enterprise, Popilius?
Pop. Fare you well. [*Advances to Cæsar.*]
Bru. What said Popilius Lena?
Cas. He wish'd to-day our enterprise might thrive.
I fear our purpose is discovered.
Bru. Look, how he makes to Cæsar: mark him.
Cas. Casca, be sudden, for we fear prevention.
Brutus, what shall be done? If this be known,
Cassius or Cæsar never shall turn back,
For I will slay myself.
Bru. Cassius, be constant:
Popilius Lena speaks not of our purposes;
For, look, he smiles, and Cæsar doth not change.
Cas. Trebonius knows his time; for, look you, Brutus,
He draws Mark Antony out of the way.
[*Exeunt Antony and Trebonius.*]
Dec. Where is Metellus Cimber? Let him go,
And presently prefer his suit to Cæsar.
Bru. He is address'd: press near and second him.
Cin. Casca, you are the first that rears your hand.
Cæs. Are we all ready? What is now amiss
That Cæsar and his senate must redress?
Met. Most high, most mighty, and most puissant Cæsar,
Metellus Cimber throws before thy seat
An humble heart,— [*Kneeling.*]
Cæs. I must prevent thee, Cimber.
These couchings and these lowly courtesies
Might fire the blood of ordinary men,
And turn pre-ordinance and first decree
Into the law of children. Be not fond,
To think that Cæsar bears such rebel blood
That will be thaw'd from the true quality
With that which melteth fools; I mean, sweet words,
Low-crooked court'sies and base spaniel-fawning.
Thy brother by decree is banished:
If thou dost bend and pray and fawn for him,
I spurn thee like a cur out of my way.
Know, Cæsar doth not wrong, nor without cause
Will he be satisfied.
Met. Is there no voice more worthy than my own,
To sound more sweetly in great Cæsar's ear
For the repealing of my banish'd brother?
Bru. I kiss thy hand, but not in flattery, Cæsar;
Desiring thee that Publius Cimber may
Have an immediate freedom of repeal.
Cæs. What, Brutus!
Cas. Pardon, Cæsar; Cæsar, pardon:
As low as to thy foot doth Cassius fall,
To beg enfranchisement for Publius Cimber.
Cæs. I could be well mov'd, if I were as you;
If I could pray to move, prayers would move me:
But I am constant as the northern star,
Of whose true-fix'd and resting quality
There is no fellow in the firmament.
The skies are painted with unnumb'red sparks,
They are all fire and every one doth shine,

that it was in the portico of Pompey's theatre, where the Senate was sitting. 3. **schedule,** written scroll. 29. **address'd,** ready. 39. **fond,** so foolish as. 41. **thaw'd from the true quality.** The idea is that the cool brain governed by reason might be visited by various intruding spirits (carrying with them heat) and so thawed. 47-48. **Know . . . satisfied.** Ben Jonson ridicules these lines in his *Discoveries,* where he says, "Caesar did never wrong but with just cause." Such may have been the original text or its reading on the stage, but the F reading is intelligible.

But there 's but one in all doth hold his place:
So in the world; 'tis furnish'd well with men,
And men are flesh and blood, and apprehensive;
Yet in the number I do know but one
That unassailable holds on his rank,
Unshak'd of motion: and that I am he,
Let me a little show it, even in this;
That I was constant Cimber should be banish'd,
And constant do remain to keep him so.
Cin. O Cæsar,—
Cæs. Hence! wilt thou lift up Olympus?
Dec. Great Cæsar,—
Cæs. Doth not Brutus bootless kneel?
Casca. Speak, hands, for me!
They stab Cæsar[, *Casca first, Brutus last*].
Cæs. Et tu, Brutè? Then fall, Cæsar! *Dies.*
Cin. Liberty! Freedom! Tyranny is dead!
Run hence, proclaim, cry it about the streets.
Cas. Some to the common pulpits, and cry out
'Liberty, freedom, and enfranchisement!'
Bru. People and senators, be not affrighted;
Fly not; stand still: ambition's debt is paid.
Casca. Go to the pulpit, Brutus.
Dec. And Cassius too.
Bru. Where 's Publius?
Cin. Here, quite confounded with this mutiny.
Met. Stand fast together, lest some friend of Cæsar's
Should chance—
Bru. Talk not of standing. Publius, good cheer;
There is no harm intended to your person,
Nor to no Roman else: so tell them, Publius.
Cas. And leave us, Publius; lest that the people,
Rushing on us, should do your age some mischief.
Bru. Do so: and let no man abide this deed,
But we the doers.

Enter TREBONIUS.

Cas. Where is Antony?
Tre. Fled to his house amaz'd:
Men, wives and children stare, cry out and run
As it were doomsday.
Bru. Fates, we will know your pleasures:
That we shall die, we know; 'tis but the time
And drawing days out, that men stand upon.
Cas. Why, he that cuts off twenty years of life
Cuts off so many years of fearing death.
Bru. Grant that, and then is death a benefit:
So are we Cæsar's friends, that have abridg'd
His time of fearing death. Stoop, Romans, stoop,
And let us bathe our hands in Cæsar's blood
Up to the elbows, and besmear our swords:
Then walk we forth, even to the market-place,
And, waving our red weapons o'er our heads,
Let 's all cry, 'Peace, freedom and liberty!'
Cas. Stoop, then, and wash. How many ages hence
Shall this our lofty scene be acted over
In states unborn and accents yet unknown!
Bru. How many times shall Cæsar bleed in sport,
That now on Pompey's basis lies along
No worthier than the dust!
Cas. So oft as that shall be,
So often shall the knot of us be call'd
The men that gave their country liberty.
Dec. What, shall we forth?
Cas. Ay, every man away:
Brutus shall lead; and we will grace his heels
With the most boldest and best hearts of Rome.

Enter a Servant.

Bru. Soft! who comes here? A friend of Antony's.
Serv. Thus, Brutus, did my master bid me kneel;
Thus did Mark Antony bid me fall down;
And, being prostrate, thus he bade me say:
Brutus is noble, wise, valiant, and honest;
Cæsar was mighty, bold, royal, and loving:
Say I love Brutus, and I honour him;
Say I fear'd Cæsar, honour'd him and lov'd him.
If Brutus will vouchsafe that Antony
May safely come to him, and be resolv'd
How Cæsar hath deserv'd to lie in death,
Mark Antony shall not love Cæsar dead
So well as Brutus living; but will follow
The fortunes and affairs of noble Brutus
Thorough the hazards of this untrod state
With all true faith. So says my master Antony.
Bru. Thy master is a wise and valiant Roman;
I never thought him worse.
Tell him, so please him come unto this place,
He shall be satisfied; and, by my honour,
Depart untouch'd.
Serv. I'll fetch him presently. *Exit Ser.*
Bru. I know that we shall have him well to friend.
Cas. I wish we may: but yet have I a mind
That fears him much; and my misgiving still
Falls shrewdly to the purpose.

Enter ANTONY.

Bru. But here comes Antony.—Welcome, Mark Antony.
Ant. O mighty Cæsar! dost thou lie so low?
Are all thy conquests, glories, triumphs, spoils,
Shrunk to this little measure? Fare thee well.
I know not, gentlemen, what you intend,
Who else must be let blood, who else is rank:
If I myself, there is no hour so fit
As Cæsar's death's hour, nor no instrument
Of half that worth as those your swords, made rich
With the most noble blood of all this world.
I do beseech ye, if you bear me hard,
Now, whilst your purpled hands do reek and smoke,
Fulfil your pleasure. Live a thousand years,
I shall not find myself so apt to die:
No place will please me so, no mean of death,
As here by Cæsar, and by you cut off,
The choice and master spirits of this age.
Bru. O Antony, beg not your death of us.
Though now we must appear bloody and cruel,
As, by our hands and this our present act,
You see we do, yet see you but our hands
And this the bleeding business they have done:
Our hearts you see not; they are pitiful;

67. **apprehensive,** capable of reason. 69. **rank,** place, in line or file, position. 74. **Olympus,** mountain dwelling of the Greek gods. 75. **bootless,** in vain. 77. **Et tu, Brutè,** and you too, Brutus? 80. **common pulpits,** public rostra. 85. **Publius,** an old senator, too confused to flee. 86. **confounded with,** overwhelmed by. **mutiny,** tumult. 96. **amaz'd,** full of consternation. 100. **drawing days out,** prolonging their lives. **stand upon,** attach importance to. 115. **Pompey's basis,** pedestal of Pompey's statue. 143. **to friend,** for a friend. 146. **Falls . . . purpose,** hits the mark precisely. 152. **let blood,** bled, i.e., killed. **rank,** diseased and in need of bleeding (with pun on *overgrown, too powerful*). 157. **bear . . . hard,** bear ill-will to. 159. **Live,** if I should live. 160. **apt,** ready. 173. **leaden,** i.e., blunt. 174-175. **Our . . . temper,** both

And pity to the general wrong of Rome—
As fire drives out fire, so pity pity—
Hath done this deed on Cæsar. For your part,
To you our swords have leaden points, Mark Antony:
†Our arms, in strength of malice, and our hearts
Of brothers' temper, do receive you in
With all kind love, good thoughts, and reverence.
Cas. Your voice shall be as strong as any man's
In the disposing of new dignities.
Bru. Only be patient till we have appeas'd
The multitude, beside themselves with fear,
And then we will deliver you the cause,
Why I, that did love Cæsar when I struck him,
Have thus proceeded.
Ant. I doubt not of your wisdom.
Let each man render me his bloody hand:
First, Marcus Brutus, will I shake with you;
Next, Caius Cassius, do I take your hand;
Now, Decius Brutus, yours; now yours, Metellus;
Yours, Cinna; and, my valiant Casca, yours;
Though last, not least in love, yours, good Trebonius.
Gentlemen all,—alas, what shall I say?
My credit now stands on such slippery ground,
That one of two bad ways you must conceit me,
Either a coward or a flatterer.
That I did love thee, Cæsar, O, 'tis true:
If then thy spirit look upon us now,
Shall it not grieve thee dearer than thy death,
To see thy Antony making his peace,
Shaking the bloody fingers of thy foes,
Most noble! in the presence of thy corse?
Had I as many eyes as thou hast wounds,
Weeping as fast as they stream forth thy blood,
It would become me better than to close
In terms of friendship with thine enemies.
Pardon me, Julius! Here wast thou bay'd, brave hart;
Here didst thou fall; and here thy hunters stand,
Sign'd in thy spoil, and crimson'd in thy lethe.
O world, thou wast the forest to this hart;
And this, indeed, O world, the heart of thee.
How like a deer, strucken by many princes,
Dost thou here lie!
Cas. Mark Antony,—
Ant. Pardon me, Caius Cassius:
The enemies of Cæsar shall say this;
Then, in a friend, it is cold modesty.
Cas. I blame you not for praising Cæsar so;
But what compact mean you to have with us?
Will you be prick'd in number of our friends;
Or shall we on, and not depend on you?
Ant. Therefore I took your hands, but was, indeed,
Sway'd from the point, by looking down on Cæsar.
Friends am I with you all and love you all,
Upon this hope, that you shall give me reasons
Why and wherein Cæsar was dangerous.
Bru. Or else were this a savage spectacle:
Our reasons are so full of good regard
That were you, Antony, the son of Cæsar,
You should be satisfied.
Ant. That 's all I seek:
And am moreover suitor that I may
Produce his body to the market-place;
And in the pulpit, as becomes a friend,
Speak in the order of his funeral.
Bru. You shall, Mark Antony.
Cas. Brutus, a word with you.
[*Aside to Bru.*] You know not what you do: do not consent
That Antony speak in his funeral:
Know you how much the people may be mov'd
By that which he will utter?
Bru. By your pardon;
I will myself into the pulpit first,
And show the reason of our Cæsar's death:
What Antony shall speak, I will protest
He speaks by leave and by permission,
And that we are contented Cæsar shall
Have all true rites and lawful ceremonies.
It shall advantage more than do us wrong.
Cas. I know not what may fall; I like it not.
Bru. Mark Antony, here, take you Cæsar's body.
You shall not in your funeral speech blame us,
But speak all good you can devise of Cæsar,
And say you do 't by our permission;
Else shall you not have any hand at all
About his funeral: and you shall speak
In the same pulpit whereto I am going,
After my speech is ended.
Ant. Be it so;
I do desire no more.
Bru. Prepare the body then, and follow us.
Exeunt. Manet Antony.
Ant. O, pardon me, thou bleeding piece of earth,
That I am meek and gentle with these butchers!
Thou art the ruins of the noblest man
That ever lived in the tide of times.
Woe to the hand that shed this costly blood!
Over thy wounds now do I prophesy,—
Which, like dumb mouths, do ope their ruby lips,
To beg the voice and utterance of my tongue—
A curse shall light upon the †limbs of men;
Domestic fury and fierce civil strife
Shall cumber all the parts of Italy;
Blood and destruction shall be so in use
And dreadful objects so familiar
That mothers shall but smile when they behold
Their infants quartered with the hands of war;
All pity chok'd with custom of fell deeds:
And Cæsar's spirit, ranging for revenge,
With Ate by his side come hot from hell,
Shall in these confines with a monarch's voice
Cry 'Havoc,' and let slip the dogs of war;
That this foul deed shall smell above the earth
With carrion men, groaning for burial.

Enter Octavius' Servant.

You serve Octavius Cæsar, do you not?
Serv. I do, Mark Antony.
Ant. Cæsar did write for him to come to Rome.
Serv. He did receive his letters, and is coming;
And bid me say to you by word of mouth—
O Cæsar!— [*Seeing the body.*]

our arms, though seeming strong in enmity, and our hearts, full of brotherly feeling. 178. **dignities,** offices of state. 181. **deliver,** report to. 192. **conceit,** judge. 204. **bay'd,** brought to bay. **hart,** stag, with pun on *heart*. 206. **Sign'd in,** marked with the signs of. **spoil,** slaughter. **lethe,** death. 213. **modesty,** moderation. 216. **prick'd in,** set down, marked off on a list. 224. **good regard,** sound consideration.

230. **order,** course. 232. **You know not what you do.** Plutarch calls attention to this as the second error which Brutus committed; the first was that he failed to have Antony killed as well as Caesar. 238. **protest,** announce. 268. **quartered,** slaughtered. 271. **Ate,** goddess of revenge. 273. **'Havoc,'** the signal for sack, pillage, and slaughter. 274. **That,** so that.

Ant. Thy heart is big, get thee apart and weep.
Passion, I see, is catching; for mine eyes,
Seeing those beads of sorrow stand in thine,
Began to water. Is thy master coming?
Serv. He lies to-night within seven leagues of Rome.
Ant. Post back with speed, and tell him what hath chanc'd:
Here is a mourning Rome, a dangerous Rome,
No Rome of safety for Octavius yet;
Hie hence, and tell him so. Yet, stay awhile;
Thou shalt not back till I have borne this corse
Into the market-place: there shall I try,
In my oration, how the people take
The cruel issue of these bloody men;
According to the which, thou shalt discourse
To young Octavius of the state of things.
Lend me your hand. *Exeunt [with Cæsar's body].*

[SCENE II. *The Forum.*]

Enter BRUTUS *and [presently] goes into the pulpit, and* CASSIUS, *with the Plebeians.*

Citizens. We will be satisfi'd! Let us be satisfi'd!
Bru. Then follow me, and give me audience, friends.
Cassius, go you into the other street,
And part the numbers.
Those that will hear me speak, let 'em stay here;
Those that will follow Cassius, go with him;
And public reasons shall be rendered
Of Cæsar's death.
First Cit. I will hear Brutus speak.
Sec. Cit. I will hear Cassius; and compare their reasons,
When severally we hear them rendered.
[*Exit Cassius, with some of the Citizens.*]
Third. Cit. The noble Brutus is ascended: silence!
Bru. Be patient till the last.

Romans, countrymen, and lovers! hear me for my cause, and be silent, that you may hear: believe me for mine honour, and have respect to mine honour, that you may believe: censure me in your wisdom, and awake your senses, that you may the better judge. If there be any in this assembly, any dear friend of Cæsar's, to him I say, that Brutus' love to Cæsar was no less than his. If then that friend demand why Brutus rose against Cæsar, this is my answer:—Not that I loved Cæsar less, but that I loved Rome more. Had you rather Cæsar were living and die all slaves, than that Cæsar were dead, to live all free men? As Cæsar loved me, I weep for him; as he was fortunate, I rejoice at it; as he was valiant, I honour him: but, as he was ambitious, I slew him. There is tears for his love; joy for his fortune; honour for his valour; and death for his ambition. Who is here so base that would be a bondman? If any, speak; for him have I offended. Who is here so rude that would not be a Roman? If any, speak; for him have I offended. Who is here so vile that will not love his country? If any, speak; for him have I offended. I pause for a reply.

All. None, Brutus, none!

Bru. Then none have I offended. I have done no more to Cæsar than you shall do to Brutus. The question of his death is enrolled in the Capitol; his glory not extenuated, wherein he was worthy, nor his offences enforced, for which he suffered death.

Enter ANTONY *[and others] with* CÆSAR'S *body.*

Here comes his body, mourned by Mark Antony: who, though he had no hand in his death, shall receive the benefit of his dying, a place in the commonwealth; as which of you shall not? With this I depart,—that, as I slew my best lover for the good of Rome, I have the same dagger for myself, when it shall please my country to need my death.

All. Live, Brutus! live, live!
First Cit. Bring him with triumph home unto his house.
Sec. Cit. Give him a statue with his ancestors.
Third Cit. Let him be Cæsar.
Fourth Cit. Cæsar's better parts
Shall be crown'd in Brutus.
First Cit. We'll bring him to his house
With shouts and clamours.
Bru. My countrymen,—
Sec. Cit. Peace, silence! Brutus speaks.
First Cit. Peace, ho!
Bru. Good countrymen, let me depart alone,
And, for my sake, stay here with Antony:
Do grace to Cæsar's corpse, and grace his speech
Tending to Cæsar's glories; which Mark Antony,
By our permission, is allow'd to make.
I do entreat you, not a man depart,
Save I alone, till Antony have spoke. *Exit.*
First Cit. Stay, ho! and let us hear Mark Antony.
Third Cit. Let him go up into the public chair;
We'll hear him. Noble Antony, go up.
Ant. For Brutus' sake, I am beholding to you.
[*Goes into the pulpit.*]
Fourth Cit. What does he say of Brutus?
Third Cit. He says, for Brutus' sake,
He finds himself beholding to us all.
Fourth Cit. 'Twere best he speak no harm of Brutus here.
First Cit. This Cæsar was a tyrant.
Third Cit. Nay, that's certain:
We are blest that Rome is rid of him.
Sec. Cit. Peace! let us hear what Antony can say.
Ant. You gentle Romans,—
Citizens. Peace, ho! let us hear him.
Ant. Friends, Romans, countrymen, lend me your ears;
I come to bury Cæsar, not to praise him.
The evil that men do lives after them;
The good is oft interred with their bones;
So let it be with Cæsar. The noble Brutus
Hath told you Cæsar was ambitious:
If it were so, it was a grievous fault,
And grievously hath Cæsar answer'd it.
Here, under leave of Brutus and the rest—
For Brutus is an honourable man;
So are they all, all honourable men—

290. **Hie,** hasten. 294. **issue,** deed.
SCENE II. 4. **part,** divide; see glossary. 10. **severally,** individually. 14. **lovers,** friends. 12-37. **Be . . . reply.** The speech of Brutus is in careful sententious prose. It is Shakespeare's attempt to reproduce in style what Plutarch means when he says, "He counterfeited that brief compendius manner of speech of the Lacedaemonians." In content the speech is original with Shakespeare. 33. **rude,** barbarous. 42-43. **The question . . . enrolled,** the considerations that necessitated his death are recorded. **extenuated,** minimized. 44. **enforced,** exaggerated. 50. **lover,** friend. 78-257. **Friends . . . such another.** Plutarch gives a brief description of Antony's oration and its effect, telling how Antony moved the audience and displayed to them Caesar's bloody garments.

Come I to speak in Cæsar's funeral.
He was my friend, faithful and just to me:
But Brutus says he was ambitious;
And Brutus is an honourable man.
He hath brought many captives home to Rome,
Whose ransoms did the general coffers fill:
Did this in Cæsar seem ambitious?
When that the poor have cried, Cæsar hath wept:
Ambition should be made of sterner stuff:
Yet Brutus says he was ambitious;
And Brutus is an honourable man.
You all did see that on the Lupercal
I thrice presented him a kingly crown,
Which he did thrice refuse: was this ambition?
Yet Brutus says he was ambitious;
And, sure, he is an honourable man.
I speak not to disprove what Brutus spoke,
But here I am to speak what I do know.
You all did love him once, not without cause:
What cause withholds you then, to mourn for him?
O judgement! thou art fled to brutish beasts,
And men have lost their reason. Bear with me;
My heart is in the coffin there with Cæsar,
And I must pause till it come back to me.
First Cit. Methinks there is much reason in his sayings.
Sec. Cit. If thou consider rightly of the matter,
Cæsar has had great wrong.
Third Cit. Has he, masters?
I fear there will a worse come in his place.
Fourth Cit. Mark'd ye his words? He would not take the crown;
Therefore 'tis certain he was not ambitious.
First Cit. If it be found so, some will dear abide it.
Sec. Cit. Poor soul! his eyes are red as fire with weeping.
Third Cit. There 's not a nobler man in Rome than Antony.
Fourth Cit. Now mark him, he begins again to speak.
Ant. But yesterday the word of Cæsar might
Have stood against the world; now lies he there,
And none so poor to do him reverence.
O masters, if I were dispos'd to stir
Your hearts and minds to mutiny and rage,
I should do Brutus wrong, and Cassius wrong,
Who, you all know, are honourable men:
I will not do them wrong; I rather choose
To wrong the dead, to wrong myself and you,
Than I will wrong such honourable men.
But here 's a parchment with the seal of Cæsar;
I found it in his closet, 'tis his will:
Let but the commons hear this testament—
Which, pardon me, I do not mean to read—
And they would go and kiss dead Cæsar's wounds
And dip their napkins in his sacred blood,
Yea, beg a hair of him for memory,
And, dying, mention it within their wills,
Bequeathing it as a rich legacy
Unto their issue.
Fourth Cit. We'll hear the will! Read it, Mark Antony.
All. The will, the will! we will hear Cæsar's will.
Ant. Have patience, gentle friends, I must not read it;
It is not meet you know how Cæsar lov'd you.
You are not wood, you are not stones, but men;
And, being men, hearing the will of Cæsar,
It will inflame you, it will make you mad:
'Tis good you know not that you are his heirs;
For, if you should, O, what would come of it!
Fourth Cit. Read the will; we'll hear it, Antony;
You shall read us the will, Cæsar's will.
Ant. Will you be patient? will you stay awhile?
I have o'ershot myself to tell you of it:
I fear I wrong the honourable men
Whose daggers have stabb'd Cæsar; I do fear it.
Fourth Cit. They were traitors: honourable men!
All. The will! the testament!
Sec. Cit. They were villains, murderers: the will! read the will.
Ant. You will compel me, then, to read the will?
Then make a ring about the corpse of Cæsar,
And let me show you him that made the will.
Shall I descend? and will you give me leave?
Several Cit. Come down.
Sec. Cit. Descend.
Third Cit. You shall have leave. [*Antony comes down.*]
Fourth Cit. A ring; stand round.
First Cit. Stand from the hearse, stand from the body.
Sec. Cit. Room for Antony, most noble Antony.
Ant. Nay, press not so upon me; stand far off.
Several Cit. Stand back; room; bear back!
Ant. If you have tears, prepare to shed them now.
You all do know this mantle: I remember
The first time ever Cæsar put it on;
'Twas on a summer's evening, in his tent,
That day he overcame the Nervii:
Look, in this place ran Cassius' dagger through:
See what a rent the envious Casca made:
Through this the well-beloved Brutus stabb'd;
And as he pluck'd his cursed steel away,
Mark how the blood of Cæsar followed it,
As rushing out of doors, to be resolv'd
If Brutus so unkindly knock'd, or no;
For Brutus, as you know, was Cæsar's angel:
Judge, O you gods, how dearly Cæsar lov'd him!
This was the most unkindest cut of all;
For when the noble Cæsar saw him stab,
Ingratitude, more strong than traitors' arms,
Quite vanquish'd him: then burst his mighty heart;
And, in his mantle muffling up his face,
Even at the base of Pompey's statue,
Which all the while ran blood, great Cæsar fell.
O, what a fall was there, my countrymen!
Then I, and you, and all of us fell down,
Whilst bloody treason flourish'd over us.
O, now you weep; and, I perceive, you feel
The dint of pity: these are gracious drops.
Kind souls, what, weep you when you but behold
Our Cæsar's vesture wounded? Look you here,
Here is himself, marr'd, as you see, with traitors.

Appian tells of an image of Caesar in wax with three and twenty wounds; and Dion furnishes hints for Antony's praise of Caesar's liberality and Caesar's betrayal by his friends. The oration is sometimes thought to illustrate the "Asiatic" or florid style as opposed to the "Greek" or classical style used by Brutus. 93. **captives.** It has been estimated that Caesar and Pompey sold a million captives into slavery.

146. **meet,** fitting that. 169. **hearse,** bier. 171. **far,** farther. 177. **Nervii,** the Belgian tribe whose defeat is described in Caesar's *Gallic War*, II, xv-xxvii. 183. **be resolv'd,** learn for certain. 185. **angel,** favorite. 187. **most unkindest,** the most familiar of Shakespeare's double superlatives. 192. **statue,** trisyllabic here.

First Cit. O piteous spectacle!
Sec. Cit. O noble Cæsar!
Third Cit. O woful day!
Fourth Cit. O traitors, villains!
First Cit. O most bloody sight!
Sec. Cit. We will be reveng'd.
All. Revenge! About! Seek! Burn! Fire! Kill! Slay!
Let not a traitor live!
Ant. Stay, countrymen.
First Cit. Peace there! hear the noble Antony.
Sec. Cit. We'll hear him, we'll follow him, we'll die with him!
Ant. Good friends, sweet friends, let me not stir you up
To such a sudden flood of mutiny.
They that have done this deed are honourable:
What private griefs they have, alas, I know not,
That made them do it: they are wise and honourable,
And will, no doubt, with reasons answer you.
I come not, friends, to steal away your hearts:
I am no orator, as Brutus is;
But, as you know me all, a plain blunt man,
That love my friend; and that they know full well
That gave me public leave to speak of him:
For I have neither wit, nor words, nor worth,
Action, nor utterance, nor the power of speech,
To stir men's blood: I only speak right on;
I tell you that which you yourselves do know;
Show you sweet Cæsar's wounds, poor poor dumb mouths,
And bid them speak for me: but were I Brutus,
And Brutus Antony, there were an Antony
Would ruffle up your spirits and put a tongue
In every wound of Cæsar that should move
The stones of Rome to rise and mutiny.
All. We'll mutiny.
First Cit. We'll burn the house of Brutus.
Third Cit. Away, then! come, seek the conspirators.
Ant. Yet hear me, countrymen; yet hear me speak.
All. Peace, ho! Hear Antony. Most noble Antony!
Ant. Why, friends, you go to do you know not what:
Wherein hath Cæsar thus deserv'd your loves?
Alas, you know not: I must tell you, then:
You have forgot the will I told you of.
All. Most true. The will! Let 's stay and hear the will.
Ant. Here is the will, and under Cæsar's seal.
To every Roman citizen he gives,
To every several man, seventy five drachmas.
Sec. Cit. Most noble Cæsar! We'll revenge his death.
Third Cit. O royal Cæsar!
Ant. Hear me with patience.
All. Peace, ho!
Ant. Moreover, he hath left you all his walks,
His private arbours and new-planted orchards,
On this side Tiber; he hath left them you,
And to your heirs for ever, common pleasures,
To walk abroad, and recreate yourselves.
Here was a Cæsar! when comes such another?
First Cit. Never, never. Come, away, away!
We'll burn his body in the holy place,
And with the brands fire the traitors' houses.
Take up the body.
Sec. Cit. Go fetch fire.
Third Cit. Pluck down benches.
Fourth Cit. Pluck down forms, windows, any thing.
Exeunt Plebeians [with the body].
Ant. Now let it work. Mischief, thou art afoot,
Take thou what course thou wilt!

Enter Servant.

How now, fellow!
Serv. Sir, Octavius is already come to Rome.
Ant. Where is he?
Serv. He and Lepidus are at Cæsar's house.
Ant. And thither will I straight to visit him:
He comes upon a wish. Fortune is merry,
And in this mood will give us any thing.
Serv. I heard him say, Brutus and Cassius
Are rid like madmen through the gates of Rome.
Ant. Belike they had some notice of the people,
How I had mov'd them. Bring me to Octavius.
Exeunt.

[SCENE III. *A street.*]

Enter CINNA *the poet, and after him the* Plebeians.

Cin. I dreamt to-night that I did feast with Cæsar,
And things unluckily charge my fantasy:
I have no will to wander forth of doors,
Yet something leads me forth.
First Cit. What is your name?
Sec. Cit. Whither are you going?
Third Cit. Where do you dwell?
Fourth Cit. Are you a married man or a bachelor?
Sec. Cit. Answer every man directly.
First Cit. Ay, and briefly.
Fourth Cit. Ay, and wisely.
Third Cit. Ay, and truly, you were best.
Cin. What is my name? Whither am I going? Where do I dwell? Am I a married man or a bachelor? Then, to answer every man directly and briefly, wisely and truly: wisely I say, I am a bachelor.
Sec. Cit. That 's as much as to say, they are fools that marry: you'll bear me a bang for that, I fear. Proceed; directly.
Cin. Directly, I am going to Cæsar's funeral.
First Cit. As a friend or an enemy?
Cin. As a friend.
Sec. Cit. That matter is answered directly.
Fourth Cit. For your dwelling—briefly.
Cin. Briefly, I dwell by the Capitol.
Third Cit. Your name, sir, truly.
Cin. Truly, my name is Cinna.
First Cit. Tear him to pieces; he 's a conspirator!
Cin. I am Cinna the poet, I am Cinna the poet!
Fourth Cit. Tear him for his bad verses, tear him for his bad verses!
Cin. I am not Cinna the conspirator.
Fourth Cit. It is no matter, his name 's Cinna; pluck

225. **wit,** understanding, intelligence. F reads *writ*, a possible reading in the sense of written speech. **worth,** stature, authority. 226. **Action,** gesture. **utterance,** good delivery. 247. **drachmas,** a coin. 252. **walks,** parks. 255. **pleasures,** pleasure gardens (in which). 264. **forms,** benches. 275. **Belike,** likely enough.

SCENE III. 20. **bear me a bang,** get a beating from me.
ACT IV. SCENE I. 1. **prick'd,** marked down on a list; appropriate to the use of the stylus on waxen tablets. 6. **spot,** puncture with a stylus. 8-9. **we shall . . . legacies,** i.e., we'll figure out a way to reduce the outlay of Caesar's estate, by altering the will. 11. **Or,** either. 14. **three-fold,**

but his name out of his heart, and turn him going.

Third Cit. Tear him, tear him! Come, brands, ho! fire-brands: to Brutus', to Cassius'; burn all: some to Decius' house, and some to Casca's; some to Ligarius': away, go! *Exeunt all the Plebeians.*

ACT IV.

[SCENE I. *A house in Rome.*]

Enter ANTONY, OCTAVIUS, *and* LEPIDUS.

Ant. These many, then, shall die; their names are prick'd.
Oct. Your brother too must die; consent you, Lepidus?
Lep. I do consent,—
Oct. Prick him down, Antony.
Lep. Upon condition Publius shall not live,
Who is your sister's son, Mark Antony.
Ant. He shall not live; look, with a spot I damn him.
But, Lepidus, go you to Cæsar's house;
Fetch the will hither, and we shall determine
How to cut off some charge in legacies.
Lep. What, shall I find you here?
Oct. Or here, or at the Capitol. *Exit Lepidus.*
Ant. This is a slight unmeritable man,
Meet to be sent on errands: is it fit,
The three-fold world divided, he should stand
One of the three to share it?
Oct. So you thought him;
And took his voice who should be prick'd to die,
In our black sentence and proscription.
Ant. Octavius, I have seen more days than you:
And though we lay these honours on this man,
To ease ourselves of divers sland'rous loads,
He shall but bear them as the ass bears gold,
To groan and sweat under the business,
Either led or driven, as we point the way;
And having brought our treasure where we will,
Then take we down his load, and turn him off,
Like to the empty ass, to shake his ears,
And graze in commons.
Oct. You may do your will;
But he 's a tried and valiant soldier.
Ant. So is my horse, Octavius; and for that
I do appoint him store of provender:
It is a creature that I teach to fight,
To wind, to stop, to run directly on,
His corporal motion govern'd by my spirit.
And, in some taste, is Lepidus but so;
He must be taught and train'd and bid go forth;
A barren-spirited fellow; one that feeds
On objects, arts, and imitations,
Which, out of use and stal'd by other men,
Begin his fashion: do not talk of him,
But as a property. And now, Octavius,
Listen great things:—Brutus and Cassius
Are levying powers: we must straight make head:
Therefore let our alliance be combin'd,
†Our best friends made, our means stretch'd;
And let us presently go sit in council,
How covert matters may be best disclos'd,
And open perils surest answered.
Oct. Let us do so: for we are at the stake,
And bay'd about with many enemies;
And some that smile have in their hearts, I fear,
Millions of mischiefs. *Exeunt.*

[SCENE II. *Camp near Sardis. Before Brutus' tent.*]

Drum. Enter BRUTUS, LUCILIUS, [LUCIUS,] *and the* army; TITINIUS *and* PINDARUS *meet them.*

Bru. Stand, ho!
Lucil. Give the word, ho! and stand.
Bru. What now, Lucilius! is Cassius near?
Lucil. He is at hand; and Pindarus is come
To do you salutation from his master.
Bru. He greets me well. Your master, Pindarus,
In his own change, or by ill officers,
Hath given me some worthy cause to wish
Things done, undone: but, if he be at hand,
I shall be satisfied.
Pin. I do not doubt
But that my noble master will appear
Such as he is, full of regard and honour.
Bru. He is not doubted. A word, Lucilius;
How he receiv'd you, let me be resolv'd.
Lucil. With courtesy and with respect enough;
But not with such familiar instances,
Nor with such free and friendly conference,
As he hath us'd of old.
Bru. Thou hast describ'd
A hot friend cooling: ever note, Lucilius,
When love begins to sicken and decay,
It useth an enforced ceremony.
There are no tricks in plain and simple faith;
But hollow men, like horses hot at hand,
Make gallant show and promise of their mettle;
Low march within.
But when they should endure the bloody spur,
They fall their crests, and, like deceitful jades,
Sink in the trial. Comes his army on?
Lucil. They mean this night in Sardis to be quarter'd;
The greater part, the horse in general,
Are come with Cassius.
Bru. Hark! he is arriv'd.
March gently on to meet him.

Enter CASSIUS *and his powers.*

Cas. Stand, ho!
Bru. Stand, ho! Speak the word along.
First Sol. Stand!
Sec. Sol. Stand!
Third Sol. Stand!
Cas. Most noble brother, you have done me wrong.
Bru. Judge me, you gods! wrong I mine enemies?
And, if not so, how should I wrong a brother?
Cas. Brutus, this sober form of yours hides wrongs;

signifying either division into three parts or as made up of Europe, Asia, and Africa. 27. **commons,** public pasture. 32. **wind,** turn (horse trainer's term). 37. **On objects, arts, and imitations,** on curiosities, artifices, and the following of fashion. 38. **stal'd,** made common or cheap. 39. **Begin his fashion,** i.e., he then chooses these outworn fashions as his fashion. 46. **How . . . disclos'd,** how hidden dangers may best be discovered. 48. **at the stake,** a figure from bearbaiting.

SCENE II. 7. **change,** i.e., in his feelings toward me. 23. **hollow,** insincere. **hot at hand,** restless when held in. 26. **jades,** worthless horses.

And when you do them—
Bru. Cassius, be content;
Speak your griefs softly: I do know you well.
Before the eyes of both our armies here,
Which should perceive nothing but love from us,
Let us not wrangle: bid them move away;
Then in my tent, Cassius, enlarge your griefs,
And I will give you audience.
Cas. Pindarus,
Bid our commanders lead their charges off
A little from this ground.
Bru. Lucilius, do you the like; and let no man
Come to our tent till we have done our conference.
Let Lucius and Titinius guard our door.
Exeunt. Mane[n]t Brutus and Cassius.

[SCENE III. *Brutus' tent.*]

Cas. That you have wrong'd me doth appear in this:
You have condemn'd and noted Lucius Pella
For taking bribes here of the Sardians;
Wherein my letters, praying on his side,
Because I knew the man, were slighted off.
Bru. You wrong'd yourself to write in such a case.
Cas. In such a time as this it is not meet
That every nice offence should bear his comment.
Bru. Let me tell you, Cassius, you yourself
Are much condemn'd to have an itching palm;
To sell and mart your offices for gold
To undeservers.
Cas. I an itching palm!
You know that you are Brutus that speak this,
Or, by the gods, this speech were else your last.
Bru. The name of Cassius honours this corruption,
And chastisement doth therefore hide his head.
Cas. Chastisement!
Bru. Remember March, the ides of March remember:
Did not great Julius bleed for justice' sake?
What villain touch'd his body, that did stab,
And not for justice? What, shall one of us,
That struck the foremost man of all this world
But for supporting robbers, shall we now
Contaminate our fingers with base bribes,
And sell the mighty space of our large honours
For so much trash as may be grasped thus?
I had rather be a dog, and bay the moon,
Than such a Roman.
Cas. Brutus, bait not me;
I'll not endure it: you forget yourself,
To hedge me in; I am a soldier, I,
Older in practice, abler than yourself
To make conditions.
Bru. Go to; you are not, Cassius.
Cas. I am.
Bru. I say you are not.
Cas. Urge me no more, I shall forget myself;
Have mind upon your health, tempt me no farther.
Bru. Away, slight man!
Cas. Is 't possible?
Bru. Hear me, for I will speak.
Must I give way and room to your rash choler?
Shall I be frighted when a madman stares?
Cas. O ye gods, ye gods! must I endure all this?
Bru. All this! ay, more: fret till your proud heart break;
Go show your slaves how choleric you are,
And make your bondmen tremble. Must I budge?
Must I observe you? must I stand and crouch
Under your testy humour? By the gods,
You shall digest the venom of your spleen,
Though it do split you; for, from this day forth,
I'll use you for my mirth, yea, for my laughter,
When you are waspish.
Cas. Is it come to this?
Bru. You say you are a better soldier:
Let it appear so; make your vaunting true,
And it shall please me well: for mine own part,
I shall be glad to learn of noble men.
Cas. You wrong me every way; you wrong me, Brutus;
I said, an elder soldier, not a better:
Did I say 'better'?
Bru. If you did, I care not.
Cas. When Cæsar liv'd, he durst not thus have mov'd me.
Bru. Peace, peace! you durst not so have tempted him.
Cas. I durst not!
Bru. No.
Cas. What, durst not tempt him!
Bru. For your life you durst not.
Cas. Do not presume too much upon my love;
I may do that I shall be sorry for.
Bru. You have done that you should be sorry for.
There is no terror, Cassius, in your threats,
For I am arm'd so strong in honesty
That they pass by me as the idle wind,
Which I respect not. I did send to you
For certain sums of gold, which you denied me:
For I can raise no money by vile means:
By heaven, I had rather coin my heart,
And drop my blood for drachmas, than to wring
From the hard hands of peasants their vile trash
By any indirection: I did send
To you for gold to pay my legions,
Which you denied me: was that done like Cassius?
Should I have answer'd Caius Cassius so?
When Marcus Brutus grows so covetous,
To lock such rascal counters from his friends,
Be ready, gods, with all your thunderbolts;
Dash him to pieces!
Cas. I denied you not.
Bru. You did.
Cas. I did not: he was but a fool that brought
My answer back. Brutus hath riv'd my heart:
A friend should bear his friend's infirmities,
But Brutus makes mine greater than they are.
Bru. I do not, till you practise them on me.
Cas. You love me not.
Bru. I do not like your faults.

SCENE III. The scene is continuous. Brutus and Cassius remain (*Manent*) on stage. 2. **noted,** publicly disgraced. **Lucius Pella,** a Roman praetor in Sardis; detail from Plutarch. 4. **on his side,** in his behalf. 5. **slighted off,** put slightingly aside. 8. **nice,** trivial. **bear his comment,** be made the object of scrutiny. 10. **condemn'd to have,** accused of having. **itching,** covetous. 11. **mart,** traffic in. 15. **corruption,** dishonesty in public office. 26. **trash.** It is a part of Brutus' stoic philosophy to despise money. 27. **bay,** bark at. 32. **make conditions,** i.e., manage affairs. 45. **observe,** pay reverence to. 71. **vile means,** may allude to Cassius' extortions of money from the Rhodians; mentioned by Plutarch. 75. **indirection,** irregular or unjust means. 80. **rascal counters,** worthless pelf. 85. **riv'd,** cleft. 102. **Dearer than**

Cas. A friendly eye could never see such faults.
Bru. A flatterer's would not, though they do appear
As huge as high Olympus.
Cas. Come, Antony, and young Octavius, come,
Revenge yourselves alone on Cassius,
For Cassius is aweary of the world;
Hated by one he loves; brav'd by his brother;
Check'd like a bondman; all his faults observ'd,
Set in a note-book, learn'd, and conn'd by rote,
To cast into my teeth. O, I could weep
My spirit from mine eyes! There is my dagger,
And here my naked breast; within, a heart
Dearer than Pluto's mine, richer than gold:
If that thou be'st a Roman, take it forth;
I, that denied thee gold, will give my heart:
Strike, as thou didst at Cæsar; for, I know,
When thou didst hate him worst, thou lovedst him better
Than ever thou lovedst Cassius.
Bru. Sheathe your dagger:
Be angry when you will, it shall have scope;
Do what you will, dishonour shall be humour.
O Cassius, you are yoked with a lamb
That carries anger as the flint bears fire;
Who, much enforced, shows a hasty spark,
And straight is cold again.
Cas. Hath Cassius liv'd
To be but mirth and laughter to his Brutus,
When grief, and blood ill-temper'd, vexeth him?
Bru. When I spoke that, I was ill-temper'd too.
Cas. Do you confess so much? Give me your hand.
Bru. And my heart too.
Cas. O Brutus!
Bru. What 's the matter?
Cas. Have not you love enough to bear with me,
When that rash humour which my mother gave me
Makes me forgetful?
Bru. Yes, Cassius; and, from henceforth,
When you are over-earnest with your Brutus,
He'll think your mother chides, and leave you so.

Enter a Poet [*followed by* LUCILIUS, TITINIUS, *and* LUCIUS].

Poet. Let me go in to see the generals;
There is some grudge between 'em, 'tis not meet
They be alone.
Lucil. You shall not come to them.
Poet. Nothing but death shall stay me.
Cas. How now! what 's the matter?
Poet. For shame, you generals! what do you mean?
Love, and be friends, as two such men should be;
For I have seen more years, I'm sure, than ye.
Cas. Ha, ha! how vilely doth this cynic rhyme!
Bru. Get you hence, sirrah; saucy fellow, hence!
Cas. Bear with him, Brutus; 'tis his fashion.
Bru. I'll know his humour, when he knows his time:
What should the wars do with these jigging fools?
Companion, hence!
Cas. Away, away, be gone! *Exit Poet.*
Bru. Lucilius and Titinius, bid the commanders
Prepare to lodge their companies to-night.
Cas. And come yourselves, and bring Messala with you
Immediately to us. [*Exeunt Lucilius and Titinius.*]
Bru. Lucius, a bowl of wine!
[*Exit Lucius.*]
Cas. I did not think you could have been so angry.
Bru. O Cassius, I am sick of many griefs.
Cas. Of your philosophy you make no use,
If you give place to accidental evils.
Bru. No man bears sorrow better. Portia is dead.
Cas. Ha! Portia!
Bru. She is dead.
Cas. How 'scaped I killing when I cross'd you so?
O insupportable and touching loss!
Upon what sickness?
Bru. Impatient of my absence,
And grief that young Octavius with Mark Antony
Have made themselves so strong:—for with her death
That tidings came;—with this she fell distract,
And, her attendants absent, swallow'd fire.
Cas. And died so?
Bru. Even so.
Cas. O ye immortal gods!

Enter Boy [LUCIUS] *with wine and tapers.*

Bru. Speak no more of her. Give me a bowl of wine.
In this I bury all unkindness, Cassius. *Drinks.*
Cas. My heart is thirsty for that noble pledge.
Fill, Lucius, till the wine o'erswell the cup;
I cannot drink too much of Brutus' love.
[*Drinks. Exit Lucius.*]

Enter TITINIUS *and* MESSALA.

Bru. Come in, Titinius! Welcome, good Messala.
Now sit we close about this taper here,
And call in question our necessities.
Cas. Portia, art thou gone?
Bru. No more, I pray you.
Messala, I have here received letters,
That young Octavius and Mark Antony
Come down upon us with a mighty power,
Bending their expedition toward Philippi.
Mes. Myself have letters of the selfsame tenure.
Bru. With what addition?
Mes. That by proscription and bills of outlawry,
Octavius, Antony, and Lepidus,
Have put to death an hundred senators.
Bru. Therein our letters do not well agree;
Mine speak of seventy senators that died
By their proscriptions, Cicero being one.
Cas. Cicero one!
Mes. Cicero is dead,
And by that order of proscription.
Had you your letters from your wife, my lord?
Bru. No, Messala.
Mes. Nor nothing in your letters writ of her?
Bru. Nothing, Messala.
Mes. That, methinks, is strange.
Bru. Why ask you? hear you aught of her in yours?
Mes. No, my lord.

Pluto's mine, i.e., more precious than the wealth of Pluto, god of the underworld (probably confused with Plutus, god of riches). 109. **dishonour . . . humour,** i.e., I'll regard insults as the result of your hot temper. 115. **ill-temper'd,** i.e., with humors. 133. **cynic,** rude fellow. 136. **time,** proper time. 146. **accidental,** incidental. 156. **swallow'd fire.** Plutarch: "Portia . . . took hot burning coals and cast them in her mouth, and kept her mouth so close that she choked herself." 165. **call in question,** examine into. 171. **tenure,** tenor. 181-195. This passage is sometimes bracketed or deleted as contradictory to and redundant of lines 143-166; perhaps the passage here was a first draft, meant to be canceled.

Bru. Now, as you are a Roman, tell me true.
Mes. Then like a Roman bear the truth I tell:
For certain she is dead, and by strange manner.
Bru. Why, farewell, Portia. We must die, Messala:
With meditating that she must die once,
I have the patience to endure it now.
Mes. Even so great men great losses should endure.
Cas. I have as much of this in art as you,
But yet my nature could not bear it so.
Bru. Well, to our work alive. What do you think
Of marching to Philippi presently?
Cas. I do not think it good.
Bru. Your reason?
Cas. This it is:
'Tis better that the enemy seek us:
So shall he waste his means, weary his soldiers,
Doing himself offence; whilst we, lying still,
Are full of rest, defence, and nimbleness.
Bru. Good reasons must, of force, give place to better.
The people 'twixt Philippi and this ground
Do stand but in a forc'd affection;
For they have grudg'd us contribution:
The enemy, marching along by them,
By them shall make a fuller number up,
Come on refresh'd, new-added, and encourag'd;
From which advantage shall we cut him off,
If at Philippi we do face him there,
These people at our back.
Cas. Hear me, good brother.
Bru. Under your pardon. You must note beside,
That we have tried the utmost of our friends,
Our legions are brim-full, our cause is ripe:
The enemy increaseth every day;
We, at the height, are ready to decline.
There is a tide in the affairs of men,
Which, taken at the flood, leads on to fortune;
Omitted, all the voyage of their life
Is bound in shallows and in miseries.
On such a full sea are we now afloat;
And we must take the current when it serves,
Or lose our ventures.
Cas. Then, with your will, go on;
We'll along ourselves, and meet them at Philippi.
Bru. The deep of night is crept upon our talk,
And nature must obey necessity;
Which we will niggard with a little rest.
There is no more to say?
Cas. No more. Good night:
Early to-morrow will we rise, and hence.
Bru. Lucius! (*Enter Lucius.*) My gown. [*Exit Lucius.*]
Farewell, good Messala:
Good night, Titinius. Noble, noble Cassius,
Good night, and good repose.
Cas. O my dear brother!
This was an ill beginning of the night:
Never come such division 'tween our souls!
Let it not, Brutus.

Enter LUCIUS *with the gown.*

Bru. Every thing is well.
Cas. Good night, my lord.
Bru. Good night, good brother.
Tit. Mes. Good night, Lord Brutus.
Bru. Farewell, every one.
Exeunt [all but Brutus and Lucius].
Give me the gown. Where is thy instrument?
Luc. Here in the tent.
Bru. What, thou speak'st drowsily?
Poor knave, I blame thee not; thou art o'er-watch'd.
Call Claudius and some other of my men;
I'll have them sleep on cushions in my tent.
Luc. Varro and Claudius!

Enter VARRO *and* CLAUDIUS.

Var. Calls my lord?
Bru. I pray you, sirs, lie in my tent and sleep;
It may be I shall raise you by and by
On business to my brother Cassius.
Var. So please you, we will stand and watch your pleasure.
Bru. I will not have it so: lie down, good sirs;
It may be I shall otherwise bethink me.
Look, Lucius, here 's the book I sought for so;
I put it in the pocket of my gown.
[*Var. and Clau. lie down.*]
Luc. I was sure your lordship did not give it me.
Bru. Bear with me, good boy, I am much forgetful.
Canst thou hold up thy heavy eyes awhile,
And touch thy instrument a strain or two?
Luc. Ay, my lord, an 't please you.
Bru. It does, my boy:
I trouble thee too much, but thou art willing.
Luc. It is my duty, sir.
Bru. I should not urge thy duty past thy might;
I know young bloods look for a time of rest.
Luc. I have slept, my lord, already.
Bru. It was well done; and thou shalt sleep again;
I will not hold thee long: if I do live,
I will be good to thee. *Music, and a song.*
This is a sleepy tune. O murd'rous slumber,
Layest thou thy leaden mace upon my boy,
That plays thee music? Gentle knave, good night;
I will not do thee so much wrong to wake thee:
If thou dost nod, thou break'st thy instrument;
I'll take it from thee; and, good boy, good night.
Let me see, let me see; is not the leaf turn'd down
Where I left reading? Here it is, I think.

Enter the Ghost of CÆSAR.

How ill this taper burns! Ha! who comes here?
I think it is the weakness of mine eyes
That shapes this monstrous apparition.
It comes upon me. Art thou any thing?
Art thou some god, some angel, or some devil,
That mak'st my blood cold and my hair to stare?
Speak to me what thou art.
Ghost. Thy evil spirit, Brutus.
Bru. Why com'st thou?
Ghost. To tell thee thou shalt see me at Philippi.
Bru. Well; then I shall see thee again?
Ghost. Ay, at Philippi.

191. **once,** at some time. 194. **art,** i.e., the acquired wisdom of stoical fortitude. 196. **alive,** concerning us as living. 209. **new-added,** reinforced. 224. **ventures,** investments (of enterprises at sea). 228. **niggard,** stint (by sleeping only briefly). 231. **gown,** dressing gown. 239. **instrument,** lute. 241. **knave,** boy. **o'er-watch'd,** tired from lack of sleep. 262. **young bloods,** youthful constitutions. 267. **murd'rous,** producing the likeness of death. (Lucius has fallen asleep at his playing.) 268. **mace,** staff, club. 275. **How . . . burns.** It is a part of the machinery of apparitions that lights burn low and blue. 280. **stare,** stand on end. 291. **false,** out of tune. 307. **betimes before,** early in the morning

Bru. Why, I will see thee at Philippi, then.
[*Exit Ghost.*]
Now I have taken heart thou vanishest:
Ill spirit, I would hold more talk with thee.
Boy, Lucius! Varro! Claudius! Sirs, awake!
Claudius!
Luc. The strings, my lord, are false.
Bru. He thinks he still is at his instrument.
Lucius, awake!
Luc. My lord?
Bru. Didst thou dream, Lucius, that thou so criedst out?
Luc. My lord, I do not know that I did cry.
Bru. Yes, that thou didst: didst thou see any thing?
Luc. Nothing, my lord.
Bru. Sleep again, Lucius. Sirrah Claudius!
[*To Var.*] Fellow thou, awake!
Var. My lord?
Clau. My lord?
Bru. Why did you so cry out, sirs, in your sleep?
Var. Clau. Did we, my lord?
Bru. Ay: saw you any thing?
Var. No, my lord, I saw nothing.
Clau. Nor I, my lord.
Bru. Go and commend me to my brother Cassius;
Bid him set on his pow'rs betimes before,
And we will follow.
Var. Clau. It shall be done, my lord.
Exeunt.

ACT V.

[SCENE I. *The plains of Philippi.*]

Enter OCTAVIUS, ANTONY, *and their* army.

Oct. Now, Antony, our hopes are answered:
You said the enemy would not come down,
But keep the hills and upper regions;
It proves not so: their battles are at hand;
They mean to warn us at Philippi here,
Answering before we do demand of them.
Ant. Tut, I am in their bosoms, and I know
Wherefore they do it: they could be content
To visit other places; and come down
With fearful bravery, thinking by this face
To fasten in our thoughts that they have courage;
But 'tis not so.

Enter a Messenger.

Mess. Prepare you, generals:
The enemy comes on in gallant show;
Their bloody sign of battle is hung out,
And something to be done immediately.
Ant. Octavius, lead your battle softly on,
Upon the left hand of the even field.
Oct. Upon the right hand I; keep thou the left.
Ant. Why do you cross me in this exigent?
Oct. I do not cross you; but I will do so. *March.*

Drum. Enter BRUTUS, CASSIUS, *and their* army
[; LUCILIUS, TITINIUS, MESSALA, *and others*].

Bru. They stand, and would have parley.
Cas. Stand fast, Titinius: we must out and talk.
Oct. Mark Antony, shall we give sign of battle?
Ant. No, Cæsar, we will answer on their charge.
Make forth; the generals would have some words.
Oct. Stir not until the signal.
Bru. Words before blows: is it so, countrymen?
Oct. Not that we love words better, as you do.
Bru. Good words are better than bad strokes, Octavius.
Ant. In your bad strokes, Brutus, you give good words:
Witness the hole you made in Cæsar's heart,
Crying 'Long live! hail, Cæsar!'
Cas. Antony,
The posture of your blows are yet unknown;
But for your words, they rob the Hybla bees,
And leave them honeyless.
Ant. Not stingless too.
Bru. O, yes, and soundless too;
For you have stol'n their buzzing, Antony,
And very wisely threat before you sting.
Ant. Villains, you did not so, when your vile daggers
Hack'd one another in the sides of Cæsar:
You show'd your teeth like apes, and fawn'd like hounds,
And bow'd like bondmen, kissing Cæsar's feet;
Whilst damned Casca, like a cur, behind
Struck Cæsar on the neck. O you flatterers!
Cas. Flatterers! Now, Brutus, thank yourself:
This tongue had not offended so to-day,
If Cassius might have rul'd.
Oct. Come, come, the cause: if arguing make us sweat,
The proof of it will turn to redder drops.
Look;
I draw a sword against conspirators;
When think you that the sword goes up again?
Never, till Cæsar's three and thirty wounds
Be well aveng'd; or till another Cæsar
Have added slaughter to the sword of traitors.
Bru. Cæsar, thou canst not die by traitors' hands,
Unless thou bring'st them with thee.
Oct. So I hope;
I was not born to die on Brutus' sword.
Bru. O, if thou wert the noblest of thy strain,
Young man, thou couldst not die more honourable.
Cas. A peevish schoolboy, worthless of such honour,
Join'd with a masker and a reveller!
Ant. Old Cassius still!
Oct. Come, Antony, away!
Defiance, traitors, hurl we in your teeth:
If you dare fight to-day, come to the field;
If not, when you have stomachs.
Exeunt Octavius, Antony, and army.
Cas. Why, now, blow wind, swell billow and swim bark!
The storm is up, and all is on the hazard.
Bru. Ho, Lucilius! hark, a word with you.
Lucil. *(Stands forth)* My lord?
[*Brutus and Lucilius converse apart.*]

before me.

ACT V. SCENE I. 5. **warn,** challenge. 7. **bosoms,** secret councils. 10. **fearful bravery,** cowardly bravado. **face,** pretense. 14. **bloody sign of battle.** Plutarch describes this as an "arming scarlet coat." 17. **even,** level or evenly divided. 19. **cross,** contradict. **exigent,** critical moment. 20. **I will do so,** i.e., as I said. 21. **parley,** conference. 24. **answer on their charge,** attack when they attack. 33. **posture,** quality. 34. **Hybla,** a mountain and a town in Sicily, famous for honey. (Antony is accused of honeyed and insincere speech.) 41. **show'd your teeth,** i.e., in smiles. 48. **the cause,** to our business.

Cas. Messala!
Mes. (*Stands forth*) What says my general?
Cas. Messala,
This is my birth-day; as this very day
Was Cassius born. Give me thy hand, Messala:
Be thou my witness that against my will,
As Pompey was, am I compell'd to set
Upon one battle all our liberties.
You know that I held Epicurus strong
And his opinion: now I change my mind,
And partly credit things that do presage.
Coming from Sardis, on our former ensign
Two mighty eagles fell, and there they perch'd,
Gorging and feeding from our soldiers' hands;
Who to Philippi here consorted us:
This morning are they fled away and gone;
And in their steads do ravens, crows and kites,
Fly o'er our heads and downward look on us,
As we were sickly prey: their shadows seem
A canopy most fatal, under which
Our army lies, ready to give up the ghost.
Mes. Believe not so.
Cas. I but believe it partly;
For I am fresh of spirit and resolv'd
To meet all perils very constantly.
Bru. Even so, Lucilius.
Cas. Now, most noble Brutus,
The gods to-day stand friendly, that we may,
Lovers in peace, lead on our days to age!
But since the affairs of men rest still incertain,
Let 's reason with the worst that may befall.
If we do lose this battle, then is this
The very last time we shall speak together:
What are you then determined to do?
Bru. Even by the rule of that philosophy
By which I did blame Cato for the death
Which he did give himself, I know not how,
But I do find it cowardly and vile,
For fear of what might fall, so to prevent
The time of life: arming myself with patience
To stay the providence of some high powers
That govern us below.
Cas. Then, if we lose this battle,
You are contented to be led in triumph
Thorough the streets of Rome?
Bru. No, Cassius, no: think not, thou noble Roman,
That ever Brutus will go bound to Rome;
He bears too great a mind. But this same day
Must end that work the ides of March begun;
And whether we shall meet again I know not.
Therefore our everlasting farewell take:
For ever, and for ever, farewell, Cassius!
If we do meet again, why, we shall smile;
If not, why then, this parting was well made.
Cas. For ever, and for ever, farewell, Brutus!
If we do meet again, we'll smile indeed;
If not, 'tis true this parting was well made.
Bru. Why, then, lead on. O, that a man might know
The end of this day's business ere it come!
But it sufficeth that the day will end,
And then the end is known. Come, ho! away! *Exeunt.*

[SCENE II. *The same. The field of battle.*]

Alarum. Enter BRUTUS *and* MESSALA.

Bru. Ride, ride, Messala, ride, and give these bills
Unto the legions on the other side. *Loud alarum.*
Let them set on at once; for I perceive
But cold demeanour in Octavius' wing,
And sudden push gives them the overthrow.
Ride, ride, Messala: let them all come down. *Exeunt.*

[SCENE III. *Another part of the field.*]

Alarums. Enter CASSIUS *and* TITINIUS.

Cas. O, look, Titinius, look, the villains fly!
Myself have to mine own turn'd enemy:
This ensign here of mine was turning back;
I slew the coward, and did take it from him.
Tit. O Cassius, Brutus gave the word too early;
Who, having some advantage on Octavius,
Took it too eagerly: his soldiers fell to spoil,
Whilst we by Antony are all enclos'd.

Enter PINDARUS.

Pin. Fly further off, my lord, fly further off;
Mark Antony is in your tents, my lord:
Fly, therefore, noble Cassius, fly far off.
Cas. This hill is far enough. Look, look, Titinius;
Are those my tents where I perceive the fire?
Tit. They are, my lord.
Cas. Titinius, if thou lovest me,
Mount thou my horse, and hide thy spurs in him,
Till he have brought thee up to yonder troops,
And here again; that I may rest assur'd
Whether yond troops are friend or enemy.
Tit. I will be here again, even with a thought. *Exit.*
Cas. Go, Pindarus, get higher on that hill;
My sight was ever thick; regard Titinius,
And tell me what thou not'st about the field.
[*Pindarus goes up*].
This day I breathed first: time is come round,
And where I did begin, there shall I end;
My life is run his compass. Sirrah, what news?
Pin. (*Above*) O my lord!
Cas. What news?
Pin. (*Above*) Titinius is enclosed round about
With horsemen, that make to him on the spur;
Yet he spurs on. Now they are almost on him.
Now, Titinius! Now some light. O, he lights too.
He 's ta'en. (*Shout.*) And, hark! they shout for joy.
Cas. Come down, behold no more.
O, coward that I am, to live so long,
To see my best friend ta'en before my face!

Enter PINDARUS [*from above*].

Come hither, sirrah:
In Parthia did I take thee prisoner;

72. **as,** redundant particle. 75. **Pompey.** The reference is to Pharsalus, and the sentence is closely repeated from Plutarch. 77. **Epicurus,** a Grecian philosopher who lived from 341 to 270 B.C., whose materialistic philosophy spurned belief in omens or superstitions. 79. **presage,** foretell events. The incident of the eagles is from Plutarch. 83. **consorted,** accompanied. 93. **Even so, Lucilius.** Brutus thus ends his private conversation with Lucilius. 102. **Cato,** Cato the Younger, Brutus' father-in-law. The justifiability of his destruction of himself was long a subject of debate. 106. **time,** term.

SCENE II. 1. **bills,** orders. 2. **side,** wing. 4. **cold demeanour,** signs of faint-heartedness. 6. **come down,** attack.

SCENE III. 3. **ensign,** bearer of the standard. 21. **thick,** imperfect,

And then I swore thee, saving of thy life,
That whatsoever I did bid thee do,
Thou shouldst attempt it. Come now, keep thine oath;
Now be a freeman: and with this good sword,
That ran through Cæsar's bowels, search this bosom.
Stand not to answer: here, take thou the hilts;
And, when my face is cover'd, as 'tis now,
Guide thou the sword. [*Pindarus stabs him.*] Cæsar, thou art reveng'd,
Even with the sword that kill'd thee. [*Dies.*]
Pin. So, I am free; yet would not so have been,
Durst I have done my will. O Cassius!
Far from this country Pindarus shall run,
Where never Roman shall take note of him. [*Exit.*]

Enter TITINIUS *with* MESSALA.

Mes. It is but change, Titinius; for Octavius
Is overthrown by noble Brutus' power,
As Cassius' legions are by Antony.
Tit. These tidings will well comfort Cassius.
Mes. Where did you leave him?
Tit. All disconsolate,
With Pindarus his bondman, on this hill.
Mes. Is not that he that lies upon the ground?
Tit. He lies not like the living. O my heart!
Mes. Is not that he?
Tit. No, this was he, Messala,
But Cassius is no more. O setting sun,
As in thy red rays thou dost sink to night,
So in his red blood Cassius' day is set;
The sun of Rome is set! Our day is gone;
Clouds, dews, and dangers come; our deeds are done!
Mistrust of my success hath done this deed.
Mes. Mistrust of good success hath done this deed.
O hateful error, melancholy's child,
Why dost thou show to the apt thoughts of men
The things that are not? O error, soon conceiv'd,
Thou never com'st unto a happy birth,
But kill'st the mother that engend'red thee!
Tit. What, Pindarus! where art thou, Pindarus?
Mes. Seek him, Titinius, whilst I go to meet
The noble Brutus, thrusting this report
Into his ears; I may say, thrusting it;
For piercing steel and darts envenomed
Shall be as welcome to the ears of Brutus
As tidings of this sight.
Tit. Hie you, Messala,
And I will seek for Pindarus the while. [*Exit Messala.*]
Why didst thou send me forth, brave Cassius?
Did I not meet thy friends? and did not they
Put on my brows this wreath of victory,
And bid me give it thee? Didst thou not hear their shouts?
Alas, thou hast misconstrued every thing!
But, hold thee, take this garland on thy brow;
Thy Brutus bid me give it thee, and I
Will do his bidding. Brutus, come apace,
And see how I regarded Caius Cassius.
By your leave, gods:—this is a Roman's part:
Come, Cassius' sword, and find Titinius' heart.
Dies.

Alarum. Enter BRUTUS, MESSALA, *young* CATO, STRATO, VOLUMNIUS, *and* LUCILIUS.

Bru. Where, where, Messala, doth his body lie?
Mes. Lo, yonder, and Titinius mourning it.
Bru. Titinius' face is upward.
Cato. He is slain.
Bru. O Julius Cæsar, thou art mighty yet!
Thy spirit walks abroad, and turns our swords
In our own proper entrails. *Low alarums.*
Cato. Brave Titinius!
Look, whe'r he have not crown'd dead Cassius!
Bru. Are yet two Romans living such as these?
The last of all the Romans, fare thee well!
It is impossible that ever Rome
Should breed thy fellow. Friends, I owe moe tears
To this dead man than you shall see me pay.
I shall find time, Cassius, I shall find time.
Come, therefore, and to Thasos send his body:
His funerals shall not be in our camp,
Lest it discomfort us. Lucilius, come;
And come, young Cato; let us to the field.
Labeo and Flavius, set our battles on:
'Tis three o'clock; and, Romans, yet ere night
We shall try fortune in a second fight. *Exeunt.*

[SCENE IV. *Another part of the field.*]

Alarum. Enter BRUTUS, MESSALA, [*young*] CATO, LUCILIUS, *and* FLAVIUS.

Bru. Yet, countrymen, O, yet hold up your heads!
[*Exit, followed by Messala and Flavius.*]
Cato. What bastard doth not? Who will go with me?
I will proclaim my name about the field:
I am the son of Marcus Cato, ho!
A foe to tyrants, and my country's friend;
I am the son of Marcus Cato, ho!

Enter Soldiers *and fight.*

Lucil. And I am Brutus, Marcus Brutus I!
Brutus, my country's friend! Know me for Brutus!
[*Young Cato falls.*]
O young and noble Cato, art thou down?
Why, now thou diest as bravely as Titinius;
And mayst be honour'd, being Cato's son.
First Sold. Yield, or thou diest.
Lucil. Only I yield to die:
There is so much that thou wilt kill me straight;
[*Offering money.*]
Kill Brutus, and be honour'd in his death.
First Sold. We must not. A noble prisoner!
Sec. Sold. Room, ho! Tell Antony, Brutus is ta'en.
First Sold. I'll tell the news. Here comes the general.

Enter ANTONY.

Brutus is ta'en, Brutus is ta'en, my lord.
Ant. Where is he?

dim. 31. **lights,** alights. 37. **Parthia,** allusion to the campaign of Crassus in Parthia, 53 B.C., in which Plutarch states that Cassius had captured Pindarus. 38. **swore thee,** made thee swear. 49. **Pindarus shall run.** Plutarch states that Pindarus was never seen again. 51. **change,** exchange. 65. **Mistrust,** i.e., Cassius' fear. 68. **apt,** impressionable. 97. **whe'r,** whether. 104. **Thasos,** an island off the coast of Thrace. 106. **discomfort,** discourage. 110. **second fight.** The second battle was, in point of fact, twenty days later.

SCENE IV. 7-8. **And I . . . Brutus.** This speech is unassigned in F. It is here assigned to Lucilius, who, in lines 12-14 below, pretends to be Brutus as an act of devotion to his master. 9. **Cato,** a son of Marcus Cato, whose death is recounted by Plutarch.

Lucil. Safe, Antony; Brutus is safe enough:
I dare assure thee that no enemy
Shall ever take alive the noble Brutus:
The gods defend him from so great a shame!
When you do find him, or alive or dead,
He will be found like Brutus, like himself.
Ant. This is not Brutus, friend; but, I assure you,
A prize no less in worth: keep this man safe;
Give him all kindness: I had rather have
Such men my friends than enemies. Go on,
And see whe'r Brutus be alive or dead;
And bring us word unto Octavius' tent
How every thing is chanc'd. *Exeunt.*

[SCENE V. *Another part of the field.*]

Enter BRUTUS, DARDANIUS, CLITUS, STRATO, *and* VOLUMNIUS.

Bru. Come, poor remains of friends, rest on this rock.
Cli. Statilius show'd the torch-light, but, my lord,
He came not back: he is or ta'en or slain.
Bru. Sit thee down, Clitus: slaying is the word;
It is a deed in fashion. Hark thee, Clitus. [*Whispers.*]
Cli. What, I, my lord? No, not for all the world.
Bru. Peace then! no words.
Cli. I'll rather kill myself.
Bru. Hark thee, Dardanius. [*Whispers.*]
Dar. Shall I do such a deed?
Cli. O Dardanius!
Dar. O Clitus!
Cli. What ill request did Brutus make to thee?
Dar. To kill him, Clitus. Look, he meditates.
Cli. Now is that noble vessel full of grief,
That it runs over even at his eyes.
Bru. Come hither, good Volumnius; list a word.
Vol. What says my lord?
Bru. Why, this, Volumnius:
The ghost of Cæsar hath appear'd to me
Two several times by night; at Sardis once,
And, this last night, here in Philippi fields:
I know my hour is come.
Vol. Not so, my lord.
Bru. Nay, I am sure it is, Volumnius.
Thou seest the world, Volumnius, how it goes;
Our enemies have beat us to the pit: *Low alarums.*
It is more worthy to leap in ourselves,
Than tarry till they push us. Good Volumnius,
Thou know'st that we two went to school together:
Even for that our love of old, I prithee,
Hold thou my sword-hilts, whilst I run on it.
Vol. That 's not an office for a friend, my lord.
Alarum still.
Cli. Fly, fly, my lord; there is no tarrying here.
Bru. Farewell to you; and you; and you, Volumnius.
Strato, thou hast been all this while asleep;
Farewell to thee too, Strato. Countrymen,
My heart doth joy that yet in all my life
I found no man but he was true to me.
I shall have glory by this losing day
More than Octavius and Mark Antony
By this vile conquest shall attain unto.
So fare you well at once; for Brutus' tongue
Hath almost ended his life's history:
Night hangs upon mine eyes; my bones would rest,
That have but labour'd to attain this hour.
Alarum. Cry within, 'Fly, fly, fly!'
Cli. Fly, my lord, fly.
Bru. Hence! I will follow.
[*Exeunt Clitus, Dardanius, and Volumnius.*]
I prithee, Strato, stay thou by thy lord:
Thou art a fellow of a good respect;
Thy life hath had some smatch of honour in it:
Hold then my sword, and turn away thy face,
While I do run upon it. Wilt thou, Strato?
Stra. Give me your hand first. Fare you well, my lord.
Bru. Farewell, good Strato. [*Runs on his sword.*]
Cæsar, now be still:
I kill'd not thee with half so good a will. *Dies.*

Alarum. Retreat. Enter ANTONY, OCTAVIUS, MESSALA, LUCILIUS, *and the army.*

Oct. What man is that?
Mes. My master's man. Strato, where is thy master?
Stra. Free from the bondage you are in, Messala:
The conquerors can but make a fire of him;
For Brutus only overcame himself,
And no man else hath honour by his death.
Lucil. So Brutus should be found. I thank thee, Brutus,
That thou hast prov'd Lucilius' saying true.
Oct. All that serv'd Brutus, I will entertain them.
Fellow, wilt thou bestow thy time with me?
Stra. Ay, if Messala will prefer me to you.
Oct. Do so, good Messala.
Mes. How died my master, Strato?
Stra. I held the sword, and he did run on it.
Mes. Octavius, then take him to follow thee,
That did the latest service to my master.
Ant. This was the noblest Roman of them all:
All the conspirators save only he
Did that they did in envy of great Cæsar;
He only, in a general honest thought
And common good to all, made one of them.
His life was gentle, and the elements
So mix'd in him that Nature might stand up
And say to all the world 'This was a man!'
Oct. According to his virtue let us use him,
With all respect and rites of burial.
Within my tent his bones to-night shall lie,
Most like a soldier, order'd honourably.
So call the field to rest; and let 's away,
To part the glories of this happy day. *Exeunt omnes.*

SCENE V. 2. **show'd the torch-light.** A scout named Statilius has gone to see if Cassius' camp is still occupied; he signals back, but is taken or slain. 23. **pit,** a trap for wild animals; also, a grave. 46. **smatch,** smack, flavor. 68-75. **This . . . man.** This famous eulogy is based upon a statement by Plutarch that Antony cast his embroidered cloak over Brutus' body and paid the cost of Brutus' burial, and upon Plutarch's statement in his summary of the character of Brutus that even Brutus' enemies confessed that he had had no other intent but to restore the ancient institutions of Rome. 73. **gentle,** a favorite word with Shakespeare meaning "true," "cultured," "affable." **elements.** Man as a microcosm was made up of earth, air, fire, and water, whose qualities were mingled in Brutus in due proportions. 80. **field,** army in the field. 81. **part,** share.

the period of tragedies

When the Globe, the most famous of the London public playhouses, was built in 1599, one-half interest in the property was assigned to the brothers Cuthbert and Richard Burbage. The other half was divided among five actor-sharers: Shakespeare, Will Kempe, Thomas Pope, Augustine Phillips, and John Heminges. Kempe left the company, however, in 1599, and subsequently became a member of the Earl of Worcester's men. His place as leading comic actor was taken by Robert Armin, an experienced man of the theatre and occasional author whose comic specialty was the role of the wise fool. We can observe in Shakespeare's plays the effects of Kempe's departure and of Armin's arrival. Kempe had apparently specialized in clownish and rustic parts, such as those of Dogberry in *Much Ado*, Launcelot Gobbo in *The Merchant of Venice*, and Bottom in *A Midsummer Night's Dream*. (We know that he played Dogberry because his name appears in the play manuscript; similar evidence links his name to the role of Peter in *Romeo and Juliet*.) For Armin, on the other hand, Shakespeare evidently created such roles as Touchstone in *As You Like It*, Feste in *Twelfth Night*, Lavatch in *All's Well that Ends Well*, and the Fool in *King Lear*.

Other shifts in personnel can sometimes be traced in Shakespeare's plays, especially changes in the number and ability of the boy actors (whose voices would suddenly start to crack at puberty). Shakespeare makes an amusing point about the relative size of two boy actors, for example, in *A Midsummer Night's Dream* and in *As You Like It;* this option may have been available to him only at certain times. On the other hand, not all changes in the company roster can be related meaningfully to Shakespeare's dramatic development. Augustine Phillips, who died in 1605, was a full actor-sharer of long standing in the company, but his "type" of role was probably not sharply differentiated from that of several of his associates. Shakespeare's plays, after all, involve many important supporting roles, and versatility in the undertaking of such parts must have been more common than specialization. (Phillips is remembered, however, for his last will and testament: he left a bequest of "a thirty shillings peece in gould" to "my Fellowe, William Shakespeare," and similar bequests to other members of the troupe.)

With the reopening of the boys' acting companies in 1598–1599, a serious economic rivalry sprang up between them and the adult companies. The Children of the Chapel Royal occupied the theatre in Blackfriars, and the Children of Paul's probably acted in their own singing school in St. Paul's churchyard. Their plays exploited a new vogue for satire. The satiric laughter was often directed at the city of London and its bourgeois inhabitants: socially ambitious tradesmen's wives, Puritan zealots, and the like. Other favorite targets included parvenu knights at court, would-be poets, and hysterical governmental officials. The price of admission at the private theatres was considerably higher than at the Globe or Rose, so that the clientele tended to be more fashionable. Sophisticated authors like Ben Jonson, George Chapman, and John Marston tended to find writing for the boy actors more literarily rewarding than writing for the adult players.

One manifestation of the rivalry between public and private theatres was the so-called War of the Theatres, or Psychomachia. In part this was a personal quarrel between Jonson on one side and Marston and Thomas Dekker on the other. Underlying this quarrel, however, was a serious hostility between a broadly based popular theatre and one that catered to the elite. Dekker, with Marston's encouragement, attacked Jonson as a literary dictator and snob, one who subverted public decency. Jonson replied with a fervent defense of the artist's right to criticize everything he sees wrong. The major plays in the exchange (1600–1601) were Jonson's *Cynthia's Revels*, Dekker's and Marston's *Satiromastix*, and Jonson's *The Poetaster*.

Shakespeare allows Hamlet to comment on the theatrical rivalry (II,ii), with seeming regret for the fact that the boys have been overly successful and that many adult troupes have been obliged to tour the provinces. Most of all, though, Hamlet's remarks deplore the needless bitterness on both sides. The tone of kindly remonstrance makes it seem unlikely that Shakespeare took an active part in the fracas. To be sure, in the Cambridge play *2 Return from Parnassus* (1601–1603) the character called Will Kempe does

THE HUNTINGTON LIBRARY, SAN MARINO, CALIFORNIA

Unlike his predecessor Will Kempe, who left Shakespeare's company in 1600, Robert Armin specialized in comic roles emphasizing subtle wit and sharp repartee.

assert that his fellow actor Shakespeare had put down the famous Ben Jonson:

> Why, heres our fellow *Shakespeare* puts them all downe, I, and *Ben Ionson* too. O that *Ben Ionson* is a pestilent fellow, and he brought vp *Horace* giuing the Poets a pill, but our fellow *Shakespeare* hath giuen him a purge that made him bewray his credit.
>
> (ll. 1809–1813)

Nevertheless, no play exists in which Shakespeare did put down Jonson, and Kempe is probably thinking instead of *Satiromastix* which was performed by Shakespeare's company. In fact, Shakespeare and Jonson remained on cordial terms despite their profound differences in artistic outlook.

Upon the death of Queen Elizabeth in 1603 and the accession to the throne of King James I, Shakespeare's company added an important new success to their already great prosperity. According to a document of instruction from King James to his Keeper of the Privy Seal, dated May 19, 1603, and endorsed as "The Players' Privilege," the acting company that had formerly been the Lord Chamberlain's men now became the King's servants. The document names Shakespeare, Richard Burbage, Augustine Phillips, John Heminges, Henry Condell, Will Sly, Robert Armin, Richard Cowley, and Lawrence Fletcher—the last an actor who had played before the king and the Scottish court in 1599 and 1601. These players are accorded the usual privileges of exercising their art anywhere within the kingdom and are henceforth to be known as the King's company. As the King's servants, the principal members of the troupe were also appointed to the honorary rank of Grooms of the Royal Chamber. We therefore find them duly recorded in the Accounts of the Master of the Wardrobe on March 15, 1604, as recipients of the customary grants of red cloth, so that they, dressed in the royal livery, might take part in the approaching coronation procession of King James. The same men are mentioned in these grants as in the Players' Privilege. Shakespeare's name stands second in the former document and first in the latter. In a somewhat similar manner the king's players, as Grooms of the Royal Chamber, were called in attendance on the Spanish ambassador at Somerset House in August 1604.

The Revels Accounts of performances at court during the winter season of 1604–1605 contain an unusually full entry listing several of Shakespeare's plays. The list includes *Othello*, *The Merry Wives of Windsor*, *Measure for Measure*, "*The plaie of Errors*," *Love's Labour's Lost*, *Henry V*, and *The Merchant of Venice*. The last play was "Againe Commanded By the Kings Maiestie," and so was performed a second time. This list also sporadically notes the names of "the poets which mayd the plaies," ascribing three of these works to "Shaxberd." (Probably the final "d" is an error for "e," since the two characters are easily confused in Elizabethan handwriting; the word represents "Shaxbere" or "Shaxpere.") The entire entry was once called into question as a possible forgery, but is now generally regarded as authentic.

Business and Family Affairs

A number of records during this period show us glimpses of Shakespeare as a man of property. On May 1, 1602, John and William Combe conveyed to Shakespeare one hundred and seven acres of arable land plus twenty acres of pasture in the parish of Old Stratford, for the sizable payment of three hundred and twenty pounds. The deed was delivered to Shakespeare's brother Gilbert and not to the poet, who was probably at that time occupied in London. On September 28th of the same year Shakespeare acquired the title to "one cottage and one garden by estimation a quarter of an acre," located opposite his home (New Place) in Stratford.

Shakespeare made still other real-estate investments in his home town. In 1605 he purchased an interest in the tithes of Stratford and adjacent villages from one Ralph Huband for the considerable sum of four hundred and forty pounds. The purchasing of tithes was a common financial transaction in Shakespeare's time, though unknown today. Tithes were originally intended for the support of the church, but had in many cases become privately owned and hence negotiable. The owners of tithes paid a fixed rental sum for the right to collect as many of these taxes as they could, up to the total amount due under the law. Shakespeare seems, on this occasion in 1605, to have bought from Ralph Huband a one-half interest, or "moiety," in certain tithes of Stratford and vicinity. Later, probably in 1609, Shakespeare was one of those who brought a bill of complaint before the Lord Chancellor, requesting that certain other titheholders be required to come into the High Court of Chancery and make answer to the complaints alleged, namely, that they had not paid their proportional part of an annual rental of £27 13s. 4d. on the whole property in the tithes to one Henry Barker. This Barker had the theoretical right to foreclose on the entire property if any one of the forty-two titheholders failed to contribute his share of the annual fee. The suit was in effect a friendly one, designed to ensure that all those who were supposed to contribute did so on an equitable and businesslike basis.

We learn from the Stratford Registers of baptism, marriage, and burial, of the changes in Shakespeare's family during this period. His father died in 1601, his brother Edmund in 1607, and his mother in 1608. On June 5, 1607, his daughter Susanna was married to Dr. John Hall in Holy Trinity Church, Stratford. Their first child and Shakespeare's first grandchild, Elizabeth, was christened in the same church on February 21, 1608.

Allusions

Allusions to Shakespeare are frequent during this period of his life. One amusing reference is not literary, but professes to tell about Shakespeare's prowess as a lover and rival of his good friend and theatrical colleague, Richard Burbage. Perhaps the joke was just a good bawdy story and should not be taken too seriously, but it is nonetheless one of the few anecdotes that date from Shakespeare's lifetime. Our informant is John Manningham, a young law student, who notes in his commonplace book in 1602 the following:

> 13 March 1601 [1602] . . . Vpon a tyme when Burbidge played Rich. 3. there was a citizen greue [grew] soe farr in liking with him, that before shee went from the play shee appointed him to come that night vnto hir by the name of Ri: the 3. Shakespeare overhearing their conclusion went before, was intertained, and at his game ere Burbidge came. Then message being brought that Rich. the 3.[d] was at the dore, Shakespeare caused returne to be made that William the Conqueror was before Rich. the 3. Shakespeare's name William.

Other allusions of the time are more literary. Shakespeare's greatness is by this time taken for granted. Anthony Scoloker, for example, in his epistle prefatory to *Diaphantus, or the Passions of Love* (1604), attempts to describe an excellent literary work in this way:

The Accompte of the Office of the Reuelles of this whole yeres Charge in An^o 1604: Untill the last of Octobar 1605:

The Chardges ...

Edmundo Tylney ...

The plaiers names	1605	The poets which mayd the plaies
By the Kings Ma^tis plaiers:	Hallamas Day being the first of Nouembar A play in the Banketinge house att Whithall Called The Moor of Venis:	
By his Ma^tis plaiers:	The Sunday ffollowinge A play of the Merry wiues of winsor:	
By his Ma^tis plaiers:	On St Stiuens night in the Hall A play Caled Mesur for Mesur:	Shaxberd:
	On St Jones night A maske ...	
By his Ma^tis plaiers:	On Inosents night The plaie of Errors:	Shaxberd:
By the Queens Ma^tis plaiers:	On Sunday ffollowinge A plaie Called How to Larne of a woman to wooe:	Heewood:
The Boyes of the Chapell:	On Newers Night A playe Cauled: All Foulles:	By George Chapman:
By his Ma^tis plaiers:	Betwin Newers Day And Twelfe day A play of Loues Labours Lost:	

The popularity of Shakespeare's plays at court is apparent from these entries in the Revels Account of 1604–1605 listing five of his seven plays performed that winter.

It should be like the *Neuer-too-well read Arcadia*, . . . or to come home to the vulgars *Element*, like *Friendly Shakespeare's Tragedies*, where the *Commedian* rides, when the *Tragedian* stands on Tip-toe: Faith it should please all, like Prince *Hamlet*.

The antiquarian William Camden includes Shakespeare's name among his list of England's greatest writers in his *Remaines of a greater Worke concerning Britaine* (1605):

These may suffice for some Poeticall descriptions of our auncient Poets, if I would come to our time, what a world could I present to you out of *Sir Philipp Sidney, Ed. Spencer, Samuel Daniel, Hugh Holland, Ben: Johnson, Th. Campion, Mich. Drayton, George Chapman, Iohn Marston, William Shakespeare*, & other most pregnant witts of these our times, whom succeeding ages may iustly admire.

A striking attempt to use Shakespeare's growing reputation and dramatic skill for political effect had some potentially very serious repercussions. Two days before the abortive rebellion of the Earl of Essex on February 7, 1601, Shakespeare's company was commissioned to perform a well-known play in its repertory about King Richard II. This play must almost surely have been Shakespeare's. Evidently the purpose of this extraordinary performance was to awaken public sympathy for Essex by suggesting that Queen Elizabeth was another Richard II, surrounded by corrupt favorites and deaf to the pleas of her subjects. Essex' avowed intention was to remove from positions of influence those men whom he considered his political enemies. Fortunately Shakespeare's company was later exonerated of any blame in the affair (see Play Introduction to *Richard II*).

Perhaps no other allusion to Shakespeare during this period, however, can suggest so well as the following quotation the extent to which Shakespeare's plays had become familiar to Englishmen everywhere. The quotation is taken from the notes of a certain Captain Keeling, commander of the East India Company's ship *Dragon*, off Sierra Leone, in the years 1607 and 1608:

1607, Sept. 5. I sent the interpreter, according to his deseir, abord the Hector whear he brooke fast, and after came abord mee, wher we gaue the tragedie of Hamlett.

30. Captain Hawkins dinned with me, wher my companions acted Kinge Richard the Second.

[March 31.] I envited Captain Hawkins to a ffishe dinner, and had Hamlet acted abord me; which I permitt to keepe my people from idlenes and unlawful games, or sleepe.

Other Drama of the Period

Even without Shakespeare, the early Jacobean drama in England would rank as one of the most creative periods in the history of all theatre. (The word "Jacobean" is derived from *Jacobus*, the Latin form of the name of King James I.) Shakespeare's earlier contemporaries—Lyly, Greene, Marlowe, Peele, Kyd—were dead or silent, but another generation of playwrights was at hand. George Chapman, John Marston, and Ben Jonson all began writing plays shortly before 1600. The names of Thomas Dekker and Thomas Heywood are perhaps to be associated with various lost plays as early as 1594, but these men are known today for the plays they wrote after 1599. Francis Beaumont, John Fletcher, Cyril Tourneur, and Thomas Middleton emerged into prominence in about 1606 or 1607. John Webster collaborated with Dekker and others in such plays as *Westward Ho* and *Sir Thomas Wyatt* around 1604, although he did not write his great tragedies until 1609–1614. Lesser talents such as Henry Chettle, Anthony Munday, Henry Porter, John Day, and William Haughton continued to pour forth an abundant supply of workmanlike plays. As Shakespeare's career developed, therefore, he enjoyed the fellowship and no doubt the rivalry of a remarkably gifted and diverse group of practicing dramatists.

Early Jacobean drama is, on the whole, strikingly different from the late Elizabethan drama that had preceded it. Other dramatists besides Shakespeare mirror his shift of focus from romantic comedies and patriotic histories to "problem" plays and tragedies. The boys' companies, reopening in 1598–1599 after virtually a decade of silence, did much to set the new tone. They avoided almost entirely the English history play with its muscularly heroic style, so unsuited for the acting capabilities of boys. Besides, sophisticated audiences were satiated with jingoistic fare, and even in the public theatres the genre had pretty well run its course. The fashion of the moment turned instead to revenge tragedy and satiric comedy.

The Jacobean revenge play owed much of its original inspiration to Thomas Kyd's *The Spanish Tragedy* (c. 1587), with its pace-setting conventions: the intervention of supernatural forces, the feigned madness of the avenger, his difficulty in ascertaining the true facts of the murder, his morbid awareness of the conflict between human injustice and divine justice, his devising of a play within the play, and his invention of ingenious methods of slaughter in the play's gory ending. Kyd may also have written an early version of *Hamlet* featuring similar motifs. Shakespeare elevated the revenge play to sublimest tragedy in his *Hamlet* (c. 1599–1601), but most followers of Kyd preferred to revel in the sensationalism of the genre. Some private-theatre dramatists, such as Marston, even subjected the conventions of the genre to caricature. Marston's revenge plays, written chiefly for Paul's boys and (after 1604) for the Children of the Queen's Revels, include *Antonio's Revenge* (1599–1601), and *The Malcontent* (1600–1604). These dramas are marked by flamboyantly overstated cynicism, and are in many ways as close to satire as to tragedy. Marston had in fact made his first reputation as a nondramatic satirist, with *The Metamorphosis of Pygmalions Image* and *The Scourge of Villanie* in 1598. His plays represent a continuation in dramatic form of the techniques of the Roman satirist. The typical Marstonian avenger, such as Malevole in *The Malcontent*, is an exaggeratedly unattractive authorial spokesman, pouring forth venomous hatred upon the loathsome and degenerate court in which he finds himself.

Similar in their exaggerated pursuit of the grotesque and the morbid are Cyril Tourneur's *The Atheist's Tragedy* (1607–1611), and a play often attributed to Tourneur, *The Revenger's Tragedy* (1606–1607). These plays are stunningly brilliant in the plotting of excruciatingly impossible situations, and in the invention of cunning Italianate forms of torture and murder. Any sympathetic identification with the characters of these plays is sacrificed in the interests of technical virtuosity. As a result, the plays are more ironic than cathartic in their effect on us as audience; we are overwhelmed by life's dark absurdities rather than ennobled by a vision of man's tragic grandeur. *The Tragedy of Hoffman, or A Revenge for a Father* by Henry Chettle (Admiral's men, 1602) is similarly grotesque and lacking in sympathy for its revenger hero. To be sure, George Chapman's *Bussy D'Ambois* (1600–1604) and its sequel *The Revenge of Bussy D'Ambois* (1607–1612) are thoughtful plays about human aspiration, in the vein of Marlowe's *Tamburlaine*, but even these plays employ a good deal of Senecan melodrama of blood.

The revenge play enjoyed a great popularity on the public stage and (in a caricatured form) on the private stage. The public theatre did, however, cater also to its Puritan-leaning audiences with more pious and moral tragic fare. *Arden of Feversham* (c. 1591) is a good early example of what has come to be called domestic or homiletic tragedy. In the studiously plain style of a broadside ballad, it sets forth the facts of an actual murder that had occurred in 1551 and had been reported in Holinshed's *Chronicles*. The play interprets those events earnestly and providentially. The most famous play in the genre of domestic tragedy is Thomas Heywood's *A Woman Killed with Kindness* (1603). It tells not of a murder but of an adultery, for which the good-hearted but offending wife must be perpetually banished by her grieving husband. The play succeeds in elevating the private sorrows of its ordinary characters to universally tragic stature. The moral stances are unambiguous: adultery is a heinous offense but can be transcended by Christian forgiveness; dueling is evil. Other plays in the vein of domestic tragedy include *A Yorkshire Tragedy* (1605–1608), *The Miseries of Enforced Marriage* (1605–1606), and *Two Lamentable Tragedies* (c. 1594–1598).

In comedy, the greatest writer of the period besides Shakespeare was Ben Jonson. His predilection was toward the private theatre, though he continued to write occasionally for the public stage as well. To an ever-increasing extent, he fixed his satirical gaze on those values and institutions which Thomas Heywood cherished: the city of London, its bourgeois citizens, its traditional approach to morality, its religious zeal. *Every Man Out of His Humour* (1599), though written for the Chamberlain's men, features a foolish uxorious citizen, his socially aspiring wife, and her fashion-mongering lover—humours types that were to appear again and again in the genre of satirical comedy known as "city comedy." (See Brian Gibbons, *Jacobean City Comedy*, 1968). *Volpone* (1605–1606), though technically not a city comedy since it purportedly takes place in Venice, castigates greed among lawyers, businessmen, and other professional types. *The Alchemist* (1610) ridicules the affectations of petty shopkeepers, lawyer's clerks, Puritan divines, and others. *Bartholomew Fair* (1614) gives us Jonson's most memorable indictment of the Puritans.

Numerous other writers contributed to humours comedy and city comedy. George Chapman probably deserves more credit than he usually receives for having helped determine the shape of humours comedy in his *The Blind Beggar of Alexandria* (1596), *An Humorous Day's Mirth* (1597), *All Fools* (1599–1604), *May-Day* (1601–1609), *The Gentleman Usher* (1602–1604), and others. Francis Beaumont, assisted perhaps by John Fletcher, ridicules London grocers and apprentices for their naive tastes in romantic chivalry in *The Knight of the Burning Pestle* (1607–1610). Some satire in this vein, to be sure, is reasonably good-humored. *Eastward Ho* (1605), by Chapman, Jonson, and Marston, is genially sympathetic toward the life-style of the small shopkeeper, even though the play contains a good deal of satire directed at social climbing and sharp business practices. Thomas Dekker's collaboration with Thomas Middleton on *The Honest Whore* (Part I, 1604) gives us an amused and yet warm portrayal of a linen draper who succeeds in business by insisting that the customer is always right. Dekker often shows a wry but generous appreciation of bourgeois ethics, as in *The Shoemakers' Holiday* (1599). Yet even he turns against the Puritans in *If This Be Not a Good Play, the Devil Is in It* (1611–1612).

Marston shows his talent for city comedy in *The Dutch Courtesan* (1603–1605). Perhaps the most ingratiating and truly funny of the writers of city comedy, however, is Middleton. His *A Trick to Catch the Old One* (1604–1607) illustrates the tendency of Jacobean comedy to move away both from Shakespeare's romantic vein and Jonson's morally satirical vein towards a more lighthearted comedy of manners anticipating the style of Restoration comedy. One of Middleton's most hilarious and philosophically unpretentious plays, though plotted with great ingenuity of situation, is *A Mad World, My Masters* (1604–1607). *Michaelmas Term*, written about the same time, exposes the sharp practices of usurers and lawyers. All these Middleton plays were written for Paul's boys.

Romantic comedy, though overshadowed by humours and city comedy during the 1600's, still held forth at the public theatres. A leading exponent was Thomas Heywood, in such plays as *The Fair Maid of the West*, or *A Girl Worth Gold* (1597–1610). Heywood also wrote English history plays designed to prove the sturdiness and historical importance of the London citizenry he so loved, as in *Edward IV* (1597–1599), *The Four Prentices of London* (c. 1600), and *If You Know Not Me You Know Nobody* (1605). Classical tragedy also continued to be written, despite the vogue of revenge tragedy. Ben Jonson rather dogmatically illustrated his classical theories of tragedy in *Sejanus* (1603) and *Cataline* (1611). Samuel Daniel wrote *Philotas* in 1604 and a revision of his *Cleopatra* in 1607. Heywood's *The Rape of Lucrece* appeared in 1606–1608. These are not, however, the immortal tragedies for which the Jacobean period is remembered.

Shakespeare's Work

Shakespeare's plays of this period reveal many Jacobean characteristics. The comedies are few in number and lack the joyous affirmation we associate with *Twelfth Night* and earlier plays. *Measure for Measure*, for example, is not about young men and women happily in love, but about premarital sex and the insoluble problems that arise when vice-prone men attempt to legislate morality for their fellow men. Angelo, self-hating and out of emotional control, is a tragic hero providentially rescued from his own worst self. The duke and Isabella must use ethically dubious means—the bed trick—to effect their virtuous aims.

COURTESY OF THE TRUSTEES, THE BRITISH MUSEUM

A woodcut from Holinshed's Chronicles *(1577) shows the "three Weird sisters" attired more like modest ladies of the court than sinister witches.*

Comedy in the play deals darkly in terms of prostitution, slander, and police inefficiency.

All's Well that Ends Well, though less grim than *Measure for Measure* in its confrontation of man's degeneracy, does apply a similar bed trick as its central plot device. Just as importantly, the obstacles to love are internal and psychological rather than external. That is, the happy union of Bertram and Helena is delayed not by parental objections or by accident (as in *Romeo and Juliet* and *A Midsummer Night's Dream*) but by Bertram's snobbish refusal to see Helena's true worth. *Troilus and Cressida* is a play in which love is paralyzed by a combination of external and internal forces. Troilus must hand Cressida over to the Greeks because his code of honor bids him put his country's cause before his own, and yet that code of "honor" is based on Paris' rape of Helen. Cressida simply gives herself up to Diomedes, knowing she is not strong enough to stand alone in a moral wilderness. The combatants in the greatest war in all history turn out to be petty bickerers, who play nasty games on one another and sulk when their reputations are impugned. The cause for which both sides fight is squalid and senseless.

Meanwhile, in *Hamlet*, Shakespeare explores similar dilemmas posed by man's carnality. Women are too often frail, men are too often importunate and brutal. How is a thoughtful person to justify his own existence? Should he struggle actively against injustice and personal wrong? How can he know what is really true, or foresee the complex results of action? How, in *Othello*, can man resist diabolical evil prompting him to destroy the very thing on which his happiness depends? Is Macbeth tempted to sin by the weird sisters and his wife, or is the choice to murder Duncan ultimately his? To what extent is man responsible for his tragic fate? Most of all, in *King Lear*, are the heavens themselves indifferent to man's bestiality? Must Cordelia die? Yet despite these overwhelmingly pessimistic questions, and the tragic consequences they imply for all human life, Shakespeare's "great" tragedies affirm at least the nobility of man's striving to know himself, and the redeeming fact that human goodness does exist (in Desdemona, Duncan, Cordelia) even if those who practice goodness are often slaughtered.

The Roman or classical tragedies are something apart from the "great" tragedies. They are more ironic in tone, more dispiriting, though they too affirm an essential nobility in man. Brutus misguidedly leads a revolution against Caesar, but dies loyal to his great principles. Timon of Athens proves the appalling ingratitude of his fellow man and resolutely cuts himself off from all human contact. Coriolanus proclaims himself an enemy of the Roman people and seeks to destroy them for their ingratitude, though he is compromised and destroyed at last by his promptings of human feeling. Antony too is pulled apart by an irreconcilable conflict. Yet in this play at least Shakespeare achieves a triumph over defeat that seems to offer a new resolution of man's tragic dilemma.

ALL'S WELL THAT ENDS WELL

All's Well that Ends Well belongs to that period of Shakespeare's creative life when he concentrated on his great tragedies and wrote little comedy. The few apparent exceptions do not fit readily into conventional dramatic genres. *Measure for Measure* (1603–1604), usually called a "problem" play, is darkly preoccupied with human carnality and injustice. *Troilus and Cressida* (c. 1601–1602), printed between the histories and the tragedies in the Folio of 1623, is a disillusioning satire of love and war somewhat akin to the "black" comedy of our modern theatre. *All's Well* shares to an extent the satiric and brooding spirit of these two plays. Its "bed trick," resembling that of *Measure for Measure*, poses ethical problems for the audience, who accordingly may regard the heroine as too much of a schemer. For these and other reasons, *All's Well* is often grouped with the "problem" plays.

Yet to no less an extent the play looks forward to Shakespeare's late romances, *Pericles*, *Cymbeline*, *The Winter's Tale*, and *The Tempest*. Here the mode of comedy turns toward the miraculous and tragicomic, with journeys of separation ending in tearful reunion, and sinful error ending in spiritual rebirth. This mode was not unknown in Shakespeare's comedies of the late 1590's: *As You Like It* ends with the sudden and implausible conversion of its villains, and *Much Ado about Nothing* offers forgiveness to the undeserving Claudio while restoring his traduced fiancée, Hero, to a new life. *Measure for Measure* follows a similar pattern of redemptive pardon for the corrupted Angelo and providential deliverance for Isabella. Both *All's Well* and *Measure for Measure*, despite their ironic commentaries on man's fallen condition, are best understood as comedies of forgiveness in a direct line of development from *Much Ado* to the romances. (See R. G. Hunter, *Shakespeare and the Comedy of Forgiveness*.)

The probable date of *All's Well* is consistent with such a transitional function. Its dates are hard to fix by external evidence, for it was neither registered nor printed until 1623, and allusions to it are scarce. Some scholars would like to think that it is the *Love's Labour's Won* intriguingly mentioned by Francis Meres in 1598, which Shakespeare might then have revised some time around 1601–1604. Portions of the play do feature the rhymed couplets, letters in sonnet form, and witty conceits that we normally associate with Shakespeare's early style. These old-fashioned effects may have been deliberate on Shakespeare's part, however, not unlike the anachronisms he later introduces in *Pericles* and *Cymbeline*. Certainly a major portion of the play dates stylistically from 1601–1604 or even later. Here the language is elliptical and compact, the images complexly interwoven, the verse rhythms free.

In any event, with its two contrasting styles poised between romance and satire, *All's Well* plaintively seeks comic reassurance amid the pessimistic ironies of Shakespeare's tragic period. It lacks many of the felicities we associate with the festive comedies of the 1590's, the love songs, the innocently hedonistic joy, the well-mated young lovers escaping from stern parents or an envious court. *All's Well* has too often been judged negatively for its failure to achieve a festive mood that Shakespeare probably did not intend. The hero, Bertram, is undeniably a cad. As the undeserving hero forgiven in spite of his waywardness, however, he plays an essential role in the comedy of forgiveness. His unworthiness renders him all the more like us, all the more in need of that generosity of spirit which Helena bestows in forgiving him.

The satiric mode in *All's Well* is conveyed chiefly through Lavatch the clown and through Parolles, the boastful cowardly knave who accompanies Bertram to the wars. Lavatch, with his bitter and riddling wit of the professional fool, gives expression to many of the satirical themes also illustrated by the exposure of Parolles. Lavatch jests about cuckoldry and the other marital difficulties that cause men to flee from women; he pokes fun at court manners, and apes the prodigal disobedience of his master Bertram. He is, like Parolles, called a "foul-mouthed and calumnious knave," although the inversion of appearance and reality is evident here as with all Shakespearean fools: Parolles is truly more fool and knave than his mocking counterpart. Parolles is all pretense. Full of sound, but hollow like the drum to which he is compared, he is a swaggerer and a fashion-monger whose clothes conceal his lack of inner substance. He is a recognizable satiric type going back to Plautus and Terence, the braggart soldier. He is, to be sure, endearing in his outrageousness; Shakespeare endows him with that vitality or "rarity" we find also in those earlier braggart soldiers, Falstaff and Pistol. Yet because Parolles lacks the self-awareness of Falstaff, we merely laugh at him rather than with him. To the impressionable young Bertram, hungry for fame, Parolles represents smartness and military style. Bertram rejects the true worth of Helena because she lacks family position, and ironically embraces the false worth of a parvenu. Parolles and Helena are foils from their first encounter, when the braggart sardonically derides virginity as unnatural and out of fashion. Parolles stands opposite also to Lafew, to the Countess, and to the King, those dignified embodiments of a disappearing chivalrous order whom the cynical younger generation hold in contempt. By offering Bertram the slick insolence of the new guise, Parolles wins for a time his friend's allegiance. Parolles is not really a tempter, for we never see him bending Bertram from his true inclination; rather, Bertram is himself too much in love with sham reputation, too rebellious against the civilized decencies of his elders. He is the Prodigal Son, or Youth in the old morality play, perversely eager to prove his own worst enemy.

Yet Bertram is not without a redeeming nobleness —he bears himself bravely in the Florentine wars—

and cannot be fooled indefinitely by his roguish companion. The exposure of Parolles is one of satiric humiliation, like that of Malvolio in *Twelfth Night* or one of Ben Jonson's "humourous" gulls. The engineers of Parolles' exposure use the language of Jonsonian satire in their devices to outwit him: their game is a "sport" done "for the love of laughter," employing a snare whereby the "fox" or the "woodcock" will entrap himself. The device of public humiliation is particularly appropriate because Parolles is himself a railing slanderer, like Lucio in *Measure for Measure*, caustically brilliant in his invective but nonetheless a slayer of men's reputations. The punishment of ridicule fits his particular crime. His callous disregard for the good name of various French military commanders is parallel to Bertram's indifference to the public shame he has heaped upon his virtuous wife. Once Parolles' bluff has been called, Bertram is in part disabused of his folly; but other more wondrous and spiritual means are needed to convince him of the wrong he has done to Helena. Indeed, Bertram's very coldness in turning away from Parolles shows a lack of that humility which he must learn by being tricked, exposed, and humiliated himself.

The fabulous romance-like aspect of *All's Well* is conveyed chiefly through its folktale plot and through the character of Helena. The story is derived from the

COURTESY OF THE TRUSTEES, THE BRITISH MUSEUM

Like Helena in All's Well that Ends Well, *Shakespeare's typical romantic heroines are enterprising, clever, and sophisticated, especially in matters of courtship and love.*

third "day" of Boccaccio's *Decameron*, a day devoted to tales of lovers obliged to overcome seemingly impossible obstacles in order to achieve love's happiness. The story was translated into English by William Painter in *The Palace of Pleasure* (1566). To win the nobly born Beltramo, Giletta of Narbona must cure the French king with her physician-father's secret remedy, and then must perform the riddling tasks assigned her by Beltramo as his means of being rid of her. Both these motifs have ancient antecedents in folklore, and, as in his late romances, Shakespeare puts great stress on the wondrous and improbable nature of these events.

All common sense warns against the likelihood of Helena's success. She is vastly below Bertram in social station or in "blood," even though she excels in "virtue." Her only hope is a desperate gamble: to cure the ailing king and so win Bertram as her reward. No one supposes at first she will even be admitted to the king, who has given up all hope of living; his "congregated college" of learned doctors "have concluded That labouring art can never ransom nature From her inaidible estate" (II,i). Helena transcends these rational doubts through resourcefulness and above all through a faith in help from above. She is willing to "hazard" all for love. She senses that her father's legacy will "be sanctified by the luckiest stars in heaven," and she manages to convince not only the Countess and Lafew (persons who do not appear in Boccaccio) but also the king himself. Believing, like Shaw's Saint Joan, that God will perform his greatest works through the humblest of his creatures, Helena inspires her listeners with faith in the impossible. Lafew is so moved by her simple eloquence that he proclaims to the king, "I have seen a medicine That's able to breathe life into stone." Soon the king too is persuaded that in Helena "some blessed spirit doth speak His powerful sound within an organ weak." Once the king's cure has been effected, even Parolles and Bertram must agree with Lafew that the age of miracles, long thought to have passed, is with them again. The king's cure by the "very hand of heaven," through the agency of a "weak and debile minister," is matter for a pious ballad or an old tale (II,iii).

The impossible tasks Helena must perform are stated as riddles, as usual in a folk tale, and must be solved by riddling or paradoxical means. Bertram writes that she must "get the ring upon my finger which never shall come off, and show me a child begotten of thy body that I am father to" (III,ii). Such a challenge invites ingenuity, as in Boccaccio, but in Shakespeare the solution also requires providential aid. Helena's first sad response is to set Bertram free and renounce her audacious pretentions. Her pilgrimage of grief takes her to Florence, where Bertram happens to be serving in the wars. Is this mere coincidence, or conscious scheming on her part? Providence in any event must be credited with introducing her to Diana, the very lady whom Bertram is importuning in love. Helena makes the most of such opportunities afforded her, never doubting that "heaven" has "fated" her both to help Diana and simultaneously to serve her own turn (IV,iv). The bed trick is a "plot," but a virtuous one, a "deceit" that is "lawful," a deed that is "not sin, and yet a sinful fact" (III,vii). Diana repeatedly plays upon these same riddles in accusing Bertram before the king: he is "guilty, and he is not guilty" (V,iii).

The conundrums, although playful and entertaining in Shakespeare's highly complicated denouement (not found in Boccaccio), also hint at paradoxes in the nature of man. Bertram's typically human waywardness justifies a cunning response. "I think 't no sin," argues Diana, "To cozen him that would unjustly win" (IV,ii). Justice among men, as in *Measure for Measure,* must take forms only roughly approximating those of heavenly justice, for man's bestial nature sometimes requires an answer in kind. Yet by a providential paradox, man's thwarted nature, which seems his fatal enemy, contributes essentially to his regeneration: by being humbled, he is enabled to rise. "The web of our life is of a mingled yarn, good and ill together," says a choric observer of Bertram. "Our virtues would be proud, if our faults whipped them not; and our crimes would despair, if they were not cherished by our virtues" (IV,iii). Man's perversity reminds him of his dependence on grace.

Helena is a romantic heroine, only metaphorically the "angel" who must "Bless this unworthy husband," reprieving him by her "prayers" from "the wrath Of greatest justice" (III,iv). Still, the spiritual overtones are not extraneous to this bittersweet comedy. Bertram typifies the "Natural rebellion" of all youth, Helena the "herb of grace" whom he has willfully rejected. However much we may sympathize with his desire to choose in love for himself, Bertram's revolt is incomprehensible to every witness except Parolles. Bertram himself confesses, too late it seems, that he has recognized Helena's precious worth. This note of "love that comes too late," wherein the penitent sinner confesses "That's good that's gone," hovers over the play with its tragicomic mood. Helena is a "jewel" thrown away and seemingly forever lost. The semblance of her death is in fact only another one of her inventive schemes, along with the bewildering contretemps of the final scene. Yet when she reappears, setting all to rights, she comes as "one that's dead" but is now "quick," alive again, merely a "shadow" of her former self. Bertram has not actually committed the evil he intended; by a providential sophistry he is innocent, like Claudio in *Much Ado* or Angelo in *Measure for Measure,* and so is reconciled to the goodness he has failed to merit. Even Parolles is given a second chance by the magnanimous Lafew. As the play's title implies, all might have miscarried through man's "rash faults" that "Make trivial price of serious things we have," were it not for a forgiving power that can make man's worst failings an instrument of his penitence and recovery.

ALL'S WELL THAT ENDS WELL

[*Dramatis Personae*

KING OF FRANCE.
DUKE OF FLORENCE.
BERTRAM, Count of Rousillon.
LAFEW, *an old lord.*
PAROLLES, *a follower of Bertram.*
Steward, } *servants to the Countess of Rousillon.*
Clown, }
A Page.

COUNTESS OF ROUSILLON, *mother to Bertram.*
HELENA, *a gentlewoman protected by the Countess.*
An old Widow of Florence.
DIANA, *daughter to the Widow.*
VIOLENTA, } *neighbours and friends to the Widow.*
MARIANA, }

Lords, Officers, Soldiers, *&c., French and Florentine.*

SCENE: *Rousillon; Paris; Florence; Marseilles.*]

ACT I.

SCENE I. [*Rousillon. The* COUNT'S *palace.*]

Enter young BERTRAM, COUNT OF ROUSILLON, *his Mother* [*the* COUNTESS], *and* HELENA, [*with*] LORD LAFEW, *all in black.*

Count. In delivering my son from me, I bury a second husband.

Ber. And I in going, madam, weep o'er my father's death anew: but I must attend his majesty's command, to whom I am now in ward, evermore in subjection.

Laf. You shall find of the king a husband, madam; you, sir, a father: he that so generally is at all times good must of necessity hold his virtue to you; whose worthiness would stir it up where it wanted rather than lack it where there is such abundance.

Count. What hope is there of his majesty's amendment?

Laf. He hath abandoned his physicians, madam; under whose practices he hath persecuted time with hope, and finds no other advantage in the process but only the losing of hope by time.

Count. This young gentlewoman had a father,—O, that 'had'! how sad a passage 'tis!—whose skill was almost as great as his honesty; had it stretched so far, would have made nature immortal, and death should have play for lack of work. Would, for the king's sake, he were living! I think it would be the death of the king's disease.

Laf. How called you the man you speak of, madam?

Count. He was famous, sir, in his profession, and it was his great right to be so: Gerard de Narbon.

Laf. He was excellent indeed, madam: the king

very lately spoke of him admiringly and mourningly: he was skilful enough to have lived still, if knowledge could be set up against mortality.

Ber. What is it, my good lord, the king languishes of?

Laf. A fistula, my lord.

Ber. I heard not of it before.

Laf. I would it were not notorious. Was this gentlewoman the daughter of Gerard de Narbon?

Count. His sole child, my lord, and bequeathed to my overlooking. I have those hopes of her good that her education promises; her dispositions she inherits, which makes fair gifts fairer; for where an unclean mind carries virtuous qualities, there commendations go with pity; they are virtues and traitors too: in her they are the better for their simpleness; she derives her honesty and achieves her goodness.

Laf. Your commendations, madam, get from her tears.

Count. 'Tis the best brine a maiden can season her praise in. The remembrance of her father never approaches her heart but the tyranny of her sorrows takes all livelihood from her cheek. No more of this, Helena; go to, no more; lest it be rather thought you affect a sorrow than have it.

Hel. I do affect a sorrow indeed, but I have it too.

Laf. Moderate lamentation is the right of the dead, excessive grief the enemy to the living.

Count. If the living be enemy to the grief, the excess makes it soon mortal.

Ber. Madam, I desire your holy wishes.

Laf. How understand we that?

Count. Be thou blest, Bertram, and succeed thy father
In manners, as in shape! thy blood and virtue
Contend for empire in thee, and thy goodness
Share with thy birthright! Love all, trust a few,
Do wrong to none: be able for thine enemy
Rather in power than use, and keep thy friend
Under thy own life's key: be check'd for silence,
But never tax'd for speech. What heaven more will,
That thee may furnish and my prayers pluck down,
Fall on thy head! Farewell, my lord;
'Tis an unseason'd courtier; good my lord,
Advise him.

Laf. He cannot want the best
That shall attend his love.

Count. Heaven bless him! Farewell, Bertram. [*Exit.*]

Ber. The best wishes that can be forged in your thoughts be servants to you! [*To Helena*] Be comfortable to my mother, your mistress, and make much of her.

Laf. Farewell, pretty lady: you must hold the credit of your father. [*Exeunt Bertram and Lafew.*]

Hel. O, were that all! I think not on my father;
And these great tears grace his remembrance more
Than those I shed for him. What was he like?
I have forgot him: my imagination
Carries no favour in 't but Bertram's.
I am undone: there is no living, none,
If Bertram be away. 'Twere all one
That I should love a bright particular star
And think to wed it, he is so above me:
In his bright radiance and collateral light
Must I be comforted, not in his sphere.
Th' ambition in my love thus plagues itself:
The hind that would be mated by the lion
Must die for love. 'Twas pretty, though a plague,
To see him every hour; to sit and draw
His arched brows, his hawking eye, his curls,
In our heart's table; heart too capable
Of every line and trick of his sweet favour:
But now he 's gone, and my idolatrous fancy
Must sanctify his reliques. Who comes here?

Enter PAROLLES.

[*Aside*] One that goes with him: I love him for his sake;
And yet I know him a notorious liar,
Think him a great way fool, solely a coward;
Yet these fix'd evils sit so fit in him,
That they take place, when virtue's steely bones
†Look bleak i' th' cold wind: withal, full oft we see
Cold wisdom waiting on superfluous folly.

Par. Save you, fair queen!

Hel. And you, monarch!

Par. No.

Hel. And no.

Par. Are you meditating on virginity?

Hel. Ay. You have some stain of soldier in you: let me ask you a question. Man is enemy to virginity; how may we barricado it against him?

Par. Keep him out.

Hel. But he assails; and our virginity, though valiant, in the defence yet is weak: unfold to us some warlike resistance.

Par. There is none: man, sitting down before you, will undermine you and blow you up.

Hel. Bless our poor virginity from underminers and blowers up! Is there no military policy, how virgins might blow up men?

Par. Virginity being blown down, man will quicklier be blown up: marry, in blowing him down again, with the breach yourselves made, you lose your city. It is not politic in the commonwealth of nature to preserve virginity. Loss of virginity is rational increase and there was never virgin got till virginity was first lost. That you were made of is metal to make virgins. Virginity by being once lost

ACT I. SCENE I. 1. **delivering,** sending. 5. **in ward.** According to a feudal custom, a lord became the guardian of a vassal's orphaned child. His jurisdiction extended even so far as the bestowal of his ward in marriage, but only to someone of equal rank. 9. **hold,** continue to devote (Brigstocke). 11. **wanted,** is lacking. 14. **amendment,** recovery. 16. **persecuted time,** i.e., he has continued to live in pain. 21. **honesty,** integrity of character. 30. **his great right,** i.e., his right in proportion to his greatness. 39. **fistula,** an ulcerous sore. 47. **dispositions,** innate qualities. 51. **simpleness,** integrity. 52. **goodness,** acquired virtues, accomplishments, in antithesis to *honesty* as innate virtue. 62-63. **I do . . . too,** i.e., I pretend grief for my father, but my tears are for Bertram's departure. 69. **How . . . that.** Attempts have been made to emend the text; the speech is regarded by some as not appropriately assigned. It can, however, be construed as it stands. Lafew asks, "What holy wishes do you desire?" The countess answers by making the wishes particular. Possibly lines 68 and 69 are in reverse order. 71-72. **thy blood . . . thee,** i.e., may your noble birth (blood) and your innate goodness (virtue) both be so great that they compete for domination over you. (In an ironic sense, "blood" also connotes passion, which will indeed struggle to overwhelm Bertram's reason.) 74-75. **be able . . . use,** i.e., be a match for your enemies in power, but do not put that power to bad use. 76. **check'd,** reproved. 77. **will,** may bestow. 96-100. **'Twere all . . . sphere.** The metaphor is based on Ptolemaic astronomy. Bertram's was a higher *sphere* (i.e., farther from the earth) than Helena's, since he was of a higher social rank. The different spheres moved collaterally, and their stars, although enjoying one another's light, could never move together. 105. **hawking,** keen. 113. **sit so fit,** are so natural and plausible (in him). 114. **take place,** find acceptance. 116. **Cold . . . folly,** i.e., naked wisdom is forced to defer to overdressed folly. 122. **stain,** tinge. 135. **blown up,** with bawdy meaning. 145. **stand,** fight, stand up. 152. **buried . . . limit.** Suicides were customarily buried at crossroads of highways, not in may be ten times found; by being ever kept, it is ever lost: 'tis too cold a companion; away with 't!

Hel. I will stand for 't a little, though therefore I die a virgin.

Par. There 's little can be said in 't; 'tis against the rule of nature. To speak on the part of virginity, is to accuse your mothers; which is most infallible disobedience. He that hangs himself is a virgin: virginity murders itself; and should be buried in highways out of all sanctified limit, as a desperate offendress against nature. Virginity breeds mites, much like a cheese; consumes itself to the very paring, and so dies with feeding his own stomach. Besides, virginity is peevish, proud, idle, made of self-love, which is the most inhibited sin in the canon. Keep it not; you cannot choose but lose by 't: out with 't! within ten year it will make itself ten, which is a goodly increase; and the principal itself not much the worse: away with 't!

Hel. How might one do, sir, to lose it to her own liking?

Par. Let me see: marry, ill, to like him that ne'er it likes. 'Tis a commodity will lose the gloss with lying; the longer kept, the less worth: off with 't while 'tis vendible; answer the time of request. Virginity, like an old courtier, wears her cap out of fashion: richly suited, but unsuitable: just like the brooch and the tooth-pick, which wear not now. Your date is better in your pie and your porridge than in your cheek: and your virginity, your old virginity, is like one of our French withered pears, it looks ill, it eats drily; marry, 'tis a withered pear; it was formerly better; marry, yet 'tis a withered pear: will you any thing with it?

Hel. †Not my virginity yet . . . . .
There shall your master have a thousand loves,
A mother and a mistress and a friend,
A phœnix, captain and an enemy,
A guide, a goddess, and a sovereign,
A counsellor, a traitress, and a dear;
His humble ambition, proud humility,
His jarring concord, and his discord dulcet,
His faith, his sweet disaster; with a world
Of pretty, fond, adoptious christendoms,
That blinking Cupid gossips. Now shall he—
I know not what he shall. God send him well!
The court 's a learning place, and he is one—

Par. What one, i' faith?

Hel. That I wish well. 'Tis pity—

Par. What 's pity?

Hel. That wishing well had not a body in 't,
Which might be felt; that we, the poorer born,
Whose baser stars do shut us up in wishes,
Might with effects of them follow our friends,
And show what we alone must think, which never
Returns us thanks.

Enter Page.

Page. Monsieur Parolles, my lord calls for you. [*Exit.*]

Par. Little Helen, farewell: if I can remember thee, I will think of thee at court.

Hel. Monsieur Parolles, you were born under a charitable star.

Par. Under Mars, I.

Hel. I especially think, under Mars.

Par. Why under Mars?

Hel. The wars have so kept you under that you must needs be born under Mars.

Par. When he was predominant.

Hel. When he was retrograde, I think, rather.

Par. Why think you so?

Hel. You go so much backward when you fight.

Par. That 's for advantage.

Hel. So is running away, when fear proposes the safety: but the composition that your valour and fear makes in you is a virtue of a good wing, and I like the wear well.

Par. I am so full of businesses, I cannot answer thee acutely. I will return perfect courtier; in the which, my instruction shall serve to naturalize thee, so thou wilt be capable of a courtier's counsel and understand what advice shall thrust upon thee; else thou diest in thine unthankfulness, and thine ignorance makes thee away: farewell. When thou hast leisure, say thy prayers; when thou hast none, remember thy friends: get thee a good husband, and use him as he uses thee: so, farewell. [*Exit.*]

Hel. Our remedies oft in ourselves do lie,
Which we ascribe to heaven: the fated sky
Gives us free scope, only doth backward pull
Our slow designs when we ourselves are dull.
What power is it which mounts my love so high,
That makes me see, and cannot feed mine eye?
The mightiest space in fortune nature brings
To join like likes and kiss like native things.
Impossible be strange attempts to those
That weigh their pains in sense and do suppose
What hath been cannot be: who ever strove
To show her merit, that did miss her love?
The king's disease—my project may deceive me,
But my intents are fix'd and will not leave me. *Exit.*

[SCENE II. *Paris. The* KING'S *palace.*]

Flourish cornets. Enter the KING OF FRANCE, *with letters, and divers Attendants.*

consecrated ground. 157-158. **self-love . . . canon,** probably a reference to the "first and great commandment" as read in the liturgy after the decalogue—i.e., that you love your neighbor as yourself. Charron characterizes self-love as "the plague of mankinde, the capitall enemie of wisdome, the true gangreene and corruption of the soul." (*Of Wisdom*, Bk. II, Ch. i.) 167. **with lying,** i.e., unused, with quibble on *lying down.* 168-169. **the time of request,** when there is demand. 170. **suited,** trimmed. 171. **tooth-pick,** usually associated with foppish manners; cf. *King John*, I, i, 190. **wear not,** are not in fashion. 172. **date,** pun on the fruit and the meaning "time of life." 179. **Not . . . yet,** the moment for surrendering my virginity has not yet arrived (?). There may be a textual omission here. 181-184. **A mother . . . a dear.** Helena here recites a series of epithets, like those used in Elizabethan love poetry to describe the beloved person. 188. **adoptious christendoms,** pet names. 189. **gossips,** is godfather to. 198. **them,** i.e., wishes. 211. **predominant,** in the ascendant, ruling; i.e., in that sign of the zodiac which is just rising above the horizon. 212. **retrograde,** moving apparently in a direction contrary to the order of the signs of the zodiac, or from east to west (Onions); cf. *1 Henry VI*, I, ii, 1-2, note. 218. **of a good wing,** strong in flight; said of a falcon or of an arrow. 219. **wear,** fashion. 223. **naturalize,** familiarize; also, deflower. 226-227. **makes . . . away,** destroys, puts an end to. 232. **fated,** invested with the power of destiny. 237-238. **The mightiest . . . things.** Helena's resolve is apparent in the change in metaphor: whereas above (ll. 96-100) she thinks of their relative positions in terms of the natural phenomenon of the celestial spheres, the space between which nothing can bridge, now she thinks of herself and Bertram as so similar in affections that they naturally will be drawn together. 239. **Impossible,** inconceivable. 240. **That weigh . . . sense,** i.e., who worry too much about the cost and effort needed to do something.

King. The Florentines and Senoys are by th' ears;
Have fought with equal fortune and continue
A braving war.
First Lord. So 'tis reported, sir.
King. Nay, 'tis most credible; we here receive it
A certainty, vouch'd from our cousin Austria,
With caution that the Florentine will move us
For speedy aid; wherein our dearest friend
Prejudicates the business and would seem
To have us make denial.
First Lord. His love and wisdom,
Approv'd so to your majesty, may plead
For amplest credence.
King. He hath arm'd our answer,
And Florence is denied before he comes:
Yet, for our gentlemen that mean to see
The Tuscan service, freely have they leave
To stand on either part.
Sec. Lord. It well may serve
A nursery to our gentry, who are sick
For breathing and exploit.
King. What 's he comes here?

Enter BERTRAM, LAFEW, *and* PAROLLES.

First Lord. It is the Count Rousillon, my good lord,
Young Bertram.
King. Youth, thou bear'st thy father's face;
Frank nature, rather curious than in haste,
Hath well compos'd thee. Thy father's moral parts
Mayst thou inherit too! Welcome to Paris.
Ber. My thanks and duty are your majesty's.
King. I would I had that corporal soundness now,
As when thy father and myself in friendship
First tried our soldiership! He did look far
Into the service of the time and was
Discipled of the bravest: he lasted long;
But on us both did haggish age steal on
And wore us out of act. It much repairs me
To talk of your good father. In his youth
He had the wit which I can well observe
To-day in our young lords; but they may jest
Till their own scorn return to them unnoted
Ere they can hide their levity in honour:
†So like a courtier, contempt nor bitterness
Were in his pride or sharpness; if they were,
His equal had awak'd them, and his honour,
Clock to itself, knew the true minute when
Exception bid him speak, and at this time
His tongue obey'd his hand: who were below him
He us'd as creatures of another place
And bow'd his eminent top to their low ranks,
Making them proud of his humility,
†In their poor praise he humbled. Such a man
Might be a copy to these younger times;
Which, followed well, would demonstrate them now
But goers backward.
Ber. His good remembrance, sir,
Lies richer in your thoughts than on his tomb;
So in approof lives not his epitaph
As in your royal speech.
King. Would I were with him! He would always say—
Methinks I hear him now; his plausive words
He scatter'd not in ears, but grafted them,
To grow there and to bear,—'Let me not live,'—
This his good melancholy oft began,
On the catastrophe and heel of pastime,
When it was out,—'Let me not live,' quoth he,
'After my flame lacks oil, to be the snuff
Of younger spirits, whose apprehensive senses
All but new things disdain; whose judgements are
Mere fathers of their garments; whose constancies
Expire before their fashions.' This he wish'd:
I after him do after him wish too,
Since I nor wax nor honey can bring home,
I quickly were dissolved from my hive,
To give some labourers room.
Sec. Lord. You're loved, sir;
They that least lend it you shall lack you first.
King. I fill a place, I know 't. How long is 't, count,
Since the physician at your father's died?
He was much fam'd.
Ber. Some six months since, my lord.
King. If he were living, I would try him yet.
Lend me an arm; the rest have worn me out
With several applications: nature and sickness
Debate it at their leisure. Welcome, count;
My son 's no dearer.
Ber. Thank your majesty.
Exeunt. Flourish.

[SCENE III. *Rousillon. The* COUNT'S *palace*.]

Enter COUNTESS, Steward, *and* Clown.

Count. I will now hear; what say you of this gentlewoman?

Stew. Madam, the care I have had to even your content, I wish might be found in the calendar of my past endeavours; for then we wound our modesty and make foul the clearness of our deservings, when of ourselves we publish them.

Count. What does this knave here? Get you gone, sirrah: the complaints I have heard of you I do not all believe: 'tis my slowness that I do not; for I know you lack not folly to commit them, and have ability enough to make such knaveries yours.

Clo. 'Tis not unknown to you, madam, I am a poor fellow.

Count. Well, sir.

Clo. No, madam, 'tis not so well that I am poor, though many of the rich are damned: but, if I may have your ladyship's good will to go to the world, Isbel the woman and I will do as we may.

Count. Wilt thou needs be a beggar?

Clo. I do beg your good will in this case.

SCENE II. 1. **Senoys,** natives of Siena. **by th' ears,** at variance, quarreling. 3. **braving war,** war of taunts and challenges. 8. **Prejudicates,** passes judgment beforehand. 10. **Approv'd,** demonstrated by proofs. 16. **nursery,** training school. 16-17. **sick For,** i.e., for want of. 17. **breathing,** vigorous exercise. 20. **curious,** careful. 26-27. **did look far Into,** understood. 27. **service,** military affairs. 30. **repairs,** refreshes. 33-35. **but they . . . honour.** Your father (says the king) had the same airy flights of satirical wit with the young lords of the present time, but they do not what he did, hide their unnoted (i.e., disregarded) levity in honor, cover petty faults with great merit (Johnson). 36. **courtier,** perfect gentleman. 39. **Clock to itself,** self-governing. 40. **Exception,** disapproval. 41. **his,** i.e., the clock's. 42. **creatures . . . place,** people of a different (i.e., more elevated) station; cf. *Hamlet*, II, ii, 556-558. 45. **humbled,** i.e., humbled himself. 50. **approof,** approbation. 53. **plausive,** pleasing (Brigstocke, citing *Hamlet*, I, iv, 30). 57. **catastrophe . . . pastime,** i.e., pastime drawing to a close. 58. **it,** i.e., pastime. **out,** over. 59. **snuff,** candle end. 60. **apprehensive,** quick to perceive. 61-62. **whose judgements . . . garments,** i.e., whose judgments are entirely given over to designing new fashions. 64. **I after . . . wish too,** I, surviving him, wish as he did. 66. **were dissolved,** optative subjunctive; see Abbott, 301. 68. **lend it.** The antecedent is *love*, implied in the verb, line 67 (New

Count. In what case?

Clo. In Isbel's case and mine own. Service is no heritage: and I think I shall never have the blessing of God till I have issue o' my body; for they say barnes are blessings.

Count. Tell me thy reason why thou wilt marry.

Clo. My poor body, madam, requires it: I am driven on by the flesh; and he must needs go that the devil drives.

Count. Is this all your worship's reason?

Clo. Faith, madam, I have other holy reasons, such as they are.

Count. May the world know them?

Clo. I have been, madam, a wicked creature, as you and all flesh and blood are; and, indeed, I do marry that I may repent.

Count. Thy marriage, sooner than thy wickedness.

Clo. I am out o' friends, madam; and I hope to have friends for my wife's sake.

Count. Such friends are thine enemies, knave.

Clo. Y' are shallow, madam, in great friends; for the knaves come to do that for me which I am aweary of. He that ears my land spares my team and gives me leave to in the crop; if I be his cuckold, he 's my drudge: he that comforts my wife is the cherisher of my flesh and blood; he that cherishes my flesh and blood loves my flesh and blood; he that loves my flesh and blood is my friend: ergo, he that kisses my wife is my friend. If men could be contented to be what they are, there were no fear in marriage; for young Charbon the puritan and old Poysam the papist, howsome'er their hearts are severed in religion, their heads are both one; they may joul horns together, like any deer i' the herd.

Count. Wilt thou ever be a foul-mouthed and calumnious knave?

Clo. A prophet I, madam; and I speak the truth the next way:

For I the ballad will repeat,
Which men full true shall find;
Your marriage comes by destiny,
Your cuckoo sings by kind.

Count. Get you gone, sir; I'll talk with you more anon.

Stew. May it please you, madam, that he bid Helen come to you: of her I am to speak.

Count. Sirrah, tell my gentlewoman I would speak with her; Helen, I mean.

Clo. Was this fair face the cause, quoth she,
Why the Grecians sacked Troy?
Fond done, done fond,
Was this King Priam's joy?
With that she sighed as she stood,
With that she sighed as she stood,
And gave this sentence then;
Among nine bad if one be good,
Among nine bad if one be good,
There 's yet one good in ten.

Count. What, one good in ten? you corrupt the song, sirrah.

Clo. One good woman in ten, madam; which is a purifying o' the song: would God would serve the world so all the year! we 'ld find no fault with the tithe-woman, if I were the parson. One in ten, quoth 'a! An we might have a good woman born but one every blazing star, or at an earthquake, 'twould mend the lottery well: a man may draw his heart out, ere 'a pluck one.

Count. You'll be gone, sir knave, and do as I command you.

Clo. That man should be at woman's command, and yet no hurt done! Though honesty be no puritan, yet it will do no hurt; it will wear the surplice of humility over the black gown of a big heart. I am going, forsooth: the business is for Helen to come hither. *Exit.*

Count. Well, now.

Stew. I know, madam, you love your gentlewoman entirely.

Count. Faith, I do: her father bequeathed her to me; and she herself, without other advantage, may lawfully make title to as much love as she finds: there is more owing her than is paid; and more shall be paid her than she 'll demand.

Stew. Madam, I was very late more near her than I think she wished me: alone she was, and did communicate to herself her own words to her own ears; she thought, I dare vow for her, they touched not any stranger sense. Her matter was, she loved your son: Fortune, she said, was no goddess, that had put such difference betwixt their two estates; Love no god, that would not extend his might, only where qualities were level; Dian no queen of virgins, that would suffer her poor knight surprised, without rescue in the first assault or ransom afterward. This she delivered in the most bitter touch of sorrow that e'er I heard virgin exclaim in: which I held my duty speedily to acquaint you withal; sithence, in the loss that may happen, it concerns you something to know it.

Count. You have discharged this honestly; keep it to yourself: many likelihoods informed me of this before, which hung so tottering in the balance that I could neither believe nor misdoubt. Pray you, leave me: stall this in your bosom; and I thank you for your honest care: I will speak with you further anon. *Exit Steward.*

Enter HELENA.

Even so it was with me when I was young:
If ever we are nature's, these are ours; this thorn
Doth to our rose of youth rightly belong;
Our blood to us, this to our blood is born;
It is the show and seal of nature's truth,
Where love's strong passion is impress'd in youth:
By our remembrances of days foregone,

Cambridge).

SCENE III. 3. **to even your content,** make my endeavors balance with your wishes (Brigstocke). 4. **calendar,** record. 7. **publish,** make known. 19-20. **go to the world,** give up the life of a celibate. 28. **barnes,** children. 34. **holy reasons,** in antithesis to the *world*, the *flesh*, and the *devil* (ll. 20, 31, 32). 45. **shallow . . . in,** a superficial judge of. 46. **ears,** plows. 48. **in,** a verb, to get in; i.e., harvest the crop. 55, 56. **Charbon, Poysam,** corruptions of *Chairbonne*, good meat, and *Poisson*, fish, the fast-day diets of Puritans and Catholics respectively. 58. **joul,** dash, knock. 63. **next,** nearest; i.e., speak the truth most directly. 89. **tithe-woman,** an allusion to the practice of paying tithes "in kind," not in money; cf. *Romeo and Juliet*, I, iv, 79. 97-100. **Though honesty . . . big heart,** a variant on the conventional slur at the Puritans who demurred at obedience to some of the rubrics and canons pertaining to public worship; some of them, to *do no hurt*, conformed in some respects such as wearing the surplice; nevertheless they wore it over the black Genevan gown customarily worn by Calvinistic Protestants on the Continent. 100. **big heart,** proud spirit. 120. **surprised,** to be surprised. 124. **sithence,** since. 135. **these,** i.e., the pangs of love, signs of which the countess sees manifested in Helena.

†Such were our faults, or then we thought them none.
Her eye is sick on 't: I observe her now.
Hel. What is your pleasure, madam?
Count. You know, Helen,
I am a mother to you.
Hel. Mine honourable mistress.
Count. Nay, a mother:
Why not a mother? When I said 'a mother,'
Methought you saw a serpent: what 's in 'mother,'
That you start at it? I say, I am your mother;
And put you in the catalogue of those
That were enwombed mine: 'tis often seen
Adoption strives with nature and choice breeds
A native slip to us from foreign seeds:
You ne'er oppress'd me with a mother's groan,
Yet I express to you a mother's care:
God's mercy, maiden! does it curd thy blood
To say I am thy mother? What 's the matter,
That this distempered messenger of wet,
The many-colour'd Iris, rounds thine eye?
Why? that you are my daughter?
Hel. That I am not.
Count. I say, I am your mother.
Hel. Pardon, madam;
The Count Rousillon cannot be my brother:
I am from humble, he from honoured name;
No note upon my parents, his all noble:
My master, my dear lord he is; and I
His servant live, and will his vassal die:
He must not be my brother.
Count. Nor I your mother?
Hel. You are my mother, madam; would you were,—
So that my lord your son were not my brother,—
Indeed my mother! or were you both our mothers,
I care no more for than I do for heaven,
So I were not his sister. Can 't no other,
But, I your daughter, he must be my brother?
Count. Yes, Helen, you might be my daughter-in-law:
God shield you mean it not! daughter and mother
So strive upon your pulse. What, pale again?
My fear hath catch'd your fondness: now I see
The myst'ry of your loneliness, and find
Your salt tears' head: now to all sense 'tis gross
You love my son; invention is asham'd,
Against the proclamation of thy passion,
To say thou dost not: therefore tell me true;
But tell me then, 'tis so; for, look, thy cheeks
Confess it, th' one to th' other; and thine eyes
See it so grossly shown in thy behaviours
That in their kind they speak it: only sin
And hellish obstinacy tie thy tongue,
That truth should be suspected. Speak, is 't so?
If it be so, you have wound a goodly clew;
If it be not, forswear 't: howe'er, I charge thee,
As heaven shall work in me for thine avail,
To tell me truly.
Hel. Good madam, pardon me!
Count. Do you love my son?
Hel. Your pardon, noble mistress!
Count. Love you my son?
Hel. Do not you love him, madam?
Count. Go not about; my love hath in 't a bond,
Whereof the world takes note: come, come, disclose
The state of your affection; for your passions
Have to the full appeach'd.
Hel. Then, I confess,
Here on my knee, before high heaven and you,
That before you, and next unto high heaven,
I love your son.
My friends were poor, but honest; so 's my love:
Be not offended; for it hurts not him
That he is lov'd of me: I follow him not
By any token of presumptuous suit;
Nor would I have him till I do deserve him;
Yet never know how that desert should be.
I know I love in vain, strive against hope;
Yet in this captious and intenible sieve
I still pour in the waters of my love
And lack not to lose still: thus, Indian-like,
Religious in mine error, I adore
The sun, that looks upon his worshipper,
But knows of him no more. My dearest madam,
Let not your hate encounter with my love
For loving where you do: but if yourself,
Whose aged honour cites a virtuous youth,
Did ever in so true a flame of liking
Wish chastely and love dearly, that your Dian
Was both herself and love; O, then, give pity
To her, whose state is such that cannot choose
But lend and give where she is sure to lose;
That seeks not to find that her search implies,
But riddle-like lives sweetly where she dies!
Count. Had you not lately an intent,—speak truly,—
To go to Paris?
Hel. Madam, I had.
Count. Wherefore? tell true.
Hel. I will tell truth; by grace itself I swear.
You know my father left me some prescriptions
Of rare and prov'd effects, such as his reading
And manifest experience had collected
For general sovereignty; and that he will'd me
In heedfull'st reservation to bestow them,
As notes whose faculties inclusive were
More than they were in note: amongst the rest
There is a remedy, approv'd, set down,
To cure the desperate languishings whereof
The king is render'd lost.
Count. This was your motive
For Paris, was it? speak.
Hel. My lord your son made me to think of this;

152. **slip,** grafting. 158. **Iris,** Juno's messenger; also the rainbow. 163. **note,** distinction. 178. **gross,** palpable, apparent. 188. **clew,** ball of thread (used figuratively). 197. **appeach'd,** informed against. 201. **friends,** kinfolk. 208. **captious,** deceptive; also, capacious. **intenible,** incapable of holding. 210. **lack . . . still,** still have enough to keep pouring without diminishing my supply. 216. **cites,** bespeaks, gives evidence of. 222. **that,** that which. 229. **manifest experience,** i.e., the practice, in antithesis to the theory (reading). 230. **general sovereignty,** general efficacy and use. 231. **In . . . them,** to use them only in special circumstances. 232-233. **As notes . . . note,** i.e., as prescriptions whose power surpassed their reputation. 241. **Happily,** haply, perhaps. 247. **Embowell'd,** emptied.

ACT II. SCENE I. 6. **After . . . soldiers,** usually explained as "after having become seasoned soldiers"; the New Cambridge editors punctuate: *After, well-entered soldiers,* taking *After* with *return.* 12-14. **let higher . . . monarchy.** *Higher Italy* has been taken to mean (1) the knightly class in antithesis to *worthy Frenchmen;* (2) Tuscany, of which Florence and Siena are cities. *The last monarchy* has been explained as the Roman monarchy; the New Cambridge editors think it refers to the decline of the house of the Medici after the death of Cosimo in 1574, citing the social demoralization of Florence. They paraphrase: "except those Tuscans (*those bated*) who adhere to the decadent fortunes and vices of the Medicis." 16. **questant,** seeker. 17. **cry you loud,** proclaim you loudly. 23. **Come . . . me.** Some stage business accom-

Else Paris and the medicine and the king
Had from the conversation of my thoughts
Happily been absent then.
Count. But think you, Helen,
If you should tender your supposed aid,
He would receive it? he and his physicians
Are of a mind; he, that they cannot help him,
They, that they cannot help: how shall they credit
A poor unlearned virgin, when the schools,
Embowell'd of their doctrine, have left off
The danger to itself?
Hel. There 's something in 't,
More than my father's skill, which was the great'st
Of his profession, that his good receipt
Shall for my legacy be sanctified
By th' luckiest stars in heaven: and, would your honour
But give me leave to try success, I 'ld venture
The well-lost life of mine on his grace's cure
By such a day and hour.
Count. Dost thou believe 't?
Hel. Ay, madam, knowingly.
Count. Why, Helen, thou shalt have my leave and love,
Means and attendants and my loving greetings
To those of mine in court: I'll stay at home
And pray God's blessing into thy attempt:
Be gone to-morrow; and be sure of this,
What I can help thee to thou shalt not miss. *Exeunt.*

ACT II.

[SCENE I. *Paris. The* KING'S *Palace.*]

Enter the KING *with divers young* Lords *taking leave for the Florentine war:* [BERTRAM] COUNT ROUSILLON, *and* PAROLLES. *Flourish cornets.*

King. Farewell, young lords; these warlike principles
Do not throw from you: and you, my lords, farewell:
Share the advice betwixt you; if both gain, all
The gift doth stretch itself as 'tis receiv'd,
And is enough for both.
First Lord. 'Tis our hope, sir,
After well ent'red soldiers, to return
And find your grace in health.
King. No, no, it cannot be; and yet my heart
Will not confess he owes the malady
That doth my life besiege. Farewell, young lords;
Whether I live or die, be you the sons
Of worthy Frenchmen: let higher Italy,—
†Those bated that inherit but the fall
Of the last monarchy,—see that you come
Not to woo honour, but to wed it; when
The bravest questant shrinks, find what you seek,
That fame may cry you loud. I say, farewell.
Sec. Lord. Health, at your bidding, serve your majesty!
King. Those girls of Italy, take heed of them:
They say, our French lack language to deny,
If they demand: beware of being captives,
Before you serve.
Both. Our hearts receive your warnings.
King. Farewell. Come hither to me. [*Exit, attended.*]
First Lord. O my sweet lord, that you will stay behind us!
Par. 'Tis not his fault, the spark.
Sec. Lord. O, 'tis brave wars!
Par. Most admirable: I have seen those wars.
Ber. I am commanded here, and kept a coil with
'Too young' and 'the next year' and ''tis too early.'
Par. An thy mind stand to 't boy, steal away bravely.
Ber. I shall stay here the forehorse to a smock,
Creaking my shoes on the plain masonry,
Till honour be bought up and no sword worn
But one to dance with! By heaven, I'll steal away.
First Lord. There 's honour in the theft.
Par. Commit it, count.
Sec. Lord. I am your accessary; and so, farewell.
Ber. I grow to you, and our parting is a tortured body.
First Lord. Farewell, captain.
Sec. Lord. Sweet Monsieur Parolles!

Par. Noble heroes, my sword and yours are kin. Good sparks and lustrous, a word, good metals: you shall find in the regiment of the Spinii one Captain Spurio, with his cicatrice, an emblem of war, here on his sinister cheek; it was this very sword entrenched it: say to him, I live; and observe his reports for me.

First Lord. We shall, noble captain. [*Exeunt Lords.*]

Par. Mars dote on you for his novices! [*To Ber.*] what will ye do?

Ber. Stay: the king.

[*Enter* KING, *assisted.* BERTRAM *and* PAROLLES *retire.*]

Par. [*To Ber.*] Use a more spacious ceremony to the noble lords; you have restrained yourself within the list of too cold an adieu: be more expressive to them: for they wear themselves in the cap of the time, there do muster true gait, eat, speak, and move under the influence of the most received star; and though the devil lead the measure, such are to be followed: after them, and take a more dilated farewell.

Ber. And I will do so.

Par. Worthy fellows; and like to prove most sinewy sword-men. *Exeunt* [*Bertram and Parolles*].

Enter LAFEW.

panies this speech for which F gives no guidance. Most editors follow either Pope, who has the king leave the stage, or Capell, who has him retire to a couch. The words may be addressed to Bertram (Pope) or to attendants (Theobald). The New Cambridge editors follow Theobald and add the stage direction, "he swoons and is carried to the couch, before which curtains are drawn." Cf. l. 50 below, note. 25. **spark,** elegant young man, a beau. 27. **kept a coil,** pestered. 30. **forehorse . . . smock,** i.e., ushering in and squiring ladies (Schmidt); the leader in a team of horses driven by a woman (New Cambridge); a *forehorse* is the lead horse of a team. 32. **Till . . . up,** till opportunity for winning honor in the wars is past. 33. **one to dance with,** light ornamental weapon. 43. **cicatrice,** scar. 44. **sinister,** left. 50. **Stay: the king.** F, without stage direction, reads: *Stay the King.* So punctuated it would mean "support or wait on the king"; Brigstocke so explains it. Pope, followed by others, punctuated: *Stay; the king,* explaining as "I shall stay; the king wills it." The Cambridge editors, taking *Stay* as a word of caution, punctuate as here and explain, "The ushers in attendance throw open the folding doors at the back of the stage, Bertram and Parolles retire close to one of the side doors, and while they are speaking together the king is borne in upon his couch to the front of the stage." 55. **muster true gait,** set the right pace. 56. **influence,** supposed flowing from the stars of an ethereal fluid acting upon the characters and destinies of men; see glossary. 57. **receiv'd,** fashionable. 59. **dilated,** expressed at length.

Laf. [*Kneeling*] Pardon, my lord, for me and for my tidings.
King. I'll fee thee to stand up.
Laf. [*Rising*] Then here 's a man stands, that has brought his pardon.
I would you had kneel'd, my lord, to ask me mercy,
And that at my bidding you could so stand up.
King. I would I had; so I had broke thy pate,
And ask'd thee mercy for 't.
Laf. Good faith, across: but, my good lord, 'tis thus;
Will you be cur'd of your infirmity?
King. No.
Laf. O, will you eat no grapes, my royal fox?
Yes, but you will my noble grapes, an if
My royal fox could reach them: I have seen a medicine
That 's able to breathe life into a stone,
Quicken a rock, and make you dance canary
With spritely fire and motion; whose simple touch
Is powerful to araise King Pepin, nay,
To give great Charlemain a pen in 's hand
And write to her a love-line.
King. What 'her' is this?
Laf. Why, Doctor She: my lord, there 's one arriv'd,
If you will see her: now, by my faith and honour,
If seriously I may convey my thoughts
In this my light deliverance, I have spoke
With one that, in her sex, her years, profession,
Wisdom and constancy, hath amaz'd me more
Than I dare blame my weakness: will you see her,
For that is her demand, and know her business?
That done, laugh well at me.
King. Now, good Lafew,
Bring in the admiration; that we with thee
May spend our wonder too, or take off thine
By wond'ring how thou took'st it.
Laf. Nay, I'll fit you,
And not be all day neither. [*Exit.*]
King. Thus he his special nothing ever prologues.

Enter [LAFEW, *with*] HELENA.

Laf. Nay, come your ways.
King. This haste hath wings indeed.
Laf. Nay, come your ways;
This is his majesty; say your mind to him:
A traitor you do look like; but such traitors
His majesty seldom fears: I am Cressid's uncle,
That dare leave two together; fare you well. *Exit.*
King. Now, fair one, does your business follow us?
Hel. Ay, my good lord.
Gerard de Narbon was my father;
In what he did profess, well found.
King. I knew him.
Hel. The rather will I spare my praises towards him;
Knowing him is enough. On 's bed of death
Many receipts he gave me; chiefly one,
Which, as the dearest issue of his practice,
And of his old experience th' only darling,
He bade me store up, as a triple eye,
Safer than mine own two, more dear; I have so;
And, hearing your high majesty is touch'd
With that malignant cause wherein the honour
Of my dear father's gift stands chief in power,
I come to tender it and my appliance
With all bound humbleness.
King. We thank you, maiden;
But may not be so credulous of cure,
When our most learned doctors leave us and
The congregated college have concluded
That labouring art can never ransom nature
From her inaidible estate; I say we must not
So stain our judgement, or corrupt our hope,
To prostitute our past-cure malady
To empirics, or to dissever so
Our great self and our credit, to esteem
A senseless help when help past sense we deem.
Hel. My duty then shall pay me for my pains:
I will no more enforce mine office on you;
Humbly entreating from your royal thoughts
A modest one, to bear me back again.
King. I cannot give thee less, to be call'd grateful:
Thou thought'st to help me; and such thanks I give
As one near death to those that wish him live:
But what at full I know, thou know'st no part,
I knowing all my peril, thou no art.
Hel. What I can do can do no hurt to try,
Since you set up your rest 'gainst remedy.
He that of greatest works is finisher
Oft does them by the weakest minister:
So holy writ in babes hath judgement shown,
When judges have been babes; great floods have flown
From simple sources, and great seas have dried
When miracles have by the great'st been denied.
Oft expectation fails and most oft there
Where most it promises, and oft it hits
Where hope is coldest and despair most fits.
King. I must not hear thee; fare thee well, kind maid;
Thy pains not us'd must by thyself be paid:
Proffers not took reap thanks for their reward.
Hel. Inspired merit so by breath is barr'd:
It is not so with Him that all things knows
As 'tis with us that square our guess by shows;
But most it is presumption in us when
The help of heaven we count the act of men.
Dear sir, to my endeavours give consent;
Of heaven, not me, make an experiment.
I am not an impostor that proclaim
Myself against the level of mine aim;
But know I think and think I know most sure
My art is not past power nor you past cure.
King. Art thou so confident? within what space

64. **I'll fee . . . up.** Those who retain this reading explain it in one of two ways: (1) the king, referring to his inability to rise, says to Lafew, "I'll fee thee to help me to stand"; (2) referring to Lafew's having knelt, he bids him rise. Lafew's speech indicates that the latter is the more likely. Some editors accept Theobald's emendation: *I see thee* . . . . 70. **Good faith, across,** a metaphor from tilting; to break a lance *across* one's opponent is the act of an unskillful tilter. 75. **medicine,** physician. 77. **canary,** lively Spanish dance. 79. **araise,** raise from the dead. 85. **deliverance,** utterance, delivery. 86. **profession,** what she professes to be. 92. **take off,** dispel. 93. **fit,** satisfy.

96. **come your ways,** come along. 100. **Cressid's uncle,** Pandarus, in the story of Troilus and Cressida, who acted as a go-between for the lovers. 105. **well found,** well skilled. 109. **issue,** product. 116. **tender,** offer. **appliance,** treatment. 120. **congregated college,** college of physicians, who kept quacks from practice. 125. **empirics,** quack doctors. 127. **past sense,** past realization or perception. 138. **set . . . rest,** stake your all; a figure from gambling. 151. **by breath,** i.e., by spoken words. 153. **square . . . shows,** make decisions on the basis of appearances; in antithesis to the king's words, line 127. 158-159. **proclaim . . . aim,** claim more than I can accomplish. 163. **great'st**

Hop'st thou my cure?
Hel. The great'st grace lending grace,
Ere twice the horses of the sun shall bring
Their fiery torcher his diurnal ring,
Ere twice in murk and occidental damp
Moist Hesperus hath quench'd her sleepy lamp,
Or four and twenty times the pilot's glass
Hath told the thievish minutes how they pass,
What is infirm from your sound parts shall fly,
Health shall live free and sickness freely die.
King. Upon thy certainty and confidence
What dar'st thou venture?
Hel. Tax of impudence,
A strumpet's boldness, a divulged shame
Traduc'd by odious ballads: my maiden's name
Sear'd otherwise; nay, worse of worst, extended
With vilest torture let my life be ended.
King. Methinks in thee some blessed spirit doth speak
His powerful sound within an organ weak:
And what impossibility would slay
In common sense, sense saves another way.
Thy life is dear; for all that life can rate
Worth name of life in thee hath estimate,
Youth, beauty, wisdom, courage, all
That happiness and prime can happy call:
Thou this to hazard needs must intimate
Skill infinite or monstrous desperate.
Sweet practiser, thy physic I will try,
That ministers thine own death if I die.
Hel. If I break time, or flinch in property
Of what I spoke, unpitied let me die,
And well deserv'd: not helping, death 's my fee;
But, if I help, what do you promise me?
King. Make thy demand.
Hel. But will you make it even?
King. Ay, by my sceptre and my hopes of heaven.
Hel. Then shalt thou give me with thy kingly hand
What husband in thy power I will command:
Exempted be from me the arrogance
To choose from forth the royal blood of France,
My low and humble name to propagate
With any branch or image of thy state;
But such a one, thy vassal, whom I know
Is free for me to ask, thee to bestow.
King. Here is my hand; the premises observ'd,
Thy will by my performance shall be serv'd:
So make the choice of thy own time, for I,
Thy resolv'd patient, on thee still rely.
More should I question thee, and more I must,
Though more to know could not be more to trust,
From whence thou cam'st, how tended on: but rest
Unquestion'd welcome and undoubted blest.
Give me some help here, ho! If thou proceed
As high as word, my deed shall match thy meed.
Flourish. Exeunt.

[SCENE II. *Rousillon. The* COUNT'S *palace.*]

Enter COUNTESS *and* Clown.

Count. Come on, sir; I shall now put you to the height of your breeding.

Clo. I will show myself highly fed and lowly taught: I know my business is but to the court.

Count. To the court! why, what place make you special, when you put off that with such contempt? But to the court!

Clo. Truly, madam, if God have lent a man any manners, he may easily put it off at court: he that cannot make a leg, put off 's cap, kiss his hand and say nothing, has neither leg, hands, lip, nor cap; and indeed such a fellow, to say precisely, were not for the court; but for me, I have an answer will serve all men.

Count. Marry, that 's a bountiful answer that fits all questions.

Clo. It is like a barber's chair that fits all buttocks, the pin-buttock, the quatch-buttock, the brawn buttock, or any buttock.

Count. Will your answer serve fit to all questions?

Clo. As fit as ten groats is for the hand of an attorney, as your French crown for your taffety punk, as Tib's rush for Tom's forefinger, as a pancake for Shrove Tuesday, a morris for May-day, as the nail to his hole, the cuckold to his horn, as a scolding quean to a wrangling knave, as the nun's lip to the friar's mouth, nay, as the pudding to his skin.

Count. Have you, I say, an answer of such fitness for all questions?

Clo. From below your duke to beneath your constable, it will fit any question.

Count. It must be an answer of most monstrous size that must fit all demands.

Clo. But a trifle neither, in good faith, if the learned should speak truth of it: here it is, and all that belongs to 't. Ask me if I am a courtier: it shall do you no harm to learn.

Count. To be young again, if we could: I will be a fool in question, hoping to be the wiser by your answer. I pray you, sir, are you a courtier?

Clo. O Lord, sir! There 's a simple putting off. More, more, a hundred of them.

Count. Sir, I am a poor friend of yours, that loves you.

Clo. O Lord, sir! Thick, thick, spare not me.

Count. I think, sir, you can eat none of this homely meat.

Clo. O Lord, sir! Nay, put me to 't, I warrant you.

Count. You were lately whipped, sir, as I think.

Clo. O Lord, sir!—spare not me.

Count. Do you cry, 'O Lord, sir!' at your whipping, and 'spare not me'? Indeed your 'O Lord, sir!' is very sequent to your whipping: you would answer very well to a whipping, if you were but bound to 't.

Clo. I ne'er had worse luck in my life in my 'O Lord, sir!' I see things may serve long, but not serve ever.

---

grace, divine grace. 168. **pilot's glass,** hourglass. 173. **Tax,** accusation. 176. **otherwise,** in other ways as well. 180-181. **what . . . way,** what common sense would regard as impossible, a higher sense (faith) can believe. 185. **prime,** youth. 190. **break,** infringe, fail to keep. **flinch in property,** fall short in any detail.

SCENE II. 1-2. **put you . . . breeding,** test your good manners. 3. **lowly taught,** taught to keep my place; or, underdisciplined. 5-6. **make you special,** do you consider special. 6. **put off,** dismiss. 19. **pin,** narrow. **quatch,** fat. 23. **French crown,** probably used quibblingly: a coin and the *corona veneris*, a scab on the head, symptomatic of the "French disease," as syphilis was sometimes called. (*Shakespeare's England*, I, 438.) 23-24. **taffety punk,** prostitute finely dressed. 24. **Tib's rush,** a possible reference to a folk custom of placing a ring made of rush on the woman's finger in a marriage without benefit of clergy. 25. **morris,** morris dance. 27. **quean,** wench. 43. **O Lord, sir,** a foppish phrase in vogue at King James' court. Farmer finds it ridiculed in other contemporary passages. 47. **Thick,** quickly.

Count. I play the noble housewife with the time,
To entertain it so merrily with a fool.

Clo. O Lord, sir! why, there 't serves well again.

Count. An end, sir; to your business. Give Helen this,
And urge her to a present answer back:
Commend me to my kinsmen and my son:
This is not much.

Clo. Not much commendation to them?

Count. Not much employment for you: you understand me?

Clo. Most fruitfully: I am there before my legs.

Count. Haste you again. *Exeunt [severally]*.

[SCENE III. *Paris. The* KING'S *palace*.]

Enter COUNT [BERTRAM], LAFEW, *and* PAROLLES.

Laf. They say miracles are past; and we have our philosophical persons, to make modern and familiar, things supernatural and causeless. Hence is it that we make trifles of terrors, ensconcing ourselves into seeming knowledge, when we should submit ourselves to an unknown fear.

Par. Why, 'tis the rarest argument of wonder that hath shot out in our latter times.

Ber. And so 'tis.

Laf. To be relinquished of the artists,—

Par. So I say.

Laf. Both of Galen and Paracelsus.

Par. So I say.

Laf. Of all the learned and authentic fellows,—

Par. Right; so I say.

Laf. That gave him out incurable,—

Par. Why, there 'tis; so say I too.

Laf. Not to be helped,—

Par. Right: as 'twere, a man assured of a—

Laf. Uncertain life, and sure death.

Par. Just, you say well; so would I have said.

Laf. I may truly say, it is a novelty to the world.

Par. It is, indeed: if you will have it in showing, you shall read it in—what do ye call there?

Laf. A showing of a heavenly effect in an earthly actor.

Par. That 's it; I would have said the very same.

Laf. Why, your dolphin is not lustier: 'fore me, I speak in respect—

Par. Nay, 'tis strange, 'tis very strange, that is the brief and the tedious of it; and he 's of a most facinerious spirit that will not acknowledge it to be the—

Laf. Very hand of heaven.

Par. Ay, so I say.

Laf. In a most weak—

Par. And debile minister; great power, great transcendence: which should, indeed, give us a further use to be made than alone the recovery of the king, as to be—

Laf. Generally thankful.

Enter KING, HELENA, *and* Attendants.

Par. I would have said it; you say well. Here comes the king.

Laf. Lustig! as the Dutchman says: I'll like a maid the better, whilst I have a tooth in my head: why, he 's able to lead her a coranto.

Par. Mort du vinaigre! is not this Helen?

Laf. 'Fore God, I think so.

King. Go, call before me all the lords in court.
[*Exit an Attendant*.]
Sit, my preserver, by thy patient's side;
And with this healthful hand, whose banish'd sense
Thou hast repeal'd, a second time receive
The confirmation of my promis'd gift,
Which but attends thy naming.

Enter three or four Lords.

Fair maid, send forth thine eye: this youthful parcel
Of noble bachelors stand at my bestowing,
O'er whom both sovereign power and father's voice
I have to use: thy frank election make;
Thou hast power to choose, and they none to forsake.

Hel. To each of you one fair and virtuous mistress
Fall, when Love please! marry, to each, but one!

Laf. [*Aside*] I 'ld give bay Curtal and his furniture,
My mouth no more were broken than these boys',
And writ as little beard.

King. Peruse them well:
Not one of those but had a noble father.

Hel. Gentlemen,
Heaven hath through me restor'd the king to health.

All. We understand it, and thank heaven for you.

Hel. I am a simple maid, and therein wealthiest,
That I protest I simply am a maid.
Please it your majesty, I have done already:
The blushes in my cheeks thus whisper me,
'We blush that thou shouldst choose; but, be refus'd,
Let the white death sit on thy cheek for ever;
We'll ne'er come there again.'

King. Make choice; and, see,
Who shuns thy love shuns all his love in me.

Hel. Now, Dian, from thy altar do I fly,
And to imperial Love, that god most high,
Do my sighs stream. *(She addresses her to a Lord.)* Sir, will you hear my suit?

First Lord. And grant it.

Hel. Thanks, sir; all the rest is mute.

Laf. [*Aside*] I had rather be in this choice than throw ames-ace for my life.

Hel. [*To another*] The honour, sir, that flames in your fair eyes,
Before I speak, too threat'ningly replies:
Love make your fortunes twenty times above
Her that so wishes and her humble love!

Sec. Lord. No better, if you please.

Hel. My wish receive,
Which great Love grant! and so, I take my leave.

Laf. [*Aside*] Do all they deny her? An they were sons of mine, I'd have them whipped; or I would send them to the Turk, to make eunuchs of.

Hel. [*To a third*] Be not afraid that I your hand

SCENE III. 4. **ensconcing,** taking refuge, fortifying. 10. **artists,** i.e., the physicians. 12. **Galen,** Greek physician of the second century. **Paracelsus,** Swiss physician of the sixteenth century. 14. **authentic fellows,** those properly licensed to practice. 25. **showing,** print. 31. **dolphin,** the fish; supposed by some to mean the dauphin of France. 34. **the brief . . . it.** Cf. the modern phrase "the short and the long of it." 35. **facinerious,** infamous. 39. **debile,** weak. 47. **Lustig,** German word for "merry." 49. **coranto,** lively dance. 50. **Mort du vinaigre,** possibly an oath by the vinegar in Christ's wounds; literally, death of the vinegar. 61. **frank election,** uninhibited choice. 65. **bay . . . furniture,** my horse and his trappings. 66. **My mouth . . . broken,** i.e., if I had all my teeth. 67. **writ,** laid claim to. 83. **all . . . mute,** I have nothing more to say to you. 85. **ames-ace,** two aces; the lowest possible throw in dice—i.e., barely escape death (New

should take;
I'll never do you wrong for your own sake:
Blessing upon your vows! and in your bed
Find fairer fortune, if you ever wed!

Laf. [*Aside*] These boys are boys of ice, they'll none have her: sure, they are bastards to the English; the French ne'er got 'em.

Hel. [*To a fourth*] You are too young, too happy, and too good,
To make yourself a son out of my blood.

Fourth Lord. Fair one, I think not so.

Laf. [*Aside*] There 's one grape yet; I am sure thy father drunk wine: but if thou be'st not an ass, I am a youth of fourteen; I have known thee already.

Hel. [*To Bertram*] I dare not say I take you; but I give
Me and my service, ever whilst I live,
Into your guiding power.—This is the man.

King. Why, then, young Bertram, take her; she 's thy wife.

Ber. My wife, my liege! I shall beseech your highness,
In such a business give me leave to use
The help of mine own eyes.

King. Know'st thou not, Bertram,
What she has done for me?

Ber. Yes, my good lord;
But never hope to know why I should marry her.

King. Thou know'st she has rais'd me from my sickly bed.

Ber. But follows it, my lord, to bring me down
Must answer for your raising? I know her well:
She had her breeding at my father's charge.
A poor physician's daughter my wife! Disdain
Rather corrupt me ever!

King. 'Tis only title thou disdain'st in her, the which
I can build up. Strange is it that our bloods,
Of colour, weight, and heat, pour'd all together,
Would quite confound distinction, yet stand off
In differences so mighty. If she be
All that is virtuous, save what thou dislik'st,
A poor physician's daughter, thou dislik'st
Of virtue for the name: but do not so:
From lowest place when virtuous things proceed,
The place is dignified by th' doer's deed:
Where great additions swell 's, and virtue none,
It is a dropsied honour. Good alone
Is good without a name. Vileness is so:
The property by what it is should go,
Not by the title. She is young, wise, fair;
In these to nature she 's immediate heir,
And these breed honour: that is honour's scorn,
Which challenges itself as honour's born
And is not like the sire: honours thrive,
When rather from our acts we them derive
Than our foregoers: the mere word 's a slave
Debosh'd on every tomb, on every grave
A lying trophy, and as oft is dumb
Where dust and damn'd oblivion is the tomb
Of honour'd bones indeed. What should be said?
If thou canst like this creature as a maid,
I can create the rest: virtue and she
Is her own dower; honour and wealth from me.

Ber. I cannot love her, nor will strive to do 't.

King. Thou wrong'st thyself, if thou shouldst strive to choose.

Hel. That you are well restor'd, my lord, I'm glad:
Let the rest go.

King. My honour 's at the stake; which to defeat,
I must produce my power. Here, take her hand,
Proud scornful boy, unworthy this good gift;
That dost in vile misprision shackle up
My love and her desert; that canst not dream,
We, poising us in her defective scale,
Shall weigh thee to the beam; that wilt not know,
It is in us to plant thine honour where
We please to have it grow. Check thy contempt:
Obey our will, which travails in thy good:
Believe not thy disdain, but presently
Do thine own fortunes that obedient right
Which both thy duty owes and our power claims;
Or I will throw thee from my care for ever
Into the staggers and the careless lapse
Of youth and ignorance; both my revenge and hate
Loosing upon thee, in the name of justice,
Without all terms of pity. Speak; thine answer.

Ber. Pardon, my gracious lord; for I submit
My fancy to your eyes: when I consider
What great creation and what dole of honour
Flies where you bid it, I find that she, which late
Was in my nobler thoughts most base, is now
The praised of the king; who, so ennobled,
Is as 'twere born so.

King. Take her by the hand,
And tell her she is thine: to whom I promise
A counterpoise, if not to thy estate
A balance more replete.

Ber. I take her hand.

King. Good fortune and the favour of the king
Smile upon this contract; whose ceremony
Shall seem expedient on the now-born brief,
And be perform'd to-night: the solemn feast
Shall more attend upon the coming space,
Expecting absent friends. As thou lov'st her,
Thy love 's to me religious; else, does err.

Exeunt. Parolles and Lafew stay behind, commenting of this wedding.

Laf. Do you hear, monsieur? a word with you.

Par. Your pleasure, sir?

Laf. Your lord and master did well to make his recantation.

Par. Recantation! My lord! my master!

Laf. Ay; is it not a language I speak?

Par. A most harsh one, and not to be understood without bloody succeeding. My master!

Laf. Are you companion to the Count Rousillon?

Par. To any count, to all counts, to what is man.

Laf. To what is count's man: count's master is of another style.

Par. You are too old, sir; let it satisfy you, you are too old.

Cambridge). 92. **Do all . . . her.** None of them have denied her, or deny her afterwards, but Bertram. The scene must be so regulated that Lafew and Parolles talk at a distance, where they may see what passes between Helena and the lords, but not hear it, so that they know not by whom the refusal is made (Johnson). 106. **drunk wine,** i.e., was red-blooded. 122-123. **Disdain . . . ever,** i.e., rather let my disdain for her ruin me forever. 134. **great additions swell 's,** pompous titles puff us up. 141. **challenges itself,** claims itself to be. 145. **Debosh'd,** debauched. 159. **misprision,** contempt. 170. **staggers,** giddy or wild conduct. 185-186. **whose . . . brief,** the consecration of which will serve as a fitting conclusion to the agreement just made. 199. **succeeding,** consequences; i.e., a duel. 203. **what is man,** i.e., any true man; or, manly. 204. **count's man,** i.e., servant (used belittlingly). 205. **too old,** i.e., for me to duel with.

Laf. I must tell thee, sirrah, I write man; to which title age cannot bring thee.

Par. What I dare too well do, I dare not do.

Laf. I did think thee, for two ordinaries, to be a pretty wise fellow; thou didst make tolerable vent of thy travel; it might pass: yet the scarfs and the bannerets about thee did manifoldly dissuade me from believing thee a vessel of too great a burthen. I have now found thee; when I lose thee again, I care not: yet art thou good for nothing but taking up; and that thou 'rt scarce worth.

Par. Hadst thou not the privilege of antiquity upon thee,—

Laf. Do not plunge thyself too far in anger, lest thou hasten thy trial; which if—Lord have mercy on thee for a hen! So, my good window of lattice, fare thee well: thy casement I need not open, for I look through thee. Give me thy hand.

Par. My lord, you give me most egregious indignity.

Laf. Ay, with all my heart; and thou art worthy of it.

Par. I have not, my lord, deserved it.

Laf. Yes, good faith, every dram of it; and I will not bate thee a scruple.

Par. Well, I shall be wiser.

Laf. Even as soon as thou canst, for thou hast to pull at a smack o' the contrary. If ever thou be'st bound in thy scarf and beaten, thou shalt find what it is to be proud of thy bondage. I have a desire to hold my acquaintance with thee, or rather my knowledge, that I may say in the default, he is a man I know.

Par. My lord, you do me most insupportable vexation.

Laf. I would it were hell-pains for thy sake, and my poor doing eternal: for doing I am past; as I will by thee, in what motion age will give me leave. *Exit.*

Par. Well, thou hast a son shall take this disgrace off me; scurvy, old, filthy, scurvy lord! Well, I must be patient; there is no fettering of authority. I'll beat him, by my life, if I can meet him with any convenience, an he were double and double a lord. I'll have no more pity of his age than I would have of—I'll beat him, an if I could but meet him again.

Enter LAFEW.

Laf. Sirrah, your lord and master 's married; there 's news for you: you have a new mistress.

Par. I most unfeignedly beseech your lordship to make some reservation of your wrongs: he is my good lord: whom I serve above is my master.

Laf. Who? God?

Par. Ay, sir.

Laf. The devil it is that 's thy master. Why dost thou garter up thy arms o' this fashion? dost make hose of thy sleeves? do other servants so? Thou wert best set thy lower part where thy nose stands. By mine honour, if I were but two hours younger, I 'ld beat thee: methinks, thou art a general offence, and every man should beat thee: I think thou wast created for men to breathe themselves upon thee.

Par. This is hard and undeserved measure, my lord.

Laf. Go to, sir; you were beaten in Italy for picking a kernel out of a pomegranate; you are a vagabond and no true traveller: you are more saucy with lords and honourable personages than the commission of your birth and virtue gives you heraldry. You are not worth another word, else I 'ld call you knave. I leave you. *Exit.*

Par. Good, very good; it is so then: good, very good; let it be concealed awhile.

Enter [BERTRAM] COUNT ROUSILLON.

Ber. Undone, and forfeited to cares for ever!

Par. What 's the matter, sweet-heart?

Ber. Although before the solemn priest I have sworn,
I will not bed her.

Par. What, what, sweet-heart?

Ber. O my Parolles, they have married me! I'll to the Tuscan wars, and never bed her.

Par. France is a dog-hole, and it no more merits
The tread of a man's foot: to th' wars!

Ber. There 's letters from my mother: what th'
import is, I know not yet.

Par. Ay, that would be known. To th' wars, my
boy, to th' wars!
He wears his honour in a box unseen,
That hugs his kicky-wicky here at home,
Spending his manly marrow in her arms,
Which should sustain the bound and high curvet
Of Mars's fiery steed. To other regions
France is a stable; we that dwell in 't jades;
Therefore, to th' war!

Ber. It shall be so: I'll send her to my house,
Acquaint my mother with my hate to her,
And wherefore I am fled; write to the king
That which I durst not speak: his present gift
Shall furnish me to those Italian fields,
Where noble fellows strike: war is no strife
To the dark house and the detested wife.

Par. Will this capriccio hold in thee? art sure?

Ber. Go with me to my chamber, and advise me.
I'll send her straight away: to-morrow
I'll to the wars, she to her single sorrow.

Par. Why, these balls bound; there 's noise in it.
'Tis hard:
A young man married is a man that 's marr'd:
Therefore away, and leave her bravely; go:
The king has done you wrong: but, hush, 'tis so.
Exit [*with Bertram*].

[SCENE IV. *Paris. The* KING'S *palace.*]

Enter HELENA *and* Clown.

Hel. My mother greets me kindly: is she well?

Clo. She is not well; but yet she has her health: she 's very merry; but yet she is not well: but thanks be given, she 's very well and wants nothing i' the world; but yet she is not well.

Hel. If she be very well, what does she ail, that

211. **ordinaries,** meals. 220. **privilege of antiquity,** referring to his advanced age. 225. **window of lattice,** sign of an alehouse. 234. **bate,** take away from. 237. **smack,** a taste, a draught. **the contrary,** i.e., of wisdom (l. 235)—folly. 241. **in the default,** when you fail. 253. **convenience,** advantage. 293. **letters,** i.e., a letter. 297. **kicky-wicky,** woman (with sexual suggestion, as also in *Spending*, *marrow* l. 298, *box* l. 296). 307. **furnish me.** Knights customarily provided themselves with trappings and armed retainers when enlisting in warlike enterprises. 310. **capriccio,** caprice. 314. **balls,** tennis balls.

SCENE IV. 2. **not well,** an adaptation of the Elizabethan euphemism by which the dead were spoken of as "well"; cf. *2 Henry IV*, V, ii, 3; *Antony and Cleopatra*, II, v, 31-33. 24. **shakes out,** referring to his loose, wagging tongue. 32. **found thee,** found you out. 34. **in yourself,** by yourself. 45. **Whose want,** the lack of which; the antecedent of she 's not very well?

Clo. Truly, she 's very well indeed, but for two things.

Hel. What two things?

Clo. One, that she 's not in heaven, whither God send her quickly! the other, that she 's in earth, from whence God send her quickly!

Enter PAROLLES.

Par. Bless you, my fortunate lady!

Hel. I hope, sir, I have your good will to have mine own good fortunes.

Par. You had my prayers to lead them on; and to keep them on, have them still. O, my knave, how does my old lady?

Clo. So that you had her wrinkles and I her money, I would she did as you say.

Par. Why, I say nothing.

Clo. Marry, you are the wiser man; for many a man's tongue shakes out his master's undoing: to say nothing, to do nothing, to know nothing, and to have nothing, is to be a great part of your title; which is within a very little of nothing.

Par. Away! th' art a knave.

Clo. You should have said, sir, before a knave th' art a knave; that 's, before me th' art a knave: this had been truth, sir.

Par. Go to, thou art a witty fool; I have found thee.

Clo. Did you find me in yourself, sir? or were you taught to find me? The search, sir, was profitable; and much fool may you find in you, even to the world's pleasure and the increase of laughter.

Par. A good knave, i' faith, and well fed.
Madam, my lord will go away to-night;
A very serious business calls on him.
The great prerogative and rite of love,
Which, as your due, time claims, he does acknowledge;
But puts it off to a compell'd restraint;
Whose want, and whose delay, is strew'd with sweets,
Which they distil now in the curbed time,
To make the coming hour o'erflow with joy
And pleasure drown the brim.

Hel. What 's his will else?

Par. That you will take your instant leave o' th' king,
And make this haste as your own good proceeding,
Strength'ned with what apology you think
May make it probable need.

Hel. What more commands he?

Par. That, having this obtain'd, you presently
Attend his further pleasure.

Hel. In every thing I wait upon his will.

Par. I shall report it so. *Exit. Par.*

Hel. I pray you. Come, sirrah. *Exit* [*with Clown*].

[SCENE V. *Paris. The* KING'S *palace.*]

Enter LAFEW *and* BERTRAM.

Laf. But I hope your lordship thinks not him a soldier.

Ber. Yes, my lord, and of very valiant approof.

Laf. You have it from his own deliverance.

Ber. And by other warranted testimony.

Laf. Then my dial goes not true: I took this lark for a bunting.

Ber. I do assure you, my lord, he is very great in knowledge and accordingly valiant.

Laf. I have then sinned against his experience and transgressed against his valour; and my state that way is dangerous, since I cannot yet find in my heart to repent. Here he comes: I pray you, make us friends; I will pursue the amity.

Enter PAROLLES.

Par. [*To Bertram*] These things shall be done, sir.

Laf. Pray you, sir, who 's his tailor?

Par. Sir?

Laf. O, I know him well, I, sir; he, sir, 's a good workman, a very good tailor.

Ber. [*Aside to Par.*] Is she gone to the king?

Par. She is.

Ber. Will she away to-night?

Par. As you'll have her.

Ber. I have writ my letters, casketed my treasure,
Given order for our horses; and to-night,
When I should take possession of the bride,
End ere I do begin.

Laf. A good traveller is something at the latter end of a dinner; but one that lies three thirds and uses a known truth to pass a thousand nothings with, should be once heard and thrice beaten. God save you, captain.

Ber. Is there any unkindness between my lord and you, monsieur?

Par. I know not how I have deserved to run into my lord's displeasure.

Laf. You have made shift to run into 't, boots and spurs and all, like him that leaped into the custard; and out of it you'll run again, rather than suffer question for your residence.

Ber. It may be you have mistaken him, my lord.

Laf. And shall do so ever, though I took him at 's prayers. Fare you well, my lord; and believe this of me, there can be no kernel in this light nut; the soul of this man is his clothes. Trust him not in matter of heavy consequence; I have kept of them tame, and know their natures. Farewell, monsieur: I have spoken better of you †than you have or will to deserve at my hand; but we must do good against evil. [*Exit.*]

Par. An idle lord, I swear.

Ber. I think so.

Par. Why, do you not know him?

Ber. Yes, I do know him well, and common speech
Gives him a worthy pass. Here comes my clog.

Enter HELENA.

Hel. I have, sir, as I was commanded from you,
Spoke with the king and have procur'd his leave
For present parting; only he desires

whose is the idea of line 42. 46. **curbed time,** usually explained as restraints of time. The New Cambridge editors explain the metaphor to be drawn from the process of distillation, *the curbed time* being conceived as the confined vessel or still in which the process is carried on. 52. **probable need,** a specious appearance of necessity (Johnson).

SCENE V. 6. **dial,** a compass, i.e., judgment. 7. **lark, bunting,** birds so nearly alike as to be confused by the casual observer; the bunting is less valuable. 30. **good traveller,** referring to their previous quarrel (II, iii, 212-213). 39-42. **You have . . . residence.** Lafew taunts Parolles with his braggartlike conduct at their previous meeting. 40. **leaped . . . custard.** Theobald points out the "foolery practised at city entertainments" of having a clown jump into a large, deep custard. 49-50. **I have . . . tame,** I have kept tame animals of this kind (New Cambridge).

Some private speech with you.
Ber. I shall obey his will.
You must not marvel, Helen, at my course,
Which holds not colour with the time, nor does
The ministration and required office
On my particular. Prepar'd I was not
For such a business; therefore am I found
So much unsettled: this drives me to entreat you
That presently you take your way for home;
And rather muse than ask why I entreat you,
For my respects are better than they seem
And my appointments have in them a need
Greater than shows itself at the first view
To you that know them not. This to my mother:
[*Giving a letter.*]
'Twill be two days ere I shall see you, so
I leave you to your wisdom.
Hel. Sir, I can nothing say,
But that I am your most obedient servant.
Ber. Come, come, no more of that.
Hel. And ever shall
With true observance seek to eke out that
Wherein toward me my homely stars have fail'd
To equal my great fortune.
Ber. Let that go:
My haste is very great: farewell; hie home.
Hel. Pray, sir, your pardon.
Ber. Well, what would you say?
Hel. I am not worthy of the wealth I owe,
Nor dare I say 'tis mine, and yet it is;
But, like a timorous thief, most fain would steal
What law does vouch mine own.
Ber. What would you have?
Hel. Something; and scarce so much: nothing, indeed.
I would not tell you what I would, my lord:
Faith, yes;
Strangers and foes do sunder, and not kiss.
Ber. I pray you, stay not, but in haste to horse.
Hel. I shall not break your bidding, good my lord.
Ber. Where are my other men, monsieur? Farewell.
Exit [*Helena*].
Go thou toward home; where I will never come
Whilst I can shake my sword or hear the drum.
Away, and for our flight.
Par. Bravely, coragio! [*Exeunt.*]

ACT III.

[SCENE I. *Florence. The* DUKE's *palace.*]

Flourish. Enter the DUKE OF FLORENCE [*attended*]; *the two Frenchmen, with a troop of soldiers.*

Duke. So that from point to point now have you heard
The fundamental reasons of this war,
Whose great decision hath much blood let forth
And more thirsts after.
First Lord. Holy seems the quarrel
Upon your grace's part; black and fearful
On the opposer.
Duke. Therefore we marvel much our cousin France
Would in so just a business shut his bosom
Against our borrowing prayers.
Sec. Lord. Good my lord,
The reasons of our state I cannot yield,
But like a common and an outward man,
That the great figure of a council frames
By self-unable motion: therefore dare not
Say what I think of it, since I have found
Myself in my incertain grounds to fail
As often as I guess'd.
Duke. Be it his pleasure.
First Lord. But I am sure the younger of our nature,
That surfeit on their ease, will day by day
Come here for physic.
Duke. Welcome shall they be;
And all the honours that can fly from us
Shall on them settle. You know your places well;
When better fall, for your avails they fell:
To-morrow to the field. *Flourish.* [*Exeunt.*]

[SCENE II. *Rousillon. The* COUNT's *palace.*]

Enter COUNTESS *and* Clown.

Count. It hath happened all as I would have had it, save that he comes not along with her.

Clo. By my troth, I take my young lord to be a very melancholy man.

Count. By what observance, I pray you?

Clo. Why, he will look upon his boot and sing; mend the ruff and sing; ask questions and sing; pick his teeth and sing. I know a man that had this trick of melancholy sold a goodly manor for a song.

Count. Let me see what he writes, and when he means to come. [*Opening a letter.*]

Clo. I have no mind to Isbel since I was at court: our old ling and our Isbels o' the country are nothing like your old ling and your Isbels o' the court: the brains of my Cupid 's knocked out, and I begin to love, as an old man loves money, with no stomach.

Count. What have we here?

Clo. E'en that you have there. *Exit.*

[*Count. reads*] *a letter.* I have sent you a daughter-in-law: she hath recovered the king, and undone me. I have wedded her, not bedded her; and sworn to make the 'not' eternal. You shall hear I am run away: know it before the report come. If there be breadth enough in the world, I will hold a long distance. My duty to you.
Your unfortunate son,
BERTRAM.

This is not well, rash and unbridled boy,
To fly the favours of so good a king;
To pluck his indignation on thy head
By the misprising of a maid too virtuous
For the contempt of empire.

Enter Clown.

Clo. O madam, yonder is heavy news within between two soldiers and my young lady!

Count. What is the matter?

71. **respects,** motives. 72. **appointments,** purposes. 80. **homely stars,** lowly origin. 97. **coragio,** courage.

ACT III. SCENE I. 3. **decision,** combat to decide an issue. 10. **yield,** communicate, produce. 11. **outward,** not having intimate knowledge of things. 12. **the great . . . council.** The New Cambridge editors explain this as an astrological metaphor, defining *figure* as a scheme or table showing the disposition of the heavens at a given time. 13. **self-unable,** impotent. **motion,** guess. 17. **nature,** kind—by birth and position; i.e., young lords. 22. **better fall,** i.e., better places fall vacant (Brigstocke). **fell,** will fall.

Clo. Nay, there is some comfort in the news, some comfort; your son will not be killed so soon as I thought he would.

Count. Why should he be killed?

Clo. So say I, madam, if he run away, as I hear he does: the danger is in standing to 't; that 's the loss of men, though it be the getting of children. Here they come will tell you more: for my part, I only hear your son was run away. [*Exit.*]

Enter HELENA *and* [*the*] *two* [French] Gentlemen.

First Gent. Save you, good madam.
Hel. Madam, my lord is gone, for ever gone!
Sec. Gent. Do not say so.
Count. Think upon patience. Pray you, gentlemen,
I have felt so many quirks of joy and grief,
That the first face of neither, on the start,
Can woman me unto 't: where is my son, I pray you?
Sec. Gent. Madam, he 's gone to serve the duke of Florence:
We met him thitherward; for thence we came,
And, after some dispatch in hand at court,
Thither we bend again.
Hel. Look on his letter, madam; here 's my passport.

[*Reads*] When thou canst get the ring upon my finger which never shall come off, and show me a child begotten of thy body that I am father to, then call me husband: but in such a 'then' I write a 'never.'

This is a dreadful sentence.
Count. Brought you this letter, gentlemen?
First Gent. Ay, madam;
And for the contents' sake are sorry for our pains.
Count. I prithee, lady, have a better cheer;
If thou engrossest all the griefs are thine,
Thou robb'st me of a moiety: he was my son;
But I do wash his name out of my blood,
And thou art all my child. Towards Florence is he?
Sec. Gent. Ay, madam.
Count. And to be a soldier?
Sec. Gent. Such is his noble purpose; and, believe 't,
The duke will lay upon him all the honour
That good convenience claims.
Count. Return you thither?
First Gent. Ay, madam, with the swiftest wing of speed.
Hel. [*Reads*] Till I have no wife, I have nothing in France.
'Tis bitter.
Count. Find you that there?
Hel. Ay, madam.

First Gent. 'Tis but the boldness of his hand, haply, which his heart was not consenting to.

Count. Nothing in France, until he have no wife!
There 's nothing here that is too good for him
But only she; and she deserves a lord
That twenty such rude boys might tend upon
And call her hourly mistress. Who was with him?
First Gent. A servant only, and a gentleman
Which I have sometime known.
Count. Parolles, was it not?
First Gent. Ay, my good lady, he.
Count. A very tainted fellow, and full of wickedness.
My son corrupts a well-derived nature
With his inducement.
First Gent. Indeed, good lady,
The fellow has a deal of that too much,
Which holds him much to have.
Count. Y' are welcome, gentlemen.
I will entreat you, when you see my son,
To tell him that his sword can never win
The honour that he loses: more I'll entreat you
Written to bear along.
Sec. Gent. We serve you, madam,
In that and all your worthiest affairs.
Count. Not so, but as we change our courtesies.
Will you draw near? *Exit* [*with Gentlemen*].
Hel. 'Till I have no wife, I have nothing in France.'
Nothing in France, until he has no wife!
Thou shalt have none, Rousillon, none in France;
Then hast thou all again. Poor lord! is 't I
That chase thee from thy country and expose
Those tender limbs of thine to the event
Of the none-sparing war? and is it I
That drive thee from the sportive court, where thou
Wast shot at with fair eyes, to be the mark
Of smoky muskets? O you leaden messengers,
That ride upon the violent speed of fire,
†Fly with false aim; move the still-peering air,
That sings with piercing; do not touch my lord.
Whoever shoots at him, I set him there;
Whoever charges on his forward breast,
I am the caitiff that do hold him to 't;
And, though I kill him not, I am the cause
His death was so effected: better 'twere
I met the ravin lion when he roar'd
With sharp constraint of hunger; better 'twere
That all the miseries which nature owes
Were mine at once. No, come thou home, Rousillon,
Whence honour but of danger wins a scar,
As oft it loses all: I will be gone;
My being here it is that holds thee hence:
Shall I stay here to do 't? no, no, although
The air of paradise did fan the house
And angels offic'd all: I will be gone,
That pitiful rumour may report my flight,
To consolate thine ear. Come, night; end, day!
For with the dark, poor thief, I'll steal away. *Exit.*

[SCENE III. *Florence. Before the* DUKE'S *palace.*]

Flourish. Enter the DUKE OF FLORENCE, [BERTRAM, COUNT] ROUSILLON, Drum *and* Trumpets, Soldiers, PAROLLES.

Duke. The general of our horse thou art; and we,
Great in our hope, lay our best love and credence
Upon thy promising fortune.
Ber. Sir, it is
A charge too heavy for my strength, but yet
We'll strive to bear it for your worthy sake
To th' extreme edge of hazard.
Duke. Then go thou forth;
And fortune play upon thy prosperous helm,
As thy auspicious mistress!
Ber. This very day,

SCENE II. 14. **ling,** salted codfish; also, lecherous man. 34. **of empire,** of even an emperor. 43. **standing to 't,** standing one's ground (with sexual pun). 53. **woman me,** i.e., make me weep. 68. **griefs are,** griefs that are. 75. **convenience,** propriety. 91. **inducement,** influence (Brigstocke). 93. **holds him,** is of use or advantage to him. 100. **Not so . . . courtesies,** i.e., only as we serve each other—I by giving you entertainment. 113. **still-peering,** always observing (?). Frequently emended to *still-piercing*. 120. **ravin,** ravenous.

SCENE III. 6. **edge of hazard,** limit of peril.

Great Mars, I put myself into thy file:
Make me but like my thoughts, and I shall prove
A lover of thy drum, hater of love. *Exeunt omnes.*

[SCENE IV. *Rousillon. The* COUNT'S *palace.*]

Enter COUNTESS *and* Steward.

Count. Alas! and would you take the letter of her?
Might you not know she would do as she has done,
By sending me a letter? Read it again.

[*Stew. reads the*] *letter.*

I am Saint Jaques' pilgrim, thither gone:
Ambitious love hath so in me offended,
That barefoot plod I the cold ground upon,
With sainted vow my faults to have amended.
Write, write, that from the bloody course of war
My dearest master, your dear son, may hie:
Bless him at home in peace, whilst I from far
His name with zealous fervour sanctify:
His taken labours bid him me forgive;
I, his despiteful Juno, sent him forth
From courtly friends, with camping foes to live,
Where death and danger dogs the heels of worth:
He is too good and fair for death and me;
Whom I myself embrace, to set him free.

Count. Ah, what sharp stings are in her mildest words!
Rinaldo, you did never lack advice so much,
As letting her pass so: had I spoke with her,
I could have well diverted her intents,
Which thus she hath prevented.
Stew. Pardon me, madam:
If I had given you this at over-night,
She might have been o'erta'en; and yet she writes,
Pursuit would be but vain.
Count. What angel shall
Bless this unworthy husband? he cannot thrive,
Unless her prayers, whom heaven delights to hear
And loves to grant, reprieve him from the wrath
Of greatest justice. Write, write, Rinaldo,
To this unworthy husband of his wife;
Let every word weigh heavy of her worth
That he does weigh too light: my greatest grief,
Though little he do feel it, set down sharply.
Dispatch the most convenient messenger:
When haply he shall hear that she is gone,
He will return; and hope I may that she,
Hearing so much, will speed her foot again,
Led hither by pure love. Which of them both
Is dearest to me, I have no skill in sense
To make distinction. Provide this messenger:
My heart is heavy and mine age is weak;
Grief would have tears, and sorrow bids me speak.
Exeunt.

[SCENE V. *Florence. Without the walls.*] *A tucket afar off.*

Enter old Widow *of Florence, her Daughter* [DIANA], VIOLENTA, *and* MARIANA, *with other* Citizens.

Wid. Nay, come; for if they do approach the city, we shall lose all the sight.

Dia. They say the French count has done most honourable service.

Wid. It is reported that he has taken their greatest commander; and that with his own hand he slew the duke's brother. [*Tucket.*] We have lost our labour; they are gone a contrary way: hark! you may know by their trumpets.

Mar. Come, let 's return again, and suffice ourselves with the report of it. Well, Diana, take heed of this French earl: the honour of a maid is her name; and no legacy is so rich as honesty.

Wid. I have told my neighbour how you have been solicited by a gentleman his companion.

Mar. I know that knave; hang him! one Parolles: a filthy officer he is in those suggestions for the young earl. Beware of them, Diana; their promises, enticements, oaths, tokens, and all these engines of lust, are not the things they go under: many a maid hath been seduced by them; and the misery is, example, that so terrible shows in the wrack of maidenhood, cannot for all that dissuade succession, but that they are limed with the twigs that threatens them. I hope I need not to advise you further; but I hope your own grace will keep you where you are, though there were no further danger known but the modesty which is so lost.

Dia. You shall not need to fear me.

Wid. I hope so.

Enter HELENA [*disguised like a Pilgrim*].

Look, here comes a pilgrim: I know she will lie at my house; thither they send one another: I'll question her. God save you, pilgrim! whither are you bound?

Hel. To Saint Jaques le Grand.
Where do the palmers lodge, I do beseech you?
Wid. At the Saint Francis here beside the port.
Hel. Is this the way?
Wid. Ay, marry, is 't. (*A march afar.*) Hark you! they come this way.
If you will tarry, holy pilgrim,
But till the troops come by,
I will conduct you where you shall be lodg'd;
The rather, for I think I know your hostess
As ample as myself.
Hel. Is it yourself?
Wid. If you shall please so, pilgrim.
Hel. I thank you, and will stay upon your leisure.
Wid. You came, I think, from France?
Hel. I did so.
Wid. Here you shall see a countryman of yours
That has done worthy service.
Hel. His name, I pray you.
Dia. The Count Rousillon: know you such a one?
Hel. But by the ear, that hears most nobly of him:
His face I know not.
Dia. Whatsome'er he is,
He 's bravely taken here. He stole from France,
As 'tis reported, for the king had married him
Against his liking: think you it is so?
Hel. Ay, surely, mere the truth: I know his lady.

9. **file,** army.
SCENE IV. 4. **Saint Jaques' pilgrim,** identified with the shrine of St. James of Compostella in Spain. 12. **taken,** undertaken. 13. **despiteful Juno,** an allusion to Juno's persecution of Hercules by assigning him the twelve labors. 17. **Whom,** i.e., *death.* 23. **at over-night,** last night.
SCENE V. *Stage Direction:* **tucket,** preliminary signal given on a trumpet. 22. **go under,** pretend to be. 23-25. **example . . . succession,** the terrifying example of what happens with the loss of virginity cannot dissuade another from a similar course. 46. **ample,** fully, completely.

Dia. There is a gentleman that serves the count
Reports but coarsely of her.
Hel. What 's his name?
Dia. Monsieur Parolles.
Hel. O, I believe with him,
In argument of praise, or to the worth
Of the great count himself, she is too mean
To have her name repeated: all her deserving
Is a reserved honesty, and that
I have not heard examin'd.
Dia. Alas, poor lady!
'Tis a hard bondage to become the wife
Of a detesting lord.
Wid. I warrant, good creature, wheresoe'er she is,
Her heart weighs sadly: this young maid might do her
A shrewd turn, if she pleas'd.
Hel. How do you mean?
May be the amorous count solicits her
In the unlawful purpose.
Wid. He does indeed;
And brokes with all that can in such a suit
Corrupt the tender honour of a maid:
But she is arm'd for him and keeps her guard
In honestest defence.
Mar. The gods forbid else!
Wid. So, now they come:

Drum and Colours. Enter [BERTRAM] COUNT ROUSILLON, PAROLLES, *and the whole army.*

That is Antonio, the duke's eldest son;
That, Escalus.
Hel. Which is the Frenchman?
Dia. He;
That with the plume: 'tis a most gallant fellow.
I would he lov'd his wife: if he were honester
He were much goodlier: is 't not a handsome gentleman?
Hel. I like him well.
Dia. 'Tis pity he is not honest: yond 's that same knave
That leads him to these places: were I his lady,
I would poison that vile rascal.
Hel. Which is he?
Dia. That jack-an-apes with scarfs: why is he melancholy?
Hel. Perchance he 's hurt i' the battle.
Par. Lose our drum! well.
Mar. He 's shrewdly vexed at something: look, he has spied us.
Wid. Marry, hang you!
Mar. And your courtesy, for a ring-carrier!
Exeunt [*Bertram, Parolles, and army*].
Wid. The troop is past. Come, pilgrim, I will bring you
Where you shall host: of enjoin'd penitents
There 's four or five, to great Saint Jaques bound,
Already at my house.
Hel. I humbly thank you:
Please it this matron and this gentle maid
To eat with us to-night, the charge and thanking
Shall be for me; and, to requite you further,
I will bestow some precepts of this virgin
Worthy the note.
Both. We'll take your offer kindly.
Exeunt.

[SCENE VI. *Camp before Florence.*]

Enter [BERTRAM] COUNT ROUSILLON *and the* [*two*] Frenchmen, *as at first.*

Sec. Lord. Nay, good my lord, put him to 't; let him have his way.

First Lord. If your lordship find him not a hilding, hold me no more in your respect.

Sec. Lord. On my life, my lord, a bubble.

Ber. Do you think I am so far deceived in him?

Sec. Lord. Believe it, my lord, in mine own direct knowledge, without any malice, but to speak of him as my kinsman, he 's a most notable coward, an infinite and endless liar, an hourly promise-breaker, the owner of no one good quality worthy your lordship's entertainment.

First Lord. It were fit you knew him; lest, reposing too far in his virtue, which he hath not, he might at some great and trusty business in a main danger fail you.

Ber. I would I knew in what particular action to try him.

First Lord. None better than to let him fetch off his drum, which you hear him so confidently undertake to do.

Sec. Lord. I, with a troop of Florentines, will suddenly surprise him; such I will have, whom I am sure he knows not from the enemy: we will bind and hoodwink him so, that he shall suppose no other but that he is carried into the leaguer of the adversaries, when we bring him to our own tents. Be but your lordship present at his examination: if he do not, for the promise of his life and in the highest compulsion of base fear, offer to betray you and deliver all the intelligence in his power against you, and that with the divine forfeit of his soul upon oath, never trust my judgement in any thing.

First Lord. O, for the love of laughter, let him fetch his drum; he says he has a stratagem for 't: when your lordship sees the bottom of his success in 't, and to what metal this counterfeit lump of ore will be melted, if you give him not John Drum's entertainment, your inclining cannot be removed. Here he comes.

Enter PAROLLES.

Sec. Lord. [*Aside to Ber.*] O, for the love of laughter, hinder not the honour of his design: let him fetch off his drum in any hand.

Ber. How now, monsieur! this drum sticks sorely in your disposition.

First Lord. A pox on 't, let it go; 'tis but a drum.

Par. 'But a drum'! is 't 'but a drum'? A drum so lost! There was excellent command,—to charge in with our horse upon our own wings, and to rend our own soldiers!

First Lord. That was not to be blamed in the command of the service: it was a disaster of war that

65. **reserved honesty,** well-guarded chastity. 66. **examin'd,** doubted. 95. **ring-carrier,** go-between. 97. **host,** lodge. **enjoin'd,** obligated by oath.
SCENE VI. 4. **hilding,** good-for-nothing. 20. **fetch off,** recapture. 26. **hoodwink,** blindfold. 27. **leaguer,** camp. 41. **John Drum's entertainment,** slang phrase for a thorough beating and unceremonious dismissal. John Marston used the phrase as title for a satirical comedy, 1600.

Cæsar himself could not have prevented, if he had been there to command.

Ber. Well, we cannot greatly condemn our success: some dishonour we had in the loss of that drum; but it is not to be recovered.

Par. It might have been recovered.

Ber. It might; but it is not now.

Par. It is to be recovered: but that the merit of service is seldom attributed to the true and exact performer, I would have that drum or another, or 'hic jacet.'

Ber. Why, if you have a stomach, to 't, monsieur: if you think your mystery in stratagem can bring this instrument of honour again into his native quarter, be magnanimous in the enterprise and go on; I will grace the attempt for a worthy exploit: if you speed well in it, the duke shall both speak of it, and extend to you what further becomes his greatness, even to the utmost syllable of your worthiness.

Par. By the hand of a soldier, I will undertake it.

Ber. But you must not now slumber in it.

Par. I'll about it this evening: and I will presently pen down my dilemmas, encourage myself in my certainty, put myself into my mortal preparation; and by midnight look to hear further from me.

Ber. May I be bold to acquaint his grace you are gone about it?

Par. I know not what the success will be, my lord; but the attempt I vow.

Ber. I know th' art valiant; and, to the possibility of thy soldiership, will subscribe for thee. Farewell.

Par. I love not many words. *Exit.*

Sec. Lord. No more than a fish loves water. Is not this a strange fellow, my lord, that so confidently seems to undertake this business, which he knows is not to be done; damns himself to do and dares better be damned than to do 't?

First Lord. You do not know him, my lord, as we do: certain it is, that he will steal himself into a man's favour and for a week escape a great deal of discoveries; but when you find him out, you have him ever after.

Ber. Why, do you think he will make no deed at all of this that so seriously he does address himself unto?

Sec. Lord. None in the world; but return with an invention and clap upon you two or three probable lies: but we have almost embossed him; you shall see his fall to-night; for indeed he is not for your lordship's respect.

First Lord. We'll make you some sport with the fox ere we case him. He was first smoked by the old lord Lafew: when his disguise and he is parted, tell me what a sprat you shall find him; which you shall see this very night.

Sec. Lord. I must go look my twigs: he shall be
caught.

Ber. Your brother he shall go along with me.

Sec. Lord. As 't please your lordship; I'll leave you.
[*Exit.*]

Ber. Now will I lead you to the house, and show
you
The lass I spoke of.

First Lord. But you say she 's honest.

Ber. That 's all the fault: I spoke with her but once
And found her wondrous cold; but I sent to her,
By this same coxcomb that we have i' th' wind,
Tokens and letters which she did re-send;
And this is all I have done. She 's a fair creature:
Will you go see her?

First Lord. With all my heart, my lord.
Exeunt.

[SCENE VII. *Florence. The* Widow's *house.*]

Enter HELENA *and* Widow.

Hel. If you misdoubt me that I am not she,
I know not how I shall assure you further,
But I shall lose the grounds I work upon.

Wid. Though my estate be fall'n, I was well born,
Nothing acquainted with these businesses;
And would not put my reputation now
In any staining act.

Hel. Nor would I wish you.
First, give me trust, the count he is my husband,
And what to your sworn counsel I have spoken
Is so from word to word; and then you cannot,
By the good aid that I of you shall borrow,
Err in bestowing it.

Wid. I should believe you;
For you have show'd me that which well approves
Y' are great in fortune.

Hel. Take this purse of gold,
And let me buy your friendly help thus far,
Which I will over-pay and pay again
When I have found it. The count he wooes your
daughter,
Lays down his wanton siege before her beauty,
Resolv'd to carry her: let her in fine consent,
As we'll direct her how 'tis best to bear it.
Now his important blood will nought deny
That she'll demand: a ring the county wears,
That downward hath succeeded in his house
From son to son, some four or five descents
Since the first father wore it: this ring he holds
In most rich choice; yet in his idle fire,
To buy his will, it would not seem too dear,
Howe'er repented after.

Wid. Now I see
The bottom of your purpose.

Hel. You see it lawful, then: it is no more,
But that your daughter, ere she seems as won,
Desires this ring; appoints him an encounter;
In fine, delivers me to fill the time,
Herself most chastely absent: after this,
To marry her, I'll add three thousand crowns
To what is past already.

Wid. I have yielded:
Instruct my daughter how she shall persever,
That time and place with this deceit so lawful
May prove coherent. Every night he comes
With musics of all sorts and songs compos'd
To her unworthiness: it nothing steads us
To chide him from our eaves; for he persists

66. **'hic jacet,'** here lies; the beginning phrase of tomb inscriptions. 68. **mystery,** skill. 80. **pen . . . dilemmas,** encourage myself in my certainty, i.e., by writing down all the contrary arguments in order to argue them out in my own favor (Brigstocke). 81-82. **mortal preparation,** extreme unction; or, death-dealing readiness. 88. **possibility,** capacity. 107. **embossed,** driven to exhaustion (hunting term). 111. **case,** strip, unmask. **smoked,** found out. 113. **sprat,** small fish. 115. **look my twigs,** a figure from catching birds by liming the twigs.
SCENE VII. 17. **it,** i.e., fortune. 19. **in fine,** at length. 21. **important,** importunate. 26. **most rich choice,** highest estimation.

As if his life lay on 't.

Hel. Why then to-night
Let us assay our plot; which, if it speed,
Is wicked meaning in a lawful deed
And lawful meaning in a lawful act,
Where both not sin, and yet a sinful fact:
But let 's about it. [*Exeunt.*]

ACT IV.

[SCENE I. *Without the Florentine camp.*]

Enter one of the Frenchmen [*the* Second Lord] *with five or six other* Soldiers, *in ambush.*

Sec. Lord. He can come no other way but by this hedge-corner. When you sally upon him, speak what terrible language you will: though you understand it not yourselves, no matter; for we must not seem to understand him, unless some one among us whom we must produce for an interpreter.

First Sold. Good captain, let me be the interpreter.

Sec. Lord. Art not acquainted with him? knows he not thy voice?

First Sold. No, sir, I warrant you.

Sec. Lord. But what linsey-woolsey hast thou to speak to us again?

First Sold. E'en such as you speak to me.

Sec. Lord. He must think us some band of strangers i' the adversary's entertainment. Now he hath a smack of all neighbouring languages; therefore we must every one be a man of his own fancy, not to know what we speak one to another; so we seem to know, is to know straight our purpose: choughs' language, gabble enough, and good enough. As for you, interpreter, you must seem very politic. But couch, ho! here he comes, to beguile two hours in a sleep, and then to return and swear the lies he forges.

[*They hide.*] *Enter* PAROLLES.

Par. Ten o'clock: within these three hours 'twill be time enough to go home. What shall I say I have done? It must be a very plausive invention that carries it: they begin to smoke me; and disgraces have of late knocked too often at my door. I find my tongue is too foolhardy; but my heart hath the fear of Mars before it and of his creatures, not daring the reports of my tongue.

Sec. Lord. This is the first truth that e'er thine own tongue was guilty of.

Par. What the devil should move me to undertake the recovery of this drum, being not ignorant of the impossibility, and knowing I had no such purpose? I must give myself some hurts, and say I got them in exploit: yet slight ones will not carry it; they will say, 'Came you off with so little?' and great ones I dare not give. Wherefore, what 's the instance? Tongue, I must put you into a butter-woman's mouth and buy myself another of Bajazet's mule, if you prattle me into these perils.

Sec. Lord. Is it possible he should know what he is, and be that he is?

Par. I would the cutting of my garments would serve the turn, or the breaking of my Spanish sword.

Sec. Lord. We cannot afford you so.

Par. Or the baring of my beard; and to say it was in stratagem.

Sec. Lord. 'Twould not do.

Par. Or to drown my clothes, and say I was stripped.

Sec. Lord. Hardly serve.

Par. Though I swore I leaped from the window of the citadel—

Sec. Lord. How deep?

Par. Thirty fathom.

Sec. Lord. Three great oaths would scarce make that be believed.

Par. I would I had any drum of the enemy's: I would swear I recovered it.

Sec. Lord. You shall hear one anon.

Par. A drum now of the enemy's,— *Alarum within.*

Sec. Lord. Throca movousus, cargo, cargo, cargo.

All. Cargo, cargo, cargo, villianda par corbo, cargo.

Par. O, ransom, ransom! do not hide mine eyes.
[*They seize and blindfold him.*]

First Sold. Boskos thromuldo boskos.

Par. I know you are the Muskos' regiment:
And I shall lose my life for want of language:
If there be here German, or Dane, low Dutch,
Italian, or French, let him speak to me; I'll
Discover that which shall undo the Florentine.

First Sold. Boskos vauvado: I understand thee, and can speak thy tongue. Kerelybonto, sir, betake thee to thy faith, for seventeen poniards are at thy bosom.

Par. O!

First Sold. O, pray, pray, pray! Manka revania dulche.

Sec. Lord. Oscorbidulchos volivorco.

First Sold. The general is content to spare thee yet;
And, hoodwink'd as thou art, will lead thee on
To gather from thee: haply thou mayst inform
Something to save thy life.

Par. O, let me live!
And all the secrets of our camp I'll show,
Their force, their purposes; nay, I'll speak that
Which you will wonder at.

First Sold. But wilt thou faithfully?

Par. If I do not, damn me.

First Sold. Acordo linta.
Come on; thou art granted space.
Exit [*with Parolles guarded*]. *A short alarum within.*

Sec. Lord. Go, tell the Count Rousillon, and my brother,
We have caught the woodcock, and will keep him muffled
Till we do hear from them.

Sec. Sold. Captain, I will.

Sec. Lord. 'A will betray us all unto ourselves:
Inform on that.

Sec. Sold. So I will, sir.

Sec. Lord. Till then I'll keep him dark and safely lock'd. *Exeunt.*

[SCENE II. *Florence. The* Widow's *house.*]

ACT IV. SCENE I. 13. **linsey-woolsey,** a fabric woven from wool and flax; figuratively, nonsense. 16. **entertainment,** employment. 22. **choughs',** small, chattering species of the crow family, the jackdaw. 45. **butter-woman's,** i.e., of a proverbial scold. 46. **of Bajazet's mule,** i.e., from a Turkish mule, since mules are notoriously mute. (Many emendations have been proposed.) 53. **afford,** let you off. 54. **baring,** shaving. 76. **Muskos',** Muscovites. 91. **gather,** get information. **haply,** perhaps. 98. **space,** time. 100. **woodcock,** proverbially stupid bird.

Enter BERTRAM *and the Maid called* DIANA.

Ber. They told me that your name was Fontibell.
Dia. No, my good lord, Diana.
Ber. Titled goddess;
And worth it, with addition! But, fair soul,
In your fine frame hath love no quality?
If the quick fire of youth light not your mind,
You are no maiden, but a monument:
When you are dead, you should be such a one
As you are now, for you are cold and stern;
And now you should be as your mother was
When your sweet self was got.
Dia. She then was honest.
Ber. So should you be.
Dia. No:
My mother did but duty; such, my lord,
As you owe to your wife.
Ber. No more o' that;
I prithee, do not strive against my vows:
I was compell'd to her; but I love thee
By love's own sweet constraint, and will for ever
Do thee all rights of service.
Dia. Ay, so you serve us
Till we serve you; but when you have our roses,
You barely leave our thorns to prick ourselves
And mock us with our bareness.
Ber. How have I sworn!
Dia. 'Tis not the many oaths that makes the truth,
But the plain single vow that is vow'd true.
What is not holy, that we swear not by,
But take the High'st to witness: then, pray you, tell me,
If I should swear by Jove's great attributes,
I lov'd you dearly, would you believe my oaths,
When I did love you ill? This has no holding,
To swear by him whom I protest to love,
That I will work against him: therefore your oaths
Are words and poor conditions, but unseal'd,
At least in my opinion.
Ber. Change it, change it;
Be not so holy-cruel: love is holy;
And my integrity ne'er knew the crafts
That you do charge men with. Stand no more off,
But give thyself unto my sick desires,
Who then recover: say thou art mine, and ever
My love as it begins shall so persever.
Dia. †I see that men may rope 's in such a snare
That we'll forsake ourselves. Give me that ring.
Ber. I'll lend it thee, my dear; but have no power
To give it from me.
Dia. Will you not, my lord?
Ber. It is an honour 'longing to our house,
Bequeathed down from many ancestors;
Which were the greatest obloquy i' th' world
In me to lose.
Dia. Mine honour 's such a ring:
My chastity 's the jewel of our house,
Bequeathed down from many ancestors;
Which were the greatest obloquy i' th' world
In me to lose: thus your own proper wisdom
Brings in the champion Honour on my part,
Against your vain assault.
Ber. Here, take my ring:
My house, mine honour, yea, my life, be thine,
And I'll be bid by thee.
Dia. When midnight comes, knock at my chamber-window:
I'll order take my mother shall not hear.
Now will I charge you in the band of truth,
When you have conquer'd my yet maiden bed,
Remain there but an hour, nor speak to me:
My reasons are most strong; and you shall know them
When back again this ring shall be deliver'd:
And on your finger in the night I'll put
Another ring, that what in time proceeds
May token to the future our past deeds.
Adieu, till then; then, fail not. You have won
A wife of me, though there my hope be done.
Ber. A heaven on earth I have won by wooing thee. [*Exit.*]
Dia. For which live long to thank both heaven and me!
You may so in the end.
My mother told me just how he would woo,
As if she sat in 's heart; she says all men
Have the like oaths: he had sworn to marry me
When his wife 's dead; therefore I'll lie with him
When I am buried. Since Frenchmen are so braid,
Marry that will, I live and die a maid:
Only in this disguise I think 't no sin
To cozen him that would unjustly win. *Exit.*

[SCENE III. *The Florentine camp.*]

Enter the two French Captains *and some two or three* Soldiers.

First Lord. You have not given him his mother's letter?

Sec. Lord. I have delivered it an hour since: there is something in 't that stings his nature; for on the reading it he changed almost into another man.

First Lord. He has much worthy blame laid upon him for shaking off so good a wife and so sweet a lady.

Sec. Lord. Especially he hath incurred the everlasting displeasure of the king, who had even tuned his bounty to sing happiness to him. I will tell you a thing, but you shall let it dwell darkly with you.

First Lord. When you have spoken it, 'tis dead, and I am the grave of it.

Sec. Lord. He hath perverted a young gentlewoman here in Florence, of a most chaste renown; and this night he fleshes his will in the spoil of her honour: he hath given her his monumental ring, and thinks himself made in the unchaste composition.

First Lord. Now, God delay our rebellion! as we are ourselves, what things are we!

Sec. Lord. Merely our own traitors. And as in the common course of all treasons, we still see them reveal themselves, till they attain to their abhorred ends, so he that in this action contrives against his own nobility, in his proper stream o'erflows himself.

First Lord. Is it not meant damnable in us, to be

SCENE II. 4. **quality,** position. 10. **got,** begotten. 11. **honest,** chaste. 27. **holding,** consistency. 30. **but unseal'd,** merely invalid. 38. **rope 's . . . snare,** entrap us in such a snare. F, Globe: *ropes, scarre.* 73. **braid,** deceitful, loose (?).

SCENE III. 22. **made,** a made man. **composition,** bargain. 24. **are ourselves,** unaided by God. 37. **company,** companion. **anatomized,** trumpeters of our unlawful intents? We shall not then have his company to-night?

Sec. Lord. Not till after midnight; for he is dieted to his hour.

First Lord. That approaches apace; I would gladly have him see his company anatomized, that he might take a measure of his own judgements, wherein so curiously he had set this counterfeit.

Sec. Lord. We will not meddle with him till he come; for his presence must be the whip of the other.

First Lord. In the mean time, what hear you of these wars?

Sec. Lord. I hear there is an overture of peace.

First Lord. Nay, I assure you, a peace concluded.

Sec. Lord. What will Count Rousillon do then? will he travel higher, or return again into France?

First Lord. I perceive, by this demand, you are not altogether of his council.

Sec. Lord. Let it be forbid, sir; so should I be a great deal of his act.

First Lord. Sir, his wife some two months since fled from his house: her pretence is a pilgrimage to Saint Jaques le Grand; which holy undertaking with most austere sanctimony she accomplished; and, there residing, the tenderness of her nature became as a prey to her grief; in fine, made a groan of her last breath, and now she sings in heaven.

Sec. Lord. How is this justified?

First Lord. The stronger part of it by her own letters, which makes her story true, even to the point of her death: her death itself, which could not be her office to say is come, was faithfully confirmed by the rector of the place.

Sec. Lord. Hath the count all this intelligence?

First Lord. Ay, and the particular confirmations, point from point, to the full arming of the verity.

Sec. Lord. I am heartily sorry that he'll be glad of this.

First Lord. How mightily sometimes we make us comforts of our losses!

Sec. Lord. And how mightily some other times we drown our gain in tears! The great dignity that his valour hath here acquired for him shall at home be encountered with a shame as ample.

First Lord. The web of our life is of a mingled yarn, good and ill together: our virtues would be proud, if our faults whipped them not; and our crimes would despair, if they were not cherished by our virtues.

Enter a [Servant *as*] Messenger.

How now! where 's your master?

Serv. He met the duke in the street, sir, of whom he hath taken a solemn leave: his lordship will next morning for France. The duke hath offered him letters of commendations to the king.

Sec. Lord. They shall be no more than needful there, if they were more than they can commend.

First Lord. They cannot be too sweet for the king's tartness. Here 's his lordship now.

Enter [BERTRAM] COUNT ROUSILLON.

How now, my lord! is 't not after midnight?

Ber. I have to-night dispatched sixteen businesses, a month's length a-piece, by an abstract of success: I have congied with the duke, done my adieu with his nearest; buried a wife, mourned for her; writ to my lady mother I am returning; entertained my convoy; and between these main parcels of dispatch effected many nicer needs: the last was the greatest, but that I have not ended yet.

Sec. Lord. If the business be of any difficulty, and this morning your departure hence, it requires haste of your lordship.

Ber. I mean, the business is not ended, as fearing to hear of it hereafter. But shall we have this dialogue between the fool and the soldier? Come, bring forth this counterfeit module, has deceived me, like a double-meaning prophesier.

Sec. Lord. Bring him forth. [*Exeunt Soldiers.*] Has sat i' the stocks all night, poor gallant knave.

Ber. No matter; his heels have deserved it, in usurping his spurs so long. How does he carry himself?

Sec. Lord. I have told your lordship already, the stocks carry him. But to answer you as you would be understood; he weeps like a wench that had shed her milk: he hath confessed himself to Morgan, whom he supposes to be a friar, from the time of his remembrance to this very instant disaster of his setting i' the stocks: and what think you he hath confessed?

Ber. Nothing of me, has 'a?

Sec. Lord. His confession is taken, and it shall be read to his face: if your lordship be in 't, as I believe you are, you must have the patience to hear it.

Enter PAROLLES [*guarded*] *with* [First Soldier *as*] *his Interpreter*.

Ber. A plague upon him! muffled! he can say nothing of me.

First Lord. Hush, hush! Hoodman comes! Portotartarosa.

First Sold. He calls for the tortures: what will you say without 'em?

Par. I will confess what I know without constraint: if ye pinch me like a pasty, I can say no more.

First Sold. Bosko chimurcho.

First Lord. Boblibindo chicurmurco.

First Sold. You are a merciful general. Our general bids you answer to what I shall ask you out of a note.

Par. And truly, as I hope to live.

First Sold. [*Reads*] 'First demand of him how many horse the duke is strong.' What say you to that?

Par. Five or six thousand; but very weak and unserviceable: the troops are all scattered, and the commanders very poor rogues, upon my reputation and credit and as I hope to live.

First Sold. Shall I set down your answer so?

Par. Do: I'll take the sacrament on 't, how and which way you will.

Ber. All 's one to him. What a past-saving slave is this!

First Lord. Y' are deceived, my lord: this is Monsieur Parolles, the gallant militarist,—that was his own phrase,—that had the whole theoric of war in the knot of his scarf, and the practice in the chape of his dagger.

Sec. Lord. I will never trust a man again for keeping

dissected. 40. **this counterfeit,** i.e., Parolles. 50. **higher,** farther. 56. **pretence,** intent. 64. **justified,** made certain. 103. **entertained my convoy,** arranged my transportation. 114. **module,** mere image. 123. **shed,** spilled. 136. **Hoodman comes,** customary call in the game of blindman's buff. 164. **chape,** scabbard-tip.

his sword clean, nor believe he can have every thing in him by wearing his apparel neatly.

First Sold. Well, that 's set down.

Par. Five or six thousand horse, I said,—I will say true,—or thereabouts, set down, for I'll speak truth.

First Lord. He 's very near the truth in this.

Ber. But I con him no thanks for 't, in the nature he delivers it.

Par. Poor rogues, I pray you, say.

First Sold. Well, that 's set down.

Par. I humbly thank you, sir: a truth 's a truth, the rogues are marvellous poor.

First Sold. [*Reads*] 'Demand of him, of what strength they are a-foot.' What say you to that?

Par. By my troth, sir, if I were to live this present hour, I will tell true. Let me see: Spurio, a hundred and fifty; Sebastian, so many; Corambus, so many; Jaques, so many; Guiltian, Cosmo, Lodowick, and Gratii, two hundred fifty each; mine own company, Chitopher, Vaumond, Bentii, two hundred fifty each: so that the muster-file, rotten and sound, upon my life, amounts not to fifteen thousand poll; half of the which dare not shake the snow from off their cassocks, lest they shake themselves to pieces.

Ber. What shall be done to him?

First Lord. Nothing, but let him have thanks. Demand of him my condition, and what credit I have with the duke.

First Sold. Well, that 's set down. [*Reads*] 'You shall demand of him, whether one Captain Dumain be i' the camp, a Frenchman; what his reputation is with the duke; what his valour, honesty, and expertness in wars; or whether he thinks it were not possible, with well-weighing sums of gold, to corrupt him to a revolt.' What say you to this? what do you know of it?

Par. I beseech you, let me answer to the particular of the inter'gatories: demand them singly.

First Sold. Do you know this Captain Dumain?

Par. I know him: 'a was a botcher's 'prentice in Paris, from whence he was whipped for getting the shrieve's fool with child,—a dumb innocent, that could not say him nay.

Ber. Nay, by your leave, hold your hands; though I know his brains are forfeit to the next tile that falls.

First Sold. Well, is this captain in the Duke of Florence's camp?

Par. Upon my knowledge, he is, and lousy.

First Lord. Nay, look not so upon me; we shall hear of your lordship anon.

First Sold. What is his reputation with the duke?

Par. The duke knows him for no other but a poor officer of mine; and writ to me this other day to turn him out o' the band: I think I have his letter in my pocket.

First Sold. Marry, we'll search.

Par. In good sadness, I do not know; either it is there, or it is upon a file with the duke's other letters in my tent.

First Sold. Here 'tis; here 's a paper: shall I read it to you?

Par. I do not know if it be it or no.

Ber. Our interpreter does it well.

First Lord. Excellently.

First Sold. [*Reads*] 'Dian, the count 's a fool, and
full of gold,'—

Par. That is not the duke's letter, sir; that is an advertisement to a proper maid in Florence, one Diana, to take heed of the allurement of one Count Rousillon, a foolish idle boy, but for all that very ruttish: I pray you, sir, put it up again.

First Sold. Nay, I'll read it first, by your favour.

Par. My meaning in 't, I protest, was very honest in the behalf of the maid; for I knew the young count to be a dangerous and lascivious boy, who is a whale to virginity and devours up all the fry it finds.

Ber. Damnable both-sides rogue!

First Sold. [*Reads*] 'When he swears oaths, bid him
drop gold, and take it;
After he scores, he never pays the score:
Half won is match well made; match, and well
make it;
He ne'er pays after-debts, take it before;
And say a soldier, Dian, told thee this,
Men are to mell with, boys are not to kiss:
For count of this, the count 's a fool, I know it,
Who pays before, but not when he does owe it.
Thine, as he vowed to thee in thine ear,
PAROLLES.'

Ber. He shall be whipped through the army with this rhyme in 's forehead.

Sec. Lord. This is your devoted friend, sir, the manifold linguist and the armipotent soldier.

Ber. I could endure any thing before but a cat, and now he 's a cat to me.

First Sold. I perceive, sir, by our general's looks, we shall be fain to hang you.

Par. My life, sir, in any case: not that I am afraid to die; but that, my offences being many, I would repent out the remainder of nature: let me live, sir, in a dungeon, i' the stocks, or any where, so I may live.

First Sold. We'll see what may be done, so you confess freely; therefore, once more to this Captain Dumain: you have answered to his reputation with the duke and to his valour: what is his honesty?

Par. He will steal, sir, an egg out of a cloister: for rapes and ravishments he parallels Nessus: he professes not keeping of oaths; in breaking 'em he is stronger than Hercules: he will lie, sir, with such volubility, that you would think truth were a fool: drunkenness is his best virtue, for he will be swine-drunk; and in his sleep he does little harm, save to his bed-clothes about him; but they know his conditions and lay him in straw. I have but little more to say, sir, of his honesty: he has every thing that an honest man should not have; what an honest man should have, he has nothing.

First Lord. I begin to love him for this.

Ber. For this description of thine honesty? A pox upon him for me, he 's more and more a cat.

First Sold. What say you to his expertness in war?

Par. Faith, sir, has led the drum before the English tragedians; to belie him, I will not, and more of his soldiership I know not; except, in that country he had the honour to be the officer at a place there called Mile-end, to instruct for the doubling of files: I would

211. **botcher's,** mender's, especially a tailor who makes repairs. 213. **shrieve's fool,** feeble-minded girl in the sheriff's custody. 240. **advertisement,** warning. 257. **mell,** meddle. 265. **armipotent,** powerful in arms. 272. **remainder of nature,** i.e., what is left of my life. 281. **Nessus,** a centaur who offered violence to the wife of Hercules. 298-299. **led . . . tragedians.** It was a custom of actors to parade the street before the performance of a play. 302. **Mile-end,** place near London where the trainbands were regularly exercised. 303. **doubling of files,**

do the man what honour I can, but of this I am not certain.

First Lord. He hath out-villained villany so far, that the rarity redeems him.

Ber. A pox on him, he 's a cat still.

First Sold. His qualities being at this poor price, I need not to ask you if gold will corrupt him to revolt.

Par. Sir, for a cardecue he will sell the fee-simple of his salvation, the inheritance of it; and cut the entail from all remainders, and a perpetual succession for it perpetually.

First Sold. What 's his brother, the other Captain Dumain?

Sec. Lord. Why does he ask him of me?

First Sold. What 's he?

Par. E'en a crow o' the same nest; not altogether so great as the first in goodness, but greater a great deal in evil: he excels his brother for a coward, yet his brother is reputed one of the best that is: in a retreat he outruns any lackey; marry, in coming on he has the cramp.

First Sold. If your life be saved, will you undertake to betray the Florentine?

Par. Ay, and the captain of his horse, Count Rousillon.

First Sold. I'll whisper with the general, and know his pleasure.

Par. [*Aside*] I'll no more drumming; a plague of all drums! Only to seem to deserve well, and to beguile the supposition of that lascivious young boy the count, have I run into this danger. Yet who would have suspected an ambush where I was taken?

First Sold. There is no remedy, sir, but you must die: the general says, you that have so traitorously discovered the secrets of your army and made such pestiferous reports of men very nobly held, can serve the world for no honest use; therefore you must die. Come, headsman, off with his head.

Par. O Lord, sir, let me live, or let me see my death!

First Sold. That shall you, and take your leave of all your friends. [*Unblinding him.*] So, look about you: know you any here?

Ber. Good morrow, noble captain.

Sec. Lord. God bless you, Captain Parolles.

First Lord. God save you, noble captain.

Sec. Lord. Captain, what greeting will you to my Lord Lafew? I am for France.

First Lord. Good captain, will you give me a copy of the sonnet you writ to Diana in behalf of the Count Rousillon? an I were not a very coward, I 'ld compel it of you: but fare you well.

Exeunt [*Bertram and Lords*].

First Sold. You are undone, captain, all but your scarf; that has a knot on 't yet.

Par. Who cannot be crushed with a plot?

First Sold. If you could find out a country where but women were that had received so much shame, you might begin an impudent nation. Fare ye well, sir; I am for France too: we shall speak of you there.

Exit [*with Soldiers*].

Par. Yet am I thankful: if my heart were great,
'Twould burst at this. Captain I'll be no more;
But I will eat and drink, and sleep as soft
As captain shall: simply the thing I am
Shall make me live. Who knows himself a braggart,
Let him fear this, for it will come to pass
That every braggart shall be found an ass.
Rust, sword! cool, blushes! and, Parolles, live
Safest in shame! being fool'd, by fool'ry thrive!
There 's place and means for every man alive.:
I'll after them. *Exit.*

[SCENE IV. *Florence. The* Widow's *house.*]

Enter HELENA, Widow, *and* DIANA.

Hel. That you may well perceive I have not wrong'd you,
One of the greatest in the Christian world
Shall be my surety; 'fore whose throne 'tis needful,
Ere I can perfect mine intents, to kneel:
Time was, I did him a desired office,
Dear almost as his life; which gratitude
Through flinty Tartar's bosom would peep forth,
And answer, thanks: I duly am inform'd
His grace is at Marseilles; to which place
We have convenient convoy. You must know,
I am supposed dead: the army breaking,
My husband hies him home; where, heaven aiding,
And by the leave of my good lord the king,
We'll be before our welcome.

Wid. Gentle madam,
You never had a servant to whose trust
Your business was more welcome.

Hel. Nor you, mistress,
Ever a friend whose thoughts more truly labour
To recompense your love: doubt not but heaven
Hath brought me up to be your daughter's dower,
As it hath fated her to be my motive
And helper to a husband. But, O strange men!
That can such sweet use make of what they hate,
When saucy trusting of the cozen'd thoughts
Defiles the pitchy night: so lust doth play
With what it loathes for that which is away.
But more of this hereafter. You, Diana,
Under my poor instructions yet must suffer
Something in my behalf.

Dia. Let death and honesty
Go with your impositions, I am yours
Upon your will to suffer.

Hel. Yet, I pray you:
But with the word the time will bring on summer,
When briers shall have leaves as well as thorns,
And be as sweet as sharp. We must away;
Our waggon is prepar'd, and time revives us:
All's well that ends well: still the fine 's the crown;
Whate'er the course, the end is the renown. *Exeunt.*

[SCENE V. *Rousillon. The* COUNT'S *palace.*]

Enter Clown, *Old Lady* [COUNTESS], *and* LAFEW.

Laf. No, no, no, your son was misled with a snipt-taffeta fellow there, whose villanous saffron would have made all the unbaked and doughy youth of a

simple dull maneuvers. 311. **cardecue,** quart d'écu, eight pence. 312. **fee-simple,** total and perpetual ownership. 333. **supposition,** judgment. 366. **great,** full or "big" with emotion or pride.

SCENE IV. 11. **breaking,** demobilizing. 20. **motive,** means; instigator. 35. **the fine 's,** the end is.

SCENE V. 2. **snipt-taffeta,** wearing notched or serrated garments of taffeta. **saffron,** vegetable coloring used in making pastry; applied here to the fashionable wearing of yellow.

nation in his colour: your daughter-in-law had been alive at this hour, and your son here at home, more advanced by the king than by that red-tailed humble-bee I speak of.

Count. I would I had not known him! It was the death of the most virtuous gentlewoman that ever nature had praise for creating. If she had partaken of my flesh, and cost me the dearest groans of a mother, I could not have owed her a more rooted love.

Laf. 'Twas a good lady, 'twas a good lady: we may pick a thousand sallets ere we light on such another herb.

Clo. Indeed, sir, she was the sweet-marjoram of the sallet, or rather, the herb of grace.

Laf. They are not herbs, you knave; they are nose-herbs.

Clo. I am no great Nebuchadnezzar, sir; I have not much skill in grass.

Laf. Whether dost thou profess thyself, a knave or a fool?

Clo. A fool, sir, at a woman's service, and a knave at a man's.

Laf. Your distinction?

Clo. I would cozen the man of his wife and do his service.

Laf. So you were a knave at his service, indeed.

Clo. And I would give his wife my bauble, sir, to do her service.

Laf. I will subscribe for thee, thou art both knave and fool.

Clo. At your service.

Laf. No, no, no.

Clo. Why, sir, if I cannot serve you, I can serve as great a prince as you are.

Laf. Who 's that? a Frenchman?

Clo. Faith, sir, 'a has an English name; but his fisnomy is more hotter in France than there.

Laf. What prince is that?

Clo. The black prince, sir; alias, the prince of darkness; alias, the devil.

Laf. Hold thee, there 's my purse: I give thee not this to suggest thee from thy master thou talkest of; serve him still.

Clo. I am a woodland fellow, sir, that always loved a great fire; and the master I speak of ever keeps a good fire. But, sure, he is the prince of the world; let his nobility remain in 's court. I am for the house with the narrow gate, which I take to be too little for pomp to enter: some that humble themselves may; but the many will be too chill and tender, and they'll be for the flowery way that leads to the broad gate and the great fire.

Laf. Go thy ways, I begin to be aweary of thee; and I tell thee so before, because I would not fall out with thee. Go thy ways: let my horses be well looked to, without any tricks.

Clo. If I put any tricks upon 'em, sir, they shall be jades' tricks; which are their own right by the law of nature. *Exit.*

Laf. A shrewd knave and an unhappy.

Count. So 'a is. My lord that 's gone made himself much sport out of him: by his authority he remains here, which he thinks is a patent for his sauciness; and, indeed, he has no pace, but runs where he will.

Laf. I like him well; 'tis not amiss. And I was about to tell you, since I heard of the good lady's death and that my lord your son was upon his return home, I moved the king my master to speak in the behalf of my daughter; which, in the minority of them both, his majesty, out of a self-gracious remembrance, did first propose: his highness hath promised me to do it: and, to stop up the displeasure he hath conceived against your son, there is no fitter matter. How does your ladyship like it?

Count. With very much content, my lord; and I wish it happily effected.

Laf. His highness comes post from Marseilles, of as able body as when he numbered thirty: he will be here to-morrow, or I am deceived by him that in such intelligence hath seldom failed.

Count. It rejoices me, that I hope I shall see him ere I die. I have letters that my son will be here to-night: I shall beseech your lordship to remain with me till they meet together.

Laf. Madam, I was thinking with what manners I might safely be admitted.

Count. You need but plead your honourable privilege.

Laf. Lady, of that I have made a bold charter; but I thank my God it holds yet.

Enter Clown.

Clo. O madam, yonder 's my lord your son with a patch of velvet on 's face: whether there be a scar under 't or no, the velvet knows; but 'tis a goodly patch of velvet: his left cheek is a cheek of two pile and a half, but his right cheek is worn bare.

Laf. A scar nobly got, or a noble scar, is a good livery of honour; so belike is that.

Clo. But it is your carbonadoed face.

Laf. Let us go see your son, I pray you: I long to talk with the young noble soldier.

Clo. Faith, there 's a dozen of 'em, with delicate fine hats and most courteous feathers, which bow the head and nod at every man. *Exeunt.*

ACT V.

[SCENE I. *Marseilles. A street.*]

Enter HELENA, Widow, *and* DIANA, *with two* Attendants.

Hel. But this exceeding posting day and night
Must wear your spirits low; we cannot help it:
But since you have made the days and nights as one
To wear your gentle limbs in my affairs,
Be bold you do so grow in my requital
As nothing can unroot you. In happy time;

Enter a Gentleman.

This man may help me to his majesty's ear,
If he would spend his power. God save you, sir.

7. **humblebee,** bumblebee. 16. **sallets,** salads. 18. **herb of grace,** rue. 19. **not herbs,** punning on "knot-herbs," from intricate knot-gardens. 20. **nose-herbs,** fragrant herbs used for bouquets, not salads. 21-22. **Nebuchadnezzar . . . grass.** In Daniel 4:28-37, King Nebuchadnezzar is reported to have gone mad and eaten grass like an ox. 24. **Whether,** which. 32. **bauble,** stick carried by a court fool (with bawdy suggestion, as in "do her service"). 41. **English name,** i.e., the Black Prince, a familiar name for the eldest son of Edward III. 42. **fisnomy,** physiognomy. 47. **suggest,** tempt. 107. **carbonadoed,** scored across with gashes (as meat for broiling).

Gent. And you.
Hel. Sir, I have seen you in the court of France.
Gent. I have been sometimes there.
Hel. I do presume, sir, that you are not fall'n
From the report that goes upon your goodness;
And therefore, goaded with most sharp occasions,
Which lay nice manners by, I put you to
The use of your own virtues, for the which
I shall continue thankful.
Gent. What 's your will?
Hel. That it will please you
To give this poor petition to the king,
And aid me with that store of power you have
To come into his presence.
Gent. The king 's not here.
Hel. Not here, sir!
Gent. Not, indeed:
He hence remov'd last night and with more haste
Than is his use.
Wid. Lord, how we lose our pains!
Hel. All's well that ends well yet,
Though time seem so adverse and means unfit.
I do beseech you, whither is he gone?
Gent. Marry, as I take it, to Rousillon;
Whither I am going.
Hel. I do beseech you, sir,
Since you are like to see the king before me,
Commend the paper to his gracious hand,
Which I presume shall render you no blame
But rather make you thank your pains for it.
I will come after you with what good speed
Our means will make us means.
Gent. This I'll do for you.
Hel. And you shall find yourself to be well thank'd,
Whate'er falls more. We must to horse again.
Go, go, provide. [*Exeunt*.]

[SCENE II. *Rousillon. Before the* COUNT'S *palace*.]

Enter Clown, *and* PAROLLES.

Par. Good Monsieur Lavatch, give my Lord Lafew this letter: I have ere now, sir, been better known to you, when I have held familiarity with fresher clothes; but I am now, sir, muddied in fortune's mood, and smell somewhat strong of her strong displeasure.

Clo. Truly, fortune's displeasure is but sluttish, if it smell so strongly as thou speakest of: I will henceforth eat no fish of fortune's buttering. Prithee, allow the wind.

Par. Nay, you need not to stop your nose, sir; I spake but by a metaphor.

Clo. Indeed, sir, if your metaphor stink, I will stop my nose; or against any man's metaphor. Prithee, get thee further.

Par. Pray you, sir, deliver me this paper.

Clo. Foh! prithee, stand away: a paper from fortune's close-stool to give to a nobleman! Look, here he comes himself.

Enter LAFEW.

Here is a purr of fortune's, sir, or of fortune's cat,—but not a musk-cat,—that has fallen into the unclean fishpond of her displeasure, and, as he says, is muddied withal: pray you, sir, use the carp as you may; for he looks like a poor, decayed, ingenious, foolish, rascally knave. I do pity his distress in my similes of comfort and leave him to your lordship. [*Exit*.]

Par. My lord, I am a man whom fortune hath cruelly scratched.

Laf. And what would you have me to do? 'Tis too late to pare her nails now. Wherein have you played the knave with fortune, that she should scratch you, who of herself is a good lady and would not have knaves thrive long under her? There 's a cardecue for you: let the justices make you and fortune friends: I am for other business.

Par. I beseech your honour to hear me one single word.

Laf. You beg a single penny more: come, you shall ha 't; save your word.

Par. My name, my good lord, is Parolles.

Laf. You beg more than 'word,' then. Cox my passion! give me your hand. How does your drum?

Par. O my good lord, you were the first that found me!

Laf. Was I, in sooth? and I was the first that lost thee.

Par. It lies in you, my lord, to bring me in some grace, for you did bring me out.

Laf. Out upon thee, knave! dost thou put upon me at once both the office of God and the devil? One brings thee in grace and the other brings thee out. [*Trumpets sound*.] The king 's coming; I know by his trumpets. Sirrah, inquire further after me; I had talk of you last night: though you are a fool and a knave, you shall eat; go to, follow.

Par. I praise God for you. [*Exeunt*.]

[SCENE III. *Rousillon. The* COUNT'S *palace*.]

Flourish. Enter KING, *Old Lady* [COUNTESS], LAFEW, *the two* French Lords, *with* Attendants.

King. We lost a jewel of her; and our esteem
Was made much poorer by it: but your son,
As mad in folly, lack'd the sense to know
Her estimation home.
Count. 'Tis past, my liege;
And I beseech your majesty to make it
Natural rebellion, done i' th' blaze of youth;
When oil and fire, too strong for reason's force,
O'erbears it and burns on.
King. My honour'd lady,
I have forgiven and forgotten all;
Though my revenges were high bent upon him,
And watch'd the time to shoot.
Laf. This I must say,
But first I beg my pardon, the young lord
Did to his majesty, his mother and his lady
Offence of mighty note; but to himself
The greatest wrong of all. He lost a wife
Whose beauty did astonish the survey

ACT V. SCENE I. 5. **bold,** sure. 15. **nice,** scrupulous.
SCENE II. 10. **allow the wind,** let me have the windward side of you. 18. **close-stool,** privy. 20. **purr,** knave, with pun on cat's noise and also on dung. 25. **ingenious,** stupid. 35. **cardecue,** quart d'écu (see IV, iii, 311). 41-42. **Parolles . . . 'word,'** a pun on Parolles' name, which suggests the French *parole*, meaning "word." 42. **Cox,** a perversion of *God's*, sometimes spelled *Cock's*.
SCENE III. 1. **our esteem,** our own value. 3-4. **know . . . home,** appreciate her value fully.

Of richest eyes, whose words all ears took captive,
Whose dear perfection hearts that scorn'd to serve
Humbly call'd mistress.
King. Praising what is lost
Makes the remembrance dear. Well, call him hither;
We are reconcil'd, and the first view shall kill
All repetition: let him not ask our pardon;
The nature of his great offence is dead,
And deeper than oblivion we do bury
Th' incensing relics of it: let him approach,
A stranger, no offender; and inform him
So 'tis our will he should.
Gent. I shall, my liege. [*Exit.*]
King. What says he to your daughter? have you spoke?
Laf. All that he is hath reference to your highness.
King. Then shall we have a match. I have letters sent me
That set him high in fame.

Enter COUNT BERTRAM.

Laf. He looks well on 't.
King. I am not a day of season,
For thou mayst see a sunshine and a hail
In me at once: but to the brightest beams
Distracted clouds give way; so stand thou forth;
The time is fair again.
Ber. My high-repented blames,
Dear sovereign, pardon to me.
King. All is whole;
Not one word more of the consumed time.
Let 's take the instant by the forward top;
For we are old, and on our quick'st decrees
Th' inaudible and noiseless foot of Time
Steals ere we can effect them. You remember
The daughter of this lord?
Ber. Admiringly, my liege, at first
I stuck my choice upon her, ere my heart
Durst make too bold a herald of my tongue:
Where the impression of mine eye infixing,
Contempt his scornful perspective did lend me,
Which warp'd the line of every other favour;
Scorn'd a fair colour, or express'd it stol'n;
Extended or contracted all proportions
To a most hideous object: thence it came
That she whom all men prais'd and whom myself,
Since I have lost, have lov'd, was in mine eye
The dust that did offend it.
King. Well excus'd:
That thou didst love her, strikes some scores away
From the great compt: but love that comes too late,
Like a remorseful pardon slowly carried,
To the great sender turns a sour offence,
Crying, 'That 's good that 's gone.' Our rash faults
Make trivial price of serious things we have,
Not knowing them until we know their grave:
Oft our displeasures, to ourselves unjust,
Destroy our friends and after weep their dust:
†Our own love waking cries to see what 's done,
While shameful hate sleeps out the afternoon.
Be this sweet Helen's knell, and now forget her.
Send forth your amorous token for fair Maudlin:
The main consents are had; and here we'll stay
To see our widower's second marriage-day.
Count. Which better than the first, O dear heaven, bless!
Or, ere they meet, in me, O nature, cesse!
Laf. Come on, my son, in whom my house's name
Must be digested, give a favour from you
To sparkle in the spirits of my daughter,
That she may quickly come. [*Bertram gives a ring.*] By my old beard,
And ev'ry hair that 's on 't, Helen, that 's dead,
Was a sweet creature: such a ring as this,
The last that e'er I took her leave at court,
I saw upon her finger.
Ber. Hers it was not.
King. Now, pray you, let me see it; for mine eye,
While I was speaking, oft was fasten'd to 't.
This ring was mine; and, when I gave it Helen,
I bade her, if her fortunes ever stood
Necessitied to help, that by this token
I would relieve her. Had you that craft, to reave her
Of what should stead her most?
Ber. My gracious sovereign,
Howe'er it pleases you to take it so,
The ring was never hers.
Count. Son, on my life,
I have seen her wear it; and she reckon'd it
At her life's rate.
Laf. I am sure I saw her wear it.
Ber. You are deceiv'd, my lord; she never saw it:
In Florence was it from a casement thrown me,
Wrapp'd in a paper, which contain'd the name
Of her that threw it: noble she was, and thought
I stood ingag'd: but when I had subscrib'd
To mine own fortune and inform'd her fully
I could not answer in that course of honour
As she had made the overture, she ceas'd
In heavy satisfaction and would never
Receive the ring again.
King. Plutus himself,
That knows the tinct and multiplying med'cine,
Hath not in nature's mystery more science
Than I have in this ring: 'twas mine, 'twas Helen's,
Whoever gave it you. Then, if you know
That you are well acquainted with yourself,
Confess 'twas hers, and by what rough enforcement
You got it from her; she call'd the saints to surety
That she would never put it from her finger,
Unless she gave it to yourself in bed,
Where you have never come, or sent it us
Upon her great disaster.
Ber. She never saw it.
King. Thou speak'st it falsely, as I love mine honour;
And mak'st conjectural fears to come into me,
Which I would fain shut out. If it should prove
That thou art so inhuman,—'twill not prove so;—
And yet I know not: thou didst hate her deadly,
And she is dead; which nothing, but to close
Her eyes myself, could win me to believe,
More than to see this ring. Take him away.
[*Guards seize Bertram.*]
My fore-past proofs, howe'er the matter fall,

22. **repetition,** mention of what is past. 32. **day of season,** i.e., of one consistent kind of weather. 36. **blames,** i.e., faults for which I am to blame. 48. **perspective,** a metaphor from the optical glass for producing distorted images. 57. **compt,** reckoning. 63. **displeasures,** offenses. 64. **weep their dust,** mourn their ashes. 66. **shameful hate,** so F; Globe: *shame full late;* Brigstocke's paraphrase: Hate has done its best and now sleeps at ease. 72. **ere they meet,** i.e., before the two marriages come to resemble one another. **cesse,** cease. 74. **digested,** amalgamated. 85. **Necessitied to,** in need of. 96. **ingag'd,** not pledged; the prefix has negative force; so F; Globe: *engaged.* 100.

Shall tax my fears of little vanity,
Having vainly fear'd too little. Away with him!
We'll sift this matter further.
Ber. If you shall prove
This ring was ever hers, you shall as easy
Prove that I husbanded her bed in Florence,
Where yet she never was. [*Exit, guarded.*]
King. I am wrapp'd in dismal thinkings.

Enter a Gentleman.

Gent. Gracious sovereign,
Whether I have been to blame or no, I know not:
Here 's a petition from a Florentine,
Who hath for four or five removes come short
To tender it herself. I undertook it,
Vanquish'd thereto by the fair grace and speech
Of the poor suppliant, who by this I know
Is here attending: her business looks in her
With an importing visage; and she told me,
In a sweet verbal brief, it did concern
Your highness with herself.

[*King reads*] *a letter.* Upon his many protestations to marry me when his wife was dead, I blush to say it, he won me. Now is the Count Rousillon a widower: his vows are forfeited to me, and my honour 's paid to him. He stole from Florence, taking no leave, and I follow him to his country for justice: grant it me, O king! in you it best lies; otherwise a seducer flourishes, and a poor maid is undone. DIANA CAPILET.

Laf. I will buy me a son-in-law in a fair, and toll for this: I'll none of him.

King. The heavens have thought well on thee, Lafew,
To bring forth this discov'ry. Seek these suitors:
Go speedily and bring again the count.
I am afeard the life of Helen, lady,
Was foully snatch'd.
Count. Now, justice on the doers!

Enter BERTRAM [*guarded*].

King. I wonder, sir, sith wives are monsters to you,
And that you fly them as you swear them lordship,
Yet you desire to marry.

Enter Widow [*and*] DIANA.

What woman 's that?
Dia. I am, my lord, a wretched Florentine,
Derived from the ancient Capilet:
My suit, as I do understand, you know,
And therefore know how far I may be pitied.
Wid. I am her mother, sir, whose age and honour
Both suffer under this complaint we bring,
And both shall cease, without your remedy.
King. Come hither, count; do you know these women?
Ber. My lord, I neither can nor will deny
But that I know them: do they charge me further?
Dia. Why do you look so strange upon your wife?
Ber. She 's none of mine, my lord.
Dia. If you shall marry,
You give away this hand, and that is mine;
You give away heaven's vows, and those are mine;
You give away myself, which is known mine;
For I by vow am so embodied yours,
That she which marries you must marry me,
Either both or none.

Laf. Your reputation comes too short for my daughter; you are no husband for her.

Ber. My lord, this is a fond and desp'rate creature,
Whom sometime I have laugh'd with: let your highness
Lay a more noble thought upon mine honour
Than for to think that I would sink it here.
King. Sir, for my thoughts, you have them ill to friend
Till your deeds gain them: fairer prove your honour
Than in my thought it lies.
Dia. Good my lord,
Ask him upon his oath, if he does think
He had not my virginity.
King. What say'st thou to her?
Ber. She 's impudent, my lord,
And was a common gamester to the camp.
Dia. He does me wrong, my lord; if I were so,
He might have bought me at a common price:
Do not believe him. O, behold this ring,
Whose high respect and rich validity
Did lack a parallel; yet for all that
He gave it to a commoner o' th' camp,
If I be one.
Count. He blushes, and 'tis hit:
Of six preceding ancestors, that gem,
Conferr'd by testament to th' sequent issue,
Hath it been ow'd and worn. This is his wife;
That ring 's a thousand proofs.
King. Methought you said
You saw one here in court could witness it.
Dia. I did, my lord, but loath am to produce
So bad an instrument: his name 's Parolles.
Laf. I saw the man to-day, if man he be.
King. Find him, and bring him hither.
[*Exit an Attendant.*]
Ber. What of him?
He 's quoted for a most perfidious slave,
With all the spots o' th' world tax'd and debosh'd;
Whose nature sickens but to speak a truth.
Am I or that or this for what he'll utter,
That will speak any thing?
King. She hath that ring of yours.
Ber. I think she has: certain it is I lik'd her,
And boarded her i' th' wanton way of youth:
She knew her distance and did angle for me,
Madding my eagerness with her restraint,
As all impediments in fancy's course
Are motives of more fancy; and, in fine,
Her infinite cunning, with her modern grace,
Subdu'd me to her rate: she got the ring;
And I had that which any inferior might
At market-price have bought.
Dia. I must be patient:
You, that have turn'd off a first so noble wife,
May justly diet me. I pray you yet;
Since you lack virtue, I will lose a husband;
Send for your ring, I will return it home,
And give me mine again.

heavy satisfaction, doleful resignation. 101. **Plutus,** the god of wealth. 102. **tinct . . . med'cine,** the alchemical process of transmuting base metals into gold. 103. **science,** knowledge. 114. **conjectural,** suspicious. 121. **fore-past,** previous. 122. **Shall . . . vanity,** i.e., will rebuke my previous fears as inadequate to the real truth. 149. **toll for,** put up for sale. 182. **to friend,** as a friend. 188. **gamester,** prostitute. 197. **sequent issue,** the next heir. 211. **boarded,** accosted (with sexual meaning). 215. **fine,** conclusion. 217. **her rate,** her terms. 221. **diet,** restrain, or, send me packing after a day's work.

Ber. I have it not.
King. What ring was yours, I pray you?
Dia. Sir, much like
The same upon your finger.
King. Know you this ring? this ring was his of late.
Dia. And this was it I gave him, being abed.
King. The story then goes false, you threw it him
Out of a casement.
Dia. I have spoke the truth.

Enter PAROLLES.

Ber. My lord, I do confess the ring was hers.
King. You boggle shrewdly, every feather starts you.
Is this the man you speak of?
Dia. Ay, my lord.
King. Tell me, sirrah, but tell me true, I charge you,
Not fearing the displeasure of your master,
Which on your just proceeding I'll keep off,
By him and by this woman here what know you?

Par. So please your majesty, my master hath been an honourable gentleman: tricks he hath had in him, which gentlemen have.

King. Come, come, to the purpose: did he love this woman?

Par. Faith, sir, he did love her; but how?

King. How, I pray you?

Par. He did love her, sir, as a gentleman loves a woman.

King. How is that?

Par. He loved her, sir, and loved her not.

King. As thou art a knave, and no knave.
What an equivocal companion is this!

Par. I am a poor man, and at your majesty's command.

Laf. He 's a good drum, my lord, but a naughty orator.

Dia. Do you know he promised me marriage?

Par. Faith, I know more than I'll speak.

King. But wilt thou not speak all thou knowest?

Par. Yes, so please your majesty. I did go between them, as I said; but more than that, he loved her: for indeed he was mad for her, and talked of Satan and of Limbo and of Furies and I know not what: yet I was in that credit with them at that time that I knew of their going to bed, and of other motions, as promising her marriage, and things which would derive me ill will to speak of; therefore I will not speak what I know.

King. Thou hast spoken all already, unless thou canst say they are married: but thou art too fine in thy evidence; therefore stand aside. This ring, you say, was yours?

Dia. Ay, my good lord.
King. Where did you buy it? or who gave it you?
Dia. It was not given me, nor I did not buy it.
King. Who lent it you?
Dia. It was not lent me neither.
King. Where did you find it, then?
Dia. I found it not.
King. If it were yours by none of all these ways,
How could you give it him?
Dia. I never gave it him.

Laf. This woman 's an easy glove, my lord; she goes off and on at pleasure.

King. This ring was mine; I gave it his first wife.
Dia. It might be yours or hers, for aught I know.
King. Take her away; I do not like her now;
To prison with her: and away with him.
Unless thou tell'st me where thou hadst this ring,
Thou diest within this hour.
Dia. I'll never tell you.
King. Take her away.
Dia. I'll put in bail, my liege.
King. I think thee now some common customer.
Dia. By Jove, if ever I knew man, 'twas you.
King. Wherefore hast thou accus'd him all this while?
Dia. Because he 's guilty, and he is not guilty:
He knows I am no maid, and he'll swear to 't;
I'll swear I am a maid, and he knows not.
Great king, I am no strumpet, by my life;
I am either maid, or else this old man's wife.
King. She does abuse our ears: to prison with her!
Dia. Good mother, fetch my bail. Stay, royal sir: [*Exit Widow.*]
The jeweller that owes the ring is sent for,
And he shall surety me. But for this lord,
Who hath abus'd me, as he knows himself,
Though yet he never harm'd me, here I quit him:
He knows himself my bed he hath defil'd;
And at that time he got his wife with child:
Dead though she be, she feels her young one kick:
So there 's my riddle: one that 's dead is quick:
And now behold the meaning.

Enter HELENA *and* Widow.

King. Is there no exorcist
Beguiles the truer office of mine eyes?
Is 't real that I see?
Hel. No, my good lord;
'Tis but the shadow of a wife you see,
The name and not the thing.
Ber. Both, both. O, pardon!
Hel. O my good lord, when I was like this maid,
I found you wondrous kind. There is your ring;
And, look you, here 's your letter; this it says:
'When from my finger you can get this ring
And are by me with child,' &c. This is done:
Will you be mine, now you are doubly won?
Ber. If she, my liege, can make me know this clearly,
I'll love her dearly, ever, ever dearly.
Hel. If it appear not plain and prove untrue,
Deadly divorce step between me and you!
O my dear mother, do I see you living?
Laf. Mine eyes smell onions; I shall weep anon:
[*To Parolles*] Good Tom Drum, lend me a handkercher: so,
I thank thee: wait on me home, I'll make sport with thee:
Let thy curtsies alone, they are scurvy ones.
King. Let us from point to point this story know,
To make the even truth in pleasure flow.
[*To Diana*] If thou be'st yet a fresh uncropped flower,
Choose thou thy husband, and I'll pay thy dower;
For I can guess that by thy honest aid
Thou kept'st a wife herself, thyself a maid.
Of that and all the progress, more and less,
Resolvedly more leisure shall express:
All yet seems well; and if it end so meet,

232. **boggle shrewdly,** startle excessively. 270. **fine,** subtle. 287. **customer,** prostitute. 294. **old man's,** Lafew's. 332. **Resolvedly,** so that all doubts are removed.

The bitter past, more welcome is the sweet. *Flourish.*

[EPILOGUE.]

[*King.*] The king's a beggar, now the play is done:
All is well ended, if this suit be won,
That you express content; which we will pay,
With strife to please you, day exceeding day:
Ours be your patience then, and yours our parts;
Your gentle hands lend us, and take our hearts.
Exeunt omnes.

MEASURE FOR MEASURE

A play Caled Mesur for Mesur" by "Shaxberd" was performed at court, for the new King James I, by "his Maiesties plaiers" on December 26, 1604. Probably it had been composed that same year, or in late 1603. The play dates from the very height of Shakespeare's tragic period, three years or so after *Hamlet*, contemporary with *Othello*, shortly before *King Lear* and *Macbeth*. This period includes very little comedy of any sort, and what there is differs markedly from the "festive" comedy of the 1590's. *Troilus and Cressida* (c. 1601–1602), hovering between satire and tragedy, bleakly portrays a hopeless love affair caught in the toils of a pointless and stalemated war. *All's Well that Ends Well* (c. 1601–1604) resembles *Measure for Measure* in its portrayal of an undeserving protagonist who must be deceived into marriage by an ethically ambiguous bed trick. *Measure for Measure*, the last such unfestive comedy from the tragic period, illustrates most clearly of all what critics usually mean by "problem comedy" or "problem play."

Its chief concern is not with the triumphs of love, as in the happy comedies, but with moral and social problems: "filthy vices" arising from sexual desire, and the abuses of judicial authority. Images of disease abound in this play. We see corruption in Vienna "boil and bubble Till it o'er-run the stew." Angelo is for most of the play a deeply torn protagonist, abhorring his own perverse sinfulness, compulsively driven to an attempted murder in order to cover up his lust for Isabella. His soliloquies are introspective, tortured, focused on the psychological horror of an intelligent mind succumbing to criminal desire. The disguised Duke, witnessing this fall into depravity and despair, can offer Angelo's intended victims no better philosophical counsel than Christian renunciation of the world and all its vain hopes. Tragedy is averted only by providential intervention and by the harsh trickery of "Craft against vice," in which the Duke becomes involved as chief manipulator and stage manager. Of the concluding marriages, two are foisted on the bridegrooms (Angelo and Lucio) against their wills, whereas that of the Duke and Isabella jars oddly with his stoical teachings and with her previous determination to be a nun. The ending thus seems arbitrary; both justice and romantic happiness are so perilously achieved in this play that they seem inconsistent with the injustice and lechery that have prevailed until the last.

Yet the very improbability of the ending, and the sense of tragedy narrowly averted, are perhaps intentional. These features are appropriate not only for "problem" comedy but for "tragicomedy" or "comedy of forgiveness," overlapping genres toward which Shakespeare gravitated in his late romances. Angelo is, like Leontes in *The Winter's Tale* (or, earlier, like Bertram in *All's Well* or Claudio in *Much Ado about Nothing*), an erring protagonist forgiven in excess of his deserving, spared by a benign overseeing providence from destroying that which is most precious to him.

The play's title, *Measure for Measure*, introduces a paradox of human justice which this "problem" play cannot wholly resolve. How is fallible man to judge the sins of his fellow mortals and still obey Christ's injunction of the Sermon on the Mount, "Judge not that ye be not judged"? Three positions emerge from the debate: absolute justice at one extreme, mercy at the other, and equity as a middle ground. Isabella speaks for mercy, and her words ring with biblical authority. Since all men would be condemned to eternal darkness were God not merciful as well as just, should not men also be merciful? The difficulty, however, is that Vienna shows all too clearly the effects of leniency under the kindly Duke. Vice is rampant; stern measures are needed. Though he has not wished to crack the whip himself, the Duke firmly endorses "strict statutes and most biting laws, The needful bits and curbs to headstrong weeds" (I,iii). To carry out necessary reform, the Duke has chosen Lord Angelo, spokesman for absolute justice, to represent him. Angelo's position is cold but consistent. Only by a literal and impartial administering of the statutes, he maintains, can the law deter potential offenders. If the judge is found guilty, he must pay the penalty as well. One difficulty here, however, is that literal enforcement of the statute on fornication seems ironically to catch the wrong culprits. Claudio and Juliet, who are about to be married and are already joined by a "true contract" of betrothal, are sentenced to the severest limit of the law, whereas the pimps and whores of Vienna's suburbs manage at first to evade punishment entirely. Angelo's deputy, Escalus, can only shake his head in dismay at this unjust result of strict justice. Angelo has not remembered fully the terms of his commission from the Duke: he was enjoined to practice both "Mortality and mercy" in Vienna, to "enforce or qualify the laws As to your soul seem good." The attributes of a ruler, like those of God, must include "terror" but also "love" (I,i).

Escalus' compassionate and pragmatic approach to law illustrates equity, or the flexible application of the law to particular cases. Because Claudio is only technically guilty (though still guilty), Escalus would pronounce for him a light sentence. Pompey and Mistress Overdone, on the other hand, require vigorous and unceasing prosecution. The problem of policing vice is compounded by the law's inefficiency as well as by man's own bestial nature, which will never be wholly tamed. Constable Elbow, like Dogberry in *Much Ado*, is a pompous user of malapropisms, less clever by far than the criminals he would arrest. His evidence against Pompey is so absurdly circumstantial that Escalus is first obliged to let off this engaging pimp with a stern warning. Yet Escalus patiently and tenaciously attends to such proceedings, unlike Angelo, whose interest in the law is too theoretical. Escalus deals with day-to-day problems effectively. He orders reforms of the system by which constables are selected, instructs Elbow in the rudiments of his office, and so proceeds ultimately to an effective arrest. Vice is not eliminated; as Pompey defiantly points out, unless someone plans to "geld and splay all the youth of the city," they "will to 't then" (II,i). Still, vice is held in check. Law can shape the outer man and hope for some inner reform. Even Pompey is taught a trade, albeit a grisly one, as an apprentice hangman. The law must use both "correction" and "instruction."

The solutions arrived at in the comic subplot do not fit the case of Angelo, for he is powerful enough to be above the Viennese law. Indeed, he tries finally to brazen it out, pitting his authority against that of the seemingly friendless Isabella, much like the biblical Elders when justly accused of immorality by the innocent Susannah. Corrupt society is on Angelo's side; only providence can rescue the defenseless. The Duke of Vienna, hovering in the background and seeing all that happens, intervenes just at those points when tragedy threatens to become irreversible. Moreover, the Duke is testing those he observes. As he says to Friar Thomas, explaining why he has delegated his power to Angelo: "Hence shall we see, If power change purpose, what our seemers be" (I,iii). The Duke obviously expects Angelo to fall. Indeed, he has known all along how Angelo has dishonorably repudiated his solemn contract to Mariana when her marriage dowry disappeared at sea (III,i). Like an all-seeing deity who keeps a reckoning of men's good and evil deeds, the Duke has found out Angelo's great weakness. As Angelo confesses, "I perceive your grace, like pow'r divine, Hath look'd upon my passes" (V,i). Paradoxically, however, this seemingly tragic story of temptation and fall yields precious benefits of remorse and humility. Angelo is profoundly grateful to be rescued from his self-made nightmare of seduction, murder, and tyranny. Knowing now that he is prone like other men to fleshly weakness, he knows also that he needs spiritual assistance and that as judge he ought to use mercy. Seen in retrospect, his panic, despair, and humiliation are curative.

The disguised Duke tests the other characters as well, intentionally misleading them to expect the worst in order to try their resolve. On a comic level, he exposes the amiable but loose-tongued Lucio as a slanderer against the Duke himself, and devises for Lucio a suitably satirical exposure and witty punishment. More seriously, as confessor to Juliet he assures her that her beloved Claudio must die on the morrow. As she ought, she penitentially accepts "shame with joy," and so is cleansed (II,iii). To Claudio, the Duke similarly offers the counsel of Christian renunciation. In one of the play's most poignantly melancholy reflections on the vanity of human striving, the Duke characterizes life as a breath, a dreamlike "after-dinner's sleep," a fever of inconstancy in which timorous man longs fretfully for what he does not have and spurns those things he has (III,i). Claudio responds as he ought, resolving to "find life" by "seeking death." He achieves this calm, however, in the face of certain execution; ironically, what he must then learn to overmaster is the desperate hope of living by means of his sister's dishonor. Claudio is broken by this test, and begs perversely for a few years of guilty life at the cost of eternal shame for himself and Isabella. The searing encounter between Claudio and Isabella puts her to the test as well, and her response seems hysterical and no doubt prudish to modern audiences. She has much to learn about the complexities of human behavior. Although she is sincere in protesting that she would lay down her life for her brother, and is correct in the play's terms to prefer virtue to mere existence, her tone is too strident. Like other major characters, she must be humbled before she can rise. She and Claudio must heed the Duke's essential admonition: "Do not satisfy your resolution with hopes that are fallible." Only then, paradoxically, can they go on to achieve earthly happiness.

In her final testing, Isabella truly achieves greatness. Here Shakespeare significantly alters his chief source, George Whetstone's *Promos and Cassandra* (1578), and the other versions of the story which Shakespeare probably also consulted—Cinthio's *Hecatommithi* and Whetstone's *Heptameron of Civill Discourses*. In all these versions, the character corresponding to Angelo does actually ravish the heroine, and in Cinthio he also murders her brother. Shakespeare, by witholding these tragically irreversible acts, not only gives to Angelo a technical innocence, but allows the Duke as *deus ex machina* to practice virtuous deception on Isabella one more time. Can she forgive the supposed murderer of her brother? Her affirmative answer confutes the Old Testament ethic of "An Angelo for Claudio, death for death" whereby "Like doth quit like, and Measure still for Measure" (V,i). Although Angelo confessedly deserves to die for what he intended, the forfeit need not be paid so long as humanity can reveal itself capable of Isabella's godlike mercy.

MEASURE FOR MEASURE

The Names of All the Actors

VINCENTIO, *the Duke.*
ANGELO, *the Deputy.*
ESCALUS, *an ancient Lord.*
CLAUDIO, *a young gentleman.*
LUCIO, *a fantastic.*
Two other gentlemen.
PROVOST.
THOMAS, } *two friars.*
PETER, }
[A Justice.]
[VARRIUS.]
ELBOW, *a simple constable.*
FROTH, *a foolish gentleman.*
CLOWN [POMPEY, *a servant to Mistress Overdone*].
ABHORSON, *an executioner.*
BARNARDINE, *a dissolute prisoner.*

ISABELLA, *sister to Claudio.*
MARIANA, *betrothed to Angelo.*
JULIET, *beloved of Claudio.*
FRANCISCA, *a nun.*
MISTRESS OVERDONE, *a bawd.*

[Lords, Officers, Citizens, Boy, *and* Attendants.]

THE SCENE: *Vienna.*

ACT I.

SCENE I. [*An apartment in the* DUKE'S *palace.*]

Enter DUKE, ESCALUS, Lords [*and* Attendants].

Duke. Escalus.
Escal. My lord.
Duke. Of government the properties to unfold,
Would seem in me t' affect speech and discourse;
Since I am put to know that your own science
Exceeds, in that, the lists of all advice
My strength can give you: then no more remains,
†But that to your sufficiency . . . . .
. . . . as your worth is able,
And let them work. The nature of our people,
Our city's institutions, and the terms
For common justice, y' are as pregnant in
As art and practice hath enriched any
That we remember. There is our commission,
From which we would not have you warp. Call hither,
I say, bid come before us Angelo. [*Exit an Attendant.*]
What figure of us think you he will bear?
For you must know, we have with special soul
Elected him our absence to supply,
Lent him our terror, dress'd him with our love,
And given his deputation all the organs
Of our own power: what think you of it?
Escal. If any in Vienna be of worth
To undergo such ample grace and honour,
It is Lord Angelo.

Enter ANGELO.

Duke. Look where he comes.
Ang. Always obedient to your grace's will,
I come to know your pleasure.
Duke. Angelo,
There is a kind of character in thy life,
That to th' observer doth thy history
Fully unfold. Thyself and thy belongings
Are not thine own so proper as to waste
Thyself upon thy virtues, they on thee.
Heaven doth with us as we with torches do,
Not light them for themselves; for if our virtues
Did not go forth of us, 'twere all alike
As if we had them not. Spirits are not finely touch'd
But to fine issues, nor Nature never lends
The smallest scruple of her excellence
But, like a thrifty goddess, she determines
Herself the glory of a creditor,
Both thanks and use. But I do bend my speech
To one that can my part in him advertise;
Hold therefore, Angelo:—
In our remove be thou at full ourself;
Mortality and mercy in Vienna
Live in thy tongue and heart: old Escalus,
Though first in question, is thy secondary.
Take thy commission.
Ang. Now, good my lord,
Let there be some more test made of my mettle,
Before so noble and so great a figure
Be stamp'd upon it.
Duke. No more evasion:
We have with a leaven'd and prepared choice
Proceeded to you; therefore take your honours.
Our haste from hence is of so quick condition
That it prefers itself and leaves unquestion'd
Matters of needful value. We shall write to you,
As time and our concernings shall importune,
How it goes with us, and do look to know
What doth befall you here. So, fare you well:
To th' hopeful execution do I leave you
Of your commissions.
Ang. Yet give leave, my lord,
That we may bring you something on the way.
Duke. My haste may not admit it;
Nor need you, on mine honour, have to do

THE NAMES OF ALL THE ACTORS. 5. **a fantastic,** one who has fanciful ideas or indulges in wild notions.

ACT I. SCENE I. 4. **t' affect . . . discourse,** to be in love with my own voice. 5. **put to know,** forced to admit. **science,** knowledge. 6. **that,** i.e., *properties of government* (l. 3). 8-9. **But . . . able.** The passage appears in F as a single line. Several unsuccessful attempts at emendation have been made; Theobald inserted after *sufficiency* the phrase *you add due diligency.* The most plausible explanation is that something has been deleted or has been inadvertently omitted by the printer. 8. **sufficiency,** fitness for office. 11-12. **terms . . . justice,** the terms of court. 17. **figure,** representation. 18. **with special soul,** with sincerest intentions or sentiments. 20. **Lent . . . terror,** commissioned him with authority to administer punishments. 21. **his deputation,** him as deputy. 24. **undergo,** bear the weight of. 36. **touch'd,** endowed. 37. **issues,** purposes. 39. **determines,** requests. 40. **Herself,** for herself. 42. **advertise,** inform. 44. **at full,** in every respect. 45-46. **Mortality . . . heart,** your word is the only law respecting sentence of life and death. 49. **mettle,** so F; Globe: *metal.* 52. **leaven'd,** fermented; i.e., well-considered. 54-55. **Our . . . itself,** the cause for my hasty departure is so urgent (*quick*) that it takes precedence over all other matters. 55. **unquestion'd,** not yet considered. 57. **importune,** make urgent. 60. **hopeful execution,** transferred modifier; i.e., I hopefully leave you. 62. **bring you something,** accompany you a short distance.

With any scruple; your scope is as mine own,
So to enforce or qualify the laws
As to your soul seems good. Give me your hand:
I'll privily away. I love the people,
But do not like to stage me to their eyes:
Though it do well, I do not relish well
Their loud applause and Aves vehement;
Nor do I think the man of safe discretion
That does affect it. Once more, fare you well.
Ang. The heavens give safety to your purposes!
Escal. Lead forth and bring you back in happiness!
Duke. I thank you. Fare you well. *Exit.*
Escal. I shall desire you, sir, to give me leave
To have free speech with you; and it concerns me
To look into the bottom of my place:
A pow'r I have, but of what strength and nature
I am not yet instructed.
Ang. 'Tis so with me. Let us withdraw together,
And we may soon our satisfaction have
Touching that point.
Escal. I'll wait upon your honour. *Exeunt.*

SCENE II. [*A street.*]

Enter LUCIO *and two other* Gentlemen.

Lucio. If the duke with the other dukes come not to composition with the King of Hungary, why then all the dukes fall upon the king.

First Gent. Heaven grant us its peace, but not the King of Hungary's!

Sec. Gent. Amen.

Lucio. Thou concludest like the sanctimonious pirate, that went to sea with the Ten Commandments, but scraped one out of the table.

Sec. Gent. 'Thou shalt not steal'?

Lucio. Ay, that he razed.

First Gent. Why, 'twas a commandment to command the captain and all the rest from their functions: they put forth to steal. There 's not a soldier of us all, that, in the thanksgiving before meat, do relish the petition well that prays for peace.

Sec. Gent. I never heard any soldier dislike it.

Lucio. I believe thee; for I think thou never wast where grace was said.

Sec. Gent. No? a dozen times at least.

First Gent. What, in metre?

Lucio. In any proportion or in any language.

First Gent. I think, or in any religion.

Lucio. Ay, why not? Grace is grace, despite of all controversy: as, for example, thou thyself art a wicked villain, despite of all grace.

First Gent. Well, there went but a pair of shears between us.

Lucio. I grant; as there may between the lists and the velvet. Thou art the list.

First Gent. And thou the velvet: thou art good velvet; thou 'rt a three-piled piece, I warrant thee: I had as lief be a list of an English kersey as be piled, as thou art piled, for a French velvet. Do I speak feelingly now?

Lucio. I think thou dost; and, indeed, with most painful feeling of thy speech: I will, out of thine own confession, learn to begin thy health; but, whilst I live, forget to drink after thee.

First Gent. I think I have done myself wrong, have I not?

Sec. Gent. Yes, that thou hast, whether thou art tainted or free.

Enter Bawd [MISTRESS OVERDONE].

Lucio. Behold, behold, where Madam Mitigation comes! I have purchased as many diseases under her roof as come to—

Sec. Gent. To what, I pray?

Lucio. Judge.

Sec. Gent. To three thousand dolours a year.

First Gent. Ay, and more.

Lucio. A French crown more.

First Gent. Thou art always figuring diseases in me; but thou art full of error; I am sound.

Lucio. Nay, not as one would say, healthy; but so sound as things that are hollow: thy bones are hollow; impiety has made a feast of thee.

First Gent. [*To the Bawd*] How now! which of your hips has the most profound sciatica?

Mrs Ov. Well, well; there 's one yonder arrested and carried to prison was worth five thousand of you all.

Sec. Gent. Who 's that, I pray thee?

Mrs Ov. Marry, sir, that 's Claudio, Signior Claudio.

First Gent. Claudio to prison? 'tis not so.

Mrs Ov. Nay, but I know 'tis so: I saw him arrested, saw him carried away; and, which is more, within these three days his head to be chopped off.

Lucio. But, after all this fooling, I would not have it so. Art thou sure of this?

Mrs Ov. I am too sure of it: and it is for getting Madam Julietta with child.

Lucio. Believe me, this may be: he promised to meet me two hours since, and he was ever precise in promise-keeping.

Sec. Gent. Besides, you know, it draws something near to the speech we had to such a purpose.

First Gent. But, most of all, agreeing with the proclamation.

Lucio. Away! let 's go learn the truth of it.
Exit [*Lucio with the Gentlemen*].

Mrs Ov. Thus, what with the war, what with the

64-65. **Nor . . . scruple,** you need have no misgivings. 68-69. **I'll privily away,** etc. This passage is usually explained as a complimentary reference to King James' dislike for crowds. The compliment is repeated in I, iii, 8-10, and in II, iv, 24-30. The fact that James issued an edict against his subjects' crowding to wish him well on his entrance to London in 1603 and the further fact that this play was presented before the king (1604) give credence to this explanation. 72. **safe,** sound, sane. 79. **the bottom . . . place,** the extent of my commission and authority.

SCENE II. 4. **its,** one of the few instances in Shakespeare of this form of the possessive; cf. *his* in glossary. 22. **in metre,** i.e., a grace in verse. 28-29. **there . . . between us,** we're of the same stuff. 31. **lists,** selvages. 33. **three-piled.** The New Cambridge editors suggest that the Gentleman quibbles in *piled* on the meaning "the downy nap [on velvet]" and the word *piled-pilled* or *peeled,* i.e., hairless, bald, as a result of venereal disease (known as the French disease; see *French velvet,* l. 36, and *French crown,* l. 52). 35. **kersey,** a coarse, cheap fabric. 36. **feelingly,** to the purpose. 37-40. **I think . . . thee.** Lucio's reply is a quibble on *feelingly;* i.e., the Gentleman speaks with most painful feeling because his mouth is affected by the French disease; hence Lucio will not drink from the same cup after him. 45. **Mitigation,** so called because her function is to relieve desire. 50. **dolours,** quibble on "dollars." 56. **sound,** resounding. 84. **the sweat,** sweating sickness; a form of the plague. 85. **custom-shrunk,** having fewer customers. 91. **peculiar,** sweat, what with the gallows and what with poverty, I am custom-shrunk.

Enter Clown [POMPEY].

How now! what's the news with you?

Pom. Yonder man is carried to prison.

Mrs Ov. Well; what has he done?

Pom. A woman.

Mrs Ov. But what 's his offence?

Pom. Groping for trouts in a peculiar river.

Mrs Ov. What, is there a maid with child by him?

Pom. No, but there 's a woman with maid by him. You have not heard of the proclamation, have you?

Mrs Ov. What proclamation, man?

Pom. All houses in the suburbs of Vienna must be plucked down.

Mrs Ov. And what shall become of those in the city?

Pom. They shall stand for seed: they had gone down too, but that a wise burgher put in for them.

Mrs Ov. But shall all our houses of resort in the suburbs be pulled down?

Pom. To the ground, mistress.

Mrs Ov. Why, here 's a change indeed in the commonwealth! What shall become of me?

Pom. Come; fear not you: good counsellors lack no clients: though you change your place, you need not change your trade; I'll be your tapster still. Courage! there will be pity taken on you: you that have worn your eyes almost out in the service, you will be considered.

Mrs Ov. What 's to do here, Thomas tapster? let 's withdraw.

Pom. Here comes Signior Claudio, led by the provost to prison; and there 's Madam Juliet. *Exeunt.*

Enter PROVOST, CLAUDIO, JULIET, Officers; LUCIO *and two* Gentlemen [follow].

Claud. Fellow, why dost thou show me thus to th' world?
Bear me to prison, where I am committed.

Prov. I do it not in evil disposition,
But from Lord Angelo by special charge.

Claud. Thus can the demigod Authority
Make us pay down for our offence by weight
The words of heaven; on whom it will, it will;
On whom it will not, so; yet still 'tis just.

Lucio. Why, how now, Claudio! whence comes this restraint?

Claud. From too much liberty, my Lucio, liberty:
As surfeit is the father of much fast,
So every scope by the immoderate use
Turns to restraint. Our natures do pursue,
Like rats that ravin down their proper bane,
A thirsty evil; and when we drink we die.

Lucio. If I could speak so wisely under an arrest, I would send for certain of my creditors: and yet, to say the truth, I had as lief have the foppery of freedom as the morality of imprisonment. What 's thy offence, Claudio?

Claud. What but to speak of would offend again.

Lucio. What, is 't murder?

Claud. No.

Lucio. Lechery?

Claud. Call it so.

Prov. Away, sir! you must go.

Claud. One word, good friend. Lucio, a word with you.

Lucio. A hundred, if they'll do you any good.
Is lechery so look'd after?

Claud. Thus stands it with me: upon a true contract
I got possession of Julietta's bed:
You know the lady; she is fast my wife,
Save that we do the denunciation lack
Of outward order: this we came not to,
Only for propagation of a dow'r
Remaining in the coffer of her friends,
From whom we thought it meet to hide our love
Till time had made them for us. But it chances
The stealth of our most mutual entertainment
With character too gross is writ on Juliet.

Lucio. With child, perhaps?

Claud. Unhappily, even so.
And the new deputy now for the duke—
Whether it be the fault and glimpse of newness,
Or whether that the body public be
A horse whereon the governor doth ride,
Who, newly in the seat, that it may know
He can command, lets it straight feel the spur;
Whether the tyranny be in his place,
Or in his eminence that fills it up,
I stagger in:—but this new governor
Awakes me all the enrolled penalties
Which have, like unscour'd armour, hung by th' wall
So long that nineteen zodiacs have gone round
And none of them been worn; and, for a name,
Now puts the drowsy and neglected act
Freshly on me: 'tis surely for a name.

Lucio. I warrant it is: and thy head stands so tickle on thy shoulders that a milkmaid, if she be in love, may sigh it off. Send after the duke and appeal to him.

Claud. I have done so, but he 's not to be found.
I prithee, Lucio, do me this kind service:
This day my sister should the cloister enter
And there receive her approbation:
Acquaint her with the danger of my state;
Implore her, in my voice, that she make friends
To the strict deputy; bid herself assay him:
I have great hope in that; for in her youth
There is a prone and speechless dialect,
Such as move men; beside, she hath prosperous art
When she will play with reason and discourse,
And well she can persuade.

privately owned (with bawdy suggestion). 98. **houses,** brothels. **suburbs,** location of the brothels in Shakespeare's London. 102. **for seed,** to preserve the species (with ribald pun). 118. **Provost,** officer charged with apprehension, custody, and punishment of offenders. 126. **words of heaven.** See Romans 9:15-18: "For he saith to Moses, I will have mercy on whom I will have mercy, and I will have compassion on whom I will have compassion. . . . Therefore hath he mercy on whom he will have mercy, and whom he will he hardeneth." 131. **scope,** freedom. 133. **ravin . . . bane,** greedily devour what is poisonous to them. 148. **so look'd after,** taken so seriously. 151. **fast my wife,** i.e., by precontract. Formal betrothal was legally regarded as making a valid marriage. Cf. IV, i, 71-75, where the duke urges Mariana to comply in the plot to save Claudio on the grounds of her precontract with Angelo. 152. **denunciation,** formal declaration. 154. **propagation,** increase. 155. **friends,** relatives. 157. **made them for us,** disposed them (*friends*) in our favor. 159. **character too gross,** letters too large. 162. **the fault . . . newness,** imperfection awaiting upon the sudden and unaccustomed brightness or flash of of novelty (Hart). 166. **straight,** at once. 169. **I stagger in,** I am certain. 172. **nineteen zodiacs,** nineteen years. 177. **tickle,** uncertain. 183. **approbation,** novitiate. 188. **prone,** eager. The phrase is taken commonly as a hendiadys—speechlessly prone, i.e., speaking eagerly without words (Onions). 189. **prosperous art,** skill or ability to gain favorable results.

Lucio. I pray she may; as well for the encouragement of the like, which else would stand under grievous imposition, as for the enjoying of thy life, who I would be sorry should be thus foolishly lost at a game of tick-tack. I'll to her.

Claud. I thank you, good friend Lucio.
Lucio. Within two hours.
Claud. Come, officer, away! *Exeunt*.

SCENE [III. *A monastery*].

Enter DUKE *and* FRIAR THOMAS.

Duke. No, holy father; throw away that thought;
Believe not that the dribbling dart of love
Can pierce a complete bosom. Why I desire thee
To give me secret harbour, hath a purpose
More grave and wrinkled than the aims and ends
Of burning youth.
Fri. T. May your grace speak of it?
Duke. My holy sir, none better knows than you
How I have ever lov'd the life removed
And held in idle price to haunt assemblies
Where youth, and cost, and witless bravery keeps.
I have deliver'd to Lord Angelo,
A man of stricture and firm abstinence,
My absolute power and place here in Vienna,
And he supposes me travell'd to Poland;
For so I have strew'd it in the common ear,
And so it is receiv'd. Now, pious sir,
You will demand of me why I do this?
Fri. T. Gladly, my lord.
Duke. We have strict statutes and most biting laws,
The needful bits and curbs to headstrong weeds,
Which for this fourteen years we have let slip;
Even like an o'ergrown lion in a cave,
That goes not out to prey. Now, as fond fathers,
Having bound up the threat'ning twigs of birch,
Only to stick it in their children's sight
For terror, not to use, in time the rod
Becomes more mock'd than fear'd; so our decrees,
Dead to infliction, to themselves are dead;
And liberty plucks justice by the nose;
The baby beats the nurse, and quite athwart
Goes all decorum.
Fri. T. It rested in your grace
To unloose this tied-up justice when you pleas'd:
And it in you more dreadful would have seem'd
Than in Lord Angelo.
Duke. I do fear, too dreadful:
Sith 'twas my fault to give the people scope,
'Twould be my tyranny to strike and gall them
For what I bid them do: for we bid this be done,
When evil deeds have their permissive pass
And not the punishment. Therefore indeed, my father,
I have on Angelo impos'd the office;
Who may, in th' ambush of my name, strike home,
†And yet my nature never in the fight
To do it slander. And to behold his sway,
I will, as 'twere a brother of your order,
Visit both prince and people: therefore, I prithee,
Supply me with the habit and instruct me
How I may formally in person bear
Like a true friar. Moe reasons for this action
At our more leisure shall I render you;
Only, this one: Lord Angelo is precise;
Stands at a guard with envy; scarce confesses
That his blood flows, or that his appetite
Is more to bread than stone: hence shall we see,
If power change purpose, what our seemers be. *Exeunt*.

SCENE [IV. *A nunnery*].

Enter ISABELLA *and* FRANCISCA, *a Nun*.

Isab. And have you nuns no farther privileges?
Fran. Are not these large enough?
Isab. Yes, truly: I speak not as desiring more;
But rather wishing a more strict restraint
Upon the sisterhood, the votarists of Saint Clare.
Lucio. (*Within*) Ho! Peace be in this place!
Isab. Who 's that which calls?
Fran. It is a man's voice. Gentle Isabella,
Turn you the key, and know his business of him;
You may, I may not; you are yet unsworn.
When you have vow'd, you must not speak with men
But in the presence of the prioress:
Then, if you speak, you must not show your face,
Or, if you show your face, you must not speak.
He calls again; I pray you, answer him. [*Exit*.]
Isab. Peace and prosperity! Who is 't that calls?

[*Enter* LUCIO.]

Lucio. Hail, virgin, if you be, as those cheek-roses
Proclaim you are no less! Can you so stead me
As bring me to the sight of Isabella,
A novice of this place and the fair sister
To her unhappy brother Claudio?
Isab. Why 'her unhappy brother'? let me ask,
The rather for I now must make you know
I am that Isabella and his sister.
Lucio. Gentle and fair, your brother kindly greets you:
Not to be weary with you, he 's in prison.
Isab. Woe me! for what?
Lucio. For that which, if myself might be his judge,
He should receive his punishment in thanks:
He hath got his friend with child.
Isab. Sir, make me not your story.
Lucio. 'Tis true.
I would not—though 'tis my familiar sin
With maids to seem the lapwing and to jest,
Tongue far from heart—play with all virgins so:
I hold you as a thing ensky'd and sainted,
By your renouncement an immortal spirit,
And to be talk'd with in sincerity,
As with a saint.
Isab. You do blaspheme the good in mocking me.
Lucio. Do not believe it. Fewness and truth, 'tis thus:

196. **tick-tack,** a form of backgammon in which pegs were driven into holes.

SCENE III. 2. **dribbling,** falling short or wide of the mark. 9. **idle,** unprofitable. 10. **cost,** costly things. 12. **stricture,** strictness. 21. **fourteen.** Claudio mentions nineteen years at I, ii, 172; probably the compositor confused xiv and xix. 28. **Dead to infliction,** dead in that they are not executed. 43. **it,** i.e., nature; so Hanmer; Globe, following F: *in*. 50. **precise,** puritanical. 51. **Stands at a guard,** acts cautiously.

SCENE IV. 30. **story,** subject for mirth. 32. **lapwing,** peewit or plover, with reference to its habit of running away from its nest in order to draw away enemies. 39. **Fewness and truth,** in few words and truly. 43. **foison,** plentiful harvest. 48. **vain though apt,** foolish though

Your brother and his lover have embrac'd:
As those that feed grow full, as blossoming time
That from the seedness the bare fallow brings
To teeming foison, even so her plenteous womb
Expresseth his full tilth and husbandry.
Isab. Some one with child by him? My cousin Juliet?
Lucio. Is she your cousin?
Isab. Adoptedly; as school-maids change their names
By vain though apt affection.
Lucio. She it is.
Isab. O, let him marry her.
Lucio. This is the point.
The duke is very strangely gone from hence;
Bore many gentlemen, myself being one,
In hand and hope of action: but we do learn
By those that know the very nerves of state,
His givings-out were of an infinite distance
From his true-meant design. Upon his place,
And with full line of his authority,
Governs Lord Angelo; a man whose blood
Is very snow-broth; one who never feels
The wanton stings and motions of the sense,
But doth rebate and blunt his natural edge
With profits of the mind, study and fast.
He—to give fear to use and liberty,
Which have for long run by the hideous law,
As mice by lions—hath pick'd out an act,
Under whose heavy sense your brother's life
Falls into forfeit: he arrests him on it;
And follows close the rigour of the statute,
To make him an example. All hope is gone,
Unless you have the grace by your fair prayer
To soften Angelo: and that 's my pith of business
'Twixt you and your poor brother.
Isab. Doth he so seek his life?
Lucio. Has censur'd him
Already; and, as I hear, the provost hath
A warrant for 's execution.
Isab. Alas! what poor ability 's in me
To do him good?
Lucio. Assay the pow'r you have.
Isab. My power? Alas, I doubt—
Lucio. Our doubts are traitors
And make us lose the good we oft might win
By fearing to attempt. Go to Lord Angelo,
And let him learn to know, when maidens sue,
Men give like gods; but when they weep and kneel,
All their petitions are as freely theirs
As they themselves would owe them.
Isab. I'll see what I can do.
Lucio. But speedily.
Isab. I will about it straight;
No longer staying but to give the mother
Notice of my affair. I humbly thank you:
Commend me to my brother: soon at night
I'll send him certain word of my success.
Lucio. I take my leave of you.
Isab. Good sir, adieu. *Exeunt.*

ACT II.

SCENE I. [*A hall in* ANGELO's *house.*]

Enter ANGELO, ESCALUS, *and* Servants, [*a*] Justice.

Ang. We must not make a scarecrow of the law,
Setting it up to fear the birds of prey,
And let it keep one shape, till custom make it
Their perch and not their terror.
Escal. Ay, but yet
Let us be keen, and rather cut a little,
Than fall, and bruise to death. Alas, this gentleman,
Whom I would save, had a most noble father!
Let but your honour know,
Whom I believe to be most strait in virtue,
That, in the working of your own affections,
Had time coher'd with place or place with wishing,
Or that the resolute acting of your blood
Could have attain'd th' effect of your own purpose,
Whether you had not sometime in your life
Err'd in this point which now you censure him,
And pull'd the law upon you.
Ang. 'Tis one thing to be tempted, Escalus,
Another thing to fall. I not deny,
The jury, passing on the prisoner's life,
May in the sworn twelve have a thief or two
Guiltier than him they try. What 's open made to justice,
That justice seizes: what knows the laws
That thieves do pass on thieves? 'Tis very pregnant,
The jewel that we find, we stoop and take 't
Because we see it; but what we do not see
We tread upon, and never think of it.
You may not so extenuate his offence
For I have had such faults; but rather tell me,
When I, that censure him, do so offend,
Let mine own judgement pattern out my death,
And nothing come in partial. Sir, he must die.

Enter PROVOST.

Escal. Be it as your wisdom will.
Ang. Where is the provost?
Prov. Here, if it like your honour.
Ang. See that Claudio
Be executed by nine to-morrow morning:
Bring him his confessor, let him be prepar'd;
For that 's the utmost of his pilgrimage. [*Exit Provost.*]
Escal. [*Aside*] Well, heaven forgive him! and forgive us all!
Some rise by sin, and some by virtue fall:
†Some run from breaks of ice, and answer none:
And some condemned for a fault alone.

Enter ELBOW, FROTH, *Clown* [POMPEY], Officers.

Elb. Come, bring them away: if these be good people in a commonweal that do nothing but use their abuses in common houses, I know no law: bring them away.

Ang. How now, sir! What 's your name? and what 's the matter?

Elb. If it please your honour, I am the poor duke's

natural. 51-52. **Bore . . . action,** kept us in expectation of some action. 60. **rebate,** abate. 72. **censur'd,** passed sentence on. 83. **owe,** possess.
ACT II. SCENE I. 2. **fear,** frighten. 6. **fall,** fell; i.e., cause to fall. 22. **what knows,** so F; Globe, following Rowe: *what know;* New Cambridge: *who knows.* There is no need to emend either the pronoun or the verb. Third person present plurals in *s* and *es* are common in Shakespeare; cf. Abbott, 333. Angelo asks here, "What does the law know of those who enforce it?" The law, he urges, is not to be identified and confused with its enforcers. 23. **pregnant,** clear. 28. **For,** because. 31. **And . . . partial,** let there be no partiality. 36. **utmost,** furthest point. 39. **Some . . . none,** i.e., some commit sin (grossly violate chastity) and escape the consequences.

constable, and my name is Elbow: I do lean upon justice, sir, and do bring in here before your good honour two notorious benefactors.

Ang. Benefactors? Well; what benefactors are they? are they not malefactors?

Elb. If it please your honour, I know not well what they are: but precise villains they are, that I am sure of; and void of all profanation in the world that good Christians ought to have.

Escal. This comes off well; here 's a wise officer.

Ang. Go to: what quality are they of? Elbow is your name? why dost thou not speak, Elbow?

Pom. He cannot, sir; he 's out at elbow.

Ang. What are you, sir?

Elb. He, sir! a tapster, sir; parcel-bawd; one that serves a bad woman; whose house, sir, was, as they say, plucked down in the suburbs; and now she professes a hot-house, which, I think, is a very ill house too.

Escal. How know you that?

Elb. My wife, sir, whom I detest before heaven and your honour,—

Escal. How? thy wife?

Elb. Ay, sir; whom, I thank heaven, is an honest woman,—

Escal. Dost thou detest her therefore?

Elb. I say, sir, I will detest myself also, as well as she, that this house, if it be not a bawd's house, it is pity of her life, for it is a naughty house.

Escal. How dost thou know that, constable?

Elb. Marry, sir, by my wife; who, if she had been a woman cardinally given, might have been accused in fornication, adultery, and all uncleanliness there.

Escal. By the woman's means?

Elb. Ay, sir, by Mistress Overdone's means: but as she spit in his face, so she defied him.

Pom. Sir, if it please your honour, this is not so.

Elb. Prove it before these varlets here, thou honourable man; prove it.

Escal. Do you hear how he misplaces?

Pom. Sir, she came in great with child; and longing, saving your honour's reverence, for stewed prunes; sir, we had but two in the house, which at that very distant time stood, as it were, in a fruit-dish, a dish of some three-pence; your honours have seen such dishes; they are not China dishes, but very good dishes,—

Escal. Go to, go to: no matter for the dish, sir.

Pom. No, indeed, sir, not of a pin; you are therein in the right: but to the point. As I say, this Mistress Elbow, being, as I say, with child, and being great-bellied, and longing, as I said, for prunes; and having but two in the dish, as I said, Master Froth here, this very man, having eaten the rest, as I said, and, as I say, paying for them very honestly; for, as you know, Master Froth, I could not give you three-pence again.

Froth. No, indeed.

Pom. Very well; you being then, if you be remembered, cracking the stones of the foresaid prunes,—

Froth. Ay, so I did indeed.

Pom. Why, very well; I telling you then, if you be remembered, that such a one and such a one were past cure of the thing you wot of, unless they kept very good diet, as I told you,—

Froth. All this is true.

Pom. Why, very well, then,—

Escal. Come, you are a tedious fool: to the purpose. What was done to Elbow's wife, that he hath cause to complain of? Come me to what was done to her.

Pom. Sir, your honour cannot come to that yet.

Escal. No, sir, nor I mean it not.

Pom. Sir, but you shall come to it, by your honour's leave. And, I beseech you, look into Master Froth here, sir; a man of fourscore pound a year; whose father died at Hallowmas: was 't not at Hallowmas, Master Froth?

Froth. All-hallond eve.

Pom. Why, very well; I hope here be truths. He, sir, sitting, as I say, in a lower chair, sir; 'twas in the Bunch of Grapes, where indeed you have a delight to sit, have you not?

Froth. I have so; because it is an open room and good for winter.

Pom. Why, very well, then; I hope here be truths.

Ang. This will last out a night in Russia,
When nights are longest there: I'll take my leave,
And leave you to the hearing of the cause;
Hoping you'll find good cause to whip them all.

Escal. I think no less. Good morrow to your
lordship. *Exit* [*Angelo*].
Now, sir, come on: what was done to Elbow's wife, once more?

Pom. Once, sir? there was nothing done to her once.

Elb. I beseech you, sir, ask him what this man did to my wife.

Pom. I beseech your honour, ask me.

Escal. Well, sir; what did this gentleman to her?

Pom. I beseech you, sir, look in this gentleman's face. Good Master Froth, look upon his honour; 'tis for a good purpose. Doth your honour mark his face?

Escal. Ay, sir, very well.

Pom. Nay, I beseech you, mark it well.

Escal. Well, I do so.

Pom. Doth your honour see any harm in his face?

Escal. Why, no.

Pom. I'll be supposed upon a book, his face is the worst thing about him. Good, then; if his face be the worst thing about him, how could Master Froth do the constable's wife any harm? I would know that of your honour.

Escal. He 's in the right. Constable, what say you to it?

Elb. First, an it like you, the house is a respected house; next, this is a respected fellow; and his mistress is a respected woman.

Pom. By this hand, sir, his wife is a more respected person than any of us all.

Elb. Varlet, thou liest; thou liest, wicked varlet! the time is yet to come that she was ever respected with man, woman, or child.

Pom. Sir, she was respected with him before he married with her.

Escal. Which is the wiser here? Justice or Iniquity? Is this true?

54. **precise,** puritanical; possibly one of Elbow's malapropisms. 55. **profanation,** malapropism for "profession." 59. **quality,** profession. 63. **parcel-bawd,** partly, i.e., he follows two trades—tapster and bawd. 67. **hot-house,** bathhouse. 69. **detest,** for "protest." 81. **cardinally,** malapropism for "carnally." 90. **misplaces,** uses words in the wrong place. 92-93. **stewed prunes,** associated with prostitutes; cf. *stews,* meaning "houses of prostitution." 99. **pin,** an insignificant trifle. 120. **done,** with sexual double meaning; cf. I, ii, 88. 121. **me,** the ethical dative. 130. **All-hallond eve,** Halloween. 132. **lower chair,** possibly easy chair (Steevens). 133. **the Bunch of Grapes,** the name of a room. It

Elb. O thou caitiff! O thou varlet! O thou wicked Hannibal! I respected with her before I was married to her! If ever I was respected with her, or she with me, let not your worship think me the poor duke's officer. Prove this, thou wicked Hannibal, or I'll have mine action of battery on thee.

Escal. If he took you a box o' the ear, you might have your action of slander too.

Elb. Marry, I thank your good worship for it. What is 't your worship's pleasure I shall do with this wicked caitiff?

Escal. Truly, officer, because he hath some offences in him that thou wouldst discover if thou couldst, let him continue in his courses till thou knowest what they are.

Elb. Marry, I thank your worship for it. Thou seest, thou wicked varlet, now, what 's come upon thee: thou art to continue now, thou varlet; thou art to continue.

Escal. Where were you born, friend?

Froth. Here in Vienna, sir.

Escal. Are you of fourscore pounds a year?

Froth. Yes, an 't please you, sir.

Escal. So. What trade are you of, sir?

Pom. A tapster; a poor widow's tapster.

Escal. Your mistress' name?

Pom. Mistress Overdone.

Escal. Hath she had any more than one husband?

Pom. Nine, sir; Overdone by the last.

Escal. Nine! Come hither to me, Master Froth. Master Froth, I would not have you acquainted with tapsters: they will draw you, Master Froth, and you will hang them. Get you gone, and let me hear no more of you.

Froth. I thank your worship. For mine own part, I never come into any room in a taphouse, but I am drawn in.

Escal. Well, no more of it, Master Froth: farewell. [*Exit Froth.*] Come you hither to me, Master tapster. What 's your name, Master tapster?

Pom. Pompey.

Escal. What else?

Pom. Bum, sir.

Escal. Troth, and your bum is the greatest thing about you; so that in the beastliest sense you are Pompey the Great. Pompey, you are partly a bawd, Pompey, howsoever you colour it in being a tapster, are you not? come, tell me true: it shall be the better for you.

Pom. Truly, sir, I am a poor fellow that would live.

Escal. How would you live, Pompey? by being a bawd? What do you think of the trade, Pompey? is it a lawful trade?

Pom. If the law would allow it, sir.

Escal. But the law will not allow it, Pompey; nor it shall not be allowed in Vienna.

Pom. Does your worship mean to geld and splay all the youth of the city?

Escal. No, Pompey.

Pom. Truly, sir, in my poor opinion, they will to 't then. If your worship will take order for the drabs and the knaves, you need not to fear the bawds.

Escal. There is pretty orders beginning, I can tell you: it is but heading and hanging.

Pom. If you head and hang all that offend that way but for ten year together, you'll be glad to give out a commission for more heads: if this law hold in Vienna ten year, I'll rent the fairest house in it after three-pence a bay: if you live to see this come to pass, say Pompey told you so.

Escal. Thank you, good Pompey; and, in requital of your prophecy, hark you, I advise you, let me not find you before me again upon any complaint whatsoever; no, not for dwelling where you do: if I do, Pompey, I shall beat you to your tent, and prove a shrewd Cæsar to you; in plain dealing, Pompey, I shall have you whipt: so, for this time, Pompey, fare you well.

Pom. I thank your worship for your good counsel: [*Aside*] but I shall follow it as the flesh and fortune shall better determine.
Whip me? No, no; let carman whip his jade:
The valiant heart 's not whipt out of his trade. *Exit.*

Escal. Come hither to me, Master Elbow; come hither, Master constable. How long have you been in this place of constable?

Elb. Seven year and a half, sir.

Escal. I thought, by your readiness in the office, you had continued in it some time. You say, seven years together?

Elb. And a half, sir.

Escal. Alas, it hath been great pains to you. They do you wrong to put you so oft upon 't: are there not men in your ward sufficient to serve it?

Elb. Faith, sir, few of any wit in such matters: as they are chosen, they are glad to choose me for them; I do it for some piece of money, and go through with all.

Escal. Look you bring me in the names of some six or seven, the most sufficient of your parish.

Elb. To your worship's house, sir?

Escal. To my house. Fare you well. [*Exit Elbow.*]
What 's o'clock, think you?

Just. Eleven, sir.

Escal. I pray you home to dinner with me.

Just. I humbly thank you.

Escal. It grieves me for the death of Claudio;
But there 's no remedy.

Just. Lord Angelo is severe.

Escal. It is but needful:
Mercy is not itself, that oft looks so;
Pardon is still the nurse of second woe:
But yet,—poor Claudio! There is no remedy.
Come, sir. *Exeunt.*

SCENE II. [*Another room in the same.*]

Enter PROVOST [*and a*] Servant.

Serv. He 's hearing of a cause; he will come straight:
I'll tell him of you.

Prov. Pray you, do. [*Exit Servant.*] I'll know
His pleasure; may be he will relent. Alas,
He hath but as offended in a dream!

was not uncommon to designate particular rooms in inns by such names. 135. **open,** public. 163. **supposed,** malapropism for "deposed," i.e., sworn. 167. **respected,** for "suspected." 180. **Justice or Iniquity,** personified characters in a morality play. 183. **Hannibal,** for "cannibal." 195. **discover,** reveal. 204. **of,** possessed of. 215. **draw,** used with multiple quibble in the senses of "disembowel," "empty"—i.e., of his belongings, and (l. 220) "cheat"—i.e., take in. 250. **heading,** beheading. 255. **bay,** division of a house included under one gable. 263. **Cæsar.** Escalus refers to Caesar's defeat of Pompey at Pharsalus.

SCENE II. 4. **He,** i.e., Claudio.

All sects, all ages smack of this vice; and he
To die for 't!

Enter ANGELO.

Ang. Now, what 's the matter, provost?
Prov. Is it your will Claudio shall die to-morrow?
Ang. Did not I tell thee yea? hadst thou not order?
Why dost thou ask again?
Prov. Lest I might be too rash:
Under your good correction, I have seen,
When, after execution, judgement hath
Repented o'er his doom.
Ang. Go to; let that be mine:
Do you your office, or give up your place,
And you shall well be spar'd.
Prov. I crave your honour's pardon.
What shall be done, sir, with the groaning Juliet?
She 's very near her hour.
Ang. Dispose of her
To some more fitter place, and that with speed.

[*Enter* Servant.]

Serv. Here is the sister of the man condemn'd
Desires access to you.
Ang. Hath he a sister?
Prov. Ay, my good lord; a very virtuous maid,
And to be shortly of a sisterhood,
If not already.
Ang. Well, let her be admitted.
[*Exit Servant.*]
See you the fornicatress be remov'd:
Let her have needful, but not lavish, means;
There shall be order for 't.

Enter LUCIO *and* ISABELLA.

Prov. 'Save your honour!
Ang. Stay a little while. [*To Isab.*] Y' are welcome: what 's your will?
Isab. I am a woeful suitor to your honour,
Please but your honour hear me.
Ang. Well; what 's your suit?
Isab. There is a vice that most I do abhor,
And most desire should meet the blow of justice;
For which I would not plead, but that I must;
For which I must not plead, but that I am
At war 'twixt will and will not.
Ang. Well; the matter?
Isab. I have a brother is condemn'd to die:
I do beseech you, let it be his fault,
And not my brother.
Prov. [*Aside*] Heaven give thee moving graces!
Ang. Condemn the fault, and not the actor of it?
Why, every fault 's condemn'd ere it be done:
Mine were the very cipher of a function,
To fine the faults whose fine stands in record,
And let go by the actor.
Isab. O just but severe law!
I had a brother, then. Heaven keep your honour!
Lucio. [*Aside to Isab.*] Give 't not o'er so: to him again, entreat him;
Kneel down before him, hang upon his gown:
You are too cold; if you should need a pin,
You could not with more tame a tongue desire it:
To him, I say!
Isab. Must he needs die?
Ang. Maiden, no remedy.
Isab. Yes; I do think that you might pardon him,
And neither heaven nor man grieve at the mercy.
Ang. I will not do 't.
Isab. But can you, if you would?
Ang. Look what I will not, that I cannot do.
Isab. But might you do 't, and do the world no wrong,
If so your heart were touch'd with that remorse
As mine is to him?
Ang. He 's sentenc'd; 'tis too late.
Lucio. [*Aside to Isab.*] You are too cold.
Isab. Too late? why, no; I, that do speak a word,
May call it back again. Well, believe this,
No ceremony that to great ones 'longs,
Not the king's crown, nor the deputed sword,
The marshal's truncheon, nor the judge's robe,
Become them with one half so good a grace
As mercy does.
If he had been as you and you as he,
You would have slipt like him; but he, like you,
Would not have been so stern.
Ang. Pray you, be gone.
Isab. I would to heaven I had your potency,
And you were Isabel! should it then be thus?
No; I would tell what 'twere to be a judge,
And what a prisoner.
Lucio. [*Aside to Isab.*] Ay, touch him; there 's the vein.
Ang. Your brother is a forfeit of the law,
And you but waste your words.
Isab. Alas, alas!
Why, all the souls that were were forfeit once;
And He that might the vantage best have took
Found out the remedy. How would you be,
If He, which is the top of judgement, should
But judge you as you are? O, think on that;
And mercy then will breathe within your lips,
Like man new made.
Ang. Be you content, fair maid;
It is the law, not I condemn your brother:
Were he my kinsman, brother, or my son,
It should be thus with him: he must die to-morrow.
Isab. To-morrow! O, that 's sudden! Spare him, spare him!
He 's not prepar'd for death. Even for our kitchens
We kill the fowl of season: shall we serve heaven
With less respect than we do minister
To our gross selves? Good, good my lord, bethink you;
Who is it that hath died for this offence?
There 's many have committed it.
Lucio. [*Aside to Isab.*] Ay, well said.
Ang. The law hath not been dead, though it hath slept:
Those many had not dar'd to do that evil,
If the first that did th' edict infringe
Had answer'd for his deed: now 'tis awake,
Takes note of what is done; and, like a prophet,
Looks in a glass, that shows what future evils,
Either new, or by remissness new-conceiv'd,

5. **sects,** classes of people, ranks. 10. **Under . . . correction,** i.e., allow me to say. 23. **fornicatress,** i.e., Juliet. 35. **let . . . fault,** i.e., let the fault die. 39. **cipher,** nonentity, a mere nothing. 40. **fine, fine,** punish, punishment. 43. **Give 't . . . so,** don't give up so soon. 61. **truncheon,** staff borne by military officers. 71. **forfeit,** person handed over to the law or to death. 76. **top of judgement,** supreme judge.

And so in progress to be hatch'd and born,
Are now to have no successive degrees,
But, ere they live, to end.
Isab. Yet show some pity.
Ang. I show it most of all when I show justice;
For then I pity those I do not know,
Which a dismiss'd offence would after gall;
And do him right that, answering one foul wrong,
Lives not to act another. Be satisfied;
Your brother dies to-morrow; be content.
Isab. So you must be the first that gives this sentence,
And he, that suffers. O, it is excellent
To have a giant's strength; but it is tyrannous
To use it like a giant.
Lucio. [*Aside to Isab.*] That 's well said.
Isab. Could great men thunder
As Jove himself does, Jove would ne'er be quiet,
For every pelting, petty officer
Would use his heaven for thunder;
Nothing but thunder! Merciful Heaven,
Thou rather with thy sharp and sulphurous bolt
Splits the unwedgeable and gnarled oak
Than the soft myrtle: but man, proud man,
Drest in a little brief authority,
Most ignorant of what he 's most assur'd,
His glassy essence, like an angry ape,
Plays such fantastic tricks before high heaven
As makes the angels weep; who, with our spleens,
Would all themselves laugh mortal.
Lucio. [*Aside to Isab.*] O, to him, to him, wench! he will relent;
He 's coming; I perceive 't.
Prov. [*Aside*] Pray heaven she win him!
Isab. We cannot weigh our brother with ourself:
Great men may jest with saints; 'tis wit in them,
But in the less foul profanation.
Lucio. [*Aside to Isab.*] Thou 'rt i' th' right, girl; more o' that.
Isab. That in the captain 's but a choleric word,
Which in the soldier is flat blasphemy.
Lucio [*Aside to Isab.*] Art avis'd o' that? more on 't.
Ang. Why do you put these sayings upon me?
Isab. Because authority, though it err like others,
Hath yet a kind of medicine in itself,
That skins the vice o' th' top. Go to your bosom;
Knock there, and ask your heart what it doth know
That 's like my brother's fault: if it confess
A natural guiltiness such as is his,
Let it not sound a thought upon your tongue
Against my brother's life.
Ang. [*Aside*] She speaks, and 'tis
Such sense, that my sense breeds with it.—Fare you well.
Isab. Gentle my lord, turn back.
Ang. I will bethink me: come again to-morrow.
Isab. Hark how I'll bribe you: good my lord, turn back.
Ang. How! bribe me?
Isab. Ay, with such gifts that heaven shall share with you.
Lucio. [*Aside to Isab.*] You had marr'd all else.
Isab. Not with fond sicles of the tested gold,
Or stones whose rates are either rich or poor
As fancy values them; but with true prayers
That shall be up at heaven and enter there
Ere sun-rise, prayers from preserved souls,
From fasting maids whose minds are dedicate
To nothing temporal.
Ang. Well; come to me to-morrow.
Lucio. [*Aside to Isab.*] Go to; 'tis well; away!
Isab. Heaven keep your honour safe!
Ang. [*Aside*] Amen:
For I am that way going to temptation,
Where prayers cross.
Isab. At what hour to-morrow
Shall I attend your lordship?
Ang. At any time 'fore noon.
Isab. 'Save your honour!
[*Exeunt Isabella, Lucio, and Provost.*]
Ang. From thee, even from thy virtue!
What 's this, what 's this? Is this her fault or mine?
The tempter or the tempted, who sins most?
Ha!
Not she; nor doth she tempt: but it is I
That, lying by the violet in the sun,
Do as the carrion does, not as the flow'r,
Corrupt with virtuous season. Can it be
That modesty may more betray our sense
Than woman's lightness? Having waste ground enough,
Shall we desire to raze the sanctuary
And pitch our evils there? O, fie, fie, fie!
What dost thou, or what art thou, Angelo?
Dost thou desire her foully for those things
That make her good? O, let her brother live:
Thieves for their robbery have authority
When judges steal themselves. What, do I love her,
That I desire to hear her speak again,
And feast upon her eyes? What is 't I dream on?
O cunning enemy, that, to catch a saint,
With saints dost bait thy hook! Most dangerous
Is that temptation that doth goad us on
To sin in loving virtue: never could the strumpet,
With all her double vigour, art and nature,
Once stir my temper; but this virtuous maid
Subdues me quite. Ever till now,
When men were fond, I smil'd and wond'red how.
Exit.

SCENE III. [*A room in a prison.*]

Enter [*severally*] DUKE [*disguised as a friar*] *and* PROVOST.

Duke. Hail to you, provost! so I think you are.
Prov. I am the provost. What 's your will, good friar?
Duke. Bound by my charity and my blest order,
I come to visit the afflicted spirits
Here in the prison. Do me the common right
To let me see them and to make me know
The nature of their crimes, that I may minister
To them accordingly.
Prov. I would do more than that, if more were needful.

Enter JULIET.

Look, here comes one: a gentlewoman of mine,
Who, falling in the flaws of her own youth,

79. **Like man new made,** i.e., new created by salvation, born again. 95. **glass,** crystal ball. 98. **successive degrees,** successors. 112. **pelting,** paltry. 120. **glassy essence,** fragile nature. 123. **laugh mortal,** i.e., excessively. 132. **avis'd,** informed. 136. **skins . . . top,** covers over with skin. 142. **sense, sense,** import, sensuality. 149. **sicles,** shekels. 168. **with virtuous season,** i.e., while all else flourishes.

Hath blister'd her report: she is with child;
And he that got it, sentenc'd; a young man
More fit to do another such offence
Than die for this.
Duke. When must he die?
Prov. As I do think, to-morrow.
I have provided for you: stay awhile, [*To Juliet*.]
And you shall be conducted.
Duke. Repent you, fair one, of the sin you carry?
Jul. I do; and bear the shame most patiently.
Duke. I'll teach you how you shall arraign your conscience,
And try your penitence, if it be sound,
Or hollowly put on.
Jul. I'll gladly learn.
Duke. Love you the man that wrong'd you?
Jul. Yes, as I love the woman that wrong'd him.
Duke. So then it seems your most offenceful act
Was mutually committed?
Jul. Mutually.
Duke. Then was your sin of heavier kind than his.
Jul. I do confess it, and repent it, father.
Duke. 'Tis meet so, daughter: but lest you do repent,
As that the sin hath brought you to this shame,
Which sorrow is always toward ourselves, not heaven,
Showing we would not spare heaven as we love it,
But as we stand in fear,—
Jul. I do repent me, as it is an evil,
And take the shame with joy.
Duke. There rest.
Your partner, as I hear, must die to-morrow,
And I am going with instruction to him.
Grace go with you, Benedicite! *Exit*.
Jul. Must die to-morrow! O injurious love,
That respites me a life, whose very comfort
Is still a dying horror!
Prov. 'Tis pity of him. *Exeunt*.

SCENE IV. [*A room in* ANGELO'S *house*.]

Enter ANGELO.

Ang. When I would pray and think, I think and pray
To several subjects. Heaven hath my empty words;
Whilst my invention, hearing not my tongue,
Anchors on Isabel: Heaven in my mouth,
As if I did but only chew his name;
And in my heart the strong and swelling evil
Of my conception. The state, whereon I studied,
Is like a good thing, being often read,
Grown sere and tedious; yea, my gravity,
Wherein—let no man hear me—I take pride,
Could I with boot change for an idle plume,
Which the air beats for vain. O place, O form,
How often dost thou with thy case, thy habit,
Wrench awe from fools and tie the wiser souls
To thy false seeming! Blood, thou art blood:
Let 's write good angel on the devil's horn;
'Tis not the devil's crest.

Enter Servant.

How now! who 's there?
Serv. One Isabel, a sister, desires access to you.
Ang. Teach her the way. [*Exit Serv*.] O heavens!
Why does my blood thus muster to my heart,
Making both it unable for itself,
And dispossessing all my other parts
Of necessary fitness?
So play the foolish throngs with one that swoons;
Come all to help him, and so stop the air
By which he should revive: and even so
The general, subject to a well-wish'd king,
Quit their own part, and in obsequious fondness
Crowd to his presence, where their untaught love
Must needs appear offence.

Enter ISABELLA.

How now, fair maid?
Isab. I am come to know your pleasure.
Ang. That you might know it, would much better please me
Than to demand what 'tis. Your brother cannot live.
Isab. Even so. Heaven keep your honour!
Ang. Yet may he live awhile; and, it may be,
As long as you or I: yet he must die.
Isab. Under your sentence?
Ang. Yea.
Isab. When, I beseech you? that in his reprieve,
Longer or shorter, he may be so fitted
That his soul sicken not.
Ang. Ha! fie, these filthy vices! It were as good
To pardon him that hath from nature stol'n
A man already made, as to remit
Their saucy sweetness that do coin heaven's image
In stamps that are forbid: 'tis all as easy
Falsely to take away a life true made
As to put metal in restrained means
To make a false one.
Isab. 'Tis set down so in heaven, but not in earth.
Ang. Say you so? then I shall pose you quickly.
Which had you rather, that the most just law
Now took your brother's life; or, to redeem him,
Give up your body to such sweet uncleanness
As she that he hath stain'd?
Isab. Sir, believe this,
I had rather give my body than my soul.
Ang. I talk not of your soul: our compell'd sins
Stand more for number than for accompt.
Isab. How say you?
Ang. Nay, I'll not warrant that; for I can speak
Against the thing I say. Answer to this:

SCENE III. 12. **report,** reputation. 31, 33, 34. **As that, as,** because. 41. **respites,** i.e., prolongs, does not forfeit. The law imposed the death penalty on the offending man but not on the woman.

SCENE IV. 7. **The state,** statecraft. 9. **sere,** withered, old. F, Globe: *fear'd*. *Fray'd* has also been proposed. 11. **boot,** profit. 15. **Blood, thou art blood,** i.e., passions are inherent in human nature. 16-17. **Let 's write . . . crest,** i.e., in our secret viciousness we may give an outwardly virtuous appearance to the devil himself, but that is not his true nature. (Angelo is punning on his own name.) 20-23. **Why . . . fitness.** According to Elizabethan psychology and physiology, this is what happens to a victim of passion. Normally the blood passes from the veins into the heart where from it "spirit" is engendered which is conveyed by the arteries to the other parts and becomes "the instrument of the soul, to perform all his actions." Under the sway of passion, however, the blood rushes (*musters*) to the heart, and the parts of the soul, having "more motion and heat than is needful for them, change and become hurtfull." (Burton, *Anatomy of Melancholy*, I, 1, ii, 2; Charron, *Of Wisdom*, Bk. I, Ch. xviii.) 27. **general,** public, multitude. 28. **part,** places. 43-44. **To . . . made,** to pardon a murderer. 44. **remit,** pardon. 45. **saucy,** wanton. 48. **metal.** Cf. I, i, 49. **restrained,** prohibited, illicit. 51. **pose,** put a question to. 57-58. **compell'd . . . accompt,** sins committed under compulsion are recorded but not charged to our spiritual accounts. 59. **that,** i.e., the idea expressed in lines 57-58. 67. **Pleas'd,** if it pleased. 68. **Were . . . charity,** the sinful act and

I, now the voice of the recorded law,
Pronounce a sentence on your brother's life:
Might there not be a charity in sin
To save this brother's life?
Isab. Please you to do 't,
I'll take it as a peril to my soul,
It is no sin at all, but charity.
Ang. Pleas'd you to do 't at peril of your soul,
Were equal poise of sin and charity.
Isab. That I do beg his life, if it be sin,
Heaven let me bear it! you granting of my suit,
If that be sin, I'll make it my morn prayer
To have it added to the faults of mine,
And nothing of your answer.
Ang. Nay, but hear me.
Your sense pursues not mine: either you are ignorant,
Or seem so craftily; and that 's not good.
Isab. Let me be ignorant, and in nothing good,
But graciously to know I am no better.
Ang. Thus wisdom wishes to appear most bright
When it doth tax itself; as these black masks
Proclaim an enshield beauty ten times louder
Than beauty could, display'd. But mark me;
To be received plain, I'll speak more gross:
Your brother is to die.
Isab. So.
Ang. And his offence is so, as it appears,
Accountant to the law upon that pain.
Isab. True.
Ang. Admit no other way to save his life,—
As I subscribe not that, nor any other,
But in the loss of question,—that you, his sister,
Finding yourself desir'd of such a person,
Whose credit with the judge, or own great place,
Could fetch your brother from the manacles
Of the all-binding law; and that there were
No earthly mean to save him, but that either
You must lay down the treasures of your body
To this suppos'd, or else to let him suffer;
What would you do?
Isab. As much for my poor brother as myself:
That is, were I under the terms of death,
Th' impression of keen whips I 'ld wear as rubies,
And strip myself to death, as to a bed
That longing have been sick for, ere I 'ld yield
My body up to shame.
Ang. Then must your brother die.
Isab. And 'twere the cheaper way:
Better it were a brother died at once,
Than that a sister, by redeeming him,
Should die for ever.
Ang. Were not you then as cruel as the sentence
That you have slander'd so?
Isab. Ignomy in ransom and free pardon
Are of two houses: lawful mercy
Is nothing kin to foul redemption.
Ang. You seem'd of late to make the law a tyrant;
And rather prov'd the sliding of your brother
A merriment than a vice.
Isab. O, pardon me, my lord; it oft falls out,
To have what we would have, we speak not what we
mean:
I something do excuse the thing I hate,
For his advantage that I dearly love.
Ang. We are all frail.
Isab. Else let my brother die,
If not a feodary, but only he
Owe and succeed thy weakness.
Ang. Nay, women are frail too.
Isab. Ay, as the glasses where they view themselves;
Which are as easy broke as they make forms.
Women! Help Heaven! men their creation mar
In profiting by them. Nay, call us ten times frail;
For we are soft as our complexions are,
And credulous to false prints.
Ang. I think it well:
And from this testimony of your own sex,—
Since I suppose we are made to be no stronger
Than faults may shake our frames,—let me be bold;
I do arrest your words. Be that you are,
That is, a woman; if you be more, you 're none;
If you be one, as you are well express'd
By all external warrants, show it now,
By putting on the destin'd livery.
Isab. I have no tongue but one: gentle my lord,
Let me entreat you speak the former language.
Ang. Plainly conceive, I love you.
Isab. My brother did love Juliet,
And you tell me that he shall die for 't.
Ang. He shall not, Isabel, if you give me love.
Isab. I know your virtue hath a license in 't,
Which seems a little fouler than it is,
To pluck on others.
Ang. Believe me, on mine honour,
My words express my purpose.
Isab. Ha! little honour to be much believ'd,
And most pernicious purpose! Seeming, seeming!
I will proclaim thee, Angelo; look for 't:
Sign me a present pardon for my brother,
Or with an outstretch'd throat I'll tell the world
aloud
What man thou art.
Ang. Who will believe thee, Isabel?
My unsoil'd name, th' austereness of my life,
My vouch against you, and my place i' th' state,
Will so your accusation overweigh,
That you shall stifle in your own report
And smell of calumny. I have begun,
And now I give my sensual race the rein:
Fit thy consent to my sharp appetite;
Lay by all nicety and prolixious blushes,
That banish what they sue for; redeem thy brother

the deed of loving charity would balance one another off. 73. **of your answer,** to which you will have to answer. 77. **graciously,** through divine grace. 79. **tax,** accuse. **these,** generically referring to any. 80. **enshield,** enshielded, protected, i.e., behind the black masks. 82. **received plain,** plainly understood. **gross,** plainly. 86. **Accountant,** accountable. 89. **subscribe,** assent to. 90. **But . . . question,** except for the sake of continuing this discussion. 97. **suppos'd,** hypothetical person. 103. **longing . . . for,** i.e., that I have been sick with longing for. 106. **died at once,** i.e., physical death as contrasted to the death of the soul through sin. 111. **Ignomy,** ignominy. 122-123. **If . . . weakness,** if he, not as a sharer of the weakness of all men, but unique in this respect, is the only man to possess this inclination to sin. 122. **feodary,** associate, i.e., one of the whole group of mankind. 123. **thy,** spoken to Angelo not as an individual but as of the class; this is plain from Angelo's response (l. 124). 126. **forms,** images. 127. **men . . . mar,** men debase their nature. 130. **credulous . . . prints,** susceptible to false impressions. 134. **I do . . . words,** I take you at your word. 140. **former,** i.e., customary. 145-147. **your virtue . . . others,** you, although virtuous, are pretending foul purposes in order to mislead (*pluck on*) me. 156. **vouch,** testimony. 160. **race,** natural or inherited disposition. 162. **prolixious,** tedious.

By yielding up thy body to my will;
Or else he must not only die the death,
But thy unkindness shall his death draw out
To ling'ring sufferance. Answer me to-morrow,
Or, by the affection that now guides me most,
I'll prove a tyrant to him. As for you,
Say what you can, my false o'erweighs your true. *Exit.*

Isab. To whom should I complain? Did I tell this,
Who would believe me? O perilous mouths,
That bear in them one and the self-same tongue,
Either of condemnation or approof;
Bidding the law make court'sy to their will;
Hooking both right and wrong to th' appetite,
To follow as it draws! I'll to my brother:
Though he hath fall'n by prompture of the blood,
Yet hath he in him such a mind of honour,
That, had he twenty heads to tender down
On twenty bloody blocks, he 'ld yield them up,
Before his sister should her body stoop
To such abhorr'd pollution.
Then, Isabel, live chaste, and, brother, die:
More than our brother is our chastity.
I'll tell him yet of Angelo's request,
And fit his mind to death, for his soul's rest. *Exit.*

ACT III.

SCENE I. [*A room in the prison.*]

Enter DUKE [*disguised as before*], CLAUDIO, *and* PROVOST.

Duke. So then you hope of pardon from Lord Angelo?

Claud. The miserable have no other medicine
But only hope:
I have hope to live, and am prepar'd to die.

Duke. Be absolute for death; either death or life
Shall thereby be the sweeter. Reason thus with life:
If I do lose thee, I do lose a thing
That none but fools would keep: a breath thou art,
Servile to all the skyey influences,
That dost this habitation, where thou keep'st,
Hourly afflict: merely, thou art death's fool;
For him thou labour'st by thy flight to shun
And yet runn'st toward him still. Thou art not noble;
For all th' accommodations that thou bear'st
Are nurs'd by baseness. Thou 'rt by no means valiant;
For thou dost fear the soft and tender fork
Of a poor worm. Thy best of rest is sleep,
And that thou oft provok'st; yet grossly fear'st
Thy death, which is no more. Thou art not thyself;
For thou exists on many a thousand grains
That issue out of dust. Happy thou art not;
For what thou hast not, still thou striv'st to get,
And what thou hast, forget'st. Thou art not certain;
For thy complexion shifts to strange effects,
After the moon. If thou art rich, thou 'rt poor;
For, like an ass whose back with ingots bows,
Thou bear'st thy heavy riches but a journey,
And death unloads thee. Friend hast thou none;
For thine own bowels, which do call thee sire,
The mere effusion of thy proper loins,
Do curse the gout, serpigo, and the rheum,
For ending thee no sooner. Thou hast nor youth nor age,
But, as it were, an after-dinner's sleep,
Dreaming on both; for all thy blessed youth
Becomes as aged, and doth beg the alms
Of palsied eld; and when thou art old and rich,
Thou hast neither heat, affection, limb, nor beauty,
To make thy riches pleasant. What 's yet in this
That bears the name of life? Yet in this life
Lie hid moe thousand deaths: yet death we fear,
That makes these odds all even.

Claud. I humbly thank you.
To sue to live, I find I seek to die;
And, seeking death, find life: let it come on.

Enter ISABELLA.

Isab. What, ho! Peace here; grace and good company!

Prov. Who 's there? come in: the wish deserves a welcome.

Duke. Dear sir, ere long I'll visit you again.

Claud. Most holy sir, I thank you.

Isab. My business is a word or two with Claudio.

Prov. And very welcome. Look, signior, here 's your sister.

Duke. Provost, a word with you.

Prov. As many as you please.

Duke. Bring me to hear them speak, where I may be conceal'd. [*Duke and Provost withdraw.*]

Claud. Now, sister, what 's the comfort?

Isab. Why,
As all comforts are; most good, most good indeed.
Lord Angelo, having affairs to heaven,
Intends you for his swift ambassador,
Where you shall be an everlasting leiger:
Therefore your best appointment make with speed;
To-morrow you set on.

Claud. Is there no remedy?

Isab. None, but such remedy as, to save a head,
To cleave a heart in twain.

Claud. But is there any?

Isab. Yes, brother, you may live:
There is a devilish mercy in the judge,
If you'll implore it, that will free your life,
But fetter you till death.

Claud. Perpetual durance?

Isab. Ay, just; perpetual durance, a restraint,
Though all the world's vastidity you had,
To a determin'd scope.

Claud. But in what nature?

Isab. In such a one as, you consenting to 't,
Would bark your honour from that trunk you bear,
And leave you naked.

Claud. Let me know the point.

Isab. O, I do fear thee, Claudio; and I quake,

---

167. **sufferance,** torture. 168. **affection,** passion.

ACT III. SCENE I. 5. **absolute,** absolutely prepared. 7-41. **If I do lose,** etc. The duke's indirect apostrophe to Life becomes merged, as the speech proceeds, with his direct instructions to Claudio. It is not easy to keep clear the distinction between the abstraction apostrophized and the young man who is the embodiment of that abstraction. 14. **accommodations,** conveniences. 23-25. **Thou . . . moon,** Life (personified) is of a temperament as variable as the constantly changing moon. 23. **certain,** steadfast. 24. **effects,** appearances, manifestations. 26. **ingots,** metal cast into molds. 31. **serpigo,** skin eruption. **rheum,** catarrh. 59. **leiger,** resident ambassador. 60. **appointment,** preparation. 67. **durance,** imprisonment. 68-70. **restraint . . . scope,** a confinement to fixed limits or bounds (i.e., to damnation), even if you had the entire vastness of the world to wander in. 72. **bark,** strip. 75. **entertain,** maintain, keep up (Onions); endure (Hart); possibly, desire. 82. **fetch,** derive. 89. **appliances,** devices, remedies. 91. **emmew,** drive a fowl into the water; misprint for *enew* (so printed by some editors). 93. **cast,** vomited. 94, 97. **prenzie,** so F; the word is

Lest thou a feverous life shouldst entertain,
And six or seven winters more respect
Than a perpetual honour. Dar'st thou die?
The sense of death is most in apprehension;
And the poor beetle, that we tread upon,
In corporal sufferance finds a pang as great
As when a giant dies.
Claud. Why give you me this shame?
Think you I can a resolution fetch
From flow'ry tenderness? If I must die,
I will encounter darkness as a bride,
And hug it in mine arms.
Isab. There spake my brother; there my father's grave
Did utter forth a voice. Yes, thou must die:
Thou art too noble to conserve a life
In base appliances. This outward-sainted deputy,
Whose settled visage and deliberate word
Nips youth i' th' head and follies doth emmew
As falcon doth the fowl, is yet a devil;
His filth within being cast, he would appear
A pond as deep as hell.
Claud. The prenzie Angelo!
Isab. O, 'tis the cunning livery of hell,
The damned'st body to invest and cover
In prenzie guards! Dost thou think, Claudio?
If I would yield him my virginity,
Thou mightst be freed.
Claud. O heavens! it cannot be.
Isab. Yes, he would give 't thee, from this rank offence,
So to offend him still. This night 's the time
That I should do what I abhor to name,
Or else thou diest to-morrow.
Claud. Thou shalt not do 't.
Isab. O, were it but my life,
I 'ld throw it down for your deliverance
As frankly as a pin.
Claud. Thanks, dear Isabel.
Isab. Be ready, Claudio, for your death to-morrow.
Claud. Yes. Has he affections in him,
That thus can make him bite the law by th' nose,
When he would force it? Sure, it is no sin;
Or of the deadly seven it is the least.
Isab. Which is the least?
Claud. If it were damnable, he being so wise,
Why would he for the momentary trick
Be perdurably fin'd? O Isabel!
Isab. What says my brother?
Claud. Death is a fearful thing.
Isab. And shamed life a hateful.
Claud. Ay, but to die, and go we know not where;
To lie in cold obstruction and to rot;
This sensible warm motion to become
A kneaded clod; and the delighted spirit
To bathe in fiery floods, or to reside
In thrilling region of thick-ribbed ice;
To be imprison'd in the viewless winds,
And blown with restless violence round about
The pendent world; or to be worse than worst
Of those that lawless and incertain thought
Imagine howling: 'tis too horrible!
The weariest and most loathed worldly life
That age, ache, penury and imprisonment
Can lay on nature is a paradise
To what we fear of death.
Isab. Alas, alas!
Claud. Sweet sister, let me live:
What sin you do to save a brother's life,
Nature dispenses with the deed so far
That it becomes a virtue.
Isab. O you beast!
O faithless coward! O dishonest wretch!
Wilt thou be made a man out of my vice?
Is 't not a kind of incest, to take life
From thine own sister's shame? What should I think?
Heaven shield my mother play'd my father fair!
For such a warped slip of wilderness
Ne'er issu'd from his blood. Take my defiance!
Die, perish! Might but my bending down
Reprieve thee from thy fate, it should proceed:
I'll pray a thousand prayers for thy death,
No word to save thee.
Claud. Nay, hear me, Isabel.
Isab. O, fie, fie, fie!
Thy sin 's not accidental, but a trade.
Mercy to thee would prove itself a bawd:
'Tis best that thou diest quickly.
Claud. O hear me, Isabella!

[DUKE *comes forward.*]

Duke. Vouchsafe a word, young sister, but one word.
Isab. What is your will?

Duke. Might you dispense with your leisure, I would by and by have some speech with you: the satisfaction I would require is likewise your own benefit.

Isab. I have no superfluous leisure; my stay must be stolen out of other affairs; but I will attend you awhile. [*Walks apart.*]

Duke. Son, I have overheard what hath passed between you and your sister. Angelo had never the purpose to corrupt her; only he hath made an assay of her virtue to practise his judgement with the disposition of natures: she, having the truth of honour in her, hath made him that gracious denial which he is most glad to receive. I am confessor to Angelo, and I know this to be true; therefore prepare yourself to death: do not satisfy your resolution with hopes that are fallible: to-morrow you must die; go to your knees and make ready.

Claud. Let me ask my sister pardon. I am so out of love with life that I will sue to be rid of it.

Duke. Hold you there: farewell. [*Claudio retires.*] Provost, a word with you!

[PROVOST *comes forward.*]

Prov. What 's your will, father?

unknown elsewhere. *Princely, priestly, primsie* are suggested conjectures. Hart connects it with "prim," i.e., overnice; the New Cambridge editors favor *proxy* (Bulloch's conjecture) for line 94 and some word corresponding with "priestly" for line 97; they offer *prosne* or *prozne* (i.e., homily). **guards,** trimmings. 115. **perdurably,** lastingly. 119. **obstruction,** cessation of the vital functions. 120. **sensible,** endowed with feeling. **motion,** organism. 121. **delighted spirit,** spirit once or now capable of delight. 122-128. **fiery . . . howling.** Keightly in his comment on *Paradise Lost,* II, 587-595, observes the currency in the Middle Ages of the idea of hell as consisting in alternations between the extremes of cold and heat; he finds it to come from the Jewish commentators. It is found in Dante's *Inferno* and in the description of hell in the *Faust-Book* (1587). 123. **thrilling,** causing one to shiver. 124. **viewless,** invisible. 126. **pendent,** hanging in space (a Ptolemaic concept). 142. **warped,** perverse. **slip,** scion. **wilderness,** worthlessness. 164-165. **to practise . . . natures,** to test his ability to judge people's characters.

Duke. That now you are come, you will be gone. Leave me awhile with the maid: my mind promises with my habit no loss shall touch her by my company.

Prov. In good time.

Exit [Provost with Claudio. Isabella comes forward].

Duke. The hand that hath made you fair hath made you good: the goodness that is cheap in beauty makes beauty brief in goodness; but grace, being the soul of your complexion, shall keep the body of it ever fair. The assault that Angelo hath made to you, fortune hath conveyed to my understanding; and, but that frailty hath examples for his falling, I should wonder at Angelo. How will you do to content this substitute, and to save your brother?

Isab. I am now going to resolve him: I had rather my brother die by the law than my son should be unlawfully born. But, O, how much is the good duke deceived in Angelo! If ever he return and I can speak to him, I will open my lips in vain, or discover his government.

Duke. That shall not be much amiss: yet, as the matter now stands, he will avoid your accusation; he made trial of you only. Therefore fasten your ear on my advisings: to the love I have in doing good a remedy presents itself. I do make myself believe that you may most uprighteously do a poor wronged lady a merited benefit; redeem your brother from the angry law; do no stain to your own gracious person; and much please the absent duke, if peradventure he shall ever return to have hearing of this business.

Isab. Let me hear you speak farther. I have spirit to do any thing that appears not foul in the truth of my spirit.

Duke. Virtue is bold, and goodness never fearful. Have you not heard speak of Mariana, the sister of Frederick the great soldier who miscarried at sea?

Isab. I have heard of the lady, and good words went with her name.

Duke. She should this Angelo have married; was affianced to her by oath, and the nuptial appointed: between which time of the contract and limit of the solemnity, her brother Frederick was wracked at sea, having in that perished vessel the dowry of his sister. But mark how heavily this befell to the poor gentlewoman: there she lost a noble and renowned brother, in his love toward her ever most kind and natural; with him, the portion and sinew of her fortune, her marriage-dowry; with both, her combinate husband, this well-seeming Angelo.

Isab. Can this be so? did Angelo so leave her?

Duke. Left her in her tears, and dried not one of them with his comfort; swallowed his vows whole, pretending in her discoveries of dishonour: in few, bestowed her on her own lamentation, which she yet wears for his sake; and he, a marble to her tears, is washed with them, but relents not.

Isab. What a merit were it in death to take this poor maid from the world! What corruption in this life, that it will let this man live! But how out of this can she avail?

Duke. It is a rupture that you may easily heal: and the cure of it not only saves your brother, but keeps you from dishonour in doing it.

Isab. Show me how, good father.

Duke. This forenamed maid hath yet in her the continuance of her first affection: his unjust unkindness, that in all reason should have quenched her love, hath, like an impediment in the current, made it more violent and unruly. Go you to Angelo; answer his requiring with a plausible obedience; agree with his demands to the point; only refer yourself to this advantage, first, that your stay with him may not be long; that the time may have all shadow and silence in it; and the place answer to convenience. This being granted in course,—and now follows all,—we shall advise this wronged maid to stead up your appointment, go in your place; if the encounter acknowledge itself hereafter, it may compel him to her recompense: and here, by this, is your brother saved, your honour untainted, the poor Mariana advantaged, and the corrupt deputy scaled. The maid will I frame and make fit for his attempt. If you think well to carry this as you may, the doubleness of the benefit defends the deceit from reproof. What think you of it?

Isab. The image of it gives me content already; and I trust it will grow to a most prosperous perfection.

Duke. It lies much in your holding up. Haste you speedily to Angelo: if for this night he entreat you to his bed, give him promise of satisfaction. I will presently to Saint Luke's: there, at the moated grange, resides this dejected Mariana. At that place call upon me; and dispatch with Angelo, that it may be quickly.

Isab. I thank you for this comfort. Fare you well, good father. *Exit.*

[SCENE II. *The street before the prison.*]

Enter [to the DUKE] ELBOW, *Clown* [POMPEY, *and*] Officers.

Elb. Nay, if there be no remedy for it, but that you will needs buy and sell men and women like beasts, we shall have all the world drink brown and white bastard.

Duke. O heavens! what stuff is here?

Pom. 'Twas never merry world since, of two usuries, the merriest was put down, and the worser allowed by order of law a furred gown to keep him warm; and furred with fox and lamb-skins too, to signify, that craft, being richer than innocency, stands for the facing.

Elb. Come your way, sir. 'Bless you, good father friar.

181. **with my habit,** as well as my priestly garb. 183. **In good time,** i.e., very well. 185-186. **the goodness . . . goodness,** the physical graces that come easily with beauty make beauty soon cease to be morally good. 187. **complexion,** character. 192. **this substitute,** i.e., the deputy, Angelo. 194. **resolve,** answer. 199. **discover his government,** expose Angelo's misconduct. 224. **limit of the solemnity,** date set for the ceremony. 231. **combinate husband,** i.e., betrothed; cf. I, ii, 151, note. 237. **bestowed . . . lamentation,** left to her grief, with quibble on *bestowed* meaning "gave in marriage." 243. **avail,** benefit. 254. **to the point,** precisely. 261-262. **if the . . . hereafter,** i.e., if she should become pregnant. 266. **scaled,** weighed. **frame,** prepare. 277. **moated grange,** a country house surrounded by a ditch. 278. **dispatch,** settle, conclude (business).

SCENE II. The scene is continuous with the previous scene. 4. **bastard,** sweet Spanish wine (used quibblingly). 6-7. **two usuries,** i.e., moneylending (*the worser*) and procuring (*the merriest*). 9. **furred . . . lamb-skins,** characteristic trimmings of usurers' gowns. 11. **facing,** trimming. 14. **brother father,** the duke's retort to Elbow's *father friar* (i.e., father brother). 41. **From our . . . free,** so F; there are no satisfactory conjectures. Some editors adopt F_2: *Free from our*, etc. 42. **His . . .**

Duke. And you, good brother father. What offence hath this man made you, sir?

Elb. Marry, sir, he hath offended the law: and, sir, we take him to be a thief too, sir; for we have found upon him, sir, a strange picklock, which we have sent to the deputy.

Duke. Fie, sirrah! a bawd, a wicked bawd!
The evil that thou causest to be done,
That is thy means to live. Do thou but think
What 'tis to cram a maw or clothe a back
From such a filthy vice: say to thyself,
From their abominable and beastly touches
I drink, I eat, array myself, and live.
Canst thou believe thy living is a life,
So stinkingly depending? Go mend, go mend.

Pom. Indeed, it does stink in some sort, sir; but yet, sir, I would prove—

Duke. Nay, if the devil have given thee proofs for sin,
Thou wilt prove his. Take him to prison, officer:
Correction and instruction must both work
Ere this rude beast will profit.

Elb. He must before the deputy, sir; he has given him warning: the deputy cannot abide a whoremaster: if he be a whoremonger, and comes before him, he were as good go a mile on his errand.

Duke. That we were all, as some would seem to be,
†From our faults, as faults from seeming, free!

Enter LUCIO.

Elb. His neck will come to your waist,—a cord, sir.

Pom. I spy comfort; I cry bail. Here 's a gentleman and a friend of mine.

Lucio. How now, noble Pompey! What, at the wheels of Cæsar? art thou led in triumph? What, is there none of Pygmalion's images, newly made woman, to be had now, for putting the hand in the pocket and extracting it clutched? What reply, ha? What sayest thou to this tune, matter and method? Is 't not drowned i' the last rain, ha? What sayest thou, Trot? Is the world as it was, man? Which is the way? Is it sad, and few words? or how? The trick of it?

Duke. Still thus, and thus; still worse!

Lucio. How doth my dear morsel, thy mistress? Procures she still, ha?

Pom. Troth, sir, she hath eaten up all her beef, and she is herself in the tub.

Lucio. Why, 'tis good; it is the right of it; it must be so: ever your fresh whore and your powdered bawd: an unshunned consequence; it must be so. Art going to prison, Pompey?

Pom. Yes, faith, sir.

Lucio. Why, 'tis not amiss, Pompey. Farewell: go say I sent thee thither. For debt, Pompey? or how?

Elb. For being a bawd, for being a bawd.

Lucio. Well, then, imprison him: if imprisonment be the due of a bawd, why, 'tis his right: bawd is he doubtless, and of antiquity too; bawd-born. Farewell, good Pompey. Commend me to the prison, Pompey: you will turn good husband now, Pompey; you will keep the house.

Pom. I hope, sir, your good worship will be my bail.

Lucio. No, indeed, will I not, Pompey; it is not the wear. I will pray, Pompey, to increase your bondage: if you take it not patiently, why, your mettle is the more. Adieu, trusty Pompey. 'Bless you, friar.

Duke. And you.

Lucio. Does Bridget paint still, Pompey, ha?

Elb. Come your ways, sir; come.

Pom. You will not bail me, then, sir?

Lucio. Then, Pompey, nor now. What news abroad, friar? what news?

Elb. Come your ways, sir; come.

Lucio. Go to kennel, Pompey; go. [*Exeunt Elbow, Pompey and Officers*.] What news, friar, of the duke?

Duke. I know none. Can you tell me of any?

Lucio. Some say he is with the Emperor of Russia; other some, he is in Rome: but where is he, think you?

Duke. I know not where; but wheresoever, I wish him well.

Lucio. It was a mad fantastical trick of him to steal from the state, and usurp the beggary he was never born to. Lord Angelo dukes it well in his absence; he puts transgression to 't.

Duke. He does well in 't.

Lucio. A little more lenity to lechery would do no harm in him: something too crabbed that way, friar.

Duke. It is too general a vice, and severity must cure it.

Lucio. Yes, in good sooth, the vice is of a great kindred; it is well allied: but it is impossible to extirp it quite, friar, till eating and drinking be put down. They say this Angelo was not made by man and woman after this downright way of creation: is it true, think you?

Duke. How should he be made, then?

Lucio. Some report a sea-maid spawned him; some, that he was begot between two stock-fishes. But it is certain that when he makes water his urine is congealed ice; that I know to be true: †and he is a motion generative; that 's infallible.

Duke. You are pleasant, sir, and speak apace.

Lucio. Why, what a ruthless thing is this in him, for the rebellion of a codpiece to take away the life of a man! Would the duke that is absent have done this? Ere he would have hanged a man for the getting a hundred bastards, he would have paid for the nursing a thousand: he had some feeling of the sport; he knew the service, and that instructed him to mercy.

Duke. I never heard the absent duke much detected for women; he was not inclined that way.

Lucio. O, sir, you are deceived.

Duke. 'Tis not possible.

Lucio. Who, not the duke? yes, your beggar of fifty; and his use was to put a ducat in her clack-dish: the duke had crotchets in him. He would be drunk too; that let me inform you.

cord. Elbow hints at Pompey's liability to hang, at the same time referring to the cord about the duke's waist—in his habit of friar. 48. **Pygmalion's images,** i.e., prostitutes. Pygmalion was a sculptor whose female statue came to life. 50. **clutch'd,** i.e., with money in it. 53. **Trot,** old bawd. 59. **in the tub,** i.e., a victim of venereal disease, so designated from the sweating-tub treatment to which victims were subjected. 62. **powdered,** salted; salt was put into the baths (cf. preceding note); hence arise the puns on *salt* meaning "wanton, lecherous." 73. **good husband,** thrifty manager. 74. **keep the house,** stay indoors (with pun). 80. **mettle,** spirit, with quibble on "metal," i.e., the irons with which he will be shackled. 108-109. **is . . . kindred,** belongs to a numerous race. 110. **extirp,** eradicate. 115. **sea-maid,** mermaid. 116. **stock-fishes,** dried codfish. 119. **motion generative,** a masculine puppet. 122. **codpiece,** an appendage to the front of close-fitting hose or breeches worn by men in the sixteenth century, often ornamented and indelicately conspicuous. 135. **clack-dish,** beggar's wooden dish with a lid, "clacked" to attract attention. **crotchets,** whims.

Duke. You do him wrong, surely.

Lucio. Sir, I was an inward of his. A shy fellow was the duke: and I believe I know the cause of his withdrawing.

Duke. What, I prithee, might be the cause?

Lucio. No, pardon; 'tis a secret must be locked within the teeth and the lips: but this I can let you understand, the greater file of the subject held the duke to be wise.

Duke. Wise! why, no question but he was.

Lucio. A very superficial, ignorant, unweighing fellow.

Duke. Either this is envy in you, folly, or mistaking: the very stream of his life and the business he hath helmed must upon a warranted need give him a better proclamation. Let him be but testimonied in his own bringings-forth, and he shall appear to the envious a scholar, a statesman and a soldier. Therefore you speak unskilfully; or if your knowledge be more it is much darkened in your malice.

Lucio. Sir, I know him, and I love him.

Duke. Love talks with better knowledge, and knowledge with dearer love.

Lucio. Come, sir, I know what I know.

Duke. I can hardly believe that, since you know not what you speak. But, if ever the duke return, as our prayers are he may, let me desire you to make your answer before him. If it be honest you have spoke, you have courage to maintain it: I am bound to call upon you; and, I pray you, your name?

Lucio. Sir, my name is Lucio; well known to the duke.

Duke. He shall know you better, sir, if I may live to report you.

Lucio. I fear you not.

Duke. O, you hope the duke will return no more; or you imagine me too unhurtful an opposite. But indeed I can do you little harm; you'll forswear this again.

Lucio. I'll be hanged first: thou art deceived in me, friar. But no more of this. Canst thou tell if Claudio die to-morrow or no?

Duke. Why should he die, sir?

Lucio. Why? For filling a bottle with a tun-dish. I would the duke we talk of were returned again: this ungenitured agent will unpeople the province with continency; sparrows must not build in his house-eaves, because they are lecherous. The duke yet would have dark deeds darkly answered; he would never bring them to light: would he were returned! Marry, this Claudio is condemned for untrussing. Farewell, good friar: I prithee, pray for me. The duke, I say to thee again, would eat mutton on Fridays. He 's not past it yet, and I say to thee, he would mouth with a beggar, though she smelt brown bread and garlic: say that I said so. Farewell. *Exit.*

Duke. No might nor greatness in mortality
Can censure 'scape; back-wounding calumny
The whitest virtue strikes. What king so strong
Can tie the gall up in the slanderous tongue?
But who comes here?

Enter ESCALUS, PROVOST, *and* [Officers *with*] *Bawd* [MISTRESS OVERDONE].

Escal. Go; away with her to prison!

Mrs Ov. Good my lord, be good to me; your honour is accounted a merciful man; good my lord.

Escal. Double and treble admonition, and still forfeit in the same kind! This would make mercy swear and play the tyrant.

Prov. A bawd of eleven years' continuance, may it please your honour.

Mrs Ov. My lord, this is one Lucio's information against me. Mistress Kate Keepdown was with child by him in the duke's time; he promised her marriage: his child is a year and a quarter old, come Philip and Jacob: I have kept it myself; and see how he goes about to abuse me!

Escal. That fellow is a fellow of much license: let him be called before us. Away with her to prison! Go to; no more words. [*Exeunt Officers with Mistress Ov.*] Provost, my brother Angelo will not be altered; Claudio must die to-morrow: let him be furnished with divines, and have all charitable preparation. If my brother wrought by my pity, it should not be so with him.

Prov. So please you, this friar hath been with him, and advised him for the entertainment of death.

Escal. Good even, good father.

Duke. Bliss and goodness on you!

Escal. Of whence are you?

Duke. Not of this country, though my chance is now
To use it for my time: I am a brother
Of gracious order, late come from the See
In special business from his holiness.

Escal. What news abroad i' the world?

Duke. None, but that there is so great a fever on goodness, that the dissolution of it must cure it: novelty is only in request; and it is as dangerous to be aged in any kind of course, as it is virtuous to be constant in any undertaking. There is scarce truth enough alive to make societies secure; but security enough to make fellowships accurst: much upon this riddle runs the wisdom of the world. This news is old enough, yet it is every day's news. I pray you, sir, of what disposition was the duke?

Escal. One that, above all other strifes, contended especially to know himself.

Duke. What pleasure was he given to?

Escal. Rather rejoicing to see another merry, than merry at any thing which professed to make him rejoice: a gentleman of all temperance. But leave we him to his events, with a prayer they may prove prosperous; and let me desire to know how you find

138. **inward,** intimate acquaintance. 144. **the greater . . . subject,** the majority of the people. 147. **unweighing,** thoughtless. 151. **upon . . . need,** if a warrant is needed. 153. **testimonied . . . bringings-forth,** proclaimed by his own public actions. 175. **too . . . opposite,** too harmless an adversary. 182. **tun-dish,** funnel. 184. **ungenitured,** sexless. 188. **darkly answered,** not made public. 190. **untrussing,** undressing. 192. **mutton,** quibble on the meaning *prostitute.* 206. **forfeit . . . kind,** guilty of the same offense. 214. **Philip and Jacob,** feast of St. Philip and St. Jacob, May 1. 232. **the See,** Rome. 256. **sinister,** unfair, unjust. 269. **straitness,** strictness. 277-278. **Pattern . . . virtue go,** so F; Johnson rewrote: *Patterning Himself . . . In grace to stand, in virtue go.* Hart emended *and* to *an* (i.e., *if*), which gives the sense, "if virtue fail elsewhere." 287-290. **How . . . things.** Probably a corrupt passage, of uncertain meaning. The gist of the meaning is man's hypocritical concealment of his guilt, in which he creates an illusion of virtue (like the deceitful spider's web) to cover over the heavy and substantial reality of guilt.

ACT IV. SCENE I. 4. **mislead,** i.e., mislead one to expect the morning. 8-9. **whose . . . discontent.** Mariana is implying a length of association impossible with the time scheme as it now stands, but this sort of compression of time is common in Shakespeare. 9. **brawling,** clamorous. 13-15. **My . . . harm.** These lines reflect the Renaissance conception

Claudio prepared. I am made to understand that you have lent him visitation.

Duke. He professes to have received no sinister measure from his judge, but most willingly humbles himself to the determination of justice: yet had he framed to himself, by the instruction of his frailty, many deceiving promises of life; which I by my good leisure have discredited to him, and now is he resolved to die.

Escal. You have paid the heavens your function, and the prisoner the very debt of your calling. I have laboured for the poor gentleman to the extremest shore of my modesty: but my brother justice have I found so severe, that he hath forced me to tell him he is indeed Justice.

Duke. If his own life answer the straitness of his proceeding, it shall become him well; wherein if he chance to fail, he hath sentenced himself.

Escal. I am going to visit the prisoner. Fare you well.

Duke. Peace be with you! [*Exeunt Escalus and Provost.*]
He who the sword of heaven will bear
Should be as holy as severe;
Pattern in himself to know,
†Grace to stand, and virtue go;
More nor less to others paying
Than by self-offences weighing.
Shame to him whose cruel striking
Kills for faults of his own liking!
Twice treble shame on Angelo,
To weed my vice and let his grow!
O, what may man within him hide,
Though angel on the outward side!
†How may likeness made in crimes,
Making practice on the times,
To draw with idle spiders' strings
Most ponderous and substantial things!
Craft against vice I must apply:
With Angelo to-night shall lie
His old betrothed but despised;
†So disguise shall, by th' disguised,
Pay with falsehood false exacting,
And perform an old contracting. *Exit.*

ACT IV.

SCENE I. [*The moated grange at* ST LUKE'S.]

Enter MARIANA, *and* BOY *singing.*

SONG.

Take, O, take those lips away,
That so sweetly were forsworn;
And those eyes, the break of day,
Lights that do mislead the morn:
But my kisses bring again, bring again;
Seals of love, but seal'd in vain, seal'd in vain.

Enter DUKE [*disguised as before*].

Mari. Break off thy song, and haste thee quick away:
Here comes a man of comfort, whose advice
Hath often still'd my brawling discontent. [*Exit Boy.*]
I cry you mercy, sir; and well could wish
You had not found me here so musical:
Let me excuse me, and believe me so,
My mirth it much displeas'd, but pleas'd my woe.

Duke. 'Tis good; though music oft hath such a charm
To make bad good, and good provoke to harm.
I pray you, tell me, hath any body inquired for me here to-day? much upon this time have I promised here to meet.

Mari. You have not been inquired after: I have sat here all day.

Enter ISABELLA.

Duke. I do constantly believe you. The time is come even now. I shall crave your forbearance a little: may be I will call upon you anon, for some advantage to yourself.

Mari. I am always bound to you. *Exit.*

Duke. Very well met, and well come.
What is the news from this good deputy?

Isab. He hath a garden circummur'd with brick,
Whose western side is with a vineyard back'd;
And to that vineyard is a planched gate,
That makes his opening with this bigger key:
This other doth command a little door
Which from the vineyard to the garden leads;
There have I made my promise
Upon the heavy middle of the night
To call upon him.

Duke. But shall you on your knowledge find this way?

Isab. I have ta'en a due and wary note upon 't:
With whispering and most guilty diligence,
In action all of precept, he did show me
The way twice o'er.

Duke. Are there no other tokens
Between you 'greed concerning her observance?

Isab. No, none, but only a repair i' th' dark;
And that I have possess'd him my most stay
Can be but brief; for I have made him know
I have a servant comes with me along,
That stays upon me, whose persuasion is
I come about my brother.

Duke. 'Tis well borne up.
I have not yet made known to Mariana
A word of this. What, ho! within! come forth!

Enter MARIANA.

I pray you, be acquainted with this maid;
She comes to do you good.

of the psychological effects of music; cf. Burton's description: "As [music] is acceptable and conducing to most, so especially to a melancholy man; provided always, his disease proceed not originally from it, that he be not some light *Inamorato*, some idle phantastick, who capers in conceit all the day long, and thinks of nothing else but how to make Jigs, Sonnets, Madrigals, in commendation of his Mistress. In such cases Musick is most pernicious, as a spur to a free horse will make him run himself blind, or break his wind . . . for Musick enchants, it will make such melancholy persons mad, and the sound of those Jigs and Horn-pipes will not be removed out of the ears a week after. *Plato* for this reason forbids Musick and wine to all young men, because they are most part amorous, lest one fire increase another. Many men are melancholy by hearing Musick, but it is a pleasing melancholy that it causeth; and therefore to such as are discontent, in woe, fear, sorrow, or dejected, it is a most present remedy; it expels cares, alters their grieved minds, and easeth in an instant." (*Anatomy of Melancholy*, II, 2, vi, 3.) 21. **constantly,** confidently. 28. **circummur'd,** walled about. 30. **planched,** made of boards. 40. **In action . . . precept,** i.e., teaching by demonstration. 42. **her observance,** what she is supposed to do. 43. **repair,** act of going or coming to a place. 44. **possess'd,** informed. **my most stay,** my stay at the longest. 47. **stays upon,** waits for.

Isab. I do desire the like.
Duke. Do you persuade yourself that I respect you?
Mari. Good friar, I know you do, and have found it.
Duke. Take, then, this your companion by the hand,
Who hath a story ready for your ear.
I shall attend your leisure: but make haste;
The vaporous night approaches.
Mari. Will 't please you walk aside?
Exit [*with Isabella*].
Duke. O place and greatness! millions of false eyes
Are stuck upon thee: volumes of report
Run with these false, and most contrarious quest
Upon thy doings: thousand escapes of wit
Make thee the father of their idle dreams
And rack thee in their fancies.

Enter MARIANA *and* ISABELLA.

Welcome, how agreed?
Isab. She'll take the enterprise upon her, father,
If you advise it.
Duke. It is not my consent,
But my entreaty too.
Isab. Little have you to say
When you depart from him, but, soft and low,
'Remember now my brother.'
Mari. Fear me not.
Duke. Nor, gentle daughter, fear you not at all.
He is your husband on a pre-contract:
To bring you thus together, 'tis no sin,
Sith that the justice of your title to him
Doth flourish the deceit. Come, let us go.
Our corn 's to reap, for yet our tithe 's to sow. *Exeunt.*

SCENE II. [*A room in the prison.*]

Enter PROVOST *and Clown* [POMPEY].

Prov. Come hither, sirrah. Can you cut off a man's head?

Pom. If the man be a bachelor, sir, I can; but if he be a married man, he 's his wife's head, and I can never cut off a woman's head.

Prov. Come, sir, leave me your snatches, and yield me a direct answer. To-morrow morning are to die Claudio and Barnardine. Here is in our prison a common executioner, who in his office lacks a helper: if you will take it on you to assist him, it shall redeem you from your gyves; if not, you shall have your full time of imprisonment and your deliverance with an unpitied whipping, for you have been a notorious bawd.

Pom. Sir, I have been an unlawful bawd time out of mind; but yet I will be content to be a lawful hangman. I would be glad to receive some instruction from my fellow partner.

Prov. What, ho! Abhorson! Where 's Abhorson, there?

Enter ABHORSON.

Abhor. Do you call, sir?

Prov. Sirrah, here 's a fellow will help you to-morrow in your execution. If you think it meet, compound with him by the year, and let him abide here with you; if not, use him for the present and dismiss him. He cannot plead his estimation with you; he hath been a bawd.

Abhor. A bawd, sir? fie upon him! he will discredit our mystery.

Prov. Go to, sir; you weigh equally; a feather will turn the scale. *Exit.*

Pom. Pray, sir, by your good favour,—for surely, sir, a good favour you have, but that you have a hanging look,—do you call, sir, your occupation a mystery?

Abhor. Ay, sir; a mystery.

Pom. Painting, sir, I have heard say, is a mystery; and your whores, sir, being members of my occupation, using painting, do prove my occupation a mystery: but what mystery there should be in hanging, if I should be hanged, I cannot imagine.

Abhor. Sir, it is a mystery.

Pom. Proof?

Abhor. Every true man's apparel fits your thief: if it be too little for your thief, your true man thinks it big enough; if it be too big for your thief, your thief thinks it little enough: so every true man's apparel fits your thief.

Enter PROVOST.

Prov. Are you agreed?

Pom. Sir, I will serve him; for I do find your hangman is a more penitent trade than your bawd; he doth oftener ask forgiveness.

Prov. You, sirrah, provide your block and your axe to-morrow four o'clock.

Abhor. Come on, bawd; I will instruct thee in my trade; follow.

Pom. I do desire to learn, sir: and I hope, if you have occasion to use me for your own turn, you shall find me yare; for truly, sir, for your kindness I owe you a good turn.

Prov. Call hither Barnardine and Claudio:
Exit [*Pompey, with Abhorson*].
Th' one has my pity; not a jot the other,
Being a murderer, though he were my brother.

Enter CLAUDIO.

Look, here 's the warrant, Claudio, for thy death:
'Tis now dead midnight, and by eight to-morrow
Thou must be made immortal. Where 's Barnardine?
Claud. As fast lock'd up in sleep as guiltless labour
When it lies starkly in the traveller's bones:
He will not wake.
Prov. Who can do good on him?
Well, go, prepare yourself. [*Knocking within.*] But, hark, what noise?

60-61. **millions . . . thee,** an allusion to the eyelike markings of the peacock's plumage, betokening pride; or, more likely, to the many eyes associated with either Fame or Jealousy as emblematically portrayed in the Renaissance. 62-63. **Run . . . doings,** i.e., run like hounds, and perversely chase after (quest) the deeds of great men. 63. **escapes,** sallies (of wit). 65. **rack,** distort. 72. **pre-contract.** Cf. I, ii, 151, note. 75. **flourish,** embellish. 76. **Our corn . . . sow,** we must first sow grain before we can expect to reap a harvest; i.e., we must get started. **tithe,** grain sown for tithe dues.

SCENE II. 6. **snatches,** smart repartee. 12. **gyves,** fetters, shackles. 24. **compound,** make an agreement. 27-28. **plead his estimation,** claim any respect on account of his reputation. 30. **mystery,** craft, occupation. 38-50. **Painting, sir . . . your thief.** Pompey's argument is: Painting is a craft, whores use painting, therefore their trade is a craft or respectable mystery. And since he belongs to a kindred occupation, both Pompey's and Overdone's occupations rank as mysteries. Abhorson replies, similarly I can show that thieves' and hangmen's trades belong to the dignity of a mystery. A fitter of apparel's occupation is a mystery

Heaven give your spirits comfort! [*Exit Claudio.*] By and by!
I hope it is some pardon or reprieve
For the most gentle Claudio.

Enter DUKE [*disguised as before*].

Welcome, father.
Duke. The best and wholesom'st spirits of the night
Envelop you, good Provost! Who call'd here of late?
Prov. None, since the curfew rung.
Duke. Not Isabel?
Prov. No.
Duke. They will, then, ere 't be long.
Prov. What comfort is for Claudio?
Duke. There 's some in hope.
Prov. It is a bitter deputy.
Duke. Not so, not so; his life is parallel'd
Even with the stroke and line of his great justice:
He doth with holy abstinence subdue
That in himself which he spurs on his pow'r
To qualify in others: were he meal'd with that
Which he corrects, then were he tyrannous;
But this being so, he 's just. [*Knocking within.*]
Now are they come. [*Exit Provost.*]
This is a gentle provost: seldom when
The steeled gaoler is the friend of men. [*Knocking within.*]
How now! what noise? That spirit 's possess'd with haste
That wounds th' unsisting postern with these strokes.

[*Enter* PROVOST].

Prov. There he must stay until the officer
Arise to let him in: he is call'd up.
Duke. Have you no countermand for Claudio yet,
But he must die to-morrow?
Prov. None, sir, none.
Duke. As near the dawning, provost, as it is,
You shall hear more ere morning.
Prov. Happily
You something know; yet I believe there comes
No countermand; no such example have we:
Besides, upon the very siege of justice
Lord Angelo hath to the public ear
Profess'd the contrary.

Enter a MESSENGER.

This is his lordship's man.
Duke. And here comes Claudio's pardon.

Mes. [*Giving a paper.*] My lord hath sent you this note; and by me this further charge, that you swerve not from the smallest article of it, neither in time, matter, or other circumstance. Good morrow; for, as I take it, it is almost day.

Prov. I shall obey him. [*Exit Messenger.*]
Duke. [*Aside*] This is his pardon, purchas'd by such sin
For which the pardoner himself is in.
Hence hath offence his quick celerity,
When it is borne in high authority:
When vice makes mercy, mercy 's so extended,
That for the fault's love is th' offender friended.
Now, sir, what news?

Prov. I told you. Lord Angelo, belike thinking me remiss in mine office, awakens me with this unwonted putting-on; methinks strangely, for he hath not used it before.

Duke. Pray you, let 's hear.

[*Prov. reads*] *the letter.*

'Whatsoever you may hear to the contrary, let Claudio be executed by four of the clock; and in the afternoon Barnardine: for my better satisfaction, let me have Claudio's head sent me by five. Let this be duly performed; with a thought that more depends on it than we must yet deliver. Thus fail not to do your office, as you will answer it at your peril.'

What say you to this, sir?

Duke. What is that Barnardine who is to be executed in the afternoon?

Prov. A Bohemian born, but here nursed up and bred; one that is a prisoner nine years old.

Duke. How came it that the absent duke had not either delivered him to his liberty or executed him? I have heard it was ever his manner to do so.

Prov. His friends still wrought reprieves for him: and, indeed, his fact, till now in the government of Lord Angelo, came not to an undoubtful proof.

Duke. It is now apparent?

Prov. Most manifest, and not denied by himself.

Duke. Hath he borne himself penitently in prison? how seems he to be touched?

Prov. A man that apprehends death no more dreadfully but as a drunken sleep; careless, reckless, and fearless of what 's past, present, or to come; insensible of mortality, and desperately mortal.

Duke. He wants advice.

Prov. He will hear none: he hath evermore had the liberty of the prison; give him leave to escape hence, he would not: drunk many times a day, if not many days entirely drunk. We have very oft awaked him, as if to carry him to execution, and showed him a seeming warrant for it: it hath not moved him at all.

Duke. More of him anon. There is written in your brow, provost, honesty and constancy: if I read it not truly, my ancient skill beguiles me; but, in the boldness of my cunning, I will lay my self in hazard. Claudio, whom here you have warrant to execute, is no greater forfeit to the law than Angelo who hath sentenced him. To make you understand this in a manifested effect, I crave but four days' respite; for the which you are to do me both a present and a dangerous courtesy.

Prov. Pray, sir, in what?

Duke. In the delaying death.

Prov. Alack, how may I do it, having the hour limited, and an express command, under penalty, to deliver his head in the view of Angelo? I may make

(a tailor's carft); a thief fits himself from every true man, therefore his business is a mystery. And I, the hangman, find the thief's apparel big enough for my use, who am a true man, so that I am also a member of the thief's occupation or mystery (Hart). Abhorson (ll. 46-50) refers to the custom of the executioner's taking the garments of those executed. 54. **he doth . . . forgiveness.** The executioner perfunctorily asked forgiveness of those whose lives he was about to take. 56. **to-morrow four o'clock.** Cf. *by eight to-morrow* (l. 67); the contradiction is accompanied by the fact that the first reference is in a prose passage, the second in a verse passage. 60. **use me . . . turn,** i.e., cut off your head. 61. **yare,** ready. 70. **starkly,** stiffly. 86. **qualify,** mitigate. **meal'd,** spotted, stained. 90. **steeled,** hardened. 92. **unsisting,** unassisting, or unresisting (?). **postern,** back door. 98. **Happily,** haply, perhaps. 101. **siege,** seat. 120. **putting-on,** urging. 125. **better satisfaction,** greater assurance. 135. **a prisoner . . . old,** nine years a prisoner. 142. **fact,** crime. 152-153. **insensible . . . mortal,** indifferent to death and without hope of immortality. 167. **forfeit to the law.** Cf. II, ii, 71, note. 169. **in a . . . effect,** by means of concrete proof.

my case as Claudio's, to cross this in the smallest.

Duke. By the vow of mine order I warrant you, if my instructions may be your guide. Let this Barnardine be this morning executed, and his head borne to Angelo.

Prov. Angelo hath seen them both, and will discover the favour.

Duke. O, death 's a great disguiser; and you may add to it. Shave the head, and tie the beard; and say it was the desire of the penitent to be so bared before his death: you know the course is common. If any thing fall to you upon this, more than thanks and good fortune, by the saint whom I profess, I will plead against it with my life.

Prov. Pardon me, good father; it is against my oath.

Duke. Were you sworn to the duke, or to the deputy?

Prov. To him, and to his substitutes.

Duke. You will think you have made no offence, if the duke avouch the justice of your dealing?

Prov. But what likelihood is in that?

Duke. Not a resemblance, but a certainty. Yet since I see you fearful, that neither my coat, integrity, nor persuasion can with ease attempt you, I will go further than I meant, to pluck all fears out of you. Look you, sir, here is the hand and seal of the duke: you know the character, I doubt not; and the signet is not strange to you.

Prov. I know them both.

Duke. The contents of this is the return of the duke: you shall anon over-read it at your pleasure; where you shall find, within these two days he will be here. This is a thing that Angelo knows not; for he this very day receives letters of strange tenour; perchance of the duke's death; perchance entering into some monastery; but, by chance, nothing of what is writ. Look, the unfolding star calls up the shepherd. Put not yourself into amazement how these things should be: all difficulties are but easy when they are known. Call your executioner, and off with Barnardine's head: I will give him a present shrift and advise him for a better place. Yet you are amazed; but this shall absolutely resolve you. Come away; it is almost clear dawn. *Exit [with Provost].*

SCENE III. [*Another room in the same.*]

Enter Clown [POMPEY].

Pom. I am as well acquainted here as I was in our house of profession: one would think it were Mistress Overdone's own house, for here be many of her old customers. First, here 's young Master Rash; he 's in for a commodity of brown paper and old ginger, nine-score and seventeen pounds; of which he made five marks, ready money: marry, then ginger was not much in request, for the old women were all dead. Then is there here one Master Caper, at the suit of Master Three-pile the mercer, for some four suits of peach-coloured satin, which now peaches him a beggar. Then have we here young Dizy, and young Master Deep-vow, and Master Copper-spur, and Master Starve-lackey the rapier and dagger man, and young Drop-heir that killed lusty Pudding, and Master Forthlight the tilter, and brave Master Shooty the great traveller, and wild Half-can that stabbed Pots, and, I think, forty more; all great doers in our trade, and are now 'for the Lord's sake.'

Enter ABHORSON.

Abhor. Sirrah, bring Barnardine hither.

Pom. Master Barnardine! you must rise and be hanged, Master Barnardine!

Abhor. What, ho, Barnardine!

Bar. (*Within*) A pox o' your throats! Who makes that noise there? What are you?

Pom. Your friends, sir; the hangman. You must be so good, sir, to rise and be put to death.

Bar. [*Within*] Away, you rogue, away! I am sleepy.

Abhor. Tell him he must awake, and that quickly too.

Pom. Pray, Master Barnardine, awake till you are executed, and sleep afterwards.

Abhor. Go in to him, and fetch him out.

Pom. He is coming, sir, he is coming; I hear his straw rustle.

Enter BARNARDINE.

Abhor. Is the axe upon the block, sirrah?

Pom. Very ready, sir.

Bar. How now, Abhorson? what 's the news with you?

Abhor. Truly, sir, I would desire you to clap into your prayers; for, look you, the warrant 's come.

Bar. You rogue, I have been drinking all night; I am not fitted for 't.

Pom. O, the better, sir; for he that drinks all night, and is hanged betimes in the morning, may sleep the sounder all the next day.

Enter DUKE [*disguised as before*].

Abhor. Look you, sir; here comes your ghostly father: do we jest now, think you?

Duke. Sir, induced by my charity, and hearing how hastily you are to depart, I am come to advise you, comfort you and pray with you.

Bar. Friar, not I: I have been drinking hard all night, and I will have more time to prepare me, or they shall beat out my brains with billets: I will not consent to die this day, that 's certain.

Duke. O, sir, you must: and therefore I beseech you
Look forward on the journey you shall go.

Bar. I swear I will not die to-day for any man's persuasion.

Duke. But hear you.

Bar. Not a word: if you have any thing to say to

185. **favour,** i.e., the difference in features. 205. **attempt,** win, influence. 218. **unfolding star,** i.e., morning star; cf. Comus: "The star that bids the shepherd fold," i.e., the evening star. 223. **present shrift,** immediate absolution for sins (after confession).

SCENE III. 5-6. **a commodity . . . ginger.** Moneylenders were in the habit of buying up refuse commodities—lustrings, hobbyhorses, brown or gray paper, sugar, spices, hops, or what not—at remnant prices which they advanced to gullible borrowers in lieu of cash at a high rate of interest. The borrower unable to sell his commodity—and hence unable to repay the loan—was often thrown into prison. This use circumvented the laws against usurious moneylending. 8. **marks.** A mark was worth about two thirds of a pound. 12. **peaches,** betrays. 15. **rapier and dagger,** a contemptuous reference to the foppery associated with these weapons as more fashionable than the sword and buckler. Hart suggests that Pompey's sneer is based on class distinctions; the upper class used the rapier and dagger to supplant the less harmful weapons of the common people. 21. **'for the Lord's sake,'** the cry of prisoners from jail windows to passers-by to give them food or alms. 49. **betimes,** early. 58. **billets,** thick sticks used as weapons. 68. **gravel,** stony. 88. **continue,** retain, live. 92. **journal,** daily. 93. **the**

me, come to my ward; for thence will not I to-day.
Exit.

Enter PROVOST.

Duke. Unfit to live or die: O gravel heart!
After him, fellows; bring him to the block.
[*Exeunt Abhorson and Pompey.*]
Prov. Now, sir, how do you find the prisoner?
Duke. A creature unprepar'd, unmeet for death;
And to transport him in the mind he is
Were damnable.
Prov. Here in the prison, father,
There died this morning of a cruel fever
One Ragozine, a most notorious pirate,
A man of Claudio's years; his beard and head
Just of his colour. What if we do omit
This reprobate till he were well inclin'd;
And satisfy the deputy with the visage
Of Ragozine, more like to Claudio?
Duke. O, 'tis an accident that heaven provides!
Dispatch it presently; the hour draws on
Prefix'd by Angelo: see this be done,
And sent according to command; whiles I
Persuade this rude wretch willingly to die.
Prov. This shall be done, good father, presently.
But Barnardine must die this afternoon:
And how shall we continue Claudio,
To save me from the danger that might come
If he were known alive?
Duke. Let this be done.
Put them in secret holds, both Barnardine and Claudio:
Ere twice the sun hath made his journal greeting
To the under generation, you shall find
Your safety manifested.
Prov. I am your free dependant.
Duke. Quick, dispatch, and send the head to Angelo. *Exit* [*Provost*].
Now will I write letters to Angelo,—
The provost, he shall bear them,—whose contents
Shall witness to him I am near at home,
And that, by great injunctions, I am bound
To enter publicly: him I'll desire
To meet me at the consecrated fount
A league below the city; and from thence,
By cold gradation and well-balanc'd form,
We shall proceed with Angelo.

Enter PROVOST.

Prov. Here is the head; I'll carry it myself.
Duke. Convenient is it. Make a swift return;
For I would commune with you of such things
That want no ear but yours.
Prov. I'll make all speed. *Exit.*
Isab. (*Within*) Peace, ho, be here!
Duke. The tongue of Isabel. She 's come to know
If yet her brother's pardon be come hither:
But I will keep her ignorant of her good,
To make her heavenly comforts of despair,
When it is least expected.

Enter ISABELLA.

Isab. Ho, by your leave!
Duke. Good morning to you, fair and gracious daughter.
Isab. The better, given me by so holy a man.
Hath yet the deputy sent my brother's pardon?
Duke. He hath releas'd him, Isabel, from the world:
His head is off and sent to Angelo.
Isab. Nay, but it is not so!
Duke. It is no other: show your wisdom, daughter,
In your close patience.
Isab. O, I will to him and pluck out his eyes!
Duke. You shall not be admitted to his sight.
Isab. Unhappy Claudio! wretched Isabel!
Injurious world! most damned Angelo!
Duke. This nor hurts him nor profits you a jot;
Forbear it therefore; give your cause to heaven.
Mark what I say, which you shall find
By every syllable a faithful verity:
The duke comes home to-morrow; nay, dry your eyes;
One of our covent, and his confessor,
Gives me this instance: already he hath carried
Notice to Escalus and Angelo,
Who do prepare to meet him at the gates,
There to give up their pow'r. If you can, pace your wisdom
In that good path that I would wish it go,
And you shall have your bosom on this wretch,
Grace of the duke, revenges to your heart,
And general honour.
Isab. I am directed by you.
Duke. This letter, then, to Friar Peter give;
'Tis that he sent me of the duke's return:
Say, by this token, I desire his company
At Mariana's house to-night. Her cause and yours
I'll perfect him withal, and he shall bring you
Before the duke, and to the head of Angelo
Accuse him home and home. For my poor self,
I am combined by a sacred vow
And shall be absent. Wend you with this letter:
Command these fretting waters from your eyes
With a light heart; trust not my holy order,
If I pervert your course. Who 's here?

Enter LUCIO.

Lucio. Good even. Friar, where 's the provost?
Duke. Not within, sir.
Lucio. O pretty Isabella, I am pale at mine heart to see thine eyes so red: thou must be patient. I am fain to dine and sup with water and bran; I dare not for my head fill my belly; one fruitful meal would set me to 't. But they say the duke will be here to-morrow. By my troth, Isabel, I loved thy brother: if the old fantastical duke of dark corners had been at home, he had lived. [*Exit Isabella.*]

under, so Hanmer; F: *yond;* Pope: *yonder;* New Cambridge: *th'under,* from W. W. Greg's suggestion (privately made) that Shakespeare wrote *ye onder. Under* may mean the antipodes, or merely the human race—the generation under heaven. Hart keeps *yond,* defining as "those beyond the prison walls." 95. **free dependant,** willing servant. 97. **to Angelo.** The New Cambridge editors think this a mistake, since Angelo was not to meet the duke *at the consecrated fount a league below the city,* but at the city gates (cf. ll. 135-137 below). The compositor's eye probably caught the phrase *to Angelo* from the end of the preceding line. 100. **great injunctions,** powerful precedent. 104. **By cold gradation,** not eagerly and passionately, as my feelings would prompt me (Schmidt). **well-balanc'd form.** Some editors retain F: *weal(e) balanced,* which Schmidt defines as "kept in a just proportion by reasons of state." 107. **Convenient,** timely. 117. **better,** i.e., comparative of *Good* in the preceding line. 123. **In your close patience,** by enduring your grief secretly. 133. **covent,** convent. 139. **bosom,** desire. 146. **perfect,** acquaint completely. 149. **combined,** bound. 157-158. **I am . . . heart,** i.e., from sighing, since sighs cost the heart loss of blood. 159. **fain,** compelled.

Duke. Sir, the duke is marvellous little beholding to your reports; but the best is, he lives not in them.

Lucio. Friar, thou knowest not the duke so well as I do: he 's a better woodman than thou takest him for.

Duke. Well, you'll answer this one day. Fare ye well.

Lucio. Nay, tarry; I'll go along with thee: I can tell thee pretty tales of the duke.

Duke. You have told me too many of him already, sir, if they be true; if not true, none were enough.

Lucio. I was once before him for getting a wench with child.

Duke. Did you such a thing?

Lucio. Yes, marry, did I: but I was fain to forswear it; they would else have married me to the rotten medlar.

Duke. Sir, your company is fairer than honest. Rest you well.

Lucio. By my troth, I'll go with thee to the lane's end: if bawdy talk offend you, we'll have very little of it. Nay, friar, I am a kind of burr; I shall stick.

Exeunt.

SCENE IV. [*A room in* ANGELO'S *house.*]

Enter ANGELO *and* ESCALUS.

Escal. Every letter he hath writ hath disvouched other.

Ang. In most uneven and distracted manner. His actions show much like to madness: pray heaven his wisdom be not tainted! And why meet him at the gates, and redeliver our authorities there?

Escal. I guess not.

Ang. And why should we proclaim it in an hour before his entering, that if any crave redress of injustice, they should exhibit their petitions in the street?

Escal. He shows his reason for that: to have a dispatch of complaints, and to deliver us from devices hereafter, which shall then have no power to stand against us.

Ang. Well, I beseech you, let it be proclaimed betimes i' the morn; I'll call you at your house: give notice to such men of sort and suit as are to meet him.

Escal. I shall, sir. Fare you well.

Ang. Good night. *Exit* [*Escalus*].

This deed unshapes me quite, makes me unpregnant
And dull to all proceedings. A deflow'red maid!
And by an eminent body that enforc'd
The law against it! But that her tender shame
Will not proclaim against her maiden loss,
How might she tongue me! Yet reason dares her no;
For my authority bears of a credent bulk,
That no particular scandal once can touch
But it confounds the breather. He should have liv'd,
Save that his riotous youth, with dangerous sense,
Might in the times to come have ta'en revenge,
By so receiving a dishonour'd life
With ransom of such shame. Would yet he had liv'd!
Alack, when once our grace we have forgot,
Nothing goes right: we would, and we would not.

Exit.

SCENE V. [*Fields without the town*].

Enter DUKE [*in his own habit*] *and* FRIAR PETER.

Duke. These letters at fit time deliver me: [*Giving letters.*]
The provost knows our purpose and our plot.
The matter being afoot, keep your instruction,
And hold you ever to our special drift;
Though sometimes you do blench from this to that,
As cause doth minister. Go call at Flavius' house,
And tell him where I stay: give the like notice
To Valencius, Rowland, and to Crassus,
And bid them bring the trumpets to the gate;
But send me Flavius first.

Fri. P. It shall be speeded well. [*Exit.*]

Enter VARRIUS.

Duke. I thank thee, Varrius; thou hast made good haste:
Come, we will walk. There 's other of our friends
Will greet us here anon, my gentle Varrius. *Exeunt.*

SCENE VI. [*Street near the city gate.*]

Enter ISABELLA *and* MARIANA.

Isab. To speak so indirectly I am loath:
I would say the truth; but to accuse him so,
That is your part: yet I am advis'd to do it;
He says, to veil full purpose.

Mari. Be rul'd by him.

Isab. Besides, he tells me that, if peradventure
He speak against me on the adverse side,
I should not think it strange; for 'tis a physic
That 's bitter to sweet end.

Mari. I would Friar Peter—

Enter [FRIAR] PETER.

Isab. O, peace! the friar is come.

Fri. P. Come, I have found you out a stand most fit,
Where you may have such vantage on the duke,
He shall not pass you. Twice have the trumpets sounded;
The generous and gravest citizens
Have hent the gates, and very near upon
The duke is ent'ring: therefore, hence, away! *Exeunt.*

ACT V.

SCENE I. [*The city gate.*]

Enter DUKE, VARRIUS, LORDS, ANGELO, ESCALUS, LUCIO, [PROVOST, Officers, *and*] Citizens *at several doors.*

Duke. My very worthy cousin, fairly met!
Our old and faithful friend, we are glad to see you.

170. **woodman,** hunter, i.e., woman hunter (Onions). 185. **medlar,** a pear that was eaten partly rotten; here, signifying a prostitute.
SCENE IV. 1. **disvouched,** contradicted. 19. **sort,** rank. **suit,** such as owe attendance. 23. **This deed,** i.e., his supposed abuse of Isabella. **unpregnant,** unapt. 28. **dares her no,** defies or taunts her with no (Hart). 29. **credent,** credible.
SCENE V. 1. **me,** for me. 4. **drift,** plot. 5. **blench,** deviate. 11. **Varrius,** not listed with the names of the actors at the end of the F text; this character has no lines to speak here or at his second appearance (V, i). 12. **walk,** stroll.

Ang.
Escal. } Happy return be to your royal grace!
Duke. Many and hearty thankings to you both.
We have made inquiry of you; and we hear
Such goodness of your justice, that our soul
Cannot but yield you forth to public thanks,
Forerunning more requital.
Ang. You make my bonds still greater.
Duke. O, your desert speaks loud; and I should wrong it,
To lock it in the wards of covert bosom,
When it deserves, with characters of brass,
A forted residence 'gainst the tooth of time
And razure of oblivion. Give me your hand,
And let the subject see, to make them know
That outward courtesies would fain proclaim
Favours that keep within. Come, Escalus,
You must walk by us on our other hand;
And good supporters are you.

Enter [Friar] Peter *and* Isabella.

Fri. P. Now is your time: speak loud and kneel before him.
Isab. Justice, O royal duke! Vail your regard
Upon a wrong'd, I would fain have said, a maid!
O worthy prince, dishonour not your eye
By throwing it on any other object
Till you have heard me in my true complaint
And given me justice, justice, justice, justice!
Duke. Relate your wrongs; in what? by whom? be brief.
Here is Lord Angelo shall give you justice:
Reveal yourself to him.
Isab. O worthy duke,
You bid me seek redemption of the devil:
Hear me yourself; for that which I must speak
Must either punish me, not being believ'd,
Or wring redress from you. Hear me, O hear me, here!
Ang. My lord, her wits, I fear me, are not firm:
She hath been a suitor to me for her brother
Cut off by course of justice,—
Isab. By course of justice!
Ang. And she will speak most bitterly and strange.
Isab. Most strange, but yet most truly, will I speak:
That Angelo 's forsworn; is it not strange?
That Angelo 's a murderer; is 't not strange?
That Angelo is an adulterous thief,
An hypocrite, a virgin-violator;
Is it not strange and strange?
Duke. Nay, it is ten times strange.
Isab. It is not truer he is Angelo
Than this is all as true as it is strange:
Nay, it is ten times true; for truth is truth
To th' end of reck'ning.
Duke. Away with her! Poor soul,
She speaks this in th' infirmity of sense.
Isab. O prince, I conjure thee, as thou believ'st
There is another comfort than this world,
That thou neglect me not, with that opinion
That I am touch'd with madness! Make not impossible
That which but seems unlike: 'tis not impossible
But one, the wicked'st caitiff on the ground,
May seem as shy, as grave, as just, as absolute
As Angelo; even so may Angelo,
In all his dressings, characts, titles, forms,
Be an arch-villain; believe it, royal prince:
If he be less, he 's nothing; but he 's more,
Had I more name for badness.
Duke. By mine honesty,
If she be mad,—as I believe no other,—
Her madness hath the oddest frame of sense,
Such a dependency of thing on thing,
As e'er I heard in madness.
Isab. O gracious duke,
Harp not on that, nor do not banish reason
For inequality; but let your reason serve
To make the truth appear where it seems hid,
And hide the false seems true.
Duke. Many that are not mad
Have, sure, more lack of reason. What would you say?
Isab. I am the sister of one Claudio,
Condemn'd upon the act of fornication
To lose his head; condemn'd by Angelo:
I, in probation of a sisterhood,
Was sent to by my brother; one Lucio
As then the messenger,—
Lucio. That 's I, an 't like your grace:
I came to her from Claudio, and desir'd her
To try her gracious fortune with Lord Angelo
For her poor brother's pardon.
Isab. That 's he indeed.
Duke. You were not bid to speak.
Lucio. No, my good lord;
Nor wish'd to hold my peace.
Duke. I wish you now, then;
Pray you, take note of it: and when you have
A business for yourself, pray heaven you then
Be perfect.
Lucio. I warrant your honour.
Duke. The warrant 's for yourself; take heed to 't.
Isab. This gentleman told somewhat of my tale,—
Lucio. Right.
Duke. It may be right; but you are i' the wrong
To speak before your time.—Proceed.
Isab. I went
To this pernicious caitiff deputy,—
Duke. That 's somewhat madly spoken.
Isab. Pardon it;
The phrase is to the matter.
Duke. Mended again. The matter; proceed.
Isab. In brief, to set the needless process by,
How I persuaded, how I pray'd, and kneel'd,
How he refell'd me, and how I replied,—
For this was of much length,—the vile conclusion
I now begin with grief and shame to utter:
He would not, but by gift of my chaste body
To his concupiscible intemperate lust,
Release my brother; and, after much debatement,
My sisterly remorse confutes mine honour,
And I did yield to him: but the next morn betimes,
His purpose surfeiting, he sends a warrant
For my poor brother's head.
Duke. This is most likely!

Scene vi. 13. **generous,** highborn. 14. **hent,** reached, occupied.
Act v. scene i. 10. **To lock . . . bosom,** to keep it locked up in my heart. 12. **forted,** fortified. 13. **razure,** effacement. 47. **in . . . sense,** out of a sick mind. 56. **characts,** symbols of office. 62. **a dependency of thing on thing,** coherence. 65. **inequality,** injustice. 92. **to . . . by,** not to dwell on unnecessary details in the story. 94. **refell'd,** refuted. 98. **concupiscible,** lustful. 103. **This . . . likely.** The duke feigns contempt for Isabella's story in order to fortify Angelo's confidence in denying Isabella.

Isab. O, that it were as like as it is true!
Duke. By heaven, fond wretch, thou know'st not what thou speak'st,
Or else thou art suborn'd against his honour
In hateful practice. First, his integrity
Stands without blemish. Next, it imports no reason
That with such vehemency he should pursue
Faults proper to himself: if he had so offended,
He would have weigh'd thy brother by himself
And not have cut him off. Some one hath set you on:
Confess the truth, and say by whose advice
Thou cam'st here to complain.
Isab. And is this all?
Then, O you blessed ministers above,
Keep me in patience, and with ripened time
Unfold the evil which is here wrapt up
In countenance! Heaven shield your grace from woe,
As I, thus wrong'd, hence unbelieved go!
Duke. I know you 'ld fain be gone. An officer!
To prison with her! Shall we thus permit
A blasting and a scandalous breath to fall
On him so near us? This needs must be a practice.
Who knew of your intent and coming hither?
Isab. One that I would were here, Friar Lodowick.
Duke. A ghostly father, belike. Who knows that Lodowick?
Lucio. My lord, I know him; 'tis a meddling friar;
I do not like the man: had he been lay, my lord,
For certain words he spake against your grace
In your retirement, I had swing'd him soundly.
Duke. Words against me! this 's a good friar, belike!
And to set on this wretched woman here
Against our substitute! Let this friar be found.
Lucio. But yesternight, my lord, she and that friar,
I saw them at the prison: a saucy friar,
A very scurvy fellow.
Fri. P. Blessed be your royal grace!
I have stood by, my lord, and I have heard
Your royal ear abus'd. First, hath this woman
Most wrongfully accus'd your substitute,
Who is as free from touch or soil with her
As she from one ungot.
Duke. We did believe no less.
Know you that Friar Lodowick that she speaks of?
Fri. P. I know him for a man divine and holy;
Not scurvy, nor a temporary meddler,
As he 's reported by this gentleman;
And, on my trust, a man that never yet
Did, as he vouches, misreport your grace.
Lucio. My lord, most villanously; believe it.
Fri. P. Well, he in time may come to clear himself;
But at this instant he is sick, my lord,
Of a strange fever. Upon his mere request,
Being come to knowledge that there was complaint
Intended 'gainst Lord Angelo, came I hither,
To speak, as from his mouth, what he doth know
Is true and false; and what he with his oath
And all probation will make up full clear,
Whensoever he 's convented. First, for this woman,
To justify this worthy nobleman,
So vulgarly and personally accus'd,
Her shall you hear disproved to her eyes,
Till she herself confess it.
Duke. Good friar, let 's hear it.
[*Isabella is carried off guarded.*]

Enter MARIANA.

Do you not smile at this, Lord Angelo?
O heaven, the vanity of wretched fools!
Give us some seats. Come, cousin Angelo;
In this I'll be impartial; be you judge
Of your own cause. Is this the witness, friar?
First, let her show her face, and after speak.
Mari. Pardon, my lord; I will not show my face
Until my husband bid me.
Duke. What, are you married?
Mari. No, my lord.
Duke. Are you a maid?
Mari. No, my lord.
Duke. A widow, then?
Mari. Neither, my lord.
Duke. Why, you are nothing then: neither maid, widow, nor wife?
Lucio. My lord, she may be a punk; for many of them are neither maid, widow, nor wife.
Duke. Silence that fellow: I would he had some cause
To prattle for himself.
Lucio. Well, my lord.
Mari. My lord, I do confess I ne'er was married;
And I confess besides I am no maid:
I have known my husband; yet my husband
Knows not that ever he knew me.
Lucio. He was drunk then, my lord: it can be no better.
Duke. For the benefit of silence, would thou wert so too!
Lucio. Well, my lord.
Duke. This is no witness for Lord Angelo.
Mari. Now I come to 't, my lord:
She that accuses him of fornication,
In self-same manner doth accuse my husband,
And charges him, my lord, with such a time
When I'll depose I had him in mine arms
With all th' effect of love.
Ang. Charges she moe than me?
Mari. Not that I know.
Duke. No? you say your husband.
Mari. Why, just, my lord, and that is Angelo,
Who thinks he knows that he ne'er knew my body,
But knows he thinks that he knows Isabel's.
Ang. This is a strange abuse. Let 's see thy face.
Mari. My husband bids me; now I will unmask.
[*Unveiling.*]
This is that face, thou cruel Angelo,
Which once thou swor'st was worth the looking on;
This is the hand which, with a vow'd contract,
Was fast belock'd in thine; this is the body
That took away the match from Isabel,
And did supply thee at thy garden-house
In her imagin'd person.
Duke. Know you this woman?
Lucio. Carnally, she says.
Duke. Sirrah, no more!

117-118. **wrapt up In countenance,** concealed by means of authority. 123. **practice,** plot. 128. **lay,** not a cleric. 142. **ungot,** unborn. 145. **temporary meddler,** meddler in temporal affairs. 157. **probation,** proof. 158. **convented,** summoned. 160. **vulgarly,** publicly. 162. **Till . . . hear it.** This line anticipates action (or a speech) which does not subsequently occur. The New Cambridge editors think the text has been tampered with here. 179. **punk,** harlot. 187. **known,** had intercourse with. 199. **Charges . . . me,** does she (Isabella) bring charges against persons besides myself? 205. **abuse,** deception. 211. **match,** meeting. 219. **proportions,** dowry. 220. **composition,** agreement.

Lucio. Enough, my lord.
Ang. My lord, I must confess I know this woman:
And five years since there was some speech of marriage
Betwixt myself and her; which was broke off,
Partly for that her promised proportions
Came short of composition, but in chief
For that her reputation was disvalued
In levity: since which time of five years
I never spake with her, saw her, nor heard from her,
Upon my faith and honour.
Mari. Noble prince,
As there comes light from heaven and words from breath,
As there is sense in truth and truth in virtue,
I am affianc'd this man's wife as strongly
As words could make up vows: and, my good lord,
But Tuesday night last gone in 's garden-house
He knew me as a wife. As this is true,
Let me in safety raise me from my knees;
Or else for ever be confixed here,
A marble monument!
Ang. I did but smile till now:
Now, good my lord, give me the scope of justice;
My patience here is touch'd. I do perceive
These poor informal women are no more
But instruments of some more mightier member
That sets them on: let me have way, my lord,
To find this practice out.
Duke. Ay, with my heart;
And punish them to your height of pleasure.
Thou foolish friar, and thou pernicious woman,
Compact with her that 's gone, think'st thou thy oaths,
Though they would swear down each particular saint,
Were testimonies against his worth and credit
That 's seal'd in approbation? You, Lord Escalus,
Sit with my cousin; lend him your kind pains
To find out this abuse, whence 'tis deriv'd.
There is another friar that set them on;
Let him be sent for.
Fri. P. Would he were here, my lord! for he indeed
Hath set the women on to this complaint:
Your provost knows the place where he abides
And he may fetch him.
Duke. Go do it instantly. [*Exit Provost*.]
And you, my noble and well-warranted cousin,
Whom it concerns to hear this matter forth,
Do with your injuries as seems you best,
In any chastisement: I for a while will leave you;
But stir not you till you have well determin'd
Upon these slanderers.
Escal. My lord, we'll do it throughly. *Exit* [*Duke*].
Signior Lucio, did not you say you knew that Friar Lodowick to be a dishonest person?
Lucio. 'Cucullus non facit monachum:' honest in nothing but in his clothes; and one that hath spoke most villanous speeches of the duke.
Escal. We shall entreat you to abide here till he come and enforce them against him: we shall find this friar a notable fellow.
Lucio. As any in Vienna, on my word.
Escal. Call that same Isabel here once again: I would speak with her. [*Exit an Attendant*.] Pray you, my lord, give me leave to question; you shall see how I'll handle her.
Lucio. Not better than he, by her own report.
Escal. Say you?
Lucio. Marry, sir, I think, if you handled her privately, she would sooner confess: perchance, publicly, she'll be ashamed.
Escal. I will go darkly to work with her.
Lucio. That 's the way; for women are light at midnight.

Enter DUKE [*disguised as a friar*], PROVOST, ISABELLA [, *and* Officers].

Escal. Come on, mistress: here 's a gentlewoman denies all that you have said.
Lucio. My lord, here comes the rascal I spoke of; here with the provost.
Escal. In very good time: speak not you to him till we call upon you.
Lucio. Mum.
Escal. Come, sir: did you set these women on to slander Lord Angelo? they have confessed you did.
Duke. 'Tis false.
Escal. How! know you where you are?
Duke. Respect to your great place! and let the devil
Be sometime honour'd for his burning throne!
Where is the duke? 'tis he should hear me speak.
Escal. The duke 's in us; and we will hear you speak:
Look you speak justly.
Duke. Boldly, at least. But, O, poor souls,
Come you to seek the lamb here of the fox?
Good night to your redress! Is the duke gone?
Then is your cause gone too. The duke 's unjust,
Thus to retort your manifest appeal,
And put your trial in the villain's mouth
Which here you come to accuse.
Lucio. This is the rascal; this is he I spoke of.
Escal. Why, thou unreverend and unhallowed friar,
Is 't not enough thou hast suborn'd these women
To accuse this worthy man, but, in foul mouth
And in the witness of his proper ear,
To call him villain? and then to glance from him
To th' duke himself, to tax him with injustice?
Take him hence; to th' rack with him! We'll touse you
Joint by joint, but we will know his purpose.
What, 'unjust'!
Duke. Be not so hot; the duke
Dare no more stretch this finger of mine than he
Dare rack his own: his subject am I not,
Nor here provincial. My business in this state
Made me a looker on here in Vienna,
Where I have seen corruption boil and bubble
Till it o'er-run the stew; laws for all faults,
But faults so countenanc'd, that the strong statutes
Stand like the forfeits in a barber's shop,
As much in mock as mark.
Escal. Slander to th' state! Away with him to prison!
Ang. What can you vouch against him, Signior Lucio?

221-222. **disvalued In levity,** discredited for lightness. 236. **informal,** rash. 242. **Compact,** in collusion. 243. **swear down,** i.e., call down to witness. 263. **'Cucullus . . . monachum,'** a cowl doesn't make a monk; a nice bit of dramatic irony. 279. **darkly,** subtly, slyly. 280. **light,** wanton, unchaste. 303. **retort,** turn back. 313. **touse,** tear. 323. **forfeits,** ie., the extracted teeth of patients (barbers also were tooth-drawers) strung and hung on the walls (Hart, who notes *most biting laws*, I, iii, 19).

Is this the man that you did tell us of?

Lucio. 'Tis he, my lord. Come hither, goodman baldpate: do you know me?

Duke. I remember you, sir, by the sound of your voice: I met you at the prison, in the absence of the duke.

Lucio. O, did you so? And do you remember what you said of the duke?

Duke. Most notedly, sir.

Lucio. Do you so, sir? And was the duke a flesh-monger, a fool, and a coward, as you then reported him to be?

Duke. You must, sir, change persons with me, ere you make that my report: you, indeed, spoke so of him; and much more, much worse.

Lucio. O thou damnable fellow! Did not I pluck thee by the nose for thy speeches?

Duke. I protest I love the duke as I love myself.

Ang. Hark, how the villain would close now, after his treasonable abuses!

Escal. Such a fellow is not to be talked withal. Away with him to prison! Where is the provost? Away with him to prison! lay bolts enough upon him: let him speak no more. Away with those giglots too, and with the other confederate companion!

Duke. [*To Provost*] Stay, sir; stay awhile.

Ang. What, resists he? Help him, Lucio.

Lucio. Come, sir; come, sir; come, sir; foh, sir! Why, you bald-pated, lying rascal, you must be hooded, must you? Show your knave's visage, with a pox to you! show your sheep-biting face, and be hanged an hour! Will 't not off?

[*Pulls off the friar's hood, and discovers the Duke.*]

Duke. Thou art the first knave that e'er mad'st a duke.
First, provost, let me bail these gentle three.
[*To Lucio*] Sneak not away, sir; for the friar and you
Must have a word anon. Lay hold on him.

Lucio. This may prove worse than hanging.

Duke. [*To Escalus*] What you have spoke I pardon: sit you down:
We'll borrow place of him. [*To Angelo*] Sir, by your leave.
Hast thou or word, or wit, or impudence,
That yet can do thee office? If thou hast,
Rely upon it till my tale be heard,
And hold no longer out.

Ang. O my dread lord,
I should be guiltier than my guiltiness,
To think I can be undiscernible,
When I perceive your grace, like pow'r divine,
Hath look'd upon my passes. Then, good prince,
No longer session hold upon my shame,
But let my trial be mine own confession:
Immediate sentence then and sequent death
Is all the grace I beg.

Duke. Come hither, Mariana.
Say, wast thou e'er contracted to this woman?

Ang. I was, my lord.

Duke. Go take her hence, and marry her instantly.
Do you the office, friar; which consummate,
Return him here again. Go with him, provost.

Exit [*Angelo, with Mariana, Friar Peter and Provost*].

Escal. My lord, I am more amaz'd at his dishonour
Than at the strangeness of it.

Duke. Come hither, Isabel.
Your friar is now your prince: as I was then
Advertising and holy to your business,
Not changing heart with habit, I am still
Attorney'd at your service.

Isab. O, give me pardon,
That I, your vassal, have employ'd and pain'd
Your unknown sovereignty!

Duke. You are pardon'd, Isabel:
And now, dear maid, be you as free to us.
Your brother's death, I know, sits at your heart;
And you may marvel why I obscur'd myself,
Labouring to save his life, and would not rather
Make rash remonstrance of my hidden pow'r
Than let him so be lost. O most kind maid,
It was the swift celerity of his death,
Which I did think with slower foot came on,
That brain'd my purpose. But, peace be with him!
That life is better life, past fearing death,
Than that which lives to fear: make it your comfort,
So happy is your brother.

Isab. I do, my lord.

Enter Angelo, Mariana, [Friar] Peter, [*and*] Provost.

Duke. For this new-married man approaching here,
Whose salt imagination yet hath wrong'd
Your well defended honour, you must pardon
For Mariana's sake: but as he adjudg'd your brother,—
Being criminal, in double violation
Of sacred chastity and of promise-breach
Thereon dependent, for your brother's life,—
The very mercy of the law cries out
Most audible, even from his proper tongue,
'An Angelo for Claudio, death for death!'
Haste still pays haste, and leisure answers leisure;
Like doth quit like, and measure still for measure.
Then, Angelo, thy fault 's thus manifested;
Which, though thou wouldst deny, denies thee vantage.
We do condemn thee to the very block
Where Claudio stoop'd to death, and with like haste.
Away with him!

Mari. O my most gracious lord,
I hope you will not mock me with a husband.

Duke. It is your husband mock'd you with a husband.
Consenting to the safeguard of your honour,
I thought your marriage fit; else imputation,
For that he knew you, might reproach your life
And choke your good to come: for his possessions,
Although by confiscation they are ours,
We do instate and widow you withal,
To buy you a better husband.

Mari. O my dear lord,
I crave no other, nor no better man.

Duke. Never crave him; we are definitive.

Mari. Gentle my liege,— [*Kneeling.*]

Duke. You do but lose your labour.
Away with him to death! [*To Lucio*] Now, sir, to you.

346. **close,** come to terms. 352. **giglots,** wanton women. 373. **undiscernible,** not to be seen through (Schmidt). 375. **passes,** demeanor, conduct. 397. **remonstrance,** manifestation. 401. **brain'd,** defeated. 406. **salt,** lecherous. 425. **imputation,** accusation, slander. 429.

Mari. O my good lord! Sweet Isabel, take my part;
Lend me your knees, and all my life to come
I'll lend you all my life to do you service.
Duke. Against all sense you do importune her:
Should she kneel down in mercy of this fact,
Her brother's ghost his paved bed would break,
And take her hence in horror.
Mari. Isabel,
Sweet Isabel, do yet but kneel by me;
Hold up your hands, say nothing; I'll speak all.
They say, best men are moulded out of faults;
And, for the most, become much more the better
For being a little bad: so may my husband.
O Isabel, will you not lend a knee?
Duke. He dies for Claudio's death.
Isab. Most bounteous sir, [*Kneeling.*]
Look, if it please you, on this man condemn'd,
As if my brother liv'd: I partly think
A due sincerity govern'd his deeds,
Till he did look on me: since it is so,
Let him not die. My brother had but justice,
In that he did the thing for which he died:
For Angelo,
His act did not o'ertake his bad intent,
And must be buried but as an intent
That perish'd by the way: thoughts are no subjects;
Intents but merely thoughts.
Mari. Merely, my lord.
Duke. Your suit 's unprofitable; stand up, I say.
I have bethought me of another fault.
Provost, how came it Claudio was beheaded
At an unusual hour?
Prov. It was commanded so.
Duke. Had you a special warrant for the deed?
Prov. No, my good lord; it was by private message.
Duke. For which I do discharge you of your office:
Give up your keys.
Prov. Pardon me, noble lord:
I thought it was a fault, but knew it not;
Yet did repent me, after more advice:
For testimony whereof, one in the prison,
That should by private order else have died,
I have reserv'd alive.
Duke. What 's he?
Prov. His name is Barnardine.
Duke. I would thou hadst done so by Claudio.
Go fetch him hither; let me look upon him.
[*Exit Provost.*]
Escal. I am sorry, one so learned and so wise
As you, Lord Angelo, have still appear'd,
Should slip so grossly, both in the heat of blood,
And lack of temper'd judgement afterward.
Ang. I am sorry that such sorrow I procure:
And so deep sticks it in my penitent heart
That I crave death more willingly than mercy;
'Tis my deserving, and I do entreat it.

Enter BARNARDINE *and* PROVOST, CLAUDIO [*muffled*], [*and*] JULIET.

Duke. Which is that Barnardine?
Prov. This, my lord.
Duke. There was a friar told me of this man.
Sirrah, thou art said to have a stubborn soul,
That apprehends no further than this world,
And squar'st thy life according. Thou 'rt condemn'd:
But, for those earthly faults, I quit them all;
And pray thee take this mercy to provide
For better times to come. Friar, advise him;
I leave him to your hand. What muffled fellow 's that?
Prov. This is another prisoner that I sav'd,
Who should have died when Claudio lost his head;
As like almost to Claudio as himself. [*Unmuffles Claudio.*]
Duke. [*To Isabella*] If he be like your brother, for his sake
Is he pardon'd; and, for your lovely sake,
Give me your hand and say you will be mine,
He is my brother too: but fitter time for that.
By this Lord Angelo perceives he 's safe;
Methinks I see a quick'ning in his eye.
Well, Angelo, your evil quits you well:
Look that you love your wife; her worth worth yours.
I find an apt remission in myself;
And yet here 's one in place I cannot pardon.
[*To Lucio*] You, sirrah, that knew me for a fool, a coward,
One all of luxury, an ass, a madman;
Wherein have I so deserv'd of you,
That you extol me thus?
Lucio. 'Faith, my lord, I spoke it but according to the trick. If you will hang me for it, you may; but I had rather it would please you I might be whipt.
Duke. Whipt first, sir, and hang'd after.
Proclaim it, provost, round about the city,
Is any woman wrong'd by this lewd fellow,
As I have heard him swear himself there 's one
Whom he begot with child, let her appear,
And he shall marry her: the nuptial finish'd,
Let him be whipt and hang'd.
Lucio. I beseech your highness, do not marry me to a whore. Your highness said even now, I made you a duke: good my lord, do not recompense me in making me a cuckold.
Duke. Upon mine honour, thou shalt marry her.
Thy slanders I forgive; and therewithal
Remit thy other forfeits. Take him to prison;
And see our pleasure herein executed.
Lucio. Marrying a punk, my lord, is pressing to death, whipping, and hanging.
Duke. Slandering a prince deserves it.
[*Exeunt Officers with Lucio.*]
She, Claudio, that you wrong'd, look you restore.
Joy to you, Mariana! Love her, Angelo:
I have confess'd her and I know her virtue.
Thanks, good friend Escalus, for thy much goodness:
There 's more behind that is more gratulate.
Thanks, provost, for thy care and secrecy:
We shall employ thee in a worthier place.
Forgive him, Angelo, that brought you home
The head of Ragozine for Claudio's:
Th' offence pardons itself. Dear Isabel,
I have a motion much imports your good;
Whereto if you'll a willing ear incline,
What 's mine is yours and what is yours is mine.
So, bring us to our palace; where we'll show
What 's yet behind, that 's meet you all should know.
[*Exeunt.*]

widow, settle a jointure upon. 487. **squar'st,** regulatest. 501. **quits,** rewards, requites. 508. **extol,** proclaim. 510. **trick,** fashion. 528-529. **pressing to death,** i.e., by having heavy weights placed on the chest. 535. **gratulate,** gratifying. 541. **motion,** proposal.

TROILUS AND CRESSIDA

Troilus and Cressida is perhaps Shakespeare's most puzzling play. From the start it had an odd and abortive career. On February 7, 1603, the printer James Roberts entered his name on the Stationers' Register to print, "when he hath gotten sufficient aucthority for yt, The booke of Troilus and Cresseda as yt is acted by my lord Chamberlens Men." Evidently the authority was not forthcoming, for in 1609 the play was re-registered to R. Bonian and H. Walley and published by them that year in quarto as "The Historie of Troylus and Cresseida. As it was acted by the Kings Maiesties seruants at the Globe. Written by William Shakespeare." Immediately afterwards, however, a second issue of this quarto text appeared with a new title: "The Famous Historie of Troylus and Cresseid. Excellently expressing the beginning of their loues, with the conceited wooing of Pandarus Prince of Licia. Written by William Shakespeare." This second issue had, moreover, a preface to the reader (something found in no other Shakespearean quarto) declaring *Troilus and Cressida* to be "a new play, neuer stal'd with the Stage, neuer clapper-clawd with the palmes of the vulger," nor "sullied with the smoaky breath of the multitude." The preface goes on to imply that the play's "grand possessors" (i.e., Shakespeare's company) had not wished to see the play released at all. This second issue, then, casts some doubt on previous assertions that the play had actually been performed by Shakespeare's company, and at the Globe. Contributing to this doubt is an epilogue by Pandarus at the conclusion of *Troilus*, evidently promising a sequel to be played some "two months hence"—a sequel that does not exist.

Furthermore, the editors of the First Folio in 1623 seem to have had difficulty in obtaining permission to print *Troilus*. Three pages of the play were actually printed to follow *Romeo and Juliet*, among the tragedies, but were then withdrawn to be replaced by *Timon of Athens*. Ultimately the play appeared in the Folio almost without pagination, unlisted in the table of contents, and placed with fitting ambiguity between the histories and tragedies. It is as though Shakespeare and his company had indeed wished to disown so uncharacteristically satirical a play of so anomalous a genre. If performed at all, it certainly was not performed long; the play's stage history is almost a total blank until the present day (except for a much-changed Restoration version by Dryden, in which Cressida remains true to Troilus and slays herself when accused of infidelity). Yet the 1609 text, evidently from Shakespeare's own copy, is a good one and unquestionably genuine. Some scholars have hypothesized that Shakespeare's company mounted a special production of the play for a private audience, such as the Inns of Court. An arrangement of this sort would have been most unusual, however, if not unique. Although Shakespeare's company often took its regular plays to court or other special audiences, no instance is positively known in which Shakespeare wrote on commission for a private showing. More likely, *Troilus* was performed publicly but was a flop. A sequel was not called for, and the company was not anxious to see it in print. The publishers of the second issue in 1609 may have been trying to capitalize on the play's public failure, by touting it as caviare to the general and hence to be appreciated only by discerning readers.

Such appeals to antipopular sentiment were common among the satirists of the years 1601–1602, when *Troilus* was probably written. Satire in the drama, catering to select courtly audiences, had received new impetus with the reopening of the boys' theatres in 1599. Jonson, Chapman, and Marston were among the authors who inclined to this coterie world of sophisticated taste. Jonson launched a series of plays he called "comicall satyres," in which he savagely rebuked the London citizenry and presumed to teach manners to the court as well. The so-called War of the Theatres among Jonson, Marston, and Dekker, although partly a personality clash of no consequence, was also a serious debate between public and private stages on the proper uses of satire. Public dramatists complained about the libelous boldness of the new satire and were galled by its runaway commercial success; even Shakespeare fretted in *Hamlet* (II,ii,353–379) about the rivalry. Yet as an artist in search of new forms, he also responded positively. He experimented with a Jonsonian type of satirical plot in the exposure of Malvolio, in *Twelfth Night* (1600–1602). *Troilus and Cressida* seems to have been another and more ambitious experiment embracing a different kind of satire, not of witty exposure but of disillusionment.

This satiric genre is hard to classify according to the conventional rubrics of tragedy, comedy, or history (as the editors of the Folio seem to indicate), but does have its own clearly defined rationale that makes special sense in terms of our modern theatre. The play is nominally tragic in that it presents the fall of great Hector and adumbrates the fall of Troy, yet its love story merely dwindles into frustrated estrangement without the death of either lover. The play is comic only as what we might call "black" comedy or comedy of the absurd. Its leering sexual titillation and its mood of spiritual paralysis link *Troilus* to the "problem" comedies *All's Well that Ends Well* (c. 1601–1604) and *Measure for Measure* (1603–1604). The play is called a "Historie" on both its early title pages, and assuredly deals with the great events of history's most famous war, but history has become essentially ironic. In this, *Troilus* represents a culmination of Shakespeare's ironic exploration of history as begun in the impasses of *Richard II* or *Henry IV* and portrayed more fully in the sustained ambiguities of *Julius Caesar* (1599). However much Shakespeare may have been influenced by the contemporary vogue of satire in the boys' theatre, his own satire of disillusion is integral to his development as an artist. *Troilus* is a fitting contemporary for *Hamlet* (c. 1599–1601). Like that play it evokes a universal disorder that may well reflect Jacobean loss of faith in the medieval hierarchies of the old Ptolemaic earth-centered cosmos.

Troilus achieves its disillusioning effect through repeated ironic juxtaposition of heroic ideals and tarnished realities. Although it deals with the greatest war in history and a renowned love affair, we as audience know that Troy and the lovers will be overthrown by cunning and infidelity. Shakespeare partly inherited from his sources this duality of epic grandness and dispiriting conclusion. To learn of the war itself, he must have known Chapman's translation of the *Iliad* (of which seven books were published in 1598), and of course Virgil's account of the destruction of Troy, but he relied more particularly on medieval romances: Raoul Lefevre's *Receuil des Histoires de Troyes* as translated and published by William Caxton, and perhaps Lydgate's *Troy Book*, derived in part from Guido delle Colonne's *Historia Trojana*. These romances were Trojan in point of view and hence tragically concerned with the fall of that city. For the bitter love story, Shakespeare went to Chaucer's *Troilus and Criseyde* (c. 1385–1386), which had been derived from the twelfth-century medieval romance of Benoit de Sainte-Maure, *Le Roman de Troie*, as amplified and retold in Boccaccio's *Il Filostrato*. Chaucer's Criseyde is an admirably self-possessed young woman, and Troilus' winning of her attractively represents the courtly love tradition upon which the story was based. Since the late fourteenth century, however, Chaucer's heroine had suffered a drastic decline in esteem. In Robert Henryson's *Testament of Cresseid*, for example, Cressida becomes a leper and beggar, the "lazar kite of Cressid's kind" to whom Pistol alludes in *Henry V*. Her name becomes synonymous with womanly infidelity, as Shakespeare wryly points out in *Troilus:* "Let all constant men be Troiluses, all false women Cressids, and all brokers-between Pandars" (III,ii). Time has a wallet at its back, and Fame has a way of magnifying human weaknesses —as Achilles also discovers. Thus Shakespeare found in his materials both chivalric splendor and a deflation of it.

Stylistically, Shakespeare exploits this juxtaposition. He employs epic conventions more than is his custom. The narrative commences, as the chorus informs us, *in medias res*, "Beginning in the middle." Epic similes adorn the formal speeches of Ulysses and Nestor. The rhetoric of persuasion plays an important role, as in *Julius Caesar* and other Roman plays. The great names of antiquity are paraded past us in a roll call of heroes. Hector above all is an epic hero, although in the fashion of medieval romance he is also the prince of chivalry. He longs to resolve the war by a challenge to single combat, in tournament, with the breaking of lances and with each warrior defending the honor of his lady fair (I,iii). The Greeks respond for a time to this stirring call to arms. Yet in the broader context of the war itself, with its unworthy causes, its frustrating irresolution, and its enervating effect on the morale of both sides, Hector's idealism cannot endure. Nor can Ulysses' ennobling vision of "degree, priority, and place" by which the heavens show man the value of harmonious order. These visions offer not reassurance but a mocking of man's hopeless descent into appetite and chaos. Epic convention becomes hollow travesty, as man's chivalric aspirations repeatedly dissolve into the sordid insinuations of Thersites or Pandarus. Despite the play's epic machinery, the gods are nowhere to be found.

A prevailing metaphor is that of disease (as also in *Hamlet*). Insubordinate conduct "infects" the body politic. The Greek commanders hope to "physic" Achilles lest his virtues, "like fair fruit in an unwholesome dish," rot untasted (II,iii). Hector similarly deplores the way his fellow-Trojans "infectiously" enslave themselves to willful appetite (II,ii). Elsewhere, love is described as an open ulcer and as an itch that must be scratched; Helen is "contaminated carrion." Thersites most of all teaches us to regard both love and war as disease-ridden, afflicted by boils, plagues, scabs, the Neapolitan "bone-ache" (syphilis), "lethargies, cold palsies, raw eyes, dirt-rotten livers, wheezing lungs, bladders full of imposthume [abscess], sciaticas," and still more (II,iii and V,i). On a similarly tawdry note, Pandarus ends the play jesting about prostitutes (Winchester geese, he calls them) and the "sweating" or venereal diseases.

The war is both glorious and absurd. It calls forth brave deeds and heroic sacrifices. Yet it is correctly labeled by the chorus a "quarrel," begun over an "old aunt" whom the Greeks have held captive and Helen, whom the Trojans abducted in reprisal. No one considers the original cause to justify the bloodletting that has ensued. Menelaus' cuckoldry is the subject of obscene mirth in the Greek camp. Among the Trojans, Troilus can argue only that one doesn't return soiled goods; since all Troy consented to Helen's abduction, Troy must continue the war to maintain its honor. The war thus assumes a grim momentum of its own. The combatants repeatedly discover that they are trapped in the ironies of a situation they helped make but can no longer unmake. Hector's challenge to single combat falls upon Ajax, his "father's sister's son." Achilles too has allegiances in the enemy's camp, since he is enamored of Priam's daughter Polyxena. In the parleys between the two sides, the warriors greet one another as long-lost brothers, though they have vowed to slaughter one another on the morrow. With fitting oxymoron, Paris comments on the paradox of this "most despiteful gentle greeting," this "noblest hateful love" (IV,i). Only barbarians such as Ajax are free of regret for a peace that seems so near and is yet so far. The war offers insidious temptations to potentially worthy men, perverting Achilles' once-honorable quest for fame into maniacal ambition and the irresistible impulse to murder Hector. Fame mocks Achilles for this craven deed, putting him down as a bully rather than a brave soldier, and insolently elevating in his stead the blockish Ajax.

Hector's tragedy is in its own way no less ironic. Even though he emerges as the most thoughtful and courageous man on both sides, and advises his fellow-Trojans to let Helen go in response to the "moral laws Of nature and of nations," he nonetheless ends the Trojan council of war by resolving to fight on with them (II,ii). This conclusion may represent in part a realization that the others will fight on in any case, and that he must therefore be loyal to them, but the choice also reflects *hubris*. Hector is not unlike Julius Caesar in the proud repudiation of his wife Andromache's ominous dreams, his sister Cassandra's mad but oracular prophecies, and his own conviction that Troy's pursuit of honor stems from a sickened appetite. He goes to his death because "the gods have heard me swear" (V,iii). His character is his fate. Even his humane compunctions, like Brutus', hold against him; he spares the life of Achilles, and is murdered as his reward. War is no place for men of scruple, as Troilus reminds his older brother. Yet by dying as a victim rather than allowing himself to become corrupted by war's savage ethic, Hector morally transcends the conflict from which, as a warrior, he could find no escape.

The lovers as well are caught in war's trap, not only Troilus and Cressida but Paris and Helen, Achilles and Polyxena. Achilles vows to Polyxena not to fight and thereby misses his cherished opportunity for fame; ironically he is aroused to vengeful action only by the death of a male friend, Patroclus, who is whispered to be his "male varlet" or "masculine whore." Paris is obliged to ask his brother Troilus to return Cressida to the Greeks, so that Paris may continue to enjoy Helen. What else can he do? "There is no help," he complains. "The bitter disposition of the time Will have it so" (IV,i). Troilus prepares his own undoing when he argues in the Trojan council of war that Helen must be kept at all cost; the cost, it turns out, is his own Cressida. He sees this irony at once: "How my achievements mock me!" (IV,ii). The love of Troilus and Cressida is dwarfed by the war, which impersonally has no regard for their private concerns. Troilus wins Cressida after many months of wooing, only to lose her the next day. Yet how could Cressida's father Calchas know of her personal situation? He wishes only to have his daughter back. And although the Trojan leaders do know of Troilus' new affair, they must pay heed first to matters of state such as the exchange of prisoners.

So too must Troilus. Perhaps the greatest irony is that he must himself choose to send Cressida to the Greeks, placing duty above personal longing. It is a noble choice, but surrounded by absurdities, and it is one that Cressida cannot comprehend. She has determined to stay no matter what the world may think; love is higher in her scale of priorities. Although Cressida was first introduced to us as a sardonic and worldly young woman, urbane, mocking, self-possessed, witty, anti-sentimental, and above all wary of emotional commitment, she does fall truly in love with Troilus. For a moment she catches a glimpse of something precious to which she would cling forever, something genuine in her unstable world. Yet it is Troilus who sends her off to the Greek camp. There she reverts to her former disillusioned self, behaving as is expected of her. Who has deserted whom? Cressida gives up rather than fight insuperable odds. She knows she cannot be true because, like too many women in her experience, she is led by "the error of our eye" and is thus a prey to male importunity (V,ii). Still, this surrender to will and appetite in her is not unsympathetic, and does not happen without inner struggle. Her weakness is emblematic of a universal disorder, and is partly caused by it. In the grim interplay of war and love, both men and women are powerless to assert their true selves. As the malcontent Thersites concludes, "Lechery, lechery, still wars and lechery: nothing else holds fashion."

TROILUS AND CRESSIDA

[*Dramatis Personae*

PRIAM, *King of Troy.*
HECTOR, TROILUS, PARIS, DEIPHOBUS, HELENUS, } *his sons.*
MARGARELON, *a bastard son of Priam.*
ÆNEAS, ANTENOR, } *Trojan commanders.*
CALCHAS, *a Trojan priest, taking part with the Greeks.*
PANDARUS, *uncle to Cressida.*
AGAMEMNON, *the Grecian general.*
MENELAUS, *his brother.*
ACHILLES, AJAX, ULYSSES, NESTOR, DIOMEDES, PATROCLUS, } *Grecian princes.*
THERSITES, *a deformed and scurrilous Grecian.*
ALEXANDER, *servant to Cressida.*
Servant to Troilus.
Servant to Paris.
Servant to Diomedes.

HELEN, *wife to Menelaus.*
ANDROMACHE, *wife to Hector.*
CASSANDRA, *daughter to Priam, a prophetess.*
CRESSIDA, *daughter to Calchas.*

Trojan *and* Greek Soldiers, *and* Attendants.

SCENE: *Troy, and the Grecian camp before it.*]

PROLOGUE.

IN Troy, there lies the scene. From isles of Greece
The princes orgulous, their high blood chaf'd,
Have to the port of Athens sent their ships,
Fraught with the ministers and instruments
Of cruel war: sixty and nine, that wore
Their crownets regal, from th' Athenian bay
Put forth toward Phrygia; and their vow is made
To ransack Troy, within whose strong immures
The ravish'd Helen, Menelaus' queen,
With wanton Paris sleeps; and that 's the quarrel.
To Tenedos they come;
And the deep-drawing barks do there disgorge
Their warlike fraughtage: now on Dardan plains
The fresh and yet unbruised Greeks do pitch
Their brave pavilions: Priam's six-gated city,
Dardan, and Tymbria, Helias, Chetas, Troien,
And Antenorides, with massy staples
And corresponsive and fulfilling bolts,
Sperr up the sons of Troy.
Now expectation, tickling skittish spirits,
On one and other side, Troyan and Greek,
Sets all on hazard: and hither am I come
A prologue arm'd, but not in confidence
Of author's pen or actor's voice, but suited
In like conditions as our argument,
To tell you, fair beholders, that our play
Leaps o'er the vaunt and firstlings of those broils,
Beginning in the middle, starting thence away
To what may be digested in a play.
Like or find fault; do as your pleasures are:
Now good or bad, 'tis but the chance of war.

[ACT I.

SCENE I. *Troy. Before Priam's palace.*]

Enter PANDARUS *and* TROILUS.

Tro. Call here my varlet; I'll unarm again:
Why should I war without the walls of Troy,
That find such cruel battle here within?
Each Troyan that is master of his heart,
Let him to field; Troilus, alas! hath none.
Pan. Will this gear ne'er be mended?
Tro. The Greeks are strong and skilful to their strength,
Fierce to their skill and to their fierceness valiant;
But I am weaker than a woman's tear,
Tamer than sleep, fonder than ignorance,
Less valiant than the virgin in the night
And skilless as unpractis'd infancy.

Pan. Well, I have told you enough of this: for my part, I'll not meddle nor make no further. He that will have a cake out of the wheat must needs tarry the grinding.

Tro. Have I not tarried?
Pan. Ay, the grinding; but you must tarry the bolting.
Tro. Have I not tarried?
Pan. Ay, the bolting, but you must tarry the leavening.
Tro. Still have I tarried.

Pan. Ay, to the leavening; but here 's yet in the word 'hereafter' the kneading, the making of the cake, the heating of the oven and the baking; nay, you must stay the cooling too, or you may chance to burn your lips.

PROLOGUE. 2. **orgulous,** proud. 4. **ministers,** agents. 6. **crownets,** coronets, i.e., garlands, chaplets; here probably the equivalent of "crown." 7. **Phrygia,** district in Asia Minor, identified by the Roman poets—hence in Renaissance poetry—with Troy. 8. **immures,** walls. 11. **Tenedos,** small island in the Aegean Sea off the coast of Asia Minor. 13. **fraughtage,** cargo. **Dardan,** Trojan, from Dardanus—son of Zeus and Electra, daughter of Atlas—according to legend, the ancestor of the Trojan race. 18. **corresponsive,** answering. 19. **Sperr,** close. 23-25. **A prologue . . . argument.** I am armed not as a belligerent actor or author, but as representing the warlike theme of the play. 27. **vaunt,** van, beginning. **firstlings,** first-fruits.

ACT I. SCENE I. 1. **varlet,** gentleman's son in the service of a knight or a prince; probably free from any connotation of contempt. 5. **none,** i.e., heart. 7-8. **The Greeks . . . valiant.** These lines illustrate the mature Shakespeare's peculiar compactness of style. The series of ideas here is like a series of involutes in their intricacy and closeness of expression and idea. When the lines are footnoted by equating *to* with "in addition to," assuming that the reader will make the substitution, they are reduced to their mere literal significance, as if the involutes had been pulled out into a straight but limp and uninteresting line. The idea is not an unusual or complex one, but its expression is compact and interesting. As one of Troilus' first utterances, it helps to make us aware of his personality and of his overwrought emotional state. 7. **to,** in addition to, but see Abbott (187), who explains "in proportion to." 16. **tarry,** wait for. 17. **bolting,** sifting.

Tro. Patience herself, what goddess e'er she be,
Doth lesser blench at suff'rance than I do.
At Priam's royal table do I sit;
And when fair Cressid comes into my thoughts,—
So, traitor! 'When she comes!' When is she thence?

Pan. Well, she looked yesternight fairer than ever I saw her look, or any woman else.

Tro. I was about to tell thee:—when my heart,
As wedged with a sigh, would rive in twain,
Lest Hector or my father should perceive me,
I have, as when the sun doth light a-scorn,
Buried this sigh in wrinkle of a smile:
But sorrow, that is couch'd in seeming gladness,
Is like that mirth fate turns to sudden sadness.

Pan. An her hair were not somewhat darker than Helen's—well, go to—there were no more comparison between the women: but, for my part, she is my kinswoman; I would not, as they term it, praise her: but I would somebody had heard her talk yesterday, as I did. I will not dispraise your sister Cassandra's wit, but—

Tro. O Pandarus! I tell thee, Pandarus,—
When I do tell thee, there my hopes lie drown'd,
Reply not in how many fathoms deep
They lie indrench'd. I tell thee I am mad
In Cressid's love: thou answer'st 'she is fair;'
Pour'st in the open ulcer of my heart
Her eyes, her hair, her cheek, her gait, her voice;
Handlest in thy discourse, O, that her hand,
In whose comparison all whites are ink,
Writing their own reproach, to whose soft seizure
The cygnet's down is harsh and spirit of sense
Hard as the palm of ploughman: this thou tell'st me,
As true thou tell'st me, when I say I love her;
But, saying thus, instead of oil and balm,
Thou lay'st in every gash that love hath given me
The knife that made it.

Pan. I speak no more than truth.

Tro. Thou dost not speak so much.

Pan. Faith, I'll not meddle in 't. Let her be as she is: if she be fair, 'tis the better for her; an she be not, she has the mends in her own hands.

Tro. Good Pandarus, how now, Pandarus!

Pan. I have had my labour for my travail; ill-thought on of her and ill-thought on of you; gone between and between, but small thanks for my labour.

Tro. What, art thou angry, Pandarus? what, with me?

Pan. Because she 's kin to me, therefore she 's not so fair as Helen: an she were not kin to me, she would be as fair on Friday as Helen is on Sunday. But what care I? I care not an she were a black-a-moor; 'tis all one to me.

Tro. Say I she is not fair?

Pan. I do not care whether you do or no. She 's a fool to stay behind her father; let her to the Greeks; and so I'll tell her the next time I see her: for my part, I'll meddle nor make no more i' the matter.

Tro. Pandarus,—

Pan. Not I.

Tro. Sweet Pandarus,—

Pan. Pray you, speak no more to me: I will leave all as I found it, and there an end.

Exit. Sound alarum.

Tro. Peace, you ungracious clamours! peace, rude sounds!
Fools on both sides! Helen must needs be fair,
When with your blood you daily paint her thus.
I cannot fight upon this argument;
It is too starv'd a subject for my sword.
But Pandarus,—O gods, how do you plague me!
I cannot come to Cressid but by Pandar;
And he 's as tetchy to be woo'd to woo,
As she is stubborn-chaste against all suit.
Tell me, Apollo, for thy Daphne's love,
What Cressid is, what Pandar, and what we?
Her bed is India; there she lies, a pearl:
Between our Ilium and where she resides,
Let it be call'd the wild and wand'ring flood,
Ourself the merchant, and this sailing Pandar
Our doubtful hope, our convoy and our bark.

Alarum. Enter ÆNEAS.

Æne. How now, Prince Troilus! wherefore not afield?

Tro. Because not there: this woman's answer sorts,
For womanish it is to be from thence.
What news, Æneas, from the field to-day?

Æne. That Paris is returned home and hurt.

Tro. By whom, Æneas?

Æne. Troilus, by Menelaus.

Tro. Let Paris bleed: 'tis but a scar to scorn;
Paris is gor'd with Menelaus' horn. *Alarum.*

Æne. Hark, what good sport is out of town to-day!

Tro. Better at home, if 'would I might' were 'may.'
But to the sport abroad: are you bound thither?

Æne. In all swift haste.

Tro. Come, go we then together.

Exeunt.

[SCENE II. *The same. A street.*]

Enter CRESSIDA *and her man* [ALEXANDER].

Cres. Who were those went by?

Alex. Queen Hecuba and Helen.

Cres. And whither go they?

Alex. Up to the eastern tower,
Whose height commands as subject all the vale,
To see the battle. Hector, whose patience
Is, as a virtue fix'd, to-day was mov'd:
He chid Andromache and struck his armorer,
And, like as there were husbandry in war,
Before the sun rose he was harness'd light,
And to the field goes he; where every flower

27-28. **Patience . . . I do.** I have a greater capacity for suffering than patience herself. 28. **blench,** shy from. 35. **As wedged,** as if entered by a wedge; cf. I, iii, 316. **rive,** split. 37. **a-scorn,** scorningly, mockingly (?). Globe emends to *a storm*. 47. **Cassandra's wit,** refers to Cassandra's gift of prophecy, bestowed on her by Apollo out of his love for her. Because she slighted his love, he added to the gift the condition that her prophecies would never be believed. 51. **indrench'd,** immersed. 55. **discourse.** Globe has comma; Q has colon. **that her hand,** that hand of hers. 57. **seizure,** clasp; i.e., hand clasp. 58. **spirit of sense,** most exquisite power of sensibility (Johnson); sense or sensibility itself (Schmidt). Spirits were thin bodily substances believed to transmit sense impressions to the soul. 68. **mends,** remedy; Johnson thought the line referred to cosmetics; Steevens paraphrased, "She may make the best of it." 83. **her father.** Cressida's father, Calchas, was a Trojan priest who, advised by the oracle of Apollo that Troy would fall, fled to the Greeks. 95. **upon this argument,** for this cause, i.e., Paris' cause, with quibbling allusion, probably, to the phrase "to fight on an empty stomach." 99. **tetchy,** fretful, peevish. 101. **Apollo,** i.e., in his role of god of music and poetry. Mention of his love for Daphne is appropriate here because she successfully eluded him; she was a nymph changed into a bay tree. 104. **Ilium,** Troy generally, but here Priam's palace. 109. **sorts,** is appropriate. 112-113. **Paris . . .**

Did, as a prophet, weep what it foresaw
In Hector's wrath.
Cres. What was his cause of anger?
Alex. The noise goes, this: there is among the Greeks
A lord of Troyan blood, nephew to Hector;
They call him Ajax.
Cres. Good; and what of him?
Alex. They say he is a very man per se,
And stands alone.

Cres. So do all men, unless they are drunk, sick, or have no legs.

Alex. This man, lady, hath robbed many beasts of their particular additions; he is as valiant as the lion, churlish as the bear, slow as the elephant: a man into whom nature hath so crowded humours that his valour is crushed into folly, his folly sauced with discretion: there is no man hath a virtue that he hath not a glimpse of, nor any man an attaint but he carries some stain of it: he is melancholy without cause, and merry against the hair: he hath the joints of every thing, but every thing so out of joint that he is a gouty Briareus, many hands and no use, or purblind Argus, all eyes and no sight.

Cres. But how should this man, that makes me smile, make Hector angry?

Alex. They say he yesterday coped Hector in the battle and struck him down, the disdain and shame whereof hath ever since kept Hector fasting and waking.

Cres. Who comes here?

Alex. Madam, your uncle Pandarus.

[*Enter* PANDARUS.]

Cres. Hector 's a gallant man.

Alex. As may be in the world, lady.

Pan. What 's that? what 's that?

Cres. Good morrow, uncle Pandarus.

Pan. Good morrow, cousin Cressid: what do you talk of? Good morrow, Alexander. How do you, cousin? When were you at Ilium?

Cres. This morning, uncle.

Pan. What were you talking of when I came? Was Hector armed and gone ere ye came to Ilium? Helen was not up, was she?

Cres. Hector was gone, but Helen was not up.

Pan. E'en so: Hector was stirring early.

Cres. That were we talking of, and of his anger.

Pan. Was he angry?

Cres. So he says here.

Pan. True, he was so: I know the cause too: he'll lay about him to-day, I can tell them that: and there 's Troilus will not come far behind him; let them take heed of Troilus, I can tell them that too.

Cres. What, is he angry too?

Pan. Who, Troilus? Troilus is the better man of the two.

Cres. O Jupiter! there 's no comparison.

Pan. What, not between Troilus and Hector? Do you know a man if you see him?

Cres. Ay, if I ever saw him before and knew him.

Pan. Well, I say Troilus is Troilus.

Cres. Then you say as I say; for, I am sure, he is not Hector.

Pan. No, nor Hector is not Troilus in some degrees.

Cres. 'Tis just to each of them; he is himself.

Pan. Himself! Alas, poor Troilus! I would he were.

Cres. So he is.

Pan. Condition, I had gone barefoot to India.

Cres. He is not Hector.

Pan. Himself! no, he 's not himself: would 'a were himself! Well, the gods are above; time must friend or end: well, Troilus, well: I would my heart were in her body. No, Hector is not a better man than Troilus.

Cres. Excuse me.

Pan. He is elder.

Cres. Pardon me, pardon me.

Pan. Th' other 's not come to 't; you shall tell me another tale, when th' other 's come to 't. Hector shall not have his wit this year.

Cres. He shall not need it, if he have his own.

Pan. Nor his qualities.

Cres. No matter.

Pan. Nor his beauty.

Cres. 'Twould not become him; his own 's better.

Pan. You have no judgement, niece: Helen herself swore th' other day, that Troilus, for a brown favour —for so 'tis, I must confess,—not brown neither,—

Cres. No, but brown.

Pan. 'Faith, to say truth, brown and not brown.

Cres. To say the truth, true and not true.

Pan. She praised his complexion above Paris.

Cres. Why, Paris hath colour enough.

Pan. So he has.

Cres. Then Troilus should have too much: if she praised him above, his complexion is higher than his; he having colour enough, and the other higher, is too flaming a praise for a good complexion. I had as lief Helen's golden tongue had commended Troilus for a copper nose.

Pan. I swear to you, I think Helen loves him better than Paris.

Cres. Then she 's a merry Greek indeed.

Pan. Nay, I am sure she does. She came to him th' other day into the compassed window,—and, you know, he has not past three or four hairs on his chin,—

Cres. Indeed, a tapster's arithmetic may soon bring his particulars therein to a total.

Pan. Why, he is very young: and yet will he, within three pound, lift as much as his brother Hector.

Cres. Is he so young a man and so old a lifter?

Pan. But to prove to you that Helen loves him: she came and puts me her white hand to his cloven chin—

Cres. Juno have mercy! how came it cloven?

Pan. Why, you know, 'tis dimpled: I think his

Menelaus, alludes to the duel (related in *Iliad,* III) between Paris and Menelaus, stopped by Venus' interference. 114. **a scar to scorn.** The phrase plays on the two ideas, a wound not sufficiently serious to be regarded, and a scar in return for Paris' scorn for Menelaus. 115. **horn,** symbol of cuckoldry, since Paris had stolen Helen from Menelaus. 116. **out of town,** outside the walls.

SCENE II. 5. **Is . . . fix'd,** is of the nature of a fixed, unshakable virtue (Deighton); the pointing follows F; Globe: *Is, as a virtue, fix'd.* 7. **husbandry,** thrift, good management. 8. **light,** i.e., in light armor. 15. **per se,** i.e., unique. 26. **attaint,** the opposite of virtue (l. 25); any defect of character. 28. **against the hair,** contrary to natural tendency. 30. **Briareus,** Greek mythological monster with fifty heads and one hundred hands. 31. **Argus,** a monster with one hundred eyes. 46. **Ilium,** the palace. 58. **lay about him,** fight vigorously. 73. **in some,** by several. 80. **I had gone,** contrary to fact subjunctive; i.e., he is himself if I have gone, etc. 100. **favour,** complexion. 115. **copper,** red. 118. **Greek,** slang for frivolous, loose in morals. 120. **compassed,** bay. 123. **tapster's,** proverbially a poor reckoner; cf. *Love's Labour's Lost,* I, ii, 43. 129. **lifter,** quibble on the meaning "thief."

smiling becomes him better than any man in all Phrygia.

Cres. O, he smiles valiantly.

Pan. Does he not?

Cres. O yes, an 'twere a cloud in autumn.

Pan. Why, go to, then: but to prove to you that Helen loves Troilus,—

Cres. Troilus will stand to the proof, if you'll prove it so.

Pan. Troilus! why, he esteems her no more than I esteem an addle egg.

Cres. If you love an addle egg as well as you love an idle head, you would eat chickens i' the shell.

Pan. I cannot choose but laugh, to think how she tickled his chin: indeed, she has a marvell's white hand, I must needs confess,—

Cres. Without the rack.

Pan. And she takes upon her to spy a white hair on his chin.

Cres. Alas, poor chin! many a wart is richer.

Pan. But there was such laughing! Queen Hecuba laughed that her eyes ran o'er.

Cres. With mill-stones.

Pan. And Cassandra laughed.

Cres. But there was more temperate fire under the pot of her eyes: did her eyes run o'er too?

Pan. And Hector laughed.

Cres. At what was all this laughing?

Pan. Marry, at the white hair that Helen spied on Troilus' chin.

Cres. An 't had been a green hair, I should have laughed too.

Pan. They laughed not so much at the hair as at his pretty answer.

Cres. What was his answer?

Pan. Quoth she, 'Here 's but two and fifty hairs on your chin, and one of them is white.'

Cres. This is her question.

Pan. That 's true; make no question of that. 'Two and fifty hairs,' quoth he, 'and one white: that white hair is my father, and all the rest are his sons.' 'Jupiter!' quoth she, 'which of these hairs is Paris my husband?' 'The forked one,' quoth he, 'pluck 't out, and give it him.' But there was such laughing! and Helen so blushed, and Paris so chafed, and all the rest so laughed, that it passed.

Cres. So let it now; for it has been a great while going by.

Pan. Well, cousin, I told you a thing yesterday; think on 't.

Cres. So I do.

Pan. I'll be sworn 'tis true; he will weep you, an 'twere a man born in April.

Cres. And I'll spring up in his tears, an 'twere a nettle against May. *Sound a retreat.*

Pan. Hark! they are coming from the field: shall we stand up here, and see them as they pass toward Ilium? good niece, do, sweet niece Cressida.

Cres. At your pleasure.

Pan. Here, here, here 's an excellent place; here we may see most bravely: I'll tell you them all by their names as they pass by; but mark Troilus above the rest.

Cres. Speak not so loud.

Enter ÆNEAS [*and passes across the stage*].

Pan. That 's Æneas: is not that a brave man? he 's one of the flowers of Troy, I can tell you: but mark Troilus; you shall see anon.

Enter ANTENOR [*and passes across the stage*].

Cres. Who 's that?

Pan. That 's Antenor: he has a shrewd wit, I can tell you; and he 's a man good enough: he 's one o' the soundest judgements in Troy, whosoever, and a proper man of person. When comes Troilus? I'll show you Troilus anon: if he see me, you shall see him nod at me.

Cres. Will he give you the nod?

Pan. You shall see.

Cres. If he do, the rich shall have more.

Enter HECTOR [*and passes across the stage*].

Pan. That 's Hector, that, that, look you, that; there 's a fellow! Go they way, Hector! There 's a brave man, niece. O brave Hector! Look how he looks! there 's a countenance! is 't not a brave man?

Cres. O, a brave man!

Pan. Is 'a not? it does a man's heart good. Look you what hacks are on his helmet! look you yonder, do you see? look you there: there 's no jesting; there 's laying on, take 't off who will, as they say: there be hacks!

Cres. Be those with swords?

Pan. Swords! any thing, he cares not; an the devil come to him, it 's all one; by God's lid, it does one's heart good. Yonder comes Paris, yonder comes Paris.

Enter PARIS [*and passes across the stage*].

Look ye yonder, niece; is 't not a gallant man too, is 't not? Why, this is brave now. Who said he came hurt home to-day? he 's not hurt: why, this will do Helen's heart good now, ha! Would I could see Troilus now! You shall see Troilus anon.

Cres. Who 's that?

Enter HELENUS [*and passes across the stage*].

Pan. That 's Helenus. I marvel where Troilus is. That 's Helenus. I think he went not forth to-day. That 's Helenus.

Cres. Can Helenus fight, uncle?

Pan. Helenus? no. Yes, he'll fight indifferent well. I marvel where Troilus is. Hark! do you not hear the people cry 'Troilus'? Helenus is a priest.

Cres. What sneaking fellow comes yonder?

Enter TROILUS [*and passes across the stage*].

Pan. Where? yonder? that 's Deiphobus. 'Tis Troilus! there 's a man, niece! Hem! Brave Troilus! the prince of chivalry!

142. **stand . . . proof,** i.e., will not shrink from the test (with bawdy pun on "stand"). 152. **rack,** torture. 175. **Two and fifty.** Priam had fifty sons. Theobald emended to *one and fifty*. Some commentators assume that the bastard Margarelon is to be included among the sons of Priam. 178. **forked,** i.e., he has cuckold's horns. 189. **an 'twere,** as if he were. 191. **against,** in expectation of. 212. **give . . . nod,** a term in the game of cards called noddy, a word which also signifies "a fool." Cressida means to call Pandarus a noddy, and says he shall by more nods be made more significantly a fool (Singer). 214. **the rich . . . more,** i.e., the fool will become more foolish. 224. **laying on,** evidence of blows exchanged. 228. **by God's lid,** an oath by God's eyelid. 271. **drayman,** one who draws a cart. 280. **minced,** simpering (playing on the idea of *spices*). 281. **date is,** time is (playing on the fruit). 283. **ward, lie,** technical terms in fencing. 295. **swell,** i.e., in pregnancy. 303. **doubt,** fear. 312. **wooing,** i.e., being wooed. 314. **That she,** that woman. 319. **Achievement . . . beseech,** i.e., to achieve

Cres. Peace, for shame, peace!

Pan. Mark him; note him. O brave Troilus! Look well upon him, niece: look you how his sword is bloodied, and his helm more hacked than Hector's, and how he looks, and how he goes! O admirable youth! he ne'er saw three and twenty. Go thy way, Troilus, go thy way! Had I a sister were a grace, or a daughter a goddess, he should take his choice. O admirable man! Paris? Paris is dirt to him; and, I warrant, Helen, to change, would give an eye to boot.

Cres. Here come more.

[Forces *pass across the stage.*]

Pan. Asses, fools, dolts! chaff and bran, chaff and bran! porridge after meat! I could live and die i' the eyes of Troilus. Ne'er look, ne'er look; the eagles are gone: crows and daws, crows and daws! I had rather be such a man as Troilus than Agamemnon and all Greece.

Cres. There is among the Greeks Achilles, a better man than Troilus.

Pan. Achilles! a drayman, a porter, a very camel.

Cres. Well, well.

Pan. 'Well, well!' Why, have you any discretion? have you any eyes? do you know what a man is? Is not birth, beauty, good shape, discourse, manhood, learning, gentleness, virtue, youth, liberality, and such like, the spice and salt that season a man?

Cres. Ay, a minced man: and then to be baked with no date in the pie, for then the man's date is out.

Pan. You are such a woman! one knows not at what ward you lie.

Cres. Upon my back, to defend my belly; upon my wit, to defend my wiles; upon my secrecy, to defend mine honesty; my mask, to defend my beauty; and you, to defend all these: and at all these wards I lie, at a thousand watches.

Pan. Say one of your watches.

Cres. Nay, I'll watch you for that; and that 's one of the chiefest of them too: if I cannot ward what I would not have hit, I can watch you for telling how I took the blow; unless it swell past hiding, and then it 's past watching.

Pan. You are such another!

Enter [Troilus'] Boy.

Boy. Sir, my lord would instantly speak with you.

Pan. Where?

Boy. At your own house; there he unarms him.

Pan. Good boy, tell him I come. [*Exit Boy.*]
I doubt he be hurt. Fare ye well, good niece.

Cres. Adieu, uncle.

Pan. I'll be with you, niece, by and by.

Cres. To bring, uncle?

Pan. Ay, a token from Troilus.

Cres. By the same token, you are a bawd.
[*Exit Pandarus.*]
Words, vows, gifts, tears, and love's full sacrifice,
He offers in another's enterprise:
But more in Troilus thousand fold I see
Than in the glass of Pandar's praise may be;
Yet hold I off. Women are angels, wooing:
Things won are done; joy's soul lies in the doing.
That she belov'd knows nought that knows not this:
Men prize the thing ungain'd more than it is:
That she was never yet that ever knew
Love got so sweet as when desire did sue.
Therefore this maxim out of love I teach:
Achievement is command; ungain'd, beseech:
Then though my heart's content firm love doth bear,
Nothing of that shall from mine eyes appear. *Exit.*

[Scene III. *The Grecian camp. Before Agamemnon's tent.*]

[*Sennet.*] *Enter* Agamemnon, Nestor, Ulysses, Diomedes, Menelaus, *with others.*

Agam. Princes,
What grief hath set the jaundice on your cheeks?
The ample proposition that hope makes
In all designs begun on earth below
Fails in the promis'd largeness: checks and disasters
Grow in the veins of actions highest rear'd,
As knots, by the conflux of meeting sap,
Infects the sound pine and divert his grain
Tortive and errant from his course of growth.
Nor, princes, is it matter new to us
That we come short of our suppose so far
That after seven years' siege yet Troy walls stand;
Sith every action that hath gone before,
Whereof we have record, trial did draw
Bias and thwart, not answering the aim,
And that unbodied figure of the thought
That gave 't surmised shape. Why then, you princes,
Do you with cheeks abash'd behold our works,
And call them shames? which are indeed nought else
But the protractive trials of great Jove
To find persistive constancy in men:
The fineness of which metal is not found
In fortune's love; for then the bold and coward,
The wise and fool, the artist and unread,
The hard and soft, seem all affin'd and kin:
But, in the wind and tempest of her frown,
Distinction, with a broad and powerful fan,
Puffing at all, winnows the light away;
And what hath mass or matter, by itself
Lies rich in virtue and unmingled.

Nest. With due observance of thy godlike seat,
Great Agamemnon, Nestor shall apply
Thy latest words. In the reproof of chance
Lies the true proof of men: the sea being smooth,
How many shallow bauble boats dare sail
Upon her patient breast, making their way
With those of nobler bulk!
But let the ruffian Boreas once enrage
The gentle Thetis, and anon behold
The strong-ribb'd bark through liquid mountains cut,
Bounding between the two moist elements,

(to win a woman) is to command her; unwon, she must be besought.
Scene iii. The scene has an epic tone; this is due to the long figurative speeches, which give it the ceremoniousness of an epic counsel. 7. **conflux,** flowing together. 9. **Tortive,** distorted. **errant,** wandering. 11. **suppose,** expectation. 13-17. **Sith . . . shape.** Delius noted that *trial* is the subject, *action* the object. Paradise paraphrases: Since trial has drawn awry and crosswise every previous action of which we have record, so that it has not corresponded to the aim of its originator nor to the impalpable shape which it assumed in thought. 14. **record,** accent on second syllable. 24. **artist,** scholar. 25. **affin'd,** related. 26. **her.** The antecedent is *fortune's* (l. 23). 30. **unmingled,** unalloyed. 31. **godlike,** because Agamemnon is king. 35. **bauble,** toy. 38. **Boreas,** the north wind. 39. **Thetis,** a sea deity, mother of Achilles. 41. **moist elements,** air and water.

Like Perseus' horse: where 's then the saucy boat
Whose weak untimber'd sides but even now
Co-rivall'd greatness? Either to harbour fled,
Or made a toast for Neptune. Even so
Doth valour's show and valour's worth divide
In storms of fortune; for in her ray and brightness
The herd hath more annoyance by the breese
Than by the tiger; but when the splitting wind
Makes flexible the knees of knotted oaks,
And flies fled under shade, why, then the thing of courage
As rous'd with rage with rage doth sympathize,
And with an accent tun'd in selfsame key
Retorts to chiding fortune.
Ulyss. Agamemnon,
Thou great commander, nerve and bone of Greece,
Heart of our numbers, soul and only spirit,
In whom the tempers and the minds of all
Should be shut up, hear what Ulysses speaks.
Besides th' applause and approbation
The which, [*To Agamemnon*] most mighty for thy place and sway,
[*To Nestor*] And thou most reverend for thy stretch'd-out life
I give to both your speeches, which were such
As Agamemnon and the hand of Greece
Should hold up high in brass, and such again
As venerable Nestor, hatch'd in silver,
Should with a bond of air, strong as the axle-tree
On which heaven rides, knit all the Greekish ears
To his experienc'd tongue, yet let it please both,
Thou great, and wise, to hear Ulysses speak.
Agam. Speak, Prince of Ithaca; and be 't of less expect
That matter needless, of importless burden,
Divide thy lips, than we are confident,
When rank Thersites opes his mastic jaws,
We shall hear music, wit and oracle.
Ulyss. Troy, yet upon his basis, had been down,
And the great Hector's sword had lack'd a master,
But for these instances.
The specialty of rule hath been neglected:
And look how many Grecian tents do stand
Hollow upon this plain, so many hollow factions.
When that the general is not like the hive
To whom the foragers shall all repair,
What honey is expected? Degree being vizarded,
Th' unworthiest shows as fairly in the mask.
The heavens themselves, the planets and this centre
Observe degree, priority and place,
Insisture, course, proportion, season, form,
Office and custom, in all line of order;
And therefore is the glorious planet Sol
In noble eminence enthron'd and spher'd
Amidst the other; whose med'cinable eye
Corrects the ill aspects of planets evil,
And posts, like the commandment of a king,
Sans check to good and bad: but when the planets
In evil mixture to disorder wander,
What plagues and what portents! what mutiny!
What raging of the sea! shaking of earth!
Commotion in the winds! frights, changes, horrors,
Divert and crack, rend and deracinate
The unity and married calm of states
Quite from their fixure! O, when degree is shak'd,
Which is the ladder to all high designs,
The enterprise is sick! How could communities,
Degrees in schools and brotherhoods in cities,
Peaceful commerce from dividable shores,
The primogenity and due of birth,
Prerogative of age, crowns, sceptres, laurels,
But by degree, stand in authentic place?
Take but degree away, untune that string,
And, hark, what discord follows! each thing meets
In mere oppugnancy: the bounded waters
Should lift their bosoms higher than the shores
And make a sop of all this solid globe:
Strength should be lord of imbecility,
And the rude son should strike his father dead:
Force should be right; or rather, right and wrong,
Between whose endless jar justice resides,
Should lose their names, and so should justice too.
Then every thing includes itself in power,
Power into will, will into appetite;
And appetite, an universal wolf,
So doubly seconded with will and power,
Must make perforce an universal prey,
And last eat up himself. Great Agamemnon,
This chaos, when degree is suffocate,
Follows the choking.
And this neglection of degree it is
That by a pace goes backward, with a purpose
It hath to climb. The general 's disdain'd
By him one step below, he by the next,
That next by him beneath; so every step,
Exampled by the first pace that is sick
Of his superior, grows to an envious fever
Of pale and bloodless emulation:
And 'tis this fever that keeps Troy on foot,
Not her own sinews. To end a tale of length,
Troy in our weakness stands, not in her strength.
Nest. Most wisely hath Ulysses here discover'd

42. **Perseus' horse,** Pegasus, a winged horse which sprang from the blood of Medusa when Perseus cut off her head. The horse was given to Bellerophon by the gods. It is associated, however, with Perseus, probably because Ovid relates that the latter hero was mounted on Pegasus when he rescued Andromeda from the sea monster. **saucy,** presumptuous, rashly venturing. 45. **toast,** rich morsel to be swallowed (Schmidt). 48. **breese,** gadfly. 51. **fled,** are fled. **thing of courage,** any courageous thing. 64. **brass,** frequently used as a type of durability. 65. **hatch'd,** thinly streaked, referring to Nestor's gray hair. 66. **bond of air,** his breath—words. 70-74. **be 't . . . oracle,** i.e., we should expect unimportant matter from you just as we should expect music, wit, and oracle from Thersites. 70. **expect,** expectation. 73. **mastic,** abusive, scouring. (Some editors emend to *mastiff*.) 78. **specialty of rule,** particular rights of supreme authority (Johnson). 80. **Hollow,** empty. 83. **Degree,** here the equivalent of authority. Below (l. 86) the word has a more cosmological import, where it reflects the Renaissance belief (inherited from Plato) that the world achieved its stability by means of the gradation of all created things. The social and political implication of this conception is that human beings are born to a designated station or degree to which they must adhere with mutual respect and the responsibilities of which they must accept if society and government are to remain stable. Renaissance writers were fond of pointing out analogies between the civil organization and any natural or cosmological manifestations of some kind of order or degree. This passage (ll. 85-134) is not only Shakespeare's fullest and most eloquent statement of this concept, but also one of the most distinguished in all Renaissance literature. 85. **this centre,** the earth. 87. **Insisture,** steady continuance in their path. 91. **med'cinable,** healing. 92. **aspects,** relative positions of the heavenly bodies as they appear to an observer on the earth's surface at a given time, and the influence attributed thereto. 94. **Sans,** without. 95. **mixture,** conjunction. 99. **deracinate,** uproot. 101. **fixure,** stability. 102. **ladder . . . designs,** means by which all lofty purposes are realized. 105. **dividable,** separated. 106. **primogenity,** the right of the eldest son to succeed to his father's estate. 111. **mere oppugnancy,** total strife. 113. **sop,** pulp. 114. **imbecility,** weakness. 116-117. **right . . . resides,** refers to the desirability of adhering to the golden mean. 117. **jar,** collision. 119-124. **Then . . . himself.** This metaphor is the converse of the figure

The fever whereof all our power is sick.
Agam. The nature of the sickness found, Ulysses,
What is the remedy?
Ulyss. The great Achilles, whom opinion crowns
The sinew and the forehand of our host,
Having his ear full of his airy fame,
Grows dainty of his worth and in his tent
Lies mocking our designs: with him Patroclus
Upon a lazy bed the livelong day
Breaks scurril jests,
And with ridiculous and awkward action,
Which, slanderer, he imitation calls,
He pageants us. Sometime, great Agamemnon,
Thy topless deputation he puts on,
And, like a strutting player, whose conceit
Lies in his hamstring, and doth think it rich
To hear the wooden dialogue and sound
'Twixt his stretch'd footing and the scaffoldage,—
Such to-be-pitied and o'er-wrested seeming
He acts thy greatness in: and when he speaks,
'Tis like a chime a-mending; with terms unsquar'd,
Which, from the tongue of roaring Typhon dropp'd,
Would seem hyperboles. At this fusty stuff
The large Achilles, on his press'd bed lolling,
From his deep chest laughs out a loud applause;
Cries 'Excellent! 'tis Agamemnon just.
Now play me Nestor; hem, and stroke thy beard,
As he being drest to some oration.'
That 's done, as near as the extremest ends
Of parallels, as like as Vulcan and his wife:
Yet god Achilles still cries 'Excellent!
'Tis Nestor right. Now play him me, Patroclus,
Arming to answer in a night alarm.'
And then, forsooth, the faint defects of age
Must be the scene of mirth; to cough and spit,
And, with a palsy-fumbling on his gorget,
Shake in and out the rivet: and at this sport
Sir Valour dies; cries 'O, enough, Patroclus;
Or give me ribs of steel! I shall split all
In pleasure of my spleen.' And in this fashion,
All our abilities, gifts, natures, shapes,
Severals and generals of grace exact,
Achievements, plots, orders, preventions,
Excitements to the field, or speech for truce,
Success or loss, what is or is not, serves
As stuff for these two to make paradoxes.
Nest. And in the imitation of these twain—
Who, as Ulysses says, opinion crowns
With an imperial voice—many are infect.
Ajax is grown self-will'd, and bears his head
In such a rein, in full as proud a place
As broad Achilles; keeps his tent like him;
Makes factious feasts; rails on our state of war,
Bold as an oracle, and sets Thersites,
A slave whose gall coins slanders like a mint,
To match us in comparisons with dirt,
To weaken and discredit our exposure,
How rank soever rounded in with danger.
Ulyss. They tax our policy, and call it cowardice,
Count wisdom as no member of the war,
Forestall prescience and esteem no act
But that of hand: the still and mental parts,
That do contrive how many hands shall strike,
When fitness calls them on, and know by measure
Of their observant toil the enemies' weight,—
Why, this hath not a finger's dignity:
They call this bed-work, mapp'ry, closet-war;
So that the ram that batters down the wall,
For the great swing and rudeness of his poise,
They place before his hand that made the engine,
Or those that with the fineness of their souls
By reason guide his execution.
Nest. Let this be granted, and Achilles' horse
Makes many Thetis' sons. [*A tucket.*]
Agam. What trumpet? look, Menelaus.
Men. From Troy.

[*Enter* ÆNEAS.]

Agam. What would you 'fore our tent?
Æne. Is this great Agamemnon's tent, I pray you?
Agam. Even this.
Æne. May one, that is a herald and a prince,
Do a fair message to his kingly ears?
Agam. With surety stronger than Achilles' arm
'Fore all the Greekish heads, which with one voice
Call Agamemnon head and general.
Æne. Fair leave and large security. How may
A stranger to those most imperial looks
Know them from eyes of other mortals?
Agam. How!
Æne. Ay;
I ask, that I might waken reverence,
And bid the cheek be ready with a blush
Modest as morning when she coldly eyes
The youthful Phœbus:
Which is that god in office, guiding men?
Which is the high and mighty Agamemnon?
Agam. This Troyan scorns us; or the men of Troy
Are ceremonious courtiers.
Æne. Courtiers as free, as debonair, unarm'd,
As bending angels; that 's their fame in peace:
But when they would seem soldiers, they have galls,

of the microcosm, or man as a little world. Here the faculties and passions of the soul are imputed to the universe and misgovernment in states is explained in physiological terms. 119. **includes,** resolves itself in the end into (Deighton); encloses within limits (*NED*, citing this passage). 132. **sick,** envious. 143. **forehand,** upper hand or advantage. 144. **airy,** unsubstantial. 145. **dainty of,** i.e., he overestimates his own worth. 148. **scurril,** indecent. 151. **pageants,** dramatizes, mimics. 152. **topless deputation,** supreme power deputed to thee (Rolfe); dignity as Jove's substitute (Schmidt). 153-154. **like . . . hamstring,** i.e., his ability as an actor is not in his faculties but in his legs; implies, perhaps, an artificial strut. 156. **'Twixt . . . scaffoldage,** between the floor and roof of the stage; i.e., he is impressed by the echo of his own voice. 159. **a-mending.** He who has been in the tower of a church while the chimes were repairing, will never wish a second time to be present at so dissonantly noisy an operation (Steevens). **terms,** notes. **unsquar'd,** unadapted to their subject as stones are unfitted to the purposes of architecture while they are yet unsquared (Steevens). 160. **Typhon,** Greek mythological monster with a hundred heads which breathed fire. He made war against the gods and was destroyed by one of Zeus' thunderbolts. 161. **fusty,** pertaining to fustian, i.e., bombastic language. 168. **Vulcan . . . wife,** the ugliest god, and Venus, the most beautiful goddess. 174. **gorget,** piece of armor for the throat. 176. **Sir Valour,** contemptuously refers to Achilles' reputation. 180. **Severals . . . exact,** well-ordered gifts, individual and general (Delius). 183. **what is or is not,** i.e., all our positive qualities and all our defects of character or conduct. 184. **paradoxes,** absurdities (Deighton). 186-187. **opinion . . . voice,** i.e., they virtually rule the Greek forces because of the high regard in which they are held. 195. **our exposure,** the danger to which we are exposed. 197. **tax,** blame, censure; see glossary. 199. **Forestall,** condemn beforehand (Paradise). **prescience,** foresight; or perhaps measures taken as a result of foresight. 202. **fitness,** readiness. 203. **their.** The antecedent is *mental parts* (l. 200). 209. **fineness . . . souls,** the idea is the opposite to mere physical action; perhaps brain-work. 212. **many Thetis' sons,** i.e., many Achilleses. *Stage Direction:* ***tucket,*** signal given on a trumpet. 235. **debonair,** gentle, meek. 237. **galls,** spirit to resent injury.

Good arms, strong joints, true swords; and, Jove's accord,
Nothing so full of heart. But peace, Æneas,
Peace, Troyan; lay thy finger on thy lips!
The worthiness of praise distains his worth,
If that the prais'd himself bring the praise forth:
But what the repining enemy commends,
That breath fame blows; that praise, sole pure, transcends.
Agam. Sir, you of Troy, call you yourself Æneas?
Æne. Ay, Greek, that is my name.
Agam. What 's your affair, I pray you?
Æne. Sir, pardon; 'tis for Agamemnon's ears.
Agam. He hears nought privately that comes from Troy.
Æne. Nor I from Troy come not to whisper him:
I bring a trumpet to awake his ear,
To set his sense on the attentive bent,
And then to speak.
Agam. Speak frankly as the wind;
It is not Agamemnon's sleeping hour:
That thou shalt know, Troyan, he is awake,
He tells thee so himself.
Æne. Trumpet, blow loud,
Send thy brass voice through all these lazy tents;
And every Greek of mettle, let him know,
What Troy means fairly shall be spoke aloud.
[*Sound trumpet.*]
We have, great Agamemnon, here in Troy
A prince call'd Hector,—Priam is his father,—
Who in this dull and long-continued truce
Is rusty grown: he bade me take a trumpet,
And to this purpose speak. Kings, princes, lords!
If there be one among the fair'st of Greece
That holds his honour higher than his ease,
That seeks his praise more than he fears his peril,
That knows his valour, and knows not his fear,
That loves his mistress more than in confession,
With truant vows to her own lips he loves,
And dare avow her beauty and her worth
In other arms than hers,—to him this challenge.
Hector, in view of Troyans and of Greeks,
Shall make it good, or do his best to do it,
He hath a lady, wiser, fairer, truer,
Than ever Greek did compass in his arms,
And will to-morrow with his trumpet call
Midway between your tents and walls of Troy,
To rouse a Grecian that is true in love:
If any come, Hector shall honour him;
If none, he'll say in Troy when he retires,
The Grecian dames are sunburnt and not worth
The splinter of a lance. Even so much.
Agam. This shall be told our lovers, Lord Æneas;
If none of them have soul in such a kind,
We left them all at home: but we are soldiers;
And may that soldier a mere recreant prove,
That means not, hath not, or is not in love!
If then one is, or hath, or means to be,
That one meets Hector; if none else, I am he.
Nest. Tell him of Nestor, one that was a man
When Hector's grandsire suck'd: he is old now;
But if there be not in our Grecian host
One noble man that hath one spark of fire,
To answer for his love, tell him from me
I'll hide my silver beard in a gold beaver
And in my vantbrace put this wither'd brawn,
And meeting him will tell him that my lady
Was fairer than his grandam and as chaste
As may be in the world: his youth in flood,
I'll prove this truth with my three drops of blood.
Æne. Now heavens forfend such scarcity of youth!
Ulyss. Amen.
Agam. Fair Lord Æneas, let me touch your hand;
To our pavilion shall I lead you, sir.
Achilles shall have word of this intent;
So shall each lord of Greece, from tent to tent:
Yourself shall feast with us before you go
And find the welcome of a noble foe.
[*Exeunt all but Ulysses and Nestor.*]
Ulyss. Nestor!
Nest. What says Ulysses?
Ulyss. I have a young conception in my brain;
Be you my time to bring it to some shape.
Nest. What is 't?
Ulyss. This 'tis:
Blunt wedges rive hard knots: the seeded pride
That hath to this maturity blown up
In rank Achilles must or now be cropp'd,
Or, shedding, breed a nursery of like evil,
To overbulk us all.
Nest. Well, and how?
Ulyss. This challenge that the gallant Hector sends,
However it is spread in general name,
Relates in purpose only to Achilles.
Nest. True, the purpose is perspicuous as substance,
Whose grossness little characters sum up:
And, in the publication, make no strain,
But that Achilles, were his brain as barren
As banks of Libya,—though, Apollo knows,
'Tis dry enough,—will, with great speed of judgement,
Ay, with celerity, find Hector's purpose
Pointing on him.
Ulyss. And wake him to the answer, think you?
Nest. Yes, 'tis most meet: whom may you else oppose,
That can from Hector bring his honour off,
If not Achilles? Though 't be a sportful combat,
Yet in the trial much opinion dwells;
For here the Troyans taste our dear'st repute
With their fin'st palate: and trust to me, Ulysses,
Our imputation shall be oddly pois'd
In this wild action; for the success,
Although particular, shall give a scantling
Of good or bad unto the general;
And in such indexes, although small pricks
To their subsequent volumes, there is seen
The baby figure of the giant mass
Of things to come at large. It is suppos'd
He that meets Hector issues from our choice;
And choice, being mutual act of all our souls,

238-239. **and, Jove's . . . heart.** *Jove annuente* (Jove being in full accord), nothing is so full of heart as they (Theobald). 269-270. **more than . . . loves,** more than enough to protest his love by false vows. 282. **sunburnt,** i.e., unattractive. 296. **beaver,** face guard of a helmet. 297. **vantbrace,** armor for the front part of the arm. 313. **Be you . . . shape,** be to my conception what time is to the embryo (Deighton). 318. **or,** either. 324-325. **substance . . . sum up,** i.e., a significant sum is recorded in small characters. 326. **make no strain,** parenthetical expression—have no difficulty in believing. 334. **his.** The antecedent is *That*. 337. **our dear'st repute,** Achilles. 338. **their fin'st palate,** Hector. 339. **imputation,** reputation. 341. **scantling,** specimen. 343. **indexes,** the characters—index fingers—placed in the margins of books to call attention to significant passages. 343-344. **small . . . volumes,** small markings in comparison with the volumes that follow. 349. **Makes . . . election,** makes her choice on the basis of merit alone. 361. **to show,** to be shown. 376. **sort,** lot. 378. **the great Myrmidon,**

Makes merit her election, and doth boil,
As 'twere from forth us all, a man distill'd
Out of our virtues; who miscarrying,
What heart receives from hence the conquering part,
To steel a strong opinion to themselves?
Which entertain'd, limbs are his instruments,
In no less working than are swords and bows
Directive by the limbs.
Ulyss. Give pardon to my speech:
Therefore 'tis meet Achilles meet not Hector.
Let us, like merchants, show our foulest wares,
And think, perchance, they'll sell; if not,
The lustre of the better yet to show,
Shall show the better. Do not consent
That ever Hector and Achilles meet;
For both our honour and our shame in this
Are dogg'd with two strange followers.
Nest. I see them not with my old eyes: what are they?
Ulyss. What glory our Achilles shares from Hector,
Were he not proud, we all should share with him:
But he already is too insolent;
And we were better parch in Afric sun
Than in the pride and salt scorn of his eyes,
Should he 'scape Hector fair: if he were foil'd,
Why then, we did our main opinion crush
In taint of our best man. No, make a lott'ry;
And, by device, let blockish Ajax draw
The sort to fight with Hector: among ourselves
Give him allowance for the better man;
For that will physic the great Myrmidon
Who broils in loud applause, and make him fall
His crest that prouder than blue Iris bends.
If the dull brainless Ajax come safe off,
We'll dress him up in voices: if he fail,
Yet go we under our opinion still
That we have better men. But, hit or miss,
Our project's life this shape of sense assumes:
Ajax employ'd plucks down Achilles' plumes.
Nest. Now,
Ulysses, I begin to relish thy advice;
And I will give a taste thereof forthwith
To Agamemnon: go we to him straight.
Two curs shall tame each other: pride alone
Must tarre the mastiffs on, as 'twere a bone.
Exeunt.

[ACT II.

SCENE I. *A part of the Grecian camp.*]

Enter AJAX *and* THERSITES.

Ajax. Thersites!

Ther. Agamemnon, how if he had boils? full, all over, generally?

Ajax. Thersites!

Ther. And those boils did run? say so: did not the general run then? were not that a botchy core?

Ajax. Dog!

Ther. Then would come some matter from him; I see none now.

Ajax. Thou bitch-wolf's son, canst thou not hear? [*Beating him*] Feel, then.

Ther. The plague of Greece upon thee, thou mongrel beef-witted lord!

Ajax. Speak then, thou vinewedst leaven, speak: I will beat thee into handsomeness.

Ther. I shall sooner rail thee into wit and holiness: but, I think, thy horse will sooner con an oration than thou learn a prayer without book. Thou canst strike, canst thou? a red murrain o' thy jade's tricks!

Ajax. Toadstool, learn me the proclamation.

Ther. Dost thou think I have no sense, thou strikest me thus?

Ajax. The proclamation!

Ther. Thou art proclaimed fool, I think.

Ajax. Do not, porpentine, do not: my fingers itch.

Ther. I would thou didst itch from head to foot and I had the scratching of thee; I would make thee the loathsomest scab in Greece. When thou art forth in the incursions, thou strikest as slow as another.

Ajax. I say, the proclamation!

Ther. Thou grumblest and railest every hour on Achilles, and thou art as full of envy at his greatness as Cerberus is at Proserpina's beauty, ay, that thou barkest at him.

Ajax. Mistress Thersites!

Ther. Thou shouldst strike him.

Ajax. Cobloaf!

Ther. He would pun thee into shivers with his fist, as a sailor breaks a biscuit.

Ajax. [*Beating him*] You whoreson cur!

Ther. Do, do.

Ajax. Thou stool for a witch!

Ther. Ay, do, do; thou sodden-witted lord! thou hast no more brain than I have in mine elbows; an asinico may tutor thee: thou scurvy-valiant ass! thou art here but to thrash Troyans; and thou art bought and sold among those of any wit, like a barbarian slave. If thou use to beat me, I will begin at thy heel, and tell what thou art by inches, thou thing of no bowels, thou!

Ajax. You dog!

Ther. You scurvy lord!

Ajax. [*Beating him*] You cur!

Ther. Mars his idiot! do, rudeness; do, camel; do, do.

[*Enter* ACHILLES *and* PATROCLUS.]

Achil. Why, how now, Ajax! wherefore do you thus?
How now, Thersites! what 's the matter, man?

Ther. You see him there, do you?

Achil. Ay; what 's the matter?

Ther. Nay, look upon him.

Achil. So I do: what 's the matter?

Ther. Nay, but regard him well.

Achil. 'Well!' why, I do so.

Ther. But yet you look not well upon him; for, whosomever you take him to be, he is Ajax.

i.e., Achilles, so called here because accompanied by a band of Myrmidon warriors—a tribe living in Thessaly. 379. **broils in,** basks in. 380. **Iris,** i.e., the rainbow. 392. **tarre,** provoke, incite.

ACT II. SCENE I. 6. **botchy core,** central hard mass of a boil or tumor. 9. **matter,** sense, with quibble. 14. **mongrel.** His mother was a Trojan; cf. II, ii, 77, note. 15. **vinewedst,** most moldy. **leaven,** dough. 19. **con,** memorize. 20. **without book,** by heart. 21. **murrain,** plague. 22. **learn me,** find out for me. 27. **porpentine,** porcupine. 32. **forth in the incursions,** abroad engaging in battle. 37. **Cerberus,** three-headed dog which guarded the entrance to Hades. **Proserpina,** queen of Hades. 41. **Cobloaf,** small round loaf; a bun. 42. **pun,** pound. 46. **stool,** privy. 49. **asinico,** little ass. 54. **of no bowels,** merciless. 58. **Mars his,** Mars'.

Achil. I know that, fool.

Ther. Ay, but that fool knows not himself.

Ajax. Therefore I beat thee.

Ther. Lo, lo, lo, lo, what modicums of wit he utters! his evasions have ears thus long. I have bobbed his brain more than he has beat my bones: I will buy nine sparrows for a penny, and his pia mater is not worth the ninth part of a sparrow. This lord, Achilles, Ajax, who wears his wit in his belly and his guts in his head, I'll tell you what I say of him.

Achil. What?

Ther. I say, this Ajax— [*Ajax offers to beat him.*]

Achil. Nay, good Ajax.

Ther. Has not so much wit—

Achil. Nay, I must hold you.

Ther. As will stop the eye of Helen's needle, for whom he comes to fight.

Achil. Peace, fool!

Ther. I would have peace and quietness, but the fool will not: he there: that he: look you there.

Ajax. O thou damned cur! I shall—

Achil. Will you set your wit to a fool's?

Ther. No, I warrant you; for a fool's will shame it.

Patr. Good words, Thersites.

Achil. What 's the quarrel?

Ajax. I bade the vile owl go learn me the tenour of the proclamation, and he rails upon me.

Ther. I serve thee not.

Ajax. Well, go to, go to.

Ther. I serve here voluntary.

Achil. Your last service was sufferance, 'twas not voluntary: no man is beaten voluntary: Ajax was here the voluntary, and you as under an impress.

Ther. E'en so; a great deal of your wit, too, lies in your sinews, or else there be liars. Hector shall have a great catch, if he knock out either of your brains: 'a were as good crack a fusty nut with no kernel.

Achil. What, with me too, Thersites?

Ther. There 's Ulysses and old Nestor, whose wit was mouldy ere your grandsires had nails on their toes, yoke you like draught-oxen and make you plough up the wars.

Achil. What, what?

Ther. Yes, good sooth: to, Achilles! to, Ajax! to!

Ajax. I shall cut out your tongue.

Ther. 'Tis no matter; I shall speak as much as thou afterwards.

Patr. No more words, Thersites; peace!

Ther. I will hold my peace when Achilles' brach bids me, shall I?

Achil. There 's for you, Patroclus.

Ther. I will see you hanged, like clotpoles, ere I come any more to your tents: I will keep where there is wit stirring and leave the faction of fools. *Exit.*

Patr. A good riddance.

Achil. Marry, this, sir, is proclaim'd through all our host:
That Hector, by the fifth hour of the sun,
Will with a trumpet 'twixt our tents and Troy
To-morrow morning call some knight to arms
That hath a stomach: and such a one that dare
Maintain—I know not what: 'tis trash. Farewell.

Ajax. Farewell. Who shall answer him?

Achil. I know not: 'tis put to lottery; otherwise
He knew his man.

Ajax. O, meaning you. I will go learn more of it.
[*Exeunt.*]

[SCENE II. *Troy. A room in Priam's palace.*]

Enter PRIAM, HECTOR, TROILUS, PARIS, *and* HELENUS.

Pri. After so many hours, lives, speeches spent,
Thus once again says Nestor from the Greeks:
'Deliver Helen, and all damage else—
As honour, loss of time, travail, expense,
Wounds, friends, and what else dear that is consum'd
In hot digestion of this cormorant war—
Shall be struck off.' Hector, what say you to 't?

Hect. Though no man lesser fears the Greeks than I
As far as toucheth my particular,
Yet, dread Priam,
There is no lady of more softer bowels,
More spongy to suck in the sense of fear,
More ready to cry out 'Who knows what follows?'
Than Hector is: the wound of peace is surety,
Surety secure; but modest doubt is call'd
The beacon of the wise, the tent that searches
To th' bottom of the worst. Let Helen go:
Since the first sword was drawn about this question,
Every tithe soul, 'mongst many thousand dismes,
Hath been as dear as Helen; I mean, of ours:
If we have lost so many tenths of ours,
To guard a thing not ours nor worth to us,
Had it our name, the value of one ten,
What merit 's in that reason which denies
The yielding of her up?

Tro. Fie, fie, my brother!
Weigh you the worth and honour of a king
So great as our dread father in a scale
Of common ounces? will you with counters sum
The past proportion of his infinite?
And buckle in a waist most fathomless
With spans and inches so diminutive
As fears and reasons? fie, for godly shame!

Hel. No marvel, though you bite so sharp at reasons,
You are so empty of them. Should not our father
Bear the great sway of his affairs with reasons,
Because your speech hath none that tells him so?

Tro. You are for dreams and slumbers, brother priest;
You fur your gloves with reason. Here are your reasons:
You know an enemy intends you harm;
You know a sword employ'd is perilous,
And reason flies the object of all harm:
Who marvels then, when Helenus beholds
A Grecian and his sword, if he do set

75. **have ears thus long,** are those of an ass. 77. **pia mater,** used loosely for "brain." 94. **set your wit to,** match wits with. 111. **fusty,** moldy. 126. **brach,** bitch hound. 128. **clotpoles,** blockheads. 134. **fifth hour,** eleven o'clock. 141. **knew,** subjunctive, would know.

SCENE II. 6. **cormorant,** gluttonous. 11. **bowels,** considered as the seat of tenderness and pity. 14. **the wound . . . surety,** i.e., a sense of security is dangerous to peace. 16. **tent,** probe. 19. **Every tithe soul,** every soul exacted by the war as a tithe. **dismes,** tenths (of men sacrificed). 23. **our name,** i.e., the name of Trojan, which Helen has not. 28. **counters,** pieces of coin-shaped metal used in calculation. 29. **past . . . infinite,** his infinitude past all comparison. 37-50. **You . . . deject.** This tirade shows Troilus to be a person in whom the passion of love has brought about a rejection of reason; he deliberately follows the rule of impulse. 38. **You . . . reason,** a hyperbolical way of saying, you demand reason—or rely on reason—for everything. 45. **chidden Mercury.** Mercury as Jove's errand boy was subject to his chiding. 46. **disorb'd,** removed from its sphere. 58-60. **the will . . . merit,** the will which attributes qualities to what it loves is foolish

The very wings of reason to his heels
And fly like chidden Mercury from Jove,
Or like a star disorb'd? Nay, if we talk of reason,
Let 's shut our gates and sleep: manhood and honour
Should have hare-hearts, would they but fat their thoughts
With this cramm'd reason: reason and respect
Make livers pale and lustihood deject.

Hect. Brother, she is not worth what she doth cost
The holding.

Tro. What 's aught, but as 'tis valued?

Hect. But value dwells not in particular will;
It holds his estimate and dignity
As well wherein 'tis precious of itself
As in the prizer: 'tis mad idolatry
To make the service greater than the god;
And the will dotes that is attributive
To what infectiously itself affects,
Without some image of th' affected merit.

Tro. I take to-day a wife, and my election
Is led on in the conduct of my will;
My will enkindled by mine eyes and ears,
Two traded pilots 'twixt the dangerous shores
Of will and judgement: how may I avoid,
Although my will distaste what it elected,
The wife I chose? there can be no evasion
To blench from this and to stand firm by honour:
We turn not back the silks upon the merchant,
When we have soil'd them, nor the remainder viands
We do not throw in unrespective sieve,
Because we now are full. It was thought meet
Paris should do some vengeance on the Greeks:
Your breath of full consent bellied his sails;
The seas and winds, old wranglers, took a truce
And did him service: he touch'd the ports desir'd,
And for an old aunt whom the Greeks held captive,
He brought a Grecian queen, whose youth and freshness
Wrinkles Apollo's, and makes stale the morning.
Why keep we her? the Grecians keep our aunt:
Is she worth keeping? why, she is a pearl,
Whose price hath launch'd above a thousand ships,
And turn'd crown'd kings to merchants.
If you'll avouch 'twas wisdom Paris went—
As you must needs, for you all cried 'Go, go,'—
If you'll confess he brought home worthy prize—
As you must needs, for you all clapp'd your hands,
And cried 'Inestimable!'—why do you now
The issue of your proper wisdoms rate,
And do a deed that never fortune did,
Beggar the estimation which you priz'd
Richer than sea and land? O, theft most base,
That we have stol'n what we do fear to keep!
But, thieves, unworthy of a thing so stol'n,
That in their country did them that disgrace,
We fear to warrant in our native place!

Cas. [*Within*] Cry, Troyans, cry!

Pri. What noise? what shriek is this?

Tro. 'Tis our mad sister, I do know her voice.

Cas. [*Within*] Cry, Troyans!

Hect. It is Cassandra.

Enter CASSANDRA, *raving*.

Cas. Cry, Troyans, cry! lend me ten thousand eyes,
And I will fill them with prophetic tears.

Hect. Peace, sister, peace!

Cas. Virgins and boys, mid-age and wrinkled eld,
Soft infancy, that nothing canst but cry,
Add to my clamours! let us pay betimes
A moiety of that mass of moan to come.
Cry, Troyans, cry! practise your eyes with tears!
Troy must not be, nor goodly Ilion stand;
Our firebrand brother, Paris, burns us all.
Cry, Troyans, cry! a Helen and a woe:
Cry, cry! Troy burns, or else let Helen go. *Exit.*

Hect. Now, youthful Troilus, do not these high strains
Of divination in our sister work
Some touches of remorse? or is your blood
So madly hot that no discourse of reason,
Nor fear of bad success in a bad cause,
Can qualify the same?

Tro. Why, brother Hector,
We may not think the justness of each act
Such and no other than event doth form it,
Nor once deject the courage of our minds,
Because Cassandra 's mad: her brain-sick raptures
Cannot distaste the goodness of a quarrel
Which hath our several honours all engag'd
To make it gracious. For my private part,
I am no more touch'd than all Priam's sons:
And Jove forbid there should be done amongst us
Such things as might offend the weakest spleen
To fight for and maintain!

Par. Else might the world convince of levity
As well my undertakings as your counsels:
But I attest the gods, your full consent
Gave wings to my propension and cut off
All fears attending on so dire a project.
For what, alas, can these my single arms?
What propugnation is in one man's valour,
To stand the push and enmity of those
This quarrel would excite? Yet, I protest,
Were I alone to pass the difficulties
And had as ample power as I have will,
Paris should ne'er retract what he hath done,
Nor faint in the pursuit.

Pri. Paris, you speak
Like one besotted on your sweet delights:
You have the honey still, but these the gall;
So to be valiant is no praise at all.

Par. Sir, I propose not merely to myself
The pleasures such a beauty brings with it;
But I would have the soil of her fair rape
Wip'd off, in honourable keeping her.
What treason were it to the ransack'd queen,
Disgrace to your great worths and shame to me,
Now to deliver her possession up

unless there is present some evidence (*image*) of the merit or qualities attributed. 61. **I take to-day a wife,** etc. Troilus, in stating Paris' case, is also stating his own credo about love. 64. **traded,** practiced, skillful in their trade. 71. **unrespective sieve,** i.e., one that cares not what is thrown into it. 77. **an old aunt,** Hesione, Priam's sister, rescued from the wrath of Poseidon by Hercules and bestowed by him on the Greek, Telamon, father of Ajax. 79. **Wrinkles Apollo's,** makes Apollo look old and ugly by comparison. 82. **Whose . . . ships,** echoes the famous line from Marlowe's *Faustus:* "Was this the face that launched a thousand ships?" 83. **turn'd . . . merchants,** made kings like merchants seeking a rare pearl. 89. **issue,** results. **rate,** condemn. 91. **Beggar,** make valueless. 105. **nothing canst,** can do nothing. 108. **practise . . . tears,** learn to weep (Schmidt). 123. **distaste,** render distasteful. 125. **gracious,** righteous, pious, holy. 128-129. **offend . . . fight,** offend to the extent of making (someone) fight. 133. **propension,** propensity. 136. **propugnation,** defense. 139. **pass,** experience, undergo. 141. **retract,** disavow. 148. **rape,** abduction. 150. **ransack'd,** carried off.

On terms of base compulsion! Can it be
That so degenerate a strain as this
Should once set footing in your generous bosoms?
There 's not the meanest spirit on our party
Without a heart to dare or sword to draw
When Helen is defended, nor none so noble
Whose life were ill bestow'd or death unfam'd
Where Helen is the subject; then, I say,
Well may we fight for her whom, we know well,
The world's large spaces cannot parallel.
Hect. Paris and Troilus, you have both said well,
And on the cause and question now in hand
Have gloz'd, but superficially; not much
Unlike young men, whom Aristotle thought
Unfit to hear moral philosophy:
The reasons you allege do more conduce
To the hot passion of distemp'red blood
Than to make up a free determination
'Twixt right and wrong, for pleasure and revenge
Have ears more deaf than adders to the voice
Of any true decision. Nature craves
All dues be rend'red to their owners: now,
What nearer debt in all humanity
Than wife is to the husband? If this law
Of nature be corrupted through affection,
And that great minds, of partial indulgence
To their benumbed wills, resist the same,
There is a law in each well-order'd nation
To curb those raging appetites that are
Most disobedient and refractory.
If Helen then be wife to Sparta's king,
As it is known she is, these moral laws
Of nature and of nations speak aloud
To have her back return'd: thus to persist
In doing wrong extenuates not wrong,
But makes it much more heavy. Hector's opinion
Is this in way of truth; yet ne'ertheless,
My spritely brethren, I propend to you
In resolution to keep Helen still,
For 'tis a cause that hath no mean dependance
Upon our joint and several dignities.
Tro. Why, there you touch'd the life of our design:
Were it not glory that we more affected
Than the performance of our heaving spleens,
I would not wish a drop of Troyan blood
Spent more in her defence. But, worthy Hector,
She is a theme of honour and renown,
A spur to valiant and magnanimous deeds,
Whose present courage may beat down our foes,
And fame in time to come canonize us;
For, I presume, brave Hector would not lose
So rich advantage of a promis'd glory
As smiles upon the forehead of this action
For the wide world's revenue.
Hect. I am yours,
You valiant offspring of great Priamus.
I have a roisting challenge sent amongst
The dull and factious nobles of the Greeks
Will strike amazement to their drowsy spirits:
I was advertis'd their great general slept,
Whilst emulation in the army crept:
This, I presume, will wake him. *Exeunt.*

[SCENE III. *The Grecian camp. Before Achilles' tent.*]

Enter THERSITES, *solus.*

Ther. How now, Thersites! what, lost in the labyrinth of thy fury! Shall the elephant Ajax carry it thus? he beats me, and I rail at him: O, worthy satisfaction! would it were otherwise; that I could beat him, whilst he railed at me. 'Sfoot, I'll learn to conjure and raise devils, but I'll see some issue of my spiteful execrations. Then there 's Achilles, a rare enginer! If Troy be not taken till these two undermine it, the walls will stand till they fall of themselves. O thou great thunder-darter of Olympus, forget that thou art Jove, the king of gods, and, Mercury, lose all the serpentine craft of thy caduceus, if ye take not that little little less than little wit from them that they have! which short-armed ignorance itself knows is so abundant scarce, it will not in circumvention deliver a fly from a spider, without drawing their massy irons and cutting the web. After this, the vengeance on the whole camp! or rather, the Neapolitan bone-ache! for that, methinks, is the curse dependant on those that war for a placket. I have said my prayers and devil Envy say Amen. What ho! my Lord Achilles!

[*Enter* PATROCLUS.]

Patr. Who 's there? Thersites! Good Thersites, come in and rail.

Ther. If I could 'a remembered a gilt counterfeit, thou wouldst not have slipped out of my contemplation: but it is no matter; thyself upon thyself! The common curse of mankind, folly and ignorance, be thine in great revenue! heaven bless thee from a tutor, and discipline come not near thee! Let thy blood be thy direction till thy death! then if she that lays thee out says thou art a fair corse, I'll be sworn and sworn upon 't she never shrouded any but lazars. Amen. Where 's Achilles?

Patr. What, art thou devout? wast thou in prayer?

Ther. Ay: the heavens hear me!

Enter ACHILLES.

Achil. Who 's there?

Patr. Thersites, my lord.

Achil. Where, where? O where? Art thou come? why, my cheese, my digestion, why hast thou not served thyself in to my table so many meals? Come, what 's Agamemnon?

Ther. Thy commander, Achilles. Then tell me,

165. **gloz'd,** commented on. 167. **moral philosophy.** Aristotle says this of political philosophy in the *Nichomachean Ethics.* Shakespeare's line is paralleled by a sentence in Bacon's *Advancement of Learning,* Book II: "Is not the opinion of Aristotle worthy to be regarded wherein he saith that young men are not fit auditors of moral philosophy?" This similarity of apparent error is advanced in support of the Baconian theory of authorship. Sir Sidney Lee (*Life of Shakespeare,* App. II) points out that both Bacon and Shakespeare relied, in all probability, on a summary paraphrase of Aristotle's *Ethics,* translated from Italian and published in 1547, in which *political* as referring to civil society is made the equivalent of *moral* as understood in the Renaissance period. 172. **adders.** Cf. *2 Henry VI,* III, ii, 76, note. 178-179. **great . . . wills,** great minds indulgent (through partiality) to their wills benumbed (i.e., rendered impotent) by appetite. 178. **of,** out of. 190. **spritely,** full of spirit. **propend,** incline. 202. **canonize,** enroll among famous persons. 206. **revenue,** accent on second syllable. 208. **roisting,** roistering, clamorous. 211. **advertis'd,** informed. **their great general,** Achilles. 212. **emulation,** ambitious or jealous rivalry.

SCENE III. 4. **worthy satisfaction,** adequate revenge (used contemptuously). 6. **'Sfoot,** an oath by God's foot. 7. **but I'll see,** rather than not see. 8. **enginer,** a sapper, one who digs countermines under the enemy's battlements (used contemptuously here). 13-14. **the serpentine . . . caduceus,** alludes to Mercury's wand, having two serpents twined round it; also to the wisdom of serpents. 18. **massy irons,**

Patroclus, what 's Achilles?

Patr. Thy lord, Thersites: then tell me, I pray thee, what 's thyself?

Ther. Thy knower, Patroclus: then tell me, Patroclus, what art thou?

Patr. Thou mayst tell that knowest.

Achil. O, tell, tell.

Ther. I'll decline the whole question. Agamemnon commands Achilles; Achilles is my lord; I am Patroclus' knower, and Patroclus is a fool.

Patr. You rascal!

Ther. Peace, fool! I have not done.

Achil. He is a privileged man. Proceed, Thersites.

Ther. Agamemnon is a fool; Achilles is a fool; Thersites is a fool, and, as aforesaid, Patroclus is a fool.

Achil. Derive this; come.

Ther. Agamemnon is a fool to offer to command Achilles; Achilles is a fool to be commanded of Agamemnon; Thersites is a fool to serve such a fool, and Patroclus is a fool positive.

Patr. Why am I a fool?

Ther. Make that demand of the Creator. It suffices me thou art. Look you, who comes here?

Enter [at a distance] AGAMEMNON, ULYSSES, NESTOR, DIOMEDES, AJAX, *and* CALCHAS.

Achil. Patroclus, I'll speak with nobody. Come in with me, Thersites. [*Exit*.]

Ther. Here is such patchery, such juggling and such knavery! all the argument is a whore and a cuckold; a good quarrel to draw emulous factions and bleed to death upon. Now, the dry serpigo on the subject! and war and lechery confound all! [*Exit*.]

Agam. Where is Achilles?

Patr. Within his tent; but ill dispos'd, my lord.

Agam. Let it be known to him that we are here.
He shent our messengers; and we lay by
Our appertainments, visiting of him:
Let him be told so; lest perchance he think
We dare not move the question of our place,
Or know not what we are.

Patr. I shall say so to him. [*Exit*.]

Ulyss. We saw him at the opening of his tent:
He is not sick.

Ajax. Yes, lion-sick, sick of proud heart: you may call it melancholy, if you will favour the man; but, by my head, 'tis pride: but why, why? let him show us the cause. A word, my lord. [*Takes Agamemnon aside*.]

Nest. What moves Ajax thus to bay at him?

Ulyss. Achilles hath inveigled his fool from him.

Nest. Who, Thersites?

Ulyss. He.

Nest. Then will Ajax lack matter, if he have lost his argument.

Ulyss. No, you see, he is his argument that has his argument, Achilles.

Nest. All the better; their fraction is more our wish than their faction: but it was a strong composure a fool could disunite.

Ulyss. The amity that wisdom knits not, folly may easily untie. Here comes Patroclus.

[*Enter* PATROCLUS.]

Nest. No Achilles with him.

Ulyss. The elephant hath joints, but none for courtesy: his legs are legs for necessity, not for flexure.

Patr. Achilles bids me say, he is much sorry,
If any thing more than your sport and pleasure
Did move your greatness and this noble state
To call upon him; he hopes it is no other
But for your health and your digestion sake,
An after-dinner's breath.

Agam. Hear you, Patroclus:
We are too well acquainted with these answers:
But his evasion, wing'd thus swift with scorn,
Cannot outfly our apprehensions.
Much attribute he hath, and much the reason
Why we ascribe it to him; yet all his virtues,
Not virtuously on his own part beheld,
Do in our eyes begin to lose their gloss,
Yea, like fair fruit in an unwholesome dish,
Are like to rot untasted. Go and tell him,
We come to speak with him; and you shall not sin,
If you do say we think him over-proud
And under-honest, in self-assumption greater
Than in the note of judgement; and worthier than himself
Here tend the savage strangeness he puts on,
Disguise the holy strength of their command,
And underwrite in an observing kind
His humorous predominance; yea, watch
His pettish lunes, his ebbs, his flows, as if
The passage and whole carriage of this action
Rode on his tide. Go tell him this, and add,
That if he overhold his price so much,
We'll none of him; but let him, like an engine
Not portable, lie under this report:
'Bring action hither, this cannot go to war:
A stirring dwarf we do allowance give
Before a sleeping giant.' Tell him so.

Patr. I shall; and bring his answer presently. [*Exit*.]

Agam. In second voice we'll not be satisfied;
We come to speak with him. Ulysses, enter you.
[*Exit Ulysses*.]

Ajax. What is he more than another?

Agam. No more than what he thinks he is.

Ajax. Is he so much? Do you not think he thinks himself a better man than I am?

Agam. No question.

Ajax. Will you subscribe his thought, and say he is?

Agam. No, noble Ajax; you are as strong, as valiant, as wise, no less noble, much more gentle, and altogether more tractable.

Ajax. Why should a man be proud? How doth

swords, in contrast to cobwebs. 20. **bone-ache,** another name for venereal disease. 22. **placket,** slit in a petticoat; an indecent way of referring to a woman. 28. **slipped,** quibble on "slip," counterfeit coin. 32. **bless thee from,** bless by protecting thee from. 36. **lazars,** lepers, from the biblical leper, Lazarus. 44. **cheese,** supposed, proverbially, to aid digestion. 55. **decline,** go through in order from beginning to end, as when inflecting a noun. 61. **privileged man.** Fools were privileged to speak without restraint. 66. **Derive,** give the origin of; the grammatical metaphor is continued here and also in line 70. 70. **positive,** i.e., absolute. 77. **patchery,** knavery. 78. **all the argument,** issue of the war. 79. **emulous,** envious. 81. **serpigo,** skin eruption. 86. **shent,** rebuked. 87. **appertainments,** rights, prerogatives. 89. **move . . . place,** raise the question of our authority. 93. **lion-sick,** sick with pride. 107. **fraction,** discord. **faction,** union. 109. **composure,** union (contemptuously). 113. **elephant hath joints.** A vulgar error mentioned often in the sixteenth century regarding natural history was to the effect that elephants had no joints. 118. **this noble state,** i.e., the distinguished men accompanying Agamemnon. 124. **apprehensions,** understanding. 125. **attribute,** credit, reputation. 134. **Than . . . judgement,** than true judges know him to be (Schmidt). 135. **tend,** wait upon. 137. **underwrite,** submit to (as observers). 138. **humorous predominance,** whim caused by unbalanced humors. 139. **lunes,** lunacies, freaks.

pride grow? I know not what pride is.

Agam. Your mind is the clearer, Ajax, and your virtues the fairer. He that is proud eats up himself: pride is his own glass, his own trumpet, his own chronicle; and whatever praises itself but in the deed, devours the deed in the praise.

Ajax. I do hate a proud man, as I hate the engendering of toads.

Nest. And yet he loves himself: is 't not strange? [*Aside.*]

Enter ULYSSES.

Ulyss. Achilles will not to the field to-morrow.
Agam. What 's his excuse?
Ulyss. He doth rely on none,
But carries on the stream of his dispose
Without observance or respect of any,
In will peculiar and in self-admission.
Agam. Why will he not upon our fair request
Untent his person and share the air with us?
Ulyss. Things small as nothing, for request's sake only,
He makes important: possess'd he is with greatness,
And speaks not to himself but with a pride
That quarrels at self-breath: imagin'd worth
Holds in his blood such swoln and hot discourse
That 'twixt his mental and his active parts
Kingdom'd Achilles in commotion rages
And batters down himself: what should I say?
He is so plaguy proud that the death-tokens of it
Cry 'No recovery.'
Agam. Let Ajax go to him.
Dear lord, go you and greet him in his tent:
'Tis said he holds you well, and will be led
At your request a little from himself.
Ulyss. O Agamemnon, let it not be so!
We'll consecrate the steps that Ajax makes
When they go from Achilles: shall the proud lord
That bastes his arrogance with his own seam
And never suffers matter of the world
Enter his thoughts, save such as do revolve
And ruminate himself, shall he be worshipp'd
Of that we hold an idol more than he?
No, this thrice worthy and right valiant lord
Shall not so stale his palm, nobly acquir'd;
Nor, by my will, assubjugate his merit,
As amply titled as Achilles is,
By going to Achilles:
That were to enlard his fat-already pride
And add more coals to Cancer when he burns
With entertaining great Hyperion.
This lord go to him! Jupiter forbid,
And say in thunder 'Achilles go to him.'
Nest. [*Aside to Dio.*] O, this is well; he rubs the vein of him.
Dio. [*Aside to Nest.*] And how his silence drinks up this applause!
Ajax. If I go to him, with my armed fist
I'll pash him o'er the face.
Agam. O, no, you shall not go.
Ajax. An 'a be proud with me, I'll pheeze his pride;
Let me go to him.
Ulyss. Not for the worth that hangs upon our quarrel.
Ajax. A paltry, insolent fellow!
Nest. [*Aside*] How he describes himself!
Ajax. Can he not be sociable?
Ulyss. [*Aside*] The raven chides blackness.
Ajax. I'll let his humours blood.

Agam. [*Aside*] He will be the physician that should be the patient.

Ajax. An all men were o' my mind,—
Ulyss. [*Aside*] Wit would be out of fashion.

Ajax. 'A should not bear it so, 'a should eat swords first: shall pride carry it?

Nest. [*Aside*] An 'twould, you 'ld carry half.
Ulyss. [*Aside*] 'A would have ten shares.
Ajax. I will knead him; I'll make him supple.

Nest. [*Aside*] He 's not yet through warm: force him with praises: pour in, pour in; his ambition is dry.

Ulyss. [*To Agam.*] My lord, you feed too much on this dislike.

Nest. Our noble general, do not do so.
Dio. You must prepare to fight without Achilles.
Ulyss. Why, 'tis this naming of him does him harm.
Here is a man—but 'tis before his face;
I will be silent.
Nest. Wherefore should you so?
He is not emulous, as Achilles is.
Ulyss. Know the whole world, he is as valiant.
Ajax. A whoreson dog, that shall palter thus with us!
Would he were a Troyan!
Nest. What a vice were it in Ajax now,—
Ulyss. If he were proud,—
Dio. Or covetous of praise,—
Ulyss. Ay, or surly borne,—
Dio. Or strange, or self-affected!
Ulyss. Thank the heavens, lord, thou art of sweet composure;
Praise him that got thee, she that gave thee suck:
Fam'd be thy tutor, and thy parts of nature
Thrice fam'd, beyond all erudition:
But he that disciplin'd thine arms to fight,
Let Mars divide eternity in twain,
And give him half: and, for thy vigour,
Bull-bearing Milo his addition yield
To sinewy Ajax. I will not praise thy wisdom,
Which, like a bourn, a pale, a shore, confines
Thy spacious and dilated parts: here 's Nestor;
Instructed by the antiquary times,
He must, he is, he cannot but be wise:
But pardon, father Nestor, were your days
As green as Ajax' and your brain so temper'd,
You should not have the eminence of him,
But be as Ajax.
Ajax. Shall I call you father?
Nest. Ay, my good son.
Dio. Be rul'd by him, Lord Ajax.
Ulyss. There is no tarrying here; the hart Achilles
Keeps thicket. Please it our great general

174. **dispose,** bent of mind. 176. **will peculiar,** i.e., his own independent will. **self-admission,** self-approbation. 184. **mental . . . parts,** his mind and body. 187. **it.** The antecedent is "pride," implied in the phrase *plaguy proud.* 195. **bastes,** moistens (as roasting meat with melted fat). **seam,** fat, grease. 201. **stale . . . acquir'd,** sully his nobly won honor. 202. **assubjugate,** reduce to subjection. 206-207. **add . . . Hyperion.** Cancer is the sign of the zodiac into which the sun enters at the beginning of summer. The lines mean "add a fire to the heat of summer." 207. **Hyperion,** the sun god. 210. **vein,** humor, disposition. 213. **pash,** smash. 215. **pheeze,** settle the matter of. 222. **let . . . blood,** bleed him (as a physician) to cure his excessive humors. 232. **through,** thoroughly. 244. **palter,** dodge. 250. **strange,** distant. 253-254. **thy . . . erudition,** i.e., your natural gifts thrice exceed what erudition can achieve. 258. **Milo,** celebrated athlete of phenomenal strength. 273. **main,** full force.

ACT III. SCENE I. 15. **in . . . grace,** i.e., in the way of salvation

To call together all his state of war;
Fresh kings are come to Troy: to-morrow
We must with all our main of power stand fast:
And here 's a lord,—come knights from east to west,
And cull their flower, Ajax shall cope the best.

Agam. Go we to council. Let Achilles sleep:
Light boats sail swift, though greater hulks draw
deep. *Exeunt.*

[ACT III.

SCENE I. *Troy. Priam's palace.*]

[*Music within*]. *Enter* [*a* Servant *and*] PANDARUS.

Pan. Friend, you! pray you, a word: do not you follow the young Lord Paris?

Serv. Ay, sir, when he goes before me.

Pan. You depend upon him, I mean?

Serv. Sir, I do depend upon the lord.

Pan. You depend upon a noble gentleman; I must needs praise him.

Serv. The lord be praised!

Pan. You know me, do you not?

Serv. Faith, sir, superficially.

Pan. Friend, know me better; I am the Lord Pandarus.

Serv. I hope I shall know your honour better.

Pan. I do desire it.

Serv. You are in the state of grace.

Pan. Grace! not so, friend; honour and lordship are my titles. What music is this?

Serv. I do but partly know, sir: it is music in parts.

Pan. Know you the musicians?

Serv. Wholly, sir.

Pan. Who play they to?

Serv. To the hearers, sir.

Pan. At whose pleasure, friend?

Serv. At mine, sir, and theirs that love music.

Pan. Command, I mean, friend.

Serv. Who shall I command, sir?

Pan. Friend, we understand not one another: I am too courtly and thou too cunning. At whose request do these men play?

Serv. That 's to 't indeed, sir: marry, sir, at the request of Paris my lord, who is there in person; with him, the mortal Venus, the heart-blood of beauty, love's invisible soul,—

Pan. Who, my cousin Cressida?

Serv. No, sir, Helen: could not you find out that by her attributes?

Pan. It should seem, fellow, thou hast not seen the Lady Cressid. I come to speak with Paris from the Prince Troilus: I will make a complimental assault upon him, for my business seethes.

Serv. Sodden business! there 's a stewed phrase indeed!

Enter PARIS *and* HELEN [*attended*].

Pan. Fair be to you, my lord, and to all this fair company! fair desires, in all fair measure, fairly guide them! especially to you, fair queen! fair thoughts be your fair pillow!

Helen. Dear lord, you are full of fair words.

Pan. You speak your fair pleasure, sweet queen. Fair prince, here is good broken music.

Par. You have broke it, cousin: and, by my life, you shall make it whole again; you shall piece it out with a piece of your performance. Nell, he is full of harmony.

Pan. Truly, lady, no.

Helen. O, sir,—

Pan. Rude, in sooth; in good sooth, very rude.

Par. Well said, my lord! well, you say so in fits.

Pan. I have business to my lord, dear queen. My lord, will you vouchsafe me a word?

Helen. Nay, this shall not hedge us out: we'll hear you sing, certainly.

Pan. Well, sweet queen, you are pleasant with me. But, marry, thus, my lord: my dear lord and most esteemed friend, your brother Troilus,—

Helen. My Lord Pandarus; honey-sweet lord,—

Pan. Go to, sweet queen, go to:—commends himself most affectionately to you,—

Helen. You shall not bob us out of our melody: if you do, our melancholy upon your head!

Pan. Sweet queen, sweet queen! that 's a sweet queen, i' faith.

Helen. And to make a sweet lady sad is a sour offence.

Pan. Nay, that shall not serve your turn; that shall it not, in truth, la. Nay, I care not for such words; no, no. And, my lord, he desires you, that if the king call for him at supper, you will make his excuse.

Helen. My Lord Pandarus,—

Pan. What says my sweet queen, my very very sweet queen?

Par. What exploit 's in hand? where sups he to-night?

Helen. Nay, but, my lord,—

Pan. What says my sweet queen? My cousin will fall out with you.

Helen. You must not know where he sups.

Par. I'll lay my life, with my disposer Cressida.

Pan. No, no, no such matter; you are wide: come, your disposer is sick.

Par. Well, I'll make's excuse.

Pan. Ay, good my lord. Why should you say Cressida? no, your poor disposer 's sick.

Par. I spy.

Pan. You spy! what do you spy? Come, give me an instrument. Now, sweet queen.

Helen. Why, this is kindly done.

Pan. My niece is horribly in love with a thing you have, sweet queen.

Helen. She shall have it, my lord, if it be not my lord Paris.

Pan. He! no, she'll none of him; they two are twain.

Helen. Falling in, after falling out, may make them three.

because he desires to be better. Pandarus answers to the idea of grace as a courtly title applicable to a duke. 35. **love's invisible soul,** the very essence or spirit of love, personified in Helen. 42. **complimental,** courteous. 43. **seethes,** boils, requires haste. 44. **stewed,** quibbling reference to stews, brothels. 52. **broken music,** music arranged for parts, with quibble. 59. **Rude,** discordant. Pandarus deprecates his musical talents. 62. **in fits,** perhaps a quibble on *fit* as "division of a song." 66. **hedge,** shut. 75. **bob,** cheat. 95. **disposer,** i.e., one who may dispose of me or order me as she wishes. (Paris is being very courtly.) 97. **wide,** wide of the mark. 111. **twain,** not in accord, having nothing in common. 112-113. **Falling . . . three.** Helen bawdily jokes that Cressida's game will result in the birth of a child, a third person.

Pan. Come, come, I'll hear no more of this; I'll sing you a song now.

Helen. Ay, ay, prithee now. By my troth, sweet lord, thou hast a fine forehead.

Pan. Ay, you may, you may.

Helen. Let thy song be love: this love will undo us all. O Cupid, Cupid, Cupid!

Pan. Love! ay, that it shall, i' faith.

Par. Ay, good now, love, love, nothing but love.

Pan. In good troth, it begins so. [*Sings.*]

Love, love, nothing but love, still love, still more!
For, O, love's bow
Shoots buck and doe:
The shaft confounds,
Not that it wounds,
But tickles still the sore.
These lovers cry Oh! oh! they die!
Yet that which seems the wound to kill,
Doth turn oh! oh! to ha! ha! he!
So dying love lives still:
Oh! oh! a while, but ha! ha! ha!
Oh! oh! groans out for ha! ha! ha!
Heigh-ho!

Helen. In love, i' faith, to the very tip of the nose.

Par. He eats nothing but doves, love, and that breeds hot blood, and hot blood begets hot thoughts, and hot thoughts beget hot deeds, and hot deeds is love.

Pan. Is this the generation of love? hot blood, hot thoughts, and hot deeds? Why, they are vipers: is love a generation of vipers? Sweet lord, who 's a-field to-day?

Par. Hector, Deiphobus, Helenus, Antenor, and all the gallantry of Troy: I would fain have armed to-day, but my Nell would not have it so. How chance my brother Troilus went not?

Helen. He hangs the lip at something: you know all, Lord Pandarus.

Pan. Not I, honey-sweet queen. I long to hear how they sped to-day. You'll remember your brother's excuse?

Par. To a hair.

Pan. Farewell, sweet queen.

Helen. Commend me to your niece.

Pan. I will, sweet queen. [*Exit.*]

Sound a retreat.

Par. They 're come from field: let us to Priam's hall,
To greet the warriors. Sweet Helen, I must woo you
To help unarm our Hector: his stubborn buckles,
With these your white enchanting fingers touch'd,
Shall more obey than to the edge of steel
Or force of Greekish sinews; you shall do more
Than all the island kings,—disarm great Hector.

Helen. 'Twill make us proud to be his servant, Paris;
Yea, what he shall receive of us in duty
Gives us more palm in beauty than we have,
Yea, overshines ourself.

Par. Sweet, above thought I love thee. *Exeunt.*

[SCENE II. *The same. Pandarus' orchard.*]

Enter PANDARUS [*and*] TROILUS' Man [*meeting*].

Pan. How now! where 's thy master? at my cousin Cressida's?

Man. No, sir; he stays for you to conduct him thither.

Pan. O, here he comes.

[*Enter* TROILUS.]

How now, how now!

Tro. Sirrah, walk off. [*Exit Man.*]

Pan. Have you seen my cousin?

Tro. No, Pandarus: I stalk about her door,
Like a strange soul upon the Stygian banks
Staying for waftage. O, be thou my Charon,
And give me swift transportance to those fields
Where I may wallow in the lily-beds
Propos'd for the deserver! O gentle Pandar,
From Cupid's shoulder pluck his painted wings,
And fly with me to Cressid!

Pan. Walk here i' th' orchard, I'll bring her straight. [*Exit.*]

Tro. I am giddy; expectation whirls me round.
Th' imaginary relish is so sweet
That it enchants my sense: what will it be,
When that the wat'ry palates taste indeed
Love's thrice repured nectar? death, I fear me,
Sounding destruction, or some joy too fine,
Too subtle-potent, tun'd too sharp in sweetness,
For the capacity of my ruder powers:
I fear it much; and I do fear besides,
That I shall lose distinction in my joys;
As doth a battle, when they charge on heaps
The enemy flying.

[*Enter* PANDARUS.]

Pan. She 's making her ready, she'll come straight: you must be witty now. She does so blush, and fetches her wind so short, as if she were frayed with a sprite: I'll fetch her. It is the prettiest villain: she fetches her breath as short as a new-ta'en sparrow. [*Exit.*]

Tro. Even such a passion doth embrace my bosom:
My heart beats thicker than a feverous pulse;
And all my powers do their bestowing lose,
Like vassalage at unawares encount'ring
The eye of majesty.

Enter PANDARUS *and* CRESSIDA.

Pan. Come, come, what need you blush? shame 's a baby. Here she is now: swear the oaths now to her that you have sworn to me. What, are you gone again? you must be watched ere you be made tame, must you? Come your ways, come your ways; an you draw backward, we'll put you i' the fills. Why do you not speak to her? Come, draw this curtain, and let 's see your picture. Alas the day, how loath you are to offend daylight! an 'twere dark, you' ld close sooner. So, so; rub on, and kiss the mistress. How now! a kiss in fee-farm! build there, carpenter; the air is sweet. Nay, you shall fight your hearts out ere I part you. The falcon as the tercel, for all the ducks i' the river: go to, go to.

Tro. You have bereft me of all words, lady.

143. **a . . . vipers.** See Matthew 3:7. 167. **island kings,** kings of Grecian islands. 170. **more palm,** i.e., more honor.

SCENE II. 10-11. **a strange . . . Charon,** refers to the Greek mythological conception of the fate of departed souls who had to wait on the banks of the Styx or the Acheron until the boatman Charon ferried them across to the infernal regions. 14. **Propos'd,** promised. 22. **wat'ry,** watering. 24. **Sounding,** swooning. 28. **lose . . . joys,** be unable to distinguish one delight from another. 32. **witty,** alert. 34. **frayed,** frightened. **sprite,** ghost. 38. **thicker,** faster. 39. **bestowing,** proper use. 48. **fills,** shafts of a cart. 49-50. **Come, draw . . . picture,** remove your veil and let us see your face. 52. **kiss the mistress,** touch the central target; term from bowls; *mistress* is analogous to "master," short for "master bowl," a small bowl placed as a mark for players to aim at. 53. **fee-farm,** grant of lands in fee, that is, forever; i.e., a kiss

Pan. Words pay no debts, give her deeds: but she'll bereave you o' the deeds too, if she call your activity in question. What, billing again? Here 's 'In witness whereof the parties interchangeably'—Come in, come in: I'll go get a fire. [*Exit.*]

Cres. Will you walk in, my lord?

Tro. O Cressid, how often have I wished me thus!

Cres. Wished, my lord! The gods grant,—O my lord!

Tro. What should they grant? what makes this pretty abruption? What too curious dreg espies my sweet lady in the fountain of our love?

Cres. More dregs than water, if my fears have eyes.

Tro. Fears make devils of cherubins; they never see truly.

Cres. Blind fear, that seeing reason leads, finds safer footing than blind reason stumbling without fear: to fear the worst oft cures the worse.

Tro. O, let my lady apprehend no fear: in all Cupid's pageant there is presented no monster.

Cres. Nor nothing monstrous neither?

Tro. Nothing, but our undertakings; when we vow to weep seas, live in fire, eat rocks, tame tigers; thinking it harder for our mistress to devise imposition enough than for us to undergo any difficulty imposed. This is the monstruosity in love, lady, that the will is infinite and the execution confined, that the desire is boundless and the act a slave to limit.

Cres. They say all lovers swear more performance than they are able and yet reserve an ability that they never perform, vowing more than the perfection of ten and discharging less than the tenth part of one. They that have the voice of lions and the act of hares, are they not monsters?

Tro. Are there such? such are not we: praise us as we are tasted, allow us as we prove; our head shall go bare till merit crown it: no perfection in reversion shall have a praise in present: we will not name desert before his birth, and, being born, his addition shall be humble. Few words to fair faith: Troilus shall be such to Cressid as what envy can say worst shall be a mock for his truth, and what truth can speak truest not truer than Troilus.

Cres. Will you walk in, my lord?

[*Enter* PANDARUS.]

Pan. What, blushing still? have you not done talking yet?

Cres. Well, uncle, what folly I commit, I dedicate to you.

Pan. I thank you for that: if my lord get a boy of you, you'll give him me. Be true to my lord: if he flinch, chide me for it.

Tro. You know now your hostages; your uncle's word and my firm faith.

Pan. Nay, I'll give my word for her too: our kindred, though they be long ere they be wooed, they are constant being won: they are burs, I can tell you; they'll stick where they are thrown.

Cres. Boldness comes to me now, and brings me heart.
Prince Troilus, I have lov'd you night and day
For many weary months.

Tro. Why was my Cressid then so hard to win?

Cres. Hard to seem won: but I was won, my lord,
With the first glance that ever—pardon me—
If I confess much, you will play the tyrant.
I love you now; but not, till now, so much
But I might master it: in faith, I lie;
My thoughts were like unbridled children, grown
Too headstrong for their mother. See, we fools!
Why have I blabb'd? who shall be true to us,
When we are so unsecret to ourselves?
But, though I lov'd you well, I woo'd you not:
And yet, good faith, I wish'd myself a man,
Or that we women had men's privilege
Of speaking first. Sweet, bid me hold my tongue,
For in this rapture I shall surely speak
The thing I shall repent. See, see, your silence,
Cunning in dumbness, from my weakness draws
My very soul of counsel! stop my mouth.

Tro. And shall, albeit sweet music issues thence.

Pan. Pretty, i' faith.

Cres. My lord, I do beseech you, pardon me;
'Twas not my purpose, thus to beg a kiss:
I am asham'd. O heavens! what have I done?
For this time will I take my leave, my lord.

Tro. Your leave, sweet Cressid!

Pan. Leave! an you take leave till to-morrow morning,—

Cres. Pray you, content you.

Tro. What offends you, lady?

Cres. Sir, mine own company.

Tro. You cannot shun
Yourself.

Cres. Let me go and try:
I have a kind of self resides with you;
But an unkind self, that itself will leave,
To be another's fool. I would be gone:
Where is my wit? I know not what I speak.

Tro. Well know they what they speak that speak so wisely.

Cres. Perchance, my lord, I show more craft than love;
And fell so roundly to a large confession,
To angle for your thoughts: but you are wise,
Or else you love not, for to be wise and love
Exceeds man's might; that dwells with gods above.

Tro. O that I thought it could be in a woman—
As, if it can, I will presume in you—
To feed for aye her lamp and flames of love;
To keep her constancy in plight and youth,
Outliving beauty's outward, with a mind
That doth renew swifter than blood decays!
Or that persuasion could but thus convince me,
That my integrity and truth to you
Might be affronted with the match and weight
Of such a winnowed purity in love;
How were I then uplifted! but, alas!
I am as true as truth's simplicity
And simpler than the infancy of truth.

Cres. In that I'll war with you.

of endless duration. 55-56. **The falcon . . . tercel,** the female hawk against the male, as in a wager; i.e., Cressida is a match for Troilus. 60. **In . . . interchangeably,** a legal formula, ending, "have set their hand and seals." 70. **abruption,** breaking off. **curious,** causing anxiety. 80-81. **no fear . . . no monster,** may refer to figures in masques or similar entertainments. 98. **tasted,** tried, proved. **allow,** acknowledge. 99-100. **no . . . reversion,** no promise of perfection to come. 104-105. **what envy . . . his truth,** the worst envy can do is to mock Troilus' loyalty. 106. **than,** Globe, by error: *that.* 141. **counsel,** my inmost thoughts. 157. **fool,** dupe; possibly with a quibble on "fool" used as a term of endearment. 168. **To . . . youth,** to keep her pledged constancy fresh. 170. **blood decays,** passions wane. 173. **affronted,** confronted, equaled.

Tro. O virtuous fight,
When right with right wars who shall be most right!
True swains in love shall in the world to come
Approve their truths by Troilus: when their rhymes,
Full of protest, of oath and big compare,
Want similes, truth tir'd with iteration,
As true as steel, as plantage to the moon,
As sun to day, as turtle to her mate,
As iron to adamant, as earth to th' centre,
Yet, after all comparisons of truth,
As truth's authentic author to be cited,
'As true as Troilus' shall crown up the verse,
And sanctify the numbers.

Cres. Prophet may you be!
If I be false, or swerve a hair from truth,
When time is old and hath forgot itself,
When waterdrops have worn the stones of Troy,
And blind oblivion swallow'd cities up,
And mighty states characterless are grated
To dusty nothing, yet let memory,
From false to false, among false maids in love,
Upbraid my falsehood! when th' have said 'as false
As air, as water, wind, or sandy earth,
As fox to lamb, as wolf to heifer's calf,
Pard to the hind, or stepdame to her son,'
'Yea,' let them say, to stick the heart of falsehood,
'As false as Cressid.'

Pan. Go to, a bargain made: seal it, seal it; I'll be the witness. Here I hold your hand, here my cousin's. If ever you prove false one to another, since I have taken such pains to bring you together, let all pitiful goers-between be called to the world's end after my name; call them all Pandars; let all constant men be Troiluses, all false women Cressids, and all brokers-between Pandars! say, amen.

Tro. Amen.

Cres. Amen.

Pan. Amen. Whereupon I will show you a chamber with a bed; which bed, because it shall not speak of your pretty encounters, press it to death: away!

Exeunt [*Troilus and Cressida*].

And Cupid grant all tongue-tied maidens here
Bed, chamber, Pandar to provide this gear! *Exit.*

[SCENE III. *The Grecian camp. Before Achilles' tent.*]

Enter ULYSSES, DIOMEDES, NESTOR, AGAMEMNON, [AJAX, MENELAUS, *and*] CALCHAS. [*Flourish.*]

Cal. Now, princes, for the service I have done,
Th' advantage of the time prompts me aloud
To call for recompense. Appear it to your mind
†That, through the sight I bear in things to come,
I have abandon'd Troy, left my possession,
Incurr'd a traitor's name; expos'd myself,
From certain and possess'd conveniences,
To doubtful fortunes; sequest'ring from me all
That time, acquaintance, custom and condition
Made tame and most familiar to my nature,
And here, to do you service, am become
As new into the world, strange, unacquainted:
I do beseech you, as in way of taste,
To give me now a little benefit,
Out of those many regist'red in promise,
Which, you say, live to come in my behalf.

Agam. What wouldst thou of us, Troyan? make demand.

Cal. You have a Troyan prisoner, call'd Antenor,
Yesterday took: Troy holds him very dear.
Oft have you—often have you thanks therefore—
Desir'd my Cressid in right great exchange,
Whom Troy hath still denied: but this Antenor,
I know, is such a wrest in their affairs
That their negotiations all must slack,
Wanting his manage; and they will almost
Give us a prince of blood, a son of Priam,
In change of him: let him be sent, great princes,
And he shall buy my daughter; and her presence
Shall quite strike off all service I have done,
In most accepted pain.

Agam. Let Diomedes bear him,
And bring us Cressid hither: Calchas shall have
What he requests of us. Good Diomed,
Furnish you fairly for this interchange:
Withal bring word if Hector will to-morrow
Be answered in his challenge: Ajax is ready.

Dio. This shall I undertake; and 'tis a burden
Which I am proud to bear.

Exit [*with Calchas.*]

ACHILLES *and* PATROCLUS *stand in their tent.*

Ulyss. Achilles stands i' th' entrance of his tent:
Please it our general to pass strangely by him,
As if he were forgot; and, princes all,
Lay negligent and loose regard upon him:
I will come last. 'Tis like he'll question me
Why such unplausive eyes are bent on him:
If so, I have derision medicinable,
To use between your strangeness and his pride,
Which his own will shall have desire to drink:
It may do good: pride hath no other glass
To show itself but pride, for supple knees
Feed arrogance and are the proud man's fees.

Agam. We'll execute your purpose, and put on
A form of strangeness as we pass along:
So do each lord, and either greet him not,
Or else disdainfully, which shall shake him more
Than if not look'd on. I will lead the way.

Achil. What, comes the general to speak with me?
You know my mind, I'll fight no more 'gainst Troy.

Agam. What says Achilles? would he aught with us?

Nest. Would you, my lord, aught with the general?

Achil. No.

Nest. Nothing, my lord.

Agam. The better.

182. **protest,** protestation. **big compare,** extravagant comparisons. 184. **plantage . . . moon,** vegetation waxing in growth with the moon. 185. **turtle,** turtledove. 186. **adamant,** loadstone (magnetic). **as earth . . . centre,** as faithfully as the earth remains in the center (its proper position in the Ptolemaic universe). 195. **characterless are grated,** i.e., all record of their greatness obliterated. 197. **From . . . love,** from one false one to another false one among maids in love who are false (Deighton). 201. **Pard,** leopard. **hind,** doe.

SCENE III. 2-3. **aloud To call,** to give vocal utterance. 4. **in things to come,** so F_4; QF_{1-3}: *in things to love*; Tannenbaum (*Shakespeare Association Bulletin*, VII, 76-77) justifies the F_4 text here on paleographical grounds: "From other errors in the Shakspere canon we know that his Roman *c* (a letter which many Elizabethans preferred to the secretary *c*) was sometimes mistaken for an *l*; also, that Shakspere's *m*, *n*, and *v* (*u*) were often indistinguishable." 8. **sequest'ring,** separating, removing. 10. **Made . . . nature,** accustomed my nature to. 16. **live to come,** i.e., are actually forthcoming. 21. **right great exchange,** i.e., exchange for distinguished captives. 23. **wrest,** tuning key. 30. **In most accepted pain,** in pains (troubles, hardships) which I have endured most willingly. 33. **Furnish you fairly,** provide yourself well. 39. **strangely,** i.e., as one who pretends to be a stranger. 43. **unplausive,** disapproving. 44. **derision,** pretended seriousness (Deighton). 48. **To show itself,** in which to see its image. 48-49. **for supple . . . fees,** arrogance feeds on obsequious bending of knees, and

Achil. Good day, good day.
Men. How do you? how do you?
Achil. What, does the cuckold scorn me?
Ajax. How now, Patroclus!
Achil. Good morrow, Ajax.
Ajax. Ha?
Achil. Good morrow.
Ajax. Ay, and good next day too. *Exeunt.*
Achil. What mean these fellows? Know they not Achilles?
Patr. They pass by strangely: they were us'd to bend,
To send their smiles before them to Achilles;
To come as humbly as they us'd to creep
To holy altars.
Achil. What, am I poor of late?
'Tis certain, greatness, once fall'n out with fortune,
Must fall out with men too: what the declin'd is
He shall as soon read in the eyes of others
As feel in his own fall; for men, like butterflies,
Show not their mealy wings but to the summer,
And not a man, for being simply man,
Hath any honour, but honour for those honours
That are without him, as place, riches, and favour,
Prizes of accident as oft as merit:
Which when they fall, as being slippery standers,
The love that lean'd on them as slippery too,
Doth one pluck down another and together
Die in the fall. But 'tis not so with me:
Fortune and I are friends: I do enjoy
At ample point all that I did possess,
Save these men's looks; who do, methinks, find out
Something not worth in me such rich beholding
As they have often given. Here is Ulysses:
I'll interrupt his reading.
How now, Ulysses!
Ulyss. Now, great Thetis' son!
Achil. What are you reading?
Ulyss. A strange fellow here
Writes me: 'That man, how dearly ever parted,
How much in having, or without or in,
Cannot make boast to have that which he hath,
Nor feels not what he owes, but by reflection;
As when his virtues aiming upon others
Heat them and they retort that heat again
To the first giver.'
Achil. This is not strange, Ulysses.
The beauty that is borne here in the face
The bearer knows not, but commends itself
To others' eyes; nor doth the eye itself,
That most pure spirit of sense, behold itself,
Not going from itself; but eye to eye oppos'd
Salutes each other with each other's form;
For speculation turns not to itself,
Till it hath travell'd and is mirror'd there
Where it may see itself. This is not strange at all.
Ulyss. I do not strain at the position,—
It is familiar,—but at the author's drift;
Who, in his circumstance, expressly proves
That no man is the lord of any thing,
Though in and of him there be much consisting,
Till he communicate his parts to others;
Nor doth he of himself know them for aught
Till he behold them formed in th' applause
Where th' are extended; who, like an arch, reverb'rate
The voice again, or, like a gate of steel
Fronting the sun, receives and renders back
His figure and his heat. I was much rapt in this;
And apprehended here immediately
Th' unknown Ajax.
Heavens, what a man is there! a very horse,
That has he knows not what. Nature, what things there are
Most abject in regard and dear in use!
What things again most dear in the esteem
And poor in worth! Now shall we see to-morrow—
An act that very chance doth throw upon him—
Ajax renown'd. O heavens, what some men do,
While some men leave to do!
How some men creep in skittish fortune's hall,
Whiles others play the idiots in her eyes!
How one man eats into another's pride,
While pride is fasting in his wantonness!
To see these Grecian lords!—why, even already
They clap the lubber Ajax on the shoulder,
As if his foot were on brave Hector's breast
And great Troy shrieking.
Achil. I do believe it; for they pass'd by me
As misers do by beggars, neither gave to me
Good word nor look: what, are my deeds forgot?
Ulyss. Time hath, my lord, a wallet at his back,
Wherein he puts alms for oblivion,
A great-siz'd monster of ingratitudes:
Those scraps are good deeds past; which are devour'd
As fast as they are made, forgot as soon
As done: perseverance, dear my lord,
Keeps honour bright: to have done is to hang
Quite out of fashion, like a rusty mail
In monumental mock'ry. Take the instant way;
For honour travels in a strait so narrow,
Where one but goes abreast: keep then the path;
For emulation hath a thousand sons
That one by one pursue: if you give way,
Or hedge aside from the direct forthright,
Like to an ent'red tide, they all rush by
And leave you hindmost;
Or, like a gallant horse fall'n in first rank,
Lie there for pavement to the abject rear,
O'er-run and trampled on: then what they do in present,
Though less than yours in past, must o'ertop yours;
For Time is like a fashionable host
That slightly shakes his parting guest by th' hand,

such knee-bending is the fee exacted by pride. 79. **mealy,** powdery. 82. **without,** external to. 84. **slippery,** inconstant. 89. **At ample point,** to the full. 91. **Something . . . beholding,** something in me not worthy of such high respect. 95. **strange fellow.** Churton Collins noted that Plato is the strange fellow. The sentiments to which Ulysses gives utterance are from the *Dialogues*. 101. **retort,** reflect. 106. **most . . . sense,** the most exquisite sense; cf. I, i, 58. 109. **speculation,** power of sight. 112. **strain at,** find difficulty in. 112, 113. **position, drift,** the generalization and the application of it. 116. **Though . . . consisting,** although in him there are qualities from which much may be expected. 120. **extended,** noised abroad, bestowed. **who.** The antecedent is *applause*. 123. **His,** the sun's. 125. **unknown Ajax,** the Ajax whose true worth is not yet generally known. 128. **abject . . . use,** lowly esteemed and yet valuable, of practical value. 132, 133. **do,** implies activity; i.e., some men are energetic, some are inactivity itself. 134. **in,** into. 136-137. **How . . . wantonness.** Achilles is he who fasts; who capriciously [in his wantonness] abstains from those active exertions which would furnish new food for his pride (Malone). 153. **instant way,** the way which lies immediately before you now. 154. **strait,** narrow pass. 157. **one by one pursue,** follow one another in single file. 158. **forthright,** straight path. 162. **abject rear,** those inferior specimens in the rear. 166. **slightly,** carelessly.

And with his arms outstretch'd, as he would fly,
Grasps in the comer: the welcome ever smiles,
And farewell goes out sighing. Let not virtue seek
Remuneration for the thing it was;
For beauty, wit,
High birth, vigour of bone, desert in service,
Love, friendship, charity, are subjects all
To envious and calumniating Time.
One touch of nature makes the whole world kin,
That all with one consent praise new-born gawds,
Though they are made and moulded of things past,
And give to dust that is a little gilt
More laud than gilt o'er-dusted.
The present eye praises the present object:
Then marvel not, thou great and complete man,
That all the Greeks begin to worship Ajax;
Since things in motion sooner catch the eye
Than what not stirs. The cry went once on thee,
And still it might, and yet it may again,
If thou wouldst not entomb thyself alive
And case thy reputation in thy tent;
Whose glorious deeds, but in these fields of late,
Made emulous missions 'mongst the gods themselves
And drave great Mars to faction.
Achil. Of this my privacy
I have strong reasons.
Ulyss. But 'gainst your privacy
The reasons are more potent and heroical:
'Tis known, Achilles, that you are in love
With one of Priam's daughters.
Achil. Ha! known!
Ulyss. Is that a wonder?
The providence that 's in a watchful state
Knows almost every grain of Pluto's gold,
Finds bottom in th' uncomprehensive deeps,
Keeps place with thought and almost, like the gods,
Does thoughts unveil in their dumb cradles.
There is a mystery—with whom relation
Durst never meddle—in the soul of state;
Which hath an operation more divine
Than breath or pen can give expressure to:
All the commerce that you have had with Troy
As perfectly is ours as yours, my lord;
And better would it fit Achilles much
To throw down Hector than Polyxena:
But it must grieve young Pyrrhus now at home,
When fame shall in our islands sound her trump,
And all the Greekish girls shall tripping sing,
'Great Hector's sister did Achilles win,
But our great Ajax bravely beat down him.'
Farewell, my lord: I as your lover speak;
The fool slides o'er the ice that you should break. [*Exit.*]
Patr. To this effect, Achilles, have I mov'd you:
A woman impudent and mannish grown
Is not more loath'd than an effeminate man
In time of action. I stand condemn'd for this;
They think my little stomach to the war
And your great love to me restrains you thus:
Sweet, rouse yourself; and the weak wanton Cupid
Shall from your neck unloose his amorous fold,
And, like a dew-drop from the lion's mane,
Be shook to air.
Achil. Shall Ajax fight with Hector?
Patr. Ay, and perhaps receive much honour by him.
Achil. I see my reputation is at stake;
My fame is shrewdly gor'd.
Patr. O, then, beware;
Those wounds heal ill that men do give themselves:
Omission to do what is necessary
Seals a commission to a blank of danger;
And danger, like an ague, subtly taints
Even then when we sit idly in the sun.
Achil. Go call Thersites hither, sweet Patroclus:
I'll send the fool to Ajax and desire him
T' invite the Troyan lords after the combat
To see us here unarm'd: I have a woman's longing,
An appetite that I am sick withal,
To see great Hector in his weeds of peace,
To talk with him and to behold his visage,
Even to my full of view.

Enter THERSITES.

A labour sav'd!
Ther. A wonder!
Achil. What?

Ther. Ajax goes up and down the field, asking for himself.

Achil. How so?

Ther. He must fight singly to-morrow with Hector, and is so prophetically proud of an heroical cudgelling that he raves in saying nothing.

Achil. How can that be?

Ther. Why, 'a stalks up and down like a peacock,—a stride and a stand: ruminates like an hostess that hath no arithmetic but her brain to set down her reckoning: bites his lip with a politic regard, as who should say 'There were wit in this head, an 'twould out;' and so there is, but it lies as coldly in him as fire in a flint, which will not show without knocking. The man 's undone for ever; for if Hector break not his neck i' the combat, he'll break 't himself in vain-glory. He knows not me: I said 'Good morrow, Ajax;' and he replies 'Thanks, Agamemnon.' What think you of this man that takes me for the general? He 's grown a very land-fish, languageless, a monster. A plague of opinion! a man may wear it on both sides, like a leather jerkin.

Achil. Thou must be my ambassador to him, Thersites.

Ther. Who, I? why, he'll answer nobody; he professes not answering: speaking is for beggars; he wears his tongue in 's arms. I will put on his presence: let Patroclus make demands to me, you shall see the pageant of Ajax.

Achil. To him, Patroclus: tell him I humbly desire the valiant Ajax to invite the most valorous Hector to

175. **nature,** i.e., in the sense of natural human weakness. 176. **gawds,** trifles, toys. 179. **More . . . dusted,** i.e., more praise than they give to merit that is old and covered by dust. 187. **case,** box up. 189-190. **emulous . . . faction,** refers to the partisanship of Olympian deities in the Trojan War; even the god of war, usually impartial, took sides. 194. **one . . . daughters,** Polyxena. It was while making request for her hand that he was fatally wounded in the heel by Paris. 196. **providence,** foresight. 197. **Pluto's.** Pluto, god of the underworld, was often confused with Plutus, god of riches. 198. **uncomprehensive,** unfathomable. 199. **Keeps place,** keeps up with, parallels. 201-202. **with . . . meddle,** that is never talked about. 205. **commerce,** i.e., dealings with Polyxena. 206. **is ours,** i.e., is known to us of the Greek council. 209. **Pyrrhus,** Achilles' son, also called Neoptolemus. 214. **lover,** friend. 215. **The fool . . . break,** the fool easily escapes dangers that to a man of your dignity would be fatal (Deighton). 220. **little stomach to,** lack of enthusiasm for. 231. **Seals . . . danger,** gives danger unlimited license. 245. **himself,** "Ajax," with a quibble on a "jakes," or latrine. 253. **hostess . . . arithmetic,** tavern keepers were proverbially poor at reckoning; cf. I, ii, 123. 254. **politic regard,** assumption of a knowing manner. 264. **land-fish,** monstrous creature,

come unarmed to my tent, and to procure safe-conduct for his person of the magnanimous and most illustrious six-or-seven-times-honoured captain-general of the Grecian army, Agamemnon, et cetera. Do this.

Patr. Jove bless great Ajax!

Ther. Hum!

Patr. I come from the worthy Achilles,—

Ther. Ha!

Patr. Who most humbly desires you to invite Hector to his tent,—

Ther. Hum!

Patr. And to procure safe-conduct from Agamemnon.

Ther. Agamemnon!

Patr. Ay, my lord.

Ther. Ha!

Patr. What say you to 't?

Ther. God b' wi' you, with all my heart.

Patr. Your answer, sir.

Ther. If to-morrow be a fair day, by eleven of the clock it will go one way or other: howsoever, he shall pay for me ere he has me.

Patr. Your answer, sir.

Ther. Fare you well, with all my heart.

Achil. Why, but he is not in this tune, is he?

Ther. No, but he 's out of tune thus. What music will be in him when Hector has knocked out his brains, I know not; but, I am sure, none, unless the fiddler Apollo get his sinews to make catlings on.

Achil. Come, thou shalt bear a letter to him straight.

Ther. Let me bear another to his horse; for that 's the more capable creature.

Achil. My mind is troubled, like a fountain stirr'd;
And I myself see not the bottom of it.
[*Exeunt Achilles and Patroclus.*]

Ther. Would the fountain of your mind were clear again, that I might water an ass at it! I had rather be a tick in a sheep than such a valiant ignorance. [*Exit.*]

[ACT IV.

SCENE I. *Troy. A street.*]

Enter, at one door, ÆNEAS, [*and* Servant *with a torch;*] *at another,* PARIS, DEIPHOBUS, ANTENOR, DIOMEDES *the Grecian, with torches.*

Par. See, ho! who is that there?
Dei. It is the Lord Æneas.
Æne. Is the prince there in person?
Had I so good occasion to lie long
As you, Prince Paris, nothing but heavenly business
Should rob my bed-mate of my company.
Dio. That 's my mind too. Good morrow, Lord Æneas.
Par. A valiant Greek, Æneas,—take his hand,—
Witness the process of your speech, wherein
You told how Diomed, a whole week by days,
Did haunt you in the field.
Æne. Health to you, valiant sir,
During all question of the gentle truce;
But when I meet you arm'd, as black defiance
As heart can think or courage execute.
Dio. The one and other Diomed embraces.
Our bloods are now in calm; and, so long, health!
But when contention and occasion meet,
By Jove, I'll play the hunter for thy life
With all my force, pursuit and policy.
Æne. And thou shalt hunt a lion, that will fly
With his face backward. In humane gentleness,
Welcome to Troy! now, by Anchises' life,
Welcome, indeed! By Venus' hand I swear,
No man alive can love in such a sort
The thing he means to kill more excellently.
Dio. We sympathise: Jove, let Æneas live,
If to my sword his fate be not the glory,
A thousand complete courses of the sun!
But, in mine emulous honour, let him die,
With every joint a wound, and that to-morrow!
Æne. We know each other well.
Dio. We do; and long to know each other worse.
Par. This is the most despiteful gentle greeting,
The noblest hateful love, that e'er I heard of.
What business, lord, so early?
Æne. I was sent for to the king; but why, I know not.
Par. His purpose meets you: 'twas to bring this Greek
To Calchas' house, and there to render him,
For the enfreed Antenor, the fair Cressid:
Let 's have your company, or, if you please,
Haste there before us: I constantly do think—
Or rather, call my thought a certain knowledge—
My brother Troilus lodges there to-night:
Rouse him and give him note of our approach,
With the whole quality wherefore: I fear
We shall be much unwelcome.
Æne. That I assure you:
Troilus had rather Troy were borne to Greece
Than Cressid borne from Troy.
Par. There is no help;
The bitter disposition of the time
Will have it so. On, lord; we'll follow you.
Æne. Good morrow, all. [*Exit with Servant.*]
Par. And tell me, noble Diomed, faith, tell me true,
Even in the soul of sound good-fellowship,
Who, in your thoughts, merits fair Helen best,
Myself or Menelaus?
Dio. Both alike:
He merits well to have her, that doth seek her,
Not making any scruple of her soilure,
With such a hell of pain and world of charge,
And you as well to keep her, that defend her,
Not palating the taste of her dishonour,
With such a costly loss of wealth and friends:

something like Caliban in *The Tempest*. 265. **opinion,** self-respect and self-conceit; used in both the favorable and unfavorable senses. 272. **put on his presence,** dramatize him. 305. **the fiddler Apollo,** i.e., as god of music. 306. **catlings,** catgut, of which strings for instruments were made.

ACT IV. SCENE I. 8. **Witness the process,** as is testified by the drift. 9. **a whole week by days,** every day for a week. 11. **question,** discussion, parley (allowed by the truce). 12. **black defiance,** parallel in structure with *Health* (l. 10). 16. **when . . . meet,** when the battle gives us opportunity. 21, 22. **Anchises' life, Venus' hand.** Diomedes, with the aid of Minerva, had wounded Venus in the hand. Anchises and Venus were Aeneas' parents. 23. **in such a sort,** to such a degree. 24. **excellently,** modifies *kill*. 25. **sympathise,** share your feeling. 28. **emulous,** ambitious; a transferred epithet. Diomedes is ambitious for such an honor. 31. **worse,** perhaps, in worse condition, wounded, or dead, or deprived of honor; may be simply oxymoron. 40. **constantly do think,** am confirmed in the thought. 44. **the . . . wherefore,** with all the reasons and circumstances. 57. **With . . . charge,** modifies *seek* (l. 55); refers to the hardships of the war.

He, like a puling cuckold, would drink up
The lees and dregs of a flat tamed piece;
You, like a lecher, out of whorish loins
Are pleas'd to breed out your inheritors:
Both merits pois'd, each weighs nor less nor more;
But he as he, the heavier for a whore.

Par. You are too bitter to your country-woman.

Dio. She 's bitter to her country: hear me, Paris:
For every false drop in her bawdy veins
A Grecian's life hath sunk; for every scruple
Of her contaminated carrion weight,
A Troyan hath been slain: since she could speak,
She hath not given so many good words breath
As for her Greeks and Troyans suff'red death.

Par. Fair Diomed, you do as chapmen do,
Dispraise the thing that you desire to buy:
But we in silence hold this virtue well,
We'll not commend what we intend to sell.
Here lies our way. *Exeunt.*

[SCENE II. *The same. Court of Pandarus' house.*]

Enter TROILUS *and* CRESSIDA.

Tro. Dear, trouble not yourself: the morn is cold.

Cres. Then, sweet my lord, I'll call mine uncle down;
He shall unbolt the gates.

Tro. Trouble him not;
To bed, to bed: sleep kill those pretty eyes,
And give as soft attachment to thy senses
As infants' empty of all thought!

Cres. Good morrow, then.

Tro. I prithee now, to bed.

Cres. Are you a-weary of me?

Tro. O Cressida! but that the busy day,
Wak'd by the lark, hath rous'd the ribald crows,
And dreaming night will hide our joys no longer,
I would not from thee.

Cres. Night hath been too brief.

Tro. Beshrew the witch! with venomous wights she stays
As tediously as hell, but flies the grasps of love
With wings more momentary-swift than thought.
You will catch cold, and curse me.

Cres. Prithee, tarry:
You men will never tarry.
O foolish Cressid! I might have still held off,
And then you would have tarried. Hark! there 's one up.

Pan. [*Within*] What, 's all the doors open here?

Tro. It is your uncle.

Cres. A pestilence on him! now will he be mocking:
I shall have such a life!

[*Enter* PANDARUS.]

Pan. How now, how now! how go maidenheads?
Here, you maid! where 's my cousin Cressid?

Cres. Go hang yourself, you naughty mocking uncle!
You bring me to do, and then you flout me too.

Pan. To do what? to do what? let her say what: what have I brought you to do?

Cres. Come, come, beshrew your heart! you'll ne'er be good,
Nor suffer others.

Pan. Ha, ha! Alas, poor wretch! ah, poor capocchia! hast not slept to-night? would he not, a naughty man, let it sleep? a bugbear take him!

Cres. Did not I tell you? Would he were knock'd i' the head! *One knocks.*
Who 's that at door? good uncle, go and see.
My lord, come you again into my chamber:
You smile and mock me, as if I meant naughtily.

Tro. Ha, ha!

Cres. Come, you are deceiv'd, I think of no such thing. *Knock.*
How earnestly they knock! Pray you, come in:
I would not for half Troy have you seen here.
Exeunt [*Troilus and Cressida*].

Pan. Who 's there? what 's the matter? will you beat down the door? How now! what 's the matter?

[*Enter* ÆNEAS.]

Æne. Good morrow, lord, good morrow.

Pan. Who 's there? my Lord Æneas! By my troth,
I knew you not: what news with you so early?

Æne. Is not Prince Troilus here?

Pan. Here! what should he do here?

Æne. Come, he is here, my lord; do not deny him:
It doth import him much to speak with me.

Pan. Is he here, say you? 'tis more than I know, I'll be sworn: for my own part, I came in late. What should he do here?

Æne. Who!—nay, then: come, come, you'll do him wrong ere you 're ware: you'll be so true to him, to be false to him: do not you know of him, but yet go fetch him hither; go.

[*Enter* TROILUS.]

Tro. How now! what 's the matter?

Æne. My lord, I scarce have leisure to salute you,
My matter is so rash: there is at hand
Paris your brother, and Deiphobus,
The Grecian Diomed, and our Antenor
Deliver'd to us; and for him forthwith,
Ere the first sacrifice, within this hour,
We must give up to Diomedes' hand
The Lady Cressida.

Tro. Is it so concluded?

Æne. By Priam and the general state of Troy:
They are at hand and ready to effect it.

Tro. How my achievements mock me!
I will go meet them: and, my Lord Æneas,
We met by chance; you did not find me here.

Æne. Good, good, my lord; the secrets of nature
Have not more gift in taciturnity.
Exeunt [*Troilus and Æneas*].

Pan. Is 't possible? no sooner got but lost? The devil take Antenor! the young prince will go mad: a plague upon Antenor! I would they had broke 's neck!

Enter CRESSIDA.

62. **tamed piece,** wine cask so long opened that the wine is flat; hence, a used woman. 66. **he as he,** the one like the other. 75. **chapmen,** bickering traders.

SCENE II. 5. **attachment,** arrest, confinement. 9. **ribald,** offensively noisy. 12. **witch,** i.e., night. **venomous wights,** malignant beings. 33. **capocchia,** dolt, fool. 58-59. **do not . . . of him,** you may pretend not to know of him. 62. **rash,** urgent, pressing. 115. **sounding,** uttering, pronouncing.

SCENE III. 1. **great morning,** broad day. 11. **would . . . help,** wish I could help to the extent that I shall pity.

Cres. How now! what 's the matter? who was here?
Pan. Ah, ah!
Cres. Why sigh you so profoundly? where 's my lord? gone! Tell me, sweet uncle, what 's the matter?
Pan. Would I were as deep under the earth as I am above!
Cres. O the gods! what 's the matter?
Pan. Prithee, get thee in: would thou hadst ne'er been born! I knew thou wouldst be his death. O, poor gentleman! A plague upon Antenor!
Cres. Good uncle, I beseech you, on my knees I beseech you, what 's the matter?
Pan. Thou must be gone, wench, thou must be gone; thou art changed for Antenor: thou must to thy father, and be gone from Troilus: 'twill be his death; 'twill be his bane; he cannot bear it.
Cres. O you immortal gods! I will not go.
Pan. Thou must.
Cres. I will not, uncle: I have forgot my father;
I know no touch of consanguinity;
No kin, no love, no blood, no soul so near me
As the sweet Troilus. O you gods divine!
Make Cressid's name the very crown of falsehood,
If ever she leave Troilus! Time, force, and death,
Do to this body what extremes you can;
But the strong base and building of my love
Is as the very centre of the earth,
Drawing all things to it. I'll go in and weep,—
Pan. Do, do.
Cres. Tear my bright hair and scratch my praised cheeks,
Crack my clear voice with sobs and break my heart
With sounding Troilus. I will not go from Troy.
[*Exeunt.*]

[SCENE III. *The same. Street before Pandarus' house.*]

Enter PARIS, TROILUS, ÆNEAS, DEIPHOBUS, ANTENOR, [*and*] DIOMEDES.

Par. It is great morning, and the hour prefix'd
For her delivery to this valiant Greek
Comes fast upon. Good my brother Troilus,
Tell you the lady what she is to do,
And haste her to the purpose.
Tro. Walk into her house;
I'll bring her to the Grecian presently:
And to his hand when I deliver her,
Think it an altar, and thy brother Troilus
A priest there off'ring to it his own heart. [*Exit.*]
Par. I know what 'tis to love;
And would, as I shall pity, I could help!
Please you walk in, my lords. *Exeunt.*

[SCENE IV. *The same. Pandarus' house.*]

Enter PANDARUS *and* CRESSIDA.

Pan. Be moderate, be moderate.
Cres. Why tell you me of moderation?
The grief is fine, full, perfect, that I taste,
And violenteth in a sense as strong
As that which causeth it: how can I moderate it?
If I could temporise with my affection,
Or brew it to a weak and colder palate,
The like allayment could I give my grief:
My love admits no qualifying dross;
No more my grief, in such a precious loss.

Enter TROILUS.

Pan. Here, here, here he comes. Ah, sweet ducks!
Cres. O Troilus! Troilus! [*Embracing him.*]
Pan. What a pair of spectacles is here! Let me embrace too. 'O heart,' as the goodly saying is,
'——O heart, heavy heart,
Why sigh'st thou without breaking?'
where he answers again,
'Because thou canst not ease thy smart
By friendship nor by speaking.'
There was never a truer rhyme. Let us cast away nothing, for we may live to have need of such a verse: we see it, we see it. How now, lambs?
Tro. Cressid, I love thee in so strain'd a purity,
That the bless'd gods, as angry with my fancy,
More bright in zeal than the devotion which
Cold lips blow to their deities, take thee from me.
Cres. Have the gods envy?
Pan. Ay, ay, ay, ay; 'tis too plain a case.
Cres. And is it true that I must go from Troy?
Tro. A hateful truth.
Cres. What, and from Troilus too?
Tro. From Troy and Troilus.
Cres. Is 't possible?
Tro. And suddenly; where injury of chance
Puts back leave-taking, justles roughly by
All time of pause, rudely beguiles our lips
Of all rejoindure, forcibly prevents
Our lock'd embrasures, strangles our dear vows
Even in the birth of our own labouring breath:
We two, that with so many thousand sighs
Did buy each other, must poorly sell ourselves
With the rude brevity and discharge of one.
Injurious Time now with a robber's haste
Crams his rich thiev'ry up, he knows not how:
As many farewells as be stars in heaven,
With distinct breath and consign'd kisses to them,
He fumbles up into a loose adieu,
And scants us with a single famish'd kiss,
Distasted with the salt of broken tears.
Æne. (*Within*) My lord, is the lady ready?
Tro. Hark! you are call'd: some say the Genius
Cries so to him that instantly must die.
Bid them have patience; she shall come anon.
Pan. Where are my tears? rain, to lay this wind, or my heart will be blown up by the root. [*Exit.*]
Cres. I must then to the Grecians?
Tro. No remedy.
Cres. A woful Cressid 'mongst the merry Greeks!
When shall we see again?
Tro. Hear me, my love: be thou but true of heart,—
Cres. I true! how now! what wicked deem is this?
Tro. Nay, we must use expostulation kindly,

SCENE IV. 3. **fine,** extreme, i.e., to the limit; this is Cressida's answer to Pandarus' exhortation to be moderate. 4. **violenteth,** is violent. 15. **spectacles,** sights, with pun on *eyeglasses*. 26. **strain'd,** purified as by filtering. 35. **injury of chance,** injurious Fortune. 38. **rejoindure,** reunion. 47. **With . . . them,** with the words of farewell and the kisses with which those words are ratified. 49. **scants us,** puts us off with. 50. **Distasted,** rendered distasteful. 52. **Genius,** attendant spirit supposed to be allotted to a person at birth. 58. **merry Greeks.** Cf. I, ii, 118. 61. **deem,** thought. 62. **expostulation,** opportunity for discourse.

For it is parting from us:
I speak not 'be thou true,' as fearing thee,
For I will throw my glove to Death himself,
That there 's no maculation in thy heart:
But 'be thou true,' say I, to fashion in
My sequent protestation; be thou true,
And I will see thee.
Cres. O, you shall be expos'd, my lord, to dangers
As infinite as imminent! but I'll be true.
Tro. And I'll grow friend with danger. Wear this sleeve.
Cres. And you this glove. When shall I see you?
Tro. I will corrupt the Grecian sentinels,
To give thee nightly visitation.
But yet be true.
Cres. O heavens! 'be true' again!
Tro. Hear why I speak it, love:
The Grecian youths are full of quality;
They 're loving, well compos'd with gifts of nature,
And swelling o'er with arts and exercise:
How novelty may move, and parts with person,
Alas, a kind of godly jealousy—
Which, I beseech you, call a virtuous sin—
Makes me afeard.
Cres. O heavens! you love me not.
Tro. Die I a villain, then!
In this I do not call your faith in question
So mainly as my merit: I cannot sing,
Nor heel the high lavolt, nor sweeten talk,
Nor play at subtle games; fair virtues all,
To which the Grecians are most prompt and pregnant:
But I can tell that in each grace of these
There lurks a still and dumb-discoursive devil
That tempts most cunningly: but be not tempted.
Cres. Do you think I will?
Tro. No.
But something may be done that we will not:
And sometimes we are devils to ourselves,
When we will tempt the frailty of our powers,
Presuming on their changeful potency.
Æne. (*Within*) Nay, good my lord,—
Tro. Come, kiss; and let us part.
Par. (*Within*) Brother Troilus!
Tro. Good brother, come you hither;
And bring Æneas and the Grecian with you.
Cres. My lord, will you be true?
Tro. Who, I? alas, it is my vice, my fault:
Whiles others fish with craft for great opinion,
I with great truth catch mere simplicity;
Whilst some with cunning gild their copper crowns,
With truth and plainness I do wear mine bare.
Fear not my truth: the moral of my wit
Is 'plain and true;' there 's all the reach of it.

[*Enter* ÆNEAS, PARIS, ANTENOR, DEIPHOBUS, *and* DIOMEDES.]

Welcome, Sir Diomed! here is the lady
Which for Antenor we deliver you:
At the port, lord, I'll give her to thy hand;
And by the way possess thee what she is.
Entreat her fair; and, by my soul, fair Greek,
If e'er thou stand at mercy of my sword,
Name Cressid, and thy life shall be as safe
As Priam is in Ilion.
Dio. Fair Lady Cressid,
So please you, save the thanks this prince expects:
The lustre in your eye, heaven in your cheek,
Pleads your fair usage; and to Diomed
You shall be mistress, and command him wholly.
Tro. Grecian, thou dost not use me courteously,
To shame the zeal of my petition to thee
In praising her: I tell thee, lord of Greece,
She is as far high-soaring o'er thy praises
As thou unworthy to be call'd her servant.
I charge thee use her well, even for my charge;
For, by the dreadful Pluto, if thou dost not,
Though the great bulk Achilles be thy guard,
I'll cut thy throat.
Dio. O, be not mov'd, Prince Troilus:
Let me be privileg'd by my place and message,
To be a speaker free; when I am hence,
I'll answer to my lust: and know you, lord,
I'll nothing do on charge: to her own worth
She shall be priz'd; but that you say 'be 't so,'
I'll speak it in my spirit and honour, 'no.'
Tro. Come, to the port. I'll tell thee, Diomed,
This brave shall oft make thee to hide thy head.
Lady, give me your hand, and, as we walk,
To our own selves bend we our needful talk.
[*Exeunt Troilus, Cressida, and Diomedes.*]
[*Trumpet within.*]
Par. Hark! Hector's trumpet.
Æne. How have we spent this morning!
The prince must think me tardy and remiss,
That swore to ride before him to the field.
Par. 'Tis Troilus' fault: come, come, to field with him.
Dei. Let us make ready straight.
Æne. Yea, with a bridegroom's fresh alacrity,
Let us address to tend on Hector's heels:
The glory of our Troy doth this day lie
On his fair worth and single chivalry. *Exeunt.*

[SCENE V. *The Grecian camp.*]

Enter AJAX, *armed;* ACHILLES, PATROCLUS, AGAMEMNON, MENELAUS, ULYSSES, NESTOR, CALCHAS, *&c.*

Agam. Here art thou in appointment fresh and fair,
Anticipating time. With starting courage,
Give with thy trumpet a loud note to Troy,
Thou dreadful Ajax; that the appalled air
May pierce the head of the great combatant
And hale him hither.
Ajax. Thou, trumpet, there 's my purse.
Now crack thy lungs, and split thy brazen pipe:
Blow, villain, till thy sphered bias cheek
Outswell the colic of puff'd Aquilon:

66. **maculation,** stain of impurity. 67. **to fashion in,** serve as introduction for. 80. **arts and exercise,** theory and practice. 81. **parts with person,** accomplishments with personal charm. 82, 83. **godly jealousy, virtuous sin,** instances of oxymoron. 88. **lavolt,** lively dance for two. 90. **prompt,** inclined. **pregnant,** ready. 92. **dumb-discoursive,** eloquently silent. 96. **will not,** do not desire. 99. **changeful potency,** power which may change to failure. 109. **moral,** maxim. 110. **reach,** sphere to which an agency or power is limited. 134. **I'll answer . . . lust,** I'll follow my own desires. 135. **on charge,** i.e., because you command it. 138. **port,** gate. 139. **brave,** boast. 142. **spent,** consumed by using. 148. **address,** get ready.

SCENE V. 1. **appointment,** equipment, accouterment. 2. **time. With.** The punctuation is that of QF; Globe, following Theobald: *time, with.* **starting courage,** bold defiance (Deighton). 6. **trumpet,** trumpeter. 9. **Aquilon,** the north wind. 20-21. **particular . . . general,** i.e., private, in his own person, not as the general of the army,

Come, stretch thy chest, and let thy eyes spout blood;
Thou blowest for Hector. [*Trumpet sounds.*]
Ulyss. No trumpet answers.
Achil. 'Tis but early days.
Agam. Is not yond Diomed, with Calchas' daughter?
Ulyss. 'Tis he, I ken the manner of his gait;
He rises on the toe: that spirit of his
In aspiration lifts him from the earth.

[*Enter* DIOMEDES, *with* CRESSIDA.]

Agam. Is this the Lady Cressid?
Dio. Even she.
Agam. Most dearly welcome to the Greeks, sweet lady.
Nest. Our general doth salute you with a kiss.
Ulyss. Yet is the kindness but particular;
'Twere better she were kiss'd in general.
Nest. And very courtly counsel: I'll begin.
So much for Nestor.
Achil. I'll take that winter from your lips, fair lady:
Achilles bids you welcome.
Men. I had good argument for kissing once.
Patr. But that 's no argument for kissing now;
For thus popp'd Paris in his hardiment,
And parted thus you and your argument.
Ulyss. O deadly gall, and theme of all our scorns!
For which we lose our heads to gild his horns.
Patr. The first was Menelaus' kiss; this, mine:
Patroclus kisses you.
Men. O, this is trim!
Patr. Paris and I kiss evermore for him.
Men. I'll have my kiss, sir. Lady, by your leave.
Cres. In kissing, do you render or receive?
Patr. Both take and give.
Cres. I'll make my match to live,
The kiss you take is better than you give;
Therefore no kiss.
Men. I'll give you boot, I'll give you three for one.
Cres. You are an odd man; give even, or give none.
Men. An odd man, lady! every man is odd.
Cres. No, Paris is not; for you know 'tis true,
That you are odd, and he is even with you.
Men. You fillip me o' th' head.
Cres. No, I'll be sworn.
Ulyss. It were no match, your nail against his horn.
May I, sweet lady, beg a kiss of you?
Cres. You may.
Ulyss. I do desire it.
Cres. Why, beg, then.
Ulyss. Why then for Venus' sake, give me a kiss,
When Helen is a maid again, and his.
Cres. I am your debtor, claim it when 'tis due.
Ulyss. Never 's my day, and then a kiss of you.
Dio. Lady, a word: I'll bring you to your father.
[*Exit with Cressida.*]
Nest. A woman of quick sense.
Ulyss. Fie, fie upon her!
There 's language in her eye, her cheek, her lip,
Nay, her foot speaks; her wanton spirits look out
At every joint and motive of her body.
O, these encounterers, so glib of tongue,
That give a coasting welcome ere it comes,
And wide unclasp the tables of their thoughts
To every ticklish reader! set them down
For sluttish spoils of opportunity
And daughters of the game.

Flourish. Enter all of Troy [HECTOR, PARIS, ÆNEAS, HELENUS, TROILUS, *and* Attendants].

All. The Troyans' trumpet.
Agam. Yonder comes the troop.
Æne. Hail, all you state of Greece! what shall be done
To him that victory commands? or do you purpose
A victor shall be known? will you the knights
Shall to the edge of all extremity
Pursue each other, or shall they be divided
By any voice or order of the field?
Hector bade ask.
Agam. Which way would Hector have it?
Æne. He cares not; he'll obey conditions.
Achil. 'Tis done like Hector; but securely done,
A little proudly, and great deal misprizing
The knight oppos'd.
Æne. If not Achilles, sir,
What is your name?
Achil. If not Achilles, nothing.
Æne. Therefore Achilles: but, whate'er, know this:
In the extremity of great and little,
Valour and pride excel themselves in Hector;
The one almost as infinite as all,
The other blank as nothing. Weigh him well,
And that which looks like pride is courtesy.
This Ajax is half made of Hector's blood:
In love whereof, half Hector stays at home;
Half heart, half hand, half Hector comes to seek
This blended knight, half Troyan and half Greek.
Achil. A maiden battle, then? O, I perceive you.

[*Enter* DIOMEDES.]

Agam. Here is Sir Diomed. Go, gentle knight,
Stand by our Ajax: as you and Lord Æneas
Consent upon the order of their fight,
So be it; either to the uttermost,
Or else a breath: the combatants being kin
Half stints their strife before their strokes begin.
[*Ajax and Hector enter the lists.*]
Ulyss. They are oppos'd already.
Agam. What Troyan is that same that looks so heavy?
Ulyss. The youngest son of Priam, a true knight,
Not yet mature, yet matchless, firm of word,
Speaking in deeds and deedless in his tongue;
Not soon provok'd nor being provok'd soon calm'd;
His heart and hand both open and both free;
For what he has he gives, what thinks he shows;
Yet gives he not till judgement guide his bounty,
Nor dignifies an impair thought with breath;
Manly as Hector, but more dangerous;

with quibble on *general*. 24. **that winter,** alludes to Nestor's old age. 28. **hardiment,** bold exploits, boldness. 37. **I'll . . . to live,** I'll wager my life. 40. **boot,** odds. 41. **odd.** Deighton sees a play here on the meaning "single," i.e., no longer having a wife. 57. **motive,** moving limb or organ. 58. **encounterers,** forward persons. 59. **a coasting,** sidelong. 61. **ticklish,** wanton. 62. **sluttish . . . opportunity,** corrupt wenches, of whose chastity every opportunity may make a prey (Johnson). 63. **daughters of the game,** i.e., prostitutes. 73. **securely,** overconfidently. 74. **misprizing,** disdaining. 78-79. **In . . . Hector,** Hector's valor excels in the extreme of greatness, his pride in the extreme of littleness. 83. **Ajax . . . blood.** Cf. II, ii, 77, note. 87. **maiden battle,** one without bloodshed. 94. **oppos'd,** facing each other ready for the contest. 103. **impair,** unsuitable.

For Hector in his blaze of wrath subscribes
To tender objects, but he in heat of action
Is more vindicative than jealous love:
They call him Troilus, and on him erect
A second hope, as fairly built as Hector.
Thus says Æneas; one that knows the youth
Even to his inches, and with private soul
Did in great Ilion thus translate him to me.
Alarum. [*Hector and Ajax fight.*]
Agam. They are in action.
Nest. Now, Ajax, hold thine own!
Tro. Hector, thou sleep'st;
Awake thee!
Agam. His blows are well dispos'd: there, Ajax!
Dio. You must no more. *Trumpets cease.*
Æne. Princes, enough, so please you.
Ajax. I am not warm yet; let us fight again.
Dio. As Hector pleases.
Hect. Why, then will I no more:
Thou art, great lord, my father's sister's son,
A cousin-german to great Priam's seed;
The obligation of our blood forbids
A gory emulation 'twixt us twain:
Were thy commixtion Greek and Troyan so
That thou couldst say 'This hand is Grecian all,
And this is Troyan; the sinews of this leg
All Greek, and this all Troy; my mother's blood
Runs on the dexter cheek, and this sinister
Bounds in my father's;' by Jove multipotent,
Thou shouldst not bear from me a Greekish member
Wherein my sword had not impressure made
Of our rank feud: but the just gods gainsay
That any drop thou borrow'dst from thy mother,
My sacred aunt, should by my mortal sword
Be drained! Let me embrace thee, Ajax:
By him that thunders, thou hast lusty arms;
Hector would have them fall upon him thus:
Cousin, all honour to thee!
Ajax. I thank thee, Hector:
Thou art too gentle and too free a man:
I came to kill thee, cousin, and bear hence
A great addition earned in thy death.
Hect. Not Neoptolemus so mirable,
On whose bright crest Fame with her loud'st Oyes
Cries 'This is he,' could promise to himself
A thought of added honour torn from Hector.
Æne. There is expectance here from both the sides,
What further you will do.
Hect. We'll answer it;
The issue is embracement: Ajax, farewell.
Ajax. If I might in entreaties find success—
As seld I have the chance—I would desire
My famous cousin to our Grecian tents.
Dio. 'Tis Agamemnon's wish, and great Achilles
Doth long to see unarm'd the valiant Hector.
Hect. Æneas, call my brother Troilus to me,
And signify this loving interview
To the expecters of our Troyan part;
Desire them home. Give me thy hand, my cousin;
I will go eat with thee and see your knights.
Ajax. Great Agamemnon comes to meet us here.
Hect. The worthiest of them tell me name by name;
But for Achilles, my own searching eyes
Shall find him by his large and portly size.
Agam. Worthy all arms! as welcome as to one
That would be rid of such an enemy;
But that 's no welcome: understand more clear.
What 's past and what 's to come is strew'd with husks
And formless ruin of oblivion;
But in this extant moment, faith and troth,
Strain'd purely from all hollow bias-drawing,
Bids thee, with most divine integrity,
From heart of very heart, great Hector, welcome.
Hect. I thank thee, most imperious Agamemnon.
Agam. [*To Troilus*] My well-fam'd lord of Troy, no less to you.
Men. Let me confirm my princely brother's greeting:
You brace of warlike brothers, welcome hither.
Hect. Who must we answer?
Æne. The noble Menelaus.
Hect. O, you, my lord? by Mars his gauntlet, thanks!
Mock not, that I affect th' untraded oath;
Your quondam wife swears still by Venus' glove:
She 's well, but bade me not commend her to you.
Men. Name her not now, sir; she 's a deadly theme.
Hect. O, pardon; I offend.
Nest. I have, thou gallant Troyan, seen thee oft
Labouring for destiny make cruel way
Through ranks of Greekish youth, and I have seen thee,
As hot as Perseus, spur thy Phrygian steed,
Despising many forfeits and subduements,
When thou hast hung thy advanced sword i' th' air,
Not letting it decline on the declined,
That I have said to some my standers by
'Lo, Jupiter is yonder, dealing life!'
And I have seen thee pause and take thy breath,
When that a ring of Greeks have hemm'd thee in,
Like an Olympian wrestling: this have I seen;
But this thy countenance, still lock'd in steel,
I never saw till now. I knew thy grandsire,
And once fought with him: he was a soldier good;
But, by great Mars, the captain of us all,
Never like thee. Let an old man embrace thee;
And, worthy warrior, welcome to our tents.
Æne. 'Tis the old Nestor.
Hect. Let me embrace thee, good old chronicle,
That hast so long walk'd hand in hand with time:
Most reverend Nestor, I am glad to clasp thee.
Nest. I would my arms could match thee in contention,
As they contend with thee in courtesy.
Hect. I would they could.
Nest. Ha!
By this white beard, I 'ld fight with thee to-morrow.
Well, welcome, welcome!—I have seen the time.
Ulyss. I wonder now how yonder city stands
When we have here her base and pillar by us.
Hect. I know your favour, Lord Ulysses, well.
Ah, sir, there 's many a Greek and Troyan dead,

107. **vindicative,** vindictive. 111. **Even . . . inches,** every inch of him. 121. **cousin-german,** blood relation. 128. **dexter,** right. **sinister,** left. 142. **Neoptolemus,** evidently intended for Achilles; this is the name of Achilles' son. **mirable,** marvelous. 143. **Oyes,** hear; call of the public crier. 150. **seld,** seldom. 156. **expecters . . . part,** Trojans awaiting the outcome. 162. **portly,** stately, dignified. 163. **as to one,** as is possible to one. 169. **Strain'd,** refined, purged. **hollow bias-drawing,** insincerities, obliquities, such as the bias gives the bowl. 178. **untraded,** unhackneyed; i.e., that his use of a new, eccentric oath is an affectation. 184. **Labouring for destiny,** employed in the service of fate, putting people to death. 187. **Despising . . . subduements,** ignoring those already vanquished, whose lives were forfeit. 195. **still,**

Since first I saw yourself and Diomed
In Ilion, on your Greekish embassy.
Ulyss. Sir, I foretold you then what would ensue:
My prophecy is but half his journey yet;
For yonder walls, that pertly front your town,
Yon towers, whose wanton tops do buss the clouds,
Must kiss their own feet.
Hect. I must not believe you:
There they stand yet, and modestly I think,
The fall of every Phrygian stone will cost
A drop of Grecian blood: the end crowns all,
And that old common arbitrator, Time,
Will one day end it.
Ulyss. So to him we leave it.
Most gentle and most valiant Hector, welcome:
After the general, I beseech you next
To feast with me and see me at my tent.
Achil. I shall forestall thee, Lord Ulysses, thou!
Now, Hector, I have fed mine eyes on thee;
I have with exact view perus'd thee, Hector,
And quoted joint by joint.
Hect. Is this Achilles?
Achil. I am Achilles.
Hect. Stand fair, I pray thee: let me look on thee.
Achil. Behold thy fill.
Hect. Nay, I have done already.
Achil. Thou art too brief: I will the second time,
As I would buy thee, view thee limb by limb.
Hect. O, like a book of sport thou 'lt read me o'er;
But there 's more in me than thou understand'st.
Why dost thou so oppress me with thine eye?
Achil. Tell me, you heavens, in which part of his body
Shall I destroy him? whether there, or there, or there?
That I may give the local wound a name
And make distinct the very breach whereout
Hector's great spirit flew: answer me, heavens!
Hect. It would discredit the blest gods, proud man,
To answer such a question: stand again:
Think'st thou to catch my life so pleasantly
As to prenominate in nice conjecture
Where thou wilt hit me dead?
Achil. I tell thee, yea.
Hect. Wert thou an oracle to tell me so,
I 'ld not believe thee. Henceforth guard thee well;
For I'll not kill thee there, nor there, nor there;
But, by the forge that stithied Mars his helm,
I'll kill thee every where, yea, o'er and o'er.
You wisest Grecians, pardon me this brag;
His insolence draws folly from my lips;
But I'll endeavour deeds to match these words,
Or may I never—
Ajax. Do not chafe thee, cousin:
And you, Achilles, let these threats alone,
Till accident or purpose bring you to 't:
You may have every day enough of Hector,
If you have stomach; the general state, I fear,
Can scarce entreat you to be odd with him.
Hect. I pray you, let us see you in the field:
We have had pelting wars, since you refus'd
The Grecians' cause.
Achil. Dost thou entreat me, Hector?
To-morrow do I meet thee, fell as death;
To-night all friends.
Hect. Thy hand upon that match.
Agam. First, all you peers of Greece, go to my tent;
There in the full convive we: afterwards,
As Hector's leisure and your bounties shall
Concur together, severally entreat him.
Beat loud the tabourines, let the trumpets blow,
That this great soldier may his welcome know.
Exeunt [all except Troilus and Ulysses].
Tro. My Lord Ulysses, tell me, I beseech you,
In what place of the field doth Calchas keep?
Ulyss. At Menelaus' tent, most princely Troilus:
There Diomed doth feast with him to-night;
Who neither looks upon the heaven nor earth,
But gives all gaze and bent of amorous view
On the fair Cressid.
Tro. Shall I, sweet lord, be bound to you so much,
After we part from Agamemnon's tent,
To bring me thither?
Ulyss. You shall command me, sir.
As gentle tell me, of what honour was
This Cressida in Troy? Had she no lover there
That wails her absence?
Tro. O, sir, to such as boasting show their scars
A mock is due. Will you walk on, my lord?
She was belov'd, she lov'd; she is, and doth:
But still sweet love is food for fortune's tooth. *Exeunt.*

[ACT V.

SCENE I. *The Grecian camp. Before Achilles' tent.*]

Enter ACHILLES *and* PATROCLUS.

Achil. I'll heat his blood with Greekish wine to-night,
Which with my scimitar I'll cool to-morrow.
Patroclus, let us feast him to the height.
Patr. Here comes Thersites.

Enter THERSITES.

Achil. How now, thou core of envy!
Thou crusty batch of nature, what 's the news?

Ther. Why, thou picture of what thou seemest, and idol of idiot-worshippers, here 's a letter for thee.

Achil. From whence, fragment?

Ther. Why, thou full dish of fool, from Troy.

Patr. Who keeps the tent now?

Ther. The surgeon's box, or the patient's wound.

Patr. Well said, adversity! and what need these tricks?

Ther. Prithee, be silent, boy; I profit not by thy talk: thou art thought to be Achilles' male varlet.

Patr. Male varlet, you rogue! what 's that?

Ther. Why, his masculine whore. Now, the rotten diseases of the south, the guts-griping, ruptures, catarrhs, loads o' gravel i' the back, lethargies, cold palsies, raw eyes, dirt-rotten livers, wheezing lungs, bladders full of imposthume, sciaticas, limekilns i' the

always. 202. **chronicle.** As an old man he is the repository of the events of the past. 219. **front,** i.e., that are the front of. 239. **book of sport,** possibly a jest book, or any book of light entertainment. 250. **prenominate,** name beforehand. **nice,** precise. 255. **stithied,** forged. 264. **general state,** Greek commanders in council. 265. **be odd,** be at odds. 267. **pelting,** paltry. 269. **fell,** fierce. 272. **convive,** feast together. 274. **entreat,** invite. 278. **keep,** dwell.

ACT V. SCENE I. 5. **crusty . . . nature,** i.e., as a batch of crusty bread. 12. **surgeon's box.** Thersites puns on *tent* (l. 11), i.e., a probe for cleansing a wound. 24. **imposthume,** abscess. 25. **limekilns,** burning sensations.

palm, incurable bone-ache, and the rivelled fee-simple of the tetter, take and take again such preposterous discoveries!

Patr. Why, thou damnable box of envy, thou, what meanest thou to curse thus?

Ther. Do I curse thee?

Patr. Why, no, you ruinous butt, you whoreson indistinguishable cur, no.

Ther. No! why art thou then exasperate, thou idle immaterial skein of sleave-silk, thou green sarcenet flap for a sore eye, thou tassel of a prodigal's purse, thou? Ah, how the poor world is pestered with such waterflies, diminutives of nature!

Patr. Out, gall!

Ther. Finch-egg!

Achil. My sweet Patroclus, I am thwarted quite
From my great purpose in to-morrow's battle.
Here is a letter from Queen Hecuba,
A token from her daughter, my fair love,
Both taxing me and gaging me to keep
An oath that I have sworn. I will not break it:
Fall Greeks; fail fame; honour or go or stay;
My major vow lies here, this I'll obey.
Come, come, Thersites, help to trim my tent:
This night in banqueting must all be spent.
Away, Patroclus! [*Exeunt Achilles and Patroclus.*]

Ther. With too much blood and too little brain, these two may run mad; but, if with too much brain and too little blood they do, I'll be a curer of madmen. Here 's Agamemnon, an honest fellow enough, and one that loves quails; but he has not so much brain as ear-wax: and the goodly transformation of Jupiter there, his brother, the bull,—the primitive statue, and oblique memorial of cuckolds; a thrifty shoeing-horn in a chain, hanging at his brother's leg,—to what form but that he is, should wit larded with malice and malice forced with wit turn him to? To an ass, were nothing; he is both ass and ox: to an ox, were nothing; he is both ox and ass. To be a dog, a mule, a cat, a fitchew, a toad, a lizard, an owl, a puttock, or a herring without a roe, I would not care; but to be Menelaus! I would conspire against destiny. Ask me not what I would be, if I were not Thersites; for I care not to be the louse of a lazar, so I were not Menelaus. Hey-day! spirits and fires!

Enter [HECTOR, TROILUS, AJAX,] AGAMEMNON, ULYSSES, NESTOR, [MENELAUS,] *and* DIOMEDES, *with lights*.

Agam. We go wrong, we go wrong.

Ajax. No, yonder 'tis;
There, where we see the lights.

Hect. I trouble you.

Ajax. No, not a whit.

Ulyss. Here comes himself to guide you.

[*Enter* ACHILLES.]

Achil. Welcome, brave Hector; welcome, princes all.

Agam. So now, fair Prince of Troy, I bid good night.
Ajax commands the guard to tend on you.

Hect. Thanks and good night to the Greeks' general.

Men. Good night, my lord.

Hect. Good night, sweet Lord Menelaus.

Ther. Sweet draught: 'sweet' quoth 'a! sweet sink, sweet sewer.

Achil. Good night and welcome, both at once, to those
That go or tarry.

Agam. Good night. *Exeunt Agamemnon [and] Menelaus.*

Achil. Old Nestor tarries; and you too, Diomed,
Keep Hector company an hour or two.

Dio. I cannot, lord; I have important business,
The tide whereof is now. Good night, great Hector.

Hect. Give me your hand.

Ulyss. [*Aside to Troilus*] Follow his torch; he goes to Calchas' tent:
I'll keep you company.

Tro. Sweet sir, you honour me.

Hect. And so, good night.

[*Exit Diomedes; Ulysses and Troilus following.*]

Achil. Come, come, enter my tent.

Exeunt [*Achilles, Hector, Ajax, and Nestor*].

Ther. That same Diomed 's a false-hearted rogue, a most unjust knave; I will no more trust him when he leers than I will a serpent when he hisses: he will spend his mouth, and promise, like Brabbler the hound; but when he performs, astronomers foretell it; it is prodigious, there will come some change; the sun borrows of the moon, when Diomed keeps his word. I will rather leave to see Hector, than not to dog him: they say he keeps a Troyan drab, and uses the traitor Calchas' tent: I'll after. Nothing but lechery! all incontinent varlets! [*Exit.*]

[SCENE II. *The same. Before Calchas' tent.*]

Enter DIOMEDES.

Dio. What, are you up here, ho? speak.

Cal. [*Within*] Who calls?

Dio. Diomed. Calchas, I think. Where 's your daughter?

Cal. [*Within*] She comes to you.

[*Enter* TROILUS *and* ULYSSES, *at a distance; after them*, THERSITES.]

Ulyss. Stand where the torch may not discover us.

Enter CRESSIDA.

Tro. Cressid comes forth to him.

Dio. How now, my charge!

Cres. Now, my sweet guardian! Hark, a word with you. [*Whispers.*]

Tro. Yea, so familiar!

Ulyss. She will sing any man at first sight.

Ther. And any man may sing her, if he can take her cliff; she 's noted.

Dio. Will you remember?

Cres. Remember! yes.

Dio. Nay, but do, then;
And let your mind be coupled with your words.

26. **rivelled,** wrinkled. **fee-simple,** absolute possession, i.e., incurable disease. 27. **tetter,** skin disease. 32. **ruinous butt,** dilapidated cask. **indistinguishable,** shapeless. 35. **sleave-silk,** floss-silk. 36. **sarcenet,** fine, soft silk. 46. **taxing,** censuring. **gaging,** binding to a promies. 48. **or . . . or,** either . . . or. 57. **quails,** cant term for prostitutes. 59-60. **transformation . . . bull,** alludes to the myth of Jupiter's rape of Europa, whom he encountered in a meadow after changing himself into a bull. Thersites has in mind the bull's horns; cf. V, vii, 10, 12. 60. **oblique memorial,** indirect reminder. 61. **shoeing-horn,** shoehorn; another joke on the cuckold's horn. 67. **fitchew,** polecat. 68.

Tro. What should she remember?
Ulyss. List.
Cres. Sweet honey Greek, tempt me no more to folly.
Ther. Roguery!
Dio. Nay, then,—
Cres. I'll tell you what,—
Dio. Foh, foh! come, tell a pin: you are forsworn.
Cres. In faith, I cannot: what would you have me do?
Ther. A juggling trick,—to be secretly open.
Dio. What did you swear you would bestow on me?
Cres. I prithee, do not hold me to mine oath;
Bid me do any thing but that, sweet Greek.
Dio. Good night.
Tro. Hold, patience!
Ulyss. How now, Troyan!
Cres. Diomed,—
Dio. No, no, good night: I'll be your fool no more.
Tro. Thy better must.
Cres. Hark, one word in your ear.
Tro. O plague and madness!
Ulyss. You are moved, prince; let us depart, I pray you,
Lest your displeasure should enlarge itself
To wrathful terms: this place is dangerous;
The time right deadly; I beseech you, go.
Tro. Behold, I pray you!
Ulyss. Nay, good my lord, go off:
You flow to great distraction; come, my lord.
Tro. I prithee, stay.
Ulyss. You have not patience; come.
Tro. I pray you, stay; by hell and all hell's torments,
I will not speak a word!
Dio. And so, good night.
Cres. Nay, but you part in anger.
Tro. Doth that grieve thee?
O withered truth!
Ulyss. How now, my lord!
Tro. By Jove,
I will be patient.
Cres. Guardian!—why, Greek!
Dio. Foh, foh! adieu; you palter.
Cres. In faith, I do not: come hither once again.
Ulyss. You shake, my lord, at something: will you go?
You will break out.
Tro. She strokes his cheek!
Ulyss. Come, come.
Tro. Nay, stay; by Jove, I will not speak a word:
There is between my will and all offences
A guard of patience: stay a little while.
Ther. How the devil Luxury, with his fat rump and potato-finger, tickles these together! Fry, lechery, fry!
Dio. But will you, then?
Cres. In faith, I will, la; never trust me else.
Dio. Give me some token for the surety of it.
Cres. I'll fetch you one. *Exit.*
Ulyss. You have sworn patience.
Tro. Fear me not, sweet lord;
I will not be myself, nor have cognition
Of what I feel: I am all patience.

Enter CRESSIDA.

Ther. Now the pledge; now, now, now!
Cres. Here, Diomed, keep this sleeve.
Tro. O beauty! where is thy faith?
Ulyss. My lord,—
Tro. I will be patient; outwardly I will.
Cres. You look upon that sleeve; behold it well.
He lov'd me—O false wench!—Give 't me again.
Dio. Whose was 't?
Cres. It is no matter, now I ha 't again.
I will not meet with you to-morrow night:
I prithee, Diomed, visit me no more.
Ther. Now she sharpens: well said, whetstone!
Dio. I shall have it.
Cres. What, this?
Dio. Ay, that.
Cres. O, all you gods! O pretty, pretty pledge!
Thy master now lies thinking in his bed
Of thee and me, and sighs, and takes my glove,
And gives memorial dainty kisses to it,
As I kiss thee. Nay, do not snatch it from me;
He that takes that doth take my heart withal.
Dio. I had your heart before, this follows it.
Tro. I did swear patience.
Cres. You shall not have it, Diomed; faith, you shall not;
I'll give you something else.
Dio. I will have this: whose was it?
Cres. It is no matter.
Dio. Come, tell me whose it was.
Cres. 'Twas one's that lov'd me better than you will.
But, now you have it, take it.
Dio. Whose was it?
Cres. By all Diana's waiting-women yond,
And by herself, I will not tell you whose.
Dio. To-morrow will I wear it on my helm,
And grieve his spirit that dares not challenge it.
Tro. Wert thou the devil, and wor'st it on thy horn,
It should be challeng'd.
Cres. Well, well, 'tis done, 'tis past: and yet it is not;
I will not keep my word.
Dio. Why, then, farewell;
Thou never shalt mock Diomed again.
Cres. You shall not go: one cannot speak a word,
But it straight starts you.
Dio. I do not like this fooling.
Ther. Nor I, by Pluto: but that that likes not you pleases me best.
Dio. What, shall I come? the hour?
Cres. Ay, come:—O Jove!—do come:—I shall be plagu'd.
Dio. Farewell till then.
Cres. Good night: I prithee, come.
[*Exit Diomedes.*]
Troilus, farewell! one eye yet looks on thee;
But with my heart the other eye doth see.
Ah, poor our sex! this fault in us I find,
The error of our eye directs our mind:
What error leads must err; O, then conclude
Minds sway'd by eyes are full of turpitude. *Exit.*
Ther. A proof of strength she could not publish more,

puttock, bird of prey of the kite kind. **herring . . . roe.** Cf. *Romeo and Juliet*, II, iv, 39. 71. **care not to be,** would as soon be. 98. **spend his mouth,** bay without scenting the game. 103. **leave to see,** cease gazing on. **him,** i.e., Diomedes.
SCENE II. 9. **sing . . . at first sight,** i.e., without previous acquaintance. 11. **cliff,** clef, key (with obscene pun on *cleft*). **noted,** set to music, with quibble on the meaning "stigmatized," i.e., in bad repute. 25. **secretly,** privately and sexually. 48. **palter,** use trickery. 55. **Luxury,** lechery. 56. **potato-finger.** Potatoes were accounted stimulants to lechery. 91. **Diana's.** Ironically, the goddess of chastity.

Unless she said 'My mind is now turn'd whore.'
Ulyss. All 's done, my lord.
Tro. It is.
Ulyss. Why stay we, then?
Tro. To make a recordation to my soul
Of every syllable that here was spoke.
But if I tell how these two did co-act,
Shall I not lie in publishing a truth?
Sith yet there is a credence in my heart,
An esperance so obstinately strong,
That doth invert th' attest of eyes and ears,
As if those organs had deceptious functions,
Created only to calumniate.
Was Cressid here?
Ulyss. I cannot conjure, Troyan.
Tro. She was not, sure.
Ulyss. Most sure she was.
Tro. Why, my negation hath no taste of madness.
Ulyss. Nor mine, my lord: Cressid was here but now.
Tro. Let it not be believ'd for womanhood!
Think, we had mothers; do not give advantage
To stubborn critics, apt, without a theme,
For depravation, to square the general sex
By Cressid's rule: rather think this not Cressid.
Ulyss. What hath she done, prince, that can soil our mothers?
Tro. Nothing at all, unless that this were she.
Ther. Will 'a swagger himself out on 's own eyes?
Tro. This she? no, this is Diomed's Cressida:
If beauty have a soul, this is not she;
If souls guide vows, if vows be sanctimonies,
If sanctimony be the gods' delight,
If there be rule in unity itself,
This is not she. O madness of discourse,
That cause sets up with and against itself!
Bi-fold authority! where reason can revolt
Without perdition, and loss assume all reason
Without revolt: this is, and is not, Cressid.
Within my soul there doth conduce a fight
Of this strange nature that a thing inseparate
Divides more wider than the sky and earth,
And yet the spacious breadth of this division
Admits no orifex for a point as subtle
As Ariachne's broken woof to enter.
Instance, O instance! strong as Pluto's gates;
Cressid is mine, tied with the bonds of heaven:
Instance, O instance! strong as heaven itself;
The bonds of heaven are slipp'd, dissolv'd, and loos'd;
And with another knot, five-finger-tied,
The fractions of her faith, orts of her love,
The fragments, scraps, the bits and greasy relics
Of her o'er-eaten faith, are bound to Diomed.
Ulyss. May worthy Troilus be half attach'd
With that which here his passion doth express?
Tro. Ay, Greek; and that shall be divulged well
In characters as red as Mars his heart
Inflam'd with Venus: never did young man fancy
With so eternal and so fix'd a soul.
Hark, Greek: as much as I do Cressid love,
So much by weight hate I her Diomed:
That sleeve is mine that he'll bear on his helm;
Were it a casque compos'd by Vulcan's skill,
My sword should bite it: not the dreadful spout
Which shipmen do the hurricano call,
Constring'd in mass by the almighty sun,
Shall dizzy with more clamour Neptune's ear
In his descent than shall my prompted sword
Falling on Diomed.
Ther. He'll tickle it for his concupy.
Tro. O Cressid! O false Cressid! false, false, false!
Let all untruths stand by thy stained name,
And they'll seem glorious.
Ulyss. O, contain yourself;
Your passion draws ears hither.

Enter ÆNEAS.

Æne. I have been seeking you this hour, my lord:
Hector, by this, is arming him in Troy;
Ajax, your guard, stays to conduct you home.
Tro. Have with you, prince. My courteous lord, adieu.
Farewell, revolted fair! and, Diomed,
Stand fast, and wear a castle on thy head!
Ulyss. I'll bring you to the gates.
Tro. Accept distracted thanks.
Exeunt Troilus, Æneas, and Ulysses.

Ther. Would I could meet that rogue Diomed! I would croak like a raven; I would bode, I would bode. Patroclus will give me any thing for the intelligence of this whore: the parrot will not do more for an almond than he for a commodious drab. Lechery, lechery; still, wars and lechery; nothing else holds fashion: a burning devil take them! *Exit.*

[SCENE III. *Troy. Before Priam's palace.*]

Enter HECTOR *and* ANDROMACHE.

And. When was my lord so much ungently temper'd,
To stop his ears against admonishment?
Unarm, unarm, and do not fight to-day.
Hect. You train me to offend you; get you in:
By all the everlasting gods, I'll go!
And. My dreams will, sure, prove ominous to the day.
Hect. No more, I say.

Enter CASSANDRA.

Cas. Where is my brother Hector?
And. Here, sister; arm'd, and bloody in intent.
Consort with me in loud and dear petition,
Pursue we him on knees; for I have dream'd
Of bloody turbulence, and this whole night
Hath nothing been but shapes and forms of slaughter.
Cas. O, 'tis true.
Hect. Ho! bid my trumpet sound.

121. **esperance,** hope. 123. **deceptious,** deceiving. 132-133. **square . . . rule,** make Cressida the standard by which all womankind is measured. 136. **Will . . . eyes,** i.e., will he succeed in deceiving his own eyes? **on,** of. 139. **sanctimonies,** sacred things. 147. **conduce,** take place. 151. **orifex,** orifice. 152. **Ariachne's broken woof,** spider web. Arachne challenged Minerva to a weaving contest; the goddess became angered, tore up Arachne's work, and turned her into a spider. 157. **five-finger-tied,** a knot tied by giving her hand to Diomedes (Johnson).

158. **orts,** refuse, fragments. 161. **half-attach'd,** half as much affected (as it appears). 170. **casque,** headpiece, helmet. 173. **Constring'd,** compressed. 177. **concupy,** lust. 187. **castle,** fortress. 192. **bode,** warn, prognosticate.

SCENE III. 21. **For,** because. **would give,** want to give. 26. **keeps the weather of,** keeps to the windward side of. 27. **the dear man,** earnest, sincere person; so Q; Globe, following Pope: *the brave man.* 34. **brushes,** hostile encounters. 37. **vice of mercy,** an instance of

Cas. No notes of sally, for the heavens, sweet brother.
Hect. Be gone, I say: the gods have heard me swear.
Cas. The gods are deaf to hot and peevish vows:
They are polluted off'rings, more abhorr'd
Than spotted livers in the sacrifice.
And. O, be persuaded! do not count it holy
To hurt by being just: it is as lawful,
For we would give much, to use violent thefts,
And rob in the behalf of charity.
Cas. It is the purpose that makes strong the vow;
But vows to every purpose must not hold:
Unarm, sweet Hector.
Hect. Hold you still, I say;
Mine honour keeps the weather of my fate:
Life every man holds dear; but the dear man
Holds honour far more precious-dear than life.

Enter TROILUS.

How now, young man! mean'st thou to fight to-day?
And. Cassandra, call my father to persuade.
Exit Cassandra.
Hect. No, faith, young Troilus; doff thy harness, youth;
I am to-day i' th' vein of chivalry:
Let grow thy sinews till their knots be strong,
And tempt not yet the brushes of the war.
Unarm thee, go, and doubt thou not, brave boy,
I'll stand to-day for thee and me and Troy.
Tro. Brother, you have a vice of mercy in you,
Which better fits a lion than a man.
Hect. What vice is that, good Troilus? chide me for it.
Tro. When many times the captive Grecian falls,
Even in the fan and wind of your fair sword,
You bid them rise, and live.
Hect. O, 'tis fair play.
Tro. Fool's play, by heaven, Hector.
Hect. How now! how now!
Tro. For the love of all the gods,
Let 's leave the hermit Pity with our mothers,
And when we have our armours buckled on,
The venom'd vengeance ride upon our swords,
Spur them to ruthful work, rein them from ruth.
Hect. Fie, savage, fie!
Tro. Hector, then 'tis wars.
Hect. Troilus, I would not have you fight to-day.
Tro. Who should withhold me?
Not fate, obedience, nor the hand of Mars
Beck'ning with fiery truncheon my retire;
Not Priamus and Hecuba on knees,
Their eyes o'ergalled with recourse of tears;
Nor you, my brother, with your true sword drawn,
Oppos'd to hinder me, should stop my way,
But by my ruin.

Enter PRIAM *and* CASSANDRA.

Cas. Lay hold upon him, Priam, hold him fast:
He is thy crutch; now if thou lose thy stay,
Thou on him leaning, and all Troy on thee,
Fall all together.
Pri. Come, Hector, come, go back:
Thy wife hath dream'd; thy mother hath had visions;
Cassandra doth foresee; and I myself
Am like a prophet suddenly enrapt
To tell thee that this day is ominous:
Therefore, come back.
Hect. Æneas is a-field;
And I do stand engag'd to many Greeks,
Even in the faith of valour, to appear
This morning to them.
Pri. Ay, but thou shalt not go.
Hect. I must not break my faith.
You know me dutiful; therefore, dear sir,
Let me not shame respect; but give me leave
To take that course by your consent and voice,
Which you do here forbid me, royal Priam.
Cas. O Priam, yield not to him!
And. Do not, dear father.
Hect. Andromache, I am offended with you:
Upon the love you bear me, get you in.
Exit Andromache.
Tro. This foolish, dreaming, superstitious girl
Makes all these bodements.
Cas. O, farewell, dear Hector!
Look, how thou diest! look, how thy eye turns pale!
Look, how thy wounds do bleed at many vents!
Hark, how Troy roars! how Hecuba cries out!
How poor Andromache shrills her dolours forth!
Behold, distraction, frenzy and amazement,
Like witless antics, one another meet,
And all cry, Hector! Hector 's dead! O Hector!
Tro. Away! away!
Cas. Farewell: yet, soft! Hector, I take my leave:
Thou dost thyself and all our Troy deceive. [*Exit.*]
Hect. You are amaz'd, my liege, at her exclaim:
Go in and cheer the town: we'll forth and fight,
Do deeds worth praise and tell you them at night.
Pri. Farewell: the gods with safety stand about thee! [*Exeunt severally Priam and Hector.*] *Alarum.*
Tro. They are at it, hark! Proud Diomed, believe,
I come to lose my arm, or win my sleeve.

Enter PANDARUS.

Pan. Do you hear, my lord? do you hear?
Tro. What now?
Pan. Here 's a letter come from yond poor girl.
Tro. Let me read.
Pan. A whoreson tisick, a whoreson rascally tisick so troubles me, and the foolish fortune of this girl; and what one thing, what another, that I shall leave you one o' these days: and I have a rheum in mine eyes too, and such an ache in my bones that, unless a man were cursed, I cannot tell what to think on 't. What says she there?
Tro. Words, words, mere words, no matter from the heart:
Th' effect doth operate another way. [*Tearing the letter.*]
Go, wind, to wind, there turn and change together.

oxymoron. 38. **better fits a lion,** alludes to the tradition of natural history where clemency is frequently ascribed to the lion. Johnson comments: "Troilus reasons not improperly, that to spare against reason, by mere instinct of pity, became rather a generous beast than a wise man." This interpretation gives point to his calling mercy a vice. 41. **fair.** *Fierce, fell, fear'd* have been suggested as emendations. Tannenbaum (*Shakespeare Association Bulletin*, VII, 81) conjectured *sure*, spelled *suer*, with long *s* mistaken for *f*, *u* for open *a*, and *e* for *i*. 48. **ruthful,** lamentable, i.e., causing lamentation. **ruth,** pity. 53. **Beck'ning . . . retire,** alludes to the practice of signaling by means of a truncheon (i.e., staff of office) that a combat should cease. **retire,** withdrawal. 55. **o'ergalled,** inflamed. 60. **stay,** prop. 73. **shame respect,** violate my filial duty. 101. **tisick,** consumptive cough. 110. **wind,** a symbol of inconstancy.

My love with words and errors still she feeds;
But edifies another with her deeds. *Exeunt.*

[SCENE IV. *Plains between Troy and the Grecian camp.*]

[*Alarum.*] *Enter* THERSITES. *Excursions.*

Ther. Now they are clapper-clawing one another; I'll go look on. That dissembling abominable varlet, Diomed, has got that same scurvy doting foolish young knave's sleeve of Troy there in his helm: I would fain see them meet; that that same young Troyan ass, that loves the whore there, might send that Greekish whoremasterly villain, with the sleeve, back to the dissembling luxurious drab, of a sleeveless errand. O' the t'other side, the policy of those crafty swearing rascals, that stale old mouse-eaten dry cheese, Nestor, and that same dog-fox, Ulysses, is not proved worth a blackberry: they set me up, in policy, that mongrel cur, Ajax, against that dog of as bad a kind, Achilles: and now is the cur Ajax prouder than the cur Achilles, and will not arm to-day; whereupon the Grecians begin to proclaim barbarism, and policy grows into an ill opinion. Soft! here comes sleeve, and t'other.

[*Enter* DIOMEDES, TROILUS *following.*]

Tro. Fly not; for shouldst thou take the river Styx,
I would swim after.

Dio. Thou dost miscall retire:
I do not fly, but advantageous care
Withdrew me from the odds of multitude:
Have at thee!

Ther. Hold thy whore, Grecian!—now for thy whore, Troyan!—now the sleeve, now the sleeve!

[*Exeunt Troilus and Diomedes, fighting.*]

Enter HECTOR.

Hect. What art thou, Greek? art thou for Hector's match?
Art thou of blood and honour?

Ther. No, no, I am a rascal; a scurvy railing knave; a very filthy rogue.

Hect. I do believe thee: live. [*Exit.*]

Ther. God-a-mercy, that thou wilt believe me; but a plague break thy neck for frighting me! What 's become of the wenching rogues? I think they have swallowed one another: I would laugh at that miracle: yet, in a sort, lechery eats itself. I'll seek them. *Exit.*

[SCENE V. *Another part of the plains.*]

Enter DIOMEDES *and* Servant.

Dio. Go, go, my servant, take thou Troilus' horse;
Present the fair steed to my lady Cressid:
Fellow, commend my service to her beauty;
Tell her I have chastis'd the amorous Troyan,
And am her knight by proof.

Serv. I go, my lord. [*Exit.*]

Enter AGAMEMNON.

Agam. Renew, renew! The fierce Polydamas
Hath beat down Menon: bastard Margarelon
Hath Doreus prisoner,
And stands colossus-wise, waving his beam,
Upon the pashed corses of the kings
Epistrophus and Cedius: Polyxenes is slain,
Amphimachus and Thoas deadly hurt,
Patroclus ta'en or slain, and Palamedes
Sore hurt and bruis'd: the dreadful Sagittary
Appals our numbers: haste we, Diomed,
To reinforcement, or we perish all.

Enter NESTOR.

Nest. Go, bear Patroclus' body to Achilles;
And bid the snail-pac'd Ajax arm for shame.
There is a thousand Hectors in the field:
Now here he fights on Galathe his horse,
And there lacks work; anon he 's there afoot,
And there they fly or die, like scaled sculls
Before the belching whale; then is he yonder,
And there the strawy Greeks, ripe for his edge,
Fall down before him, like the mower's swath:
Here, there, and every where, he leaves and takes,
Dexterity so obeying appetite
That what he will he does, and does so much
That proof is call'd impossibility.

Enter ULYSSES.

Ulyss. O, courage, courage, princes! great Achilles
Is arming, weeping, cursing, vowing vengeance:
Patroclus' wounds have rous'd his drowsy blood,
Together with his mangled Myrmidons,
That noseless, handless, hack'd and chipp'd, come to him,
Crying on Hector. Ajax hath lost a friend
And foams at mouth, and he is arm'd and at it,
Roaring for Troilus, who hath done to-day
Mad and fantastic execution,
Engaging and redeeming of himself
With such a careless force and forceless care
As if that luck, in very spite of cunning,
Bade him win all.

Enter AJAX.

Ajax. Troilus! thou coward Troilus! *Exit.*

Dio. Ay, there, there.

Nest. So, so, we draw together. *Exit.*

Enter ACHILLES.

Achil. Where is this Hector?
Come, come, thou boy-queller, show thy face;
Know what it is to meet Achilles angry:
Hector! where 's Hector? I will none but Hector.
Exit.

[SCENE VI. *Another part of the plains.*]

Enter AJAX.

Ajax. Troilus, thou coward Troilus, show thy head!

Enter DIOMEDES.

SCENE IV. 1. **clapper-clawing,** mauling, thrashing; cf. the use of this term in the Preface to the second issue of Q (see Introduction). 9. **sleeveless,** futile. 18. **proclaim barbarism,** set up the authority of ignorance, to declare that they will be governed by policy no longer (Johnson). 21. **miscall retire,** call my retirement by a wrong name. 22-23. **advantageous . . . multitude,** care for my own advantage prompted me to withdraw from facing heavy odds. 28. **for Hector's match,** ready for a match with Hector.

SCENE V. 9. **colossus-wise,** i.e., like the statue of Apollo at Rhodes, which, according to an unfounded tradition, was said to have its feet placed on two moles which formed the harbor entrance so that ships passed between its legs. It was demolished by an earthquake in the

Dio. Troilus, I say! where 's Troilus?
Ajax. What wouldst thou?
Dio. I would correct him.
Ajax. Were I the general, thou shouldst have my office
Ere that correction. Troilus, I say! what, Troilus!

Enter TROILUS.

Tro. O traitor Diomed! turn thy false face, thou traitor,
And pay thy life thou owest me for my horse!
Dio. Ha, art thou there?
Ajax. I'll fight with him alone: stand, Diomed.
Dio. He is my prize; I will not look upon.
Tro. Come, both you cogging Greeks; have at you both! [*Exeunt, fighting.*]

[*Enter* HECTOR.]

Hect. Yea, Troilus? O, well fought, my youngest brother!

Enter ACHILLES.

Achil. Now do I see thee, ha! have at thee, Hector! [*They fight; Achilles tires.*]
Hect. Pause, if thou wilt.
Achil. I do disdain thy courtesy, proud Troyan:
Be happy that my arms are out of use:
My rest and negligence befriends thee now,
But thou anon shalt hear of me again;
Till when, go seek thy fortune. *Exit.*
Hect. Fare thee well:
I would have been much more a fresher man,
Had I expected thee. How now, my brother!

Enter TROILUS.

Tro. Ajax hath ta'en Æneas: shall it be?
No, by the flame of yonder glorious heaven,
He shall not carry him: I'll be ta'en too,
Or bring him off: fate, hear me what I say!
I reck not though I end my life to-day. *Exit.*

Enter one in armour.

Hect. Stand, stand, thou Greek; thou art a goodly mark:
No? wilt thou not? I like thy armour well;
I'll frush it and unlock the rivets all,
But I'll be master of it: wilt thou not, beast, abide?
Why, then fly on, I'll hunt thee for thy hide. *Exeunt.*

[SCENE VII. *Another part of the plains.*]

Enter ACHILLES, *with* Myrmidons.

Achil. Come here about me, you my Myrmidons;
Mark what I say. Attend me where I wheel:
Strike not a stroke, but keep yourselves in breath:
And when I have the bloody Hector found,
Empale him with your weapons round about;
In fellest manner execute your aims.
Follow me, sirs, and my proceedings eye:
It is decreed Hector the great must die. *Exeunt.*

Enter THERSITES; MENELAUS [*and*] PARIS [*fighting*].

Ther. The cuckold and the cuckold-maker are at it. Now, bull! now, dog! 'Loo, Paris, 'loo! now my double-horned Spartan! 'loo, Paris, 'loo! The bull has the game: ware horns, ho! *Exeunt Paris and Menelaus.*

Enter Bastard [MARGARELON].

Mar. Turn, slave, and fight.
Ther. What art thou?
Mar. A bastard son of Priam's.
Ther. I am a bastard too; I love bastards: I am a bastard begot, bastard instructed, bastard in mind, bastard in valour, in every thing illegitimate. One bear will not bite another, and wherefore should one bastard? Take heed, the quarrel 's most ominous to us: if the son of a whore fight for a whore, he tempts judgement: farewell, bastard. [*Exit.*]
Mar. The devil take thee, coward! *Exit.*

[SCENE VIII. *Another part of the plains.*]

Enter HECTOR.

Hect. Most putrefied core, so fair without,
Thy goodly armour thus hath cost thy life.
Now is my day's work done; I'll take good breath:
Rest, sword; thou hast thy fill of blood and death.
[*Puts off his helmet and hangs his shield behind him.*]

Enter ACHILLES *and* Myrmidons.

Achil. Look, Hector, how the sun begins to set;
How ugly night comes breathing at his heels:
Even with the vail and dark'ning of the sun,
To close the day up, Hector's life is done.
Hect. I am unarm'd; forego this vantage, Greek.
Achil. Strike, fellows, strike; this is the man I seek. [*Hector falls.*]
So, Ilion, fall thou next! now, Troy, sink down!
Here lies thy heart, thy sinews, and thy bone.
On, Myrmidons, and cry you all amain,
'Achilles hath the mighty Hector slain.' *Retreat* [*sounded*].
Hark! a retire upon our Grecian part.
Myr. The Troyan trumpets sound the like, my lord.
Achil. The dragon wing of night o'erspreads the earth,
And, stickler-like, the armies separates.
My half-supp'd sword, that frankly would have fed,
Pleas'd with this dainty bait, thus goes to bed. [*Sheathes his sword.*]
Come, tie his body to my horse's tail;
Along the field I will the Troyan trail. *Exeunt.*

[SCENE IX. *Another part of the plains.*]

Enter AGAMEMNON, AJAX, MENELAUS, NESTOR, DIOMEDES, *and the rest, marching.* [*Shouts within.*]

Agam. Hark! Hark! what shout is that?
Nest. Peace, drums!
Sold. (*Within*) Achilles! Achilles! Hector 's slain! Achilles!
Dio. The bruit is, Hector 's slain, and by Achilles.

third century B.C. **beam,** sword. 14. **Sagittary,** literally, the archer; a centaur, i.e., a monster half man, half horse, who according to medieval legends fought in the Trojan War against the Greeks. 22. **sculls,** schools (of fish). 40. **forceless care,** easy dexterity (Deighton). 45. **boy-queller,** boy killer; i.e., he has slain Patroclus.
SCENE VI. 11. **cogging,** deceitful. 29. **frush,** bruise.

SCENE VII. 10. **'Loo,** cry to incite dogs to the chase. 11. **double-horned,** cuckolded and bull-like. 12. **has the game,** wins.
SCENE VIII. 18. **stickler-like,** like an umpire.

Ajax. If it be so, yet bragless let it be;
Great Hector was a man as good as he.
Agam. March patiently along: let one be sent
To pray Achilles see us at our tent.
If in his death the gods have us befriended,
Great Troy is ours, and our sharp wars are ended.
Exeunt.

[SCENE X. *Another part of the plains.*]

Enter ÆNEAS, PARIS, ANTENOR, [*and*] DEIPHOBUS.

Æne. Stand, ho! yet are we masters of the field:
Never go home; here starve we out the night.

Enter TROILUS.

Tro. Hector is slain.
All. Hector! the gods forbid!
Tro. He 's dead; and at the murderer's horse's tail,
In beastly sort, dragg'd through the shameful field.
Frown on, you heavens, effect your rage with speed!
Sit, gods, upon your thrones, and smile at Troy!
I say, at once let your brief plagues be mercy,
And linger not our sure destructions on!
Æne. My lord, you do discomfort all the host.
Tro. You understand me not that tell me so:
I do not speak of flight, of fear, of death,
But dare all imminence that gods and men
Address their dangers in. Hector is gone:
Who shall tell Priam so, or Hecuba?
Let him that will a screech-owl aye be call'd,
Go in to Troy, and say there, Hector 's dead:
There is a word will Priam turn to stone;
Make wells and Niobes of the maids and wives,
Cold statues of the youth, and, in a word,
Scare Troy out of itself. But, march away:
Hector is dead; there is no more to say.
Stay yet. You vile abominable tents,
Thus proudly pight upon our Phrygian plains,
Let Titan rise as early as he dare.
I'll through and through you! and, thou great-siz'd coward,
No space of earth shall sunder our two hates:
I'll haunt thee like a wicked conscience still,
That mouldeth goblins swift as frenzy's thoughts.
Strike a free march to Troy! with comfort go:
Hope of revenge shall hide our inward woe.
[*Exeunt Æneas and Trojans.*

Enter PANDARUS.

Pan. But hear you, hear you!
Tro. Hence, broker-lackey! ignomy and shame
Pursue thy life, and live aye with thy name!
Exeunt all but Pandarus.

Pan. A goodly medicine for my aching bones! O world! world! world! thus is the poor agent despised! O traitors and bawds, how earnestly are you set a-work, and how ill requited! why should our endeavour be so loved and the performance so loathed? what verse for it? what instance for it? Let me see:

Full merrily the humble-bee doth sing,
Till he hath lost his honey and his sting;
And being once subdu'd in armed tail,
Sweet honey and sweet notes together fail.

Good traders in the flesh, set this in your painted cloths.

As many as be here of pandar's hall,
Your eyes, half out, weep out at Pandar's fall;
Or if you cannot weep, yet give some groans,
Though not for me, yet for your aching bones.
Brethren and sisters of the hold-door trade,
Some two months hence my will shall here be made:
It should be now, but that my fear is this,
Some galled goose of Winchester would hiss:
Till then I'll sweat and seek about for eases,
And at that time bequeathe you my diseases. [*Exit.*]

SCENE IX. 5. **bragless,** without gloating.
SCENE X. 13. **imminence,** impending evil. 16. **screech-owl,** traditional prognosticator of death. 19. **Niobes.** Niobe boasted that her six sons and six daughters made her superior to Latona, mother of Apollo and Diana, for which she was punished by seeing them put to death by the arrows of these two deities. While weeping she was changed into a stone, but her tears continued to flow from the rock. 24. **pight,** pitched. 28. **conscience,** almost synonymous with imagination; it carries the double suggestion that the sense of guilt makes the imagination conjure up goblins. 34. **live . . . name.** Cf. III, ii, 208-210. 46. **your painted cloths,** hangings worked or painted with designs. 52. **hold-door trade,** prostitution. 55. **galled . . . Winchester,** one having a venereal disease; so called because the brothels of Southwark were under the jurisdiction of the bishop of Winchester.

HAMLET, PRINCE OF DENMARK

A recurring motif in *Hamlet* is of a seemingly healthy exterior concealing inward sickness. Mere pretense of virtue, as Hamlet warns his mother, "will but skin and film the ulcerous place, Whiles rank corruption, mining all within, Infects unseen" (III,iv). His mother's shameful deed "takes off the rose From the fair forehead of an innocent love And sets a blister there." Polonius confesses, when he is about to use his daughter as a decoy for Hamlet, that "with devotion's visage And pious action we do sugar o'er The devil himself"; and his observation elicits a more anguished *mea culpa* from Claudius in an aside: "How smart a lash that speech doth give my conscience! The harlot's cheek, beautied with plast'ring art, Is not more ugly to the thing that helps it Than is my deed to my most painted word" (III,i).

This motif of concealed evil and disease continually reminds us that, in both a specific and a broader sense, "Something is rotten in the state of Denmark." The specific source of contamination is a poison: the poison with which Claudius has killed Hamlet Senior, the poison in the players' version of this same murder, and the two poisons (envenomed sword and poisoned drink) with which Claudius and Laertes plot to rid themselves of young Hamlet. More generally, the poison is man's evil nature seeking to destroy his better nature, as in the archetypal murder of Abel by Cain. "O my offence is rank, it smells to heaven," laments Claudius, "It hath the primal curse upon 't, A brother's murther" (III,iii). Hamlet Senior and Claudius typify what is best and worst in man, the sun-god Hyperion compared to a satyr. Claudius is a "serpent" and a "mildew'd ear Blasting his wholesome brother" (III,iv). Too many men, finding this quality in themselves, are perversely drawn in spite of their better qualities to "some vicious mole of nature" in themselves over which they have no control. "Their virtues else—be they as pure as grace, As infinite as man may undergo—Shall in the general censure take corruption From that particular fault." The "dram of evil" pollutes "all the noble substance" (I,iv). Thus poison spreads outward to infect individual men, just as bad men can infect an entire court or nation.

Hamlet, his mind attuned to philosophical matters, is keenly and poetically aware of man's fallen condition. He is, moreover, a shrewd observer of the Danish court, one familiar with its ways and at the same time newly returned from abroad, looking at Denmark with a stranger's eyes. What particularly darkens his view of man, however, is not so much the general condition of mankind as Hamlet's knowledge of a dreadful secret. Even before he learns of his father's murder, Hamlet senses that something is more deeply amiss than his mother's overhasty marriage to her deceased husband's brother. This is serious enough, to be sure, for it violates a widely held taboo (parallel to the marriage of a widower to his deceased wife's sister, long regarded as incestuous by the English), and is thus accurately referred to as "incest" by Hamlet and his father's ghost. The appalling spectacle of Gertrude's "wicked speed, to post With such dexterity to incestuous sheets" overwhelms Hamlet with revulsion at carnal appetite and greatly intensifies the emotional crisis any son goes through when forced to contemplate his father's death and mother's remarriage. Still, the Ghost's revelation is of something far worse, something Hamlet has subconsciously feared and suspected. "O my prophetic soul! My uncle!" Now Hamlet has confirming evidence for his intuition that the world itself is "an unweeded garden That grows to seed; things rank and gross in nature Possess it merely" (I,ii).

Something is indeed rotten in the state of Denmark. The monarch on whom the health and safety of the kingdom should depend is the perpetrator of a lie and an unspeakable crime. Yet few persons know his secret: Hamlet, Horatio only belatedly, Claudius himself, and ourselves as audience. Many ironies and misunderstandings of the play cannot be understood without a proper awareness of this gap between Hamlet's knowledge and most others' ignorance of the murder. For, according to their own lights, Polonius and the rest behave as courtiers normally behave, obeying and flattering a king whom they acknowledge their legitimate ruler. Hamlet, for his part, is so obsessed with the secret murder that he overreacts to those around him, rejecting well-meant overtures of friendship and becoming embittered, callous, brutal, and even violent. His antisocial behavior gives the others good reason to fear him as a menace to the state. Nevertheless, we share with Hamlet a knowledge of the truth, and know that he is right whereas the others are at best unhappily deceived by their own blind complicity in evil.

Rosencrantz and Guildenstern, for instance, are boyhood friends of Hamlet but are now dependent on the favor of King Claudius. Despite their seeming concern for their onetime comrade, and Hamlet's initial pleasure in receiving them, they are faceless courtiers whose very names, like their personalities, are virtually interchangeable. "Thanks, Rosencrantz and gentle Guildenstern," says the king, and "Thanks, Guildenstern and gentle Rosencrantz" echoes the queen (II,ii). They cannot understand why Hamlet increasingly mocks their overtures of friendship, whereas Hamlet cannot stomach their subservience to the king. The secret murder divides Hamlet from them, since only he knows of it. As the confrontation between Hamlet and Claudius grows more deadly, Rosencrantz and Guildenstern, not knowing the true cause, can only interpret Hamlet's behavior as dangerous madness. The wild display he puts on at the players' performance, and the killing of Polonius, are evidence of a treasonous threat to the crown, eliciting from them staunch assertions of the

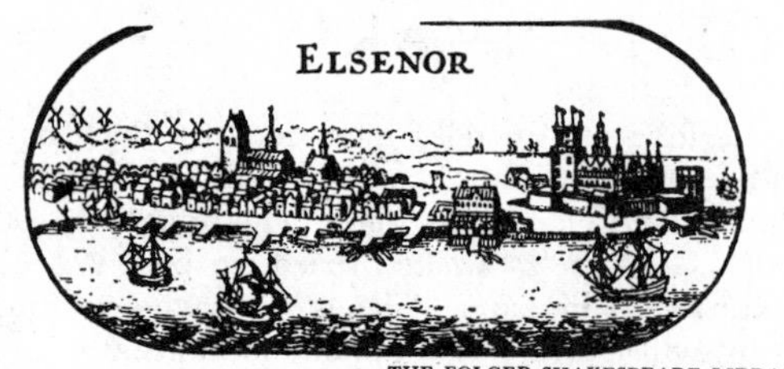

Elsinore, the Danish seaport and castle, scene of Hamlet.

divine right of kings. "Most holy and religious fear it is To keep those many many bodies safe That live and feed upon your majesty," professes Guildenstern, and Rosencrantz reiterates the theme: "The cess of majesty Dies not alone; but, like a gulf, doth draw What's near it with it" (III,iii). These sentiments of Elizabethan orthodoxy, which would pass for true current in Shakespeare's history plays, are here undercut by a devastating irony, since they are spoken unwittingly in defense of a murderer. This irony pursues Rosencrantz and Guildenstern to their graves, for they are killed performing what they see as their duty to convey Hamlet safely to England. They are as ignorant of Claudius' secret orders for the murder of Hamlet in England as they are of Claudius' real reason for wishing to be rid of his stepson. That Hamlet should ingeniously remove the secret commission from Rosencrantz and Guildenstern's packet and substitute an order for their execution is ironically fitting, even though they are guiltless of having plotted Hamlet's death. "Why, man, they did make love to this employment," says Hamlet to Horatio. "They are not near my conscience; their defeat Does by their own insinuation grow" (V,ii). In other words, they have condemned themselves by officiously interceding in deadly affairs of which they had no comprehension.

Polonius too must die for meddling. It seems a harsh fate, since he too wishes no physical harm to Hamlet, and is only trying to ingratiate himself with Claudius. Yet Polonius' complicity in jaded court politics is more deep than his fatuous parental sententiousness might lead one to suppose. His famous advice to his son, often quoted out of context as though it were wise counsel, is in fact a worldly gospel of self-interest and concern for appearances. Like his son Laertes he cynically presumes that Hamlet's affection for Ophelia cannot be serious, since princes are not free to marry ladies of the court; accordingly, Polonius obliges his daughter to return the love letters she so cherishes. Polonius' spies are everywhere, seeking to entrap Polonius' own son in fleshly sin or to discover symptoms of Hamlet's presumed lovesickness. Polonius cuts a ridiculous figure as a prattling busybody, but he has actually helped Claudius to the throne and is an essential instrument of royal policy. His ineffectuality and lack of knowledge of the murder do not really lessen the degree of his guilty involvement.

Ophelia is more innocent than her father and brother, and more truly affectionate toward Hamlet. Nevertheless her pitiable story suggests that weak-willed acquiescence becomes poisoned by the evil to which it surrenders. Ophelia is much like Gertrude, who has yielded to Claudius' importunity without ever knowing fully what awful price Claudius has paid for her and for the throne. The resemblance between Ophelia and Gertrude confirms Hamlet's tendency to generalize about feminine weakness—"Frailty, thy name is woman"—and prompts his misogynistic outburst against Ophelia when he realizes she too is spying on him. His rejection of love and friendship (except for Horatio's) seems paranoid in character, and yet is at least partially justified by the fact that so many of the court are in fact conspiring to learn his secret.

It is their oversimplification of his dilemma and their facile analyses that vex Hamlet as much as the meddling. When they presume to diagnose his malady, the courtiers actually reveal more about themselves than about Hamlet. Rosencrantz and Guildenstern think in political terms reflecting their own ambitious natures, and Hamlet takes mordant delight in leading them on. "Sir, I lack advancement," he mockingly answers Rosencrantz' questioning as to the cause of his distemper. Rosencrantz is immediately taken in: "How can that be, when you have the voice of the king himself for your succession in Denmark?" (III,ii). Actually Hamlet does hold a grudge against Claudius for having "Popp'd in between th' election and my hopes" (V,ii), using the Danish custom of "election" by the chief lords of the realm to deprive young Hamlet of the succession that would normally have been his. Nevertheless, it is a gross oversimplification to suppose that political frustration is the key to Hamlet's sorrow. To speculate thus is more presumptuous than to attempt playing the recorder without having studied that musical instrument. "Why, look you now, how unworthy a thing you would make of me!" Hamlet protests to Rosencrantz and Guildenstern. "You would play upon me; you would seem to know my stops; you would pluck out the heart of my mystery" (III,ii). Yet the worst offender in such distortion of complex truth is Polonius, whose diagnosis of lovesickness appears to have been inspired by recollections of Polonius' own far-off youth. ("Truly in my youth I suffered much extremity for love; very near this," II,ii). Polonius' incredibly fatuous complacency in his own powers of analysis—"If circumstances lead me, I will find Where truth is hid, though it were hid indeed Within the centre"—reads like a parody of Hamlet's struggle to discover what is true and what is not.

Thus, although Hamlet may seem to react with excessive bitterness toward those who are set to watch over him, the corruption he decries in Denmark is both real and universal. "The time is out of joint," he laments. "O cursed spite That ever I was born to set it right!" (I,v). How is he to proceed in setting things right? Ever since the nineteenth century it has been fashionable to discover reasons for Hamlet's delaying in revenge. The basic Romantic approach is to find a defect, or tragic flaw, in Hamlet himself. In Coleridge's words, Hamlet suffers from "an overbalance in the contemplative faculty," and is "one who vacillates from sensibility and procrastinates from thought, and loses the power of action in the energy of resolve." More recent psychological interpretations, like that of Freud's disciple, Ernest Jones, are still Romantic in character in that they too seek to explain Hamlet's failure of will. In Jones' interpretation, Hamlet is the victim of an Oedipal trauma; he has longed unconsciously to possess his mother, but cannot bring himself to punish the hated uncle who has supplanted him in his incestuous and forbidden desire. Such interpretations suggest at least that Hamlet continues to serve as a mirror in which analysts who would pluck out the heart of his mystery see an image of themselves—just as Rosencrantz and Guildenstern read politics, and Polonius lovesickness, into Hamlet's distress.

We must ask, however, not only whether the answers to Hamlet's supposed delay are valid but whether the question being asked is itself valid. Is the delay unnecessary or excessive? The question did not even arise until the nineteenth century. Earlier audiences were evidently satisfied that Hamlet must test the Ghost's credibility, since apparitions can tell half-truths to deceive men, and that once Hamlet has confirmed the Ghost's word he proceeds as resolutely as his canny adversary allows. More recent criticism, perhaps reflecting a modern absorption in existentialist philosophy, has proposed that Hamlet's dilemma of action is not a matter of personal failure but of the absurdity of action itself in a corrupt world. Does what Hamlet is asked to do make any sense, given the bestial nature of man and the impossibility of knowing what is right? In part it is a matter of style: Claudius' Denmark is crassly vulgar, and to combat this vulgarity on its own terms seems to require the sort of bad histrionics Hamlet derides in actors who mouth their lines or tear a passion to tatters. Hamlet's dilemma of action can best be studied in the play by comparing him with various characters who are obliged to act in situations similar to his own, and who respond in meaningfully different ways.

Three young men—Hamlet, Laertes, and Fortinbras—are called upon to avenge their fathers' violent deaths. Ophelia too has lost a father by violent means, and her madness and death are another kind of reaction to such a loss. The responses of Laertes and Fortinbras offer implicit object lessons to Hamlet, and in both cases the lesson seems to be the futility of positive and forceful action. Laertes thinks he has received an unambiguous mandate to revenge, since Hamlet has undoubtedly slain Polonius and helped to deprive Ophelia of her sanity. Accordingly Laertes comes back to Denmark in a fury, stirring the rabble to an insurrectionist mood with his demagoguery and spouting Senecan rant about dismissing conscience "to the profoundest pit" in his quest for vengeance (IV,v). When Claudius asks what Laertes would do to Hamlet "To show yourself your father's son in deed More than in words," Laertes fires back: "To cut his throat i' th' church!" (IV,vii). This resolution is wholly understandable. The pity is, however, that Laertes has only superficially identified the murderer in the case. He is too easily deceived by Claudius because he has jumped to easy and fallacious conclusions, and so is doomed to become a pawn in Claudius' sly maneuverings. Too late he sees his error and must die for it, begging and receiving Hamlet's forgiveness. Before we accuse Hamlet of thinking too deliberately before acting, we must consider that Laertes has not thought enough.

Fortinbras of Norway, as his name implies ("strong in arms"), is one who believes in decisive action. At the play's beginning we learn that his father has been slain in battle by old Hamlet, and that Fortinbras has collected an army to win back by force the territory fairly won by the Danes in that encounter. Like Hamlet, young Fortinbras does not succeed his father to the throne, but must now contend with an uncle-king. When this uncle, at Claudius' instigation, forbids Fortinbras to march against the Danes, and rewards him for his restraint with a huge annual income and a commission to fight the Poles instead, Fortinbras cannily embraces the new opportunity. He pockets the money, marches against Poland, and waits for occasion to deliver Denmark as well into his hands. Clearly this is more of a success story than that of Laertes, and Hamlet does after all give his blessing to the "election" of Fortinbras to the Danish throne. Fortinbras is the man of the hour, the representative of a restored political stability. Yet Hamlet's admiration for this man on horseback is qualified by a profound ironic reservation. The spectacle of Fortinbras marching against Poland "to gain a little patch of ground That hath in it no profit but the name" prompts Hamlet to berate himself for inaction, but he cannot ignore the absurdity of the effort. "Two thousand souls and twenty thousand ducats Will not debate the question of this straw." The soldiers will risk their very lives "Even for an egg-shell" (IV,iv). It is only one step from this view of the vanity of ambitious striving to the speculation that great Caesar or Alexander, dead and turned to dust, may one day produce the loam or clay with which to stop the bunghole of a beer barrel. Fortinbras epitomizes the ongoing political order after Hamlet's death, but is that order of any consequence to us after we have experienced with Hamlet the futility of all human endeavor?

To ask such a question is to seek more passive or self-abnegating answers to the riddle of life, and Hamlet is much attuned to such inquiries. Even before he learns of his father's murder he meditates on suicide, wishing "that the Everlasting had not fix'd His canon 'gainst self-slaughter" (I,ii). Once again, as with the alternative of action, other characters serve as foils to Hamlet, revealing both the attractions and perils of withdrawal. Ophelia is destroyed by meekly acquiescing in others' desires. Whether she commits suicide is uncertain, but the very possibility reminds us that Hamlet has considered and reluctantly rejected this despairing path as forbidden by Christian teaching. He has also playacted at the madness to which Ophelia succumbs. Gertrude identifies herself with Ophelia, and like her has surrendered her will to male importunity. We suspect she knows little of the actual murder but dares not think how deeply she may be implicated. Her death may possibly be a suicide also, one of atonement. A more attractive alternative to action for Hamlet is acting, and he is full of advice to the visiting players. Yet playacting is, he recognizes, an escape for him, a way of unpacking his heart with words, of narcissistically verbalizing his situation without doing something to remedy it. Acting and talking remind him too much of Polonius, who was an actor in his youth and who continues to be, like Hamlet, an inveterate punster.

Of the passive responses in the play, the stoicism of Horatio is by far the most attractive to Hamlet. "More an antique Roman than a Dane," Horatio is, as Hamlet praises him, immune to flattering or to opportunities for cheap self-advancement. He is "As one, in suff'ring all, that suffers nothing, A man that fortune's buffets and rewards Hast ta'en with equal thanks" (III,ii). Such a person has a sure defense against the worst that life can offer. Hamlet can trust and love Horatio as he can no one else. Yet even here there are limits, for Horatio's skeptical and Roman philosophy cuts him off from a Christian and metaphysical overview. "There are more things in heaven and earth, Horatio, Than are dreamt of in your philosophy" (I,v). After they have beheld together the skulls of Yorick's graveyard, Horatio cannot share with Hamlet the exulting Christian perception that, although human life is indeed vain, providence will reveal a pattern transcending human sorrow.

Hamlet's path must lie somehow between the rash suddenness of Laertes or the astute *realpolitik* of Fortinbras on the one hand, and the passivity of Ophelia or Gertrude and the stoic resignation of Horatio on the other. Accordingly, he alternates between action and inaction in his attempts to fulfill his mission, finding neither satisfactory. The Ghost has commanded Hamlet to revenge, but has not explained how this is to be done; indeed, Gertrude is to be left passively to heaven and her conscience. If this method will suffice for her (and Christian wisdom taught that such a purgation was as thorough as it was sure), why not for Claudius? If Claudius must be killed, should it be while he is at his sin rather than at his prayers? The play is full of questions, stemming chiefly from the enigmatic commands of the Ghost. "Say, why is this? wherefore? what should we do?" (I,iv). Hamlet is not incapable of action; he shows unusual strength and cunning on the pirate ship, or in his duel with Laertes ("I shall win at the odds"), or especially in his slaying of Polonius. Here is forthright action of the sort Laertes espouses. Yet when the corpse behind his mother's arras turns out to be Polonius rather than Claudius, Hamlet knows he has offended heaven. Even if Polonius deserves what he got, Hamlet has made himself into a cruel "scourge" of providence who must accordingly suffer retribution as well as deal it out. Inconsiderate action has not accomplished what the Ghost commanded.

The Ghost in fact does not appear to speak for providence. His message is of revenge, a pagan concept basic to all primitive societies but at odds with Christian teaching. His wish that Claudius be sent to hell and that Gertrude be more gently treated is not the judgment of an impartial deity but the emotional reaction of a murdered man's restless spirit. This is not to say that Hamlet is being tempted to perform a damnable act, as he fears possible, but that the Ghost's command cannot readily be reconciled with a complex and balanced view of justice. If Hamlet were to spring on Claudius in the fullness of his vice and cut his throat, we would pronounce Hamlet a murderer. What Hamlet learns instead is that he must become the instrument of providence according to *its* plans, not his own. After his return from England, he senses triumphantly that all will be for the best if he allows providence to decide the time and place for his final act. Under these conditions, rash action will be right. "Prais'd be rashness for it, let us know, Our indiscretion sometime serves us well, When our deep plots do pall: and that should teach us There 's a divinity that shapes our ends, Rough-hew them how we will" (V,ii). Passivity too is now a proper course, for Hamlet puts himself wholly at the disposal of providence. What had seemed so impossible when Hamlet tried to formulate his own design now proves elementary once he trusts to heaven's justice. Rashness and passivity are perfectly fused. Hamlet is revenged without having to commit premeditated murder, and is relieved of his painful existence without having to commit suicide.

Providence does indeed accomplish all that Hamlet desires, by a route so circuitous that no man could ever have foreseen or devised it. Polonius' death, as it turns out, was instrumental after all, for it led to Laertes' angry return to Denmark and the challenge to a duel. Every seemingly unrelated event has its place; "There 's a special providence in the fall of a sparrow." Repeatedly the characters stress the role of seeming accident leading to just retribution. Horatio sums up a pattern "Of accidental judgements, casual slaughters . . . And, in this upshot, purposes mistook Fall'n on th' inventors' heads." Laertes confesses himself "a woodcock to mine own springe." As Hamlet had said earlier, of Rosencrantz and Guildenstern, " 'tis the sport to have the enginer Hoist with his own petar" (III,iv). Thus, too, Claudius' poisoned cup, intended for Hamlet, kills the queen for whom Claudius had done such evil.

Divine justice has supplanted all human agencies

of revenge. Yet in its origins *Hamlet* is a revenge story, and these traditions have left some residual savagery in the play. In the *Historia Danica* of Saxo Grammaticus, 1180–1208, and in the rather free translation of Saxo into French by Belleforest, *Histoires Tragiques* (1576), Hamlet is cunning and bloodily resolute throughout. He kills an eavesdropper without a qualm during the interview with his mother, and exchanges letters on his way to England with characteristic shrewdness. Ultimately he returns to Denmark, sets fire to his uncle's hall, slays its courtly inhabitants, and claims his rightful throne from a grateful people. The Ghost, absent in this account, may well have been supplied by Thomas Kyd, author of *The Spanish Tragedy* (c. 1587) and seemingly of a lost *Hamlet* play in existence by 1589. The extant *Spanish Tragedy* bears many resemblances to our *Hamlet*, and suggests what the lost *Hamlet* may well have contained: a sensational murder, a Senecan Ghost demanding revenge, the avenger hampered by court intrigue, his resort to a feigned madness, his difficulty in authenticating the ghostly vision. A German version of *Hamlet*, called *Der bestrafte Brudermord* (1710), based seemingly on the older *Hamlet*, includes such details as the play within the play, the sparing of the king at his prayers in order to damn his soul, Ophelia's madness, the fencing match with poisoned swords and poisoned drink, and the final catastrophe of vengeance and death. Similarly, the early pirated first quarto of *Hamlet* (1603) offers some passages seemingly based on the older play by Kyd.

Although this evidence suggests that Shakespeare received most of his plot material intact, his transformation of that material was nonetheless immeasurable. To be sure, Kyd's *Spanish Tragedy* contains many rhetorical passages on the inadequacy of human justice, but the overall effect is still sensational and the outcome is a triumph for the pagan spirit of revenge. So too in general with the many revenge plays of the 1590's and 1600's which Kyd's dramatic genius had inspired, including Shakespeare's own *Titus Andronicus* (c. 1589–1591). *Hamlet*, written in about 1599–1601 (it is not mentioned by Frances Meres in 1598, and was entered in the Stationers' Register in 1602), is unparalleled in its philosophical richness. Its ending is truly cathartic, for Hamlet dies not as a bloodied avenger but as one who has affirmed the tragic dignity of man. His courage and faith, maintained in the face of great odds, atone for the dismal corruption in which Denmark has festered. His resolutely honest inquiries have taken him beyond the revulsion and doubt that express so eloquently, among other matters, the fearful response of Shakespeare's own generation to a seeming breakdown of established political, theological, and astronomical values. Hamlet finally perceives that "if it be not now, yet it will come," and that "the readiness is all" (V,ii). His discovery in no way denies the tragic circumstance of life, but does provide a philosophic consolation by which man may rise above despair.

HAMLET, PRINCE OF DENMARK

[*Dramatis Personae*

Claudius, King of Denmark.
Hamlet, *son to the late, and nephew to the present king.*
Polonius, *lord chamberlain.*
Horatio, *friend to Hamlet.*
Laertes, *son to Polonius.*
Voltimand,
Cornelius,
Rosencrantz,
Guildenstern,
Osric,
A Gentleman, } *courtiers.*
A Priest.
Marcellus,
Bernardo, } *officers.*
Francisco, *a soldier.*
Reynaldo, *servant to Polonius.*
Players.
Two Clowns, *grave-diggers.*
Fortinbras, Prince of Norway.
A Captain.
English Ambassadors.

Gertrude, Queen of Denmark, *and mother to Hamlet.*
Ophelia, *daughter to Polonius.*

Lords, Ladies, Officers, Soldiers, Sailors, Messengers, *and other* Attendants.
Ghost of Hamlet's Father.

Scene: *Denmark.*]

[ACT I.

SCENE I. *Elsinore. A platform before the castle.*]

Enter Bernardo *and* Francisco, *two sentinals.*

Ber. Who 's there?
Fran. Nay, answer me: stand, and unfold yourself.
Ber. Long live the king!
Fran. Bernardo?
Ber. He.
Fran. You come most carefully upon your hour.
Ber. 'Tis now struck twelve; get thee to bed, Francisco.
Fran. For this relief much thanks: 'tis bitter cold,
And I am sick at heart.
Ber. Have you had quiet guard?
Fran. Not a mouse stirring.
Ber. Well, good night.
If you do meet Horatio and Marcellus,
The rivals of my watch, bid them make haste.

Enter Horatio *and* Marcellus.

Fran. I think I hear them. Stand, ho! Who is there?
Hor. Friends to this ground.

Mar. And liegemen to the Dane.
Fran. Give you good night.
Mar. O, farewell, honest soldier:
Who hath reliev'd you?
Fran. Bernardo hath my place.
Give you good night. *Exit Fran.*
Mar. Holla! Bernardo!
Ber. Say,
What, is Horatio there?
Hor. A piece of him.
Ber. Welcome, Horatio: welcome, good Marcellus.
Mar. What, has this thing appear'd again to-night?
Ber. I have seen nothing.
Mar. Horatio says 'tis but our fantasy,
And will not let belief take hold of him
Touching this dreaded sight, twice seen of us:
Therefore I have entreated him along
With us to watch the minutes of this night;
That if again this apparition come,
He may approve our eyes and speak to it.
Hor. Tush, tush, 'twill not appear.
Ber. Sit down awhile;
And let us once again assail your ears,
That are so fortified against our story
What we have two nights seen.
Hor. Well, sit we down,
And let us hear Bernardo speak of this.
Ber. Last night of all,
When yond same star that 's westward from the pole
Had made his course t' illume that part of heaven
Where now it burns, Marcellus and myself,
The bell then beating one,—

Enter Ghost.

Mar. Peace, break thee off; look, where it comes again!
Ber. In the same figure, like the king that 's dead.
Mar. Thou art a scholar; speak to it, Horatio.
Ber. Looks 'a not like the king? mark it, Horatio.
Hor. Most like: it harrows me with fear and wonder.
Ber. It would be spoke to.
Mar. Speak to it, Horatio.
Hor. What art thou that usurp'st this time of night,
Together with that fair and warlike form
In which the majesty of buried Denmark
Did sometimes march? by heaven I charge thee, speak!
Mar. It is offended.
Ber. See, it stalks away!
Hor. Stay! speak, speak! I charge thee, speak!
Exit Ghost.
Mar. 'Tis gone, and will not answer.
Ber. How now, Horatio! you tremble and look pale:
Is not this something more than fantasy?
What think you on 't?
Hor. Before my God, I might not this believe
Without the sensible and true avouch
Of mine own eyes.
Mar. Is it not like the king?
Hor. As thou art to thyself:
Such was the very armour he had on
When he the ambitious Norway combated;
So frown'd he once, when, in an angry parle,
He smote the sledded Polacks on the ice.
'Tis strange.
Mar. Thus twice before, and jump at this dead hour,
With martial stalk hath he gone by our watch.
Hor. In what particular thought to work I know not;
But in the gross and scope of my opinion,
This bodes some strange eruption to our state.
Mar. Good now, sit down, and tell me, he that knows,
Why this same strict and most observant watch
So nightly toils the subject of the land,
And why such daily cast of brazen cannon,
And foreign mart for implements of war;
Why such impress of shipwrights, whose sore task
Does not divide the Sunday from the week;
What might be toward, that this sweaty haste
Doth make the night joint-labourer with the day:
Who is 't that can inform me?
Hor. That can I;
At least, the whisper goes so. Our last king,
Whose image even but now appear'd to us,
Was, as you know, by Fortinbras of Norway,
Thereto prick'd on by a most emulate pride,
Dar'd to the combat; in which our valiant Hamlet—
For so this side of our known world esteem'd him—
Did slay this Fortinbras; who, by a seal'd compact,
Well ratified by law and heraldry,
Did forfeit, with his life, all those his lands
Which he stood seiz'd of, to the conqueror:
Against the which, a moiety competent
Was gaged by our king; which had return'd
To the inheritance of Fortinbras,
Had he been vanquisher; as, by the same comart,
And carriage of the article design'd,
His fell to Hamlet. Now, sir, young Fortinbras,
Of unimproved mettle hot and full,
Hath in the skirts of Norway here and there
Shark'd up a list of lawless resolutes,
For food and diet, to some enterprise
That hath a stomach in 't; which is no other—
As it doth well appear unto our state—
But to recover of us, by strong hand
And terms compulsatory, those foresaid lands
So by his father lost: and this, I take it,
Is the main motive of our preparations,
The source of this our watch and the chief head
Of this post-haste and romage in the land.
Ber. I think it be no other but e'en so:

ACT I. SCENE I. *Stage Direction:* **platform,** a level space on the battlements of the royal castle at Elsinore, a Danish seaport; now Helsingör. 2. **me.** This is emphatic, since Francisco is the sentry. 3. **Long live the king,** either a password or greeting; Horatio and Marcellus use a different one in line 15. 13. **rivals,** partners. 16. **Give you,** God give you. 29. **approve,** corroborate. 36. **pole,** polestar. 42. **scholar.** Exorcisms were performed in Latin, which Horatio as an educated man would be able to speak. 44. **harrows,** lacerates the feelings. 45. **It . . . to.** A ghost could not speak until spoken to. 48. **buried Denmark,** the buried King of Denmark. 63. **smote,** defeated. **sledded Polacks,** Polanders using sledges. The Earl of Rochester (1761) explained *sleaded* (Q_1F) or *sledded* (Q_2) as "loaded with lead" and *pollax* ($Q_{1,2}$F) as "pole-ax," the idea being that the elder Hamlet dashed his pole-ax against the ice while engaged in a parley; this is upheld by Schmidt and others. 65. **jump,** exactly. 68. **gross and scope,** general drift. 70. **Good now,** an expression denoting entreaty or expostulation. 72. **toils,** causes or makes to toil. **subject,** people, subjects. 73. **cast,** casting, founding. 74. **mart,** buying and selling, traffic. 75. **impress,** impressment. 83. **prick'd on,** incited. **emulate,** rivaling. 87. **law and heraldry,** heraldic law, governing combat. 89. **seiz'd,** possessed. 90. **moiety competent,** adequate or sufficient portion. 93. **comart,** joint bargain. 94. **carriage,** import, bearing. 96. **unimproved,** not turned to account. **hot and full,** full of fight. 98. **Shark'd up,** got together in haphazard fashion. **resolutes,** desperadoes. 99. **food and diet,** no

Well may it sort that this portentous figure
Comes armed through our watch; so like the king
That was and is the question of these wars.
Hor. A mote it is to trouble the mind's eye.
In the most high and palmy state of Rome,
A little ere the mightiest Julius fell,
The graves stood tenantless and the sheeted dead
Did squeak and gibber in the Roman streets:
†As stars with trains of fire and dews of blood,
Disasters in the sun; and the moist star
Upon whose influence Neptune's empire stands
Was sick almost to doomsday with eclipse:
And even the like precurse of fear'd events,
As harbingers preceding still the fates
And prologue to the omen coming on,
Have heaven and earth together demonstrated
Unto our climatures and countrymen.—

Enter Ghost.

But soft, behold! lo, where it comes again!
I'll cross it, though it blast me. Stay, illusion!
If thou hast any sound, or use of voice,
Speak to me! *It spreads his arms.*
If there be any good thing to be done,
That may to thee do ease and grace to me,
Speak to me!
If thou art privy to thy country's fate,
Which, happily, foreknowing may avoid,
O, speak!
Or if thou hast uphoarded in thy life
Extorted treasure in the womb of earth,
For which, they say, you spirits oft walk in death,
The cock crows.
Speak of it: stay, and speak! Stop it, Marcellus.
Mar. Shall I strike at it with my partisan?
Hor. Do, if it will not stand.
Ber. 'Tis here!
Hor. 'Tis here!
Mar. 'Tis gone! [*Exit Ghost.*]
We do it wrong, being so majestical,
To offer it the show of violence;
For it is, as the air, invulnerable,
And our vain blows malicious mockery.
Ber. It was about to speak, when the cock crew.
Hor. And then it started like a guilty thing
Upon a fearful summons. I have heard,
The cock, that is the trumpet to the morn,
Doth with his lofty and shrill-sounding throat
Awake the god of day; and, at his warning,
Whether in sea or fire, in earth or air,
Th' extravagant and erring spirit hies
To his confine: and of the truth herein
This present object made probation.
Mar. It faded on the crowing of the cock.
Some say that ever 'gainst that season comes
Wherein our Saviour's birth is celebrated,
The bird of dawning singeth all night long:
And then, they say, no spirit dare stir abroad;
The nights are wholesome; then no planets strike,
No fairy takes, nor witch hath power to charm,
So hallow'd and so gracious is that time.
Hor. So have I heard and do in part believe it.
But, look, the morn, in russet mantle clad,
Walks o'er the dew of yon high eastward hill:
Break we our watch up; and by my advice,
Let us impart what we have seen to-night
Unto young Hamlet; for, upon my life,
This spirit, dumb to us, will speak to him.
Do you consent we shall acquaint him with it,
As needful in our loves, fitting our duty?
Mar. Let 's do 't, I pray; and I this morning know
Where we shall find him most conveniently. *Exeunt.*

[SCENE II. *A room of state in the castle.*]

Flourish. Enter CLAUDIUS, KING OF DENMARK, GERTRUDE *the* QUEEN, Councilors, POLONIUS *and his Son* LAERTES, HAMLET, *cum aliis* [*including* VOLTIMAND *and* CORNELIUS].

King. Though yet of Hamlet our dear brother's death
The memory be green, and that it us befitted
To bear our hearts in grief and our whole kingdom
To be contracted in one brow of woe,
Yet so far hath discretion fought with nature
That we with wisest sorrow think on him,
Together with remembrance of ourselves.
Therefore our sometime sister, now our queen,
Th' imperial jointress to this warlike state,
Have we, as 'twere with a defeated joy,—
With an auspicious and a dropping eye,
With mirth in funeral and with dirge in marriage,
In equal scale weighing delight and dole,—
Taken to wife: nor have we herein barr'd
Your better wisdoms, which have freely gone
With this affair along. For all, our thanks.
Now follows, that you know, young Fortinbras,
Holding a weak supposal of our worth,
Or thinking by our late dear brother's death
Our state to be disjoint and out of frame,
Colleagued with this dream of his advantage,
He hath not fail'd to pester us with message,
Importing the surrender of those lands
Lost by his father, with all bands of law,
To our most valiant brother. So much for him.
Now for ourself and for this time of meeting:
Thus much the business is: we have here writ
To Norway, uncle of young Fortinbras,—
Who, impotent and bed-rid, scarcely hears
Of this his nephew's purpose,—to suppress
His further gait herein; in that the levies,
The lists and full proportions, are all made

pay but their keep. 107. **romage,** bustle, commotion. 109. **sort,** suit. 112. **mote,** speck of dust. 113. **palmy state,** triumphant sovereignty. 117. **stars . . . fire,** i.e., comets. 118. **Disasters,** unfavorable aspects. **moist star,** the moon, governing tides. 119. **Neptune's empire,** the sea. 120. **sick . . . doomsday.** See Matthew 24:20; Revelation 6:12. 121. **precurse,** heralding. **fear'd,** Collier: *feard;* Q_2: *feare;* Globe: *fierce,* after Q_4: *fearce.* 127. **cross,** meet, face; thus bringing down the evil influence on the person who crosses it. 129. *Stage Direction:* ***It,*** the Ghost, or perhaps Horatio. 133-139. **If . . . it.** Horatio recites the traditional reasons why ghosts might walk. 140. **partisan,** long-handled spear with a blade having lateral projections. 147. **cock crew.** According to traditional ghost lore, spirits returned to their confines at cockcrow.

154. **extravagant and erring,** wandering. Both words mean the same thing. 155. **confine,** place of confinement. 156. **probation,** proof, trial. 158. **'gainst,** just before. 162. **planets strike.** It was thought that planets were malignant and might strike travelers by night. 164. **gracious,** full of goodness.

SCENE II. *Stage Direction:* ***cum aliis,*** with others. 9. **jointress,** woman possessed of a jointure, or, joint tenancy of an estate. 17. **that,** that which. 18. **weak supposal,** low estimate. 20. **disjoint,** distracted, out of joint. **frame,** order. 21. **Colleagued,** added to. **dream . . . advantage,** visionary hope of success. 23. **Importing,** purporting, pertaining to. 31. **gait,** proceeding.

Out of his subject: and we here dispatch
You, good Cornelius, and you, Voltimand,
For bearers of this greeting to old Norway;
Giving to you no further personal power
To business with the king, more than the scope
Of these delated articles allow.
Farewell, and let your haste commend your duty.
Cor.
Vol. } In that and all things will we show our duty.
King. We doubt it nothing: heartily farewell.
[*Exeunt Voltimand and Cornelius.*]
And now, Laertes, what 's the news with you?
You told us of some suit; what is 't, Laertes?
You cannot speak of reason to the Dane,
And lose your voice: what wouldst thou beg, Laertes,
That shall not be my offer, not thy asking?
The head is not more native to the heart,
The hand more instrumental to the mouth,
Than is the throne of Denmark to thy father.
What wouldst thou have, Laertes?
Laer. My dread lord,
Your leave and favour to return to France;
From whence though willingly I came to Denmark,
To show my duty in your coronation,
Yet now, I must confess, that duty done,
My thoughts and wishes bend again toward France
And bow them to your gracious leave and pardon.
King. Have you your father's leave? What says Polonius?
Pol. He hath, my lord, wrung from me my slow leave
By laboursome petition, and at last
Upon his will I seal'd my hard consent:
I do beseech you, give him leave to go.
King. Take thy fair hour, Laertes; time be thine,
And thy best graces spend it at thy will!
But now, my cousin Hamlet, and my son,—
Ham. [*Aside*] A little more than kin, and less than kind.
King. How is it that the clouds still hang on you?
Ham. Not so, my lord; I am too much in the sun.
Queen. Good Hamlet, cast thy nighted colour off,
And let thine eye look like a friend on Denmark.
Do not for ever with thy vailed lids
Seek for thy noble father in the dust:
Thou know'st 'tis common; all that lives must die,
Passing through nature to eternity.
Ham. Ay, madam, it is common.
Queen. If it be,
Why seems it so particular with thee?
Ham. Seems, madam! nay, it is; I know not 'seems.'
'Tis not alone my inky cloak, good mother,
Nor customary suits of solemn black,
Nor windy suspiration of forc'd breath,
No, nor the fruitful river in the eye,
Nor the dejected 'haviour of the visage,
Together with all forms, moods, shapes of grief,
That can denote me truly: these indeed seem,
For they are actions that a man might play:
But I have that within which passeth show;
These but the trappings and the suits of woe.
King. 'Tis sweet and commendable in your nature, Hamlet,
To give these mourning duties to your father:
But, you must know, your father lost a father;
That father lost, lost his, and the survivor bound
In filial obligation for some term
To do obsequious sorrow: but to persever
In obstinate condolement is a course
Of impious stubbornness; 'tis unmanly grief;
It shows a will most incorrect to heaven,
A heart unfortified, a mind impatient,
An understanding simple and unschool'd:
For what we know must be and is as common
As any the most vulgar thing to sense,
Why should we in our peevish opposition
Take it to heart? Fie! 'tis a fault to heaven,
A fault against the dead, a fault to nature,
To reason most absurd; whose common theme
Is death of fathers, and who still hath cried,
From the first corse till he that died to-day,
'This must be so.' We pray you, throw to earth
This unprevailing woe, and think of us
As of a father: for let the world take note,
You are the most immediate to our throne;
And with no less nobility of love
Than that which dearest father bears his son,
Do I impart toward you. For your intent
In going back to school in Wittenberg,
It is most retrograde to our desire:
And we beseech you, bend you to remain
Here, in the cheer and comfort of our eye,
Our chiefest courtier, cousin, and our son.
Queen. Let not thy mother lose her prayers, Hamlet:
I pray thee, stay with us; go not to Wittenberg.
Ham. I shall in all my best obey you, madam.
King. Why, 'tis a loving and a fair reply:
Be as ourself in Denmark. Madam, come;
This gentle and unforc'd accord of Hamlet
Sits smiling to my heart: in grace whereof,
No jocund health that Denmark drinks to-day,
But the great cannon to the clouds shall tell,
And the king's rouse the heaven shall bruit again,
Re-speaking earthly thunder. Come away.
Flourish. Exeunt all but Hamlet.
Ham. O, that this too too sullied flesh would melt,
Thaw and resolve itself into a dew!
Or that the Everlasting had not fix'd
His canon 'gainst self-slaughter! O God! God!
How weary, stale, flat and unprofitable,
Seem to me all the uses of this world!
Fie on 't! ah fie! 'tis an unweeded garden,
That grows to seed; things rank and gross in nature
Possess it merely. That it should come to this!
But two months dead: nay, not so much, not two:
So excellent a king; that was, to this,

33. **Out of his subject,** at the expense of Norway's subjects (collectively). 38. **delated,** expressly stated. 44. **the Dane,** Danish king. 45. **lose your voice,** speak in vain. 47. **native,** closely connected, related. 48. **instrumental,** serviceable. 56. **leave and pardon,** permission to depart. 64. **cousin,** any kin not of the immediate family. 65. **A little . . . kind,** my relation to you has become more than kinship warrants; it has also become unnatural. 67. **I am . . . sun.** The senses seem to be: I am too much out of doors, I am too much in the sun of your grace (ironical), I am too much of a son to you. Johnson suggested an allusion to the proverb, "Out of heaven's blessing into the warm sun," i.e., Hamlet is out of house and home in being deprived of the kingship. 74. **Ay . . . common,** it is common, but it hurts nevertheless; possibly a reference to the commonplace quality of the queen's remark. 78. **customary suits,** suits prescribed by custom for mourning. 79. **windy suspiration,** heavy sighing. 92. **obsequious,** dutiful. 93. **condolement,** sorrowing. 95. **incorrect,** untrained, uncorrected. 99. **vulgar thing,** common experience. 107. **unprevailing,** unavailing. 109. **most immediate,** next in succession. 110. **nobility,** high degree. 112. **impart.** The object is apparently *love* (l. 110). 113. **Wittenberg,** famous German university founded in 1502. 114. **retrograde,** contrary. 115. **bend you,** incline

Hyperion to a satyr; so loving to my mother
That he might not beteem the winds of heaven
Visit her face too roughly. Heaven and earth!
Must I remember? why, she would hang on him,
As if increase of appetite had grown
By what it fed on: and yet, within a month—
Let me not think on 't—Frailty, thy name is woman!—
A little month, or ere those shoes were old
With which she followed my poor father's body,
Like Niobe, all tears:—why she, even she—
O God! a beast, that wants discourse of reason,
Would have mourn'd longer—married with my uncle,
My father's brother, but no more like my father
Than I to Hercules: within a month:
Ere yet the salt of most unrighteous tears
Had left the flushing in her galled eyes,
She married. O, most wicked speed, to post
With such dexterity to incestuous sheets!
It is not nor it cannot come to good:
But break, my heart; for I must hold my tongue.

Enter HORATIO, MARCELLUS, *and* BERNARDO.

Hor. Hail to your lordship!
Ham. I am glad to see you well:
Horatio!—or I do forget myself.
Hor. The same, my lord, and your poor servant ever.
Ham. Sir, my good friend; I'll change that name with you:
And what make you from Wittenberg, Horatio?
Marcellus?
Mar. My good lord—
Ham. I am very glad to see you. Good even, sir.
But what, in faith, make you from Wittenberg?
Hor. A truant disposition, good my lord.
Ham. I would not hear your enemy say so,
Nor shall you do my ear that violence,
To make it truster of your own report
Against yourself: I know you are no truant.
But what is your affair in Elsinore?
We'll teach you to drink deep ere you depart.
Hor. My lord, I came to see your father's funeral.
Ham. I prithee, do not mock me, fellow-student;
I think it was to see my mother's wedding.
Hor. Indeed, my lord, it follow'd hard upon.
Ham. Thrift, thrift, Horatio! the funeral bak'd meats
Did coldly furnish forth the marriage tables.
Would I had met my dearest foe in heaven
Or ever I had seen that day, Horatio!
My father!—methinks I see my father.
Hor. Where, my lord?
Ham. In my mind's eye, Horatio.
Hor. I saw him once; 'a was a goodly king.
Ham. 'A was a man, take him for all in all,
I shall not look upon his like again.
Hor. My lord, I think I saw him yesternight.
Ham. Saw? who?
Hor. My lord, the king your father.
Ham. The king my father!
Hor. Season your admiration for a while
With an attent ear, till I may deliver,
Upon the witness of these gentlemen,
This marvel to you.
Ham. For God's love, let me hear.
Hor. Two nights together had these gentlemen,
Marcellus and Bernardo, on their watch,
In the dead waste and middle of the night,
Been thus encount'red. A figure like your father,
Armed at point exactly, cap-a-pe,
Appears before them, and with solemn march
Goes slow and stately by them: thrice he walk'd
By their oppress'd and fear-surprised eyes,
Within his truncheon's length; whilst they, distill'd
Almost to jelly with the act of fear,
Stand dumb and speak not to him. This to me
In dreadful secrecy impart they did;
And I with them the third night kept the watch:
Where, as they had deliver'd, both in time,
Form of the thing, each word made true and good,
The apparition comes: I knew your father;
These hands are not more like.
Ham. But where was this?
Mar. My lord, upon the platform where we watch'd.
Ham. Did you not speak to it?
Hor. My lord, I did;
But answer made it none: yet once methought
It lifted up it head and did address
Itself to motion, like as it would speak;
But even then the morning cock crew loud,
And at the sound it shrunk in haste away,
And vanish'd from our sight.
Ham. 'Tis very strange.
Hor. As I do live, my honour'd lord, 'tis true;
And we did think it writ down in our duty
To let you know of it.
Ham. Indeed, indeed, sirs, but this troubles me.
Hold you the watch to-night?
Mar., *Ber.* We do, my lord.
Ham. Arm'd, say you?
Mar., *Ber.* Arm'd, my lord.
Ham. From top to toe?
Mar., *Ber.* My lord, from head to foot.
Ham. Then saw you not his face?
Hor. O, yes, my lord; he wore his beaver up.
Ham. What, look'd he frowningly?
Hor. A countenance more in sorrow than in anger.
Ham. Pale or red?
Hor. Nay, very pale.
Ham. And fix'd his eyes upon you?
Hor. Most constantly.
Ham. I would I had been there.

yourself; imperative. 127. **rouse,** draft of liquor. **heaven,** so Q_2; F and Globe: *heavens.* **bruit again,** echo. 129. **sullied,** so Furness and Cambridge; Qq: *sallied;* F and Globe: *solid.* 137. **merely,** completely, entirely. 140. **Hyperion,** god of the sun in the older regime of ancient gods. 141. **beteem,** allow. 149. **Niobe,** Tantalus' daughter, who boasted that she had more sons and daughters than Leto; for this Apollo and Artemis slew her children. She was turned into stone by Zeus on Mount Sipylus. 150. **discourse of reason,** process or faculty of reason. 155. **galled,** irritated. 157. **dexterity,** facility. 163. **I'll . . . you,** I'll be your servant, you shall be my friend (Johnson); also explained as "I'll exchange the name of friend with you." 179. **hard,** close. 180. **bak'd meats,** meat pies. 182. **dearest,** direst. The adjective *dear* in Shakespeare has two different origins: O. E. *deore,* "beloved," and O. E. *deor,* "fierce." *Dearest* is the superlative of the second. 187. **'A,** he. 192. **Season your admiration,** restrain your astonishment. 200. **cap-a-pe,** from head to foot. 203. **oppress'd,** distressed. 204. **truncheon,** officer's staff. **distill'd,** softened, weakened. 205. **act,** action. 216. **it,** its. 222. **writ down.** Q_1 has *right done,* regarded as an evidence of stenographic reporting. 230. **beaver,** visor on the helmet.

Hor. It would have much amaz'd you.
Ham. Very like, very like. Stay'd it long?
Hor. While one with moderate haste might tell a hundred.
Mar., *Ber.* Longer, longer.
Hor. Not when I saw 't.
Ham. His beard was grizzled,—no?
Hor. It was, as I have seen it in his life,
A sable silver'd.
Ham. I will watch to-night;
Perchance 'twill walk again.
Hor. I warr'nt it will.
Ham. If it assume my noble father's person,
I'll speak to it, though hell itself should gape
And bid me hold my peace. I pray you all,
If you have hitherto conceal'd this sight,
Let it be tenable in your silence still;
And whatsoever else shall hap to-night,
Give it an understanding, but no tongue:
I will requite your loves. So, fare you well:
Upon the platform, 'twixt eleven and twelve,
I'll visit you.
All. Our duty to your honour.
Ham. Your loves, as mine to you: farewell.
Exeunt [*all but Hamlet*].
My father's spirit in arms! all is not well;
I doubt some foul play: would the night were come!
Till then sit still, my soul: foul deeds will rise,
Though all the earth o'erwhelm them, to men's eyes.
Exit.

[SCENE III. *A room in Polonius' house.*]

Enter LAERTES *and* OPHELIA, *his Sister.*

Laer. My necessaries are embark'd: farewell:
And, sister, as the winds give benefit
And convoy is assistant, do not sleep,
But let me hear from you.
Oph. Do you doubt that?
Laer. For Hamlet and the trifling of his favour,
Hold it a fashion and a toy in blood,
A violet in the youth of primy nature,
Forward, not permanent, sweet, not lasting,
The perfume and suppliance of a minute;
No more.
Oph. No more but so?
Laer. Think it no more:
For nature, crescent, does not grow alone
In thews and bulk, but, as this temple waxes,
The inward service of the mind and soul
Grows wide withal. Perhaps he loves you now,
And now no soil nor cautel doth besmirch
The virtue of his will: but you must fear,
His greatness weigh'd, his will is not his own;
For he himself is subject to his birth:
He may not, as unvalued persons do,
Carve for himself; for on his choice depends
The safety and health of this whole state;
And therefore must his choice be circumscrib'd
Unto the voice and yielding of that body
Whereof he is the head. Then if he says he loves you,
It fits your wisdom so far to believe it
As he in his particular act and place
May give his saying deed; which is no further
Than the main voice of Denmark goes withal.
Then weigh what loss your honour may sustain,
If with too credent ear you list his songs,
Or lose your heart, or your chaste treasure open
To his unmast'red importunity.
Fear it, Ophelia, fear it, my dear sister,
And keep you in the rear of your affection,
Out of the shot and danger of desire.
The chariest maid is prodigal enough,
If she unmask her beauty to the moon:
Virtue itself 'scapes not calumnious strokes:
The canker galls the infants of the spring,
Too oft before their buttons be disclos'd,
And in the morn and liquid dew of youth
Contagious blastments are most imminent.
Be wary then; best safety lies in fear:
Youth to itself rebels, though none else near.
Oph. I shall the effect of this good lesson keep,
As watchman to my heart. But, good my brother,
Do not, as some ungracious pastors do,
Show me the steep and thorny way to heaven;
Whiles, like a puff'd and reckless libertine,
Himself the primrose path of dalliance treads,
And recks not his own rede.

Enter POLONIUS.

Laer. O, fear me not.
I stay too long: but here my father comes.
A double blessing is a double grace;
Occasion smiles upon a second leave.
Pol. Yet here, Laertes? aboard, aboard, for shame!
The wind sits in the shoulder of your sail,
And you are stay'd for. There; my blessing with thee!
And these few precepts in thy memory
Look thou character. Give thy thoughts no tongue,
Nor any unproportion'd thought his act.
Be thou familiar, but by no means vulgar.
Those friends thou hast, and their adoption tried,
Grapple them to thy soul with hoops of steel;
But do not dull thy palm with entertainment
Of each new-hatch'd, unfledg'd comrade. Beware
Of entrance to a quarrel, but being in,
Bear 't that th' opposed may beware of thee.
Give every man thy ear, but few thy voice;
Take each man's censure, but reserve thy judgement.
Costly thy habit as thy purse can buy,

242. **sable,** black color. 256. **doubt,** fear.
SCENE III. 3. **convoy is assistant,** means of conveyance are available. 6. **fashion,** custom, prevailing usage. **toy in blood,** passing amorous fancy. 7. **primy,** in its prime. 8. **Forward,** precocious. 9. **suppliance of a minute,** diversion to fill up a minute. 10. **so.** Q_2F place a period after this word. The punctuation concerns the extent to which Ophelia is obedient to Laertes' suggestion. 11. **crescent,** growing, waxing. 12. **thews,** bodily strength. **temple,** body. 15. **soil,** blemish. **cautel,** crafty device. 17. **greatness weigh'd,** high position considered. 23. **voice and yielding,** assent, approval. 27. **deed,** effect. 30. **credent,** credulous. 32. **unmast'red,** unrestrained. 36. **chariest,** most scrupulously modest. 39. **The canker . . . spring,** the cankerworm destroys the young plants of spring. 40. **buttons,** buds. **disclos'd,** opened. 41. **liquid dew,** i.e., time when dew is fresh. 42. **blastments,** blights. 47. **ungracious,** graceless. 49. **puff'd,** bloated. 51. **recks,** heeds. **rede,** counsel. 53. **double,** i.e., Laertes has already bade his father good-by. 54. **Occasion,** opportunity. 58. **precepts.** Many parallels have been found to the series of maxims which follows, one of the closest being that in Lyly's *Euphues*. 59. **Look,** so Q_2; Globe, following F: *See*. **character,** inscribe. 60. **unproportion'd,** inordinate. 61. **vulgar,** common. 65. **unfledg'd,** immature. 71. **express'd in fancy,** fantastical in design. 74. **Are . . . that.** Onions defines *chief* as "in chief," "mainly," "principally." *Chief* is usually taken as a substantive meaning "head," "eminence." 77. **husbandry,** thrift. 81. **season,** mature. 94. **put on,** impressed on. 99, 103. **tenders,** offers. 102. **Unsifted,** untried. 106. **tenders,** promises to pay. 107. **sterling,** legal currency.

But not express'd in fancy; rich, not gaudy;
For the apparel oft proclaims the man,
And they in France of the best rank and station
†Are of a most select and generous chief in that.
Neither a borrower nor a lender be;
For loan oft loses both itself and friend,
And borrowing dulleth edge of husbandry.
This above all: to thine own self be true,
And it must follow, as the night the day,
Thou canst not then be false to any man.
Farewell: my blessing season this in thee!

Laer. Most humbly do I take my leave, my lord.

Pol. The time invites you; go; your servants tend.

Laer. Farewell, Ophelia; and remember well
What I have said to you.

Oph. 'Tis in my memory lock'd,
And you yourself shall keep the key of it.

Laer. Farewell. *Exit Laertes.*

Pol. What is 't, Ophelia, he hath said to you?

Oph. So please you, something touching the Lord Hamlet.

Pol. Marry, well bethought:
'Tis told me, he hath very oft of late
Given private time to you; and you yourself
Have of your audience been most free and bounteous:
If it be so, as so 't is put on me,
And that in way of caution, I must tell you,
You do not understand yourself so clearly
As it behoves my daughter and your honour.
What is between you? give me up the truth.

Oph. He hath, my lord, of late made many tenders
Of his affection to me.

Pol. Affection! pooh! you speak like a green girl,
Unsifted in such perilous circumstance.
Do you believe his tenders, as you call them?

Oph. I do not know, my lord, what I should think.

Pol. Marry, I will teach you: think yourself a baby;
That you have ta'en these tenders for true pay,
Which are not sterling. Tender yourself more dearly;
Or—not to crack the wind of the poor phrase,
Running it thus—you'll tender me a fool.

Oph. My lord, he hath importun'd me with love
In honourable fashion.

Pol. Ay, fashion you may call it; go to, go to.

Oph. And hath given countenance to his speech, my lord,
With almost all the holy vows of heaven.

Pol. Ay, springes to catch woodcocks. I do know,
When the blood burns, how prodigal the soul
Lends the tongue vows: these blazes, daughter,
Giving more light than heat, extinct in both,
Even in their promise, as it is a-making,
You must not take for fire. From this time
Be somewhat scanter of your maiden presence;
Set your entreatments at a higher rate
Than a command to parley. For Lord Hamlet,
Believe so much in him, that he is young,
And with a larger tether may he walk
Than may be given you: in few, Ophelia,
Do not believe his vows; for they are brokers,
Not of that dye which their investments show,
But mere implorators of unholy suits,
Breathing like sanctified and pious bawds,
The better to beguile. This is for all:
I would not, in plain terms, from this time forth,
Have you so slander any moment leisure,
As to give words or talk with the Lord Hamlet.
Look to 't, I charge you: come your ways.

Oph. I shall obey, my lord. *Exeunt.*

[Scene iv. *The platform.*]

Enter Hamlet, Horatio, *and* Marcellus.

Ham. The air bites shrewdly; it is very cold.

Hor. It is a nipping and an eager air.

Ham. What hour now?

Hor. I think it lacks of twelve.

Mar. No, it is struck.

Hor. Indeed? I heard it not: then it draws near the season
Wherein the spirit held his wont to walk.

A flourish of trumpets, and two pieces go off.

What does this mean, my lord?

Ham. The king doth wake to-night and takes his rouse,
Keeps wassail, and the swagg'ring up-spring reels;
And, as he drains his draughts of Rhenish down,
The kettle-drum and trumpet thus bray out
The triumph of his pledge.

Hor. Is it a custom?

Ham. Ay, marry, is 't:
But to my mind, though I am native here
And to the manner born, it is a custom
More honour'd in the breach than the observance.
This heavy-headed revel east and west
Makes us traduc'd and tax'd of other nations:
They clepe us drunkards, and with swinish phrase
Soil our addition; and indeed it takes
From our achievements, though perform'd at height,
The pith and marrow of our attribute.
So, oft it chances in particular men,
That for some vicious mole of nature in them,
As, in their birth—wherein they are not guilty,
Since nature cannot choose his origin—
By the o'ergrowth of some complexion,
Oft breaking down the pales and forts of reason,
Or by some habit that too much o'er-leavens
The form of plausive manners, that these men,
Carrying, I say, the stamp of one defect,
Being nature's livery, or fortune's star,—
Their virtues else—be they as pure as grace,

Tender, hold. 108. **crack the wind,** i.e., run it until it is broken-winded. 109. **tender . . . fool,** show me a fool (for a daughter). 112. **fashion,** mere form, pretense. 113. **countenance,** credit, support. 115. **springes,** snares. **woodcocks,** birds easily caught; type of stupidity. 122. **entreatments,** conversations, interviews. 123. **command to parley,** mere invitation to talk. 124. **so . . . him,** this much concerning him. 126. **in few,** briefly. 127. **brokers,** go-betweens, procurers. 128. **dye,** color or sort. **investments,** clothes. 129. **implorators of,** solicitors of. 130. **Breathing,** speaking. **bawds,** so Theobald. Many editors follow the Q_2 reading, *bonds*, which would mean "agreements." 133. **slander,** bring disgrace or reproach upon.

Scene iv. 8. **wake,** stay awake, hold revel. **rouse,** carouse, drinking bout. 9. **wassail,** carousal. **up-spring,** last and wildest dance at German merry-makings (Elze). **reels,** reels through. 10. **Rhenish,** Rhine wine. 12. **triumph . . . pledge,** his glorious achievement as a drinker. 15. **to . . . born,** destined by birth to be subject to the custom in question (Onions). 17-38. **This . . . scandal.** The omission of this passage from F may be due to deference to the queen of James I, who was a Danish princess. 19. **clepe,** call. **with swinish phrase,** by calling us swine. 20. **addition,** reputation. 22. **attribute,** reputation. 24. **mole of nature,** natural blemish in one's constitution. 28. **pales,** palings (as of a fortification). 29. **o'er-leavens,** induces a change throughout (as yeast works in bread). 30. **plausive,** pleasing. 32. **nature's livery,** endowment from nature. **fortune's star,** the position in which one is placed by fortune; a reference to astrology. The two phrases are aspects of the same thing.

As infinite as man may undergo—
Shall in the general censure take corruption
From that particular fault: the dram of †eale
Doth all the noble substance †of a doubt
To his own scandal.

Enter Ghost.

Hor. Look, my lord, it comes!
Ham. Angels and ministers of grace defend us!
Be thou a spirit of health or goblin damn'd,
Bring with thee airs from heaven or blasts from hell,
Be thy intents wicked or charitable,
Thou com'st in such a questionable shape
That I will speak to thee: I'll call thee Hamlet,
King, father, royal Dane: O, answer me!
Let me not burst in ignorance; but tell
Why thy canoniz'd bones, hearsed in death,
Have burst their cerements; why the sepulchre,
Wherein we saw thee quietly interr'd,
Hath op'd his ponderous and marble jaws,
To cast thee up again. What may this mean,
That thou, dead corse, again in complete steel
Revisit'st thus the glimpses of the moon,
Making night hideous; and we fools of nature
So horridly to shake our disposition
With thoughts beyond the reaches of our souls?
Say, why is this? wherefore? what should we do?
[*Ghost*] *beckons* [*Hamlet*].
Hor. It beckons you to go away with it,
As if it some impartment did desire
To you alone.
Mar. Look, with what courteous action
It waves you to a more removed ground:
But do not go with it.
Hor. No, by no means.
Ham. It will not speak; then I will follow it.
Hor. Do not, my lord!
Ham. Why, what should be the fear?
I do not set my life at a pin's fee;
And for my soul, what can it do to that,
Being a thing immortal as itself?
It waves me forth again: I'll follow it.
Hor. What if it tempt you toward the flood, my lord,
Or to the dreadful summit of the cliff
That beetles o'er his base into the sea,
And there assume some other horrible form,
Which might deprive your sovereignty of reason
And draw you into madness? think of it:
The very place puts toys of desperation,
Without more motive, into every brain
That looks so many fathoms to the sea
And hears it roar beneath.
Ham. It waves me still.
Go on; I'll follow thee.
Mar. You shall not go, my lord.
Ham. Hold off your hands!
Hor. Be rul'd; you shall not go.
Ham. My fate cries out,
And makes each petty artere in this body
As hardy as the Nemean lion's nerve.
Still am I call'd. Unhand me, gentlemen.
By heaven, I'll make a ghost of him that lets me!
I say, away! Go on; I'll follow thee.
Exeunt Ghost and Hamlet.
Hor. He waxes desperate with imagination.
Mar. Let 's follow; 'tis not fit thus to obey him.
Hor. Have after. To what issue will this come?
Mar. Something is rotten in the state of Denmark.
Hor. Heaven will direct it.
Mar. Nay, let 's follow him. *Exeunt.*

[SCENE V. *Another part of the platform.*]

Enter GHOST *and* HAMLET.

Ham. Whither wilt thou lead me? speak; I'll go no further.
Ghost. Mark me.
Ham. I will.
Ghost. My hour is almost come,
When I to sulphurous and tormenting flames
Must render up myself.
Ham. Alas, poor ghost!
Ghost. Pity me not, but lend thy serious hearing
To what I shall unfold.
Ham. Speak; I am bound to hear.
Ghost. So art thou to revenge, when thou shalt hear.
Ham. What?
Ghost. I am thy father's spirit,
Doom'd for a certain term to walk the night,
And for the day confin'd to fast in fires,
Till the foul crimes done in my days of nature
Are burnt and purg'd away. But that I am forbid
To tell the secrets of my prison-house,
I could a tale unfold whose lightest word
Would harrow up thy soul, freeze thy young blood,
Make thy two eyes, like stars, start from their spheres,
Thy knotted and combined locks to part
And each particular hair to stand an end,
Like quills upon the fretful porpentine:
But this eternal blazon must not be
To ears of flesh and blood. List, list, O, list!
If thou didst ever thy dear father love—
Ham. O God!
Ghost. Revenge his foul and most unnatural murder.
Ham. Murder!
Ghost. Murder most foul, as in the best it is;
But this most foul, strange and unnatural.
Ham. Haste me to know 't, that I, with wings as swift

36-38. **the dram . . . scandal,** a famous crux; *dram of eale* has had various interpretations, the preferred one being probably, "a dram of evil." The following emendations of *of a doubt* have been offered: (1) *oft adoubt* or *adout* (often erase or "do out"), (2) *antidote* (counteract). Dowden suggests that *scandal* may be a verb to be read with *Doth*, giving the general interpretation, "Out of a mere doubt or suspicion the dram of evil degrades in reputation all the noble substance to its own [substance]." 39. **ministers of grace,** messengers of God. 43. **questionable,** inviting question or conversation. 47. **canoniz'd,** buried according to the canons of the church. **hearsed,** coffined. 48. **cerements,** grave-clothes. 49. **interr'd,** so Qq; F: *enurn'd;* Globe: *inurn'd.* 53. **glimpses of the moon,** the earth by night. 54. **fools of nature,** mere men, limited to natural knowledge. 59. **impartment,** communication. 61. **removed,** remote. 71. **beetles o'er,** overhangs threateningly. 73. **deprive . . . reason,** take away the sovereignty of your reason. It was thought that evil spirits would sometimes assume the form of departed spirits in order to work madness in a human creature. 75. **toys of desperation,** freakish notions of suicide. 82. **artere,** artery. 83. **Nemean lion's.** The Nemean lion was one of the monsters slain by Hercules. **nerve,** sinew, tendon. The point is that the arteries which were carrying the spirits out into the body were functioning and were as stiff and hard as the sinews of the lion. 85. **lets,** hinders. 89. **issue,** outcome. 91. **it,** i.e., the outcome.

SCENE V. 1. **Whither,** Q_2: *Whether;* F and Globe: *Where.* 11. **fast,** probably, do without food. It has been sometimes taken in the sense of doing general penance. 17. **spheres,** orbits. 18. **knotted,** perhaps,

As meditation or the thoughts of love,
May sweep to my revenge.
Ghost. I find thee apt;
And duller shouldst thou be than the fat weed
That roots itself in ease on Lethe wharf,
Wouldst thou not stir in this. Now, Hamlet, hear:
'Tis given out that, sleeping in my orchard,
A serpent stung me; so the whole ear of Denmark
Is by a forged process of my death
Rankly abus'd: but know, thou noble youth,
The serpent that did sting thy father's life
Now wears his crown.
Ham. O my prophetic soul!
My uncle!
Ghost. Ay, that incestuous, that adulterate beast,
With witchcraft of his wit, with traitorous gifts,—
O wicked wit and gifts, that have the power
So to seduce!—won to his shameful lust
The will of my most seeming-virtuous queen:
O Hamlet, what a falling-off was there!
From me, whose love was of that dignity
That it went hand in hand even with the vow
I made to her in marriage, and to decline
Upon a wretch whose natural gifts were poor
To those of mine!
But virtue, as it never will be moved,
Though lewdness court it in a shape of heaven,
So lust, though to a radiant angel link'd,
Will sate itself in a celestial bed,
And prey on garbage.
But, soft! methinks I scent the morning air;
Brief let me be. Sleeping within my orchard,
My custom always of the afternoon,
Upon my secure hour thy uncle stole,
With juice of cursed hebona in a vial,
And in the porches of my ears did pour
The leperous distilment; whose effect
Holds such an enmity with blood of man
That swift as quicksilver it courses through
The natural gates and alleys of the body,
And with a sudden vigour it doth posset
And curd, like eager droppings into milk,
The thin and wholesome blood: so did it mine;
And a most instant tetter bark'd about,
Most lazar-like, with vile and loathsome crust,
All my smooth body.
Thus was I, sleeping, by a brother's hand
Of life, of crown, of queen, at once dispatch'd:
Cut off even in the blossoms of my sin,
Unhous'led, disappointed, unanel'd,
No reck'ning made, but sent to my account
With all my imperfections on my head:
O, horrible! O, horrible! most horrible!
If thou hast nature in thee, bear it not;
Let not the royal bed of Denmark be
A couch for luxury and damned incest.
But, howsomever thou pursues this act,
Taint not thy mind, nor let thy soul contrive
Against thy mother aught: leave her to heaven
And to those thorns that in her bosom lodge,
To prick and sting her. Fare thee well at once!
The glow-worm shows the matin to be near,
And 'gins to pale his uneffectual fire:
Adieu, adieu, adieu! remember me. [*Exit.*]
Ham. O all you host of heaven! O earth! what else?
And shall I couple hell? O, fie! Hold, hold, my heart;
And you, my sinews, grow not instant old,
But bear me stiffly up. Remember thee!
Ay, thou poor ghost, whiles memory holds a seat
In this distracted globe. Remember thee!
Yea, from the table of my memory
I'll wipe away all trivial fond records,
All saws of books, all forms, all pressures past,
That youth and observation copied there;
And thy commandment all alone shall live
Within the book and volume of my brain,
Unmix'd with baser matter: yes, by heaven!
O most pernicious woman!
O villain, villain, smiling, damned villain!
My tables,—meet it is I set it down,
That one may smile, and smile, and be a villain;
At least I am sure it may be so in Denmark: [*Writing.*]
So, uncle, there you are. Now to my word;
It is 'Adieu, adieu! remember me.'
I have sworn 't.

Enter HORATIO *and* MARCELLUS.

Hor. My lord, my lord,—
Mar. Lord Hamlet,—
Hor. Heavens secure him!
Ham. So be it!
Mar. Hillo, ho, ho, my lord!
Ham. Hillo, ho, ho, boy! come, bird, come.
Mar. How is 't, my noble lord?
Hor. What news, my lord?
Ham. O, wonderful!
Hor. Good my lord, tell it.
Ham. No; you will reveal it.
Hor. Not I, my lord, by heaven.
Mar. Nor I, my lord.
Ham. How say you, then; would heart of man once think it?
But you'll be secret?
Hor., *Mar.* Ay, by heaven, my lord.
Ham. There 's ne'er a villain dwelling in all Denmark
But he 's an arrant knave.
Hor. There needs no ghost, my lord, come from the grave
To tell us this.
Ham. Why, right; you are in the right;

intricately arranged (Onions). **combined,** tied, bound. 20. **fretful,** so Q_1F; Q_2: *fearefull,* which is defensible. **porpentine,** porcupine. 21. **eternal blazon,** promulgation or proclamation of eternity, revelation of the hereafter. 25. **unnatural,** i.e., pertaining to fratricide. 32. **fat weed.** Many suggestions have been offered as to the particular plant intended, including asphodel; probably, a general figure for plants growing along rotting wharves and piles. 33. **Lethe wharf,** bank of the river of forgetfulness in Hades. 42. **adulterate,** adulterous. 61. **secure,** confident, unsuspicious. 62. **hebona,** generally supposed to mean henbane. Elze conjectured *hemlock;* Nicholson, *ebenus,* meaning "yew." 64. **leperous,** causing leprosy. 68. **posset,** coagulate, curdle. 69. **eager,** sour, acid. 72. **lazar-like,** leperlike. 75. **dispatch'd,** suddenly bereft. 77. **Unhous'led,** without having received the sacrament. **disappointed,** unready, without equipment for the last journey. **unanel'd,** without having received extreme unction. 80. **O . . . horrible.** Many editors give this line to Hamlet; Garrick and Sir Henry Irving spoke it in that part. 83. **luxury,** lechery. 85. **Taint . . . mind,** probably, deprave not thy character, do nothing except in the pursuit of a natural revenge. 89. **matin,** morning. 90. **uneffectual fire,** cold light. 93. **couple,** add. 97. **distracted globe,** confused head. 100. **saws,** wise sayings. **pressures,** impressions stamped. 107. **tables,** probably a small portable writing-tablet carried at the belt. 110. **word,** watchword. 115. **Hillo, ho, ho,** a falconer's call to a hawk in air. 124. **arrant,** thoroughgoing.

And so, without more circumstance at all,
I hold it fit that we shake hands and part:
You, as your business and desire shall point you;
For every man has business and desire,
Such as it is; and for my own poor part,
Look you, I'll go pray.
Hor. These are but wild and whirling words, my lord.
Ham. I am sorry they offend you, heartily;
Yes, 'faith, heartily.
Hor. There 's no offence, my lord.
Ham. Yes, by Saint Patrick, but there is, Horatio,
And much offence too. Touching this vision here,
It is an honest ghost, that let me tell you:
For your desire to know what is between us,
O'ermaster 't as you may. And now, good friends,
As you are friends, scholars and soldiers,
Give me one poor request.
Hor. What is 't, my lord? we will.
Ham. Never make known what you have seen to-night.
Hor. } *Mar.* } My lord, we will not.
Ham. Nay, but swear 't.
Hor. In faith,
My lord, not I.
Mar. Nor I, my lord, in faith.
Ham. Upon my sword.
Mar. We have sworn, my lord, already.
Ham. Indeed, upon my sword, indeed.
Ghost cries under the stage.
Ghost. Swear.
Ham. Ah, ha, boy! say'st thou so? art thou there, truepenny?
Come on—you hear this fellow in the cellarage—
Consent to swear.
Hor. Propose the oath, my lord.
Ham. Never to speak of this that you have seen,
Swear by my sword.
Ghost. [*Beneath*] Swear.
Ham. Hic et ubique? then we'll shift our ground.
Come hither, gentlemen,
And lay your hands again upon my sword:
Swear by my sword,
Never to speak of this that you have heard.
Ghost. [*Beneath*] Swear by his sword.
Ham. Well said, old mole! canst work i' th' earth so fast?
A worthy pioner! Once more remove, good friends.
Hor. O day and night, but this is wondrous strange!
Ham. And therefore as a stranger give it welcome.
There are more things in heaven and earth, Horatio,
Than are dreamt of in your philosophy.
But come;
Here, as before, never, so help you mercy,
How strange or odd soe'er I bear myself,
As I perchance hereafter shall think meet
To put an antic disposition on,
That you, at such times seeing me, never shall,
With arms encumb'red thus, or this head-shake,
Or by pronouncing of some doubtful phrase,
As 'Well, well, we know,' or 'We could, an if we would,'
Or 'If we list to speak,' or 'There be, an if they might,'
Or such ambiguous giving out, to note
That you know aught of me: this not to do,
So grace and mercy at your most need help you,
Swear.
Ghost. [*Beneath*] Swear.
Ham. Rest, rest, perturbed spirit! [*They swear*]. So, gentlemen,
With all my love I do commend me to you:
And what so poor a man as Hamlet is
May do, t' express his love and friending to you,
God willing, shall not lack. Let us go in together;
And still your fingers on your lips, I pray.
The time is out of joint: O cursed spite,
That ever I was born to set it right!
Nay, come, let 's go together. *Exeunt.*

[ACT II.

SCENE I. *A room in Polonius' house.*]

Enter old POLONIUS *with his man* [REYNALDO].

Pol. Give him this money and these notes, Reynaldo.
Rey. I will, my lord.
Pol. You shall do marvellous wisely, good Reynaldo,
Before you visit him, to make inquire
Of his behaviour.
Rey. My lord, I did intend it.
Pol. Marry, well said; very well said. Look you, sir,
Inquire me first what Danskers are in Paris;
And how, and who, what means, and where they keep,
What company, at what expense; and finding
By this encompassment and drift of question
That they do know my son, come you more nearer
Than your particular demands will touch it:
Take you, as 'twere, some distant knowledge of him;
As thus, 'I know his father and his friends,
And in part him:' do you mark this, Reynaldo?
Rey. Ay, very well, my lord.
Pol. 'And in part him; but' you may say 'not well:
But, if 't be he I mean, he 's very wild;
Addicted so and so:' and there put on him
What forgeries you please; marry, none so rank
As may dishonour him; take heed of that;
But, sir, such wanton, wild and usual slips
As are companions noted and most known
To youth and liberty.
Rey. As gaming, my lord.

136. **Saint Patrick.** St. Patrick was keeper of Purgatory and patron saint of all blunders and confusion. 138. **honest,** i.e., a real ghost and not an evil spirit. 147. **sword,** i.e., the hilt in the form of a cross. 150. **truepenny,** good old boy, or the like. 156. **Hic et ubique?** Here and everywhere? 159-160. F and Globe transpose these lines. 161. **by his sword.** F and Globe omit. 163. **pioner,** digger, miner. 172. **antic,** fantastic. 174. **encumb'red,** folded or entwined. 178. **giving out,** profession of knowledge. **to note,** to give a sign. 186. **friending,** friendliness.

ACT II. SCENE I. *Stage Direction:* Q_2 has *Polonius with his man or two;* possible confusion for *Montano*, name of Reynaldo in Q_1. 7. **Danskers.** Danke was a common variant for "Denmark"; hence "Dane." 8. **keep,** dwell. 10. **encompassment,** roundabout talking. **drift,** gradual approach or course. 11-12. **come . . . it,** i.e., you will find out more this way than by asking pointed questions. 13. **Take,** assume, pretend. 19. **put on,** impute to. 20. **forgeries,** invented tales. 22. **wanton,** sportive, unrestrained. 25. **fencing,** indicative of the ill repute of professional fencers and fencing schools in Elizabethan times. 26. **Drabbing,** associating with immoral women. 30. **incontinency,** habitual loose behavior. Malone's interpretation would make this habitual incontinency the *scandal* described; Hudson would read *open to* as *open of*, meaning "open in his practice of." 31. **quaintly,** delicately, ingeniously. 32. **taints of liberty,** blemishes due to freedom. 34. **unreclaimed,** untamed. 35. **general assault,** tendency that assails all

Pol. Ay, or drinking, fencing, swearing, quarrelling,
Drabbing: you may go so far.
Rey. My lord, that would dishonour him.
Pol. 'Faith, no; as you may season it in the charge.
You must not put another scandal on him,
That he is open to incontinency;
That 's not my meaning: but breathe his faults so quaintly
That they may seem the taints of liberty,
The flash and outbreak of a fiery mind,
A savageness in unreclaimed blood,
Of general assault.
Rey. But, my good lord,—
Pol. Wherefore should you do this?
Rey. Ay, my lord,
I would know that.
Pol. Marry, sir, here 's my drift;
And, I believe, it is a fetch of wit:
You laying these slight sullies on my son,
As 'twere a thing a little soil'd i' th' working,
Mark you,
Your party in converse, him you would sound,
Having ever seen in the prenominate crimes
The youth you breathe of guilty, be assur'd
He closes with you in this consequence;
'Good sir,' or so, or 'friend,' or 'gentleman,'
According to the phrase or the addition
Of man and country.
Rey. Very good, my lord.
Pol. And then, sir, does 'a this—'a does—what was I about to say? By the mass, I was about to say something: where did I leave?
Rey. At 'closes in the consequence,' at 'friend or so,' and 'gentleman.'
Pol. At 'closes in the consequence,' ay, marry;
He closes thus: 'I know the gentleman;
I saw him yesterday, or t' other day,
Or then, or then; with such, or such; and, as you say,
There was 'a gaming; there o'ertook in 's rouse;
There falling out at tennis:' or perchance,
'I saw him enter such a house of sale,'
Videlicet, a brothel, or so forth.
See you now;
Your bait of falsehood takes this carp of truth:
And thus do we of wisdom and of reach,
With windlasses and with assays of bias,
By indirections find directions out:
So by my former lecture and advice,
Shall you my son. You have me, have you not?
Rey. My lord, I have.
Pol. God bye ye; fare ye well.
Rey. Good my lord!
Pol. Observe his inclination in yourself.
Rey. I shall, my lord.
Pol. And let him ply his music.
Rey. Well, my lord.
Pol. Farewell! *Exit Reynaldo.*

Enter OPHELIA.

How now, Ophelia! what 's the matter?
Oph. O, my lord, my lord, I have been so affrighted!
Pol. With what, i' th' name of God?
Oph. My lord, as I was sewing in my closet,
Lord Hamlet, with his doublet all unbrac'd;
No hat upon his head; his stockings foul'd,
Ungart'red, and down-gyved to his ankle;
Pale as his shirt; his knees knocking each other;
And with a look so piteous in purport
As if he had been loosed out of hell
To speak of horrors,—he comes before me.
Pol. Mad for thy love?
Oph. My lord, I do not know;
But truly, I do fear it.
Pol. What said he?
Oph. He took me by the wrist and held me hard;
Then goes he to the length of all his arm;
And, with his other hand thus o'er his brow,
He falls to such perusal of my face
As 'a would draw it. Long stay'd he so;
At last, a little shaking of mine arm
And thrice his head thus waving up and down,
He rais'd a sigh so piteous and profound
As it did seem to shatter all his bulk
And end his being: that done, he lets me go:
And, with his head over his shoulder turn'd,
He seem'd to find his way without his eyes;
For out o' doors he went without their helps,
And, to the last, bended their light on me.
Pol. Come, go with me: I will go seek the king.
This is the very ecstasy of love,
Whose violent property fordoes itself
And leads the will to desperate undertakings
As oft as any passion under heaven
That does afflict our natures. I am sorry.
What, have you given him any hard words of late?
Oph. No, my good lord, but, as you did command,
I did repel his letters and denied
His access to me.
Pol. That hath made him mad.
I am sorry that with better heed and judgement
I had not quoted him: I fear'd he did but trifle,
And meant to wrack thee; but, beshrew my jealousy!
By heaven, it is as proper to our age
To cast beyond ourselves in our opinions
As it is common for the younger sort
To lack discretion. Come, go we to the king:
This must be known; which, being kept close, might move
More grief to hide than hate to utter love.
Come. *Exeunt.*

[SCENE II. *A room in the castle.*]

Flourish. Enter KING *and* QUEEN, ROSENCRANTZ, *and* GUILDENSTERN [*with others*].

untrained youth. 38. **fetch of wit,** clever trick. The F reading, *fetch of warrant*, would mean "a warranted device." 43. **ever,** at any time. **prenominate,** before-mentioned. 45. **closes . . . consequence,** agrees with you in this conclusion. 49-51. **And then . . . leave.** Malone's arrangement of Q_2F as prose is probably correct, since Polonius is represented as letting his mind wander in confusion. 58. **o'ertook in 's rouse,** overcome by drink. 61. **Videlicet,** namely. 64. **reach,** capacity, ability. 65. **windlasses,** i.e., circuitous paths. **assays of bias,** attempts that resemble the course of the bowl, which, being weighted on one side, has a curving motion. 66. **indirections,** devious courses. **directions,** straight courses, i.e., the truth. 67. **lecture,** admonition. 69. **bye ye,** be with you. 71. **Observe . . . yourself,** in your own person, not by spies (Johnson), or conform your own conduct to his inclination (Clarendon Press); or test him by studying yourself. 73. **ply his music,** probably to be taken literally. 77. **closet,** private chamber. 78. **doublet,** close-fitting coat. **unbrac'd,** unfastened. 80. **down-gyved,** fallen to the ankles (like gyves or fetters). 95. **bulk,** body. 103. **property,** nature. **fordoes,** destroys. 112. **quoted,** observed. 113. **beshrew my jealousy,** curse my suspicions. 115. **cast beyond,** overshoot, miscalculate. 118-119. **might . . . love,** i.e., I might cause more grief to others by hiding the knowledge of Hamlet's love to Ophelia than hatred to me and mine by telling of it.

King. Welcome, dear Rosencrantz and Guildenstern!
Moreover that we much did long to see you,
The need we have to use you did provoke
Our hasty sending. Something have you heard
Of Hamlet's transformation; so call it,
Sith nor th' exterior nor the inward man
Resembles that it was. What it should be,
More than his father's death, that thus hath put him
So much from th' understanding of himself,
I cannot dream of: I entreat you both,
That, being of so young days brought up with him,
And sith so neighbour'd to his youth and haviour,
That you vouchsafe your rest here in our court
Some little time: so by your companies
To draw him on to pleasures, and to gather,
So much as from occasion you may glean,
Whether aught, to us unknown, afflicts him thus,
That, open'd, lies within our remedy.
Queen. Good gentlemen, he hath much talk'd of you;
And sure I am two men there are not living
To whom he more adheres. If it will please you
To show us so much gentry and good will
As to expend your time with us awhile,
For the supply and profit of our hope,
Your visitation shall receive such thanks
As fits a king's remembrance.
Ros. Both your majesties
Might, by the sovereign power you have of us,
Put your dread pleasures more into command
Than to entreaty.
Guil. But we both obey,
And here give up ourselves, in the full bent
To lay our service freely at your feet,
To be commanded.
King. Thanks, Rosencrantz and gentle Guildenstern.
Queen. Thanks, Guildenstern and gentle Rosencrantz:
And I beseech you instantly to visit
My too much changed son. Go, some of you,
And bring these gentlemen where Hamlet is.
Guil. Heavens make our presence and our practices
Pleasant and helpful to him!
Queen. Ay, amen!
Exeunt Rosencrantz and Guildenstern [*with some Attendants*].

Enter POLONIUS.

Pol. Th' ambassadors from Norway, my good lord,
Are joyfully return'd.
King. Thou still hast been the father of good news.
Pol. Have I, my lord? I assure my good liege,
I hold my duty, as I hold my soul,
Both to my God and to my gracious king:
And I do think, or else this brain of mine
Hunts not the trail of policy so sure
As it hath us'd to do, that I have found
The very cause of Hamlet's lunacy.
King. O, speak of that; that do I long to hear.
Pol. Give first admittance to th' ambassadors;
My news shall be the fruit to that great feast.
King. Thyself do grace to them, and bring them in.
[*Exit Polonius*.]
He tells me, my dear Gertrude, he hath found
The head and source of all your son's distemper.
Queen. I doubt it is no other but the main;
His father's death, and our o'erhasty marriage.
King. Well, we shall sift him.

Enter Ambassadors [VOLTIMAND *and* CORNELIUS, *with* POLONIUS].

Welcome, my good friends!
Say, Voltimand, what from our brother Norway?
Volt. Most fair return of greetings and desires.
Upon our first, he sent out to suppress
His nephew's levies; which to him appear'd
To be a preparation 'gainst the Polack;
But, better look'd into, he truly found
It was against your highness: whereat griev'd,
That so his sickness, age and impotence
Was falsely borne in hand, sends out arrests
On Fortinbras; which he, in brief, obeys;
Receives rebuke from Norway, and in fine
Makes vow before his uncle never more
To give th' assay of arms against your majesty.
Whereon old Norway, overcome with joy,
Gives him three score thousand crowns in annual fee,
And his commission to employ those soldiers,
So levied as before, against the Polack:
With an entreaty, herein further shown, [*Giving a paper*.]
That it might please you to give quiet pass
Through your dominions for this enterprise,
On such regards of safety and allowance
As therein are set down.
King. It likes us well;
And at our more consider'd time we'll read,
Answer, and think upon this business.
Meantime we thank you for your well-took labour:
Go to your rest; at night we'll feast together:
Most welcome home! *Exeunt Ambassadors*.
Pol. This business is well ended.
My liege, and madam, to expostulate
What majesty should be, what duty is,
Why day is day, night night, and time is time,
Were nothing but to waste night, day and time.
Therefore, since brevity is the soul of wit,
And tediousness the limbs and outward flourishes,
I will be brief: your noble son is mad:
Mad call I it; for, to define true madness,
What is 't but to be nothing else but mad?
But let that go.
Queen. More matter, with less art.
Pol. Madam, I swear I use no art at all.
That he is mad, 'tis true: 'tis true 'tis pity;
And pity 'tis 'tis true: a foolish figure;
But farewell it, for I will use no art.
Mad let us grant him, then: and now remains
That we find out the cause of this effect,

SCENE II. 2. **Moreover that,** besides the fact that. 6. **Sith,** since. 11. **of . . . days,** from such early youth. 13. **vouchsafe your rest,** please to stay. 22. **gentry,** courtesy. 24. **supply and profit,** aid and successful outcome. 30. **in . . . bent,** to the utmost degree of our mental capacity. 56. **doubt,** fear. **main,** chief point, principal concern. 67. **borne in hand,** deluded. 69. **in fine,** in the end. 71. **assay,** assault, trial (of arms). 73. **three score,** so Q_2; Globe, following F: *three*. 79. **safety and allowance,** pledges of safety to the country and terms of permission for the troops to pass. 80. **likes,** pleases. 81. **consider'd,** suitable for deliberation. 90. **wit,** sound sense or judgment. 91. **flourishes,** ostentation embellishments. 98. **figure,** figure of speech. 105. **Perpend,** consider. 120. **ill . . . numbers,** unskilled at writing verses. 121. **reckon,** number metrically, scan (Yale). 124. **machine,** bodily frame. 126. **more above,** moreover. 127. **fell out,** occurred. **means,** opportunities (of access). 136. **play'd . . . table-book,** i.e., remained shut up, concealed his information. 137. **given . . . winking,** given my heart a signal to keep silent. 140. **bespeak,** address. 141. **out . . . star,** above thee in position. 146. **repelled,** so Q_2; F and Globe:

Or rather say, the cause of this defect,
For this effect defective comes by cause:
Thus it remains, and the remainder thus.
Perpend.
I have a daughter—have while she is mine—
Who, in her duty and obedience, mark,
Hath given me this: now gather, and surmise. [*Reads the*] *letter*. 'To the celestial and my soul's idol, the most beautified Ophelia,'—
That 's an ill phrase, a vile phrase; 'beautified' is a vile phrase: but you shall hear. Thus: [*Reads.*]
'In her excellent white bosom, these, &c.'
Queen. Came this from Hamlet to her?
Pol. Good madam, stay awhile; I will be faithful. [*Reads.*]
'Doubt thou the stars are fire;
Doubt that the sun doth move;
Doubt truth to be a liar;
But never doubt I love.
'O dear Ophelia, I am ill at these numbers; I have not art to reckon my groans: but that I love thee best, O most best, believe it. Adieu.
'Thine evermore, most dear lady, whilst this machine is to him, HAMLET.'
This, in obedience, hath my daughter shown me,
And more above, hath his solicitings,
As they fell out by time, by means and place,
All given to mine ear.
King. But how hath she
Receiv'd his love?
Pol. What do you think of me?
King. As of a man faithful and honourable.
Pol. I would fain prove so. But what might you think,
When I had seen this hot love on the wing—
As I perceiv'd it, I must tell you that,
Before my daughter told me—what might you,
Or my dear majesty your queen here, think,
If I had play'd the desk or table-book,
Or given my heart a winking, mute and dumb,
Or look'd upon this love with idle sight;
What might you think? No, I went round to work,
And my young mistress thus I did bespeak:
'Lord Hamlet is a prince, out of thy star;
This must not be:' and then I prescripts gave her,
That she should lock herself from his resort,
Admit no messengers, receive no tokens.
Which done, she took the fruits of my advice;
And he, repelled—a short tale to make—
Fell into a sadness, then into a fast,
Thence to a watch, thence into a weakness,
Thence to a lightness, and, by this declension,
Into the madness wherein now he raves,
And all we mourn for.
King. Do you think 'tis this?
Queen. It may be, very like.
Pol. Hath there been such a time—I would fain know that—
That I have positively said ''Tis so,'
When it prov'd otherwise?
King. Not that I know.
Pol. [*Pointing to his head and shoulder*] Take this from this, if this be otherwise:
If circumstances lead me, I will find
Where truth is hid, though it were hid indeed
Within the centre.
King. How may we try it further?
Pol. You know, sometimes he walks four hours together
Here in the lobby.
Queen. So he does indeed.
Pol. At such a time I'll loose my daughter to him:
Be you and I behind an arras then;
Mark the encounter: if he love her not
And be not from his reason fall'n thereon,
Let me be no assistant for a state,
But keep a farm and carters.
King. We will try it.

Enter HAMLET [*reading on a book*].

Queen. But, look, where sadly the poor wretch comes reading.
Pol. Away, I do beseech you both, away:
Exeunt King and Queen [*with Attendants*].
I'll board him presently. O, give me leave.
How does my good Lord Hamlet?
Ham. Well, God-a-mercy.
Pol. Do you know me, my lord?
Ham. Excellent well; you are a fishmonger.
Pol. Not I, my lord.
Ham. Then I would you were so honest a man.
Pol. Honest, my lord!

Ham. Ay, sir; to be honest, as this world goes, is to be one man picked out of ten thousand.

Pol. That 's very true, my lord.

Ham. For if the sun breed maggots in a dead dog, being a good kissing carrion,—Have you a daughter?

Pol. I have, my lord.

Ham. Let her not walk i' the sun: conception is a blessing: but as your daughter may conceive—Friend, look to 't.

Pol. [*Aside*] How say you by that? Still harping on my daughter: yet he knew me not at first; 'a said I was a fishmonger: 'a is far gone, far gone: and truly in my youth I suffered much extremity for love; very near this. I'll speak to him again. What do you read, my lord?

Ham. Words, words, words.

Pol. What is the matter, my lord?

Ham. Between who?

Pol. I mean, the matter that you read, my lord.

Ham. Slanders, sir: for the satirical rogue says here that old men have grey beards, that their faces are wrinkled, their eyes purging thick amber and plum-tree gum and that they have a plentiful lack of wit, together with most weak hams: all which, sir, though I most powerfully and potently believe, yet I hold it not honesty to have it thus set down, for yourself, sir,

repulsed. 148. **watch,** state of sleeplessness. 149. **lightness,** light-headedness. **declension,** decline, deterioration. 152. **like,** so Q_2; Globe, following F: *likely*. 159. **centre,** middle point of the earth. 163. **arras,** hanging, tapestry. 165. **thereon,** on that account. 170. **board,** accost. 174. **fishmonger,** an opprobrious expression meaning "bawd," "procurer." 182. **good kissing carrion,** i.e., a good piece of flesh for kissing (?). Many editors, including Globe, emend to *God kissing carrion*, signifying the sun god shining on a dead body. 185. **i' the sun,** in the sunshine of princely favors (Chambers). **conception,** quibble on "understanding" and "pregnancy." 188. **by,** concerning. 195. **matter,** substance. 196. **Between who.** Hamlet deliberately takes *matter* as meaning "basis of dispute"; modern usage demands *whom* instead of *who*. 200. **purging,** discharging. 205. **honesty,** decency.

should be old as I am, if like a crab you could go backward.

Pol. [*Aside*] Though this be madness, yet there is method in 't.—Will you walk out of the air, my lord?

Ham. Into my grave.

Pol. Indeed, that 's out of the air. [*Aside*] How pregnant sometimes his replies are! a happiness that often madness hits on, which reason and sanity could not so prosperously be delivered of. I will leave him, and suddenly contrive the means of meeting between him and my daughter.—My honourable lord, I will most humbly take my leave of you.

Ham. You cannot, sir, take from me any thing that I will more willingly part withal: except my life, except my life, except my life.

Enter GUILDENSTERN *and* ROSENCRANTZ.

Pol. Fare you well, my lord.

Ham. These tedious old fools!

Pol. You go to seek the Lord Hamlet; there he is.

Ros. [*To Polonius*] God save you, sir! [*Exit Polonius.*]

Guil. My honoured lord!

Ros. My most dear lord!

Ham. My excellent good friends! How dost thou, Guildenstern? Ah, Rosencrantz! Good lads, how do ye both?

Ros. As the indifferent children of the earth.

Guil. Happy, in that we are not over-happy;
On Fortune's cap we are not the very button.

Ham. Nor the soles of her shoe?

Ros. Neither, my lord.

Ham. Then you live about her waist, or in the middle of her favours?

Guil. 'Faith, her privates we.

Ham. In the secret parts of Fortune? O, most true; she is a strumpet. What 's the news?

Ros. None, my lord, but that the world 's grown honest.

Ham. Then is doomsday near: but your news is not true. Let me question more in particular: what have you, my good friends, deserved at the hands of Fortune, that she sends you to prison hither?

Guil. Prison, my lord!

Ham. Denmark 's a prison.

Ros. Then is the world one.

Ham. A goodly one; in which there are many confines, wards and dungeons, Denmark being one o' the worst.

Ros. We think not so, my lord.

Ham. Why, then, 'tis none to you; for there is nothing either good or bad, but thinking makes it so: to me it is a prison.

Ros. Why then, your ambition makes it one; 'tis too narrow for your mind.

Ham. O God, I could be bounded in a nutshell and count myself a king of infinite space, were it not that I have bad dreams.

Guil. Which dreams indeed are ambition, for the very substance of the ambitious is merely the shadow of a dream.

Ham. A dream itself is but a shadow.

Ros. Truly, and I hold ambition of so airy and light a quality that it is but a shadow's shadow.

Ham. Then are our beggars bodies, and our monarchs and outstretched heroes the beggars' shadows. Shall we to the court? for, by my fay, I cannot reason.

Ros.
Guil. } We'll wait upon you.

Ham. No such matter: I will not sort you with the rest of my servants, for, to speak to you like an honest man, I am most dreadfully attended. But, in the beaten way of friendship, what make you at Elsinore?

Ros. To visit you, my lord; no other occasion.

Ham. Beggar that I am, I am even poor in thanks; but I thank you: and sure, dear friends, my thanks are too dear a halfpenny. Were you not sent for? Is it your own inclining? Is it a free visitation? Come, come, deal justly with me: come, come; nay, speak.

Guil. What should we say, my lord?

Ham. Why, any thing, but to the purpose. You were sent for; and there is a kind of confession in your looks which your modesties have not craft enough to colour: I know the good king and queen have sent for you.

Ros. To what end, my lord?

Ham. That you must teach me. But let me conjure you, by the rights of our fellowship, by the consonancy of our youth, by the obligation of our ever-preserved love, and by what more dear a better proposer could charge you withal, be even and direct with me, whether you were sent for, or no?

Ros. [*Aside to Guil.*] What say you?

Ham. [*Aside*] Nay, then, I have an eye of you.—If you love me, hold not off.

Guil. My lord, we were sent for.

Ham. I will tell you why; so shall my anticipation prevent your discovery, and your secrecy to the king and queen moult no feather. I have of late—but wherefore I know not—lost all my mirth, forgone all custom of exercises; and indeed it goes so heavily with my disposition that this goodly frame, the earth, seems to me a sterile promontory, this most excellent canopy, the air, look you, this brave o'erhanging firmament, this majestical roof fretted with golden fire, why, it appeareth nothing to me but a foul and pestilent congregation of vapours. What a piece of work is a man! how noble in reason! how infinite in faculties! in form and moving how express and ad-

213. **happiness,** felicity of expression. 214. **prosperously,** successfully. 231. **indifferent,** ordinary. 238. **privates,** i.e., ordinary men (with sexual pun on *private parts*). 252. **confines,** places of confinement. 264. **very . . . ambitious,** that seemingly most substantial thing which the ambitious pursue (Hudson). 272. **fay,** faith. **reason,** argue. 273. **wait upon,** accompany. 274. **sort,** class. 276. **dreadfully attended,** poorly provided with servants. 277. **in the . . . friendship,** as a matter of course among friends. 282. **a,** i.e., at a. 294. **conjure,** adjure, entreat. 295. **consonancy of our youth,** the fact that we are of the same age. 297. **better proposer,** one more skillful in finding proposals. 305. **prevent your discovery,** forestall your disclosure. 313. **fretted,** adorned. 317. **faculties,** capacity. 318. **express,** well-framed (?), exact (?). 319. **apprehension,** understanding. 321. **quintessence,** the fifth essence of ancient philosophy, supposed to be the substance of the heavenly bodies and to be latent in all things. 329. **lenten,** meager.

330. **coted,** overtook and passed beyond. 334. **foil and target,** sword and shield; see *target* in glossary. 336. **humorous man,** actor who takes the part of the humor characters. 338. **tickle o' the sere,** easy on the trigger. 338-340. **the lady . . . for 't,** the lady (fond of talking) shall have opportunity to talk, blank verse or no blank verse. 344. **residence,** remaining in one place. 346. **inhibition,** formal prohibition (from acting plays in the city or, possibly, at court). 347. **innovation,** the new fashion in satirical plays performed by boy actors in the "private" theatres. 352-379. **How . . . load too.** The passage (omitted from Qq) is the famous one dealing with the War of the Theatres (1599-1602), namely, the rivalry between the children's companies and the adult actors. 354. **aery,** nest. 355. **eyases,** young hawks. 355-356. **cry . . . question,** speak in a high key dominating conversation (Clarendon Press); clamor forth the height of controversy (Dowden); probably "excel" (cf. l. 459); perhaps intended to decry leaders of the dramatic

mirable! in action how like an angel! in apprehension how like a god! the beauty of the world! the paragon of animals! And yet, to me, what is this quintessence of dust? man delights not me: no, nor woman neither, though by your smiling you seem to say so.

Ros. My lord, there was no such stuff in my thoughts.

Ham. Why did you laugh then, when I said 'man delights not me'?

Ros. To think, my lord, if you delight not in man, what lenten entertainment the players shall receive from you: we coted them on the way; and hither are they coming, to offer you service.

Ham. He that plays the king shall be welcome; his majesty shall have tribute of me; the adventurous knight shall use his foil and target; the lover shall not sigh gratis; the humorous man shall end his part in peace; the clown shall make those laugh whose lungs are tickle o' the sere; and the lady shall say her mind freely, or the blank verse shall halt for 't. What players are they?

Ros. Even those you were wont to take delight in, the tragedians of the city.

Ham. How chances it they travel? their residence, both in reputation and profit, was better both ways.

Ros. I think their inhibition comes by the means of the late innovation.

Ham. Do they hold the same estimation they did when I was in the city? are they so followed?

Ros. No, indeed, are they not.

Ham. How comes it? do they grow rusty?

Ros. Nay, their endeavour keeps in the wonted pace: but there is, sir, an aery of children, little eyases, that cry out on the top of question, and are most tyrannically clapped for 't: these are now the fashion, and so berattle the common stages—so they call them—that many wearing rapiers are afraid of goose-quills and dare scarce come thither.

Ham. What, are they children? who maintains 'em? how are they escoted? Will they pursue the quality no longer than they can sing? will they not say afterwards, if they should grow themselves to common players—as it is most like, if their means are no better—their writers do them wrong, to make them exclaim against their own succession?

Ros. 'Faith, there has been much to do on both sides; and the nation holds it no sin to tarre them to controversy: there was, for a while, no money bid for argument, unless the poet and the player went to cuffs in the question.

Ham. Is 't possible?

Guil. O, there has been much throwing about of brains.

Ham. Do the boys carry it away?

Ros. Ay, that they do, my lord; Hercules and his load too.

Ham. It is not very strange; for my uncle is king of Denmark, and those that would make mows at him while my father lived, give twenty, forty, fifty, a hundred ducats a-piece for his picture in little. 'Sblood, there is something in this more than natural, if philosophy could find it out.

A flourish [of trumpets within].

Guil. There are the players.

Ham. Gentlemen, you are welcome to Elsinore. Your hands, come then: the appurtenance of welcome is fashion and ceremony: let me comply with you in this garb, lest my extent to the players, which, I tell you, must show fairly outwards, should more appear like entertainment than yours. You are welcome: but my uncle-father and aunt-mother are deceived.

Guil. In what, my dear lord?

Ham. I am but mad north-north-west: when the wind is southerly I know a hawk from a handsaw.

Enter POLONIUS.

Pol. Well be with you, gentlemen!

Ham. Hark you, Guildenstern; and you too: at each ear a hearer: that great baby you see there is not yet out of his swaddling-clouts.

Ros. Happily he is the second time come to them; for they say an old man is twice a child.

Ham. I will prophesy he comes to tell me of the players; mark it.—You say right, sir: o' Monday morning; 'twas then indeed.

Pol. My lord, I have news to tell you.

Ham. My lord, I have news to tell you. When Roscius was an actor in Rome,—

Pol. The actors are come hither, my lord.

Ham. Buz, buz!

Pol. Upon my honour,—

Ham. Then came each actor on his ass,—

Pol. The best actors in the world, either for tragedy, comedy, history, pastoral, pastoral-comical, historical-pastoral, tragical-historical, tragical-comical-historical-pastoral, scene individable, or poem unlimited: Seneca cannot be too heavy, nor Plautus too light. For the law of writ and the liberty, these are the only men.

Ham. O Jephthah, judge of Israel, what a treasure hadst thou!

Pol. What a treasure had he, my lord?

Ham. Why,

'One fair daughter, and no more,
The which he loved passing well.'

Pol. [*Aside*] Still on my daughter.

Ham. Am I not i' the right, old Jephthah?

profession. 356. **tyrannically,** outrageously. 358. **berattle,** berate. **common stages,** public theatres. 359. **many wearing rapiers,** many men of fashion, who were afraid to patronize the common players for fear of being satirized by the poets who wrote for the children. 360. **goose-quills,** i.e., pens of satirists. 362. **escoted,** maintained. 363. **quality,** acting profession. 363-364. **no longer . . . sing,** i.e., until their voices change. 365. **common,** regular, adult. 368. **succession,** future careers. 370. **tarre,** set on (as dogs). 372. **argument,** probably, plot for a play. 373. **went to cuffs,** came to blows. **question,** controversy. 377. **carry it away,** win the day. 378-379. **Hercules . . . load,** regarded as an allusion to the sign of the Globe Theatre, which was Hercules bearing the world on his shoulder. 381. **mows,** grimaces. 382. **ducats,** gold coins worth 9s. 4d. 383. **in little,** in miniature. 390. **comply,** observe the formalities of courtesy. **garb,** manner. 391. **extent,** showing of kindness. 396. **I am . . . north-north-west,** I am only partly mad, i.e., in only one point of the compass. 397. **handsaw.** Hanmer's proposed reading *hernshaw* would mean "heron"; *handsaw* may be an early corruption of *hernshaw.* Another view regards *hawk* as the variant of *hack,* a tool of the pickax type, and *handsaw* as a saw operated by hand. 401. **swaddling-clouts,** cloths in which to wrap a newborn baby. 407. **o' Monday morning,** said to mislead Polonius. 410. **Roscius,** a famous Roman actor. 412. **Buz, buz,** according to Blackstone, an interjection used at Oxford to denote stale news. 418. **scene individable,** a play observing the unity of place. **poem unlimited,** a play disregarding the unities of time and place. 419. **Seneca,** writer of Latin tragedies, model of early Elizabethan writers of tragedy. **Plautus,** writer of Latin comedy. 420. **law . . . liberty,** pieces written according to rules and without rules, i.e., "classical" and "romantic" dramas (Chambers). 422. **Jephthah . . . Israel.** Jephthah had to sacrifice his daughter; see Judges 11.

Pol. If you call me Jephthah, my lord, I have a daughter that I love passing well.

Ham. Nay, that follows not.

Pol. What follows, then, my lord?

Ham. Why,

'As by lot, God wot,'

and then, you know,

'It came to pass, as most like it was,'—

the first row of the pious chanson will show you more; for look, where my abridgement comes.

Enter the Players.

You are welcome, masters; welcome, all. I am glad to see thee well. Welcome, good friends. O, old friend! why, thy face is valanced since I saw thee last: comest thou to beard me in Denmark? What, my young lady and mistress! By 'r lady, your ladyship is nearer to heaven than when I saw you last, by the altitude of a chopine. Pray God, your voice, like a piece of uncurrent gold, be not cracked within the ring. Masters, you are all welcome. We'll e'en to 't like French falconers, fly at any thing we see: we'll have a speech straight: come, give us a taste of your quality; come, a passionate speech.

First Play. What speech, my good lord?

Ham. I heard thee speak me a speech once, but it was never acted; or, if it was, not above once; for the play, I remember, pleased not the million; 'twas caviary to the general: but it was—as I received it, and others, whose judgements in such matters cried in the top of mine—an excellent play, well digested in the scenes, set down with as much modesty as cunning. I remember, one said there were no sallets in the lines to make the matter savoury, nor no matter in the phrase that might indict the author of affectation; but called it an honest method, as wholesome as sweet, and by very much more handsome than fine. One speech in 't I chiefly loved: 'twas Æneas' tale to Dido; and thereabout of it especially, where he speaks of Priam's slaughter: if it live in your memory, begin at this line: let me see, let me see—

'The rugged Pyrrhus, like th' Hyrcanian beast,'—

'tis not so:—it begins with Pyrrhus:—

'The rugged Pyrrhus, he whose sable arms,
Black as his purpose, did the night resemble
When he lay couched in the ominous horse,
Hath now this dread and black complexion smear'd
With heraldry more dismal; head to foot
Now is he total gules; horridly trick'd
With blood of fathers, mothers, daughters, sons,
Bak'd and impasted with the parching streets,
That lend a tyrannous and a damned light
To their lord's murder: roasted in wrath and fire,
And thus o'er-sized with coagulate gore,
With eyes like carbuncles, the hellish Pyrrhus
Old grandsire Priam seeks.'

So, proceed you.

Pol. 'Fore God, my lord, well spoken, with good accent and good discretion.

First Play. 'Anon he finds him
Striking too short at Greeks; his antique sword,
Rebellious to his arm, lies where it falls,
Repugnant to command: unequal match'd,
Pyrrhus at Priam drives; in rage strikes wide;
But with the whiff and wind of his fell sword
Th' unnerved father falls. Then senseless Ilium,
Seeming to feel this blow, with flaming top
Stoops to his base, and with a hideous crash
Takes prisoner Pyrrhus' ear: for, lo! his sword,
Which was declining on the milky head
Of reverend Priam, seem'd i' th' air to stick:
So, as a painted tyrant, Pyrrhus stood,
And like a neutral to his will and matter,
Did nothing.
But, as we often see, against some storm,
A silence in the heavens, the rack stand still,
The bold winds speechless and the orb below
As hush as death, anon the dreadful thunder
Doth rend the region, so, after Pyrrhus' pause,
Aroused vengeance sets him new a-work;
And never did the Cyclops' hammers fall
On Mars's armour forg'd for proof eterne
With less remorse than Pyrrhus' bleeding sword
Now falls on Priam.
Out, out, thou strumpet, Fortune! All you gods,
In general synod, take away her power;
Break all the spokes and fellies from her wheel,
And bowl the round nave down the hill of heaven,
As low as to the fiends!'

Pol. This is too long.

Ham. It shall to the barber's, with your beard. Prithee, say on: he 's for a jig or a tale of bawdry, or he sleeps: say on: come to Hecuba.

First Play. 'But who, ah woe! had seen the mobled queen—'

Ham. 'The mobled queen?'

Pol. That 's good; 'mobled queen' is good.

First Play. 'Run barefoot up and down, threat'ning the flames
With bisson rheum; a clout upon that head
Where late the diadem stood, and for a robe,
About her lank and all o'er-teemed loins,
A blanket, in the alarm of fear caught up;
Who this had seen, with tongue in venom steep'd,
'Gainst Fortune's state would treason have pronounc'd:
But if the gods themselves did see her then
When she saw Pyrrhus make malicious sport
In mincing with his sword her husband's limbs,
The instant burst of clamour that she made,
Unless things mortal move them not at all,

431. **passing,** surpassingly. 437. **like,** probable. 438. **row,** stanza. **chanson,** ballad. 439. **abridgement comes,** opportunity comes for cutting short the conversation. 442. **valanced,** fringed (with a beard). 447. **chopine,** kind of shoe raised by the thickness of the heel; worn in Italy, particularly at Venice. 448. **uncurrent,** not passable as lawful coinage. 449. **cracked within the ring.** In the center of coins were rings enclosing the sovereign's head; if the coin was cracked within this ring, it was unfit for currency. 457. **caviary to the general,** not relished by the multitude. 459. **cried in the top of,** spoke with greater authority than. 461. **cunning,** skill. 462. **sallets,** salads; here, spicy improprieties. 464. **indict,** convict. 466-467. **as wholesome . . . fine.** Its beauty was not that of elaborate ornament, but that of order and proportion (Chambers). 468. **Æneas' tale to Dido.** The lines recited by the player are imitated from Marlowe and Nashe's *Dido Queen of Carthage* (II, i, 214 ff.). They are written in such a way that the conventionality of the play within a play is raised above that of ordinary drama. 472. **Pyrrhus,** a Greek hero in the Trojan War. **Hyrcanian beast,** the tiger; see Virgil, *Aeneid*, IV, 266. 476. **ominous horse,** Trojan horse. 479. **gules,** red; a heraldic term. **trick'd,** spotted, smeared. 481. **impasted,** made into a paste. 484. **o'er-sized,** covered as with size or glue. 493. **Repugnant,** disobedient. 496. **Then senseless Ilium,** insensate Troy. 502. **painted tyrant,** tyrant in a picture. 503. **matter,** task. 505. **against,** before. 506. **rack,** mass of clouds. 509. **region,** sky. 512. **proof eterne,** eternal resistance to assault. 516. **synod,** assembly. 517. **fellies,** pieces of wood forming the rim of a wheel. 518. **nave,** hub. 522. **jig,** comic performance given at the end or in an interval of a play.

Would have made milch the burning eyes of heaven,
And passion in the gods.'

Pol. Look, whe'r he has not turned his colour and has tears in 's eyes. Prithee, no more.

Ham. 'Tis well; I'll have thee speak out the rest soon. Good my lord, will you see the players well bestowed? Do you hear, let them be well used; for they are the abstract and brief chronicles of the time: after your death you were better have a bad epitaph than their ill report while you live.

Pol. My lord, I will use them according to their desert.

Ham. God's bodykins, man, much better: use every man after his desert, and who shall 'scape whipping? Use them after your own honour and dignity: the less they deserve, the more merit is in your bounty. Take them in.

Pol. Come, sirs.

Ham. Follow him, friends: we'll hear a play to-morrow. [*Aside to First Player.*] Dost thou hear me, old friend; can you play the Murder of Gonzago?

First Play. Ay, my lord.

Ham. We'll ha 't to-morrow night. You could, for a need, study a speech of some dozen or sixteen lines, which I would set down and insert in 't, could you not?

First Play. Ay, my lord.

Ham. Very well. Follow that lord; and look you mock him not.—My good friends, I'll leave you till night: you are welcome to Elsinore.

Exeunt Pol. and Players.

Ros. Good my lord! *Exeunt* [*Ros. and Guil*].

Ham. Ay, so, God bye to you.—Now I am alone.
Guildenstern.] Now I am alone.
O, what a rogue and peasant slave am I!
Is it not monstrous that this player here,
But in a fiction, in a dream of passion,
Could force his soul so to his own conceit
That from her working all his visage wann'd,
Tears in his eyes, distraction in 's aspect,
A broken voice, and his whole function suiting
With forms to his conceit? and all for nothing!
For Hecuba!
What 's Hecuba to him, or he to Hecuba,
That he should weep for her? What would he do,
Had he the motive and the cue for passion
That I have? He would drown the stage with tears
And cleave the general ear with horrid speech,
Make mad the guilty and appal the free,
Confound the ignorant, and amaze indeed
The very faculties of eyes and ears.
Yet I,
A dull and muddy-mettled rascal, peak,
Like John-a-dreams, unpregnant of my cause,
And can say nothing; no, not for a king,
Upon whose property and most dear life
A damn'd defeat was made. Am I a coward?
Who calls me villain? breaks my pate across?
Plucks off my beard, and blows it in my face?
Tweaks me by the nose? gives me the lie i' th' throat,
As deep as to the lungs? who does me this?
Ha!
'Swounds, I should take it: for it cannot be
But I am pigeon-liver'd and lack gall
To make oppression bitter, or ere this
I should have fatted all the region kites
With this slave's offal: bloody, bawdy villain!
Remorseless, treacherous, lecherous, kindless villain!
O, vengeance!
Why, what an ass am I! This is most brave,
That I, the son of a dear father murder'd,
Prompted to my revenge by heaven and hell,
Must, like a whore, unpack my heart with words,
And fall a-cursing, like a very drab,
A stallion!
Fie upon 't! foh! About, my brains! Hum, I have heard
That guilty creatures sitting at a play
Have by the very cunning of the scene
Been struck so to the soul that presently
They have proclaim'd their malefactions;
For murder, though it have no tongue, will speak
With most miraculous organ. I'll have these players
Play something like the murder of my father
Before mine uncle: I'll observe his looks;
I'll tent him to the quick: if 'a do blench,
I know my course. The spirit that I have seen
May be the devil: and the devil hath power
T' assume a pleasing shape; yea, and perhaps
Out of my weakness and my melancholy,
As he is very potent with such spirits,
Abuses me to damn me: I'll have grounds
More relative than this: the play 's the thing
Wherein I'll catch the conscience of the king. *Exit.*

[ACT III.

SCENE I. *A room in the castle.*]

Enter KING, QUEEN, POLONIUS, OPHELIA, ROSENCRANTZ, GUILDENSTERN, Lords.

King. And can you, by no drift of conference,
Get from him why he puts on this confusion,
Grating so harshly all his days of quiet
With turbulent and dangerous lunacy?

Ros. He does confess he feels himself distracted;
But from what cause 'a will by no means speak.

Guil. Nor do we find him forward to be sounded,
But, with a crafty madness, keeps aloof,
When we would bring him on to some confession
Of his true state.

Queen. Did he receive you well?

Ros. Most like a gentleman.

523. **bawdry,** indecency. **Hecuba,** wife of Priam, king of Troy. 525. **mobled,** muffled. 529. **bisson rheum,** blinding tears. **clout,** piece of cloth. 531. **o'er-teemed,** worn out with bearing children. 534. **pronounc'd,** proclaimed. 540. **milch,** moist with tears. 542. **turned,** changed. 548. **abstract,** summary account. 554. **bodykins,** diminutive form of the oath, "by God's body." 567. **dozen or sixteen lines.** Critics have amused themselves by trying to locate Hamlet's lines. Lucianus' speech, III, ii, 266, ff., is the best guess. 576. **peasant,** base. 580. **wann'd,** grew pale. 582-583. **his whole . . . conceit,** his whole being responded with forms to suit his thought. 594. **muddy-mettled,** dull-spirited. **peak,** mope, pine. 595. **John-a-dreams,** an expression occurring elsewhere in Elizabethan literature to indicate a dreamer. **unpregnant of,** not quickened by. 597. **property,** proprietorship (of crown and life). 605. **pigeon-liver'd.** The pigeon was supposed to secrete no gall; if Hamlet, so he says, had had gall, he would have felt the bitterness of oppression, and avenged it. 607. **region kites,** kites of the air. 609. **kindless,** unnatural. 615. **drab,** prostitute. 616. **stallion,** prostitute (male or female). Many editors, including Globe, follow F reading of *scullion.* 617. **About,** about it, or turn thou right about. 626. **tent,** probe. **blench,** quail, flinch. 628. **May be the devil.** Hamlet's suspicion is properly grounded in the belief of the time. 631. **spirits,** humors. 633. **relative,** closely related, definite. **this,** i.e., the ghost's story.

ACT III. SCENE I. 1. **drift of conference,** device of conversation; so Q_2; Globe, following F: *circumstance.* 7. **forward,** willing.

Guil. But with much forcing of his disposition.
Ros. Niggard of question; but, of our demands,
Most free in his reply.
Queen. Did you assay him
To any pastime?
Ros. Madam, it so fell out, that certain players
We o'er-raught on the way: of these we told him;
And there did seem in him a kind of joy
To hear of it: they are here about the court,
And, as I think, they have already order
This night to play before him.
Pol. 'Tis most true:
And he beseech'd me to entreat your majesties
To hear and see the matter.
King. With all my heart; and it doth much content me
To hear him so inclin'd.
Good gentlemen, give him a further edge,
And drive his purpose into these delights.
Ros. We shall, my lord.
Exeunt Rosencrantz and Guildenstern.
King. Sweet Gertrude, leave us too;
For we have closely sent for Hamlet hither,
That he, as 'twere by accident, may here
Affront Ophelia:
Her father and myself, lawful espials,
Will so bestow ourselves that, seeing, unseen,
We may of their encounter frankly judge,
And gather by him, as he is behav'd,
If 't be th' affliction of his love or no
That thus he suffers for.
Queen. I shall obey you.
And for your part, Ophelia, I do wish
That your good beauties be the happy cause
Of Hamlet's wildness: so shall I hope your virtues
Will bring him to his wonted way again,
To both your honours.
Oph. Madam, I wish it may. [*Exit Queen.*]
Pol. Ophelia, walk you here. Gracious, so please you,
We will bestow ourselves. [*To Ophelia*] Read on this book;
That show of such an exercise may colour
Your loneliness. We are oft to blame in this,—
'Tis too much prov'd—that with devotion's visage
And pious action we do sugar o'er
The devil himself.
King. [*Aside*] O, 'tis too true!
How smart a lash that speech doth give my conscience!
The harlot's cheek, beautied with plast'ring art,
Is not more ugly to the thing that helps it
Than is my deed to my most painted word:
O heavy burthen!
Pol. I hear him coming: let 's withdraw, my lord.
[*Exeunt King and Polonius.*]

Enter HAMLET.

Ham. To be, or not to be: that is the question:
Whether 'tis nobler in the mind to suffer
The slings and arrows of outrageous fortune,
Or to take arms against a sea of troubles,
And by opposing end them? To die: to sleep;
No more; and by a sleep to say we end
The heart-ache and the thousand natural shocks
That flesh is heir to, 'tis a consummation
Devoutly to be wish'd. To die, to sleep;
To sleep: perchance to dream: ay, there 's the rub;
For in that sleep of death what dreams may come
When we have shuffled off this mortal coil,
Must give us pause: there 's the respect
That makes calamity of so long life;
For who would bear the whips and scorns of time,
Th' oppressor's wrong, the proud man's contumely,
The pangs of despis'd love, the law's delay,
The insolence of office and the spurns
That patient merit of th' unworthy takes,
When he himself might his quietus make
With a bare bodkin? who would fardels bear,
To grunt and sweat under a weary life,
But that the dread of something after death,
The undiscover'd country from whose bourn
No traveller returns, puzzles the will
And makes us rather bear those ills we have
Than fly to others that we know not of?
Thus conscience does make cowards of us all;
And thus the native hue of resolution
Is sicklied o'er with the pale cast of thought,
And enterprises of great pitch and moment
With this regard their currents turn awry,
And lose the name of action.—Soft you now!
The fair Ophelia! Nymph, in thy orisons
Be all my sins remember'd.
Oph. Good my lord,
How does your honour for this many a day?
Ham. I humbly thank you; well, well, well.
Oph. My lord, I have remembrances of yours,
That I have longed long to re-deliver;
I pray you, now receive them.
Ham. No, not I;
I never gave you aught.
Oph. My honour'd lord, you know right well you did;
And, with them, words of so sweet breath compos'd
As made the things more rich: their perfume lost,
Take these again; for to the noble mind
Rich gifts wax poor when givers prove unkind.
There, my lord.
Ham. Ha, ha! are you honest?
Oph. My lord?
Ham. Are you fair?
Oph. What means your lordship?

12. **forcing of his disposition,** i.e., against his will. 13. **Niggard of question,** sparing of conversation. 14. **assay,** try to win. 17. **o'er-raught,** overtook. 26. **edge,** incitement. 28. **too,** so F; Q_2: *two*. 29. **closely,** secretly. 31. **Affront,** confront. 32. **lawful espials,** legitimate spies. 40. **wildness,** madness. 43. **Gracious,** your grace (addressed to the king). 45. **exercise,** act of devotion. (The book she reads is one of devotion.) **colour,** give a plausible appearance to. 52. **to,** compared to. **thing,** i.e., the cosmetic. 59. **sea.** The mixed metaphor of this speech has often been commented on; Theobald's emendation *siege* has sometimes been spoken on the stage. 67. **shuffled,** sloughed, cast. **coil,** usually means "turmoil"; here, possibly "body" (conceived of as wound about the soul like rope); *clay*, *soil*, *veil*, have been suggested as emendations. 68. **respect,** consideration. 69. **of . . . life,** so long-lived. 70. **time,** the world. 72. **despis'd,** rejected. 73. **office,** office-holders. **spurns,** insults. 75. **quietus,** acquittance; here, death. 76. **bare bodkin,** mere dagger; *bare* is sometimes understood as "unsheathed." **fardels,** burdens. 79. **bourn,** boundary. 83. **conscience,** probably, inhibition by the faculty of reason restraining the will from doing wrong. 84. **native hue,** natural color; metaphor derived from the color of the face. 85. **sicklied o'er,** given a sickly tinge. **cast,** shade of color. 86. **pitch,** height (as of a falcon's flight). **moment,** importance. 87. **regard,** respect, consideration. **currents,** courses. 89. **orisons,** prayers. 103-108. **are you . . . beauty.** *Honest* meaning "truthful" (l. 103) and "chaste" (l. 107), and *fair* meaning "just, honorable" (l. 105) and "beautiful" (l. 107) are not mere quibbles; the speech has the irony of a *double entendre*. 108. **your honesty,** your chastity. **discourse to,** familiar inter-

Ham. That if you be honest and fair, your honesty should admit no discourse to your beauty.

Oph. Could beauty, my lord, have better commerce than with honesty?

Ham. Ay, truly; for the power of beauty will sooner transform honesty from what it is to a bawd than the force of honesty can translate beauty into his likeness: this was sometime a paradox, but now the time gives it proof. I did love you once.

Oph. Indeed, my lord, you made me believe so.

Ham. You should not have believed me; for virtue cannot so inoculate our old stock but we shall relish of it: I loved you not.

Oph. I was the more deceived.

Ham. Get thee to a nunnery: why wouldst thou be a breeder of sinners? I am myself indifferent honest; but yet I could accuse me of such things that it were better my mother had not borne me: I am very proud, revengeful, ambitious, with more offences at my beck than I have thoughts to put them in, imagination to give them shape, or time to act them in. What should such fellows as I do crawling between earth and heaven? We are arrant knaves, all; believe none of us. Go thy ways to a nunnery. Where 's your father?

Oph. At home, my lord.

Ham. Let the doors be shut upon him, that he may play the fool no where but in 's own house. Farewell.

Oph. O, help him, you sweet heavens!

Ham. If thou dost marry, I'll give thee this plague for thy dowry: be thou as chaste as ice, as pure as snow, thou shalt not escape calumny. Get thee to a nunnery, go: farewell. Or, if thou wilt needs marry, marry a fool; for wise men know well enough what monsters you make of them. To a nunnery, go, and quickly too. Farewell.

Oph. O heavenly powers, restore him!

Ham. I have heard of your paintings too, well enough; God hath given you one face, and you make yourselves another: you jig, you amble, and you lisp; you nick-name God's creatures, and make your wantonness your ignorance. Go to, I'll no more on 't; it hath made me mad. I say, we will have no moe marriage: those that are married already, all but one, shall live; the rest shall keep as they are. To a nunnery, go. *Exit.*

Oph. O, what a noble mind is here o'er-thrown!
The courtier's, soldier's, scholar's, eye, tongue, sword;
Th' expectancy and rose of the fair state,
The glass of fashion and the mould of form,
Th' observ'd of all observers, quite, quite down!
And I, of ladies most deject and wretched,
That suck'd the honey of his music vows,
Now see that noble and most sovereign reason,
Like sweet bells jangled, out of time and harsh;
That unmatch'd form and feature of blown youth
Blasted with ecstasy: O, woe is me,
T' have seen what I have seen, see what I see!

Enter KING *and* POLONIUS.

King. Love! his affections do not that way tend;
Nor what he spake, though it lack'd form a little,
Was not like madness. There 's something in his soul,
O'er which his melancholy sits on brood;
And I do doubt the hatch and the disclose
Will be some danger: which for to prevent,
I have in quick determination
Thus set it down: he shall with speed to England,
For the demand of our neglected tribute:
Haply the seas and countries different
With variable objects shall expel
This something-settled matter in his heart,
Whereon his brains still beating puts him thus
From fashion of himself. What think you on 't?

Pol. It shall do well: but yet do I believe
The origin and commencement of his grief
Sprung from neglected love. How now, Ophelia!
You need not tell us what Lord Hamlet said;
We heard it all. My lord, do as you please;
But, if you hold it fit, after the play
Let his queen mother all alone entreat him
To show his grief: let her be round with him;
And I'll be plac'd, so please you, in the ear
Of all their conference. If she find him not,
To England send him, or confine him where
Your wisdom best shall think.

King. It shall be so:
Madness in great ones must not unwatch'd go. *Exeunt.*

[SCENE II. *A hall in the castle.*]

Enter HAMLET *and three of the* Players.

Ham. Speak the speech, I pray you, as I pronounced it to you, trippingly on the tongue: but if you mouth it, as many of your players do, I had as lief the town-crier spoke my lines. Nor do not saw the air too much with your hand, thus, but use all gently; for in the very torrent, tempest, and, as I may say, whirlwind of your passion, you must acquire and beget a temperance that may give it smoothness. O, it offends me to the soul to hear a robustious periwig-pated fellow tear a passion to tatters, to very rags, to split the ears of the groundlings, who for the most part are capable of nothing but inexplicable dumb-shows and noise: I would have such a fellow whipped for o'er-doing Termagant; it out-herods Herod: pray you, avoid it.

First Play. I warrant your honour.

Ham. Be not too tame neither, but let your own discretion be your tutor: suit the action to the word, the word to the action; with this special observance, that you o'er-step not the modesty of nature: for any

course with. 110. **commerce,** intercourse. 115. **the time,** the present age. 119. **inoculate,** graft (metaphorical). 120. **but . . . it,** i.e., that we do not still have about us a taste of the old stock; i.e., retain our sinfulness. 124. **indifferent honest,** moderately virtuous. 128. **beck,** command. 145. **monsters,** an allusion to the horns of a cuckold. 148. **your,** indefinite use. 150. **jig,** move with jerky motion; probably allusion to the *jig*, or song and dance, of the current stage. 152-153. **make . . . ignorance,** i.e., excuse your wantonness on the ground of your ignorance. 156. **one,** i.e., the king. 160. **expectancy and rose,** source of hope. 161. **The glass . . . form,** the mirror of fashion and the pattern of courtly behavior. 162. **observ'd . . . observers,** i.e., the center of attention in the court. 167. **blown,** blooming. 168. **ecstasy,** madness. 174. **doubt,** fear. **disclose,** disclosure or revelation (by chipping of the shell). 180. **variable,** various. 181. **something-settled,** somewhat settled. 183. **From . . . himself,** out of his natural manner. 191. **round,** blunt.

SCENE II. 4. **your,** indefinite use. 8. **your,** so Q_2; F and Globe omit. 10. **robustious,** violent, boisterous. **periwig-pated,** wearing a wig. 12. **groundlings,** those who stood in the yard of the theatre. 13. **capable of,** susceptible of being influenced by. 14. **inexplicable,** of no significance worth explaining. 16. **Termagant,** a god of the Saracens; a character in the St. Nicholas play, where one of his worshipers, leaving him in charge of goods, returns to find them stolen; whereupon he beats the god (or idol), which howls vociferously. **Herod,** Herod of Jewry; a character in *The Slaughter of the Innocents* and other cycle plays. The part was played with great noise and fury.

thing so overdone is from the purpose of playing, whose end, both at the first and now, was and is, to hold, as 't were, the mirror up to nature; to show virtue her own feature, scorn her own image, and the very age and body of the time his form and pressure. Now this overdone, or come tardy off, though it make the unskilful laugh, cannot but make the judicious grieve; the censure of the which one must in your allowance o'erweigh a whole theatre of others. O, there be players that I have seen play, and heard others praise, and that highly, not to speak it profanely, that, neither having the accent of Christians nor the gait of Christian, pagan, nor man, have so strutted and bellowed that I have thought some of nature's journeymen had made men and not made them well, they imitated humanity so abominably.

First Play. I hope we have reformed that indifferently with us, sir.

Ham. O, reform it altogether. And let those that play your clowns speak no more than is set down for them; for there be of them that will themselves laugh, to set on some quantity of barren spectators to laugh too; though, in the mean time, some necessary question of the play be then to be considered: that 's villanous, and shows a most pitiful ambition in the fool that uses it. Go, make you ready. [*Exeunt Players.*]

Enter POLONIUS, GUILDENSTERN, *and* ROSENCRANTZ.

How now, my lord! will the king hear this piece of work?

Pol. And the queen too, and that presently.

Ham. Bid the players make haste. [*Exit Polonius.*]
Will you two help to hasten them?

Ros.
Guil. } We will, my lord.

Exeunt they two.

Ham. What ho! Horatio!

Enter HORATIO.

Hor. Here, sweet lord, at your service.

Ham. Horatio, thou art e'en as just a man
As e'er my conversation cop'd withal.

Hor. O, my dear lord,—

Ham. Nay, do not think I flatter;
For what advancement may I hope from thee
That no revenue hast but thy good spirits,
To feed and clothe thee? Why should the poor be flatter'd?
No, let the candied tongue lick absurd pomp,
And crook the pregnant hinges of the knee
Where thrift may follow fawning. Dost thou hear?
Since my dear soul was mistress of her choice
And could of men distinguish her election,
S' hath seal'd thee for herself; for thou hast been
As one, in suff'ring all, that suffers nothing,
A man that fortune's buffets and rewards
Hast ta'en with equal thanks: and blest are those
Whose blood and judgement are so well commeddled,
That they are not a pipe for fortune's finger
To sound what stop she please. Give me that man
That is not passion's slave, and I will wear him
In my heart's core, ay, in my heart of heart,
As I do thee.—Something too much of this.—
There is a play to-night before the king;
One scene of it comes near the circumstance
Which I have told thee of my father's death:
I prithee, when thou seest that act afoot,
Even with the very comment of thy soul
Observe my uncle: if his occulted guilt
Do not itself unkennel in one speech,
It is a damned ghost that we have seen,
And my imaginations are as foul
As Vulcan's stithy. Give him heedful note;
For I mine eyes will rivet to his face,
And after we will both our judgements join
In censure of his seeming.

Hor. Well, my lord:
If 'a steal aught the whilst this play is playing,
And 'scape detecting, I will pay the theft.

Enter trumpets and kettledrums, KING, QUEEN, POLONIUS, OPHELIA [, ROSENCRANTZ, GUILDENSTERN, *and others*].

Ham. They are coming to the play; I must be idle: Get you a place.

King. How fares our cousin Hamlet?

Ham. Excellent, i' faith; of the chameleon's dish: I eat the air, promise-crammed: you cannot feed capons so.

King. I have nothing with this answer, Hamlet; these words are not mine.

Ham. No, nor mine now. [*To Polonius*] My lord, you played once i' the university, you say?

Pol. That did I, my lord; and was accounted a good actor.

Ham. What did you enact?

Pol. I did enact Julius Cæsar: I was killed i' the Capitol; Brutus killed me.

Ham. It was a brute part of him to kill so capital a calf there. Be the players ready?

Ros. Ay, my lord; they stay upon your patience.

Queen. Come hither, my dear Hamlet, sit by me.

Ham. No, good mother, here 's metal more attractive.

Pol. [*To the King*] O, ho! do you mark that?

Ham. Lady, shall I lie in your lap?

[*Lying down at Ophelia's feet.*]

Oph. No, my lord.

Ham. I mean, my head upon your lap?

Oph. Ay, my lord.

Ham. Do you think I meant country matters?

Oph. I think nothing, my lord.

Ham. That 's a fair thought to lie between maids' legs.

Oph. What is, my lord?

27. **pressure,** stamp, impressed character. 28. **come tardy off,** inadequately done. 31. **the censure . . . one,** the judgment of even one of whom. 38. **journeymen,** laborers not yet masters in their trade. 40. **abominably.** Q_2F: *abhominably*, a word thought to be derived from *ab homine*, a circumstance which brings out better the contrast with *humanity*. 41. **indifferently,** fairly, tolerably. 44. **of,** i.e., some among them. 46. **barren,** i.e., of wit. 59. **just,** honest, honorable. 63. **revenue,** accent on second syllable. 66. **pregnant,** pliant. 67. **thrift,** profit. 69-70. Text follows Q_2; Globe, following F, places comma after *distinguish* and reads *Hath*. 74. **commeddled,** so Q_2; Globe, following F: *commingled*. 76. **stop,** hole in a wind instrument for controlling the sound. 84. **very . . . soul,** inward and sagacious criticism (Dowden). 85. **occulted,** hidden. 87. **damned,** in league with Satan. 89. **stithy,** smithy, place of *stiths* (anvils). 92. **censure . . . seeming,** judgment of his appearance or behavior. 95. **idle,** crazy, or not attending to anything serious. 98. **chameleon's dish.** Chameleons were supposed to feed on air. (Hamlet deliberately misinterprets the King's "fares" as "feeds.") 101. **have . . . with,** make nothing of. 102. **are not mine,**

Ham. Nothing.

Oph. You are merry, my lord.

Ham. Who, I?

Oph. Ay, my lord.

Ham. O God, your only jig-maker. What should a man do but be merry? for, look you, how cheerfully my mother looks, and my father died within's two hours.

Oph. Nay, 'tis twice two months, my lord.

Ham. So long? Nay then, let the devil wear black, for I'll have a suit of sables. O heavens! die two months ago, and not forgotten yet? Then there's hope a great man's memory may outlive his life half a year: but, by 'r lady, 'a must build churches, then; or else shall 'a suffer not thinking on, with the hobby-horse, whose epitaph is 'For, O, for, O, the hobby-horse is forgot.'

The trumpets sound. Dumb show follows.

Enter a King *and a* Queen [*very lovingly*]; *the* Queen *embracing him, and he her.* [*She kneels, and makes show of protestation unto him.*] *He takes her up, and declines his head upon her neck: he lies him down upon a bank of flowers: she, seeing him asleep, leaves him. Anon comes in another man, takes off his crown, kisses it, pours poison in the sleeper's ears, and leaves him. The* Queen *returns; finds the* King *dead, makes passionate action. The* Poisoner, *with some three or four come in again, seem to condole with her. The dead body is carried away. The* Poisoner *wooes the* Queen *with gifts: she seems harsh awhile, but in the end accepts love.* [*Exeunt.*]

Oph. What means this, my lord?

Ham. Marry, this is miching mallecho; it means mischief.

Oph. Belike this show imports the argument of the play.

Enter Prologue.

Ham. We shall know by this fellow: the players cannot keep counsel; they'll tell all.

Oph. Will 'a tell us what this show meant?

Ham. Ay, or any show that you'll show him: be not you ashamed to show, he'll not shame to tell you what it means.

Oph. You are naught, you are naught: I'll mark the play.

Pro. For us, and for our tragedy,
Here stooping to your clemency,
We beg your hearing patiently. [*Exit.*]

Ham. Is this a prologue, or the posy of a ring?

Oph. 'Tis brief, my lord.

Ham. As woman's love.

Enter [*two* Players *as*] King *and* Queen.

P. King. Full thirty times hath Phœbus' cart gone round
Neptune's salt wash and Tellus' orbed ground,
And thirty dozen moons with borrowed sheen
About the world have times twelve thirties been,
Since love our hearts and Hymen did our hands
Unite commutual in most sacred bands.

P. Queen. So many journeys may the sun and moon
Make us again count o'er ere love be done!
But, woe is me, you are so sick of late,
So far from cheer and from your former state,
That I distrust you. Yet, though I distrust,
Discomfort you, my lord, it nothing must:
For women's fear and love holds quantity;
In neither aught, or in extremity.
Now, what my love is, proof hath made you know;
And as my love is siz'd, my fear is so:
Where love is great, the littlest doubts are fear;
Where little fears grow great, great love grows there.

P. King. 'Faith, I must leave thee, love, and shortly too;
My operant powers their functions leave to do:
And thou shalt live in this fair world behind,
Honour'd, belov'd; and haply one as kind
For husband shalt thou—

P. Queen. O, confound the rest!
Such love must needs be treason in my breast:
In second husband let me be accurst!
None wed the second but who kill'd the first.

Ham. [*Aside*] Wormwood, wormwood.

P. Queen. The instances that second marriage move
Are base respects of thrift, but none of love:
A second time I kill my husband dead,
When second husband kisses me in bed.

P. King. I do believe you think what now you speak;
But what we do determine oft we break.
Purpose is but the slave to memory,
Of violent birth, but poor validity:
Which now, like fruit unripe, sticks on the tree;
But fall, unshaken, when they mellow be.
Most necessary 'tis that we forget
To pay ourselves what to ourselves is debt:
What to ourselves in passion we propose,
The passion ending, doth the purpose lose.
The violence of either grief or joy
Their own enactures with themselves destroy:
Where joy most revels, grief doth most lament;
Grief joys, joy grieves, on slender accident.
This world is not for aye, nor 'tis not strange
That even our loves should with our fortunes change;
For 'tis a question left us yet to prove,
Whether love lead fortune, or else fortune love.
The great man down, you mark his favourite flies;
The poor advanc'd makes friends of enemies.
And hitherto doth love on fortune tend;
For who not needs shall never lack a friend,
And who in want a hollow friend doth try,
Directly seasons him his enemy.
But, orderly to end where I begun,
Our wills and fates do so contrary run
That our devices still are overthrown;

do not respond to what I asked. 123. **country,** with a bawdy pun. 132. **your only,** only your. **jig-maker,** composer of jigs (song and dance). 138. **suit of sables,** garments trimmed with the fur of the sable, with a quibble on *sable* meaning "black." 143. **suffer . . . on,** undergo oblivion. 144-145. **'For . . . forgot,'** verse of a song occurring also in *Love's Labour's Lost,* III, i, 30. The hobbyhorse was a character in the Morris Dance. 147. **miching mallecho,** sneaking mischief. 158. **naught,** indecent. 160. **stooping,** bowing. 162. **posy,** motto. 166. **salt wash,** the sea. **Tellus,** goddess of the earth (*orbed ground*). 167. **borrowed,** i.e., reflected. 169. **Hymen,** god of matrimony. 170. **commutual,** mutually. 175. **distrust,** am anxious about. 176. After this line Q_2 has *For women feare too much, euen as they loue.* 177. **hold quantity,** keeps proportion between. 184. **operant,** active. **leave,** cease. 207. **enactures,** fulfillments. 210. **aye,** ever. 218. **who,** whoever. 219. **seasons,** matures, ripens.

Our thoughts are ours, their ends none of our own:
So think thou wilt no second husband wed;
But die thy thoughts when thy first lord is dead.

P. Queen. Nor earth to me give food, nor heaven light!
Sport and repose lock from me day and night!
To desperation turn my trust and hope!
An anchor's cheer in prison be my scope!
Each opposite that blanks the face of joy
Meet what I would have well and it destroy!
Both here and hence pursue me lasting strife,
If, once a widow, ever I be wife!

Ham. If she should break it now!

P. King. 'Tis deeply sworn. Sweet, leave me here awhile;
My spirits grow dull, and fain I would beguile
The tedious day with sleep. [*Sleeps.*]

P. Queen. Sleep rock thy brain;
And never come mischance between us twain! *Exit.*

Ham. Madam, how like you this play?

Queen. The lady doth protest too much, methinks.

Ham. O, but she'll keep her word.

King. Have you heard the argument? Is there no offence in 't?

Ham. No, no, they do but jest, poison in jest; no offence i' the world.

King. What do you call the play?

Ham. The Mouse-trap. Marry, how? Tropically. This play is the image of a murder done in Vienna: Gonzago is the duke's name; his wife, Baptista: you shall see anon; 't is a knavish piece of work: but what o' that? your majesty and we that have free souls, it touches us not: let the galled jade winch, our withers are unwrung.

Enter LUCIANUS.

This is one Lucianus, nephew to the king.

Oph. You are as good as a chorus, my lord.

Ham. I could interpret between you and your love, if I could see the puppets dallying.

Oph. You are keen, my lord, you are keen.

Ham. It would cost you a groaning to take off my edge.

Oph. Still better, and worse.

Ham. So you mistake your husbands. Begin, murderer; pox, leave thy damnable faces, and begin. Come: the croaking raven doth bellow for revenge.

Luc. Thoughts black, hands apt, drugs fit, and time agreeing;
Confederate season, else no creature seeing;
Thou mixture rank, of midnight weeds collected,
With Hecate's ban thrice blasted, thrice infected,
Thy natural magic and dire property,
On wholesome life usurp immediately.
[*Pours the poison into the sleeper's ears.*]

Ham. 'A poisons him i' the garden for his estate. His name 's Gonzago: the story is extant, and written in very choice Italian: you shall see anon how the murderer gets the love of Gonzago's wife.

Oph. The king rises.

Ham. What, frighted with false fire!

Queen. How fares my lord?

Pol. Give o'er the play.

King. Give me some light: away!

Pol. Lights, lights, lights!

Exeunt all but Hamlet and Horatio.

Ham. Why, let the strucken deer go weep,
The hart ungalled play;
For some must watch, while some must sleep:
Thus runs the world away.

Would not this, sir, and a forest of feathers—if the rest of my fortunes turn Turk with me—with two Provincial roses on my razed shoes, get me a fellowship in a cry of players, sir?

Hor. Half a share.

Ham. A whole one, I.
For thou dost know, O Damon dear,
This realm dismantled was
Of Jove himself; and now reigns here
A very, very—pajock.

Hor. You might have rhymed.

Ham. O good Horatio, I'll take the ghost's word for a thousand pound. Didst perceive?

Hor. Very well, my lord.

Ham. Upon the talk of the poisoning?

Hor. I did very well note him.

Ham. Ah, ha! Come, some music! come, the recorders!
For if the king like not the comedy,
Why then, belike, he likes it not, perdy.
Come, some music!

Enter ROSENCRANTZ *and* GUILDENSTERN.

Guil. Good my lord, vouchsafe me a word with you.

Ham. Sir, a whole history.

Guil. The king, sir,—

Ham. Ay, sir, what of him?

Guil. Is in his retirement marvellous distempered.

Ham. With drink, sir?

Guil. No, my lord, rather with choler.

Ham. Your wisdom should show itself more richer to signify this to his doctor; for, for me to put him to his purgation would perhaps plunge him into far more choler.

Guil. Good my lord, put your discourse into some frame and start not so wildly from my affair.

Ham. I am tame, sir: pronounce.

Guil. The queen, your mother, in most great affliction of spirit, hath sent me to you.

Ham. You are welcome.

Guil. Nay, good my lord, this courtesy is not of the right breed. If it shall please you to make me a whole-

223. **ends,** results. 229. **An anchor's,** an anchorite's. **cheer,** fare; sometimes printed as *chair*. 230. **opposite,** adverse thing. **blanks,** causes to *blanch* or grow pale. 248. **Tropically,** figuratively. The Q_1 reading, *trapically*, suggests a pun on *trap* in *Mouse-trap* (l. 247). 249. **Gonzago.** In 1538 Luigi Gonzago murdered the Duke of Urbano by pouring poisoned lotion in his ears. 253. **galled jade,** horse whose hide is rubbed by saddle or harness. **winch,** wince. **withers,** the part between the horse's shoulder blades. **unwrung,** not wrung or twisted. 255. **chorus.** In many Elizabethan plays the action was explained by an actor known as the "chorus"; at a puppet show the actor who explained the action was known as an "interpreter," as indicated by the lines following. 258. **dallying,** with sexual suggestion, continued in *keen* (sexually aroused), *groaning* (i.e., in pregnancy), and *edge* (i.e., sexual desire or impetuosity). 261. **Still . . . worse,** more keen, less decorous (Caldecott). 262. **mistake,** err in taking. 263. **pox,** an imprecation. 267. **Confederate,** conspiring (to assist the murderer). 269. **Hecate,** the goddess of witchcraft. **ban,** curse. 277. **false fire,** fireworks, or a blank discharge. 282-285. **Why . . . away,** probably from an old ballad, with allusion to the popular belief that a wounded deer retires to weep and die. Cf. *As You Like It*, II, i, 66. 286. **this,** i.e., the play. **feathers,** allusion to the plumes which Elizabethan actors were fond of wearing. 287. **turn Turk with,** go back on. 288. **two Provincial roses,** rosettes of ribbon like the roses of Provins near Paris, or else the roses of Provence. **razed,** cut, slashed (by way of ornament). 289. **fellowship . . . players,** partnership in a theatrical company. **cry,** pack (as of hounds). 290. **Half a share,** allusion to the custom in dramatic companies of dividing the ownership into a number of shares among the householders. 292-295. **For . . . very,** probably from an old

some answer, I will do your mother's commandment: if not, your pardon and my return shall be the end of my business.

Ham. Sir, I cannot.

Guil. What, my lord?

Ham. Make you a wholesome answer; my wit 's diseased: but, sir, such answer as I can make, you shall command; or, rather, as you say, my mother: therefore no more, but to the matter: my mother, you say,—

Ros. Then thus she says; your behaviour hath struck her into amazement and admiration.

Ham. O wonderful son, that can so 'stonish a mother! But is there no sequel at the heels of this mother's admiration? Impart.

Ros. She desires to speak with you in her closet, ere you go to bed.

Ham. We shall obey, were she ten times our mother. Have you any further trade with us?

Ros. My lord, you once did love me.

Ham. And do still, by these pickers and stealers.

Ros. Good my lord, what is your cause of distemper? you do, surely, bar the door upon your own liberty, if you deny your griefs to your friend.

Ham. Sir, I lack advancement.

Ros. How can that be, when you have the voice of the king himself for your succession in Denmark?

Ham. Ay, sir, but 'While the grass grows,'—the proverb is something musty.

Enter the Players *with recorders.*

O, the recorders! let me see one. To withdraw with you:—why do you go about to recover the wind of me, as if you would drive me into a toil?

Guil. O, my lord, if my duty be too bold, my love is too unmannerly.

Ham. I do not well understand that. Will you play upon this pipe?

Guil. My lord, I cannot.

Ham. I pray you.

Guil. Believe me, I cannot.

Ham. I do beseech you.

Guil. I know no touch of it, my lord.

Ham. 'Tis as easy as lying: govern these ventages with your fingers and thumb, give it breath with your mouth, and it will discourse most eloquent music. Look you, these are the stops.

Guil. But these cannot I command to any utterance of harmony; I have not the skill.

Ham. Why, look you now, how unworthy a thing you make of me! You would play upon me; you would seem to know my stops; you would pluck out the heart of my mystery; you would sound me from my lowest note to the top of my compass: and there is much music, excellent voice, in this little organ; yet cannot you make it speak. 'Sblood, do you think I am easier to be played on than a pipe? Call me what instrument you will, though you can fret me, you cannot play upon me.

Enter POLONIUS.

God bless you, sir!

Pol. My lord, the queen would speak with you, and presently.

Ham. Do you see yonder cloud that 's almost in shape of a camel?

Pol. By the mass, and 'tis like a camel, indeed.

Ham. Methinks it is like a weasel.

Pol. It is backed like a weasel.

Ham. Or like a whale?

Pol. Very like a whale.

Ham. Then I will come to my mother by and by. [*Aside*] They fool me to the top of my bent.—I will come by and by.

Pol. I will say so. [*Exit.*]

Ham. By and by is easily said.
Leave me, friends. [*Exeunt all but Hamlet.*]
'Tis now the very witching time of night,
When churchyards yawn and hell itself breathes out
Contagion to this world: now could I drink hot blood,
And do such bitter business as the day
Would quake to look on. Soft! now to my mother.
O heart, lose not thy nature; let not ever
The soul of Nero enter this firm bosom:
Let me be cruel, not unnatural:
I will speak daggers to her, but use none;
My tongue and soul in this be hypocrites;
How in my words somever she be shent,
To give them seals never, my soul, consent! *Exit.*

[SCENE III. *A room in the castle.*]

Enter KING, ROSENCRANTZ, *and* GUILDENSTERN.

King. I like him not, nor stands it safe with us
To let his madness range. Therefore prepare you;
I your commission will forthwith dispatch,
And he to England shall along with you:
The terms of our estate may not endure
Hazard so near us as doth hourly grow
Out of his brows.

Guil. We will ourselves provide:
Most holy and religious fear it is
To keep those many many bodies safe
That live and feed upon your majesty.

Ros. The single and peculiar life is bound,
With all the strength and armour of the mind,
To keep itself from noyance; but much more
That spirit upon whose weal depend and rest
The lives of many. The cess of majesty
Dies not alone; but, like a gulf, doth draw
What 's near it with it: it is a massy wheel,

ballad having to do with Damon and Pythias. 293. **dismantled,** stripped, divested. 295. **pajock,** peacock (a bird with a bad reputation). Skeat suggested that the word was *patchock*, diminutive of *patch*, clown. 303. **recorders,** wind instruments of the flute kind. 305. **perdy,** corruption of *par dieu*. 315. **choler,** bilious disorder, with quibble on the sense "anger." 321. **frame,** order. 328. **wholesome,** sensible. 337. **matter,** matter in hand. 349. **pickers and stealers,** hands, so called from the catechism, "to keep my hands from picking and stealing." 356. **voice,** support. 358. **'While . . . grows.'** The rest of the proverb is "the silly horse starves." Hamlet may be destroyed while he is waiting for the succession to the kingdom (Malone). 360. **withdraw,** speak in private. 361. **recover the wind,** get to the windward side. 362. **toil,** snare. 363-364. **if . . . unmannerly,** if I am using an unmannerly boldness, it is my love which occasions it. 373. **ventages,** stops of the recorders. 384. **compass,** range of voice. 385. **organ,** musical instrument, i.e., the pipe. 388. **fret,** quibble on meaning "irritate" and the piece of wood, gut, or metal which regulates the fingering. 401. **top of my bent,** limit of endurance, i.e., extent to which a bow may be bent. 402. **by and by,** immediately. 406. **witching time,** i.e., time when spells are cast. 412. **Nero,** murderer of his mother, Agrippina. 416. **shent,** rebuked. 417. **give them seals,** confirm with deeds.

SCENE III. 3. **dispatch,** prepare. 5. **terms,** condition, circumstances. **estate,** state. 7. **brows,** effronteries. 11. **single and peculiar,** individual and private. 13. **noyance,** harm. 15. **cess,** decease. 16. **gulf,** whirlpool.

Fix'd on the summit of the highest mount,
To whose huge spokes ten thousand lesser things
Are mortis'd and adjoin'd; which, when it falls,
Each small annexment, petty consequence,
Attends the boist'rous ruin. Never alone
Did the king sigh, but with a general groan.
King. Arm you, I pray you, to this speedy voyage;
For we will fetters put about this fear,
Which now goes too free-footed.
Ros. We will haste us.
Exeunt Gentlemen [*Ros. and Guil*].

Enter POLONIUS.

Pol. My lord, he 's going to his mother's closet:
Behind the arras I'll convey myself,
To hear the process; I'll warrant she'll tax him home:
And, as you said, and wisely was it said,
'Tis meet that some more audience than a mother,
Since nature makes them partial, should o'erhear
The speech, of vantage. Fare you well, my liege:
I'll call upon you ere you go to bed,
And tell you what I know.
King. Thanks, dear my lord.
Exit [*Polonius*].

O, my offence is rank, it smells to heaven;
It hath the primal eldest curse upon 't,
A brother's murder. Pray can I not,
Though inclination be as sharp as will:
My stronger guilt defeats my strong intent;
And, like a man to double business bound,
I stand in pause where I shall first begin,
And both neglect. What if this cursed hand
Were thicker than itself with brother's blood,
Is there not rain enough in the sweet heavens
To wash it white as snow? Whereto serves mercy
But to confront the visage of offence?
And what 's in prayer but this two-fold force,
To be forestalled ere we come to fall,
Or pardon'd being down? Then I'll look up;
My fault is past. But, O, what form of prayer
Can serve my turn? 'Forgive me my foul murder'?
That cannot be: since I am still possess'd
Of those effects for which I did the murder,
My crown, mine own ambition and my queen.
May one be pardon'd and retain th' offence?
In the corrupted currents of this world
Offence's gilded hand may shove by justice,
And oft 'tis seen the wicked prize itself
Buys out the law: but 'tis not so above;
There is no shuffling, there the action lies
In his true nature; and we ourselves compell'd,
Even to the teeth and forehead of our faults,
To give in evidence. What then? what rests?
Try what repentance can: what can it not?
Yet what can it when one can not repent?
O wretched state! O bosom black as death!
O limed soul, that, struggling to be free,
Art more engag'd! Help, angels! Make assay!
Bow, stubborn knees; and, heart with strings of steel,
Be soft as sinews of the new-born babe!
All may be well. [*He kneels*.]

Enter HAMLET.

Ham. Now might I do it pat, now he is praying;
And now I'll do 't. And so 'a goes to heaven;
And so am I reveng'd. That would be scann'd:
A villain kills my father; and for that,
I, his sole son, do this same villain send
To heaven.
Why, this is hire and salary, not revenge.
'A took my father grossly, full of bread;
With all his crimes broad blown, as flush as May;
And how his audit stands who knows save heaven?
But in our circumstance and course of thought,
'Tis heavy with him: and am I then reveng'd,
To take him in the purging of his soul,
When he is fit and season'd for his passage?
No!
Up, sword; and know thou a more horrid hent:
When he is drunk asleep, or in his rage,
Or in th' incestuous pleasure of his bed;
At game, a-swearing, or about some act
That has no relish of salvation in 't;
Then trip him, that his heels may kick at heaven,
And that his soul may be as damn'd and black
As hell, whereto it goes. My mother stays:
This physic but prolongs thy sickly days. *Exit*.
King. [*Rising*] My words fly up, my thoughts remain below:
Words without thoughts never to heaven go. *Exit*.

[SCENE IV. *The Queen's closet*.]

Enter [QUEEN] GERTRUDE *and* POLONIUS.

Pol. 'A will come straight. Look you lay home to him:
Tell him his pranks have been too broad to bear with,
And that your grace hath screen'd and stood between
Much heat and him. I'll sconce me even here.
Pray you, be round with him.
Ham. (*Within*) Mother, mother, mother!
Queen. I'll warrant you,
Fear me not: withdraw, I hear him coming.
[*Polonius hides behind the arras*.]

Enter HAMLET.

Ham. Now, mother, what 's the matter?
Queen. Hamlet, thou hast thy father much offended.
Ham. Mother, you have my father much offended.

22. **Attends,** participates in. 24. **Arm,** prepare. 25. **about,** so Q_2; Globe, following F: *upon*. 28. **arras,** screen of tapestry placed around the walls of household apartments. **convey,** implication of secrecy; *convey* was often used to mean "steal." 29. **process,** proceedings. **tax him home,** reprove him severely. 33. **of vantage,** from an advantageous place. 37. **primal eldest curse,** the curse of Cain, the first to kill his brother. 39. **sharp as will,** i.e., his desire is as strong as his determination. 47. **confront,** oppose directly. 49. **forestalled,** prevented. 55. **ambition,** i.e., realization of ambition. 56. **offence,** benefit accruing from offense. 57. **currents,** courses. 58. **gilded hand,** hand offering gold as a bribe. 59. **wicked prize,** prize won by wickedness. 61. **shuffling,** escape by trickery. **lies,** is sustainable. 63. **teeth and forehead,** very face. 64. **rests,** remains. 68. **limed,** caught as with birdlime. 69. **engag'd,** embedded. **assay,** trial. 73. **pat,** opportunely. 75. **would be scann'd,** needs to be looked into. 79. **hire and salary,** so F; Q_2: *base and silly*, which can be defended; Wilson: *bait and salary*. 80. **full of bread,** enjoying his worldly pleasures (see Ezekiel 16:49). 81. **broad blown,** in full bloom. **flush,** lusty. 83. **in . . . course,** as we see it in our mortal situation. 86. **fit . . . passage,** i.e., reconciled to heaven by forgiveness of his sins. 88. **hent,** seizing; or, more probably, occasion of seizure. 89. **drunk asleep,** in a drunken sleep. 96. **physic,** purging (by prayer).

SCENE IV. 1. **lay,** thrust. 2. **broad,** unrestrained. 4. **Much heat,** i.e., the king's anger. **sconce,** hide. 5. **round,** blunt. 9-10. **thy father, my father,** i.e., Claudius, the elder Hamlet. 14. **rood,** cross. 37. **braz'd,** brazened, hardened. 44. **sets a blister,** brands as a harlot.

Queen. Come, come, you answer with an idle tongue.
Ham. Go, go, you question with a wicked tongue.
Queen. Why, how now, Hamlet!
Ham. What 's the matter now?
Queen. Have you forgot me?
Ham. No, by the rood, not so:
You are the queen, your husband's brother's wife;
And—would it were not so!—you are my mother.
Queen. Nay, then, I'll set those to you that can speak.
Ham. Come, come, and sit you down; you shall not budge;
You go not till I set you up a glass
Where you may see the inmost part of you.
Queen. What wilt thou do? thou wilt not murder me?
Help, help, ho!
Pol. [*Behind*] What, ho! help, help, help!
Ham. [*Drawing*] How now! a rat? Dead, for a ducat, dead! [*Makes a pass through the arras.*]
Pol. [*Behind*] O, I am slain! [*Falls and dies.*]
Queen. O me, what hast thou done?
Ham. Nay, I know not:
Is it the king?
Queen. O, what a rash and bloody deed is this!
Ham. A bloody deed! almost as bad, good mother,
As kill a king, and marry with his brother.
Queen. As kill a king!
Ham. Ay, lady, it was my word.
[*Lifts up the arras and discovers Polonius.*]
Thou wretched, rash, intruding fool, farewell!
I took thee for thy better: take thy fortune;
Thou find'st to be too busy is some danger.
Leave wringing of your hands: peace! sit you down,
And let me wring your heart; for so I shall,
If it be made of penetrable stuff,
If damned custom have not braz'd it so
That it be proof and bulwark against sense.
Queen. What have I done, that thou dar'st wag thy tongue
In noise so rude against me?
Ham. Such an act
That blurs the grace and blush of modesty,
Calls virtue hypocrite, takes off the rose
From the fair forehead of an innocent love
And sets a blister there, makes marriage-vows
As false as dicers' oaths: O, such a deed
As from the body of contraction plucks
The very soul, and sweet religion makes
A rhapsody of words: heaven's face does glow
O'er this solidity and compound mass
With heated visage, as against the doom
Is thought-sick at the act.
Queen. Ay me, what act,
That roars so loud, and thunders in the index?
Ham. Look here, upon this picture, and on this.
The counterfeit presentment of two brothers.
See, what a grace was seated on this brow;
Hyperion's curls; the front of Jove himself;
An eye like Mars, to threaten and command;
A station like the herald Mercury
New-lighted on a heaven-kissing hill;
A combination and a form indeed,
Where every god did seem to set his seal,
To give the world assurance of a man:
This was your husband. Look you now, what follows:
Here is your husband; like a mildew'd ear,
Blasting his wholesome brother. Have you eyes?
Could you on this fair mountain leave to feed,
And batten on this moor? Ha! have you eyes?
You cannot call it love; for at your age
The hey-day in the blood is tame, it 's humble,
And waits upon the judgement: and what judgement
Would step from this to this? Sense, sure, you have,
Else could you not have motion; but sure, that sense
Is apoplex'd; for madness would not err,
Nor sense to ecstasy was ne'er so thrall'd
But it reserv'd some quantity of choice,
To serve in such a difference. What devil was 't
That thus hath cozen'd you at hoodman-blind?
Eyes without feeling, feeling without sight,
Ears without hands or eyes, smelling sans all,
Or but a sickly part of one true sense
Could not so mope.
O shame! where is thy blush? Rebellious hell,
If thou canst mutine in a matron's bones,
To flaming youth let virtue be as wax,
And melt in her own fire: proclaim no shame
When the compulsive ardour gives the charge,
Since frost itself as actively doth burn
And reason pandars will.
Queen. O Hamlet, speak no more:
Thou turn'st mine eyes into my very soul;
And there I see such black and grained spots
As will not leave their tinct.
Ham. Nay, but to live
In the rank sweat of an enseamed bed,
Stew'd in corruption, honeying and making love
Over the nasty sty,—
Queen. O, speak to me no more;
These words, like daggers, enter in mine ears;
No more, sweet Hamlet!
Ham. A murderer and a villain;
A slave that is not twentieth part the tithe
Of your precedent lord; a vice of kings;
A cutpurse of the empire and the rule,
That from a shelf the precious diadem stole,
And put it in his pocket!
Queen. No more!

Enter GHOST.

Ham. A king of shreds and patches,—

46. **contraction,** the marriage contract. 47. **religion,** religious vows. 48. **rhapsody,** senseless string. 48-51. **heaven's . . . act,** heaven's face blushes to look down upon this world, compounded of the four elements, with hot face as though the day of doom were near, and thought-sick at the deed (i.e., Gertrude's marriage). 50. **heated,** so Q_2; Globe, following F: *tristful.* **doom,** Last Judgment. 52. **index,** prelude or preface. 54. **counterfeit presentment,** portrayed representation. 56. **Hyperion,** the sun god. **front,** brow. 58. **station,** manner of standing. 62. **assurance,** pledge, guarantee. 64. **mildew'd ear.** See Genesis 41:5-7. 67. **batten,** grow fat. **moor,** barren upland. 69. **hey-day,** state of excitement. 71-72. **Sense . . . motion.** Sense and motion are functions of the middle or sensible soul, the possession of sense being the basis of motion. 73. **apoplex'd,** paralyzed. Mental derangement was thus of three sorts: apoplexy, ecstasy, and diabolic possession. 74. **thrall'd,** enslaved. 75. **quantity of choice,** fragment of the power to choose. 77. **cozen'd,** tricked, cheated. **hoodman-blind,** blindman's buff. 79. **sans,** without. 81. **mope,** be in a depressed, spiritless state, act aimlessly. 83. **mutine,** mutiny, rebel. 86. **gives the charge,** delivers the attack. 88. **reason pandars will.** The normal and proper situation was one in which reason guided the will in the direction of good; here, reason is perverted and leads in the direction of evil. 90. **grained,** dyed in grain. 92. **enseamed,** loaded with grease, greased. 98. **precedent lord,** i.e., the elder Hamlet. **vice of kings,** buffoon of kings; a reference to the Vice, or clown, of the morality plays and interludes. 102. **shreds and patches,** i.e., motley, the traditional costume of the Vice.

Save me, and hover o'er me with your wings,
You heavenly guards! What would your gracious figure?
Queen. Alas, he 's mad!
Ham. Do you not come your tardy son to chide,
That, laps'd in time and passion, lets go by
Th' important acting of your dread command?
O, say!
Ghost. Do not forget: this visitation
Is but to whet thy almost blunted purpose.
But, look, amazement on thy mother sits:
O, step between her and her fighting soul:
Conceit in weakest bodies strongest works:
Speak to her, Hamlet.
Ham. How is it with you, lady?
Queen. Alas, how is 't with you,
That you do bend your eye on vacancy
And with th' incorporal air do hold discourse?
Forth at your eyes your spirits wildly peep;
And, as the sleeping soldiers in th' alarm,
Your bedded hair, like life in excrements,
Start up, and stand an end. O gentle son,
Upon the heat and flame of thy distemper
Sprinkle cool patience. Whereon do you look?
Ham. On him, on him! Look you, how pale he glares!
His form and cause conjoin'd, preaching to stones,
Would make them capable.—Do not look upon me;
Lest with this piteous action you convert
My stern effects: then what I have to do
Will want true colour; tears perchance for blood.
Queen. To whom do you speak this?
Ham. Do you see nothing there?
Queen. Nothing at all; yet all that is I see.
Ham. Nor did you nothing hear?
Queen. No, nothing but ourselves.
Ham. Why, look you there! look, how it steals away!
My father, in his habit as he liv'd!
Look, where he goes, even now, out at the portal!
Exit Ghost.
Queen. This is the very coinage of your brain:
This bodiless creation ecstasy
Is very cunning in.
Ham. Ecstasy!
My pulse, as yours, doth temperately keep time,
And makes as healthful music: it is not madness
That I have utt'red: bring me to the test,
And I the matter will re-word, which madness
Would gambol from. Mother, for love of grace,
Lay not that flattering unction to your soul,
That not your trespass, but my madness speaks:
It will but skin and film the ulcerous place,
Whiles rank corruption, mining all within,
Infects unseen. Confess yourself to heaven;
Repent what 's past; avoid what is to come;
And do not spread the compost on the weeds,
To make them ranker. Forgive me this my virtue;
For in the fatness of these pursy times
Virtue itself of vice must pardon beg,
Yea, curb and woo for leave to do him good.
Queen. O Hamlet, thou hast cleft my heart in twain.
Ham. O, throw away the worser part of it,
And live the purer with the other half.
Good night: but go not to my uncle's bed;
Assume a virtue, if you have it not.
That monster, custom, who all sense doth eat,
Of habits devil, is angel yet in this,
That to the use of actions fair and good
He likewise gives a frock or livery,
That aptly is put on. Refrain to-night,
And that shall lend a kind of easiness
To the next abstinence: the next more easy;
For use almost can change the stamp of nature,
†And either . . . the devil, or throw him out
With wondrous potency. Once more, good night:
And when you are desirous to be bless'd,
I'll blessing beg of you. For this same lord,
[*Pointing to Polonius.*]
I do repent: but heaven hath pleas'd it so,
To punish me with this and this with me,
That I must be their scourge and minister.
I will bestow him, and will answer well
The death I gave him. So, again, good night.
I must be cruel, only to be kind:
Thus bad begins and worse remains behind.
One wòrd more, good lady.
Queen. What shall I do?
Ham. Not this, by no means, that I bid you do:
Let the bloat king tempt you again to bed;
Pinch wanton on your cheek; call you his mouse;
And let him, for a pair of reechy kisses,
Or paddling in your neck with his damn'd fingers,
Make you to ravel all this matter out,
That I essentially am not in madness,
But mad in craft. 'Twere good you let him know;
For who, that 's but a queen, fair, sober, wise,
Would from a paddock, from a bat, a gib,
Such dear concernings hide? who would do so?
No, in despite of sense and secrecy,
Unpeg the basket on the house's top,
Let the birds fly, and, like the famous ape,
To try conclusions, in the basket creep,
And break your own neck down.
Queen. Be thou assur'd, if words be made of breath,
And breath of life, I have no life to breathe
What thou hast said to me.
Ham. I must to England; you know that?
Queen. Alack,
I had forgot: 'tis so concluded on.
Ham. There 's letters seal'd: and my two schoolfellows,
Whom I will trust as I will adders fang'd,

107. **laps'd . . . passion,** having suffered time to slip and passion to cool (Johnson); also explained as "engrossed in casual events and lapsed into mere fruitless passion, so that he no longer entertains a rational purpose." 108. **important,** urgent. 112. **amazement,** frenzy, distraction. 118. **incorporal,** immaterial. 121. **bedded,** laid in smooth layers. **excrements.** The hair was considered an excrement or voided part of the body. 122. **an,** on. 126. **conjoin'd,** united. 128-129. **convert . . . effects,** divert me from my stern duty. For *effects* Singer conjectures *affects* (affections of the mind). 130. **want true colour,** lack good reason so that (with a play on the normal sense of *colour*) I shall shed tears instead of blood. 143. **re-word,** repeat in words. 144. **gambol,** skip away. 145. **unction,** ointment used medicinally or as a rite; suggestion that forgiveness for sin may not be so easily achieved. 148. **mining,** working under the surface. 150. **what is to come,** i.e., the sins of the future. 151. **compost,** manure. 152. **this my virtue,** my virtuous talk in reproving you. 153. **fatness,** grossness. **pursy,** short-winded, corpulent. 155. **curb,** bow, bend the knee. 169. Defective line usually emended by inserting *master* after *either*, following Q_4 and early editors. 171. **be bless'd,** become blessed, i.e., repentant. 182. **bloat,** bloated. 184. **reechy,** dirty, filthy. 187. **essentially,** in my essential nature. 190. **paddock,** toad. **gib,** tomcat. 191. **dear concernings,** important affairs. 194. **the famous ape.** A letter from Sir John Suckling seems to supply other details of the story, otherwise not identified: "It is the story of the jackanapes and the partridges; thou starest after a beauty till it be lost to thee, then let'st out another, and starest after that till it is gone too." 195. **con-**

They bear the mandate; they must sweep my way,
And marshal me to knavery. Let it work;
For 'tis the sport to have the enginer
Hoist with his own petar: and 't shall go hard
But I will delve one yard below their mines,
And blow them at the moon: O, 'tis most sweet,
When in one line two crafts directly meet.
This man shall set me packing:
I'll lug the guts into the neighbour room.
Mother, good night. Indeed this counsellor
Is now most still, most secret and most grave,
Who was in life a foolish prating knave.
Come, sir, to draw toward an end with you.
Good night, mother.

Exeunt [severally; Hamlet dragging in Polonius].

[ACT IV.

SCENE I. *A room in the castle.*]

Enter KING *and* QUEEN, *with* ROSENCRANTZ *and* GUILDENSTERN.

King. There 's matter in these sighs, these profound heaves:
You must translate: 'tis fit we understand them.
Where is your son?

Queen. Bestow this place on us a little while.

[Exeunt Rosencrantz and Guildenstern.]

Ah, mine own lord, what have I seen to-night!

King. What, Gertrude? How does Hamlet?

Queen. Mad as the sea and wind, when both contend
Which is the mightier: in his lawless fit,
Behind the arras hearing something stir,
Whips out his rapier, cries, 'A rat, a rat!'
And, in this brainish apprehension, kills
The unseen good old man.

King. O heavy deed!
It had been so with us, had we been there:
His liberty is full of threats to all;
To you yourself, to us, to every one.
Alas, how shall this bloody deed be answer'd?
It will be laid to us, whose providence
Should have kept short, restrain'd and out of haunt,
This mad young man: but so much was our love,
We would not understand what was most fit;
But, like the owner of a foul disease,
To keep it from divulging, let it feed
Even on the pith of life. Where is he gone?

Queen. To draw apart the body he hath kill'd:
O'er whom his very madness, like some ore
Among a mineral of metals base,
Shows itself pure; 'a weeps for what is done.

King. O Gertrude, come away!
The sun no sooner shall the mountains touch,
But we will ship him hence: and this vile deed
We must, with all our majesty and skill,
Both countenance and excuse. Ho, Guildenstern!

Enter ROSENCRANTZ *and* GUILDENSTERN.

Friends both, go join you with some further aid:
Hamlet in madness hath Polonius slain,
And from his mother's closet hath he dragg'd him:
Go seek him out; speak fair, and bring the body
Into the chapel. I pray you, haste in this.

[Exeunt Rosencrantz and Guildenstern.]

Come, Gertrude, we'll call up our wisest friends;
And let them know, both what we mean to do,
†And what 's untimely done . . . .
Whose whisper o'er the world's diameter,
As level as the cannon to his blank,
Transports his pois'ned shot, may miss our name,
And hit the woundless air. O, come away!
My soul is full of discord and dismay. *Exeunt.*

[SCENE II. *Another room in the castle.*]

Enter HAMLET.

Ham. Safely stowed.

Ros., *Guil.* (*Within*) Hamlet! Lord Hamlet!

Ham. But soft, what noise? who calls on Hamlet? O, here they come.

Enter ROSENCRANTZ *and* GUILDENSTERN.

Ros. What have you done, my lord, with the dead body?

Ham. Compounded it with dust, whereto 'tis kin.

Ros. Tell us where 'tis, that we may take it thence And bear it to the chapel.

Ham. Do not believe it.

Ros. Believe what?

Ham. That I can keep your counsel and not mine own. Besides, to be demanded of a sponge! what replication should be made by the son of a king?

Ros. Take you me for a sponge, my lord?

Ham. Ay, sir, that soaks up the king's countenance, his rewards, his authorities. But such officers do the king best service in the end: he keeps them, like an ape an apple, in the corner of his jaw; first mouthed, to be last swallowed: when he needs what you have gleaned, it is but squeezing you, and, sponge, you shall be dry again.

Ros. I understand you not, my lord.

Ham. I am glad of it: a knavish speech sleeps in a foolish ear.

Ros. My lord, you must tell us where the body is, and go with us to the king.

Ham. The body is with the king, but the king is not with the body. The king is a thing—

Guil. A thing, my lord!

clusions, experiments. 204. **sweep my way,** clear my path. 206. **enginer,** constructor of military works, or possibly, artilleryman. 207. **Hoist,** blown up. **petar,** defined as a small engine of war used to blow in a door or make a breach, and as a case filled with explosive materials. 210. **two crafts,** two acts of guile, with quibble on the sense of "two ships." 211. **set me packing,** set me to making schemes, and set me to lugging (him), and, also, send me off in a hurry. 216. **draw,** come, with quibble on literal sense.

ACT IV. SCENE I. 11. **brainish,** headstrong, passionate. **apprehension,** conception, imagination. 17. **providence,** foresight. 18. **short,** i.e., on a short tether. **out of haunt,** secluded. 22. **divulging,** becoming evident. 26. **mineral,** mine. 40. Defective line; Capell and others: *so, haply, slander;* Theobald and others: *for, haply, slander;* other conjectures. 41. **diameter,** extent from side to side. 42. **level,** straight. **blank,** white spot in the center of a target. 44. **woundless,** invulnerable.

SCENE II. 11. **keep your counsel.** Hamlet is aware of their treachery but says nothing about it. 13. **replication,** reply. 17. **authorities,** authoritative backing. 19. **like . . . apple,** so Farmer; F: *like an ape* (Globe); Q_2: *like an apple.* 29-30. **The body . . . body.** There are many interpretations; possibly, "The body lies in death with the king, my father; but my father walks disembodied" (Dowden); or "Claudius has the bodily possession of kingship, but kingliness, or justice of inheritance, is not with him." Yale editor explains, "The King is still alive (i.e., with *his* body), but he is not with the dead body (i.e., Polonius)."

Ham. Of nothing: bring me to him. Hide fox, and all after. *Exeunt.*

[SCENE III. *Another room in the castle.*]

Enter KING, *and two or three.*

King. I have sent to seek him, and to find the body.
How dangerous is it that this man goes loose!
Yet must not we put the strong law on him:
He 's lov'd of the distracted multitude,
Who like not in their judgement, but their eyes;
And where 'tis so, th' offender's scourge is weigh'd,
But never the offence. To bear all smooth and even,
This sudden sending him away must seem
Deliberate pause: diseases desperate grown
By desperate appliance are reliev'd,
Or not at all.

Enter ROSENCRANTZ, [GUILDENSTERN,] *and all the rest.*

How now! what hath befall'n?
Ros. Where the dead body is bestow'd, my lord,
We cannot get from him.
King. But where is he?
Ros. Without, my lord; guarded, to know your pleasure.
King. Bring him before us.
Ros. Ho! bring in the lord.

They enter [*with* HAMLET].

King. Now, Hamlet, where 's Polonius?
Ham. At supper.
King. At supper! where?

Ham. Not where he eats, but where 'a is eaten: a certain convocation of politic worms are e'en at him. Your worm is your only emperor for diet: we fat all creatures else to fat us, and we fat ourselves for maggots: your fat king and your lean beggar is but variable service, two dishes, but to one table: that 's the end.

King. Alas, alas!

Ham. A man may fish with the worm that hath eat of a king, and eat of the fish that hath fed of that worm.

King. What dost thou mean by this?

Ham. Nothing but to show you how a king may go a progress through the guts of a beggar.

King. Where is Polonius?

Ham. In heaven; send thither to see: if your messenger find him not there, seek him i' the other place yourself. But if indeed you find him not within this month, you shall nose him as you go up the stairs into the lobby.

King. Go seek him there, [*To some Attendants.*]
Ham. 'A will stay till you come. [*Exeunt Attendants.*]
King. Hamlet, this deed, for thine especial safety,—
Which we do tender, as we dearly grieve
For that which thou hast done,—must send thee hence
With fiery quickness: therefore prepare thyself;
The bark is ready, and the wind at help,
Th' associates tend, and everything is bent
For England.
Ham. For England!
King. Ay, Hamlet.
Ham. Good.
King. So is it, if thou knew'st our purposes.

Ham. I see a cherub that sees them. But, come; for England! Farewell, dear mother.

King. Thy loving father, Hamlet.

Ham. My mother: father and mother is man and wife; man and wife is one flesh; and so, my mother. Come, for England! *Exit.*

King. Follow him at foot; tempt him with speed aboard;
Delay it not; I'll have him hence to-night:
Away! for every thing is seal'd and done
That else leans on th' affair: pray you, make haste.
[*Exeunt all but the King.*]
And, England, if my love thou hold'st at aught—
As my great power thereof may give thee sense,
Since yet thy cicatrice looks raw and red
After the Danish sword, and thy free awe
Pays homage to us— thou mayst not coldly set
Our sovereign process; which imports at full,
By letters congruing to that effect,
The present death of Hamlet. Do it, England;
For like the hectic in my blood he rages,
And thou must cure me: till I know 'tis done,
Howe'er my haps, my joys were ne'er begun. *Exit.*

[SCENE IV. *A plain in Denmark.*]

Enter FORTINBRAS *with his Army over the stage.*

For. Go, captain, from me greet the Danish king;
Tell him that, by his license, Fortinbras
Craves the conveyance of a promis'd march
Over his kingdom. You know the rendezvous.
If that his majesty would aught with us,
We shall express our duty in his eye;
And let him know so.
Cap. I will do 't, my lord.
For. Go softly on. [*Exeunt all but Captain.*]

Enter HAMLET, ROSENCRANTZ, [GUILDENSTERN,] *&c.*

Ham. Good sir, whose powers are these?
Cap. They are of Norway, sir.
Ham. How purpos'd, sir, I pray you?
Cap. Against some part of Poland.
Ham. Who commands them, sir?
Cap. The nephew to old Norway, Fortinbras.
Ham. Goes it against the main of Poland, sir,
Or for some frontier?
Cap. Truly to speak, and with no addition,
We go to gain a little patch of ground
That hath in it no profit but the name.

32-33. **Hide . . . after,** an old signal cry in the game of hide-and-seek.
SCENE III. 4. **distracted,** i.e., without power of forming logical judgments. 6. **scourge,** punishment. **weigh'd,** taken into consideration. 9. **Deliberate pause,** considered action. 21. **convocation . . . worms,** allusion to the Diet of Worms (1521). **politic,** crafty. 25. **variable service,** a variety of dishes. 33. **progress,** royal journey of state. 43. **tender,** regard, hold dear. 50. **cherub.** Cherubim are angels of knowledge (Dowden). 56. **at foot,** close behind, at heel. 62. **cicatrice,** scar. 63. **free awe,** voluntary show of respect. 68. **hectic,** fever. 70. **haps,** fortunes.

SCENE IV. 2. **license,** leave. 3. **conveyance,** escort, convoy. 6. **in his eye,** in his presence. 8. **softly,** slowly. 15. **main,** country itself. 20. **farm it,** take a lease of it. 22. **fee,** fee simple. 26. **debate . . . straw,** settle this trifling matter. 27. **imposthume,** purulent abscess or swelling. 32. **occasions,** incidents, events. **inform against,** generally defined as "show," "betray" (i.e., his tardiness); more probably *inform* means "take shape," as in *Macbeth*, II, i, 48. 34. **market of his time,** the best use he makes of his time, or, that for which he sells his time (Johnson). 39. **fust,** grow moldy. 58. **Excitements of,** incentives to. 61. **trick,** toy, trifle. 62. **plot,** i.e., of ground.

To pay five ducats, five, I would not farm it;
Nor will it yield to Norway or the Pole
A ranker rate, should it be sold in fee.
Ham. Why, then the Polack never will defend it.
Cap. Yes, it is already garrison'd.
Ham. Two thousand souls and twenty thousand ducats
Will not debate the question of this straw:
This is th' imposthume of much wealth and peace,
That inward breaks, and shows no cause without
Why the man dies. I humbly thank you, sir.
Cap. God be wi' you, sir. [*Exit.*]
Ros. Will 't please you go, my lord?
Ham. I'll be with you straight. Go a little before.
[*Exeunt all except Hamlet.*]
How all occasions do inform against me,
And spur my dull revenge! What is a man,
If his chief good and market of his time
Be but to sleep and feed? a beast, no more.
Sure, he that made us with such large discourse,
Looking before and after, gave us not
That capability and god-like reason
To fust in us unus'd. Now, whether it be
Bestial oblivion, or some craven scruple
Of thinking too precisely on th' event,
A thought which, quarter'd, hath but one part wisdom
And ever three parts coward, I do not know
Why yet I live to say 'This thing 's to do;'
Sith I have cause and will and strength and means
To do 't. Examples gross as earth exhort me:
Witness this army of such mass and charge
Led by a delicate and tender prince,
Whose spirit with divine ambition puff'd
Makes mouths at the invisible event,
Exposing what is mortal and unsure
To all that fortune, death and danger dare,
Even for an egg-shell. Rightly to be great
Is not to stir without great argument,
But greatly to find quarrel in a straw
When honour 's at the stake. How stand I then,
That have a father kill'd, a mother stain'd,
Excitements of my reason and my blood,
And let all sleep? while, to my shame, I see
The imminent death of twenty thousand men,
That, for a fantasy and trick of fame,
Go to their graves like beds, fight for a plot
Whereon the numbers cannot try the cause,
Which is not tomb enough and continent
To hide the slain? O, from this time forth,
My thoughts be bloody, or be nothing worth! *Exit.*

[SCENE V. *Elsinore. A room in the castle.*]

Enter HORATIO, [QUEEN] GERTRUDE, *and a* Gentleman.

Queen. I will not speak with her.
Gent. She is importunate, indeed distract:
Her mood will needs be pitied.
Queen. What would she have?
Gent. She speaks much of her father; says she hears
There 's tricks i' th' world; and hems, and beats her heart;
Spurns enviously at straws; speaks things in doubt,
That carry but half sense: her speech is nothing,
Yet the unshaped use of it doth move
The hearers to collection; they yawn at it,
And botch the words up fit to their own thoughts;
Which, as her winks, and nods, and gestures yield them,
Indeed would make one think there might be thought,
Though nothing sure, yet much unhappily.
Hor. 'Twere good she were spoken with: for she may strew
Dangerous conjectures in ill-breeding minds.
Queen. Let her come in. [*Exit Gentleman.*]
[*Aside*] To my sick soul, as sin's true nature is,
Each toy seems prologue to some great amiss:
So full of artless jealousy is guilt,
It spills itself in fearing to be spilt.

Enter OPHELIA [*distracted*].

Oph. Where is the beauteous majesty of Denmark?
Queen. How now, Ophelia!
Oph. (*She sings*) How should I your true love know
From another one?
By his cockle hat and staff,
And his sandal shoon.
Queen. Alas, sweet lady, what imports this song?
Oph. Say you? nay, pray you, mark.
He is dead and gone, lady, (*Song*)
He is dead and gone;
At his head a grass-green turf,
At his heels a stone.
O, ho!
Queen. Nay, but, Ophelia,—
Oph. Pray you, mark
[*Sings*] White his shroud as the mountain snow,—

Enter KING.

Queen. Alas, look here, my lord.
Oph. Larded all with flowers; (*Song*)
Which bewept to the grave did not go
With true-love showers.
King. How do you, pretty lady?
Oph. Well, God 'ild you! They say the owl was a baker's daughter. Lord, we know what we are, but know not what we may be. God be at your table!
King. Conceit upon her father.
Oph. Pray let 's have no words of this; but when they ask you what it means, say you this:
To-morrow is Saint Valentine's day, (*Song*)
All in the morning betime,
And I a maid at your window,
To be your Valentine.
Then up he rose, and donn'd his clothes,

SCENE V. 5. **tricks,** deceptions. **heart,** i.e., breast. 6. **Spurns . . . straws,** kicks spitefully at small objects in her path. 8. **unshaped,** unformed, artless. 9. **collection,** inference, a guess at some sort of meaning. **yawn,** wonder; so Q_2; Globe, following F: *aim*. 10. **botch,** patch. 11. **yield,** deliver, bring forth (her words). 13. **much unhappily,** expressive of much unhappiness. 15. **ill-breeding minds,** minds bent on mischief. 18. **great amiss,** calamity, disaster. 19-20. **So . . . spilt,** guilt is so full of suspicion that it unskillfully betrays itself in fearing to be betrayed (Onions). 25. **cockle hat,** hat with cockleshell stuck in it as a sign that the wearer had been a pilgrim to the shrine of St. James of Compostella. The pilgrim's garb was a conventional disguise for lovers. 26. **shoon,** shoes. 37. **Larded . . . flowers,** so Q_2; Globe, following F: *Larded with sweet flowers*. **Larded,** decorated. 38. **not,** so Q_2F; Globe, following Pope, omits. 41. **God 'ild,** God yield or reward. 42. **owl,** reference to a monkish legend that a baker's daughter was turned into an owl for refusing bread to the Saviour; quoted by Douce. 51. **Valentine.** This song alludes to the belief that the first girl seen by a man on the morning of this day was his valentine or truelove (Halliwell).

And dupp'd the chamber-door;
Let in the maid, that out a maid
Never departed more.

King. Pretty Ophelia!

Oph. Indeed, la, without an oath, I'll make an end on 't:

[*Sings*] By Gis and by Saint Charity,
Alack, and fie for shame!
Young men will do 't, if they come to 't;
By cock, they are to blame.
Quoth she, before you tumbled me,
You promis'd me to wed.
So would I ha' done, by yonder sun,
An thou hadst not come to my bed.

King. How long hath she been thus?

Oph. I hope all will be well. We must be patient: but I cannot choose but weep, to think they would lay him i' the cold ground. My brother shall know of it: and so I thank you for your good counsel. Come, my coach! Good night, ladies; good night, sweet ladies; good night, good night. [*Exit*.]

King. Follow her close; give her good watch, I pray you. [*Exit Horatio*.]
O, this is the poison of deep grief; it springs
All from her father's death. O Gertrude, Gertrude,
When sorrows come, they come not single spies,
But in battalions. First, her father slain:
Next, your son gone; and he most violent author
Of his own just remove: the people muddied,
Thick and unwholesome in their thoughts and whispers,
For good Polonius' death; and we have done but greenly,
In hugger-mugger to inter him: poor Ophelia
Divided from herself and her fair judgement,
Without the which we are pictures, or mere beasts:
Last, and as much containing as all these,
Her brother is in secret come from France;
Feeds on his wonder, keeps himself in clouds,
And wants not buzzers to infect his ear
With pestilent speeches of his father's death;
Wherein necessity, of matter beggar'd,
Will nothing stick our person to arraign
In ear and ear. O my dear Gertrude, this,
Like to a murd'ring-piece, in many places
Gives me superfluous death. *A noise within*.

Queen. Alack, what noise is this?

King. Where are my Switzers? Let them guard the door.

Enter a Messenger.

What is the matter?

Mess. Save yourself, my lord:
The ocean, overpeering of his list,
Eats not the flats with more impiteous haste
Than young Laertes, in a riotous head,
O'erbears your officers. The rabble call him lord;
And, as the world were now but to begin,
Antiquity forgot, custom not known,
The ratifiers and props of every word,
They cry 'Choose we: Laertes shall be king:'
Caps, hands, and tongues, applaud it to the clouds:
'Laertes shall be king, Laertes king!' *A noise within*.

Queen. How cheerfully on the false trail they cry!
O, this is counter, you false Danish dogs!

King. The doors are broke.

Enter LAERTES *with others*.

Laer. Where is this king? Sirs, stand you all without.

Danes. No, let 's come in.

Laer. I pray you, give me leave.

Danes. We will, we will. [*They retire without the door*.]

Laer. I thank you: keep the door. O thou vile king,
Give me my father!

Queen. Calmly, good Laertes.

Laer. That drop of blood that 's calm proclaims me bastard,
Cries cuckold to my father, brands the harlot
Even here, between the chaste unsmirched brow
Of my true mother.

King. What is the cause, Laertes,
That thy rebellion looks so giant-like?
Let him go, Gertrude; do not fear our person:
There 's such divinity doth hedge a king,
That treason can but peep to what it would,
Acts little of his will. Tell me, Laertes,
Why thou art thus incens'd. Let him go, Gertrude.
Speak, man.

Laer. Where is my father?

King. Dead.

Queen. But not by him.

King. Let him demand his fill.

Laer. How came he dead? I'll not be juggled with:
To hell, allegiance! vows, to the blackest devil!
Conscience and grace, to the profoundest pit!
I dare damnation. To this point I stand,
That both the worlds I give to negligence,
Let come what comes; only I'll be reveng'd
Most throughly for my father.

King. Who shall stay you?

Laer. My will, not all the world's:
And for my means, I'll husband them so well,
They shall go far with little.

King. Good Laertes,
If you desire to know the certainty
Of your dear father, is 't writ in your revenge,
That, swoopstake, you will draw both friend and foe,
Winner and loser?

Laer. None but his enemies.

King. Will you know them then?

Laer. To his good friends thus wide I'll ope my arms;
And like the kind life-rend'ring pelican,
Repast them with my blood.

King. Why, now you speak
Like a good child and a true gentleman.
That I am guiltless of your father's death,
And am most sensibly in grief for it,

53. **dupp'd,** opened. 59. **Gis,** Jesus. 62. **cock,** perversion of "God" in oaths. 83. **greenly,** foolishly. 84. **hugger-mugger,** secret haste. 89. **in clouds,** invisible. 90. **buzzers,** gossipers. 92. **of matter beggar'd,** unprovided with facts. 93. **nothing stick,** not hesitate. 94. **In ear and ear,** in everybody's ears. 95. **murd'ring-piece,** small cannon or mortar; suggestion of numerous missiles fired. 97. **Switzers,** Swiss guards, mercenaries. 99. **overpeering,** overflowing. **list,** shore. 105. **word,** promise. 110. **counter,** a hunting term meaning to follow the trail in a direction opposite to that which the game has taken. 124. **peep to,** i.e., look at from afar off. **would,** wishes to do. 134. **give to negligence.** He despises both the here and the hereafter. 137. **My will.** He will not be stopped except by his own will. 142. **swoopstake,** literally, drawing the whole stake at once, i.e., indiscriminately. 146. **pelican,** reference to the belief that the pelican feeds its young with its own blood. 147. **Repast,** feed. 151. **'pear,** so Q_2; Globe, following F: *pierce*. 154. **heat,** probably the heat generated by the passion of grief. 172. **wheel,** spinning wheel as accompaniment to the song (Onions); refrain (Steevens). **false steward.** The story is unknown. 175. **rosemary,**

It shall as level to your judgement 'pear
As day does to your eye.

A noise within: 'Let her come in.'

Laer. How now! what noise is that?

Enter OPHELIA.

O heat, dry up my brains! tears seven times salt,
Burn out the sense and virtue of mine eye!
By heaven, thy madness shall be paid with weight,
Till our scale turn the beam. O rose of May!
Dear maid, kind sister, sweet Ophelia!
O heavens! is 't possible, a young maid's wits
Should be as mortal as an old man's life?
Nature is fine in love, and where 'tis fine,
It sends some precious instance of itself
After the thing it loves.

Oph. *(Song)*

They bore him barefac'd on the bier;
Hey non nonny, nonny, hey nonny;
And in his grave rain'd many a tear:—
Fare you well, my dove!

Laer. Hadst thou thy wits, and didst persuade revenge,
It could not move thus.

Oph. [*Sings*] You must sing a-down a-down,
An you call him a-down-a.
O, how the wheel becomes it! It is the false steward, that stole his master's daughter.

Laer. This nothing 's more than matter.

Oph. There 's rosemary, that 's for remembrance; pray you, love, remember: and there is pansies, that 's for thoughts.

Laer. A document in madness, thoughts and remembrance fitted.

Oph. There 's fennel for you, and columbines: there 's rue for you; and here 's some for me: we may call it herb of grace o' Sundays: O, you must wear your rue with a difference. There 's a daisy: I would give you some violets, but they withered all when my father died: they say 'a made a good end,—

[*Sings*] For bonny sweet Robin is all my joy.

Laer. Thought and affliction, passion, hell itself,
She turns to favour and to prettiness.

Oph. And will 'a not come again? *(Song)*
And will 'a not come again?
No, no, he is dead:
Go to thy death-bed:
He never will come again.

His beard was as white as snow,
All flaxen was his poll:
He is gone, he is gone,
And we cast away moan:
God ha' mercy on his soul!
And of all Christian souls, I pray God. God be wi' you.
[*Exit.*]

Laer. Do you see this, O God?

King. Laertes, I must commune with your grief,
Or you deny me right. Go but apart,
Make choice of whom your wisest friends you will,
And they shall hear and judge 'twixt you and me:
If by direct or by collateral hand
They find us touch'd, we will our kingdom give,
Our crown, our life, and all that we call ours,
To you in satisfaction; but if not,
Be you content to lend your patience to us,
And we shall jointly labour with your soul
To give it due content.

Laer. Let this be so;
His means of death, his obscure funeral—
No trophy, sword, nor hatchment o'er his bones,
No noble rite nor formal ostentation—
Cry to be heard, as 'twere from heaven to earth,
That I must call 't in question.

King. So you shall;
And where th' offence is let the great axe fall.
I pray you, go with me. *Exeunt.*

[SCENE VI. *Another room in the castle.*]

Enter HORATIO *and others.*

Hor. What are they that would speak with me?

Gent. Sea-faring men, sir: they say they have letters for you.

Hor. Let them come in. [*Exit Gent.*]
I do not know from what part of the world
I should be greeted, if not from lord Hamlet.

Enter Sailors.

First Sail. God bless you, sir.

Hor. Let him bless thee too.

First Sail. 'A shall, sir, an 't please him. There 's a letter for you, sir; it comes from the ambassador that was bound for England; if your name be Horatio, as I am let to know it is.

Hor. [*Reads*] 'Horatio, when thou shalt have overlooked this, give these fellows some means to the king: they have letters for him. Ere we were two days old at sea, a pirate of very warlike appointment gave us chase. Finding ourselves too slow of sail, we put on a compelled valour, and in the grapple I boarded them: on the instant they got clear of our ship; so I alone became their prisoner. They have dealt with me like thieves of mercy: but they knew what they did; I am to do a good turn for them. Let the king have the letters I have sent; and repair thou to me with as much speed as thou wouldest fly death. I have words to speak in thine ear will make thee dumb; yet are they much too light for the bore of the matter. These good fellows will bring thee where I am. Rosencrantz and Guildenstern hold their course for England: of them I have much to tell thee. Farewell.

'He that thou knowest thine, HAMLET.'

Come, I will give you way for these your letters;
And do 't the speedier, that you may direct me
To him from whom you brought them. *Exeunt.*

---

used as a symbol of remembrance both at weddings and at funerals. 177. **pansies,** emblems of love and courtship. Cf. French *pensées.* 178. **document,** piece of instruction or lesson. 180. **fennel,** emblem of flattery. **columbines,** emblem of unchastity (?) or ingratitude (?) 181. **rue,** emblem of repentance. It was usually mingled with holy water and then known as *herb of grace.* F and Globe: *herb-grace.* Ophelia is probably playing on the two meanings of *rue,* "repentant" and "even for ruth (pity)"; the former signification is for the queen, the latter for herself. 184. **daisy,** emblem of dissembling, faithlessness. **violets,** emblems of faithfulness. 187. **For . . . joy,** probably a line from a Robin Hood ballad. 188. **Thought,** melancholy thought. 190. **And . . . again.** This song appeared in the songbooks as "The Merry Milkmaids' Dumps." 196. **poll,** head. 198. **cast away,** shipwrecked. 203. **right,** my rights. 206. **collateral,** indirect. 207. **touch'd,** implicated. 214. **hatchment,** tablet displaying the armorial bearings of a deceased person.

SCENE VI. 14. **means,** means of access. 21. **thieves of mercy,** merciful thieves. 27. **bore,** caliber, importance.

[SCENE VII. *Another room in the castle.*]

Enter KING *and* LAERTES.

King. Now must your conscience my acquittance seal,
And you must put me in your heart for friend,
Sith you have heard, and with a knowing ear,
That he which hath your noble father slain
Pursued my life.
Laer. It well appears: but tell me
Why you proceeded not against these feats,
So criminal and so capital in nature,
As by your safety, wisdom, all things else,
You mainly were stirr'd up.
King. O, for two special reasons;
Which may to you, perhaps, seem much unsinew'd,
But yet to me th' are strong. The queen his mother
Lives almost by his looks; and for myself—
My virtue or my plague, be it either which—
She 's so conjunctive to my life and soul,
That, as the star moves not but in his sphere,
I could not but by her. The other motive,
Why to a public count I might not go,
Is the great love the general gender bear him;
Who, dipping all his faults in their affection,
Would, like the spring that turneth wood to stone,
Convert his gyves to graces; so that my arrows,
Too slightly timber'd for so loud a wind,
Would have reverted to my bow again,
And not where I had aim'd them.
Laer. And so have I a noble father lost;
A sister driven into desp'rate terms,
Whose worth, if praises may go back again,
Stood challenger on mount of all the age
For her perfections: but my revenge will come.
King. Break not your sleeps for that: you must not think
That we are made of stuff so flat and dull
That we can let our beard be shook with danger
And think it pastime. You shortly shall hear more:
I lov'd your father, and we love ourself;
And that, I hope, will teach you to imagine—

Enter a Messenger *with letters.*

How now! what news?
Mess. Letters, my lord, from Hamlet:
These to your majesty; this to the queen.
King. From Hamlet! who brought them?
Mess. Sailors, my lord, they say; I saw them not:
They were given me by Claudio; he receiv'd them
Of him that brought them.
King. Laertes, you shall hear them.
Leave us. [*Exit Messenger.*]
[*Reads*] 'High and mighty, You shall know I am set naked on your kingdom. To-morrow shall I beg leave to see your kingly eyes: when I shall, first asking your pardon thereunto, recount the occasion of my sudden and more strange return. 'HAMLET.'
What should this mean? Are all the rest come back?
Or is it some abuse, and no such thing?
Laer. Know you the hand?
King. 'Tis Hamlet's character. 'Naked!'
And in a postscript here, he says 'alone.'
Can you devise me?
Laer. I 'm lost in it, my lord. But let him come;
It warms the very sickness in my heart,
That I shall live and tell him to his teeth,
'Thus didst thou.'
King. If it be so, Laertes—
As how should it be so? how otherwise?—
Will you be rul'd by me?
Laer. Ay, my lord;
So you will not o'errule me to a peace.
King. To thine own peace. If he be now return'd,
As checking at his voyage, and that he means
No more to undertake it, I will work him
To an exploit, now ripe in my device,
Under the which he shall not choose but fall:
And for his death no wind of blame shall breathe,
But even his mother shall uncharge the practice
And call it accident.
Laer. My lord, I will be rul'd;
The rather, if you could devise it so
That I might be the organ.
King. It falls right.
You have been talk'd of since your travel much,
And that in Hamlet's hearing, for a quality
Wherein, they say, you shine: your sum of parts
Did not together pluck such envy from him
As did that one, and that, in my regard,
Of the unworthiest siege.
Laer. What part is that, my lord?
King. A very riband in the cap of youth,
Yet needful too; for youth no less becomes
The light and careless livery that it wears
Than settled age his sables and his weeds,
Importing health and graveness. Two months since,
Here was a gentleman of Normandy:—
I have seen myself, and serv'd against, the French,
And they can well on horseback: but this gallant
Had witchcraft in 't; he grew unto his seat;
And to such wondrous doing brought his horse,
As had he been incorps'd and demi-natur'd
With the brave beast: so far he topp'd my thought,
That I, in forgery of shapes and tricks,
Come short of what he did.
Laer. A Norman was 't?
King. A Norman.
Laer. Upon my life, Lamord.
King. The very same.

SCENE VII. 1. **conscience,** knowledge that this is true. 7. **criminal,** so Q_2; Globe, following F: *crimeful.* **capital,** punishable by death. 9. **mainly,** greatly. 10. **unsinew'd,** weak. 14. **conjunctive,** comformable (the next line suggesting planetary conjunction). 15. **sphere,** the hollow sphere in which, according to Ptolemaic astronomy, the planets were supposed to move. 17. **count,** account, reckoning. 18. **general gender,** common people. 20. **spring,** i.e., one heavily charged with lime. 21. **gyves,** fetters; here, faults, or possibly, punishments inflicted (on him). 22. **slightly timber'd,** light. **loud,** strong. For *loud a wind* Jennens would retain the Q_2 reading *loved Arm'd*, explaining, "one so loved and armed with the affections of the people"; for *so loud a wind* Elze suggests *solid arms* to agree with his reading *grieves* (for *gyves*) in line 21. 26. **terms,** state, condition. 27. **go back,** i.e., to Ophelia's former virtues. 28. **on mount,** set up on high (Onions), mounted (on horseback). **of all the age,** qualifies *challenger* and not *mount.* 37. **to the queen.** One hears no more of the letter to the queen. 40. **Claudio.** This character does not appear in the play. 44. **naked,** unprovided (with retinue). 54. **devise,** explain to. 59. **As . . . otherwise?** How can this (Hamlet's return) be true? (yet) how otherwise than true (since we have the evidence of his letter)? Some editors read *How should it not be so*, etc., making the words refer to Laertes' desire to meet with Hamlet. 63. **checking at,** used in falconry of a hawk's leaving the quarry to fly at a chance bird, turn aside. 68. **uncharge the practice,** acquit the stratagem of being a plot. 71. **organ,** agent, instrument. 77. **siege,** rank. 81. **sables,** rich garments. 85. **can well,** are skilled. 88. **incorps'd and demi-natur'd,** of one body and nearly of one nature (like the centaur). 89. **topp'd,** surpassed. 90. **forgery,** invention. 93. **Lamord.** This refers possibly to Pietro Monte,

Laer. I know him well: he is the brooch indeed
And gem of all the nation.
King. He made confession of you,
And gave you such a masterly report
For art and exercise in your defence
And for your rapier most especial,
That he cried out, 'twould be a sight indeed,
If one could match you: the scrimers of their nation,
He swore, had neither motion, guard, nor eye,
If you oppos'd them. Sir, this report of his
Did Hamlet so envenom with his envy
That he could nothing do but wish and beg
Your sudden coming o'er, to play with you.
Now, out of this,—
Laer. What out of this, my lord?
King. Laertes, was your father dear to you?
Or are you like the painting of a sorrow,
A face without a heart?
Laer. Why ask you this?
King. Not that I think you did not love your father;
But that I know love is begun by time;
And that I see, in passages of proof,
Time qualifies the spark and fire of it.
There lives within the very flame of love
A kind of wick or snuff that will abate it;
And nothing is at a like goodness still;
For goodness, growing to a plurisy,
Dies in his own too much: that we would do,
We should do when we would; for this 'would' changes
And hath abatements and delays as many
As there are tongues, are hands, are accidents;
And then this 'should' is like a spendthrift sigh,
That hurts by easing. But, to the quick o' th' ulcer:—
Hamlet comes back: what would you undertake,
To show yourself your father's son in deed
More than in words?
Laer. To cut his throat i' th' church.
King. No place, indeed, should murder sanctuarize;
Revenge should have no bounds. But, good Laertes,
Will you do this, keep close within your chamber.
Hamlet return'd shall know you are come home:
We'll put on those shall praise your excellence
And set a double varnish on the fame
The Frenchman gave you, bring you in fine together
And wager on your heads: he, being remiss,
Most generous and free from all contriving,
Will not peruse the foils; so that, with ease,
Or with a little shuffling, you may choose
A sword unbated, and in a pass of practice
Requite him for your father.
Laer. I will do 't:
And, for that purpose, I'll anoint my sword.
I bought an unction of a mountebank,
So mortal that, but dip a knife in it,
Where it draws blood no cataplasm so rare,
Collected from all simples that have virtue
Under the moon, can save the thing from death
That is but scratch'd withal: I'll touch my point
With this contagion, that, if I gall him slightly,
It may be death.
King. Let 's further think of this;
Weigh what convenience both of time and means
May fit us to our shape: if this should fail,
And that our drift look through our bad performance,
'Twere better not assay'd: therefore this project
Should have a back or second, that might hold,
If this should blast in proof. Soft! let me see:
We'll make a solemn wager on your cunnings:
I ha 't:
When in your motion you are hot and dry—
As make your bouts more violent to that end—
And that he calls for drink, I'll have prepar'd him
A chalice for the nonce, whereon but sipping,
If he by chance escape your venom'd stuck,
Our purpose may hold there. But stay, what noise?

Enter QUEEN.

Queen. One woe doth tread upon another's heel,
So fast they follow: your sister 's drown'd, Laertes.
Laer. Drown'd! O, where?
Queen. There is a willow grows askant the brook,
That shows his hoar leaves in the glassy stream;
There with fantastic garlands did she make
Of crow-flowers, nettles, daisies, and long purples
That liberal shepherds give a grosser name,
But our cold maids do dead men's fingers call them:
There, on the pendent boughs her crownet weeds
Clamb'ring to hang, an envious sliver broke;
When down her weedy trophies and herself
Fell in the weeping brook. Her clothes spread wide;
And, mermaid-like, awhile they bore her up:
Which time she chanted snatches of old lauds;
As one incapable of her own distress,
Or like a creature native and indued
Unto that element: but long it could not be
Till that her garments, heavy with their drink,
Pull'd the poor wretch from her melodious lay
To muddy death.
Laer. Alas then, she is drown'd?
Queen. Drown'd, drown'd.
Laer. Too much of water hast thou, poor Ophelia,
And therefore I forbid my tears: but yet
It is our trick; nature her custom holds,
Let shame say what it will: when these are gone,
The woman will be out. Adieu, my lord:
I have a speech of fire, that fain would blaze,
But that this folly drowns it. *Exit.*
King. Let 's follow, Gertrude:
How much I had to do to calm his rage!

instructor to Louis XII's master of the horse (Hudson). 96. **confession,** grudging admission of superiority. 98. **art and exercise,** skillful exercise. **defence,** science of defense in sword practice. 101. **scrimers,** fencers. 106. **play,** fence. 113. **passages of proof,** proved instances. 118. **plurisy,** excess, plethora. 119. **in his own too much,** of its own excess. 121. **abatements,** diminutions. 122. **accidents,** occurrences, incidents. 123. **spendthrift,** an allusion to the belief that each sigh cost the heart a drop of blood. 124. **quick o' th' ulcer,** heart of the difficulty. 128. **sanctuarize,** protect from punishment; allusion to the right of sanctuary with which certain religious places were invested. 139. **unbated,** not blunted, having no button. **pass of practice,** treacherous thrust. 142. **mountebank,** quack doctor. 144. **cataplasm,** plaster or poultice. 145. **simples,** herbs. 146. **Under the moon,** i.e., when collected by moonlight to add to their medicinal value. 148. **gall,** graze, wound. 151. **shape,** part we propose to act. 152. **drift . . . performance,** intention be disclosed by our bungling. 155. **blast in proof,** burst in the test (like a cannon). 156. **cunnings,** skills. The F reading, *commings*, is explained by Caldecott and Knight as "bouts at fence." 161. **chalice,** cup. 162. **stuck,** thrust (from *stoccado*). 167. **willow,** for its significance of forsaken love. **askant,** aslant. 168. **hoar,** white (i.e., on the underside). 169. **make,** so Q_2; Globe, following F, *come*. 170. **crow-flowers,** buttercups. **long purples,** early purple orchis. 171. **liberal,** probably, free-spoken. 173. **crownet,** coronet; made into a chaplet. 174. **sliver,** branch. 175. **weedy,** i.e., of plants. 178. **lauds,** hymns. 179. **incapable,** lacking capacity to apprehend. 180. **indued,** endowed with qualities fitting her for living in water. 188. **trick,** way. 189-190. **when . . . out,** when my tears are all shed, the woman in me will be satisfied.

Now fear I this will give it start again;
Therefore let 's follow. *Exeunt.*

[ACT V.

SCENE I. *A churchyard.*]

Enter two Clowns [*with spades, &c.*].

First Clo. Is she to be buried in Christian burial when she wilfully seeks her own salvation?

Sec. Clo. I tell thee she is; therefore make her grave straight: the crowner hath sat on her, and finds it Christian burial.

First Clo. How can that be, unless she drowned herself in her own defence?

Sec. Clo. Why, 'tis found so.

First Clo. It must be 'se offendendo;' it cannot be else. For here lies the point: if I drown myself wittingly, it argues an act: and an act hath three branches; it is, to act, to do, and to perform: argal, she drowned herself wittingly.

Sec. Clo. Nay, but hear you, goodman delver,—

First Clo. Give me leave. Here lies the water; good: here stands the man; good: if the man go to this water, and drown himself, it is, will he, nill he, he goes,—mark you that; but if the water come to him and drown him, he drowns not himself: argal, he that is not guilty of his own death shortens not his own life.

Sec. Clo. But is this law?

First Clo. Ay, marry, is 't; crowner's quest law.

Sec. Clo. Will you ha' the truth on 't? If this had not been a gentlewoman, she should have been buried out o' Christian burial.

First Clo. Why, there thou say'st: and the more pity that great folk should have countenance in this world to drown or hang themselves, more than their even Christian. Come, my spade. There is no ancient gentlemen but gardeners, ditchers, and grave-makers: they hold up Adam's profession.

Sec. Clo. Was he a gentleman?

First Clo. 'A was the first that ever bore arms.

Sec. Clo. Why, he had none.

First Clo. What, art a heathen? How dost thou understand the Scripture? The Scripture says 'Adam digged:' could he dig without arms? I'll put another question to thee: if thou answerest me not to the purpose, confess thyself—

Sec. Clo. Go to.

First Clo. What is he that builds stronger than either the mason, the shipwright, or the carpenter?

Sec. Clo. The gallows-maker; for that frame outlives a thousand tenants.

First Clo. I like thy wit well, in good faith: the gallows does well; but how does it well? it does well to those that do ill: now thou dost ill to say the gallows is built stronger than the church: argal, the gallows may do well to thee. To 't again, come.

Sec. Clo. 'Who builds stronger than a mason, a shipwright, or a carpenter?'

First Clo. Ay, tell me that, and unyoke.

Sec. Clo. Marry, now I can tell.

First Clo. To 't.

Sec. Clo. Mass, I cannot tell.

Enter HAMLET *and* HORATIO [*at a distance.*]

First Clo. Cudgel thy brains no more about it, for your dull ass will not mend his pace with beating; and, when you are asked this question next, say 'a grave-maker:' the houses he makes lasts till doomsday. Go, get thee in, and fetch me a stoup of liquor.
[*Exit Sec. Clown.*]
Song. [*He digs.*]

In youth, when I did love, did love,
Methought it was very sweet,
To contract—O—the time, for—a—my behove,
O, methought, there—a—was nothing—a—meet.

Ham. Has this fellow no feeling of his business, that 'a sings at grave-making?

Hor. Custom hath made it in him a property of easiness.

Ham. 'Tis e'en so: the hand of little employment hath the daintier sense.

First Clo. *Song.*

But age, with his stealing steps,
Hath claw'd me in his clutch,
And hath shipped me into the land,
As if I had never been such. [*Throws up a skull.*]

Ham. That skull had a tongue in it, and could sing once: how the knave jowls it to the ground, as if 'twere Cain's jaw-bone, that did the first murder! This might be the pate of a politician, which this ass now o'er-reaches; one that would circumvent God, might it not?

Hor. It might, my lord.

Ham. Or of a courtier; which could say 'Good morrow, sweet lord! How dost thou, sweet lord?' This might be my lord such-a-one, that praised my lord such-a-one's horse, when he meant to beg it; might it not?

Hor. Ay, my lord.

Ham. Why, e'en so: and now my Lady Worm's; chapless, and knocked about the mazzard with a sexton's spade: here 's fine revolution, an we had the trick to see 't. Did these bones cost no more the breeding, but to play at loggats with 'em? mine ache to think on 't.

First Clo. *Song.*

A pick-axe, and a spade, a spade,
For and a shrouding sheet:
O, a pit of clay for to be made
For such a guest is meet. [*Throws up another skull.*]

ACT V. SCENE I. *Stage Direction:* **Clowns.** The word *clown* was used to denote peasants as well as humorous characters; here applied to the rustic type of clown. 4. **straight,** straightway, immediately; Johnson interprets "from east to west in a direct line, parallel with the church." **crowner,** coroner. 9. **'se offendendo,'** for *se defendendo*, term used in verdicts of justifiable homicide. 11. **wittingly,** intentionally. 12. **three branches,** parody of legal phraseology. 13. **argal,** corruption of *ergo*, therefore. 15. **delver,** digger. 24. **quest,** inquest. 29. **there thou say'st,** that's right. 31. **countenance,** privilege. 32. **even,** fellow. 35. **hold up,** maintain, continue. 44. **confess thyself,** "and be hanged" completes the proverb. 45. **Go to,** perhaps, "begin," or some other form of concession. 59. **unyoke,** after this great effort you may unharness the team of your wits (Dowden). 62. **Mass,** by the Mass. 68. **in, and,** so Q_2; F: *to Yaughan*, probably a London tavern keeper. **stoup,** two-quart measure. 69. **In . . . love.** This and the two following stanzas, with nonsensical variations, are from a poem attributed to Lord Vaux and printed in *Tottel's Miscellany* (1557). The *O* and *ah* are possibly grunts of the digger or (Clarendon Press) represent drawling notes. 71. **behove,** benefit. 76. **property of easiness,** a peculiarity that now is easy. 81. **into,** so Q_2; Globe, following F: *intil*. 84. **jowls,** dashes. 85. **Cain's jaw-bone,** allusion to the old tradition that Cain slew Abel with the jawbone of an ass. 87. **politician,** schemer, plotter. **o'er-reaches,** quibble on the literal sense and the sense "circumvent"; the F reading, *o'er Offices*, Onions

Ham. There 's another: why may not that be the skull of a lawyer? Where be his quiddities now, his quillities, his cases, his tenures, and his tricks? why does he suffer this mad knave now to knock him about the sconce with a dirty shovel, and will not tell him of his action of battery? Hum! This fellow might be in 's time a great buyer of land, with his statutes, his recognizances, his fines, his double vouchers, his recoveries: is this the fine of his fines, and the recovery of his recoveries, to have his fine pate full of fine dirt? will his vouchers vouch him no more of his purchases, and double ones too, than the length and breadth of a pair of indentures? The very conveyances of his lands will scarcely lie in this box; and must the inheritor himself have no more, ha?

Hor. Not a jot more, my lord.

Ham. Is not parchment made of sheep-skins?

Hor. Ay, my lord, and of calf-skins too.

Ham. They are sheep and calves which seek out assurance in that. I will speak to this fellow. Whose grave 's this, sirrah?

First Clo. Mine, sir.

[*Sings*] O, a pit of clay for to be made
For such a guest is meet.

Ham. I think it be thine, indeed; for thou liest in 't.

First Clo. You lie out on 't, sir, and therefore 't is not yours: for my part, I do not lie in 't, yet it is mine.

Ham. Thou dost lie in 't, to be in 't and say it is thine: 'tis for the dead, not for the quick; therefore thou liest.

First Clo. 'Tis a quick lie, sir; 'twill away again, from me to you.

Ham. What man dost thou dig it for?

First Clo. For no man, sir.

Ham. What woman, then?

First Clo. For none, neither.

Ham. Who is to be buried in 't?

First Clo. One that was a woman, sir; but, rest her soul, she 's dead.

Ham. How absolute the knave is! we must speak by the card, or equivocation will undo us. By the Lord, Horatio, these three years I have taken note of it; the age is grown so picked that the toe of the peasant comes so near the heel of the courtier, he galls his kibe. How long hast thou been a grave-maker?

First Clo. Of all the days i' the year, I came to 't that day that our last king Hamlet overcame Fortinbras.

Ham. How long is that since?

First Clo. Cannot you tell that? every fool can tell that: it was the very day that young Hamlet was born; he that is mad, and sent into England.

Ham. Ay, marry, why was he sent into England?

First Clo. Why, because 'a was mad: 'a shall recover his wits there; or, if 'a do not, 'tis no great matter there.

Ham. Why?

First Clo. 'Twill not be seen in him there; there the men are as mad as he.

Ham. How came he mad?

First Clo. Very strangely, they say.

Ham. How strangely?

First Clo. Faith, e'en with losing his wits.

Ham. Upon what ground?

First Clo. Why, here in Denmark: I have been sexton here, man and boy, thirty years.

Ham. How long will a man lie i' the earth ere he rot?

First Clo. Faith, if 'a be not rotten before 'a die—as we have many pocky corses now-a-days, that will scarce hold the laying in—'a will last you some eight year or nine year: a tanner will last you nine year.

Ham. Why he more than another?

First Clo. Why, sir, his hide is so tanned with his trade, that 'a will keep out water a great while; and your water is a sore decayer of your whoreson dead body. Here 's a skull now hath lain you i' th' earth three and twenty years.

Ham. Whose was it?

First Clo. A whoreson mad fellow's it was: whose do you think it was?

Ham. Nay, I know not.

First Clo. A pestilence on him for a mad rogue! 'a poured a flagon of Rhenish on my head once. This same skull, sir, was Yorick's skull, the king's jester.

Ham. This?

First Clo. E'en that.

Ham. Let me see. [*Takes the skull.*] Alas, poor Yorick! I knew him, Horatio: a fellow of infinite jest, of most excellent fancy: he hath borne me on his back a thousand times; and now, how abhorred in my imagination it is! my gorge rises at it. Here hung those lips that I have kissed I know not how oft. Where be your gibes now? your gambols? your songs? your flashes of merriment, that were wont to set the table on a roar? Not one now, to mock your own grinning? quite chap-fallen? Now get you to my lady's chamber, and tell her, let her paint an inch thick, to this favour she must come; make her laugh at that. Prithee, Horatio, tell me one thing.

Hor. What 's that, my lord?

Ham. Dost thou think Alexander looked o' this fashion i' the earth?

Hor. E'en so.

Ham. And smelt so? pah! [*Puts down the skull.*]

Hor. E'en so, my lord.

Ham. To what base uses we may return, Horatio! Why may not imagination trace the noble dust of Alexander, till 'a find it stopping a bung-hole?

Hor. 'Twere to consider too curiously, to consider so.

Ham. No, faith, not a jot; but to follow him thither with modesty enough, and likelihood to lead it: as thus: Alexander died, Alexander was buried, Alex-

defines as "lords it over by virtue of his office." 97. **chapless,** having no lower jaw. 98. **mazzard,** head. 100. **loggats,** a game in which six sticks are thrown to lie as near as possible to a stake fixed in the ground, or block of wood on a floor. 103. **For and,** and moreover. 107. **quiddities,** subtleties, quibbles. 108. **quillities,** verbal niceties, subtle distinctions. **tenures,** the holding of a piece of property or office or the conditions or period of such holding. 110. **sconce,** head. 114. **statutes, recognizances,** legal terms connected with the transfer of land. 115. **vouchers,** persons called on to warrant a tenant's title. **recoveries,** process for transfer of entailed estate. 116. **fine.** The four uses of this word are as follows: (1) end, (2) legal process, (3) elegant, (4) small. 119. **indentures,** conveyances or contracts. 121. **inheritor,** possessor, owner. 124. **calf-skins,** parchments. 126. **assurance in that,** safety in legal parchments. 148. **absolute,** positive, decided. 149. **by the card,** with precision, i.e., by the mariner's card on which the points of the compass were marked. **equivocation,** ambiguity in the use of terms. 152. **picked,** refined, fastidious. 153. **galls,** chafes. **kibe,** chilblain. 177. **thirty years.** This statement with that in line 160 shows Hamlet's age to be thirty years. 181. **pocky,** rotten, diseased. 189-190. **hath . . . earth,** so Q_2 (*lien*); F (Globe): *this skull has lain in the earth.* 227. **curiously,** minutely.

ander returneth into dust; the dust is earth; of earth we make loam; and why of that loam, whereto he was converted, might they not stop a beer-barrel?

Imperious Cæsar, dead and turn'd to clay,
Might stop a hole to keep the wind away:
O, that that earth, which kept the world in awe,
Should patch a wall t' expel the winter's flaw!
But soft! but soft awhile! here comes the king,

Enter KING, QUEEN, LAERTES, *and the* Corse [*of* OPHELIA, *in procession, with* Priest, Lords, *etc.*].

The queen, the courtiers: who is this they follow?
And with such maimed rites? This doth betoken
The corse they follow did with desp'rate hand
Fordo it own life: 'twas of some estate.
Couch we awhile, and mark. [*Retiring with Horatio.*]
Laer. What ceremony else?
Ham. That is Laertes,
A very noble youth: mark.
Laer. What ceremony else?
First Priest. Her obsequies have been as far enlarg'd
As we have warranty: her death was doubtful;
And, but that great command o'ersways the order,
She should in ground unsanctified have lodg'd
Till the last trumpet; for charitable prayers,
Shards, flints and pebbles should be thrown on her:
Yet here she is allow'd her virgin crants,
Her maiden strewments and the bringing home
Of bell and burial.
Laer. Must there no more be done?
First Priest. No more be done:
We should profane the service of the dead
To sing a requiem and such rest to her
As to peace-parted souls.
Laer. Lay her i' th' earth:
And from her fair and unpolluted flesh
May violets spring! I tell thee, churlish priest,
A minist'ring angel shall my sister be,
When thou liest howling.
Ham. What, the fair Ophelia!
Queen. Sweets to the sweet: farewell!
[*Scattering flowers.*]
I hop'd thou shouldst have been my Hamlet's wife;
I thought thy bride-bed to have deck'd, sweet maid,
And not have strew'd thy grave.
Laer. O, treble woe
Fall ten times treble on that cursed head,
Whose wicked deed thy most ingenious sense
Depriv'd thee of! Hold off the earth awhile,
Till I have caught her once more in mine arms:
[*Leaps into the grave.*]
Now pile your dust upon the quick and dead,
Till of this flat a mountain you have made,
T' o'ertop old Pelion, or the skyish head
Of blue Olympus.
Ham. [*Advancing*] What is he whose grief
Bears such an emphasis? whose phrase of sorrow
Conjures the wand'ring stars, and makes them stand
Like wonder-wounded hearers? This is I,
Hamlet the Dane. [*Leaps into the grave.*]
Laer. The devil take thy soul!
[*Grappling with him.*]
Ham. Thou pray'st not well.
I prithee, take thy fingers from my throat;
For, though I am not splenitive and rash,
Yet have I in me something dangerous,
Which let thy wisdom fear: hold off thy hand.
King. Pluck them asunder.
Queen. Hamlet, Hamlet!
All. Gentlemen,—
Hor. Good my lord, be quiet.
[*The Attendants part them, and they come out of the grave.*]
Ham. Why, I will fight with him upon this theme
Until my eyelids will no longer wag.
Queen. O my son, what theme?
Ham. I lov'd Ophelia: forty thousand brothers
Could not, with all their quantity of love,
Make up my sum. What wilt thou do for her?
King. O, he is mad, Laertes.
Queen. For love of God, forbear him.
Ham. 'Swounds, show me what thou 'lt do:
Woo 't weep? woo 't fight? woo 't fast? woo 't tear thyself?
Woo 't drink up eisel? eat a crocodile?
I'll do 't. Dost thou come here to whine?
To outface me with leaping in her grave?
Be buried quick with her, and so will I:
And, if thou prate of mountains, let them throw
Millions of acres on us, till our ground,
Singeing his pate against the burning zone,
Make Ossa like a wart! Nay, an thou 'lt mouth,
I'll rant as well as thou.
Queen. This is mere madness:
And thus awhile the fit will work on him;
Anon, as patient as the female dove,
When that her golden couplets are disclos'd,
His silence will sit drooping.
Ham. Hear you, sir;
What is the reason that you use me thus?
I lov'd you ever: but it is no matter;
Let Hercules himself do what he may,
The cat will mew and dog will have his day.
King. I pray thee, good Horatio, wait upon him.
Exit Hamlet and Horatio.
[*To Laertes*] Strengthen your patience in our last night's speech;
We'll put the matter to the present push.
Good Gertrude, set some watch over your son.
This grave shall have a living monument:

234. **loam,** clay paste for brickmaking. 236. **Imperious,** imperial. 239. **flaw,** gust of wind; see glossary. 244. **Fordo,** destroy. **it,** its. 245. **Couch,** hide, lurk. 249. **enlarg'd,** extended, referring to the fact that suicides are not given full burial rites. 254. **Shards,** broken bits of pottery. 255. **crants,** garlands customarily hung upon the biers of unmarried women. 256. **strewments,** traditional strewing of flowers. 256-257. **bringing . . . burial,** the laying to rest of the body, to the sound of the bell. 261. **peace-parted,** allusion to the text, "Lord, now lettest thou thy servant depart in peace." 265. **howling,** i.e., in hell. 271. **ingenious sense,** mind endowed with finest qualities. 276. **Pelion.** Olympus, Pelion, and Ossa are mountains in the north of Thessaly. 279. **wand'ring stars,** planets. 284. **splenitive,** quick-tempered. 285. **in me something,** so Q_2; F (Globe): *something in me.* 290. **wag,** move (not used ludicrously). 293. **quantity.** Dowden suggests that the word is used in a deprecatory sense (little bits, fragments). 296. **forbear,** leave alone. 297. **'Swounds,** oath, "God's wounds." 298. **Woo 't,** wilt thou. 299. **eisel,** vinegar. Some editors have taken this to be the name of a river, such as the Yssel, the Weissel, and the Nile. 305. **burning zone,** sun's orbit. 310. **golden couplets.** The pigeon lays two eggs; the young when hatched are covered with golden down (Dowden). 317. **in,** by recalling. 318. **present push,** immediate test. 320. **living,** lasting; also refers (for Laertes' benefit) to the plot against Hamlet.

SCENE II. 6. **mutines,** mutineers. **bilboes,** shackles. **Rashly,** goes with line 12. 9. **pall,** fail. 11. **Rough-hew,** shape roughly. Dowden suggests that it may mean "bungle." 13. **sea-gown,** "a sea-gown, or a

An hour of quiet shortly shall we see;
Till then, in patience our proceeding be. *Exeunt.*

[SCENE II. *A hall in the castle.*]

Enter HAMLET *and* HORATIO.

Ham. So much for this, sir: now shall you see the other;
You do remember all the circumstance?
Hor. Remember it, my lord!
Ham. Sir, in my heart there was a kind of fighting,
That would not let me sleep: methought I lay
Worse than the mutines in the bilboes. Rashly,
And prais'd be rashness for it, let us know,
Our indiscretion sometime serves us well,
When our deep plots do pall: and that should learn us
There 's a divinity that shapes our ends,
Rough-hew them how we will,—
Hor. That is most certain.
Ham. Up from my cabin,
My sea-gown scarf'd about me, in the dark
Grop'd I to find out them; had my desire,
Finger'd their packet, and in fine withdrew
To mine own room again; making so bold,
My fears forgetting manners, to unseal
Their grand commission; where I found, Horatio,—
O royal knavery!—an exact command,
Larded with many several sorts of reasons
Importing Denmark's health and England's too,
With, ho! such bugs and goblins in my life,
That, on the supervise, no leisure bated,
No, not to stay the grinding of the axe,
My head should be struck off.
Hor. Is 't possible?
Ham. Here 's the commission: read it at more leisure.
But wilt thou hear me how I did proceed?
Hor. I beseech you.
Ham. Being thus be-netted round with villanies,—
Ere I could make a prologue to my brains,
They had begun the play—I sat me down,
Devis'd a new commission, wrote it fair:
I once did hold it, as our statists do,
A baseness to write fair and labour'd much
How to forget that learning, but, sir, now
It did me yeoman's service: wilt thou know
Th' effect of what I wrote?
Hor. Ay, good my lord.
Ham. An earnest conjuration from the king,
As England was his faithful tributary,
As love between them like the palm might flourish,
As peace should still her wheaten garland wear
And stand a comma 'tween their amities,
And many such-like 'As'es of great charge,
That, on the view and knowing of these contents,
Without debatement further, more or less,
He should the bearers put to sudden death,
Not shriving-time allow'd.
Hor. How was this seal'd?
Ham. Why, even in that was heaven ordinant.
I had my father's signet in my purse,
Which was the model of that Danish seal;
Folded the writ up in the form of th' other,
Subscrib'd it, gave 't th' impression, plac'd it safely,
The changeling never known. Now, the next day
Was our sea-fight; and what to this was sequent
Thou know'st already.
Hor. So Guildenstern and Rosencrantz go to 't.
Ham. Why, man, they did make love to this employment;
They are not near my conscience; their defeat
Does by their own insinuation grow:
'Tis dangerous when the baser nature comes
Between the pass and fell incensed points
Of mighty opposites.
Hor. Why, what a king is this!
Ham. Does it not, think thee, stand me now upon—
He that hath kill'd my king and whor'd my mother,
Popp'd in between th' election and my hopes,
Thrown out his angle for my proper life,
And with such coz'nage—is 't not perfect conscience,
To quit him with this arm? and is 't not to be damn'd,
To let this canker of our nature come
In further evil?
Hor. It must be shortly known to him from England
What is the issue of the business there.
Ham. It will be short: the interim is mine;
And a man's life 's no more than to say 'One.'
But I am very sorry, good Horatio,
That to Laertes I forgot myself;
For, by the image of my cause, I see
The portraiture of his: I'll court his favours:
But, sure, the bravery of his grief did put me
Into a tow'ring passion.
Hor. Peace! who comes here?

Enter a Courtier [OSRIC].

Osr. Your lordship is right welcome back to Denmark.

Ham. I humbly thank you, sir. [To *Hor.*] Dost know this water-fly?

Hor. No, my good lord.

Ham. Thy state is the more gracious; for 'tis a vice to know him. He hath much land, and fertile: let a beast be lord of beasts, and his crib shall stand at the king's mess: 'tis a chough; but, as I say, spacious in the possession of dirt.

Osr. Sweet lord, if your lordship were at leisure, I should impart a thing to you from his majesty.

coarse, high-collered, and short-sleeved gowne, reaching down to the mid-leg, and used most by seamen and saylors" (Cotgrave, quoted by Singer). 15. **Finger'd,** pilfered, filched. **in fine,** finally. 20. **Larded,** enriched. 22. **such . . . life,** such imaginary dangers if I were allowed to live. **bugs,** bugbears. 23. **supervise,** perusal. **leisure bated,** delay allowed. 30-31. **prologue . . . play,** i.e., before I could begin to think, my mind had made its decision. 33. **statists,** statesmen. 34. **fair,** in a clear hand. 36. **yeoman's,** i.e., faithful. 41. **wheaten garland,** symbol of peace. 42. **comma,** smallest break or separation (Gollancz). Here *amity* begins and *amity* ends the period, and *peace* stands between like a dependent clause (Dowden). The comma indicates continuity, link. 43. **'As'es,** the "whereases" of a formal document, with play on the word *ass.* **charge,** import, and burden. 47. **shriving-time,** time for absolution. 48. **ordinant,** directing. 54. **sequent,** subsequent. 59. **insinuation,** interference. 61. **pass,** thrust. **fell incensed,** fiercely angered. 63. **stand,** become incumbent. 65. **election.** The Danish throne was filled by election. 66. **angle,** fishing line. 67. **coz'nage,** trickery. 68. **quit,** repay. 69. **canker,** ulcer, or possibly the worm which destroys buds and leaves. 79. **bravery,** bravado. 84. **water-fly,** vain or busily idle person. 88. **lord of beasts.** Cf. Genesis 1:26, 28. 89. **his crib . . . mess,** he shall eat at the king's table, i.e., be one of the group of persons (usually four) constituting a *mess* at a banquet. 90. **chough,** probably, chattering jackdaw; also explained as *chuff,* provincial boor or churl.

Ham. I will receive it, sir, with all diligence of spirit. Put your bonnet to his right use; 'tis for the head.

Osr. I thank your lordship, it is very hot.

Ham. No, believe me, 'tis very cold; the wind is northerly.

Osr. It is indifferent cold, my lord, indeed.

Ham. But yet methinks it is very sultry and hot for my complexion.

Osr. Exceedingly, my lord; it is very sultry,—as 'twere,—I cannot tell how. But, my lord, his majesty bade me signify to you that 'a has laid a great wager on your head: sir, this is the matter,—

Ham. I beseech you, remember—

[*Hamlet moves him to put on his hat.*]

Osr. Nay, good my lord; for mine ease, in good faith. Sir, here is newly come to court Laertes; believe me, an absolute gentleman, full of most excellent differences, of very soft society and great showing: indeed, to speak feelingly of him, he is the card or calendar of gentry, for you shall find in him the continent of what part a gentleman would see.

Ham. Sir, his definement suffers no perdition in you; though, I know, to divide him inventorially would dozy the arithmetic of memory, †and yet but yaw neither, in respect of his quick sail. But, in the verity of extolment, I take him to be a soul of great article; and his infusion of such dearth and rareness, as, to make true diction of him, his semblable is his mirror; and who else would trace him, his umbrage, nothing more.

Osr. Your lordship speaks most infallibly of him.

Ham. The concernancy, sir? why do we wrap the gentleman in our more rawer breath?

Osr. Sir?

Hor. [*Aside to Ham.*] Is 't not possible to understand in another tongue? You will do 't, sir, really.

Ham. What imports the nomination of this gentleman?

Osr. Of Laertes?

Hor. [*Aside to Ham.*] His purse is empty already; all 's golden words are spent.

Ham. Of him, sir.

Osr. I know you are not ignorant—

Ham. I would you did, sir; yet, in faith, if you did, it would not much approve me. Well, sir?

Osr. You are not ignorant of what excellence Laertes is—

Ham. I dare not confess that, lest I should compare with him in excellence; but, to know a man well, were to know himself.

Osr. I mean, sir, for his weapon; but in the imputation laid on him by them, in his meed he 's unfellowed.

Ham. What 's his weapon?

Osr. Rapier and dagger.

Ham. That 's two of his weapons: but, well.

Osr. The king, sir, hath wagered with him six Barbary horses: against the which he has impawned, as I take it, six French rapiers and poniards, with their assigns, as girdle, hangers, and so: three of the carriages, in faith, are very dear to fancy, very responsive to the hilts, most delicate carriages, and of very liberal conceit.

Ham. What call you the carriages?

Hor. [*Aside to Ham.*] I knew you must be edified by the margent ere you had done.

Osr. The carriages, sir, are the hangers.

Ham. The phrase would be more german to the matter, if we could carry cannon by our sides: I would it might be hangers till then. But, on: six Barbary horses against six French swords, their assigns, and three liberal-conceited carriages; that 's the French bet against the Danish. Why is this 'impawned,' as you call it?

Osr. The king, sir, hath laid, that in a dozen passes between yourself and him, he shall not exceed you three hits: he hath laid on twelve for nine; and it would come to immediate trial, if your lordship would vouchsafe the answer.

Ham. How if I answer 'no'?

Osr. I mean, my lord, the opposition of your person in trial.

Ham. Sir, I will walk here in the hall: if it please his majesty, it is the breathing time of day with me; let the foils be brought, the gentleman willing, and the king hold his purpose, I will win for him an I can; if not, I will gain nothing but my shame and the odd hits.

Osr. Shall I re-deliver you e'en so?

Ham. To this effect, sir; after what flourish your nature will.

Osr. I commend my duty to your lordship.

Ham. Yours, yours. [*Exit Osric.*] He does well to commend it himself; there are no tongues else for 's turn.

Hor. This lapwing runs away with the shell on his head.

Ham. 'A did comply, sir, with his dug, before 'a sucked it. Thus has he—and many more of the same breed that I know the drossy age dotes on—only got the tune of the time and out of an habit of encounter; a kind of yesty collection, which carries them through and through the most †fann'd and winnowed opinions; and do but blow them to their trial, the bubbles are out.

Enter a Lord.

Lord. My lord, his majesty commended him to you by young Osric, who brings back to him, that you attend him in the hall: he sends to know if your pleasure hold to play with Laertes, or that you will take longer time.

Ham. I am constant to my purposes; they follow

100. **indifferent,** somewhat. 108. **remember,** i.e., remember thy courtesy; conventional phrase for "Be covered." 109. **mine ease,** conventional reply declining the invitation of "Remember thy courtesy." 112. **soft,** gentle. 113. **showing,** distinguished appearance. 114. **feelingly,** with just perception. **card,** chart, map. 115. **gentry,** good breeding. 117. **definement,** definition. **perdition,** loss, diminution. 118. **divide him inventorially,** i.e., enumerate his graces. 119. **dozy,** dizzy. 120. **yaw,** to move unsteadily (of a ship). Dowden's note: To enumerate in detail the perfections of Laertes would bewilder the computations of memory, yet for all that—in spite of the calculations—the enumeration would stagger to and fro (and so fall behind) in comparison with Laertes' quick sailing (or, possibly, considering *its* quick sail, which ought to steady the ship). 122. **article,** moment or importance. 123. **infusion,** infused temperament, character imparted by nature. **dearth and rareness,** rarity. 124. **semblable,** true likeness. 125. **trace,** follow. 126. **umbrage,** shadow. 128. **concernancy,** import. 129. **breath,** speech. 131-132. **Is 't . . . tongue?** i.e., can one converse with Osric only in this outlandish jargon? 133. **nomination,** naming. 141. **approve,** commend. 146-147. **but . . . himself,** but to know a man as excellent were to know Laertes. 149. **imputation,** reputation. 150. **meed,** merit. 155-156. **he has impawned,** he has wagered. 158. **hangers,** straps on the sword belt from which the sword hung. 159. **dear to fancy,** fancifully made. **responsive,** probably, well balanced; corresponding closely (Onions). 160. **delicate,** i.e., in workmanship. **liberal conceit,** elaborate design. 163. **margent,** margin of a book, place for explanatory notes. 165. **german,** germain, appropriate.

the king's pleasure: if his fitness speaks, mine is ready; now or whensoever, provided I be so able as now.

Lord. The king and queen and all are coming down.

Ham. In happy time.

Lord. The queen desires you to use some gentle entertainment to Laertes before you fall to play.

Ham. She well instructs me. [*Exit Lord.*]

Hor. You will lose this wager, my lord.

Ham. I do not think so; since he went into France, I have been in continual practice; I shall win at the odds. But thou wouldst not think how ill all 's here about my heart: but it is no matter.

Hor. Nay, good my lord,—

Ham. It is but foolery; but it is such a kind of gain-giving, as would perhaps trouble a woman.

Hor. If your mind dislike any thing, obey it: I will forestal their repair hither, and say you are not fit.

Ham. Not a whit, we defy augury: there 's a special providence in the fall of a sparrow. If it be now, 'tis not to come; if it be not to come, it will be now; if it be not now, yet it will come: the readiness is all: since no man of aught he leaves knows, what is 't to leave betimes? Let be.

A table prepared. [*Enter*] *Trumpets, Drums, and* Officers *with cushions;* KING, QUEEN, [OSRIC,] *and all the State; foils, daggers,* [*and wine borne in;*] *and* LAERTES.

King. Come, Hamlet, come, and take this hand
from me. [*The King puts Laertes' hand into Hamlet's.*]

Ham. Give me your pardon, sir: I have done you
wrong;
But pardon 't, as you are a gentleman.
This presence knows,
And you must needs have heard, how I am punish'd
With a sore distraction. What I have done,
That might your nature, honour and exception
Roughly awake, I here proclaim was madness.
Was 't Hamlet wrong'd Laertes? Never Hamlet:
If Hamlet from himself be ta'en away,
And when he 's not himself does wrong Laertes,
Then Hamlet does it not, Hamlet denies it.
Who does it, then? His madness: if 't be so,
Hamlet is of the faction that is wrong'd;
His madness is poor Hamlet's enemy.
Sir, in this audience,
Let my disclaiming from a purpos'd evil
Free me so far in your most generous thoughts,
That I have shot mine arrow o'er the house,
And hurt my brother.

Laer. I am satisfied in nature,
Whose motive, in this case, should stir me most
To my revenge: but in my terms of honour
I stand aloof; and will no reconcilement,
Till by some elder masters, of known honour,
I have a voice and precedent of peace,
To keep my name ungor'd. But till that time,
I do receive your offer'd love like love,
And will not wrong it.

Ham. I embrace it freely;
And will this brother's wager frankly play.
Give us the foils. Come on.

Laer. Come, one for me.

Ham. I'll be your foil, Laertes: in mine ignorance
Your skill shall, like a star i' th' darkest night,
Stick fiery off indeed.

Laer. You mock me, sir.

Ham. No, by this hand.

King. Give them the foils, young Osric. Cousin
Hamlet,
You know the wager?

Ham. Very well, my lord;
Your grace has laid the odds o' th' weaker side.

King. I do not fear it; I have seen you both:
But since he is better'd, we have therefore odds.

Laer. This is too heavy, let me see another.

Ham. This likes me well. These foils have all a
length? [*They prepare to play.*]

Osr. Ay, my good lord.

King. Set me the stoups of wine upon that table.
If Hamlet give the first or second hit,
Or quit in answer of the third exchange,
Let all the battlements their ordnance fire;
The king shall drink to Hamlet's better breath;
And in the cup an union shall he throw,
Richer than that which four successive kings
In Denmark's crown have worn. Give me the cups;
And let the kettle to the trumpet speak,
The trumpet to the cannoneer without,
The cannons to the heavens, the heavens to earth,
'Now the king drinks to Hamlet.' Come, begin:
Trumpets the while.
And you, the judges, bear a wary eye.

Ham. Come on, sir.

Laer. Come, my lord. [*They play.*]

Ham. One.

Laer. No.

Ham. Judgement.

Osr. A hit, a very palpable hit.

Drum, trumpets, and shot. Flourish. A piece goes off.

Laer. Well; again.

King. Stay; give me drink. Hamlet, this pearl is
thine;
Here 's to thy health. Give him the cup.

Ham. I'll play this bout first; set it by awhile.
Come. [*They play.*] Another hit; what say you?

Laer. A touch, a touch, I do confess 't.

King. Our son shall win.

Queen. He 's fat, and scant of breath.
Here, Hamlet, take my napkin, rub thy brows:
The queen carouses to thy fortune, Hamlet.

Ham. Good madam!

181. **breathing time,** exercise period. 193. **lapwing,** peewit; note its wiliness in drawing a visitor away from its nest and its supposed habit of running about when newly hatched with its head in the shell; Ruth Cline suggests allusion to Osric's hat. 195. **did comply . . . dug,** paid compliments to his mother's breast. 197. **drossy,** frivolous. 198. **tune,** temper, mood. 199. **out of an,** so Q_2; F (Globe): *outward.* **habit of encounter,** demeanor of social intercourse. **yesty,** frothy. 201. **fann'd and winnowed,** select and refined. Q_2: *prophane and trennowed;* F: *fond and winnowed* (trivial and sensible; so Globe, following W. J. Craig); text follows Warburton. 202. **blow . . . out,** i.e., put them to the test, and their ignorance is exposed. 214. **In happy time,** a phrase of courtesy. 226. **gain-giving,** misgiving. 233. **all,** all that matters. 239. **presence,** royal assembly. 242. **exception,** disapproval. 255. **brother.** With reference to the F reading, *mother,* Dowden calls attention to Gertrude's request to *use some gentle entertainment* to Laertes. **nature,** i.e., he is personally satisfied, but his honor must be satisfied by the rules of the code of honor. 260. **voice,** authoritative pronouncement. 266. **foil,** quibble on the two senses, "background which sets something off," and "blunted rapier for fencing." 268. **Stick fiery off,** stand out brilliantly. 283. **union,** pearl. 286. **kettle,** kettledrum. 293. **pearl,** i.e., the poison. 297. **confess 't,** Q_2: *confest;* F (Globe): *confess.* 298. **fat,** not physically fit, out of training. Some earlier editors speculated that the term applied to the corpulence of Richard Burbage, who originally played the part, but the allusion now appears unlikely. *Fat* may also suggest "sweaty." 300. **carouses,** drinks a toast.

King. Gertrude, do not drink.
Queen. I will, my lord; I pray you, pardon me. [*Drinks.*]
King. [*Aside*] It is the poison'd cup: it is too late.
Ham. I dare not drink yet, madam; by and by.
Queen. Come, let me wipe thy face.
Laer. My lord, I'll hit him now.
King. I do not think 't.
Laer. [*Aside*] And yet 'tis almost 'gainst my conscience.
Ham. Come, for the third, Laertes: you but dally;
I pray you, pass with your best violence;
I am afeard you make a wanton of me.
Laer. Say you so? come on. [*They play.*]
Osr. Nothing, neither way.
Laer. Have at you now!
[*Laertes wounds Hamlet; then, in scuffling, they change rapiers, and Hamlet wounds Laertes.*]
King. Part them; they are incens'd.
Ham. Nay, come, again. [*The Queen falls.*]
Osr. Look to the queen there, ho!
Hor. They bleed on both sides. How is it, my lord?
Osr. How is 't, Laertes?
Laer. Why, as a woodcock to mine own springe, Osric;
I am justly kill'd with mine own treachery.
Ham. How does the queen?
King. She swounds to see them bleed.
Queen. No, no, the drink, the drink,—O my dear Hamlet,—
The drink, the drink! I am poison'd. [*Dies.*]
Ham. O villany! Ho! let the door be lock'd:
Treachery! Seek it out. [*Laertes falls.*]
Laer. It is here, Hamlet: Hamlet, thou art slain;
No medicine in the world can do thee good;
In thee there is not half an hour of life;
The treacherous instrument is in thy hand,
Unbated and envenom'd: the foul practice
Hath turn'd itself on me; lo, here I lie,
Never to rise again: thy mother 's poison'd:
I can no more: the king, the king 's to blame.
Ham. The point envenom'd too!
Then, venom, to thy work. [*Stabs the King.*]
All. Treason! treason!
King. O, yet defend me, friends; I am but hurt.
Ham. Here, thou incestuous, murd'rous, damned Dane,
Drink off this potion. Is thy union here?
Follow my mother. [*King dies.*]
Laer. He is justly serv'd;
It is a poison temper'd by himself.
Exchange forgiveness with me, noble Hamlet:
Mine and my father's death come not upon thee,
Nor thine on me! [*Dies.*]
Ham. Heaven make thee free of it! I follow thee.
I am dead, Horatio. Wretched queen, adieu!
You that look pale and tremble at this chance,
That are but mutes or audience to this act,
Had I but time—as this fell sergeant, Death,
Is strict in his arrest—O, I could tell you—
But let it be. Horatio, I am dead;
Thou livest; report me and my cause aright
To the unsatisfied.
Hor. Never believe it:
I am more an antique Roman than a Dane:
Here 's yet some liquor left.
Ham. As th' art a man,
Give me the cup: let go; by heaven, I'll ha 't.
O God! Horatio, what a wounded name,
Things standing thus unknown, shall live behind me!
If thou didst ever hold me in thy heart,
Absent thee from felicity awhile,
And in this harsh world draw thy breath in pain,
To tell my story. *A march afar off.*
What warlike noise is this?
Osr. Young Fortinbras, with conquest come from Poland,
To the ambassadors of England gives
This warlike volley.
Ham. O, I die, Horatio;
The potent poison quite o'er-crows my spirit:
I cannot live to hear the news from England;
But I do prophesy th' election lights
On Fortinbras: he has my dying voice;
So tell him, with th' occurrents, more and less,
Which have solicited. The rest is silence. [*Dies.*]
Hor. Now cracks a noble heart. Good night, sweet prince;
And flights of angels sing thee to thy rest!
Why does the drum come hither? [*March within.*]

Enter FORTINBRAS, *with the* [English] Ambassadors [*and others*].

Fort. Where is this sight?
Hor. What is it you would see?
If aught of woe or wonder, cease your search.
Fort. This quarry cries on havoc. O proud Death,
What feast is toward in thine eternal cell,
That thou so many princes at a shot
So bloodily hast struck?
First Amb. The sight is dismal;
And our affairs from England come too late:
The ears are senseless that should give us hearing,
To tell him his commandment is fulfill'd,
That Rosencrantz and Guildenstern are dead:
Where should we have our thanks?
Hor. Not from his mouth,
Had it th' ability of life to thank you:
He never gave commandment for their death.
But since, so jump upon this bloody question,
You from the Polack wars, and you from England,
Are here arriv'd, give order that these bodies
High on a stage be placed to the view;
And let me speak to th' yet unknowing world
How these things came about: so shall you hear
Of carnal, bloody, and unnatural acts,
Of accidental judgements, casual slaughters,
Of deaths put on by cunning and forc'd cause,
And, in this upshot, purposes mistook

310. **wanton,** spoiled child. 313. *Stage Direction:* ***in scuffling, they change rapiers.*** Occurs in F. According to a widespread stage tradition, Hamlet receives a scratch, realizes that Laertes' sword is unbated, and accordingly forces an exchange. 317. **woodcock,** as type of stupidity or as decoy. **springe,** trap, snare. 319. **swounds,** swoons. 328. **Unbated,** not blunted with a button. 339. **temper'd,** mixed. 346. **mutes,** performers in a play who speak no words. 347. **sergeant,** sheriff's officer. Chambers takes the word to mean the officer who enforces a judgment of a tribunal or the commands of a person in authority. 352. **Roman.** It was the Roman custom to follow masters in death (Yale). 355. **God,** so Q_2; F (Globe): *good*. 364. **o'er-crows,** triumphs over. 368. **occurrents,** events, incidents. 369. **solicited,** moved, urged. 375. **quarry,** heap of dead. **cries on havoc,** proclaims a general slaughter. 383. **his mouth,** i.e., the king's. 386. **jump,** precisely. **question,** dispute. 389. **stage,** platform. 400. **of memory,** traditional, remembered. 403. **voice . . . more,** vote will influence still others. 406. **On,** on account of,

Fall'n on th' inventors' heads: all this can I
Truly deliver.
Fort. Let us haste to hear it,
And call the noblest to the audience.
For me, with sorrow I embrace my fortune:
I have some rights of memory in this kingdom,
Which now to claim my vantage doth invite me.
Hor. Of that I shall have also cause to speak,
And from his mouth whose voice will draw on more:
But let this same be presently perform'd,
Even while men's minds are wild; lest more
mischance,
On plots and errors, happen.
Fort. Let four captains
Bear Hamlet, like a soldier, to the stage;
For he was likely, had he been put on,
To have prov'd most royal: and, for his passage,
The soldiers' music and the rites of war
Speak loudly for him.
Take up the bodies: such a sight as this
Becomes the field, but here shows much amiss.
Go, bid the soldiers shoot.
Exeunt [marching, bearing off the dead bodies; after which a peal of ordnance is shot off].

or possibly, on top of, in addition to. 409. **royal,** so Q_2; F (Globe): *royally.* **passage,** death. 413. **field,** i.e., of battle.

OTHELLO, THE MOOR OF VENICE

Othello differs in several respects from the other three major Shakespearean tragedies with which it is usually ranked. Written seemingly about the time of its performance at court by the King's men on November 1, 1604, after *Hamlet* (c. 1599–1601) and before *King Lear* (c. 1605) and *Macbeth* (c. 1606–1607), *Othello* shares with these other plays a fascination with evil in its most virulent and universal aspect. These plays study the devastating effects of ambitious pride, ingratitude, wrath, jealousy, and vengeful hate—the deadly sins of the spirit—with only a passing interest in the domestic or political strife to which Shakespeare's other tragedies are generally devoted. Of the four, *Othello* is the narrowest in frame of reference. Its taut narrative of jealousy in love limits its scope to the arena of men's actions. There are no supernatural visitations as in *Hamlet* and *Macbeth*, and few appeals to ideas of divine justice as compared with *King Lear;* the macrocosm does not play a visible role. Nor is the state seriously shaken by Othello's tragedy. The fair-minded Duke of Venice remains firmly in control, and his deputy Lodovico oversees a just conclusion on Cyprus.

By the same token, *Othello* contains less philosophical generalization about man and his place in the cosmos. The imagery focuses instead on degrading bestiality and monstrosity: goats, monkeys, wolves, baboons, guinea hens, wildcats, spiders, flies, asses, dogs, copulating horses and sheep, serpents, toads; also green-eyed monsters, devils, blackness, poisons, money-purses, tarnished jewels, music untuned, and light extinguished. The story is immediate and direct, retaining the sensational atmosphere of its Italian prose source by Giovanni Baptista Giraldi Cinthio, in his *Hecatommithi* of 1565 (translated into French in 1584). Events move even more swiftly than in Cinthio, for Shakespeare has compressed the story into two or three nights and days (although with an intervening sea journey and with an elastic use of stage time to allow for the maturing of long-term plans, as when we learn that Iago has begged Emilia "a hundred times" to steal Desdemona's handkerchief, or that Iago has accused Cassio of making love to Desdemona "a thousand times"). *Othello* does not have a fully developed double plot as in *King Lear* or a comparatively large group of characters serving as foils to the protagonist as in *Hamlet*. *Othello's* cast is small and the plot is concentrated to an unusual degree on Othello, Desdemona, and Iago. What *Othello* may lose in cosmic breadth it gains in dramatic intensity.

Daringly, Shakespeare opens his play about a love tragedy not with a direct and sympathetic portrayal of the lovers themselves, but with a scene of vicious insinuation about their marriage. The images employed by Iago to describe the coupling of Othello and Desdemona are revoltingly animalistic, sodomistic. "Even now, now, very now, an old black ram Is tupping your white ewe," he taunts Desdemona's father Brabantio. ("Tupping" is a word used specifically for the copulating of sheep.) "You'll have your daughter covered with a Barbary horse; you'll have your nephews neigh to you"; "Your daughter and the Moor are now making the beast with two backs"; "the devil will make a grandsire of you." This degraded view reduces the marriage to one of utter carnality, with repeated emphasis on the word "gross": Desdemona has yielded "to the gross clasps of a lascivious Moor," and has made "a gross revolt" against her family and society. Iago's second thematic emphasis, one that is habitual with him, is on money. "What, ho, Brabantio! thieves! thieves! thieves! Look to your house, your daughter, and your bags!" The implication is of a sinister bond between thievery in sex and thievery in gold. Sex and money are both commodities to be protected by watchful fathers against libidinous and opportunistic children.

We as audience make plentiful allowance for Iago's bias in all this, since he has admitted to Roderigo his knavery and resentment of Othello. Even so, the carnal image of love we must confront is a calculatedly disturbing one. What are our own prejudices about a black man and a white woman? Othello is unquestionably a black man, referred to as the "thick-lips," with a "sooty bosom"; Elizabethan usage applied the term "Moor" to Africans without attempting to distinguish between Arabian and Negroid peoples. From the ugly start of the play, Othello and Desdemona have to prove the worth of their love in the face of preset attitudes against miscegenated marriage. Brabantio takes refuge in the thought that Othello must have bewitched Desdemona. His basic assumption—one to be echoed later by Iago and by Othello himself—is that a miscegenated marriage is unnatural by definition. In confronting and accusing Othello he repeatedly appeals "to all things of sense" (that is, to common sense) and asks if it is not "gross in sense" (self-evident) that Othello has practiced magic on her, since nothing else could prompt human nature so to leave its natural path. "For nature so preposterously to err, Being not deficient, blind, or lame of sense, Sans witchcraft could not" (I,ii–iii). We as audience do not endorse Brabantio's view, and in fact partly recognize in him the type of imperious father who conventionally opposes romantic love. It is sadly ironic that he should now prefer Roderigo as his son-in-law, evidently concluding that any white Venetian would be preferable to the prince of blacks. Still, Brabantio has been hospitable to the Moor and trusting of his daughter. He is a sorrowful rather than ridiculous figure, and the charge he levels at the married pair, however much based on *a priori* assumptions of what is "natural" in human behavior, remains to be answered.

After all, we find ourselves wondering, what did attract Othello and Desdemona to one another? Even though he certainly did not use witchcraft, may Othello not have employed a subtler kind of enchantment in the exotic character of his life-history, his travel accounts "of the Cannibals that each other eat, The Anthropophagi, and men whose heads Do grow beneath their shoulders" (I,iii)? These "passing strange" events fascinate Desdemona as they do everyone including the Duke of Venice ("I think this tale would win my daughter too"). Othello has not practiced unfairly on her—"This only is the witchcraft I have us'd." Yet may he not represent for Desdemona a radical novelty, being a man at once less devious and more mysterious than the dissolute Venetian swaggerers like Roderigo who follow her about? Was her deceiving of her father by means of the elopement a protest, an escape from conventionality? Why has she been attracted to a man so much older than herself? For his part, Othello gives the impression of being inexperienced with women, at least of Desdemona's rank and complexion, and thus is both intrigued and flattered by her attentions. "She lov'd me for the dangers I had pass'd, And I lov'd her that she did pity them." Desdemona fulfills a place in Othello's ego. Does she also represent a kind of status for him in Venetian society, where he has been employed as a military commander but treated nonetheless as something of an alien?

These subtle but impertinent ways of doubting the motivations of Othello and Desdemona are thrust upon us by the play's opening, and are later crucial to Iago's strategy of breeding mistrust. Just as importantly, however, these insinuations are refuted by Othello and especially by Desdemona. Whatever others may think, she never gives any slightest indication of regarding her husband as different or exotic because he is black. She is utterly fond of him, admiring, and faithful. We believe her when she says that she does not even know what it means to be unfaithful; the word "whore" is not in her vocabulary. She is defenseless against the charges brought against her because she does not even comprehend them, cannot believe that anyone would imagine such things. Her love is of that transcendent purity common to several late Shakespearean heroines such as Cordelia in *King Lear* and Hermione in *The Winter's Tale*, whose names are synonymous with grace. Her "preferring" Othello to her father, like Cordelia's placing her duty to a husband before that to a father, is not ungrateful but natural and proper. And Othello, however much he may regard Desdemona as an extention of himself (he calls her "my fair warrior"), does cherish Desdemona as she deserves. "I cannot speak enough of this content," he exclaims when he rejoins her on Cyprus. "It stops me here; it is too much of joy" (II,i). The very passionate intensity of his love prepares the way for his tragedy, for he knows only too well that "when I love thee not, Chaos is come again" (III,iii). Iago speaks truly when he observes that Othello "Is of a constant, loving, noble nature" (II,i). Othello's tragedy is not that he is easily duped, but that his strong faith can be destroyed at such terrible cost. Othello never forgets how much he is losing. The threat to his love is not its lack of wholesomeness, but the kind of insidious thinking which assumes that a black-white marriage cannot succeed because it is unnatural. The fear of such an inherent flaw exists in Othello's mind, but the human instrument of this vicious gospel is Iago.

Iago belongs to a select group of villains in Shakespeare who take delight in evil for its own sake: Aaron the Moor in *Titus Andronicus*, Richard III, Don John in *Much Ado*, Iago, Edmund in *King Lear*. They are not, like Macbeth or like Claudius in *Hamlet*, men driven by ambition to commit crimes they clearly recognize as morally wrong. Although Edmund does belatedly try to make amends, these villains are essentially conscienceless, sinister, and amused at their own cunning. As Bernard Spivack observes (in *Shakespeare and the Allegory of Evil*), they are related to one another by a stage metaphor of personified evil derived from the Vice of the morality play. Like that engaging tempter of Mankind, they take the audience into their confidence, boast in soliloquy of their cleverness, exult in the triumph of evil, and improvise plans with incredible daring and resourcefulness. They are all superb actors, deceiving virtually every character on stage until late in the game with their protean and hypocritical display. They take pleasure in this "sport" and amaze us by their virtuosity. The role is essentially comic, although it is the grim and ironic comedy of vice. We know that we are to condemn morally even while we applaud the skill and technique.

This tradition of vice comedy may best explain a puzzling feature of Iago, noted long ago and memorably phrased by Coleridge as "the motive hunting of a motiveless malignity." Iago does offer plausible motives for what he does. Despite his resemblance to the morality Vice, he is no allegorized abstraction but an ensign in the army, a junior field officer who hates being outranked by a theoretician or staff officer. As an old-school professional he also resents that he has not been promoted on the basis of seniority, the "old gradation." Even his efforts at using influence with Othello have come to naught, and Iago can scarcely be blamed for supposing that Cassio's friendship with Othello has won him special favor. Thus Iago has reason to plot against Cassio as well as Othello. Nevertheless a further dimension is needed to explain the gloating, the utter lack of moral reflection, the concentration on destroying Desdemona (who has not wronged Iago), the absorption in ingenious methods of plotting, the finesse and the style. Probably the tradition of the stage Machiavel, as in Marlowe's *Jew of Malta*, adds an ingredient; this tradition was readily assimilated with that of the Vice.

Iago's machinations yield him both "sport" and "profit" (I,iii); that is, he inherently enjoys his evildoing, although he is also driven by a motive. This duality of Vice-like behavior in human garb creates a restless sense of a dark metaphysical reality lying behind his visible exterior. Even his stated motives do not always make sense. When in an outburst of hatred he soliloquizes that "I hate the Moor; And it is thought abroad, that 'twixt my sheets H' as done my office," Iago goes on to concede the unlikelihood of this charge. "I know not if 't be true; But I, for mere suspicion in that kind, Will do as if for surety" (I,iii). The charge is so absurd, in fact, that we have to look into Iago himself for the origin of this jealous paranoia. The answer may be partly emblematic: as the personification of sexual jealousy, Iago suffers with ironic appropriateness from the evil he preaches, and without external cause. Emilia understands that jealousy is not a rational affliction but a self-induced disease of the mind. Jealous persons, she tells Desdemona, "are not ever jealous for the cause, But jealous for they are jealous: 'tis a monster Begot upon itself, born on itself" (III,iv). Iago's own testimonial bears this out, for his jealousy is at once wholly irrational and agonizingly self-destructive. "I do suspect the lusty Moor Hath leap'd into my seat; the thought whereof Doth, like a poisonous mineral, gnaw my inwards" (II,i). In light of this nightmare, we can see that even his seemingly plausible resentment of Cassio's promotion is a form of jealousy, or envy.

Othello comes to regard Iago as a "demi-devil" who has tempted Othello to damn himself "beneath all depth in hell"; Lodovico speaks of Iago in the closing lines of the play as a "hellish villain"; and Iago himself boasts that "When devils will the blackest sins put on, They do suggest at first with heavenly shows, As I do now" (II,iii). Conversely, Desdemona is in Emilia's words an "angel," purely chaste; "So come my soul to bliss, as I speak true" (V,ii). When Desdemona lands on Cyprus, she is greeted in words that echo the *Ave Maria:* "Hail to thee, lady! and the grace of heaven . . . Enwheel thee round!" (II,i). These images introduce metaphorically a conflict of good and evil in which Othello, typical of fallen man, has chosen evil and destroyed the good at the prompting of a diabolical counselor. Here again we see the heritage of the morality play, especially the later morality in which the Mankind figure was sometimes damned rather than saved. Even so, to allegorize *Othello* is to do serious violence to its clash of human passion. In dramatic terms, the theological issue of salvation or damnation is not relevant; the play does not attempt to preach homiletically about the dangers of jealousy. The metaphysical dimensions of a homiletic tradition are still present but have been transmuted into human drama. Recognizing these limitations, we can perhaps see a spiritual analogy in Iago's devillike method of undoing his victims.

His trick resembles that of the similarly diabolical Don John in *Much Ado:* an optical illusion by which the blameless heroine is impugned as an adulteress. The concealed Othello must watch Cassio boasting of sexual triumphs, and believe he is talking about Desdemona. Like the devil, Iago is given power over men's frail senses, especially of seeing. Yet he must prepare Othello to see what Iago wants him to see, as Don John prepares Claudio, since the hoodwinking depends on fixed preconceptions. Iago practices on

Othello with an *a priori* logic used before on Brabantio and Roderigo, urging the proneness of all mortals to sin and the unnaturalness of a black-white marriage. All women have appetites; Desdemona is a woman; hence Desdemona has appetites. "The wine she drinks is made of grapes," he scoffs to Roderigo. "If she had been blessed, she would never have loved the Moor" (II,i). She is a Venetian, and "In Venice they do let heaven see the pranks They dare not show their husbands" (III,iii). Therefore she too is a hypocrite; "she did deceive her father." Most of all, it stands to reason that she must long for a man of her own race. As Iago succeeds in getting Othello to ponder: "And yet, how nature erring from itself . . . " This proposition that Nature teaches all persons, including Desdemona, to seek a harmonious matching of "clime, complexion, and degree" strikes a responsive chord in Othello, since he knows that he is black and alien. "Haply, for I am black And have not those soft parts of conversation That chamberers have . . . " Then, too, he is sensitive that he is considerably older than she, "declin'd Into the vale of years" (III,iii), "the young affects In me defunct" (I,iii). And so, if one must conclude from the preceding that Desdemona will seek a lover, the only question is who. "This granted,—as it is a most pregnant and unforced position—who stands so eminent in the degree of this fortune as Cassio does?" (II,i). Once Othello has accepted this syllogistic sequence of proofs, specious not through any lapse in logic but because the axiomatic assumptions about human nature are degraded and do not apply to Desdemona, Othello has arrived at an unshakable conclusion to which all subsequent evidence must be forced as "a foregone conclusion." "Villain, be sure thou prove my love a whore," he commissions Iago (III,iii). Desdemona's innocent pleading for Cassio only makes things look worse. Cassio's reputed muttering while asleep, like the handkerchief seen in his possession or his giddy talk about his mistress Bianca, "speaks against her [Desdemona] with the other proofs."

The increasing surrender of Othello's judgment to passion can be measured in three successive trial scenes in the play: the entirely fair trial of Othello himself by the Venetian senate concerning the elopement, Othello's trial of Cassio for drinking and rioting (when, ominously, Othello's "blood begins my safer guides to rule"), and finally the prejudged sentencing of Desdemona without any opportunity for her to defend herself. In a corollary decline, Othello falls from the Christian compassion of the opening scenes (he customarily confesses to heaven "the vices of my blood," I,iii) to the pagan savagery of his vengeful and ritual execution of his wife. "My heart is turned to stone" (IV,i), he vows, and at the play's end he grievingly characterizes himself as a "base Judean" who "threw a pearl away Richer than all his tribe." (The First Folio reading of "Iudean" or "Judean" refers perhaps to Judas Iscariot or to Herod; some editors prefer the quarto reading of "Indian.") Iago knows that he must persuade Othello to sentence and execute Desdemona himself, for only by this active commitment to evil will Othello damn himself. In nothing does Iago so resemble the devil as in his wish to see Othello destroy the innocence and goodness on which his happiness depends.

The fate of some of the lesser characters echoes that of Othello, for Iago's universally evil intent is to "enmesh them all" (II,iii). Cassio in particular is, like Othello, an admirable man with a single but fatally vulnerable weakness, in his case fleshly appetite for wine and women. These seem like genial flaws, but lead to disaster because they put Cassio at the mercy of his remorseless enemy. Ironically, Iago is himself the apostle of absolute self-control: "Our bodies are our gardens, to the which our wills are gardeners" (I,iii). Thus, Cassio's tragedy is anything but a straightforward homily on the virtues of temperance. Similarly, Bianca is undone not through any simple cause-and-effect punishment of her sexual conduct—she is, after all, fond of Cassio and loyal to him, even if he will not marry her—but because Iago is able to turn appearances against her. With his usual appeal to *a priori* logic and guilt by association, he builds a case that she and Cassio are in cahoots: "I do suspect this trash To be a party in this injury . . . This is the fruit of whoring" (V,i). Roderigo is another of Iago's victims, a contemptible one, led by the nose because he too has surrendered reason to passion. Even Emilia cannot escape Iago's evil influence, and steals the handkerchief for him despite her knowing what it means to Desdemona. Seemingly little flaws are magnified into disasters by a remorseless evil intelligence. Men must be ceaselessly circumspect; a good reputation is sooner lost than recovered. Emilia is a normally virtuous woman—she would be faithless in marriage, she tells Desdemona, only for a very high price—and yet her one small compromise with her conscience results in a murder. Like Othello she offers atonement too late, by denouncing her husband. Desdemona is the only person in the play too good to be struck down through some inner flaw, which may explain why Iago is committed above all else to seeing that she be destroyed.

As a tragic hero, Othello obtains self-knowledge at a terrible price. He knows finally that what he has destroyed was ineffably good. The discovery is too late for him to be able to make amends, and he dies at his own hand by way of atonement. Despite the tragic loss, however, his reaffirmation of faith in Desdemona's goodness undoes what the devillike Iago had most hoped to achieve: the separation of Othello from a belief in goodness. In this important sense, Othello's self-knowledge is cathartic and a compensation for the terrible price he has paid. The very existence of a person as good as Desdemona gives the lie to Iago's creed that everyone has his price. She is the sacrificial victim who must die for Othello's tragically human loss of faith, and, by so dying, rekindle that faith.

OTHELLO, THE MOOR OF VENICE

The Names of the Actors

OTHELLO, *the Moor.*
BRABANTIO, [*a senator,*] *father to Desdemona.*
CASSIO, *an honourable lieutenant* [*to Othello*].
IAGO, [*Othello's ancient,*] *a villain.*
RODERIGO, *a gulled gentleman.*
DUKE OF VENICE.
Senators [*of Venice*].
MONTANO, *governor of Cyprus.*
LODOVICO *and* GRATIANO, [*kinsmen to Brabantio,*] *two noble Venetians.*
Sailors.
Clown.

DESDEMONA, [*daughter to Brabantio and*] *wife to Othello.*
EMILIA, *wife to Iago.*
BIANCA, *a courtezan* [*and mistress to Cassio*].

[Messenger, Herald, Officers, Gentlemen, Musicians, *and* Attendants.]

[SCENE: *Venice: a Sea-port in Cyprus.*]

ACT I.

SCENE I. [*Venice. A street.*]

Enter RODERIGO *and* IAGO.

Rod. Tush! never tell me; I take it much unkindly
That thou, Iago, who hast had my purse
As if the strings were thine, shouldst know of this.
Iago. 'Sblood, but you'll not hear me:
If ever I did dream of such a matter,
Abhor me.
Rod. Thou told'st me thou didst hold him in thy hate.
Iago. Despise me, if I do not. Three great ones of the city,
In personal suit to make me his lieutenant,
Off-capp'd to him: and, by the faith of man,
I know my price, I am worth no worse a place:
But he, as loving his own pride and purposes,
Evades them, with a bombast circumstance
Horribly stuff'd with epithets of war;
And, in conclusion,
Nonsuits my mediators; for, 'Certes,' says he,
'I have already chose my officer.'
And what was he?
Forsooth, a great arithmetician,
One Michael Cassio, a Florentine,
†A fellow almost damn'd in a fair wife;
That never set a squadron in the field,
Nor the division of a battle knows
More than a spinster; unless the bookish theoric,
Wherein the toged consuls can propose
As masterly as he: mere prattle, without practice,
Is all his soldiership. But he, sir, had th' election:
And I, of whom his eyes had seen the proof
At Rhodes, at Cyprus and on other grounds
Christian and heathen, must be be-lee'd and calm'd
By debitor and creditor: this counter-caster,
He, in good time, must his lieutenant be,
And I—God bless the mark!—his Moorship's ancient.
Rod. By heaven, I rather would have been his hangman.
Iago. Why, there 's no remedy; 'tis the curse of service,
Preferment goes by letter and affection,
And not by old gradation, where each second
Stood heir to th' first. Now, sir, be judge yourself,
Whether I in any just term am affin'd
To love the Moor.
Rod. I would not follow him then.
Iago. O, sir, content you;
I follow him to serve my turn upon him:
We cannot all be masters, nor all masters
Cannot be truly follow'd. You shall mark
Many a duteous and knee-crooking knave,
That, doting on his own obsequious bondage,
Wears out his time, much like his master's ass,
For nought but provender, and when he 's old, cashier'd:
Whip me such honest knaves. Others there are
Who, trimm'd in forms and visages of duty,
Keep yet their hearts attending on themselves,
And, throwing but shows of service on their lords,
Do well thrive by them and when they have lin'd their coats
Do themselves homage: these fellows have some soul;
And such a one do I profess myself. For, sir,
It is as sure as you are Roderigo,
Were I the Moor, I would not be Iago:
In following him, I follow but myself;
Heaven is my judge, not I for love and duty,
But seeming so, for my peculiar end:
For when my outward action doth demonstrate
The native act and figure of my heart
In compliment extern, 'tis not long after
But I will wear my heart upon my sleeve
For daws to peck at: I am not what I am.
Rod. What a full fortune does the thick-lips owe,
If he can carry 't thus!
Iago. Call up her father,
Rouse him: make after him, poison his delight,
Proclaim him in the streets; incense her kinsmen,

ACT I. SCENE I. 4. **'Sblood,** an oath, "by God's blood." 8. **great ones of the city.** Iago means to indicate his importance in the community; this is suggested also by his use of the word *worth* in line 11. 10. **him,** Othello. 16. **Nonsuits,** rejects. 19. **arithmetician,** a man whose military knowledge was merely theoretical, based on books of tactics. 21. **A . . . wife.** Cassio does not seem to be married, but his counterpart in Shakespeare's source did have a wife. See also IV, i, 127. 23. **division,** disposition of a battle line. 24. **theoric,** theory. 25. **toged,** wearing the toga. **propose,** discuss. 29. **Rhodes, Cyprus,** islands in the Mediterranean south of Asia Minor, long subject to contention between the Venetians and the Turks. 31. **counter-caster,** a sort of bookkeeper; contemptuous term. 32. **in good time,** forsooth. 33. **God bless the mark,** anciently, a pious interjection to avert evil omens. **ancient,** standardbearer, ensign. 37. **old gradation,** seniority. Iago here expresses a characteristic prejudice of professional soldiers. 39. **affin'd,** bound. 57. **Were . . . Iago.** Were I in the position of the Moor, I should not feel as Iago feels. 63. **compliment extern,** outward civility. 66. **thick-lips.** Elizabethans often applied the term "Moor" to Negroes.

And, though he in a fertile climate dwell,
Plague him with flies: though that his joy be joy,
Yet throw such changes of vexation on 't,
As it may lose some colour.
Rod. Here is her father's house; I'll call aloud.
Iago. Do, with like timorous accent and dire yell
As when, by night and negligence, the fire
Is spied in populous cities.
Rod. What, ho, Brabantio! Signior Brabantio, ho!
Iago. Awake! what, ho, Brabantio! thieves! thieves! thieves!
Look to your house, your daughter and your bags!
Thieves! thieves!

BRABANTIO [*appears*] *above* [*at a window*].

Bra. What is the reason of this terrible summons?
What is the matter there?
Rod. Signior, is all your family within?
Iago. Are your doors lock'd?
Bra. Why, wherefore ask you this?
Iago. 'Zounds, sir, y' are robb'd; for shame, put on your gown;
Your heart is burst, you have lost half your soul;
Even now, now, very now, an old black ram
Is tupping your white ewe. Arise, arise;
Awake the snorting citizens with the bell,
Or else the devil will make a grandsire of you:
Arise, I say.
Bra. What, have you lost your wits?
Rod. Most reverend signior, do you know my voice?
Bra. Not I: what are you?
Rod. My name is Roderigo.
Bra. The worser welcome:
I have charg'd thee not to haunt about my doors:
In honest plainness thou hast heard me say
My daughter is not for thee; and now, in madness,
Being full of supper and distemp'ring draughts,
Upon malicious bravery, dost thou come
To start my quiet.
Rod. Sir, sir, sir,—
Bra. But thou must needs be sure
My spirit and my place have in them power
To make this bitter to thee.
Rod. Patience, good sir.
Bra. What tell'st thou me of robbing? this is Venice;
My house is not a grange.
Rod. Most grave Brabantio,
In simple and pure soul I come to you.

Iago. 'Zounds, sir, you are one of those that will not serve God, if the devil bid you. Because we come to do you service and you think we are ruffians, you'll have your daughter covered with a Barbary horse; you'll have your nephews neigh to you; you'll have coursers for cousins and gennets for germans.

Bra. What profane wretch art thou?

Iago. I am one, sir, that comes to tell you your daughter and the Moor are now making the beast with two backs.

Bra. Thou art a villain.
Iago. You are—a senator.
Bra. This thou shalt answer; I know thee, Roderigo.
Rod. Sir, I will answer any thing. But, I beseech you,
If 't be your pleasure and most wise consent,
As partly I find it is, that your fair daughter,
At this odd-even and dull watch o' th' night,
Transported, with no worse nor better guard
But with a knave of common hire, a gondolier,
To the gross clasps of a lascivious Moor,—
If this be known to you and your allowance,
We then have done you bold and saucy wrongs;
But if you know not this, my manners tell me
We have your wrong rebuke. Do not believe
That, from the sense of all civility,
I thus would play and trifle with your reverence:
Your daughter, if you have not given her leave,
I say again, hath made a gross revolt;
Tying her duty, beauty, wit and fortunes
In an extravagant and wheeling stranger
Of here and every where. Straight satisfy yourself:
If she be in her chamber or your house,
Let loose on me the justice of the state
For thus deluding you.
Bra. Strike on the tinder, ho!
Give me a taper! call up all my people!
This accident is not unlike my dream:
Belief of it oppresses me already.
Light, I say! light! *Exit* [*above*].
Iago. Farewell; for I must leave you:
It seems not meet, nor wholesome to my place,
To be produc'd—as, if I stay, I shall—
Against the Moor: for, I do know, the state,
However this may gall him with some check,
Cannot with safety cast him, for he 's embark'd
With such loud reason to the Cyprus wars,
Which even now stand in act, that, for their souls,
Another of his fathom they have none,
To lead their business: in which regard,
Though I do hate him as I do hell-pains,
Yet, for necessity of present life,
I must show out a flag and sign of love,
Which is indeed but sign. That you shall surely find him,
Lead to the Sagittary the raised search:
And there will I be with him. So, farewell. *Exit.*

Enter [*below*] BRABANTIO, *with* Servants *and torches.*

Bra. It is too true an evil: gone she is;
And what 's to come of my despised time
Is nought but bitterness. Now, Roderigo,
Where didst thou see her? O unhappy girl!
With the Moor, say'st thou? Who would be a father!
How didst thou know 'twas she? O, she deceives me
Past thought! What said she to you? Get moe tapers:
Raise all my kindred. Are they married, think you?
Rod. Truly, I think they are.
Bra. O heaven! How got she out? O treason of the blood!
Fathers, from hence trust not your daughters' minds
By what you see them act. Is there not charms
By which the property of youth and maidhood
May be abus'd? Have you not read, Roderigo,

75. **timorous,** frightening. 90. **snorting,** snoring. 100. **bravery,** defiance, bravado. 101. **start,** disrupt. 106. **grange,** isolated farmhouse. 112. **nephews,** grandsons. 113. **gennets,** small Spanish horses. 114. **germans,** near relatives. 124. **odd-even,** between night and morning. 128. **allowance,** permission. 132. **from,** contrary to. 137. **extravagant,** wandering. **wheeling,** wandering, vagabond. 141. **tinder,** charred linen kept in a metal box, and ignited by a spark from flint and steel. 143. **accident,** occurrence, event. 149. **check,** rebuke. 150. **cast,** dismiss. 152. **stand in act,** are going on. 153. **fathom,** ability. 159. **Sagittary,** probably an inn. 160. *Stage Direction.* In Q, Brabantio enters "in his nightgown," i.e., dressing gown. 167. **moe,** more. 172. **Is,** are. 173. **property,** special quality. 176. **you,** Roderigo. 183. **officers of night,** police.

SCENE II. 5. **yerk'd,** stabbed. 12. **magnifico,** Venetian grandee

Of some such thing?
Rod. Yes, sir, I have indeed.
Bra. Call up my brother. O, would you had had her!
Some one way, some another. Do you know
Where we may apprehend her and the Moor?
Rod. I think I can discover him, if you please
To get good guard and go along with me.
Bra. Pray you, lead on. At every house I'll call;
I may command at most. Get weapons, ho!
And raise some special officers of night.
On, good Roderigo: I will deserve your pains. *Exeunt.*

SCENE II. [*Another street.*]

Enter OTHELLO, IAGO, Attendants *with torches.*

Iago. Though in the trade of war I have slain men,
Yet do I hold it very stuff o' th' conscience
To do no contriv'd murder: I lack iniquity
Sometime to do me service: nine or ten times
I had thought t' have yerk'd him here under the ribs.
Oth. 'Tis better as it is.
Iago. Nay, but he prated,
And spoke such scurvy and provoking terms
Against your honour
That, with the little godliness I have,
I did full hard forbear him. But, I pray you, sir,
Are you fast married? Be assur'd of this,
That the magnifico is much belov'd,
And hath in his effect a voice potential
As double as the duke's: he will divorce you;
Or put upon you what restraint and grievance
The law, with all his might to enforce it on,
Will give him cable.
Oth. Let him do his spite;
My services which I have done the signiory
Shall out-tongue his complaints. 'Tis yet to know,—
Which, when I know that boasting is an honour,
I shall promulgate—I fetch my life and being
From men of royal siege, and my demerits
May speak unbonneted to as proud a fortune
As this that I have reach'd: for know, Iago,
But that I love the gentle Desdemona,
I would not my unhoused free condition
Put into circumscription and confine
For the sea's worth. But, look! what lights come yond?
Iago. Those are the raised father and his friends:
You were best go in.
Oth. Not I; I must be found:
My parts, my title and my perfect soul
Shall manifest me rightly. Is it they?
Iago. By Janus, I think no.

Enter CASSIO [*and certain* Officers] *with torches.*

Oth. The servants of the duke, and my lieutenant.
The goodness of the night upon you, friends!
What is the news?
Cas. The duke does greet you, general,
And he requires your haste-post-haste appearance,
Even on the instant.
Oth. What is the matter, think you?
Cas. Something from Cyprus, as I may divine:
It is a business of some heat: the galleys
Have sent a dozen sequent messengers
This very night at one another's heels,
And many of the consuls, rais'd and met,
Are at the duke's already: you have been hotly call'd for;
When, being not at your lodging to be found,
The senate hath sent about three several quests
To search you out.
Oth. 'Tis well I am found by you.
I will but spend a word here in the house,
And go with you. [*Exit.*]
Cas. Ancient, what makes he here?
Iago. 'Faith, he to-night hath boarded a land carack:
If it prove lawful prize, he 's made for ever.
Cas. I do not understand.
Iago. He 's married.
Cas. To who?

[*Enter* OTHELLO.]

Iago. Marry, to—Come, captain, will you go?
Oth. Have with you.
Cas. Here comes another troop to seek for you.

Enter BRABANTIO, RODERIGO, *with* Officers *and torches.*

Iago. It is Brabantio. General, be advis'd;
He comes to bad intent.
Oth. Holla! stand there!
Rod. Signior, it is the Moor.
Bra. Down with him, thief!
[*They draw on both sides.*]
Iago. You, Roderigo! come, sir, I am for you.
Oth. Keep up your bright swords, for the dew will rust them.
Good signior, you shall more command with years
Than with your weapons.
Bra. O thou foul thief, where hast thou stow'd my daughter?
Damn'd as thou art, thou hast enchanted her;
For I'll refer me to all things of sense,
If she in chains of magic were not bound,
Whether a maid so tender, fair and happy,
So opposite to marriage that she shunn'd
The wealthy curled darlings of our nation,
Would ever have, t' incur a general mock,
Run from her guardage to the sooty bosom
Of such a thing as thou, to fear, not to delight.
Judge me the world, if 'tis not gross in sense
That thou hast practis'd on her with foul charms,
Abus'd her delicate youth with drugs or minerals
That weaken motion: I'll have 't disputed on;
'Tis probable and palpable to thinking.
I therefore apprehend and do attach thee
For an abuser of the world, a practiser
Of arts inhibited and out of warrant.
Lay hold upon him: if he do resist,
Subdue him at his peril.

(i.e., Brabantio). 13. **effect,** influence. **potential,** powerful. 14. **double,** twice as influential as most men's. 18. **signiory,** Venetian government. 22. **siege,** rank. **demerits,** deserts. 23. **unbonneted,** on equal terms. 31. **perfect soul,** unflawed conscience. 41. **sequent,** successive. 43. **consuls,** senators. 46. **several,** separate. 50. **carack,** large merchant ship. 63. **things of sense,** commonsense understandings of the natural order. 70. **guardage,** guardianship. 72. **gross in sense,** easily discernible in apprehension or perception. 74. **minerals,** medicine, poison. 75. **motion,** thought, reason. **disputed on,** argued in court by professional counsel. 78. **abuser of the world,** corrupter of society. 79. **inhibited,** prohibited.

Oth. Hold your hands,
Both you of my inclining, and the rest:
Were it my cue to fight, I should have known it
Without a prompter. Wither will you that I go
To answer this your charge?
Bra. To prison, till fit time
Of law and course of direct session
Call thee to answer.
Oth. What if I do obey?
How may the duke be therewith satisfied,
Whose messengers are here about my side,
Upon some present business of the state
To bring me to him?
First Off. 'Tis true, most worthy signior;
The duke 's in council, and your noble self,
I am sure, is sent for.
Bra. How! the duke in council!
In this time of the night! Bring him away:
Mine 's not an idle cause: the duke himself,
Or any of my brothers of the state,
Cannot but feel this wrong as 'twere their own;
For if such actions may have passage free,
Bond-slaves and pagans shall our statesmen be.
Exeunt.

SCENE III. [*A council-chamber.*]

Enter DUKE, Senators, *and* Officers [*set at a table, with lights and* Attendants].

Duke. There is no composition in these news
That gives them credit.
First Sen. Indeed, they are disproportion'd;
My letters say a hundred and seven galleys.
Duke. And mine, a hundred forty.
Sec. Sen. And mine, two hundred:
But though they jump not on a just account,—
As in these cases, where the aim reports,
'Tis oft with difference—yet do they all confirm
A Turkish fleet, and bearing up to Cyprus.
Duke. Nay, it is possible enough to judgement:
I do not so secure me in the error,
But the main article I do approve
In fearful sense.
Sailor. (*Within*) What, ho! what, ho! what, ho!
First Off. A messenger from the galleys.

Enter Sailor.

Duke. Now, what 's the business?
Sail. The Turkish preparation makes for Rhodes;
So was I bid report here to the state
By Signior Angelo.
Duke. How say you by this change?
First Sen. This cannot be,
By no assay of reason: 'tis a pageant,
To keep us in false gaze. When we consider
Th' importancy of Cyprus to the Turk,
And let ourselves again but understand,
That as it more concerns the Turk than Rhodes,
So may he with more facile question bear it,
For that it stands not in such warlike brace,
But altogether lacks th' abilities
That Rhodes is dress'd in: if we make thought of this,
We must not think the Turk is so unskilful
To leave that latest which concerns him first,
Neglecting an attempt of ease and gain,
To wake and wage a danger profitless.
Duke. Nay, in all confidence, he 's not for Rhodes.
First Off. Here is more news.

Enter a Messenger.

Mess. The Ottomites, reverend and gracious,
Steering with due course toward the isle of Rhodes,
Have there injointed them with an after fleet.
First Sen. Ay, so I thought. How many, as you guess?
Mess. Of thirty sail: and now they do re-stem
Their backward course, bearing with frank appearance
Their purposes toward Cyprus. Signior Montano,
Your trusty and most valiant servitor,
With his free duty recommends you thus,
And prays you to believe him.
Duke. 'Tis certain, then, for Cyprus.
Marcus Luccicos, is not he in town?
First Sen. He 's now in Florence.
Duke. Write from us to him; post-post-haste dispatch.
First Sen. Here comes Brabantio and the valiant Moor.

Enter BRABANTIO, OTHELLO, CASSIO, IAGO, RODERIGO, *and* Officers.

Duke. Valiant Othello, we must straight employ you
Against the general enemy Ottoman.
[*To Brabantio*] I did not see you; welcome, gentle signior;
We lack'd your counsel and your help to-night.
Bra. So did I yours. Good your grace, pardon me;
Neither my place nor aught I heard of business
Hath rais'd me from my bed, nor doth the general care
Take hold on me, for my particular grief
Is of so flood-gate and o'erbearing nature
That it engluts and swallows other sorrows
And it is still itself.
Duke. Why, what 's the matter?
Bra. My daughter! O, my daughter!
Duke and Sen. Dead?
Bra. Ay, to me;
She is abus'd, stol'n from me, and corrupted
By spells and medicines bought of mountebanks;
For nature so preposterously to err,
Being not deficient, blind, or lame of sense,
Sans witchcraft could not.
Duke. Whoe'er he be that in this foul proceeding
Hath thus beguil'd your daughter of herself
And vou of her, the bloody book of law
You shall yourself read in the bitter letter
After your own sense, yea, though our proper son
Stood in your action.

82. **inclining,** following, party. 86. **course of direct session,** regular legal proceedings. 99. **Bond-slaves and pagans,** contemptuous references to Othello's past history.

SCENE III. 2. **disproportion'd,** inconsistent. 5. **jump,** agree. 6. **aim,** conjecture. 10. **secure me,** feel myself secure. 11. **main article,** i.e., that the Turkish fleet is threatening. **approve,** accept. 18. **assay,** test. 23. **more facile question,** greater facility of effort. 24. **brace,** state of defense. 37. **re-stem,** steer again. 57. **engluts,** engulfs. 70. **Stood . . . action,** was under your accusation. 83. **pith,** strength, vigor. 89. **patience,** sufferance, permission. 95-96. **motion . . . herself,** inward impulses blushed at themselves. 103. **vouch,** assert. 111-112. **Did . . . affections.** The possibility of such enchantment is accepted by the

Bra. Humbly I thank your grace.
Here is the man, this Moor, whom now, it seems,
Your special mandate for the state-affairs
Hath hither brought.
Duke and Sen. We are very sorry for 't.
Duke. [*To Othello*] What, in your own part, can you say to this?
Bra. Nothing, but this is so.
Oth. Most potent, grave, and reverend signiors,
My very noble and approv'd good masters,
That I have ta'en away this old man's daughter,
It is most true; true, I have married her:
The very head and front of my offending
Hath this extent, no more. Rude am I in my speech,
And little bless'd with the soft phrase of peace;
For since these arms of mine had seven years' pith,
Till now some nine moons wasted, they have us'd
Their dearest action in the tented field,
And little of this great world can I speak,
More than pertains to feats of broil and battle,
And therefore little shall I grace my cause
In speaking for myself. Yet, by your gracious patience,
I will a round unvarnish'd tale deliver
Of my whole course of love; what drugs, what charms,
What conjuration and what mighty magic,
For such proceeding I am charg'd withal,
I won his daughter.
Bra. A maiden never bold;
Of spirit so still and quiet, that her motion
Blush'd at herself; and she, in spite of nature,
Of years, of country, credit, every thing,
To fall in love with what she fear'd to look on!
It is a judgement maim'd and most imperfect
That will confess perfection so could err
Against all rules of nature, and must be driven
To find out practices of cunning hell,
Why this should be. I therefore vouch again
That with some mixtures pow'rful o'er the blood,
Or with some dram conjur'd to this effect,
He wrought upon her.
Duke. To vouch this, is no proof,
Without more wider and more overt test
Than these thin habits and poor likelihoods
Of modern seeming do prefer against him.
First Sen. But, Othello, speak:
Did you by indirect and forced courses
Subdue and poison this young maid's affections?
Or came it by request and such fair question
As soul to soul affordeth?
Oth. I do beseech you,
Send for the lady to the Sagittary,
And let her speak of me before her father:
If you do find me foul in her report,
The trust, the office I do hold of you,
Not only take away, but let your sentence
Even fall upon my life.
Duke. Fetch Desdemona hither.
Oth. Ancient, conduct them; you best know the place. [*Exeunt Iago and Attendants.*]
And, till she come, as truly as to heaven
I do confess the vices of my blood,
So justly to your grave ears I'll present
How I did thrive in this fair lady's love,
And she in mine.
Duke. Say it, Othello.
Oth. Her father lov'd me; oft invited me;
Still question'd me the story of my life,
From year to year, the battles, sieges, fortunes,
That I have pass'd.
I ran it through, even from my boyish days,
To th' very moment that he bade me tell it;
Wherein I spake of most disastrous chances,
Of moving accidents by flood and field,
Of hair-breadth scapes i' th' imminent deadly breach,
Of being taken by the insolent foe
And sold to slavery, of my redemption thence
And portance in my travels' history:
Wherein of antres vast and deserts idle,
Rough quarries, rocks and hills whose heads touch heaven,
It was my hint to speak,—such was the process;
And of the Cannibals that each other eat,
The Anthropophagi and men whose heads
Do grow beneath their shoulders. This to hear
Would Desdemona seriously incline:
But still the house-affairs would draw her thence:
Which ever as she could with haste dispatch,
She 'ld come again, and with a greedy ear
Devour up my discourse: which I observing,
Took once a pliant hour, and found good means
To draw from her a prayer of earnest heart
That I would all my pilgrimage dilate,
Whereof by parcels she had something heard,
But not intentively: I did consent,
And often did beguile her of her tears,
When I did speak of some distressful stroke
That my youth suffer'd. My story being done,
She gave me for my pains a world of sighs:
She swore, in faith, 'twas strange, 'twas passing strange,
'Twas pitiful, 'twas wondrous pitiful:
She wish'd she had not heard it, yet she wish'd
That heaven had made her such a man: she thank'd me,
And bade me, if I had a friend that lov'd her,
I should but teach him how to tell my story,
And that would woo her. Upon this hint I spake:
She lov'd me for the dangers I had pass'd,
And I lov'd her that she did pity them.
This only is the witchcraft I have us'd:
Here comes the lady; let her witness it.

Enter DESDEMONA, IAGO, [*and*] Attendants.

Duke. I think this tale would win my daughter too.
Good Brabantio,
Take up this mangled matter at the best:
Men do their broken weapons rather use
Than their bare hands.
Bra. I pray you, hear her speak:
If she confess that she was half the wooer,
Destruction on my head, if my bad blame

court; it would be as readily accepted by an Elizabethan audience. The English Parliament of the year 1604 denounced by law the employment of magic to secure love. 136. **imminent,** i.e., impending parts when a gap has been made in a fortification. 139. **portance,** conduct. 140. **antres,** caverns. **idle,** barren, unprofitable. 142. **hint,** occasion. 143. **eat,** ate. 144. **Anthropophagi,** man-eaters, a term from Pliny's *Natural History.* 144-145. **whose . . . shoulders.** Tales of tribes of headless men appear in Pliny and in the voyages of travelers, such as Ralegh's *Discovery of Guiana.* 153. **dilate,** relate in detail. 155. **intentively,** with full attention.

Light on the man! Come hither, gentle mistress:
Do you perceive in all this noble company
Where most you owe obedience?
Des. My noble father,
I do perceive here a divided duty:
To you I am bound for life and education;
My life and education both do learn me
How to respect you; you are the lord of duty;
I am hitherto your daughter: but here 's my husband,
And so much duty as my mother show'd
To you, preferring you before her father,
So much I challenge that I may profess
Due to the Moor my lord.
Bra. God be with you! I have done.
Please it your grace, on to the state-affairs:
I had rather to adopt a child than get it.
Come hither, Moor:
I here do give thee that with all my heart
Which, but thou hast already, with all my heart
I would keep from thee. For your sake, jewel,
I am glad at soul I have no other child;
For thy escape would teach me tyranny,
To hang clogs on them. I have done, my lord.
Duke. Let me speak like yourself, and lay a sentence,
Which, as a grise or step, may help these lovers
Into your favour.
When remedies are past, the griefs are ended
By seeing the worst, which late on hopes depended.
To mourn a mischief that is past and gone
Is the next way to draw new mischief on.
What cannot be preserv'd when fortune takes,
Patience her injury a mock'ry makes.
The robb'd that smiles steals something from the thief;
He robs himself that spends a bootless grief.
Bra. So let the Turk of Cyprus us beguile;
We lose it not, so long as we can smile.
He bears the sentence well that nothing bears
But the free comfort which from thence he hears,
But he bears both the sentence and the sorrow
That, to pay grief, must of poor patience borrow.
These sentences, to sugar, or to gall,
Being strong on both sides, are equivocal:
But words are words; I never yet did hear
That the bruis'd heart was pierced through the ear.
I humbly beseech you, proceed to th' affairs of state.

Duke. The Turk with a most mighty preparation makes for Cyprus. Othello, the fortitude of the place is best known to you; and though we have there a substitute of most allowed sufficiency, yet opinion, a sovereign mistress of effects, throws a more safer voice on you: you must therefore be content to slubber the gloss of your new fortunes with this more stubborn and boisterous expedition.

Oth. The tyrant custom, most grave senators,
Hath made the flinty and steel couch of war
My thrice-driven bed of down: I do agnize
A natural and prompt alacrity
I find in hardness, and do undertake
These present wars against the Ottomites.
Most humbly therefore bending to your state,
I crave fit disposition for my wife,
Due reference of place and exhibition,
With such accommodation and besort
As levels with her breeding.
Duke. If you please,
Be 't at her father's.
Bra. I'll not have it so.
Oth. Nor I.
Des. Nor I; I would not there reside,
To put my father in impatient thoughts
By being in his eye. Most gracious duke,
To my unfolding lend your prosperous ear;
And let me find a charter in your voice,
T' assist my simpleness.
Duke. What would you, Desdemona?
Des. That I did love the Moor to live with him,
My downright violence and storm of fortunes
May trumpet to the world: my heart 's subdu'd
Even to the very quality of my lord:
I saw Othello's visage in his mind,
And to his honours and his valiant parts
Did I my soul and fortunes consecrate.
So that, dear lords, if I be left behind,
A moth of peace, and he go to the war,
The rites for why I love him are bereft me,
And I a heavy interim shall support
By his dear absence. Let me go with him.
Oth. Let her have your voices.
Vouch with me, heaven, I therefore beg it not,
To please the palate of my appetite,
Nor to comply with heat—the young affects
In me defunct—and proper satisfaction,
But to be free and bounteous to her mind:
And heaven defend your good souls, that you think
I will your serious and great business scant
When she is with me: no, when light-wing'd toys
Of feather'd Cupid seel with wanton dullness
My speculative and offic'd instruments,
That my disports corrupt and taint my business,
Let housewives make a skillet of my helm,
And all indign and base adversities
Make head against my estimation!
Duke. Be it as you shall privately determine,
Either for her stay or going: th' affair cries haste,
And speed must answer it.
First Sen. You must away to-night.
Oth. With all my heart.
Duke. At nine i' th' morning here we'll meet again.
Othello, leave some officer behind,
And he shall our commission bring to you;
With such things else of quality and respect
As doth import you.
Oth. So please your grace, my ancient;

181. **divided duty.** Desdemona recognizes that she still owes a duty to her father even after marriage. 190. **on to,** i.e., proceed with. 191. **get,** beget. 195. **For your sake,** on your account. 199. **like yourself,** i.e., as you would, in your proper temper. **sentence,** maxim. 200. **grise,** step. 202-220. **When . . . state.** The sententious matter in this passage is cast into rhyme, as not infrequently in Shakespeare. 205. **next,** nearest. 213. **comfort,** i.e., the consolation that it may be borne with patience. 223. **fortitude,** strength. 225. **allowed,** acknowledged. 225-226. **opinion . . . on you,** public opinion, an important determiner of affairs, chooses you as the best man. 228. **slubber,** soil, sully. 232. **thrice-driven,** thrice sifted. **agnize,** know in myself. 234. **hardness,** hardship. 238. **exhibition,** allowance. 239. **besort,** suitable company. 245. **prosperous,** propitious. 246. **charter,** privilege. 247. **simpleness,** simplicity. 258. **rites.** Some editors read *rights*. 264. **affects,** inclinations, desires. 270. **seel,** in falconry, to make blind by sewing up the eyes of the hawk in training. 271. **speculative . . . instruments,** ability to see and reason clearly. 272. **That,** so that. **disports,** pastime. **taint,** impair. 273. **skillet,** defined as "a small kettle"; usually means "a frying pan of the older style." 274. **indign,** unworthy, shameful. 275. **estimation,** reputation. 284. **import,** concern. 290. **delighted,**

A man he is of honesty and trust:
To his conveyance I assign my wife,
With what else needful your good grace shall think
To be sent after me.

Duke. Let it be so.
Good night to every one. [*To Brab.*] And, noble signior,
If virtue no delighted beauty lack,
Your son-in-law is far more fair than black.

First Sen. Adieu, brave Moor; use Desdemona well.

Bra. Look to her, Moor, if thou hast eyes to see:
She has deceiv'd her father, and may thee.

Exeunt [*Duke, Senators, Officers, &c.*].

Oth. My life upon her faith! Honest Iago,
My Desdemona must I leave to thee:
I prithee, let thy wife attend on her;
And bring them after in the best advantage.
Come, Desdemona; I have but an hour
Of love, of worldly matters and direction,
To spend with thee: we must obey the time.

Exit [*with Desdemona*].

Rod. Iago,—

Iago. What say'st thou, noble heart?

Rod. What will I do, thinkest thou?

Iago. Why, go to bed, and sleep.

Rod. I will incontinently drown myself.

Iago. If thou dost, I shall never love thee after. Why, thou silly gentleman!

Rod. It is silliness to live when to live is torment; and then have we a prescription to die when death is our physician.

Iago. O villanous! I have looked upon the world for four times seven years; and since I could distinguish betwixt a benefit and an injury, I never found man that knew how to love himself. Ere I would say, I would drown myself for the love of a guinea-hen, I would change my humanity with a baboon.

Rod. What should I do? I confess it is my shame to be so fond; but it is not in my virtue to amend it.

Iago. Virtue! a fig! 'tis in ourselves that we are thus or thus. Our bodies are our gardens, to the which our wills are gardeners; so that if we will plant nettles, or sow lettuce, set hyssop and weed up thyme, supply it with one gender of herbs, or distract it with many, either to have it sterile with idleness, or manured with industry, why, the power and corrigible authority of this lies in our wills. If the balance of our lives had not one scale of reason to poise another of sensuality, the blood and baseness of our natures would conduct us to most preposterous conclusions: but we have reason to cool our raging motions, our carnal stings, our unbitted lusts, whereof I take this that you call love to be a sect or scion.

Rod. It cannot be.

Iago. It is merely a lust of the blood and a permission of the will. Come, be a man. Drown thyself! drown cats and blind puppies. I have professed me thy friend and I confess me knit to thy deserving with cables of perdurable toughness; I could never better stead thee than now. Put money in thy purse; follow thou the wars; defeat thy favour with an usurped beard; I say, put money in thy purse. It cannot be that Desdemona should long continue her love to the Moor,—put money in thy purse,—nor he his to her: it was a violent commencement in her, and thou shalt see an answerable sequestration:—put but money in thy purse. These Moors are changeable in their wills:—fill thy purse with money:—the food that to him now is as luscious as locusts, shall be to him shortly as bitter as coloquintida. She must change for youth: when she is sated with his body, she will find the error of her choice: she must have change, she must: therefore put money in thy purse. If thou wilt needs damn thyself, do it a more delicate way than drowning. Make all the money thou canst: if sanctimony and a frail vow betwixt an erring barbarian and a super-subtle Venetian be not too hard for my wits and all the tribe of hell, thou shalt enjoy her; therefore make money. A pox of drowning thyself! it is clean out of the way: seek thou rather to be hanged in compassing thy joy than to be drowned and go without her.

Rod. Wilt thou be fast to my hopes, if I depend on the issue?

Iago. Thou art sure of me:—go, make money:—I have told thee often, and I re-tell thee again and again, I hate the Moor: my cause is hearted; thine hath no less reason. Let us be conjunctive in our revenge against him; if thou canst cuckold him, thou dost thyself a pleasure, me a sport. There are many events in the womb of time which will be delivered. Traverse! go, provide thy money. We will have more of this to-morrow. Adieu.

Rod. Where shall we meet i' the morning?

Iago. At my lodging.

Rod. I'll be with thee betimes.

Iago. Go to; farewell. Do you hear, Roderigo?

Rod. What say you?

Iago. No more of drowning, do you hear?

Rod. I am changed: I'll go sell all my land. *Exit.*

Iago. Thus do I ever make my fool my purse;
For I mine own gain'd knowledge should profane,
If I would time expend with such a snipe,
But for my sport and profit. I hate the Moor;
And it is thought abroad, that 'twixt my sheets
H' as done my office: I know not if 't be true;
But I, for mere suspicion in that kind,
Will do as if for surety. He holds me well;
The better shall my purpose work on him.
Cassio 's a proper man: let me see now:
To get his place and to plume up my will
In double knavery—How, how?—Let 's see:—
After some time, to abuse Othello's ears
That he is too familiar with his wife.

delightful. 295. **Honest Iago,** an evidence of Iago's carefully built reputation. 306. **incontinently,** immediately. 320. **virtue,** strength. 325. **hyssop,** an herb of the mint family. 327. **gender,** kind. 328. **idleness,** want of cultivation. 329. **corrigible authority,** the power to correct. 334-335. **reason . . . motions.** Iago understands the warfare between reason and sensuality, but his ethics are totally inverted; reason works in him not good, as it should according to natural law, but evil, which he has chosen for his good. 335. **motions,** appetites. **unbitted,** uncontrolled. 337. **sect,** cutting. 344. **perdurable,** very durable. 346. **defeat thy favour,** disguise and disfigure thy face. 351. **answerable sequestration,** a separation corresponding. 354. **locusts,** of doubtful meaning; defined as fruit of the carob tree (Matthew 3:4), as honeysuckle, and as lollipops or sugar-sticks. 355. **coloquintida,** colocynth, or bitter apple, a purgative. 362. **erring,** wandering, vagabond. 374. **hearted,** fixed in the heart. 375. **conjunctive,** united. 379. **Traverse,** go (military term). 391. **snipe,** gull, fool. 392-410. **I hate . . . light.** This is the passage about which Coleridge used his famous phrase, "the motive-hunting of a motiveless malignity." 399. **plume up,** glorify, gratify. 402. **he,** i.e., Cassio.

He hath a person and a smooth dispose
To be suspected, fram'd to make women false.
The Moor is of a free and open nature,
That thinks men honest that but seem to be so,
And will as tenderly be led by th' nose
As asses are.
I have 't. It is engend'red. Hell and night
Must bring this monstrous birth to the world's light.
[*Exit.*]

ACT II.

SCENE I. [*A Sea-port in Cyprus. An open place near the quay.*]

Enter MONTANO *and two* Gentlemen.

Mon. What from the cape can you discern at sea?
First Gent. Nothing at all: it is a high-wrought flood;
I cannot, 'twixt the heaven and the main,
Descry a sail.
Mon. Methinks the wind hath spoke aloud at land;
A fuller blast ne'er shook our battlements:
If it hath ruffian'd so upon the sea,
What ribs of oak, when mountains melt on them,
Can hold the mortise? What shall we hear of this?
Sec. Gent. A segregation of the Turkish fleet:
For do but stand upon the foaming shore,
The chidden billow seems to pelt the clouds;
The wind-shak'd surge, with high and monstrous mane,
Seems to cast water on the burning bear,
And quench the guards of th' ever-fixed pole:
I never did like molestation view
On the enchafed flood.
Mon. If that the Turkish fleet
Be not enshelter'd and embay'd, they are drown'd;
It is impossible they bear it out.

Enter a [*third*] Gentleman.

Third Gent. News, lads! our wars are done.
The desperate tempest hath so bang'd the Turks,
That their designment halts: a noble ship of Venice
Hath seen a grievous wrack and sufferance
On most part of their fleet.
Mon. How! is this true?
Third Gent. The ship is here put in,
A Veronesa; Michael Cassio,
Lieutenant to the warlike Moor Othello,
Is come on shore: the Moor himself at sea,
And is in full commission here for Cyprus.
Mon. I am glad on 't; 'tis a worthy governor.
Third Gent. But this same Cassio, though he speak of comfort
Touching the Turkish loss, yet he looks sadly,
And prays the Moor be safe; for they were parted
With foul and violent tempest.
Mon. Pray heavens he be;
For I have serv'd him, and the man commands
Like a full soldier. Let 's to the seaside, ho!
As well to see the vessel that 's come in
As to throw out our eyes for brave Othello,
Even till we make the main and th' aerial blue
An indistinct regard.
Third Gent. Come, let 's do so;
For every minute is expectancy
Of more arrivance.

Enter CASSIO.

Cas. Thanks, you the valiant of this warlike isle,
That so approve the Moor! O, let the heavens
Give him defence against the elements,
For I have lost him on a dangerous sea.
Mon. Is he well shipp'd?
Cas. His bark is stoutly timber'd, and his pilot
Of very expert and approv'd allowance;
Therefore my hopes, not surfeited to death,
Stand in bold cure. [*A cry*] *within* 'A sail, a sail, a sail!'

[*Enter a fourth* Gentleman.]

Cas. What noise?
Fourth Gent. The town is empty; on the brow o' th' sea
Stand ranks of people, and they cry 'A sail!'
Cas. My hopes do shape him for the governor.
[*Guns heard.*]
Sec. Gent. They do discharge their shot of courtesy:
Our friends at least.
Cas. I pray you, sir, go forth,
And give us truth who 'tis that is arriv'd.
Sec. Gent. I shall. *Exit.*
Mon. But, good lieutenant, is your general wiv'd?
Cas. Most fortunately: he hath achiev'd a maid
That paragons description and wild fame;
One that excels the quirks of blazoning pens,
And in th' essential vesture of creation
Does tire the ingener.

Enter [*second*] Gentleman.

How now! who has put in?
Sec. Gent. 'Tis one Iago, ancient to the general.
Cas. Has had most favourable and happy speed:
Tempests themselves, high seas and howling winds,
The gutter'd rocks and congregated sands,—
Traitors ensteep'd to clog the guiltless keel,—
As having sense of beauty, do omit
Their mortal natures, letting go safely by
The divine Desdemona.
Mon. What is she?
Cas. She that I spake of, our great captain's captain,
Left in the conduct of the bold Iago,
Whose footing here anticipates our thoughts
A se'nnight's speed. Great Jove, Othello guard,
And swell his sail with thine own pow'rful breath,
That he may bless this bay with his tall ship,
Make love's quick pants in Desdemona's arms,
Give renew'd fire to our extincted spirits,
And bring all Cyprus comfort!

Enter DESDEMONA, IAGO, RODERIGO, *and* EMILIA, [*with* Attendants].

O, behold,
The riches of the ship is come on shore!
You men of Cyprus, let her have your knees.

403. **dispose,** external manner. 405. **free,** frank. 409. **Hell and night.** Note Iago's allegiance to the devil.
ACT II. SCENE I. *Stage Direction.* One of the gentlemen who enters at this point may be "above," in the gallery, looking out and reporting things that Montano cannot see. 7. **ruffian'd,** raged. 9. **mortise,** the socket hollowed out in fitting timbers. 10. **segregation,** dispersion. 14. **bear,** a constellation. 15. **quench the guards,** overwhelm the stars near the polestar. 17. **enchafed,** angry. 22. **designment,** enterprise. 23. **sufferance,** disaster. 36. **full,** perfect. 39-40. **make . . . regard,** cause the blue of the sea and the air to grow indistinguishable in our view. 42. **arrivance,** arrival. 49. **allowance,** reputation. 62. **paragons,** surpasses. 63. **quirks,** witty conceits. **blazoning,** setting forth honorably in words. 64. **vesture of creation,** the real qualities with which creation has invested her (Johnson). 65. **ingener,** inventor,

Hail to thee, lady! and the grace of heaven,
Before, behind thee and on every hand,
Enwheel thee round!

Des. I thank you, valiant Cassio.
What tidings can you tell me of my lord?

Cas. He is not yet arriv'd: nor know I aught
But that he 's well and will be shortly here.

Des. O, but I fear—How lost you company?

Cas. The great contention of the sea and skies
Parted our fellowship—But, hark! a sail.
(*Within*) 'A sail, a sail!' [*Guns heard.*]

Sec. Gent. They give their greeting to the citadel:
This likewise is a friend.

Cas. See for the news. [*Exit Gentleman.*]
Good ancient, you are welcome. [*To Emilia*] Welcome, mistress:
Let it not gall your patience, good Iago,
That I extend my manners; 'tis my breeding
That gives me this bold show of courtesy. [*Kissing her.*]

Iago. Sir, would she give you so much of her lips
As of her tongue she oft bestows on me,
You would have enough.

Des. Alas, she has no speech.

Iago. In faith, too much;
I find it still, when I have list to sleep:
Marry, before your ladyship, I grant,
She puts her tongue a little in her heart,
And chides with thinking.

Emil. You have little cause to say so.

Iago. Come on, come on; you are pictures out of doors,
Bells in your parlours, wild-cats in your kitchens,
Saints in your injuries, devils being offended,
Players in your housewifery, and housewives in your beds.

Des. O, fie upon thee, slanderer!

Iago. Nay, it is true, or else I am a Turk:
You rise to play and go to bed to work.

Emil. You shall not write my praise.

Iago. No, let me not.

Des. What wouldst thou write of me, if thou shouldst praise me?

Iago. O gentle lady, do not put me to 't;
For I am nothing, if not critical.

Des. Come on, assay. There 's one gone to the harbour?

Iago. Ay, madam.

Des. I am not merry; but I do beguile
The thing I am, by seeming otherwise.
Come, how wouldst thou praise me?

Iago. I am about it; but indeed my invention
Comes from my pate as birdlime does from frieze;
It plucks out brains and all: but my Muse labours,
And thus she is deliver'd.
If she be fair and wise, fairness and wit,
The one 's for use, the other useth it.

Des. Well praised! How if she be black and witty?

Iago. If she be black, and thereto have a wit,
She'll find a white that shall her blackness fit.

Des. Worse and worse.

Emil. How if fair and foolish?

Iago. She never yet was foolish that was fair;
For even her folly help'd her to an heir.

Des. These are old fond paradoxes to make fools laugh i' the alehouse. What miserable praise hast thou for her that 's foul and foolish?

Iago. There 's none so foul and foolish thereunto,
But does foul pranks which fair and wise ones do.

Des. O heavy ignorance! thou praisest the worst best. But what praise couldst thou bestow on a deserving woman indeed, one that, in the authority of her merit, did justly put on the vouch of very malice itself?

Iago. She that was ever fair and never proud,
Had tongue at will and yet was never loud,
Never lack'd gold and yet went never gay,
Fled from her wish and yet said 'Now I may,'
She that being ang'red, her revenge being nigh,
Bade her wrong stay and her displeasure fly,
She that in wisdom never was so frail
To change the cod's head for the salmon's tail,
She that could think and ne'er disclose her mind,
See suitors following and not look behind,
She was a wight, if ever such wight were,—

Des. To do what?

Iago. To suckle fools and chronicle small beer.

Des. O most lame and impotent conclusion! Do not learn of him, Emilia, though he be thy husband. How say you, Cassio? is he not a most profane and liberal counsellor?

Cas. He speaks home, madam: you may relish him more in the soldier than in the scholar.

Iago. [*Aside*] He takes her by the palm: ay, well said, whisper: with as little a web as this will I ensnare as great a fly as Cassio. Ay, smile upon her, do; I will gyve thee in thine own courtship. You say true; 'tis so, indeed: if such tricks as these strip you out of your lieutenantry, it had been better you had not kissed your three fingers so oft, which now again you are most apt to play the sir in. Very good; well kissed! an excellent courtesy! 'tis so, indeed. Yet again your fingers to your lips? would they were clyster-pipes for your sake! [*Trumpet within.*] The Moor! I know his trumpet.

Cas. 'Tis truly so.

Des. Let 's meet him and receive him.

Cas. Lo, where he comes!

Enter OTHELLO *and* Attendants.

Oth. O my fair warrior!

Des. My dear Othello!

Oth. It gives me wonder great as my content
To see you here before me. O my soul's joy!
If after every tempest come such calms,
May the winds blow till they have waken'd death!
And let the labouring bark climb hills of seas
Olympus-high and duck again as low
As hell 's from heaven! If it were now to die,
'Twere now to be most happy; for, I fear,
My soul hath her content so absolute
That not another comfort like to this
Succeeds in unknown fate.

praiser. 69. **gutter'd,** jagged, trenched. 70. **ensteep'd,** lying under water. 72. **mortal,** deadly. 77. **se'nnight's,** week's. 113. **housewives,** huzzies. 120. **critical,** censorious. 127. **birdlime,** sticky substance smeared on twigs to catch small birds. **frieze,** coarse woolen cloth. 134. **white,** a fair person, with word-play on "wight." 139. **fond,** foolish. 148. **put on the vouch,** compel the approval. 156. **To change . . . tail,** to exchange a delicacy for mere refuse. 161. **chronicle small beer,** keep petty household accounts. 165. **liberal,** licentious. 166. **speaks home,** i.e., without reserve. 171. **gyve,** fetter, shackle. 172. **courtship,** courtesy. 175. **kissed your three fingers.** He kisses his own hand as a token of reverence. 176. **the sir,** i.e., the fine gentleman. 179. **clyster-pipes,** tubes used for enemas.

Des. The heavens forbid
But that our loves and comforts should increase,
Even as our days do grow!
Oth. Amen to that, sweet powers!
I cannot speak enough of this content;
It stops me here; it is too much of joy:
And this, and this, the greatest discords be [*Kissing her.*]
That e'er our hearts shall make!
Iago. [*Aside*] O, you are well tun'd now!
But I'll set down the pegs that make this music,
As honest as I am.
Oth. Come, let us to the castle.
News, friends; our wars are done, the Turks are drown'd.
How does my old acquaintance of this isle?
Honey, you shall be well desir'd in Cyprus;
I have found great love amongst them. O my sweet,
I prattle out of fashion, and I dote
In mine own comforts. I prithee, good Iago,
Go to the bay and disembark my coffers:
Bring thou the master to the citadel;
He is a good one, and his worthiness
Does challenge much respect. Come, Desdemona,
Once more, well met at Cyprus.

Exeunt Othello and Desdemona [and all but Iago and Roderigo].

Iago. [To an Attendant] Do thou meet me presently at the harbour. [To Rod.] Come hither. If thou be'st valiant,—as, they say, base men being in love have then a nobility in their natures more than is native to them,—list me. The lieutenant tonight watches on the court of guard:—first, I must tell thee this—Desdemona is directly in love with him.

Rod. With him! why, 'tis not possible.

Iago. Lay thy finger thus, and let thy soul be instructed. Mark me with what violence she first loved the Moor, but for bragging and telling her fantastical lies: and will she love him still for prating? let not thy discreet heart think it. Her eye must be fed; and what delight shall she have to look on the devil? When the blood is made dull with the act of sport, there should be, again to inflame it and to give satiety a fresh appetite, loveliness in favour, sympathy in years, manners and beauties; all which the Moor is defective in: now, for want of these required conveniences, her delicate tenderness will find itself abused, begin to heave the gorge, disrelish and abhor the Moor; very nature will instruct her in it and compel her to some second choice. Now, sir, this granted,—as it is a most pregnant and unforced position—who stands so eminent in the degree of this fortune as Cassio does? a knave very voluble; no further conscionable than in putting on the mere form of civil and humane seeming, for the better compassing of his salt and most hidden loose affection? why, none; why, none: a slipper and subtle knave, a finder of occasions, that has an eye can stamp and counterfeit advantages, though true advantage never present itself; a devilish knave. Besides, the knave is handsome, young, and hath all those requisites in him that folly and green minds look after: a pestilent complete knave; and the woman hath found him already.

Rod. I cannot believe that in her; she 's full of most blessed condition.

Iago. Blessed fig's-end! the wine she drinks is made of grapes: if she had been blessed, she would never have loved the Moor. Blessed pudding! Didst thou not see her paddle with the palm of his hand? didst not mark that?

Rod. Yes, that I did; but that was but courtesy.

Iago. Lechery, by this hand; an index and obscure prologue to the history of lust and foul thoughts. They met so near with their lips that their breaths embraced together. Villanous thoughts, Roderigo! when these mutualities so marshal the way, hard at hand comes the master and main exercise, the incorporate conclusion, Pish! But, sir, be you ruled by me: I have brought you from Venice. Watch you to-night; for the command, I'll lay 't upon you. Cassio knows you not. I'll not be far from you: do you find some occasion to anger Cassio, either by speaking too loud, or tainting his discipline; or from what other course you please, which the time shall more favourably minister.

Rod. Well.

Iago. Sir, he is rash and very sudden in choler, and haply may strike at you: provoke him, that he may; for even out of that will I cause these of Cyprus to mutiny; whose qualification shall come into no true taste again but by the displanting of Cassio. So shall you have a shorter journey to your desires by the means I shall then have to prefer them; and the impediment most profitably removed, without the which there were no expectation of our prosperity.

Rod. I will do this, if I can bring it to any opportunity.

Iago. I warrant thee. Meet me by and by at the citadel: I must fetch his necessaries ashore. Farewell.

Rod. Adieu. *Exit.*

Iago. That Cassio loves her, I do well believe 't;
That she loves him, 'tis apt and of great credit:
The Moor, howbeit that I endure him not,
Is of a constant, loving, noble nature,
And I dare think he'll prove to Desdemona
A most dear husband. Now, I do love her too;
Not out of absolute lust, though peradventure
I stand accountant for as great a sin,
But partly led to diet my revenge,
For that I do suspect the lusty Moor
Hath leap'd into my seat; the thought whereof
Doth, like a poisonous mineral, gnaw my inwards;
And nothing can or shall content my soul
Till I am even'd with him, wife for wife,
Or failing so, yet that I put the Moor
At least into a jealousy so strong
That judgement cannot cure. Which thing to do,
If this poor trash of Venice, whom I trash
For his quick hunting, stand the putting on,
I'll have our Michael Cassio on the hip,
Abuse him to the Moor in the rank garb—
For I fear Cassio with my night-cap too—
Make the Moor thank me, love me and reward me,
For making him egregiously an ass
And practising upon his peace and quiet

202. **set down the pegs,** lower the pitch of the strings, i.e., disturb the harmony. 219. **court of guard,** guardhouse. 242. **conscionable,** conscientious. 244. **salt,** licentious. 246. **slipper,** slippery. 275. **tainting,** disparaging. 283. **qualification,** appeasement. 291. **by and by,** immediately. 296. **apt,** probable. **credit,** credibility. 312. **trash,** worthless thing (Roderigo). **trash,** hold in check. This use of the word is as a hunting term. 313. **putting on,** incitement to quarrel. 314. **on the hip,** at my mercy (wrestling term).

SCENE II. 3. **mere perdition,** complete destruction. 10. **offices,** rooms where food and drink were kept.

Even to madness. 'Tis here, but yet confus'd:
Knavery's plain face is never seen till us'd. *Exit.*

SCENE II. [*A street.*]

Enter Othello's Herald *with a proclamation.*

Her. It is Othello's pleasure, our noble and valiant general, that, upon certain tidings now arrived, importing the mere perdition of the Turkish fleet, every man put himself into triumph; some to dance, some to make bonfires, each man to what sport and revels his addiction leads him: for, besides these beneficial news, it is the celebration of his nuptial. So much was his pleasure should be proclaimed. All offices are open, and there is full liberty of feasting from this present hour of five till the bell have told eleven. Heaven bless the isle of Cyprus and our noble general Othello! *Exit.*

[SCENE III. *A hall in the castle.*]

Enter OTHELLO, DESDEMONA, CASSIO, *and* Attendants.

Oth. Good Michael, look you to the guard to-night:
Let 's teach ourselves that honourable stop,
Not to outsport discretion.

Cas. Iago hath direction what to do;
But, notwithstanding, with my personal eye
Will I look to 't.

Oth. Iago is most honest.
Michael, good night: to-morrow with your earliest
Let me have speech with you. [*To Desdemona*] Come, my dear love,
The purchase made, the fruits are to ensue;
That profit 's yet to come 'tween me and you.
Good night. *Exit* [*Othello, with Desdemona and Attendants*].

Enter IAGO.

Cas. Welcome, Iago; we must to the watch.

Iago. Not this hour, lieutenant; 'tis not yet ten o' the clock. Our general cast us thus early for the love of his Desdemona; who let us not therefore blame: he hath not yet made wanton the night with her; and she is sport for Jove.

Cas. She 's a most exquisite lady.

Iago. And, I'll warrant her, full of game.

Cas. Indeed, she 's a most fresh and delicate creature.

Iago. What an eye she has! methinks it sounds a parley of provocation.

Cas. An inviting eye; and yet methinks right modest.

Iago. And when she speaks, is it not an alarum to love?

Cas. She is indeed perfection.

Iago. Well, happiness to their sheets! Come, lieutenant, I have a stoup of wine; and here without are a brace of Cyprus gallants that would fain have a measure to the health of black Othello.

Cas. Not to-night, good Iago: I have very poor and unhappy brains for drinking: I could well wish courtesy would invent some other custom of entertainment.

Iago. O, they are our friends; but one cup: I'll drink for you.

Cas. I have drunk but one cup to-night, and that was craftily qualified too, and, behold, what innovation it makes here: I am unfortunate in the infirmity, and dare not task my weakness with any more.

Iago. What, man! 'tis a night of revels: the gallants desire it.

Cas. Where are they?

Iago. Here at the door; I pray you, call them in.

Cas. I'll do 't; but it dislikes me. *Exit.*

Iago. If I can fasten but one cup upon him,
With that which he hath drunk to-night already,
He'll be as full of quarrel and offence
As my young mistress' dog. Now, my sick fool Roderigo,
Whom love hath turn'd almost the wrong side out,
To Desdemona hath to-night carous'd
Potations pottle-deep; and he 's to watch:
Three lads of Cyprus, noble swelling spirits,
That hold their honours in a wary distance,
The very elements of this warlike isle,
Have I to-night fluster'd with flowing cups,
And they watch too. Now, 'mongst this flock of drunkards,
Am I to put our Cassio in some action
That may offend the isle.—But here they come:

Enter CASSIO, MONTANO, *and* Gentlemen [; *servants following with wine*].

If consequence do but approve my dream,
My boat sails freely, both with wind and stream.

Cas. 'Fore God, they have given me a rouse already.

Mon. Good faith, a little one; not past a pint, as I am a soldier.

Iago. Some wine, ho!
[*Sings*] And let me the canakin clink, clink;
And let me the canakin clink:
A soldier 's a man;
A life 's but a span;
Why, then, let a soldier drink.
Some wine, boys!

Cas. 'Fore God, an excellent song.

Iago. I learned it in England, where, indeed, they are most potent in potting: your Dane, your German, and your swag-bellied Hollander—Drink, ho!—are nothing to your English.

Cas. Is your Englishman so expert in his drinking?

Iago. Why, he drinks you, with facility, your Dane dead drunk; he sweats not to overthrow your Almain; he gives your Hollander a vomit, ere the next pottle can be filled.

Cas. To the health of our general!

Mon. I am for it, lieutenant; and I'll do you justice.

Iago. O sweet England! [*Sings.*]
King Stephen was a worthy peer,

SCENE III. 2. **stop,** restraint. 14. **cast,** dismissed. 30. **stoup,** measure of liquor, two quarts. 41. **qualified,** diluted. 42. **innovation,** disturbance. **here,** i.e., in Cassio's head. 56. **pottle-deep,** to the bottom of the tankard. 58. **hold . . . distance,** i.e., are extremely sensitive of their honor. 59. **very elements,** true representatives. 61. **watch,** are members of the guard. 64. **approve,** confirm. 67. **rouse,** full draft of liquor. 71. **canakin,** small drinking vessel. 86. **Almain,** German. 89-90. **I'll . . . justice,** i.e., drink as much as you. 92-99. **King . . . thee,** a version of a popular ballad, found also in the *Percy Folio.*

His breeches cost him but a crown;
He held them sixpence all too dear,
With that he call'd the tailor lown.

He was a wight of high renown,
And thou art but of low degree:
'Tis pride that pulls the country down;
Then take thine auld cloak about thee.

Some wine, ho!

Cas. Why, this is a more exquisite song than the other.

Iago. Will you hear 't again?

Cas. No; for I hold him to be unworthy of his place that does those things. Well, God 's above all; and there be souls must be saved, and there be souls must not be saved.

Iago. It 's true, good lieutenant.

Cas. For mine own part,—no offence to the general, nor any man of quality,—I hope to be saved.

Iago. And so do I too, lieutenant.

Cas. Ay, but, by your leave, not before me; the lieutenant is to be saved before the ancient. Let 's have no more of this; let 's to our affairs.—God forgive us our sins!—Gentlemen, let 's look to our business. Do not think, gentlemen, I am drunk: this is my ancient; this is my right hand, and this is my left: I am not drunk now; I can stand well enough, and speak well enough.

All. Excellent well.

Cas. Why, very well then; you must not think then that I am drunk. *Exit.*

Mon. To th' platform, masters; come, let 's set the watch.

Iago. You see this fellow that is gone before;
He 's a soldier fit to stand by Cæsar
And give direction: and do but see his vice;
'Tis to his virtue a just equinox,
The one as long as th' other: 'tis pity of him.
I fear the trust Othello puts him in,
On some odd time of his infirmity,
Will shake this island.

Mon. But is he often thus?

Iago. 'Tis evermore the prologue to his sleep:
He'll watch the horologe a double set,
If drink rock not his cradle.

Mon. It were well
The general were put in mind of it.
Perhaps he sees it not; or his good nature
Prizes the virtue that appears in Cassio,
And looks not on his evils: is not this true?

Enter RODERIGO.

Iago. [*Aside to him*] How now, Roderigo!
I pray you, after the lieutenant; go. [*Exit Roderigo.*]

Mon. And 'tis great pity that the noble Moor
Should hazard such a place as his own second
With one of an ingraft infirmity:
It were an honest action to say
So to the Moor.

Iago. Not I, for this fair island:
I do love Cassio well; and would do much
To cure him of this evil—But, hark! what noise?
[*Cry within:* 'Help! help!']

Enter CASSIO, *pursuing* RODERIGO.

Cas. 'Zounds, you rogue! you rascal!

Mon. What 's the matter, lieutenant?

Cas. A knave teach me my duty!
I'll beat the knave into a twiggen bottle.

Rod. Beat me!

Cas. Dost thou prate, rogue? [*Striking Roderigo.*]

Mon. Nay, good lieutenant; [*Staying him.*]
I pray you, sir, hold your hand.

Cas. Let me go, sir,
Or I'll knock you o'er the mazzard.

Mon. Come, come, you 're drunk.

Cas. Drunk! [*They fight.*]

Iago. [*Aside to Roderigo*] Away, I say; go out, and cry a mutiny. [*Exit Roderigo.*]
Nay, good lieutenant,—God's will, gentlemen;—
Help, ho!—Lieutenant,—sir,—Montano,—sir;—
Help, masters!—Here 's a goodly watch indeed! [*Bell rings.*]
Who 's that which rings the bell?—Diablo, ho!
The town will rise: God's will, lieutenant, hold!
You'll be asham'd for ever.

Enter OTHELLO *and* Attendants.

Oth. What is the matter here?

Mon. 'Zounds, I bleed still; I am hurt to th' death.
He dies! [*Thrusts at Cassio.*]

Oth. Hold, for your lives!

Iago. Hold, ho! Lieutenant,—sir,—Montano,—gentlemen,—
Have you forgot all sense of place and duty?
Hold! the general speaks to you; hold, for shame!

Oth. Why, how now, ho! from whence ariseth this?
Are we turn'd Turks, and to ourselves do that
Which heaven hath forbid the Ottomites?
For Christian shame, put by this barbarous brawl:
He that stirs next to carve for his own rage
Holds his soul light; he dies upon his motion.
Silence that dreadful bell: it frights the isle
From her propriety. What is the matter, masters?
Honest Iago, that looks dead with grieving,
Speak, who began this? on thy love, I charge thee.

Iago. I do not know: friends all but now, even now,
In quarter, and in terms like bride and groom
Devesting them for bed; and then, but now—
As if some planet had unwitted men—
Swords out, and tilting one at other's breast,
In opposition bloody. I cannot speak
Any beginning to this peevish odds;
And would in action glorious I had lost
Those legs that brought me to a part of it!

Oth. How comes it, Michael, you are thus forgot?

Cas. I pray you, pardon me; I cannot speak.

Oth. Worthy Montano, you were wont be civil;
The gravity and stillness of your youth
The world hath noted, and your name is great
In mouths of wisest censure: what 's the matter,
That you unlace your reputation thus
And spend your rich opinion for the name
Of a night-brawler? give me answer to it.

Mon. Worthy Othello, I am hurt to danger:

95. **lown,** lout, loon. 129. **equinox,** equal length of days and nights; used figuratively to mean "counterpart." 135. **horologe,** clock. **double set,** twice around. 145. **ingraft,** ingrafted, inveterate. 152. **twiggen,** covered with woven twigs. 155. **mazzard,** head. 161. **Diablo,** the Devil; a scrap of Spanish. 162. **rise,** grow riotous. 170. **turn'd Turks,** changed completely for the worse; proverbial. 173. **carve for,** indulge. 176. **propriety,** proper state or condition. 180. **In quarter,** on terms. 185. **peevish odds,** childish quarrel. 193. **censure,** judgment. 194.

Your officer, Iago, can inform you,—
While I spare speech, which something now offends me,—
Of all that I do know: nor know I aught
By me that 's said or done amiss this night;
Unless self-charity be sometimes a vice,
And to defend ourselves it be a sin
When violence assails us.

Oth. Now, by heaven,
My blood begins my safer guides to rule;
And passion, having my best judgement collied,
Assays to lead the way: if I once stir,
Or do but lift this arm, the best of you
Shall sink in my rebuke. Give me to know
How this foul rout began, who set it on;
And he that is approv'd in this offence,
Though he had twinn'd with me, both at a birth,
Shall lose me. What! in a town of war,
Yet wild, the people's hearts brimful of fear,
To manage private and domestic quarrel,
In night, and on the court and guard of safety!
'Tis monstrous. Iago, who began 't?

Mon. If partially affin'd, or leagu'd in office,
Thou dost deliver more or less than truth,
Thou art no soldier.

Iago. Touch me not so near:
I had rather have this tongue cut from my mouth
Than it should do offence to Michael Cassio;
Yet, I persuade myself, to speak the truth
Shall nothing wrong him. Thus it is, general.
Montano and myself being in speech,
There comes a fellow crying out for help;
And Cassio following him with determin'd sword,
To execute upon him. Sir, this gentleman
Steps in to Cassio, and entreats his pause:
Myself the crying fellow did pursue,
Lest by his clamour—as it so fell out—
The town might fall in fright: he, swift of foot,
Outran my purpose; and I return'd the rather
For that I heard the clink and fall of swords,
And Cassio high in oath; which till to-night
I ne'er might say before. When I came back—
For this was brief—I found them close together,
At blow and thrust; even as again they were
When you yourself did part them.
More of this matter cannot I report:
But men are men; the best sometimes forget:
Though Cassio did some little wrong to him,
As men in rage strike those that wish them best,
Yet surely Cassio, I believe, receiv'd
From him that fled some strange indignity,
Which patience could not pass.

Oth. I know, Iago,
Thy honesty and love doth mince this matter,
Making it light to Cassio. Cassio, I love thee;
But never more be officer of mine.

Enter DESDEMONA, *attended.*

Look, if my gentle love be not rais'd up!
I'll make thee an example.

Des. What 's the matter?

Oth. All 's well now, sweeting; come away to bed.
Sir, for your hurts, myself will be your surgeon:
Lead him off. [*To Montano, who is led off.*]
Iago, look with care about the town,
And silence those whom this vile brawl distracted.
Come, Desdemona: 'tis the soldiers' life
To have their balmy slumbers wak'd with strife.

Exit [*with all but Iago and Cassio*].

Iago. What, are you hurt, lieutenant?

Cas. Ay, past all surgery.

Iago. Marry, God forbid!

Cas. Reputation, reputation, reputation! O, I have lost my reputation! I have lost the immortal part of myself, and what remains is bestial. My reputation, Iago, my reputation!

Iago. As I am an honest man, I thought you had received some bodily wound; there is more sense in that than in reputation. Reputation is an idle and most false imposition; oft got without merit, and lost without deserving: you have lost no reputation at all, unless you repute yourself such a loser. What, man! there are ways to recover the general again: you are but now cast in his mood, a punishment more in policy than in malice; even so as one would beat his offenceless dog to affright an imperious lion: sue to him again, and he 's yours.

Cas. I will rather sue to be despised than to deceive so good a commander with so slight, so drunken, and so indiscreet an officer. Drunk? and speak parrot? and squabble? swagger? swear? and discourse fustian with one's own shadow? O thou invisible spirit of wine, if thou hast no name to be known by, let us call thee devil!

Iago. What was he that you followed with your sword? What had he done to you?

Cas. I know not.

Iago. Is 't possible?

Cas. I remember a mass of things, but nothing distinctly; a quarrel, but nothing wherefore. O God, that men should put an enemy in their mouths to steal away their brains! that we should, with joy, pleasance, revel and applause, transform ourselves into beasts!

Iago. Why, but you are now well enough: how came you thus recovered?

Cas. It hath pleased the devil drunkenness to give place to the devil wrath: one unperfectness shows me another, to make me frankly despise myself.

Iago. Come, you are too severe a moraler: as the time, the place, and the condition of this country stands, I could heartily wish this had not befallen; but, since it is as it is, mend it for your own good.

Cas. I will ask him for my place again; he shall tell me I am a drunkard! Had I as many mouths as Hydra, such an answer would stop them all. To be now a sensible man, by and by a fool, and presently a beast! O strange! Every inordinate cup is unblessed and the ingredient is a devil.

Iago. Come, come, good wine is a good familiar creature, if it be well used: exclaim no more against it. And, good lieutenant, I think you think I love you.

Cas. I have well approved it, sir. I drunk!

Iago. You or any man living may be drunk at a time, man. I'll tell you what you shall do. Our general's wife is now the general: I may say so in this respect, for that he hath devoted and given up himself

unlace, degrade. 206. **collied,** darkened. 211. **approv'd in,** found guilty of. 216. **court and guard,** spot and guarding place, i.e., the main guardhouse. 218. **affin'd,** bound by a tie. 228. **execute,** give effect to (his anger). 281. **speak parrot,** talk nonsense; *discourse fustian,* below, has the same meaning. 299. **unperfectness,** imperfection. 308. **Hydra,** the Lernaean Hydra, a monster with many heads, slain by Hercules as the second of his twelve labors. 311. **unblessed,** accursed. 317. **approved,** proved.

to the contemplation, mark, and denotement of her parts and graces: confess yourself freely to her; importune her help to put you in your place again: she is of so free, so kind, so apt, so blessed a disposition, she holds it a vice in her goodness not to do more than she is requested: this broken joint between you and her husband entreat her to splinter; and, my fortunes against any lay worth naming, this crack of your love shall grow stronger than it was before.

Cas. You advise me well.

Iago. I protest, in the sincerity of love and honest kindness.

Cas. I think it freely; and betimes in the morning I will beseech the virtuous Desdemona to undertake for me: I am desperate of my fortunes if they check me here.

Iago. You are in the right. Good night, lieutenant;
I must to the watch.

Cas. Good night, honest Iago. *Exit Cassio.*

Iago. And what 's he then that says I play the villain?
When this advice is free I give and honest,
Probal to thinking and indeed the course
To win the Moor again? For 'tis most easy
Th' inclining Desdemona to subdue
In any honest suit: she 's fram'd as fruitful
As the free elements. And then for her
To win the Moor—were 't to renounce his baptism,
All seals and symbols of redeemed sin,
His soul is so enfetter'd to her love,
That she may make, unmake, do what she list,
Even as her appetite shall play the god
With his weak function. How am I then a villain
To counsel Cassio to this parallel course,
Directly to his good? Divinity of hell!
When devils will the blackest sins put on,
They do suggest at first with heavenly shows,
As I do now: for whiles this honest fool
Plies Desdemona to repair his fortunes
And she for him pleads strongly to the Moor,
I'll pour this pestilence into his ear,
That she repeals him for her body's lust;
And by how much she strives to do him good,
She shall undo her credit with the Moor.
So will I turn her virtue into pitch,
And out of her own goodness make the net
That shall enmesh them all.

Enter RODERIGO.

How now, Roderigo!

Rod. I do follow here in the chase, not like a hound that hunts, but one that fills up the cry. My money is almost spent; I have been to-night exceedingly well cudgelled; and I think the issue will be, I shall have so much experience for my pains, and so, with no money at all and a little more wit, return again to Venice.

Iago. How poor are they that have not patience!
What wound did ever heal but by degrees?
Thou know'st we work by wit, and not by witchcraft;
And wit depends on dilatory time.
Does 't not go well? Cassio hath beaten thee,
And thou, by that small hurt, hast cashier'd Cassio:
Though other things grow fair against the sun,
Yet fruits that blossom first will first be ripe:
Content thyself awhile. By th' mass, 'tis morning;
Pleasure and action make the hours seem short.
Retire thee; go where thou art billeted:
Away, I say; thou shalt know more hereafter:
Nay, get thee gone. *Exit Roderigo.*
Two things are to be done:
My wife must move for Cassio to her mistress;
I'll set her on;
Myself the while to draw the Moor apart,
And bring him jump when he may Cassio find
Soliciting his wife: ay, that 's the way:
Dull not device by coldness and delay. *Exit.*

ACT III.

SCENE I. [*Before the castle.*]

Enter CASSIO [*and*] Musicians.

Cas. Masters, play here; I will content your pains;
Something that 's brief; and bid 'Good morrow, general.' [*They play.*]

[*Enter*] Clown.

Clo. Why, masters, have your instruments been in Naples, that they speak i' the nose thus?

First Mus. How, sir, how!

Clo. Are these, I pray you, wind-instruments?

First Mus. Ay, marry, are they, sir.

Clo. O, thereby hangs a tail.

First Mus. Whereby hangs a tale, sir?

Clo. Marry, sir, by many a wind-instrument that I know. But, masters, here 's money for you: and the general so likes your music, that he desires you, for love's sake, to make no more noise with it.

First Mus. Well, sir, we will not.

Clo. If you have any music that may not be heard, to 't again: but, as they say, to hear music the general does not greatly care.

First Mus. We have none such, sir.

Clo. Then put up your pipes in your bag, for I'll away: go; vanish into air; away! *Exeunt Musicians.*

Cas. Dost thou hear, my honest friend?

Clo. No, I hear not your honest friend; I hear you.

Cas. Prithee, keep up thy quillets. There 's a poor piece of gold for thee: if the gentlewoman that attends the general's wife be stirring, tell her there 's one Cassio entreats her a little favour of speech: wilt thou do this?

Clo. She is stirring, sir: if she will stir hither, I shall seem to notify unto her.

Cas. Do, good my friend. *Exit Clown.*

Enter Iago.

In happy time, Iago.

Iago. You have not been a-bed, then?

Cas. Why, no; the day had broke
Before we parted. I have made bold, Iago,
To send in to your wife: my suit to her
Is, that she will to virtuous Desdemona

323. **denotement,** observation; QF: *devotement,* which is possibly correct. 329. **splinter,** bind with splints. 330. **lay,** stake, wager. 337. **check,** repulse. 344. **Probal,** probable. 346. **inclining,** favorably disposed. **subdue,** persuade. 355. **parallel,** probably, corresponding to his best interest. 357. **put on,** further. 358. **suggest,** tempt. 363. **repeals him,** i.e., attempts to get him restored. 371. **cry,** pack. 381. **cashier'd,** dismissed from service. 392. **jump,** precisely.

ACT III. SCENE I. 1. **content,** reward. 4. **speak i' the nose,** i.e., like Neapolitans, who spoke a nasal dialect (with a joke on syphilis, which attacks the nose). 9. **tale,** pun on *tail*, a wind instrument of sorts.

Procure me some access.
Iago. I'll send her to you presently;
And I'll devise a mean to draw the Moor
Out of the way, that your converse and business
May be more free.
Cas. I humbly thank you for 't. *Exit [Iago].*
I never knew
A Florentine more kind and honest.

Enter EMILIA.

Emil. Good morrow, good lieutenant: I am sorry
For your displeasure; but all will sure be well.
The general and his wife are talking of it;
And she speaks for you stoutly: the Moor replies,
That he you hurt is of great fame in Cyprus
And great affinity and that in wholesome wisdom
He might not but refuse you, but he protests he loves
you
And needs no other suitor but his likings
To take the safest occasion by the front
To bring you in again.
Cas. Yet, I beseech you,
If you think fit, or that it may be done,
Give me advantage of some brief discourse
With Desdemona alone.
Emil. Pray you, come in:
I will bestow you where you shall have time
To speak your bosom freely.
Cas. I am much bound to you. *[Exeunt.]*

SCENE II. [*A room in the castle.*]

Enter OTHELLO, IAGO, *and* Gentlemen.

Oth. These letters give, Iago, to the pilot;
And by him do my duties to the senate:
That done, I will be walking on the works;
Repair there to me.
Iago. Well, my good lord, I'll do 't.
Oth. This fortification, gentlemen, shall we see 't?
Gent. We'll wait upon your lordship. *Exeunt.*

SCENE III. [*The garden of the castle.*]

Enter DESDEMONA, CASSIO, *and* EMILIA.

Des. Be thou assur'd, good Cassio, I will do
All my abilities in thy behalf.
Emil. Good madam, do: I warrant it grieves my
husband,
As if the case were his.
Des. O, that 's an honest fellow. Do not doubt,
Cassio,
But I will have my lord and you again
As friendly as you were.
Cas. Bounteous madam,
Whatever shall become of Michael Cassio,
He 's never any thing but your true servant.
Des. I know 't; I thank you. You do love my lord:
You have known him long; and be you well assur'd
He shall in strangeness stand no farther off
Than in a politic distance.
Cas. Ay, but, lady,
That policy may either last so long,
Or feed upon such nice and waterish diet,
Or breed itself so out of circumstance,
That, I being absent and my place supplied,
My general will forget my love and service.
Des. Do not doubt that; before Emilia here
I give thee warrant of thy place: assure thee,
If I do vow a friendship, I'll perform it
To the last article: my lord shall never rest;
I'll watch him tame and talk him out of patience;
His bed shall seem a school, his board a shrift;
I'll intermingle every thing he does
With Cassio's suit: therefore be merry, Cassio;
For thy solicitor shall rather die
Than give thy cause away.

Enter OTHELLO *and* IAGO [*at a distance*].

Emil. Madam, here comes my lord.
Cas. Madam, I'll take my leave.
Des. Why, stay, and hear me speak.
Cas. Madam, not now: I am very ill at ease,
Unfit for mine own purposes.
Des. Well, do your discretion. *Exit Cassio.*
Iago. Ha! I like not that.
Oth. What dost thou say?
Iago. Nothing, my lord: or if—I know not what.
Oth. Was not that Cassio parted from my wife?
Iago. Cassio, my lord! No, sure, I cannot think it,
That he would steal away so guilty-like,
Seeing you coming.
Oth. I do believe 'twas he.
Des. How now, my lord!
I have been talking with a suitor here,
A man that languishes in your displeasure.
Oth. Who is 't you mean?
Des. Why, your lieutenant, Cassio. Good my lord,
If I have any grace or power to move you,
His present reconciliation take;
For if he be not one that truly loves you,
That errs in ignorance and not in cunning,
I have no judgement in an honest face:
I prithee, call him back.
Oth. Went he hence now?
Des. Ay, sooth; so humbled
That he hath left part of his grief with me,
To suffer with him. Good love, call him back.
Oth. Not now, sweet Desdemon; some other time.
Des. But shall 't be shortly?
Oth. The sooner, sweet, for you.
Des. Shall 't be to-night at supper?
Oth. No, not to-night.
Des. To-morrow dinner, then?
Oth. I shall not dine at home;
I meet the captains at the citadel.
Des. Why, then, to-morrow night; or Tuesday
morn;
On Tuesday noon, or night; on Wednesday morn:
I prithee, name the time, but let it not
Exceed three days: in faith, he 's penitent;
And yet his trespass, in our common reason—

49. **affinity,** kindred, family connection. 52. **by the front,** i.e., by the forelock.
SCENE II. 3. **works,** earthworks, fortifications.
SCENE III. 12. **strangeness,** distant behavior. 16. **breed . . . circumstance,** increase itself so on account of accidents. 19. **doubt,** fear.

23. **watch him tame,** tame him by keeping him from sleeping (a term from falconry). 24. **shrift,** confessional. 28. **away,** up. 64. **common reason,** everyday judgments.

Save that, they say, the wars must make examples
Out of their best—is not almost a fault
T' incur a private check. When shall he come?
Tell me, Othello: I wonder in my soul,
What you would ask me, that I should deny,
Or stand so mamm'ring on. What! Michael Cassio,
That came a-wooing with you, and so many a time,
When I have spoke of you dispraisingly,
Hath ta'en your part; to have so much to do
To bring him in! Trust me, I could do much,—
Oth. Prithee, no more: let him come when he will;
I will deny thee nothing.
Des. Why, this is not a boon;
'Tis as I should entreat you wear your gloves,
Or feed on nourishing dishes, or keep you warm,
Or sue to you to do a peculiar profit
To your own person: nay, when I have a suit
Wherein I mean to touch your love indeed,
It shall be full of poise and difficult weight
And fearful to be granted.
Oth. I will deny thee nothing:
Whereon, I do beseech thee, grant me this,
To leave me but a little to myself.
Des. Shall I deny you? no: farewell, my lord.
Oth. Farewell, my Desdemona: I'll come to thee straight.
Des. Emilia, come. Be as your fancies teach you;
Whate'er you be, I am obedient.
Exit [*with Emilia*].
Oth. Excellent wretch! Perdition catch my soul,
But I do love thee! and when I love thee not,
Chaos is come again.
Iago. My noble lord,—
Oth. What dost thou say, Iago?
Iago. Did Michael Cassio, when you woo'd my lady,
Know of your love?
Oth. He did, from first to last: why dost thou ask?
Iago. But for a satisfaction of my thought;
No further harm.
Oth. Why of thy thought, Iago?
Iago. I did not think he had been acquainted with her.
Oth. O, yes; and went between us very oft.
Iago. Indeed!
Oth. Indeed! ay, indeed: discern'st thou aught in that?
Is he not honest?
Iago. Honest, my lord!
Oth. Honest! ay, honest.
Iago. My lord, for aught I know.
Oth. What dost thou think?
Iago. Think, my lord!
Oth. Think, my lord!
By heaven, he echoes me,
As if there were some monster in his thought
Too hideous to be shown. Thou dost mean something:
I heard thee say even now, thou lik'st not that,
When Cassio left my wife: what didst not like?
And when I told thee he was of my counsel
In my whole course of wooing, thou criedst 'Indeed!'
And didst contract and purse thy brow together,
As if thou then hadst shut up in thy brain
Some horrible conceit: if thou dost love me,
Show me thy thought.
Iago. My lord, you know I love you.
Oth. I think thou dost;
And, for I know thou 'rt full of love and honesty,
And weigh'st thy words before thou giv'st them breath,
Therefore these stops of thine fright me the more:
For such things in a false disloyal knave
Are tricks of custom, but in a man that 's just
They 're close delations, working from the heart
That passion cannot rule.
Iago. For Michael Cassio,
I dare be sworn I think that he is honest.
Oth. I think so too.
Iago. Men should be what they seem;
Or those that be not, would they might seem none!
Oth. Certain, men should be what they seem.
Iago. Why, then, I think Cassio 's an honest man.
Oth. Nay, yet there 's more in this:
I prithee, speak to me as to thy thinkings,
As thou dost ruminate, and give thy worst of thoughts
The worst of words.
Iago. Good my lord, pardon me:
Though I am bound to every act of duty,
I am not bound to that all slaves are free to.
Utter my thoughts? Why, say they are vile and false;
As where 's that palace whereinto foul things
Sometimes intrude not? who has a breast so pure,
But some uncleanly apprehensions
Keep leets and law-days and in sessions sit
With meditations lawful?
Oth. Thou dost conspire against thy friend, Iago,
If thou but think'st him wrong'd and mak'st his ear
A stranger to thy thoughts.
Iago. I do beseech you—
Though I perchance am vicious in my guess,
As, I confess, it is my nature's plague
To spy into abuses, and oft my jealousy
Shapes faults that are not—that your wisdom yet,
From one that so imperfectly conceits,
Would take no notice, nor build yourself a trouble
Out of his scattering and unsure observance.
It were not for your quiet nor your good,
Nor for my manhood, honesty, or wisdom,
To let you know my thoughts.
Oth. What dost thou mean?
Iago. Good name in man and woman, dear my lord,
Is the immediate jewel of their souls:
Who steals my purse steals trash; 'tis something, nothing;
'Twas mine, 'tis his, and has been slave to thousands;
But he that filches from me my good name
Robs me of that which not enriches him
And makes me poor indeed.
Oth. By heaven, I'll know thy thoughts.
Iago. You cannot, if my heart were in your hand;
Nor shall not, whilst 'tis in my custody.
Oth. Ha!

70. **mamm'ring on,** wavering. 82. **poise,** weight, heaviness. 90. **wretch,** term of affectionate endearment with a connotation of pity. 123. **close delations,** secret or involuntary accusations; Q: *denotements,* which is close to the sense. 140. **Keep leets,** hold courts. **law-days,** court-days. 145. **vicious,** wrong. 147. **jealousy,** suspicion of evil. 149. **conceits,** judges. 173. **fineless,** boundless. 182. **exsufflicate and blown,** unsubstantial and inflated, flyblown. 198. **secure,** free from uneasiness. 200. **self-bounty,** inherent or natural goodness. 209. **seeming,** false appearance. 210. **seel,** blind (a term from falconry). 219. **reach,** meaning. 232. **will,** sensuality. 233. **disproportion,**

Iago. O, beware, my lord, of jealousy;
It is the green-ey'd monster which doth mock
The meat it feeds on: that cuckold lives in bliss
Who, certain of his fate, loves not his wronger;
But, O, what damned minutes tells he o'er
Who dotes, yet doubts, suspects, yet strongly loves!
Oth. O misery!
Iago. Poor and content is rich and rich enough,
But riches fineless is as poor as winter
To him that ever fears he shall be poor.
Good God, the souls of all my tribe defend
From jealousy!
Oth. Why, why is this?
Think'st thou I 'ld make a life of jealousy,
To follow still the changes of the moon
With fresh suspicions? No; to be once in doubt
Is once to be resolv'd: exchange me for a goat,
When I shall turn the business of my soul
To such exsufflicate and blown surmises,
Matching thy inference. 'Tis not to make me jealous
To say my wife is fair, feeds well, loves company,
Is free of speech, sings, plays and dances well;
Where virtue is, these are more virtuous:
Nor from mine own weak merits will I draw
The smallest fear or doubt of her revolt;
For she had eyes, and chose me. No, Iago;
I'll see before I doubt; when I doubt, prove;
And on the proof, there is no more but this,—
Away at once with love or jealousy!
Iago. I am glad of this; for now I shall have reason
To show the love and duty that I bear you
With franker spirit: therefore, as I am bound,
Receive it from me. I speak not yet of proof.
Look to your wife; observe her well with Cassio;
Wear your eye thus, not jealous nor secure:
I would not have your free and noble nature,
Out of self-bounty, be abus'd; look to 't:
I know our country disposition well;
In Venice they do let heaven see the pranks
They dare not show their husbands; their best conscience
Is not to leave 't undone, but keep 't unknown.
Oth. Dost thou say so?
Iago. She did deceive her father, marrying you;
And when she seem'd to shake and fear your looks,
She lov'd them most,
Oth. And so she did.
Iago. Why, go to then;
She that, so young, could give out such a seeming,
To seel her father's eyes up close as oak—
He thought 'twas witchcraft—but I am much to blame;
I humbly do beseech you of your pardon
For too much loving you.
Oth. I am bound to thee for ever.
Iago. I see this hath a little dash'd your spirits.
Oth. Not a jot, not a jot.
Iago. I' faith, I fear it has.
I hope you will consider what is spoke
Comes from my love. But I do see y' are mov'd:
I am to pray you not to strain my speech
To grosser issues nor to larger reach
Than to suspicion.
Oth. I will not.
Iago. Should you do so, my lord,
My speech should fall into such vile success
As my thoughts aim not at. Cassio 's my worthy friend—
My lord, I see y' are mov'd.
Oth. No, not much mov'd:
I do not think but Desdemona 's honest.
Iago. Long live she so! and long live you to think so!
Oth. And yet, how nature erring from itself,—
Iago. Ay, there 's the point: as—to be bold with you—
Not to affect many proposed matches
Of her own clime, complexion, and degree,
Whereto we see in all things nature tends—
Foh! one may smell in such a will most rank,
Foul disproportion, thoughts unnatural.
But pardon me; I do not in position
Distinctly speak of her; though I may fear
Her will, recoiling to her better judgement,
May fall to match you with her country forms
And happily repent.
Oth. Farewell, farewell:
If more thou dost perceive, let me know more;
Set on thy wife to observe: leave me, Iago.
Iago. [*Going*] My lord, I take my leave.
Oth. Why did I marry? This honest creature doubtless
Sees and knows more, much more, than he unfolds.
Iago. [*Returning*] My Lord, I would I might entreat your honour
To scan this thing no farther; leave it to time:
Although 'tis fit that Cassio have his place,
For, sure, he fills it up with great ability,
Yet, if you please to hold him off awhile,
You shall by that perceive him and his means:
Note, if your lady strain his entertainment
With any strong or vehement importunity;
Much will be seen in that. In the mean time,
Let me be thought too busy in my fears—
As worthy cause I have to fear I am—
And hold her free, I do beseech your honour.
Oth. Fear not my government.
Iago. I once more take my leave. *Exit.*
Oth. This fellow 's of exceeding honesty,
And knows all qualities, with a learned spirit,
Of human dealings. If I do prove her haggard,
Though that her jesses were my dear heartstrings,
I 'ld whistle her off and let her down the wind,
To prey at fortune. Haply, for I am black
And have not those soft parts of conversation
That chamberers have, or for I am declin'd
Into the vale of years,—yet that 's not much—
She 's gone. I am abus'd: and my relief
Must be to loathe her. O curse of marriage,
That we can call these delicate creatures ours,
And not their appetites! I had rather be a toad,
And live upon the vapour of a dungeon,
Than keep a corner in the thing I love

abnormality. 234. **position,** general argument. 236. **recoiling to,** falling back upon, or recoiling against. 237. **fall . . . forms,** happen to compare you with Venetian norms of handsomeness. 238. **repent,** i.e., of her marriage. 250. **strain his entertainment,** urge his reinstatement. 255. **hold her free,** regard her as innocent. 256. **government,** self-control. 260. **haggard,** a wild female duck. 261. **jesses,** straps fastened around the legs of a trained hawk. 263. **at fortune,** at random. 265. **chamberers,** gallants.

For others' uses. Yet, 'tis the plague of great ones;
Prerogativ'd are they less than the base;
'Tis destiny unshunnable, like death:
Even then this forked plague is fated to us
When we do quicken. Look where she comes:

Enter DESDEMONA *and* EMILA.

If she be false, O, then heaven mocks itself!
I'll not believe 't.
Des. How now, my dear Othello!
Your dinner, and the generous islanders
By you invited, do attend your presence.
Oth. I am to blame.
Des. Why do you speak so faintly?
Are you not well?
Oth. I have a pain upon my forehead here.
Des. 'Faith, that 's with watching; 'twill away again:
Let me but bind it hard, within this hour
It will be well.
Oth. Your napkin is too little:
[*He puts the handkerchief from him; and it drops.*]
Let it alone. Come, I'll go in with you.
Des. I am very sorry that you are not well.
Exit [*with Othello*].
Emil. I am glad I have found this napkin:
This was her first remembrance from the Moor:
My wayward husband hath a hundred times
Woo'd me to steal it; but she so loves the token,
For he conjur'd her she should ever keep it,
That she reserves it evermore about her
To kiss and talk to. I'll have the work ta'en out,
And give 't Iago: what he will do with it
Heaven knows, not I;
I nothing but to please his fantasy.

Enter Iago.

Iago. How now! what do you here alone?
Emil. Do not you chide; I have a thing for you.
Iago. A thing for me? it is a common thing—
Emil. Ha!
Iago. To have a foolish wife.
Emil. O, is that all? What will you give me now
For that same handkerchief?
Iago. What handkerchief?
Emil. What handkerchief!
Why, that the Moor first gave to Desdemona;
That which so often you did bid me steal.
Iago. Hast stol'n it from her?
Emil. No, 'faith; she let it drop by negligence,
And, to th' advantage, I, being here, took 't up.
Look, here it is.
Iago. A good wench; give it me.
Emil. What will you do with 't, that you have been so earnest
To have me filch it?
Iago. [*Snatching it*] Why, what is that to you?
Emil. If it be not for some purpose of import,
Give 't me again: poor lady, she'll run mad
When she shall lack it.
Iago. Be not acknown on 't; I have use for it.
Go, leave me. *Exit Emilia.*
I will in Cassio's lodging lose this napkin,
And let him find it. Trifles light as air
Are to the jealous confirmations strong
As proofs of holy writ: this may do something.
The Moor already changes with my poison:
Dangerous conceits are, in their natures, poisons,
Which at the first are scarce found to distaste,
But with a little act upon the blood,
Burn like the mines of sulphur. I did say so:

Enter OTHELLO.

Look, where he comes! Not poppy, nor mandragora,
Nor all the drowsy syrups of the world,
Shall ever medicine thee to that sweet sleep
Which thou owedst yesterday.
Oth. Ha! ha! false to me?
Iago. Why, how now, general! no more of that.
Oth. Avaunt! be gone! thou hast set me on the rack;
I swear 'tis better to be much abus'd
Than but to know 't a little.
Iago. How now, my lord!
Oth. What sense had I of her stol'n hours of lust?
I saw 't not, thought it not, it harm'd not me:
I slept the next night well, fed well, was free and merry;
I found not Cassio's kisses on her lips:
He that is robb'd, not wanting what is stol'n,
Let him not know 't, and he 's not robb'd at all.
Iago. I am sorry to hear this.
Oth. I had been happy, if the general camp,
Pioners and all, had tasted her sweet body,
So I had nothing known. O, now, for ever
Farewell the tranquil mind! farewell content!
Farewell the plumed troop, and the big wars,
That make ambition virtue! O, farewell!
Farewell the neighing steed, and the shrill trump,
The spirit-stirring drum, th' ear-piercing fife,
The royal banner, and all quality,
Pride, pomp and circumstance of glorious war!
And, O you mortal engines, whose rude throats
Th' immortal Jove's dread clamours counterfeit,
Farewell! Othello's occupation 's gone!
Iago. Is 't possible, my lord?
Oth. Villain, be sure thou prove my love a whore,
Be sure of it; give me the ocular proof;
Or, by the worth of mine eternal soul,
Thou hadst been better have been born a dog
Than answer my wak'd wrath!
Iago. Is 't come to this?
Oth. Make me to see 't; or, at the least, so prove it,
That the probation bear no hinge nor loop
To hang a doubt on; or woe upon thy life!
Iago. My noble lord,—
Oth. If thou dost slander her and torture me,
Never pray more; abandon all remorse;
On horror's head horrors accumulate;
Do deeds to make heaven weep, all earth amaz'd;
For nothing canst thou to damnation add
Greater than that.
Iago. O grace! O heaven forgive me!
Are you a man? have you a soul or sense?

274. **Prerogativ'd,** privileged. 276. **forked,** an allusion to the horns of the cuckold. 277. **quicken,** receive life. 280. **generous,** noble. 285. **watching,** working late. 296. **work ta'en out,** design copied. 302. **common thing** (with bawdy suggestion). 319. **Be . . . on 't,** do not confess knowledge of it. 328. **act,** action, working. 346. **Pioners,** sappers, a low grade of soldiers. 354. **circumstance,** attendant fact; here, formal display; see glossary. 355. **mortal engines,** i.e., cannon. 370. **horrors,** object of *accumulate*. 399. **bolster,** lie together. 404. **salt,** wanton, sensual. 406. **imputation,** i.e., opinion founded on strong circumstantial evidence (Schmidt). 428. **foregone conclusion,** previous

God be wi' you; take mine office. O wretched fool,
That liv'st to make thine honesty a vice!
O monstrous world! Take note, take note, O world,
To be direct and honest is not safe.
I thank you for this profit; and from hence
I'll love no friend, sith love breeds such offence.
Oth. Nay, stay: thou shouldst be honest.
Iago. I should be wise, for honesty 's a fool
And loses that it works for.
Oth. By the world,
I think my wife be honest and think she is not;
I think that thou art just and think thou art not.
I'll have some proof. Her name, that was as fresh
As Dian's visage, is now begrim'd and black
As mine own face. If there be cords, or knives,
Poison, or fire, or suffocating streams,
I'll not endure it. Would I were satisfied!
Iago. I see, sir, you are eaten up with passion:
I do repent me that I put it to you.
You would be satisfied?
Oth. Would! nay, I will.
Iago. And may: but, how? how satisfied, my lord?
Would you, the supervisor, grossly gape on—
Behold her topp'd?
Oth. Death and damnation! O!
Iago. It were a tedious difficulty, I think,
To bring them to that prospect: damn them then,
If ever mortal eyes do see them bolster
More than their own! What then? how then?
What shall I say? Where 's satisfaction?
It is impossible you should see this,
Were they as prime as goats, as hot as monkeys,
As salt as wolves in pride, and fools as gross
As ignorance made drunk. But yet, I say,
If imputation and strong circumstances,
Which lead directly to the door of truth,
Will give you satisfaction, you may have 't.
Oth. Give me a living reason she 's disloyal.
Iago. I do not like the office:
But, sith I am ent'red in this cause so far,
Prick'd to 't by foolish honesty and love,
I will go on. I lay with Cassio lately;
And, being troubled with a raging tooth,
I could not sleep.
There are a kind of men so loose of soul,
That in their sleeps will mutter their affairs:
One of this kind is Cassio:
In sleep I heard him say 'Sweet Desdemona,
Let us be wary, let us hide our loves;'
And then, sir, would he gripe and wring my hand,
Cry 'O sweet creature!' and then kiss me hard,
As if he pluck'd up kisses by the roots
That grew upon my lips: then laid his leg
Over my thigh, and sigh'd, and kiss'd; and then
Cried 'Cursed fate that gave thee to the Moor!'
Oth. O monstrous! monstrous!
Iago. Nay, this was but his dream.
Oth. But this denoted a foregone conclusion:
'Tis a shrewd doubt, though it be but a dream.
Iago. And this may help to thicken other proofs
That do demonstrate thinly.
Oth. I'll tear her all to pieces.
Iago. Nay, but be wise: yet we see nothing done;
She may be honest yet. Tell me but this,
Have you not sometimes seen a handkerchief
Spotted with strawberries in your wife's hand?
Oth. I gave her such a one; 'twas my first gift.
Iago. I know not that: but such a handkerchief—
I am sure it was your wife's—did I to-day
See Cassio wipe his beard with.
Oth. If it be that,—
Iago. If it be that, or any that was hers,
It speaks against her with the other proofs.
Oth. O, that the slave had forty thousand lives!
One is too poor, too weak for my revenge.
Now do I see 'tis true. Look here, Iago;
All my fond love thus do I blow to heaven.
'Tis gone.
Arise, black vengeance, from the hollow hell!
Yield up, O love, thy crown and hearted throne
To tyrannous hate! Swell, bosom, with thy fraught,
For 'tis of aspics' tongues!
Iago. Yet be content.
Oth. O, blood, blood, blood!
Iago. Patience, I say; your mind perhaps may change.
Oth. Never, Iago. Like to the Pontic sea,
Whose icy current and compulsive course
Ne'er feels retiring ebb, but keeps due on
To the Propontic and the Hellespont,
Even so my bloody thoughts, with violent pace,
Shall ne'er look back, ne'er ebb to humble love,
Till that a capable and wide revenge
Swallow them up. Now, by yond marble heaven,
[*Kneels*] In the due reverence of a sacred vow
I here engage my words.
Iago. Do not rise yet.
[*Kneels*] Witness, you ever-burning lights above,
You elements that clip us round about,
Witness that here Iago doth give up
The execution of his wit, hands, heart,
To wrong'd Othello's service! Let him command,
And to obey shall be in me remorse,
What bloody business ever. [*They rise.*]
Oth. I greet thy love,
Not with vain thanks, but with acceptance bounteous,
And will upon the instant put thee to 't:
Within these three days let me hear thee say
That Cassio 's not alive.
Iago. My friend is dead; 'tis done at your request:
But let her live.
Oth. Damn her, lewd minx! O, damn her! damn her!
Come, go with me apart; I will withdraw,
To furnish me with some swift means of death
For the fair devil. Now art thou my lieutenant.
Iago. I am your own for ever. *Exeunt.*

SCENE IV. [*Before the castle.*]

Enter DESDEMONA, EMILIA, *and* Clown.

Des. Do you know, sirrah, where Lieutenant Cassio lies?

Clo. I dare not say he lies any where.

trial or experience (not used in our sense). 448. **hearted,** fixed in the heart. 449. **fraught,** freight, burden. 450. **aspics',** venomous serpents'. 453-456. **Pontic . . . Propontic . . . Hellespont.** Steevens refers to Holland's *Pliny*, bk. II, ch. 97 (1601): "And the sea Pontus euermore floweth and runneth out into Propontic, but the sea neuer retireth backe againe within Pontus [the Black Sea]." 460. **marble,** i.e., gleaming like marble. 466. **execution,** exercise. 468. **remorse,** pity for Othello's wrongs.

Des. Why, man?

Clo. He 's a soldier, and for one to say a soldier lies, is stabbing.

Des. Go to: where lodges he?

Clo. To tell you where he lodges, is to tell you where I lie.

Des. Can any thing be made of this?

Clo. I know not where he lodges, and for me to devise a lodging and say he lies here or he lies there, were to lie in mine own throat.

Des. Can you inquire him out, and be edified by report?

Clo. I will catechize the world for him; that is, make questions, and by them answer.

Des. Seek him, bid him come hither: tell him I have moved my lord on his behalf, and hope all will be well.

Clo. To do this is within the compass of man's wit; and therefore I will attempt the doing it. *Exit Clo.*

Des. Where should I lose that handkerchief, Emilia?

Emil. I know not, madam.

Des. Believe me, I had rather have lost my purse
Full of crusadoes: and, but my noble Moor
Is true of mind and made of no such baseness
As jealous creatures are, it were enough
To put him to ill thinking.

Emil. Is he not jealous?

Des. Who, he? I think the sun where he was born
Drew all such humours from him.

Emil. Look, where he comes.

Enter OTHELLO.

Des. I will not leave him now till Cassio
Be call'd to him.—How is 't with you, my lord?

Oth. Well, my good lady. [*Aside*] O, hardness to dissemble!—
How do you, Desdemona?

Des. Well, my good lord.

Oth. Give me your hand: this hand is moist, my lady.

Des. It yet hath felt no age nor known no sorrow.

Oth. This argues fruitfulness and liberal heart:
Hot, hot, and moist: this hand of yours requires
A sequester from liberty, fasting and prayer,
Much castigation, exercise devout;
For here 's a young and sweating devil here,
That commonly rebels. 'Tis a good hand,
A frank one.

Des. You may, indeed, say so;
For 'twas that hand that gave away my heart.

Oth. A liberal hand: the hearts of old gave hands;
But our new heraldry is hands, not hearts.

Des. I cannot speak of this. Come now, your promise.

Oth. What promise, chuck?

Des. I have sent to bid Cassio come speak with you.

Oth. I have a salt and sorry rheum offends me;
Lend me thy handkerchief.

Des. Here, my lord.

Oth. That which I gave you.

Des. I have it not about me.

Oth. Not?

Des. No, indeed, my lord.

Oth. That 's a fault.
That handkerchief
Did an Egyptian to my mother give;
She was a charmer, and could almost read
The thoughts of people: she told her, while she kept it,
'Twould make her amiable and subdue my father
Entirely to her love, but if she lost it
Or made a gift of it, my father's eye
Should hold her loathed and his spirits should hunt
After new fancies: she, dying, gave it me;
And bid me, when my fate would have me wive,
To give it her. I did so: and take heed on 't;
Make it a darling like your precious eye;
To lose 't or give 't away were such perdition
As nothing else could match.

Des. Is 't possible?

Oth. 'Tis true: there 's magic in the web of it:
A sibyl, that had numb'red in the world
The sun to course two hundred compasses,
In her prophetic fury sew'd the work;
The worms were hallow'd that did breed the silk;
And it was dy'd in mummy which the skilful
Conserv'd of maidens' hearts.

Des. Indeed! is 't true?

Oth. Most veritable; therefore look to 't well.

Des. Then would to God that I had never seen 't!

Oth. Ha! wherefore?

Des. Why do you speak so startingly and rash?

Oth. Is 't lost? is 't gone? speak, is it out o' th' way?

Des. Heaven bless us!

Oth. Say you?

Des. It is not lost; but what an if it were?

Oth. How!

Des. I say, it is not lost.

Oth. Fetch 't, let me see 't.

Des. Why, so I can, sir, but I will not now.
This is a trick to put me from my suit:
Pray you, let Cassio be receiv'd again.

Oth. Fetch me the handkerchief: my mind misgives.

Des. Come, come;
You'll never meet a more sufficient man.

Oth. The handkerchief!

Des. I pray, talk me of Cassio.

Oth. The handkerchief!

Des. A man that all his time
Hath founded his good fortunes on your love,
Shar'd dangers with you,—

Oth. The handkerchief!

Des. In sooth, you are to blame.

Oth. Away! *Exit Othello.*

Emil. Is not this man jealous?

Des. I ne'er saw this before.
Sure, there 's some wonder in this handkerchief:
I am most unhappy in the loss of it.

Emil. 'Tis not a year or two shows us a man:
They are all but stomachs, and we all but food;
They eat us hungerly, and when they are full,

SCENE IV. 26. **crusadoes,** Portuguese gold coins. 40. **sequester,** separation, sequestration. 47. **new . . . hearts.** This is thought by Warburton and some later critics to allude to the creation of a new order of baronets by King James I in 1611, the arms for which were a hand gules on a field argent, More probably, however, it is a current expression referring to marriages in which there is a joining of hands without the giving of hearts. 51. **sorry rheum,** distressful head cold. 56. **Egyptian,** gypsy. 70-71. **had numb'red . . . compasses.** "We say, I counted the clock to strike four; so she numbered the sun to course, to run two hundred compasses, two hundred annual circuits" (Johnson).

They belch us.

Enter IAGO *and* CASSIO.

Look you, Cassio and my husband!
Iago. There is no other way; 'tis she must do 't:
And, lo, the happiness! go, and importune her.
Des. How now, good Cassio! what 's the news with
you?
Cas. Madam, my former suit: I do beseech you
That by your virtuous means I may again
Exist, and be a member of his love
Whom I with all the office of my heart
Entirely honour: I would not be delay'd.
If my offence be of such mortal kind
That nor my service past, nor present sorrows,
Nor purpos'd merit in futurity,
Can ransom me into his love again,
But to know so must be my benefit;
So shall I clothe me in a forc'd content,
And shut myself up in some other course,
To fortune's alms.
Des. Alas, thrice-gentle Cassio!
My advocation is not now in tune;
My lord is not my lord; nor should I know him,
Were he in favour as in humour alter'd.
So help me every spirit sanctified,
As I have spoken for you all my best
And stood within the blank of his displeasure
For my free speech! you must awhile be patient:
What I can do I will; and more I will
Than for myself I dare: let that suffice you.
Iago. Is my lord angry?
Emil. He went hence but now,
And certainly in strange unquietness.
Iago. Can he be angry? I have seen the cannon,
When it hath blown his ranks into the air,
And, like the devil, from his very arm
Puff'd his own brother:—and can he be angry?
Something of moment then: I will go meet him:
There 's matter in 't indeed, if he be angry.
Des. I prithee, do so. *Exit* [*Iago*].
Something, sure, of state,
Either from Venice, or some unhatch'd practice
Made demonstrable here in Cyprus to him,
Hath puddled his clear spirit; and in such cases
Men's natures wrangle with inferior things,
Though great ones are their object. 'Tis even so;
For let our finger ache, and it indues
Our other healthful members even to a sense
Of pain: nay, we must think men are not gods,
Nor of them look for such observancy
As fits the bridal. Beshrew me much, Emilia,
I was, unhandsome warrior as I am,
Arraigning his unkindness with my soul;
But now I find I had suborn'd the witness,
And he 's indicted falsely.
Emil. Pray heaven it be state-matters, as you think,
And no conception nor no jealous toy
Concerning you.
Des. Alas the day! I never gave him cause.
Emil. But jealous souls will not be answer'd so;
They are not ever jealous for the cause,
But jealous for they are jealous: 'tis a monster
Begot upon itself, born on itself.
Des. Heaven keep that monster from Othello's
mind!
Emil. Lady, amen.
Des. I will go seek him. Cassio, walk here about:
If I do find him fit, I'll move your suit
And seek to effect it to my uttermost.
Cas. I humbly thank your ladyship.
Exit [*Desdemona with Emilia*].

Enter BIANCA.

Bian. Save you, friend Cassio!
Cas. What make you from home?
How is 't with you, my most fair Bianca?
I' faith, sweet love, I was coming to your house.
Bian. And I was going to your lodging, Cassio.
What, keep a week away? seven days and nights?
Eight score eight hours? and lovers' absent hours,
More tedious than the dial eight score times?
O weary reck'ning!
Cas. Pardon me, Bianca:
I have this while with leaden thoughts been press'd;
But I shall, in a more continuate time,
Strike off this score of absence. Sweet Bianca,
[*Giving her Desdemona's handkerchief*.]
Take me this work out.
Bian. O Cassio, whence came this?
This is some token from a newer friend:
To the felt absence now I feel a cause:
Is 't come to this? Well, well.
Cas. Go to, woman!
Throw your vile guesses in the devil's teeth,
From whence you have them. You are jealous now
That this is from some mistress, some remembrance:
No, in good troth, Bianca.
Bian. Why, whose is it?
Cas. I know not, sweet: I found it in my chamber.
I like the work well: ere it be demanded—
As like enough it will—I would have it copied:
Take it, and do 't; and leave me for this time.
Bian. Leave you! wherefore?
Cas. I do attend here on the general;
And think it no addition, nor my wish,
To have him see me woman'd.
Bian. Why, I pray you?
Cas. Not that I love you not.
Bian. But that you do not love me.
I pray you, bring me on the way a little,
And say if I shall see you soon at night.
Cas. 'Tis but a little way that I can bring you;
For I attend here: but I'll see you soon.
Bian. 'Tis very good; I must be circumstanc'd.
Exeunt omnes.

ACT IV.

SCENE I. [*Cyprus. Before the castle.*]

Enter OTHELLO *and* IAGO.

74. **mummy,** medicinal or magical preparation drained from the flesh of mummified bodies. 75. **Conserv'd of,** preserved out of. 119. **to know . . . benefit,** to know that my case is hopeless will end my vain endeavor. 123. **advocation,** advocacy. 128. **blank,** white spot in the center of a target; here, range. 143. **puddled,** sullied the purity of. 146. **indues,** brings to the same condition. 151. **unhandsome,** unfair. 156. **conception,** mere fancy. 178. **continuate,** uninterrupted. Q: *conuenient*. 180. **Take . . . out,** i.e., copy this embroidery for me. 201. **circumstanc'd,** governed by circumstances.

Iago. Will you think so?
Oth. Think so, Iago!
Iago. What,
To kiss in private?
Oth. An unauthoriz'd kiss.
Iago. Or to be naked with her friend in bed
An hour or more, not meaning any harm?
Oth. Naked in bed, Iago, and not mean harm!
It is hypocrisy against the devil:
They that mean virtuously, and yet do so,
The devil their virtue tempts, and they tempt heaven.
Iago. So they do nothing, 'tis a venial slip:
But if I give my wife a handkerchief,—
Oth. What then?
Iago. Why, then, 'tis hers, my lord; and, being hers,
She may, I think, bestow 't on any man.
Oth. She is protectress of her honour too:
May she give that?
Iago. Her honour is an essence that 's not seen;
They have it very oft that have it not:
But, for the handkerchief,—
Oth. By heaven, I would most gladly have forgot it.
Thou said'st—O, it comes o'er my memory,
As doth the raven o'er the infected house,
Boding to all—he had my handkerchief.
Iago. Ay, what of that?
Oth. That 's not so good now.
Iago. What,
If I had said I had seen him do you wrong?
Or heard him say,—as knaves be such abroad,
Who having, by their own importunate suit,
Or voluntary dotage of some mistress,
Convinced or supplied them, cannot choose
But they must blab—
Oth. Hath he said any thing?
Iago. He hath, my lord; but be you well assur'd,
No more than he'll unswear.
Oth. What hath he said?
Iago. 'Faith, that he did—I know not what he did.
Oth. What? what?
Iago. Lie—
Oth. With her?
Iago. With her, on her; what you will.

Oth. Lie with her! lie on her! We say lie on her, when they belie her. Lie with her! that 's fulsome.—Handkerchief—confessions—handkerchief!—To confess, and be hanged for his labour;—first, to be hanged, and then to confess.—I tremble at it. Nature would not invest herself in such shadowing passion without some instruction. It is not words that shakes me thus. Pish! Noses, ears, and lips.—Is 't possible?—Confess—handkerchief!—O devil! *Falls in a trance.*

Iago. Work on,
My medicine, work! Thus credulous fools are caught;
And many worthy and chaste dames even thus,
All guiltless, meet reproach. What, ho! my lord!
My lord, I say! Othello!

Enter CASSIO.

How now, Cassio!
Cas. What 's the matter?
Iago. My lord is fall'n into an epilepsy:
This is his second fit; he had one yesterday.
Cas. Rub him about the temples.
Iago. No, forbear;
The lethargy must have his quiet course:
If not, he foams at mouth and by and by
Breaks out to savage madness. Look, he stirs:
Do you withdraw yourself a little while,
He will recover straight: when he is gone,
I would on great occasion speak with you. [*Exit Cassio*].
How is it, general? have you not hurt your head?
Oth. Dost thou mock me?
Iago. I mock you! no, by heaven.
Would you would bear your fortune like a man!
Oth. A horned man 's a monster and a beast.
Iago. There 's many a beast then in a populous city,
And many a civil monster.
Oth. Did he confess it?
Iago. Good sir, be a man;
Think every bearded fellow that 's but yok'd
May draw with you: there 's millions now alive
That nightly lie in those unproper beds
Which they dare swear peculiar: your case is better.
O, 'tis the spite of hell, the fiend's arch-mock,
To lip a wanton in a secure couch,
And to suppose her chaste! No, let me know;
And knowing what I am, I know what she shall be.
Oth. O, thou art wise; 'tis certain.
Iago. Stand you awhile apart;
Confine yourself but in a patient list.
Whilst you were here o'erwhelmed with your grief—
A passion most unsuiting such a man—
Cassio came hither: I shifted him away,
And laid good 'scuse upon your ecstasy,
Bade him anon return and here speak with me;
The which he promis'd. Do but encave yourself,
And mark the fleers, the gibes, and notable scorns,
That dwell in every region of his face;
For I will make him tell the tale anew,
Where, how, how oft, how long ago, and when
He hath, and is again to cope your wife:
I say, but mark his gesture. Marry, patience;
Or I shall say y' are all in all in spleen,
And nothing of a man.
Oth. Dost thou hear, Iago?
I will be found most cunning in my patience;
But—dost thou hear?—most bloody.
Iago. That 's not amiss;
But yet keep time in all. Will you withdraw?
[*Othello retires.*]
Now will I question Cassio of Bianca,
A housewife that by selling her desires
Buys herself bread and clothes: it is a creature
That dotes on Cassio; as 'tis the strumpet's plague
To beguile many and be beguil'd by one:
He, when he hears of her, cannot refrain
From the excess of laughter. Here he comes:

Enter CASSIO.

As he shall smile, Othello shall go mad;

ACT IV. SCENE I. 9. **So,** so long as. 21. **raven . . . house,** allusion to the belief that the raven hovered over a house of sickness or infection. 28. **Convinced or supplied,** i.e., mistresses gained by importunity and those who doted voluntarily. 40-42. **Nature . . . instruction,** i.e., my jealousy cannot be merely the result of natural imagination, but must have some foundation in fact. 54. **lethargy,** unconscious condition.

65. **civil,** i.e., in civilized society. 68. **draw with you,** i.e., share your fate as cuckold. 69. **unproper,** not belonging exclusively to an individual. The meaning "improper" is post-Shakespearean. 70. **peculiar,** private, one's own. 76. **patient list,** within the bounds of patience; see glossary. 82. **encave,** conceal. 83. **fleers,** sneers. 93. **keep time,** use judgment and order. 102. **unbookish,** uninstructed.

And his unbookish jealousy must conster
Poor Cassio's smiles, gestures and light behaviour,
Quite in the wrong. How do you now, lieutenant?

Cas. The worser that you give me the addition
Whose want even kills me.

Iago. Ply Desdemona well, and you are sure on 't.
[*Speaking lower*] Now, if this suit lay in Bianca's power,
How quickly should you speed!

Cas. Alas, poor caitiff!

Oth. Look, how he laughs already!

Iago. I never knew woman love man so.

Cas. Alas, poor rogue! I think, i' faith, she loves me.

Oth. Now he denies it faintly, and laughs it out.

Iago. Do you hear, Cassio?

Oth. Now he importunes him
To tell it o'er: go to; well said, well said.

Iago. She gives it out that you shall marry her:
Do you intend it?

Cas. Ha, ha, ha!

Oth. Do you triumph, Roman? do you triumph?

Cas. I marry her! what? a customer! Prithee, bear some charity to my wit; do not think it so unwholesome. Ha, ha, ha!

Oth. So, so, so, so: they laugh that win.

Iago. 'Faith, the cry goes that you shall marry her.

Cas. Prithee, say true.

Iago. I am a very villain else.

Oth. Have you scored me? Well.

Cas. This is the monkey's own giving out: she is persuaded I will marry her, out of her own love and flattery, not out of my promise.

Oth. Iago beckons me; now he begins the story.

Cas. She was here even now; she haunts me in every place. I was the other day talking on the sea-bank with certain Venetians; and thither comes the bauble, and, by this hand, she falls me thus about my neck—

Oth. Crying, 'O dear Cassio!' as it were: his gesture imports it.

Cas. So hangs, and lolls, and weeps upon me; so shakes, and pulls me: ha, ha, ha!

Oth. Now he tells how she plucked him to my chamber. O, I see that nose of yours, but not that dog I shall throw it to.

Cas. Well, I must leave her company.

Iago. Before me! look, where she comes.

Enter Bianca.

Cas. 'Tis such another fitchew! marry, a perfumed one.—What do you mean by this haunting of me?

Bian. Let the devil and his dam haunt you! What did you mean by that same handkerchief you gave me even now? I was a fine fool to take it. I must take out the work?—A likely piece of work, that you should find it in your chamber, and not know who left it there! This is some minx's token, and I must take out the work? There; give it your hobby-horse: wheresoever you had it, I'll take out no work on 't.

Cas. How now, my sweet Bianca! how now! how now!

Oth. By heaven, that should be my handkerchief!

Bian. An you'll come to supper to-night, you may; an you will not, come when you are next prepared for. *Exit.*

Iago. After her, after her.

Cas. 'Faith, I must; she'll rail in the street else.

Iago. Will you sup there?

Cas. Yes, I intend so.

Iago. Well, I may chance to see you; for I would very fain speak with you.

Cas. Prithee, come; will you?

Iago. Go to; say no more. [*Exit Cassio.*]

Oth. [*Advancing*] How shall I murder him, Iago?

Iago. Did you perceive how he laughed at his vice?

Oth. O Iago!

Iago. And did you see the handkerchief?

Oth. Was that mine?

Iago. Yours, by this hand: and to see how he prizes the foolish woman your wife! she gave it him, and he hath given it his whore.

Oth. I would have him nine years a-killing. A fine woman! a fair woman! a sweet woman!

Iago. Nay, you must forget that.

Oth. Ay, let her rot, and perish, and be damned to-night; for she shall not live: no, my heart is turned to stone; I strike it, and it hurts my hand. O, the world hath not a sweeter creature: she might lie by an emperor's side and command him tasks.

Iago. Nay, that 's not your way.

Oth. Hang her! I do but say what she is: so delicate with her needle: an admirable musician: O! she will sing the savageness out of a bear: of so high and plenteous wit and invention:—

Iago. She 's the worse for all this.

Oth. O, a thousand thousand times: and then, of so gentle a condition!

Iago. Ay, too gentle.

Oth. Nay, that 's certain: but yet the pity of it, Iago! O Iago, the pity of it, Iago!

Iago. If you are so fond over her iniquity, give her patent to offend; for, if it touch not you, it comes near nobody.

Oth. I will chop her into messes: cuckold me!

Iago. O, 'tis foul in her.

Oth. With mine officer!

Iago. That 's fouler.

Oth. Get me some poison, Iago; this night: I'll not expostulate with her, lest her body and beauty unprovide my mind again: this night, Iago.

Iago. Do it not with poison, strangle her in her bed, even the bed she hath contaminated.

Oth. Good, good: the justice of it pleases: very good.

Iago. And for Cassio, let me be his undertaker: you shall hear more by midnight.

Oth. Excellent good. [*A trumpet within.*] What
trumpet is that same?

Iago. I warrant something from Venice.

Enter Lodovico, Desdemona, *and* Attendants.

'Tis Lodovico.
This comes from the duke: and, see, your wife 's with him.

Lod. God save you, worthy general!

conster, construe. 105. **addition,** title. 121. **Roman.** The epithet arises from the association of the Romans with the idea of triumph. 122. **customer,** prostitute. 130. **scored me,** made up my reckoning, or branded me. 139. **bauble,** plaything. 149. **Before me!** On my soul! 150. **fitchew,** polecat (because of her strong perfume; also, slang word for a prostitute). 160. **hobby-horse,** harlot. 197. **your way,** i.e., the way you should think of her. 209. **patent,** license. 211. **messes,** dishes of food. 218. **unprovide,** weaken, unfit. 224. **let . . . undertaker,** i.e., let me settle with him.

Oth. With all my heart, sir.
Lod. The duke and the senators of Venice greet you.
[*Gives him a letter.*]
Oth. I kiss the instrument of their pleasures.
[*Opens the letter, and reads.*]
Des. And what 's the news, good cousin Lodovico?
Iago. I am very glad to see you, signior;
Welcome to Cyprus.
Lod. I thank you. How does Lieutenant Cassio?
Iago. Lives, sir.
Des. Cousin, there 's fall'n between him and my lord
An unkind breach: but you shall make all well.
Oth. Are you sure of that?
Des. My lord?
Oth. [*Reads*] 'This fail you not to do, as you will—'
Lod. He did not call; he 's busy in the paper.
Is there division 'twixt my lord and Cassio?
Des. A most unhappy one: I would do much
T' atone them, for the love I bear to Cassio.
Oth. Fire and brimstone!
Des. My lord?
Oth. Are you wise?
Des. What, is he angry?
Lod. May be the letter mov'd him;
For, as I think, they do command him home,
Deputing Cassio in his government.
Des. Trust me, I am glad on 't.
Oth. Indeed!
Des. My lord?
Oth. I am glad to see you mad.
Des. Why, sweet Othello,—
Oth. [*Striking her*] Devil!
Des. I have not deserv'd this.
Lod. My lord, this would not be believ'd in Venice,
Though I should swear I saw 't: 'tis very much:
Make her amends; she weeps.
Oth. O devil, devil!
If that the earth could teem with woman's tears,
Each drop she falls would prove a crocodile.
Out of my sight!
Des. I will not stay to offend you. [*Going*].
Lod. Truly, an obedient lady:
I do beseech your lordship, call her back.
Oth. Mistress!
Des. My lord?
Oth. What would you with her, sir?
Lod. Who, I, my lord?
Oth. Ay; you did wish that I would make her turn:
Sir, she can turn, and turn, and yet go on,
And turn again; and she can weep, sir, weep;
And she 's obedient, as you say, obedient,
Very obedient. Proceed you in your tears.
Concerning this, sir,—O well-painted passion!—
I am commanded home. Get you away;
I'll send for you anon. Sir, I obey the mandate,
And will return to Venice. Hence, avaunt!
[*Exit Desdemona.*]
Cassio shall have my place. And, sir, to-night,
I do entreat that we may sup together:
You are welcome, sir, to Cyprus.—Goats and monkeys! *Exit.*

Lod. Is this the noble Moor whom our full senate
Call all in all sufficient? Is this the nature
Whom passion could not shake? whose solid virtue
The shot of accident, nor dart of chance,
Could neither graze nor pierce?
Iago. He is much chang'd.
Lod. Are his wits safe? is he not light of brain?
Iago. He 's that he is: I may not breathe my censure
What he might be: if what he might he is not,
I would to heaven he were!
Lod. What, strike his wife!
Iago. 'Faith, that was not so well; yet would I knew
That stroke would prove the worst!
Lod. Is it his use?
Or did the letters work upon his blood,
And new-create this fault?
Iago. Alas, alas!
It is not honesty in me to speak
What I have seen and known. You shall observe him,
And his own courses will denote him so
That I may save my speech: do but go after,
And mark how he continues.
Lod. I am sorry that I am deceiv'd in him. *Exeunt.*

SCENE II. [*A room in the castle.*]

Enter OTHELLO *and* EMILIA.

Oth. You have seen nothing then?
Emil. Nor ever heard, nor ever did suspect.
Oth. Yes, you have seen Cassio and she together.
Emil. But then I saw no harm, and then I heard
Each syllable that breath made up between them.
Oth. What, did they never whisper?
Emil. Never, my lord.
Oth. Nor send you out o' th' way?
Emil. Never.
Oth. To fetch her fan, her gloves, her mask, nor nothing?
Emil. Never, my lord.
Oth. That 's strange.
Emil. I durst, my lord, to wager she is honest,
Lay down my soul at stake: if you think other,
Remove your thought; it doth abuse your bosom.
If any wretch have put this in your head,
Let heaven requite it with the serpent's curse!
For, if she be not honest, chaste, and true,
There 's no man happy; the purest of their wives
Is foul as slander.
Oth. Bid her come hither: go.
Exit Emilia.
She says enough; yet she 's a simple bawd
That cannot say as much. This is a subtle whore,
A closet lock and key of villanous secrets:
And yet she'll kneel and pray; I have seen her do 't.

Enter DESDEMONA *and* EMILIA.

Des. My lord, what is your will?
Oth. Pray, chuck, come hither.
Des. What is your pleasure?
Oth. Let me see your eyes;
Look in my face.

248. **government,** office. 257. **prove a crocodile,** i.e., by weeping crocodile tears; it was believed the crocodile shed tears over the body of the man he was eating. 268. **well-painted passion,** well-simulated emotion. 286. The purpose of Othello's recall is not clear.

SCENE II. 16. **serpent's curse.** Cf. Genesis 3:14. 22. **closet lock and key,** complete storeroom. 27. **Some . . . function,** i.e., set to work in your chosen profession, that of bawd. 28. **procreants,** mating couples. 30. **mystery,** trade, occupation. 48. **they,** heavenly powers. 54-55. **A . . . at.** Othello possibly thinks of himself as a man set in a pillory at whom the scornful world points in mockery. There seems to

Des. What horrible fancy 's this?
Oth. [*To Emilia*] Some of your function, mistress;
Leave procreants alone and shut the door;
Cough, or cry 'hem', if any body come:
Your mystery, your mystery: nay, dispatch.
Exit Emilia.
Des. Upon my knees, what doth your speech import?
I understand a fury in your words,
But not the words.
Oth. Why, what art thou?
Des. Your wife, my lord; your true
And loyal wife.
Oth. Come, swear it, damn thyself;
Lest, being like one of heaven, the devils themselves
Should fear to seize thee: therefore be double damn'd:
Swear thou art honest.
Des. Heaven doth truly know it.
Oth. Heaven truly knows that thou art false as hell.
Des. To whom, my lord? with whom? how am I false?
Oth. O Desdemon! away! away! away!
Des. Alas the heavy day! Why do you weep?
Am I the motive of these tears, my lord?
If haply you my father do suspect
An instrument of this your calling back,
Lay not your blame on me: if you have lost him,
Why, I have lost him too.
Oth. Had it pleas'd heaven
To try me with affliction; had they rain'd
All kinds of sores and shames on my bare head,
Steep'd me in poverty to the very lips,
Given to captivity me and my utmost hopes,
I should have found in some place of my soul
A drop of patience: but, alas, to make me
A fixed figure for the time of scorn
To point his slow unmoving finger at!
Yet could I bear that too; well, very well:
But there, where I have garner'd up my heart,
Where either I must live, or bear no life;
The fountain from the which my current runs,
Or else dries up; to be discarded thence!
Or keep it as a cistern for foul toads
To knot and gender in! Turn thy complexion there,
Patience, thou young and rose-lipp'd cherubin,—
Ay, there, look grim as hell!
Des. I hope my noble lord esteems me honest.
Oth. O, ay; as summer flies are in the shambles,
That quicken even with blowing. O thou weed,
Who art so lovely fair and smell'st so sweet
That the sense aches at thee, would thou hadst ne'er been born!
Des. Alas, what ignorant sin have I committed?
Oth. Was this fair paper, this most goodly book,
Made to write 'whore' upon? What committed!
Committed! O thou public commoner!
I should make very forges of my cheeks,
That would to cinders burn up modesty,
Did I but speak thy deeds. What committed!
Heaven stops the nose at it and the moon winks,
The bawdy wind that kisses all it meets
Is hush'd within the hollow mine of earth,
And will not hear it. What committed!
Impudent strumpet!
Des. By heaven, you do me wrong.
Oth. Are not you a strumpet?
Des. No, as I am a Christian:
If to preserve this vessel for my lord
From any other foul unlawful touch
Be not to be a strumpet, I am none.
Oth. What, not a whore?
Des. No, as I shall be sav'd.
Oth. Is 't possible?
Des. O, heaven forgive us!
Oth. I cry you mercy, then:
I took you for that cunning whore of Venice
That married with Othello. [*Raising his voice*] You, mistress,
That have the office opposite to Saint Peter,
And keep the gate of hell!

Enter EMILIA.

You, you, ay, you!
We have done our course; there 's money for your pains:
I pray you, turn the key and keep our counsel. *Exit.*
Emil. Alas, what does this gentleman conceive?
How do you, madam? how do you, my good lady?
Des. 'Faith, half asleep.
Emil. Good madam, what 's the matter with my lord?
Des. With who?
Emil. Why, with my lord, madam.
Des. Who is thy lord?
Emil. He that is yours, sweet lady.
Des. I have none: do not talk to me, Emilia;
I cannot weep; nor answers have I none,
But what should go by water. Prithee, tonight
Lay on my bed my wedding sheets: remember;
And call thy husband hither.
Emil. Here 's a change indeed! *Exit.*
Des. 'Tis meet I should be us'd so, very meet.
How have I been behav'd, that he might stick
The small'st opinion on my least misuse?

Enter IAGO *and* EMILIA.

Iago. What is your pleasure, madam? How is 't with you?
Des. I cannot tell. Those that do teach young babes
Do it with gentle means and easy tasks:
He might have chid me so; for, in good faith,
I am a child to chiding.
Iago. What is the matter, lady?
Emil. Alas, Iago, my lord hath so bewhor'd her,
Thrown such despite and heavy terms upon her,
As true hearts cannot bear.
Des. Am I that name, Iago?
Iago. What name, fair lady?
Des. Such as she said my lord did say I was.
Emil. He call'd her whore: a beggar in his drink
Could not have laid such terms upon his callet.
Iago. Why did he so?
Des. I do not know; I am sure I am none such.
Iago. Do not weep, do not weep. Alas the day!

be a comparison with the sundial, whose gnomon, or indicator, becomes the finger of scornful time. For *unmoving* some editors adopt the F reading, *and moving*. 62. **gender,** engender. **Turn thy complexion,** grow pale. At such an object do thou, patience, thyself change color; at this do thou, even thou, rosy cherub as thou art, look grim as hell (Johnson). 66. **shambles,** slaughterhouse. 67. **quicken,** come to life. 73. **commoner,** prostitute. 83. **vessel,** body; I Thessalonians 4:4. 104. **go by water,** be expressed by tears. 109. **misuse,** evil conduct. 116. **despite,** contempt, scorn. 121. **callet,** lewd woman.

Emil. Hath she forsook so many noble matches,
Her father and her country and her friends,
To be call'd whore? would it not make one weep?
Des. It is my wretched fortune.
Iago. Beshrew him for 't!
How comes this trick upon him?
Des. Nay, heaven doth know.
Emil. I will be hang'd, if some eternal villain,
Some busy and insinuating rogue,
Some cogging, cozening slave, to get some office,
Have not devis'd this slander; I will be hang'd else.
Iago. Fie, there is no such man; it is impossible.
Des. If any such there be, heaven pardon him!
Emil. A halter pardon him! and hell gnaw his bones!
Why should he call her whore? who keeps her company?
What place? what time? what form? what likelihood?
The Moor 's abus'd by some most villanous knave,
Some base notorious knave, some scurvy fellow.
O heaven, that such companions thou 'ldst unfold,
And put in every honest hand a whip
To lash the rascals naked through the world
Even from the east to th' west!
Iago. Speak within door.
Emil. O, fie upon them! Some such squire he was
That turn'd your wit the seamy side without,
And made you to suspect me with the Moor.
Iago. You are a fool; go to.
Des. Alas, Iago,
What shall I do to win my lord again?
Good friend, go to him; for, by this light of heaven,
I know not how I lost him. Here I kneel:
If e'er my will did trespass 'gainst his love,
Either in discourse of thought or actual deed,
Or that mine eyes, mine ears, or any sense,
Delighted them in any other form;
Or that I do not yet, and ever did,
And ever will—though he do shake me off
To beggarly divorcement—love him dearly,
Comfort forswear me! Unkindness may do much;
And his unkindness may defeat my life,
But never taint my love. I cannot say 'whore:'
It doth abhor me now I speak the word;
To do the act that might the addition earn
Not the world's mass of vanity could make me.
Iago. I pray you, be content; 'tis but his humour:
The business of the state does him offence,
And he does chide with you.
Des. If 'twere no other,—
Iago. 'Tis but so, I warrant.
[*Trumpets within.*]
Hark, how these instruments summon to supper!
The messengers of Venice stay the meat:
Go in, and weep not; all things shall be well.
Exeunt Desdemona and Emilia.

Enter RODERIGO.

How now, Roderigo!
Rod. I do not find that thou dealest justly with me.
Iago. What in the contrary?
Rod. Every day thou daffest me with some device, Iago; and rather, as it seems to me now, keepest from me all conveniency than suppliest me with the least advantage of hope. I will indeed no longer endure it, nor am I yet persuaded to put up in peace what already I have foolishly suffered.

Iago. Will you hear me, Roderigo?

Rod. 'Faith, I have heard too much, for your words and performances are no kin together.

Iago. You charge me most unjustly.

Rod. With nought but truth. I have wasted myself out of my means. The jewels you have had from me to deliver to Desdemona would half have corrupted a votarist: you have told me she hath received them and returned me expectations and comforts of sudden respect and acquaintance, but I find none.

Iago. Well; go to; very well.

Rod. Very well! go to! I cannot go to, man; nor 'tis not very well: nay, I think it is scurvy, and begin to find myself fopped in it.

Iago. Very well.

Rod. I tell you 'tis not very well. I will make myself known to Desdemona: if she will return me my jewels, I will give over my suit and repent my unlawful solicitation; if not, assure yourself I will seek satisfaction of you.

Iago. You have said now.

Rod. Ay, and said nothing but what I protest intendment of doing.

Iago. Why, now I see there 's mettle in thee, and even from this instant do build on thee a better opinion than ever before. Give me thy hand, Roderigo: thou hast taken against me a most just exception; but yet, I protest, I have dealt most directly in thy affair.

Rod. It hath not appeared.

Iago. I grant indeed it hath not appeared, and your suspicion is not without wit and judgement. But, Roderigo, if thou hast that in thee indeed, which I have greater reason to believe now than ever, I mean purpose, courage and valour, this night show it: if thou the next night following enjoy not Desdemona, take me from this world with treachery and devise engines for my life.

Rod. Well, what is it? is it within reason and compass?

Iago. Sir, there is especial commission come from Venice to depute Cassio in Othello's place.

Rod. Is that true? why, then Othello and Desdemona return again to Venice.

Iago. O, no; he goes into Mauritania and takes away with him the fair Desdemona, unless his abode be lingered here by some accident: wherein none can be so determinate as the removing of Cassio.

Rod. How do you mean, removing of him?

Iago. Why, by making him uncapable of Othello's place; knocking out his brains.

Rod. And that you would have me to do?

Iago. Ay, if you dare do yourself a profit and a right. He sups to-night with a harlotry, and thither will I go to him: he knows not yet of his honourable fortune. If you will watch his going thence, which I will fashion to fall out between twelve and one, you may

132. **cogging,** cheating. 144. **Speak . . . door,** i.e., not so loud; Q: *dores*. 163. **addition,** title. 170. **stay the meat,** are waiting for supper. 176. **daffest me,** puttest me off with an excuse. 178. **conveniency,** advantage, opportunity. 181. **put up,** submit to. 190. **votarist,** nun. 197. **fopped,** fooled, duped. 204. **You . . . now,** well said, quite right (Schmidt). 206. **intendment,** purpose, intention. 221. **engines for,** plots against. 229. **Mauritania,** Roman name of northwest Africa, supposed land of the Moors. 232. **determinate,** decisive. 239. **harlotry,** courtesan. 249. **high,** quite.

SCENE III. 12. **incontinent,** immediately. 20. **stubbornness,** rough-take him at your pleasure: I will be near to second your attempt, and he shall fall between us. Come, stand not amazed at it, but go along with me; I will show you such a necessity in his death that you shall think yourself bound to put it on him. It is now high supper-time, and the night grows to waste: about it.

Rod. I will hear further reason for this.

Iago. And you shall be satisfied. *Exeunt.*

SCENE III. [*Another room in the castle.*]

Enter OTHELLO, LODOVICO, DESDEMONA, EMILIA, *and* Attendants.

Lod. I do beseech you, sir, trouble yourself no further.
Oth. O, pardon me; 'twill do me good to walk.
Lod. Madam, good night; I humbly thank your ladyship.
Des. Your honour is most welcome.
Oth. Will you walk, sir?
O,—Desdemona,—
Des. My lord?

Oth. Get you to bed on th' instant; I will be returned forthwith: dismiss your attendant there: look 't be done.

Des. I will, my lord.
Exit [*Othello, with Lodovico and Attendants*].
Emil. How goes it now? he looks gentler than he did.
Des. He says he will return incontinent:
He hath commanded me to go to bed,
And bade me to dismiss you.
Emil. Dismiss me!
Des. It was his bidding; therefore, good Emilia,
Give me my nightly wearing, and adieu:
We must not now displease him.
Emil. I would you had never seen him!
Des. So would not I: my love doth so approve him,
That even his stubbornness, his checks, his frowns,—
Prithee, unpin me,—have grace and favour in them.
Emil. I have laid those sheets you bade me on the bed.
Des. All 's one. Good faith, how foolish are our minds!
If I do die before thee, prithee, shroud me
In one of those same sheets.
Emil. Come, come, you talk.
Des. My mother had a maid call'd Barbary:
She was in love, and he she lov'd prov'd mad
And did forsake her: she had a song of 'willow;'
An old thing 'twas, but it express'd her fortune,
And she died singing it: that song to-night
Will not go from my mind; I have much to do,
But to go hang my head all at one side,
And sing it like poor Barbary. Prithee, dispatch.
Emil. Shall I go fetch your night-gown?
Des. No, unpin me here.
This Lodovico is a proper man.
Emil. A very handsome man.
Des. He speaks well.

Emil. I know a lady in Venice would have walked barefoot to Palestine for a touch of his nether lip.

Des. [*Singing*] The poor soul sat sighing by a sycamore tree,
Sing all a green willow;
Her hand on her bosom, her head on her knee,
Sing willow, willow, willow:
The fresh streams ran by her, and murmur'd her moans;
Sing willow, willow, willow;
Her salt tears fell from her, and soft'ned the stones;—
Lay by these:—
[*Singing*] Sing willow, willow, willow;
Prithee, hie thee; he'll come anon:—
[*Singing*] Sing all a green willow must be my garland.
Let nobody blame him; his scorn I approve,—
Nay, that 's not next.—Hark! who is 't that knocks?
Emil. It 's the wind.
Des. [*Singing*] I call'd my love false love; but what said he then?
Sing willow, willow, willow:
If I court moe women, you'll couch with moe men.—
So, get thee gone; good night. Mine eyes do itch;
Doth that bode weeping?
Emil. 'Tis neither here nor there.
Des. I have heard it said so. O, these men, these men!
Dost thou in conscience think,—tell me, Emilia,—
That there be women do abuse their husbands
In such gross kind?
Emil. There be some such, no question.
Des. Wouldst thou do such a deed for all the world?
Emil. Why, would not you?
Des. No, by this heavenly light!

Emil. Nor I neither by this heavenly light; I might do 't as well i' the dark.

Des. Wouldst thou do such a deed for all the world?
Emil. The world 's a huge thing: it is a great price
For a small vice.
Des. In troth, I think thou wouldst not.

Emil. In troth, I think I should; and undo 't when I had done. Marry, I would not do such a thing for a joint-ring, nor for measures of lawn, nor for gowns, petticoats, nor caps, nor any petty exhibition; but, for all the whole world,—why, who would not make her husband a cuckold to make him a monarch? I should venture purgatory for 't.

Des. Beshrew me, if I would do such a wrong
For the whole world.

Emil. Why, the wrong is but a wrong i' the world; and having the world for your labour, 'tis a wrong in your own world, and you might quickly make it right.

Des. I do not think there is any such woman.

Emil. Yes, a dozen; and as many to the vantage as would store the world they played for.
But I do think it is their husbands' faults
If wives do fall: say that they slack their duties,
And pour our treasures into foreign laps,
Or else break out in peevish jealousies,
Throwing restraint upon us; or say they strike us,
Or scant our former having in despite;

ness, harshness. **checks,** rebukes. 32. **But to,** not to. 34. **night-gown,** dressing-gown. 41-57. **The poor soul,** etc. Desdemona's song is a popular ballad apparently well known in Shakespeare's time. In the versions preserved the forsaken lover is a man. Shakespeare has changed it to apply to Desdemona, and has made it personal by introducing the pathetic little sketch of Barbary, her mother's maid. 73. **joint-ring,** a ring made in separable halves as a lover's token. 75. **exhibition,** gift, present. 85-86. **to the vantage,** in addition, to boot. 89. **pour . . . laps,** i.e., are unfaithful. 92. **scant . . . despite,** reduce our allowance to spite us.

Why, we have galls, and though we have some grace,
Yet have we some revenge. Let husbands know
Their wives have sense like them: they see and smell
And have their palates both for sweet and sour,
As husbands have. What is it that they do
When they change us for others? Is it sport?
I think it is: and doth affection breed it?
I think it doth: is 't frailty that thus errs?
It is so too: and have not we affections,
Desires for sport, and frailty, as men have?
Then let them use us well: else let them know,
The ills we do, their ills instruct us so.
Des. Good night, good night: heaven me such uses send,
Not to pick bad from bad, but by bad mend! *Exeunt.*

ACT V.

SCENE I. [*Cyprus. A street.*]

Enter IAGO *and* RODERIGO.

Iago. Here stand behind this bulk; straight will he come:
Wear thy good rapier bare, and put it home:
Quick, quick; fear nothing; I'll be at thy elbow:
It makes us, or it mars us; think on that,
And fix most firm thy resolution.
Rod. Be near at hand; I may miscarry in 't.
Iago. Here, at thy hand: be bold, and take thy stand. [*Retires.*]
Rod. I have no great devotion to the deed;
And yet he hath given me satisfying reasons:
'Tis but a man gone. Forth, my sword: he dies.
Iago. I have rubb'd this young quat almost to the sense,
And he grows angry. Now, whether he kill Cassio,
Or Cassio him, or each do kill the other,
Every way makes my gain: live Roderigo,
He calls me to a restitution large
Of gold and jewels that I bobb'd from him,
As gifts to Desdemona;
It must not be: if Cassio do remain,
He hath a daily beauty in his life
That makes me ugly; and, besides, the Moor
May unfold me to him; there stand I in much peril:
No, he must die. But so: I hear him coming.

Enter CASSIO.

Rod. I know his gait, 'tis he.—Villain, thou diest! [*Makes a pass at Cassio.*]
Cas. That thrust had been mine enemy indeed,
But that my coat is better than thou know'st:
I will make proof of thine. [*Draws, and wounds Roderigo.*]
Rod. O, I am slain!
[*Iago from behind wounds Cassio in the leg, and exit.*]
Cas. I am maim'd for ever. Help, ho! murder! murder! [*Falls.*]

Enter OTHELLO.

Oth. The voice of Cassio: Iago keeps his word.
Rod. O, villain that I am!
Oth. It is even so.
Cas. O, help, ho! light! a surgeon!
Oth. 'Tis he:—O brave Iago, honest and just,
That hast such noble sense of thy friend's wrong!
Thou teachest me. Minion, your dear lies dead,
And your unblest fate hies: strumpet, I come.
Forth of my heart those charms, thine eyes, are blotted;
Thy bed, lust-stain'd, shall with lust's blood be spotted. *Exit Othello.*

Enter LODOVICO *and* GRATIANO.

Cas. What, ho! no watch? no passage? murder! murder!
Gra. 'Tis some mischance; the cry is very direful.
Cas. O, help!
Lod. Hark!
Rod. O wretched villain!
Lod. Two or three groan: it is a heavy night:
These may be counterfeits: let 's think 't unsafe
To come in to the cry without more help.
Rod. Nobody come? then shall I bleed to death.
Lod. Hark!

Enter IAGO [*with a light*].

Gra. Here 's one comes in his shirt, with light and weapons.
Iago. Who 's there? whose noise is this that cries on murder?
Lod. We do not know.
Iago. Did not you hear a cry?
Cas. Here, here! for heaven's sake, help me!
Iago. What 's the matter?
Gra. This is Othello's ancient, as I take it.
Lod. The same indeed; a very valiant fellow.
Iago. What are you here that cry so grievously?
Cas. Iago? O, I am spoil'd, undone by villains!
Give me some help.
Iago. O me, lieutenant! what villains have done this?
Cas. I think that one of them is hereabout,
And cannot make away.
Iago. O treacherous villains!
What are you there? come in, and give some help.
[*To Lodovico and Gratiano.*]
Rod. O, help me here!
Cas. That 's one of them.
Iago. O murd'rous slave! O villain! [*Stabs Roderigo.*]
Rod. O damn'd Iago! O inhuman dog!
Iago. Kill men i' th' dark!—Where be these bloody thieves?—
How silent is this town!—Ho! murder! murder!—
What may you be? are you of good or evil?
Lod. As you shall prove us, praise us.
Iago. Signior Lodovico?
Lod. He, sir.
Iago. I cry you mercy. Here 's Cassio hurt by villains.
Gra. Cassio!
Iago. How is 't, brother!
Cas. My leg is cut in two.

93. **have galls,** are capable of resenting injury and insult. **grace,** i.e., to forgive.
ACT V. SCENE I. 1. **bulk,** framework projecting from the front of a shop. 11. **quat,** pimple, pustule; used contemptuously. **to the sense,** to the quick. 16. **bobb'd,** filched cunningly. 25. **coat,** coat of mail. 37. **passage,** people passing. 42. **heavy,** thick, cloudy. 48. **cries on,** cries out. 65. **What,** who. 82. **chair,** sedan chair. 85. **trash,** worthless thing, i.e., Bianca. 106. **gastness,** terror, ghastliness. 129.

Iago. Marry, heaven forbid!
Light, gentlemen: I'll bind it with my shirt.

Enter BIANCA.

Bian. What is the matter, ho? who is 't that cried?
Iago. Who is 't that cried?
Bian. O my dear Cassio! my sweet Cassio!
O Cassio, Cassio, Cassio!
Iago. O notable strumpet! Cassio, may you suspect
Who they should be that have thus mangled you?
Cas. No.
Gra. I am sorry to find you thus: I have been to seek you.
Iago. Lend me a garter. So. O, for a chair,
To bear him easily hence!
Bian. Alas, he faints! O Cassio, Cassio, Cassio!
Iago. Gentlemen all, I do suspect this trash
To be a party in this injury.
Patience awhile, good Cassio. Come, come;
Lend me a light. Know we this face or no?
Alas, my friend and my dear countryman
Roderigo! no:—yes, sure:—O heaven! Roderigo.
Gra. What, of Venice?
Iago. Even he, sir: did you know him?
Gra. Know him! ay.
Iago. Signior Gratiano? I cry your gentle pardon;
These bloody accidents must excuse my manners,
That so neglected you.
Gra. I am glad to see you.
Iago. How do you, Cassio? O, a chair, a chair!
Gra. Roderigo!
Iago. He, he, 'tis he. [*A chair brought in.*] O, that 's well said; the chair.
Some good man bear him carefully from hence;
I'll fetch the general's surgeon. [*To Bianca*] For you, mistress,
Save you your labour. He that lies slain here, Cassio,
Was my dear friend: what malice was between you?
Cas. None in the world; nor do I know the man.
Iago. [*To Bian.*] What, look you pale? O, bear him out o' th' air. [*Cassio and Roderigo are borne off.*]
Stay you, good gentlemen. Look you pale, mistress?
Do you perceive the gastness of her eye?
Nay, if you stare, we shall hear more anon.
Behold her well; I pray you, look upon her:
Do you see, gentlemen? nay, guiltiness will speak,
Though tongues were out of use.

[*Enter* EMILIA.]

Emil. 'Las, what 's the matter? what 's the matter, husband?
Iago. Cassio hath here been set on in the dark
By Roderigo and fellows that are scap'd:
He 's almost slain, and Roderigo dead.
Emil. Alas, good gentleman! alas, good Cassio!
Iago. This is the fruit of whoring. Prithee, Emilia,
Go know of Cassio where he supp'd to-night.
[*To Bianca*] What, do you shake at that?
Bian. He supp'd at my house; but I therefore shake not.
Iago. O, did he so? I charge you, go with me.
Emil. Fie, fie upon thee, strumpet!
Bian. I am no strumpet; but of life as honest
As you that thus abuse me.
Emil. As I! foh! fie upon thee!
Iago. Kind gentlemen, let 's go see poor Cassio dress'd.
Come, mistress, you must tell 's another tale.
Emilia, run you to the citadel,
And tell my lord and lady what hath happ'd.
Will you go on afore? [*Aside*] This is the night
That either makes me or fordoes me quite. *Exeunt.*

SCENE II. [*A bedchamber in the castle.*]

Enter OTHELLO [*with a light*]; DESDEMONA *in her bed.*

Oth. It is the cause, it is the cause, my soul,—
Let me not name it to you, you chaste stars!—
It is the cause. Yet I'll not shed her blood;
Nor scar that whiter skin of hers than snow,
And smooth as monumental alabaster.
Yet she must die, else she'll betray more men.
Put out the light, and then put out the light:
If I quench thee, thou flaming minister,
I can again thy former light restore,
Should I repent me: but once put out thy light,
Thou cunning'st pattern of excelling nature,
I know not where is that Promethean heat
That can thy light relume. When I have pluck'd the rose,
I cannot give it vital growth again,
It needs must wither: I'll smell thee on the tree. [*Kissing her.*]
O balmy breath, that dost almost persuade
Justice to break her sword! One more, one more.
Be thus when thou art dead, and I will kill thee,
And love thee after. One more, and that 's the last:
So sweet was ne'er so fatal. I must weep,
But they are cruel tears: this sorrow 's heavenly;
It strikes where it doth love. She wakes.
Des. Who 's there? Othello?
Oth. Ay, Desdemona.
Des. Will you come to bed, my lord?
Oth. Have you pray'd to-night, Desdemon?
Des. Ay, my lord.
Oth. If you bethink yourself of any crime
Unreconcil'd as yet to heaven and grace,
Solicit for it straight.
Des. Alack, my lord, what may you mean by that?
Oth. Well, do it, and be brief; I will walk by:
I would not kill thy unprepared spirit;
No; heaven forfend! I would not kill thy soul.
Des. Talk you of killing?
Oth. Ay, I do.
Des. Then heaven
Have mercy on me!
Oth. Amen, with all my heart!
Des. If you say so, I hope you will not kill me.
Oth. Hum!
Des. And yet I fear you; for you 're fatal then
When your eyes roll so: why I should fear I know not,
Since guiltiness I know not; but yet I feel I fear.

fordoes, undoes, ruins. Iago's uneasiness is again apparent in this scene.

SCENE II. 1. **It is the cause,** i.e., the cause of justice on which Othello must act, Desdemona's deed, which is too unmentionable to be named to the chaste stars. 12. **Promethean heat,** divine fire; allusion to the theft of fire from heaven by Prometheus. 13. **relume,** rekindle. 21. **this . . . heavenly,** this tenderness, with which I lament the punishment which justice compels me to inflict, is a holy passion (Johnson).

Oth. Think on thy sins.
Des. They are loves I bear to you.
Oth. Ay, and for that thou diest.
Des. That death 's unnatural that kills for loving.
Alas, why gnaw you so your nether lip?
Some bloody passion shakes your very frame:
These are portents; but yet I hope, I hope,
They do not point on me.
Oth. Peace, and be still!
Des. I will so. What 's the matter?
Oth. That handkerchief which I so lov'd and gave thee
Thou gav'st to Cassio.
Des. No, by my life and soul!
Send for the man, and ask him.
Oth. Sweet soul, take heed,
Take heed of perjury; thou art on thy deathbed.
Des. Ay, but not yet to die.
Oth. Yes, presently:
Therefore confess thee freely of thy sin;
For to deny each article with oath
Cannot remove nor choke the strong conception
That I do groan withal. Thou art to die.
Des. Then Lord have mercy on me!
Oth. I say, amen.
Des. And have you mercy too! I never did
Offend you in my life; never lov'd Cassio
But with such general warranty of heaven
As I might love; I never gave him token.
Oth. By heaven, I saw my handkerchief in 's hand.
O perjur'd woman! thou dost stone my heart,
And makes me call what I intend to do
A murder, which I thought a sacrifice:
I saw the handkerchief.
Des. He found it then;
I never gave it him: send for him hither;
Let him confess a truth.
Oth. He hath confess'd.
Des. What, my lord?
Oth. That he hath us'd thee.
Des. How? unlawfully?
Oth. Ay.
Des. He will not say so.
Oth. No, his mouth is stopp'd;
Honest Iago hath ta'en order for 't.
Des. O! my fear interprets: what, is he dead?
Oth. Had all his hairs been lives, my great revenge
Had stomach for them all.
Des. Alas! he is betray'd and I undone.
Oth. Out, strumpet! weep'st thou for him to my face?
Des. O, banish me, my lord, but kill me not!
Oth. Down, strumpet!
Des. Kill me to-morrow: let me live to-night!
Oth. Nay, if you strive,—
Des. But half an hour!
Oth. Being done, there is no pause.
Des. But while I say one prayer!
Oth. It is too late. *Smothers her.*
Emil. (At the door) My lord, my lord! what, ho! my lord, my lord!
Oth. What noise is this? Not dead? not yet quite dead?
I that am cruel am yet merciful;
I would not have thee linger in thy pain:
So, so.
Emil. (Within) What, ho! my lord, my lord!
Oth. Who 's there?
Emil. [*Within*] O, good my lord, I would speak a word with you!
Oth. Yes: 'tis Emilia. By and by. She 's dead.
'Tis like she comes to speak of Cassio's death.—
The noise was here. Ha! no more moving?
Still as the grave. Shall she come in? were 't good?—
I think she stirs again:—no. What 's best to do?
If she come in, she'll sure speak to my wife:
My wife! my wife! what wife? I have no wife.
O, insupportable! O heavy hour!
Methinks it should be now a huge eclipse
Of sun and moon, and that th' affrighted globe
Should yawn at alteration.
Emil. [*Within*] I do beseech you
That I may speak with you, O, good my lord!
Oth. I had forgot thee: O, come in, Emilia:
Soft; by and by. Let me the curtains draw.
Where art thou? [*Closes bed-curtains and opens door.*]

Enter EMILIA.

What 's the matter with thee now?
Emil. O, my good lord, yonder 's foul murders done!
Oth. What, now?
Emil. But now, my lord.
Oth. It is the very error of the moon;
She comes more nearer earth than she was wont,
And makes men mad.
Emil. Cassio, my lord, hath kill'd a young Venetian
Call'd Roderigo.
Oth. Roderigo kill'd!
And Cassio kill'd!
Emil. No, Cassio is not kill'd.
Oth. Not Cassio kill'd! then murder 's out of tune,
And sweet revenge grows harsh.
Des. O, falsely, falsely murder'd!
Emil. Alas, what cry is that?
Oth. That! what?
Emil. Out, and alas! that was my lady's voice.
Help! help, ho! help! O lady, speak again!
Sweet Desdemona! O sweet mistress, speak!
Des. A guiltless death I die.
Emil. O, who hath done this deed?
Des. Nobody; I myself. Farewell:
Commend me to my kind lord: O, farewell! [*Dies.*]
Oth. Why, how should she be murd'red?
Emil. Alas, who knows?
Oth. You heard her say herself, it was not I.
Emil. She said so: I must needs report the truth.
Oth. She 's, like a liar, gone to burning hell:
'Twas I that kill'd her.
Emil. O, the more angel she,
And you the blacker devil!
Oth. She turn'd to folly, and she was a whore.

55. **conception,** plan, intention. 63. **stone,** turn to stone, harden; Othello means that he will be tempted to kill her in sheer anger because of her perjury. 72. **ta'en order,** taken measures. 82. **Being . . . pause,** i.e., when the execution of the deed has once begun, there is no stopping. 88. **So, so.** The stage tradition, dating apparently from the time of Garrick, is for Othello to stab Desdemona. There is, however, no necessity for assuming such an action, and it is more likely that he renews his attempt to smother her (Parrott). 101. **yawn,** gape in amazement, i.e., there would be an earthquake, since according to Pliny, earthquakes often happen during eclipses. **at alteration,** at the change. 109. **error,** aberration, irregularity. 132. **folly,** unchastity. 145. **chrysolite,** the golden stone; a name given to various

Emil. Thou dost belie her, and thou art a devil.
Oth. She was false as water.
Emil. Thou art rash as fire, to say
That she was false: O, she was heavenly true!
Oth. Cassio did top her; ask thy husband else.
O, I were damn'd beneath all depth in hell,
But that I did proceed upon just grounds
To this extremity. Thy husband knew it all.
Emil. My husband!
Oth. Thy husband.
Emil. That she was false to wedlock?
Oth. Ay, with Cassio. Nay, had she been true,
If heaven would make me such another world
Of one entire and perfect chrysolite,
I 'ld not have sold her for it.
Emil. My husband!
Oth. Ay, 'twas he that told me first:
An honest man he is, and hates the slime
That sticks on filthy deeds.
Emil. My husband!
Oth. What needs this iterance, woman? I say thy husband.
Emil. O mistress, villany hath made mocks with love!
My husband say that she was false!
Oth. He, woman;
I say thy husband: dost understand the word?
My friend, thy husband, honest, honest Iago.
Emil. If he say so, may his pernicious soul
Rot half a grain a day! he lies to th' heart:
She was too fond of her most filthy bargain.
Oth. Ha!
Emil. Do thy worst:
This deed of thine is no more worthy heaven
Than thou wast worthy her.
Oth. Peace, you were best.
Emil. Thou hast not half that power to do me harm
As I have to be hurt. O gull! O dolt!
As ignorant as dirt! thou hast done a deed—
I care not for thy sword; I'll make thee known,
Though I lost twenty lives.—Help! help, ho! help!
The Moor hath kill'd my mistress! Murder! murder!

Enter MONTANO, GRATIANO, *and* IAGO [*with others*].

Mon. What is the matter? How now, general!
Emil. O, are you come, Iago? you have done well,
That men must lay their murders on your neck.
Gra. What is the matter?
Emil. Disprove this villain, if thou be'st a man:
He says thou told'st him that his wife was false:
I know thou didst not, thou 'rt not such a villain:
Speak, for my heart is full.
Iago. I told him what I thought, and told no more
Than what he found himself was apt and true.
Emil. But did you ever tell him she was false?
Iago. I did.
Emil. You told a lie; an odious, damned lie;
Upon my soul, a lie, a wicked lie.
She false with Cassio!—did you say with Cassio?
Iago. With Cassio, mistress. Go to, charm your tongue.
Emil. I will not charm my tongue; I am bound to speak:
My mistress here lies murdered in her bed,—
All. O heavens forfend!
Emil. And your reports have set the murder on.
Oth. Nay, stare not, masters: it is true, indeed.
Gra. 'Tis a strange truth.
Mon. O monstrous act!
Emil. Villany, villany, villany!
I think upon 't, I think: I smell 't: O villany!—
I thought so then:—I'll kill myself for grief:—
O villany, villany!
Iago. What, are you mad? I charge you, get you home.
Emil. Good gentlemen, let me have leave to speak:
'Tis proper I obey him, but not now.
Perchance, Iago, I will ne'er go home.
Oth. O! O! O! [*He falls on the bed.*]
Emil. Nay, lay thee down and roar;
For thou hast kill'd the sweetest innocent
That e'er did lift up eye.
Oth. [*Rising*] O, she was foul!
I scarce did know you, uncle: there lies your niece,
Whose breath, indeed, these hands have newly stopp'd:
I know this act shows horrible and grim.
Gra. Poor Desdemon! I am glad thy father 's dead:
Thy match was mortal to him, and pure grief
Shore his old thread in twain: did he live now,
This sight would make him do a desperate turn,
Yea, curse his better angel from his side,
And fall to reprobation.
Oth. 'Tis pitiful; but yet Iago knows
That she with Cassio hath the act of shame
A thousand times committed; Cassio confess'd it:
And she did gratify his amorous works
With that recognizance and pledge of love
Which I first gave her; I saw it in his hand:
It was a handkerchief, an antique token
My father gave my mother.
Emil. O heaven! O heavenly pow'rs!
Iago. Come, hold your peace.
Emil. 'Twill out, 'twill out: I peace!
No, I will speak as liberal as the north:
Let heaven and men and devils, let them all,
All, all, cry shame against me, yet I'll speak.
Iago. Be wise, and get you home.
Emil. I will not. [*Iago offers to stab Emilia.*]
Gra. Fie!
Your sword upon a woman?
Emil. O thou dull Moor! that handkerchief thou speak'st of
I found by fortune and did give my husband;
For often, with a solemn earnestness,
More than indeed belong'd to such a trifle,
He begg'd of me to steal it.
Iago. Villanous whore!
Emil. She give it Cassio! no, alas! I found it,
And I did give 't my husband.
Iago. Filth, thou liest!
Emil. By heaven, I do not, I do not, gentlemen.

precious stones of green color. 150. **iterance,** iteration, repetition. 151. **made mocks with,** derided, made sport of. 163. **to be hurt,** i.e., to endure hurting. 177. **apt,** natural, likely. 183. **charm,** keep silent. 192. **then,** i.e., at some earlier time, probably IV, ii, 130-144, when she suspected the machinations of *some eternal villain:* she did not, however, know that villain to be Iago until this moment. 206. **Shore,** cut. 209. **reprobation,** damnation, rejection by God; so Q; F: *reprobance,* possibly to be preferred. 214. **recognizance,** token. 217. **My . . . mother.** This statement is hardly consistent with that in III, iv, 56. 220. **liberal as the north,** freely as the north wind. 226. **fortune,** chance.

O murd'rous coxcomb! what should such a fool
Do with so good a wife?
Oth. Are there no stones in heaven
But what serves for the thunder?—Precious villain!
[*He runs at Iago: Iago, from behind, stabs Emilia, and exit.*]
Gra. The woman falls; sure, he hath kill'd his wife.
Emil. Ay, ay: O, lay me by my mistress' side.
Gra. He 's gone, but his wife 's kill'd.
Mon. 'Tis a notorious villain. Take you this weapon,
Which I have here recover'd from the Moor:
Come, guard the door without; let him not pass,
But kill him rather. I'll after that same villain,
For 'tis a damned slave.
Exit [*with all but Othello and Emilia*].
Oth. I am not valiant neither,
But every puny whipster gets my sword:
But why should honour outlive honesty?
Let it go all.
Emil. What did thy song bode, lady?
Hark, canst thou hear me? I will play the swan,
And die in music. [*Singing*] Willow, willow, willow.—
Moor, she was chaste; she lov'd thee, cruel Moor;
So come my soul to bliss, as I speak true;
So speaking as I think, I die, I die. [*Dies.*]
Oth. I have another weapon in this chamber;
It is a sword of Spain, the ice-brook's temper:—
O, here it is. Uncle, I must come forth.
Gra. [*Within*] If thou attempt it, it will cost thee dear:
Thou hast no weapon, and perforce must suffer.
Oth. Look in upon me then and speak with me,
Or, naked as I am, I will assault thee.

[*Enter* GRATIANO.]

Gra. What is the matter?
Oth. Behold, I have a weapon;
A better never did itself sustain
Upon a soldier's thigh: I have seen the day,
That, with this little arm and this good sword,
I have made my way through more impediments
Than twenty times your stop: but, O vain boast!
Who can control his fate? 'tis not so now.
Be not afraid, though you do see me weapon'd;
Here is my journey's end, here is my butt,
And very sea-mark of my utmost sail.
Do you go back dismay'd? 'tis a lost fear;
Man but a rush against Othello's breast,
And he retires. Where should Othello go?
Now, how dost thou look now? O ill-starr'd wench!
Pale as thy smock! when we shall meet at compt,
This look of thine will hurl my soul from heaven,
And fiends will snatch at it. Cold, cold, my girl!
Even like thy chastity. O cursed, cursed slave!
Whip me, ye devils,
From the possession of this heavenly sight!
Blow me about in winds! roast me in sulphur!
Wash me in steep-down gulfs of liquid fire!
O Desdemon! Dead Desdemon! dead!
Oh! Oh!

Enter LODOVICO, CASSIO [*carried in a chair*], MONTANO, *and* IAGO [*prisoner*], *with* Officers.

Lod. Where is this rash and most unfortunate man?
Oth. That 's he that was Othello: here I am.
Lod. Where is that viper? bring the villain forth.
Oth. I look down towards his feet; but that 's a fable.
If that thou be'st a devil, I cannot kill thee.
[*Wounds Iago.*]
Lod. Wrench his sword from him.
Iago. I bleed, sir; but not kill'd.
Oth. I am not sorry neither: I 'ld have thee live;
For, in my sense, 'tis happiness to die.
Lod. O thou Othello, that wert once so good,
Fall'n in the practice of a damned slave,
What shall be said to thee?
Oth. Why, any thing:
An honourable murderer, if you will;
For nought I did in hate, but all in honour.
Lod. This wretch hath part confess'd his villany:
Did you and he consent in Cassio's death?
Oth. Ay.
Cas. Dear general, I never gave you cause.
Oth. I do believe it, and I ask you pardon.
Will you, I pray, demand that demi-devil
Why he hath thus ensnar'd my soul and body?
Iago. Demand me nothing: what you know, you know:
From this time forth I never will speak word.
Lod. What, not to pray?
Gra. Torments will ope your lips.
Oth. Well, thou dost best.
Lod. Sir, you shall understand what hath befall'n,
Which, as I think, you know not. Here is a letter
Found in the pocket of the slain Roderigo;
And here another: the one of them imports
The death of Cassio to be undertook
By Roderigo.
Oth. O villain!
Cas. Most heathenish and most gross!
Lod. Now here 's another discontented paper,
Found in his pocket too; and this, it seems,
Roderigo meant t' have sent this damned villain;
But that belike Iago in the interim
Came in and satisfied him.
Oth. O thou pernicious caitiff!—
How came you, Cassio, by that handkerchief
That was my wife's?
Cas. I found it in my chamber:
And he himself confess'd but even now
That there he dropp'd it for a special purpose
Which wrought to his desire.
Oth. O fool! fool! fool!
Cas. There is besides in Roderigo's letter,
How he upbraids Iago, that he made him
Brave me upon the watch; whereon it came
That I was cast: and even but now he spake,
After long seeming dead, Iago hurt him,
Iago set him on.
Lod. You must forsake this room, and go with us:
Your power and your command is taken off,
And Cassio rules in Cyprus. For this slave,

233. **coxcomb,** fool; addressed to Othello. 234. **stones in heaven,** thunderbolts. It was supposed that real stones fell with the thunder and caused the damage. 244. **whipster,** contemptible fellow. 245. **honour outlive honesty.** Othello realizes that he has done a shameful deed; he asks why his reputation for valor should endure. 253. **ice-brook's temper,** usually defined as "tempered in ice-cold water." F has *Ice brookes,* Q: *Isebrookes;* Onions notes that *Isebrooke* is the Elizabethan form for *Innsbruck,* once noted for fine steel. 258. **naked,** unarmed. 264. **stop,** power. 267. **butt,** mark for archery, goal, limit. 268. **sea-mark,** beacon (marking his destination or limit). 270. **Man,** provide, as in manning a gun. **rush,** reed. 273. **compt,** account, judgment day. 286. **towards his feet,** i.e., to see if they were cloven like a devil's. 314. **discontented,** expressing dissatisfaction. 318. **caitiff,** wretch. 326. **Brave,** defy. 327. **cast,** dismissed. 331. **taken off,** taken away.

If there be any cunning cruelty
That can torment him much and hold him long,
It shall be his. You shall close prisoner rest,
Till that the nature of your fault be known
To the Venetian state. Come, bring him away.
Oth. Soft you; a word or two before you go.
I have done the state some service, and they know 't.
No more of that. I pray you, in your letters,
When you shall these unlucky deeds relate,
Speak of me as I am; nothing extenuate,
Nor set down aught in malice: then must you speak
Of one that lov'd not wisely but too well;
Of one not easily jealous, but being wrought,
Perplex'd in the extreme; of one whose hand,
Like the base Judean, threw a pearl away
Richer than all his tribe; of one whose subdu'd eyes,
Albeit unused to the melting mood,
Drop tears as fast as the Arabian trees
Their medicinable gum. Set you down this;
And say besides, that in Aleppo once,
Where a malignant and a turban'd Turk
Beat a Venetian and traduc'd the state,
I took by th' throat the circumcised dog,
And smote him, thus. [*Stabs himself.*]
Lod. O bloody period!
Gra. All that is spoke is marr'd.
Oth. I kiss'd thee ere I kill'd thee: no way but this;
Killing myself, to die upon a kiss.
[*Falls on the bed, and*] *dies.*
Cas. This did I fear, but thought he had no weapon;
For he was great of heart.
Lod. [*To Iago*] O Spartan dog,
More fell than anguish, hunger, or the sea!
Look on the tragic loading of this bed;
This is thy work: the object poisons sight;
Let it be hid. Gratiano, keep the house,
And seize upon the fortunes of the Moor,
For they succeed on you. To you, lord governor,
Remains the censure of this hellish villain;
The time, the place, the torture: O, enforce it!
Myself will straight aboard; and to the state
This heavy act with heavy heart relate. *Exeunt.*

342. **extenuate,** diminish, depreciate; the idea is contrasted with the thought of *malice* in the following line. 346. **Perplex'd,** confounded, distracted. 347. **Judean,** infidel or disbeliever. There may be a reference to Herod, who slew Miriamne in a fit of jealousy, or to Judas Iscariot, the betrayer of Christ. The reading is much disputed, and some editors (including Globe) prefer the Q reading of *Indian.* 350-351. **tears . . . gum.** Back of the comparison of tears to Arabian gums lies Pliny's description of the aromatic wealth of Arabia. 351. **medicinable,** so F. Some editors, including Globe, prefer Q reading, *med'cinal.* 352. **Aleppo,** a Turkish city where the Venetians had special trading privileges. It is stated that it was immediate death for a Christian to strike a Turk in Aleppo; Othello risked his life for the honor of Venice. 357. **period,** termination, conclusion. 361. **Spartan dog.** Spartan dogs were noted for their savagery.

KING LEAR

In *King Lear*, Shakespeare pushes to its limit the hypothesis of a malign or at least indifferent universe in which man's life is meaningless and brutal. Few plays other than *Hamlet* and *Macbeth* approach *King Lear* in evoking the wretchedness of human existence, and even they cannot match the devastating spectacle of Gloucester blinded or Cordelia dead in Lear's arms. The responses of the chief characters are correspondingly searing. "Is man no more than this?" rages Lear. "Unaccommodated man is no more but such a poor, bare, forked animal as thou art" (III,iv). Life he calls a "great stage of fools," an endless torment: "the first time that we smell the air, We wawl and cry" (IV,vi). Gloucester's despair takes the form of accusing the gods of gleeful malice toward man: "As flies to wanton boys, are we to th' gods, They kill us for their sport" (IV,i). Gloucester's ministering son Edgar can offer him no greater consolation than stoic resolve: "Men must endure Their going hence, even as their coming hither: Ripeness is all" (V,ii). These statements need not be read as choric expressions of "meaning" for the play as a whole, but they do attest to the depth of suffering. In no other Shakespearean play does injustice appear to triumph so ferociously, for so long, and with such impunity. Will the heavens countenance this reign of injustice on earth? Retribution is late in coming and is not certainly the work of the heavens themselves. For, at the last, we must confront the wanton death of the innocent Cordelia, a death no longer willed even by the villain who arranged her execution. "Is this the promis'd end?" asks Kent, stressing the unparalleled horror of the catastrophe.

Throughout its earlier history, in fact, the ancient story of King Lear had always ended happily. In the popular folktale of Cinderella, to which the legend of Lear's daughters bears a significant resemblance, the youngest and virtuous daughter triumphs over her two older wicked sisters and is married to her princely wooer. Geoffrey of Monmouth's *Historia Regum Britanniae* (c. 1136), the earliest known version of the Lear story, records that after Lear is overthrown by his sons-in-law (more than by his daughters), he is restored to his throne by the intervention of the French king and is allowed to enjoy his kingdom and Cordelia's love until his natural death. (Cordelia, as his successor, is later dethroned and murdered by her wicked nephews, but that is another story.) Subsequent Tudor versions of the Lear story with which Shakespeare was familiar—John Higgins' account in *The First parte of the Mirour for Magistrates* (1574), Holinshed's *Chronicles* (1587), Spenser's *The Faerie Queene*, II,x,27–32, and a play called *The True Chronicle History of King Leir* (by 1594, published 1605)—all retain the happy ending. The tragic pattern may have been suggested instead by Shakespeare's probable source for the Gloucester-Edgar-Edmund plot, Sir Philip Sidney's *Arcadia*, II,10, in which the Paphlagonian king is the victim of filial ingratitude and deceit. Shakespeare's genius linked the two plots, employing in both the themes of exile, cruel persecution, and the barrenness of human existence.

Yet even Shakespeare's great authority was not sufficient to put down the craving for a romantic solution. Nahum Tate's adaptation (1681), which banished the Fool as indecorous for a trágedy and united Edgar and Cordelia in marriage, placing Lear once again on his throne, actually held the English stage for about 150 years. David Garrick restored some of Shakespeare's lines, and Edmund Kean restored the tragic ending, but not until 1838 was Shakespeare's play again performed more or less as he wrote it. Dr. Johnson evidently spoke for most eighteenth-century audiences when he confessed that he could not bring himself to read Shakespeare's text. Cordelia's slaughter violated that age's longing for "poetic justice." Her death implied a wanton universe and so counseled philosophic despair. Today, however, the relentless honesty of Shakespeare's tragic vision, and his refusal to accept easy answers, convince us that Shakespeare was right to defy the conventions of his source. He evidently wrote *King Lear* some time before it was performed at court in December of 1606, probably in 1605 and certainly no earlier than 1603–1604; Edgar's speeches as Tom o' Bedlam contain references to Samuel Harsnett's *Declaration of Egregious Popishe Impostures* which was registered for publication in March of 1603. Thus *King Lear* was probably written between *Othello* (c. 1603–1604) and *Macbeth* (c. 1606–1607), when Shakespeare was at the very height of his tragic power.

It seems a paradox that Shakespeare should have chosen for this supremely mature work a fable derived from folklore and legend, with many of the wondrous and implausible circumstances of popular romance. A prose rendition might almost begin, "Once upon a time there was a king who had three daughters. . . ." In part, Shakespeare's purpose seems to have been to arouse romantic expectations only to crush them by aborting the conventional happy ending, thus setting up a dramatic tension between an idealized world of make-believe and the actual world of disappointed hopes. Just as importantly, however, the folktale element focuses our attention on the archetypal situations with which the story is concerned: rivalry between siblings, fear of parental rejection, and, conversely, parental fear of children's ingratitude. The "unrealistic" contrast between Cordelia and her wicked sisters, or between Edgar and Edmund, is something we accept as a convention of storytelling because it expresses so vividly the psychic truth of rivalry between brothers and sisters. We identify with Cordelia and Edgar as virtuous children whose worth is misunderstood, and who are losing to hated siblings the contest for parental approval. (In folklore the rejecting parent is usually a stepparent, to signify our conviction that he or she is not a true parent at all.) Similarly, we accept as a convention of storytelling the equally "unrealistic" device by which Lear tests the love of his daughters. Here we identify with Lear's universal longing to be loved and appreciated in return for the kindnesses he has performed. This identification is particularly strong for middle-aged readers or viewers of Shakespeare with grown children of their own. Is it too much to ask, after parents have provided for their children and grown old, that those children should express their gratitude and look after the parents?

The difficulty is that the parable of Lear and his children presents two contrasting viewpoints, that of the unappreciated child and that of the unwanted aging parent. Tragic misunderstanding is inevitable and outweighs the question of assessing blame. From Lear's point of view, Cordelia's silence is a truculent scanting of obedience. What he has devised is, after all, only a prearranged formality, with Cordelia to receive the richest third of England. Cannot such a ceremony be answered with the conventional hyperbole of courtly language, to which the king's ear is attuned? Don't parents have a right to be verbally reassured of their children's love? How can children be so laconic about such a precious matter? For her part, however, Cordelia senses that Lear is demanding love as payment for his parental kindliness, *quid pro quo*. True love ought rather to be selfless, as the King of France tells Burgundy: "Love's not love When it is mingled with regards that stand Aloof from th' entire point." Is Cordelia being asked to prefer Lear before her own husband-to-be? Is this the price she must pay for her upbringing? Lear's ego seems fully capable of demanding this self-sacrifice from his daughters, especially his favorite, Cordelia: he has given them his whole kingdom, now let them care for him as befits his royal rank and patriarchal role. The "second childishness" of old age can often bring with it such a self-centered longing to monopolize the lives of one's children, and to be oneself a child again. Besides, as king, Lear has long grown accustomed to flattery and absolute obedience. Goneril and Regan are content to flatter and promise obedience, knowing they will turn him out once he has relinquished his authority. Cordelia, of course, refuses to lie in this fashion, but she also will not yield to Lear's implicit request for her undivided affection. Part of her must be loyal to her own husband and her children, in the natural cycle of the generations. "When I shall wed, That lord whose hand must take my plight shall carry Half my love with him, half my care and duty." Marriage will not prevent her from loving, honoring, and obeying her father as is fit, but will establish a new priority. To

Lear, as to many fathers contemplating a daughter's marriage, this savors of desertion.

Lear is sadly deficient in self-knowledge. As Regan drily observes, "he hath ever but slenderly known himself," and has grown ever more changeable and imperious with age. By dividing his kingdom in three, ostensibly so that "future strife May be prevented now," he instead guarantees a civil war and French invasion. His intention of setting aside his regal authority while still retaining "The name, and all th' additions to a king," betrays an abysmal lack of comprehension of the realities of power. He hearkens to poisoned flattery but interprets well-intended criticism, whether from Cordelia or Kent, as treason. These failures in no sense justify what Lear's ungrateful children do to him; as he later says, just before going mad, "I am a man More sinn'd against than sinning" (III,ii). They are, however, tokens of his worldly insolence from which he must fall. The process is a painful one, but since it brings self-discovery it is not without its compensations. Indeed a central paradox of the play is that by no other way could Lear have learned what human suffering and need are all about.

Lear's Fool is instrumental in elucidating this paradox. The Fool offers Lear advice in palatable form as mere foolery or entertainment, and thus obtains a hearing when Kent and Cordelia have been angrily dismissed. Beneath his seemingly innocent jibes, however, are plain warnings of the looming disaster Lear blindly refuses to acknowledge. The Fool knows, as indeed any fool could tell, that Goneril and Regan are remorseless and unnatural. The real fool, therefore, is Lear himself, for having placed himself in their power. In a metaphor of which the Renaissance was incessantly fond—as in Erasmus' *In Praise of Folly*, Cervantes' *Don Quixote*, and Shakespeare's own earlier *As You Like It* and *Twelfth Night*—folly and wisdom exchange places. By a similar inversion of logic, the Fool offers his coxcomb to Kent for siding with Lear in his exile, "for taking one's part that 's out of favour" (I,iv). Worldly wisdom is to serve those whose fortunes are on the rise, as does the obsequious and servile Oswald. Indeed, the sinister progress of the first half of the play seems to confirm the Fool's contention that kindness and love are a sure way to exile and poverty. "Let go thy hold when a great wheel runs down a hill, lest it break thy neck with following; but the great one that goes upward, let him draw thee after" (II,iv). Yet the Fool resolves to ignore his own cynical advice: "I would have none but knaves follow it, since a fool gives it." Beneath his mocking, the Fool expresses the deeper truth that it is better to be a "fool" and suffer than to win on the world's terms. The greatest fools in the truest sense are those who prosper through cruelty and so become hardened in sin. As the Fool puts it, deriving a seemingly contrary lesson from Lear's rejection of Cordelia: "Why, this fellow has banished two on 's daughters, and did the third a blessing against his will" (I,iv).

These paradoxes find a parallel in Christian teaching, although the play is nominally pagan in setting. (The lack of explicit Christian reference may be in part the result of a recent Parliamentary order banning references to "God" on stage as blasphemous.) Christianity does not hold a monopoly on the idea that one must lose the world to win a better world, but its expressions of that idea were plentifully available to Shakespeare: "Blessed are the meek, for they shall inherit the earth" (the Sermon on the Mount); "Go and sell that thou hast, and give to the poor, and thou shalt have treasure in heaven" (Matthew 19:21); "He hath put down the mighty from their seats, and exalted them of low degree" (Luke 1:52). Cordelia's vision of true love is of this exalted spiritual order. She is, as the King of France extols her, "most rich, being poor; Most choice, forsaken; and most lov'd, despis'd" (I,i). This is the sense in which Lear has bestowed on her an unintended blessing, by exiling her from a worldly prosperity that is inherently pernicious. Now, with poetic fitness, Lear must learn the same lesson himself. He does so, paradoxically, at the very moment he goes mad, parting ways with the conventional truths of the corrupted world. "My wits begin to turn," he says, and then speaks his first kind words to the Fool, who is his companion in the storm. Lear senses companionship with a fellow mortal who is cold and outcast as he is. In his madness he perceives both the worth of this insight and the need for suffering to attain it: "The art of our necessities is strange, That can make vile things precious" (III,ii). Misery teaches Lear things he never could know as king about other "Poor naked wretches" who "bide the pelting of this pitiless storm." How are such poor persons to be fed and clothed? "O, I have ta'en Too little care of this! Take physic, pomp; Expose thyself to feel what wretches feel, That thou mayst shake the superflux to them, And show the heavens more just" (III,iv). This vision of perfect justice is visionary and utopian, utterly mad in fact, but it is also spiritual wisdom dearly bought.

Gloucester learns a similar truth and expresses it in much the same way. Like Lear he had driven into exile a virtuous child and has placed himself in the power of the wicked. Enlightenment comes only through suffering. Just as Lear achieves spiritual wisdom when he goes mad, Gloucester achieves spiritual vision when he is physically blinded. His eyes having been ground out by the heel of Cornwall's boot, Gloucester asks for Edmund only to learn that Edmund has betrayed him for siding with Lear in the approaching civil war. Gloucester's response, however, is not to accuse Edmund of treachery but to beg forgiveness of the wronged Edgar. No longer does Gloucester need eyes to see this truth; "I stumbled when I saw." Although the discovery is shattering, Gloucester perceives, as does Lear, that adversity is a blessing in disguise since prosperity had previously caused him to be so spiritually blind. "Full oft 'tis seen, Our means secure us, and our mere defects

Prove our commodities." And this realization leads him, as it does Lear, to express a longing for utopian social justice in which arrogant men will be humbled and the poor raised up by their redistributed wealth. "Heavens, deal so still! Let the superfluous and lust-dieted man, That slaves your ordinance, that will not see Because he does not feel, feel your pow'r quickly; So distribution should undo excess, And each man have enough" (IV,i).

To say that Lear and Gloucester learn something precious is not, however, to deny that they are also devastated and broken by their savage humiliation. Indeed, Gloucester is driven to a despairing attempt at suicide, and Lear remains obsessed with the rotten stench of his own mortality, "bound Upon a wheel of fire" (IV,vii). Every value, every decency that we like to associate with civilization is grotesquely inverted during the storm scenes. Justice, for example, is portrayed in two sharply contrasting scenes: the mere "form of justice" by which Cornwall condemns Gloucester for treason (III,vii), and the earnestly play-acted trial by which the mad Lear arraigns Goneril and Regan of filial ingratitude (III,vi). The appearance and the reality of justice have exchanged places, as have folly and wisdom or blindness and seeing. The trial of Gloucester is correct in outward show, for Cornwall possesses the legal authority to try his subjects, and at least goes through the motions of interrogating his prisoner. The outcome is, however, cruelly predetermined. In the playacting trial concurrently taking place in a wretched hovel, the outward appearance of justice is pathetically absurd. Here justice on earth is personified by a madman (Lear), Edgar disguised as another madman (Tom o' Bedlam), and a Fool, the latter two addressed by Lear as "Thou robed man of justice" and "thou, his yokefellow of equity." They are caught up in a pastime of illusion, using a footstool to represent Lear's ungrateful daughters. Yet true justice is here and not inside the manor house.

Similar contrasts invert the values of loyalty, obedience, and family bonds. Edmund becomes, in the language of the villains, the "loyal" son whose loyalty is demonstrated by turning on his own "traitorous" father. Cornwall becomes a new father to Edmund ("thou shalt find a dearer father in my love"). Conversely, a servant who tries to restrain Cornwall from criminally blinding Gloucester is, in Regan's eyes, monstrously insubordinate. "A peasant stand up thus!"

All these inversions are subsumed in the inversion of the word "natural." Edmund is the "natural" son of Gloucester, meaning literally that he is illegitimate. Figuratively he therefore represents a violation of traditional moral order. In appearance he is smooth and plausible, but in reality he is an archdeceiver like the Vice in the morality play, a superb actor who boasts to the audience in soliloquy of his protean villainy. (See the Introduction to *Othello* for a comparison with Iago.) "Nature" is his goddess, and by this he means something like a naturalistic universe in which the race goes to the swiftest and in which conscience, morality, and religion are empty myths. Whereas Lear invokes Nature as a goddess who will punish ungrateful daughters and defend rejected fathers (I,iv), and whereas Gloucester believes in a cosmic correspondence between eclipses of the moon or sun and mutinous discords among men (I,ii), Edmund scoffs at all such metaphysical speculations. He spurns, in other words, the Boethian conception of a divine harmony uniting the cosmos and man, with man at the Ptolemaic center of the universe. As a rationalist, Edmund echoes Jacobean challenges of the older world order in politics and religion as well as in science. He is a Machiavellian, atheist, Epicurean, everything inimical to traditional Elizabethan order. To him, "natural" means precisely what Lear and Gloucester call "unnatural."

His creed provides the play with its supreme test. Which idea of "natural" is true? Do the heavens exist, and will they let Edmund and his cohorts get away with their evil? The question is frequently asked, but the answers are ambiguous. "If you do love old men," Lear implores the gods, "if your sweet sway Allow obedience, if you yourselves are old, Make it your cause" (II,iv). His exhortations mount into frenzied rant, until finally the heavens do send down a terrible storm—on Lear himself. Witnesses agree that the absence of divine order in the universe would have the gravest consequences. "If that the heavens do not their visible spirits Send quickly down to tame these vile offences," says Albany of Lear's ordeal, "It will come, Humanity must perforce prey on itself, Like monsters of the deep" (IV,ii). And Cornwall's servants have perceived earlier the dire implications of their masters' evil deeds. "I'll never care what wickedness I do, If this man come to good," says one, and his fellow agrees: "If she [Regan] live long, And in the end meet the old course of death, Women will all turn monsters" (III,vii). Yet these servants do in fact obey their own best instincts, turning on Cornwall and ministering to Gloucester despite danger to themselves. Similarly, Albany abandons his mild attempts at conciliation and uses his power for good. The crimes of the villains are punished, and Albany sees divine cause in this. Just as plausibly, however, one can postulate a fundamental decency in humankind that has at last asserted itself, revulsed by what it has seen. In part, too, villainy destroys itself, for Edmund's insatiable ambition extends past Cornwall to the English throne, and Goneril and Regan would willingly kill one another to be Edmund's queen. Whatever force oversees the restoration of at least some semblance of justice cannot prevent the death of Cordelia. Yet her ability to forgive and cherish her father, and Edgar's comparable ministering to Gloucester, give the lie to Edmund's "natural" or amoral view of humanity. Cordelia and Edgar show that, with or without the gods, mankind can atone for its own vicious tendencies by a will to believe in goodness.

KING LEAR

[*Dramatis Personae*

LEAR, King of Britain.
KING OF FRANCE.
DUKE OF BURGUNDY.
DUKE OF CORNWALL.
DUKE OF ALBANY.
EARL OF KENT.
EARL OF GLOUCESTER.
EDGAR, *son to Gloucester.*
EDMUND, *bastard son to Gloucester.*
CURAN, *a courtier.*
Old Man, *tenant to Gloucester.*
Doctor.
Fool.
OSWALD, *steward to Goneril.*
A Captain employed by Edmund.
Gentleman attendant on Cordelia.
A Herald.
Servants to Cornwall.

GONERIL, REGAN, CORDELIA, } *daughters to Lear.*

Knights of Lear's train, Captains, Messengers, Soldiers, *and* Attendants.

SCENE: *Britain.*]

ACT I.

SCENE I. [*King Lear's palace.*]

Enter KENT, GLOUCESTER, *and* EDMUND.

Kent. I thought the king had more affected the Duke of Albany than Cornwall.

Glou. It did always seem so to us: but now, in the division of the kingdom, it appears not which of the dukes he values most; for equalities are so weighed, that curiosity in neither can make choice of either's moiety.

Kent. Is not this your son, my lord?

Glou. His breeding, sir, hath been at my charge: I have so often blushed to acknowledge him, that now I am brazed to 't.

Kent. I cannot conceive you.

Glou. Sir, this young fellow's mother could: whereupon she grew round-wombed, and had, indeed, sir, a son for her cradle ere she had a husband for her bed. Do you smell a fault?

Kent. I cannot wish the fault undone, the issue of it being so proper.

Glou. But I have a son, sir, by order of law, some year elder than this, who yet is no dearer in my account: though this knave came something saucily to the world before he was sent for, yet was his mother fair; there was good sport at his making, and the whoreson must be acknowledged. Do you know this noble gentleman, Edmund?

Edm. No, my lord.

Glou. My lord of Kent: remember him hereafter as my honourable friend.

Edm. My services to your lordship.

Kent. I must love you, and sue to know you better.

Edm. Sir, I shall study deserving.

Glou. He hath been out nine years, and away he shall again. The king is coming.

Sennet. Enter KING LEAR, CORNWALL, ALBANY, GONERIL, REGAN, CORDELIA, *and* Attendants.

Lear. Attend the lords of France and Burgundy,
Gloucester.

Glou. I shall, my lord. *Exit* [*with Edmund*].

Lear. Meantime we shall express our darker purpose.
Give me the map there. Know that we have divided
In three our kingdom: and 'tis our fast intent
To shake all cares and business from our age;
Conferring them on younger strengths, while we
Unburthen'd crawl toward death. Our son of Cornwall,
And you, our no less loving son of Albany,
We have this hour a constant will to publish
Our daughters' several dowers, that future strife
May be prevented now. The princes, France and Burgundy,
Great rivals in our youngest daughter's love,
Long in our court have made their amorous sojourn,
And here are to be answer'd. Tell me, my daughters,—
Since now we will divest us, both of rule,
Interest of territory, cares of state,—
Which of you shall we say doth love us most?
That we our largest bounty may extend
Where nature doth with merit challenge. Goneril,
Our eldest-born, speak first.

Gon. Sir, I love you more than word can wield the matter;
Dearer than eye-sight, space, and liberty;
Beyond what can be valued, rich or rare;
No less than life, with grace, health, beauty, honour;
As much as child e'er lov'd, or father found;
A love that makes breath poor, and speech unable;
Beyond all manner of so much I love you.

Cor. [*Aside*] What shall Cordelia speak? Love, and be silent.

Lear. Of all these bounds, even from this line to this,
With shadowy forests and with champains rich'd,
With plenteous rivers and wide-skirted meads,
We make thee lady: to thine and Albany's issue
Be this perpetual. What says our second daughter,
Our dearest Regan, wife of Cornwall? Speak.

Reg. Sir, I am made
Of that self mettle as my sister,
And prize me at her worth. In my true heart
I find she names my very deed of love;
Only she comes too short: that I profess
Myself an enemy to all other joys,

ACT I. SCENE I. 5. **equalities,** equivalences (in the lands assigned). 6. **curiosity,** nicety, close scrutiny. 11. **brazed,** hardened. 39. **fast intent,** firm intention. 44. **constant,** fixed. 54. **Where . . . challenge,** where both natural affection and merit claim it as due. 56. **wield the matter,** avail in expressing. 64. **bounds.** The division of Lear's kingdom seems to be a traditional one; it appears also in *1 Henry IV*, III, i, 70 ff. 65. **shadowy,** shady. **champains,** plains. 73. **deed of love,** love in very deed. 74. **that,** in that.

Which the most precious square of sense possesses;
And find I am alone felicitate
In your dear highness' love.
Cor. [*Aside*] Then poor Cordelia!
And yet not so; since, I am sure, my love 's
More ponderous than my tongue.
Lear. To thee and thine hereditary ever
Remain this ample third of our fair kingdom;
No less in space, validity, and pleasure,
Than that conferr'd on Goneril. Now, our joy,
Although our last and least; to whose young love
The vines of France and milk of Burgundy
Strive to be interess'd; what can you say to draw
A third more opulent than your sisters? Speak.
Cor. Nothing, my lord.
Lear. Nothing!
Cor. Nothing.
Lear. Nothing will come of nothing: speak again.
Cor. Unhappy that I am, I cannot heave
My heart into my mouth: I love your majesty
According to my bond; no more nor less.
Lear. How, how, Cordelia! mend your speech a little,
Lest you may mar your fortunes.
Cor. Good my lord,
You have begot me, bred me, lov'd me: I
Return those duties back as are right fit,
Obey you, love you, and most honour you.
Why have my sisters husbands, if they say
They love you all? Haply, when I shall wed,
That lord whose hand must take my plight shall carry
Half my love with him, half my care and duty:
Sure, I shall never marry like my sisters,
To love my father all.
Lear. But goes thy heart with this?
Cor. Ay, my good lord.
Lear. So young, and so untender?
Cor. So young, my lord, and true.
Lear. Let it be so; thy truth, then, be thy dower.
For, by the sacred radiance of the sun,
The mysteries of Hecate, and the night;
By all the operation of the orbs
From whom we do exist, and cease to be;
Here I disclaim all my paternal care,
Propinquity and property of blood,
And as a stranger to my heart and me
Hold thee, from this, for ever. The barbarous Scythian,
Or he that makes his generation messes
To gorge his appetite, shall to my bosom
Be as well neighbour'd, pitied, and reliev'd,
As thou my sometime daughter.
Kent. Good my liege,—
Lear. Peace, Kent!
Come not between the dragon and his wrath.
I lov'd her most, and thought to set my rest
On her kind nursery. Hence, and avoid my sight!
So be my grave my peace, as here I give
Her father's heart from her! Call France; who stirs?
Call Burgundy. Cornwall and Albany,
With my two daughters' dowers digest this third:
Let pride, which she calls plainness, marry her.
I do invest you jointly with my power,
Pre-eminence, and all the large effects
That troop with majesty. Ourself, by monthly course,
With reservation of an hundred knights,
By you to be sustain'd, shall our abode
Make with you by due turns. Only we shall retain
The name, and all th' addition to a king;
The sway, revenue, execution of the rest,
Beloved sons, be yours: which to confirm,
This coronet part between you.
Kent. Royal Lear,
Whom I have ever honour'd as my king,
Lov'd as my father, as my master follow'd,
As my great patron thought on in my prayers,—
Lear. The bow is bent and drawn, make from the shaft.
Kent. Let it fall rather, though the fork invade
The region of my heart: be Kent unmannerly,
When Lear is mad. What wouldst thou do, old man?
Think'st thou that duty shall have dread to speak,
When power to flattery bows? To plainness honour 's bound,
When majesty falls to folly. Reserve thy state,
And, in thy best consideration, check
This hideous rashness: answer my life my judgement,
Thy youngest daughter does not love thee least;
Nor are those empty-hearted whose low sounds
Reverb no hollowness.
Lear. Kent, on thy life, no more.
Kent. My life I never held but as a pawn
To wage against thine enemies; nor fear to lose it,
Thy safety being motive.
Lear. Out of my sight!
Kent. See better, Lear; and let me still remain
The true blank of thine eye.
Lear. Now, by Apollo,—
Kent. Now, by Apollo, king,
Thou swear'st thy gods in vain.
Lear. O, vassal! miscreant!
[*Laying his hand on his sword.*]
Alb., *Corn.* Dear sir, forbear.
Kent. Do;
Kill thy physician, and the fee bestow
Upon thy foul disease. Revoke thy gift;
Or, whilst I can vent clamour from my throat,
I'll tell thee thou dost evil.
Lear. Hear me, recreant!
On thine allegiance, hear me!
That thou hast sought to make us break our vows,
Which we durst never yet, and with strain'd pride
To come betwixt our sentence and our power,
Which nor our nature nor our place can bear,
Our potency made good, take thy reward.
Five days we do allot thee, for provision
To shield thee from disasters of the world;
And on the sixth to turn thy hated back
Upon our kingdom: if, on the tenth day following,

76. **square of sense,** criterion of the senses. 77. **felicitate,** made happy. 83. **validity,** value. 85. **least,** smallest. 86. **vines,** vineyards. **milk,** pastures. 87. **to be interess'd,** to a right in. 95. **bond,** duty, obligation. 102. **Haply,** perhaps. 103. **plight,** pledge. 112. **Hecate,** goddess of witchcraft. 118. **this,** this time forth. **Scythian,** typical of barbarity from the time of Herodotus. 119. **makes . . . messes,** makes meals of his children. 125. **set my rest,** repose myself; a phrase from a game of cards meaning "to stake all." 126. **nursery,** nursing. 127. **So . . . peace, as,** let me rest peacefully in my grave, only as. 133. **effects,** outward shows. 141. **coronet,** i.e., the crown intended for Cordelia. 145. **make from,** get out of the way of. 146. **fall,** strike. **fork,** barbed head of an arrow. 150-151. **To . . . folly.** Allegiance demands frankness when kingship stoops to folly. 151. **Reserve thy state,** retain your royal authority. 153. **answer my life,** let my life answer. 157. **pawn,** stake, wager. 158. **wage,** hazard, wager. 161. **blank,** white center of the target. 162. **by Apollo.** The play of *King*

Thy banish'd trunk be found in our dominions,
The moment is thy death. Away! by Jupiter,
This shall not be revok'd.

Kent. Fare thee well, king: sith thus thou wilt appear,
Freedom lives hence, and banishment is here.
[*To Cordelia*] The gods to their dear shelter take thee, maid,
That justly think'st, and hast most rightly said!
[*To Regan and Goneril*] And your large speeches may your deeds approve,
That good effects may spring from words of love.
Thus Kent, O princes, bids you all adieu;
He'll shape his old course in a country new. *Exit.*

Flourish. Enter GLOUCESTER, *with* FRANCE *and* BURGUNDY; Attendants.

Glou. Here's France and Burgundy, my noble lord.

Lear. My lord of Burgundy,
We first address toward you, who with this king
Hath rivall'd for our daughter: what, in the least,
Will you require in present dower with her,
Or cease your quest of love?

Bur. Most royal majesty,
I crave no more than hath your highness offer'd,
Nor will you tender less.

Lear. Right noble Burgundy,
When she was dear to us, we did hold her so;
But now her price is fall'n. Sir, there she stands:
If aught within that little seeming substance,
Or all of it, with our displeasure piec'd,
And nothing more, may fitly like your grace,
She 's there, and she is yours.

Bur. I know no answer.

Lear. Will you, with those infirmities she owes,
Unfriended, new-adopted to our hate,
Dow'r'd with our curse, and stranger'd with our oath,
Take her, or leave her?

Bur. Pardon me, royal sir;
Election makes not up on such conditions.

Lear. Then leave her, sir; for, by the pow'r that made me,
I tell you all her wealth. [*To France*] For you, great king,
I would not from your love make such a stray,
To match you where I hate; therefore beseech you
T' avert your liking a more worthier way
Than on a wretch whom nature is asham'd
Almost t' acknowledge hers.

France. This is most strange,
That she, whom even but now was your best object,
The argument of your praise, balm of your age,
The best, the dearest, should in this trice of time
Commit a thing so monstrous, to dismantle
So many folds of favour. Sure, her offence
Must be of such unnatural degree,
That monsters it, or your fore-vouch'd affection
Fall'n into taint: which to believe of her,
Must be a faith that reason without miracle
Should never plant in me.

Cor. I yet beseech your majesty,—
If for I want that glib and oily art,
To speak and purpose not; since what I well intend,
I'll do 't before I speak,—that you make known
It is no vicious blot, murder, or foulness,
No unchaste action, or dishonoured step,
That hath depriv'd me of your grace and favour;
But even for want of that for which I am richer,
A still-soliciting eye, and such a tongue
As I am glad I have not, though not to have it
Hath lost me in your liking.

Lear. Better thou
Hadst not been born than not t' have pleas'd me better.

France. Is it but this,—a tardiness in nature
Which often leaves the history unspoke
That it intends to do? My lord of Burgundy,
What say you to the lady? Love 's not love
When it is mingled with regards that stands
Aloof from th' entire point. Will you have her?
She is herself a dowry.

Bur. Royal king,
Give but that portion which yourself propos'd,
And here I take Cordelia by the hand,
Duchess of Burgundy.

Lear. Nothing: I have sworn; I am firm.

Bur. I am sorry, then, you have so lost a father
That you must lose a husband.

Cor. Peace be with Burgundy!
Since that respects of fortune are his love,
I shall not be his wife.

France. Fairest Cordelia, that art most rich, being poor;
Most choice, forsaken; and most lov'd, despis'd!
Thee and thy virtues here I seize upon:
Be it lawful I take up what 's cast away.
Gods, gods! 'tis strange that from their cold'st neglect
My love should kindle to inflam'd respect.
Thy dow'rless daughter, king, thrown to my chance,
Is queen of us, of ours, and our fair France:
Not all the dukes of wat'rish Burgundy
Can buy this unpriz'd precious maid of me.
Bid them farewell, Cordelia, though unkind:
Thou losest here, a better where to find.

Lear. Thou hast her, France: let her be thine; for we
Have no such daughter, nor shall ever see
That face of hers again. Therefore be gone
Without our grace, our love, our benison.
Come, noble Burgundy.

Flourish. Exeunt [*all but France, Goneril, Regan, and Cordelia*].

France. Bid farewell to your sisters.

Cor. The jewels of our father, with wash'd eyes
Cordelia leaves you: I know you what you are;
And like a sister am most loath to call
Your faults as they are nam'd. Love well our father:
To your professed bosoms I commit him:
But yet, alas, stood I within his grace,
I would prefer him to a better place.
So, farewell to you both.

Lear is rather carefully pagan in all its externals. 172. **strain'd,** excessive. 175. **Our potency made good,** our authority being maintained. 180. **trunk,** body. 193. **address,** address ourself. 201. **seeming,** probably, specious, insincere; taken also with *little* to mean "seemingly small." 202. **piec'd,** added. 207. **stranger'd,** estranged. 209. **Election . . . conditions,** no choice is possible under such conditions. 212. **make such a stray,** stray so far. 218. **argument,** theme. 223. **monsters,** makes monstrous. **fore-vouch'd,** hitherto affirmed. 224. **taint,** decay. 234. **still-soliciting,** ever-begging. 242. **regards,** considerations. 261. **wat'rish,** well-watered (with rivers); used contemptuously, water being the symbol of fickleness. 262. **unpriz'd,** not appreciated or priceless. 264. **here . . . where,** used as nouns. 275. **professed,** i.e., full of professions (avowals).

Reg. Prescribe not us our duty.
Gon. Let your study
Be to content your lord, who hath receiv'd you
At fortune's alms. You have obedience scanted,
And well are worth the want that you have wanted.
Cor. Time shall unfold what plighted cunning hides:
Who covers faults, at last shame them derides.
Well may you prosper!
France. Come, my fair Cordelia.
Exeunt France and Cordelia.

Gon. Sister, it is not little I have to say of what most nearly appertains to us both. I think our father will hence to-night.

Reg. That 's most certain, and with you; next month with us.

Gon. You see how full of changes his age is; the observation we have made of it hath not been little: he always loved our sister most; and with what poor judgement he hath now cast her off appears too grossly.

Reg. 'Tis the infirmity of his age: yet he hath ever but slenderly known himself.

Gon. The best and soundest of his time hath been but rash; then must we look from his age to receive not alone the imperfections of long-engraffed condition, but therewithal the unruly waywardness that infirm and choleric years bring with them.

Reg. Such unconstant starts are we like to have from him as this of Kent's banishment.

Gon. There is further compliment of leave-taking between France and him. Pray you, let us hit together: if our father carry authority with such disposition as he bears, this last surrender of his will but offend us.

Reg. We shall further think of it.

Gon. We must do something, and i' the heat. *Exeunt.*

SCENE II. [*The Earl of Gloucester's castle.*]

Enter Bastard [EDMUND, *with a letter*].

Edm. Thou, nature, art my goddess; to thy law
My services are bound. Wherefore should I
Stand in the plague of custom, and permit
The curiosity of nations to deprive me,
For that I am some twelve or fourteen moonshines
Lag of a brother? Why bastard? wherefore base?
When my dimensions are as well compact,
My mind as generous, and my shape as true,
As honest madam's issue? Why brand they us
With base? with baseness? bastardy? base, base?
Who, in the lusty stealth of nature, take
More composition and fierce quality
Than doth, within a dull, stale, tired bed,
Go to th' creating a whole tribe of fops,
Got 'tween asleep and wake? Well, then,
Legitimate Edgar, I must have your land:
Our father's love is to the bastard Edmund
As to th' legitimate: fine word,—legitimate!
Well, my legitimate, if this letter speed,
And my invention thrive, Edmund the base
Shall top th' legitimate. I grow; I prosper:
Now, gods, stand up for bastards!

Enter GLOUCESTER.

Glou. Kent banish'd thus! and France in choler parted!
And the king gone to-night! prescrib'd his pow'r!
Confin'd to exhibition! All this done
Upon the gad! Edmund, how now! what news?
Edm. So please your lordship, none.
[*Putting up the letter.*]
Glou. Why so earnestly seek you to put up that letter?
Edm. I know no news, my lord.
Glou. What paper were you reading?
Edm. Nothing, my lord.

Glou. No? What needed, then, that terrible dispatch of it into your pocket? the quality of nothing hath not such need to hide itself. Let 's see: come, if it be nothing, I shall not need spectacles.

Edm. I beseech you, sir, pardon me: it is a letter from my brother, that I have not all o'er-read; and for so much as I have perused, I find it not fit for your o'er-looking.

Glou. Give me the letter, sir.

Edm. I shall offend, either to detain or give it. The contents, as in part I understand them, are to blame.

Glou. Let 's see, let 's see.

Edm. I hope, for my brother's justification, he wrote this but as an essay or taste of my virtue.

Glou. (*Reads*) 'This policy and reverence of age makes the world bitter to the best of our times; keeps our fortunes from us till our oldness cannot relish them. I begin to find an idle and fond bondage in the oppression of aged tyranny; who sways, not as it hath power, but as it is suffered. Come to me, that of this I may speak more. If our father would sleep till I waked him, you should enjoy half his revenue for ever, and live the beloved of your brother,
EDGAR.'
Hum—conspiracy!—'Sleep till I waked him,—you should enjoy half his revenue,'—My son Edgar! Had he a hand to write this? a heart and brain to breed it in?—When came this to you? who brought it?

Edm. It was not brought me, my lord; there 's the cunning of it; I found it thrown in at the casement of my closet.

Glou. You know the character to be your brother's?

Edm. If the matter were good, my lord, I durst swear it were his; but, in respect of that, I would fain think it were not.

Glou. It is his.

Edm. It is his hand, my lord; but I hope his heart is not in the contents.

281. **At,** i.e., priced at. 282. **well . . . wanted,** well deserve the lack of affection which you yourself have shown; *want* may, however, refer to her dowry. 283. **plighted,** pleated, enfolded. 295. **grossly,** obviously. 298. **time,** lifetime. 301. **long-engraffed condition,** long-implanted habit. 308. **hit,** agree. 310. **offend,** harm, injure. 312. **i' the heat,** i.e., while the iron is hot.

SCENE II. 1. **nature,** i.e., the material world, governed by mechanistic forces rather than by divine hierarchy. 3. **plague,** vexatious injustice. Warburton suggested *plage* meaning "place," "boundary." 4. **curiosity,** nicety, fastidiousness. 5. **moonshines,** months. 6. **Lag of,** later than. 7. **dimensions,** bodily parts or proportions. **compact,** knit together. 8. **generous,** befitting a nobleman. 12. **composition,** completeness. 15. **Got,** begotten. 24. **prescrib'd,** limited. 25. **exhibition,** allowance. 26. **Upon the gad,** suddenly, as if pricked by a gad. 32. **terrible,** terrified. 47. **essay,** assay, trial. 48. **policy and reverence of,** i.e., policy of reverencing; hendiadys, a construction common in *King Lear*. 65. **closet,** private room. 77. **declined,** having become feeble. 82. **detested,** detestable. 89. **where,** whereas.

Glou. Has he never before sounded you in this business?

Edm. Never, my lord: but I have heard him oft maintain it to be fit, that, sons at perfect age, and fathers declined, the father should be as ward to the son, and the son manage his revenue. 79

Glou. O villain, villain! His very opinion in the letter! Abhorred villain! Unnatural, detested, brutish villain! worse than brutish! Go, sirrah, seek him; I'll apprehend him: abominable villain! Where is he?

Edm. I do not well know, my lord. If it shall please you to suspend your indignation against my brother till you can derive from him better testimony of his intent, you should run a certain course; where, if you violently proceed against him, mistaking his purpose, it would make a great gap in your own honour, and shake in pieces the heart of his obedience. I dare pawn down my life for him, that he hath writ this to feel my affection to your honour, and to no other pretence of danger. 95

Glou. Think you so?

Edm. If your honour judge it meet, I will place you where you shall hear us confer of this, and by an auricular assurance have your satisfaction; and that without any further delay than this very evening. 101

Glou. He cannot be such a monster—

Edm. Nor is not, sure.

Glou. To his father, that so tenderly and entirely loves him. Heaven and earth! Edmund, seek him out; wind me into him, I pray you: frame the business after your own wisdom. I would unstate myself, to be in a due resolution.

Edm. I will seek him, sir, presently; convey the business as I shall find means, and acquaint you withal. 111

Glou. These late eclipses in the sun and moon portend no good to us: though the wisdom of nature can reason it thus and thus, yet nature finds itself scourged by the sequent effects: love cools, friendship falls off, brothers divide: in cities, mutinies; in countries, discord; in palaces, treason; and the bond cracked 'twixt son and father. This villain of mine comes under the prediction; there 's son against father: the king falls from bias of nature; there 's father against child. We have seen the best of our time: machinations, hollowness, treachery, and all ruinous disorders, follow us disquietly to our graves. Find out this villain, Edmund; it shall lose thee nothing; do it carefully. And the noble and true-hearted Kent banished! his offence, honesty! 'Tis strange. *Exit.* 127

Edm. This is the excellent foppery of the world, that, when we are sick in fortune,—often the surfeits of our own behaviour,—we make guilty of our disasters the sun, the moon, and stars: as if we were villains on necessity; fools by heavenly compulsion; knaves, thieves, and treachers, by spherical predominance; drunkards, liars, and adulterers, by an enforced obedience of planetary influence; and all that we are evil in, by a divine thrusting on: an admirable evasion of whoremaster man, to lay his goatish disposition on the charge of a star! My father compounded with my mother under the Dragon's Tail; and my nativity was under Ursa Major; so that it follows, I am rough and lecherous. Fut, I should have been that I am, had the maidenliest star in the firmament twinkled on my bastardizing. Edgar—

Enter EDGAR.

and pat he comes like the catastrophe of the old comedy: my cue is villanous melancholy, with a sigh like Tom o' Bedlam. O, these eclipses do portend these divisions! fa, sol, la, mi.

Edg. How now, brother Edmund! what serious contemplation are you in? 151

Edm. I am thinking, brother, of a prediction I read this other day, what should follow these eclipses.

Edg. Do you busy yourself with that?

Edm. I promise you, the effects he writes of succeed unhappily; as of unnaturalness between the child and the parent; death, dearth, dissolutions of ancient amities; divisions in state, menaces and maledictions against king and nobles; needless diffidences, banishment of friends, dissipation of cohorts, nuptial breaches, and I know not what. 163

Edg. How long have you been a sectary astronomical?

Edm. Come, come; when saw you my father last?

Edg. Why, the night gone by.

Edm. Spake you with him?

Edg. Ay, two hours together. 170

Edm. Parted you in good terms? Found you no displeasure in him by word nor countenance?

Edg. None at all.

Edm. Bethink yourself wherein you may have offended him: and at my entreaty forbear his presence until some little time hath qualified the heat of his displeasure; which at this instant so rageth in him, that with the mischief of your person it would scarcely allay.

Edg. Some villain hath done me wrong. 180

Edm. That 's my fear. I pray you, have a continent forbearance till the speed of his rage goes slower; and, as I say, retire with me to my lodging, from whence I will fitly bring you to hear my lord speak: pray ye, go; there 's my key: if you do stir abroad, go armed.

Edg. Armed, brother!

Edm. Brother, I advise you to the best; go armed: I am no honest man if there be any good meaning toward you: I have told you what I have seen and heard; but faintly, nothing like the image and horror of it: pray you, away.

Edg. Shall I hear from you anon?

Edm. I do serve you in this business. *Exit* [*Edgar*].

A credulous father! and a brother noble,
Whose nature is so far from doing harms,

95. **pretence,** intention, purpose. 106. **wind me into him,** insinuate yourself into his confidence; *me* is an ethical dative. 108. **unstate myself,** give up my position and dignity. **due resolution,** actual certainty. 109. **convey,** manage with secrecy. 112-127. **These . . . strange.** The fact that there were eclipses of the sun and moon in the autumn of 1605 has been regarded as an indication of the date of the play; also the references to discord, mutinies, and treason have been thought to refer to the Gunpowder Plot (Nov. 5, 1605). 114. **wisdom of nature,** natural science. 115. **sequent,** consequent, following. 128. **foppery,** foolishness. 131. **disasters,** unfavorable aspects. 134. **treachers,** traitors. **spherical predominance,** ascendancy of planets. Edmund's denial of planetary influence must be set down as a sort of religious infidelity. 145. **catastrophe,** conclusion. 148. **Tom o' Bedlam.** See II, iii, 14, note below. 157. **succeed,** come to pass. 161. **diffidences,** distrust of others. 162. **dissipation of cohorts,** the falling away of supporters. 164. **sectary astronomical,** student of astrology. 175. **qualified,** moderated. 178. **mischief of,** harm to. 179. **allay,** be allayed. 182. **continent,** restraining.

That he suspects none; on whose foolish honesty
My practices ride easy! I see the business.
Let me, if not by birth, have lands by wit:
All with me 's meet that I can fashion fit. *Exit.*

SCENE III. [*The Duke of Albany's palace.*]

Enter GONERIL, *and* [OSWALD, *her*] *steward.*

Gon. Did my father strike my gentleman for chiding of his fool?

Osw. Yes, madam.

Gon. By day and night he wrongs me; every hour
He flashes into one gross crime or other,
That sets us all at odds: I'll not endure it:
His knights grow riotous, and himself upbraids us
On every trifle. When he returns from hunting,
I will not speak with him; say I am sick:
If you come slack of former services,
You shall do well; the fault of it I'll answer.

Osw. He 's coming, madam; I hear him. [*Horns within.*]

Gon. Put on what weary negligence you please,
You and your fellows; I 'ld have it come to question:
If he distaste it, let him to my sister,
Whose mind and mine, I know, in that are one,
Not to be over-rul'd. Idle old man,
That still would manage those authorities
That he hath given away! Now, by my life,
Old fools are babes again; and must be us'd
With checks as flatteries,—when they are seen abus'd.
Remember what I have said.

Osw. Well, madam.

Gon. And let his knights have colder looks among you;
What grows of it, no matter; advise your fellows so:
I would breed from hence occasions, and I shall
That I may speak: I'll write straight to my sister,
To hold my very course. Prepare for dinner. *Exeunt.*

SCENE IV. [*A hall in the same.*]

Enter KENT [*disguised*].

Kent. If but as well I other accents borrow,
That can my speech defuse, my good intent
May carry through itself to that full issue
For which I raz'd my likeness. Now, banish'd Kent,
If thou canst serve where thou dost stand condemn'd,
So may it come, thy master, whom thou lov'st,
Shall find thee full of labours.

Horns within. Enter LEAR, [Knights,] *and* Attendants.

Lear. Let me not stay a jot for dinner; go get it ready. [*Exit an Attendant.*] How now! what art thou?

Kent. A man, sir.

Lear. What dost thou profess? what wouldst thou with us?

Kent. I do profess to be no less than I seem; to serve him truly that will put me in trust; to love him that is honest; to converse with him that is wise, and says little; to fear judgement; to fight when I cannot choose; and to eat no fish.

Lear. What art thou?

Kent. A very honest-hearted fellow, and as poor as the king.

Lear. If thou be'st as poor for a subject as he 's for a king, thou art poor enough. What wouldst thou?

Kent. Service.

Lear. Who wouldst thou serve?

Kent. You.

Lear. Dost thou know me, fellow?

Kent. No, sir; but you have that in your countenance which I would fain call master.

Lear. What 's that?

Kent. Authority.

Lear. What services canst thou do?

Kent. I can keep honest counsel, ride, run, mar a curious tale in telling it, and deliver a plain message bluntly: that which ordinary men are fit for, I am qualified in; and the best of me is diligence.

Lear. How old art thou?

Kent. Not so young, sir, to love a woman for singing, nor so old to dote on her for any thing: I have years on my back forty eight.

Lear. Follow me; thou shalt serve me: if I like thee no worse after dinner, I will not part from thee yet. Dinner, ho, dinner! Where 's my knave? my fool? Go you, and call my fool hither. [*Exit an Attendant.*]

Enter Steward [OSWALD].

You, you, sirrah, where 's my daughter?

Osw. So please you,— *Exit.*

Lear. What says the fellow there? Call the clotpoll back. [*Exit a Knight.*] Where 's my fool, ho? I think the world 's asleep.

[*Enter* Knight.]

How now! where 's that mongrel?

Knight. He says, my lord, your daughter is not well.

Lear. Why came not the slave back to me when I called him?

Knight. Sir, he answered me in the roundest manner, he would not.

Lear. He would not!

Knight. My lord, I know not what the matter is; but, to my judgement, your highness is not entertained with that ceremonious affection as you were wont; there 's a great abatement of kindness appears as well in the general dependants as in the duke himself also and your daughter.

Lear. Ha! sayest thou so?

Knight. I beseech you, pardon me, my lord, if I be mistaken; for my duty cannot be silent when I think your highness wronged.

Lear. Thou but rememberest me of mine own conception: I have perceived a most faint neglect of late; which I have rather blamed as mine own jealous

SCENE III. 14. **distaste,** dislike. 16. **Idle,** foolish, silly. 20. **With . . . abus'd,** with rebukes instead of flattery, when they (old men) act unselfknowingly (as Lear does). 24-25. **I would . . . speak,** I wish to create incidents from this sort of thing, and thus give me the opportunity to speak to Lear.

SCENE IV. 2. **defuse,** confuse; hence, disguise. 4. **raz'd,** erased. 12. **What . . . profess?** What is thy profession? 16. **judgement,** i.e., God's judgment. 18. **eat no fish.** Warburton's explanation is usually followed: Roman Catholics, who observed the custom of eating fish on Fridays, were thought of as enemies of the government. 51. **clotpoll,** blockhead. 72. **rememberest,** remindest. 74. **faint,** slight, or indifferent, half-hearted. 75. **jealous curiosity,** overscrupulous regard for minutiae. 76. **very pretence,** true intention, purpose. 92. **bandy,** strike a ball to and fro, as in tennis; here figurative, give and take. 95. **foot-ball player.** Football was a rough, dangerous, public sport without organization or officials, and under statutory ban; it was played in the curiosity than as a very pretence and purpose of unkindness: I will look further into 't. But where 's my fool? I have not seen him this two days.

Knight. Since my young lady 's going into France, sir, the fool hath much pined away.

Lear. No more of that; I have noted it well. Go you, and tell my daughter I would speak with her. [*Exit an Attendant.*] Go you, call hither my fool.

[*Exit an Attendant.*]

Enter Steward [OSWALD].

O, you sir, you, come you hither, sir: who am I, sir?

Osw. My lady's father.

Lear. 'My lady's father'! my lord's knave: you whoreson dog! you slave! you cur!

Osw. I am none of these, my lord; I beseech your pardon.

Lear. Do you bandy looks with me, you rascal?

[*Striking him.*]

Osw. I'll not be strucken, my lord.

Kent. Nor tripped neither, you base foot-ball player.

[*Tripping up his heels.*]

Lear. I thank thee, fellow; thou servest me, and I'll love thee.

Kent. Come, sir, arise, away! I'll teach you differences: away, away! If you will measure your lubber's length again, tarry: but away! go to; have you wisdom? so. [*Pushes Oswald out.*]

Lear. Now, my friendly knave, I thank thee: there 's earnest of thy service. [*Giving Kent money.*]

Enter Fool.

Fool. Let me hire him too: here 's my coxcomb.

[*Offering Kent his cap.*]

Lear. How now, my pretty knave! how dost thou?

Fool. Sirrah, you were best take my coxcomb.

Kent. Why, fool?

Fool. Why, for taking one's part that 's out of favour: nay, an thou canst not smile as the wind sits, thou 'lt catch cold shortly: there, take my coxcomb: why, this fellow has banished two on 's daughters, and did the third a blessing against his will; if thou follow him, thou must needs wear my coxcomb. How now, nuncle! Would I had two coxcombs and two daughters!

Lear. Why, my boy?

Fool. If I gave them all my living, I 'ld keep my coxcombs myself. There 's mine; beg another of thy daughters.

Lear. Take heed, sirrah; the whip.

Fool. Truth 's a dog must to kennel; he must be whipped out, when Lady the brach may stand by the fire and stink.

Lear. A pestilent gall to me!

Fool. Sirrah, I'll teach thee a speech.

Lear. Do.

Fool. Mark it, nuncle:

Have more than thou showest,
Speak less than thou knowest,
Lend less than thou owest,
Ride more than thou goest,
Learn more than thou trowest,
Set less than thou throwest;
Leave thy drink and thy whore,
And keep in-a-door,
And thou shalt have more
Than two tens to a score.

Kent. This is nothing, fool.

Fool. Then 'tis like the breath of an unfee'd lawyer; you gave me nothing for 't. Can you make no use of nothing, nuncle?

Lear. Why, no, boy; nothing can be made out of nothing.

Fool. [*To Kent*] Prithee, tell him, so much the rent of his land comes to: he will not believe a fool.

Lear. A bitter fool!

Fool. Dost thou know the difference, my boy, between a bitter fool and a sweet one?

Lear. No, lad; teach me.

Fool. That lord that counsell'd thee
To give away thy land,
Come place him here by me,
Do thou for him stand:
The sweet and bitter fool
Will presently appear;
The one in motley here,
The other found out there.

Lear. Dost thou call me fool, boy?

Fool. All thy other titles thou hast given away; that thou wast born with.

Kent. This is not altogether fool, my lord.

Fool. No, faith, lords and great men will not let me; if I had a monopoly out, they would have part on 't: and ladies too, they will not let me have all the fool to myself; they'll be snatching. Give me an egg, nuncle, and I'll give thee two crowns.

Lear. What two crowns shall they be?

Fool. Why, after I have cut the egg i' the middle, and eat up the meat, the two crowns of the egg. When thou clovest thy crown i' the middle, and gavest away both parts, thou borest thine ass on thy back o'er the dirt: thou hadst little wit in thy bald crown, when thou gavest thy golden one away. If I speak like myself in this, let him be whipped that first finds it so.

[*Singing*] Fools had ne'er less grace in a year;
For wise men are grown foppish,
And know not how their wits to wear,
Their manners are so apish.

Lear. When were you wont to be so full of songs, sirrah?

Fool. I have used it, nuncle, e'er since thou madest thy daughters thy mothers: for when thou gavest them the rod, and put'st down thine own breeches,

[*Singing*] Then they for sudden joy did weep,
And I for sorrow sung,
That such a king should play bo-peep,
And go the fools among.

Prithee, nuncle, keep a schoolmaster that can teach thy fool to lie: I would fain learn to lie.

streets by the rowdiest element of the population. 97. **differences,** distinctions in rank. 105. **coxcomb,** fool's cap. 112. **smile . . . sits,** i.e., play along with those in power. 115. **banished,** i.e., alienated. 117. **nuncle,** contraction of "mine uncle," customary address of the licensed fool to his superior. 120. **living,** property. 125. **brach,** a female hound. 131. **showest,** seemest to have. 133. **owest,** ownest. 134. **goest,** i.e., on foot. 136. **Set . . . throwest,** stake less at dice than you have a chance to throw, i.e., don't bet all you can. 138. **in-a-door,** at home. 154. **That lord.** A lord, Skalliger, in the old play of *King Leir* is apparently referred to; no such advice is given to Lear in this play. 160. **motley,** the particolored dress of the fool. 167. **monopoly.** This allusion would be well understood, since the granting of monopolies by King James was a current abuse. **out,** taken out, granted. 179. **like myself,** i.e., like a fool. 181. **grace in a year,** favor at any time. 182. **foppish,** foolish. 191-194. **Then . . . among.** These lines, and probably others below, are no doubt taken from old songs.

Lear. An you lie, sirrah, we'll have you whipped.

Fool. I marvel what kin thou and thy daughters are: they'll have me whipped for speaking true, thou 'lt have me whipped for lying; and sometimes I am whipped for holding my peace. I had rather be any kind o' thing than a fool: and yet I would not be thee, nuncle; thou hast pared thy wit o' both sides, and left nothing i' the middle: here comes one o' the parings.

Enter GONERIL.

Lear. How now, daughter! what makes that frontlet on? Methinks you are too much of late i' the frown.

Fool. Thou wast a pretty fellow when thou hadst no need to care for her frowning; now thou art an O without a figure: I am better than thou art now; I am a fool, thou art nothing. [*To Gon.*] Yes, forsooth, I will hold my tongue; so your face bids me, though you say nothing. Mum, mum,

He that keeps nor crust nor crum,
Weary of all, shall want some.

[*Pointing to Lear*] That 's a sheal'd peascod.

Gon. Not only, sir, this your all-licens'd fool,
But other of your insolent retinue
Do hourly carp and quarrel; breaking forth
In rank and not-to-be-endured riots. Sir,
I had thought, by making this well known unto you,
To have found a safe redress; but now grow fearful,
By what yourself too late have spoke and done,
That you protect this course, and put it on
By your allowance; which if you should, the fault
Would not 'scape censure, nor the redresses sleep,
Which, in the tender of a wholesome weal,
Might in their working do you that offence,
Which else were shame, that then necessity
Will call discreet proceeding.

Fool. For, you know, nuncle,
The hedge-sparrow fed the cuckoo so long,
That it had it head bit off by it young.
So, out went the candle, and we were left darkling.

Lear. Are you our daughter?

Gon. Come, sir,
I would you would make use of your good wisdom,
Whereof I know you are fraught; and put away
These dispositions, which of late transport you
From what you rightly are.

Fool. May not an ass know when the cart draws the horse? Whoop, Jug! I love thee.

Lear. Does any here know me? This is not Lear:
Does Lear walk thus? speak thus? Where are his eyes?
Either his notion weakens, his discernings
Are lethargied—Ha! waking? 'tis not so.
Who is it that can tell me who I am?

Fool. Lear's shadow.

Lear. I would learn that; for, by the marks of sovereignty, knowledge, and reason, I should be false persuaded I had daughters.

Fool. Which they will make an obedient father.

Lear. Your name, fair gentlewoman?

Gon. This admiration, sir, is much o' th' savour
Of other your new pranks. I do beseech you
To understand my purposes aright:
As you are old and reverend, should be wise.
Here do you keep a hundred knights and squires;
Men so disorder'd, so debosh'd and bold,
That this our court, infected with their manners,
Shows like a riotous inn: epicurism and lust
Makes it more like a tavern or a brothel
Than a grac'd palace. The shame itself doth speak
For instant remedy: be then desir'd
By her, that else will take the thing she begs,
A little to disquantity your train;
And the remainders, that shall still depend,
To be such men as may besort your age,
Which know themselves and you.

Lear. Darkness and devils!
Saddle my horses; call my train together.
Degenerate bastard! I'll not trouble thee:
Yet have I left a daughter.

Gon. You strike my people; and your disorder'd rabble
Make servants of their betters.

Enter ALBANY.

Lear. Woe, that too late repents,—[*To Alb.*] O, sir, are you come?
Is it your will? Speak, sir. Prepare my horses.
Ingratitude, thou marble-hearted fiend,
More hideous when thou show'st thee in a child
Than the sea-monster!

Alb. Pray, sir, be patient.

Lear. [*To Gon.*] Detested kite! thou liest:
My train are men of choice and rarest parts,
That all particulars of duty know,
And in the most exact regard support
The worships of their name. O most small fault,
How ugly didst thou in Cordelia show!
Which, like an engine, wrench'd my frame of nature
From the fix'd place; drew from my heart all love,
And added to the gall. O Lear, Lear, Lear!
Beat at this gate, that let thy folly in, [*Striking his head.*]
And thy dear judgement out! Go, go, my people.

Alb. My lord, I am guiltless, as I am ignorant
Of what hath moved you.

Lear. It may be so, my lord.
Hear, nature, hear; dear goddess, hear!
Suspend thy purpose, if thou didst intend
To make this creature fruitful!
Into her womb convey sterility!
Dry up in her the organs of increase;
And from her derogate body never spring
A babe to honour her! If she must teem,
Create her child of spleen; that it may live,
And be a thwart disnatur'd torment to her!
Let it stamp wrinkles in her brow of youth;
With cadent tears fret channels in her cheeks;
Turn all her mother's pains and benefits
To laughter and contempt; that she may feel
How sharper than a serpent's tooth it is

208. **frontlet,** a band worn on the forehead; forehead; here, frowning visage. 212. **O without a figure,** cipher of no value unless joined to a figure. 219. **sheal'd peascod,** shelled pea pod. 221. **other,** others. 227. **put it on,** encourage it. 228. **allowance,** approval. 229. **redresses sleep,** punishment for the riotous conduct of Lear's attendants lie dormant. 230. **tender . . . weal,** preservation of the peace of the state. 232-233. **necessity . . . proceeding,** i.e., everyone will justify the action of chastisement as prudent under the circumstances. 236. **it.** The second and third *it's* are possessives. 237. **darkling,** in the dark. 241. **fraught,** filled. 245. **Whoop, Jug! I love thee,** regarded as a quotation from an old song; used by the Fool to cover up his impertinence. *Jug,* probably, Joan. 248. **notion,** intellectual power. 255. **Which,** whom. 258. **admiration,** wonderment. 263. **debosh'd,** debauched. 265. **epicurism,** luxury. 267. **grac'd,** honorable. 270. **disquantity,** diminish. 271. **depend,** be dependents. 272. **besort,** befit. 283. **sea-monster,** possible allusion to the hippopotamus, reputed in Egyptian mythology to be a monster of ingratitude; the whale has also been suggested. W. J. Craig suggests that no particular monster is

To have a thankless child! Away, away! *Exit.*
Alb. Now, gods that we adore, whereof comes this?
Gon. Never afflict yourself to know more of it;
But let his disposition have that scope
That dotage gives it.

Enter LEAR.

Lear. What, fifty of my followers at a clap!
Within a fortnight!
Alb. What 's the matter, sir?
Lear. I'll tell thee: [*To Gon.*] Life and death! I am asham'd
That thou hast power to shake my manhood thus;
That these hot tears, which break from me perforce,
Should make thee worth them. Blasts and fogs upon thee!
Th' untented woundings of a father's curse
Pierce every sense about thee! Old fond eyes,
Beweep this cause again, I'll pluck ye out,
And cast you, with the waters that you loose,
To temper clay. Yea, is it come to this?
Ha! Let it be so: I have another daughter,
Who, I am sure, is kind and comfortable:
When she shall hear this of thee, with her nails
She'll flay thy wolvish visage. Thou shalt find
That I'll resume the shape which thou dost think
I have cast off for ever: thou shalt, I warrant thee.
Exit [*Lear, with Kent, and Attendants*].
Gon. Do you mark that, my lord?
Alb. I cannot be so partial, Goneril,
To the great love I bear you,—
Gon. Pray you, content. What, Oswald, ho!
[*To the Fool*] You, sir, more knave than fool, after your master.
Fool. Nuncle Lear, nuncle Lear, tarry and take the fool with thee.
A fox, when one has caught her,
And such a daughter,
Should sure to the slaughter,
If my cap would buy a halter:
So the fool follows after. *Exit.*
Gon. This man hath had good counsel:—a hundred knights!
'Tis politic and safe to let him keep
At point a hundred knights: yes, that, on every dream,
Each buzz, each fancy, each complaint, dislike,
He may enguard his dotage with their pow'rs,
And hold our lives in mercy. Oswald, I say!
Alb. Well, you may fear too far.
Gon. Safer than trust too far:
Let me still take away the harms I fear,
Not fear still to be taken: I know his heart.
What he hath utter'd I have writ my sister:
If she sustain him and his hundred knights,
When I have show'd th' unfitness,—

Enter Steward [OSWALD].

How now, Oswald!
What, have you writ that letter to my sister?
Osw. Ay, madam.
Gon. Take you some company, and away to horse:
Inform her full of my particular fear;
And thereto add such reasons of your own
As may compact it more. Get you gone;
And hasten your return. [*Exit Oswald.*] No, no, my lord,
This milky gentleness and course of yours
Though I condemn not, yet, under pardon,
You are much more attask'd for want of wisdom
Than prais'd for harmful mildness.
Alb. How far your eyes may pierce I cannot tell:
Striving to better, oft we mar what 's well.
Gon. Nay, then—
Alb. Well, well; th' event. *Exeunt.*

[SCENE V. *Court before the same.*]

Enter LEAR, KENT, *and* Fool.

Lear. Go you before to Gloucester with these letters. Acquaint my daughter no further with any thing you know than comes from her demand out of the letter. If your diligence be not speedy, I shall be there afore you.

Kent. I will not sleep, my lord, till I have delivered your letter. *Exit.*

Fool. If a man's brains were in 's heels, were 't not in danger of kibes?

Lear. Ay, boy.

Fool. Then, I prithee, be merry; thy wit shall not go slip-shod.

Lear. Ha, ha, ha!

Fool. Shalt see thy other daughter will use thee kindly; for though she 's as like this as a crab 's like an apple, yet I can tell what I can tell.

Lear. What canst tell, boy?

Fool. She will taste as like this as a crab does to a crab. Thou canst tell why one's nose stands i' the middle on 's face?

Lear. No.

Fool. Why, to keep one's eyes of either side 's nose; that what a man cannot smell out, he may spy into.

Lear. I did her wrong—

Fool. Canst tell how an oyster makes his shell?

Lear. No.

Fool. Nor I neither; but I can tell why a snail has a house.

Lear. Why?

Fool. Why, to put 's head in; not to give it away to his daughters, and leave his horns without a case.

Lear. I will forget my nature. So kind a father! Be my horses ready?

Fool. Thy asses are gone about 'em. The reason why the seven stars are no moe than seven is a pretty reason.

Lear. Because they are not eight?

Fool. Yes, indeed: thou wouldst make a good fool.

meant, but that the allusion is to the monsters of classical mythology. 287. **in . . . regard,** with extreme care. 288. **worships,** honors. 290. **engine,** possibly machines for razing houses. 302. **derogate,** debased. 303. **teem,** increase. 305. **thwart,** contrary. **disnatur'd,** without natural affection. 307. **cadent,** falling. 322. **untented,** not cleansed with lint, and therefore liable to fester. 323. **fond,** foolish. 324. **Beweep,** if you weep for. 328. **comfortable,** willing to comfort. 347. **At point,** under arms. 348. **buzz,** idle rumor. 349. **enguard,** surround with a guard. 353. **taken,** overtaken (by the *harms*). 362. **compact,** confirm.

364. **This . . . yours,** the cowardly weakness of your course. 366. **attask'd,** taken to task, blamed. 371. **th' event,** time will show.

SCENE V. 9. **kibes,** chilblains, or ulcerated sores on the heels. 12. **slip-shod,** in slippers. There are no brains, thinks the Fool, in Lear's heels when they are on their way to visit Regan. 15. **kindly,** double sense: according to filial nature and according to her own nature. 16. **a crab 's . . . apple,** seems proverbial for "a crab-apple's an apple." 25. **her.** Lear again thinks of Cordelia. 38. **seven stars,** the Pleiades.

Lear. To take 't again perforce! Monster ingratitude!

Fool. If thou wert my fool, nuncle, I 'ld have thee beaten for being old before thy time.

Lear. How 's that?

Fool. Thou shouldst not have been old till thou hadst been wise.

Lear. O, let me not be mad, not mad, sweet heaven!
Keep me in temper: I would not be mad!

[*Enter*] Gentleman.

How now! are the horses ready?

Gent. Ready, my lord.

Lear. Come, boy.

Fool. She that 's a maid now, and laughs at my departure,
Shall not be a maid long, unless things be cut shorter.

Exeunt.

ACT II.

SCENE I. [*The Earl of Gloucester's castle.*]

Enter Bastard [EDMUND] *and* CURAN, *severally.*

Edm. Save thee, Curan.

Cur. And you, sir. I have been with your father, and given him notice that the Duke of Cornwall and Regan his duchess will be here with him this night.

Edm. How comes that?

Cur. Nay, I know not. You have heard of the news abroad; I mean the whispered ones, for they are yet but ear-kissing arguments?

Edm. Not I: pray you, what are they?

Cur. Have you heard of no likely wars toward, 'twixt the Dukes of Cornwall and Albany?

Edm. Not a word.

Cur. You may do, then, in time. Fare you well, sir.

Exit.

Edm. The duke be here to-night? The better! best!
This weaves itself perforce into my business.
My father hath set guard to take my brother;
And I have one thing, of a queasy question,
Which I must act: briefness and fortune, work!
Brother, a word; descend: brother, I say!

Enter EDGAR.

My father watches: O sir, fly this place;
Intelligence is given where you are hid;
You have now the good advantage of the night:
Have you not spoken 'gainst the Duke of Cornwall?
He 's coming hither; now, i' th' night, i' th' haste,
And Regan with him: have you nothing said
Upon his party 'gainst the Duke of Albany?
Advise yourself.

Edg. I am sure on 't, not a word.

Edm. I hear my father coming: pardon me;
In cunning I must draw my sword upon you:
Draw; seem to defend yourself; now quit you well.
Yield! come before my father!—Light, ho, here!
Fly, brother.—Torches, torches!—So, farewell.

Exit Edgar.

Some blood drawn on me would beget opinion [*Wounds his arm.*]
Of my more fierce endeavour: I have seen drunkards
Do more than this in sport. Father, father!
Stop, stop! No help?

Enter GLOUCESTER, *and* Servants *with torches.*

Glou. Now, Edmund, where 's the villain?

Edm. Here stood he in the dark, his sharp sword out,
Mumbling of wicked charms, conjuring the moon
To stand auspicious mistress,—

Glou. But where is he?

Edm. Look, sir, I bleed.

Glou. Where is the villain, Edmund?

Edm. Fled this way, sir. When by no means he could—

Glou. Pursue him, ho! Go after. [*Exeunt some Servants.*] By no means what?

Edm. Persuade me to the murder of your lordship;
But that I told him, the revenging gods
'Gainst parricides did all the thunder bend;
Spoke, with how manifold and strong a bond
The child was bound to th' father; sir, in fine,
Seeing how loathly opposite I stood
To his unnatural purpose, in fell motion,
With his prepared sword, he charges home
My unprovided body, latch'd mine arm:
But when he saw my best alarum'd spirits,
Bold in the quarrel's right, rous'd to th' encounter,
Or whether gasted by the noise I made,
Full suddenly he fled.

Glou. Let him fly far:
Not in this land shall he remain uncaught;
And found—dispatch. The noble duke my master,
My worthy arch and patron, comes to-night:
By his authority I will proclaim it,
That he which finds him shall deserve our thanks,
Bringing the murderous coward to the stake;
He that conceals him, death.

Edm. When I dissuaded him from his intent,
And found him pight to do it, with curst speech
I threaten'd to discover him: he replied,
'Thou unpossessing bastard! dost thou think,
If I would stand against thee, would the reposal
Of any trust, virtue, or worth in thee
Make thy words faith'd? No: what I should deny,—
As this I would; ay, though thou didst produce
My very character,—I 'ld turn it all
To thy suggestion, plot, and damned practice:
And thou must make a dullard of the world,
If they not thought the profits of my death
Were very pregnant and potential spirits

58. **cut shorter,** a bawdy joke addressed to the audience, implying universal carnality.

ACT II. SCENE I. 1. **Save thee,** i.e., God save thee. 8. **ear-kissing arguments,** lightly whispered topics. 19. **queasy question,** hazardous or ticklish, nature. 20. **briefness,** promptitude. 28. **Upon his party 'gainst,** i.e., concerning Cornwall's feud with Albany. 29. **Advise yourself,** probably, recollect. 31. **cunning,** pretense. 32. **quit you.** acquit yourself. 35. **beget,** create (for me). 50. **fine,** conclusion, 51. **loathly opposite,** loathingly opposed. 52. **fell motion,** deadly thrust. 54. **latch'd,** wounded. 55. **best alarum'd,** thoroughly aroused to action as by a trumpet. 57. **gasted,** frightened. 60. **dispatch,** I will dispatch him. 61. **arch,** chief. 64. **stake,** an allusion to tying prisoners to a stake, or a figure from bearbaiting. 67. **pight,** determined. **curst,** angry. 69. **unpossessing,** unable to inherit, beggarly. 70. **I would,** I should. **reposal,** placing. 72. **faith'd,** believed. 74. **character,** written testimony. 75. **practice,** plot. 76. **make . . . world,** think the world an idiot. 77. **If . . . thought,** if they had not thought. 78. **pregnant,** teeming (with urgings). **potential spirits,** potent evil spirits. 79. **fast'ned,** confirmed. 80. **got,** begot. 99. **consort,** set, company. 101. **put . . . on,** incited him to. 102. **expense and waste,** squandering. 109. **bewray his practice,** expose Edgar's plot. 114. **in my strength,** by my power and authority. **For,** as for. 121. **threading,** passing

To make thee seek it.'
Glou. O strange and fast'ned villain!
Would he deny his letter, said he? I never got him.
Tucket within.
Hark, the duke's trumpets! I know not why he comes.
All ports I'll bar; the villain shall not 'scape;
The duke must grant me that: besides, his picture
I will send far and near, that all the kingdom
May have due note of him; and of my land,
Loyal and natural boy, I'll work the means
To make thee capable.

Enter CORNWALL, REGAN, *and* Attendants.

Corn. How now, my noble friend! since I came hither,
Which I can call but now, I have heard strange news.
Reg. If it be true, all vengeance comes too short
Which can pursue th' offender. How dost, my lord?
Glou. O, madam, my old heart is crack'd, it's crack'd!
Reg. What, did my father's godson seek your life?
He whom my father nam'd? your Edgar?
Glou. O, lady, lady, shame would have it hid!
Reg. Was he not companion with the riotous knights
That tended upon my father?
Glou. I know not, madam: 'tis too bad, too bad.
Edm. Yes, madam, he was of that consort.
Reg. No marvel, then, though he were ill affected:
'Tis they have put him on the old man's death,
To have th' expense and waste of his revenues.
I have this present evening from my sister
Been well inform'd of them; and with such cautions,
That if they come to sojourn at my house,
I'll not be there.
Corn. Nor I, assure thee, Regan.
Edmund, I hear that you have shown your father
A child-like office.
Edm. It was my duty, sir.
Glou. He did bewray his practice; and receiv'd
This hurt you see, striving to apprehend him.
Corn. Is he pursued?
Glou. Ay, my good lord.
Corn. If he be taken, he shall never more
Be fear'd of doing harm: make your own purpose,
How in my strength you please. For you, Edmund,
Whose virtue and obedience doth this instant
So much commend itself, you shall be ours:
Natures of such deep trust we shall much need;
You we first seize on.
Edm. I shall serve you, sir,
Truly, however else.
Glou. For him I thank your grace.
Corn. You know not why we came to visit you,—
Reg. Thus out of season, threading dark-ey'd night:
Occasions, noble Gloucester, of some prize,
Wherein we must have use of your advice:
Our father he hath writ, so hath our sister,
Of differences, which I least thought it fit
To answer from our home; the several messengers
From hence attend dispatch. Our good old friend,
Lay comforts to your bosom; and bestow
Your needful counsel to our businesses,
Which craves the instant use.
Glou. I serve you, madam:
Your graces are right welcome. *Exeunt. Flourish.*

SCENE II. [*Before Gloucester's castle.*]

Enter KENT *and Steward* [OSWALD], *severally.*

Osw. Good dawning to thee, friend: art of this house?

Kent. Ay.

Osw. Where may we set our horses?

Kent. I' the mire.

Osw. Prithee, if thou lovest me, tell me.

Kent. I love thee not.

Osw. Why, then, I care not for thee.

Kent. If I had thee in Lipsbury pinfold, I would make thee care for me.

Osw. Why dost thou use me thus? I know thee not.

Kent. Fellow, I know thee.

Osw. What dost thou know me for?

Kent. A knave; a rascal; an eater of broken meats; a base, proud, shallow, beggarly, three-suited, hundred-pound, filthy, worsted-stocking knave; a lily-livered, action-taking, whoreson, glass-gazing, superserviceable, finical rogue; one-trunk-inheriting slave; one that wouldst be a bawd, in way of good service, and art nothing but the composition of a knave, beggar, coward, pandar, and the son and heir of a mongrel bitch: one whom I will beat into clamorous whining, if thou deniest the least syllable of thy addition.

Osw. Why, what a monstrous fellow art thou, thus to rail on one that is neither known of thee nor knows thee!

Kent. What a brazen-faced varlet art thou, to deny thou knowest me! Is it two days since I tripped up thy heels, and beat thee before the king? Draw, you rogue: for, though it be night, yet the moon shines; I'll make a sop o' the moonshine of you: draw, you whoreson cullionly barber-monger, draw.
[*Drawing his sword.*]

Osw. Away! I have nothing to do with thee.

Kent. Draw, you rascal: you come with letters against the king; and take Vanity the puppet's part against the royalty of her father: draw, you rogue, or I'll so carbonado your shanks: draw, you rascal; come your ways.

Osw. Help, ho! murder! help!

Kent. Strike, you slave; stand, rogue, stand; you neat slave, strike. [*Beating him.*]

Osw. Help, ho! murder! murder!

through (as thread through the eye of a needle). 122. **prize,** price, significance. 125. **which,** the letter. 127. **attend dispatch,** wait to be dispatched.

SCENE II. 9. **Lipsbury pinfold.** This phrase is unexplained. *Pinfold* means "pound for stray animals." Critics have tried to see in it an allusion to the prize ring; Nares supposes the allusion may be to the teeth within the pinfold of the lips. 17. **three-suited,** probable allusion to three suits a year allowed to servants. **hundred-pound,** possible allusion to the minimum property qualification for the status of gentleman; sometimes seen as a reference to James I's wholesale creation of knights. **worsted-stocking,** too poor and menial to wear silk stockings. 18. **action-taking,** settling quarrels by resort to law instead of arms, cowardly. 19. **glass-gazing,** fond of looking in the mirror. **superserviceable,** officious. 20. **finical,** excessively particular, probably, in dress. **one-trunk-inheriting,** possessing effects sufficient for one trunk only. 26. **addition,** title. 35. **sop o' the moonshine,** supposed punning allusion to a dish called "eggs in moonshine." 36. **cullionly barber-monger,** base frequenter of barber shops, fop. 39-40. **Vanity the puppet's part.** Vanity was a character in the morality plays. 41. **carbonado,** cut you crosswise like meat for broiling. 45. **neat,** foppish.

Enter Bastard [EDMUND, *with his rapier drawn*], CORNWALL, REGAN, GLOUCESTER, Servants.

Edm. How now! What 's the matter? Part!

Kent. With you, goodman boy, if you please: come, I'll flesh ye: come on, young master.

Glou. Weapons! arms! What 's the matter here?

Corn. Keep peace, upon your lives;
He dies that strikes again. What is the matter?

Reg. The messengers from our sister and the king.

Corn. What is your difference? speak.

Osw. I am scarce in breath, my lord.

Kent. No marvel, you have so bestirred your valour. You cowardly rascal, nature disclaims in thee: a tailor made thee.

Corn. Thou art a strange fellow: a tailor make a man?

Kent. A tailor, sir: a stone-cutter or a painter could not have made him so ill, though they had been but two years o' the trade.

Corn. Speak yet, how grew your quarrel?

Osw. This ancient ruffian, sir, whose life I have spared at suit of his gray beard,—

Kent. Thou whoreson zed! thou unnecessary letter! My lord, if you will give me leave, I will tread this unbolted villain into mortar, and daub the walls of a jakes with him. Spare my gray beard, you wagtail?

Corn. Peace, sirrah!
You beastly knave, know you no reverence?

Kent. Yes, sir; but anger hath a privilege.

Corn. Why art thou angry?

Kent. That such a slave as this should wear a sword,
Who wears no honesty. Such smiling rogues as these,
Like rats, oft bite the holy cords a-twain
Which are too intrinse t' unloose; smooth every passion
That in the natures of their lords rebel;
Bring oil to fire, snow to their colder moods;
Renege, affirm, and turn their halcyon beaks
With every gale and vary of their masters,
Knowing nought, like dogs, but following.
A plague upon your epileptic visage!
Smile you my speeches, as I were a fool?
Goose, if I had you upon Sarum plain,
I 'ld drive ye cackling home to Camelot.

Corn. What, art thou mad, old fellow?

Glou. How fell you out? say that.

Kent. No contraries hold more antipathy
Than I and such a knave.

Corn. Why dost thou call him knave? What is his fault?

Kent. His countenance likes me not.

Corn. No more, perchance, does mine, nor his, nor hers.

Kent. Sir, 'tis my occupation to be plain:
I have seen better faces in my time
Than stands on any shoulder that I see
Before me at this instant.

Corn. This is some fellow,
Who, having been prais'd for bluntness, doth affect
A saucy roughness, and constrains the garb
Quite from his nature: he cannot flatter, he,
An honest mind and plain, he must speak truth!
An they will take it, so; if not, he 's plain.
These kind of knaves I know, which in this plainness
Harbour more craft and more corrupter ends
Than twenty silly ducking observants
That stretch their duties nicely.

Kent. Sir, in good faith, in sincere verity,
Under th' allowance of your great aspect,
Whose influence, like the wreath of radiant fire
On flick'ring Phœbus' front,—

Corn. What mean'st by this?

Kent. To go out of my dialect, which you discommend so much. I know, sir, I am no flatterer: he that beguiled you in a plain accent was a plain knave; which for my part I will not be, though I should win your displeasure to entreat me to 't.

Corn. What was th' offence you gave him?

Osw. I never gave him any:
It pleas'd the king his master very late
To strike at me, upon his misconstruction;
When he, compact, and flattering his displeasure,
Tripp'd me behind; being down, insulted, rail'd,
And put upon him such a deal of man,
That worthied him, got praises of the king
For him attempting who was self-subdu'd;
And, in the fleshment of this dread exploit,
Drew on me here again.

Kent. None of these rogues and cowards
But Ajax is their fool.

Corn. Fetch forth the stocks!
You stubborn ancient knave, you reverent braggart,
We'll teach you—

Kent. Sir, I am too old to learn:
Call not your stocks for me: I serve the king;
On whose employment I was sent to you:
You shall do small respect, show too bold malice
Against the grace and person of my master,
Stocking his messenger.

Corn. Fetch forth the stocks! As I have life and honour,
There shall he sit till noon.

Reg. Till noon! till night, my lord; and all night too.

Kent. Why, madam, if I were your father's dog,
You should not use me so.

Reg. Sir, being his knave, I will.

Corn. This is a fellow of the self-same colour
Our sister speaks of. Come, bring away the stocks!

Stocks brought out.

Glou. Let me beseech your grace not to do so:
His fault is much, and the good king his master
Will check him for 't: your purpos'd low correction

47. **matter.** Kent takes the secondary meaning, "cause for quarrel." 48. **goodman boy,** contemptuously. 60. **disclaims in,** disowns. 69. **zed,** the letter Z, a Greek character; in the spelling of English words, known but unnecessary, and often not included in dictionaries. 71. **unbolted,** unsifted; hence, coarse. 72. **jakes,** privy. 73. **wagtail,** name of a bird; epithet to denote pertness. 75. **beastly,** in literal sense, beast-like. 80. **holy cords,** natural bonds of affection. 81. **intrinse,** defined as "entangled" and as "very tightly drawn." **smooth,** flatter, humor. 84. **Renege,** deny. **halcyon beaks.** The halcyon or kingfisher, if hung up, would turn his beak against the wind. 85. **vary,** variation. 87. **epileptic,** indication of Oswald's visage, pale with fright and distorted with a grin. 89-90. **Sarum . . . Camelot.** The allusion is to Sarum plain, the Salisbury plain (where large flocks of geese were bred), and to Camelot, the seat of King Arthur and his Round Table, said to have been at Cadbury and at Winchester. 101. **some,** a (sort of). 103-104. **constrains . . . nature,** distorts plainness to the point of caricature. 109. **ducking observants,** bowing, obsequious courtiers. 110. **nicely,** punctiliously. 111. **Sir, in good faith,** etc., Kent assumes the speech of courtly decorum. 124. **misconstruction,** misunderstanding (me). 125. **compact,** joined, united with him. 127. **put . . . man,** acted like such a hero. 128. **worthied,** won reputation. 129. **attempting,** assailing. 130. **fleshment,** excitement resulting from a first success. 132. **Ajax is their fool,** Ajax, traditional braggart, is outdone by them in boasting. 138. **grace . . . master,** who as a messenger Kent represented. 161.

Is such as basest and contemned'st wretches
For pilf'rings and most common trespasses
Are punish'd with: the king must take it ill,
That he, so slightly valued in his messenger,
Should have him thus restrain'd.

Corn. I'll answer that.

Reg. My sister may receive it much more worse,
To have her gentleman abus'd, assaulted,
For following her affairs. Put in his legs.
[*Kent is put in the stocks.*]
Come, my lord, away.
Exit [*with all but Gloucester and Kent*].

Glou. I am sorry for thee, friend; 'tis the duke's pleasure,
Whose disposition, all the world well knows,
Will not be rubb'd nor stopp'd: I'll entreat for thee.

Kent. Pray, do not, sir: I have watch'd and travell'd hard;
Some time I shall sleep out, the rest I'll whistle.
A good man's fortune may grow out at heels:
Give you good morrow!

Glou. The duke 's to blame in this; 'twill be ill taken. *Exit.*

Kent. Good king, that must approve the common saw,
Thou out of heaven's benediction com'st
To the warm sun!
Approach, thou beacon to this under globe,
That by thy comfortable beams I may
Peruse this letter! Nothing almost sees miracles
But misery: I know 'tis from Cordelia,
Who hath most fortunately been inform'd
Of my obscured course; and shall find time
†From this enormous state, seeking to give
Losses their remedies. All weary and o'er-watch'd,
Take vantage, heavy eyes, not to behold
This shameful lodging.
Fortune, good night: smile once more; turn thy wheel! [*Sleeps.*]

[SCENE III. *The same.*]

Enter EDGAR.

Edg. I heard myself proclaim'd;
And by the happy hollow of a tree
Escap'd the hunt. No port is free; no place,
That guard, and most unusual vigilance,
Does not attend my taking. Whiles I may 'scape,
I will preserve myself: and am bethought
To take the basest and most poorest shape
That ever penury, in contempt of man,
Brought near to beast: my face I'll grime with filth;
Blanket my loins; elf all my hairs in knots;
And with presented nakedness out-face
The winds and persecutions of the sky.
The country gives me proof and precedent
Of Bedlam beggars, who, with roaring voices,
Strike in their numb'd and mortified bare arms
Pins, wooden pricks, nails, sprigs of rosemary;
And with this horrible object, from low farms,
Poor pelting villages, sheep-cotes, and mills,
Sometime with lunatic bans, sometime with prayers,
Enforce their charity. Poor Turlygod! poor Tom!
That's something yet: Edgar I nothing am. *Exit.*

[SCENE IV. *The same. Kent still in the stocks.*]

Enter LEAR, Fool, *and* Gentleman.

Lear. 'Tis strange that they should so depart from home,
And not send back my messenger.

Gent. As I learn'd,
The night before there was no purpose in them
Of this remove.

Kent. Hail to thee, noble master!

Lear. Ha!
Mak'st thou this shame thy pastime?

Kent. No, my lord.

Fool. Ha, ha! he wears cruel garters. Horses are tied by the heads, dogs and bears by the neck, monkeys by the loins, and men by the legs: when a man 's over-lusty at legs, then he wears wooden nether-stocks.

Lear. What 's he that hath so much thy place mistook
To set thee here?

Kent. It is both he and she;
Your son and daughter.

Lear. No.

Kent. Yes.

Lear. No, I say.

Kent. I say, yea.

Lear. No, no, they would not.

Kent. Yes, they have.

Lear. By Jupiter, I swear, no.

Kent. By Juno, I swear, ay.

Lear. They durst not do 't;
They could not, would not do 't; 'tis worse than murder,
To do upon respect such violent outrage:
Resolve me, with all modest haste, which way
Thou mightst deserve, or they impose, this usage,
Coming from us.

Kent. My lord, when at their home
I did commend your highness' letters to them,
Ere I was risen from the place that show'd
My duty kneeling, came there a reeking post,
Stew'd in his haste, half breathless, panting forth
From Goneril his mistress salutations;
Deliver'd letters, spite of intermission,
Which presently they read: on whose contents,
They summon'd up their meiny, straight took horse;

rubb'd, hindered, obstructed; term from bowls. 163. **sleep out,** sleep through. 165. **Give you,** i.e., God give you. 167. **approve,** prove true. **saw,** proverb: "To run out of God's blessing into the warm sun," meaning "to go from better to worse." 175-177. **and . . . remedies,** an obscure passage. Daniel's conjecture of *she'll* for *shall* makes a sort of sense. 177. **o'er-watch'd,** exhausted with watching.

SCENE III. The scene is continuous; Kent is still in the stocks. 3. **port,** means of exit. 5. **attend,** watch, wait for. 6. **am bethought,** it has occurred to me. 10. **elf,** tangle into elf-locks. 14. **Bedlam beggars,** called also "Tom o' Bedlams" and "Abraham men"; they were lunatic patients of Bethlehem Hospital turned out to beg for their bread. Dekker in the *Bellman of London*, 1608, gives a description of their characteristics which closely parallels the one in the text. 15. **mortified,** numbed, insensible. 16. **wooden pricks,** skewers. 17. **object,** appearance. **low,** lowly. 18. **pelting,** paltry, petty. 19. **bans,** curses. 20. **Turlygod,** meaning unknown; Warburton proposed *Turlipin*, the name of an order of mad beggars in France. 21. **nothing,** probably, not at all, in no respect.

SCENE IV. 4. **remove,** change of residence (of royalty). 7. **cruel.** Q: *crewell*, a double meaning: (1) "unkind," (2) "crewel," a thin yarn of which garters were made. 11. **nether-stocks,** stockings. 24. **upon respect,** deliberately. 28. **commend,** deliver, commit. 33. **spite of intermission,** in spite of interrupting me. 35. **meiny,** household.

Commanded me to follow, and attend
The leisure of their answer; gave me cold looks:
And meeting here the other messenger,
Whose welcome, I perceiv'd, had poison'd mine,—
Being the very fellow which of late
Display'd so saucily against your highness,—
Having more man than wit about me, drew:
He rais'd the house with loud and coward cries.
Your son and daughter found this trespass worth
The shame which here it suffers.

Fool. Winter 's not gone yet, if the wild-geese fly that way.

Fathers that wear rags
  Do make their children blind;
But fathers that bear bags
  Shall see their children kind.
Fortune, that arrant whore,
Ne'er turns the key to th' poor.

But, for all this, thou shalt have as many dolours for thy daughters as thou canst tell in a year.

Lear. O, how this mother swells up toward my heart!
Hysterica passio, down, thou climbing sorrow,
Thy element 's below! Where is this daughter?

Kent. With the earl, sir, here within.

Lear. Follow me not;
Stay here. *Exit.*

Gent. Made you no more offence but what you speak of?

Kent. None.
How chance the king comes with so small a number?

Fool. An thou hadst been set i' the stocks for that question, thou'dst well deserved it.

Kent. Why, fool?

Fool. We'll set thee to school to an ant, to teach thee there 's no labouring i' the winter. All that follow their noses are led by their eyes but blind men; and there 's not a nose among twenty but can smell him that 's stinking. Let go thy hold when a great wheel runs down a hill, lest it break thy neck with following; but the great one that goes upward, let him draw thee after. When a wise man gives thee better counsel, give me mine again: I would have none but knaves follow it, since a fool gives it.

That sir which serves and seeks for gain,
  And follows but for form,
Will pack when it begins to rain,
  And leave thee in the storm.
But I will tarry; the fool will stay,
  And let the wise man fly:
The knave turns fool that runs away;
  The fool no knave, perdy.

Kent. Where learned you this, fool?

Fool. Not i' th' stocks, fool.

Enter LEAR *and* GLOUCESTER.

Lear. Deny to speak with me? They are sick? they are weary?
They have travell'd all the night? Mere fetches;
The images of revolt and flying off.
Fetch me a better answer.

Glou. My dear lord,
You know the fiery quality of the duke;
How unremoveable and fix'd he is
In his own course.

Lear. Vengeance! plague! death! confusion!
Fiery? what quality? Why, Gloucester, Gloucester,
I 'ld speak with the Duke of Cornwall and his wife.

Glou. Well, my good lord, I have inform'd them so.

Lear. Inform'd them! Dost thou understand me, man?

Glou. Ay, my good lord.

Lear. The king would speak with Cornwall; the dear father
Would with his daughter speak, commands her service:
Are they inform'd of this? My breath and blood!
Fiery? the fiery duke? Tell the hot duke that—
No, but not yet: may be he is not well:
Infirmity doth still neglect all office
Whereto our health is bound; we are not ourselves
When nature, being oppress'd, commands the mind
To suffer with the body: I'll forbear;
And am fallen out with my more headier will,
To take the indispos'd and sickly fit
For the sound man. Death on my state! wherefore
[*Looking on Kent.*]
Should he sit here? This act persuades me
That this remotion of the duke and her
Is practice only. Give me my servant forth.
Go tell the duke and 's wife I 'ld speak with them,
Now, presently: bid them come forth and hear me,
Or at their chamber-door I'll beat the drum
Till it cry sleep to death.

Glou. I would have all well betwixt you. *Exit.*

Lear. O me, my heart, my rising heart! but, down!

Fool. Cry to it, nuncle, as the cockney did to the eels when she put 'em i' the paste alive; she knapped 'em o' the coxcombs with a stick, and cried 'Down, wantons, down!' 'Twas her brother that, in pure kindness to his horse, buttered his hay.

Enter CORNWALL, REGAN, GLOUCESTER, [*and*] Servants.

Lear. Good morrow to you both.

Corn. Hail to your grace!
Kent here set at liberty.

Reg. I am glad to see your highness.

Lear. Regan, I think you are; I know what reason
I have to think so: if thou shouldst not be glad,
I would divorce me from thy mother's tomb,
Sepulchring an adultress. [*To Kent*] O, are you free?
Some other time for that. Beloved Regan,
Thy sister 's naught: O Regan, she hath tied
Sharp-tooth'd unkindness, like a vulture, here:
[*Points to his heart.*]
I can scarce speak to thee; thou 'lt not believe
With how deprav'd a quality—O Regan!

Reg. I pray you, sir, take patience: I have hope

41. **Display'd,** behaved ostentatiously. 42. **drew,** i.e., my sword. 49. **blind,** i.e., indifferent. 50. **bags,** i.e., of gold. 53. **turns the key,** i.e., opens the door. 55. **dolours,** griefs, with pun on "dollars." **tell,** count. 56, 57. **mother, Hysterica passio,** i.e., hysteria, giving the sensation of choking or suffocating. 58. **element's,** proper place is. 64. **chance,** chances it. 69-73. **All . . . stinking,** i.e., one who is out of favor can be easily detected (he smells of misfortune), and so is easily avoided by timeservers. 81. **pack,** take himself off. 90. **fetches,** pretexts, dodges. 91. **flying off,** desertion. 111-112. **am . . . take,** now disapprove of my more impetuous will in taking. 115. **remotion,** removal. 120. **cry sleep to death,** i.e., put an end to sleep. 123. **cockney,** i.e., a Londoner, ignorant of ways of cooking eels. 124. **paste,** pastry pie. 125. **knapped,** rapped. **coxcombs,** heads. 126. **wantons,** playful creatures. 127-128. **'Twas . . . hay.** Another city ignorance; the act is well-intended, but horses do not like greasy hay. 150. **confine,** assigned boundary. 151. **discretion,** discreet person.

You less know how to value her desert
Than she to scant her duty.
  Lear.   Say, how is that?
  Reg. I cannot think my sister in the least
Would fail her obligation: if, sir, perchance
She have restrain'd the riots of your followers,
'Tis on such ground, and to such wholesome end,
As clears her from all blame.
  Lear. My curses on her!
  Reg.   O, sir, you are old;
Nature in you stands on the very verge
Of her confine: you should be rul'd and led
By some discretion, that discerns your state
Better than you yourself. Therefore, I pray you,
That to our sister you do make return;
Say you have wrong'd her, sir.
  Lear.   Ask her forgiveness?
Do you but mark how this becomes the house:
'Dear daughter, I confess that I am old;   [*Kneeling*.]
Age is unnecessary: on my knees I beg
That you'll vouchsafe me raiment, bed, and food.'
  Reg. Good sir, no more; these are unsightly tricks:
Return you to my sister.
  Lear.   [*Rising*] Never, Regan:
She hath abated me of half my train;
Look'd black upon me; struck me with her tongue,
Most serpent-like, upon the very heart:
All the stor'd vengeances of heaven fall
On her ingrateful top! Strike her young bones,
You taking airs, with lameness!
  Corn.   Fie, sir, fie!
  Lear. You nimble lightnings, dart your blinding flames
Into her scornful eyes! Infect her beauty,
You fen-suck'd fogs, drawn by the pow'rful sun,
To fall and blast her pride!
  Reg. O the blest gods! so will you wish on me,
When the rash mood is on.
  Lear. No, Regan, thou shalt never have my curse:
Thy tender-hefted nature shall not give
Thee o'er to harshness: her eyes are fierce; but thine
Do comfort and not burn. 'Tis not in thee
To grudge my pleasures, to cut off my train,
To bandy hasty words, to scant my sizes,
And in conclusion to oppose the bolt
Against my coming in: thou better know'st
The offices of nature, bond of childhood,
Effects of courtesy, dues of gratitude;
Thy half o' th' kingdom hast thou not forgot,
Wherein I thee endow'd.
  Reg.   Good sir, to th' purpose.
  Lear. Who put my man i' th' stocks?   *Tucket within.*
  Corn.   What trumpet 's that?
  Reg. I know 't, my sister's: this approves her letter,
That she would soon be here.

Enter Steward [OSWALD].

                Is your lady come?
  Lear. This is a slave, whose easy-borrowed pride
Dwells in the fickle grace of her he follows.
Out, varlet, from my sight!
  Corn.   What means your grace?
  Lear. Who stock'd my servant? Regan, I have good hope
Thou didst not know on 't.

Enter GONERIL.

                Who comes here? O heavens,
If you do love old men, if your sweet sway
Allow obedience, if you yourselves are old,
Make it your cause; send down, and take my part!
[*To Gon*.] Art not asham'd to look upon this beard?
O Regan, will you take her by the hand?
  Gon. Why not by th' hand, sir? How have I offended?
All 's not offence that indiscretion finds
And dotage terms so.
  Lear.   O sides, you are too tough;
Will you yet hold? How came my man i' th' stocks?
  Corn. I set him there, sir: but his own disorders
Deserv'd much less advancement.
  Lear.   You! did you?
  Reg. I pray you, father, being weak, seem so.
If, till the expiration of your month,
You will return and sojourn with my sister,
Dismissing half your train, come then to me:
I am now from home, and out of that provision
Which shall be needful for your entertainment.
  Lear. Return to her, and fifty men dismiss'd?
No, rather I abjure all roofs, and choose
To wage against the enmity o' th' air;
To be a comrade with the wolf and owl,—
Necessity's sharp pinch! Return with her?
Why, the hot-blooded France, that dowerless took
Our youngest born, I could as well be brought
To knee his throne, and, squire-like, pension beg
To keep base life afoot. Return with her?
Persuade me rather to be slave and sumpter
To this detested groom.   [*Pointing at Oswald*.]
  Gon.   At your choice, sir.
  Lear. I prithee, daughter, do not make me mad:
I will not trouble thee, my child; farewell:
We'll no more meet, no more see one another:
But yet thou art my flesh, my blood, my daughter;
Or rather a disease that 's in my flesh,
Which I must needs call mine: thou art a boil,
A plague-sore, or embossed carbuncle,
In my corrupted blood. But I'll not chide thee;
Let shame come when it will, I do not call it:
I do not bid the thunder-bearer shoot,
Nor tell tales of thee to high-judging Jove:
Mend when thou canst; be better at thy leisure:
I can be patient; I can stay with Regan,
I and my hundred knights.
  Reg.   Not altogether so:
I look'd not for you yet, nor am provided
For your fit welcome. Give ear, sir, to my sister;
For those that mingle reason with your passion
Must be content to think you old, and so—
But she knows what she does.

155. **how . . . house,** how this would be suitable to our position. 165. **ingrateful top,** ungrateful head. **young bones,** i.e., unborn child. 166. **taking,** infectious. 169. **fen-suck'd.** It was supposed that the sun sucked up poisons from fens or marshes. 174. **tender-hefted,** set in a tender, delicate frame (Wright); gentle. 178. **sizes,** allowances. 186. **approves,** confirms. 188. **easy-borrowed,** put on without justification; hyphen comes from Theobald; perhaps *easy* has an independent meaning, "cool," "impudent." 191. **stock'd,** put into the stocks.

195. **Make . . . cause,** make my cause yours. 200. **sides . . . tough.** This is not figurative but indicates belief in an actual swelling of the heart so that it might break through the sides. 212. **wage,** wage war. 215. **hot-blooded,** passionate, angry. In I, ii, 23, France is said to have "in choler parted," his blood heated by passion. 217. **knee,** fall on my knees before. 219. **sumpter,** pack horse; hence, drudge. 227. **embossed,** swollen, tumid. 230. **thunder-bearer,** Jupiter.

Lear. Is this well spoken?
Reg. I dare avouch it, sir: what, fifty followers?
Is it not well? What should you need of more?
Yea, or so many, sith that both charge and danger
Speak 'gainst so great a number? How, in one house,
Should many people, under two commands,
Hold amity? 'Tis hard; almost impossible.
Gon. Why might not you, my lord, receive attendance
From those that she calls servants or from mine?
Reg. Why not, my lord? If then they chanc'd to slack ye,
We could control them. If you will come to me,—
For now I spy a danger,—I entreat you
To bring but five and twenty: to no more
Will I give place or notice.
Lear. I gave you all—
Reg. And in good time you gave it.
Lear. Made you my guardians, my depositaries;
But kept a reservation to be followed
With such a number. What, must I come to you
With five and twenty, Regan? said you so?
Reg. And speak 't again, my lord; no more with me.
Lear. Those wicked creatures yet do look well-favour'd,
When others are more wicked; not being the worst
Stands in some rank of praise. [*To Gon.*] I'll go with thee:
Thy fifty yet doth double five-and-twenty,
And thou art twice her love.
Gon. Hear me, my lord:
What need you five and twenty, ten, or five,
To follow in a house where twice so many
Have a command to tend you?
Reg. What need one?
Lear. O, reason not the need! Our basest beggars
Are in the poorest thing superfluous:
Allow not nature more than nature needs,
Man's life is cheap as beast's: thou art a lady;
If only to go warm were gorgeous,
Why, nature needs not what thou gorgeous wear'st,
Which scarcely keeps thee warm. But, for true need,—
You heavens, give me that patience, patience I need!
You see me here, you gods, a poor old man,
As full of grief as age; wretched in both!
If it be you that stirs these daughters' hearts
Against their father, fool me not so much
To bear it tamely; touch me with noble anger,
And let not women's weapons, water-drops,
Stain my man's cheeks! No, you unnatural hags,
I will have such revenges on you both,
That all the world shall—I will do such things,—
What they are, yet I know not; but they shall be
The terrors of the earth. You think I'll weep;
No, I'll not weep:
I have full cause of weeping; but this heart
Shall break into a hundred thousand flaws,
Or ere I'll weep. O fool, I shall go mad!

Storm and tempest. Exeunt [*Lear, Gloucester, Kent, and Fool*].

Corn. Let us withdraw; 'twill be a storm.
Reg. This house is little: the old man and 's people
Cannot be well bestow'd.
Gon. 'Tis his own blame; hath put himself from rest,
And must needs taste his folly.
Reg. For his particular, I'll receive him gladly,
But not one follower.
Gon. So am I purpos'd.
Where is my lord of Gloucester?
Corn. Follow'd the old man forth: he is return'd.

Enter GLOUCESTER.

Glou. The king is in high rage.
Corn. Whither is he going?
Glou. He calls to horse; but will I know not whither.
Corn. 'Tis best to give him way; he leads himself.
Gon. My lord, entreat him by no means to stay.
Glou. Alack, the night comes on, and the high winds
Do sorely ruffle; for many miles about
There 's scarce a bush.
Reg. O, sir, to wilful men,
The injuries that they themselves procure
Must be their schoolmasters. Shut up your doors:
He is attended with a desperate train;
And what they may incense him to, being apt
To have his ear abus'd, wisdom bids fear.
Corn. Shut up your doors, my lord; 'tis a wild night:
My Regan counsels well: come out o' th' storm.

Exeunt.

ACT III.

SCENE I. [*A heath.*]

Storm still. Enter KENT *and a* Gentleman, *severally.*

Kent. Who 's there, besides foul weather?
Gent. One minded like the weather, most unquietly.
Kent. I know you. Where 's the king?
Gent. Contending with the fretful elements;
Bids the wind blow the earth into the sea,
Or swell the curled waters 'bove the main,
That things might change or cease; tears his white hair,
Which the impetuous blasts, with eyeless rage,
Catch in their fury, and make nothing of;
Strives in his little world of man to out-scorn
The to-and-fro-conflicting wind and rain.
This night, wherein the cub-drawn bear would couch,
The lion and the belly-pinched wolf
Keep their fur dry, unbonneted he runs,
And bids what will take all.
Kent. But who is with him?

240. **avouch,** swear by. 242. **sith that,** since. **charge,** expense. 245. **Hold amity,** maintain friendship. 248. **slack,** be careless in their attendance on. 252. **notice,** countenance. 254. **my guardians.** Lear understands his contract to be that the daughters were guardians, or stewardesses, of his realm under him. 261. **Stands . . . praise,** is at least relatively worthy of praise. 265. **follow,** attend on. 266. **tend,** wait on. 267. **reason,** scrutinize. 268. **Are . . . superfluous,** have some wretched possession they can dispense with. 269. **Allow,** if you allow. **needs,** i.e., to survive. 271-273. **If . . . warm,** i.e., if fashions in clothes were determined only by the need for warmth, this natural standard wouldn't justify the rich robes you wear to be gorgeous—which don't serve well for warmth in any case. 278. **fool,** humiliate. 279. **To bear,** as to make me bear. 288. **flaws,** fragments; also, gusts of passion. 292. **bestow'd,** lodged. 293. **blame,** fault. **from rest,** i.e., out of the house; also, lacking peace of mind. 295. **For his particular,** as for him individually. 304. **ruffle,** bluster. 308. **desperate train,** body of desperate followers. 309. **incense him to,** incite him to undertake. 309-310. **being . . . abus'd,** being inclined to hearken to wild counsel.

ACT III. SCENE I. 6. **main,** mainland. 10. **little world of man,** the microcosm; allusion to the theory that man is an epitome of the macrocosm, or universe, and moves in accordance with its laws and influences. 12. **cub-drawn,** famished, with udders sucked dry (and hence

Gent. None but the fool; who labours to out-jest
His heart-struck injuries.
Kent. Sir, I do know you;
And dare, upon the warrant of my note,
Commend a dear thing to you. There is division,
Although as yet the face of it is cover'd
With mutual cunning, 'twixt Albany and Cornwall;
Who have—as who have not, that their great stars
Thron'd and set high?—servants, who seem no less,
Which are to France the spies and speculations
Intelligent of our state; what hath been seen,
Either in snuffs and packings of the dukes,
Or the hard rein which both of them have borne
Against the old kind king; or something deeper,
Whereof perchance these are but furnishings;
But, true it is, from France there comes a power
Into this scattered kingdom; who already,
Wise in our negligence, have secret feet
In some of our best ports, and are at point
To show their open banner. Now to you:
If on my credit you dare build so far
To make your speed to Dover, you shall find
Some that will thank you, making just report
Of how unnatural and bemadding sorrow
The king hath cause to plain.
I am a gentleman of blood and breeding;
And, from some knowledge and assurance, offer
This office to you.
Gent. I will talk further with you.
Kent. No, do not.
For confirmation that I am much more
Than my out-wall, open this purse, and take
What it contains. If you shall see Cordelia,—
As fear not but you shall,—show her this ring;
And she will tell you who that fellow is
That yet you do not know. Fie on this storm!
I will go seek the king.
Gent. Give me your hand: have you no more to say?
Kent. Few words, but, to effect, more than all yet;
That, when we have found the king,—in which your pain
That way, I'll this,—he that first lights on him
Holla the other. *Exeunt* [*severally*].

SCENE II. [*Another part of the heath.*]

Storm still. Enter LEAR *and* Fool.

Lear. Blow, winds, and crack your cheeks! rage! blow!
You cataracts and hurricanoes, spout
Till you have drench'd our steeples, drown'd the cocks!
You sulph'rous and thought-executing fires,
Vaunt-couriers of oak-cleaving thunderbolts,
Singe my white head! And thou, all-shaking thunder,
Strike flat the thick rotundity o' th' world!
Crack nature's moulds, all germens spill at once,
That makes ingrateful man!

Fool. O nuncle, court holy-water in a dry house is better than this rain-water out o' door. Good nuncle, in, ask thy daughters' blessing: here 's a night pities neither wise men nor fools.

Lear. Rumble thy bellyful! Spit, fire! spout, rain!
Nor rain, wind, thunder, fire, are my daughters:
I tax not you, you elements, with unkindness;
I never gave you kingdom, call'd you children,
You owe me no subscription: then let fall
Your horrible pleasure; here I stand, your slave,
A poor, infirm, weak, and despis'd old man:
But yet I call you servile ministers,
That will with two pernicious daughters join
Your high engender'd battles 'gainst a head
So old and white as this. O! O! 'tis foul!

Fool. He that has a house to put 's head in has a good head-piece.

The cod-piece that will house
Before the head has any,
The head and he shall louse;
So beggars marry many.
The man that makes his toe
What he his heart should make
Shall of a corn cry woe,
And turn his sleep to wake.

For there was never yet fair woman but she made mouths in a glass.

Lear. No, I will be the pattern of all patience;
I will say nothing.

Enter KENT.

Kent. Who 's there?

Fool. Marry, here 's grace and a cod-piece; that 's a wise man and a fool.

Kent. Alas, sir, are you here? things that love night
Love not such nights as these; the wrathful skies
Gallow the very wanderers of the dark,
And make them keep their caves: since I was man,
Such sheets of fire, such bursts of horrid thunder,
Such groans of roaring wind and rain, I never
Remember to have heard: man's nature cannot carry
Th' affliction nor the fear.
Lear. Let the great gods,
That keep this dreadful pudder o'er our heads,
Find out their enemies now. Tremble, thou wretch,
That hast within thee undivulged crimes,
Unwhipp'd of justice: hide thee, thou bloody hand;
Thou perjur'd, and thou simular of virtue
That art incestuous: caitiff, to pieces shake,
That under covert and convenient seeming
Hast practis'd on man's life: close pent-up guilts,
Rive your concealing continents, and cry
These dreadful summoners grace. I am a man
More sinn'd against than sinning.
Kent. Alack, bare-headed!

ravenous). **couch,** lie close. 18. **upon . . . note,** on the strength of what I know. 19. **Commend,** entrust. 24. **speculations,** scouts, spies. Johnson conjectured *speculators*. 26. **snuffs,** quarrels. **packings,** intrigues. 29. **furnishings,** outward shows. 31. **scattered,** divided. 33. **at point,** ready. 38. **bemadding,** distracting. 39. **plain,** complain of. 45. **out-wall,** exterior. 52. **to effect,** to the purpose. 53-54. **your pain That way,** laborious quest (take you) that way.

SCENE II. 2. **hurricanoes,** waterspouts. 3. **cocks,** weathercocks. 4. **thought-executing,** probably, acting with the quickness of thought. 5. **Vaunt-couriers,** forerunners. 8. **germens,** germs, seeds. **spill,** destroy. 10. **court holy-water,** flattery. 18. **subscription,** allegiance. 23. **high engender'd battles,** battalions levied in the heavens. 27-34. **The cod-piece . . . wake,** a man who cohabits sexually but improvidently can expect penury; and one who elevates what is base above what is noble can expect misery also (as Lear has done with his daughters). **cod-piece,** front part of close-fitting hose worn by men; hence, the sexual member. 44. **Gallow,** frighten, terrify. 50. **pudder,** turmoil. 54. **simular,** pretender. 56. **seeming,** hypocrisy. 58. **Rive,** split. **continents,** covering. 58-59. **cry . . . grace,** pray for mercy at the hands of the officers of divine justice. A *summoner* was the police officer of an ecclesiastical court.

Gracious my lord, hard by here is a hovel;
Some friendship will it lend you 'gainst the tempest:
Repose you there; while I to this hard house—
More harder than the stones whereof 'tis rais'd;
Which even but now, demanding after you,
Denied me to come in—return, and force
Their scanted courtesy.

Lear. My wits begin to turn.
Come on, my boy: how dost, my boy? art cold?
I am cold myself. Where is this straw, my fellow?
The art of our necessities is strange,
That can make vile things precious. Come, your hovel.
Poor fool and knave, I have one part in my heart
That 's sorry yet for thee.

Fool. [*Singing*] He that has and a little tiny wit,—
With hey, ho, the wind and the rain,—
Must make content with his fortunes fit,
Though the rain it raineth every day.

Lear. True, boy. Come, bring us to this hovel. *Exit* [*with Kent*].

Fool. This is a brave night to cool a courtezan.
I'll speak a prophecy ere I go:
When priests are more in word than matter;
When brewers mar their malt with water;
When nobles are their tailors' tutors;
No heretics burn'd, but wenches' suitors;
When every case in law is right;
No squire in debt, nor no poor knight;
When slanders do not live in tongues;
Nor cutpurses come not to throngs;
When usurers tell their gold i' th' field;
And bawds and whores do churches build;
Then shall the realm of Albion
Come to great confusion:
Then comes the time, who lives to see 't,
That going shall be us'd with feet.
This prophecy Merlin shall make; for I live before his time. *Exit.*

SCENE III. [*Gloucester's castle.*]

Enter GLOUCESTER *and* EDMUND.

Glou. Alack, alack, Edmund, I like not this unnatural dealing. When I desired their leave that I might pity him, they took from me the use of mine own house; charged me, on pain of perpetual displeasure, neither to speak of him, entreat for him, or any way sustain him.

Edm. Most savage and unnatural!

Glou. Go to; say you nothing. There is division between the dukes; and a worse matter than that: I have received a letter this night; 'tis dangerous to be spoken; I have locked the letter in my closet: these injuries the king now bears will be revenged home; there is part of a power already footed: we must incline to the king. I will look him, and privily relieve him: go you and maintain talk with the duke, that my charity be not of him perceived: if he ask for me, I am ill, and gone to bed. If I die for it, as no less is threatened me, the king my old master must be relieved. There is strange things toward, Edmund; pray you, be careful. *Exit.*

Edm. This courtesy, forbid thee, shall the duke
Instantly know; and of that letter too:
This seems a fair deserving, and must draw me
That which my father loses; no less than all:
The younger rises when the old doth fall. *Exit.*

SCENE IV. [*The heath. Before a hovel.*]

Enter LEAR, KENT, *and* Fool.

Kent. Here is the place, my lord; good my lord, enter:
The tyranny of the open night 's too rough
For nature to endure. *Storm still.*

Lear. Let me alone.

Kent. Good my lord, enter here.

Lear. Wilt break my heart?

Kent. I had rather break mine own. Good my lord, enter.

Lear. Thou think'st 'tis much that this contentious storm
Invades us to the skin: so 'tis to thee;
But where the greater malady is fix'd,
The lesser is scarce felt. Thou 'ldst shun a bear;
But if thy flight lay toward the roaring sea,
Thou 'ldst meet the bear i' th' mouth. When the mind 's free,
The body 's delicate: the tempest in my mind
Doth from my senses take all feeling else
Save what beats there. Filial ingratitude!
Is it not as this mouth should tear this hand
For lifting food to 't? But I will punish home:
No, I will weep no more. In such a night
To shut me out! Pour on; I will endure.
In such a night as this! O Regan, Goneril!
Your old kind father, whose frank heart gave all,—
O, that way madness lies; let me shun that;
No more of that.

Kent. Good my lord, enter here.

Lear. Prithee, go in thyself; seek thine own ease:
This tempest will not give me leave to ponder
On things would hurt me more. But I'll go in.
[*To the Fool*] In, boy; go first. You houseless poverty,—
Nay, get thee in. I'll pray, and then I'll sleep.
Exit [*Fool into the hovel*].
Poor naked wretches, wheresoe'er you are,
That bide the pelting of this pitiless storm,
How shall your houseless heads and unfed sides,
Your loop'd and window'd raggedness, defend you

63. **hard,** cruel. 65. **Which,** i.e., the owners of the house. **demanding,** I inquiring. 80-95. **I'll . . . time.** Omitted in Q and usually regarded as an interpolation in the text of F. Merlin was a magician of King Arthur's court; a prophecy of Merlin, somewhat like these lines, is found in Holinshed and other places. 81. **matter,** i.e., the truth of the Gospel. 89. **tell,** count. **i' th' field,** i.e., openly. 92. **confusion,** i.e., the ironic result of an impossible reform. 94. **going,** i.e., walking (an anticlimax suggesting normality).

SCENE III. 14. **footed,** landed. 15. **look,** look for. 22. **courtesy, forbid thee,** i.e., this kindness to Lear you were forbidden to show. 24. **fair deserving,** meritorious action.

SCENE IV. 8. **greater malady.** There was a familiar belief that one passion might drive out or allay another. 28-36. **Poor naked wretches,** etc. Lear's error has been a violation of that law of nature which is called justice. His sufferings have brought him round to a complete recognition and expression of general distributive justice. 29. **bide,** endure. 31. **loop'd and window'd,** full of openings like windows and loopholes. 33. **Take physic, pomp,** cure yourself, O distempered great man. 35. **superflux,** superfluity, a word suggestive of the ethics of ownership in society. 58. **over four-inched bridges,** i.e., take mad risks. **course,** chase. 59. **five wits,** the five mental faculties: common wit, imagination, fantasy, judgment, memory. 61. **star-blasting,** blighting by influence of the stars. **taking,** pestilence. 65. **pass,** evil plight. 69. **pendulous,** suspended. 77. **pelican,** greedy; a reference

From seasons such as these? O, I have ta'en
Too little care of this! Take physic, pomp;
Expose thyself to feel what wretches feel,
That thou mayst shake the superflux to them,
And show the heavens more just.

Edg. [*Within*] Fathom and half, fathom and half! Poor Tom! *Enter Fool* [*from the hovel*].

Fool. Come not in here, nuncle, here 's a spirit. Help me, help me!

Kent. Give me thy hand. Who 's there?

Fool. A spirit, a spirit: he says his name 's poor Tom.

Kent. What art thou that dost grumble there i' the straw? Come forth.

Enter EDGAR [*disguised as a madman*].

Edg. Away! the foul fiend follows me!
Through the sharp hawthorn blows the cold wind.
Hum! go to thy bed, and warm thee.

Lear. Didst thou give all to thy daughters?
And art thou come to this?

Edg. Who gives any thing to poor Tom? whom the foul fiend hath led through fire and through flame, through ford and whirlpool, o'er bog and quagmire; that hath laid knives under his pillow, and halters in his pew; set ratsbane by his porridge; made him proud of heart, to ride on a bay trotting-horse over four-inched bridges, to course his own shadow for a traitor. Bless thy five wits! Tom 's a-cold,—O, do de, do de, do de. Bless thee from whirlwinds, star-blasting, and taking! Do poor Tom some charity, whom the foul fiend vexes: there could I have him now,—and there,—and there again, and there. *Storm still.*

Lear. What, have his daughters brought him to this pass?
Couldst thou save nothing? Wouldst thou give 'em all?

Fool. Nay, he reserved a blanket, else we had been all shamed.

Lear. Now, all the plagues that in the pendulous air
Hang fated o'er men's faults light on thy daughters!

Kent. He hath no daughters, sir.

Lear. Death, traitor! nothing could have subdu'd nature
To such a lowness but his unkind daughters.
Is it the fashion, that discarded fathers
Should have thus little mercy on their flesh?
Judicious punishment! 'twas this flesh begot
Those pelican daughters.

Edg. Pillicock sat on Pillicock-hill:
Halloo, halloo, loo, loo!

Fool. This cold night will turn us all to fools and madmen.

Edg. Take heed o' the foul fiend: obey thy parents; keep thy word's justice; swear not; commit not with man's sworn spouse; set not thy sweet heart on proud array. Tom 's a-cold.

Lear. What hast thou been?

Edg. A serving-man, proud in heart and mind; that curled my hair; wore gloves in my cap; served the lust of my mistress' heart, and did the act of darkness with her; swore as many oaths as I spake words, and broke them in the sweet face of heaven: one that slept in the contriving of lust, and waked to do it: wine loved I deeply, dice dearly; and in woman out-paramoured the Turk: false of heart, light of ear, bloody of hand; hog in sloth, fox in stealth, wolf in greediness, dog in madness, lion in prey. Let not the creaking of shoes nor the rustling of silks betray thy poor heart to woman: keep thy foot out of brothels, thy hand out of plackets, thy pen from lenders' books, and defy the foul fiend.
Still through the hawthorn blows the cold wind:
Says suum, mun, nonny.
Dolphin my boy, boy, sessa! let him trot by.
Storm still.

Lear. Thou wert better in a grave than to answer with thy uncovered body this extremity of the skies. Is man no more than this? Consider him well. Thou owest the worm no silk, the beast no hide, the sheep no wool, the cat no perfume. Ha! here 's three on 's are sophisticated! Thou art the thing itself: unaccommodated man is no more but such a poor, bare, forked animal as thou art. Off, off, you lendings! come, unbutton here. [*Tearing off his clothes.*]

Fool. Prithee, nuncle, be contented; 'tis a naughty night to swim in. Now a little fire in a wild field were like an old lecher's heart; a small spark, all the rest on 's body cold. Look, here comes a walking fire.

Enter GLOUCESTER, *with a torch.*

Edg. This is the foul Flibbertigibbet: he begins at curfew, and walks till the first cock; he gives the web and the pin, squints the eye, and makes the hare-lip; mildews the white wheat, and hurts the poor creature of earth.
S. Withold footed thrice the 'old;
He met the night-mare, and her nine-fold;
Bid her alight,
And her troth plight,
And, aroint thee, witch, aroint thee!

Kent. How fares your grace?

Lear. What 's he?

Kent. Who 's there? What is 't you seek?

Glou. What are you there? Your names?

Edg. Poor Tom; that eats the swimming frog, the toad, the tadpole, the wall-newt and the water; that in the fury of his heart, when the foul fiend rages, eats cow-dung for sallets; swallows the old rat and the ditch-dog; drinks the green mantle of the standing pool; who is whipped from tithing to tithing, and stock-punished, and imprisoned; who hath had three suits to his back, six shirts to his body, horse to ride, and weapon to wear;
But mice and rats, and such small deer,
Have been Tom's food for seven long year.

to the belief that young pelicans fed on the blood of their mother's breasts. 78. **Pillicock,** from an old rhyme (suggested by *pelican*). *Pillicock* seems to have been used to mean "darling." 83. **commit not,** i.e., adultery. 88. **gloves,** as his mistress' favors. 95. **light of ear,** foolishly credulous (Schmidt), frivolous (Onions). 99. **plackets,** slits in skirts. 100. **pen . . . books,** sign a contract for a loan. 103-104. **suum . . . sessa,** imitative of the wind. 104. **Dolphin my boy,** a slang phrase, or bit of song. 110. **cat,** civet cat. 111. **sophisticated,** clad in the trappings of civilized life; Schmidt defines as "adulterated." 112. **unaccommodated man,** man unprovided with clothes and necessaries; also, man without social modification. 120. **Flibbertigibbet,** a fiend whose name Shakespeare borrowed from Harsnet's *Declaration* (1603).

121. **first cock,** midnight. 122. **web and the pin,** cataract of the eye. **squints,** makes to squint or cross. 124. **white wheat,** approaching ripeness. 125. **S. Withold,** understood as a corruption of St. Vitalis, who is said to have been invoked against nightmare. **footed thrice the 'old,** thrice traversed the wold (tract of hilly upland). 126. **nine-fold,** nine familiars; suggestive also certainly of nine foals. 129. **aroint thee,** begone. 135. **wall-newt,** lizard. 136. **water,** i.e., water newt. 137. **sallets,** salads. 139. **mantle,** scum. 140. **tithing to tithing,** i.e., from one ward or parish to another. **stock-punished,** punished by being put into the stocks. 144. **deer,** probably, animals generally.

Beware my follower. Peace, Smulkin; peace, thou fiend!

Glou. What, hath your grace no better company?
Edg. The prince of darkness is a gentleman:
Modo he 's call'd, and Mahu.
Glou. Our flesh and blood, my lord, is grown so vile
That it doth hate what gets it.
Edg. Poor Tom 's a-cold.
Glou. Go in with me: my duty cannot suffer
T' obey in all your daughters' hard commands:
Though their injunction be to bar my doors,
And let this tyrannous night take hold upon you,
Yet have I ventured to come seek you out,
And bring you where both fire and food is ready.
Lear. First let me talk with this philosopher.
What is the cause of thunder?
Kent. Good my lord, take his offer; go into th' house.
Lear. I'll talk a word with this same learned Theban.
What is your study?
Edg. How to prevent the fiend, and to kill vermin.
Lear. Let me ask you one word in private.
Kent. Importune him once more to go, my lord;
His wits begin t' unsettle.
Glou. Canst thou blame him? *Storm still.*
His daughters seek his death; ah, that good Kent!
He said it would be thus, poor banish'd man!
Thou sayest the king grows mad; I'll tell thee, friend,
I am almost mad myself: I had a son,
Now outlaw'd from my blood; he sought my life,
But lately, very late: I lov'd him, friend:
No father his son dearer: truth to tell thee,
The grief hath craz'd my wits. What a night 's this!
I do beseech your grace,—
Lear. O, cry you mercy, sir.
Noble philosopher, your company.
Edg. Tom 's a-cold.
Glou. In, fellow, there, into th' hovel: keep thee warm.
Lear. Come, let 's in all.
Kent. This way, my lord.
Lear. With him;
I will keep still with my philosopher.
Kent. Good my lord, soothe him; let him take the fellow.
Glou. Take him you on.
Kent. Sirrah, come on; go along with us.
Lear. Come, good Athenian.
Glou. No words, no words: hush.
Edg. Child Rowland to the dark tower came,
His word was still,—Fie, foh, and fum,
I smell the blood of a British man. *Exeunt.*

SCENE V. [*Gloucester's castle.*]

Enter CORNWALL *and* EDMUND.

Corn. I will have my revenge ere I depart his house.

Edm. How, my lord, I may be censured, that nature thus gives way to loyalty, something fears me to think of.

Corn. I now perceive, it was not altogether your brother's evil disposition made him seek his death; but a provoking merit, set a-work by a reproveable badness in himself.

Edm. How malicious is my fortune, that I must repent to be just! This is the letter he spoke of, which approves him an intelligent party to the advantages of France. O heavens! that this treason were not, or not I the detector!

Corn. Go with me to the duchess.

Edm. If the matter of this paper be certain, you have mighty business in hand.

Corn. True or false, it hath made thee Earl of Gloucester. Seek out where thy father is, that he may be ready for our apprehension.

Edm. [*Aside*] If I find him comforting the king, it will stuff his suspicion more fully.—I will persevere in my course of loyalty, though the conflict be sore between that and my blood.

Corn. I will lay trust upon thee; and thou shalt find a dearer father in my love. *Exeunt.*

SCENE VI. [*A chamber in a farmhouse adjoining the castle.*]

Enter KENT *and* GLOUCESTER.

Glou. Here is better than the open air; take it thankfully. I will piece out the comfort with what addition I can: I will not be long from you.

Kent. All the power of his wits have given way to his impatience: the gods reward your kindness!

Exit [*Gloucester*].

Enter LEAR, EDGAR, *and* FOOL.

Edg. Frateretto calls me; and tells me Nero is an angler in the lake of darkness. Pray, innocent, and beware the foul fiend.

Fool. Prithee, nuncle, tell me whether a madman be a gentleman or a yeoman?

Lear. A king, a king!

Fool. No, he 's a yeoman that has a gentleman to his son; for he 's a mad yeoman that sees his son a gentleman before him.

Lear. To have a thousand with red burning spits
Come hizzing in upon 'em,—
Edg. The foul fiend bites my back.

Fool. He 's mad that trusts in the tameness of a wolf, a horse's health, a boy's love, or a whore's oath.

Lear. It shall be done; I will arraign them straight.
[*To Edgar*] Come, sit thou here, most learned justice;
[*To the Fool*] Thou, sapient sir, sit here. Now, you she foxes!
Edg. Look, where he stands and glares!
Want'st thou eyes at trial, madam?
Come o'er the bourn, Bessy, to me,—

146. **Smulkin,** another name occurring in Harsnet. 149. **Modo, Mahu,** two superior fiends in Harsnet. 151. **gets,** begets. 162. **learned Theban,** possibly a current phrase to indicate a philosopher. 182. **soothe,** humor, indulge. 187. **Child Rowland,** etc., fragments of the ballad *Child Rowland and Burd Ellen*. The theme of Browning's *Childe Roland to the Dark Tower Came* is derived from these lines.

SCENE V. 8. **provoking merit,** etc., i.e., an evil justice (in Edgar) incited by the badness of Gloucester. 12. **approves him,** proves him to be. **intelligent,** aware (in the legal sense). 25. **blood,** natural feeling.

SCENE VI. 7. **Frateretto,** another of the fiends from Harsnet. 8. **Nero is an angler,** pointed out as an allusion to Rabelais, ii, 30, where Nero is described as a fiddler and Trajan as an angler. 9. **innocent,** simpleton, fool. 17. **hizzing,** hissing. (Lear is contemplating revenge.) 23. **justice,** judge. 25. **he,** perhaps Lear, or one of Edgar's devils. 26. **Want'st . . . trial,** meaning doubtful. Possibly Edgar alludes to the staring fiend. 27. **Come . . . me,** first line of a ballad by William Birche (1558). (The Fool makes a ribald reply; see *hath a leak*.) 32. **Hoppedance.** Harsnet mentions "Hobberdidance." 33. **white,** unsmoked (contrasted with *black devil*). **Croak,** make a rumbling sound in the stomach to denote hunger. 37. **evidence,** witnesses. 39.

Fool. Her boat hath a leak,
And she must not speak
Why she dares not come over to thee.

Edg. The foul fiend haunts poor Tom in the voice of a nightingale. Hoppedance cries in Tom's belly for two white herring. Croak not, black angel; I have no food for thee.

Kent. How do you, sir? Stand you not so amaz'd.
Will you lie down and rest upon the cushions?

Lear. I'll see their trial first. Bring in the evidence.
[*To Edgar*] Thou robed man of justice, take thy place;
[*To the Fool*] And thou, his yoke-fellow of equity,
Bench by his side: [*To Kent*] you are o' th' commission,
Sit you too.

Edg. Let us deal justly.
Sleepest or wakest thou, jolly shepherd?
Thy sheep be in the corn;
And for one blast of thy minikin mouth,
Thy sheep shall take no harm.
Pur! the cat is gray.

Lear. Arraign her first; 'tis Goneril. I here take my oath before this honourable assembly, she kicked the poor king her father.

Fool. Come hither, mistress. Is your name Goneril?

Lear. She cannot deny it.

Fool. Cry you mercy, I took you for a joint-stool.

Lear. And here 's another, whose warp'd looks proclaim
What store her heart is made on. Stop her there!
Arms, arms, sword, fire! Corruption in the place!
False justicer, why hast thou let her 'scape?

Edg. Bless thy five wits!

Kent. O pity! Sir, where is the patience now,
That you so oft have boasted to retain?

Edg. [*Aside*] My tears begin to take his part so much,
They'll mar my counterfeiting.

Lear. The little dogs and all,
Tray, Blanch, and Sweet-heart, see, they bark at me.

Edg. Tom will throw his head at them.
Avaunt, you curs!
Be thy mouth or black or white,
Tooth that poisons if it bite;
Mastiff, greyhound, mongrel grim,
Hound or spaniel, brach or lym,
Or bobtail tike or trundle-tail,
Tom will make him weep and wail:
For, with throwing thus my head,
Dogs leap'd the hatch, and all are fled.
Do de, de, de. Sessa! Come, march to wakes and fairs and market-towns. Poor Tom, thy horn is dry.

Lear. Then let them anatomize Regan; see what breeds about her heart. Is there any cause in nature that makes these hard hearts? [*To Edgar*] You, sir, I entertain for one of my hundred; only I do not like the fashion of your garments: you will say they are Persian; but let them be changed.

Kent. Now, good my lord, lie here and rest awhile.

Lear. Make no noise, make no noise; draw the curtains: so, so. We'll go to supper i' th' morning. So, so, so.

Fool. And I'll go to bed at noon.

Enter GLOUCESTER.

Glou. Come hither, friend: where is the king my master?

Kent. Here, sir; but trouble him not, his wits are gone.

Glou. Good friend, I prithee, take him in thy arms;
I have o'erheard a plot of death upon him:
There is a litter ready; lay him in 't,
And drive toward Dover, friend, where thou shalt meet
Both welcome and protection. Take up thy master:
If thou shouldst dally half an hour, his life,
With thine, and all that offer to defend him,
Stand in assured loss: take up, take up;
And follow me, that will to some provision
Give thee quick conduct.

Kent. Oppressed nature sleeps:
This rest might yet have balm'd thy broken sinews,
Which, if convenience will not allow,
Stand in hard cure. [*To the Fool*] Come, help to bear thy master;
Thou must not stay behind.

Glou. Come, come, away.
Exeunt [*all but Edgar*].

Edg. When we our betters see bearing our woes,
We scarcely think our miseries our foes.
Who alone suffers suffers most i' th' mind,
Leaving free things and happy shows behind:
But then the mind much sufferance doth o'erskip,
When grief hath mates, and bearing fellowship.
How light and portable my pain seems now,
When that which makes me bend makes the king bow,
He childed as I fathered! Tom, away!
Mark the high noises; and thyself bewray,
When false opinion, whose wrong thoughts defile thee,
In thy just proof, repeals and reconciles thee.
What will hap more to-night, safe 'scape the king!
Lurk, lurk. [*Exit.*]

SCENE VII. [*Gloucester's castle.*]

Enter CORNWALL, REGAN, GONERIL, *Bastard* [EDMUND], *and* Servants.

Corn. Post speedily to my lord your husband; show him this letter: the army of France is landed. Seek out the traitor Gloucester. [*Exeunt some of the Servants.*]

Reg. Hang him instantly.

Gon. Pluck out his eyes.

Corn. Leave him to my displeasure. Edmund, keep you our sister company: the revenges we are bound to

yoke-fellow, partner. 40. **Bench,** sit on the judgment seat. **o' th' commission,** a justice of peace. 45. **minikin,** pretty, dainty. 47. **Pur.** Perhaps for the sound of a cat, or the name of a demon, or both. There is a fiend in Harsnet named Purre. 55. **joint-stool,** chair made by a joiner, possibly ornamented. Proverbially this phrase meant "I beg your pardon for failing to notice you." The reference is also presumably to a real stool on stage. 57. **store,** material. 58. **Corruption in the place,** i.e., there is iniquity or bribery in this court. 72. **lym,** lymmer, a species of bloodhound which runs by scent. 73. **tike,** small dog, cur. **trundle-tail,** curly tail. 76. **hatch,** lower half of a divided door. 77. **Sessa,** away! **wakes,** parish feasts. 79. **horn,** horn bottle used by beggars to beg for drinks. 86. **Persian,** rich, gorgeous attire (ironic). 96. **upon,** against. 102. **Stand in assured loss,** will assuredly be lost. 105. **balm'd,** cured, healed. **sinews,** nerves. 106. **convenience,** fortunate circumstance. 107. **Stand . . . cure,** will be hard to cure. 109. **our woes,** woes like ours. 110. **our foes,** i.e., ours alone. 113. **sufferance,** suffering. 114. **bearing,** tribulation. 115. **portable,** endurable. 117. **He . . . fathered,** he has found the same cruelty in his children which I found in my father. 118. **bewray,** betray, reveal. 120. **In . . . proof,** in vindication of your just conduct. **repeals,** recalls, restores.

take upon your traitorous father are not fit for your beholding. Advise the duke, where you are going, to a most festinate preparation: we are bound to the like. Our posts shall be swift and intelligent betwixt us. Farewell, dear sister: farewell, my lord of Gloucester.

Enter Steward [Oswald].

How now! where 's the king?
Osw. My lord of Gloucester hath convey'd him hence:
Some five or six and thirty of his knights,
Hot questrists after him, met him at gate;
Who, with some other of the lord's dependants,
Are gone with him toward Dover; where they boast
To have well-armed friends.
Corn. Get horses for your mistress.
[*Exit Oswald.*]
Gon. Farewell, sweet lord, and sister.
Corn. Edmund, farewell.
Exit [*Goneril with Edmund*].
Go seek the traitor Gloucester,
Pinion him like a thief, bring him before us.
[*Exeunt other Servants.*]
Though well we may not pass upon his life
Without the form of justice, yet our power
Shall do a court'sy to our wrath, which men
May blame, but not control. Who 's there? the traitor?

Enter Gloucester *and* Servants.

Reg. Ingrateful fox! 'tis he.
Corn. Bind fast his corky arms.
Glou. What means your graces? Good my friends, consider
You are my guests: do me no foul play, friends.
Corn. Bind him, I say. [*Servants bind him.*]
Reg. Hard, hard. O filthy traitor!
Glou. Unmerciful lady as you are, I'm none.
Corn. To this chair bind him. Villain, thou shalt find— [*Regan plucks his beard.*]
Glou. By the kind gods, 'tis most ignobly done
To pluck me by the beard.
Reg. So white, and such a traitor!
Glou. Naughty lady,
These hairs, which thou dost ravish from my chin,
Will quicken, and accuse thee: I am your host:
With robbers' hands my hospitable favours
You should not ruffle thus. What will you do?
Corn. Come, sir, what letters had you late from France?
Reg. Be simple answer'd, for we know the truth.
Corn. And what confederacy have you with the traitors
Late footed in the kingdom?
Reg. To whose hands you have sent the lunatic king:
Speak.
Glou. I have a letter guessingly set down,
Which came from one that 's of a neutral heart,
And not from one oppos'd.
Corn. Cunning.
Reg. And false.
Corn. Where hast thou sent the king?
Glou. To Dover.
Reg. Wherefore to Dover? Wast thou not charg'd at peril—
Corn. Wherefore to Dover? Let him answer that.
Glou. I am tied to th' stake, and I must stand the course.
Reg. Wherefore to Dover?
Glou. Because I would not see thy cruel nails
Pluck out his poor old eyes; nor thy fierce sister
In his anointed flesh stick boarish fangs.
The sea, with such a storm as his bare head
In hell-black night endur'd, would have buoy'd up,
And quench'd the stelled fires:
Yet, poor old heart, he holp the heavens to rain.
If wolves had at thy gate howl'd that stern time,
Thou shouldst have said 'Good porter, turn the key.'
All cruels else subscribe: but I shall see
The winged vengeance overtake such children.
Corn. See 't shalt thou never. Fellows, hold the chair.
Upon these eyes of thine I'll set my foot.
Glou. He that will think to live till he be old,
Give me some help! O cruel! O you gods!
Reg. One side will mock another; th' other too.
Corn. If you see vengeance,—
First Serv. Hold your hand, my lord:
I have serv'd you ever since I was a child;
But better service have I never done you
Than now to bid you hold.
Reg. How now, you dog!
First Serv. If you did wear a beard upon your chin,
I'd shake it on this quarrel. What do you mean?
Corn. My villain! [*They draw and fight.*]
First Serv. Nay, then, come on, and take the chance of anger.
Reg. Give me thy sword. A peasant stand up thus!
[*Takes a sword, and runs at him behind.*] *Kills him.*
First Serv. O, I am slain! My lord, you have one eye left
To see some mischief on him. O! [*Dies.*]
Corn. Lest it see more, prevent it. Out, vile jelly!
Where is thy lustre now?
Glou. All dark and comfortless. Where 's my son Edmund?
Edmund, enkindle all the sparks of nature,
To quit this horrid act.
Reg. Out, treacherous villain!
Thou call'st on him that hates thee: it was he
That made the overture of thy treasons to us;
Who is too good to pity thee.
Glou. O my follies! then Edgar was abus'd.
Kind gods, forgive me that, and prosper him!
Reg. Go thrust him out at gates, and let him smell
His way to Dover. *Exit* [*one*] *with Gloucester.* How is 't, my lord? how look you?

Scene vii. 9-10. **Advise . . . to,** i.e., advise him to make. 10. **festinate,** hasty. 11. **bound,** ready. 12. **intelligent,** serviceable in bearing intelligence. 13. **my . . . Gloucester,** i.e., Edmund. In line 15 the reference is to Gloucester himself. 17. **questrists,** searchers. 24. **pass upon,** pass sentence upon. 29. **corky,** withered with age. 39. **quicken,** come to life. 40. **hospitable favours.** Gloucester appeals to the sacredness of hospitality; the meaning is "the features of me, your host." 42. **late,** lately. 43. **simple answer'd,** i.e., straightforward in your answers. 45. **footed,** landed. 54. **tied to th' stake,** like a bear to be baited with dogs. 60. **buoy'd,** lifted itself. 61. **stelled,** fixed; sometimes defined as "starry." 63. **stern,** so F; Q: *heard that dearn.* Many editors follow Capell, *howl'd that dearn,* in which *dearn* means "dire," "dreary." 64. **turn the key,** i.e., let them in. 65. **All . . . subscribe,** all other cruel creatures show forgiveness except you. 78. **villain,** servant, bondman. 87. **quit,** requite. 89. **overture,** disclosure. 98. **Untimely,** inopportunely. 101. **old,** customary, natural.

Corn. I have receiv'd a hurt: follow me, lady.
Turn out that eyeless villain; throw this slave
Upon the dunghill. Regan, I bleed apace:
Untimely comes this hurt: give me your arm.
Exeunt [*Cornwall, led by Regan*].

Sec. Serv. I'll never care what wickedness I do,
If this man come to good.

Third Serv. If she live long,
And in the end meet the old course of death,
Women will all turn monsters.

Sec. Serv. Let 's follow the old earl, and get the Bedlam
To lead him where he would: his roguish madness
Allows itself to any thing.

Third Serv. Go thou: I'll fetch some flax and whites of eggs
To apply to his bleeding face. Now, heaven help him!
[*Exeunt severally.*]

ACT IV.

SCENE I. [*The heath.*]

Enter EDGAR.

Edg. Yet better thus, and known to be contemn'd,
Than still contemn'd and flatter'd. To be worst,
The lowest and most dejected thing of fortune,
Stands still in esperance, lives not in fear:
The lamentable change is from the best;
The worst returns to laughter. Welcome, then,
Thou unsubstantial air that I embrace!
The wretch that thou hast blown unto the worst
Owes nothing to thy blasts. But who comes here?

Enter GLOUCESTER, *and an* Old Man.

My father, poorly led? World, world, O world!
But that thy strange mutations make us hate thee,
Life would not yield to age.

Old Man. O, my good lord, I have been your tenant, and your father's tenant, these fourscore years.

Glou. Away, get thee away; good friend, be gone:
Thy comforts can do me no good at all;
Thee they may hurt.

Old Man. You cannot see your way.

Glou. I have no way, and therefore want no eyes;
I stumbled when I saw: full oft 'tis seen,
Our means secure us, and our mere defects
Prove our commodities. O dear son Edgar,
The food of thy abused father's wrath!
Might I but live to see thee in my touch,
I 'ld say I had eyes again!

Old Man. How now! Who 's there?

Edg. [*Aside*] O gods! Who is 't can say 'I am at the worst'?
I am worse than e'er I was.

Old Man. 'Tis poor mad Tom.

Edg. [*Aside*] And worse I may be yet: the worst is not
So long as we can say 'This is the worst.'

Old Man. Fellow, where goest?

Glou. Is it a beggar-man?

Old Man. Madman and beggar too.

Glou. He has some reason, else he could not beg.
I' th' last night's storm I such a fellow saw;
Which made me think a man a worm: my son
Came then into my mind; and yet my mind
Was then scarce friends with him: I have heard more since.
As flies to wanton boys, are we to th' gods,
They kill us for their sport.

Edg. [*Aside*] How should this be?
Bad is the trade that must play fool to sorrow,
Ang'ring itself and others.—Bless thee, master!

Glou. Is that the naked fellow?

Old Man. Ay, my lord.

Glou. Then, prithee, get thee gone: if, for my sake,
Thou wilt o'ertake us, hence a mile or twain,
I' th' way toward Dover, do it for ancient love;
And bring some covering for this naked soul,
Which I'll entreat to lead me.

Old Man. Alack, sir, he is mad.

Glou. 'Tis the times' plague, when madmen lead the blind.
Do as I bid thee, or rather do thy pleasure;
Above the rest, be gone.

Old Man. I'll bring him the best 'parel that I have,
Come on 't what will. *Exit.*

Glou. Sirrah, naked fellow,—

Edg. Poor Tom 's a-cold. [*Aside*] I cannot daub it further.

Glou. Come hither, fellow.

Edg. [*Aside*] And yet I must.—Bless thy sweet eyes, they bleed.

Glou. Know'st thou the way to Dover?

Edg. Both stile and gate, horse-way and foot-path. Poor Tom hath been scared out of his good wits: bless thee, good man's son, from the foul fiend! five fiends have been in poor Tom at once; of lust, as Obidicut; Hobbididance, prince of dumbness; Mahu, of stealing; Modo, of murder; Flibbertigibbet, of mopping and mowing, who since possesses chambermaids and waiting-women. So, bless thee, master!

Glou. Here, take this purse, thou whom the heavens' plagues
Have humbled to all strokes: that I am wretched
Makes thee the happier: heavens, deal so still!
Let the superfluous and lust-dieted man,
That slaves your ordinance, that will not see
Because he does not feel, feel your pow'r quickly;
So distribution should undo excess,
And each man have enough. Dost thou know Dover?

Edg. Ay, master.

Glou. There is a cliff, whose high and bending head
Looks fearfully in the confined deep:
Bring me but to the very brim of it,
And I'll repair the misery thou dost bear
With something rich about me: from that place
I shall no leading need.

Edg. Give me thy arm:

103. **Bedlam,** Bedlamite, lunatic.

ACT IV. SCENE I. 3. **dejected . . . of,** debased or humbled by. 4. **esperance,** hope. 6. **The worst . . . laughter,** i.e., every terrible extreme must turn some day to better fortune. 11. **mutations,** changes, variations. 12. **age,** aging and death. 22. **Our means secure us,** our prosperity makes us overconfident. **mere defects,** sheer afflictions. 23. **commodities,** benefits. 51. **'parel,** apparel. 54. **daub it further,** keep up the disguise. 62-64. **Obidicut . . . Flibbertigibbet,** fiends borrowed, as before, from Harsnet. 65. **mopping and mowing,** making grimaces and mouths. 70. **superfluous,** having a superfluity. **lust-dieted,** probably, feeding luxuriously. 71. **slaves your ordinance,** i.e., makes the laws of heaven his slaves. 73. **distribution,** the principle of distributive justice in ethics.

Poor Tom shall lead thee. *Exeunt.*

SCENE II. [*Before the Duke of Albany's palace.*]

Enter GONERIL [*and*] *Bastard* [EDMUND].

Gon. Welcome, my lord: I marvel our mild husband
Not met us on the way.

[*Enter*] *Steward* [OSWALD].

Now, where 's your master?
Osw. Madam, within; but never man so chang'd.
I told him of the army that was landed;
He smil'd at it: I told him you were coming;
His answer was 'The worse:' of Gloucester's treachery,
And of the loyal service of his son,
When I inform'd him, then he call'd me sot,
And told me I had turn'd the wrong side out:
What most he should dislike seems pleasant to him;
What like, offensive.
Gon. [*To Edm.*] Then shall you go no further.
It is the cowish terror of his spirit,
That dares not undertake: he'll not feel wrongs
Which tie him to an answer. Our wishes on the way
May prove effects. Back, Edmund, to my brother;
Hasten his musters and conduct his pow'rs:
I must change names at home, and give the distaff
Into my husband's hands. This trusty servant
Shall pass between us: ere long you are like to hear,
If you dare venture in your own behalf,
A mistress's command. Wear this; spare speech;
[*Giving a favour.*]
Decline your head: this kiss, if it durst speak,
Would stretch thy spirits up into the air:
Conceive, and fare thee well.
Edm. Yours in the ranks of death. *Exit.*
Gon. My most dear Gloucester!
O, the difference of man and man!
To thee a woman's services are due:
My fool usurps my body.
Osw. Madam, here comes my lord. [*Exit.*]

Enter ALBANY.

Gon. I have been worth the whistle.
Alb. O Goneril!
You are not worth the dust which the rude wind
Blows in your face. I fear your disposition:
That nature, which contemns its origin,
Cannot be bordered certain in itself;
She that herself will sliver and disbranch
From her material sap, perforce must wither
And come to deadly use.
Gon. No more; the text is foolish.
Alb. Wisdom and goodness to the vile seem vile:
Filths savour but themselves. What have you done?
Tigers, not daughters, what have you perform'd?
A father, and a gracious aged man,
Whose reverence even the head-lugg'd bear would lick,
Most barbarous, most degenerate! have you madded.
Could my good brother suffer you to do it?
A man, a prince, by him so benefited!
If that the heavens do not their visible spirits
Send quickly down to tame these vile offences,
It will come,
Humanity must perforce prey on itself,
Like monsters of the deep.
Gon. Milk-liver'd man!
That bear'st a cheek for blows, a head for wrongs:
Who hast not in thy brows an eye discerning
Thine honour from thy suffering; that not know'st
Fools do those villains pity who are punish'd
Ere they have done their mischief. Where 's thy drum?
France spreads his banners in our noiseless land,
With plumed helm thy state begins to threat;
Whilst thou, a moral fool, sits still, and cries
'Alack, why does he so?'
Alb. See thyself, devil!
Proper deformity seems not in the fiend
So horrid as in woman.
Gon. O vain fool!
Alb. Thou changed and self-cover'd thing, for shame,
Be-monster not thy feature. Were 't my fitness
To let these hands obey my blood,
They are apt enough to dislocate and tear
Thy flesh and bones: howe'er thou art a fiend,
A woman's shape doth shield thee.
Gon. Marry, your manhood, mew!

Enter a Messenger.

Alb. What news?
Mess. O, my good lord, the Duke of Cornwall 's dead;
Slain by his servant, going to put out
The other eye of Gloucester.
Alb. Gloucester's eyes!
Mess. A servant that he bred, thrill'd with remorse,
Oppos'd against the act, bending his sword
To his great master; who, thereat enrag'd,
Flew on him, and amongst them fell'd him dead;
But not without that harmful stroke, which since
Hath pluck'd him after.
Alb. This shows you are above,
You justicers, that these our nether crimes
So speedily can venge! But, O poor Gloucester!
Lost he his other eye?
Mess. Both, both, my lord.
This letter, madam, craves a speedy answer;
'Tis from your sister.
Gon. [*Aside*] One way I like this well;
But being widow, and my Gloucester with her,
May all the building in my fancy pluck
Upon my hateful life: another way,

SCENE II. 1. **Welcome.** Goneril, who has just arrived home from Gloucester escorted by Edmund, bids him brief welcome before he must return. **mild,** used ironically. 8. **sot,** fool. 9. **turn'd the wrong side out,** put a wrong interpretation on the matter. 12. **cowish,** cowardly. 13-14. **he'll . . . answer,** i.e., in his cowardice he will ignore injuries he ought to resent. 14. **Our . . . way,** my wishes expressed to you on the way. 15. **prove effects,** come to pass. 17. **change names,** i.e., exchange the roles of master and mistress of the household. **distaff,** spinning staff, symbolizing the wife's role. 24. **Conceive,** understand, take my meaning; with sexual double entendre, continuing from *stretch thy spirits* in the previous line. 29. **whistle.** She alludes to the proverb: "It is a poor dog that is not worth the whistling." 33. **bordered,** kept within bounds. 34. **sliver,** tear off. 35. **material sap,** nourishing substance. 39. **savour but,** care only for. 42. **head-lugg'd,** dragged by the head and infuriated. 43. **madded,** driven mad. 47. **offences,** offenders. 50. **Milk-liver'd,** cowardly. 54. **Fools,** only fools. 55. **thy drum,** i.e., your military preparations. 56. **noiseless,** peaceful, having none of the bustle of war. 58. **moral,** moralizing. 60. **Proper,** i.e., the deformity appropriate to the fiend. 62. **self-cover'd,** having the true self concealed. 63. **Be-monster . . . feature,** do not, being

The news is not so tart.—I'll read, and answer. [*Exit.*]
Alb. Where was his son when they did take his eyes?
Mess. Come with my lady hither.
Alb. He is not here.
Mess. No, my good lord; I met him back again.
Alb. Knows he the wickedness?
Mess. Ay, my good lord; 'twas he inform'd against him;
And quit the house on purpose, that their punishment
Might have the freer course.
Alb. Gloucester, I live
To thank thee for the love thou show'dst the king,
And to revenge thine eyes. Come hither, friend:
Tell me what more thou know'st. *Exeunt.*

SCENE [III. *The French camp near Dover.*]

Enter KENT *and a* Gentleman.

Kent. Why the King of France is so suddenly gone back know you no reason?

Gent. Something he left imperfect in the state, which since his coming forth is thought of; which imports to the kingdom so much fear and danger, that his personal return was most required and necessary.

Kent. Who hath he left behind him general?

Gent. The Marshal of France, Monsieur La Far.

Kent. Did your letters pierce the queen to any demonstration of grief?

Gent. Ay, sir; she took them, read them in my presence;
And now and then an ample tear trill'd down
Her delicate cheek: it seem'd she was a queen
Over her passion; who, most rebel-like,
Sought to be king o'er her.
Kent. O, then it moved her.
Gent. Not to a rage: patience and sorrow strove
Who should express her goodliest. You have seen
Sunshine and rain at once: her smiles and tears
†Were like a better way: those happy smilets,
That play'd on her ripe lip, seem'd not to know
What guests were in her eyes; which parted thence,
As pearls from diamonds dropp'd. In brief,
Sorrow would be a rarity most beloved,
If all could so become it.
Kent. Made she no verbal question?
Gent. 'Faith, once or twice she heav'd the name of 'father'
Pantingly forth, as if it press'd her heart;
Cried 'Sisters! sisters! Shame of ladies! sisters!
Kent! father! sisters! What, i' th' storm? i' th' night?
Let pity not be believ'd!' There she shook
The holy water from her heavenly eyes,
And clamour moisten'd: then away she started
To deal with grief alone.
Kent. It is the stars,
The stars above us, govern our conditions;
Else one self mate and make could not beget
Such different issues. You spoke not with her since?
Gent. No.
Kent. Was this before the king return'd?
Gent. No, since.
Kent. Well, sir, the poor distressed Lear 's i' th' town;
Who sometime, in his better tune, remembers
What we are come about, and by no means
Will yield to see his daughter.
Gent. Why, good sir?
Kent. A sovereign shame so elbows him: his own unkindness,
That stripp'd her from his benediction, turn'd her
To foreign casualties, gave her dear rights
To his dog-hearted daughters, these things sting
His mind so venomously, that burning shame
Detains him from Cordelia.
Gent. Alack, poor gentleman!
Kent. Of Albany's and Cornwall's powers you heard not?
Gent. 'Tis so, they are afoot.
Kent. Well, sir, I'll bring you to our master Lear,
And leave you to attend him: some dear cause
Will in concealment wrap me up awhile;
When I am known aright, you shall not grieve
Lending me this acquaintance. I pray you, go
Along with me. *Exeunt.*

SCENE [IV. *The same. A tent.*]

Enter, with drum and colours, CORDELIA, Doctor, *and* Soldiers.

Cor. Alack, 'tis he: why, he was met even now
As mad as the vex'd sea; singing aloud;
Crown'd with rank fumiter and furrow-weeds,
With har-docks, hemlock, nettles, cuckoo-flow'rs,
Darnel, and all the idle weeds that grow
In our sustaining corn. A century send forth;
Search every acre in the high-grown field,
And bring him to our eye. [*Exit an Officer.*] What can man's wisdom
In the restoring his bereaved sense?
He that helps him take all my outward worth.
Doct. There is means, madam:
Our foster-nurse of nature is repose,
The which he lacks; that to provoke in him,
Are many simples operative, whose power
Will close the eye of anguish.
Cor. All blest secrets,
All you unpublish'd virtues of the earth,
Spring with my tears! be aidant and remediate
In the good man's distress! Seek, seek for him;
Lest his ungovern'd rage dissolve the life
That wants the means to lead it.

Enter Messenger.

Mess. News, madam;

fiend, take on the outward form of a fiend. **my fitness,** suitable for me. 66. **howe'er,** although. 68. **mew,** an exclamation of disgust. 73. **thrill'd,** deeply moved. **remorse,** pity. 74-75. **bending . . . To,** directing his sword against. 88. **tart,** painful. 91. **back,** going back.
SCENE III. 5. **imports,** portends. 14. **trill'd,** trickled. 21. **like a better way,** possibly, better than this. **smilets,** smiles. 22. **ripe,** probably, red (W. J. Craig). 27. **heav'd,** breathed out. 36. **Else . . . make,** otherwise, one couple (husband and wife). 41. **better tune,** saner moments. 44. **elbows,** thrusts away, or possibly, stands at his elbow. 45. **turn'd,** expelled.

SCENE IV. 3. **fumiter,** the weed "earth-smoke." **furrow-weeds,** weeds growing in the furrows of plowed land. 4. **har-docks,** perhaps burdocks, or hoar-docks, white-leaved. **cuckoo-flow'rs,** possibly, cowslips. 5. **Darnel,** a weed of the grass kind. The plants mentioned in this passage are probably selected because of their bitter and poisonous quality. 6. **sustaining,** giving sustenance. **century,** usually interpreted as a troop of 100 men, as in the Roman army; also taken to mean "sentry" or "scout." 8. **wisdom,** science. 9. **bereaved,** snatched away. 14. **simples,** medicinal plants. **operative,** effective. 16. **unpublish'd,** little known. 17. **aidant and remediate,** helpful and remedial.

The British pow'rs are marching hitherward.
Cor. 'Tis known before; our preparation stands
In expectation of them. O dear father,
It is thy business that I go about;
Therefore great France
My mourning and importun'd tears hath pitied.
No blown ambition doth our arms incite,
But love, dear love, and our ag'd father's right:
Soon may I hear and see him! *Exeunt.*

SCENE [V. *Gloucester's castle.*]

Enter REGAN *and Steward* [OSWALD].

Reg. But are my brother's pow'rs set forth?
Osw. Ay, madam.
Reg. Himself in person there?
Osw. Madam, with much ado:
Your sister is the better soldier.
Reg. Lord Edmund spake not with your lord at home?
Osw. No, madam.
Reg. What might import my sister's letter to him?
Osw. I know not, lady.
Reg. 'Faith, he is posted hence on serious matter.
It was great ignorance, Gloucester's eyes being out,
To let him live: where he arrives he moves
All hearts against us: Edmund, I think, is gone,
In pity of his misery, to dispatch
His nighted life; moreover, to descry
The strength o' th' enemy.
Osw. I must needs after him, madam, with my letter.
Reg. Our troops set forth to-morrow: stay with us;
The ways are dangerous.
Osw. I may not, madam:
My lady charg'd my duty in this business.
Reg. Why should she write to Edmund? Might not you
Transport her purposes by word? Belike,
Something—I know not what: I'll love thee much,
Let me unseal the letter.
Osw. Madam, I had rather—
Reg. I know your lady does not love her husband;
I am sure of that: and at her late being here
She gave strange œillades and most speaking looks
To noble Edmund. I know you are of her bosom.
Osw. I, madam?
Reg. I speak in understanding; y' are, I know 't:
Therefore I do advise you, take this note:
My lord is dead; Edmund and I have talk'd;
And more convenient is he for my hand
Than for your lady's: you may gather more.
If you do find him, pray you, give him this;
And when your mistress hears thus much from you,
I pray, desire her call her wisdom to her.
So, fare you well.
If you do chance to hear of that blind traitor,
Preferment falls on him that cuts him off.
Osw. Would I could meet him, madam! I should show
What party I do follow.
Reg. Fare thee well. *Exeunt.*

SCENE [VI. *Fields near Dover.*]

Enter GLOUCESTER, *and* EDGAR [*dressed like a peasant*].

Glou. When shall I come to th' top of that same hill?
Edg. You do climb up it now: look, how we labour.
Glou. Methinks the ground is even.
Edg. Horrible steep.
Hark, do you hear the sea?
Glou. No, truly.
Edg. Why, then, your other senses grow imperfect
By your eyes' anguish.
Glou. So may it be, indeed:
Methinks thy voice is alter'd; and thou speak'st
In better phrase and matter than thou didst.
Edg. Y' are much deceiv'd: in nothing am I chang'd
But in my garments.
Glou. Methinks y' are better spoken.
Edg. Come on, sir; here 's the place: stand still. How fearful
And dizzy 'tis, to cast one's eyes so low!
The crows and choughs that wing the midway air
Show scarce so gross as beetles: half way down
Hangs one that gathers samphire, dreadful trade!
Methinks he seems no bigger than his head:
The fishermen, that walk upon the beach,
Appear like mice; and yond tall anchoring bark,
Diminish'd to her cock; her cock, a buoy
Almost too small for sight: the murmuring surge,
That on th' unnumb'red idle pebbles chafes,
Cannot be heard so high. I'll look no more;
Lest my brain turn, and the deficient sight
Topple down headlong.
Glou. Set me where you stand.
Edg. Give me your hand: you are now within a foot
Of th' extreme verge: for all beneath the moon
Would I not leap upright.
Glou. Let go my hand.
Here, friend, 's another purse; in it a jewel
Well worth a poor man's taking: fairies and gods
Prosper it with thee! Go thou farther off;
Bid me farewell, and let me hear thee going.
Edg. Now fare ye well, good sir.
Glou. With all my heart.
Edg. Why I do trifle thus with his despair
Is done to cure it.
Glou. [*Kneeling*] O you mighty gods!
This world I do renounce, and, in your sights,
Shake patiently my great affliction off:
If I could bear it longer, and not fall

26. **importun'd,** importunate. 27. **blown,** puffed up with pride. (Cordelia is at pains to stress that France is invading England not for territorial advantage.)

SCENE V. 6. **import,** to bear as its purport, to express (Onions). 8. **is posted,** has hurried. 9. **ignorance,** error. 18. **charg'd,** ordered strictly. 20. **word,** word of mouth. **Belike,** it may be. 24. **late,** recent. 25. **œillades,** amorous glances. 26. **of her bosom,** in her confidence. 29. **take this note,** take note of this. 30. **have talk'd,** are affianced to one another (W. J. Craig). 32. **gather more,** i.e., infer what I am trying to suggest. 35. **call her wisdom,** recall herself to her senses. 38. **Preferment,** advancement.

SCENE VI. 13. **choughs,** jackdaws. **midway,** halfway down. 14. **gross,** large. 15. **samphire,** an herb called sea-fennel and the herb of St. Pierre, used for pickles. 19. **Diminish'd . . . cock,** reduced to the size of her cock-boat. 21. **unnumb'red,** innumerable. 23-24. **the deficient sight Topple,** my failing sight topple me. 27. **upright,** i.e., up and down, much less forward. 38. **opposeless,** irresistible. 39. **snuff,** useless residue; the metaphor is taken from the smoking wick of a candle. 42. **conceit,** imagination. 47. **pass,** die. 53. **at each,** end to end. 57. **bourn,** limit, boundary. 58. **a-height,** on high.

To quarrel with your great opposeless wills,
My snuff and loathed part of nature should
Burn itself out. If Edgar live, O, bless him!
Now, fellow, fare thee well. [*He falls forward.*]
Edg. Gone, sir: farewell.—
And yet I know not how conceit may rob
The treasury of life, when life itself
Yields to the theft: had he been where he thought,
By this, had thought been past.—Alive or dead?
Ho, you sir! friend! Hear you, sir! speak!—
Thus might he pass indeed: yet he revives.
What are you, sir?
Glou. Away, and let me die.
Edg. Hadst thou been aught but gossamer, feathers, air,
So many fathom down precipitating,
Thou 'dst shiver'd like an egg: but thou dost breathe;
Hast heavy substance; bleed'st not; speak'st; art sound.
Ten masts at each make not the altitude
Which thou hast perpendicularly fell:
Thy life 's a miracle. Speak yet again.
Glou. But have I fall'n, or no?
Edg. From the dread summit of this chalky bourn.
Look up a-height; the shrill-gorg'd lark so far
Cannot be seen or heard: do but look up.
Glou. Alack, I have no eyes.
Is wretchedness depriv'd that benefit,
To end itself by death? 'Twas yet some comfort,
When misery could beguile the tyrant's rage,
And frustrate his proud will.
Edg. Give me your arm:
Up: so. How is 't? Feel you your legs? You stand.
Glou. Too well, too well.
Edg. This is above all strangeness.
Upon the crown o' th' cliff, what thing was that
Which parted from you?
Glou. A poor unfortunate beggar.
Edg. As I stood here below, methought his eyes
Were two full moons; he had a thousand noses,
Horns whelk'd and waved like the enridged sea:
It was some fiend; therefore, thou happy father,
Think that the clearest gods, who make them honours
Of men's impossibilities, have preserved thee.
Glou. I do remember now: henceforth I'll bear
Affliction till it do cry out itself
'Enough, enough,' and die. That thing you speak of,
I took it for a man; often 'twould say
'The fiend, the fiend:' he led me to that place.
Edg. Bear free and patient thoughts. But who comes here?

Enter LEAR [*fantastically dressed with wild flowers*].

The safer sense will ne'er accommodate
His master thus.
Lear. No, they cannot touch me for coining;
I am the king himself.
Edg. O thou side-piercing sight!

Lear. Nature 's above art in that respect. There 's your press-money. That fellow handles his bow like a crow-keeper: draw me a clothier's yard. Look, look, a mouse! Peace, peace; this piece of toasted cheese will do 't. There 's my gauntlet; I'll prove it on a giant. Bring up the brown bills. O, well flown, bird! i' the clout, i' the clout: hewgh! Give the word.

Edg. Sweet marjoram.
Lear. Pass.
Glou. I know that voice.

Lear. Ha! Goneril, with a white beard! They flattered me like a dog; and told me I had white hairs in my beard ere the black ones were there. To say 'ay' and 'no' to every thing that I said!—'Ay' and 'no' too was no good divinity. When the rain came to wet me once, and the wind to make me chatter; when the thunder would not peace at my bidding; there I found 'em, there I smelt 'em out. Go to, they are not men o' their words: they told me I was every thing; 'tis a lie, I am not ague-proof.

Glou. The trick of that voice I do well remember:
Is 't not the king?
Lear. Ay, every inch a king:
When I do stare, see how the subject quakes.
I pardon that man's life. What was thy cause?
Adultery?
Thou shalt not die: die for adultery! No:
The wren goes to 't, and the small gilded fly
Does lecher in my sight.
Let copulation thrive; for Gloucester's bastard son
Was kinder to his father than my daughters
Got 'tween the lawful sheets.
To 't, luxury, pell-mell! for I lack soldiers.
Behold yond simp'ring dame,
Whose face between her forks presages snow;
That minces virtue, and does shake the head
To hear of pleasure's name;
The fitchew, nor the soiled horse, goes to 't
With a more riotous appetite.
Down from the waist they are Centaurs,
Though women all above:
But to the girdle do the gods inherit,
Beneath is all the fiends';
There 's hell, there 's darkness, there is the sulphurous pit,
Burning, scalding, stench, consumption; fie, fie, fie! pah, pah! Give me an ounce of civet, good apothecary, to sweeten my imagination: there 's money for thee.

Glou. O, let me kiss that hand!
Lear. Let me wipe it first; it smells of mortality.
Glou. O ruin'd piece of nature! This great world
Shall so wear out to nought. Dost thou know me?

Lear. I remember thine eyes well enough. Dost thou squiny at me? No, do thy worst, blind Cupid; I'll not love. Read thou this challenge; mark but the penning of it.

Glou. Were all thy letters suns, I could not see one.

shrill-gorg'd, shrill-throated. 63. **beguile,** outwit. 71. **whelk'd,** explained as "twisted"; also as "swollen, as with whelks or knobs." **enridged,** furrowed. 73. **clearest,** most righteous. 74. **men's impossibilities,** things impossible to men. 80. **free,** probably, free from despair. 81. **safer,** saner. **accommodate,** furnish, accoutre. 83. **touch,** arrest, prosecute. **coining,** minting coins (a royal prerogative). 87. **press-money,** bonus given soldiers when they were pressed into service. 89. **clothier's yard,** arrow the length of a cloth yard. 91. **prove it on,** maintain it against. 92. **brown bills,** soldiers carrying pikes, or the pikes themselves. **well flown, bird.** Lear may think he is hawking, or he may be speaking of the flight of an arrow. 93. **clout,** target. **word,** password. 102. **no good divinity,** not good theology, contrary to biblical teaching; see II Cor. 1:18 and James 5:12. 104. **peace,** hold its peace. 108. **trick,** peculiar characteristic. 119. **luxury,** lust. 121. **Whose . . . snow,** whose frosty countenance seems to suggest frigidity between her legs. 122. **minces,** affects. 123. **pleasure's,** i.e., sexual pleasure's. 124. **fitchew,** polecat. **soiled horse,** horse turned out to grass. 126. **Centaurs,** fabulous monsters, half man, half horse. 128. **But,** only. **inherit,** possess. 137. **piece,** masterpiece. 140. **squiny,** squint, look askance.

Edg. [*Aside*] I would not take this from report; it is,
And my heart breaks at it.

Lear. Read.

Glou. What, with the case of eyes?

Lear. O, ho, are you there with me? No eyes in your head, nor no money in your purse? Your eyes are in a heavy case, your purse in a light: yet you see how this world goes.

Glou. I see it feelingly.

Lear. What, art mad? A man may see how this world goes with no eyes. Look with thine ears: see how yond justice rails upon yond simple thief. Hark, in thine ear: change places; and, handy-dandy, which is the justice, which is the thief? Thou hast seen a farmer's dog bark at a beggar?

Glou. Ay, sir.

Lear. And the creature run from the cur? There thou mightst behold the great image of authority: a dog 's obeyed in office.
Thou rascal beadle, hold thy bloody hand!
Why dost thou lash that whore? Strip thy own back;
Thou hotly lusts to use her in that kind
For which thou whipp'st her. The usurer hangs the
cozener.
Through tatter'd clothes small vices do appear;
Robes and furr'd gowns hide all. Plate sin with gold,
And the strong lance of justice hurtless breaks;
Arm it in rags, a pigmy's straw does pierce it.
None does offend, none, I say, none; I'll able 'em:
Take that of me, my friend, who have the power
To seal th' accuser's lips. Get thee glass eyes;
And, like a scurvy politician, seem
To see the things thou dost not. Now, now, now, now:
Pull off my boots: harder, harder: so.

Edg. O, matter and impertinency mix'd!
Reason in madness!

Lear. If thou wilt weep my fortunes, take my eyes.
I know thee well enough; thy name is Gloucester:
Thou must be patient; we came crying hither:
Thou know'st, the first time that we smell the air,
We wawl and cry. I will preach to thee: mark.

Glou. Alack, alack the day!

Lear. When we are born, we cry that we are come
To this great stage of fools: this' a good block;
It were a delicate stratagem, to shoe
A troop of horse with felt: I'll put 't in proof;
And when I have stol'n upon these son-in-laws,
Then, kill, kill, kill, kill, kill, kill!

Enter a Gentleman [*with* Attendants].

Gent. O, here he is: lay hand upon him. Sir,
Your most dear daughter—

Lear. No rescue? What, a prisoner? I am even
The natural fool of fortune. Use me well;
You shall have ransom. Let me have surgeons;
I am cut to th' brains.

Gent. You shall have any thing.

Lear. No seconds? all myself?
Why, this would make a man a man of salt,
To use his eyes for garden water-pots,
Ay, and laying autumn's dust.

Gent. Good sir,—

Lear. I will die bravely, like a smug bridegroom.
What!
I will be jovial: come, come; I am a king,
Masters, know you that.

Gent. You are a royal one, and we obey you.

Lear. Then there 's life in 't. Come, an you get it, you shall get it by running. Sa, sa, sa, sa.
Exit [*running; Attendants follow*].

Gent. A sight most pitiful in the meanest wretch,
Past speaking of in a king! Thou hast one daughter,
Who redeems nature from the general curse
Which twain have brought her to.

Edg. Hail, gentle sir.

Gent. Sir, speed you: what 's your will?

Edg. Do you hear aught, sir, of a battle toward?

Gent. Most sure and vulgar: every one hears that,
Which can distinguish sound.

Edg. But, by your favour,
How near 's the other army?

Gent. Near and on speedy foot; the main descry
Stands on the hourly thought.

Edg. I thank you, sir: that 's all.

Gent. Though that the queen on special cause is
here,
Her army is mov'd on.

Edg. I thank you, sir. *Exit* [*Gent.*].

Glou. You ever-gentle gods, take my breath from
me;
Let not my worser spirit tempt me again
To die before you please!

Edg. Well pray you, father.

Glou. Now, good sir, what are you?

Edg. A most poor man, made tame to fortune's
blows;
Who, by the art of known and feeling sorrows,
Am pregnant to good pity. Give me your hand,
I'll lead you to some biding.

Glou. Hearty thanks:
The bounty and the benison of heaven
To boot, and boot!

Enter Steward [OSWALD].

Osw. A proclaim'd prize! Most
happy!
That eyeless head of thine was first fram'd flesh
To raise my fortunes. Thou old unhappy traitor,
Briefly thyself remember: the sword is out
That must destroy thee.

Glou. Now let thy friendly hand
Put strength enough to 't. [*Edgar interposes.*]

Osw. Wherefore, bold peasant,
Dar'st thou support a publish'd traitor? Hence;
Lest that th' infection of his fortune take
Like hold on thee. Let go his arm.

Edg. Chill not let go, zir, without vurther 'casion.

Osw. Let go, slave, or thou diest!

Edg. Good gentleman, go your gait, and let poor volk pass. An chud ha' bin zwaggered out of my life,

147. **case,** mere sockets. 148. **are . . . me?** Is that your situation? 157. **handy-dandy,** take your choice of hands, as in a well-known child's game. 161-171. **And the . . . pierce it.** Into these ravings should be read the conception of a state resting upon authority solely, and this state fallen into ruin because the holders of this divinely constituted authority are themselves corrupt. 167. **cozener,** cheater. 172. **able,** give warrant to. 175. **politician,** opportunist. 187. **this',** this is. **block,** probably, hat, from the form on which it was molded.

189. **in proof,** to the test. 199. **man of salt,** of salt tears. 212. **speed you,** God speed you. 214. **vulgar,** in everyone's mouth, generally known. 215. **Which,** who. 217-218. **the main . . . thought,** the full view of the main body is expected every hour. 226. **feeling,** heartfelt, deep. 227. **pregnant,** prone. 228. **biding,** abiding place. 230. **To boot, and boot,** i.e., in addition (to my thanks), I wish you the bounty of heaven. 231. **fram'd flesh,** born. 233. **thyself remember,** confess thy sins. 239. **Chill,** I will. Edgar adopts a dialect, apparently of the

'twould not ha' bin zo long as 'tis by a vortnight. Nay, come not near th' old man; keep out, che vor ye, or ise try whether your costard or my ballow be the harder: chill be plain with you.

Osw. Out, dunghill!

Edg. Chill pick your teeth, zir: come; no matter vor your foins. [*They fight, and Edgar knocks him down.*]

Osw. Slave, thou hast slain me: villain, take my purse:
If ever thou wilt thrive, bury my body;
And give the letters which thou find'st about me
To Edmund Earl of Gloucester; seek him out
Upon the English party: O, untimely death! [*Dies.*]

Edg. I know thee well: a serviceable villain;
As duteous to the vices of thy mistress
As badness would desire.

Glou. What, is he dead?

Edg. Sit you down, father; rest you.
Let 's see these pockets: the letters that he speaks of
May be my friends. He 's dead; I am only sorry
He had no other death's-man. Let us see:
Leave, gentle wax; and, manners, blame us not:
To know our enemies' minds, we rip their hearts;
Their papers, is more lawful. (*Reads the letter.*) 'Let our reciprocal vows be remembered. You have many opportunities to cut him off: if your will want not, time and place will be fruitfully offered. There is nothing done, if he return the conqueror: then am I the prisoner, and his bed my gaol; from the loathed warmth whereof deliver me, and supply the place for your labour.

'Your—wife, so I would say—
'Affectionate servant, GONERIL.'

O indistinguish'd space of woman's will!
A plot upon her virtuous husband's life;
And the exchange my brother! Here, in the sands,
Thee I'll rake up, the post unsanctified
Of murderous lechers: and in the mature time
With this ungracious paper strike the sight
Of the death-practis'd duke: for him 'tis well
That of thy death and business I can tell.

Glou. The king is mad: how stiff is my vile sense,
That I stand up, and have ingenious feeling
Of my huge sorrows! Better I were distract:
So should my thoughts be sever'd from my griefs,
And woes by wrong imaginations lose
The knowledge of themselves.

Edg. Give me your hand:
Drum afar off.
Far off, methinks, I hear the beaten drum:
Come, father, I'll bestow you with a friend. *Exeunt.*

SCENE VII. [*A tent in the French camp.*]

Enter CORDELIA, KENT, [DOCTOR,] *and* Gentleman.

Cor. O thou good Kent, how shall I live and work,
To match thy goodness? My life will be too short,
And every measure fail me.

Kent. To be acknowledg'd, madam, is o'er-paid.
All my reports go with the modest truth;
Nor more nor clipp'd, but so.

Cor. Be better suited:
These weeds are memories of those worser hours:
I prithee, put them off.

Kent. Pardon, dear madam;
Yet to be known shortens my made intent:
My boon I make it, that you know me not
Till time and I think meet.

Cor. Then be 't so, my good lord. [*To the Doctor*] How does the king?

Doct. Madam, sleeps still.

Cor. O you kind gods,
Cure this great breach in his abused nature!
Th' untun'd and jarring senses, O, wind up
Of this child-changed father!

Doct. So please your majesty
That we may wake the king: he hath slept long.

Cor. Be govern'd by your knowledge, and proceed
I' th' sway of your own will. Is he array'd?

Enter LEAR *in a chair carried by* Servants.

Gent. Ay, madam; in the heaviness of sleep
We put fresh garments on him.

Doct. Be by, good madam, when we do awake him;
I doubt not of his temperance.

Cor. Very well. [*Music.*]

Doct. Please you, draw near. Louder the music there!

Cor. O my dear father! Restoration hang
Thy medicine on my lips; and let this kiss
Repair those violent harms that my two sisters
Have in thy reverence made!

Kent. Kind and dear princess!

Cor. Had you not been their father, these white flakes
Did challenge pity of them. Was this a face
To be oppos'd against the warring winds?
To stand against the deep dread-bolted thunder?
In the most terrible and nimble stroke
Of quick, cross lightning? to watch—poor perdu!—
With this thin helm? Mine enemy's dog,
Though he had bit me, should have stood that night
Against my fire; and wast thou fain, poor father,
To hovel thee with swine, and rogues forlorn,
In short and musty straw? Alack, alack!
'Tis wonder that thy life and wits at once
Had not concluded all. He wakes; speak to him.

Doct. Madam, do you; 'tis fittest.

Cor. How does my royal lord? How fares your majesty?

Lear. You do me wrong to take me out o' th' grave:
Thou art a soul in bliss; but I am bound
Upon a wheel of fire, that mine own tears
Do scald like molten lead.

Cor. Sir, do you know me?

Lear. You are a spirit, I know: when did you die?

Cor. Still, still, far wide!

Doct. He 's scarce awake: let him alone awhile.

south country. 242. **go your gait,** go your own way. 243. **An chud,** if I could. 246. **che vor ye,** I warn you. 247. **ise,** I shall. **costard,** an apple, slang for "head." **ballow,** cudgel. 249. **dunghill,** person of the lowest extraction. 251. **foins,** thrusts in fencing. 263. **death's-man,** executioner. 264. **Leave,** by your leave. 270. **fruitfully,** amply, fully. 276. **servant,** lover. 278. **indistinguish'd . . . will,** incalculable range of woman's appetite. 281. **rake up,** cover up. 283. **ungracious,** wicked. 284. **death-practis'd,** whose death is plotted. 286. **stiff,** obstinate. **sense,** consciousness. 287. **ingenious,** conscious. 288. **distract,** distracted, crazy.

SCENE VII. 6. **clipp'd,** curtailed. **suited,** dressed. 7. **memories,** remembrances. 9. **made intent,** carefully thought-out purpose. 17. **child-changed,** changed (in mind) by children's cruelty. 24. **temperance,** sanity. 33. **dread-bolted,** furnished with the dreadful thunderstone. 35. **perdu,** soldier placed in a position of peculiar danger. 42. **concluded all,** come to an end all together.

Lear. Where have I been? Where am I? Fair daylight?
I am mightily abus'd. I should e'en die with pity,
To see another thus. I know not what to say.
I will not swear these are my hands: let 's see;
I feel this pin prick. Would I were assur'd
Of my condition!
Cor. O, look upon me, sir,
And hold your hand in benediction o'er me:
You must not kneel.
Lear. Pray, do not mock me:
I am a very foolish fond old man,
Fourscore and upward, not an hour more nor less;
And, to deal plainly,
I fear I am not in my perfect mind.
Methinks I should know you, and know this man;
Yet I am doubtful: for I am mainly ignorant
What place this is; and all the skill I have
Remembers not these garments; nor I know not
Where I did lodge last night. Do not laugh at me;
For, as I am a man, I think this lady
To be my child Cordelia.
Cor. And so I am, I am.
Lear. Be your tears wet? yes, 'faith. I pray, weep not:
If you have poison for me, I will drink it.
I know you do not love me; for your sisters
Have, as I do remember, done me wrong:
You have some cause, they have not.
Cor. No cause, no cause.
Lear. Am I in France?
Kent. In your own kingdom, sir.
Lear. Do not abuse me.
Doct. Be comforted, good madam: the great rage,
You see, is kill'd in him: and yet it is danger
To make him even o'er the time he has lost.
Desire him to go in; trouble him no more
Till further settling.
Cor. Will 't please your highness walk?
Lear. You must bear with me:
Pray you now, forget and forgive: I am old and foolish. *Exeunt* [*all but Kent and Gentleman*].

Gent. Holds it true, sir, that the Duke of Cornwall was so slain?

Kent. Most certain, sir.

Gent. Who is conductor of his people?

Kent. As 'tis said, the bastard son of Gloucester.

Gent. They say Edgar, his banished son, is with the Earl of Kent in Germany.

Kent. Report is changeable. 'Tis time to look about; the powers of the kingdom approach apace.

Gent. The arbitrement is like to be bloody. Fare you well, sir. [*Exit*.]

Kent. My point and period will be throughly wrought,
Or well or ill, as this day's battle 's fought. *Exit*.

ACT V.

SCENE I. [*The British camp, near Dover*.]

Enter, with drum and colours, EDMUND, REGAN, *Gentlemen, and* Soldiers.

Edm. Know of the duke if his last purpose hold,
Or whether since he is advis'd by aught
To change the course: he 's full of alteration
And self-reproving: bring his constant pleasure.
[*To a Gentleman, who goes out*.]
Reg. Our sister's man is certainly miscarried.
Edm. 'Tis to be doubted, madam.
Reg. Now, sweet lord,
You know the goodness I intend upon you:
Tell me—but truly—but then speak the truth,
Do you not love my sister?
Edm. In honour'd love.
Reg. But have you never found my brother's way
To the forfended place?
Edm. That thought abuses you.
Reg. I am doubtful that you have been conjunct
And bosom'd with her, as far as we call hers.
Edm. No, by mine honour, madam.
Reg. I never shall endure her: dear my lord,
Be not familiar with her.
Edm. Fear me not:
She and the duke her husband!

Enter, with drum and colours, ALBANY, GONERIL, [*and*] Soldiers.

Gon. [*Aside*] I had rather lose the battle than that sister
Should loosen him and me.
Alb. Our very loving sister, well be-met.
Sir, this I hear; the king is come to his daughter,
With others whom the rigour of our state
Forc'd to cry out. Where I could not be honest,
I never yet was valiant: for this business,
It toucheth us, as France invades our land,
Not bolds the king, with others, whom, I fear,
Most just and heavy causes make oppose.
Edm. Sir, you speak nobly.
Reg. Why is this reason'd?
Gon. Combine together 'gainst the enemy;
For these domestic and particular broils
Are not the question here.
Alb. Let 's then determine
With th' ancient of war on our proceeding.
Edm. I shall attend you presently at your tent.
Reg. Sister, you'll go with us?
Gon. No.
Reg. 'Tis most convenient; pray you, go with us.
Gon. [*Aside*] O, ho, I know the riddle.—I will go.

[*As they are going out*,] *enter* EDGAR [*disguised*].

Edg. [*To Albany*] If e'er your grace had speech with man so poor,
Hear me one word.
Alb. I'll overtake you.—Speak.
Exeunt both the armies.
Edg. Before you fight the battle, ope this letter.
If you have victory, let the trumpet sound
For him that brought it: wretched though I seem,

65. **mainly,** perfectly. 77. **abuse,** deceive. 80. **even o'er,** give an account of, go over in his mind. 82. **settling,** composing of his mind. 94. **powers,** armies. 95. **arbitrement,** decision by arms. 98. **period,** end aimed at.

ACT V. SCENE I. 1. **Know,** inquire. 2. **advis'd,** persuaded. 4. **constant pleasure,** settled decision. 5. **miscarried,** lost, perished. 6. **doubted,** feared. 9. **honour'd,** honorable. 11. **forfended,** forbidden. **abuses,** deceives; also, degrades. 12. **doubtful,** fearful. **conjunct,** joined (both sexually and in spirit). 13. **bosom'd with her,** in her confidence; suggesting also her embraces. 23. **honest,** honorable. 26. **Not . . . others,** not because France encourages the king and others. 27. **heavy causes,** weighty reasons. **make oppose,** compel to fight (against us). 28. **reason'd,** argued. 32. **ancient of war,** veteran soldiers. 36. **convenient,** proper, befitting. 44. **avouched,** formally asserted. **miscarry,** perish, come to destruction. 50. **o'erlook,** peruse. 53. **discovery,** reconnoitering. 54. **greet the time,** face the situation.

I can produce a champion that will prove
What is avouched there. If you miscarry,
Your business of the world hath so an end,
And machination ceases. Fortune love you!
Alb. Stay till I have read the letter.
Edg. I was forbid it.
When time shall serve, let but the herald cry,
And I'll appear again.
Alb. Why, fare thee well: I will o'erlook thy paper.
Exit [*Edgar*].

Enter EDMUND.

Edm. The enemy 's in view; draw up your powers.
Here is the guess of their true strength and forces
By diligent discovery; but your haste
Is now urg'd on you.
Alb. We will greet the time. *Exit.*
Edm. To both these sisters have I sworn my love;
Each jealous of the other, as the stung
Are of the adder. Which of them shall I take?
Both? one? or neither? Neither can be enjoy'd,
If both remain alive: to take the widow
Exasperates, makes mad her sister Goneril;
And hardly shall I carry out my side,
Her husband being alive. Now then we'll use
His countenance for the battle; which being done,
Let her who would be rid of him devise
His speedy taking off. As for the mercy
Which he intends to Lear and to Cordelia,
The battle done, and they within our power,
Shall never see his pardon; for my state
Stands on me to defend, not to debate. *Exit.*

SCENE II. [*A field between the two camps.*]

Alarum within. Enter, with drum and colours, LEAR, CORDELIA, *and* Soldiers, *over the stage; and exeunt.*

Enter EDGAR *and* GLOUCESTER.

Edg. Here, father, take the shadow of this tree
For your good host; pray that the right may thrive:
If ever I return to you again,
I'll bring you comfort.
Glou. Grace go with you, sir!
Exit [*Edgar*].

Alarum and retreat within. Enter EDGAR.

Edg. Away, old man; give me thy hand; away!
King Lear hath lost, he and his daughter ta'en:
Give me thy hand; come on.
Glou. No further, sir; a man may rot even here.
Edg. What, in ill thoughts again? Men must endure
Their going hence, even as their coming hither:
Ripeness is all: come on.
Glou. And that's true too. *Exeunt.*

SCENE III. [*The British camp near Dover.*]

Enter, in conquest, with drum and colours, EDMUND; LEAR *and* CORDELIA, *as prisoners;* Soldiers, Captain, [&c.].

Edm. Some officers take them away: good guard,
Until their greater pleasures first be known
That are to censure them.
Cor. We are not the first
Who, with best meaning, have incurr'd the worst.
For thee, oppressed king, am I cast down;
Myself could else out-frown false fortune's frown.
Shall we not see these daughters and these sisters?
Lear. No, no, no, no! Come, let 's away to prison:
We two alone will sing like birds i' th' cage:
When thou dost ask me blessing, I'll kneel down,
And ask of thee forgiveness: so we'll live,
And pray, and sing, and tell old tales, and laugh
At gilded butterflies, and hear poor rogues
Talk of court news; and we'll talk with them too,
Who loses and who wins; who 's in, who 's out;
And take upon 's the mystery of things,
As if we were God's spies: and we'll wear out,
In a wall'd prison, packs and sects of great ones,
That ebb and flow by th' moon.
Edm. Take them away.
Lear. Upon such sacrifices, my Cordelia,
The gods themselves throw incense. Have I caught thee?
He that parts us shall bring a brand from heaven,
And fire us hence like foxes. Wipe thine eyes;
The good-years shall devour them, flesh and fell,
Ere they shall make us weep: we'll see 'em starv'd first.
Come. *Exit* [*with Cordelia, guarded*].
Edm. Come hither, captain; hark.
Take thou this note [*giving a paper*]; go follow them to prison:
One step I have advanc'd thee; if thou dost
As this instructs thee, thou dost make thy way
To noble fortunes: know thou this, that men
Are as the time is: to be tender-minded
Does not become a sword: thy great employment
Will not bear question; either say thou 'lt do 't,
Or thrive by other means.
Capt. I'll do 't, my lord.
Edm. About it; and write happy when th' hast done.
Mark, I say, instantly; and carry it so
As I have set it down.
Capt. I cannot draw a cart, nor eat dried oats;
If it be man's work, I'll do 't. *Exit Captain.*

Flourish. Enter ALBANY, GONERIL, REGAN, [*another* Captain, *and*] Soldiers.

Alb. Sir, you have show'd to-day your valiant strain,
And fortune led you well: you have the captives
Who were the opposites of this day's strife:
I do require them of you, so to use them
As we shall find their merits and our safety
May equally determine.
Edm. Sir, I thought it fit
To send the old and miserable king
To some retention and appointed guard;
Whose age had charms in it, whose title more,
To pluck the common bosom on his side,

56. **jealous,** suspicious. 61. **carry out my side,** fulfill my ambition, and satisfy her. 63. **countenance,** backing. 68-69. **my state . . . debate,** my position depends upon maintenance by force, not on debate.
SCENE II. 11. **Ripeness,** fulfillment of one's allotted years.
SCENE III. 13. **gilded butterflies,** courtiers. 17. **wear out,** outlast. 18-19. **packs . . . moon,** i.e., followers and cliques attached to persons of high station, whose fortunes change erratically and constantly. 23. **fire . . . foxes,** i.e., as foxes are driven out of their holes by fire and smoke; reminiscent of Samson's stratagem, Judges 15:4. 24. **good-years,** apparently a general word for evil; thought sometimes to be the name of a disease. Compare, however, the story of Pharaoh's dream, Genesis 41. **flesh and fell,** flesh and skin. 33. **bear question,** admit of discussion. 35. **write happy,** call yourself happy. 47. **retention,** custody. 49. **common bosom,** the aflection of the mob.

And turn our impress'd lances in our eyes
Which do command them. With him I sent the queen;
My reason all the same; and they are ready
To-morrow, or at further space, t' appear
Where you shall hold your session. At this time
We sweat and bleed: the friend hath lost his friend;
And the best quarrels, in the heat, are curs'd
By those that feel their sharpness:
The question of Cordelia and her father
Requires a fitter place.

Alb. Sir, by your patience,
I hold you but a subject of this war,
Not as a brother.

Reg. That 's as we list to grace him.
Methinks our pleasure might have been demanded,
Ere you had spoke so far. He led our powers;
Bore the commission of my place and person;
The which immediacy may well stand up,
And call itself your brother.

Gon. Not so hot:
In his own grace he doth exalt himself,
More than in your addition.

Reg. In my rights,
By me invested, he compeers the best.

Gon. That were the most, if he should husband you.

Reg. Jesters do oft prove prophets.

Gon. Holla, holla!
That eye that told you so look'd but a-squint.

Reg. Lady, I am not well; else I should answer
From a full-flowing stomach. General,
Take thou my soldiers, prisoners, patrimony;
Dispose of them, of me; the walls is thine:
Witness the world, that I create thee here
My lord and master.

Gon. Mean you to enjoy him?

Alb. The let-alone lies not in your good will.

Edm. Nor in thine, lord.

Alb. Half-blooded fellow, yes.

Reg. [*To Edmund*] Let the drum strike, and prove my title thine.

Alb. Stay yet; hear reason. Edmund, I arrest thee
On capital treason; and, in thy attaint,
This gilded serpent [*pointing to Gon.*]. For your claim, fair sister,
I bar it in the interest of my wife;
'Tis she is sub-contracted to this lord,
And I, her husband, contradict your banes.
If you will marry, make your loves to me,
My lady is bespoke.

Gon. An interlude!

Alb. Thou art arm'd, Gloucester: let the trumpet sound:
If none appear to prove upon thy person
Thy heinous, manifest, and many treasons,
There is my pledge [*throwing down a glove*]; I'll make it on thy heart,
Ere I taste bread, thou art in nothing less
Than I have here proclaim'd thee.

Reg. Sick, O, sick!

Gon. [*Aside*] If not, I'll ne'er trust medicine.

Edm. There 's my exchange [*throwing down a glove*]: what in the world he is
That names me traitor, villain-like he lies:
Call by the trumpet: he that dares approach,
On him, on you, who not? I will maintain
My truth and honour firmly.

Alb. A herald, ho!

Edm. A herald, ho, a herald!

Alb. Trust to thy single virtue; for thy soldiers,
All levied in my name, have in my name
Took their discharge.

Reg. My sickness grows upon me.

Alb. She is not well; convey her to my tent.
[*Exit Regan, led.*]

Enter a Herald.

Come hither, herald,—Let the trumpet sound,—
And read out this.

Capt. Sound, trumpet! *A trumpet sounds.*

Her. (*Reads*) 'If any man of quality or degree within the lists of the army will maintain upon Edmund, supposed Earl of Gloucester, that he is a manifold traitor, let him appear by the third sound of the trumpet: he is bold in his defence.'

Edm. Sound! *First trumpet.*

Her. Again! *Second trumpet.*

Her. Again! *Third trumpet.*
Trumpet answers within.

Enter EDGAR, [*at the third sound,*] armed [*with a trumpeter before him*].

Alb. Ask him his purposes, why he appears
Upon this call o' th' trumpet.

Her. What are you?
Your name, your quality? and why you answer
This present summons?

Edg. Know, my name is lost;
By treason's tooth bare-gnawn and canker-bit:
Yet am I noble as the adversary
I come to cope.

Alb. Which is that adversary?

Edg. What 's he that speaks for Edmund Earl of Gloucester?

Edm. Himself: what say'st thou to him?

Edg. Draw thy sword,
That, if my speech offend a noble heart,
Thy arm may do thee justice: here is mine.
Behold, it is the privilege of mine honours,
My oath, and my profession: I protest,
Maugre thy strength, place, youth, and eminence,
Despite thy victor sword and fire-new fortune,
Thy valour and thy heart, thou art a traitor;
False to thy gods, thy brother, and thy father;
Conspirant 'gainst this high-illustrious prince;
And, from th' extremest upward of thy head
To the descent and dust below thy foot,
A most toad-spotted traitor. Say thou 'No,'
This sword, this arm, and my best spirits, are bent
To prove upon thy heart, whereto I speak,
Thou liest.

Edm. In wisdom I should ask thy name;

50. **impress'd lances,** weapons of troops impressed into service. 53. **space,** time. 58. **question,** cause. 61. **list,** please. 65. **immediacy,** next in authority, or nearness of his being my agent. 69. **compeers,** is equal with. 72. **That . . . a-squint,** reference to a proverb: Love being jealous makes a good eye look asquint. 74. **full-flowing stomach,** full tide of angry rejoinder. 76. **the walls is thine,** probably a phrase signifying complete surrender; many conjectures. 80. **Half-blooded,** partly of mean blood. 83. **in thy attaint,** i.e., as partner in your treason. 87. **banes,** banns. 89. **interlude,** play, i.e., you are melodramatic. 93. **make,** prove. 96. **medicine,** i.e., poison. 119. **What,**

But, since thy outside looks so fair and warlike,
And that thy tongue some say of breeding breathes,
What safe and nicely I might well delay
By rule of knighthood, I disdain and spurn:
Back do I toss these treasons to thy head;
With the hell-hated lie o'erwhelm thy heart;
Which, for they yet glance by and scarcely bruise,
This sword of mine shall give them instant way,
Where they shall rest for ever. Trumpets, speak!
Alarums. Fight. [*Edmund falls.*]
Alb. Save him, save him!
Gon. This is practice, Gloucester:
By th' law of war thou wast not bound to answer
An unknown opposite; thou art not vanquish'd,
But cozen'd and beguil'd.
Alb. Shut your mouth, dame,
Or with this paper shall I stop it. Hold, sir;
Thou worse than any name, read thine own evil:
No tearing, lady; I perceive you know it.
Gon. Say, if I do, the laws are mine, not thine:
Who can arraign me for 't?
Alb. Most monstrous! oh!
Know'st thou this paper?
Gon. Ask me not what I know. *Exit.*
Alb. Go after her: she 's desperate; govern her.
[*Exit an Officer.*]
Edm. What you have charg'd me with, that have I done;
And more, much more; the time will bring it out:
'Tis past, and so am I. But what art thou
That hast this fortune on me? If thou 'rt noble,
I do forgive thee.
Edg. Let 's exchange charity.
I am no less in blood than thou art, Edmund;
If more, the more th' hast wrong'd me.
My name is Edgar, and thy father's son.
The gods are just, and of our pleasant vices
Make instruments to plague us:
The dark and vicious place where thee he got
Cost him his eyes.
Edm. Th' hast spoken right, 'tis true;
The wheel is come full circle; I am here.
Alb. Methought thy very gait did prophesy
A royal nobleness: I must embrace thee:
Let sorrow split my heart, if ever I
Did hate thee or thy father!
Edg. Worthy prince, I know 't.
Alb. Where have you hid yourself?
How have you known the miseries of your father?
Edg. By nursing them, my lord. List a brief tale;
And when 'tis told, O, that my heart would burst!
The bloody proclamation to escape,
That follow'd me so near,—O, our lives' sweetness!
That we the pain of death would hourly die
Rather than die at once!—taught me to shift
Into a madman's rags; t' assume a semblance
That very dogs disdain'd: and in this habit
Met I my father with his bleeding rings,
Their precious stones new lost; became his guide,
Led him, begg'd for him, sav'd him from despair;
Never,—O fault!—reveal'd myself unto him,
Until some half-hour past, when I was arm'd:
Not sure, though hoping, of this good success,
I ask'd his blessing, and from first to last
Told him our pilgrimage: but his flaw'd heart,
Alack, too weak the conflict to support!
'Twixt two extremes of passion, joy and grief,
Burst smilingly.
Edm. This speech of yours hath mov'd me,
And shall perchance do good: but speak you on;
You look as you had something more to say.
Alb. If there be more, more woeful, hold it in;
For I am almost ready to dissolve,
Hearing of this.
Edg. This would have seem'd a period
To such as love not sorrow; but another,
To amplify too much, would make much more,
And top extremity.
Whilst I was big in clamour came there in a man,
Who, having seen me in my worst estate,
Shunn'd my abhorr'd society; but then, finding
Who 'twas that so endur'd, with his strong arms
He fasten'd on my neck, and bellow'd out
As he 'ld burst heaven; threw him on my father;
Told the most piteous tale of Lear and him
That ever ear receiv'd: which in recounting
His grief grew puissant, and the strings of life
Began to crack: twice then the trumpets sounded,
And there I left him tranc'd.
Alb. But who was this?
Edg. Kent, sir, the banish'd Kent; who in disguise
Follow'd his enemy king, and did him service
Improper for a slave.

Enter a Gentleman [*with a bloody knife*].

Gent. Help, help, O, help!
Edg. What kind of help?
Alb. Speak, man.
Edg. What means this bloody knife?
Gent. 'Tis hot, it smokes;
It came even from the heart of—O, she 's dead!
Alb. Who dead? speak, man.
Gent. Your lady, sir, your lady: and her sister
By her is poisoned; she confesses it.
Edm. I was contracted to them both: all three
Now marry in an instant.
Edg. Here comes Kent.
Alb. Produce the bodies, be they alive or dead:
This judgement of the heavens, that makes us tremble,
Touches us not with pity. [*Exit Gentleman.*]

Enter KENT.

O, is this he?
The time will not allow the compliment
Which very manners urges.
Kent. I am come
To bid my king and master aye good night:
Is he not here?
Alb. Great thing of us forgot!
Speak, Edmund, where 's the king? and where 's Cordelia?

who. 122. **canker-bit,** withered, i.e., bitten by the caterpillar. 131. **Maugre,** in spite of. 132. **fire-new,** freshly gained. 136. **upward,** top. 138. **toad-spotted,** venomous, or having spots of infamy. 141. **wisdom,** prudence; i.e., Edmund might have demanded that his adversary be his equal in rank. 143. **say,** flavor, indication; possibly for "assay," proof.

146. **head,** i.e., to thy teeth. 147. **hell-hated,** hated as hell is hated. 161. **govern,** restrain. 165. **fortune,** victory, success. 170. **pleasant,** pleasurable. 172. **got,** begot. 174. **wheel,** wheel of fortune. 189. **rings,** sockets. 196. **flaw'd,** cracked, damaged by a flaw. 204. **a period,** the limit. 218. **tranc'd,** entranced, senseless.

See'st thou this object, Kent?
Goneril's and Regan's bodies [*are*] *brought out.*
Kent. Alack, why thus?
Edm. Yet Edmund was belov'd:
The one the other poison'd for my sake,
And after slew herself.
Alb. Even so. Cover their faces.
Edm. I pant for life: some good I mean to do,
Despite of mine own nature. Quickly send,
Be brief in it, to th' castle; for my writ
Is on the life of Lear and on Cordelia:
Nay, send in time.
Alb. Run, run, O, run!
Edg. To who, my lord? Who has the office? send
Thy token of reprieve.
Edm. Well thought on: take my sword,
Give it the captain.
Edg. Haste thee, for thy life.
[*Exit Officer*].
Edm. He hath commission from thy wife and me
To hang Cordelia in the prison, and
To lay the blame upon her own despair,
That she fordid herself.
Alb. The gods defend her! Bear him hence awhile.
[*Edmund is borne off.*]

Enter Lear, *with* Cordelia *in his arms* [; Gentleman *and others following*].

Lear. Howl, howl, howl, howl! O, you are men of stones:
Had I your tongues and eyes, I 'ld use them so
That heaven's vault should crack. She 's gone for ever!
I know when one is dead, and when one lives;
She 's dead as earth. Lend me a looking-glass;
If that her breath will mist or stain the stone,
Why, then she lives.
Kent. Is this the promis'd end?
Edg. Or image of that horror?
Alb. Fall, and cease!
Lear. This feather stirs; she lives! if it be so,
It is a chance which does redeem all sorrows
That ever I have felt.
Kent. [*Kneeling*] O my good master!
Lear. Prithee, away.
Edg. 'Tis noble Kent, your friend.
Lear. A plague upon you, murderers, traitors all!
I might have sav'd her; now she 's gone for ever!
Cordelia, Cordelia! stay a little. Ha!
What is 't thou say'st? Her voice was ever soft,
Gentle, and low, an excellent thing in woman.
I kill'd the slave that was a-hanging thee.
Capt. 'Tis true, my lords, he did.
Lear. Did I not, fellow?
I have seen the day, with my good biting falchion
I would have made them skip: I am old now,
And these same crosses spoil me. Who are you?
Mine eyes are not o' th' best: I'll tell you straight.
Kent. If Fortune brag of two she lov'd and hated,
One of them we behold.
Lear. This is a dull sight. Are you not Kent?
Kent. The same,
Your servant Kent. Where is your servant Caius?
Lear. He 's a good fellow, I can tell you that;
He'll strike, and quickly too: he 's dead and rotten.
Kent. No, my good lord; I am the very man,—
Lear. I'll see that straight.
Kent. That, from your first of difference and decay,
Have follow'd your sad steps.
Lear. You are welcome hither.
Kent. Nor no man else: all 's cheerless, dark, and deadly.
Your eldest daughters have fordone themselves,
And desperately are dead.
Lear. Ay, so I think.
Alb. He knows not what he says: and vain it is
That we present us to him.
Edg. Very bootless.

Enter a Messenger.

Mess. Edmund is dead, my lord.
Alb. That 's but a trifle here.
You lords and noble friends, know our intent.
What comfort to this great decay may come
Shall be applied: for us, we will resign,
During the life of this old majesty,
To him our absolute power: [*To Edgar and Kent*] you, to your rights;
With boot, and such addition as your honours
Have more than merited. All friends shall taste
The wages of their virtue, and all foes
The cup of their deservings. O, see, see!
Lear. And my poor fool is hang'd! No, no, no life!
Why should a dog, a horse, a rat, have life,
And thou no breath at all? Thou 'lt come no more,
Never, never, never, never, never!
Pray you, undo this button: thank you, sir.
Do you see this? Look on her, look, her lips,
Look there, look there! *He dies.*
Edg. He faints! My lord, my lord!
Kent. Break, heart; I prithee, break!
Edg. Look up, my lord.
Kent. Vex not his ghost: O, let him pass! he hates him
That would upon the rack of this tough world
Stretch him out longer.
Edg. He is gone, indeed.
Kent. The wonder is, he hath endur'd so long:
He but usurp'd his life.
Alb. Bear them from hence. Our present business
Is general woe. [*To Kent and Edgar*] Friends of my soul, you twain
Rule in this realm, and the gor'd state sustain.
Kent. I have a journey, sir, shortly to go;
My master calls me, I must not say no.
Edg. The weight of this sad time we must obey;
Speak what we feel, not what we ought to say.
The oldest hath borne most: we that are young
Shall never see so much, nor live so long.
Exeunt, with a dead march.

249. **office,** commission. 255. **fordid,** destroyed. 262. **mist,** becloud. **stone,** crystal (of which the mirror is made). 263. **end,** Last Judgment. 264. **image,** duplicate. **Fall, and cease.** Let the heavens fall and all things cease. 276. **falchion,** sword; properly, a sword curved at the point with the edge on the convex side. 278. **these . . . spoil me,** all these misfortunes weaken me. 279. **I'll tell you straight,** I'll admit to you; or, I'll recognize you in a moment. 280. **two,** i.e., Lear, and a hypothetical individual whose misfortunes are without parallel. **lov'd and hated,** i.e., first raised and then lowered. 282. **dull sight,** melancholy spectacle; and (Lear's) clouded vision. 283. **Caius,** Kent's disguise name. 287. **see that straight,** attend to that soon; or, comprehend that soon. 288. **first of difference,** beginning of your change for the worst. 292. **desperately,** in despair. 305. **my poor fool,** i.e., Cordelia. It has sometimes been wrongly thought that this refers to the Fool, but *fool,* as here used, is a term of endearment.

TIMON OF ATHENS

T*imon of Athens* is Shakespeare's most relentless study in misanthropy. It expresses with *King Lear* a moral outrage at human depravity, but refuses to soften its anger with compassionate tears. Timon learns only bitterness from his encounters with avarice and ingratitude. The play is based on Thomas North's translation of Plutarch's *Lives*, and ultimately (through intermediary sources) on the dialogue *Timon*, or *The Misanthrope*, by the Greek satirist Lucian. Like Shakespeare's other Roman or classical plays, most of which were also based on Plutarch (*Julius Caesar*, *Antony and Cleopatra*, *Coriolanus*), *Timon* is dominated by an ironic mood. The political and social world in all these plays (and in *Troilus and Cressida* as well) is marked by an atmosphere of enervation and futility. Political conflicts end in stalemate or a victory for opportunists; the populace is fickle and craven; private virtues of noble men must yield to crass considerations of statecraft. Banishment is a common affliction ungratefully meted out to those who have given their lives in selfless public service (as also in the early *Titus Andronicus*). Shakespeare's misanthropic vision is therefore not new in *Timon*. The Roman or classical plays are prominent throughout Shakespeare's tragic period, running concurrently with the great tragedies of evil (*Hamlet*, *Othello*, *King Lear*, *Macbeth*) and counterpointing their moral Christian perspective with a more sardonic and dispiriting comment on life's tragic absurdity. Except for *Antony and Cleopatra*, the Roman and classical plays offer little cathartic vision as in the tragedies of evil. *Timon* appears to have been written some time between 1605 and 1608, and is often grouped with *King Lear* (c. 1605) on grounds of stylistic and thematic similarity. Whatever its exact date, *Timon* certainly belongs to the period of Shakespeare's most unsparing portrayal of human villainy and corruption.

Like *Troilus and Cressida*, *Timon* defies the conventional categories of tragedy, comedy, and history. In terms of Northrop Frye's *Anatomy of Criticism*, *Timon* stands chiefly between tragedy and satire: that is, its mythic connotations are those of dying and sterility, as at the end of the cycle of the seasons, rather than those of renewal and growth. The play is tragic in portraying a fall from greatness, satiric in exposing an unfeeling society. Yet satire is potentially comic as well, and we are invited to laugh bitterly at the hypocrisies of Timon's fair-weather friends. Even history claims its share in the play's Folio title, *The Life of Timon of Athens*. Accordingly, *Timon* ought to be read with the expectations of satire and ironic history as well as of tragedy.

As a genre, in fact, the play resembles those works which the Painter and the Poet wish to offer Timon himself: a "moral painting" and a "satire against the softness of prosperity" (I,i and V,i). Such a genre is deliberately old-fashioned, reminiscent of the "hybrid" morality plays of the 1570's and '80's like Thomas Lupton's *All for Money* (c. 1577) or Thomas Lodge and Robert Greene's *A Looking Glass for London and England* (1587–1591), which inveigh against usury and the neglect of military heroes. John Marston's later quasi-morality, *Histriomastix* (c. 1599), proclaims the decline of civilization through worldly insolence. Ben Jonson's *Volpone* (1605–1606), though a "comical" rather than "tragical" satire, similarly castigates human greed. The *Parnassus* trilogy (1598–1603) indulges in a massive venting of spleen against a Philistine culture. *Timon* follows this tradition of social satire, both English and classical in flavor. Like most satire of the 1600's, both dramatic and nondramatic, it is crabbed in style, features a railing protagonist, and denounces through exaggerated caricature an ugly array of types representing a broad social spectrum. *Timon* is distinctly not in Shakespeare's "popular" vein. It may not even have been produced; the text, not printed until the 1623 Folio, appears to have been taken from the author's unfinished manuscript, with contradictory uncancelled lines (see Timon's will, V,iv,70–73), unresolved discrepancies as to the amount of money Timon gives or requests, and passages of half-versified prose.

Timon's theme, the universality of human greed, lends itself to satiric treatment. Avarice is not terrifying, like the spiritual sins of envy or prideful ambition as portrayed in *Othello* and *Macbeth*, but is disgusting, ludicrous, and incredibly tenacious. Those who sponge off Timon and then desert him are quick to return when he is rumored to have found gold in his exile. Greed is also self-deceiving. Infinite are the excuses offered for failing to come to Timon's aid: one friend rates Timon as a bad credit risk, another happens to be short of ready cash at the moment, a third insists that Timon's generosity to him wasn't as great as people suppose, and so on. No wonder Timon is tempted, like Volpone and Mosca, to expose such hypocrites at their own game, arranging a farewell banquet in which he rewards their crass expectations with a mocking litany of curses and a dinner of water and stones.

Appropriately for this satire of exposure, the characters are virtually all types or "humours," social abstractions in a generic portrayal of avarice. Several represent the crafts and professions, and are abstractly labeled as such: the Poet, the Painter, the Jeweller, the Merchant. Others are "flattering lords" or "false friends" or "thieves." Apemantus is "a churlish philosopher," recognized as a "humourous" type through his dominant trait of personality (caused, according to the quasi-medical theory of "humours," by a dominance of one of the four bodily fluids, blood, phlegm, bile, or black bile). Timon himself becomes a "humourous" type in his conversion to misanthropy, "infected," as Apemantus says, by "A poor unmanly melancholy sprung From change of fortune" (IV,iii). Character types are often associated, as in *Volpone*, with the traits of various beasts: lion, fox, ass, wolf, bear, and most of all the dog. The image of disease is equally pervasive. Generic portrayal of this sort is basically static, a vivid and one-sided lampoon or caricature allowing for little subtlety or change (except for Timon's own violent shift from philanthropy to misanthropy). The dramatic situation is also unusually static for Shakespeare. Timon is involved in no torn family loyalties, and faces no hard choice between duty and affection. He simply retires from the ungrateful world and breathes upon it his dying curse. Alcibiades does offer, to be sure, the alternative of vengeful action toward that ungrateful world, but even this alternative is seen by Timon as something to be avoided.

There are no villains in *Timon*, another sure sign that it lacks the terrifying evil of *Othello* or *Macbeth*. What is depressing about greed, in fact, is its normality. Those who desert Timon have many prudent arguments on their side. After all, his original generosity is excessive and reckless. If his friends take advantage of him, they can at least say they have tried to warn him. Even a fool can see what lies in store. Much of Timon's wealth goes into drunken and gluttonous debauchery, into "feasts, pomps, and vainglories." Timon does not know how to use prosperity wisely, and even his loyal servants deplore the "riot." He is deaf to the friendly counsel of his steward, Flavius. For one who is so openhanded, Timon is surprisingly churlish with his creditors. And is he not presumptuous to assume that his friends will come to his aid when such vast sums are needed? Are they to be blamed for not emulating his prodigal decline into poverty? Clearly Timon expects too much, naively having failed to learn the economic facts of life. Everyone knows that charity begins at home and that commerce is a god worshiped by all; need he be so shocked at this? As bystanders, we share with Timon's choric servants the certainty that his large requests for help will be refused. And yet, no matter how stupid or blind Timon may be, the desertion of him is still monstrous. Timon differs from us chiefly in being an idealist, in expecting that men will repay kindness with gratitude. We know, as do Timon's sympathetic servants, that most men are not like that—the more's the pity.

Timon thus tears himself apart in a rage at what we consider the way of the world. We find his misanthropy intemperate, and yet we cannot help being moved by his sweeping indictment of man's pettiness and inhumanity. Timon's furor carries him beyond satire to the tragic splendor of King Lear. He is, like Lear, all the more clear-sighted for being near to madness. Wisdom and folly exchange places, as Apemantus' friend the Fool has already pointed out (II,ii). In Timon's mad vision beggars and lords are interchangeable, distinguished only by wealth and position. Love of gold, he sees, inverts everything decent in human life, making "black white, foul fair, Wrong right, base noble, old young, coward valiant" (IV,iii). True thieves and whores are at least more honest than their counterparts in everyday life, the respectable citizens of Athens and their wives; accordingly, Timon mockingly rewards the true thieves and insults the hypocrites. His curse embraces the cosmos as well as humanity, inverting all semblance of hierarchical order: obedience must turn to rebellion, fidelity to incontinence, virginity to lasciviousness. "Degrees, observances, customs, and laws" must "Decline to your confounding contraries" (IV,i). Clothing and cosmetics must be stripped away, as in *King Lear*, so that man's monstrosity may be revealed for what it truly is.

Three persons serve as chief foils to Timon in his estrangement from humanity. Apemantus the cynic, who first taught Timon to rail at greed, now counsels him to find stoic contentment in renunciation of desire, or, conversely, to thrive as a flatterer by preying on those who have undone him (IV,iii). Alcibiades, the military commander banished by an ungrateful Athenian senate for presuming to beg the life of one who had rashly shed blood in a quarrel, offers Timon the means to active revenge against his enemies. Timon, although resembling both men as railer and as victim of ingratitude, rejects their counsels as too politic, too worldly. His stand is unflinching, absolute, so lacking in compromise that his sole choice can be to curse, die, and hope for oblivion. Only Flavius, his steward, offers brief consolation. Flavius comes to him, like Kent to King Lear, offering disinterested love and service in exile. Flavius even speaks in paradoxes reminiscent of *King Lear*, calling Timon "My dearest lord, bless'd to be most accurs'd, Rich only to be wretched" (IV,ii). These are precious words, showing that humanity is not utterly irredeemable. Still, this consolation is evidently too late to offset the nightmarish truth that Timon has learned. Timon experiences little of the compassionate love that comes to Lear in his madness, but he at least faces the bleakness of human existence with unbending honesty.

This and my food are equals; there 's no odds:
Feasts are too proud to give thanks to the gods.

Apemantus' grace.

Immortal gods, I crave no pelf;
I pray for no man but myself:
Grant I may never prove so fond,
To trust man on his oath or bond;
Or a harlot, for her weeping;
Or a dog, that seems a-sleeping;
Or a keeper with my freedom;
Or my friends, if I should need 'em.
Amen. So fall to 't:
Rich men sin, and I eat root. [*Eats and drinks.*]
Much good †dich thy good heart, Apemantus!

Tim. Captain Alcibiades, your heart 's in the field now.

Alcib. My heart is ever at your service, my lord.

Tim. You had rather be at a breakfast of enemies than a dinner of friends.

Alcib. So they were bleeding-new, my lord, there 's no meat like 'em: I could wish my best friend at such a feast.

Apem. Would all those flatterers were thine enemies then, that then thou mightst kill 'em and bid me to 'em!

First Lord. Might we but have that happiness, my lord, that you would once use our hearts, whereby we might express some part of our zeals, we should think ourselves for ever perfect.

Tim. O, no doubt, my good friends, but the gods themselves have provided that I shall have much help from you: how had you been my friends else? why have you that charitable title from thousands, did not you chiefly belong to my heart? I have told more of you to myself than you can with modesty speak in your own behalf; and thus far I confirm you. O you gods, think I, what need we have any friends, if we should ne'er have need of 'em? they were the most needless creatures living, should we ne'er have use for 'em, and would most resemble sweet instruments hung up in cases that keeps their sounds to themselves. Why, I have often wished myself poorer, that I might come nearer to you. We are born to do benefits: and what better or properer can we call our own than the riches of our friends? O, what a precious comfort 'tis, to have so many, like brothers, commanding one another's fortunes! O joy's e'en made away ere 't can be born! Mine eyes cannot hold out water, methinks: to forget their faults, I drink to you.

Apem. Thou weep'st to make them drink, Timon.

Sec. Lord. Joy had the like conception in our eyes
And at that instant like a babe sprung up.

Apem. Ho, ho! I laugh to think that babe a bastard.

Third Lord. I promise you, my lord, you mov'd me
much.

Apem. Much! *Sound tucket.*

Tim. What means that trump?

Enter Servant.

How now?

Serv. Please you, my lord, there are certain ladies most desirous of admittance.

Tim. Ladies! what are their wills?

Serv. There comes with them a forerunner, my lord, which bears that office, to signify their pleasures.

Tim. I pray, let them be admitted.

Enter Cupid.

Cup. Hail to thee, worthy Timon, and to all
That of his bounties taste! The five best senses
Acknowledge thee their patron; and come freely
To gratulate thy plenteous bosom: th' ear,
Taste, touch and smell, pleased from thy table rise;
They only now come but to feast thine eyes.

Tim. They 're welcome all; let 'em have kind
admittance:
Music, make their welcome! [*Exit Cupid.*]

First Lord. You see, my lord, how ample y' are
belov'd.

[*Music.*] *Enter* Cupid, *with a mask of* Ladies [*as*] *Amazons, with lutes in their hands, dancing and playing.*

Apem. Hoy-day, what a sweep of vanity comes this
way!
They dance! they are mad women.
Like madness is the glory of this life,
As this pomp shows to a little oil and root.
We make ourselves fools, to disport ourselves;
And spend our flatteries, to drink those men
Upon whose age we void it up again,
With poisonous spite and envy.
Who lives that 's not depraved or depraves?
Who dies, that bears not one spurn to their graves
Of their friends' gift?
I should fear those that dance before me now
Would one day stamp upon me: 't has been done;
Men shut their doors against a setting sun.

The Lords *rise from table, with much adoring of* Timon; *and to show their loves, each single out an* Amazon, *and all dance, men with women, a lofty strain or two to the hautboys, and cease.*

Tim. You have done our pleasures much grace, fair
ladies,
Set a fair fashion on our entertainment,
Which was not half so beautiful and kind;
You have added worth unto 't and lustre,
And entertain'd me with mine own device;
I am to thank you for 't.

First Lady. My lord, you take us even at the best.

Apem. 'Faith, for the worst is filthy; and would not hold taking, I doubt me.

Tim. Ladies, there is an idle banquet attends you:
Please you to dispose yourselves.

All Ladies. Most thankfully, my lord.

Exeunt [*Cupid and Ladies*].

my tears. 126. **pleasures,** wishes. 137. **sweep of vanity,** troop of vain creatures. 138. **they are mad women.** Steevens quotes Stubbes' *Anatomy of Abuses:* "*Dauncers* thought to be *mad men,*" and again: "And as in all feasts and pastimes dauncing is the last, so it is the extream of all other vice." 139-140. **Like madness . . . root.** The word *like* in this place does not express *resemblance*, but *equality*. Apemantus does not mean to say that the glory of this life was like madness, but it was *just as much madness* in the eye of reason, as the pomp appeared to be when compared to the frugal repast of a philosopher (M. Mason). 142-144. **And . . . envy,** and lavish our flatteries in order to drink the health of those upon whom, when old, we cast up our surfeit in the shape of poisonous spite and envy. 145. **depraved,** vilified, slandered. 147. **gift,** giving. 150. **Men . . . sun.** Cf. North's Plutarch (*Life of Pompey*), where is related Pompey's retort to Sulla's threat of resistance: Pompey "told him frankly again how men did honour the rising, not the setting of the sun." 153. **kind,** favorable (Onions); suitable (Deighton). 155. **with mine own device.** The mask appears to have been designed by Timon to surprise his guests (Johnson). 158. **would . . . taking,** i.e., is too rotten with venereal disease. 160. **idle,** trifling, slight.

Tim. Flavius.
Flav. My lord?
Tim. The little casket bring me hither.
Flav. Yes, my lord. More jewels yet! [*Aside.*]
There is no crossing him in 's humour;
Else I should tell him well, i' faith, I should,
When all 's spent, he 'ld be cross'd then, an he could.
'Tis pity bounty had not eyes behind,
That man might ne'er be wretched for his mind. *Exit.*
First Lord. Where be our men?
Serv. Here, my lord, in readiness.
Sec. Lord. Our horses!

Enter FLAVIUS [*with the casket*].

Tim. O my friends,
I have one word to say to you: look you, my good lord,
I must entreat you, honour me so much
As to advance this jewel; accept it and wear it,
Kind my lord.
First Lord. I am so far already in your gifts,—
All. So are we all.

Enter a Servant.

Serv. My lord, there are certain nobles of the senate
Newly alighted, and come to visit you.
Tim. They are fairly welcome.
Flav. I beseech your honour,
Vouchsafe me a word; it does concern you near.
Tim. Near! why then, another time I'll hear thee:
I prithee, let 's be provided to show them entertainment.
Flav. [*Aside*] I scarce know how.

Enter another Servant.

Sec. Serv. May it please your honour, Lord Lucius,
Out of his free love, hath presented to you
Four milk-white horses, trapp'd in silver.
Tim. I shall accept them fairly; let the presents
Be worthily entertain'd.

Enter a third Servant.

How now! what news?
Third Serv. Please you, my lord, that honourable gentleman, Lord Lucullus, entreats your company to-morrow to hunt with him, and has sent your honour two brace of greyhounds.
Tim. I'll hunt with him; and let them be receiv'd,
Not without fair reward.
Flav. [*Aside*] What will this come to?
He commands us to provide, and give great gifts,
And all out of an empty coffer:
Nor will he know his purse, or yield me this,
To show him what a beggar his heart is,
Being of no power to make his wishes good:
His promises fly so beyond his state
That what he speaks is all in debt; he owes
For ev'ry word: he is so kind that he now
Pays interest for 't; his land 's put to their books.
Well, would I were gently put out of office
Before I were forc'd out!
Happier is he that has no friend to feed
Than such that do e'en enemies exceed.
I bleed inwardly for my lord. *Exit.*
Tim. You do yourselves
Much wrong, you bate too much of your own merits:
Here, my lord, a trifle of our love.
Sec. Lord. With more than common thanks I will receive it.
Third Lord. O, he 's the very soul of bounty!
Tim. And now I remember, my lord, you gave
Good words the other day of a bay courser
I rode on: 'tis yours, because you lik'd it.
Sec. Lord. O, I beseech you, pardon me, my lord, in that.
Tim. You may take my word, my lord; I know, no man
Can justly praise but what he does affect:
I weigh my friend's affection with mine own;
I'll tell you true. I'll call to you.
All Lords. O, none so welcome.
Tim. I take all and your several visitations
So kind to heart, 'tis not enough to give;
Methinks, I could deal kingdoms to my friends,
And ne'er be weary. Alcibiades,
Thou art a soldier, therefore seldom rich;
It comes in charity to thee: for all thy living
Is 'mongst the dead, and all the lands thou hast
Lie in a pitch'd field.
Alcib. Ay, defil'd land, my lord.
First Lord. We are so virtuously bound—
Tim. And so
Am I to you.
Sec. Lord. So infinitely endear'd—
Tim. All to you. Lights, more lights!
First Lord. The best of happiness,
Honour and fortunes, keep with you, Lord Timon!
Tim. Ready for his friends.
Exeunt lords [*and all but Apemantus and Timon*].
Apem. What a coil 's here!
Serving of becks and jutting-out of bums!
I doubt whether their legs be worth the sums
That are given for 'em. Friendship 's full of dregs:
Methinks, false hearts should never have sound legs.
Thus honest fools lay out their wealth on court'sies.
Tim. Now, Apemantus, if thou wert not sullen,
I would be good to thee.
Apem. No, I'll nothing: for if I should be bribed too, there would be none left to rail upon thee, and then thou wouldst sin the faster. Thou givest so long, Timon, I fear me thou wilt give away thyself in paper shortly: what need these feasts, pomps and vain-glories?
Tim. Nay, an you begin to rail on society once, I am sworn not to give regard to you. Farewell; and come with better music. *Exit.*
Apem. So:
Thou wilt not hear me now; thou shalt not then:
I'll lock thy heaven from thee.

167. **tell him well,** use plain language; so F; Globe, following Rowe: *tell him—well.* Editors adopting Rowe's punctuation think such direct language indecorous for a servant; but see the steward's speeches at II, ii, 8, *I must be round with him,* and II, ii, 142-147, *At many . . . I . . . pray'd you,* etc. 168. **cross'd,** quibbling on the meanings "thwarted" and "provided with coins having on them the representation of a cross." 170. **for his mind,** on account of his generous inclinations. 176. **advance,** make more worthy; i.e., by possessing it; cf. I, i, 170-172.

200. **yield me this,** grant me opportunity. 202. **Being,** modifies *heart.* 203. **state,** estate. 212. **bate too much of,** belittle too much. 223. **call to,** call on (Malone); appeal to (Delius). 231. **defil'd land,** quibble on "pitch'd field." (Cf. *Ecclesiasticus* 13:1: "He that toucheth pitch shall be defiled.") 237. **becks,** nods, bows. **bums,** posteriors. 238. **their legs,** curtsies. 248. **paper,** bonds, promises to pay.

ACT II. SCENE I. 7. **moe,** more. 10. **No porter.** Johnson thought a line was lost here "in which the behaviour of a surly porter was

O, that men's ears should be
To counsel deaf, but not to flattery! *Exit.*

[ACT II.

SCENE I. *A Senator's house.*]

Enter a Senator [*with papers in his hand*].

Sen. And late, five thousand: to Varro and to Isidore
He owes nine thousand; besides my former sum,
Which makes it five and twenty. Still in motion
Of raging waste? It cannot hold; it will not.
If I want gold, steal but a beggar's dog,
And give it Timon, why, the dog coins gold.
If I would sell my horse, and buy twenty moe
Better than he, why, give my horse to Timon,
Ask nothing, give it him, it foals me, straight,
And able horses. No porter at his gate,
But rather one that smiles and still invites
All that pass by. It cannot hold; no reason
Can sound his state in safety. Caphis, ho!
Caphis, I say!

Enter CAPHIS.

Caph. Here, sir; what is your pleasure?
Sen. Get on your cloak, and haste you to Lord Timon;
Importune him for my moneys; be not ceas'd
With slight denial, nor then silenc'd when—
'Commend me to your master'—and the cap
Plays in the right hand, thus: but tell him,
My uses cry to me, I must serve my turn
Out of mine own; his days and times are past
And my reliances on his fracted dates
Have smit my credit: I love and honour him,
But must not break my back to heal his finger;
Immediate are my needs, and my relief
Must not be toss'd and turn'd to me in words,
But find supply immediate. Get you gone:
Put on a most importunate aspect,
A visage of demand; for, I do fear,
When every feather sticks in his own wing,
Lord Timon will be left a naked gull,
Which flashes now a phœnix. Get you gone.
Caph. I go, sir.
Sen. 'I go, sir!'—Take the bonds along with you,
And have the dates in compt.
Caph. I will, sir.
Sen. Go. *Exeunt.*

[SCENE II. *The same. Before Timon's house.*]

Enter Steward [FLAVIUS] *with many bills in his hand.*

Flav. No care, no stop! so senseless of expense,
That he will neither know how to maintain it,
Nor cease his flow of riot: takes no account
How things go from him, nor resumes no care
Of what is to continue: never mind
Was to be so unwise, to be so kind.
What shall be done? he will not hear, till feel:
I must be round with him, now he comes from hunting.
Fie, fie, fie, fie!

Enter CAPHIS [*and the* Servants *of*] ISIDORE *and* VARRO.

Caph. Good even, Varro: what,
You come for money?
Var. Serv. Is 't not your business too?
Caph. It is: and yours too, Isidore?
Isid. Serv. It is so.
Caph. Would we were all discharg'd!
Var. Serv. I fear it.
Caph. Here comes the lord.

Enter TIMON *and his train* [*with* ALCIBIADES].

Tim. So soon as dinner 's done, we'll forth again,
My Alcibiades. With me? what is your will?
Caph. My lord, here is a note of certain dues.
Tim. Dues! Whence are you?
Caph. Of Athens here, my lord.
Tim. Go to my steward.
Caph. Please it your lordship, he hath put me off
To the succession of new days this month:
My master is awak'd by great occasion
To call upon his own, and humbly prays you
That with your other noble parts you'll suit
In giving him his right.
Tim. Mine honest friend,
I prithee, but repair to me next morning.
Caph. Nay, good my lord,—
Tim. Contain thyself, good friend.
Var. Serv. One Varro's servant, my good lord,—
Isid. Serv. From Isidore;
He humbly prays your speedy payment.
Caph. If you did know, my lord, my master's wants—
Var. Serv. 'Twas due on forfeiture, my lord, six weeks
And past.
Isid. Serv. Your steward puts me off, my lord;
And I am sent expressly to your lordship.
Tim. Give me breath.
I do beseech you, good my lords, keep on;
I'll wait upon you instantly.
[*Exeunt Alcibiades and Lords.*]
[*To Flav.*] Come hither: pray you,
How goes the world, that I am thus encount'red
With clamorous demands of date-broke bonds,
And the detention of long-since-due debts,
Against my honour?
Flav. Please you, gentlemen,
The time is unagreeable to this business:
Your importunacy cease till after dinner,
That I may make his lordship understand
Wherefore you are not paid.
Tim. Do so, my friends. See them well entertain'd.
[*Exit.*]

described." As Farmer pointed out, sternness was characteristic of a porter; Mason added, further, that *one* does not refer to *porter* but means "a person." 13. **sound,** so F; i.e., by sounding find it to be safe; Globe, following Johnson: *found.* 16. **be not ceas'd,** do not allow yourself to be silenced. 20. **uses,** needs. 22. **fracted,** broken; i.e., failure to meet payments on notes due; cf. II, ii, 38, *date-broke bonds.* 27. **immediate,** immediately. 30. **When . . . wing,** when everything is in the hands of its rightful possessor. 31. **gull,** quibble on the meanings "unfledged bird" and "dupe." 35. **in compt,** in reckoning; Theobald's addition to text.

SCENE II. 2. **know how,** set his mind to knowing how. 6. **Was . . . kind,** to be so unwise in order to be so kind. 12. **discharg'd,** paid. **fear it,** am apprehensive about our being paid. 20. **this month,** for a month; i.e., he has put me off from one day to another all month. 23. **with . . . parts,** in conformity to your otherwise noble nature.

Flav. Pray, draw near. *Exit.*

Enter APEMANTUS *and* Fool.

Caph. Stay, stay, here comes the fool with Apemantus: let 's ha' some sport with 'em.

Var. Serv. Hang him, he'll abuse us.

Isid. Serv. A plague upon him, dog!

Var. Serv. How dost, fool?

Apem. Dost dialogue with thy shadow?

Var. Serv. I speak not to thee.

Apem. No, 'tis to thyself. [*To the Fool*] Come away.

Isid. Serv. There 's the fool hangs on your back already.

Apem. No, thou stand'st single, th' art not on him
yet.

Caph. Where 's the fool now?

Apem. He last asked the question. Poor rogues, and usurers' men! bawds between gold and want!

All Serv. What are we, Apemantus?

Apem. Asses.

All Serv. Why?

Apem. That you ask me what you are, and do not know yourselves. Speak to 'em, fool.

Fool. How do you, gentlemen?

All Serv. Gramercies, good fool: how does your mistress?

Fool. She 's e'en setting on water to scald such chickens as you are. Would we could see you at Corinth!

Apem. Good! gramercy.

Enter Page.

Fool. Look you, here comes my mistress' page.

Page. [*To the Fool*] Why, how now, captain! what do you in this wise company? How dost thou, Apemantus?

Apem. Would I had a rod in my mouth, that I might answer thee profitably.

Page. Prithee, Apemantus, read me the superscription of these letters: I know not which is which.

Apem. Canst not read?

Page. No.

Apem. There will little learning die then, that day thou art hanged. This is to Lord Timon; this to Alcibiades. Go; thou wast born a bastard, and thou 't die a bawd.

Page. Thou wast whelped a dog, and thou shalt famish a dog's death. Answer not: I am gone. *Exit.*

Apem. E'en so thou outrunnest grace. Fool, I will go with you to Lord Timon's.

Fool. Will you leave me there?

Apem. If Timon stay at home. You three serve three usurers?

All Serv. Ay; would they served us!

Apem. So would I,—as good a trick as ever hangman served thief.

Fool. Are you three usurers' men?

All Serv. Ay, fool.

Fool. I think no usurer but has a fool to his servant: my mistress is one, and I am her fool. When men come to borrow of your masters, they approach sadly, and go away merry; but they enter my mistress' house merrily, and go away sadly: the reason of this?

Var. Serv. I could render one.

Apem. Do it then, that we may account thee a whoremaster and a knave; which notwithstanding, thou shalt be no less esteemed.

Var. Serv. What is a whoremaster, fool?

Fool. A fool in good clothes, and something like thee. 'Tis a spirit: sometime 't appears like a lord; sometime like a lawyer; sometime like a philosopher, with two stones moe than 's artificial one: he is very often like a knight; and, generally, in all shapes that man goes up and down in from fourscore to thirteen, this spirit walks in.

Var. Serv. Thou art not altogether a fool.

Fool. Nor thou altogether a wise man: as much foolery as I have, so much wit thou lackest.

Apem. That answer might have become Apemantus.

All Serv. Aside, aside; here comes Lord Timon.

Enter TIMON *and Steward* [FLAVIUS].

Apem. Come with me, fool, come.

Fool. I do not always follow lover, elder brother and woman; sometime the philosopher.

[*Exeunt Apemantus and Fool.*]

Flav. Pray you, walk near: I'll speak with you
anon. *Exeunt* [*Servants*].

Tim. You make me marvel: wherefore ere this time
Had you not fully laid my state before me,
That I might so have rated my expense,
As I had leave of means?

Flav. You would not hear me,
At many leisures I propos'd.

Tim. Go to:
Perchance some single vantages you took,
When my indisposition put you back;
And that unaptness made your minister,
Thus to excuse yourself.

Flav. O my good lord,
At many times I brought in my accounts,
Laid them before you; you would throw them off,
And say, you found them in mine honesty.
When, for some trifling present, you have bid me
Return so much, I have shook my head and wept;
Yea, 'gainst th' authority of manners, pray'd you
To hold your hand more close: I did endure
Not seldom, nor no slight checks, when I have
Prompted you in the ebb of your estate
And your great flow of debts. My lov'd lord,
†Though you hear now, too late—yet now 's a time—
The greatest of your having lacks a half
To pay your present debts.

Tim. Let all my land be sold.

Flav. 'Tis all engag'd, some forfeited and gone;
And what remains will hardly stop the mouth
Of present dues: the future comes apace:
What shall defend the interim? and at length
How goes our reck'ning?

Tim. To Lacedæmon did my land extend.

Flav. O my good lord, the world is but a word:

69. **Gramercies,** many thanks. 71. **She 's . . . scald,** allusion to the sweating-tub treatment for venereal disease. 73. **Corinth,** house of ill fame. 79. **rod,** stick (to use for a beating). 93. **outrunnest grace,** run away from profitable teaching. 94. **to Lord Timon's.** The error which some commentators assume to be here is more likely to be in their assumption that the scene is laid at Timon's house; since F supplies no scene indications, the action could as well be assumed to take place in a court or street before Timon's house. 115. **a spirit,** i.e., one that can assume various shapes (Deighton). 117. **artificial one,** i.e., philosopher's stone. (The "two stones" are testicles.) 135. **rated,** regulated. 136. **As . . . means,** as my means permitted. 138. **single vantages,** occasional opportunities. 152. **yet now 's a time,** i.e., late as it is, it is necessary that you be made acquainted with it (Ritson). 155. **engag'd,** i.e., mortgaged. 158. **at length,** at the last; i.e., what will happen at the final reckoning. 167. **offices,** parts of the house-buildings devoted to purely household matters, especially the kitchen

Were it all yours to give it in a breath,
How quickly were it gone!
Tim. You tell me true.
Flav. If you suspect my husbandry or falsehood,
Call me before th' exactest auditors
And set me on the proof. So the gods bless me,
When all our offices have been oppress'd
With riotous feeders, when our vaults have wept
With drunken spilth of wine, when every room
Hath blaz'd with lights and bray'd with minstrelsy,
I have retir'd me to a wasteful cock,
And set mine eyes at flow.
Tim. Prithee, no more.
Flav. Heavens, have I said, the bounty of this lord!
How many prodigal bits have slaves and peasants
This night englutted! Who is not Timon's?
What heart, head, sword, force, means, but is Lord Timon's?
Great Timon, noble, worthy, royal Timon!
Ah, when the means are gone that buy this praise,
The breath is gone whereof this praise is made:
Feast-won, fast-lost; one cloud of winter show'rs,
These flies are couch'd.
Tim. Come, sermon me no further:
No villanous bounty yet hath pass'd my heart;
Unwisely, not ignobly, have I given.
Why dost thou weep? Canst thou the conscience lack,
To think I shall lack friends? Secure thy heart;
If I would broach the vessels of my love,
And try the argument of hearts by borrowing,
Men and men's fortunes could I frankly use
As I can bid thee speak.
Flav. Assurance bless your thoughts!
Tim. And, in some sort, these wants of mine are crown'd,
That I account them blessings; for by these
Shall I try friends: you shall perceive how you
Mistake my fortunes; I am wealthy in my friends.
Within there! Flaminius! Servilius!

Enter three servants [FLAMINIUS, SERVILIUS, *and another*].

Servants. My lord? my lord?

Tim. I will dispatch you severally; you to Lord Lucius; to Lord Lucullus you: I hunted with his honour to-day: you, to Sempronius: commend me to their loves, and, I am proud, say, that my occasions have found time to use 'em toward a supply of money: let the request be fifty talents.

Flam. As you have said, my lord.
Flav. [*Aside*] Lord Lucius and Lucullus? hum!
Tim. Go you, sir, to the senators—
Of whom, even to the state's best health, I have
Deserv'd this hearing—bid 'em send o' th' instant
A thousand talents to me.
Flav. I have been bold—
For that I knew it the most general way—
To them to use your signet and your name;
But they do shake their heads, and I am here
No richer in return.
Tim. Is 't true? can 't be?
Flav. They answer, in a joint and corporate voice,
That now they are at fall, want treasure, cannot
Do what they would; are sorry—you are honourable,—
But yet they could have wish'd—they know not—
Something hath been amiss—a noble nature
May catch a wrench—would all were well—'tis pity;—
And so, intending other serious matters,
After distasteful looks and these hard fractions,
With certain half-caps and cold-moving nods
They froze me into silence.
Tim. You gods, reward them!
Prithee, man, look cheerly. These old fellows
Have their ingratitude in them hereditary:
Their blood is cak'd, 'tis cold, it seldom flows;
'Tis lack of kindly warmth they are not kind;
And nature, as it grows again toward earth,
Is fashion'd for the journey, dull and heavy.
[*To a Serv.*] Go to Ventidius. [*To Flav.*] Prithee, be not sad,
Thou art true and honest; ingeniously I speak,
No blame belongs to thee. [*To Ser.*] Ventidius lately
Buried his father; by whose death he 's stepp'd
Into a great estate: when he was poor,
Imprison'd and in scarcity of friends,
I clear'd him with five talents: greet him from me;
Bid him suppose some good necessity
Touches his friend, which craves to be remember'd
With those five talents [*Exit Ser.*]. [*To Flav.*] That had, give 't these fellows
To whom 'tis instant due. Nev'r speak, or think,
That Timon's fortunes 'mong his friends can sink.
Flav. I would I could not think it: that thought is bounty's foe;
Being free itself, it thinks all others so. *Exeunt.*

[ACT III.

SCENE I. *A room in Lucullus' house.*]

FLAMINIUS *waiting to speak with a* Lord, [LUCULLUS,] *from his Master; enters a* Servant *to him.*

Serv. I have told my lord of you; he is coming down to you.

Flam. I thank you, sir.

Enter LUCULLUS.

Serv. Here 's my lord.

Lucul. [*Aside*] One of Lord Timon's men? a gift, I warrant. Why, this hits right; I dreamt of a silver basin and ewer to-night. Flaminius, honest Flaminius; you are very respectively welcome, sir. Fill me some wine. [*Exit Servant.*] And how does that honourable, complete, free-hearted gentleman of Athens, thy very bountiful good lord and master?

Flam. His health is well, sir.

Lucul. I am right glad that his health is well, sir: and what hast thou there under thy cloak, pretty Flaminius?

(Onions). 169. **spilth,** spilling. 170. **bray'd with minstrelsy,** echoed with the raucous noise of paid entertainers. 171. **retir'd me to,** turned myself into. **cock,** faucet. 175-177. **Who is not Timon's,** etc. Flavius is scornfully recalling the empty pledges of loyalty that he has overheard during these extravagant feasts. 181. **couch'd,** lying concealed. 191. **That,** so that. 196. **severally,** on different errands. 206. **state's best health,** i.e., for my services in behalf of the state's welfare; cf. IV, iii, 93-95, where Alcibiades refers to Timon's sword and fortune offered in the defense of Athens. 210. **To . . . name,** i.e., Timon's friends have drawn on his fortune to pay their debts. 213. **joint . . . voice,** in unanimous agreement. 220. **fractions,** broken sentences. 230. **ingeniously,** frankly. 238. **That had,** when you have that. 241. **that thought,** i.e., the thought that his fortunes cannot sink when he has friends to sustain them.

ACT III. SCENE I. 7. **respectively,** with due respect.

Flam. 'Faith, nothing but an empty box, sir; which, in my lord's behalf, I come to entreat your honour to supply; who, having great and instant occasion to use fifty talents, hath sent to your lordship to furnish him, nothing doubting your present assistance therein.

Lucul. La, la, la la! 'nothing doubting,' says he? Alas, good lord! a noble gentleman 'tis, if he would not keep so good a house. Many a time and often I ha' dined with him, and told him on 't, and come again to supper to him, of purpose to have him spend less, and yet he would embrace no counsel, take no warning by my coming. Every man has his fault, and honesty is his: I ha' told him on 't, but I could ne'er get him from 't.

Enter Servant, *with wine.*

Serv. Please your lordship, here is the wine.

Lucul. Flaminius, I have noted thee always wise. Here 's to thee.

Flam. Your lordship speaks your pleasure.

Lucul. I have observed thee always for a towardly prompt spirit—give thee thy due—and one that knows what belongs to reason; and canst use the time well, if the time use thee well: good parts in thee. [*To Serv.*] Get you gone, sirrah [*Exit Serv.*]. Draw nearer, honest Flaminius. Thy lord 's a bountiful gentleman: but thou art wise; and thou knowest well enough, although thou comest to me, that this is no time to lend money, especially upon bare friendship, without security. Here 's three solidares for thee: good boy, wink at me, and say thou sawest me not. Fare thee well.

Flam. Is 't possible the world should so much differ,
And we alive that liv'd? Fly, damned baseness,
To him that worships thee! [*Throwing the money back.*]

Lucul. Ha! now I see thou art a fool, and fit for thy master. *Exit Lucullus.*

Flam. May these add to the number that may scald thee!
Let molten coin be thy damnation,
Thou disease of a friend, and not himself!
Has friendship such a faint and milky heart,
It turns in less than two nights? O you gods,
I feel my master's passion! this slave,
Unto his honour, has my lord's meat in him:
Why should it thrive and turn to nutriment,
When he is turn'd to poison?
O, may diseases only work upon 't!
And, when he 's sick to death, let not that part of nature
Which my lord paid for, be of any power
To expel sickness, but prolong his hour! *Exit.*

[SCENE II. *A public place.*]

Enter LUCIUS, *with three* Strangers.

Luc. Who, the Lord Timon? he is my very good friend, and an honourable gentleman.

First Stran. We know him for no less, though we are but strangers to him. But I can tell you one thing, my lord, and which I hear from common rumours: now Lord Timon's happy hours are done and past, and his estate shrinks from him.

Luc. Fie, no, do not believe it; he cannot want for money.

Sec. Stran. But believe you this, my lord, that, not long ago, one of his men was with the Lord Lucullus to borrow so many talents, nay, urged extremely for 't and showed what necessity belonged to 't, and yet was denied.

Luc. How!

Sec. Stran. I tell you, denied, my lord.

Luc. What a strange case was that! now, before the gods, I am ashamed on 't. Denied that honourable man! there was very little honour showed in 't. For my own part, I must needs confess, I have received some small kindnesses from him, as money, plate, jewels and such-like trifles, nothing comparing to his; yet, had he mistook him and sent to me, I should ne'er have denied his occasion so many talents.

Enter SERVILIUS.

Ser. See, by good hap, yonder 's my lord; I have sweat to see his honour. My honoured lord,— [*To Lucius.*]

Luc. Servilius! you are kindly met, sir. Fare thee well: commend me to thy honourable virtuous lord, my very exquisite friend.

Ser. May it please your honour, my lord hath sent—

Luc. Ha! what has he sent? I am so much endeared to that lord; he 's ever sending: how shall I thank him, thinkest thou? And what has he sent now?

Ser. Has only sent his present occasion now, my lord; requesting your lordship to supply his instant use with so many talents.

Luc. I know his lordship is but merry with me;
†He cannot want fifty five hundred talents.

Ser. But in the mean time he wants less, my lord.
If his occasion were not virtuous,
I should not urge it half so faithfully.

Luc. Dost thou speak seriously, Servilius?

Ser. Upon my soul, 'tis true, sir.

Luc. What a wicked beast was I to disfurnish myself against such a good time, when I might ha' shown myself honourable! how unluckily it happened, that I should purchase the day before for a little part, and undo a great deal of honour! Servilius, now, before the gods, I am not able to do,—the more beast, I say:—I was sending to use Lord Timon myself, these gentlemen can witness; but I would not, for the wealth of Athens, I had done 't now. Commend me bountifully to his good lordship; and I hope his honour will conceive the fairest of me, because I have no power to be kind: and tell him this from me, I

24. **keep . . . house,** be so lavish in his housekeeping. 26-27. **of purpose . . . him,** purposely to urge him. 29. **honesty,** liberality. 35. **Your lordship . . . pleasure,** a complimentary reply: it pleases your lordship to say so. 37. **towardly prompt,** quick to meet another's thoughts (Deighton). 46. **solidares,** small coins. 54-55. **May . . . damnation.** Stories appear to be common of avaricious men punished with tortures by means of molten metal. Steevens cites three: Mithridates' treatment of M. Aquilius; Lazarus' description in the *Kalender of Shepherdes* (see Oskar Sommer's reprint of the Paris edition, 1503, e_4, verso) of covetous men in hell being thrown into kettles of boiling lead and oil; and a black-letter ballad entitled *The Dead Man's Song.* Mason cites the story of Crassus and the Parthians, who are said to have poured molten gold down his throat. 58. **turns,** sours, with quibble on the idea of "turn" as in turncoat. 59. **feel . . . passion,** feel the anger which my master is going to feel.

SCENE II. 25. **mistook,** i.e., mistakenly sent to me, who owe him less. 28. **I have sweat,** i.e., I have been hurrying. 36. **endeared,** bound by obligation. 43. **He cannot . . . talents,** probably an indication of Shakespeare's uncertainty over the value of this currency. 45. **were not virtuous,** were due to a fault instead of a virtue, i.e., generosity. 52-53. **purchase . . . part,** several attempts at emendation: Theobald read *dirt* for *part*, Johnson, *park;* Jackson transposes the *and* count it one of my greatest afflictions, say, that I cannot pleasure such an honourable gentleman. Good Servilius, will you befriend me so far, as to use mine own words to him?

Ser. Yes, sir, I shall.

Luc. I'll look you out a good turn, Servilius.

Exit Servilius.

True, as you said, Timon is shrunk indeed;
And he that 's once denied will hardly speed. *Exit.*

First Stran. Do you observe this, Hostilius?

Sec. Stran. Ay, too well.

First Stran. Why, this is the world's soul; and just of the same piece
Is every flatterer's spirit. Who can call him
His friend that dips in the same dish? for, in
My knowing, Timon has been this lord's father,
And kept his credit with his purse,
Supported his estate; nay, Timon's money
Has paid his men their wages: he ne'er drinks,
But Timon's silver treads upon his lip;
And yet—O, see the monstrousness of man
When he looks out in an ungrateful shape!—
He does deny him, in respect of his,
What charitable men afford to beggars.

Third Stran. Religion groans at it.

First Stran. For mine own part,
I never tasted Timon in my life,
Nor came any of his bounties over me,
To mark me for his friend; yet, I protest,
For his right noble mind, illustrious virtue
And honourable carriage,
Had his necessity made use of me,
I would have put my wealth into donation,
And the best half should have return'd to him,
So much I love his heart: but, I perceive,
Men must learn now with pity to dispense;
For policy sits above conscience. *Exeunt.*

[SCENE III. *A room in Sempronius' house.*]

Enter a third Servant [*of Timon's*] *with* SEMPRONIUS, *another of Timon's Friends.*

Sem. Must he needs trouble me in 't,—hum! —'bove all others?
He might have tried Lord Lucius or Lucullus;
And now Ventidius is wealthy too,
Whom he redeem'd from prison: all these
Owe their estates unto him.

Serv. My lord,
They have all been touch'd and found base metal, for
They have all denied him.

Sem. How! have they denied him?
Has Ventidius and Lucullus denied him?
And does he send to me? Three? hum!
It shows but little love or judgement in him:
Must I be his last refuge? His friends, like physicians,
†Thrive, give him over: must I take th' cure upon me?
Has much disgrac'd me in 't; I 'm angry at him,
That might have known my place: I see no sense for 't,
But his occasions might have woo'd me first;
For, in my conscience, I was the first man
That e'er received gift from him:
And does he think so backwardly of me now,
That I'll requite it last? No:
So it may prove an argument of laughter
To th' rest, and 'mongst lords I be thought a fool.
I 'ld rather than the worth of thrice the sum,
Had sent to me first, but for my mind's sake;
I'd such a courage to do him good. But now return,
And with their faint reply this answer join;
Who bates mine honour shall not know my coin. *Exit.*

Serv. Excellent! Your lordship 's a goodly villain. The devil knew not what he did when he made man politic; he crossed himself by 't: and I cannot think but, in the end, the villanies of man will set him clear. How fairly this lord strives to appear foul! takes virtuous copies to be wicked, like those that under hot ardent zeal would set whole realms on fire:
Of such a nature is his politic love.
This was my lord's best hope; now all are fled,
Save only the gods: now his friends are dead,
Doors, that were ne'er acquainted with their wards
Many a bounteous year, must be employ'd
Now to guard sure their master.
And this is all a liberal course allows;
Who cannot keep his wealth must keep his house. *Exit.*

[SCENE IV. *The same. A hall in Timon's house.*]

Enter [*two of*] *Varro's* Men, *meeting* [*Lucius'* Servant *and*] *others, all* [*being servants of*] *Timon's creditors, to wait for his coming out. Then enter* TITUS *and* HORTENSIUS.

First Var. Serv. Well met; good morrow, Titus and Hortensius.

Tit. The like to you, kind Varro.

Hor. Lucius!
What, do we meet together?

Luc. Serv. Ay, and I think
One business does command us all; for mine
Is money.

Tit. So is theirs and ours.

Enter PHILOTUS.

Luc. Serv. And Sir Philotus too!

Phi. Good day at once.

Luc. Serv. Welcome, good brother.
What do you think the hour?

Phi. Labouring for nine.

Luc. Serv. So much?

Phi. Is not my lord seen yet?

Luc. Serv. Not yet.

Phi. I wonder on 't; he was wont to shine at seven.

Luc. Serv. Ay, but the days are wax'd shorter with him:

---

following this phrase to read *and for a little part;* Onions (citing *NED*) defines *purchase* as "exert oneself," which removes all difficulties. 63. **pleasure,** gratify. 71. **soul,** real essence, vital principle. 81-82. **He . . . beggars.** Considering his possessions, he (Lucius) denies Timon the mere pittance that a charitable man would give a beggar. 90. **put . . . donation,** treated all my wealth as a gift.

SCENE III. 6. **touch'd,** metaphor derived from testing metals with a touchstone to see if they are gold. 12. **Thrive, give,** many emendations: Pope: *Three give;* Theobald: *Thriv'd, give;* Hanmer: *Tried give;* Johnson: *Thrice give;* Mitford: *Have given;* Deighton explains the difficulty as an ellipsis: physicians (who) thrive, give. 23. **Had,** i.e., he had. **my mind's sake,** for the sake of my own satisfaction. 24. **courage,** desire. 26. **Who bates,** whoever abates. 29. **crossed,** foiled (by making man his rival in treachery). 31. **fairly,** completely, plausibly; probably a quibble on these two meanings plus the antithesis to *foul.* 32. **copies,** patterns, examples. 38. **wards,** bolts; i.e., were never locked. 42. **keep his house,** stay indoors; with quibble.

SCENE IV. 10. **to shine at seven.** This metaphor of the sun, continued in the next speech, ironically echoes Timon's figure earlier (I, ii, 150).

You must consider that a prodigal course
Is like the sun's; but not, like his, recoverable.
I fear 'tis deepest winter in Lord Timon's purse;
That is, one may reach deep enough, and yet
Find little.

Phi. I am of your fear for that.

Tit. I'll show you how t' observe a strange event.
Your lord sends now for money.

Hor. Most true, he does.

Tit. And he wears jewels now of Timon's gift,
For which I wait for money.

Hor. It is against my heart.

Luc. Serv. Mark, how strange it shows,
Timon in this should pay more than he owes:
And e'en as if your lord should wear rich jewels,
And send for money for 'em.

Hor. I'm weary of this charge, the gods can witness:
I know my lord hath spent of Timon's wealth,
And now ingratitude makes it worse than stealth.

First Var. Serv. Yes, mine 's three thousand crowns: what 's yours?

Luc. Serv. Five thousand mine.

First Var. Serv. 'Tis much deep: and it should seem by th' sum,
Your master's confidence was above mine;
Else, surely, his had equall'd.

Enter FLAMINIUS.

Tit. One of Lord Timon's men.

Luc. Serv. Flaminius! Sir, a word: pray, is my lord ready to come forth?

Flam. No, indeed, he is not.

Tit. We attend his lordship; pray, signify so much.

Flam. I need not tell him that; he knows you are too diligent. [*Exit.*]

Enter Steward [FLAVIUS] *in a cloak, muffled.*

Luc. Serv. Ha! is not that his steward muffled so?
He goes away in a cloud: call him, call him.

Tit. Do you hear, sir?

Sec. Var. Serv. By your leave, sir,—

Flav. What do ye ask of me, my friend?

Tit. We wait for certain money here, sir.

Flav. Ay,
If money were as certain as your waiting,
'Twere sure enough.
Why then preferr'd you not your sums and bills,
When your false masters eat of my lord's meat?
Then they could smile and fawn upon his debts
And take down th' int'rest into their glutt'nous maws.
You do yourselves but wrong to stir me up;
Let me pass quietly:
Believe 't, my lord and I have made an end;
I have no more to reckon, he to spend.

Luc. Serv. Ay, but this answer will not serve.

Flav. If 'twill not serve, 'tis not so base as you;
For you serve knaves. [*Exit.*]

First Var. Serv. How! what does his cashiered worship mutter?

Sec. Var. Serv. No matter what; he 's poor, and that 's revenge enough. Who can speak broader than he that has no house to put his head in? such may rail against great buildings.

Enter SERVILIUS.

Tit. O, here 's Servilius; now we shall know some answer.

Ser. If I might beseech you, gentlemen, to repair some other hour, I should derive much from 't; for, take 't of my soul, my lord leans wondrously to discontent: his comfortable temper has forsook him; he 's much out of health, and keeps his chamber.

Luc. Serv. Many do keep their chambers are not sick:
And, if it be so far beyond his health,
Methinks he should the sooner pay his debts,
And make a clear way to the gods.

Ser. Good gods!

Tit. We cannot take this for answer, sir.

Flam. (*Within*) Servilius, help! My lord! my lord!

Enter TIMON, *in a rage.*

Tim. What, are my doors oppos'd against my passage?
Have I been ever free, and must my house
Be my retentive enemy, my gaol?
The place which I have feasted, does it now,
Like all mankind, show me an iron heart?

Luc. Serv. Put in now, Titus.

Tit. My lord, here is my bill.

Luc. Serv. Here 's mine.

Hor. And mine, my lord.

Both Var. Serv. And ours, my lord.

Phi. All our bills.

Tim. Knock me down with 'em: cleave me to the girdle.

Luc. Serv. Alas, my lord,—

Tim. Cut my heart in sums.

Tit. Mine, fifty talents.

Tim. Tell out my blood.

Luc. Serv. Five thousand crowns, my lord.

Tim. Five thousand drops pays that. What yours?—and yours?

First Var. Serv. My lord,—

Sec. Var. Serv. My lord,—

Tim. Tear me, take me, and the gods fall upon you! *Exit Timon.*

Hor. 'Faith, I perceive our masters may throw their caps at their money: these debts may well be called desperate ones, for a madman owes 'em. *Exeunt.*

Enter TIMON [*and* FLAVIUS].

Tim. They have e'en put my breath from me, the slaves.
Creditors? devils!

Flav. My dear lord,—

Tim. What if it should be so?

Flav. My lord,—

Tim. I'll have it so. My steward!

Flav. Here, my lord.

Tim. So fitly? Go, bid all my friends again,
Lucius, Lucullus, and Sempronius:
All:
I'll once more feast the rascals.

21. **against my heart,** contrary to my feelings. 27. **stealth,** theft. 42. **in a cloud,** quibble on the meanings "muffled" and "in a surly humor." 64. **broader,** quibble on "more freely" and "more in the open." 69. **repair,** return. 71. **comfortable,** cheerful. 77. **make . . . gods,** i.e., pay all his debts before he dies. 83. **place . . . feasted,** Timon's misanthropy extends to the personification of his own house, where he has been so lavish. 91. **Knock, cleave.** Timon plays on *bills* as weapons.

SCENE V. 5. **compassion to the senate,** i.e., may the senate have compassion. 12. **stepp'd into the law,** incurred the penalties of the law. 14. **setting . . . aside,** not considering his ill-fated action. 17. **buys out,**

Flav. O my lord,
You only speak from your distracted soul;
There 's not so much left, to furnish out
A moderate table.
Tim. Be it not in thy care; go,
I charge thee, invite them all: let in the tide
Of knaves once more; my cook and I'll provide.
Exeunt.

[SCENE V. *The same. The senate-house.*]

Enter three Senators *at one door*, ALCIBIADES *meeting them, with* Attendants.

First Sen. My lord, you have my voice to 't; the fault 's
Bloody; 'tis necessary he should die:
Nothing emboldens sin so much as mercy.
Sec. Sen. Most true; the law shall bruise him.
Alcib. Honour, health, and compassion to the senate!
First Sen. Now, captain?
Alcib. I am an humble suitor to your virtues;
For pity is the virtue of the law,
And none but tyrants use it cruelly.
It pleases time and fortune to lie heavy
Upon a friend of mine, who, in hot blood,
Hath stepp'd into the law, which is past depth
To those that, without heed, do plunge into 't.
He is a man, setting his fate aside,
Of comely virtues:
Nor did he soil the fact with cowardice—
An honour in him which buys out his fault—
But with a noble fury and fair spirit,
Seeing his reputation touch'd to death,
He did oppose his foe:
And with such sober and unnoted passion
He did behave his anger, ere 'twas spent,
As if he had but prov'd an argument.
First Sen. You undergo too strict a paradox,
Striving to make an ugly deed look fair:
Your words have took such pains as if they labour'd
To bring manslaughter into form and set quarrelling
Upon the head of valour; which indeed
Is valour misbegot and came into the world
When sects and factions were newly born:
He 's truly valiant that can wisely suffer
The worst that man can breathe, and make his wrongs
His outsides, to wear them like his raiment, carelessly,
And ne'er prefer his injuries to his heart,
To bring it into danger.
If wrongs be evils and enforce us kill,
What folly 'tis to hazard life for ill!
Alcib. My lord,—
First Sen. You cannot make gross sins look clear:
To revenge is no valour, but to bear.
Alcib. My lords, then, under favour, pardon me,
If I speak like a captain.
Why do fond men expose themselves to battle,
And not endure all threats? sleep upon 't,
And let the foes quietly cut their throats,
Without repugnancy? If there be
Such valour in the bearing, what make we
Abroad? why then, women are more valiant
That stay at home, if bearing carry it,
And the ass more captain than the lion, the felon
Loaden with irons wiser than the judge,
If wisdom be in suffering. O my lords,
As you are great, be pitifully good:
Who cannot condemn rashness in cold blood?
To kill, I grant, is sin's extremest gust;
But, in defence, by mercy, 'tis most just.
To be in anger is impiety;
But who is man that is not angry?
Weigh but the crime with this.
Sec. Sen. You breathe in vain.
Alcib. In vain! his service done
At Lacedæmon and Byzantium
Were a sufficient briber for his life.
First Sen. What 's that?
Alcib. I say, my lords, h' as done fair service,
And slain in fight many of your enemies:
How full of valour did he bear himself
In the last conflict, and made plenteous wounds!
Sec. Sen. He has made too much plenty with 'em;
He 's a sworn rioter: he has a sin that often
Drowns him, and takes his valour prisoner:
If there were no foes, that were enough
To overcome him: in that beastly fury
He has been known to commit outrages,
And cherish factions: 'tis inferr'd to us,
His days are foul and his drink dangerous.
First Sen. He dies.
Alcib. Hard fate! he might have died in war.
My lords, if not for any parts in him—
Though his right arm might purchase his own time
And be in debt to none—yet, more to move you,
Take my deserts to his, and join 'em both:
And, for I know your reverend ages love
Security, I'll pawn my victories, all
My honours to you, upon his good returns.
If by this crime he owes the law his life,
Why, let the war receive 't in valiant gore;
For law is strict, and war is nothing more.
First Sen. We are for law: he dies; urge it no more,
On height of our displeasure: friend or brother,
He forfeits his own blood that spills another.
Alcib. Must it be so? it must not be. My lords,
I do beseech you, know me.
Sec. Sen. How!
Alcib. Call me to your remembrances.
Third Sen. What!
Alcib. I cannot think but your age has forgot me;
It could not else be, I should prove so base,
To sue, and be denied such common grace:
My wounds ache at you.
First Sen. Do you dare our anger?
'Tis in few words, but spacious in effect;
We banish thee for ever.
Alcib. Banish me!

redeems. 22. **behave,** control. 24. **undergo,** take upon yourself to demonstrate. 27. **bring . . . form,** make murder appear orderly, or according to form. 34. **prefer,** advance; metaphor from the practice of recommending someone for honor or advancement. 45. **repugnancy,** resistance. 54. **sin's extremest gust,** the relish of extremest sin; Malone defined *gust* as outburst. 55. **by mercy,** by a merciful interpretation of law (Malone). 61. **briber,** pleader. 77. **Though . . . time,** his ability in war should purchase his freedom, i.e., let him die a natural death. 97. **spacious in effect,** of great import, with quibble on the limitless world to which Alcibiades is banished.

Banish your dotage; banish usury,
That makes the senate ugly.

First Sen. If, after two days' shine, Athens contain thee,
Attend our weightier judgement. And, not to swell our spirit,
He shall be executed presently. *Exeunt [Senators].*

Alcib. Now the gods keep you old enough; that you may live
Only in bone, that none may look on you!
I 'm worse than mad: I have kept back their foes,
While they have told their money and let out
Their coin upon large interest, I myself
Rich only in large hurts. All those for this?
Is this the balsam that the usuring senate
Pours into captains' wounds? Banishment!
It comes not ill; I hate not to be banish'd;
It is a cause worthy my spleen and fury,
That I may strike at Athens. I'll cheer up
My discontented troops, and lay for hearts.
'Tis honour with most lands to be at odds:
Soldiers should brook as little wrongs as gods. *Exit.*

[SCENE VI. *The same. A banqueting-room in Timon's house.*]

[*Music. Tables set out:* Servants *attending.*] *Enter divers* Friends [*of* TIMON] *at several doors.*

First Lord. The good time of day to you, sir.

Sec. Lord. I also wish it to you. I think this honourable lord did but try us this other day.

First Lord. Upon that were my thoughts tiring, when we encountered: I hope it is not so low with him as he made it seem in the trial of his several friends.

Sec. Lord. It should not be, by the persuasion of his new feasting.

First Lord. I should think so: he hath sent me an earnest inviting, which many my near occasions did urge me to put off; but he hath conjured me beyond them, and I must needs appear.

Sec. Lord. In like manner was I in debt to my importunate business, but he would not hear my excuse. I am sorry, when he sent to borrow of me, that my provision was out.

First Lord. I am sick of that grief too, as I understand how all things go.

Sec. Lord. Every man here 's so. What would he have borrowed of you?

First Lord. A thousand pieces.

Sec. Lord. A thousand pieces!

First Lord. What of you?

Sec. Lord. He sent to me, sir,—Here he comes.

Enter TIMON *and* Attendants.

Tim. With all my heart, gentlemen both; and how fare you?

First Lord. Ever at the best, hearing well of your lordship.

Sec. Lord. The swallow follows not summer more willing than we your lordship.

Tim. [*Aside*] Nor more willingly leaves winter; such summer-birds are men.—Gentlemen, our dinner will not recompense this long stay: feast your ears with the music awhile, if they will fare so harshly o' the trumpet's sound; we shall to 't presently.

First Lord. I hope it remains not unkindly with your lordship that I returned you an empty messenger.

Tim. O, sir, let it not trouble you.

Sec. Lord. My noble lord,—

Tim. Ah, my good friend, what cheer?

Sec. Lord. My most honourable lord, I am e'en sick of shame, that, when your lordship this other day sent to me, I was so unfortunate a beggar.

Tim. Think not on 't, sir.

Sec. Lord. If you had sent but two hours before,—

Tim. Let it not cumber your better remembrance. (*The banquet brought in.*) Come, bring in all together.

Sec. Lord. All covered dishes!

First Lord. Royal cheer, I warrant you.

Third Lord. Doubt not that, if money and the season can yield it.

First Lord. How do you? What 's the news?

Third Lord. Alcibiades is banished: hear you of it?

First and Sec. Lord. Alcibiades banished!

Third Lord. 'Tis so, be sure of it.

First Lord. How! how!

Sec. Lord. I pray you, upon what?

Tim. My worthy friends, will you draw near?

Third Lord. I'll tell you more anon. Here 's a noble feast toward.

Sec. Lord. This is the old man still.

Third Lord. Will 't hold? will 't hold?

Sec. Lord. It does: but time will—and so—

Third Lord. I do conceive.

Tim. Each man to his stool, with that spur as he would to the lip of his mistress: your diet shall be in all places alike. Make not a city feast of it, to let the meat cool ere we can agree upon the first place: sit, sit. The gods require our thanks.

You great benefactors, sprinkle our society with thankfulness. For your own gifts, make yourselves praised: but reserve still to give, lest your deities be despised. Lend to each man enough, that one need not lend to another; for, were your godheads to borrow of men, men would forsake the gods. Make the meat be beloved more than the man that gives it. Let no assembly of twenty be without a score of villains: if there sit twelve women at the table, let a dozen of them be—as they are. †The rest of your fees, O gods—the senators of Athens, together with the common lag of people—what is amiss in them, you gods, make suitable for destruction. For these my present friends, as they are to me nothing, so in nothing bless them, and to nothing are they welcome.

Uncover, dogs, and lap.

[*The dishes are uncovered and seen to be full of warm water.*]

105. **Only in bone,** i.e., mere skeletons. 115. **lay for hearts,** endeavor to win their affection. 116. **at odds,** at variance, in disagreement.

SCENE VI. 5. **tiring,** preying upon, i.e., busily engaged. 8-9. **by the . . . feasting,** i.e., as his new feasting persuades me to believe. 11-12. **near occasions,** urgent necessities or business. 38. **to 't,** i.e., to the dinner. 47-48. **so unfortunate a beggar,** so unfortunate as to be out of ready resources. 69. **This . . . still,** this is the same (generous) Timon. 75. **city feast,** formal occasion. 77. **first place,** place of honor. 89. **fees,** i.e., as for the rest of your gifts or benefactions. 90. **lag,** dregs, followers. 91-92. **what . . . destruction,** what doesn't at present deserve destroying, make suitable for destruction. Timon suggests by implication that only the wrong is right; right is amiss and must be corrected and brought into line with all other evil so that it may fulfill its destiny, which is destruction. 99. **mouth-friends,** i.e., those who had fed off Timon and flattered him. **smoke,** i.e., steam, "hot air." 100. **Is your perfection,** suits you perfectly. 101. **stuck and spangled,** bespattered and decorated. 106. **time's flies,** fair-weather insects. 107. **Cap and knee slaves,** men obsequious with their caps and

Some speak. What does his lordship mean?
Some other. I know not.
Tim. May you a better feast never behold,
You knot of mouth-friends! smoke and luke-warm water
Is your perfection. This is Timon's last;
Who, stuck and spangled with your flatteries,
Washes it off, and sprinkles in your faces
Your reeking villany. [*Throwing the water in their faces.*]
Live loath'd and long,
Most smiling, smooth, detested parasites,
Courteous destroyers, affable wolves, meek bears,
You fools of fortune, trencher-friends, time's flies,
Cap and knee slaves, vapours, and minute-jacks!
Of man and beast the infinite malady
Crust you quite o'er! What, dost thou go?
Soft! take thy physic first—thou too—and thou;—
Stay, I will lend thee money, borrow none.
[*Throws the dishes at them, and drives them out.*]
What, all in motion? Henceforth be no feast,
Whereat a villain 's not a welcome guest.
Burn, house! sink, Athens! henceforth hated be
Of Timon, man, and all humanity! *Exit.*

Enter the Senators, *with other* Lords.

First Lord. How now, my lords!
Sec. Lord. Know you the quality of Lord Timon's fury?
Third Lord. Push! did you see my cap?
Fourth Lord. I have lost my gown.
First Lord. He 's but a mad lord, and nought but humour sways him. He gave me a jewel th' other day, and now he has beat it out of my hat: did you see my jewel?
Third Lord. Did you see my cap?
Sec. Lord. Here 'tis.
Fourth Lord. Here lies my gown.
First Lord. Let 's make no stay.
Sec. Lord. Lord Timon 's mad.
Third Lord. I feel 't upon my bones.
Fourth Lord. One day he gives us diamonds, next day stones. *Exeunt the Senators* [*etc.*].

[ACT IV.

SCENE I. *Without the walls of Athens.*]

Enter TIMON.

Tim. Let me look back upon thee. O thou wall,
That girdles in those wolves, dive in the earth,
And fence not Athens! Matrons, turn incontinent!
Obedience fail in children! slaves and fools,
Pluck the grave wrinkled senate from the bench,
And minister in their steads! to general filths
Convert o' th' instant, green virginity,
Do 't in your parents' eyes! bankrupts, hold fast;
Rather than render back, out with your knives,
And cut your trusters' throats! bound servants, steal!
Large-handed robbers your grave masters are,
And pill by law. Maid, to thy master's bed;
Thy mistress is o' th' brothel! Son of sixteen,
Pluck the lin'd crutch from thy old limping sire,
With it beat out his brains! Piety, and fear,
Religion to the gods, peace, justice, truth,
Domestic awe, night-rest, and neighbourhood,
Instruction, manners, mysteries, and trades,
Degrees, observances, customs, and laws,
Decline to your confounding contraries,
And let confusion live! Plagues, incident to men,
Your potent and infectious fevers heap
On Athens, ripe for stroke! Thou cold sciatica,
Cripple our senators, that their limbs may halt
As lamely as their manners! Lust and liberty
Creep in the minds and marrows of our youth,
That 'gainst the stream of virtue they may strive,
And drown themselves in riot! Itches, blains,
Sow all th' Athenian bosoms; and their crop
Be general leprosy! Breath infect breath,
That their society, as their friendship, may
Be merely poison! Nothing I'll bear from thee,
But nakedness, thou detestable town!
Take thou that too, with multiplying bans!
Timon will to the woods; where he shall find
Th' unkindest beast more kinder than mankind.
The gods confound—hear me, you good gods all—
Th' Athenians both within and out that wall!
And grant, as Timon grows, his hate may grow
To the whole race of mankind, high and low!
Amen. *Exit.*

[SCENE II. *Athens. A room in Timon's house.*]

Enter Steward [FLAVIUS], *with two or three* Servants.

First Serv. Hear you, master steward, where 's our master?
Are we undone? cast off? nothing remaining?
Flav. Alack, my fellows, what should I say to you?
Let me be recorded by the righteous gods,
I am as poor as you.
First Serv. Such a house broke!
So noble a master fall'n! All gone! and not
One friend to take his fortune by the arm,
And go along with him!
Sec. Serv. As we do turn our backs
From our companion thrown into his grave,
So his familiars to his buried fortunes
Slink all away, leave their false vows with him,
Like empty purses pick'd; and his poor self,
A dedicated beggar to the air,
With his disease of all-shunn'd poverty,
Walks, like contempt, alone. More of our fellows.

Enter other Servants.

Flav. All broken implements of a ruin'd house.
Third Serv. Yet do our hearts wear Timon's livery;
That see I by our faces; we are fellows still,

curtsies. **minute-jacks,** fickle persons, jacks (i.e., mannikins which strike a bell on the outside of a clock) which vary with every minute. 108. **the infinite malady,** every loathsome disease, infinite as the number is (Deighton). 115. Most editions including Globe leave this line without punctuation; F has comma after *man.* 119. **Push,** pshaw.

ACT IV. SCENE I. 3. **fence,** quibble on the meanings "enclose" and "defend." 6. **general filths,** common prostitutes. 12. **pill,** pillage. 14. **lin'd,** stuffed, padded. 15-21. **Piety . . . live,** another of Timon's statements contrary to the accepted ethics of the age; such contraries come more and more to be the burden of his misanthropic reflection. 17. **Domestic awe,** respect for the head of a household. **neighbourhood,** neighborliness. 20. **Decline,** i.e., may all these virtues give way to their opposites. 25. **liberty,** licentiousness. 32. **merely,** i.e., unadulterated, nothing but.

SCENE II. 10. **his familiars . . . fortunes,** those familiar with him when he was fortunate. 13. **dedicated . . . air,** a beggar dedicated to homelessness.

Serving alike in sorrow: leak'd is our bark,
And we, poor mates, stand on the dying deck,
Hearing the surges threat: we must all part
Into this sea of air.
Flav. Good fellows all,
The latest of my wealth I'll share amongst you.
Wherever we shall meet, for Timon's sake,
Let 's yet be fellows; let 's shake our heads, and say,
As 'twere a knell unto our master's fortunes,
'We have seen better days.' Let each take some;
Nay, put out all your hands. Not one word more:
Thus part we rich in sorrow, parting poor.
[*Servants*] *embrace, and part several ways.*
O, the fierce wretchedness that glory brings us!
Who would not wish to be from wealth exempt,
Since riches point to misery and contempt?
Who would be so mock'd with glory? or to live
But in a dream of friendship?
To have his pomp and all what state compounds
But only painted, like his varnish'd friends?
Poor honest lord, brought low by his own heart,
Undone by goodness! Strange, unusual blood,
When man's worst sin is, he does too much good!
Who, then, dares to be half so kind again?
For bounty, that makes gods, does still mar men.
My dearest lord, bless'd, to be most accurs'd,
Rich, only to be wretched, thy great fortunes
Are made thy chief afflictions. Alas, kind lord!
He 's flung in rage from this ingrateful seat
Of monstrous friends, nor has he with him to
Supply his life, or that which can command it.
I'll follow and inquire him out:
I'll ever serve his mind with my best will;
Whilst I have gold, I'll be his steward still. *Exit.*

[SCENE III. *Woods and cave, near the sea-shore.*]

Enter TIMON, in the *woods.*

Tim. O blessed breeding sun, draw from the earth
Rotten humidity; below thy sister's orb
Infect the air! Twinn'd brothers of one womb,
Whose procreation, residence, and birth,
Scarce is dividant, touch them with several fortunes;
The greater scorns the lesser: not nature,
To whom all sores lay siege, can bear great fortune,
But by contempt of nature.
Raise me this beggar, and deny 't that lord;
The senator shall bear contempt hereditary,
The beggar native honour.
It is the pasture lards the rother's sides,
The want that makes him lean. Who dares, who dares,
In purity of manhood stand upright,
And say 'This man 's a flatterer'? if one be,
So are they all; for every grise of fortune
Is smooth'd by that below: the learned pate
Ducks to the golden fool: all 's obliquy;
There 's nothing level in our cursed natures,
But direct villany. Therefore, be abhorr'd
All feasts, societies, and throngs of men!
His semblable, yea, himself, Timon disdains:
Destruction fang mankind! Earth, yield me roots!
[*Digging.*]
Who seeks for better of thee, sauce his palate
With thy most operant poison! What is here?
Gold? yellow, glittering, precious gold? No, gods,
I am no idle votarist: roots, you clear heavens!
Thus much of this will make black white, foul fair,
Wrong right, base noble, old young, coward valiant.
Ha, you gods! why this? what this, you gods? Why, this
Will lug your priests and servants from your sides,
Pluck stout men's pillows from below their heads:
This yellow slave
Will knit and break religions, bless th' accurs'd,
Make the hoar leprosy ador'd, place thieves
And give them title, knee and approbation
With senators on the bench: this is it
That makes the wappen'd widow wed again;
She, whom the spital-house and ulcerous sores
Would cast the gorge at, this embalms and spices
To th' April day again. Come, damned earth,
Thou common whore of mankind, that puts odds
Among the rout of nations, I will make thee
Do thy right nature. (*March afar off.*) Ha! a drum?
Th' art quick,
But yet I'll bury thee: thou 'lt go, strong thief,
When gouty keepers of thee cannot stand.
Nay, stay thou out for earnest. [*Keeping some gold.*]

Enter ALCIBIADES, *with drum and fife, in warlike manner; and* PHRYNIA *and* TIMANDRA.

Alcib. What art thou there? speak.
Tim. A beast, as thou art. The canker gnaw thy heart,
For showing me again the eyes of man!
Alcib. What is thy name? Is man so hateful to thee,
That art thyself a man?
Tim. I am Misanthropos, and hate mankind.
For thy part, I do wish thou wert a dog,
That I might love thee something.
Alcib. I know thee well;
But in thy fortunes am unlearn'd and strange.
Tim. I know thee too; and more than that I know thee,
I not desire to know. Follow thy drum;
With man's blood paint the ground, gules, gules:
Religious canons, civil laws are cruel;
Then what should war be? This fell whore of thine
Hath in her more destruction than thy sword,
For all her cherubin look.
Phr. Thy lips rot off!

33. **or to live,** i.e., or who would live. 35. **all . . . compounds,** that which constitutes dignity. 46-47. **nor . . . life,** he has nothing to maintain himself. 49. **serve his mind,** execute his wishes.

SCENE III. 2. **Rotten humidity,** damp causing rot (Rolfe). **thy sister's,** i.e., the moon. Apollo, god of the sun, was twin brother to Diana, goddess of the moon. 5. **dividant,** separate. **touch,** test. 6, 8. **nature,** quibble on the meanings "human nature" and "beings of like nature" (Deighton, who thinks Timon conceives of great fortune as a sore). 10. **bear contempt hereditary,** endure contempt as something inherited, i.e., proper to their position. 12. **rother's,** ox's. 16. **grise,** step. 17. **smooth'd,** flattered. 18. **all 's obliquy,** i.e., deviating from the right; so F; Globe, following Pope: *all is oblique.* The image in this passage cumulates by the logic of suggestion. Timon thinks first of the conduct of an individual toward his superior, then of another: he sees them as forming a series which becomes "the ladder to all high design" set askew, and he sums up the image in the phrase, *all's obliquy.* 19. **level,** direct; the contrary to *obliquy.* 22. **His semblable,** his own kind. 23. **fang,** seize. 25. **operant,** active, potent. 27. **no idle votarist,** no trifler in my vows. 32. **Pluck . . . heads.** Pulling away the pillow from under a man's head would supposedly cause suffocation; the implication is that gold will kill even strong (stout) men. 35. **place thieves,** give thievery a recognized status. 38. **wappen'd,** worn out; possible misprint for *wapper'd,* fatigued. 40. **cast the gorge,** vomit. 40-41. **embalms . . . again,** restores to the freshness of an April day. 42-43. **Thou . . . nations,** i.e., gold stirs up strife among nations and makes them behave like individuals that make up the rabble. 44. **thy right nature,** i.e., the *right nature* of the *common whore of mankind;* Timon is anticipating the use he put the gold to later in the scene (Deighton).

Tim. I will not kiss thee; then the rot returns
To thine own lips again.
Alcib. How came the noble Timon to this change?
Tim. As the moon does, by wanting light to give:
But then renew I could not, like the moon;
There were no suns to borrow of.
Alcib. Noble Timon,
What friendship may I do thee?
Tim. None, but to
Maintain my opinion.
Alcib. What is it, Timon?
Tim. Promise me friendship, but perform none: if thou wilt not promise, the gods plague thee, for thou art a man! if thou dost perform, confound thee, for thou art a man!
Alcib. I have heard in some sort of thy miseries.
Tim. Thou saw'st them, when I had prosperity.
Alcib. I see them now; then was a blessed time.
Tim. As thine is now, held with a brace of harlots.
Timan. Is this th' Athenian minion, whom the world
Voic'd so regardfully?
Tim. Art thou Timandra?
Timan. Yes.
Tim. Be a whore still: they love thee not that use thee;
Give them diseases, leaving with thee their lust.
Make use of thy salt hours: season the slaves
For tubs and baths; bring down rose-cheeked youth
To the tub-fast and the diet.
Timan. Hang thee, monster!
Alcib. Pardon him, sweet Timandra; for his wits
Are drown'd and lost in his calamities.
I have but little gold of late, brave Timon,
The want whereof doth daily make revolt
In my penurious band: I have heard, and griev'd,
How cursed Athens, mindless of thy worth,
Forgetting thy great deeds, when neighbour states,
But for thy sword and fortune, trod upon them,—
Tim. I prithee, beat thy drum, and get thee gone.
Alcib. I am thy friend, and pity thee, dear Timon.
Tim. How dost thou pity him whom thou dost trouble?
I had rather be alone.
Alcib. Why, fare thee well.
Here is some gold for thee.
Tim. Keep it, I cannot eat it.
Alcib. When I have laid proud Athens on a heap,—
Tim. Warr'st thou 'gainst Athens?
Alcib. Ay, Timon, and have cause.
Tim. The gods confound them all in thy conquest;
And thee after, when thou hast conquered!
Alcib. Why me, Timon?
Tim. That, by killing of villains,
Thou wast born to conquer my country.
Put up thy gold: go on,—here 's gold,—go on;
Be as a planetary plague, when Jove
Will o'er some high-vic'd city hang his poison
In the sick air: let not thy sword skip one:
Pity not honour'd age for his white beard;
He is an usurer: strike me the counterfeit matron;
It is her habit only that is honest,
Herself 's a bawd: let not the virgin's cheek
Make soft thy trenchant sword; for those milk-paps,
That through the window-bars bore at men's eyes,
Are not within the leaf of pity writ,
But set them down horrible traitors: spare not the babe,
Whose dimpled smiles from fools exhaust their mercy;
Think it a bastard, whom the oracle
Hath doubtfully pronounc'd thy throat shall cut,
And mince it sans remorse: swear against objects;
Put armour on thine ears and on thine eyes;
Whose proof, nor yells of mothers, maids, nor babes,
Nor sight of priests in holy vestments bleeding,
Shall pierce a jot. There 's gold to pay thy soldiers:
Make large confusion; and, thy fury spent,
Confounded be thyself! Speak not, be gone.
Alcib. Hast thou gold yet? I'll take the gold thou givest me,
Not all thy counsel.
Tim. Dost thou, or dost thou not, heaven's curse upon thee!
Phr. and Timan. Give us some gold, good Timon: hast thou more?
Tim. Enough to make a whore forswear her trade,
And to make whores, a bawd. Hold up, you sluts,
Your aprons mountant: you are not oathable,—
Although, I know, you'll swear, terribly swear
Into strong shudders and to heavenly agues
Th' immortal gods that hear you,—spare your oaths,
I'll trust to your conditions: be whores still;
And he whose pious breath seeks to convert you,
Be strong in whore, allure him, burn him up;
Let your close fire predominate his smoke,
And be no turncoats: yet may your pains, six months,
Be quite contrary: and thatch your poor thin roofs
With burthens of the dead;—some that were hang'd,
No matter:—wear them, betray with them: whore still;
Paint till a horse may mire upon your face:
A pox of wrinkles!
Phr. and Timan. Well, more gold: what then?
Believe 't, that we'll do any thing for gold.
Tim. Consumptions sow
In hollow bones of man; strike their sharp shins,
And mar men's spurring. Crack the lawyer's voice,
That he may never more false title plead,
Nor sound his quillets shrilly: hoar the flamen,
That scolds against the quality of flesh,
And not believes himself: down with the nose,
Down with it flat; take the bridge quite away

53. **Misanthropos,** hater of mankind. 59. **gules,** heraldic name for "red." 76. **in some sort,** i.e., I have heard something. 81. **regardfully,** respectfully. 85. **salt,** lecherous. 86. **tubs and baths,** allusion to the treatments for venereal diseases, as is also *tub-fast* (l. 87). 93. **mindless,** careless, unmindful. 108. **planetary plague,** allusion to the superstitious belief in the malignant influence of planets. 109. **high-vic'd,** extremely vicious. 116. **window-bars,** i.e., laced bodices. 119. **exhaust,** draw forth. 122. **mince,** slash, cut in small pieces; not uncommonly applied to murdering persons (*NED*). **sans,** without. **objects,** objections (to your cruelty). 133-134. **Enough . . . bawd,** enough to make a whore leave whoring and a bawd leave making whores (Johnson). 135. **mountant,** rising; a heraldic term (with sexual pun; see also *erection* at l. 164). **oathable,** to be believed on your oath (Deighton). 142. **close,** possible quibble on the meanings "secret," i.e., concealed disease, and "concentrated." 143-144. **yet . . . contrary,** various explanations: six months in houses of correction (Steevens); six months recuperating from the ravaging effects of your profession (Warburton); Deighton conjectures the reading *paint-sized mouths;* the sense of the whole passage may be construed as, "Cheer up! in six months you will have achieved murder." 148. **A pox of wrinkles,** don't worry about the wrinkles; i.e., because the paint will cover them. 151-152. **Consumptions . . . bones,** i.e., may the bones of men be made hollow by the disease of pox (syphilis). 155. **hoar,** make rotten. **flamen,** priest. 156. **quality of flesh,** fleshly desire. 157. **down . . . nose,** an effect of syphilis.

Of him that, his particular to foresee,
Smells from the general weal: make curl'd-pate ruffians bald;
And let the unscarr'd braggarts of the war
Derive some pain from you: plague all;
That your activity may defeat and quell
The source of all erection. There 's more gold:
Do you damn others, and let this damn you,
And ditches grave you all!

Phr. and Timan. More counsel with more money, bounteous Timon.

Tim. More whore, more mischief first; I have given you earnest.

Alcib. Strike up the drum towards Athens! Farewell, Timon:
If I thrive well, I'll visit thee again.

Tim. If I hope well, I'll never see thee more.

Alcib. I never did thee harm.

Tim. Yes, thou spok'st well of me.

Alcib. Call'st thou that harm?

Tim. Men daily find it. Get thee away, and take
Thy beagles with thee.

Alcib. We but offend him. Strike!

[*Drum beats.*] *Exeunt* [*Alcibiades, Phrynia, and Timandra*].

Tim. That nature, being sick of man's unkindness,
Should yet be hungry! Common mother, thou, [*Digging.*]
Whose womb unmeasurable, and infinite breast,
Teems, and feeds all; whose self-same mettle,
Whereof thy proud child, arrogant man, is puff'd,
Engenders the black toad and adder blue,
The gilded newt and eyeless venom'd worm,
With all th' abhorred births below crisp heaven
Whereon Hyperion's quick'ning fire doth shine;
Yield him, who all thy human sons doth hate,
From forth thy plenteous bosom, one poor root!
Ensear thy fertile and conceptious womb,
Let it no more bring out ingrateful man!
Go great with tigers, dragons, wolves, and bears;
Teem with new monsters, whom thy upward face
Hath to the marbled mansion all above
Never presented!—O, a root,—dear thanks!—
Dry up thy marrows, vines, and plough-torn leas;
Whereof ingrateful man, with liquorish draughts
And morsels unctuous, greases his pure mind,
That from it all consideration slips!

Enter APEMANTUS.

More man? plague, plague!

Apem. I was directed hither: men report
Thou dost affect my manners, and dost use them.

Tim. 'Tis, then, because thou dost not keep a dog,
Whom I would imitate: consumption catch thee!

Apem. This is in thee a nature but infected;
A poor unmanly melancholy sprung
From change of fortune. Why this spade? this place?
This slave-like habit? and these looks of care?
Thy flatterers yet wear silk, drink wine, lie soft;
Hug their diseas'd perfumes, and have forgot
That ever Timon was. Shame not these woods,
By putting on the cunning of a carper.
Be thou a flatterer now, and seek to thrive
By that which has undone thee: hinge thy knee,
And let his very breath, whom thou 'lt observe,
Blow off thy cap; praise his most vicious strain,
And call it excellent: thou wast told thus;
Thou gav'st thine ears like tapsters that bade welcome
To knaves and all approachers: 'tis most just
That thou turn rascal; hadst thou wealth again,
Rascals should have 't. Do not assume my likeness.

Tim. Were I like thee, I 'ld throw away myself.

Apem. Thou hast cast away thyself, being like thyself;
A madman so long, now a fool. What, think'st
That the bleak air, thy boisterous chamberlain,
Will put thy shirt on warm? will these moss'd trees,
That have outliv'd the eagle, page thy heels,
And skip when thou point'st out? will the cold brook,
Candied with ice, caudle thy morning taste,
To cure thy o'er-night's surfeit? Call the creatures
Whose naked natures live in all the spite
Of wreakful heaven, whose bare unhoused trunks,
To the conflicting elements expos'd,
Answer mere nature; bid them flatter thee;
O, thou shalt find—

Tim. A fool of thee: depart.

Apem. I love thee better now than e'er I did.

Tim. I hate thee worse.

Apem. Why?

Tim. Thou flatter'st misery.

Apem. I flatter not; but say thou art a caitiff.

Tim. Why dost thou seek me out?

Apem. To vex thee.

Tim. Always a villain's office or a fool's.
Dost please thyself in 't?

Apem. Ay.

Tim. What! a knave too?

Apem. If thou didst put this sour-cold habit on
To castigate thy pride, 'twere well: but thou
Dost it enforcedly; thou 'ldst courtier be again,
Wert thou not beggar. Willing misery
Outlives incertain pomp, is crown'd before:
The one is filling still, never complete;
The other, at high wish: best state, contentless,
Hath a distracted and most wretched being,
Worse than the worst, content.
Thou shouldst desire to die, being miserable.

Tim. Not by his breath that is more miserable.
Thou art a slave, whom Fortune's tender arm
With favour never clasp'd; but bred a dog.
Hadst thou, like us from our first swath, proceeded
The sweet degrees that this brief world affords
To such as may the passive drugs of it
Freely command, thou wouldst have plung'd thyself
In general riot; melted down thy youth
In different beds of lust; and never learn'd
The icy precepts of respect, but followed
The sug'red game before thee. But myself,

159. **his particular to foresee,** in order to look out for his own interests. 160. **Smells from,** metaphor from hounds following the scent of game; *to smell from* is to leave or lose the scent. 174. **find it,** i.e., find it harmful to be well spoken of. 175. **beagles,** i.e., beagle hounds, fawning followers—the prostitutes. 182. **newt,** a small salamander. **eyeless venom'd worm,** the blindworm; cf. *Macbeth*, IV, i, 16; *A Midsummer Night's Dream*, II, ii, 11. 184. **Hyperion's,** i.e., the sun's. 187. **Ensear,** dry up. 196. **consideration,** regard for others, or for other things than sensual pleasures (Deighton); possibly, reflection, rationality; cf. *Henry V*, I, i, 28. 202. **but infected,** i.e., he isn't to the manner born; his pessimism is induced by misery; it is not philosophical, hence it is insincere. 207. **diseas'd perfumes,** diseased perfumed mistresses (Malone). 209. **By . . . carper.** Apemantus objects not to Timon's philosophy but to his behavior. 221-223. **think'st . . . warm,** alludes to the practice of having a servant warm one's garment by the fire. 226. **caudle,** provide with a caudle, i.e., a hot spiced drink. 228. **in,** exposed

Who had the world as my confectionary,
The mouths, the tongues, the eyes and hearts of men
At duty, more than I could frame employment,
That numberless upon me stuck as leaves
Do on the oak, have with one winter's brush
Fell from their boughs and left me open, bare
For every storm that blows: I, to bear this,
That never knew but better, is some burden:
Thy nature did commence in sufferance, time
Hath made thee hard in 't. Why shouldst thou hate men?
They never flatter'd thee: what hast thou given?
If thou wilt curse, thy father, that poor rag,
Must be thy subject, who in spite put stuff
To some she beggar and compounded thee
Poor rogue hereditary. Hence, be gone!
If thou hadst not been born the worst of men,
Thou hadst been a knave and flatterer.

Apem. Art thou proud yet?

Tim. Ay, that I am not thee.

Apem. I, that I was
No prodigal.

Tim. I, that I am one now:
Were all the wealth I have shut up in thee,
I 'ld give thee leave to hang it. Get thee gone.
That the whole life of Athens were in this!
Thus would I eat it. [*Eating a root.*]

Apem. Here; I will mend thy feast.
[*Offering him a root.*]

Tim. First mend my company, take away thyself.

Apem. So I shall mend mine own, by th' lack of thine.

Tim. 'Tis not well mended so, it is but botch'd;
If not, I would it were.

Apem. What wouldst thou have to Athens?

Tim. Thee thither in a whirlwind. If thou wilt,
Tell them there I have gold; look, so I have.

Apem. Here is no use for gold.

Tim. The best and truest;
For here it sleeps, and does no hired harm.

Apem. Where liest o' nights, Timon?

Tim. Under that 's above me.
Where feed'st thou o' days, Apemantus?

Apem. Where my stomach finds meat; or, rather, where I eat it.

Tim. Would poison were obedient and knew my mind!

Apem. Where wouldst thou send it?

Tim. To sauce thy dishes.

Apem. The middle of humanity thou never knewest, but the extremity of both ends: when thou wast in thy gilt and thy perfume, they mocked thee for too much curiosity; in thy rags thou knowest none, but art despised for the contrary. There 's a medlar for thee, eat it.

Tim. On what I hate I feed not.

Apem. Dost hate a medlar?

Tim. Ay, though it look like thee.

Apem. An th' hadst hated meddlers sooner, thou shouldst have loved thyself better now. What man didst thou ever know unthrift that was beloved after his means?

Tim. Who, without those means thou talkest of, didst thou ever know beloved?

Apem. Myself.

Tim. I understand thee; thou hadst some means to keep a dog.

Apem. What things in the world canst thou nearest compare to thy flatterers?

Tim. Women nearest; but men, men are the things themselves. What wouldst thou do with the world, Apemantus, if it lay in thy power?

Apem. Give it the beasts, to be rid of the men.

Tim. Wouldst thou have thyself fall in the confusion of men, and remain a beast with the beasts?

Apem. Ay, Timon.

Tim. A beastly ambition, which the gods grant thee t' attain to! If thou wert the lion, the fox would beguile thee: if thou wert the lamb, the fox would eat thee: if thou wert the fox, the lion would suspect thee, when peradventure thou wert accused by the ass: if thou wert the ass, thy dulness would torment thee, and still thou livedst but as a breakfast to the wolf: if thou wert the wolf, thy greediness would afflict thee, and oft thou shouldst hazard thy life for thy dinner: wert thou the unicorn, pride and wrath would confound thee and make thine own self the conquest of thy fury: wert thou a bear, thou wouldst be killed by the horse: wert thou a horse, thou wouldst be seized by the leopard: wert thou a leopard, thou wert german to the lion and the spots of thy kindred were jurors on thy life: all thy safety were remotion and thy defence absence. What beast couldst thou be, that were not subject to a beast? and what a beast art thou already, that seest not thy loss in transformation!

Apem. If thou couldst please me with speaking to me, thou mightst have hit upon it here: the commonwealth of Athens is become a forest of beasts.

Tim. How has the ass broke the wall, that thou art out of the city?

Apem. Yonder comes a poet and a painter: the plague of company light upon thee! I will fear to catch it and give way: when I know not what else to do, I'll see thee again.

Tim. When there is nothing living but thee, thou shalt be welcome. I had rather be a beggar's dog than Apemantus.

Apem. Thou art the cap of all the fools alive.

Tim. Would thou wert clean enough to spit upon!

Apem. A plague on thee! thou art too bad to curse.

Tim. All villains that do stand by thee are pure.

Apem. There is no leprosy but what thou speak'st.

Tim. If I name thee.
I'll beat thee, but I should infect my hands.

Apem. I would my tongue could rot them off!

Tim. Away, thou issue of a mangy dog!
Choler does kill me that thou art alive;
I swound to see thee.

Apem. Would thou wouldst burst!

Tim. Away,

to. 229. **wreakful,** revengeful. 231. **Answer,** cope with or correspond with. 244. **is filling still,** is always filling, i.e., is never filled. 245. **at high wish,** as full as could be wished. 245-247. **best . . . content.** Best states (or conditions) without content have a wretched existence, an existence worse than that of the worst states that are content. 251. **bred a dog,** i.e., thou wert bred up like a dog. 252. **swath,** swaddling clothes. **proceeded.** To proceed B.A., M.A., etc., is the English academic idiom for taking a degree. 254. **drugs,** drudges; obsolete form. 257. **different,** various. 262. **At duty,** subservient to my wishes. 266. **I, to bear this,** that I should bear this. 280. **hang it,** i.e., hang yourself. 303. **curiosity,** fastidiousness. 305. **medlar,** fruit like a small brown-skinned apple; proverbial for a type of rottenness; used here, as often, for the sake of a quibble. 312. **after his means,** after his means were gone; or, according to his means. 344. **german,** related to. 346. **remotion,** in a state of constantly going elsewhere. 363. **cap,** acme, summit.

Thou tedious rogue! I am sorry I shall lose
A stone by thee. [*Throws a stone at him.*]
Apem. Beast!
Tim. Slave!
Apem. Toad!
Tim. Rogue, rogue, rogue!
I am sick of this false world, and will love nought
But even the mere necessities upon 't.
Then, Timon, presently prepare thy grave;
Lie where the light foam of the sea may beat
Thy grave-stone daily: make thine epitaph,
That death in me at others' lives may laugh.
[*To the gold*] O thou sweet king-killer, and dear divorce
'Twixt natural son and sire! thou bright defiler
Of Hymen's purest bed! thou valiant Mars!
Thou ever young, fresh, lov'd and delicate wooer,
Whose blush doth thaw the consecrated snow
That lies on Dian's lap! thou visible god,
That sold'rest close impossibilities,
And mak'st them kiss! that speak'st with every tongue,
To every purpose! O thou touch of hearts!
Think, thy slave man rebels, and by thy virtue
Set them into confounding odds, that beasts
May have the world in empire!
Apem. Would 'twere so!
But not till I am dead. I'll say th' hast gold:
Thou wilt be throng'd to shortly.
Tim. Throng'd to!
Apem. Ay.
Tim. Thy back, I prithee.
Apem. Live, and love thy misery.
Tim. Long live so, and so die. I am quit.
Apem. Moe things like men! Eat, Timon, and abhor them. *Exit Apemantus.*

Enter the Banditti.

First Ban. Where should he have this gold? It is some poor fragment, some slender ort of his remainder: the mere want of gold, and the falling-from of his friends, drove him into this melancholy.

Sec. Ban. It is noised he hath a mass of treasure.

Third Ban. Let us make the assay upon him: if he care not for 't, he will supply us easily; if he covetously reserve it, how shall 's get it?

Sec. Ban. True; for he bears it not about him, 'tis hid.

First Ban. Is not this he?
Banditti. Where?
Sec. Ban. 'Tis his description.
Third Ban. He; I know him.
Banditti. Save thee, Timon.
Tim. Now, thieves?
Banditti. Soldiers, not thieves.
Tim. Both too; and women's sons.
Banditti. We are not thieves, but men that much do want.
Tim. Your greatest want is, you want much of meat.
Why should you want? Behold, the earth hath roots;
Within this mile break forth a hundred springs;
The oaks bear mast, the briers scarlet hips;
The bounteous housewife, nature, on each bush
Lays her full mess before you. Want! why want?
First Ban. We cannot live on grass, on berries, water,
As beasts and birds and fishes.
Tim. Nor on the beasts themselves, the birds, and fishes;
You must eat men. Yet thanks I must you con
That you are thieves profess'd, that you work not
In holier shapes: for there is boundless theft
In limited professions. Rascal thieves,
Here 's gold. Go, suck the subtle blood o' th' grape,
Till the high fever seethe your blood to froth,
And so 'scape hanging: trust not the physician;
His antidotes are poison, and he slays
Moe than you rob: take wealth and lives together;
Do villany, do, since you protest to do 't,
Like workmen. I'll example you with thievery:
The sun 's a thief, and with his great attraction
Robs the vast sea: the moon 's an arrant thief,
And her pale fire she snatches from the sun:
The sea 's a thief, whose liquid surge resolves
The moon into salt tears: the earth 's a thief,
That feeds and breeds by a composture stol'n
From gen'ral excrement: each thing 's a thief:
The laws, your curb and whip, in their rough power
Has uncheck'd theft. Love not yourselves: away,
Rob one another. There 's more gold. Cut throats:
All that you meet are thieves: to Athens go,
Break open shops; nothing can you steal,
But thieves do lose it: steal less for this
I give you, and gold confound you howsoe'er!
Amen.

Third Ban. Has almost charmed me from my profession, by persuading me to it.

First Ban. 'Tis in the malice of mankind that he thus advises us; not to have us thrive in our mystery.

Sec. Ban. I'll believe him as an enemy, and give over my trade.

First Ban. Let us first see peace in Athens: there is no time so miserable but a man may be true. *Exeunt Thieves.*

Enter the Steward [FLAVIUS] *to* TIMON.

Flav. O you gods!
Is yond despis'd and ruinous man my lord?
Full of decay and failing? O monument
And wonder of good deeds evilly bestow'd!
What an alteration of honour
Has desp'rate want made!
What viler thing upon the earth than friends
Who can bring noblest minds to basest ends!
How rarely does it meet with this time's guise,
When man was wish'd to love his enemies!
Grant I may ever love, and rather woo
Those that would mischief me than those that do!
Has caught me in his eye: I will present

388. **impossibilities,** things incapable of being united. 390. **touch,** touchstone. 397. **I am quit,** finally he (Apemantus) is going. 400. **ort,** fragment. 401-402. **falling-from.** Cf. *falling-off*, *Hamlet*, I, v, 47. 406. **make the assay,** see whether or not we can find out if Timon has any money. 419. **Your . . . meat,** you talk about wanting much, but in reality all you want is to satisfy your voracious appetites (Deighton); or possibly, your greatest defect is that you inordinately desire much of this world's goods. 422. **mast,** fruit, i.e., acorns. **hips,** fruit of the rosebush. 428. **thanks . . . con,** I must offer you thanks. 432. **subtle,** treacherous in its influence; cf. *2 Henry IV*, IV, iii, 103-122, on the virtues of sack. 438. **example you with,** give you instances of. 439-445. **The sun 's a thief,** etc. Parallels to this passage have been pointed out by Steevens (the play *Albumazar*, licensed 1615) and by Farmer (Puttenham's *Arte of English Poesie*, 1589, where Ronsard's translation of Anacreon's ode in this vein is quoted with an English translation). The idea is the converse of the Renaissance commonplace of the

My honest grief unto him; and, as my lord,
Still serve him with my life. My dearest master!
Tim. Away! what art thou?
Flav. Have you forgot me, sir?
Tim. Why dost ask that? I have forgot all men;
Then, if thou grant'st th' art a man, I have forgot thee.
Flav. An honest poor servant of yours.
Tim. Then I know thee not:
I never had honest man about me, I; all
I kept were knaves, to serve in meat to villains.
Flav. The gods are witness,
Nev'r did poor steward wear a truer grief
For his undone lord than mine eyes for you.
Tim. What, dost thou weep? Come nearer. Then I love thee,
Because thou art a woman, and disclaim'st
Flinty mankind; whose eyes do never give
But thorough lust and laughter. Pity 's sleeping:
Strange times, that weep with laughing, not with weeping!
Flav. I beg of you to know me, good my lord,
T' accept my grief and whilst this poor wealth lasts
To entertain me as your steward still.
Tim. Had I a steward
So true, so just, and now so comfortable?
It almost turns my dangerous nature mild.
Let me behold thy face. Surely, this man
Was born of woman.
Forgive my general and exceptless rashness,
You perpetual-sober gods! I do proclaim
One honest man—mistake me not—but one;
No more, I pray,—and he 's a steward.
How fain would I have hated all mankind!
And thou redeem'st thyself: but all, save thee,
I fell with curses.
Methinks thou art more honest now than wise;
For, by oppressing and betraying me,
Thou mightst have sooner got another service:
For many so arrive at second masters,
Upon their first lord's neck. But tell me true—
For I must ever doubt, though ne'er so sure—
Is not thy kindness subtle, covetous,
If not a usuring kindness, and, as rich men deal gifts,
Expecting in return twenty for one?
Flav. No, my most worthy master; in whose breast
Doubt and suspect, alas, are plac'd too late:
You should have fear'd false times when you did feast:
Suspect still comes where an estate is least.
That which I show, heaven knows, is merely love,
Duty and zeal to your unmatched mind,
Care of your food and living; and, believe it,
My most honour'd lord,
For any benefit that points to me,
Either in hope or present, I 'ld exchange
For this one wish, that you had power and wealth
To requite me, by making rich yourself.
Tim. Look thee, 'tis so! Thou singly honest man,
Here, take: the gods out of my misery
Have sent thee treasure. Go, live rich and happy;
But thus condition'd: thou shalt build from men;
Hate all, curse all, show charity to none,
But let the famish'd flesh slide from the bone,
Ere thou relieve the beggar; give to dogs
What thou deniest to men; let prisons swallow 'em,
Debts wither 'em to nothing; be men like blasted woods,
And may diseases lick up their false bloods!
And so farewell and thrive.
Flav. O, let me stay,
And comfort you, my master.
Tim. If thou hat'st curses,
Stay not; fly, whilst thou art blest and free:
Ne'er see thou man, and let me ne'er see thee.
Exit [Flavius; Timon retires to his cave].

[ACT V.

SCENE I. *The woods. Before Timon's cave.*]

Enter Poet *and* Painter. [TIMON *watching them from his cave.*]

Pain. As I took note of the place, it cannot be far where he abides.

Poet. What 's to be thought of him? does the rumour hold for true, that he 's so full of gold?

Pain. Certain: Alcibiades reports it; Phrynia and Timandra had gold of him: he likewise enriched poor straggling soldiers with great quantity: 'tis said he gave unto his steward a mighty sum.

Poet. Then this breaking of his has been but a try for his friends.

Pain. Nothing else: you shall see him a palm in Athens again, and flourish with the highest. Therefore 'tis not amiss we tender our loves to him, in this supposed distress of his: it will show honestly in us; and is very likely to load our purposes with what they travail for, if it be a just and true report that goes of his having.

Poet. What have you now to present unto him?

Pain. Nothing at this time but my visitation: only I will promise him an excellent piece.

Poet. I must serve him so too, tell him of an intent that 's coming toward him.

Pain. Good as the best. Promising is the very air o' the time: it opens the eyes of expectation: performance is ever the duller for his act; and, but in the plainer and simpler kind of people, the deed of saying is quite out of use. To promise is most courtly and fashionable: performance is a kind of will or testament which argues a great sickness in his judgement that makes it. *Enter Timon from his cave.*

Tim. [*Aside*] Excellent workman! thou canst not paint a man so bad as is thyself.

Poet. I am thinking what I shall say I have provided for him: it must be a personating of himself; a satire against the softness of prosperity, with a discovery of the infinite flatteries that follow youth and opulency.

concept of gratitude in nature. It has the dramatic effect here of illustrating Timon's misanthropy. 440. **arrant,** thoroughgoing. 442-443. **whose . . . tears,** alludes to the superstitious belief that the moon produced moisture and that it influenced the tides; cf. *Shakespeare's England*, I, 458. 444. **composture,** compost, manure. 465. **ruinous,** brought to ruin. 472. **guise,** habit, custom. 475. **would,** i.e., have a will to, profess to. 491. **give,** give forth tears. 498. **comfortable,** comforting. 502. **exceptless,** making no exception. 519. **suspect,** suspicion. 533. **thus condition'd,** upon this condition. **from,** away from.

ACT V. SCENE I. 12. **palm,** person of honor. 15-16. **show honestly,** appear to be seemly or worthy. 17. **travail,** labor, with quibble on the meaning "journey." 25. **air,** style. 27. **but in,** excepting among. 28. **deed of saying,** action and words going together; a type of candor. 35. **personating,** representation. Warburton points out that the poet's intention is to satirize Timon's case, not Timon.

Tim. [*Aside*] Must thou needs stand for a villain in thine own work? wilt thou whip thine own faults in other men? Do so, I have gold for thee.

Poet. Nay, let 's seek him:
Then do we sin against our own estate,
When we may profit meet, and come too late.

Pain. True;
When the day serves, before black-corner'd night,
Find what thou want'st by free and offer'd light.
Come.

Tim. [*Aside*] I'll meet you at the turn. What a god 's gold,
That he is worshipp'd in a baser temple
Than where swine feed!
'Tis thou that rigg'st the bark and plough'st the foam,
Settlest admired reverence in a slave:
To thee be worship! and thy saints for aye
Be crown'd with plagues that thee alone obey!
Fit I meet them. [*Coming forward.*]

Poet. Hail, worthy Timon!

Pain. Our late noble master!

Tim. Have I once liv'd to see two honest men?

Poet. Sir,
Having often of your open bounty tasted,
Hearing you were retir'd, your friends fall'n off,
Whose thankless natures—O abhorred spirits!—
Not all the whips of heaven are large enough:
What! to you,
Whose star-like nobleness gave life and influence
To their whole being! I am rapt and cannot cover
The monstrous bulk of this ingratitude
With any size of words.

Tim. Let it go naked, men may see 't the better:
You that are honest, by being what you are,
Make them best seen and known.

Pain. He and myself
Have travail'd in the great show'r of your gifts,
And sweetly felt it.

Tim. Ay, you are honest men.

Pain. We are hither come to offer you our service.

Tim. Most honest men! Why, how shall I requite you?
Can you eat roots, and drink cold water? no.

Both. What we can do, we'll do, to do you service.

Tim. Y' are honest men: y' have heard that I have gold;
I am sure you have: speak truth; y' are honest men.

Pain. So it is said, my noble lord; but therefore
Came not my friend nor I.

Tim. Good honest men! Thou draw'st a counterfeit
Best in all Athens: th' art, indeed, the best;
Thou counterfeit'st most lively.

Pain. So, so, my lord.

Tim. E'en so, sir, as I say. And, for thy fiction,
Why, thy verse swells with stuff so fine and smooth
That thou art even natural in thine art.
But, for all this, my honest-natur'd friends,
I must needs say you have a little fault:
Marry, 'tis not monstrous in you, neither wish I
You take much pains to mend.

Both. Beseech your honour
To make it known to us.

Tim. You'll take it ill.

Both. Most thankfully, my lord.

Tim. Will you, indeed?

Both. Doubt it not, worthy lord.

Tim. There 's never a one of you but trusts a knave,
That mightily deceives you.

Both. Do we, my lord?

Tim. Ay, and you hear him cog, see him dissemble,
Know his gross patchery, love him, feed him,
Keep in your bosom: yet remain assur'd
That he 's a made-up villain.

Pain. I know none such, my lord.

Poet. Nor I.

Tim. Look you, I love you well; I'll give you gold,
Rid me these villains from your companies:
Hang them or stab them, drown them in a draught,
Confound them by some course, and come to me,
I'll give you gold enough.

Both. Name them, my lord, let 's know them.

Tim. You that way and you this, but two in company;
Each man apart, all single and alone,
Yet an arch-villain keeps him company.
If where thou art two villains shall not be,
Come not near him. If thou wouldst not reside
But where one villain is, then him abandon.
Hence, pack! there 's gold; you came for gold, ye slaves:
[*To Painter*] You have work'd for me; there 's payment: hence!
[*To Poet*] You are an alchemist; make gold of that.
Out, rascal dogs!

Exeunt [*both, beaten out by Timon, who retires to his cave*].

Enter Steward [FLAVIUS] *and two* Senators.

Fla. It is in vain that you would speak with Timon;
For he is set so only to himself
That nothing but himself which looks like man
Is friendly with him.

First Sen. Bring us to his cave:
It is our part and promise to th' Athenians
To speak with Timon.

Sec. Sen. At all times alike
Men are not still the same: 'twas time and griefs
That fram'd him thus: time, with his fairer hand,
Offering the fortunes of his former days,
The former man may make him. Bring us to him,
And chance it as it may.

Flav. Here is his cave.
Peace and content be here! Lord Timon! Timon!
Look out, and speak to friends: th' Athenians,
By two of their most reverend senate, greet thee:
Speak to them, noble Timon.

Enter TIMON *out of his cave.*

Tim. Thou sun, that comforts, burn! Speak, and be hang'd:
For each true word, a blister! and each false
Be as a cauterizing to the root o' th' tongue,
Consuming it with speaking!

39. **stand for,** serve as a model for. 44. **estate,** worldly well-being. 47. **black-corner'd night,** night which darkens corners; i.e., makes it hard to find things. 49. **at the turn,** i.e., trick for trick in a cheating game. 51. **temple,** the human body. 54. **admired . . . slave,** wondering awe in a slave for his master. 66. **star-like . . . influence,** an astrological metaphor: whose nobility of character was of such power as to influence men's destinies. 67. **rapt,** literally, caught, possessed; equivalent to the loose use today of "overwhelmed." 83. **counterfeit,** picture, likeness, with quibble in line 85. 88. **natural,** i.e., true to your own nature, which is deceitful (playing on the meaning that art can triumph over nature in verisimilitude). 98. **cog,** cheat. 99. **patchery,** knavery. 105. **draught,** cesspool, sink. 115-117. **there 's**

First Sen. Worthy Timon,—
Tim. Of none but such as you, and you of Timon.
First Sen. The senators of Athens greet thee, Timon.
Tim. I thank them; and would send them back the plague,
Could I but catch it for them.
First Sen. O, forget
What we are sorry for ourselves in thee.
The senators with one consent of love
Entreat thee back to Athens; who have thought
On special dignities, which vacant lie
For thy best use and wearing.
Sec. Sen. They confess
Toward thee forgetfulness too general, gross:
Which now the public body, which doth seldom
Play the recanter, feeling in itself
A lack of Timon's aid, hath sense withal
Of it own fail, restraining aid to Timon;
And send forth us, to make their sorrow'd render,
Together with a recompense more fruitful
Than their offence can weigh down by the dram;
Ay, even such heaps and sums of love and wealth
As shall to thee blot out what wrongs were theirs
And write in thee the figures of their love,
Ever to read them thine.
Tim. You witch me in it;
Surprise me to the very brink of tears:
Lend me a fool's heart and a woman's eyes,
And I'll beweep these comforts, worthy senators.
First Sen. Therefore, so please thee to return with us
And of our Athens, thine and ours, to take
The captainship, thou shalt be met with thanks,
Allow'd with absolute power and thy good name
Live with authority: so soon we shall drive back
Of Alcibiades th' approaches wild,
Who, like a boar too savage, doth root up
His country's peace.
Sec. Sen. And shakes his threat'ning sword
Against the walls of Athens.
First Sen. Therefore, Timon,—
Tim. Well, sir, I will; therefore, I will, sir; thus:
If Alcibiades kill my countrymen,
Let Alcibiades know this of Timon,
That Timon cares not. But if he sack fair Athens,
And take our goodly aged men by th' beards,
Giving our holy virgins to the stain
Of contumelious, beastly, mad-brain'd war,
Then let him know, and tell him Timon speaks it,
In pity of our aged and our youth,
I cannot choose but tell him, that I care not,
And let him take 't at worst; for their knives care not,
While you have throats to answer: for myself,
There 's not a whittle in th' unruly camp
But I do prize it at my love before
The reverend'st throat in Athens. So I leave you
To the protection of the prosperous gods,
As thieves to keepers.
Flav. Stay not, all 's in vain.
Tim. Why, I was writing of my epitaph;
It will be seen to-morrow: my long sickness
Of health and living now begins to mend,
And nothing brings me all things. Go, live still;
Be Alcibiades your plague, you his,
And last so long enough!
First Sen. We speak in vain.
Tim. But yet I love my country, and am not
One that rejoices in the common wrack,
As common bruit doth put it.
First Sen. That 's well spoke.
Tim. Commend me to my loving countrymen,—
First Sen. These words become your lips as they pass thorough them.
Sec. Sen. And enter in our ears like great triumphers
In their applauding gates.
Tim. Commend me to them,
And tell them that, to ease them of their griefs,
Their fears of hostile strokes, their aches, losses,
Their pangs of love, with other incident throes
That nature's fragile vessel doth sustain
In life's uncertain voyage, I will some kindness do them:
I'll teach them to prevent wild Alcibiades' wrath.
First Sen. I like this well; he will return again.
Tim. I have a tree, which grows here in my close,
That mine own use invites me to cut down,
And shortly must I fell it: tell my friends,
Tell Athens, in the sequence of degree
From high to low throughout, that whoso please
To stop affliction, let him take his haste,
Come hither, ere my tree hath felt the axe,
And hang himself. I pray you, do my greeting.
Flav. Trouble him no further; thus you still shall find him.
Tim. Come not to me again: but say to Athens,
Timon hath made his everlasting mansion
Upon the beached verge of the salt flood;
Who once a day with his embossed froth
The turbulent surge shall cover: thither come,
And let my grave-stone be your oracle.
Lips, let sour words go by and language end:
What is amiss plague and infection mend!
Graves only be men's works and death their gain!
Sun, hide thy beams! Timon hath done his reign.
Exit Timon [into his cave].
First Sen. His discontents are unremoveably
Coupled to nature.
Sec. Sen. Our hope in him is dead: let us return,
And strain what other means is left unto us
In our dear peril.
First Sen. It requires swift foot. *Exeunt.*

[SCENE II. *Before the walls of Athens.*]

Enter two other Senators *with a* Messenger.

First Sen. Thou hast painfully discover'd: are his files
As full as thy report?
Mess. I have spoke the least:
Besides, his expedition promises
Present approach.

. . . that. Timon gives not gold but abuse to the least sincere of his visitors. He refers here to the beating he is giving them. 120. **set . . . himself,** so self-absorbed. 142. **What . . . thee,** those wrongs which we regret having done you. 151. **it,** its. 152. **render,** rendering, i.e., of their apologies. 158. **them,** i.e., the Athenians, the *public body* (l. 148). **witch,** bewitch. 183. **whittle,** small clasp-knife. 186. **prosperous,** causing prosperity. 189-190. **my long . . . living,** another of Timon's paradoxical distortions. 206. **prevent,** probably quibble on the meanings "frustrate" and "anticipate" (Deighton). 220. **embossed,** foaming.

Sec. Sen. We stand much hazard, if they bring not
Timon.
Mess. I met a courier, one mine ancient friend;
Whom, though in general part we were oppos'd,
†Yet our old love made a particular force,
And made us speak like friends: this man was riding
From Alcibiades to Timon's cave,
With letters of entreaty, which imported
His fellowship i' th' cause against your city,
In part for his sake mov'd.

Enter the other Senators [*from* TIMON].

First Sen. Here come our brothers.
Third Sen. No talk of Timon, nothing of him expect.
The enemies' drum is heard, and fearful scouring
Doth choke the air with dust: in, and prepare:
Ours is the fall, I fear; our foes the snare. *Exeunt.*

[SCENE III. *The woods. Timon's cave, and a rude tomb seen.*]

Enter a Soldier *in the woods, seeking* TIMON.

Sold. By all description this should be the place.
Who 's here? speak, ho! No answer! What is this?
'Timon is dead, who hath outstretch'd his span:
Some beast read this; there does not live a man.'
Dead, sure; and this his grave. What 's on this tomb
I cannot read; the character I'll take with wax:
Our captain hath in every figure skill,
An ag'd interpreter, though young in days:
Before proud Athens he 's set down by this,
Whose fall the mark of his ambition is. *Exit.*

[SCENE IV. *Before the walls of Athens.*]

Trumpets sound. Enter ALCIBIADES *with his powers before Athens.*

Alcib. Sound to this coward and lascivious town
Our terrible approach. *Sound a parley.*

The Senators *appear on the walls.*

Till now you have gone on and fill'd the time
With all licentious measure, making your wills
The scope of justice; till now myself and such
As slept within the shadow of your power
Have wander'd with our travers'd arms and breath'd
Our sufferance vainly: now the time is flush,
When crouching marrow in the bearer strong
Cries of itself 'No more:' now breathless wrong
Shall sit and pant in your great chairs of ease,
And pursy insolence shall break his wind
With fear and horrid flight.
First Sen. Noble and young,
When thy first griefs were but a mere conceit,
Ere thou hadst power or we had cause of fear,
We sent to thee, to give thy rages balm,
To wipe out our ingratitude with loves
Above their quantity.
Sec. Sen. So did we woo
Transformed Timon to our city's love
By humble message and by promis'd means:
We were not all unkind, nor all deserve
The common stroke of war.
First Sen. These walls of ours
Were not erected by their hands from whom
You have receiv'd your griefs; nor are they such
That these great tow'rs, trophies and schools should
fall
For private faults in them.
Sec. Sen. Nor are they living
Who were the motives that you first went out;
Shame that they wanted cunning, in excess
Hath broke their hearts. March, noble lord,
Into our city with thy banners spread:
By decimation, and a tithed death—
If thy revenges hunger for that food
Which nature loathes—take thou the destin'd tenth,
And by the hazard of the spotted die
Let die the spotted.
First Sen. All have not offended;
For those that were, it is not square to take
On those that are, revenges: crimes, like lands,
Are not inherited. Then, dear countryman,
Bring in thy ranks, but leave without thy rage:
Spare thy Athenian cradle and those kin
Which in the bluster of thy wrath must fall
With those that have offended: like a shepherd,
Approach the fold and cull th' infected forth,
But kill not all together.
Sec. Sen. What thou wilt,
Thou rather shalt enforce it with thy smile
Than hew to 't with thy sword.
First Sen. Set but thy foot
Against our rampir'd gates, and they shall ope;
So thou wilt send thy gentle heart before,
To say thou 'lt enter friendly.
Sec. Sen. Throw thy glove,
Or any token of thine honour else,
That thou wilt use the wars as thy redress
And not as our confusion, all thy powers
Shall make their harbour in our town, till we
Have seal'd thy full desire.
Alcib. Then there 's my glove;
Descend, and open your uncharged ports:
Those enemies of Timon's and mine own
Whom you yourselves shall set out for reproof
Fall and no more: and, to atone your fears
With my more noble meaning, not a man
Shall pass his quarter, or offend the stream
Of regular justice in your city's bounds,
But shall be render'd to your public laws
At heaviest answer.
Both. 'Tis most nobly spoken.
Alcib. Descend, and keep your words.
[*The Senators descend, and open the gates.*]

SCENE II. 7. **in general part,** on public issues; i.e., we were in opposite factions, but we were still personal friends. The antithesis is between *general* and *particular* (l. 8). 13. **In . . . mov'd,** undertaken partly on Timon's behalf. 15. **scouring,** hurrying along.

SCENE III. 6. **the . . . wax,** I'll take an impression of the inscription in wax. 7. **every figure,** all kinds of writing.

SCENE IV. 4-5. **making . . . justice,** equating justice to your wills. 7. **travers'd,** a term in military drill, arms inactive (Rolfe); folded (Onions). 7-8. **breath'd Our sufferance,** voiced our sufferings. 9. **marrow,** resolution. 10. **breathless wrong,** i.e., those wronged and out of breath because they have exerted themselves. 12. **pursy,** short-winded and corpulent. 13. **Noble and young,** addressed to Alcibiades, probably in contrast to senators, the old men. 24. **they.** The antecedent is *griefs*. 26. **them,** i.e., those *from whom you have received your griefs*. 27. **motives . . . out,** the instigators that prompted you to go out. 28. **in excess,** modifies *shame*. 31. **decimation, tithed death,** selection of every tenth to die; the two phrases mean the same thing. 34. **spotted die,** lot; cf. *Julius Caesar*, IV, i, 6. 35. **the spotted,** the corrupt, wicked. 39. **without,** outside. 47. **rampir'd,** barricaded. 55. **uncharged,** unattacked. 57. **reproof,** disgrace, guilt. 58. **atone,** square, put into agreement. 59. **man,** i.e., soldier of mine. 60. **pass his quarter,** pass outside his barracks; a guarantee against pillage.

Enter [Soldier *as*] *a Messenger.*

Sold. My noble general, Timon is dead;
Entomb'd upon the very hem o' th' sea;
And on his grave-stone this insculpture, which
With wax I brought away, whose soft impression
Interprets for my poor ignorance.
Alcib. (*Reads the epitaph*) 'Here lies a wretched corse, of wretched soul bereft:
Seek not my name: a plague consume you wicked caitiffs left!
Here lie I, Timon; who, alive, all living men did hate:
Pass by and curse thy fill, but pass and stay not here thy gait.'
These well express in thee thy latter spirits:
Though thou abhorr'dst in us our human griefs,
Scorn'dst our brain's flow and those our droplets which
From niggard nature fall, yet rich conceit
Taught thee to make vast Neptune weep for aye
On thy low grave, on faults forgiven. Dead
Is noble Timon: of whose memory
Hereafter more. Bring me into your city,
And I will use the olive with my sword,
Make war breed peace, make peace stint war, make each
Prescribe to other as each other's leech.
Let our drums strike. *Exeunt.*

76. **brain's flow,** tears.

MACBETH

Macbeth is perhaps the last in a series of four great Shakespearean tragedies concerned with spiritual evil, as distinguished from domestic or political strife. The play was certainly in existence by April 20, 1611, when Simon Forman saw it at the Globe, but the style and some rather tenuous topical clues suggest a date around 1606–1607: King James' accession to the English throne in 1603, his reassertion of the power of the royal touch to cure the "king's evil" in 1604–1605 (see IV,iii), the trial of the Gunpowder Plot conspirators (to which the Porter may allude in his remarks about "equivocators") in March of 1606, and a seeming reference in a play called *The Puritan*, published in 1607, to Banquo's ghost sitting "at the upper end of the table." As the possible culmination, then, of an analysis of evil begun with *Hamlet* (c. 1599–1601) and extending through *Othello* (c. 1603–1604) and *King Lear* (c. 1605), *Macbeth* offers a terse and gloomy vision of a particular man's encounter with the powers of darkness. However much Macbeth may possess freedom of will and be personally responsible for his own fate, his tragic doom seems relentlessly unavoidable.

To an extent not found in the other tragedies, the issue is stated in terms of salvation versus damnation. Macbeth knows before he acts that Duncan's virtues "Will plead like angels, trumpet-tongu'd, against The deep damnation of his taking-off" (I,vii). After the deed, he is equally aware that he has "Put rancours in the vessel of my peace . . . and mine eternal jewel Given to the common enemy of man" (III,i). Increasingly he is described by his enemies as a devil himself, a "hell-hound." He is, like Marlowe's Doctor Faustus before him, one who has knowingly sold his soul for self-gain. And although as a mortal he still has time to repent his crimes, horrible as they are, Macbeth cannot find the words to be penitent. "Wherefore could not I pronounce 'Amen'?" he implores his wife after they have committed the murder. "I had most need of blessing, and 'Amen' Stuck in my throat" (II,ii). Macbeth's own answer seems to be that he has launched himself into evil in such an inexorable fashion that he cannot turn back. Sentence has been pronounced: "Glamis hath murder'd sleep, and therefore Cawdor Shall sleep no more; Macbeth shall sleep no more."

Macbeth is not a conventional morality play (even less so than *Doctor Faustus*), and is not concerned primarily with preaching against sinfulness or demonstrating that Macbeth is finally damned for what he does. A homiletic tradition has been transformed into an intensely human psychological study of the effects of evil on a particular man and, to a lesser extent, on his wife. That homiletic tradition nevertheless provides as its legacy a spiritual and cosmic framework for understanding how evil operates. A perverse ambition seemingly inborn in Macbeth himself is abetted by dark forces dwelling in the universe, waiting to catch him off guard. Among Shakespeare's tragedies, indeed, *Macbeth* is remarkable for its focus on evil in the protagonist, and on his relationship to those sinister forces tempting him. In no other Shakespearean play must we identify to such an extent with the evildoer himself. We are sharers in Macbeth's inclination toward brutality, as well as in his humane resistance of that urge. We must witness and account for his downfall through two phases: the soul-struggle leading up to the crime, and the despairing aftermath with its vain quest for security through continued violence. Evil is thus presented in two aspects, as insidious suggestion leading us on toward an illusory promise of gain, and then as frenzied addiction for the hated thing by which we are possessed.

In the first phase, up to the crime, we wonder to what extent the powers of darkness are a determining factor in what Macbeth does. Can he avoid the fate the witches proclaim? Evidently he and Lady Macbeth have previously considered murdering Duncan; the witches appear after the thought, not before. Lady Macbeth reminds her wavering husband that he was the first to "break this enterprise" to her, on some previous occasion when "Nor time nor place Did then adhere, and yet you would make both" (I,vii). Elizabethans would understand that evil spirits such as witches appear when summoned, whether by our conscious or unconscious minds. Macbeth is ripe for their insinuations. A mind free of taint would see no sinister invitation in their prophecy of greatness to come. And in a saner moment Macbeth knows that his restless desire to interfere with destiny is arrogant and useless. "If chance will have me king, why, chance may crown me, Without my stir" (I,iii). Banquo, his companion, serves as his dramatic opposite by consistently displaying the correct attitude toward the witches. "Speak then to me," he addresses them, "who neither beg nor fear Your favours nor your hate." Like Horatio in *Hamlet*, Banquo is stoically indifferent to the blandishments of fortune as well as to its buffets. Indeed, promises of success are often more ruinous than setbacks—as in the seemingly paradoxical instance of the farmer, cited by Macbeth's Porter, who "hanged himself on the expectation of plenty." It is by showing Macbeth that he is two-thirds of his way to the throne that the witches tempt him to seize the last third at whatever cost. "Glamis, and Thane of Cawdor! The greatest is behind."

Banquo comprehends the nature of temptation. "To win us to our harm," he observes, "The instruments of darkness tell us truths, Win us with honest trifles, to betray 's In deepest consequence." The devil can speak true, and his strategy is to invite us into a trap we help prepare. Without our active consent in evil (as Othello also learns) we cannot fall. Yet in what sense are the witches trifling with Macbeth, or prevaricating? When they address him as one "that shalt be king hereafter," they are stating a certainty, for they can "look into the seeds of time, And say which grain will grow and which will not," as Banquo says. They know that Banquo will be "Lesser than Macbeth, and greater, Not so happy, yet much happier," since Banquo will beget a race of kings and Macbeth will not. How then do they know that Macbeth will be king? If we consider for a moment the hypothetical question, what if Macbeth does *not* murder Duncan, we can perceive the very center of the relationship between character and fate; for the only valid answer is that the question remains hypothetical, Macbeth *does* kill Duncan, the witches are right in their prediction. It is idle to speculate that providence would have found another way to make Macbeth king, for the witches' prophecy is self-fulfilling in the very way they foresee. Character is fate; they know Macbeth's fatal weakness, and know they can "enkindle" him to seize the crown by laying irresistible temptations before him. This does not mean that they predetermine his choice, but rather that Macbeth's choice is predictable and therefore unavoidable, even though not preordained. He has free choice, but that choice will in fact go only one way—as with Adam and Eve in Milton's *Paradise Lost*, and in the great medieval exegetical tradition from which it was derived.

The powers of evil cannot predetermine Macbeth's choice, but they can importantly influence the external conditions affecting that choice. By a series of apparently circumstantial events, calculatedly timed, they can repeatedly assail him just when he is about to rally to the call of conscience. The witches, armed with supernatural knowledge, inform Macbeth he is to be the Thane of Cawdor shortly before the king's ambassadors confirm the new title. Duncan chooses this very night to lodge under Macbeth's roof. And just when Macbeth resolves to abandon even this unparalleled opportunity, his wife intervenes on the side of the witches. He performs the murder in part to keep his word to her and prove he is no coward (like Donwald, the slayer of King Duff in one of Shakespeare's chief sources from Holinshed's *Chronicles*). Not only the opportunities presented to Macbeth but the obstacles put in his way are cannily timed to overwhelm his conscience. When King Duncan announces that his son Malcolm is now Prince of Cumberland and official heir to the throne (I,iv), the unintended threat to Macbeth arouses him from a mood of gratitude and acceptance to one of hostility. These are mitigating circumstances in our judgment of Macbeth, and even though they cannot excuse him they certainly increase our sympathetic identification.

We are moved too by the poetic intensity of Macbeth's moral vision. His soliloquies are memorable as poetry, not merely because Shakespeare wrote them but because Macbeth is a sensitively aware man. The horror, indeed, of his crime is that his cultivated self is revulsed by what he cannot prevent himself from doing. He understands with a terrible clarity not only the moral wrong of what he is about to do, but also the inescapably destructive consequences for himself. He is as reluctant as we to see the crime committed, and yet he goes to it in a sad and rational deliberateness rather than in a self-blinding fury. There is no seeming loss of perspective, and yet there is total alienation of the act from the doer's moral consciousness. The arguments for and against murdering Duncan, as Macbeth perceptively appraises them, are overwhelmingly opposed to the deed. Duncan is his king and his guest, both sacred obligations. The king is virtuous and able. He has shown every favor to Macbeth, thereby removing any sane motivation for striving after further promotion. Furthermore, all human history shows that murders of this sort "return To plague th' inventor" (I,vii). Finally, judgment in "the life to come" remains to be considered. On the other side of the ledger is nothing but Macbeth's "Vaulting ambition, which o'erleaps itself"—an empty, motiveless refusal to be content with all his present good fortune since there is more that beckons. Who could weigh the issues so dispassionately and still choose the wrong? The answer apparently is that we could, for Macbeth strikes us as typically human both in his understanding and in his totally perverse ambition.

Macbeth's clarity of vision is contrasted with that of his wife. He is always seeing visions or hearing voices—a dagger in the air, the ghost of Banquo, a voice crying "Sleep no more!"—and she is always denying them. "The sleeping and the dead Are but as pictures," she insists. He knows that "all great Neptune's ocean" cannot wash the blood from his hands; "No, this my hand will rather The multitudinous seas incarnadine, Making the green one red." To Lady Macbeth, contrastingly, "A little water clears us of this deed: How easy is it, then!" (II,ii). He knows that the murder of Duncan is but the beginning: "We have scorch'd the snake, not kill'd it." Lady Macbeth would prefer to believe that "What's done is done" (III,ii). Paradoxically, she is the one who must finally endure visions of the most agonizing sort, sleepwalking in her madness and trying to rub away the "damned spot" that before seemed so easy to remove. This relationship between Macbeth and Lady Macbeth owes much to traditions of the contrast between male and female temperaments, including the archetypal relationship of Adam and Eve. The man is the more rational of the two but knowingly shares his wife's sin through a uxorious fondness for her. She has failed to foresee the long-range consequences of sinful action and so becomes a temptress to her husband. The fall of man takes place in an incongruous atmosphere of domestic intimacy and mutual concern; Lady Macbeth is motivated by ambition for her husband in much the same way that he sins to win her approbation.

The fatal disharmony flawing this domestic accord is conveyed through images of sexual inversion. Lady Macbeth prepares for her ordeal with the incantation, "Come, you spirits That tend on mortal thoughts, unsex me here . . . Come to my woman's breasts, And take my milk for gall" (I,v). When she accuses her husband of unmanly cowardice, and vows she would dash out the brains of her own infant for such effeminacy as he has displayed, he extols her with "Bring forth men-children only; For thy undaunted mettle should compose Nothing but males" (I,vii). She takes the initiative, devising and then carrying out the plan to drug Duncan's chamberguards with wine. This assumption of the dominant male role by the woman would again bring to the Elizabethan mind numerous medieval parallels deploring the ascendancy of passion over reason: Eve choosing for Adam, Noah's wife taking command of the ark, the Wife of Bath dominating her husbands, Venus emasculating Mars, and others.

In *Macbeth*, sexual inversion also draws a parallel between Lady Macbeth and the witches or weird sisters, the bearded women. Their sexual inversion betokens disorder in nature, for they can sail in a sieve, and "look not like th' inhabitants o' th' earth, And yet are on 't" (I,iii). Habitually they speak in paradoxes: "When the battle's lost and won," "Fair is foul, and foul is fair." Shakespeare probably drew on numerous sources to depict them: Holinshed's *Chronicles* (in which he conflated two accounts, one of Duncan and Macbeth, and the other of King Duff slain by Donwald with the help of his wife), King James' writings on witchcraft, Harsnet's *Declaration of Egregious Popishe Impostures* (used also for *King Lear*), and the accounts of the Scottish witch trials published around 1590. In the last, particularly, Shakespeare could have found mention of witches raising storms and sailing in sieves to endanger vessels at sea, performing threefold rituals blaspheming the Trinity, and brewing witches' broth. Holinshed's *Chronicles* refer to the weird sisters as "goddesses of destinie," thus relating them to Clotho, Lachesis, and Atropos who spin, pull, and cut the thread of fate; but in *Macbeth* the sisters' power to control fortune is curtailed, and they are portrayed as witches according to popular contemporary understanding. The popularity of witchlore tempted Shakespeare's company to expand the witch scenes with spectacle of song and dance, and the Folio text we have evidently contains interpolations derived in part from Middleton's *The Witch* (see especially III,v and part of IV,i containing mention of Middleton's songs "Come away" and "Black spirits"). Nevertheless, Shakespeare's original theme of a disharmony in nature remains clearly visible.

Other image patterns reinforce the same theme. The murder of Duncan, like that of Julius Caesar, is accompanied by signs of the heavens' anger. Various observers report that chimneys blow down during the unruly night, that owls clamor and attack falcons, that the earth shakes, and that Duncan's horses devour each other. (Some of these prodigies are from Holinshed.) Owls appear repeatedly in the imagery, along with other creatures associated with nighttime and horror: the wolf, serpents, scorpions, bats, toads, beetles, crows, rooks. Darkness itself assumes tangible and menacing shapes of hidden stars or extinguished candles, a thick blanket shrouded "in the dunnest smoke of hell," an entombment of the earth in place of "living light," a scarf to hoodwink the eye of "pitiful day," and a bloody and invisible hand to tear to pieces the lives of virtuous men. Sleep correspondingly is transformed from "great nature's second course" and a "nourisher" of life that "knits up the ravell'd sleave of care" (II,ii) into "death's counterfeit" and a living hell for Lady Macbeth. Life becomes a sterility for Macbeth, a denial of harvest, the lees or dregs of the wine and "the sear, the yellow leaf." By the same token life is unreal, "a walking shadow, a poor player That struts and frets his hour upon the stage And then is heard no more" (V,v). This theme of empty illusion carries over into the recurring metaphor of borrowed or ill-fitting garments that belie the wearer. For Macbeth is an actor, a hypocrite, whose "False face must hide what the false heart doth know" (I,vii) and who must "look like the innocent flower, But be the serpent under 't" (I,v). Even the show of grief is an assumed mask whereby evildoers deceive the virtuous, so much so that Malcolm, Donalbain, and Macduff learn to conceal their true feeling rather than be thought to "show an unfelt sorrow."

Blood is at once a literal sign of disorder, an emblem of Macbeth's remorseless butchery, a "damned spot" on the conscience, and a promise of divine vengeance: "It will have blood; they say, blood will have blood" (III,iv). This emphasis on corrupted blood also suggests disease, in which Macbeth's tyranny is a sickness to his country as well as to himself. Scotland bleeds (IV,iii), needing a physician, and so Macduff and his allies call themselves "the med'cine of the sickly weal" (V,ii). Lady Macbeth's disease is incurable, beyond the practice of a doctor, something spiritually corrupt wherein "the patient Must minister to himself." Conversely, the English King Edward is renowned for his divine gift of curing the "king's evil," or scrofula.

Throughout, the defenders of righteousness are associated with positive images of natural order. Duncan rewards his subjects by saying, "I have begun to plant thee, and will labour To make thee full of growing" (I,iv). His arrival at Inverness Castle is heralded by signs of summer, sweet air, and "the temple-haunting martlet" (I,vi). He is a fatherly figure, so much so that even Lady Macbeth balks at the act of seeming parricide. Macduff too is a father and husband whose family is butchered, desecrated. Banquo is above all a patriarchal figure, ancestor of the royal line governing Scotland and England when the play was written. These harmonies are restorative. Scotland's peace is violated for a time, and in that bloody interim "to do harm Is often laudable, to do good sometime Accounted dangerous folly" (IV,ii), but the sense of an overriding stability to which Scotland will return is far more omnipresent than in *King Lear*. Even the witches' riddling prophecies, "the equivocation of the fiend" luring Macbeth into further atrocities with the vain promise of security, anticipate a divinely inspired retribution. Man's fall is unavoidable, but the concern of providence is no less sure.

MACBETH

[*Dramatis Personae*

DUNCAN, King of Scotland.
MALCOLM, DONALBAIN, } *his sons.*
MACBETH, BANQUO, } *generals of the king's army.*
MACDUFF, LENNOX, ROSS, MENTEITH, ANGUS, CAITHNESS, } *noblemen of Scotland.*
FLEANCE, *son to Banquo.*
SIWARD, Earl of Northumberland, *general of the English forces.*
Young SIWARD, *his son.*
SEYTON, *an officer attending on Macbeth.*
Boy, *son to Macduff.*
An English Doctor.
A Scottish Doctor.
A Soldier.
A Porter.
An Old Man.

LADY MACBETH.
LADY MACDUFF.
Gentlewoman attending on Lady Macbeth.

HECATE.
Three Witches.
Apparitions.

Lords, Gentlemen, Officers, Soldiers, Murderers, Attendants, *and* Messengers.

SCENE: *Scotland: England.*]

ACT I.

SCENE I. [*A desert place.*]

Thunder and lightning. Enter three Witches.

First Witch. When shall we three meet again
In thunder, lightning, or in rain?
Sec. Witch. When the hurlyburly 's done,
When the battle 's lost and won.
Third Witch. That will be ere the set of sun.
First Witch. Where the place?
Sec. Witch. Upon the heath.
Third Witch. There to meet with Macbeth.
First Witch. I come, Graymalkin!
Sec. Witch. Paddock calls.
Third Witch. Anon.
All. Fair is foul, and foul is fair:
Hover through the fog and filthy air. *Exeunt.*

SCENE II. [*A camp near Forres.*]

Alarum within. Enter King [DUNCAN], MALCOLM, DONALBAIN, LENNOX, *with* Attendants, *meeting a bleeding* Captain.

Dun. What bloody man is that? He can report,
As seemeth by his plight, of the revolt
The newest state.
Mal. This is the sergeant
Who like a good and hardy soldier fought
'Gainst my captivity. Hail, brave friend!
Say to the king the knowledge of the broil
As thou didst leave it.
Capt. Doubtful it stood;
As two spent swimmers, that do cling together
And choke their art. The merciless Macdonwald—
Worthy to be a rebel, for to that
The multiplying villainies of nature
Do swarm upon him—from the western isles
Of kerns and gallowglasses is supplied;
And Fortune, on his damned quarrel smiling,
Show'd like a rebel's whore: but all 's too weak:
For brave Macbeth—well he deserves that name—
Disdaining Fortune, with his brandish'd steel,
Which smok'd with bloody execution,
Like valour's minion carved out his passage
Till he fac'd the slave;
†Which ne'er shook hands, nor bade farewell to him,
Till he unseam'd him from the nave to th' chops,
And fix'd his head upon our battlements.
Dun. O valiant cousin! worthy gentleman!
Capt. As whence the sun 'gins his reflection
Shipwracking storms and direful thunders break,
So from that spring whence comfort seem'd to come
Discomfort swells. Mark, king of Scotland, mark:
No sooner justice had with valour arm'd
Compell'd these skipping kerns to trust their heels,
But the Norweyan lord surveying vantage,
With furbish'd arms and new supplies of men
Began a fresh assault.
Dun. Dismay'd not this
Our captains, Macbeth and Banquo?
Capt. Yes;
As sparrows eagles, or the hare the lion.
If I say sooth, I must report they were
As cannons overcharg'd with double cracks, so they
Doubly redoubled strokes upon the foe:
Except they meant to bathe in reeking wounds,
Or memorize another Golgotha,
I cannot tell.
But I am faint, my gashes cry for help.
Dun. So well thy words become thee as thy wounds;
They smack of honour both. Go get him surgeons.
[*Exit Captain, attended.*]
Who comes here?

Enter ROSS *and* ANGUS.

Mal. The worthy Thane of Ross.
Len. What a haste looks through his eyes! So should he look
That seems to speak things strange.
Ross. God save the king!
Dun. Whence cam'st thou, worthy thane?
Ross. From Fife, great king;
Where the Norweyan banners flout the sky
And fan our people cold. Norway himself,
With terrible numbers,
Assisted by that most disloyal traitor
The Thane of Cawdor, began a dismal conflict;
Till that Bellona's bridegroom, lapp'd in proof,
Confronted him with self-comparisons,
Point against point rebellious, arm 'gainst arm,
Curbing his lavish spirit: and, to conclude,
The victory fell on us.
Dun. Great happiness!
Ross. That now
Sweno, the Norways' king, craves composition;
Nor would we deign him burial of his men
Till he disbursed at Saint Colme's inch
Ten thousand dollars to our general use.
Dun. No more that Thane of Cawdor shall deceive
Our bosom interest: go pronounce his present death,
And with his former title greet Macbeth.
Ross. I'll see it done.
Dun. What he hath lost noble Macbeth hath won.
Exeunt.

SCENE III. [*A heath near Forres.*]

Thunder. Enter the three Witches.

First Witch. Where hast thou been, sister?
Sec. Witch. Killing swine.
Third Witch. Sister, where thou?
First Witch. A sailor's wife had chestnuts in her lap,
And munch'd, and munch'd, and munch'd:—'Give me,' quoth I:
'Aroint thee, witch!' the rump-fed ronyon cries.
Her husband 's to Aleppo gone, master o' th' Tiger:
But in a sieve I'll thither sail,
And, like a rat without a tail,
I'll do, I'll do, and I'll do.
Sec. Witch. I'll give thee a wind.
First Witch. Th' art kind.

ACT I. SCENE I. 3. **hurlyburly,** tumult. 8. **Graymalkin,** gray cat, name of the witch's familiar spirit. 9. **Paddock,** toad; also, a familiar. 10. **Anon,** at once.

SCENE II. *Stage Direction:* ***Alarum,*** noise of battle. 3. **sergeant,** i.e., staff officer. There may be no inconsistency with his rank of "captain" in the stage direction and speech prefixes in F. 6. **broil,** battle. 8. **spent,** tired out. 9. **choke their art,** render their skill useless. 10. **to that,** in addition to. 12. **western isles,** the Hebrides and perhaps Ireland. 13. **kerns,** light-armed Irish foot soldiers. **gallowglasses,** retainers of Irish chiefs, armed with axes. 19. **minion,** darling. 21. **Which,** who, i.e., Macbeth. 22. **nave,** navel. **chops,** jaws. 26. **break,** supplied by Pope. 28. **Mark,** listen, take heed. 31. **surveying vantage,** seeing an opportunity. 37. **cracks,** discharges of cannon. 40. **memorize,** make memorable or famous. **Golgotha,** "place of a skull," where the Saviour was crucified (Mark 15:22). 45. **Thane,** Scottish title of honor, roughly equivalent to *earl.* 47. **seems to speak,** probably, "is about to speak." 49. **flout,** mock, insult. 53. **dismal,** disastrous, calamitous. 54. **Bellona's bridegroom,** i.e., Macbeth. Bellona was the Roman goddess of war. **lapp'd in proof,** clad in well-tested armor. 55. **self-comparisons,** matching counter-thrusts. 57. **lavish,** insolent, unrestrained. 59. **Norways',** Norwegians'. **composition,** agreement, treaty of peace. 61. **Saint Colme's inch,** Inchcolm, the Isle of St. Columba in the Firth of Forth. 62. **dollars,** Spanish or Dutch coins. **general,** public. 64. **bosom,** close and affectionate. **present,** immediate.

SCENE III. 5. **munch'd,** chewed with closed lips. 6. **Aroint thee,** avaunt, begone. **rump-fed,** fed on refuse, or fat-rumped. **ronyon,** mangy creature; a term of contempt. 7. **Tiger,** a ship's name. 8. **in a sieve.** Sailing in sieves was one of the things confessed by the witches in the Scottish witchcraft trials. 9. **without a tail.** A familiar or transformed witch could be recognized by some bodily defect.

Third Witch. And I another.
First Witch. I myself have all the other,
And the very ports they blow,
All the quarters that they know
I' th' shipman's card.
I'll drain him dry as hay:
Sleep shall neither night nor day
Hang upon his pent-house lid;
He shall live a man forbid:
Weary sev'nights nine times nine
Shall he dwindle, peak and pine:
Though his bark cannot be lost,
Yet it shall be tempest-tost.
Look what I have.
Sec. Witch. Show me, show me.
First Witch. Here I have a pilot's thumb,
Wrack'd as homeward he did come. *Drum within.*
Third Witch. A drum, a drum!
Macbeth doth come.
All. The weird sisters, hand in hand,
Posters of the sea and land,
Thus do go about, about:
Thrice to thine and thrice to mine
And thrice again, to make up nine.
Peace! the charm 's wound up.

Enter MACBETH *and* BANQUO.

Macb. So foul and fair a day I have not seen.
Ban. How far is 't call'd to Forres? What are these
So wither'd and so wild in their attire,
That look not like th' inhabitants o' th' earth,
And yet are on 't? Live you? or are you aught
That man may question? You seem to understand me,
By each at once her choppy finger laying
Upon her skinny lips: you should be women,
And yet your beards forbid me to interpret
That you are so.
Macb. Speak, if you can: what are you?
First Witch. All hail, Macbeth! hail to thee, Thane of Glamis!
Sec. Witch. All hail, Macbeth! hail to thee, Thane of Cawdor!
Third Witch. All hail, Macbeth, that shalt be king hereafter!
Ban. Good sir, why do you start; and seem to fear
Things that do sound so fair? I' th' name of truth,
Are ye fantastical, or that indeed
Which outwardly ye show? My noble partner
You greet with present grace and great prediction
Of noble having and of royal hope,
That he seems rapt withal: to me you speak not.
If you can look into the seeds of time,
And say which grain will grow and which will not,
Speak then to me, who neither beg nor fear
Your favours nor your hate.
First Witch. Hail!
Sec. Witch. Hail!
Third Witch. Hail!
First Witch. Lesser than Macbeth, and greater.
Sec. Witch. Not so happy, yet much happier.
Third Witch. Thou shalt get kings, though thou be none:
So all hail, Macbeth and Banquo!
First Witch. Banquo and Macbeth, all hail!
Macb. Stay, you imperfect speakers, tell me more:
By Sinel's death I know I am Thane of Glamis;
But how of Cawdor? the Thane of Cawdor lives,
A prosperous gentleman; and to be king
Stands not within the prospect of belief,
No more than to be Cawdor. Say from whence
You owe this strange intelligence? or why
Upon this blasted heath you stop our way
With such prophetic greeting? Speak, I charge you.
Witches vanish.
Ban. The earth hath bubbles, as the water has,
And these are of them. Whither are they vanish'd?
Macb. Into the air; and what seem'd corporal melted
As breath into the wind. Would they had stay'd!
Ban. Were such things here as we do speak about?
Or have we eaten on the insane root
That takes the reason prisoner?
Macb. Your children shall be kings.
Ban. You shall be king.
Macb. And Thane of Cawdor too: went it not so?
Ban. To th' selfsame tune and words. Who 's here?

Enter ROSS *and* ANGUS.

Ross. The king hath happily receiv'd, Macbeth,
The news of thy success; and when he reads
Thy personal venture in the rebels' fight,
His wonders and his praises do contend
Which should be thine or his: silenc'd with that,
In viewing o'er the rest o' th' selfsame day,
He finds thee in the stout Norweyan ranks,
Nothing afeard of what thyself didst make,
Strange images of death. As thick as tale
Came post with post; and every one did bear
Thy praises in his kingdom's great defence,
And pour'd them down before him.
Ang. We are sent
To give thee from our royal master thanks;
Only to herald thee into his sight,
Not pay thee.
Ross. And, for an earnest of a greater honour,
He bade me, from him, call thee Thane of Cawdor:
In which addition, hail, most worthy thane!
For it is thine.
Ban. What, can the devil speak true?
Macb. The Thane of Cawdor lives: why do you dress me
In borrowed robes?
Ang. Who was the thane lives yet;
But under heavy judgement bears that life
Which he deserves to lose. Whether he was combin'd

15. **they blow,** i.e., to which they (the winds) blow. The witches can control a ship's destination this way. 17. **shipman's card,** compass card, or a chart. 20. **pent-house lid,** eyelid. 21. **forbid,** accursed. 22. **sev'nights,** weeks. 32. **weird,** connected with fate. 33. **Posters of,** travelers over. 44. **choppy,** chapped. 53. **fantastical,** creatures of fantasy or imagination. 54. **show,** appear. 55. **grace,** honor. 66. **happy,** fortunate. 67. **get,** beget. 70. **imperfect,** incomplete. 71. **Sinel's.** Sinel was Macbeth's father. **Glamis,** now a village near Perth; pronounced by the Scots as a monosyllable rhyming with "alms." 81. **corporal,** bodily. 84. **insane root,** root causing insanity. The root of hemlock may be referred to since the eating of it was supposed to cause men to see visions. 90. **reads,** considers. 92-93. **His . . . that,** i.e., your wondrous deeds so outdo any praise he could offer that he is silenced. 97-98. **As thick . . . post,** as fast as could be counted came messenger after messenger. 106. **addition,** title. 108-129. **The . . . gentlemen.** Ross has informed Duncan (I, ii, 48-62) of Cawdor's overthrow, and that Macbeth had defeated him; yet both here seem ignorant of the event. 112. **line,** strengthen. 126. **In**

With those of Norway, or did line the rebel
With hidden help and vantage, or that with both
He labour'd in his country's wrack, I know not;
But treasons capital, confess'd and prov'd,
Have overthrown him.
Macb. [*Aside*] Glamis, and Thane of Cawdor!
The greatest is behind. [*To Ross and Angus*] Thanks for
your pains.
[*To Ban.*] Do you not hope your children shall be
kings,
When those that gave the Thane of Cawdor to me
Promis'd no less to them?
Ban. That trusted home
Might yet enkindle you unto the crown,
Besides the Thane of Cawdor. But 'tis strange:
And oftentimes, to win us to our harm,
The instruments of darkness tell us truths,
Win us with honest trifles, to betray 's
In deepest consequence.
Cousins, a word, I pray you.
Macb. [*Aside*] Two truths are told,
As happy prologues to the swelling act
Of the imperial theme.—I thank you, gentlemen.
[*Aside*] This supernatural soliciting
Cannot be ill, cannot be good: if ill,
Why hath it given me earnest of success,
Commencing in a truth? I am Thane of Cawdor:
If good, why do I yield to that suggestion
Whose horrid image doth unfix my hair
And make my seated heart knock at my ribs,
Against the use of nature? Present fears
Are less than horrible imaginings:
My thought, whose murder yet is but fantastical,
Shakes so my single state of man that function
Is smother'd in surmise, and nothing is
But what is not.
Ban. Look, how our partner 's rapt.
Macb. [*Aside*] If chance will have me king, why,
chance may crown me,
Without my stir.
Ban. New honours come upon him,
Like our strange garments, cleave not to their mould
But with the aid of use.
Macb. [*Aside*] Come what come may,
Time and the hour runs through the roughest day.
Ban. Worthy Macbeth, we stay upon your leisure.
Macb. Give me your favour: my dull brain was
wrought
With things forgotten. Kind gentlemen, your pains
Are regist'red where every day I turn
The leaf to read them. Let us toward the king.
[*To Ban.*] Think upon what hath chanc'd, and, at
more time,
The interim having weigh'd it, let us speak
Our free hearts each to other.
Ban. Very gladly.
Macb. Till then, enough. Come, friends. *Exeunt.*

SCENE IV. [*Forres. The palace.*]

Flourish. Enter King [DUNCAN], LENNOX, MALCOLM, DONALBAIN, *and* Attendants.

Dun. Is execution done on Cawdor? Are not
Those in commission yet return'd?
Mal. My liege,
They are not yet come back. But I have spoke
With one that saw him die: who did report
That very frankly he confess'd his treasons,
Implor'd your highness' pardon and set forth
A deep repentance: nothing in his life
Became him like the leaving it; he died
As one that had been studied in his death
To throw away the dearest thing he ow'd,
As 'twere a careless trifle.
Dun. There 's no art
To find the mind's construction in the face:
He was a gentleman on whom I built
An absolute trust.

Enter MACBETH, BANQUO, ROSS, *and* ANGUS.

O worthiest cousin!
The sin of my ingratitude even now
Was heavy on me: thou art so far before
That swiftest wing of recompense is slow
To overtake thee. Would thou hadst less deserv'd,
That the proportion both of thanks and payment
Might have been mine! only I have left to say,
More is thy due than more than all can pay.
Macb. The service and the loyalty I owe,
In doing it, pays itself. Your highness' part
Is to receive our duties; and our duties
Are to your throne and state children and servants,
Which do but what they should, by doing every thing
Safe toward your love and honour.
Dun. Welcome hither:
I have begun to plant thee, and will labour
To make thee full of growing. Noble Banquo,
That hast no less deserv'd, nor must be known
No less to have done so, let me infold thee
And hold thee to my heart.
Ban. There if I grow,
The harvest is your own.
Dun. My plenteous joys,
Wanton in fulness, seek to hide themselves
In drops of sorrow. Sons, kinsmen, thanes,
And you whose places are the nearest, know
We will establish our estate upon
Our eldest, Malcolm, whom we name hereafter
The Prince of Cumberland; which honour must
Not unaccompanied invest him only,
But signs of nobleness, like stars, shall shine
On all deservers. From hence to Inverness,
And bind us further to you.
Macb. The rest is labour, which is not us'd for you:
I'll be myself the harbinger and make joyful
The hearing of my wife with your approach;

deepest consequence, in the profoundly important sequel. 129. **imperial theme,** theme of empire. 130. **supernatural soliciting,** temptation by supernatural beings. 135. **unfix my hair,** make it stand on end. 140. **single state of man,** whole being; an obvious allusion to the doctrine of the microcosm, according to which the being of man is a counterpart of the macrocosm, or universe. 140-142. **function . . . not,** power of action is lost in speculation and only unreal imaginings have (for me) any reality. 144. **stir,** bestirring (myself). **come,** i.e., which have come. 145. **strange,** new. 149. **favour,** pardon. 153. **at more time,** at a time of greater leisure. 155. **Our free hearts,** our hearts freely.

SCENE IV. 2. **commission,** those having warrant to see to the execution of Cawdor. 10. **ow'd,** owned. 11. **careless,** uncared for. 27. **Safe toward,** securely directed toward. 37. **establish our estate,** fix the succession of our state. 42. **Inverness,** the seat of Macbeth's castle. 45. **harbinger,** forerunner, messenger.

So humbly take my leave.
Dun. My worthy Cawdor!
Macb. [*Aside*] The Prince of Cumberland! that is a step
On which I must fall down, or else o'erleap,
For in my way it lies. Stars, hide your fires;
Let not light see my black and deep desires:
The eye wink at the hand; yet let that be,
Which the eye fears, when it is done, to see. *Exit.*
Dun. True, worthy Banquo; he is full so valiant,
And in his commendations I am fed;
It is a banquet to me. Let 's after him,
Whose care is gone before to bid us welcome:
It is a peerless kinsman. *Flourish. Exeunt.*

SCENE V. [*Inverness. Macbeth's castle.*]

Enter Macbeth's Wife, *alone, with a letter.*

Lady M. 'They met me in the day of success; and I have learned by the perfectest report, they have more in them than mortal knowledge. When I burned in desire to question them further, they made themselves air, into which they vanished. Whiles I stood rapt in the wonder of it, came missives from the king, who all-hailed me "Thane of Cawdor;" by which title, before, these weird sisters saluted me, and referred me to the coming on of time, with "Hail, king that shalt be!" This have I thought good to deliver thee, my dearest partner of greatness, that thou mightst not lose the dues of rejoicing, by being ignorant of what greatness is promised thee. Lay it to thy heart, and farewell.'
Glamis thou art, and Cawdor; and shalt be
What thou art promis'd: yet do I fear thy nature;
It is too full o' th' milk of human kindness
To catch the nearest way: thou wouldst be great;
Art not without ambition, but without
The illness should attend it: what thou wouldst highly,
That wouldst thou holily; wouldst not play false,
And yet wouldst wrongly win: thou 'ldst have, great Glamis,
That which cries 'Thus thou must do,' if thou have it;
And that which rather thou dost fear to do
Than wishest should be undone. Hie thee hither,
That I may pour my spirits in thine ear;
And chastise with the valour of my tongue
All that impedes thee from the golden round,
Which fate and metaphysical aid doth seem
To have thee crown'd withal.

Enter Messenger.

What is your tidings?
Mess. The king comes here to-night.
Lady M. Thou 'rt mad to say it:
Is not thy master with him? who, were 't so,
Would have inform'd for preparation.
Mess. So please you, it is true: our thane is coming:
One of my fellows had the speed of him,
Who, almost dead for breath, had scarcely more
Than would make up his message.
Lady M. Give him tending;
He brings great news. *Exit Messenger.*
The raven himself is hoarse
That croaks the fatal entrance of Duncan
Under my battlements. Come, you spirits
That tend on mortal thoughts, unsex me here,
And fill me from the crown to the toe top-full
Of direst cruelty! make thick my blood;
Stop up th' access and passage to remorse,
That no compunctious visitings of nature
Shake my fell purpose, nor keep peace between
Th' effect and it! Come to my woman's breasts,
And take my milk for gall, you murd'ring ministers,
Wherever in your sightless substances
You wait on nature's mischief! Come, thick night,
And pall thee in the dunnest smoke of hell,
That my keen knife see not the wound it makes,
Nor heaven peep through the blanket of the dark,
To cry 'Hold, hold!'

Enter MACBETH.

Great Glamis! worthy Cawdor!
Greater than both, by the all-hail hereafter!
Thy letters have transported me beyond
This ignorant present, and I feel now
The future in the instant.
Macb. My dearest love,
Duncan comes here to-night.
Lady M. And when goes hence?
Macb. To-morrow, as he purposes.
Lady M. O, never
Shall sun that morrow see!
Your face, my thane, is as a book where men
May read strange matters. To beguile the time,
Look like the time; bear welcome in your eye,
Your hand, your tongue: look like th' innocent flower,
But be the serpent under 't. He that 's coming
Must be provided for: and you shall put
This night's great business into my dispatch;
Which shall to all our nights and days to come
Give solely sovereign sway and masterdom.
Macb. We will speak further.
Lady M. Only look up clear;
To alter favour ever is to fear:
Leave all the rest to me. *Exeunt.*

SCENE VI. [*Before Macbeth's castle.*]

Hautboys and torches. Enter King [DUNCAN], MALCOLM, DONALBAIN, BANQUO, LENNOX, MACDUFF, ROSS, ANGUS, *and* Attendants.

50. **in my way it lies.** Prince of Cumberland was the title of the heir apparent to Duncan's throne. The monarchy was not hereditary, and Macbeth had a right to believe that he himself might be chosen as Duncan's successor; he here states the issue as to whether or not he will interfere with the course of circumstance. 52. **eye wink at the hand,** blind itself to the hand's deed.

SCENE V. 7. **missives,** messengers. 18. **milk of human kindness,** gentleness of human nature. Macbeth is Duncan's *peerless kinsman* (I, iv, 58), and this is another testimony to the uprightness of his character when the play begins. 21. **illness,** ruthlessness. 25-26. **And that . . . undone,** i.e., your fears to achieve what you desire exceed your wish to see the thing accomplished. 29. **golden round,** the crown. 30. **metaphysical,** supernatural. 34. **inform'd for preparation,** sent me word so that I might get things ready. 36. **had the speed of,** outstripped. 42. **tend . . . thoughts,** are the instruments of deadly or murderous thoughts. The spirits conveying various passions were the tools of thought. **mortal,** deadly. 44-45. **make . . . remorse.** By making the blood thick it would be less able to flow out in generous passions and thus awaken remorse or pity. 46. **compunctious . . . nature,** natural feelings of pity and conscience. 47. **fell,** fierce. 49. **for gall,** in exchange for gall. **murd'ring ministers,** evil angels. 50. **sightless,** invisible. 51. **wait on,** attend, assist. 52. **pall,** envelope. **dunnest,** darkest. 59. **instant,** present. 69. **dispatch,** management. 72. **look up clear,** give the appearance of being untroubled. 73. **To . . . fear,** to show a troubled countenance is to incur risk.

SCENE VI. 3. **gentle senses,** a case of transferred epithet. It is the

Dun. This castle hath a pleasant seat; the air
Nimbly and sweetly recommends itself
Unto our gentle senses.
Ban. This guest of summer,
The temple-haunting martlet, does approve,
By his lov'd mansionry, that the heaven's breath
Smells wooingly here: no jutty, frieze,
Buttress, nor coign of vantage, but this bird
Hath made his pendent bed and procreant cradle:
Where they most breed and haunt, I have observ'd,
The air is delicate.

Enter LADY [MACBETH].

Dun. See, see, our honour'd hostess!
The love that follows us sometime is our trouble,
Which still we thank as love. Herein I teach you
How you shall bid God 'ild us for your pains,
And thank us for your trouble.
Lady M. All our service
In every point twice done and then done double
Were poor and single business to contend
Against those honours deep and broad wherewith
Your majesty loads our house: for those of old,
And the late dignities heap'd up to them,
We rest your hermits.
Dun. Where 's the Thane of Cawdor?
We cours'd him at the heels, and had a purpose
To be his purveyor: but he rides well;
And his great love, sharp as his spur, hath holp him
To his home before us. Fair and noble hostess,
We are your guest to-night.
Lady M. Your servants ever
Have theirs, themselves and what is theirs, in compt,
To make their audit at your highness' pleasure,
Still to return your own.
Dun. Give me your hand;
Conduct me to mine host: we love him highly,
And shall continue our graces towards him.
By your leave, hostess. *Exeunt.*

SCENE VII. [*Macbeth's castle.*]

Hautboys [*and*] *torches. Enter a* Sewer, *and divers* Servants *with dishes and service,* [*and pass*] *over the stage. Then enter* MACBETH.

Macb. If it were done when 'tis done, then 'twere well
It were done quickly: if th' assassination
Could trammel up the consequence, and catch
With his surcease success; that but this blow
Might be the be-all and the end-all here,
But here, upon this bank and shoal of time,
We 'ld jump the life to come. But in these cases
We still have judgement here; that we but teach
Bloody instructions, which, being taught, return
To plague th' inventor: this even-handed justice
Commends th' ingredients of our poison'd chalice
To our own lips. He 's here in double trust;
First, as I am his kinsman and his subject,
Strong both against the deed; then, as his host,
Who should against his murderer shut the door,
Not bear the knife myself. Besides, this Duncan
Hath borne his faculties so meek, hath been
So clear in his great office, that his virtues
Will plead like angels, trumpet-tongu'd, against
The deep damnation of his taking-off;
And pity, like a naked new-born babe,
Striding the blast, or heaven's cherubim, hors'd
Upon the sightless couriers of the air,
Shall blow the horrid deed in every eye,
That tears shall drown the wind. I have no spur
To prick the sides of my intent, but only
Vaulting ambition, which o'erleaps itself
And falls on th' other.

Enter LADY [MACBETH].

How now! what news?
Lady M. He has almost supp'd: why have you left the chamber?
Macb. Hath he ask'd for me?
Lady M. Know you not he has?
Macb. We will proceed no further in this business:
He hath honour'd me of late; and I have bought
Golden opinions from all sorts of people,
Which would be worn now in their newest gloss,
Not cast aside so soon.
Lady M. Was the hope drunk
Wherein you dress'd yourself? hath it slept since?
And wakes it now, to look so green and pale
At what it did so freely? From this time
Such I account thy love. Art thou afeard
To be the same in thine own act and valour
As thou art in desire? Wouldst thou have that
Which thou esteem'st the ornament of life,
And live a coward in thine own esteem,
Letting 'I dare not' wait upon 'I would,'
Like the poor cat i' th' adage?
Macb. Prithee, peace:
I dare do all that may become a man;
Who dares do more is none.
Lady M. What beast was 't, then,
That made you break this enterprise to me?
When you durst do it, then you were a man;
And, to be more than what you were, you would
Be so much more the man. Nor time nor place
Did then adhere, and yet you would make both:
They have made themselves, and that their fitness now
Does unmake you. I have given suck, and know
How tender 'tis to love the babe that milks me:
I would, while it was smiling in my face,

air which seems gentle to the senses. 6. **jutty,** projection of wall or building. 7. **coign of vantage,** convenient corner, i.e., for nesting. 10. **delicate,** delicious. 11. **follows,** attends. **sometime,** sometimes. 13. **God 'ild us,** God reward us, i.e., thank us. Duncan means that, since he is there because he loves them, they should thank him even for the trouble he causes them. 16. **single,** small, inconsiderable. 16-17. **contend Against,** vie with. 20. **rest,** remain. **hermits,** i.e., those who will pray for you like hermits or beadsmen. 22. **purveyor,** an officer sent ahead of the king to provide for his entertainment; here, forerunner. 26. **in compt,** under obligation (to serve the king).

SCENE VII. *Stage Direction:* ***Hautboys,*** wooden double-reed musical instruments. **Sewer,** chief servant who directed the placing of dishes on the table, or the servant who acted as taster and guard against poison. 3. **trammel up,** entangle in a net, prevent. 4. **surcease,** cessation. 6. **shoal,** so Theobald; F: *schoole*, which may be construed with *bank* (meaning bench) and with lines 8-10. 17. **faculties,** prerogatives. 20. **taking-off,** murder. 28. **other,** i.e., the other side of my intent. 45. **adage,** "The cate would eate fyshe, and would not wet her feete" (Heywood). 47-51. **beast . . . man,** if you are a man, it must have been a beast that prompted you to *break* (disclose) this enterprise to me; if it is unmanly to do the deed, it was unmanly to suggest it. 52. **adhere,** agree, suit. 53. **that their fitness,** their very suitability.

Have pluck'd my nipple from his boneless gums,
And dash'd the brains out, had I so sworn as you
Have done to this.

Macb. If we should fail?

Lady M. We fail!
But screw your courage to the sticking-place,
And we'll not fail. When Duncan is asleep—
Whereto the rather shall his day's hard journey
Soundly invite him—his two chamberlains
Will I with wine and wassail so convince
That memory, the warder of the brain,
Shall be a fume, and the receipt of reason
A limbeck only: when in swinish sleep
Their drenched natures lie as in a death,
What cannot you and I perform upon
Th' unguarded Duncan? what not put upon
His spongy officers, who shall bear the guilt
Of our great quell?

Macb. Bring forth men-children only;
For thy undaunted mettle should compose
Nothing but males. Will it not be receiv'd,
When we have mark'd with blood those sleepy two
Of his own chamber and us'd their very daggers,
That they have done 't?

Lady M. Who dares receive it other,
As we shall make our griefs and clamour roar
Upon his death?

Macb. I am settled, and bend up
Each corporal agent to this terrible feat.
Away, and mock the time with fairest show:
False face must hide what the false heart doth know.

Exeunt.

ACT II.

SCENE I. [*Court of Macbeth's castle.*]

Enter BANQUO, *and* FLEANCE, [*with*] *a torch before him.*

Ban. How goes the night, boy?

Fle. The moon is down; I have not heard the clock.

Ban. And she goes down at twelve.

Fle. I take 't, 'tis later, sir.

Ban. Hold, take my sword. There 's husbandry in heaven;
Their candles are all out. Take thee that too.
A heavy summons lies like lead upon me,
And yet I would not sleep: merciful powers,
Restrain in me the cursed thoughts that nature
Gives way to in repose!

Enter MACBETH, *and a* Servant *with a torch.*

Give me my sword.
Who 's there?

Macb. A friend.

Ban. What, sir, not yet at rest? The king 's a-bed:
He hath been in unusual pleasure, and
Sent forth great largess to your offices.
This diamond he greets your wife withal,
By the name of most kind hostess; and shut up
In measureless content.

Macb. Being unprepar'd,
Our will became the servant to defect;
Which else should free have wrought.

Ban. All 's well.
I dreamt last night of the three weird sisters:
To you they have show'd some truth.

Macb. I think not of them:
Yet, when we can entreat an hour to serve,
We would spend it in some words upon that business,
If you would grant the time.

Ban. At your kind'st leisure.

Macb. If you shall cleave to my consent, when 'tis,
It shall make honour for you.

Ban. So I lose none
In seeking to augment it, but still keep
My bosom franchis'd and allegiance clear,
I shall be counsell'd.

Macb. Good repose the while!

Ban. Thanks, sir: the like to you!

Exit Banquo [*with Fleance*].

Macb. Go bid thy mistress, when my drink is ready,
She strike upon the bell. Get thee to bed. *Exit* [*Servant*].
Is this a dagger which I see before me,
The handle toward my hand? Come, let me clutch thee.
I have thee not, and yet I see thee still.
Art thou not, fatal vision, sensible
To feeling as to sight? or art thou but
A dagger of the mind, a false creation,
Proceeding from the heat-oppressed brain?
I see thee yet, in form as palpable
As this which now I draw.
Thou marshall'st me the way that I was going;
And such an instrument I was to use.
Mine eyes are made the fools o' th' other senses,
Or else worth all the rest; I see thee still,
And on thy blade and dudgeon gouts of blood,
Which was not so before. There 's no such thing:
It is the bloody business which informs
Thus to mine eyes. Now o'er the one half-world
Nature seems dead, and wicked dreams abuse
The curtain'd sleep; witchcraft celebrates
Pale Hecate's offerings, and wither'd murder,
Alarum'd by his sentinel, the wolf,
Whose howl 's his watch, thus with his stealthy pace,
With Tarquin's ravishing strides, towards his design
Moves like a ghost. Thou sure and firm-set earth,
Hear not my steps, which way they walk, for fear
Thy very stones prate of my whereabout,
And take the present horror from the time,
Which now suits with it. Whiles I threat, he lives:
Words to the heat of deeds too cold breath gives.

A bell rings.

60. **sticking-place,** the notch into which is fitted the string of a cross-bow cranked taut for shooting. 64. **wassail,** carousal, drink. **convince,** overpower. 65-67. **warder . . . only.** The brain was divided into three ventricles, imagination in front, memory at the back, and between them the seat of reason. The fumes of wine would deaden memory and judgment. 67. **limbeck,** alembic, still. 70. **put upon,** attribute to. 71. **spongy,** drunken. 72. **quell,** murder. 74. **receiv'd,** as truth. 77. **other,** otherwise. 79. **settled,** determined. 79-80. **bend . . . feat.** The language all the way through the passage about the deed is not primarily figurative, but drawn from current psychology. A stiffly maintained head of passion is necessary for action. *To alter favour ever is to fear* (I, v, 73); hence, the bodily agents must be immovable, the blood thick, and the passage to remorse closed.

ACT II. SCENE I. 4. **husbandry,** economy. 6. **summons,** i.e., to sleep. 14. **largess,** gifts, gratuities. **offices,** servants' quarters. 18. **Our will . . . defect,** our good will (to entertain the king handsomely) was limited by our meager means (at such short notice). 25. **If . . . 'tis,** if you give me your support when the fulfillment occurs. 28. **franchis'd,** free (from guilt). **clear,** unstained. 46. **dudgeon,** hilt of a dagger. **gouts,** drops. 52. **Hecate's.** Hecate was the goddess of

I go, and it is done; the bell invites me.
Hear it not, Duncan; for it is a knell
That summons thee to heaven or to hell. *Exit.*

SCENE II. [*The same.*]

Enter LADY [MACBETH].

Lady M. That which hath made them drunk hath made me bold;
What hath quench'd them hath given me fire. Hark! Peace!
It was the owl that shriek'd, the fatal bellman,
Which gives the stern'st good-night. He is about it:
The doors are open; and the surfeited grooms
Do mock their charge with snores: I have drugg'd their possets,
That death and nature do contend about them,
Whether they live or die.
Macb. [*Within*] Who 's there? what, ho!
Lady M. Alack, I am afraid they have awak'd,
And 'tis not done. Th' attempt and not the deed
Confounds us. Hark! I laid their daggers ready;
He could not miss 'em. Had he not resembled
My father as he slept, I had done 't.

Enter MACBETH.

My husband!
Macb. I have done the deed. Didst thou not hear a noise?
Lady M. I heard the owl scream and the crickets cry.
Did not you speak?
Macb. When?
Lady M. Now.
Macb. As I descended?
Lady M. Ay.
Macb. Hark!
Who lies i' th' second chamber?
Lady M. Donalbain.
Macb. This is a sorry sight. [*Looking on his hands.*]
Lady M. A foolish thought, to say a sorry sight.
Macb. There 's one did laugh in 's sleep, and one cried 'Murder!'
That they did wake each other: I stood and heard them:
But they did say their prayers, and address'd them
Again to sleep.
Lady M. There are two lodg'd together.
Macb. One cried 'God bless us!' and 'Amen' the other;
As they had seen me with these hangman's hands.
List'ning their fear, I could not say 'Amen,'
When they did say 'God bless us!'
Lady M. Consider it not so deeply.
Macb. But wherefore could not I pronounce 'Amen'?
I had most need of blessing, and 'Amen'
Stuck in my throat.
Lady M. These deeds must not be thought
After these ways; so, it will make us mad.
Macb. Methought I heard a voice cry 'Sleep no more!
Macbeth does murder sleep,' the innocent sleep,
Sleep that knits up the ravell'd sleave of care,
The death of each day's life, sore labour's bath,
Balm of hurt minds, great nature's second course,
Chief nourisher in life's feast,—
Lady M. What do you mean?
Macb. Still it cried 'Sleep no more!' to all the house:
'Glamis hath murder'd sleep, and therefore Cawdor
Shall sleep no more; Macbeth shall sleep no more.'
Lady M. Who was it that thus cried? Why, worthy thane,
You do unbend your noble strength, to think
So brainsickly of things. Go get some water,
And wash this filthy witness from your hand.
Why did you bring these daggers from the place?
They must lie there: go carry them; and smear
The sleepy grooms with blood.
Macb. I'll go no more:
I am afraid to think what I have done;
Look on 't again I dare not.
Lady M. Infirm of purpose!
Give me the daggers: the sleeping and the dead
Are but as pictures: 'tis the eye of childhood
That fears a painted devil. If he do bleed,
I'll gild the faces of the grooms withal;
For it must seem their guilt. *Exit. Knock within.*
Macb. Whence is that knocking?
How is 't with me, when every noise appals me?
What hands are here? ha! they pluck out mine eyes.
Will all great Neptune's ocean wash this blood
Clean from my hand? No, this my hand will rather
The multitudinous seas incarnadine,
Making the green one red.

Enter LADY [MACBETH].

Lady M. My hands are of your colour; but I shame
To wear a heart so white. (*Knock.*) I hear a knocking
At the south entry: retire we to our chamber:
A little water clears us of this deed:
How easy is it, then! Your constancy
Hath left you unattended. (*Knock.*) Hark! more knocking.
Get on your nightgown, lest occasion call us,
And show us to be watchers. Be not lost
So poorly in your thoughts.
Macb. To know my deed, 'twere best not know myself. (*Knock.*)
Wake Duncan with thy knocking! I would thou couldst! *Exeunt.*

---

witchcraft. 55. **Tarquin's.** Tarquin was a Roman tyrant who ravished Lucrece. 59-60. **take . . . with it,** and thus shatter the horrible silence which is so suited to this evil hour(?).

SCENE II. 3. **bellman,** night-watch. 4. **stern'st good-night,** i.e., a notice to condemned criminals that they are to be executed in the morning. 5. **grooms,** servants. 6. **possets,** hot milk poured on ale or wine and spiced, a bedtime drink common at the time. 21. **sorry,** wretched. 25. **address'd them,** settled themselves. 29. **List'ning,** listening to. 37. **ravell'd sleave,** tangled skein. 39. **second course.** Ordinary feasts had two courses; only the more elaborate ones had three; hence, the second course was the *chief nourisher* and the conclusion of the feast. 46. **brainsickly,** insanely, madly. 56-57. **gild . . . guilt.** The pun would be more obvious to Shakespeare's audience than to us, for gold was ordinarily thought of as red. 62. **incarnadine,** make red. 63. **one red,** one all-pervading red. F has *Making the Greene one, Red,* which some editors have followed. 64. **shame,** am ashamed. 68-69. **Your . . . unattended,** your firmness has deserted you. 70. **nightgown,** dressing gown. 72. **poorly,** dejectedly. 73. **To . . . deed.** It were better to be lost in my thoughts than to have consciousness of my deed.

SCENE III. [*The same.*]

Knocking within. Enter a Porter.

Porter. Here 's a knocking indeed! If a man were porter of hell-gate, he should have old turning the key. (*Knock.*) Knock, knock, knock! Who 's there, i' the name of Beelzebub? Here 's a farmer, that hanged himself on the expectation of plenty: come in time; have napkins enow about you; here you'll sweat for 't. (*Knock.*) Knock, knock! Who 's there, in the other devil's name? Faith, here 's an equivocator, that could swear in both the scales against either scale; who committed treason enough for God's sake, yet could not equivocate to heaven: O, come in, equivocator. (*Knock.*) Knock, knock, knock! Who 's there? Faith, here 's an English tailor come hither, for stealing out of a French hose: come in, tailor; here you may roast your goose. (*Knock.*) Knock, knock; never at quiet! What are you? But this place is too cold for hell. I'll devil-porter it no further: I had thought to have let in some of all professions that go the primrose way to the everlasting bonfire. (*Knock.*) Anon, anon! I pray you, remember the porter. [*Opens the gate.*]

Enter MACDUFF *and* LENNOX.

Macd. Was it so late, friend, ere you went to bed,
That you do lie so late?

Port. 'Faith, sir, we were carousing till the second cock: and drink, sir, is a great provoker of three things.

Macd. What three things does drink especially provoke?

Port. Marry, sir, nose-painting, sleep, and urine. Lechery, sir, it provokes, and unprovokes; it provokes the desire, but it takes away the performance: therefore, much drink may be said to be an equivocator with lechery: it makes him, and it mars him; it sets him on, and it takes him off; it persuades him, and disheartens him; makes him stand to, and not stand to; in conclusion, equivocates him in a sleep, and, giving him the lie, leaves him.

Macd. I believe drink gave thee the lie last night.

Port. That it did, sir, i' the very throat on me: but I requited him for his lie; and, I think, being too strong for him, though he took up my legs sometime, yet I made a shift to cast him.

Macd. Is thy master stirring?

Enter MACBETH.

Our knocking has awak'd him; here he comes.

Len. Good morrow, noble sir.

Macb. Good morrow, both.

Macd. Is the king stirring, worthy thane?

Macb. Not yet.

Macd. He did command me to call timely on him:
I have almost slipp'd the hour.

Macb. I'll bring you to him.

Macd. I know this is a joyful trouble to you;
But yet 'tis one.

Macb. The labour we delight in physics pain.
This is the door.

Macd. I'll make so bold to call,
For 'tis my limited service. *Exit Macd.*

Len. Goes the king hence to-day?

Macb. He does: he did appoint so.

Len. The night has been unruly: where we lay,
Our chimneys were blown down; and, as they say,
Lamentings heard i' th' air; strange screams of death,
And prophesying with accents terrible
Of dire combustion and confus'd events
New hatch'd to th' woeful time: the obscure bird
Clamour'd the livelong night: some say, the earth
Was feverous and did shake.

Macb. 'Twas a rough night.

Len. My young remembrance cannot parallel
A fellow to it.

Enter MACDUFF.

Macd. O horror, horror, horror! Tongue nor heart
Cannot conceive nor name thee!

Macb. }
Len. } What 's the matter?

Macd. Confusion now hath made his masterpiece!
Most sacrilegious murder hath broke ope
The Lord's anointed temple, and stole thence
The life o' th' building!

Macb. What is 't you say? the life?

Len. Mean you his majesty?

Macd. Approach the chamber, and destroy your sight
With a new Gorgon: do not bid me speak;
See, and then speak yourselves.
Exeunt Macbeth and Lennox.
Awake, awake!
Ring the alarum-bell. Murder and treason!
Banquo and Donalbain! Malcolm! awake!
Shake off this downy sleep, death's counterfeit,
And look on death itself! up, up, and see
The great doom's image! Malcolm! Banquo!
As from your graves rise up, and walk like sprites,
To countenance this horror! Ring the bell. *Bell rings.*

Enter LADY [MACBETH].

Lady M. What 's the business,
That such a hideous trumpet calls to parley
The sleepers of the house? speak, speak!

Macd. O gentle lady,
'Tis not for you to hear what I can speak:
The repetition, in a woman's ear,
Would murder as it fell.

Enter BANQUO.

O Banquo, Banquo,
Our royal master's murder'd!

Lady M. Woe, alas!

SCENE III. 3. **old,** colloquial use, meaning "plenty of." 5-6. **Here 's a farmer . . . plenty.** This is thought to allude to the conditions of the year 1606 when there were abundant harvests and low prices. (The farmer, who has hoarded in anticipation of a scarcity, will be justly punished by a crop surplus and low prices.) 7. **come in time,** you have come in good time. 10. **equivocator.** This is regarded as an allusion to the trial of the Jesuit Henry Garnet for treason in the spring of 1606, and to the doctrine of equivocation said to have been presented in his defense; according to this doctrine a lie was not a lie if the utterer had in his mind a different meaning in which the utterance was true. 17. **French hose,** very narrow breeches and therefore hard for the tailor to steal cloth from when he made them. 18. **goose,** tailor's smoothing iron. 27. **cock,** cockcrow. 46. **cast,** throw (with pun on "vomit"). 51. **timely,** betimes, early. 52. **slipp'd,** let slip. 55. **physics,** cures. 57. **limited,** appointed. 64. **obscure bird,** owl, the bird of darkness. 71. **Confusion,** destruction. 73. **The Lord's anointed temple,** allusion to the king as God's anointed representative. 77. **Gorgon,** allusion to the monsters of Greek mythology whose look turned the beholders to stone. 85. **countenance,** be in keeping with. 98. **mortality,** mortal life. 100. **lees,** dregs. 101. **vault,** wine-vault; also, earth. 107.

What, in our house?
Ban. Too cruel any where.
Dear Duff, I prithee, contradict thyself,
And say it is not so.

Enter MACBETH, LENNOX, *and* ROSS.

Macb. Had I but died an hour before this chance,
I had liv'd a blessed time; for, from this instant,
There 's nothing serious in mortality:
All is but toys: renown and grace is dead;
The wine of life is drawn, and the mere lees
Is left this vault to brag of.

Enter MALCOLM *and* DONALBAIN.

Don. What is amiss?
Macb. You are, and do not know 't:
The spring, the head, the fountain of your blood
Is stopp'd; the very source of it is stopp'd.
Macd. Your royal father 's murder'd.
Mal. O, by whom?
Len. Those of his chamber, as it seem'd, had done 't:
Their hands and faces were all badg'd with blood;
So were their daggers, which unwip'd we found
Upon their pillows:
They star'd, and were distracted; no man's life
Was to be trusted with them.
Macb. O, yet I do repent me of my fury,
That I did kill them.
Macd. Wherefore did you so?
Macb. Who can be wise, amaz'd, temp'rate and furious,
Loyal and neutral, in a moment? No man:
Th' expedition of my violent love
Outrun the pauser, reason. Here lay Duncan,
His silver skin lac'd with his golden blood;
And his gash'd stabs look'd like a breach in nature
For ruin's wasteful entrance: there, the murderers,
Steep'd in the colours of their trade, their daggers
Unmannerly breech'd with gore: who could refrain,
That had a heart to love, and in that heart
Courage to make 's love known?
Lady M. Help me hence, ho!
Macd. Look to the lady.
Mal. [*Aside to Don.*] Why do we hold our tongues,
That most may claim this argument for ours?
Don. [*Aside to Mal.*] What should be spoken here, where our fate,
Hid in an auger-hole, may rush, and seize us?
Let 's away;
Our tears are not yet brew'd.
Mal. [*Aside to Don.*] Nor our strong sorrow
Upon the foot of motion.
Ban. Look to the lady:
[*Lady Macbeth is carried out.*]
And when we have our naked frailties hid,
That suffer in exposure, let us meet,
And question this most bloody piece of work,
To know it further. Fears and scruples shake us:
In the great hand of God I stand; and thence
Against the undivulg'd pretence I fight
Of treasonous malice.
Macd. And so do I.
All. So all.
Macb. Let 's briefly put on manly readiness,
And meet i' th' hall together.
All. Well contented.
Exeunt [*all but Malcolm and Donalbain*].
Mal. What will you do? Let 's not consort with them:
To show an unfelt sorrow is an office
Which the false man does easy. I'll to England.
Don. To Ireland, I; our separated fortune
Shall keep us both the safer: where we are,
There 's daggers in men's smiles: the near in blood,
The nearer bloody.
Mal. This murderous shaft that 's shot
Hath not yet lighted, and our safest way
Is to avoid the aim. Therefore, to horse;
And let us not be dainty of leave-taking,
But shift away: there 's warrant in that theft
Which steals itself, when there 's no mercy left. *Exeunt.*

SCENE IV. [*Outside Macbeth's castle.*]

Enter ROSS *with an* old Man.

Old M. Threescore and ten I can remember well:
Within the volume of which time I have seen
Hours dreadful and things strange; but this sore night
Hath trifled former knowings.
Ross. Ah, good father,
Thou seest, the heavens, as troubled with man's act,
Threatens his bloody stage: by th' clock, 'tis day,
And yet dark night strangles the travelling lamp:
Is 't night's predominance, or the day's shame,
That darkness does the face of earth entomb,
When living light should kiss it?
Old M. 'Tis unnatural,
Even like the deed that 's done. On Tuesday last,
A falcon, tow'ring in her pride of place,
Was by a mousing owl hawk'd at and kill'd.
Ross. And Duncan's horses—a thing most strange and certain—
Beauteous and swift, the minions of their race,
Turn'd wild in nature, broke their stalls, flung out,
Contending 'gainst obedience, as they would make
War with mankind.
Old M. 'Tis said they eat each other.
Ross. They did so, to th' amazement of mine eyes
That look'd upon 't.

Enter MACDUFF.

Here comes the good Macduff.
How goes the world, sir, now?

badg'd, marked as with a badge or emblem. 116. **expedition,** haste. 122. **breech'd,** covered to the hilts with gore (as with breeches). 124. **Help me hence, ho!** This timely fainting of Lady Macbeth is usually taken as pretense in order to make a diversion in behalf of her husband, but it need not be so understood. 126. **argument,** topic, business. 128. **in an auger-hole,** in some obscure place. 131. **Upon . . . . motion,** yet in motion. 132. **frailties hid,** bodies clothed. 135. **scruples,** doubts. 136-138. **and thence . . . malice.** With God's help I will fight against the as-yet-unknown purpose which prompted this treason. 139. **manly readiness,** men's clothing, or armor. 143. **easy,** easily. 146. **near,** nearer, i.e., the nearer in relationship the greater the danger of being murdered. 148. **lighted,** descended.

SCENE IV. 4. **trifled . . . knowings,** made trivial all former knowledge. 7. **travelling lamp,** i.e., the sun. 8. **predominance,** ascendancy, superior influence (of a heavenly body). 12. **tow'ring,** soaring (term in falconry). **place,** pitch, highest point in the falcon's flight. 14. **horses,** pronounced as one syllable, indicating the old form of the plural then in common use. 15. **minions,** darlings.

Macd. Why, see you not?
Ross. Is 't known who did this more than bloody deed?
Macd. Those that Macbeth hath slain.
Ross. Alas, the day!
What good could they pretend?
Macd. They were suborn'd:
Malcolm and Donalbain, the king's two sons,
Are stol'n away and fled; which puts upon them
Suspicion of the deed.
Ross. 'Gainst nature still!
Thriftless ambition, that wilt ravin up
Thine own life's means! Then 'tis most like
The sovereignty will fall upon Macbeth.
Macd. He is already nam'd, and gone to Scone
To be invested.
Ross. Where is Duncan's body?
Macd. Carried to Colmekill,
The sacred storehouse of his predecessors,
And guardian of their bones.
Ross. Will you to Scone?
Macd. No, cousin, I'll to Fife.
Ross. Well, I will thither.
Macd. Well, may you see things well done there: adieu!
Lest our old robes sit easier than our new!
Ross. Farewell, father.
Old M. God's benison go with you; and with those
That would make good of bad, and friends of foes!
Exeunt omnes.

ACT III.

SCENE I. [*Forres. The palace.*]

Enter BANQUO.

Ban. Thou hast it now: king, Cawdor, Glamis, all,
As the weird women promis'd, and, I fear,
Thou play'dst most foully for 't: yet it was said
It should not stand in thy posterity,
But that myself should be the root and father
Of many kings. If there come truth from them—
As upon thee, Macbeth, their speeches shine—
Why, by the verities on thee made good,
May they not be my oracles as well,
And set me up in hope? But hush! no more.

Sennet sounded. Enter MACBETH, *as king*, LADY [MACBETH], LENNOX, ROSS, LORDS, *and* Attendants.

Macb. Here 's our chief guest.
Lady M. If he had been forgotten,
It had been as a gap in our great feast,
And all-thing unbecoming.
Macb. To-night we hold a solemn supper, sir,
And I'll request your presence.
Ban. Let your highness
Command upon me; to the which my duties
Are with a most indissoluble tie
For ever knit.
Macb. Ride you this afternoon?
Ban. Ay, my good lord.
Macb. We should have else desir'd your good advice,
Which still hath been both grave and prosperous,
In this day's council; but we'll take to-morrow.
Is 't far you ride?
Ban. As far, my lord, as will fill up the time
'Twixt this and supper: go not my horse the better,
I must become a borrower of the night
For a dark hour or twain.
Macb. Fail not our feast.
Ban. My lord, I will not.
Macb. We hear, our bloody cousins are bestow'd
In England and in Ireland, not confessing
Their cruel parricide, filling their hearers
With strange invention: but of that to-morrow,
When therewithal we shall have cause of state
Craving us jointly. Hie you to horse: adieu,
Till you return at night. Goes Fleance with you?
Ban. Ay, my good lord: our time does call upon 's.
Macb. I wish your horses swift and sure of foot;
And so I do commend you to their backs.
Farewell. *Exit Banquo.*
Let every man be master of his time
Till seven at night: to make society
The sweeter welcome, we will keep ourself
Till supper-time alone: while then, God be with you!
Exeunt Lords. [*Manet Macbeth, and a servant.*]
Sirrah, a word with you: attend those men
Our pleasure?
Serv. They are, my lord, without the palace gate.
Macb. Bring them before us. *Exit Servant.*
To be thus is nothing;
But to be safely thus.—Our fears in Banquo
Stick deep; and in his royalty of nature
Reigns that which would be fear'd: 'tis much he dares;
And, to that dauntless temper of his mind,
He hath a wisdom that doth guide his valour
To act in safety. There is none but he
Whose being I do fear: and, under him,
My Genius is rebuk'd; as, it is said,
Mark Antony's was by Cæsar. He chid the sisters
When first they put the name of king upon me,
And bade them speak to him: then prophet-like
They hail'd him father to a line of kings:
Upon my head they plac'd a fruitless crown,
And put a barren sceptre in my gripe,
Thence to be wrench'd with an unlineal hand,
No son of mine succeeding. If 't be so,
For Banquo's issue have I fil'd my mind;
For them the gracious Duncan have I murder'd;
Put rancours in the vessel of my peace
Only for them; and mine eternal jewel

24. **pretend,** hope for. **suborn'd,** procured to do an evil action. 28. **Thriftless,** wasteful. **ravin up,** devour ravenously. 31. **nam'd,** elected. **Scone,** ancient royal city of Scotland near Perth. The stone of Scone, on which Jacob rested this head at Bethel, was carried to England by Edward I. It has ever since formed a part of the coronation chair of English kings in Westminster Abbey. 33. **Colmekill,** Icolmkill, i.e., Cell of St. Columba, the barren islet of Iona in the Western Islands, a sacred spot where the kings were buried; here called a *storehouse.* 40. **benison,** blessing.

ACT III. SCENE I. 7. **shine,** are brilliantly manifest. 13. **all-thing,** in every way. 14. **solemn,** ceremonious. 30. **bestow'd,** lodged. 33. **invention,** falsehood. 34. **cause of state,** questions of state. 44. **while,** till. 48-49. **To . . . thus.** This is explained in several ways, of which the following is perhaps correct: "To be thus (i.e., on the throne) is nothing unless we are safely on the throne." 52-54. **to that . . . safety.** Macbeth here attributes to Banquo the perfect virtue of courage. 56. **My Genius.** This passage is a borrowing from Plutarch's *Life of Antony;* Antony's good angel was abashed before that of Octavius. Cf. *Antony and Cleopatra,* II, iii. 62. **gripe,** grasp. 65. **fil'd,** defiled. 68-69. **mine . . . man.** Macbeth had understood his bargain when he professed a willingness to

Given to the common enemy of man,
To make them kings, the seeds of Banquo kings!
Rather than so, come fate into the list,
And champion me to th' utterance! Who 's there?

Enter Servant *and two* Murderers.

Now go to the door, and stay there till we call.
Exit Servant.
Was it not yesterday we spoke together?
Murderers. It was, so please your highness.
Macb. Well then, now
Have you consider'd of my speeches? Know
That it was he in the times past which held you
So under fortune, which you thought had been
Our innocent self: this I made good to you
In our last conference, pass'd in probation with you,
How you were borne in hand, how cross'd, the instruments,
Who wrought with them, and all things else that might
To half a soul and to a notion craz'd
Say 'Thus did Banquo.'
First Mur. You made it known to us.
Macb. I did so, and went further, which is now
Our point of second meeting. Do you find
Your patience so predominant in your nature
That you can let this go? Are you so gospell'd
To pray for this good man and for his issue,
Whose heavy hand hath bow'd you to the grave
And beggar'd yours for ever?
First Mur. We are men, my liege.
Macb. Ay, in the catalogue ye go for men;
As hounds and greyhounds, mongrels, spaniels, curs,
Shoughs, water-rugs and demi-wolves are clept
All by the name of dogs: the valued file
Distinguishes the swift, the slow, the subtle,
The housekeeper, the hunter, every one
According to the gift which bounteous nature
Hath in him clos'd, whereby he does receive
Particular addition, from the bill
That writes them all alike: and so of men.
Now, if you have a station in the file,
Not i' th' worst rank of manhood, say 't;
And I will put that business in your bosoms,
Whose execution takes your enemy off,
Grapples you to the heart and love of us,
Who wear our health but sickly in his life,
Which in his death were perfect.
Sec. Mur. I am one, my liege,
Whom the vile blows and buffets of the world
Hath so incens'd that I am reckless what
I do to spite the world.
First Mur. And I another
So weary with disasters, tugg'd with fortune,
That I would set my life on any chance,
To mend it, or be rid on 't.
Macb. Both of you
Know Banquo was your enemy.
Both Mur. True, my lord.
Macb. So is he mine; and in such bloody distance,
That every minute of his being thrusts
Against my near'st of life: and though I could
With barefac'd power sweep him from my sight
And bid my will avouch it, yet I must not,
For certain friends that are both his and mine,
Whose loves I may not drop, but wail his fall
Who I myself struck down; and thence it is,
That I to your assistance do make love,
Masking the business from the common eye
For sundry weighty reasons.
Sec. Mur. We shall, my lord,
Perform what you command us.
First Mur. Though our lives—
Macb. Your spirits shine through you. Within this hour at most
I will advise you where to plant yourselves;
Acquaint you with the perfect spy o' th' time,
The moment on 't; for 't must be done to-night,
And something from the palace; always thought
That I require a clearness: and with him—
To leave no rubs nor botches in the work—
Fleance his son, that keeps him company,
Whose absence is no less material to me
Than is his father's, must embrace the fate
Of that dark hour. Resolve yourselves apart:
I'll come to you anon.
Both Mur. We are resolv'd, my lord.
Macb. I'll call upon you straight: abide within.
Exeunt [*Murderers*].
It is concluded. Banquo, thy soul's flight,
If it find heaven, must find it out to-night. [*Exit.*]

SCENE II. [*The palace.*]

Enter MACBETH'S LADY *and a* Servant.

Lady M. Is Banquo gone from court?
Serv. Ay, madam, but returns again to-night.
Lady M. Say to the king, I would attend his leisure
For a few words.
Serv. Madam, I will. *Exit.*
Lady M. Nought 's had, all 's spent,
Where our desire is got without content:
'Tis safer to be that which we destroy
Than by destruction dwell in doubtful joy.

Enter MACBETH.

How now, my lord! why do you keep alone,
Of sorriest fancies your companions making,
Using those thoughts which should indeed have died
With them they think on? Things without all remedy
Should be without regard: what 's done is done.
Macb. We have scorch'd the snake, not kill'd it:
She'll close and be herself, whilst our poor malice
Remains in danger of her former tooth.

jump the life to come (I, vii, 7); he here acknowledges it. 71. **list,** lists, place of combat. 72. **champion me,** fight with me in single combat. **to th' utterance,** to the last extremity; French *à l'outrance*. 80. **probation,** proof, i.e., in detail. 81. **borne in hand,** deceived by false promises. **cross'd,** thwarted. 83. **half a soul,** a half-wit. **notion,** mind. 88. **gospell'd,** imbued with the gospel spirit. 94. **Shoughs,** a kind of shaggy dog, called also *shocks*. **water-rugs,** rough water dogs (?). **demi-wolves,** apparently a crossbreed with the wolf. **clept,** called. 95. **valued file,** list classified according to value. 97. **housekeeper,** watchdog. 100. **Particular . . . bill,** particular qualification apart from the catalog. 112. **tugg'd with,** pulled about by (as in wrestling). 116. **distance,** hostility. 118. **near'st of life,** most vital interests. 120. **avouch,** warrant, i.e., destroy him as an act of royal will. 128. **Your . . . you,** i.e., the spirits of defiance and revenge rise into their faces. 130. **perfect spy o' th' time,** knowledge or espial of the exact time; many conjectures. 132. **thought,** being borne in mind. 133. **clearness,** freedom from suspicion.

SCENE II. 9. **sorriest,** most despicable. 13. **scorch'd,** slashed, cut. Many editors, including Globe, follow Theobald's emendation to *scotch'd*. 14. **close,** heal. **poor,** feeble.

But let the frame of things disjoint, both the worlds suffer,
Ere we will eat our meal in fear and sleep
In the affliction of these terrible dreams
That shake us nightly: better be with the dead,
Whom we, to gain our peace, have sent to peace,
Than on the torture of the mind to lie
In restless ecstasy. Duncan is in his grave;
After life's fitful fever he sleeps well;
Treason has done his worst: nor steel, nor poison,
Malice domestic, foreign levy, nothing,
Can touch him further.
Lady M. Come on;
Gentle my lord, sleek o'er your rugged looks;
Be bright and jovial among your guests to-night.
Macb. So shall I, love; and so, I pray, be you:
Let your remembrance apply to Banquo;
Present him eminence, both with eye and tongue:
†Unsafe the while, that we
Must lave our honours in these flattering streams,
And make our faces vizards to our hearts,
Disguising what they are.
Lady M. You must leave this.
Macb. O, full of scorpions is my mind, dear wife!
Thou know'st that Banquo, and his Fleance, lives.
Lady M. But in them nature's copy 's not eterne.
Macb. There 's comfort yet; they are assailable;
Then be thou jocund: ere the bat hath flown
His cloister'd flight, ere to black Hecate's summons
The shard-borne beetle with his drowsy hums
Hath rung night's yawning peal, there shall be done
A deed of dreadful note.
Lady M. What 's to be done?
Macb. Be innocent of the knowledge, dearest chuck,
Till thou applaud the deed. Come, seeling night,
Scarf up the tender eye of pitiful day;
And with thy bloody and invisible hand
Cancel and tear to pieces that great bond
Which keeps me pale! Light thickens; and the crow
Makes wing to th' rooky wood:
Good things of day begin to droop and drowse;
Whiles night's black agents to their preys do rouse.
Thou marvell'st at my words: but hold thee still:
Things bad begun make strong themselves by ill.
So, prithee, go with me. *Exeunt.*

SCENE III. [*A park near the palace.*]

Enter three Murderers.

First Mur. But who did bid thee join with us?
Third Mur. Macbeth.
Sec. Mur. He needs not our mistrust, since he delivers
Our offices and what we have to do
To the direction just.
First Mur. Then stand with us.
The west yet glimmers with some streaks of day.
Now spurs the lated traveller apace
To gain the timely inn; and near approaches
The subject of our watch.
Third Mur. Hark! I hear horses.
Ban. (*Within*) Give us a light there, ho!
Sec. Mur. Then 'tis he: the rest
That are within the note of expectation
Already are i' th' court.
First Mur. His horses go about.
Third Mur. Almost a mile: but he does usually,
So all men do, from hence to th' palace gate
Make it their walk.

Enter BANQUO *and* FLEANCE, *with a torch.*

Sec. Mur. A light, a light!
Third Mur. 'Tis he.
First Mur. Stand to 't.
Ban. It will be rain to-night.
First Mur. Let it come down.
[*They set upon Banquo.*]
Ban. O, treachery! Fly, good Fleance, fly, fly, fly!
Thou mayst revenge. O slave! [*Dies. Fleance escapes.*]
Third Mur. Who did strike out the light?
First Mur. Was 't not the way?
Third Mur. There 's but one down; the son is fled.
Sec. Mur. We have lost
Best half of our affair.
First Mur. Well, let 's away, and say how much is done. *Exeunt.*

SCENE IV. [*The same. Hall in the palace.*]

Banquet prepared. Enter MACBETH, LADY [MACBETH], ROSS, LENNOX, Lords, *and* Attendants.

Macb. You know your own degrees; sit down: at first
And last the hearty welcome.
Lords. Thanks to your majesty.
Macb. Ourself will mingle with society,
And play the humble host.
Our hostess keeps her state, but in best time
We will require her welcome.
Lady M. Pronounce it for me, sir, to all our friends;
For my heart speaks they are welcome.

Enter First Murderer [*at the door*].

Macb. See, they encounter thee with their hearts' thanks.
Both sides are even: here I'll sit i' th' midst:
Be large in mirth; anon we'll drink a measure
The table round. [*Goes to First Murderer.*] There 's blood upon thy face.
Mur. 'Tis Banquo's then.
Macb. 'Tis better thee without than he within.
Is he dispatch'd?
Mur. My lord, his throat is cut; that I did for him.

16. **frame of things,** universe. **both the worlds suffer,** heaven and earth perish. 27. **sleek o'er,** smooth. 31. **Present him eminence,** distinguish him with favor. 32-33. **Unsafe . . . streams,** we are unsafe so long as we have to keep our dignities unsullied by means of flattery. The text is possibly corrupt. 34. **vizards,** masks. 38. **nature's copy,** lease of life (i.e., by copyhold); possibly, man. **eterne,** perpetual. 42. **shard-borne,** borne on shards, or horny wing cases. 43. **yawning,** drowsy. 44. **note,** significance. 45. **chuck,** term of endearment. 46. **seeling,** eye-closing. Night is pictured here as a falconer sewing up the eyes of day lest it should struggle against the deed that is to be done (Parrott). 47. **Scarf up,** blindfold. 49. **bond,** Banquo's lease of life. 51. **rooky,** full of rooks.

SCENE III. 2-3. **He . . . offices,** we need not mistrust this man, since he can state exactly our duties (as told us by Macbeth). 4. **To,** according to. **just,** exactly. That is, they know he comes from Macbeth, since he has instructions identical with theirs. 6. **lated,** belated. 10. **note of expectation,** list of those expected. 19. **way,** i.e., thing to do.

SCENE IV. 1. **degrees,** ranks. 1-2. **at first And last,** from the beginning to the end (of the feast). 6. **require,** request. 14. **'Tis better . . . within.** It is better for it to be on the outside of thee than on the inside of him; sometimes explained as "better that his blood should be on thy face than he in this room." 23. **casing,** enveloping. 24-25.

Macb. Thou art the best o' th' cut-throats: yet he 's good
That did the like for Fleance: if thou didst it,
Thou art the nonpareil.
Mur. Most royal sir,
Fleance is 'scap'd.
Macb. Then comes my fit again: I had else been perfect,
Whole as the marble, founded as the rock,
As broad and general as the casing air:
But now I am cabin'd, cribb'd, confin'd, bound in
To saucy doubts and fears. But Banquo 's safe?
Mur. Ay, my good lord: safe in a ditch he bides,
With twenty trenched gashes on his head;
The least a death to nature.
Macb. Thanks for that.
There the grown serpent lies; the worm that 's fled
Hath nature that in time will venom breed,
No teeth for th' present. Get thee gone: to-morrow
We'll hear, ourselves, again. *Exit Murderer.*
Lady M. My royal lord,
You do not give the cheer: the feast is sold
That is not often vouch'd, while 'tis a-making,
'Tis given with welcome: to feed were best at home;
From thence the sauce to meat is ceremony;
Meeting were bare without it.

Enter the Ghost of Banquo, and sits in Macbeth's place.

Macb. Sweet remembrancer!
Now, good digestion wait on appetite,
And health on both!
Len. May 't please your highness sit.
Macb. Here had we now our country's honour roof'd,
Were the grac'd person of our Banquo present;
Who may I rather challenge for unkindness
Than pity for mischance!
Ross. His absence, sir,
Lays blame upon his promise. Please 't your highness
To grace us with your royal company.
Macb. The table 's full.
Len. Here is a place reserv'd, sir.
Macb. Where?
Len. Here, my good lord. What is 't that moves your highness?
Macb. Which of you have done this?
Lords. What, my good lord?
Macb. Thou canst not say I did it: never shake
Thy gory locks at me.
Ross. Gentlemen rise; his highness is not well.
Lady M. Sit, worthy friends: my lord is often thus,
And hath been from his youth: pray you, keep seat;
The fit is momentary; upon a thought
He will again be well: if much you note him,
You shall offend him and extend his passion:
Feed, and regard him not.—Are you a man?
Macb. Ay, and a bold one, that dare look on that
Which might appal the devil.
Lady M. O proper stuff!
This is the very painting of your fear:
This is the air-drawn dagger which, you said,
Led you to Duncan. O, these flaws and starts,
Impostors to true fear, would well become
A woman's story at a winter's fire,
Authoriz'd by her grandam. Shame itself!
Why do you make such faces? When all 's done,
You look but on a stool.
Macb. Prithee, see there! behold! look! lo! how say you?
Why, what care I? If thou canst nod, speak too.
If charnel-houses and our graves must send
Those that we bury back, our monuments
Shall be the maws of kites. [*Ghost vanishes.*]
Lady M. What, quite unmann'd in folly?
Macb. If I stand here, I saw him.
Lady M. Fie, for shame!
Macb. Blood hath been shed ere now, i' th' olden time,
Ere humane statute purg'd the gentle weal;
Ay, and since too, murders have been perform'd
Too terrible for the ear: the time has been,
That, when the brains were out, the man would die,
And there an end; but now they rise again,
With twenty mortal murders on their crowns,
And push us from our stools: this is more strange
Than such a murder is.
Lady M. My worthy lord,
Your noble friends do lack you.
Macb. I do forget.
Do not muse at me, my most worthy friends;
I have a strange infirmity, which is nothing
To those that know me. Come, love and health to all;
Then I'll sit down. Give me some wine; fill full.

Enter Ghost.

I drink to th' general joy o' th' whole table,
And to our dear friend Banquo, whom we miss;
Would he were here! to all, and him, we thirst,
And all to all.
Lords. Our duties, and the pledge.
Macb. [*Seeing Ghost.*] Avaunt! and quit my sight! let the earth hide thee!
Thy bones are marrowless, thy blood is cold;
Thou hast no speculation in those eyes
Which thou dost glare with!
Lady M. Think of this, good peers,
But as a thing of custom: 'tis no other;
Only it spoils the pleasure of the time.
Macb. What man dare, I dare:
Approach thou like the rugged Russian bear,
The arm'd rhinoceros, or th' Hyrcan tiger;
Take any shape but that, and my firm nerves
Shall never tremble: or be alive again,
And dare me to the desert with thy sword;
†If trembling I inhabit then, protest me

bound in To, confined along with. 25. **saucy,** sharp (Koppel); impudent (Schmidt). 26. **bides,** lies. 29. **worm,** small serpent. 32. **hear, ourselves,** talk it over. 33. **is sold,** i.e., seems grudgingly given, as by an innkeeper. 34. **vouch'd,** i.e., accompanied with assurances of welcome. 35. **to feed . . . home,** i.e., mere eating is best done at home. 40. **roof'd,** under one roof. 41. **grac'd,** gracious. 42. **Who may I,** whom I hope I may. 55. **upon a thought,** in a moment. 57. **extend,** prolong. 60. **O proper stuff!** O veritable nonsense! 64. **to,** compared with. 73. **maws,** stomachs, i.e., our only tombs will be the stomachs of birds of prey. 76. **humane.** This spelling carried both meanings: "appertaining to mankind" and "befitting man." **purg'd . . . weal,** cleansed the commonwealth of violence and made it gentle. 81. **mortal murders,** deadly wounds. 84. **lack,** miss. 91. **thirst,** desire to drink. 92. **all to all,** all good wishes to all. 95. **speculation,** light of living intellect; also defined as "power of sight." 100-101. **bear . . . tiger.** Bears of Russia and tigers of Hyrcania were types of ferocity. 101. **arm'd,** sheathed in armor. 105. **If . . . then,** if then I tremble (i.e., put on trembling as a garment). Some editors prefer the reading due to Pope and Steevens: *If trembling I inhibit thee.*

The baby of a girl. Hence, horrible shadow!
Unreal mock'ry, hence! [*Ghost vanishes.*]
Why, so: being gone,
I am a man again. Pray you, sit still.
Lady M. You have displac'd the mirth, broke the good meeting,
With most admir'd disorder.
Macb. Can such things be,
And overcome us like a summer's cloud,
Without our special wonder? You make me strange
Even to the disposition that I owe,
When now I think you can behold such sights,
And keep the natural ruby of your cheeks,
When mine is blanch'd with fear.
Ross. What sights, my lord?
Lady M. I pray you, speak not; he grows worse and worse;
Question enrages him. At once, good night:
Stand not upon the order of your going,
But go at once.
Len. Good night; and better health
Attend his majesty!
Lady M. A kind good night to all!
Exeunt Lords.
Macb. It will have blood; they say, blood will have blood:
Stones have been known to move and trees to speak;
Augurs and understood relations have
By magot-pies and choughs and rooks brought forth
The secret'st man of blood. What is the night?
Lady M. Almost at odds with morning, which is which.
Macb. How say'st thou, that Macduff denies his person
At our great bidding?
Lady M. Did you send to him, sir?
Macb. I hear it by the way; but I will send:
There 's not a one of them but in his house
I keep a servant fee'd. I will to-morrow,
And betimes I will, to the weird sisters:
More shall they speak; for now I am bent to know,
By the worst means, the worst. For mine own good,
All causes shall give way: I am in blood
Stepp'd in so far that, should I wade no more,
Returning were as tedious as go o'er:
Strange things I have in head, that will to hand;
Which must be acted ere they may be scann'd.
Lady M. You lack the season of all natures, sleep.
Macb. Come, we'll to sleep. My strange and self-abuse
Is the initiate fear that wants hard use:
We are yet but young in deed. *Exeunt.*

SCENE V. [*A Heath.*]

Thunder. Enter the three Witches, *meeting* HECATE.

First Witch. Why, how now, Hecate! you look angerly.
Hec. Have I not reason, beldams as you are,
Saucy and overbold? How did you dare
To trade and traffic with Macbeth
In riddles and affairs of death;
And I, the mistress of your charms,
The close contriver of all harms,
Was never call'd to bear my part,
Or show the glory of our art?
And, which is worse, all you have done
Hath been but for a wayward son,
Spiteful and wrathful, who, as others do,
Loves for his own ends, not for you.
But make amends now: get you gone,
And at the pit of Acheron
Meet me i' th' morning: thither he
Will come to know his destiny:
Your vessels and your spells provide,
Your charms and every thing beside.
I am for th' air; this night I'll spend
Unto a dismal and a fatal end:
Great business must be wrought ere noon:
Upon the corner of the moon
There hangs a vap'rous drop profound;
I'll catch it ere it come to ground:
And that distill'd by magic sleights
Shall raise such artificial sprites
As by the strength of their illusion
Shall draw him on to his confusion:
He shall spurn fate, scorn death, and bear
His hopes 'bove wisdom, grace and fear:
And you all know, security
Is mortals' chiefest enemy.
Music and a song.
Hark! I am call'd; my little spirit, see,
Sits in a foggy cloud, and stays for me. [*Exit.*]
Sing within, 'Come away, come away,' &c.
First Witch. Come, let 's make haste; she'll soon be back again. *Exeunt.*

SCENE VI. [*Forres. The palace.*]

Enter LENNOX *and another* Lord.

Len. My former speeches have but hit your thoughts,
Which can interpret farther: only, I say,
Things have been strangely borne. The gracious Duncan
Was pitied of Macbeth: marry, he was dead:
And the right-valiant Banquo walk'd too late;
Whom, you may say, if 't please you, Fleance kill'd,
For Fleance fled: men must not walk too late.
Who cannot want the thought how monstrous
It was for Malcolm and for Donalbain
To kill their gracious father? damned fact!
How it did grieve Macbeth! did he not straight
In pious rage the two delinquents tear,
That were the slaves of drink and thralls of sleep?

106. **baby of a girl,** a baby girl. 109. **displac'd,** banished. 110. **admir'd,** wondered at. 112-113. **You make . . . owe,** you cause me to feel I do not know my own nature (which I had presumed to be that of a brave man). 119. **Stand . . . order,** do not wait for the ceremonies. 123. **Stones,** thought to be an allusion to rocking-stones or great stones so balanced on their foundations that they can be rocked with little effort. 124. **Augurs,** probably, auguries. **understood relations,** comprehended reports or utterances. 125. **magot-pies,** magpies. **choughs,** jackdaws. 130. **by the way,** casually. 132. **fee'd,** i.e., to spy. 140. **ere . . . scann'd,** i.e., even before thinking about them carefully, at once. 141. **season,** seasoning, relish. 142. **self-abuse,** self-delusion. 143. **initiate,** of the beginner. **use,** experience.

SCENE V. Practically all critics agree that this scene is not by Shakespeare. 2. **beldams,** hags. 7. **close,** secret. 15. **Acheron,** a river of hell. 24. **profound,** ready to drop (?), of deep significance (?). 27. **artificial,** produced by magical arts. 32. **security,** confidence, overconfidence.

SCENE VI. 8. **want the thought,** help thinking. 13. **thralls,** slaves.

Was not that nobly done? Ay, and wisely too;
For 'twould have anger'd any heart alive
To hear the men deny 't. So that, I say,
He has borne all things well: and I do think
That had he Duncan's sons under his key—
As, an 't please heaven, he shall not—they should find
What 'twere to kill a father; so should Fleance.
But, peace! for from broad words and 'cause he fail'd
His presence at the tyrant's feast, I hear
Macduff lives in disgrace: sir, can you tell
Where he bestows himself?
Lord. The son of Duncan,
From whom this tyrant holds the due of birth,
Lives in the English court, and is receiv'd
Of the most pious Edward with such grace
That the malevolence of fortune nothing
Takes from his high respect: thither Macduff
Is gone to pray the holy king, upon his aid
To wake Northumberland and warlike Siward:
That, by the help of these—with Him above
To ratify the work—we may again
Give to our tables meat, sleep to our nights,
Free from our feasts and banquets bloody knives,
Do faithful homage and receive free honours:
All which we pine for now: and this report
Hath so exasperate the king that he
Prepares for some attempt of war.
Len. Sent he to Macduff?
Lord. He did: and with an absolute 'Sir, not I,'
The cloudy messenger turns me his back,
And hums, as who should say 'You'll rue the time
That clogs me with this answer.'
Len. And that well might
Advise him to a caution, t' hold what distance
His wisdom can provide. Some holy angel
Fly to the court of England and unfold
His message ere he come, that a swift blessing
May soon return to this our suffering country
Under a hand accurs'd!
Lord. I'll send my prayers with him.
Exeunt.

ACT IV.

SCENE I. [*A cavern. In the middle, a boiling cauldron.*]

Thunder. Enter the three Witches.

First Witch. Thrice the brinded cat hath mew'd.
Sec. Witch. Thrice and once the hedge-pig whin'd.
Third Witch. Harpier cries 'Tis time, 'tis time.
First Witch. Round about the cauldron go;
In the poison'd entrails throw.
†Toad, that under cold stone
Days and nights has thirty one
Swelt'red venom sleeping got,
Boil thou first i' th' charmed pot.
All. Double, double toil and trouble;
Fire burn, and cauldron bubble.
Sec. Witch. Fillet of a fenny snake,
In the cauldron boil and bake;
Eye of newt and toe of frog,
Wool of bat and tongue of dog,
Adder's fork and blind-worm's sting,
Lizard's leg and howlet's wing,
For a charm of pow'rful trouble,
Like a hell-broth boil and bubble.
All. Double, double toil and trouble;
Fire burn and cauldron bubble.
Third Witch. Scale of dragon, tooth of wolf,
Witches' mummy, maw and gulf
Of the ravin'd salt-sea shark,
Root of hemlock digg'd i' th' dark,
Liver of blaspheming Jew,
Gall of goat, and slips of yew
Sliver'd in the moon's eclipse,
Nose of Turk and Tartar's lips,
Finger of birth-strangled babe
Ditch-deliver'd by a drab,
Make the gruel thick and slab:
Add thereto a tiger's chaudron,
For th' ingredients of our cauldron.
All. Double, double toil and trouble;
Fire burn and cauldron bubble.
Sec. Witch. Cool it with a baboon's blood,
Then the charm is firm and good.

Enter HECATE *to the other three Witches.*

Hec. O, well done! I commend your pains;
And every one shall share i' th' gains:
And now about the cauldron sing,
Like elves and fairies in a ring,
Enchanting all that you put in.
Music and a song: 'Black spirits,' &c.
[*Hecate retires.*]
Sec. Witch. By the pricking of my thumbs,
Something wicked this way comes.
Open, locks,
Whoever knocks!

Enter MACBETH.

Macb. How now, you secret, black, and midnight hags!
What is 't you do?
All. A deed without a name.
Macb. I conjure you, by that which you profess,
Howe'er you come to know it, answer me:
Though you untie the winds and let them fight
Against the churches; though the yesty waves
Confound and swallow navigation up;
Though bladed corn be lodg'd and trees blown down;
Though castles topple on their warders' heads;
Though palaces and pyramids do slope
Their heads to their foundations; though the treasure
Of nature's germens tumble all together,
Even till destruction sicken; answer me
To what I ask you.

21. **from,** on account of. **broad,** open, plain. 22. **tyrant's,** usurper's. 27. **Edward,** Edward the Confessor. 30. **upon his aid,** in aid of Malcolm. 35. **Free . . . feasts,** free our feasts from. 36. **free,** freely bestowed, or the honors pertaining to freemen. 40. **absolute,** curt, peremptory. 41. **cloudy,** angry. 48-49. **suffering country Under,** country suffering under.

ACT IV. SCENE I. 1. **brinded,** marked with streaks (as by fire), brindled. 2. **hedge-pig,** hedgehog. 3. **Harpier,** form doubtful, probably intended for "harpy." 6. **cold,** two syllables. 8. **venom.** The toad was commonly thought to be venomous. 12. **fenny,** swamp. 16. **fork,** forked tongue. **blind-worm,** a harmless kind of lizard, also called slowworm. 17. **howlet's,** owl's. 23. **gulf,** gullet. 24. **ravin'd,** ravenous. 28. **Sliver'd,** broken off (as a branch). 31. **drab,** harlot. 32. **slab,** viscous, thick. 33. **chaudron,** entrails. 39-43. **O . . . in.** These lines are universally regarded as non-Shakespearean. 53. **yesty,** foamy. 55. **bladed,** in the ear. **corn,** general name for wheat and other grains. **lodg'd,** thrown down, laid. 59. **nature's germens,** seed or elements, from which nature operates. 60. **sicken,** be surfeited.

First Witch. Speak.
Sec. Witch. Demand.
Third Witch. We'll answer.
First Witch. Say, if th' hadst rather hear it from our mouths,
Or from our masters?
Macb. Call 'em; let me see 'em.
First Witch. Pour in sow's blood, that hath eaten
Her nine farrow; grease that 's sweaten
From the murderer's gibbet throw
Into the flame.
All. Come, high or low;
Thyself and office deftly show!

Thunder. First Apparition: *an armed Head.*

Macb. Tell me, thou unknown power,—
First Witch. He knows thy thought:
Hear his speech, but say thou nought.
First App. Macbeth! Macbeth! Macbeth! beware Macduff;
Beware the Thane of Fife. Dismiss me. Enough.
He descends.
Macb. Whate'er thou art, for thy good caution, thanks;
Thou hast harp'd my fear aright: but one word more,—
First Witch. He will not be commanded: here 's another,
More potent than the first.

Thunder. Second Apparition: *a bloody Child.*

Sec. App. Macbeth! Macbeth! Macbeth!
Macb. Had I three ears, I 'ld hear thee.
Sec. App. Be bloody, bold, and resolute; laugh to scorn
The pow'r of man, for none of woman born
Shall harm Macbeth. *Descends.*
Macb. Then live, Macduff: what need I fear of thee?
But yet I'll make assurance double sure,
And take a bond of fate: thou shalt not live;
That I may tell pale-hearted fear it lies,
And sleep in spite of thunder.

Thunder. Third Apparition: *a Child crowned, with a tree in his hand.*

What is this
That rises like the issue of a king,
And wears upon his baby-brow the round
And top of sovereignty?
All. Listen, but speak not to 't.
Third App. Be lion-mettled, proud; and take no care
Who chafes, who frets, or where conspirers are:
Macbeth shall never vanquish'd be until
Great Birnam wood to high Dunsinane hill
Shall come against him. *Descends.*
Macb. That will never be:
Who can impress the forest, bid the tree
Unfix his earth-bound root? Sweet bodements! good!
Rebellion's head, rise never till the wood
Of Birnam rise, and our high-plac'd Macbeth
Shall live the lease of nature, pay his breath
To time and mortal custom. Yet my heart
Throbs to know one thing: tell me, if your art
Can tell so much: shall Banquo's issue ever
Reign in this kingdom?
All. Seek to know no more.
Macb. I will be satisfied: deny me this,
And an eternal curse fall on you! Let me know.
Why sinks that cauldron? and what noise is this?
Hautboys.
First Witch. Show!
Sec. Witch. Show!
Third Witch. Show!
All. Show his eyes, and grieve his heart;
Come like shadows, so depart!

A show of Eight Kings, *and Banquo [the] last [King], with a glass in his hand.*

Macb. Thou art too like the spirit of Banquo: down!
Thy crown does sear mine eye-balls. And thy hair,
Thou other gold-bound brow, is like the first.
A third is like the former. Filthy hags!
Why do you show me this? A fourth! Start, eyes!
What, will the line stretch out to th' crack of doom?
Another yet! A seventh! I'll see no more:
And yet the eighth appears, who bears a glass
Which shows me many more; and some I see
That two-fold balls and treble sceptres carry:
Horrible sight! Now, I see, 'tis true;
For the blood-bolter'd Banquo smiles upon me,
And points at them for his. [*Apparitions vanish.*] What, is this so?
First Witch. Ay, sir, all this is so: but why
Stands Macbeth thus amazedly?
Come, sisters, cheer we up his sprites,
And show the best of our delights:
I'll charm the air to give a sound,
While you perform your antic round;
That this great king may kindly say,
Our duties did his welcome pay.
Music. The Witches dance, and vanish.
Macb. Where are they? Gone? Let this pernicious hour
Stand aye accursed in the calendar!
Come in, without there!

Enter LENNOX.

Len. What 's your grace's will?
Macb. Saw you the weird sisters?
Len. No, my lord.
Macb. Came they not by you?
Len. No, indeed, my lord.
Macb. Infected be the air whereon they ride;
And damn'd all those that trust them! I did hear
The galloping of horse: who was 't came by?

65. **nine farrow,** litter of nine. **sweaten,** sweated. 68. **office,** function. *Stage Direction:* ***armed Head.*** This symbolizes the head of Macbeth cut off by Macduff and presented by him to Malcolm. 74. **harp'd,** hit, touched. 76. *Stage Direction:* ***bloody Child.*** This symbolizes Macduff (see V, viii, 15-16). 83. **double,** doubly. 84. **take a bond of,** get a guarantee from (i.e., by killing Macduff, to make doubly sure he can do no harm). 86. *Stage Direction:* ***Child . . . hand.*** This third apparition symbolizes Malcolm, the royal child. 88-89. **round . . . sovereignty,** seems to allude to the shape of a crown as made up of a lower round and a top part, and also to the rounding out and culmination in sovereignty. 93. **Birnam, Dunsinane.** Birnam is a hill near Dunkeld, twelve miles from Dunsinane, which is seven miles from Perth. 95. **impress,** like soldiers. 96. **bodements,** prophecies. 99. **lease of nature,** natural period, full life-span. 106. **noise,** music. 112. **Thou . . . Banquo.** This would be the first in the succession of Scottish kings down to James I, therefore Fleance, whose coronation was the thing most dreaded by Macbeth. 116. **Start,** bulge from their sockets. 117. **crack of doom,** possibly, thunder announcing Doomsday. 121. **two-fold balls,** a probable reference to the double coronation of James at Scone and Westminster, as king of England and Scotland. **treble**

Len. 'Tis two or three, my lord, that bring you word
Macduff is fled to England.
Macb. Fled to England!
Len. Ay, my good lord.
Macb. Time, thou anticipat'st my dread exploits:
The flighty purpose never is o'ertook
Unless the deed go with it: from this moment
The very firstlings of my heart shall be
The firstlings of my hand. And even now,
To crown my thoughts with acts, be it thought and done:
The castle of Macduff I will surprise;
Seize upon Fife; give to th' edge o' th' sword
His wife, his babes, and all unfortunate souls
That trace him in his line. No boasting like a fool:
This deed I'll do before this purpose cool.
But no more sights!—Where are these gentlemen?
Come, bring me where they are. *Exeunt.*

SCENE II. [*Fife. Macduff's castle.*]

Enter MACDUFF'S WIFE, *her* Son, *and* ROSS.

L. Macd. What had he done, to make him fly the land?
Ross. You must have patience, madam.
L. Macd. He had none:
His flight was madness: when our actions do not,
Our fears do make us traitors.
Ross. You know not
Whether it was his wisdom or his fear.
L. Macd. Wisdom! to leave his wife, to leave his babes,
His mansion and his titles in a place
From whence himself does fly? He loves us not;
He wants the natural touch: for the poor wren,
The most diminutive of birds, will fight,
Her young ones in her nest, against the owl.
All is the fear and nothing is the love;
As little is the wisdom, where the flight
So runs against all reason.
Ross. My dearest coz,
I pray you, school yourself: but for your husband,
He is noble, wise, judicious, and best knows
The fits o' th' season. I dare not speak much further;
But cruel are the times, when we are traitors
And do not know ourselves, when we hold rumour
From what we fear, yet know not what we fear,
But float upon a wild and violent sea
Each way and move. I take my leave of you:
Shall not be long but I'll be here again:
Things at the worst will cease, or else climb upward
To what they were before. My pretty cousin,
Blessing upon you!
L. Macd. Father'd he is, and yet he 's fatherless.
Ross. I am so much a fool, should I stay longer,
It would be my disgrace and your discomfort:
I take my leave at once. *Exit Ross.*
L. Macd. Sirrah, your father 's dead:
And what will you do now? How will you live?
Son. As birds do, mother.
L. Macd. What, with worms and flies?
Son. With what I get, I mean; and so do they.
L. Macd. Poor bird! thou 'ldst never fear the net nor lime,
The pitfall nor the gin.
Son. Why should I, mother? Poor birds they are not set for.
My father is not dead, for all your saying.
L. Macd. Yes, he is dead: how wilt thou do for a father?
Son. Nay, how will you do for a husband?
L. Macd. Why, I can buy me twenty at any market.
Son. Then you'll buy 'em to sell again.
L. Macd. Thou speak'st with all thy wit; and yet, i' faith,
With wit enough for thee.
Son. Was my father a traitor, mother?
L. Macd. Ay, that he was.
Son. What is a traitor?
L. Macd. Why, one that swears and lies.
Son. And be all traitors that do so?
L. Macd. Every one that does so is a traitor, and must be hanged.
Son. And must they all be hanged that swear and lie?
L. Macd. Every one.
Son. Who must hang them?
L. Macd. Why, the honest men.
Son. Then the liars and swearers are fools, for there are liars and swearers enow to beat the honest men and hang up them.
L. Macd. Now, God help thee, poor monkey! But how wilt thou do for a father?
Son. If he were dead, you 'ld weep for him: if you would not, it were a good sign that I should quickly have a new father.
L. Macd. Poor prattler, how thou talk'st!

Enter a Messenger.

Mess. Bless you, fair dame! I am not to you known,
Though in your state of honour I am perfect.
I doubt some danger does approach you nearly:
If you will take a homely man's advice,
Be not found here; hence, with your little ones.
To fright you thus, methinks, I am too savage;
To do worse to you were fell cruelty,
Which is too nigh your person. Heaven preserve you!
I dare abide no longer. *Exit Mess.*
L. Macd. Whither should I fly?
I have done no harm. But I remember now
I am in this earthly world; where to do harm
Is often laudable, to do good sometime
Accounted dangerous folly: why then, alas,

---

sceptres, almost certainly refers to James' assumed title of King of Great Britain, France, and Ireland. 123. **blood-bolter'd,** having his hair matted with blood. 125-135. **Ay . . . there.** These lines are also held to be spurious. 130. **antic round,** grotesque dance in a circle. 145. **flighty,** fleeting. 147-148. **firstlings . . . hand,** my impulses will be acted on immediately. 153. **trace,** follow. **line,** family succession.

SCENE II. 2. **He had none.** Patience was the virtue by which the faculties were controlled; hence, *His flight was madness* (l. 3). 7. **titles,** possessions. 9. **wants,** lacks. **touch,** affection, feeling. 17. **fits o' th' season,** violent disorders of the time. 19. **know ourselves,** know ourselves (or possibly, each other) to be traitors. Owing to Macbeth's system of espionage even good men have grown suspicious of each other. **hold,** accept, believe. 22. **Each . . . move,** many emendations; Theobald: *Each way and wave;* Capell: *And move each way;* Cambridge eds: *Each way and none.* 23. **Shall,** it shall. 34. **lime,** birdlime. 35. **gin,** snare. 36. **they,** the snares. 47. **swears and lies,** swears allegiance and breaks his oath. 66. **in . . . honour,** with your honorable rank. **perfect,** perfectly acquainted. 67. **doubt,** fear.

Do I put up that womanly defence,
To say I have done no harm?

Enter Murderers.

What are these faces?
First Mur. Where is your husband?
L. Macd. I hope, in no place so unsanctified
Where such as thou mayst find him.
First Mur. He 's a traitor.
Son. Thou liest, thou shag-ear'd villain!
First Mur. What, you egg!
[*Stabbing him.*]
Young fry of treachery!
Son. He has kill'd me, mother:
Run away, I pray you! [*Dies.*]
Exit [*Lady Macduff*] *crying* 'Murder!'
[*followed by Murderers*].

SCENE III. [*England. Before the King's palace.*]

Enter MALCOLM *and* MACDUFF.

Mal. Let us seek out some desolate shade, and there
Weep our sad bosoms empty.
Macd. Let us rather
Hold fast the mortal sword, and like good men
Bestride our down-fall'n birthdom: each new morn
New widows howl, new orphans cry, new sorrows
Strike heaven on the face, that it resounds
As if it felt with Scotland and yell'd out
Like syllable of dolour.
Mal. What I believe I'll wail,
What know believe, and what I can redress,
As I shall find the time to friend, I will.
What you have spoke, it may be so perchance.
This tyrant, whose sole name blisters our tongues,
Was once thought honest: you have lov'd him well;
He hath not touch'd you yet. I am young; but something
You may deserve of him through me, and wisdom
To offer up a weak poor innocent lamb
T' appease an angry god.
Macd. I am not treacherous.
Mal. But Macbeth is.
A good and virtuous nature may recoil
In an imperial charge. But I shall crave your pardon;
That which you are my thoughts cannot transpose:
Angels are bright still, though the brightest fell:
Though all things foul would wear the brows of grace,
Yet grace must still look so.
Macd. I have lost my hopes.
Mal. Perchance even there where I did find my doubts.
Why in that rawness left you wife and child,
Those precious motives, those strong knots of love,
Without leave-taking? I pray you,
Let not my jealousies be your dishonours,
But mine own safeties. You may be rightly just,
Whatever I shall think.
Macd. Bleed, bleed, poor country!
Great tyranny! lay thou thy basis sure,
For goodness dare not check thee: wear thou thy wrongs;
The title is affeer'd! Fare thee well, lord:
I would not be the villain that thou think'st
For the whole space that 's in the tyrant's grasp,
And the rich East to boot.
Mal. Be not offended:
I speak not as in absolute fear of you.
I think our country sinks beneath the yoke;
It weeps, it bleeds; and each new day a gash
Is added to her wounds: I think withal
There would be hands uplifted in my right;
And here from gracious England have I offer
Of goodly thousands: but, for all this,
When I shall tread upon the tyrant's head,
Or wear it on my sword, yet my poor country
Shall have more vices than it had before,
More suffer and more sundry ways than ever,
By him that shall succeed.
Macd. What should he be?
Mal. It is myself I mean: in whom I know
All the particulars of vice so grafted
That, when they shall be open'd, black Macbeth
Will seem as pure as snow, and the poor state
Esteem him as a lamb, being compar'd
With my confineless harms.
Macd. Not in the legions
Of horrid hell can come a devil more damn'd
In evils to top Macbeth.
Mal. I grant him bloody,
Luxurious, avaricious, false, deceitful,
Sudden, malicious, smacking of every sin
That has a name: but there 's no bottom, none,
In my voluptuousness: your wives, your daughters,
Your matrons and your maids, could not fill up
The cistern of my lust, and my desire
All continent impediments would o'erbear
That did oppose my will: better Macbeth
Than such an one to reign.
Macd. Boundless intemperance
In nature is a tyranny; it hath been
Th' untimely emptying of the happy throne
And fall of many kings. But fear not yet
To take upon you what is yours: you may
Convey your pleasures in a spacious plenty,
And yet seem cold, the time you may so hoodwink.
We have willing dames enough; there cannot be
That vulture in you, to devour so many
As will to greatness dedicate themselves,
Finding it so inclin'd.
Mal. With this there grows
In my most ill-compos'd affection such
A stanchless avarice that, were I king,
I should cut off the nobles for their lands,
Desire his jewels and this other's house:
And my more-having would be as a sauce
To make me hunger more; that I should forge

82. **shag-ear'd,** i.e., shaggy-haired. 83. **egg,** used contemptuously of the young. 84. **fry,** spawn.
SCENE III. 2. **Weep . . . empty.** Up to line 117 Malcolm suspects Macduff of being an emissary of Macbeth sent thither to ensnare him; he is testing out Macduff. 4. **Bestride,** stand over in defense. **birthdom,** fatherland. 10. **to friend,** for my friend. 12. **sole,** mere. 19. **recoil,** fall away, degenerate. 20. **imperial charge,** royal command. 24. **so,** like grace. 26. **rawness,** haste, unpreparedness. 34. **affeer'd,** confirmed, certified. 43. **England,** king of England. 48. **sundry,** various. 49. **What,** who. 52. **open'd,** unfolded (like buds). 55. **my confineless harms,** the boundless injuries I shall inflict. 58. **Luxurious,** lustful. 59. **Sudden,** violent, passionate. 64. **continent,** restraining. 67. **nature,** man's nature. 69. **yet,** nevertheless. 71. **Convey,** manage with secrecy. 72. **the time . . . hoodwink,** you may so deceive the age. 77. **ill-compos'd affection,** evil disposition. 78. **stanchless,** insatiable. 86. **summer-seeming,** passing away with youth, transitory. 88.

Quarrels unjust against the good and loyal,
Destroying them for wealth.
Macd. This avarice
Sticks deeper, grows with more pernicious root
Than summer-seeming lust, and it hath been
The sword of our slain kings: yet do not fear;
Scotland hath foisons to fill up your will,
Of your mere own: all these are portable,
With other graces weigh'd.
Mal. But I have none: the king-becoming graces,
As justice, verity, temp'rance, stableness,
Bounty, perseverance, mercy, lowliness,
Devotion, patience, courage, fortitude,
I have no relish of them, but abound
In the division of each several crime,
Acting it many ways. Nay, had I pow'r, I should
Pour the sweet milk of concord into hell,
Uproar the universal peace, confound
All unity on earth.
Macd. O Scotland, Scotland!
Mal. If such a one be fit to govern, speak:
I am as I have spoken.
Macd. Fit to govern!
No, not to live. O nation miserable,
With an untitled tyrant bloody-scept'red,
When shalt thou see thy wholesome days again,
Since that the truest issue of thy throne
By his own interdiction stands accurs'd,
And does blaspheme his breed? Thy royal father
Was a most sainted king: the queen that bore thee,
Oft'ner upon her knees than on her feet,
Died every day she liv'd. Fare thee well!
These evils thou repeat'st upon thyself
Hath banish'd me from Scotland. O my breast,
Thy hope ends here!
Mal. Macduff, this noble passion,
Child of integrity, hath from my soul
Wip'd the black scruples, reconcil'd my thoughts
To thy good truth and honour. Devilish Macbeth
By many of these trains hath sought to win me
Into his power, and modest wisdom plucks me
From over-credulous haste: but God above
Deal between thee and me! for even now
I put myself to thy direction, and
Unspeak mine own detraction, here abjure
The taints and blames I laid upon myself,
For strangers to my nature. I am yet
Unknown to woman, never was forsworn,
Scarcely have coveted what was mine own,
At no time broke my faith, would not betray
The devil to his fellow, and delight
No less in truth than life: my first false speaking
Was this upon myself: what I am truly,
Is thine and my poor country's to command:
Whither indeed, before thy here-approach,
Old Siward, with ten thousand warlike men,
Already at a point, was setting forth.
Now we'll together; and the chance of goodness
Be like our warranted quarrel! Why are you silent?
Macd. Such welcome and unwelcome things at once
'Tis hard to reconcile.

Enter a Doctor.

Mal. Well; more anon.—Comes the king forth, I
pray you?
Doct. Ay, sir; there are a crew of wretched souls
That stay his cure: their malady convinces
The great assay of art; but at his touch—
Such sanctity hath heaven given his hand—
They presently amend.
Mal. I thank you, doctor. *Exit [Doctor].*
Macd. What 's the disease he means?
Mal. 'Tis call'd the evil:
A most miraculous work in this good king;
Which often, since my here-remain in England,
I have seen him do. How he solicits heaven,
Himself best knows: but strangely-visited people,
All swoln and ulcerous, pitiful to the eye,
The mere despair of surgery, he cures,
Hanging a golden stamp about their necks,
Put on with holy prayers: and 'tis spoken,
To the succeeding royalty he leaves
The healing benediction. With this strange virtue,
He hath a heavenly gift of prophecy,
And sundry blessings hang about his throne,
That speak him full of grace.

Enter Ross.

Macd. See, who comes here?
Mal. My countryman; but yet I know him not.
Macd. My ever-gentle cousin, welcome hither.
Mal. I know him now. Good God, betimes
remove
The means that makes us strangers!
Ross. Sir, amen.
Macd. Stands Scotland where it did?
Ross. Alas, poor country!
Almost afraid to know itself. It cannot
Be call'd our mother, but our grave; where nothing,
But who knows nothing, is once seen to smile;
Where sighs and groans and shrieks that rend the air
Are made, not mark'd; where violent sorrow seems
A modern ecstasy: the dead man's knell
Is there scarce ask'd for who; and good men's lives
Expire before the flowers in their caps,
Dying or ere they sicken.
Macd. O, relation
Too nice, and yet too true!
Mal. What 's the newest grief?
Ross. That of an hour's age doth hiss the speaker:
Each minute teems a new one.
Macd. How does my wife?
Ross. Why, well.
Macd. And all my children?
Ross. Well too.
Macd. The tyrant has not batter'd at their peace?
Ross. No; they were well at peace when I did leave
'em.
Macd. Be not a niggard of your speech: how goes 't?
Ross. When I came hither to transport the tidings,

foisons, resources. 89. **your mere own,** what is absolutely your own. **portable,** bearable. 90. **With,** against. 91. **king-becoming graces.** The list which follows is a typical enumeration of the princely virtues of the Renaissance. 95. **relish of,** flavor or trace of. 104. **untitled,** lacking rightful title. 107. **interdiction,** authoritative exclusion. 108. **blaspheme,** slander, defame. 111. **Died . . . liv'd,** lived a life of daily mortification (Delius). 118. **trains,** plots, artifices. 126. **forsworn,** perjured. 135. **at a point,** ready, prepared. 136. **chance of goodness,** chance of success. 141. **crew,** company. 142. **convinces,** conquers. 143. **assay of art,** efforts of medical skill. 146. **evil,** disease, i.e., scrofula. The passage is an obvious compliment to James I, who claimed the miraculous power of the royal touch. 150. **strangely-visited,** afflicted by strange diseases. 153. **stamp,** coin (hung around the necks of the persons touched). 166. **nothing,** nobody. 167. **once,** ever. 170. **modern ecstasy,** commonplace excitement. 175. **hiss,** cause to be hissed. 176. **teems,** teems with. 177. **children,** three syllables.

Which I have heavily borne, there ran a rumour
Of many worthy fellows that were out;
Which was to my belief witness'd the rather,
For that I saw the tyrant's power a-foot:
Now is the time of help; your eye in Scotland
Would create soldiers, make our women fight,
To doff their dire distresses.
Mal. Be 't their comfort
We are coming thither: gracious England hath
Lent us good Siward and ten thousand men;
An older and a better soldier none
That Christendom gives out.
Ross. Would I could answer
This comfort with the like! But I have words
That would be howl'd out in the desert air,
Where hearing should not latch them.
Macd. What concern they?
The general cause? or is it a fee-grief
Due to some single breast?
Ross. No mind that 's honest
But in it shares some woe; though the main part
Pertains to you alone.
Macd. If it be mine,
Keep it not from me, quickly let me have it.
Ross. Let not your ears despise my tongue for ever,
Which shall possess them with the heaviest sound
That ever yet they heard.
Macd. Hum! I guess at it.
Ross. Your castle is surpris'd; your wife and babes
Savagely slaughter'd: to relate the manner,
Were, on the quarry of these murder'd deer,
To add the death of you.
Mal. Merciful heaven!
What, man! ne'er pull your hat upon your brows;
Give sorrow words: the grief that does not speak
Whispers the o'er-fraught heart and bids it break.
Macd. My children too?
Ross. Wife, children, servants, all
That could be found.
Macd. And I must be from thence!
My wife kill'd too?
Ross. I have said.
Mal. Be comforted:
Let 's make us med'cines of our great revenge,
To cure this deadly grief.
Macd. He has no children. All my pretty ones?
Did you say all? O hell-kite! All?
What, all my pretty chickens and their dam
At one fell swoop?
Mal. Dispute it like a man.
Macd. I shall do so;
But I must also feel it as a man:
I cannot but remember such things were,
That were most precious to me. Did heaven look on,
And would not take their part? Sinful Macduff,
They were all struck for thee! naught that I am,
Not for their own demerits, but for mine,
Fell slaughter on their souls. Heaven rest them now!
Mal. Be this the whetstone of your sword: let grief
Convert to anger; blunt not the heart, enrage it.
Macd. O, I could play the woman with mine eyes
And braggart with my tongue! But, gentle heavens,
Cut short all intermission; front to front
Bring thou this fiend of Scotland and myself;
Within my sword's length set him; if he 'scape,
Heaven forgive him too!
Mal. This tune goes manly.
Come, go we to the king; our power is ready;
Our lack is nothing but our leave: Macbeth
Is ripe for shaking, and the pow'rs above
Put on their instruments. Receive what cheer you
may:
The night is long that never finds the day. *Exeunt.*

ACT V.

SCENE I. [*Dunsinane. Ante-room in the castle.*]

Enter a Doctor of Physic *and a* Waiting-Gentlewoman.

Doct. I have two nights watched with you, but can perceive no truth in your report. When was it she last walked?

Gent. Since his majesty went into the field, I have seen her rise from her bed, throw her nightgown upon her, unlock her closet, take forth paper, fold it, write upon 't, read it, afterwards seal it, and again return to bed; yet all this while in a most fast sleep.

Doct. A great perturbation in nature, to receive at once the benefit of sleep, and do the effects of watching! In this slumbery agitation, besides her walking and other actual performances, what, at any time, have you heard her say?

Gent. That, sir, which I will not report after her.

Doct. You may to me: and 'tis most meet you should.

Gent. Neither to you nor any one, having no witness to confirm my speech.

Enter LADY [MACBETH], *with a taper.*

Lo you, here she comes! This is her very guise; and, upon my life, fast asleep. Observe her; stand close.

Doct. How came she by that light?

Gent. Why, it stood by her: she has light by her continually; 'tis her command.

Doct. You see, her eyes are open.

Gent. Ay, but their sense are shut.

Doct. What is it she does now? Look, how she rubs her hands.

Gent. It is an accustomed action with her, to seem thus washing her hands: I have known her continue in this a quarter of an hour.

Lady M. Yet here 's a spot.

Doct. Hark! she speaks: I will set down what comes from her, to satisfy my remembrance the more strongly.

Lady M. Out, damned spot! out, I say!—One: two:

182. **heavily,** sadly. 183. **out,** in arms. 188. **doff,** put off, get rid of. 189. **England,** the king of England. 192. **gives out,** tells of, proclaims. 195. **latch,** catch the sound of. 196. **fee-grief,** a grief with an individual owner. 206. **quarry,** heap of slaughtered deer at a hunt. 209-210. **the . . . break.** The conception of the broken heart is to be taken literally. 210. **Whispers,** whispers to. **o'er-fraught,** overburdened. 214. **Let 's . . . revenge.** This line expresses a current thought about revenge, not sanctioned by Christianity, but bearing a sort of sanction from the philosophy of Seneca and other ancients. 216. **He has no children,** i.e., no father would do such a thing (?). 220. **Dispute,** fight on the issue; not reason upon it. 229. **Convert,** change. 232. **intermission,** delay. 237. **Our . . . leave,** we need only to take our leave, or possibly, we need only permission to depart. 239. **Put on their instruments,** set us on as their instruments.

ACT V. SCENE I. 12. **effects of watching,** deeds characteristic of waking. 29. **sense are shut,** so F. Globe emends to *is*, but *sense* is plural here. 60. **sorely charged,** heavily burdened with passions. 71. **on 's,** of his. 84. **annoyance,** i.e., harming herself. 86. **mated,** bewildered, why, then 'tis time to do 't.—Hell is murky!—Fie, my lord, fie! a soldier, and afeard? What need we fear who knows it, when none can call our power to account?—Yet who would have thought the old man to have had so much blood in him.

Doct. Do you mark that?

Lady M. The Thane of Fife had a wife: where is she now?—What, will these hands ne'er be clean?—No more o' that, my lord, no more o' that: you mar all with this starting.

Doct. Go to, go to; you have known what you should not.

Gent. She has spoke what she should not, I am sure of that: heaven knows what she has known.

Lady M. Here 's the smell of the blood still: all the perfumes of Arabia will not sweeten this little hand. Oh, oh, oh!

Doct. What a sigh is there! The heart is sorely charged.

Gent. I would not have such a heart in my bosom for the dignity of the whole body.

Doct. Well, well, well,—

Gent. Pray God it be, sir.

Doct. This disease is beyond my practice: yet I have known those which have walked in their sleep who have died holily in their beds.

Lady M. Wash your hands, put on your nightgown; look not so pale.—I tell you yet again, Banquo 's buried; he cannot come out on 's grave.

Doct. Even so?

Lady M. To bed, to bed! there 's knocking at the gate: come, come, come, come, give me your hand. What 's done cannot be undone.—To bed, to bed, to bed! *Exit Lady.*

Doct. Will she go now to bed?

Gent. Directly.

Doct. Foul whisp'rings are abroad: unnatural deeds
Do breed unnatural troubles: infected minds
To their deaf pillows will discharge their secrets:
More needs she the divine than the physician.
God, God forgive us all! Look after her;
Remove from her the means of all annoyance,
And still keep eyes upon her. So, good night:
My mind she has mated, and amaz'd my sight.
I think, but dare not speak.

Gent. Good night, good doctor. *Exeunt.*

SCENE II. [*The country near Dunsinane.*]

Drum and colours. Enter MENTEITH, CAITHNESS, ANGUS, LENNOX, [*and*] Soldiers.

Ment. The English pow'r is near, led on by Malcolm,
His uncle Siward and the good Macduff:
Revenges burn in them; for their dear causes
Would to the bleeding and the grim alarm
Excite the mortified man.

Ang. Near Birnam wood
Shall we well meet them; that way are they coming.

Caith. Who knows if Donalbain be with his brother?

Len. For certain, sir, he is not: I have a file
Of all the gentry: there is Siward's son,
And many unrough youths that even now
Protest their first of manhood.

Ment. What does the tyrant?

Caith. Great Dunsinane he strongly fortifies:
Some say he 's mad; others that lesser hate him
Do call it valiant fury: but, for certain,
He cannot buckle his distemper'd cause
Within the belt of rule.

Ang. Now does he feel
His secret murders sticking on his hands;
Now minutely revolts upbraid his faith-breach;
Those he commands move only in command,
Nothing in love: now does he feel his title
Hang loose about him, like a giant's robe
Upon a dwarfish thief.

Ment. Who then shall blame
His pester'd senses to recoil and start,
When all that is within him does condemn
Itself for being there?

Caith. Well, march we on,
To give obedience where 'tis truly ow'd:
Meet we the med'cine of the sickly weal,
And with him pour we in our country's purge
Each drop of us.

Len. Or so much as it needs,
To dew the sovereign flower and drown the weeds.
Make we our march towards Birnam. *Exeunt, marching.*

SCENE III. [*Dunsinane. A room in the castle.*]

Enter MACBETH, Doctor, *and* Attendants.

Macb. Bring me no more reports; let them fly all:
Till Birnam wood remove to Dunsinane,
I cannot taint with fear. What 's the boy Malcolm?
Was he not born of woman? The spirits that know
All mortal consequences have pronounc'd me thus:
'Fear not, Macbeth; no man that 's born of woman
Shall e'er have power upon thee.' Then fly, false thanes,
And mingle with the English epicures:
The mind I sway by and the heart I bear
Shall never sag with doubt nor shake with fear.

Enter Servant.

The devil damn thee black, thou cream-fac'd loon!
Where got'st thou that goose look?

Serv. There is ten thousand—

Macb. Geese, villain?

Serv. Soldiers, sir.

Macb. Go, prick thy face, and over-red thy fear,
Thou lily-liver'd boy. What soldiers, patch?
Death of thy soul! those linen cheeks of thine

stupefied.

SCENE II. 4. **alarm,** call to battle. 5. **Excite,** incite. **mortified,** paralyzed. 8. **file,** list, roster. 10. **unrough,** beardless. 11. **Protest,** assert publicly. 18. **minutely,** happening every minute. 23. **pester'd,** troubled, embarrassed. **recoil,** fall away, degenerate. 27. **med'cine,** i.e., Malcolm. 30. **dew,** bedew.

SCENE III. 1. **them,** the thanes. 3. **taint,** become imbued with (an undesirable quality). 5. **mortal consequences,** what befalls man. Cuningham prefers either *consequents* or (following Singer) *consequence,* both of which are metrically better than the text. 8. **epicures,** luxury-loving persons. Holinshed refers to the introduction of luxurious habits of living by the English into Scotland. 9. **sway by,** am directed or swayed by. 11. **loon,** stupid fellow. 14. **over-red,** redden over. The servant's blood has all retired into his lower abdomen on account of his fear, so that he is very pale and there is no blood in his liver, where his courage should have resided—hence, *lily-liver'd* (l. 15). 15. **patch,** domestic fool; here used contemptuously.

Are counsellors to fear. What soldiers, whey-face?
Serv. The English force, so please you.
Macb. Take thy face hence. [*Exit Servant.*]
Seyton!—I am sick at heart,
When I behold—Seyton, I say!—This push
Will cheer me ever, or disseat me now.
I have liv'd long enough: my way of life
Is fall'n into the sear, the yellow leaf;
And that which should accompany old age,
As honour, love, obedience, troops of friends,
I must not look to have; but, in their stead,
Curses, not loud but deep, mouth-honour, breath,
Which the poor heart would fain deny, and dare not.
Seyton!

Enter SEYTON.

Sey. What is your gracious pleasure?
Macb. What news more?
Sey. All is confirm'd, my lord, which was reported.
Macb. I'll fight till from my bones my flesh be hack'd.
Give me my armour.
Sey. 'Tis not needed yet.
Macb. I'll put it on.
Send out moe horses; skirr the country round;
Hang those that talk of fear. Give me mine armour.
How does your patient, doctor?
Doct. Not so sick, my lord,
As she is troubled with thick-coming fancies,
That keep her from her rest.
Macb. Cure her of that.
Canst thou not minister to a mind diseas'd,
Pluck from the memory a rooted sorrow,
Raze out the written troubles of the brain
And with some sweet oblivious antidote
Cleanse the stuff'd bosom of that perilous stuff
Which weighs upon the heart?
Doct. Therein the patient
Must minister to himself.
Macb. Throw physic to the dogs; I'll none of it.
Come, put mine armour on; give me my staff.
Seyton, send out. Doctor, the thanes fly from me.
Come, sir, dispatch. If thou couldst, doctor, cast
The water of my land, find her disease,
And purge it to a sound and pristine health,
I would applaud thee to the very echo,
That should applaud again.—Pull 't off, I say.—
What rhubarb, senna, or what purgative drug,
Would scour these English hence? Hear'st thou of them?
Doct. Ay, my good lord; your royal preparation
Makes us hear something.
Macb. Bring it after me.
I will not be afraid of death and bane,
Till Birnam forest come to Dunsinane.
Doct. [*Aside*] Were I from Dunsinane away and clear,
Profit again should hardly draw me here. *Exeunt.*

SCENE IV. [*Country near Birnam wood.*]

Drum and colours. Enter MALCOLM, SIWARD, MACDUFF, *Siward's* Son, MENTEITH, CAITHNESS, ANGUS, [LENNOX, ROSS,] *and* Soldiers, *marching.*

Mal. Cousins, I hope the days are near at hand
That chambers will be safe.
Ment. We doubt it nothing.
Siw. What wood is this before us?
Ment. The wood of Birnam.
Mal. Let every soldier hew him down a bough
And bear 't before him: thereby shall we shadow
The numbers of our host and make discovery
Err in report of us.
Soldiers. It shall be done.
Siw. We learn no other but the confident tyrant
Keeps still in Dunsinane, and will endure
Our setting down before 't.
Mal. 'Tis his main hope:
For where there is advantage to be given,
Both more and less have given him the revolt,
And none serve with him but constrained things
Whose hearts are absent too.
Macd. Let our just censures
Attend the true event, and put we on
Industrious soldiership.
Siw. The time approaches
That will with due decision make us know
What we shall say we have and what we owe.
Thoughts speculative their unsure hopes relate,
But certain issue strokes must arbitrate:
Towards which advance the war. *Exeunt, marching.*

SCENE V. [*Dunsinane. Within the castle.*]

Enter MACBETH, SEYTON, *and* Soldiers, *with drum and colours.*

Macb. Hang out our banners on the outward walls:
The cry is still 'They come:' our castle's strength
Will laugh a siege to scorn: here let them lie
Till famine and the ague eat them up:
Were they not forc'd with those that should be ours,
We might have met them dareful, beard to beard,
And beat them backward home. *A cry within of women.*
What is that noise?
Sey. It is the cry of women, my good lord. [*Exit.*]
Macb. I have almost forgot the taste of fears:
The time has been, my senses would have cool'd
To hear a night-shriek; and my fell of hair
Would at a dismal treatise rouse and stir
As life were in 't: I have supp'd full with horrors;
Direness, familiar to my slaughterous thoughts,
Cannot once start me.

[*Enter* SEYTON.]

Wherefore was that cry?

17. **counsellors to fear,** i.e., they suggest fear in conformity with psychological doctrine; I, v, 73. 20. **push,** crisis, onset. 21. **cheer . . . disseat,** so F; Dyce: *chair;* others: *disease* (so F_2). 35. **skirr,** scour. 43. **oblivious,** causing forgetfulness. 48. **staff,** lance; probably not the general's baton. 50. **cast,** technical term for "diagnose." 54. **Pull 't off,** referring to some part of the armor. 55. **senna,** purgative drug; F: *Cyme,* evidently misprint for "cynne," a common spelling of the word. 58. **it,** the armor.

SCENE IV. 2. **chambers,** i.e., men may sleep safely in their bedchambers. 14. **censures.** The older soldier recalls them to their task; in this he is seconded by Siward.

SCENE V. 1. **Hang . . . banners.** Keightley's punctuation is attractive: *Hang out our banners! On the outward walls,* etc. 5. **forc'd,** reinforced. 10. **The time has been.** Macbeth here lays claim to that callousness which comes from *hard use* (III, iv, 143). 11. **my fell of hair,** the hair of my scalp. 12. **dismal treatise,** sinister story. 14. **slaughterous thoughts,** thoughts of murder. 17. **She . . . hereafter.** Her death should have been deferred to some more peaceful hour

Sey. The queen, my lord, is dead.
Macb. She should have died hereafter;
There would have been a time for such a word.
To-morrow, and to-morrow, and to-morrow,
Creeps in this petty pace from day to day
To the last syllable of recorded time,
And all our yesterdays have lighted fools
The way to dusty death. Out, out, brief candle!
Life 's but a walking shadow, a poor player
That struts and frets his hour upon the stage
And then is heard no more: it is a tale
Told by an idiot, full of sound and fury,
Signifying nothing.

Enter a Messenger.

Thou com'st to use thy tongue; thy story quickly.
Mess. Gracious my lord,
I should report that which I say I saw,
But know not how to do it.
Macb. Well, say, sir.
Mess. As I did stand my watch upon the hill,
I look'd toward Birnam, and anon, methought,
The wood began to move.
Macb. Liar and slave!
Mess. Let me endure your wrath, if 't be not so:
Within this three mile may you see it coming;
I say, a moving grove.
Macb. If thou speak'st false,
Upon the next tree shalt thou hang alive,
Till famine cling thee: if thy speech be sooth,
I care not if thou dost for me as much.
I pull in resolution, and begin
To doubt th' equivocation of the fiend
That lies like truth: 'Fear not, till Birnam wood
Do come to Dunsinane:' and now a wood
Comes toward Dunsinane. Arm, arm, and out!
If this which he avouches does appear,
There is nor flying hence nor tarrying here.
I 'gin to be aweary of the sun,
And wish th' estate o' th' world were now undone.
Ring the alarum-bell! Blow, wind! come, wrack!
At least we'll die with harness on our back. *Exeunt.*

SCENE VI. [*Dunsinane. Before the castle.*]

Drum and colours. Enter MALCOLM, SIWARD, MACDUFF, *and their* Army, *with boughs.*

Mal. Now near enough: your leavy screens throw down,
And show like those you are. You, worthy uncle,
Shall, with my cousin, your right-noble son,
Lead our first battle: worthy Macduff and we
Shall take upon 's what else remains to do,
According to our order.
Siw. Fare you well.
Do we but find the tyrant's power to-night,
Let us be beaten, if we cannot fight.
Macd. Make all our trumpets speak; give them all breath,
Those clamorous harbingers of blood and death.
Exeunt. Alarums continued.

SCENE VII. [*Another part of the field.*]

Enter MACBETH.

Macb. They have tied me to a stake; I cannot fly,
But, bear-like, I must fight the course. What 's he
That was not born of woman? Such a one
Am I to fear, or none.

Enter young SIWARD.

Yo. Siw. What is thy name?
Macb. Thou 'lt be afraid to hear it.
Yo. Siw. No; though thou call'st thyself a hotter name
Than any is in hell.
Macb. My name 's Macbeth.
Yo. Siw. The devil himself could not pronounce a title
More hateful to mine ear.
Macb. No, nor more fearful.
Yo. Siw. Thou liest, abhorred tyrant; with my sword
I'll prove the lie thou speak'st.
Fight, and young Siward slain.
Macb. Thou wast born of woman.
But swords I smile at, weapons laugh to scorn,
Brandish'd by man that 's of a woman born. *Exit.*

Alarums. Enter MACDUFF.

Macd. That way the noise is. Tyrant, show thy face!
If thou be'st slain and with no stroke of mine,
My wife and children's ghosts will haunt me still.
I cannot strike at wretched kerns, whose arms
Are hir'd to bear their staves: either thou, Macbeth,
Or else my sword with an unbattered edge
I sheathe again undeeded. There thou shouldst be;
By this great clatter, one of greatest note
Seems bruited. Let me find him, fortune!
And more I beg not. *Exit. Alarums.*

Enter MALCOLM *and* SIWARD.

Siw. This way, my lord; the castle 's gently rend'red:
The tyrant's people on both sides do fight;
The noble thanes do bravely in the war;
The day almost itself professes yours,
And little is to do.
Mal. We have met with foes
That strike beside us.
Siw. Enter, sir, the castle.
Exeunt. Alarum.

[SCENE VIII. *Another part of the field.*]

Enter MACBETH.

Macb. Why should I play the Roman fool, and die

(Johnson); or, she would have died some day. 18. **such a word,** i.e., as death. 19-28. **To-morrow . . . nothing.** The first sentence is not easy to construe, but the whole passage is clear. 40. **cling,** cause to shrivel up. **sooth,** truth. 42. **pull in,** explained as "check," "restrain." Johnson conjectured *pall,* grow stale, fail—a preferable reading. 51. **wrack,** ruin.

SCENE VII. 2. **bear-like . . . course.** This is a simile from the sport of bearbaiting, in which the bear was tied to a stake and dogs were set upon him; the *course* was a bout or round. 17. **kerns,** properly, Irish foot soldiers; here applied contemptuously to the rank and file. 18. **staves,** spears. 22. **bruited,** noised abroad, announced.

SCENE VIII. 1. **Roman fool.** Shakespeare had staged deep arguments from Plutarch on the propriety of suicide when he wrote *Julius Caesar,* and was probably now reading on the same issue in the *Life of Antony.* He here seems to give voice to the northern temper. Macbeth is a man in whom the impulse to live is overmastering.

On mine own sword? whiles I see lives, the gashes
Do better upon them.

Enter MACDUFF.

Macd. Turn, hell-hound, turn!
Macb. Of all men else I have avoided thee:
But get thee back; my soul is too much charg'd
With blood of thine already.
Macd. I have no words:
My voice is in my sword: thou bloodier villain
Than terms can give thee out! *Fight. Alarum.*
Macb. Thou losest labour:
As easy mayst thou the intrenchant air
With thy keen sword impress as make me bleed:
Let fall thy blade on vulnerable crests;
I bear a charmed life, which must not yield
To one of woman born.
Macd. Despair thy charm;
And let the angel whom thou still hast serv'd
Tell thee, Macduff was from his mother's womb
Untimely ripp'd.
Macb. Accursed be that tongue that tells me so,
For it hath cow'd my better part of man!
And be these juggling fiends no more believ'd,
That palter with us in a double sense;
That keep the word of promise to our ear,
And break it to our hope. I'll not fight with thee.
Macd. Then yield thee, coward,
And live to be the show and gaze o' th' time:
We'll have thee, as our rarer monsters are,
Painted upon a pole, and underwrit,
'Here may you see the tyrant.'
Macb. I will not yield,
To kiss the ground before young Malcolm's feet,
And to be baited with the rabble's curse.
Though Birnam wood be come to Dunsinane,
And thou oppos'd, being of no woman born,
Yet I will try the last. Before my body
I throw my warlike shield. Lay on, Macduff,
And damn'd be him that first cries 'Hold, enough!'
Exeunt, fighting. Alarums.

Enter fighting, and MACBETH *slain.* [*Exit Macduff with Macbeth's body.*]
Retreat, and flourish. Enter, with drums and colours, MALCOLM, SIWARD, ROSS, Thanes, *and* Soldiers.

Mal. I would the friends we miss were safe arriv'd.
Siw. Some must go off: and yet, by these I see,
So great a day as this is cheaply bought.
Mal. Macduff is missing, and your noble son.
Ross. Your son, my lord, has paid a soldier's debt:
He only liv'd but till he was a man;
The which no sooner had his prowess confirm'd
In the unshrinking station where he fought,
But like a man he died.
Siw. Then he is dead?
Ross. Ay, and brought off the field: your cause of sorrow
Must not be measur'd by his worth, for then
It hath no end.
Siw. Had he his hurts before?
Ross. Ay, on the front.
Siw. Why then, God's soldier be he!
Had I as many sons as I have hairs,
I would not wish them to a fairer death:
And so, his knell is knoll'd.
Mal. He 's worth more sorrow,
And that I'll spend for him.
Siw. He 's worth no more:
They say he parted well, and paid his score:
And so, God be with him! Here comes newer comfort.

Enter MACDUFF, *with* MACBETH'S *head.*

Macd. Hail, king! for so thou art: behold, where stands
Th' usurper's cursed head; the time is free:
I see thee compass'd with thy kingdom's pearl,
That speak my salutation in their minds;
Whose voices I desire aloud with mine:
Hail, King of Scotland!
All. Hail, King of Scotland! *Flourish.*
Mal. We shall not spend a large expense of time
Before we reckon with your several loves,
And make us even with you. My thanes and kinsmen,
Henceforth be earls, the first that ever Scotland
In such an honour nam'd. What 's more to do,
Which would be planted newly with the time,
As calling home our exil'd friends abroad
That fled the snares of watchful tyranny;
Producing forth the cruel ministers
Of this dead butcher and his fiend-like queen,
Who, as 'tis thought, by self and violent hands
Took off her life; this, and what needful else
That calls upon us, by the grace of Grace,
We will perform in measure, time and place:
So, thanks to all at once and to each one,
Whom we invite to see us crown'd at Scone.
Flourish. Exeunt omnes.

9. **intrenchant,** invulnerable, indivisible. 14. **angel,** evil angel, Macbeth's genius. 18. **cow'd . . . man,** subdued my soul, or spirit, or mind. Macbeth's invulnerability was, in some measure, his belief in his invulnerability. 20. **palter . . . sense,** equivocate with us. 26. **Painted upon a pole,** i.e., painted on a board suspended on a pole. 30-34. **Though . . . enough.** Macbeth's recoil to courage would be explained in the psychology of the time as the setting up in him of a new impulse of passion. His repugnance to submission drives out his craven fear. 42. **unshrinking station,** post from which he did not shrink. 55. **free,** released from tyranny. 56. **thy kingdom's pearl,** the flower of thy kingdom. 63. **Henceforth be earls,** a detail from Holinshed. *Earl* was an English title. 70. **self and violent,** her own violent.

THOUGH MACB WAS EVIL, HAD NOBILITY + DEPTH

ANTONY AND CLEOPATRA

Shakespeare probably wrote *Antony and Cleopatra* in 1606 or 1607; it was registered for publication on May 20, 1608, and apparently influenced a revision of Samuel Daniel's *Cleopatra* that was published "newly altered" in 1607. *Antony and Cleopatra* was thus roughly contemporary with *King Lear* and *Macbeth*. Yet the contrast between those dark tragedies of evil and this Roman tragedy of love and political struggle is immense. Unlike *Macbeth*, with its taut focus on a murderer and his wife, *Antony and Cleopatra* moves back and forth across the Mediterranean in its epic sweep of characters and events, weaving together the fates of Pompey, Octavius Caesar, Octavia, and Lepidus with those of the protagonists. *King Lear* gives proper names to fourteen characters, *Macbeth* to eighteen; *Antony and Cleopatra* to thirty-one. The Roman play requires no less than forty-two separate scenes, of which most occur in what modern editors label Acts III and IV—although no play is less suited to the classical rigors of five-act structure, and these divisions are not found in the reliable Folio text of 1623. Indeed, it is as though Shakespeare resolved at the height of his career to show that he could dispense entirely with the classical "rules," which had never taken serious hold of the English popular stage in any case. The flouting of the unities is so extreme that John Dryden, in his *All for Love or The World Well Lost* (1678), undertook not so much to revise Shakespeare as to start afresh on the same subject. Dryden's play is restricted to the last few hours of the protagonists' lives, at Cleopatra's tomb in Alexandria, with a severely limited cast of characters and much of the narrative revealed through recollection. Although a substantial achievement in its own right, *All for Love* surely reveals that Shakespeare knew what he was doing, for Dryden has excised a good deal of the panorama, the excitement, the "infinite variety."

Shakespeare departs also from the somber tone of his tragedies of evil, pursuing instead the ironies found in his other Roman plays. As protagonists, Antony and Cleopatra lack tragic stature, or so it first appears: she is a tawny gypsy temptress and he a "strumpet's fool," a once-great general now bound in "strong Egyptian fetters" and lost in "dotage." Several scenes, especially those set in Egypt, are comic and delightfully bawdy: Charmian learning her fortune from the soothsayer, Cleopatra practicing her charms in vain to keep Antony from leaving Egypt or raunchily daydreaming of being Antony's horse "to bear the weight of Antony" (I,v), Cleopatra flying into a magnificent rage at the news of Antony's marriage to Octavia and then consoling herself with catty reflections on Octavia's reported low voice and shortness of stature ("I think so, Charmian: dull of tongue, and dwarfish," III,iii). In its comic texture the play somewhat resembles *Romeo and Juliet*, an earlier play about a younger pair of lovers. For *Antony* is, after all, about lovers, not like *Othello* about the jealous end of love. In its depiction of two contrasting worlds, also, *Antony* recalls the movement of several earlier comedies from the realistic world of political conniving to a dream world of exotic adventure. Accordingly, the vision of life presented is often ambivalent and ironic as much as it is tragic. The sense of relative values separating Egypt and Rome prevents us from identifying fully with either, and underscores instead the mystery and paradox of man's seemingly irreconcilable quest for pleasure and honor. The ending is neither a triumph nor a defeat for the lovers, but something of both. Cathartic affirmation comes not through revelation of man's dignity in the face of a hostile universe, but through an almost comic perception of the absurdity of worldly striving which can be transfigured only by our dreams.

The Roman point of view opens the play, and never entirely loses its force as an ideal. At first it seems decidedly superior to that of Egypt. Demetrius and Philo, disinterested choric figures even though they are also Roman soldiers, lament the decline of Antony into Circean enslavement. Their tragic concept is of the Fall of Princes, all the more soberly edifying because of the heights from which Antony has toppled. "You shall see in him The triple pillar of the world transform'd Into a strumpet's fool." Egypt is enchanting but clearly enervating—a bizarre assemblage of soothsayers, eunuchs, and waiting-gentlewomen who wish to be "married to three kings in a forenoon, and widow them all." Their mirth is all bawdry, tinged with practices Roman custom views as unnatural. Prevailing images are of procreation in various shapes, sleep (mandragora, Lethe), the oriental opulence of Cleopatra's barge (a golden poop, purple sails, silver oars, divers-colored fans), Epicurean feasting, and drinking. As Enobarbus says, "Mine, and most of our fortunes, to-night, shall be—drunk to bed" (I,ii).

Antony, for all his reckless defiance of Rome, agrees in his more reflective moments with what Demetrius and Philo have said. "A Roman thought hath struck him," Cleopatra observantly remarks, and Antony has indeed determined that "I must from this enchanting queen break off" (I,ii). His later return to Cleopatra is at least in part a surrender, a betrayal of his marriage vows to Octavia and his political assurances to Caesar. In the ensuing battles, Antony submits himself dangerously to Cleopatra's governance, and this inversion of male and female roles is clearly emblematic of a deeper disorder. As Enobarbus concludes bitterly, Antony "would make his will Lord of his reason," and so has subverted his "judgement" (III,xiii) to passion.

From the beginning, Cleopatra has instinctively sought dominance over Antony in the war of the sexes. When Antony first came to her on the River Cydnus, we learn, he was so overcome in all his senses that he was "barber'd ten time o'er," like Samson in the hands of Delilah (II,ii). Cleopatra boasts that she "angled" for Antony on that occasion, catching him the way fishermen "betray" fish, and that when she had "drunk him to his bed" she "put my tires and mantles on him, whilst I wore his sword Philippan" (II,v). Caesar, affronted by such transvestite debauchery, charges that Antony "is not more manlike Than Cleopatra, nor the queen of Ptolemy More womanly than he" (I,iv). During the battle scenes, Antony's followers complain that "Photinus an eunuch" and Cleopatra's maids manage the war: "So our leader's led, And we are women's men" (III,vii). Antony confesses too late that they were right. He becomes a "doting mallard," one whose heart is "tied by th' strings" to Cleopatra's rudder when her ships retreat in the first naval engagement (III,xi). In the mythic images used to raise their relationship to heroic proportions, Antony is Mars to Cleopatra's Venus (I,v), but not as the correct embodiment of masterful soldiership and beauteous feminine companionship; instead, they are the sensual objects of Olympian ridicule. Similarly Antony is like Hercules, not in his prime but with the shirt of Nessus on his back—a poisoned shirt given Hercules by his wife in a mistaken hope of thereby assuring his love for her (IV,xii). Antony's soldiers understandably believe that the god Hercules has deserted his reputed descendant and onetime champion (IV,iii).

Despite Antony's shameful violation of manhood, honor, attention to duty, self-knowledge, and all that Rome stands for, however, the end of his story is anything but a one-sided endorsement for the Roman point of view. The actual Rome, disfigured by political conniving, falls far short of the ideal. Antony has a point when he protests that "Kingdoms are clay" (I,i). Alliances are unstable and are governed by mere political expediency. At first, Antony's wife Fulvia and his brother Lucius have fought one another until forced to unite against the greater threat of Octavius Caesar. Similarly, Antony and Caesar come together only because Pompey has become dangerously powerful at sea and has won the favor of the fickle mob, "Our slippery people." This *detente* is not meant to last. As Enobarbus bluntly puts it, "if you borrow one another's love for the instant, you may, when you hear no more words of Pompey, return it again" (II,ii). Enobarbus is rebuked for his unstatesmanlike tone, but no one denies the validity of what he says. In this cynical negotiation, Octavia is a pawn between husband and brother, shabbily treated by both. Caesar coldly bargains away the happiness of the one person whom he is able to love; Antony, although hating false promises and so resolving to be loyal to Octavia, knows within himself that it won't work. To make matters worse for the fair-minded Antony, he has received great favors from Pompey which he must now uncharitably repudiate in the interests of politics. Pompey does not miss the opportunity to remind Antony of his ingratitude, but the prevailing mood is not so much one of bitterness as of ironic futility. Old friendships must be sacrificed; no one seems wholly to blame, no one can stop the game. Pompey is as much in the wrong as anyone, and as powerless. Despite his idealistic hope of rescuing Rome from political infighting, he has had to ally himself with pirates who offer him sinister temptations. He could be "lord of all the world" if he would only murder on occasion, but Pompey is destined to be trapped between lofty ends and ignoble means. Lepidus is still another dismaying victim of political callousness, used condescendingly by Caesar and permitted to drink himself into oblivion, until he is cashiered on a trumped-up charge and imprisoned for life.

Octavius Caesar embodies most of all the ironic limits of political ambition. He has avoided enslavement to passion at the very real cost of enslaving himself to duty. His ideal warrior is one who, driven by military necessity, would "drink The stale [urine] of horses, and the gilded puddle Which beasts would cough at" (I,iv). As a general he is Antony's opposite in every way. He attacks only when he has the advantage, and places those who have deserted Antony in his own front lines so "That Antony may seem to spend his fury Upon himself" (IV,vi). He controls his supplies cannily, believing it a "waste" to feast his army (IV,i). He of course declines Antony's offers of single combat. Antony meantime recklessly accepts Caesar's gambit to fight at sea, feasts debauchingly in one "gaudy night" after another, and generously refuses to blame or penalize those who leave him. His sending Enobarbus' belongings after him into Caesar's camp convinces that honest soldier he has made a fatal error; for, however imprudent Antony's chivalry may be, it is unquestionably noble and great-hearted. Caesar is a superb general and political genius, but he is also a military automaton, a logistical reckoner, a Machiavel. In his personal life he is no less austere and puritanical. He deplores loosening his tongue with alcohol. About women he is deeply cynical, firmly believing that "want will perjure The ne'er-touch'd vestal" (III,xii). Between him and Cleopatra there is a profound antipathy, based in part on his revulsion at her earlier affair with his namesake and

THE HUNTINGTON LIBRARY, SAN MARINO, CALIFORNIA

Asps from *Historia Animalium* by Conrad Gesner, 1603 (Huntington)

predecessor, Julius Caesar (III,vi). Cleopatra may entertain briefly the notion of trying to seduce this new Caesar (III,xiii), for like Charmian she loves long life "better than figs," but if so she soon discovers that she and Caesar are not compatible. All that he represents she must instead grandly repudiate, choosing death and an eternity with Antony as her way to "call great Caesar ass Unpolicied" (V,ii).

Cleopatra's greatness is elusive, all the more enthralling because so mysterious. She rises above her counterpart in Shakespeare's source, Plutarch's *Lives*, where she is an impressive queenly woman but still essentially a temptress causing the lamentable fall of the hero. Shakespeare's Cleopatra is that, but is also something indefinable that can be gotten at only through paradox. Her very character is the essence of contradiction: she knows how "to chide, to laugh, to weep," to be sullen or violent, like a skillful actor keeping Antony continually off guard. Dispassionately examined, she is a woman no longer young who abuses messengers like an oriental despot, who lies about her wealth when captured by Caesar (what is she planning to do with that wealth, anyway?), and who may take her own life only when she realizes that the alternative is public shame and captivity. Yet the myth of her charm is eternal. Observers evoking her splendor do not describe her person directly, but rather her effects and surroundings: Enobarbus says simply that "For her own person, It beggar'd all description," and goes on to catalogue her cloth-of-gold pavilion and her mermaid-like attendants. Most of all, she is paradox: she makes defect perfection, age cannot wither her, and "vilest things Become themselves in her, that the holy priests Bless her when she is riggish" (II,ii). She is the Lucretian Venus, holy and sluttish. In her, "fancy" exceeds "nature." When she protests that she will not go to Rome to behold herself in a wretched play and thus see "Some squeaking Cleopatra boy my greatness I' th' posture of a whore" (V,ii), we realize that Shakespeare is calling attention to his own art as well, pointing out how Elizabethan boy actors on a bare stage can transform reality into a dream that we believe. Cleopatra's mystery is like that of poetic art itself. The "real" world pales into insignificance of a "little O, the earth," something "no better than a sty," full of illusory shadows that "mock our eyes with air"; and Caesar's triumph vanishes with it. In its place, Antony and Cleopatra raise up a vision of themselves as lovers who, through art, have indeed become eternal. Together they will overpicture Venus and Mars, and will be so renowned that "Dido and her Aeneas shall want troops, And all the haunt be ours" (IV,xiv). Antony is no longer dying Hercules but the god of Cleopatra's dream whose "legs bestrid the ocean: his rear'd arm Crested the world: his voice was propertied As all the tuned spheres" (V,ii). These are the "immortal longings" for which Cleopatra goes willingly to death, dressed in her "best attires" like a queen; for she will accept nothing less than greatness.

ANTONY AND CLEOPATRA

[*Dramatis Personae*

MARK ANTONY, OCTAVIUS CÆSAR, M. ÆMILIUS LEPIDUS, — *triumvirs.*
SEXTUS POMPEIUS.
DOMITIUS ENOBARBUS, VENTIDIUS, EROS, SCARUS, DECRETAS, DEMETRIUS, PHILO, — *friends to Antony.*

MECÆNAS, AGRIPPA, DOLABELLA, PROCULEIUS, THIDIAS, GALLUS, — *friends to Cæsar.*

MENAS, MENECRATES, VARRIUS, — *friends to Pompey.*
TAURUS, *lieutenant-general to Cæsar.*
CANIDIUS, *lieutenant-general to Antony.*
An Officer in Ventidius' army.
An Ambassador from Antony to Cæsar.
ALEXAS, MARDIAN, *a Eunuch,* SELEUCUS, DIOMEDES, — *attendants on Cleopatra.*
A Soothsayer.
A Clown.

CLEOPATRA, Queen of Egypt.
OCTAVIA, *sister to Cæsar and wife to Antony.*
CHARMIAN, IRAS, — *attendants on Cleopatra.*

Officers, Soldiers, Messengers, *and* other Attendants.

SCENE: *In several parts of the Roman empire.*]

ACT I.

SCENE I. [*Alexandria. A room in Cleopatra's palace.*]

Enter DEMETRIUS *and* PHILO.

Phi. Nay, but this dotage of our general's
O'erflows the measure: those his goodly eyes,
That o'er the files and musters of the war
Have glow'd like plated Mars, now bend, now turn,
The office and devotion of their view
Upon a tawny front: his captain's heart,
Which in the scuffles of great fights hath burst
The buckles on his breast, reneges all temper,

And is become the bellows and the fan
To cool a gipsy's lust.

Flourish. Enter ANTONY, CLEOPATRA, *her Ladies, the Train, with Eunuchs fanning her.*

Look, where they come:
Take but good note, and you shall see in him
The triple pillar of the world transform'd
Into a strumpet's fool: behold and see.
Cleo. If it be love indeed, tell me how much.
Ant. There 's beggary in the love that can be reckon'd.
Cleo. I'll set a bourn how far to be belov'd.
Ant. Then must thou needs find out new heaven, new earth.

Enter a Messenger.

Mess. News, my good lord, from Rome.
Ant. Grates me: the sum.
Cleo. Nay, hear them, Antony:
Fulvia perchance is angry; or, who knows
If the scarce-bearded Cæsar have not sent
His pow'rful mandate to you, 'Do this, or this;
Take in that kingdom, and enfranchise that;
Perform 't, or else we damn thee.'
Ant. How, my love!
Cleo. Perchance! nay, and most like:
You must not stay here longer, your dismission
Is come from Cæsar; therefore hear it, Antony.
Where 's Fulvia's process? Cæsar's I would say? both?
Call in the messengers. As I am Egypt's queen,
Thou blushest, Antony; and that blood of thine
Is Cæsar's homager: else so thy cheek pays shame
When shrill-tongu'd Fulvia scolds. The messengers!
Ant. Let Rome in Tiber melt, and the wide arch
Of the rang'd empire fall! Here is my space.
Kingdoms are clay: our dungy earth alike
Feeds beast as man: the nobleness of life
Is to do thus; when such a mutual pair [*Embracing.*]
And such a twain can do 't, in which I bind,
On pain of punishment, the world to weet
We stand up peerless.
Cleo. Excellent falsehood!
Why did he marry Fulvia, and not love her?
I'll seem the fool I am not; Antony
Will be himself.
Ant. But stirr'd by Cleopatra.
Now, for the love of Love and her soft hours,
Let 's not confound the time with conference harsh:
There 's not a minute of our lives should stretch
Without some pleasure now. What sport to-night?
Cleo. Hear the ambassadors.
Ant. Fie, wrangling queen!
Whom every thing becomes, to chide, to laugh,
To weep; whose every passion fully strives
To make itself, in thee, fair and admir'd!
No messenger, but thine; and all alone
To-night we'll wander through the streets and note
The qualities of people. Come, my queen;
Last night you did desire it.—Speak not to us.
Exeunt [*Ant. and Cleo.*] *with the train.*
Dem. Is Cæsar with Antonius priz'd so slight?
Phi. Sir, sometimes, when he is not Antony,
He comes too short of that great property
Which still should go with Antony.
Dem. I am full sorry
That he approves the common liar, who
Thus speaks of him at Rome: but I will hope
Of better deeds to-morrow. Rest you happy! *Exeunt.*

[SCENE II. *The same. Another room.*]

Enter ENOBARBUS, LAMPRIUS, *a* Soothsayer, RANNIUS, LUCILLIUS, CHARMIAN, IRAS, MARDIAN *the Eunuch, and* ALEXAS.

Char. Lord Alexas, sweet Alexas, most any thing Alexas, almost most absolute Alexas, where 's the soothsayer that you praised so to the queen? O, that I knew this husband, which, you say, must charge his horns with garlands!
Alex. Soothsayer!
Sooth. Your will?
Char. Is this the man? Is 't you, sir, that know things?
Sooth. In nature's infinite book of secrecy
A little I can read.
Alex. Show him your hand.
Eno. Bring in the banquet quickly; wine enough
Cleopatra's health to drink.
Char. Good sir, give me good fortune.
Sooth. I make not, but foresee.
Char. Pray, then, foresee me one.
Sooth. You shall be yet far fairer than you are.
Char. He means in flesh.
Iras. No, you shall paint when you are old.
Char. Wrinkles forbid!
Alex. Vex not his prescience; be attentive.
Char. Hush!
Sooth. You shall be more beloving than beloved.
Char. I had rather heat my liver with drinking.
Alex. Nay, hear him.
Char. Good now, some excellent fortune! Let me be married to three kings in a forenoon, and widow them all: let me have a child at fifty, to whom Herod of Jewry may do homage: find me to marry me with Octavius Cæsar, and companion me with my mistress.
Sooth. You shall outlive the lady whom you serve.
Char. O excellent! I love long life better than figs.
Sooth. You have seen and prov'd a fairer former fortune
Than that which is to approach.
Char. Then belike my children shall have no names: prithee, how many boys and wenches must I have?
Sooth. If every of your wishes had a womb,
And fertile every wish, a million.
Char. Out, fool! I forgive thee for a witch.
Alex. You think none but your sheets are privy to your wishes.

ACT I. SCENE I. 4. **plated,** clothed in armor. 5. **office,** service. 6. **tawny,** yellowish brown. 8. **reneges,** renounces. **temper,** self-restraint. 10. **gipsy's,** suggests that Cleopatra was an Egyptian, and also used as an opprobrious epithet. 12. **triple,** third; allusion to the Triumvirate composed of Antony, Lepidus, and Octavius Caesar. 16. **bourn,** boundary. 18. **Grates me,** it vexes me. **the sum,** i.e., be brief. 20. **Fulvia,** Antony's wife, of whom Cleopatra is jealous. 23. **Take in,** conquer. **enfranchise,** set free. 26. **dismission,** dismissal. 28. **process,** summons. 31. **homager,** vassal. 34. **rang'd,** ordered, or possibly, extended. 37. **mutual,** exchanging equal love. 39. **weet,** wit, know. 43. **stirr'd,** moved, excited. The meaning depends somewhat on lines 40-42, which Johnson thought were spoken as an aside. 60. **approves,** corroborates.

SCENE II. 11. **banquet,** dessert. 23. **with drinking,** with wine rather than love. 28. **Herod of Jewry,** the blustering tyrant who massacred the children of Judea. 29. **find me,** by examining my hand. 32. **better than figs,** probably a proverbial expression, with phallic suggestion. Malone and many other commentators interpret the sooth-

Char. Nay, come, tell Iras hers.

Alex. We'll know all our fortunes.

Eno. Mine, and most of our fortunes, to-night, shall be—drunk to bed.

Iras. There 's a palm presages chastity, if nothing else.

Char. E'en as the o'erflowing Nilus presageth famine.

Iras. Go, you wild bedfellow, you cannot soothsay.

Char. Nay, if an oily palm be not a fruitful prognostication, I cannot scratch mine ear. Prithee, tell her but a worky-day fortune.

Sooth. Your fortunes are alike.

Iras. But how, but how? give me particulars.

Sooth. I have said.

Iras. Am I not an inch of fortune better than she?

Char. Well, if you were but an inch of fortune better than I, where would you choose it?

Iras. Not in my husband's nose.

Char. Our worser thoughts heavens mend! Alexas,—come, his fortune, his fortune! O, let him marry a woman that cannot go, sweet Isis, I beseech thee! and let her die too, and give him a worse! and let worse follow worse, till the worst of all follow him laughing to his grave, fifty-fold a cuckold! Good Isis, hear me this prayer, though thou deny me a matter of more weight; good Isis, I beseech thee!

Iras. Amen. Dear goddess, hear that prayer of the people! for, as it is a heart-breaking to see a handsome man loose-wived, so it is a deadly sorrow to behold a foul knave uncuckolded: therefore, dear Isis, keep decorum, and fortune him accordingly!

Char. Amen.

Alex. Lo, now, if it lay in their hands to make me a cuckold, they would make themselves whores, but they 'ld do 't!

Enter CLEOPATRA.

Eno. Hush! here comes Antony.
Char. Not he; the queen.
Cleo. Saw you my lord?
Eno. No, lady.
Cleo. Was he not here?
Char. No, madam.
Cleo. He was dispos'd to mirth; but on the sudden
A Roman thought hath struck him. Enobarbus!
Eno. Madam?
Cleo. Seek him, and bring him hither. Where 's Alexas?
Alex. Here, at your service. My lord approaches.

Enter ANTONY *with a* Messenger [*and* Attendants].

Cleo. We will not look upon him: go with us.
Exeunt [*all but Antony, Messenger, and Attendants*].
Mess. Fulvia thy wife first came into the field.
Ant. Against my brother Lucius?
Mess. Ay:
But soon that war had end, and the time 's state
Made friends of them, jointing their force 'gainst Cæsar;
Whose better issue in the war, from Italy,
Upon the first encounter, drave them.
Ant. Well, what worst?
Mess. The nature of bad news infects the teller.
Ant. When it concerns the fool or coward. On:
Things that are past are done with me. 'Tis thus;
Who tells me true, though in his tale lie death,
I hear him as he flatter'd.
Mess. Labienus—
This is stiff news—hath, with his Parthian force,
Extended Asia from Euphrates;
His conquering banner shook from Syria
To Lydia and to Ionia;
Whilst—
Ant. Antony, thou wouldst say,—
Mess. O, my lord!
Ant. Speak to me home, mince not the general tongue:
Name Cleopatra as she is call'd in Rome;
Rail thou in Fulvia's phrase; and taunt my faults
With such full license as both truth and malice
Have power to utter. O, then we bring forth weeds,
When our quick minds lie still; and our ills told us
Is as our earing. Fare thee well awhile.
Mess. At your noble pleasure. *Exit Mess.*
Ant. From Sicyon, ho, the news! Speak there!
First Att. The man from Sicyon,—is there such an one?
Sec. Att. He stays upon your will.
Ant. Let him appear.
These strong Egyptian fetters I must break,
Or lose myself in dotage.

Enter another Messenger, *with a letter.*

What are you?
Sec. Mess. Fulvia thy wife is dead.
Ant. Where died she?
Sec. Mess. In Sicyon:
Her length of sickness, with what else more serious
Importeth thee to know, this bears. [*Gives a letter.*]
Ant. Forbear me. [*Exit Sec. Messenger.*]
There 's a great spirit gone! Thus did I desire it:
What our contempts doth often hurl from us,
We wish it ours again; the present pleasure,
By revolution low'ring, does become
The opposite of itself: she 's good, being gone;
The hand could pluck her back that shov'd her on.
I must from this enchanting queen break off:
Ten thousand harms, more than the ills I know,
My idleness doth hatch. How now! Enobarbus!

Enter ENOBARBUS.

Eno. What 's your pleasure, sir?

Ant. I must with haste from hence.

Eno. Why, then, we kill all our women: we see how mortal an unkindness is to them; if they suffer our departure, death 's the word.

Ant. I must be gone.

Eno. Under a compelling occasion, let women die:

sayer's words in terms of the outcome of the play. 36. **have no names,** be illegitimate. 38. **every of,** every one of. 40. **I forgive . . . witch,** probably I forgive thee because thou art a wizard; possibly, I have no opinion of your powers as a soothsayer. 53. **oily palm,** sweaty or moist palm; indication of a wanton disposition. 55. **worky-day,** ordinary. 61, 63. **inch, nose,** with bawdy suggestion; see also *go*, l. 66. 67. **Isis,** Egyptian goddess of earth and fertility. 87. **Roman thought.** Schmidt explains as "a thought of Rome"; possibly to be explained as "a thought of duty and virtue." 96. **jointing,** uniting. 103. **Labienus,** emissary of Brutus and Cassius to Orodes, King of Parthia; after Philippi he became the commander of the Parthian forces. 105. **Extended,** seized upon; legal phrase. **Euphrates,** accented on first syllable. 109. **general tongue,** common report. 111. **Fulvia's phrase.** Plutarch says she was of a "peevish, crooked, and troublesome nature." 114-115. **our ills . . . earing,** telling us our faults improves us as plowing improves land run to weeds. 117. **Sicyon,** ancient city of Greece. 125. **Forbear me,** leave me. 129. **By revolution low'ring,** growing worse by the revolution of time. 131. **could,** would be willing to.

it were pity to cast them away for nothing; though, between them and a great cause, they should be esteemed nothing. Cleopatra, catching but the least noise of this, dies instantly; I have seen her die twenty times upon far poorer moment: I do think there is mettle in death, which commits some loving act upon her, she hath such a celerity in dying.

Ant. She is cunning past man's thought.

Eno. Alack, sir, no; her passions are made of nothing but the finest part of pure love: we cannot call her winds and waters sighs and tears; they are greater storms and tempests than almanacs can report: this cannot be cunning in her; if it be, she makes a shower of rain as well as Jove.

Ant. Would I had never seen her!

Eno. O, sir, you had then left unseen a wonderful piece of work; which not to have been blest withal would have discredited your travel.

Ant. Fulvia is dead.

Eno. Sir?

Ant. Fulvia is dead.

Eno. Fulvia!

Ant. Dead.

Eno. Why, sir, give the gods a thankful sacrifice. When it pleaseth their deities to take the wife of a man from him, it shows to man the tailors of the earth; comforting therein, that when old robes are worn out, there are members to make new. If there were no more women but Fulvia, then had you indeed a cut, and the case to be lamented: this grief is crowned with consolation; your old smock brings forth a new petticoat: and indeed the tears live in an onion that should water this sorrow.

Ant. The business she hath broached in the state
Cannot endure my absence.

Eno. And the business you have broached here cannot be without you; especially that of Cleopatra's, which wholly depends on your abode.

Ant. No more light answers. Let our officers
Have notice what we purpose. I shall break
The cause of our expedience to the queen,
And get her leave to part. For not alone
The death of Fulvia, with more urgent touches,
Do strongly speak to us; but the letters too
Of many our contriving friends in Rome
Petition us at home: Sextus Pompeius
Hath given the dare to Cæsar, and commands
The empire of the sea: our slippery people,
Whose love is never link'd to the deserver
Till his deserts are past, begin to throw
Pompey the Great and all his dignities
Upon his son; who, high in name and power,
Higher than both in blood and life, stands up
For the main soldier: whose quality, going on,
The sides o' th' world may danger: much is breeding,
Which, like the courser's hair, hath yet but life,
And not a serpent's poison. Say, our pleasure,
To such whose place is under us, requires
Our quick remove from hence.

Eno. I shall do 't. [*Exeunt.*]

[SCENE III. *The same. Another room.*]

Enter CLEOPATRA, CHARMIAN, ALEXAS, *and* IRAS.

Cleo. Where is he?

Char. I did not see him since.

Cleo. See where he is, who 's with him, what he does:
I did not send you: if you find him sad,
Say I am dancing; if in mirth, report
That I am sudden sick: quick, and return. [*Exit Alexas.*]

Char. Madam, methinks, if you did love him dearly,
You do not hold the method to enforce
The like from him.

Cleo. What should I do, I do not?

Char. In each thing give him way, cross him in nothing.

Cleo. Thou teachest like a fool; the way to lose him.

Char. Tempt him not so too far; I wish, forbear:
In time we hate that which we often fear.

Enter ANTONY.

But here comes Antony.

Cleo. I am sick and sullen.

Ant. I am sorry to give breathing to my purpose,—

Cleo. Help me away, dear Charmian; I shall fall:
It cannot be thus long, the sides of nature
Will not sustain it.

Ant. Now, my dearest queen,—

Cleo. Pray you, stand farther from me.

Ant. What 's the matter?

Cleo. I know, by that same eye, there 's some good news.
What says the married woman? You may go:
Would she had never given you leave to come!
Let her not say 'tis I that keep you here:
I have no power upon you; hers you are.

Ant. The gods best know,—

Cleo. O, never was there queen
So mightily betray'd! yet at the first
I saw the treasons planted.

Ant. Cleopatra,—

Cleo. Why should I think you can be mine and true,
Though you in swearing shake the throned gods,
Who have been false to Fulvia? Riotous madness,
To be entangled with those mouth-made vows,
Which break themselves in swearing!

Ant. Most sweet queen,—

Cleo. Nay, pray you, seek no colour for your going,
But bid farewell, and go: when you sued staying,
Then was the time for words: no going then;
Eternity was in our lips and eyes,
Bliss in our brows' bent; none our parts so poor,
But was a race of heaven: they are so still,
Or thou, the greatest soldier of the world,

146. **upon . . . moment,** for less important reasons. 150. **cunning,** clever in dissembling. 169-172. **it shows . . . new.** Many explanations of this obscure passage; Johnson's is as good as any: "It shows man the tailors of the earth comforting him in this . . . that the deities have made other women to take her place." *Members* may, however, mean "persons." 172-180. **cut, case, broached,** with bawdy puns. 182. **abode,** staying. 185. **expedience,** haste. 187. **urgent touches,** pressing feelings or motives. 189. **Of . . . friends,** from many friends working in our interest. 190. **at home,** i.e., to come home. **Sextus Pompeius,** son of Pompey the Great and now leader of the party opposed to Caesar. 194-196. **throw . . . Upon,** bestow . . . upon. 197. **blood and life,** mettle and vitality. 198. **main,** principal. 199. **sides,** frame. **danger,** endanger. 200. **like . . . hair,** allusion to the popular belief that a horsehair put into water will turn to a snake.

SCENE III. 8. **like,** same. **I do not,** that I am not doing. 10. Collier, followed by many editors, punctuates this line with commas after *teachest* and *fool*. 14. **breathing,** utterance. 16. **sides of nature,** i.e., her body cannot contain her swelling heart, and she will die. Enobarbus has already borne testimony to her use of this device. 20. **married woman,** i.e., Fulvia. 32. **colour,** pretext. 37. **race of heaven,** of

Art turn'd the greatest liar.
Ant. How now, lady!
Cleo. I would I had thy inches; thou shouldst know
There were a heart in Egypt.
Ant. Hear me, queen:
The strong necessity of time commands
Our services awhile; but my full heart
Remains in use with you. Our Italy
Shines o'er with civil swords: Sextus Pompeius
Makes his approaches to the port of Rome:
Equality of two domestic powers
Breed scrupulous faction: the hated, grown to strength,
Are newly grown to love: the condemn'd Pompey,
Rich in his father's honour, creeps apace
Into the hearts of such as have not thriv'd
Upon the present state, whose numbers threaten;
And quietness, grown sick of rest, would purge
By any desperate change: my more particular,
And that which most with you should safe my going,
Is Fulvia's death.
Cleo. Though age from folly could not give me freedom,
It does from childishness: can Fulvia die?
Ant. She 's dead, my queen:
Look here, and at thy sovereign leisure read
The garboils she awak'd; at the last, best:
See when and where she died.
Cleo. O most false love!
Where be the sacred vials thou shouldst fill
With sorrowful water? Now I see, I see,
In Fulvia's death, how mine receiv'd shall be.
Ant. Quarrel no more, but be prepar'd to know
The purposes I bear; which are, or cease,
As you shall give th' advice. By the fire
That quickens Nilus' slime, I go from hence
Thy soldier, servant; making peace or war
As thou affects.
Cleo. Cut my lace, Charmian, come;
But let it be: I am quickly ill, and well,
So Antony loves.
Ant. My precious queen, forbear;
And give true evidence to his love, which stands
An honourable trial.
Cleo. So Fulvia told me.
I prithee, turn aside and weep for her;
Then bid adieu to me, and say the tears
Belong to Egypt: good now, play one scene
Of excellent dissembling; and let it look
Like perfect honour.
Ant. You'll heat my blood: no more.
Cleo. You can do better yet; but this is meetly.
Ant. Now, by my sword,—
Cleo. And target. Still he mends;
But this is not the best. Look, prithee, Charmian,
How this Herculean Roman does become
The carriage of his chafe.
Ant. I'll leave you, lady.
Cleo. Courteous lord, one word.
Sir, you and I must part, but that 's not it:
Sir, you and I have lov'd, but there 's not it;
That you know well: something it is I would,—
O, my oblivion is a very Antony,
And I am all forgotten.
Ant. But that your royalty
Holds idleness your subject, I should take you
For idleness itself.
Cleo. 'Tis sweating labour
To bear such idleness so near the heart
As Cleopatra this. But, sir, forgive me;
Since my becomings kill me, when they do not
Eye well to you: your honour calls you hence;
Therefore be deaf to my unpitied folly,
And all the gods go with you! upon your sword
Sit laurel victory! and smooth success
Be strew'd before your feet!
Ant. Let us go. Come;
Our separation so abides, and flies,
That thou, residing here, go'st yet with me,
And I, hence fleeting, here remain with thee.
Away! *Exeunt.*

[SCENE IV. *Rome. Cæsar's house.*]

Enter OCTAVIUS [CÆSAR], *reading a letter*, LEPIDUS, *and their* Train.

Cæs. You may see, Lepidus, and henceforth know,
It is not Cæsar's natural vice to hate
Our great competitor: from Alexandria
This is the news: he fishes, drinks, and wastes
The lamps of night in revel; is not more manlike
Than Cleopatra; nor the queen of Ptolemy
More womanly than he; hardly gave audience, or
Vouchsaf'd to think he had partners: you shall find there
A man who is the abstract of all faults
That all men follow.
Lep. I must not think there are
Evils enow to darken all his goodness:
His faults in him seem as the spots of heaven,
More fiery by night's blackness; hereditary,
Rather than purchas'd; what he cannot change,
Than what he chooses.
Cæs. You are too indulgent. Let us grant, it is not
Amiss to tumble on the bed of Ptolemy;
To give a kingdom for a mirth; to sit
And keep the turn of tippling with a slave;
To reel the streets at noon, and stand the buffet
With knaves that smell of sweat: say this becomes him,—
As his composure must be rare indeed
Whom these things cannot blemish,—yet must Antony
No way excuse his foils, when we do bear

heavenly origin; defined also as "smack or flavor of heaven." 44. **in use,** i.e., in usufruct, for use. 48. **scrupulous,** cautious, or carping. 53. **purge,** be restored to activity (as by medicinal purgation). 55. **safe,** make safe. 61. **garboils,** disturbances, commotions. 63. **sacred vials,** alluding to the supposed custom of the Romans of putting bottles filled with tears in the tombs of the departed. 71. **lace,** cord fastening up the bodice. 73. **So,** if only. 74. **evidence,** testimony, i.e., by her behavior. 78. **Egypt,** the queen of Egypt. 81. **meetly,** fairly good. 84. **Herculean.** Antony claimed descent from Anton, son of Hercules. 84-85. **does . . . chafe,** lends grace to his angry deportment. 90-91. **my . . . forgotten,** my forgetful memory is like Antony, and, like him, has forgotten my power over it. 91-92. **your . . . subject,** if you did not consciously employ trifling (banter) to serve your royal purposes. 97. **Eye,** appear to the eye.

SCENE IV. 3. **competitor,** associate. 6. **Ptolemy,** allusion to Cleopatra's brother, to whom she had been married according to Egyptian custom. She was supposed to have poisoned him. 9. **abstract,** epitome. 19. **keep . . . of,** take turns. 20. **reel,** stagger along. 22. **composure,** composition, temperament. 24. **foils,** blemishes.

So great weight in his lightness. If he fill'd
His vacancy with his voluptuousness,
Full surfeits, and the dryness of his bones,
Call on him for 't: but to confound such time,
That drums him from his sport, and speaks as loud
As his own state and ours,—'tis to be chid
As we rate boys, who, being mature in knowledge,
Pawn their experience to their present pleasure,
And so rebel to judgement.

Enter a Messenger.

Lep. Here 's more news.
Mess. Thy biddings have been done; and every hour,
Most noble Cæsar, shalt thou have report
How 'tis abroad. Pompey is strong at sea;
And it appears he is belov'd of those
That only have fear'd Cæsar: to the ports
The discontents repair, and men's reports
Give him much wrong'd.
Cæs. I should have known no less.
It hath been taught us from the primal state,
That he which is was wish'd until he were;
And the ebb'd man, ne'er lov'd till ne'er worth love,
Comes dear'd by being lack'd. This common body,
Like to a vagabond flag upon the stream,
Goes to and back, lackeying the varying tide,
To rot itself with motion.
Mess. Cæsar, I bring thee word,
Menecrates and Menas, famous pirates,
Make the sea serve them, which they ear and wound
With keels of every kind: many hot inroads
They make in Italy; the borders maritime
Lack blood to think on 't, and flush youth revolt:
No vessel can peep forth, but 'tis as soon
Taken as seen; for Pompey's name strikes more
Than could his war resisted.
Cæs. Antony,
Leave thy lascivious wassails. When thou once
Was beaten from Modena, where thou slew'st
Hirtius and Pansa, consuls, at thy heel
Did famine follow; whom thou fought'st against,
Though daintily brought up, with patience more
Than savages could suffer: thou didst drink
The stale of horses, and the gilded puddle
Which beasts would cough at: thy palate then did deign
The roughest berry on the rudest hedge;
Yea, like the stag, when snow the pasture sheets,
The barks of trees thou brows'd; on the Alps
It is reported thou didst eat strange flesh,
Which some did die to look on: and all this—
It wounds thine honour that I speak it now—
Was borne so like a soldier, that thy cheek
So much as lank'd not.
Lep. 'Tis pity of him.
Cæs. Let his shames quickly
Drive him to Rome; 'tis time we twain
Did show ourselves i' th' field; and to that end
Assemble we immediate council: Pompey
Thrives in our idleness.
Lep. To-morrow, Cæsar,
I shall be furnish'd to inform you rightly
Both what by sea and land I can be able
To front this present time.
Cæs. Till which encounter,
It is my business too. Farewell.
Lep. Farewell, my lord: what you shall know meantime
Of stirs abroad, I shall beseech you, sir,
To let me be partaker.
Cæs. Doubt not, sir;
I knew it for my bond. *Exeunt.*

[SCENE V. *Alexandria. Cleopatra's palace.*]

Enter CLEOPATRA, CHARMIAN, IRAS, *and* MARDIAN.

Cleo. Charmian!
Char. Madam?
Cleo. Ha, ha!
Give me to drink mandragora.
Char. Why, madam?
Cleo. That I might sleep out this great gap of time
My Antony is away.
Char. You think of him too much.
Cleo. O, 'tis treason!
Char. Madam, I trust, not so.
Cleo. Thou, eunuch Mardian!
Mar. What 's your highness' pleasure?
Cleo. Not now to hear thee sing; I take no pleasure
In aught an eunuch has: 'tis well for thee,
That, being unseminar'd, thy freer thoughts
May not fly forth of Egypt. Hast thou affections?
Mar. Yes, gracious madam.
Cleo. Indeed!
Mar. Not in deed, madam; for I can do nothing
But what indeed is honest to be done:
Yet have I fierce affections, and think
What Venus did with Mars.
Cleo. O Charmian,
Where think'st thou he is now? Stands he, or sits he?
Or does he walk? or is he on his horse?
O happy horse, to bear the weight of Antony!
Do bravely, horse! for wot'st thou whom thou mov'st?
The demi-Atlas of this earth, the arm
And burgonet of men. He 's speaking now,
Or murmuring 'Where 's my serpent of old Nile?'
For so he calls me: now I feed myself
With most delicious poison. Think on me,
That am with Phœbus' amorous pinches black,
And wrinkled deep in time? Broad-fronted Cæsar,
When thou wast here above the ground, I was
A morsel for a monarch: and great Pompey
Would stand and make his eyes grow in my brow;
There would he anchor his aspect and die
With looking on his life.

Enter ALEXAS.

Alex. Sovereign of Egypt, hail!

25. **lightness,** levity, with play on literal meaning. 25-28. **If . . . for 't,** if he filled his idle hours with voluptuousness, let his own physical deterioration pay him for it. 31. **rate,** berate. 40. **Give him,** represent him as. 42. **That . . . were,** that the man in power was desired until he obtained it. 43. **ebb'd,** decayed in fortune. 44. **Comes dear'd,** becomes endeared. 45. **flag,** iris. 46. **lackeying,** following like a lackey. 49. **ear,** plow. 52. **Lack blood,** turn pale. **flush,** lusty. 54. **strikes,** destroys. 56. **wassails,** carousals. 56-71. **When . . . not,** a passage closely following Plutarch. 62. **stale,** urine. **gilded,** covered with red or yellow slime. 71. **lank'd,** became thin. 84. **bond,** bounden duty.

SCENE V. 4. **mandragora,** juice of the mandrake (a narcotic). 11. **unseminar'd,** deprived of virility. 23. **demi-Atlas.** She disregards Lepidus as a triumvir. 24. **burgonet,** light casque or steel cap. 29. **Cæsar,** Julius Caesar. 33. **aspect,** look, glance. 36. **med'cine,** drug, elixir; possibly, physician. 37. **tinct,** color. 48. **arm-gaunt,**

Cleo. How much unlike art thou Mark Antony!
Yet, coming from him, that great med'cine hath
With his tinct gilded thee.
How goes it with my brave Mark Antony?
Alex. Last thing he did, dear queen,
He kiss'd,—the last of many doubled kisses,—
This orient pearl. His speech sticks in my heart.
Cleo. Mine ear must pluck it thence.
Alex. 'Good friend,' quoth he,
'Say, the firm Roman to great Egypt sends
This treasure of an oyster; at whose foot,
To mend the petty present, I will piece
Her opulent throne with kingdoms; all the east,
Say thou, shall call her mistress.' So he nodded,
†And soberly did mount an arm-gaunt steed,
Who neigh'd so high, that what I would have spoke
Was beastly dumb'd by him.
Cleo. What, was he sad or merry?
Alex. Like to the time o' th' year between the extremes
Of hot and cold, he was nor sad nor merry.
Cleo. O well-divided disposition! Note him,
Note him, good Charmian, 'tis the man; but note him:
He was not sad, for he would shine on those
That make their looks by his; he was not merry,
Which seem'd to tell them his remembrance lay
In Egypt with his joy; but between both:
O heavenly mingle! Be'st thou sad or merry,
The violence of either thee becomes,
So does it no man else. Met'st thou my posts?
Alex. Ay, madam, twenty several messengers:
Why do you send so thick?
Cleo. Who 's born that day
When I forget to send to Antony,
Shall die a beggar. Ink and paper, Charmian.
Welcome, my good Alexas. Did I, Charmian,
Ever love Cæsar so?
Char. O that brave Cæsar!
Cleo. Be chok'd with such another emphasis!
Say, the brave Antony.
Char. The valiant Cæsar!
Cleo. By Isis, I will give thee bloody teeth,
If thou with Cæsar paragon again
My man of men.
Char. By your most gracious pardon,
I sing but after you.
Cleo. My salad days,
When I was green in judgement: cold in blood,
To say as I said then! But, come, away;
Get me ink and paper:
He shall have every day a several greeting,
Or I'll unpeople Egypt. *Exeunt*.

[ACT II.

SCENE I. *Messina. Pompey's house.*]

Enter POMPEY, MENECRATES, *and* MENAS, *in warlike manner*.

Pom. If the great gods be just, they shall assist
The deeds of justest men.
Mene. Know, worthy Pompey,
That what they do delay, they not deny.
Pom. Whiles we are suitors to their throne, decays
The thing we sue for.
Mene. We, ignorant of ourselves,
Beg often our own harms, which the wise pow'rs
Deny us for our good; so find we profit
By losing of our prayers.
Pom. I shall do well:
The people love me, and the sea is mine;
My powers are crescent, and my auguring hope
Says it will come to th' full. Mark Antony
In Egypt sits at dinner, and will make
No wars without doors: Cæsar gets money where
He loses hearts: Lepidus flatters both,
Of both is flatter'd; but he neither loves,
Nor either cares for him.
Men. Cæsar and Lepidus
Are in the field: a mighty strength they carry.
Pom. Where have you this? 'tis false.
Men. From Silvius, sir.
Pom. He dreams: I know they are in Rome together,
Looking for Antony. But all the charms of love,
Salt Cleopatra, soften thy wan'd lip!
Let witchcraft join with beauty, lust with both!
Tie up the libertine in a field of feasts,
Keep his brain fuming; Epicurean cooks
Sharpen with cloyless sauce his appetite;
That sleep and feeding may prorogue his honour
Even till a Lethe'd dulness!

Enter VARRIUS.

How now, Varrius!
Var. This is most certain that I shall deliver:
Mark Antony is every hour in Rome
Expected: since he went from Egypt 'tis
A space for further travel.
Pom. I could have given less matter
A better ear. Menas, I did not think
This amorous surfeiter would have donn'd his helm
For such a petty war: his soldiership
Is twice the other twain: but let us rear
The higher our opinion, that our stirring
Can from the lap of Egypt's widow pluck
The ne'er-lust-wearied Antony.
Men. I cannot hope
Cæsar and Antony shall well greet together:
His wife that 's dead did trespasses to Cæsar;
His brother warr'd upon him; although, I think,
Not mov'd by Antony.
Pom. I know not, Menas,
How lesser enmities may give way to greater.
Were 't not that we stand up against them all,
'Twere pregnant they should square between themselves;
For they have entertained cause enough
To draw their swords: but how the fear of us

gaunt from bearing arms in warlike service, or with gaunt limbs; many emendations. 50. **dumb'd,** silenced. 71. **paragon,** compare on equal terms. 73-75. **My salad . . . then.** The F punctuation puts a comma after *judgement* instead of a colon. This is correct from the simple fact that hot and dry, not cold and wet (*green*), represent the elementary condition of judgment. She means to say that she spoke as she did then because she was in her salad days, when her judgment was green and her blood cold.

ACT II. SCENE I. 10. **crescent,** on the increase. **auguring,** prophesying. 21. **Salt,** wanton. **wan'd,** faded, withered. 23. **Tie . . . feasts,** probably, as an animal might be staked out in a rich pasture. 25. **cloyless,** which will not satiate. 26. **prorogue,** defer the operation of. 27. **Lethe'd,** oblivious. 31. **space,** time enough. 36. **opinion,** of ourselves. 37. **Egypt's widow,** Cleopatra, widow of the young king Ptolemy. 41. **His brother,** Lucius Antonius. **warr'd,** so F_2; F: *wan'd*. 45. **pregnant,** likely. **square,** quarrel, or fight.

May cement their divisions and bind up
The petty difference, we yet not know.
Be 't as our gods will have 't! It only stands
Our lives upon to use our strongest hands.
Come, Menas. *Exeunt.*

[SCENE II. *Rome. The house of Lepidus.*]

Enter ENOBARBUS *and* LEPIDUS.

Lep. Good Enobarbus, 'tis a worthy deed,
And shall become you well, to entreat your captain
To soft and gentle speech.
Eno. I shall entreat him
To answer like himself: if Cæsar move him,
Let Antony look over Cæsar's head
And speak as loud as Mars. By Jupiter,
Were I the wearer of Antonius' beard,
I would not shave 't to-day.
Lep. 'Tis not a time
For private stomaching.
Eno. Every time
Serves for the matter that is then born in 't.
Lep. But small to greater matters must give way.
Eno. Not if the small come first.
Lep. Your speech is passion:
But, pray you, stir no embers up. Here comes
The noble Antony.

Enter ANTONY *and* VENTIDIUS.

Eno. And yonder, Cæsar.

Enter CÆSAR, MECÆNAS, *and* AGRIPPA.

Ant. If we compose well here, to Parthia:
Hark, Ventidius.
Cæs. I do not know,
Mecænas; ask Agrippa.
Lep. Noble friends,
That which combin'd us was most great, and let not
A leaner action rend us. What 's amiss,
May it be gently heard: when we debate
Our trivial difference loud, we do commit
Murder in healing wounds: then, noble partners,
The rather, for I earnestly beseech,
Touch you the sourest points with sweetest terms,
Nor curstness grow to th' matter.
Ant. 'Tis spoken well.
Were we before our armies, and to fight,
I should do thus. *Flourish.*
Cæs. Welcome to Rome.
Ant. Thank you.
Cæs. Sit.
Ant. Sit, sir.
Cæs. Nay, then.
Ant. I learn, you take things ill which are not so,
Or being, concern you not.
Cæs. I must be laugh'd at,
If, or for nothing or a little, I
Should say myself offended, and with you
Chiefly i' th' world; more laugh'd at, that I should
Once name you derogately, when to sound your name
It not concern'd me.
Ant. My being in Egypt, Cæsar,
What was 't to you?
Cæs. No more than my residing here at Rome
Might be to you in Egypt: yet, if you there
Did practise on my state, your being in Egypt
Might be my question.
Ant. How intend you, practis'd?
Cæs. You may be pleas'd to catch at mine intent
By what did here befal me. Your wife and brother
Made wars upon me; and their contestation
Was theme for you, you were the word of war.
Ant. You do mistake your business; my brother never
Did urge me in his act: I did inquire it;
And have my learning from some true reports,
That drew their swords with you. Did he not rather
Discredit my authority with yours;
And make the wars alike against my stomach,
Having alike your cause? Of this my letters
Before did satisfy you. If you'll patch a quarrel,
As matter whole you have not to make it with,
It must not be with this.
Cæs. You praise yourself
By laying defects of judgement to me; but
You patch'd up your excuses.
Ant. Not so, not so;
I know you could not lack, I am certain on 't,
Very necessity of this thought, that I,
Your partner in the cause 'gainst which he fought,
Could not with graceful eyes attend those wars
Which fronted mine own peace. As for my wife,
I would you had her spirit in such another:
The third o' th' world is yours; which with a snaffle
You may pace easy, but not such a wife.
Eno. Would we had all such wives, that the men might go to wars with the women!
Ant. So much uncurbable, her garboils, Cæsar,
Made out of her impatience, which not wanted
Shrewdness of policy too, I grieving grant
Did you too much disquiet: for that you must
But say, I could not help it.
Cæs. I wrote to you
When rioting in Alexandria; you
Did pocket up my letters, and with taunts
Did gibe my missive out of audience.
Ant. Sir,
He fell upon me ere admitted: then
Three kings I had newly feasted, and did want
Of what I was i' th' morning: but next day
I told him of myself; which was as much
As to have ask'd him pardon. Let this fellow
Be nothing of our strife; if we contend,
Out of our question wipe him.
Cæs. You have broken
The article of your oath; which you shall never
Have tongue to charge me with.
Lep. Soft, Cæsar!
Ant. No,
Lepidus, let him speak:
The honour is sacred which he talks on now,

50-51. **It . . . upon,** it solely and vitally concerns our lives.

SCENE II. 8. **I would not shave 't.** Since plucking the beard was a symbolic act for starting a fight, this means that, if he were Antony, he would not avoid a contest. 9. **stomaching,** giving way to resentment. 15. **compose,** come to an agreement. **to Parthia,** I shall go to Parthia. 25. **curstness,** ill-humor. **grow to,** be added to (the real business). 34. **derogately,** disparagingly. 40. **question,** business. 44. **theme for you,** had you for theme, or supplied you with a ground for your intrigues (Cuningham). 46. **urge . . . act,** claim that he was fighting in my behalf. **inquire,** inquire into. 51. **Having . . . cause,** I having the same cause of resentment that you had. 52. **patch a quarrel,** make a quarrel out of shreds and patches, since you have no real ground.

Supposing that I lack'd it. But, on, Cæsar;
The article of my oath.
Cæs. To lend me arms and aid when I requir'd them;
The which you both denied.
Ant. Neglected, rather;
And then when poisoned hours had bound me up
From mine own knowledge. As nearly as I may,
I'll play the penitent to you: but mine honesty
Shall not make poor my greatness, nor my power
Work without it. Truth is, that Fulvia,
To have me out of Egypt, made wars here;
For which myself, the ignorant motive, do
So far ask pardon as befits mine honour
To stoop in such a case.
Lep. 'Tis noble spoken.
Mec. If it might please you, to enforce no further
The griefs between ye: to forget them quite
Were to remember that the present need
Speaks to atone you.
Lep. Worthily spoken, Mecænas.
Eno. Or, if you borrow one another's love for the instant, you may, when you hear no more words of Pompey, return it again: you shall have time to wrangle in when you have nothing else to do.
Ant. Thou art a soldier only: speak no more.
Eno. That truth should be silent I had almost forgot.
Ant. You wrong this presence; therefore speak no more.
Eno. Go to, then; your considerate stone.
Cæs. I do not much dislike the matter, but
The manner of his speech: for 't cannot be
We shall remain in friendship, our conditions
So diff'ring in their acts. Yet, if I knew
What hoop should hold us stanch, from edge to edge
O' th' world I would pursue it.
Agr. Give me leave, Cæsar,—
Cæs. Speak, Agrippa.
Agr. Thou hast a sister by the mother's side,
Admir'd Octavia: great Mark Antony
Is now a widower.
Cæs. Say not so, Agrippa:
If Cleopatra heard you, your reproof
Were well deserv'd of rashness.
Ant. I am not married, Cæsar: let me hear Agrippa further speak.
Agr. To hold you in perpetual amity,
To make you brothers, and to knit your hearts
With an unslipping knot, take Antony
Octavia to his wife; whose beauty claims
No worse a husband than the best of men;
Whose virtue and whose general graces speak
That which none else can utter. By this marriage,
All little jealousies, which now seem great,
And all great fears, which now import their dangers,
Would then be nothing: truths would be tales,
Where now half tales be truths: her love to both
Would, each to other and all loves to both,
Draw after her. Pardon what I have spoke;
For 'tis a studied, not a present thought,
By duty ruminated.
Ant. Will Cæsar speak?
Cæs. Not till he hears how Antony is touch'd
With what is spoke already.
Ant. What power is in Agrippa,
If I would say, 'Agrippa, be it so,'
To make this good?
Cæs. The power of Cæsar, and
His power unto Octavia.
Ant. May I never
To this good purpose, that so fairly shows,
Dream of impediment! Let me have thy hand:
Further this act of grace; and from this hour
The heart of brothers govern in our loves
And sway our great designs!
Cæs. There's my hand.
A sister I bequeath you, whom no brother
Did ever love so dearly: let her live
To join our kingdoms and our hearts; and never
Fly off our loves again!
Lep. Happily, amen!
Ant. I did not think to draw my sword 'gainst Pompey;
For he hath laid strange courtesies and great
Of late upon me: I must thank him only,
Lest my remembrance suffer ill report;
At heel of that, defy him.
Lep. Time calls upon 's:
Of us must Pompey presently be sought,
Or else he seeks out us.
Ant. Where lies he?
Cæs. About the mount Mesena.
Ant. What is his strength by land?
Cæs. Great and increasing: but by sea
He is an absolute master.
Ant. So is the fame.
Would we had spoke together! Haste we for it:
Yet, ere we put ourselves in arms, dispatch we
The business we have talk'd of.
Cæs. With most gladness;
And do invite you to my sister's view,
Whither straight I'll lead you.
Ant. Let us, Lepidus,
Not lack your company.
Lep. Noble Antony,
Not sickness should detain me.
Flourish. Exeunt. Mane[n]t Enobarbus, Agrippa, Mecænas.
Mec. Welcome from Egypt, sir.
Eno. Half the heart of Cæsar, worthy Mecænas! My honourable friend, Agrippa!
Agr. Good Enobarbus!
Mec. We have cause to be glad that matters are so well digested. You stayed well by 't in Egypt.
Eno. Ay, sir; we did sleep day out of countenance, and made the night light with drinking.
Mec. Eight wild-boars roasted whole at a breakfast, and but twelve persons there; is this true?
Eno. This was but as a fly by an eagle: we had much more monstrous matter of feast, which worthily deserved noting.
Mec. She 's a most triumphant lady, if report be square to her.

60. **graceful eyes attend,** regard favorably. 63-64. **which . . . wife,** which you may put through its paces easily with a snaffle-bit, but you cannot so control such a wife. 67. **garboils,** brawls. 74. **missive,** messenger. 93-94. **my power . . . it.** He seems to mean that he will not exert his power unless his greatness (*honour*) is recognized as intact. 112. **your . . . stone,** I shall continue to reflect, but be as silent as a stone.

121. **Octavia,** full sister, not half-sister, of Octavius. 135. **import,** carry with them. 146. **unto,** over. 155. **Fly . . . again,** desert each other again. 160. **At heel of,** immediately after. 163. **Mesena,** i.e., Misenum, an Italian port. 170. **my sister's view,** to see my sister. 182. **light,** giddy and frivolous, with pun on the commoner meaning. 190. **square,** just.

Eno. When she first met Mark Antony, she pursed up his heart, upon the river of Cydnus.

Agr. There she appeared indeed; or my reporter devised well for her.

Eno. I will tell you.
The barge she sat in, like a burnish'd throne,
Burn'd on the water: the poop was beaten gold;
Purple the sails, and so perfumed that
The winds were love-sick with them; the oars were silver,
Which to the tune of flutes kept stroke, and made
The water which they beat to follow faster,
As amorous of their strokes. For her own person,
It beggar'd all description: she did lie
In her pavilion—cloth-of-gold of tissue—
O'er-picturing that Venus where we see
The fancy outwork nature: on each side her
Stood pretty dimpled boys, like smiling Cupids,
With divers-colour'd fans, whose wind did seem
To glow the delicate cheeks which they did cool,
And what they undid did.

Agr. O, rare for Antony!

Eno. Her gentlewomen, like the Nereides,
So many mermaids, tended her i' th' eyes,
And made their bends adornings: at the helm
A seeming mermaid steers: the silken tackle
Swell with the touches of those flower-soft hands,
That yarely frame the office. From the barge
A strange invisible perfume hits the sense
Of the adjacent wharfs. The city cast
Her people out upon her; and Antony,
Enthron'd i' th' market-place, did sit alone,
Whistling to th' air; which, but for vacancy,
Had gone to gaze on Cleopatra too
And made a gap in nature.

Agr. Rare Egyptian!

Eno. Upon her landing, Antony sent to her,
Invited her to supper: she replied,
It should be better he became her guest;
Which she entreated: our courteous Antony,
Whom ne'er the word of 'No' woman heard speak,
Being barber'd ten times o'er, goes to the feast,
And for his ordinary pays his heart
For what his eyes eat only.

Agr. Royal wench!
She made great Cæsar lay his sword to bed:
He plough'd her, and she cropp'd.

Eno. I saw her once
Hop forty paces through the public street;
And having lost her breath, she spoke, and panted,
That she did make defect perfection,
And, breathless, pow'r breathe forth.

Mec. Now Antony must leave her utterly.

Eno. Never; he will not:
Age cannot wither her, nor custom stale
Her infinite variety: other women cloy
The appetites they feed; but she makes hungry
Where most she satisfies: for vilest things
Become themselves in her; that the holy priests
Bless her when she is riggish.

Mec. If beauty, wisdom, modesty, can settle
The heart of Antony, Octavia is
A blessed lottery to him.

Agr. Let us go.
Good Enobarbus, make yourself my guest
Whilst you abide here.

Eno. Humbly, sir, I thank you.

Exeunt.

[SCENE III. *The same. Cæsar's house.*]

Enter ANTONY, CÆSAR, OCTAVIA *between them* [, *and* Attendants].

Ant. The world and my great office will sometimes
Divide me from your bosom.

Octa. All which time
Before the gods my knee shall bow my prayers
To them for you.

Ant. Good night, sir. My Octavia,
Read not my blemishes in the world's report:
I have not kept my square; but that to come
Shall be all done by th' rule. Good night, dear lady.
Good night, sir.

Cæs. Good night. *Exit* [*with Octavia*].

Enter Soothsayer.

Ant. Now, sirrah; you do wish yourself in Egypt?

Sooth. Would I had never come from thence, nor you
Thither!

Ant. If you can, your reason?

Sooth. I see it in
My motion, have it not in my tongue: but yet
Hie you to Egypt again.

Ant. Say to me,
Whose fortunes shall rise higher, Cæsar's or mine?

Sooth. Cæsar's.
Therefore, O Antony, stay not by his side:
Thy demon, that 's thy spirit which keeps thee, is
Noble, courageous, high, unmatchable,
Where Cæsar's is not; but, near him, thy angel
Becomes a fear, as being o'erpow'r'd: therefore
Make space enough between you.

Ant. Speak this no more.

Sooth. To none but thee; no more, but when to thee.
If thou dost play with him at any game,
Thou art sure to lose; and, of that natural luck,
He beats thee 'gainst the odds: thy lustre thickens,
When he shines by: I say again, thy spirit
Is all afraid to govern thee near him;
But, he away, 'tis noble.

Ant. Get thee gone:
Say to Ventidius I would speak with him:
Exit [*Soothsayer*].
He shall to Parthia. Be it art or hap,
He hath spoken true: the very dice obey him;
And in our sports my better cunning faints
Under his chance: if we draw lots, he speeds;
His cocks do win the battle still of mine,

192. **upon . . . Cydnus,** upon the banks of, or more probably, on the river of Cydnus, by the spectacle described below. 204. **cloth-of-gold of tissue,** cloth made of gold thread and silk woven together (Onions). 205. **that Venus,** usually thought to refer to the Venus Anadyomene of Apelles. 209. **glow,** cause to glow. 212. **tended her i' th' eyes,** waited in her sight. 213. **made . . . adornings,** made their graceful bowings beautiful, as in a work of art. 216. **yarely,** nimbly, briskly. 218. **wharfs,** banks. 221. **but for vacancy,** except that it would have created a vacuum. 230. **ordinary,** meal, supper. 232. **Cæsar,** Julius Caesar, by whom Cleopatra had a son named Caesarion. 233. **cropp'd,** bore fruit (a son). 245. **riggish,** wanton. 248. **lottery,** prize.

SCENE III. 6. **kept my square,** kept within my duty. 13-14. **in My motion,** probably refers to the motions of his spirits; might be rendered as "instinctively." 19. **demon,** guardian spirit, in accordance with the doctrine that each of us is attended by a special angel, or by two angels, a good and a bad. Macbeth declares his genius is rebuked by that of

When it is all to nought; and his quails ever
Beat mine, inhoop'd, at odds. I will to Egypt:
And though I make this marriage for my peace,
I' th' east my pleasure lies.

Enter VENTIDIUS.

O, come, Ventidius,
You must to Parthia: your commission 's ready;
Follow me, and receive 't. *Exeunt.*

[SCENE IV. *The same. A street.*]

Enter LEPIDUS, MECÆNAS, *and* AGRIPPA.

Lep. Trouble yourselves no further: pray you, hasten
Your generals after.
Agr. Sir, Mark Antony
Will e'en but kiss Octavia, and we'll follow.
Lep. Till I shall see you in your soldier's dress,
Which will become you both, farewell.
Mec. We shall,
As I conceive the journey, be at Mount
Before you, Lepidus.
Lep. Your way is shorter;
My purposes do draw me much about:
You'll win two days upon me.
Mec. } *Agr.* } Sir, good success!
Lep. Farewell. *Exeunt.*

[SCENE V. *Alexandria. Cleopatra's palace.*]

Enter CLEOPATRA, CHARMIAN, IRAS, *and* ALEXAS.

Cleo. Give me some music; music, moody food
Of us that trade in love.
All. The music, ho!

Enter MARDIAN *the Eunuch.*

Cleo. Let it alone; let 's to billiards: come, Charmian.
Char. My arm is sore; best play with Mardian.
Cleo. As well a woman with an eunuch play'd
As with a woman. Come, you'll play with me, sir?
Mar. As well as I can, madam.
Cleo. And when good will is show'd, though 't come too short,
The actor may plead pardon. I'll none now:
Give me mine angle; we'll to th' river: there,
My music playing far off, I will betray
Tawny-finn'd fishes; my bended hook shall pierce
Their slimy jaws; and, as I draw them up,
I'll think them every one an Antony,
And say 'Ah, ha! y' are caught.'
Char. 'Twas merry when
You wager'd on your angling; when your diver
Did hang a salt-fish on his hook, which he
With fervency drew up.
Cleo. That time,—O times!—
I laugh'd him out of patience; and that night
I laugh'd him into patience: and next morn,
Ere the ninth hour, I drunk him to his bed;
Then put my tires and mantles on him, whilst
I wore his sword Philippan.

Enter a Messenger.

O, from Italy!
Ram thou thy fruitful tidings in mine ears,
That long time have been barren.
Mess. Madam, madam,—
Cleo. Antonio 's dead!—If thou say so, villain,
Thou kill'st thy mistress: but well and free,
If thou so yield him, there is gold, and here
My bluest veins to kiss; a hand that kings
Have lipp'd, and trembled kissing.
Mess. First, madam, he is well.
Cleo. Why, there 's more gold.
But, sirrah, mark, we use
To say the dead are well: bring it to that,
The gold I give thee will I melt and pour
Down thy ill-uttering throat.
Mess. Good madam, hear me.
Cleo. Well, go to, I will;
But there 's no goodness in thy face: if Antony
Be free and healthful,—so tart a favour
To trumpet such good tidings! If not well,
Thou shouldst come like a Fury crown'd with snakes,
Not like a formal man.
Mess. Will 't please you hear me?
Cleo. I have a mind to strike thee ere thou speak'st:
Yet, if thou say Antony lives, is well,
Or friends with Cæsar, or not captive to him,
I'll set thee in a shower of gold, and hail
Rich pearls upon thee.
Mess. Madam, he 's well.
Cleo. Well said.
Mess. And friends with Cæsar.
Cleo. Th' art an honest man.
Mess. Cæsar and he are greater friends than ever.
Cleo. Make thee a fortune from me.
Mess. But yet, madam,—
Cleo. I do not like 'But yet,' it does allay
The good precedence; fie upon 'But yet'!
'But yet' is as a gaoler to bring forth
Some monstrous malefactor. Prithee, friend,
Pour out the pack of matter to mine ear,
The good and bad together: he 's friends with Cæsar;
In state of health thou say'st; and thou say'st free.
Mess. Free, madam! no; I made no such report:
He 's bound unto Octavia.
Cleo. For what good turn?
Mess. For the best turn i' th' bed.
Cleo. I am pale, Charmian.
Mess. Madam, he 's married to Octavia.
Cleo. The most infectious pestilence upon thee!
Strikes him down.
Mess. Good madam, patience.
Cleo. What say you? Hence,
Strikes him.

Banquo as "Mark Antony's was by Caesar" (*Macbeth*, III, i, 54-57). This play and *Macbeth* were probably written about the same time. 27. **thickens,** grows dim. 30. **he away, 'tis,** Pope's emendation of F: *he alway 'tis.* 32. **hap,** accident, chance. 34. **cunning,** skill. 35. **chance,** luck. 36. **still,** always. 37. **When . . . nought,** when the odds are everything to nothing (in my favor). 38. **inhoop'd.** The birds were inclosed in hoops to make them fight.

SCENE IV. 6. **Mount,** Mount Misenum. 8. **about,** roundabout.

SCENE V. 3. **billiards.** There were no billiards in those days. 8. **too short,** a bawdy joke. 10. **angle,** rod and line. 17. **salt-fish . . . hook,** an incident recorded in Plutarch; an ancient jest. 22. **tires,** probably, headdresses, though it may be general for "attire." 23. **Philippan,** apparently named for the victory of Philippi. 38. **tart a favour,** sour a visage. 41. **formal man,** ordinary man, or in form of man. 51. **good precedence,** the good news which preceded it.

Horrible villain! or I'll spurn thine eyes
Like balls before me; I'll unhair thy head:
She hales him up and down.
Thou shalt be whipp'd with wire, and stew'd in brine,
Smarting in ling'ring pickle.
Mess. Gracious madam,
I that do bring the news made not the match.
Cleo. Say 'tis not so, a province I will give thee,
And make thy fortunes proud: the blow thou hadst
Shall make thy peace for moving me to rage;
And I will boot thee with what gift beside
Thy modesty can beg.
Mess. He 's married, madam.
Cleo. Rogue, thou hast liv'd too long. *Draw a knife.*
Mess. Nay, then I'll run.
What mean you, madam? I have made no fault. *Exit.*
Char. Good madam, keep yourself within yourself:
The man is innocent.
Cleo. Some innocents 'scape not the thunderbolt.
Melt Egypt into Nile! and kindly creatures
Turn all to serpents! Call the slave again:
Though I am mad, I will not bite him: call.
Char. He is afeard to come.
Cleo. I will not hurt him.
[Exit Charmian.]
These hands do lack nobility, that they strike
A meaner than myself; since I myself
Have given myself the cause.

Enter [CHARMIAN *and*] *the* Messenger *again.*

Come hither, sir.
Though it be honest, it is never good
To bring bad news: give to a gracious message
An host of tongues; but let ill tidings tell
Themselves when they be felt.
Mess. I have done my duty.
Cleo. Is he married?
I cannot hate thee worser than I do,
If thou again say 'Yes.'
Mess. He 's married, madam.
Cleo. The gods confound thee! dost thou hold there still?
Mess. Should I lie, madam?
Cleo. O, I would thou didst,
So half my Egypt were submerg'd and made
A cistern for scal'd snakes! Go, get thee hence:
Hadst thou Narcissus in thy face, to me
Thou wouldst appear most ugly. He is married?
Mess. I crave your highness' pardon.
Cleo. He is married?
Mess. Take no offence that I would not offend you:
To punish me for what you make me do
Seems much unequal: he 's married to Octavia.
Cleo. O, that his fault should make a knave of thee,
That art not what th' art sure of! Get thee hence:
The merchandise which thou hast brought from Rome
Are all too dear for me: lie they upon thy hand,
And be undone by 'em! *[Exit Messenger.]*
Char. Good your highness, patience.
Cleo. In praising Antony, I have disprais'd Cæsar.
Char. Many times, madam.
Cleo. I am paid for 't now.
Lead me from hence;
I faint: O Iras, Charmian! 'tis no matter.
Go to the fellow, good Alexas; bid him
Report the feature of Octavia, her years,
Her inclination, let him not leave out
The colour of her hair: bring me word quickly.
[Exit Alexas.]
Let him for ever go:—let him not—Charmian,
Though he be painted one way like a Gorgon,
The other way 's a Mars. Bid you Alexas [*To Mardian.*]
Bring me word how tall she is. Pity me, Charmian,
But do not speak to me. Lead me to my chamber.
Exeunt.

[SCENE VI. *Near Misenum.*]

Flourish. Enter POMPEY [*and* MENAS] *at one door, with drum and trumpet: at another,* CÆSAR, LEPIDUS, ANTONY, ENOBARBUS, MECÆNAS, AGRIPPA, *with* Soldiers *marching.*

Pom. Your hostages I have, so have you mine;
And we shall talk before we fight.
Cæs. Most meet
That first we come to words; and therefore have we
Our written purposes before us sent;
Which, if thou hast considered, let us know
If 'twill tie up thy discontented sword,
And carry back to Sicily much tall youth
That else must perish here.
Pom. To you all three,
The senators alone of this great world,
Chief factors for the gods, I do not know
Wherefore my father should revengers want,
Having a son and friends; since Julius Cæsar,
Who at Philippi the good Brutus ghosted,
There saw you labouring for him. What was 't
That mov'd pale Cassius to conspire; and what
Made all-honour'd, honest Roman, Brutus,
With the arm'd rest, courtiers of beauteous freedom,
To drench the Capitol; but that they would
Have one man but a man? And that is it
Hath made me rig my navy; at whose burthen
The anger'd ocean foams; with which I meant
To scourge th' ingratitude that despiteful Rome
Cast on my noble father.
Cæs. Take your time.
Ant. Thou canst not fear us, Pompey, with thy sails;
We'll speak with thee at sea: at land, thou know'st
How much we do o'er-count thee.
Pom. At land, indeed,
Thou dost o'er-count me of my father's house:
But, since the cuckoo builds not for himself,
Remain in 't as thou mayst.
Lep. Be pleas'd to tell us—
For this is from the present—how you take
The offers we have sent you.

71. **boot thee with,** give thee into the bargain. 84. **the cause,** i.e., by loving Antony. 94. **So,** even though. 96. **Narcissus,** a pattern of beauty. 99. **Take . . . offend you,** be not offended that I hesitate to offend you (by telling bad news). 101. **unequal,** unjust. 103. **That . . . of.** Many interpretations and conjectures; Cuningham: that art not thyself the thing of which thou art so hatefully positive; Gollancz: that art not the evil thing of which thou art so certain. Cuningham suggests *act* for *art*, which would indicate that Cleopatra had in mind the censure of Antony, which appears again in line 107. 113. **inclination,** disposition. 116-117. **Though . . . Mars.** This alludes to a type of picture known as a perspective, which shows different objects when looked at from different points of view.

SCENE VI. 2. **meet,** suitable. 10. **factors,** agents. 13. **ghosted,** haunted. 24. **fear,** frighten. 27. **Thou . . . house.** Plutarch informs

Cæs. There 's the point.
Ant. Which do not be entreated to, but weigh
What it is worth embrac'd.
Cæs. And what may follow,
To try a larger fortune.
Pom. You have made me offer
Of Sicily, Sardinia; and I must
Rid all the sea of pirates; then, to send
Measures of wheat to Rome; this 'greed upon,
To part with unhack'd edges, and bear back
Our targes undinted.
Cæs. Ant. Lep. That 's our offer.
Pom. Know, then,
I came before you here a man prepar'd
To take this offer: but Mark Antony
Put me to some impatience: though I lose
The praise of it by telling, you must know,
When Cæsar and your brother were at blows,
Your mother came to Sicily and did find
Her welcome friendly.
Ant. I have heard it, Pompey;
And am well studied for a liberal thanks
Which I do owe you.
Pom. Let me have your hand:
I did not think, sir, to have met you here.
Ant. The beds i' th' east are soft; and thanks to you,
That call'd me timelier than my purpose hither;
For I have gain'd by 't.
Cæs. Since I saw you last,
There's is a change upon you.
Pom. Well, I know not
What counts harsh fortune casts upon my face;
But in my bosom shall she never come,
To make my heart her vassal.
Lep. Well met here.
Pom. I hope so, Lepidus. Thus we are agreed:
I crave our composition may be written,
And seal'd between us.
Cæs. That 's the next to do.
Pom. We'll feast each other ere we part; and let 's
Draw lots who shall begin.
Ant. That will I, Pompey.
Pom. No, Antony, take the lot: but, first
Or last, your fine Egyptian cookery
Shall have the fame. I have heard that Julius Cæsar
Grew fat with feasting there.
Ant. You have heard much.
Pom. I have fair meanings, sir.
Ant. And fair words to them.
Pom. Then so much have I heard:
And I have heard, Apollodorus carried—
Eno. No more of that: he did so.
Pom. What, I pray you?
Eno. A certain queen to Cæsar in a mattress.
Pom. I know thee now: how far'st thou, soldier?
Eno. Well;
And well am like to do; for, I perceive,
Four feasts are toward.
Pom. Let me shake thy hand;
I never hated thee: I have seen thee fight,
When I have envied thy behaviour.
Eno. Sir,
I never lov'd you much; but I ha' prais'd ye,
When you have well deserv'd ten times as much
As I have said you did.
Pom. Enjoy thy plainness,
It nothing ill becomes thee.
Aboard my galley I invite you all:
Will you lead, lords?
Cæs. Ant. Lep. Show 's the way, sir.
Pom. Come.

Exeunt. Mane[n]t Enobarbus and Menas.

Men. [*Aside*] Thy father, Pompey, would ne'er have made this treaty.—You and I have known, sir.

Eno. At sea, I think.

Men. We have, sir.

Eno. You have done well by water.

Men. And you by land.

Eno. I will praise any man that will praise me; though it cannot be denied what I have done by land.

Men. Nor what I have done by water.

Eno. Yes, something you can deny for your own safety: you have been a great thief by sea.

Men. And you by land.

Eno. There I deny my land service. But give me your hand, Menas: if our eyes had authority, here they might take two thieves kissing.

Men. All men's faces are true, whatsom-e'er their hands are.

Eno. But there is never a fair woman has a true face.

Men. No slander; they steal hearts.

Eno. We came hither to fight with you.

Men. For my part, I am sorry it is turned to a drinking. Pompey doth this day laugh away his fortune.

Eno. If he do, sure, he cannot weep 't back again.

Men. Y' have said, sir. We looked not for Mark Antony here: pray you, is he married to Cleopatra?

Eno. Cæsar's sister is called Octavia.

Men. True, sir; she was the wife of Caius Marcellus.

Eno. But she is now the wife of Marcus Antonius.

Men. Pray ye, sir?

Eno. 'Tis true.

Men. Then is Cæsar and he for ever knit together.

Eno. If I were bound to divine of this unity, I would not prophesy so.

Men. I think the policy of that purpose made more in the marriage than the love of the parties.

Eno. I think so too. But you shall find, the band that seems to tie their friendship together will be the very strangler of their amity: Octavia is of a holy, cold, and still conversation.

Men. Who would not have his wife so?

Eno. Not he that himself is not so; which is Mark Antony. He will to his Egyptian dish again: then shall the sighs of Octavia blow the fire up in Cæsar; and, as I said before, that which is the strength of their amity shall prove the immediate author of their variance. Antony will use his affection where it is: he married but his occasion here.

us that Antony bought the elder Pompey's house at auction and later refused to pay for it; *o'er-count* has possibly the suggestion of cheating. 30. **from the present,** away from the business. 33. **embrac'd,** if accepted. 38. **edges,** swords. 39. **targes,** shields. 48. **well studied,** well prepared by thinking. 52. **timelier,** earlier. 55. **What . . . face.** The figure is from casting accounts or reckonings. 59. **composition,** agreement. 69-71. **Apollodorus . . . mattress.** This alludes to a tale told by Plutarch according to which Cleopatra had herself done up in a mattress and carried secretly on the shoulders of Apollodorus into a palace to meet Julius Caesar. 74. **toward,** coming up. 86. **known,** known each other. 120. **Pray ye?** Are you in earnest? 124. **divine of,** prophesy about. 129. **strangler,** destroyer. Later folios have *stranger,* which Rowe changed to *estranger.* 140. **occasion,** according to his personal interests.

Men. And thus it may be. Come, sir, will you aboard? I have a health for you.

Eno. I shall take it, sir: we have used our throats in Egypt.

Men. Come, let 's away. *Exeunt.*

[SCENE VII. *On board Pompey's galley, off Misenum.*]

Music plays. Enter two or three Servants *with a banquet.*

First Serv. Here they'll be, man. Some o' their plants are ill-rooted already; the least wind i' the world will blow them down.

Sec. Serv. Lepidus is high-coloured.

First Serv. They have made him drink alms-drink.

Sec. Serv. As they pinch one another by the disposition, he cries out 'No more;' reconciles them to his entreaty, and himself to the drink.

First Serv. But it raises the greater war between him and his discretion.

Sec. Serv. Why, this it is to have a name in great men's fellowship: I had as lief have a reed that will do me no service as a partisan I could not heave.

First Serv. To be called into a huge sphere, and not to be seen to move in 't, are the holes where eyes should be, which pitifully disaster the cheeks.

A sennet sounded. Enter CÆSAR, ANTONY, POMPEY, LEPIDUS, AGRIPPA, MECÆNAS, ENOBARBUS, MENAS, *with other captains.*

Ant. [*To Cæsar*] Thus do they, sir: they take the flow o' th' Nile
By certain scales i' th' pyramid; they know,
By th' height, the lowness, or the mean, if dearth
Or foison follow: the higher Nilus swells,
The more it promises: as it ebbs, the seedsman
Upon the slime and ooze scatters his grain,
And shortly comes to harvest.

Lep. Y' have strange serpents there.

Ant. Ay, Lepidus.

Lep. Your serpent of Egypt is bred now of your mud by the operation of your sun: so is your crocodile.

Ant. They are so.

Pom. Sit,—and some wine! A health to Lepidus!

Lep. I am not so well as I should be, but I'll ne'er out.

Eno. Not till you have slept; I fear me you'll be in till then.

Lep. Nay, certainly, I have heard the Ptolemies' pyramises are very goodly things; without contradiction, I have heard that.

Men. [*Aside to Pom.*] Pompey, a word.

Pom. [*Aside to Men.*] Say in mine ear: what is 't?

Men. [*Aside to Pom.*] Forsake thy seat, I do beseech thee, captain,
And hear me speak a word.

Pom. [*Aside to Men.*] Forbear me till anon.
[*Menas*] *whispers in 's ear.*
This wine for Lepidus!

Lep. What manner o' thing is your crocodile?

Ant. It is shaped, sir, like itself; and it is as broad as it hath breadth: it is just so high as it is, and moves with it own organs: it lives by that which nourisheth it; and the elements once out of it, it transmigrates.

Lep. What colour is it of?

Ant. Of it own colour too.

Lep. 'Tis a strange serpent.

Ant. 'Tis so. And the tears of it are wet.

Cæs. Will this description satisfy him?

Ant. With the health that Pompey gives him, else he is a very epicure.

Pom. [*Aside to Men.*] Go hang, sir, hang! Tell me of that? away!
Do as I bid you.—Where 's this cup I call'd for?

Men. [*Aside to Pom.*] If for the sake of merit thou wilt hear me,
Rise from thy stool.

Pom. [*Aside to Men.*] I think th' art mad. The matter? [*Rises, and walks aside.*]

Men. I have ever held my cap off to thy fortunes.

Pom. Thou hast serv'd me with much faith. What 's else to say?—
Be jolly, lords.

Ant. These quick-sands, Lepidus,
Keep off them, for you sink.

Men. Wilt thou be lord of all the world?

Pom. What say'st thou?

Men. Wilt thou be lord of the whole world? That 's twice.

Pom. How should that be?

Men. But entertain it,
And, though thou think me poor, I am the man
Will give thee all the world.

Pom. Hast thou drunk well?

Men. No, Pompey, I have kept me from the cup.
Thou art, if thou dar'st be, the earthly Jove:
Whate'er the ocean pales, or sky inclips,
Is thine, if thou wilt ha 't.

Pom. Show me which way.

Men. These three world-sharers, these competitors,
Are in thy vessel: let me cut the cable;
And, when we are put off, fall to their throats:
All there is thine.

Pom. Ah, this thou shouldst have done,
And not have spoke on 't! In me 'tis villany;
In thee 't had been good service. Thou must know,
'Tis not my profit that does lead mine honour;
Mine honour, it. Repent that e'er thy tongue
Hath so betray'd thine act: being done unknown,
I should have found it afterwards well done;
But must condemn it now. Desist, and drink.

Men. [*Aside*] For this,
I'll never follow thy pall'd fortunes more.
Who seeks, and will not take when once 'tis offer'd,
Shall never find it more.

SCENE VII. *Stage Direction:* **banquet,** a course of the feast, probably, dessert. 2. **plants,** soles of the feet, with pun on usual sense. 6. **alms-drink.** Malone thought this meant his share and the others' too; more probably, the leavings, ordinarily saved for alms-people, besides his own share; Cuningham suggests "drinks taken as a work of charity, i.e., to further the reconciliation." 7. **pinch . . . disposition,** chafe one another, fall to bickering. Lepidus stops them but has to join them in fresh bumpers of drink. 14. **partisan,** long-bladed spear having one or more cutting edges, used by infantry. 18. **disaster,** disfigure; an astrological term following *sphere*, two lines above. 23. **foison,** plenty. 29. **Your,** colloquial use; not readily translatable. 36. **I'll ne'er out,** I'll never refuse a toast. 38. **in,** in for it; also in drink. 40. **pyramises,** pyramids. 49. **it own,** its own. 51. **elements . . . it,** i.e., at its dissolution; the word *elements* may, however, mean "vital elements." 55. **tears,** allusion to the ancient belief that the crocodile wept over its victim before devouring it. 63. **held my cap off,** been a faithful servant. 69. **But entertain it,** only accept it. 74. **pales,** impales, fences in. **inclips,** embraces. 76. **competitors,** partners. 83. **Mine honour, it,** i.e., my honor has to come before my personal advancement. 88. **pall'd,** decayed, waning. 99. **go on**

Pom. This health to Lepidus!
Ant. Bear him ashore. I'll pledge it for him, Pompey.
Eno. Here 's to thee, Menas!
Men. Enobarbus, welcome!
Pom. Fill till the cup be hid.
Eno. There 's a strong fellow, Menas.
[*Pointing to the Attendant who carries off Lepidus.*]
Men. Why?
Eno. 'A bears the third part of the world, man; see'st not?
Men. The third part, then, is drunk: would it were all,
That it might go on wheels!
Eno. Drink thou; increase the reels.
Men. Come.
Pom. This is not yet an Alexandrian feast.
Ant. It ripens towards it. Strike the vessels, ho!
Here is to Cæsar!
Cæs. I could well forbear 't.
It 's monstrous labour, when I wash my brain,
And it grows fouler.
Ant. Be a child o' th' time.
Cæs. Possess it, I'll make answer:
But I had rather fast from all four days
Than drink so much in one.
Eno. Ha, my brave emperor!
[*To Antony.*]
Shall we dance now the Egyptian Bacchanals,
And celebrate our drink?
Pom. Let 's ha 't, good soldier.
Ant. Come, let 's all take hands,
Till that the conquering wine hath steep'd our sense
In soft and delicate Lethe.
Eno. All take hands.
Make battery to our ears with the loud music:
The while I'll place you: then the boy shall sing;
The holding every man shall bear as loud
As his strong sides can volley.
Music plays. Enobarbus places them hand in hand.

THE SONG.

Come, thou monarch of the vine,
Plumpy Bacchus with pink eyne!
In thy fats our cares be drown'd,
With thy grapes our hairs be crown'd:
Cup us, till the world go round,
Cup us, till the world go round!

Cæs. What would you more? Pompey, good night. Good brother,
Let me request you off: our graver business
Frowns at this levity. Gentle lords, let 's part;
You see we have burnt our cheeks: strong Enobarb
Is weaker than the wine; and mine own tongue
Splits what it speaks: the wild disguise hath almost
Antick'd us all. What needs more words? Good night.
Good Antony, your hand.
Pom. I'll try you on the shore.
Ant. And shall, sir: give 's your hand.
Pom. O Antony,
You have my father's house,—But, what? we are friends.
Come, down into the boat.
Eno. Take heed you fall not.
[*Exeunt all but Enobarbus and Menas.*]
Menas, I'll not on shore.
Men. No, to my cabin.
These drums! these trumpets, flutes! what!
Let Neptune hear we bid a loud farewell
To these great fellows: sound and be hang'd, sound out!
Sound a flourish, with drums.
Eno. Ho! says 'a. There 's my cap.
Men. Ho! Noble captain, come. *Exeunt.*

[ACT III.

SCENE I. *A plain in Syria.*]

Enter VENTIDIUS *as it were in triumph* [*with* SILIUS, *and other* Romans, Officers, *and* Soldiers], *the dead body of* PACORUS *borne before him.*

Ven. Now, darting Parthia, art thou struck; and now
Pleas'd fortune does of Marcus Crassus' death
Make me revenger. Bear the king's son's body
Before our army. Thy Pacorus, Orodes,
Pays this for Marcus Crassus.
Sil. Noble Ventidius,
Whilst yet with Parthian blood thy sword is warm,
The fugitive Parthians follow; spur through Media,
Mesopotamia, and the shelters whither
The routed fly: so thy grand captain Antony
Shall set thee on triumphant chariots and
Put garlands on thy head.
Ven. O Silius, Silius,
I have done enough; a lower place, note well,
May make too great an act: for learn this, Silius;
Better to leave undone, than by our deed
Acquire too high a fame when him we serve 's away.
Cæsar and Antony have ever won
More in their officer than person: Sossius,
One of my place in Syria, his lieutenant,
For quick accumulation of renown,
Which he achiev'd by th' minute, lost his favour.
Who does i' th' wars more than his captain can
Becomes his captain's captain: and ambition,
The soldier's virtue, rather makes choice of loss,
Than gain which darkens him.
I could do more to do Antonius good,
But 'twould offend him; and in his offence
Should my performance perish.
Sil. Thou hast, Ventidius, that
Without the which a soldier, and his sword,
Grants scarce distinction. Thou wilt write to Antony?
Ven. I'll humbly signify what in his name,

wheels, go fast or easily; proverbial. 100. **increase the reels,** increase the reeling and whirling of drunkenness. Steevens conjectured, *And grease the wheels.* 103. **Strike the vessels,** tap the casks; also explained as "clash your drinking vessels together." 105. **wash my brain,** drink copiously. 106. **And it grows.** F has *grow,* with which reading *And* would mean "if." 107. **Possess it,** have your way; or, drink it off. 114. **Lethe,** forgetfulness. 117. **holding,** refrain, burden. 121. **pink eyne,** winking, half-shut eyes. 122. **fats,** vats, vessels. 131. **disguise,** drunkenness. 132. **Antick'd,** made like buffoons.

ACT III. SCENE I. 1. **darting Parthia,** Orodes, King of Parthia. The Parthians were famous for archery and for the Parthian dart which they discharged as they fled. Pacorus was the son of Orodes. 2. **Marcus Crassus' death.** Crassus, member of the first triumvirate with Pompey and Julius Caesar, was overthrown and treacherously murdered by Orodes in 53 B.C. 12. **lower place,** i.e., one of lower rank. 20. **lost his favour.** No authority has been discovered for this somewhat improbable charge against Antony. 24. **darkens him,** deprives him of luster or renown. 29. **Grants scarce distinction,** can scarcely be distinguished (i.e., Ventidius has discretion).

That magical word of war, we have effected;
How, with his banners and his well-paid ranks,
The ne'er-yet-beaten horse of Parthia
We have jaded out o' th' field.
Sil. Where is he now?
Ven. He purposeth to Athens: whither, with what haste
The weight we must convey with 's will permit,
We shall appear before him. On, there; pass along!
Exeunt.

[SCENE II. *Rome. An ante-chamber in Cæsar's house.*]

Enter AGRIPPA *at one door*, ENOBARBUS *at another*.

Agr. What, are the brothers parted?
Eno. They have dispatch'd with Pompey, he is gone;
The other three are sealing. Octavia weeps
To part from Rome; Cæsar is sad; and Lepidus,
Since Pompey's feast, as Menas says, is troubled
With the green sickness.
Agr. 'Tis a noble Lepidus.
Eno. A very fine one: O, how he loves Cæsar!
Agr. Nay, but how dearly he adores Mark Antony!
Eno. Cæsar? Why, he 's the Jupiter of men.
Agr. What 's Antony? The god of Jupiter.
Eno. Spake you of Cæsar? How! the non-pareil!
Agr. O Antony! O thou Arabian bird!
Eno. Would you praise Cæsar, say 'Cæsar:' go no further.
Agr. Indeed, he plied them both with excellent praises.
Eno. But he loves Cæsar best; yet he loves Antony:
Hoo! hearts, tongues, figures, scribes, bards, poets, cannot
Think, speak, cast, write, sing, number, hoo!
His love to Antony. But as for Cæsar,
Kneel down, kneel down, and wonder.
Agr. Both he loves.
Eno. They are his shards, and he their beetle.
[*Trumpets within.*] So;
This is to horse. Adieu, noble Agrippa.
Agr. Good fortune, worthy soldier; and farewell.

Enter CÆSAR, ANTONY, LEPIDUS, *and* OCTAVIA.

Ant. No further, sir.
Cæs. You take from me a great part of myself;
Use me well in 't. Sister, prove such a wife
As my thoughts make thee, and as my farthest band
Shall pass on thy approof. Most noble Antony,
Let not the piece of virtue, which is set
Betwixt us as the cement of our love,
To keep it builded, be the ram to batter
The fortress of it; for better might we
Have lov'd without this mean, if on both parts
This be not cherish'd.
Ant. Make me not offended
In your distrust.
Cæs. I have said.
Ant. You shall not find,
Though you be therein curious, the least cause
For what you seem to fear: so, the gods keep you,
And make the hearts of Romans serve your ends!
We will here part.
Cæs. Farewell, my dearest sister, fare thee well:
The elements be kind to thee, and make
Thy spirits all of comfort! fare thee well.
Oct. My noble brother!
Ant. The April 's in her eyes: it is love's spring,
And these the showers to bring it on. Be cheerful.
Oct. Sir, look well to my husband's house; and—
Cæs. What,
Octavia?
Oct. I'll tell you in your ear.
Ant. Her tongue will not obey her heart, nor can
Her heart inform her tongue,—the swan's down-feather,
That stands upon the swell at full of tide,
And neither way inclines.
Eno. [*Aside to Agr.*] Will Cæsar weep?
Agr. [*Aside to Eno.*] He has a cloud in 's face.
Eno. [*Aside to Agr.*] He were the worse for that, were he a horse;
So is he, being a man.
Agr. [*Aside to Eno.*] Why, Enobarbus,
When Antony found Julius Cæsar dead,
He cried almost to roaring; and he wept
When at Philippi he found Brutus slain.
Eno. [*Aside to Agr.*] That year, indeed, he was troubled with a rheum;
What willingly he did confound he wail'd,
Believe 't, till I wept too.
Cæs. No, sweet Octavia,
You shall hear from me still; the time shall not
Out-go my thinking on you.
Ant. Come, sir, come;
I'll wrestle with you in my strength of love:
Look, here I have you; thus I let you go,
And give you to the gods.
Cæs. Adieu; be happy!
Lep. Let all the number of the stars give light
To thy fair way!
Cæs. Farewell, farewell! *Kisses Octavia.*
Ant. Farewell! *Trumpets sound. Exeunt.*

[SCENE III. *Alexandria. Cleopatra's palace.*]

Enter CLEOPATRA, CHARMIAN, IRAS, *and* ALEXAS.

Cleo. Where is the fellow?
Alex. Half afeard to come.
Cleo. Go to, go to.

Enter the Messenger *as before*.

Come hither, sir.
Alex. Good majesty,
Herod of Jewry dare not look upon you
But when you are well pleas'd.
Cleo. That Herod's head

34. **jaded,** driven, exhausted, beaten. 36. **with 's,** with us.
SCENE II. 1. **parted,** departed. 2. **dispatch'd,** concluded the business. 3. **sealing,** bringing matters to a conclusion. 6. **green sickness,** a kind of anemia supposed to affect young women; used ironically, Lee thinks, with reference to the love (?) Lepidus bore to Caesar and Antony. 11. **non-pareil,** one having no equal. 12. **Arabian bird,** the fabled phoenix, which arose fresh from its ashes and of which there was only one. 17. **cast,** calculate. **number,** write verses. 20. **shards,** wings (by means of which the dull Lepidus might rise from earth). 26-27. **as my . . . approof,** such as my utmost bond shall be justified on what thou shalt prove to be. 28. **piece,** masterpiece. 48. **swan's down-feather.** The figure seems to refer to a condition of inertia due to conflicting passions; it may have some reference to Octavia's affections divided between husband and brother. 51. **cloud in 's face,** phrase applied to some marking in a horse's face which was regarded as a blemish. 57. **rheum,** running at the eyes; used of any discharge of mucus from the

I'll have: but how, when Antony is gone
Through whom I might command it? Come thou near.
Mess. Most gracious majesty,—
Cleo. Didst thou behold Octavia?
Mess. Ay, dread queen.
Cleo. Where?
Mess. Madam, in Rome;
I look'd her in the face, and saw her led
Between her brother and Mark Antony.
Cleo. Is she as tall as me?
Mess. She is not, madam.
Cleo. Didst hear her speak? is she shrill-tongu'd or low?
Mess. Madam, I heard her speak; she is low-voic'd.
Cleo. That 's not so good: he cannot like her long.
Char. Like her! O Isis! 'tis impossible.
Cleo. I think so, Charmian: dull of tongue, and dwarfish!
What majesty is in her gait? Remember,
If e'er thou look'dst on majesty.
Mess. She creeps:
Her motion and her station are as one;
She shows a body rather than a life,
A statue than a breather.
Cleo. Is this certain?
Mess. Or I have no observance.
Char. Three in Egypt
Cannot make better note.
Cleo. He 's very knowing;
I do perceive 't: there 's nothing in her yet:
The fellow has good judgement.
Char. Excellent.
Cleo. Guess at her years, I prithee.
Mess. Madam,
She was a widow,—
Cleo. Widow! Charmian, hark.
Mess. And I do think she 's thirty.
Cleo. Bear'st thou her face in mind? is 't long or round?
Mess. Round even to faultiness.
Cleo. For the most part, too, they are foolish that are so.
Her hair, what colour?
Mess. Brown, madam: and her forehead
As low as she would wish it.
Cleo. There 's gold for thee.
Thou must not take my former sharpness ill:
I will employ thee back again; I find thee
Most fit for business: go make thee ready;
Our letters are prepar'd. [*Exit Messenger.*]
Char. A proper man.
Cleo. Indeed, he is so: I repent me much
That so I harried him. Why, methinks, by him,
This creature 's no such thing.
Char. Nothing, madam.
Cleo. The man hath seen some majesty, and should know.
Char. Hath he seen majesty? Isis else defend,
And serving you so long!
Cleo. I have one thing more to ask him yet, good Charmian:
But 'tis no matter; thou shalt bring him to me
Where I will write. All may be well enough.
Char. I warrant you, madam. *Exeunt.*

[SCENE IV. *Athens. A room in Antony's house.*]

Enter ANTONY *and* OCTAVIA.

Ant. Nay, nay, Octavia, not only that,—
That were excusable, that, and thousands more
Of semblable import,—but he hath wag'd
New wars 'gainst Pompey; made his will, and read it
To public ear:
Spoke scantly of me: when perforce he could not
But pay me terms of honour, cold and sickly
He vented them; most narrow measure lent me:
When the best hint was given him, he not took 't,
Or did it from his teeth.
Oct. O my good lord,
Believe not all; or, if you must believe,
Stomach not all. A more unhappy lady,
If this division chance, ne'er stood between,
Praying for both parts:
The good gods will mock me presently,
When I shall pray, 'O, bless my lord and husband!'
Undo that prayer, by crying out as loud,
'O, bless my brother!' Husband win, win brother,
Prays, and destroys the prayer; no midway
'Twixt these extremes at all.
Ant. Gentle Octavia,
Let your best love draw to that point, which seeks
Best to preserve it: if I lose mine honour,
I lose myself: better I were not yours
Than yours so branchless. But, as you requested,
Yourself shall go between 's: the mean time, lady,
I'll raise the preparation of a war
Shall stain your brother: make your soonest haste;
So your desires are yours.
Oct. Thanks to my lord.
The Jove of power make me most weak, most weak,
Your reconciler! Wars 'twixt you twain would be
As if the world should cleave, and that slain men
Should solder up the rift.
Ant. When it appears to you where this begins,
Turn your displeasure that way; for our faults
Can never be so equal, that your love
Can equally move with them. Provide your going;
Choose your own company, and command what cost
Your heart has mind to. *Exeunt.*

[SCENE V. *The same. Another room.*]

Enter ENOBARBUS *and* EROS.

Eno. How now, friend Eros!
Eros. There 's strange news come, sir.
Eno. What, man?

head. 58. **wail'd,** bewailed. 61. **Out-go,** outstrip; the phrase is also interpreted as "I shall think of you while life lasts."

SCENE III. 22. **station,** manner of standing. 24. **breather,** living being. 25. **observance,** ability to observe. 32. **face . . . round.** Physiognomy taught that very round faces denoted silliness. 37. **As . . . it.** Low foreheads were attributes of ugliness. **as she would wish it,** as could be (cant phrase). 43. **harried,** maltreated. **by,** according to. 44. **such,** very remarkable.

SCENE IV. 3. **semblable,** similar. 4-5. **made . . . ear.** Plutarch states that Octavius read Antony's will, not his own. In Shakespeare's version, Antony is accusing Caesar of catering to public opinion by showing the populace what benefits they might expect from him. 6. **scantly,** grudgingly. 10. **from his teeth,** from the teeth only, not from the heart. 12. **Stomach,** resent. 14. **parts,** sides. 24. **branchless,** pruned (of honor). 27. **stain,** eclipse (his preparations). **soonest,** quickest.

Eros. Cæsar and Lepidus have made wars upon Pompey.
Eno. This is old: what is the success?
Eros. Cæsar, having made use of him in the wars 'gainst Pompey, presently denied him rivality; would not let him partake in the glory of the action: and not resting here, accuses him of letters he had formerly wrote to Pompey; upon his own appeal, seizes him: so the poor third is up, till death enlarge his confine.
Eno. Then, world, thou hast a pair of chaps, no more;
And throw between them all the food thou hast,
They'll grind the one the other. Where 's Antony?
Eros. He 's walking in the garden—thus; and spurns
The rush that lies before him; cries, 'Fool Lepidus!'
And threats the throat of that his officer
That murd'red Pompey.
Eno. Our great navy 's rigg'd.
Ero. For Italy and Cæsar. More, Domitius;
My lord desires you presently: my news
I might have told hereafter.
Eno. 'Twill be naught:
But let it be. Bring me to Antony.
Eros. Come, sir. *Exeunt.*

[SCENE VI. *Rome. Cæsar's house.*]

Enter AGRIPPA, MECÆNAS, *and* CÆSAR.

Cæs. Contemning Rome, he has done all this, and more,
In Alexandria: here 's the manner of 't:
I' th' market-place, on a tribunal silver'd,
Cleopatra and himself in chairs of gold
Were publicly enthron'd: at the feet sat
Cæsarion, whom they call my father's son,
And all the unlawful issue that their lust
Since then hath made between them. Unto her
He gave the stablishment of Egypt; made her
Of lower Syria, Cyprus, Lydia,
Absolute queen.
Mec. This in the public eye?
Cæs. I' th' common show-place, where they exercise.
His sons he there proclaim'd the kings of kings:
Great Media, Parthia, and Armenia,
He gave to Alexander; to Ptolemy he assign'd
Syria, Cilicia, and Phœnicia: she
In th' habiliments of the goddess Isis
That day appear'd; and oft before gave audience,
As 'tis reported, so.
Mec. Let Rome be thus
Inform'd.
Agr. Who, queasy with his insolence
Already, will their good thoughts call from him.
Cæs. The people knows it; and have now receiv'd
His accusations.
Agr. Who does he accuse?
Cæs. Cæsar: and that, having in Sicily
Sextus Pompeius spoil'd, we had not rated him
His part o' th' isle: then does he say, he lent me
Some shipping unrestor'd: lastly, he frets
That Lepidus of the triumvirate
Should be depos'd; and, being, that we detain
All his revenue.
Agr. Sir, this should be answer'd.
Cæs. 'Tis done already, and the messenger gone.
I have told him, Lepidus was grown too cruel;
That he his high authority abus'd,
And did deserve his change: for what I have conquer'd,
I grant him part; but then, in his Armenia,
And other of his conquer'd kingdoms, I
Demand the like.
Mec. He'll never yield to that.
Cæs. Nor must not then be yielded to in this.

Enter OCTAVIA *with her train.*

Oct. Hail, Cæsar, and my lord! hail, most dear Cæsar!
Cæs. That ever I should call thee castaway!
Oct. You have not call'd me so, nor have you cause.
Cæs. Why have you stol'n upon us thus? You come not
Like Cæsar's sister: the wife of Antony
Should have an army for an usher, and
The neighs of horse to tell of her approach
Long ere she did appear; the trees by th' way
Should have borne men; and expectation fainted,
Longing for what it had not; nay, the dust
Should have ascended to the roof of heaven,
Rais'd by your populous troops: but you are come
A market-maid to Rome; and have prevented
The ostentation of our love, which, left unshown,
Is often left unlov'd: we should have met you
By sea and land; supplying every stage
With an augmented greeting.
Oct. Good my lord,
To come thus was I not constrain'd, but did it
On my free will. My lord, Mark Antony,
Hearing that you prepar'd for war, acquainted
My grieved ear withal; whereon, I begg'd
His pardon for return.
Cæs. Which soon he granted,
Being an abstract 'tween his lust and him.
Oct. Do not say so, my lord.
Cæs. I have eyes upon him,
And his affairs come to me on the wind.
Where is he now?
Oct. My lord, in Athens.
Cæs. No, my most wronged sister; Cleopatra
Hath nodded him to her. He hath given his empire
Up to a whore; who now are levying
The kings o' th' earth for war: he hath assembled
Bocchus, the king of Libya; Archelaus,
Of Cappadocia; Philadelphos, king
Of Paphlagonia; the Thracian king, Adallas;
King Malchus of Arabia; King of Pont;

SCENE V. 9. **rivality,** rights of a partner. 12. **his own appeal,** Caesar's own accusation. 13. **up,** shut up (in prison). 14. **pair of chaps,** two jaws (destined to grind each other). **no more.** The meaning is "no more than one pair." 18. **rush,** strewn rushes. 20. **Pompey.** Pompey met defeat in Sicily, escaped thence to the East with designs against Antony, and was supposed to have been murdered by Antony's orders; here Antony blames his officer.

SCENE VI. 3. **tribunal,** seat of eminence. 9. **stablishment,** settled possession. The first 19 lines of this scene reflect the point of view of imperial Rome, with which Plutarch is strongly in sympathy, namely, the impiety of the establishment of independent kingdoms on Roman soil. 20. **queasy,** disgusted, i.e., the Roman people. 50. **populous,** numerous. 52. **ostentation,** public display. 61. **abstract,** shortcut. 69-76. **Bocchus . . . sceptres.** The list of powers is from Plutarch and is somewhat confused, as here, in North's translation. *Libya* is here correctly given; in line 10 Shakespeare followed North in writing *Lydia.* 81. **negligent danger,** danger neglected, or danger through negligence. 88-89. **makes . . . Of us,** make us their minister

Herod of Jewry; Mithridates, king
Of Comagene; Polemon and Amyntas,
The kings of Mede and Lycaonia,
With a more larger list of sceptres.
Oct. Ay me, most wretched,
That have my heart parted betwixt two friends
That do afflict each other!
Cæs. Welcome hither:
Your letters did withhold our breaking forth;
Till we perceiv'd, both how you were wrong led,
And we in negligent danger. Cheer your heart:
Be you not troubled with the time, which drives
O'er your content these strong necessities;
But let determin'd things to destiny
Hold unbewail'd their way. Welcome to Rome;
Nothing more dear to me. You are abus'd
Beyond the mark of thought: and the high gods,
To do you justice, makes his ministers
Of us and those that love you. Best of comfort;
And ever welcome to us.
Agr. Welcome, lady.
Mec. Welcome, dear madam.
Each heart in Rome does love and pity you:
Only th' adulterous Antony, most large
In his abominations, turns you off;
And gives his potent regiment to a trull,
That noises it against us.
Oct. Is it so, sir?
Cæs. Most certain. Sister, welcome: pray you,
Be ever known to patience: my dear'st sister! *Exeunt.*

[SCENE VII. *Near Actium. Antony's camp.*]

Enter CLEOPATRA *and* ENOBARBUS.

Cleo. I will be even with thee, doubt it not.
Eno. But why, why, why?
Cleo. Thou hast forspoke my being in these wars,
And say'st it is not fit.
Eno. Well, is it, is it?
Cleo. If not denounc'd against us, why should not we
Be there in person?
Eno. [*Aside*] Well, I could reply:
If we should serve with horse and mares together,
The horse were merely lost; the mares would bear
A soldier and his horse.
Cleo. What is 't you say?
Eno. Your presence needs must puzzle Antony;
Take from his heart, take from his brain, from 's time,
What should not then be spar'd. He is already
Traduc'd for levity; and 'tis said in Rome
That Photinus, an eunuch and your maids
Manage this war.
Cleo. Sink Rome, and their tongues rot
That speak against us! A charge we bear i' th' war,
And, as the president of my kingdom, will
Appear there for a man. Speak not against it;
I will not stay behind.

Enter ANTONY *and* CANIDIUS.

Eno. Nay, I have done.
Here comes the emperor.
Ant. Is it not strange, Canidius,
That from Tarentum and Brundusium
He could so quickly cut the Ionian sea,
And take in Toryne?—You have heard on 't, sweet?
Cleo. Celerity is never more admir'd
Than by the negligent.
Ant. A good rebuke,
Which might have well becom'd the best of men,
To taunt at slackness. Canidius, we
Will fight with him by sea.
Cleo. By sea! what else?
Can. Why will my lord do so?
Ant. For that he dares us to 't.
Eno. So hath my lord dar'd him to single fight.
Can. Ay, and to wage this battle at Pharsalia,
Where Cæsar fought with Pompey: but these offers,
Which serve not for his vantage, he shakes off;
And so should you.
Eno. Your ships are not well mann'd;
Your mariners are muleters, reapers, people
Ingross'd by swift impress; in Cæsar's fleet
Are those that often have 'gainst Pompey fought:
Their ships are yare; yours, heavy: no disgrace
Shall fall you for refusing him at sea,
Being prepar'd for land.
Ant. By sea, by sea.
Eno. Most worthy sir, you therein throw away
The absolute soldiership you have by land;
Distract your army, which doth most consist
Of war-mark'd footmen; leave unexecuted
Your own renowned knowledge; quite forego
The way which promises assurance; and
Give up yourself merely to chance and hazard,
From firm security.
Ant. I'll fight at sea.
Cleo. I have sixty sails, Cæsar none better.
Ant. Our overplus of shipping will we burn;
And, with the rest full-mann'd, from th' head of Actium
Beat th' approaching Cæsar. But if we fail,
We then can do 't at land.

Enter a Messenger.

Thy business?
Mess. The news is true, my lord; he is descried;
Cæsar has taken Toryne.
Ant. Can he be there in person? 'tis impossible;
Strange that his power should be. Canidius,
Our nineteen legions thou shalt hold by land,
And our twelve thousand horse. We'll to our ship:
Away, my Thetis!

Enter a Soldier.

How now, worthy soldier!

of justice. 89. **Best of comfort,** i.e., may you have, etc. 95. **regiment,** government, rule. **trull,** worthless woman or prostitute. 96. **noises it,** is clamorous.

SCENE VII. 3. **forspoke,** spoken against. 5-6. **If not . . . person.** Cuningham suggests that this means "even if the war were not declared against me (which it is)," etc. This is better than the more obvious meaning, since historically the war was declared against Cleopatra and not Antony. 9. **merely,** utterly. 15. **That . . . maids.** So F, without punctuation. Shakespeare uses *an eunuch* to describe Mardian, not Photinus. 17. **A charge . . . war.** Plutarch states that Cleopatra wished to go to the war to prevent Antony from being reconciled to Octavia; she bribed Canidius to argue for her, so that Antony consented. Plutarch says it was predestined that the government of all the world should fall into Octavius Caesar's hands. 36. **muleters,** F: *Militers;* F_2: *Muliters. Militers* may mean "soldiers." *Muleters* are mule-drivers, peasants. 37. **Ingross'd,** collected. **impress,** impressment. 39. **yare,** easily managed. 61. **Thetis,** sea goddess.

Sold. O noble emperor, do not fight by sea;
Trust not to rotten planks: do you misdoubt
This sword and these my wounds? Let th' Egyptians
And the Phœnicians go a-ducking: we
Have us'd to conquer, standing on the earth,
And fighting foot to foot.
Ant. Well, well; away!
Exeunt Antony, Cleopatra, and Enobarbus.
Sold. By Hercules, I think I am i' th' right.
Can. Soldier, thou art: but his whole action grows
Not in the power on 't: so our leader 's led,
And we are women's men.
Sold. You keep by land
The legions and the horse whole, do you not?
Can. Marcus Octavius, Marcus Justeius,
Publicola, and Cælius, are for sea:
But we keep whole by land. This speed of Cæsar's
Carries beyond belief.
Sold. While he was yet in Rome,
His power went out in such distractions as
Beguil'd all spies.
Can. Who 's his lieutenant, hear you?
Sold. They say, one Taurus.
Can. Well I know the man.

Enter a Messenger.

Mess. The emperor calls Canidius.
Can. With news the time 's with labour, and throws forth,
Each minute, some. *Exeunt.*

[SCENE VIII. *A plain near Actium.*]

Enter CÆSAR [*and* TAURUS] *with his army, marching.*

Cæs. Taurus!
Taur. My lord?
Cæs. Strike not by land; keep whole: provoke not battle,
Till we have done at sea. Do not exceed
The prescript of this scroll: our fortune lies
Upon this jump. *Exit* [*with army*].

[SCENE IX. *Another part of the plain.*]

Enter ANTONY *and* ENOBARBUS.

Ant. Set we our squadrons on yond side o' th' hill,
In eye of Cæsar's battle; from which place
We may the number of the ships behold,
And so proceed accordingly. *Exit* [*with Eno.*]

[SCENE X. *Another part of the plain.*]

CANIDIUS *marcheth with his land army one way over the stage; and* TAURUS, *the lieutenant of* CÆSAR, *the other way. After their going in, is heard the noise of a sea-fight.*

Alarum. Enter ENOBARBUS.

Eno. Naught, naught, all naught! I can behold no longer:
Th' Antoniad, the Egyptian admiral,
With all their sixty, fly and turn the rudder:
To see 't mine eyes are blasted.

Enter SCARUS.

Scar. Gods and goddesses,
All the whole synod of them!
Eno. What 's thy passion?
Scar. The greater cantle of the world is lost
With very ignorance; we have kiss'd away
Kingdoms and provinces.
Eno. How appears the fight?
Scar. On our side like the token'd pestilence,
Where death is sure. Yon ribaudred nag of Egypt,—
Whom leprosy o'ertake!—i' th' midst o' th' fight,
When vantage like a pair of twins appear'd,
Both as the same, or rather ours the elder,
The breese upon her, like a cow in June,
Hoists sails and flies.
Eno. That I beheld:
Mine eyes did sicken at the sight, and could not
Endure a further view.
Scar. She once being loof'd,
The noble ruin of her magic, Antony,
Claps on his sea-wing, and, like a doting mallard,
Leaving the fight in height, flies after her:
I never saw an action of such shame;
Experience, manhood, honour, ne'er before
Did violate so itself.
Eno. Alack, alack!

Enter CANIDIUS.

Can. Our fortune on the sea is out of breath,
And sinks most lamentably. Had our general
Been what he knew himself, it had gone well:
O, he has given example for our flight,
Most grossly, by his own!
Eno. Ay, are you thereabouts?
Why, then, good night indeed.
Can. Toward Peloponnesus are they fled.
Scar. 'Tis easy to 't; and there I will attend
What further comes.
Can. To Cæsar will I render
My legions and my horse: six kings already
Show me the way of yielding.
Eno. I'll yet follow
The wounded chance of Antony, though my reason
Sits in the wind against me. [*Exeunt.*]

[SCENE XI. *Alexandria. Cleopatra's palace.*]

Enter ANTONY *with* Attendants.

Ant. Hark! the land bids me tread no more upon 't;
It is asham'd to bear me! Friends, come hither.

69-70. **his . . . on 't,** usually taken to mean "his whole action proceeds not from the source of its possible power." Johnson interpreted, with some propriety, "his whole conduct becomes ungoverned by the right, or by reason." Canidius shows, like the others, a soldier's disgust with Antony's infatuation, and is less definitely a traitor than in Plutarch. 76. **Carries beyond,** surpasses (like an arrow in archery). 77. **distractions,** detachments. 81-82. **With news . . . some,** more news is born every minute; *throws,* gives birth to.
SCENE VIII. 5. **prescript,** direction.
SCENE X. 2. **Antoniad,** the name of Cleopatra's admiral or chief galley of her fleet. 5. **synod,** assembly of the gods. 6. **cantle,** corner; hence, piece or part. 9. **token'd pestilence.** Certain red spots appeared on the bodies of the plague-smitten, which were, according to Steevens, called "God's tokens," i.e., of death. Shakespeare had many ways of fighting battles on the stage; all had to be more or less indirect. In this one two old soldiers on the hill give their report. 10. **ribaudred nag,** foul, obscene jade. 13. **elder,** more advanced. 14. **breese,** gadfly (with a pun on "breeze"). 18. **loof'd,** luffed, brought close to the wind (with a pun on "aloofed," becoming distant). 20. **mallard,** drake. 29. **thereabouts,** of that opinion. 32. **to 't,** to get to it. 33. **render,** surrender. 36. **wounded chance,** broken fortunes. 37. **Sits . . . against,** is in opposition to.

I am so lated in the world, that I
Have lost my way forever: I have a ship
Laden with gold; take that, divide it; fly,
And make your peace with Cæsar.
All. Fly! not we.
Ant. I have fled myself; and have instructed cowards
To run and show their shoulders. Friends, be gone;
I have myself resolv'd upon a course
Which has no need of you; be gone:
My treasure 's in the harbour, take it. O,
I follow'd that I blush to look upon:
My very hairs do mutiny; for the white
Reprove the brown for rashness, and they them
For fear and doting. Friends, be gone: you shall
Have letters from me to some friends that will
Sweep your way for you. Pray you, look not sad,
Nor make replies of loathness: take the hint
Which my despair proclaims; let that be left
Which leaves itself: to the sea-side straightway:
I will possess you of that ship and treasure.
Leave me, I pray, a little: pray you now:
Nay, do so; for, indeed, I have lost command,
Therefore I pray you: I'll see you by and by. *Sits down.*

Enter CLEOPATRA *led by* CHARMIAN, [IRAS,] *and* EROS.

Eros. Nay, gentle madam, to him, comfort him.
Iras. Do, most dear queen.
Char. Do! why: what else?
Cleo. Let me sit down. O Juno!
Ant. No, no, no, no, no.
Eros. See you here, sir?
Ant. O fie, fie, fie!
Char. Madam!
Iras. Madam, O good empress!
Eros. Sir, sir,—
Ant. Yes, my lord, yes; he at Philippi kept
His sword e'en like a dancer; while I struck
The lean and wrinkled Cassius; and 'twas I
That the mad Brutus ended: he alone
Dealt on lieutenantry, and no practice had
In the brave squares of war: yet now—No matter.
Cleo. Ah, stand by.
Eros. The queen, my lord, the queen.
Iras. Go to him, madam, speak to him:
He is unqualitied with very shame.
Cleo. Well then, sustain me: O!
Eros. Most noble sir, arise; the queen approaches;
Her head 's declin'd, and death will seize her, but
Your comfort makes the rescue.
Ant. I have offended reputation,
A most unnoble swerving.
Eros. Sir, the queen.
Ant. O, whither hast thou led me, Egypt? See,
How I convey my shame out of thine eyes
By looking back what I have left behind
'Stroy'd in dishonour.
Cleo. O my lord, my lord,
Forgive my fearful sails! I little thought
You would have follow'd.
Ant. Egypt, thou knew'st too well
My heart was to thy rudder tied by th' strings,
And thou shouldst tow me after: o'er my spirit
Thy full supremacy thou knew'st, and that
Thy beck might from the bidding of the gods
Command me.
Cleo. O, my pardon!
Ant. Now I must
To the young man send humble treaties, dodge
And palter in the shifts of lowness; who
With half the bulk o' th' world play'd as I pleas'd,
Making and marring fortunes. You did know
How much you were my conqueror; and that
My sword, made weak by my affection, would
Obey it on all cause.
Cleo. Pardon, pardon!
Ant. Fall not a tear, I say; one of them rates
All that is won and lost: give me a kiss;
Even this repays me. We sent our schoolmaster;
Is 'a come back? Love, I am full of lead.
Some wine, within there, and our viands! Fortune knows
We scorn her most when most she offers blows. *Exeunt.*

[SCENE XII. *Egypt. Cæsar's camp.*]

Enter CÆSAR, AGRIPPA, [THIDIAS,] *and* DOLABELLA, *with others.*

Cæs. Let him appear that 's come from Antony.
Know you him?
Dol. Cæsar, 'tis his schoolmaster:
An argument that he is pluck'd, when hither
He sends so poor a pinion of his wing,
Which had superfluous kings for messengers
Not many moons gone by.

Enter Ambassador *from Antony.*

Cæs. Approach, and speak.
Amb. Such as I am, I come from Antony:
I was of late as petty to his ends
As is the morn-dew on the myrtle-leaf
To his grand sea.
Cæs. Be 't so: declare thine office.
Amb. Lord of his fortunes he salutes thee, and
Requires to live in Egypt: which not granted,
He lessens his requests; and to thee sues
To let him breathe between the heavens and earth,
A private man in Athens: this for him.
Next, Cleopatra does confess thy greatness;
Submits her to thy might; and of thee craves
The circle of the Ptolemies for her heirs,
Now hazarded to thy grace.
Cæs. For Antony,
I have no ears to his request. The queen

SCENE XI. 3. **lated,** belated, benighted. 8. **show their shoulders,** common expression for "show their backs." 18. **loathness,** unwillingness. 23. **lost command.** Johnson rightly interpreted this as "lost command of emotion"; the usual interpretation is "lost command of his troops." 35. **my lord,** sometimes thought to be addressed to an imaginary interlocutor or, in bitterness, to Caesar; probably it is to Eros (ironically). **he,** i.e., Octavius, to whom Plutarch attributes poor soldiership at Philippi. 36. **sword . . . dancer,** seems to allude to swords worn for ornament only, as by dancers. 39. **Dealt on lieutenantry,** let his subordinates do the fighting. 40. **squares,** squadrons. 44. **unqualitied,** not himself. 47. **but,** unless. 51-54. **See . . . dishonour,** see how I avert my eyes from yours and reflect on the ruin of my fortunes and honor. 62. **treaties,** propositions for settlement. 63. **palter,** use trickery. 69. **Fall,** let fall. **rates,** equals. 71. **schoolmaster,** identified historically as Euphronius, tutor to Antony's children by Cleopatra.

SCENE XII. 8-10. **as petty . . . sea,** as insignificant compared to his great ends as is the dewdrop on the myrtle leaf compared to the grand sea; several interpretations. 12. **Requires,** asks. 14. **breathe,** i.e., live. 18. **circle,** crown.

Of audience nor desire shall fail, so she
From Egypt drive her all-disgraced friend,
Or take his life there: this if she perform,
She shall not sue unheard. So to them both.
Amb. Fortune pursue thee!
Cæs. Bring him through the bands.
[*Exit Ambassador.*]
[*To Thidias*] To try thy eloquence, now 'tis time: dispatch;
From Antony win Cleopatra: promise,
And in our name, what she requires; add more,
From thine invention, offers: women are not
In their best fortunes strong; but want will perjure
The ne'er-touch'd vestal: try thy cunning, Thidias;
Make thine own edict for thy pains, which we
Will answer as a law.
Thid. Cæsar, I go.
Cæs. Observe how Antony becomes his flaw,
And what thou think'st his very action speaks
In every power that moves.
Thid. Cæsar, I shall. *Exeunt.*

[SCENE XIII. *Alexandria. Cleopatra's palace.*]

Enter CLEOPATRA, ENOBARBUS, CHARMIAN, *and* IRAS.

Cleo. What shall we do, Enobarbus?
Eno. Think, and die.
Cleo. Is Antony or we in fault for this?
Eno. Antony only, that would make his will
Lord of his reason. What though you fled
From that great face of war, whose several ranges
Frighted each other? why should he follow?
The itch of his affection should not then
Have nick'd his captainship; at such a point,
When half to half the world oppos'd, he being
The meered question: 'twas a shame no less
Than was his loss, to course your flying flags,
And leave his navy gazing.
Cleo. Prithee, peace.

Enter the Ambassador *with* ANTONY.

Ant. Is that his answer?
Amb. Ay, my lord.
Ant. The queen shall then have courtesy, so she
Will yield us up.
Amb. He says so.
Ant. Let her know 't.
To the boy Cæsar send this grizzled head,
And he will fill thy wishes to the brim
With principalities.
Cleo. That head, my lord?
Ant. To him again: tell him he wears the rose
Of youth upon him; from which the world should note
Something particular: his coin, ships, legions,
May be a coward's; whose ministers would prevail
Under the service of a child as soon
As i' th' command of Cæsar: I dare him therefore
To lay his gay comparisons apart,
And answer me declin'd, sword against sword,
Ourselves alone. I'll write it: follow me.
[*Exeunt Antony and Ambassador.*]
Eno. [*Aside*] Yes, like enough, high-battled Cæsar will
Unstate his happiness, and be stag'd to th' show,
Against a sworder! I see men's judgements are
A parcel of their fortunes; and things outward
Do draw the inward quality after them,
To suffer all alike. That he should dream,
Knowing all measures, the full Cæsar will
Answer his emptiness! Cæsar, thou hast subdu'd
His judgement too.

Enter a Servant.

Ser. A messenger from Cæsar.
Cleo. What, no more ceremony? See, my women!
Against the blown rose may they stop their nose
That kneel'd unto the buds. Admit him, sir.
[*Exit Servant.*]
Eno. [*Aside*] Mine honesty and I begin to square.
The loyalty well held to fools does make
Our faith mere folly: yet he that can endure
To follow with allegiance a fall'n lord
Does conquer him that did his master conquer,
And earns a place i' th' story.

Enter THIDIAS.

Cleo. Cæsar's will?
Thid. Hear it apart.
Cleo. None but friends: say boldly.
Thid. So, haply, are they friends to Antony.
Eno. He needs as many, sir, as Cæsar has;
Or needs not us. If Cæsar please, our master
Will leap to be his friend: for us, you know
Whose he is we are, and that is, Cæsar's.
Thid. So.
Thus then, thou most renown'd: Cæsar entreats,
Not to consider in what case thou stand'st,
Further than he is Cæsar.
Cleo. Go on: right royal.
Thid. He knows that you embrace not Antony
As you did love, but as you fear'd him.
Cleo. O!
Thid. The scars upon your honour, therefore, he
Does pity, as constrained blemishes,
Not as deserv'd.
Cleo. He is a god, and knows
What is most right: mine honour was not yielded,
But conquer'd merely.
Eno. [*Aside*] To be sure of that,
I will ask Antony. Sir, sir, thou art so leaky,
That we must leave thee to thy sinking, for
Thy dearest quit thee. *Exit Eno.*
Thid. Shall I say to Cæsar
What you require of him? for he partly begs
To be desir'd to give. It much would please him,
That of his fortunes you should make a staff

32. **Make . . . pains,** decree thine own reward. 34. **becomes his flaw,** bears his misfortune and disgrace. 36. **power that moves,** faculty or passion that manifests itself.

SCENE XIII. 1. **Think, and die,** take thought on our situation, and die. 3-4. **his . . . reason.** Since *will* might operate against *reason*, they were often thought of as opposing forces. 5. **ranges,** ranks, lines (of ships). 8. **nick'd,** cut short (from being nicked), or (from gaming) got the better of, since a *nick* was a winning throw in games of chance (Cuningham). 10. **meered question,** sole ground of quarrel (if we suppose the word is coined from *mere*). Many conjectures, including Johnson: *mooted;* Cuningham: *moved* (or *meued*); Rowe: *meer*. 11. **course,** pursue (as in hunting). 15. **so,** if. 26. **gay comparisons,** the wealth and splendor just mentioned (to be compared to Antony's poverty). 27. **declin'd,** in fortune. 29. **high-battled,** provided with noble armies. 30. **Unstate,** strip of dignity. **stag'd,** exhibited publicly. 31. **sworder,** gladiator. 32. **parcel of,** of a piece with (Steevens). 41. **square,** quarrel. 52. **Whose . . . Cæsar's,** i.e., whoever can command Antony—as Caesar can—may also command us (?). 55. **Cæsar,** a

To lean upon: but it would warm his spirits,
To hear from me you had left Antony,
†And put yourself under his shrowd,
The universal landlord.
Cleo. What 's your name?
Thid. My name is Thidias.
Cleo. Most kind messenger,
Say to great Cæsar this: in deputation
I kiss his conqu'ring hand: tell him, I am prompt
To lay my crown at 's feet, and there to kneel:
Tell him, from his all-obeying breath I hear
The doom of Egypt.
Thid. 'Tis your noblest course.
Wisdom and fortune combating together,
If that the former dare but what it can,
No chance may shake it. Give me grace to lay
My duty on your hand.
Cleo. Your Cæsar's father oft,
When he hath mus'd of taking kingdoms in,
Bestow'd his lips on that unworthy place,
As it rain'd kisses.

Enter ANTONY *and* ENOBARBUS.

Ant. Favours, by Jove that thunders!
What art thou, fellow?
Thid. One that but performs
The bidding of the fullest man, and worthiest
To have command obey'd.
Eno. [*Aside*] You will be whipp'd.
Ant. Approach, there! Ah, you kite! Now, gods and devils!
Authority melts from me: of late, when I cried 'Ho!'
Like boys unto a muss, kings would start forth,
And cry 'Your will?' Have you no ears? I am
Antony yet.

Enter a Servant [*followed by others*].

Take hence this Jack, and whip him.
Eno. [*Aside*] 'Tis better playing with a lion's whelp
Than with an old one dying.
Ant. Moon and stars!
Whip him. Were 't twenty of the greatest tributaries
That do acknowledge Cæsar, should I find them
So saucy with the hand of she here,—what 's her name,
Since she was Cleopatra? Whip him, fellows,
Till, like a boy, you see him cringe his face,
And whine aloud for mercy: take him hence.
Thid. Mark Antony!
Ant. Tug him away: being whipp'd,
Bring him again: this Jack of Cæsar's shall
Bear us an errand to him.
Exeunt [*Servants*] *with Thidias.*
You were half blasted ere I knew you: ha!
Have I my pillow left unpress'd in Rome,
Forborne the getting of a lawful race,
And by a gem of women, to be abus'd
By one that looks on feeders?
Cleo. Good my lord,—
Ant. You have been a boggler ever:
But when we in our viciousness grow hard—
O misery on 't!—the wise gods seel our eyes;
In our own filth drop our clear judgements; make us
Adore our errors; laugh at 's, while we strut
To our confusion.
Cleo. O, is 't come to this?
Ant. I found you as a morsel cold upon
Dead Cæsar's trencher; nay, you were a fragment
Of Cneius Pompey's; besides what hotter hours,
Unregist'red in vulgar fame, you have
Luxuriously pick'd out: for, I am sure,
Though you can guess what temperance should be,
You know not what it is.
Cleo. Wherefore is this?
Ant. To let a fellow that will take rewards
And say 'God quit you!' be familiar with
My playfellow, your hand; this kingly seal
And plighter of high hearts! O, that I were
Upon the hill of Basan, to outroar
The horned herd! for I have savage cause;
And to proclaim it civilly, were like
A halter'd neck which does the hangman thank
For being yare about him.

Enter a Servant *with* THIDIAS.

Is he whipp'd?
Ser. Soundly, my lord.
Ant. Cried he? and begg'd 'a pardon?
Ser. He did ask favour.
Ant. If that thy father live, let him repent
Thou wast not made his daughter; and be thou sorry
To follow Cæsar in his triumph, since
Thou hast been whipp'd for following him: henceforth
The white hand of a lady fever thee,
Shake thou to look on 't. Get thee back to Cæsar,
Tell him thy entertainment: look, thou say
He makes me angry with him; for he seems
Proud and disdainful, harping on what I am,
Not what he knew I was: he makes me angry;
And at this time most easy 'tis to do 't,
When my good stars, that were my former guides,
Have empty left their orbs, and shot their fires
Into th' abysm of hell. If he mislike
My speech and what is done, tell him he has
Hipparchus, my enfranched bondman, whom
He may at pleasure whip, or hang, or torture,
As he shall like, to quit me: urge it thou:
Hence with thy stripes, begone! *Exit Thidias.*
Cleo. Have you done yet?
Ant. Alack, our terrene moon
Is now eclips'd; and it portends alone
The fall of Antony!
Cleo. I must stay his time.
Ant. To flatter Cæsar, would you mingle eyes
With one that ties his points?
Cleo. Not know me yet?
Ant. Cold-hearted toward me?

noble person. 71. **shrowd,** shelter, protection. 74. **Say . . . deputation.** Punctuation of the text follows Theobald in putting a larger stop after *this;* F has a comma at the end of the line, where we should put a colon, which gives a better sense. **deputation,** by deputy. 77. **all-obeying,** obeyed by all. 87. **fullest,** most complete in all respects. 89. **kite,** Cleopatra (?). 91. **muss,** scramble. 93. **Jack,** contemptuous epithet. 100. **cringe,** transitive use. 108. **abus'd,** betrayed. 109. **feeders,** servants. 110. **boggler,** waverer; often used of shying horses. 112. **seel,** blind; a term in falconry for closing the eyes of wild hawks by sewing their eyelids together. 120. **Luxuriously,** lustfully. 121. **temperance,** probably, chastity. 127. **hill of Basan,** allusion to Psalms 68:15, and 22:12; apparently to the Prayer Book version. Antony imagines himself as the greatest horned beast, i.e., cuckold, of that herd. 131. **yare,** ready, quick. 138. **fever,** put thee in a fever (imperative). 146. **orbs,** spheres. 149. **Hipparchus.** According to Plutarch the man was a deserter. **enfranched,** enfranchised. 151. **quit,** requite. 153. **terrene,** earthly, i.e., Cleopatra eclipsed like the moon. 157. **his,** Caesar's. **points,** laces by which articles of clothing were secured.

Cleo. Ah, dear, if I be so,
From my cold heart let heaven engender hail,
And poison it in the source; and the first stone
Drop in my neck: as it determines, so
Dissolve my life! The next Cæsarion smite!
Till by degrees the memory of my womb,
Together with my brave Egyptians all,
By the discandying of this pelleted storm,
Lie graveless, till the flies and gnats of Nile
Have buried them for prey!
Ant. I am satisfied.
Cæsar sits down in Alexandria; where
I will oppose his fate. Our force by land
Hath nobly held; our sever'd navy too
Have knit again, and fleet, threat'ning most sea-like.
Where hast thou been, my heart? Dost thou hear, lady?
If from the field I shall return once more
To kiss these lips, I will appear in blood;
I and my sword will earn our chronicle:
There 's hope in 't yet.
Cleo. That 's my brave lord!
Ant. I will be treble-sinew'd, hearted, breath'd,
And fight maliciously: for when mine hours
Were nice and lucky, men did ransom lives
Of me for jests; but now I'll set my teeth,
And send to darkness all that stop me. Come,
Let 's have one other gaudy night: call to me
All my sad captains; fill our bowls once more;
Let 's mock the midnight bell.
Cleo. It is my birth-day:
I had thought t' have held it poor; but, since my lord
Is Antony again, I will be Cleopatra.
Ant. We will yet do well.
Cleo. Call all his noble captains to my lord.
Ant. Do so, we'll speak to them; and to-night I'll force
The wine peep through their scars. Come on, my queen;
There 's sap in 't yet. The next time I do fight,
I'll make Death love me; for I will contend
Even with his pestilent scythe.
Exeunt [all but Enobarbus].
Eno. Now he'll outstare the lightning. To be furious,
Is to be frighted out of fear; and in that mood
The dove will peck the estridge; and I see still,
A diminution in our captain's brain
Restores his heart: when valour preys on reason,
It eats the sword it fights with. I will seek
Some way to leave him. *Exit.*

[ACT IV.

SCENE I. *Before Alexandria. Cæsar's camp.*]

Enter CÆSAR, AGRIPPA, *and* MECÆNAS, *with his army;* CÆSAR *reading a letter.*

Cæs. He calls me boy; and chides, as he had power
To beat me out of Egypt; my messenger
He hath whipp'd with rods; dares me to personal combat,
Cæsar to Antony: let the old ruffian know
I have many other ways to die; meantime
Laugh at his challenge.
Mec. Cæsar must think,
When one so great begins to rage, he 's hunted
Even to falling. Give him no breath, but now
Make boot of his distraction: never anger
Made good guard for itself.
Cæs. Let our best heads
Know, that to-morrow the last of many battles
We mean to fight: within our files there are,
Of those that serv'd Mark Antony but late,
Enough to fetch him in. See it done:
And feast the army; we have store to do 't,
And they have earn'd the waste. Poor Antony! *Exeunt.*

[SCENE II. *Alexandria. Cleopatra's palace.*]

Enter ANTONY, CLEOPATRA, ENOBARBUS, CHARMIAN, IRAS, ALEXAS, *with others.*

Ant. He will not fight with me, Domitius.
Eno. No.
Ant. Why should he not?
Eno. He thinks, being twenty times of better fortune,
He is twenty men to one.
Ant. To-morrow, soldier,
By sea and land I'll fight: or I will live,
Or bathe my dying honour in the blood
Shall make it live again. Woo 't thou fight well?
Eno. I'll strike, and cry 'Take all.'
Ant. Well said; come on.
Call forth my household servants: let 's to-night
Be bounteous at our meal.

Enter three or four Servitors.

Give me thy hand,
Thou hast been rightly honest;—so hast thou;—
Thou,—and thou,—and thou:—you have serv'd me well,
And kings have been your fellows.
Cleo. [*Aside to Eno.*] What means this?
Eno. [*Aside to Cleo.*] 'Tis one of those odd tricks which sorrow shoots
Out of the mind.
Ant. And thou art honest too.
I wish I could be made so many men,
And all of you clapp'd up together in
An Antony, that I might do you service
So good as you have done.
All. The gods forbid!
Ant. Well, my good fellows, wait on me to-night:
Scant not my cups; and make as much of me
As when mine empire was your fellow too,
And suffer'd my command.
Cleo. [*Aside to Eno.*] What does he mean?

161. **determines,** comes to an end, melts. 163. **memory of my womb,** offspring. 165. **discandying,** melting. **pelleted,** falling in pellets. 171. **fleet,** float. 175. **chronicle,** place in history. 183. **gaudy,** festive. 185. **birth-day.** Plutarch notes that Cleopatra, to clear herself of suspicion, made at this juncture more of Antony than she ever had, and that the celebration of her birthday was part of her program. 195-200. **Now . . . with.** Enobarbus is a choral spokesman; hence, this soliloquy is significant. Enobarbus analyzes for us Antony's psychological and ethical state and does so in Aristotelian terms. Note the two aphorisms, *To be furious*, etc., and *when valour preys*, etc. Antony's recoil to valor is factitious and lacks the balance or steadying power of reason.

ACT IV. SCENE I. 9. **boot,** advantage. 14. **fetch him in,** capture him. SCENE II. 7. **Woo 't,** wilt. 8. **'Take all,'** apparently a gaming phrase

Eno. [*Aside to Cleo.*] To make his followers weep.
Ant. Tend me to-night;
May be it is the period of your duty:
Haply you shall not see me more; or if,
A mangled shadow: perchance to-morrow
You'll serve another master. I look on you
As one that takes his leave. Mine honest friends,
I turn you not away; but, like a master
Married to your good service, stay till death:
Tend me to-night two hours, I ask no more,
And the gods yield you for 't!
Eno. What mean you, sir,
To give them this discomfort? Look, they weep;
And I, an ass, am onion-ey'd: for shame,
Transform us not to women.
Ant. Ho, ho, ho!
Now the witch take me, if I meant it thus!
Grace grow where those drops fall! My hearty friends,
You take me in too dolorous a sense;
For I spake to you for your comfort; did desire you
To burn this night with torches: know, my hearts,
I hope well of to-morrow; and will lead you
Where rather I'll expect victorious life
Than death and honour. Let 's to supper, come,
And drown consideration. *Exeunt.*

[SCENE III. *The same. Before the palace.*]

Enter a company of Soldiers.

First Sold. Brother, good night: to-morrow is the day.
Sec. Sold. It will determine one way: fare you well.
Heard you of nothing strange about the streets?
First Sold. Nothing. What news?
Sec. Sold. Belike 'tis but a rumour. Good night to you.
First Sold. Well, sir, good night.

They meet other Soldiers.

Sec. Sold. Soldiers, have careful watch.
Third Sold. And you. Good night, good night.
They place themselves in every corner of the stage.
Fourth Sold. Here we: and if to-morrow
Our navy thrive, I have an absolute hope
Our landmen will stand up.
Third Sold. 'Tis a brave army,
And full of purpose.
Music of the hautboys is under the stage.
Fourth Sold. Peace! what noise?
First Sold. List, list!
Sec. Sold. Hark!
First Sold. Music i' th' air.
Third Sold. Under the earth.
Fourth Sold. It signs well, does it not?
Third Sold. No.
First Sold. Peace, I say!
What should this mean?
Sec. Sold. 'Tis the god Hercules, whom Antony lov'd,
Now leaves him.
First Sold. Walk; let 's see if other watchmen
Do hear what we do. [*They advance to another post.*]
Sec. Sold. How now, masters.
All. (*Speak together*) How now!
How now! do you hear this?
First Sold. Ay; is 't not strange?
Third Sold. Do you hear, masters? do you hear?
First Sold. Follow the noise so far as we have quarter;
Let 's see how it will give off.
All. Content. 'Tis strange. *Exeunt.*

[SCENE IV. *The same. A room in the palace.*]

Enter ANTONY *and* CLEOPATRA, *with* [CHARMIAN *and*] *others* [*attending*].

Ant. Eros! mine armour, Eros!
Cleo. Sleep a little.
Ant. No, my chuck. Eros, come; mine armour, Eros!

Enter EROS [*with armour*].

Come, good fellow, put mine iron on:
If fortune be not ours to-day, it is
Because we brave her: come.
Cleo. Nay, I'll help too.
What 's this for?
Ant. Ah, let be, let be! thou art
The armourer of my heart: false, false; this, this.
Cleo. Sooth, la, I'll help: thus it must be.
Ant. Well, well;
We shall thrive now. Seest thou, my good fellow?
Go put on thy defences.
Eros. Briefly, sir.
Cleo. Is not this buckled well?
Ant. Rarely, rarely:
He that unbuckles this, till we do please
To daff 't for our repose, shall hear a storm.
Thou fumblest, Eros; and my queen 's a squire
More tight at this than thou: dispatch. O love,
That thou couldst see my wars to-day, and knew'st
The royal occupation! thou shouldst see
A workman in 't.

Enter an armed Soldier.

Good morrow to thee; welcome:
Thou look'st like him that knows a warlike charge:
To business that we love we rise betime,
And go to 't with delight.
Sold. A thousand, sir,
Early though 't be, have on their riveted trim,
And at the port expect you. *Shout. Trumpets flourish.*

Enter Captains *and* Soldiers.

Capt. The morn is fair. Good morrow, general.
All. Good morrow, general.
Ant. 'Tis well blown, lads:
This morning, like the spirit of a youth

meaning "If you beat me, you get everything." 25. **period,** end. 33. **yield,** reward.
SCENE III. 13. **Music . . . earth.** This strange bit is from Plutarch, who, however, makes the music the symbol of the departure of the god of Antony's "singular devotion," namely Bacchus. Shakespeare tells us that it is the god Hercules, whom Antony claimed as his ancestor and whom he imitated. 14. **signs well,** is a good sign. 23. **give off,** cease, end. **Content,** all right, agreed.
SCENE IV. 2. **chuck,** term of endearment. 7. **false,** wrong. 13. **daff 't,** doff it, take it off. 15. **tight,** deft, skillful. 20. **betime,** betimes, early. 22. **riveted trim,** armor. 25. **well blown,** probably refers to the flourish of trumpets above, but has been thought to refer to the blossoming or breaking forth of the morning.

That means to be of note, begins betimes.
So, so; come, give me that: this way; well said.
Fare thee well, dame, whate'er becomes of me:
This is a soldier's kiss: rebukeable [*Kisses her.*]
And worthy shameful check it were, to stand
On more mechanic compliment; I'll leave thee
Now, like a man of steel. You that will fight,
Follow me close; I'll bring you to 't. Adieu.
Exeunt [*Antony, Eros, Captains, and Soldiers*].
Char. Please you, retire to your chamber.
Cleo. Lead me.
He goes forth gallantly. That he and Cæsar might
Determine this great war in single fight!
Then, Antony,—but now—Well, on. *Exeunt.*

[SCENE V. *Alexandria. Antony's camp.*]

Trumpets sound. Enter ANTONY *and* EROS [; *a* Soldier *meeting them*].

Sold. The gods make this a happy day to Antony!
Ant. Would thou and those thy scars had once prevail'd
To make me fight at land!
Sold. Hadst thou done so,
The kings that have revolted, and the soldier
That has this morning left thee, would have still
Follow'd thy heels.
Ant. Who 's gone this morning?
Sold. Who!
One ever near thee: call for Enobarbus,
He shall not hear thee; or from Cæsar's camp
Say 'I am none of thine.'
Ant. What sayest thou?
Sold. Sir,
He is with Cæsar.
Eros. Sir, his chests and treasure
He has not with him.
Ant. Is he gone?
Sold. Most certain.
Ant. Go, Eros, send his treasure after; do it;
Detain no jot, I charge thee: write to him—
I will subscribe—gentle adieus and greetings;
Say that I wish he never find more cause
To change a master. O, my fortunes have
Corrupted honest men! Dispatch.—Enobarbus!
Exit [*with Eros and Soldier*].

[SCENE VI. *Alexandria. Cæsar's camp.*]

Flourish. Enter AGRIPPA, CÆSAR, *with* ENOBARBUS, *and* DOLABELLA.

Cæs. Go forth, Agrippa, and begin the fight:
Our will is Antony be took alive;
Make it so known.
Agr. Cæsar, I shall. [*Exit.*]
Cæs. The time of universal peace is near:
Prove this a prosp'rous day, the three-nook'd world
Shall bear the olive freely.

Enter a Messenger.

Mess. Antony
Is come into the field.
Cæs. Go charge Agrippa
Plant those that have revolted in the vant,
That Antony may seem to spend his fury
Upon himself. *Exeunt* [*all but Enobarbus*].
Eno. Alexas did revolt; and went to Jewry on
Affairs of Antony; there did dissuade
Great Herod to incline himself to Cæsar,
And leave his master Antony: for this pains
Cæsar hath hang'd him. Canidius and the rest
That fell away have entertainment, but
No honourable trust. I have done ill;
Of which I do accuse myself so sorely,
That I will joy no more.

Enter a Soldier *of* CÆSAR'S.

Sold. Enobarbus, Antony
Hath after thee sent all thy treasure, with
His bounty overplus: the messenger
Came on my guard; and at thy tent is now
Unloading of his mules.
Eno. I give it you.
Sold. Mock not, Enobarbus.
I tell you true: best you saf'd the bringer
Out of the host; I must attend mine office,
Or would have done 't myself. Your emperor
Continues still a Jove. *Exit.*
Eno. I am alone the villain of the earth,
And feel I am so most. O Antony,
Thou mine of bounty, how wouldst thou have paid
My better service, when my turpitude
Thou dost so crown with gold! This blows my heart:
If swift thought break it not, a swifter mean
Shall outstrike thought: but thought will do 't, I feel.
I fight against thee! No: I will go seek
Some ditch wherein to die; the foul'st best fits
My latter part of life. *Exit.*

[SCENE VII. *Field of battle between the camps.*]

Alarum. Drums and trumpets. Enter AGRIPPA [*and others*].

Agr. Retire, we have engag'd ourselves too far:
Cæsar himself has work, and our oppression
Exceeds what we expected. *Exit* [*with soldiers*].

Alarums. Enter ANTONY, *and* SCARUS *wounded.*

Scar. O my brave emperor, this is fought indeed!
Had we done so at first, we had droven them home
With clouts about their heads.
Ant. Thou bleed'st apace.
Scar. I had a wound here that was like a T,
But now 'tis made an H. [*Sound retreat*] *far off.*
Ant. They do retire.
Scar. We'll beat 'em into bench-holes: I have yet

31. **check,** reproof. 31-32. **stand On,** be particular about, insist on. 32. **mechanic,** vulgar.
SCENE V. 14. **subscribe,** sign.
SCENE VI. 5. **The . . . near.** This is Plutarch's theme and the justification of imperial Rome; it was handed down as a political and historical belief to the Renaissance. 6. **three-nook'd,** three-cornered; thought to refer to the division of power among the triumvirs, and also to the main regions of the Roman world, East, West, and Africa. 9. **vant,** van, front lines. 13. **dissuade,** i.e., from Antony. 17. **entertainment,** employment. 26. **best you saf'd,** it were best you safeguarded. 34. **blows,** causes his heart to swell with passions. 35. **mean,** i.e., he will stab himself. 36. **thought,** probably in the sense of sorrow. **do 't,** i.e., break his heart.
SCENE VII. 2. **oppression,** difficulty. 6. **clouts,** bandages, or blows and knocks. **apace,** fast. 8. **H,** i.e., the bottom of the *T* has been cut across; some see in this a pun on the pronunciation of *H* like modern

Room for six scotches more.

Enter EROS.

Eros. They are beaten, sir; and our advantage serves
For a fair victory.
Scar. Let us score their backs,
And snatch 'em up, as we take hares, behind!
'Tis sport to maul a runner.
Ant. I will reward thee
Once for thy spritely comfort, and ten-fold
For thy good valour. Come thee on.
Scar. I'll halt after. *Exeunt.*

[SCENE VIII. *Under the walls of Alexandria.*]

Alarum. Enter ANTONY *again in a march;* SCARUS, *with others.*

Ant. We have beat him to his camp: run one before,
And let the queen know of our gests. To-morrow,
Before the sun shall see 's, we'll spill the blood
That has to-day escap'd. I thank you all;
For doughty-handed are you, and have fought
Not as you serv'd the cause, but as 't had been
Each man 's like mine; you have shown all Hectors.
Enter the city, clip your wives, your friends,
Tell them your feats; whilst they with joyful tears
Wash the congealment from your wounds, and kiss
The honour'd gashes whole. [*To Scarus.*] Give me thy hand;

Enter CLEOPATRA [*attended*].

To this great fairy I'll commend thy acts,
Make her thanks bless thee. [*To Cleo.*] O thou day o' th' world,
Chain mine arm'd neck; leap thou, attire and all,
Through proof of harness to my heart, and there
Ride on the pants triumphing!
Cleo. Lord of lords!
O infinite virtue, com'st thou smiling from
The world's great snare uncaught?
Ant. My nightingale,
We have beat them to their beds. What, girl! though grey
Do something mingle with our younger brown, yet ha' we
A brain that nourishes our nerves, and can
Get goal for goal of youth. Behold this man;
Commend unto his lips thy favouring hand:
Kiss it, my warrior: he hath fought to-day
As if a god, in hate of mankind, had
Destroy'd in such a shape.
Cleo. I'll give thee, friend,
An armour all of gold; it was a king's.
Ant. He has deserv'd it, were it carbuncled
Like holy Phœbus' car. Give me thy hand:
Through Alexandria make a jolly march;
Bear our hack'd targets like the men that owe them:
Had our great palace the capacity
To camp this host, we all would sup together,
And drink carouses to the next day's fate,
Which promises royal peril. Trumpeters,
With brazen din blast you the city's ear;
Make mingle with our rattling tabourines;
That heaven and earth may strike their sounds together,
Applauding our approach. *Exeunt.*

[SCENE IX. *Cæsar's camp.*]

Enter a Sentry *and his company.* ENOBARBUS *follows.*

First Sold. If we be not reliev'd within this hour,
We must return to th' court of guard: the night
Is shiny; and they say we shall embattle
By th' second hour i' th' morn.
Sec. Sold. This last day was
A shrewd one to 's.
Eno. O, bear me witness, night,—
Third Sold. What man is this?
Sec. Sold. Stand close, and list him.
Eno. Be witness to me, O thou blessed moon,
When men revolted shall upon record
Bear hateful memory, poor Enobarbus did
Before thy face repent!
First Sold. Enobarbus!
Third Sold. Peace!
Hark further.
Eno. O sovereign mistress of true melancholy,
The poisonous damp of night disponge upon me,
That life, a very rebel to my will,
May hang no longer on me: throw my heart
Against the flint and hardness of my fault;
Which, being dried with grief, will break to powder,
And finish all foul thoughts. O Antony,
Nobler than my revolt is infamous,
Forgive me in thine own particular;
But let the world rank me in register
A master-leaver and a fugitive:
O Antony! O Antony! [*Dies*].
Sec. Sold. Let 's speak
To him.
First Sold. Let 's hear him, for the things he speaks
May concern Cæsar.
Third Sold. Let 's do so. But he sleeps.
First Sold. Swoons rather; for so bad a prayer as his
Was never yet for sleep.
Sec. Sold. Go we to him.
Third Sold. Awake, sir, awake; speak to us.
Sec. Sold. Hear you, sir?
First Sold. The hand of death hath raught him.
(*Drums afar off.*) Hark! the drums
Demurely wake the sleepers. Let us bear him
To th' court of guard; he is of note: our hour
Is fully out.
Third Sold. Come on, then;
He may recover yet. *Exeunt* [*with the body*].

---

ache. 10. **scotches,** cuts.

SCENE VIII. 2. **gests,** deeds. 7. **shown,** shown yourselves. 8. **clip,** embrace. 10. **congealment,** clotted blood. 12. **fairy,** enchantress. 15. **proof of harness,** proof-armor, tested armor. 16. **pants,** heartbeats. 21. **nerves,** sinews, tendons, i.e., parts of the body in which strength resides, the brain being the source of true courage. 22. **Get . . . of,** stay competitively equal with. 28. **carbuncled,** set with carbuncles; apparently a vague recollection of Ovid, *Metamorphoses*, ii, where the yoke of Phoebus' car is said to be set with chrysolites (Furness). 37. **mingle,** union, mingling. **tabourines,** drums.

SCENE IX. 2. **court of guard,** guardroom. 3. **embattle,** fall in for the combat. 12. **mistress . . . melancholy,** the moon, so addressed because of her influence in causing lunacy. 13. **disponge,** pour down. 17. **dried with grief.** Enobarbus has passed into the condition of despair, his spirits having descended into his bowels, leaving his heart dry. 30. **raught,** reached. 31. **Demurely,** with subdued sound (Onions).

[SCENE X. *Between the two camps.*]

Enter ANTONY *and* SCARUS, *with their Army.*

Ant. Their preparation is to-day by sea;
We please them not by land.
Scar. For both, my lord.
Ant. I would they 'ld fight i' th' fire or i' th' air;
We 'ld fight there too. But this it is; our foot
Upon the hills adjoining to the city
Shall stay with us: order for sea is given;
†They have put forth the haven . . .
Where their appointment we may best discover,
And look on their endeavour. *Exeunt.*

[SCENE XI. *Another part of the same.*]

Enter CÆSAR, *and his Army.*

Cæs. But being charg'd, we will be still by land,
Which, as I take 't, we shall; for his best force
Is forth to man his galleys. To the vales,
And hold our best advantage. *Exeunt.*

[SCENE XII. *Another part of the same.*]

Enter ANTONY *and* SCARUS.

Ant. Yet they are not join'd: where yond pine does stand,
I shall discover all: I'll bring thee word
Straight, how 'tis like to go. *Exit.*
Scar. Swallows have built
In Cleopatra's sails their nests: the augurers
Say they know not, they cannot tell; look grimly,
And dare not speak their knowledge. Antony
Is valiant, and dejected; and, by starts,
His fretted fortunes give him hope, and fear,
Of what he has, and has not.
Alarum afar off, as at a sea-fight.

Enter ANTONY.

Ant. All is lost;
This foul Egyptian hath betrayed me:
My fleet hath yielded to the foe; and yonder
They cast their caps up and carouse together
Like friends long lost. Triple-turn'd whore! 'tis thou
Hast sold me to this novice; and my heart
Makes only wars on thee. Bid them all fly;
For when I am reveng'd upon my charm,
I have done all. Bid them all fly; begone. [*Exit Scarus.*]
O sun, thy uprise shall I see no more:
Fortune and Antony part here; even here
Do we shake hands. All come to this? The hearts
That spaniel'd me at heels, to whom I gave
Their wishes, do discandy, melt their sweets
On blossoming Cæsar; and this pine is bark'd,
That overtopp'd them all. Betray'd I am:
O this false soul of Egypt! this grave charm,—
Whose eye beck'd forth my wars, and call'd them home;
Whose bosom was my crownet, my chief end,—
Like a right gipsy, hath, at fast and loose,
Beguil'd me to the very heart of loss.
What, Eros, Eros!

Enter CLEOPATRA.

Ah, thou spell! Avaunt!
Cleo. Why is my lord enrag'd against his love?
Ant. Vanish, or I shall give thee thy deserving,
And blemish Cæsar's triumph. Let him take thee,
And hoist thee up to the shouting plebeians:
Follow his chariot, like the greatest spot
Of all thy sex; most monster-like, be shown
For poor'st diminutives, for dolts; and let
Patient Octavia plough thy visage up
With her prepared nails. *Exit Cleopatra.*
'Tis well th' art gone,
If it be well to live: but better 'twere
Thou fell'st into my fury, for one death
Might have prevented many. Eros, ho!
The shirt of Nessus is upon me: teach me,
Alcides, thou mine ancestor, thy rage:
Let me lodge Lichas on the horns o' th' moon;
And with those hands, that grasp'd the heaviest club,
Subdue my worthiest self. The witch shall die:
To the young Roman boy she hath sold me, and I fall
Under this plot; she dies for 't. Eros, ho! *Exit.*

[SCENE XIII. *Alexandria. Cleopatra's palace.*]

Enter CLEOPATRA, CHARMIAN, IRAS, [*and*] MARDIAN.

Cleo. Help me, my women! O, he's more mad
Than Telamon for his shield; the boar of Thessaly
Was never so emboss'd.
Char. To th' monument!
There lock yourself, and send him word you are dead.
The soul and body rive not more in parting
Than greatness going off.
Cleo. To th' monument!
Mardian, go tell him I have slain myself;
Say, that the last I spoke was 'Antony,'
And word it, prithee, piteously: hence, Mardian,
And bring me how he takes my death. To th' monument! *Exeunt.*

[SCENE XIV. *The same. Another room.*]

Enter ANTONY *and* EROS.

Ant. Eros, thou yet behold'st me?
Eros. Ay, noble lord.
Ant. Sometime we see a cloud that 's dragonish;
A vapour sometime like a bear or lion,
A tower'd citadel, a pendent rock,

SCENE X. 6-8. **order . . . Where.** Line 7 is probably incomplete; but if *order . . . haven* is treated as parenthetical, *Where* (whither) may be taken to refer to *hills* (l. 5) and the passage construed. 7. **forth,** forth from.

SCENE XI. 1. **But being,** unless we are.

SCENE XII. 3-5. **Swallows . . . tell.** This gives a slight indication of how Shakespeare used his source. The swallows are mentioned in connection with Actium. Plutarch said that in that place swallows built under the poop of Cleopatra's galley and that others came and drove them away; it is interpreted as an evil omen. But this allusion Shakespeare took not from the text, but from the marginal note. The note says, "An ill signe, foreshewed by swallowes breding in Cleopatraes shippe." 13. **Triple-turn'd,** three times faithless (to Pompey, Julius Caesar, and now Antony). 16. **charm,** charmer. 22. **discandy,** melt. 23. **bark'd,** stripped. 25. **grave charm,** destructive witchcraft. 26. **beck'd,** beckoned. 27. **crownet,** coronet. 28. **right,** veritable. **gipsy,** double sense: Egyptian and gypsy (rogue). **fast and loose,** a cheating game the name of which is still proverbial. 35. **spot,** disgrace. 36. **shown,** exhibited. 37. **diminutives,** undersized creatures; i.e., the populace. 43. **Nessus.** When Hercules had fatally wounded the centaur Nessus for trying to rape Hercules' wife Deianira, Nessus vengefully gave his blood-soaked shirt to Deianira as a supposed

A forked mountain, or blue promontory
With trees upon 't, that nod unto the world,
And mock our eyes with air: thou hast seen these
signs;
They are black vesper's pageants.

Eros. Ay, my lord.

Ant. That which is now a horse, even with a
thought
The rack dislimns, and makes it indistinct,
As water is in water.

Eros. It does, my lord.

Ant. My good knave Eros, now thy captain is
Even such a body: here I am Antony;
Yet cannot hold this visible shape, my knave.
I made these wars for Egypt; and the queen,—
Whose heart I thought I had, for she had mine;
Which whilst it was mine had annex'd unto 't
A million moe, now lost,—she, Eros, has
Pack'd cards with Cæsar, and false-play'd my glory
Unto an enemy's triumph.
Nay, weep not, gentle Eros; there is left us
Ourselves to end ourselves.

Enter MARDIAN.

O, thy vile lady!
She has robb'd me of my sword.

Mar. No, Antony;
My mistress lov'd thee, and her fortunes mingled
With thine entirely.

Ant. Hence, saucy eunuch; peace!
She hath betray'd me and shall die the death.

Mar. Death of one person can be paid but once,
And that she has discharg'd: what thou wouldst do
Is done unto thy hand: the last she spake
Was 'Antony! most noble Antony!'
Then in the midst a tearing groan did break
The name of Antony; it was divided
Between her heart and lips: she rend'red life,
Thy name so buried in her.

Ant. Dead, then?

Mar. Dead.

Ant. Unarm, Eros; the long day's task is done,
And we must sleep. [*To Mar.*] That thou depart'st
hence safe,
Does pay thy labour richly; go. *Exit Mardian.*
Off, pluck off:
The seven-fold shield of Ajax cannot keep
The battery from my heart. O, cleave, my sides!
Heart, once be stronger than thy continent,
Crack thy frail case! Apace, Eros, apace.
No more a soldier: bruised pieces, go;
You have been nobly borne. From me awhile.
Exit Eros.
I will o'ertake thee, Cleopatra, and
Weep for my pardon. So it must be, for now
All length is torture: since the torch is out,
Lie down, and stray no farther: now all labour
Mars what it does; yea, very force entangles
Itself with strength: seal then, and all is done.
Eros!—I come, my queen:—Eros!—Stay for me:
Where souls do couch on flowers, we'll hand in hand,
And with our sprightly port make the ghosts gaze:
Dido and her Æneas shall want troops,
And all the haunt be ours. Come, Eros, Eros!

Enter EROS.

Eros. What would my lord?

Ant. Since Cleopatra died,
I have liv'd in such dishonour, that the gods
Detest my baseness. I, that with my sword
Quarter'd the world, and o'er green Neptune's back
With ships made cities, condemn myself to lack
The courage of a woman; less noble mind
Than she which by her death our Cæsar tells
'I am conqueror of myself.' Thou art sworn, Eros,
That, when the exigent should come, which now
Is come indeed, when I should see behind me
Th' inevitable prosecution of
Disgrace and horror, that, on my command,
Thou then wouldst kill me: do 't; the time is come:
Thou strik'st not me, 'tis Cæsar thou defeat'st.
Put colour in thy cheek.

Eros. The gods withhold me!
Shall I do that which all the Parthian darts,
Though enemy, lost aim, and could not?

Ant. Eros,
Wouldst thou be window'd in great Rome and see
Thy master thus with pleach'd arms, bending down
His corrigible neck, his face subdu'd
To penetrative shame, whilst the wheel'd seat
Of fortunate Cæsar, drawn before him, branded
His baseness that ensu'd?

Eros. I would not see 't.

Ant. Come, then; for with a wound I must be cur'd.
Draw that thy honest sword, which thou hast worn
Most useful for thy country.

Eros. O, sir, pardon me!

Ant. When I did make thee free, swor'st thou not
then
To do this when I bade thee? Do it at once;
Or thy precedent services are all
But accidents unpurpos'd. Draw, and come.

Eros. Turn from me, then, that noble countenance,
Wherein the worship of the whole world lies.

Ant. Lo thee! [*Turning from him.*]

Eros. My sword is drawn.

Ant. Then let it do at once
The thing why thou hast drawn it.

Eros. My dear master,
My captain, and my emperor, let me say,
Before I strike this bloody stroke, farewell.

Ant. 'Tis said, man; and farewell.

Eros. Farewell, great chief. Shall I strike now?

Ant. Now, Eros.

Eros. Why, there then: thus I do escape the sorrow
Of Antony's death. *Kills himself.*

love-charm for her husband. The poison gave Hercules (or Alcides) such agony that he cast his page Lichas high into the air.

SCENE XIII. 2. **Telamon,** Ajax Telamon, who after the capture of Troy went mad and slew himself when he was not awarded the shield and armor of Achilles. **boar of Thessaly,** the boar sent by Diana to ravage the fields of Calydon, and slain by Meleager. 3. **emboss'd,** foaming at the mouth, or driven to extremity. 5. **rive,** split, sever. 10. **bring me,** i.e., word.

SCENE XIV. 10. **rack,** floating vapor or cloud. **dislimns,** effaces. 12. **knave,** boy. 33. **rend'red,** gave up. 38. **seven-fold shield.** The shield of Ajax was made of brass and was reinforced with seven thicknesses of ox hide. 39. **battery from my heart,** ordinarily taken to mean the swelling of his heart denoted in its beating. Cuningham thinks it means the battery of calamity from outside. 46. **length,** length of life. 51. **couch,** lie. 53. **Dido . . . troops,** i.e., Antony and Cleopatra will be the most distinguished lovers there; they will outshine even Dido and Aeneas. 60. **less noble mind,** being a less noble-minded person. 63. **exigent,** exigency, decisive moment. 65. **prosecution,** pursuit. 72. **window'd,** placed in a window to look on. 73. **pleach'd,** folded. 74. **corrigible,** submissive to correction. 76. **branded,** rendered conspicuous as by a brand. 77. **ensu'd,** followed. 83. **precedent,** former.

Ant. Thrice-nobler than myself!
Thou teachest me, O valiant Eros, what
I should, and thou couldst not. My queen and Eros
Have by their brave instruction got upon me
A nobleness in record: but I will be
A bridegroom in my death, and run into 't
As to a lover's bed. Come, then; and, Eros,
Thy master dies thy scholar: to do thus
[*Falling on his sword.*]
I learn'd of thee. How! not dead? not dead?
The guard, ho! O, dispatch me!

Enter [DECRETAS *and*] *a* [*Company of the*] Guard.

First Guard. What 's the noise?
Ant. I have done my work ill, friends: O, make an end
Of what I have begun.
Sec. Guard. The star is fall'n.
First Guard. And time is at his period.
All. Alas, and woe!
Ant. Let him that loves me strike me dead.
First Guard. Not I.
Sec. Guard. Nor I.
Third Guard. Nor any one. *Exeunt* [*Guard*].
Decr. Thy death and fortunes bid thy followers fly.
This sword but shown to Cæsar, with this tidings,
Shall enter me with him.

Enter DIOMEDES.

Dio. Where 's Antony?
Decr. There, Diomed, there.
Dio. Lives he?
Wilt thou not answer, man? [*Exit Decretas.*]
Ant. Art thou there, Diomed? Draw thy sword, and give me
Sufficing strokes for death.
Dio. Most absolute lord,
My mistress Cleopatra sent me to thee.
Ant. When did she send thee?
Dio. Now, my lord.
Ant. Where is she?
Dio. Lock'd in her monument. She had a prophesying fear
Of what hath come to pass: for when she saw—
Which never shall be found—you did suspect
She had dispos'd with Cæsar, and that your rage
Would not be purg'd, she sent you word she was dead;
But, fearing since how it might work, hath sent
Me to proclaim the truth; and I am come,
I dread, too late.
Ant. Too late, good Diomed: call my guard, I prithee.
Dio. What, ho, the emperor's guard! The guard, what, ho!
Come, your lord calls!

Enter four or five of the Guard *of* ANTONY.

Ant. Bear me, good friends, where Cleopatra bides;
'Tis the last service that I shall command you.
First Guard. Woe, woe are we, sir, you may not live to wear
All your true followers out.
All. Most heavy day!
Ant. Nay, good my fellows, do not please sharp fate
To grace it with your sorrows: bid that welcome
Which comes to punish us, and we punish it
Seeming to bear it lightly. Take me up:
I have led you oft: carry me now, good friends,
And have my thanks for all. *Exeunt, bearing Antony.*

[SCENE XV. *The same. A monument.*]

Enter CLEOPATRA, *and her maids aloft, with* CHARMIAN *and* IRAS.

Cleo. O Charmian, I will never go from hence.
Char. Be comforted, dear madam.
Cleo. No, I will not:
All strange and terrible events are welcome,
But comforts we despise; our size of sorrow,
Proportion'd to our cause, must be as great
As that which makes it.

Enter [*below*] DIOMEDES.

How now! is he dead?
Dio. His death 's upon him, but not dead.
Look out o' th' other side your monument;
His guard have brought him thither.

Enter [*below*] ANTONY, *and the* Guard [*bearing him*].

Cleo. O sun,
Burn the great sphere thou mov'st in! darkling stand
The varying shore o' th' world. O Antony,
Antony, Antony! Help, Charmian, help, Iras, help;
Help, friends below; let 's draw him hither.
Ant. Peace!
Not Cæsar's valour hath o'erthrown Antony,
But Antony's hath triumph'd on itself.
Cleo. So it should be, that none but Antony
Should conquer Antony; but woe 'tis so!
Ant. I am dying, Egypt, dying; only
I here importune death awhile, until
Of many thousand kisses the poor last
I lay upon thy lips.
Cleo. I dare not, dear,—
Dear my lord, pardon,—I dare not,
Lest I be taken: not th' imperious show
Of the full-fortun'd Cæsar ever shall
Be brooch'd with me; if knife, drugs, serpents, have
Edge, sting, or operation, I am safe:
Your wife Octavia, with her modest eyes
And still conclusion, shall acquire no honour
Demuring upon me. But come, come, Antony,—
Help me, my women,—we must draw thee up:
Assist, good friends.
Ant. O, quick, or I am gone.
Cleo. Here 's sport indeed! How heavy weighs my lord!
Our strength is all gone into heaviness,

98-99. **got . . . record,** won for themselves (upon me) a noble place in the story (Cuningham). 104. *Stage Direction:* **Decretas,** so spelled usually in F. Often emended to *Dercetas,* as in Globe. 113. **enter me with,** recommend me to. 123. **dispos'd with,** come to terms with. 136. **To grace,** by gracing or honoring.

SCENE XV. 4. **our size of sorrow,** i.e., the size of our sorrow. 10. **sphere.** The sun is here thought of as fixed in a great sphere with which it revolved around the earth. **darkling,** in darkness. 11. **varying shore,** varying between night and day. Presumably if the sun had burned its sphere, earth's shore would no longer vary between light and darkness. 23. **imperious,** imperial. 25. **brooch'd,** adorned (as with a brooch). 28. **still conclusion,** composed and quiet judgment. 29. **Demuring,** looking demurely, i.e., with affected modesty. 33. **heaviness,** sadness, with play on *weight.* 39. **Quicken,** come back to life.

That makes the weight: had I great Juno's power,
The strong-wing'd Mercury should fetch thee up,
And set thee by Jove's side. Yet come a little,—
Wishers were ever fools,—O, come, come, come;
They heave Antony aloft to Cleopatra.
And welcome, welcome! die when thou hast liv'd:
Quicken with kissing: had my lips that power,
Thus would I wear them out.

All. A heavy sight!

Ant. I am dying, Egypt, dying:
Give me some wine, and let me speak a little.

Cleo. No, let me speak; and let me rail so high,
That the false huswife Fortune break her wheel,
Provok'd by my offence.

Ant. One word, sweet queen:
Of Cæsar seek your honour, with your safety. O!

Cleo. They do not go together.

Ant. Gentle, hear me:
None about Cæsar trust but Proculeius.

Cleo. My resolution and my hands I'll trust;
None about Cæsar.

Ant. The miserable change now at my end
Lament nor sorrow at; but please your thoughts
In feeding them with those my former fortunes
Wherein I liv'd, the greatest prince o' th' world,
The noblest; and do now not basely die,
Not cowardly put off my helmet to
My countryman,—a Roman by a Roman
Valiantly vanquish'd. Now my spirit is going;
I can no more.

Cleo. Noblest of men, woo 't die?
Hast thou no care of me? shall I abide
In this dull world, which in thy absence is
No better than a sty? O, see, my women, [*Antony dies.*]
The crown o' th' earth doth melt. My lord!
O, wither'd is the garland of the war,
The soldier's pole is fall'n: young boys and girls
Are level now with men; the odds is gone,
And there is nothing left remarkable
Beneath the visiting moon. [*Faints.*]

Char. O, quietness, lady!

Iras. She's dead too, our sovereign.

Char. Lady!

Iras. Madam!

Char. O madam, madam, madam!

Iras. Royal Egypt,
Empress!

Char. Peace, peace, Iras!

Cleo. No more, but e'en a woman, and commanded
By such poor passion as the maid that milks
And does the meanest chares. It were for me
To throw my sceptre at the injurious gods;
To tell them that this world did equal theirs
Till they had stol'n our jewel. All 's but naught;
Patience is sottish, and impatience does
Become a dog that 's mad: then is it sin
To rush into the secret house of death,
Ere death dare come to us? How do you, women?
What, what! good cheer! Why, how now, Charmian!
My noble girls! Ah, women, women, look,
Our lamp is spent, it 's out! Good sirs, take heart:
We'll bury him; and then, what 's brave, what 's noble,
Let 's do 't after the high Roman fashion,
And make death proud to take us. Come, away:
This case of that huge spirit now is cold:
Ah, women, women! come; we have no friend
But resolution, and the briefest end.
Exeunt, [*those above*] *bearing off Antony's body.*

[ACT V.

SCENE I. *Alexandria. Cæsar's camp.*]

Enter CÆSAR, AGRIPPA, DOLABELLA, MECÆNAS, [GALLUS, PROCULEIUS,] *with his council of war.*

Cæs. Go to him, Dolabella, bid him yield;
Being so frustrate, tell him he mocks
The pauses that he makes.

Dol. Cæsar, I shall. [*Exit.*]

Enter DECRETAS, *with the sword of* ANTONY.

Cæ. Wherefore is that? and what art thou that dar'st
Appear thus to us?

Decr. I am call'd Decretas;
Mark Antony I serv'd, who best was worthy
Best to be serv'd: whilst he stood up and spoke,
He was my master; and I wore my life
To spend upon his haters. If thou please
To take me to thee, as I was to him
I'll be to Cæsar; if thou pleasest not,
I yield thee up my life.

Cæs. What is 't thou say'st?

Decr. I say, O Cæsar, Antony is dead.

Cæs. The breaking of so great a thing should make
A greater crack: †the round world
Should have shook lions into civil streets,
And citizens to their dens: the death of Antony
Is not a single doom; in the name lay
A moiety of the world.

Decr. He is dead, Cæsar;
Not by a public minister of justice,
Nor by a hired knife; but that self hand,
Which writ his honour in the acts it did,
Hath, with the courage which the heart did lend it,
Splitted the heart. This is his sword;
I robb'd his wound of it; behold it stain'd
With his most noble blood.

Cæs. Look you sad, friends?
The gods rebuke me, but it is tidings
To wash the eyes of kings.

Agr. And strange it is,
That nature must compel us to lament
Our most persisted deeds.

Mer. His taints and honours
Wag'd equal with him.

Agr. A rarer spirit never
Did steer humanity: but you, gods, will give us

44. **huswife,** used in a bad sense meaning "hussy," "wanton." 57. **a Roman by a Roman.** Shakespeare follows Plutarch very closely in his account of Antony's death, and repeats simply and admiringly the rhetoric of his source. 65. **pole,** lodestar; also explained as "banner or standard." 66. **odds,** distinctive quality or measure. 67. **remarkable,** distinguished, noteworthy. 75. **chares,** chores, drudgery. 79. **sottish,** merely stupid. 85. **Good sirs,** addressed to the women.

ACT V. SCENE I. 2. **frustrate,** helpless, baffled. 2-3. **mocks . . . makes,** makes himself ridiculous by his delays. 15-17. **the round . . . dens,** that is, Antony's death ought to have produced more striking inversions. 16. **civil,** city. 21. **self,** same. 27. **but it is,** if it be not. 30. **persisted,** persistently desired or pursued. 31. **Wag'd equal,** were equal (with him), contended equally. 32. **humanity,** human nature.

Some faults to make us men. Cæsar is touch'd.
Mec. When such a spacious mirror 's set before him,
He needs must see himself.
Cæs. O Antony!
I have followed thee to this; but we do launch
Diseases in our bodies: I must perforce
Have shown to thee such a declining day,
Or look on thine; we could not stall together
In the whole world: but yet let me lament,
With tears as sovereign as the blood of hearts,
That thou, my brother, my competitor
In top of all design, my mate in empire,
Friend and companion in the front of war,
The arm of mine own body, and the heart
Where mine his thoughts did kindle,—that our stars,
Unreconcilable, should divide
Our equalness to this. Hear me, good friends,—
But I will tell you at some meeter season:

Enter an Egyptian.

The business of this man looks out of him;
We'll hear him what he says. Whence are you?
Egyp. A poor Egyptian yet. The queen my mistress,
Confin'd in all she has, her monument,
Of thy intents desires instruction,
That she preparedly may frame herself
To th' way she 's forc'd to.
Cæs. Bid her have good heart:
She soon shall know of us, by some of ours,
How honourable and how kindly we
Determine for her; for Cæsar cannot live
To be ungentle.
Egyp. So the gods preserve thee! *Exit.*
Cæs. Come hither, Proculeius. Go and say,
We purpose her no shame: give her what comforts
The quality of her passion shall require,
Lest, in her greatness, by some mortal stroke
She do defeat us; for her life in Rome
Would be eternal in our triumph: go,
And with your speediest bring us what she says,
And how you find of her.
Pro. Cæsar, I shall. *Exit Pro.*
Cæs. Gallus, go you along. [*Exit Gallus.*] Where 's Dolabella,
To second Proculeius?
All. Dolabella!
Cæs. Let him alone, for I remember now
How he 's employ'd: he shall in time be ready.
Go with me to my tent; where you shall see
How hardly I was drawn into this war;
How calm and gentie I proceeded still
In all my writings: go with me, and see
What I can show in this. *Exeunt.*

[SCENE II. *Alexandria. A room in the monument.*]

Enter CLEOPATRA, CHARMIAN, IRAS, *and* MARDIAN.

Cleo. My desolation does begin to make
A better life. 'Tis paltry to be Cæsar;
Not being Fortune, he 's but Fortune's knave,
A minister of her will: and it is great
To do that thing that ends all other deeds;
Which shackles accidents and bolts up change;
Which sleeps, and never palates more the dung,
The beggar's nurse and Cæsar's.

Enter [to the gates of the monument] PROCULEIUS [, GALLUS, *and* Soldiers].

Pro. Cæsar sends greeting to the Queen of Egypt;
And bids thee study on what fair demands
Thou mean'st to have him grant thee.
Cleo. What 's thy name?
Pro. My name is Proculeius.
Cleo. Antony
Did tell me of you, bade me trust you; but
I do not greatly care to be deceiv'd,
That have no use for trusting. If your master
Would have a queen his beggar, you must tell him,
That majesty, to keep decorum, must
No less beg than a kingdom: if he please
To give me conquer'd Egypt for my son,
He gives me so much of mine own, as I
Will kneel to him with thanks.
Pro. Be of good cheer;
Y' are fall'n into a princely hand, fear nothing:
Make your full reference freely to my lord,
Who is so full of grace, that it flows over
On all that need: let me report to him
Your sweet dependency; and you shall find
A conqueror that will pray in aid for kindness,
Where he for grace is kneel'd to.
Cleo. Pray you, tell him
I am his fortune's vassal, and I send him
The greatness he has got. I hourly learn
A doctrine of obedience; and would gladly
Look him i' th' face.
Pro. This I'll report, dear lady.
Have comfort, for I know your plight is pitied
Of him that caus'd it.
[*Here some of the Guard ascend the monument by a ladder placed against it, and, having descended, come behind Cleopatra. Some of the Guard unbar and open the gates.*]
You see how easily she may be surpris'd:
[*To the Guard*] Guard her till Cæsar come.
Iras. Royal queen!
Char. O Cleopatra! thou art taken, queen.
Cleo. Quick, quick, good hands. [*Drawing a dagger.*]
Pro. Hold, worthy lady, hold:
[*Seizes and disarms her.*]
Do not yourself such wrong, who are in this
Reliev'd, but not betray'd.
Cleo. What, of death too,
That rids our dogs of languish?
Pro. Cleopatra,
Do not abuse my master's bounty by

36. **launch,** lance. 39. **stall,** dwell. 42. **competitor,** associate (probably with slight sense of rivalry). 43. **In . . . design,** in height of, i.e., in all-daring, enterprise. 49. **meeter,** more fitting. 55-56. **frame . . . to,** conform or mold to. 59. **Determine,** decide. 65. **life in Rome,** presence in Rome alive. 66. **eternal in our triumph,** would be eternally recorded in our triumph (Schmidt); may be merely intensive, i.e., would contribute in the highest degree to our triumph (Cuningham).
SCENE II. 1-2. **My . . . life.** Cleopatra tells what she means in the lines which follow; she contemplates a deed which will show her contempt of fortune. 3. **knave,** servant. 6. **bolts up,** fetters or locks up. 7-8. **Which . . . Cæsar's.** To commit suicide would be to render oneself independent of accident and change, i.e., to sleep and rely no more on the fruits of life (the dungy earth) which sustain both Caesar and the beggar. 14. **care . . . deceiv'd,** whether I am deceived or not. 27. **pray in aid,** beg assistance; a legal term meaning "to call in the assistance of an outside person." 29-30. **I send . . . got,** I own his superiority

Th' undoing of yourself: let the world see
His nobleness well acted, which your death
Will never let come forth.

Cleo. Where art thou, death?
Come hither, come! come, come, and take a queen
Worth many babes and beggars!

Pro. O, temperance, lady!

Cleo. Sir, I will eat no meat, I'll not drink, sir;
If idle talk will once be necessary,
I'll not sleep neither: this mortal house I'll ruin,
Do Cæsar what he can. Know, sir, that I
Will not wait pinion'd at your master's court;
Nor once be chastis'd with the sober eye
Of dull Octavia. Shall they hoist me up
And show me to the shouting varletry
Of censuring Rome? Rather a ditch in Egypt
Be gentle grave unto me! rather on Nilus' mud
Lay me stark naked, and let the water-flies
Blow me into abhorring! rather make
My country's high pyramides my gibbet,
And hang me up in chains!

Pro. You do extend
These thoughts of horror further than you shall
Find cause in Cæsar.

Enter DOLABELLA.

Dol. Proculeius,
What thou hast done thy master Cæsar knows,
And he hath sent for thee: for the queen,
I'll take her to my guard.

Pro. So, Dolabella,
It shall content me best: be gentle to her.
[*To Cleo.*] To Cæsar I will speak what you shall
please,
If you'll employ me to him.

Cleo. Say, I would die.

Exit Proculeius [*with Soldiers*].

Dol. Most noble empress, you have heard of me?

Cleo. I cannot tell.

Dol. Assuredly you know me.

Cleo. No matter, sir, what I have heard or known.
You laugh when boys or women tell their dreams;
Is 't not your trick?

Dol. I understand not, madam.

Cleo. I dream'd there was an Emperor Antony:
O, such another sleep, that I might see
But such another man!

Dol. If it might please ye,—

Cleo. His face was as the heav'ns; and therein stuck
A sun and moon, which kept their course, and lighted
The little O, the earth.

Dol. Most sovereign creature,—

Cleo. His legs bestrid the ocean: his rear'd arm
Crested the world: his voice was propertied
As all the tuned spheres, and that to friends;
But when he meant to quail and shake the orb,
He was as rattling thunder. For his bounty,
There was no winter in 't; an autumn 'twas
That grew the more by reaping: his delights
Were dolphin-like; they show'd his back above
The element they liv'd in: in his livery
Walk'd crowns and crownets; realms and islands
were
As plates dropp'd from his pocket.

Dol. Cleopatra!

Cleo. Think you there was, or might be, such a man
As this I dream'd of?

Dol. Gentle madam, no.

Cleo. You lie, up to the hearing of the gods.
But, if there be nor ever were one such,
It 's past the size of dreaming: nature wants stuff
To vie strange forms with fancy; yet, t' imagine
An Antony, were nature's piece 'gainst fancy,
Condemning shadows quite.

Dol. Hear me, good madam.
Your loss is as yourself, great; and you bear it
As answering to the weight: would I might never
O'ertake pursu'd success, but I do feel,
By the rebound of yours, a grief that smites
My very heart at root.

Cleo. I thank you, sir.
Know you what Cæsar means to do with me?

Dol. I am loath to tell you what I would you
knew.

Cleo. Nay, pray you, sir,—

Dol. Though he be honourable,—

Cleo. He'll lead me, then, in triumph?

Dol. Madam, he will; I know 't. *Flourish.*

Enter PROCULEIUS, CÆSAR, GALLUS, MECÆNAS,
[SELEUCUS,] *and others of his train.*

All. Make way there: Cæsar!

Cæs. Which is the Queen of Egypt?

Dol. It is the emperor, madam. *Cleopatra kneels.*

Cæs. Arise, you shall not kneel:
I pray you, rise; rise, Egypt.

Cleo. Sir, the gods
Will have it thus; my master and my lord
I must obey.

Cæs. Take to you no hard thoughts:
The record of what injuries you did us,
Though written in our flesh, we shall remember
As things but done by chance.

Cleo. Sole sir o' th' world,
I cannot project mine own cause so well
To make it clear; but do confess I have
Been laden with like frailties which before
Have often sham'd our sex.

Cæs. Cleopatra, know,
We will extenuate rather than enforce:
If you apply yourself to our intents,
Which towards you are most gentle, you shall find
A benefit in this change; but if you seek
To lay on me a cruelty, by taking
Antony's course, you shall bereave yourself
Of my good purposes, and put your children
To that destruction which I'll guard them from,
If thereon you rely. I'll take my leave.

Cleo. And may, through all the world: 'tis yours;
and we,

with complete submission (Johnson). 34. *Stage Direction:* the bracketed reconstruction of this sequence is conjectural. 42. **languish,** lingering disease. 48. **temperance,** moderation. 50. **If . . . necessary,** even if for this once I must resort to speech. 53. **pinion'd,** bound. 56. **varletry,** rabble. 60. **abhorring,** abhorrence, abomination. 61. **pyramides,** possibly obelisks. 83. **Crested,** formed a crest for. 83-84. **propertied . . . friends,** endowed with qualities which, when he spoke to friends, recalled the music of the spheres. 85. **quail,** make quail, overawe. **orb,** world. 92. **plates,** pieces of money. 97. **past . . . dreaming,** no dream can come up to it. 98. **To vie . . . fancy,** to equal the strange forms produced by fancy. 99. **piece,** masterpiece. 103. **but I do,** if I do not. 125. **enforce,** lay stress upon. 126. **If . . . intents,** if you fall in with my plans. 130. **bereave,** deprive. 134. **And may,** may take your leave throughout the world.

Your scutcheons and your signs of conquest, shall
Hang in what place you please. Here, my good lord.
Cæs. You shall advise me in all for Cleopatra.
Cleo. This is the brief of money, plate, and jewels,
I am possess'd of: 'tis exactly valued;
Not petty things admitted. Where 's Seleucus?
Sel. Here, madam.
Cleo. This is my treasurer: let him speak, my lord,
Upon his peril, that I have reserv'd
To myself nothing. Speak the truth, Seleucus.
Sel. Madam,
I had rather seal my lips, than, to my peril,
Speak that which is not.
Cleo. What have I kept back?
Sel. Enough to purchase what you have made known.
Cæs. Nay, blush not Cleopatra; I approve
Your wisdom in the deed.
Cleo. See, Cæsar! O, behold,
How pomp is followed! mine will now be yours;
And, should we shift estates, yours would be mine.
The ingratitude of this Seleucus does
Even make me wild: O slave, of no more trust
Than love that 's hir'd! What, goest thou back? thou shalt
Go back, I warrant thee; but I'll catch thine eyes,
Though they had wings: slave, soulless villain, dog!
O rarely base!
Cæs. Good queen, let us entreat you.
Cleo. O Cæsar, what a wounding shame is this,
That thou, vouchsafing here to visit me,
Doing the honour of thy lordliness
To one so meek, that mine own servant should
Parcel the sum of my disgraces by
Addition of his envy! Say, good Cæsar,
That I some lady trifles have reserv'd,
Immoment toys, things of such dignity
As we greet modern friends withal; and say,
Some nobler token I have kept apart
For Livia and Octavia, to induce
Their mediation; must I be unfolded
With one that I have bred? The gods! it smites me
Beneath the fall I have. [*To Seleucus*] Prithee, go hence;
Or I shall show the cinders of my spirits
Through th' ashes of my chance: wert thou a man,
Thou wouldst have mercy on me.
Cæs. Forbear, Seleucus. [*Exit Seleucus.*]
Cleo. Be it known, that we, the greatest, are misthought
For things that others do; and, when we fall,
We answer others' merits in our name,
Are therefore to be pitied.
Cæs. Cleopatra,
Not what you have reserv'd, nor what acknowledg'd,
Put we i' th' roll of conquest: still be 't yours,
Bestow it at your pleasure; and believe,
Cæsar 's no merchant, to make prize with you
Of things that merchants sold. Therefore be cheer'd;
Make not your thoughts your prisons: no, dear queen;
For we intend so to dispose you as
Yourself shall give us counsel. Feed, and sleep:
Our care and pity is so much upon you,
That we remain your friend; and so, adieu.
Cleo. My master, and my lord!
Cæs. Not so. Adieu.
Flourish. Exeunt Cæsar and his train.
Cleo. He words me, girls, he words me, that I should not
Be noble to myself: but, hark thee, Charmian.
[*Whispers Charmian.*]
Iras. Finish, good lady; the bright day is done,
And we are for the dark.
Cleo. Hie thee again:
I have spoke already, and it is provided;
Go put it to the haste.
Char. Madam, I will.

Enter DOLABELLA.

Dol. Where 's the queen?
Char. Behold, sir. [*Exit.*]
Cleo. Dolabella!
Dol. Madam, as thereto sworn by your command,
Which my love makes religion to obey,
I tell you this: Cæsar through Syria
Intends his journey; and within three days
You with your children will he send before:
Make your best use of this: I have perform'd
Your pleasure and my promise.
Cleo. Dolabella,
I shall remain your debtor.
Dol. I your servant.
Adieu, good queen; I must attend on Cæsar.
Cleo. Farewell, and thanks. *Exit* [*Dolabella*].
Now, Iras, what think'st thou?
Thou, an Egyptian puppet, shall be shown
In Rome, as well as I: mechanic slaves
With greasy aprons, rules, and hammers, shall
Uplift us to the view; in their thick breaths,
Rank of gross diet, shall we be enclouded,
And forc'd to drink their vapour.
Iras. The gods forbid!
Cleo. Nay, 'tis most certain, Iras: saucy lictors
Will catch at us, like strumpets; and scald rhymers
Ballad us out o' tune: the quick comedians,
Extemporally will stage us, and present
Our Alexandrian revels; Antony
Shall be brought drunken forth, and I shall see
Some squeaking Cleopatra boy my greatness
I' th' posture of a whore.
Iras. O the good gods!
Cleo. Nay, that 's certain.
Iras. I'll never see 't; for, I am sure, my nails
Are stronger than mine eyes.
Cleo. Why, that 's the way
To fool their preparation, and to conquer
Their most absurd intents.

Enter CHARMIAN.

Now, Charmian!
Show me, my women, like a queen: go fetch
My best attires: I am again for Cydnus,
To meet Mark Antony: sirrah Iras, go.

135. **scutcheons,** shields showing armorial bearings. 138. **brief,** list or schedule. 140. **Not petty things admitted,** petty things omitted. 151. **mine,** my followers. 163. **Parcel,** specify or particularize. 165. **lady,** ladylike, feminine. 166. **Immoment,** of no moment. 167. **modern,** common. 169. **Livia,** Caesar's wife. 170-171. **unfolded With,** exposed by. 174. **chance,** her misfortunes, through which her resentment will show like fire through ashes. 175. **Forbear,** withdraw. 176. **misthought,** misjudged. 178. **We . . . name,** we are accountable in our name for the deserts (misdeeds) of others. 191. **He words me.** Cleopatra sees through Caesar's treachery exactly as in the source, where, however, such subtlety is not meant to detract from Caesar's nobility. 193. **Finish,** end, die. 195. **it,** the asp. 199. **religion,** sacred duty. 208. **an Egyptian puppet,** thought to be an allusion to Elizabethan puppet shows, of which there were many. 214. **lictors,** minor officials in

Now, noble Charmian, we'll dispatch indeed;
And, when thou hast done this chare, I'll give thee leave
To play till doomsday. Bring our crown and all.
Wherefore 's this noise? [*Exit Iras.*] *A noise within.*

Enter a Guardsman.

Guard. Here is a rural fellow
That will not be denied your highness' presence:
He brings you figs.

Cleo. Let him come in. *Exit Guardsman.*
What poor an instrument
May do a noble deed! he brings me liberty.
My resolution 's plac'd, and I have nothing
Of woman in me: now from head to foot
I am marble-constant; now the fleeting moon
No planet is of mine.

Enter Guardsman, *and* Clown [*bringing in a basket*].

Guard. This is the man.

Cleo. Avoid, and leave him. *Exit Guardsman.*
Hast thou the pretty worm of Nilus there,
That kills and pains not?

Clown. Truly, I have him: but I would not be the party that should desire you to touch him, for his biting is immortal; those that do die of it do seldom or never recover.

Cleo. Rememberest thou any that have died on 't?

Clown. Very many, men and women too. I heard of one of them no longer than yesterday: a very honest woman, but something given to lie; as a woman should not do, but in the way of honesty: how she died of the biting of it, what pain she felt: truly, she makes a very good report o' the worm; but he that will believe all that they say, shall never be saved by half that they do: but this is most falliable, the worm 's an odd worm.

Cleo. Get thee hence; farewell.

Clown. I wish you all joy of the worm.
[*Setting down his basket.*]

Cleo. Farewell.

Clown. You must think this, look you, that the worm will do his kind.

Cleo. Ay, ay; farewell.

Clown. Look you, the worm is not to be trusted but in the keeping of wise people; for, indeed, there is no goodness in the worm.

Cleo. Take thou no care; it shall be heeded.

Clown. Very good. Give it nothing, I pray you, for it is not worth the feeding.

Cleo. Will it eat me?

Clown. You must not think I am so simple but I know the devil himself will not eat a woman: I know that a woman is a dish for the gods, if the devil dress her not. But, truly, these same whoreson devils do the gods great harm in their women; for in every ten that they make, the devils mar five.

Cleo. Well, get thee gone; farewell.

Clown. Yes, forsooth: I wish you joy o' the worm.
Exit.

[*Enter* Iras *with a robe, crown, &c.*]

Cleo. Give me my robe, put on my crown; I have
Immortal longings in me: now no more
The juice of Egypt's grape shall moist this lip:
Yare, yare, good Iras; quick. Methinks I hear
Antony call; I see him rouse himself
To praise my noble act; I hear him mock
The luck of Cæsar, which the gods give men
To excuse their after wrath: husband, I come:
Now to that name my courage prove my title!
I am fire and air; my other elements
I give to baser life. So; have you done?
Come then, and take the last warmth of my lips.
Farewell, kind Charmian; Iras, long farewell.
[*Kisses them. Iras falls and dies.*]
Have I the aspic in my lips? Dost fall?
If thou and nature can so gently part,
The stroke of death is as a lover's pinch,
Which hurts, and is desir'd. Dost thou lie still?
If thus thou vanishest, thou tell'st the world
It is not worth leave-taking.

Char. Dissolve, thick cloud, and rain; that I may say,
The gods themselves do weep!

Cleo. This proves me base:
If she first meet the curled Antony,
He'll make demand of her, and spend that kiss
Which is my heaven to have. Come, thou mortal wretch, [*To an asp, which she applies to her breast.*]
With thy sharp teeth this knot intrinsicate
Of life at once untie: poor venomous fool,
Be angry, and dispatch. O, couldst thou speak,
That I might hear thee call great Cæsar ass
Unpolicied!

Char. O eastern star!

Cleo. Peace, peace!
Dost thou not see my baby at my breast,
That sucks the nurse asleep?

Char. O, break! O, break!

Cleo. As sweet as balm, as soft as air, as gentle,—
O Antony!—Nay, I will take thee too:
[*Applying another asp to her arm.*]
What should I stay— *Dies.*

Char. In this wild world? So, fare thee well.
Now boast thee, death, in thy possession lies
A lass unparallel'd. Downy windows, close;
And golden Phœbus never be beheld
Of eyes again so royal! Your crown 's awry;
I'll mend it, and then play.

Enter the Guard, *rustling in.*

First Guard. Where is the queen?

Char. Speak softly, wake her not.

First Guard. Cæsar hath sent—

Char. Too slow a messenger.
[*Applies an asp.*]
O, come apace, dispatch! I partly feel thee.

First Guard. Approach, ho! All 's not well: Cæsar 's beguil'd.

attendance on Roman magistrates. 215. **scald,** scurvy, mean. 220. **boy,** allusion to the practice of having women's parts acted by boys on the Elizabethan stage. 231. **chare,** task. 238. **plac'd,** fixed. 240. **marble-constant,** firm as marble. 242. **Avoid,** withdraw. 243. **worm,** snake. 247. **immortal,** blunder for "mortal." 259. **falliable,** blunder for "infallible"; so F; Globe: *fallible.* 264. **his kind,** i.e., his natural function. 284. **Immortal longings,** longings for immortality. 286. **Yare,** quick. 290. **their after wrath,** i.e., the wrath of the gods visited on those who have been insolently proud of their good fortune. 296. **aspic,** asp, venomous serpent. 304. **curled,** freshly barbered. 305. **He'll . . . kiss,** he will inquire of her concerning me and kiss her for giving him intelligence (Johnson). 306. **wretch,** creature. 307. **intrinsicate,** intricate. 311. **Unpolicied,** outwitted. 316. **What,** why. 326. **beguil'd,** cheated.

Sec. Guard. There 's Dolabella sent from Cæsar; call him.
First Guard. What work is here! Charmian, is this well done?
Char. It is well done, and fitting for a princess
Descended of so many royal kings.
Ah, soldier! *Charmian dies.*

Enter DOLABELLA.

Dol. How goes it here?
Sec. Guard. All dead.
Dol. Cæsar, thy thoughts
Touch their effects in this: thyself art coming
To see perform'd the dreaded act which thou
So sought'st to hinder.

Enter CÆSAR *and all his train, marching.*

All. A way there, a way for Cæsar!
Dol. O sir, you are too sure an augurer;
That you did fear is done.
Cæs. Bravest at the last,
She levell'd at our purposes, and, being royal,
Took her own way. The manner of their deaths?
I do not see them bleed.
Dol. Who was last with them?
First Guard. A simple countryman, that brought her figs:
This was his basket.
Cæs. Poison'd, then.
First Guard. O Cæsar,
This Charmian liv'd but now; she stood and spake:
I found her trimming up the diadem
On her dead mistress; tremblingly she stood
And on the sudden dropp'd.
Cæs. O noble weakness!
If they had swallow'd poison, 'twould appear
By external swelling: but she looks like sleep,
As she would catch another Antony
In her strong toil of grace.
Dol. Here, on her breast,
There is a vent of blood and something blown:
The like is on her arm.
First Guard. This is an aspic's trail: and these fig-leaves
Have slime upon them, such as th' aspic leaves
Upon the caves of Nile.
Cæs. Most probable
That so she died; for her physician tells me
She hath pursu'd conclusions infinite
Of easy ways to die. Take up her bed;
And bear her women from the monument:
She shall be buried by her Antony:
No grave upon the earth shall clip in it
A pair so famous. High events as these
Strike those that make them: and their story is
No less in pity than his glory which
Brought them to be lamented. Our army shall
In solemn show attend this funeral;
And then to Rome. Come, Dolabella, see
High order in this great solemnity. *Exeunt omnes.*

333. **Touch their effects,** meet with realization. 337. **augurer,** foreteller of future events. 352. **something blown,** somewhat swollen. 358. **conclusions,** experiments. 363-366. **High . . . lamented,** the very causers of events, like the present, cannot help being touch'd by them: and the pitifulness of them will set them as high in fame as conquest will the person that wrought them (Steevens).

CORIOLANUS

Coriolanus may be Shakespeare's last tragedy. Even though external evidence is scarce as to its actual date, the style suggests a time around 1608. If so, Shakespeare's final statement on man's tragic destiny is disillusioned, wry, almost anticlimactic, in the vein of his Roman and classical tragedies rather than of his great tragedies of evil (*Hamlet*, *Othello*, *King Lear*, *Macbeth*). The play is based on Plutarch's *Lives of the Noble Grecians and Romans* as translated by Sir Thomas North, the source Shakespeare used so extensively during his tragic period. As in the presumably earlier Plutarchan plays, *Julius Caesar*, *Timon of Athens*, and *Antony and Cleopatra*, and in the non-Plutarchan *Titus Andronicus* and *Troilus and Cressida*, Shakespeare's ancient political world is one of constant upheaval. In the clash of ideologies, the plebeian mob turns giddily from one idol to the next, and strong men rise briefly only to be supplanted by a rival. The result of unceasing change is political stalemate. The great men of the ancient world seem fascinatingly alive to us, but they also seem blind to their own limitations, fatally proud, and hemmed in by circumstance. Their virtues and their defects are inseparable and indeed often identical, for private virtues serve these tragic heroes poorly in the amoral and pitiless arena of politics. Their human natures cannot easily be moved from a tragic predilection for catastrophe, and so their downfall proceeds inexorably from what Aristotle, writing of Greek tragedy, termed a flaw, or *hamartia*, in their characters. The ending is usually one of tragic waste, ironic rather than cathartic in its effect.

Coriolanus admirably captures this conflict dividing personal nobleness from political reality. The play returns to a basic political problem studied before in *Julius Caesar:* the rivalry in ancient Rome between republican and aristocratic rule. *Coriolanus*, although written later than *Julius Caesar*, analyzes an earlier period of Roman history, for the Junius Brutus who defends republicanism in this play is the famous ancestor of the Marcus Brutus who kills Julius Caesar. In *Coriolanus* we witness the birth of republicanism, in *Julius Caesar* its demise. Shakespeare views both events with ironic detachment.

Republicanism was potentially a matter of controversy on the Jacobean stage, insofar as spectators might draw analogies between it and parliamentary efforts to curb the power of the English throne. The differences are real, of course, especially in *Julius Caesar*, where Caesar's claim to absolute rule has no sanction of divine right and Brutus' republicanism is ineffably genteel rather than populist. *Coriolanus*, however, hits closer to home. Republicanism is identified as a peoples' movement. Popular unrest over famine and high prices leads to rioting and the expression of democratic sentiments such as were heard and feared by the authorities in England. Riots over scarcity of grain occurred in Northamptonshire, Warwickshire, and Leicestershire during the summer of 1607. King James I, who had come to the throne in 1603, took a dim view of Puritan efforts to democratize church government and of corresponding challenges in Parliament on behalf of the common law. From its perspective of ancient Rome, distant in time and place, *Coriolanus* appraises the conflict in terms that bear no precise relation to Jacobean England and yet have a timeless relevance. Without taking sides, the play dwells on the ambiguity of the struggle and on the indecisive, self-defeating results ironically achieved by both parties.

As in *Julius Caesar*, men of both sides are passionately sincere but driven to shortsighted extremism. The tribunes insist on behalf of the mob that the peoples' voice is to be the ultimate law of Rome. Coriolanus, in angry response, sees republicanism and its elected tribunes as the enemies of hierarchical prerogative, threatening the very existence of the state. Which view is correct? Is the peoples' voice a brave force of resistance against aristocratic hauteur and class privilege, as exemplified by Coriolanus, or is republicanism a grab for power by demagogues willing to risk anarchy and a weakening of national defense? Shakespeare seems to offer no unequivocal answer. Like Plutarch, he explores the weaknesses and strengths of both parties. He uses a dramatic structure, as in *Julius Caesar*, of sustained ambiguity. If any conclusion emerges, it is that violent political struggle leads only to an undoing of those civilized institutions which moderate men, caught in the middle, strive vainly to preserve.

The citizens play a dominant role in *Coriolanus*. The action begins, as in *Julius Caesar*, with a mob scene, setting a tone of ominous instability. The mob is too easily swayed. Lacking any consistent political philosophy of its own, it will follow whatever charismatic orator catches its fancy. It despises Coriolanus one moment and adulates him the next. Its own members agree that the mob is a "many-headed multitude," directionless, irresponsible. Other characters besides Coriolanus protest the offensive stench of the crowd, "stinking" breaths, "reechy" necks, "stinking greasy caps," and unclean teeth. The Roman citizens are a "herd," "apron-men," "garlic-eaters," curs, hares, foxes, geese, a "cockle of rebellion, insolence, sedition." This deliberately repulsive portraiture merely intensifies what is true also of the other Roman plays and the English history plays. Nowhere in Shakespeare does mob action lead to anything constructive or even politically acceptable. Nevertheless the mob in *Coriolanus*, as elsewhere in Shakespeare, does not bear chief responsibility for disaster. Individually its members are good-natured, slow to be aroused, quick to forget injury, too credulous indeed for their own good. They have to be prompted again and again by the tribunes to press forward with their resentment. Many citizens, left to themselves, are wise and patient. They are a neutral force, dangerous only when whipped up to collective frenzy by demagogic persuasion.

Much blame would seem to fall then on the tribunes, and indeed the play's moderating and choral spokesmen such as Menenius are deeply mistrustful of Junius Brutus and Sicinius Velutus. These tribunes are willing to risk the consequences of mob violence to achieve their ends, especially when they urge the "rabble of Plebeians" to "bustle about Coriolanus" (III,i). Ignoring Menenius' pleas that "This is the way to kindle, not to quench," and that "Confusion's near," the tribunes deliberately goad Coriolanus to anger. Their strategy is to foment clamor, and "with a din confus'd Enforce the present execution," shouting down reason with hysteria (III,iii). They carefully stage each confrontation with Coriolanus, rehearsing the citizens in what they are to do, cannily timing their provocations. They talk like conspirators. Shakespeare's audience, accustomed to governmental warnings against mob violence, would probably have understood the menace posed by the tribunes, and would have savored the irony that Rome is weakened rather than strengthened by their machinations.

Still, Shakespeare's portrayal of the tribunes is remarkably sympathetic. They honestly fear that Coriolanus seeks "one sole throne Without assistance" (IV,vi), and that as consul he will do everything in his ability to suppress the peoples' liberties. This is no idle fear; Coriolanus' own friends merely counsel him to attack the tribunes after he has achieved power, not before. Although the tribunes do arouse the people to actions they would not otherwise take, the tribunes believe they are doing so in the peoples' best interests, providing leadership for a constituency that has hitherto lacked a voice. They fervently believe in a government "by the consent of all" that can hold aristocratic insolence in check through the "lawful censure" of the commons. "What is the city but the people?" (III,i). Moreover, they are not revolutionaries by temperament and gladly abandon mob tactics once they have made their point. Their achievements mock them when Rome proves defenseless against the return of Coriolanus, but even here they can argue with some reason that Rome would have achieved peace had it not been for Coriolanus' lawless vengeance.

Perhaps then Coriolanus must bear the prime responsibility for provoking republican extremism through his contempt of the citizenry. From his first appearance, he antagonizes us as well as the populace with his curt, insulting manner. He addresses the people as "dissentious rogues" itching with scabby diseases, and dismisses them as "curs" who are "beneath abhorring." His hatred amounts to revulsion, and we fear he is all too ready to employ his sword on "thousands of these quarter'd slaves." When denied the consulship by the tribunes, in fact, he draws his sword in the marketplace, relishing the opportunity for a military solution. His tendency to forget names betrays a coldness. Although he professes not to speak merely in anger, he is too easily baited by the tribunes, too quick to speak his mind. Even those who admire his virtues concede that "to seem to affect the malice and displeasure of the people is as bad as that which he dislikes, to flatter them for their love" (II,ii). Coriolanus is glad to hear of the impending Volscian attack on Rome, for he prefers war to peace and sees conscription as a way of channeling revolutionary energies against an outward foe. He professes a love of his country, but because his attachment is to a dying patrician order he is ready to turn traitor against the new Rome he so abhors.

Nevertheless, the portrayal of Coriolanus, as of the tribunes, is delicately balanced. We admire Coriolanus' hatred of hypocrisy. He is scrupulously honest, refusing all spoils of war except those to which his fellow soldiers are entitled. Despite his pride in family and name, he genuinely dislikes to hear himself praised. Though he disdains to lead cowardly citizen-soldiers, and shines most in single deeds of valor rather than in generalship, he is charismatic and even popular among valiant soldiers like himself. He is generous in praising the achievements of his colleagues. Even in matters of statecraft he shows resoluteness and integrity. He has a consistent political philosophy, one bolstered by Menenius' comparison of the state to a body in which the members must harmoniously interact (I,i). Jacobean spectators would recognize in this analogy the orthodox appeal to order and degree they heard regularly from pulpit and throne. Coriolanus firmly believes that the ancient prerogatives of the aristocracy are Rome's only safe bulwark against chaos. By granting power to the tribunes, in his view, the senate has sealed its doom. He sees the people as their own worst enemies, insatiable and irrational in their demands, unable to comprehend the subtleties of managing a vast commonwealth, instinctively envious of their betters. Such base mortals require subjection to their masters, though they cannot be expected to realize this themselves. Coriolanus knows that such conservatism is out of fashion, and that the current trend is to appease popular demands with compromise, but he can see no end to the compromises that will be needed once the tribunes have established their prerogatives. He prefers a battle to the death, and welcomes the danger to himself. If his courage and consistency are "too absolute," if he is "too noble for the world," he would prefer to believe that the fault lies in that world rather than in him.

Between the extremes of republicanism and aristocratic rule, the middle position of compromise offers many attractions. Menenius sanely desires to see "On both sides more respect," and pleads with those who would be "truly your country's friend" to "temp'rately proceed to what you would Thus violently redress" (III,i). Although his sympathies are patrician, he acknowledges the tribunes' power as a political reality which must be dealt with. He finds fault with Coriolanus for not having "temporiz'd." Menenius is a bluff, honest fellow who chorically directs our sympathies, like the equally outspoken Enobarbus in *Antony and Cleopatra*. Yet compromise always has its ridiculous aspect. Menenius increasingly assumes the self-contradictory and sardonically amusing role of the appeaser, like the choric York of *Richard II*, urging actions that are repugnant to him personally. At the last, after having denounced the tribunes for betraying Rome, he must go as their ambassador to beg mercy of Coriolanus. When Aufidius' guardsmen scoff at him for having been turned away by Coriolanus, Menenius is beyond caring for their taunts. He does in fact hold to a consistent principle, the survival of his beloved city at whatever cost to his pride. He and Rome blunder pragmatically through, though not without loss of dignity.

Coriolanus' mother Volumnia is caught in an even more ironic dilemma. She of course shares her son's aristocratic pride, having taught him a code of death before dishonor. The emotional bond between mother and son is extraordinarily, even distressingly, close. She speaks of him metaphorically as her husband, and of his warlike prowess as a vicarious substitute for "the embracements of his bed" (I,iii). Throughout, Coriolanus' deeds of war are love-offerings to his mother. Every citizen of Rome knows that whatever Coriolanus has done for his country he also did "to please his mother" (I,i). The conflict arises from her desire to have him famous not only in war but in politics. Here she must, like Menenius, espouse the compromise and "policy" that they all hate. She and Menenius stage Coriolanus' public appearances with as much care as the tribunes rehearse their plebeians. They "prompt" Coriolanus to "perform a part" for which he has no aptitude (III,ii); as he later says, capitulating to his mother for the last time, "Like a dull actor now, I have forgot my part, and I am out" (V,iii). This integrity has its admirable side, but brings disaster to Volumnia's plans. She is defeated by the very pride she has engendered in him, and he is defeated by her overriding ambition for him. To win her praise he must put away his true disposition, becoming effeminate and emasculated like a "harlot" or "an eunuch." To satisfy her quest for fame he must give up his attack on Rome, perjure himself to Aufidius, and die a condemned traitor to the Volscian state. Volumnia's crushing love for her son proves ironically fatal to everything they have cherished.

Coriolanus' relationship to Aufidius is one of love as well as hate, and it too poses a fatal conflict. Despite their rivalry to the death, these two military heroes are singularly attracted to one another. Coriolanus confesses "I sin in envying his nobility," and considers Aufidius "a lion That I am proud to hunt" (I,i). Coriolanus' fate is to love his enemy and hate his birthplace. Aufidius, in turn, greets Coriolanus with more joy "Than when I first my wedded mistress saw Bestride my threshold" (IV,v). Yet Aufidius has always resented Coriolanus' superiority in battle, and has planned to overcome him by fair means or foul. In their brief military alliance, Coriolanus proves too attractive a rival, overshadowing the achievements of Aufidius. For these reasons Aufidius secretly exults in Coriolanus' fatal dilemma, since the Volscian general prefers vengeance to victory over Rome. In a final disillusioning scene he stages one more public outcry at Coriolanus, goading him into a proud rage, and then with his fellow conspirators ingloriously performs an execution "whereat valour will weep." Aufidius' virtues, like those of Coriolanus, have been betrayed by his worst instincts. Throughout, the Volscians have been cunning enemies, lying in wait for Rome to tear herself apart. The laws governing the relations between states are brutally competitive, characterized by the "slippery turns" of fortune that ironically bring together former enemies as allies and then turn them against one another. In this world of sudden reversals, Coriolanus' last act is something he could never have foreseen: saving the Roman state and its tribunes from a destruction he himself had wished on it. As Coriolanus wrily observes of his own destiny, "The gods look down, and this unnatural scene They laugh at."

CORIOLANUS

[*Dramatis Personae*

CAIUS MARCIUS, *afterwards* CAIUS MARCIUS CORIOLANUS.
TITUS LARTIUS, } *generals against the Volscians.*
COMINIUS, }
MENENIUS AGRIPPA, *friend to Coriolanus.*
SICINIUS VELUTUS, } *tribunes of the people.*
JUNIUS BRUTUS, }
Young MARCIUS, *son to Coriolanus.*
A Roman Herald.
TULLUS AUFIDIUS, *general of the Volscians.*
Lieutenant to Aufidius.
Conspirators with Aufidius.
A Citizen of Antium.
Two Volscian Guards.

VOLUMNIA, *mother to Coriolanus.*
VIRGILIA, *wife to Coriolanus.*
VALERIA, *friend to Virgilia.*
Gentlewoman, *attending on Virgilia.*

Roman *and* Volscian Senators, Patricians, Ædiles, Lictors, Soldiers, Citizens, Messengers, Servants to Aufidius, *and other* Attendants.

SCENE: *Rome and the neighbourhood; Corioli and the neighbourhood; Antium.*]

ACT I.

SCENE I. [*Rome. A street.*]

Enter a company of mutinous Citizens, *with staves, clubs, and other weapons.*

First Cit. Before we proceed any further, hear me speak.

All. Speak, speak.

First Cit. You are all resolved rather to die than to famish?

All. Resolved, resolved.

First Cit. First, you know Caius Marcius is chief enemy to the people.

All. We know 't, we know 't.

First Cit. Let us kill him, and we'll have corn at our own price. Is 't a verdict?

All. No more talking on 't; let it be done: away, away!

Sec. Cit. One word, good citizens.

First Cit. We are accounted poor citizens, the patricians good. What authority surfeits on would relieve us: if they would yield us but the superfluity, while it were wholesome, we might guess they relieved us humanely; but they think we are too dear: the leanness that afflicts us, the object of our misery, is as an inventory to particularize their abundance; our sufferance is a gain to them. Let us revenge this with our pikes, ere we become rakes: for the gods know I speak this in hunger for bread, not in thirst for revenge.

Sec. Cit. Would you proceed especially against Caius Marcius?

All. Against him first: he 's a very dog to the commonalty.

Sec. Cit. Consider you what services he has done for his country?

First Cit. Very well; and could be content to give him good report for 't, but that he pays himself with being proud.

Sec. Cit. Nay, but speak not maliciously.

First Cit. I say unto you, what he hath done famously, he did it to that end: though soft-conscienced men can be content to say it was for his country, he did it to please his mother, and to be partly proud; which he is, even to the altitude of his virtue.

Sec. Cit. What he cannot help in his nature, you account a vice in him. You must in no way say he is covetous.

First Cit. If I must not, I need not be barren of accusations; he hath faults, with surplus, to tire in repetition. (*Shouts within.*) What shouts are these? The other side o' the city is risen: why stay we prating here? to the Capitol!

All. Come, come.

First Cit. Soft! who comes here?

Enter MENENIUS AGRIPPA.

Sec. Cit. Worthy Menenius Agrippa; one that hath always loved the people.

First Cit. He 's one honest enough: would all the rest were so!

Men. What work 's, my countrymen, in hand? where go you
With bats and clubs? The matter? speak, I pray you.

First Cit. Our business is not unknown to the senate; they have had inkling this fortnight what we intend to do, which now we'll show 'em in deeds. They say poor suitors have strong breaths: they shall know we have strong arms too.

Men. Why, masters, my good friends, mine honest neighbours,
Will you undo yourselves?

First Cit. We cannot, sir, we are undone already.

Men. I tell you, friends, most charitable care
Have the patricians of you. For your wants,
Your suffering in this dearth, you may as well
Strike at the heaven with your staves as lift them
Against the Roman state, whose course will on
The way it takes, cracking ten thousand curbs
Of more strong link asunder than can ever
Appear in your impediment. For the dearth,
The gods, not the patricians, make it, and
Your knees to them, not arms, must help. Alack,
You are transported by calamity
Thither where more attends you, and you slander
The helms o' th' state, who care for you like fathers,
When you curse them as enemies.

First Cit. Care for us! True, indeed! They ne'er cared for us yet: suffer us to famish, and their storehouses crammed with grain; make edicts for usury, to support usurers; repeal daily any wholesome act established against the rich, and provide more piercing statutes daily, to chain up and restrain the poor. If the wars eat us not up, they will; and there 's all the love they bear us.

Men. Either you must
Confess yourselves wondrous malicious,
Or be accus'd of folly. I shall tell you
A pretty tale: it may be you have heard it;
But, since it serves my purpose, I will venture
To stale 't a little more.

First Cit. Well, I'll hear it, sir: yet you must not think to fob off our disgrace with a tale: but, an 't please you, deliver.

Men. There was a time when all the body's members
Rebell'd against the belly, thus accus'd it:
That only like a gulf it did remain
I' th' midst o' th' body, idle and unactive,
Still cupboarding the viand, never bearing
Like labour with the rest, where th' other instruments
Did see and hear, devise, instruct, walk, feel,
And, mutually participate, did minister
Unto the appetite and affection common
Of the whole body. The belly answer'd—

First Cit. Well, sir, what answer made the belly?

Men. Sir, I shall tell you. With a kind of smile,
Which ne'er came from the lungs, but even thus—
For, look you, I may make the belly smile
As well as speak—it tauntingly replied
To th' discontented members, the mutinous parts
That envied his receipt; even so most fitly
As you malign our senators for that
They are not such as you.

First Cit. Your belly's answer? What!
The kingly-crowned head, the vigilant eye,
The counsellor heart, the arm our soldier,
Our steed the leg, the tongue our trumpeter,
With other muniments and petty helps
In this our fabric, if that they—

Men. What then?
'Fore me, this fellow speaks! What then? what then?

First Cit. Should by the cormorant belly be restrain'd,
Who is the sink o' th' body,—

Men. Well, what then?

First Cit. The former agents, if they did complain,
What could the belly answer?

Men. I will tell you;
If you'll bestow a small—of what you have little—
Patience awhile, you'll hear the belly's answer.

First Cit. Y' are long about it.

Men. Note me this, good friend;

ACT I. SCENE I. 10. **corn,** grain, such as wheat or barley. 11. **Is 't a verdict?** Are we agreed? 12. **on 't,** of it, about it. 16. **good,** rich. 19. **we are too dear,** cost more than we are worth; explained also as too precious. 20. **object,** sight. 21-22. **is as . . . abundance,** serves as a catalog to point out in detail how rich they are. 22. **sufferance,** suffering. 23. **pikes,** spears, lances; pitchforks. 24. **rakes,** i.e., as lean as rakes. 33. **good report,** credit. 40. **partly proud,** partly out of pride. 40-41. **even . . . to virtue,** i.e., he is as proud as he is brave. 49. **Capitol,** the Temple of Jupiter on Capitoline Hill; used here to stand for the Senate building. 51. **Soft,** stay, stop (an interjection). 57. **bats,** stout staves. 61. **suitors,** petitioners. 69. **dearth,** famine. 72. **cracking,** breaking. 74. **in your impediment,** in any hindrance you may be able to offer. 77. **transported,** carried out of control. 79. **helms,** helmsmen. 83-84. **grain . . . usury.** Two causes of quarrel are merged by Shakespeare. The Senate fought long but finally failed to redress the grievances of the debtors. The plebeians withdrew to Mons Sacer, after which occurred the first fight against the Volscians; then arose the issue over grain. Marcius steadily opposed the plebeians. Menenius Agrippa, who was sent by the Senate to Mons Sacer, is spoken of by Plutarch as the chief man among certain of the pleasantest old men. 95. **stale 't,** make it stale by repeating it; F: *scale*, defended by some editors as meaning "disperse" or "scatter." 97. **fob off,** set aside by a trick. **disgrace,** hardship. 98. **an 't,** if it. **deliver,** tell your tale. 101. **gulf,** whirlpool. 103. **Still,** always. **cupboarding,** stow-

Your most grave belly was deliberate,
Not rash like his accusers, and thus answer'd:
'True is it, my incorporate friends,' quoth he,
'That I receive the general food at first,
Which you do live upon; and fit it is,
Because I am the store-house and the shop
Of the whole body: but, if you do remember,
I send it through the rivers of your blood,
Even to the court, the heart, to th' seat o' th' brain;
And, through the cranks and offices of man,
The strongest nerves and small inferior veins
From me receive that natural competency
Whereby they live: and though that all at once,
You, my good friends,'—this says the belly, mark me,—

First Cit. Ay, sir; well, well.

Men. 'Though all at once cannot
See what I do deliver out to each,
Yet I can make my audit up, that all
From me do back receive the flour of all,
And leave me but the bran.' What say you to 't?

First Cit. It was an answer: how apply you this?

Men. The senators of Rome are this good belly,
And you the mutinous members; for examine
Their counsels and their cares, digest things rightly
Touching the weal o' th' common, you shall find
No public benefit which you receive
But it proceeds or comes from them to you
And no way from yourselves. What do you think,
You, the great toe of this assembly?

First Cit. I the great toe! why the great toe?

Men. For that, being one o' th' lowest, basest, poorest,
Of this most wise rebellion, thou go'st foremost:
Thou rascal, that art worst in blood to run,
Lead'st first to win some vantage.
But make you ready your stiff bats and clubs:
Rome and her rats are at the point of battle;
The one side must have bale.

Enter Caius Marcius.

Hail, noble Marcius!

Mar. Thanks. What 's the matter, you dissentious rogues,
That, rubbing the poor itch of your opinion,
Make yourselves scabs?

First Cit. We have ever your good word.

Mar. He that will give good words to thee will flatter
Beneath abhorring. What would you have, you curs,
That like nor peace nor war? the one affrights you,
The other makes you proud. He that trusts to you,
Where he should find you lions, finds you hares;
Where foxes, geese: you are no surer, no,
Than is the coal of fire upon the ice,
Or hailstone in the sun. Your virtue is
To make him worthy whose offence subdues him
And curse that justice did it. Who deserves greatness
Deserves your hate; and your affections are
A sick man's appetite, who desires most that
Which would increase his evil. He that depends
Upon your favours swims with fins of lead
And hews down oaks with rushes. Hang ye! Trust ye?
With every minute you do change a mind,
And call him noble that was now your hate,
Him vile that was your garland. What 's the matter,
That in these several places of the city
You cry against the noble senate, who,
Under the gods, keep you in awe, which else
Would feed on one another? What 's their seeking?

Men. For corn at their own rates; whereof, they say,
The city is well stor'd.

Mar. Hang 'em! They say!
They'll sit by th' fire, and presume to know
What 's done i' th' Capitol; who 's like to rise,
Who thrives and who declines; side factions and give out
Conjectural marriages; making parties strong
And feebling such as stand not in their liking
Below their cobbled shoes. They say there 's grain enough!
Would the nobility lay aside their ruth,
And let me use my sword, I 'ld make a quarry
With thousands of these quarter'd slaves, as high
As I could pick my lance.

Men. Nay, these are almost thoroughly persuaded;
For though abundantly they lack discretion,
Yet are they passing cowardly. But, I beseech you,
What says the other troop?

Mar. They are dissolv'd: hang 'em!
They said they were an-hungry; sigh'd forth proverbs,
That hunger broke stone walls, that dogs must eat,
That meat was made for mouths, that the gods sent not
Corn for the rich men only: with these shreds
They vented their complainings; which being answer'd,
And a petition granted them, a strange one—
To break the heart of generosity,
And make bold power look pale—they threw their caps
As they would hang them on the horns o' th' moon,
Shouting their emulation.

Men. What is granted them?

Mar. Five tribunes to defend their vulgar wisdoms,
Of their own choice: one 's Junius Brutus,
Sicinius Velutus, and I know not—'Sdeath!
The rabble should have first unroof'd the city,
Ere so prevail'd with me: it will in time
Win upon power and throw forth greater themes
For insurrection's arguing.

Men. This is strange.

Mar. Go, get you home, you fragments!

ing away. 104. **Like,** equal. **where,** whereas. 107. **participate,** participating. 116. **his receipt,** what he received. 122. **muniments,** furnishings, or defenses. 124. **'Fore me,** an oath. 125. **cormorant,** ravenous, rapacious. 134. **incorporate,** belonging to one body. 141. **cranks,** winding passages. **offices,** service rooms of a household; kitchen, etc. 142. **nerves,** sinews. 155. **common,** commons, people. 163. **rascal,** lean deer not worth the hunting; hence the modern meanings. **in blood,** in vigor, condition (hunting term). 165. **stiff bats,** stout cudgels. 167. **have bale,** get the worst of it, receive injury. 168. **dissentious,** rebellious. 170. **scabs,** scurvy fellows, rascals; with play on literal meaning. 173. **nor . . . nor,** neither . . . nor. 179. **make him worthy,** glorify that person. **subdues,** i.e., subjects to punishment. 188. **garland,** object of highest honor and praise. The fickleness of the mob is an ancient theme and is fundamental to the play. 191. **which,** who. 192. **seeking,** demand. 197. **side,** take sides with; or possibly arrange factions on sides. 199. **feebling,** making weak. 200. **cobbled,** mended. 201. **ruth,** tender-heartedness. 202. **quarry,** heap of slain. 203. **quarter'd,** slaughtered. 204. **pick,** pitch. 212. **shreds,** bits, scraps (of wisdom). 215. **generosity,** the nobles. 218. **emulation,** envy of superiors. 219. **tribunes,** official representatives of the people's interests. 221. **'Sdeath,** an oath, by God's death. 224. **Win upon,** gain advantage over.

Enter a Messenger, *hastily.*

Mess. Where 's Caius Marcius?
Mar. Here: what 's the matter?
Mess. The news is, sir, the Volsces are in arms.
Mar. I am glad on 't: then we shall ha' means to vent
Our musty superfluity. See, our best elders.

Enter Sicinius Velutus, Junius Brutus, Cominius, Titus Lartius, *with other* Senators.

First Sen. Marcius, 'tis true that you have lately told us;
The Volsces are in arms.
Mar. They have a leader,
Tullus Aufidius, that will put you to 't.
I sin in envying his nobility,
And were I any thing but what I am,
I would wish me only he.
Com. You have fought together.
Mar. Were half to half the world by th' ears and he
Upon my party, I 'ld revolt, to make
Only my wars with him: he is a lion
That I am proud to hunt.
First Sen. Then, worthy Marcius,
Attend upon Cominius to these wars.
Com. It is your former promise.
Mar. Sir, it is;
And I am constant. Titus Lartius, thou
Shalt see me once more strike at Tullus' face.
What, art thou stiff? stand'st out?
Tit. No, Caius Marcius;
I'll lean upon one crutch and fight with t' other,
Ere stay behind this business.
Men. O, true-bred!
First Sen. Your company to th' Capitol; where, I know,
Our greatest friends attend us.
Tit. [*To Com.*] Lead you on.
[*To Mar.*] Follow Cominius; we must follow you;
Right worthy you priority.
Com. Noble Marcius!
First Sen. [*To the Citizens*] Hence to your homes; be gone!
Mar. Nay, let them follow:
The Volsces have much corn; take these rats thither
To gnaw their garners. Worshipful mutiners,
Your valour puts well forth: pray, follow. *Exeunt.*

Citizens steal away. Mane[n]t Sicinius and Brutus.

Sic. Was ever man so proud as is this Marcius?
Bru. He has no equal.
Sic. When we were chosen tribunes for the people,—
Bru. Mark'd you his lip and eyes?
Sic. Nay, but his taunts.
Bru. Being mov'd, he will not spare to gird the gods.
Sic. Be-mock the modest moon.
Bru. The present wars devour him: he is grown
Too proud to be so valiant.
Sic. Such a nature,
Tickled with good success, disdains the shadow
Which he treads on at noon: but I do wonder
His insolence can brook to be commanded
Under Cominius.
Bru. Fame, at the which he aims,
In whom already he 's well grac'd, can not
Better be held nor more attain'd than by
A place below the first: for what miscarries
Shall be the general's fault, though he perform
To th' utmost of a man, and giddy censure
Will then cry out of Marcius 'O, if he
Had borne the business!'
Sic. Besides, if things go well,
Opinion that so sticks on Marcius shall
Of his demerits rob Cominius.
Bru. Come:
Half all Cominius' honours are to Marcius,
Though Marcius earn'd them not, and all his faults
To Marcius shall be honours, though indeed
In aught he merit not.
Sic. Let 's hence, and hear
How the dispatch is made, and in what fashion,
More than his singularity, he goes
Upon this present action.
Bru. Let 's along. *Exeunt.*

[Scene ii. *Corioli. The Senate-house.*]

Enter Tullus Aufidius *with* Senators *of Corioles.*

First Sen. So, your opinion is, Aufidius,
That they of Rome are ent'red in our counsels
And know how we proceed.
Auf. Is it not yours?
What ever have been thought on in this state,
That could be brought to bodily act ere Rome
Had circumvention? 'Tis not four days gone
Since I heard thence; these are the words: I think
I have the letter here; yes, here it is.
[*Reads*] 'They have press'd a power, but it is not known
Whether for east or west: the dearth is great;
The people mutinous; and it is rumour'd,
Cominius, Marcius your old enemy,
Who is of Rome worse hated than of you,
And Titus Lartius, a most valiant Roman,
These three lead on this preparation
Whither 'tis bent: most likely 'tis for you:
Consider of it.'
First Sen. Our army 's in the field:
We never yet made doubt but Rome was ready
To answer us.
Auf. Nor did you think it folly
To keep your great pretences veil'd till when
They needs must show themselves; which in the hatching,
It seem'd, appear'd to Rome. By the discovery
We shall be short'ned in our aim, which was
To take in many towns ere almost Rome
Should know we were afoot.
Sec. Sen. Noble Aufidius,
Take your commission; hie you to your bands:

233. **put you to 't,** i.e., to the test. 237. **by th' ears,** at variance. 245. **stiff,** i.e., with age. **stand'st out,** refuse to engage. 251. **Right . . . priority,** you being right worthy of priority. 254. **Worshipful mutiners,** mock politeness. 255. **puts well forth,** begins to bud, shows a fair promise (said ironically). 260. **gird,** gird at, scoff at. 261. **modest,** i.e., as representing Diana. 263. **Too proud to be,** too proud of being. 268. **whom,** which. 272. **giddy censure,** thoughtless opinion. 276. **demerits,** merits, deserts. 277. **are to,** belong to. 281. **dispatch,** execution of the business. 282. **More . . . singularity,** i.e., apart from his special peculiarities.

Scene ii. 2. **ent'red in,** acquainted with. 6. **circumvention,** i.e., warning enabling them to circumvent. **gone,** ago. 9. **press'd a power,** raised an army. 20. **pretences,** intentions. 24. **take in,** capture. 28. **set down before 's,** lay siege to us. **remove,** raising of the siege.

Scene iii. 8. **all gaze,** i.e., the gaze of all. 14. **like,** likely. 16. **bound with oak,** i.e., as a badge to signify that he had saved the life of

Let us alone to guard Corioles:
If they set down before 's, for the remove
Bring up your army; but, I think, you'll find
Th' have not prepar'd for us.

Auf. O, doubt not that;
I speak from certainties. Nay, more,
Some parcels of their power are forth already,
And only hitherward. I leave your honours.
If we and Caius Marcius chance to meet,
'Tis sworn between us we shall ever strike
Till one can do no more.

All. The gods assist you!

Auf. And keep your honours safe!

First Sen. Farewell.

Sec. Sen. Farewell.

All. Farewell. *Exeunt omnes.*

[SCENE III. *Rome. A room in Marcius' house.*]

Enter VOLUMNIA *and* VIRGILIA, *mother and wife to Marcius: they set them down on two low stools, and sew.*

Vol. I pray you, daughter, sing; or express yourself in a more comfortable sort: if my son were my husband, I should freelier rejoice in that absence wherein he won honour than in the embracements of his bed where he would show most love. When yet he was but tender-bodied and the only son of my womb, when youth with comeliness plucked all gaze his way, when for a day of kings' entreaties a mother should not sell him an hour from her beholding, I, considering how honour would become such a person, that it was no better than picture-like to hang by the wall, if renown made it not stir, was pleased to let him seek danger where he was like to find fame. To a cruel war I sent him; from whence he returned, his brows bound with oak. I tell thee, daughter, I sprang not more in joy at first hearing he was a man-child than now in first seeing he had proved himself a man.

Vir. But had he died in the business, madam; how then?

Vol. Then his good report should have been my son; I therein would have found issue. Hear me profess sincerely: had I a dozen sons, each in my love alike and none less dear than thine and my good Marcius, I had rather had eleven die nobly for their country than one voluptuously surfeit out of action.

Enter a Gentlewoman.

Gent. Madam, the Lady Valeria is come to visit you.

Vir. Beseech you, give me leave to retire myself.

Vol. Indeed, you shall not.
Methinks I hear hither your husband's drum,
See him pluck Aufidius down by th' hair,
As children from a bear, the Volsces shunning him:
Methinks I see him stamp thus, and call thus:
'Come on, you cowards! you were got in fear,
Though you were born in Rome:' his bloody brow
With his mail'd hand then wiping, forth he goes,
Like to a harvest-man that 's task'd to mow
Or all or lose his hire.

Vir. His bloody brow! O Jupiter, no blood!

Vol. Away, you fool! it more becomes a man
Than gilt his trophy: the breasts of Hecuba,
When she did suckle Hector, look'd not lovelier
Than Hector's forehead when it spit forth blood
At Grecian sword, contemning. Tell Valeria,
We are fit to bid her welcome. *Exit Gent.*

Vir. Heavens bless my lord from fell Aufidius!

Vol. He'll beat Aufidius' head below his knee
And tread upon his neck.

Enter VALERIA, *with an* Usher *and* Gentlewoman.

Val. My ladies both, good day to you.

Vol. Sweet madam.

Vir. I am glad to see your ladyship.

Val. How do you both? you are manifest housekeepers. What are you sewing here? A fine spot, in good faith. How does your little son?

Vir. I thank your ladyship; well, good madam.

Vol. He had rather see the swords, and hear a drum, than look upon his schoolmaster.

Val. O' my word, the father's son: I'll swear, 'tis a very pretty boy. O' my troth, I looked upon him o' Wednesday half an hour together: has such a confirmed countenance. I saw him run after a gilded butterfly; and when he caught it, he let it go again; and after it again; and over and over he comes, and up again; catched it again; or whether his fall enraged him, or how 'twas, he did so set his teeth and tear it; O, I warrant, how he mammocked it!

Vol. One on 's father's moods.

Val. Indeed, la, 'tis a noble child.

Vir. A crack, madam.

Val. Come, lay aside your stitchery; I must have you play the idle huswife with me this afternoon.

Vir. No, good madam; I will not out of doors.

Val. Not out of doors!

Vol. She shall, she shall.

Vir. Indeed, no, by your patience; I'll not over the threshold till my lord return from the wars.

Val. Fie, you confine yourself most unreasonably: come, you must go visit the good lady that lies in.

Vir. I will wish her speedy strength, and visit her with my prayers; but I cannot go thither.

Vol. Why, I pray you?

Vir. 'Tis not to save labour, nor that I want love.

Val. You would be another Penelope: yet, they say, all the yarn she spun in Ulysses' absence did but fill Ithaca full of moths. Come; I would your cambric were sensible as your finger, that you might leave pricking it for pity. Come, you shall go with us.

Vir. No, good madam, pardon me; indeed, I will not forth.

Val. In truth, la, go with me; and I'll tell you excellent news of your husband.

Vir. O, good madam, there can be none yet.

Val. Verily, I do not jest with you; there came news from him last night.

Vir. Indeed, madam?

a Roman citizen. The *cruel war* was that against the Latins and Tarquin the Proud. 22. **good report,** reputation. As a typical Roman matron Volumnia lifts the public cause above her private love. 32. **hear hither,** i.e., penetrating hither. 36. **got,** begot. 39. **task'd,** set the task. 43. **Than gilt his trophy,** i.e., than gilding sets off his monument. 46. **At . . . Tell.** Capell's emendation; F: *At Grecian sword.* **contemning,** tell. The emended text suggests the brow and blood of Hector as scorning the Grecian sword. 48. **fell,** cruel. 54. **manifest,** notorious.

55. **house-keepers,** stay-at-homes. **sewing,** embroidering. 56. **spot,** pattern, figure. 63. **O' my troth,** mild oath. 71. **mammocked,** tore into fragments. 72. **on 's,** of his. 74. **crack,** boy (suggestion of pertness). 75. **stitchery,** needlework. 76. **huswife,** housewife, with play on sense of "hussy." 92. **Penelope,** faithful wife of Ulysses, King of Ithaca and hero of Homer's *Odyssey.* 95. **cambric,** fine white linen.

Val. In earnest, it 's true; I heard a senator speak it. Thus it is: the Volsces have an army forth; against whom Cominius the general is gone, with one part of our Roman power: your lord and Titus Lartius are set down before their city Corioles; they nothing doubt prevailing and to make it brief wars. This is true, on mine honour; and so, I pray, go with us.

Vir. Give me excuse, good madam; I will obey you in every thing hereafter.

Vol. Let her alone, lady: as she is now, she will but disease our better mirth.

Val. In troth, I think she would. Fare you well, then. Come, good sweet lady. Prithee, Virgilia, turn thy solemness out o' door, and go along with us.

Vir. No, at a word, madam; indeed, I must not. I wish you much mirth.

Val. Well, then, farewell. *Exeunt Ladies.*

[SCENE IV. *Before Corioli.*]

Enter MARCIUS, TITUS LARTIUS, *with drum and colours, with* Captains *and* Soldiers, *as before the city* [*of*] *Corioles. To them a* Messenger.

Mar. Yonder comes news. A wager they have met.
Lart. My horse to yours, no.
Mar. 'Tis done.
Lart. Agreed.
Mar. Say, has our general met the enemy?
Mess. They lie in view; but have not spoke as yet.
Lart. So, the good horse is mine.
Mar. I'll buy him of you.
Lart. No, I'll nor sell nor give him: lend you him I will
For half a hundred years. Summon the town.
Mar. How far off lie these armies?
Mess. Within this mile and half.
Mar. Then shall we hear their 'larum, and they ours.
Now, Mars, I prithee, make us quick in work,
That we with smoking swords may march from hence,
To help our fielded friends! Come, blow thy blast.

They sound a parley. Enter two Senators *with others on the walls of Corioles.*

Tullus Aufidius, is he within your walls?
First Sen. No, nor a man that fears you less than he,
That 's lesser than a little *(Drum afar off.)* Hark! our drums
Are bringing forth our youth. We'll break our walls,
Rather than they shall pound us up: our gates,
Which yet seem shut, we have but pinn'd with rushes;
They'll open of themselves. *(Alarum far off.)* Hark you, far off!
There is Aufidius; list, what work he makes
Amongst your cloven army.
Mar. O, they are at it!
Lart. Their noise be our instruction. Ladders, ho!

Enter the army of the Volsces.

Mar. They fear us not, but issue forth their city.
Now put your shields before your hearts, and fight
With hearts more proof than shields. Advance, brave Titus:
They do disdain us much beyond our thoughts,
Which makes me sweat with wrath. Come on, my fellows:
He that retires, I'll take him for a Volsce,
And he shall feel mine edge.

Alarum. The Romans *are beat back to their trenches. Enter* MARCIUS, *cursing.*

Mar. All the contagion of the south light on you,
You shames of Rome! you herd of—Boils and plagues
Plaster you o'er, that you may be abhorr'd
Farther than seen and one infect another
Against the wind a mile! You souls of geese,
That bear the shapes of men, how have you run
From slaves that apes would beat! Pluto and hell!
All hurt behind; backs red, and faces pale
With flight and agued fear! Mend and charge home,
Or, by the fires of heaven, I'll leave the foe
And make my wars on you: look to 't: come on;
If you'll stand fast, we'll beat them to their wives,
As they us to our trenches. Follow 's!

Another alarum; [*the* Volsces *fly,*] *and* MARCIUS *follows them to* [*the*] *gates.*

So, now the gates are ope: now prove good seconds:
'Tis for the followers fortune widens them,
Not for the fliers: mark me, and do the like.
Enter the gates and is shut in.
First Sol. Fool-hardiness; not I.
Sec. Sol. Nor I.
First Sol. See, they have shut him in.
All. To th' pot, I warrant him.
Alarum continues.

Enter TITUS LARTIUS.

Lart. What is become of Marcius?
All. Slain, sir, doubtless.
First Sol. Following the fliers at the very heels,
With them he enters; who, upon the sudden,
Clapp'd to their gates: he is himself alone,
To answer all the city.
Lart. O noble fellow!
Who sensibly outdares his senseless sword,
And, when it bows, stand'st up. Thou art left, Marcius:
A carbuncle entire, as big as thou art,
Were not so rich a jewel. Thou wast a soldier
Even to Cato's wish, not fierce and terrible
Only in strokes; but, with thy grim looks and
The thunder-like percussion of thy sounds,
Thou mad'st thine enemies shake, as if the world
Were feverous and did tremble.

Enter MARCIUS, *bleeding, assaulted by the enemy.*

First Sol. Look, sir.
Lart. O, 'tis Marcius!
Let 's fetch him off, or make remain alike.
They fight, and all enter the city.

---

117. **disease our better mirth,** trouble our mirth which would be greater without her. 120. **out o' door,** out-of-doors; with quibble.
SCENE IV. 2. **My horse to yours,** i.e., I'll bet my horse against yours they have not met in battle. 7. **Summon the town,** i.e., by trumpet, to parley. 9. **'larum,** call to arms. 12. **fielded,** in the field. 17. **pound,** shut up as in a pound. 21. **cloven,** explained as split in two and routed; possibly refers to the divided formation of the Roman forces. 25. **proof,** impenetrable. 29. **edge,** sword. 30. **south,** south wind as source of contagion. 34. **Against . . . mile,** i.e., so great that it will carry a mile against the wind. 38. **agued,** i.e., operating like an ague, trembling. **Mend,** do better, or possibly reform (your ranks). **home,** to the utmost. 42. **Follow 's,** i.e., follow me. 43. **seconds,** supporters. 47. **pot,** i.e., to certain destruction. 51. **himself alone,** quite alone. 53-54. **Who . . . up,** who, though endowed with feeling, dares more than his insensible sword; it might bend to fear, he would not. 54. **left,** abandoned. 57. **Cato's,** so Theobald; F: *Calues*. The reference

[SCENE V. *Corioli. A street.*]

Enter certain Romans, *with spoils.*

First Rom. This will I carry to Rome.
Sec. Rom. And I this.
Third Rom. A murrain on 't! I took this for silver.
Exeunt. Alarum continues still afar off.

Enter MARCIUS *and* TITUS [LARTIUS] *with a trumpet.*

Mar. See here these movers that do prize their hours
At a crack'd drachma! Cushions, leaden spoons,
Irons of a doit, doublets that hangmen would
Bury with those that wore them, these base slaves,
Ere yet the fight be done, pack up: down with them!
And hark, what noise the general makes! To him!
There is the man of my soul's hate, Aufidius,
Piercing our Romans: then, valiant Titus, take
Convenient numbers to make good the city;
Whilst I, with those that have the spirit, will haste
To help Cominius.
Lart. Worthy sir, thou bleed'st;
Thy exercise hath been too violent
For a second course of fight.
Mar. Sir, praise me not;
My work hath yet not warm'd me: fare you well:
The blood I drop is rather physical
Than dangerous to me: to Aufidius thus
I will appear, and fight.
Lart. Now the fair goddess, Fortune,
Fall deep in love with thee; and her great charms
Misguide thy opposers' swords! Bold gentleman,
Prosperity be thy page!
Mar. Thy friend no less
Than those she placeth highest! So, farewell.
Lart. Thou worthiest Marcius! [*Exit Marcius.*]
Go sound thy trumpet in the market-place;
Call thither all the officers o' th' town,
Where they shall know our mind: away! *Exeunt.*

[SCENE VI. *Near the camp of Cominius.*]

Enter COMINIUS, *as it were in retire, with soldiers.*

Com. Breathe you, my friends: well fought; we are come off
Like Romans, neither foolish in our stands,
Nor cowardly in retire: believe me, sirs,
We shall be charg'd again. Whiles we have struck,
By interims and conveying gusts we have heard
The charges of our friends. Ye Roman gods!
Lead their successes as we wish our own,
That both our powers, with smiling fronts encount'ring,
May give you thankful sacrifice.

Enter a Messenger.

Thy news?
Mess. The citizens of Corioles have issued,
And given to Lartius and to Marcius battle:
I saw our party to their trenches driven,
And then I came away.
Com. Though thou speakest truth,
Methinks thou speak'st not well. How long is 't since?
Mess. Above an hour, my lord.
Com. 'Tis not a mile; briefly we heard their drums:
How couldst thou in a mile confound an hour,
And bring thy news so late?
Mess. Spies of the Volsces
Held me in chase, that I was forc'd to wheel
Three or four miles about, else had I, sir,
Half an hour since brought my report.

Enter MARCIUS.

Com. Who 's yonder,
That does appear as he were flay'd? O gods!
He has the stamp of Marcius; and I have
Before-time seen him thus.
Mar. Come I too late?
Com. The shepherd knows not thunder from a tabor
More than I know the sound of Marcius' tongue
From every meaner man.
Mar. Come I too late?
Com. Ay, if you come not in the blood of others,
But mantled in your own.
Mar. O, let me clip ye
In arms as sound as when I woo'd, in heart
As merry as when our nuptial day was done,
And tapers burn'd to bedward!
Com. Flower of warriors,
How is 't with Titus Lartius?
Mar. As with a man busied about decrees:
Condemning some to death, and some to exile;
Ransoming him, or pitying, threat'ning th' other;
Holding Corioles in the name of Rome,
Even like a fawning greyhound in the leash,
To let him slip at will.
Com. Where is that slave
Which told me they had beat you to your trenches?
Where is he? call him hither.
Mar. Let him alone;
He did inform the truth: but for our gentlemen,
The common file—a plague! tribunes for them!—
The mouse ne'er shunn'd the cat as they did budge
From rascals worse than they.
Com. But how prevail'd you?
Mar. Will the time serve to tell? I do not think.
Where is the enemy? are you lords o' th' field?
If not, why cease you till you are so?
Com. Marcius,
We have at disadvantage fought and did
Retire to win our purpose.
Mar. How lies their battle? know you on which side
They have plac'd their men of trust?
Com. As I guess, Marcius,
Their bands i' th' vaward are the Antiates,
Of their best trust; o'er them Aufidius,
Their very heart of hope.
Mar. I do beseech you,

is to Marcus Cato, celebrated in Plutarch as a staunch soldier and exponent of Roman ethics. 62. **make remain alike,** remain to share his fate.

SCENE V. 3. **murrain,** plague. *Stage Direction:* ***trumpet,*** trumpeter. 5. **movers,** active persons; here used ironically. **prize their hours,** value their time. 6. **drachma,** Greek coin. 7. **of a doit,** worth a coin of small value. 7-8. **would . . . them,** i.e., hangmen, entitled to the clothes of persons put to death, would not have them. 13. **make good,** hold. 17. **second course,** usually explained as bout in fighting; more probably, reference to second course in banquet. 19. **physical,** curative. 24. **Thy friend no less,** i.e., may she be no less thy friend.

SCENE VI. 1. **are come off,** have left the field of battle. 5. **By . . . gusts,** at intervals and borne to us on the wind. 16. **briefly,** recently. 23. **stamp,** outward look. 25. **tabor,** drum. 29. **mantled,** covered. **clip,** embrace. 36. **pitying,** remitting his ransom (Johnson). 53. **vaward,** vanguard. **Antiates,** inhabitants of Antium.

By all the battles wherein we have fought,
By th' blood we have shed together, by th' vows
We have made to endure friends, that you directly
Set me against Aufidius and his Antiates;
And that you not delay the present, but,
Filling the air with swords advanc'd and darts,
We prove this very hour.
  Com. Though I could wish
You were conducted to a gentle bath
And balms applied to you, yet dare I never
Deny your asking: take your choice of those
That best can aid your action.
  Mar. Those are they
That most are willing. If any such be here—
As it were sin to doubt—that love this painting
Wherein you see me smear'd; if any fear
Lesser his person than an ill report;
If any think brave death outweighs bad life
And that his country 's dearer than himself;
Let him alone, or so many so minded,
Wave thus, to express his disposition,
And follow Marcius.

They all shout and wave their swords, take him up in their arms, and cast up their caps.

O, me alone! make you a sword of me?
If these shows be not outward, which of you
But is four Volsces? none of you but is
Able to bear against the great Aufidius
A shield as hard as his. A certain number,
Though thanks to all, must I select from all: the rest
Shall bear the business in some other fight,
As cause will be obey'd. Please you to march;
†And four shall quickly draw out my command,
Which men are best inclin'd.
  Com. March on, my fellows:
Make good this ostentation, and you shall
Divide in all with us. *Exeunt.*

[SCENE VII. *The gates of Corioli.*]

TITUS LARTIUS, *having set a guard upon Corioles, going with drum and trumpet toward* COMINIUS *and* CAIUS MARCIUS, *enters with a* Lieutenant, *other* Soldiers, *and a* Scout.

  Lart. So, let the ports be guarded: keep your duties,
As I have set them down. If I do send, dispatch
Those centuries to our aid; the rest will serve
For a short holding: if we lose the field,
We cannot keep the town.
  Lieu. Fear not our care, sir.
  Lart. Hence, and shut your gates upon 's.
Our guider, come; to th' Roman camp conduct us.
Exeunt.

[SCENE VIII. *A field of battle.*]

Alarum as in battle. Enter MARCIUS *and* AUFIDIUS *at several doors.*

  Mar. I'll fight with none but thee; for I do hate thee
Worse than a promise-breaker.
  Auf. We hate alike:
Not Afric owns a serpent I abhor
More than thy fame and envy. Fix thy foot.
  Mar. Let the first budger die the other's slave,
And the gods doom him after!
  Auf. If I fly, Marcius,
Holloa me like a hare.
  Mar. Within these three hours, Tullus,
Alone I fought in your Corioles walls,
And made what work I pleas'd: 'tis not my blood
Wherein thou seest me mask'd; for thy revenge
Wrench up thy power to th' highest.
  Auf. Wert thou the Hector
That was the whip of your bragg'd progeny,
Thou shouldst not scape me here.

Here they fight, and certain Volsces come in the aid of Aufidius. Marcius fights till they be driven in breathless.

Officious, and not valiant, you have sham'd me
In your condemned seconds. [*Exeunt.*]

[SCENE IX. *The Roman camp.*]

Flourish. Alarum. A retreat is sounded. Enter, at one door, COMINIUS *with the* Romans; *at another door* MARCIUS, *with his arm in a scarf.*

  Com. If I should tell thee o'er this thy day's work,
Thou 'ldst not believe thy deeds: but I'll report it
Where senators shall mingle tears with smiles,
Where great patricians shall attend and shrug,
I' th' end admire, where ladies shall be frighted,
And, gladly quak'd, hear more; where the dull tribunes,
That, with the fusty plebeians, hate thine honours,
Shall say against their hearts 'We thank the gods
Our Rome hath such a soldier.'
Yet cam'st thou to a morsel of this feast,
Having fully din'd before.

Enter TITUS [LARTIUS] *with his power, from the pursuit.*

  Lart. O general,
Here is the steed, we the caparison:
Hadst thou beheld—
  Mar. Pray now, no more: my mother,
Who has a charter to extol her blood,
When she does praise me grieves me. I have done
As you have done; that 's what I can; induc'd
As you have been; that 's for my country:
He that has but effected his good will
Hath overta'en mine act.
  Com. You shall not be
The grave of your deserving; Rome must know
The value of her own: 'twere a concealment
Worse than a theft, no less than a traducement,
To hide your doings; and to silence that,

58. **endure,** continue. 60. **the present,** now. 76. **O . . . me.** F has a comma after *alone*, colon after *me*. Herford's explanation: Yes, make me your weapon indeed! Follow me up as strenuously as the hand the sword. Some editors place question mark after *alone*. 77. **outward,** external, deceptive. 83. **As . . . obey'd,** as necessity shall require. 84. **four.** Capell conjectured *I;* i.e., I shall choose from the whole force.

SCENE VII. 3. **centuries,** companies.

SCENE VIII. *Stage Direction:* **several,** different. 3. **Afric,** famous for serpents, because when drops of blood fell from the head of the Gorgon slain by Perseus, they turned to snakes. 11. **Hector,** the most famous of the Trojan warriors; allusion to supposed descent of the Romans from the Trojans. 12. **whip,** possibly the scourge that urged the Trojans to deeds of valor; also explained (by Johnson) as the whip with which the Trojans scourged the Greeks. **progeny,** ancestors. 15. **condemned seconds,** despised efforts at assistance.

SCENE IX. 6. **gladly quak'd,** glad to be frightened. 7. **fusty,** moldy, ill-smelling. 8. **against their hearts,** unwillingly. 12. **caparison,**

Which, to the spire and top of praises vouch'd,
Would seem but modest: therefore, I beseech you—
In sign of what you are, not to reward
What you have done—before our army hear me.
Mar. I have some wounds upon me, and they smart
To hear themselves remember'd.
Com. Should they not,
Well might they fester 'gainst ingratitude,
And tent themselves with death. Of all the horses,
Whereof we have ta'en good and good store, of all
The treasure in this field achiev'd and city,
We render you the tenth, to be ta'en forth,
Before the common distribution, at
Your only choice.
Mar. I thank you, general;
But cannot make my heart consent to take
A bribe to pay my sword: I do refuse it;
And stand upon my common part with those
That have beheld the doing.

A long flourish. They all cry 'Marcius! Marcius!' *cast up their caps and lances: Cominius and Lartius stand bare.*

Mar. May these same instruments, which you profane,
Never sound more! when drums and trumpets shall
I' th' field prove flatterers, let courts and cities be
Made all of false-fac'd soothing!
When steel grows soft as the parasite's silk,
Let him be made an overture for th' wars!
No more, I say! For that I have not wash'd
My nose that bled, or foil'd some debile wretch,—
Which, without note, here 's many else have done,—
You shout me forth
In acclamations hyperbolical;
As if I lov'd my little should be dieted
In praises sauc'd with lies.
Com. Too modest are you;
More cruel to your good report than grateful
To us that give you truly: by your patience,
If 'gainst yourself you be incens'd, we'll put you,
Like one that means his proper harm, in manacles,
Then reason safely with you. Therefore, be it known,
As to us, to all the world, that Caius Marcius
Wears this war's garland: in token of the which,
My noble steed, known to the camp, I give him,
With all his trim belonging; and from this time,
For what he did before Corioles, call him,
With all th' applause and clamour of the host,
Caius Marcius Coriolanus! Bear
Th' addition nobly ever!

Flourish. Trumpets sound, and drums.

All. Caius Marcius Coriolanus!
Cor. I will go wash;
And when my face is fair, you shall perceive
Whether I blush or no: howbeit, I thank you.
I mean to stride your steed, and at all times
To undercrest your good addition
To th' fairness of my power.
Com. So, to our tent;
Where, ere we do repose us, we will write
To Rome of our success. You, Titus Lartius,
Must to Corioles back: send us to Rome
The best, with whom we may articulate,
For their own good and ours.
Lart. I shall, my lord.
Cor. The gods begin to mock me. I, that now
Refus'd most princely gifts, am bound to beg
Of my lord general.
Com. Take 't; 'tis yours. What is 't?
Cor. I sometime lay here in Corioles
At a poor man's house; he us'd me kindly:
He cried to me; I saw him prisoner;
But then Aufidius was within my view,
And wrath o'erwhelm'd my pity: I request you
To give my poor host freedom.
Com. O, well begg'd!
Were he the butcher of my son, he should
Be free as is the wind. Deliver him, Titus.
Lart. Marcius, his name?
Cor. By Jupiter! forgot.
I am weary; yea, my memory is tir'd.
Have we no wine here?
Com. Go we to our tent:
The blood upon your visage dries; 'tis time
It should be look'd to: come. *Exeunt.*

[SCENE X. *The camp of the Volsces.*]

A flourish. Cornets. Enter TULLUS AUFIDIUS, *bloody, with two or three* Soldiers.

Auf. The town is ta'en!
First Sol. 'Twill be deliver'd back on good condition.
Auf. Condition!
I would I were a Roman; for I cannot,
Being a Volsce, be that I am. Condition!
What good condition can a treaty find
I' th' part that is at mercy? Five times, Marcius,
I have fought with thee; so often hast thou beat me,
And wouldst do so, I think, should we encounter
As often as we eat. By th' elements,
If e'er again I meet him beard to beard,
He 's mine, or I am his: mine emulation
Hath not that honour in 't it had; for where
I thought to crush him in an equal force,
True sword to sword, I'll potch at him some way
Or wrath or craft may get him.
First Sol. He 's the devil.
Auf. Bolder, though not so subtle. My valour 's poison'd
With only suff'ring stain by him; for him
Shall fly out of itself: nor sleep nor sanctuary,
Being naked, sick, nor fane nor Capitol,
The prayers of priests nor times of sacrifice,
Embarquements all of fury, shall lift up
Their rotten privilege and custom 'gainst
My hate to Marcius: where I find him, were it

trappings of a steed. 14. **charter . . . blood,** right to praise her child. 18. **effected,** manifested in action. 19-20. **You . . . deserving,** you shall not conceal your merit. 22. **traducement,** calumny, slander. 31. **tent,** cure by probing. 32. **good and good,** excellent ones and plenty of them. 44. **soothing,** flattery. 46. **him,** i.e., the silk. **an overture,** a covering. So F; Globe, following Steevens: *a coverture.* 47. **For that,** because. 48. **debile,** weak. 49. **note,** notice taken. 52. **my little,** the little I have done. 52-53. **dieted In,** fed on. 55. **give,** report. 57. **means,** intends. **proper,** own. 60. **garland,** principal glory. 62. **trim,** trappings. 72. **undercrest,** wear (as a crest). 77. **best,** i.e., in blood among the Volscians. **articulate,** come to terms. 80. **bound to,** about to.

SCENE X. 2. **condition,** terms; Aufidius plays on the word (ll. 3, 5) with the additional sense of state or quality. 15. **potch,** thrust. 16. **Or . . . craft,** in which either wrath or craft. 18. **stain,** tarnishment, eclipse. 19. **fly out,** shall deviate from its own native generosity (Johnson). 22. **Embarquements,** embargoes, restraints.

At home, upon my brother's guard, even there,
Against the hospitable canon, would I
Wash my fierce hand in 's heart. Go you to th' city;
Learn how 'tis held; and what they are that must
Be hostages for Rome.

First Sol. Will not you go?

Auf. I am attended at the cypress grove: I pray you—
'Tis south the city mills—bring me word thither
How the world goes, that to the pace of it
I may spur on my journey.

First Sol. I shall, sir. [*Exeunt.*]

ACT II.

[SCENE I. *Rome. A public place.*]

Enter MENENIUS *with the two Tribunes of the people,* SICINIUS *and* BRUTUS.

Men. The augurer tells me we shall have news to-night.

Bru. Good or bad?

Men. Not according to the prayer of the people, for they love not Marcius.

Sic. Nature teaches beasts to know their friends.

Men. Pray you, who does the wolf love?

Sic. The lamb.

Men. Ay, to devour him; as the hungry plebeians would the noble Marcius.

Bru. He 's a lamb indeed, that baas like a bear.

Men. He 's a bear indeed, that lives like a lamb. You two are old men: tell me one thing that I shall ask you.

Both. Well, sir.

Men. In what enormity is Marcius poor in, that you two have not in abundance?

Bru. He 's poor in no one fault, but stored with all.

Sic. Especially in pride.

Bru. And topping all others in boasting.

Men. This is strange now: do you two know how you are censured here in the city, I mean of us o' the right-hand file? do you?

Both. Why, how are we censured?

Men. Because you talk of pride now,—will you not be angry?

Both. Well, well, sir, well.

Men. Why, 'tis no great matter; for a very little thief of occasion will rob you of a great deal of patience: give your dispositions the reins, and be angry at your pleasures; at the least, if you take it as a pleasure to you in being so. You blame Marcius for being proud?

Bru. We do it not alone, sir.

Men. I know you can do very little alone; for your helps are many, or else your actions would grow wondrous single: your abilities are too infant-like for doing much alone. You talk of pride: O that you could turn your eyes toward the napes of your necks, and make but an interior survey of your good selves! O that you could!

Both. What then, sir?

Men. Why, then you should discover a brace of unmeriting, proud, violent, testy magistrates, alias fools, as any in Rome.

Sic. Menenius, you are known well enough too.

Men. I am known to be a humorous patrician, and one that loves a cup of hot wine with not a drop of allaying Tiber in 't; said to be something imperfect in favouring the first complaint; hasty and tinder-like upon too trivial motion; one that converses more with the buttock of the night than with the forehead of the morning: what I think I utter, and spend my malice in my breath. Meeting two such wealsmen as you are—I cannot call you Lycurguses—if the drink you give me touch my palate adversely, I make a crooked face at it. I can 't say your worships have delivered the matter well, when I find the ass in compound with the major part of your syllables: and though I must be content to bear with those that say you are reverend grave men, yet they lie deadly that tell you you have good faces. If you see this in the map of my microcosm, follows it that I am known well enough too? what harm can your bisson conspectuities glean out of this character, if I be known well enough too?

Bru. Come, sir, come, we know you well enough.

Men. You know neither me, yourselves, nor any thing. You are ambitious for poor knaves' caps and legs: you wear out a good wholesome forenoon in hearing a cause between an orange-wife and a forset-seller; and then rejourn the controversy of three pence to a second day of audience. When you are hearing a matter between party and party, if you chance to be pinched with the colic, you make faces like mummers; set up the bloody flag against all patience; and, in roaring for a chamber-pot, dismiss the controversy bleeding, the more entangled by your hearing: all the peace you make in their cause is, calling both the parties knaves. You are a pair of strange ones.

Bru. Come, come, you are well understood to be a perfecter giber for the table than a necessary bencher in the Capitol.

Men. Our very priests must become mockers, if they shall encounter such ridiculous subjects as you are. When you speak best unto the purpose, it is not worth the wagging of your beards; and your beards deserve not so honourable a grave as to stuff a botcher's cushion, or to be entombed in an ass's pack-saddle. Yet you must be saying, Marcius is proud; who, in a cheap estimation, is worth all your predecessors since Deucalion, though peradventure some of the best of 'em were hereditary hangmen. God-den to your worships: more of your conversation would infect my brain, being the herdsmen of the

26. **hospitable canon,** law of hospitality. 30. **attended,** waited for.

ACT II. SCENE I. 25. **censured,** judged. 26. **file,** body of persons; i.e., the party of aristocrats. 31-32. **very . . . occasion,** very slight occasion acting like a thief. 40. **single,** poor, feeble. 42-43. **turn . . . necks,** allusion to the fable of Aesop according to which Jupiter provided each man with two bags; one, worn in front and always in sight, contained his neighbors' faults; the other, worn at his own back and out of sight, contained his own. 53. **allaying Tiber,** water which dilutes. 54. **something . . . complaint,** somewhat easily influenced by the first version that reaches his ears. 56-57. **one . . . morning,** i.e., he is better acquainted with the last hour of the night than with the first hour of the morning. 59. **wealsmen,** statesmen. 60. **Lycurguses,** used ironically; Lycurgus was the famous Spartan lawgiver. 63-65. **I find . . . syllables,** I find assininity in nearly everything you say. 67-68. **good faces,** probably, honest faces and handsome faces. 68-69. **map of my microcosm,** my face, or chart of my little world (as opposed to the macrocosm or great world). 70. **bisson conspectuities,** purblind faculty of sight. 77. **caps and legs,** doffing caps and making obeisances to indicate servility. 78. **orange-wife,** woman who sells oranges. 79. **forset-seller,** one who sells taps for drawing liquor from barrels. 83. **mummers,** masked actors or buffoons; possibly actors in mummings, or rural plays, at Christmas. 84. **set . . . flag,** declare violent war. 91-92. **perfecter . . . Capitol,** better at after-dinner jests than at sitting in the Senate as a councilor. 98. **botcher's,** of one who patches old beastly plebeians: I will be bold to take my leave of you. *Brutus and Sicinius [go] aside.*

Enter VOLUMNIA, VIRGILIA, *and* VALERIA.

How now, my as fair as noble ladies,—and the moon, were she earthly, no nobler,—whither do you follow your eyes so fast?

Vol. Honourable Menenius, my boy Marcius approaches; for the love of Juno, let 's go.

Men. Ha! Marcius coming home!

Vol. Ay, worthy Menenius; and with most prosperous approbation.

Men. Take my cap, Jupiter, and I thank thee. Hoo! Marcius coming home!

Vol. Vir. Nay, 'tis true.

Vol. Look, here 's a letter from him: the state hath another, his wife another; and, I think, there 's one at home for you.

Men. I will make my very house reel to-night: a letter for me!

Vir. Yes, certain, there 's a letter for you; I saw 't.

Men. A letter for me! it gives me an estate of seven years' health; in which time I will make a lip at the physician: the most sovereign prescription in Galen is but empiricutic, and, to this preservative, of no better report than a horse-drench. Is he not wounded? he was wont to come home wounded.

Vir. O, no, no, no.

Vol. O, he is wounded; I thank the gods for 't.

Men. So do I too, if it be not too much: brings 'a victory in his pocket? the wounds become him.

Vol. On 's brows: Menenius, he comes the third time home with the oaken garland.

Men. Has he disciplined Aufidius soundly?

Vol. Titus Lartius writes, they fought together, but Aufidius got off.

Men. And 'twas time for him too, I'll warrant him that: an he had stayed by him, I would not have been so fidiused for all the chests in Corioles, and the gold that 's in them. Is the senate possessed of this?

Vol. Good ladies, let 's go. Yes, yes, yes; the senate has letters from the general, wherein he gives my son the whole name of the war: he hath in this action outdone his former deeds doubly.

Val. In troth, there 's wondrous things spoke of him.

Men. Wondrous! ay, I warrant you, and not without his true purchasing.

Vir. The gods grant them true!

Vol. True! pow, waw.

Men. True! I'll be sworn they are true. Where is he wounded? [*To the Tribunes*] God save your good worships! Marcius is coming home: he has more cause to be proud. Where is he wounded?

Vol. I' the shoulder and i' the left arm: there will be large cicatrices to show the people, when he shall stand for his place. He received in the repulse of Tarquin seven hurts i' the body.

Men. One i' the neck, and two i' the thigh,—there 's nine that I know.

Vol. He had, before this last expedition, twenty-five wounds upon him.

Men. Now it 's twenty-seven: every gash was an enemy's grave. (*A shout and flourish.*) Hark! the trumpets.

Vol. These are the ushers of Marcius: before him he carries noise, and behind him he leaves tears:
Death, that dark spirit, in 's nervy arm doth lie;
Which, being advanc'd, declines, and then men die.

A sennet. Trumpets sound. Enter COMINIUS *the general, and* TITUS LARTIUS; *between them,* CORIOLANUS, *crowned with an oaken garland; with* Captains *and* Soldiers, *and a* Herald.

Her. Know, Rome, that all alone Marcius did fight
Within Corioles gates: where he hath won,
With fame, a name to Caius Marcius; these
In honour follows Coriolanus.
Welcome to Rome, renowned Coriolanus!
Sound. Flourish.

All. Welcome to Rome, renowned Coriolanus!

Cor. No more of this; it does offend my heart:
Pray now, no more.

Com. Look, sir, your mother!

Cor. O,
You have, I know, petition'd all the gods
For my prosperity! *Kneels.*

Vol. Nay, my good soldier, up;
My gentle Marcius, worthy Caius, and
By deed-achieving honour newly nam'd,—
What is it?—Coriolanus must I call thee?—
But, O, thy wife!

Cor. My gracious silence, hail!
Wouldst thou have laugh'd had I come coffin'd home,
That weep'st to see me triumph? Ah, my dear,
Such eyes the widows in Corioles wear,
And mothers that lack sons.

Men. Now, the gods crown thee!

Cor. And live you yet? [*To Valeria*] O my sweet lady, pardon.

Vol. I know not where to turn: O, welcome home:
And welcome, general: and y' are welcome all.

Men. A hundred thousand welcomes. I could weep
And I could laugh, I am light and heavy. Welcome.
A curse begin at very root on 's heart,
That is not glad to see thee! You are three
That Rome should dote on: yet, by the faith of men,
We have some old crab-trees here at home that will not
Be grafted to your relish. Yet welcome, warriors:
We call a nettle but a nettle and
The faults of fools but folly.

Com. Ever right.

Cor. Menenius ever, ever.

clothes or boots. 102. **Deucalion,** the Greek Noah with whose name was connected the tradition of a flood. 103. **God-den,** good evening. 114. **prosperous approbation,** positive success. 115. **Take . . . Jupiter,** i.e., he tosses his cap in the air. 126-127. **make a lip,** make a contemptuous face. 128. **Galen,** Greek physician; he was not born until six hundred years after the time of Coriolanus. **empiricutic,** empirical, quacklike. **to,** compared to. 137. **On 's brows,** reference to the garland of oak leaves as a token of victory; see I, iii, 16. 144. **fidiused,** coined word from Aufidius. 146. **possessed,** informed. 149. **name,** credit, reputation. 157. **pow, waw,** pish. 164. **cicatrices,** scars. 165. **stand for his place,** seek the consulship. 166. **repulse of Tarquin.** Plutarch tells us that Marcius fought his first battle against King Tarquin the Proud in 499 B.C. on the occasion of Tarquin's last attempt to regain the kingdom. 177. **nervy,** sinewy. 181. **to,** added to. 192. **My gracious silence.** Old Arden editor suggests that this form of address was suggested by Plutarch's reference to Numa's designation of one of the muses as Tacita, or "Lady Silence." 197. **And . . . pardon.** F assigns to Cominius; some editors would also include in the speech, now assigned to Coriolanus, the words *I . . . turn.* 205. **crab-trees;** i.e., sour-natured old men. 206. **grafted to your relish,** improved by grafting until they like you. 209. **Menenius ever,** same old Menenius.

Herald. Give way there, and go on!
Cor. [*To Volumnia and Virgilia*] Your hand, and yours:
Ere in our own house I do shade my head,
The good patricians must be visited;
From whom I have receiv'd not only greetings,
But with them change of honours.
Vol. I have liv'd
To see inherited my very wishes
And the buildings of my fancy: only
There 's one thing wanting, which I doubt not but
Our Rome will cast upon thee.
Cor. Know, good mother,
I had rather be their servant in my way
Than sway with them in theirs.
Com. On, to the Capitol!

Flourish. Cornets. Exeunt in state, as before. Brutus and Sicinius [*come forward*].

Bru. All tongues speak of him, and the bleared sights
Are spectacled to see him: your prattling nurse
Into a rapture lets her baby cry
While she chats him: the kitchen malkin pins
Her richest lockram 'bout her reechy neck,
Clamb'ring the walls to eye him: stalls, bulks, windows,
Are smother'd up, leads fill'd, and ridges hors'd
With variable complexions, all agreeing
In earnestness to see him: seld-shown flamens
Do press among the popular throngs and puff
To win a vulgar station: our veil'd dames
Commit the war of white and damask in
Their nicely-gawded cheeks to th' wanton spoil
Of Phœbus' burning kisses: such a pother
As if that whatsoever god who leads him
Were slily crept into his human powers
And gave him graceful posture.
Sic. On the sudden,
I warrant him consul.
Bru. Then our office may,
During his power, go sleep.
Sic. He cannot temp'rately transport his honours
From where he should begin and end, but will
Lose those he hath won.
Bru. In that there 's comfort.
Sic. Doubt not
The commoners, for whom we stand, but they
Upon their ancient malice will forget
With the least cause these his new honours, which
That he will give them make I as little question
As he is proud to do 't.
Bru. I heard him swear,
Were he to stand for consul, never would he
Appear i' th' market-place nor on him put
The napless vesture of humility;
Nor, showing, as the manner is, his wounds
To th' people, beg their stinking breaths.
Sic. 'Tis right.
Bru. It was his word: O, he would miss it rather
Than carry it but by the suit of the gentry to him
And the desire of the nobles.
Sic. I wish no better
Than have him hold that purpose and to put it
In execution.
Bru. 'Tis most like he will.
Sic. It shall be to him then as our good wills,
A sure destruction.
Bru. So it must fall out
To him or our authorities. For an end,
We must suggest the people in what hatred
He still hath held them; that to 's power he would
Have made them mules, silenc'd their pleaders and
Dispropertied their freedoms, holding them,
In human action and capacity,
Of no more soul nor fitness for the world
Than camels in the war, who have their provand
Only for bearing burdens, and sore blows
For sinking under them.
Sic. This, as you say, suggested
At some time when his soaring insolence
Shall touch the people—which time shall not want,
If he be put upon 't; and that 's as easy
As to set dogs on sheep—will be his fire
To kindle their dry stubble; and their blaze
Shall darken him for ever.

Enter a Messenger.

Bru. What 's the matter?
Mess. You are sent for to the Capitol. 'Tis thought
That Marcius shall be consul:
I have seen the dumb men throng to see him and
The blind to hear him speak: matrons flung gloves,
Ladies and maids their scarfs and handkerchers,
Upon him as he pass'd: the nobles bended,
As to Jove's statue, and the commons made
A shower and thunder with their caps and shouts:
I never saw the like.
Bru. Let 's to the Capitol;
And carry with us ears and eyes for th' time,
But hearts for the event.
Sic. Have with you. *Exeunt.*

[SCENE II. *The same. The Capitol.*]

Enter two Officers, *to lay cushions, as it were in the Capitol.*

First Off. Come, come, they are almost here. How many stand for consulships?

Sec. Off. Three, they say: but 'tis thought of every one Coriolanus will carry it.

First Off. That 's a brave fellow; but he 's vengeance proud, and loves not the common people.

Sec. Off. Faith, there have been many great men that have flattered the people, who ne'er loved them;

214. **change of honours,** promotion. 215. **inherited,** realized. 220. **sway,** bear rule. 223. **rapture,** fit. 224. **chats,** gossips about. **malkin,** untidy servantmaid. 225. **lockram,** coarse linen fabric. **reechy,** dirty, filthy. 226. **bulks,** structures projecting from the front of a shop. 227. **leads,** roofs. **hors'd,** bestridden (as a horse). 228. **variable,** various. **complexions,** types. 229. **seld-shown,** rarely seen. **flamens,** priests of ancient Rome. 230. **popular,** plebeian, vulgar. 231. **vulgar station,** place in the crowd. 232-234. **Commit . . . kisses,** i.e., fine ladies expose themselves to the sun's rays. 233. **nicely-gawded,** daintily adorned. 234. **pother,** hubbub. 240-241. **He . . . end,** i.e., he cannot, as a temperate man could, carry his honors throughout his course. 245. **which,** i.e., provocation, cause. 246-247. **That . . . do 't,** i.e., I have no doubt that he will be proud to give provocation. 250. **napless,** threadbare. 254. **but,** otherwise than. 258. **as . . . wills,** as we should have it. 260. **authorities,** offices. **For an end,** to cut the matter short. 261. **suggest,** insinuate to (with implication of evil). 263. **made them mules,** made beasts of burden of them. 264. **Dispropertied,** alienated, deprived (them) of. 267. **provand,** provisions, food. 272. **put upon 't,** urged, incited to it. 273. **will . . . fire,** i.e., the spark that kindles his hatred. 285. **time,** present spectacle. 286. **hearts for the event,** i.e., their deeper desires and purposes will be for what is to follow.
SCENE II. 3. **of,** by. 4. **will carry it,** will win (the consulship).

and there be many that they have loved, they know not wherefore: so that, if they love they know not why, they hate upon no better a ground: therefore, for Coriolanus neither to care whether they love or hate him manifests the true knowledge he has in their disposition; and out of his noble carelessness lets them plainly see 't.

First Off. If he did not care whether he had their love or no, he waved indifferently 'twixt doing them neither good nor harm: but he seeks their hate with greater devotion than they can render it him; and leaves nothing undone that may fully discover him their opposite. Now, to seem to affect the malice and displeasure of the people is as bad as that which he dislikes, to flatter them for their love.

Sec. Off. He hath deserved worthily of his country: and his ascent is not by such easy degrees as those who, having been supple and courteous to the people, bonneted, without any further deed to have them at all into their estimation and report: but he hath so planted his honours in their eyes, and his actions in their hearts, that for their tongues to be silent, and not confess so much, were a kind of ingrateful injury; to report otherwise, were a malice, that, giving itself the lie, would pluck reproof and rebuke from every ear that heard it.

First Off. No more of him; he 's a worthy man: make way, they are coming.

A sennet. Enter the Patricians *and the* Tribunes *of the people,* Lictors *before them;* CORIOLANUS, MENENIUS, COMINIUS *the Consul.* SICINIUS *and* BRUTUS *take their places by themselves.* CORIOLANUS *stands.*

Men. Having determin'd of the Volsces and
To send for Titus Lartius, it remains,
As the main point of this our after-meeting,
To gratify his noble service that
Hath thus stood for his country: therefore, please you,
Most reverend and grave elders, to desire
The present consul, and last general
In our well-found successes, to report
A little of that worthy work perform'd
By Caius Marcius Coriolanus, whom
We met here both to thank and to remember
With honours like himself.
First Sen. Speak, good Cominius:
Leave nothing out for length, and make us think
Rather our state 's defective for requital
Than we to stretch it out. [*To the Tribunes*] Masters o' th' people,
We do request your kindest ears, and after,
Your loving motion toward the common body,
To yield what passes here.
Sic. We are convented
Upon a pleasing treaty, and have hearts
Inclinable to honour and advance
The theme of our assembly.
Bru. Which the rather
We shall be blest to do, if he remember
A kinder value of the people than
He hath hereto priz'd them at.
Men. That 's off, that 's off;
I would you rather had been silent. Please you
To hear Cominius speak?
Bru. Most willingly;
But yet my caution was more pertinent
Than the rebuke you give it.
Men. He loves your people;
But tie him not to be their bedfellow.
Worthy Cominius, speak.
Coriolanus rises and offers to go away.
Nay, keep your place.
First Sen. Sit, Coriolanus; never shame to hear
What you have nobly done.
Cor. Your honours' pardon:
I had rather have my wounds to heal again
Than hear say how I got them.
Bru. Sir, I hope
My words disbench'd you not.
Cor. No, sir: yet oft,
When blows have made me stay, I fled from words.
You sooth'd not, therefore hurt not: but your people,
I love them as they weigh.
Men. Pray now, sit down.
Cor. I had rather have one scratch my head i' th' sun
When the alarum were struck than idly sit
To hear my nothings monster'd. *Exit Corio.*
Men. Masters of the people,
Your multiplying spawn how can he flatter—
That 's thousand to one good one—when you now see
He had rather venture all his limbs for honour
Than one on 's ears to hear it? Proceed, Cominius.
Com. I shall lack voice: the deeds of Coriolanus
Should not be utter'd feebly. It is held
That valour is the chiefest virtue, and
Most dignifies the haver: if it be,
The man I speak of cannot in the world
Be singly counterpois'd. At sixteen years,
When Tarquin made a head for Rome, he fought
Beyond the mark of others: our then dictator,
Whom with all praise I point at, saw him fight,
When with his Amazonian chin he drove
The bristled lips before him: he bestrid
An o'er-press'd Roman and i' th' consul's view
Slew three opposers: Tarquin's self he met,
And struck him on his knee: in that day's feats,
When he might act the woman in the scene,
He prov'd best man i' th' field, and for his meed
Was brow-bound with the oak. His pupil age
Man-ent'red thus, he waxed like a sea,
And in the brunt of seventeen battles since
He lurch'd all swords of the garland. For this last,
Before and in Corioles, let me say,

15. **in,** concerning. 19. **waved indifferently,** would waver impartially. 23. **opposite,** adversary. 30. **bonneted,** took their hats off. 37. **giving . . . lie,** manifesting its own falsehood. 40. *Stage Direction:* **Lictors,** officials attendant upon Roman magistrates. 41. **determin'd of,** reached a decision concerning. 44. **gratify,** reward, requite. 48. **well-found,** fortunately met with. 51. **remember,** commemorate. 55. **stretch it out.** If *it* refers to the state, the meaning is "straining its resources for proper reward"; if *it* refers to *requital,* the meaning is "in our endeavors to extend reward until it match desert." 58. **yield,** grant. **passes,** is voted. **convented,** summoned, convened. 59. **treaty,** proposal. 61. **theme,** i.e., Coriolanus. 63. **kinder value,** more favorable estimation. 64. **That 's off,** that is not the question. 75. **disbench'd,** made (you) leave your seat. 78. **as they weigh,** according to their deserts. 80. **alarum were struck,** battle signal sounded. 81. **monster'd,** pointed at as wonderful. 83. **That 's . . . one,** in which there are a thousand bad ones to one good one. 89. **haver,** possessor. 91. **singly counterpois'd,** equaled by a single one. 93. **mark,** ability, reach. **dictator,** wartime leader. 95. **Amazonian,** beardless (like the female warriors, the Amazons). 97. **o'er-press'd,** overthrown. 99. **on,** to. 103. **Man-ent'red,** i.e., entered in the fashion of a man. 105. **lurch'd,** robbed, cheated.

I cannot speak him home: he stopp'd the fliers;
And by his rare example made the coward
Turn terror into sport: as weeds before
A vessel under sail, so men obey'd
And fell below his stem: his sword, death's stamp,
Where it did mark, it took; from face to foot
He was a thing of blood, whose every motion
Was tim'd with dying cries: alone he ent'red
The mortal gate of th' city, which he painted
With shunless destiny; aidless came off,
And with a sudden re-inforcement struck
Corioles like a planet: now all 's his:
When, by and by, the din of war gan pierce
His ready sense; then straight his doubled spirit
Re-quick'ned what in flesh was fatigate,
And to the battle came he; where he did
Run reeking o'er the lives of men, as if
'Twere a perpetual spoil: and till we call'd
Both field and city ours, he never stood
To ease his breast with panting.
Men. Worthy man!
First Sen. He cannot but with measure fit the honours
Which we devise him.
Com. Our spoils he kick'd at,
And look'd upon things precious as they were
The common muck of the world: he covets less
Than misery itself would give; rewards
His deeds with doing them, and is content
To spend the time to end it.
Men. He 's right noble:
Let him be call'd for.
First Sen. Call Coriolanus.
Off. He doth appear.

Enter Coriolanus.

Men. The senate, Coriolanus, are well pleas'd
To make thee consul.
Cor. I do owe them still
My life and services.
Men. It then remains
That you do speak to the people.
Cor. I do beseech you,
Let me o'erleap that custom, for I cannot
Put on the gown, stand naked and entreat them,
For my wounds' sake, to give their suffrage: please you
That I may pass this doing.
Sic. Sir, the people
Must have their voices; neither will they bate
One jot of ceremony.
Men. Put them not to 't:
Pray you, go fit you to the custom and
Take to you, as your predecessors have,
Your honour with your form.
Cor. It is a part
That I shall blush in acting, and might well
Be taken from the people.
Bru. [*To Sic.*] Mark you that?
Cor. To brag unto them, thus I did, and thus;
Show them th' unaching scars which I should hide,
As if I had receiv'd them for the hire
Of their breath only!
Men. Do not stand upon 't.
We recommend to you, tribunes of the people,
Our purpose to them: and to our noble consul
Wish we all joy and honour.
Senators. To Coriolanus come all joy and honour!
Flourish cornets. Then exeunt. Mane[n]t Sicinius and Brutus.
Bru. You see how he intends to use the people.
Sic. May they perceive 's intent! He will require them,
As if he did contemn what he requested
Should be in them to give.
Bru. Come, we'll inform them
Of our proceedings here: on th' market-place,
I know, they do attend us. [*Exeunt.*]

[scene iii. *The same. The Forum.*]

Enter seven or eight Citizens.

First Cit. Once, if he do require our voices, we ought not to deny him.

Sec. Cit. We may, sir, if we will.

Third Cit. We have power in ourselves to do it, but it is a power that we have no power to do; for if he show us his wounds and tell us his deeds, we are to put our tongues into those wounds and speak for them; so, if he tell us his noble deeds, we must also tell him our noble acceptance of them. Ingratitude is monstrous, and for the multitude to be ingrateful, were to make a monster of the multitude; of the which we being members, should bring ourselves to be monstrous members.

First Cit. And to make us no better thought of, a little help will serve; for once we stood up about the corn, he himself stuck not to call us the many-headed multitude.

Third Cit. We have been called so of many; not that our heads are some brown, some black, some abram, some bald, but that our wits are so diversely coloured: and truly I think if all our wits were to issue out of one skull, they would fly east, west, north, south, and their consent of one direct way should be at once to all the points o' the compass.

Sec. Cit. Think you so? Which way do you judge my wit would fly?

Third Cit. Nay, your wit will not so soon out as another man's will; 'tis strongly wedged up in a block-head, but if it were at liberty, 'twould, sure, southward.

Sec. Cit. Why that way?

Third Cit. To lose itself in a fog, where being three parts melted away with rotten dews, the fourth would return for conscience sake, to help to get thee a wife.

Sec. Cit. You are never without your tricks: you may, you may.

Third Cit. Are you all resolved to give your voices? But that 's no matter, the greater part carries it. I say,

107. **speak him home,** praise him properly. 111. **stem,** main timber of the prow of a ship. 112. **took,** took possession, slew. 114. **tim'd,** kept time with; Johnson explains: "The cries of the slaughter'd regularly followed his motion as music and a dancer accompany each other." 115-116. **painted . . . destiny,** stained with the blood of those who could not escape their doom (Brooke). 118. **like a planet,** reference to the power of striking or blasting believed to belong to the planets. 121. **fatigate,** wearied. 124. **spoil,** slaughter. 127. **with measure,** becomingly. 133. **end it,** i.e., kill time. 143. **pass,** neglect, disregard. **doing,** action. 145. **Put . . . to 't,** do not force the issue. 146. **fit you,** accommodate yourself. 148. **with your form,** i.e., with the accompanying conventionalities. 154. **breath,** votes. **stand upon 't,** make a point of it. 155. **recommend,** commit, consign. 160. **require,** ask, request. 161. **contemn,** scorn.

Scene iii. 1. **Once,** once for all. 16. **stuck not,** did not hesitate. 20. **abram,** auburn. 24. **consent of,** agreement upon. 32. **southward,** if he would incline to the people, there was never a worthier man.

Enter CORIOLANUS *in a gown of humility, with* MENENIUS.

Here he comes, and in the gown of humility: mark his behaviour. We are not to stay all together, but to come by him where he stands, by ones, by twos, and by threes. He 's to make his requests by particulars; wherein every one of us has a single honour, in giving him our own voices with our own tongues: therefore follow me, and I'll direct you how you shall go by him.

All. Content, content. [*Exeunt citizens.*]

Men. O sir, you are not right: have you not known
The worthiest men have done 't?
Cor. What must I say?
'I pray, sir,'—Plague upon 't! I cannot bring
My tongue to such a pace:—'Look, sir, my wounds!
I got them in my country's service, when
Some certain of your brethren roar'd and ran
From th' noise of our own drums.'
Men. O me, the gods!
You must not speak of that: you must desire them
To think upon you.
Cor. Think upon me! hang 'em!
I would they would forget me, like the virtues
Which our divines lose by 'em.
Men. You'll mar all:
I'll leave you: pray you, speak to 'em, I pray you,
In wholesome manner. *Exit.*
Cor. Bid them wash their faces
And keep their teeth clean.

Enter three of the Citizens.

So, here comes a brace.
You know the cause, sir, of my standing here.

Third Cit. We do, sir; tell us what hath brought you to 't.

Cor. Mine own desert.

Sec. Cit. Your own desert?

Cor. Ay, but not mine own desire.

Third Cit. How not your own desire?

Cor. No, sir, 'twas never my desire yet to trouble the poor with begging.

Third Cit. You must think, if we give you any thing, we hope to gain by you.

Cor. Well then, I pray, your price o' the consulship?

First Cit. The price is to ask it kindly.

Cor. Kindly! Sir, I pray, let me ha 't: I have wounds to show you, which shall be yours in private. Your good voice, sir; what say you?

Sec. Cit. You shall ha 't, worthy sir.

Cor. A match, sir. There 's in all two worthy voices begged. I have your alms: adieu.

Third Cit. But this is something odd.

Sec. Cit. An 'twere to give again,—but 'tis no matter. *Exeunt* [*the three Citizens*].

Enter two other Citizens.

Cor. Pray you now, if it may stand with the tune of your voices that I may be consul, I have here the customary gown.

Fourth Cit. You have deserved nobly of your country, and you have not deserved nobly.

Cor. Your enigma?

Fourth Cit. You have been a scourge to her enemies, you have been a rod to her friends; you have not indeed loved the common people.

Cor. You should account me the more virtuous that I have not been common in my love. I will, sir, flatter my sworn brother, the people, to earn a dearer estimation of them; 'tis a condition they account gentle: and since the wisdom of their choice is rather to have my hat than my heart, I will practise the insinuating nod and be off to them most counterfeitly; that is, sir, I will counterfeit the bewitchment of some popular man and give it bountiful to the desirers. Therefore, beseech you, I may be consul.

Fifth Cit. We hope to find you our friend; and therefore give you our voices heartily.

Fourth Cit. You have received many wounds for your country.

Cor. I will not seal your knowledge with showing them. I will make much of your voices, and so trouble you no farther.

Both Cit. The gods give you joy, sir, heartily! [*Exeunt.*]

Cor. Most sweet voices!
Better it is to die, better to starve,
Than crave the hire which first we do deserve.
Why in this woolvish toge should I stand here,
To beg of Hob and Dick, that does appear,
Their needless vouches? Custom calls me to 't:
What custom wills, in all things should we do 't,
The dust on antique time would lie unswept,
And mountainous error be too highly heapt
For truth to o'er-peer. Rather than fool it so,
Let the high office and the honour go
To one that would do thus. I am half through;
The one part suffer'd, the other will I do.

Enter three Citizens *more.*

Here come moe voices.
Your voices: for your voices I have fought;
Watch'd for your voices; for your voices bear
Of wounds two dozen odd; battles thrice six
I have seen and heard of; for your voices have
Done many things, some less, some more: your voices:
Indeed, I would be consul.

Sixth Cit. He has done nobly, and cannot go without any honest man's voice.

Seventh Cit. Therefore let him be consul: the gods give him joy, and make him good friend to the people!

All Cit. Amen, amen. God save thee, noble consul! [*Exeunt.*]

Cor. Worthy voices!

Enter MENENIUS, *with* BRUTUS *and* SICINIUS.

Men. You have stood your limitation; and the tribunes

allusion to the south wind bringing pestilence. 39. **you may,** go on, say what you like. 48. **by particulars,** one by one, in detail. 49. **single,** separate, individual. 57. **to such a pace,** i.e., gentle pace. 64. **lose by 'em,** vainly seek to propagate in them by preaching (Yale). 67. **brace,** pair (contemptuous). 91. **stand with,** be consistent with. 103. **dearer estimation of them,** higher esteem on their part. 107. **be off,** doff my hat. **counterfeitly,** hypocritically. 108. **bewitchment,** sorcery, hocus-pocus. 109. **popular man,** demagogue. **bountiful,** bountifully. 115. **seal,** confirm. 122. **woolvish toge.** The meaning seems to be wolf's toga with apparent allusion to wolf in sheep's clothing; *woolless* has also been suggested. 123. **Hob and Dick,** typical names for rustics. 124. **vouches,** confirmations. 128. **o'er-peer,** peep over (tradition). **fool it,** play the fool. 132. **moe voices,** more votes. 134. **Watch'd,** kept watches (in camp). 146. **limitation,** allotted time.

Endue you with the people's voice: remains
That, in th' official marks invested, you
Anon do meet the senate.
Cor. Is this done?
Sic. The custom of request you have discharg'd:
The people do admit you, and are summon'd
To meet anon, upon your approbation.
Cor. Where? at the senate-house?
Sic. There, Coriolanus.
Cor. May I change these garments?
Sic. You may, sir.
Cor. That I'll straight do; and, knowing myself again,
Repair to th' senate-house.
Men. I'll keep you company. Will you along?
Bru. We stay here for the people.
Sic. Fare you well.
Exeunt Coriolanus and Menenius.
He has it now, and by his looks methinks
'Tis warm at 's heart.
Bru. With a proud heart he wore his humble weeds.
Will you dismiss the people?

Enter the Plebeians.

Sic. How now, my masters! have you chose this man?
First Cit. He has our voices, sir.
Bru. We pray the gods he may deserve your loves.
Sec. Cit. Amen, sir: to my poor unworthy notice,
He mock'd us when he begg'd our voices.
Third Cit. Certainly
He flouted us downright.
First Cit. No, 'tis his kind of speech: he did not mock us.
Sec. Cit. Not one amongst us, save yourself, but says
He us'd us scornfully: he should have show'd us
His marks of merit, wounds receiv'd for 's country.
Sic. Why, so he did, I am sure.
Citizens. No, no; no man saw 'em.
Third Cit. He said he had wounds, which he could show in private;
And with his hat, thus waving it in scorn,
'I would be consul,' says he: 'aged custom,
But by your voices, will not so permit me;
Your voices therefore.' When we granted that,
Here was 'I thank you for your voices: thank you:
Your most sweet voices: now you have left your voices,
I have no further with you.' Was not this mockery?
Sic. Why either were you ignorant to see 't,
Or, seeing it, of such childish friendliness
To yield your voices?
Bru. Could you not have told him
As you were lesson'd, when he had no power,
But was a petty servant to the state,
He was your enemy, ever spake against
Your liberties and the charters that you bear
I' th' body of the weal; and now, arriving
A place of potency and sway o' th' state,
If he should still malignantly remain
Fast foe to th' plebii, your voices might
Be curses to yourselves? You should have said
That as his worthy deeds did claim no less
Than what he stood for, so his gracious nature
Would think upon you for your voices and
Translate his malice towards you into love,
Standing your friendly lord.
Sic. Thus to have said,
As you were fore-advis'd, had touch'd his spirit
And tried his inclination; from him pluck'd
Either his gracious promise, which you might,
As cause had call'd you up, have held him to;
Or else it would have gall'd his surly nature,
Which easily endures not article
Tying him to aught; so putting him to rage,
You should have ta'en th' advantage of his choler
And pass'd him unelected.
Bru. Did you perceive
He did solicit you in free contempt
When he did need your loves, and do you think
That his contempt shall not be bruising to you,
When he hath power to crush? Why, had your bodies
No heart among you? or had you tongues to cry
Against the rectorship of judgement?
Sic. Have you
Ere now denied the asker? and now again
Of him that did not ask, but mock, bestow
Your sued-for tongues?
Third Cit. He 's not confirm'd; we may deny him yet.
Sec. Cit. And will deny him:
I'll have five hundred voices of that sound.
First Cit. I twice five hundred and their friends to piece 'em.
Bru. Get you hence instantly, and tell those friends,
They have chose a consul that will from them take
Their liberties; make them of no more voice
Than dogs that are as often beat for barking
As therefore kept to do so.
Sic. Let them assemble,
And on a safer judgement all revoke
Your ignorant election; enforce his pride,
And his old hate unto you; besides, forget not
With what contempt he wore the humble weed,
How in his suit he scorn'd you; but your loves,
Thinking upon his services, took from you
Th' apprehension of his present portance,
Which most gibingly, ungravely, he did fashion
After the inveterate hate he bears you.
Bru. Lay
A fault on us, your tribunes; that we labour'd,
No impediment between, but that you must
Cast your election on him.
Sic. Say, you chose him
More after our commandment than as guided
By your own true affections, and that your minds,
Pre-occupied with what you rather must do
Than what you should, made you against the grain
To voice him consul: lay the fault on us.
Bru. Ay, spare us not. Say we read lectures to you,

147. **Endue,** endow (as with some quality). **remains,** it remains. 160. **'Tis . . . heart,** it warms his heart. 182. **ignorant,** too dull. 188. **charters,** privileges. 189. **weal,** commonwealth. **arriving,** attaining. 192. **plebeii,** plebeians; common people of ancient Rome. 196. **think upon,** esteem. 199. **touch'd,** tested (as gold and silver were tested with the touchstone). 202. **call'd you up,** aroused you. 204. **article,** stipulation, condition. 208. **free,** frank. 212. **heart,** i.e., as seat of courage. 212-213. **cry . . . judgement.** He asks if their tongues rebelled against the supremacy of their judgments or reason. 215. **Of,** upon. 220. **piece,** add to, reinforce. 227. **enforce,** lay stress upon. 232. **apprehension,** physical perception. **portance,** behavior. 234. **After,** in accord with. 236. **No impediment between,** without admitting any impediment. 246-253. **The . . . ancestor.** Plutarch recites noble names from the roll of the house of the Marcians; Shakespeare, declaring them ancestors to Marcius, has put down names of persons who lived long after his hero. 251-252. **And . . . censor.** The bracketed

How youngly he began to serve his country,
How long continued, and what stock he springs of,
The noble house o' th' Marcians, from whence came
That Ancus Marcius, Numa's daughter's son,
Who, after great Hostilius, here was king;
Of the same house Publius and Quintus were,
That our best water brought by conduits hither;
And [Censorinus,] nobly named so,
Twice being [by the people chosen] censor,
Was his great ancestor.
Sic. One thus descended,
That hath beside well in his person wrought
To be set high in place, we did commend
To your remembrances: but you have found,
Scaling his present bearing with his past,
That he 's your fixed enemy, and revoke
Your sudden approbation.
Bru. Say, you ne'er had done 't—
Harp on that still—but by our putting on:
And presently, when you have drawn your number,
Repair to th' Capitol.
All. We will so: almost all
Repent in their election. *Exeunt Plebeians.*
Bru. Let them go on;
This mutiny were better put in hazard,
Than stay, past doubt, for greater:
If, as his nature is, he fall in rage
With their refusal, both observe and answer
The vantage of his anger.
Sic. To th' Capitol, come:
We will be there before the stream o' th' people;
And this shall seem, as partly 'tis, their own,
Which we have goaded onward. *Exeunt.*

ACT III.

[SCENE I. *Rome. A street.*]

Cornets. Enter CORIOLANUS, MENENIUS, *all the Gentry,* COMINIUS, TITUS LARTIUS, *and other* Senators.

Cor. Tullus Aufidius then had made new head?
Lart. He had, my lord; and that it was which caus'd
Our swifter composition.
Cor. So then the Volsces stand but as at first,
Ready, when time shall prompt them, to make road
Upon 's again.
Com. They are worn, lord consul, so,
That we shall hardly in our ages see
Their banners wave again.
Cor. Saw you Aufidius?
Lart. On safe-guard he came to me; and did curse
Against the Volsces, for they had so vilely
Yielded the town: he is retir'd to Antium.
Cor. Spoke he of me?
Lart. He did, my lord.
Cor. How? what?
Lart. How often he had met you, sword to sword;
That of all things upon the earth he hated
Your person most, that he would pawn his fortunes
To hopeless restitution, so he might
Be call'd your vanquisher.
Cor. At Antium lives he?
Lart. At Antium.
Cor. I wish I had a cause to seek him there,
To oppose his hatred fully. Welcome home.

Enter SICINIUS *and* BRUTUS.

Behold, these are the tribunes of the people,
The tongues o' th' common mouth: I do despise them;
For they do prank them in authority,
Against all noble sufferance.
Sic. Pass no further.
Cor. Ha! what is that?
Bru. It will be dangerous to go on: no further.
Cor. What makes this change?
Men. The matter?
Com. Hath he not pass'd the noble and the common?
Bru. Cominius, no.
Cor. Have I had children's voices?
First Sen. Tribunes, give way; he shall to th' market-place.
Bru. The people are incens'd against him.
Sic. Stop,
Or all will fall in broil.
Cor. Are these your herd?
Must these have voices, that can yield them now
And straight disclaim their tongues? What are your offices?
You being their mouths, why rule you not their teeth?
Have you not set them on?
Men. Be calm, be calm.
Cor. It is a purpos'd thing, and grows by plot,
To curb the will of the nobility:
Suffer 't, and live with such as cannot rule
Nor ever will be rul'd.
Bru. Call 't not a plot:
The people cry you mock'd them, and of late,
When corn was given them gratis, you repin'd;
Scandal'd the suppliants for the people, call'd them
Time-pleasers, flatterers, foes to nobleness.
Cor. Why, this was known before.
Bru. Not to them all.
Cor. Have you inform'd them sithence?
Bru. How! I inform them!
Com. You are like to do such business.
Bru. Not unlike,
Each way, to better yours.
Cor. Why then should I be consul? By yond clouds,
Let me deserve so ill as you, and make me
Your fellow tribune.
Sic. You show too much of that
For which the people stir: if you will pass
To where you are bound, you must inquire your way,
Which you are out of, with a gentler spirit,
Or never be so noble as a consul,
Nor yoke with him for tribune.

parts of these lines have been supplied by editors from Plutarch. Some editors follow Delius, who inserts in line 251 the words: *Censorinus who that was so surnam'd.* 257. **Scaling,** estimating, balancing. 260. **putting on,** urging. 261. **drawn,** assembled, collected. 263. **in,** of. 264. **put in hazard,** risk (infinitive). 267-268. **answer The vantage,** make use.

ACT III. SCENE I. 1. **made new head,** raised another army. 5. **road,** raid, attack. 16. **To hopeless restitution,** beyond hope of redemption.

23. **prank them,** dress themselves up. 24. **Against . . . sufferance,** beyond the power of nobility to suffer. 30. **children's voices,** votes like those of children; i.e., to be given and taken away lightly. 35. **tongues,** votes. 38. **purpos'd,** schemed, got up for the occasion. 44. **Scandal'd,** defamed. 47. **sithence,** since. 48. **You . . . business,** assigned by Theobald to Coriolanus. 48-49. **Not . . . yours,** not unlikely to prove, in any case, a better way than yours. 52. **that,** i.e., the quality of tyranny.

Men. Let 's be calm.
Com. The people are abus'd; set on. This palt'ring
Becomes not Rome, nor has Coriolanus
Deserv'd this so dishonour'd rub, laid falsely
I' th' plain way of his merit.
Cor. Tell me of corn!
This was my speech, and I will speak 't again—
Men. Not now, not now.
First Sen. Not in this heat, sir, now.
Cor. Now, as I live, I will. My nobler friends,
I crave their pardons:
For the mutable, rank-scented many, let them
Regard me as I do not flatter, and
Therein behold themselves: I say again,
In soothing them, we nourish 'gainst our senate
The cockle of rebellion, insolence, sedition,
Which we ourselves have plough'd for, sow'd, and scatter'd,
By mingling them with us, the honour'd number,
Who lack not virtue, no, nor power, but that
Which they have given to beggars.
Men. Well, no more.
First Sen. No more words, we beseech you.
Cor. How! no more!
As for my country I have shed my blood,
Not fearing outward force, so shall my lungs
Coin words till their decay against those measles,
Which we disdain should tetter us, yet sought
The very way to catch them.
Bru. You speak o' th' people,
As if you were a god to punish, not
A man of their infirmity.
Sic. 'Twere well
We let the people know 't.
Men. What, what? his choler?
Cor. Choler!
Were I as patient as the midnight sleep,
By Jove, 'twould be my mind!
Sic. It is a mind
That shall remain a poison where it is,
Not poison any further.
Cor. Shall remain!
Hear you this Triton of the minnows? mark you
His absolute 'shall'?
Com. 'Twas from the canon.
Cor. 'Shall'!
O good but most unwise patricians! why,
You grave but reckless senators, have you thus
Given Hydra here to choose an officer,
That with his peremptory 'shall,' being but
The horn and noise o' th' monster's, wants not spirit
To say he'll turn your current in a ditch,
And make your channel his? If he have power,
Then vail your ignorance; if none, awake
Your dangerous lenity. If you are learn'd,
Be not as common fools; if you are not,
Let them have cushions by you. You are plebeians,
If they be senators: and they are no less,
When, both your voices blended, the great'st taste
Most palates theirs. They choose their magistrate,
And such a one as he, who puts his 'shall,'
His popular 'shall,' against a graver bench
Than ever frown'd in Greece. By Jove himself!
It makes the consuls base: and my soul aches
To know, when two authorities are up,
Neither supreme, how soon confusion
May enter 'twixt the gap of both and take
The one by th' other.
Com. Well, on to th' market-place.
Cor. Whoever gave that counsel, to give forth
The corn o' th' storehouse gratis, as 'twas us'd
Sometime in Greece,—
Men. Well, well, no more of that.
Cor. Though there the people had more absolute pow'r,
I say, they nourish'd disobedience, fed
The ruin of the state.
Bru. Why, shall the people give
One that speaks thus their voice?
Cor. I'll give my reasons,
More worthier than their voices. They know the corn
Was not our recompense, resting well assur'd
They ne'er did service for 't: being press'd to th' war,
Even when the navel of the state was touch'd,
They would not thread the gates. This kind of service
Did not deserve corn gratis. Being i' th' war,
Their mutinies and revolts, wherein they show'd
Most valour, spoke not for them: th' accusation
Which they have often made against the senate,
All cause unborn, could never be the native
Of our so frank donation. Well, what then?
How shall this bosom multiplied digest
The senate's courtesy? Let deeds express
What 's like to be their words: 'We did request it;
We are the greater poll, and in true fear
They gave us our demands.' Thus we debase
The nature of our seats and make the rabble
Call our cares fears; which will in time
Break ope the locks o' th' senate and bring in
The crows to peck the eagles.
Men. Come, enough.
Bru. Enough, with over-measure.
Cor. No, take more:
What may be sworn by, both divine and human,
Seal what I end withal! This double worship,
Where one part does disdain with cause, the other
Insult without all reason, where gentry, title, wisdom,
Cannot conclude but by the yea and no
Of general ignorance,—it must omit
Real necessities, and give way the while
To unstable slightness: purpose so barr'd, it follows,
Nothing is done to purpose. Therefore, beseech you,—
You that will be less fearful than discreet,
That love the fundamental part of state
More than you doubt the change on 't, that prefer
A noble life before a long, and wish

58. **set on,** incited. 60. **dishonour'd,** dishonoring. 66-68. **For . . . themselves,** as for the changeable, rank-scented multitude, let them learn what they are from my unflattering attitude of hostility. 66. **many.** F: *Meynie*, retained by some editors as the word *meiny*, household retinue, multitude. 70. **cockle,** a weed (darnel); thought to be the same as the scriptural tares. 78. **measles,** loathsome disease spots. 79. **tetter,** affect with tetter (skin eruption). 86. **mind,** resolved opinion. 89. **Triton of the minnows,** god of the little fishes; Triton was Neptune's son and trumpeter. 90. **from the canon,** beyond the law. 93. **Given,** permitted. **Hydra,** many-headed monster slain by Hercules; here the mob. 95. **horn and noise,** noisy horn; see allusion to Triton above. 98. **vail your ignorance,** let your ignorant yielding of power to him bow down. 98-99. **awake . . . lenity,** arouse yourselves from your dangerous mildness. 101. **cushions,** seats. 102-104. **and . . . theirs,** and they are to all intents and purposes senators if, when their voices are mingled with yours, the resulting action savors of them rather than of you. 109. **up,** established. 111. **gap of both,** cleavage between the two. 121. **our recompense,** reward from us. 123. **navel,** vital center. 124. **thread,** pass through. 129. **unborn,** nonexistent. **native,** natural source or origin. Sometimes emended to *motive*, as in

†To jump a body with a dangerous physic
That 's sure of death without it, at once pluck out
The multitudinous tongue; let them not lick
The sweet which is their poison: your dishonour
Mangles true judgement and bereaves the state
Of that integrity which should become 't,
Not having the power to do the good it would,
For th' ill which doth control 't.
Bru. Has said enough.
Sic. Has spoken like a traitor, and shall answer
As traitors do.
Cor. Thou wretch, despite o'erwhelm thee!
What should the people do with these bald tribunes?
On whom depending, their obedience fails
To th' greater bench: in a rebellion,
When what 's not meet, but what must be, was law,
Then were they chosen: in a better hour,
Let what is meet be said it must be meet,
And throw their power i' th' dust.
Bru. Manifest treason!
Sic. This a consul? no.
Bru. The ædiles, ho!

Enter an Ædile.

Let him be apprehended.
Sic. Go, call the people: [*Exit Ædile*] in whose name myself
Attach thee as a traitorous innovator,
A foe to th' public weal: obey, I charge thee,
And follow to thine answer.
Cor. Hence, old goat!
Senators, &c. We'll surety him.
Com. Aged sir, hands off.
Cor. Hence, rotten thing! or I shall shake thy bones
Out of thy garments.
Sic. Help, ye citizens!

Enter a rabble of Plebeians, with the Ædiles.

Men. On both sides more respect.
Sic. Here 's he that would take from you all your power.
Bru. Seize him, ædiles!
Citizens. Down with him! down with him!
Sec. Sen. Weapons, weapons, weapons!
They all bustle about Coriolanus, [*crying*]
'Tribunes!' 'Patricians!' 'Citizens!' 'What, ho!'
'Sicinius!' 'Brutus!' 'Coriolanus!' 'Citizens!'
'Peace, peace, peace!' 'Stay, hold, peace!'
Men. What is about to be? I am out of breath;
Confusion 's near; I cannot speak. You, tribunes
To th' people! Coriolanus, patience!
Speak, good Sicinius.
Sic. Hear me, people; peace!
Citizens. Let 's hear our tribune: peace! Speak, speak, speak.
Sic. You are at point to lose your liberties:
Marcius would have all from you; Marcius,
Whom late you have nam'd for consul.
Men. Fie, fie, fie!
This is the way to kindle, not to quench.
First Sen. To unbuild the city and to lay all flat.
Sic. What is the city but the people?
Citizens. True,
The people are the city.
Bru. By the consent of all, we were establish'd
The people's magistrates.
Citizens. You so remain.
Men. And so are like to do.
Com. That is the way to lay the city flat;
To bring the roof to the foundation,
And bury all, which yet distinctly ranges,
In heaps and piles of ruin.
Sic. This deserves death.
Bru. Or let us stand to our authority,
Or let us lose it. We do here pronounce,
Upon the part o' th' people, in whose power
We were elected theirs, Marcius is worthy
Of present death.
Sic. Therefore lay hold of him;
Bear him to th' rock Tarpeian, and from thence
Into destruction cast him.
Bru. Ædiles, seize him!
Citizens. Yield, Marcius, yield!
Men. Hear me one word;
Beseech you, tribunes, hear me but a word.
Æd. Peace, peace!
Men. [*To Brutus*] Be that you seem, truly your country's friend,
And temp'rately proceed to what you would
Thus violently redress.
Bru. Sir, those cold ways,
That seem like prudent helps, are very poisonous
Where the disease is violent. Lay hands upon him,
And bear him to the rock.
Cor. No, I'll die here.
Coriolanus draws his sword.
There 's some among you have beheld me fighting:
Come, try upon yourselves what you have seen me.
Men. Down with that sword! Tribunes, withdraw awhile.
Bru. Lay hands upon him.
Men. Help Marcius, help,
You that be noble; help him, young and old!
Citizens. Down with him, down with him!
In this mutiny, the Tribunes, the Ædiles, and the People, are beat in.
Men. Go, get you to your house; be gone, away!
All will be naught else.
Sec. Sen. Get you gone.
Com. Stand fast;
We have as many friends as enemies.
Men. Shall it be put to that?
First Sen. The gods forbid!
I prithee, noble friend, home to thy house;
Leave us to cure this cause.
Men. For 'tis a sore upon us,

Globe. 131. **bosom multiplied,** many-bosomed beast. Sometimes emended to *bisson multitude,* as in Globe. 140. **over-measure,** excess. 141-142. **What . . . Seal,** may all divine and human sanctities approve. 142. **double worship,** divided authority. 145. **conclude,** come to a final conclusion. 148. **slightness,** trivialities. **purpose so barr'd,** planning being thus obstructed. 150. **less . . . discreet,** less actuated by fear than by foresight. 151-152. **That . . . on 't,** that love the essentials of our government more than you fear the troubles arising when attempt is made to change it. 154. **jump,** risk. 157. **sweet,** i.e., power. 161. **Has,** he has. 164. **despite,** scorn. 167. **bench,** senators collectively. 168. **what 's . . . be,** unfitting but inevitable necessity. 173. **ædiles,** officers attached to the tribunes. 177. **answer,** defense, answer to a charge. 178. **surety,** go bail for. 206. **distinctly ranges,** stretches out in proper order. 213. **rock Tarpeian,** famous precipice on the Capitoline Hill in ancient Rome from which persons condemned for treason were thrown down. 225. **seen me,** i.e., seen me do. 231. **naught else,** lost or ruined otherwise.

You cannot tent yourself: be gone, beseech you.
Com. Come, sir, along with us.
Cor. I would they were barbarians— as they are,
Though in Rome litter'd—not Romans—as they are not,
Though calved i' th' porch o' th' Capitol—
Men. Be gone;
Put not your worthy rage into your tongue;
One time will owe another.
Cor. On fair ground
I could beat forty of them.
Men. I could myself
Take up a brace o' th' best of them; yea, the two tribunes.
Com. But now 'tis odds beyond arithmetic;
And manhood is call'd foolery, when it stands
Against a falling fabric. Will you hence,
Before the tag return? whose rage doth rend
Like interrupted waters and o'erbear
What they are us'd to bear.
Men. Pray you, be gone:
I'll try whether my old wit be in request
With those that have but little: this must be patch'd
With cloth of any colour.
Com. Nay, come away.
Exeunt Coriolanus and Cominius [*with others*].
A Patrician. This man has marr'd his fortune.
Men. His nature is too noble for the world:
He would not flatter Neptune for his trident,
Or Jove for 's power to thunder. His heart 's his mouth:
What his breast forges, that his tongue must vent;
And, being angry, does forget that ever
He heard the name of death. *A noise within.*
Here 's goodly work!
A Patrician. I would they were a-bed!
Men. I would they were in Tiber! What the vengeance!
Could he not speak 'em fair?

Enter Brutus *and* Sicinius, *with the rabble again.*

Sic. Where is this viper
That would depopulate the city and
Be every man himself?
Men. You worthy tribunes,—
Sic. He shall be thrown down the Tarpeian rock
With rigorous hands: he hath resisted law,
And therefore law shall scorn him further trial
Than the severity of the public power
Which he so sets at nought.
First Cit. He shall well know
The noble tribunes are the people's mouths,
And we their hands.
Citizens. He shall, sure on 't.
Men. Sir, sir,—
Sic. Peace!
Men. Do not cry havoc, where you should but hunt
With modest warrant.
Sic. Sir, how comes 't that you
Have holp to make this rescue?
Men. Hear me speak:
As I do know the consul's worthiness,
So can I name his faults,—
Sic. Consul! what consul?
Men. The consul Coriolanus.
Bru. He consul!
Citizens. No, no, no, no, no.
Men. If, by the tribunes' leave, and yours, good people,
I may be heard, I would crave a word or two;
The which shall turn you to no further harm
Than so much loss of time.
Sic. Speak briefly then;
For we are peremptory to dispatch
This viperous traitor: to eject him hence
Were but one danger, and to keep him here
Our certain death: therefore it is decreed
He dies to-night.
Men. Now the good gods forbid
That our renowned Rome, whose gratitude
Towards her deserved children is enroll'd
In Jove's own book, like an unnatural dam
Should now eat up her own!
Sic. He 's a disease that must be cut away.
Men. O, he 's a limb that has but a disease;
Mortal, to cut it off; to cure it, easy.
What has he done to Rome that 's worthy death?
Killing our enemies, the blood he hath lost—
Which, I dare vouch, is more than that he hath,
By many an ounce—he dropp'd it for his country;
And what is left, to lose it by his country,
Were to us all, that do 't and suffer it,
A brand to th' end o' th' world.
Sic. This is clean kam.
Bru. Merely awry: when he did love his country,
It honour'd him.
Men. The service of the foot
Being once gangren'd, is not then respected
For what before it was.
Bru. We'll hear no more.
Pursue him to his house, and pluck him thence;
Lest his infection, being of catching nature,
Spread further.
Men. One word more, one word.
This tiger-footed rage, when it shall find
The harm of unscann'd swiftness, will too late
Tie leaden pounds to 's heels. Proceed by process;
Lest parties, as he is belov'd, break out,
And sack great Rome with Romans.
Bru. If it were so,—
Sic. What do ye talk?
Have we not had a taste of his obedience?
Our ædiles smote? ourselves resisted? Come.
Men. Consider this: he has been bred i' th' wars
Since 'a could draw a sword, and is ill school'd
In bolted language; meal and bran together
He throws without distinction. Give me leave,
I'll go to him, and undertake to bring him

236. **tent,** treat, cure. 242. **One . . . another,** i.e., this occasion of the people's rebelling will be made up for on another occasion. 244. **Take up,** cope with. 245. **arithmetic,** computation. 248. **tag,** rabble. 249. **interrupted,** obstructed. 252-253. **this . . . colour,** we cannot be particular, we must use the roughest remedies. 259. **does,** he does. 263. **viper,** used in allusion to the parent-devouring attributes of the viper. 269. **severity,** i.e., exposure to severity. 275. **cry havoc,** originally to give the order to pillage. 276. **modest warrant,** i.e., as moderation warrants. 286. **peremptory,** determined. 293. **Jove's own book,** explained by Gordon as the rolls and registers of the Capitol, which was Jupiter's temple. 304. **brand,** i.e., of infamy. **clean kam,** quite perverse. 306-308. **The . . . was.** This speech is sometimes assigned to Sicinius or to Brutus; if spoken by Menenius, it is to be understood as ironical. 313. **unscann'd,** inconsiderate. 314. **pounds,** weights. **process,** legal method. 322. **bolted,** refined.

Scene ii. 2. **wheel,** instrument of torture and death by which the

Where he shall answer, by a lawful form,
In peace, to his utmost peril.
First Sen. Noble tribunes,
It is the humane way: the other course
Will prove too bloody, and the end of it
Unknown to the beginning.
Sic. Noble Menenius,
Be you then as the people's officer.
Masters, lay down your weapons.
Bru. Go not home.
Sic. Meet on the market-place. We'll attend you there:
Where, if you bring not Marcius, we'll proceed
In our first way.
Men. I'll bring him to you.
[*To the Senators*] Let me desire your company: he must come,
Or what is worst will follow.
First Sen. Pray you, let 's to him. *Exeunt omnes.*

[SCENE II. *A room in Coriolanus' house.*]

Enter CORIOLANUS *with* Nobles.

Cor. Let them pull all about mine ears, present me
Death on the wheel or at wild horses' heels,
Or pile ten hills on the Tarpeian rock,
That the precipitation might down stretch
Below the beam of sight, yet will I still
Be thus to them.
A Patrician. You do the nobler.
Cor. I muse my mother
Does not approve me further, who was wont
To call them woollen vassals, things created
To buy and sell with groats, to show bare heads
In congregations, to yawn, be still and wonder,
When one but of my ordinance stood up
To speak of peace or war.

Enter VOLUMNIA.

I talk of you:
Why did you wish me milder? would you have me
False to my nature? Rather say I play
The man I am.
Vol. O, sir, sir, sir,
I would have had you put your power well on,
Before you had worn it out.
Cor. Let go.
Vol. You might have been enough the man you are,
With striving less to be so: lesser had been
The thwartings of your dispositions, if
You had not show'd them how ye were dispos'd
Ere they lack'd power to cross you.
Cor. Let them hang.
Vol. Ay, and burn too.

Enter MENENIUS *with the* Senators.

Men. Come, come, you have been too rough, something too rough;
You must return and mend it.
First Sen. There 's no remedy;
Unless, by not so doing, our good city
Cleave in the midst, and perish.
Vol. Pray, be counsell'd:
†I have a heart as little apt as yours,
But yet a brain that leads my use of anger
To better vantage.
Men. Well said, noble woman!
Before he should thus stoop to th' herd, but that
The violent fit o' th' time craves it as physic
For the whole state, I would put mine armour on,
Which I can scarcely bear.
Cor. What must I do?
Men. Return to th' tribunes.
Cor. Well, what then? what then?
Men. Repent what you have spoke.
Cor. For them? I cannot do it to the gods;
Must I then do 't to them?
Vol. You are too absolute;
Though therein you can never be too noble,
But when extremities speak. I have heard you say,
Honour and policy, like unsever'd friends,
I' th' war do grow together: grant that, and tell me,
In peace what each of them by th' other lose,
That they combine not there.
Cor. Tush, tush!
Men. A good demand.
Vol. If it be honour in your wars to seem
The same you are not, which, for your best ends,
You adopt your policy, how is it less or worse,
That it shall hold companionship in peace
With honour, as in war, since that to both
It stands in like request?
Cor. Why force you this?
Vol. Because that now it lies you on to speak
To th' people; not by your own instruction,
Nor by th' matter which your heart prompts you,
But with such words that are but roted in
Your tongue, though but bastards and syllables
Of no allowance to your bosom's truth.
Now, this no more dishonours you at all
Than to take in a town with gentle words,
Which else would put you to your fortune and
The hazard of much blood.
I would dissemble with my nature where
My fortunes and my friends at stake requir'd
I should do so in honour: I am in this,
Your wife, your son, these senators, the nobles;
And you will rather show our general louts
How you can frown than spend a fawn upon 'em,
For the inheritance of their loves and safeguard
Of what that want might ruin.
Men. Noble lady!
Come, go with us; speak fair: you may salve so,
Not what is dangerous present, but the loss
Of what is past.
Vol. I prithee now, my son,

victim's limbs were broken. 5. **beam,** range. 9. **woollen,** coarsely clad. 11. **yawn,** i.e., with amazement. 12. **ordinance,** rank. 18. **Let go,** enough. 23. **Ere . . . you,** i.e., until you became consul and had power to crush them. 29. **apt,** compliant. 39. **absolute,** arbitrary. 41. **But . . . speak,** except when necessity requires. 42. **Honour and policy,** the search for fame and the proper consideration of stratagem and craft; these are the two cardinal points in the teaching of leaders in war as it was presented in books on the art of war. 46-51. **If . . . request.** Volumnia endeavors to carry over the principles of the art of war into the conduct of peacetime. 52. **lies you on,** is your duty. 55. **are but roted in,** have learned by rote; so Malone; F: *roated;* Johnson conjectured *rooted.* 57. **Of no allowance to,** unsanctioned by. 59. **take in,** capture. 60. **fortune,** i.e., of war. 64-65. **I . . . wife,** in this I represent your wife. 66. **general louts,** vulgar clowns. 68. **safeguard,** for the defense. 71-72. **Not . . . past,** not only the present danger but what has been lost already.

Go to them, with this bonnet in thy hand;
And thus far having stretch'd it—here be with them—
Thy knee bussing the stones—for in such business
Action is eloquence, and the eyes of th' ignorant
More learned than the ears—waving thy head,
Which often, thus, correcting thy stout heart,
Now humble as the ripest mulberry
That will not hold the handling: or say to them,
Thou art their soldier, and being bred in broils
Hast not the soft way which, thou dost confess,
Were fit for thee to use as they to claim,
In asking their good loves, but thou wilt frame
Thyself, forsooth, hereafter theirs, so far
As thou hast power and person.

Men. This but done,
Even as she speaks, why, their hearts were yours;
For they have pardons, being ask'd, as free
As words to little purpose.

Vol. Prithee now,
Go, and be rul'd: although I know thou hadst rather
Follow thine enemy in a fiery gulf
Than flatter him in a bower.

Enter COMINIUS.

Here is Cominius.

Com. I have been i' th' market-place; and, sir, 'tis fit
You make strong party, or defend yourself
By calmness or by absence: all 's in anger.

Men. Only fair speech.

Com. I think 'twill serve, if he
Can thereto frame his spirit.

Vol. He must, and will.
Prithee now, say you will, and go about it.

Cor. Must I go show them my unbarb'd sconce? Must I
With my base tongue give to my noble heart
A lie that it must bear? Well, I will do 't:
Yet, were there but this single plot to lose,
This mould of Marcius, they to dust should grind it
And throw 't against the wind. To th' market-place!
You have put me now to such a part which never
I shall discharge to th' life.

Com. Come, come, we'll prompt you.

Vol. I prithee now, sweet son, as thou hast said
My praises made thee first a soldier, so,
To have my praise for this, perform a part
Thou hast not done before.

Cor. Well, I must do 't:
Away, my disposition, and possess me
Some harlot's spirit! my throat of war be turn'd,
Which quired with my drum, into a pipe
Small as an eunuch, or the virgin voice
That babies lulls asleep! the smiles of knaves
Tent in my cheeks, and schoolboys' tears take up
The glasses of my sight! a beggar's tongue
Make motion through my lips, and my arm'd knees,
Who bow'd but in my stirrup, bend like his
That hath receiv'd an alms! I will not do 't,
Lest I surcease to honour mine own truth
And by my body's action teach my mind
A most inherent baseness.

Vol. At thy choice, then:
To beg of thee, it is my more dishonour
Than thou of them. Come all to ruin; let
Thy mother rather feel thy pride than fear
Thy dangerous stoutness, for I mock at death
With as big heart as thou. Do as thou list.
Thy valiantness was mine, thou suck'dst it from me,
But owe thy pride thyself.

Cor. Pray, be content:
Mother, I am going to the market-place;
Chide me no more. I'll mountebank their loves,
Cog their hearts from them, and come home belov'd
Of all the trades in Rome. Look, I am going:
Commend me to my wife. I'll return consul;
Or never trust to what my tongue can do
I' th' way of flattery further.

Vol. Do your will. *Exit Vol.*

Com. Away! the tribunes do attend you: arm yourself
To answer mildly; for they are prepar'd
With accusations, as I hear, more strong
Than are upon you yet.

Cor. The word is 'mildly.' Pray you, let us go:
Let them accuse me by invention, I
Will answer in mine honour.

Men. Ay, but mildly.

Cor. Well, mildly be it then. Mildly! *Exeunt.*

[SCENE III. *The same. The Forum.*]

Enter SICINIUS *and* BRUTUS.

Bru. In this point charge him home, that he affects
Tyrannical power: if he evade us there,
Enforce him with his envy to the people,
And that the spoil got on the Antiates
Was ne'er distributed.

Enter an Ædile.

What, will he come?

Æd. He 's coming.

Bru. How accompanied?

Æd. With old Menenius, and those senators
That always favour'd him.

Sic. Have you a catalogue
Of all the voices that we have procur'd
Set down by th' poll?

Æd. I have; 'tis ready.

Sic. Have you collected them by tribes?

Æd. I have.

Sic. Assemble presently the people hither;
And when they hear me say 'It shall be so
I' th' right and strength o' th' commons,' be it either
For death, for fine, or banishment, then let them,
If I say fine, cry 'Fine;' if death, cry 'Death.'
Insisting on the old prerogative
And power i' th' truth o' th' cause.

Æd. I shall inform them.

73-78. **Go . . . heart.** Volumnia seems to act out the part—designating his bonnet, showing how far to stretch his bow, bending her knee, and waving her head from side to side; it has also been suggested that *stretch'd it* means "gone thus far." 75. **bussing,** kissing. 78. **Which . . . thus,** i.e., often repeated thus. 80. **or . . . them.** We should say, "and say to them." 83. **as they,** as for them. 94. **make strong party,** get forces together. 99. **unbarb'd sconce,** unhelmeted head. 102. **this single plot,** i.e., his own person. 103. **mould,** bodily form. 106. **discharge to th' life,** perform convincingly. 112. **harlot's,** lewd person's. 113. **quired,** harmonized. 116. **Tent,** lodge. **take up,** fill up. 117. **glasses,** eyeballs. 121. **surcease,** cease. 125. **Than . . . them,** than for thee to beg of them. 127. **stoutness,** obstinate pride. 130. **owe,** own. 132. **mountebank,** win over with the tricks of a mountebank. 133. **Cog,** cheat. 138. **attend,** await.

SCENE III. 1. **charge him home,** call upon him to give answer thoroughly or effectively. 3. **Enforce him,** urge him (to action or desperation). 10. **Set . . . poll,** set down by individual names; to have set them down by hundreds would have given the plebeians fewer votes,

Bru. And when such time they have begun to cry,
Let them not cease, but with a din confus'd
Enforce the present execution
Of what we chance to sentence.
Æd. Very well.
Sic. Make them be strong and ready for this hint,
When we shall hap to give 't them.
Bru. Go about it. [*Exit Ædile.*]
Put him to choler straight: he hath been us'd
†Ever to conquer, and to have his worth
Of contradiction: being once chaf'd, he cannot
Be rein'd again to temperance; then he speaks
What 's in his heart; and that is there which looks
With us to break his neck.
Sic. Well, here he comes.

Enter CORIOLANUS, MENENIUS, *and* COMINIUS, *with others* [Senators *and* Patricians].

Men. Calmly, I do beseech you.
Cor. Ay, as an ostler, that for th' poorest piece
Will bear the knave by th' volume. Th' honour'd gods
Keep Rome in safety, and the chairs of justice
Supplied with worthy men! plant love among 's!
Throng our large temples with the shows of peace,
And not our streets with war!
First Sen. Amen, amen.
Men. A noble wish.

Enter the Ædile, *with the* Plebeians.

Sic. Draw near, ye people.
Æd. List to your tribunes. Audience! peace, I say!
Cor. First, hear me speak.
Both Tri. Well, say. Peace, ho!
Cor. Shall I be charg'd no further than this present?
Must all determine here?
Sic. I do demand,
If you submit you to the people's voices,
Allow their officers and are content
To suffer lawful censure for such faults
As shall be prov'd upon you?
Cor. I am content.
Men. Lo, citizens, he says he is content:
The warlike service he has done, consider; think
Upon the wounds his body bears, which show
Like graves i' th' holy churchyard.
Cor. Scratches with briers,
Scars to move laughter only.
Men. Consider further,
That when he speaks not like a citizen,
You find him like a soldier: do not take
His rougher accents for malicious sounds,
But, as I say, such as become a soldier,
Rather than envy you.
Com. Well, well, no more.
Cor. What is the matter
That being pass'd for consul with full voice,
I am so dishonour'd that the very hour
You take it off again?
Sic. Answer to us.
Cor. Say, then: 'tis true, I ought so.
Sic. We charge you, that you have contriv'd to take
From Rome all season'd office and to wind
Yourself into a power tyrannical;
For which you are a traitor to the people.
Cor. How! traitor?
Men. Nay, temperately; your promise.
Cor. The fires i' th' lowest hell fold-in the people!
Call me their traitor! Thou injurious tribune!
Within thine eyes sat twenty thousand deaths,
In thy hands clutch'd as many millions, in
Thy lying tongue both numbers, I would say
'Thou liest' unto thee with a voice as free
As I do pray the gods.
Sic. Mark you this, people?
Citizens. To th' rock, to th' rock with him!
Sic. Peace!
We need not put new matter to his charge:
What you have seen him do and heard him speak,
Beating your officers, cursing yourselves,
Opposing laws with strokes and here defying
Those whose great power must try him; even this,
So criminal and in such capital kind,
Deserves th' extremest death.
Bru. But since he hath
Serv'd well for Rome,—
Cor. What do you prate of service?
Bru. I talk of that, that know it.
Cor. You?
Men. Is this the promise that you made your mother?
Com. Know, I pray you,—
Cor. I'll know no further:
Let them pronounce the steep Tarpeian death,
Vagabond exile, flaying, pent to linger
But with a grain a day, I would not buy
Their mercy at the price of one fair word;
Nor check my courage for what they can give,
To have 't with saying 'Good morrow.'
Sic. For that he has,
As much as in him lies, from time to time
Envied against the people, seeking means
To pluck away their power, as now at last
Given hostile strokes, and that not in the presence
Of dreaded justice, but on the ministers
That doth distribute it; in the name o' th' people
And in the power of us the tribunes, we,
Ev'n from this instant, banish him our city,
In peril of precipitation
From off the rock Tarpeian never more
To enter our Rome gates: i' th' people's name,
I say it shall be so.
Citizens. It shall be so, it shall be so; let him away:
He 's banish'd, and it shall be so.
Com. Hear me, my masters, and my common friends,—
Sic. He 's sentenc'd: no more hearing.
Com. Let me speak:

since in that case there would have been a property qualification. 11. **tribes,** alluding to the division of the Roman people into tribes, a democratic division. 26. **worth,** full quota or portion (Malone); many interpretations and emendations of this passage; Malone's seems best. 29. **looks,** promises, tends. 32. **piece,** coin, piece of money. 33. **bear . . . volume,** endure being called knave by the volume (i.e., to any extent). 40. **Audience!** Listen, give heed! 42. **this present,** i.e., occasion. 43. **determine,** cease, come to an end. 45. **Allow,** acknowledge. 55. **accents,** so Theobald; F: *Actions*. 57. **Rather . . . you,** rather than such as show malice toward you. 62. **so,** to do so. 64. **season'd,** established. 68. **fold-in,** enclose, encircle. 69. **injurious,** abusive. 70-72. **Within . . . numbers.** Understand "although" before each of the three clauses. 81. **capital,** death-deserving. 89-90. **pent . . . day,** imprisoned to starve with but a small particle of food a day. 93. **To . . . saying,** i.e., if I might have it with saying. 94. **in him lies,** he could. 95. **Envied against,** showed malice toward.

I have been consul, and can show for Rome
Her enemies' marks upon me. I do love
My country's good with a respect more tender,
More holy and profound, than mine own life,
My dear wife's estimate, her womb's increase,
And treasure of my loins; then if I would
Speak that,—
Sic. We know your drift: speak what?
Bru. There 's no more to be said, but he is banish'd,
As enemy to the people and his country:
It shall be so.
Citizens. It shall be so, it shall be so.
Cor. You common cry of curs! whose breath I hate
As reek o' th' rotten fens, whose loves I prize
As the dead carcasses of unburied men
That do corrupt my air, I banish you!
And here remain with your uncertainty!
Let every feeble rumour shake your hearts!
Your enemies, with nodding of their plumes,
Fan you into despair! Have the power still
To banish your defenders; till at length
Your ignorance, which finds not till it feels,
Making but reservation of yourselves,
Still your own foes, deliver you as most
Abated captives to some nation
That won you without blows! Despising,
For you, the city, thus I turn my back:
There is a world elsewhere.
Exeunt Coriolanus, Cominius[*, Menenius, Senators, and Patricians*].
Æd. The people's enemy is gone, is gone!
Citizens. Our enemy is banish'd! he is gone! Hoo! hoo! *They all shout, and throw up their caps.*
Sic. Go, see him out at gates, and follow him,
As he hath follow'd you, with all despite;
Give him deserv'd vexation. Let a guard
Attend us through the city.
Citizens. Come, come; let 's see him out at gates; come.
The gods preserve our noble tribunes! Come. *Exeunt.*

ACT IV.

[SCENE I. *Rome. Before a gate of the city.*]

Enter CORIOLANUS, VOLUMNIA, VIRGILIA, MENENIUS, COMINIUS, *with the young Nobility of Rome.*

Cor. Come, leave your tears: a brief farewell: the beast
With many heads butts me away. Nay, mother,
Where is your ancient courage? you were us'd
To say extremities was the trier of spirits;
That common chances common men could bear;
That when the sea was calm all boats alike
Show'd mastership in floating; fortune's blows,
When most struck home, being gentle wounded, craves
A noble cunning: you were us'd to load me
With precepts that would make invincible
The heart that conn'd them.
Vir. O heavens! O heavens!
Cor. Nay, I prithee, woman,—
Vol. Now the red pestilence strike all trades in Rome,
And occupations perish!
Cor. What, what, what!
I shall be lov'd when I am lack'd. Nay, mother,
Resume that spirit, when you were wont to say,
If you had been the wife of Hercules,
Six of his labours you 'ld have done, and sav'd
Your husband so much sweat. Cominius,
Droop not; adieu. Farewell, my wife, my mother:
I'll do well yet. Thou old and true Menenius,
Thy tears are salter than a younger man's,
And venomous to thine eyes. My sometime general,
I have seen thee stern, and thou hast oft beheld
Heart-hard'ning spectacles; tell these sad women
'Tis fond to wail inevitable strokes,
As 'tis to laugh at 'em. My mother, you wot well
My hazards still have been your solace: and
Believe 't not lightly—though I go alone,
Like to a lonely dragon, that his fen
Makes fear'd and talk'd of more than seen—your son
Will or exceed the common or be caught
With cautelous baits and practice.
Vol. My first son,
Whither wilt thou go? Take good Cominius
With thee awhile: determine on some course,
More than a wild exposture to each chance
That starts i' th' way before thee.
Cor. O the gods!
Com. I'll follow thee a month, devise with thee
Where thou shalt rest, that thou mayst hear of us
And we of thee: so if the time thrust forth
A cause for thy repeal, we shall not send
O'er the vast world to seek a single man,
And lose advantage, which doth ever cool
I' th' absence of the needer.
Cor. Fare ye well:
Thou hast years upon thee; and thou art too full
Of the wars' surfeits, to go rove with one
That 's yet unbruis'd: bring me but out at gate.
Come, my sweet wife, my dearest mother, and
My friends of noble touch, when I am forth,
Bid me farewell, and smile. I pray you, come.
While I remain above the ground, you shall
Hear from me still, and never of me aught
But what is like me formerly.
Men. That 's worthily
As any ear can hear. Come, let 's not weep.
If I could shake off but one seven years
From these old arms and legs, by the good gods,
I 'ld with thee every foot.
Cor. Give me thy hand:
Come. *Exeunt.*

---

114. **estimate,** reputation. 120. **cry,** pack. 124. **remain,** remain you. **uncertainty,** inconstancy, fickleness. 129. **finds . . . feels,** learns only through experience. 130. **Making . . . yourselves,** seeking only to preserve yourselves. (Globe has "not" for "but," following Capell.) 132. **Abated,** humbled.

ACT IV. SCENE I. 1-2. **beast . . . heads,** comparison of the mob to a beast with many heads is derived from Horace, *Epistolae,* Bk. I, i, 76, *Bellua multorum es capitum.* 7-9. **fortune's . . . cunning.** The sentence starts as if fortune's blows were to be the subject, but the construction breaks and *being gentle wounded* is made to serve; this type of broken structure is called anacoluthon. Johnson gives the meaning as, "When fortune strikes her hardest blows, to be wounded, and yet continue calm, requires a generous policy." 13. **red pestilence,** allusion to the red spots which presaged death to those striken with the plague. 14. **occupations,** trades, handicrafts. 15. **lack'd,** missed. 26. **fond,** foolish. 27. **wot,** know. 30. **fen,** lurking place; note ellipsis: that his lonely lurking place makes him feared, etc. 32. **or . . . common,** either exceed the ordinary deeds of men. 33. **cautelous,** crafty, deceitful.

[SCENE II. *The same. A street near the gate.*]

Enter the two Tribunes, SICINIUS *and* BRUTUS, *with the* Ædile.

Sic. Bid them all home; he 's gone, and we'll no further.
The nobility are vex'd, whom we see have sided
In his behalf.
Bru. Now we have shown our power,
Let us seem humbler after it is done
Than when it was a-doing.
Sic. Bid them home:
Say their great enemy is gone, and they
Stand in their ancient strength.
Bru. Dismiss them home. [*Exit Ædile.*]
Here comes his mother.

Enter VOLUMNIA, VIRGILIA, *and* MENENIUS.

Sic. Let 's not meet her.
Bru. Why?
Sic. They say she 's mad.
Bru. They have ta'en note of us: keep on your way.
Vol. O, y' are well met: th' hoarded plague o' th' gods
Requite your love!
Men. Peace, peace; be not so loud.
Vol. If that I could for weeping, you should hear,—
Nay, and you shall hear some. [*To Brutus*] Will you be gone?
Vir. [*To Sicinius*] You shall stay too: I would I had the power
To say so to my husband.
Sic. Are you mankind?
Vol. Ay, fool; is that a shame? Note but this fool.
Was not a man my father? Hadst thou foxship
To banish him that struck more blows for Rome
Than thou hast spoken words?
Sic. O blessed heavens!
Vol. More noble blows than ever thou wise words;
And for Rome's good. I'll tell thee what; yet go:
Nay, but thou shalt stay too: I would my son
Were in Arabia, and thy tribe before him,
His good sword in his hand.
Sic. What then?
Vir. What then!
He 'ld make an end of thy posterity.
Vol. Bastards and all.
Good man, the wounds that he does bear for Rome!
Men. Come, come, peace.
Sic. I would he had continued to his country
As he began, and not unknit himself
The noble knot he made.
Bru. I would he had.
Vol. 'I would he had'! 'Twas you incens'd the rabble:
Cats, that can judge as fitly of his worth
As I can of those mysteries which heaven
Will not have earth to know.
Bru. Pray, let 's go.
Vol. Now, pray, sir, get you gone:
You have done a brave deed. Ere you go, hear this:—
As far as doth the Capitol exceed
The meanest house in Rome, so far my son—
This lady's husband here, this, do you see?—
Whom you have banish'd, does exceed you all.
Bru. Well, well, we'll leave you.
Sic. Why stay we to be baited
With one that wants her wits? *Exeunt Tribunes.*
Vol. Take my prayers with you.
I would the gods had nothing else to do
But to confirm my curses! Could I meet 'em
But once a-day, it would unclog my heart
Of what lies heavy to 't.
Men. You have told them home;
And, by my troth, you have cause. You'll sup with me?
Vol. Anger 's my meat; I sup upon myself,
And so shall starve with feeding. Come, let 's go:
Leave this faint puling and lament as I do,
In anger, Juno-like. Come, come, come.
Men. Fie, fie, fie! *Exeunt.*

[SCENE III. *A highway between Rome and Antium.*]

Enter a Roman *and a* Volsce [*meeting*].

Rom. I know you well, sir, and you know me: your name, I think, is Adrian.

Vols. It is so, sir: truly, I have forgot you.

Rom. I am a Roman; and my services are, as you are, against 'em: know you me yet?

Vols. Nicanor? no.

Rom. The same, sir.

Vols. You had more beard when I last saw you; but your favour is well appeared by your tongue. What 's the news in Rome? I have a note from the Volscian state, to find you out there: you have well saved me a day's journey.

Rom. There hath been in Rome strange insurrections; the people against the senators, patricians, and nobles.

Vols. Hath been! is it ended, then? Our state thinks not so: they are in a most warlike preparation, and hope to come upon them in the heat of their division.

Rom. The main blaze of it is past, but a small thing would make it flame again: for the nobles receive so to heart the banishment of that worthy Coriolanus, that they are in a ripe aptness to take all power from the people and to pluck from them their tribunes for ever. This lies glowing, I can tell you, and is almost mature for the violent breaking out.

Vols. Coriolanus banished!

Rom. Banished, sir.

Vols. You will be welcome with this intelligence, Nicanor.

Rom. The day serves well for them now. I have heard it said, the fittest time to corrupt a man's wife is when she 's fallen out with her husband. Your noble

first, one and only. 36. **exposture,** exposure. 46. **wars' surfeits,** evil results of military service. 47. **bring,** conduct. 49. **noble touch,** approved nobility (from the use of the touchstone with precious metals). 53. **worthily,** worthily spoken.

SCENE II. 2. **sided,** enlisted. 9. **mad,** probably angry, furious. 14. **some,** a part. 16. **mankind,** defined as masculine, of the male sex; also as infuriated (beyond human nature). 18. **foxship,** ingratitude (Onions), or craftiness. 24. **Arabia,** type of a desert. 32. **noble knot,** i.e., the obligation under which he had laid his country. 43-44. **baited With,** worried or harassed by. 48. **heavy to 't,** heavy upon it. **told them home,** told them the complete truth. 51. **starve with feeding,** i.e., she feeds only on herself, but eating only this food, she may die. 52. **Leave . . . puling,** cease this weak complaining (addressed to Virgilia).

SCENE III. 9. **appeared,** made to appear, manifested. (Globe emends to *approved*, following Steevens.) 26. **glowing,** i.e., like a spark.

Tullus Aufidius will appear well in these wars, his great opposer, Coriolanus, being now in no request of his country.

Vols. He cannot choose. I am most fortunate, thus accidentally to encounter you: you have ended my business, and I will merrily accompany you home.

Rom. I shall, between this and supper, tell you most strange things from Rome; all tending to the good of their adversaries. Have you an army ready, say you?

Vols. A most royal one; the centurions and their charges, distinctly billeted, already in the entertainment, and to be on foot at an hour's warning.

Rom. I am joyful to hear of their readiness, and am the man, I think, that shall set them in present action. So, sir, heartily well met, and most glad of your company.

Vols. You take my part from me, sir; I have the most cause to be glad of yours.

Rom. Well, let us go together. *Exeunt.*

[SCENE IV. *Antium. Before Aufidius' house.*]

Enter CORIOLANUS *in mean apparel, disguised and muffled.*

Cor. A goodly city is this Antium. City,
'Tis I that made thy widows: many an heir
Of these fair edifices 'fore my wars
Have I heard groan and drop: then know me not,
Lest that thy wives with spits and boys with stones
In puny battle slay me.

Enter a Citizen.

Save you, sir.

Cit. And you.

Cor. Direct me, if it be your will,
Where great Aufidius lies: is he in Antium?

Cit. He is, and feasts the nobles of the state
At his house this night.

Cor. Which is his house, beseech you?

Cit. This, here before you.

Cor. Thank you, sir: farewell. *Exit Citizen.*
O world, thy slippery turns! Friends now fast sworn,
Whose double bosoms seems to wear one heart,
Whose hours, whose bed, whose meal, and exercise,
Are still together, who twin, as 'twere, in love
Unseparable, shall within this hour,
On a dissension of a doit, break out
To bitterest enmity: so, fellest foes,
Whose passions and whose plots have broke their sleep
To take the one the other, by some chance,
Some trick not worth an egg, shall grow dear friends
And interjoin their issues. So with me:
My birth-place hate I, and my love 's upon
This enemy town. I'll enter: if he slay me,
He does fair justice; if he give me way,
I'll do his country service. *Exit.*

[SCENE V. *The same. A hall in Aufidius' house.*]

Music plays. Enter a Servingman.

First Serv. Wine, wine, wine! What service is here! I think our fellows are asleep. [*Exit.*]

Enter another Servingman.

Sec. Serv. Where 's Cotus? my master calls for him. Cotus! *Exit.*

Enter CORIOLANUS.

Cor. A goodly house: the feast smells well; but I
Appear not like a guest.

Enter the first Servingman.

First Serv. What would you have, friend? whence are you? Here 's no place for you: pray, go to the door. *Exit.*

Cor. I have deserv'd no better entertainment,
In being Coriolanus.

Enter second Servant.

Sec. Serv. Whence are you, sir? Has the porter his eyes in his head, that he gives entrance to such companions? Pray, get you out.

Cor. Away!

Sec. Serv. Away! get you away.

Cor. Now th' art troublesome.

Sec. Serv. Are you so brave? I'll have you talked with anon.

Enter third Servingman. *The first meets him.*

Third Serv. What fellow 's this?

First Serv. A strange one as ever I looked on: I cannot get him out o' the house: prithee, call my master to him. [*Exit.*]

Third Serv. What have you to do here, fellow? Pray you, avoid the house.

Cor. Let me but stand; I will not hurt your hearth.

Third Serv. What are you?

Cor. A gentleman.

Third Serv. A marvellous poor one.

Cor. True, so I am.

Third Serv. Pray you, poor gentleman, take up some other station; here 's no place for you; pray you, avoid: come.

Cor. Follow your function, go, and batten on cold bits. *Pushes him away from him.*

Third Serv. What, you will not? Prithee, tell my master what a strange guest he has here.

Sec. Serv. And I shall. *Exit Sec. Serv.*

Third Serv. Where dwellest thou?

Cor. Under the canopy.

Third Serv. Under the canopy!

Cor. Ay.

Third Serv. Where 's that?

Cor. I' the city of kites and crows.

Third Serv. I' the city of kites and crows! What an ass it is! Then thou dwellest with daws too?

Cor. No, I serve not thy master.

Third Serv. How, sir! do you meddle with my master?

Cor. Ay; 'tis an honester service than to meddle with thy mistress.
Thou prat'st, and prat'st; serve with thy trencher,
hence! *Beats him away.* [*Exit third Servingman.*]

37. **in no request of,** unvalued by. 39. **choose,** do otherwise. 48. **distinctly billeted,** separately enrolled. 55. **my part,** the words I should say.

SCENE IV. 3. **'fore my wars,** facing me in battle. 15. **twin,** are like twins. 17. **dissension of a doit,** paltry dispute. 18. **fellest,** fiercest. 20. **To . . . other,** i e., plots by which the one tries to get the better of the other. 21. **trick,** trifle. 22. **issues,** children; fortunes.

SCENE V. 34. **avoid,** get out. 35. **function,** proper duty. **batten,** grow fat on. 41. **canopy,** i.e., of heaven. 48. **daws,** jackdaws, types of foolishness. 67. **tackle 's,** rigging is. 77. **memory,** reminder. 84. **Whoop'd,** driven with hoots. 89. **full quit of,** fully evened with. 91. **wreak,** vengeance. 92-93. **maims Of shame,** dishonoring mutilations.

Enter Aufidius *with the* [*second*] Servingman.

Auf. Where is this fellow?

Sec. Serv. Here, sir: I 'ld have beaten him like a dog, but for disturbing the lords within. [*Exit.*]

Auf. Whence com'st thou? what wouldst thou? thy name?
Why speak'st not? speak, man: what 's thy name?

Cor. If, Tullus, [*Unmuffling.*]
Not yet thou know'st me, and, seeing me, dost not
Think me for the man I am, necessity
Commands me name myself.

Auf. What is thy name?

Cor. A name unmusical to the Volscians' ears,
And harsh in sound to thine.

Auf. Say, what 's thy name?
Thou hast a grim appearance, and thy face
Bears a command in 't; though thy tackle 's torn,
Thou show'st a noble vessel: what 's thy name?

Cor. Prepare thy brow to frown: know'st thou me yet?

Auf. I know thee not: thy name?

Cor. My name is Caius Marcius, who hath done
To thee particularly and to all the Volsces
Great hurt and mischief; thereto witness may
My surname, Coriolanus: the painful service,
The extreme dangers and the drops of blood
Shed for my thankless country are requited
But with that surname; a good memory,
And witness of the malice and displeasure
Which thou shouldst bear me: only that name remains;
The cruelty and envy of the people,
Permitted by our dastard nobles, who
Have all forsook me, hath devour'd the rest;
And suffer'd me by th' voice of slaves to be
Whoop'd out of Rome. Now this extremity
Hath brought me to thy hearth; not out of hope—
Mistake me not—to save my life, for if
I had fear'd death, of all the men i' th' world
I would have 'voided thee, but in mere spite,
To be full quit of those my banishers,
Stand I before thee here. Then if thou hast
A heart of wreak in thee, that wilt revenge
Thine own particular wrongs and stop those maims
Of shame seen through thy country, speed thee straight,
And make my misery serve thy turn: so use it
That my revengeful services may prove
As benefits to thee, for I will fight
Against my cank'red country with the spleen
Of all the under fiends. But if so be
Thou dar'st not this and that to prove more fortunes
Th' art tir'd, then, in a word, I also am
Longer to live most weary, and present
My throat to thee and to thy ancient malice;
Which not to cut would show thee but a fool,
Since I have ever followed thee with hate,
Drawn tuns of blood out of thy country's breast,
And cannot live but to thy shame, unless
It be to do thee service.

Auf. O Marcius, Marcius!
Each word thou hast spoke hath weeded from my heart
A root of ancient envy. If Jupiter
Should from yond cloud speak divine things,
And say ''Tis true,' I 'ld not believe them more
Than thee, all noble Marcius. Let me twine
Mine arms about that body, where against
My grained ash an hundred times hath broke,
And scarr'd the moon with splinters: here I clip
The anvil of my sword, and do contest
As hotly and as nobly with thy love
As ever in ambitious strength I did
Contend against thy valour. Know thou first,
I lov'd the maid I married; never man
Sigh'd truer breath; but that I see thee here,
Thou noble thing! more dances my rapt heart
Than when I first my wedded mistress saw
Bestride my threshold. Why, thou Mars! I tell thee,
We have a power on foot; and I had purpose
Once more to hew thy target from thy brawn,
Or lose mine arm for 't: thou hast beat me out
Twelve several times, and I have nightly since
Dreamt of encounters 'twixt thyself and me;
We have been down together in my sleep,
Unbuckling helms, fisting each other's throat,
And wak'd half dead with nothing. Worthy Marcius,
Had we no other quarrel else to Rome, but that
Thou art thence banish'd, we would muster all
From twelve to seventy, and, pouring war
Into the bowels of ungrateful Rome,
Like a bold flood o'er-beat. O, come, go in,
And take our friendly senators by th' hands;
Who now are here, taking their leaves of me,
Who am prepar'd against your territories,
Though not for Rome itself.

Cor. You bless me, gods!

Auf. Therefore, most absolute sir, if thou wilt have
The leading of thine own revenges, take
Th' one half of my commission; and set down—
As best thou art experienc'd, since thou know'st
Thy country's strength and weakness,—thine own ways;
Whether to knock against the gates of Rome,
Or rudely visit them in parts remote,
To fright them, ere destroy. But come in:
Let me commend thee first to those that shall
Say yea to thy desires. A thousand welcomes!
And more a friend than e'er an enemy;
Yet, Marcius, that was much. Your hand: most welcome!

Exeunt [*Coriolanus and Aufidius*]. *Enter two of the Servingmen.*

First Serv. Here 's a strange alteration!

Sec. Serv. By my hand, I had thought to have strucken him with a cudgel; and yet my mind gave me his clothes made a false report of him.

First Serv. What an arm he has! he turned me about with his finger and his thumb, as one would set up a top.

Sec. Serv. Nay, I knew by his face that there was

93. **through,** throughout. 97. **cank'red,** infected with evils (from the action of the cankerworm). 98. **under fiends,** fiends of the underworld, or possibly subordinate fiends. 99. **prove more fortunes,** try your fortunes further. 105. **tuns,** large barrels. 109. **root of ancient envy,** source of ancient malice. 114. **grained ash,** spear with ashen shaft showing a strong grain. 116. **anvil,** i.e., Coriolanus has been as an anvil for his sword. 125. **power on foot,** force in the field. 126. **brawn,** muscle of the arm; here, arm. 131. **fisting,** clutching. 137. **o'er-beat,** overflow, surge over. (Globe emends to *o'er-bear.*) 142. **absolute,** perfect. 144. **set down,** determine upon. 157. **gave,** misgave or told. 161. **set up,** set going.

something in him: he had, sir, a kind of face, methought,—I cannot tell how to term it.

First Serv. He had so; looking as it were—would I were hanged, but I thought there was more in him than I could think.

Sec. Serv. So did I, I'll be sworn: he is simply the rarest man i' the world.

First Serv. I think he is: but a greater soldier than he, you wot one.

Sec. Serv. Who, my master?

First Serv. Nay, it 's no matter for that.

Sec. Serv. Worth six on him.

First Serv. Nay, not so neither: but I take him to be the greater soldier.

Sec. Serv. Faith, look you, one cannot tell how to say that: for the defence of a town, our general is excellent.

First Serv. Ay, and for an assault too.

Enter the third Servingman.

Third Serv. O slaves, I can tell you news,—news, you rascals!

First and Sec. Serv. What, what, what? let's partake.

Third Serv. I would not be a Roman, of all nations; I had as lieve be a condemned man.

First and Sec. Serv. Wherefore? wherefore?

Third Serv. Why, here 's he that was wont to thwack our general, Caius Marcius.

First Serv. Why do you say 'thwack our general'?

Third Serv. I do not say 'thwack our general;' but he was always good enough for him.

Sec. Serv. Come, we are fellows and friends: he was ever too hard for him; I have heard him say so himself.

First Serv. He was too hard for him directly, to say the troth on 't: before Corioles he scotched him and notched him like a carbonado.

Sec. Serv. An he had been cannibally given, he might have boiled and eaten him too.

First Serv. But, more of thy news?

Third Serv. Why, he is so made on here within, as if he were son and heir to Mars; set at upper end o' the table; no question asked him by any of the senators, but they stand bald before him: our general himself makes a mistress of him; sanctifies himself with 's hand and turns up the white o' the eye to his discourse. But the bottom of the news is, our general is cut i' the middle and but one half of what he was yesterday; for the other has half, by the entreaty and grant of the whole table. He'll go, he says, and sowl the porter of Rome gates by the ears: he will mow all down before him, and leave his passage polled.

Sec. Serv. And he 's as like to do 't as any man I can imagine.

Third Serv. Do 't? he will do 't; for, look you, sir, he has as many friends as enemies; which friends, sir, as it were, durst not, look you, sir, show themselves, as we term it, his friends whilst he 's in directitude.

First Serv. Directitude! what 's that?

Third Serv. But when they shall see, sir, his crest up again, and the man in blood, they will out of their burrows, like conies after rain, and revel all with him.

First Serv. But when goes this forward?

Third Serv. To-morrow; to-day; presently; you shall have the drum struck up this afternoon: 'tis, as it were, a parcel of their feast, and to be executed ere they wipe their lips.

Sec. Serv. Why, then we shall have a stirring world again. This peace is nothing, but to rust iron, increase tailors, and breed ballad-makers.

First Serv. Let me have war, say I; it exceeds peace as far as day does night; it 's spritely, waking, audible, and full of vent. Peace is a very apoplexy, lethargy; mulled, deaf, sleepy, insensible; a getter of more bastard children than war 's a destroyer of men.

Sec. Serv. 'Tis so: and as war, in some sort, may be said to be a ravisher, so it cannot be denied but peace is a great maker of cuckolds.

First Serv. Ay, and it makes men hate one another.

Third Serv. Reason; because they then less need one another. The wars for my money. I hope to see Romans as cheap as Volscians. They are rising, they are rising.

All. In, in, in, in! *Exeunt.*

[SCENE VI. *Rome. A public place.*]

Enter the two Tribunes, SICINIUS *and* BRUTUS.

Sic. We hear not of him, neither need we fear him;
His remedies are tame: the present peace
And quietness of the people, which before
Were in wild hurry. Here do we make his friends
Blush that the world goes well, who rather had,
Though they themselves did suffer by 't, behold
Dissentious numbers pest'ring streets than see
Our tradesmen singing in their shops and going
About their functions friendly.

Bru. We stood to 't in good time. (*Enter Menenius.*) Is this Menenius?

Sic. 'Tis he, 'tis he: O, he is grown most kind of late.
Hail, sir!

Men. Hail to you both!

Sic. Your Coriolanus
Is not much miss'd, but with his friends:
The commonwealth doth stand, and so would do,
Were he more angry at it.

Men. All 's well; and might have been much better, if
He could have temporiz'd.

Sic. Where is he, hear you?

Men. Nay, I hear nothing: his mother and his wife
Hear nothing from him.

Enter three or four Citizens.

Citizens. The gods preserve you both!

Sic. God-den, our neighbours.

Bru. God-den to you all, god-den to you all.

168-180. **So did . . . too.** The First Servingman is craftily ambiguous in alluding to a "greater soldier." Instead of *one* in line 171, Dyce suggested *on;* according to this, *you wot on* would mean you know whom I mean, i.e., Aufidius. 173. **Nay . . . that,** I won't commit myself; never mind about names. 174, 176. **him,** i.e., Coriolanus according to Dyce; Aufidius according to the text. 178-179. **our general,** i.e., Aufidius. 183. **let's partake,** let's share it. 197. **directly,** plainly, pointedly. 198. **scotched,** scored, gashed. 199. **carbonado,** meat scored across for broiling. 201. **boiled,** so F; Pope, followed by Globe: *broiled.* 203. **made on,** flattered, made much of. 208. **sanctifies . . . hand,** touches his hand as if it were a relic. 208-209. **turns . . . eye,** i.e., as an expression of veneration. 212. **other,** i.e., Coriolanus. **entreaty and grant,** requesting and granting. 213. **sowl,** drag; F: *sole.* 215. **polled,** stripped (properly of branches or foliage). 222. **directitude,** blundering form; Malone conjectured *discreditude,* which suggests the meaning. 226. **conies,** rabbits. 231. **parcel,** part. 237. **spritely, waking,** so Pope (*sprightly*); F: *sprightly walking.* 238. **vent,** excitement, activity. 239. **mulled,** insipid. 247. **Reason,** i.e., this is the reason. 250. **rising,**

First Cit. Ourselves, our wives, and children, on our knees,
Are bound to pray for you both.
Sic. Live, and thrive!
Bru. Farewell, kind neighbours: we wish'd Coriolanus
Had lov'd you as we did.
Citizens. Now the gods keep you!
Both Tri. Farewell, farewell. *Exeunt Citizens.*
Sic. This is a happier and more comely time
Than when these fellows ran about the streets,
Crying confusion.
Bru. Caius Marcius was
A worthy officer i' th' war; but insolent,
O'ercome with pride, ambitious past all thinking,
Self-loving,—
Sic. And affecting one sole throne,
Without assistance.
Men. I think not so.
Sic. We should by this, to all our lamentation,
If he had gone forth consul, found it so.
Bru. The gods have well prevented it, and Rome
Sits safe and still without him.

Enter an Ædile.

Æd. Worthy tribunes,
There is a slave, whom we have put in prison,
Reports, the Volsces with two several powers
Are ent'red in the Roman territories,
And with the deepest malice of the war
Destroy what lies before 'em.
Men. 'Tis Aufidius,
Who, hearing of our Marcius' banishment,
Thrusts forth his horns again into the world;
Which were inshell'd when Marcius stood for Rome,
And durst not once peep out.
Sic. Come, what talk you
Of Marcius?
Bru. Go see this rumourer whipp'd. It cannot be
The Volsces dare break with us.
Men. Cannot be?
We have record that very well it can,
And three examples of the like hath been
Within my age. But reason with the fellow,
Before you punish him, where he heard this,
Lest you shall chance to whip your information
And beat the messenger who bids beware
Of what is to be dreaded.
Sic. Tell not me:
I know this cannot be.
Bru. Not possible.

Enter a Messenger.

Mess. The nobles in great earnestness are going
All to the senate-house: some news is come
That turns their countenances.
Sic. 'Tis this slave;—
Go whip him 'fore the people's eyes:—his raising;
Nothing but his report.
Mess. Yes, worthy sir,
The slave's report is seconded; and more,
More fearful, is deliver'd.
Sic. What more fearful?
Mess. It is spoke freely out of many mouths—
How probable I do not know—that Marcius,
Join'd with Aufidius, leads a power 'gainst Rome,
And vows revenge as spacious as between
The young'st and oldest thing.
Sic. This is most likely!
Bru. Rais'd only, that the weaker sort may wish
Good Marcius home again.
Sic. The very trick on 't.
Men. This is unlikely:
He and Aufidius can no more atone
Than violent'st contrariety.

Enter [a second] Messenger.

Sec. Mess. You are sent for to the senate:
A fearful army, led by Caius Marcius
Associated with Aufidius, rages
Upon our territories; and have already
O'erborne their way, consum'd with fire, and took
What lay before them.

Enter Cominius.

Com. O, you have made good work!
Men. What news? what news?
Com. You have holp to ravish your own daughters and
To melt the city leads upon your pates,
To see your wives dishonour'd to your noses,—
Men. What 's the news? what 's the news?
Com. Your temples burned in their cement, and
Your franchises, whereon you stood, confin'd
Into an auger's bore.
Men. Pray now, your news?
You have made fair work, I fear me.—Pray, your news?—
If Marcius should be join'd with Volscians,—
Com. If!
He is their god: he leads them like a thing
Made by some other deity than nature,
That shapes man better; and they follow him,
Against us brats, with no less confidence
Than boys pursuing summer butterflies,
Or butchers killing flies.
Men. You have made good work,
You and your apron-men; you that stood so much
Upon the voice of occupation and
The breath of garlic-eaters!
Com. He'll shake
Your Rome about your ears.
Men. As Hercules
Did shake down mellow fruit. You have made fair work!
Bru. But is this true, sir?
Com. Ay; and you'll look pale

i.e., from table.
Scene vi. 2. **His . . . tame,** his means (of revenge) are rendered ineffectual (?). 4. **hurry,** commotion. 7. **pest'ring,** crowding. 13. **but with,** except among. 27. **comely,** gracious. 29. **Crying confusion,** starting trouble. 34. **by this,** by this time. **to all our lamentation,** to the lamentation of all of us. 35. **gone forth,** i.e., as consul. **found,** have found. 44. **Thrusts . . . again,** i.e., like a snail. 45. **inshell'd,** i.e., in the shell like a snail's horns. 46. **what,** why. 59. **turns,** changes the color of. 68. **young'st . . . thing,** every living thing. 69. **Rais'd,** invented, stirred up; see *raising,* line 60 above. 78. **O'erborne their way,** carried all before them. 82. **leads,** roofs of lead (melted by fire). 83. **to,** before. 85. **cement,** material of which the temples were made; accent on first syllable. 86. **franchises,** political rights. 93. **brats,** mere children. 96. **apron-men,** mechanics in aprons. 97. **voice of occupation,** votes of the laboring men. 99-100. **Hercules . . . fruit,** allusion to the eleventh labor of Hercules, the stealing of the golden apples of Hesperides.

Before you find it other. All the regions
Do smilingly revolt; and who resists
Are mock'd for valiant ignorance,
And perish constant fools. Who is 't can blame him?
Your enemies and his find something in him.
Men. We are all undone, unless
The noble man have mercy.
Com. Who shall ask it?
The tribunes cannot do 't for shame; the people
Deserve such pity of him as the wolf
Does of the shepherds: for his best friends, if they
Should say 'Be good to Rome,' they charg'd him even
As those should do that had deserv'd his hate,
And therein show'd like enemies.
Men. 'Tis true:
If he were putting to my house the brand
That should consume it, I have not the face
To say 'Beseech you, cease.' You have made fair hands,
You and your crafts! you have crafted fair!
Com. You have brought
A trembling upon Rome, such as was never
So incapable of help.
Both Tri. Say not we brought it.
Men. How! Was 't we? we lov'd him; but, like beasts
And cowardly nobles, gave way unto your clusters,
Who did hoot him out o' th' city.
Com. But I fear
They'll roar him in again. Tullus Aufidius,
The second name of men, obeys his points
As if he were his officer: desperation
Is all the policy, strength and defence,
That Rome can make against them.

Enter a troop of Citizens.

Men. Here come the clusters.
And is Aufidius with him? You are they
That made the air unwholesome, when you cast
Your stinking greasy caps in hooting at
Coriolanus' exile. Now he 's coming;
And not a hair upon a soldier's head
Which will not prove a whip: as many coxcombs
As you threw caps up will he tumble down,
And pay you for your voices. 'Tis no matter;
If he could burn us all into one coal,
We have deserv'd it.
Citizens. Faith, we hear fearful news.
First Cit. For mine own part,
When I said, banish him, I said, 'twas pity.
Sec. Cit. And so did I.
Third Cit. And so did I; and, to say the truth, so did very many of us: that we did, we did for the best; and though we willingly consented to his banishment, yet it was against our will.
Com. Y' are goodly things, you voices!
Men. You have made
Good work, you and your cry! Shall 's to the Capitol?
Com. O, ay, what else? *Exeunt both.*
Sic. Go, masters, get you home; be not dismay'd:
These are a side that would be glad to have
This true which they so seem to fear. Go home,
And show no sign of fear.
First Cit. The gods be good to us! Come, masters, let 's home. I ever said we were i' the wrong when we banished him.
Sec. Cit. So did we all. But, come, let 's home.
Exeunt Citizens.
Bru. I do not like this news.
Sic. Nor I.
Bru. Let 's to the Capitol. Would half my wealth
Would buy this for a lie!
Sic. Pray, let 's go. *Exeunt Tribunes.*

[SCENE VII. *A camp, at a small distance from Rome.*]

Enter AUFIDIUS *with his* Lieutenant.

Auf. Do they still fly to th' Roman?
Lieu. I do not know what witchcraft 's in him, but
Your soldiers use him as the grace 'fore meat,
Their talk at table, and their thanks at end;
And you are dark'ned in this action, sir,
Even by your own.
Auf. I cannot help it now,
Unless, by using means, I lame the foot
Of our design. He bears himself more proudlier,
Even to my person, than I thought he would
When first I did embrace him: yet his nature
In that 's no changeling; and I must excuse
What cannot be amended.
Lieu. Yet I wish, sir,—
I mean for your particular,—you had not
Join'd in commission with him; but either
Had borne the action of yourself, or else
To him had left it solely.
Auf. I understand thee well; and be thou sure,
When he shall come to his account, he knows not
What I can urge against him. Although it seems,
And so he thinks, and is no less apparent
To th' vulgar eye, that he bears all things fairly,
And shows good husbandry for the Volscian state,
Fights dragon-like, and does achieve as soon
As draw his sword; yet he hath left undone
That which shall break his neck or hazard mine,
Whene'er we come to our account.
Lieu. Sir, I beseech you, think you he'll carry Rome?
Auf. All places yield to him ere he sits down;
And the nobility of Rome are his:
The senators and patricians love him too:
The tribunes are no soldiers; and their people

102. **other,** otherwise. 103. **smilingly,** gladly, willingly. **who,** whoever. 112. **they charg'd him even,** they would be enjoining him just. 117. **made . . . hands,** done fine work (ironic). 118. **crafted fair,** advanced the interests of the crafts or occupations and showed your craft or cunning (ironical). 124. **roar . . . again,** roar with pain when he returns. 125. **second . . . men,** second greatest name among men. **points,** instructions. 126-127. **desperation . . . defence,** policy, strength, and defense amount only to a desperate hope. 137. **coal,** cinder or ashes. 148. **Shall 's,** shall we go. 151. **side,** party.

SCENE VII. 5. **you . . . action,** your glory is dimmed in this undertaking. 6. **your own,** i.e., followers. 7. **using means,** resorting to treachery. 11. **changeling,** inconstant person. 15. **borne . . . yourself,** taken the whole command yourself. 18-26. **When . . . account.** Attempt has been made to explain this from Plutarch's treatment of the first demands of the Volsces, which the Romans were given thirty days to answer. This may be correct; there is, however, an undercurrent in the play which shows that Aufidius was not sincere. 21. **bears . . . fairly,** behaves honorably in all things. 28. **sits down,** besieges. 34. **osprey,** fish hawk, said to have power of fascinating fishes; F: *asprey.* 37. **Carry . . . even,** bear his honors temperately. 43. **casque,** as sym-

Will be as rash in the repeal, as hasty
To expel him thence. I think he'll be to Rome
As is the osprey to the fish, who takes it
By sovereignty of nature. First he was
A noble servant to them; but he could not
Carry his honours even: whether 'twas pride,
Which out of daily fortune ever taints
The happy man; whether defect of judgement,
To fail in the disposing of those chances
Which he was lord of; or whether nature,
Not to be other than one thing, not moving
From th' casque to th' cushion, but commanding peace
Even with the same austerity and garb
As he controll'd the war; but one of these—
As he hath spices of them all, not all,
For I dare so far free him—made him fear'd,
So hated, and so banish'd: but he has a merit,
To choke it in the utt'rance. So our virtues
Lie in th' interpretation of the time:
And power, unto itself most commendable,
†Hath not a tomb so evident as a chair
T' extol what it hath done.
One fire drives out one fire; one nail, one nail;
Rights by rights falter, strengths by strengths do fail.
Come, let 's away. When, Caius, Rome is thine,
Thou art poor'st of all; then shortly art thou mine.
Exeunt.

ACT V.

[SCENE I. *Rome. A public place.*]

Enter MENENIUS, COMINIUS; SICINIUS, BRUTUS, *the two Tribunes; with others.*

Men. No, I'll not go: you hear what he hath said
Which was sometime his general; who loved him
In a most dear particular. He call'd me father:
But what o' that? Go, you that banish'd him;
A mile before his tent fall down, and knee
The way into his mercy: nay, if he coy'd
To hear Cominius speak, I'll keep at home.
Com. He would not seem to know me.
Men. Do you hear?
Com. Yet one time he did call me by my name:
I urg'd our old acquaintance, and the drops
That we have bled together. Coriolanus
He would not answer to; forbad all names;
He was a kind of nothing, titleless,
Till he had forg'd himself a name o' th' fire
Of burning Rome.
Men. Why, so: you have made good work!
A pair of tribunes that have rack'd for Rome,
To make coals cheap,—a noble memory!
Com. I minded him how royal 'twas to pardon
When it was less expected: he replied,
It was a bare petition of a state
To one whom they had punish'd.
Men. Very well:
Could he say less?
Com. I offer'd to awaken his regard
For 's private friends: his answer to me was,
He could not stay to pick them in a pile
Of noisome musty chaff: he said 'twas folly,
For one poor grain or two, to leave unburnt,
And still to nose th' offence.
Men. For one poor grain or two!
I am one of those; his mother, wife, his child,
And this brave fellow too, we are the grains:
You are the musty chaff; and you are smelt
Above the moon: we must be burnt for you.
Sic. Nay, pray, be patient: if you refuse your aid
In this so never-needed help, yet do not
Upbraid 's with our distress. But, sure, if you
Would be your country's pleader, your good tongue,
More than the instant army we can make,
Might stop our countryman.
Men. No, I'll not meddle.
Sic. Pray you, go to him.
Men. What should I do?
Bru. Only make trial what your love can do
For Rome, towards Marcius.
Men. Well, and say that Marcius
Return me, as Cominius is return'd,
Unheard; what then?
But as a discontented friend, grief-shot
With his unkindness? say 't be so?
Sic. Yet your good will
Must have that thanks from Rome, after the measure
As you intended well.
Men. I'll undertake 't:
I think he'll hear me. Yet, to bite his lip
And hum at good Cominius, much unhearts me.
He was not taken well; he had not din'd:
The veins unfill'd, our blood is cold, and then
We pout upon the morning, are unapt
To give or to forgive; but when we have stuff'd
These pipes and these conveyances of our blood
With wine and feeding, we have suppler souls
Than in our priest-like fasts: therefore I'll watch him
Till he be dieted to my request,
And then I'll set upon him.
Bru. You know the very road into his kindness,
And cannot lose your way.
Men. Good faith, I'll prove him,
Speed how it will. I shall ere long have knowledge
Of my success. *Exit.*
Com. He'll never hear him.
Sic. Not?
Com. I tell you, he does sit in gold, his eye
Red as 'twould burn Rome; and his injury
The gaoler to his pity. I kneel'd before him;

bol of the warrior. **cushion,** as symbol of the senator. 44. **austerity and garb,** austere behavior. 46. **spices,** traces. 48-49. **he . . . utt'rance,** he has a merit to counterbalance every fault you urge against him; Johnson: He has a merit for no other purpose than to destroy it by boasting it. 52-53. **Hath . . . done,** has no means of being immortalized (and hence engraved on one's tomb) so certain as the public rostrum, from which deeds of honor are publicly proclaimed.

ACT V. SCENE I. 3. **dear particular,** private affection. 5. **knee,** crawl on knee. 6. **coy'd,** showed reluctance, or disdained. 12. **forbad all names,** prohibited the use of all names in addressing him. 16. **rack'd,** striven; F: *wrack'd*; some editors: *wreck'd fair*. 20. **bare,** mere, paltry. 23. **offer'd,** attempted. 28. **nose th' offence,** smell the offensive stuff. 34. **In . . . help,** in this strait where help is needed as never before. 37. **instant army,** i.e., army we can raise at this instant; existent army (Onions). 41. **towards,** in relation to. 46-47. **after . . . As,** in proportion that. 49. **hum,** i.e., as expression of dissatisfaction. 56. **watch him,** observe him; also suggested that there is an allusion to falconry, the hawk being kept awake and without food to tame it. 62. **Not?** Do you think not? 63. **in gold,** on a golden throne. 63-64. **eye Red,** betokening anger.

'Twas very faintly he said 'Rise;' dismiss'd me
Thus, with his speechless hand: what he would do,
He sent in writing after me; what he would not,
Bound with an oath to yield to his conditions:
So that all hope is vain,
Unless his noble mother, and his wife;
Who, as I hear, mean to solicit him
For mercy to his country. Therefore, let 's hence,
And with our fair entreaties haste them on. *Exeunt.*

[SCENE II. *Entrance of the Volscian camp before Rome.*]

Enter MENENIUS *to the* Watch *on guard.*

Sentinal. Stay: whence are you?
Sec. Sen. Stand, and go back.
Men. You guard like men; 'tis well: but, by your leave,
I am an officer of state, and come
To speak with Coriolanus.
First Sen. From whence?
Men. From Rome.
First Sen. You may not pass, you must return: our general
Will no more hear from thence.
Sec. Sen. You'll see your Rome embrac'd with fire before
You'll speak with Coriolanus.
Men. Good my friends,
If you have heard your general talk of Rome,
And of his friends there, it is lots to blanks,
My name hath touch'd your ears: it is Menenius.
First Sen. Be it so; go back: the virtue of your name
Is not here passable.
Men. I tell thee, fellow,
Thy general is my lover: I have been
The book of his good acts, whence men have read
His fame unparallel'd, haply amplified;
For I have ever †verified my friends,
Of whom he 's chief, with all the size that verity
Would without lapsing suffer: nay, sometimes,
Like to a bowl upon a subtle ground,
I have tumbled past the throw; and in his praise
Have almost stamp'd the leasing: therefore, fellow,
I must have leave to pass.

First Sen. Faith, sir, if you had told as many lies in his behalf as you have uttered words in your own, you should not pass here; no, though it were as virtuous to lie as to live chastely. Therefore, go back.

Men. Prithee, fellow, remember my name is Menenius, always factionary on the party of your general.

Sec. Sen. Howsoever you have been his liar, as you say you have, I am one that, telling true under him, must say, you cannot pass. Therefore, go back.

Men. Has he dined, canst thou tell? for I would not speak with him till after dinner.

First Sen. You are a Roman, are you?

Men. I am, as thy general is.

First Sen. Then you should hate Rome, as he does. Can you, when you have pushed out your gates the very defender of them, and, in a violent popular ignorance, given your enemy your shield, think to front his revenges with the easy groans of old women, the virginal palms of your daughters, or with the palsied intercession of such a decayed dotant as you seem to be? Can you think to blow out the intended fire your city is ready to flame in, with such weak breath as this? No, you are deceived; therefore, back to Rome, and prepare for your execution: you are condemned, our general has sworn you out of reprieve and pardon.

Men. Sirrah, if thy captain knew I were here, he would use me with estimation.

First Sen. Come, my captain knows you not.

Men. I mean, thy general.

First Sen. My general cares not for you. Back, I say, go; lest I let forth your half-pint of blood; back,—that 's the utmost of your having: back.

Men. Nay, but, fellow, fellow,—

Enter CORIOLANUS *with* AUFIDIUS.

Cor. What 's the matter?

Men. Now, you companion, I'll say an errand for you: you shall know now that I am in estimation; you shall perceive that a Jack guardant cannot office me from my son Coriolanus: guess, but by my entertainment with him, if thou standest not i' the state of hanging, or of some death more long in spectatorship, and crueller in suffering; behold now presently, and swoon for what 's to come upon thee. [*To Cor.*] The glorious gods sit in hourly synod about thy particular prosperity, and love thee no worse than thy old father Menenius does! O my son, my son! thou art preparing fire for us; look thee, here 's water to quench it. I was hardly moved to come to thee; but being assured none but myself could move thee, I have been blown out of your gates with sighs; and conjure thee to pardon Rome, and thy petitionary countrymen. The good gods assuage thy wrath, and turn the dregs of it upon this varlet here,—this, who, like a block, hath denied my access to thee.

Cor. Away!

Men. How! away?

Cor. Wife, mother, child, I know not. My affairs
Are servanted to others: though I owe
My revenge properly, my remission lies
In Volscian breasts. That we have been familiar,
Ingrate forgetfulness shall poison, rather
Than pity note how much. Therefore, be gone.
Mine ears against your suits are stronger than

66. **faintly,** coldly, indifferently. 68-69. **what . . . conditions,** a baffling crux. By *what he would not* (do) is meant such things as burning Rome; the following paraphrase yields a sort of meaning: what he would not do he bound up with the proviso that we should take an oath to yield to his conditions (before we learned what they were). 71. **Unless,** unless in, except from.

SCENE II. 10. **lots to blanks,** all the world to nothing; there is a dispute as to whether *lots* means prizes or merely all numbers in the lottery. 13. **passable,** current. 14. **lover,** friend. 17. **verified,** spoken the truth about (Malone); *magnified*, *amplified*, *glorified* have been conjectured. 18. **size,** exaggeration. 19. **lapsing,** lying. 20. **subtle,** deceptively smooth (Onions). 21. **throw,** distance aimed at. 22. **stamp'd,** given currency to. **leasing,** lying. 30. **factionary,** active as a partisan. 33-34. **telling . . . him,** telling the truth in his service. 43. **violent popular ignorance,** folly of mob violence. 44. **front,** meet. 45. **easy groans,** i.e., groans which are easily provoked. 45-46. **virginal . . . daughters,** uplifted hands of your virgin daughters. 47. **dotant,** dotard, doddering old man. 53. **out of,** beyond the reach of. 55. **estimation,** esteem. 61-62. **utmost of your having,** all you are going to get. 65. **say an errand,** deliver a message. 67. **Jack guardant,** common fellow on guard; *guardant* is a heraldic term. 68. **office,** drive by virtue of your office. 71. **spectatorship,** in presence of spectators. 85. **block,** impediment and blockhead. 89. **servanted,** subjected. **owe,** own. 90. **remission,** power to forgive. 91-93. **That**

Your gates against my force. Yet, for I lov'd thee,
Take this along; I writ it for thy sake, [*Gives a letter.*]
And would have sent it. Another word, Menenius,
I will not hear thee speak. This man, Aufidius,
Was my belov'd in Rome: yet thou behold'st!

Auf. You keep a constant temper.

Exeunt. Mane[n]t the Guard and Menenius.

First Sen. Now, sir, is your name Menenius?

Sec. Sen. 'Tis a spell, you see, of much power: you know the way home again.

First Sen. Do you hear how we are shent for keeping your greatness back?

Sec. Sen. What cause, do you think, I have to swoon?

Men. I neither care for the world nor your general: for such things as you, I can scarce think there 's any, y' are so slight. He that hath a will to die by himself fears it not from another: let your general do his worst. For you, be that you are, long; and your misery increase with your age! I say to you, as I was said to, Away! *Exit.*

First Sen. A noble fellow, I warrant him.

Sec. Sen. The worthy fellow is our general: he 's the rock, the oak not to be wind-shaken. *Exit Watch.*

[SCENE III. *The tent of Coriolanus.*]

Enter CORIOLANUS *and* AUFIDIUS [*with others*].

Cor. We will before the walls of Rome to-morrow
Set down our host. My partner in this action,
You must report to th' Volscian lords, how plainly
I have borne this business.

Auf. Only their ends
You have respected; stopp'd your ears against
The general suit of Rome; never admitted
A private whisper, no, not with such friends
That thought them sure of you.

Cor. This last old man,
Whom with a crack'd heart I have sent to Rome,
Lov'd me above the measure of a father;
Nay, godded me, indeed. Their latest refuge
Was to send him; for whose old love I have,
Though I show'd sourly to him, once more offer'd
The first conditions, which they did refuse
And cannot now accept; to grace him only
That thought he could do more, a very little
I have yielded to: fresh embassies and suits,
Nor from the state nor private friends, hereafter
Will I lend ear to. Ha! what shout is this? *Shout within.*
Shall I be tempted to infringe my vow
In the same time 'tis made? I will not.

Enter VIRGILIA, VOLUMNIA, VALERIA, *young* MARCIUS, *with* Attendants.

My wife comes foremost; then the honour'd mould
Wherein this trunk was fram'd, and in her hand
The grandchild to her blood. But, out, affection!
All bond and privilege of nature, break!
Let it be virtuous to be obstinate.
What is that curt'sy worth? or those doves' eyes,
Which can make gods forsworn? I melt, and am not
Of stronger earth than others. My mother bows;
As if Olympus to a molehill should
In supplication nod: and my young boy
Hath an aspect of intercession, which
Great nature cries 'Deny not.' Let the Volsces
Plough Rome, and harrow Italy: I'll never
Be such a gosling to obey instinct, but stand,
As if a man were author of himself
And knew no other kin.

Vir. My lord and husband!

Cor. These eyes are not the same I wore in Rome.

Vir. The sorrow that delivers us thus chang'd
Makes you think so.

Cor. Like a dull actor now,
I have forgot my part, and I am out,
Even to a full disgrace. Best of my flesh,
Forgive my tyranny; but do not say
For that 'Forgive our Romans.' O, a kiss
Long as my exile, sweet as my revenge!
Now, by the jealous queen of heaven, that kiss
I carried from thee, dear; and my true lip
Hath virgin'd it e'er since. You gods! I prate,
And the most noble mother of the world
Leave unsaluted: sink, my knee, i' th' earth; *Kneels.*
Of thy deep duty more impression show
Than that of common sons.

Vol. O, stand up blest!
Whilst, with no softer cushion than the flint,
I kneel before thee; and unproperly
Show duty, as mistaken all this while
Between the child and parent. [*Kneels.*]

Cor. What's this?
Your knees to me? to your corrected son?
Then let the pebbles on the hungry beach
Fillip the stars; then let the mutinous winds
Strike the proud cedars 'gainst the fiery sun;
Murd'ring impossibility, to make
What cannot be, slight work.

Vol. Thou art my warrior;
I holp to frame thee. Do you know this lady?

Cor. The noble sister of Publicola,
The moon of Rome, chaste as the icicle
That 's curdied by the frost from purest snow
And hangs on Dian's temple: dear Valeria!

Vol. This is a poor epitome of yours,
Which by th' interpretation of full time
May show like all yourself.

Cor. The god of soldiers,

. . . **much,** that we have been friends I shall allow Rome's ingratitude to obliterate, or convert into hostility, rather than grow pitiful by remembering what friends we were. 104. **shent,** blamed. 111. **die by himself,** destroy himself. 112. **For,** as for. **that,** what. 113. **long,** for a long time.

SCENE III. 3. **plainly,** openly. 6. **general suit,** petitions of all Rome. 11. **godded,** deified. 18. **Nor . . . nor,** neither . . . nor. 34. **harrow,** literal use, carrying strongly the meaning "distress, harass." 35. **gosling,** young goose; here, fool. 38-40. **These . . . so.** Coriolanus says, "I see with different eyes from those I wore in Rome." Virgilia replies, taking his words literally, "Our sorrow has changed us past recognition." 41. **I am out,** I am at a loss. 48. **prate,** talk idly; so Theobald; F: *pray.* 51. **more . . . show,** i.e., sink deeper into the ground and display thy duty more plainly. 54. **unproperly,** improperly, i.e., unnaturally. 55. **as mistaken,** i.e., as if the obligation to show reverence had been mistaken. 57. **corrected,** submissive to correction. 58. **hungry,** unfertile (Onions), barren. 59. **Fillip,** flip, strike. 61. **Murd'ring,** removing. 62. **slight work,** an easy task. 65. **moon of Rome,** allusion to Diana, goddess of chastity. 66. **curdied,** congealed. 67. **Valeria.** According to Plutarch it was this noble lady who suggested the visit of the women to the camp of Coriolanus. 68. **poor epitome,** reference to the son of Coriolanus. 69. **by . . . time,** when time shall have fully developed his powers.

With the consent of supreme Jove, inform
Thy thoughts with nobleness; that thou mayst prove
To shame unvulnerable, and stick i' th' wars
Like a great sea-mark, standing every flaw,
And saving those that eye thee!
Vol. Your knee, sirrah.
Cor. That 's my brave boy!
Vol. Even he, your wife, this lady, and myself,
Are suitors to you.
Cor. I beseech you, peace:
Or, if you 'ld ask, remember this before:
The thing I have forsworn to grant may never
Be held by you denials. Do not bid me
Dismiss my soldiers, or capitulate
Again with Rome's mechanics: tell me not
Wherein I seem unnatural: desire not
T' allay my rages and revenges with
Your colder reasons.
Vol. O, no more, no more!
You have said you will not grant us any thing;
For we have nothing else to ask, but that
Which you deny already: yet we will ask;
That, if you fail in our request, the blame
May hang upon your hardness: therefore hear us.
Cor. Aufidius, and you Volsces, mark; for we'll
Hear nought from Rome in private. Your request?
Vol. Should we be silent and not speak, our raiment
And state of bodies would bewray what life
We have led since thy exile. Think with thyself
How more unfortunate than all living women
Are we come hither: since that thy sight, which should
Make our eyes flow with joy, hearts dance with comforts,
Constrains them weep and shake with fear and sorrow;
Making the mother, wife and child to see
The son, the husband and the father tearing
His country's bowels out. And to poor we
Thine enmity's most capital: thou barr'st us
Our prayers to the gods, which is a comfort
That all but we enjoy; for how can we,
Alas, how can we for our country pray,
Whereto we are bound, together with thy victory,
Whereto we are bound? alack, or we must lose
The country, our dear nurse, or else thy person,
Our comfort in the country. We must find
An evident calamity, though we had
Our wish, which side should win: for either thou
Must, as a foreign recreant, be led
With manacles through our streets, or else
Triumphantly tread on thy country's ruin,
And bear the palm for having bravely shed
Thy wife and children's blood. For myself, son,
I purpose not to wait on fortune till
These wars determine: if I cannot persuade thee
Rather to show a noble grace to both parts
Than seek the end of one, thou shalt no sooner
March to assault thy country than to tread—
Trust to 't, thou shalt not—on thy mother's womb,
That brought thee to this world.
Vir. Ay, and mine,
That brought you forth this boy, to keep your name
Living to time.
Young Mar. 'A shall not tread on me;
I'll run away till I am bigger, but then I'll fight.
Cor. Not of a woman's tenderness to be,
Requires nor child nor woman's face to see.
I have sat too long. [*Rising.*]
Vol. Nay, go not from us thus.
If it were so that our request did tend
To save the Romans, thereby to destroy
The Volsces whom you serve, you might condemn us,
As poisonous of your honour: no; our suit
Is, that you reconcile them: while the Volsces
May say 'This mercy we have show'd;' the Romans,
'This we receiv'd;' and each in either side
Give the all-hail to thee, and cry 'Be blest
For making up this peace!' Thou know'st, great son,
The end of war 's uncertain, but this certain,
That, if thou conquer Rome, the benefit
Which thou shalt thereby reap is such a name,
Whose repetition will be dogg'd with curses;
Whose chronicle thus writ: 'The man was noble,
But with his last attempt he wip'd it out;
Destroy'd his country, and his name remains
To th' ensuing age abhorr'd.' Speak to me, son:
Thou hast affected the fine strains of honour,
To imitate the graces of the gods;
To tear with thunder the wide cheeks o' th' air,
And yet to charge thy sulphur with a bolt
That should but rive an oak. Why dost not speak?
Think'st thou it honourable for a noble man
Still to remember wrongs? Daughter, speak you:
He cares not for your weeping. Speak thou, boy:
Perhaps thy childishness will move him more
Than can our reasons. There 's no man in the world
More bound to 's mother; yet here he lets me prate
Like one i' th' stocks. Thou hast never in thy life
Show'd thy dear mother any courtesy,
When she, poor hen, fond of no second brood,
Has cluck'd thee to the wars and safely home,
Loaden with honour. Say my request 's unjust,
And spurn me back: but if it be not so,
Thou art not honest; and the gods will plague thee,
That thou restrain'st from me the duty which
To a mother's part belongs. He turns away:
Down, ladies; let us shame him with our knees.
To his surname Coriolanus 'longs more pride
Than pity to our prayers. Down: an end;
This is the last: so we will home to Rome,
And die among our neighbours. Nay, behold 's:
This boy, that cannot tell what he would have,

73. **stick,** stand out. 80-81. **The . . . denials,** it would be unjust to regard me as refusing to grant what I have no longer the power of granting (Wright). 109. **or,** either. 112. **evident,** certain. 117. **bear the palm,** i.e., the emblem of victory. 120. **determine,** come to an end. 121. **parts,** sides. 129. **Not . . . be,** if a man is not to yield to a womanly tenderness. 146. **attempt,** undertaking. **it,** i.e., the nobility. 151. **cheeks o' th' air,** supposed reference to pictures of cherubs on old maps, or possibly pictures of the winds. 152. **sulphur,** supposed source of lightning. 159-160. **prate . . . stocks,** talk uselessly like a prisoner in the stocks who has power to do nothing else. 162. **fond of,** desirous of. 163. **cluck'd,** marshaled as a hen her brood; F: *clock'd*. 171. **an end,** let us be done. 175. **fellowship,** company. 176. **reason,** argue for. 180. **dispatch,** dismissal, leave to go. 191. **convenient,** fitting, proper. 196. **sweat compassion,** weep with pity. 199. **Stand to,** stand by. 202. **former fortune,** fortune great as formerly. 204. **better witness,** i.e., formal document of peace. 205. **counter-seal'd,**

But kneels and holds up hands for fellowship,
Does reason our petition with more strength
Than thou hast to deny 't. Come, let us go:
This fellow had a Volscian to his mother;
His wife is in Corioles and his child
Like him by chance. Yet give us our dispatch:
I am hush'd until our city be afire,
And then I'll speak a little.
[He] holds her by the hand, silent.

Cor. O mother, mother!
What have you done? Behold, the heavens do ope,
The gods look down, and this unnatural scene
They laugh at. O my mother, mother! O!
You have won a happy victory to Rome;
But, for your son,—believe it, O, believe it,
Most dangerously you have with him prevail'd,
If not most mortal to him. But, let it come.
Aufidius, though I cannot make true wars,
I'll frame convenient peace. Now, good Aufidius,
Were you in my stead, would you have heard
A mother less? or granted less, Aufidius?

Auf. I was mov'd withal.

Cor. I dare be sworn you were:
And, sir, it is no little thing to make
Mine eyes to sweat compassion. But, good sir,
What peace you'll make, advise me: for my part,
I'll not to Rome, I'll back with you; and pray you,
Stand to me in this cause. O mother! wife!

Auf. *[Aside]* I am glad thou hast set thy mercy and thy honour
At difference in thee: out of that I'll work
Myself a former fortune.
[The Ladies make signs to Coriolanus.]

Cor. Ay, by and by;
[To Volumnia, Virgilia, &c.]
But we will drink together; and you shall bear
A better witness back than words, which we,
On like conditions, will have counter-seal'd.
Come, enter with us. Ladies, you deserve
To have a temple built you: all the swords
In Italy, and her confederate arms,
Could not have made this peace. *Exeunt.*

[SCENE IV. *Rome. A public place.*]

Enter MENENIUS *and* SICINIUS.

Men. See you yond coign o' the Capitol, yond corner-stone?

Sic. Why, what of that?

Men. If it be possible for you to displace it with your little finger, there is some hope the ladies of Rome, especially his mother, may prevail with him. But I say there is no hope in 't: our throats are sentenced and stay upon execution.

Sic. Is 't possible that so short a time can alter the condition of a man?

Men. There is differency between a grub and a butterfly; yet your butterfly was a grub. This Marcius is grown from man to dragon: he has wings; he 's more than a creeping thing.

Sic. He loved his mother dearly.

Men. So did he me: and he no more remembers his mother now than an eight-year-old horse. The tartness of his face sours ripe grapes: when he walks, he moves like an engine, and the ground shrinks before his treading: he is able to pierce a corslet with his eye; talks like a knell, and his hum is a battery. He sits in his state, as a thing made for Alexander. What he bids be done is finished with his bidding. He wants nothing of a god but eternity and a heaven to throne in.

Sic. Yes, mercy, if you report him truly.

Men. I paint him in the character. Mark what mercy his mother shall bring from him: there is no more mercy in him than there is milk in a male tiger; that shall our poor city find: and all this is long of you.

Sic. The gods be good unto us!

Men. No, in such a case the gods will not be good unto us. When we banished him, we respected not them; and, he returning to break our necks, they respect not us.

Enter a Messenger.

Mess. Sir, if you 'ld save your life, fly to your house:
The plebeians have got your fellow-tribune
And hale him up and down, all swearing, if
The Roman ladies bring not comfort home,
They'll give him death by inches.

Enter another Messenger.

Sic. What 's the news?

Sec. Mess. Good news, good news; the ladies have prevail'd,
The Volscians are dislodg'd, and Marcius gone:
A merrier day did never yet greet Rome,
No, not th' expulsion of the Tarquins.

Sic. Friend,
Art thou certain this is true? is 't most certain?

Sec. Mess. As certain as I know the sun is fire:
Where have you lurk'd, that you make doubt of it?
Ne'er through an arch so hurried the blown tide,
As the recomforted through th' gates. Why, hark you!
Trumpets; hautboys; drums beat; all together.
The trumpets, sackbuts, psalteries and fifes,
Tabors and cymbals and the shouting Romans,
Make the sun dance. Hark you! *A shout within.*

Men. This is good news:
I will go meet the ladies. This Volumnia
Is worth of consuls, senators, patricians,
A city full; of tribunes, such as you,
A sea and land full. You have pray'd well to-day:
This morning for ten thousand of your throats
I 'ld not have given a doit. Hark, how they joy!
Sound still, with the shouts.

sealed with an additional seal as a further sanction. 208. **confederate arms,** weapons of the allies.

SCENE IV. 1. **coign,** corner. 21-22. **talks . . . battery,** his voice is a signal of death and his hum (exclamation) is as loud as a battery (a battle assault). 22-23. **as . . . Alexander,** as if it were the throne of Alexander the Great (who, of course, is too late to be referred to in a play of this period). 26. **throne,** be enthroned. 28. **in the character,** to the life. 44. **dislodg'd,** gone from their camp. 50. **Ne'er . . . tide.** The Yale editor sees in this an allusion to the rush of the tide through the arches of the old London Bridge. **blown,** swollen. 52. **sackbuts,** bass trumpets with a slide like that of a trombone. **psalteries,** stringed instruments played by plucking the strings. 53. **Tabors,** drums. 54. **sun dance.** According to popular superstition the sun danced on Easter Day.

Sic. First, the gods bless you for your tidings; next,
Accept my thankfulness.
Sec. Mess. Sir, we have all
Great cause to give great thanks.
Sic. They are near the city?
Sec. Mess. Almost at point to enter.
Sic. We'll meet them,
And help the joy. *Exeunt.*

[SCENE V. *The same. A street near the gate.*]

Enter two Senators *with Ladies* [VOLUMNIA, VIRGILIA, VALERIA] *passing over the stage, with other Lords.*

First Sen. Behold our patroness, the life of Rome!
Call all your tribes together, praise the gods,
And make triumphant fires; strew flowers before them:
Unshout the noise that banish'd Marcius,
Repeal him with the welcome of his mother;
Cry 'Welcome, ladies, welcome!'
All. Welcome, ladies,
Welcome! *A flourish with drums and trumpets.* [*Exeunt.*]

[SCENE VI. *Antium. A public place.*]

Enter TULLUS AUFIDIUS, *with* Attendants.

Auf. Go tell the lords o' th' city I am here:
Deliver them this paper: having read it,
Bid them repair to th' market-place; where I,
Even in theirs and in the commons' ears,
Will vouch the truth of it. Him I accuse
The city ports by this hath enter'd and
Intends t' appear before the people, hoping
To purge himself with words: dispatch.
[*Exeunt Attendants.*]

Enter three or four Conspirators *of* AUFIDIUS' *faction.*

Most welcome!
First Con. How is it with our general?
Auf. Even so
As with a man by his own alms empoison'd,
And with his charity slain.
Sec. Con. Most noble sir,
If you do hold the same intent wherein
You wish'd us parties, we'll deliver you
Of your great danger.
Auf. Sir, I cannot tell:
We must proceed as we do find the people.
Third Con. The people will remain uncertain whilst
'Twixt you there 's difference; but the fall of either
Makes the survivor heir of all.
Auf. I know it;
And my pretext to strike at him admits
A good construction. I rais'd him, and I pawn'd
Mine honour for his truth: who being so heighten'd,
He watered his new plants with dews of flattery,
Seducing so my friends; and, to this end,
He bow'd his nature, never known before
But to be rough, unswayable and free.
Third Con. Sir, his stoutness
When he did stand for consul, which he lost
By lack of stooping,—
Auf. That I would have spoke of:
Being banish'd for 't, he came unto my hearth;
Presented to my knife his throat: I took him;
Made him joint-servant with me; gave him way
In all his own desires; nay, let him choose
Out of my files, his projects to accomplish,
My best and freshest men; serv'd his designments
In mine own person; holp to reap the fame
Which he did end all his; and took some pride
To do myself this wrong: till, at the last,
I seem'd his follower, not partner, and
He wag'd me with his countenance, as if
I had been mercenary.
First Con. So he did, my lord:
The army marvell'd at it, and, in the last,
When he had carried Rome and that we look'd
For no less spoil than glory,—
Auf. There was it:
For which my sinews shall be stretch'd upon him.
At a few drops of women's rheum, which are
As cheap as lies, he sold the blood and labour
Of our great action: therefore shall he die,
And I'll renew me in his fall. But, hark!
Drums and trumpets sound, with great shouts of the People.
First Con. Your native town you enter'd like a post,
And had no welcomes home; but he returns,
Splitting the air with noise.
Sec. Con. And patient fools,
Whose children he hath slain, their base throats tear
With giving him glory.
Third Con. Therefore, at your vantage,
Ere he express himself, or move the people
With what he would say, let him feel your sword,
Which we will second. When he lies along,
After your way his tale pronounc'd shall bury
His reasons with his body.
Auf. Say no more:
Here come the lords.

Enter the Lords *of the city.*

All the Lords. You are most welcome home.
Auf. I have not deserv'd it.
But, worthy lords, have you with heed perus'd
What I have written to you?
Lords. We have.
First Lord. And grieve to hear 't.
What faults he made before the last, I think

SCENE V. 4. **Unshout,** recall, or cancel by more shouting.

SCENE VI. 5. **Him,** he whom. 6. **by this,** by this time. 20. **pretext,** intention. 21. **construction,** interpretation. 23. **new plants,** i.e., Volscians. 27. **stoutness,** obstinacy. 34. **files,** men in depth from front to rear in a military formation in line; here generally ranks, troops. 37. **Which . . . his,** which he did gather in as all his own. 40. **wag'd,** remunerated. **countenance,** patronage, favor. 43. **carried,** virtually carried, or might have carried. 45. **my . . . stretch'd.** I shall exert all my strength. 46. **rheum,** tears. 50. **post,** messenger. 54. **at your vantage,** at an opportune moment for you. 57. **lies along,** lies low. 58. **your . . . pronounc'd,** your statement of the case. 65. **fines,** penalties. 67-68. **answering . . . charge,** rewarding us with our own expenses (Johnson). 68. **treaty,** compromise. 69. **yielding,** i.e., complete victory for us. 72. **infected,** affected, or possibly contaminated. 75. **prosperously . . . attempted,** my warlike enterprise has been prosperous. 96. **twist,** skein. 102. **No more,** say no more; also explained

Might have found easy fines: but there to end
Where he was to begin and give away
The benefit of our levies, answering us
With our own charge, making a treaty where
There was a yielding,—this admits no excuse.
Auf. He approaches: you shall hear him.

Enter CORIOLANUS, *marching with drum and colours; the Commoners being with him.*

Cor. Hail, lords! I am return'd your soldier,
No more infected with my country's love
Than when I parted hence, but still subsisting
Under your great command. You are to know
That prosperously I have attempted and
With bloody passage led your wars even to
The gates of Rome. Our spoils we have brought home
Do more than counterpoise a full third part
The charges of the action. We have made peace
With no less honour to the Antiates
Than shame to th' Romans: and we here deliver,
Subscrib'd by th' consuls and patricians,
Together with the seal o' th' senate, what
We have compounded on.
Auf. Read it not, noble lords;
But tell the traitor, in the highest degree
He hath abus'd your powers.
Cor. Traitor! how now!
Auf. Ay, traitor, Marcius!
Cor. Marcius!
Auf. Ay, Marcius, Caius Marcius: dost thou think
I'll grace thee with that robbery, thy stol'n name
Coriolanus in Corioles?
You lords and heads o' th' state, perfidiously
He has betray'd your business, and given up,
For certain drops of salt, your city Rome,
I say 'your city,' to his wife and mother;
Breaking his oath and resolution like
A twist of rotten silk, never admitting
Counsel o' th' war, but at his nurse's tears
He whin'd and roar'd away your victory,
That pages blush'd at him and men of heart
Look'd wond'ring each at other.
Cor. Hear'st thou, Mars?
Auf. Name not the god, thou boy of tears!
Cor. Ha!
Auf. No more.
Cor. Measureless liar, thou hast made my heart
Too great for what contains it. Boy! O slave!
Pardon me, lords, 'tis the first time that ever
I was forc'd to scold. Your judgements, my grave lords,
Must give this cur the lie: and his own notion—
Who wears my stripes impress'd upon him; that
Must bear my beating to his grave—shall join
To thrust the lie unto him.
First Lord. Peace, both, and hear me speak.
Cor. Cut me to pieces, Volsces; men and lads,
Stain all your edges on me. Boy! false hound!
If you have writ your annals true, 'tis there,
That, like an eagle in a dove-cote, I
Flutter'd your Volscians in Corioles:
Alone I did it. Boy!
Auf. Why, noble lords,
Will you be put in mind of his blind fortune,
Which was your shame, by this unholy braggart,
'Fore your own eyes and ears?
All Consp. Let him die for 't.
All the people. 'Tear him to pieces.' 'Do it presently.' 'He killed my son.' 'My daughter.' 'He killed my cousin Marcus.' 'He killed my father.'
Sec. Lord. Peace, ho! no outrage: peace!
The man is noble and his fame folds-in
This orb o' th' earth. His last offences to us
Shall have judicious hearing. Stand, Aufidius,
And trouble not the peace.
Cor. O that I had him,
With six Aufidiuses, or more, his tribe,
To use my lawful sword!
Auf. Insolent villain!
All Consp. Kill, kill, kill, kill, kill him!
Draw the Conspirators, and kill Marcius, who falls. Aufidius stands on him.
Lords. Hold, hold, hold, hold!
Auf. My noble masters, hear me speak.
First Lord. O Tullus,—
Sec. Lord. Thou hast done a deed whereat valour will weep.
Third Lord. Tread not upon him. Masters all, be quiet;
Put up your swords.
Auf. My lords, when you shall know—as in this rage,
Provok'd by him, you cannot—the great danger
Which this man's life did owe you, you'll rejoice
That he is thus cut off. Please it your honours
To call me to your senate, I'll deliver
Myself your loyal servant, or endure
Your heaviest censure.
First Lord. Bear from hence his body;
And mourn you for him: let him be regarded
As the most noble corse that ever herald
Did follow to his urn.
Sec. Lord. His own impatience
Takes from Aufidius a great part of blame.
Let 's make the best of it.
Auf. My rage is gone;
And I am struck with sorrow. Take him up.
Help, three o' th' chiefest soldiers; I'll be one.
Beat thou the drum, that it speak mournfully:
Trail your steel pikes. Though in this city he
Hath widow'd and unchilded many a one,
Which to this hour bewail the injury,
Yet he shall have a noble memory.
Assist.

Exeunt, bearing the body of Marcius. A dead march sounded.

as no more than a boy of tears. 104. **Too . . . it,** swollen with rage so that his breast cannot contain it. 107. **notion,** understanding, mind. 116. **Flutter'd,** so F_{3-4}; F_{1-2}: *Flatter'd,* retained by Schmidt with the meaning fluttered or scared; Onions also retains it. 118. **blind fortune,** luck in a reckless undertaking, or gift of Fortune, the blind goddess. 126. **folds-in,** overspreads (Johnson). 128. **judicious,** judicial, or possibly rational, fair. 139. **Which . . . owe you,** which while this man lived was owing to you, would sooner or later have befallen you (Deighton). 145-146. **herald . . . urn.** In Shakespeare's day a herald marshaled the funeral procession of noblemen deceased and proclaimed their rank and station. 150. **I'll be one.** The play thus closes with the eulogy of Aufidius, whose admiration for Coriolanus has been no less in evidence throughout the play than his jealousy and implacable enmity. 152. **Trail . . . pikes.** Mournful music, trailing pikes and banners were customary in a soldier's burial. 153. **unchilded,** slain the children of.

the period of romances

In the summer of 1608, Shakespeare's acting company signed a twenty-one-year lease for the use of the Blackfriars playhouse, an indoor and rather intimate, artificially lighted theatre inside the city of London, close to St. Paul's cathedral. A private theatre had existed on this spot since 1576, when the Children of the Chapel and then Paul's boys began acting their courtly plays for paying spectators in a building that had once belonged to the Dominicans, or Black Friars. James Burbage had begun construction in 1596 of the so-called Second Blackfriars theatre in the same building. Although James encountered opposition from the residents of the area and died before he could complete the work, James' son Richard did succeed in opening the new theatre in 1600. At first he leased it (for twenty-one years) to a children's company; but when that company was suppressed in 1608 for offending the French ambassador in a play by George Chapman, Burbage seized the opportunity to take back the unexpired lease and set up Blackfriars as the winter playhouse for his adult company, the King's men. By this time the adult troupes could plainly see that they needed to cater more directly to courtly audiences than they once had done. Their popular audiences were becoming increasingly disenchanted with the drama. Puritan fulminations against the stage gained in effect, especially when many playwrights refused to disguise their satirical hostility toward Puritans and the London bourgeoisie.

Several of Shakespeare's late plays may have been acted both at the Globe and at Blackfriars. The plays he wrote after 1608–1609, *Cymbeline*, *The Winter's Tale*, and *The Tempest*, all show the distinct influence of the dramaturgy of the private theatres. Also, we know that an increasing number of Shakespeare's plays were acted at the court of King James. *Othello*, *King Lear*, and *The Tempest* are named in court revels accounts, and *Macbeth* attentively flatters the Scottish royal ancestry of King James as though for a court performance. On the other hand, Shakespeare's plays certainly continued to be acted at the Globe to the very end of his career. The 1609 quarto of *Pericles* advertises that it was acted "by his Maiesties Seruants, at the Globe on the Banck-side." The 1608 quarto of *King Lear* mentions a performance at court and assigns the play to "his Maiesties seruants playing vsually at the Gloabe on the Bancke-side." Simon Forman saw *Macbeth*, *Cymbeline*, and *The Winter's Tale* at the Globe. Finally, a performance of *Henry VIII* on June 29, 1613, resulted in the burning of the Globe to the ground, though it was rebuilt soon after.

Shakespeare's last plays, written with a view to Blackfriars and the court as well as to the Globe, are usually called romances or tragicomedies or sometimes both. The term romance suggests a return to the kind of story Robert Greene had derived from Greek romance: tales of adventure, long separation, and tearful reunion, involving shipwreck, capture by pirates, riddling prophecies, children set adrift in boats or abandoned on foreign shores, the illusion of death and subsequent restoration to life, the revelation of the identity of long-lost children by birthmarks, and the like. The term tragicomedy suggests a play in which the protagonist commits a seemingly fatal error or crime, or (as in *Pericles*) suffers an extraordinarily adverse fortune to test his patience; in either event he must experience agonies of contrition and bereavement until he is miraculously delivered from his tribulations. The tone is deeply melancholy and resigned, although suffused also with a sense of gratitude for the harmonies that are mysteriously restored.

The appropriateness of such plays to the elegant atmosphere of Blackfriars and the court is subtle but real. Although one might suppose at first that old-fashioned naiveté would seem out of place in a sophisticated milieu, the naiveté is only superficial. Tragicomedy and pastoral romance were, in the period from 1606 to 1610, beginning to enjoy a fashionable courtly revival. The leading practitioners of the new genre were Beaumont and Fletcher, though Shakespeare made a highly significant contribution. Perhaps sophisticated audiences responded to pastoral and romantic drama as the nostalgic evocation of an idealized past, a chivalric "golden world" fleetingly recovered through an artistic journey back to naiveté and innocence. The evocation of such a world demands the kind of studied but informal artifice we find in many tragicomic plays of the period: the elaborate masques and allegorical shows, the descents of enthroned gods from the heavens (as in *Cymbeline*), the use of quaint Chorus figures like Old Gower or Time (in *Pericles* and *The Winter's Tale*), the quasi-operatic blend of music and spectacle. At their best, such plays powerfully compel belief in the artistic world thus artificially created. The very improbability of the story becomes, paradoxically, part of the means by which an audience must "awake its faith" in a mysterious truth.

Shakespeare did not merely ape the new fashion in tragicomedy and romance. In fact, he may have done much to establish it. His *Pericles*, written seemingly in about 1606–1608 for the public stage before Shakespeare's company acquired Blackfriars, anticipated many important features not only of Shakespeare's own later romances but of Beaumont and Fletcher's *The Maid's Tragedy* and *Philaster* (c. 1608–1611). Still, Shakespeare was on the verge of retirement, and the future belonged to Beaumont and Fletcher. Gradually Shakespeare disengaged himself, spending more and more time in Stratford. His last-known stint as an actor was in *Sejanus* in 1603. Some time in 1611 or 1612 he probably gave up his lodgings in London, though he still may have returned for such occasions as the opening performance of *Henry VIII* in 1613. He continued to be one of the proprietors of the newly rebuilt Globe, but his involvement in its day-to-day operations dwindled.

Literary Allusions

Shakespeare's reputation among his contemporaries was undiminished in his late years, even though Beaumont and Fletcher were the new rage at the Globe and Blackfriars. Among those who apostrophized Shakespeare was John Davies of Hereford in *The Scourge of Folly* (S. R. 1610):

To our English Terence, Mr. Will. Shake-speare.

Some say (good *Will*) which I, in sport, do sing,
Had'st thou not plaid some Kingly parts in sport,
Thou hadst bin a companion for a *King;*
And, beene a King among the meaner sort.
Some others raile; but, raile as they thinke fit,
Thou hast no rayling, but, a raigning Wit:
And honesty *thou sow'st, which they do reape;*
So, to increase their Stocke *which they do keepe.*

The following sonnet is from *Runne and a Great Cast* (1614) by Thomas Freeman:

To Master W. Shakespeare.

Shakespeare, that nimble *Mercury* thy braine,
Lulls many hundred *Argus*-eyes asleepe,
So fit, for all thou fashionest thy vaine,
At th' *horse-foote* fountaine thou hast drunk full deepe,
Vertues or vices theame to thee all one is:
Who loues chaste life, there's *Lucrece* for a Teacher:
Who list read lust there's *Venus* and *Adonis*,
True modell of a most lasciuious leatcher.
Besides in plaies thy wit windes like *Meander:*
Whence needy new-composers borrow more
Then *Terence* doth from *Plautus* or *Menander*.
But to praise thee aright I want thy store:
Then let thine owne works thine owne worth upraise,
And help t' adorne thee with deserued Baies.

Ben Jonson took a more critical view, though he also admired Shakespeare greatly. In the Induction to his *Bartholomew Fair* (1631 edition), Jonson compared the imaginary world he presented in his play with the more improbable fantasies of romantic drama:

If there bee neuer a *Seruant-monster* i' the Fayre; who can helpe it? he [the author, Jonson] sayes; nor a nest of *Antiques?* Hee is loth to make Nature afraid in his *Playes*, like those

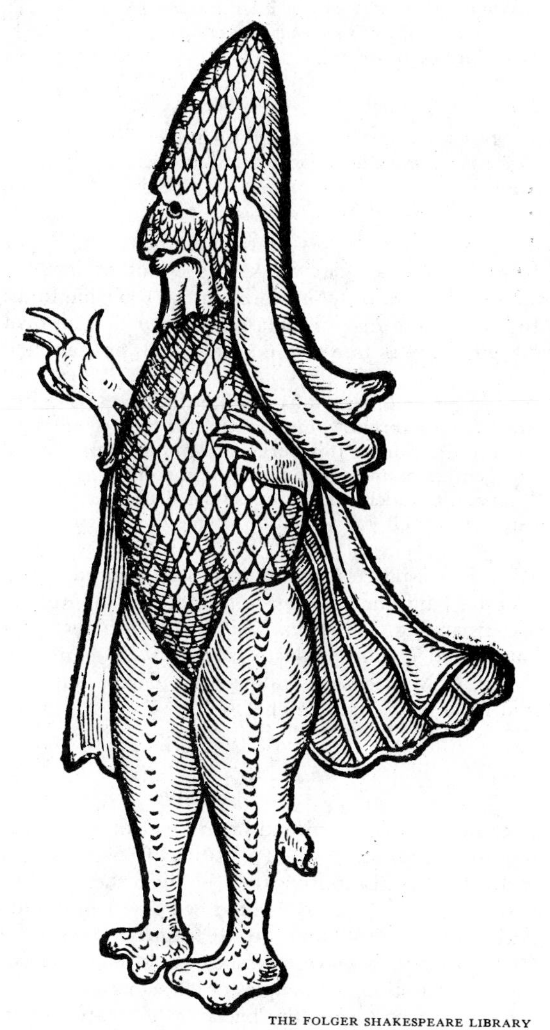

THE FOLGER SHAKESPEARE LIBRARY

This contemporary illustration of a mythical beast may have given Shakespeare an idea for his conception of Caliban.

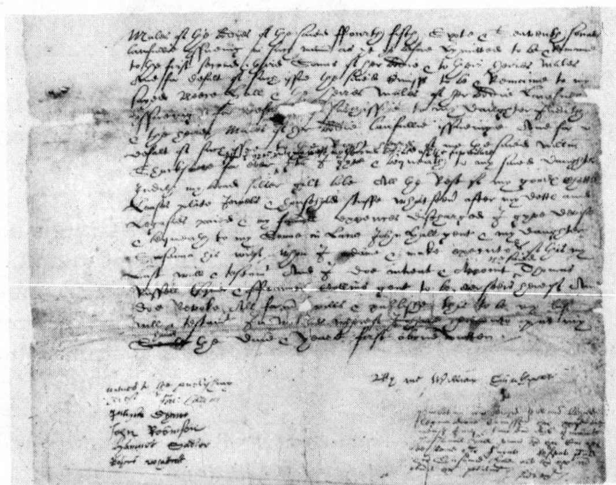

TRANSCRIPTS OF CROWN-COPYRIGHT RECORDS IN THE PUBLIC RECORD OFFICE APPEAR BY PERMISSION OF THE CONTROLLER OF H. M. STATIONERY OFFICE

As with so many other things in his life, the curious terms of Shakespeare's will have led to endless and provocative conjecture.

that beget *Tales*, *Tempests*, and such like
Drolleries, to mixe his head with other mens
heeles.

From this, one judges that Jonson had in mind not only *The Tempest* but Shakespeare's other late romances. He similarly protested in the Prologue to his 1616 edition of *Every Man in His Humour* that his own playwriting was free of the usual romantic claptrap:

Where neither *Chorus* wafts you ore the seas;
Nor creaking throne comes downe, the boys to please;
Nor nimble squibbe [fireworks] is seene, to make afear'd
The gentlewomen; nor roul'd bullet heard
To say, it thunders; nor tempestuous drumme
Rumbles, to tell you when the storme doth come.

Still, Shakespeare's reputation was assured. John Webster paid due homage, in his note To the Reader accompanying *The White Devil* (1612), to "the right happy and copious industry of M. *Shake-speare*, M. *Decker*, & M. *Heywood*," along with Chapman, Jonson, Beaumont, and Fletcher.

Latest Records

Shakespeare's last recorded investment in real estate was the purchase of a house in Blackfriars, London, in 1613. There is no indication he lived there, for he had retired to Stratford. He did not pay the full purchase price of £140, and the mortgage deed executed for the unpaid balance furnishes one of the six absolutely unquestioned examples of his signature.

John Combe, a wealthy bachelor of Stratford and Shakespeare's friend, left him a legacy of five pounds in his will at the time of Combe's death in 1613. At about the same time, John's kinsman William Combe began a controversial attempt to enclose Welcombe Common—that is, to convert narrow strips of arable land to pasture. Presumably Combe was interested in a more efficient means of using the land. Enclosure was, however, an explosive issue, since many people feared they would lose the right to farm the land and be evicted to make room for cattle and sheep. Combe attempted to guarantee Shakespeare and other titheholders that they would lose no money. He offered similar assurances to the Stratford Council, but the townspeople were adamantly opposed. Shakespeare was consulted by letter as a leading titheholder. The letter is lost, but presumably it set forth the Council's reasons for objecting to enclosure. Shakespeare's views on the controversy remain unknown. Eventually the case went to the Privy Council, where Combe was ordered to restore the land to its original use.

One of the most interesting documents from the later period consists of the records of a lawsuit entered into in 1612 by Stephen Belott against his father-in-law Christopher Mountjoy, a Huguenot maker of woman's ornamental headdresses who resided on Silver Street, St. Olave's parish, London. Belott sought to secure the payment of a dower promised him at the time of his marriage to Mountjoy's daughter. In this suit Shakespeare was summoned as a witness and made deposition on five interrogatories. From this document we learn that Shakespeare was a lodger in Mountjoy's house at the time of the marriage in 1604 and probably for some time before that, since he states in his testimony that he had known Mountjoy for more than ten years. Shakespeare admitted that, at the solicitation of Mountjoy's wife, he had acted as an intermediary in the arrangement of the marriage between Belott and Mountjoy's daughter. Shakespeare declared himself unable, however, to recall the exact amount of the portion or the date on which it was to have been paid. Shakespeare's signature to his deposition is undoubtedly authentic, and one of the best samples of his handwriting that we have.

In January of 1615 or 1616, Shakespeare drew up his last will and testament with the assistance of his lawyer Francis Collins, who had aided him earlier in some of his transactions in real estate. On March 25, 1616, Shakespeare revised his will in order to provide for the marriage of his daughter Judith and Thomas Quiney in that same year. Shakespeare's three quavering signatures, one on each page of this document, suggest that he was in failing health. The cause of his death on April 23 is not known. An intriguing bit of Stratford gossip is reported by John Ward, vicar of Holy Trinity in Stratford from 1662 to 1689, in his diary: "Shakespear, Drayton, and Ben Jhonson, had a merry meeting, and itt seems drank too hard, for Shakespear died of a feavour there contracted." The report comes fifty years after Shakespeare's death, however, and is hardly an expert medical opinion.

The will disposes of all the property of which

Shakespeare is known to have died possessed, the greater share of it going to his daughter Susanna. His recently married daughter Judith received a dowry, a provision for any children that might be born of her marriage, and other gifts. Ten pounds went to the poor of Stratford, Shakespeare's sword to Mr. Thomas Combe, 28s. 8d. apiece to Shakespeare's fellow actors Heminges, Burbage, and Condell to buy them mourning rings, and other small bequests to various other friends and relatives.

An interlineation contains the bequest of Shakespeare's "second best bed with the furniture," that is, the hangings, to his wife. Anne's name appears nowhere else in the will. Some scholars, beginning with Edmond Malone, have taken this reference as proof of an unhappy marriage, confirming earlier indications such as the hasty wedding to a woman who was William's senior by eight years, and his prolonged residence in London for twenty years or more seemingly without his family. The evidence is inconclusive, however. Shakespeare certainly supported his family handsomely, acquired much property in Stratford, and retired there when he might have remained still in London. Although he showed no great solicitude for Anne's well-being in the will, her rights were protected by law; a third of her husband's estate went to her without having to be mentioned in the will. New Place was to be the home of Shakespeare's favorite daughter Susanna, wife of the distinguished Dr. John Hall. Anne Shakespeare would make her home with her daughter, and with her dower rights secured by law would be quite as wealthy as she would need to be.

The date of Shakespeare's death, April 23, 1616, is inscribed on his monument. This elaborate structure, still standing in the chancel of Trinity Church, Stratford, was erected some time before 1623 by the London stonecutting firm of Gheerart Janssen and his sons. Janssen's shop was in Southwark, near the Globe, and may have been familiar to the actors. The bust of Shakespeare is a conventional sort of statuary for its time. Still, it is one of the only two contemporary likenesses we have. The other is the Droeshout engraving of Shakespeare in the Folio of 1623.

The epitaph on the monument reads as follows:

Ivdicio Pylivm, genio Socratem, arte Maronem:
Terra tegit, popvlvs maeret, Olympvs habet.
Stay Passenger, why goest thov by so fast?
Read if thov canst, whom enviovs Death hath plast,
With in this monvment Shakspeare: with whome,
Quick natvre dide: whose name doth deck y^s^ Tombe,
Far more then cost: sieh all, y^t^ He hath writt,
Leaves living art, bvt page, to serve his witt.
Obiit anno domini 1616
Aetatis—53 die 23 April.

These lines, which seem to indicate, as well as anything could, the high reputation in which Shakespeare was held as a poet at the time of his death, are not so well known as those inscribed over Shakespeare's grave near the north wall of the chancel. A local tradition assigns them to Shakespeare himself and implies that he wrote them "to suit the capacity of clerks and sextons," whom he wished apparently to frighten out of the idea of opening the grave to make room for a new occupant:

HOLY TRINITY CHURCH, STRATFORD. BY PERMISSION OF THE VICAR AND CHURCHWARDENS

The monument over Shakespeare's grave at Stratford, complete with death's head, coat of arms, bust, and epitaph.

Good frend for Iesvs sake forbeare,
To digg the dvst encloased heare.
Bleste be y[e] man y[t] spares thes stones,
And cvrst be he y[t] moves my bones.

Whether Shakespeare actually wrote these lines cannot, however, be determined.

Other Dramatists

The most significant new development in the drama of the period from about 1608 to 1616, apart from Shakespeare's new interest in romance and tragicomedy, was the emergence of the famous literary partners Francis Beaumont and John Fletcher. Beaumont, the son of a distinguished lawyer, studied for a while at Oxford and then at the Inner Temple before drifting into a literary career. In 1613 he married an heiress and retired almost completely from the theatre. John Fletcher was the son of Richard Fletcher, Queen Elizabeth's chaplain and later Bishop of London. The young man probably studied at Cambridge. The father died in 1596 heavily in debt, leaving the young Fletcher to support a family of eight children. Fletcher became a professional writer, earning his living as chief dramatist for the King's men. He was Shakespeare's successor. Fletcher's cousins Giles and Phineas Fletcher gained some reputation as poets. Beaumont and Fletcher, who were close friends, regarded themselves also as poets and as members of the "tribe of Ben"—the disciples of the great Ben Jonson who often gathered together at the Mermaid Tavern for an evening of witty literary conversation.

What things have we seen
Done at the Mermaid! heard words that have been
So nimble, and so full of subtle flame,
As if that every one from whence they came
Had meant to put his whole wit in a jest,
And had resolv'd to live a fool the rest
Of his dull life!

(*Master Francis Beaumont's Letter to Ben Jonson*)

Beaumont and Fletcher actually collaborated on only about seven plays: *The Woman Hater*, a comedy (1606), *The Maid's Tragedy*, a tragedy (1608–1611), *Philaster*, a tragicomedy (1608–1610), *Cupid's Revenge*, a tragedy (c. 1607–1612), *The Coxcomb*, a comedy (1608–1610), *A King and No King*, a tragicomedy (1611), *The Scornful Lady*, a tragicomedy (1613–1616), and perhaps one or two others. They may have collaborated on *The Knight of the Burning Pestle* (c. 1607–1610), though it was chiefly Beaumont's. Beaumont also wrote a *Mask of the Inner Temple and Gray's Inn* (1613). Fletcher unassisted wrote *The Faithful Shepherdess* (1608–1609), *The Night Walker* (c. 1611), *Bonduca* (1611–1614), *Valentinian* (1610–1614), and others. He also collaborated with several other writers, including Massinger, Middleton, Field, and Rowley. Importantly, he may have collaborated with Shakespeare on *The Two Noble Kinsmen* (1613–1616), and conceivably *Henry VIII*. Eventually, most of these various dramatic enterprises were gathered together in 1647 as the works of Beaumont and Fletcher. They have remained known as such ever since, partly because the original collaboration of these two men did so much to set a new style in coterie drama.

The plays they wrote together, such as *The Maid's Tragedy* and *Philaster*, offer an interesting comparison with Shakespeare's contemporary writing in a similar genre. Beaumont and Fletcher often employ exotic settings, like Rhodes or Sicily. In such an environment, refined aristocratic characters are caught in dynastic struggles or in a rarified conflict between love and honor. They must cope with stereotyped villains such as tyrants or shamelessly lustful courtiers. The sentiments are lofty, the rhetoric is mannered; elaborately contrived situations are offered with no pretense of versimilitude. The characters live according to lofty chivalric codes, and despise ill breeding above all else. In the plotting of the tragicomic reversal, the audience is sometimes deliberately deceived into believing something that is not true, so that the sudden happy outcome arrives as a theatrically contrived surprise. Disguising and masking are common motifs. The audience is deliberately made aware throughout of the play's theatrical artifice, statuesque scene-building, and titillating sensationalism.

Although Shakespeare wrote no tragedies during his last years, great tragedy did continue to appear on the Jacobean stage. John Webster wrote his two most splendid plays, *The White Devil* and *The Duchess of Malfi*, between 1609 and 1614. Both contain elements of the still-popular revenge tradition. They also manage to achieve a vision of triumphant human dignity in defeat that merits comparison with Shakespeare's greatest tragic achievement. Still to come were *The Changeling* (1622) by Middleton and Rowley, *Women Beware Women* (c. 1620–1627) by Middleton, *'Tis Pity She's a Whore* (1629?–1633) by John Ford, and others. Although these tragedies are more concerned with the grotesque than Shakespeare's great tragedies, more obsessed with abnormal human psychology (incest, werewolfism, and the like), technically more "degenerate," they are nonetheless sublime achievements in art. The genius of the age for tragedy did not die with Shakespeare. During Shakespeare's last years Chapman was also writing his best tragedies, including *Charles Duke of Byron* in 1608, *The Revenge of Bussy D'Ambois* in about 1610, and *Chabot, Admiral of France* between 1611 and 1622. Jonson's *Cataline His Conspiracy*, a classical tragedy, appeared in 1611, Marston's *The Insatiate Countess* in about 1610.

PERICLES

Pericles is a deceptively simple play. On the printed page it may seem naive and trivial, especially when compared with its contemporaries *King Lear*, *Macbeth*, *Timon of Athens*, and *Antony and Cleopatra*. It purports to be the work of a medieval poet, John Gower, who as chorus-figure apologizes to his sophisticated Jacobean audience ("born in these latter times When wit's more ripe") for the "lame feet of my rhyme" and the quaintness of his ditty. The narrative offers a series of implausible and disjointed sea voyages, separations, hairbreadth escapes, and reunions. Thrilling circumstances abound: Pericles fleeing the wrath of Antiochus, his wife Thaisa giving birth to Marina on board ship in the midst of a gigantic storm, and Marina later being rescued by pirates from a would-be murderer only to be sold by her new captors to a house of prostitution. Time leaps forward in sequential segments from Pericles' own youth to that of his daughter Marina. The action takes place in lands remote, shifting constantly back and forth among six eastern Mediterranean localities: Antioch, Tyre, Tarsus, Pentapolis, Ephesus, and Mytilene. Conventional devices of plot include the expounding of riddles, the discovery of incest at court, the exposure of infants to the hostile elements, the miraculous restoration of life after seeming death, the appearance of the gods in a vision, and recognition of long-lost loved ones by means of signs or tokens.

These are the attributes of popular romance, a distinctly old-fashioned genre in 1606–1608 when *Pericles* was apparently written. Robert Greene had composed prose romances of this sort in the 1580's and early 1590's, including *Pandosto*, Shakespeare's source for *The Winter's Tale*. Sir Philip Sidney's *Arcadia* had endowed romance with noble eloquence and literary fashionableness, but that too was in the late 1580's. One source for *Pericles* itself, a prose history of Apollonius of Tyre by Laurence Twine, was registered for publication in 1576, although no edition exists before that of 1594 or 1595. Earlier accounts of Apollonius (as the hero was originally named), going back to Greek romance, include a ninth-century *Historia Apollonii Regis Tyri*, Godfrey of Viterbo's *Pantheon* (c. 1186), John Gower's *Confessio Amantis* (c. 1383–1393) and the *Gesta Romanorum*. Why did Shakespeare's company resuscitate such an old war-horse in 1606–1608?

The puzzle is aggravated by questions of authorship and textual reliability. The editors of the First Folio did not include *Pericles* in the canon of Shakespeare's plays. Perhaps they experienced copyright difficulties or could not lay their hands on the prompt-book, but it is also possible they either suspected or knew that Shakespeare was not sole author. Printed editions were available to them: the first quarto of 1609 and the subsequent quartos of 1609, 1611, and 1619, each based on the preceding edition. The first quarto was, however, a bad text with occasionally glaring contradictions. In Act I, scene ii, for example, Pericles' lords wish him a safe journey when no one has yet spoken of his departure, and Helicanus rebukes these same lords for flattery even though they have not said anything remotely sycophantic. Other scenes present similar difficulties, especially in the first two acts. The characters do not always seem consistent: Cleon is condemned in Act V for having tried to murder Marina, even though our earlier impression of him is of a man who is genuinely horrified at his wife's villainy. He weakly bends to the will of Dionyza, but is no murderer. Such inconsistencies and errors, and the naiveté of the whole, have led generally to three hypotheses: that Shakespeare worked with a collaborator such as Thomas Heywood or George Wilkins, that he revised an older play and left the first two acts pretty much as they were, or that he wrote the entire play which was then "pirated" by two unemployed actors whose portions differed markedly in accuracy.

To complicate matters still further, a prose version of the story called *The Painfull Aduentures of Pericles* by George Wilkins appeared in 1608, purporting to be "the true History of the Play of Pericles"—that is, to be a prose account of a dramatic performance. This redaction is indeed close at times to the play we have, but at other times it departs widely. The departures of the later work are sometimes explained with the hypothesis that Wilkins based his account on an older play, one to which Wilkins might have contributed himself; another and more current opinion favors the notion that Wilkins took what he needed from the play we have, borrowing also from Twine's prose version or from his own imagination. Apparently, then, *Pericles* was such a popular stage success that it inspired Wilkins' *Painfull Aduentures* in 1608, a new reprint in 1607 of Twine's *Patterne of Painefull Aduentures* on which the play itself had been partly based, and a botched surreptitious quarto edition of the play in 1609. Shakespeare's sole authorship must remain in doubt, although the incongruities, especially in the first two acts, are sometimes explained as the result of faulty memorial reporting and compositorial error.

The naiveté of *Pericles* is probably deliberate. Its romantic motifs continue on into that group of plays known generally as the late romances: *Cymbeline* (c. 1608–1610), *The Winter's Tale* (c. 1610–1611), and *The Tempest* (c. 1610–1611). Nor are these motifs entirely new in *Pericles:* the "problem" comedies *All's Well that Ends Well* and *Measure for Measure* use a tragicomic structure in which miraculous cures or providential interventions triumph over the semblance of death. *Pericles* occupies an integral place, then, in the development of Shakespearean comedy during the "tragic" period. To that development it offers a new emphasis on the simplicity of folk legend. Of the four late romances, *Pericles*, the earliest, is also the nearest in tone to romance of the 1580's. The play seems to have constituted a revival of that old genre, and was so immensely popular that it did much to establish the vogue of tragicomedy exploited by Beaumont and Fletcher.

The Chorus, old Gower, gives to the episodic materials of the play a unified point of view. He speaks with the authority of one who has told the story before, even though his *Confessio Amantis* (c. 1383–1393) was probably not Shakespeare's immediate source. Gower adopts a kind of Chaucerian persona, appealing to "what mine authors say" and apologizing for his rude simplicity. Like the chorus of *Henry V*, he repeatedly urges his auditors to transcend the limitations of his naive art form, using the power of imagination to bridge gaps in time and to suppose the stage a storm-tossed ship or the city of Antioch. His appearances divide the action into seven episodic segments, surely a more authentic structure than the five "acts" conventionally employed by later editions. He offers moral appraisals of his various characters, often before we have had a chance to see them, contrasting the good with the bad. Most importantly, he presides as a sort of benign deity over the changing fortunes of his characters, assuring us that as narrator he will not allow the virtuous to come to grief or the wicked to escape punishment. He thus paces our expectations and provides a comic reassurance appropriate to romance. He promises to "show you those in trouble's reign, Losing a mite, a mountain gain." To the virtuous he will ultimately give his "benison." Under his direction, the vacillations of fortune take on a predictable rhythm, whereby the rewards of virtuous conduct may be delayed but cannot eventually fail. Pericles, he tells us, will suffer adversity "Till fortune, tir'd with doing bad, Threw him ashore, to give him glad" (II, Chorus). This pattern is repeated not once but several times.

The characters are almost all morally black and white and one-dimensional. They are often presented in contrasting pairs, as "foils," to illustrate a type of human depravity and its ideal opposite, such as tyranny and true monarchy. For example, both Antiochus and Simonides seem to welcome the various suitors who flock to their courts, seeking the hand in marriage of the two kings' daughters. Antiochus does so deceitfully, however, since he is his daughter's incestuous lover. Pericles learns in Antioch the danger of perceiving too much about the private affairs of a suspicious and vengeful tyrant like Antiochus. Simonides is, on the other hand, a true prince, beloved by the simplest of his subjects, generous, lacking in envy, courteous to strangers, and more impressed with inner substance than with outward show. He approves of Pericles as a son-in-law, though (like Prospero in *The Tempest*) he imposes artificial restraints on the lovers to make their eventual triumph of love seem all the more sweet. Antiochus and his daughter are eventually shrivelled up by a fire from heaven, whereas Simonides and Thaisa earn the just rewards of gracious hospitality. Another opposing pair of characters, Thaliard and Helicanus, are conventionally typed as false and true courtiers. Thaliard, ordered by Antiochus to murder Pericles, is evasive and self-serving; Helicanus, when offered the opportunity to supplant Pericles as ruler of Tyre, loyally awaits his master's return.

THE FOLGER SHAKESPEARE LIBRARY

Gambling in a brothel during the time of Elizabeth.

Pericles is conceived in these same conventional terms as a prince of chivalry, young, brave, admirable both as a romantic wooer and as a resolute adventurer. His visit to the city of Tarsus, which has recently been toppled from wealth to poverty, shows him practicing the generosity that befits his lofty rank and innately noble qualities. Even when fortune strips him of his finery, his princely bearing is evident to discerning observers like King Simonides and Thaisa. Pericles thus differs markedly from the flawed tragicomic protagonists more often found in the late romances, such as Posthumus in *Cymbeline* and Leontes in *The Winter's Tale*, who bring grief upon themselves and must suffer agonizing contrition before gaining an unexpected second chance. Pericles is virtually without fault, a hero of romance rather than of tragedy. His soliloquies and eloquent speeches are not darkly introspective and psychological, like Leontes'. Although he grieves in sackcloth and ashes, he does so for undeserved misfortune rather than for his own follies. The play accordingly has little to say about man's perverse instinct for self-destruction. If Pericles does have one defect, it is his excessive despair in his grief, his withdrawal into absolute silence. He must learn a more affirmative and patient response from his courageous daughter Marina, whereupon his trials will have run their necessary course. Even his learning such a lesson is of less importance than the sublime sense of mystery and joy that accompanies his reunion with Marina.

In several ways, Marina is a typical heroine of Shakespeare's late romances. Her name, like that of Perdita in *The Winter's Tale*, signifies loss and recovery. Marina is the gift of the sea, that mysterious power of fortune in *Pericles* which takes with one hand even while it gives with the other. Just as the sea tosses Pericles on the coast of Pentapolis and then returns to him the suit of armor in which he will joust for the love of fair Thaisa, so in another storm at sea Thaisa apparently dies giving birth to Marina. The child is a "fresh new seafarer" on the troubled voyage of life. The sea parts her from her mother and father and leads to the misunderstandings whereby Marina is supposed dead, but the sea also eventually deposits Pericles on the coast of Mytilene where he finds his long-lost daughter. Like Perdita, again, Marina is associated with flowers and with Tellus, the goddess of the earth. The inscription on her monument, when she is supposed dead, speaks of elemental strife between the sea and the shore caused by her death, in which the angry sea gods "Make raging battery upon shores of flint" (IV,iv). She is a princess from folk legend, like Snow White or like Imogen in *Cymbeline*, who must flee the envious wrath of a witchlike stepmother and queen. Her true mother, Thaisa, another princess in a folk tale, is washed ashore in a treasure-filled chest, smelling sweetly and betokening some miraculous change of fortune.

Most important, Marina is one who can preach conversion to the sinful and cure distempered souls. She recovers her husband-to-be, Lysimachus, from the brothels of Mytilene, and even converts pimps and prostitutes by her innocent faith. As one with a strange power to bring new life to dead hope, she resembles a number of mysterious artist-figures and magicians in the late romances. One such is Cerimon, who restores life to Thaisa. Like him, or like Paulina in *The Winter's Tale,* whose devices are "lawful" though seemingly magical, Marina offers cures that can be rationally explained and yet appear to be miraculous. To Pericles, her ministrations seem "the rarest dream that e'er dull sleep Did mock sad fools withal" (V,i). Yet what she has taught him, by her own example, is simple patience; she has suffered even more than he, but nevertheless knows how to endure, how to "look Like Patience gazing on kings' graves and smiling Extremity out of act."

Through her we understand finally why providence has allowed so much misfortune to afflict the virtuous: only by such testing can men learn to conquer time and death. Time will always remain "the king of men; He's both their parent, and he is their grave, And gives them what he will, not what they crave" (II,iii). Nevertheless, providence can turn the accidents of time and fortune to good purpose for those who are Joblike in their patient faith. Even pirates unknowingly take part in a divine plan, rescuing Marina from the clutches of the evil Dionyza. As Gower puts it, those who are "assail'd with fortune fierce and keen" are also "Led on by heaven, and crown'd with joy at last" (Epilogue). To Pericles, such a delayed reward is ample compensation for his sorrows, almost indeed an unbearable joy. "No more, you gods!" he movingly pleads, "Your present kindness Makes my past miseries sports."

PERICLES

[*Dramatis Personae*

ANTIOCHUS, King of Antioch.
PERICLES, Prince of Tyre.
HELICANUS, ESCANES, } *two lords of Tyre.*
SIMONIDES, King of Pentapolis.
CLEON, *governor of Tarsus.*
LYSIMACHUS, *governor of Mytilene.*
CERIMON, *a lord of Ephesus.*
THALIARD, *a lord of Antioch.*
PHILEMON, *servant to Cerimon.*
LEONINE, *servant to Dionyza.*
Marshal.
A Pandar.
BOULT, *his servant.*

The Daughter of Antiochus.
DIONYZA, *wife to Cleon.*
THAISA, *daughter to Simonides.*
MARINA, *daughter to Pericles and Thaisa.*
LYCHORIDA, *nurse to Marina.*
A Bawd.

Lords, Knights, Gentlemen, Sailors, Pirates, Fishermen, *and* Messengers.

DIANA.

GOWER, as Chorus.

SCENE: *In various eastern Mediterranean countries.*]

[ACT I.]

Enter GOWER.

[*Before the palace of Antioch.*]

To sing a song that old was sung,
From ashes ancient Gower is come;
Assuming man's infirmities,
To glad your ear, and please your eyes.
It hath been sung at festivals,
On ember-eves and holy-ales;
And lords and ladies in their lives
Have read it for restoratives:
The purchase is to make men glorious;
Et bonum quo antiquius, eo melius.
If you, born in these latter times,
When wit 's more ripe, accept my rhymes,
And that to hear an old man sing
May to your wishes pleasure bring,
I life would wish, and that I might
Waste it for you, like taper-light.
This Antioch, then, Antiochus the Great
Built up, this city, for his chiefest seat;
The fairest in all Syria,
I tell you what mine authors say:
This king unto him took a peer,

Who died and left a female heir,
So buxom, blithe, and full of face,
As heaven had lent her all his grace;
With whom the father liking took,
And her to incest did provoke:
Bad child; worse father! to entice his own
To evil should be done by none:
But custom what they did begin
Was with long use account'd no sin.
The beauty of this sinful dame
Made many princes thither frame,
To seek her as a bed-fellow,
In marriage-pleasures play-fellow:
Which to prevent he made a law,
To keep her still, and men in awe,
That whoso ask'd her for his wife,
His riddle told not, lost his life:
So for her many a wight did die,
As yon grim looks do testify.
What now ensues, to the judgement of your eye
I give, my cause who best can justify. *Exit.*

[SCENE I. *Antioch. A room in the palace.*]

Enter ANTIOCHUS, PRINCE PERICLES, *and followers.*

Ant. Young prince of Tyre, you have at large receiv'd
The danger of the task you undertake.
Per. I have, Antiochus, and, with a soul
Embold'ned with the glory of her praise,
Think death no hazard in this enterprise.
Ant. Music! Bring in our daughter, clothed like a bride,
For the embracements even of Jove himself;
At whose conception, till Lucina reign'd,
Nature this dowry gave, to glad her presence,
The senate-house of planets all did sit,
To knit in her their best perfections.

[*Music.*] *Enter* Antiochus' Daughter.

Per. See where she comes, apparell'd like the spring,
Graces her subjects, and her thoughts the king
Of every virtue gives renown to men!
Her face the book of praises, where is read
Nothing but curious pleasures, as from thence
Sorrow were ever ras'd, and testy wrath
Could never be her mild companion.
You gods that made me man, and sway in love,
That have inflam'd desire in my breast
To taste the fruit of yon celestial tree,
Or die in the adventure, be my helps,
As I am son and servant to your will,
To compass such a boundless happiness!
Ant. Prince Pericles,—
Per. That would be son to great Antiochus.
Ant. Before thee stands this fair Hesperides,
With golden fruit, but dangerous to be touch'd;
For death-like dragons here affright thee hard:
Her face, like heaven, enticeth thee to view
Her countless glory, which desert must gain;
And which, without desert, because thine eye
Presumes to reach, all the whole heap must die.
Yon sometimes famous princes, like thyself,
Drawn by report, advent'rous by desire,
Tell thee, with speechless tongues and semblance pale,
That without covering, save yon field of stars,
Here they stand martyrs, slain in Cupid's wars;
And with dead cheeks advise thee to desist
For going on death's net, whom none resist.
Per. Antiochus, I thank thee, who hath taught
My frail mortality to know itself,
And by those fearful objects to prepare
This body, like to them, to what I must;
For death remembered should be like a mirror,
Who tells us life 's but breath, to trust it error.
I'll make my will then, and, as sick men do
Who know the world, see heaven, but, feeling woe,
Gripe not at earthly joys as erst they did;
So I bequeath a happy peace to you
And all good men, as every prince should do;
My riches to the earth from whence they came;
But my unspotted fire of love to you.
[*To the daughter of Antiochus.*]
Thus ready for the way of life or death,
I wait the sharpest blow, Antiochus.
Ant. Scorning advice, read the conclusion, then:
Which read and not expounded, 'tis decreed,
As these before thee thou thyself shalt bleed.
Daugh. Of all say'd yet, mayst thou prove prosperous!
Of all say'd yet, I wish thee happiness!
Per. Like a bold champion, I assume the lists,
Nor ask advice of any other thought
But faithfulness and courage.
[*He reads*] *the riddle.*

I am no viper, yet I feed
On mother's flesh which did me breed.
I sought a husband, in which labour
I found that kindness in a father:
He 's father, son, and husband mild;
I mother, wife, and yet his child.
How they may be, and yet in two,
As you will live, resolve it you.

Sharp physic is the last: but, O you powers
That gives heaven countless eyes to view men's acts,
Why cloud they not their sights perpetually,
If this be true, which makes me pale to read it?
Fair glass of light, I lov'd you, and could still,
Were not this glorious casket stor'd with ill:
But I must tell you, now my thoughts revolt;

ACT I. PROLOGUE. 1. **old,** of old. 2. **ancient Gower,** the fourteenth-century poet, John Gower, who related the adventures of Apollonius of Tyre (of which *Pericles* is a version) in his *Confessio Amantis*. The stylistic affectations of the Gower parts are mainly due to the dramatist's attempt to reproduce the archaic language of an earlier century. 3. **Assuming man's infirmities,** taking on a mortal body. 6. **ember-eves,** evenings before the ember days—the periodic fast days which coincide with the four changes of the seasons. **holy-ales,** i.e., church ales or festivals. 10. **Et . . . melius,** a good thing is better for being older. 11-13. **If . . . that.** The construction of the clause is parallel; *if*, if that, a conjunction of common occurrence, is to be understood with *that* after *And*. 16. **Waste,** spend. 21. **peer,** consort. 23. **full of face,** florid (Onions); replete with every facial charm (Deighton). 29-30. **But . . . sin,** custom—familiarity—bred of long use, made what they began accounted no sin. 32. **frame,** direct their steps. 36. **and men,** and to keep men. 38. **His riddle told not,** if his (Antiochus') riddle were not solved. 40. **yon grim looks.** Gower points to the heads of unsuccessful suitors placed on the palace gate. 42. **who.** The antecedent is *your eye*. **justify,** witness (Deighton).

SCENE I. 8. **Lucina,** goddess of childbirth, in her capacity as goddess of light; the line may mean, "during the period of gestation," i.e., from her conception until her birth. 9-11. **Nature . . . perfections,** i.e., Nature bestowed on her a favorable aspect of all the planets, so that all perfect qualities would be combined in her. 14. **gives,** which gives. 18. **her mild companion,** companion of her mildness. 27. **Hesperides,** correctly speaking, nymphs who guarded the golden fruit belonging to Juno. The name was frequently applied to the garden where these fruits grew. Here it implies that the princess is the embodi-

For he 's no man on whom perfections wait
That, knowing sin within, will touch the gate.
You are a fair viol, and your sense the strings;
Who, finger'd to make man his lawful music,
Would draw heaven down, and all the gods, to hearken;
But being play'd upon before your time,
Hell only danceth at so harsh a chime.
Good sooth, I care not for you.

Ant. Prince Pericles, touch not, upon thy life,
For that 's an article within our law,
As dangerous as the rest. Your time 's expir'd:
Either expound now, or receive your sentence.

Per. Great king,
Few love to hear the sins they love to act;
'Twould braid yourself too near for me to tell it.
Who has a book of all that monarchs do,
He 's more secure to keep it shut than shown:
For vice repeated is like the wand'ring wind,
Blows dust in others' eyes, to spread itself;
And yet the end of all is bought thus dear,
The breath is gone, and the sore eyes see clear
To stop the air would hurt them. The blind mole casts
Copp'd hills towards heaven, to tell the earth is throng'd
By man's oppression; and the poor worm doth die for 't.
Kings are earth's gods; in vice their law 's their will;
And if Jove stray, who dares say Jove doth ill?
It is enough you know; and it is fit,
What being more known grows worse, to smother it.
All love the womb that their first being bred,
Then give my tongue like leave to love my head.

Ant. [*Aside*] Heaven, that I had thy head! he has found the meaning:
But I will gloze with him.—Young prince of Tyre,
Though by the tenour of our strict edict,
Your exposition misinterpreting,
We might proceed to cancel of your days;
Yet hope, succeeding from so fair a tree
As your fair self, doth tune us otherwise:
Forty days longer we do respite you;
If by which time our secret be undone,
This mercy shows we'll joy in such a son:
And until then your entertain shall be
As doth befit our honour and your worth.

[*Exeunt.*] *Manet Pericles solus.*

Per. How courtesy would seem to cover sin,
When what is done is like an hypocrite,
The which is good in nothing but in sight!
If it be true that I interpret false,
Then were it certain you were not so bad
As with foul incest to abuse your soul;
Where now you 're both a father and a son,
By your untimely claspings with your child,
Which pleasures fits a husband, not a father;
And she an eater of her mother's flesh,
By the defiling of her parent's bed;
And both like serpents are, who though they feed
On sweetest flowers, yet they poison breed.
Antioch, farewell! for wisdom sees, those men
Blush not in actions blacker than the night,
Will shun no course to keep them from the light.
One sin, I know, another doth provoke;
Murder 's as near to lust as flame to smoke:
Poison and treason are the hands of sin,
Ay, and the targets, to put off the shame:
Then, lest my life be cropp'd to keep you clear,
By flight I'll shun the danger which I fear. *Exit.*

Enter ANTIOCHUS.

Ant. He hath found the meaning, for which we mean
To have his head.
He must not live to trumpet forth my infamy,
Nor tell the world Antiochus doth sin
In such a loathed manner;
And therefore instantly this prince must die;
For by his fall my honour must keep high.
Who attends us there?

Enter THALIARD.

Thal. Doth your highness call?

Ant. Thaliard,
You are of our chamber, Thaliard, and our mind partakes
Her private actions to your secrecy;
And for your faithfulness we will advance you.
Thaliard, behold, here 's poison, and here 's gold;
We hate the prince of Tyre, and thou must kill him:
It fits thee not to ask the reason why,
Because we bid it. Say, is it done?

Thal. My lord,
'Tis done.

Ant. Enough.

Enter a Messenger.

Let your breath cool yourself, telling your haste.

Mess. My lord, prince Pericles is fled. [*Exit.*]

Ant. As thou
Wilt live, fly after: and like an arrow shot
From a well-experienc'd archer hits the mark
His eye doth level at, so thou ne'er return
Unless thou say 'Prince Pericles is dead.'

Thal. My lord,
If I can get him within my pistol's length,
I'll make him sure enough: so, farewell to your highness.

Ant. Thaliard, adieu! [*Exit Thal.*] Till Pericles be dead,
My heart can lend no succour to my head. [*Exit.*]

ment of all things rich; that she is without price. 29. **death-like dragons,** alludes to the dragon which guarded the garden of the Hesperides. 40. **For going on,** from entering. 44. **must,** must expect. 49. **Gripe,** clutch. 56. **conclusion,** problem, riddle. 59, 60. **say'd,** assayed, attempted. 61. **assume the lists,** undertake the combat. 64-65. **I am no viper,** etc. Seager (*Shakespeare's Natural History*, p. 331) quotes from Bartholomew, Trevisa's translation: "Viper is a manner kind of serpents that is full venomous, and hath that name for she bringeth forth brood by strength; for when her womb draweth to the time of whelping, the whelps abideth not convenable time nor kind passing, but gnaweth and fretteth the sides of their mother, and they come so into this world with strength and with the death of the mother." 79-80. **For . . . gate,** he, however perfect, is no man who, knowing sin to be within, will touch the gate. Pericles is thinking of his own manhood and the loss of dignity he would suffer by a possible alliance with the contaminated princess. 88. **an article,** i.e., one of the conditions under which the riddle was attempted; cf. *Prologue*, 34-35. 93. **braid,** upbraid. 97. **to spread itself,** to allow itself free action. 101. **Copp'd,** peaked. **throng'd,** beset. 102. **worm,** creature; a common term of pity. 105. **you know,** i.e., that you know that I know your riddle. 110. **gloze,** talk smoothly and speciously. 112. **Your exposition misinterpreting,** since your exposition interprets wrongly. 114. **succeeding from,** resulting from. 119. **entertain,** entertainment. 121. **would seem,** speciously endeavors (Deighton); perhaps, doth seem. 128. **untimely,** ill-fitting. 134. **men,** i.e., men who. 152. **of our chamber,** our chamberlain. **partakes,** imparts. 171. **My . . . head,** I can have no confidence in anything which my thoughts can contrive.

[SCENE II. *Tyre. A room in the palace.*]

Enter PERICLES.

Per. [*To Lords without*] Let none disturb us.—Why should this change of thoughts,
The sad companion, dull-ey'd melancholy,
Be my so us'd a guest as not an hour,
In the day's glorious walk, or peaceful night,
The tomb where grief should sleep, can breed me quiet?
Here pleasures court mine eyes, and mine eyes shun them,
And danger, which I fear'd, is at Antioch,
Whose arm seems far too short to hit me here:
Yet neither pleasure's art can joy my spirits,
Nor yet the other's distance comfort me.
Then it is thus: the passions of the mind,
That have their first conception by mis-dread,
Have after-nourishment and life by care;
And what was first but fear what might be done,
Grows elder now and cares it be not done.
And so with me: the great Antiochus,
'Gainst whom I am too little to contend,
Since he 's so great can make his will his act,
Will think me speaking, though I swear to silence;
Nor boots it me to say I honour him,
If he suspect I may dishonour him:
And what may make him blush in being known,
He'll stop the course by which it might be known;
With hostile forces he'll o'erspread the land,
And with th' ostent of war will look so huge,
Amazement shall drive courage from the state;
Our men be vanquish'd ere they do resist,
And subjects punish'd that ne'er thought offence:
Which care of them, not pity of myself,
Who am no more but as the tops of trees,
Which fence the roots they grow by and defend them,
Makes both my body pine and soul to languish,
And punish that before that he would punish.

Enter [HELICANUS *and*] *all the* Lords *to* PERICLES.

First Lord. Joy and all comfort in your sacred breast!
Sec. Lord. And keep your mind, till you return to us,
Peaceful and comfortable!
Hel. Peace, peace, and give experience tongue.
They do abuse the king that flatter him:
For flattery is the bellows blows up sin;
The thing the which is flattered, but a spark,
To which that blast gives heat and stronger glowing;
Whereas reproof, obedient and in order,
Fits kings, as they are men, for they may err.
When Signior Sooth here does proclaim a peace,
He flatters you, makes war upon your life.
Prince, pardon me, or strike me, if you please;
I cannot be much lower than my knees. [*Kneels.*]
Per. All leave us else; but let your cares o'erlook
What shipping and what lading 's in our haven,
And then return to us. [*Exeunt Lords.*] Helicanus, thou
Hast moved us: what seest thou in our looks?
Hel. An angry brow, dread lord.
Per. If there be such a dart in princes' frowns,
How durst thy tongue move anger to our face?
Hel. How dares the plants look up to heaven, from whence
They have their nourishment?
Per. Thou knowest I have power
To take thy life from thee.
Hel. I have ground the axe myself;
Do you but strike the blow.
Per. Rise, prithee, rise. [*He rises.*]
Sit down: thou art no flatterer:
I thank thee for 't; and heaven forbid
That kings should let their ears hear their faults hid:
Fit counsellor and servant for a prince,
Who by thy wisdom makes a prince thy servant,
What wouldst thou have me do?
Hel. To bear with patience
Such griefs as you yourself do lay upon yourself.
Per. Thou speak'st like a physician, Helicanus,
That ministers a potion unto me
That thou wouldst tremble to receive thyself.
Attend me, then: I went to Antioch,
Where as thou know'st, against the face of death,
I sought the purchase of a glorious beauty,
From whence an issue I might propagate,
†Are arms to princes, and bring joys to subjects.
Her face was to mine eye beyond all wonder;
The rest—hark in thine ear—as black as incest:
Which by my knowledge found, the sinful father
Seem'd not to strike, but smooth: but thou know'st this,
'Tis time to fear when tyrants seem to kiss.
Which fear so grew in me, I hither fled,
Under the covering of a careful night,
Who seem'd my good protector; and, being here,
Bethought me what was past, what might succeed.
I knew him tyrannous; and tyrants' fears
Decrease not, but grow faster than the years:
And should he doubt it, as no doubt he doth,
That I should open to the list'ning air
How many worthy princes' bloods were shed,
To keep his bed of blackness unlaid ope,
To lop that doubt, he'll fill this land with arms,
And make pretence of wrong that I have done him;
When all, for mine, if I may call offence,
Must feel war's blow, who spares not innocence:
Which love to all, of which thyself art one,
Who now reprov'st me for 't,—
Hel. Alas, sir!
Per. Drew sleep out of mine eyes, blood from my cheeks,
Musings into my mind, with thousand doubts
How I might stop this tempest ere it came;
And finding little comfort to relieve them,
I thought it princely charity to grieve them.

SCENE II. 1. **change of thoughts,** usually explained as altered disposition of mind. *Change* more likely means succession; perhaps this is a figure from the change of a peal of bells. The altered disposition does not disturb Pericles' quiet so much as the recurrence of the thoughts which he recounts in the subsequent lines (cf. I, ii, 79-98, where the details are repeated). This passage both in its analysis of the passion of fear and in its recital of the substance of Pericles' fears corresponds to the sixteenth-century doctrine regarding fearful melancholy. Burton describes how persons suffering from this passion are subject to torment and perplexity of thoughts "which so much, so continually, tortures and crucifies their souls." Cf. R. Anderson, *Elizabethan Psychology and Shakespeare's Plays*, p. 96. 15. **cares,** takes care. 18. **so great can,** so great that he can. 23. **it,** structurally redundant; the antecedent is the clause *what . . . known* (l. 22). 25. **ostent,** display. 31. **fence,** shield, shelter. 33. **he,** i.e., Antiochus. 35. **till you return to us.** Here the lords of Tyre appear to know of Pericles' departure. In the next scene we find that he left *unlicensed of their loves*, i.e., without their knowledge. The prose narratives which recount the same story state that his departure was accomplished secretly. This is one of the several inconsistencies of this rather garbled

Hel. Well, my lord, since you have given me leave to speak,
Freely will I speak. Antiochus you fear,
And justly too, I think, you fear the tyrant,
Who either by public war or private treason
Will take away your life.
Therefore, my lord, go travel for a while,
Till that his rage and anger be forgot,
Or till the Destinies do cut his thread of life.
Your rule direct to any; if to me,
Day serves not light more faithful than I'll be.
Per. I do not doubt thy faith;
But should he wrong my liberties in my absence?
Hel. We'll mingle our bloods together in the earth,
From whence we had our being and our birth.
Per. Tyre, I now look from thee then, and to Tarsus
Intend my travel, where I'll hear from thee;
And by whose letters I'll dispose myself.
The care I had and have of subjects' good
On thee I lay, whose wisdom's strength can bear it.
I'll take thy word for faith, not ask thine oath:
Who shuns not to break one will sure crack both:
But in our orbs we'll live so round and safe,
That time of both this truth shall ne'er convince,
Thou show'dst a subject's shine, I a true prince.
Exeunt.

[SCENE III. *Tyre. An ante-chamber in the palace.*]

Enter THALIARD *solus.*

Thal. So, this is Tyre, and this the court. Here must I kill King Pericles; and if I do it not, I am sure to be hanged at home: 'tis dangerous. Well, I perceive he was a wise fellow, and had good discretion, that, being bid to ask what he would of the king, desired he might know none of his secrets: now do I see he had some reason for 't; for if a king bid a man be a villain, he 's bound by the indenture of his oath to be one. Husht! here comes the lords of Tyre.

Enter HELICANUS [*and*] ESCANES, *with other* Lords [*of Tyre*].

Hel. You shall not need, my fellow peers of Tyre,
Further to question me of your king's departure:
His seal'd commission, left in trust with me,
Does speak sufficiently he 's gone to travel.
Thal. [*Aside*] How! the king gone!
Hel. If further yet you will be satisfied,
Why, as it were unlicens'd of your loves,
He would depart, I'll give some light unto you.
Being at Antioch——
Thal. [*Aside*] What from Antioch?
Hel. Royal Antiochus—on what cause I know not—
Took some displeasure at him; at least he judg'd so:
And doubting lest he had err'd or sinn'd,
To show his sorrow, he 'ld correct himself;
So puts himself unto the shipman's toil,
With whom each minute threatens life or death.
Thal. [*Aside*] Well, I perceive
I shall not be hang'd now, although I would;
But since he 's gone, † the king's ears it must please:
He 'scap'd the land, to perish at the seas.
I'll present myself.—Peace to the lords of Tyre!
Hel. Lord Thaliard from Antiochus is welcome.
Thal. From him I come
With message unto princely Pericles;
But since my landing I have understood
Your lord has betook himself to unknown travels,
My message must return from whence it came.
Hel. We have no reason to desire it,
Commended to our master, not to us:
Yet, ere you shall depart, this we desire,
As friends to Antioch, we may feast in Tyre. *Exeunt.*

[SCENE IV. *Tarsus. A room in the Governor's house.*]

Enter CLEON, *the governor of Tarsus, with* [DIONYZA] *his Wife, and others.*

Cle. My Dionyza, shall we rest us here,
And by relating tales of others' griefs,
See if 'twill teach us to forget our own?
Dio. That were to blow at fire in hope to quench it;
For who digs hills because they do aspire
Throws down one mountain to cast up a higher.
O my distressed lord, even such our griefs are;
Here they are but felt, and seen with mischief's eyes,
But like to groves, being topp'd, they higher rise.
Cle. O Dionyza,
Who wanteth food, and will not say he wants it,
Or can conceal his hunger till he famish?
Our tongues and sorrows do sound deep
Our woes into the air; our eyes do weep,
Till lungs fetch breath that may proclaim them louder;
That, if heaven slumber while their creatures want,
They may awake their helps to comfort them.
I'll then discourse our woes, felt several years,
And wanting breath to speak help me with tears.
Dio. I'll do my best, sir.
Cle. This Tarsus, o'er which I have the government,
A city on whom Plenty held full hand,
For Riches strew'd herself even in her streets;
Whose towers bore heads so high they kiss'd the clouds,
And strangers ne'er beheld but wond'red at;
Whose men and dames so jetted and adorn'd,
Like one another's glass to trim them by:
Their tables were stor'd full, to glad the sight,
And not so much to feed on as delight;
All poverty was scorn'd, and pride so great,
The name of help grew odious to repeat.
Dio. O, 'tis too true.
Cle. But see what heaven can do! By this our change,
These mouths, who but of late, earth, sea, and air,

text. 37. **give experience tongue,** let the experienced speak. 62. **hear . . . hid,** hear words that gloss over their faults. 66. **Such griefs . . . upon yourself,** such griefs as are only in your imagination (Deighton). 74. **Are,** which are, or such as are, the antecedent being in the plural idea of *issue*, i.e., sons. 92. **for . . . offence,** for my offense—if I may call it offense. 100. **grieve,** grieve for. 104. **treason,** treachery. 112. **he,** Antiochus. **my liberties,** royal rights and prerogatives (Schmidt). 117. **by . . . myself,** i.e., I'll act upon the advices of your letters.

SCENE III. 17. **unlicens'd of your loves,** without your loving assent (Deighton); cf. I, ii, 35, note. 24. **toil,** travail, hence dangers. 27. **would,** i.e., would have been. 28. **the king's ears it must please,** so Dyce; Q reads *the Kings seas must please*. Other emendations offered.

SCENE IV. 5. **digs,** removes. **aspire,** mount up. 8. **mischief's,** calamity's. 15. **them,** i.e., *woes* (l. 14). 19. **help me,** i.e., you help me. 23. **Riches,** a singular concept, probably derived from the French *richesse*, equivalent to "plenty"; Deighton explains the image as that of the cornucopia being held aloft over the city. 26. **jetted,** strutted.

Were all too little to content and please,
Although they gave their creatures in abundance,
As houses are defil'd for want of use,
They are now starv'd for want of exercise:
Those palates who, not yet two summers younger,
Must have inventions to delight the taste,
Would now be glad of bread, and beg for it:
Those mothers who, to nousle up their babes,
Thought nought too curious, are ready now
To eat those little darlings whom they lov'd.
So sharp are hunger's teeth, that man and wife
Draw lots who first shall die to lengthen life:
Here stands a lord, and there a lady weeping;
Here many sink, yet those which see them fall
Have scarce strength left to give them burial.
Is not this true?
Dio. Our cheeks and hollow eyes do witness it.
Cle. O, let those cities that of Plenty's cup
And her prosperities so largely taste,
With their superfluous riots, hear these tears!
The misery of Tarsus may be theirs.

Enter a Lord.

Lord. Where 's the lord governor?
Cle. Here.
Speak out thy sorrows which thou bring'st in haste,
For comfort is too far for us to expect.
Lord. We have descried, upon our neighbouring shore,
A portly sail of ships make hitherward.
Cle. I thought as much.
One sorrow never comes but brings an heir,
That may succeed as his inheritor;
And so in ours: some neighbouring nation,
Taking advantage of our misery,
Hath stuff'd these hollow vessels with their power,
To beat us down, the which are down already;
And make a conquest of unhappy me,
Whereas no glory 's got to overcome.
Lord. That 's the least fear; for, by the semblance
Of their white flags display'd, they bring us peace,
And come to us as favourers, not as foes.
Cle. Thou speak'st like him 's untutor'd to repeat:
Who makes the fairest show means most deceit.
But bring they what they will and what they can,
What need we fear?
The ground 's the lowest, and we are half way there.
Go tell their general we attend him here,
To know for what he comes, and whence he comes,
And what he craves.
Lord. I go, my lord. [*Exit.*]
Cle. Welcome is peace, if he on peace consist;
If wars, we are unable to resist.

Enter PERICLES *with* Attendants.

Per. Lord governor, for so we hear you are,
Let not our ships and number of our men
Be like a beacon fir'd t' amaze your eyes.
We have heard your miseries as far as Tyre,
And seen the desolation of your streets:
Nor come we to add sorrow to your tears,
But to relieve them of their heavy load;
And these our ships, you happily may think
Are like the Trojan horse was stuff'd within
With bloody veins, expecting overthrow,
Are stor'd with corn to make your needy bread,
And give them life whom hunger starv'd half dead.
All. The gods of Greece protect you!
And we'll pray for you. [*They kneel.*]
Per. Arise, I pray you, rise:
We do not look for reverence, but for love,
And harbourage for ourself, our ships, and men.
Cle. The which when any shall not gratify,
Or pay you with unthankfulness in thought,
Be it our wives, our children, or ourselves,
The curse of heaven and men succeed their evils!
Till when,—the which I hope shall ne'er be seen,—
Your grace is welcome to our town and us.
Per. Which welcome we'll accept; feast here awhile,
Until our stars that frown lend us a smile. *Exeunt.*

[ACT II.]

Enter GOWER.

Gow. Here have you seen a mighty king
His child, I wis, to incest bring;
A better prince and benign lord,
That will prove awful both in deed and word.
Be quiet then as men should be,
Till he hath pass'd necessity.
I'll show you those in trouble's reign,
Losing a mite, a mountain gain.
The good in conversation,
To whom I give my benison,
Is still at Tarsus, where each man
Thinks all is writ he speken can;
And, to remember what he does,
Build his statue to make him glorious:
But tidings to the contrary
Are brought your eyes; what need speak I?

DUMB SHOW.

Enter at one door PERICLES *talking with* CLEON; *all the train with them. Enter at another door a* Gentleman, *with a letter to* PERICLES; PERICLES *shows the letter to* CLEON; PERICLES *gives the* Messenger *a reward, and knights him. Exit* PERICLES *at one door, and* CLEON *at another.*

Good Helicane, that stay'd at home
Not to eat honey like a drone
From others' labours; for though he strive
To killen bad, keep good alive;
And to fulfil his prince' desire,
Sends word of all that haps in Tyre:
How Thaliard came full bent with sin
And had intent to murder him;
And that in Tarsus was not best
Longer for him to make his rest.
He, doing so, put forth to seas,

40. **inventions,** novelties. 42. **nousle,** train (Onions); a corruption of *nursle,* to cherish (Deighton). 54. **superfluous,** i.e., prodigal. **tears,** sound of weeping. 61. **portly,** majestic, stately. 70. **Whereas . . . overcome,** where there is no glory to be gained. 74. **like . . . repeat,** like one who has never been taught how to recite. 83. **on peace consist,** is disposed toward peace. 94. **expecting overthrow,** may modify *you* (l. 92). 95. **your needy bread,** bread which you need.

ACT II. PROLOGUE. 2. **I wis,** certainly. 6. **necessity,** those hardships imposed by fate. 7. **those,** i.e., those who. 10. **benison,** blessing. 12. **writ,** holy writ. **he speken can,** which he speaks; an archaic affectation. 13. **remember,** commemorate. 19. **for,** difficult to explain as the text stands; some emend to *forth,* others omit. 28. **been,** are. 35. **of man, of pelf,** partitive genitives to be construed with *All.* 38. **glad,** gladness.
SCENE I. *Stage Direction:* ***Pentapolis.*** This fictitious name occurs in

Where when men been, there 's seldom ease;
For now the wind begins to blow;
Thunder above and deeps below
Make such unquiet, that the ship
Should house him safe is wrack'd and split;
And he, good prince, having all lost,
By waves from coast to coast is tost:
All perishen of man, of pelf,
Ne aught escapend but himself;
Till fortune, tir'd with doing bad,
Threw him ashore, to give him glad:
And here he comes. What shall be next,
Pardon old Gower,—this 'longs the text. [*Exit.*]

[SCENE I. *Pentapolis. An open place by the sea-side.*]

Enter PERICLES, *wet.*

Per. Yet cease your ire, you angry stars of heaven!
Wind, rain, and thunder, remember, earthly man
Is but a substance that must yield to you;
And I, as fits my nature, do obey you:
Alas, the seas hath cast me on the rocks,
Wash'd me from shore to shore, and left me breath
Nothing to think on but ensuing death:
Let it suffice the greatness of your powers
To have bereft a prince of all his fortunes;
And having thrown him from your wat'ry grave,
Here to have death in peace is all he'll crave.

Enter three Fishermen.

First Fish. What, ho, Pilch!

Sec. Fish. Ha, come and bring away the nets!

First Fish. What, Patch-breech, I say!

Third Fish. What say you, master?

First Fish. Look how thou stirrest now! come away, or I'll fetch thee with a wanion.

Third Fish. 'Faith, master, I am thinking of the poor men that were cast away before us even now.

First Fish. Alas, poor souls, it grieved my heart to hear what pitiful cries they made to us to help them, when, well-a-day, we could scarce help ourselves.

Third Fish. Nay, master, said not I as much when I saw the porpoise how he bounced and tumbled? they say they're half fish, half flesh: a plague on them, they ne'er come but I look to be washed. Master, I marvel how the fishes live in the sea.

First Fish. Why, as men do a-land; the great ones eat up the little ones: I can compare our rich misers to nothing so fitly as to a whale; 'a plays and tumbles, driving the poor fry before him, and at last devours them all at a mouthful: such whales have I heard on o' the land, who never leave gaping till they 've swallowed the whole parish, church, steeple, bells, and all.

Per. [*Aside*] A pretty moral.

Third Fish. But, master, if I had been the sexton, I would have been that day in the belfry.

Sec. Fish. Why, man?

Third Fish. Because he should have swallowed me too: and when I had been in his belly, I would have kept such a jangling of the bells, that he should never have left, till he cast bells, steeple, church, and parish, up again. But if the good King Simonides were of my mind,—

Per. [*Aside*] Simonides!

Third Fish. We would purge the land of these drones, that rob the bee of her honey.

Per. [*Aside*] How from the finny subject of the sea
These fishers tell the infirmities of men;
And from their wat'ry empire recollect
All that may men approve or men detect!—
Peace be at your labour, honest fishermen.

Sec. Fish. Honest! good fellow, what 's that? If it be a day fits you, †search out of the calendar, and nobody look after it.

Per. May see the sea hath cast upon your coast.

Sec. Fish. What a drunken knave was the sea to cast thee in our way!

Per. A man whom both the waters and the wind,
In that vast tennis-court, hath made the ball
For them to play upon, entreats you pity him;
He asks of you, that never us'd to beg.

First Fish. No, friend, cannot you beg? Here 's them in our country of Greece gets more with begging than we can do with working.

Sec. Fish. Canst thou catch any fishes, then?

Per. I never practised it.

Sec. Fish. Nay, then thou wilt starve, sure; for here 's nothing to be got now-a-days, unless thou canst fish for 't.

Per. What I have been I have forgot to know;
But what I am, want teaches me to think on:
A man throng'd up with cold: my veins are chill,
And have no more of life than may suffice
To give my tongue that heat to ask your help;
Which if you shall refuse, when I am dead,
For that I am a man, pray you see me buried.

First Fish. Die quoth-a? Now gods forbid 't! And I have a gown here; come, put it on; keep thee warm. Now, afore me, a handsome fellow! Come, thou shalt go home, and we'll have flesh for holidays, fish for fasting-days, and moreo'er puddings and flap-jacks, and thou shalt be welcome.

Per. I thank you, sir.

Sec. Fish. Hark you, my friend; you said you could not beg.

Per. I did but crave.

Sec. Fish. But crave! Then I'll turn craver too, and so I shall 'scape whipping.

Per. Why, are all your beggars whipped, then?

Sec. Fish. O, not all, my friend, not all; for if all your beggars were whipped, I would wish no better office than to be beadle. But, master, I'll go draw up the net. [*Exit with Third Fisherman.*]

Per. [*Aside*] How well this honest mirth becomes
their labour!

First Fish. Hark you, sir, do you know where ye are?

Per. Not well.

the earlier versions of the Apollonius story. 12, 14. **Pilch, Patch-breech,** nicknames derived from the clothes they wear; *Pilch,* a leather garment. 13. **bring away,** bring here. 17. **wanion,** vengeance. 23. **well-a-day,** alas. 26. **the porpoise.** These actions of porpoises were recognized prognostications of stormy weather. 52. **subject,** subjects or people, used collectively, so that *the finny subject of the sea* would be the fish, i.e., residents. 54. **recollect,** gather up. 56-59. **Peace . . . after it.** Most commentators think something lost—some reference to the *day* to occasion the fisherman's reply. Steevens attempted to reconstruct the passage, adding to Pericles' speech the line, *The day is rough and thwarts your occupation.* Deighton prefixed to the last line of Pericles' speech the exclamation *Hoy-day!* 60. **May,** you may. 79. **that heat,** warmth enough to enable him to move his tongue, now almost cleaving to the roof of his mouth (Deighton); heat was thought of as the source of motion. 84. **afore me,** a mild oath.

First Fish. Why, I'll tell you: this is called Pentapolis, and our king the good Simonides.

Per. The good Simonides, do you call him?

First Fish. Ay, sir; and he deserves so to be called for his peaceable reign and good government.

Per. He is a happy king, since he gains from his subjects the name of good by his government. How far is his court distant from this shore?

First Fish. Marry, sir, half a day's journey: and I'll tell you, he hath a fair daughter, and to-morrow is her birth-day; and there are princes and knights come from all parts of the world to just and tourney for her love.

Per. Were my fortunes equal to my desires, I could wish to make one there.

First Fish. O, sir, things must be as they may; and what a man cannot get, he may lawfully deal for—†his wife's soul.

Enter the two [*other*] Fishermen, *drawing up a net.*

Sec. Fish. Help, master, help! here 's a fish hangs in the net, like a poor man's right in the law; 'twill hardly come out. Ha! bots on 't, 'tis come at last, and 'tis turned to a rusty armour.

Per. An armour, friends! I pray you, let me see it.
Thanks, fortune, yet, that, after all my crosses,
Thou givest me somewhat to repair myself;
And though it was mine own, part of my heritage,
Which my dead father did bequeath to me,
With this strict charge, even as he left his life,
'Keep it, my Pericles; it hath been a shield
'Twixt me and death;'—and pointed to this brace;—
'For that it sav'd me, keep it; in like necessity—
The which the gods protect thee from!—may defend
thee.'
It kept where I kept, I so dearly lov'd it;
Till the rough seas, that spares not any man,
Took it in rage, though calm'd have given 't again:
I thank thee for 't: my shipwrack now 's no ill,
Since I have here my father gave in his will.

First Fish. What mean you, sir?

Per. To beg of you, kind friends, this coat of worth,
For it was sometime target to a king;
I know it by this mark. He lov'd me dearly,
And for his sake I wish the having of it;
And that you 'ld guide me to your sovereign's court,
Where with it I may appear a gentleman;
And if that ever my low fortune 's better,
I'll pay your bounties; till then rest your debtor.

First Fish. Why, wilt thou tourney for the lady?

Per. I'll show the virtue I have borne in arms.

First Fish. Why, do 'e take it, and the gods give thee good on 't!

Sec. Fish. Ay, but hark you, my friend; 'twas we that made up this garment through the rough seams of the waters: there are certain condolements, certain vails. I hope, sir, if you thrive, you'll remember from whence you had it.

Per. Believe 't, I will.
By your furtherance I am cloth'd in steel;
And, spite of all the rapture of the sea,
This jewel holds his building on my arm:
Unto thy value I will mount myself
Upon a courser, whose delightful steps
Shall make the gazer joy to see him tread.
Only, my friend, I yet am unprovided
Of a pair of bases.

Sec. Fish. We'll sure provide: thou shalt have my best gown to make thee a pair; and I'll bring thee to the court myself.

Per. Then honour be but a goal to my will,
This day I'll rise, or else add ill to ill. [*Exeunt.*]

[SCENE II. *The same. A public way leading to the lists. A pavilion by the side of it for the reception of the King, Princess, Lords, & c.*]

Enter SIMONIDES, *with attendance, and* THAISA.

Sim. Are the knights ready to begin the triumph?

First Lord. They are, my liege;
And stay your coming to present themselves.

Sim. Return them, we are ready; and our daughter,
In honour of whose birth these triumphs are,
Sits here, like beauty's child, whom nature gat
For men to see, and seeing wonder at. [*Exit a Lord.*]

Thai. It pleaseth you, my royal father, to express
My commendations great, whose merit 's less.

Sim. It 's fit it should be so; for princes are
A model, which heaven makes like to itself:
As jewels lose their glory if neglected,
So princes their renowns if not respected.
'Tis now your honour, daughter, to entertain
The labour of each knight in his device.

Thai. Which, to preserve mine honour, I'll perform.

The first Knight passes by [*and his* Squire *presents his shield to the* Princess].

Sim. Who is the first that doth prefer himself?

Thai. A knight of Sparta, my renowned father;
And the device he bears upon his shield
Is a black Ethiope reaching at the sun:
The word, 'Lux tua vita mihi.'

Sim. He loves you well that holds his life of you.
The Second Knight [*passes over*].
Who is the second that presents himself?

Thai. A prince of Macedon, my royal father;
And the device he bears upon his shield
Is an arm'd knight that 's conquer'd by a lady;
The motto thus, in Spanish, 'Piu por dulzura que por
fuerza.' *Third Knight* [*passes over*].

Sim. And what 's the third?

Thai. The third of Antioch;
And his device, a wreath of chivalry;
The word, 'Me pompæ provexit apex.'
Fourth Knight [*passes over*].

Sim. What is the fourth?

Thai. A burning torch that 's turned upside down;
The word, 'Quod me alit, me extinguit.'

116. **just,** joust, tilt in a tournament. 118. **to make one,** i.e., to take part in the tourney. 121. **his wife's soul.** A difficult line. The text may be imperfect here. 124. **bots on 't,** plague take it (*bots*, disease of horses). 129. **And though,** even though (Deighton). 140. **my father gave,** what my father gave. 142. **coat,** refers to *armour*, line 126. 156-157. **condolements,** possibly confused with "dole" (Onions). 157. **vails,** perquisites, tips. 161. **rapture,** plundering. 162. **This . . . arm,** this jewel on my arm will provide a means, i.e., to buy a courser. 167. **bases,** pleated skirts of cloth, velvet or rich brocade, appended to the doublet and reaching from the waist to the knee.

SCENE II. 1. **triumph,** festive entertainment. 4. **Return,** reply to. 8-9. **to . . . less,** to praise me out of proportion to my desert. 14. **entertain,** review; so Qq; Globe, following Steevens: *explain*. 17. **prefer,** introduce. 21. **'Lux . . . mihi.'** Thy light is my life. 27. **'Piu . . . fuerza,'** more by gentleness than by force. 30. **'Me . . . apex.'** The highest summit of honor has led me on. 33. **'Quod . . . extinguit.'**

Sim. Which shows that beauty hath his power and will,
Which can as well inflame as it can kill.

Fifth Knight [*passes over*].

Thai. The fifth, an hand environed with clouds,
Holding out gold that 's by the touchstone tried;
The motto thus, 'Sic spectanda fides.'

Sixth Knight [, *Pericles, passes over*].

Sim. And what 's
The sixth and last, the which the knight himself
With such a graceful courtesy deliver'd?
Thai. He seems to be a stranger; but his present is
A withered branch, that 's only green at top;
The motto, 'In hac spe vivo.'
Sim. A pretty moral;
From the dejected state wherein he is,
He hopes by you his fortunes yet may flourish.
First Lord. He had need mean better than his outward show
Can any way speak in his just commend;
For by his rusty outside he appears
To have practis'd more the whipstock than the lance.
Sec. Lord. He well may be a stranger, for he comes
To an honour'd triumph strangely furnished.
Third Lord. And on set purpose let his armour rust
Until this day, to scour it in the dust.
Sim. Opinion 's but a fool, that makes us scan
The outward habit by the inward man.
But stay, the knights are coming: we will withdraw
Into the gallery. [*Exeunt.*]

Great shouts [*within*], *and all cry* 'The mean knight!'

[SCENE III. *The same. A hall of state: a banquet prepared.*]

Enter the KING [SIMONIDES, THAISA, Marshal, Ladies, Lords], *and* Knights *from tilting.*

Sim. Knights,
To say you 're welcome were superfluous.
To place upon the volume of your deeds,
As in a title-page, your worth in arms,
Were more than you expect, or more than 's fit,
Since every worth in show commends itself.
Prepare for mirth, for mirth becomes a feast:
You are princes and my guests.
Thai. But you, my knight and guest;
To whom this wreath of victory I give,
And crown you king of this day's happiness.
Per. 'Tis more by fortune, lady, than by merit.
Sim. Call it by what you will, the day is yours;
And here, I hope, is none that envies it.
In framing an artist, art hath thus decreed,
To make some good, but others to exceed;
And you are her labour'd scholar. Come, queen o' th' feast,—
For, daughter, so you are,—here take your place:
Marshal the rest, as they deserve their grace.
Knights. We are honour'd much by good Simonides.
Sim. Your presence glads our days: honour we love;
For who hates honour hates the gods above.
Marshal. Sir, yonder is your place.
Per. Some other is more fit.
First Knight. Contend not, sir; for we are gentlemen
Have neither in our hearts nor outward eyes
Envied the great nor shall the low despise.
Per. You are right courteous knights.
Sim. Sit, sir, sit.—
[*Aside*] By Jove, I wonder, that is king of thoughts,
These cates resist me, he not thought upon.
Thai. [*Aside*] By Juno, that is queen of marriage,
All viands that I eat do seem unsavoury,
Wishing him my meat. [*To Sim.*] Sure, he 's a gallant gentleman.
Sim. [*To Thai.*] He 's but a country gentleman;
Has done no more than other knights have done;
Has broken a staff or so; so let it pass.
Thai. [*Aside*] To me he seems like diamond to glass.
Per. [*Aside*] Yon king 's to me like to my father's picture,
Which tells me in that glory once he was;
Had princes sit, like stars, about his throne,
And he the sun, for them to reverence;
None that beheld him, but, like lesser lights,
Did vail their crowns to his supremacy:
Where now his son 's like a glow-worm in the night,
The which hath fire in darkness, none in light:
Whereby I see that Time 's the king of men,
He 's both their parent, and he is their grave,
And gives them what he will, not what they crave.
Sim. What, are you merry, knights?
Knights. Who can be other in this royal presence?
Sim. Here, with a cup that 's stor'd unto the brim,—
As you do love, fill to your mistress' lips,—
We drink this health to you.
Knights. We thank your grace.
Sim. Yet pause awhile:
Yon knight doth sit too melancholy,
As if the entertainment in our court
Had not a show might countervail his worth.
Note it not you, Thaisa?
Thai. What is 't
To me, my father?
Sim. O, attend, my daughter:
Princes in this should live like gods above,
Who freely give to every one that come
To honour them:
And princes not doing so are like to gnats,
Which make a sound, but kill'd are wond'red at.
Therefore to make his entrance more sweet,
Here, say we drink this standing-bowl of wine to him.
Thai. Alas, my father, it befits not me
Unto a stranger knight to be so bold:
He may my proffer take for an offence,
Since men take women's gifts for impudence.
Sim. How!
Do as I bid you, or you'll move me else.
Thai. [*Aside*] Now, by the gods, he could not please me better.
Sim. And furthermore tell him, we desire to know of him,

That which feeds my flame puts out my light. 38. **'Sic spectanda fides.'** Thus is faith to be tried. 44. **'In . . . vivo.'** In this hope I live. 51. **whipstock,** i e., as if he were accustomed to driving work horses.

SCENE III. 6. **every . . . itself,** everything worthy manifests its own worth. 16. **To make,** to exceed. The two infinitives are not strictly parallel. Some are to be made good, but others are to be made excellent. 17. **her labour'd scholar,** the one on whom art has bestowed the most pains. 28-29. **By . . . upon.** Malone assigned the speech to Pericles; followed by Globe. Cambridge marks speeches (ll. 28-47) as asides. 29. **These cates resist me,** these delicacies are distasteful to me. **he,** so Qq; Globe, following Malone: *she*. **not,** so Qq; Globe, following Mason: *but*. 51. **fill to,** fill and drink to. 56. **countervail,** equal. 65. **standing-bowl,** bowl resting on a pedestal.

Of whence he is, his name and parentage.
Thai. The king my father, sir, has drunk to you.—
Per. I thank him.
Thai. Wishing it so much blood unto your life.
Per. I thank both him and you, and pledge him freely.
Thai. And further he desires to know of you,
Of whence you are, your name and parentage.
Per. A gentleman of Tyre; my name, Pericles;
My education been in arts and arms;
Who, looking for adventures in the world,
Was by the rough seas reft of ships and men,
And after shipwrack driven upon this shore.
Thai. He thanks your grace; names himself Pericles,
A gentleman of Tyre,
Who only by misfortune of the seas
Bereft of ships and men, cast on this shore.
Sim. Now, by the gods, I pity his misfortune,
And will awake him from his melancholy.
Come, gentlemen, we sit too long on trifles,
And waste the time, which looks for other revels.
Even in your armours, as you are address'd,
Will very well become a soldier's dance.
I will not have excuse, with saying this
Loud music is too harsh for ladies' heads,
Since they love men in arms as well as beds. *They dance.*
So, this was well ask'd, 'twas so well perform'd.
Come, sir;
Here's a lady that wants breathing too:
And I have heard, you knights of Tyre
Are excellent in making ladies trip;
And that their measures are as excellent.
Per. In those that practise them they are, my lord.
Sim. O, that 's as much as you would be denied
Of your fair courtesy. *They dance.*
Unclasp, unclasp:
Thanks, gentlemen, to all; all have done well,
[*To Per.*] But you the best.—Pages and lights, to conduct
These knights unto their several lodgings! [*To Per.*]
Yours, sir,
We have given order to be next our own.
Per. I am at your grace's pleasure.
Sim. Princes, it is too late to talk of love;
And that 's the mark I know you level at:
Therefore each one betake him to his rest;
To-morrow all for speeding do their best. [*Exeunt.*]

[SCENE IV. *Tyre. A room in the Governor's house.*]

Enter HELICANUS *and* ESCANES.

Hel. No, Escanes, know this of me,
Antiochus from incest liv'd not free:
For which, the most high gods not minding longer
To withhold the vengeance that they had in store,
Due to this heinous capital offence,
Even in the height and pride of all his glory,
When he was seated in a chariot
Of an inestimable value, and his daughter with him,
A fire from heaven came and shrivell'd up
Their bodies, even to loathing; for they so stunk,
That all those eyes ador'd them ere their fall
Scorn now their hand should give them burial.
Esca. 'Twas very strange.
Hel. And yet but justice; for though
This king were great, his greatness was no guard
To bar heaven's shaft, but sin had his reward.
Esca. 'Tis very true.

Enter two or three Lords.

First Lord. See, not a man in private conference
Or council has respect with him but he.
Sec. Lord. It shall no longer grieve without reproof.
Third Lord. And curs'd be he that will not second it.
First Lord. Follow me, then. Lord Helicane, a word.
Hel. With me? and welcome: happy day, my lords.
First Lord. Know that our griefs are risen to the top,
And now at length they overflow their banks.
Hel. Your griefs! for what? wrong not your prince you love.
First Lord. Wrong not yourself, then, noble Helicane;
But if the prince do live, let us salute him,
Or know what ground 's made happy by his breath.
If in the world he live, we'll seek him out;
If in his grave he rest, we'll find him there;
And be resolv'd he lives to govern us,
Or dead, give 's cause to mourn his funeral,
And leave us to our free election.
Sec. Lord. Whose death 's indeed the strongest in our censure:
And knowing this kingdom is without a head,—
Like goodly buildings left without a roof
Soon fall to ruin,—your noble self,
That best know how to rule and how to reign,
We thus submit unto,—our sovereign.
All. Live, noble Helicane!
Hel. For honour's cause, forbear your suffrages:
If that you love Prince Pericles, forbear.
Take I your wish, I leap into the seas,
Where 's hourly trouble for a minute's ease.
A twelvemonth longer, let me entreat you
To forbear the absence of your king;
If in which time expir'd, he not return,
I shall with aged patience bear your yoke.
But if I cannot win you to this love,
Go search like nobles, like noble subjects,
And in your search spend your adventurous worth;
Whom if you find, and win unto return,
You shall like diamonds sit about his crown.
First Lord. To wisdom he 's a fool that will not yield;
And since Lord Helicane enjoineth us,
We with our travels will endeavour it.
Hel. Then you love us, we you, and we'll clasp hands:
When peers thus knit, a kingdom ever stands. [*Exeunt.*]

[SCENE V. *Pentapolis. A room in the palace.*]

Enter the KING [SIMONIDES] *reading of a letter, at one door: the* Knights *meet him.*

---

94. **address'd,** accoutered. 95. **Will . . . become.** The subject is *you* understood. 97. **Loud music,** noise of armor (Malone). 101. **breathing,** exercise. 106-107. **that 's . . . courtesy,** that 's the equivalent of your denial of your accomplishment.

SCENE IV. 3. **minding,** intending. 11. **eyes,** eyes which. 18. **he,** Escanes. 19. **without reproof,** i.e., such grievance cannot continue without some bad results. 34. **Whose . . . censure,** according to our judgment it is more likely that he is dead. 41. **suffrages,** petitions, requests. 43. **Take . . . wish,** if I should act on your wish. 49. **to this love,** to this regard for my request.

First Knight. Good morrow to the good Simonides.
Sim. Knights, from my daughter this I let you know,
That for this twelvemonth she'll not undertake
A married life.
Her reason to herself is only known,
Which from her by no means can I get.
Sec. Knight. May we not get access to her, my lord?
Sim. 'Faith, by no means; she hath so strictly tied
Her to her chamber, that 'tis impossible.
One twelve moons more she'll wear Diana's livery;
This by the eye of Cynthia hath she vow'd,
And on her virgin honour will not break it.
Third Knight. Loath to bid farewell, we take our leaves. [*Exeunt Knights.*]
Sim. So,
They are well dispatch'd; now to my daughter's letter:
She tells me here, she'll wed the stranger knight,
Or never more to view nor day nor light.
'Tis well, mistress; your choice agrees with mine;
I like that well: nay, how absolute she 's in 't,
Not minding whether I dislike or no!
Well, I do commend her choice;
And will no longer have it be delay'd.
Soft! here he comes: I must dissemble it.

Enter Pericles.

Per. All fortune to the good Simonides!
Sim. To you as much, sir! I am beholding to you
For your sweet music this last night: I do
Protest my ears were never better fed
With such delightful pleasing harmony.
Per. It is your grace's pleasure to commend;
Not my desert.
Sim. Sir, you are music's master.
Per. The worst of all her scholars, my good lord.
Sim. Let me ask you one thing:
What do you think of my daughter, sir?
Per. A most virtuous princess.
Sim. And she is fair too, is she not?
Per. As a fair day in summer, wondrous fair.
Sim. Sir, my daughter thinks very well of you;
Ay, so well, that you must be her master,
And she will be your scholar: therefore look to it.
Per. I am unworthy for her schoolmaster.
Sim. She thinks not so; peruse this writing else.
Per. [*Aside*] What 's here?
A letter, that she loves the knight of Tyre!
'Tis the king's subtilty to have my life.—
O, seek not to entrap me, gracious lord,
A stranger and distressed gentleman,
That never aim'd so high to love your daughter,
But bent all offices to honour her.
Sim. Thou hast bewitch'd my daughter, and thou art
A villain.
Per. By the gods, I have not:
Never did thought of mine levy offence;
Nor never did my actions yet commence
A deed might gain her love or your displeasure.
Sim. Traitor, thou liest.
Per. Traitor!
Sim. Ay, traitor.
Per. Even in his throat—unless it be the king—
That calls me traitor, I return the lie.
Sim. [*Aside*] Now, by the gods, I do applaud his courage.
Per. My actions are as noble as my thoughts,
That never relish'd of a base descent.
I came unto your court for honour's cause,
And not to be a rebel to her state;
And he that otherwise accounts of me,
This sword shall prove he 's honour's enemy.
Sim. No?
Here comes my daughter, she can witness it.

Enter Thaisa.

Per. Then, as you are as virtuous as fair,
Resolve your angry father, if my tongue
Did e'er solicit, or my hand subscribe
To any syllable that made love to you.
Thai. Why, sir, say if you had,
Who takes offence at that would make me glad?
Sim. Yea, mistress, are you so peremptory?
(*Aside*) I am glad on 't with all my heart.—
I'll tame you; I'll bring you in subjection.
Will you, not having my consent,
Bestow your love and your affections
Upon a stranger? (*Aside*) who, for aught I know,
May be, nor can I think the contrary,
As great in blood as I myself.—
Therefore hear you, mistress; either frame
Your will to mine,—and you, sir, hear you,
Either be rul'd by me, or I'll make you—
Man and wife.
Nay, come, your hands and lips must seal it too:
And being join'd, I'll thus your hopes destroy;
And for further grief,—God give you joy!
What, are you both pleas'd?
Thai. Yes, if you love me, sir.
Per. Even as my life my blood that fosters it.
Sim. What, are you both agreed?
Both. Yes, if 't please your majesty.
Sim. It pleaseth me so well, that I will see you wed;
And then with what haste you can get you to bed.
Exeunt.

[ACT III.]

Enter Gower.

Gow. Now sleep yslaked hath the rout;
No din but snores the house about,
Made louder by the o'er-fed breast
Of this most pompous marriage-feast.
The cat, with eyne of burning coal,
Now couches fore the mouse's hole;
And crickets sing at the oven's mouth,
E'er the blither for their drouth.
Hymen hath brought the bride to bed,
Where, by the loss of maidenhead,
A babe is moulded. Be attent,
And time that is so briefly spent

Scene v. 19. **absolute,** unconditional, positive. 38-39. **her . . . scholar.** In the prose versions of the story there is a lapse of time between the scholar-master proposal and the marriage proposal, although Simonides' dissimulation is essentially the same in all versions. The telescoping may be due here to the dramatist or to the person who transmitted the text. 41. **else,** i.e., if you don't believe me.

Act iii. prologue. 1. **yslaked,** laid to rest; an archaic affectation. 3. **breast,** lungs, i.e., breathing because of the overeating at the marriage feast. 11. **attent,** attentive.

With your fine fancies quaintly eche:
What 's dumb in show I'll plain with speech.

[DUMB SHOW.]

Enter, PERICLES *and* SIMONIDES, *at one door, with* Attendants; *a* Messenger *meets them, kneels, and gives* PERICLES *a letter:* PERICLES *shows it* SIMONIDES; *the* Lords *kneel to him* [PERICLES]. *Then enter* THAISA *with child, with* LYCHORIDA *a nurse. The* KING *shows her the letter; she rejoices: she and* PERICLES *take leave of her father, and depart* [*with* LYCHORIDA *and their* Attendants. *Then exeunt* SIMONIDES *and the rest.*]

By many a dern and painful perch
Of Pericles the careful search,
By the four opposing coigns
Which the world together joins,
Is made with all due diligence
That horse and sail and high expense
Can stead the quest. At last from Tyre,
Fame answering the most strange inquire,
To th' court of King Simonides
Are letters brought, the tenour these:
Antiochus and his daughter dead;
The men of Tyrus on the head
Of Helicanus would set on
The crown of Tyre, but he will none:
The mutiny he there hastes t' appease;
Says to 'em, if King Pericles
Come not home in twice six moons,
He, obedient to their dooms,
Will take the crown. The sum of this,
Brought hither to Pentapolis,
Y-ravished the regions round,
And every one with claps can sound,
'Our heir-apparent is a king!
Who dream'd, who thought of such a thing?'
Brief, he must hence depart to Tyre:
His queen with child makes her desire—
Which who shall cross?—along to go:
Omit we all their dole and woe:
Lychorida, her nurse, she takes,
And so to sea. Their vessel shakes
On Neptune's billow; half the flood
Hath their keel cut: but fortune's mood
Varies again; the grisled north
Disgorges such a tempest forth,
That, as a duck for life that dives,
So up and down the poor ship drives:
The lady shrieks, and well-a-near
Does fall in travail with her fear:
And what ensues in this fell storm
Shall for itself itself perform.
I nill relate, action may
Conveniently the rest convey;
Which might not what by me is told.
In your imagination hold
This stage the ship, upon whose deck
The sea-tost Pericles appears to speak. [*Exit.*]

[SCENE I.]

Enter PERICLES, *on shipboard.*

Per. Thou god of this great vast, rebuke these surges,
Which wash both heaven and hell; and thou, that hast
Upon the winds command, bind them in brass,
Having call'd them from the deep! O, still
Thy deaf'ning, dreadful thunders; gently quench
Thy nimble, sulphurous flashes! O, how, Lychorida,
How does my queen? Thou stormest venomously;
Wilt thou spit all thyself? The seaman's whistle
Is as a whisper in the ears of death,
Unheard. Lychorida!—Lucina, O
Divinest patroness, and midwife gentle
To those that cry by night, convey thy deity
Aboard our dancing boat; make swift the pangs
Of my queen's travails!

Enter LYCHORIDA [*with an Infant*].

Now, Lychorida!
Lyc. Here is a thing too young for such a place,
Who, if it had conceit, would die, as I
Am like to do: take in your arms this piece
Of your dead queen.
Per. How, how, Lychorida!
Lyc. Patience, good sir; do not assist the storm.
Here 's all that is left living of your queen,
A little daughter: for the sake of it,
Be manly, and take comfort.
Per. O you gods!
Why do you make us love your goodly gifts,
And snatch them straight away? We here below
Recall not what we give, and therein may
Use honour with you.
Lyc. Patience, good sir,
Even for this charge.
Per. Now, mild may be thy life!
For a more blustrous birth had never babe:
Quiet and gentle thy conditions! for
Thou art the rudeliest welcome to this world
That ever was prince's child. Happy what follows!
Thou hast as chiding a nativity
As fire, air, water, earth, and heaven can make,
To herald thee from the womb: even at the first
Thy loss is more than can thy portage quit,
With all thou canst find here. Now, the good gods
Throw their best eyes upon 't!

Enter two Sailors.

First Sail. What courage, sir? God save you!
Per. Courage enough: I do not fear the flaw;
It hath done to me the worst. Yet, for the love
Of this poor infant, this fresh-new sea-farer,
I would it would be quiet.

First Sail. Slack the bolins there! Thou wilt not, wilt thou? Blow, and split thyself.

Sec. Sail. But sea-room, an the brine and cloudy billow kiss the moon, I care not.

First Sail. Sir, your queen must overboard: the sea

---

13. **eche,** eke out. 14. **plain,** make plain. 15. **dern,** dark, drear. **perch,** measure of land. 17. **coigns,** compass points. 35. **Y-ravished,** delighted. 47. **grisled,** fearful, horrible. 51. **well-a-near,** a cry of lamentation. 55. **nill,** will not.

SCENE I. 1. **vast,** expanse. 6. **sulphurous flashes.** Lightning was apparently thought to be sulphurous; cf. *Measure for Measure,* II, ii, 115; *King Lear,* III, ii, 4; *The Tempest,* I, ii, 204. 10. **Lucina.** Cf. I, i, 8, note. 16. **conceit,** understanding (of its precarious position). 26. **Use honour,** share, or are entitled to equal honor. 27. **charge,** i.e., care of the infant. 35. **portage,** port dues. 43. **bolins,** bowlines. 63. **e'er-remaining.** Qq: *ayre-remaining;* Malone-Steevens: *aye-remaining.* W. Bell conjectured *air-retaining lamps,* i.e., lampreys. 67. **My . . . jewels,** i.e., my casket of jewels. 68. **satin coffer,** perhaps a satin-lined coffer; or one containing satins and clothes of state. 72. **bi-**

works high, the wind is loud, and will not lie till the ship be cleared of the dead.

Per. That 's your superstition.

First Sail. Pardon us, sir; with us at sea it hath been still observed; and we are strong in custom. Therefore briefly yield her; for she must overboard straight.

Per. As you think meet. Most wretched queen!

Lyc. Here she lies, sir.

Per. A terrible childbed hast thou had, my dear;
No light, no fire: th' unfriendly elements
Forgot thee utterly; nor have I time
To give thee hallow'd to thy grave, but straight
Must cast thee, scarcely coffin'd, in the ooze;
Where, for a monument upon thy bones,
And e'er-remaining lamps, the belching whale
And humming water must o'erwhelm thy corpse,
Lying with simple shells. O Lychorida,
Bid Nestor bring me spices, ink and paper,
My casket and my jewels; and bid Nicander
Bring me the satin coffer: lay the babe
Upon the pillow: hie thee, whiles I say
A priestly farewell to her: suddenly, woman.
[*Exit Lychorida.*]

Sec. Sail. Sir, we have a chest beneath the hatches, caulked and bitumed ready.

Per. I thank thee. Mariner, say what coast is this?

Sec. Sail. We are near Tarsus.

Per. Thither, gentle mariner,
Alter thy course for Tyre. When canst thou reach it?

Sec. Sail. By break of day, if the wind cease.

Per. O, make for Tarsus!
There will I visit Cleon, for the babe
Cannot hold out to Tyrus: there I'll leave it
At careful nursing. Go thy ways, good mariner:
I'll bring the body presently. *Exeunt.*

[SCENE II. *Ephesus. A room in Cerimon's house.*]

Enter Lord CERIMON, *with a Servant* [*and some Persons who have been shipwrecked*].

Cer. Philemon, ho!

Enter PHILEMON.

Phil. Doth my lord call?

Cer. Get fire and meat for these poor men:
'T has been a turbulent and stormy night. [*Exit Phil.*]

Serv. I have been in many; but such a night as this,
Till now, I ne'er endured.

Cer. Your master will be dead ere you return;
There 's nothing can be minist'red to nature
That can recover him. [*To another*] Give this to the 'pothecary,
And tell me how it works. [*Exeunt all but Cerimon.*]

Enter two Gentlemen.

First Gent. Good morrow.

Sec. Gent. Good morrow to your lordship.

Cer. Gentlemen,
Why do you stir so early?

First Gent. Sir,
Our lodgings, standing bleak upon the sea,
Shook as the earth did quake;
The very principals did seem to rend,
And all-to topple: pure surprise and fear
Made me to quit the house.

Sec. Gent. That is the cause we trouble you so early;
'Tis not our husbandry.

Cer. O, you say well.

First Gent. But I much marvel that your lordship, having
Rich tire about you, should at these early hours
Shake off the golden slumber of repose.
'Tis most strange,
Nature should be so conversant with pain,
Being thereto not compell'd.

Cer. I hold it ever,
Virtue and cunning were endowments greater
Than nobleness and riches: careless heirs
May the two latter darken and expend;
But immortality attends the former,
Making a man a god. 'Tis known, I ever
Have studied physic, through which secret art,
By turning o'er authorities, I have,
Together with my practice, made familiar
To me and to my aid the blest infusions
That dwell in vegetives, in metals, stones;
And I can speak of the disturbances
That nature works, and of her cures; which doth give me
A more content in course of true delight
Than to be thirsty after tottering honour,
Or tie my treasure up in silken bags,
To please the fool and death.

Sec. Gent. Your honour has through Ephesus pour'd forth
Your charity, and hundreds call themselves
Your creatures, who by you have been restor'd:
And not your knowledge, your personal pain, but even
Your purse, still open, hath built Lord Cerimon
Such strong renown as time shall never raze.

Enter two or three [Servants] *with a chest.*

First Serv. So; lift there.

Cer. What's that?

First Serv. Sir, even now
Did the sea toss upon our shore this chest:
'Tis of some wrack.

Cer. Set 't down, let 's look upon 't.

Sec. Gent. 'Tis like a coffin, sir.

Cer. Whate'er it be,
'Tis wondrous heavy. Wrench it open straight:
If the sea's stomach be o'ercharg'd with gold,
†'Tis a good constraint of fortune it belches upon us.

Sec. Gent. 'Tis so, my lord.

Cer. How close 'tis caulk'd and bitumed!
Did the sea cast it up?

First Serv. I never saw so huge a billow, sir,
As toss'd it upon shore.

Cer. Wrench it open;

tumed, smeared with pitch. 76. **Alter . . . Tyre,** change your course, which has been for Tyre.
SCENE II. 8-9. **There 's . . . him,** i.e., only supernatural ministrations can restore him. 16. **principals,** main timbers of houses. 17. **all-to topple,** topple down completely. 25. **Nature . . . pain,** any human being should care to have so much to do with painful matters (Deighton). 27. **cunning,** knowledge, skill. 29. **expend,** squander.

35. **infusions,** medicinal properties. 39. **course,** pursuit. 42. **the fool and death,** probably alludes to the frequency of these figures in the old Dance of Death motifs. 45. **Your creatures,** people created anew because of your restoratives. 55. **'Tis . . . us.** Possible textual corruption. It may mean: it is fortunate that it is compelled to vomit upon us.

Soft! it smells most sweetly in my sense.
Sec. Gent. A delicate odour.
Cer. As ever hit my nostril. So, up with it.
O you most potent gods! what 's here? a corse!
First Gent. Most strange!
Cer. Shrouded in cloth of state; balm'd and entreasur'd
With full bags of spices! A passport too!
Apollo, perfect me in the characters! [*Reads from a scroll.*]
'Here I give to understand,
If e'er this coffin drives a-land,
I, King Pericles, have lost
This queen, worth all our mundane cost.
Who finds her, give her burying;
She was the daughter of a king:
Besides this treasure for a fee,
The gods requite his charity!'
If thou livest, Pericles, thou hast a heart
That even cracks for woe! This chanc'd to-night.
Sec. Gent. Most likely, sir.
Cer. Nay, certainly to-night;
For look how fresh she looks! They were too rough
That threw her in the sea. Make a fire within:
Fetch hither all my boxes in my closet. [*Exit a Servant.*]
Death may usurp on nature many hours,
And yet the fire of life kindle again
The o'erpress'd spirits. †I heard of an Egyptian
That had nine hours lien dead,
Who was by good appliance recovered.

Enter one with [*boxes,*] *napkins, and fire.*

Well said, well said; the fire and cloths.
The rough and woeful music that we have,
Cause it to sound, beseech you.
The viol once more: how thou stirr'st, thou block!
The music there!—I pray you, give her air.
Gentlemen,
This queen will live: nature awakes; a warmth
Breathes out of her: she hath not been entranc'd
Above five hours: see how she gins to blow
Into life's flower again!
First Gent. The heavens,
Through you, increase our wonder and set up
Your fame for ever.
Cer. She is alive; behold,
Her eyelids, cases to those heavenly jewels
Which Pericles hath lost,
Begin to part their fringes of bright gold;
The diamonds of a most praised water
Doth appear, to make the world twice rich. Live,
And make us weep to hear your fate, fair creature,
Rare as you seem to be. *She moves.*
Thai. O dear Diana,
Where am I? Where 's my lord? What world is this?
Sec. Gent. Is not this strange?
First Gent. Most rare.
Cer. Hush, my gentle neighbours!
Lend me your hands; to the next chamber bear her.
Get linen: now this matter must be look'd to,
For her relapse is mortal. Come, come;
And Æsculapius guide us!
They carry her away. Exeunt omnes.

[SCENE III. *Tarsus. A room in Cleon's house.*]

Enter PERICLES *at Tarsus, with* CLEON *and* DIONYZA [*and* LYCHORIDA *with* MARINA *in her arms*].

Per. Most honour'd Cleon, I must needs be gone;
My twelve months are expir'd, and Tyrus stands
In a litigious peace. You, and your lady,
Take from my heart all thankfulness! The gods
Make up the rest upon you!
Cle. Your shafts of fortune, though they hurt you mortally,
Yet glance full wond'ringly on us.
Dion. O your sweet queen!
That the strict fates had pleas'd you had brought her hither,
To have bless'd mine eyes with her!
Per. We cannot but obey
The powers above us. Could I rage and roar
As doth the sea she lies in, yet the end
Must be as 'tis. My gentle babe Marina, whom,
For she was born at sea, I have nam'd so, here
I charge your charity withal, leaving her
The infant of your care; beseeching you
To give her princely training, that she may be
Manner'd as she is born.
Cle. Fear not, my lord, but think
Your grace, that fed my country with your corn,
For which the people's prayers still fall upon you,
Must in your child be thought on. If neglection
Should therein make me vile, the common body,
By you reliev'd, would force me to my duty:
But if to that my nature need a spur,
The gods revenge it upon me and mine,
To the end of generation!
Per. I believe you;
Your honour and your goodness teach me to 't,
Without your vows. Till she be married, madam,
By bright Diana, whom we honour, all
Unscissar'd shall this hair of mine remain,
Though I show ill in 't. So I take my leave.
Good madam, make me blessed in your care
In bringing up my child.
Dion. I have one myself,
Who shall not be more dear to my respect
Than yours, my lord.
Per. Madam, my thanks and prayers.
Cle. We'll bring your grace e'en to the edge o' th' shore,
Then give you up to the mask'd Neptune and
The gentlest winds of heaven.
Per. I will embrace
Your offer. Come, dearest madam. O, no tears,
Lychorida, no tears:

---

67. **perfect . . . characters,** enable me to read the writing; may refer to the possibility of their being in a foreign tongue. 71. **cost,** wealth. 79. **rough,** hasty. 88-91. **The . . . there.** According to Burton (*Anatomy*, II, ii, vi. 3) music has animating power, "because the spirits about the heart take in that trembling and dancing air into the body, are moved together, and stirred up with it." On the power of music to revive, cf. *King Lear*, IV, vii, 25, and *The Winter's Tale*, V, iii, 98. There is some dispute as to whether *viol* designates a musical instrument or a phial of medicine. Q_{1-3}: *violl;* $Q_{4-6}F_3$: *viall;* F_4: *vial.* Judging from the emphasis in Burton on "the trembling and dancing air," the stringed instrument is the more likely because of the viol's peculiar vibrancy. 95. **blow,** bloom. 102. **water,** luster. 111. **Æsculapius,** god of medicine.

SCENE III. 3. **litigious,** disturbed by disputes. 7. **wond'ringly,** so Q; Globe, following Steevens: *wanderingly*. 25. **of generation,** i.e., of my generation—my descendants. 36. **mask'd Neptune,** alludes to his deceitful aspect of calm.

SCENE IV. 6. **eaning time,** time of delivery.

ACT IV. PROLOGUE. 6. **fast-growing scene,** alludes to the interval

Look to your little mistress, on whose grace
You may depend hereafter. Come, my lord. [*Exeunt.*]

[SCENE IV. *Ephesus. A room in Cerimon's house.*]

Enter CERIMON *and* THAISA.

Cer. Madam, this letter, and some certain jewels,
Lay with you in your coffer: which are
At your command. Know you the character?
Thai. It is my lord's.
That I was shipp'd at sea, I well remember,
Even on my eaning time; but whether there
Delivered, by the holy gods,
I cannot rightly say. But since King Pericles,
My wedded lord, I ne'er shall see again,
A vestal livery will I take me to,
And never more have joy.
Cer. Madam, if this you purpose as ye speak,
Diana's temple is not distant far,
Where you may abide till your date expire.
Moreover, if you please, a niece of mine
Shall there attend you.
Thai. My recompense is thanks, that 's all;
Yet my good will is great, though the gift small. *Exeunt.*

[ACT IV.]

Enter GOWER.

Gow. Imagine Pericles arriv'd at Tyre,
Welcom'd and settled to his own desire.
His woeful queen we leave at Ephesus,
Unto Diana there a votaress.
Now to Marina bend your mind,
Whom our fast-growing scene must find
At Tarsus, and by Cleon train'd
In music, letters; who hath gain'd
Of education all the grace,
Which makes her both the heart and place
Of general wonder. But, alack,
That monster Envy, oft the wrack
Of earned praise, Marina's life
Seeks to take off by treason's knife.
And in this kind hath our Cleon
One daughter, and a wench full grown,
Even ripe for marriage-rite; this maid
Hight Philoten: and it is said
For certain in our story, she
Would ever with Marina be:
Be 't when she weav'd the sleided silk
With fingers long, small, white as milk;
Or when she would with sharp needle wound
The cambric, which she made more sound
By hurting it; or when to th' lute
She sung, and made the night-bird mute,
That still records with moan; or when
She would with rich and constant pen
Vail to her mistress Dian; still
This Philoten contends in skill
With absolute Marina: so
With the dove of Paphos might the crow
Vie feathers white. Marina gets
All praises, which are paid as debts,
And not as given. This so darks
In Philoten all graceful marks,
That Cleon's wife, with envy rare,
A present murderer does prepare
For good Marina, that her daughter
Might stand peerless by this slaughter.
The sooner her vile thoughts to stead,
Lychorida, our nurse, is dead:
And cursed Dionyza hath
The pregnant instrument of wrath
Prest for this blow. The unborn event
I do commend to your content:
Only I carry winged time
Post on the lame feet of my rhyme;
Which never could I so convey,
Unless your thoughts went on my way.
Dionyza does appear,
With Leonine, a murderer. *Exit.*

[SCENE I. *Tarsus. An open place near the sea-shore.*]

Enter DIONYZA *with* LEONINE.

Dion. Thy oath remember; thou hast sworn to do 't:
'Tis but a blow, which never shall be known.
Thou canst not do a thing in the world so soon,
To yield thee so much profit. Let not conscience,
Which is but cold, inflaming love i' thy bosom,
Inflame too nicely; nor let pity, which
Even women have cast off, melt thee, but be
A soldier to thy purpose.
Leon. I will do 't; but yet she is a goodly creature.
Dion. The fitter, then, the gods should have her.
†Here she comes weeping for her only mistress' death.
Thou art resolv'd?
Leon. I am resolv'd.

Enter MARINA, *with a basket of flowers.*

Mar. No, I will rob Tellus of her weed,
To strew thy green with flowers: the yellows, blues,
The purple violets, and marigolds,
Shall as a carpet hang upon thy grave,
While summer-days doth last. Ay me! poor maid,
Born in a tempest, when my mother died,
This world to me is like a lasting storm,
Whirring me from my friends.
Dion. How now, Marina! why do you keep alone?
How chance my daughter is not with you? Do not
Consume your blood with sorrowing: have you
A nurse of me. Lord, how your favour 's chang'd
With this unprofitable woe!
Come, give me your flowers, ere the sea mar it.

of years between acts; cf. ll. 47-50, below. 10-11. **both . . . wonder,** the focal point of the admiration of all. 14. **treason's,** treachery's. 15. **in this kind,** similarly; i.e., like Pericles, Cleon has a daughter, etc. 18. **Hight,** is called. 21. **sleided silk,** floss silk; cf. *Troilus and Cressida,* V, i, 35. 27. **records,** sings. 28. **constant,** loyal. 29. **Vail,** do homage to. 32. **Paphos,** city sacred to Venus. 33. **Vie feathers white,** contend with in whiteness of plumage. 38. **present,** transferred modifier; i.e., forthwith prepares. 45. **Prest,** prepared.
SCENE I. 4-6. **Let . . . nicely,** Knight's emendation of Q: *in flaming, thy loue bosome;* Deighton emended, *or flaming love thy bosom Enslave too nicely* and commented: Dionyza mentions three possible hindrances, conscience, love, pity, as likely to deter Leonine, and an obvious antithesis between *cold conscience* and *flaming love* seems to be intended. 6. **nicely,** scrupulously. 11. **only mistress',** Nicholson: *only nurse's;* Percy: *old nurse's.* 14. **Tellus,** goddess of the earth. 15. **green,** grave. 24. **with sorrowing,** i.e., with sighs; cf. *blood-drinking sighs, 2 Henry VI,* III, ii, 63. 27. **ere . . . it,** before your tears mar your face; often emended to *on the sea margent.*

Walk with Leonine; the air is quick there,
And it pierces and sharpens the stomach. Come,
Leonine, take her by the arm, walk with her.
Mar. No, I pray you;
I'll not bereave you of your servant.
Dion. Come, come;
I love the king your father, and yourself,
With more than foreign heart. We every day
Expect him here: when he shall come and find
Our paragon to all reports thus blasted,
He will repent the breadth of his great voyage;
Blame both my lord and me, that we have taken
No care to your best courses. Go, I pray you,
Walk, and be cheerful once again; reserve
That excellent complexion, which did steal
The eyes of young and old. Care not for me;
I can go home alone.
Mar. Well, I will go;
But yet I have no desire to it.
Dion. Come, come, I know 'tis good for you.
Walk half an hour, Leonine, at the least:
Remember what I have said.
Leon. I warrant you, madam.
Dion. I'll leave you, my sweet lady, for a while:
Pray, walk softly, do not heat your blood:
What! I must have a care of you.
Mar. My thanks, sweet madam.
[*Exit Dionyza.*]
Is this wind westerly that blows?
Leon. South-west.
Mar. When I was born, the wind was north.
Leon. Was 't so?
Mar. My father, as nurse says, did never fear,
But cried 'Good seamen!' to the sailors, galling
His kingly hands, haling ropes;
And, clasping to the mast, endur'd a sea
That almost burst the deck.
Leon. When was this?
Mar. When I was born:
Never was waves nor wind more violent;
And from the ladder-tackle washes off
A canvas-climber. 'Ha!' says one, 'wolt out?'
And with a dropping industry they skip
From stem to stern: the boatswain whistles, and
The master calls, and trebles their confusion.
Leon. Come, say your prayers.
Mar. What mean you?
Leon. If you require a little space for prayer,
I grant it: pray; but be not tedious,
For the gods are quick of ear, and I am sworn
To do my work with haste.
Mar. Why will you kill me?
Leon. To satisfy my lady.
Mar. Why would she have me kill'd?
Now, as I can remember, by my troth,
I never did her hurt in all my life:
I never spake bad word, nor did ill turn
To any living creature: believe me, la,
I never kill'd a mouse, nor hurt a fly:
I trod upon a worm against my will,
But I wept for it. How have I offended,
Wherein my death might yield her any profit,
Or my life imply her any danger?
Leon. My commission
Is not to reason of the deed, but do 't.
Mar. You will not do 't for all the world, I hope.
You are well favoured, and your looks foreshow
You have a gentle heart. I saw you lately,
When you caught hurt in parting two that fought:
Good sooth, it show'd well in you: do so now:
Your lady seeks my life; come you between,
And save poor me, the weaker.
Leon. I am sworn,
And will dispatch. [*He seizes her.*]

Enter Pirates.

First Pirate. Hold, villain! [*Leonine runs away.*]
Sec. Pirate. A prize! a prize!
Third Pirate. Half-part, mates, half-part.
Come, let 's have her aboard suddenly.
Exeunt [*Pirates with Marina*].

Enter LEONINE.

Leon. These roguing thieves serve the great pirate Valdes;
And they have seiz'd Marina. Let her go:
There 's no hope she will return. I'll swear she 's dead,
And thrown into the sea. But I'll see further:
Perhaps they will but please themselves upon her,
Not carry her aboard. If she remain,
Whom they have ravish'd must by me be slain. *Exit.*

[SCENE II. *Mytilene. A brothel.*]

Enter the three Bawds [Pandar, Bawd, *and* BOULT].

Pand. Boult!

Boult. Sir?

Pand. Search the market narrowly; Mytilene is full of gallants. We lost too much money this mart by being too wenchless.

Bawd. We were never so much out of creatures. We have but poor three, and they can do no more than they can do; and they with continual action are even as good as rotten.

Pand. Therefore let 's have fresh ones, whate'er we pay for them. If there be not a conscience to be used in every trade, we shall never prosper.

Bawd. Thou sayest true: 'tis not our bringing up of poor bastards,—as, I think, I have brought up some eleven—

Boult. Ay, to eleven; and brought them down again. But shall I search the market?

Bawd. What else, man? The stuff we have, a strong wind will blow it to pieces, they are so pitifully sodden.

Pand. Thou sayest true; they 're too unwholesome, o' conscience. The poor Transylvanian is dead, that lay with the little baggage.

Boult. Ay, she quickly pooped him; she made him roast-meat for worms. But I'll go search the market. *Exit.*

Pand. Three or four thousand chequins were as pretty a proportion to live quietly, and so give over.

34. **more . . . heart,** more than a foreigner usually does, i.e., as his countrymen do. 36. **paragon . . . reports,** the equal in repute to anyone. 39. **to your best courses,** to bring you up well. 40. **reserve,** preserve. 62. **'wolt out?'** Do you want to get out? 63. **with . . . industry,** dripping wet as they labored. 88. **caught hurt,** received an injury. 95. **Half-part,** shares. 97. **Valdes.** Malone thought this name was derived from that of Don Pedro de Valdes, a Spanish admiral captured by Sir Francis Drake.

SCENE II. 5. **this mart,** at the last market time. 28. **chequins,** zecchinos, Italian coins. 37. **keep . . . hatched,** keep the lower halfdoor

Bawd. Why to give over, I pray you? is it a shame to get when we are old?

Pand. O, our credit comes not in like the commodity, nor the commodity wages not with the danger: therefore, if in our youths we could pick up some pretty estate, 'twere not amiss to keep our door hatched. Besides, the sore terms we stand upon with the gods will be strong with us for giving o'er.

Bawd. Come, other sorts offend as well as we.

Pand. As well as we! ay, and better too; we offend worse. Neither is our profession any trade; it 's no calling. But here comes Boult.

Enter BOULT, *with the* Pirates *and* MARINA.

Boult. [*To Marina*] Come your ways. My masters, you say she 's a virgin?

First Pirate. O, sir, we doubt it not.

Boult. Master, I have gone through for this piece, you see: if you like her, so; if not, I have lost my earnest.

Bawd. Boult, has she any qualities?

Boult. She has a good face, speaks well, and has excellent good clothes: there 's no farther necessity of qualities can make her be refused.

Bawd. What 's her price, Boult?

Boult. It cannot be bated one doit of a thousand pieces.

Pand. Well, follow me, my masters, you shall have your money presently. Wife, take her in; instruct her what she has to do, that she may not be raw in her entertainment. [*Exeunt Pandar and Pirates.*]

Bawd. Boult, take you the marks of her, the colour of her hair, complexion, height, her age, with warrant of her virginity; and cry 'He that will give most shall have her first.' Such a maidenhead were no cheap thing, if men were as they have been. Get this done as I command you.

Boult. Performance shall follow. *Exit.*

Mar. Alack that Leonine was so slack, so slow!
He should have struck, not spoke; or that these pirates,
Not enough barbarous, had not o'erboard thrown me
For to seek my mother!

Bawd. Why lament you, pretty one?

Mar. That I am pretty.

Bawd. Come, the gods have done their part in you.

Mar. I accuse them not.

Bawd. You are light into my hands, where you are like to live.

Mar. The more my fault
To scape his hands where I was like to die.

Bawd. Ay, and you shall live in pleasure.

Mar. No.

Bawd. Yes, indeed shall you, and taste gentlemen of all fashions: you shall fare well; you shall have the difference of all complexions. What! do you stop your ears?

Mar. Are you a woman?

Bawd. What would you have me be, an I be not a woman?

Mar. An honest woman, or not a woman.

Bawd. Marry, whip thee, gosling: I think I shall have something to do with you. Come, you 're a young foolish sapling, and must be bowed as I would have you.

Mar. The gods defend me!

Bawd. If it please the gods to defend you by men, then men must comfort you, men must feed you, men must stir you up. Boult 's returned.

[*Enter* BOULT.]

Now, sir, hast thou cried her through the market?

Boult. I have cried her almost to the number of her hairs; I have drawn her picture with my voice.

Bawd. And I prithee tell me, how dost thou find the inclination of the people, especially of the younger sort?

Boult. 'Faith, they listened to me as they would have hearkened to their father's testament. There was a Spaniard's mouth so watered, and he went to bed to her very description.

Bawd. We shall have him here to-morrow with his best ruff on.

Boult. To-night, to-night. But, mistress, do you know the French knight that cowers i' the hams?

Bawd. Who, Monsieur Veroles?

Boult. Ay, he: he offered to cut a caper at the proclamation; but he made a groan at it, and swore he would see her to-morrow.

Bawd. Well, well; as for him, he brought his disease hither: here he does but repair it. I know he will come in our shadow, to scatter his crowns in the sun.

Boult. Well, if we had of every nation a traveller, we should lodge them with this sign.

Bawd. [*To Mar.*] Pray you, come hither awhile. You have fortunes coming upon you. Mark me: you must seem to do that fearfully which you commit willingly, despise profit where you have most gain. To weep that you live as ye do makes pity in your lovers: seldom but that pity begets you a good opinion, and that opinion a mere profit.

Mar. I understand you not.

Boult. O, take her home, mistress, take her home: these blushes of hers must be quenched with some present practice.

Bawd. Thou sayest true, i' faith so they must; for your bride goes to that with shame which is her way to go with warrant.

Boult. 'Faith, some do, and some do not. But, mistress, if I have bargained for the joint,—

Bawd. Thou mayst cut a morsel off the spit.

Boult. I may so.

Bawd. Who should deny it? Come, young one, I like the manner of your garments well.

Boult. Ay, by my faith, they shall not be changed yet.

Bawd. Boult, spend thou that in the town: report what a sojourner we have; you'll lose nothing by custom. When nature framed this piece, she meant thee a good turn; therefore say what a paragon she is, and thou hast the harvest out of thine own report.

Boult. I warrant you, mistress, thunder shall not so awake the beds of eels as my giving out her beauty stirs

(the hatch) closed. 47. **gone through,** made a bid. 52-53. **there 's . . . refused,** i.e., there is no requirement that she cannot meet. 77. **are light,** have chanced to light. 79. **fault,** misfortune. 85. **difference,** variety. 108. **and,** as if. 120. **repair,** quibble on the meanings "return with" and "mend" in an ironic sense, hence "made worse."

128. **despise,** parallel with *do* (l. 127). 134. **take her home,** talk plainly, i.e., be direct with her. 155. **beds of eels.** Seager (*Natural History*, p. 98) quotes *Hortus Sanitatus:* the eel "is disturbed by the sound of thunder."

up the lewdly-inclined. I'll bring home some to-night.
Bawd. Come your ways; follow me.
Mar. If fires be hot, knives sharp, or waters deep,
Untied I still my virgin knot will keep.
Diana, aid my purpose!
Bawd. What have we to do with Diana? Pray you, will you go with us? *Exeunt.*

[SCENE III. *Tarsus. A room in Cleon's house.*]

Enter CLEON *and* DIONYZA.

Dion. Why, are you foolish? Can it be undone?
Cle. O Dionyza, such a piece of slaughter
The sun and moon ne'er look'd upon!
Dion. I think
You'll turn a child again.
Cle. Were I chief lord of all this spacious world,
I 'ld give it to undo the deed. O lady,
Much less in blood than virtue, yet a princess
To equal any single crown o' th' earth
I' th' justice of compare! O villain Leonine!
Whom thou hast pois'ned too:
If thou hadst drunk to him, 't had been a kindness
Becoming well thy fact: what canst thou say
When noble Pericles shall demand his child?
Dion. That she is dead. Nurses are not the fates,
To foster it, nor ever to preserve.
She died at night; I'll say so. Who can cross it?
Unless you play the pious innocent,
And for an honest attribute cry out
'She died by foul play.'
Cle. O, go to. Well, well,
Of all the faults beneath the heavens, the gods
Do like this worst.
Dion. Be one of those that thinks
The petty wrens of Tarsus will fly hence,
And open this to Pericles. I do shame
To think of what a noble strain you are,
And of how coward a spirit.
Cle. To such proceeding
Who ever but his approbation added,
Though not his prime consent, he did not flow
From honourable sources.
Dion. Be it so, then:
Yet none does know, but you, how she came dead,
Nor none can know, Leonine being gone.
She did distain my child, and stood between
Her and her fortunes: none would look on her,
But cast their gazes on Marina's face;
Whilst ours was blurted at and held a malkin
Not worth the time of day. It pierc'd me thorough;
And though you call my course unnatural,
You not your child well loving, yet I find
It greets me as an enterprise of kindness
Perform'd to your sole daughter.
Cle. Heavens forgive it!
Dion. And as for Pericles,
What should he say? We wept after her hearse,
And yet we mourn: her monument
Is almost finish'd, and her epitaphs
In glitt'ring golden characters express
A general praise to her, and care in us
At whose expense 'tis done.
Cle. Thou art like the harpy,
Which, to betray, dost, with thine angel's face,
Seize with thine eagle's talents.
Dion. Ye're like one that superstitiously
Do swear to th' gods that winter kills the flies:
But yet I know you'll do as I advise. [*Exeunt.*]

[SCENE IV.]

[*Enter* GOWER, *before the monument of* MARINA *at Tarsus.*]

Gow. Thus time we waste, and long leagues make short;
Sail seas in cockles, have and wish but for 't;
Making, to take your imagination,
From bourn to bourn, region to region.
By you being pardoned, we commit no crime
To use one language in each several clime
Where our scenes seem to live. I do beseech you
To learn of me, who stand i' th' gaps to teach you,
The stages of our story. Pericles
Is now again thwarting the wayward seas,
Attended on by many a lord and knight,
To see his daughter, all his life's delight.
Old Helicanus goes along. Behind
Is left to govern it, you bear in mind,
Old Escanes, whom Helicanus late
Advanc'd in time to great and high estate.
Well-sailing ships and bounteous winds have brought
This king to Tarsus,—think his pilot thought;
So with his steerage shall your thoughts grow on,—
To fetch his daughter home, who first is gone.
Like motes and shadows see them move awhile;
Your ears unto your eyes I'll reconcile.

[DUMB SHOW.]

Enter PERICLES, *at one door, with all his train;* CLEON *and* DIONYZA, *at the other.* CLEON *shows* PERICLES *the tomb; whereat* PERICLES *makes lamentation, puts on sackcloth, and in a mighty passion departs.* [*Then exeunt* CLEON *and* DIONYZA.]

See how belief may suffer by foul show!
This borrowed passion stands for true old woe;
And Pericles, in sorrow all devour'd,
With sighs shot through, and biggest tears o'ershow'r'd,
Leaves Tarsus and again embarks. He swears
Never to wash his face, nor cut his hairs:
He puts on sackcloth, and to sea. He bears
A tempest, which his mortal vessel tears,
And yet he rides it out. Now please you wit
The epitaph is for Marina writ
By wicked Dionyza.
[*Reads the inscription on Marina's monument.*]

'The fairest, sweetest, and best lies here,
Who withered in her spring of year.

SCENE III. 9. **I' . . . compare,** if justly compared. 11. **drunk to him,** taken a drink of the poison with him. 14. **Nurses . . . fates,** i.e., nurses have not the power of the fates to control life and death. 18. **for . . . attribute,** for the epithet "honest" to be attached to your name. 27. **prime,** original. 31. **distain,** defile, dishonor; i.e., my child appeared so by comparison. 34. **malkin,** diminutive of Moll, contemptuous name for a woman servant. 35. **time of day,** greeting.

48. **talents,** talons. 50. **Do . . . flies,** you blame the death of flies on winter, thus exculpating the gods.

SCENE IV. 2. **cockles,** cockleshells, i.e., as supernatural creatures do; alludes to the imaginary crossing of the seas between scenes of the play. **have . . . for 't,** have something if we but wish it. **and,** so Q; Globe, following Dyce: *an.* 8. **who . . . gaps,** who bridges the gaps of time and space between scenes. 18. **think . . . thought,** think or imag-

She was of Tyrus the king's daughter,
On whom foul death hath made this slaughter;
Marina was she call'd; and at her birth,
Thetis, being proud, swallow'd some part o' th'
earth:
Therefore the earth, fearing to be o'erflowed,
Hath Thetis' birth-child on the heavens bestowed:
Wherefore she does, and swears she'll never stint,
Make raging battery upon shores of flint.'

No visor does become black villany
So well as soft and tender flattery.
Let Pericles believe his daughter 's dead,
And bear his courses to be ordered
By Lady Fortune; while our scene must play
His daughter's woe and heavy well-a-day
In her unholy service. Patience, then,
And think you now are all in Mytilene. *Exit.*

[SCENE V. *Mytilene. A street before the brothel.*]

Enter [from the brothel] two Gentlemen.

First Gent. Did you ever hear the like?

Sec. Gent. No, nor never shall do in such a place as this, she being once gone.

First Gent. But to have divinity preached there! did you ever dream of such a thing?

Sec. Gent. No, no. Come, I am for no more bawdy-houses: shall 's go hear the vestals sing?

First Gent. I'll do any thing now that is virtuous; but I am out of the road of rutting for ever. *Exeunt.*

[SCENE VI. *The same. A room in the brothel.*]

Enter three Bawds [Pandar, Bawd, *and* BOULT].

Pand. Well, I had rather than twice the worth of her she had ne'er come here.

Bawd. Fie, fie upon her! she 's able to freeze the god Priapus, and undo a whole generation. We must either get her ravished, or be rid of her. When she should do for clients her fitment, and do me the kindness of our profession, she has me her quirks, her reasons, her master reasons, her prayers, her knees; that she would make a puritan of the devil, if he should cheapen a kiss of her.

Boult. 'Faith, I must ravish her, or she'll disfurnish us of all our cavaliers, and make our swearers priests.

Pand. Now, the pox upon her green-sickness for me!

Bawd. 'Faith, there 's no way to be rid on 't but by the way to the pox. Here comes the Lord Lysimachus disguised.

Boult. We should have both lord and lown, if the peevish baggage would but give way to customers.

Enter LYSIMACHUS.

Lys. How now! How a dozen of virginities?

Bawd. Now, the gods to-bless your honour!

Boult. I am glad to see your honour in good health.

Lys. You may so; 'tis the better for you that your resorters stand upon sound legs. How now! wholesome iniquity have you that a man may deal withal, and defy the surgeon?

Bawd. We have here one, sir, if she would—but there never came her like in Mytilene.

Lys. If she 'ld do the deed of darkness, thou wouldst say.

Bawd. Your honour knows what 'tis to say well enough.

Lys. Well, call forth, call forth.

Boult. For flesh and blood, sir, white and red, you shall see a rose; and she were a rose indeed, if she had but—

Lys. What, prithee?

Boult. O, sir, I can be modest.

Lys. That dignifies the renown of a bawd, no less than it gives a good report to a number to be chaste.

[*Exit Boult.*]

Bawd. Here comes that which grows to the stalk; never plucked yet, I can assure you.

[*Enter* BOULT *with* MARINA.]

Is she not a fair creature?

Lys. 'Faith, she would serve after a long voyage at sea. Well, there 's for you: leave us.

Bawd. I beseech your honour, give me leave: a word, and I'll have done presently.

Lys. I beseech you, do.

Bawd. [*To Marina*] First, I would have you note, this is an honourable man.

Mar. I desire to find him so, that I may worthily note him.

Bawd. Next, he 's the governor of this country, and a man whom I am bound to.

Mar. If he govern the country, you are bound to him indeed; but how honourable he is in that, I know not.

Bawd. Pray you, without any more virginal fencing, will you use him kindly? He will line your apron with gold.

Mar. What he will do graciously, I will thankfully receive.

Lys. Ha' you done?

Bawd. My lord, she 's not paced yet: you must take some pains to work her to your manage. Come, we will leave his honour and her together. Go thy ways.

[*Exeunt Bawd, Pandar, and Boult.*]

Lys. Now, pretty one, how long have you been at this trade?

Mar. What trade, sir?

Lys. Why, I cannot name 't but I shall offend.

Mar. I cannot be offended with my trade.
Please you to name it.

Lys. How long have you been of this profession?

Mar. E'er since I can remember.

Lys. Did you go to 't so young? Were you a gamester at five or at seven?

Mar. Earlier too, sir, if now I be one.

Lys. Why, the house you dwell in proclaims you to be a creature of sale.

Mar. Do you know this house to be a place of such

ine his voyage (instead of tracing it). 19. **his steerage,** the steering of his ship. 30. **mortal vessel,** human body. 31. **wit,** know. 39. **Thetis,** sea nymph; alludes to Marina's being born at sea. 42-43. **Wherefore . . . flint,** on account of which she (Thetis) continuously beats upon rocky shores. 47. **bear,** endure, allow.

SCENE V. 7. **shall 's,** shall we; originally expressing necessity, *shall* was sometimes used as an impersonal verb.

SCENE VI. 4. **Priapus,** god of lechery. 6. **fitment,** duty. 10. **cheapen,** bargain for. 19. **lown,** stupid fellow. 25. **to-bless,** bless completely. 42-44. **dignifies . . . chaste,** i.e., modesty gives renown to a bawd as well as attesting the chastity of many women. 54, 56. **note,** quibble on the meanings "observe" and "set down as having a good or bad character." 68, 69. **paced, manage,** terms used in training horses.

resort, and will come into 't? I hear say you're of honourable parts, and are the governor of this place.

Lys. Why, hath your principal made known unto you who I am?

Mar. Who is my principal?

Lys. Why, your herb-woman: she that sets seeds and roots of shame and iniquity. O, you have heard something of my power, and so stand aloof for more serious wooing. But I protest to thee, pretty one, my authority shall not see thee, or else look friendly upon thee. Come, bring me to some private place: come, come.

Mar. If you were born to honour, show it now;
If put upon you, make the judgement good
That thought you worthy of it.

Lys. How 's this? how 's this? Some more; be sage.

Mar. For me,
That am a maid, though most ungentle fortune
Have plac'd me in this sty, where, since I came,
Diseases have been sold dearer than physic,
O, that the gods
Would set me free from this unhallowed place,
Though they did change me to the meanest bird
That flies i' th' purer air!

Lys. I did not think
Thou couldst have spoke so well; ne'er dream'd thou
couldst.
Had I brought hither a corrupted mind,
Thy speech had alter'd it. Hold, here 's gold for thee:
Persever in that clear way thou goest,
And the gods strengthen thee!

Mar. The good gods preserve you!

Lys. For me, be you thoughten
That I came with no ill intent; for to me
The very doors and windows savour vilely.
Fare thee well. Thou art a piece of virtue, and
I doubt not but thy training hath been noble.
Hold, here 's more gold for thee.
A curse upon him, die he like a thief,
That robs thee of thy goodness! If thou dost
Hear from me, it shall be for thy good.

[*Enter* BOULT.]

Boult. I beseech your honour, one piece for me.

Lys. Avaunt, thou damned door-keeper!
Your house, but for this virgin that doth prop it,
Would sink and overwhelm you. Away! [*Exit.*]

Boult. How 's this? We must take another course with you. If your peevish chastity, which is not worth a breakfast in the cheapest country under the cope, shall undo a whole household, let me be gelded like a spaniel. Come your ways.

Mar. Whither would you have me?

Boult. I must have your maidenhead taken off, or the common hangman shall execute it. Come your ways. We'll have no more gentlemen driven away. Come your ways, I say.

Enter Bawd.

Bawd. How now! what 's the matter?

Boult. Worse and worse, mistress; she has here spoken holy words to the Lord Lysimachus.

Bawd. O abominable!

Boult. She makes our profession as it were to stink afore the face of the gods.

Bawd. Marry, hang her up for ever!

Boult. The nobleman would have dealt with her like a nobleman, and she sent him away as cold as a snowball; saying his prayers too.

Bawd. Boult, take her away; use her at thy pleasure: crack the glass of her virginity, and make the rest malleable.

Boult. An if she were a thornier piece of ground than she is, she shall be ploughed.

Mar. Hark, hark, you gods!

Bawd. She conjures: away with her! Would she had never come within my doors! Marry, hang you! She 's born to undo us. Will you not go the way of women-kind? Marry, come up, my dish of chastity with rosemary and bays! [*Exit.*]

Boult. Come, mistress; come your ways with me.

Mar. Whither wilt thou have me?

Boult. To take from you the jewel you hold so dear.

Mar. Prithee, tell me one thing first.

Boult. Come now, your one thing.

Mar. What canst thou wish thine enemy to be?

Boult. Why, I could wish him to be my master, or rather, my mistress.

Mar. Neither of these are so bad as thou art,
Since they do better thee in their command.
Thou hold'st a place, for which the pained'st fiend
Of hell would not in reputation change:
Thou art the damned doorkeeper to every
Coistrel that comes inquiring for his Tib;
To the choleric fisting of every rogue
Thy ear is liable; thy food is such
As hath been belch'd on by infected lungs.

Boult. What would you have me do? go to the wars, would you? where a man may serve seven years for the loss of a leg, and have not money enough in the end to buy him a wooden one?

Mar. Do any thing but this thou doest. Empty
Old receptacles, or common shores, of filth;
Serve by indenture to the common hangman:
Any of these ways are yet better than this;
For what thou professest, a baboon, could he speak,
Would own a name too dear. O, that the gods
Would safely deliver me from this place!
Here, here 's gold for thee.
If that thy master would gain by me,
Proclaim that I can sing, weave, sew, and dance,
With other virtues, which I'll keep from boast;
And I will undertake all these to teach.
I doubt not but this populous city will
Yield many scholars.

Boult. But can you teach all this you speak of?

Mar. Prove that I cannot, take me home again,
And prostitute me to the basest groom
That doth frequent your house.

Boult. Well, I will see what I can do for thee: if I can place thee, I will.

Mar. But amongst honest women.

Boult. 'Faith, my acquaintance lies little amongst them. But since my master and mistress have bought you, there 's no going but by their consent: therefore I will make them acquainted with your purpose, and

96. **shall not see thee,** i.e., I'll wink at your offenses, not enforce the laws against prostitutes. 115. **be you thoughten,** let it seem to you. 132. **cope,** the firmament. 159. **Marry, come up,** i.e., hoity-toity. 160. **rosemary and bays,** customary garnishes for certain foods. 176. **Coistrel,** knave. **Tib,** common woman. 177. **choleric fisting,** angry blows. 190. **too dear,** i.e., that he could not afford.

I doubt not but I shall find them tractable enough.
Come, I'll do for thee what I can; come your ways.
Exeunt.

[ACT V.]

Enter GOWER.

Gow. Marina thus the brothel 'scapes, and chances
Into an honest house, our story says.
She sings like one immortal, and she dances
As goddess-like to her admired lays;
Deep clerks she dumbs; and with her neele composes
Nature's own shape, of bud, bird, branch, or berry,
That even her art sisters the natural roses;
Her inkle, silk, twin with the rubied cherry:
That pupils lacks she none of noble race,
Who pour their bounty on her; and her gain
She gives the cursed bawd. Here we her place;
And to her father turn our thoughts again,
Where we left him, on the sea. We there him lost;
Whence, driven before the winds, he is arriv'd
Here where his daughter dwells; and on this coast
Suppose him now at anchor. The city striv'd
God Neptune's annual feast to keep: from whence
Lysimachus our Tyrian ship espies,
His banners sable, trimm'd with rich expense;
And to him in his barge with fervour hies.
In your supposing once more put your sight
Of heavy Pericles; think this his bark:
Where what is done in action, more, if might,
Shall be discover'd; please you, sit and hark. *Exit.*

[SCENE I. *On board Pericles' ship, off Mytilene. A close pavilion on deck, with a curtain before it; Pericles within it, reclined on a couch.*]

Enter HELICANUS. *To him two* Sailors [, *one belonging to the Tyrian vessel, the other to a barge of Mytilene that is alongside*].

Tyr. Sail. [*To the Sailor of Mytilene*] Where is lord Helicanus? he can resolve you.
O, here he is.
Sir, there is a barge put off from Mytilene,
And in it is Lysimachus the governor,
Who craves to come aboard. What is your will?
Hel. That he have his. Call up some gentlemen.
Tyr. Sail. Ho, gentlemen! my lord calls.

Enter two or three Gentlemen.

First Gent. Doth your lordship call?
Hel. Gentlemen, there is some of worth would come aboard;
I pray, greet him fairly.
[*Exeunt the Gentlemen and the two Sailors.*]

Enter [*as from the barge*] LYSIMACHUS [*and* Lords; *with the* Gentlemen *and the two* Sailors].

Tyr. Sail. Sir,
This is the man that can, in aught you would,
Resolve you.
Lys. Hail, reverend sir! the gods preserve you!
Hel. And you, sir, to outlive the age I am,
And die as I would do.
Lys. You wish me well.
Being on shore, honouring of Neptune's triumphs,
Seeing this goodly vessel ride before us,
I made to it, to know of whence you are.
Hel. First, what is your place?
Lys. I am the governor of this place you lie before.
Hel. Sir,
Our vessel is of Tyre, in it the king;
A man who for this three months hath not spoken
To any one, nor taken sustenance
But to prorogue his grief.
Lys. Upon what ground is his distemperature?
Hel. 'Twould be too tedious to repeat;
But the main grief springs from the loss
Of a beloved daughter and a wife.
Lys. May we not see him?
Hel. You may;
But bootless is your sight: he will not speak
To any.
Lys. Yet let me obtain my wish.
Hel. Behold him. [*Pericles discovered.*] This was a goodly person,
Till the disaster that, one mortal night,
Drove him to this.
Lys. Sir king, all hail! the gods preserve you!
Hail, royal sir!
Hel. It is in vain; he will not speak to you.
First Lord. Sir,
We have a maid in Mytilene, I durst wager,
Would win some words of him.
Lys. 'Tis well bethought.
She questionless with her sweet harmony
And other chosen attractions, would allure,
And make a batt'ry through his deafen'd parts,
Which now are midway stopp'd:
She is all happy as the fairest of all,
And, with her fellow maids, is now upon
The leafy shelter that abuts against
The island's side.
[*Whispers a Lord, who goes off to bring Marina.*]
Hel. Sure, all 's effectless; yet nothing we'll omit
That bears recovery's name. But, since your kindness
We have stretch'd thus far, let us beseech you
That for our gold we may provision have,
Wherein we are not destitute for want,
But weary for the staleness.
Lys. O, sir, a courtesy
Which if we should deny, the most just gods
For every graff would send a caterpillar,
And so inflict our province. Yet once more
Let me entreat to know at large the cause
Of your king's sorrow.
Hel. Sit, sir, I will recount it to you:
But, see, I am prevented.

[*Enter, as though from the barge,* Lord, *with* MARINA, *and a young* Lady.]

Lys. O, here's

ACT V. PROLOGUE. 5. **dumbs,** silences. **neele,** needle. 8. **inkle,** kind of tape; also linen or yarn from which it is made. 21. **supposing,** imagination.

SCENE I. 9. **some,** a certain one; the Old English pronoun *sum;* cf. Abbott, 21. 26. **prorogue,** prolong. 48. **midway stopp'd,** i.e., the spirits of hearing are stopped midway by grief. 60. **graff,** scion, shoot.

The lady that I sent for. Welcome, fair one!
Is 't not a goodly presence?
Hel. She 's a gallant lady.
Lys. She 's such a one, that, were I well assur'd
Came of a gentle kind and noble stock,
I 'ld wish no better choice, and think me rarely wed.
Fair one, all goodness that consists in bounty
Expect even here, where is a kingly patient:
If that thy prosperous and artificial feat
Can draw him but to answer thee in aught,
Thy sacred physic shall receive such pay
As thy desires can wish.
Mar. Sir, I will use
My utmost skill in his recovery,
Provided
That none but I and my companion maid
Be suffered to come near him.
Lys. Come, let us leave her;
And the gods make her prosperous!
[*They stand aside.*] *The song* [*by Marina*].
Lys. Mark'd he your music?
Mar. No, nor look'd on us.
Lys. See, she will speak to him.
Mar. Hail, sir! my lord, lend ear.
Per. Hum, ha!
Mar. I am a maid,
My lord, that ne'er before invited eyes,
But have been gaz'd on like a comet: she speaks,
My lord, that, may be, hath endur'd a grief
Might equal yours, if both were justly weigh'd.
Though wayward fortune did malign my state,
My derivation was from ancestors
Who stood equivalent with mighty kings:
But time hath rooted out my parentage,
And to the world and awkward casualties
Bound me in servitude. [*Aside*] I will desist;
But there is something glows upon my cheek,
And whispers in mine ear 'Go not till he speak.'
Per. My fortunes—parentage—good parentage—
To equal mine!—was it not thus? what say you?
Mar. I said, my lord, if you did know my parentage,
You would not do me violence.
Per. I do think so. Pray you, turn your eyes upon me.
You are like something that—What countrywoman?
Here of these shores?
Mar. No, nor of any shores:
Yet I was mortally brought forth, and am
No other than I appear.
Per. I am great with woe, and shall deliver weeping.
My dearest wife was like this maid, and such a one
My daughter might have been: my queen's square brows;
Her stature to an inch; as wand-like straight;
As silver-voic'd; her eyes as jewel-like
And cas'd as richly; in pace another Juno;
Who starves the ears she feeds, and makes them hungry,
The more she gives them speech. Where do you live?
Mar. Where I am but a stranger: from the deck
You may discern the place.
Per. Where were you bred?
And how achiev'd you these endowments, which
You make more rich to owe?
Mar. If I should tell my history, it would seem
Like lies disdain'd in the reporting.
Per. Prithee, speak:
Falseness cannot come from thee; for thou lookest
Modest as Justice, and thou seemest a palace
For the crown'd Truth to dwell in: I will believe thee,
And make my senses credit thy relation
To points that seem impossible; for thou lookest
Like one I lov'd indeed. What were thy friends?
Didst thou not say, when I did push thee back—
Which was when I perceiv'd thee—that thou cam'st
From good descending?
Mar. So indeed I did.
Per. Report thy parentage. I think thou said'st
Thou hadst been toss'd from wrong to injury,
And that thou thought'st thy griefs might equal mine,
If both were opened.
Mar. Some such thing
I said, and said no more but what my thoughts
Did warrant me was likely.
Per. Tell thy story;
If thine considered prove the thousandth part
Of my endurance, thou art a man, and I
Have suffered like a girl: yet thou dost look
Like Patience gazing on kings' graves, and smiling
Extremity out of act. What were thy friends?
How lost thou them? Thy name, my most kind virgin?
Recount, I do beseech thee: come, sit by me.
Mar. My name is Marina.
Per. O, I am mock'd,
And thou by some incensed god sent hither
To make the world to laugh at me.
Mar. Patience, good sir,
Or here I'll cease.
Per. Nay, I'll be patient.
Thou little know'st how thou dost startle me,
To call thyself Marina.
Mar. The name
Was given me by one that had some power,
My father, and a king.
Per. How! a king's daughter?
And call'd Marina?
Mar. You said you would believe me;
But, not to be a troubler of your peace,
I will end here.
Per. But are you flesh and blood?
Have you a working pulse? and are no fairy?
Motion! Well; speak on. Where were you born?
And wherefore call'd Marina?
Mar. Call'd Marina
For I was born at sea.
Per. At sea! what mother?
Mar. My mother was the daughter of a king;
Who died the minute I was born,
As my good nurse Lychorida hath oft
Delivered weeping.
Per. O, stop there a little!
[*Aside*] This is the rarest dream that e'er dull sleep
Did mock sad fools withal: this cannot be:
My daughter 's buried.—Well: where were you bred?
I'll hear you more, to th' bottom of your story,

72. **prosperous,** producing favorable results. **artificial,** skillful. 80. *Stage Direction:* ***The song.*** On the restorative effects of music, cf. III, ii, 88-91, note. 86. **ne'er . . . eyes,** never before had to ask to be looked at. 94. **awkward,** adverse. 101. **You . . . violence.** This may refer to something lost from the text. The older prose story of Twine records that Apollonius struck his daughter, angry at her addressing him. 139-140. **smiling . . . act,** smiling extreme calamity out of existence, making it dissolve. 209-210. Many emendations; text will make sense if *The heir of kingdoms* is in apposition with the preceding phrase. K. Deighton would read *and so be another life*, etc.

And never interrupt you.
Mar. You scorn: believe me, 'twere best I did give o'er.
Per. I will believe you by the syllable
Of what you shall deliver. Yet, give me leave:
How came you in these parts? where were you bred?
Mar. The king my father did in Tarsus leave me;
Till cruel Cleon, with his wicked wife,
Did seek to murder me: and having woo'd
A villain to attempt it, who having drawn to do 't,
A crew of pirates came and rescued me;
Brought me to Mytilene. But, good sir,
Whither will you have me? Why do you weep? It may be,
You think me an impostor: no, good faith;
I am the daughter to King Pericles,
If good King Pericles be.
Per. Ho, Helicanus!
Hel. Calls my lord?
Per. Thou art a grave and noble counsellor,
Most wise in general: tell me, if thou canst,
What this maid is, or what is like to be,
That thus hath made me weep?
Hel. I know not; but
Here's the regent, sir, of Mytilene
Speaks nobly of her.
Lys. She would never tell
Her parentage; being demanded that,
She would sit still and weep.
Per. O Helicanus, strike me, honour'd sir;
Give me a gash, put me to present pain;
Lest this great sea of joys rushing upon me
O'erbear the shores of my mortality,
And drown me with their sweetness. O, come hither,
Thou that beget'st him that did thee beget;
Thou that wast born at sea, buried at Tarsus,
And found at sea again! O Helicanus,
Down on thy knees, thank the holy gods as loud
As thunder threatens us: this is Marina.
What was thy mother's name? tell me but that,
For truth can never be confirm'd enough,
Though doubts did ever sleep.
Mar. First, sir, I pray,
What is your title?
Per. I am Pericles of Tyre: but tell me now
My drown'd queen's name, as in the rest you said
Thou hast been godlike perfect,
†The heir of kingdoms and another like
To Pericles thy father.
Mar. Is it no more to be your daughter than
To say my mother's name was Thaisa?
Thaisa was my mother, who did end
The minute I began.
Per. Now, blessing on thee! rise; thou art my child.
Give me fresh garments. Mine own, Helicanus;
She is not dead at Tarsus, as she should have been,
By savage Cleon: she shall tell thee all;
When thou shalt kneel, and justify in knowledge
She is thy very princess.—Who is this?
Hel. Sir, 'tis the governor of Mytilene,
Who, hearing of your melancholy state,
Did come to see you.
Per. I embrace you.
Give me my robes. I am wild in my beholding.
O heavens bless my girl! But, hark, what music?
Tell Helicanus, my Marina, tell him
O'er, point by point, for yet he seems to doubt,
How sure you are my daughter. But, what music?
Hel. My lord, I hear none.
Per. None!
The music of the spheres! List, my Marina.
Lys. It is not good to cross him; give him way.
Per. Rarest sounds! Do ye not hear?
Lys. Music, my lord?
Per. I hear most heavenly music!
It nips me unto list'ning, and thick slumber
Hangs upon mine eyes: let me rest. [*Sleeps.*]
Lys. A pillow for his head:
So, leave him all. Well, my companion friends,
If this but answer to my just belief,
I'll well remember you. [*Exeunt all but Pericles.*]

DIANA [*appears to* PERICLES *as in a vision*].

Dia. My temple stands in Ephesus: hie thee thither,
And do upon mine altar sacrifice.
There, when my maiden priests are met together,
Before the people all,
Reveal how thou at sea didst lose thy wife:
To mourn thy crosses, with thy daughter's, call
And give them repetition to the life.
Or perform my bidding, or thou livest in woe;
Do 't, and happy; by my silver bow!
Awake, and tell thy dream. [*Disappears.*]
Per. Celestial Dian, goddess argentine,
I will obey thee. Helicanus!

[*Enter* HELICANUS, LYSIMACHUS, *and* MARINA.]

Hel. Sir?
Per. My purpose was for Tarsus, there to strike
The inhospitable Cleon; but I am
For other service first: toward Ephesus
Turn our blown sails; eftsoons I'll tell thee why.
[*To Lysimachus*] Shall we refresh us, sir, upon your shore,
And give you gold for such provision
As our intents will need?
Lys. Sir,
With all my heart; and, when you come ashore,
I have another suit.
Per. You shall prevail,
Were it to woo my daughter; for it seems
You have been noble towards her.
Lys. Sir, lend me your arm.
Per. Come, my Marina. *Exeunt.*

[SCENE II. *Enter* GOWER, *before the temple of* DIANA *at Ephesus.*]

Gow. Now our sands are almost run;
More a little, and then dumb.
This, my last boon, give me,
For such kindness must relieve me,
That you aptly will suppose

219. **justify in knowledge,** be made certain (that). 224. **wild in my beholding,** i.e., in ecstasy at what I see. 231. **music . . . spheres,** a Ptolemaic notion first conceived of by Pythagoras, Greek philosopher and mathematician. He thought of the spheres—orbs—in which heavenly bodies moved as separated by intervals according to the laws of musical harmony, their motion producing sounds of exceptional beauty, rarely heard by mortals. 235. **nips me,** arrests my attention. 248. **Or,** either. 251. **argentine,** silvery in appearance, as appropriate to the moon goddess. 256. **eftsoons,** shortly.

What pageantry, what feats, what shows,
What minstrelsy, and pretty din,
The regent made in Mytilin
To greet the king. So he thrived,
That he is promis'd to be wived
To fair Marina; but in no wise
Till he had done his sacrifice,
As Dian bade: whereto being bound,
The interim, pray you, all confound.
In feather'd briefness sails are fill'd,
And wishes fall out as they 're will'd.
At Ephesus, the temple see,
Our king and all his company.
That he can hither come so soon,
Is by your fancies' thankful doom. [*Exit.*]

[SCENE III. *The temple of Diana at Ephesus;* THAISA *standing near the altar, as high priestess; a number of Virgins on each side;* CERIMON *and other Inhabitants of Ephesus attending.*]

[*Enter* PERICLES, *with his train;* LYSIMACHUS, HELICANUS, MARINA, *and a* Lady.]

Per. Hail, Dian! to perform thy just command,
I here confess myself the king of Tyre;
Who, frighted from my country, did wed
At Pentapolis the fair Thaisa.
At sea in childbed died she, but brought forth
A maid-child call'd Marina; who, O goddess,
Wears yet thy silver livery. She at Tarsus
Was nurs'd with Cleon; who at fourteen years
He sought to murder: but her better stars
Brought her to Mytilene; 'gainst whose shore
Riding, her fortunes brought the maid aboard us,
Where, by her own most clear remembrance, she
Made known herself my daughter.
Thai. Voice and favour!
You are, you are—O royal Pericles! [*Faints.*]
Per. What means the nun? she dies! help, gentlemen!
Cer. Noble sir,
If you have told Diana's altar true,
This is your wife.
Per. Reverend appearer, no;
I threw her overboard with these very arms.
Cer. Upon this coast, I warrant you.
Per. 'Tis most certain.
Cer. Look to the lady; O, she 's but overjoy'd.
Early in blustering morn this lady was
Thrown upon this shore. I op'd the coffin,
Found there rich jewels; recovered her, and plac'd her
Here in Diana's temple.
Per. May we see them?
Cer. Great sir, they shall be brought you to my house,
Whither I invite you. Look, Thaisa is
Recovered.
Thai. O, let me look!
If he be none of mine, my sanctity
Will to my sense bend no licentious ear,
But curb it, spite of seeing. O, my lord,
Are you not Pericles? Like him you spake,
Like him you are: did you not name a tempest,
A birth, and death?
Per. The voice of dead Thaisa!
Thai. That Thaisa am I, supposed dead
And drown'd.
Per. Immortal Dian!
Thai. Now I know you better.
When we with tears parted Pentapolis,
The king my father gave you such a ring. [*Shows a ring.*]
Per. This, this: no more, you gods! your present kindness
Makes my past miseries sports: you shall do well,
That on the touching of her lips I may
Melt and no more be seen. O, come, be buried
A second time within these arms.
Mar. My heart
Leaps to be gone into my mother's bosom.
[*Kneels to Thaisa.*]
Per. Look, who kneels here! Flesh of thy flesh, Thaisa;
Thy burden at the sea, and call'd Marina
For she was yielded there.
Thai. Blest, and mine own!
Hel. Hail, madam, and my queen!
Thai. I know you not.
Per. You have heard me say, when I did fly from Tyre,
I left behind an ancient substitute:
Can you remember what I call'd the man?
I have nam'd him oft.
Thai. 'Twas Helicanus then.
Per. Still confirmation:
Embrace him, dear Thaisa; this is he.
Now do I long to hear how you were found;
How possibly preserv'd: and who to thank,
Besides the gods, for this great miracle.
Thai. Lord Cerimon, my lord; this man,
Through whom the gods have shown their power; that can
From first to last resolve you.
Per. Reverend sir,
The gods can have no mortal officer
More like a god than you. Will you deliver
How this dead queen re-lives?
Cer. I will, my lord.
Beseech you, first go with me to my house,
Where shall be shown you all was found with her;
How she came placed here in the temple;
No needful thing omitted.
Per. Pure Dian, bless thee for thy vision! I
Will offer night-oblations to thee. Thaisa,
This prince, the fair-betrothed of your daughter,
Shall marry her at Pentapolis. And now
This ornament
Makes me look dismal will I clip to form;
And what this fourteen years no razor touch'd,
To grace thy marriage-day, I'll beautify.
Thai. Lord Cerimon hath letters of good credit, sir,
My father 's dead.
Per. Heavens make a star of him! Yet there, my queen,
We'll celebrate their nuptials, and ourselves
Will in that kingdom spend our following days:
Our son and daughter shall in Tyrus reign.

SCENE II. 14. **confound,** omit. 15. **feather'd,** winged.
SCENE III. 18. **Reverend appearer,** reverend one who appears here. 29-30. **my . . . ear,** passion will not persuade me to give over my holy vows. 41. **sports,** jests. 42. **That,** if. 48. **yielded,** born. 62. **mortal officer,** human agent. 70. **night-oblations,** nightly sacrifices. 73. **ornament,** i.e., hair and beard (text probably corrupt).

Lord Cerimon, we do our longing stay
To hear the rest untold: sir, lead 's the way. [*Exeunt.*]

[*Enter* GOWER.]

Gow. In Antiochus and his daughter you have heard
Of monstrous lust the due and just reward:
In Pericles, his queen and daughter, seen,
Although assail'd with fortune fierce and keen,
Virtue preserv'd from fell destruction's blast,
Led on by heaven, and crown'd with joy at last:
In Helicanus may you well descry
A figure of truth, of faith, of loyalty:
In reverend Cerimon there well appears
The worth that learned charity aye wears:
For wicked Cleon and his wife, when fame
Had spread their cursed deed, the honour'd name
Of Pericles, to rage the city turn,
That him and his they in his palace burn;
The gods for murder seemed so content
To punish them; although not done, but meant.
So, on your patience evermore attending,
New joy wait on you! Here our play has ending.
[*Exit.*]

83. **we . . . stay,** we will let our desires await satisfaction.

CYMBELINE

The genre of *Cymbeline* can be suggested by such critical terms as romance, tragicomedy, and the comedy of forgiveness. As in *Pericles*, *The Winter's Tale*, and other late plays, Shakespeare turns to the improbable fictions of romance: a poison-wielding stepmother-queen envious of her fair and virtuous stepdaughter (cf. *Snow White*), lost sons recognized by the inevitable cliché of a birthmark, the reunion of many persons long separated by exile and wandering, the intervention of the gods by means of a riddling and inane prophecy. These are the distinguishing features of English romance in the 1580's, a titillating vogue exploited by Robert Greene and other professional writers of the period. From two romantic plays of the 1580's—*Sir Clyomon and Sir Clamydes* and *The Rare Triumphs of Love and Fortune*—Shakespeare may in fact have drawn source material. Why did he turn to such old-fashioned models in 1608–1610? The choice has puzzled many critics, and has prompted them to speak condescendingly of Shakespeare's dotage or to assign parts of the play (notably the descent of Jupiter) to some other dramatist.

Shakespeare nevertheless courted the improbabilities, even the deliberate absurdities, of romance with intensely serious artistic purpose. In part he was responding to a new literary fashion, evident especially in the private theatres, for a tragicomedy of refined sensibility—a literary fashion that had also produced Beaumont and Fletcher's *Philaster*. This play of about 1609 features, like *Cymbeline*, a rapidly moving and ingeniously woven plot of separation and reunion, a king's daughter betrothed by her father to a churl and then wrongly accused of infidelity, a young maiden in male disguise, and other comparable details. Whether *Cymbeline* preceded or followed *Philaster* is a matter difficult to determine, since *Cymbeline* can be dated only approximately in 1608–1610 on grounds of style; but in any case Shakespeare's fascination with romance goes back at least to *All's Well that Ends Well* (c. 1601–1604) and *Pericles* (c. 1606–1608). His experiments in the genre must be viewed as innovative and unique. Despite the affinities to Fletcherian tragicomedy, Shakespeare never indulges in the cloying sensationalism, the exaggerated heightening of exotic emotion, and (except in *The Winter's Tale*) the trickery of concealing essential information from the audience, such as we find in works of the Beaumont and Fletcher canon. Shakespeare's interest in romantic improbability is instead related to the profoundly serious motif of redemption, of an unexpected and undeserved second chance for erring mankind.

The tragic possibilities are manifold. Cymbeline, like Lear (another king from British mythic history in Holinshed's *Chronicles*), tyrannically repulses a virtuous daughter and rewards the vicious members of his family with predictably unhappy consequences. Posthumus Leonatus, like Othello, commands the death of his beloved mistress because he believes a groundless but cunningly presented accusation of her infidelity; finally, concluding too late that he has destroyed the only precious jewel capable of giving order to his life, he despairingly longs for death. Whereas Lear and Othello must suffer the tragic consequences of their choice, however, Cymbeline and Posthumus are spared. Some benign force, integral to the world of this play, prevents fallible men from pursuing their misguided intentions to the point of irreversible injury. Posthumus relies for his vengeance on the virtuous Pisanio, who cannot bring himself to slay Imogen. The queen's box of "poison," given ultimately to Imogen by the well-meaning but duped Pisanio, is in fact only a sleeping potion concocted by that kindly manipulator behind the scenes, Doctor Cornelius. These fortunate avoidances of disaster recall other such narrow escapes in *Much Ado about Nothing*, *All's Well that Ends Well*, and *Measure for Measure*. They also anticipate similarly providential events in *The Winter's Tale*.

Because *Cymbeline* begins with dilemmas like those of *King Lear* and *Othello*, the prevailing tone seems at first tragic. (In fact, the editors of the 1623 Folio printed the play among the tragedies.) The king's behavior toward Imogen and her virtuous but humbly ranked lover Posthumus is deplorably tyrannical. Fair-minded observers condemn the wicked queen's domineering power over Cymbeline, and laugh up their sleeves at the queen's cowardly and ridiculous son Cloten. Good men like Belarius have been forced to flee the envious court for lifelong banishment, dwelling in caves. Indeed, the romantic pattern of exile and wandering reflects the need to escape from a court dominated by the wicked queen. One by one, honest persons of the play—Posthumus, Imogen, Pisanio—leave society in disfavor to be reunited in the wild landscape of Belarius and his stepsons. Italy is no better a place than the English court. Its evil genius is Iachimo, apostle of animal appetite, duplicity, and a cynical indifference to human values.

Despite the prevailing tragic mood at first, however, there are promises of brighter prospects. Posthumus' birth is attended by romantic and wondrous circumstances that would appear to single him out for an extraordinary career. In the very first scene, moreover, we learn that the king's only two sons were stolen from their nursery in their infancy—an obvious hint that they will turn up sooner or later. Cloten, too, strikes us as a ludicrously amusing suitor of Imogen, the type of buffoonish and witless rival appropriate to a love comedy. As the embodiment of pure superficiality, whose sole preoccupation is with clothes, he is fittingly exposed and ridiculed. Even his death is grotesquely comic.

Another technique used to protect us from undue fear of tragic outcome is that of the simultaneous and ironic juxtaposition of sorrow and hope. For instance, when Arviragus and Guiderius mourn the "death" of Imogen with an exquisite song on the vanity of human striving, we respond to the appropriateness of the sentiment and yet qualify it with our consoling knowledge that she has really taken a sleeping potion. Similarly, when Posthumus jests eloquently about death with his jailer, and prepares to find his only freedom in surcease, we cannot ignore Jupiter's assurance of eventual redress in the action immediately preceding. As in *Measure for Measure*, tragic suffering and regret are framed in the benignly ironic context of a providential design we alone can fully appreciate.

The cumulative effect of this tragicomedy, then, is that we feel simultaneously threatened and consoled. The chief source of anxiety is Posthumus' renunciation of Imogen. The sensationalism of the plot derives in part from its affinities to the "wager" motif in several Italianate *novelle*, such as the ninth tale of the second day in Boccaccio's *Decameron*. The psychological portrait of Posthumus' wavering and fall, like that of Othello or Leontes, is intense and ugly, fraught with grotesque images of sexual coupling. Posthumus conjures up the imagined sexual triumph of Iachimo in animalistic terms: "Perchance he spoke not, but, Like a full-acorn'd boar, a German one, Cried 'O!' and mounted" (II,v). Like Othello, he insists on being proved a cuckold; once he has experienced jealousy, he can expect only one conclusion. He longs "to tear her limb-meal," and like Lear he would violently destroy "the woman's part in me." It is this essential perversity of man's fallen nature, vividly exemplified in a man who is in most respects noble, that threatens disaster and demands either a tragic ending or the unexpected second chance of tragicomedy. Posthumus receives that second chance, but meantime he has raised a familiarly Shakespearean question as to the extent of his responsibility for his fall. How could he have avoided the false accusation of Imogen?

Powerful forces militate against Posthumus. Iachimo is a plausible villain, in the vein of Don John (*Much Ado about Nothing*), Iago, and Edmund. Like them he plots to arouse envy and dissension in others, by means of appearance falsely presented to the senses. Although we can postulate a human motive for him as a quarrelsome and lecherous man, his chief motive is delight in the evil effects he produces. His contention is that every woman has her price (and every man, too). When he discovers in Imogen a purity that will not yield to his insinuations, he seeks to destroy her as a dangerous refutation of his low premise about human nature. He states the confrontation between them in cosmic spiritual terms: "Though this a heavenly angel, hell is here" (II,ii). We do not see him gleefully boasting to the audience, or dominating the play to the extent Iago does; moreover, he himself experiences the beneficent change brought about by the play's happy ending, and speaks eloquently in praise of Imogen's virtue. As befits a tragicomedy, he is more sinister than potent, almost at times a travesty of a tragic villain. Nevertheless, in the temptation scenes his function and method are those of a diabolical emissary approaching man through his frail senses. His use of the ring as evidence recalls the motif of the handkerchief in *Othello*. Iachimo creates a minutely circumstantial inference of Imogen's transgression, and lets Posthumus' inclination to believe the worst do the rest.

As in the case of Othello, then, Posthumus must bear the blame for loss of faith. The tempter can prevail upon his senses, but man's own wavering heart must choose evil. Trustworthy observers perceive Posthumus' fallacy and indicate the correct response; as Philario says, "This is not strong enough to be liev'd Of one persuaded well of" (II,iv). True faith would urge that, being what she is, Imogen could not do the thing alleged. She is, like Helena and Desdemona before her, another Patient Griselda: a virtuous woman who responds to her undeserved tribulations with long-suffering forbearance (though even her patience has a limit). She overbalances faithlessness with her forgiveness. Her perseverance in virtue confounds Iachimo's thesis and enables Posthumus to be rescued from his worst self. Iachimo and she are spiritual contestants for the allegiance of Posthumus' faith; and she triumphs not through Posthumus' choice (which is for evil) but through her own unassailable goodness.

The story of King Cymbeline's long-lost sons is similarly tragicomic, and is even more explicitly indebted to the conventions of romance with its motifs of banishment, wandering, and eventual recognition and reunion. The sylvan setting of this romantic narrative lends to the second half of the play an aura of primal vigor and mystery (as also in *The Winter's Tale*). Arviragus and Guiderius remind us of medieval legends about Parzival:—that is, like Parzival they are young princes raised in a wilderness whose lack of courtly training cannot suppress the "invisible instinct" prompting them to assert their royal blood. Ignoring their stepfather's warnings about the ingratitude and decadence of the society from which he has fled into banishment and taken these princes with him, they long to prove themselves in deeds of chivalry. They are a rejuvenating force in this play, bringing together the ideals of medieval knighthood and the unsullied strength of their sylvan world. Cloten, that effete semblance of a courtier and their foil in every respect, is appropriately destroyed by these agents of "divine Nature." Conversely, they cherish Imogen as one of their own, and grieve for her seeming death with the vivid immediacy of those who have lived with the rhythms of nature. To them she is an earth goddess, and her awakening brings a restoration of natural vigor nicely complementing the spiritual grace she embodies for Posthumus. Her name to them is appropriately "Fidele." Old Belarius' reconciliation with Cymbeline signifies an end to political injustice, still another consequence of man's fallen condition for which grace must be provided.

The war plot, derived in part from Holinshed, contributes also to the process of spiritual rebirth. It sets in motion a series of apparently random events, including the return to Britain of Posthumus and Iachimo, without which the play's happy conclusion would be impossible. Although the war itself is destructive and is supported chiefly by Cloten and the queen (whose patriotic utterances show us just how hollow a thing patriotism can be), the war does lead ultimately to new life for Britain as well as for the romantic lovers. The king, no longer misled by evil counselors, finds reconciliation with his true daughter and her husband. The final scene, in which the seeming accidents of fortune are finally unraveled, is a structural tour de force of comic discovery. The playwright, by this studiously artificial control of his materials, creates a world of the play in which seeming accident is benign. His spokesman as *deus ex machina* (literally illustrating that term, for Jupiter "descends" from the stage roof by means of some mechanical device) is Jupiter. The scene (V,iv) of this divine intervention is so blatantly unrealistic that, as we have seen, many critics have wished to exonerate Shakespeare of having written it; but this very unreality is the keynote of the play's ending. Jupiter places the suffering we have witnessed in a cosmic perspective: "Whom best I love I cross: to make my gift, The more delay'd, delighted. Be content." In the tragicomic view, suffering is merely a manifestation of a design to test and strengthen us, engineered and supervised by a loving deity. The test indeed affirms Imogen's strength, shows Posthumus a reason to cherish what he would otherwise destroy, and even reclaims the evil agent by whom the test had been administered.

CYMBELINE

[*Dramatis Personae*

CYMBELINE, King of Britain.
CLOTEN, *son to the Queen by a former husband.*
POSTHUMUS LEONATUS, *a gentleman, husband to Imogen.*
BELARIUS, *a banished lord, disguised under the name of Morgan.*
GUIDERIUS, ARVIRAGUS, } *sons to Cymbeline, disguised under the names of Polydore and Cadwal, supposed sons to Morgan.*
PHILARIO, *friend to Posthumus,* IACHIMO, *friend to Philario,* } *Italians.*
CAIUS LUCIUS, *general of the Roman forces.*
PISANIO, *servant to Posthumus.*
CORNELIUS, *a physician.*
A Roman Captain.
Two British Captains.
A Frenchman, *friend to Philario.*
Two Lords of Cymbeline's court.
Two Gentlemen of the same.
Two Gaolers.

QUEEN, *wife to Cymbeline.*
IMOGEN, *daughter to Cymbeline by a former queen.*
HELEN, *a lady attending on Imogen.*

Lords, Ladies, Roman Senators, Tribunes, a Soothsayer, a Dutchman, a Spaniard, Musicians, Officers, Captains, Soldiers, Messengers, *and other* attendants.

Apparitions.

SCENE: *Britain; Rome.*]

ACT I.

SCENE I. [*Britain. The garden of Cymbeline's palace.*]

Enter two Gentlemen.

First Gent. You do not meet a man but frowns: our bloods
No more obey the heavens than our courtiers
Still seem as does the king's.
Sec. Gent. But what 's the matter?
First Gent. His daughter, and the heir of 's kingdom, whom
He purpos'd to his wife's sole son—a widow
That late he married—hath referr'd herself
Unto a poor but worthy gentleman: she 's wedded;
Her husband banish'd; she imprison'd: all
Is outward sorrow; though I think the king
Be touch'd at very heart.
Sec. Gent. None but the king?
First Gent. He that hath lost her too; so is the queen,
That most desir'd the match; but not a courtier,
Although they wear their faces to the bent

Of the king's looks, hath a heart that is not
Glad at the thing they scowl at.
Sec. Gent. And why so?
First Gent. He that hath miss'd the princess is a thing
Too bad for bad report: and he that hath her—
I mean, that married her, alack, good man!
And therefore banish'd—is a creature such
As, to seek through the regions of the earth
For one his like, there would be something failing
In him that should compare. I do not think
So fair an outward and such stuff within
Endows a man but he.
Sec. Gent. You speak him far.
First Gent. I do extend him, sir, within himself,
Crush him together rather than unfold
His measure duly.
Sec. Gent. What 's his name and birth?
First Gent. I cannot delve him to the root: his father
Was call'd Sicilius, who did join his honour
Against the Romans with Cassibelan,
But had his titles by Tenantius whom
He serv'd with glory and admir'd success,
So gain'd the sur-addition Leonatus;
And had, besides this gentleman in question,
Two other sons, who in the wars o' th' time
Died with their swords in hand; for which their father,
Then old and fond of issue, took such sorrow
That he quit being, and his gentle lady,
Big of this gentleman our theme, deceas'd
As he was born. The king he takes the babe
To his protection, calls him Posthumus Leonatus,
Breeds him and makes him of his bed-chamber,
Puts to him all the learnings that his time
Could make him the receiver of; which he took,
As we do air, fast as 'twas minist'red,
And in 's spring became a harvest, liv'd in court—
Which rare it is to do—most prais'd, most lov'd,
A sample to the youngest, to th' more mature
A glass that feated them, and to the graver
A child that guided dotards; to his mistress,
For whom he now is banish'd, her own price
Proclaims how she esteem'd him and his virtue;
By her election may be truly read
What kind of man he is.
Sec. Gent. I honour him
Even out of your report. But, pray you, tell me,
Is she sole child to th' king?
First Gent. His only child.
He had two sons: if this be worth your hearing,
Mark it: the eldest of them at three years old,
I' th' swathing-clothes the other, from their nursery
Were stol'n, and to this hour no guess in knowledge
Which way they went.
Sec. Gent. How long is this ago?
First Gent. Some twenty years.
Sec. Gent. That a king's children should be so convey'd,
So slackly guarded, and the search so slow,
That could not trace them!
First Gent. Howso'er 'tis strange,
Or that the negligence may well be laugh'd at,
Yet is it true, sir.
Sec. Gent. I do well believe you.
First Gent. We must forbear: here comes the gentleman,
The queen, and princess. *Exeunt.*

Enter the QUEEN, POSTHUMUS, *and* IMOGEN.

Queen. No, be assur'd you shall not find me, daughter,
After the slander of most stepmothers,
Evil-ey'd unto you: you 're my prisoner, but
Your gaoler shall deliver you the keys
That lock up your restaint. For you, Posthumus,
So soon as I can win th' offended king,
I will be known your advocate: marry, yet
The fire of rage is in him, and 'twere good
You lean'd unto his sentence with what patience
Your wisdom may inform you.
Post. Please your highness,
I will from hence to-day.
Queen. You know the peril.
I'll fetch a turn about the garden, pitying
The pangs of barr'd affections, though the king
Hath charg'd you should not speak together. *Exit.*
Imo. O
Dissembling courtesy! How fine this tyrant
Can tickle where she wounds! My dearest husband,
I something fear my father's wrath; but nothing—
Always reserv'd my holy duty—what
His rage can do on me: you must be gone;
And I shall here abide the hourly shot
Of angry eyes, not comforted to live,
But that there is this jewel in the world
That I may see again.
Post. My queen! my mistress!
O lady, weep no more, lest I give cause
To be suspected of more tenderness
Than doth become a man. I will remain
The loyal'st husband that did e'er plight troth:
My residence in Rome at one Philario's,
Who to my father was a friend, to me
Known but by letter: thither write, my queen,
And with mine eyes I'll drink the words you send,
Though ink be made of gall.

Enter QUEEN.

Queen. Be brief, I pray you:
If the king come, I shall incur I know not
How much of his displeasure. [*Aside*] Yet I'll move him
To walk this way: I never do him wrong,
But he does buy my injuries, to be friends;
Pays dear for my offences. [*Exit.*]
Post. Should we be taking leave
As long a term as yet we have to live,
The loathness to depart would grow. Adieu!
Imo. Nay, stay a little:
Were you but riding forth to air yourself,
Such parting were too petty. Look here, love;
This diamond was my mother's: take it, heart;
But keep it till you woo another wife,

ACT I. SCENE I. 6. **referr'd,** handed over (married). 13-14. **bent . . . looks,** inclination of the king's mind, as indicated by his looks. 24. **speak . . . far,** go far in praising him. 25. **I . . . himself,** I magnify his virtues within the limits of what he actually is. 29. **join his honour,** give his honorable assistance. 30. **Cassibelan,** according to Holinshed, Lud's younger brother and successor. 31. **Tenantius,** son of King Lud and apparently regarded as Cymbeline's predecessor. 33. **sur-addition,** additional title. 37. **fond of issue,** devoted to his children. 38. **quit being,** left existence, died. 39. **Big,** great with young. 40. **king he,** pleonastic subject. 41. **Posthumus,** accent on second syllable. 43. **time,** age. 48. **sample,** example. 49. **glass . . . them,** mirror that reflected their features. 78. **lean'd unto,** deferred to. 105. **But . . . friends,** that he does not reward me for the injuries I have done him in order that I may be friends with him. The statement

When Imogen is dead.
Post. How, how: another?
You gentle gods, give me but this I have,
And sear up my embracements from a next
With bonds of death! [*Putting on the ring.*] Remain, remain thou here
While sense can keep it on. And, sweetest, fairest,
As I my poor self did exchange for you,
To your so infinite loss, so in our trifles
I still win of you: for my sake wear this;
It is a manacle of love; I'll place it
Upon this fairest prisoner.
[*Putting a bracelet upon her arm.*]
Imo. O the gods!
When shall we see again?

Enter CYMBELINE *and* Lords.

Post. Alack, the king!
Cym. Thou basest thing, avoid! hence, from my sight!
If after this command thou fraught the court
With thy unworthiness, thou diest: away!
Thou 'rt poison to my blood.
Post. The gods protect you!
And bless the good remainders of the court!
I am gone. *Exit.*
Imo. There cannot be a pinch in death
More sharp than this is.
Cym. O disloyal thing,
That shouldst repair my youth, thou heap'st
A year's age on me.
Imo. I beseech you, sir,
Harm not yourself with your vexation:
I am senseless of your wrath; a touch more rare
Subdues all pangs, all fears.
Cym. Past grace? obedience?
Imo. Past hope, and in despair; that way, past grace.
Cym. That mightst have had the sole son of my queen!
Imo. O blessed, that I might not! I chose an eagle,
And did avoid a puttock.
Cym. Thou took'st a beggar; wouldst have made my throne
A seat for baseness.
Imo. No; I rather added
A lustre to it.
Cym. O thou vile one!
Imo. Sir,
It is your fault that I have lov'd Posthumus:
You bred him as my playfellow, and he is
A man worth any woman, overbuys me
Almost the sum he pays.
Cym. What, art thou mad?
Imo. Almost, sir: heaven restore me! Would I were
A neat-herd's daughter, and my Leonatus
Our neighbour shepherd's son!

Enter QUEEN.

Cym. Thou foolish thing!—
[*To Queen*] They were again together: you have done
Not after our command. Away with her,
And pen her up.
Queen. Beseech your patience. Peace,
Dear lady daughter, peace! Sweet sovereign,
Leave us to ourselves; and make yourself some comfort
Out of your best advice.
Cym. Nay, let her languish
A drop of blood a day; and, being aged,
Die of this folly! *Exit* [*with Lords*].
Queen. Fie! you must give way.

Enter PISANIO.

Here is your servant. How now, sir! What news?
Pis. My lord your son drew on my master.
Queen. Ha!
No harm, I trust, is done?
Pis. There might have been,
But that my master rather play'd than fought
And had no help of anger: they were parted
By gentlemen at hand.
Queen. I am very glad on 't.
Imo. Your son 's my father's friend; he takes his part.
To draw upon an exile! O brave sir!
I would they were in Afric both together;
Myself by with a needle, that I might prick
The goer-back. Why came you from your master?
Pis. On his command: he would not suffer me
To bring him to the haven; left these notes
Of what commands I should be subject to,
When 't pleas'd you to employ me.
Queen. This hath been
Your faithful servant: I dare lay mine honour
He will remain so.
Pis. I humbly thank your highness.
Queen. Pray, walk awhile.
Imo. About some half-hour hence,
I pray you, speak with me: you shall at least
Go see my lord aboard: for this time leave me. *Exeunt.*

SCENE [II. *The same. A public place*].

Enter CLOTEN *and two* Lords.

First Lord. Sir, I would advise you to shift a shirt; the violence of action hath made you reek as a sacrifice: where air comes out, air comes in: there 's none abroad so wholesome as that you vent.

Clo. If my shirt were bloody, then to shift it. Have I hurt him?

Sec. Lord. [*Aside*] No, 'faith; not so much as his patience.

First Lord. Hurt him! his body 's a passable carcass, if he be not hurt: it is a throughfare for steel, if it be not hurt.

Sec. Lord. [*Aside*] His steel was in debt; it went o' the backside the town.

Clo. The villain would not stand me.

Sec. Lord. [*Aside*] No; but he fled forward still, toward your face.

First Lord. Stand you! You have land enough of

gives an idea of the doting quality of the king. 116. **sear up,** dry up, blight; suggestion also of *cere*, cover with wax, as the linen of a shroud. 124. **see,** see each other (reciprocal sense). 126. **fraught,** burden. 129. **remainders,** those who remain. 135. **a touch more rare,** a more exquisite feeling of pain. (Imogen is so wretched at Leonatus' banishment that she has lost all fear of her father.) 140. **puttock,** kite, bird of prey the name of which was often used as a contemptuous epithet.

146-147. **overbuys . . . pays,** pays more for me than I am worth by almost as much as, in giving himself, he has given for me. 149. **neat-herd's,** cowherd's. 153. **Beseech,** I beseech. 156. **best advice,** most mature reflection. 176. **walk,** go aside, withdraw.

SCENE II. 10. **passable,** penetrable, with pun on *tolerable*. 11. **throughfare,** thoroughfare.

your own: but he added to your having; gave you some ground.

Sec. Lord. [*Aside*] As many inches as you have oceans. Puppies!

Clo. I would they had not come between us.

Sec. Lord. [*Aside*] So would I, till you had measured how long a fool you were upon the ground.

Clo. And that she should love this fellow and refuse me!

Sec. Lord. [*Aside*] If it be a sin to make a true election, she is damned.

First Lord. Sir, as I told you always, her beauty and her brain go not together: she 's a good sign, but I have seen small reflection of her wit.

Sec. Lord. [*Aside*] She shines not upon fools, lest the reflection should hurt her.

Clo. Come, I'll to my chamber. Would there had been some hurt done!

Sec. Lord. [*Aside*] I wish not so; unless it had been the fall of an ass, which is no great hurt.

Clo. You'll go with us?

First Lord. I'll attend your lordship.

Clo. Nay, come, let 's go together.

Sec. Lord. Well, my lord. *Exeunt.*

SCENE [III. *A room in Cymbeline's palace*].

Enter IMOGEN *and* PISANIO.

Imo. I would thou grew'st unto the shores o' th'
haven,
And questioned'st every sail: if he should write,
And I not have it, 'twere a paper lost,
As offer'd mercy is. What was the last
That he spake to thee?

Pis. It was his queen, his queen!

Imo. Then wav'd his handkerchief?

Pis. And kiss'd it, madam.

Imo. Senseless linen! happier therein than I!
And that was all?

Pis. No, madam; for so long
As he could make me with this eye or ear
Distinguish him from others, he did keep
The deck, with glove, or hat, or handkerchief,
Still waving, as the fits and stirs of 's mind
Could best express how slow his soul sail'd on,
How swift his ship.

Imo. Thou shouldst have made him
As little as a crow, or less, ere left
To after-eye him.

Pis. Madam, so I did.

Imo. I would have broke mine eye-strings; crack'd
them, but
To look upon him, till the diminution
Of space had pointed him sharp as my needle,
Nay, followed him, till he had melted from
The smallness of a gnat to air, and then
Have turn'd mine eye and wept. But, good Pisanio,
When shall we hear from him?

Pis. Be assur'd, madam,
With his next vantage.

Imo. I did not take my leave of him, but had
Most pretty things to say: ere I could tell him
How I would think on him at certain hours
Such thoughts and such, or I could make him swear
The shes of Italy should not betray
Mine interest and his honour, or have charg'd him,
At the sixth hour of morn, at noon, at midnight,
T' encounter me with orisons, for then
I am in heaven for him; or ere I could
Give him that parting kiss which I had set
Betwixt two charming words, comes in my father
And like the tyrannous breathing of the north
Shakes all our buds from growing.

Enter a Lady.

Lady. The queen, madam,
Desires your highness' company.

Imo. Those things I bid you do, get them dispatch'd.
I will attend the queen.

Pis. Madam, I shall. *Exeunt.*

SCENE [IV. *Rome. Philario's house*].

Enter PHILARIO, IACHIMO, *a* Frenchman, *a* Dutchman, *and a* Spaniard.

Iach. Believe it, sir, I have seen him in Britain: he was then of a crescent note, expected to prove so worthy as since he hath been allowed the name of; but I could then have looked on him without the help of admiration, though the catalogue of his endowments had been tabled by his side and I to peruse him by items.

Phi. You speak of him when he was less furnished than now he is with that which makes him both without and within.

French. I have seen him in France: we had very many there could behold the sun with as firm eyes as he.

Iach. This matter of marrying his king's daughter, wherein he must be weighed rather by her value than his own, words him, I doubt not, a great deal from the matter.

French. And then his banishment.

Iach. Ay, and the approbation of those that weep this lamentable divorce under her colours are wonderfully to extend him; be it but to fortify her judgement, which else an easy battery might lay flat, for taking a beggar without less quality. But how comes it he is to sojourn with you? How creeps acquaintance?

Phi. His father and I were soldiers together; to whom I have been often bound for no less than my life.

Enter POSTHUMUS.

Here comes the Briton: let him be so entertained amongst you as suits, with gentlemen of your knowing, to a stranger of his quality.—I beseech you all, be better known to this gentleman, whom I commend to you as a noble friend of mine: how worthy he is I will

30. **election,** choice; a theological expression. 33. **sign,** semblance, appearance.

SCENE III. 3-4. **'twere . . . is,** i.e., the loss of such a letter would be as unfortunate as a pardon offered but failing to arrive before the execution. 7. **Senseless,** without feeling. 15. **left,** you left off. 16. **after-eye,** look after. 29. **shes,** women. 32. **encounter,** join. **orisons,** prayers. 35. **charming,** having magical potency. 36. **north,** north wind.

SCENE IV. 2. **crescent note,** growing reputation of importance. 7. **tabled,** set down in a list. 10. **makes . . . within,** establishes him as regards both his fortune and his character. 16-17. **words . . . matter,** causes him to be described as other (and better) than he is. 20-21. **under her colours,** in Imogen's party, influenced by her. 21. **extend him,** increase his reputation. 24. **without less,** with less (double negative). 29. **knowing,** knowledge, *savoir faire*. 30. **stranger,** foreigner. **quality,** rank. 34. **story,** give an account of. 36. **known together,** leave to appear hereafter, rather than story him in his own hearing.

French. Sir, we have known together in Orleans.

Post. Since when I have been debtor to you for courtesies, which I will be ever to pay and yet pay still.

French. Sir, you o'er-rate my poor kindness: I was glad I did atone my countryman and you; it had been pity you should have been put together with so mortal a purpose as then each bore, upon importance of so slight and trivial a nature.

Post. By your pardon, sir, I was then a young traveller; rather shunned to go even with what I heard than in my every action to be guided by others' experiences: but upon my mended judgement—if I offend not to say it is mended—my quarrel was not altogether slight.

French. 'Faith, yes, to be put to the arbitrement of swords, and by such two that would by all likelihood have confounded one the other, or have fallen both.

Iach. Can we, with manners, ask what was the difference?

French. Safely, I think: 'twas a contention in public, which may, without contradiction, suffer the report. It was much like an argument that fell out last night, where each of us fell in praise of our country mistresses; this gentleman at that time vouching—and upon warrant of bloody affirmation—his to be more fair, virtuous, wise, chaste, constant-qualified and less attemptable than any the rarest of our ladies in France.

Iach. That lady is not now living, or this gentleman's opinion by this worn out.

Post. She holds her virtue still and I my mind.

Iach. You must not so far prefer her 'fore ours of Italy.

Post. Being so far provoked as I was in France, I would abate her nothing, though I profess myself her adorer, not her friend.

Iach. As fair and as good—a kind of hand-in-hand comparison—had been something too fair and too good for any lady in Britain. If she went before others I have seen, as that diamond of yours outlustres many I have beheld, I could not but believe she excelled many: but I have not seen the most precious diamond that is, nor you the lady.

Post. I praised her as I rated her: so do I my stone.

Iach. What do you esteem it at?

Post. More than the world enjoys.

Iach. Either your unparagoned mistress is dead, or she 's outprized by a trifle.

Post. You are mistaken: the one may be sold, or given, or if there were wealth enough for the purchase, or merit for the gift: the other is not a thing for sale, and only the gift of the gods.

Iach. Which the gods have given you?

Post. Which, by their graces, I will keep.

Iach. You may wear her in title yours: but, you know, strange fowl light upon neighbouring ponds. Your ring may be stolen too: so your brace of unprizable estimations; the one is but frail and the other casual; a cunning thief, or a that way accomplished courtier, would hazard the winning both of first and last.

Post. Your Italy contains none so accomplished a courtier to convince the honour of my mistress, if, in the holding or loss of that, you term her frail. I do nothing doubt you have store of thieves; notwithstanding, I fear not my ring.

Phi. Let us leave here, gentlemen.

Post. Sir, with all my heart. This worthy signior, I thank him, makes no stranger of me; we are familiar at first.

Iach. With five times so much conversation, I should get ground of your fair mistress, make her go back, even to the yielding, had I admittance and opportunity to friend.

Post. No, no.

Iach. I dare thereupon pawn the moiety of my estate to your ring; which, in my opinion, o'ervalues it something: but I make my wager rather against your confidence than her reputation: and, to bar your offence herein too, I durst attempt it against any lady in the world.

Post. You are a great deal abused in too bold a persuasion; and I doubt not you sustain what y' are worthy of by your attempt.

Iach. What 's that?

Post. A repulse: though your attempt, as you call it, deserve more; a punishment too.

Phi. Gentlemen, enough of this: it came in too suddenly; let it die as it was born, and, I pray you, be better acquainted.

Iach. Would I had put my estate and my neighbour's on the approbation of what I have spoke!

Post. What lady would you choose to assail?

Iach. Yours; whom in constancy you think stands so safe. I will lay you ten thousands ducats to your ring, that, commend me to the court where your lady is, with no more advantage than the opportunity of a second conference, and I will bring from thence that honour of hers which you imagine so reserved.

Post. I will wage against your gold, gold to it: my ring I hold dear as my finger; 'tis part of it.

Iach. You are a friend, and therein the wiser. If you buy ladies' flesh at a million a dram, you cannot preserve it from tainting: but I see you have some religion in you, that you fear.

Post. This is but a custom in your tongue; you bear a graver purpose, I hope.

Iach. I am the master of my speeches, and would undergo what 's spoken, I swear.

Post. Will you? I shall but lend my diamond till your return: let there be covenants drawn between 's: my mistress exceeds in goodness the hugeness of your unworthy thinking: I dare you to this match: here 's my ring.

Phi. I will have it no lay.

Iach. By the gods, it is one. If I bring you no sufficient testimony that I have enjoyed the dearest

been acquainted. 39-40. **which . . . still,** for which I shall be forever in debt and yet be paying always. 42. **atone,** set at one, reconcile. 44. **put together,** i.e., in a duel. 45. **importance,** matter, occasion. 59. **suffer the report,** be reported or told. 60. **our country,** i.e., of our own country's (with bawdy pun). 63. **bloody affirmation,** affirming the truth with his blood. 65. **constant-qualified,** endowed with constancy. **attemptable,** open to attempts on their virtue. 68. **by this,** by now. 99. **unprizable,** invaluable. **estimations,** things highly esteemed. 104. **to,** as to. **convince,** overcome. 105. **in . . . that,** on the question of holding or losing her honor. 109. **leave,** leave off, cease. 115. **go back,** succumb, give way. 116. **to friend,** as my friend. 124-125. **abused . . . persuasion,** deceived by too bold an opinion. 134. **approbation,** attestation, confirmation. 144. **wage,** lay as a wager. 146. **You . . . wiser,** i.e., you know her too well to bet your ring on her. 159. **I . . . lay,** I will not let it be a wager.

bodily part of your mistress, my ten thousand ducats are yours; so is your diamond too: if I come off, and leave her in such honour as you have trust in, she your jewel, this your jewel, and my gold are yours: provided I have your commendation for my more free entertainment.

Post. I embrace these conditions; let us have articles betwixt us. Only, thus far you shall answer: if you make your voyage upon her and give me directly to understand you have prevailed, I am no further your enemy; she is not worth our debate: if she remain unseduced, you not making it appear otherwise, for your ill opinion and the assault you have made to her chastity you shall answer me with your sword.

Iach. Your hand; a covenant: we will have these things set down by lawful counsel, and straight away for Britain, lest the bargain should catch cold and starve: I will fetch my gold and have our two wagers recorded.

Post. Agreed. [*Exeunt Posthumus and Iachimo.*]
French. Will this hold, think you?
Phil. Signior Iachimo will not from it. Pray, let us follow 'em. *Exeunt.*

SCENE [V. *Britain. A room in Cymbeline's palace*].

Enter QUEEN, Ladies, *and* CORNELIUS.

Queen. Whiles yet the dew 's on ground, gather those flowers;
Make haste: who has the note of them?
First Lady. I, madam.
Queen. Dispatch. *Exeunt Ladies.*
Now, master doctor, have you brought those drugs?
Cor. Pleaseth your highness, ay: here they are, madam: [*Presenting a small box.*]
But I beseech your grace, without offence,—
My conscience bids me ask—wherefore you have
Commanded of me these most poisonous compounds,
Which are the movers of a languishing death;
But though slow, deadly?
Queen. I wonder, doctor,
Thou ask'st me such a question. Have I not been
Thy pupil long? Hast thou not learn'd me how
To make perfumes? distil? preserve? yea, so
That our great king himself doth woo me oft
For my confections? Having thus far proceeded,—
Unless thou think'st me devilish—is 't not meet
That I did amplify my judgement in
Other conclusions? I will try the forces
Of these thy compounds on such creatures as
We count not worth the hanging, but none human,
To try the vigour of them and apply
Allayments to their act, and by them gather
Their several virtues and effects.
Cor. Your highness
Shall from this practice but make hard your heart:
Besides, the seeing these effects will be
Both noisome and infectious.
Queen. O, content thee.

Enter PISANIO.

[*Aside*] Here comes a flattering rascal; upon him
Will I first work: he 's for his master,
And enemy to my son. How now, Pisanio!
Doctor, your service for this time is ended;
Take your own way.
Cor. [*Aside*] I do suspect you, madam;
But you shall do no harm.
Queen. [*To Pisanio*] Hark thee, a word.
Cor. [*Aside*] I do not like her. She doth think she has
Strange ling'ring poisons: I do know her spirit,
And will not trust one of her malice with
A drug of such damn'd nature. Those she has
Will stupify and dull the sense awhile;
Which first, perchance, she'll prove on cats and dogs,
Then afterward up higher: but there is
No danger in what show of death it makes,
More than the locking-up the spirits a time,
To be more fresh, reviving. She is fool'd
With a most false effect; and I the truer,
So to be false with her.
Queen. No further service, doctor,
Until I send for thee.
Cor. I humbly take my leave. *Exit.*
Queen. Weeps she still, say'st thou? Dost thou think in time
She will not quench and let instructions enter
Where folly now possesses? Do thou work:
When thou shalt bring me word she loves my son,
I'll tell thee on the instant thou art then
As great as is thy master, greater, for
His fortunes all lie speechless and his name
Is at last gasp: return he cannot, nor
Continue where he is: to shift his being
Is to exchange one misery with another,
And every day that comes comes to decay
A day's work in him. What shalt thou expect,
To be depender on a thing that leans,
Who cannot be new built, nor has no friends,
So much as but to prop him? [*The Queen drops the box: Pisanio takes it up.*] Thou tak'st up
Thou know'st not what; but take it for thy labour:
It is a thing I made, which hath the king
Five times redeem'd from death: I do not know
What is more cordial. Nay, I prithee, take it;
It is an earnest of a farther good
That I mean to thee. Tell thy mistress how
The case stands with her; do 't as from thyself.
Think what a chance thou changest on, but think
Thou hast thy mistress still, to boot, my son,
Who shall take notice of thee: I'll move the king
To any shape of thy preferment such
As thou 'lt desire; and then myself, I chiefly,
That set thee on to this desert, am bound
To load thy merit richly. Call my women:
Think on my words. *Exit Pisanio.*

167. **commendation,** introduction (to Imogen). **entertainment,** welcome. 178. **counsel,** legal adviser.
SCENE V. 2. **note,** list. 12. **learn'd,** taught. 15. **confections,** compounds of drugs. 18. **conclusions,** experiments. 22. **Allayments,** antidotes. **act,** action. **them,** i.e., the experiments. **gather,** collect a record of. 26. **content thee,** do not trouble thyself. 38. **prove,** test. 41. **locking-up the spirits.** This was the current theory of medicine with reference to potions whose effects were temporary, such as the one employed here and that in *Romeo and Juliet.* 43. **truer,** more honest. 47. **quench,** become cool. 54. **shift his being,** change his abode. 56-57. **And . . . him,** i.e., and every new day brings to him a day of inaction and frustration. 58. **leans,** is about to fall. 64. **cordial,** restorative. 68. **chance . . . on,** opportunity you here discover to change service (?). 76. **shak'd,** shaken (in his loyalty). 77. **remembrancer of her,** one who reminds her. 78. **hand-fast,** marriage contract. 79. **unpeople her,** deprive her of the services of. 80. **liegers,** ambassadors. 81. **Except . . . humour,** unless she change her mind (about not accepting Cloten). 84. **closet,** private chamber.

A sly and constant knave,
Not to be shak'd; the agent for his master
And the remembrancer of her to hold
The hand-fast to her lord. I have given him that
Which, if he take, shall quite unpeople her
Of liegers for her sweet, and which she after,
Except she bend her humour, shall be assur'd
To taste of too.

Enter PISANIO *and* Ladies.

So, so: well done, well done:
The violets, cowslips, and the primroses,
Bear to my closet. Fare thee well, Pisanio;
Think on my words. *Exeunt Queen and Ladies.*

Pis. And shall do:
But when to my good lord I prove untrue,
I'll choke myself: there 's all I'll do for you. *Exit.*

SCENE [VI. *The same. Another room in the palace*].

Enter IMOGEN *alone.*

Imo. A father cruel, and a step-dame false;
A foolish suitor to a wedded lady,
That hath her husband banish'd;—O, that husband!
My supreme crown of grief! and those repeated
Vexations of it! Had I been thief-stol'n,
As my two brothers, happy! but most miserable
Is the desire that 's glorious: blessed be those,
How mean soe'er, that have their honest wills,
Which seasons comfort. Who may this be? Fie!

Enter PISANIO *and* IACHIMO.

Pis. Madam, a noble gentleman of Rome,
Comes from my lord with letters.

Iach. Change you, madam?
The worthy Leonatus is in safety
And greets your highness dearly. [*Presents a letter.*]

Imo. Thanks, good sir:
You 're kindly welcome.

Iach. [*Aside*] All of her that is out of door most rich!
If she be furnish'd with a mind so rare,
She is alone th' Arabian bird, and I
Have lost the wager. Boldness be my friend!
Arm me, audacity, from head to foot!
Or, like the Parthian, I shall flying fight;
Rather, directly fly.

Imo. (*Reads*) 'He is one of the noblest note, to whose kindnesses I am most infinitely tied. Reflect upon him accordingly, as you value your trust— LEONATUS.'
So far I read aloud:
But even the very middle of my heart
Is warm'd by th' rest, and takes it thankfully.
You are as welcome, worthy sir, as I
Have words to bid you, and shall find it so
In all that I can do.

Iach. Thanks, fairest lady.
What, are men mad? Hath nature given them eyes
To see this vaulted arch, and the rich crop
Of sea and land, which can distinguish 'twixt
The fiery orbs above and the twinn'd stones
Upon the number'd beach? and can we not
Partition make with spectacles so precious
'Twixt fair and foul?

Imo. What makes your admiration?

Iach. It cannot be i' th' eye, for apes and monkeys
'Twixt two such shes would chatter this way and
Contemn with mows the other; nor i' th' judgement,
For idiots in this case of favour would
Be wisely definite; nor i' th' appetite;
Sluttery to such neat excellence oppos'd
Should make desire vomit emptiness,
Not so allur'd to feed.

Imo. What is the matter, trow?

Iach. The cloyed will,
That satiate yet unsatisfied desire, that tub
Both fill'd and running, ravening first the lamb
Longs after for the garbage.

Imo. What, dear sir,
Thus raps you? Are you well?

Iach. Thanks, madam; well. [*To Pisanio*] Beseech you, sir, desire
My man's abode where I did leave him:
He 's strange and peevish.

Pis. I was going, sir,
To give him welcome. *Exit.*

Imo. Continues well my lord? His health, beseech you?

Iach. Well, madam.

Imo. Is he dispos'd to mirth? I hope he is.

Iach. Exceeding pleasant; none a stranger there
So merry and so gamesome: he is call'd
The Briton reveller.

Imo. When he was here,
He did incline to sadness, and oft-times
Not knowing why.

Iach. I never saw him sad.
There is a Frenchman his companion, one
An eminent monsieur, that, it seems, much loves
A Gallian girl at home; he furnaces
The thick sighs from him, whiles the jolly Briton—
Your lord, I mean—laughs from 's free lungs, cries 'O,
Can my sides hold, to think that man, who knows
By history, report, or his own proof,
What woman is, yea, what she cannot choose
But must be, will 's free hours languish for
Assured bondage?'

Imo. Will my lord say so?

Iach. Ay, madam, with his eyes in flood with laughter:
It is a recreation to be by
And hear him mock the Frenchman. But, heavens know,
Some men are much to blame.

Imo. Not he, I hope.

Iach. Not he: but yet heaven's bounty towards him might
Be us'd more thankfully. In himself, 'tis much;

SCENE VI. 6-7. **most . . . glorious,** i.e., greatest wretchedness comes from longing for a sublime but unachievable happiness. 8. **honest wills,** simple desires. 9. **seasons comfort,** gives happiness its proper quality. 11. **Comes,** who comes. **Change you,** do you change color? 15. **out of door,** external. 17. **Arabian bird,** the phoenix; pattern of rarity and beauty. 20. **Parthian,** an allusion to the Parthian shot, the Parthians being proverbial in ancient times for discharging a flight of arrows as they fled. 33. **crop,** harvest, produce. 35. **twinn'd,** exactly alike. 36. **number'd,** abounding (in stones). 37. **Partition,** distinction. **spectacles,** organs of vision. 40. **this way,** i.e., toward Imogen. 41. **mows,** grimaces, wry faces. 42. **in . . . favour,** in presence of a face of such beauty. 43. **definite,** resolute. 44. **Sluttery,** the condition of being sluttish or unclean. 45-46. **Should . . . feed,** desire would refuse to satisfy itself and turn away in disgust. 48-49. **That . . . desire, that tub . . . running,** in apposition with *will.* 49. **ravening,** devouring greedily. 51. **raps,** transports. 52-53. **desire . . . abode,** bid my servant remain. 66. **Gallian,** Gallic, French. **furnaces,** gives forth like a furnace.

In you, which I account his beyond all talents,
Whilst I am bound to wonder, I am bound
To pity too.
Imo. What do you pity, sir?
Iach. Two creatures heartily.
Imo. Am I one, sir?
You look on me: what wrack discern you in me
Deserves your pity?
Iach. Lamentable! What,
To hide me from the radiant sun and solace
I' th' dungeon by a snuff?
Imo. I pray you, sir,
Deliver with more openness your answers
To my demands. Why do you pity me?
Iach. That others do—
I was about to say—enjoy your——But
It is an office of the gods to venge it,
Not mine to speak on 't.
Imo. You do seem to know
Something of me, or what concerns me: pray you,—
Since doubting things go ill often hurts more
Than to be sure they do; for certainties
Either are past remedies, or, timely knowing,
The remedy then born—discover to me
What both you spur and stop.
Iach. Had I this cheek
To bathe my lips upon; this hand, whose touch,
Whose every touch, would force the feeler's soul
To th' oath of loyalty; this object, which
Takes prisoner the wild motion of mine eye,
Fixing it only here; should I, damn'd then,
Slaver with lips as common as the stairs
That mount the Capitol; join gripes with hands
Made hard with hourly falsehood—falsehood, as
With labour; then by-peeping in an eye
Base and illustrous as the smoky light
That 's fed with stinking tallow; it were fit
That all the plagues of hell should at one time
Encounter such revolt.
Imo. My lord, I fear,
Has forgot Britain.
Iach. And himself. Not I,
Inclin'd to this intelligence, pronounce
The beggary of his change; but 'tis your graces
That from my mutest conscience to my tongue
Charms this report out.
Imo. Let me hear no more.
Iach. O dearest soul! your cause doth strike my heart
With pity, that doth make me sick. A lady
So fair, and fasten'd to an empery,
Would make the great'st king double,—to be partner'd
With tomboys hir'd with that self exhibition
Which your own coffers yield! with diseas'd ventures
That play with all infirmities for gold
Which rottenness can lend nature! such boil'd stuff
As well might poison poison! Be reveng'd;
Or she that bore you was no queen, and you
Recoil from your great stock.
Imo. Reveng'd!
How should I be reveng'd? If this be true,—
As I have such a heart that both mine ears
Must not in haste abuse—if it be true,
How should I be reveng'd?
Iach. Should he make me
Live, like Diana's priest, betwixt cold sheets,
Whiles he is vaulting variable ramps,
In your despite, upon your purse? Revenge it.
I dedicate myself to your sweet pleasure,
More noble than that runagate to your bed,
And will continue fast to your affection,
Still close as sure.
Imo. What, ho, Pisanio!
Iach. Let me my service tender on your lips.
Imo. Away! I do condemn mine ears that have
So long attended thee. If thou wert honourable,
Thou wouldst have told this tale for virtue, not
For such an end thou seek'st,—as base as strange.
Thou wrong'st a gentleman, who is as far
From thy report as thou from honour, and
Solicits here a lady that disdains
Thee and the devil alike. What ho, Pisanio!
The king my father shall be made acquainted
Of thy assault: if he shall think it fit,
A saucy stranger in his court to mart
As in a Romish stew and to expound
His beastly mind to us, he hath a court
He little cares for and a daughter who
He not respects at all. What, ho, Pisanio!
Iach. O happy Leonatus! I may say:
The credit that thy lady hath of thee
Deserves thy trust, and thy most perfect goodness
Her assur'd credit. Blessed live you long!
A lady to the worthiest sir that ever
Country call'd his! and you his mistress, only
For the most worthiest fit! Give me your pardon.
I have spoke this, to know if your affiance
Were deeply rooted; and shall make your lord,
That which he is, new o'er: and he is one
The truest manner'd; such a holy witch
That he enchants societies into him;
Half all men's hearts are his.
Imo. You make amends.
Iach. He sits 'mongst men like a descended god:
He hath a kind of honour sets him off,
More than a mortal seeming. Be not angry,
Most mighty princess, that I have adventur'd
To try your taking of a false report; which hath
Honour'd with confirmation your great judgement
In the election of a sir so rare,
Which you know cannot err: the love I bear him
Made me to fan you thus, but the gods made you,
Unlike all others, chaffless. Pray, your pardon.
Imo. All 's well, sir: take my pow'r i' th' court for yours.
Iach. My humble thanks. I had almost forgot
T' entreat your grace but in a small request,

80. **talents,** natural endowments, or wealth. 86. **solace,** take delight. 87. **snuff,** burning candlewick. 98. **remedy then born,** i.e., is then born. 99. **spur and stop,** disclose and then conceal. 108. **by-peeping,** giving sidelong glances. 109. **illustrous,** not lustrous. 112. **Encounter,** meet. **revolt,** inconstancy. 113-114. **Not . . . pronounce,** though not inclined to disclose this information, I must report. 116. **mutest,** most silent. 120. **empery,** empire. 121. **double,** as having twice the majesty. **partner'd,** put on a level with. 122. **tomboys,** wantons. **self,** same. **exhibition,** allowance. 123. **ventures,** adventuresses. 125. **boil'd stuff,** i.e., women treated by "sweating" for venereal disease. 128. **Recoil,** fall away, degenerate. 133. **priest,** priestess. 134. **ramps,** prostitutes. 137. **runagate,** renegade. 139. **close,** secret. 142. **attended,** listened to. 151. **saucy,** insolent. **to mart,** should bargain. 152. **stew,** house of prostitution. 160. **sir,** man. 163. **affiance,** fidelity. 165. **new o'er,** refreshed and renewed by, made over again by. 166. **witch,** charmer, fascinating person; used of men as well as women. 167. **into,** unto. 176. **Which,** who. 177. **fan,** test; figure from winnowing of grain. 178. **chaffless,** without

And yet of moment too, for it concerns
Your lord; myself and other noble friends
Are partners in the business.
Imo. Pray, what is 't?
Iach. Some dozen Romans of us and your lord—
The best feather of our wing—have mingled sums
To buy a present for the emperor;
Which I, the factor for the rest, have done
In France: 'tis plate of rare device, and jewels
Of rich and exquisite form; their values great;
And I am something curious, being strange,
To have them in safe stowage: may it please you
To take them in protection?
Imo. Willingly;
And pawn mine honour for their safety: since
My lord hath interest in them, I will keep them
In my bedchamber.
Iach. They are in a trunk,
Attended by my men: I will make bold
To send them to you, only for this night;
I must aboard to-morrow.
Imo. O, no, no.
Iach. Yes, I beseech; or I shall short my word
By length'ning my return. From Gallia
I cross'd the seas on purpose and on promise
To see your grace.
Imo. I thank you for your pains:
But not away to-morrow!
Iach. O, I must, madam:
Therefore I shall beseech you, if you please
To greet your lord with writing, do 't to-night:
I have outstood my time; which is material
To th' tender of our present.
Imo. I will write.
Send your trunk to me; it shall safe be kept,
And truly yielded you. You 're very welcome. *Exeunt.*

ACT II.

SCENE I. [*Britain. Before Cymbeline's palace.*]

Enter CLOTEN *and the two* Lords.

Clo. Was there ever man had such luck! when I kissed the jack, upon an up-cast to be hit away! I had a hundred pound on 't: and then a whoreson jackanapes must take me up for swearing; as if I borrowed mine oaths of him and might not spend them at my pleasure.

First Lord. What got he by that? You have broke his pate with your bowl.

Sec. Lord. [*Aside*] If his wit had been like him that broke it, it would have run all out.

Clo. When a gentleman is disposed to swear, it is not for any standers-by to curtail his oaths, ha?

Sec. Lord. No, my lord; [*Aside*] nor crop the ears of them.

Clo. Whoreson dog! I gave him satisfaction! Would he had been one of my rank!

Sec. Lord. [*Aside*] To have smelt like a fool.

Clo. I am not vexed more at any thing in the earth: a pox on 't! I had rather not be so noble as I am; they dare not fight with me, because of the queen my mother: every Jack-slave hath his bellyful of fighting, and I must go up and down like a cock that nobody can match.

Sec. Lord. [*Aside*] You are cock and capon too; and you crow, cock, with your comb on.

Clo. Sayest thou?

Sec. Lord. It is not fit your lordship should undertake every companion that you give offence to.

Clo. No, I know that: but it is fit I should commit offence to my inferiors.

Sec. Lord. Ay, it is fit for your lordship only.

Clo. Why, so I say.

First Lord. Did you hear of a stranger that 's come to court to-night?

Clo. A stranger, and I not know on 't!

Sec. Lord. [*Aside*] He 's a strange fellow himself, and knows it not.

First Lord. There 's an Italian come; and, 'tis thought, one of Leonatus' friends.

Clo. Leonatus! a banished rascal; and he 's another, whatsoever he be. Who told you of this stranger?

First Lord. One of your lordship's pages.

Clo. Is it fit I went to look upon him? is there no derogation in 't?

Sec. Lord. You cannot derogate, my lord.

Clo. Not easily, I think.

Sec. Lord. [*Aside*] You are a fool granted; therefore your issues, being foolish, do not derogate.

Clo. Come, I'll go see this Italian: what I have lost to-day at bowls I'll win to-night of him. Come, go.

Sec. Lord. I'll attend your lordship.

Exeunt [*Cloten and First Lord*].

That such a crafty devil as is his mother
Should yield the world this ass! a woman that
Bears all down with her brain; and this her son
Cannot take two from twenty, for his heart,
And leave eighteen. Alas, poor princess,
Thou divine Imogen, what thou endur'st,
Betwixt a father by thy step-dame govern'd,
A mother hourly coining plots, a wooer
More hateful than the foul expulsion is
Of thy dear husband, than that horrid act
Of the divorce he 'ld make! The heavens hold firm
The walls of thy dear honour, keep unshak'd
That temple, thy fair mind, that thou mayst stand,
T' enjoy thy banish'd lord and this great land! *Exit.*

SCENE II. [*Imogen's bedchamber in Cymbeline's palace: a trunk in one corner of it.*]

Enter IMOGEN *in her bed, and a* Lady [*attending*].

Imo. Who 's there? my woman Helen?
Lady. Please you, madam.
Imo. What hour is it?

chaff, perfect. 188. **factor,** agent. 191. **curious,** anxious. **strange,** a foreigner. 196. **bedchamber.** Bedchambers were often used for storage of treasure in Elizabethan England. 200. **short my word,** impair my promise. 208. **tender of our present,** offering of our gift.

ACT II. SCENE I. 2. **kissed the jack,** touched and lay near the small bowl used as target in the game of bowls. **up-cast,** throw in the game of bowls. 4. **take me up,** take me to task. 12. **curtail,** shorten, abridge. The word is a corruption of *curtal,* formed to suggest the bobbing of a dog's tail; hence, *crop the ears* (of the *oaths*) below. 17. **rank,** social class; taken, in the aside which follows, to mean "rankness." 22. **Jack-slave,** lowborn fellow. 25. **capon,** castrated rooster, perhaps used quibblingly for "cap on," i.e., with fool's cap or coxcomb. 27. **Sayest thou?** What dost thou say? 29. **undertake,** engage with, give satisfaction. 47. **derogation,** action unbecoming his position. 51. **issues,** deeds, actions. 59. **Bears all down,** triumphs over everyone. 60. **for his heart,** for the life of him.

SCENE II. *Stage Direction:* **in her bed.** On the Elizabethan stage a bed would be "thrust out" at this point, and the trunk carried on.

Lady. Almost midnight, madam.
Imo. I have read three hours then: mine eyes are weak:
Fold down the leaf where I have left: to bed:
Take not away the taper, leave it burning;
And if thou canst awake by four o' th' clock,
I prithee, call me. Sleep hath seiz'd me wholly.
[*Exit Lady.*]
To your protection I commend me, gods.
From fairies and the tempters of the night
Guard me, beseech ye.
Sleeps. Iachimo [*comes*] *from the trunk.*
Iach. The crickets sing, and man's o'er-labour'd sense
Repairs itself by rest. Our Tarquin thus
Did softly press the rushes, ere he waken'd
The chastity he wounded. Cytherea,
How bravely thou becom'st thy bed, fresh lily,
And whiter than the sheets! That I might touch!
But kiss; one kiss! Rubies unparagon'd,
How dearly they do 't! 'Tis her breathing that
Perfumes the chamber thus: the flame o' th' taper
Bows toward her, and would under-peep her lids,
To see th' enclosed lights, now canopied
Under these windows, white and azure lac'd
With blue of heaven's own tinct. But my design,
To note the chamber: I will write all down:
Such and such pictures; there the window; such
Th' adornment of her bed; the arras; figures,
Why, such and such; and the contents o' th' story.
Ah, but some natural notes about her body,
Above ten thousand meaner moveables
Would testify, t' enrich mine inventory.
O sleep, thou ape of death, lie dull upon her!
And be her sense but as a monument,
Thus in a chapel lying! Come off, come off:
[*Taking off her bracelet.*]
As slippery as the Gordian knot was hard!
'Tis mine; and this will witness outwardly,
As strongly as the conscience does within,
To th' madding of her lord. On her left breast
A mole cinque-spotted, like the crimson drops
I' th' bottom of a cowslip: here 's a voucher,
Stronger than ever law could make: this secret
Will force him think I have pick'd the lock and ta'en
The treasure of her honour. No more. To what end?
Why should I write this down, that 's riveted,
Screw'd to my memory? She hath been reading late
The tale of Tereus; here the leaf 's turn'd down
Where Philomel gave up. I have enough:
To th' trunk again, and shut the spring of it.
Swift, swift, you dragons of the night, that dawning
May bare the raven's eye! I lodge in fear;
Though this a heavenly angel, hell is here.
Clock strikes.
One, two, three: time, time!
[*Goes into the trunk.*] *Exeunt.*

SCENE III. [*An ante-chamber adjoining Imogen's apartments.*]

Enter CLOTEN *and* Lords.

First Lord. Your lordship is the most patient man in loss, the most coldest that ever turned up ace.

Clo. It would make any man cold to lose.

First Lord. But not every man patient after the noble temper of your lordship. You are most hot and furious when you win.

Clo. Winning will put any man into courage. If I could get this foolish Imogen, I should have gold enough. It 's almost morning, is 't not?

First Lord. Day, my lord.

Clo. I would this music would come: I am advised to give her music o' mornings; they say it will penetrate.

Enter Musicians.

Come on; tune: if you can penetrate her with your fingering, so; we'll try with tongue too: if none will do, let her remain; but I'll never give o'er. First, a very excellent good-conceited thing; after, a wonderful sweet air, with admirable rich words to it: and then let her consider.

SONG.

Hark, hark! the lark at heaven's gate sings,
And Phœbus 'gins arise,
His steeds to water at those springs
On chalic'd flow'rs that lies;
And winking Mary-buds begin
To ope their golden eyes:
With every thing that pretty is,
My lady sweet, arise:
Arise, arise.

Clo. So, get you gone. If this penetrate, I will consider your music the better: if it do not, it is a vice in her ears, which horse-hairs and calves'-guts, nor the voice of unpaved eunuch to boot, can never amend. [*Exeunt Musicians.*]

Enter CYMBELINE *and* QUEEN.

Sec. Lord. Here comes the king.

Clo. I am glad I was up so late; for that 's the reason I was up so early: he cannot choose but take this service I have done fatherly.—Good morrow to your majesty and to my gracious mother.

Cym. Attend you here the door of our stern daughter? Will she not forth?

Clo. I have assail'd her with musics, but she vouchsafes no notice.

Cym. The exile of her minion is too new;
She hath not yet forgot him: some more time
Must wear the print of his remembrance out,
And then she 's yours.
Queen. You are most bound to th' king,
Who lets go by no vantages that may

SCENE II. 9. **fairies,** evil fairies. 12. **Our Tarquin,** the Roman Sextus Tarquinius in the story of Lucrece. 13. **press the rushes.** Elizabethan floors were strewn with rushes. 14. **Cytherea,** Venus. 22. **windows,** eyelids. 23. **tinct,** color. 26. **arras,** hangings of tapestry. 27. **story,** subject set forth in embroidery on the tapestry. 29. **meaner moveables,** lesser furnishings. 34. **Gordian knot.** According to prophecy whoever untied the knot binding the yoke to the pole of the chariot of Gordius, peasant king of Phrygia, should be king of all Asia. Alexander severed the knot with his sword. 37. **madding,** maddening, making mad. 38. **cinque-spotted,** with five spots. 45. **Tereus,** mythical king of Thrace, who dishonored Philomela, sister of his wife, Procne. He had Philomela's tongue cut out so that she could not tell the story, but she wove it into a tapestry. 49. **raven's eye.** The raven was supposed to wake at early dawn. 50. **this,** this is. 51. **time, time.** Iachimo remembers that Imogen is to be called at four. Presumably the bed and trunk (with Iachimo inside) are carried off stage.

SCENE III. 2. **most coldest,** coolest, most deliberate. 4. **cold,** gloomy, dispirited. 13. **penetrate,** affect (with bawdy double meaning; see also *stand,* erection, and *understand the case,* penetrate the woman's sex, ll. 75, 80). 16. **so,** it is well. 26. **Mary-buds,** buds of marigolds.

Prefer you to his daughter. Frame yourself
To orderly solicits, and be friended
With aptness of the season; make denials
Increase your services; so seem as if
You were inspir'd to do those duties which
You tender to her; that you in all obey her,
Save when command to your dismission tends,
And therein you are senseless.
Clo. Senseless! not so.

[*Enter a* Messenger.]

Mess. So like you, sir, ambassadors from Rome;
The one is Caius Lucius.
Cym. A worthy fellow,
Albeit he comes on angry purpose now;
But that 's no fault of his: we must receive him
According to the honour of his sender;
And towards himself, his goodness forespent on us,
We must extend our notice. Our dear son,
When you have given good morning to your mistress,
Attend the queen and us; we shall have need
T' employ you towards this Roman. Come, our
queen. *Exeunt* [*all but Cloten*].
Clo. If she be up, I'll speak with her; if not,
Let her lie still and dream. [*Knocks*] By your leave, ho!
I know her women are about her: what
If I do line one of their hands? 'Tis gold
Which buys admittance; oft it doth; yea, and makes
Diana's rangers false themselves, yield up
Their deer to th' stand o' th' stealer; and 'tis gold
Which makes the true man kill'd and saves the thief;
Nay, sometime hangs both thief and true man: what
Can it not do and undo? I will make
One of her women lawyer to me, for
I yet not understand the case myself.
By your leave. *Knocks.*

Enter a Lady.

Lady. Who 's there that knocks?
Clo. A gentleman.
Lady. No more?
Clo. Yes, and a gentlewoman's son.
Lady. That 's more
Than some, whose tailors are as dear as yours,
Can justly boast of. What 's your lordship's
pleasure?
Clo. Your lady's person: is she ready?
Lady. Ay,
To keep her chamber.
Clo. There is gold for you;
Sell me your good report.
Lady. How! my good name? or to report of you
What I shall think is good?—The princess!

Enter IMOGEN.

Clo. Good morrow, fairest sister; your sweet hand.
[*Exit Lady.*]
Imo. Good morrow, sir. You lay out too much pains
For purchasing but trouble: the thanks I give
Is telling you that I am poor of thanks
And scarce can spare them.
Clo. Still, I swear I love you.
Imo. If you but said so, 'twere as deep with me:
If you swear still, your recompense is still
That I regard it not.
Clo. This is no answer.
Imo. But that you shall not say I yield being silent,
I would not speak. I pray you, spare me: 'faith,
I shall unfold equal discourtesy
To your best kindness: one of your great knowing
Should learn, being taught, forbearance.
Clo. To leave you in your madness, 'twere my sin:
I will not.
Imo. Fools are not mad folks.
Clo. Do you call me fool?
Imo. As I am mad, I do:
If you'll be patient, I'll no more be mad;
That cures us both. I am much sorry, sir,
You put me to forget a lady's manners,
By being so verbal: and learn now, for all,
That I, which know my heart, do here pronounce,
By th' very truth of it, I care not for you,
And am so near the lack of charity—
To accuse myself—I hate you; which I had rather
You felt than make 't my boast.
Clo. You sin against
Obedience, which you owe your father. For
The contract you pretend with that base wretch,
One bred of alms and foster'd with cold dishes,
With scraps o' th' court, it is no contract, none:
And though it be allow'd in meaner parties—
Yet who than he more mean?—to knit their souls,
On whom there is no more dependency
But brats and beggary, in self-figur'd knot;
Yet you are curb'd from that enlargement by
The consequence o' th' crown, and must not soil
The precious note of it with a base slave,
A hilding for a livery, a squire's cloth,
A pantler, not so eminent.
Imo. Profane fellow!
Wert thou the son of Jupiter and no more
But what thou art besides, thou wert too base
To be his groom: thou wert dignified enough,
Even to the point of envy, if 'twere made
Comparative for your virtues, to be styl'd
The under-hangman of his kingdom, and hated
For being preferr'd so well.
Clo. The south-fog rot him!
Imo. He never can meet more mischance than come
To be but nam'd of thee. His mean'st garment,
That ever hath but clipp'd his body, is dearer
In my respect than all the hairs above thee,
Were they all made such men. How now, Pisanio!

Enter PISANIO.

Clo. 'His garment!' Now the devil—

32. **consider,** reward. 33. **horse-hairs,** of the fiddlebow. 34. **calves'-guts,** fiddlestrings. **unpaved,** unstoned, castrated. 39. **fatherly,** as a father. 51. **Prefer,** recommend. **Frame,** conform. 52. **solicits,** solicitings. 57. **dismission,** dismissal, rejection. 58. **senseless,** insensible (to her commands). Cloten understands the word as meaning "stupid." 59. **So like you,** if you please. 64. **forespent,** previously bestowed. 72. **line,** i.e., with gold. 74. **rangers,** nymphs (vowed to chastity). **false,** verb meaning "turn false." 75. **stand,** station of huntsman waiting for game. 88. **good report,** favorable speech. The Lady understands another meaning of the expression, namely "reputation," "good name." 102. **knowing,** knowledge, discernment; ironical. 111. **By . . . verbal.** If the phrase refers to Cloten, the meaning of *verbal* is "verbose"; if to Imogen, "plain-spoken." 117. **For,** as for. 124. **self-figur'd,** self-contracted. 125. **enlargement,** liberty. 126. **consequence,** succession. 128. **hilding,** good-for-nothing fellow. **for,** fit for. **cloth,** dress, livery. 129. **pantler,** pantry-servant. 134. **Comparative for,** proportioned to, comparing with. 136. **south-fog.** The south wind was supposed to be charged with poisonous vapors and diseases. 139. **clipp'd,** embraced.

Imo. To Dorothy my woman hie thee presently—
Clo. 'His garment!'
Imo. I am sprited with a fool,
Frighted, and ang'red worse: go bid my woman
Search for a jewel that too casually
Hath left mine arm: it was thy master's: 'shrew me,
If I would lose it for a revenue
Of any king's in Europe. I do think
I saw 't this morning: confident I am
Last night 'twas on mine arm; I kiss'd it:
I hope it be not gone to tell my lord
That I kiss aught but he.
Pis. 'Twill not be lost.
Imo. I hope so: go and search. [*Exit Pisanio.*]
Clo. You have abus'd me:
'His meanest garment!'
Imo. Ay, I said so, sir:
If you will make 't an action, call witness to 't.
Clo. I will inform your father.
Imo. Your mother too:
She 's my good lady, and will conceive, I hope,
But the worst of me. So, I leave you, sir,
To th' worst of discontent. *Exit.*
Clo. I'll be reveng'd:
'His meanest garment!' Well. *Exit.*

SCENE IV. [*Rome. Philario's house.*]

Enter POSTHUMUS *and* PHILARIO.

Post. Fear it not, sir: I would I were so sure
To win the king as I am bold her honour
Will remain hers.
Phi. What means do you make to him?
Post. Not any, but abide the change of time,
Quake in the present winter's state and wish
That warmer days would come: in these fear'd hopes,
I barely gratify your love; they failing,
I must die much your debtor.
Phi. Your very goodness and your company
O'erpays all I can do. By this, your king
Hath heard of great Augustus: Caius Lucius
Will do 's commission throughly: and I think
He'll grant the tribute, send th' arrearages,
Or look upon our Romans, whose remembrance
Is yet fresh in their grief.
Post. I do believe,
Statist though I am none, nor like to be,
That this will prove a war; and you shall hear
The legions now in Gallia sooner landed
In our not-fearing Britain than have tidings
Of any penny tribute paid. Our countrymen
Are men more order'd than when Julius Cæsar
Smil'd at their lack of skill, but found their courage
Worthy his frowning at: their discipline,
Now mingled with their courages, will make known
To their approvers they are people such
That mend upon the world.

Enter IACHIMO.

Phi. See! Iachimo!
Post. The swiftest harts have posted you by land;
And winds of all the corners kiss'd your sails,
To make your vessel nimble.
Phi. Welcome, sir.
Post. I hope the briefness of your answer made
The speediness of your return.
Iach. Your lady
Is one of the fairest that I have look'd upon.
Post. And therewithal the best; or let her beauty
Look through a casement to allure false hearts
And be false with them.
Iach. Here are letters for you.
Post. Their tenour good, I trust.
Iach. 'Tis very like.
Phi. Was Caius Lucius in the Britain court
When you were there?
Iach. He was expected then,
But not approach'd.
Post. All is well yet.
Sparkles this stone as it was wont? or is 't not
Too dull for your good wearing?
Iach. If I had lost it,
I should have lost the worth of it in gold.
I'll make a journey twice as far, t' enjoy
A second night of such sweet shortness which
Was mine in Britain, for the ring is won.
Post. The stone 's too hard to come by.
Iach. Not a whit,
Your lady being so easy.
Post. Make not, sir,
Your loss your sport: I hope you know that we
Must not continue friends.
Iach. Good sir, we must,
If you keep covenant. Had I not brought
The knowledge of your mistress home, I grant
We were to question farther: but I now
Profess myself the winner of her honour,
Together with your ring; and not the wronger
Of her or you, having proceeded but
By both your wills.
Post. If you can make 't apparent
That you have tasted her in bed, my hand
And ring is yours; if not, the foul opinion
You had of her pure honour gains or loses
Your sword or mine, or masterless leaves both
To who shall find them.
Iach. Sir, my circumstances,
Being so near the truth as I will make them,
Must first induce you to believe: whose strength
I will confirm with oath; which, I doubt not,
You'll give me leave to spare, when you shall find
You need it not.
Post. Proceed.
Iach. First, her bedchamber,—
Where, I confess, I slept not, but profess
Had that was well worth watching—it was hang'd
With tapestry of silk and silver; the story
Proud Cleopatra, when she met her Roman,
And Cydnus swell'd above the banks, or for
The press of boats or pride: a piece of work
So bravely done, so rich, that it did strive
In workmanship and value; which I wonder'd
Could be so rarely and exactly wrought,

144. **sprited,** haunted. 156. **action,** action at law. 158. **my good lady,** patroness (ironical). **conceive,** believe, think.
SCENE IV. 2. **bold,** confident. 3. **means,** approach. 6. **fear'd,** mixed with fear. 13. **arrearages,** arrears, parts of the tribute due but unpaid. 14. **Or look,** before he will look. 16. **Statist,** statesman. 21. **more order'd,** better disciplined and governed. 25. **approvers,** those who test (their courage). 26. **mend upon,** improve. 52. **question,** debate; here, settle matters by a duel. 71. **Cydnus,** a river in Cilicia, the scene of the meeting of Antony and Cleopatra which is described in *Antony and Cleopatra*, II, ii, 191-231. 83-85. **the cutter . . .**

Since the true life on 't was—
Post. This is true;
And this you might have heard of here, by me,
Or by some other.
Iach. More particulars
Must justify my knowledge.
Post. So they must,
Or do your honour injury.
Iach. The chimney
Is south the chamber, and the chimney-piece
Chaste Dian bathing: never saw I figures
So likely to report themselves: the cutter
Was as another nature, dumb; outwent her,
Motion and breath left out.
Post. This is a thing
Which you might from relation likewise reap,
Being, as it is, much spoke of.
Iach. The roof o' th' chamber
With golden cherubins is fretted: her andirons—
I had forgot them—were two winking Cupids
Of silver, each on one foot standing, nicely
Depending on their brands.
Post. This is her honour!
Let it be granted you have seen all this—and praise
Be given to your remembrance—the description
Of what is in her chamber nothing saves
The wager you have laid.
Iach. Then, if you can,
[*Showing the bracelet.*]
Be pale: I beg but leave to air this jewel; see!
And now 'tis up again: it must be married
To that your diamond; I'll keep them.
Post. Jove!
Once more let me behold it: is it that
Which I left with her?
Iach. Sir—I thank her—that:
She stripp'd it from her arm; I see her yet;
Her pretty action did outsell her gift,
And yet enrich'd it too: she gave it me, and said
She priz'd it once.
Post. May be she pluck'd it off
To send it me.
Iach. She writes so to you, doth she?
Post. O, no, no, no! 'tis true. Here, take this too;
[*Gives the ring.*]
It is a basilisk unto mine eye,
Kills me to look on 't. Let there be no honour
Where there is beauty; truth, where semblance; love,
Where there 's another man: the vows of women
Of no more bondage be, to where they are made,
Than they are to their virtues; which is nothing.
O, above measure false!
Phi. Have patience, sir,
And take your ring again; 'tis not yet won:
It may be probable she lost it; or
Who knows if one of her women, being corrupted,
Hath stol'n it from her?
Post. Very true;
And so, I hope, he came by 't. Back my ring:
Render to me some corporal sign about her,
More evident than this; for this was stol'n.
Iach. By Jupiter, I had it from her arm.
Post. Hark you, he swears; by Jupiter he swears.
'Tis true:—nay, keep the ring—'tis true: I am sure
She would not lose it: her attendants are
All sworn and honourable:—they induc'd to steal it!
And by a stranger!—No, he hath enjoy'd her:
The cognizance of her incontinency
Is this: she hath bought the name of whore thus
dearly.
There, take thy hire; and all the fiends of hell
Divide themselves between you!
Phi. Sir, be patient:
This is not strong enough to be believ'd
Of one persuaded well of—
Post. Never talk on 't;
She hath been colted by him.
Iach. If you seek
For further satisfying, under her breast—
Worthy the pressing—lies a mole, right proud
Of that most delicate lodging: by my life,
I kiss'd it; and it gave me present hunger
To feed again, though full. You do remember
This stain upon her?
Post. Ay, and it doth confirm
Another stain, as big as hell can hold,
Were there no more but it.
Iach. Will you hear more?
Post. Spare your arithmetic: never count the turns;
Once, and a million!
Iach. I'll be sworn—
Post. No swearing.
If you will swear you have not done 't, you lie;
And I will kill thee, if thou dost deny
Thou'st made me cuckold.
Iach. I'll deny nothing.
Post. O, that I had her here, to tear her limb-meal!
I will go there and do 't, i' th' court, before
Her father. I'll do something— *Exit.*
Phi. Quite besides
The government of patience! You have won:
Let 's follow him, and pervert the present wrath
He hath against himself.
Iach. With all my heart. *Exeunt.*

[SCENE V. *Another room in Philario's house.*]

Enter POSTHUMUS.

Post. Is there no way for men to be but women
Must be half-workers? We are all bastards;
And that most venerable man which I
Did call my father, was I know not where
When I was stamp'd; some coiner with his tools
Made me a counterfeit: yet my mother seem'd
The Dian of that time: so doth my wife
The nonpareil of this. O, vengeance, vengeance!
Me of my lawful pleasure she restrain'd
And pray'd me oft forbearance; did it with
A pudency so rosy the sweet view on 't
Might well have warm'd old Saturn; that I thought
her
As chaste as unsunn'd snow. O, all the devils!
This yellow Iachimo, in an hour,—was 't not?—

out, the sculptor, though unable to impart voice, was like nature; indeed surpassed her but for motion and breath. 86. **relation,** hearsay. 88. **fretted,** adorned with carved or embossed work in decorative patterns (Onions). 91. **Depending,** leaning. **brands,** torches, i.e., of the Cupids. 97. **up,** put up, pocketed. 102. **outsell,** exceed in value. 111. **bondage,** obligation. 127. **cognizance,** mark or token by which a thing is recognized. 133. **colted,** enjoyed sexually. 147. **limb-meal,** limb from limb. 149. **besides,** beyond. 151. **pervert,** turn, divert.

SCENE V. 1. **be,** exist. 8. **nonpareil,** one that has no equal. 11. **pudency,** modesty.

Or less,—at first?—perchance he spoke not, but,
Like a full-acorn'd boar, a German one,
Cried 'O!' and mounted; found no opposition
But what he look'd for should oppose and she
Should from encounter guard. Could I find out
The woman's part in me! For there 's no motion
That tends to vice in man, but I affirm
It is the woman's part: be it lying, note it,
The woman's; flattering, hers; deceiving, hers;
Lust and rank thoughts, hers, hers; revenges, hers;
Ambitions, covetings, change of prides, disdain,
Nice longing, slanders, mutability,
All faults that may be nam'd, nay, that hell knows,
Why, hers, in part or all; but rather, all;
For even to vice
They are not constant, but are changing still
One vice, but of a minute old, for one
Not half so old as that. I'll write against them,
Detest them, curse them: yet 'tis greater skill
In a true hate, to pray they have their will:
The very devils cannot plague them better. *Exit.*

ACT III.

SCENE I. [*Britain. A hall in Cymbeline's palace.*]

Enter in state, CYMBELINE, QUEEN, CLOTEN, *and* Lords *at one door, and at another*, CAIUS LUCIUS *and* Attendants.

Cym. Now say, what would Augustus Cæsar with us?
Luc. When Julius Cæsar, whose remembrance yet
Lives in men's eyes and will to ears and tongues
Be theme and hearing ever, was in this Britain
And conquer'd it, Cassibelan, thine uncle,—
Famous in Cæsar's praises, no whit less
Than in his feats deserving it—for him
And his succession granted Rome a tribute,
Yearly three thousand pounds, which by thee lately
Is left untender'd.
Queen. And, to kill the marvel,
Shall be so ever.
Clo. There be many Cæsars,
Ere such another Julius. Britain's a world
By itself; and we will nothing pay
For wearing our own noses.
Queen. That opportunity
Which then they had to take from 's, to resume
We have again. Remember, sir, my liege,
The kings your ancestors, together with
The natural bravery of your isle, which stands
As Neptune's park, ribbed and paled in
With rocks unscaleable and roaring waters,
With sands that will not bear your enemies' boats,
But suck them up to th' topmast. A kind of conquest
Cæsar made here; but made not here his brag
Of 'Came' and 'saw' and 'overcame:' with shame—
The first that ever touch'd him—he was carried
From off our coast, twice beaten; and his shipping—
Poor ignorant baubles!—on our terrible seas,
Like egg-shells mov'd upon their surges, crack'd
As easily 'gainst our rocks: for joy whereof
The fam'd Cassibelan, who was once at point—
O giglot fortune!—to master Cæsar's sword,
Made Lud's town with rejoicing fires bright
And Britons strut with courage.

Clo. Come, there 's no more tribute to be paid: our kingdom is stronger than it was at that time; and, as I said, there is no moe such Cæsars: other of them may have crook'd noses, but to owe such straight arms, none.

Cym. Son, let your mother end.

Clo. We have yet many among us can gripe as hard as Cassibelan: I do not say I am one; but I have a hand. Why tribute? why should we pay tribute? If Cæsar can hide the sun from us with a blanket, or put the moon in his pocket, we will pay him tribute for light; else, sir, no more tribute, pray you now.

Cym. You must know,
Till the injurious Romans did extort
This tribute from us, we were free: Cæsar's ambition,
Which swell'd so much that it did almost stretch
The sides o' th' world, against all colour here
Did put the yoke upon 's; which to shake off
Becomes a warlike people, whom we reckon
Ourselves to be.
Clo. and Lords. We do.
Cym. Say, then to Cæsar,
Our ancestor was that Mulmutius which
Ordain'd our laws, whose use the sword of Cæsar
Hath too much mangled; whose repair and franchise
Shall, by the power we hold, be our good deed,
Though Rome be therefore angry: Mulmutius made
our laws,
Who was the first of Britain which did put
His brows within a golden crown and call'd
Himself a king.
Luc. I am sorry, Cymbeline,
That I am to pronounce Augustus Cæsar—
Cæsar, that hath moe kings his servants than
Thyself domestic officers—thine enemy:
Receive it from me, then: war and confusion
In Cæsar's name pronounce I 'gainst thee: look
For fury not to be resisted. Thus defied,
I thank thee for myself.
Cym. Thou art welcome, Caius.
Thy Cæsar knighted me; my youth I spent
Much under him; of him I gather'd honour;
Which he to seek of me again, perforce,
Behoves me keep at utterance. I am perfect
That the Pannonians and Dalmatians for
Their liberties are now in arms; a precedent
Which not to read would show the Britons cold:
So Cæsar shall not find them.
Luc. Let proof speak.

Clo. His majesty bids you welcome. Make pastime with us a day or two, or longer: if you seek us afterwards in other terms, you shall find us in our salt-water girdle: if you beat us out of it, it is yours; if you

25. **change of prides,** varying vanities (in dress, etc.). 26. **Nice,** fastidious. **mutability,** inconstancy. 32. **write against,** denounce. 33. **skill,** reason.

ACT III. SCENE I. 10. **kill the marvel,** end the surprise (by making nonpayment a regular practice). 19. **paled,** fenced. 27. **ignorant,** silly, unskilled. 30. **Cassibelan.** The incident referred to is recorded of Nennius, brother of Cassibelan, in Holinshed. 30-31. **at point . . . to master,** on the point . . . of mastering. 31. **giglot,** lewd, wanton. 32. **Lud's town,** London. 37. **owe,** own. 40. **gripe,** grasp (a sword). 48. **injurious,** malicious, or insolent. 51. **against all colour,** in opposition to all reason. 53. **whom,** which. 55. **Mulmutius.** Holinshed gives an account of the beneficent reign of Mulmutius. 57. **franchise,** free exercise. 64. **moe,** more. **his,** as his. 72. **he to seek,** since he seeks it. 73. **keep at utterance,** defend to the last extremity. **perfect,** well fall in the adventure, our crows shall fare the better for you; and there 's an end.

Luc. So, sir.

Cym. I know your master's pleasure and he mine:
All the remain is 'Welcome!' *Exeunt.*

SCENE II. [*Another room in the palace.*]

Enter PISANIO, *reading of a letter.*

Pis. How! of adultery? Wherefore write you not
What monsters her accuse? Leonatus!
O master! what a strange infection
Is fall'n into thy ear! What false Italian,
As poisonous-tongu'd as handed, hath prevail'd
On thy too ready hearing? Disloyal! No:
She 's punish'd for her truth, and undergoes,
More goddess-like than wife-like, such assaults
As would take in some virtue. O my master!
Thy mind to her is now as low as were
Thy fortunes. How! that I should murder her?
Upon the love and truth and vows which I
Have made to thy command? I, her? her blood?
If it be so to do good service, never
Let me be counted serviceable. How look I,
That I should seem to lack humanity
So much as this fact comes to? [*Reading*] 'Do 't: the letter
That I have sent her, by her own command
Shall give thee opportunity.' O damn'd paper!
Black as the ink that 's on thee! Senseless bauble,
Art thou a feodary for this act, and look'st
So virgin-like without? Lo, here she comes.

Enter IMOGEN.

I am ignorant in what I am commanded.

Imo. How now, Pisanio!

Pis. Madam, here is a letter from my lord.

Imo. Who? thy lord? that is my lord, Leonatus!
O, learn'd indeed were that astronomer
That knew the stars as I his characters;
He 'ld lay the future open. You good gods,
Let what is here contain'd relish of love,
Of my lord's health, of his content, yet not
That we two are asunder; let that grieve him:
Some griefs are med'cinable; that is one of them,
For it doth physic love: of his content,
All but in that! Good wax, thy leave. Blest be
You bees that make these locks of counsel! Lovers
And men in dangerous bonds pray not alike:
Though forfeiters you cast in prison, yet
You clasp young Cupid's tables. Good news, gods!

[*Reads*] 'Justice, and your father's wrath, should he take me in his dominion, could not be so cruel to me, as you, O the dearest of creatures, would even renew me with your eyes. Take notice that I am in Cambria, at Milford-Haven: what your own love will out of this advise you, follow. So he wishes you all happiness, that remains loyal to his vow, and your, increasing in love, LEONATUS POSTHUMUS.'

O, for a horse with wings! Hear'st thou, Pisanio?
He is at Milford-Haven: read, and tell me
How far 'tis thither. If one of mean affairs
May plod it in a week, why may not I
Glide thither in a day? Then, true Pisanio,—
Who long'st, like me, to see thy lord; who long'st,—
O, let me bate,—but not like me—yet long'st,
But in a fainter kind:—O, not like me;
For mine 's beyond beyond—say, and speak thick;
Love's counsellor should fill the bores of hearing,
To th' smothering of the sense—how far it is
To this same blessed Milford: and by th' way
Tell me how Wales was made so happy as
T' inherit such a haven: but first of all,
How we may steal from hence, and for the gap
That we shall make in time, from our hence-going
And our return, to excuse: but first, how get hence:
Why should excuse be born or ere begot?
We'll talk of that hereafter. Prithee, speak,
How many score of miles may we well rid
'Twixt hour and hour?

Pis. One score 'twixt sun and sun,
Madam, 's enough for you: [*Aside*] and too much too.

Imo. Why, one that rode to 's execution, man,
Could never go so slow: I have heard of riding wagers,
Where horses have been nimbler than the sands
That run i' th' clock's behalf. But this is fool'ry:
Go bid my woman feign a sickness; say
She'll home to her father: and provide me presently
A riding-suit, no costlier than would fit
A franklin's housewife.

Pis. Madam, you 're best consider.

Imo. I see before me, man: nor here, nor here,
Nor what ensues, but have a fog in them,
That I cannot look through. Away, I prithee;
Do as I bid thee: there 's no more to say;
Accessible is none but Milford way. *Exeunt.*

SCENE III. [*Wales: a mountainous country with a cave.*]

Enter [*from the cave*] BELARIUS; GUIDERIUS, *and* ARVIRAGUS [*following*].

Bel. A goodly day not to keep house, with such
Whose roof 's as low as ours! Stoop, boys; this gate
Instructs you how t' adore the heavens and bows you
To a morning's holy office: the gates of monarchs
Are arch'd so high that giants may jet through
And keep their impious turbans on, without
Good morrow to the sun. Hail, thou fair heaven!
We house i' th' rock, yet use thee not so hardly
As prouder livers do.

Gui. Hail, heaven!

Arv. Hail, heaven!

Bel. Now for our mountain sport: up to yond hill;
Your legs are young; I'll tread these flats. Consider,
When you above perceive me like a crow,
That it is place which lessens and sets off:
And you may then revolve what tales I have told you
Of courts, of princes, of the tricks in war:

aware. 87. **remain,** remainder, rest.

SCENE II. 9. **take in,** cause to yield, conquer. 10. **to,** compared to. 21. **feodary,** accomplice. 28. **characters,** handwriting. 36. **locks of counsel,** waxen seals enclosing confidential matters. 38. **forfeiters,** those who forfeit their bonds. The contrast is between the waxen seals on forfeited bonds and on love letters. 39. **tables,** tablets. 44. **Cambria,** Wales. 52. **mean affairs,** ordinary business. 58. **thick,** quickly, fast. 69. **rid,** cover. 75. **i' th' clock's behalf,** i.e., doing the service of a clock. 79. **franklin's,** yeoman's. A *franklin* was a farmer who owned his own land but was not of noble birth. **you 're best,** you had better.

SCENE III. *Stage Direction:* ***from the cave,*** i.e., through one of the tiring-house doors. 1. **keep house,** stay at home. 3. **bows you,** makes you bow. 5. **jet,** walk pompously, strut. 13. **place,** position.

This service is not service, so being done,
But being so allow'd: to apprehend thus,
Draws us a profit from all things we see;
And often, to our comfort, shall we find
The sharded beetle in a safer hold
Than is the full-wing'd eagle. O, this life
Is nobler than attending for a check,
Richer than doing nothing for a bauble,
Prouder than rustling in unpaid-for silk:
Such gain the cap of him that makes him fine,
Yet keeps his book uncross'd: no life to ours.

Gui. Out of your proof you speak: we, poor unfledg'd,
Have never wing'd from view o' th' nest, nor know not
What air 's from home. Haply this life is best,
If quiet life be best; sweeter to you
That have a sharper known; well corresponding
With your stiff age: but unto us it is
A cell of ignorance; travelling a-bed;
A prison for a debtor, that not dares
To stride a limit.

Arv. What should we speak of
When we are old as you? when we shall hear
The rain and wind beat dark December, how,
In this our pinching cave, shall we discourse
The freezing hours away? We have seen nothing;
We are beastly, subtle as the fox for prey,
Like warlike as the wolf for what we eat;
Our valour is to chase what flies; our cage
We make a quire, as doth the prison'd bird,
And sing our bondage freely.

Bel. How you speak!
Did you but know the city's usuries
And felt them knowingly; the art o' th' court,
As hard to leave as keep; whose top to climb
Is certain falling, or so slipp'ry that
The fear 's as bad as falling; the toil o' th' war,
A pain that only seems to seek out danger
I' th' name of fame and honour; which dies i' th' search,
And hath as oft a sland'rous epitaph
As record of fair act; nay, many times,
Doth ill deserve by doing well; what 's worse,
Must court'sy at the censure:—O boys, this story
The world may read in me: my body 's mark'd
With Roman swords, and my report was once
First with the best of note: Cymbeline lov'd me,
And when a soldier was the theme, my name
Was not far off: then was I as a tree
Whose boughs did bend with fruit: but in one night,
A storm or robbery, call it what you will,
Shook down my mellow hangings, nay, my leaves,
And left me bare to weather.

Gui. Uncertain favour!

Bel. My fault being nothing—as I have told you oft—
But that two villains, whose false oaths prevail'd
Before my perfect honour, swore to Cymbeline
I was confederate with the Romans: so
Follow'd my banishment, and this twenty years
This rock and these demesnes have been my world;
Where I have liv'd at honest freedom, paid
More pious debts to heaven than in all
The fore-end of my time. But up to th' mountains!
This is not hunters' language: he that strikes
The venison first shall be the lord o' th' feast;
To him the other two shall minister;
And we will fear no poison, which attends
In place of greater state. I'll meet you in the valleys.

Exeunt [Guiderius and Arviragus].

How hard it is to hide the sparks of nature!
These boys know little they are sons to th' king;
Nor Cymbeline dreams that they are alive.
They think they are mine; and though train'd up thus meanly
I' th' cave wherein they bow, their thoughts do hit
The roofs of palaces, and nature prompts them
In simple and low things to prince it much
Beyond the trick of others. This Polydore,
The heir of Cymbeline and Britain, who
The king his father call'd Guiderius,—Jove!
When on my three-foot stool I sit and tell
The warlike feats I have done, his spirits fly out
Into my story: say 'Thus mine enemy fell,
And thus I set my foot on 's neck;' even then
The princely blood flows in his cheek, he sweats,
Strains his young nerves and puts himself in posture
That acts my words. The younger brother, Cadwal,
Once Arviragus, in as like a figure,
Strikes life into my speech and shows much more
His own conceiving.—Hark, the game is rous'd!—
O Cymbeline! heaven and my conscience knows
Thou didst unjustly banish me: whereon,
At three and two years old, I stole these babes;
Thinking to bar thee of succession, as
Thou reft'st me of my lands. Euriphile,
Thou wast their nurse; they took thee for their mother,
And every day do honour to her grave:
Myself, Belarius, that am Morgan call'd,
They take for natural father. The game is up. *Exit.*

SCENE IV. [*Country near Milford-Haven.*]

Enter PISANIO *and* IMOGEN.

Imo. Thou told'st me, when we came from horse, the place
Was near at hand: ne'er long'd my mother so
To see me first, as I have now. Pisanio! man!
Where is Posthumus? What is in thy mind,
That makes thee stare thus? Wherefore breaks that sigh
From th' inward of thee? One, but painted thus,
Would be interpreted a thing perplex'd
Beyond self-explication: put thyself
Into a haviour of less fear, ere wildness

17. **allow'd,** acknowledged. 20. **sharded,** covered with shards or the sheaths of insects' wings. 22. **attending,** doing service (at court). **check,** rebuke. 23. **bauble,** so Rowe; F: *Babe;* Hanmer: *bribe.* 25-26. **Such . . . uncross'd,** such a one is adulated by elegant fops without having to pay his bill. 27. **proof,** experience. **we, poor unfledg'd.** The youths of royal blood have born in them a taste for kingly courts and noble deeds. 29. **air 's from,** air there is away from. 33. **a-bed,** i.e., in dreams only. 35. **stride a limit,** overpass a bound. 41. **Like,** equally. 58. **note,** distinction, importance. 63. **hangings,** hanging fruit. 70. **demesnes,** domains, regions. 73. **fore-end,** earlier part. 83. **bow,** stoop in entering. 85. **prince,** play the prince. 86. **trick,** capability. 94. **nerves,** sinews, parts of the body in which the chief strength lies. 96. **in . . . figure,** acting his part equally well. 103. **reft'st,** didst deprive. 107. **up,** roused.

SCENE IV. 9. **haviour,** behavior. 15. **drug-damn'd,** condemned for its drugs and poisons. **out-craftied,** outwitted. 17. **take . . . extremity,** reduce somewhat the shock. 32. **pandar,** accomplice. 37. **worms,** serpents. 44. **charge,** lead, burden (figurative). 51. **jay,**

Vanquish my staider senses. What 's the matter?
Why tender'st thou that paper to me, with
A look untender? If 't be summer news,
Smile to 't before; if winterly, thou need'st
But keep that count'nance still. My husband's hand!
That drug-damn'd Italy hath out-craftied him,
And he 's at some hard point. Speak, man: thy tongue
May take off some extremity, which to read
Would be even mortal to me.
  Pis. Please you, read;
And you shall find me, wretched man, a thing
The most disdain'd of fortune.

Imo. (*Reads*) 'Thy mistress, Pisanio, hath played the strumpet in my bed; the testimonies whereof lie bleeding in me. I speak not out of weak surmises, but from proof as strong as my grief and as certain as I expect my revenge. That part thou, Pisanio, must act for me, if thy faith be not tainted with the breach of hers. Let thine own hands take away her life: I shall give thee opportunity at Milford-Haven. She hath my letter for the purpose: where, if thou fear to strike and to make me certain it is done, thou art the pandar to her dishonour and equally to me disloyal.'

  Pis. What shall I need to draw my sword? the paper
Hath cut her throat already. No, 'tis slander,
Whose edge is sharper than the sword, whose tongue
Outvenoms all the worms of Nile, whose breath
Rides on the posting winds and doth belie
All corners of the world: kings, queens and states,
Maids, matrons, nay, the secrets of the grave
This viperous slander enters. What cheer, madam?
  Imo. False to his bed! What is it to be false?
To lie in watch there and to think on him?
To weep 'twixt clock and clock? if sleep charge nature,
To break it with a fearful dream of him
And cry myself awake? that 's false to 's bed, is it?
  Pis. Alas, good lady!
  Imo. I false! Thy conscience witness: Iachimo,
Thou didst accuse him of incontinency;
Thou then look'dst like a villain; now methinks
Thy favour 's good enough. Some jay of Italy
†Whose mother was her painting, hath betray'd him:
Poor I am stale, a garment out of fashion;
And, for I am richer than to hang by th' walls,
I must be ripp'd:—to pieces with me!—O,
Men's vows are women's traitors! All good seeming,
By thy revolt, O husband, shall be thought
Put on for villany; not born where 't grows,
But worn a bait for ladies.
  Pis. Good madam, hear me.
  Imo. True honest men being heard, like false Æneas,
Were in his time thought false, and Sinon's weeping
Did scandal many a holy tear, took pity
From most true wretchedness: so thou, Posthumus,
Wilt lay the leaven on all proper men;
Goodly and gallant shall be false and perjur'd
From thy great fail. Come, fellow, be thou honest:
Do thou thy master's bidding: when thou see'st him,
A little witness my obedience: look!
I draw the sword myself: take it, and hit
The innocent mansion of my love, my heart:
Fear not; 'tis empty of all things but grief:
Thy master is not there, who was indeed
The riches of it: do his bidding; strike.
Thou mayst be valiant in a better cause;
But now thou seem'st a coward.
  Pis. Hence, vile instrument!
Thou shalt not damn my hand.
  Imo. Why, I must die;
And if I do not by thy hand, thou art
No servant of thy master's. Against self-slaughter
There is a prohibition so divine
That cravens my weak hand. Come, here 's my heart.
Something 's afore 't. Soft, soft! we'll no defence;
Obedient as the scabbard. What is here?
The scriptures of the loyal Leonatus,
All turn'd to heresy? Away, away,
Corrupters of my faith! you shall no more
Be stomachers to my heart. Thus may poor fools
Believe false teachers: though those that are betray'd
Do feel the treason sharply, yet the traitor
Stands in worse case of woe.
And thou, Posthumus, thou that didst set up
My disobedience 'gainst the king my father
And make me put into contempt the suits
Of princely fellows, shalt hereafter find
It is no act of common passage, but
A strain of rareness: and I grieve myself
To think, when thou shalt be disedg'd by her
That now thou tirest on, how thy memory
Will then be pang'd by me. Prithee, dispatch:
The lamb entreats the butcher: where 's thy knife?
Thou art too slow to do thy master's bidding,
When I desire it too.
  Pis. O gracious lady,
Since I receiv'd command to do this business
I have not slept one wink.
  Imo. Do 't, and to bed then.
  Pis. I'll wake mine eye-balls blind first.
  Imo. Wherefore then
Didst undertake it? Why hast thou abus'd
So many miles with a pretence? this place?
Mine action and thine own? our horses' labour?
The time inviting thee? the perturb'd court,
For my being absent? whereunto I never
Purpose return. Why hast thou gone so far,
To be unbent when thou hast ta'en thy stand,
Th' elected deer before thee?
  Pis. But to win time
To lose so bad employment; in the which
I have consider'd of a course. Good lady,
Hear me with patience.
  Imo. Talk thy tongue weary; speak:
I have heard I am a strumpet; and mine ear,
Therein false struck, can take no greater wound,
Nor tent to bottom that. But speak.

flashy or light woman. 52. **Whose . . . painting,** explained as "who owed her beauty to her painted face"; i.e., a creature born and made up of the paint pot (Dowden); also as "whose painted face was the sum of her woman-like qualities." 60. **Æneas,** thought of as the pattern of faithless love because of his desertion of Dido. 61. **Sinon's.** The Greek Sinon by his guile persuaded the Trojans to introduce within the walls of Troy the wooden horse filled with armed men. 64. **lay the leaven on,** taint, corrupt. 66. **fail,** fault, offense. 80. **cravens,** renders cowardly. 81. **Something 's,** i.e., Posthumus' letter. 83. **scriptures,** writings. It suggests the ordinary meaning, which is played on in what follows; also, the letters which she has from Leonatus have been as Holy Writ to her. 86. **stomachers,** ornamental coverings for the breast. 90. **set up,** incite, encourage. 94-95. **It . . . rareness,** that my choice of you is no act of ordinary occurrence but a rare and high-pitched impulse (of the heart). 96. **disedg'd,** surfeited. 97. **tirest on,** tearest or devourest (as a bird of prey). 98. **pang'd,** pained. 104. **blind,** so Hanmer; Johnson: *out;* F omits. 111. **unbent,** with unbent bow. 112. **elected,** chosen. 118. **Nor . . . that,** nor probe that to the bottom.

Pis. Then, madam,
I thought you would not back again.
Imo. Most like;
Bringing me here to kill me.
Pis. Not so, neither:
But if I were as wise as honest, then
My purpose would prove well. It cannot be
But that my master is abus'd:
Some villain, ay, and singular in his art,
Hath done you both this cursed injury.
Imo. Some Roman courtezan.
Pis. No, on my life.
I'll give but notice you are dead and send him
Some bloody sign of it; for 'tis commanded
I should do so: you shall be miss'd at court,
And that will well confirm it.
Imo. Why, good fellow,
What shall I do the while? where bide? how live?
Or in my life what comfort, when I am
Dead to my husband?
Pis. If you'll back to th' court—
Imo. No court, no father; nor no more ado
†With that harsh, noble, simple nothing,
That Cloten, whose love-suit hath been to me
As fearful as a siege.
Pis. If not at court,
Then not in Britain must you bide.
Imo. Where then?
Hath Britain all the sun that shines? Day, night,
Are they not but in Britain? I' th' world's volume
Our Britain seems as of it, but not in 't;
In a great pool a swan's nest: prithee, think
There 's livers out of Britain.
Pis. I am most glad
You think of other place. Th' ambassador,
Lucius the Roman, comes to Milford-Haven
To-morrow: now, if you could wear a mind
Dark as your fortune is, and but disguise
That which, t' appear itself, must not yet be
But by self-danger, you should tread a course
†Pretty and full of view; yea, haply, near
The residence of Posthumus; so nigh at least
That though his actions were not visible, yet
Report should render him hourly to your ear
As truly as he moves.
Imo. O, for such means!
Though peril to my modesty, not death on 't,
I would adventure.
Pis. Well, then, here 's the point:
You must forget to be a woman; change
Command into obedience: fear and niceness—
The handmaids of all women, or, more truly,
Woman it pretty self—into a waggish courage;
Ready in gibes, quick-answer'd, saucy and
As quarrelous as the weasel; nay, you must
Forget that rarest treasure of your cheek,
Exposing it—but, O, the harder heart!
Alack, no remedy!—to the greedy touch
Of common-kissing Titan, and forget
Your laboursome and dainty trims, wherein
You made great Juno angry.
Imo. Nay, be brief:
I see into thy end, and am almost
A man already.
Pis. First, make yourself but like one.
Fore-thinking this, I have already fit—
'Tis in my cloak-bag—doublet, hat, hose, all
That answer to them: would you in their serving,
And with what imitation you can borrow
From youth of such a season, 'fore noble Lucius
Present yourself, desire his service, tell him
Wherein you 're happy,—which will make him know,
If that his head have ear in music,—doubtless
With joy he will embrace you, for he 's honourable
And doubling that, most holy. Your means abroad,
You have me, rich; and I will never fail
Beginning nor supplyment.
Imo. Thou art all the comfort
The gods will diet me with. Prithee, away:
There 's more to be consider'd; but we'll even
All that good time will give us: this attempt
I am soldier to, and will abide it with
A prince's courage. Away, I prithee.
Pis. Well, madam, we must take a short farewell,
Lest, being miss'd, I be suspected of
Your carriage from the court. My noble mistress,
Here is a box; I had it from the queen:
What 's in 't is precious; if you are sick at sea,
Or stomach-qualm'd at land, a dram of this
Will drive away distemper. To some shade,
And fit you to your manhood. May the gods
Direct you to the best!
Imo. Amen: I thank thee. *Exeunt [severally].*

SCENE V. [*A room in Cymbeline's palace.*]

Enter CYMBELINE, QUEEN, CLOTEN, LUCIUS, [Attendants,] *and* Lords.

Cym. Thus far; and so farewell.
Luc. Thanks, royal sir.
My emperor hath wrote, I must from hence;
And am right sorry that I must report ye
My master's enemy.
Cym. Our subjects, sir,
Will not endure his yoke; and for ourself
To show less sovereignty than they, must needs
Appear unkinglike.
Luc. So, sir: I desire of you
A conduct over-land to Milford-Haven.
Madam, all joy befal your grace!
Queen. And you!
Cym. My lords, you are appointed for that office;
The due of honour in no point omit.
So farewell, noble Lucius.
Luc. Your hand, my lord.
Clo. Receive it friendly; but from this time forth
I wear it as your enemy.
Luc. Sir, the event
Is yet to name the winner: fare you well.
Cym. Leave not the worthy Lucius, good my lords,

135. **With . . . nothing.** This line has puzzled commentators, and there are many emendations; but there seems no reason not to read it straight on and regard it as a good example of Imogen's admirable use of epithets. 147. **Dark,** obscure, mean. 148. **That which,** i.e., the fact that she is a woman. 150. **Pretty,** fair, advantageous. **full of view,** promising. 158. **Command,** i.e., as befitting one of royal birth. **niceness,** coyness, reserve. 160. **it,** its. **waggish,** roguish, masculine.

162. **quarrelous,** quarrelsome. 164. **harder,** too hard. 166. **common-kissing,** kissing everybody and everything. **Titan,** god of the sun. 167. **laboursome . . . trims,** elaborate and dainty apparel. 168. **angry,** i.e., jealous. 171. **Fore-thinking,** foreseeing, anticipating. **fit,** ready. 173. **in their serving,** employing them. 175. **such a season,** i.e., of such an age as you will represent. 176. **his service,** i.e., employment in his service. 177. **happy,** gifted, skillful. 180. **Your means abroad,** as to

Till he have cross'd the Severn. Happiness!
Exeunt Lucius etc.
Queen. He goes hence frowning: but it honours us
That we have given him cause.
Clo. 'Tis all the better;
Your valiant Britons have their wishes in it.
Cym. Lucius hath wrote already to the emperor
How it goes here. It fits us therefore ripely
Our chariots and our horsemen be in readiness:
The pow'rs that he already hath in Gallia
Will soon be drawn to head, from whence he moves
His war for Britain.
Queen. 'Tis not sleepy business;
But must be look'd to speedily and strongly.
Cym. Our expectation that it would be thus
Hath made us forward. But, my gentle queen,
Where is our daughter? She hath not appear'd
Before the Roman, nor to us hath tender'd
The duty of the day: she looks us like
A thing more made of malice than of duty:
We have noted it. Call her before us; for
We have been too slight in sufferance.
[*Exit a Messenger.*]
Queen. Royal sir,
Since the exile of Posthumus, most retir'd
Hath her life been; the cure whereof, my lord,
'Tis time must do. Beseech your majesty,
Forbear sharp speeches to her: she 's a lady
So tender of rebukes that words are strokes
And strokes death to her.

Enter Messenger.

Cym. Where is she, sir? How
Can her contempt be answer'd?
Mess. Please you, sir,
Her chambers are all lock'd; and there 's no answer
That will be given to th' loudest noise we make.
Queen. My lord, when last I went to visit her,
She pray'd me to excuse her keeping close,
Whereto constrain'd by her infirmity,
She should that duty leave unpaid to you,
Which daily she was bound to proffer: this
She wish'd me to make known; but our great court
Made me to blame in memory.
Cym. Her doors lock'd?
Not seen of late? Grant, heavens, that which I fear
Prove false! *Exit.*
Queen. Son, I say, follow the king.
Clo. That man of hers, Pisanio, her old servant,
I have not seen these two days.
Queen. Go, look after. *Exit* [*Cloten*].
Pisanio, thou that stand'st so for Posthumus!
He hath a drug of mine; I pray his absence
Proceed by swallowing that, for he believes
It is a thing most precious. But for her,
Where is she gone? Haply, despair hath seiz'd her,
Or, wing'd with fervour of her love, she 's flown
To her desir'd Posthumus: gone she is
To death or to dishonour; and my end
Can make good use of either: she being down,
I have the placing of the British crown.

Enter CLOTEN.

How now, my son?
Clo. 'Tis certain she is fled.
Go in and cheer the king: he rages; none
Dare come about him.
Queen. [*Aside*] All the better: may
This night forestall him of the coming day! *Exit Queen.*
Clo. I love and hate her: for she 's fair and royal,
And that she hath all courtly parts more exquisite
Than lady, ladies, woman; from every one
The best she hath, and she, of all compounded,
Outsells them all; I love her therefore: but
Disdaining me and throwing favours on
The low Posthumus slanders so her judgement
That what 's else rare is chok'd; and in that point
I will conclude to hate her, nay, indeed,
To be reveng'd upon her. For when fools
Shall—

Enter PISANIO.

Who is here? What, are you packing,
sirrah?
Come hither: ah, you precious pandar! Villain,
Where is thy lady? In a word; or else
Thou art straightway with the fiends.
Pis. O, good my lord!
Clo. Where is thy lady? or, by Jupiter,—
I will not ask again. Close villain,
I'll have this secret from thy heart, or rip
Thy heart to find it. Is she with Posthumus?
From whose so many weights of baseness cannot
A dram of worth be drawn.
Pis. Alas, my lord,
How can she be with him? When was she miss'd?
He is in Rome.
Clo. Where is she, sir? Come nearer;
No farther halting: satisfy me home
What is become of her.
Pis. O, my all-worthy lord!
Clo. All-worthy villain!
Discover where thy mistress is at once,
At the next word: no more of 'worthy lord!'
Speak, or thy silence on the instant is
Thy condemnation and thy death.
Pis. Then, sir,
This paper is the history of my knowledge
Touching her flight. [*Presenting a letter.*]
Clo. Let 's see 't. I will pursue her
Even to Augustus' throne.
Pis. [*Aside*] Or this, or perish.
She 's far enough; and what he learns by this
May prove his travel, not her danger.
Clo. Hum!
Pis. [*Aside*] I'll write to my lord she 's dead. O
Imogen,
Safe mayst thou wander, safe return again!
Clo. Sirrah, is this letter true?
Pis. Sir, as I think.
Clo. It is Posthumus' hand; I know 't. Sirrah, if thou wouldst not be a villain, but do me true service, undergo those employments wherein I should have

your means while you are abroad. 184. **even,** keep even with, profit by. 186. **soldier to,** enlisted to, devoted to. 190. **Your carriage,** having removed you.

SCENE V. 8. **conduct,** safe-conduct, escort. 10. **office,** duty (as escorts of Lucius). 14. **event,** outcome. 22. **fits,** befits. **ripely,** speedily. 25. **drawn to head,** brought together, levied. 32. **looks us,** seems to us. 35. **slight in sufferance,** careless in permitting it. 42. **answer'd,** accounted for. 46. **close,** in private. 50. **great court,** important courtly business. 56. **stand'st so for,** strongly support. 58. **by,** from. 69. **forestall,** deprive. 70. **for,** because. 71. **that,** because. **parts,** endowments, graces. 74. **Outsells,** outvalues, excels. 80. **packing,** plotting. 82. **In a word,** answer in a word. 85. **Close,** secretive. 88. **whose so many,** so many of whose. 92. **home,** completely. 95. **Discover,** disclose.

cause to use thee with a serious industry, that is, what villany soe'er I bid thee do, to perform it directly and truly, I would think thee an honest man: thou shouldst neither want my means for thy relief nor my voice for thy preferment.

Pis. Well, my good lord.

Clo. Wilt thou serve me? for since patiently and constantly thou hast stuck to the bare fortune of that beggar Posthumus, thou canst not, in the course of gratitude, but be a diligent follower of mine: wilt thou serve me?

Pis. Sir, I will.

Clo. Give me thy hand; here 's my purse. Hast any of thy late master's garments in thy possession?

Pis. I have, my lord, at my lodging, the same suit he wore when he took leave of my lady and mistress.

Clo. The first service thou dost me, fetch that suit hither: let it be thy first service; go.

Pis. I shall, my lord. *Exit.*

Clo. Meet thee at Milford-Haven!—I forgot to ask him one thing; I'll remember 't anon:—even there, thou villain Posthumus, will I kill thee. I would these garments were come. She said upon a time—the bitterness of it I now belch from my heart—that she held the very garment of Posthumus in more respect than my noble and natural person, together with the adornment of my qualities. With that suit upon my back, will I ravish her: first kill him, and in her eyes; there shall she see my valour, which will then be a torment to her contempt. He on the ground, my speech of insultment ended on his dead body, and when my lust hath dined,—which, as I say, to vex her I will execute in the clothes that she so praised,—to the court I'll knock her back, foot her home again. She hath despised me rejoicingly, and I'll be merry in my revenge.

Enter PISANIO [*with the clothes*].

Be those the garments?

Pis. Ay, my noble lord.

Clo. How long is 't since she went to Milford-Haven?

Pis. She can scarce be there yet.

Clo. Bring this apparel to my chamber; that is the second thing that I have commanded thee: the third is, that thou wilt be a voluntary mute to my design. Be but duteous, and true preferment shall tender itself to thee. My revenge is now at Milford: would I had wings to follow it! Come, and be true. *Exit.*

Pis. Thou bid'st me to my loss: for true to thee
Were to prove false, which I will never be,
To him that is most true. To Milford go,
And find not her whom thou pursuest. Flow, flow,
You heavenly blessings, on her! This fool's speed
Be cross'd with slowness; labour be his meed! *Exit.*

SCENE VI. [*Wales. Before the cave of Belarius.*]

Enter IMOGEN *alone* [*in boy's clothes*].

Imo. I see a man's life is a tedious one:
I have tir'd myself, and for two nights together
Have made the ground my bed. I should be sick,
But that my resolution helps me. Milford,
When from the mountain-top Pisanio show'd thee,
Thou wast within a ken: O Jove! I think
Foundations fly the wretched; such, I mean,
Where they should be reliev'd. Two beggars told me
I could not miss my way: will poor folks lie,
That have afflictions on them, knowing 'tis
A punishment or trial? Yes; no wonder,
When rich ones scarce tell true. To lapse in fulness
Is sorer than to lie for need, and falsehood
Is worse in kings than beggars. My dear lord!
Thou art one o' th' false ones. Now I think on thee,
My hunger 's gone; but even before, I was
At point to sink for food. But what is this?
Here is a path to 't: 'tis some savage hold:
I were best not call; I dare not call: yet famine,
Ere clean it o'erthrow nature, makes it valiant.
Plenty and peace breeds cowards: hardness ever
Of hardiness is mother. Ho! who 's here?
If any thing that 's civil, speak; if savage,
Take or lend. Ho! No answer? Then I'll enter.
Best draw my sword; and if mine enemy
But fear the sword like me, he'll scarcely look on 't.
Such a foe, good heavens! *Exit* [*to the cave*].

Enter BELARIUS, GUIDERIUS, *and* ARVIRAGUS.

Bel. You, Polydore, have prov'd best woodman and
Are master of the feast: Cadwal and I
Will play the cook and servant; 'tis our match:
The sweat of industry would dry and die,
But for the end it works to. Come; our stomachs
Will make what 's homely savoury: weariness
Can snore upon the flint, when resty sloth
Finds the down pillow hard. Now peace be here,
Poor house, that keep'st thyself!

Gui. I am throughly weary.

Arv. I am weak with toil, yet strong in appetite.

Gui. There is cold meat i' th' cave; we'll browse on that,
Whilst what we have kill'd be cook'd.

Bel. [*Looking into the cave*] Stay; come not in.
But that it eats our victuals, I should think
Here were a fairy.

Gui. What 's the matter, sir?

Bel. By Jupiter, an angel! or, if not,
An earthly paragon! Behold divineness
No elder than a boy!

Enter IMOGEN.

Imo. Good masters, harm me not:
Before I enter'd here, I call'd; and thought
To have begg'd or bought what I have took: good troth,
I have stol'n nought, nor would not, though I had found
Gold strew'd i' th' floor. Here 's money for my meat:
I would have left it on the board so soon
As I had made my meal, and parted
With pray'rs for the provider.

Gui. Money, youth?

145. **insultment,** contemptuous triumph (Onions). 149. **foot,** kick.
SCENE VI. 6. **within a ken,** within sight. 7. **Foundations,** quibbling use, denoting fixed places and charitable institutions (Schmidt). 13. **sorer,** worse, more wicked. 18. **hold,** stronghold, fastness. 20. **clean,** altogether. 21. **hardness,** hardship. 22. **hardiness,** hardihood, bravery. 24. **Take or lend,** take my life or give me food. Dowden explains: "Take what I have before you lend me food." 28. **woodman,** huntsman. 30. **match,** agreement, bargain. 34. **resty,** sluggish, indolent. 64. **in,** into. 71. **I bid . . . buy,** I bid for you as one who would have you. 77. **prize,** value, i.e., she would not have been heir to the throne. 79. **wrings,** writhes. 85-86. **laying . . . multitudes,** disregarding the valueless gift of the fickle mob (as spectators). 87. **out-peer,** excel.

Arv. All gold and silver rather turn to dirt!
As 'tis no better reckon'd, but of those
Who worship dirty gods.
Imo. I see you 're angry:
Know, if you kill me for my fault, I should
Have died had I not made it.
Bel. Whither bound?
Imo. To Milford-Haven.
Bel. What 's your name?
Imo. Fidele, sir. I have a kinsman who
Is bound for Italy; he embark'd at Milford;
To whom being going, almost spent with hunger,
I am fall'n in this offence.
Bel. ' Prithee, fair youth,
Think us no churls, nor measure our good minds
By this rude place we live in. Well encounter'd!
'Tis almost night: you shall have better cheer
Ere you depart; and thanks to stay and eat it.
Boys, bid him welcome.
Gui. Were you a woman, youth,
I should woo hard but be your groom. In honesty,
I bid for you as I 'ld buy.
Arv. I'll make 't my comfort
He is a man; I'll love him as my brother:
And such a welcome as I 'ld give to him
After long absence, such is yours: most welcome!
Be sprightly, for you fall 'mongst friends.
Imo. 'Mongst friends,
If brothers. [*Aside*] Would it had been so, that they
Had been my father's sons! then had my prize
Been less, and so more equal ballasting
To thee, Posthumus.
Bel. He wrings at some distress.
Gui. Would I could free 't!
Arv. Or I, whate'er it be,
What pain it cost, what danger. Gods!
Bel. Hark, boys. [*Whispering.*]
Imo. Great men,
That had a court no bigger than this cave,
That did attend themselves and had the virtue
Which their own conscience seal'd them—laying by
That nothing-gift of differing multitudes—
Could not out-peer these twain. Pardon me, gods!
I 'ld change my sex to be companion with them,
Since Leonatus 's false.
Bel. It shall be so.
Boys, we'll go dress our hunt. Fair youth, come in:
Discourse is heavy, fasting; when we have supp'd,
We'll mannerly demand thee of thy story,
So far as thou wilt speak it.
Gui. Pray, draw near.
Arv. The night to th' owl and morn to th' lark less
welcome.
Imo. Thanks, sir.
Arv. I pray, draw near. *Exeunt.*

SCENE [VII. *Rome. A public place*].

Enter two Roman Senators *and* Tribunes.

First Sen. This is the tenour of the emperor's writ:
That since the common men are now in action
'Gainst the Pannonians and Dalmatians,
And that the legions now in Gallia are
Full weak to undertake our wars against
The fall'n-off Britons, that we do incite
The gentry to this business. He creates
Lucius proconsul: and to you the tribunes,
For this immediate levy, he commends
His absolute commission. Long live Cæsar!
First Tri. Is Lucius general of the forces?
Sec. Sen. Ay.
First Tri. Remaining now in Gallia?
First Sen. With those legions
Which I have spoke of, whereunto your levy
Must be supplyant: the words of your commission
Will tie you to the numbers and the time
Of their dispatch.
First Tri. We will discharge our duty.
Exeunt.

ACT IV.

SCENE I. [*Wales: near the cave of Belarius.*]

Enter CLOTEN *alone.*

Clo. I am near to the place where they should meet, if Pisanio have mapped it truly. How fit his garments serve me! Why should his mistress, who was made by him that made the tailor, not be fit too? the rather—saving reverence of the word—for 'tis said a woman's fitness comes by fits. Therein I must play the workman. I dare speak it to myself—for it is not vain-glory for a man and his glass to confer in his own chamber—I mean, the lines of my body are as well drawn as his; no less young, more strong, not beneath him in fortunes, beyond him in the advantage of the time, above him in birth, alike conversant in general services, and more remarkable in single oppositions: yet this imperceiverant thing loves him in my despite. What mortality is! Posthumus, thy head, which now is growing upon thy shoulders, shall within this hour be off; thy mistress enforced; thy garments cut to pieces before her face: and all this done, spurn her home to her father; who may haply be a little angry for my so rough usage; but my mother, having power of his testiness, shall turn all into my commendations. My horse is tied up safe: out, sword, and to a sore purpose! Fortune, put them into my hand! This is the very description of their meeting-place: and the fellow dares not deceive me. *Exit.*

SCENE II. [*Before the cave of Belarius.*]

Enter BELARIUS, GUIDERIUS, ARVIRAGUS, *and* IMOGEN *from the cave.*

Bel. [*To Imogen*] You are not well: remain here in
the cave;
We'll come to you after hunting.
Arv. [*To Imogen*] Brother, stay here:

90. **hunt,** game taken in the hunt.
SCENE VII. 6. **fall'n-off,** revolted. 9. **commends,** delivers, presents. F has *commands*, which may be retained with the meaning, "commands to be given." 14. **supplyant,** reinforcing, auxiliary.
ACT IV. SCENE I. 6. **saving reverence,** asking pardon. 7. **fitness,** i.e., sexual inclination. **fits,** sudden, transitory states, with pun on the fit of the tailor. 13. **advantage of the time,** superiority in social opportunity. 14. **alike . . . services,** equally versed in military matters. 15. **single oppositions,** single combat. 16. **imperceiverant,** dull of perception; possibly, giddy, thoughtless; F: *imperseuerant*, which would be the correct form of a word meaning "changeable." 17. **What,** what a thing. 24. **power of,** power over.

Are we not brothers?
Imo. So man and man should be;
But clay and clay differs in dignity,
Whose dust is both alike. I am very sick.
Gui. Go you to hunting; I'll abide with him.
Imo. So sick I am not, yet I am not well;
But not so citizen a wanton as
To seem to die ere sick: so please you, leave me;
Stick to your journal course: the breach of custom
Is breach of all. I am ill, but your being by me
Cannot amend me; society is no comfort
To one not sociable: I am not very sick,
Since I can reason of it. Pray you, trust me here:
I'll rob none but myself; and let me die,
Stealing so poorly.
Gui. I love thee; I have spoke it:
How much the quantity, the weight as much,
As I do love my father.
Bel. What! how! how!
Arv. If it be sin to say so, sir, I yoke me
In my good brother's fault: I know not why
I love this youth; and I have heard you say,
Love's reason 's without reason: the bier at door,
And a demand who is 't shall die, I 'ld say
'My father, not this youth.'
Bel. [*Aside*] O noble strain!
O worthiness of nature! breed of greatness!
Cowards father cowards and base things sire base:
Nature hath meal and bran, contempt and grace.
I 'm not their father; yet who this should be,
Doth miracle itself, lov'd before me.—
'Tis the ninth hour o' th' morn.
Arv. Brother, farewell.
Imo. I wish ye sport.
Arv. You health. So please you, sir.
Imo. [*Aside*] These are kind creatures. Gods, what lies I have heard!
Our courtiers say all 's savage but at court:
Experience, O, thou disprov'st report!
Th' imperious seas breed monsters, for the dish
Poor tributary rivers as sweet fish.
I am sick still; heart-sick. Pisanio,
I'll now taste of thy drug. [*Swallows some.*]
Gui. I could not stir him:
He said he was gentle, but unfortunate;
Dishonestly afflicted, but yet honest.
Arv. Thus did he answer me: yet said, hereafter
I might know more.
Bel. To th' field, to th' field!
We'll leave you for this time: go in and rest.
Arv. We'll not be long away.
Bel. Pray, be not sick,
For you must be our housewife.
Imo. Well or ill,
I am bound to you. *Exit* [*to the cave*].
Bel. And shalt be ever.
This youth, howe'er distress'd, appears he hath had
Good ancestors.
Arv. How angel-like he sings!
Gui. But his neat cookery! he cut our roots
In characters,
And sauc'd our broths, as Juno had been sick
And he her dieter.
Arv. Nobly he yokes
A smiling with a sigh, as if the sigh
Was that it was, for not being such a smile;
The smile mocking the sigh, that it would fly
From so divine a temple, to commix
With winds that sailors rail at.
Gui. I do note
That grief and patience, rooted in him both,
Mingle their spurs together.
Arv. Grow, patience!
And let the stinking elder, grief, untwine
His perishing root with the increasing vine!
Bel. It is great morning. Come, away!—Who 's there?

Enter CLOTEN.

Clo. I cannot find those runagates; that villain
Hath mock'd me. I am faint.
Bel. 'Those runagates!'
Means he not us? I partly know him: 'tis
Cloten, the son o' th' queen. I fear some ambush.
I saw him not these many years, and yet
I know 'tis he. We are held as outlaws: hence!
Gui. He is but one: you and my brother search
What companies are near: pray you, away;
Let me alone with him. [*Exeunt Belarius and Arviragus.*]
Clo. Soft! What are you
That fly me thus? some villain mountaineers?
I have heard of such. What slave art thou?
Gui. A thing
More slavish did I ne'er than answering
A slave without a knock.
Clo. Thou art a robber,
A law-breaker, a villain: yield thee, thief.
Gui. To who? to thee? What art thou? Have not I
An arm as big as thine? a heart as big?
Thy words, I grant, are bigger, for I wear not
My dagger in my mouth. Say what thou art,
Why I should yield to thee?
Clo. Thou villain base,
Know'st me not by my clothes?
Gui. No, nor thy tailor, rascal,
Who is thy grandfather: he made those clothes,
Which, as it seems, make thee.
Clo. Thou precious varlet,
My tailor made them not.
Gui. Hence, then, and thank
The man that gave them thee. Thou art some fool;
I am loath to beat thee.
Clo. Thou injurious thief,
Hear but my name, and tremble.
Gui. What 's thy name?
Clo. Cloten, thou villain.
Gui. Cloten, thou double villain, be thy name,
I cannot tremble at it: were it Toad, or Adder, Spider,
'Twould move me sooner.
Clo. To thy further fear,
Nay, to thy mere confusion, thou shalt know
I am son to th' queen.
Gui. I am sorry for 't; not seeming

SCENE II. 8. **citizen,** effeminate. **wanton,** spoiled or pampered person. 10. **journal,** daily. 17. **How much,** however much. 35. **imperious,** imperial. 36. **as sweet fish,** breed as sweet fish (for eating) as the sea. 38. **stir,** i.e., to tell about himself. 39. **gentle,** well born. 53. **that,** what. 58. **spurs,** roots of a tree (used of projecting roots). 59. **elder,** elder tree. **untwine,** cease to twine. 60. **perishing,** baleful. 61. **great morning,** broad day. 69. **companies,** companions. 81. **Know'st . . . clothes.** Cloten is dressed as one from the court. 86. **injurious,** malicious, insulting. 92. **mere,** utter. 97. **proper,** own. 106. **absolute,** positive. 107. **very Cloten,** Cloten himself. 109. **fell,**

So worthy as thy birth.
Clo. Art not afeard?
Gui. Those that I reverence those I fear, the wise:
At fools I laugh, not fear them.
Clo. Die the death!
When I have slain thee with my proper hand,
I'll follow those that even now fled hence,
And on the gates of Lud's-town set your heads:
Yield, rustic mountaineer. *Fight, and exeunt.*

Enter BELARIUS *and* ARVIRAGUS.

Bel. No company's abroad?
Arv. None in the world: you did mistake him, sure.
Bel. I cannot tell: long is it since I saw him,
But time hath nothing blurr'd those lines of favour
Which then he wore; the snatches in his voice,
And burst of speaking, were as his: I am absolute
'Twas very Cloten.
Arv. In this place we left them:
I wish my brother make good time with him,
You say he is so fell.
Bel. Being scarce made up,
I mean, to man, he had not apprehension
Of roaring terrors: for the effect of judgement
Is oft the cause of fear.

Enter GUIDERIUS [*with* CLOTEN's *head*].

But see, thy brother.
Gui. This Cloten was a fool, an empty purse;
There was no money in 't: not Hercules
Could have knock'd out his brains, for he had none:
Yet I not doing this, the fool had borne
My head as I do his.
Bel. What hast thou done?
Gui. I am perfect what: cut off one Cloten's head,
Son to the queen, after his own report;
Who call'd me traitor, mountaineer, and swore
With his own single hand he 'ld take us in,
Displace our heads where—thank the gods!—they grow,
And set them on Lud's-town.
Bel. We are all undone.
Gui. Why, worthy father, what have we to lose,
But that he swore to take, our lives? The law
Protects not us: then why should we be tender
To let an arrogant piece of flesh threat us,
Play judge and executioner all himself,
For we do fear the law? What company
Discover you abroad?
Bel. No single soul
Can we set eye on; but in all safe reason
He must have some attendants. Though his humour
Was nothing but mutation, ay, and that
From one bad thing to worse; not frenzy, not
Absolute madness could so far have rav'd
To bring him here alone; although perhaps
It may be heard at court that such as we
Cave here, hunt here, are outlaws, and in time
May make some stronger head; the which he hearing—
As it is like him—might break out, and swear
He 'ld fetch us in; yet is 't not probable
To come alone, either he so undertaking,
Or they so suffering: then on good ground we fear,
If we do fear this body hath a tail
More perilous than the head.
Arv. Let ordinance
Come as the gods foresay it: howsoe'er,
My brother hath done well.
Bel. I had no mind
To hunt this day: the boy Fidele's sickness
Did make my way long forth.
Gui. With his own sword,
Which he did wave against my throat, I have ta'en
His head from him: I'll throw 't into the creek
Behind our rock; and let it to the sea,
And tell the fishes he 's the queen's son, Cloten:
That 's all I reck. *Exit.*
Bel. I fear 'twill be reveng'd:
Would, Polydore, thou hadst not done 't! though valour
Becomes thee well enough.
Arv. Would I had done 't,
So the revenge alone pursu'd me! Polydore,
I love thee brotherly, but envy much
Thou hast robb'd me of this deed: I would revenges,
That possible strength might meet, would seek us through
And put us to our answer.
Bel. Well, 'tis done:
We'll hunt no more to-day, nor seek for danger
Where there 's no profit. I prithee, to our rock;
You and Fidele play the cooks: I'll stay
Till hasty Polydore return, and bring him
To dinner presently.
Arv. Poor sick Fidele!
I'll willingly to him: to gain his colour
I 'ld let a parish of such Clotens blood,
And praise myself for charity. *Exit.*
Bel. O thou goddess,
Thou divine Nature, how thyself thou blazon'st
In these two princely boys! They are as gentle
As zephyrs blowing below the violet,
Not wagging his sweet head; and yet as rough,
Their royal blood enchaf'd, as the rud'st wind,
That by the top doth take the mountain pine,
And make him stoop to th' vale. 'Tis wonder
That an invisible instinct should frame them
To royalty unlearn'd, honour untaught,
Civility not seen from other, valour
That wildly grows in them, but yields a crop
As if it had been sow'd. Yet still it 's strange
What Cloten's being here to us portends,
Or what his death will bring us.

Enter GUIDERIUS.

Gui. Where 's my brother?
I have sent Cloten's clotpoll down the stream,
In embassy to his mother: his body 's hostage
For his return. *Solemn music.*
Bel. My ingenious instrument!
Hark, Polydore, it sounds! But what occasion
Hath Cadwal now to give it motion? Hark!
Gui. Is he at home?

fierce. 110. **apprehension,** comprehension, conception. 111. **effect,** result. The F reading, *defect*, is retained by the Arden editors and others as meaning "defectiveness in the use of judgment." 118. **perfect,** well aware. 125. **that,** that which. 126. **tender,** quick, keen. 138. **Cave,** live in a cave. 141. **fetch us in,** capture us. 145. **ordinance,** what is ordained. 149. **make . . . forth,** make my wandering from the cave seem long. 154. **reck,** care. 160. **That . . . meet,** that strength such as ours might resist. **seek us through,** call us to account. 167. **gain his colour,** restore him to health. 168. **let . . . blood,** let a parish full of such Clotens suffer death. 184. **clotpoll,** head.

Bel. He went hence even now.
Gui. What does he mean? since death of my dear'st mother
It did not speak before. All solemn things
Should answer solemn accidents. The matter?
Triumphs for nothing and lamenting toys
Is jollity for apes and grief for boys.
Is Cadwal mad?

Enter ARVIRAGUS, *with* IMOGEN, [*as*] *dead, bearing her in his arms.*

Bel. Look, here he comes,
And brings the dire occasion in his arms
Of what we blame him for.
Arv. The bird is dead
That we have made so much on. I had rather
Have skipp'd from sixteen years of age to sixty,
To have turn'd my leaping-time into a crutch,
Than have seen this.
Gui. O sweetest, fairest lily!
My brother wears thee not the one half so well
As when thou grew'st thyself.
Bel. O melancholy!
Who ever yet could sound thy bottom? find
The ooze, to show what coast thy sluggish crare
Might eas'liest harbour in? Thou blessed thing!
Jove knows what man thou mightst have made; but I,
Thou diedst, a most rare boy, of melancholy.
How found you him?
Arv. Stark, as you see:
Thus smiling, as some fly had tickled slumber,
Not as death's dart, being laugh'd at; his right cheek
Reposing on a cushion.
Gui. Where?
Arv. O' th' floor;
His arms thus leagu'd: I thought he slept, and put
My clouted brogues from off my feet, whose rudeness
Answer'd my steps too loud.
Gui. Why, he but sleeps:
If he be gone, he'll make his grave a bed;
With female fairies will his tomb be haunted,
And worms will not come to thee.
Arv. With fairest flowers
Whilst summer lasts and I live here, Fidele,
I'll sweeten thy sad grave: thou shalt not lack
The flower that 's like thy face, pale primrose, nor
The azur'd harebell, like thy veins, no, nor
The leaf of eglantine, whom not to slander,
Out-sweet'ned not thy breath: the ruddock would,
With charitable bill,—O bill, sore-shaming
Those rich-left heirs that let their fathers lie
Without a monument!—bring thee all this;
Yea, and furr'd moss besides, when flow'rs are none,
To winter-ground thy corse.
Gui. Prithee, have done;
And do not play in wench-like words with that
Which is so serious. Let us bury him,
And not protract with admiration what
Is now due debt. To th' grave!
Arv. Say, where shall 's lay him?
Gui. By good Euriphile, our mother.
Arv. Be 't so:
And let us, Polydore, though now our voices
Have got the mannish crack, sing him to th' ground,
As once our mother; use like note and words,
Save that Euriphile must be Fidele.
Gui. Cadwal,
I cannot sing: I'll weep, and word it with thee;
For notes of sorrow out of tune are worse
Than priests and fanes that lie.
Arv. We'll speak it, then.
Bel. Great griefs, I see, med'cine the less; for Cloten
Is quite forgot. He was a queen's son, boys;
And though he came our enemy, remember
He was paid for that: though mean and mighty, rotting
Together, have one dust, yet reverence,
That angel of the world, doth make distinction
Of place 'tween high and low. Our foe was princely;
And though you took his life, as being our foe,
Yet bury him as a prince.
Gui. Pray you, fetch him hither.
Thersites' body is as good as Ajax',
When neither are alive.
Arv. If you'll go fetch him,
We'll say our song the whilst. Brother, begin.
[*Exit Belarius.*]
Gui. Nay, Cadwal, we must lay his head to th' east;
My father hath a reason for 't.
Arv. 'Tis true.
Gui. Come on then, and remove him.
Arv. So. Begin.

SONG.

Gui. Fear no more the heat o' th' sun,
Nor the furious winter's rages;
Thou thy worldly task hast done,
Home art gone, and ta'en thy wages:
Golden lads and girls all must,
As chimney-sweepers, come to dust.

Arv. Fear no more the frown o' th' great;
Thou art past the tyrant's stroke;
Care no more to clothe and eat;
To thee the reed is as the oak:
The sceptre, learning, physic, must
All follow this, and come to dust.

Gui. Fear no more the lightning-flash,
Arv. Nor th' all-dreaded thunder-stone;
Gui. Fear not slander, censure rash;
Arv. Thou hast finish'd joy and moan:
Both. All lovers young, all lovers must
Consign to thee, and come to dust.

Gui. No exorciser harm thee!
Arv. Nor no witchcraft charm thee!
Gui. Ghost unlaid forbear thee!
Arv. Nothing ill come near thee!
Both. Quiet consummation have;
And renowned be thy grave!

192. **answer,** correspond to. **accidents,** events. 198. **on,** of. 205. **crare,** skiff, small boat, so Sympson (Steevens); F: *care,* which may be retained as meaning "a vessel in search of a harbor." 209. **Stark,** stiff in death. 213. **leagu'd,** folded. 214. **clouted brogues,** heavy shoes studded with nails. 224. **ruddock,** robin redbreast. 229. **winter-ground,** cover so as to protect from frost. 230. **wench-like,** womanish.

242. **fanes,** temples. 252. **Thersites' . . . Ajax'.** Thersites was the base scoffer in the *Iliad;* Ajax, a Greek hero. 255. **lay . . . east.** Opposite to the Christian custom. Shakespeare may wish to suggest that the play is pagan, or he may know that the Earthly Paradise or Happy Isles were located across the Western ocean. 271. **thunder-stone,** thunderbolt (the supposed solid body accompanying a stroke of lightning). 275.

Enter BELARIUS, *with the body of* CLOTEN.

Gui. We have done our obsequies: come, lay him down.
Bel. Here 's a few flow'rs; but 'bout midnight, more:
The herbs that have on them cold dew o' th' night
Are strewings fitt'st for graves. Upon their faces.
You were as flow'rs, now wither'd: even so
These herblets shall, which we upon you strew.
Come on, away: apart upon our knees.
The ground that gave them first has them again:
Their pleasures here are past, so is their pain.
Exeunt [Belarius, Guiderius, and Arviragus].
Imo. (*Awakes*) Yes, sir, to Milford-Haven; which is the way?—
I thank you.—By yond bush?—Pray, how far thither?
'Ods pittikins! can it be six mile yet?—
I have gone all night. 'Faith, I'll lie down and sleep.
But, soft! no bedfellow!—O gods and goddesses!
[*Seeing the body of Cloten.*]
These flow'rs are like the pleasures of the world;
This bloody man, the care on 't. I hope I dream;
For so I thought I was a cave-keeper,
And cook to honest creatures: but 'tis not so;
'Twas but a bolt of nothing, shot at nothing,
Which the brain makes of fumes: our very eyes
Are sometimes like our judgements, blind. Good faith,
I tremble still with fear: but if there be
Yet left in heaven as small a drop of pity
As a wren's eye, fear'd gods, a part of it!
The dream 's here still: even when I wake, it is
Without me, as within me; not imagin'd, felt.
A headless man! The garments of Posthumus!
I know the shape of 's leg: this is his hand;
His foot Mercurial; his Martial thigh;
The brawns of Hercules: but his Jovial face—
Murder in heaven?—How!—'Tis gone. Pisanio,
All curses madded Hecuba gave the Greeks,
And mine to boot, be darted on thee! Thou,
Conspir'd with that irregulous devil, Cloten,
Hast here cut off my lord. To write and read
Be henceforth treacherous! Damn'd Pisanio
Hath with his forged letters,—damn'd Pisanio—
From this most bravest vessel of the world
Struck the main-top! O Posthumus! alas,
Where is thy head? where 's that? Ay me! where 's that?
Pisanio might have kill'd thee at the heart,
And left this head on. How should this be? Pisanio?
'Tis he and Cloten: malice and lucre in them
Have laid this woe here. O, 'tis pregnant, pregnant!
The drug he gave me, which he said was precious
And cordial to me, have I not found it
Murd'rous to th' senses? That confirms it home:
This is Pisanio's deed, and Cloten: O!
Give colour to my pale cheek with thy blood,
That we the horrider may seem to those
Which chance to find us: O, my lord, my lord!
[*Falls on the body.*]

Enter LUCIUS, Captains, *and a* Soothsayer *to them.*

Cap. The legions garrison'd in Gallia,
After your will, have cross'd the sea, attending
You here at Milford-Haven with your ships:
They are in readiness.
Luc. But what from Rome?
Cap. The senate hath stirr'd up the confiners
And gentlemen of Italy, most willing spirits,
That promise noble service: and they come
Under the conduct of bold Iachimo,
Syenna's brother.
Luc. When expect you them?
Cap. With the next benefit o' th' wind.
Luc. This forwardness
Makes our hopes fair. Command our present numbers
Be muster'd; bid the captains look to 't. Now, sir,
What have you dream'd of late of this war's purpose?
Sooth. Last night the very gods show'd me a vision—
I fast and pray'd for their intelligence—thus:
I saw Jove's bird, the Roman eagle, wing'd
From the spongy south to this part of the west,
There vanish'd in the sunbeams: which portends—
Unless my sins abuse my divination—
Success to th' Roman host.
Luc. Dream often so,
And never false. Soft, ho! what trunk is here
Without his top? The ruin speaks that sometime
It was a worthy building. How! a page!
Or dead, or sleeping on him? But dead rather;
For nature doth abhor to make his bed
With the defunct, or sleep upon the dead.
Let 's see the boy's face.
Cap. He 's alive, my lord.
Luc. He'll then instruct us of this body. Young one,
Inform us of thy fortunes, for it seems
They crave to be demanded. Who is this
Thou mak'st thy bloody pillow? Or who was he
That, otherwise than noble nature did,
Hath alter'd that good picture? What 's thy interest
In this sad wrack? How came 't? Who is 't?
What art thou?
Imo. I am nothing: or if not,
Nothing to be were better. This was my master,
A very valiant Briton and a good,
That here by mountaineers lies slain. Alas!
There is no more such masters: I may wander
From east to occident, cry out for service,
Try many, all good, serve truly, never
Find such another master.
Luc. 'Lack, good youth!
Thou mov'st no less with thy complaining than
Thy master in bleeding: say his name, good friend.
Imo. Richard du Champ. [*Aside*] If I do lie and do
No harm by it, though the gods hear, I hope
They'll pardon it.—Say you, sir?
Luc. Thy name?
Imo. Fidele, sir.
Luc. Thou dost approve thyself the very same:
Thy name well fits thy faith, thy faith thy name.
Wilt take thy chance with me? I will not say

Consign, co-sign, share a similar fate. 276. **exorciser,** conjurer. 280. **consummation,** end, death. 287. **herblets,** small herbs, flowers. 293. **'Ods pittikins,** God's pity (diminutive oath). 298. **cave-keeper,** one who dwells in a cave. 301. **fumes,** vapors engendered of humors which, according to current theory, rose up into the brain and, by affecting imagination in the forechamber of the brain, caused dreams. 310. **Mercurial,** nimble and swift like the foot of Mercury. **Martial,** powerful for war like that of Mars. 311. **brawns,** muscles; here, arms. **Jovial,** Jove-like. 313. **Hecuba,** wife of Priam, King of Troy. 315. **irregulous,** lawless. 325. **pregnant,** evident. 329. **Cloten,** Cloten's. 334. **After,** according to. 337. **confiners,** inhabitants. 341. **Syenna's,** of the ruler of Sienna. 347. **fast,** fasted. 360. **instruct,** inform.

Thou shalt be so well master'd, but, be sure,
No less belov'd. The Roman emperor's letters,
Sent by a consul to me, should not sooner
Than thine own worth prefer thee: go with me.
Imo. I'll follow, sir. But first, an 't please the gods,
I'll hide my master from the flies, as deep
As these poor pickaxes can dig; and when
With wild wood-leaves and weeds I ha' strew'd his grave,
And on it said a century of prayers,
Such as I can, twice o'er, I'll weep and sigh;
And leaving so his service, follow you,
So please you entertain me.
Luc. Ay, good youth;
And rather father thee than master thee.
My friends,
The boy hath taught us manly duties: let us
Find out the prettiest daisied plot we can,
And make him with our pikes and partisans
A grave: come, arm him. Boy, he's preferr'd
By thee to us, and he shall be interr'd
As soldiers can. Be cheerful; wipe thine eyes:
Some falls are means the happier to arise. *Exeunt.*

SCENE III. [*A room in Cymbeline's palace.*]

Enter CYMBELINE, Lords, [Attendants,] *and* PISANIO.

Cym. Again; and bring me word how 'tis with her.
[*Exit an Attendant.*]
A fever with the absence of her son,
A madness, of which her life 's in danger. Heavens,
How deeply you at once do touch me! Imogen,
The great part of my comfort, gone; my queen
Upon a desperate bed, and in a time
When fearful wars point at me; her son gone,
So needful for this present: it strikes me, past
The hope of comfort. But for thee, fellow,
Who needs must know of her departure and
Dost seem so ignorant, we'll enforce it from thee
By a sharp torture.
Pis. Sir, my life is yours;
I humbly set it at your will; but, for my mistress,
I nothing know where she remains, why gone,
Nor when she purposes return. Beseech your highness,
Hold me your loyal servant.
First Lord. Good my liege,
The day that she was missing he was here:
I dare be bound he 's true and shall perform
All parts of his subjection loyally. For Cloten,
There wants no diligence in seeking him,
And will, no doubt, be found.
Cym. The time is troublesome.
[*To Pisanio*] We'll slip you for a season; but our jealousy
Does yet depend.
First Lord. So please your majesty,
The Roman legions, all from Gallia drawn,
Are landed on your coast, with a supply
Of Roman gentlemen, by the senate sent.
Cym. Now for the counsel of my son and queen!
I am amaz'd with matter.
First Lord. Good my liege,
Your preparation can affront no less
Than what you hear of: come more, for more you 're ready:
The want is but to put those pow'rs in motion
That long to move.
Cym. I thank you. Let 's withdraw;
And meet the time as it seeks us. We fear not
What can from Italy annoy us; but
We grieve at chances here. Away!
Exeunt [*all but Pisanio*].
Pis. I heard no letter from my master since
I wrote him Imogen was slain: 'tis strange:
Nor hear I from my mistress, who did promise
To yield me often tidings; neither know I
What is betid to Cloten; but remain
Perplex'd in all. The heavens still must work.
Wherein I am false I am honest; not true, to be true.
These present wars shall find I love my country,
Even to the note o' th' king, or I'll fall in them.
All other doubts, by time let them be clear'd:
Fortune brings in some boats that are not steer'd. *Exit.*

SCENE IV. [*Wales: before the cave of Belarius.*]

Enter BELARIUS, GUIDERIUS, *and* ARVIRAGUS.

Gui. The noise is round about us.
Bel. Let us from it.
Arv. What pleasure, sir, find we in life, to lock it
From action and adventure?
Gui. Nay, what hope
Have we in hiding us? This way, the Romans
Must or for Britons slay us, or receive us
For barbarous and unnatural revolts
During their use, and slay us after.
Bel. Sons,
We'll higher to the mountains; there secure us.
To the king's party there 's no going: newness
Of Cloten's death—we being not known, not muster'd
Among the bands—may drive us to a render
Where we have liv'd, and so extort from 's that
Which we have done, whose answer would be death
Drawn on with torture.
Gui. This is, sir, a doubt
In such a time nothing becoming you,
Nor satisfying us.
Arv. It is not likely
That when they hear the Roman horses neigh,
Behold their quarter'd fires, have both their eyes
And ears so cloy'd importantly as now,
That they will waste their time upon our note,
To know from whence we are.
Bel. O, I am known
Of many in the army: many years,
Though Cloten then but young, you see, not wore him
From my remembrance. And, besides, the king
Hath not deserv'd my service nor your loves;

386. **prefer,** recommend. 391. **century,** hundred. 399. **partisans,** long-handled weapons with pointed and sharp-edged heads; halberds. 400. **arm,** take up into the arms.

SCENE III. 6. **desperate bed,** bed of dangerous illness. 11. **enforce,** force, compel. 19. **subjection,** duty. 22. **slip you,** let you go. **jealousy,** suspicion. 23. **depend,** impend, threaten. 28. **matter,** business, pressure of affairs. 29. **preparation,** military force. **affront,** confront in combat. 30. **come more,** if more come. 31. **want is but,** sole thing needed is. 34. **annoy,** injure. 40. **betid,** happened. 44. **note,** knowledge, recognition.

SCENE IV. 4. **This way,** by this course of conduct. 6. **revolts,** deserters, rebels. 7. **During their use,** while they are making use of us. 11. **render,** rendering of an account, relation. 13. **answer,** something done in punishment of an act. 18. **quarter'd fires,** regularly disposed,

Who find in my exile the want of breeding,
The certainty of this hard life; aye hopeless
To have the courtesy your cradle promis'd,
But to be still hot summer's tanlings and
The shrinking slaves of winter.
Gui. Than be so
Better to cease to be. Pray, sir, to th' army:
I and my brother are not known; yourself
So out of thought, and thereto so o'ergrown,
Cannot be question'd.
Arv. By this sun that shines,
I'll thither: what thing is 't that I never
Did see man die! scarce ever look'd on blood,
But that of coward hares, hot goats, and venison!
Never bestrid a horse, save one that had
A rider like myself, who ne'er wore rowel
Nor iron on his heel! I am asham'd
To look upon the holy sun, to have
The benefit of his blest beams, remaining
So long a poor unknown.
Gui. By heavens, I'll go:
If you will bless me, sir, and give me leave,
I'll take the better care, but if you will not,
The hazard therefore due fall on me by
The hands of Romans!
Arv. So say I: amen.
Bel. No reason I, since of your lives you set
So slight a valuation, should reserve
My crack'd one to more care. Have with you, boys!
If in your country wars you chance to die,
That is my bed too, lads, and there I'll lie:
Lead, lead. [*Aside*] The time seems long; their blood thinks scorn,
Till it fly out and show them princes born. *Exeunt.*

ACT V.

SCENE I. [*Britain. The Roman camp.*]

Enter POSTHUMUS *alone* [*with a bloody handkerchief*].

Post. Yea, bloody cloth, I'll keep thee, for I wish'd
Thou shouldst be colour'd thus. You married ones,
If each of you should take this course, how many
Must murder wives much better than themselves
For wrying but a little! O Pisanio!
Every good servant does not all commands:
No bond but to do just ones. Gods! if you
Should have ta'en vengeance on my faults, I never
Had liv'd to put on this: so had you sav'd
The noble Imogen to repent, and struck
Me, wretch more worth your vengeance. But, alack,
You snatch some hence for little faults; that 's love,
To have them fall no more: you some permit
†To second ills with ills, each elder worse,
And make them dread it, to the doers' thrift.
But Imogen is your own: do your best wills,
And make me blest to obey! I am brought hither
Among th' Italian gentry, and to fight
Against my lady's kingdom: 'tis enough
That, Britain, I have kill'd thy mistress; peace!
I'll give no wound to thee. Therefore, good heavens,
Hear patiently my purpose: I'll disrobe me
Of these Italian weeds and suit myself
As does a Briton peasant: so I'll fight
Against the part I come with; so I'll die
For thee, O Imogen, even for whom my life
Is every breath a death; and thus, unknown,
Pitied nor hated, to the face of peril
Myself I'll dedicate. Let me make men know
More valour in me than my habits show.
Gods, put the strength o' th' Leonati in me!
To shame the guise o' th' world, I will begin
The fashion, less without and more within. *Exit.*

SCENE II. [*Field of battle between the British and Roman camps.*]

Enter LUCIUS, IACHIMO, *and the* Roman Army *at one door, and the Briton army at another,* LEONATUS POSTHUMUS *following, like a poor soldier. They march over and go out. Then enter again, in skirmish,* IACHIMO *and* POSTHUMUS: *he vanquisheth and disarmeth* IACHIMO, *and then leaves him.*

Iach. The heaviness and guilt within my bosom
Takes off my manhood: I have belied a lady,
The princess of this country, and the air on 't
Revengingly enfeebles me; or could this carl,
A very drudge of nature's, have subdu'd me
In my profession? Knighthoods and honours, borne
As I wear mine, are titles but of scorn.
If that thy gentry, Britain, go before
This lout as he exceeds our lords, the odds
Is that we scarce are men and you are gods. *Exit.*

The battle continues; the Britons *fly;* CYMBELINE *is taken: then enter, to his rescue,* BELARIUS, GUIDERIUS, *and* ARVIRAGUS.

Bel. Stand, stand! We have th' advantage of the ground;
The lane is guarded: nothing routs us but
The villany of our fears.
Gui., *Arv.* Stand, stand, and fight!

Enter POSTHUMUS, *and seconds the* Britons: *they rescue* CYMBELINE, *and exeunt. Then enter* LUCIUS, IACHIMO, *and* IMOGEN.

Luc. Away, boy, from the troops, and save thyself;
For friends kill friends, and the disorder 's such
As war were hoodwink'd.
Iach. 'Tis their fresh supplies.
Luc. It is a day turn'd strangely: or betimes
Let 's re-inforce, or fly. *Exeunt.*

SCENE III. [*Another part of the field.*]

Enter POSTHUMUS *and a* Briton Lord.

Lord. Cam'st thou from where they made the stand?
Post. I did:

or simply camp fires. 20. **our note,** noting us. 26-28. **Who . . . promis'd,** you who find in exile want of breeding and the certain results of this hard life, perpetually without hope of ever finding the refinement promised you by your high birth. 29. **tanlings,** those tanned by the sun. 33. **o'ergrown,** i.e., with hair and beard; or, replaced in their thoughts. 37. **hot,** lecherous. 39. **rowel,** wheel of a spur.

ACT V. SCENE I. 5. **wrying,** swerving from the right course. 7. **bond but,** obligation except. 9. **put on,** incite, encourage. 12-13. **that 's . . . more,** that is an act of kindness, since it makes them sin no more. 14. **second,** follow up. **elder,** subsequent sin. 15. **dread . . . thrift.** The guilty, by knowing of the further progress of evil, repent before committing more crimes. 25. **part,** party, side. 32. **guise,** custom.

SCENE II. 3. **on 't,** of it. 4. **carl,** churl, peasant. 8. **go before,** excel. 16. **hoodwink'd,** blindfolded.

Though you, it seems, come from the fliers.
Lord. I did.
Post. No blame be to you, sir; for all was lost,
But that the heavens fought: the king himself
Of his wings destitute, the army broken,
And but the backs of Britons seen, all flying
Through a strait lane; the enemy full-hearted,
Lolling the tongue with slaught'ring, having work
More plentiful than tools to do 't, struck down
Some mortally, some slightly touch'd, some falling
Merely through fear; that the strait pass was damm'd
With dead men hurt behind, and cowards living
To die with length'ned shame.
Lord. Where was this lane?
Post. Close by the battle, ditch'd, and wall'd with turf;
Which gave advantage to an ancient soldier,
An honest one, I warrant; who deserv'd
So long a breeding as his white beard came to,
In doing this for 's country: athwart the lane,
He, with two striplings—lads more like to run
The country base than to commit such slaughter;
With faces fit for masks, or rather fairer
Than those for preservation cas'd, or shame,—
Made good the passage; cried to those that fled,
'Our Britain's harts die flying, not our men:
To darkness fleet souls that fly backwards. Stand;
Or we are Romans and will give you that
Like beasts which you shun beastly, and may save,
But to look back in frown: stand, stand.' These three,
Three thousand confident, in act as many—
For three performers are the file when all
The rest do nothing—with this word 'Stand, stand,'
Accommodated by the place, more charming
With their own nobleness, which could have turn'd
A distaff to a lance, gilded pale looks,
Part shame, part spirit renew'd; that some, turn'd coward
But by example—O, a sin in war,
Damn'd in the first beginners!—gan to look
The way that they did, and to grin like lions
Upon the pikes o' th' hunters. Then began
A stop i' th' chaser, a retire, anon
A rout, confusion thick; forthwith they fly
Chickens, the way which they stoop'd eagles; slaves,
The strides they victors made: and now our cowards,
Like fragments in hard voyages, became
The life o' th' need: having found the back-door open
Of the unguarded hearts, heavens, how they wound!
Some slain before; some dying; some their friends
O'er-borne i' th' former wave: ten, chas'd by one,
Are now each one the slaughter-man of twenty:
Those that would die or ere resist are grown
The mortal bugs o' th' field.
Lord. This was strange chance:
A narrow lane, an old man, and two boys.
Post. Nay, do not wonder at it: you are made
Rather to wonder at the things you hear
Than to work any. Will you rhyme upon 't,
And vent it for a mock'ry? Here is one:
'Two boys, an old man twice a boy, a lane,
Preserv'd the Britons, was the Romans' bane.'
Lord. Nay, be not angry, sir.
Post. 'Lack, to what end?
Who dares not stand his foe, I'll be his friend;
For if he'll do as he is made to do,
I know he'll quickly fly my friendship too.
You have put me into rhyme.
Lord. Farewell; you 're angry. *Exit.*
Post. Still going? This is a lord! O noble misery,
To be i' th' field, and ask 'what news?' of me!
To-day how many would have given their honours
To have sav'd their carcases! took heel to do 't,
And yet died too! I, in mine own woe charm'd,
Could not find Death where I did hear him groan,
Nor feel him where he struck: being an ugly monster,
'Tis strange he hides him in fresh cups, soft beds,
Sweet words; or hath moe ministers than we
That draw his knives i' th' war. Well, I will find him:
For being now a favourer to the Briton,
No more a Briton. I have resum'd again
The part I came in: fight I will no more,
But yield me to the veriest hind that shall
Once touch my shoulder. Great the slaughter is
Here made by th' Roman; great the answer be
Britons must take. For me, my ransom 's death;
On either side I come to spend my breath;
Which neither here I'll keep nor bear again,
But end it by some means for Imogen.

Enter two [British] Captains *and* Soldiers.

First Cap. Great Jupiter be prais'd! Lucius is taken.
'Tis thought the old man and his sons were angels.
Sec. Cap. There was a fourth man, in a silly habit,
That gave th' affront with them.
First Cap. So 'tis reported:
But none of 'em can be found. Stand! who 's there?
Post. A Roman,
Who had not now been drooping here, if seconds
Had answer'd him.
Sec. Cap. Lay hands on him; a dog!
A leg of Rome shall not return to tell
What crows have peck'd them here. He brags his service
As if he were of note: bring him to th' king.

Enter CYMBELINE, BELARIUS, GUIDERIUS, ARVIRAGUS, PISANIO, [Soldiers, Attendants,] *and* Roman Captives. *The* Captains *present* POSTHUMUS *to* CYMBELINE, *who delivers him over to a* Gaoler. [*Then exeunt omnes.*]

SCENE IV. [*A British prison.*]

Enter POSTHUMUS *and* [*two*] Gaoler[s].

First Gaol. You shall not now be stol'n, you have locks upon you;
So graze as you find pasture.
Sec. Gaol. Ay, or a stomach.
[*Exeunt Gaolers.*]

SCENE III. 7. **strait,** narrow. **full-hearted,** full of courage and confidence. 17. **breeding,** life. 20. **base,** prisoner's base, a game in which rapid running is the means to victory. 22. **cas'd,** covered. **shame,** modesty, shyness. 25. **fleet,** hasten. 26. **are Romans,** i.e., will act like Romans. 27. **beastly,** like cowards. **save,** prevent. 28. **But . . . frown,** only by looking back in defiance. 30. **file,** rank (of soldiers). 32. **more charming,** persuading others (to turn and fight). 34. **gilded,** imparted a flush or color. 35. **Part . . . part,** in some . . . in others. 37. **gan,** began. 38. **grin,** bare the teeth. 40. **chaser,** pursuer. 42. **stoop'd,** swooped over (like eagles). 42-43. **slaves . . . made,** retracing, as slaves, the steps they took as victors. 44. **fragments,** scraps, fragments of food. 45. **The . . . need,** support for life in time of necessity. 50. **or ere,** rather than. 51. **mortal bugs,** deadly bugbears. 56. **vent,** air. 59. **'Lack,** alack; exclamation expressing sorrow. 60.

Post. Most welcome, bondage! for thou art a way,
I think, to liberty: yet am I better
Than one that 's sick o' th' gout; since he had rather
Groan so in perpetuity than be cur'd
By th' sure physician, Death, who is the key
T' unbar these locks. My conscience, thou art fetter'd
More than my shanks and wrists: you good gods, give me
The penitent instrument to pick that bolt,
Then, free for ever! Is 't enough I am sorry?
So children temporal fathers do appease;
Gods are more full of mercy. Must I repent?
I cannot do it better than in gyves,
Desir'd more than constrain'd: to satisfy,
If of my freedom 'tis the main part, take
No stricter render of me than my all.
I know you are more clement than vile men,
Who of their broken debtors take a third,
A sixth, a tenth, letting them thrive again
On their abatement: that 's not my desire:
For Imogen's dear life take mine; and though
'Tis not so dear, yet 'tis a life; you coin'd it:
'Tween man and man they weigh not every stamp;
Though light, take pieces for the figure's sake:
You rather mine, being yours: and so, great pow'rs,
If you will take this audit, take this life,
And cancel these cold bonds. O Imogen!
I'll speak to thee in silence. [*Sleeps.*]

Solemn music. Enter, as in an apparition, SICILIUS LEONATUS, *father to Posthumus, an old man, attired like a warrior; leading in his hand an ancient matron, his wife, and mother to Posthumus, with music before them: then, after other music, follows the two young* LEONATI, *brothers to Posthumus, with wounds as they died in the wars. They circle* POSTHUMUS *round, as he lies sleeping.*

Sici. No more, thou thunder-master, show
Thy spite on mortal flies:
With Mars fall out, with Juno chide,
That thy adulteries
Rates and revenges.
Hath my poor boy done aught but well,
Whose face I never saw?
I died whilst in the womb he stay'd
Attending nature's law:
Whose father then, as men report
Thou orphans' father art,
Thou shouldst have been, and shielded him
From this earth-vexing smart.

Moth. Lucina lent not me her aid,
But took me in my throes;
That from me was Posthumus ript,
Came crying 'mongst his foes,
A thing of pity!

Sici. Great nature, like his ancestry,
Moulded the stuff so fair,
That he deserv'd the praise o' th' world,
As great Sicilius' heir.

First Bro. When once he was mature for man,
In Britain where was he
That could stand up his parallel;
Or fruitful object be
In eye of Imogen, that best
Could deem his dignity?

Moth. With marriage wherefore was he mock'd,
To be exil'd, and thrown
From Leonati seat, and cast
From her his dearest one,
Sweet Imogen?

Sici. Why did you suffer Iachimo,
Slight thing of Italy,
To taint his nobler heart and brain
With needless jealousy;
And to become the geck and scorn
O' th' other's villany?

Sec. Bro. For this from stiller seats we came,
Our parents and us twain,
That striking in our country's cause
Fell bravely and were slain,
Our fealty and Tenantius' right
With honour to maintain.

First Bro. Like hardiment Posthumus hath
To Cymbeline perform'd:
Then, Jupiter, thou king of gods,
Why hast thou thus adjourn'd
The graces for his merits due,
Being all to dolours turn'd?

Sici. Thy crystal window ope; look out;
No longer exercise
Upon a valiant race thy harsh
And potent injuries.

Moth. Since, Jupiter, our son is good,
Take off his miseries.

Sici. Peep through thy marble mansion; help;
Or we poor ghosts will cry
To th' shining synod of the rest
Against thy deity.

Both Bro. Help, Jupiter; or we appeal,
And from thy justice fly.

JUPITER *descends in thunder and lightning, sitting upon an eagle: he throws a thunderbolt. The Ghosts fall on their knees.*

Jup. No more, you petty spirits of region low,
Offend our hearing; hush! How dare you ghosts
Accuse the thunderer, whose bolt, you know,
Sky-planted batters all rebelling coasts?
Poor shadows of Elysium, hence, and rest

stand, withstand. 61. **made,** inclined. 64. **going,** fleeing. **noble misery,** false nobility. 68. **charm'd,** i.e., made invulnerable. 74. **being . . . favourer,** i.e., since Death now favors. 79. **answer,** retaliation. 86. **silly,** simple. 90. **seconds,** supporters.

SCENE IV. 14. **gyves,** fetters. 15. **constrain'd,** forced upon me. 17. **stricter render,** sterner repayment. 24. **stamp,** coin. 25. **pieces,** coins. **for . . . sake,** for the sake of the image stamped upon it (i.e., the image of the gods). 43. **Lucina,** goddess of childbirth. 67. **geck,** dupe. 69. **stiller seats,** quieter abodes (the Elysian fields). 75. **hardiment,** bold exploit. 78. **adjourn'd,** deferred. 89. **synod,** assembly of the gods.

Upon your never-withering banks of flow'rs:
Be not with mortal accidents opprest;
No care of yours it is; you know 'tis ours.
Whom best I love I cross; to make my gift,
The more delay'd, delighted. Be content;
Your low-laid son our godhead will uplift:
His comforts thrive, his trials well are spent.
Our Jovial star reign'd at his birth, and in
Our temple was he married. Rise, and fade.
He shall be lord of lady Imogen,
And happier much by his affliction made.
This tablet lay upon his breast, wherein
Our pleasure his full fortune doth confine:
And so, away: no farther with your din
Express impatience, lest you stir up mine.
Mount, eagle, to my palace crystalline. *Ascends.*

Sici. He came in thunder; his celestial breath
Was sulphurous to smell: the holy eagle
Stoop'd, as to foot us: his ascension is
More sweet than our blest fields: his royal bird
Prunes the immortal wing and cloys his beak,
As when his god is pleas'd.

All. Thanks, Jupiter!

Sici. The marble pavement closes, he is enter'd
His radiant roof. Away! and, to be blest,
Let us with care perform his great behest.
[*The Ghosts*] *vanish.*

Post. [*Waking*] Sleep, thou hast been a grandsire, and begot
A father to me; and thou hast created
A mother and two brothers: but, O scorn!
Gone! they went hence so soon as they were born:
And so I am awake. Poor wretches that depend
On greatness' favour dream as I have done,
Wake and find nothing. But, alas, I swerve:
Many dream not to find, neither deserve,
And yet are steep'd in favours; so am I,
That have this golden chance and know not why.
What fairies haunt this ground? A book? O rare one!
Be not, as is our fangled world, a garment
Nobler than that it covers: let thy effects
So follow, to be most unlike our courtiers,
As good as promise.

(*Reads*) 'When as a lion's whelp shall, to himself unknown, without seeking find, and be embraced by a piece of tender air; and when from a stately cedar shall be lopped branches, which, being dead many years, shall after revive, be jointed to the old stock and freshly grow; then shall Posthumus end his miseries, Britain be fortunate and flourish in peace and plenty.'

'Tis still a dream, or else such stuff as madmen
Tongue and brain not; either both or nothing;
Or senseless speaking or a speaking such
As sense cannot untie. Be what it is,
The action of my life is like it, which
I'll keep, if but for sympathy.

Enter Gaoler.

First Gaol. Come, sir, are you ready for death?

Post. Over-roasted rather; ready long ago.

First Gaol. Hanging is the word, sir: if you be ready for that, you are well cooked.

Post. So, if I prove a good repast to the spectators, the dish pays the shot.

First Gaol. A heavy reckoning for you, sir. But the comfort is, you shall be called to no more payments, fear no more tavern-bills; which are often the sadness of parting, as the procuring of mirth: you come in faint for want of meat, depart reeling with too much drink; sorry that you have paid too much, and sorry that you are paid too much; purse and brain both empty; the brain the heavier for being too light, the purse too light, being drawn of heaviness: of this contradiction you shall now be quit. O, the charity of a penny cord! it sums up thousands in a trice: you have no true debitor and creditor but it; of what 's past, is, and to come, the discharge: your neck, sir, is pen, book and counters; so the acquittance follows.

Post. I am merrier to die than thou art to live.

First Gaol. Indeed, sir, he that sleeps feels not the tooth-ache: but a man that were to sleep your sleep, and a hangman to help him to bed, I think he would change places with his officer; for, look you, sir, you know not which way you shall go.

Post. Yes, indeed do I, fellow.

First Gaol. Your death has eyes in 's head then; I have not seen him so pictured: you must either be directed by some that take upon them to know, or to take upon yourself that which I am sure you do not know, or jump the after inquiry on your own peril: and how you shall speed in your journey's end, I think you'll never return to tell one.

Post. I tell thee, fellow, there are none want eyes to direct them the way I am going, but such as wink and will not use them.

First Gaol. What an infinite mock is this, that a man should have the best use of eyes to see the way of blindness! I am sure hanging 's the way of winking.

Enter a Messenger.

Mess. Knock off his manacles; bring your prisoner to the king.

Post. Thou bring'st good news; I am called to be made free.

First Gaol. I'll be hang'd then.

Post. Thou shalt be then freer than a gaoler; no bolts for the dead. *Exeunt* [*all but the First Gaoler.*]

First Gaol. Unless a man would marry a gallows and beget young gibbets, I never saw one so prone. Yet, on my conscience, there are verier knaves desire to live, for all he be a Roman: and there be some of them too that die against their wills; so should I, if I were one. I would we were all of one mind, and one mind good; O, there were desolation of gaolers and gallowses! I speak against my present profit, but my wish hath a preferment in 't. [*Exit.*]

SCENE V. [*Cymbeline's tent.*]

Enter CYMBELINE, BELARIUS, GUIDERIUS, ARVIRAGUS, PISANIO, [Officers, Attendants,] *and* Lords.

102. **delighted,** delighted in. 105. **Jovial star,** the planet Jupiter, the happiest of all stars to be born under. 110. **confine,** precisely state. 116. **foot,** seize (in his talons). 118. **Prunes,** preens, arranges the feathers with the beak. **cloys,** claws, strokes with the claw (Schmidt). 120. **marble pavement,** heavens (above the Elizabethan stage). 125. **scorn,** mockery. 129. **swerve,** mistake, go astray. 133. **book,** tablet or scroll. 134. **fangled,** characterized by fopperies or gaudiness. 138. **When as,** when. 147. **Tongue,** speak of. **brain,** understand. 149. **Be what it is,** let it be what it may. 158. **shot,** tavern reckoning. 168. **drawn,** tapped, emptied. 171. **debitor and creditor,** accounting book. 172. **discharge,** payment. 173. **counters,** round pieces of metal used for calculating. 189. **jump,** gamble on. 190. **how . . . speed,**

Cym. Stand by my side, you whom the gods have made
Preservers of my throne. Woe is my heart
That the poor soldier that so richly fought,
Whose rags sham'd gilded arms, whose naked breast
Stepp'd before targes of proof, cannot be found:
He shall be happy that can find him, if
Our grace can make him so.
Bel. I never saw
Such noble fury in so poor a thing;
Such precious deeds in one that promis'd nought
But beggary and poor looks.
Cym. No tidings of him?
Pis. He hath been search'd among the dead and living,
But no trace of him.
Cym. To my grief, I am
The heir of his reward; [*To Belarius, Guiderius, and Arviragus*] which I will add
To you, the liver, heart and brain of Britain,
By whom I grant she lives. 'Tis now the time
To ask of whence you are. Report it.
Bel. Sir,
In Cambria are we born, and gentlemen:
Further to boast were neither true nor modest,
Unless I add, we are honest.
Cym. Bow your knees.
Arise my knights o' th' battle: I create you
Companions to our person and will fit you
With dignities becoming your estates.

Enter CORNELIUS *and* Ladies.

There 's business in these faces. Why so sadly
Greet you our victory? you look like Romans,
And not o' th' court of Britain.
Cor. Hail, great king!
To sour your happiness, I must report
The queen is dead.
Cym. Who worse than a physician
Would this report become? But I consider,
By med'cine life may be prolong'd, yet death
Will seize the doctor too. How ended she?
Cor. With horror, madly dying, like her life,
Which, being cruel to the world, concluded
Most cruel to herself. What she confess'd
I will report, so please you: these her women
Can trip me, if I err; who with wet cheeks
Were present when she finish'd.
Cym. Prithee, say.
Cor. First, she confess'd she never lov'd you, only
Affected greatness got by you, not you:
Married your royalty, was wife to your place;
Abhorr'd your person.
Cym. She alone knew this;
And, but she spoke it dying, I would not
Believe her lips in opening it. Proceed.
Cor. Your daughter, whom she bore in hand to love
With such integrity, she did confess
Was as a scorpion to her sight; whose life,
But that her flight prevented it, she had
Ta'en off by poison.
Cym. O most delicate fiend!
Who is 't can read a woman? Is there more?
Cor. More, sir, and worse. She did confess she had
For you a mortal mineral: which, being took,
Should by the minute feed on life and ling'ring
By inches waste you: in which time she purpos'd,
By watching, weeping, tendance, kissing, to
O'ercome you with her show, and in time,
When she had fitted you with her craft, to work
Her son into th' adoption of the crown:
But, failing of her end by his strange absence,
Grew shameless-desperate; open'd, in despite
Of heaven and men, her purposes; repented
The evils she hatch'd were not effected; so
Despairing died.
Cym. Heard you all this, her women?
Ladies. We did, so please your highness.
Cym. Mine eyes
Were not in fault, for she was beautiful;
Mine ears, that heard her flattery; nor my heart,
That thought her like her seeming; it had been vicious
To have mistrusted her: yet, O my daughter!
That it was folly in me, thou mayst say,
And prove it in thy feeling. Heaven mend all!

Enter LUCIUS, IACHIMO, [*the* Soothsayer,] *and other* Roman Prisoners, [*guarded;* POSTHUMUS] LEONATUS *behind, and* IMOGEN.

Thou com'st not, Caius, now for tribute; that
The Britons have raz'd out, though with the loss
Of many a bold one; whose kinsmen have made suit
That their good souls may be appeas'd with slaughter
Of you their captives, which ourself have granted:
So think of your estate.
Luc. Consider, sir, the chance of war: the day
Was yours by accident; had it gone with us,
We should not, when the blood was cool, have threaten'd
Our prisoners with the sword. But since the gods
Will have it thus, that nothing but our lives
May be call'd ransom, let it come: sufficeth
A Roman with a Roman's heart can suffer:
Augustus lives to think on 't: and so much
For my peculiar care. This one thing only
I will entreat; my boy, a Briton born,
Let him be ransom'd: never master had
A page so kind, so duteous, diligent,
So tender over his occasions, true,
So feat, so nurse-like: let his virtue join
With my request, which I'll make bold your highness
Cannot deny; he hath done no Briton harm,
Though he have serv'd a Roman: save him, sir,
And spare no blood beside.
Cym. I have surely seen him:
His favour is familiar to me. Boy,
Thou hast look'd thyself into my grace,
†And art mine own. I know not why, wherefore,
To say 'live, boy:' ne'er thank thy master; live:
And ask of Cymbeline what boon thou wilt,

how you will succeed. 193. **wink,** close. 208. **prone,** ready, eager. 214. **gallowses,** gallows, or possibly, hangmen.

SCENE V. 5. **targes of proof,** shields of steel hardened to withstand certain tests. 35. **trip,** refute, contradict. 38. **Affected,** desired. 42. **opening,** revealing. 43. **bore in hand,** pretended with false appearances. 47. **Ta'en off,** ended. **delicate,** subtle. 50. **mortal mineral,** deadly poison. 51. **by the minute,** minute by minute. 53. **tendance,** attentiveness. 55. **fitted,** prepared. 56. **adoption,** right of an adopted heir. 58. **shameless-desperate,** shamelessly desperate. **open'd,** revealed. 68. **prove,** experience. **feeling,** suffering. 70. **raz'd out,** erased. 83. **peculiar,** particular, individual. 87. **occasions,** particular wants or requirements. 88. **feat,** adroit, neat.

Fitting my bounty and thy state, I'll give it;
Yea, though thou do demand a prisoner,
The noblest ta'en.
Imo. I humbly thank your highness.
Luc. I do not bid thee beg my life, good lad;
And yet I know thou wilt.
Imo. No, no: alack,
There 's other work in hand: I see a thing
Bitter to me as death: your life, good master,
Must shuffle for itself.
Luc. The boy disdains me,
He leaves me, scorns me: briefly die their joys
That place them on the truth of girls and boys.
Why stands he so perplex'd?
Cym. What wouldst thou, boy?
I love thee more and more: think more and more
What 's best to ask. Know'st him thou look'st on? speak,
Wilt have him live? Is he thy kin? thy friend?
Imo. He is a Roman; no more kin to me
Than I to your highness; who, being born your vassal,
Am something nearer.
Cym. Wherefore ey'st him so?
Imo. I'll tell you, sir, in private, if you please
To give me hearing.
Cym. Ay, with all my heart,
And lend my best attention. What 's thy name?
Imo. Fidele, sir.
Cym. Thou 'rt my good youth, my page;
I'll be thy master: walk with me; speak freely.
[*Cymbeline and Imogen converse apart.*]
Bel. Is not this boy reviv'd from death?
Arv. One sand another
Not more resembles that sweet rosy lad
Who died, and was Fidele. What think you?
Gui. The same dead thing alive.
Bel. Peace, peace! see further; he eyes us not; forbear;
Creatures may be alike: were 't he, I am sure
He would have spoke to us.
Gui. But we saw him dead.
Bel. Be silent; let 's see further.
Pis. [*Aside*] It is my mistress:
Since she is living, let the time run on
To good or bad. [*Cymbeline and Imogen come forward.*]
Cym. Come, stand thou by our side;
Make thy demand aloud. [*To Iachimo*] Sir, step you forth;
Give answer to this boy, and do it freely;
Or, by our greatness and the grace of it,
Which is our honour, bitter torture shall
Winnow the truth from falsehood.—On, speak to him.
Imo. My boon is, that this gentleman may render
Of whom he had this ring.
Post. [*Aside*] What 's that to him?
Cym. That diamond upon your finger, say
How came it yours?
Iach. Thou 'lt torture me to leave unspoken that
Which, to be spoke, would torture thee.
Cym. How! me?
Iach. I am glad to be constrain'd to utter that
Which torments me to conceal. By villany
I got this ring: 'twas Leonatus' jewel;
Whom thou didst banish; and—which more may grieve thee,
As it doth me—a nobler sir ne'er liv'd
'Twixt sky and ground. Wilt thou hear more, my lord?
Cym. All that belongs to this.
Iach. That paragon, thy daughter,—
For whom my heart drops blood, and my false spirits
Quail to remember—Give me leave; I faint.
Cym. My daughter! what of her? Renew thy strength:
I had rather thou shouldst live while nature will
Than die ere I hear more: strive, man, and speak.
Iach. Upon a time,—unhappy was the clock
That struck the hour!—it was in Rome,—accurs'd
The mansion where!—'twas at a feast,—O, would
Our viands had been poison'd, or at least
Those which I heav'd to head!—the good Posthumus—
What should I say? he was too good to be
Where ill men were; and was the best of all
Amongst the rar'st of good ones,—sitting sadly,
Hearing us praise our loves of Italy
For beauty that made barren the swell'd boast
Of him that best could speak, for feature, laming
The shrine of Venus, or straight-pight Minerva,
Postures beyond brief nature, for condition,
A shop of all the qualities that man
Loves woman for, besides that hook of wiving,
Fairness which strikes the eye—
Cym. I stand on fire:
Come to the matter.
Iach. All too soon I shall,
Unless thou wouldst grieve quickly. This Posthumus,
Most like a noble lord in love and one
That had a royal lover, took his hint;
And, not dispraising whom we prais'd,—therein
He was as calm as virtue—he began
His mistress' picture; which by his tongue being made,
And then a mind put in 't, either our brags
Were crack'd of kitchen-trulls, or his description
Prov'd us unspeaking sots.
Cym. Nay, nay, to th' purpose.
Iach. Your daughter's chastity—there it begins.
He spake of her, as Dian had hot dreams,
And she alone were cold: whereat I, wretch,
Made scruple of his praise; and wager'd with him
Pieces of gold 'gainst this which then he wore
Upon his honour'd finger, to attain
In suit the place of 's bed and win this ring
By hers and mine adultery. He, true knight,
No lesser of her honour confident
Than I did truly find her, stakes this ring;
And would so, had it been a carbuncle
Of Phœbus' wheel, and might so safely, had it
Been all the worth of 's car. Away to Britain
Post I in this design: well may you, sir,
Remember me at court; where I was taught
Of your chaste daughter the wide difference
'Twixt amorous and villanous. Being thus quench'd
Of hope, not longing, mine Italian brain

103. **thing,** i.e., the ring on Iachimo's finger. 157. **heav'd to head,** raised to lips. 163. **laming,** making seem crippled. 164. **shrine,** image. **straight-pight,** erect. 165. **Postures,** forms, attitudes. **beyond brief nature,** immortal. **condition,** temper of mind. 166. **shop,** store. 167. **hook of wiving,** the incentive to matrimony. 177. **crack'd of,** boasted in praise of. **kitchen-trulls,** kitchen maids. 178. **unspeaking sots,** speechless blockheads. 180. **as,** as if. 189. **would so,** would have done so. 196. **not longing,** though not of my desire. 200.

'Gan in your duller Britain operate
Most vilely; for my vantage, excellent:
And, to be brief, my practice so prevail'd,
That I return'd with simular proof enough
To make the noble Leonatus mad,
By wounding his belief in her renown
With tokens thus, and thus; averring notes
Of chamber-hanging, pictures, this her bracelet,—
O cunning, how I got it!—nay, some marks
Of secret on her person, that he could not
But think her bond of chastity quite crack'd,
I having ta'en the forfeit. Whereupon—
Methinks, I see him now—
Post. [*Advancing*] Ay, so thou dost,
Italian fiend! Ay me, most credulous fool,
Egregious murderer, thief, any thing
That 's due to all the villains past, in being,
To come! O, give me cord, or knife, or poison,
Some upright justicer! Thou, king, send out
For torturers ingenious: it is I
That all th' abhorred things o' th' earth amend
By being worse than they. I am Posthumus,
That kill'd thy daughter:—villain-like, I lie—
That caus'd a lesser villain than myself,
A sacrilegious thief, to do 't: the temple
Of virtue was she; yea, and she herself.
Spit, and throw stones, cast mire upon me, set
The dogs o' th' street to bay me: every villain
Be call'd Posthumus Leonatus; and
Be villany less than 'twas! O Imogen!
My queen, my life, my wife! O Imogen,
Imogen, Imogen!
Imo. Peace, my lord; hear, hear—
Post. Shall 's have a play of this? Thou scornful page,
There lie thy part. [*Striking her: she falls.*]
Pis. O, gentlemen, help!
Mine and your mistress! O, my lord Posthumus!
You ne'er kill'd Imogen till now. Help, help!
Mine honour'd lady!
Cym. Does the world go round?
Post. How comes these staggers on me?
Pis. Wake, my mistress!
Cym. If this be so, the gods do mean to strike me
To death with mortal joy.
Pis. How fares my mistress?
Imo. O, get thee from my sight;
Thou gav'st me poison: dangerous fellow, hence!
Breathe not where princes are.
Cym. The tune of Imogen!
Pis. Lady,
The gods throw stones of sulphur on me, if
That box I gave you was not thought by me
A precious thing: I had it from the queen.
Cym. New matter still?
Imo. It poison'd me.
Cor. O gods!
I left out one thing which the queen confess'd,
Which must approve thee honest: 'If Pisanio
Have' said she 'given his mistress that confection
Which I gave him for cordial, she is serv'd
As I would serve a rat.'
Cym. What 's this, Cornelius?
Cor. The queen, sir, very oft importun'd me
To temper poisons for her, still pretending
The satisfaction of her knowledge only
In killing creatures vile, as cats and dogs,
Of no esteem: I, dreading that her purpose
Was of more danger, did compound for her
A certain stuff, which, being ta'en, would cease
The present pow'r of life, but in short time
All offices of nature should again
Do their due functions. Have you ta'en of it?
Imo. Most like I did, for I was dead.
Bel. My boys,
There was our error.
Gui. This is, sure, Fidele.
Imo. Why did you throw your wedded lady from you?
Think that you are upon a rock; and now
Throw me again. [*Embracing him.*]
Post. Hang there like fruit, my soul,
Till the tree die!
Cym. How now, my flesh, my child!
What, mak'st thou me a dullard in this act?
Wilt thou not speak to me?
Imo. [*Kneeling*] Your blessing, sir.
Bel. [*To Guiderius and Arviragus*] Though you did love this youth, I blame ye not;
You had a motive for 't.
Cym. My tears that fall
Prove holy water on thee! Imogen,
Thy mother 's dead.
Imo. I am sorry for 't, my lord.
Cym. O, she was naught; and long of her it was
That we meet here so strangely: but her son
Is gone, we know not how nor where.
Pis. My lord,
Now fear is from me, I'll speak troth. Lord Cloten,
Upon my lady's missing, came to me
With his sword drawn; foam'd at the mouth, and swore,
If I discover'd not which way she was gone,
It was my instant death. By accident,
I had a feigned letter of my master's
Then in my pocket; which directed him
To seek her on the mountains near to Milford;
Where, in a frenzy, in my master's garments,
Which he enforc'd from me, away he posts
With unchaste purpose and with oath to violate
My lady's honour: what became of him
I further know not.
Gui. Let me end the story:
I slew him there.
Cym. Marry, the gods forfend!
I would not thy good deeds should from my lips
Pluck a hard sentence: prithee, valiant youth,
Deny 't again.
Gui. I have spoke it, and I did it.
Cym. He was a prince.
Gui. A most incivil one: the wrongs he did me
Were nothing prince-like; for he did provoke me
With language that would make me spurn the sea,
If it could so roar to me: I cut off 's head;
And am right glad he is not standing here
To tell this tale of mine.

simular, simulated, or pretended. 216-217. **That . . . they.** The thought is that great crimes make lesser ones look better by comparison. 233. **staggers,** dizziness, bewilderment. 238. **tune,** sound of voice. 246. **confection,** composition of drugs. 262. **rock,** cliff, rocky eminence. Dowden conjectures: *upon a lock*, a wrestling embrace. 263. *Stage Direction:* ***Embracing him,*** added by Hanmer and making clear a passage regarded as obscure. 271. **long of,** on account of. 274. **troth,** truth. 277. **discover'd,** disclosed.

Cym. I am sorry for thee:
By thine own tongue thou art condemn'd, and must
Endure our law: thou 'rt dead.
Imo. That headless man
I thought had been my lord.
Cym. Bind the offender,
And take him from our presence.
Bel. Stay, sir king:
This man is better than the man he slew,
As well descended as thyself; and hath
More of thee merited than a band of Clotens
Had ever scar for. [*To the Guard*] Let his arms alone;
They were not born for bondage.
Cym. Why, old soldier,
Wilt thou undo the worth thou art unpaid for,
By tasting of our wrath? How of descent
As good as we?
Arv. In that he spake too far.
Cym. And thou shalt die for 't.
Bel. We will die all three:
But I will prove that two on 's are as good
As I have given out him. My sons, I must,
For mine own part, unfold a dangerous speech,
Though, haply, well for you.
Arv. Your danger 's ours.
Gui. And our good his.
Bel. Have at it then, by leave.
Thou hadst, great king, a subject who
Was call'd Belarius.
Cym. What of him? he is
A banish'd traitor.
Bel. He it is that hath
Assum'd this age; indeed a banish'd man;
I know not how a traitor.
Cym. Take him hence:
The whole world shall not save him.
Bel. Not too hot:
First pay me for the nursing of thy sons;
And let it be confiscate all, so soon
As I have receiv'd it.
Cym. Nursing of my sons!
Bel. I am too blunt and saucy: here 's my knee:
Ere I arise, I will prefer my sons;
Then spare not the old father. Mighty sir,
These two young gentlemen, that call me father
And think they are my sons, are none of mine;
They are the issue of your loins, my liege,
And blood of your begetting.
Cym. How! my issue!
Bel. So sure as you your father's. I, old Morgan,
Am that Belarius whom you sometime banish'd:
Your pleasure was my mere offence, my punishment
Itself, and all my treason; that I suffer'd
Was all the harm I did. These gentle princes—
For such and so they are—these twenty years
Have I train'd up: those arts they have as I
Could put into them; my breeding was, sir, as
Your highness knows. Their nurse, Euriphile,
Whom for the theft I wedded, stole these children
Upon my banishment: I mov'd her to 't,
Having receiv'd the punishment before,
For that which I did then: beaten for loyalty
Excited me to treason: their dear loss,
The more of you 'twas felt, the more it shap'd
Unto my end of stealing them. But, gracious sir,
Here are your sons again; and I must lose
Two of the sweet'st companions in the world.
The benediction of these covering heavens
Fall on their heads like dew! for they are worthy
To inlay heaven with stars.
Cym. Thou weep'st, and speak'st.
The service that you three have done is more
Unlike than this thou tell'st. I lost my children:
If these be they, I know not how to wish
A pair of worthier sons.
Bel. Be pleas'd awhile.
This gentleman, whom I call Polydore,
Most worthy prince, as yours, is true Guiderius:
This gentleman, my Cadwal, Arviragus,
Your younger princely son; he, sir, was lapp'd
In a most curious mantle, wrought by th' hand
Of his queen mother, which for more probation
I can with ease produce.
Cym. Guiderius had
Upon his neck a mole, a sanguine star;
It was a mark of wonder.
Bel. This is he;
Who hath upon him still that natural stamp:
It was wise nature's end in the donation,
To be his evidence now.
Cym. O, what, am I
A mother to the birth of three? Ne'er mother
Rejoic'd deliverance more. Blest pray you be,
That, after this strange starting from your orbs,
You may reign in them now! O Imogen,
Thou hast lost by this a kingdom.
Imo. No, my lord;
I have got two worlds by 't. O my gentle brothers,
Have we thus met? O, never say hereafter
But I am truest speaker: you call'd me brother,
When I was but your sister; I you brothers,
When ye were so indeed.
Cym. Did you e'er meet?
Arv. Ay, my good lord.
Gui. And at first meeting lov'd;
Continu'd so, until we thought he died.
Cor. By the queen's dram she swallow'd.
Cym. O rare instinct!
When shall I hear all through? This fierce
abridgement
Hath to it circumstantial branches, which
Distinction should be rich in. Where? how liv'd you?
And when came you to serve our Roman captive?
How parted with your brothers? how first met them?
Why fled you from the court? and whither? These,
And your three motives to the battle, with
I know not how much more, should be demanded;
And all the other by-dependencies,
From chance to chance: but nor the time nor place
Will serve our long inter'gatories. See,
Posthumus anchors upon Imogen,
And she, like harmless lightning, throws her eye
On him, her brothers, me, her master, hitting
Each object with a joy: the counterchange

312. **given out,** reported. 315. **by leave,** with your permission. 319. **Assum'd,** reached, attained. 326. **prefer,** promote. 360. **lapp'd,** enfolded. 371. **orbs,** orbits. 383-384. **circumstantial . . . in,** separate narratives which ought to be followed out in all their rich details (Herford). 388. **your three motives,** the motives of you three. 390. **by-dependencies,** attendant circumstances. 391. **chance to chance,** event to event. 396-397. **the counterchange . . . all,** the exchange is in all and severally in each. 405. **forlorn,** lost, not to be found. 409. **beseeming,** appearance. **fitment,** makeshift. 412. **made you finish,** put an end to you. 413. **sinks,** causes to sink. 420. **doom'd,** pro-

Is severally in all. Let 's quit this ground,
And smoke the temple with our sacrifices.
[*To Belarius*] Thou art my brother; so we'll hold thee
ever.

Imo. You are my father too, and did relieve me,
To see this gracious season.

Cym. All o'erjoy'd,
Save these in bonds: let them be joyful too,
For they shall taste our comfort.

Imo. My good master,
I will yet do you service.

Luc. Happy be you!

Cym. The forlorn soldier, that so nobly fought,
He would have well becom'd this place, and grac'd
The thankings of a king.

Post. I am, sir,
The soldier that did company these three
In poor beseeming; 'twas a fitment for
The purpose I then follow'd. That I was he,
Speak, Iachimo: I had you down and might
Have made you finish.

Iach. [*Kneeling*] I am down again:
But now my heavy conscience sinks my knee,
As then your force did. Take that life, beseech you,
Which I so often owe: but your ring first;
And here the bracelet of the truest princess
That ever swore her faith.

Post. Kneel not to me:
The pow'r that I have on you is to spare you;
The malice towards you to forgive you: live,
And deal with others better.

Cym. Nobly doom'd!
We'll learn our freeness of a son-in-law;
Pardon 's the word to all.

Arv. You holp us, sir,
As you did mean indeed to be our brother;
Joy'd are we that you are.

Post. Your servant, princes. Good my lord of Rome,
Call forth your soothsayer: as I slept, methought
Great Jupiter, upon his eagle back'd,
Appear'd to me, with other spritely shows
Of mine own kindred: when I wak'd, I found
This label on my bosom; whose containing
Is so from sense in hardness, that I can
Make no collection of it: let him show
His skill in the construction.

Luc. Philarmonus!

Sooth. Here, my good lord.

Luc. Read, and declare the meaning.

Sooth. (*Reads*) 'When as a lion's whelp shall, to himself unknown, without seeking find, and be embraced by a piece of tender air; and when from a stately cedar shall be lopped branches, which, being dead many years, shall after revive, be jointed to the old stock, and freshly grow; then shall Posthumus end his miseries, Britain be fortunate and flourish in peace and plenty.'
Thou, Leonatus, art the lion's whelp;
The fit and apt construction of thy name,
Being Leo-natus, doth import so much.
[*To Cymbeline*] The piece of tender air, thy virtuous
daughter,
Which we call 'mollis aer;' and 'mollis aer'
We term it 'mulier:' which 'mulier' I divine
Is this most constant wife; who, even now,
Answering the letter of the oracle,
Unknown to you, unsought, were clipp'd about
With this most tender air.

Cym. This hath some seeming.

Sooth. The lofty cedar, royal Cymbeline,
Personates thee: and thy lopp'd branches point
Thy two sons forth; who, by Belarius stol'n,
For many years thought dead, are now reviv'd,
To the majestic cedar join'd, whose issue
Promises Britain peace and plenty.

Cym. Well;
My peace we will begin. And, Caius Lucius,
Although the victor, we submit to Cæsar,
And to the Roman empire; promising
To pay our wonted tribute, from the which
We were dissuaded by our wicked queen;
Whom heavens, in justice, both on her and hers,
Have laid most heavy hand.

Sooth. The fingers of the pow'rs above do tune
The harmony of this peace. The vision
Which I made known to Lucius, ere the stroke
Of this yet scarce-cold battle, at this instant
Is full accomplish'd; for the Roman eagle,
From south to west on wing soaring aloft,
Lessen'd herself, and in the beams o' th' sun
So vanish'd: which foreshow'd our princely
eagle,
Th' imperial Cæsar, should again unite
His favour with the radiant Cymbeline,
Which shines here in the west.

Cym. Laud we the gods;
And let our crooked smokes climb to their nostrils
From our blest altars. Publish we this peace
To all our subjects. Set we forward: let
A Roman and a British ensign wave
Friendly together: so through Lud's-town march:
And in the temple of great Jupiter
Our peace we'll ratify; seal it with feasts.
Set on there! Never was a war did cease,
Ere bloody hands were wash'd, with such a peace.

Exeunt.

nounced judgment, decreed. 421. **freeness,** liberality, generosity. 428. **spritely,** ghostly, in the form of spirits. **shows,** appearances. 430. **label,** tablet. 430-431. **whose . . . hardness,** whose meaning is so remote from sense in its difficulty. 432. **collection of,** inference or deduction from. 445. **Leo-natus,** one born of the lion. 447. **'mollis aer,'** tender air; a fanciful derivation of Latin *mulier*, woman. 452. **This . . . seeming,** this seems well founded (Gollancz). 476. **Laud,** praise. 484. **Set on there!** Forward march!

THE WINTER'S TALE

The Winter's Tale (c. 1610–1611), with its almost symmetrical division into two halves of bleak tragedy and comic romance, illustrates perhaps more clearly than any other Shakespearean play the genre of tragicomedy. To be sure, all the late romances feature journeys of separation, apparent deaths, and tearful reconciliations. Marina and Thaisa in *Pericles*, Imogen in *Cymbeline*, and Ferdinand in *The Tempest*, all supposed irrecoverably lost, are brought back to life by apparently miraculous devices. Of the four late romances, however, *The Winter's Tale* uses the most formal structure to evoke the antithesis of tragedy and romance. It is sharply divided into contrasting halves by a gap of sixteen years. The tragic first half takes place almost entirely in Sicilia, whereas the action of the second half is limited for the most part to Bohemia. At the court of Sicilia we see tyrannical jealousy producing a spiritual climate of "winter In storm perpetual"; in Bohemia we witness a pastoral landscape and a sheepshearing "in the sweet o' the year," "When daffodils begin to peer."

Although this motif of a renewing journey from jaded court to idealized countryside reminds us of *As You Like It* and other early comedies, we sense in the late romances and especially in *The Winter's Tale* a new preoccupation with man's tragic folly. The vision of human depravity is world-weary and pessimistic, as though infected by the gloomy spirit of the great tragedies. And because man is so bent on destroying himself, the restoration is at once more urgently needed and more miraculous than in the "festive" world of early comedy. Renewal is mythically associated with the seasonal cycle from winter to summer.

King Leontes' tragedy seems at first irreversible and terrifying, like that of Shakespeare's greatest tragic protagonists. He suffers from irrational jealousy, as does Othello, and attempts to destroy the person on whom all his happiness depends. Unlike Othello, however, Leontes needs no diabolical tempter such as Iago to poison his mind against Queen Hermione. Leontes is undone by his own fantasies. No differences in race or age can explain Leontes' fears of estrangement from Hermione. She is not imprudent in her conduct, like her counterpart in Robert Greene's *Pandosto* (1588), the prose romance from which Shakespeare drew his narrative. Although Hermione is graciously fond of Leontes' dear friend Polixenes, and urges him to stay longer in Sicilia, she does so only with a hospitable warmth demanded by the occasion and encouraged by her husband. In every way, then, Shakespeare strips away from Leontes the motive and the occasion for plausible doubting of his wife. All observers in the Sicilian court are incredulous and shocked at the king's accusations. Even so, Leontes is neither an unsympathetic nor an unbelievable character. Like Othello, Leontes cherishes his wife and perceives with a horrifying intensity what a fearful cost he must pay for his suspicions. Not only his marriage, but his lifelong friendship with Polixenes, his sense of pride in his children, and his enjoyment of his subjects' warm regard, all must be sacrificed to a single overwhelming compulsion.

Whatever may be the psychological cause of this obsession, it manifests itself as a revulsion against all sexual behavior. Like mad Lear, Leontes imagines lechery to be the unavoidable fact of the human condition, the lowest common denominator to which all persons (including Hermione) must stoop. He is persuaded that "It is a bawdy planet," in which cuckolded man has "his pond fish'd by his next neighbour, by Sir Smile, his neighbour" (I,ii). Leontes' tortured soliloquies are laden with what today we would call Freudian images, of unattended "gates" letting in and out the enemy "with bag and baggage," and of a "dagger" that must be "muzzl'd Lest it should bite its master." As in *King Lear*, order is inverted to disorder, sanity to madness, legitimacy to illegitimacy. Sexual misconduct is emblematic of a universal malaise: "Why, then the world and all that's in 't is nothing, The covering sky is nothing, Bohemia nothing, My wife is nothing." Other characters too see the trial of Hermione as a testing of humanity's worth: if Hermione prove false, Antigonus promises, he will treat his own wife as a stable-horse and will "geld" his three daughters (II,i). Prevailing images are of spiders, venom, infection, sterility, and the "dungy" earth.

Cosmic order is never really challenged, however. Leontes' fantasies of universal disorder are chimerical. His wife is in fact chaste, Polixenes true, and the king's courtiers loyal. Camillo refuses to carry out Leontes' order to murder Polixenes, not only because he knows murder to be wrong but because history offers not one example of a man "that had struck anointed kings And flourish'd after" (I,ii). The cosmos of this play is one in which crimes are invariably and swiftly punished. The Delphic oracle vindicates Hermione and gives Leontes stern warning. When Leontes persists in his madness, his son Mamillius' death follows as an immediate consequence. As Leontes at once perceives, "Apollo's angry, and the heavens themselves Do strike at my injustice" (III,ii). Leontes paradoxically welcomes the lengthy contrition he must undergo, for it confirms a pattern in the universe of just cause and effect. Although as tragic protagonist he has discovered the truth about Hermione moments too late, and so must pay richly for his error, Leontes has at least recovered faith in Hermione's transcendent goodness. His nightmare now over, he accepts and embraces suffering as a necessary atonement.

The transition to romance is therefore anticipated to an extent by the play's first half, even though the tone of the last two acts is strikingly different. Old Father Time comes on stage as Chorus, like Gower in *Pericles*, to remind us of the conscious artifice of the dramatist. He can "o'erthrow law" and carry us over sixteen years as if we had merely dreamed out the interim. Shakespeare flaunts the improbability of his story by giving Bohemia a seacoast (much to the distress of Ben Jonson), and by employing animals on stage ("*Exit pursued by a bear*"). The narrative uses many typical devices of romance: a babe abandoned to the elements, a princess brought up by shepherds, a prince disguised as a swain, a sea voyage, and a recognition scene. Love is threatened not by the internal psychic obstacle of jealousy, but by the external obstacles of parental opposition and a seeming disparity of social rank between the lovers. Comedy easily finds solutions for such difficulties by the unraveling of illusion. This comic world also properly includes clownish shepherds, coy shepherdesses, and Autolycus, the roguish pedlar, whose songs help set the mood of jollity and whose machinations contribute in an unforeseen manner to the working out of the love plot.

The conventional romantic ending is infused, however, with a sadness and a mystery not usually found in comedy. In Shakespeare's most notable departure from his source, Greene's *Pandosto*, Hermione is brought back to life. All observers view this event, and the rediscovery of Perdita, as grossly implausible, "so like an old tale that the verity of it is in strong suspicion" (V,ii). The play's very title, *The Winter's Tale*, reinforces this sense of naive improbability. Why does Shakespeare stress this riddling paradox of an unbelievable reality, and why does he deliberately mislead his audience into believing that Hermione has in fact died (III,iii), using a kind of theatrical trickery found in no other Shakespearean play? The answer may well be that, in Paulina's words, we must awake our faith, accepting mysteriously a narrative of death and return to life that cannot ultimately be comprehended by reason. On the rational level we are told that Hermione has been kept in hiding for sixteen years, in order to bring Leontes' contrition to fulfillment. Such an explanation seems psychologically incomprehensible, however, for it casts both Hermione and her keeper Paulina in the role of sadistic punishers of the king. Instead we are drawn toward an emblematic interpretation, bearing in mind that it is more an evocative hint than a complete truth. Throughout the play, Hermione has been repeatedly associated with "Grace" and with the goddess Proserpina, whose return from the underworld, after "Three crabbed months had sour'd themselves to death" (I,ii), signals the coming of spring. Perdita, also associated with Proserpina (IV,iv), is welcomed by her father "As is the spring to th' earth" (V,i). Paulina has a similarly emblematic role, that of Conscience, patiently guiding the king to a divinely appointed renewal of his joy. Paulina speaks of herself as an artist-figure, like Prospero in *The Tempest*, performing wonders of illusion though she rejects the assistance of wicked powers. These emblematic hints do not rob the story of its movingly human drama, but they do lend a transcendent significance to Leontes' bittersweet story of sinful error, affliction, and an unexpected second happiness.

THE WINTER'S TALE

The Names of the Actors

LEONTES, King of Sicilia.
MAMILLIUS, *young prince of Sicilia.*
CAMILLO, ANTIGONUS, CLEOMENES, DION, *four Lords of Sicilia.*
POLIXENES, King of Bohemia.
FLORIZEL, Prince of Bohemia.
ARCHIDAMUS, *a lord of Bohemia.*
Old Shepherd, *reputed father of Perdita.*
Clown, *his son.*
AUTOLYCUS, *a rogue.*
[A Mariner.]
[A Gaoler.]

HERMIONE, *queen to Leontes.*
PERDITA, *daughter to Leontes and Hermione.*
PAULINA, *wife to Antigonus.*
EMILIA, *a lady* [*attending on Hermione*].

[MOPSA, [DORCAS, *Shepherdesses.*]

Other Lords *and* Gentlemen, [Ladies, Officers,] *and* Servants, Shepherds, *and* Shepherdesses.

[Time, *as* Chorus.]

[SCENE: *Sicilia, and Bohemia.*]

ACT I.

SCENE I. [*Antechamber in* LEONTES' *palace.*]

Enter CAMILLO *and* ARCHIDAMUS.

Arch. If you shall chance, Camillo, to visit Bohemia, on the like occasion whereon my services are now on foot, you shall see, as I have said, great difference betwixt our Bohemia and your Sicilia.

Cam. I think, this coming summer, the King of Sicilia means to pay Bohemia the visitation which he justly owes him.

Arch. Wherein our entertainment shall shame us we will be justified in our loves; for indeed—

Cam. Beseech you,—

Arch. Verily, I speak it in the freedom of my knowledge: we cannot with such magnificence—in so rare—I know not what to say. We will give you sleepy drinks, that your senses, unintelligent of our insufficience, may, though they cannot praise us, as little accuse us.

Cam. You pay a great deal too dear for what 's given freely.

Arch. Believe me, I speak as my understanding instructs me and as mine honesty puts it to utterance.

Cam. Sicilia cannot show himself over-kind to Bohemia. They were trained together in their childhoods; and there rooted betwixt them then such an affection, which cannot choose but branch now. Since their more mature dignities and royal necessities made separation of their society, their encounters, though not personal, have been royally attorneyed with interchange of gifts, letters, loving embassies; that they have seemed to be together, though absent, shook hands, as over a vast, and embraced, as it were, from the ends of opposed winds. The heavens continue their loves!

Arch. I think there is not in the world either malice or matter to alter it. You have an unspeakable comfort of your young prince Mamillius: it is a gentleman of the greatest promise that ever came into my note.

Cam. I very well agree with you in the hopes of him: it is a gallant child; one that indeed physics the subject, makes old hearts fresh: they that went on crutches ere he was born desire yet their life to see him a man.

Arch. Would they else be content to die?

Cam. Yes; if there were no other excuse why they should desire to live.

Arch. If the king had no son, they would desire to live on crutches till he had one. *Exeunt.*

SCENE II. [*A room of state in the same.*]

Enter LEONTES, HERMIONE, MAMILLIUS, POLIXENES, CAMILLO [, *and* Attendants].

Pol. Nine changes of the wat'ry star hath been
The shepherd's note since we have left our throne
Without a burthen: time as long again
Would be fill'd up, my brother, with our thanks;
And yet we should, for perpetuity,
Go hence in debt: and therefore, like a cipher,
Yet standing in rich place, I multiply
With one 'We thank you' many thousands moe
That go before it.
Leon. Stay your thanks a while;
And pay them when you part.
Pol. Sir, that 's to-morrow.
I am question'd by my fears, of what may chance
Or breed upon our absence; that may blow
No sneaping winds at home, to make us say
'This is put forth too truly:' besides, I have stay'd
To tire your royalty.
Leon. We are tougher, brother,
Than you can put us to 't.
Pol. No longer stay.
Leon. One sev'n-night longer.
Pol. Very sooth, to-morrow.
Leon. We'll part the time between 's then; and in that
I'll no gainsaying.
Pol. Press me not, beseech you, so.
There is no tongue that moves, none, none i' th' world,
So soon as yours could win me: so it should now,
Were there necessity in your request, although
'Twere needful I denied it. My affairs
Do even drag me homeward: which to hinder
Were in your love a whip to me; my stay
To you a charge and trouble: to save both,
Farewell, our brother.
Leon. Tongue-tied our queen? speak you.
Her. I had thought, sir, to have held my peace until
You had drawn oaths from him not to stay. You, sir,
Charge him too coldly. Tell him, you are sure
All in Bohemia 's well; this satisfaction
The by-gone day proclaim'd: say this to him,
He 's beat from his best ward.
Leon. Well said, Hermione.
Her. To tell, he longs to see his son, were strong:
But let him say so then, and let him go;
But let him swear so, and he shall not stay,
We'll thwack him hence with distaffs.
Yet of your royal presence I'll adventure
The borrow of a week. When at Bohemia
You take my lord, I'll give him my commission
To let him there a month behind the gest
Prefix'd for 's parting: yet, good deed, Leontes,
I love thee not a jar o' th' clock behind
What lady-she her lord. You'll stay?
Pol. No, madam.
Her. Nay, but you will?
Pol. I may not, verily.
Her. Verily!
You put me off with limber vows; but I,
Though you would seek t' unsphere the stars with oaths,
Should yet say 'Sir, no going.' Verily,
You shall not go: a lady's 'Verily' is
As potent as a lord's. Will you go yet?
Force me to keep you as a prisoner,
Not like a guest; so you shall pay your fees
When you depart, and save your thanks. How say you?
My prisoner? or my guest? by your dread 'Verily,'
One of them you shall be.
Pol. Your guest, then, madam:
To be your prisoner should import offending;
Which is for me less easy to commit
Than you to punish.
Her. Not your gaoler, then,
But your kind hostess. Come, I'll question you
Of my lord's tricks and yours when you were boys:
You were pretty lordings then?
Pol. We were, fair queen,
Two lads that thought there was no more behind
But such a day to-morrow as to-day,
And to be boy eternal.
Her. Was not my lord

ACT I. SCENE I. 30. **attorneyed,** carried out by deputy. 33. **vast,** boundless, desolate space. 37. **of,** in the person of. 40. **note,** observation. 43. **physics the subject,** acts as a cordial to the people.

SCENE II. 1. **wat'ry star,** moon. 6-7. **like . . . place,** like a zero at the end of a number, multiplying its quantity. 11-14. **I am . . . truly,** i.e., I am anxious what may happen during my absence from Bohemia, worried that my absence may provoke my enemies to say that my leaving was very opportune for them. 13. **sneaping,** biting. 16. **Than . . . to 't,** than anything you can do to try us. 17. **sev'n-night,** common expression for "week." 19. **I'll no gainsaying,** I will have no refusal. 25. **your love a whip,** to make your love a punishment. 33. **ward,** defense. 39. **borrow,** borrowing. 41. **gest,** time allotted for a halt. 42. **good deed,** a mild oath. 43. **jar,** tick. 47. **limber,** limp. 53. **fees.** Persons leaving prison were obliged to pay for their lodging whether guilty or not. 57. **import,** imply. 63. **behind,** to come. 68. **chang'd,** exchanged. 74-75. **imposition . . . ours,** original sin, although imposed upon us by heredity, was swept clean away (Furness). 80. **Grace to boot,** i.e., Heaven help me. 85. **fault,** offense. 96. **heat,**

The verier wag o' th' two?
Pol. We were as twinn'd lambs that did frisk i' th' sun,
And bleat the one at th' other: what we chang'd
Was innocence for innocence; we knew not
The doctrine of ill-doing, nor dream'd
That any did. Had we pursu'd that life,
And our weak spirits ne'er been higher rear'd
With stronger blood, we should have answer'd heaven
Boldly 'not guilty;' the imposition clear'd
Hereditary ours.
Her. By this we gather
You have tripp'd since.
Pol. O my most sacred lady!
Temptations have since then been born to 's; for
In those unfledg'd days was my wife a girl;
Your precious self had then not cross'd the eyes
Of my young play-fellow.
Her. Grace to boot!
Of this make no conclusion, lest you say
Your queen and I are devils: yet go on;
Th' offences we have made you do we'll answer,
If you first sinn'd with us and that with us
You did continue fault and that you slipp'd not
With any but with us.
Leon. Is he won yet?
Her. He'll stay, my lord.
Leon. At my request he would not.
Hermione, my dearest, thou never spok'st
To better purpose.
Her. Never?
Leon. Never, but once.
Her. What! have I twice said well? when was 't before?
I prithee tell me; cram 's with praise, and make 's
As fat as tame things: one good deed dying tongueless
Slaughters a thousand waiting upon that.
Our praises are our wages: you may ride 's
With one soft kiss a thousand furlongs ere
With spur we heat an acre. But to th' goal:
My last good deed was to entreat his stay:
What was my first? it has an elder sister,
Or I mistake you: O, would her name were Grace!
But once before I spoke to th' purpose: when?
Nay, let me have 't; I long.
Leon. Why, that was when
Three crabbed months had sour'd themselves to death,
Ere I could make thee open thy white hand
And clap thyself my love: then didst thou utter
'I am yours for ever.'
Her. 'Tis grace indeed.
Why, lo you now, I have spoke to th' purpose twice:
The one for ever earn'd a royal husband;
Th' other for some while a friend.
Leon. [*Aside*] Too hot, too hot!
To mingle friendship far is mingling bloods.
I have tremor cordis on me: my heart dances;
But not for joy; not joy. This entertainment
May a free face put on, derive a liberty
From heartiness, from bounty, fertile bosom,
And well become the agent; 't may, I grant;
But to be paddling palms and pinching fingers,
As now they are, and making practis'd smiles,
As in a looking-glass, and then to sigh, as 'twere
The mort o' th' deer; O, that is entertainment
My bosom likes not, nor my brows! Mamillius,
Art thou my boy?
Mam. Ay, my good lord.
Leon. I' fecks!
Why, that 's my bawcock. What, hast smutch'd thy nose?
They say it is a copy out of mine. Come, captain,
We must be neat; not neat, but cleanly, captain:
And yet the steer, the heifer and the calf
Are all call'd neat.—Still virginalling
Upon his palm!—How now, you wanton calf!
Art thou my calf?
Mam. Yes, if you will, my lord.
Leon. Thou want'st a rough pash and the shoots that I have,
To be full like me: yet they say we are
Almost as like as eggs; women say so,
That will say any thing: but were they false
As o'er-dy'd blacks, as wind, as waters, false
As dice are to be wish'd by one that fixes
No bourn 'twixt his and mine, yet were it true
To say this boy were like me. Come, sir page,
Look on me with your welkin eye: sweet villain!
Most dear'st! my collop! Can thy dam?—may 't be?—
Affection! thy intention stabs the centre:
Thou dost make possible things not so held,
Communicat'st with dreams;—how can this be?—
With what 's unreal thou coactive art,
And fellow'st nothing: then 'tis very credent
Thou mayst co-join with something; and thou dost,
And that beyond commission, and I find it,
And that to the infection of my brains
And hard'ning of my brows.
Pol. What means Sicilia?
Her. He something seems unsettled.
Pol. How, my lord!
What cheer? how is 't with you, best brother?
Her. You look
As if you held a brow of much distraction:
Are you mov'd, my lord?
Leon. No, in good earnest.
How sometimes nature will betray its folly,
Its tenderness, and make itself a pastime
To harder bosoms! Looking on the lines
Of my boy's face, methoughts I did recoil
Twenty-three years, and saw myself unbreech'd,
In my green velvet coat, my dagger muzzled,
Lest it should bite its master, and so prove,
As ornaments oft do, too dangerous:
How like, methought, I then was to this kernel,
This squash, this gentleman. Mine honest friend,

traverse (as a horse driven by the spur). 104. **clap,** clasp hands, plight troth. 110. **tremor cordis,** fluttering of the heart. 118. **mort,** note sounded on a horn at the death of a deer. 120. **I' fecks,** in faith. 121. **bawcock,** French, *beau coq,* fine fellow. 123. **not . . . cleanly.** Leontes changes the word because *neat* reminds him of the cuckold's horns. 125. **virginalling,** playing on the virginals, a keyed instrument of the piano class; here, touching hands. 128. **pash,** head. **shoots,** horns; an allusion to the cuckold's horns. 132. **o'er-dy'd blacks,** probably, black garments whose fabric is destroyed by dye. 134. **bourn,** boundary. 136. **welkin,** sky-blue. 137. **collop,** piece of meat; here, a term of endearment. 138-143. **Affection . . . something.** Lustful passion, your power pierces to the very center, the soul of man. You deal in matters normally considered fantastic; you partake of the nature of dreams. How can this be? You collaborate with unreality, and create imagined fantasies. It's likely, then, that such imaginings may also become real. 144. **commission,** what is lawful. 154. **recoil,** go back in memory. 160. **squash,** unripe peascod.

Will you take eggs for money?
Mam. No, my lord, I'll fight.
Leon. You will! why, happy man be 's dole! My brother,
Are you so fond of your young prince as we
Do seem to be of ours?
Pol. If at home, sir,
He 's all my exercise, my mirth, my matter,
Now my sworn friend and then mine enemy,
My parasite, my soldier, statesman, all:
He makes a July's day short as December,
And with his varying childness cures in me
Thoughts that would thick my blood.
Leon. So stands this squire
Offic'd with me: we two will walk, my lord,
And leave you to your graver steps. Hermione,
How thou lov'st us, show in our brother's welcome;
Let what is dear in Sicily be cheap:
Next to thyself and my young rover, he 's
Apparent to my heart.
Her. If you would seek us,
We are yours i' th' garden: shall 's attend you there?
Leon. To your own bents dispose you: you'll be found,
Be you beneath the sky. [*Aside*] I am angling now,
Though you perceive me not how I give line.
Go to, go to!
How she holds up the neb, the bill to him!
And arms her with the boldness of a wife
To her allowing husband!
[*Exeunt Polixenes, Hermione, and Attendants.*]
Gone already!
Inch-thick, knee-deep, o'er head and ears a fork'd one!
Go, play, boy, play: thy mother plays, and I
Play too, but so disgrac'd a part, whose issue
Will hiss me to my grave: contempt and clamour
Will be my knell. Go, play, boy, play. There have been,
Or I am much deceiv'd, cuckolds ere now;
And many a man there is, even at this present,
Now while I speak this, holds his wife by th' arm,
That little thinks she has been sluic'd in 's absence
And his pond fish'd by his next neighbour, by
Sir Smile, his neighbour: nay, there 's comfort in 't
Whiles other men have gates and those gates open'd,
As mine, against their will. Should all despair
That have revolted wives, the tenth of mankind
Would hang themselves. Physic for 't there 's none;
It is a bawdy planet, that will strike
Where 'tis predominant; and 'tis powerful, think it,
From east, west, north and south: be it concluded,
No barricado for a belly; know 't;
It will let in and out the enemy
With bag and baggage: many thousand on 's
Have the disease, and feel 't not. How now, boy!
Mam. I am like you, they say.
Leon. Why, that 's some comfort.
What, Camillo there?
Cam. Ay, my good lord.
Leon. Go play, Mamillius; thou 'rt an honest man.
[*Exit Mamillius.*]
Camillo, this great sir will yet stay longer.
Cam. You had much ado to make his anchor hold:
When you cast out, it still came home.
Leon. Didst note it?
Cam. He would not stay at your petitions; made
His business more material.
Leon. Didst perceive it?
[*Aside*] They 're here with me already, whisp'ring, rounding
'Sicilia is a so-forth:' 'tis far gone,
When I shall gust it last. How came 't, Camillo,
That he did stay?
Cam. At the good queen's entreaty.
Leon. At the queen's be 't: 'good' should be pertinent;
But, so it is, it is not. Was this taken
By any understanding pate but thine?
For thy conceit is soaking, will draw in
More than the common blocks: not noted, is 't,
But of the finer natures? by some severals
Of head-piece extraordinary? lower messes
Perchance are to this business purblind? say.
Cam. Business, my lord! I think most understand
Bohemia stays here longer.
Leon. Ha!
Cam. Stays here longer.
Leon. Ay, but why?
Cam. To satisfy your highness and the entreaties
Of our most gracious mistress.
Leon. Satisfy!
Th' entreaties of your mistress! satisfy!
Let that suffice. I have trusted thee, Camillo,
With all the nearest things to my heart, as well
My chamber-councils, wherein, priest-like, thou
Hast cleans'd my bosom, I from thee departed
Thy penitent reform'd: but we have been
Deceiv'd in thy integrity, deceiv'd
In that which seems so.
Cam. Be it forbid, my lord!
Leon. To bide upon 't, thou art not honest, or,
If thou inclin'st that way, thou art a coward,
Which hoxes honesty behind, restraining
From course requir'd; or else thou must be counted
A servant grafted in my serious trust
And therein negligent; or else a fool
That seest a game play'd home, the rich stake drawn,
And tak'st it all for jest.
Cam. My gracious lord,
I may be negligent, foolish and fearful;
In every one of these no man is free,
But that his negligence, his folly, fear,
Among the infinite doings of the world,
Sometime puts forth. In your affairs, my lord,
If ever I were wilful-negligent,
It was my folly; if industriously
I play'd the fool, it was my negligence,
Not weighing well the end; if ever fearful
To do a thing, where I the issue doubted,

161. **take eggs for money,** proverbial for "be imposed upon." 163. **happy . . . dole,** proverbial, "may good fortune be his lot." 170. **childness,** childishness. 171. **thick my blood.** Melancholy thoughts would thicken the blood. 172. **Offic'd,** placed in particular function. 178. **shall 's,** shall we. 179. **To . . . you,** do with yourselves according to the inclinations of your minds. 183. **neb,** beak; here, nose. 184. **arms her with,** assumes. 188. **issue,** outcome. 201. **strike,** blast, destroy by a malign influence. 202. **predominant,** in the ascendant (used of a planet). 216. **material,** important. 217-219. **They 're . . . last,** referring to the king's fear of public disgrace and shame. Note *contempt and clamour*, line 189. 217. **rounding,** whispering. 219. **gust,** taste; here, hear of. 221. **pertinent,** i.e., appropriately applied. 222. **so,** as. **taken,** perceived. 224. **soaking,** very receptive. 225. **blocks,** blockheads. 227. **lower messes,** persons of a lower rank. 228. **pur-**

Whereof the execution did cry out
Against the non-performance, 'twas a fear
Which oft infects the wisest: these, my lord,
Are such allow'd infirmities that honesty
Is never free of. But, beseech your grace,
Be plainer with me; let me know my trespass
By its own visage: if I then deny it,
'Tis none of mine.
Leon. Ha' not you seen, Camillo,—
But that 's past doubt, you have, or your eye-glass
Is thicker than a cuckold's horn,—or heard,—
For to a vision so apparent rumor
Cannot be mute,—or thought,—for cogitation
Resides not in that man that does not think,—
My wife is slippery? If thou wilt confess,
Or else be impudently negative,
To have nor eyes nor ears nor thought, then say
My wife 's a hobby-horse, deserves a name
As rank as any flax-wench that puts to
Before her troth-plight: say 't and justify 't.
Cam. I would not be a stander-by to hear
My sovereign mistress clouded so, without
My present vengeance taken: 'shrew my heart,
You never spoke what did become you less
Than this; which to reiterate were sin
As deep as that, though true.
Leon. Is whispering nothing?
Is leaning cheek to cheek? is meeting noses?
Kissing with inside lip? stopping the career
Of laughter with a sigh?—a note infallible
Of breaking honesty—horsing foot on foot?
Skulking in corners? wishing clocks more swift?
Hours, minutes? noon, midnight? and all eyes
Blind with the pin and web but theirs, theirs only,
That would unseen be wicked? is this nothing?
Why, then the world and all that 's in 't is nothing;
The covering sky is nothing; Bohemia nothing;
My wife is nothing; nor nothing have these nothings,
If this be nothing.
Cam. Good my lord, be cur'd
Of this diseas'd opinion, and betimes;
For 'tis most dangerous.
Leon. Say it be, 'tis true.
Cam. No, no, my lord.
Leon. It is; you lie, you lie:
I say thou liest, Camillo, and I hate thee,
Pronounce thee a gross lout, a mindless slave,
Or else a hovering temporizer, that
Canst with thine eyes at once see good and evil,
Inclining to them both: were my wife's liver
Infected as her life, she would not live
The running of one glass.
Cam. Who does infect her?
Leon. Why, he that wears her like her medal, hanging
About his neck, Bohemia: who, if I
Had servants true about me, that bare eyes
To see alike mine honour as their profits,
Their own particular thrifts, they would do that
Which should undo more doing: ay, and thou,
His cupbearer,—whom I from meaner form
Have bench'd and rear'd to worship, who mayst see
Plainly as heaven sees earth and earth sees heaven,
How I am gall'd,—mightst bespice a cup,
To give mine enemy a lasting wink;
Which draught to me were cordial.
Cam. Sir, my lord,
I could do this, and that with no rash potion,
But with a ling'ring dram that should not work
Maliciously like poison: but I cannot
Believe this crack to be in my dread mistress,
So sovereignly being honourable.
I have lov'd thee,—
Leon. †Make that thy question, and go rot!
Dost think I am so muddy, so unsettled,
To appoint myself in this vexation, sully
The purity and whiteness of my sheets,
Which to preserve is sleep, which being spotted
Is goads, thorns, nettles, tails of wasps,
Give scandal to the blood o' th' prince my son,
Who I do think is mine and love as mine,
Without ripe moving to 't? Would I do this?
Could man so blench?
Cam. I must believe you, sir:
I do; and will fetch off Bohemia for 't;
Provided that, when he 's remov'd, your highness
Will take again your queen as yours at first,
Even for your son's sake; and thereby for sealing
The injury of tongues in courts and kingdoms
Known and allied to yours.
Leon. Thou dost advise me
Even so as I mine own course have set down:
I'll give no blemish to her honour, none.
Cam. My lord,
Go then; and with a countenance as clear
As friendship wears at feasts, keep with Bohemia
And with your queen. I am his cupbearer:
If from me he have wholesome beverage,
Account me not your servant.
Leon. This is all:
Do 't and thou hast the one half of my heart;
Do 't not, thou split'st thine own.
Cam. I'll do 't, my lord.
Leon. I will seem friendly, as thou hast advis'd me. *Exit.*
Cam. O miserable lady! But, for me,
What case stand I in? I must be the poisoner
Of good Polixenes; and my ground to do 't
Is the obedience to a master, one
Who in rebellion with himself will have
All that are his so too. To do this deed,
Promotion follows. If I could find example
Of thousands that had struck anointed kings
And flourish'd after, I 'ld not do 't; but since
Nor brass nor stone nor parchment bears not one,
Let villany itself forswear 't. I must
Forsake the court: to do 't, or no, is certain
To me a break-neck. Happy star reign now!
Here comes Bohemia.

blind, blind. 237. **chamber-councils,** private affairs. 242. **bide,** insist. 244. **hoxes,** hocks, cuts the hamstrings of. 254. **puts forth,** appears. 256. **industriously,** of set purpose. 268. **eye-glass,** lens of the eye. 270. **vision,** thing visible. 277. **flax-wench,** common slut. 286. **career,** full course. 288. **honesty,** chastity. **horsing,** setting. 291. **pin and web,** cataract of the eye. 302. **hovering,** wavering. 306. **glass,** hour-glass. 311. **thrifts,** gains. 314. **bench'd,** raised to authority. 317. **lasting wink,** death. 323. **So . . . honourable,** being so supremely honorable. 324. **that,** i.e., the dishonesty of Hermione. 326. **appoint,** equip, array. 332. **ripe,** urgent. 334. **fetch off,** do away with; or, with deliberate ambiguity, rescue. 337. **for sealing,** silencing. 352. **case,** position. 359-360. **but . . . one,** but since recorded history shows no instances of men who have killed a king and prospered afterwards. 363. **break-neck,** destruction, ruin.

Enter POLIXENES.

Pol. This is strange: methinks
My favour here begins to warp. Not speak?
Good day, Camillo.
Cam. Hail, most royal sir!
Pol. What is the news i' th' court?
Cam. None rare, my lord.
Pol. The king hath on him such a countenance
As he had lost some province and a region
Lov'd as he loves himself: even now I met him
With customary compliment; when he,
Wafting his eyes to th' contrary and falling
A lip of much contempt, speeds from me and
So leaves me to consider what is breeding
That changeth thus his manners.
Cam. I dare not know, my lord.
Pol. How! dare not! do not. Do you know, and dare not?
Be intelligent to me: 'tis thereabouts;
For, to yourself, what you do know, you must,
And cannot say, you dare not. Good Camillo,
Your chang'd complexions are to me a mirror
Which shows me mine chang'd too; for I must be
A party in this alteration, finding
Myself thus alter'd with 't.
Cam. There is a sickness
Which puts some of us in distemper, but
I cannot name the disease; and it is caught
Of you that yet are well.
Pol. How! caught of me!
Make me not sighted like the basilisk:
I have look'd on thousands, who have sped the better
By my regard, but kill'd none so. Camillo,—
As you are certainly a gentleman, thereto
Clerk-like experienc'd, which no less adorns
Our gentry than our parents' noble names,
In whose success we are gentle,—I beseech you,
If you know aught which does behove my knowledge
Thereof to be inform'd, imprison 't not
In ignorant concealment.
Cam. I may not answer.
Pol. A sickness caught of me, and yet I well!
I must be answer'd. Dost thou hear, Camillo?
I conjure thee, by all the parts of man
Which honour does acknowledge, whereof the least
Is not this suit of mine, that thou declare
What incidency thou dost guess of harm
Is creeping toward me; how far off, how near;
Which way to be prevented, if to be;
If not, how best to bear it.
Cam. Sir, I will tell you;
Since I am charg'd in honour and by him
That I think honourable: therefore mark my counsel,
Which must be ev'n as swiftly followed as
I mean to utter it, or both yourself and me
Cry lost, and so good night!
Pol. On, good Camillo.
Cam. I am appointed him to murder you.
Pol. By whom, Camillo?
Cam. By the king.
Pol. For what?
Cam. He thinks, nay, with all confidence he swears,
As he had seen 't or been an instrument
To vice you to 't, that you have touch'd his queen
Forbiddenly.
Pol. O, then my best blood turn
To an infected jelly and my name
Be yok'd with his that did betray the Best!
Turn then my freshest reputation to
A savour that may strike the dullest nostril
Where I arrive, and my approach be shunn'd,
Nay, hated too, worse than the great'st infection
That e'er was heard or read!
Cam. Swear his thought over
By each particular star in heaven and
By all their influences, you may as well
Forbid the sea for to obey the moon
As or by oath remove or counsel shake
The fabric of his folly, whose foundation
Is pil'd upon his faith and will continue
The standing of his body.
Pol. How should this grow?
Cam. I know not: but I am sure 'tis safer to
Avoid what 's grown than question how 'tis born.
If therefore you dare trust my honesty,
That lies enclosed in this trunk which you
Shall bear along impawn'd, away to-night!
Your followers I will whisper to the business,
And will by twos and threes at several posterns
Clear them o' th' city. For myself, I'll put
My fortunes to your service, which are here
By this discovery lost. Be not uncertain;
For, by the honour of my parents, I
Have utt'red truth: which if you seek to prove,
I dare not stand by; nor shall you be safer
Than one condemn'd by the king's own mouth, thereon
His execution sworn.
Pol. I do believe thee:
I saw his heart in 's face. Give me thy hand:
Be pilot to me and thy places shall
Still neighbour mine. My ships are ready and
My people did expect my hence departure
Two days ago. This jealousy
Is for a precious creature: as she 's rare,
Must it be great, and as his person 's mighty,
Must it be violent, and as he does conceive
He is dishonour'd by a man which ever
Profess'd to him, why, his revenges must
In that be made more bitter. Fear o'ershades me:
Good expedition be my friend, and comfort
†The gracious queen, part of his theme, but nothing
Of his ill-ta'en suspicion! Come, Camillo;
I will respect thee as a father if
Thou bear'st my life off hence: let us avoid.
Cam. It is in mine authority to command
The keys of all the posterns: please your highness
To take the urgent hour. Come, sir, away. *Exeunt.*

---

365. **warp,** change, grow askew. 372. **Wafting . . . contrary,** turning his eyes in an opposite direction. 378. **Be . . . thereabouts,** be intelligible—it must be something of this nature: that you know and dare not tell (Furness). 381. **chang'd,** grown pale. 388. **basilisk,** a fabled serpent whose gaze was fatal. 394. **whose success,** succession from whom. **gentle,** wellborn. 403. **incidency,** threatening development. 412. **him,** i.e., by Leontes. 416. **vice,** impel. 419. **his . . . Best,** a reference to Judas. 424. **Swear . . . over,** deny his suspicion with oaths. 431. **standing,** life, existence. **How . . . grow?** How could this suspicion have arisen? 435. **trunk,** body. 436. **impawn'd,** i.e., as a pledge of good faith. 438. **posterns,** gates. 441. **discovery,** revelation, disclosure. 443. **prove,** test. 444. **stand by,** affirm publicly; stay. 448. **places,** official functions. 456. **Profess'd,** openly professed friendship. 458-460. **Good . . . suspicion,** may my hasty departure prove

ACT II.

SCENE I. [*A room in* LEONTES' *palace.*]

Enter HERMIONE, MAMILLIUS, [*and*] Ladies.

Her. Take the boy to you: he so troubles me,
'Tis past enduring.
First Lady. Come, my gracious lord,
Shall I be your playfellow?
Mam. No, I'll none of you.
First Lady. Why, my sweet lord?
Mam. You'll kiss me hard and speak to me as if
I were a baby still. I love you better.
Sec. Lady. And why so, my lord?
Mam. Not for because
Your brows are blacker; yet black brows, they say,
Become some women best, so that there be not
Too much hair there, but in a semicircle,
Or a half-moon made with a pen.
Sec. Lady. Who taught' this?
Mam. I learnt it out of women's faces. Pray now
What colour are your eyebrows?
First Lady. Blue, my lord.
Mam. Nay, that 's a mock: I have seen a lady's nose
That has been blue, but not her eyebrows.
First Lady. Hark ye;
The queen your mother rounds apace: we shall
Present our services to a fine new prince
One of these days; and then you 'ld wanton with us,
If we would have you.
Sec. Lady. She is spread of late
Into a goodly bulk: good time encounter her!
Her. What wisdom stirs amongst you? Come, sir, now
I am for you again: pray you, sit by us,
And tell 's a tale.
Mam. Merry or sad shall 't be?
Her. As merry as you will.
Mam. A sad tale 's best for winter: I have one
Of sprites and goblins.
Her. Let 's have that, good sir.
Come on, sit down: come on, and do your best
To fright me with your sprites; you 're powerful at it.
Mam. There was a man—
Her. Nay, come, sit down; then on.
Mam. Dwelt by a churchyard: I will tell it softly;
Yond crickets shall not hear it.
Her. Come on, then,
And give 't me in mine ear.

[*Enter*] LEONTES, ANTIGONUS, Lords.

Leon. Was he met there? his train? Camillo with him?
First Lord. Behind the tuft of pines I met them; never
Saw I men scour so on their way: I ey'd them
Even to their ships.
Leon. How blest am I
In my just censure, in my true opinion!
Alack, for lesser knowledge! how accurs'd
In being so blest! There may be in the cup
A spider steep'd, and one may drink, depart,
And yet partake no venom, for his knowledge
Is not infected: but if one present
Th' abhorr'd ingredient to his eye, make known
How he hath drunk, he cracks his gorge, his sides,
With violent hefts. I have drunk, and seen the spider.
Camillo was his help in this, his pandar:
There is a plot against my life, my crown;
All 's true that is mistrusted: that false villain
Whom I employ'd was pre-employ'd by him:
He has discover'd my design, and I
Remain a pinch'd thing; yea, a very trick
For them to play at will. How came the posterns
So easily open?
First Lord. By his great authority;
Which often hath no less prevail'd than so
On your command.
Leon. I know 't too well.
Give me the boy: I am glad you did not nurse him:
Though he does bear some signs of me, yet you
Have too much blood in him.
Her. What is this? sport?
Leon. Bear the boy hence; he shall not come about her;
Away with him! and let her sport herself
With that she 's big with; for 'tis Polixenes
Has made thee swell thus. [*Mamillius is led out.*]
Her. But I 'ld say he had not,
And I'll be sworn you would believe my saying,
Howe'er you lean to th' nayward.
Leon. You, my lords,
Look on her, mark her well; be but about
To say 'she is a goodly lady,' and
The justice of your hearts will thereto add
''Tis pity she 's not honest, honourable:'
Praise her but for this her without-door form,
Which on my faith deserves high speech, and straight
The shrug, the hum or ha, these petty brands
That calumny doth use—O, I am out—
That mercy does, for calumny will sear
Virtue itself: these shrugs, these hums and ha's,
When you have said 'she 's goodly,' come between
Ere you can say 'she 's honest:' but be 't known,
From him that has most cause to grieve it should be,
She 's an adulteress.
Her. Should a villain say so,
The most replenish'd villain in the world,
He were as much more villain: you, my lord,
Do but mistake.
Leon. You have mistook, my lady,
Polixenes for Leontes: O thou thing!
Which I'll not call a creature of thy place,
Lest barbarism, making me the precedent,
Should a like language use to all degrees
And mannerly distinguishment leave out
Betwixt the prince and beggar: I have said
She 's an adulteress; I have said with whom:
More, she 's a traitor and Camillo is

my best course, and bring what comfort it may to the gracious queen, who must also be the object of the king's suspicions but who is guiltless of them. 462. **avoid,** depart.

ACT II. SCENE I. 11. **taught',** taught you (elided). 18. **wanton,** sport, play. 25. **A sad tale 's best for winter.** This may have some connection with the title, *The Winter's Tale.* 31. **crickets,** meaning court ladies "with their tittering and chirping laughter" (Furnivall).

38. **Alack, for lesser knowledge,** i.e., would that what I know weren't true. 45. **hefts,** heavings, retchings. 50. **discover'd,** disclosed. 51. **pinch'd,** tortured, ridiculous. 62. **I 'ld,** I need only. 64. **nayward,** disbelief. 69. **without-door,** outward. 72. **out,** wrong. 73. **does,** uses. 83. **place,** position. 86. **mannerly distinguishment,** polite distinctions.

A federary with her, and one that knows
What she should shame to know herself
But with her most vile principal, that she 's
A bed-swerver, even as bad as those
That vulgars give bold'st titles, ay, and privy
To this their late escape.
Her. No, by my life,
Privy to none of this. How will this grieve you,
When you shall come to clearer knowledge, that
You thus have publish'd me! Gentle my lord,
You scarce can right me throughly then to say
You did mistake.
Leon. No; if I mistake
In those foundations which I build upon,
The centre is not big enough to bear
A school-boy's top. Away with her! to prison!
He who shall speak for her is afar off guilty
But that he speaks.
Her. There 's some ill planet reigns:
I must be patient till the heavens look
With an aspect more favourable. Good my lords,
I am not prone to weeping, as our sex
Commonly are; the want of which vain dew
Perchance shall dry your pities: but I have
That honourable grief lodg'd here which burns
Worse than tears drown: beseech you all, my lords,
With thoughts so qualified as your charities
Shall best instruct you, measure me; and so
The king's will be perform'd!
Leon. Shall I be heard?
Her. Who is 't that goes with me? Beseech your highness,
My women may be with me; for you see
My plight requires it. Do not weep, good fools;
There is no cause: when you shall know your mistress
Has deserv'd prison, then abound in tears
As I come out: this action I now go on
Is for my better grace. Adieu, my lord:
I never wish'd to see you sorry; now
I trust I shall. My women, come; you have leave.
Leon. Go, do our bidding; hence!
[*Exit Queen, guarded; with Ladies.*]
First Lord. Beseech your highness, call the queen again.
Ant. Be certain what you do, sir, lest your justice
Prove violence; in the which three great ones suffer,
Yourself, your queen, your son.
First Lord. For her, my lord,
I dare my life lay down and will do 't, sir,
Please you t' accept it, that the queen is spotless
I' th' eyes of heaven and to you; I mean,
In this which you accuse her.
Ant. If it prove
†She 's otherwise, I'll keep my stables where
I lodge my wife; I'll go in couples with her;
Than when I feel and see her no farther trust her;
For every inch of woman in the world,
Ay, every dram of woman's flesh is false,
If she be.
Leon. Hold your peaces.
First Lord. Good my lord,—
Ant. It is for you we speak, not for ourselves:
You are abus'd and by some putter-on
That will be damn'd for 't; would I knew the villain,
†I would land-damn him. Be she honour-flaw'd,
I have three daughters; the eldest is eleven;
The second and the third, nine, and some five;
If this prove true, they'll pay for 't: by mine honour,
I'll geld 'em all; fourteen they shall not see,
To bring false generations: they are co-heirs;
And I had rather glib myself than they
Should not produce fair issue.
Leon. Cease; no more.
You smell this business with a sense as cold
As is a dead man's nose: but I do see 't and feel 't,
As you feel doing thus; and see withal
The instruments that feel.
Ant. If it be so,
We need no grave to bury honesty:
There 's not a grain of it the face to sweeten
Of the whole dungy earth.
Leon. What! lack I credit?
First Lord. I had rather you did lack than I, my lord,
Upon this ground; and more it would content me
To have her honour true than your suspicion,
Be blam'd for 't how you might.
Leon. Why, what need we
Commune with you of this, but rather follow
Our forceful instigation? Our prerogative
Calls not your counsels, but our natural goodness
Imparts this; which if you, or stupified
Or seeming so in skill, cannot or will not
Relish a truth like us, inform yourselves
We need no more of your advice: the matter,
The loss, the gain, the ord'ring on 't, is all
Properly ours.
Ant. And I wish, my liege,
You had only in your silent judgment tried it,
Without more overture.
Leon. How could that be?
Either thou art most ignorant by age,
Or thou wert born a fool. Camillo's flight,
Added to their familiarity,
Which was as gross as ever touch'd conjecture,
That lack'd sight only, nought for approbation
But only seeing, all other circumstances
Made up to th' deed, doth push on this proceeding:
Yet, for a greater confirmation,
For in an act of this importance 'twere
Most piteous to be wild, I have dispatch'd in post
To sacred Delphos, to Apollo's temple,
Cleomenes and Dion, whom you know
Of stuff'd sufficiency: now from the oracle
They will bring all; whose spiritual counsel had,
Shall stop or spur me. Have I done well?
First Lord. Well done, my lord.
Leon. Though I am satisfied and need no more
Than what I know, yet shall the oracle
Give rest to th' minds of others, such as he
Whose ignorant credulity will not
Come up to th' truth. So have we thought it good
From our free person she should be confin'd,
Lest that the treachery of the two fled hence

90. **federary,** confederate, accomplice. 94. **vulgars,** common people. 102. **centre,** center of the earth and of the universe. 104. **afar off,** indirectly. 115. **heard,** obeyed. 121. **action,** indictment. 134. **stables,** usually regarded as equivalent to *kennels*; but Moorman suggests "station"—*stabilis statio*—interpreting the passage, "I'll keep my station in the same place where my wife is lodged." 135. **couples,** i.e., like hounds. 141. **putter-on,** instigator. 143. **land-damn him,** possibly, make a hell on earth for him or abuse with rancor; many conjectures. 145. **some,** about. 148. **false generations,** illegitimate children. 149. **glib,** geld. 153. **As . . . thus,** possibly expressed by a gesture. 159.

Be left her to perform. Come, follow us;
We are to speak in public; for this business
Will raise us all.
Ant. [*Aside*] To laughter, as I take it,
If the good truth were known. *Exeunt.*

SCENE II. [*A prison.*]

Enter PAULINA, *a* Gentleman [*and* Attendants].

Paul. The keeper of the prison, call to him;
Let him have knowledge who I am. [*Exit Gent.*]
Good lady,
No court in Europe is too good for thee;
What dost thou then in prison?

[*Enter* Gentleman, *with the*] Gaoler.

Now, good sir,
You know me, do you not?
Gaol. For a worthy lady
And one who much I honour.
Paul. Pray you then,
Conduct me to the queen.
Gaol. I may not, madam:
To the contrary I have express commandment.
Paul. Here 's ado,
To lock up honesty and honour from
Th' access of gentle visitors! Is 't lawful, pray you,
To see her women? any of them? Emilia?
Gaol. So please you, madam,
To put apart these your attendants, I
Shall bring Emilia forth.
Paul. I pray now, call her.
Withdraw yourselves. [*Exeunt Gentleman and Attendants.*]
Gaol. And, madam,
I must be present at your conference.
Paul. Well, be 't so, prithee. [*Exit Gaoler.*]
Here 's such ado to make no stain a stain
As passes colouring.

[*Enter* Gaoler, *with*] EMILIA.

Dear gentlewoman,
How fares our gracious lady?
Emil. As well as one so great and so forlorn
May hold together: on her frights and griefs,
Which never tender lady hath borne greater,
She is something before her time deliver'd.
Paul. A boy?
Emil. A daughter, and a goodly babe,
Lusty and like to live: the queen receives
Much comfort in 't; says 'My poor prisoner,
I am innocent as you.'
Paul. I dare be sworn:
These dangerous unsafe lunes i' th' king, beshrew
them!
He must be told on 't, and he shall: the office
Becomes a woman best; I'll take 't upon me:
If I prove honey-mouth'd, let my tongue blister
And never to my red-look'd anger be
The trumpet any more. Pray you, Emilia,
Commend my best obedience to the queen:
If she dares trust me with her little babe,
I'll show 't the king and undertake to be
Her advocate to th' loud'st. We do not know
How he may soften at the sight o' th' child:
The silence often of pure innocence
Persuades when speaking fails.
Emil. Most worthy madam,
Your honour and your goodness is so evident
That your free undertaking cannot miss
A thriving issue: there is no lady living
So meet for this great errand. Please your ladyship
To visit the next room, I'll presently
Acquaint the queen of your most noble offer;
Who but to-day hammer'd of this design,
But durst not tempt a minister of honour,
Lest she should be denied.
Paul. Tell her, Emilia,
I'll use that tongue I have: if wit flow from 't
As boldness from my bosom, let 't not be doubted
I shall do good.
Emil. Now be you blest for it!
I'll to the queen: please you, come something nearer.
Gaol. Madam, if 't please the queen to send the
babe,
I know not what I shall incur to pass it,
Having no warrant.
Paul. You need not fear it, sir:
This child was prisoner to the womb and is
By law and process of great nature thence
Freed and enfranchis'd, not a party to
The anger of the king nor guilty of,
If any be, the trespass of the queen.
Gaol. I do believe it.
Paul. Do not you fear: upon mine honour, I
Will stand betwixt you and danger. *Exeunt.*

SCENE III. [*A room in* LEONTES' *palace.*]

Enter LEONTES, Servants, ANTIGONUS, *and* Lords.

Leon. Nor night nor day no rest: it is but weakness
To bear the matter thus; mere weakness. If
The cause were not in being,—part o' th' cause,
She th' adulteress; for the harlot king
Is quite beyond mine arm, out of the blank
And level of my brain, plot-proof; but she
I can hook to me: say that she were gone,
Given to the fire, a moiety of my rest
Might come to me again. Who 's there?
First Serv. My lord?
Leon. How does the boy?
First Serv. He took good rest to-night;
'Tis hop'd his sickness is discharg'd.
Leon. To see his nobleness!
Conceiving the dishonour of his mother,
He straight declin'd, droop'd, took it deeply,
Fasten'd and fix'd the shame on 't in himself,
Threw off his spirit, his appetite, his sleep,
And downright languish'd. Leave me solely: go,
See how he fares. [*Exit Serv.*] Fie, fie! no thought of
him:
The very thought of my revenges that way
Recoil upon me: in himself too mighty,

Upon this ground, in this matter. 164. **Calls not,** doesn't need. 164-165. **but . . . this,** but out of the goodness of my heart I tell you this. 166. **skill,** reason. 172. **overture,** disclosure. 176. **touch'd conjecture,** verified suspicion. 177. **approbation,** proof. 185. **stuff'd sufficiency,** abundant capabilities. 186. **had,** having been obtained. 191. **he,** probably, any person. 198. **raise,** rouse.

SCENE II. 23. **on,** in consequence of. 30. **lunes,** fits of lunacy. 49. **hammer'd of,** earnestly deliberated. 57. **pass it,** let it pass. 63. **If any be,** if there be any guilt.

SCENE III. 4. **harlot,** lewd. 5. **blank,** the center of a target.

And in his parties, his alliance; let him be
Until a time may serve: for present vengeance,
Take it on her. Camillo and Polixenes
Laugh at me, make their pastime at my sorrow:
They should not laugh if I could reach them, nor
Shall she within my power.

Enter PAULINA [*with a baby*].

First Lord. You must not enter.
Paul. Nay, rather, good my lords, be second to me:
Fear you his tyrannous passion more, alas,
Than the queen's life? a gracious innocent soul,
More free than he is jealous.
Ant. That 's enough.
Sec. Serv. Madam, he hath not slept to-night; commanded
None should come at him.
Paul. Not so hot, good sir:
I come to bring him sleep. 'Tis such as you,
That creep like shadows by him and do sigh
At each his needless heavings, such as you
Nourish the cause of his awaking: I
Do come with words as medicinal as true,
Honest as either, to purge him of that humour
That presses him from sleep.
Leon. What noise there, ho?
Paul. No noise, my lord; but needful conference
About some gossips for your highness.
Leon. How!
Away with that audacious lady! Antigonus,
I charg'd thee that she should not come about me:
I knew she would.
Ant. I told her so, my lord,
On your displeasure's peril and on mine,
She should not visit you.
Leon. What, canst not rule her?
Paul. From all dishonesty he can: in this,
Unless he take the course that you have done,
Commit me for committing honour, trust it,
He shall not rule me.
Ant. La you now, you hear:
When she will take the rein I let her run;
But she'll not stumble.
Paul. Good my liege, I come;
And, I beseech you, hear me, who professes
Myself your loyal servant, your physician,
Your most obedient counsellor, yet that dare
Less appear so in comforting your evils,
Than such as most seem yours: I say, I come
From your good queen.
Leon. Good queen!
Paul. Good queen, my lord,
Good queen; I say good queen;
And would by combat make her good, so were I
A man, the worst about you.
Leon. Force her hence.
Paul. Let him that makes but trifles of his eyes
First hand me: on mine own accord I'll off;
But first I'll do my errand. The good queen,
For she is good, hath brought you forth a daughter;
Here 'tis; commends it to your blessing.
[*Laying down the baby.*]
Leon. Out!
A mankind witch! Hence with her, out o' door:
A most intelligencing bawd!
Paul. Not so:
I am as ignorant in that as you
In so entitling me, and no less honest
Than you are mad; which is enough, I'll warrant,
As this world goes, to pass for honest.
Leon. Traitors!
Will you not push her out? Give her the bastard.
Thou dotard! thou art woman-tir'd, unroosted
By thy dame Partlet here. Take up the bastard;
Take 't up, I say; give 't to thy crone.
Paul. For ever
Unvenerable be thy hands, if thou
Tak'st up the princess by that forced baseness
Which he has put upon 't!
Leon. He dreads his wife.
Paul. So I would you did; then 'twere past all doubt
You 'ld call your children yours.
Leon. A nest of traitors!
Ant. I am none, by this good light.
Paul. Nor I, nor any
But one that 's here, and that 's himself, for he
The sacred honour of himself, his queen's,
His hopeful son's, his babe's, betrays to slander,
Whose sting is sharper than the sword's; and will not—
For, as the case now stands, it is a curse
He cannot be compell'd to 't—once remove
The root of his opinion, which is rotten
As ever oak or stone was sound.
Leon. A callet
Of boundless tongue, who late hath beat her husband
And now baits me! This brat is none of mine;
It is the issue of Polixenes:
Hence with it, and together with the dam
Commit them to the fire!
Paul. It is yours;
And, might we lay th' old proverb to your charge,
So like you, 'tis the worse. Behold, my lords,
Although the print be little, the whole matter
And copy of the father, eye, nose, lip,
The trick of 's frown, his forehead, nay, the valley,
The pretty dimples of his chin and cheek,
His smiles,
The very mould and frame of hand, nail, finger:
And thou, good goddess Nature, which hast made it
So like to him that got it, if thou hast
The ordering of the mind too, 'mongst all colours
No yellow in 't, lest she suspect, as he does,
Her children not her husband's!
Leon. A gross hag!
And, lozel, thou art worthy to be hang'd,
That wilt not stay her tongue.
Ant. Hang all the husbands
That cannot do that feat, you'll leave yourself
Hardly one subject.
Leon. Once more, take her hence.
Paul. A most unworthy and unnatural lord
Can do no more.

23. **Take it,** let it be taken. 27. **be second to,** aid, second. 41. **gossips,** godfathers and godmothers. 49. **Commit,** i.e., to prison. 56-57. **comforting . . . yours,** encouraging your evil courses, than those flatterers who seem to be your most loyal servants. 67. **mankind,** masculine, violent; here used as an adjective. 68. **intelligencing,** acting as go-between. 74. **woman-tir'd,** henpecked, from "tire" in falconry, meaning "tear." **unroosted,** driven from perch. 75. **Partlet,** name of the hen in *Reynard the Fox*, who appears as *Pertelote* in the *Nun's Priest's Tale* of Chaucer. 78. **forced baseness,** false attribution of illegitimacy. 79. **He . . . wife,** he (Antigonus) is afraid of his wife

Leon. I'll ha' thee burnt.
Paul. I care not:
It is an heretic that makes the fire,
Not she which burns in 't. I'll not call you tyrant;
But this most cruel usage of your queen,
Not able to produce more accusation
Than your own weak-hing'd fancy, something savours
Of tyranny and will ignoble make you,
Yea, scandalous to the world.
Leon. On your allegiance,
Out of the chamber with her! Were I a tyrant,
Where were her life? she durst not call me so,
If she did know me one. Away with her!
Paul. I pray you, do not push me; I'll be gone.
Look to your babe, my lord; 'tis yours: Jove send her
A better guiding spirit! What needs these hands?
You, that are thus so tender o'er his follies,
Will never do him good, not one of you.
So, so: farewell; we are gone. *Exit.*
Leon. Thou, traitor, hast set on thy wife to this.
My child? away with 't! Even thou, that hast
A heart so tender o'er it, take it hence
And see it instantly consum'd with fire;
Even thou and none but thou. Take it up straight:
Within this hour bring me word 'tis done,
And by good testimony, or I'll seize thy life,
With what thou else call'st thine. If thou refuse
And wilt encounter with my wrath, say so;
The bastard brains with these my proper hands
Shall I dash out. Go, take it to the fire;
For thou set'st on thy wife.
Ant. I did not, sir:
These lords, my noble fellows, if they please,
Can clear me in 't.
Lords. We can: my royal liege,
He is not guilty of her coming hither.
Leon. You 're liars all.
First Lord. Beseech your highness, give us better credit:
We have always truly serv'd you, and beseech
So to esteem of us, and on our knees we beg,
As recompense of our dear services
Past and to come, that you do change this purpose,
Which being so horrible, so bloody, must
Lead on to some foul issue: we all kneel.
Leon. I am a feather for each wind that blows:
Shall I live on to see this bastard kneel
And call me father? better burn it now
Than curse it then. But be it; let it live.
It shall not neither. You, sir, come you hither;
You that have been so tenderly officious
With Lady Margery, your midwife there,
To save this bastard's life,—for 'tis a bastard,
So sure as this beard 's grey,—what will you adventure
To save this brat's life?
Ant. Any thing, my lord,
That my ability may undergo
And nobleness impose: at least thus much:
I'll pawn the little blood which I have left
To save the innocent: any thing possible.
Leon. It shall be possible. Swear by this sword
Thou wilt perform my bidding.
Ant. I will, my lord.
Leon. Mark and perform it, see'st thou? for the fail
Of any point in 't shall not only be
Death to thyself but to thy lewd-tongu'd wife,
Whom for this time we pardon. We enjoin thee,
As thou art liege-man to us, that thou carry
This female bastard hence and that thou bear it
To some remote and desert place quite out
Of our dominions, and that there thou leave it,
Without more mercy, to it own protection
And favour of the climate. As by strange fortune
It came to us, I do in justice charge thee,
On thy soul's peril and thy body's torture,
That thou commend it strangely to some place
Where chance may nurse or end it. Take it up.
Ant. I swear to do this, though a present death
Had been more merciful. Come on, poor babe:
Some powerful spirit instruct the kites and ravens
To be thy nurses! Wolves and bears, they say,
Casting their savageness aside have done
Like offices of pity. Sir, be prosperous
In more than this deed does require! And blessing
Against this cruelty fight on thy side,
Poor thing, condemn'd to loss! *Exit [with the baby].*
Leon. No, I'll not rear
Another's issue.

Enter a Servant.

Serv. Please your highness, posts
From those you sent to th' oracle are come
An hour since: Cleomenes and Dion,
Being well arriv'd from Delphos, are both landed,
Hasting to th' court.
First Lord. So please you, sir, their speed
Hath been beyond account.
Leon. Twenty three days
They have been absent: 'tis good speed: foretells
The great Apollo suddenly will have
The truth of this appear. Prepare you, lords;
Summon a session, that we may arraign
Our most disloyal lady, for, as she hath
Been publicly accus'd, so shall she have
A just and open trial. While she lives
My heart will be a burthen to me. Leave me,
And think upon my bidding. *Exeunt.*

ACT III.

SCENE I. [*A sea-port in Sicilia.*]

Enter CLEOMENES *and* DION.

Cleo. The climate 's delicate, the air most sweet,
Fertile the isle, the temple much surpassing
The common praise it bears.
Dion. I shall report,
For most it caught me, the celestial habits,
Methinks I so should term them, and the reverence
Of the grave wearers. O, the sacrifice!

(Paulina). 90. **callet,** lewd woman. 96. **old proverb.** The sense of the proverb is given by Overbury ("Character of a Sergeant"): "The devil calls him his white son; he's so like him, that he is the worse for it." 107. **yellow,** suggestive of jealousy. 109. **lozel,** worthless person, scoundrel. 127. **What . . . hands.** She is being pushed from the room. 170. **fail,** failure. 178. **it,** its. 182. **commend,** deliver, commit. **strangely,** as a foreigner. 192. **loss,** destruction.

ACT III. SCENE I. 2. **isle.** Shakespeare follows Greene's *Pandosto* in erroneously placing Delphi on an island.

How ceremonious, solemn and unearthly
It was i' th' off'ring!
Cleo. But of all, the burst
And the ear-deaf'ning voice o' th' oracle,
Kin to Jove's thunder, so surpris'd my sense,
That I was nothing.
Dion. If th' event o' th' journey
Prove as successful to the queen,—O be 't so!—
As it hath been to us rare, pleasant, speedy,
The time is worth the use on 't.
Cleo. Great Apollo
Turn all to th' best! These proclamations,
So forcing faults upon Hermione,
I little like.
Dion. The violent carriage of it
Will clear or end the business: when the oracle,
Thus by Apollo's great divine seal'd up,
Shall the contents discover, something rare
Even then will rush to knowledge. Go: fresh horses!
And gracious be the issue! *Exeunt.*

SCENE II. [*A court of Justice.*]

Enter LEONTES, Lords, [*and*] Officers.

Leon. This sessions, to our great grief we pronounce,
Even pushes 'gainst our heart: the party tried
The daughter of a king, our wife, and one
Of us too much belov'd. Let us be clear'd
Of being tyrannous, since we so openly
Proceed in justice, which shall have due course,
Even to the guilt or the purgation.
Produce the prisoner.
Off. It is his highness' pleasure that the queen
Appear in person here in court. Silence!

[*Enter*] HERMIONE, *as to her trial,* [PAULINA, *and*] Ladies.

Leon. Read the indictment.

Off. [*Reads*] Hermione, queen to the worthy Leontes, king of Sicilia, thou art here accused and arraigned of high treason, in committing adultery with Polixenes, king of Bohemia, and conspiring with Camillo to take away the life of our sovereign lord the king, thy royal husband: the pretence whereof being by circumstances partly laid open, thou, Hermione, contrary to the faith and allegiance of a true subject, didst counsel and aid them, for their better safety, to fly away by night.

Her. Since what I am to say must be but that
Which contradicts my accusation and
The testimony on my part no other
But what comes from myself, it shall scarce boot me
To say 'not guilty:' mine integrity
Being counted falsehood, shall, as I express it,
Be so receiv'd. But thus: if pow'rs divine
Behold our human actions, as they do,
I doubt not then but innocence shall make
False accusation blush and tyranny
Tremble at patience. You, my lord, best know,
Who least will seem to do so, my past life
Hath been as continent, as chaste, as true,
As I am now unhappy; which is more
Than history can pattern, though devis'd
And play'd to take spectators. For behold me
A fellow of the royal bed, which owe
A moiety of the throne, a great king's daughter,
The mother to a hopeful prince, here standing
To prate and talk for life and honour 'fore
Who please to come and hear. For life, I prize it
As I weigh grief, which I would spare: for honour,
'Tis a derivative from me to mine,
And only that I stand for. I appeal
To your own conscience, sir, before Polixenes
Came to your court, how I was in your grace,
How merited to be so; since he came,
With what encounter so uncurrent I
Have strain'd t' appear thus: if one jot beyond
The bound of honour, or in act or will
That way inclining, hard'ned be the hearts
Of all that hear me, and my near'st of kin
Cry fie upon my grave!
Leon. I ne'er heard yet
That any of these bolder vices wanted
Less impudence to gainsay what they did
Than to perform it first.
Her. That 's true enough;
Though 'tis a saying, sir, not due to me.
Leon. You will not own it.
Her. †More than mistress of
Which comes to me in name of fault, I must not
At all acknowledge. For Polixenes,
With whom I am accus'd, I do confess
I lov'd him as in honour he requir'd,
With such a kind of love as might become
A lady like me, with a love even such,
So and no other, as yourself commanded:
Which not to have done I think had been in me
Both disobedience and ingratitude
To you and toward your friend, whose love had spoke,
Even since it could speak, from an infant, freely
That it was yours. Now, for conspiracy,
I know not how it tastes; though it be dish'd
For me to try how: all I know of it
Is that Camillo was an honest man;
And why he left your court, the gods themselves,
Wotting no more than I, are ignorant.
Leon. You knew of his departure, as you know
What you have underta'en to do in 's absence.
Her. Sir,
You speak a language that I understand not:
My life stands in the level of your dreams,
Which I'll lay down.
Leon. Your actions are my dreams;
You had a bastard by Polixenes,
And I but dream'd it. As you were past all shame,—
Those of your fact are so—so past all truth:
Which to deny concerns more than avails; for as
Thy brat hath been cast out, like to itself,

8. **burst,** utterance. 14. **worth . . . on 't,** well employed. 17. **carriage,** execution, management. 19. **divine,** here applied to a priest of the heathen religion. 21. **fresh horses.** This indicates that the scene is laid at some point on the return journey.

SCENE II. 1. **sessions,** sitting of a court of justice. **pronounce,** declare. 7. **purgation,** clearing from the accusation. 18. **pretence,** purpose, design. 26. **boot,** avail. 38. **take,** please. 39. **owe,** own. 43-46. **For . . . for,** as for life, it is only grief to me, and I would willingly dismiss it; as for honor, it is transmitted by descent from me to mine, and that only I maintain. 50-51. **With . . . thus,** (I ask) by what behavior so improper I have exceeded bounds so that I appear thus (in disgrace). 59. **due,** applicable. 60-62. **More . . . acknowledge,** I will not acknowledge that I am answerable for more than what may be called faults; i.e., she is not guilty of the *bolder vices* of line 56. 82. **level,** aim, range (in archery). 86. **Those . . . fact,** all those who do what you did. 87. **Which . . . avails,** to deny this is more trouble than it is

No father owning it,—which is, indeed,
More criminal in thee than it,—so thou
Shalt feel our justice, in whose easiest passage
Look for no less than death.
Her. Sir, spare your threats:
The bug which you would fright me with I seek.
To me can life be no commodity:
The crown and comfort of my life, your favour,
I do give lost; for I do feel it gone,
But know not how it went. My second joy
And first-fruits of my body, from his presence
I am barr'd, like one infectious. My third comfort,
Starr'd most unluckily, is from my breast,
The innocent milk in it most innocent mouth,
Hal'd out to murder: myself on every post
Proclaim'd a strumpet: with immodest hatred
The child-bed privilege denied, which 'longs
To women of all fashion; lastly, hurried
Here to this place, i' th' open air, before
I have got strength of limit. Now, my liege,
Tell me what blessings I have here alive,
That I should fear to die? Therefore proceed.
But yet hear this; mistake me not; no life,
I prize it not a straw, but for mine honour,
Which I would free, if I shall be condemn'd
Upon surmises, all proofs sleeping else
But what your jealousies awake, I tell you
'Tis rigour and not law. Your honours all,
I do refer me to the oracle:
Apollo be my judge!
First Lord. This your request
Is altogether just: therefore bring forth,
And in Apollo's name, his oracle. [*Exeunt certain Officers.*]
Her. The Emperor of Russia was my father:
O that he were alive, and here beholding
His daughter's trial! that he did but see
The flatness of my misery, yet with eyes
Of pity, not revenge!

[*Enter* Officers, *with*] CLEOMENES [*and*] DION.

Off. You here shall swear upon this sword of justice,
That you, Cleomenes and Dion, have
Been both at Delphos, and from thence have brought
This seal'd-up oracle, by the hand deliver'd
Of great Apollo's priest and that since then
You have not dar'd to break the holy seal
Nor read the secrets in 't.
Cleo. Dion. All this we swear.
Leon. Break up the seals and read.
Off. [*Reads*] Hermione is chaste; Polixenes blameless; Camillo a true subject; Leontes a jealous tyrant; his innocent babe truly begotten; and the king shall live without an heir, if that which is lost be not found.
Lords. Now blessed be the great Apollo!
Her. Praised!
Leon. Hast thou read truth?
Off. Ay, my lord; even so
As it is here set down.
Leon. There is no truth at all i' th' oracle:
The sessions shall proceed: this is mere falsehood.

[*Enter* Servant.]

Serv. My lord the king, the king!
Leon. What is the business?
Serv. O sir, I shall be hated to report it!
The prince your son, with mere conceit and fear
Of the queen's speed, is gone.
Leon. How! gone!
Serv. Is dead.
Leon. Apollo 's angry; and the heavens themselves
Do strike at my injustice. [*Hermione swoons.*] How now there!
Paul. This news is mortal to the queen: look down
And see what death is doing.
Leon. Take her hence:
Her heart is but o'ercharg'd: she will recover:
I have too much believ'd mine own suspicion:
Beseech you, tenderly apply to her
Some remedies for life.
[*Exeunt Paulina and Ladies, with Hermione.*]
Apollo, pardon
My great profaneness 'gainst thine oracle!
I'll reconcile me to Polixenes,
New woo my queen, recall the good Camillo,
Whom I proclaim a man of truth, of mercy;
For, being transported by my jealousies
To bloody thoughts and to revenge, I chose
Camillo for the minister to poison
My friend Polixenes: which had been done,
But that the good mind of Camillo tardied
My swift command, though I with death and with
Reward did threaten and encourage him,
Not doing it and being done: he, most humane
And fill'd with honour, to my kingly guest
Unclasp'd my practice, quit his fortunes here,
Which you knew great, and to the hazard
Of all incertainties himself commended,
No richer than his honour: how he glisters
Through my rust! and how his piety
Does my deeds make the blacker!

[*Enter* PAULINA.]

Paul. Woe the while!
O, cut my lace, lest my heart, cracking it,
Break too!
First Lord. What fit is this, good lady?
Paul. What studied torments, tyrant, hast for me?
What wheels? racks? fires? what flaying? boiling?
In leads or oils? what old or newer torture
Must I receive, whose every word deserves
To taste of thy most worst? Thy tyranny
Together working with thy jealousies,
Fancies too weak for boys, too green and idle
For girls of nine, O, think what they have done
And then run mad indeed, stark mad! for all
Thy by-gone fooleries were but spices of it.
That thou betray'dst Polixenes, 'twas nothing;
That did but show thee, of a fool, inconstant
And damnable ingrateful: nor was 't much,

worth. 88. **like to itself,** as it ought to be (since it has no father). 93. **bug,** bogey, imaginary object of terror. 94. **commodity,** asset. 96. **give,** reckon as. 100. **Starr'd,** fated. 101. **it,** its. 103. **immodest,** immoderate. 105. **fashion,** rank. 107. **strength of limit,** limited strength. 110. **no life,** i.e., I do not ask for life. 115. **rigour,** tyranny, injustice. 120. **Emperor of Russia.** In *Pandosto* it is the wife of Egistus (Polixenes) who is daughter of the Emperor of Russia. 123. **flatness,** absoluteness. 146. **speed,** success. 154. **Apollo, pardon.** The suddenness of Leontes' conversion is characteristic of Shakespeare's treatment of conscience, and connects itself with the current psychological theory of the sudden predominance of one emotion. 163. **tardied,** delayed in executing. 166. **Not . . . done,** i.e., reward if he did it, and death if he did not. 168. **Unclasp'd my practice,** disclosed my conspiracy. 171. **No richer than,** with no riches except. 185. **spices,** foretastes, samples. 187. **of,** for.

That wouldst have poison'd good Camillo's honour,
To have him kill a king; poor trespasses,
More monstrous standing by: whereof I reckon
The casting forth to crows thy baby-daughter
To be or none or little; though a devil
Would have shed water out of fire ere done 't:
Nor is 't directly laid to thee, the death
Of the young prince, whose honourable thoughts,
Thoughts high for one so tender, cleft the heart
That could conceive a gross and foolish sire
Blemish'd his gracious dam: this is not, no,
Laid to thy answer: but the last,—O lords,
When I have said, cry 'woe!'—the queen, the queen,
The sweet'st, dear'st creature 's dead, and vengeance for 't
Not dropp'd down yet.

First Lord. The higher pow'rs forbid!

Paul. I say she 's dead; I'll swear 't. If word nor oath
Prevail not, go and see: if you can bring
Tincture or lustre in her lip, her eye,
Heat outwardly or breath within, I'll serve you
As I would do the gods. But, O thou tyrant!
Do not repent these things, for they are heavier
Than all thy woes can stir: therefore betake thee
To nothing but despair. A thousand knees
Ten thousand years together, naked, fasting,
Upon a barren mountain, and still winter
In storm perpetual, could not move the gods
To look that way thou wert.

Leon. Go on, go on:
Thou canst not speak too much; I have deserv'd
All tongues to talk their bitt'rest.

First Lord. Say no more:
Howe'er the business goes, you have made fault
I' th' boldness of your speech.

Paul. I am sorry for 't:
All faults I make, when I shall come to know them,
I do repent. Alas! I have show'd too much
The rashness of a woman: he is touch'd
To th' noble heart. What 's gone and what 's past help
Should be past grief: do not receive affliction
At my petition; I beseech you, rather
Let me be punish'd, that have minded you
Of what you should forget. Now, good my liege,
Sir, royal sir, forgive a foolish woman:
The love I bore your queen—lo, fool again!—
I'll speak of her no more, nor of your children;
I'll not remember you of my own lord,
Who is lost too: take your patience to you,
And I'll say nothing.

Leon. Thou didst speak but well
When most the truth; which I receive much better
Than to be pitied of thee. Prithee, bring me
To the dead bodies of my queen and son:
One grave shall be for both: upon them shall
The causes of their death appear, unto
Our shame perpetual. Once a day I'll visit
The chapel where they lie, and tears shed there
Shall be my recreation: so long as nature
Will bear up with this exercise, so long
I daily vow to use it. Come and lead me
To these sorrows. *Exeunt.*

SCENE III. [*Bohemia. A desert country near the sea.*]

Enter ANTIGONUS [*and*] *a* Mariner, [*with a*] *Babe.*

Ant. Thou art perfect then, our ship hath touch'd upon
The deserts of Bohemia?

Mar. Ay, my lord; and fear
We have landed in ill time: the skies look grimly
And threaten present blusters. In my conscience,
The heavens with that we have in hand are angry
And frown upon 's.

Ant. Their sacred wills be done! Go, get aboard;
Look to thy bark: I'll not be long before
I call upon thee.

Mar. Make your best haste, and go not
Too far i' th' land: 'tis like to be loud weather;
Besides, this place is famous for the creatures
Of prey that keep upon 't.

Ant. Go thou away:
I'll follow instantly.

Mar. I am glad at heart
To be so rid o' th' business. *Exit.*

Ant. Come, poor babe:
I have heard, but not believ'd, the spirits o' th' dead
May walk again: if such thing be, thy mother
Appear'd to me last night, for ne'er was dream
So like a waking. To me comes a creature,
Sometimes her head on one side, some another;
I never saw a vessel of like sorrow,
So fill'd and so becoming: in pure white robes,
Like very sanctity, she did approach
My cabin where I lay; thrice bow'd before me,
And gasping to begin some speech, her eyes
Became two spouts: the fury spent, anon
Did this break from her: 'Good Antigonus,
Since fate, against thy better disposition,
Hath made thy person for the thrower-out
Of my poor babe, according to thine oath,
Places remote enough are in Bohemia,
There weep and leave it crying; and, for the babe
Is counted lost for ever, Perdita,
I prithee, call 't. For this ungentle business,
Put on thee by my lord, thou ne'er shalt see
Thy wife Paulina more.' And so, with shrieks,
She melted into air. Affrighted much,
I did in time collect myself and thought
This was so and no slumber. Dreams are toys:
Yet for this once, yea, superstitiously,
I will be squar'd by this. I do believe
Hermione hath suffer'd death, and that
Apollo would, this being indeed the issue
Of King Polixenes, it should here be laid,
Either for life or death, upon the earth
Of its right father. Blossom, speed thee well!
[*He lays down the baby.*]

191. **More . . . by,** when more monstrous sins are at hand for comparison. 194. **shed . . . fire,** wept from his fiery eyes. 210. **woes can stir,** penance can remove. 225. **my petition.** She has bid him, in lines 210-211, to betake himself to despair. 231. **remember,** remind.

SCENE III. 1. **perfect,** certain. 2. **deserts of Bohemia,** i.e., on the seacoast. Shakespeare's famous blunder is in his source, which he merely repeats. 21. **vessel,** creature. 22. **becoming,** apparently, imbued with grace and fitness. The association of the word with *fill'd* has caused Moorman to suspect that we have here a typographical error for *beteeming*, meaning "overflowing." 33. **Perdita,** i.e., the lost girl. 41. **squar'd,** directed in my course. 47. **character,** written account, the same which subsequently served to identify Perdita. **there these.** The reference is to the ornaments found by the shepherd (ll. 120-126). 48. **breed,** keep, support. **pretty,** pretty one. 49. **rest,** remain, i.e., a

There lie, and there thy character: there these;
Which may, if fortune please, both breed thee, pretty,
And still rest thine. The storm begins: poor wretch,
That for thy mother's fault art thus expos'd
To loss and what may follow! Weep I cannot,
But my heart bleeds; and most accurs'd am I
To be by oath enjoin'd to this. Farewell!
The day frowns more and more: thou 'rt like to have
A lullaby too rough: I never saw
The heavens so dim by day. A savage clamour!
Well may I get aboard! This is the chase:
I am gone for ever. *Exit, pursued by a bear.*

[*Enter a*] Shepherd.

Shep. I would there were no age between sixteen and three-and-twenty, or that youth would sleep out the rest; for there is nothing in the between but getting wenches with child, wronging the ancientry, stealing, fighting—Hark you now! Would any but these boiled brains of nineteen and two-and-twenty hunt this weather? They have scared away two of my best sheep, which I fear the wolf will sooner find than the master: if any where I have them, 'tis by the seaside, browsing of ivy. Good luck, an 't be thy will! what have we here? Mercy on 's, a barne; a very pretty barne! A boy or a child, I wonder? A pretty one; a very pretty one: sure, some 'scape: though I am not bookish, yet I can read waiting-gentlewoman in the 'scape. This has been some stair-work, some trunk-work, some behind-door-work: they were warmer that got this than the poor thing is here. I'll take it up for pity: yet I'll tarry till my son come; he hallooed but even now. Whoa, ho, hoa!

Enter Clown.

Clo. Hilloa, loa!

Shep. What, art so near? If thou 'lt see a thing to talk on when thou art dead and rotten, come hither. What ailest thou, man?

Clo. I have seen two such sights, by sea and by land! but I am not to say it is a sea, for it is now the sky: betwixt the firmament and it you cannot thrust a bodkin's point.

Shep. Why, boy, how is it?

Clo. I would you did but see how it chafes, how it rages, how it takes up the shore! but that 's not to the point. O, the most piteous cry of the poor souls! sometimes to see 'em, and not to see 'em; now the ship boring the moon with her main-mast, and anon swallowed with yest and froth, as you 'ld thrust a cork into a hogshead. And then for the land-service, to see how the bear tore out his shoulder-bone; how he cried to me for help and said his name was Antigonus, a nobleman. But to make an end of the ship, to see how the sea flap-dragoned it: but, first, how the poor souls roared, and the sea mocked them; and how the poor gentleman roared and the bear mocked him, both roaring louder than the sea or weather.

Shep. Name of mercy, when was this, boy?

Clo. Now, now: I have not winked since I saw these sights: the men are not yet cold under water, nor the bear half dined on the gentleman: he 's at it now.

Shep. Would I had been by, to have helped the old man!

Clo. I would you had been by the ship side, to have helped her: there your charity would have lacked footing.

Shep. Heavy matters! heavy matters! but look thee here, boy. Now bless thyself: thou mettest with things dying, I with things new-born. Here 's a sight for thee; look thee, a bearing-cloth for a squire's child! look thee here; take up, take up, boy; open 't. So, let 's see: it was told me I should be rich by the fairies. This is some changeling: open 't. What 's within, boy?

Clo. You 're a made old man: if the sins of your youth are forgiven you, you 're well to live. Gold! all gold!

Shep. This is fairy gold, boy, and 'twill prove so: up with 't, keep it close: home, home, the next way. We are lucky, boy; and to be so still requires nothing but secrecy. Let my sheep go: come, good boy, the next way home.

Clo. Go you the next way with your findings. I'll go see if the bear be gone from the gentleman and how much he hath eaten: they are never curst but when they are hungry: if there be any of him left, I'll bury it.

Shep. That 's a good deed. If thou mayest discern by that which is left of him what he is, fetch me to the sight of him.

Clo. Marry, will I; and you shall help to put him i' the ground.

Shep. 'Tis a lucky day, boy, and we'll do good deeds on 't. *Exeunt.*

ACT IV.

SCENE I.

Enter TIME, *the* Chorus.

Time. I, that please some, try all, both joy and terror
Of good and bad, that makes and unfolds error,
Now take upon me, in the name of Time,
To use my wings. Impute it not a crime
To me or my swift passage, that I slide
O'er sixteen years and leave the growth untried
Of that wide gap, since it is in my pow'r
To o'erthrow law and in one self-born hour
To plant and o'erwhelm custom. Let me pass
The same I am, ere ancient'st order was
Or what is now receiv'd: I witness to
The times that brought them in; so shall I do
To th' freshest things now reigning and make stale
The glistering of this present, as my tale
Now seems to it. Your patience this allowing,
I turn my glass and give my scene such growing
As you had slept between: Leontes leaving,

residue remain. 57. **This . . . chase.** Antigonus here sees the pursuing bear. 63. **ancientry,** old people. 64. **boiled brains,** hot-headed youths. 69. **ivy.** *Pandosto* has this detail, stating that the shepherd sought his sheep browsing on sea ivy. 70. **barne,** child. 71. **child,** female infant. 73. **'scape,** escapade, especially a transgression of the laws of chastity. 90. **takes up,** swallows. 95. **yest,** foam. 97. **land-service,** military service; here, doings on land; used blunderingly. 100. **flap-dragoned,** swallowed as one would a flapdragon, i.e., a raisin or the like snatched up out of burning brandy in the game of snapdragon. 119. **bearing-cloth,** child's christening robe. 125. **well to live,** well to do.

ACT IV. SCENE I. 2. **makes and unfolds,** make and unfold. 6. **growth untried,** progress unknown. 8. **self-born,** selfsame. 14. **glistering,** glistening freshness.

Th' effects of his fond jealousies so grieving
That he shuts up himself, imagine me,
Gentle spectators, that I now may be
In fair Bohemia; and remember well,
I mention'd a son o' th' king's, which Florizel
I now name to you; and with speed so pace
To speak of Perdita, now grown in grace
Equal with wond'ring: what of her ensues
I list not prophesy; but let Time's news
Be known when 'tis brought forth. A shepherd's daughter,
And what to her adheres, which follows after,
Is th' argument of Time. Of this allow,
If ever you have spent time worse ere now;
If never, yet that Time himself doth say
He wishes earnestly you never may. *Exit.*

SCENE II. [*Bohemia. The palace of* POLIXENES.]

Enter POLIXENES *and* CAMILLO.

Pol. I pray thee, good Camillo, be no more importunate: 'tis a sickness denying thee any thing; a death to grant this.

Cam. It is fifteen years since I saw my country: though I have for the most part been aired abroad, I desire to lay my bones there. Besides, the penitent king, my master, hath sent for me; to whose feeling sorrows I might be some allay, or I o'erween to think so, which is another spur to my departure.

Pol. As thou lovest me, Camillo, wipe not out the rest of thy services by leaving me now: the need I have of thee thine own goodness hath made; better not to have had thee than thus to want thee: thou, having made me businesses which none without thee can sufficiently manage, must either stay to execute them thyself or take away with thee the very services thou hast done; which if I have not enough considered, as too much I cannot, to be more thankful to thee shall be my study, and my profit therein the heaping friendships. Of that fatal country, Sicilia, prithee speak no more; whose very naming punishes me with the remembrance of that penitent, as thou callest him, and reconciled king, my brother; whose loss of his most precious queen and children are even now to be afresh lamented. Say to me, when sawest thou the Prince Florizel, my son? Kings are no less unhappy, their issue not being gracious, than they are in losing them when they have approved their virtues.

Cam. Sir, it is three days since I saw the prince. What his happier affairs may be, are to me unknown: but I have missingly noted, he is of late much retired from court and is less frequent to his princely exercises than formerly he hath appeared.

Pol. I have considered so much, Camillo, and with some care; so far that I have eyes under my service which look upon his removedness; from whom I have this intelligence, that he is seldom from the house of a most homely shepherd; a man, they say, that from very nothing, and beyond the imagination of his neighbours, is grown into an unspeakable estate.

Cam. I have heard, sir, of such a man, who hath a daughter of most rare note: the report of her is extended more than can be thought to begin from such a cottage.

Pol. That 's likewise part of my intelligence; but, I fear, the angle that plucks our son thither. Thou shalt accompany us to the place; where we will, not appearing what we are, have some question with the shepherd; from whose simplicity I think it not uneasy to get the cause of my son's resort thither. Prithee, be my present partner in this business, and lay aside the thoughts of Sicilia.

Cam. I willingly obey your command.

Pol. My best Camillo! We must disguise ourselves. *Exit* [*with Camillo*].

SCENE III. [*A road near the* Shepherd's *cottage.*]

Enter AUTOLYCUS, *singing.*

When daffodils begin to peer,
With heigh! the doxy over the dale,
Why, then comes in the sweet o' the year;
For the red blood reigns in the winter's pale.

The white sheet bleaching on the hedge,
With heigh! the sweet birds, O, how they sing!
Doth set my pugging tooth on edge;
For a quart of ale is a dish for a king.

The lark, that tirra-lyra chants,
With heigh! with heigh! the thrush and the jay,
Are summer songs for me and my aunts,
While we lie tumbling in the hay.

I have served Prince Florizel and in my time wore three-pile; but now I am out of service:

But shall I go mourn for that, my dear?
The pale moon shines by night:
And when I wander here and there,
I then do most go right.

If tinkers may have leave to live,
And bear the sow-skin budget,
Then my account I well may give,
And in the stocks avouch it.

My traffic is sheets; when the kite builds, look to lesser linen. My father named me Autolycus; who being, as I am, littered under Mercury, was likewise a snapper-up of unconsidered trifles. With die and drab I purchased this caparison, and my revenue is the silly cheat. Gallows and knock are too powerful on the highway: beating and hanging are terrors to me: for the life to come, I sleep out the thought of it. A prize! a prize!

Enter Clown.

SCENE II. 6. **been . . . abroad,** lived in foreign lands. 9. **allay,** means of abatement. **o'erween,** am presumptuous. 22. **heaping,** heaping up of. 32. **approved,** proved. 35. **missingly,** i.e., noting the prince's absence. 40-41. **eyes . . . service,** i.e., servants. 41. **removedness,** absence. 52. **angle,** fish-hook.

SCENE III. 2. **doxy,** beggar's mistress. 4. **pale,** paleness; enclosure. 7. **pugging,** thievish. 11. **aunts,** whores. 14. **three-pile,** three-pile velvet, i.e., velvet having very rich pile or nap. 20. **budget,** tool-bag. 23. **kite.** The kite was supposed to carry off small pieces of linen with which to construct its nest. 27-29. **With . . . cheat,** with dice and women I got this outfit (his rags), and the simple fool is the source of my revenue. *Cheat* is also defined as "petty thieving." 29. **knock,** resistance which a highwayman encounters (Johnson); possibly the whipping post. 33. **every . . . tods,** every eleven rams yield a *tod*, i.e., a bulk of wool weighing twenty-eight pounds. 36. **springe,** snare. 37. **cock,** woodcock. The woodcock was proverbially stupid. 38.

Clo. Let me see: every 'leven wether tods; every tod yields pound and odd shilling; fifteen hundred shorn, what comes the wool to?

Aut. [*Aside*] If the springe hold, the cock 's mine.

Clo. I cannot do 't without counters. Let me see; what am I to buy for our sheep-shearing feast? Three pound of sugar, five pound of currants, rice,—what will this sister of mine do with rice? But my father hath made her mistress of the feast, and she lays it on. She hath made me four and twenty nosegays for the shearers, three-man-song-men all, and very good ones; but they are most of them means and bases; but one puritan amongst them, and he sings psalms to hornpipes. I must have saffron to colour the warden pies; mace; dates?—none, that 's out of my note; nutmegs, seven; a race or two of ginger, but that I may beg; four pound of prunes, and as many of raisins o' the sun.

Aut. O that ever I was born! [*Grovelling on the ground.*]

Clo. I' the name of me—

Aut. O, help me, help me! pluck but off these rags; and then, death, death!

Clo. Alack, poor soul! thou hast need of more rags to lay on thee, rather than have these off.

Aut. O sir, the loathsomeness of them offends me more than the stripes I have received, which are mighty ones and millions.

Clo. Alas, poor man! a million of beating may come to a great matter.

Aut. I am robbed, sir, and beaten; my money and apparel ta'en from me, and these detestable things put upon me.

Clo. What, by a horseman, or a footman?

Aut. A footman, sweet sir, a footman.

Clo. Indeed, he should be a footman by the garments he has left with thee: if this be a horseman's coat, it hath seen very hot service. Lend me thy hand, I'll help thee: come, lend me thy hand.

Aut. O, good sir, tenderly, O!

Clo. Alas, poor soul!

Aut. O, good sir, softly, good sir! I fear, sir, my shoulder-blade is out.

Clo. How now! canst stand?

Aut. [*Picking his pocket*] Softly, dear sir; good sir, softly. You ha' done me a charitable office.

Clo. Dost lack any money? I have a little money for thee.

Aut. No, good sweet sir; no, I beseech you, sir: I have a kinsman not past three quarters of a mile hence, unto whom I was going; I shall there have money, or any thing I want: offer me no money, I pray you; that kills my heart.

Clo. What manner of fellow was he that robbed you?

Aut. A fellow, sir, that I have known to go about with troll-my-dames: I knew him once a servant of the prince: I cannot tell, good sir, for which of his virtues it was, but he was certainly whipped out of the court.

Clo. His vices, you would say; there 's no virtue whipped out of the court: they cherish it to make it stay there; and yet it will no more but abide.

Aut. Vices, I would say, sir. I know this man well: he hath been since an ape-bearer; then a process-server, a bailiff; then he compassed a motion of the Prodigal Son, and married a tinker's wife within a mile where my land and living lies; and, having flown over many knavish professions, he settled only in rogue: some call him Autolycus.

Clo. Out upon him! prig, for my life, prig: he haunts wakes, fairs and bear-baitings.

Aut. Very true, sir; he, sir, he; that 's the rogue that put me into this apparel.

Clo. Not a more cowardly rogue in all Bohemia: if you had but looked big and spit at him, he 'ld have run.

Aut. I must confess to you, sir, I am no fighter: I am false of heart that way; and that he knew, I warrant him.

Clo. How do you now?

Aut. Sweet sir, much better than I was; I can stand and walk: I will even take my leave of you, and pace softly towards my kinsman's.

Clo. Shall I bring thee on the way?

Aut. No, good-faced sir; no, sweet sir.

Clo. Then fare thee well: I must go buy spices for our sheep-shearing. *Exit.*

Aut. Prosper you, sweet sir! Your purse is not hot enough to purchase your spice. I'll be with you at your sheep-shearing too: if I make not this cheat bring out another and the shearers prove sheep, let me be unrolled and my name put in the book of virtue!

Song. Jog on, jog on, the foot-path way,
And merrily hent the stile-a:
A merry heart goes all the day,
Your sad tires in a mile-a. *Exit.*

SCENE IV. [*The* Shepherd's *cottage.*]

Enter FLORIZEL [*and*] PERDITA.

Flo. These your unusual weeds to each part of you
Do give a life: no shepherdess, but Flora
Peering in April's front. This your sheep-shearing
Is as a meeting of the petty gods,
And you the queen on 't.
Per. Sir, my gracious lord,
To chide at your extremes it not becomes me:
O, pardon, that I name them! Your high self,
The gracious mark o' th' land, you have obscur'd
With a swain's wearing, and me, poor lowly maid,
Most goddess-like prank'd up: but that our feasts
In every mess have folly and the feeders
Digest it with a custom, I should blush
To see you so attir'd, sworn, I think,
To show myself a glass.
Flo. I bless the time
When my good falcon made her flight across
Thy father's ground.

counters, token coins used in reckoning. 44. **three-man-song-men,** singers of catches or rounds. 45. **means,** tenors. 47. **psalms to hornpipes,** psalms to merry tunes. 49. **warden,** made of the warden pear. 50. **note,** apparently, list; yet if the clown could not read, it would mean "observation" or "memory." **race,** root. 52. **o' the sun,** dried in the sun. 54. **me—,** possibly the beginning of *mercy*. 92. **troll-my-dames,** a game in which the object was to "troll" balls through arches set on a board. 99. **abide,** make a temporary stay. 101. **ape-bearer,** one who carries a monkey about for exhibition. 102-103. **compassed a motion,** got possession of a puppet-show. 108. **prig,** thief. 128. **cheat,** swindle, fraud. 130. **unrolled,** taken off the roll (of rogues and vagabonds). 132. **Jog on.** Written to a popular tune of the day. 133. **hent,** take.

SCENE IV. 6. **extremes,** extravagant statements. 8. **mark,** example, pattern. 12. **with a custom,** from habit. 13. **sworn,** perhaps should read *swoon*. 14. **To . . . glass,** to show me myself as in a mirror.

Per. Now Jove afford you cause!
To me the difference forges dread; your greatness
Hath not been us'd to fear. Even now I tremble
To think your father, by some accident,
Should pass this way as you did: O, the Fates!
How would he look, to see his work so noble
Vilely bound up? What would he say? Or how
Should I, in these my borrowed flaunts, behold
The sternness of his presence?
Flo. Apprehend
Nothing but jollity. The gods themselves,
Humbling their deities to love, have taken
The shapes of beasts upon them: Jupiter
Became a bull, and bellow'd; the green Neptune
A ram, and bleated; and the fire-rob'd god,
Golden Apollo, a poor humble swain,
As I seem now. Their transformations
Were never for a piece of beauty rarer,
Nor in a way so chaste, since my desires
Run not before mine honour, nor my lusts
Burn hotter than my faith.
Per. O, but, sir,
Your resolution cannot hold, when 'tis
Oppos'd, as it must be, by th' pow'r of the king:
One of these two must be necessities,
Which then will speak, that you must change this purpose,
Or I my life.
Flo. Thou dearest Perdita,
With these forc'd thoughts, I prithee, darken not
The mirth o' th' feast. Or I'll be thine, my fair,
Or not my father's. For I cannot be
Mine own, not any thing to any, if
I be not thine. To this I am most constant,
Though destiny say no. Be merry, gentle;
Strangle such thoughts as these with any thing
That you behold the while. Your guests are coming:
Lift up your countenance, as it were the day
Of celebration of that nuptial which
We two have sworn shall come.
Per. O lady Fortune,
Stand you auspicious!
Flo. See, your guests approach:
Address yourself to entertain them sprightly,
And let 's be red with mirth.

[*Enter*] Shepherd, Clown; POLIXENES, CAMILLO [*disguised*]; MOPSA, DORCAS; Servants.

Shep. Fie, daughter! when my old wife liv'd, upon
This day she was both pantler, butler, cook,
Both dame and servant; welcom'd all, serv'd all;
Would sing her song and dance her turn; now here,
At upper end o' th' table, now i' th' middle;
On his shoulder, and his; her face o' fire
With labour and the thing she took to quench it,
She would to each one sip. You are retir'd,
As if you were a feasted one and not
The hostess of the meeting: pray you, bid
These unknown friends to 's welcome; for it is
A way to make us better friends, more known.
Come, quench your blushes and present yourself
That which you are, mistress o' th' feast: come on,
And bid us welcome to your sheep-shearing,
As your good flock shall prosper.
Per. [*To Pol.*] Sir, welcome:
It is my father's will I should take on me
The hostess-ship o' th' day. [*To Cam.*] You 're welcome, sir.
Give me those flow'rs there, Dorcas. Reverend sirs,
For you there 's rosemary and rue; these keep
Seeming and savour all the winter long:
Grace and remembrance be to you both,
And welcome to our shearing!
Pol. Shepherdess,—
A fair one are you—well you fit our ages
With flow'rs of winter.
Per. Sir, the year growing ancient,
Not yet on summer's death, nor on the birth
Of trembling winter, the fairest flow'rs o' th' season
Are our carnations and streak'd gillyvors,
Which some call nature's bastards: of that kind
Our rustic garden 's barren; and I care not
To get the slips of them.
Pol. Wherefore, gentle maiden,
Do you neglect them?
Per. For I have heard it said
There is an art which in their piedness shares
With great creating nature.
Pol. Say there be;
Yet nature is made better by no mean
But nature makes that mean: so, over that art
Which you say adds to nature, is an art
That nature makes. You see, sweet maid, we marry
A gentler scion to the wildest stock,
And make conceive a bark of baser kind
By bud of nobler race: this is an art
Which does mend nature, change it rather, but
The art itself is nature.
Per. So it is.
Pol. Then make your garden rich in gillyvors,
And do not call them bastards.
Per. I'll not put
The dibble in earth to set one slip of them;
No more than were I painted I would wish
This youth should say 'twere well and only therefore
Desire to breed by me. Here 's flow'rs for you;
Hot lavender, mints, savory, marjoram;
The marigold, that goes to bed wi' th' sun
And with him rises weeping: these are flow'rs
Of middle summer, and I think they are given
To men of middle age. Y' are very welcome.
Cam. I should leave grazing, were I of your flock,
And only live by gazing.
Per. Out, alas!
You 'ld be so lean, that blasts of January
Would blow you through and through. [*To Flo.*] Now, my fair'st friend,
I would I had some flow'rs o' th' spring that might
Become your time of day; [*To Shepherdesses*] and yours, and yours,
That wear upon your virgin branches yet
Your maidenheads growing: O Proserpina,

17. **difference,** of rank. 22. **bound up,** like a book. 23. **flaunts,** finery. 41. **forc'd,** far-fetched, unnatural. 56. **pantler,** servant in charge of the pantry. 65. **to 's,** of ours. 75. **Seeming,** outward form. 82. **gillyvors,** gillyflower—a kind of carnation. 83. **nature's bastards.** As indicated in lines 86-88, they are a result of artificial breeding. 92-97. **You . . . nature,** ironical allusion to the union of the prince with the shepherdess. 104. **Hot,** eager, ardent; here, aromatic. 116. **Proserpina,** stolen away by Pluto when, according to Ovid, she was gathering flowers in her garden. 118. **Dis's waggon,** Pluto's chariot. 119. **take,** charm. 122. **Cytherea's,** Venus'. 123. **unmarried,** i.e., too early for summer. Cf. Milton's *Lycidas:* "The rathe primrose that forsaken dies." 126. **crown imperial,** handsome fritillary, a flower from the Levant, cultivated in English gardens. 127. **flow'r-de-luce,** *fleur-de-lis.* 134. **Whitsun pastorals,** alluding to English morris dances

For the flow'rs now, that frighted thou let'st fall
From Dis's waggon! daffodils,
That come before the swallow dares, and take
The winds of March with beauty; violets dim,
But sweeter than the lids of Juno's eyes
Or Cytherea's breath; pale primroses,
That die unmarried, ere they can behold
Bright Phœbus in his strength—a malady
Most incident to maids; bold oxlips and
The crown imperial; lilies of all kinds,
The flow'r-de-luce being one! O, these I lack,
To make you garlands of, and my sweet friend,
To strew him o'er and o'er!
Flo. What, like a corse?
Per. No, like a bank for love to lie and play on;
Not like a corse; or if, not to be buried,
But quick and in mine arms. Come, take your flow'rs:
Methinks I play as I have seen them do
In Whitsun pastorals: sure this robe of mine
Does change my disposition.
Flo. What you do
Still betters what is done. When you speak, sweet,
I 'ld have you do it ever: when you sing,
I 'ld have you buy and sell so, so give alms,
Pray so; and, for the ord'ring your affairs,
To sing them too: when you do dance, I wish you
A wave o' th' sea, that you might ever do
Nothing but that; move still, still so,
And own no other function: each your doing,
So singular in each particular,
Crowns what you are doing in the present deeds,
That all your acts are queens.
Per. O Doricles,
Your praises are too large: but that your youth,
And the true blood which peepeth fairly through 't,
Do plainly give you out an unstain'd shepherd,
With wisdom I might fear, my Doricles,
You woo'd me the false way.
Flo. I think you have
As little skill to fear as I have purpose
To put you to 't. But come; our dance, I pray:
Your hand, my Perdita: so turtles pair,
That never mean to part.
Per. I'll swear for 'em.
Pol. This is the prettiest low-born lass that ever
Ran on the green-sward: nothing she does or seems
But smacks of something greater than herself,
Too noble for this place.
Cam. He tells her something
That makes her blood look out: good sooth, she is
The queen of curds and cream.
Clo. Come on, strike up!
Dor. Mopsa must be your mistress: marry, garlic,
To mend her kissing with!
Mop. Now, in good time!
Clo. Not a word, a word; we stand upon our
manners.
Come, strike up!
[*Music.*] *Here a dance of Shepherds and Shepherdesses.*
Pol. Pray, good shepherd, what fair swain is this
Which dances with your daughter?
Shep. They call him Doricles; and boasts himself
To have a worthy feeding: but I have it
Upon his own report and I believe it;
He looks like sooth. He says he loves my daughter:
I think so too; for never gaz'd the moon
Upon the water as he'll stand and read
As 'twere my daughter's eyes: and, to be plain,
I think there is not half a kiss to choose
Who loves another best.
Pol. She dances featly.
Shep. So she does any thing; though I report it,
That should be silent: if young Doricles
Do light upon her, she shall bring him that
Which he not dreams of.

Enter Servant.

Serv. O master, if you did but hear the pedlar at the door, you would never dance again after a tabor and pipe; no, the bagpipe could not move you: he sings several tunes faster than you'll tell money; he utters them as he had eaten ballads and all men's ears grew to his tunes.

Clo. He could never come better; he shall come in. I love a ballad but even too well, if it be doleful matter merrily set down, or a very pleasant thing indeed and sung lamentably.

Ser. He hath songs for man or woman, of all sizes; no milliner can so fit his customers with gloves: he has the prettiest love-songs for maids; so without bawdry, which is strange; with such delicate burthens of dildos and fadings, 'jump her and thump her;' and where some stretch-mouthed rascal would, as it were, mean mischief and break a foul gap into the matter, he makes the maid to answer 'Whoop, do me no harm, good man;' puts him off, slights him, with 'Whoop, do me no harm, good man.'

Pol. This is a brave fellow.

Clo. Believe me, thou talkest of an admirable conceited fellow. Has he any unbraided wares?

Serv. He hath ribbons of all the colours i' the rainbow; points more than all the lawyers in Bohemia can learnedly handle, though they come to him by the gross: inkles, caddisses, cambrics, lawns: why, he sings 'em over as they were gods or goddesses; you would think a smock were a she-angel, he so chants to the sleeve-hand and the work about the square on 't.

Clo. Prithee bring him in; and let him approach singing.

Per. Forewarn him that he use no scurrilous words in 's tunes. [*Exit Servant.*]

Clo. You have of these pedlars, that have more in them than you 'ld think, sister.

Per. Ay, good brother, or go about to think.

Enter Autolycus, *singing.*

Lawn as white as driven snow;
Cyprus black as e'er was crow;
Gloves as sweet as damask roses;
Masks for faces and for noses;
Bugle bracelet, necklace amber,

often performed at Whitsuntide. 143. **each your doing,** each thing you do. 145. **what . . . deed,** what you are at present doing. 152. **skill,** reason, cause. 154. **turtles,** turtledoves, as symbols of faithful love. 169. **feeding,** pasturage. 171. **sooth,** truth. 176. **featly,** gracefully. 184. **tell,** count. 187. **better,** at a better time. 195. **burthens,** refrains. **dildos and fadings,** words used as part of the refrains of ballads (but with bawdy double meaning, as in *jump her, thump her, do me,* etc.). 198. **gap,** a gross parenthesis (Staunton). 204. **unbraided,** unfaded. 206. **points,** laces for fastening clothes; also, headings in an argument. 208. **inkles,** kind of tape. **caddisses,** worsted tapes used for garters. 212. **sleeve-hand,** wristband. **square,** the embroidered bosom of a garment. 217. **You . . . pedlars,** you'll find pedlars. 221. **Cyprus,** crepe. 224. **Bugle bracelet,** bracelet of black gloss beads.

Perfume for a lady's chamber;
Golden quoifs and stomachers,
For my lads to give their dears:
Pins and poking-sticks of steel,
What maids lack from head to heel:
Come buy of me, come; come buy, come buy;
Buy, lads, or else you lasses cry:
Come buy.

Clo. If I were not in love with Mopsa, thou shouldst take no money of me; but being enthralled as I am, it will also be the bondage of certain ribbons and gloves.

Mop. I was promised them against the feast; but they come not too late now.

Dor. He hath promised you more than that, or there be liars.

Mop. He hath paid you all he promised you: may be, he has paid you more, which will shame you to give him again.

Clo. Is there no manners left among maids? will they wear their plackets where they should bear their faces? Is there not milking-time, when you are going to bed, or kiln-hole, to whistle off these secrets, but you must be tittle-tattling before all our guests? 'tis well they are whispering: clamour your tongues, and not a word more.

Mop. I have done. Come, you promised me a tawdry-lace and a pair of sweet gloves.

Clo. Have I not told thee how I was cozened by the way and lost all my money?

Aut. And indeed, sir, there are cozeners abroad; therefore it behoves men to be wary.

Clo. Fear not thou, man, thou shalt lose nothing here.

Aut. I hope so, sir; for I have about me many parcels of charge.

Clo. What hast here? ballads?

Mop. Pray now, buy some: I love a ballad in print o' life, for then we are sure they are true.

Aut. Here 's one to a very doleful tune, how a usurer's wife was brought to bed of twenty money-bags at a burthen and how she longed to eat adders' heads and toads carbonadoed.

Mop. Is it true, think you?

Aut. Very true, and but a month old.

Dor. Bless me from marrying a usurer!

Aut. Here 's the midwife's name to 't, one Mistress Tale-porter, and five or six honest wives that were present. Why should I carry lies abroad?

Mop. Pray you now, buy it.

Clo. Come on, lay it by: and let 's first see moe ballads; we'll buy the other things anon.

Aut. Here 's another ballad of a fish, that appeared upon the coast on Wednesday the fourscore of April, forty thousand fathom above water, and sung this ballad against the hard hearts of maids: it was thought she was a woman and was turned into a cold fish for she would not exchange flesh with one that loved her: the ballad is very pitiful and as true.

Dor. Is it true too, think you?

Aut. Five justices' hands at it, and witnesses more than my pack will hold.

Clo. Lay it by too: another.

Aut. This is a merry ballad, but a very pretty one.

Mop. Let 's have some merry ones.

Aut. Why, this is a passing merry one and goes to the tune of 'Two maids wooing a man:' there 's scarce a maid westward but she sings it; 'tis in request, I can tell you.

Mop. We can both sing it: if thou 'lt bear a part, thou shalt hear; 'tis in three parts.

Dor. We had the tune on 't a month ago.

Aut. I can bear my part; you must know 'tis my occupation; have at it with you.

SONG.

A. Get you hence, for I must go
Where it fits not you to know.
D. Whither? *M.* O, whither? *D.* Whither?
M. It becomes thy oath full well,
Thou to me thy secrets tell.
D. Me too, let me go thither.
M. Or thou goest to th' grange or mill.
D. If to either, thou dost ill.
A. Neither. *D.* What, neither? *A.* Neither.
D. Thou hast sworn my love to be.
M. Thou hast sworn it more to me:
Then whither goest? say, whither?

Clo. We'll have this song out anon by ourselves: my father and the gentlemen are in sad talk, and we'll not trouble them. Come, bring away thy pack after me. Wenches, I'll buy for you both. Pedlar, let 's have the first choice. Follow me, girls.

[*Exit with Dorcas and Mopsa.*]

Aut. And you shall pay well for 'em. [*Follows.*] *Song.*
Will you buy any tape,
Or lace for your cape,
My dainty duck, my dear-a?
Any silk, any thread,
And toys for your head,
Of the new'st and fin'st, fin'st wear-a?
Come to the pedlar;
Money 's a medler,
That doth utter all men's ware-a. *Exit.*

[*Enter* Servant.]

Serv. Master, there is three carters, three shepherds, three neat-herds, three swine-herds, that have made themselves all men of hair, they call themselves Saltiers, and they have a dance which the wenches say is a gallimaufry of gambols, because they are not in 't; but they themselves are o' the mind, if it be not too rough for some that know little but bowling, it will please plentifully.

Shep. Away! we'll none on 't: here has been too much homely foolery already. I know, sir, we weary you.

Pol. You weary those that refresh us: pray, let 's see these four threes of herdsmen.

Serv. One three of them, by their own report, sir, hath danced before the king; and not the worst of the three but jumps twelve foot and a half by the squier.

226. **quoifs,** close-fitting caps. 228. **poking-sticks,** rods used for stiffening the plaits of ruffs. 237. **against,** before. 242. **paid you,** i.e., made you pregnant. 245. **plackets,** slits in petticoats. 248. **kiln-hole,** fire hole in a kiln used in making malt; evidently a customary gossiping place. 250. **clamour,** silence. 253. **tawdry-lace,** cheap and showy lace, or neckerchief, much worn by women in Shakespeare's time; so called from St. Audrey's Fair or because St. Audrey suffered a tumor in the throat from wearing rich necklaces. **sweet,** with perfume. 261. **parcels of charge,** valuable parcels. 264. **o' life,** on my life, dearly. 268. **carbonadoed,** scored across and grilled. 279. **ballad of a fish.** Such a ballad was actually entered in the Stationers' Register in 1604. 330. **utter,** put on the market. 333. **men of hair,** dressed in skins.

Shep. Leave your prating: since these good men are pleased, let them come in; but quickly now.
Serv. Why, they stay at door, sir. [*Exit.*]

Here a dance of twelve Satyrs.

Pol. O, father, you'll know more of that hereafter.
[*To Cam.*] Is it not too far gone? 'Tis time to part them.
He 's simple and tells much. [*To Flor.*] How now, fair shepherd!
Your heart is full of something that does take
Your mind from feasting. Sooth, when I was young
And handed love as you do, I was wont
To load my she with knacks: I would have ransack'd
The pedlar's silken treasury and have pour'd it
To her acceptance; you have let him go
And nothing marted with him. If your lass
Interpretation should abuse and call this
Your lack of love or bounty, you were straited
For a reply, at least if you make a care
Of happy holding her.
Flo. Old sir, I know
She prizes not such trifles as these are:
The gifts she looks from me are pack'd and lock'd
Up in my heart; which I have given already,
But not deliver'd. O, hear me breathe my life
Before this ancient sir, who, it should seem,
Hath sometime lov'd! I take thy hand, this hand,
As soft as dove's down and as white as it,
Or Ethiopian's tooth, or the fann'd snow that 's bolted
By th' northern blasts twice o'er.
Pol. What follows this?
How prettily th' young swain seems to wash
The hand was fair before! I have put you out:
But to your protestation; let me hear
What you profess.
Flo. Do, and be witness to 't.
Pol. And this my neighbour too?
Flo. And he, and more
Than he, and men, the earth, the heavens, and all:
That, were I crown'd the most imperial monarch,
Thereof most worthy, were I the fairest youth
That ever made eye swerve, had force and knowledge
More than was ever man's, I would not prize them
Without her love; for her employ them all;
Commend them and condemn them to her service
Or to their own perdition.
Pol. Fairly offer'd.
Cam. This shows a sound affection.
Shep. But, my daughter,
Say you the like to him?
Per. I cannot speak
So well, nothing so well; no, nor mean better:
By th' pattern of mine own thoughts I cut out
The purity of his.
Shep. Take hands, a bargain!
And, friends unknown, you shall bear witness to 't:
I give my daughter to him, and will make
Her portion equal his.
Flo. O, that must be
I' th' virtue of your daughter: one being dead,
I shall have more than you can dream of yet;
Enough then for your wonder. But, come on,
Contract us 'fore these witnesses.
Shep. Come, your hand;
And, daughter, yours.
Pol. Soft, swain, awhile, beseech you;
Have you a father?
Flo. I have: but what of him?
Pol. Knows he of this?
Flo. He neither does nor shall.
Pol. Methinks a father
Is at the nuptial of his son a guest
That best becomes the table. Pray you once more,
Is not your father grown incapable
Of reasonable affairs? is he not stupid
With age and alt'ring rheums? can he speak? hear?
Know man from man? dispute his own estate?
Lies he not bed-rid? and again does nothing
But what he did being childish?
Flo. No, good sir;
He has his health and ampler strength indeed
Than most have of his age.
Pol. By my white beard,
You offer him, if this be so, a wrong
Something unfilial: reason my son
Should choose himself a wife, but as good reason
The father, all whose joy is nothing else
But fair posterity, should hold some counsel
In such a business.
Flo. I yield all this;
But for some other reasons, my grave sir,
Which 'tis not fit you know, I not acquaint
My father of this business.
Pol. Let him know 't.
Flo. He shall not.
Pol. Prithee, let him.
Flo. No, he must not.
Shep. Let him, my son: he shall not need to grieve
At knowing of thy choice.
Flo. Come, come, he must not.
Mark our contract.
Pol. Mark your divorce, young sir,
[*Discovering himself.*]
Whom son I dare not call; thou art too base
To be acknowledg'd: thou a sceptre's heir,
That thus affects a sheep-hook! Thou old traitor,
I am sorry that by hanging thee I can
But shorten thy life one week. And thou, fresh piece
Of excellent witchcraft, who of force must know
The royal fool thou cop'st with,—
Shep. O, my heart!
Pol. I'll have thy beauty scratch'd with briers, and made
More homely than thy state. For thee, fond boy,
If I may ever know thou dost but sigh
That thou no more shalt see this knack, as never
I mean thou shalt, we'll bar thee from succession;
Not hold thee of our blood, no, not our kin,
Far than Deucalion off: mark thou my words:
Follow us to the court. Thou churl, for this time,

334. **Saltiers,** for "satyrs." 336. **gallimaufry,** jumble. 339. **bowling,** a game played mainly by the aristocracy, who might find the satyr dance too rough. 346. **danced before the king.** Thorndike (*Influence of Beaumont and Fletcher on Shakespeare*, pp. 32-34) argues that this masque of satyrs was borrowed from Jonson's *Masque of Oberon*, acted at Court, January 1, 1611. This play would, then, be dated after that event. 348. **squier,** foot rule. 358. **handed,** handled. 359. **knacks,** knickknacks. 362. **marted,** trafficked. 363. **Interpretation should abuse,** should interpret wrongly. 364. **straited,** embarrassed. 374. **bolted,** sifted. 409. **alt'ring rheums,** weakening colds. 416. **reason,** it is reasonable. 436. **fond,** foolish. 438. **knack,** knickknack, referring to Perdita. 441. **Far,** F: *farre*, meaning "farther." **Deucalion,** the Noah of classical mythology.

Though full of our displeasure, yet we free thee
From the dead blow of it. And you, enchantment,—
Worthy enough a herdsman; yea, him too,
That makes himself, but for our honour therein,
Unworthy thee,—if ever henceforth thou
These rural latches to his entrance open,
Or hoop his body more with thy embraces,
I will devise a death as cruel for thee
As thou art tender to 't. *Exit.*

Per. Even here undone!
I was not much afeard; for once or twice
I was about to speak and tell him plainly,
The selfsame sun that shines upon his court
Hides not his visage from our cottage but
Looks on alike. [*To Flo.*] Will 't please you, sir, be gone?
I told you what would come of this: beseech you,
Of your own state take care: this dream of mine,—
Being now awake, I'll queen it no inch farther,
But milk my ewes and weep.

Cam. Why, how now, father!
Speak ere thou diest.

Shep. I cannot speak, nor think,
Nor dare to know that which I know. [*To Flo.*] O sir!
You have undone a man of fourscore three,
That thought to fill his grave in quiet, yea,
To die upon the bed my father died,
To lie close by his honest bones: but now
Some hangman must put on my shroud and lay me
Where no priest shovels in dust. O cursed wretch,
That knew'st this was the prince, and wouldst adventure
To mingle faith with him! Undone! undone!
If I might die within this hour, I have liv'd
To die when I desire. *Exit.*

Flo. Why look you so upon me?
I am but sorry, not afeard; delay'd,
But nothing alt'red: what I was, I am;
More straining on for plucking back, not following
My leash unwillingly.

Cam. Gracious my lord,
You know your father's temper: at this time
He will allow no speech, which I do guess
You do not purpose to him; and as hardly
Will he endure your sight as yet, I fear:
Then, till the fury of his highness settle,
Come not before him.

Flo. I not purpose it.
I think, Camillo?

Cam. Even he, my lord.

Per. How often have I told you 'twould be thus!
How often said, my dignity would last
But till 'twere known!

Flo. It cannot fail but by
The violation of my faith; and then
Let nature crush the sides o' th' earth together
And mar the seeds within! Lift up thy looks:
From my succession wipe me, father; I
Am heir to my affection.

Cam. Be advis'd.

Flo. I am, and by my fancy: if my reason
Will thereto be obedient, I have reason;
If not, my senses, better pleas'd with madness,
Do bid it welcome.

Cam. This is desperate, sir.

Flo. So call it: but it does fulfil my vow;
I needs must think it honesty. Camillo,
Not for Bohemia, nor the pomp that may
Be thereat glean'd, for all the sun sees or
The close earth wombs or the profound seas hide
In unknown fathoms, will I break my oath
To this my fair belov'd: therefore, I pray you,
As you have ever been my father's honour'd friend,
When he shall miss me,—as, in faith, I mean not
To see him any more,—cast your good counsels
Upon his passion: let myself and fortune
Tug for the time to come. This you may know
And so deliver, I am put to sea
With her who here I cannot hold on shore;
And most opportune to our need I have
A vessel rides fast by, but not prepar'd
For this design. What course I mean to hold
Shall nothing benefit your knowledge, nor
Concern me the reporting.

Cam. O my lord!
I would your spirit were easier for advice,
Or stronger for your need.

Flo. Hark, Perdita. [*Drawing her aside.*]
I'll hear you by and by.

Cam. He 's irremoveable,
Resolv'd for flight. Now were I happy, if
His going I could frame to serve my turn,
Save him from danger, do him love and honour,
Purchase the sight again of dear Sicilia
And that unhappy king, my master, whom
I so much thirst to see.

Flo. Now, good Camillo;
I am so fraught with curious business that
I leave out ceremony.

Cam. Sir, I think
You have heard of my poor services, i' th' love
That I have borne your father?

Flo. Very nobly
Have you deserv'd: it is my father's music
To speak your deeds, not little of his care
To have them recompens'd as thought on.

Cam. Well, my lord,
If you may please to think I love the king
And through him what is nearest to him, which is
Your gracious self, embrace but my direction:
If your more ponderous and settled project
May suffer alteration, on mine honour,
I'll point you where you shall have such receiving
As shall become your highness; where you may
Enjoy your mistress, for the whom, I see,
There 's no disjunction to be made, but by—
As heavens forfend!—your ruin; marry her,
And, with my best endeavours in your absence,
Your discontenting father strive to qualify
And bring him up to liking.

Flo. How, Camillo,
May this, almost a miracle, be done?
That I may call thee something more than man

444. **enchantment,** referring to Perdita. 445. **yea, him,** i.e., worthy of him (Florizel). 456. **alike,** indifferently. 465. **died,** i.e., died on. 468. **Where . . . dust.** It was the duty of the priest in the burial service to cast earth on the body while saying, "Earth to earth." The shepherd's meaning is that he will be deprived of the rite of Christian burial. 475. **straining on,** i.e., like a hound on the leash. 489. **mar the seeds,** a frequent figure in Shakespeare for the destruction of life. 507. **Tug,** content. 513. **Shall . . . knowledge,** shall not profit you to know. 524. **curious,** demanding care. 542. **discontenting,** discontented, displeased. **qualify,** appease, pacify. 543. **bring . . . to,** raise him to the pitch of. 548. **unthought-on,** unexpected. 561. **divides him,** probably, is divided in his speech. 564. **Faster,** firmer. 571. **point you**

And after that trust to thee.
Cam. Have you thought on
A place whereto you'll go?
Flo. Not any yet:
But as th' unthought-on accident is guilty
To what we wildly do, so we profess
Ourselves to be the slaves of chance and flies
Of every wind that blows.
Cam. Then list to me:
This follows, if you will not change your purpose
But undergo this flight, make for Sicilia,
And there present yourself and your fair princess,
For so I see she must be, 'fore Leontes:
She shall be habited as it becomes
The partner of your bed. Methinks I see
Leontes opening his free arms and weeping
His welcomes forth; asks thee the son forgiveness,
As 'twere i' th' father's person; kisses the hands
Of your fresh princess; o'er and o'er divides him
'Twixt his unkindness and his kindness; th' one
He chides to hell and bids the other grow
Faster than thought or time.
Flo. Worthy Camillo,
What colour for my visitation shall I
Hold up before him?
Cam. Sent by the king your father
To greet him and to give him comforts. Sir,
The manner of your bearing towards him, with
What you as from your father shall deliver,
Things known betwixt us three, I'll write you down:
The which shall point you forth at every sitting
What you must say; that he shall not perceive
But that you have your father's bosom there
And speak his very heart.
Flo. I am bound to you:
There is some sap in this.
Cam. A course more promising
Than a wild dedication of yourselves
To unpath'd waters, undream'd shores, most certain
To miseries enough; no hope to help you,
But as you shake off one to take another;
Nothing so certain as your anchors, who
Do their best office, if they can but stay you
Where you'll be loath to be: besides you know
Prosperity 's the very bond of love,
Whose fresh complexion and whose heart together
Affliction alters.
Per. One of these is true:
I think affliction may subdue the cheek,
But not take in the mind.
Cam. Yea, say you so?
There shall not at your father's house these seven years
Be born another such.
Flo. My good Camillo,
She 's as forward of her breeding as
†She is i' th' rear o' our birth.
Cam. I cannot say 'tis pity
She lacks instructions, for she seems a mistress
To most that teach.
Per. Your pardon, sir; for this
I'll blush you thanks.
Flo. My prettiest Perdita!
But O, the thorns we stand upon! Camillo,
Preserver of my father, now of me,
The medicine of our house, how shall we do?
We are not furnish'd like Bohemia's son,
Nor shall appear in Sicilia.
Cam. My lord,
Fear none of this: I think you know my fortunes
Do all lie there: it shall be so my care
To have you royally appointed as if
The scene you play were mine. For instance, sir,
That you may know you shall not want, one word.
[*They talk aside.*]

Enter AUTOLYCUS.

Aut. Ha, ha! what a fool Honesty is! and Trust, his sworn brother, a very simple gentleman! I have sold all my trumpery; not a counterfeit stone, not a ribbon, glass, pomander, brooch, table-book, ballad, knife, tape, glove, shoe-tie, bracelet, horn-ring, to keep my pack from fasting: they throng who should buy first, as if my trinkets had been hallowed and brought a benediction to the buyer: by which means I saw whose purse was best in picture; and what I saw, to my good use I remembered. My clown, who wants but something to be a reasonable man, grew so in love with the wenches' song, that he would not stir his pettitoes till he had both tune and words; which so drew the rest of the herd to me that all their other senses stuck in ears: you might have pinched a placket, it was senseless; 'twas nothing to geld a codpiece of a purse; I could have filed keys off that hung in chains: no hearing, no feeling, but my sir's song, and admiring the nothing of it. So that in this time of lethargy I picked and cut most of their festival purses; and had not the old man come in with whoo-bub against his daughter and the king's son and scared my choughs from the chaff, I had not left a purse alive in the whole army. [*Camillo, Florizel, and Perdita come forward.*]

Cam. Nay, but my letters, by this means being there
So soon as you arrive, shall clear that doubt.
Flo. And those that you'll procure from King Leontes—
Cam. Shall satisfy your father.
Per. Happy be you!
All that you speak shows fair.
Cam. Who have we here?
[*Seeing Autolycus.*]
We'll make an instrument of this, omit
Nothing may give us aid.
Aut. If they have overheard me now, why, hanging.
Cam. How now, good fellow! why shak'st thou so?
Fear not, man; here 's no harm intended to thee.
Aut. I am a poor fellow, sir.

Cam. Why, be so still; here 's nobody will steal that from thee: yet for the outside of thy poverty we must make an exchange; therefore discase thee instantly,—thou must think there 's a necessity in 't,—and change garments with this gentleman: though the penny-

forth, indicate to you. 586. **subdue the cheek,** i.e., with tears. 587. **take in,** overcome. 591. **o' our,** so Neilson; Rowe: *o' her*; Globe, following F, omits *o'*. 597. **medicine,** physician. 599. **appear,** i.e., as such. 602. **appointed,** equipped. 609. **pomander,** ball composed of perfume. **table-book,** notebook. 615. **best in picture,** i.e., to look at. 619. **pettitoes,** pig's feet; here, feet. 621. **stuck in ears,** were occupied with their ears. 622. **pinched a placket,** stolen a petticoat; or, pinched a behind. 623. **geld a codpiece,** cut loose from the pouch worn at the front of a man's breeches. 626. **my sir's,** the Clown's. 629. **whoo-bub,** hubbub. 630. **choughs . . . chaff,** jackdaws from the chaff; here, the Clown's from his allurements. 636. **this,** i.e., Autolycus. 646. **discase,** undress.

worth on his side be the worst, yet hold thee, there 's some boot. [*Gives money*.]

Aut. I am a poor fellow, sir. [*Aside*] I know ye well enough.

Cam. Nay, prithee, dispatch: the gentleman is half flayed already.

Aut. Are you in earnest, sir? [*Aside*] I smell the trick on 't.

Flo. Dispatch, I prithee.

Aut. Indeed, I have had earnest; but I cannot with conscience take it.

Cam. Unbuckle, unbuckle.
[*Florizel and Autolycus exchange garments*.]
Fortunate mistress,—let my prophecy
Come home to ye!—you must retire yourself
Into some covert: take your sweetheart's hat
And pluck it o'er your brows, muffle your face,
Dismantle you, and, as you can, disliken
The truth of your own seeming; that you may—
For I do fear eyes over—to shipboard
Get undescried.

Per. I see the play so lies
That I must bear a part.

Cam. No remedy.
Have you done there?

Flo. Should I now meet my father,
He would not call me son.

Cam. Nay, you shall have no hat.
[*Giving it to Perdita*.]
Come, lady, come. Farewell, my friend.

Aut. Adieu, sir.

Flo. O Perdita, what have we twain forgot!
Pray you, a word.

Cam. [*Aside*] What I do next, shall be to tell the king
Of this escape and whither they are bound;
Wherein my hope is I shall so prevail
To force him after: in whose company
I shall review Sicilia, for whose sight
I have a woman's longing.

Flo. Fortune speed us!
Thus we set on, Camillo, to th' sea-side.

Cam. The swifter speed the better.
Exit [*with Florizel and Perdita*].

Aut. I understand the business, I hear it: to have an open ear, a quick eye, and a nimble hand, is necessary for a cut-purse; a good nose is requisite also, to smell out work for the other senses. I see this is the time that the unjust man doth thrive. What an exchange had this been without boot! What a boot is here with this exchange! Sure the gods do this year connive at us, and we may do any thing extempore. The prince himself is about a piece of iniquity, stealing away from his father with his clog at his heels: if I thought it were a piece of honesty to acquaint the king withal, I would not do 't: I hold it the more knavery to conceal it; and therein am I constant to my profession.

Enter Clown *and* Shepherd.

Aside, aside; here is more matter for a hot brain: every lane's end, every shop, church, session, hanging, yields a careful man work.

Clo. See, see; what a man you are now! There is no other way but to tell the king she 's a changeling and none of your flesh and blood.

Shep. Nay, but hear me.

Clo. Nay, but hear me.

Shep. Go to, then.

Clo. She being none of your flesh and blood, your flesh and blood has not offended the king; and so your flesh and blood is not to be punished by him. Show those things you found about her, those secret things, all but what she has with her: this being done, let the law go whistle: I warrant you.

Shep. I will tell the king all, every word, yea, and his son's pranks too; who, I may say, is no honest man, neither to his father nor to me, to go about to make me the king's brother-in-law.

Clo. Indeed, brother-in-law was the farthest off you could have been to him and then your blood had been the dearer by I know how much an ounce.

Aut. [*Aside*] Very wisely, puppies!

Shep. Well, let us to the king: there is that in this fardel will make him scratch his beard.

Aut. [*Aside*] I know not what impediment this complaint may be to the flight of my master.

Clo. Pray heartily he be at palace.

Aut. [*Aside*] Though I am not naturally honest, I am so sometimes by chance: let me pocket up my pedlar's excrement. [*Takes off his false beard*.] How now, rustics! whither are you bound?

Shep. To the palace, an it like your worship.

Aut. Your affairs there, what, with whom, the condition of that fardel, the place of your dwelling, your names, your ages, of what having, breeding, and any thing that is fitting to be known, discover.

Clo. We are but plain fellows, sir.

Aut. A lie; you are rough and hairy. Let me have no lying: it becomes none but tradesmen, and they often give us soldiers the lie: but we pay them for it with stamped coin, not stabbing steel; therefore they do not give us the lie.

Clo. Your worship had like to have given us one, if you had not taken yourself with the manner.

Shep. Are you a courtier, an 't like you, sir?

Aut. Whether it like me or no, I am a courtier. Seest thou not the air of the court in these enfoldings? hath not my gait in it the measure of the court? receives not thy nose court-odour from me? reflect I not on thy baseness court-contempt? Thinkest thou, for that I insinuate, or †toaze from thee thy business, I am therefore no courtier? I am courtier cap-a-pe; and one that will either push on or pluck back thy business there: whereupon I command thee to open thy affair.

Shep. My business, sir, is to the king.

Aut. What advocate hast thou to him?

Shep. I know not, an 't like you.

Clo. Advocate 's the court-word for a pheasant: say you have none.

Shep. None, sir; I have no pheasant, cock nor hen.

Aut. How blessed are we that are not simple men!
Yet nature might have made me as these are,
Therefore I will not disdain.

650. **boot,** something to boot (giving him money). 654. **flayed,** skinned; here, undressed. 659. **earnest,** advance payment. 661. **prophecy,** i.e., that Perdita will be fortunate. 663. **covert,** secret place. 665-666. **disliken . . . seeming,** disguise your outward appearance. 667. **eyes over,** overseeing eyes. 691. **connive at,** look indulgently at. 694. **clog,** encumbrance, referring to Perdita. 699. **hot,** active, ardent. 704. **changeling,** child left by the fairies. 719. **go about,** make it his object. 727. **fardel,** bundle, burden. 733. **excrement,** hair, beard. 740. **having,** property. 745. **they . . . lie,** i.e., they sell it to us (Johnson). 750-751. **taken . . . manner,** taken with the thing stolen in your pos-

Clo. This cannot be but a great courtier.

Shep. His garments are rich, but he wears them not handsomely.

Clo. He seems to be the more noble in being fantastical: a great man, I'll warrant; I know by the picking on 's teeth.

Aut. The fardel there? what 's i' the fardel? Wherefore that box?

Shep. Sir, there lies such secrets in this fardel and box, which none must know but the king; and which he shall know within this hour, if I may come to the speech of him.

Aut. Age, thou hast lost thy labour.

Shep. Why, sir?

Aut. The king is not at the palace; he is gone aboard a new ship to purge melancholy and air himself: for, if thou beest capable of things serious, thou must know the king is full of grief.

Shep. So 'tis said, sir; about his son, that should have married a shepherd's daughter.

Aut. If that shepherd be not in hand-fast, let him fly: the curses he shall have, the tortures he shall feel, will break the back of man, the heart of monster.

Clo. Think you so, sir?

Aut. Not he alone shall suffer what wit can make heavy and vengeance bitter; but those that are germane to him, though removed fifty times, shall all come under the hangman: which though it be great pity, yet it is necessary. An old sheep-whistling rogue, a ram-tender, to offer to have his daughter come into grace! Some say he shall be stoned; but that death is too soft for him, say I: draw our throne into a sheep-cote! all deaths are too few, the sharpest too easy.

Clo. Has the old man e'er a son, sir, do you hear, an 't like you, sir?

Aut. He has a son, who shall be flayed alive; then 'nointed over with honey, set on the head of a wasp's nest; then stand till he be three quarters and a dram dead; then recovered again with aqua-vitæ or some other hot infusion; then, raw as he is, and in the hottest day prognostication proclaims, shall he be set against a brick-wall, the sun looking with a southward eye upon him, where he is to behold him with flies blown to death. But what talk we of these traitorly rascals, whose miseries are to be smiled at, their offences being so capital? Tell me, for you seem to be honest plain men, what you have to the king: being something gently considered, I'll bring you where he is aboard, tender your persons to his presence, whisper him in your behalfs; and if it be in man besides the king to effect your suits, here is man shall do it.

Clo. He seems to be of great authority: close with him, give him gold; and though authority be a stubborn bear, yet he is oft led by the nose with gold: show the inside of your purse to the outside of his hand, and no more ado. Remember 'stoned,' and 'flayed alive.'

Shep. An 't please you, sir, to undertake the business for us, here is that gold I have: I'll make it as much more and leave this young man in pawn till I bring it you.

Aut. After I have done what I promised?

Shep. Ay, sir.

Aut. Well, give me the moiety. Are you a party in this business?

Clo. In some sort, sir: but though my case be a pitiful one, I hope I shall not be flayed out of it.

Aut. O, that 's the case of the shepherd's son: hang him, he'll be made an example.

Clo. Comfort, good comfort! We must to the king and show our strange sights: he must know 'tis none of your daughter nor my sister; we are gone else. Sir, I will give you as much as this old man does when the business is performed, and remain, as he says, your pawn till it be brought you.

Aut. I will trust you. Walk before toward the sea-side; go on the right hand: I will but look upon the hedge and follow you.

Clo. We are blest in this man, as I may say, even blest.

Shep. Let 's before as he bids us: he was provided to do us good. *Exeunt [Shepherd and Clown].*

Aut. If I had a mind to be honest, I see Fortune would not suffer me: she drops booties in my mouth. I am courted now with a double occasion, gold and a means to do the prince my master good; which who knows how that may turn back to my advancement? I will bring these two moles, these blind ones, aboard him: if he think it fit to shore them again and that the complaint they have to the king concerns him nothing, let him call me rogue for being so far officious; for I am proof against that title and what shame else belongs to 't. To him will I present them: there may be matter in it. *[Exit.]*

ACT V.

SCENE I. [*A room in* LEONTES' *palace.*]

Enter LEONTES, CLEOMENES, DION, PAULINA, [*and*] *Servants.*

Cleo. Sir, you have done enough, and have perform'd
A saint-like sorrow: no fault could you make,
Which you have not redeem'd; indeed, paid down
More penitence than done trespass: at the last,
Do as the heavens have done, forget your evil;
With them forgive yourself.

Leon. Whilst I remember
Her and her virtues, I cannot forget
My blemishes in them, and so still think of
The wrong I did myself; which was so much,
That heirless it hath made my kingdom and
Destroy'd the sweet'st companion that e'er man
Bred his hopes out of.

Paul. True, too true, my lord:
If, one by one, you wedded all the world,
Or from the all that are took something good,
To make a perfect woman, she you kill'd
Would be unparallel'd.

Leon. I think so. Kill'd!
She I kill'd! I did so: but thou strik'st me
Sorely, to say I did; it is as bitter
Upon thy tongue as in my thought: now, good now,

session (a legal phrase); hence, caught yourself in the act. 759. **toaze,** tear (used figuratively). 761. **cap-a-pe,** head to foot. 768. **pheasant.** The rustics suppose that Autolycus has asked them what gift they propose to present, as a bribe. 779. **picking on 's teeth,** a stylish thing to do in Shakespeare's time. 794. **hand-fast,** custody. 800. **germane,** related. 824. **being . . . considered,** if I receive a gentlemanly consideration, i.e., a bribe. 825. **tender . . . persons,** introduce you. 830. **close with him,** accept his offer. 845. **case,** condition, and skin. 855. **look . . . hedge,** i.e., relieve myself.

Say so but seldom.
Cleo. Not at all, good lady:
You might have spoken a thousand things that would
Have done the time more benefit and grac'd
Your kindness better.
Paul. You are one of those
Would have him wed again.
Dion. If you would not so,
You pity not the state, nor the remembrance
Of his most sovereign name; consider little
What dangers, by his highness' fail of issue,
May drop upon his kingdom and devour
Incertain lookers on. What were more holy
Than to rejoice the former queen is well?
What holier than, for royalty's repair,
For present comfort and for future good,
To bless the bed of majesty again
With a sweet fellow to 't?
Paul. There is none worthy,
Respecting her that 's gone. Besides, the gods
Will have fulfill'd their secret purposes;
For has not the divine Apollo said,
Is 't not the tenour of his oracle,
That King Leontes shall not have an heir
Till his lost child be found? which that it shall,
Is all as monstrous to our human reason
As my Antigonus to break his grave
And come again to me; who, on my life,
Did perish with the infant. 'Tis your counsel
My lord should to the heavens be contrary,
Oppose against their wills. [*To Leontes.*] Care not for issue;
The crown will find an heir: great Alexander
Left his to th' worthiest; so his successor
Was like to be the best.
Leon. Good Paulina,
Who hast the memory of Hermione,
I know, in honour, O, that ever I
Had squar'd me to thy counsel! then, even now,
I might have look'd upon my queen's full eyes,
Have taken treasure from her lips—
Paul. And left them
More rich for what they yielded.
Leon. Thou speak'st truth.
No more such wives; therefore, no wife: one worse,
And better us'd, would make her sainted spirit
Again possess her corpse, and on this stage,
Where we 're offenders now, appear soul-vex'd,
†And begin, 'Why to me?'
Paul. Had she such power,
She had just cause.
Leon. She had; and would incense me
To murder her I married.
Paul. I should so.
Were I the ghost that walk'd, I 'ld bid you mark
Her eye, and tell me for what dull part in 't
You chose her; then I 'ld shriek, that even your ears
Should rift to hear me; and the words that follow'd
Should be 'Remember mine.'
Leon. Stars, stars,
And all eyes else dead coals! Fear thou no wife;
I'll have no wife, Paulina.
Paul. Will you swear
Never to marry but by my free leave?
Leon. Never, Paulina; so be blest my spirit!
Paul. Then, good my lords, bear witness to his oath.
Cleo. You tempt him over-much.
Paul. Unless another,
As like Hermione as is her picture,
Affront his eye.
Cleo. Good madam,—
Paul. I have done.
Yet, if my lord will marry,—if you will, sir,
No remedy, but you will,—give me the office
To choose you a queen: she shall not be so young
As was your former; but she shall be such
As, walk'd your first queen's ghost, it should take joy
To see her in your arms.
Leon. My true Paulina,
We shall not marry till thou bid'st us.
Paul. That
Shall be when your first queen 's again in breath;
Never till then.

Enter a Servant.

Serv. One that gives out himself Prince Florizel,
Son of Polixenes, with his princess, she
The fairest I have yet beheld, desires access
To your high presence.
Leon. What with him? he comes not
Like to his father's greatness: his approach,
So out of circumstance and sudden, tells us
'Tis not a visitation fram'd, but forc'd
By need and accident. What train?
Serv. But few,
And those but mean.
Leon. His princess, say you, with him?
Serv. Ay, the most peerless piece of earth, I think,
That e'er the sun shone bright on.
Paul. O Hermione,
As every present time doth boast itself
Above a better gone, so must thy grave
Give way to what 's seen now! Sir, you yourself
Have said and writ so, but your writing now
Is colder than that theme, 'She had not been,
Nor was not to be equall'd;'—thus your verse
Flow'd with her beauty once: 'tis shrewdly ebb'd,
To say you have seen a better.
Serv. Pardon, madam:
The one I have almost forgot,—your pardon,—
The other, when she has obtain'd your eye,
Will have your tongue too. This is a creature,
Would she begin a sect, might quench the zeal
Of all professors else, make proselytes
Of who she but bid follow.
Paul. How! not women?
Serv. Women will love her, that she is a woman
More worth than any man; men, that she is
The rarest of all women.
Leon. Go, Cleomenes;
Yourself, assisted with your honour'd friends,
Bring them to our embracement. Still, 'tis strange
Exit [*Cleomenes and others*].

ACT V. SCENE I. 27. **fail,** failure. 29. **Incertain,** not knowing what to think or do (Schmidt). 30. **well,** happy, at rest. 35. **Respecting,** in comparison with. 52. **squar'd me,** adjusted or regulated myself. 58. **possess her corpse,** i.e., return to earth (*this stage*) in her human shape. 60. **'Why to me?'** i.e., why this offense to me? 66. **rift,** split. 75. **Affront,** confront. 92. **train,** retinue. 108. **professors else,** believers in other sects. 113. **assisted with,** accompanied by. 123. **Unfurnish,** deprive, divest. 127. **hit,** exactly reproduced. 137.

He thus should steal upon us.
Paul. Had our prince,
Jewel of children, seen this hour, he had pair'd
Well with this lord: there was not full a month
Between their births.
Leon. Prithee, no more; cease; thou know'st
He dies to me again when talk'd of: sure,
When I shall see this gentleman, thy speeches
Will bring me to consider that which may
Unfurnish me of reason. They are come.

Enter FLORIZEL, PERDITA, CLEOMENES, *and others.*

Your mother was most true to wedlock, prince;
For she did print your royal father off,
Conceiving you: were I but twenty one,
Your father's image is so hit in you,
His very air, that I should call you brother,
As I did him, and speak of something wildly
By us perform'd before. Most dearly welcome!
And your fair princess,—goddess!—O, alas!
I lost a couple, that 'twixt heaven and earth
Might thus have stood begetting wonder as
You, gracious couple, do: and then I lost—
All mine own folly—the society,
Amity too, of your brave father, whom,
Though bearing misery, I desire my life
Once more to look on him.
Flo. By his command
Have I here touch'd Sicilia and from him
Give you all greetings that a king, at friend,
Can send his brother: and, but infirmity
Which waits upon worn times hath something seiz'd
His wish'd ability, he had himself
The lands and waters 'twixt your throne and his
Measur'd to look upon you; whom he loves—
He bade me say so—more than all the sceptres
And those that bear them living.
Leon. O my brother,
Good gentleman! the wrongs I have done thee stir
Afresh within me, and these thy offices,
So rarely kind, are as interpreters
Of my behind-hand slackness. Welcome hither,
As is the spring to th' earth. And hath he too
Expos'd this paragon to th' fearful usage,
At least ungentle, of the dreadful Neptune,
To greet a man not worth her pains, much less
Th' adventure of her person?
Flo. Good my lord,
She came from Libya.
Leon. Where the warlike Smalus,
That noble honour'd lord, is fear'd and lov'd?
Flo. Most royal sir, from thence; from him, whose daughter
His tears proclaim'd his, parting with her: thence,
A prosperous south-wind friendly, we have cross'd,
To execute the charge my father gave me
For visiting your highness: my best train
I have from your Sicilian shores dismiss'd;
Who for Bohemia bend, to signify
Not only my success in Libya, sir,
But my arrival and my wife's in safety
Here where we are.
Leon. The blessed gods
Purge all infection from our air whilst you
Do climate here! You have a holy father,
A graceful gentleman; against whose person,
So sacred as it is, I have done sin:
For which the heavens, taking angry note,
Have left me issueless; and your father 's blest,
As he from heaven merits it, with you
Worthy his goodness. What might I have been,
Might I a son and daughter now have look'd on,
Such goodly things as you!

Enter a Lord.

Lord. Most noble sir,
That which I shall report will bear no credit,
Were not the proof so nigh. Please you, great sir,
Bohemia greets you from himself by me;
Desires you to attach his son, who has—
His dignity and duty both cast off—
Fled from his father, from his hopes, and with
A shepherd's daughter.
Leon. Where 's Bohemia? speak.
Lord. Here in your city; I now came from him:
I speak amazedly; and it becomes
My marvel and my message. To your court
Whiles he was hast'ning, in the chase, it seems,
Of this fair couple, meets he on the way
The father of this seeming lady and
Her brother, having both their country quitted
With this young prince.
Flo. Camillo has betray'd me;
Whose honour and whose honesty till now
Endur'd all weathers.
Lord. Lay 't so to his charge:
He 's with the king your father.
Leon. Who? Camillo?
Lord. Camillo, sir; I spake with him; who now
Has these poor men in question. Never saw I
Wretches so quake: they kneel, they kiss the earth;
Forswear themselves as often as they speak:
Bohemia stops his ears, and threatens them
With divers deaths in death.
Per. O my poor father!
The heaven sets spies upon us, will not have
Our contract celebrated.
Leon. You are married?
Flo. We are not, sir, nor are we like to be;
The stars, I see, will kiss the valleys first:
The odds for high and low 's alike.
Leon. My lord,
Is this the daughter of a king?
Flo. She is,
When once she is my wife.
Leon. That 'once,' I see by your good father's speed,
Will come on very slowly. I am sorry,
Most sorry, you have broken from his liking
Where you were tied in duty, and as sorry
Your choice is not so rich in worth as beauty,
That you might well enjoy her.
Flo. Dear, look up:

my life, while I live. 140. **at friend,** friendly. 142. **worn times,** old age. 149. **offices,** messages of good will. 156. **adventure,** hazard. 170. **climate,** dwell, reside (in this clime). 171. **graceful,** full of grace, gracious. 182. **attach,** arrest. 187. **amazedly,** perplexedly. **it,** i.e., my manner of speaking. 188. **marvel,** astonishment, wonder. 198. **in question,** under interrogation. 207. **The . . . alike.** Fortune is the same for the high and low. 214. **worth,** rank.

Though Fortune, visible an enemy,
Should chase us with my father, pow'r no jot
Hath she to change our loves. Beseech you, sir,
Remember since you ow'd no more to time
Than I do now: with thought of such affections,
Step forth mine advocate; at your request
My father will grant precious things as trifles.

Leon. Would he do so, I 'ld beg your precious mistress,
Which he counts but a trifle.

Paul. Sir, my liege,
Your eye hath too much youth in 't: not a month
'Fore your queen died, she was more worth such gazes
Than what you look on now.

Leon. I thought of her,
Even in these looks I made. [*To Florizel.*] But your petition
Is yet unanswer'd. I will to your father:
Your honour not o'erthrown by your desires,
I am friend to them and you: upon which errand
I now go toward him; therefore follow me
And mark what way I make: come, good my lord.

Exeunt.

SCENE II. [*Before* LEONTES' *palace.*]

Enter AUTOLYCUS *and a* Gentleman.

Aut. Beseech you, sir, were you present at this relation?

First Gent. I was by at the opening of the fardel, heard the old shepherd deliver the manner how he found it: whereupon, after a little amazedness, we were all commanded out of the chamber; only this methought I heard the shepherd say, he found the child.

Aut. I would most gladly know the issue of it.

First Gent. I make a broken delivery of the business; but the changes I perceived in the king and Camillo were very notes of admiration: they seemed almost, with staring on one another, to tear the cases of their eyes; there was speech in their dumbness, language in their very gesture; they looked as they had heard of a world ransomed, or one destroyed: a notable passion of wonder appeared in them; but the wisest beholder, that knew no more but seeing, could not say if the importance were joy or sorrow; but in the extremity of the one, it must needs be.

Enter another Gentleman.

Here comes a gentleman that haply knows more. The news, Rogero?

Sec. Gent. Nothing but bonfires: the oracle is fulfilled; the king's daughter is found: such a deal of wonder is broken out within this hour that ballad-makers cannot be able to express it.

Enter another Gentleman.

Here comes the Lady Paulina's steward: he can deliver you more. How goes it now, sir? this news which is called true is so like an old tale, that the verity of it is in strong suspicion: has the king found his heir?

Third Gent. Most true, if ever truth were pregnant by circumstance: that which you hear you'll swear you see, there is such unity in the proofs. The mantle of Queen Hermione's, her jewel about the neck of it, the letters of Antigonus found with it which they know to be his character, the majesty of the creature in resemblance of the mother, the affection of nobleness which nature shows above her breeding, and many other evidences proclaim her with all certainty to be the king's daughter. Did you see the meeting of the two kings?

Sec. Gent. No.

Third Gent. Then have you lost a sight, which was to be seen, cannot be spoken of. There might you have beheld one joy crown another, so and in such manner that it seemed Sorrow wept to take leave of them, for their joy waded in tears. There was casting up of eyes, holding up of hands, with countenance of such distraction that they were to be known by garment, not by favour. Our king, being ready to leap out of himself for joy of his found daughter, as if that joy were now become a loss, cries 'O, thy mother, thy mother!' then asks Bohemia forgiveness; then embraces his son-in-law; then again worries he his daughter with clipping her; now he thanks the old shepherd, which stands by like a weather-bitten conduit of many kings' reigns. I never heard of such another encounter, which lames report to follow it and undoes description to do it.

Sec. Gent. What, pray you, became of Antigonus, that carried hence the child?

Third Gent. Like an old tale still, which will have matter to rehearse, though credit be asleep and not an ear open. He was torn to pieces with a bear: this avouches the shepherd's son; who has not only his innocence, which seems much, to justify him, but a handkerchief and rings of his that Paulina knows.

First Gent. What became of his bark and his followers?

Third Gent. Wracked the same instant of their master's death and in the view of the shepherd: so that all the instruments which aided to expose the child were even then lost when it was found. But O, the noble combat that 'twixt joy and sorrow was fought in Paulina! She had one eye declined for the loss of her husband, another elevated that the oracle was fulfilled: she lifted the princess from the earth, and so locks her in embracing, as if she would pin her to her heart that she might no more be in danger of losing.

First Gent. The dignity of this act was worth the audience of kings and princes; for by such was it acted.

Third Gent. One of the prettiest touches of all and that which angled for mine eyes, caught the water though not the fish, was when, at the relation of the queen's death, with the manner how she came to 't bravely confessed and lamented by the king, how attentiveness wounded his daughter; till, from one sign of dolour to another, she did, with an 'Alas,' I would fain say, bleed tears, for I am sure my heart wept blood. Who was most marble there changed colour; some swooned, all sorrowed: if all the world

219. **since,** when. 230. **Your . . . desires,** i.e., if your chaste honor, etc.
SCENE II. 2. **relation,** narrative, account. Shakespeare has chosen to solve the plot of the young lovers by reporting the solution in conversation. 12-13. **notes of admiration,** exclamations of wonder.

14-15. **cases of their eyes,** eyelids. 19. **no . . . seeing,** nothing except what he could see. 20. **importance,** import, meaning. 34. **pregnant by circumstance,** made cogent by circumstantial evidence (Moorman). 39. **character,** handwriting. 40. **affection of,** natural disposition to.

could have seen 't, the woe had been universal.

First Gent. Are they returned to the court?

Third Gent. No: the princess hearing of her mother's statue, which is in the keeping of Paulina,—a piece many years in doing and now newly performed by that rare Italian master, Julio Romano, who, had he himself eternity and could put breath into his work, would beguile Nature of her custom, so perfectly he is her ape: he so near to Hermione hath done Hermione that they say one would speak to her and stand in hope of answer: thither with all greediness of affection are they gone, and there they intend to sup.

Sec. Gent. I thought she had some great matter there in hand; for she hath privately twice or thrice a day, ever since the death of Hermione, visited that removed house. Shall we thither and with our company piece the rejoicing?

First Gent. Who would be thence that has the benefit of access? every wink of an eye some new grace will be born: our absence makes us unthrifty to our knowledge. Let 's along. *Exeunt [Gentlemen].*

Aut. Now, had I not the dash of my former life in me, would preferment drop on my head. I brought the old man and his son aboard the prince; told him I heard them talk of a fardel and I know not what: but he at that time, over-fond of the shepherd's daughter, so he then took her to be, who began to be much sea-sick, and himself little better, extremity of weather continuing, this mystery remained undiscovered. But 'tis all one to me; for had I been the finder out of this secret, it would not have relished among my other discredits.

Enter Shepherd *and* Clown.

Here come those I have done good to against my will, and already appearing in the blossoms of their fortune.

Shep. Come, boy; I am past moe children, but thy sons and daughters will be all gentlemen born.

Clo. You are well met, sir. You denied to fight with me this other day, because I was no gentleman born. See you these clothes? say you see them not and think me still no gentleman born: you were best say these robes are not gentlemen born: give me the lie, do, and try whether I am not now a gentleman born.

Aut. I know you are now, sir, a gentleman born.

Clo. Ay, and have been so any time these four hours.

Shep. And so have I, boy.

Clo. So you have: but I was a gentleman born before my father; for the king's son took me by the hand, and called me brother; and then the two kings called my father brother; and then the prince my brother and the princess my sister called my father father; and so we wept, and there was the first gentleman-like tears that ever we shed.

Shep. We may live, son, to shed many more.

Clo. Ay; or else 'twere hard luck, being in so preposterous estate as we are.

Aut. I humbly beseech you, sir, to pardon me all the faults I have committed to your worship and to give me your good report to the prince my master.

Shep. Prithee, son, do; for we must be gentle, now we are gentlemen.

Clo. Thou wilt amend thy life?

Aut. Ay, an it like your good worship.

Clo. Give me thy hand: I will swear to the prince thou art as honest a true fellow as any is in Bohemia.

Shep. You may say it, but not swear it.

Clo. Not swear it, now I am a gentleman? Let boors and franklins say it, I'll swear it.

Shep. How if it be false, son?

Clo. If it be ne'er so false, a true gentleman may swear it in the behalf of his friend: and I'll swear to the prince thou art a tall fellow of thy hands and that thou wilt not be drunk; but I know thou art no tall fellow of thy hands and that thou wilt be drunk: but I'll swear it, and I would thou wouldst be a tall fellow of thy hands.

Aut. I will prove so, sir, to my power.

Clo. Ay, by any means prove a tall fellow: if I do not wonder how thou darest venture to be drunk, not being a tall fellow, trust me not. Hark! the kings and the princes, our kindred, are going to see the queen's picture. Come, follow us: we'll be thy good masters. *Exeunt.*

SCENE III. [*A chapel in* PAULINA'S *house.*]

Enter LEONTES, POLIXENES, FLORIZEL, PERDITA, CAMILLO, PAULINA, Lords, *&c.*

Leon. O grave and good Paulina, the great comfort
That I have had of thee!
Paul. What, sovereign sir,
I did not well I meant well. All my services
You have paid home: but that you have vouchsaf'd,
With your crown'd brother and these your contracted
Heirs of your kingdoms, my poor house to visit,
It is a surplus of your grace, which never
My life may last to answer.
Leon. O Paulina,
We honour you with trouble: but we came
To see the statue of our queen: your gallery
Have we pass'd through, not without much content
In many singularities; but we saw not
That which my daughter came to look upon,
The statue of her mother.
Paul. As she liv'd peerless,
So her dead likeness, I do well believe,
Excels whatever yet you look'd upon
Or hand of man hath done; therefore I keep it
Lonely, apart. But here it is: prepare
To see the life as lively mock'd as ever
Still sleep mock'd death: behold, and say 'tis well.
[*Paulina draws a curtain, and discovers*] *Hermione* [*standing*] *like a statue.*
I like your silence, it the more shows off
Your wonder: but yet speak; first, you, my liege.
Comes it not something near?
Leon. Her natural posture!
Chide me, dear stone, that I may say indeed
Thou art Hermione; or rather, thou art she
In thy not chiding, for she was as tender
As infancy and grace. But yet, Paulina,
Hermione was not so much wrinkled, nothing

52. **countenance,** bearing, demeanor. 60. **conduit,** fountain (weeping tears). 98. **marble,** hardhearted. 105. **performed,** completed. 106. **Julio Romano,** Italian painter and sculptor of the sixteenth century; an anachronism in this play. 108. **custom,** trade. 117. **piece,** add to, augment. 121. **unthrifty to,** not likely to increase. 132. **relished,** found acceptance. 159. **preposterous,** blunder for "prosperous." 173. **franklins,** farmers who owned their own land.

SCENE III. 12. **singularities,** rarities, curiosities.

So aged as this seems.
Pol. O, not by much.
Paul. So much the more our carver's excellence;
Which lets go by some sixteen years and makes her
As she liv'd now.
Leon. As now she might have done,
So much to my good comfort, as it is
Now piercing to my soul. O, thus she stood,
Even with such life of majesty, warm life,
As now it coldly stands, when first I woo'd her!
I am asham'd: does not the stone rebuke me
For being more stone than it? O royal piece,
There 's magic in thy majesty, which has
My evils conjur'd to remembrance and
From thy admiring daughter took the spirits,
Standing like stone with thee.
Per. And give me leave,
And do not say 'tis superstition, that
I kneel and then implore her blessing. Lady,
Dear queen, that ended when I but began,
Give me that hand of yours to kiss.
Paul. O, patience!
The statue is but newly fix'd, the colour 's
Not dry.
Cam. My lord, your sorrow was too sore laid on,
Which sixteen winters cannot blow away,
So many summers dry: scarce any joy
Did ever so long live; no sorrow
But kill'd itself much sooner.
Pol. Dear my brother,
Let him that was the cause of this have pow'r
To take off so much grief from you as he
Will piece up in himself.
Paul. Indeed, my lord,
If I had thought the sight of my poor image
Would thus have wrought you,—for the stone is mine—
I 'ld not have show'd it.
Leon. Do not draw the curtain.
Paul. No longer shall you gaze on 't, lest your fancy
May think anon it moves.
Leon. Let be, let be.
Would I were dead, but that, methinks, already—
What was he that did make it? See, my lord,
Would you not deem it breath'd? and that those veins
Did verily bear blood?
Pol. Masterly done:
The very life seems warm upon her lip.
Leon. The fixture of her eye has motion in 't,
As we are mock'd with art.
Paul. I'll draw the curtain:
My lord 's almost so far transported that
He'll think anon it lives.
Leon. O sweet Paulina,
Make me to think so twenty years together!
No settled senses of the world can match
The pleasure of that madness. Let 't alone.
Paul. I am sorry, sir, I have thus far stirr'd you: but
I could afflict you farther.
Leon. Do, Paulina;
For this affliction has a taste as sweet
As any cordial comfort. Still, methinks,
There is an air comes from her: what fine chisel
Could ever yet cut breath? Let no man mock me,
For I will kiss her.
Paul. Good my lord, forbear:
The ruddiness upon her lip is wet;
You'll mar it if you kiss it, stain your own
With oily painting. Shall I draw the curtain?
Leon. No, not these twenty years.
Per. So long could I
Stand by, a looker on.
Paul. Either forbear,
Quit presently the chapel, or resolve you
For more amazement. If you can behold it,
I'll make the statue move indeed, descend
And take you by the hand: but then you'll think—
Which I protest against—I am assisted
By wicked powers.
Leon. What you can make her do,
I am content to look on: what to speak,
I am content to hear; for 'tis as easy
To make her speak as move.
Paul. It is requir'd
You do awake your faith. Then all stand still;
On: those that think it is unlawful business
I am about, let them depart.
Leon. Proceed:
No foot shall stir.
Paul. Music, awake her; strike! [*Music.*]
'Tis time; descend; be stone no more; approach;
Strike all that look upon with marvel. Come,
I'll fill your grave up: stir, nay, come away,
Bequeath to death your numbness, for from him
Dear life redeems you. You perceive she stirs:
[*Hermione comes down.*]
Start not; her actions shall be holy as
You hear my spell is lawful: do not shun her
Until you see her die again; for then
You kill her double. Nay, present your hand:
When she was young you woo'd her; now in age
Is she become the suitor?
Leon. O, she 's warm!
If this be magic, let it be an art
Lawful as eating.
Pol. She embraces him.
Cam. She hangs about his neck:
If she pertain to life let her speak too.
Pol. Ay, and make it manifest where she has liv'd,
Or how stol'n from the dead.
Paul. That she is living,
Were it but told you, should be hooted at
Like an old tale: but it appears she lives,
Though yet she speak not. Mark a little while.
Please you to interpose, fair madam: kneel
And pray your mother's blessing. Turn, good lady;
Our Perdita is found.
Her. You gods, look down
And from your sacred vials pour your graces
Upon my daughter's head! Tell me, mine own,
Where hast thou been preserv'd? where liv'd? how found
Thy father's court? for thou shalt hear that I,
Knowing by Paulina that the oracle
Gave hope thou wast in being, have preserv'd
Myself to see the issue.
Paul. There 's time enough for that;

67. **fixture,** color and setting. 72. **settled,** sane, calm. 96. **On,** let us proceed. 107. **double,** twice over.

Lest they desire upon this push to trouble
Your joys with like relation. Go together,
You precious winners all; your exultation
Partake to every one. I, an old turtle,
Will wing me to some wither'd bough and there
My mate, that 's never to be found again,
Lament till I am lost.
Leon. O, peace, Paulina!
Thou shouldst a husband take by my consent,
As I by thine a wife: this is a match,
And made between 's by vows. Thou hast found mine;
But how, is to be question'd; for I saw her,
As I thought, dead, and have in vain said many
A prayer upon her grave. I'll not seek far—
For him, I partly know his mind—to find thee
An honourable husband. Come, Camillo,
And take her by the hand, whose worth and honesty
Is richly noted and here justified
By us, a pair of kings. Let 's from this place.
What! look upon my brother: both your pardons,
That e'er I put between your holy looks
My ill suspicion. This your son-in-law
And son unto the king, whom, heavens directing,
Is troth-plight to your daughter. Good Paulina,
Lead us from hence, where we may leisurely
Each one demand and answer to his part
Perform'd in this wide gap of time since first
We were dissever'd: hastily lead away. *Exeunt.*

129. **push,** exciting moment. 130. **like relation,** similar narrative. 132. **Partake to,** share with, communicate. 141. **far,** farther. 145. **noted,** reputed. 147. **What . . . brother,** addressed to Hermione.

THE TEMPEST

In *The Tempest* Shakespeare creates sublimely and perhaps for the last time an idealized world of his imagination, a place of magical rejuvenation like the forests of *A Midsummer Night's Dream* and *As You Like It.* The journey to Shakespeare's island is to a visionary realm existing only in art, where everything is controlled by the artist. Yet the journey is no mere escape from reality, for the island shows men what they ought to be. Even its location juxtaposes the "real" world with an idealized landscape: like Plato's New Atlantis or Thomas More's Utopia, Shakespeare's island is to be found both somewhere and nowhere. On the narrative level it is certainly located in the Mediterranean Sea, since King Alonso and his party are shipwrecked during their return from Africa to Naples, following the marriage of Alonso's daughter to the King of Tunis. Yet there are also insistent overtones of the New World, the Western Hemisphere, where Thomas More had situated his island of Utopia. Ariel fetches dew at Prospero's command from the "Bermoothes," or Bermudas (I,ii). Caliban's name is an anagram of "cannibal," calling to mind those dark and fascinating savages brought back to Jacobean England by adventurers to America. And one inspiration for Shakespeare's story (for which no direct literary source has been found) may well have been various accounts of an actual shipwreck in the Bermudas of the *Sea Venture,* in 1609, carrying supplies and settlers to the new Virginian colonies. Shakespeare certainly borrowed details from Sylvester Jourdain's *A Discovery of the Barmudas, otherwise called the Isle of Divels,* published in 1610, and from William Strachey's *A true Reportory of the Wracke and Redemption . . . from the Ilands of the Bermudas,* which Shakespeare must have seen in manuscript since it is dated 1610 but was not published until after his death. He evidently wrote the play shortly after reading these works, for *The Tempest* was acted at court in 1611. His fascination with the Western Hemisphere gave him not the "actual" location of his story, which remains Mediterranean, but a state of mind associated with newness and hope. Miranda sees on the island a "brave new world" in which mankind appears beauteous; and, although her wonderment must be tempered both by Prospero's melancholy rejoinder (" 'Tis new to thee") and by Aldous Huxley's ironic use of her phrase (in his satirical novel called *Brave New World*), the island still endures as a restorative vision. Even though we experience it only fleetingly, as in a dream, this nonexistent realm assumes a permanence which only the artist can create.

Prospero rules as the artist-figure over this imaginary world, conjuring up trials and visions with which to test men's intentions and guide them toward a renewed faith in goodness. To his island come an assortment of men who, because they require different sorts of ordeals, are separated by Prospero and Ariel into three groups: King Alonso and those accompanying him; Alonso's son Ferdinand; and Stephano and Trinculo. Prospero's authority over them, though strong, has certain clearly defined limits. As Duke of Milan he was bookishly inattentive to political matters, and thus was vulnerable to the Machiavellian conniving of his younger brother Antonio. Only in this world apart, the artist's world, do his powers derived from learning find their proper sphere. Because he cannot control the world beyond his isle, he must wait for "strange, bountiful Fortune (Now my dear lady)" to bring his enemies to his shore. Moreover, he eschews the black arts of diabolism. His is a "white" magic, always devoted to good and merciful ends: rescuing Ariel from the spell of the witch Sycorax, curbing the appetite of Caliban, spying on Antonio and Sebastian in the role of Conscience. He believes that Fortune has delivered his enemies into his hands so that he may forgive and restore them, not be revenged. Such a use of power imitates the divine, though Prospero is no god. His chief power, learned from books and exercised through Ariel, is to control the elements so as to create illusion—of separation, of death, of the gods' blessing. Yet since he is a man, even this power is an immense burden. Prospero's responsibilities cause him to behave managerially and to be resented by the spirits of the isle. Even Ariel longs to be free, and it is with genuine relief as well as melancholy that Prospero finally lays aside his demanding role as creative moral intelligence.

Alonso and the members of his court party variously illustrate the unregenerate world left behind in Naples and Milan. We first see them on shipboard, panicky and desperate, their titles and their finery mocked by the roaring of the waves. Futile worldly ambition seems destined for a watery grave. Yet death by water in this play is a transfiguration rather than an end, a mystical rebirth as in the regenerative cycle of the seasons from winter to summer. Ariel suggests this in his song about a drowned father: "Those are pearls that were his eyes. Nothing of him that doth fade But doth suffer a sea-change Into something rich and strange" (I,ii). Still, this miracle is not apparent at first to those who are caught in the illusion of death. As in T. S. Eliot's *The Waste Land*, which repeatedly alludes to *The Tempest*, self-blinded men fear an apparent disaster that is ironically the prelude to reawakening.

Prospero creates this illusion of loss to test his enemies and cause them to reveal their true selves. Only Gonzalo, no enemy at all but one who long ago aided Prospero and Miranda when they were banished from Milan, responds affirmatively. He alone notices that his garments and those of his shipwrecked companions have miraculously been left unharmed by the salt water. His ideal commonwealth (II,i), drawn from an essay by Montaigne, naively postulates a natural goodness in man and makes no allowance for the dark propensities of Caliban, but at least Gonzalo's cheerfulness is in refreshing contrast to the jaded sneers of his companions. Sebastian and Antonio react to the magic isle, as to Gonzalo's commonwealth, with cynical rejection of faith in the miraculous. Confident that they are unobserved, they seize the opportunity of Alonso's sleeping to plot a murder and political coup. This attempt is not only despicable but madly ludicrous, for they are all shipwrecked and no longer have any kingdoms over which to quarrel. Even more ironically, however, Sebastian and Antonio are being observed despite their insolent belief in their self-sufficiency. The villains must be taught that an unseen omniscient power does keep track of their misdeeds. They will probably revert to type when returned to their usual habitat, but even they are at last briefly moved to a faith in the unseen (III,iii). Alonso, more worthy than they even though burdened with sin, responds to his situation with guilt and despair, for he assumes that his son Ferdinand's death is the just punishment of the gods for Alonso's part in the earlier overthrow of Prospero. He must be led, by Prospero's curative illusions, through the purgative experience of contrition to the reward he thinks impossible and undeserved: reunion with his lost son.

Alonso is thus, like Posthumus in *Cymbeline* or Leontes in *The Winter's Tale*, a tragicomic figure—sinful, contrite, forgiven. Alonso's son Ferdinand must also undergo ordeals and visions devised by Prospero to test his worth, but much more on the level of romantic comedy. Ferdinand is young, innocent, and hopeful, well-matched to Miranda. Prospero obviously approves from the start of his prospective son-in-law. Yet Prospero invents difficulties, imposing tasks of logbearing (much like those assigned to Caliban) and issuing stern warnings against premarital lust. These illusions of parental opposition conform to the comic mode, in which parents are expected to cross their children in matters of the heart. More seriously, however, Prospero is convinced by long experience that prizes too easily won are too lightly esteemed. Manifold are the temptations urging Ferdinand to surrender to the "natural" rhythms of the isle, and to fulfill his desire like Caliban. Because there are no churches on the island, Prospero must create the illusion of ceremony by his art. The marriage of Ferdinand and Miranda accordingly unites the best of both worlds: the natural innocence of the island, which teaches them to avoid the corruptions of civilization at its worst, and the higher law of nature achieved through moral wisdom at its best. To this marriage, the goddesses Iris, Ceres, and Juno bring promises of bounteous harvest, of "refreshing show'rs," of celestial harmony, and of a springtime brought back to the earth by Proserpina's return from Hades (IV,i). In Ferdinand and Miranda, "nurture" is wedded to "nature." This bond unites spirit and flesh, legitimizing erotic pleasure by subordinating it to a cosmic moral order in the universe.

At the lowest level of this same cosmic and moral framework are Stephano and Trinculo. Their comic scenes juxtapose them with Caliban, for he represents untutored nature whereas they represent the unnatural depths to which men brought up in civilized society can fall. In this they also resemble Sebastian and Antonio, who have learned in supposedly civilized Italy the arts of intrigue and political murder. The antics of Stephano and Trinculo burlesque the conduct of their presumed betters, thereby exposing to ridicule the self-deceptions of ambitious men. The clowns desire to exploit the natural wonders of the isle by taking Caliban back to England or Naples to be shown in carnivals, or by plying him with strong drink and whetting his resentment against authority. These plottings are in vain, however, for like Sebastian and Antonio the clowns are being watched. They teach Caliban to cry out for "freedom," by which they mean license to do as one pleases, but are foiled by Ariel as comic nemesis. Because they are degenerate buffoons, their exposure is appropriately humiliating and satirical, with little attempt at spiritual recovery. They are irredeemable, the dregs of a corrupted civilization.

In contrast with them, Caliban is almost an attractive and sympathetic character. Although he grumbles and curses at his servitude, he is dangerous only when aroused by the clowns and their strong drink. Even his desire to rape Miranda and people the isle with little Calibans is a natural procreative instinct. His sensitivity to natural beauty, as in his descriptions of the "nimble marmoset" or the dreaming music he so often hears (II,ii and III,ii), is entirely appropriate to this child of nature. He is, to be sure, the child of a witch also, and is called many harsh names such as "Abhorred slave" and "a born devil, on whose nature Nurture can never stick." Yet he protests with some justification that the island was his in the first place, and that Prospero and Miranda are the interlopers and exploiters. His very existence calls radically into question the value of Western civilization, which has shown itself capable of limitless depravity. What profit has Caliban derived from learning Prospero's language other than, as he puts it, to "know how to curse"? With instinctive cunning he senses that books are his chief enemy, and plots to destroy them first in his attempt at rebellion. The unspoiled natural world does indeed offer to civilized man a perspective obtainable in no other way. Ultimately, however, Shakespeare's play celebrates man's highest achievement in the union of the island with the civilized world, as in the marriage of Ferdinand and Miranda. Even Caliban is at last reconciled to this solution. Prospero speaks of him as a "thing of darkness I Acknowledge mine," and Caliban vows to "be wise hereafter And seek for grace" (V,i). This synthesis suggests that the natural man within all of us is more contented, better understood, and more truly free when harmonized with reason.

Caliban is a part of humanity, Ariel is not. Ariel can comprehend what compassion and forgiveness would be like, "were I human," and takes part amusedly in Prospero's designs to castigate or reform his fellow man, but Ariel longs to be free in quite another sense from that meant by Caliban. Ariel takes no part in the final integration of human society. This woodland spirit belongs to a magic world of song, music, and illusion which the artist borrows for his use but which exists eternally outside of him. Like the elements of air, earth, fire, and water in which it mysteriously dwells, this force is morally neutral but incredibly vital. From it the artist achieves his powers of imagination, enabling him to bedim the noontide sun or call forth the dead from their graves. These visions are illusory in the profound sense that all life is illusory, an "insubstantial pageant" melted into thin air. Prospero the artist cherishes his own humanity, as a promise of surcease from his labors. Yet the artifact created by the artist endures, existing apart from time and place as does Ariel: "Then to the elements Be free, and fare thou well!" No doubt it is a romantic fiction to associate the dramatist Shakespeare with Prospero's farewell to his art, but it is an almost irresistible idea because we are so moved by the sense of completion and yet humility, the exultation and yet the calm.

THE TEMPEST

Names of the Actors

ALONSO; King of Naples.
SEBASTIAN, *his brother.*
PROSPERO, the right Duke of Milan.
ANTONIO, *his brother, the usurping* Duke of Milan.
FERDINAND, *son to the King of Naples.*
GONZALO, *an honest old Counsellor.*
ADRIAN *and* / FRANCISCO, } *Lords.*
CALIBAN, *a savage and deformed Slave.*
TRINCULO, *a Jester.*
STEPHANO, *a drunken Butler.*
Master of a Ship.
Boatswain.
Mariners.

MIRANDA, *daughter to Prospero.*

ARIEL, *an airy Spirit.*
IRIS, / CERES, / JUNO, / Nymphs, / Reapers, } *[presented by] Spirits.*

[Other Spirits attending on Prospero.]

THE SCENE: *An uninhabited island.*

ACT I.

SCENE I. [*On a ship at sea:*] *a tempestuous noise of thunder and lightning heard.*

Enter a Ship-Master *and* a Boatswain.

Mast. Boatswain!

Boats. Here, master: what cheer?

Mast. Good, speak to the mariners: fall to 't, yarely, or we run ourselves aground: bestir, bestir. *Exit.*

Enter Mariners.

Boats. Heigh, my hearts! cheerly, cheerly, my hearts! yare, yare! Take in the topsail. Tend to the master's whistle. Blow, till thou burst thy wind, if room enough!

Enter ALONSO, SEBASTIAN, ANTONIO, FERDINAND, GONZALO, *and others.*

Alon. Good boatswain, have care. Where 's the master? Play the men.

Boats. I pray now, keep below.

Ant. Where is the master, bos'n?

Boats. Do you not hear him? You mar our labour: keep your cabins: you do assist the storm.

Gon. Nay, good, be patient.

Boats. When the sea is. Hence! What cares these roarers for the name of king? To cabin: silence! trouble us not.

Gon. Good, yet remember whom thou hast aboard.

Boats. None that I more love than myself. You are a counsellor; if you can command these elements to silence, and work the peace of the present, we will not hand a rope more; use your authority: if you cannot, give thanks you have lived so long, and make yourself ready in your cabin for the mischance of the hour, if it so hap. Cheerly, good hearts! Out of our way, I say. *Exit.*

Gon. I have great comfort from this fellow: methinks he hath no drowning mark upon him; his complexion is perfect gallows. Stand fast, good Fate, to his hanging: make the rope of his destiny our cable, for our own doth little advantage. If he be not born to be hanged, our case is miserable. *Exeunt.*

Enter Boatswain.

Boats. Down with the topmast! yare! lower, lower! Bring her to try with main-course. *(A cry within.)* A plague upon this howling! they are louder than the weather or our office.

Enter SEBASTIAN, ANTONIO, *and* GONZALO.

Yet again! what do you here? Shall we give o'er and drown? Have you a mind to sink?

Seb. A pox o' your throat, you bawling, blasphemous, incharitable dog!

Boats. Work you then.

Ant. Hang, cur! hang, you whoreson, insolent noisemaker! We are less afraid to be drowned than thou art.

Gon. I'll warrant him for drowning; though the ship were no stronger than a nutshell and as leaky as an unstanched wench.

Boats. Lay her a-hold, a-hold! set her two courses off to sea again! lay her off!

Enter Mariners *wet.*

Mariners. All lost! to prayers, to prayers! all lost! [*Exeunt.*]

Boats. What, must our mouths be cold?

Gon. The king and prince at prayers! let 's assist them,
For our case is as theirs.

Seb. I 'm out of patience.

Ant. We are merely cheated of our lives by drunkards:
This wide-chapp'd rascal—would thou mightst lie drowning
The washing of ten tides!

Gon. He'll be hang'd yet,
Though every drop of water swear against it
And gape at wid'st to glut him.

A confused noise within: 'Mercy on us!'—
'We split, we split!'—'Farewell my wife and children!'—
'Farewell, brother!'—'We split, we split, we split!'
[*Exit Boats.*]

Ant. Let 's all sink wi' th' king.

Seb. Let 's take leave of him. *Exit* [*with Ant.*]

Gon. Now would I give a thousand furlongs of sea for an acre of barren ground, long heath, brown furze, any thing. The wills above be done! but I would fain die a dry death. *Exit.*

SCENE II. [*The island. Before* PROSPERO'S *cell.*]

Enter PROSPERO *and* MIRANDA.

Mir. If by your art, my dearest father, you have
Put the wild waters in this roar, allay them.
The sky, it seems, would pour down stinking pitch,
But that the sea, mounting to th' welkin's cheek,
Dashes the fire out. O, I have suffered
With those that I saw suffer: a brave vessel,
Who had, no doubt, some noble creature in her,
Dash'd all to pieces. O, the cry did knock
Against my very heart. Poor souls, they perish'd.
Had I been any god of power, I would
Have sunk the sea within the earth or ere
It should the good ship so have swallow'd and
The fraughting souls within her.

Pros. Be collected:
No more amazement: tell your piteous heart
There 's no harm done.

Mir. O, woe the day!

Pros. No harm.
I have done nothing but in care of thee,
Of thee, my dear one, thee, my daughter, who
Art ignorant of what thou art, nought knowing
Of whence I am, nor that I am more better
Than Prospero, master of a full poor cell,
And thy no greater father.

Mir. More to know
Did never meddle with my thoughts.

Pros. 'Tis time
I should inform thee farther. Lend thy hand,
And pluck my magic garment from me. So:
[*Lays down his mantle.*]
Lie there, my art. Wipe thou thine eyes; have comfort.
The direful spectacle of the wrack, which touch'd
The very virtue of compassion in thee,
I have with such provision in mine art
So safely ordered that there is no soul—
No, not so much perdition as an hair
Betid to any creature in the vessel
Which thou heard'st cry, which thou saw'st sink. Sit down;
For thou must now know farther.

Mir. You have often
Begun to tell me what I am, but stopp'd

ACT I. SCENE I. 1. **Boatswain,** under-officer in a ship, having to do with sails and rigging and the supervision of the crew at work. 3. **Good,** probably, good friend. 3-4. **fall . . . yarely,** set to work nimbly. 8. **Tend,** attend. 9. **Blow,** addressed to the wind. **if room enough,** as long as we have sea-room enough. 11. **Play the,** act like. 19. **cares,** described as a singular verb used with a plural subject on account of haste; also as an old northern plural of the verb in *s.* **roarers,** waves or winds, or both; allusion to *roarer* meaning "bully," "blusterer." 24-25. **work . . . present,** calm the storm. 25. **hand,** handle. 32. **complexion . . . gallows,** appearance shows he was born to be hanged. 35. **doth little advantage,** is of little benefit. 38. **Bring . . . course,** heave to and sail her close to the wind by means of the mainsail. 40. **they . . . office,** the passengers make more noise than the winds or than we do at work. 49. **warrant him for drowning,** guarantee that he will never be drowned. 51. **unstanched,** wide open. 52. **a-hold,** close to the wind. 53. **courses,** sails; i.e., they would set her foresail as well as her mainsail. 56. **must . . . cold,** let us heat up our mouths with liquor. 59. **merely,** absolutely, entirely. 60. **wide-chapp'd,** with mouth wide open. 60-61. **lie . . . tides.** Pirates were hanged on the shore and left until three tides had come in. 63. **glut,** swallow. 64. **split,** i.e., on the rocks. 69. **long heath,** defined as "open barren ground"; also as "heather." 70. **furze,** broom, or gorse (a prickly shrub); F: *firrs,* taken to mean "firs" (New Cambridge).

SCENE II. 3. **stinking pitch,** suggestion of heat. 4. **But that,** were it not that. **welkin's cheek,** sky's face. 13. **fraughting,** forming the cargo. 14. **amazement,** consternation. 20. **full,** very, exceedingly.

And left me to a bootless inquisition,
Concluding 'Stay: not yet.'
Pros. The hour 's now come;
The very minute bids thee ope thine ear;
Obey and be attentive. Canst thou remember
A time before we came unto this cell?
I do not think thou canst, for then thou wast not
Out three years old.
Mir. Certainly, sir, I can.
Pros. By what? by any other house or person?
Of any thing the image tell me that
Hath kept with thy remembrance.
Mir. 'Tis far off
And rather like a dream than an assurance
That my remembrance warrants. Had I not
Four or five women once that tended me?
Pros. Thou hadst, and more, Miranda. But how is it
That this lives in thy mind? What seest thou else
In the dark backward and abysm of time?
If thou rememb'rest aught ere thou cam'st here,
How thou cam'st here thou mayst.
Mir. But that I do not.
Pros. Twelve year since, Miranda, twelve year since,
Thy father was the Duke of Milan and
A prince of power.
Mir. Sir, are not you my father?
Pros. Thy mother was a piece of virtue, and
She said thou wast my daughter; and thy father
Was Duke of Milan; and thou his only heir
And princess no worse issued.
Mir. O the heavens!
What foul play had we, that we came from thence?
Or blessed was 't we did?
Pros. Both, both, my girl:
By foul play, as thou say'st, were we heav'd thence,
But blessedly holp hither.
Mir. O, my heart bleeds
To think o' th' teen that I have turn'd you to,
Which is from my remembrance! Please you, farther.
Pros. My brother and thy uncle, call'd Antonio—
I pray thee, mark me—that a brother should
Be so perfidious!—he whom next thyself
Of all the world I lov'd and to him put
The manage of my state; as at that time
Through all the signories it was the first
And Prospero the prime duke, being so reputed
In dignity, and for the liberal arts
Without a parallel; those being all my study,
The government I cast upon my brother
And to my state grew stranger, being transported
And rapt in secret studies. Thy false uncle—
Dost thou attend me?
Mir. Sir, most heedfully.
Pros. Being once perfected how to grant suits,
How to deny them, who t' advance and who
To trash for over-topping, new created
The creatures that were mine, I say, or chang'd 'em,
Or else new form'd 'em; having both the key
Of officer and office, set all hearts i' th' state
To what tune pleas'd his ear; that now he was
The ivy which had hid my princely trunk,
And suck'd my verdure out on 't. Thou attend'st not.
Mir. O, good sir, I do.
Pros. I pray thee, mark me.
I, thus neglecting worldly ends, all dedicated
To closeness and the bettering of my mind
With that which, but by being so retir'd,
O'er-priz'd all popular rate, in my false brother
Awak'd an evil nature; and my trust,
Like a good parent, did beget of him
A falsehood in its contrary as great
As my trust was; which had indeed no limit,
A confidence sans bound. He being thus lorded,
Not only with what my revenue yielded,
But what my power might else exact, like one
†Who having into truth, by telling of it,
Made such a sinner of his memory,
To credit his own lie, he did believe
He was indeed the duke; out o' th' substitution,
And executing th' outward face of royalty,
With all prerogative: hence his ambition growing—
Dost thou hear?
Mir. Your tale, sir, would cure deafness.
Pros. To have no screen between this part he play'd
And him he play'd it for, he needs will be
Absolute Milan. Me, poor man, my library
Was dukedom large enough: of temporal royalties
He thinks me now incapable; confederates—
So dry he was for sway—wi' th' King of Naples
To give him annual tribute, do him homage,
Subject his coronet to his crown and bend
The dukedom yet unbow'd—alas, poor Milan!—
To most ignoble stooping.
Mir. O the heavens!
Pros. Mark his condition and th' event; then tell me
If this might be a brother.
Mir. I should sin
To think but nobly of my grandmother:
Good wombs have borne bad sons.
Pros. Now the condition.
This King of Naples, being an enemy
To me inveterate, hearkens my brother's suit;
Which was, that he, in lieu o' th' premises
Of homage and I know not how much tribute,
Should presently extirpate me and mine
Out of the dukedom and confer fair Milan
With all the honours on my brother: whereon,
A treacherous army levied, one midnight
Fated to th' purpose did Antonio open
The gates of Milan, and, i' th' dead of darkness,
The ministers for th' purpose hurried thence

22. **meddle,** mingle. 24. **So,** used with a gesture, meaning "good," "very well." 28. **provision,** foresight. 29. **no soul,** i.e., lost; many emendations. 30. **perdition,** loss. 35. **bootless inquisition,** profitless inquiry. 41. **Out,** fully. 45-46. **assurance . . . warrants,** certainty that my memory guarantees. 56. **piece,** masterpiece. 59. **issued,** born. 64. **teen . . . to,** trouble I've caused you to remember. 65. **from,** i.e., has no place in. 71. **signories,** states of northern Italy. 73. **liberal arts,** allusion to the learned studies of the Middle Ages. 76. **state,** position as ruler. 77. **secret studies,** magic, the occult. 79. **perfected,** grown skillful. 81. **trash,** check a hound by tying a weight to its neck. **over-topping,** running too far ahead of the pack. 83. **key,** tool for tuning stringed instruments, with suggestion of the usual meaning. 90. **closeness,** retirement, seclusion. 91-92. **but . . . rate,** except that it was done in retirement, (would have) surpassed in value all popular estimate. 93. **Awak'd.** *I* in line 89 is the subject. 95. **in its contrary,** of an opposite kind. 97. **lorded,** raised to lordship. 100-102. **Who . . . lie,** a difficult passage; the meaning is: He had lied so long that he believed his own lies. New Cambridge editors read *minted* for *into*, interpreting the passage as a figure from coining of baser metals, so that *telling* means "counting," *substitution* means "the substituting of baser metals for gold," and *executing . . . royalty* means "stamping the coins." 103. **out o',** as a result of. 109. **Absolute Milan,** actual duke of Milan. 110. **royalties,** prerogatives and rights of a sovereign. 111. **confederates,** conspires. 112. **dry,** thirsty. 117. **condition,** pact. **event,** outcome. 123. **in . . . premises,** in return for the stipulations.

Me and thy crying self.
Mir. Alack, for pity!
I, not rememb'ring how I cried out then,
Will cry it o'er again: it is a hint
That wrings mine eyes to 't.
Pros. Hear a little further
And then I'll bring thee to the present business
Which now 's upon 's; without the which this story
Were most impertinent.
Mir. Wherefore did they not
That hour destroy us?
Pros. Well demanded, wench:
My tale provokes that question. Dear, they durst not,
So dear the love my people bore me, nor set
A mark so bloody on the business, but
With colours fairer painted their foul ends.
In few, they hurried us aboard a bark,
Bore us some leagues to sea; where they prepar'd
A rotten carcass of a butt, not rigg'd,
Nor tackle, sail, nor mast; the very rats
Instinctively have quit it: there they hoist us,
To cry to th' sea that roar'd to us, to sigh
To th' winds whose pity, sighing back again,
Did us but loving wrong.
Mir. Alack, what trouble
Was I then to you!
Pros. O, a cherubin
Thou wast that did preserve me. Thou didst smile,
Infused with a fortitude from heaven,
When I have deck'd the sea with drops full salt,
Under my burthen groan'd; which rais'd in me
An undergoing stomach, to bear up
Against what should ensue.
Mir. How came we ashore?
Pros. By Providence divine.
Some food we had and some fresh water that
A noble Neapolitan, Gonzalo,
Out of his charity, who being then appointed
Master of this design, did give us, with
Rich garments, linens, stuffs and necessaries,
Which since have steaded much; so, of his gentleness,
Knowing I lov'd my books, he furnish'd me
From mine own library with volumes that
I prize above my dukedom.
Mir. Would I might
But ever see that man!
Pros. Now I arise: [*Resumes his mantle.*]
Sit still, and hear the last of our sea-sorrow.
Here in this island we arriv'd; and here
Have I, thy schoolmaster, made thee more profit
Than other princesses can that have more time
For vainer hours and tutors not so careful.
Mir. Heavens thank you for 't! And now, I pray you, sir,
For still 'tis beating in my mind, your reason
For raising this sea-storm?
Pros. Know thus far forth.
By accident most strange, bountiful Fortune,
Now my dear lady, hath mine enemies
Brought to this shore; and by my prescience
I find my zenith doth depend upon
A most auspicious star, whose influence
If now I court not but omit, my fortunes
Will ever after droop. Here cease more questions:
Thou art inclin'd to sleep; 'tis a good dulness,
And give it way: I know thou canst not choose.
[*Miranda sleeps.*]
Come away, servant, come. I am ready now.
Approach, my Ariel, come.

Enter ARIEL.

Ari. All hail, great master! grave sir, hail! I come
To answer thy best pleasure; be 't to fly,
To swim, to dive into the fire, to ride
On the curl'd clouds, to thy strong bidding task
Ariel and all his quality.
Pros. Hast thou, spirit,
Perform'd to point the tempest that I bade thee?
Ari. To every article.
I boarded the king's ship; now on the beak,
Now in the waist, the deck, in every cabin,
I flam'd amazement: sometime I 'ld divide,
And burn in many places; on the topmast,
The yards and boresprit, would I flame distinctly,
Then meet and join. Jove's lightnings, the precursors
O' th' dreadful thunder-claps, more momentary
And sight-outrunning were not; the fire and cracks
Of sulphurous roaring the most mighty Neptune
Seem to besiege and make his bold waves tremble,
Yea, his dread trident shake.
Pros. My brave spirit!
Who was so firm, so constant, that this coil
Would not infect his reason?
Ari. Not a soul
But felt a fever of the mad and play'd
Some tricks of desperation. All but mariners
Plung'd in the foaming brine and quit the vessel,
Then all afire with me: the king's son, Ferdinand,
With hair up-staring,—then like reeds, not hair,—
Was the first man that leap'd; cried, 'Hell is empty,
And all the devils are here.'
Pros. Why, that 's my spirit!
But was not this nigh shore?
Ari. Close by, my master.
Pros. But are they, Ariel, safe?
Ari. Not a hair perish'd;
On their sustaining garments not a blemish,
But fresher than before: and, as thou bad'st me,
In troops I have dispers'd them 'bout the isle.
The king's son have I landed by himself;
Whom I left cooling of the air with sighs
In an odd angle of the isle and sitting,
His arms in this sad knot. [*Folds his arms.*]
Pros. Of the king's ship
The mariners say how thou hast dispos'd
And all the rest o' th' fleet.
Ari. Safely in harbour
Is the king's ship; in the deep nook, where once
Thou call'dst me up at midnight to fetch dew
From the still-vex'd Bermoothes, there she 's hid:

134. **hint,** occasion. 138. **impertinent,** irrelevant. 139. **wench,** used as a term of affectionate address. 144. **few,** few words. 146. **butt,** tub; Globe: *boat*. 151. **loving wrong,** figure of speech called oxymoron, in which, to emphasize a contrast, contradictory terms are associated; the *wrong* done by sea and winds was wrought by seeming sympathy. 152. **cherubin,** plural used as singular; applied to an angelic woman. 155. **deck'd,** covered (with salt tears). 156. **which,** i.e., the smile. 157. **undergoing stomach,** courage to undergo. 181. **zenith,** height of fortune; astrological term. 185. **dulness,** drowsiness. 187. **Come away,** come. 192. **task,** make demands upon. 193. **quality,** fellow-spirits. 194. **point,** i.e., to the smallest detail. 196. **beak,** prow. 197. **waist,** midship. **deck,** poopdeck at the stern. 200. **boresprit,** bowsprit. **distinctly,** separately. 202. **momentary,** instantaneous. 209. **fever of the mad,** i.e., such as madmen feel. 213. **up-staring,** standing on end. 218. **sustaining garments,** garments that buoyed them up in the sea. 223. **angle,** corner. 227. **nook,** bay. 228. **fetch**

The mariners all under hatches stow'd;
Who, with a charm join'd to their suff'red labour,
I have left asleep: and for the rest o' th' fleet
Which I dispers'd, they all have met again
And are upon the Mediterranean flote,
Bound sadly home for Naples,
Supposing that they saw the king's ship wrack'd
And his great person perish.
Pros. Ariel, thy charge
Exactly is perform'd: but there 's more work.
What is the time o' th' day?
Ari. Past the mid season.
Pros. At least two glasses. The time 'twixt six and now
Must by us both be spent most preciously.
Ari. Is there more toil? Since thou dost give me pains,
Let me remember thee what thou hast promis'd,
Which is not yet perform'd me.
Pros. How now? moody?
What is 't thou canst demand?
Ari. My liberty.
Pros. Before the time be out? no more!
Ari. I prithee,
Remember I have done thee worthy service;
Told thee no lies, made thee no mistakings, serv'd
Without or grudge or grumblings: thou didst promise
To bate me a full year.
Pros. Dost thou forget
From what a torment I did free thee?
Ari. No.
Pros. Thou dost, and think'st it much to tread the ooze
Of the salt deep,
To run upon the sharp wind of the north,
To do me business in the veins o' th' earth
When it is bak'd with frost.
Ari. I do not, sir.
Pros. Thou liest, malignant thing! Hast thou forgot
The foul witch Sycorax, who with age and envy
Was grown into a hoop? hast thou forgot her?
Ari. No, sir.
Pros. Thou hast. Where was she born? speak; tell me.
Ari. Sir, in Argier.
Pros. O, was she so? I must
Once in a month recount what thou hast been,
Which thou forget'st. This damn'd witch Sycorax,
For mischiefs manifold and sorceries terrible
To enter human hearing, from Argier,
Thou know'st, was banish'd: for one thing she did
They would not take her life. Is not this true?
Ari. Ay, sir.
Pros. This blue-ey'd hag was hither brought with child
And here was left by th' sailors. Thou, my slave,
As thou report'st thyself, wast then her servant;
And, for thou wast a spirit too delicate
To act her earthy and abhorr'd commands,
Refusing her grand hests, she did confine thee,
By help of her more potent ministers
And in her most unmitigable rage,
Into a cloven pine; within which rift
Imprison'd thou didst painfully remain
A dozen years; within which space she died
And left thee there; where thou did'st vent thy groans
As fast as mill-wheels strike. Then was this island—
Save for the son that she did litter here,
A freckled whelp hag-born—not honour'd with
A human shape.
Ari. Yes, Caliban her son.
Pros. Dull thing, I say so; he, that Caliban
Whom now I keep in service. Thou best know'st
What torment I did find thee in; thy groans
Did make wolves howl and penetrate the breasts
Of ever angry bears: it was a torment
To lay upon the damn'd, which Sycorax
Could not again undo: it was mine art,
When I arriv'd and heard thee, that made gape
The pine and let thee out.
Ari. I thank thee, master.
Pros. If thou more murmur'st, I will rend an oak
And peg thee in his knotty entrails till
Thou hast howl'd away twelve winters.
Ari. Pardon, master;
I will be correspondent to command
And do my spiriting gently.
Pros. Do so, and after two days
I will discharge thee.
Ari. That 's my noble master!
What shall I do? say what; what shall I do?
Pros. Go make thyself like a nymph o' th' sea: be subject
To no sight but thine and mine, invisible
To every eyeball else. Go take this shape
And hither come in 't: go, hence with diligence!
Exit [Ariel].
Awake, dear heart, awake! thou hast slept well;
Awake!
Mir. The strangeness of your story put
Heaviness in me.
Pros. Shake it off. Come on;
We'll visit Caliban my slave, who never
Yields us kind answer.
Mir. 'Tis a villain, sir,
I do not love to look on.
Pros. But, as 'tis,
We cannot miss him: he does make our fire,
Fetch in our wood and serves in offices
That profit us. What, ho! slave! Caliban!
Thou earth, thou! speak.
Cal. (*Within*) There 's wood enough within.
Pros. Come forth, I say! there 's other business for thee:
Come, thou tortoise! when?

Enter ARIEL *like a water-nymph.*

Fine apparition! My quaint Ariel,

dew, for some incantation. 229. **Bermoothes,** Bermudas; a possible reference to *A Discovery of the Barmudas* (1609), one of the sources of the play. 234. **flote,** sea, or possibly, flotilla, i.e., making for the Mediterranean flotilla (New Cambridge). 240. **glasses,** i.e., hour-glasses. 243. **remember,** remind. 248. **mistakings,** errors. 250. **bate . . . year,** remit me a year of service. Ariel, as a spirit, longs for freedom; as a spirit, he is also incapable of affection or gratitude as entertained by human beings. 261. **Argier,** Algiers. 266. **one thing she did,** allusion not explained; taken by New Cambridge editors as evidence of a cut in the play. Lamb suggested that Shakespeare was thinking of the witch who saved Algiers from Charles v in 1541 by raising a storm that dispersed his fleet. 269. **blue-ey'd,** usually interpreted as referring to dark circles under the eyes. Staunton suggested *blear-eyed*. 274. **hests,** commands. 283. **freckled,** spotted. 297. **correspondent,** responsive, submissive. 311. **miss,** do without.

Hark in thine ear. [*Whispers.*]
Ari. My lord, it shall be done. *Exit.*
Pros. Thou poisonous slave, got by the devil himself
Upon thy wicked dam, come forth!

Enter CALIBAN.

Cal. As wicked dew as e'er my mother brush'd
With raven's feather from unwholesome fen
Drop on you both! a south-west blow on ye
And blister you all o'er!
Pros. For this, be sure, to-night thou shalt have cramps,
Side-stitches that shall pen thy breath up; urchins
Shall, for that vast of night that they may work,
All exercise on thee; thou shalt be pinch'd
As thick as honeycomb, each pinch more stinging
Than bees that made 'em.
Cal. I must eat my dinner.
This island 's mine, by Sycorax my mother,
Which thou tak'st from me. When thou cam'st first,
Thou strok'st me and made much of me, wouldst give me
Water with berries in 't, and teach me how
To name the bigger light, and how the less,
That burn by day and night: and then I lov'd thee
And show'd thee all the qualities o' th' isle,
The fresh springs, brine-pits, barren place and fertile:
Curs'd be I that did so! All the charms
Of Sycorax, toads, beetles, bats, light on you!
For I am all the subjects that you have,
Which first was mine own king: and here you sty me
In this hard rock, whiles you do keep from me
The rest o' th' island.
Pros. Thou most lying slave,
Whom stripes may move, not kindness! I have us'd thee,
Filth as thou art, with humane care, and lodg'd thee
In mine own cell, till thou didst seek to violate
The honour of my child.
Cal. O ho, O ho! would 't had been done!
Thou didst prevent me; I had peopled else
This isle with Calibans.
Mir. Abhorred slave,
Which any print of goodness wilt not take,
Being capable of all ill! I pitied thee,
Took pains to make thee speak, taught thee each hour
One thing or other: when thou didst not, savage,
Know thine own meaning, but wouldst gabble like
A thing most brutish, I endow'd thy purposes
With words that made them known. But thy vile race,
Though thou didst learn, had that in 't which good natures
Could not abide to be with; therefore wast thou
Deservedly confin'd into this rock,
Who hadst deserv'd more than a prison.
Cal. You taught me language; and my profit on 't
Is, I know how to curse. The red plague rid you
For learning me your language!
Pros. Hag-seed, hence!
Fetch us in fuel; and be quick, thou 'rt best,
To answer other business. Shrug'st thou, malice?
If thou neglect'st or dost unwillingly
What I command, I'll rack thee with old cramps,
Fill all thy bones with aches, make thee roar
That beasts shall tremble at thy din.
Cal. No, pray thee.
[*Aside*] I must obey: his art is of such pow'r,
It would control my dam's god, Setebos,
And make a vassal of him.
Pros. So, slave; hence! *Exit Caliban.*

Enter FERDINAND; *and* ARIEL, *invisible, playing and singing.*

ARIEL'S *song.*

Come unto these yellow sands,
And then take hands:
Courtsied when you have and kiss'd
The wild waves whist,
Foot it featly here and there;
And, sweet sprites, the burthen bear.
Burthen (*dispersedly*). Hark, hark!
Bow-wow.
The watch-dogs bark:
Bow-wow.
Ari. Hark, hark! I hear
The strain of strutting chanticleer
Cry, Cock-a-diddle-dow.
Fer. Where should this music be? i' th' air or th' earth?
It sounds no more: and, sure, it waits upon
Some god o' th' island. Sitting on a bank,
Weeping again the king my father's wrack,
This music crept by me upon the waters,
Allaying both their fury and my passion
With its sweet air: thence I have follow'd it,
Or it hath drawn me rather. But 'tis gone.
No, it begins again.

ARIEL'S *song.*

Full fathom five thy father lies;
Of his bones are coral made;
Those are pearls that were his eyes:
Nothing of him that doth fade
But doth suffer a sea-change
Into something rich and strange.
Sea-nymphs hourly ring his knell:
Burthen. Ding-dong.
[*Ari.*] Hark! now I hear them,—Ding-dong, bell.
Fer. The ditty does remember my drown'd father.
This is no mortal business, nor no sound
That the earth owes. I hear it now above me.
Pros. The fringed curtains of thine eye advance
And say what thou seest yond.
Mir. What is 't? a spirit?
Lord, how it looks about! Believe me, sir,
It carries a brave form. But 'tis a spirit.
Pros. No, wench; it eats and sleeps and hath such senses
As we have, such. This gallant which thou seest
Was in the wrack; and, but he 's something stain'd

321. **wicked,** mischievous, harmful. 323. **south-west,** i.e., wind (bringing disease). 326. **urchins,** hedgehogs; here, suggesting goblins. 327. **vast,** long hours. 328. **exercise,** practice, work. 334. **berries.** Strachey's *Repertory*, one of the sources, says that the Bermudas were full of thickets of "goodly Cedar . . . the Berries whereof, our men seething, straining, and letting stand some three or foure daies, made a kind of pleasant drinke." 338. **brine-pits,** salt springs. 342. **sty,** put in sty. 351-362. **Abhorred . . . prison.** Sometimes assigned to Prospero (as in Globe). 357-358. **endow'd . . . known,** enabled you to make known what was going on in your mind. 358. **race,** natural disposition. 364. **red plague,** bubonic plague. **rid,** destroy, with play on *red.* 365. **Hag-seed,** hag's offspring. 369. **old,** plenty of. 370. **aches,** pronounced "aitches." 373. **Setebos,** mentioned in Eden's *History of Travel* (1577) as a deity, or devil, of the Patagonians. 376-378. **Come . . . kiss'd,** three motions before the dance—take hands, curtsy, kiss (New Cambridge). 379. **whist,** silent. 380. **featly,** neatly. 381.

With grief that 's beauty's canker, thou mightst call him
A goodly person: he hath lost his fellows
And strays about to find 'em.
Mir. I might call him
A thing divine, for nothing natural
I ever saw so noble.
Pros. [*Aside*] It goes on, I see,
As my soul prompts it. Spirit, fine spirit! I'll free thee
Within two days for this.
Fer. Most sure, the goddess
On whom these airs attend! Vouchsafe my pray'r
May know if you remain upon this island;
And that you will some good instruction give
How I may bear me here: my prime request,
Which I do last pronounce, is, O you wonder!
If you be maid or no?
Mir. No wonder, sir;
But certainly a maid.
Fer. My language! heavens!
I am the best of them that speak this speech,
Were I but where 'tis spoken.
Pros. How? the best?
What wert thou, if the King of Naples heard thee?
Fer. A single thing, as I am now, that wonders
To hear thee speak of Naples. He does hear me;
And that he does I weep: myself am Naples,
Who with mine eyes, never since at ebb, beheld
The king my father wrack'd.
Mir. Alack, for mercy!
Fer. Yes, faith, and all his lords; the Duke of Milan
And his brave son being twain.
Pros. [*Aside*] The Duke of Milan
And his more braver daughter could control thee,
If now 'twere fit to do 't. At the first sight
They have chang'd eyes. Delicate Ariel,
I'll set thee free for this. [*To Fer.*] A word, good sir;
I fear you have done yourself some wrong: a word.
Mir. Why speaks my father so ungently? This
Is the third man that e'er I saw, the first
That e'er I sigh'd for: pity move my father
To be inclin'd my way!
Fer. O, if a virgin,
And your affection not gone forth, I'll make you
The queen of Naples.
Pros. Soft, sir! one word more.
[*Aside*] They are both in either's pow'rs; but this swift business
I must uneasy make, lest too light winning
Make the prize light. [*To Fer.*] One word more; I charge thee
That thou attend me: thou dost here usurp
The name thou ow'st not; and hast put thyself
Upon this island as a spy, to win it
From me, the lord on 't.
Fer. No, as I am a man.
Mir. There 's nothing ill can dwell in such a temple:
If the ill spirit have so fair a house,
Good things will strive to dwell with 't.
Pros. Follow me.
Speak not you for him; he 's a traitor. [*To Fer.*] Come;
I'll manacle thy neck and feet together:
Sea-water shalt thou drink; thy food shall be
The fresh-brook mussels, wither'd roots and husks
Wherein the acorn cradled. Follow.
Fer. No;
I will resist such entertainment till
Mine enemy has more pow'r.
He draws, and is charmed from moving.
Mir. O dear father,
Make not too rash a trial of him, for
He 's gentle and not fearful.
Pros. What? I say,
My foot my tutor? [*To Fer.*] Put thy sword up, traitor;
Who mak'st a show but dar'st not strike, thy conscience
Is so possess'd with guilt: come, from thy ward,
For I can here disarm thee with this stick
And make thy weapon drop.
Mir. Beseech you, father.
Pros. Hence! hang not on my garments.
Mir. Sir, have pity;
I'll be his surety.
Pros. Silence! one word more
Shall make me chide thee, if not hate thee. What!
An advocate for an impostor! hush!
Thou think'st there is no more such shapes as he,
Having seen but him and Caliban: foolish wench!
To th' most of men this is a Caliban
And they to him are angels.
Mir. My affections
Are then most humble; I have no ambition
To see a goodlier man.
Pros. [*To Fer.*] Come on; obey:
Thy nerves are in their infancy again
And have no vigour in them.
Fer. So they are;
My spirits, as in a dream, are all bound up.
My father's loss, the weakness which I feel,
The wrack of all my friends, nor this man's threats,
To whom I am subdu'd, are but light to me,
Might I but through my prison once a day
Behold this maid: all corners else o' th' earth
Let liberty make use of; space enough
Have I in such a prison.
Pros. [*Aside*] It works. [*To Fer.*] Come on.
Thou hast done well, fine Ariel! [*To Fer.*] Follow me.
[*To Ari.*] Hark what thou else shalt do me.
Mir. Be of comfort;
My father 's of a better nature, sir,
Than he appears by speech: this is unwonted
Which now came from him.
Pros. Thou shalt be as free
As mountain winds: but then exactly do
All points of my command.
Ari. To th' syllable.
Pros. Come, follow. [*To Mir.*] Speak not for him.
Exeunt.

burthen, refrain. 382. **dispersedly,** i.e., from all parts of the stage. 405. **remember,** commemorate. 407. **owes,** owns. 415. **canker,** cankerworm (feeding on buds and leaves). 419. **It goes on,** my charm works. 423. **remain,** dwell. 425. **bear me,** conduct myself. 429. **best,** i.e., in birth. 432. **single,** solitary, with a suggestion of feebleness. 438. **son,** the only reference to a son of Antonio. 439. **control,** confute. 441. **chang'd eyes,** exchanged amorous glances. 443. **done . . . wrong,** are mistaken. 451. **uneasy,** difficult. 451, 452. **light, light,** easy, cheap. 454. **ow'st,** ownest. 465. **entertainment,** treatment. 468. **gentle,** wellborn, high-spirited. **not fearful,** not dangerous (because incapable of treachery). 469. **foot,** subordinate. Miranda (the foot) presumes to instruct Prospero (the head). 471. **ward,** defensive posture (in fencing). 472. **stick,** his wand. 484. **nerves,** sinews. 491-492. **all . . . of,** those who are free may have all the rest of the world.

ACT II.

SCENE I. [*Another part of the island.*]

Enter ALONSO, SEBASTIAN, ANTONIO, GONZALO, ADRIAN, FRANCISCO, *and others.*

Gon. Beseech you, sir, be merry; you have cause,
So have we all, of joy; for our escape
Is much beyond our loss. Our hint of woe
Is common; every day some sailor's wife,
The masters of some merchant and the merchant
Have just our theme of woe; but for the miracle,
I mean our preservation, few in millions
Can speak like us: then wisely, good sir, weigh
Our sorrow with our comfort.
Alon. Prithee, peace.
Seb. [*To Ant.*] He receives comfort like cold porridge.
Ant. [*To Seb.*] The visitor will not give him o'er so.
Seb. Look, he 's winding up the watch of his wit; by and by it will strike.
Gon. Sir,—
Seb. [*To Ant.*] One: tell.
Gon. When every grief is entertain'd that 's offer'd,
Comes to the entertainer—
Seb. A dollar.
Gon. Dolour comes to him, indeed: you have spoken truer than you purposed.
Seb. You have taken it wiselier than I meant you should.
Gon. Therefore, my lord,—
Ant. Fie, what a spendthrift is he of his tongue!
Alon. I prithee, spare.
Gon. Well, I have done: but yet,—
Seb. He will be talking.
Ant. Which, of he or Adrian, for a good wager, first begins to crow?
Seb. The old cock.
Ant. The cockerel.
Seb. Done. The wager?
Ant. A laughter.
Seb. A match!
Adr. Though this island seem to be desert,—
Seb. Ha, ha, ha! So, you 're paid.
Adr. Uninhabitable and almost inaccessible,—
Seb. Yet,—
Adr. Yet,—
Ant. He could not miss 't.
Adr. It must needs be of subtle, tender and delicate temperance.
Ant. Temperance was a delicate wench.
Seb. Ay, and a subtle; as he most learnedly delivered.
Adr. The air breathes upon us here most sweetly.
Seb. As if it had lungs and rotten ones.
Ant. Or as 'twere perfumed by a fen.
Gon. Here is every thing advantageous to life.
Ant. True; save means to live.
Seb. Of that there 's none, or little.
Gon. How lush and lusty the grass looks! how green!
Ant. The ground indeed is tawny.
Seb. With an eye of green in 't.
Ant. He misses not much.
Seb. No; he doth but mistake the truth totally.
Gon. But the rarity of it is,—which is indeed almost beyond credit,—
Seb. As many vouched rarities are.
Gon. That our garments, being, as they were, drenched in the sea, hold notwithstanding their freshness and glosses, being rather new-dyed than stained with salt water.
Ant. If but one of his pockets could speak, would it not say he lies?
Seb. Ay, or very falsely pocket up his report.
Gon. Methinks our garments are now as fresh as when we put them on first in Afric, at the marriage of the king's fair daughter Claribel to the King of Tunis.
Seb. 'Twas a sweet marriage, and we prosper well in our return.
Adr. Tunis was never graced before with such a paragon to their queen.
Gon. Not since widow Dido's time.
Ant. Widow! a pox o' that! How came that widow in? widow Dido!
Seb. What if he had said 'widower Æneas' too? Good Lord, how you take it!
Adr. 'Widow Dido' said you? you make me study of that: she was of Carthage, not of Tunis.
Gon. This Tunis, sir, was Carthage.
Adr. Carthage?
Gon. I assure you, Carthage.
Seb. His word is more than the miraculous harp; he hath raised the wall and houses too.
Ant. What impossible matter will he make easy next?
Seb. I think he will carry this island home in his pocket and give it his son for an apple.
Ant. And, sowing the kernels of it in the sea, bring forth more islands.
Gon. Ay.
Ant. Why, in good time.
Gon. [*To Alon.*] Sir, we were talking that our garments seem now as fresh as when we were at Tunis at the marriage of your daughter, who is now queen.
Ant. And the rarest that e'er came there.
Seb. Bate, I beseech you, widow Dido.
Ant. O, widow Dido! ay, widow Dido.
Gon. Is not, sir, my doublet as fresh as the first day I wore it? I mean, in a sort.
Ant. That sort was well fished for.
Gon. When I wore it at your daughter's marriage?
Alon. You cram these words into mine ears against
The stomach of my sense. Would I had never
Married my daughter there! for, coming thence,

ACT II. SCENE I. 3. **hint of,** occasion for. 5. **merchant, merchant,** merchant vessel, merchant. 11. **visitor,** one taking nourishment to the sick. 15. **tell,** keep count. 18. **dollar,** widely circulated coin, the German *Thaler* and the Spanish *piece of eight*. 28-29. **Which . . . crow,** which of the two, Gonzalo or Adrian, do you bet will speak (crow) first? 30. **old cock,** i.e., Gonzalo. 33. **laughter,** sitting of eggs. When Adrian (the *cockerel*) begins to speak (l. 35), Sebastian loses the bet and pays with a *laugh* (*Ha, ha, ha!* l. 36) for a *laughter*. 34. **A match,** a bargain; agreed. 40. **He . . . miss 't,** i.e., even if it is uninhabitable and inaccessible, he could not refrain from talking about it. 42. **temperance,** temperature. 43. **Temperance,** a Puritan name for women, thought also to refer to Temperance, a character in Chapman's *May Day* (1611). 54. **tawny,** dull brown. 55. **eye,** tinge. 65. **pockets,** i.e., because they are muddy. 76. **widow Dido,** queen of Carthage deserted by Aeneas, and thus not really a widow. 86. **miraculous harp,** allusion to Amphion's harp with which he raised the walls of Thebes; Gonzalo has exceeded that deed by rebuilding a modern Carthage. 95. **in good time,** vague expression of agreement or approbation. 100. **Bate,** except. 104. **sort,** lucky catch after much angling; probable suggestion of the age of the garment, with a play on *sort* in line 103. 109. **rate,** opinion. 113-122. **Sir . . . land,** Francisco's only speech. 120. **that . . . bow'd,** that hung out over its wave-worn foot. 125.

My son is lost and, in my rate, she too,
Who is so far from Italy remov'd
I ne'er again shall see her. O thou mine heir
Of Naples and of Milan, what strange fish
Hath made his meal on thee?
Fran. Sir, he may live:
I saw him beat the surges under him,
And ride upon their backs; he trod the water,
Whose enmity he flung aside, and breasted
The surge most swoln that met him; his bold head
'Bove the contentious waves he kept, and oar'd
Himself with his good arms in lusty stroke
To th' shore, that o'er his wave-worn basis bow'd,
As stooping to relieve him: I not doubt
He came alive to land.
Alon. No, no, he 's gone.
Seb. Sir, you may thank yourself for this great loss,
That would not bless our Europe with your daughter,
But rather loose her to an African;
Where she at least is banish'd from your eye,
Who hath cause to wet the grief on 't.
Alon. Prithee, peace.
Seb. You were kneel'd to and importun'd otherwise
By all of us, and the fair soul herself
Weigh'd between loathness and obedience, at
Which end o' th' beam should bow. We have lost your son,
I fear, for ever: Milan and Naples have
Moe widows in them of this business' making
Than we bring men to comfort them:
The fault 's your own.
Alon. So is the dear'st o' th' loss.
Gon. My lord Sebastian,
The truth you speak doth lack some gentleness
And time to speak it in: you rub the sore,
When you should bring the plaster.
Seb. Very well.
Ant. And most chirurgeonly.
Gon. It is foul weather in us all, good sir,
When you are cloudy.
Seb. [*To Ant.*] Foul weather?
Ant. [*To Seb.*] Very foul.
Gon. Had I plantation of this isle, my lord,—
Ant. He 'ld sow 't with nettle-seed.
Seb. Or docks, or mallows.
Gon. And were the king on 't, what would I do?
Seb. 'Scape being drunk for want of wine.
Gon. I' th' commonwealth I would by contraries
Execute all things; for no kind of traffic
Would I admit; no name of magistrate;
Letters should not be known; riches, poverty,
And use of service, none; contract, succession,
Bourn, bound of land, tilth, vineyard, none;
No use of metal, corn, or wine, or oil;
No occupation; all men idle, all;
And women too, but innocent and pure;
No sovereignty;—
Seb. Yet he would be king on 't.
Ant. The latter end of his commonwealth forgets the beginning.
Gon. All things in common nature should produce
Without sweat or endeavour: treason, felony,
Sword, pike, knife, gun, or need of any engine,
Would I not have; but nature should bring forth,
Of it own kind, all foison, all abundance,
To feed my innocent people.
Seb. No marrying 'mong his subjects?
Ant. None, man; all idle: whores and knaves.
Gon. I would with such perfection govern, sir,
T' excel the golden age.
Seb. 'Save his majesty!
Ant. Long live Gonzalo!
Gon. And,—do you mark me, sir?
Alon. Prithee, no more: thou dost talk nothing to me.

Gon. I do well believe your highness; and did it to minister occasion to these gentlemen, who are of such sensible and nimble lungs that they always use to laugh at nothing.

Ant. 'Twas you we laughed at.

Gon. Who in this kind of merry fooling am nothing to you: so you may continue and laugh at nothing still.

Ant. What a blow was there given!

Seb. An it had not fallen flat-long.

Gon. You are gentlemen of brave mettle; you would lift the moon out of her sphere, if she would continue in it five weeks without changing.

Enter Ariel [*invisible*] *playing solemn music.*

Seb. We would so, and then go a bat-fowling.

Ant. Nay, good my lord, be not angry.

Gon. No, I warrant you; I will not adventure my discretion so weakly. Will you laugh me asleep, for I am very heavy?

Ant. Go sleep, and hear us.
[*All sleep except Alon., Seb., and Ant.*]
Alon. What, all so soon asleep! I wish mine eyes
Would, with themselves, shut up my thoughts: I find
They are inclin'd to do so.
Seb. Please you, sir,
Do not omit the heavy offer of it:
It seldom visits sorrow; when it doth,
It is a comforter.
Ant. We two, my lord,
Will guard your person while you take your rest,
And watch your safety.
Alon. Thank you. Wondrous heavy.
[*Alonso sleeps. Exit Ariel.*]
Seb. What a strange drowsiness possesses them!
Ant. It is the quality o' th' climate.
Seb. Why
Doth it not then our eyelids sink? I find not
Myself dispos'd to sleep.

loose, so F; Globe: *lose.* 127. **Who,** which (eye). 129-131. **the fair . . . bow,** Claribel herself was poised uncertain between unwillingness and obedience as to which end of the scale should sink. 140. **chirurgeonly,** like a skilled surgeon. 143. **plantation,** colonization; subsequent play on the literal meaning. 147-156. **I' th' . . . sovereignty.** This passage on man in his primitive state is based on Montaigne, *Essays,* I, xxx, perhaps derived from Florio's translation (1603). 150. **Letters,** learning. 151. **use of service,** custom of employing servants. **succession,** holding of property by right of inheritance. 152. **Bourn,** boundaries. **bound of land,** landmarks. **tilth,** tillage of soil. 161. **engine,** instrument of warfare. 163. **it,** its. **foison,** plenty. 173. **minister occasion,** furnish opportunity. 174. **sensible,** sensitive. 181. **flat-long,** with the flat of the sword. 182. **mettle,** temper, nature. 183. **lift . . . sphere.** As a planet in the old astronomy, the moon had a crystal sphere in which she moved. Gonzalo means that they would lift the moon out of her sphere if she remained steady in it. 185. **bat-fowling,** hunting birds at night with lantern and stick; also, gulling a simpleton. Gonzalo is the simpleton (or fowl), and Sebastian will use the moon as his lantern. 187. **adventure,** risk. 190. **Go . . . us,** let our laughing send you to sleep, or, go to sleep and hear us laugh at you. 194. **omit,** neglect. **heavy,** drowsy.

Ant. Nor I; my spirits are nimble.
They fell together all, as by consent;
They dropp'd, as by a thunder-stroke. What might,
Worthy Sebastian? O, what might?—No more:—
And yet methinks I see it in thy face,
What thou shouldst be: th' occasion speaks thee, and
My strong imagination sees a crown
Dropping upon thy head.
Seb. What, art thou waking?
Ant. Do you not hear me speak?
Seb. I do; and surely
It is a sleepy language and thou speak'st
Out of thy sleep. What is it thou didst say?
This is a strange repose, to be asleep
With eyes wide open; standing, speaking, moving,
And yet so fast asleep.
Ant. Noble Sebastian,
Thou let'st thy fortune sleep—die, rather; wink'st
Whiles thou art waking.
Seb. Thou dost snore distinctly;
There 's meaning in thy snores.
Ant. I am more serious than my custom: you
Must be so too, if heed me; which to do
Trebles thee o'er.
Seb. Well, I am standing water.
Ant. I'll teach you how to flow.
Seb. Do so: to ebb
Hereditary sloth instructs me.
Ant. O,
If you but knew how you the purpose cherish
Whiles thus you mock it! how, in stripping it,
You more invest it! Ebbing men, indeed,
Most often do so near the bottom run
By their own fear or sloth.
Seb. Prithee, say on:
The setting of thine eye and cheek proclaim
A matter from thee, and a birth indeed
Which throes thee much to yield.
Ant. Thus, sir:
Although this lord of weak remembrance, this,
Who shall be of as little memory
When he is earth'd, hath here almost persuaded,—
For he 's a spirit of persuasion, only
Professes to persuade,—the king his son 's alive,
'Tis as impossible that he 's undrown'd
As he that sleeps here swims.
Seb. I have no hope
That he 's undrown'd.
Ant. O, out of that 'no hope'
What great hope have you! no hope that way is
Another way so high a hope that even
Ambition cannot pierce a wink beyond,
But doubt discovery there. Will you grant with me
That Ferdinand is drown'd?
Seb. He 's gone.
Ant. Then, tell me,
Who 's the next heir of Naples?
Seb. Claribel.
Ant. She that is queen of Tunis; she that dwells
Ten leagues beyond man's life; she that from Naples
Can have no note, unless the sun were post—
The man i' th' moon 's too slow—till new-born chins
Be rough and razorable; she that from whom
We all were sea-swallow'd, though some cast again,
And by that destiny to perform an act
Whereof what 's past is prologue, what to come
In yours and my discharge.
Seb. What stuff is this! how say you?
'Tis true, my brother's daughter 's queen of Tunis;
So is she heir of Naples; 'twixt which regions
There is some space.
Ant. A space whose ev'ry cubit
Seems to cry out, 'How shall that Claribel
Measure us back to Naples? Keep in Tunis,
And let Sebastian wake.' Say, this were death
That now hath seiz'd them; why, they were no
worse
Than now they are. There be that can rule Naples
As well as he that sleeps; lords that can prate
As amply and unnecessarily
As this Gonzalo; I myself could make
A chough of as deep chat. O, that you bore
The mind that I do! what a sleep were this
For your advancement! Do you understand me?
Seb. Methinks I do.
Ant. And how does your content
Tender your own good fortune?
Seb. I remember
You did supplant your brother Prospero.
Ant. True:
And look how well my garments sit upon me;
Much feater than before: my brother's servants
Were then my fellows; now they are my men.
Seb. But, for your conscience?
Ant. Ay, sir; where lies that? if 'twere a kibe,
'Twould put me to my slipper: but I feel not
This deity in my bosom: twenty consciences,
That stand 'twixt me and Milan, candied be they
And melt ere they molest! Here lies your brother,
No better than the earth he lies upon,
If he were that which now he 's like, that 's dead;
Whom I, with this obedient steel, three inches of it,
Can lay to bed for ever; whiles you, doing thus,
To the perpetual wink for aye might put
This ancient morsel, this Sir Prudence, who
Should not upbraid our course. For all the rest,
They'll take suggestion as a cat laps milk;
They'll tell the clock to any business that
We say befits the hour.
Seb. Thy case, dear friend,
Shall be my precedent; as thou got'st Milan,
I'll come by Naples. Draw thy sword: one stroke
Shall free thee from the tribute which thou payest;
And I the king shall love thee.
Ant. Draw together;
And when I rear my hand, do you the like,
To fall it on Gonzalo. [*They draw.*]
Seb. O, but one word!

203. **consent,** agreement as to a course of action. 207. **speaks,** calls upon, proclaims (thee) king. 216. **wink'st,** shuts the eyes. 217. **distinctly,** with separate and individual sounds. 221. **Trebles thee o'er,** makes thee three times as great. **standing water,** water which neither flows nor ebbs. 224. **purpose,** i.e., of being king. 225. **stripping it,** stripping off all pretense, revealing it. 226. **Ebbing men,** men whose fortunes ebb, leaving them stranded. 229. **setting,** set expression. 230. **matter,** matter of importance. 231. **throes,** pains. 232. **this lord,** Gonzalo. **remembrance,** power of remembering. 234. **earth'd,** buried. 236. **Professes to persuade,** he was a privy councilor. 240. **that way,** i.e., in regard to Ferdinand's being saved. 242-243. **Ambition . . . there,** ambition itself cannot see any further than that hope (of the crown) without doubting the reality of the objects it sees. 247. **Ten . . . life,** it would take more than a lifetime to get there. 248. **note,** intimation. **post,** messenger. 249-250. **till . . . razorable,** till babies born today will be old enough to shave. **from,** on our voyage from. 251. **cast,** were disgorged, with pun on *casting* (of parts for a play). 254. **discharge,** performance, i.e., to get done. 259.

Enter Ariel [*invisible*], *with music and song.*

Ari. My master through his art foresees the danger
That you, his friend, are in; and sends me forth—
For else his project dies—to keep them living.
Sings in Gonzalo's ear.

While you here do snoring lie,
Open-ey'd conspiracy
His time doth take.
If of life you keep a care,
Shake off slumber, and beware:
Awake, awake!

Ant. Then let us both be sudden.
Gon. [*Wakes*] Now, good angels
Preserve the king. [*The others wake.*]
Alon. Why, how now? ho, awake! Why are you drawn?
Wherefore this ghastly looking?
Gon. What 's the matter?
Seb. Whiles we stood here securing your repose,
Even now, we heard a hollow burst of bellowing
Like bulls, or rather lions: did 't not wake you?
It struck mine ear most terribly.
Alon. I heard nothing.
Ant. O, 'twas a din to fright a monster's ear,
To make an earthquake! sure, it was the roar
Of a whole herd of lions.
Alon. Heard you this, Gonzalo?
Gon. Upon mine honour, sir, I heard a humming,
And that a strange one too, which did awake me:
I shak'd you, sir, and cried: as mine eyes open'd,
I saw their weapons drawn: there was a noise,
That 's verily. 'Tis best we stand upon our guard,
Or that we quit this place: let 's draw our weapons.
Alon. Lead off this ground; and let 's make further search
For my poor son.
Gon. Heavens keep him from these beasts!
For he is, sure, i' th' island.
Alon. Lead away.
Ari. Prospero my lord shall know what I have done:
So, king, go safely on to seek thy son. *Exeunt.*

Scene II. [*Another part of the island.*]

Enter Caliban *with a burden of wood. A noise of thunder heard.*

Cal. All the infections that the sun sucks up
From bogs, fens, flats, on Prosper fall and make him
By inch-meal a disease! His spirits hear me
And yet I needs must curse. But they'll nor pinch,
Fright me with urchin-shows, pitch me i' th' mire,
Nor lead me, like a firebrand, in the dark
Out of my way, unless he bid 'em; but
For every trifle are they set upon me;
Sometime like apes that mow and chatter at me
And after bite me, then like hedgehogs which
Lie tumbling in my barefoot way and mount
Their pricks at my footfall; sometime am I
All wound with adders who with cloven tongues
Do hiss me into madness.

Enter Trinculo.

Lo, now, lo!
Here comes a spirit of his, and to torment me
For bringing wood in slowly. I'll fall flat;
Perchance he will not mind me. [*Lies down.*]

Trin. Here 's neither bush nor shrub, to bear off any weather at all, and another storm brewing; I hear it sing i' the wind: yond same black cloud, yond huge one, looks like a foul bombard that would shed his liquor. If it should thunder as it did before, I know not where to hide my head: yond same cloud cannot choose but fall by pailfuls. What have we here? a man or a fish? dead or alive? A fish: he smells like a fish; a very ancient and fish-like smell; a kind of not of the newest Poor-John. A strange fish! Were I in England now, as once I was, and had but this fish painted, not a holiday fool there but would give a piece of silver: there would this monster make a man; any strange beast there makes a man: when they will not give a doit to relieve a lame beggar, they will lay out ten to see a dead Indian. Legged like a man! and his fins like arms! Warm o' my troth! I do now let loose my opinion; hold it no longer: this is no fish, but an islander, that hath lately suffered by a thunderbolt. [*Thunder.*] Alas, the storm is come again! my best way is to creep under his gaberdine; there is no other shelter hereabout: misery acquaints a man with strange bed-fellows. I will here shroud till the dregs of the storm be past. [*Creeps under Caliban's garment.*]

Enter Stephano, *singing* [, *a bottle in his hand*].

Ste. I shall no more to sea, to sea,
Here shall I die ashore—
This is a very scurvy tune to sing at a man's funeral: well, here 's my comfort. *Drinks.*
[*Sings.*]
The master, the swabber, the boatswain and I,
The gunner and his mate
Lov'd Mall, Meg and Marian and Margery,
But none of us car'd for Kate;
For she had a tongue with a tang,
Would cry to a sailor, Go hang!
She lov'd not the savour of tar nor of pitch,
Yet a tailor might scratch her where'er she did itch:
Then to sea, boys, and let her go hang!

This is a scurvy tune too: but here 's my comfort. *Drinks.*

Cal. Do not torment me: Oh!

Ste. What 's the matter? Have we devils here? Do you put tricks upon 's with savages and men of Ind, ha? I have not 'scaped drowning to be afeard now of your four legs; for it hath been said, As proper a man as ever went on four legs cannot make him give

Measure us, find (her) way. 259-260. **Keep . . . wake,** let her stay in Tunis, and let Sebastian wake (to his good fortune). 265-266. **I . . . chat,** I could teach a jackdaw to talk as wisely. 269. **content,** desire, contentment. 270. **Tender,** provide for; or, regard. 273. **feater,** more becomingly. 276. **kibe,** sore on the heel. 279. **candied,** frozen, congealed. 289. **tell the clock,** answer appropriately. 302. **time,** opportunity. 306. **sudden,** swift in action. 317. **humming,** i.e., Ariel's song.

Scene ii. 3. **inch-meal,** little by little. 9. **mow,** make faces. 19. **bear off,** keep off. 22. **foul bombard,** dirty leathern bottle. 29. **Poor-John,** salted hake, type of poor fare. **fish.** Malone cites a license issued by the Master of the Revels (1632) "to shew a strange fish for half a yeare." 30. **painted,** i.e., on a sign set up outside a booth or tent at a fair. 33. **make a man,** i.e., make his fortune. 35. **doit,** small coin. 40. **gaberdine,** cloak, loose upper garment. 43. **shroud,** take shelter. **dregs,** last remains. 61. **Ind,** India, or, vaguely, the East.

ground; and it shall be said so again while Stephano breathes at' nostrils.

Cal. The spirit torments me; Oh!

Ste. This is some monster of the isle with four legs, who hath got, as I take it, an ague. Where the devil should he learn our language? I will give him some relief, if it be but for that. If I can recover him and keep him tame and get to Naples with him, he 's a present for any emperor that ever trod on neat's-leather.

Cal. Do not torment me, prithee; I'll bring my wood home faster.

Ste. He 's in his fit now and does not talk after the wisest. He shall taste of my bottle: if he have never drunk wine afore, it will go near to remove his fit. If I can recover him and keep him tame, I will not take too much for him; he shall pay for him that hath him, and that soundly.

Cal. Thou dost me yet but little hurt; thou wilt anon, I know it by thy trembling: now Prosper works upon thee.

Ste. Come on your ways; open your mouth; here is that which will give language to you, cat: open your mouth; this will shake your shaking, I can tell you, and that soundly. [*Gives Caliban drink.*] You cannot tell who 's your friend: open your chaps again.

Trin. I should know that voice: it should be—but he is drowned; and these are devils: O defend me!

Ste. Four legs and two voices: a most delicate monster! His forward voice now is to speak well of his friend; his backward voice is to utter foul speeches and to detract. If all the wine in my bottle will recover him, I will help his ague. Come. [*Gives drink.*] Amen! I will pour some in thy other mouth.

Trin. Stephano!

Ste. Doth thy other mouth call me? Mercy, mercy! This is a devil, and no monster: I will leave him; I have no long spoon.

Trin. Stephano! If thou beest Stephano, touch me and speak to me; for I am Trinculo—be not afeard—thy good friend Trinculo.

Ste. If thou beest Trinculo, come forth: I'll pull thee by the lesser legs: if any be Trinculo's legs, these are they. [*Pulls him out.*] Thou art very Trinculo indeed! How camest thou to be the siege of this moon-calf? can he vent Trinculos?

Trin. I took him to be killed with a thunder-stroke. But art thou not drowned, Stephano? I hope now thou art not drowned. Is the storm overblown? I hid me under the dead moon-calf's gaberdine for fear of the storm. And art thou living, Stephano? O Stephano, two Neapolitans 'scaped!

Ste. Prithee, do not turn me about; my stomach is not constant.

Cal. [*Aside*] These be fine things, an if they be not
sprites.
That 's a brave god and bears celestial liquor.
I will kneel to him.

Ste. How didst thou 'scape? How camest thou hither? swear by this bottle how thou camest hither. I escaped upon a butt of sack which the sailors heaved o'erboard—by this bottle, which I made of the bark of a tree with mine own hands since I was cast ashore.

Cal. I'll swear upon that bottle to be thy true subject; for the liquor is not earthly.

Ste. Here; swear then how thou escapedst.

Trin. Swum ashore, man, like a duck: I can swim like a duck, I'll be sworn.

Ste. Here, kiss the book. Though thou canst swim like a duck, thou art made like a goose. [*Gives drink.*]

Trin. O Stephano, hast any more of this?

Ste. The whole butt, man: my cellar is in a rock by the sea-side where my wine is hid. How now, moon-calf! how does thine ague?

Cal. Hast thou not dropp'd from heaven?

Ste. Out o' the moon, I do assure thee: I was the man i' the moon when time was.

Cal. I have seen thee in her and I do adore thee:
My mistress show'd me thee and thy dog and thy
bush.

Ste. Come, swear to that; kiss the book: I will furnish it anon with new contents: swear. [*Gives drink.*]

Trin. By this good light, this is a very shallow monster! I afeard of him! A very weak monster! The man i' the moon! A most poor credulous monster! Well drawn, monster, in good sooth!

Cal. I'll show thee every fertile inch o' th' island;
And I will kiss thy foot: I prithee, be my god.

Trin. By this light, a most perfidious and drunken monster! when 's god 's asleep, he'll rob his bottle.

Cal. I'll kiss thy foot; I'll swear myself thy subject.

Ste. Come on then; down, and swear.

Trin. I shall laugh myself to death at this puppy-headed monster. A most scurvy monster! I could find in my heart to beat him,—

Ste. Come, kiss.

Trin. But that the poor monster 's in drink: an abominable monster!

Cal. I'll show thee the best springs; I'll pluck thee
berries;
I'll fish for thee and get thee wood enough.
A plague upon the tyrant that I serve!
I'll bear him no more sticks, but follow thee,
Thou wondrous man.

Trin. A most ridiculous monster, to make a wonder of a poor drunkard!

Cal. I prithee, let me bring thee where crabs grow;
And I with my long nails will dig thee pig-nuts;
Show thee a jay's nest and instruct thee how
To snare the nimble marmoset; I'll bring thee
To clust'ring filberts and sometimes I'll get thee
Young scamels from the rock. Wilt thou go with me?

Ste. I prithee now, lead the way without any more talking. Trinculo, the king and all our company else being drowned, we will inherit here: here; bear my bottle: fellow Trinculo, we'll fill him by and by again.

Cal. (*Sings drunkenly*)
Farewell, master; farewell, farewell!

Trin. A howling monster; a drunken monster!

Cal. No more dams I'll make for fish;
Nor fetch in firing

71. **recover,** restore. 73. **neat's-leather,** leather from the skin of an ox or cow. 80. **take too much,** i.e., no sum can be too much. 83. **trembling,** suggestion of demonic possession. 87. **cat . . . mouth,** allusion to the proverb, "Good liquor will make a cat speak." 103. **long spoon,** allusion to the proverb, "He that sups with the devil has need of a long spoon." 111. **siege,** excrement. **moon-calf,** monster, abortion (supposed to be caused by the influence of the moon). 120. **not constant,** unsteady. 126. **butt of sack,** barrel of Canary wine. 134. **kiss the book.** He gives him the bottle instead of the Bible on which to make his oath. 142. **when time was,** once upon a time. 144. **dog . . . bush.** See *A Midsummer Night's Dream*, V, i, 136. 150. **Well drawn.** Caliban takes a good draft of the wine. 171. **crabs,** crab

At requiring;
Nor scrape trenchering, nor wash dish:
'Ban, 'Ban, Cacaliban
Has a new master: get a new man.
Freedom, hey-day! hey-day, freedom! freedom, hey-day, freedom!
Ste. O brave monster! Lead the way. *Exeunt.*

ACT III.

SCENE I. [*Before* PROSPERO'S *cell.*]

Enter FERDINAND, *bearing a log.*

Fer. There be some sports are painful, and their labour
Delight in them sets off: some kinds of baseness
Are nobly undergone and most poor matters
Point to rich ends. This my mean task
Would be as heavy to me as odious, but
The mistress which I serve quickens what 's dead
And makes my labours pleasures: O, she is
Ten times more gentle than her father 's crabbed,
And he 's compos'd of harshness. I must remove
Some thousands of these logs and pile them up,
Upon a sore injunction: my sweet mistress
Weeps when she sees me work, and says, such baseness
Had never like executor. I forget:
But these sweet thoughts do even refresh my labours,
†Most busy lest, when I do it.

Enter MIRANDA; *and* PROSPERO [*at a distance, unseen*].

Mir. Alas, now, pray you,
Work not so hard: I would the lightning had
Burnt up those logs that you are enjoin'd to pile!
Pray, set it down and rest you: when this burns,
'Twill weep for having wearied you. My father
Is hard at study; pray now, rest yourself;
He 's safe for these three hours.
Fer. O most dear mistress,
The sun will set before I shall discharge
What I must strive to do.
Mir. If you'll sit down,
I'll bear your logs the while: pray, give me that;
I'll carry it to the pile.
Fer. No, precious creature;
I had rather crack my sinews, break my back,
Than you should such dishonour undergo,
While I sit lazy by.
Mir. It would become me
As well as it does you: and I should do it
With much more ease; for my good will is to it,
And yours it is against.
Pros. [*Aside*] Poor worm, thou art infected!
This visitation shows it.
Mir. You look wearily.
Fer. No, noble mistress; 'tis fresh morning with me
When you are by at night. I do beseech you—
Chiefly that I might set it in my prayers—
What is your name?
Mir. Miranda.—O my father,
I have broke your hest to say so!
Fer. Admir'd Miranda!
Indeed the top of admiration! worth
What 's dearest to the world! Full many a lady
I have ey'd with best regard and many a time
Th' harmony of their tongues hath into bondage
Brought my too diligent ear: for several virtues
Have I lik'd several women; never any
With so full soul, but some defect in her
Did quarrel with the noblest grace she ow'd
And put it to the foil: but you, O you,
So perfect and so peerless, are created
Of every creature's best!
Mir. I do not know
One of my sex; no woman's face remember,
Save, from my glass, mine own; nor have I seen
More that I may call men than you, good friend,
And my dear father: how features are abroad,
I am skilless of; but, by my modesty,
The jewel in my dower, I would not wish
Any companion in the world but you,
Nor can imagination form a shape,
Besides yourself, to like of. But I prattle
Something too wildly and my father's precepts
I therein do forget.
Fer. I am in my condition
A prince, Miranda; I do think, a king;
I would, not so!—and would no more endure
This wooden slavery than to suffer
The flesh-fly blow my mouth. Hear my soul speak:
The very instant that I saw you, did
My heart fly to your service; there resides,
To make me slave to it; and for your sake
Am I this patient log-man.
Mir. Do you love me?
Fer. O heaven, O earth, bear witness to this sound
And crown what I profess with kind event
If I speak true! if hollowly, invert
What best is boded me to mischief! I
Beyond all limit of what else i' th' world
Do love, prize, honour you.
Mir. I am a fool
To weep at what I am glad of.
Pros. [*Aside*] Fair encounter
Of two most rare affections! Heavens rain grace
On that which breeds between 'em!
Fer. Wherefore weep you?
Mir. At mine unworthiness that dare not offer
What I desire to give, and much less take
What I shall die to want. But this is trifling;
And all the more it seeks to hide itself,
The bigger bulk it shows. Hence, bashful cunning!
And prompt me, plain and holy innocence!
I am your wife, if you will marry me;
If not, I'll die your maid: to be your fellow
You may deny me; but I'll be your servant,
Whether you will or no.
Fer. My mistress, dearest;
And I thus humble ever.
Mir. My husband, then?

apples. 172. **pig-nuts,** earth-chestnuts. 174. **marmoset,** small monkey. 176. **scamels,** not explained. Keightley conjectured *seamels* (sea-gulls); Theobald: *stannels* (kestrels); New Cambridge editors call attention to the fact that "seamews" occurs in Strachey's letter. 179. **inherit,** take possession. 187. **trenchering,** trenchers, wooden plates.

ACT III. SCENE I. 11. **sore,** grievous, severe. 15. **Most . . . lest,** unexplained; Spedding suggests *Most busiest when idlest;* New Cambridge editors suggest *busy-idlest,* employed in trifles. 45. **ow'd,** owned. 46. **put . . . foil,** disgraced it; a wrestling phrase. 53. **skilless,** ignorant. 70. **hollowly,** insincerely, falsely.

Fer. Ay, with a heart as willing
As bondage e'er of freedom: here 's my hand.
Mir. And mine, with my heart in 't: and now farewell
Till half an hour hence.
Fer. A thousand thousand!
Exeunt [*Fer. and Mir. severally*].
Pros. So glad of this as they I cannot be,
Who are surpris'd withal; but my rejoicing
At nothing can be more. I'll to my book,
For yet ere supper-time must I perform
Much business appertaining. *Exit.*

SCENE II. [*Another part of the island.*]

Enter CALIBAN, STEPHANO, *and* TRINCULO.

Ste. Tell not me; when the butt is out, we will drink water; not a drop before: therefore bear up, and board 'em. Servant-monster, drink to me.

Trin. Servant-monster! the folly of this island! They say there 's but five upon this isle: we are three of them; if th' other two be brained like us, the state totters.

Ste. Drink, servant-monster, when I bid thee: thy eyes are almost set in thy head.

Trin. Where should they be set else? he were a brave monster indeed, if they were set in his tail.

Ste. My man-monster hath drown'd his tongue in sack: for my part, the sea cannot drown me; I swam, ere I could recover the shore, five and thirty leagues off and on. By this light, thou shalt be my lieutenant, monster, or my standard.

Trin. Your lieutenant, if you list; he 's no standard.

Ste. We'll not run, Monsieur Monster.

Trin. Nor go neither; but you'll lie like dogs and yet say nothing neither.

Ste. Moon-calf, speak once in thy life, if thou beest a good moon-calf.

Cal. How does thy honour? Let me lick thy shoe.
I'll not serve him; he is not valiant.

Trin. Thou liest, most ignorant monster: I am in case to justle a constable. Why, thou deboshed fish, thou, was there ever man a coward that hath drunk so much sack as I to-day? Wilt thou tell a monstrous lie, being but half a fish and half a monster?

Cal. Lo, how he mocks me! wilt thou let him, my lord?

Trin. 'Lord' quoth he. That a monster should be such a natural!

Cal. Lo, lo, again! bite him to death, I prithee.

Ste. Trinculo, keep a good tongue in your head: if you prove a mutineer,—the next tree! The poor monster 's my subject and he shall not suffer indignity.

Cal. I thank my noble lord. Wilt thou be pleased to hearken once again to the suit I made to thee?

Ste. Marry, will I: kneel and repeat it; I will stand, and so shall Trinculo.

Enter ARIEL, *invisible.*

Cal. As I told thee before, I am subject to a tyrant, a sorcerer, that by his cunning hath cheated me of the island.

Ari. Thou liest.

Cal. Thou liest, thou jesting monkey, thou: I would my valiant master would destroy thee! I do not lie.

Ste. Trinculo, if you trouble him any more in 's tale, by this hand, I will supplant some of your teeth.

Trin. Why, I said nothing.

Ste. Mum, then, and no more. Proceed.

Cal. I say, by sorcery he got this isle;
From me he got it. If thy greatness will
Revenge it on him,—for I know thou dar'st,
But this thing dare not,—
Ste. That 's most certain.
Cal. Thou shalt be lord of it and I'll serve thee.
Ste. How now shall this be compass'd?
Canst thou bring me to the party?
Cal. Yea, yea, my lord: I'll yield him thee asleep,
Where thou mayst knock a nail into his head.
Ari. Thou liest; thou canst not.
Cal. What a pied ninny 's this! Thou scurvy patch!
I do beseech thy greatness, give him blows
And take his bottle from him: when that 's gone
He shall drink nought but brine; for I'll not show him
Where the quick freshes are.

Ste. Trinculo, run into no further danger: interrupt the monster one word further, and, by this hand, I'll turn my mercy out o' doors and make a stock-fish of thee.

Trin. Why, what did I? I did nothing. I'll go farther off.

Ste. Didst thou not say he lied?

Ari. Thou liest.

Ste. Do I so? take thou that. [*Beats Trin.*] As you like this, give me the lie another time.

Trin. I did not give the lie. Out o' your wits and hearing too? A pox o' your bottle! this can sack and drinking do. A murrain on your monster, and the devil take your fingers!

Cal. Ha, ha, ha!

Ste. Now, forward with your tale. [*To Trin.*] Prithee, stand further off.

Cal. Beat him enough: after a little time
I'll beat him too.
Ste. Stand farther. Come, proceed.
Cal. Why, as I told thee, 'tis a custom with him,
I' th' afternoon to sleep: there thou mayst brain him,
Having first seiz'd his books, or with a log
Batter his skull, or paunch him with a stake,
Or cut his wezand with thy knife. Remember
First to possess his books; for without them
He 's but a sot, as I am, nor hath not
One spirit to command: they all do hate him
As rootedly as I. Burn but his books.
He has brave utensils,—for so he calls them,—
Which, when he has a house, he'll deck withal.
And that most deeply to consider is
The beauty of his daughter; he himself
Calls her a nonpareil: I never saw a woman,
But only Sycorax my dam and she;
But she as far surpasseth Sycorax
As great'st does least.

SCENE II. 3. **bear up,** put the helm up so as to bring the ship into the wind. **board 'em,** climb aboard; both phrases refer to drinking. 10. **thy eyes . . . head,** current description of drunkenness meaning that the eyes are fixed in a stare, or dimmed by drink. 19. **standard,** standard-bearer. 20. **standard,** something that stands up. 29. **case,** condition. 30. **deboshed,** debauched. 37. **natural,** idiot. 71. **pied ninny,** fool in motley. **patch,** common word for *fool*. 75. **quick freshes,** running springs. 79. **stock-fish,** dried cod beaten before boiling. 88. **murrain,** plague. 99. **wezand,** windpipe. 101. **sot,** fool. 108. **nonpareil,** one having no equal. 126. **troll the catch,** sing the

Ste. Is it so brave a lass?

Cal. Ay, lord; she will become thy bed, I warrant.
And bring thee forth brave brood.

Ste. Monster, I will kill this man: his daughter and I will be king and queen,—save our graces!—and Trinculo and thyself shall be viceroys. Dost thou like the plot, Trinculo?

Trin. Excellent.

Ste. Give me thy hand: I am sorry I beat thee; but, while thou livest, keep a good tongue in thy head.

Cal. Within this half hour will he be asleep:
Wilt thou destroy him then?

Ste. Ay, on mine honour.

Ari. This will I tell my master.

Cal. Thou mak'st me merry; I am full of pleasure:
Let us be jocund: will you troll the catch
You taught me but while-ere?

Ste. At thy request, monster, I will do reason, any reason. Come on, Trinculo, let us sing. *Sings.*

Flout 'em and scout 'em
And scout 'em and flout 'em;
Thought is free.

Cal. That 's not the tune.

Ariel plays the tune on a tabor and pipe.

Ste. What is this same?

Trin. This is the tune of our catch, played by the picture of Nobody.

Ste. If thou beest a man, show thyself in thy likeness: if thou beest a devil, take 't as thou list.

Trin. O, forgive me my sins!

Ste. He that dies pays all debts: I defy thee. Mercy upon us!

Cal. Art thou afeard?

Ste. No, monster, not I.

Cal. Be not afeard; the isle is full of noises,
Sounds and sweet airs, that give delight and hurt not.
Sometimes a thousand twangling instruments
Will hum about mine ears, and sometime voices
That, if I then had wak'd after long sleep,
Will make me sleep again: and then, in dreaming,
The clouds methought would open and show riches
Ready to drop upon me, that, when I wak'd,
I cried to dream again.

Ste. This will prove a brave kingdom to me, where I shall have my music for nothing.

Cal. When Prospero is destroyed.

Ste. That shall be by and by: I remember the story.

Trin. The sound is going away; let 's follow it, and after do our work.

Ste. Lead, monster; we'll follow. I would I could see this taborer; he lays it on.

Trin. Wilt come? I'll follow, Stephano. *Exeunt.*

SCENE III. [*Another part of the island.*]

Enter ALONSO, SEBASTIAN, ANTONIO, GONZALO, ADRIAN, FRANCISCO, *&c.*

Gon. By 'r lakin, I can go no further, sir;
My old bones ache: here 's a maze trod indeed
Through forth-rights and meanders! By your patience,
I needs must rest me.

Alon. Old lord, I cannot blame thee,
Who am myself attach'd with weariness,
To th' dulling of my spirits: sit down, and rest.
Even here I will put off my hope and keep it
No longer for my flatterer: he is drown'd
Whom thus we stray to find, and the sea mocks
Our frustrate search on land. Well, let him go.

Ant. [*Aside to Seb.*] I am right glad that he 's so out of hope.
Do not, for one repulse, forego the purpose
That you resolv'd t' effect.

Seb. [*Aside to Ant.*] The next advantage
Will we take throughly.

Ant. [*Aside to Seb.*] Let it be to-night;
For, now they are oppress'd with travel, they
Will not, nor cannot, use such vigilance
As when they are fresh.

Seb. [*Aside to Ant.*] I say, to-night: no more.

Solemn and strange music.

Alon. What harmony is this? My good friends, hark!

Gon. Marvellous sweet music!

[*Enter*] PROSPERO *on the top, invisible. Enter several strange Shapes, bringing in a banquet; they dance about it with gentle actions of salutations; and, inviting the King, &c. to eat, they depart.*

Alon. Give us kind keepers, heavens! What were these?

Seb. A living drollery. Now I will believe
That there are unicorns, that in Arabia
There is one tree, the phœnix' throne, one phœnix
At this hour reigning there.

Ant. I'll believe both;
And what does else want credit, come to me,
And I'll be sworn 'tis true: travellers ne'er did lie,
Though fools at home condemn 'em.

Gon. If in Naples
I should report this now, would they believe me?
If I should say, I saw such islanders—
For, certes, these are people of the island—
Who, though they are of monstrous shape, yet, note,
Their manners are more gentle-kind than of
Our human generation you shall find
Many, nay, almost any.

Pros. [*Aside*] Honest lord,
Thou hast said well; for some of you there present
Are worse than devils.

Alon. I cannot too much muse
Such shapes, such gesture and such sound, expressing,
Although they want the use of tongue, a kind
Of excellent dumb discourse.

Pros. [*Aside*] Praise in departing.

Fran. They vanish'd strangely.

Seb. No matter, since
They have left their viands behind; for we have stomachs.
Will 't please you taste of what is here?

Alon. Not I.

Gon. Faith, sir, you need not fear. When we were boys,
Who would believe that there were mountaineers

---

round. 127. **while-ere,** a while since. 130. **scout,** deride. New Cambridge editors emend, *cout* (befool). 133. *Stage Direction:* **tabor,** small drum. 136. **picture of Nobody,** a figure with head, arms, and legs, but no trunk, used by John Trundle, bookseller and printer.

SCENE III. 1. **By 'r lakin,** by our Lady. 3. **forth-rights and meanders,** paths straight and crooked. 19. *Stage Direction:* **on the top,** in the gallery above the stage or some higher point. 20. **keepers,** guardian angels. 21. **drollery,** puppet show. 30. **certes,** certainly. 39. **Praise in departing.** Save your praise until the end of the performance.

Dew-lapp'd like bulls, whose throats had hanging at 'em
Wallets of flesh? or that there were such men
Whose heads stood in their breasts? which now we find
Each putter-out of five for one will bring us
Good warrant of.
Alon. I will stand to and feed,
Although my last: no matter, since I feel
The best is past. Brother, my lord the duke,
Stand to and do as we.

Thunder and lightning. Enter ARIEL, *like a harpy; claps his wings upon the table; and, with a quaint device, the banquet vanishes.*

Ari. You are three men of sin, whom Destiny,
That hath to instrument this lower world
And what is in 't, the never-surfeited sea
Hath caus'd to belch up you; and on this island
Where man doth not inhabit; you 'mongst men
Being most unfit to live. I have made you mad;
And even with such-like valour men hang and drown
Their proper selves. [*Alon., Seb. &c. draw their swords.*]
You fools! I and my fellows
Are ministers of Fate: the elements,
Of whom your swords are temper'd, may as well
Wound the loud winds, or with bemock'd-at stabs
Kill the still-closing waters, as diminish
One dowle that 's in my plume: my fellow-ministers
Are like invulnerable. If you could hurt,
Your swords are now too massy for your strengths
And will not be uplifted. But remember—
For that 's my business to you—that you three
From Milan did supplant good Prospero;
Expos'd unto the sea, which hath requit it,
Him and his innocent child: for which foul deed
The pow'rs, delaying, not forgetting, have
Incens'd the seas and shores, yea, all the creatures,
Against your peace. Thee of thy son, Alonso,
They have bereft; and do pronounce by me
Ling'ring perdition, worse than any death
Can be at once, shall step by step attend
You and your ways; whose wraths to guard you from—
Which here, in this most desolate isle, else falls
Upon your heads—is nothing but heart's sorrow
And a clear life ensuing.

He vanishes in thunder; then, to soft music, enter the Shapes again, and dance, with mocks and mows, and carrying out the table.

Pros. Bravely the figure of this harpy hast thou
Perform'd, my Ariel; a grace it had, devouring:
Of my instruction hast thou nothing bated
In what thou hadst to say: so, with good life
And observation strange, my meaner ministers
Their several kinds have done. My high charms work
And these mine enemies are all knit up
In their distractions; they now are in my pow'r;
And in these fits I leave them, while I visit
Young Ferdinand, whom they suppose is drown'd,
And his and mine lov'd darling. [*Exit above.*]
Gon. I' th' name of something holy, sir, why stand you
In this strange stare?
Alon. O, it is monstrous, monstrous!
Methought the billows spoke and told me of it;
The winds did sing it to me, and the thunder,
That deep and dreadful organ-pipe, pronounc'd
The name of Prosper: it did bass my trespass.
Therefore my son i' th' ooze is bedded, and
I'll seek him deeper than e'er plummet sounded
And with him there lie mudded. *Exit.*
Seb. But one fiend at a time,
I'll fight their legions o'er.
Ant. I'll be thy second.
Exeunt [*Seb. and Ant.*].
Gon. All three of them are desperate: their great guilt,
Like poison given to work a great time after,
Now 'gins to bite the spirits. I do beseech you
That are of suppler joints, follow them swiftly
And hinder them from what this ecstasy
May now provoke them to.
Adr. Follow, I pray you. *Exeunt omnes.*

ACT IV.

SCENE I. [*Before* PROSPERO'S *cell.*]

Enter PROSPERO, FERDINAND, *and* MIRANDA.

Pros. If I have too austerely punish'd you,
Your compensation makes amends, for I
Have given you here a third of mine own life,
Or that for which I live; who once again
I tender to thy hand: all thy vexations
Were but my trials of thy love, and thou
Hast strangely stood the test: here, afore Heaven,
I ratify this my rich gift. O Ferdinand,
Do not smile at me that I boast her off,
For thou shalt find she will outstrip all praise
And make it halt behind her.
Fer. I do believe it
Against an oracle.
Pros. Then, as my gift and thine own acquisition
Worthily purchas'd, take my daughter: but
If thou dost break her virgin-knot before
All sanctimonious ceremonies may
With full and holy rite be minist'red,
No sweet aspersion shall the heavens let fall
To make this contract grow; but barren hate,
Sour-ey'd disdain and discord shall bestrew
The union of your bed with weeds so loathly
That you shall hate it both: therefore take heed,
As Hymen's lamps shall light you.

45. **Dew-lapp'd,** having a dewlap, or fold of skin hanging from the neck, as cattle; often supposed to refer to people afflicted with goiter. 48. **putter-out . . . one,** one who invests money, or gambles on the risks of travel on the condition that, if he returns safely, he is to receive five times the amount deposited; hence, any traveler. 52. *Stage Direction: **harpy,*** a fabulous monster with a woman's face and vulture's body supposed to be a minister of divine vengeance. ***quaint device,*** ingenious stage contrivance. 54. **to,** as. 59. **such-like valour,** i.e., the reckless valor derived from madness. 62. **temper'd,** composed. 64. **still-closing,** always closing again when parted. 65. **dowle,** soft, fine feather. **plume,** plumage (?) (Onions). 66. **like,** likewise, similarly. **If,** even if. 71. **requit,** requited, avenged. 82. **clear,** unspotted, innocent. 84. **devouring,** i.e., ravishing (?). 85. **bated,** abated, diminished. 86. **so . . . life,** with faithful reproduction. 87. **observation strange,** rare attention to detail. **meaner,** i.e., subordinate to Ariel. 99. **bass my trespass,** proclaimed my trespass like a bass note in music. 106. **bite the spirits,** i.e., conscience troubles them.

ACT IV. SCENE I. 7. **strangely,** extraordinarily. 12. **Against an oracle,** even if an oracle should declare otherwise. 16. **sanctimonious,** sacred. 18. **aspersion,** dew, shower. 23. **Hymen's.** Hymen was the

Fer. As I hope
For quiet days, fair issue and long life,
With such love as 'tis now, the murkiest den,
The most opportune place, the strong'st suggestion
Our worser genius can, shall never melt
Mine honour into lust, to take away
The edge of that day's celebration
When I shall think, or Phœbus' steeds are founder'd,
Or Night kept chain'd below.
Pros. Fairly spoke.
Sit then and talk with her; she is thine own.
What, Ariel! my industrious servant, Ariel!

Enter ARIEL.

Ari. What would my potent master? here I am.
Pros. Thou and thy meaner fellows your last service
Did worthily perform; and I must use you
In such another trick. Go bring the rabble,
O'er whom I give thee pow'r, here to this place:
Incite them to quick motion; for I must
Bestow upon the eyes of this young couple
Some vanity of mine art: it is my promise,
And they expect it from me.
Ari. Presently?
Pros. Ay, with a twink.
Ari. Before you can say 'come' and 'go,'
And breathe twice and cry 'so, so,'
Each one, tripping on his toe,
Will be here with mop and mow.
Do you love me, master? no?
Pros. Dearly, my delicate Ariel. Do not approach
Till thou dost hear me call.
Ari. Well, I conceive. *Exit.*
Pros. Look thou be true; do not give dalliance
Too much the rein: the strongest oaths are straw
To th' fire i' th' blood: be more abstemious,
Or else, good night your vow!
Fer. I warrant you, sir;
The white cold virgin snow upon my heart
Abates the ardour of my liver.
Pros. Well.
Now come, my Ariel! bring a corollary,
Rather than want a spirit: appear, and pertly!
No tongue! all eyes! be silent. *Soft music.*

Enter IRIS.

Iris. Ceres, most bounteous lady, thy rich leas
Of wheat, rye, barley, vetches, oats and pease;
Thy turfy mountains, where live nibbling sheep,
And flat meads thatch'd with stover, them to keep;
Thy banks with pioned and twilled brims,
Which spongy April at thy hest betrims,
To make cold nymphs chaste crowns; and thy broom-groves,
Whose shadow the dismissed bachelor loves,
Being lass-lorn; thy pole-clipt vineyard;
And thy sea-marge, sterile and rocky-hard,
Where thou thyself dost air;—the queen o' th' sky,
Whose wat'ry arch and messenger am I,
Bids thee leave these, and with her sovereign grace,
Juno descends.
Here on this grass-plot, in this very place,
To come and sport: her peacocks fly amain:
Approach, rich Ceres, her to entertain.

Enter CERES.

Cer. Hail, many-colour'd messenger, that ne'er
Dost disobey the wife of Jupiter;
Who with thy saffron wings upon my flow'rs
Diffusest honey-drops, refreshing show'rs,
And with each end of thy blue bow dost crown
My bosky acres and my unshrubb'd down,
Rich scarf to my proud earth; why hath thy queen
Summon'd me hither, to this short-grass'd green?
Iris. A contract of true love to celebrate;
And some donation freely to estate
On the blest lovers.
Cer. Tell me, heavenly bow,
If Venus or her son, as thou dost know,
Do now attend the queen? Since they did plot
The means that dusky Dis my daughter got,
Her and her blind boy's scandal'd company
I have forsworn.
Iris. Of her society
Be not afraid: I met her deity
Cutting the clouds towards Paphos and her son
Dove-drawn with her. Here thought they to have done
Some wanton charm upon this man and maid,
Whose vows are, that no bed-right shall be paid
Till Hymen's torch be lighted: but in vain;
Mars's hot minion is return'd again;
Her waspish-headed son has broke his arrows,
Swears he will shoot no more but play with sparrows
And be a boy right out.

[JUNO *alights.*]

Cer. Highest queen of state,
Great Juno, comes; I know her by her gait.
Juno. How does my bounteous sister? Go with me
To bless this twain, that they may prosperous be
And honour'd in their issue. *They sing:*

Juno. Honour, riches, marriage-blessing,
Long continuance, and increasing,
Hourly joys be still upon you!
Juno sings her blessings on you.

Cer. Earth's increase, foison plenty,
Barns and garners never empty,
Vines with clust'ring bunches growing,
Plants with goodly burthen bowing;

Spring come to you at the farthest
In the very end of harvest!
Scarcity and want shall shun you;
Ceres' blessing so is on you.

Greek and Roman god of marriage. 27. **genius,** evil genius, or evil attendant spirit. 30. **founder'd,** broken down, made lame. 37. **rabble,** band, i.e., the *meaner fellows* of line 35. 41. **vanity,** illusion. 47. **mop and mow,** gestures and grimaces. 56. **liver,** as the seat of the passions. 57. **corollary,** supernumerary. 58. **pertly,** briskly. 63. **stover,** fodder for cattle. 64. **pioned and twilled,** unexplained; excavated(?) or trenched(?) (Onions), ridged (New Cambridge), grown over with peonies and lilies (Hanmer). 66. **broom-groves,** groves of broom (?). 68. **pole-clipt,** hedged in with poles. 71. **wat'ry arch,** rainbow. 72. *Stage Direction:* ***Juno descends,*** i.e., starts her descent from the "heavens" above the stage (?). 74. **amain,** with full force or speed. 81. **bosky,** covered with shrubs. **unshrubb'd down,** shrubless upland. 89. **Dis . . . got.** Pluto, god of the infernal regions, carried off Persephone, daughter of Ceres, to be his bride in Hades. 90. **scandal'd,** scandalous. 93. **Paphos,** a town in the island of Cyprus, sacred to Venus. 98. **Mars's . . . minion,** Venus, the beloved of Mars. 99. **waspish-headed,** fiery, hot-headed (?). 110. **foison plenty,** plentiful harvest.

Fer. This is a most majestic vision, and
Harmonious charmingly. May I be bold
To think these spirits?
Pros. Spirits, which by mine art
I have from their confines call'd to enact
My present fancies.
Fer. Let me live here ever;
So rare a wond'red father and a wise
Makes this place Paradise.
Juno and Ceres whisper, and send Iris on employment.
Pros. Sweet, now, silence!
Juno and Ceres whisper seriously;
There 's something else to do: hush, and be mute,
Or else our spell is marr'd.
Iris. You nymphs, call'd Naiads, of the windring brooks,
With your sedg'd crowns and ever-harmless looks,
Leave your crisp channels and on this green land
Answer your summons; Juno does command:
Come, temperate nymphs, and help to celebrate
A contract of true love; be not too late.

Enter certain Nymphs.

You sunburnt sicklemen, of August weary,
Come hither from the furrow and be merry:
Make holiday; your rye-straw hats put on
And these fresh nymphs encounter every one
In country footing.

Enter certain Reapers, properly habited: they join with the Nymphs in a graceful dance; towards the end whereof PROSPERO *starts suddenly, and speaks; after which, to a strange, hollow, and confused noise, they heavily vanish.*

Pros. [*Aside*] I had forgot that foul conspiracy
Of the beast Caliban and his confederates
Against my life: the minute of their plot
Is almost come. [*To the Spirits.*] Well done! avoid; no more!
Fer. This is strange: your father 's in some passion
That works him strongly.
Mir. Never till this day
Saw I him touch'd with anger so distemper'd.
Pros. You do look, my son, in a mov'd sort,
As if you were dismay'd: be cheerful, sir.
Our revels now are ended. These our actors,
As I foretold you, were all spirits and
Are melted into air, into thin air:
And, like the baseless fabric of this vision,
The cloud-capp'd tow'rs, the gorgeous palaces,
The solemn temples, the great globe itself,
Yea, all which it inherit, shall dissolve
And, like this insubstantial pageant faded,
Leave not a rack behind. We are such stuff
As dreams are made on, and our little life
Is rounded with a sleep. Sir, I am vex'd;
Bear with my weakness; my old brain is troubled:
Be not disturb'd with my infirmity:
If you be pleas'd, retire into my cell
And there repose: a turn or two I'll walk,
To still my beating mind.
Fer. Mir. We wish your peace. *Exeunt.*
Pros. Come with a thought. I thank thee, Ariel: come.

Enter ARIEL.

Ari. Thy thoughts I cleave to. What 's thy pleasure?
Pros. Spirit,
We must prepare to meet with Caliban.
Ari. Ay, my commander: when I presented Ceres,
I thought to have told thee of it, but I fear'd
Lest I might anger thee.
Pros. Say again, where didst thou leave these varlets?
Ari. I told you, sir, they were red-hot with drinking;
So full of valour that they smote the air
For breathing in their faces; beat the ground
For kissing of their feet; yet always bending
Towards their project. Then I beat my tabor;
At which, like unback'd colts, they prick'd their ears,
Advanc'd their eyelids, lifted up their noses
As they smelt music: so I charm'd their ears
That calf-like they my lowing follow'd through
Tooth'd briers, sharp furzes, pricking goss and thorns,
Which ent'red their frail shins: at last I left them
I' th' filthy-mantled pool beyond your cell,
There dancing up to th' chins, that the foul lake
O'erstunk their feet.
Pros. This was well done, my bird.
Thy shape invisible retain thou still:
The trumpery in my house, go bring it hither,
For stale to catch these thieves.
Ari. I go, I go. *Exit.*
Pros. A devil, a born devil, on whose nature
Nurture can never stick; on whom my pains,
Humanely taken, all, all lost, quite lost;
And as with age his body uglier grows,
So his mind cankers. I will plague them all,
Even to roaring.

Enter ARIEL, *loaden with glistering apparel, &c.*

Come, hang them on this line.

[PROSPERO *and* ARIEL *remain, invisible.*] *Enter* CALIBAN, STEPHANO, *and* TRINCULO, *all wet.*

Cal. Pray you, tread softly, that the blind mole may not
Hear a foot fall: we now are near his cell.
Ste. Monster, your fairy, which you say is a harmless fairy, has done little better than played the Jack with us.
Trin. Monster, I do smell all horse-piss; at which my nose is in great indignation.
Ste. So is mine. Do you hear, monster? If I should take a displeasure against you, look you,—
Trin. Thou wert but a lost monster.
Cal. Good my lord, give me thy favour still.
Be patient, for the prize I'll bring thee to

123. **wond'red,** wonder-performing. 128. **windring,** wandering (?) or winding (?). 130. **crisp,** curled, rippled. 132. **temperate,** chaste. 138. **country footing,** country dancing. 142. **avoid,** depart, withdraw. 144. **works,** affects. 145. **distemper'd,** vexed. 146. **sort,** state, condition. 154. **it inherit,** occupy it. 156. **rack,** mass of cloud driven before the wind in the upper air (Onions). 164. **with a thought,** on the instant. 167. **presented,** acted the part of, or introduced. 176. **unback'd,** unbroken, unridden. 177. **Advanc'd,** lifted up. 180. **goss,** gorse, a prickly shrub. 182. **filthy-mantled,** covered with a vegetable coating, slimy. 184. **feet,** New Cambridge conjectures: *sweat.* **bird,** used as a term of endearment. 186. **trumpery,** cheap goods, the "glistering apparel" mentioned in the following stage direction. 187. **stale,** decoy. 193. **line,** probably, lime tree. 198. **played the Jack,** done a mean trick. *Jack* has a double meaning, "knave" and "will-o-the-wisp." 206. **hoodwink,** cover up; hawking term. 221. **king Stephano,** allusion to the old ballad beginning, "King Stephen was a worthy peer." 226. **frippery,** place where cast-off clothes are sold. 231. **luggage,** impedimenta, heavy stuff to be carried. 236. **jerkin,** jacket made of leather.

Shall hoodwink this mischance: therefore speak softly.
All 's hush'd as midnight yet.

Trin. Ay, but to lose our bottles in the pool,—

Ste. There is not only disgrace and dishonour in that, monster, but an infinite loss.

Trin. That 's more to me than my wetting: yet this is your harmless fairy, monster.

Ste. I will fetch off my bottle, though I be o'er ears for my labour.

Cal. Prithee, my king, be quiet. See'st thou here,
This is the mouth o' th' cell: no noise, and enter.
Do that good mischief which may make this island
Thine own for ever, and I, thy Caliban,
For aye thy foot-licker.

Ste. Give me thy hand. I do begin to have bloody thoughts.

Trin. O king Stephano! O peer! O worthy Stephano! look what a wardrobe here is for thee!

Cal. Let it alone, thou fool; it is but trash.

Trin. O, ho, monster! we know what belongs to a frippery. O king Stephano!

Ste. Put off that gown, Trinculo; by this hand, I'll have that gown.

Trin. Thy grace shall have it.

Cal. The dropsy drown this fool! what do you mean
To dote thus on such luggage? Let 's alone
And do the murder first: if he awake,
From toe to crown he'll fill our skins with pinches,
Make us strange stuff.

Ste. Be you quiet, monster. Mistress line, is not this my jerkin? [*Takes it down.*] Now is the jerkin under the line: now, jerkin, you are like to lose your hair and prove a bald jerkin.

Trin. Do, do: we steal by line and level, an 't like your grace.

Ste. I thank thee for that jest; here 's a garment for 't: wit shall not go unrewarded while I am king of this country. 'Steal by line and level' is an excellent pass of pate; there 's another garment for 't.

Trin. Monster, come, put some lime upon your fingers, and away with the rest.

Cal. I will have none on 't: we shall lose our time,
And all be turn'd to barnacles, or to apes
With foreheads villanous low.

Ste. Monster, lay to your fingers: help to bear this away where my hogshead of wine is, or I'll turn you out of my kingdom: go to, carry this.

Trin. And this.

Ste. Ay, and this.

A noise of hunters heard. Enter divers Spirits, in shape of dogs and hounds, hunting them about, PROSPERO *and* ARIEL *setting them on.*

Pros. Hey, Mountain, hey!

Ari. Silver! there it goes, Silver!

Pros. Fury, Fury! there, Tyrant, there! hark! hark!
[*Cal., Ste., and Trin. are driven out.*]
Go charge my goblins that they grind their joints
With dry convulsions, shorten up their sinews
With aged cramps, and more pinch-spotted make them
Than pard or cat o' mountain.

Ari. Hark, they roar!

Pros. Let them be hunted soundly. At this hour
Lies at my mercy all mine enemies:
Shortly shall all my labours end, and thou
Shalt have the air at freedom: for a little
Follow, and do me service. *Exeunt.*

ACT V.

SCENE I. [*Before* PROSPERO's *cell.*]

Enter PROSPERO *in his magic robes, and* ARIEL.

Pros. Now does my project gather to a head:
My charms crack not; my spirits obey; and time
Goes upright with his carriage. How 's the day?

Ari. On the sixth hour; at which time, my lord,
You said our work should cease.

Pros. I did say so,
When first I rais'd the tempest. Say, my spirit,
How fares the king and 's followers?

Ari. Confin'd together
In the same fashion as you gave in charge,
Just as you left them; all prisoners, sir,
In the line-grove which weather-fends your cell;
They cannot budge till your release. The king,
His brother and yours, abide all three distracted
And the remainder mourning over them,
Brimful of sorrow and dismay; but chiefly
Him that you term'd, sir, 'The good old lord, Gonzalo;'
His tears runs down his beard, like winter's drops
From eaves of reeds. Your charm so strongly works 'em
That if you now beheld them, your affections
Would become tender.

Pros. Dost thou think so, spirit?

Ari. Mine would, sir, were I human.

Pros. And mine shall.
Hast thou, which art but air, a touch, a feeling
Of their afflictions, and shall not myself,
One of their kind, that relish all as sharply,
Passion as they, be kindlier mov'd than thou art?
Though with their high wrongs I am struck to th' quick,
Yet with my nobler reason 'gainst my fury
Do I take part: the rarer action is
In virtue than in vengeance: they being penitent,
The sole drift of my purpose doth extend
Not a frown further. Go release them, Ariel:
My charms I'll break, their senses I'll restore,
And they shall be themselves.

Ari. I'll fetch them, sir. *Exit.*

Pros. Ye elves of hills, brooks, standing lakes and groves,
And ye that on the sands with printless foot
Do chase the ebbing Neptune and do fly him
When he comes back; you demi-puppets that

237. **under the line,** under the lime tree, with punning allusion, probably, to the equinoctial line. 238. **lose your hair,** a reference to tropical fevers experienced by seamen, causing loss of hair. 239. **by line and level,** i.e., by means of instruments, or, methodically, like dishonest carpenters and masons; with pun on *line,* above. 244. **pass of pate,** sally of wit. 246. **lime,** birdlime. 249. **barnacles,** barnacle geese, formerly supposed to be hatched from seashells attached to trees and to fall thence into the water; possibly, the ordinary meaning is intended. 260. **convulsions,** cramps. 262. **pard,** panther or leopard. **cat o' mountain,** wildcat.

ACT V. SCENE I. 2. **crack not,** are flawless (from alchemy). 3. **carriage,** burden; i.e., Time is unstooped, runs smoothly. **How 's the day?** What time is it? 10. **line-grove,** grove of lime trees. **weather-fends,** protects from the weather. 11. **your release,** you release them. 17. **eaves of reed,** thatch. 23. **all,** quite. 27. **rarer,** nobler. 33-57. **Ye . . . book.** This famous passage is an embellished paraphrase of Golding's translation of Ovid's *Metamorphoses*, vii, 197-219. 36. **demi-puppets,** elves and fairies; literally, puppets of half-size.

By moonshine do the green sour ringlets make,
Whereof the ewe not bites, and you whose pastime
Is to make midnight mushrumps, that rejoice
To hear the solemn curfew; by whose aid,
Weak masters though ye be, I have bedimm'd
The noontide sun, call'd forth the mutinous winds,
And 'twixt the green sea and the azur'd vault
Set roaring war: to the dread rattling thunder
Have I given fire and rifted Jove's stout oak
With his own bolt; the strong-bas'd promontory
Have I made shake and by the spurs pluck'd up
The pine and cedar: graves at my command
Have wak'd their sleepers, op'd, and let 'em forth
By my so potent art. But this rough magic
I here abjure, and, when I have requir'd
Some heavenly music, which even now I do,
To work mine end upon their senses that
This airy charm is for, I'll break my staff,
Bury it certain fathoms in the earth,
And deeper than did ever plummet sound
I'll drown my book. *Solemn music.*

Here enters ARIEL *before: then* ALONSO, *with a frantic gesture, attended by* GONZALO; SEBASTIAN *and* ANTONIO *in like manner, attended by* ADRIAN *and* FRANCISCO: *they all enter the circle which* PROSPERO *had made, and there stand charmed; which* PROSPERO *observing, speaks*:

A solemn air and the best comforter
To an unsettled fancy cure thy brains,
Now useless, boil'd within thy skull! There stand,
For you are spell-stopp'd.
Holy Gonzalo, honourable man,
Mine eyes, ev'n sociable to the show of thine,
Fall fellowly drops. The charm dissolves apace,
And as the morning steals upon the night,
Melting the darkness, so their rising senses
Begin to chase the ignorant fumes that mantle
Their clearer reason. O good Gonzalo,
My true preserver, and a loyal sir
To him thou follow'st! I will pay thy graces
Home both in word and deed. Most cruelly
Didst thou, Alonso, use me and my daughter:
Thy brother was a furtherer in the act.
Thou art pinch'd for 't now, Sebastian. Flesh and blood,
You, brother mine, that entertain'd ambition,
Expell'd remorse and nature; who, with Sebastian,
Whose inward pinches therefore are most strong,
Would here have kill'd your king; I do forgive thee,
Unnatural though thou art. Their understanding
Begins to swell, and the approaching tide
Will shortly fill the reasonable shore
That now lies foul and muddy. Not one of them
That yet looks on me, or would know me: Ariel,
Fetch me the hat and rapier in my cell:
I will discase me, and myself present
As I was sometime Milan: quickly, spirit;
Thou shalt ere long be free. [*Exit Ariel and return immediately.*]

ARIEL *sings and helps to attire him.*

Where the bee sucks, there suck I:
In a cowslip's bell I lie;
There I couch when owls do cry.
On the bat's back I do fly
After summer merrily.
Merrily, merrily shall I live now
Under the blossom that hangs on the bough.

Pros. Why, that 's my dainty Ariel! I shall miss thee;
But yet thou shalt have freedom: so, so, so.
To the king's ship, invisible as thou art:
There shalt thou find the mariners asleep
Under the hatches; the master and the boatswain
Being awake, enforce them to this place,
And presently, I prithee.
Ari. I drink the air before me, and return
Or ere your pulse twice beat. *Exit.*
Gon. All torment, trouble, wonder and amazement
Inhabits here: some heavenly power guide us
Out of this fearful country!
Pros. Behold, sir king,
The wronged Duke of Milan, Prospero:
For more assurance that a living prince
Does now speak to thee, I embrace thy body;
And to thee and thy company I bid
A hearty welcome.
Alon. Whe'r thou be'st he or no,
Or some enchanted trifle to abuse me,
As late I have been, I not know: thy pulse
Beats as of flesh and blood; and, since I saw thee,
Th' affliction of my mind amends, with which,
I fear, a madness held me: this must crave,
An if this be at all, a most strange story.
Thy dukedom I resign and do entreat
Thou pardon me my wrongs. But how should Prospero
Be living and be here?
Pros. First, noble friend,
Let me embrace thine age, whose honour cannot
Be measur'd or confin'd.
Gon. Whether this be
Or be not, I'll not swear.
Pros. You do yet taste
Some subtilties o' th' isle, that will not let you
Believe things certain. Welcome, my friends all!
[*Aside to Seb. and Ant.*] But you, my brace of lords, were I so minded,
I here could pluck his highness' frown upon you
And justify you traitors: at this time
I will tell no tales.
Seb. [*Aside*] The devil speaks in him.
Pros. No.
For you, most wicked sir, whom to call brother
Would even infect my mouth, I do forgive
Thy rankest fault; all of them; and require
My dukedom of thee, which perforce, I know,
Thou must restore.
Alon. If thou be'st Prospero,
Give us particulars of thy preservation;
How thou hast met us here, who three hours since
Were wrack'd upon this shore; where I have lost—
How sharp the point of this remembrance is!—
My dear son Ferdinand.
Pros. I am woe for 't, sir.
Alon. Irreparable is the loss, and Patience

37. **green sour ringlets,** fairy rings, circles of grass produced by fungus within the soil. 44-45. **to . . . fire,** the dread rattling thunderbolt I have discharged. 47. **spurs,** roots. 60. **boil'd,** made hot with humors. 63. **sociable,** sympathetic. **show,** appearance. 67. **ignorant fumes.** The fumes which rose up into the brain to produce sleep brought with them unconsciousness. 85. **discase,** undress. 96. **so, so, so,** that will do very well. 112. **trifle,** trick of magic. 124. **subtilties,** illusions. 128. **justify you,** prove you to be. 139. **woe,** sorry. 145. **late,** i.e., as

Says it is past her cure.
Pros. I rather think
You have not sought her help, of whose soft grace
For the like loss I have her sovereign aid
And rest myself content.
Alon. You the like loss!
Pros. As great to me as late; and, supportable
To make the dear loss, have I means much weaker
Than you may call to comfort you, for I
Have lost my daughter.
Alon. A daughter?
O heavens, that they were living both in Naples,
The king and queen there! that they were, I wish
Myself were mudded in that oozy bed
Where my son lies. When did you lose your daughter?
Pros. In this last tempest. I perceive, these lords
At this encounter do so much admire
That they devour their reason and scarce think
Their eyes do offices of truth, their words
Are natural breath: but, howsoev'r you have
Been justled from your senses, know for certain
That I am Prospero and that very duke
Which was thrust forth of Milan, who most strangely
Upon this shore, where you were wrack'd, was
landed,
To be the lord on 't. No more yet of this;
For 'tis a chronicle of day by day,
Not a relation for a breakfast nor
Befitting this first meeting. Welcome, sir;
This cell 's my court: here have I few attendants
And subjects none abroad: pray you, look in.
My dukedom since you have given me again,
I will requite you with as good a thing;
At least bring forth a wonder, to content ye
As much as me my dukedom.

Here PROSPERO *discovers* FERDINAND *and* MIRANDA, *playing at chess.*

Mir. Sweet lord, you play me false.
Fer. No, my dearest love,
I would not for the world.
Mir. Yes, for a score of kingdoms you should
wrangle,
And I would call it fair play.
Alon. If this prove
A vision of the Island, one dear son
Shall I twice lose.
Seb. A most high miracle!
Fer. Though the seas threaten, they are merciful;
I have curs'd them without cause. [*Kneels.*]
Alon. Now all the blessings
Of a glad father compass thee about!
Arise, and say how thou cam'st here.
Mir. O, wonder!
How many goodly creatures are there here!
How beauteous mankind is! O brave new world,
That has such people in 't!
Pros. 'Tis new to thee.
Alon. What is this maid with whom thou wast at
play?
Your eld'st acquaintance cannot be three hours:
Is she the goddess that hath sever'd us,
And brought us thus together?
Fer. Sir, she is mortal;
But by immortal Providence she 's mine:
I chose her when I could not ask my father
For his advice, nor thought I had one. She
Is daughter to this famous Duke of Milan,
Of whom so often I have heard renown,
But never saw before; of whom I have
Receiv'd a second life; and second father
This lady makes him to me.
Alon. I am hers:
But, O, how oddly will it sound that I
Must ask my child forgiveness!
Pros. There, sir, stop:
Let us not burthen our remembrance with
A heaviness that 's gone.
Gon. I have inly wept
Or should have spoke ere this. Look down, you gods,
And on this couple drop a blessed crown!
For it is you that have chalk'd forth the way
Which brought us hither.
Alon. I say, Amen, Gonzalo!
Gon. Was Milan thrust from Milan, that his issue
Should become kings of Naples? O, rejoice
Beyond a common joy, and set it down
With gold on lasting pillars: In one voyage
Did Claribel her husband find at Tunis
And Ferdinand, her brother, found a wife
Where he himself was lost, Prospero his dukedom
In a poor isle and all of us ourselves
When no man was his own.
Alon. [*To Fer. and Mir.*] Give me your
hands:
Let grief and sorrow still embrace his heart
That doth not wish you joy!
Gon. Be it so! Amen!

Enter ARIEL, *with the* Master *and* Boatswain *amazedly following.*

O, look, sir, look, sir! here is more of us:
I prophesied, if a gallows were on land,
This fellow could not drown. Now, blasphemy,
That swear'st grace o'erboard, not an oath on shore?
Hast thou no mouth by land? What is the news?
Boats. The best news is, that we have safely found
Our king and company; the next, our ship—
Which, but three glasses since, we gave out split—
Is tight and yare and bravely rigg'd as when
We first put out to sea.
Ari. [*Aside to Pros.*] Sir, all this service
Have I done since I went.
Pros. [*Aside to Ari.*] My tricksy spirit!
Alon. These are not natural events; they strengthen
From strange to stranger. Say, how came you hither?
Boats. If I did think, sir, I were well awake,
I 'ld strive to tell you. We were dead of sleep,
And—how we know not—all clapp'd under hatches;
Where but even now with strange and several noises
Of roaring, shrieking, howling, jingling chains,
And moe diversity of sounds, all horrible,
We were awak'd; straightway, at liberty;
Where we, in all her trim, freshly beheld
Our royal, good and gallant ship, our master
Cap'ring to eye her: on a trice, so please you,

great to me as it is recent. 155. **devour,** render null, destroy. 171. *Stage Direction:* ***discovers,*** by opening a curtain rear-stage. 174. **score,** double meaning: game or wager in which the score is reckoned by kingdoms, and also twenty kingdoms. **wrangle,** meaning (1) contend in a game or wager, and (2) argue or contend in words. 186. **eld'st,** earliest. 213. **own,** i.e., master of his senses. 223. **glasses,** hours. 224. **yare,** ready.

Even in a dream, were we divided from them
And were brought moping hither.
Ari. [*Aside to Pros.*] Was 't well done?
Pros. [*Aside to Ari.*] Bravely, my diligence. Thou shalt be free.
Alon. This is as strange a maze as e'er men trod;
And there is in this business more than nature
Was ever conduct of: some oracle
Must rectify our knowledge.
Pros. Sir, my liege,
Do not infest your mind with beating on
The strangeness of this business; at pick'd leisure
Which shall be shortly, single I'll resolve you,
Which to you shall seem probable, of every
These happen'd accidents; till when, be cheerful
And think of each thing well. [*Aside to Ari.*] Come hither, spirit:
Set Caliban and his companions free;
Untie the spell. [*Exit Ariel.*] How fares my gracious sir?
There are yet missing of your company
Some few odd lads that you remember not.

Enter ARIEL, *driving in* CALIBAN, STEPHANO *and* TRINCULO, *in their stolen apparel.*

Ste. Every man shift for all the rest, and let no man take care for himself; for all is but fortune. Coragio, bully-monster, coragio!

Trin. If these be true spies which I wear in my head, here 's a goodly sight.

Cal. O Setebos, these be brave spirits indeed!
How fine my master is! I am afraid
He will chastise me.
Seb. Ha, ha!
What things are these, my lord Antonio?
Will money buy 'em?
Ant. Very like; one of them
Is a plain fish, and, no doubt, marketable.
Pros. Mark but the badges of these men, my lords,
Then say if they be true. This mis-shapen knave,
His mother was a witch, and one so strong
That could control the moon, make flows and ebbs,
And deal in her command without her power.
These three have robb'd me; and this demi-devil—
For he 's a bastard one—had plotted with them
To take my life. Two of these fellows you
Must know and own; this thing of darkness I
Acknowledge mine.
Cal. I shall be pinch'd to death.
Alon. Is not this Stephano, my drunken butler?
Seb. He is drunk now: where had he wine?
Alon. And Trinculo is reeling ripe: where should they
Find this grand liquor that hath gilded 'em?
How cam'st thou in this pickle?

Trin. I have been in such a pickle since I saw you last that, I fear me, will never out of my bones: I shall not fear fly-blowing.

Seb. Why, how now, Stephano!
Ste. O, touch me not; I am not Stephano, but a cramp.
Pros. You 'ld be king o' the isle, sirrah?
Ste. I should have been a sore one then.
Alon. This is a strange thing as e'er I look'd on.
[*Pointing to Caliban.*]
Pros. He is as disproportion'd in his manners
As in his shape. Go, sirrah, to my cell;
Take with you your companions; as you look
To have my pardon, trim it handsomely.
Cal. Ay, that I will; and I'll be wise hereafter
And seek for grace. What a thrice-double ass
Was I, to take this drunkard for a god
And worship this dull fool!
Pros. Go to; away!
Alon. Hence, and bestow your luggage where you found it.
Seb. Or stole it, rather. [*Exeunt Cal., Ste., and Trin.*]
Pros. Sir, I invite your highness and your train
To my poor cell, where you shall take your rest
For this one night; which, part of it, I'll waste
With such discourse as, I not doubt, shall make it
Go quick away; the story of my life
And the particular accidents gone by
Since I came to this isle: and in the morn
I'll bring you to your ship and so to Naples,
Where I have hope to see the nuptial
Of these our dear-belov'd solemnized;
And thence retire me to my Milan, where
Every third thought shall be my grave.
Alon. I long
To hear the story of your life, which must
Take the ear strangely.
Pros. I'll deliver all;
And promise you calm seas, auspicious gales
And sail so expeditious that shall catch
Your royal fleet far off. [*Aside to Ari.*] My Ariel, chick,
That is thy charge: then to the elements
Be free, and fare thou well!—Please you, draw near.
Exeunt omnes.

EPILOGUE.

SPOKEN BY PROSPERO.

Now my charms are all o'erthrown,
And what strength I have 's mine own,
Which is most faint: now, 'tis true,
I must be here confin'd by you,
Or sent to Naples. Let me not,
Since I have my dukedom got
And pardon'd the deceiver, dwell
In this bare island by your spell;
But release me from my bands
With the help of your good hands:
Gentle breath of yours my sails
Must fill, or else my project fails,
Which was to please. Now I want
Spirits to enforce, art to enchant,
And my ending is despair,
Unless I be reliev'd by prayer,
Which pierces so that it assaults
Mercy itself and frees all faults.
As you from crimes would pardon'd be,
Let your indulgence set me free. *Exit.*

244. **conduct,** guide, leader. 246. **infest,** harass, disturb. 247. **pick'd.** chosen. 258. **Coragio,** courage. **bully-monster,** gallant monster. 267. **badges,** emblems of cloth or silver worn on the arms of retainers. Prospero refers here to the stolen clothes as emblems of their villainy. 271. **deal . . . power,** wield the moon's power, either without her authority, or beyond her influence. 280. **gilded,** flushed, made drunk. 284. **fly-blowing,** i.e., rotting after death (since he's pickled). 305. **accidents,** occurrences, events. 313. **Take,** take effect upon. **deliver,** declare, relate.

EPILOGUE. 10. **hands,** applause.

THE FAMOUS HISTORY OF THE LIFE OF KING HENRY THE EIGHTH

However much we may like to think of *The Tempest* (c. 1610–1611) as Shakespeare's farewell to his art, celebrating his retirement to Stratford in 1611 or 1612, his career was in fact not quite finished. He wrote all or part of *The Famous History of the Life of King Henry the Eighth* in 1613, and he evidently collaborated with John Fletcher (and possibly Beaumont) in *The Two Noble Kinsmen* (1613–1616). *Henry VIII* was performed by the King's men at the Globe playhouse on June 29, 1613, as a "new" play. During this performance, small cannon (called "chambers") were discharged to welcome Henry VIII and his fellow-masquers to Wolsey's house (I,iv), accidentally setting fire to the thatch roof and burning the Globe to the ground in less than an hour. (It was rebuilt.) The letter reporting this incident refers to the play by the title *All Is True*, but its identification with the extant play of *Henry VIII* is virtually certain.

Less certain is the attribution of the entire play to Shakespeare, although doubts on the subject did not arise until the nineteenth century. Alfred Lord Tennyson was the first to suspect that much of the play is metrically non-Shakespearean. His friend James Spedding took up the suggestion in his study, *Who Wrote Shakespeare's Henry VIII?* His conclusions, based on the assumption that Fletcher's mannered blank verse is generally endstopped and much given to double or "feminine" endings, assigned only I,i-ii, II,iii-iv, III,ii (through line 203), and V,i to Shakespeare, attributing all the rest to Fletcher. These metrical tests have been confirmed by subsequent researchers and augmented by other methods of statistical analysis. The result is perhaps a more comprehensive case for joint authorship than for most other plays of doubtful attribution. Moreover, the dual texture of style noted by Tennyson is undeniably there, as for example in the shift from the dense, elliptical grammar and compact images of the first two scenes to the conversational fluency of scenes three and four.

Against these arguments, however, the case for Shakespeare's sole authorship is impressive. Although Shakespeare did apparently collaborate with Fletcher during his last years in *The Two Noble Kinsmen*, that play was excluded from the 1623 Folio whereas *Henry VIII* was included as Shakespeare's final history play. Spedding's hypothesis of joint authorship would rob from Shakespeare several of the play's most famous scenes, such as the farewell speeches of Buckingham, Wolsey, and Queen Katharine, and conversely would credit Fletcher with a dramatic power not shown elsewhere. The "Fletcherian" style may well have been the result of Shakespeare's having known the work of the younger man who became Shakespeare's heir as chief writer for the King's men. No external evidence or tradition during Shakespeare's day links the play with Fletcher. Scholarly "disintegration" of the text dates only from the nineteenth century, where it should be seen as part of a broader effort to "disintegrate" many other plays and thereby rescue Shakespeare from scenes presumed unworthy of his genius. Most such efforts on Shakespeare's behalf are now happily out of fashion, and it is safest to assume in the case of *Henry VIII* that the Folio editors knew what they were doing.

What then was Shakespeare's purpose in this unexpected return to the genre of the English history play? He had set it aside fourteen years earlier, in 1599, bringing to completion in *Henry V* an eight-play saga on England's civil wars of the fifteenth century. Why turn in 1613 to a historical subject so separated in time from that of Shakespeare's earlier interest and potentially so controversial because of its relation to the religious battle between Catholics and Protestants? Or is *Henry VIII* the result of a premature dotage, with its supposedly tedious fifth act anticlimactically following the deaths of the play's most important characters, Wolsey and Katharine? The play has indeed troubled critics, although it succeeds masterfully on stage and has attracted the greatest Shakespearean actors from Betterton, Kemble, Mrs. Siddons, and Kean to Sybil Thorndike, Charles Laughton, and Flora Robson. Perhaps *Henry VIII*, like *Pericles* and other "failures" of Shakespeare's last years, needs to be regarded as an experimental work, blending conventional genres (especially history and romance) and stressing masquelike stage effects in the opulent manner of court entertainment. Since its thematic focus is also one of courtly celebration, expressing gratitude for Queen Elizabeth's Protestant rule and her cousin James' succession to the English throne, the play may best be seen as an updating of the English history play to meet a new mood of 1613. This return to a type of drama long since abandoned by Shakespeare resembles his similar fascination during his late years with the once-forgotten genre of romance.

In some ways, *Henry VIII* is deliberately unlike Shakespeare's earlier history plays, and so should not be judged by their standards. The prologue is at pains to stress that the play will contain no merriment or bawdry, no "fellow In a long motley coat." And indeed the play is unusually lacking in a comic subplot devoted to the antics of engaging commoners. To be sure, the views of the commons are not ignored, for Queen Katharine champions their hatred of Wolsey's taxes. In the fifth act they put in a brief appearance, crowding bumptiously forward at the christening of the Princess Elizabeth (V,iv). Even here, however, the tone is one of condescending amusement at their childish eagerness to see their future queen. They do not perform even the simplest of choric functions, as they do in *Richard III* or *Richard II*.

These factors may well reflect the increasing influence of the court on Shakespeare and the King's men. Ever since they became the King's men in 1603, when James I came to the throne, Shakespeare's company had enjoyed a closer relationship with the throne than before. *Measure for Measure* and *Macbeth*, among other of Shakespeare's plays, seem to contain flattering allusions to the new monarch. Moreover, faced with increasing competition from the boys' acting companies, who, since reopening in 1599, had attracted a courtly and sophisticated clientele, Shakespeare's company acquired the lease of Blackfriars in 1608 and henceforth used this "private" theatre as their winter playhouse. Shakespeare's late plays are accordingly staged with public, private, and courtly conditions of performance in mind. The late romances show the influence of Inigo Jones' lavish designs for court masques, as in *Cymbeline*'s use of machinery for celestial ascents and descents. *Henry VIII* reflects similar conditions of staging in its masquing scene (I,iv), in the pageantlike trial of Katharine and the baptism of Elizabeth, and in the vision of white-robed figures dancing before the dying Katharine (IV,ii). This affinity to courtly entertainment should not be overstressed, for Shakespeare's company remained a public company throughout his career, and its stage was always fluidly bare of scenery when compared with Jones' highly ingenious devices and use of scenic perspective. Nonetheless, *Henry VIII* should be viewed as a history play for a somewhat more selective audience than that of his earlier histories. The play's ornate and fulsome compliments to Elizabeth and King James have a courtly flavor. The year 1613 saw the politically important marriage of the Elector Palatinate to James' daughter Elizabeth, who was often flatteringly compared with her namesake Queen Elizabeth; and, although *Henry VIII* is not among the plays known to have been performed for this occasion, the marriage itself would have given added significance to the play's celebration of Tudor and Stuart rule.

Shakespeare's earlier histories may also imply homage to the Elizabethan establishment in their way, but even here *Henry VIII* produces a different emphasis. Shakespeare's earlier histories had focused chiefly on the education of the ideal prince and on the dilemmas of power he must face. *Henry VIII* is less a "mirror for magistrates" in this sense and more a dramatic expression of gratitude. *Henry VIII* is not really a patriotic play in a broadly popular sense. It lacks triumphant battle oratory and military excitement. It voices thanksgiving for a particular ruling family rather than pride in the English people. *Henry VIII* is above all the remarkable story of how Elizabeth came to be queen. The story is certainly not without its ironies, for providence works in mysterious ways, and Elizabeth's parents were complex personalities. Shakespeare reveals an increasing psychological interest in analysis of motive, as in other late and anomalous history plays such as Ford's *Perkin Warbeck*. Yet the unifying impulse of the play remains the celebration of the birth of Elizabeth.

COURTESY OF THE TRUSTEES, THE BRITISH MUSEUM

Henry VIII playing the harp, with his jester, Will Sommers; from a Psalter written for Henry by John Mallard.

This rising action in the play is counterpointed by a series of tragic falls, which indeed seem at first to be the play's chief concern. These falls proceed in remorseless succession—Buckingham, Katharine, Wolsey. In the edifying manner of that staple of medieval tragedy, the "Fall of Princes," these deaths preach useful lessons on statecraft and personal conduct. All these persons stoically exemplify the art of holy dying. They forgive their enemies and regret such sins as they have committed, and yet they also speak with dying prophecy of God's retribution that will light on offenders' heads. The prevailing mood in the falls of Buckingham and Katharine is one of pity, for both are innocent persons trampled underfoot by the ruthless Wolsey.

Cardinal Wolsey is the most interesting character of the three, and the most illustrative of another truism of medieval tragedy: the Wheel of Fortune. Even as he succeeds in toppling one victim after another, dispatching Surrey to Ireland, wheedling his way into the king's favor, reversing England's foreign policy with bewildering speed from pro-French to pro-Empire and back again, all the while amassing a vast personal fortune and negotiating for supreme power within the Roman church, we sense that he is preparing his own ultimate catastrophe. Fortune raises up insolent worldly persons of this sort, but an overseeing providential power is at work and will manifest itself through the king. Wolsey, in a nobly contrite farewell speech, sees the moral lesson of his fall: had he served God zealously, God would not "Have left me naked to mine enemies" (III,ii). Wolsey knows he has ventured beyond his depth in scheming, "Like little wanton boys that swim on bladders." Shakespeare's appraisal of this controversial man is mixed, partly because his chief source, Holinshed's *Chronicles*, incorporated both anti-Wolseyan diatribes and George Cavendish's appreciative account of Wolsey's last days. Still, the portraiture remains consistent throughout, for Wolsey is always intelligent and munificent (as in his founding of Cardinal College, later Christ Church, at Oxford) even though he employs his talents for Machiavellian ends. His chief villainy is his clerical meddling on behalf of Rome, his finagling to gain the papacy, and most of all his sending of England's precious wealth overseas for subversive purposes. Yet even this villainy has a function in the rising action of the story, for, had not Wolsey schemed against Queen Katharine in his plot to marry King Henry to the French Duchess of Alençon, Henry might never have met Elizabeth's mother Anne. An overriding cosmic irony converts the worst intents of traitors into beneficent purposes.

King Henry and Anne Bullen, who as Elizabeth's parents play the roles most essential to England's bright future, are to some extent ironically unaware of the great destiny they are performing. Henry especially, like Wolsey, is examined with some skepticism. His pious insistence that "conscience" alone banishes him from Katharine's bed elicits a tellingly wry observation, *sotto voce*, from the Duke of Suffolk: "No, his conscience Has crept too near another lady" (II,ii). As Henry neglectfully condones Wolsey's abuses of authority and credulously accepts perjured testimony against Buckingham, we catch glimpses of the whimsical tyrant whom history has revealed to us. These criticisms are muted, however, for Henry is after all Elizabeth's father. He is not only exonerated from most wrongdoing, but steps boldly forward at the play's end as champion of religious reform. Anne too is ambivalently treated. In her scene with the Old Lady (II,iii), we are reminded of the all-too-apparent reasons there are for suspecting that Anne is a schemer, a high-class auctioneer of her beauty who knows that Henry will pay handsomely. Yet in her own person Anne refutes these insinuations. All the characters of the play, whether they stand to profit or lose by Anne's marriage, speak admiringly of her beauty and honor. Although her speeches are few, her appearances are sumptuously staged with Anne at the center of a profoundly meaningful pageant.

The religious issue is presented with a similar tact and ambiguity, for it too is both controversial and of profound significance to England's future. Our sympathies are charitably disposed toward Katharine, whose innocent fall is a sad price that must be paid for England's happiness. Shakespeare significantly refuses to associate her with the decaying order of Catholicism, as he might have done. On the other hand, Bishop Gardiner, the villain of Act V, is undeniably a Catholic and persecutor of heretics, a dangerous man whose overthrow by Henry and the Protestant Cranmer signals the beginning of a new era in religion. Even though Shakespeare tactfully omits the relationship between Katharine's divorce and the Reformation, his audience would have had little difficulty making the connection in Act V between Cranmer's Protestant victory and the birth of Elizabeth. These two rising actions coalesce and give perspective to the pitiable falls from greatness which have necessarily contributed to a happy and even miraculous conclusion. History and tragicomic romance fulfill a common purpose in *Henry VIII*.

THE FAMOUS HISTORY OF THE LIFE OF KING HENRY THE EIGHTH

[*Dramatis Personae*

KING HENRY the Eighth.
CARDINAL WOLSEY.
CARDINAL CAMPEIUS.
CAPUCIUS, *Ambassador from the Emperor Charles V.*
CRANMER, Archbishop of Canterbury.
DUKE OF NORFOLK.
DUKE OF BUCKINGHAM.
DUKE OF SUFFOLK.
EARL OF SURREY.
Lord Chamberlain.
Lord Chancellor.
GARDINER, Bishop of Winchester.
Bishop of Lincoln.
LORD ABERGAVENNY.
LORD SANDS.
SIR HENRY GUILDFORD.
SIR THOMAS LOVELL.
SIR ANTHONY DENNY.
SIR NICHOLAS VAUX.
Secretaries to Wolsey.
CROMWELL, *Servant to Wolsey.*
GRIFFITH, *Gentleman-usher to Queen Katharine.*
Three Gentlemen.
DOCTOR BUTTS, *Physician to the King.*
Garter King-at-Arms.
Surveyor to the Duke of Buckingham.
BRANDON, *and* a Sergeant-at-Arms.
Door-keeper of the Council-chamber. Porter, *and* his Man.
Page to Gardiner. A Crier.

QUEEN KATHARINE, *wife to King Henry, afterwards divorced.*
ANNE BULLEN, *her Maid of Honour, afterwards* Queen.
An Old Lady, *friend to Anne Bullen.*
PATIENCE, *woman to Queen Katharine.*

Several Lords and Ladies in the Dumb Shows; Women attending upon the Queen; Scribes, Officers, Guards, *and other* Attendants. Spirits.

SCENE: *London; Westminster; Kimbolton.*]

THE PROLOGUE.

I COME no more to make you laugh: things now,
That bear a weighty and a serious brow,
Sad, high, and working, full of state and woe,
Such noble scenes as draw the eye to flow,
We now present. Those that can pity, here
May, if they think it well, let fall a tear;

The subject will deserve it. Such as give
Their money out of hope they may believe,
May here find truth too. Those that come to see
Only a show or two, and so agree
The play may pass, if they be still and willing,
I'll undertake may see away their shilling
Richly in two short hours. Only they
That come to hear a merry bawdy play,
A noise of targets, or to see a fellow
In a long motley coat guarded with yellow,
Will be deceiv'd; for, gentle hearers, know
To rank our chosen truth with such a show
As fool and fight is, beside forfeiting
Our own brains, and the opinion that we bring,
To make that only true we now intend,
Will leave us never an understanding friend.
Therefore, for goodness' sake, and as you are known
The first and happiest hearers of the town,
Be sad, as we would make ye: think ye see
The very persons of our noble story
As they were living; think you see them great,
And follow'd with the general throng and sweat
Of thousand friends; then in a moment, see
How soon this mightiness meets misery:
And, if you can be merry then, I'll say
A man may weep upon his wedding-day.

ACT I.

SCENE I. [*London. An ante-chamber in the palace.*]

Enter the DUKE OF NORFOLK *at one door; at the other, the* DUKE OF BUCKINGHAM *and the* LORD ABERGAVENNY.

Buck. Good morrow, and well met. How have ye done
Since last we saw in France?
Nor. I thank your grace,
Healthful; and ever since a fresh admirer
Of what I saw there.
Buck. An untimely ague
Stay'd me a prisoner in my chamber when
Those suns of glory, those two lights of men,
Met in the vale of Andren.
Nor. 'Twixt Guynes and Arde:
I was then present, saw them salute on horseback;
Beheld them, when they lighted, how they clung
In their embracement, as they grew together;
Which had they, what four thron'd ones could have weigh'd
Such a compounded one?
Buck. All the whole time
I was my chamber's prisoner.
Nor. Then you lost
The view of earthly glory: men might say,
Till this time pomp was single, but now married
To one above itself. Each following day
Became the next day's master, till the last
Made former wonders its. To-day the French,
All clinquant, all in gold, like heathen gods,
Shone down the English; and, to-morrow, they
Made Britain India: every man that stood
Show'd like a mine. Their dwarfish pages were
As cherubins, all gilt: the madams too,
Not us'd to toil, did almost sweat to bear
The pride upon them, that their very labour
Was to them as a painting: now this masque
Was cried incomparable; and th' ensuing night
Made it a fool and beggar. The two kings,
Equal in lustre, were now best, now worst,
As presence did present them; him in eye,
Still him in praise: and, being present both,
'Twas said they saw but one; and no discerner
Durst wag his tongue in censure. When these suns—
For so they phrase 'em—by their heralds challeng'd
The noble spirits to arms, they did perform
Beyond thought's compass; that former fabulous story,
Being now seen possible enough, got credit,
That Bevis was believ'd.
Buck. O, you go far.
Nor. As I belong to worship and affect
In honour honesty, the tract of ev'ry thing
Would by a good discourser lose some life,
Which action's self was tongue to. All was royal;
To the disposing of it nought rebell'd,
Order gave each thing view; the office did
Distinctly his full function.
Buck. Who did guide,
I mean, who set the body and the limbs
Of this great sport together, as you guess?
Nor. One, certes, that promises no element
In such a business.
Buck. I pray you, who, my lord?
Nor. All this was ord'red by the good discretion
Of the right reverend Cardinal of York.
Buck. The devil speed him! no man's pie is freed
From his ambitious finger. What had he
To do in these fierce vanities? I wonder
That such a keech can with his very bulk
Take up the rays o' th' beneficial sun
And keep it from the earth.
Nor. Surely, sir,
There 's in him stuff that puts him to these ends;
For, being not propp'd by ancestry, whose grace
Chalks successors their way, nor call'd upon
For high feats done to th' crown; neither allied
To eminent assistants; but, spider-like,
Out of his self-drawing web, 'a gives us note,
The force of his own merit makes his way;
A gift that heaven gives for him, which buys
A place next to the king.
Aber. I cannot tell

PROLOGUE. 3. **working,** exciting the emotions, full of pathos. 15. **targets,** shields. 16. **guarded,** trimmed. 17. **deceiv'd,** disappointed. 20. **opinion,** reputation. 21. **intend,** i.e., to play.

ACT I. SCENE I. 2. **saw,** i.e., saw each other. 4. **what I saw there.** Norfolk's description is of the famous meeting of Henry VIII and Francis I of France. It was near Calais, at the Field of the Cloth of Gold, so called because of the magnificence of the display. 7. **vale of Andren.** The name, more properly Ardre, appears as Andren in Holinshed. 10. **as,** as if. 19. **clinquant,** glittering. 21. **India,** i.e., the West Indies. 23. **madams,** ladies. 26. **Was . . . painting,** i.e., flushed them as though with cosmetics. 30. **As . . . them,** i.e., when they appeared. 30-31. **him . . . praise,** i.e., the one in view at the moment received the praise. 38. **Bevis,** hero of the fourteenth-century romance, *Bevis of Hampton.* The splendor depicted in the poem is the point of the allusion here. 39. **belong to worship,** am of noble rank. 40. **tract,** course (of events). 42. **Which . . . to,** i.e., the event itself was its own best description. 43. **rebell'd,** jarred. 44-45. **Order . . . function,** everything appeared in its proper place, and every official performed his function without confusion. 48-49. **One . . . business,** i.e., one whose mean origin would indicate that he lacked the *savoir faire* required for managing business of such a regal nature. 54. **fierce,** extravagant. 55. **keech,** fat of a slaughtered animal rolled into a lump; applied to Wolsey as a

What heaven hath given him,—let some graver eye
Pierce into that; but I can see his pride
Peep through each part of him: whence has he that,
If not from hell? the devil is a niggard,
Or has given all before, and he begins
A new hell in himself.

Buck. Why the devil,
Upon this French going out, took he upon him,
Without the privity o' th' king, t' appoint
Who should attend on him? He makes up the file
Of all the gentry; for the most part such
To whom as great a charge as little honour
He meant to lay upon: and his own letter,
The honourable board of council out,
Must fetch him in he papers.

Aber. I do know
Kinsmen of mine, three at the least, that have
By this so sicken'd their estates, that never
They shall abound as formerly.

Buck. O, many
Have broke their backs with laying manors on 'em
For this great journey. What did this vanity
But minister communication of
A most poor issue?

Nor. Grievingly I think,
The peace between the French and us not values
The cost that did conclude it.

Buck. Every man,
After the hideous storm that follow'd, was
A thing inspir'd; and, not consulting, broke
Into a general prophecy: That this tempest,
Dashing the garment of this peace, aboded
The sudden breach on 't.

Nor. Which is budded out;
For France hath flaw'd the league, and hath attach'd
Our merchants' goods at Bourdeaux.

Aber. Is it therefore
Th' ambassador is silenc'd?

Nor. Marry, is 't.

Aber. A proper title of a peace; and purchas'd
At a superfluous rate!

Buck. Why, all this business
Our reverend cardinal carried.

Nor. Like it your grace,
The state takes notice of the private difference
Betwixt you and the cardinal. I advise you—
And take it from a heart that wishes towards you
Honour and plenteous safety—that you read
The cardinal's malice and his potency
Together; to consider further that
What his high hatred would effect wants not
A minister in his power. You know his nature,
That he 's revengeful, and I know his sword
Hath a sharp edge: it 's long and, 't may be said,
It reaches far, and where 'twill not extend,
Thither he darts it. Bosom up my counsel,
You'll find it wholesome. Lo, where comes that rock
That I advise your shunning.

Enter CARDINAL WOLSEY, *the purse borne before him, certain of the* Guard, *and two* Secretaries *with papers. The* CARDINAL *in his passage fixeth his eye on* BUCKINGHAM, *and* BUCKINGHAM *on him, both full of disdain.*

Wol. The Duke of Buckingham's surveyor, ha?
Where 's his examination?

First Secr. Here, so please you.

Wol. Is he in person ready?

First Secr. Ay, please your grace.

Wol. Well, we shall then know more; and Buckingham
Shall lessen this big look. *Exeunt Cardinal and his Train.*

Buck. This butcher's cur is venom-mouth'd, and I
Have not the power to muzzle him; therefore best
Not wake him in his slumber. A beggar's book
Outworths a noble's blood.

Nor. What, are you chaf'd?
Ask God for temp'rance; that 's th' appliance only
Which your disease requires.

Buck. I read in 's looks
Matter against me; and his eye revil'd
Me, as his abject object: at this instant
He bores me with some trick: he 's gone to th' king;
I'll follow and outstare him.

Nor. Stay, my lord,
And let your reason with your choler question
What 'tis you go about: to climb steep hills
Requires slow pace at first: anger is like
A full-hot horse, who being allow'd his way,
Self-mettle tires him. Not a man in England
Can advise me like you: be to yourself
As you would to your friend.

Buck. I'll to the king;
And from a mouth of honour quite cry down
This Ipswich fellow's insolence; or proclaim
There 's difference in no persons.

Nor. Be advis'd;
Heat not a furnace for your foe so hot
That it do singe yourself: we may outrun,
By violent swiftness, that which we run at,
And lose by over-running. Know you not,
The fire that mounts the liquor till 't run o'er,
In seeming to augment it wastes it? Be advis'd:
I say again, there is no English soul
More stronger to direct you than yourself,
If with the sap of reason you would quench,
Or but allay, the fire of passion.

Buck. Sir,
I am thankful to you; and I'll go along
By your prescription: but this top-proud fellow,
Whom from the flow of gall I name not but
From sincere motions, by intelligence,
And proofs as clear as founts in July when
We see each grain of gravel, I do know

butcher's son. 60. **Chalks . . . way,** indicates the path noble descendants are to follow. 63. **gives us note,** lets us know. 73. **going out,** expedition, display. 74. **privity,** being privy to something. 77-78. **To . . . upon,** i.e., the cardinal imposed charges for defraying the expenses of the costly interview on those noblemen to whom he gave places of little honor. 79. **out,** not consulted. 80. **Must . . . papers,** compels the cooperation of every person he cites. 84. **laying . . . 'em,** i.e., pawning estates for wardrobes. 86-87. **minister . . . issue,** provide occasion for gossip of little value. 88. **not values,** is not worth. 91. **consulting,** i.e., each other. 93. **aboded,** foretold. 95. **attach'd.** seized. 99. **superfluous rate,** excessive price. 100. **carried,** supervised. **Like it,** may it please. 104. **read,** interpret. 107-108. **wants . . . power,** is not without agents under his control. 112. **Bosom up,** take to heart and shut up in your bosom. 115. **surveyor,** overseer of a household or estate. 116. **examination,** deposition. 119. **big,** haughty. 120. **butcher's cur,** another dig at Wolsey's reputed lowly origin. 122. **book,** book-learning. 123. **chaf'd,** angry. 124. **appliance only,** only remedy. 128. **bores,** undermines. 138. **fellow's,** usually refers to the servant class; hence here contemptuously glances at Wolsey's low origin.

To be corrupt and treasonous.
Nor. Say not 'treasonous.'
Buck. To th' king I'll say 't; and make my vouch as strong
As shore of rock. Attend. This holy fox,
Or wolf, or both,—for he is equal rav'nous
As he is subtle, and as prone to mischief
As able to perform 't; his mind and place
Infecting one another, yea, reciprocally—
Only to show his pomp as well in France
As here at home, suggests the king our master
To this last costly treaty, th' interview,
That swallowed so much treasure, and like a glass
Did break i' th' wrenching.
Nor. Faith, and so it did.
Buck. Pray, give me favour, sir. This cunning cardinal
The articles o' th' combination drew
As himself pleas'd; and they were ratified
As he cried 'Thus let be': to as much end
As give a crutch to th' dead: but our count-cardinal
Has done this, and 'tis well; for worthy Wolsey,
Who cannot err, he did it. Now this follows,—
Which, as I take it, is a kind of puppy
To th' old dam, treason,—Charles the emperor,
Under pretence to see the queen his aunt,—
For 'twas indeed his colour, but he came
To whisper Wolsey,—here makes visitation:
His fears were, that the interview betwixt
England and France might, through their amity,
Breed him some prejudice; for from this league
Peep'd harms that menac'd him: he privily
Deals with our cardinal; and, as I trow,—
Which I do well; for I am sure the emperor
Paid ere he promis'd; whereby his suit was granted
Ere it was ask'd; but when the way was made,
And pav'd with gold, the emperor thus desir'd,
That he would please to alter the king's course,
And break the foresaid peace. Let the king know,
As soon he shall by me, that thus the cardinal
Does buy and sell his honour as he pleases,
And for his own advantage.
Nor. I am sorry
To hear this of him; and could wish he were
Something mistaken in 't.
Buck. No, not a syllable:
I do pronounce him in that very shape
He shall appear in proof.

Enter BRANDON, *a* Sergeant-at-arms *before him, and two or three of the* Guard.

Bran. Your office, sergeant; execute it.
Serg. Sir,
My lord the Duke of Buckingham, and Earl
Of Hereford, Stafford, and Northampton, I
Arrest thee of high treason, in the name
Of our most sovereign king.
Buck. Lo, you, my lord,
The net has fall'n upon me! I shall perish
Under device and practice.
Bran. I am sorry
To see you ta'en from liberty, to look on
The business present: 'tis his highness' pleasure
You shall to th' Tower.
Buck. It will help me nothing
To plead mine innocence; for that dye is on me
Which makes my whit'st part black. The will of heav'n
Be done in this and all things! I obey.
O my Lord Aberga'ny, fare you well!
Bran. Nay, he must bear you company. The king [*To Abergavenny.*]
Is pleas'd you shall to th' Tower, till you know
How he determines further.
Aber. As the duke said,
The will of heaven be done, and the king's pleasure
By me obey'd!
Bran. Here is a warrant from
The king t' attach Lord Montacute; and the bodies
Of the duke's confessor, John de la Car,
One Gilbert Peck, his chancellor,—
Buck. So, so;
These are the limbs o' th' plot: no more, I hope.
Bran. A monk o' th' Chartreux.
Buck. O, Nicholas Hopkins?
Bran. He.
Buck. My surveyor is false; the o'er-great cardinal
Hath show'd him gold; my life is spann'd already:
I am the shadow of poor Buckingham,
Whose figure even this instant cloud puts on,
By dark'ning my clear sun. My lord, farewell. *Exeunt.*

SCENE II. [*The same. The council-chamber.*]

Cornets. Enter KING HENRY, *leaning on the* CARDINAL'S *shoulder, the* Nobles, *and* SIR THOMAS LOVELL; *the* CARDINAL *places himself under the* KING'S *feet on his right side.*

King. My life itself, and the best heart of it,
Thanks you for this great care: I stood i' th' level
Of a full-charg'd confederacy, and give thanks
To you that chok'd it. Let be call'd before us
That gentleman of Buckingham's; in person
I'll hear him his confessions justify;
And point by point the treasons of his master
He shall again relate.

A noise within, crying 'Room for the Queen!' *Enter the* QUEEN [KATHARINE], *ushered by the* DUKE OF NORFOLK, *and* [*the* DUKE OF] SUFFOLK: *she kneels.* [*The*] KING *riseth from his state, takes her up, kisses and placeth her by him.*

Q. Kath. Nay, we must longer kneel: I am a suitor.
King. Arise, and take place by us: half your suit
Never name to us; you have half our power:

164. **suggests,** incites. 167. **wrenching,** rough handling, rinsing. 168. **favour,** attention. 169. **articles o' th' combination,** terms of the peace treaty. 178. **colour,** pretext. 195. **Something mistaken,** somewhat misunderstood. 197. **He . . . proof,** experience shall prove him. 204. **device and practice,** stratagems and plots. 217. **attach,** arrest. 218, 219. **John de la Car, Gilbert Peck.** The names are from Holinshed's account: "Maister Iohn de la Car *alias* de la Court, the dukes confessor, and sir Gilbert Perke, priest, the duke's chancellor." Pooler thinks *Peck* and *Perke* are errors for *clerk* (i.e., clergyman). The official papers connected with the trial of the duke give the names *John Delacourt* and *Robert Gilbert, clerk.* 221. **Chartreux,** Charterhouse (Carthusian). 223. **spann'd,** measured.

SCENE II. 2. **level,** i.e., was the target of a conspiracy. 3. **full-charg'd,** well-aimed. 5. **That . . . Buckingham's.** Cf. I, i, 222, *my surveyor is false.* 6. **justify,** prove, confirm. 8. *Stage Direction:* **state,** chair of state, a raised seat with a canopy. 21. **flaw'd,** damaged. 32. **to them 'longing,** in their employ. 33. **spinsters,** spinners. **carders,** those who comb wool for impurities. **fullers,** those who beat wool to clean it. 37. **danger serves,** is attendant among them. 42. **front . . . file,** take my place at the head of others who share the responsibility.

The other moiety, ere you ask, is given;
Repeat your will and take it.
Q. Kath. Thank your majesty.
That you would love yourself, and in that love
Not unconsidered leave your honour, nor
The dignity of your office, is the point
Of my petition.
King. Lady mine, proceed.
Q. Kath. I am solicited, not by a few,
And those of true condition, that your subjects
Are in great grievance: there have been commissions
Sent down among 'em, which hath flaw'd the heart
Of all their loyalties: wherein, although,
My good lord cardinal, they vent reproaches
Most bitterly on you, as putter on
Of these exactions, yet the king our master—
Whose honour heaven shield from soil!—even he escapes not
Language unmannerly, yea, such which breaks
The sides of loyalty, and almost appears
In loud rebellion.
Nor. Not almost appears,
It doth appear; for, upon these taxations,
The clothiers all, not able to maintain
The many to them 'longing, have put off
The spinsters, carders, fullers, weavers, who,
Unfit for other life, compell'd by hunger
And lack of other means, in desperate manner
Daring th' event to th' teeth, are all in uproar,
And danger serves among them.
King. Taxation!
Wherein? and what taxation? My lord cardinal,
You that are blam'd for it alike with us,
Know you of this taxation?
Wol. Please you, sir,
I know but of a single part, in aught
Pertains to th' state; and front but in that file
Where others tell steps with me.
Q. Kath. No, my lord,
You know no more than others; but you frame
Things that are known alike; which are not wholesome
To those which would not know them, and yet must
Perforce be their acquaintance. These exactions,
Whereof my sovereign would have note, they are
Most pestilent to th' hearing; and, to bear 'em,
The back is sacrifice to th' load. They say
They are devis'd by you; or else you suffer
Too hard an exclamation.
King. Still exaction!
The nature of it? in what kind, let 's know,
Is this exaction?
Q. Kath. I am much too venturous
In tempting of your patience; but am bold'ned
Under your promis'd pardon. The subjects' grief
Comes through commissions, which compels from each
The sixth part of his substance, to be levied
Without delay; and the pretence for this
Is nam'd, your wars in France: this makes bold mouths:
Tongues spit their duties out, and cold hearts freeze
Allegiance in them; their curses now
Live where their prayers did: and it 's come to pass,
This tractable obedience is a slave
To each incensed will. I would your highness
Would give it quick consideration, for
There is no primer business.
King. By my life,
This is against our pleasure.
Wol. And for me,
I have no further gone in this than by
A single voice; and that not pass'd me but
By learned approbation of the judges. If I am
Traduc'd by ignorant tongues, which neither know
My faculties nor person, yet will be
The chronicles of my doing, let me say
'Tis but the fate of place, and the rough brake
That virtue must go through. We must not stint
Our necessary actions, in the fear
To cope malicious censurers; which ever,
As rav'nous fishes, do a vessel follow
That is new-trimm'd, but benefit no further
Than vainly longing. What we oft do best,
By sick interpreters, once weak ones, is
Not ours, or not allow'd; what worst, as oft,
Hitting a grosser quality, is cried up
For our best act. If we shall stand still,
In fear our motion will be mock'd or carp'd at,
We should take root here where we sit, or sit
State-statues only.
King. Things done well,
And with a care, exempt themselves from fear;
Things done without example, in their issue
Are to be fear'd. Have you a precedent
Of this commission? I believe, not any.
We must not rend our subjects from our laws,
And stick them in our will. Sixth part of each?
A trembling contribution! Why, we take
From every tree lop, bark, and part o' th' timber;
And, though we leave it with a root, thus hack'd,
The air will drink the sap. To every county
Where this is question'd send our letters, with
Free pardon to each man that has denied
The force of this commission: pray, look to 't;
I put it to your care.
Wol. A word with you.
[*To the Secretary.*]
Let there be letters writ to every shire,
Of the king's grace and pardon. The grieved commons
Hardly conceive of me; let it be nois'd
That through our intercession this revokement
And pardon comes: I shall anon advise you
Further in the proceeding. *Exit Secretary.*

Enter Surveyor.

Q. Kath. I am sorry that the Duke of Buckingham

44-46. **You . . . them,** in a sense you know no more than others; but you devise measures known to all (the council) which are so evil that men would rather not know. 49. **pestilent,** offensive. 52. **exclamation,** reproach. 64-65. **is . . . will,** gives way to angry defiance. 67. **no primer business,** no business more urgent. 70. **single voice,** i.e., my part in this was only to cast one vote in the council. 75. **place,** office. **brake,** thicket. 80. **new-trimm'd,** made seaworthy; hence ravenous fishes follow it in vain. 82. **sick interpreters,** i.e., those who explain our conduct out of malicious envy. **once,** at one time or another. 83. **Not . . . allow'd,** either not credited to us, or disapproved of. 84. **Hitting . . . quality,** being understood, or appreciated, by more vulgar natures, i.e., the indiscriminate praise achievements less fine because their grosser minds understand them. 86. **In fear,** for fear that. 88. **State-statues,** mere statues of statesmen. 90. **issue,** consequences. 94. **stick . . . will,** i.e., make our subjects the creatures of our will rather than servants of the law. 95. **trembling,** causing to tremble. 96. **lop,** branches. 99. **question'd,** debated. 105. **Hardly conceive,** have a bad opinion. 106. **our,** a presumption on the part of Wolsey; the plural pronoun is in the manner of royalty.

Is run in your displeasure.
King. It grieves many:
The gentleman is learn'd, and a most rare speaker;
To nature none more bound; his training such,
That he may furnish and instruct great teachers,
And never seek for aid out of himself. Yet see,
When these so noble benefits shall prove
Not well dispos'd, the mind growing once corrupt,
They turn to vicious forms, ten times more ugly
Than ever they were fair. This man so complete,
Who was enroll'd 'mongst wonders, and when we,
Almost with ravish'd list'ning, could not find
His hour of speech a minute; he, my lady,
Hath into monstrous habits put the graces
That once were his, and is become as black
As if besmear'd in hell. Sit by us; you shall hear—
This was his gentleman in trust—of him
Things to strike honour sad. Bid him recount
The fore-recited practices; whereof
We cannot feel too little, hear too much.
Wol. Stand forth, and with bold spirit relate what you,
Most like a careful subject, have collected
Out of the Duke of Buckingham.
King. Speak freely.
Surv. First, it was usual with him—every day
It would infect his speech—that if the king
Should without issue die, he'll carry it so
To make the sceptre his: these very words
I've heard him utter to his son-in-law,
Lord Aberga'ny; to whom by oath he menac'd
Revenge upon the cardinal.
Wol. Please your highness, note
This dangerous conception in this point.
Not friended by his wish, to your high person
His will is most malignant; and it stretches
Beyond you, to your friends.
Q. Kath. My learn'd lord cardinal,
Deliver all with charity.
King. Speak on:
How grounded he his title to the crown,
Upon our fail? to this point hast thou heard him
At any time speak aught?
Surv. He was brought to this
By a vain prophecy of Nicholas Henton.
King. What was that Henton?
Surv. Sir, a Chartreux friar,
His confessor; who fed him every minute
With words of sovereignty.
King. How know'st thou this?
Surv. Not long before your highness sped to France,
The duke being at the Rose, within the parish
Saint Lawrence Poultney, did of me demand
What was the speech among the Londoners
Concerning the French journey: I replied,
Men fear'd the French would prove perfidious,
To the king's danger. Presently the duke
Said, 'twas the fear, indeed; and that he doubted
'Twould prove the verity of certain words
Spoke by a holy monk; 'that oft,' says he,
'Hath sent to me, wishing me to permit
John de la Car, my chaplain, a choice hour
To hear from him a matter of some moment:
Whom after under the confession's seal
He solemnly had sworn, that what he spoke
My chaplain to no creature living, but
To me, should utter, with demure confidence
This pausingly ensu'd: Neither the king nor 's heirs,
Tell you the duke, shall prosper: bid him strive
To gain the love o' th' commonalty: the duke
Shall govern England.'
Q. Kath. If I know you well,
You were the duke's surveyor, and lost your office
On the complaint o' th' tenants: take good heed
You charge not in your spleen a noble person
And spoil your nobler soul: I say, take heed;
Yes, heartily beseech you.
King. Let him on.
Go forward.
Surv. On my soul, I'll speak but truth.
I told my lord the duke, by th' devil's illusions
The monk might be deceiv'd; and that 'twas dangerous for him
To ruminate on this so far, until
It forg'd him some design, which, being believ'd,
It was much like to do: he answer'd, 'Tush,
It can do me no damage;' adding further,
That, had the king in his last sickness fail'd,
The cardinal's and Sir Thomas Lovell's heads
Should have gone off.
King. Ha! what, so rank? Ah ha!
There 's mischief in this man: canst thou say further?
Surv. I can, my liege.
King. Proceed.
Surv. Being at Greenwich,
After your highness had reprov'd the duke
About Sir William Bulmer,—
King. I remember
Of such a time: being my sworn servant,
The duke retain'd him his. But on; what hence?
Surv. 'If,' quoth he, 'I for this had been committed,
As, to the Tower, I thought, I would have play'd
The part my father meant to act upon
Th' usurper Richard; who, being at Salisbury,
Made suit to come in 's presence; which if granted,
As he made semblance of his duty, would
Have put his knife into him.'
King. A giant traitor!
Wol. Now, madam, may his highness live in freedom,
And this man out of prison?
Q. Kath. God mend all!

110. **Is run in,** has incurred. 112. **To . . . bound,** none more indebted to nature for talents. 114. **out of himself,** beyond the treasures of his own mind (Johnson). 120-121. **could . . . minute,** when he spoke, an hour seemed but a minute. 122. **habits,** garments, i.e., shapes. 130. **collected,** learned by spying. 132-138. **First . . . cardinal.** The substance of this speech is directly from Holinshed: "This Kneuet, being had in examination before the cardinall, disclosed all the dukes life. And first he vttered, that the duke was accustomed, by waie of talke, to saie how he meant so to vse the matter, that he would attaine to the crowne, *if king Henrie* chanced to *die without issue:* & that he had talke and conference of that matter on a time with George Neuill, lord of Aburgauennie, vnto whome he had giuen his daughter in marriage; and also that he threatned to punish the cardinall for his manifold misdooings, being without cause his mortall enemie." 140. **Not . . . wish,** if his wish (that the king die childless) is ungratified. 145. **fail,** i.e., if we should die without an heir. 147, 148. **Henton,** so F; Globe, following Pope: *Hopkins*. Holinshed calls the monk "one Nicholas Hopkins, a monke of an house of the Chartreus order beside Bristow, called *Henton*." 151-171. **Not . . . England.** This passage parallels Holinshed often in phrasing as well as in substance. 152. **the Rose,** a manor house. 158. **doubted,** feared, suspected. 181. **forg'd,** caused him to frame; *which* refers vaguely to what the monk has told him. 198. **semblance,** pretense. 204. **stretch'd,** i.e., to his full height. 205. **mounting,** raising. 209. **irresolute,** unfulfilled. **period,** aim, goal. 210. **attach'd,** arrested. 211. **present,** immediate.

Scene iii. 1. **spells of France.** Holinshed mentions the offense

King. There 's something more would out of thee; what say'st?

Surv. After 'the duke his father,' with 'the knife,'
He stretch'd him, and, with one hand on his dagger,
Another spread on 's breast, mounting his eyes,
He did discharge a horrible oath; whose tenour
Was,—were he evil us'd, he would outgo
His father by as much as a performance
Does an irresolute purpose.

King. There 's his period,
To sheathe his knife in us. He is attach'd;
Call him to present trial: if he may
Find mercy in the law, 'tis his; if none,
Let him not seek 't of us: by day and night,
He's traitor to th' height. *Exeunt.*

SCENE III. [*An ante-chamber in the palace*.]

Enter LORD CHAMBERLAIN *and* LORD SANDS.

Cham. Is 't possible the spells of France should juggle
Men into such strange mysteries?

Sands. New customs,
Though they be never so ridiculous,
Nay, let 'em be unmanly, yet are follow'd.

Cham. As far as I see, all the good our English
Have got by the late voyage is but merely
A fit or two o' th' face; but they are shrewd ones;
For when they hold 'em, you would swear directly
Their very noses had been counsellors
To Pepin or Clotharius, they keep state so.

Sands. They have all new legs, and lame ones: one would take it,
That never saw 'em pace before, the spavin
Or springhalt reign'd among 'em.

Cham. Death! my lord,
Their clothes are after such a pagan cut to 't,
That, sure, th' have worn out Christendom.

Enter SIR THOMAS LOVELL.

How now!
What news, Sir Thomas Lovell?

Lov. Faith, my lord,
I hear of none, but the new proclamation
That 's clapp'd upon the court-gate.

Cham. What is 't for?

Lov. The reformation of our travell'd gallants,
That fill the court with quarrels, talk, and tailors.

Cham. I 'm glad 'tis there: now I would pray our monsieurs
To think an English courtier may be wise,
And never see the Louvre.

Lov. They must either,
For so run the conditions, leave those remnants
Of fool and feather that they got in France,
With all their honourable points of ignorance
Pertaining thereunto, as fights and fireworks,
Abusing better men than they can be,
Out of a foreign wisdom, renouncing clean
The faith they have in tennis, and tall stockings,
Short blist'red breeches, and those types of travel,
And understand again like honest men;
Or pack to their old playfellows: there, I take it,
They may, 'cum privilegio,' 'oui' away
The lag end of their lewdness and be laugh'd at.

Sands. 'Tis time to give 'em physic, their diseases
Are grown so catching.

Cham. What a loss our ladies
Will have of these trim vanities!

Lov. Ay, marry,
There will be woe indeed, lords: the sly whoresons
Have got a speeding trick to lay down ladies;
A French song and a fiddle has no fellow.

Sands. The devil fiddle 'em! I am glad they are going,
For, sure, there 's no converting of 'em: now
An honest country lord, as I am, beaten
A long time out of play, may bring his plain-song
And have an hour of hearing; and, by 'r lady,
Held current music too.

Cham. Well said, Lord Sands;
Your colt's tooth is not cast yet.

Sands. No, my lord;
Nor shall not, while I have a stump.

Cham. Sir Thomas,
Whither were you a-going?

Lov. To the cardinal's:
Your lordship is a guest too.

Cham. O, 'tis true:
This night he makes a supper, and a great one,
To many lords and ladies; there will be
The beauty of this kingdom, I'll assure you.

Lov. That churchman bears a bounteous mind indeed,
A hand as fruitful as the land that feeds us;
His dews fall every where.

Cham. No doubt he 's noble;
He had a black mouth that said other of him.

Sands. He may, my lord; has wherewithal: in him
Sparing would show a worse sin than ill doctrine;
Men of his way should be most liberal;
They are set here for examples.

Cham. True, they are so;
But few now give so great ones. My barge stays;
Your lordship shall along. Come, good Sir Thomas,
We shall be late else; which I would not be,
For I was spoke to, with Sir Henry Guildford
This night to be comptrollers.

Sands. I am your lordship's. *Exeunt.*

---

taken at the "French vices and brags" of some of Henry's courtiers who returned from the continent "all French in eating, drinking, and apparell." 2. **mysteries,** mummeries; artificial fashions (Douce). 7. **A . . . face,** artificial cast of countenance (Johnson). 10. **Pepin, Clotharius,** kings of ancient France in the sixth and seventh centuries. **keep state,** maintain a position of dignified demeanor. 11. **new legs,** new forms of saluting and new legs to salute with (Pooler); *leg* frequently means an obeisance made by drawing back one leg and bending the other. 12. **spavin,** disease of horses causing swelling of joints and lameness. 13. **springhalt,** lameness in a horse. 15. **th' have . . . Christendom,** they have exhausted the repertory of Christian fashions. 23. **Louvre,** ancient palace of the kings of France in Paris, now famous as an art museum. 25. **fool and feather,** probably alludes to the extravagant feather trimming worn in men's hats. 27. **fireworks,** whoring. 31. **blist'red,** puffed. **types,** emblems. 34. **'cum privilegio,'** with exclusive right. 35. **lag . . . lewdness,** the last days of their worthless lives. 38. **trim vanities,** fashionable and vain courtiers. 40. **lay down,** seduce; bring to bed of a child (Onions). 41. **fellow,** equal. 45. **plain-song,** simple chant or air. 47. **Held current music,** regarded as in the height of fashion. 48. **colt's tooth,** lecherousness of youth. 49. **stump,** i.e., of a tooth (with a bawdy pun). 58. **He . . . mouth,** a person must have an evil habit of speech. 60. **Sparing,** frugality. 66. **spoke to,** asked. 67. **comptrollers,** officers in a great household to act as managers in general; here, something like masters of ceremonies.

SCENE IV. [*A Hall in York Place.*]

Hautboys. A small table under a state for the CARDINAL, *a longer table for the guests. Then enter* ANNE BULLEN *and divers other* Ladies *and* Gentlemen *as guests, at one door; at another door, enter* SIR HENRY GUILDFORD.

Guild. Ladies, a general welcome from his grace
Salutes ye all; this night he dedicates
To fair content and you: none here, he hopes,
In all this noble bevy, has brought with her
One care abroad; he would have all as merry
As, first, good company, good wine, good welcome,
Can make good people.

Enter LORD CHAMBERLAIN, LORD SANDS, *and* [SIR THOMAS] LOVELL.

O my lord, y' are tardy:
The very thought of this fair company
Clapp'd wings to me.
Cham. You are young, Sir Harry Guildford.
Sands. Sir Thomas Lovell, had the cardinal
But half my lay thoughts in him, some of these
Should find a running banquet ere they rested,
I think would better please 'em: by my life,
They are a sweet society of fair ones.
Lov. O, that your lordship were but now confessor
To one or two of these!
Sands. I would I were;
They should find easy penance.
Lov. Faith, how easy?
Sands. As easy as a down-bed would afford it.
Cham. Sweet ladies, will it please you sit? Sir Harry,
Place you that side; I'll take the charge of this:
His grace is ent'ring. Nay, you must not freeze;
Two women plac'd together makes cold weather:
My Lord Sands, you are one will keep 'em waking;
Pray, sit between these ladies.
Sands. By my faith,
And thank your lordship. By your leave, sweet ladies:
If I chance to talk a little wild, forgive me;
I had it from my father.
Anne. Was he mad, sir?
Sands. O, very mad, exceeding mad, in love too:
But he would bite none; just as I do now,
He would kiss you twenty with a breath. [*Kisses her.*]
Cham. Well said, my lord.
So, now y' are fairly seated. Gentlemen,
The penance lies on you, if these fair ladies
Pass away frowning.
Sands. For my little cure,
Let me alone.

Hautboys. Enter CARDINAL WOLSEY, *and takes his state.*

Wol. Y' are welcome, my fair guests: that noble lady,
Or gentleman, that is not freely merry,
Is not my friend: this, to confirm my welcome;
And to you all, good health. [*Drinks.*]
Sands. Your grace is noble:
Let me have such a bowl may hold my thanks,
And save me so much talking.
Wol. My Lord Sands,
I am beholding to you: cheer your neighbours.
Ladies, you are not merry: gentlemen,
Whose fault is this?
Sands. The red wine first must rise
In their fair cheeks, my lord; then we shall have 'em
Talk us to silence.
Anne. You are a merry gamester,
My Lord Sands.
Sands. Yes, if I make my play.
Here 's to your ladyship: and pledge it, madam,
For 'tis to such a thing,—
Anne. You cannot show me.
Sands. I told your grace they would talk anon.
Drum and trumpet, chambers discharged.
Wol. What 's that?
Cham. Look out there, some of ye. [*Exit Servant.*]
Wol. What warlike voice,
And to what end, is this? Nay, ladies, fear not;
By all the laws of war y' are privileg'd.

Enter a Servant.

Cham. How now! what is 't?
Serv. A noble troop of strangers;
For so they seem: th' have left their barge and landed;
And hither make, as great ambassadors
From foreign princes.
Wol. Good lord chamberlain,
Go, give 'em welcome; you can speak the French tongue;
And, pray, receive 'em nobly, and conduct 'em
Into our presence, where this heaven of beauty
Shall shine at full upon them. Some attend him.
[*Exit Chamberlain, attended.*] *All rise, and tables removed.*
You have now a broken banquet; but we'll mend it.
A good digestion to you all: and once more
I show'r a welcome on ye; welcome all.

Hautboys. Enter KING *and others, as masquers, habited like shepherds, ushered by the* LORD CHAMBERLAIN. *They pass directly before the* CARDINAL, *and gracefully salute him.*

A noble company! what are their pleasures?
Cham. Because they speak no English, thus they pray'd
To tell your grace, that, having heard by fame
Of this so noble and so fair assembly
This night to meet here, they could do no less,
Out of the great respect they bear to beauty,
But leave their flocks; and, under your fair conduct,
Crave leave to view these ladies and entreat
An hour of revels with 'em.
Wol. Say, lord chamberlain,
They have done my poor house grace; for which I pay 'em
A thousand thanks, and pray 'em take their pleasures.
Choose Ladies; King and Anne Bullen.

SCENE IV. *Stage Direction:* ***a state,*** a canopy. 11. **lay,** secular. 12. **running banquet,** hasty meal (with bawdy double meaning, continued in *confess, easy penance,* etc.). 20. **Place,** assign places. 30. **with a breath,** at one breath. 33. **cure,** i.e., cure of souls; the phrase continues the ecclesiastical metaphor of line 15. 39. **may,** which may. 46. **make my play,** win my game. 49. *Stage Direction:* ***chambers,*** small pieces of cannon. 52. **y' are privileg'd,** i.e., entitled to immunity in the event of conflict. 70. **your fair conduct,** your kind permission. 89. **unhappily,** unfavorably. 95. **take you out,** lead you out of the company for a dance. 108. **best in favour,** prettiest. **knock it,** strike up.

ACT II. SCENE I. This scene provides the dramatist the opportunity to incorporate into the play not only the substance of Holinshed's account of Buckingham's trial, but also his comment upon it, particularly Holinshed's censure of Wolsey. *Stage Direction:* **several,** different. 2. **the hall,** i.e., Westminster Hall, where the trial was held. 15. **contrary,** i.e., contrary side. 18. **vivâ voce,** so that their voices can be heard.

King. The fairest hand I ever touch'd! O beauty,
Till now I never knew thee! *Music. Dance.*
Wol. My lord!
Cham. Your grace?
Wol. Pray, tell 'em thus much from me:
There should be one amongst 'em, by his person,
More worthy this place than myself; to whom,
If I but knew him, with my love and duty
I would surrender it.
Cham. I will, my lord.
Whisper [*with the Masquers*].
Wol. What say they?
Cham. Such a one, they all confess,
There is indeed; which they would have your grace
Find out, and he will take it.
Wol. Let me see, then.
By all your good leaves, gentlemen; here I'll make
My royal choice.
King. Ye have found him, cardinal:
[*Unmasking.*]
You hold a fair assembly; you do well, lord:
You are a churchman, or, I'll tell you, cardinal,
I should judge now unhappily.
Wol. I am glad
Your grace is grown so pleasant.
King. My lord chamberlain,
Prithee, come hither: what fair lady 's that?
Cham. An't please your grace, Sir Thomas Bullen's daughter,—
The Viscount Rochford,—one of her highness' women.
King. By heaven, she is a dainty one. Sweetheart,
I were unmannerly, to take you out,
And not to kiss you. A health, gentlemen!
Let it go round.
Wol. Sir Thomas Lovell, is the banquet ready
I' th' privy chamber?
Lov. Yes, my lord.
Wol. Your grace,
I fear, with dancing is a little heated.
King. I fear, too much.
Wol. There 's fresher air, my lord,
In the next chamber.
King. Lead in your ladies, ev'ry one: sweet partner,
I must not yet forsake you: let 's be merry,
Good my lord cardinal: I have half a dozen healths
To drink to these fair ladies, and a measure
To lead 'em once again; and then let 's dream
Who 's best in favour. Let the music knock it.
Exeunt with trumpets.

ACT II

SCENE I. [*Westminster. A street.*]

Enter two Gentlemen, *at several doors.*

First Gent. Whither away so fast?
Sec. Gent. O, God save ye!
Ev'n to the hall, to hear what shall become
Of the great Duke of Buckingham.
First Gent. I'll save you
That labour, sir. All 's now done, but the ceremony
Of bringing back the prisoner.
Sec. Gent. Were you there?
First Gent. Yes, indeed, was I.
Sec. Gent. Pray, speak what has happen'd.
First Gent. You may guess quickly what.
Sec. Gent. Is he found guilty?
First Gent. Yes, truly is he, and condemn'd upon 't.
Sec. Gent. I am sorry for 't.
First Gent. So are a number more.
Sec. Gent. But, pray, how pass'd it?
First Gent. I'll tell you in a little. The great duke
Came to the bar; where to his accusations
He pleaded still not guilty and alleg'd
Many sharp reasons to defeat the law.
The king's attorney on the contrary
Urg'd on the examinations, proofs, confessions
Of divers witnesses; which the duke desir'd
To have brought vivâ voce to his face:
At which appear'd against him his surveyor;
Sir Gilbert Peck his chancellor; and John Car,
Confessor to him; with that devil-monk,
Hopkins, that made this mischief.
Sec. Gent. That was he
That fed him with his prophecies?
First Gent. The same.
All these accus'd him strongly; which he fain
Would have flung from him, but, indeed, he could not:
And so his peers, upon this evidence,
Have found him guilty of high treason. Much
He spoke, and learnedly, for life; but all
Was either pitied in him or forgotten.
Sec. Gent. After all this, how did he bear himself?
First Gent. When he was brought again to th' bar, to hear
His knell rung out, his judgement, he was stirr'd
With such an agony, he sweat extremely,
And something spoke in choler, ill, and hasty:
But he fell to himself again, and sweetly
In all the rest show'd a most noble patience.
Sec. Gent. I do not think he fears death.
First Gent. Sure, he does not:
He never was so womanish; the cause
He may a little grieve at.
Sec. Gent. Certainly
The cardinal is the end of this.
First Gent. 'Tis likely,
By all conjectures: first, Kildare's attainder,
Then deputy of Ireland; who remov'd,
Earl Surrey was sent thither, and in haste too,
Lest he should help his father.
Sec. Gent. That trick of state
Was a deep envious one.
First Gent. At his return
No doubt he will requite it. This is noted,

29. **pitied . . . forgotten,** either produced no effect or produced only ineffectual pity (Malone). 32. **judgement,** sentence. 36. **In all the rest,** for the remaining time. 41-44. **first . . . father.** The incident is in Holinshed: "Bicause [Wolsey] doubted [Buckingham's] freends, kinnesmen, and alies, and cheeflie the earle of Surrie, lord admerall, (which had married the dukes daughter,) he thought good first to send him some whither out of the waie, least he might cast a trumpe in his waie. . . . At length there was occasion offered him to compasse his purpose, by occasion of the earle of Kildare his comming out of Ireland. . . . Such accusations were framed against [Kildare] . . . that he was committed to prison, and then by the cardinall's good preferment, the earle of Surrie was sent into Ireland as the King's deputy, in lieu of the said earle of Kildare; there to remaine rather as an exile than as lieutenant to the king, euen at the cardinall's pleasure, as he himselfe well perceived." 44. **father,** father-in-law.

And generally, whoever the king favours,
The card'nal instantly will find employment,
And far enough from court too.
Sec. Gent. All the commons
Hate him perniciously, and, o' my conscience,
Wish him ten fathom deep: this duke as much
They love and dote on; call him bounteous Buckingham,
The mirror of all courtesy;—

Enter BUCKINGHAM *from his arraignment; tipstaves before him; the axe with the edge towards him; halberds on each side: accompanied with* SIR THOMAS LOVELL, SIR NICHOLAS VAUX, SIR WALTER SANDS, *and common people, &c.*

First Gent. Stay there, sir,
And see the noble ruin'd man you speak of.
Sec. Gent. Let 's stand close, and behold him.
Buck. All good people,
You that thus far have come to pity me,
Hear what I say, and then go home and lose me.
I have this day receiv'd a traitor's judgement,
And by that name must die: yet, heaven bear witness,
And if I have a conscience, let it sink me,
Even as the axe falls, if I be not faithful!
The law I bear no malice for my death;
'T has done, upon the premises, but justice:
But those that sought it I could wish more Christians:
Be what they will, I heartily forgive 'em:
Yet let 'em look they glory not in mischief,
Nor build their evils on the graves of great men;
For then my guiltless blood must cry against 'em.
For further life in this world I ne'er hope,
Nor will I sue, although the king have mercies
More than I dare make faults. You few that lov'd me,
And dare be bold to weep for Buckingham,
His noble friends and fellows, whom to leave
Is only bitter to him, only dying,
Go with me, like good angels, to my end;
And, as the long divorce of steel falls on me,
Make of your prayers one sweet sacrifice,
And lift my soul to heaven. Lead on, o' God's name.
Lov. I do beseech your grace, for charity,
If ever any malice in your heart
Were hid against me, now to forgive me frankly.
Buck. Sir Thomas Lovell, I as free forgive you
As I would be forgiven: I forgive all;
There cannot be those numberless offences
'Gainst me, that I cannot take peace with: no black envy
Shall mark my grave. Commend me to his grace;
And, if he speak of Buckingham, pray, tell him
You met him half in heaven: my vows and prayers
Yet are the king's; and, till my soul forsake,
Shall cry for blessings on him: may he live
Longer than I have time to tell his years!
Ever belov'd and loving may his rule be!
And when old time shall lead him to his end,
Goodness and he fill up one monument!
Lov. To th' water side I must conduct your grace;
Then give my charge up to Sir Nicholas Vaux,
Who undertakes you to your end.
Vaux. Prepare there,
The duke is coming: see the barge be ready;
And fit it with such furniture as suits
The greatness of his person.
Buck. Nay, Sir Nicholas,
Let alone; my state now will but mock me.
When I came hither, I was lord high constable
And Duke of Buckingham; now, poor Edward Bohun:
Yet I am richer than my base accusers,
That never knew what truth meant: I now seal it;
And with that blood will make 'em one day groan for 't.
My noble father, Henry of Buckingham,
Who first rais'd head against usurping Richard,
Flying for succour to his servant Banister,
Being distress'd, was by that wretch betray'd,
And without trial fell; God's peace be with him!
Henry the Seventh succeeding, truly pitying
My father's loss, like a most royal prince,
Restor'd me to my honours, and, out of ruins,
Made my name once more noble. Now his son,
Henry the Eighth, life, honour, name and all
That made me happy at one stroke has taken
For ever from the world. I had my trial,
And, must needs say, a noble one; which makes me
A little happier than my wretched father:
Yet thus far we are one in fortunes: both
Fell by our servants, by those men we lov'd most;
A most unnatural and faithless service!
Heaven has an end in all: yet, you that hear me,
This from a dying man receive as certain:
Where you are liberal of your loves and counsels
Be sure you be not loose; for those you make friends
And give your hearts to, when they once perceive
The least rub in your fortunes, fall away
Like water from ye, never found again
But where they mean to sink ye. All good people,
Pray for me! I must now forsake ye: the last hour
Of my long weary life is come upon me.
Farewell:
And when you would say something that is sad,
Speak how I fell. I have done; and God forgive me!
Exeunt Duke and Train.
First Gent. O, this is full of pity! Sir, it calls,
I fear, too many curses on their heads
That were the authors.
Sec. Gent. If the duke be guiltless,
'Tis full of woe: yet I can give you inkling
Of an ensuing evil, if it fall,
Greater than this.
First Gent. Good angels keep it from us!
What may it be? You do not doubt my faith, sir?
Sec. Gent. This secret is so weighty, 'twill require
A strong faith to conceal it.
First Gent. Let me have it;
I do not talk much.
Sec. Gent. I am confident;
You shall, sir: did you not of late days hear

50. **perniciously,** i.e., with deadly hatred. 53. *Stage Direction:* ***tipstaves,*** bailiffs. ***halberds,*** halberdiers with long-handled weapons. **Walter,** "William" in Holinshed. 57. **lose,** forget. 63. **premises,** evidence. 76. **divorce,** that which causes separation. 84-85. **There . . . with,** i.e., I can make peace with any number of those who have offended me. 89. **forsake,** leave my body. 91. **tell,** count. 105. **seal,** ratify. 108. **rais'd head,** gathered an army. 119. **a noble one,** i.e., trial by his peers. Buckingham's father had been executed by Richard III. 127. **loose,** wanting in restraint. 143. **faith,** ability to keep a secret. 147. **shall,** i.e., shall hear it. 149. **held,** lasted. 158. **scruple.** Katharine had been betrothed to Henry's older brother, Prince Arthur, which according to the laws of the precontract would make illegal her marriage with any close relative after Arthur's death. Henry's marriage to Katharine was made possible by a papal dispensation. 160. **Cardinal**

A buzzing of a separation
Between the king and Katharine?
First Gent. Yes, but it held not:
For when the king once heard it, out of anger
He sent command to the lord mayor straight
To stop the rumour, and allay those tongues
That durst disperse it.
Sec. Gent. But that slander, sir,
Is found a truth now: for it grows again
Fresher than e'er it was; and held for certain
The king will venture at it. Either the cardinal,
Or some about him near, have, out of malice
To the good queen, possess'd him with a scruple
That will undo her: to confirm this too,
Cardinal Campeius is arriv'd, and lately;
As all think, for this business.
First Gent. 'Tis the cardinal;
And merely to revenge him on the emperor
For not bestowing on him, at his asking,
The archbishopric of Toledo, this is purpos'd.
Sec. Gent. I think you have hit the mark: but is 't not cruel
That she should feel the smart of this? The cardinal
Will have his will, and she must fall.
First Gent. 'Tis woful.
We are too open here to argue this;
Let 's think in private more. *Exeunt.*

SCENE II. [*An ante-chamber in the palace.*]

Enter LORD CHAMBERLAIN, *reading this letter.*

Cham. 'My lord, the horses your lordship sent for, with all the care I had, I saw well chosen, ridden, and furnished. They were young and handsome, and of the best breed in the north. When they were ready to set out for London, a man of my lord cardinal's, by commission and main power, took 'em from me; with this reason: His master would be served before a subject, if not before the king; which stopped our mouths, sir.'
I fear he will indeed: well, let him have them:
He will have all, I think.

Enter, to the LORD CHAMBERLAIN, *the* DUKES OF NORFOLK *and* SUFFOLK.

Nor. Well met, my lord chamberlain.
Cham. Good day to both your graces.
Suf. How is the king employ'd?
Cham. I left him private,
Full of sad thoughts and troubles.
Nor. What 's the cause?
Cham. It seems the marriage with his brother's wife
Has crept too near his conscience.
Suf. No, his conscience
Has crept too near another lady.
Nor. 'Tis so:
This is the cardinal's doing, the king-cardinal:
That blind priest, like the eldest son of Fortune,
Turns what he list. The king will know him one day.
Suf. Pray God he do! he'll never know himself else.
Nor. How holily he works in all his business!
And with what zeal! for, now he has crack'd the league
Between us and the emperor, the queen's great nephew,
He dives into the king's soul, and there scatters
Dangers, doubts, wringing of the conscience,
Fears, and despairs; and all these for his marriage:
And out of all these to restore the king,
He counsels a divorce; a loss of her
That, like a jewel, has hung twenty years
About his neck, yet never lost her lustre;
Of her that loves him with that excellence
That angels love good men with; even of her
That, when the greatest stroke of fortune falls,
Will bless the king: and is not this course pious?
Cham. Heaven keep me from such counsel! 'Tis most true
These news are every where; every tongue speaks 'em,
And every true heart weeps for 't: all that dare
Look into these affairs see this main end,
The French king's sister. Heaven will one day open
The king's eyes, that so long have slept upon
This bold bad man.
Suf. And free us from his slavery.
Nor. We had need pray,
And heartily, for our deliverance;
Or this imperious man will work us all
From princes into pages: all men's honours
Lie like one lump before him, to be fashion'd
Into what pitch he please.
Suf. For me, my lords,
I love him not, nor fear him; there 's my creed:
As I am made without him, so I'll stand,
If the king please; his curses and his blessings
Touch me alike, th' are breath I not believe in.
I knew him, and I know him; so I leave him
To him that made him proud, the pope.
Nor. Let 's in;
And with some other business put the king
From these sad thoughts, that work too much upon him:
My lord, you'll bear us company?
Cham. Excuse me;
The king has sent me otherwhere: besides,
You'll find a most unfit time to disturb him:
Health to your lordships.
Nor. Thanks, my good lord chamberlain.
Exit Lord Chamberlain; and the King draws the curtain and sits reading pensively.
Suf. How sad he looks! sure, he is much afflicted.
King. Who 's there, ha?
Nor. Pray God he be not angry.
King. Who 's there, I say? How dare you thrust yourselves
Into my private meditations?
Who am I? ha?
Nor. A gracious king that pardons all offences
Malice ne'er meant: our breach of duty this way
Is business of estate; in which we come

Campeius, Cardinal Lorenzo Campeggio, sent from Rome to confer on the legality of the king's marriage. 162. **to . . . emperor.** The queen was the aunt of Charles v, Holy Roman Emperor and King of Spain.
SCENE II. 3. **ridden,** broken in, trained. 6. **commission,** warrant. 7. **main,** mighty; i.e., by force. 29. **for,** on account of. 32-33. **like . . . neck,** refers to the custom among gentlemen of wearing a jewel on a chain or ribbon around the neck. 42. **The . . . sister,** i.e., the Duchess of Alençon; see III, ii, 86. 50. **pitch,** degree of dignity; i.e., the cardinal reduces all men of rank to one lump which he will refashion into creatures of whatever stature he pleases. 52. **As . . . him,** refers to his rank conferred by the king. The speaker was elevated to the dukedom on his marriage with the king's sister, dowager queen of France. 62. *Stage Direction:* **curtain.** The king is probably in the "discovery space" rear stage. 70. **estate,** public weal.

To know your royal pleasure.
King. Ye are too bold:
Go to; I'll make ye know your times of business:
Is this an hour for temporal affairs, ha?

Enter WOLSEY *and* CAMPEIUS, *with a commission.*

Who 's there? my good lord cardinal? O my Wolsey,
The quiet of my wounded conscience;
Thou art a cure fit for a king. [*To Camp.*] You 're welcome,
Most learned reverend sir, into our kingdom:
Use us and it. [*To Wol.*] My good lord, have great care
I be not found a talker.
Wol. Sir, you cannot.
I would your grace would give us but an hour
Of private conference.
King. [*To Nor. and Suf.*] We are busy; go.
Nor. [*Aside to Suf.*] This priest has no pride in him?
Suf. [*Aside to Nor.*] Not to speak of:
I would not be so sick though for his place:
But this cannot continue.
Nor. [*Aside to Suf.*] If it do,
I'll venture one have-at-him.
Suf. [*Aside to Nor.*] I another.
Exeunt Nor. and Suf.
Wol. Your grace has given a precedent of wisdom
Above all princes, in committing freely
Your scruple to the voice of Christendom:
Who can be angry now? what envy reach you?
The Spaniard, tied by blood and favour to her,
Must now confess, if they have any goodness,
The trial just and noble. All the clerks,
I mean the learned ones, in Christian kingdoms
Have their free voices: Rome, the nurse of judgement,
Invited by your noble self, hath sent
One general tongue unto us, this good man,
This just and learned priest, Card'nal Campeius;
Whom once more I present unto your highness.
King. And once more in mine arms I bid him welcome,
And thank the holy conclave for their loves:
They have sent me such a man I would have wish'd for.
Cam. Your grace must needs deserve all strangers' loves,
You are so noble. To your highness' hand
I tender my commission; by whose virtue,
The court of Rome commanding, you, my lord
Cardinal of York, are join'd with me their servant
In the unpartial judging of this business.
King. Two equal men. The queen shall be acquainted
Forthwith for what you come. Where 's Gardiner?
Wol. I know your majesty has always lov'd her
So dear in heart, not to deny her that
A woman of less place might ask by law:
Scholars allow'd freely to argue for her.
King. Ay, and the best she shall have; and my favour
To him that does best: God forbid else. Cardinal,
Prithee, call Gardiner to me, my new secretary:
I find him a fit fellow. [*Wolsey goes to the door.*]

Enter GARDINER.

Wol. [*Aside to Gard.*] Give me your hand: much joy and favour to you;
You are the king's now.
Gard. [*Aside to Wol.*] But to be commanded
For ever by your grace, whose hand has rais'd me.
King. Come hither, Gardiner. *Walks and whispers.*
Cam. My Lord of York, was not one Doctor Pace
In this man's place before him?
Wol. Yes, he was.
Cam. Was he not held a learned man?
Wol. Yes, surely.
Cam. Believe me, there 's an ill opinion spread then
Even of yourself, lord cardinal.
Wol. How! of me?
Cam. They will not stick to say you envied him,
And fearing he would rise, he was so virtuous,
Kept him a foreign man still; which so griev'd him,
That he ran mad and died.
Wol. Heav'n's peace be with him!
That 's Christian care enough: for living murmurers
There 's places of rebuke. He was a fool;
For he would needs be virtuous: that good fellow,
If I command him, follows my appointment:
I will have none so near else. Learn this, brother,
We live not to be grip'd by meaner persons.
King. Deliver this with modesty to th' queen.
Exit Gardiner.
The most convenient place that I can think of
For such receipt of learning is Black-Friars;
There ye shall meet about this weighty business.
My Wolsey, see it furnish'd. O, my lord,
Would it not grieve an able man to leave
So sweet a bedfellow? But, conscience, conscience!
O, 'tis a tender place; and I must leave her. *Exeunt.*

SCENE III. [*An ante-chamber of the* Queen's *apartments.*]

Enter ANNE BULLEN *and an* Old Lady.

Anne. Not for that neither: here 's the pang that pinches:
His highness having liv'd so long with her, and she
So good a lady that no tongue could ever
Pronounce dishonour of her; by my life,
She never knew harm-doing: O, now, after
So many courses of the sun enthroned,
Still growing in a majesty and pomp, the which
To leave a thousand-fold more bitter than
'Tis sweet at first t' acquire,—after this process,
To give her the avaunt! it is a pity
Would move a monster.
Old L. Hearts of most hard temper
Melt and lament for her.
Anne. O, God's will! much better
She ne'er had known pomp: though 't be temporal,

79. **talker,** i.e., rather than a doer. 83. **sick,** i.e., sick with pride. **for his place,** even for his high office. 88. **voice of Christendom,** i.e., the pope, through his representative Campeius. 96. **general tongue,** spokesman. 100. **conclave,** college of cardinals. 109. **Gardiner,** Stephen Gardiner, Wolsey's secretary; he later became one of the most influential members of the king's council. 111. **that,** that which.

122. **Doctor Pace,** a brilliant foreign diplomat of Henry's reign. His abilities are said to have provoked Wolsey's envy to the extent that the latter kept him away from court on foreign errands (cf. ll. 128-129). 127. **stick,** hesitate. 139. **Black-Friars,** convent buildings in London surrendered to the crown in Henry VIII's time.

SCENE III. 14. **quarrel,** quarreler; the abstract for the concrete

Yet, if that quarrel, Fortune, do divorce
It from the bearer, 'tis a sufferance panging
As soul and body's severing.
Old L. Alas, poor lady!
She 's a stranger now again.
Anne. So much the more
Must pity drop upon her. Verily,
I swear, 'tis better to be lowly born,
And range with humble livers in content,
Than to be perk'd up in a glist'ring grief,
And wear a golden sorrow.
Old L. Our content
Is our best having.
Anne. By my troth and maidenhead,
I would not be a queen.
Old L. Beshrew me, I would,
And venture maidenhead for 't; and so would you,
For all this spice of your hypocrisy:
You, that have so fair parts of woman on you,
Have too a woman's heart; which ever yet
Affected eminence, wealth, sovereignty;
Which, to say sooth, are blessings; and which gifts,
Saving your mincing, the capacity
Of your soft cheveril conscience would receive,
If you might please to stretch it.
Anne. Nay, good troth.
Old L. Yes, troth, and troth; you would not be a queen?
Anne. No, not for all the riches under heaven.
Old L. 'Tis strange: a three-pence bow'd would hire me,
Old as I am, to queen it: but, I pray you,
What think you of a duchess? have you limbs
To bear that load of title?
Anne. No, in truth.
Old L. Then you are weakly made: pluck off a little;
I would not be a young count in your way,
For more than blushing comes to: if your back
Cannot vouchsafe this burthen, 'tis too weak
Ever to get a boy.
Anne. How you do talk!
I swear again, I would not be a queen
For all the world.
Old L. In faith, for little England
You 'ld venture an emballing: I myself
Would for Carnarvonshire, although there 'long'd
No more to th' crown but that. Lo, who comes here?

Enter LORD CHAMBERLAIN.

Cham. Good morrow, ladies. What were 't worth to know
The secret of your conference?
Anne. My good Lord,
Not your demand; it values not your asking:
Our mistress' sorrows we were pitying.
Cham. It was a gentle business, and becoming
The action of good women: there is hope
All will be well.
Anne. Now, I pray God, amen!
Cham. You bear a gentle mind, and heav'nly blessings
Follow such creatures. That you may, fair lady,
Perceive I speak sincerely, and high note 's
Ta'en of your many virtues, the king's majesty
Commends his good opinion of you, and
Does purpose honour to you no less flowing
Than Marchioness of Pembroke; to which title
A thousand pound a year, annual support,
Out of his grace he adds.
Anne. I do not know
What kind of my obedience I should tender;
More than my all is nothing: nor my prayers
Are not words duly hallowed, nor my wishes
More worth than empty vanities; yet prayers and wishes
Are all I can return. Beseech your lordship,
Vouchsafe to speak my thanks and my obedience,
As from a blushing handmaid, to his highness;
Whose health and royalty I pray for.
Cham. Lady,
I shall not fail t' approve the fair conceit
The king hath of you. [*Aside*] I have perus'd her well;
Beauty and honour in her are so mingled
That they have caught the king: and who knows yet
But from this lady may proceed a gem
To lighten all this isle?—I'll to the king,
And say I spoke with you. *Exit Lord Chamberlain.*
Anne. My honour'd lord.
Old L. Why, this it is; see, see!
I have been begging sixteen years in court,
Am yet a courtier beggarly, nor could
Come pat betwixt too early and too late
For any suit of pounds; and you, O fate!
A very fresh fish here—fie, fie, fie upon
This compell'd fortune!—have your mouth fill'd up
Before you open it.
Anne. This is strange to me.
Old L. How tastes it? is it bitter? forty pence, no.
There was a lady once, 'tis an old story,
That would not be a queen, that would she not,
For all the mud in Egypt: have you heard it?
Anne. Come, you are pleasant.
Old L. With your theme, I could
O'ermount the lark. The Marchioness of Pembroke!
A thousand pounds a year for pure respect!
No other obligation! By my life,
That promises moe thousands: honour's train
Is longer than his foreskirt. By this time
I know your back will bear a duchess: say,
Are you not stronger than you were?
Anne. Good lady,
Make yourself mirth with your particular fancy,
And leave me out on 't. Would I had no being,
If this salute my blood a jot: it faints me,
To think what follows.
The queen is comfortless, and we forgetful
In our long absence: pray, do not deliver
What here y' have heard to her.
Old L. What do you think me? *Exeunt.*

(Johnson). 15. **panging,** causing sorrow. 21. **perk'd up,** trimmed out. 23. **having,** possession. 31. **Saving,** despite. **mincing,** coyness. 32. **cheveril,** kid leather; used as a type of flexibility. 36. **bow'd,** crooked and therefore worthless; with sexual pun on *bawd*, continued in *queen* (quean, whore), *bear*, *count* (female pudenda), *way*, *emballing*. 40. **pluck off,** come lower. 47. **emballing,** investing with the ball as emblem of royalty. 52. **values not,** is not worth. 62. **flowing,** abundant. 83. **courtier beggarly,** a poor courtier, and in a beggarly posture; used quibblingly. 85. **suit of pounds,** request for money. 87. **compell'd,** unsought. 92. **mud in Egypt,** the wealth of Egypt, referring to the overflowing of the Nile as the source of Egypt's productivity. 103. **salute,** act upon.

SCENE IV. [*A hall in Black-Friars.*]

Trumpets, sennet, and cornets. Enter two Vergers, *with short silver wands; next them, two* Scribes, *in the habit of doctors; after them, the* [ARCH]BISHOP OF CANTERBURY *alone; after him, the* BISHOPS OF LINCOLN, ELY, ROCHESTER, *and* SAINT ASAPH; *next them, with some small distance, follows a* Gentleman *bearing the purse, with the great seal, and a cardinal's hat; then two* Priests, *bearing each a silver cross; then a* Gentleman-usher *bare-headed, accompanied with a* Sergeant-at-arms *bearing a silver mace; then two* Gentlemen *bearing two great silver pillars; after them, side by side, the two* CARDINALS; *two* Noblemen *with the sword and mace. The* KING *takes place under the cloth of state; the two* CARDINALS *sit under him as judges. The* QUEEN *takes place some distance from the* KING. *The* Bishops *place themselves on each side the court, in manner of a consistory; below them, the* Scribes. *The* Lords *sit next the* Bishops. *The rest of the* Attendants *stand in convenient order about the stage.*

Wol. Whilst our commission from Rome is read,
Let silence be commanded.
King. What 's the need?
It hath already publicly been read,
And on all sides th' authority allow'd;
You may, then, spare that time.
Wol. Be 't so. Proceed.
Scribe. Say, Henry King of England, come into the court.
Crier. Henry King of England, &c.
King. Here.
Scribe. Say, Katharine Queen of England, come into the court.
Crier. Katharine Queen of England, &c.

The Queen makes no answer, rises out of her chair, goes about the court, comes to the King, and kneels at his feet; then speaks.

Q. Kath. Sir, I desire you do me right and justice;
And to bestow your pity on me: for
I am a most poor woman, and a stranger,
Born out of your dominions; having here
No judge indifferent, nor no more assurance
Of equal friendship and proceeding. Alas, sir,
In what have I offended you? what cause
Hath my behaviour given to your displeasure,
That thus you should proceed to put me off,
And take your good grace from me? Heaven witness,
I have been to you a true and humble wife,
At all times to your will conformable;
Ever in fear to kindle your dislike,
Yea, subject to your countenance, glad or sorry
As I saw it inclin'd: when was the hour
I ever contradicted your desire,
Or made it not mine too? Or which of your friends
Have I not strove to love, although I knew
He were mine enemy? what friend of mine
That had to him deriv'd your anger, did I
Continue in my liking? nay, gave notice
He was from thence discharg'd? Sir, call to mind
That I have been your wife, in this obedience,
Upward of twenty years, and have been blest
With many children by you: if, in the course
And process of this time, you can report,
And prove it too, against mine honour aught,
My bond to wedlock, or my love and duty,
Against your sacred person, in God's name,
Turn me away; and let the foul'st contempt
Shut door upon me, and so give me up
To the sharp'st kind of justice. Please you, sir,
The king, your father, was reputed for
A prince most prudent, of an excellent
And unmatch'd wit and judgement: Ferdinand,
My father, king of Spain, was reckon'd one
The wisest prince that there had reign'd by many
A year before: it is not to be question'd
That they had gather'd a wise council to them
Of every realm, that did debate this business,
Who deem'd our marriage lawful: wherefore I humbly
Beseech you, sir, to spare me, till I may
Be by my friends in Spain advis'd; whose counsel
I will implore: if not, i' th' name of God,
Your pleasure be fulfill'd!
Wol. You have here, lady,
And of your choice, these reverend fathers; men
Of singular integrity and learning,
Yea, the elect o' th' land, who are assembled
To plead your cause: it shall be therefore bootless
That longer you desire the court; as well
For your own quiet, as to rectify
What is unsettled in the king.
Cam. His grace
Hath spoken well and justly: therefore, madam,
It 's fit this royal session do proceed;
And that, without delay, their arguments
Be now produc'd and heard.
Q. Kath. Lord cardinal,
To you I speak.
Wol. Your pleasure, madam?
Q. Kath. Sir,
I am about to weep; but, thinking that
We are a queen, or long have dream'd so, certain
The daughter of a king, my drops of tears
I'll turn to sparks of fire.
Wol. Be patient yet.
Q. Kath. I will, when you are humble; nay, before,
Or God will punish me. I do believe,
Induc'd by potent circumstances, that
You are mine enemy, and make my challenge
You shall not be my judge: for it is you
Have blown this coal betwixt my lord and me;
Which God's dew quench! Therefore I say again,
I utterly abhor, yea, from my soul
Refuse you for my judge; whom, yet once more,
I hold my most malicious foe, and think not
At all a friend to truth.
Wol. I do profess
You speak not like yourself; who ever yet
Have stood to charity, and display'd th' effects
Of disposition gentle, and of wisdom
O'ertopping woman's pow'r. Madam, you do me wrong:
I have no spleen against you; nor injustice

SCENE IV. *Stage Direction:* (1) **Vergers,** those who carry the verge or emblem of office; particularly attendants on a church dignitary. (13) ***cloth of state,*** canopy. (17) ***consistory,*** college of cardinals presided over by the pope. 37. **many children.** The queen gave birth to five children, only one of whom (later Queen Mary) survived infancy. 62. **That . . . court,** that you wish the court inquiry to be prolonged. 71. **certain,** certainly. 77. **make my challenge,** i.e., I request that, etc. 96. **wound,** show up; i.e., demonstrate me a falsifier. 99. **re-**

For you or any: how far I have proceeded,
Or how far further shall, is warranted
By a commission from the consistory,
Yea, the whole consistory of Rome. You charge me
That I have blown this coal: I do deny it:
The king is present: if it be known to him
That I gainsay my deed, how may he wound,
And worthily, my falsehood! yea, as much
As you have done my truth. If he know
That I am free of your report, he knows
I am not of your wrong. Therefore in him
It lies to cure me: and the cure is, to
Remove these thoughts from you: the which before
His highness shall speak in, I do beseech
You, gracious madam, to unthink your speaking
And to say so no more.
Q. Kath. My lord, my lord,
I am a simple woman, much too weak
T' oppose your cunning. Y' are meek and humble-mouth'd;
You sign your place and calling, in full seeming,
With meekness and humility; but your heart
Is cramm'd with arrogancy, spleen, and pride.
You have, by fortune and his highness' favours,
Gone slightly o'er low steps and now are mounted
Where pow'rs are your retainers, and your words,
Domestics to you, serve your will as 't please
Yourself pronounce their office. I must tell you,
You tender more your person's honour than
Your high profession spiritual: that again
I do refuse you for my judge; and here,
Before you all, appeal unto the pope,
To bring my whole cause 'fore his holiness,
And to be judg'd by him.
She curtsies to the King, and offers to depart.
Cam. The queen is obstinate,
Stubborn to justice, apt to accuse it, and
Disdainful to be tried by 't: 'tis not well.
She 's going away.
King. Call her again.
Crier. Katharine Queen of England, come into the court.
Grif. Madam, you are call'd back.
Q. Kath. What need you note it? pray you, keep your way:
When you are call'd, return. Now, the Lord help,
They vex me past my patience! Pray you, pass on:
I will not tarry; no, nor ever more
Upon this business my appearance make
In any of their courts. *Exeunt Queen, and her Attendants.*
King. Go thy ways, Kate:
That man i' th' world who shall report he has
A better wife, let him in nought be trusted,
For speaking false in that: thou art, alone,
If thy rare qualities, sweet gentleness,
Thy meekness saint-like, wife-like government,
Obeying in commanding, and thy parts
Sovereign and pious else, could speak thee out,
The queen of earthly queens: she 's noble born;
And, like her true nobility, she has
Carried herself towards me.
Wol. Most gracious sir,
In humblest manner I require your highness,
That it shall please you to declare, in hearing
Of all these ears,—for where I am robb'd and bound,
There must I be unloos'd, although not there
At once and fully satisfied,—whether ever I
Did broach this business to your highness; or
Laid any scruple in your way, which might
Induce you to the question on 't? or ever
Have to you, but with thanks to God for such
A royal lady, spake one the least word that might
Be to the prejudice of her present state,
Or touch of her good person?
King. My lord cardinal,
I do excuse you; yea, upon mine honour,
I free you from 't. You are not to be taught
That you have many enemies, that know not
Why they are so, but, like to village-curs,
Bark when their fellows do: by some of these
The queen is put in anger. Y' are excus'd:
But will you be more justified? you ever
Have wish'd the sleeping of this business; never desir'd
It to be stirr'd; but oft have hind'red, oft,
The passages made toward it: on my honour,
I speak my good lord card'nal to this point,
And thus far clear him. Now, what mov'd me to 't,
I will be bold with time and your attention:
Then mark th' inducement. Thus it came; give heed to 't:
My conscience first receiv'd a tenderness,
Scruple, and prick, on certain speeches utter'd
By th' Bishop of Bayonne, then French ambassador;
Who had been hither sent on the debating
A marriage 'twixt the Duke of Orleans and
Our daughter Mary: i' th' progress of this business,
Ere a determinate resolution, he,
I mean the bishop, did require a respite;
Wherein he might the king his lord advertise
Whether our daughter were legitimate,
Respecting this our marriage with the dowager,
Sometimes our brother's wife. This respite shook
The bosom of my conscience, enter'd me,
Yea, with a spitting power, and made to tremble
The region of my breast; which forc'd such way,
That many maz'd considerings did throng
And press'd in with this caution. First, methought
I stood not in the smile of heaven; who had
Commanded nature, that my lady's womb,
If it conceiv'd a male child by me, should
Do no more offices of life to 't than
The grave does to th' dead; for her male issue
Or died where they were made, or shortly after
This world had air'd them: hence I took a thought,
This was a judgement on me; that my kingdom,
Well worthy the best heir o' th' world, should not
Be gladded in 't by me: then follows, that
I weigh'd the danger which my realms stood in
By this my issue's fail; and that gave to me
Many a groaning throe. Thus hulling in
The wild sea of my conscience, I did steer
Toward this remedy, whereupon we are
Now present here together; that 's to say,

port, adverse report. 103. **in,** regarding. 112. **slightly,** easily. 113. **pow'rs . . . retainers,** you command the service of people of rank. 116. **tender,** are concerned for. 138. **government,** behavior. 140. **speak thee out,** declare you as you are. 153. **one the least,** a single. 155. **touch,** sullying. 166. **speak,** describe. 178. **advertise,** inform. 182. **bosom,** depths. 183. **spitting,** piercing. 185. **maz'd considerings,** conflicting and confused thoughts. 198. **By . . . fail,** by my lacking a son. 199. **hulling,** drifting with sails furled.

I meant to rectify my conscience,—which
I then did feel full sick, and yet not well,—
By all the reverend fathers of the land
And doctors learn'd: first I began in private
With you, my Lord of Lincoln; you remember
How under my oppression I did reek,
When I first mov'd you.
Lin. Very well, my liege.
King. I have spoke long: be pleas'd yourself to say
How far you satisfied me.
Lin. So please your highness,
The question did at first so stagger me,
Bearing a state of mighty moment in 't
And consequence of dread, that I committed
The daring'st counsel which I had to doubt;
And did entreat your highness to this course
Which you are running here.
King. I then mov'd you,
My Lord of Canterbury; and got your leave
To make this present summons: unsolicited
I left no reverend person in this court;
But by particular consent proceeded
Under your hands and seals: therefore, go on;
For no dislike i' th' world against the person
Of the good queen, but the sharp thorny points
Of my alleged reasons, drive this forward:
Prove but our marriage lawful, by my life
And kingly dignity, we are contented
To wear our mortal state to come with her,
Katharine our queen, before the primest creature
That 's paragon'd o' th' world.
Cam. So please your highness,
The queen being absent, 'tis a needful fitness
That we adjourn this court till further day:
Meanwhile must be an earnest motion
Made to the queen, to call back her appeal
She intends unto his holiness.
King. [*Aside*] I may perceive
These cardinals trifle with me: I abhor
This dilatory sloth and tricks of Rome.
My learn'd and well-beloved servant, Cranmer,
Prithee, return: with thy approach, I know,
My comfort comes along.—Break up the court:
I say, set on. *Exeunt in manner as they entered.*

ACT III.

SCENE I. [*London. The* QUEEN's *apartments.*]

The QUEEN *and her Women, as at work.*

Q. Kath. Take thy lute, wench: my soul grows sad with troubles;
Sing, and disperse 'em, if thou canst: leave working.

SONG.

Orpheus with his lute made trees,
And the mountain tops that freeze,
Bow themselves when he did sing:
To his music plants and flowers
Ever sprung; as sun and showers
There had made a lasting spring.

Every thing that heard him play,
Even the billows of the sea,
Hung their heads, and then lay by.
In sweet music is such art,
Killing care and grief of heart
Fall asleep, or hearing, die.

Enter a Gentleman.

Q. Kath. How now!
Gent. An 't please your grace, the two great cardinals
Wait in the presence.
Q. Kath. Would they speak with me?
Gent. They will'd me say so, madam.
Q. Kath. Pray their graces
To come near. [*Exit Gent.*] What can be their business
With me, a poor weak woman, fall'n from favour?
I do not like their coming. Now I think on 't,
They should be good men; their affairs as righteous:
But all hoods make not monks.

Enter the two Cardinals, WOLSEY *and* CAMPEIUS.

Wol. Peace to your highness!
Q. Kath. Your graces find me here part of a housewife.
I would be all, against the worst may happen.
What are your pleasures with me, reverend lords?
Wol. May it please you, noble madam, to withdraw
Into your private chamber, we shall give you
The full cause of our coming.
Q. Kath. Speak it here;
There 's nothing I have done yet, o' my conscience,
Deserves a corner: would all other women
Could speak this with as free a soul as I do!
My lords, I care not, so much I am happy
Above a number, if my actions
Were tried by ev'ry tongue, ev'ry eye saw 'em,
Envy and base opinion set against 'em,
I know my life so even. If your business
Seek me out, and that way I am wife in,
Out with it boldly: truth loves open dealing.
Wol. Tanta est erga te mentis integritas, regina serenissima,—
Q. Kath. O, good my lord, no Latin;
I am not such a truant since my coming,
As not to know the language I have liv'd in:
A strange tongue makes my cause more strange, suspicious;
Pray, speak in English: here are some will thank you,
If you speak truth, for their poor mistress' sake;
Believe me, she has had much wrong: lord cardinal,
The willing'st sin I ever yet committed
May be absolv'd in English.

---

204. **yet,** still. 208. **reek,** sweat. 209. **mov'd,** mentioned the business. 213. **Bearing . . . moment,** relating to matters of the greatest consequence to the state. 214. **consequence of dread,** outcome fearful to contemplate. 214-215. **I . . . doubt,** I distrusted the most daring advice I could give (i.e., to seek an immediate dissolution of the marriage; instead, Lincoln urged a hearing in court). 222. **Under . . . seals,** i.e., with your signed agreement. 229. **primest,** most excellent. 230. **paragon'd,** set forth as a perfect model. 233. **motion,** appeal. 238. **Cranmer.** Thomas Cranmer, a University fellow, first attracted the king's notice with the advice that the marriage question should be resolved by the universities, not the pope. He became a useful and pliant churchman in fulfilling the king's wishes and was made Archbishop of Canterbury at the death of Warham.

ACT III. SCENE I. 3. **Orpheus with his lute,** alludes to the myth of Orpheus, who played on his lyre so beautifully that wild beasts, rocks, and trees listened to him. 11. **lay by,** subsided. 17. **presence,** presence chamber. 22. **their affairs,** the business they come on. 23. **hoods . . . monks,** an old proverb, usually in Latin; cf. *Measure for Measure,* V, i, 263. 24-25. **part of . . . all.** *Part of a housewife* refers to her being engaged in embroidery; *I would be all,* i.e., a complete housewife, in case I am divorced and obliged to earn my own living—a jesting exaggeration of the dangers before her (Pooler). 34. **a number,**

Wol. Noble lady,
I am sorry my integrity should breed,
And service to his majesty and you,
So deep suspicion, where all faith was meant.
We come not by the way of accusation,
To taint that honour every good tongue blesses,
Nor to betray you any way to sorrow,
You have too much, good lady; but to know
How you stand minded in the weighty difference
Between the king and you; and to deliver,
Like free and honest men, our just opinions
And comforts to your cause.
Cam. Most honour'd madam,
My Lord of York, out of his noble nature,
Zeal and obedience he still bore your grace,
Forgetting, like a good man, your late censure
Both of his truth and him, which was too far,
Offers, as I do, in a sign of peace,
His service and his counsel.
Q. Kath. [*Aside*] To betray me.—
My lords, I thank you both for your good wills;
Ye speak like honest men; pray God, ye prove so!
But how to make ye suddenly an answer,
In such a point of weight, so near mine honour,—
More near my life, I fear,—with my weak wit,
And to such men of gravity and learning,
In truth, I know not. I was set at work
Among my maids: full little, God knows, looking
Either for such men or such business.
For her sake that I have been,—for I feel
The last fit of my greatness,—good your graces,
Let me have time and counsel for my cause:
Alas, I am a woman, friendless, hopeless!
Wol. Madam, you wrong the king's love with these fears:
Your hopes and friends are infinite.
Q. Kath. In England
But little for my profit: can you think, lords,
That any Englishman dare give me counsel?
Or be a known friend, 'gainst his highness' pleasure,
Though he be grown so desperate to be honest,
And live a subject? Nay, forsooth, my friends,
They that must weigh out my afflictions,
They that my trust must grow to, live not here:
They are, as all my other comforts, far hence
In mine own country, lords.
Cam. I would your grace
Would leave your griefs, and take my counsel.
Q. Kath. How, sir?
Cam. Put your main cause into the king's protection;
He 's loving and most gracious: 'twill be much
Both for your honour better and your cause;
For if the trial of the law o'ertake ye,
You'll part away disgrac'd.
Wol. He tells you rightly.
Q. Kath. Ye tell me what ye wish for both,—my ruin:
Is this your Christian counsel? out upon ye!
Heaven is above all yet; there sits a judge
That no king can corrupt.
Cam. Your rage mistakes us.
Q. Kath. The more shame for ye: holy men I thought ye,
Upon my soul, two reverend cardinal virtues;
But cardinal sins and hollow hearts I fear ye:
Mend 'em, for shame, my lords. Is this your comfort?
The cordial that ye bring a wretched lady,
A woman lost among ye, laugh'd at, scorn'd?
I will not wish ye half my miseries;
I have more charity: but say, I warn'd ye;
Take heed, for heaven's sake, take heed, lest at once
The burthen of my sorrows fall upon ye.
Wol. Madam, this is a mere distraction;
You turn the good we offer into envy.
Q. Kath. Ye turn me into nothing: woe upon ye
And all such false professors! would you have me—
If you have any justice, any pity;
If ye be any thing but churchmen's habits—
Put my sick cause into his hands that hates me?
Alas, has banish'd me his bed already,
His love, too long ago! I am old, my lords,
And all the fellowship I hold now with him
Is only my obedience. What can happen
To me above this wretchedness? all your studies
Make me a curse like this.
Cam. Your fears are worse.
Q. Kath. Have I liv'd thus long—let me speak myself,
Since virtue finds no friends—a wife, a true one?
A woman, I dare say without vain-glory,
Never yet branded with suspicion?
Have I with all my full affections
Still met the king? lov'd him next heav'n? obey'd him?
Been, out of fondness, superstitious to him?
Almost forgot my prayers to content him?
And am I thus rewarded? 'tis not well, lords.
Bring me a constant woman to her husband,
One that ne'er dream'd a joy beyond his pleasure;
And to that woman, when she has done most,
Yet will I add an honour, a great patience.
Wol. Madam, you wander from the good we aim at.
Q. Kath. My lord, I dare not make myself so guilty,
To give up willingly that noble title
Your master wed me to: nothing but death
Shall e'er divorce my dignities.
Wol. Pray, hear me.
Q. Kath. Would I had never trod this English earth,
Or felt the flatteries that grow upon it!
Ye have angels' faces, but heaven knows your hearts.
What will become of me now, wretched lady!
I am the most unhappy woman living.
Alas, poor wenches, where are now your fortunes!
Shipwrack'd upon a kingdom, where no pity,
No friends, no hope; no kindred weep for me;

many. 36. **Envy,** malice. **opinion,** rumor. 37. **even,** constant, upright. 38. **Seek me out,** concerns me. **that . . . in,** my conduct as a wife. 40-41. **Tanta est erga,** etc. There is toward you such wholeheartedness, most serene queen. Holinshed relates that the cardinals spoke to her in Latin and were requested to speak English, but there is no Latin dialogue in the Chronicle. It is the dramatist's invention. 49. **willing'st,** most deliberate. 63. **still bore,** has always borne. 77. **For . . . been,** for the sake of the queenly person I once was. 78. **fit,** brief space, short spell; Pooler suggests a possible play on the meaning "canto," part of a poem. 86. **to be honest,** as to be open in support of me. 88. **weigh out,** compensate for. 103. **two . . . virtues,** i.e., the embodiment of all good, playing on the Aristotelian virtues, called the cardinal virtues—justice, temperance, fortitude, and prudence—sometimes catalogued as twelve. 104. **cardinal sins,** i.e., the seven deadly sins. 110. **at once,** presently. 117. **If . . . habits,** alludes to the proverb quoted in line 23 above. 123-124. **all . . . curse,** i.e., all your efforts make my life more wretched, as though accursed. **worse,** i.e., than your wretchedness. 125. **speak,** describe. 131. **superstitious to him,** devoted to him to the point of idolatry.

Almost no grave allow'd me: like the lily,
That once was mistress of the field and flourish'd,
I'll hang my head and perish.
Wol. If your grace
Could but be brought to know our ends are honest,
You 'ld feel more comfort: why should we, good lady,
Upon what cause, wrong you? alas, our places,
The way of our profession is against it:
We are to cure such sorrows, not to sow 'em.
For goodness' sake, consider what you do;
How you may hurt yourself, ay, utterly
Grow from the king's acquaintance, by this carriage.
The hearts of princes kiss obedience,
So much they love it; but to stubborn spirits
They swell, and grow as terrible as storms.
I know you have a gentle, noble temper,
A soul as even as a calm: pray, think us
Those we profess, peace-makers, friends, and servants.
Cam. Madam, you'll find it so. You wrong your virtues
With these weak women's fears: a noble spirit,
As yours was put into you, ever casts
Such doubts, as false coin, from it. The king loves you;
Beware you lose it not: for us, if you please
To trust us in your business, we are ready
To use our utmost studies in your service.
Q. Kath. Do what ye will, my lords: and, pray, forgive me,
If I have us'd myself unmannerly;
You know I am a woman, lacking wit
To make a seemly answer to such persons.
Pray, do my service to his majesty:
He has my heart yet; and shall have my prayers
While I shall have my life. Come, reverend fathers,
Bestow your counsels on me: she now begs,
That little thought, when she set footing here,
She should have bought her dignities so dear. *Exeunt.*

SCENE II. [*Ante-chamber to the* KING'S *apartment.*]

Enter the DUKE OF NORFOLK, DUKE OF SUFFOLK, LORD SURREY, *and* LORD CHAMBERLAIN.

Nor. If you will now unite in your complaints,
And force them with a constancy, the cardinal
Cannot stand under them: if you omit
The offer of this time, I cannot promise
But that you shall sustain moe new disgraces,
With these you bear already.
Sur. I am joyful
To meet the least occasion that may give me
Remembrance of my father-in-law, the duke,
To be reveng'd on him.
Suf. Which of the peers
Have uncontemn'd gone by him, or at least
Strangely neglected? when did he regard
The stamp of nobleness in any person
Out of himself?
Cham. My lords, you speak your pleasures:
What he deserves of you and me I know;
What we can do to him, though now the time
Gives way to us, I much fear. If you cannot
Bar his access to th' king, never attempt
Any thing on him; for he hath a witchcraft
Over the king in 's tongue.
Nor. O, fear him not;
His spell in that is out: the king hath found
Matter against him that for ever mars
The honey of his language. No, he 's settled,
Not to come off, in his displeasure.
Sur. Sir,
I should be glad to hear such news as this
Once every hour.
Nor. Believe it, this is true:
In the divorce his contrary proceedings
Are all unfolded; wherein he appears
As I would wish mine enemy.
Sur. How came
His practices to light?
Suf. Most strangely.
Sur. O, how, how?
Suf. The cardinal's letters to the pope miscarried,
And came to th' eye o' th' king: wherein was read,
How that the cardinal did entreat his holiness
To stay the judgement o' th' divorce; for if
It did take place, 'I do,' quoth he, 'perceive
My king is tangled in affection to
A creature of the queen's, Lady Anne Bullen.'
Sur. Has the king this?
Suf. Believe it.
Sur. Will this work?
Cham. The king in this perceives him, how he coasts
And hedges his own way. But in this point
All his tricks founder, and he brings his physic
After his patient's death: the king already
Hath married the fair lady.
Sur. Would he had!
Suf. May you be happy in your wish, my lord!
For, I profess, you have it.
Sur. Now, all my joy
Trace the conjunction!
Suf. My amen to 't!
Nor. All men's!
Suf. There 's order given for her coronation:
Marry, this is yet but young, and may be left
To some ears unrecounted. But, my lords,
She is a gallant creature, and complete
In mind and feature: I persuade me, from her
Will fall some blessing to this land, which shall
In it be memoriz'd.
Sur. But, will the king
Digest this letter of the cardinal's?
The Lord forbid!
Nor. Marry, amen!
Suf. No, no;
There be moe wasps that buzz about his nose
Is stol'n away to Rome; hath ta'en no leave;
Has left the cause o' th' king unhandled; and
Has left the cause o' the king unhandled; and
Is posted, as the agent of our cardinal,
To second all his plot. I do assure you
The king cried Ha! at this.
Cham. Now, God incense him,

161. **carriage,** conduct.
SCENE II. 3-4. **if . . . time,** if you let this opportunity pass. 8. **my father-in-law.** Cf. II, i, 41-44, note. 13. **Out of,** excepting. 20. **out,** finished. 23. **come off,** escape. **his,** the king's. 26. **his contrary proceedings,** private practices opposed to public procedure (Johnson). 36. **creature,** dependent. 38. **coasts,** goes a roundabout way. 45. **Trace,** follow. 52. **memoriz'd,** caused to be remembered; cf. *Macbeth,* I, ii, 40. 53. **Digest,** put up with. 64. **in his opinions,** with unchanged

And let him cry Ha! louder!
Nor. But, my lord,
When returns Cranmer?
Suf. He is return'd in his opinions; which
Have satisfied the king for his divorce,
Together with all famous colleges
Almost in Christendom: shortly, I believe,
His second marriage shall be publish'd, and
Her coronation. Katharine no more
Shall be call'd queen, but princess dowager
And widow to Prince Arthur.
Nor. This same Cranmer 's
A worthy fellow, and hath ta'en much pain
In the king's business.
Suf. He has; and we shall see him
For it an archbishop.
Nor. So I hear.
Suf. 'Tis so.

Enter Wolsey *and* Cromwell.

The cardinal!
Nor. Observe, observe, he 's moody.
Wol. The packet, Cromwell,
Gave 't you the king?
Crom. To his own hand, in 's bedchamber.
Wol. Look'd he o' th' inside of the paper?
Crom. Presently
He did unseal them: and the first he view'd,
He did it with a serious mind; a heed
Was in his countenance. You he bade
Attend him here this morning.
Wol. Is he ready
To come abroad?
Crom. I think, by this he is.
Wol. Leave me awhile. *Exit Cromwell.*
[*Aside*] It shall be to the Duchess of Alençon,
The French king's sister: he shall marry her.
Anne Bullen! No; I'll no Anne Bullens for him:
There 's more in 't than fair visage. Bullen!
No, we'll no Bullens. Speedily I wish
To hear from Rome. The Marchioness of Pembroke!
Nor. He 's discontented.
Suf. May be, he hears the king
Does whet his anger to him.
Sur. Sharp enough,
Lord, for thy justice!
Wol. [*Aside*] The late queen's gentlewoman, a knight's daughter,
To be her mistress' mistress! the queen's queen!
This candle burns not clear: 'tis I must snuff it;
Then out it goes. What though I know her virtuous
And well deserving? yet I know her for
A spleeny Lutheran; and not wholesome to
Our cause, that she should lie i' th' bosom of
Our hard-rul'd king. Again, there is sprung up
An heretic, an arch one, Cranmer; one
Hath crawl'd into the favour of the king,
And is his oracle.
Nor. He is vex'd at something.
Sur. I would 'twere something that would fret the string,
The master-cord on 's heart!

Enter King, *reading of a schedule*[, *and* Lovell].

Suf. The king, the king!
King. What piles of wealth hath he accumulated
To his own portion! and what expense by th' hour
Seems to flow from him! How, i' th' name of thrift,
Does he rake this together! Now, my lords,
Saw you the cardinal?
Nor. My lord, we have
Stood here observing him: some strange commotion
Is in his brain: he bites his lip, and starts;
Stops on a sudden, looks upon the ground,
Then lays his finger on his temple; straight
Springs out into fast gait; then stops again,
Strikes his breast hard, and anon he casts
His eye against the moon: in most strange postures
We have seen him set himself.
King. It may well be;
There is a mutiny in 's mind. This morning
Papers of state he sent me to peruse,
As I requir'd: and wot you what I found
There,—on my conscience, put unwittingly?
Forsooth, an inventory, thus importing;
The several parcels of his plate, his treasure,
Rich stuffs, and ornaments of household; which
I find at such proud rate, that it out-speaks
Possession of a subject.
Nor. It 's heaven's will:
Some spirit put this paper in the packet,
To bless your eye withal.
King. If we did think
His contemplation were above the earth,
And fix'd on spiritual object, he should still
Dwell in his musings: but I am afraid
His thinkings are below the moon, not worth
His serious considering.
King takes his seat; whispers Lovell, who goes to the Cardinal [*Wolsey*].
Wol. Heaven forgive me!
Ever God bless your highness!
King. Good my lord,
You are full of heavenly stuff, and bear the inventory
Of your best graces in your mind; the which
You were now running o'er: you have scarce time
To steal from spiritual leisure a brief span
To keep your earthly audit: sure, in that
I deem you an ill husband, and am glad
To have you therein my companion.
Wol. Sir,
For holy offices I have a time; a time
To think upon the part of business which
I bear i' th' state; and nature does require
Her times of preservation, which perforce
I, her frail son, amongst my brethren mortal,
Must give my tendance to.
King. You have said well.
Wol. And ever may your highness yoke together,
As I will lend you cause, my doing well
With my well saying!
King. 'Tis well said again;
And 'tis a kind of good deed to say well:

opinions; or, having sent ahead his written opinions. 66. **colleges,** i.e., the opinions of the colleges. 99. **spleeny,** staunch, contentious. 101. **hard-rul'd,** hard to manage. 103. **Hath,** who hath. 106. **on 's,** of his. 125. **parcels,** items. 127-128. **out-speaks . . . subject,** describes possessions exceeding what a subject should have. 142. **ill husband,** unthrifty manager. 148. **amongst my brethren mortal,** i.e., in my human capacity, as contrasted with my divinity.

And yet words are no deeds. My father lov'd you:
He said he did; and with his deed did crown
His word upon you. Since I had my office,
I have kept you next my heart; have not alone
Employ'd you where high profits might come home,
But par'd my present havings, to bestow
My bounties upon you.
Wol. [*Aside*] What should this mean?
Sur. [*Aside*] The Lord increase this business!
King. Have I not made you
The prime man of the state? I pray you, tell me,
If what I now pronounce you have found true:
And, if you may confess it, say withal,
If you are bound to us or no. What say you?
Wol. My sovereign, I confess your royal graces,
Show'r'd on me daily, have been more than could
My studied purposes requite; which went
Beyond all man's endeavours: my endeavours
Have ever come too short of my desires,
Yet fil'd with my abilities: mine own ends
Have been mine so that evermore they pointed
To th' good of your most sacred person and
The profit of the state. For your great graces
Heap'd upon me, poor undeserver, I
Can nothing render but allegiant thanks,
My pray'rs to heaven for you, my loyalty,
Which ever has and ever shall be growing,
Till death, that winter, kill it.
King. Fairly answer'd;
A loyal and obedient subject is
Therein illustrated: the honour of it
Does pay the act of it; as, i' th' contrary,
The foulness is the punishment. I presume
That, as my hand has open'd bounty to you,
My heart dropp'd love, my pow'r rain'd honour, more
On you than any; so your hand and heart,
Your brain, and every function of your power,
Should, notwithstanding that your bond of duty,
As 'twere in love's particular, be more
To me, your friend, than any.
Wol. I do profess
That for your highness' good I ever labour'd
More than mine own; †that am, have, and will be—
Though all the world should crack their duty to you,
And throw it from their soul; though perils did
Abound, as thick as thought could make 'em, and
Appear in forms more horrid,—yet my duty,
As doth a rock against the chiding flood,
Should the approach of this wild river break,
And stand unshaken yours.
King. 'Tis nobly spoken:
Take notice, lords, he has a loyal breast,
For you have seen him open 't. Read o'er this;
[*Giving him papers.*]
And after, this: and then to breakfast with
What appetite you have.
Exit King, frowning upon the Cardinal [*Wolsey*]*; the Nobles throng after him, smiling and whispering.*
Wol. What should this mean?
What sudden anger 's this? how have I reap'd it?
He parted frowning from me, as if ruin
Leap'd from his eyes: so looks the chafed lion
Upon the daring huntsman that has gall'd him;
Then makes him nothing. I must read this paper;
I fear, the story of his anger. 'Tis so;
This paper has undone me: 'tis th' accompt
Of all that world of wealth I have drawn together
For mine own ends; indeed, to gain the popedom,
And fee my friends in Rome. O negligence!
Fit for a fool to fall by: what cross devil
Made me put this main secret in the packet
I sent the king? Is there no way to cure this?
No new device to beat this from his brains?
I know 'twill stir him strongly; yet I know
A way, if it take right, in spite of fortune
Will bring me off again. What 's this? 'To th' Pope!'
The letter, as I live, with all the business
I writ to 's holiness. Nay then, farewell!
I have touch'd the highest point of all my greatness;
And, from that full meridian of my glory,
I haste now to my setting: I shall fall
Like a bright exhalation in the evening,
And no man see me more.

Enter to WOLSEY, *the* DUKES OF NORFOLK *and* SUFFOLK, *the* EARL OF SURREY, *and the* LORD CHAMBERLAIN.

Nor. Hear the king 's pleasure, cardinal: who commands you
To render up the great seal presently
Into our hands; and to confine yourself
To Asher House, my Lord of Winchester's,
Till you hear further from his highness.
Wol. Stay:
Where 's your commission, lords? words cannot carry
Authority so weighty.
Suf. Who dare cross 'em,
Bearing the king's will from his mouth expressly?
Wol. Till I find more than will or words to do it,
I mean your malice, know, officious lords,
I dare and must deny it. Now I feel
Of what coarse metal ye are moulded, envy:
How eagerly ye follow my disgraces,
As if it fed ye! and how sleek and wanton
Ye appear in every thing may bring my ruin!
Follow your envious courses, men of malice;
You have Christian warrant for 'em, and, no doubt,
In time will find their fit rewards. That seal,
You ask with such a violence, the king,
Mine and your master, with his own hand gave me;
Bade me enjoy it, with the place and honours,
During my life; and, to confirm his goodness,
Tied it by letters-patents: now, who'll take it?
Sur. The king, that gave it.
Wol. It must be himself, then.
Sur. Thou art a proud traitor, priest.
Wol. Proud lord, thou liest:
Within these forty hours Surrey durst better
Have burnt that tongue than said so.
Sur. Thy ambition,
Thou scarlet sin, robb'd this bewailing land

159. **par'd . . . havings,** reduced my own wealth. 167-168. **more . . . requite,** more than I could devise means to repay. 171. **fil'd,** kept pace. 172. **so that,** only to the extent that. 176. **allegiant,** loyal. 181. **illustrated,** made evident. 181-182. **the . . . it,** analogous to "Virtue is its own reward." 188-189. **notwithstanding . . . particular,** over and above your duty as a subject, as in the case of friends. 192. **that am, have, and will be,** auxiliary verbs and completed by *unshaken* (l. 199). 206. **chafed,** angry. 208. **makes him nothing,** destroys him (the hunter). 215. **main,** weighty. 226. **exhalation,** any astronomical phenomenon, such as a meteor or a falling star. 255. **Thou scarlet sin,** refers to his cardinal's cassock, described as scarlet; cf. III, i, 103-104. 272. **That,** I that. 274. **mate,** rival, vie with. 280. **jaded,** cowed.

Of noble Buckingham, my father-in-law:
The heads of all thy brother cardinals,
With thee and all thy best parts bound together,
Weigh'd not a hair of his. Plague of your policy!
You sent me deputy for Ireland;
Far from his succour, from the king, from all
That might have mercy on the fault thou gav'st him;
Whilst your great goodness, out of holy pity,
Absolv'd him with an axe.

Wol. This, and all else
This talking lord can lay upon my credit,
I answer is most false. The duke by law
Found his deserts: how innocent I was
From any private malice in his end,
His noble jury and foul cause can witness.
If I lov'd many words, lord, I should tell you
You have as little honesty as honour,
That in the way of loyalty and truth
Toward the king, my ever royal master,
Dare mate a sounder man than Surrey can be,
And all that love his follies.

Sur. By my soul,
Your long coat, priest, protects you; thou shouldst feel
My sword i' th' life-blood of thee else. My lords,
Can ye endure to hear this arrogance?
And from this fellow? If we live thus tamely,
To be thus jaded by a piece of scarlet,
Farewell nobility; let his grace go forward,
And dare us with his cap like larks.

Wol. All goodness
Is poison to thy stomach.

Sur. Yes, that goodness
Of gleaning all the land's wealth into one,
Into your own hands, card'nal, by extortion;
The goodness of your intercepted packets
You writ to th' pope against the king: your goodness,
Since you provoke me, shall be most notorious.
My Lord of Norfolk, as you are truly noble,
As you respect the common good, the state
Of our despis'd nobility, our issues,
Who, if he live, will scarce be gentlemen,
Produce the grand sum of his sins, the articles
Collected from his life. I'll startle you
Worse than the sacring bell, when the brown wench
Lay kissing in your arms, lord cardinal.

Wol. How much, methinks, I could despise this man,
But that I am bound in charity against it!

Nor. Those articles, my lord, are in the king's hand:
But, thus much, they are foul ones.

Wol. So much fairer
And spotless shall mine innocence arise,
When the king knows my truth.

Sur. This cannot save you:
I thank my memory, I yet remember
Some of these articles; and out they shall.
Now, if you can blush and cry 'guilty,' cardinal,
You'll show a little honesty.

Wol. Speak on, sir;
I dare your worst objections: if I blush,
It is to see a nobleman want manners.

Sur. I had rather want those than my head. Have at you!
First, that, without the king's assent or knowledge,
You wrought to be a legate; by which power
You maim'd the jurisdiction of all bishops.

Nor. Then, that in all you writ to Rome, or else
To foreign princes, 'Ego et Rex meus'
Was still inscrib'd; in which you brought the king
To be your servant.

Suf. Then that, without the knowledge
Either of king or council, when you went
Ambassador to the emperor, you made bold
To carry into Flanders the great seal.

Sur. Item, you sent a large commission
To Gregory de Cassado, to conclude,
Without the king's will or the state's allowance,
A league between his highness and Ferrara.

Suf. That, out of mere ambition, you have caus'd
Your holy hat to be stamp'd on the king's coin.

Sur. Then that you have sent innumerable substance—
By what means got, I leave to your own conscience—
To furnish Rome, and to prepare the ways
You have for dignities; to the mere undoing
Of all the kingdom. Many more there are;
Which, since they are of you, and odious,
I will not taint my mouth with.

Cham. O my lord,
Press not a falling man too far! 'tis virtue:
His faults lie open to the laws; let them,
Not you, correct him. My heart weeps to see him
So little of his great self.

Sur. I forgive him.

Suf. Lord cardinal, the king's further pleasure is,
Because all those things you have done of late,
By your power legative, within this kingdom,
Fall into th' compass of a præmunire,
That therefore such a writ be sued against you;
To forfeit all your goods, lands, tenements,
Chattels, and whatsoever, and to be
Out of the king's protection. This is my charge.

Nor. And so we'll leave you to your meditations
How to live better. For your stubborn answer
About the giving back the great seal to us,
The king shall know it, and, no doubt, shall thank you.
So fare you well, my little good lord cardinal.

Exeunt all but Wolsey.

Wol. So farewell to the little good you bear me.
Farewell! a long farewell, to all my greatness!
This is the state of man: to-day he puts forth
The tender leaves of hopes; to-morrow blossoms,
And bears his blushing honours thick upon him;
The third day comes a frost, a killing frost,
And, when he thinks, good easy man, full surely
His greatness is a-ripening, nips his root,
And then he falls, as I do. I have ventur'd,
Like little wanton boys that swim on bladders,
This many summers in a sea of glory,

282. **dare . . . larks,** dazzle us with his cardinal's hat as birds with a mirror or a piece of scarlet cloth. 295. **sacring bell,** bell rung at the most solemn portions of the mass. 300. **thus much,** (I can say) this much. 311-332. **You wrought,** etc. This and the following items are transcribed from Holinshed. 314. **'Ego et Rex meus,'** I and my king. Pooler remarks that in Latin the first person always came before any nouns parallel with it and that Wolsey's offense consisted in mentioning himself at all. 324. **mere,** sheer. 328. **To furnish Rome,** implying that Wolsey made gifts to Rome as bribes to obtain his own advancement. 339. **legative,** as a papal legate. 340. **præmunire,** a form of writ for prosecuting certain offenses punishable by forfeiture and imprisonment; also, the offense or penalty. 341. **sued,** moved.

But far beyond my depth: my high-blown pride
At length broke under me and now has left me,
Weary and old with service, to the mercy
Of a rude stream, that must for ever hide me.
Vain pomp and glory of this world, I hate ye:
I feel my heart new open'd. O, how wretched
Is that poor man that hangs on princes' favours!
There is, betwixt that smile we would aspire to,
That sweet aspect of princes, and their ruin,
More pangs and fears than wars or women have:
And when he falls, he falls like Lucifer,
Never to hope again.

Enter CROMWELL, *standing amazed.*

Why, how now, Cromwell!
Crom. I have no power to speak, sir.
Wol. What, amaz'd
At my misfortunes? can thy spirit wonder
A great man should decline? Nay, an you weep,
I am fall'n indeed.
Crom. How does your grace?
Wol. Why, well;
Never so truly happy, my good Cromwell.
I know myself now; and I feel within me
A peace above all earthly dignities,
A still and quiet conscience. The king has cur'd me,
I humbly thank his grace; and from these shoulders,
These ruin'd pillars, out of pity, taken
A load would sink a navy, too much honour:
O, 'tis a burden, Cromwell, 'tis a burden
Too heavy for a man that hopes for heaven!
Crom. I am glad your grace has made that right use of it.
Wol. I hope I have: I am able now, methinks,
Out of a fortitude of soul I feel,
To endure more miseries and greater far
Than my weak-hearted enemies dare offer.
What news abroad?
Crom. The heaviest and the worst
Is your displeasure with the king.
Wol. God bless him!
Crom. The next is, that Sir Thomas More is chosen
Lord chancellor in your place.
Wol. That 's somewhat sudden:
But he 's a learned man. May he continue
Long in his highness' favour, and do justice
For truth's sake and his conscience; that his bones,
When he has run his course and sleeps in blessings,
May have a tomb of orphans' tears wept on 'em!
What more?
Crom. That Cranmer is return'd with welcome,
Install'd lord archbishop of Canterbury.
Wol. That 's news indeed.
Crom. Last, that the Lady Anne,
Whom the king hath in secrecy long married,
This day was view'd in open as his queen,
Going to chapel; and the voice is now
Only about her coronation.
Wol. There was the weight that pull'd me down. O Cromwell,
The king has gone beyond me: all my glories
In that one woman I have lost for ever:
No sun shall ever usher forth mine honours,
Or gild again the noble troops that waited
Upon my smiles. Go, get thee from me, Cromwell;
I am a poor fall'n man, unworthy now
To be thy lord and master: seek the king;
That sun, I pray, may never set! I have told him
What and how true thou art: he will advance thee;
Some little memory of me will stir him—
I know his noble nature—not to let
Thy hopeful service perish too: good Cromwell,
Neglect him not; make use now, and provide
For thine own future safety.
Crom. O my lord,
Must I, then, leave you? must I needs forgo
So good, so noble and so true a master?
Bear witness, all that have not hearts of iron,
With what a sorrow Cromwell leaves his lord.
The king shall have my service; but my pray'rs
For ever and for ever shall be yours.
Wol. Cromwell, I did not think to shed a tear
In all my miseries; but thou hast forc'd me,
Out of thy honest truth, to play the woman.
Let 's dry our eyes: and thus far hear me, Cromwell;
And, when I am forgotten, as I shall be,
And sleep in dull cold marble, where no mention
Of me more must be heard of, say, I taught thee,
Say, Wolsey, that once trod the ways of glory,
And sounded all the depths and shoals of honour,
Found thee a way, out of his wrack, to rise in;
A sure and safe one, though thy master miss'd it.
Mark but my fall, and that that ruin'd me.
Cromwell, I charge thee, fling away ambition:
By that sin fell the angels; how can man, then,
The image of his Maker, hope to win by it?
Love thyself last: cherish those hearts that hate thee;
Corruption wins not more than honesty.
Still in thy right hand carry gentle peace,
To silence envious tongues. Be just, and fear not:
Let all the ends thou aim'st at be thy country's,
Thy God's, and truth's; then if thou fall'st, O Cromwell,
Thou fall'st a blessed martyr! Serve the king;
And,—prithee, lead me in:
There take an inventory of all I have,
To the last penny; 'tis the king's: my robe,
And my integrity to heaven, is all
I dare now call mine own. O Cromwell, Cromwell!
Had I but serv'd my God with half the zeal
I serv'd my king, he would not in mine age
Have left me naked to mine enemies.
Crom. Good sir, have patience.
Wol. So I have. Farewell
The hopes of court! my hopes in heaven do dwell.
Exeunt.

ACT IV.

SCENE I. [*A street in Westminster.*]

Enter two Gentlemen, *meeting one another.*

First Gent. Y' are well met once again.
Sec. Gent. So are you.

408. **gone beyond,** overreached. 452. **robe,** clerical garb.
ACT IV. SCENE I. 8. **royal,** noble. 9. **let . . . rights,** to give them due credit (Pooler). **forward,** i.e., eager to do. 12. **better taken,** more enjoyed. 16. **By custom,** i.e., of having certain offices in the coronation performed by members of families, as a hereditary right. 27. **late,** recent. 31. **main assent,** general agreement. 36. *Stage Direction:* (4) ***Music,*** musicians. (5) **Garter,** i.e., Garter King of Arms. (11) ***Collars of SS,*** golden chains of office made of flat, broad

First Gent. You come to take your stand here, and behold
The Lady Anne pass from her coronation?
Sec. Gent. 'Tis all my business. At our last encounter,
The Duke of Buckingham came from his trial.
First Gent. 'Tis very true: but that time offer'd sorrow;
This, general joy.
Sec. Gent. 'Tis well: the citizens,
I am sure, have shown at full their royal minds—
As, let 'em have their rights, they are ever forward—
In celebration of this day with shows,
Pageants and sights of honour.
First Gent. Never greater,
Nor, I'll assure you, better taken, sir.
Sec. Gent. May I be bold to ask what that contains,
That paper in your hand?
First Gent. Yes; 'tis the list
Of those that claim their offices this day
By custom of the coronation.
The Duke of Suffolk is the first, and claims
To be high-steward; next, the Duke of Norfolk,
He to be earl marshal: you may read the rest.
Sec. Gent. I thank you, sir: had I not known those customs,
I should have been beholding to your paper.
But, I beseech you, what 's become of Katharine,
The princess dowager? how goes her business?
First Gent. That I can tell you too. The Archbishop
Of Canterbury, accompanied with other
Learned and reverend fathers of his order,
Held a late court at Dunstable, six miles off
From Ampthill where the princess lay; to which
She was often cited by them, but appear'd not:
And, to be short, for not appearance and
The king's late scruple, by the main assent
Of all these learned men she was divorc'd,
And the late marriage made of none effect:
Since which she was remov'd to Kimbolton,
Where she remains now sick.
Sec. Gent. Alas, good lady! [*Trumpets.*]
The trumpets sound: stand close, the queen is coming.
Hautboys.

THE ORDER OF THE CORONATION.

1. *A lively flourish of Trumpets.*
2. Then, two Judges.
3. Lord Chancellor, *with purse and mace before him.*
4. Choristers, *singing. Music.*
5. Mayor of London, *bearing the mace. Then* Garter, *in his coat of arms, and on his head he wore a gilt copper crown.*
6. Marquess Dorset, *bearing a sceptre of gold, on his head a demi-coronal of gold. With him, the* Earl of Surrey, *bearing the rod of silver with the dove, crowned with an earl's coronet. Collars of SS.*
7. Duke of Suffolk, *in his robe of estate, his coronet on his head, bearing a long white wand, as high-steward. With him, the* Duke of Norfolk, *with the rod of marshalship, a coronet on his head. Collars of SS.*
8. *A canopy borne by four of the* Cinqueports; *under it, the* Queen *in her robe; in her hair richly adorned with pearl, crowned. On each side her, the* Bishops of London *and* Winchester.
9. *The old* Duchess of Norfolk, *in a coronal of gold, wrought with flowers, bearing the* Queen's *train.*
10. *Certain* Ladies *or* Countesses, *with plain circlets of gold without flowers.*

Exeunt, first passing over the stage in order and state, and then a great flourish of trumpets.

Sec. Gent. A royal train, believe me. These I know:
Who 's that that bears the sceptre?
First Gent. Marquess Dorset:
And that the Earl of Surrey, with the rod.
Sec. Gent. A bold brave gentleman. That should be
The Duke of Suffolk?
First Gent. 'Tis the same: high-steward.
Sec. Gent. And that my Lord of Norfolk?
First Gent. Yes.
Sec. Gent. Heaven bless thee!
[*Looking on the Queen.*]
Thou hast the sweetest face I ever look'd on.
Sir, as I have a soul, she is an angel;
Our king has all the Indies in his arms,
And more and richer, when he strains that lady:
I cannot blame his conscience.
First Gent. They that bear
The cloth of honour over her, are four barons
Of the Cinque-ports.
Sec. Gent. Those men are happy; and so are all are near her.
I take it, she that carries up the train
Is that old noble lady, Duchess of Norfolk.
First Gent. It is; and all the rest are countesses.
Sec. Gent. Their coronets say so. These are stars indeed;
And sometimes falling ones.
First Gent. No more of that.
[*Exit procession.*]

Enter a third Gentleman.

First Gent. God save you, sir! where have you been broiling?
Third Gent. Among the crowd i' th' Abbey; where a finger
Could not be wedg'd in more: I am stifled
With the mere rankness of their joy.
Sec. Gent. You saw
The ceremony?
Third Gent. That I did.
First Gent. How was it?
Third Gent. Well worth the seeing.
Sec. Gent. Good sir, speak it to us.
Third Gent. As well as I am able. The rich stream
Of lords and ladies, having brought the queen
To a prepar'd place in the choir, fell off
A distance from her; while her grace sat down
To rest awhile, some half an hour or so,
In a rich chair of state, opposing freely
The beauty of her person to the people.
Believe me, sir, she is the goodliest woman
That ever lay by man: which when the people
Had the full view of, such a noise arose
As the shrouds make at sea in a stiff tempest,
As loud, and to as many tunes: hats, cloaks,—
Doublets, I think,—flew up; and had their faces
Been loose, this day they had been lost. Such joy

S-shaped links, ornately decorated; their significance is uncertain. (16) **Cinqueports,** i.e., barons of the Cinque-ports, a group of seaport towns (originally five) situated on the southeast coast of England, in ancient times furnishing the chief part of the English navy, in return for which they had many privileges and franchises. (17) ***in her hair,*** with hair loosely hanging (customary for brides). 46. **strains,** embraces. 56. **broiling,** suffering great heat. 67. **opposing,** present in full view.

I never saw before. Great-bellied women,
That had not half a week to go, like rams
In the old time of war, would shake the press,
And make 'em reel before 'em. No man living
Could say 'This is my wife' there; all were woven
So strangely in one piece.
Sec. Gent. But, what follow'd?
Third Gent. At length her grace rose, and with modest paces
Came to the altar; where she kneel'd, and saint-like
Cast her fair eyes to heaven and pray'd devoutly.
Then rose again and bow'd her to the people:
When by the Archbishop of Canterbury
She had all the royal makings of a queen;
As holy oil, Edward Confessor's crown,
The rod, and bird of peace, and all such emblems
Laid nobly on her: which perform'd, the choir,
With all the choicest music of the kingdom,
Together sung 'Te Deum.' So she parted,
And with the same full state pac'd back again
To York-place, where the feast is held.
First Gent. Sir,
You must no more call it York-place, that 's past;
For, since the cardinal fell, that title 's lost:
'Tis now the king's, and call'd Whitehall.
Third Gent. I know it;
But 'tis so lately alter'd, that the old name
Is fresh about me.
Sec. Gent. What two reverend bishops
Were those that went on each side of the queen?
Third Gent. Stokesly and Gardiner; the one of Winchester,
Newly preferr'd from the king's secretary,
The other, London.
Sec. Gent. He of Winchester
Is held no great good lover of the archbishop's,
The virtuous Cranmer.
Third Gent. All the land knows that:
However, yet there is no great breach; when it comes,
Cranmer will find a friend will not shrink from him.
Sec. Gent. Who may that be, I pray you?
Third Gent. Thomas Cromwell;
A man in much esteem with th' king, and truly
A worthy friend. The king has made him master
O' th' jewel house,
And one, already, of the privy council.
Sec. Gent. He will deserve more.
Third Gent. Yes, without all doubt.
Come, gentlemen, ye shall go my way, which
Is to th' court, and there ye shall be my guests:
Something I can command. As I walk thither,
I'll tell ye more.
Both. You may command us, sir.
Exeunt.

SCENE II. [*Kimbolton.*]

Enter KATHARINE, *Dowager, sick; led between* GRIFFITH, *her gentleman usher, and* PATIENCE, *her woman.*

Grif. How does your grace?
Kath. O Griffith, sick to death!
My legs, like loaden branches, bow to th' earth,
Willing to leave their burthen. Reach a chair:
So; now, methinks, I feel a little ease.
Didst thou not tell me, Griffith, as thou led'st me,
That the great child of honour, Cardinal Wolsey,
Was dead?
Grif. Yes, madam; but I think your grace,
Out of the pain you suffer'd, gave no ear to 't.
Kath. Prithee, good Griffith, tell me how he died:
If well, he stepp'd before me, happily
For my example.
Grif. Well, the voice goes, madam:
For after the stout Earl Northumberland
Arrested him at York, and brought him forward,
As a man sorely tainted, to his answer,
He fell sick suddenly, and grew so ill
He could not sit his mule.
Kath. Alas, poor man!
Grif. At last, with easy roads, he came to Leicester,
Lodg'd in the abbey; where the reverend abbot,
With all his covent, honourably receiv'd him;
To whom he gave these words, 'O, father abbot,
An old man, broken with the storms of state,
Is come to lay his weary bones among ye;
Give him a little earth for charity!'
So went to bed; where eagerly his sickness
Pursu'd him still: and, three nights after this,
About the hour of eight, which he himself
Foretold should be his last, full of repentance,
Continual meditations, tears, and sorrows,
He gave his honours to the world again,
His blessed part to heaven, and slept in peace.
Kath. So may he rest; his faults lie gently on him!
Yet thus far, Griffith, give me leave to speak him,
And yet with charity. He was a man
Of an unbounded stomach, ever ranking
Himself with princes; one that, by suggestion,
Tied all the kingdom: simony was fair-play;
His own opinion was his law: i' th' presence
He would say untruths; and be ever double
Both in his words and meaning. He was never,
But where he meant to ruin, pitiful:
His promises were, as he then was, mighty;
But his performance, as he is now, nothing:
Of his own body he was ill, and gave
The clergy ill example.
Grif. Noble madam,
Men's evil manners live in brass; their virtues
We write in water. May it please your highness
To hear me speak his good now?
Kath. Yes, good Griffith;
I were malicious else.
Grif. This cardinal,
Though from an humble stock, undoubtedly
Was fashion'd to much honour from his cradle.
He was a scholar, and a ripe and good one;
Exceeding wise, fair-spoken, and persuading:
Lofty and sour to them that lov'd him not;
But to those men that sought him sweet as summer.
And though he were unsatisfied in getting,

77. **rams,** battering rams. 78. **press,** crowd. 91. **music,** i.e., musicians. 101-102. **Gardiner . . . secretary.** Gardiner, secretary to the king, was made bishop of Winchester at the fall of Wolsey; he continued to act as secretary for several years. 107. **will,** who will. 116. **Something . . . command,** I can provide refreshment.

SCENE II. 11. **the voice goes,** i.e., people say. 19. **covent,** convent, monastery. 24. **eagerly,** sharply. 33-44. **He was a man,** etc. This characterization of Wolsey and that recited by Griffith below are

Which was a sin, yet in bestowing, madam,
He was most princely: ever witness for him
Those twins of learning that he rais'd in you,
Ipswich and Oxford! one of which fell with him,
Unwilling to outlive the good that did it;
The other, though unfinish'd, yet so famous,
So excellent in art, and still so rising,
That Christendom shall ever speak his virtue.
His overthrow heap'd happiness upon him;
For then, and not till then, he felt himself,
And found the blessedness of being little:
And, to add greater honours to his age
Than man could give him, he died fearing God.
Kath. After my death I wish no other herald,
No other speaker of my living actions,
To keep mine honour from corruption,
But such an honest chronicler as Griffith.
Whom I most hated living, thou hast made me,
With thy religious truth and modesty,
Now in his ashes honour: peace be with him!
Patience, be near me still; and set me lower:
I have not long to trouble thee. Good Griffith,
Cause the musicians play me that sad note
I nam'd my knell, whilst I sit meditating
On that celestial harmony I go to. *Sad and solemn music.*
Grif. She is asleep: good wench, let 's sit down quiet,
For fear we wake her: softly, gentle Patience.

The vision. Enter, solemnly tripping one after another, six personages, clad in white robes, wearing on their heads garlands of bays, and golden vizards on their faces; branches of bays or palm in their hands. They first congee unto her, then dance; and, at certain changes, the first two hold a spare garland over her head; at which the other four make reverent curtsies; then the two that held the garland deliver the same to the other next two, who observe the same order in their changes, and holding the garland over her head: which done, they deliver the same garland to the last two, who likewise observe the same order: at which, as it were by inspiration, she makes in her sleep signs of rejoicing, and holdeth up her hands to heaven: and so in their dancing vanish, carrying the garland with them. The music continues.

Kath. Spirits of peace, where are ye? are ye all gone,
And leave me here in wretchedness behind ye?
Grif. Madam, we are here.
Kath. It is not you I call for:
Saw ye none enter since I slept?
Grif. None, madam.
Kath. No? Saw you not, even now, a blessed troop
Invite me to a banquet; whose bright faces
Cast thousand beams upon me, like the sun?
They promis'd me eternal happiness;
And brought me garlands, Griffith, which I feel
I am not worthy yet to wear: I shall, assuredly.
Grif. I am most joyful, madam, such good dreams
Possess your fancy.
Kath. Bid the music leave,
They are harsh and heavy to me. *Music ceases.*
Pat. Do you note
How much her grace is alter'd on the sudden?
How long her face is drawn? how pale she looks,
And of an earthy cold? Mark her eyes!
Grif. She is going, wench: pray, pray.
Pat. Heaven comfort her!

Enter a Messenger.

Mess. An 't like your grace,—
Kath. You are a saucy fellow:
Deserve we no more reverence?
Grif. You are to blame,
Knowing she will not lose her wonted greatness,
To use so rude behaviour; go to, kneel.
Mess. I humbly do entreat your highness' pardon;
My haste made me unmannerly. There is staying
A gentleman, sent from the king, to see you.
Kath. Admit him entrance, Griffith: but this fellow
Let me ne'er see again. *Exit Messenger*

Enter LORD CAPUCIUS [*admitted by* GRIFFITH].

If my sight fail not,
You should be lord ambassador from the emperor,
My royal nephew, and your name Capucius.
Cap. Madam, the same; your servant.
Kath. O, my lord,
The times and titles now are alter'd strangely
With me since first you knew me. But, I pray you,
What is your pleasure with me?
Cap. Noble lady,
First, mine own service to your grace; the next,
The king's request that I would visit you;
Who grieves much for your weakness, and by me
Sends you his princely commendations,
And heartily entreats you take good comfort.
Kath. O my good lord, that comfort comes too late;
'Tis like a pardon after execution:
That gentle physic, given in time, had cur'd me;
But now I am past all comforts here, but prayers.
How does his highness?
Cap. Madam, in good health.
Kath. So may he ever do! and ever flourish,
When I shall dwell with worms, and my poor name
Banish'd the kingdom! Patience, is that letter,
I caus'd you write, yet sent away?
Pat. No, madam. [*Giving it to Katharine.*]
Kath. Sir, I most humbly pray you to deliver
This to my lord the king.
Cap. Most willing, madam.
Kath. In which I have commended to his goodness
The model of our chaste loves, his young daughter:
The dews of heaven fall thick in blessings on her!
Beseeching him to give her virtuous breeding,—
She is young, and of a noble modest nature,
I hope she will deserve well,—and a little
To love her for her mother's sake, that lov'd him,
Heaven knows how dearly. My next poor petition
Is, that his noble grace would have some pity
Upon my wretched women, that so long
Have follow'd both my fortunes faithfully:
Of which there is not one, I dare avow,
And now I should not lie, but will deserve,
For virtue and true beauty of the soul,
For honesty and decent carriage,
A right good husband, let him be a noble:

closely paralleled in Holinshed both in substance and phrasing. 35. **suggestion,** crafty dealing (Wright). 37. **presence,** i.e., of the king. 55. **getting,** acquiring wealth. 58. **rais'd in you,** built in your cities. 63. **his virtue,** i.e., Wolsey's. 73. **Whom,** object of both verbs, *hated* and *honour.* 74. **modesty,** moderation. 82. *Stage Direction:* (4) **congee,** make a conge, a leave-taking. 102. **lose,** forget. 127. **that letter.** The contents, recited below, are in Holinshed. 141. **both my fortunes,** i.e., good and ill.

And, sure, those men are happy that shall have 'em.
The last is, for my men; they are the poorest,
But poverty could never draw 'em from me;
That they may have their wages duly paid 'em,
And something over to remember me by:
If heaven had pleas'd to have given me longer life
And able means, we had not parted thus.
These are the whole contents: and, good my lord,
By that you love the dearest in this world,
As you wish Christian peace to souls departed,
Stand these poor people's friend, and urge the king
To do me this last right.

Cap. By heaven, I will,
Or let me lose the fashion of a man!

Kath. I thank you, honest lord. Remember me
In all humility unto his highness:
Say his long trouble now is passing
Out of this world; tell him, in death I bless'd him,
For so I will. Mine eyes grow dim. Farewell,
My lord. Griffith, farewell. Nay, Patience,
You must not leave me yet: I must to bed;
Call in more women. When I am dead, good wench,
Let me be us'd with honour: strew me over
With maiden flowers, that all the world may know
I was a chaste wife to my grave: embalm me,
Then lay me forth: although unqueen'd, yet like
A queen, and daughter to a king, inter me.
I can no more. *Exeunt, leading Katharine.*

ACT V.

SCENE I. [*London. A gallery in the palace.*]

Enter GARDINER, Bishop of Winchester, *a* Page *with a torch before him, met by* SIR THOMAS LOVELL.

Gar. It 's one o'clock, boy, is 't not?

Boy. It hath struck.

Gar. These should be hours for necessities,
Not for delights; times to repair our nature
With comforting repose, and not for us
To waste these times. Good hour of night, Sir Thomas!
Whither so late?

Lov. Came you from the king, my lord?

Gar. I did, Sir Thomas; and left him at primero
With the Duke of Suffolk.

Lov. I must to him too,
Before he go to bed. I'll take my leave.

Gar. Not yet, Sir Thomas Lovell. What 's the matter?
It seems you are in haste: an if there be
No great offence belongs to 't, give your friend
Some touch of your late business: affairs, that walk,
As they say spirits do, at midnight, have
In them a wilder nature than the business
That seeks dispatch by day.

Lov. My lord, I love you;
And durst commend a secret to your ear
Much weightier than this work. The queen 's in labour,
They say, in great extremity; and fear'd
She'll with the labour end.

Gar. The fruit she goes with
I pray for heartily, that it may find
Good time, and live: but for the stock, Sir Thomas,
I wish it grubb'd up now.

Lov. Methinks I could
Cry the amen; and yet my conscience says
She 's a good creature, and, sweet lady, does
Deserve our better wishes.

Gar. But, sir, sir,
Hear me, Sir Thomas: y' are a gentleman
Of mine own way; I know you wise, religious;
And, let me tell you, it will ne'er be well,
'Twill not, Sir Thomas Lovell, take 't of me,
Till Cranmer, Cromwell, her two hands, and she,
Sleep in their graves.

Lov. Now, sir, you speak of two
The most remark'd i' th' kingdom. As for Cromwell,
Beside that of the jewel house, is made master
O' th' rolls, and the king's secretary; further, sir,
Stands in the gap and trade of moe preferments,
With which the time will load him. Th' archbishop
Is the king's hand and tongue; and who dare speak
One syllable against him?

Gar. Yes, yes, Sir Thomas,
There are that dare; and I myself have ventur'd
To speak my mind of him: and indeed this day,
Sir, I may tell it you, I think I have
Incens'd the lords o' th' council, that he is,
For so I know he is, they know he is,
A most arch heretic, a pestilence
That does infect the land: with which they moved
Have broken with the king; who hath so far
Given ear to our complaint, of his great grace
And princely care foreseeing those fell mischiefs
Our reasons laid before him, hath commanded
To-morrow morning to the council-board
He be convented. He 's a rank weed, Sir Thomas,
And we must root him out. From your affairs
I hinder you too long: good night, Sir Thomas.

Lov. Many good nights, my lord: I rest your servant. *Exeunt Gardiner and Page.*

Enter KING *and* SUFFOLK.

King. Charles, I will play no more to-night;
My mind 's not on 't; you are too hard for me.

Suf. Sir, I did never win of you before.

King. But little, Charles;
Nor shall not, when my fancy 's on my play.
Now, Lovell, from the queen what is the news?

Lov. I could not personally deliver to her
What you commanded me, but by her woman
I sent your message; who return'd her thanks
In the great'st humbleness, and desir'd your highness
Most heartily to pray for her.

King. What say'st thou, ha?
To pray for her? what, is she crying out?

Lov. So said her woman; and that her suff'rance made
Almost each pang a death.

ACT V. SCENE I. 7. **primero,** gambling card game. 13. **touch,** hint. 28. **way,** religious faith (opposed to Protestant reform). 31. **hands,** i.e., henchmen. 33. **remark'd,** under the public eye. 36. **trade,** beaten path. 37. **the time,** tendencies of the age (Pooler). 43. **Incens'd,** instigated; Onions conjectures *insensed*, i.e., made to understand. 46-47. **with . . . king,** they, moved with this idea, have disclosed it to the king. 47. **who,** an English adaptation of the Latin construction of the relative equivalent to *and he who;* it is the subject of both

King. Alas, good lady!
Suf. God safely quit her of her burthen, and
With gentle travail, to the gladding of
Your highness with an heir!
King. 'Tis midnight, Charles;
Prithee, to bed; and in thy pray'rs remember
Th' estate of my poor queen. Leave me alone;
For I must think of that which company
Would not be friendly to.
Suf. I wish your highness
A quiet night; and my good mistress will
Remember in my prayers.
King. Charles, good night. *Exit Suffolk.*

Enter SIR ANTHONY DENNY.

Well, sir, what follows?
Den. Sir, I have brought my lord the archbishop,
As you commanded me.
King. Ha! Canterbury?
Den. Ay, my good lord.
King. 'Tis true: where is he, Denny?
Den. He attends your highness' pleasure.
King. Bring him to us. [*Exit Denny.*]
Lov. [*Aside*] This is about that which the bishop
spake:
I am happily come hither.

Enter CRANMER *and* DENNY.

King. Avoid the gallery. (*Lovell seems to stay.*) Ha! I have said. Be gone.
What! *Exeunt Lovell and Denny.*
Cran. [*Aside*] I am fearful: wherefore frowns he
thus?
'Tis his aspect of terror. All 's not well.
King. How now, my lord! you do desire to know
Wherefore I sent for you.
Cran. [*Kneeling*] It is my duty
T' attend your highness' pleasure.
King. Pray you, arise,
My good and gracious Lord of Canterbury.
Come, you and I must walk a turn together;
I have news to tell you: come, come, give me your
hand.
Ah, my good lord, I grieve at what I speak,
And am right sorry to repeat what follows:
I have, and most unwillingly, of late
Heard many grievous, I do say, my lord,
Grievous complaints of you; which, being consider'd,
Have mov'd us and our council, that you shall
This morning come before us; where, I know,
You cannot with such freedom purge yourself,
But that, till further trial in those charges
Which will require your answer, you must take
Your patience to you, and be well contented
To make your house our Tow'r: you a brother of us,
It fits we thus proceed, or else no witness
Would come against you.
Cran. [*Kneeling*] I humbly thank your
highness;
And am right glad to catch this good occasion
Most throughly to be winnowed, where my chaff
And corn shall fly asunder: for, I know,
There 's none stands under more calumnious
tongues
Than I myself, poor man.
King. Stand up, good Canterbury:
Thy truth and thy integrity is rooted
In us, thy friend: give me thy hand, stand up:
Prithee, let 's walk. Now, by my holidame,
What manner of man are you? My lord, I look'd
You would have given me your petition, that
I should have ta'en some pains to bring together
Yourself and your accusers; and to have heard you,
Without indurance, further.
Cran. Most dread liege,
The good I stand on is my truth and honesty:
If they shall fail, I, with mine enemies,
Will triumph o'er my person; which I weigh not,
Being of those virtues vacant. I fear nothing
What can be said against me.
King. Know you not
How your state stands i' th' world, with the whole
world?
Your enemies are many, and not small; their practices
Must bear the same proportion; and not ever
The justice and the truth o' th' question carries
The due o' th' verdict with it: at what ease
Might corrupt minds procure knaves as corrupt
To swear against you? such things have been done.
You are potently oppos'd; and with a malice
Of as great size. Ween you of better luck,
I mean, in perjur'd witness, than your master,
Whose minister you are, whiles here he liv'd
Upon this naughty earth? Go to, go to;
You take a precipice for no leap of danger,
And woo your own destruction.
Cran. God and your majesty
Protect mine innocence, or I fall into
The trap is laid for me!
King. Be of good cheer;
They shall no more prevail than we give way to.
Keep comfort to you; and this morning see
You do appear before them: if they shall chance,
In charging you with matters, to commit you,
The best persuasions to the contrary
Fail not to use, and with what vehemency
Th' occasion shall instruct you: if entreaties
Will render you no remedy, this ring
Deliver them, and your appeal to us
There make before them. Look, the good man weeps!
He 's honest, on mine honour. God's blest mother!
I swear he is true-hearted; and a soul
None better in my kingdom. Get you gone,
And do as I have bid you. (*Exit Cranmer.*) He has
strangled
His language in his tears.

Enter Old Lady [, LOVELL *following*].

Gent. (*Within*) Come back: what mean
you?
Old L. I'll not come back; the tidings that I bring
Will make my boldness manners. Now, good angels
Fly o'er thy royal head, and shade thy person
Under their blessed wings!

verbs *hath . . . Given* and *hath commanded* (l. 50). 50. **hath,** that he hath. 52. **convented,** summoned. 84. **the bishop,** i.e., Gardiner. 85. **Avoid,** vacate. 106. **brother,** fellow member of the council. 121. **indurance,** imprisonment. 124-125. **which . . . vacant,** I don't value my person if it is void of those virtues (*truth* and *honesty*). 129-131. **and . . . it,** the innocence of a person does not always insure his acquittal (Pooler). 135. **Ween you of,** do you expect. 136. **master,** i.e., Christ. 146. **commit,** i.e., to prison.

King. Now, by thy looks
I guess thy message. Is the queen deliver'd?
Say, ay; and of a boy.
Old L. Ay, ay, my liege;
And of a lovely boy: the God of heaven
Both now and ever bless her! 'tis a girl,
Promises boys hereafter. Sir, your queen
Desires your visitation, and to be
Acquainted with this stranger: 'tis as like you
As cherry is to cherry.
King. Lovell!
Lov. Sir?
King. Give her an hundred marks. I'll to the queen.
Exit King.
Old L. An hundred marks! By this light, I'll ha' more.
An ordinary groom is for such payment.
I will have more, or scold it out of him.
Said I for this, the girl was like to him?
I'll have more, or else unsay 't; and now,
While 'tis hot, I'll put it to the issue.
Exit Lady [*with Lovell*].

SCENE II. [*Before the council-chamber.*]

Enter CRANMER, Archibishop of Canterbury [; *Pursuivants, Pages, &c. attending at the door*].

Cran. I hope I am not too late; and yet the gentleman,
That was sent to me from the council, pray'd me
To make great haste. All fast? what means this? Ho!
Who waits there? Sure, you know me?

Enter Keeper.

Keep. Yes, my lord;
But yet I cannot help you.
Cran. Why?
Keep. Your grace must wait till you be call'd for.

Enter DOCTOR BUTTS.

Cran. So.
Butts. [*Aside*] This is a piece of malice. I am glad
I came this way so happily: the king
Shall understand it presently. *Exit Butts.*
Cran. [*Aside*] 'Tis Butts,
The king's physician: as he pass'd along,
How earnestly he cast his eyes upon me!
Pray heaven, he sound not my disgrace! For certain,
This is of purpose laid by some that hate me—
God turn their hearts! I never sought their malice—
To quench mine honour: they would shame to make me
Wait else at door, a fellow-counsellor,
'Mong boys, grooms, and lackeys. But their pleasures
Must be fulfill'd, and I attend with patience.

Enter the KING *and* BUTTS *at a window above.*

Butts. I'll show your grace the strangest sight—
King. What 's that, Butts?
Butts. I think your highness saw this many a day.
King. Body o' me, where is it?
Butts. There, my lord:
The high promotion of his grace of Canterbury;
Who holds his state at door, 'mongst pursuivants,
Pages, and footboys.
King. Ha! 'tis he, indeed:
Is this the honour they do one another?
'Tis well there 's one above 'em yet. I had thought
They had parted so much honesty among 'em,
At least, good manners, as not thus to suffer
A man of his place, and so near our favour,
To dance attendance on their lordships' pleasures,
And at the door too, like a post with packets.
By holy Mary, Butts, there 's knavery:
Let 'em alone, and draw the curtain close:
We shall hear more anon.
[*They conceal themselves behind the curtain. Cranmer remains waiting at the door, below.*]

[SCENE III. *The Council-Chamber.*]

A council table brought in with chairs and stools, and placed under the state. Enter LORD CHANCELLOR; *places himself at the upper end of the table on the left hand; a seat being left void above him, as for* CANTERBURY'S *seat.* DUKE OF SUFFOLK, DUKE OF NORFOLK, SURREY, LORD CHAMBERLAIN, GARDINER, *seat themselves in order on each side.* CROMWELL *at lower end, as secretary.* [Keeper *at the door.*]

Chan. Speak to the business, master secretary:
Why are we met in council?
Crom. Please your honours,
The chief cause concerns his grace of Canterbury.
Gar. Has he had knowledge of it?
Crom. Yes.
Nor. Who waits there?
Keep. Without, my noble lords?
Gar. Yes.
Keep. My lord archbishop:
And has done half an hour, to know your pleasures.
Chan. Let him come in.
Keep. Your grace may enter now.
Cranmer approaches the council table.
Chan. My good lord archbishop, I 'm very sorry
To sit here at this present, and behold
That chair stand empty: but we all are men,
In our own natures frail, and capable
Of our flesh; few are angels: out of which frailty
And want of wisdom, you, that best should teach us,
Have misdemean'd yourself, and not a little,
Toward the king first, then his laws, in filling
The whole realm, by your teaching and your chaplains,
For so we are inform'd, with new opinions,
Divers and dangerous; which are heresies,
And, not reform'd, may prove pernicious.
Gar. Which reformation must be sudden too,
My noble lords; for those that tame wild horses
Pace 'em not in their hands to make 'em gentle,
But stop their mouths with stubborn bits, and spur 'em,
Till they obey the manage. If we suffer,
Out of our easiness and childish pity
To one man's honour, this contagious sickness,

SCENE II. The source for this and the following scene is Foxe's *Acts and Monuments.* Holinshed does not relate these events. 3. **fast,** locked. 13. **sound,** proclaim (Pooler); possibly, ascertain, as with a sounding line. 19. *Stage Direction: at a* ***window above.*** The gallery over the stage, representing a peephole through which the council could be spied upon. The Folio text makes no scene division between this and the following scene, so that the council would assemble under the view and in the hearing of the king. 28. **parted,** shared.

SCENE III. *Stage Direction:* ***state,*** canopy. 5. **Without,** outside the door. (Cranmer may never actually exit; the stage has now become

Farewell all physic: and what follows then?
Commotions, uproars, with a general taint
Of the whole state: as, of late days, our neighbours,
The upper Germany, can dearly witness,
Yet freshly pitied in our memories.
Cran. My good lords, hitherto, in all the progress
Both of my life and office, I have labour'd,
And with no little study, that my teaching
And the strong course of my authority
Might go one way, and safely; and the end
Was ever, to do well: nor is there living,
I speak it with a single heart, my lords,
A man that more detests, more stirs against,
Both in his private conscience and his place,
Defacers of a public peace, than I do.
Pray heaven, the king may never find a heart
With less allegiance in it! Men that make
Envy and crooked malice nourishment
Dare bite the best. I do beseech your lordships,
That, in this case of justice, my accusers,
Be what they will, may stand forth face to face,
And freely urge against me.
Suf. Nay, my lord,
That cannot be: you are a counsellor,
And, by that virtue, no man dare accuse you.
Gar. My lord, because we have business of more moment,
We will be short with you. 'Tis his highness' pleasure,
And our consent, for better trial of you,
From hence you be committed to the Tower;
Where, being but a private man again,
You shall know many dare accuse you boldly,
More than, I fear, you are provided for.
Cran. Ah, my good Lord of Winchester, I thank you;
You are always my good friend; if your will pass,
I shall both find your lordship judge and juror,
You are so merciful: I see your end;
'Tis my undoing: love and meekness, lord,
Become a churchman better than ambition:
Win straying souls with modesty again,
Cast none away. That I shall clear myself,
Lay all the weight ye can upon my patience,
I make as little doubt, as you do conscience
In doing daily wrongs. I could say more,
But reverence to your calling makes me modest.
Gar. My lord, my lord, you are a sectary,
That 's the plain truth: your painted gloss discovers,
To men that understand you, words and weakness.
Crom. My Lord of Winchester, y' are a little,
By your good favour, too sharp; men so noble,
However faulty, yet should find respect
For what they have been: 'tis a cruelty
To load a falling man.
Gar. Good master secretary,
I cry your honour mercy; you may, worst
Of all this table, say so.
Crom. Why, my lord?
Gar. Do not I know you for a favourer
Of this new sect? ye are not sound.
Crom. Not sound?
Gar. Not sound, I say.
Crom. Would you were half so honest!
Men's prayers then would seek you, not their fears.
Gar. I shall remember this bold language.
Crom. Do.
Remember your bold life too.
Chan. This is too much;
Forbear, for shame, my lords.
Gar. I have done.
Crom. And I.
Chan. Then thus for you, my lord: it stands agreed,
I take it, by all voices, that forthwith
You be convey'd to th' Tower a prisoner;
There to remain till the king's further pleasure
Be known unto us: are you all agreed, lords?
All. We are.
Cran. Is there no other way of mercy,
But I must needs to th' Tower, my lords?
Gar. What other
Would you expect? you are strangely troublesome.
Let some o' th' guard be ready there.

Enter the Guard.

Cran. For me?
Must I go like a traitor thither?
Gar. Receive him,
And see him safe i' th' Tower.
Cran. Stay, good my lords,
I have a little yet to say. Look there, my lords;
By virtue of that ring, I take my cause
Out of the gripes of cruel men, and give it
To a most noble judge, the king my master.
Cham. This is the king's ring.
Sur. 'Tis no counterfeit.
Suf. 'Tis the right ring, by heav'n: I told ye all,
When we first put this dangerous stone a-rolling,
'Twould fall upon ourselves.
Nor. Do you think, my lords,
The king will suffer but the little finger
Of this man to be vex'd?
Chan. 'Tis now too certain:
How much more is his life in value with him?
Would I were fairly out on 't!
Crom. My mind gave me,
In seeking tales and informations
Against this man, whose honesty the devil
And his disciples only envy at,
Ye blew the fire that burns ye: now have at ye!

Enter KING, *frowning on them; takes his seat.*

Gar. Dread sovereign, how much are we bound to heaven
In daily thanks, that gave us such a prince;
Not only good and wise, but most religious:
One that, in all obedience, makes the church
The chief aim of his honour; and, to strengthen
That holy duty, out of dear respect,
His royal self in judgement comes to hear
The cause betwixt her and this great offender.
King. You were ever good at sudden commendations,
Bishop of Winchester. But know, I come not
To hear such flattery now, and in my presence;
They are too thin and bare to hide offences.

the room into which he has been waiting to be admitted.) 11-12. **capable . . . flesh,** susceptible to the weaknesses of the flesh. 22. **Pace . . . hands,** i.e., don't lead them. 29-30. **our . . . Germany,** refers to the Peasants' Wars, 1524; possibly to the massacre of the Anabaptists in 1535. 38. **single,** honest; not given to double-dealing. 59. **pass** prevail. 67. **I . . . conscience,** I have as little doubt (of my blamelessness) as you have scruples. 71. **discovers,** reveals. 109. **gave,** told.

To me you cannot reach, you play the spaniel,
And think with wagging of your tongue to win me;
But, whatsoe'er thou tak'st me for, I 'm sure
Thou hast a cruel nature and a bloody.
[*To Cranmer*] Good man, sit down. Now let me see the proudest
He, that dares most, but wag his finger at thee:
By all that 's holy, he had better starve
Than but once think this place becomes thee not.

Sur. May it please your grace,—

King. No, sir, it does not please me.
I had thought I had had men of some understanding
And wisdom of my council; but I find none.
Was it discretion, lords, to let this man,
This good man,—few of you deserve that title,—
This honest man, wait like a lousy footboy
At chamber-door? and one as great as you are?
Why, what a shame was this! Did my commission
Bid ye so far forget yourselves? I gave ye
Power as he was a counsellor to try him,
Not as a groom: there 's some of ye, I see,
More out of malice than integrity,
Would try him to the utmost, had ye mean;
Which ye shall never have while I live.

Chan. Thus far,
My most dread sovereign, may it like your grace
To let my tongue excuse all. What was purpos'd
Concerning his imprisonment, was rather,
If there be faith in men, meant for his trial,
And fair purgation to the world, than malice,
I 'm sure, in me.

King. Well, well, my lords, respect him;
Take him, and use him well, he 's worthy of it.
I will say thus much for him, if a prince
May be beholding to a subject, I
Am, for his love and service, so to him.
Make me no more ado, but all embrace him:
Be friends, for shame, my lords! My Lord of Canterbury,
I have a suit which you must not deny me;
That is, a fair young maid that yet wants baptism,
You must be godfather, and answer for her.

Cran. The greatest monarch now alive may glory
In such an honour: how may I deserve it,
That am a poor and humble subject to you?

King. Come, come, my lord, you 'ld spare your spoons: you shall have two noble partners with you; the old Duchess of Norfolk, and Lady Marquess Dorset: will these please you?
Once more, my Lord of Winchester, I charge you,
Embrace and love this man.

Gar. With a true heart
And brother-love I do it.

Cran. And let heaven
Witness, how dear I hold this confirmation.

King. Good man, those joyful tears show thy true heart:
The common voice, I see, is verified
Of thee, which says thus, 'Do my Lord of Canterbury
A shrewd turn, and he is your friend for ever.'
Come, lords, we trifle time away; I long
To have this young one made a Christian.
As I have made ye one, lords, one remain;
So I grow stronger, you more honour gain. *Exeunt.*

SCENE [IV. *The palace yard*].

Noise and tumult within. Enter Porter *and his* Man.

Port. You'll leave your noise anon, ye rascals: do you take the court for Parish-garden? ye rude slaves, leave your gaping.

(*Within*) Good master porter, I belong to the larder.

Port. Belong to the gallows, and be hanged, ye rogue! is this a place to roar in? Fetch me a dozen crab-tree staves, and strong ones: these are but switches to 'em. I'll scratch your heads: you must be seeing christenings? do you look for ale and cakes here, you rude rascals?

Man. Pray, sir, be patient: 'tis as much impossible—
Unless we sweep 'em from the door with cannons—
To scatter 'em, as 'tis to make 'em sleep
On May-day morning; which will never be:
We may as well push against Powle's, as stir 'em.

Port. How got they in, and be hang'd?

Man. Alas, I know not; how gets the tide in?
As much as one sound cudgel of four foot—
You see the poor remainder—could distribute,
I made no spare, sir.

Port. You did nothing, sir.

Man. I am not Samson, nor Sir Guy, nor Colbrand,
To mow 'em down before me: but if I spar'd any
That had a head to hit, either young or old,
He or she, cuckold or cuckold-maker,
Let me ne'er hope to see a chine again;
And that I would not for a cow, God save her!

(*Within*) Do you hear, master porter?

Port. I shall be with you presently, good master puppy. Keep the door close, sirrah.

Man. What would you have me do?

Port. What should you do, but knock 'em down by the dozens? Is this Moorfields to muster in? or have we some strange Indian with the great tool come to court, the women so besiege us? Bless me, what a fry of fornication is at door! On my Christian conscience, this one christening will beget a thousand; here will be father, godfather, and all together.

Man. The spoons will be the bigger, sir. There is a fellow somewhat near the door, he should be a brazier by his face, for, o' my conscience, twenty of the dog-days now reign in 's nose; all that stand about him are under the line, they need no other penance: that fire-drake did I hit three times on the head, and three times was his nose discharged against me; he stands there, like a mortar-piece, to blow us. There was a haberdasher's wife of small wit near him, that railed upon me till her pinked porringer fell off her head, for kindling such a combustion in the state. I missed the meteor once, and hit that woman; who cried out 'Clubs!' when I might see from far some

---

167-168. **you 'ld . . . spoons,** said jestingly; spoons were a common christening gift. 178. **shrewd,** malicious.

SCENE IV. 2. **Parish-garden,** Paris-garden, a bear garden on the Bankside. 3. **gaping,** shouting. 5. **larder,** pantry, i.e., he was a servant of the palace household. 11. **ale and cakes,** refreshments appropriate to christenings and other festivals. 15. **May-day morning,** allusion to the custom of rising before dawn on May day for early morning festivities. 16. **Powle's,** St. Paul's Cathedral. 22. **Samson,** Biblical character of great strength. **Sir Guy, Colbrand.** Cf. *King John* I, i, 225, note. 26. **chine,** backbone; hence a joint of beef or other meat. 33. **Moorfields,** training ground for the militia. 34. **some strange Indian,** allusion to the Elizabethan excitement over exhibited Indians; cf. *The Tempest*, II, ii, 29-35. 35. **tool,** genitals. 37. **fry of fornication,** swarm of would-be fornicators. 42. **brazier,** forty truncheoners draw to her succour, which were the hope o' the Strand, where she was quartered. They fell on; I made good my place: at length they came to the broom-staff to me; I defied 'em still: when suddenly a file of boys behind 'em, loose shot, delivered such a shower of pebbles, that I was fain to draw mine honour in, and let 'em win the work: the devil was amongst 'em, I think, surely.

Port. These are the youths that thunder at a playhouse, and fight for bitten apples; that no audience, but the tribulation of Tower-hill, or the limbs of Limehouse, their dear brothers, are able to endure. I have some of 'em in Limbo Patrum, and there they are like to dance these three days; besides the running banquet of two beadles that is to come.

Enter LORD CHAMBERLAIN.

Cham. Mercy o' me, what a multitude are here!
They grow still too; from all parts they are coming,
As if we kept a fair here! Where are these porters,
These lazy knaves? Y' have made a fine hand, fellows:
There 's a trim rabble let in: are all these
Your faithful friends o' th' suburbs? We shall have
Great store of room, no doubt, left for the ladies,
When they pass back from the christening.
Port. An 't please your honour,
We are but men; and what so many may do,
Not being torn a-pieces, we have done:
An army cannot rule 'em.
Cham. As I live,
If the king blame me for 't, I'll lay ye all
By th' heels, and suddenly; and on your heads
Clap round fines for neglect: y' are lazy knaves;
And here ye lie baiting of bombards, when
Ye should do service. Hark! the trumpets sound;
Th' are come already from the christening:
Go, break among the press, and find a way out
To let the troop pass fairly; or I'll find
A Marshalsea shall hold ye play these two months.
Port. Make way there for the princess.
Man. You great fellow,
Stand close up, or I'll make your head ache.
Port. You i' th' camlet, get up o' th' rail;
I'll peck you o'er the pales else. *Exeunt.*

SCENE [V. *The palace*].

Enter trumpets, sounding; then two Aldermen, LORD MAYOR, GARTER, CRANMER, DUKE OF NORFOLK *with his marshal's staff,* DUKE OF SUFFOLK, *two* Noblemen *bearing great standing-bowls for the christening-gifts; then four* Noblemen *bearing a canopy, under which the* DUCHESS OF NORFOLK, *godmother, bearing the child richly habited in a mantle, &c., train borne by a* Lady; *then follows the* MARCHIONESS DORSET, *the other godmother, and Ladies. The troop pass once about the stage, and* GARTER *speaks.*

Gart. Heaven, from thy endless goodness, send prosperous life, long, and ever happy, to the high and mighty princess of England, Elizabeth!

Flourish. Enter KING *and Guard.*

Cran. [*Kneeling*] And to your royal grace, and the good queen,
My noble partners, and myself, thus pray:
All comfort, joy, in this most gracious lady,
Heaven ever laid up to make parents happy,
May hourly fall upon ye!
King. Thank you, good lord archbishop:
What is her name?
Cran. Elizabeth.
King. Stand up, lord.
[*The King kisses the child.*]
With this kiss take my blessing: God protect thee!
Into whose hand I give thy life.
Cran. Amen.
King. My noble gossips, y' have been too prodigal:
I thank ye heartily; so shall this lady,
When she has so much English.
Cran. Let me speak, sir,
For heaven now bids me; and the words I utter
Let none think flattery, for they'll find 'em truth.
This royal infant—heaven still move about her!—
Though in her cradle, yet now promises
Upon this land a thousand thousand blessings,
Which time shall bring to ripeness: she shall be—
But few now living can behold that goodness—
A pattern to all princes living with her,
And all that shall succeed: Saba was never
More covetous of wisdom and fair virtue
Than this pure soul shall be: all princely graces,
That mould up such a mighty piece as this is,
With all the virtues that attend the good,
Shall still be doubled on her: truth shall nurse her,
Holy and heavenly thoughts still counsel her:
She shall be lov'd and fear'd: her own shall bless her;
Her foes shake like a field of beaten corn,
And hang their heads with sorrow: good grows with her:
In her days every man shall eat in safety,
Under his own vine, what he plants; and sing
The merry songs of peace to all his neighbours:
God shall be truly known; and those about her
From her shall read the perfect ways of honour,
And by those claim their greatness, not by blood.
Nor shall this peace sleep with her: but as when
The bird of wonder dies, the maiden phœnix,
Her ashes new create another heir,
As great in admiration as herself;
So shall she leave her blessedness to one,
When heaven shall call her from this cloud of darkness,
Who from the sacred ashes of her honour
Shall star-like rise, as great in fame as she was,
And so stand fix'd: peace, plenty, love, truth, terror,
That were the servants to this chosen infant,
Shall then be his, and like a vine grow to him:

a worker in brass. 43. **dog-days,** midsummer, when the sun is near Sirius, the Dog Star. 44. **line,** equator. 45. **fire-drake,** fiery dragon. 48. **mortar-piece,** short piece of cannon. 50. **pinked porringer,** small close-fitting cap ornamented with perforations. 54. **truncheoners,** men armed with cudgels. 65-66. **tribulation . . . Limehouse,** probably places in London known for their boisterousness. 67. **Limbo Patrum,** prison; resting place of the pre-Christian patriarchs who had to remain there until the coming of Christ. 69. **running banquet,** whipping following imprisonment, taking *banquet* as the dessert after a meal. 85. **baiting of bombards,** drinking from leathern bottles. 90. **Marshalsea,** prison in Southwark. 94. **pales,** fence.

SCENE V. 13. **gossips,** godparents. 24. **Saba,** Queen of Sheba. 31. **own,** i.e., own people. 44. **one,** James I.

Wherever the bright sun of heaven shall shine,
His honour and the greatness of his name
Shall be, and make new nations: he shall flourish,
And, like a mountain cedar, reach his branches
To all the plains about him: our children's children
Shall see this, and bless heaven.

King. Thou speakest wonders.

Cran. She shall be, to the happiness of England,
An aged princess; many days shall see her,
And yet no day without a deed to crown it.
Would I had known no more! but she must die,
She must, the saints must have her; yet a virgin,
A most unspotted lily shall she pass
To th' ground, and all the world shall mourn her.

King. O lord archbishop,
Thou hast made me now a man! never, before
This happy child, did I get any thing:
This oracle of comfort has so pleas'd me,
That when I am in heaven I shall desire
To see what this child does, and praise my Maker.
I thank ye all. To you, my good lord mayor,
And your good brethren, I am much beholding;
I have receiv'd much honour by your presence,
And ye shall find me thankful. Lead the way, lords:
Ye must all see the queen, and she must thank ye,
She will be sick else. This day, no man think
'Has business at his house; for all shall stay:
This little one shall make it holiday. *Exeunt.*

EPILOGUE.

'Tis ten to one this play can never please
All that are here: some come to take their ease,
And sleep an act or two; but those, we fear,
W' have frighted with our trumpets; so, 'tis clear,
They'll say 'tis naught: others, to hear the city
Abus'd extremely, and to cry 'That 's witty!'
Which we have not done neither: that, I fear,
All the expected good w' are like to hear
For this play at this time, is only in
The merciful construction of good women;
For such a one we show'd 'em: if they smile,
And say 'twill do, I know, within a while
All the best men are ours; for 'tis ill hap,
If they hold when their ladies bid 'em clap.

66. **get,** beget. 76. **'Has,** he has. **stay,** come to a halt.

EPILOGUE. 10. **construction,** interpretation. 14. **hold,** hold back.

CANON, DATES, AND EARLY TEXTS

By "canon" we mean a listing of plays that can be ascribed to Shakespeare on the basis of reliable evidence. Such evidence is either "internal," derived from matters of style or poetics in the plays themselves (see General Introduction, above, pp. 38–43), or "external," derived from outside the play. The latter includes any reference by Shakespeare's contemporaries to his plays, any allusions in the plays themselves to contemporary events, the entering of Shakespeare's plays for publication in the Stationers' Register (S. R.), actual publication of the plays, and records of early performances. These matters of external evidence are also essential in attempting to date the plays.

The greatest single source of information is the First Folio text of Shakespeare's plays, sponsored by Shakespeare's fellow-actors John Heminges and Henry Condell and published in 1623. It contains all the plays included in this present edition of Shakespeare except *Pericles*, and offers strong presumptive evidence of being a complete and accurate compilation of Shakespeare's work by men who knew him and cherished his memory. It provides the only texts we have for the following plays: *The Comedy of Errors, The Two Gentlemen of Verona, The Taming of the Shrew, 1 Henry VI, King John, As You Like It, Twelfth Night, Julius Caesar, All's Well that Ends Well, Measure for Measure, Timon of Athens, Macbeth, Antony and Cleopatra, Coriolanus, Cymbeline, The Winter's Tale, The Tempest,* and *Henry VIII*. This includes nearly half the known canon of Shakespeare's plays. Our debt to the First Folio is incalculable, and confirms our impression of its reliability.

The information of the First Folio is further confirmed by contemporary references. In 1598, a divine and minor writer of the period named Francis Meres wrote in his *Palladis Tamia:*

> As the soule of *Euphorbus* was thought to liue in *Pythagoras:* so the sweete wittie soule of *Ouid* liues in mellifluous & hony-tongued *Shakespeare*, witnes his *Venus* and *Adonis*, his *Lucrece*, his sugred Sonnets among his priuate friends, &c.
>
> As *Plautus* and *Seneca* are accounted the best for Comedy and Tragedy among the Latines: so *Shakespeare* among the English is the most excellent in both kinds for the stage; for Comedy, witness his *Gentlemen of Verona*, his *Errors*, his *Loue labors lost*, his *Loue labours wonne*, his *Midsummers night dreame*, & his *Merchant of Venice:* for Tragedy his *Richard the* 2. *Richard* the *3. Henry the* 4. *King Iohn*, *Titus Andronicus* and his *Romeo* and *Iuliet.*

Though this list was meant to offer praise, not to be an exhaustive catalogue, it is remarkably full. If the tantalizing *Loue labours wonne* refers to *The Taming of the Shrew*, Meres' list of comedies is entirely complete down to 1598. Naturally the list does not include the great "festive" comedies, *Much Ado about Nothing*, *As You Like it*, and *Twelfth Night*, since these were written at or slightly later than the time of Meres' comment. Meres correctly names all of Shakespeare's history plays except the *Henry VI* trilogy and of course the later histories *Henry V* (1599) and *Henry VIII* (1613). He names both of Shakespeare's early tragedies not based on English history: *Titus Andronicus* and *Romeo and Juliet*. He tells us about the important nondramatic poems, which did not appear in the First Folio since that volume is devoted exclusively to plays. Not much can be made of the order in which Meres names the plays, however, for we learn from other sources that *Richard III* clearly precedes *Richard II* in date of composition and *King John* precedes the *Henry IV* plays.

Other writers of the 1590's add further confirming evidence. John Weever, in an epigram "*Ad Gulielmum Shakespeare*," published in 1599, refers to "Rose-checkt *Adonis*" and "Faire fire-hot *Venus*," to "Chaste *Lucretia*" and "Prowd lust-stung *Tarquine*," and to "*Romea Richard*, more whose names I know not." Richard Barnfield, in *Poems in Divers Humors*, 1598, praises Shakespeare for "*Venus*" and "*Lucrece*." Both Thomas Nashe and Robert Greene seemingly refer to the *Henry VI* plays, missing from Meres' list. Nashe, in his *Pierce Penilesse* (1592), speculates how it would "haue ioyed braue *Talbot* (the terror of the French) to thinke that after he had lyne two hundred yeares in his Tombe, hee should triumphe againe on the Stage." Talbot is the hero of *1 Henry VI*, and we know of no other play on the subject. Greene, in his *Greenes Groats-worth of Wit* (1592), lashes out at an "vpstart Crow, beautified with our feathers, that with his *Tygers hart wrapt in a Players hyde*, supposes he is as well able to bombast out a blanke verse as the best of you: and beeing an absolute *Iohannes fac totum*, is in his owne conceit the onely Shake-scene in a countrey." The line about "Tygers hart" is deliberately misquoted from *3 Henry VI*, I,iv,137. (It is possible that this famous attack on Shakespeare was actually written not by Greene himself but by Henry Chettle, his literary executor.)

The Comedy of Errors (c. 1589–1593)

The earliest known edition of *The Comedy of Errors* is in the First Folio of 1623. It is first mentioned, however, on Innocents Day, December 28, 1594, when a "Comedy of Errors (like to *Plautus* his *Menechmus*)" was performed by professional actors as part of the Christmas Revels at Gray's Inn. The evening's festivities are set down in *Gesta Grayorum*, a contemporary account of the revels, though not published until 1688. According to this record, the evening was marred by such tumult and disorder that the invited guests from the Inner Temple refused to stay; thereafter, the night became known as "The Night of Errors." References to sorcery and enchantment in the play leave little doubt that it was Shakespeare's.

Scholars generally agree that the play was not newly written for this occasion. Internally, the play seems early: its characterization is slight, for example, and its punning wit reminds us of *Love's Labour's Lost* and *The Two Gentlemen of Verona*. Topical clues are suggestive but not conclusive. Chief of these is the joke about France being "armed and reverted, making war against her heir" (III,ii). Unquestionably this refers to France's civil wars between Henry of Navarre and his Catholic opposition. Since Henry became a Catholic and the King of France in 1593, most scholars prefer a date before 1593. Peter Alexander (*Shakespeare's Life and Art*, 1961) has even argued for a date prior to 1589, since Henry III died in that year leaving Henry of Navarre as nominal king rather than heir. The sad truth is that we probably cannot attach too much weight to either conclusion. Allusions to the French civil wars during the early 1590's were common but also imprecise; the joke would have seemed relevant at almost any time up to 1595. The same is probably true of the allusion to Spain's sending "whole armadoes of caracks" (III,ii). This is often taken to refer to the Spanish Armada, 1588, but may instead refer to the Portuguese *Madre de Dios* captured and brought to England in 1592 or to a similar venture. In short, it is virtually impossible to prove that *The Comedy of Errors* precedes *Love's Labour's Lost*, *The Two Gentlemen of Verona*, or *The Taming of the Shrew*.

A lost play called *The Historie of Error* was acted before the queen by the Children of Paul's at Hampton Court on New Year's night, 1577. About this play we know nothing other than its suggestive title, and speculation that Shakespeare may have adapted it has been generally abandoned.

The Folio text, based probably on Shakespeare's own manuscript, is generally a good text although characters' names are frequently confused in the stage directions and speech prefixes.

Love's Labour's Lost (c. 1588–1589, revised 1596–1597?)

Love's Labour's Lost first appeared in a quarto dated 1598, without entry in the Stationers' Register. Its title page reads:

> A PLEASANT Conceited Comedie CALLED, Loues labors lost. As it vvas presented before her Highnes this last Christmas. Newly corrected and augmented *By W. Shakespere*. Imprinted at London by *W. W.* for *Cutbert Burby*. 1598.

Because the phrase "newly corrected and augmented" also appears on the title page of the good quarto of *Romeo and Juliet*, issued in 1599 to correct a pirated quarto of 1597, many scholars suspect that *Love's Labour's Lost* may similarly have appeared in a bad quarto that is now lost. Such a circumstance would explain why the existing quarto of *Love's Labour's Lost* was not registered: if the play had already been published, even in a pirated version, relicensing would have been unnecessary. (The *Romeo and Juliet* good quarto was not registered for this reason.)

The text shows clear signs of revision. Two long passages (IV,iii,296–304 and 318–351; V,ii,828–832 and 851–864) give duplicatory readings of the same speeches, suggesting the printer mistakenly copied both the canceled version in his copy and the revision. Speech-headings are unusually confused, sometimes referring to characters by their personal names (Navarre, Armado, Holofernes) and at other times by their generic titles (King, Braggart, Pedant). Some of these errors, notably the long uncanceled passages, suggest that the printer (who was new and relatively inexperienced) was copying from Shakespeare's working draft or foul papers. Whether Shakespeare wrote this draft on one occasion or whether he revised an earlier version is, however, a matter on which scholars disagree. The Folio text was set from the quarto, and thus gives us no additional information as to when or in what stages the play was written.

Francis Meres refers to the play in October of 1598. The performance before Queen Elizabeth "last Christmas" was probably in late 1597. Robert Tofte tells us in his *Alba* (1598) that "Loues Labour Lost, I once did see a Play Ycleped so." His phrasing suggests a performance seen some time in the past, although he could mean that he saw it only once. Apart from these allusions, dating of the play must rely on its presumed internal allusions to contemporary events. Unfortunately, the play has attracted a lot of highly speculative topical hypotheses. One such describes a "School of Night" to which Sir Walter Ralegh, Matthew Roydon, George Chapman, and others are supposed to have belonged. No objective evidence exists to prove the existence of such a school. Ralegh was tried for atheism but aquitted. Other topical hypotheses are discussed briefly in the Introduction to the play, pp. 100–102 above. Some allusions to the historical King of Navarre and to his supporters the Duc de Biron and the Duc de Longueville are undeniable. These allusions tend to argue for an early date (c. 1588–1589) when these persons had not yet become the chief figures in a bloody religious civil war in France and hence inappropriate subjects for light comedy. The influence of John Lyly and the children's drama also argues for an early date. If, on the other hand, the Muscovite masque in V,ii contains a reference to the Gray's Inn revels of 1594, as several scholars have urged, some portions of the play may be from after that date. The hypothesis that Shakespeare revived an old play of his shortly before publication in 1598, although not universally accepted, offers at least a plausible explanation of the "newly corrected and augmented" on the title page.

The Two Gentlemen of Verona (*c. 1590–1594*)

The Two Gentlemen of Verona was not published until the First Folio of 1623. Other than Francis Meres' listing of it in 1598, evidence as to dating is scarce. No convincing allusions to contemporary events have been found. From the internal evidence of style, most scholars prefer an early date, though some believe that the play was composed in various stages. (Numerous factual inconsistencies in the text lend support to this theory.) The influence of John Lyly is still perceptible in the play's overly ingenious wit-combat.

An unusual feature of the text, its grouping of characters' names at the beginning of each scene, seems to indicate that the manuscript was copied at some point by the scrivener Ralph Crane, probably from a theatre prompt-book.

The Taming of the Shrew (*c. 1592–1594*)

The Taming of the Shrew was not printed until the First Folio of 1623. Francis Meres does not mention the play in 1598, unless it is the mysterious "*Loue labours wonne*" on his list. (Meres is not totally accurate, for he omits *Henry VI* from the history plays.) The play must have existed prior to 1598, however, for its style is comparable with that of *The Two Gentlemen* and other early comedies. Moreover, a play called *The Taming of A Shrew* appeared in print in 1594 (S. R. May 1594). Although the relationship of that text to Shakespeare's play has been hotly debated, the prevailing view today is that it represents an imitation by some rival dramatist, who relied chiefly on his memory and who changed characters' names and the location to make the play seem his. Or it may be simply a bad quarto put together by memorial reconstruction. In either case, Shakespeare's play would have to be dated earlier than May 1594.

The title page of *A Shrew* proclaims that "it was sundry times acted by the *Right honorable the Earle of* Pembrook his seruants." Quite possibly this derivative version was merely trying to capitalize on the original's stage success, and was in fact describing performances of Shakespeare's play. Henslowe's record of a performance of "*the Tamynge of A Shrowe*" in 1594 at Newington Butts, a mile south of London Bridge, may also refer to Shakespeare's play; certainly the minute distinction between "A Shrew" and "The Shrew" is one that the official records of the time would overlook. The Admiral's men and the Lord Chamberlain's men were playing at Newington Butts at the time, either jointly or alternatingly. Since Shakespeare's company, the Chamberlain's, later owned *The Shrew*, they may well have owned and acted it on this occasion in 1594, having obtained it from the Earl of Pembroke's men when that company disbanded in 1593. Many of Pembroke's leading players joined the Chamberlain's, Shakespeare quite possibly among them. (The possibility that he came to the Chamberlain's from Lord Strange's men today seems less certain than it once did.) It is entirely possible, then, that *The Shrew* was acted by Pembroke's men in 1592–1593 and subsequently passed along to the Chamberlain's.

The Folio text of this play is now generally thought to have been printed from Shakespeare's working manuscript.

A Midsummer Night's Dream (*c. 1594–1595*)

A Midsummer Night's Dream was entered on the Stationers' Register by Thomas Fisher on October 8, 1600, and printed by him that same year in quarto:

> A Midsommer nights dreame. As it hath beene sundry times pub*lickely acted, by the Right honoura*ble, the Lord Chamberlaine his *seruants. Written by William Shakespeare.* Imprinted at London, for *Thomas Fisher*, and are to be soulde at his shoppe, at the Signe of the White Hart, in *Fleetestreete*. 1600.

This text appears to have been set up from Shakespeare's working manuscript. Its inconsistencies in time scheme and other irregularities may reflect some revision, although the inconsistencies are not noticeable in performance. A second quarto appeared in 1619, though falsely dated 1600; it was a reprint of the first quarto, with some minor corrections and many new errors. A copy of this second quarto, evidently with some added stage directions and other minor changes from a theatrical manuscript in the company's possession, served as the basis for the Folio text of 1623. Essentially, the first quarto remains the authoritative text.

Other than Francis Meres' listing of the play in 1598, external clues as to date are elusive. The description of unruly weather (II,i) has been related to the bad summer of 1594, but complaints about the weather are perennial. On the assumption that the play celebrates some noble wedding of the period, scholars have come up with a number of suitable marriages. Chief are those of Sir Thomas Heneage to Mary, Countess of Southampton, in 1594, of William Stanley, Earl of Derby, to Elizabeth Vere, daughter of the Earl of Oxford, in 1595, and of Thomas, son of Lord Berkeley, to Elizabeth, daughter of Lord Carey, in 1596. The Countess of Southampton was the widowed mother of the young Earl of Southampton, to whom Shakespeare had dedicated his *Venus and Adonis* and *The Rape of Lucrece*. No one has ever convincingly proven, however, that the play was written for any occasion other than commercial public performance. The play makes perfect sense for a general audience, and does not need to depend on references to any private marriage. Shakespeare was, after all, in the business of writing plays for his fellow actors, who earned their livelihood chiefly by public acting before large paying audiences. In any event the search for a court marriage is a circular argument in terms of dating; suitable court marriages can be found for any year of the decade. In the last analysis, the play has to be dated on the basis of its stylistic affinity to plays like *Romeo and Juliet* and *Richard II*, works of the "lyric" midcentury period. The "Pyramus and Thisbe" performance in *A Midsummer Night's Dream* would seem to bear an obvious relation to *Romeo and Juliet*, although no one can say for sure which came first.

The Henry the Sixth Plays (c. 1589–1592)

Shortened versions of *2* and *3 Henry VI* appeared in 1594 and 1595. One was titled as follows:

> THE First part of the Contention betwixt the two famous Houses of Yorke and Lancaster, with the death of the good Duke Humphrey: And the banishment and death of the Duke of *Suffolke*, and the Tragicall end of the proud Cardinall of *VVinchester*, vvith the notable Rebellion of *Iacke Cade: And the Duke of Yorkes first claime vnto the Crowne.* LONDON Printed by Thomas Creed, for Thomas Millington, and are to be sold at his shop vnder Saint Peters Church in Cornwall. 1594.

Its sequel was titled as follows:

> The true Tragedie of Richard *Duke of Yorke, and the death* of good King Henrie the Sixt, *with the whole contention betweene* the two Houses Lancaster and Yorke, as it was sundrie times acted by the Right Honourable the Earle of Pembrooke his seruants. Printed at London by P. S. [Peter Short] for Thomas Milling*ton, and are to be sold at his shoppe vnder Saint Peters Church in Cornwal.* 1595.

Once thought to be source plays for Shakespeare's *2* and *3 Henry VI*, these quartos have lately been demonstrated by Peter Alexander and Madeleine Doran to be bad quartos or memorial reconstructions of Shakespeare's texts, put together by actors for sale to a printer or for acting in the provinces. As such, they have little textual authority. In 1619 they were combined in a reprint by William Jaggard called *The Whole Contention betweene the two Famous Houses, Lancaster and Yorke*. These texts are considerably shorter than the Folio versions of 1623, which appeared there under the titles "The second Part of Henry the Sixt, with the death of the Good Duke HVMFREY," and "The third Part of Henry the Sixt, with the death of the Duke of YORKE." The Folio texts seem to have been based on authorial manuscripts, although it has been argued that both plays were printed from pages of the second and third quartos of each play as corrected by reference to a theatrical manuscript in the author's own handwriting (in the case of *2 Henry VI*) or to a scribal transcript of Shakespeare's manuscript to which a prompter had added his annotations (in the case of *3 Henry VI*).

The text of *1 Henry VI*, based seemingly on an authorial manuscript that had been annotated in the theatre and possibly recopied, was first published in the Folio of 1623. It alone of the three parts was registered for publication at this time. The Stationers' Register entry refers to this play as "The thirde parte of Henry the sixt." These circumstances once led to the assumption that *1 Henry VI* was written after the other two plays, especially since those two plays do not often recall events of *1 Henry VI*—for example, they make no mention of its hero, Lord Talbot. The seeming fact that the 1594 and 1595 quartos were pirated editions would, however, explain their publication before *1 Henry VI* and the necessity of registering Part I later. In other ways, *1 Henry VI* has shown itself to be no hasty afterthought, but a play with thematic unity throughout and a sense of direction anticipating the remainder of the series. Hence, scholars now tend to support Dr. Johnson's commonsense hunch that the three plays in this historical tetralogy were written in order.

Scholars also generally agree now that the entire series is Shakespeare's own work, or at the very least dominated by his artistic conception of the whole. The once-prevailing hypotheses of multiple authorship, though not forgotten, rest on questionable internal evidence such as vocabulary or versification. What sounds like Greene or Peele in these very early plays may simply be the result of those men's undoubted influence on Shakespeare during his apprenticeship. Greene's famous diatribe at Shakespeare (see below) suggests that he was keenly aware of Shakespeare's facility for learning quickly from his contemporaries. The inconsistencies in these early plays, especially in Part I—mislineation, defective verse, inaccuracy in speech prefixes, confusion about time, discrepancy in facts—may be the result not of multiple authorship but of reliance on various sources, hasty composition, and problems of transcription.

Several contemporary allusions to the *Henry VI* plays help considerably with dating the series. Thomas Nashe wrote in his *Pierce Penilesse* (registered August 1592) that it would "have ioyed braue *Talbot* (the terror of the French) to thinke that after he had lyne two hundred yeares in his Tombe, hee should triumphe againe on the Stage." Probably he was referring to Shakespeare's play. The reference in Henslowe's diary to a "ne" (new?) performance of *Harey the vi* in March of 1592 may or may not refer to Shakespeare's work, however, for this performance was by Lord Strange's men whereas Shakespeare's *Henry VI* series is associated elsewhere with Pembroke's men. In any event, *3 Henry VI* must have been completed by the time of Robert Greene's death in September of 1592, when Greene (or his literary executor, Chettle) alludes plainly to it (I,iv,137) in his angry remark about "an vpstart Crow, beautified with our feathers, that with his *Tygers hart wrapt in a Players hyde*, supposes he is as well able to bombast out a blanke verse as the best of you." These contemporary references are confirmed by allusions in the texts themselves, for all the *Henry VI* plays seem to contain echos of Books I–III of Spenser's *Faerie Queene* (printed 1590), whereas

3 Henry VI seems to have influenced parts of *The Troublesome Raigne of King John* (printed 1591). An inclusive date of 1589–1591 or 1592 ought to account for the entire series.

Richard the Third (c. 1591–1594)

A quarto edition of *Richard III*, registered by Andrew Wise on October 20, 1597, appeared later that same year with the following title:

THE TRAGEDY OF King Richard the third. Containing, His treacherous Plots against his brother Clarence: the pittiefull murther of his innocent nephewes: his tyrannicall vsurpation: with the whole course of his detested life, and most deserued death. As it hath beene lately Acted by the Right honourable the Lord Chamberlaine his seruants. AT LONDON Printed by Valentine Sims, for Andrew Wise, dwelling in Paules Chu[r]ch-yard, at the Signe of the Angell. 1597.

This text, one of the most perplexing in all Shakespeare, was once thought to be an authentic text set up either from a prompter's copy or from the author's foul papers. Today it is generally regarded as a memorial reconstruction of a peculiar kind, one in which the entire acting company banded together to reconstruct a play of which the only copy had apparently been lost. This quarto was reprinted in 1598, 1602, 1605, 1612, 1622, 1629, and 1634, each reprint successively more error-laden than the previous one. The Folio text of 1623 seems to have been set mainly from a copy of the sixth quarto (1622) which had been sporadically corrected against an independent manuscript—possibly Shakespeare's own manuscript or a copy of it. Parts of the Folio text, however, were set from an uncorrected copy of the third quarto (1602). The Folio text is thus the most authoritative, but must be approached with extreme caution.

The play is mentioned by Francis Meres in 1598. John Weever names a "*Richard*" in his *Epigrammes*, published in 1599. Most scholars date *Richard III* 1592–1594, on the basis of its style and its close affinity to the *Henry VI* series (completed probably in 1591). The play may have been influenced by the anonymous *The True Tragedy of Richard III*, registered in June 1594 but probably written in 1590–1592 or even earlier. Shakespeare's play may also have been influenced by Kyd's *Spanish Tragedy* (c. 1587) and by Marlowe's dramas (he died in 1593).

King John (c. 1594–1595)

The Life and Death of King John, as it is called in the original text, first appeared in the Folio of 1623. That text appears to have been set up from Shakespeare's foul papers, which may have been corrected with reference to a prompt-book (especially in the final two acts). Apart from Meres' listing of the play in 1598, dating clues are scarce. Editors have suggested dates ranging from 1590 to 1598, and have proposed topical allusions to bolster their various arguments. The consensus today is that *King John* was probably written shortly before or after *Richard II* in about 1594–1595, or 1596. Many editors assume that Shakespeare would have preferred to write this historically independent play in the interim between his two four-play series (*Henry VI* through *Richard III* and *Richard II* through *Henry V*), rather than interrupt the flow of composition on either of those series. This suggestion is scarcely provable, however. In any case, the link between *Richard II* and *1 Henry IV* is not so close as to preclude interruption.

A major critic of the consensus view is E. A. J. Honigmann, editor of the Arden *King John* (1954), who argues for a date in 1590 preceding the publication in 1591 of *The Troublesome Raigne of King John* (which he regards as a bad quarto). This argument has aroused controversy but little acceptance.

Titus Andronicus (c. 1589–1591)

On February 6, 1594, "a Noble Roman Historye of Tytus Andronicus" was entered in the Stationers' Register to John Danter, along with "the ballad thereof." The entry probably, though not certainly, refers to Shakespeare's play. Later in that same year, at any rate, Danter published a quarto volume with the following title:

THE MOST LAmentable Romaine Tragedie of Titus Andronicus: As it was Plaide by the Right Honourable the Earle of *Darbie*, Earle of *Pembrooke*, and Earle of *Sussex* their Seruants. LONDON, Printed by Iohn Danter, and are to be sold by *Edward White & Thomas Millington*, at the little North doore of Paules at the signe of the Gunne. 1594.

This text seems to have been set from Shakespeare's foul papers. A second quarto appeared in 1600, adding the name of the Lord Chamberlain's company to those who had acted the play. It was set up from a slightly damaged copy of the first quarto. Although the second quarto made some improvements, these were probably by the compositor and not the author. A third quarto (1611), set up from the second, contributed new errors. The Folio text of 1623 was derived from the third quarto, but with an authentic added scene (III,ii) from a manuscript source and with additional stage directions that suggest a playhouse prompt-book. One theory is that the copy used by the Folio printers, the third quarto, had been corrected from an annotated copy of the second quarto that had been used as a prompt-book. Despite these improvements, the first quarto clearly remains the authoritative text.

The date of *Titus* must be prior to 1594. Henslowe's *Diary* records a performance of a "Titus & Ondronicous" by the Earl of Sussex' men on January 24, 1594, and indicates it was "ne" or new. This could certainly mean a new play, but it could also mean it was newly revised or newly acquired. Since the players on this occasion, Sussex' men, were listed third on the 1594 title page after Derby's and Pembroke's men, they may just have acquired *Titus*. Two allusions may point to an earlier date: *A Knack to Know a Knave* (performed in 1592) and *The Troublesome Raigne of King John* (published 1591) may contain echoes of *Titus*. Stylistic considerations favor a date around 1590 or even earlier.

The authorship of *Titus* would appear at first glance to be beyond question. Although the 1594 quarto does not mention Shakespeare's name (a common omission in such early texts, especially since the author was as yet relatively unknown), Francis Meres assigns the play to Shakespeare in 1598 and the Folio editors include it in the 1623 edition. Doubts began to arise, however, when Edward Ravenscroft observed in 1687 that he had been "told by some anciently conversant with the Stage, that it was not Originally his, but brought by a private Authour to be Acted, and he only gave some Master-touches to one or two of the Principal Parts or Characters." This remark touched off a controversy that continues today; for example, J. Dover Wilson in his New Cambridge Shakespeare (1948) and J. C. Maxwell in his Arden edition (1953) still argue for the presence of Peele, in the first act especially. Nevertheless, Ravenscroft's testimonial is suspect both because it came one hundred years after the fact and because Ravenscroft himself was embarked on an adaptation of *Titus* and so might wish to denigrate the original. The efforts at assigning portions of the play to Shakespeare's contemporaries have generally been motivated by a wish to rescue Shakespeare's reputation from the violent and garish effects of this play. Most recent criticism prefers to regard the play as an interesting Senecan experiment by a young artist, with many shrewdly characteristic Shakespearean touches. The external evidence of the Elizabethan period, at any rate, is entirely on the side of awarding the play wholly to Shakespeare.

Henslowe's *Diary* records the performance of a "Tittus & Vespacia" on April 11, 1592, a "ne" play by Strange's men. Despite the similarity of the title, this play was probably on an independent subject.

Romeo and Juliet (*1594–1596*)

A corrupt and unregistered quarto of *Romeo and Juliet* appeared in 1597 with the following title:

AN EXCELLENT conceited Tragedie OF Romeo and Iuliet, As it hath been often (with great applause) plaid publiquely, by the right Honourable the L. of *Hunsdon* his Seruants. LONDON, Printed by Iohn Danter. 1597.

This was a pirated edition issued by an unscrupulous publisher, no doubt to capitalize on the play's great popularity. It seems to have been memorially reconstructed by two or more actors, and possibly thereafter used as a prompt-book. Its appearance seems to have caused the issuance two years later of a clearly authoritative version:

THE MOST EXcellent and lamentable Tragedie, of Romeo and *Iuliet. Newly corrected, augmented, and amended:* As it hath bene sundry times publiquely acted, by the right Honourable the Lord Chamberlaine his Seruants. LONDON Printed by Thomas Creede, for Cuthbert Burby, and are to be sold at his shop near the Exchange. 1599.

This text is some 800 lines longer than the first, and corrects errors in that earlier version. Oddly, however, it seems at times to have been contaminated by the first quarto, as though the manuscript source for the second quarto (probably the author's foul papers) was defective at some point. A passage from I,ii,53 to I,iii,34 was apparently set directly from the first quarto. (On this matter, see George W. Williams' old-spelling edition of the play, Duke U. Press, 1964.) Despite this contamination, however, the second quarto is the authoritative text. It served as the basis for the third quarto (1609) which in turn served as copy for the fourth quarto (1622) and the Folio of 1623. A fifth quarto appeared in 1637.

Francis Meres assigns the play to Shakespeare in 1598. So does John Weever in his *Epigrammes* of 1599. Internal evidence on dating is not reliable. The Nurse observes that " 'Tis since the earthquake now eleven years"; but suitable earthquakes have been discovered in 1580, 1583, 1584, and 1585, giving us a wide choice of dates even if we accept the dubious proposition that the Nurse is speaking accurately. Astronomical reckoning of the position of the moon at the time the play purportedly takes place ("a fortnight and odd days" before Lammastide, August 1) indicates the year 1596; again, however, we have no reason to assume Shakespeare cared about this sort of internal accuracy. More suggestive perhaps is the argument that Danter's unauthorized publication in 1597 was seeking to exploit a popular new play, one the acting company certainly did not yet wish to see published since it was a money-maker. Danter assigns the play to Lord Hunsdon's servants, a name that Shakespeare's company could have used only from July 22, 1596 (when the old Lord Chamberlain, Henry Carey, first Lord Hunsdon, died) to April 17, 1597 (when George Carey, second Lord Hunsdon, was appointed to his father's erstwhile position as Lord Chamberlain). Danter could simply have been using the name of the company at the time he pirated the play, but he may also indicate performance in late 1596. Stylistically, the play is clearly of the "lyric" period of *A Midsummer Night's Dream* and *Richard II.* There are also stylistic affinities to the sonnets and to the narrative poems of 1593–1594. A date between 1594 and 1596 is likely, especially toward the latter end of this period. Whether the play comes before or after *A Midsummer Night's Dream* is, however, a matter of conjecture.

Venus and Adonis (1592–1593)

On April 18, 1593, "a booke intituled, Venus and Adonis" was entered to Richard Field on the Stationers' Register, and was published by him the same year. The quarto contains a dedication written by Shakespeare to the Earl of Southampton. The text seems to have been carefully supervised through the press, and based on the author's fair copy. The poem was very popular, and was reprinted nine times before Shakespeare's death. The Folio of 1623, being limited to plays, did not include it or any other nondramatic poems. Contemporary references are numerous: Francis Meres and Richard Barnfield in 1598, Gabriel Harvey in 1598–1601, and John Weever in 1599, among others. Shakespeare probably wrote this poem shortly before its publication, since his intention was to present it to Southampton. The theatres closed from June 1592 to May 1594, giving Shakespeare a period of enforced leisure in which to write poetry.

The Rape of Lucrece (1593–1594)

Shakespeare promised a "graver labour" to Southampton in his dedication of *Venus and Adonis*, 1593, and *The Rape of Lucrece* is almost surely that promised sequel. It was registered in the Stationers' Register by John Harrison on May 9, 1594, and issued that same year as "printed by Richard Field, for Iohn Harrison." Although not quite as popular as *Venus and Adonis*, the poem was reprinted five times during Shakespeare's lifetime. Contemporaries of Shakespeare who allude favorably to the poem include W. Har and Michael Drayton in 1594, William Covell in 1595, Francis Meres in 1598, Gabriel Harvey in 1598–1601, John Weever in 1599, and others. The date of composition of the poem is well fixed between the publication of *Venus and Adonis* in 1593 and that of *The Rape of Lucrece* itself in 1594.

Minor Poems

The early editions of the minor poems, with questions of dating and canon, are discussed in the Introduction, p. 458 above. The title page of the second edition of *The Passionate Pilgrim*, which is the first complete edition extant, reads as follows:

THE PASSIONATE PILGRIME. *By W. Shakespeare.* AT LONDON Printed for W. Iaggard, and are to be sold by W. Leake, at the Grey-hound in Paules Churchyard. 1599.

The Phoenix and the Turtle first appeared in a volume with the following title:

LOVES MARTYR: OR, ROSALINS COMPLAINT. *Allegorically shadowing the truth of Loue,* in the constant Fate of the Phoenix *and Turtle.* . . . by ROBERT CHESTER. . . . *To these are added some new compositions, of seuerall moderne Writers whose names are subscribed to their seuerall workes, vpon the first subiect: viz. the* Phoenix *and* Turtle.

The date 1601 appears on a separate title page. One poem is signed "William Shake-speare," others John Marston, George Chapman, and Ben Jonson.

A Lover's Complaint first appeared in Thomas Thorpe's 1609 edition of the sonnets. The poem is not mentioned on the title page of the volume, but has its own head-title on sig. K^v: "A Louers complaint. By William Shake-speare." For the dubious nature of this attribution, see Introduction.

The Sonnets

On May 20, 1609, "Thomas Thorpe Entred for his copie vnder thandes of master Wilson and master Lownes Warden a Booke called Shakespeares sonnettes." In the same year appeared the following volume:

SHAKE-SPEARES SONNETS. Neuer before Imprinted. AT LONDON By *G. Eld* for *T. T.* and are to be solde by *Iohn Wright*, dwelling at Christ Church gate. 1609.

Some copies of this same edition are marked to be sold by William Aspley rather than John Wright; evidently Thorpe had set up two sellers to distribute the volume. The sonnets were not reprinted until John Benson's rearranged edition of 1640, possibly because the first edition had been suppressed or because sonnets were no longer in vogue. The 1609 edition does not give us a good text; it may rest on an authoritative manuscript, but the edition itself is marred by misprints. Clearly it was not supervised through the press as were *Venus and Adonis* and *The Rape of Lucrece*. All the evidence suggests that it was pirated from a manuscript that had been in private circulation (as we know from Francis Meres' 1598 allusion to Shakespeare's "sugred Sonnets among his priuate friends"). Two sonnets, 138 and 144, had appeared in 1599 in *The Passionate Pilgrim*. On questions of dating and order of the sonnets, see Introduction, pp. 468–471 above.

The Merchant of Venice (1594–1598)

The Stationers' Register for July 22, 1598, contains an entry on behalf of the printer James Roberts for "a booke of the Marchaunt of Venyce, or otherwise called the Jewe of Venyce, Prouided, that yt bee not prynted by the said James Robertes or anye other whatsoeuer without lycence first had from the Right honorable the lord Chamberlen." Roberts evidently enjoyed a close connection with the Chamberlain's men, and seemingly was granted the special favor of registering the play at this time even though the company did not wish to see the play published until later. In 1600, at any rate, Roberts transferred his rights as publisher to Thomas Heyes and printed the volume for him with the following title:

The most excellent Historie of the *Merchant of Venice*. VVith the extreame crueltie of *Shylocke* the Iewe towards the sayd Merchant, in cutting a iust pound of his flesh: and the obtayning of *Portia* by the choyse of three chests. *As it hath beene diuers times acted by the Lord Chamberlaine his Seruants.* Written by William Shakespeare. AT LONDON, Printed by *I. R.* for Thomas Heyes, and are to be sold in Paules Church-yard, at the signe of the Greene Dragon. 1600.

This 1600 text was generally a good one, based seemingly on the author's papers. It served as copy for the second quarto of 1619 (printed by William Jaggard for Thomas Pavier, and fraudulently dated 1600), and for the Folio of 1623.

Francis Meres mentions the play in 1598. Establishing an earlier limit for dating has proven not so easy. Many scholars have urged a connection with the Roderigo Lopez affair of 1594 (see Introduction, pp. 502–505 above). The supposed allusion to Lopez in the lines about "a wolf, who, hang'd for human slaughter" (IV,i,134) may simply indicate, however, that wolves were actually hanged for attacking men in Shakespeare's day (as dogs were for killing sheep). Besides, the Lopez case remained so notorious throughout the 1590's that even a proven allusion to it in *The Merchant* would not limit the play to 1594 or 1595. Marlowe's *The Jew of Malta* was revived in 1594 to exploit anti-Lopez sentiment, but was also revived in 1596. There may, on the other hand, be an allusion in I,i,27 to the *St. Andrew*, a Spanish ship captured at Cadiz in 1596. Any date between 1594 and early 1598 is possible, though the latter half of this period is more likely.

Much Ado about Nothing (1598–1599)

"The Commedie of muche A doo about nothing a booke" was entered in the Stationers' Register on August 4, 1600, along with *As You Like It*, *Henry V*, and Ben Jonson's *Every Man in His Humour*, all marked as plays of "My lord chamberlens men" and all "to be staied"—that is, not published without further permission. Earlier in the same memorandum, written on a spare page in the Register, occurs the name of the printer James Roberts, whose registration of *The Merchant of Venice* in 1598 was similarly stayed pending further permission to publish. Evidently the Chamberlain's men were attempting to prevent unauthorized publication of these very popular plays. They were too late to forestall the appearance of a bad quarto of *Henry V* in August of 1600, but they did manage to control release of the others. *Much Ado about Nothing* appeared later that same year in a seemingly authorized version:

Much adoe about Nothing. *As it hath been sundrie times publikely* acted by the right honourable, the Lord Chamberlaine his seruants. *Written by William Shakespeare.* LONDON Printed by V. S. [Valentine Sims] for Andrew Wise, and William Aspley. 1600.

Once thought to have been set up from a theatrical prompt-book, and then used itself in the theatre as a prompt-book before serving as copy for the Folio version, this 1600 quarto text is now generally regarded as having been set from Shakespeare's own foul papers. The names of the actors Will Kempe and Richard Cowley appear among the speech prefixes in IV,ii, indicating that an actual stage production was very close at hand, but other irregularities in speech prefixes and scene headings read more like a manuscript in the last stages of revision than a prompt-book for a finished production. The Folio text was based on the 1600 quarto.

Francis Meres does not mention the play in September of 1598, unless (and this seems unlikely) it is his "*Loue labours wonne*." Will Kempe, who played Dogberry, left the Chamberlain's men in 1599. The likeliest date, then, is the winter of 1598–1599, though publication was not until 1600.

The Merry Wives of Windsor (1597–1601)

The Stationers' Register for January 18, 1602, carries an entry for "A booke called An excellent and pleasant conceited commedie of Sir John Faulstof and the merry wyves of Windesor," by assignment from John Busby to Arthur Johnson. Later that year, Thomas Creed printed the following quarto:

A Most pleasaunt and excellent conceited Comedie, of Syr *Iohn Falstaffe*, and the merrie Wiues of *Windsor*. Entermixed with sundrie variable and pleasing humors, of Syr *Hugh* the Welch Knight, Iustice *Shallow*, and his wise Cousin M. *Slender*. With the swaggering vaine of Auncient *Pistoll*, and Corporall *Nym*. By *William Shakespeare*. As it hath bene diuers times Acted by the right Honorable my Lord Chamberlaines seruants. Both before her Maiestie, and else-where. LONDON Printed by T. C. for Arthur Iohnson, and are to be sold at his shop in Powles Church-yard, at the signe of the Flower de Leuse and the Crowne. 1602.

This text is now generally regarded as a bad quarto, memorially reconstructed perhaps by the actors who played the Host and Falstaff, and then shortened for touring in the provinces. A second quarto in 1619, printed by William Jaggard for Thomas Pavier, was based on it. The Folio text of 1623, however, was taken from a manuscript evidently copied by Ralph Crane (hence the "massed entries" of characters' names at the beginnings of scenes), and based ultimately on a theatrical prompt-book. It is the most authoritative text. Several interesting variant readings occur in the bad quarto, despite its unreliability, and seem to indicate original readings that were altered in the Folio version for reasons of prudence. We find "garmombles" in place of the Folio "germans" at IV,v,80, and "Brook" in place of the Folio "Broome" throughout as the disguise name for the jealous Ford. "Garmombles" is often interpreted as an unflattering allusion to Frederick, Count Mompelgard (see Introduction, pp. 558–560 above). "Brook" is a seeming dig at the family name of the powerful Henry Brooke, eighth Lord Cobham, whose intervention probably led to the similar changing of "Oldcastle" to "Falstaff" in *Henry IV*.

On dating, two irreconcilable choices are still very much alive: 1597, when the Lord Chamberlain was elected to the Order of the Garter, and 1600–1601, after *Henry V* (1599) in which Nym had been introduced. The S. R. entry in January of 1602 provides a forward limit in time. See more on the Order of the Garter in the Introduction.

As You Like It (*1598–1600*)

"As you like yt, a booke" was entered in the Stationers' Register on August 4, 1600, along with *Much Ado about Nothing*, *Henry V*, and Jonson's *Every Man in His Humour*, all labeled as "My lord chamberlens mens plaies" and all ordered "to be staied" from publication until further notice. Evidently the Chamberlain's men were anxious to protect their rights to these very popular plays. Despite their efforts *Henry V* was pirated that same month. *As You Like It* did not appear in print, however, until the Folio of 1623. The Folio text is a good one, based seemingly on a theatrical prompt-book or a transcript of one.

Francis Meres does not mention the play in September of 1598. The play contains an unusually clear allusion to Marlowe's *Hero and Leander* ("Who ever lov'd that lov'd not at first sight?" III,v,82), first published in 1598. Almost certainly *As You Like It* was written between 1598 and the summer of 1600, either before or after *Much Ado about Nothing*.

Twelfth Night (*1600–1602*)

Twelfth Night was registered in 1623 and first published in the Folio of that year, in a good text set up from a theatre prompt-book or possibly a transcript of it. The play was first mentioned, however, on Candlemas Day, February 2, 1602, in the following entry from the *Diary* of a Middle Temple law student or barrister named John Manningham:

> At our feast wee had a play called "Twelue Night, or What you Will," much like the Commedy of Errores, or Menechmi in Plautus, but most like and neere to that in Italian called *Inganni*. A good practise in it to make the Steward beleeve his Lady widdowe was in love with him, by counterfeyting a letter as from his Lady in generall termes, telling him what shee liked best in him, and prescribing his gesture in smiling, his apparaile, & c., and then when he came to practise making him beleeue they tooke him to be mad.

This entry was once suspected to be a forgery of John Payne Collier, who published the *Diary* in 1831, but its authenticity is now generally accepted. The date accords with several possible allusions in the play itself. When Fabian jokes about "a pension of thousands to be paid from the Sophy" (II,v,198), he seems to be recalling Sir Anthony Shirley's reception by the Shah of Persia (the Sophy) in 1599–1600. An account of this visit was entered in the S. R. in November of 1601. Viola's description of Feste as "wise enough to play the fool" (III,i,67) may recall a poem beginning "True it is, he plays the fool indeed" published in 1600–1601 by Robert Armin (who played the role of Feste). Maria's comparison of Malvolio's smiling face to "the new map with the augmentation of the Indies" (III,ii,85) refers to new maps of about 1600 in which America (the Indies) was increased in size. Leslie Hotson (*The First Night of Twelfth Night*, 1954) has argued for a first performance at court on Twelfth Night in January of 1601, when Queen Elizabeth entertained Don Virginio Orsino, Duke of Bracciano, but this hypothesis has not gained general acceptance partly because the role of Orsino in the play would scarcely flatter such a noble visitor and partly because there is no proof that any of Shakespeare's plays were originally commissioned for private performance. Nevertheless, a date between 1600 and early 1602 seems most likely. Francis Meres does not mention the play in 1598.

Richard the Second (*c. 1595–1596*)

On August 29, 1597, "The Tragedye of Richard the Second" was entered in the Stationers' Register by Andrew Wise, and was published by him later that same year:

> THE Tragedie of King Richard the second. *As it hath beene publikely acted by the right Honourable the Lorde Chamberlaine his Seruants.* LONDON Printed by Valentine Simmes for Androw Wise, and are to be sold at his shop in Paules church yard at the signe of the Angel. 1597.

This is a good text, printed evidently from the author's papers or a transcript of them. Wise issued two more quartos of this popular play in 1598, each set from the previous quarto, and then in 1603 transferred his rights in the play to Matthew Law. This publisher issued in 1608 a fourth quarto "With new additions of the Parliament Sceane, and the deposing of King Richard" (according to the title page in some copies). The deposition scene had indeed been omitted from the earlier quartos, probably through censorship. A fifth quarto appeared in 1615, based on the fourth. All the quartos after the first attribute the play to Shakespeare. The added deposition scene in quartos four and five seems to have been memorially reconstructed. The Folio text of 1623 gives a better version of the deposition scene, perhaps because the printers of the Folio had access to the manuscript prompt-book for this portion of the text. (Some scholars maintain that the Folio text was derived from an earlier quarto or quartos that had been used as a promptbook.) In any event, most of the Folio was probably set from quarto three, and perhaps from the final two leaves of quarto five, so that the most authoritative text for all but the deposition scene is the first quarto.

Francis Meres mentions the play in 1598. Clearly it had been written and performed prior to the Stationers' Register entry in August of 1597. Its earliest probable date is 1595, since the play is seemingly indebted to Samuel Daniel's poem *The First Fowre Bookes of the Civile Wars* published in that year. Shakespeare follows Daniel, for example, in increasing the queen's age from eleven (according to the chronicles) to maturity, and in other significant details. On December 9, 1595, Sir Edward Hoby invited Sir Robert Cecil to his house in Cannon Row "where as late as it shal please you a gate for your supper shal be open: & K. Richard present him selfe to your vewe." Although it is by no means certain that this passage refers to a private performance of Shakespeare's play, stylistic considerations favor a date around 1595 rather than 1597. If, as some scholars contend, Daniel's *Civile Wars* was written after Shakespeare's play rather than before it, *Richard II* might be as early as 1594.

The Henry the Fourth Plays (*c. 1596–1598*)

On February 25, 1598, "The historye of Henry the iiijth with his battaile of Shrewsburye against Henry Hottspurre of the Northe with the conceipted mirthe of Sir John Ffalstoff" was entered in the Stationers' Register by Andrew Wise. Later that year appeared the following quarto:

THE HISTORY OF HENRIE THE FOVRTH; With the battell at Shrewsburie, *betweene the King and Lord* Henry Percy, surnamed Henrie Hotspur of the North. *With the humorous conceits of Sir* Iohn Falstalffe. AT LONDON, Printed by *P. S.* [Peter Short] for *Andrew Wise*, dwelling in Paules Churchyard, at the signe of the Angell. 1598.

Actually this was not the first quarto, for an earlier fragment of eight pages has survived, part of a text that served as copy for the first complete extant quarto. Together these quartos make up an excellent authoritative text, based seemingly on the author's papers. Four more quartos appeared before the Folio of 1623, each based on the previous quarto. The Folio itself was based on the last of these.

"The second parte of the history of Kinge Henry the iiijth with the humours of Sir John Falstaff: Wrytten by master Shakespere" was entered in the Stationers' Register by Andrew Wise and William Aspley on August 23, 1600. It was published later that year as

THE Second part of Henrie the fourth, continuing to his death, *and coronation of Henrie* the fift. With the humours of sir Iohn Fal*staffe, and swaggering* Pistoll. *As it hath been sundrie times publikely* acted by the right honourable, the Lord Chamberlaine his seruants. *Written by William Shakespeare.* LONDON Printed by V. S. [Valentine Sims] for Andrew Wise, and William Aspley. 1600.

One scene, III,i, was omitted from Sims' first printing [Qa] of this quarto, whereupon Sims reset two leaves as four new leaves [Qb] including not only the omitted III,i but II,iv,370–421 and III,ii,1–113. Qb is therefore the best copy text for III,i and Qa for those portions that were reset. In addition, still other scenes were omitted from both versions of the 1600 quarto; they were later restored in the First Folio. No further quartos appeared prior to the Folio of 1623—an odd fact in view of *1 Henry IV*'s continued popularity, but perhaps the result of a large printing of *2 Henry IV* in anticipation of heavy sales. At any rate, this text seems to have been based on Shakespeare's papers and was a reliable one except for the omissions. Of the omitted passages, some may have been the result of shortening for performance, but some suggest political censorship. The Folio text restores the omitted readings. The relationship of Folio to quarto text is extraordinarily difficult to determine; perhaps the Folio compositors were using a manuscript that had been transcribed either from an extensively annotated copy of the quarto or from a quarto and a manuscript source jointly compared. The quarto version omits much profanity found in the Folio version. Despite the greater fullness of the Folio text, the quarto remains the substantive text for virtually all but the omitted passages.

Both plays show signs of revision in the use of characters' names, most notably that of Falstaff. Plainly the original version of the plays called him Sir John Oldcastle, after one of the prince's companions in the anonymous *Famous Victories of Henry the Fifth* (c. 1588) The speech-prefix "Old." is left standing at I,ii, 138 in the quarto of *2 Henry IV*, several lines of verse are one syllable short evidently because "Oldcastle" has been altered to "Falstaff," and Falstaff is jokingly referred to as "my old lad of the castle" (*1 Henry IV*, I,ii,47–48). Moreover, there are several contemporary allusions to a play about a fat knight named Oldcastle. Apparently Henry Brooke, Lord Cobham, a living descendant of the Lollard martyr Oldcastle of Henry V's reign, took umbrage at the profane use Shakespeare had made of this revered name, whereupon Shakespeare's company shifted to another less controversial name from the chronicles, Sir John Fastolfe (called "Falstaff" in the Folio text of Shakespeare's *1 Henry VI* and assigned a cowardly role in the French wars of that play). The revision also changed the names of Oldcastle's cronies from Harvey and Russell to Bardolph and Peto.

Cobham was Lord Chamberlain from July 1596 until his death in March 1597, during which interval Shakespeare's company bore the name of Lord Hunsdon's men. Quite possibly the difficulty over the name Oldcastle erupted during that period, for *1 Henry IV* seems to have been written and performed in late 1596 and early 1597 not long after Shakespeare had finished *Richard II* (c. 1595–1596). *2 Henry IV* must have been written before the end of 1598, so that Shakespeare could then begin *Henry V* in early 1599. Since *2 Henry IV* was originally performed using the names Oldcastle and Russell, however, we are inclined to date it somewhat earlier, in 1597, before the squabble over the names broke out. Scholars who prefer a date in 1597 for *The Merry Wives* also date *2 Henry IV* early in 1597, since it almost surely introduced Shallow and Pistol before they appeared in *The Merry Wives*. Francis Meres refers in 1598 to "*Henry the* 4" without specifying one or two parts. Publication of *1 Henry IV* in 1598 assured the Elizabethan public that the changes in names to Falstaff, Bardolph, and Peto had taken place; similarly, a revised epilogue to the 1600 quarto of *2 Henry IV* protests that "Oldcastle died a martyr, and this [Falstaff] is not the man," as though by way of apology or disclaimer. A play defending the reputation of the Lollard Oldcastle and attacking Falstaff, called *The History of the Life of Sir John Oldcastle, Lord Cobham, with his Martyrdom*, had been performed by the rival Admiral's men in 1599.

Henry the Fifth (*1599*)

An entry in the Stationers' Register for August 4, 1600, provides that "Henry the ffift" and three other plays belonging to the Chamberlain's men are "to be staied" from publication until further permission is granted. Evidently the Chamberlain's men were anxious to prevent unauthorized publication. They did not succeed, however, in preventing the appearance of a pirated text of *Henry V*. An entry in the Stationers' Register for August 14 assigns to Thomas Pavier an already published work entitled "The historye of Henry the Vth with the battell of Agencourt." The quarto volume to which this entry refers is the following:

THE CHRONICLE History of Henry the fift, With his battell fought at *Agin Court* in *France*. Togither with *Auntient Pistoll. As it hath bene sundry times playd by the Right honorable the Lord Chamberlaine his seruants.* LONDON *Printed by Thomas Creede*, for Tho. Millington, and Iohn Busby. And are to be sold at his house in Carter Lane, next the Powle head. 1600.

This text is manifestly corrupt. It is considerably shorter than the Folio version, and completely omits the choruses and three entire scenes (I,i, III,i, and IV,ii). The remainder seems to have been put together by memorial reconstruction. This bad quarto served as the basis for a second quarto printed by Thomas Creed for Thomas Pavier in 1602, and a third printed by William Jaggard for Thomas Pavier in 1619 but fraudulently dated 1608. The Folio text was printed seemingly from pages of the second and third quartos, reprinted from the bad first quarto, but fortunately those pages had been corrected by reference to an independent source—probably Shakespeare's own papers. The Folio text is thus the most reliable version.

Francis Meres does not mention the play in 1598, though he does mention "*Henry the* 4." The epilogue to *2 Henry IV* (written probably in 1597) promises that "our humble author will continue the story, with Sir John in it, and make you merry with fair Katharine of France"; and since the prediction is not really accurate regarding Falstaff, we can be reasonably certain that Shakespeare had not yet begun *Henry V* in 1597. An allusion in the Chorus of Act V to "the general of our gracious empress," who may in good time come home from Ireland with "rebellion broached on his sword," has been taken by virtually all editors to refer to the Earl of Essex, who left in March of 1599 to quell the Irish rebellion headed by Tyrone. Although Essex returned on September 28 of that same year having failed utterly in his assignment, the departure of such a charismatic figure could have inspired Shakespeare's praising remark. A minority view holds that the choruses (which do not appear in the bad quarto of 1600) could have been written later in 1601 for Essex' far more victorious successor, Lord Mountjoy (see Warren D. Smith's article on *Henry V* in *JEGP*, 1954). Still, Essex was more center stage during those exciting years, more likely to have been the subject of adulation. In any case the play itself must have been written before August of 1600, most probably in 1599. The reference to "this wooden O" in the Chorus of Act I is often thought to be Shakespeare's compliment to the company's new theatre, the Globe, ready for their use probably in 1599.

Julius Caesar (*1599*)

Julius Caesar was first published in the Folio of 1623. The text is an excellent one, based evidently on a theatre prompt-book or a transcript of it. In the Folio the play is included among the tragedies and entitled *The Tragedie of Julius Caesar*, although the table of contents lists it as *The Life and death of Julius Caesar.*

First performance must have occurred in 1599 or slightly earlier. On September 21, 1599, a Swiss visitor named Thomas Platter crossed the River Thames after lunch with a company of spectators to see "the tragedy of the first Emperor Julius Caesar" performed in a thatched-roofed building. The description fits the Globe, the Rose, and the Swan, but the last of these was not in regular use. The Admiral's men at the Rose are not known to have had a Caesar play, whereas the Chamberlain's men certainly had Shakespeare's play about this time. They had only recently moved from their Theatre in the north-east suburbs of London to the Globe south of the river, and *Julius Caesar* and *Henry V* were probably new plays for the occasion.

John Weever, in *The Mirror of Martyrs*, 1601, is surely referring to Shakespeare's play when he describes "the many-headed multitude" listening first to "*Brutus* speach, that *Caesar* was ambitious," and then to "eloquent *Mark Antonie*." (The dedication to Weever's book claims he wrote it "some two yeares agoe," in 1599; but since this book has been shown to be heavily indebted to a work that first appeared in 1600, Weever's allusion is not as helpful in limiting the date as was once thought.) Ben Jonson's *Every Man in His Humour*, acted in 1599, may also contain allusions to Shakespeare's play.

All's Well that Ends Well (*c. 1601–1604*)

All's Well that Ends Well was first registered in November of 1623 and published in the Folio of that same year. The text contains numerous inconsistencies and vague stage directions indicating an early stage of the author's working papers, but these errors are not as extensive as once thought and the text is basically sound. Information on the date of the play is sparse. Francis Meres does not mention it in 1598 unless it is the intriguing *Loue labours wonne* on his list. Its themes and style are more suggestive of the period of *Hamlet* and the "problem" plays, *Measure for Measure* and *Troilus and Cressida*. Accordingly, the common assumption today is that the play was written some time around 1601–1604. The role of Lavatch is clearly designed for Robert Armin, who did not join Shakespeare's company until 1599. Scholars once argued that *All's Well* is an early play later revised, but this means of explaining the inconsistencies in the text no longer seems necessary.

Measure for Measure (*1603–1604*)

Measure for Measure first appeared in the Folio of 1623. The text was evidently set from Ralph Crane's copy of Shakespeare's own draft; the usual inconsistencies of composition have not yet been smoothed away by use in the theatre. The first recorded performance was on December 26, 1604, St. Stephen's Night, when "a play Caled Mesur for Mesur" by "Shaxberd" was acted in the banqueting hall at Whitehall "by his Maiesties plaiers." Shakespeare's company, previously the Lord Chamberlain's men, had become the King's men after the accession to the throne of James I in 1603.

Several allusions in the play seem to point to the summer of 1604, when the theatres, having been closed for a year because of the plague, were reopened. A reference to the King of Hungary (I,ii) may reflect anxieties in England over James' negotiations for a settlement with Spain; censorship would forbid a direct mentioning of Spain. Mistress Overdone's complaint about the war, the "sweat" (plague), the "gallows" (public executions), and poverty (I,ii) are all suggestive of events in 1603–1604, when war with Spain and the plague were still very much in evidence. Duke Vincentio's reticent habits have been seen as a flattering reference to James' well-known dislike of crowds. Stylistically the play is clearly later than *Twelfth Night* (1600–1602), so that a date close to the first recorded performance in 1604 is a necessity even if we cannot be positive about all the supposed allusions to King James.

Troilus and Cressida (*c. 1601–1602*)

The textual history of *Troilus and Cressida* is complicated. On February 7, 1603, James Roberts entered on the Stationers' Register, "when he hath gotten sufficient aucthority for yt, The booke of Troilus and Cresseda as yt is acted by my lord Chamberlens Men." On January 28, 1609, however, a new entry appeared on the Register as though the first had never been made: "Richard Bonion Henry Walleys. Entred for their Copy vnder thandes of Master Segar deputy to Sir George Bucke and master warden Lownes a booke called the history of Troylus and Cressida." Later that year appeared the first quarto with the following title:

THE Historie of Troylus and Cresseida. *As it was acted by the Kings Maiesties* seruants at the Globe.
Written by William Shakespeare. LONDON Imprinted by *G. Eld* for *R Bonian* and *H. Walley*, and are to be sold at the spred Eagle in Paules Church-yeard, ouer against the great North doore. 1609.

In a second issue of this quarto appearing also in 1609, the title leaf A1 was replaced by two new leaves containing a new title and an epistle. The title reads:

THE Famous Historie of Troylus *and* Cresseid.
Excellently expressing the beginning of their loues, with the conceited wooing of *Pandarus* Prince of *Licia*.
Written by William Shakespeare.

The epistle is addressed "A neuer writer, to an euer reader. Newes," and begins, "Eternall reader, you haue heere a new play, neuer stal'd with the Stage, neuer clapper-clawd with the palmes of the vulger, and yet passing full of the palme comicall."

The Folio editors originally intended *Troilus and Cressida* to follow *Romeo and Juliet*. After three pages had been set up in this position, however, the play was removed (perhaps owing to copyright difficulties) and *Timon of Athens* inserted instead. Later, *Troilus* was placed between the Histories and the Tragedies, almost entirely without pagination. See Play Introduction, pp. 862–864, for some possible explanation of the unusual publishing history.

The quarto text was evidently set from a transcript of Shakespeare's foul papers, made either by Shakespeare himself or by a scribe. The first three pages of the Folio text, those originally intended to follow *Romeo and Juliet*, were set from the first quarto. The remaining pages, however, seem to have been based on the quarto after it had been collated with a manuscript source (probably the author's draft). As a result both the quarto and Folio texts have independent textual authority. Most recent editors, however, use the quarto version as their copy text, especially since the quarto version may represent Shakespeare's revision of the play whereas the Folio returns to the earlier stage of the author's draft.

The odd implication that the play may not have been publicly performed, and the failure of Shakespeare's company to provide the sequel promised at the end of *Troilus*, suggest that the play was written not long before the first Stationers' Register entry of February 1603. Certainly the play was not an old favorite in the company's repertoire. Failure as a stage play might have led to an attempt at quick publication, aimed at sophisticated readers. The current fad for satire would also have provided a motive for prompt publication. Stylistically, *Troilus* belongs to the period of *Hamlet* (c. 1599–1601). A seeming allusion in the Prologue of *Troilus* to the "arm'd" Prologue of Jonson's *Poetaster* (1601) helps set a probable early limit for date of composition. Chapman's *The Seaven Bookes of Homers Iliads*, a source of information about the Trojan war, had appeared in 1598.

Hamlet (*c. 1599–1601*)

Like everything else about *Hamlet*, the textual problem is complicated. On July 26, 1602, James Roberts entered in the Stationers' Register "A booke called the Revenge of Hamlett Prince Denmarke as yt was latelie Acted by the Lord Chamberleyne his servantes." For some reason, however, Roberts did not print his copy of *Hamlet* until 1604, by which time had appeared the following unauthorized edition:

THE Tragicall Historie of HAMLET *Prince of Denmarke*. By William Shake-speare. As it hath beene diuerse times acted by his Highnesse seruants in the Cittie of London: as also in the two Vniuersities of Cambridge and Oxford, and else-where. At London printed for N. L. [Nicholas Ling] and Iohn Trundell. 1603.

This edition, the bad quarto of *Hamlet*, seems to have been memorially reconstructed by actors who toured the provinces (note the references to Cambridge, Oxford, etc.), with some recollection of an earlier *Hamlet* play (the *Ur-Hamlet*) written before 1589 and acted during the 1590's.

The authorized quarto of *Hamlet* appeared in 1604. Roberts, the printer, seems to have reached some agreement with Ling, one of the publishers of the bad quarto, for their initials are now paired on the title page:

THE Tragicall Historie of HAMLET, *Prince of Denmarke*. By William Shakespeare. Newly imprinted and enlarged to almost as much againe as it was, according to the true and perfect Coppie. AT LONDON, Printed by I. R. [James Roberts] for N. L. [Nicholas Ling] and are to be sold at his shoppe vnder Saint Dunstons Church in Fleetstreet. 1604.

Some copies of this edition are dated 1605. This text was based seemingly on Shakespeare's own papers, but is marred by printing errors and is at times contaminated by the bad quarto—presumably when the printers found Shakespeare's manuscript unreadable. This quarto served as copy for a third quarto in 1611, Ling having meanwhile transferred his rights in the play to John Smethwick. A fourth quarto, undated but before 1623, was based on the third.

The Folio text of 1623 is derived from a manuscript source independent of that used for the second quarto. The Folio text omits more than two hundred lines found in the quarto, but it also supplies some clearly authentic passages. The consensus today is that the Folio text was set from a prompt-book in use at the time of the Folio printing, or a transcript of it. On the other hand, some textual scholars argue that the Folio text was set from an annotated copy of the second quarto rather than directly from a prompt-book. Since in either case the Folio text evidently contains changes and additions made by actors during years of repeated performance, the text of the Folio is not as close to Shakespeare's own draft as is the second quarto. Nevertheless, the Folio and even the bad quarto supply some authentic readings.

Hamlet must have been produced before the Stationers' Register entry of July 26, 1602. Francis Meres does not mention the play in 1598. Gabriel Harvey attributes the "tragedie of Hamlet, Prince of Denmarke" to Shakespeare in a marginal note in Harvey's copy of Speght's Chaucer; Harvey acquired the book in 1598, but could have written the note any time between then and 1601 or even 1603. More helpful in dating is Hamlet's clear reference to the so-called "War of the Theatres," the rivalry between the adult actors and the boy actors who had newly reopened in 1598–1599 after nearly a decade of inactivity. The Children of the Chapel Royal began acting at Blackfriars in 1598, and provided such keen competition in 1599–1601 that the adult actors were at times forced to tour the provinces (see *Hamlet*, II,ii,343–379). Revenge tragedy was also in fashion during these years: Marston's *Antonio's Revenge*, for example, dates from 1599–1601, and *The Malcontent* is from about the same time or slightly later.

Othello (*c. 1603–1604*)

On October 6, 1621, Thomas Walkley entered in the Stationers' Register "The Tragedie of Othello, the moore of Venice," and published the play in the following year:

THE Tragœdy of Othello, The Moore of Venice. *As it hath beene diuerse times acted at the* Globe, and at the Black Friers, by *his Maiesties Seruants. Written by*

VVilliam Shakespeare. LONDON, Printed by *N. O.* [Nicholas Okes] for *Thomas Walkley*, and are to be sold at his shop, at the Eagle and Child, in Brittans Bursse. 1622.

This text is a good one, although it is some 160 lines shorter than the Folio text of 1623 and appears to have been set up from a shortened version of the play—perhaps intended for provincial touring. The Folio text may have been set up from a copy of the quarto that had been corrected with reference to an authoritative manuscript, either a prompt-book or foul papers. The Folio text consciously eliminates some profanities found in the earlier text. Generally, modern editors base their work on the Folio text, with an awareness that the quarto text is of considerable importance as well.

The earliest mention of the play is on "Hallamas Day, being the first of Nouembar," 1604, when "the Kings Maiesties plaiers" performed "A Play in the Banketinge house att Whit Hall Called The Moor of Venis." The play is attributed to "Shaxberd." The authenticity of this Revels account, first printed by Peter Cunningham in 1842, was once challenged, but it is now accepted as genuine. On stylistic grounds the play is usually dated in 1603 or 1604, although arguments are sometimes presented for a date as early as 1601 or 1602.

King Lear (c. 1605)

On November 26, 1607, Nathaniel Butter and John Busby entered on the Stationers' Register "A booke called. Master William Shakespeare his historye of Kinge Lear, as yt was played before the Kinges maiestie at Whitehall vppon Sainct Stephens night at Christmas Last, by his maiesties servantes playinge vsually at the Globe on the Banksyde." Next year appeared the following quarto:

M. William Shak-speare: *HIS* True Chronicle Historie of the life and death of King LEAR and his three Daughters. *With the vnfortunate life of* Edgar, *sonne* and heire to the Earle of Gloster, and his sullen and assumed humor of TOM of Bedlam: *As it was played before the Kings Maiestie at Whitehall vpon S.* Stephans *night in Christmas Hollidayes.* By his Maiesties seruants playing vsually at the Gloabe on the Bancke-side. LONDON, Printed for *Nathaniel Butter*, and are to be sold at his shop in *Pauls* Church-yard at the signe of the Pide Bull neere St. *Austins* Gate. 1608.

This quarto is often called the "Pied Bull" quarto in reference to its place of sale. Twelve copies exist today, in ten different "states," because proofreading was being carried on while the sheets were being run off in the press; the copies variously combine corrected and uncorrected sheets. A second quarto, printed in 1619 by William Jaggard for Thomas Pavier with the fraudulent date of 1608, was based on a copy of the first quarto combining corrected and uncorrected sheets.

The Folio text of 1623 was also set up from a copy of the first quarto in a state of partial correction. The copy used for this occasion, however, had been carefully emended by reference to some authoritative manuscript, probably a prompt-book of a version of the play cut for performance. Although some 300 lines are deleted, some 100 other lines are added, and in general the Folio text gives evidence of being substantially closer to Shakespeare's original than any of its predecessors. The first quarto itself was not a "bad" quarto in the usual sense, but it does seem to have been based on a careless copy of Shakespeare's draft to which some actors were somehow a party. Whether the actors thus involved were the entire company putting together a text on tour to replace a missing prompt-book, or a single reporter, or the boys who played Goneril and Regan, is a matter of dispute; but in any event this quarto text is not generally as reliable as the Folio text except (obviously) for those 300 or so lines which the Folio omits. The modern tendency is to follow the Folio text except where it is manifestly defective or corrupt.

The Stationers' Register entry for November 26, 1607, describes a performance at court on the previous St. Stephen's night, December 26, 1606. The title page of the first quarto confirms this performance on St. Stephen's night. Such a performance at court was not likely to have been the first, however. Shakespeare's repeated use of Samuel Harsnett's *Declaration of Egregious Popishe Impostures*, registered on March 16, 1603, sets an early limit for composition of the play. Other circumstances point to the existence of the play by May of 1605. In that month, an old play called *The True Chronicle History of King Leir* was entered in the Stationers' Register as a "Tragecall historie," a phrase suggesting the influence of Shakespeare's play since the old *King Leir* does not end tragically. Moreover, the title page of the old *King Leir*, issued in 1605, proclaims the text to be "as it hath bene diuers and sundry times lately acted." In view of the unlikelihood that such an old play (written before 1594) would be revived in 1605, scholars have suggested that the title page was the publisher's way of trying to capitalize on the recent popularity of Shakespeare's play. In this case, the likeliest date for the composition of Shakespeare's *King Lear* would be in the winter of 1604–1605. Shakespeare certainly used the old *King Leir* as a chief source, but he need not have waited for its publication in 1605 if, as seems perfectly plausible, his company owned the prompt-book. On the other hand, Gloucester's mentioning of "These late eclipses in the sun and moon" (I,ii) seems to refer to an eclipse of the moon in September and of the sun in October of 1605, and we are left wondering if Shakespeare was so foresighted as to have anticipated these events.

Timon of Athens (c. 1605–1608)

Timon of Athens first appeared in the Folio of 1623. The text seems to have been based on an unusually early draft of the author's papers, with manifest inconsistencies still present that would have been straightened out in a final draft. The play seems to have been a last-minute substitution in the Folio, to replace *Troilus and Cressida* when for some reason (probably copyright difficulties) that play had to be removed from its original position following *Romeo and Juliet*. The Folio editors possibly had not intended to use *Timon* at all. The manuscript used by the printers seems to have been copied over in places by a second hand, as though the manuscript was too illegible for the printer to use.

Dating of the play is unusually difficult. In its unfinished state the play was probably never acted, and therefore left no trace until it was registered for publication on November 8, 1623. Stylistically it seems close to the late tragedies. Its pessimism reminds us of *King Lear*, and its use of Plutarch suggests *Antony and Cleopatra*. Theories of multiple authorship, once common, are no longer regarded as substantial.

Macbeth (c. 1606–1607)

Macbeth was first printed in the Folio of 1623. It was set up from a prompt-book or a transcript of one. The text is unusually short, and seems to have been cut for reasons of censorship or for some special performance. Moreover, all of III,v and parts of IV,i (39–43, 125–132) appear to be interpolations, containing songs from Middleton's *The Witch*.

An astrologer named Simon Forman, in his manuscript *The Booke of Plaies and Notes thereof per Formans for Common Pollicie*, records the first known performance of *Macbeth* on April 20, 1611, at the Globe Theatre. The play must have been in existence by 1607, however, for allusions to it seemingly occur in *Lingua* and *The Puritan* (both published in 1607) and in *The Knight of the Burning Pestle* (probably acted in 1607). On the other hand, the play itself seemingly alludes to James I's royal succession in 1603, and to the trial of the notorious Gunpowder Plot conspirators in March of 1606.

Antony and Cleopatra (1606–1607)

On May 20, 1608, Edward Blount entered on the Stationers' Register "A booke Called Anthony. and Cleopatra," along with "A booke called. The booke of Pericles prynce of Tyre." Blount was friendly with Shakespeare's company, and his entry may have been a "staying entry" designed to prevent some unscrupulous publisher from pirating these texts. If so, the tactic did not succeed with *Pericles*, issued in 1609 by another publisher, but it did succeed with *Antony and Cleopatra*. The play was first printed in the Folio of 1623. It is a good text, set evidently from Shakespeare's own draft after it had been prepared for stage presentation (though not yet actually used as a prompt-book).

The year 1608 is thus the latest possible date for *Antony and Cleopatra*. Evidently it was written in 1606–1607, however, for a "newly altered" edition in 1607 of Samuel Daniel's play *Cleopatra* seems to have been influenced by Shakespeare's play. Shakespeare himself had probably consulted the original edition of *Cleopatra*, published in 1594, or the slightly revised edition of 1599, but Daniel's more thorough revision in 1607 shows signs of his having seen Shakespeare's play in the interim. Also, a play by Barnabe Barnes called *The Devil's Charter*, 1607, may contain a parody of Cleopatra's death by asps.

Coriolanus (c. 1608)

Coriolanus was first printed in the Folio of 1623. Its text was set from the author's own manuscript or a transcript of it. Although printing errors are numerous, they are for the most part easy to correct. Dating of the play is uncertain. No early performance is on record. The late style and some possible allusions point to some time around 1608. Menenius' fable of the belly (I,i,99 ff.) is probably indebted to William Camden's *Remaines*, published 1605. Echoes of the play may appear in Robert Armin's *The Italian Taylor and his Boy* and Ben Jonson's *Epicoene*, both from 1609. Thus a date in 1608 is plausible but only approximate.

Pericles (c. 1606–1608)

On May 20, 1608, Edward Blount entered in the Stationers' Register "A booke called. the booke of Pericles prynce of Tyre." He also entered *Antony and Cleopatra* at this time, possibly hoping to forestall illegal publishing of these two texts. If so, the plan succeeded with *Antony* but not with *Pericles*. A corrupt quarto of this play was printed in 1609 by William White:

> THE LATE, And much admired Play, Called Pericles, Prince of Tyre. With the true Relation of the whole Historie, aduentures, and fortunes of the said Prince: As also, The no lesse strange, and worthy accidents, in the Birth and Life, of his Daughter MARIANA. As it hath been diuers and sundry times acted by his Maiesties Seruants, at the Globe on the Banck-side. By William Shakespeare. Imprinted at London for *Henry Gosson*, and are to be sold at the signe of the Sunne in Pater-noster row, &c. 1609.

Blount was a friend of the players, and the text he registered is likely to have been the prompt-copy. (This would explain why it is referred to as "A booke called the booke of Pericles" in the S. R., since prompt-copies were known technically as "books.") White's text, on the other hand, is a memorially constructed text and at times unintelligible. Two reporters may have been at work, and the printing was done by at least three compositors. See Play Introduction, pp. 1153–1155 above, for some examples of inconsistency in the text. Unfortunately, this bad text is the best we have. Subsequent quartos appeared in 1609, 1611, 1619, and 1630, but each was set up from the previous edition, and all attempts in them at improvement are editorial rather than authorial. *Pericles* did not appear at all in the Folio of 1623, perhaps because the editors suspected it to be partly non-Shakespearean, or because they did not possess a reliable text. Arguments for multiple authorship, though based essentially on internal evidence of the play's manifest inconsistencies, are still taken seriously by scholars. The defects of the first two acts are generally more extensive than those found even in such bad quartos as *Hamlet* or *Romeo and Juliet*. Philip Edwards has argued, on the other hand (*Shakespeare Survey 5*), that the differences between the first two acts and the last three can be accounted for by memorial reporting and compositorial error. This matter is still in dispute.

A play of *Pericles* (though probably differing textually from the one we have today) must have been in existence by the date of the Stationers' Register entry in May of 1608. A play of *Pericles* was seen by the Venetian Ambassador to England, Zorzi Giustinian, some time during his official stay from January 5, 1606, to November 23, 1608. George Wilkins' *The Painfull Aduentures of Pericles Prince of Tyre*, published in 1608, was certainly derived in part from a play about Pericles: its title page offers the work "as it was lately presented by the worthy and ancient Poet John Gower," and the final sentence of the Argument urges the reader "to receive this Historie in the same maner as it was under the habite of ancient *Gower* the famous English Poet, by the Kings Majesties Players excellently presented." The play to which Wilkins refers may have been Shakespeare's, or perhaps some earlier version—just how early, no one can say. As it stands, however, the play appears to represent the beginning of Shakespeare's fascination with the genre of romance. As such, its date is usually set between 1606 and 1608.

Cymbeline (c. 1608–1610)

Cymbeline was first printed in the Folio of 1623, where it was included among the tragedies. The text, a good one, was evidently set either from a careful transcript of Shakespeare's own papers or from a theatrical prompt-book that had incorporated many authorial stage directions. The first recorded performance was in 1611. Dr. Simon Forman, a quack astrologer, jotted down a description of *Cymbeline* in his commonplace book for that year; and, although he did not record the actual date he saw the play, he must have done so some time between April and his sudden death on September 8 of that year. Stylistically the play appears to follow *Pericles* (c. 1606–1608) and to precede *The Winter's Tale* (c. 1610–1611). Dating must be considered approximate.

The Winter's Tale (c. 1610–1611)

The Winter's Tale was first printed in the Folio of 1623. Its text is a good one, taken evidently from Ralph Crane's transcript of Shakespeare's own draft. As in most other Crane transcriptions, the stage directions are sparse and the characters' names are grouped at the beginning of each scene. The first recorded performance was on May 15, 1611, when the quack astrologer Simon Forman saw the play at the Globe and recorded a summary of it in his commonplace book. Another performance that year at court, on November 5, is recorded in the *Revels Account*, and still another during the winter of 1612–1613. Quite possibly the play was new at the time Forman saw it. It apparently contains an allusion to the dance of ten or twelve satyrs in Jonson's *Masque of Oberon*, performed at court on January 1, 1611. A 1623 entry in the *Office book* of Sir Henry Herbert, Master of the Revels, refers to *The Winter's Tale* as "an olde playe . . . formerly allowed of by Sir George Bucke." Bucke (or Buc) was first appointed Master of the Revels in 1610, but had occasionally licensed plays before that date during his predecessor's illness, so that the backward limit of 1610 cannot be considered absolute. Still, matters of style confirm the likelihood that Forman was seeing a new play in 1611.

The Tempest (c. 1610–1611)

The Tempest was first printed in the Folio of 1623. It occupies first place in the volume, and is a scrupulously prepared text from a transcript by Ralph Crane of a theatre prompt-book or of Shakespeare's draft after it had been annotated for production. Shakespeare's colleagues may have placed it first in the Folio because they considered it his most recent complete play. The first recorded performance was at court on November 1, 1611: "Hallomas nyght was presented att Whithall before ye kinges Maiestie a play Called the Tempest." The actors were "the Kings players" (*Revels Account*). The play was again presented at court during the winter of 1612–1613, this time "before the Princes Highnes the Lady Elizabeth and the Prince Pallatyne Elector." The festivities for this important betrothal and wedding were sumptuous, and included at least thirteen other plays. Various arguments have been put forward that Shakespeare composed parts of *The Tempest*, especially the masque, for this occasion, but there is absolutely no evidence that the play was singled out for special prominence among the many plays presented, and the masque is integral to the play as it stands. Probably the 1611 production was of a fairly new play. Simon Forman, who saw *Cymbeline* and *The Winter's Tale* in 1611, does not mention *The Tempest*. He died in September of 1611. According to every stylistic test, such as run-on and hypermetric lines, the play is very late. Shakespeare probably knew Sylvester Jourdain's *A Discovery of the Barmudas*, published in 1610, and William Strachey's *A true Reportory of the Wracke and Redemption*, dated July 1610 although not published until 1625.

King Henry the Eighth (1613)

The Life of King Henry the Eight was first printed in the Folio of 1623. Its text is a good one, set from a careful transcript of Shakespeare's own manuscript. The stage directions are unusually elaborate. The first recorded performance was on June 29, 1613. A letter of July 2 in that year from Sir Henry Wotton to Sir Edmund Bacon tells of a performance of "a new play, called *All Is True*, representing some principal pieces of the reign of Henry VIII." During this performance, as King Henry was arriving as a masquer at the house of Cardinal Wolsey (I,iv), "certain chambers being shot off at his entry, some of the paper, or other stuff, wherewith one of them was stopped, did light on the thatch, where being thought at first but an idle smoke, and their eyes more attentive to the show, it kindled inwardly, and ran round like a train, consuming within less than an hour the whole house to the very grounds." The identification of this *All Is True* with Shakespeare's play is certain. Other accounts include a letter from Thomas Lorkin to Sir Thomas Puckering, June 1613, asserting the fire to have started "while Bourbege his companie were acting at y[e] Globe the play of Hen: 8," a letter of 8 July from John Chamberlain to Sir Ralph Winwood, and an account in Stow's *Annales* as continued by Edmund Howe (1618).

Wotton calls it a new play, and stylistic considerations confirm this characterization. The play may also have helped provide entertainment for the betrothal and marriage of James I's daughter Elizabeth to the Elector Palatinate earlier in 1613, though *Henry VIII* is not listed among the many plays acted on this occasion.

On the controversy over John Fletcher's purported share in the authorship of *Henry VIII*, see Play Introduction, pp. 1271–1273 above.

SOURCES

The Comedy of Errors

The Comedy of Errors is based chiefly on the *Menaechmi* of Plautus (c. 254–184 B.C.). Shakespeare appears to have used the Latin, which was available to him in numerous Renaissance texts. He may also have known in manuscript the translation into English by "W. W." (William Warner), published in 1595, S. R. 1594.

Two twins have become separated when their father, a Syracusan merchant, loses one of them in Epidamnum. The lost twin is raised by a citizen of that town. The action is set in Epidamnum years later, where Menaechmus the Citizen, in the company of the parasite Peniculus, is seen quarreling with his wife and arranging to lunch with the courtesan Erotium. To the city of Epidamnum comes Menaechmus' long-separated twin brother, Menaechmus Sosicles of Syracuse, accompanied by his servant Messenio. The confusion begins when Menaechmus Sosicles is mistaken for his twin by Erotium's cook, Cylindrus, and then by Erotium herself, who invites him to lunch and to her bed. She bids him take a cloak (which Menaechmus the Citizen had given her that morning) to the dyer's for alteration. A short time later, Peniculus too mistakes Menaechmus Sosicles for the Epidamnian twin, upbraids him for having dined while the parasite was absent, and threatens to tell Menaechmus' wife of his carryings-on. Erotium's maid brings Menaechmus Sosicles a chain or bracelet to be mended at the goldsmith's. Menaechmus the Citizen now returns home from a busy day to a furious wife and a vindictive Peniculus. Among other matters the wife demands the return of her cloak which, as she suspects, her husband did in fact steal from her and give to Erotium. The husband, locked out of his own house by his angry wife, must now confront Erotium, who insists that she gave her chain and the cloak to him. The Citizen goes to seek the help of his friends. Menaechmus Sosicles shows up at this point and is angrily abused by the wife and by her father, both of whom consider the supposed husband to be mad. They send for a doctor, who arrives after Menaechmus Sosicles has fled; they instead detain Menaechmus the Citizen as a madman. Messenio the servant now returns to his supposed master and fights manfully with his captors. Finally the two twins confront one another and unravel the mystery.

Shakespeare creates the two Dromios in place of Messenio, plays down the role of the courtesan, dignifies the part of the wife, invents the sympathetic role of Luciana her sister, eliminates the parasite and the wife's father, and replaces the courtesan's maid and cook with comic servants like Luce or Nell, the kitchen-wench in the household of Antipholus of Ephesus. The conventional doctor, Medicus, becomes the zany Dr. Pinch. The setting is Ephesus rather than Epidamnum. Plautus' detached ironic tone and his matter-of-fact depiction of courtesans and parasites are replaced by a thematic emphasis on patience and loyalty in marriage. The name "Dromio" may have come from John Lyly's *Mother Bombie*.

The dual identity of the servants, and the superb confusion of Act III when Antipholus of Ephesus is locked out of his own house, are derived in good part from Plautus' *Amphitruo*. The relevant part of the story is as follows. While Jupiter makes love to Amphitryon's wife Alcmena, disguised as her husband, Mercury guards the door in the guise of Amphitryon's slave Sosia. The real Sosia approaches, but is so bewildered by Mercury's inventive wit that he begins to doubt his own identity. Later, at Jupiter's behest, Mercury again poses as Sosia to dupe Amphitryon and deny him entrance to his own house. Ultimately, after Alcmena has given birth to twins, one by Jupiter (Hercules) and one by Amphitryon (Iphiclus), Jupiter tells Amphitryon the truth.

The "framing" action of *The Comedy of Errors*, concerning old Ægeon's painful separation from his wife and their eventual reunion, is derived not from Plautus but from the story of Apollonius of Tyre. Shakespeare later used this story for *Pericles*, and for that play his sources were chiefly two: the *Confessio Amantis* by John Gower, Book VIII, and Laurence Twine's *The Patterne of Painefull Aduentures*, translated from a French version based in turn on a popular story in the *Gesta Romanorum*. Perhaps Shakespeare was acquainted with these same versions when he wrote *The Comedy of Errors;* Twine's account was entered in the Stationers' Register in 1576, although the earliest extant edition dates from around 1594–1595. Gower's account had been printed by Caxton in 1493 and reprinted in 1532 and 1554.

In Gower's *Confessio*, Apollonius' wife Lucina gives birth to a daughter on board ship and, having apparently died in childbirth, is put into a chest and committed to the sea. Washing ashore at Ephesus, she is restored by the physician Cerimon. She becomes a priestess in the Temple of Diana. Years later, Apollonius comes to Ephesus, is first reunited with his daughter Thaisa, and then is told in a vision to go to the Temple. There he discovers the "Abbess" to be his long-lost wife. Shakespeare has added the business of the threatened hanging from which Ægeon is finally rescued.

Love's Labour's Lost

No main source exists for *Love's Labour's Lost*. For his conception of an "academy" of aristocratic scholars, Shakespeare may have drawn on a knowledge of Pierre de la Primaudaye's *L'Académie françoise* (1577), translated into English in 1586, in which the ideals of scholarly withdrawal are discussed. The notion was, however, commonplace. Certain historical facts about Henry of Navarre may well have provided Shakespeare a model for the play's action, especially the visit of Catherine de' Medici with her daughter and the famous *l'escadron volant* to Henry's court in 1578, and a similar visit in 1586 (see Play Introduction, pp. 100–102 above). Published accounts of these visits were not available when Shakespeare wrote his play, but he may well have heard the gossip. John Lyly provided Shakespeare a literary model for the saucy boyish wit of Moth, Boyet, and others; and Armado and Moth are often thought to resemble Sir Tophas and the page Epiton in Lyly's *Endymion*. Traditions of the *Commedia dell' Arte* provided Shakespeare with stock comic models, especially those of the *dottore* or pedant (Holofernes), his parasite (Nathaniel, the curate), the *capitano* or braggart soldier (Armado), and the rustic servant (Costard). All of these types are individualized and rendered in English terms, however. Many literary quarrels in England of the 1590's have been adduced as possible sources for Shakespeare's play, especially the Nashe-Harvey controversy, but the evidence remains inconclusive.

The Two Gentlemen of Verona

Shakespeare appears to have combined two kinds of stories in *The Two Gentlemen of Verona*, one of romantic love triumphing over inconstancy and one of perfect friendship triumphing over perfidy. For the story of the deserted heroine and her inconstant lover, Shakespeare's main source was evidently *Diana*, a pastoral by Jorge de Montemayor (published c. 1559). This work was translated into French in 1578 and 1587, and was published in English in 1598 by Bartholomew Yonge. Yonge states that he began his translation some nineteen years earlier. Possibly then Shakespeare saw it in manuscript, or he may have relied on the French translation. A play, now lost, was performed at court in 1585 called *The history of felix & philiomena* (i.e., Felismena). It must surely have been based on Montemayor's prose pastoral, and may have provided Shakespeare with a dramatic model.

In *Diana*, the story of Felix and Felismena is one of many narratives set in contrast to the central story of Diana the shepherdess. Felismena tells her own story (in Book II). While she is living with her grandmother, her parents having died, Felismena is courted by a young gentleman named Don Felix. His father, determined to prevent the marriage, sends Don Felix off to the court of the Princess Augusta Caesarina. Felismena follows after, apparelled as a young man named Valerius. Stopping at an inn, she is invited by the host of the inn to hear some music, whereupon she happens to overhear the faithless Felix courting a lady named Celia. Disguised as Valerius, Felismena ingratiates herself with Felix' servant Fabius and takes service with Don Felix. She is sent on embassages to Celia, with whom she converses about Felix' first love. Celia falls in love with "Valerius," like Olivia in *Twelfth Night*, and subsequently dies of unrequited passion. Hereupon the distraught Felix disappears. Later, in Book VII, we hear how Felismena disguised as an Amazonian shepherdess rescues Felix from his attackers and is reconciled to him. Felix acknowledges her beauty to be superior to that of Celia.

In Sir Philip Sidney's *Arcadia* (1590), Zelmane follows Felismena's example by disguising herself as a page (Daiphantus) in the service of her beloved Pyrocles. When she falls ill and is on the verge of death, Zelmane's identity is revealed to Pyrocles. The *Arcadia* also offers a noble example of perfect friendship in the relation between Pyrocles and Musidorus.

The story of perfect friendship has many antecedents, including the fourteenth-century *Amis and Amiloun*, and Richard Edwards' play about *Damon and Pythias* (1565). The falling-out of sworn friends over a woman is the central theme of Chaucer's *The Knight's Tale* and of John Lyly's *Euphues* (1578). Perhaps the most suggestive example of perfect friendship is the story of Titus and Gisippus as it appears in Book II, Chapter XII, of Sir Thomas Elyot's *The Governour* (1531). Elyot derived his account from Day X, Novel VIII, of Boccaccio's *Decameron*. Titus and Gisippus were proverbially famous as friends, like Damon and Pythias, and other Renaissance versions of the story were available (including a Latin school play of 1546[?] and a children's play at court in 1577, both now lost). Perhaps Shakespeare knew the story as a commonplace rather than having to depend on one particular literary source.

Elyot's version tells of two look-alike friends dwelling in Athens of whom one, Gisippus, is persuaded by his kindred and acquaintances to marry. Despite a preference for the study of philosophy, he finds his fiancée most attractive. When, however, his Roman-born friend Titus falls desperately in love with the same lady and confesses as much to Gisippus, the husband-to-be generously proposes that Titus take his place on the wedding night. Because the binding element of the marriage contract is the bestowing of the ring in bed, and the undoing of the girdle of virginity, the lady is now Titus' legal wife and returns with him to Rome. Gisippus, accused by the Athenians of having mismanaged the affair, follows his friend to Rome and is there wrongly accused of a murder. Titus' turn has now arrived to be magnanimous, and he insists that he be punished for the murder. Eventually the real culprit, touched by this selflessness, confesses the crime, allowing Titus to return with Gisippus to Athens and forcibly restore him to his rightful possessions.

Valentine's sojourn in the forest and his leadership of a band of outlaws would seem to be indebted to Robin Hood tradition, although no single source has been found. An analogue to the outlaw episode does appear in Henry Wotton's *A Courtlie Controversie of Cupids Cautels* (1578), where it is linked to a story of perfidy in friendship. Valentine's unwelcome rival Thurio may owe something to the braggart soldier, Captain Spavento, of the *Commedia dell' Arte* tradition.

Silvia's father, the Duke, is a similarly conventional comic stage type.

One final analogue worthy of note is a German play, *Julio und Hyppolita*, from a collection called *Englische Comedien und Tragedien* (1620). It may have been derived from performances by English players around 1600. Although some of its lines are suggestively close to those of Shakespeare's play, we cannot determine which version is prior to the other.

The Taming of the Shrew

Most recent critics agree that the play called *The Taming of A Shrew*, published in 1594, is an imitation of Shakespeare's play and not an earlier version or source for what he wrote. An exception is Geoffrey Bullough, *Narrative and Dramatic Sources of Shakespeare*, who prefers the theory that *A Shrew* is an inaccurate text of an old play which Shakespeare used as his main source. Apart from this controversial question, all critics agree that Shakespeare's play consists of three elements, each with its own source: the romantic love-plot of Lucentio and Bianca, the wife-taming plot of Petruchio and Kate, and the framing plot or "Induction" of Christophero Sly.

The romantic love-plot is derived from George Gascoigne's *Supposes*, a neoclassical comedy performed at Gray's Inn in 1566. Gascoigne's play was a rather close translation of Ariosto's *I Suppositi* (1509), which in turn was based on Terence's *Eunuchus* and Plautus' *Captivi*. The heroine of Gascoigne's version (as of Ariosto's) is Polynesta, the resourceful daughter of Damon, a widower of Ferrara. Two suiters vie for Polynesta's hand: Dr. Cleander, an aged and miserly lawyer, and Erostrato, a Sicilian gentleman who has purportedly come to Ferrara to study. In fact, however, this "Erostrato" is the servant Dulippo in disguise, having changed places with his master. (These disguisings are the "supposes" of the title.) As a servant in Damon's household, "Dulippo" has secretly become the lover of Polynesta, and has made her pregnant. Balia, the nurse or duenna, is their go-between. Meanwhile, "Erostrato" takes great delight in outwitting Dr. Cleander and his unattractive parasite, Pasiphilo. The feigned Erostrato's ruse is to produce a rich father who will guarantee a handsome dowry and thereby outbid Cleander in the contest for Polynesta's hand. The "father" he produces, however, is actually an old Sienese stranger, who is persuaded that he is in danger in Ferrara unless he cloaks his identity. Complications arise when Damon learns of his daughter's affair and throws the lover, "Dulippo," into a dungeon. The crafty Pasiphilo overhears this compromising information and resolves to cause mischief for all the principals. Moreover, when Erostrato's real father Philogano arrives in Ferrara, he is barred from his son's house by the feigned Philogano and resolves to get help. His clever servant, Litio, suggests employing the famous lawyer Cleander. All is happily resolved when the real Dulippo proves to be the son of Dr. Cleander, and the real Erostrato is revealed to be rich and socially eligible for Polynesta's hand in marriage. Cleander is even reconciled to his parasite, Pasiphilo.

Shakespeare has almost entirely eliminated the satire of the law in his source. Gremio is aged and wealthy, but no shyster. The lover is not imprisoned in a dungeon. The parasite is gone, as also in *The Comedy of Errors*. Bianca does not consummate her affair with Lucentio as does Polynesta, and hence has no need for a go-between like Balia. Shakespeare adapts a sophisticated neoclassical comedy, racy and cosmopolitan, to the moral standards of his public theatre. The witless Hortensio, the tutoring in Latin, and the music lesson are Shakespeare's invention.

The wife-taming plot of Petruchio and Kate reflects an ancient comic antifeminist tradition, still extant today in the Scottish folksong "The Cooper of Fife" or "The Wife Wrapped in Wether's Skin" (Child's *Ballads*, V, 277). Richard Hosley has argued (in *Huntington Library Quarterly*, 1964) that Shakespeare's likeliest source was *A Merry Jest of a Shrewde and Curste Wyfe, Lapped in Morrelles Skin, for her Good behavyour* (printed c. 1550). In this version, the husband beats his shrewish wife with birch rods until she bleeds and faints, whereupon he wraps her in the raw salted skin of an old plough-horse named Morel. Like Kate, this shrewish wife has a gentle younger sister who is their father's favorite. This father warns the man who proposes to marry his older daughter that she is shrewish, but the suitor goes ahead and subsequently tames his wife with Morel's skin. Thereafter, at a celebratory dinner, everyone is impressed by the thoroughness of the taming.

Shakespeare avoids the antifeminist extremes of this story, despite the similarity of the narrative. Instead, he seems to have had in mind the more humanistic spirit of Erasmus' *A Mery Dialogue Declarynge the Propertyes of Shrowde Shrewes, and Honest Wyues* (translated 1557) and Vives' *The Office and Duty of an Husband* (translated 1553). Specific elements of the wife-taming plot have been traced to other possible sources. The scolding of a tailor occurs in Gerard Legh's *Accidence of Armory* (1562); a wife agrees with her husband's assertion of a patent falsehood in Don Juan Manuel's *El Conde Lucanor* (by 1350); and three husbands wager on the obedience of their wives in *The Book of the Knight of La Tour-Landry* (printed 1484).

The "Induction" story, of the beggar duped into believing himself a rich lord, is an old tale occurring in the *Arabian Nights*. An interesting analogue occurs in Heuterus' *De Rebus Burgundicis* (1584), translated into the French of S. Goulart (1606?) and thence into the English of Edward Grimeston (1607). According to Heuterus, in 1440 Philip the Good of Burgundy actually entertained a drunken beggar in his palace "to make triall of the vanity of our life," plying him with fine clothes, bed, a feast, and the performance of "a pleasant Comedie."

A Midsummer Night's Dream

No single source has been discovered that unites the various elements we find in *A Midsummer Night's Dream*, but the four main strands of action can be individually discussed in terms of sources. The four strands are: (1) the marriage of Duke Theseus and Queen Hippolyta, (2) the romantic tribulations and triumphs of the four young lovers, (3) the quarrel of King Oberon and Queen Titania, together with the fairies' manipulations of human affairs, and (4) the "rude mechanicals" and their play of "Pyramus and Thisbe."

For his conception of Theseus, Shakespeare went chiefly to Chaucer's *Knight's Tale* and to Thomas North's 1579 translation of The Life of Theseus in Plutarch's *Lives of the Noble Grecians and Romanes*. Chaucer's Theseus is a duke of "wysdom" and "chivalrie," renowned for his conquest of the Amazons and his marriage to Hippolyta. Plutarch provides information concerning Theseus' other conquests (to which Oberon alludes in II,i), including that of Antiopa. Shakespeare could have learned more about Theseus from Chaucer's *The Legend of Good Women* and from Ovid's *Metamorphoses*. He seems to have blended all or some of these impressions together with his own ideal of a noble yet popular Renaissance ruler.

The romantic narrative of the four lovers appears to be original with Shakespeare, although one can find many analogous situations of misunderstanding and rivalry in love. Chaucer's *Knight's Tale* tells of two friends battling over one woman. Shakespeare's own *The Two Gentlemen of Verona* gives us four lovers, properly matched at first until one of the men shifts his attentions to his friend's lady-love; eventually all is righted when the false lover recovers his senses. Parallel situations arise in Sidney's *Arcadia* and in Montemayor's *Diana*, a source for *The Two Gentlemen*. What Shakespeare adds in *A Midsummer* is the intervention of the fairies in human love affairs.

Shakespeare's knowledge of fairy lore must have been extensive, and is hard to trace exactly. Doubtless much of it was from oral traditions. In Chaucer's *Merchant's Tale*, Pluto and Proserpina as king and queen of the fairies intervene in the affairs of old January, his young wife May, and her lover Damyan. Fairies appear on stage in Lyly's *Endymion* (1588), protecting true lovers and tormenting those who are morally tainted. Shakespeare later reflects this tradition in *The Merry Wives of Windsor* (1597–1601). The name Oberon probably comes from the French romance *Huon of Bordeaux* (translated by Lord Berners by about 1540), where Oberon is a dwarfish fairy king from the mysterious East who practices enchantment in a haunted wood. In Spenser's *The Faerie Queene*, Oberon is the Elfin father of Queen Gloriana (II,x,75–76). Greene's *James IV* (c. 1591) also features Oberon as the fairy king, and a lost play called *Huon of Bordeaux* was performed by Sussex' men at about this same time. The name Titania comes from Ovid's *Metamorphoses*, where it is used as a synonym for both the enchantress Circe and the chaste goddess Diana. The name Titania does not appear in Golding's translation, suggesting that Shakespeare found it in the original. Puck or Robin Goodfellow is essentially the product of oral tradition, although Reginald Scot's *The Discoverie of Witchcraft* (1584) discusses Robin in pejorative terms as an incubus or hobgoblin in whom intelligent people no longer believe.

Scot also reports the story of a man who finds an ass' head placed on his shoulders by enchantment. Similar legends of transformation occur in Apuleius' *The Golden Ass* (translated by William Adlington, 1566) and in the well-known story of the ass' ears bestowed by Phoebus on King Midas for his presumption. Perhaps the most suggestive possible source for Shakespeare's clownish actors, however, is Anthony Munday's play *John a Kent and John a Cumber* (c. 1587–1590). In it a group of rude artisans, led by the intrepid Turnop, stage a ludicrous interlude written by their churchwarden in praise of his millhorse. Turnop's prologue is a medley of lofty comparisons. The entertainment is presented before noble spectators, who are graciously amused. *John a Kent* also features a lot of magic trickery, a boy named Shrimp whose role is comparable to that of Puck, and a multiple love plot.

"Pyramus and Thisbe" itself is based on the *Metamorphoses* (IV,67 ff.). Other versions Shakespeare may have known include Chaucer's *The Legend of Good Women*, a poem by William Griffith in 1562, George Pettie's *A Petite Palace of Pettie His Pleasure* (1576), *A Gorgeous Gallery of Gallant Inventions* (1578), and "A New Sonet of Pyramus and Thisbe" from Clement Robinson's *A Handefull of Pleasant Delites* (1584). Several of these, especially the last three, are bad enough to have given Shakespeare materials to lampoon, though the sweep of his parody goes beyond the particular story of Pyramus and Thisbe. The occasionally stilted phraseology of Golding's translation of *The Metamorphoses* contributed to the fun. According to Kenneth Muir (*Shakespeare's Sources*, 1957), Shakespeare must also have known Thomas Mouffet's *Of the Silkewormes and their Flies* (published 1599, but possibly circulated earlier in manuscript), which contains perhaps the most ridiculous of all versions of the Pyramus and Thisbe story.

The Henry the Sixth Plays

The chief source for the entire *Henry VI* trilogy is Edward Hall's *The Union of the Two Noble and Illustre Famelies of Lancastre and Yorke* (1548), a work written to glorify the Tudor monarchs by demonstrating how their lineage reconciled the fatally warring factions of Lancaster and York. Shakespeare also drew many particulars from the second edition of Raphael Holinshed's *The Chronicles of England, Scotlande, and Irelande*

(1587), from John Foxe's *Actes and Monuments of Martyrs* (1583 edition), and probably from others. Richard Grafton's *Chronicle* plagiarized so heavily from Hall that one cannot always be sure which of the two Shakespeare may have consulted.

To intensify Hall's theme of the horrors of civil dissension, Shakespeare takes considerable liberties with the chronicles. He frequently disregards chronological order, telescopes events of many years into a single sequence, invents scenes and characters, and transfers details from one historical scene to another. The artistic unity of each play is his overriding consideration, not historical accuracy.

In *1 Henry VI*, for example, Shakespeare shows the English losing Orleans to the French and then retaking the city (I,v–II,i). In point of fact, Orleans was never retaken once it had fallen. Shakespeare has transferred events from the recapture of Le Mans to his partly invented account of Orleans. Talbot's visit to the Countess of Auvergne (II,iii) is fictitious. The scene in the Temple Garden when the leaders of Lancaster and York pluck red and white roses (II,iv) is fictitious in a different sense: antagonisms between the two factions certainly did exist, but not in the allegorically schematized fashion here visualized. In III,ii Shakespeare shows us Rouen lost and recaptured in a day, whereas in fact the city was (like Orleans) never recovered. Shakespeare's intention is to suggest that France is lost through England's political divisions at home, not through any failure on the part of Lord Talbot. Shakespeare exalts Talbot's might and chivalry (hence the scene with the Countess of Auvergne), and contrastingly overstates the cowardice of Fastolfe (or Falstaff, as he is called in the Folio text). Joan la Pucelle is another exaggeratedly evil foil to Talbot; Shakespeare combines her worst traits in Hall and Holinshed. The play covers the events of about three decades. When Henry v died in 1522, his son was less than a year old; by the time of Talbot's fall in 1453 the king was over thirty.

In *2 Henry VI* Shakespeare accentuates the threat of popular unrest in a number of ways. One of his most prominent techniques is to conflate reports of the Jack Cade rebellion in 1450 with those of the Peasants' Revolt in 1381, bringing together the most unattractive features of each. Shakespeare ridicules the peasants' Utopian aims, and omits a list of sympathetic demands. Similarly, the dispute between the Armorer and his apprentice (I,iii) is put into a context of courtly politics that we do not find in the chronicles. Simpcox' name and his lameness (II,i) are added to stress the farcical nature of this "miracle." (Shakespeare could have found this account in Thomas More's *Dyaloge . . . of the Veneracyon and Worshyp of Ymages*, 1529, or in Foxe's *Actes and Monuments.*) Although the indictment of Suffolk (III,ii) was historically an act of the House of Commons, Shakespeare portrays it as a near riot in which the people hammer at the king's very door with their strident demands. In every way, *2 Henry VI* stresses the fickleness, inhumanity, and ignorance of men caught up in a mob. Despite all this, however, the play alters its sources less than does *1 Henry VI.* And for all its disapproval of mob unrest, Shakespeare's play is considerably less hostile toward the populace than an anonymous contemporary play, *The Life and Death of Jack Straw* (1590–1593).

3 Henry VI similarly alters its sources less than does *1 Henry VI.* The alterations are chiefly those of telescoping and highlighting for emphasis. The ritual killings, which form such an integral part of the spectacle in *3 Henry VI*, are cleverly adapted or rearranged from chronicle accounts. Concerning the death of the Duke of York (I, iv), for example, Hall reports merely that York died fighting manfully, whereas Holinshed tells us that the remorseless Clifford caused the dead York's head to be stricken off, "and set on it a crowne of paper, fixed it on a pole, and presented it to the queene." Shakespeare's version goes still further: Queen Margaret mocks York while he is still alive by putting a paper crown on his head. The ritual killing of the Lancastrian Prince Edward (V,v) is similarly enhanced. Throughout, Shakespeare's purpose is to intensify the scourgelike role of the Yorkist Edward iv and his brethren. Among the three, Richard of Gloucester is the most ominous. Shakespeare introduces crook-backed Richard into the fighting (II,i) when historically this man was abroad.

According to Andrew Cairncross, *3 Henry VI* contains occasional allusions to *The Faerie Queene* (see II,i,9 ff. and *FQ* I,v2), to *A Myrroure for Magistrates* (especially "Richard, Duke of York" and "King Henry the Sixth"), and to Brooke's *Romeus and Juliet* (see V,iv,1–33 and *Romeus* ll. 1359–1377). David Riggs argues (*Shakespeare's Heroical Histories: Henry VI and Its Literary Tradition*, 1971) that Marlowe's *Tamburlaine* was an important source for Shakespeare's *Henry VI* plays, and that behind *Tamburlaine* lay a classical rhetorical tradition of praise for heroism. Shakespeare would have thoroughly absorbed this tradition through the Tudor grammar-school curriculum.

Richard the Third

Richard III, like the *Henry VI* series, is based chiefly on Edward Hall's *The Union of the Noble and Illustre Famelies of Lancastre and Yorke* (1548) and also on Holinshed's *Chronicles* (1587 edition). Both of these historical compilations were, however, deeply indebted for their hostile view of Richard iii to Polydore Vergil and Thomas More. Vergil, a papal tax collector who came to England in 1501, spent many years under the patronage of Henry vii writing in Latin his *Anglica Historia* (first published in Basle, 1534). This work portrayed Richard as negatively as possible in order to glorify the claim of the Tudor monarch who had deposed Richard in 1485. Vergil argued that England's suffering was a divinely sent scourge, intended to cleanse England of her rebelliousness and prepare her for the providential reward of Tudor rule.

Thomas More's *The History of King Richard III*, left unfinished in 1513, was published in two slightly differing versions, one in English (1557) and one in Latin (1566). Thomas More obtained much information and possibly an early draft of his narrative from Cardinal Morton, in whose household More lived as a youth. Morton had figured in the struggles of Richard III's reign—he was the Bishop of Ely from whom Richard requested the strawberries (III,iv)—and had become a bitter enemy of the Yorkist king. Thomas More's own purpose in writing the life of Richard III was surely not to glorify Henry VII, with whom More had a very strained relationship, but to characterize the evil of political opportunism. His portrait of Richard becomes that of the generic tyrant, behaving as such tyrants behaved in the various literary models from Renaissance Italy with which More was doubtless familiar. The result was, in any case, one-sided. The historical Richard seems to have been no worse than many another late medieval ruler, and had indeed some admirable ideas on efficiency in government. More's blackened portrait, because it served the purposes of the Tudor state, became part of the legend and was available to Shakespeare in many redactions.

Apart from Hall's and Holinshed's chronicles, those of Robert Fabyan (first published in 1516) and the *Annales* of John Stow (1580, 1592) may have provided Shakespeare further details. Another possible source is *A Myrroure for Magistrates* (first published in 1559), where for example in the Complaint of George, Duke of Clarence we find the riddling prophecy about "G" (see I,i). A second edition of the *Myrroure* (1563) contains the Complaints of Edward IV, Anthony Woodvile (Lord Rivers), Hastings, Buckingham, Shore's Wife, and others. Shakespeare's particular indebtedness to the *Myrroure* is not great, though he certainly was familiar with it. The same is probably true of the Latin tragedy *Richardus Tertius* by Thomas Legge (1579) at Cambridge. It contains an interesting scene of Richard's wooing of the Lady Anne, not reported in the chronicles. The anonymous *The True Tragedy of Richard III* (published 1594, written c. 1590–1592) may have been useful in its fusing of Senecan revenge motifs with English history, and in its focus on the single figure of Richard. The Richard of this anonymous play is something of a Marlovian overreacher, a believer in Fortune who meets his nemesis in the devoutly Christian Earl of Richmond. Opinion is divided as to whether Shakespeare actually used the play, chiefly because by 1590 he could find the legend of Richard III set forth in so many works.

King John

To understand Shakespeare's use of sources in *King John*, we must first understand the play's relationship to the anonymous *The Troublesome Raigne of King John*, published in 1591. According to E. A. J. Honigmann (in his edition of *King John*, 1954), *Troublesome Raigne* is a bad quarto derived piratically from Shakespeare's text rather than a source for it. *Troublesome Raigne* does indeed show features of a bad quarto. Moreover, a 1611 reprint of this play is attributed to "W. Sh.," and another in 1622 to "W. Shakespeare." The Folio editors did not register *King John* for publication in 1623, as though assuming it had already been published in some form. Nevertheless, most scholars still hold to the view that *Troublesome Raigne* is a source. Its early date, by 1591, would mean a still earlier date for a play on which it was based. Honigmann's argument for dating *King John* in 1590 has not won acceptance.

If, on the other hand, we accept the argument that Shakespeare was substantially rewriting an earlier play on King John, the pattern of his indebtedness becomes clear on two points: (1) *Troublesome Raigne* was his main though not his only source, and (2) Shakespeare consciously toned down the earlier play's anti-Catholic excesses and scurrilous humor. His characters are more thoughtful and complex, the paradoxes of kingship more disturbing. Shakespeare's alteration of a crude and chauvinistic source play into a subtle exploration of political rule anticipates his similar transformation of the irrepressible *Famous Victories of Henry V* (c. 1586–1587) into the *Henry IV* plays and *Henry V*.

Briefly, some differences between *Troublesome Raigne* and *King John* are as follows. In *Troublesome Raigne*, John is a hero and a martyr for his defiance of Rome. His claim to the English throne is unquestioned. The barons who rise against him are Catholic-inspired. Vice is rampant in monasteries and other Catholic institutions. An abbot is discovered to be hiding a nun in his treasure chest. John is poisoned by a monk who is in league with the abbot and who receives absolution for his deed. The Bastard, John's loyal supporter, is an invincible foe of Catholic corruption and treason. In Shakespeare, on the other hand, John's claim to the throne is dynastically questionable, and his treatment of his nephew Arthur is reprehensible. The barons' opposition to him is prompted by a genuine moral revulsion. Although they learn belatedly that rebellion is more destructive than the evil it seeks to correct, since rebellion provides a fatal opportunity for foreign opportunists like the French Dauphin, the barons are not simply Catholic traitors. The Bastard must struggle too with his conscience over John's treatment of Arthur. The Catholic Church is often guilty of Machiavellianism, as are virtually all the kings and political leaders in the play, but the church shows no signs of moral decadence. John is poisoned by a monk, but without any evidence of conspiracy.

These contrasting estimates of King John reflect two views of him that were held concurrently in Tudor England. One, the older and more critical, is that of medieval historians generally and Polydore

Vergil in particular. The other, a more favorable estimate, is essentially a Protestant defense of John, a rewriting of history in order to view him (despite his failures) as a martyr of Catholic oppression and hence a forerunner of the Reformation. William Tyndale began this revisionist view of John in his *The Obedience of a Cristen Man* (1528). The case was vividly expounded by John Bale in his *King Johan*, a play begun before 1536 and rewritten in 1538 and 1561. Whether the author of *Troublesome Raigne*, or Shakespeare, consulted Bale is uncertain, but the author of *Troublesome Raigne* was certainly heir to the Protestant tradition. John Foxe's *Actes and Monuments* (1583 edition) gave further currency to the Protestant view. Richard Grafton and Raphael Holinshed took a similar line in their chronicles, and thus passed on the tradition to *Troublesome Raigne*.

Shakespeare's play, though based primarily for its materials on *Troublesome Raigne*, adopts the more critical attitude toward John of the older non-Protestant line. Shakespeare also directly consulted (according to Honigmann) Holinshed, Foxe, the *Historia Maior* of Matthew Paris (published 1571), and perhaps the Latin manuscript *Wakefield Chronicle*.

Titus Andronicus

Although we do not today possess any work that Shakespeare could have used for his immediate source in *Titus*, we do have an eighteenth-century chapbook called *The History of Titus Andronicus* that may tell us substantially what that source was like. This chapbook is extensively similar to Shakespeare's play, and its differences (according to Ralph Sargent, in *Studies in Philology*, 1949) can best be explained by the hypothesis that a closely-related prose version served as Shakespeare's chief source. This hypothesis is now generally accepted. Some scholars even argue that the Stationers' Register entry in 1594 to John Danter for "a Noble Roman Historye of Tytus Andronicus" with "the ballad thereof" refers to just such a prose account. Of this we cannot be certain, for Danter did after all publish the play in that same year, and the ballad seems to owe some of its details to the play (though based chiefly on the prose version). Still, the existence of a prose *History of Titus* when Shakespeare wrote his play seems likely.

The prose *History*, as it survives today, is a fictitious medley of revenge stories inspired by Seneca and Ovid. It is set in the last days of the Roman Empire, but contains no recognizable historical characters or events. Titus Andronicus is a Roman senator who defends Rome against the Goths in a protracted ten-year struggle, losing twenty-two of his own sons in the conflict. He slays the Gothic King Tottilius in battle and captures the queen, Attava. When Tottilius' two sons Alaricus and Abonus continue the assault on Rome, the Roman Emperor wearies of the conflict and resolves to marry Attava against the advice of his general, Andronicus. The queen, naturally regarding Titus as an enemy, proceeds to obtain powerful positions for her own kinsmen. She succeeds in having Titus banished, but he is recalled by popular insistence. Attava conducts an amour with her nameless Moorish servant and has a black child by him. Discovery of the child leads to the Moor's banishment, but he too is later recalled. Attava opposes the marriage of Titus' daughter Lavinia to the Emperor's only son (by a former marriage), since she desires the possession of the empire for her own sons. The remainder of the story proceeds much as in the play, except that we do not learn what happens to Rome after Titus' death. Shakespeare's chief additions include Titus' candidacy for and rejection of the throne, the struggle between Saturninus and Bassianus, the sacrifice of Tamora's son Alarbus, and a greatly magnified role for Aaron the Moor.

Although the prose version itself made use of Ovid and Seneca, Shakespeare very probably consulted these authors directly as well. The play contains many explicit references to classical authors, most notably when Lavinia turns the pages of Ovid's *Metamorphoses* to the story of Philomela's rape (IV,i). In Ovid's famous account (book VI,526 ff.), King Tereus of Thrace rapes Philomela, cuts out her tongue (but not her hands) to prevent her from revealing the crime, and keeps her prisoner. She nevertheless manages to weave her story into a tapestry and send it to her sister, Procne, who liberates Philomela and plots with her to serve Tereus' and Procne's son Itys to him at a banquet.

A similar grisly feast takes place in Seneca's *Thyestes*, from which Shakespeare may well have drawn some particulars. Atreus, the wronged avenger, murders the two sons of Thyestes and serves them to him. As in Shakespeare's play, there are two sons rather than one. Of these two sons, one is guilty of ambition, whereas Ovid's Itys is an innocent victim. The slayer is a male avenger, not (as in Ovid) the mother of the slain victim. Senecan conventions of underworld Revenge spirits and the like are also present in the play, though they may have reached Shakespeare by way of Kyd's *The Spanish Tragedy* and other Senecan plays of the late 1580's. Both Ovid and Seneca were commonly taught in Elizabethan grammar schools, though both were also available in English translation: Ovid by Golding (1567) and Seneca by Jasper Heywood (1560). Marlowe's *Tamburlaine* and *The Jew of Malta* certainly had an influence, especially on Shakespeare's conception of Aaron the Moor.

Two continental plays about Titus, the German *Tragaedia von Tito Andronico* (1620) and the Dutch *Aran en Titus* by Jan Vos (1641), were once thought to have been derived from an English play before 1594 which might then have served as a source for Shakespeare. In the German play the name of Titus' son Lucius is Vespasian, and this fact caused scholars to wonder if the "Tittus & Vespasia" acted in April 1592 by Strange's men (as mentioned in Henslowe's diary) was about Titus Andronicus. Lucius' part is small for such prominence in a title, however, and the prevailing opinion today is that Henslowe's play was on an independent subject.

Romeo and Juliet

Shakespeare's chief source for *Romeo and Juliet* was a long narrative poem by Arthur Brooke called *The Tragicall Historye of Romeus and Juliet, written first in Italian by Bandell, and nowe in Englishe by Ar. Br.* (1562). Other English versions of this popular legend were available to Shakespeare, especially in William Painter's *The Palace of Pleasure* (1566), but Shakespeare shows only a passing indebtedness to it. Brooke mentions having seen (prior to 1562) a play about the two lovers, but such an old play is not likely to have been of much service to Shakespeare. Nor does he appear to have consulted extensively the various continental versions that lay behind Brooke's poem. Still, these versions help explain the genesis of the story.

The use of a sleeping potion to escape an unwelcome marriage goes back at least to the *Ephesiaca* of Xenophon of Ephesus (by the fifth century A.D.). Masuccio of Salerno, in his *Il Novellino* (1476), seems to have been the first to combine this sleeping potion story with an ironic aftermath of misunderstanding and suicide (as found in the Pyramus and Thisbe story of Ovid's *Metamorphoses*). In Masuccio's account, the lovers Mariotto and Giannozza of Siena are secretly married by a friar. When Mariotto kills a prominent citizen of Siena in a quarrel, he is banished to Alexandria. Giannozza, to avoid marriage with a suitor of her father's choosing, takes a sleeping potion given her by the friar, and is buried as though dead. She is thereupon taken from the tomb by the friar and sent on her way to Alexandria. Mariotto, however, having failed to hear from her because the messenger is intercepted by pirates, returns in disguise to her tomb where he is discovered and executed. Giannozza, hearing this sad news, retires to a Sienese convent and dies of a broken heart.

In Luigi da Porto's *Hystoria nouellamente ritrouata di due Nobili Amanti* (published c. 1530), based on Masuccio's account, the scene shifts to Verona. Despite the feuding of their two families, the Montecchi and the Cappelletti, Romeo and Guilietta meet and fall in love at a carnival ball. Romeo at once forgets his unrequited passion for a scornful lady. Friar Lorenzo, an experimenter in magic, secretly marries the lovers. Romeo tries to avoid brawling with the Cappelletti, but when some of his own kinsmen suffer defeat, he kills Theobaldo Cappelletti. After Romeo's departure for Mantua, Guilietta's family arranges a match for her with the Count of Lodrone. Friar Lorenzo gives Guilietta a sleeping potion and sends a letter to Romeo by a fellow friar, but this messenger is unable to find Romeo in Mantua. Romeo, hearing of Guilietta's supposed death from her servant Peter, returns to Verona with a poison he already possesses. Guilietta awakens in time to converse with Romeo before he dies. Then, refusing the friar's advice to retire to a convent, she dies by stopping her own breath. This story provides no equivalents for Mercutio and the Nurse, although a young man named Marcuccio appears briefly at the Cappelletti's ball.

Da Porto's version inspired that of Matteo Bandello in his *Novelle* of 1554. Some details are added: Romeo goes to the ball in a vizard, he has a servant named Pietro, a rope ladder is given to the Nurse enabling Romeo to visit Julietta's chamber before their marriage, Romeo obtains a poison from one Spolentino, etc. The young man at the ball, Marcuccio, is now named Mercutio but is still a minor figure. This Bandello version was translated into French by Pierre Boaistuau in his *Histoires Tragiques* (1559); Boaistuau adds the apothecary (who is racked and hanged for his part in the tragedy), and has Romeo die before Juliet awakens and slays herself with Romeo's dagger.

Despite Arthur Brooke's implication on the title page that his version is based on Bandello, the narrative poem *Romeus and Juliet* is taken from Boaistuau. Brooke's is a severely pious work written in "Poulter's Measure," couplets with alternating lines of six and seven feet. Brooke openly disapproves of the lovers' carnality and haste, although fortunately the story itself remains sympathetic to Romeus and Juliet. Brooke stresses the role of star-crossed fortune and the antithesis of love and hate. He reduces Juliet's age from eighteen (as in Bandello) to sixteen. (Shakespeare further reduced her age to less than fourteen.) Brooke's narrative is generally close to Shakespeare's, though with important exceptions. Shakespeare compresses the time scheme from some nine months to a few days. In Brooke, for example, some two weeks elapse between the masked ball and Romeus' encounter with Juliet in her garden, and about two months elapse between the marriage and Tybalt's death. In Shakespeare, Capulet moves the wedding up from Thursday to Wednesday, thereby complicating the time schedule for the lovers. Shakespeare also unifies his play by such devices as introducing Tybalt and Paris early in the story; in Brooke, Tybalt appears only at the time he is slain, and Juliet's proposed marriage to Count Paris emerges as a threat only after Romeus' banishment. Shakespeare's greatest transformation is of the characters. Brooke's Juliet is scheming. His Mercutio remains a shadowy figure as in Bandello et al. Brooke's Nurse is unattractive, although she does occasionally hint at comic greatness: for example, she garrulously confides to Romeus the details of Juliet's infancy, and then keeps Juliet on tenterhooks while she prates about Romeus' fine qualities (ll. 631–714). Even if Shakespeare's play is incomparably superior to Brooke's drably-versified poem, the indebtedness is extensive.

Venus and Adonis

Venus and Adonis was Shakespeare's contribution to the vogue of Ovidian and erotic poetry in the 1580's and '90's that included Thomas Lodge's *Scilla's Metamor-*

phosis (1589), Michael Drayton's *Endimion and Phoebe* (published 1595), Christopher Marlowe's *Hero and Leander* (registered 1593), and John Marston's *Metamorphosis of Pygmalions Image* (1598). On Shakespeare's combining of three passages from Ovid's *Metamorphoses*, see Introduction, pp. 425–426 above. A disdainful Adonis had evidently become a commonplace in the 1590's, for it appears in *Hero and Leander*, ll. 12–14, Spenser's *Faerie Queene*, III,i,35, and elsewhere.

The Rape of Lucrece

Shakespeare's chief source for *The Rape of Lucrece* was Ovid's *Fasti* (II, 721–852), which had not yet been translated into English. He also seems to have known Livy's *History of Rome*, I, 57–59 (which had been translated by William Painter in his *The Palace of Pleasure*, 1566), and Chaucer's *The Legend of Good Women* (which is, like Shakespeare's poem, indebted to Ovid and Livy). Shakespeare's version is considerably longer than any of these sources. Ovid, Livy, and Chaucer give narrative, swift-moving accounts; Shakespeare follows instead the literary tradition of the "Complaint," as in *A Myrroure for Magistrates* and in Samuel Daniel's *The Complaint of Rosamond*.

The Minor Poems

Of the minor poems, the most interesting in terms of sources is "The Phoenix and the Turtle." It is sometimes related to Chaucer's *The Parlement of Fowles*, an allegorical treatment of an assembly of birds. No indebtedness can be proved, however. Instead, as F. T. Price has shown in his Arden edition of *The Poems*, Shakespeare's chief "source" was the very anthology to which he contributed this remarkable piece. Called *Loves Martyr*, assembled by one Robert Chester, it contains some execrable verse but was built around a single vivid and intriguing emblem: the union in death of two mythic birds expressing a love beyond human reason. The idea was sufficiently compelling to attract not only Shakespeare but Jonson, Chapman, and Marston. The cooperation of these highly sophisticated writers may have been prompted by some kind of private joke in the style of "high camp," but Shakespeare's venture into fantasy produced extraordinary results.

The Sonnets

See the Introduction, pp. 468–471 above, for a discussion of the sonnet vogue in England of the 1590's, and the previous history of the sonnet in England and on the continent.

The Merchant of Venice

Shakespeare's chief source for *The Merchant of Venice* was the first story of the fourth day of *Il Pecorone* (The Dunce) by Ser Giovanni Fiorentino. This collection of tales dates from the late fourteenth century but was first published in 1558 at Milan and was not translated into English in Shakespeare's time. Behind Ser Giovanni's story lies an old tradition of a bond given for human flesh, as found in Persia, India, and the Twelve Tables of Roman Law. This legend first appears in English in the thirteenth-century *Cursor Mundi*, with a Jew as the creditor. A thirteenth-century version of the *Gesta Romanorum* adds a romantic love plot, though the evil money-lender in this case is not Jewish. The hero pawns his own flesh to a merchant in order to win a lady. He succeeds on his third attempt, having learned to avoid a magic spell that had previously put him to sleep and cost him a hundred mark of florins. When he goes to pay his forfeit, the lady follows after disguised as a knight and foils the evil merchant with a quibbling distinction between flesh and blood.

Ser Giovanni's story tells of Giannetto, the adventurous youngest son of a Florentine merchant, who goes to live with his father's dearest friend Ansaldo in Venice. This worthy merchant gives him money to seek his fortune at sea. Unbeknownst to Ansaldo, Giannetto twice risks everything to woo the lady of Belmonte, but is twice given a sleeping medicine and is stripped of all his wealth while asleep. Returning destitute to Venice, he is twice forgiven by Ansaldo and given the means to seek his fortune again. For the third such voyage, however, Ansaldo is driven to borrow ten thousand ducats from a Jew on the condition of forfeiting a pound of flesh. This time, one of the lady's maids warns Giannetto not to drink his wine, and he possesses the lady as his wife. Some time later, remembering that the day of Ansaldo's forfeiture has arrived, Giannetto explains the predicament to his wife and is sent by her to Venice with a hundred thousand ducats. He arrives after the forfeiture has fallen due. The lady, however, following after in the disguise of a lawyer, decrees that the Jew may have no blood and must take no more or no less than one pound of flesh. The Jew is jeered at and receives no money. The "lawyer" refuses payment other than the ring Giannetto has received from his lady. Giving it up unwillingly, he returns to Belmonte where his lady vexes him about the ring but finally relents and tells him all. The story provides no casket episode, courtship of Nerissa by Gratiano, elopement of Jessica, or clowning of Launcelot Gobbo. The Jew's motive is not malicious.

Shakespeare may also have known "The Ballad of Gernutus," a popular work that seems to be older than the play. It has no love plot, but dwells on the unnatural cruelty of a Jewish Venetian usurer who takes a bond of flesh for "a merry ieast." Anthony Munday's prose *Zelauto* (1580), though its villain is a Christian rather than a Jewish moneylender, also features a bond of this sort, taken purportedly as a mere sport but with hidden malice. Truculento, the villain, takes the bond of two young men, Rodolfo and his friend Strabino, as surety for a loan. If they forfeit the loan, the young men are to lose their lands and their right eyes as well. The villain has a daughter, Brisana, whom he permits to marry Rodolfo since Truculento expects to marry Rodolfo's sister Cornelia himself. When Cornelia instead marries Strabino, Truculento angrily takes the young men to court to demand his bond. The two brides disguise themselves as scholars and go to court, where they appeal for mercy and then foil Truculento by means of the legal quibble about blood.

Another possible source for the courtroom scene is *The Orator*, translated into English in 1596 from the French of Alexandre Sylvain. An oration, entitled "Of a Jew, who would for his debt have a pound of the flesh of a Christian," uses many specious arguments also employed by Shylock, and is forthrightly confuted in "The Christians Answere."

Shylock's relationship to his daughter finds obvious earlier parallels in Marlowe's *The Jew of Malta* (c. 1589), in which Barabas' daughter Abigail loves a Christian and ultimately renounces her faith, and in *Zelauto*. The actual elopement, however, is closer to the fourteenth story in Masuccio's fifteenth-century *Il Novellino* (not translated in Shakespeare's day).

The casket-choosing episode, not found in *Il Pecorone*, was a widespread legend occurring for example in the story of *Barlaam and Josophat* (ninth-century Greek, translated into Latin by the thirteenth), Vincent of Beauvais' *Speculum Historiale*, the *Legenda Aurea*, Boccaccio's *Decameron* (Day X, Story 1), John Gower's *Confessio Amantis*, and—closest to Shakespeare—the *Gesta Romanorum* (translated into English in 1577 by Richard Robinson and "bettered" by him in 1595). In this last account, the choice is between a gold, silver, and lead casket, each with its own inscription. The first two are like Shakespeare's; the third reads, "Thei that chese me, shulle fynde [in] me that God hathe disposid." The chooser is a maiden, however, and she is not preceded by other contestants.

An old play called *The Jew* is referred to by Stephen Gosson in 1579 as containing "the greedinesse of worldly chusers, and bloody mindes of Usurers." Scholars have speculated that this was a source play for Shakespeare, but actually we have too little to go on for a reliable judgment. Gosson was surely not referring to Robert Wilson's *The Three Ladies of London* (c. 1581), in any case, for its Jewish figure named Gerontus (cf. Gernutus in the ballad) is an exemplary person. Besides, the probable date of this play is later than Gosson's remark.

Much Ado about Nothing

Shakespeare's probable chief source for the Hero-Claudio plot of *Much Ado* was, as C. T. Prouty has demonstrated, the twenty-second story from the *Novelle* of Matteo Bandello (Lucca, 1554). Shakespeare may have read the Italian original as well as François de Belleforest's French translation, *Histoires Tragiques* (1569 edition). The story of the maiden falsely accused was, however, much older than Bandello. Perhaps the earliest that has been found is the Greek romance *Chaereas and Callirrhoe*, fourth or fifth century A.D., in which the hero Chaereas, warned by envious rivals of his wife's purported infidelity, watches at dusk while an elegantly attired stranger is admitted by the maid to the house where Callirrhoe lies. Chaereas rushes madly in and strikes mistakenly at his wife in the dark, but is acquitted of murder when the maid confesses her part in a conspiracy to delude Chaereas. Callirrhoe is buried in a deathlike trance but awakens in time to be carried off by pirates. The story reappears in a fifteenth-century Spanish romance, *Tirante el Blanco*, in which the Princess Blanche is seemingly courted by a repulsive Negro. This Spanish version probably inspired Ariosto's *Orlando Furioso* (1516), Canto V, to which all subsequent Renaissance versions are ultimately indebted.

In Ariosto's account, as translated into English by Sir John Harington (1591), the narrator is Dalinda, maid to the virtuous Scottish Princess Genevra. Dalinda tells how she has fallen guiltily in love with Polynesso, Duke of Albany, an evil man who often makes love to Dalinda in her mistress' rooms but who longs to marry Genevra himself. Consequently, he arranges for Genevra's noble Italian suitor, Ariodante, and Ariodante's brother Lurcanio, to witness the duke's ascent to Genevra's window by a rope ladder. The woman who admits the duke is of course not Genevra but Dalinda disguised as her mistress, having been duped into believing that the duke merely wishes to satisfy his craving for Genevra by making love to her image. Lurcanio publicly accuses the innocent Genevra and offers to fight anyone who defends her cause (cf. Claudio's quarrel with Leonato). The evil duke tries to get rid of Dalinda, but all is finally put to rights by Renaldo (the hero of *Orlando Furioso*) and Ariodante. This account gives an unusually vivid motivation for the maid and the villain—a clearer motivation, in fact, than in Shakespeare's play. A lost dramatic version, *Ariodante and Genevora*, was performed at the English court in 1583.

Shakespeare probably consulted not only Ariosto but also Spenser's *The Faerie Queene* (II,iv), based on Ariosto. Spenser's emphasis is on the blind rage of Phedon, a young squire in love with Claribell. Phedon is tricked by his erstwhile friend Philemon and by Claribell's maid Pryene into believing Claribell false. Pryene's motive in dressing up as Claribell is to prove she is as beautiful as her mistress. When, after having slain Claribell for her supposed perfidy, Phedon learns the truth, he poisons Philemon and furiously pursues Pryene until he is utterly possessed by a mad frenzy.

Shakespeare's greatest debt is, however, to Bandello's story. Here the setting is Messina. Fenicia, the daughter of Lionato de' Lionati (cf. Shakespeare's Leonato), wins the love of Sir Timbreo, a knight in the service of King Piero of Arragon (cf. Shakespeare's Don Pedro of Arragon). As is the custom, Timbreo seeks Fenicia's hand in marriage through the matchmaking offices of a noble emissary. Unfortunately, Timbreo's friend Girondo also falls in love with

Fenicia and plots with a mischief-loving courtier (cf. Don John) to poison Timbreo's mind against Fenicia. Girondo escorts Timbreo to a garden where they see Girondo's servant, elegantly dressed, enter Fenicia's window. No maid takes part in the ruse, however, nor indeed is any woman seen at the window. When Fenicia is wrongly accused, she falls into a deathlike trance and is pronounced dead by a doctor, but is revived. Her father, believing in her innocence, sends her off to a country retreat and circulates the report that she is in fact dead. Soon both Timbreo and Girondo are stricken with remorse. Timbreo magnanimously spares his friend's life, and both confess the truth to Fenicia's family. A year later, Timbreo marries a wife chosen for him by Lionato, who turns out of course to be Fenicia. Girondo marries her sister Belfiore.

A lost play, *Panecia* (1574–1575), may have been based on Bandello's work. One other version Shakespeare may have known is George Whetstone's *The Rocke of Regard* (1576), based on Ariosto and Bandello. It contains a suggestive parallel to Claudio's rejection of Hero in church. Various Italian plays in the tradition of Pasqualigo's *Il Fedele* (1579), and also a version perhaps by Munday, *Fedele and Fortunio* (published 1585), are analogous in situation, though Shakespeare need not have known any of them.

For the Beatrice-Benedick plot no source has been discovered, apart from Shakespeare's own earlier fascination with wit-combat and candid wooing in *Love's Labour's Lost* and *The Taming of the Shrew*. Nor has a plausible source been found for Dogberry and the watch.

The Merry Wives of Windsor

The Merry Wives is indebted to no single source that combines the various elements found in the play: the courtship of Anne Page, the hoodwinking of Falstaff by the merry wives, the horse-stealing business, and the various "humours" portraitures. Nor in fact does any one element derive from a single source. The entire play is brilliantly improvised.

Many analogues exist to the courtship of Anne Page, for it is essentially a Plautine sort of plot in which parents and unwelcome wooers are outwitted by resourceful young people. The Bianca-Lucentio plot of Shakespeare's own *The Taming of the Shrew* is a good enough instance. Similarly, analogues have been found to the discomfiture of Falstaff. In Ser Giovanni Fiorentino's *Il Pecorone* (Day 1, Novelle 2), for example, a student twice cuckolds the very professor who is instructing him in the art of love. Comically, the student reports back to the professor at every turn and is coached in his next move. He doesn't know that the lady is the professor's wife, but the professor begins to suspect and so follows after. On the first occasion the student escapes detection by hiding under a pile of newly washed linen. The second time he slips out the door, whereupon the neighbors arrive and, finding no intruder, berate the professor for his mad suspicions. The wife's brothers even search the linen pile at the professor's suggestion but find nothing. They thrash the professor and chain him up as a madman. Next day, intending once again to report to the professor what had happened, the student discovers the truth. This version differs markedly from Shakespeare's in that the husband is the chief comic butt. Nevertheless Shakespeare may well have known it. Although *Il Pecorone* was not translated into English in the sixteenth century, Shakespeare had already used it as his chief source for *The Merchant of Venice*.

In "Two Lovers of Pisa" from *Tarletons Newes Out of Purgatorie* (1590), the husband is again the one who is duped. An old doctor, wedded to a beautiful young wife, becomes by chance the confidential adviser of a young man who has fallen in love with the wife. The young man reports to the husband his successes and plans in detail. The lover thrice escapes detection (when warned by the lady's maid of the husband's approach) by hiding in a vat of feathers, in a false ceiling, and in an old chest full of legal documents. When on the third occasion the jealous husband sets fire to his own house, the lover is saved by the husband's order to carry out the chest of documents. At last the lover reveals his knowledge of the husband's identity, and everyone laughs at the old fool. Elsewhere, Tarleton's book has suggestive references to Robin Goodfellow and other prankish spirits that may have influenced the concluding scene of *The Merry Wives*.

The story "Of Two Brethren and Their Wives" in *Riche his Farewell to Militairie profession* (1581) features two wives, one of "light disposition" and much given to adultery, the other a tedious scold. The first wife desires to rid herself of her two erstwhile lovers, a doctor and a lawyer, in order to enjoy a new liaison with a soldier. Accordingly she pretends to encourage the lawyer's advances, but when the lawyer comes to her she feigns the approach of her husband and enjoins the lawyer to hide in a large mail bag. Meanwhile, the merry wife has arranged for the doctor to come and pick up the mail bag, on the assumption that she will be hiding in it. The doctor thus carries off the lawyer, nearly suffocating from his close confinement, into the country, where the doctor expects to enjoy his rendezvous. Instead, the soldier accosts them, cudgeling first the body in the bag and then the seeming porter. The lawyer is no less astonished to discover where he has arrived than is the doctor to discover what he has been carrying.

For the background of Shakespeare's horse-stealing episodes and "humours" portraits, see Introduction pp. 558–560 above. The explicit comparison between Falstaff's ludicrous fate in Windsor Forest and the legend of Actaeon is ultimately indebted to Ovid's *Metamorphoses*, III,138–252. Actaeon, grandson of Cadmus and a mighty hunter, happens to disturb Diana and her nymphs while they are bathing naked. Transformed by the vengeful Diana into a horned stag, he is hunted to death by his own hounds.

As You Like It

Shakespeare's chief source for *As You Like It* was Thomas Lodge's graceful pastoral romance, *Rosalynde: Euphues Golden Legacie* (1590). Lodge was indebted in turn to *The Tale of Gamelyn*, a fourteenth-century poem wrongly included by some medieval scribes as "The Cook's Tale" in Chaucer's *Canterbury Tales*. *Gamelyn* was not printed until 1721, but Lodge clearly had access to a manuscript of it. Although Shakespeare may not have known it directly, his play still retains the hearty spirit of this Robin Hood legend. (In later Robin Hood ballads, Gamelyn or Gandelyn is identified with Will Scarlet, a member of Robin Hood's band.)

Gamelyn, the youngest of three brothers, is denied his inheritance by his churlish eldest brother John. When Gamelyn demands his rights, John orders his men to beat Gamelyn, but the young man arms himself with a pestle and proves a formidable fighter. After defeating the champion wrestler in a local wrestling match (a lower-class sport befitting the social milieu of this story), Gamelyn returns home to find himself locked out by his brother. He kills the porter, flings the man's body down a well, and feasts his companions day and night for a week. John feigns a reconciliation and slyly asks if he can bind Gamelyn hand and foot merely to satisfy an oath he has sworn over the death of the porter. Gamelyn trustingly agrees and is made prisoner. After his bonds have been secretly loosed by Adam the Spencer (the steward), Gamelyn pretends to remain bound until the propitious moment for revenge and escape. The moment arrives during a feast of monks who churlishly refuse to help Gamelyn. With Adam's help he fells many of them, ties up his brother, and escapes to the woods where he and Adam are rescued from hunger by a band of merry outlaws. As their chief, Gamelyn becomes a champion of the poor and an enemy of rich churchmen. His brother, now sheriff, brands Gamelyn an outlaw and manages to imprison him, but Gamelyn's second brother, Sir Ote, stands bail for him. On the day of the trial, Gamelyn frees Sir Ote and hangs the sheriff and the jury. Gamelyn finally obtains his inheritance and becomes chief officer of the king's royal forests. This story is uninfluenced by the pastoral tradition and contains no love plot. Its Robin Hood traditions are very much present, nonetheless, in Shakespeare's contrasting portrayal of a tyrannical court and of a just society in banishment.

Lodge retains the primitive vigor of *Gamelyn*, but adds generous infusions of pastoral sentiment in the manner of Sidney's *Arcadia* and sententious moralizing in the manner of John Lyly's *Euphues*. The style is also heavily influenced by Lyly's exquisitely balanced, antithetical, and ornamented prose. For his pastoralism Lodge was indebted not only to Sidney but to the ancient pastoral tradition that included the Greek Theocritus and the Roman Virgil, the Italian Sannazaro (*Arcadia*) and the Portuguese Jorge de Montemayor (*Diana*). Pastoralism by Lodge's time had become thoroughly imbued with artificial conventions: abject lovers writing sonnets to their disdainful mistresses, princes and princesses in shepherds' disguise, idealized landscapes, stylized debate as to the relative merits of love and friendship, youth and age, city life and country life, and so on. Some of these conventions were derived also from the vogue of sonneteering and can thus be described as the stereotypes of "Petrarchism." Lodge accepts these conventions at face value and gives us typically pastoral lovers even in his hero and heroine, although the elements he derived from *Gamelyn* certainly add a contrasting note of violence and danger.

Lodge's account begins much like that of *Gamelyn*. Saladyne, the envious eldest brother, bribes the champion wrestler to do away with Rosader (Orlando) in the wrestling match. Rosader succeeds instead in killing the wrestler and in winning the heart of Rosalynde, daughter of the banished King Gerismond. When she sends him a jewel, Rosader is not at all at a loss for words; indeed, he composes a Petrarchan sonnet on the spot. The usurping King Torismond (no relation to Gerismond), despite his evil nature, is impressed by Rosader's grace and martial prowess. Rosader returns home with friends, breaks open the door and feasts his company. The wily Saladyne overwhelms Rosader in his sleep and binds him to a post, but Rosader is untied by Adam and makes havoc among the eldest brother's guests as in *Gamelyn*. In this case, however, the guests are Saladyne's kindred and allies, all of whom have refused to help Rosader. The Sheriff tries to arrest Rosader and Adam, but they make good their escape to the Forest of Arden (near Lyons in France). They are saved from starvation by the kindly King Gerismond and his exiled followers. Rosalynde and King Torismond's daughter Alinda have meanwhile been banished from court and have taken abode in the forest under the names of Ganymede and Aliena. They befriend old Corydon (Corin) and young Montanus (Silvius) who is hopelessly in love with the haughty Phoebe. "Ganymede" poses as a woman to test Rosader in his wooing, and they are joined in a mock-marriage. Saladyne, now repenting of his evil deeds, comes to the forest, is saved by his brother from a lion, and falls in love with Alinda (whom he helps to rescue from ruffians). The denouement is as in Shakespeare, although the triumphant return to society is more complete: King Torismond is slain, Gerismond is restored to his throne, Rosader is named heir-apparent, and all the friends are appropriately rewarded.

Despite Shakespeare's extensive indebtedness to this charming romance, there is a crucial difference: Lodge's pastoral world is never subjected to a wry or satirical exploration. Lodge offers no equivalent for Touchstone, the fool who sees the absurdity of both country and city, Jaques the malcontent traveler, William and Audrey the clownishly simple peasants, or Sir Oliver Martext the ridiculous hedge-priest. Nor does Lodge tell of Le Beau, the court butterfly. Shakespeare's added characters are virtually all foils to the conventional pastoral vision he found in his source.

Twelfth Night

John Manningham's description of a performance of *Twelfth Night* on February 2, 1602, at the Middle Temple, compares the play to Plautus' *The Menaechmi* and to an Italian play called *Inganni*. The comment offers a helpful hint on sources. *The Menaechmi* had been the chief source for Shakespeare's earlier *The Comedy of Errors*, and that farce of mistaken identity clearly resembles *Twelfth Night* in the hilarious mix-ups resulting from the confusion of two look-alike twins. Shakespeare undoubtedly profited from his earlier experimenting with this sort of comedy. *Twelfth Night* had no need to be directly indebted to *The Menaechmi*, however, for Renaissance Italian comedy offered many imitations of Plautus from which Shakespeare could have taken his *Twelfth Night* plot. These include *Gl'Inganni* (1562) by Nicolò Secchi, another *Gl'Inganni* (1592) by Curzio Gonzaga, and most importantly an anonymous *Gl'Ingannati* (published 1537). This last play was translated into French by Charles Estienne as *Les Abusés* (1543), and adapted into Spanish by Lope de Rueda in *Los Engaños* (1567). A Latin version, *Laelia*, based on the French, was performed at Cambridge in the 1590's but never printed. Obviously, *Gl'Ingannati* was widely known, and Manningham was probably referring to it in his diary. To trace Shakespeare's own reading in this matter is difficult, owing to the large number of versions available to him, but we can note the suggestive points of comparison in each.

Both *Inganni* plays feature a brother and a sister mistaken for one another. In the later of these plays (by Gonzaga, 1592), the sister uses the disguise name of "Cesare." In Secchi's *Inganni* (1562), the disguised sister is in love with her master, who is told that a woman the exact age of his supposed page is secretly in love with him. Another play by Secchi, *L'Interesse* (1581), has a comic duel involving the disguised heroine. Of the Italian plays here considered, however, *Gl'Ingannati* (1537) is closest to Shakespeare's play. A short prefatory entertainment included with it in most editions features the name Malevolti. In the play itself, the heroine Lelia disguises herself as a page in the service of Flaminio, whom she secretly loves, and is sent on embassies to Flaminio's disdainful mistress Isabella. This lady falls in love with "Fabio," as Lelia calls herself. Lelia's father Virginio, learning of her disguise and resolving to marry her to old Gherardo (Isabella's father), seeks out Lelia but instead mistakenly arrests her long-lost twin brother, Fabrizio, who has just arrived in Modena. Fabrizio is locked up as a madman in Isabella's room, whereupon Isabella takes the opportunity to betroth herself to the person she mistakes for "Fabio." A recognition scene clears up everything and leads to the marriages of Fabrizio to Isabella and Flaminio to Lelia. This story lacks the subplot of Malvolio, Sir Toby et al. Nor is there a shipwreck.

Bandello based one of the stories in his *Novelle* (1554) on *Gl'Ingannati*, and this prose version was then translated into French by Belleforest in his *Histoires Tragiques* (1579 edition). Shakespeare may well have read both, for he consulted these collections of stories in writing *Much Ado about Nothing*. His most direct source, however, seems to have been the story "Of Apolonius and Silla" in *Riche his Farewell to Militarie profession* (1581), derived from Belleforest. Its heroine, Silla, is washed ashore near Constantinople, where, disguised as "Silvio," she takes service with Duke Apolonius. When she is sent on embassies to the lady Julina, this wealthy widow falls in love with "Silvio." The real Silvio, her twin brother, arrives and is invited by Julina to a dinner rendezvous. The next day he departs on his quest for Silla, leaving Julina pregnant. When Apolonius learns of "Silvio's" apparent success with Julina, he throws the page into prison and angrily charges him with hateful abominations. Julina is understandably distressed to learn that the supposed father of her child is in actuality a woman. Finally all is resolved when Silvio returns to marry Julina. The story has only the merest hint of a Malvolio subplot. Shakespeare has minimized the moral predicaments in his source: Sebastian does not get Olivia with child before their marriage, nor does he desert her. Correspondingly, Viola is not thrown into prison. Shakespeare studiously avoids Riche's stern moralizing about the bestiality of lust. He changes the setting to Illyria, though in fact the flavor is Elizabethan English.

Shakespeare's reading may also have included the anonymous play *Sir Clyomon and Sir Clamydes* (c. 1570–1583), Sidney's *Arcadia* (1590), and Emmanuel Forde's prose romance *Parismus* (1598) in which one "Violetta" borrows the disguise of a page. The Malvolio plot may conceivably have reflected an incident at court in which the Comptroller of the Household, Sir William Knollys, interrupted a noisy party late at night dressed only in his nightshirt and a pair of spectacles, with a copy of Aretine in his hand. A similar confrontation between revelry and sobriety occurred in 1598: Ambrose Willoughby quieted a disturbance after the queen had gone to bed, and was afterwards thanked by her for doing his duty. Such incidents were no doubt common, however, and there is no compelling reason to suppose Shakespeare was sketching from real-life situations.

Richard the Second

Shakespeare's primary source for *Richard II* was the 1587 edition of Holinshed's *Chronicles* covering the years 1398 to 1400. As in his earlier *Henry VI* plays and *Richard III*, Shakespeare departs from historical accuracy in the interests of artistic design. Queen

Isabel's part is almost wholly invented, for historically she was a child of eleven at the time the events in this play occurred. Her "Garden Scene" is a fine piece of invention, bringing together images of order and disorder that are woven into the rest of the play. The Duchess of York's role is entirely original; Holinshed reports the scene in which York's son Aumerle (the Earl of Rutland) rides to the king and begs for mercy while his father simultaneously denounces him as a traitor, but the Duchess is never mentioned. Shakespeare has added the poignant conflict between husband and wife. Northumberland's role as conspirator against Richard and as hatchetman for Bolingbroke is greatly enlarged; for example, Holinshed never names the persons who engage in the original plotting against Richard. Another invention is the meeting between John of Gaunt and the Duchess of Gloucester (I,ii). In fact, most of Gaunt's character and behavior has no basis in Holinshed at all. Shakespeare creates him to fill the role of thoughtfully conservative statesman, agonized by his son's banishment but doggedly obedient to his monarch. Finally, and most importantly, Shakespeare has greatly enlarged the role and the poetic nature of King Richard, especially in the final two acts.

Many of these alterations are Shakespeare's own; others derive from his reading in other sources. Samuel Daniel's *The First Fowre Bookes of the Civile Wars*, 1595, may have had an important influence. Although we cannot discount the possibility that Shakespeare's play may have been written first, the consensus today is that he knew Daniel's poem. It gave him the idea of the queen's maturity and grief (although not the Garden Scene), and the final meeting of king and queen. Daniel's Hotspur is unhistorically a young man, as in II,iii of Shakespeare's play. Like Shakespeare, Daniel sees York as a man of "a mild temperateness." Daniel's Richard and Bolingbroke ride together into London, not separately as in Holinshed. In Daniel's poem, Bolingbroke's indirect manner of insinuating his desire for Richard's death ("And wisht that some would so his life esteeme As rid him of these feares wherein he stood") is verbally close to Shakespeare's depiction of this scene. Richard's final soliloquies in these two works show an unmistakable similarity to one another.

Richard II's reign was an explosively controversial subject in the 1590's, and produced other plays of varying political coloration that Shakespeare must have known. *The Life and Death of Jack Straw* (anonymous, 1590–1593) gives a distortedly friendly portrait of Richard in his handling of the Peasants' Revolt of 1381, with a blatant whitewashing of governmental policy. Contrastingly, the anonymous play *Thomas of Woodstock*, sometimes known as *1 Richard II* (1591–1595), is almost a rallying cry to open rebellion against tyranny. Many verbal echoes link this latter play with Shakespeare's *Richard II*, and, although scholars have difficulty in determining which was written first, the wary consensus is that Shakespeare borrowed from *Woodstock*. Such a hypothesis would explain some of the mysterious references to Woodstock's death in the first act of *Richard II*, since the anonymous play deals with historical events preceding those of Shakespeare's play. Shakespeare's debt to *Jack Straw*, on the other hand, is slight even though he probably knew it. Marlowe's *Edward II* (c. 1592), although dealing with another reign, probably taught Shakespeare much about construction of a play in which a deplorably weak king gains sympathy in his suffering while his successful deposer becomes morally tainted by his act.

Other sources have been proposed, so many in fact that Shakespeare's task of writing the play has been compared to that of a historical researcher. More probably he had read several possible sources at one time or another and assimilated them without any formal program of research. He had certainly read Edward Hall's *Union of the Two Noble Famelies*, a chief source for his earlier history plays, but in *Richard II* he seems to have recalled little more than its overall thematic pattern. Shakespeare must have known the complaints of Mowbray and Richard in *A Myrroure for Magistrates*, but the verbal echoes are slight in this case. The same is essentially true of *The Cronycles of Englande* by John Froissart, translated by Lord Berners (1525), and two French eye-witness accounts available to Shakespeare only in manuscript: the anonymous *Chronicque de la Traïson et Mort de Richart Deux Roy Dengleterre* and Jean Créton's *Histoire du Roy d'Angleterre Richard*. The Froissart *Cronycles* perhaps give some hints for Gaunt's refusal to avenge Gloucester's death, for Richard's insensitivity at Gaunt's death, and for Northumberland's role as conspirator. The *Traïson* is notably sympathetic to Richard in his decline, although Shakespeare might also have found this sympathy in Daniel's *Civile Wars*.

Shakespeare's second tetralogy is considerably less wedded to Tudor orthodoxy than his first, less intent on proving a providential design in England's suffering. The second tetralogy does not lead forward by any direct link to the reign of the Tudors, as the first had done. Henry A. Kelly has recently shown (*Divine Providence in the England of Shakespeare's Histories*, 1970), that Shakespeare does not follow a single "Tudor myth" but allows spokesmen for both pro-Lancastrian and anti-Lancastrian sentiment to repeat arguments found in the various chronicles. This practice is especially evident in *Richard II*, in which some spokesmen eloquently warn of the disasters that will follow Bolingbroke's assumption of the throne, while other spokesmen are sympathetic to Bolingbroke's takeover as a political necessity.

The Henry the Fourth Plays

Shakespeare's chief source of information for both *Henry IV* plays was the 1587 edition of Holinshed's *Chronicles*, but Shakespeare also found an important guiding spirit in Samuel Daniel's *The First Fowre*

Bookes of the Civile Wars (1595). Following Daniel, Shakespeare readjusts the age of Hotspur (who was historically older than Henry IV) to match that of Prince Hal. Daniel's Hotspur is, like Shakespeare's, dauntless and wrongheaded, a turbulent yet noble spirit. The theme of a Nemesis of rebellion afflicting Henry IV for his usurpation owes much to Daniel's presentation, although the idea of Nemesis is to be found also in Holinshed. Both Daniel and Holinshed err in confusing the Edmund Mortimer whom Glendower captured with his nephew Edmund Mortimer, claimant to the throne; Shakespeare perpetuates this error. Hal's killing of Hotspur is unhistorical, since both Holinshed and Daniel report only that Hal bravely helped rescue his father from attack, and that Hotspur was killed in the melee. Shakespeare invents the scenes in which we see Mortimer as a devoted husband and Hotspur as a fond wit-combatant with his wife Kate; Holinshed merely informs us that these two men were married. Shakespeare greatly expands Glendower's fascination with magic and poetry, changing him from a ruthless barbarian (in Holinshed) into a cranky but charismatic Welshman. Hotspur, despite hints from Daniel, is chiefly Shakespeare's creation. In *2 Henry IV*, Shakespeare puts Northumberland in a more dishonorable position than in Holinshed, and vastly emphasizes the perfidious dastardy of Prince John. Seemingly, Shakespeare wanted to stress the coldness and cynicism of Machiavellian politicians on both sides of the rebellion, as a contrast with the more enlightened policy to which Prince Hal must aspire.

The most impressive transformations are those of Hal and Falstaff. Shakespeare knew many legends of Hal's wild youth, some of them probably from John Stow's *The Chronicles of England* (1580) and *The Annales of England* (1592), others doubtlessly from oral tradition. Sir Thomas Elyot's *The Governour* (1531) gives an account of Hal's encounter with the Lord Chief Justice that is reproduced almost verbatim by Stow. Most of these stories were also available in Holinshed. Shakespeare's readiest source, however, was a rowdy and chauvinistic play called *The Famous Victories of Henry the Fifth*, registered 1594 but usually ascribed to Richard Tarleton around 1587 or 1588. This play covers all the events of the *Henry IV* plays and *Henry V* in one chaotic sequence. Prince Hal has three companions, Sir John Oldcastle, Tom, and Ned (cf. Ned Poins), in whose company he robs the king's receivers of £1,000, visits the old tavern in East Cheap, sorely grieves his father, and strikes the Lord Chief Justice. A crucial difference is that this Hal is truly unregenerate. He not only robs and wenches, but endorses the idea of plundering the rich and encourages his companions to look forward to unrestricted license when he is king. The blow he delivers the Chief Justice is a blow for freedom. Hal seems actively to desire his father's death. Yet he does reform, and banishes his companions beyond a ten-mile limit with a promise to assist them if they mend their ways. Although this reform is crude and sudden, Hal's reputation for the common touch stands him in good stead when he goes to war against the French. He is followed by a comic crew of London artisans and thieves who prove invincible against the effete enemy.

This play suggests the unsophisticated nature of the legends Shakespeare inherited about Hal's riotous youth, and the extent of the transformation. Shakespeare invents entirely Mistress Quickly and Doll Tearsheet. Pistol bears only the faintest resemblance to any of the rowdies in the anonymous play. Shallow and Silence have no counterparts in Shakespeare's sources, although *Famous Victories* does show a farcical scene of impressment. Most of all, Shakespeare's portrayal of Falstaff is essentially his own. Sir John Oldcastle of the anonymous play is a minor character, not even Hal's closest companion. To an extent, Falstaff owes something to the tradition of the guileful and inventive Vice of the Tudor morality play (especially when Falstaff is called jestingly "that reverend vice, that grey iniquity"), but the morality play influence is general rather than specific. To label Falstaff a "Vice" is to reduce him to comic tempter and villain. Falstaff is partly also an allowed fool, a parasite, and a *miles gloriosus* or braggart soldier, but he transcends all these conventionalized types with his own unique vitality.

The *Henry IV* plays may also reveal some acquaintance with the anonymous play *Thomas of Woodstock* (c. 1591–1595), which Shakespeare may also have used in *Richard II*, and with the complaints of Owen Glendower and Northumberland in *A Myrroure for Magistrates* (1559). In neither case is the debt extensive.

Henry the Fifth

Shakespeare's principal source of information for *Henry V*, as for *Richard II* and the *Henry IV* plays, was the 1587 edition of Holinshed's *Chronicles*. In his account of Henry V, however, Raphael Holinshed had depended so heavily on Edward Hall's *The Union of the Two Noble and Illustre Famelies of Lancastre and Yorke* (1548) that we sometimes have difficulty knowing whether Shakespeare consulted Holinshed or Hall. He was certainly familiar with both. Shakespeare's sources were unanimous in acclaiming Henry V as a hero-king. Samuel Daniel's *The First Fowre Bookes of the Civile Wars* (1595), which Shakespeare may have used for his account of the treasonous plot against Henry (II,ii), also praises the king in fulsome terms.

Shakespeare follows the order of events laid down in Holinshed and Hall: the personal rivalry between Henry and the French Dauphin, Henry's request for reassurance from the clergy as to the legitimacy of the war, the maneuvering of the clergy to forestall a bill in Parliament threatening to seize many of their lands, the foiling of a plot against Henry's life, the siege of Harfleur, the glorious victory at Agincourt. Both Holinshed and Hall offer Shakespeare many particulars about the English claim to France: in both accounts, the archbishop quotes the law *In terram Salicam mulieres ne succedant,* and goes on lengthily about King Pharamond, the rivers Elbe and Sala, King Pepin, Hugh Capet, the Book of Numbers, and the rest. On the other hand, Shakespeare omits a three-year campaign that historically intervened between Agincourt and the peace treaty of Troyes. He passes over the Lollard controversy in England, with the execution of Sir John Oldcastle. And, of course, he adds unforgettable characters that we do not find in the chronicles—Welshmen, Irishmen, Scots, common soldiers, thieves—who show the unity of the British nation under King Henry's charismatic leadership.

For many of his additions to the chronicles, Shakespeare was indebted to the anonymous *The Famous Victories of Henry the Fifth* (c. 1588). This old play, not registered until 1594 and not printed until 1598, exists today only in a corrupt text; quite possibly Shakespeare knew a fuller and more authentic version that would have given him still more material. Other plays may have existed on the subject, for the Admiral's men acted a "harey the v" in 1595 and 1596 that may or may not have been *The Famous Victories.* In any event, the relationship between *Henry V* and *Famous Victories* is at times highly suggestive. *Famous Victories* omits Henry's long campaign between Agincourt and the final peace treaty, as does Shakespeare's play. The archbishop of *Famous Victories* discusses the French claim just before the arrival of the French ambassador with the tennis balls. (In Holinshed, the tennis-ball incident occurs first, at Kenilworth, whereas the archbishop's lecture occurs some time later at a meeting of Parliament in Leicester.) Henry assures the French ambassador that he has "free libertie and license to speake." To the Dauphin's insolent gift, taunting Henry about his wild youth, the king suavely replies that "My lord prince Dolphin is very pleasaunt with me," and promises to repay the insult with balls of brass and iron. (Holinshed mentions this apparently nonhistorical legend only briefly.) When the French noblemen assembled at the French court hear of Henry's arrival on their shores, they tremble with fear even though the Dauphin recklessly scoffs at so young and wild-headed a king. Henry is accompanied to France by a ludicrous assortment of London artisans and thieves, such as John Cobler, who bids farewell to his wife in a comic scene reminiscent of Pistol's parting from the Hostess, and Dericke, who comically turns the tables on a French soldier much as Pistol deals with Monsieur le Fer. When King Henry wooes Katharine of France, he protests to her that he cannot speak flatteringly because he is a plain soldier. She asks in return: "How should I love him, that hath dealt so hardly With my father?" Despite these resemblances, however, Shakespeare's *Henry V* is incomparably superior to the old play and contains many original scenes and characters such as King Henry's touring of his camp incognito, the quarrel between Henry and Williams, and above all the scenes involving Fluellen and his fellow-captains.

Other possible sources that have been suggested include the *Henrici Quinti Angliae Regis Gesta* written by a chaplain in Henry v's army, the *Vita et Gesta Henrici Quinti* erroneously ascribed to Thomas Elmham, the *Vita Henrici Quinti* by "Titus Livius," translated 1513 (in which the French brag about their horses and armor), a ballad called "The Battle of Agincourt" (c. 1530), and *The Annals of Cornelius Tacitus,* translated 1598 (in which Germanicus walks disguised through his camp at night "to sounde the souldiers minde," and hears his leadership praised).

Julius Caesar

Julius Caesar represents Shakespeare's first extensive use of Plutarch, in Thomas North's translation (based on the French of Jacques Amyot) of the *Lives of the Noble Grecians and Romanes* (1579 and 1595). Plutarch was to become Shakespeare's most often-used source in the 1600's, even though prior to 1599 he had consulted it only briefly for information on Theseus in *A Midsummer Night's Dream.* In *Julius Caesar,* he borrows many details from three lives: Caesar, Brutus, and Antonius. He uses many particular traits of character, such as Caesar's belief that it is "better to dye once, then alwayes to be affrayed of death," Brutus' determination to "frame his manners of life by the rules of virtue and study of philosophy," Cassius' choleric disposition and his "hating Caesar privately more than he did the tyranny openly," and Antonius' inclination to "rioting and banqueting."

The events of the play are substantially present in Plutarch, especially in the Life of Julius Caesar. Antonius runs the course on the feast of Lupercal to cure barrenness, and offers the diadem to Caesar. Flavius and Marullus despoil the images of Caesar. Caesar observes that he mistrusts "pale and lean men" like Brutus and Cassius, not "fat fellows." Papers are thrown by the conspirators where Brutus can find them, proclaiming "Thou sleepest, Brutus, and art not Brutus indeed." Caesar's death is preceded by prodigies: a slave's hand burns but is unconsumed, a sacrificial beast is found to contain no heart. When Caesar encounters the soothsayer who previously had warned him of his fate, and boasts that "the Ides of March be come," the soothsayer has the last word: "so they be, but yet are they not past." Brutus' wife Portia complains to him of being treated "like a harlot," not like a partner. Brutus commits what Plutarch calls two serious errors when he forbids his fellow-conspirators to kill Antonius, and when he permits Antonius to speak at Caesar's funeral. Cinna the Poet is slain by an angry crowd mistaking him for Cinna the conspirator. A ghost appears to Brutus shortly before the last battle saying "I am thy ill angel, Brutus, and thou shalt see me by the city of Phillippes," to which Brutus replies "Well, I shall see thee then." Antonius says of the vanquished conspirators that "there was none but Brutus only that was moved to do it, as thinking the act commendable of itself: but that all the other conspirators did conspire his death for some private malice or envy." Shakespeare's indebtedness to Plutarch is more extensive than these few examples can indicate.

Of course Shakespeare reshapes and selects, as in his history plays. He compresses into one day Caesar's triumphant procession, the disrobing of the images, and the offer of the crown to Caesar on the Lupercal, when in fact these events were chronologically separate. Casca is by and large an invented character, and Octavius' role is considerably enlarged. Brutus' servant Lucius is a minor but effective addition, illustrating Brutus' capacity for warmth and humanity. Brutus' two speeches after the assassination (as mentioned by Plutarch) become one, and Antonius' speech is made to follow immediately after. (In Plutarch, Antonius speaks the following day, after the reading of the will.) Shakespeare accentuates the irrationality and vacillation of the mob, for in Plutarch the people are never much swayed by Brutus' rhetoric even though they respectfully allow him to speak. The unforgettable speeches of both Brutus and Antonius are not set down at all in Plutarch. More compression of time occurs after the assassination: in Plutarch, Octavius does not arrive in Rome until some six weeks afterward, and does not agree to the formation of the Triumvirate until after more than a year of quarreling has taken place. The inexorable buildup of tension in Shakespeare's play is the result of careful selection from a vast amount of material.

Although Shakespeare depended heavily on Plutarch, he was also aware of later and conflicting traditions about Caesar. On the one hand, Dante's *Divine Comedy* consigns Brutus and Cassius to the lowest circle of hell along with Judas Iscariot and other betrayers of their masters. Chaucer's *Monk's Tale*, from the *Canterbury Tales*, similarly portrays Caesar as the manly and uncorruptible victim of envious attackers. On the other hand, Montaigne stresses the *hubris* of Caesar in aspiring to divinity. (Shakespeare could have read Montaigne in the French original or in John Florio's English translation.) A pro-Brutus view could also be found in the Latin *Julius Caesar* of Marc-Antoine Muret (1553) and the French *César* of Jacques Grévin (1561). That Shakespeare knew these works is unlikely, but they kept alive a tradition with which he was certainly familiar. Possibly he knew Lucan's account of Caesar in the *Pharsalia* and Cicero's letters and orations, which were republican in tenor. Other possible sources that have been suggested include the *Chronicle of the Romanes Warres* by Appian of Alexandria (translated 1578), the anonymous play *Caesar's Revenge* (published 1606–1607, performed in the early 1590's at Oxford), Thomas Kyd's *Cornelia* (translated from the French Senecan tragedy by Garnier), and *Il Cesare* by Orlando Pescetti (1594). The result of Shakespeare's acquaintance with both pro- and anti-Caesar traditions is that he shows much that is both good and deplorable in Caesar and in the conspirators as well.

All's Well that Ends Well

Shakespeare's only known source for *All's Well* is the tale of Giglietta of Nerbone from Boccaccio's *Decameron* (c. 1348–1358), as translated into English by William Painter in *The Palace of Pleasure* (1566, 1575). Painter may have based his translation on a French intermediary by Antoine le Maçon, and Shakespeare possibly knew the Italian and French versions although the English was the most available to him. All three are essentially the same except for the forms of the proper names.

In Painter's account, Giletta is the daughter of Gerardo of Narbona, physician to the ailing Count of Rossiglione. Giletta falls in love with the count's son, Beltramo. When the count dies, Beltramo is "left under the royall custody of the king" and is sent to Paris. Giletta's father dies soon after, and she, refusing many favorable offers of marriage, journeys to Paris and cures the king of a fistula. The king has promised her any husband as her reward, but is loath to give her Beltramo. The young man, no less reluctant, goes through with the marriage ceremony but then escapes into Italy before the marriage is consummated. In Italy he joins the Florentines in a military campaign against the Senois (Sienese). His deserted wife, now countess, returns home and governs the domain of Rossiglione with great skill. When she writes to Beltramo, offering to depart if her presence displeases him, Beltramo sets for her the "impossible" demand of obtaining his ring and begetting a son by him. Hereupon she calls together the leaders of her domain and announces her intention of going on a pilgrimage of renunciation. Despite her people's great lamentation, she departs for Florence where she inquires after Beltramo and discovers that he is paying court to a poor gentlewoman (unnamed) who dwells with her mother. Giletta offers to obtain a dowry for this daughter if she will demand the ring from Beltramo and arrange an assignation so that Giletta may secretly take her place in Beltramo's bed. Beltramo reluctantly agrees to give up the cherished ring, and Giletta becomes his lover on not one but numerous occasions. When she is pregnant, she rewards the daughter with a dowry and then remains living in Florence until she is delivered of two sons. Beltramo has meanwhile been called home by his people. Giletta arrives home in time for a great feast, at which she prostrates herself before Beltramo and proves that she has performed the terms of his "impossible" task. Beltramo is persuaded by her constancy and wit to be true to his promise and reclaim her as his wife.

Shakespeare has retained the folktale spirit of this story, with its ancient motifs of curing the king and of performing impossible tasks. Shakespeare nevertheless provides a significant change of emphasis. He adds characters, such as the Countess of Rousillon and Lafew, whose strong compassion and dignity help us to see more clearly the patient goodness of Helena and the perverse waywardness of Bertram. The king becomes a more significant character, and a spokesman for faith in the miraculous. Lavatch, the countess' fool, quizzically expounds questions of moral consequence that are absent in Painter. Conversely, the added character Parolles highlights the callowness and insensitivity of Bertram, and conveniently serves as a scapegoat when Bertram mends his ways. Shakespeare simultaneously darkens Bertram's character and intensifies Helena's best qualities. Because she is not rich, as in Painter, she represents innate virtue or "gentleness" in contrast with Bertram's hereditary nobility. The king is not reluctant to bestow Helena on Bertram, as in Painter, but is instead astonished at Bertram's willful refusal of so good a fortune. Other courtiers join the king in this sentiment. Accordingly, Helena's request for Bertram's hand in marriage does not seem so presumptuous as in Painter. Bertram is not the wise judge who finally concedes the justice of Helena's claim, as in Painter, but an evasive and self-seeking liar to the very end. Far more than the Beltramo of Painter's tale, Bertram is the unworthy hero of a comedy of forgiveness, spared the consequences of his own worst self by a benign king and a patient wife.

Shakespeare also gives his play a dramatic unity of construction and an economy of time not found in the sources. Characters such as the king and Diana are not introduced and then discarded once their primary role has been discharged, but are brought importantly into the denouement. As in his use of other Italianate fictional sources, Shakespeare compresses the time sequence: for example, Helena vows to cure the king in two days rather than eight (as in Painter), and Helena sleeps with Bertram only once rather than often. No convincing source has been found for the comic exposure of Parolles.

Measure for Measure

Stories about corrupt magistrates are ancient and universal, but Shakespeare's particular story in *Measure for Measure* seems to go back to an actual incident in the sixteenth-century Italian court of Don Ferdinando de Gonzaga. A Hungarian student named Joseph Macarius, writing from Vienna, tells about an Italian citizen accused of murder whose wife submitted to the embraces of the magistrate in hopes of saving her husband. When the magistrate executed her husband despite her having fulfilled her bargain, she appealed to the duke who ordered the magistrate to give her a dowry and marry her. Thereafter the duke ordered the magistrate to be executed. This incident seems to have inspired a Senecan drama by Claude Rouillet called *Philanira* (1556), a French translation of this play (1563), a Novella in the *Hecatommithi* of G. B. Giraldi Cinthio (1565), and a play by Cinthio called *Epitia* (posthumously published in 1583). Shakespeare may have known both the prose and the dramatic versions by Cinthio.

In Cinthio's story, the wise Emperor Maximian appoints his friend Juriste to govern Innsbruck, warning him to rule justly or expect no mercy from the emperor. Juriste rules long and well, to the satisfaction of his master and the people of Innsbruck. When a young man named Vico is brought before him for ravishing a virgin, Juriste assigns the mandatory sentence of death. Vico's sister, Epitia, an extraordinarily beautiful virgin of eighteen, pleads for Vico's life, urging that his deed was one of passion and that he stands ready to marry the girl he forced. The judge, secretly inflamed with lust for Epitia, promises to consider the matter carefully. She reports this seemingly encouraging news to Vico, who urges her to persevere. When, however, the judge proposes to take her chastity in return for her brother's life, Epitia is mortified and refuses unless Juriste will marry her. During another interim in these negotiations, Vico begs his sister to save his life at any cost. She then submits to Juriste on the condition that he will both marry her and spare Vico. Next morning, however, the jailer brings her the body of her decapitated brother. She lays her complaint before the emperor, who confronts Juriste with his guilt. Conscience-stricken, Juriste confesses and begs for mercy. At first Epitia demands strict justice, but when the emperor compels Juriste to marry her and then be beheaded, she reveals "her natural kindness" and begs successfully for the life of her wronger.

Shakespeare may also have consulted Cinthio's play *Epitia*, but his chief source was George Whetstone's two-part play *Promos and Cassandra* (1578). Here the corrupt judge is Promos, administrator of the city of Julio under the King of Hungary. The law forbidding adultery has lain in abeyance for some years when a young gentleman named Andrugio is arrested and condemned for "incontinency." His sister Cassandra, as in Cinthio, lays down her precious chastity in response to her brother's piteous entreaties. Promos gives his assurance that he will marry her and save Andrugio's life. When Promos instead treacherously orders the execution of Andrugio, the jailer secretly substitutes the head of a felon, newly executed and so mutilated as to be unrecognizable even by Cassandra. (This rescue is seen as an intervention "by the prouidence of God.") The king sentences Promos as in Cinthio, but in this play the king refuses Cassandra's pleas for the life of her new husband until Andrugio reveals himself to be still alive and offers to die for Promos. The king forgives Andrugio on condition that he marry Polina, whom he wronged. The play also features a courtesan named Lamia and her man, Rosko, who ingratiate themselves with the corrupt officer (Phallax) in charge of investigating their case. Phallax is ultimately caught and dismissed from office while Lamia is publicly carted. Whetstone wrote a prose version of this story in the *Heptameron of Civill*

Discourses (1582), which Shakespeare may have consulted. Shakespeare was also indebted for a few details to a version in Thomas Lupton's *Too Good to be True* (1581).

Even though Shakespeare's play is closer to Whetstone than to Cinthio, Shakespeare has changed much. He adds the motif of the duke's mysterious disguise. (A not very compelling analogue to this motif occurs in Sir Thomas Elyot's *The Image of Governance*, 1541.) Shakespeare introduces the use of the bed-trick, as in his presumably earlier play *All's Well that Ends Well*. Most importantly, Shakespeare stresses the moral and legal complexity of his story. Isabella is almost a nun, intent on renouncing the world. Conversely Lucio, an invented character, is an engaging cynic, hedonist, and slanderer. Claudio is at best only technically guilty of fornication. Isabella does not surrender her chastity. Her breakdown in the scene with Claudio intensifies her emotional crisis and renders all the more triumphant her final ability to forgive Angelo. Angelo himself is made puritanical in temperament, and is spared the actual consequences of his worst intentions so that he can be worthy of being forgiven. Isabella need not marry Angelo, since he has not actually seduced her; she is thus free to marry the duke. No felon need be executed in Claudio's stead, for providence provides a natural death in the prison. In the subplot, despite hints from Whetstone, Pompey is a brilliantly original innovation, Elbow a characteristically Shakespearean clown modeled on the earlier Dogberry of *Much Ado about Nothing*, and Escalus a significant spokesman for a moderate and practical course of equity in the law.

Troilus and Cressida

Shakespeare had access to Homer for information about the Trojan War, since George Chapman's translation of *The Seaven Bookes of Homers Iliads* had appeared in 1598, and earlier English translations of the entire *Iliad* were also available. Shakespeare ends his play with the death of Hector, as does Homer, and portrays Achilles from a Homeric vantage point. Thersites and Nestor are based ultimately on Homer. Ajax' ludicrous boastfulness may owe something to Homer's Ajax Telamon, as well as to Ovid's account of the quarrel between Ulysses and Ajax over Achilles' armor (*Metamorphoses*, xii–xiii). Yet for Shakespeare and for most Englishmen of his time, the chief sources of information about the Trojan war were medieval romances. These were all pro-Trojan in their bias, since Englishmen traced their own mythic history to the lineage of Aeneas and tended to look on Homer as suspiciously pro-Greek. Medieval European culture generally was far more oriented to Roman than to Greek civilization; Greek texts went almost unread. In these circumstances, a pro-Trojan legend of the war emerged and grew to considerable length.

The central work in this genre was Benoit de Sainte-Maure's *Roman de Troie* (c. 1160), a romance freely based on earlier accounts of supposed eyewitnesses named Dictys the Cretan and Dares the Phrygian. Benoit not only narrates the war from Troy's point of view but introduces the love story of Troilus, "Breseida," and Diomedes. Benoit found a slight hint for this story in the *Iliad*, where two Trojan maidens named Chryseis and Briseis are captured and given to Agamemnon and Achilles respectively. When Chryseis' father calls down a plague on the Greeks for refusing to return Chryseis, Agamemnon reluctantly gives her up but then seizes Briseis from Achilles, thereby precipitating Achilles' angry retirement to his tent and all that disastrously follows. Benoit freely transforms this situation into the rivalry of Troilus and Diomed, who appear in Homer but in entirely different roles.

Benoit's *Roman de Troie* became the inspiration for many subsequent medieval accounts of the Trojan War. Guido delle Colonne translated Benoit in his *Historia Trojana* (completed 1287). Boccaccio based his *Il Filostrato* (c. 1338) on Guido and Benoit, but with significant alterations: the love story became the focus of attention, and Pandarus assumed the important role of go-between. (In Homer, Pandarus is a fierce warrior.) Chaucer based his *Troilus and Criseyde* (c. 1385–1386) on Boccaccio, giving still greater attention to the states of mind of the two lovers and endowing Pandarus with a humorous disposition. Shakespeare certainly knew Chaucer's masterpiece. He also consulted, however, at least two other medieval accounts of the war: John Lydgate's *The Historye Sege and Dystruccyon of Troye* (first printed 1513), based on Guido and Chaucer and known also as the *Troy Book*, and William Caxton's *The Recuyell of the Historyes of Troye* (printed 1474, the first book printed in English), a translation from the French of Raoul Lefevre who had followed Guido rather closely. In Caxton, for example, Shakespeare found materials for the Trojan debate about returning Helen, and for Hector's visit to the Greek camp. In addition, Shakespeare was certainly familiar with the degeneration of Cressida's character since the time of Chaucer, as reflected for example in Robert Henryson's *The Testament of Cresseid* (published 1532), in which Cressida is punished for her faithlessness by leprosy and poverty.

Shakespeare pays a good deal more attention to the war than does Chaucer, and portrays the lovers as caught in a deadening conflict beyond their control. Shakespeare's Cressida is more sardonic and experienced in the ways of the world than is Chaucer's heroine, even though Shakespeare's Cressida is unmarried. The subtle and elaborate code of courtly love evoked by Chaucer has almost completely disappeared, leaving in its wake a more dispiriting impression of wantonness in love. Shakespeare's Troilus is still a faithful and earnest lover, as in Chaucer, but more betrayed by his own chauvinistic ideals about honor and patriotism. Pandarus is more leering, giddy, vapid, and coarse than his Chaucerian counterpart. Diomedes is also changed for the worse, being more hard and cynical.

Among the non-Chaucerian characters, Achilles is made to appear more guilty and brutalized than in any of Shakespeare's sources: Achilles orders his Myrmidons to murder the unarmed Hector, even though Hector had previously spared Achilles in battle. Lydgate and Caxton report that Achilles' Myrmidons kill Troilus, not Hector, whereas in Homer Achilles kills Hector in battle and only then unchivalrously subjects the dead man's body to outrage. Shakespeare deglamorizes the war just as he deglamorizes the love story. He also compresses the time scheme, as he did with so many of his sources. The play begins only a short time before Cressida surrenders to Troilus; she is transferred to the Greeks immediately after she and Troilus become lovers; her surrender to Diomedes follows quickly after her transfer. This telescoping provides not only dramatic unity but a sense of sudden and violent change.

Other plays on Troilus and Cressida are known to have existed, such as a "new" play acted by the Admiral's men in 1596 and another by Dekker and Chettle in 1599. Shakespeare may have known and even written in response to such productions by rival theatrical companies, but nothing is known about these now-lost plays.

Hamlet

The ultimate source of the *Hamlet* story is Saxo Grammaticus' *Historia Danica* (1180–1208), the saga of one Amlothi or (as Saxo calls him) Amlethus. The outline of the story is essentially that of Shakespeare's play, even though the emphasis of the Danish saga is overwhelmingly on cunning, brutality, and bloody revenge. Amlethus' father is Horwendil, a governor of Jutland, who bravely kills the King of Norway in single combat and thereby wins the hand in marriage of Gerutha, daughter of the King of Denmark. This good fortune goads the envious Feng into slaying his brother Horwendil and marrying Gerutha, "capping unnatural murder with incest." Though the deed is known to everyone, Feng invents excuses and soon wins the approbation of the fawning courtiers. Young Amlethus vows revenge, but perceiving his uncle's cunning he feigns madness. His mingled words of craft and candor awaken suspicions that he may be playing a game of deception.

Two attempts are made to lure Amlethus into betraying his sanity. The first plan is to tempt him into lechery, on the theory that one who lusts for women cannot be truly insane. Feng causes an attractive woman to be placed in a forest where Amlethus will meet her as though by chance; but Amlethus, secretly warned of the trap by a kindly foster brother, spirits the young lady off to a hideaway where they can make love unobserved by Feng's agents. She confesses the plot to Amlethus. In a second stratagem, a courtier who is reported to be "gifted with more assurance than judgment" hides himself under some straw in the queen's chamber in order to overhear her private conversations with Amlethus. The hero, suspecting just such a trap, feigns madness and begins crowing like a noisy rooster, bouncing up and down on the straw until he finds the eavesdropper. Amlethus stabs the man to death, drags him forth, cuts the body into morsels, boils the morsels, and flings them "through the mouth of an open sewer for the swine to eat." Thereupon he returns to his mother to accuse her of being an infamous harlot. He wins her over to repentant virtue and even cooperation. When Feng, returning from a journey, looks around for his counselor, Amlethus jestingly (but in part truly) suggests that the man went to the sewer and fell in.

Feng now sends Amlethus to the King of Britain, with secret orders for his execution. However, Amlethus finds the letter to the British king in the coffers of the two unnamed retainers accompanying him on the journey, and substitutes a new letter ordering their execution instead. The new letter, purportedly written and signed by Feng, goes on to urge that the King of Britain marry his daughter to a young Dane being sent from the Danish court. By this means Amlethus gains an English wife and rids himself of the escorts. A year later Amlethus returns to Jutland, gets the entire court drunk, flings a tapestry (knitted for him by his mother) over the prostrate courtiers, secures the tapestry with stakes, and then sets fire to the palace. Feng escapes this holocaust, but Amlethus cuts him down with the king's own sword. (Amlethus exchanges swords because his own has been rendered useless by his enemies.) Subsequently, Amlethus convinces the people of the justice of his cause and is chosen King of Jutland. After ruling for several years, he returns to Britain, marries a Scottish queen, fights a battle with his first father-in-law, is betrayed by his second wife, and is finally killed in battle.

In Saxo's account we thus find the prototypes of Hamlet, Claudius, Gertrude, Polonius, Ophelia, Rosencrantz, and Guildenstern. Several episodes are close in narrative detail to Shakespeare's play: the original murder and incestuous marriage, the feigned madness, the woman used as a decoy, the eavesdropping counselor, and especially the trip to England. A translation of Saxo into French by François de Belleforest, in *Histoires Tragiques* (1576 edition), adds a few details such as Gertrude's adultery before the murder, and Hamlet's melancholy. Belleforest's version is longer than Saxo's, with more psychological and moral observation and more dialogue. Shakespeare may have consulted it.

Shakespeare need not have depended extensively on these older versions of his story, however. His main source was almost certainly an old play of *Hamlet*. Much evidence proves the existence of such a play. Henslowe's *Diary* records a performance, not marked as "new," of a *Hamlet* at Newington Butts on June 11, 1594, by "my Lord Admeralle men" or "my Lorde Chamberlen men," probably the latter. Thomas Lodge's *Wits Miserie, and the Worlds Madnesse* (1596) refers to "the Visard of the ghost which cried so miserably at the Theator, like an oister wife, Hamlet, revenge." And Thomas Nashe, in his *Epistle* prefixed to Greene's *Menaphon* (1589), offers the following observation:

It is a common practise now a dayes amongst a sort of shifting companions, that runne through euery Art and thriue by none, to leaue the trade of *Nouerint*, whereto they were borne, and busie themselues with the endeuours of Art, that could scarcely Latinize their neck verse if they should haue neede; yet English *Seneca* read by Candlelight yeelds many good sentences, as *Blood is a begger*, and so forth; and if you intreate him faire in a frostie morning, hee will affoord you whole *Hamlets*, I should say handfuls of Tragical speeches. But O griefe! *Tempus edax rerum*, whats that will last alwayes? The Sea exhaled by droppes will in continuance bee drie, and *Seneca*, let blood line by line and page by page, at length must needes die to our Stage; which makes his famished followers to imitate the Kidde in Æsop, who, enamoured with the Foxes newfangles, forsooke all hopes of life to leape into a newe occupation; and these men, renouncing all possibilities of credite or estimation, to intermeddle with Italian Translations . . .

Nashe's testimonial describes a *Hamlet* play, written in the Senecan style by some person born to the trade of "Noverint" or scrivener who has turned to hack writing and translation. The description has often been fitted to Thomas Kyd, though this identification is not certain. (Nashe could be punning on Kyd's name when he refers to "the Kidde in Æsop.") Certainly Thomas Kyd's *The Spanish Tragedy* (c. 1587) shows many affinities with Shakespeare's play, and provides many Senecan ingredients missing from Saxo and Belleforest: the ghost, the difficulty in ascertaining whether the ghost's words are believable, the resulting need for delay and a feigning of madness, the moral perplexities afflicting a sensitive man called upon to revenge, the play within the play, the clever reversals and ironically-caused deaths in the catastrophe, the rhetoric of tragical passion. Whether or not Kyd in fact wrote the *Ur-Hamlet*, his extant play enables us to see more clearly what that lost play must have contained. The pirated first quarto of *Hamlet* (1603) also offers a few seemingly authentic details that are not found in the good second quarto but are found in the earlier sources and may have been a part of the *Ur-Hamlet*. For example, after Hamlet has killed Corambis (corresponding to Polonius), the queen vows to assist Hamlet in his strategies against the king; and later, when Hamlet has returned to England, the queen sends him a message by Horatio warning him to be careful.

One last document sheds important light on the *Ur-Hamlet*. A German play, *Der bestrafte Brudermord* (*Fratricide Punished*), from a now-lost manuscript dated 1710, seems to have been based on a text used by English actors traveling in Germany in 1586 and afterwards. Though changed by translation and manuscript transmission, and too entirely different from Shakespeare's play to have been based on it, this German version may well have been based on Shakespeare's source-play. Polonius' name in this text, Corambus, is the same as the Corambis of the bad quarto of 1603.

Der bestrafte Brudermord begins with a prologue in the Senecan manner, followed by the appearance of the ghost to Francisco, Horatio, and sentinels of the watch. Within the palace, meanwhile, the king carouses. Hamlet joins the watch, confiding to Horatio that he is "sick at heart" over his father's death and mother's hasty remarriage. The ghost appears to Hamlet, tells him how the juice of hebona was poured into his ear, and urges revenge. When Hamlet swears Horatio and Francisco to silence, the ghost (now invisible) says several times "We swear," his voice following the men as they move from place to place. Hamlet reveals to Horatio the entire circumstance of the murder. Later, in a formal session of the court, the new king speaks hypocritically of his brother's death and explains the reasons for his marriage to the queen. Hamlet is forbidden to return to Wittenberg, though Corambus' son Leonhardus has already set out for France.

Some time afterward, Corambus reports the news of Hamlet's madness to the king and queen, and presumes on the basis of his own youthful passions to diagnose Hamlet's malady as love-sickness. Concealed, he and the king overhear Hamlet tell Ophelia to "go to a nunnery." When players arrive from Germany, Hamlet instructs them in the natural style of acting, and then requests them to perform a play before the king about the murder of King Pyrrus by his brother. (Death is again inflicted by hebona poured in the ear.) After the king's guilty reaction to the play, Hamlet finds him alone at prayers but postpones the killing lest the king's soul be sent to heaven. Hamlet kills Corambus behind the tapestry in the queen's chamber, and is visited again by the ghost (who says nothing, however). Ophelia, her mind deranged, thinks herself in love with a court butterfly named Phantasmo. (This creature is also involved in a comic action to help the clown Jens with a tax problem.)

The king sends Hamlet to England with two unnamed courtiers who are verbally instructed to kill Hamlet after their arrival. A contrary wind takes them instead to an island near Dover, where Hamlet foils his two enemies by kneeling between them and asking them to shoot him on signal; at the proper moment, he ducks and they shoot one another. He finishes them off with their own swords, and discovers letters on their persons ordering Hamlet's execution by the English king if the original plot should fail. When Hamlet returns to Denmark, the king arranges a duel between him and Corambus' son Leonhardus. If Leonhardus' poisoned dagger misses its mark, a beaker of wine containing finely ground oriental diamond dust is to do the rest. Hamlet is informed of the impending duel by Phantasmo (cf. Osric), whom Hamlet taunts condescendingly and calls "Signora Phantasmo." Shortly before the duel takes place, Ophelia is reported to have thrown herself off a hill to her death. The other deaths occur much as in Shakespeare's play. The dying Hamlet bids that the crown be conveyed to his cousin, Duke Fortempras of Norway, of whom we have not heard earlier.

From the extensive similarities between *Hamlet* and this German play, we can see that Shakespeare inherited his narrative material almost intact, though in a jumble and so pitifully mangled that the modern reader can only laugh at the contrast. No source study in Shakespeare reveals so clearly the extent of Shakespeare's wholesale borrowing of plot, and the incredible transformation he achieved in reordering his materials.

Othello

Shakespeare's main source for *Othello* was the seventh story from the third day of G. B. Giraldi Cinthio's *Hecatommithi*, 1565. Cinthio was available in French but not in English translation during Shakespeare's lifetime. The verbal echoes in Shakespeare's play are usually closer to the Italian original than to Gabriel Chappuys' French version of 1584. Cinthio's account seems to have been based on an actual incident occurring in Venice around 1508.

Cinthio tells of a valiant Moor, highly regarded by the Venetian Republic for his warlike skill, with whom a virtuous and beautiful lady named Disdemona falls in love. She is attracted to him not by physical desire but by his fine qualities. He responds with no less ardor to her beauty and nobleness of mind. Despite her parents' disapproval of such a marriage, they dwell in Venice for some time in peaceful harmony. When the Moor is sent by the Signory of Venice to take command of the garrison on Cyprus, Disdemona insists on accompanying him. Traveling with them on the boat are an Ensign (whom Shakespeare calls Iago), the Ensign's attractive wife (Emilia), and a Captain (Cassio). Disdemona is fond of the young wife; the Moor values the friendship of both the Captain and the Ensign. Beneath the valorous manner of this Ensign, however, lurks an evil heart. He falls passionately in love with Disdemona, and, jealously imagining that she prefers the Captain, resolves to accuse her of adultery with the Captain and thereby destroy them both.

Even before he has time to act, however, the Moor demotes the Captain for wounding a soldier on guard duty. (The Ensign has no part in fomenting this disgrace.) When Disdemona petitions her husband to restore the Captain to his former favor, the Ensign insinuates that she has reasons for pleading thus. The poisonous suggestion does its work. Urged by the tormented Moor to speak candidly of what he knows, the Ensign offers his opinion that Disdemona is tired of the Moor because of his skin color. When the Ensign further affirms that the Captain has confessed making love to Disdemona, the Moor demands ocular proof. This test is not easy for the Ensign, since the lady is in fact so chaste. One day, however, when she is visiting the Ensign's wife and is playing with the Ensign's three-year-old daughter, the Ensign manages to steal from her sash a Moorish handkerchief. She is unhappy to discover it missing, for she knows the Moor often asks her for it. The Ensign drops off the handkerchief at the Captain's house, who finds it, knows it to be Disdemona's, and returns it to her house. Unluckily he hears the Moor coming and runs away, fearing the Moor's continued displeasure. The Moor, sure that he has recognized the Captain running away thus, commissions the Ensign to question the Captain about the matter. The Ensign thereupon engages the Captain in conversation while the Moor is within view but out of earshot; the Ensign discusses idle matters but afterwards affirms to the Moor that the Captain spoke of his love-making and confessed receiving the handkerchief from Disdemona. When the Moor then asks Disdemona for the handkerchief and observes her blushing confusion, he resolves to kill her and the Captain. To confirm further the Captain's possession of the handkerchief, the Ensign takes the Moor past a window of the Captain's house where a woman of the Captain's household is embroidering a copy of the handkerchief. Disdemona, deeply troubled by her disintegrating marriage, seeks the confidence of the Ensign's wife who knows everything about her husband's villainy but is too fearful of him to say anything.

The Ensign, paid by the Moor to dispatch the Captain, assaults him one night as the Captain is leaving the house of a courtesan, manages to cut off a leg, then runs away and returns with the crowd as though attracted by the noise. Despite this serious wound, the Captain lives. Disdemona's grieving for him confirms the Moor in his resolve to rid the world of her. He adopts the Ensign's plan for the murder: the Ensign hides in a closet, makes a noise to attract Disdemona, and finishes her off with a sand-filled stocking that leaves no marks. The two men then lay her in bed, smash her skull, and make it appear that a ceiling timber has fallen on her head. They do not get away with this murder, however, for the Moor begins to loathe the Ensign and strips him of his rank. In retaliation, the Ensign informs the Captain that it was the Moor who attacked the Captain and murdered Disdemona. Returning to Venice, the Captain brings charges against the Moor and presents the Ensign as an eyewitness. The Moor is summoned, tortured, and banished perpetually, though he confesses nothing. Eventually he is killed by Disdemona's kinsmen. The Ensign escapes punishment only to become later involved in another crime, for which he is tortured and so weakened that he dies soon after.

Many of Shakespeare's changes focus on the Ensign, or Iago. Shakespeare strips away the Ensign's simple motive of lust for Disdemona and jealous hate of the Captain, though traces of a perverse desire to cuckold Othello linger on in Iago's psyche. At the same time, Shakespeare adds the apparently specious motive of resentment over Cassio's promotion in Iago's place. (Iago's gleeful and partly unmotivated viciousness show him to be related to the Vice of the morality-play tradition.) Shakespeare adds entirely the opening scene in which Iago arouses the prejudices of Desdemona's father Brabantio. The father does not appear in the story, other than in the briefest mention that Disdemona's parents oppose the marriage. Roderigo is a brilliantly invented character who reveals Iago's skill in manipulation. Iago's soliloquies are entirely Shakespearean. Iago, unlike the Ensign of the story, is responsible for Cassio's first disgrace on the night of the watch. Cassio's weakness for wine and for Bianca are Shakespearean additions; the story notes that the Captain visits a courtesan, but the fact is utterly unexceptional. Emilia is a more complex figure than the Ensign's wife: Shakespeare implicates her in the stealing of the handkerchief, but also accentuates her love for Desdemona and her brave denunciation of her husband when at last she knows the full truth. Othello's ritual slaying of Desdemona avoids the appalling butchery of the source story. Shakespeare's ending is more unified, and brings both Othello and Iago to account for the deeds they have committed in this play. As usual, Shakespeare compresses the time element, though occasional traces of a longer time span do show through. Most importantly, Shakespeare transforms a sensational murder story into a moving tragedy of love.

King Lear

The *Lear* story goes back into ancient legend. The motif of two wicked sisters and a virtuous youngest sister reminds us of Cinderella. Lear himself appears to come from Celtic mythology. Geoffrey of Monmouth, a Welshman in close contact with Celtic legend, included a Lear or Leir as one of the pseudo-historical kings in his *Historia Regum Britanniae* (c. 1136). This fanciful mixture of history and legend traces a supposed line of descent from Brut, great-grandson of Aeneas of Troy, through Locrine, Bladud, Leir, Gorboduc, Ferrex and Porrex, Lud, Cymbeline, Bonduca, Vortigern, Arthur, etc., to the historical kings of England. The Tudor monarchs made much of their purported claim to such an ancient dynasty, and in Shakespeare's day this mythology had a quasi-official status demanding a certain reverential suspension of disbelief.

King Leir, according to Geoffrey, is the father of three daughters, Gonorilla, Regan, and Cordeilla, among whom he intends to divide his kingdom. To determine who deserves most, he asks them who loves him most. The two eldest sisters protest undying devotion; but Cordeilla, perceiving how the others flatter and deceive him, renounces hyperbole and promises only to love him as a daughter should love a father. Furious, the king denies Cordeilla her third of the kingdom but permits her to marry Aganippus, King of the Franks, without dowry. Thereafter Leir bestows his two eldest daughters on the Dukes of Albania and Cornubia (Albany and Cornwall), together with half the island during his lifetime and the possession of the remainder after his death. In due course his two sons-in-law rebel against Leir and seize his power. Thereafter Maglaunus, Duke of Albania, agrees to maintain Leir with sixty retainers, but after two years of chafing at this arrangement Gonorilla insists that the number be reduced to thirty. Angrily the king goes to Henvin, Duke of Cornubia, where all goes well for a time; within a year, however, Regan demands that Leir reduce his retinue to five knights. When Gonorilla refuses to take him back with more than one retainer, Leir crosses into France and is generously received by Cordeilla and Aganippus. An invasion restores Leir to his throne. Three years later he and Aganippus die, after which Cordeilla rules successfully for five years until overthrown by the sons of Maglaunus and Henvin. In prison she commits suicide.

This story, as part of England's mythic genealogy, was repeated in various Tudor versions such as *The First parte of the Mirour for Magistrates* (1574), William Warner's *Albions England* (1586), and Holinshed's *Chronicles*. Warner refers to the king's sons-in-law as "the Prince of Albany" and "the Cornish prince"; Holinshed refers to them as "the Duke of Albania" and "the Duke of Cornwall," but reports that it is Cornwall who marries the eldest daughter Gonorilla. *The Mirour* closer to Shakespeare in these details, speaks of "Gonerell" as married to "Albany" and of "Cordila" as married to "the king of Fraunce." Spenser's *The Faerie Queene* (II,x,27–32) reports that "Cordeill" or "Cordelia" ends her life by hanging herself. Other retellings appear in Gerard Legh's *Accidence of Armory* and William Camden's *Remaines*. All of these accounts leave the story virtually unchanged.

Shakespeare's immediate source for *King Lear*, however, was an old play called *The True Chronicle History of King Leir*. It was published in 1605 but plainly is much earlier in style. The Stationers' Register for May 14, 1594, lists "A booke called the Tragecall historie of kinge Leir and his Three Daughters &c.," and a short time earlier Henslowe's *Diary* records the performance of a "Kinge Leare" at the Rose theatre on April 6 and 8, 1594. The actors were the Queen's or Sussex' men, probably the Queen's. The play may have been written as early as 1588. Peele, Greene, Lodge, and Kyd have all been suggested as possible authors. Shakespeare probably knew the play before its publication in 1605.

This play of *Leir* ends happily, with the restoration of Leir to his throne. Essentially the play is a legendary history with a strong element of romance. The two wicked sisters are warned of the king's plans for dividing his kingdom by a sycophantish courtier named Skalliger (cf. Oswald). Cordella receives the ineffectual support of an honest courtier, Perillus (cf. Kent), but is disinherited by her angry father. Trusting herself to God's mercy and setting forth alone to live by her own labor, Cordella is found by the Gallian king and his bluff companion Mumford, who have come to England disguised as palmers to see if the English king's daughters are as beautiful as reported. The king hears Cordella's sad story, falls in love with her at first sight, and woos her (still wearing his disguise) in the name of the Gallian king. When she virtuously suggests the palmer woo for himself, he throws off his disguise and marries her forthwith.

Meanwhile the other sons-in-law, Cornwall and Cambria (i.e., Albany), draw lots for their shares of the kingdom. Leir announces that he will sojourn with Cornwall and Gonorill first. Cornwall treats the king with genuine solicitude, but Gonorill, abetted by Skalliger, tauntingly drives her father away. The king acknowledges to his loyal companion Perillus that he has wronged Cordella. Regan, who rules her mild husband as she pleases, receives the king with seeming tenderness but secretly hires an assassin to end his life. (Gonorill is partner in this plot.) The suborned agent, frightened into remorse by a providentially sent thunderstorm, shows his intended victim the letter ordering the assassination.

The Gallian king and Cordella, who have previously sent ambassadors to Leir urging him to come to France, now decide to journey with Mumford into Britain disguised as countryfolk. Before they can do so, however, Leir and Perillus arrive in France, in mariners' garb, where they encounter Cordella and her party dressed as countryfolk. Cordella recognizes Leir's voice, and father and daughter are tearfully reunited. The Gallian king invades England and restores Leir to his throne.

Shakespeare has changed much in the sheer narrative outline of his source. He discards not only the happy ending but the attempted assassination and the numerous romancelike uses of disguise (although Tom o'Bedlam, in an added plot, repeatedly uses disguise). Shakespeare eliminates the humorous Mumford and replaces Perillus with both Kent and the Fool. He turns Cornwall into a villain and Albany into a belated champion of justice. He creates the storm scene out of a mere suggestion about providential thunder.

Most of all, he adds the parallel plot of Gloucester, Edgar, and Edmund. Here Shakespeare derived some of his material from Sidney's *Arcadia* (1590). In Book II, chapter 10 of this greatest of all Elizabethan prose romances, the two heroes Pyrocles and Musidorus encounter a son leading his blind old father. The old man tells his pitiful tale. He is the deposed King of Paphlagonia, father of a bastard son named Plexirtus who, he now bitterly realizes, turned the king against his true son Leonatus—the very son who is now his guide and guardian. The true son, having managed to escape his father's order of execution, has been forced to live poorly as a soldier, while the bastard son has proceeded to usurp his father's throne. In his wretchedness, the king has been succored by his forgiving true son and has been prevented from casting himself off the top of a hill. At the conclusion of this narrative, the villain Plexirtus arrives and attacks Leonatus; reinforcements arrive on both sides, but eventually Plexirtus is driven off, enabling the king to return to his court and bestow the crown on Leonatus. He thereupon dies, his heart having been stretched beyond the limits of endurance.

Other parts of *The Arcadia* may have given Shakespeare further suggestions. Edmund is decidedly indebted to the Vice of the morality-play tradition. For Tom o' Bedlam's mad language, Shakespeare consulted Samuel Harsnett's *Declaration of Egregious Popishe Impostures*, 1603. (See K. Muir's Arden edition of *King Lear*, pp. 253–256, for an extensive comparison.)

Timon of Athens

Shakespeare certainly made use of a brief passage from the Life of Antonius in Thomas North's translation of Plutarch's *Lives of the Noble Grecians and Romanes* (1579). This passage is a digression used to illustrate Antonius' own embittered withdrawal from society, in which he compares himself to a famous misanthrope of Athens. As Plutarch reports Timon's story, citing Plato and Aristophanes as his sources, Timon is a hater of mankind because he has been victimized by deception and ingratitude. Timon shuns all company but that of young Alcibiades. When asked by Apemantus why he favors this youth, Timon replies that he knows Alcibiades will some day do great mischief to the Athenians. On another occasion, Timon mounts a public rostrum and invites his Athenian listeners to come hang themselves on a fig tree growing in his yard before he cuts it down (see V,i,208–215). When Timon dies he is buried upon the seashore (V,i,216–221). Plutarch transcribes two epitaphs, one by the poet Callimachus and one by Timon himself, both of which appear word for word in Shakespeare's play (V,iv,70–73). (Shakespeare probably meant to cancel one, for dramatically they are inconsistent with one another.) Plutarch thus provides Shakespeare not only with several incidents in the life of Timon but with the link connecting Timon, Alcibiades, and Apemantus.

Oddly, Shakespeare seems to have absorbed little from Plutarch's Life of Alcibiades, though that account does tell how the general leaves Athens in disgrace and sides with her enemies but ultimately relents when he sees that the Athenians are sorry for the injury they have done him. Alcibiades is a handsome young man and fond of women; his concubine Timandra buries him. Despite these scattered hints, however, Plutarch's life of Alcibiades provides no basis for Shakespeare's plot.

The comedy of Timon by Aristophanes, to which Plutarch alludes, has not survived. Nor has Plato's description. Apparently these accounts were based on a historical figure of fifth-century Athens, Timon the son of Echecratides. Allusions to him in classical literature are common enough to suggest that his name had become synonymous with misanthropy. The fullest surviving classical record of this Timon legend is a dialogue by Lucian of Samosata (c. 125–180 A.D.) called *Timon*, or *The Misanthrope*. No English translation was available in Shakespeare's lifetime, but he could have read Lucian in Italian, Latin, or French translation.

The dialogue begins as Timon, impoverished and abandoned by his fair-weather friends, calls upon Zeus to punish such injustice. Zeus hears this diatribe and learns from Hermes the sad tale of Timon's victimization by his ungrateful fellow man. Aware that he has been neglectful of this case, Zeus orders Hermes to descend with Plutus (Riches) and restore Timon to prosperity. Although Plutus fears he will be treated improvidently as before, Zeus is insistent. Plutus confesses to Hermes, as they descend, how he deceives men. Hermes and Plutus find Timon digging, accompanied by Poverty, Toil, Endurance. and other such allegorical companions. Poverty and his fellows are reluctant to leave Timon, for they know he has been happier with them than in his former days; and Timon too protests he wants nothing to do with prosperity. Still, the will of the gods must be obeyed, and Timon discovers treasure where he is digging.

Just as he mordantly predicts, opportunists now seek him out. One is Gnathonides the flatterer, a former recipient of Timon's hospitality who only recently has repaid that kindness by offering Timon a noose. Philiades once received from Timon a farm as a dowry for his daughters, but has spurned Timon in his poverty; now he makes a pretence of offering money, knowing Timon not to be in need. A third petitioner is the orator Demea, whose debt Timon once paid to obtain his release from jail; now, having insulted Timon in his poverty, Demea comes with a fulsome and patently fictitious decree he has composed in Timon's honor. Fourth is Thrasicles, a hypocritical philosopher who preaches self-denial but drinks to excess, and who professes to come now not for his own benefit but for those to whom he will gladly distribute Timon's new wealth. Timon drives them off one by one and then resorts to throwing stones at the ever-increasing crowd of flatterers.

Many details here are suggestive of Shakespeare's play and are not in Plutarch: Timon's generosity to former friends (including the payment of a debt and the providing of a marriage dowry), his friends' ungrateful response when he is in need, the finding of gold in the ground followed by the reappearance of the friends, the insincere offer of money, the flattering composition in praise of Timon. The personified abstractions are parablelike, as is Shakespeare's play. Yet verbal parallels between Shakespeare and Lucian are tenuous at best. Probably Shakespeare knew some later version based on Lucian. Renaissance works inspired by Lucian are not hard to find, but none seems to be the direct source for Shakespeare. He is not likely to have known an Italian play called the *Timone* of Boiardo (c. 1487).

More suggestive is an English academic play written at Cambridge and preserved in the Dyce MSS. In this version, Timon's servant Laches warns against the effects of prodigality. When one friend, Eutrapelus, experiences financial trouble, Timon gives him five talents. Laches is driven out by Timon, but returns disguised as a soldier to serve his master. At a final banquet, Timon mocks his guests with stones painted to resemble artichokes. When he finds gold, Timon's false mistress shows her readiness to take it. Even a farcical comic subplot reminds us that Shakespeare's *Timon* contains an unrelated and perhaps vestigial Fool scene. Yet this academic play may have been written after Shakespeare's play, though surely not based on it (since *Timon* was not published until 1623), and the likeliest explanation for the similarities is a common source. Perhaps Shakespeare knew and used a play now lost.

Apemantus does not have a prominent role in any of the versions here discussed, though he is mentioned in Plutarch. Apemantus bears a resemblance to many satirical railers and crabbed philosophers in Renaissance literature, such as Diogenes in John Lyly's play of *Campaspe* (1584) and Jaques in Shakespeare's *As You Like It*.

Macbeth

Shakespeare's chief source for *Macbeth* was Holinshed's *Chronicles* (1587 edition). Holinshed had gone for most of his material to Hector Boece, *Scotorum Historiae* (1526–1527), who in turn was indebted to a fourteenth-century priest named John of Fordun and to a fifteenth-century chronicler, Andrew of Wyntoun. By the time Holinshed found it, the story of Macbeth had become more fiction than fact. The historical Macbeth, who ruled from 1040 to 1057, did take the throne by killing Duncan, but in a civil conflict between two clans contending for the kingship. Contemporary observers credit him with having been a good ruler. Although he was defeated by the Earl of Northumbria (the Siward of Shakespeare's play) at Birnam Wood in 1054, the earl was forced by his own losses to retire, and Macbeth ruled three years longer before being slain by Duncan's son Malcolm. Banquo and Fleance are fictional characters apparently invented by Boece.

As Holinshed tells the story, Duncane is a king of too soft and gentle a nature, negligent in punishing his enemies and thereby an unwitting encourager of sedition. It falls to Makbeth, a critic of this soft line, and to Banquho the Thane of Lochaber, to defend Scotland against her enemies: first Makdowald (Macdonwald in Shakespeare) with his Irish kerns and gallowglasses, and then Sueno, King of Norway.

(Shakespeare fuses these battles into one.) Shortly thereafter, Makbeth and Banquho encounter "three women in strange and wild apparell, resembling creatures of elder world," who predict their futures as in the play. Although Makbeth and Banquho jest about the matter, common opinion later maintains that "these women were either the weird sisters, that is (as ye would say) the goddesses of destinie, or else some nymphs or feiries, indued with knowledge of prophesie." Certainly Makbeth soon becomes the Thane of Cawdor, whereupon, jestingly reminded of the three sisters' promise by Banquho, he resolves to seek the throne. His way is blocked, however, by Duncane's naming of his eldest but still underage son Malcolme to be Prince of Cumberland and heir to the throne. Makbeth's resentment at this is understandable, since Scottish law provides that he himself should be heir until Malcolm is of age. Accordingly, Makbeth begins to plot with his associates how to usurp the kingdom by force. His "verie ambitious" wife urges him on because of her "vnquenchable desire" to be queen. Banquho is one among many trusted friends with whose support Makbeth slays the king at Inverness or at Botgosvane. (No mention is made of a visit to Makbeth's castle.) Malcolme and Donald Bane, the dead king's sons, fly for their safety to Cumberland, where Malcolme is well received by Edward the Confessor of England.

For some ten years Makbeth rules well, using great liberality and correcting the laxity of his predecessor's reign. Inevitably, however, the weird sisters' promise of a posterity to Banquho goads Makbeth into ordering the murder of his onetime companion. Fleance escapes Makbeth's henchmen in the dark, and afterward founds the lineage of the Stuart kings. (This genealogy is fictitious.) Makbeth's tyrannical bent further causes him to build Dunsinane fortress. When Mackduffe refuses to help, the king turns against him and would kill him except that "a certeine witch, whom hee had in great trust," tells the king he need never fear a man born of woman nor any vanquishment till Birnam Wood come to Dunsinane. Mackduffe flees for his safety into England and joins Malcolme, whereupon Makbeth's agents slaughter Mackduffe's wife and children at Fife. Malcolme, fearing that Mackduffe may be an agent of Makbeth, dissemblingly professes to be a voluptuary, miser, and tyrant; but when Mackduffe responds as he should in righteous sorrow at Scotland's evil condition, Malcolme reveals his steadfast commitment to the cause of right. These leaders return to Scotland and defeat Makbeth at Birnam Wood, with their soldiers carrying branches before them. Mackduffe, proclaiming that he is a man born of no woman since he was "ripped out" of his mother's womb, slays Makbeth.

Despite extensive similarities, Shakespeare has made some important changes. Duncan is no longer an ineffectual king. Macbeth can no longer justify his claim to the throne. Most importantly, Banquo is no longer partner to a broadly-based though secret conspiracy against Duncan. Banquo is, after all, ancestor of James I (at least according to this legendary history), so that his hands must be kept scrupulously clean; King James disapproved of all tyrannicides, whatever the circumstances. Macbeth is no longer a just lawgiver. The return of Banquo's ghost to Macbeth's banqueting table is an added scene. Macbeth hears the prophecy about Birnam Wood and Macduff from the weird sisters, not, as in Holinshed, from some witch. Lady Macbeth's role is considerably enhanced, and her sleepwalking scene is original. Shakespeare compresses the time element, as he usually does.

To assist him in some of these alterations, Shakespeare turned to another story in Holinshed's chronicle of Scotland: the murder of King Duff by Donwald. King Duff, never suspecting any treachery in Donwald, often visits his castle. On one occasion Donwald's wife, bearing great malice towards the king, shows Donwald "the meanes wherby he might soonest accomplish" the murder. The husband and wife ply Duff and his few chamberlains with much to eat and drink. Donwald abhors the act "greatlie in heart," but perseveres "through instigation of his wife." Four of Donwald's servants actually commit the murder under his instruction. Next morning, Donwald breaks into the king's chamber and slays the chamberlains as though believing them guilty. Donwald is so overzealous in his investigation of the murder that many lords begin to suspect him of having done it. For six months afterward, the sun refuses to appear by day and the moon by night.

The chronicle accounts in Holinshed of Malcolm and Edward the Confessor supplied Shakespeare with further details. A more important supplementary source may have been George Buchanan's *Rerum Scoticarum Historia* (1582), a Latin history not translated in Shakespeare's lifetime, presenting a more complex psychological portrait of the protagonist than in Holinshed. Finally, Shakespeare may have known King James I's *Daemonologie* (1597), Samuel Harsnett's *Declaration of Egregious Popishe Impostures* (1603), and accounts of the Scottish witch trials published around 1590.

Antony and Cleopatra

In writing *Antony and Cleopatra*, Shakespeare relied to an unusual extent on his chief source, The Life of Marcus Antonius in Plutarch's *Lives of Noble Grecians and Romanes* (translated by Sir Thomas North, 1579). Perhaps the best-known example in all Shakespeare of his skillful point-by-point utilization of source material is in the following (see *Antony and Cleopatra*, II,ii,196–223):

She disdained to set forward otherwise, but to take her barge in the river of Cydnus, the poope whereof was of gold, the sailes of purple, and the owers of silver, which kept stroke in rowing after the sounde of the musicke of flutes, howboyes, citherns, violls, and such other instruments as they played upon in the barge. And now for the person of her selfe: she was layed under a pavillion of cloth of gold of tissue, apparelled and attired like the goddesse Venus, commonly drawen in picture: and hard by her, on either hand of her, pretie faire boyes apparelled as painters doe set forth god Cupide, with litle fannes in their hands, with the which they fanned wind upon her. Her Ladies and gentlewomen also, the fairest of them were apparelled like the nymphes Nereides (which are the mermaides of the waters) and like the Graces, some stearing the helme, others tending the tackle and ropes of the barge, out of the which there came a wonderfull passing sweete savor of perfumes, that perfumed the wharfes side, pestered with innumerable multitudes of people. Some of them followed the barge all alongest the rivers side: others also ranne out of the citie to see her comming in. So that in thend, there ranne such multitudes of people one after an other to see her, that Antonius was left post alone in the market place, in his Imperiall seate to geve audience.

Plutarch reports the other fabulous stories as well: eight wild boars roasted whole for only twelve guests (II,ii,183), Cleopatra teasing Antony by causing an old dried salt fish to be placed on his fishing line (II,iv,17), Menas the pirate suggesting to Pompey that they cut the anchor cable with all their noble guests still aboard (II,vii), Cleopatra's sudden changes from weeping to laughing, and her willingness to be flattered by those who tell her Antony has married Octavia solely out of necessity (III,iii), Octavius' tenderness for his sister, the ill-omened nesting of swallows in Cleopatra's sails (IV,xii), Antony's disregarding the advice of a valiant captain not to fight at sea (III,vii), Cleopatra's study of swift means of death, Antony's jealous reaction to the embassy of the young Thyreus or Thidias (III,xiii), the suicide of Antony's servant Eros (IV,xiv), Cleopatra's difficulty in lifting Antony up to her tomb or monument (IV,xv), his warning that she should trust none but Proculeius, Cleopatra's deception of Caesar through persuading him that she desires to live, the countryman with the basket of figs, Cleopatra's death "attired and araied in her royall robes" attended by Charmian and Iras, and much more.

Despite these extensive and detailed borrowings, Shakespeare partly turned elsewhere for his estimate of his main characters. To Plutarch, Antony is the tragic victim of infatuation. For all Cleopatra's cultivation and fascination—she knows several languages, and rules her country with royal bearing—she is the source of Antony's downfall. Plutarch's attitude is, like Enobarbus', admiring but ironic. "In the ende," he writes, "the horse of the minde as Plato termeth it, that is so hard of rayne (I meane the unreyned lust of concupiscence) did put out of Antonius heade, all honest and commendable thoughtes." This "Roman" view is present in *Antony and Cleopatra*, to be sure, but is counterbalanced by the "Egyptian" view. Shakespeare's play sets up a debate among conflicting traditions as found in various medieval and Renaissance treatments of this famous story. The moralistic view condemning vice was popular in medieval texts, such as *De Casibus Virorum Illustrium* and its continuation, Lydgate's *The Fall of Princes*. The view of Cleopatra as love's martyr was to be found in Chaucer's *The Legend of Good Women*. And finally, the view of Antony and Cleopatra as heroic protagonists rising above their guilt found expression in several neo-Senecan dramas of the later sixteenth century. Most important for Shakespeare were *The Tragedie of Antonie*, translated from Robert Garnier's *Marc Antoine* by Mary Herbert, Countess of Pembroke in about 1590 (published 1592 and 1595), and *The Tragedy of Cleopatra* by Samuel Daniel, 1593, a companion play dealing mainly with the very end of Cleopatra's life. Garnier's play had been based on Étienne Jodelle's *Cleopâtra Captive*, 1552, the first regular French tragedy. Shakespeare certainly gained from works like these a sense of tragic greatness in his protagonists. Another influential work may have been the *Chronicle of the Romanes Warres* by Appian of Alexandria (translated 1578).

Enobarbus, interestingly, is almost entirely original with Shakespeare. Plutarch mentions only the fact that such a man deserts Antony.

Coriolanus

Coriolanus probably represents Shakespeare's last use of Plutarch's *Lives of the Noble Grecians and Romanes*, as translated by Sir Thomas North (1579). The Life of Caius Martius Coriolanus provided most of the plot material for Shakespeare's play, just as The Life of Antonius had provided most of the material for *Antony and Cleopatra*. Plutarch's Coriolanus is a man of exceeding nobility but also of excessive impatience and churlish incivility. In war he practices *Virtus*, or "valliantnes" as North translates it. He wins his title of Coriolanus by storming the city of Corioles almost singlehanded. He is the son of a widow whose good opinion he cherishes; as Plutarch reports, "he thought nothing made him so happie and honorable, as that his mother might heare every bodie praise and commend him, that she might allwayes see him returne with a crowne upon his head, and that she might still embrace him with teares ronning downe her cheekes for joye." Coriolanus vehemently disapproves of leniency toward the populace as an invitation to anarchy. He is naturally an enemy of the people's first tribunes, Junius Brutus and Sicinius Vellutus, who, in Plutarch's estimation, "had only bene the causers and procurers of this sedition."

When Coriolanus stands for consul, and follows the custom of appearing in the marketplace clad only in a poor gown, the people remember his martial prowess; on the day of the election itself, however, they recall their old hate of him and refuse his candidacy. Coriolanus, in his typically choleric and intemperate fashion, makes no attempt to conceal his outrage at this insult. (Plutarch comments editorially on his behavior as "the fruites of selfe will and obstinacie.") When he is banished, Coriolanus goes in disguise to Antium, to the house of Tullus Aufidius, his great rival, knowing perfectly well that "Tullus dyd more malice and envie him, then he dyd all the Romaines besides." Coriolanus and Tullus have long been admiring rivals: "they were ever at the encounter one against another, like lustie coragious youthes, striving in all emulation of honour, and had encountered many times together." Returning vengefully to Rome, Coriolanus is "determined at the first to persist in his obstinate and inflexible rancker," but finally relents through "naturall affection" and receives his wife and mother. Volumnia's oration to him, reported in full by Plutarch, causes Coriolanus to cry out: "you have wonne a happy victorie for your countrie, but mortall and unhappy for your sonne."

Shakespeare's changes simultaneously enhance the haughtiness of Coriolanus and the fickleness of the people, thereby increasing the distance between the two sides. Shakespeare's Coriolanus is revolted by the custom of wearing a robe and showing his wounds to the people, and shows his contempt more snarlingly than in Plutarch. He is, unlike Plutarch's protagonist, reluctant to seek office, and has to be persuaded to it by his mother and friends. Shakespeare minimizes the legitimate griefs of the Roman people—they are severely oppressed by usurers in Plutarch's account—and accentuates their fickleness. Shakespeare shows them as being manipulated against Coriolanus by the scheming tribunes, whereas in Plutarch the people make up their own minds to oppose Coriolanus for the consulship. Shakespeare also magnifies the roles of Volumnia and of Menenius. Volumnia, though she is mentioned by Plutarch, takes no active part in the story until Coriolanus attacks Rome; Menenius' function in Plutarch is chiefly that of relating the fable of the belly. Shakespeare compresses and rearranges events as he usually does: for example, in Plutarch the people actually leave Rome to demonstrate their grievances, and agree to return only when granted the election of tribunes to represent their interests, whereas in Shakespeare the tribunes have already been elected when the play begins. In Shakespeare, Coriolanus is banished as the result of a dispute over his consulship, not (as in Plutarch) as the result of an insurrection over scarcity of grain.

Shakespeare probably also knew the story of Coriolanus in Livy's *Romane Historie*, Book II, as translated by Philemon Holland (1600). Other versions of the story were available to him, including the *Roman Histories* of Lucius Florus. Plutarch seems to have provided Shakespeare, however, with virtually everything he needed. Even Shakespeare's alterations of Plutarch tend to enhance rather than correct Plutarch's overall thesis and appraisal of the characters in his history.

Pericles

Shakespeare derived his *Pericles* from the ancient Greek romance of Apollonius of Tyre. He had used the story once before, in *The Comedy of Errors*. Medieval versions of this enduringly popular legend include the ninth-century Latin *Historia Apollonii Regis Tyri*, Godfrey of Viterbo's *Pantheon* (c. 1186), the *Gesta Romanorum*, John Gower's *Confessio Amantis* (c. 1383–1393), and an English chronicle of *Appolyn of Thyre* translated for the printer Wynkyn de Worde by Robert Copland from a French source (1510). Shakespeare (and possibly the author of a lost earlier dramatic version) were chiefly indebted to Gower's *Confessio* and to Laurence Twine's *The Patterne of Painefull Aduentures*, a prose version registered in 1576 but existing today only in two editions from about 1594–1595 and 1607.

The order of events in Twine is much the same as in Shakespeare: the hero Apollonius' difficulty with the incestuous King Antiochus, his relieving of the city of Tharsus, his shipwreck at Pentapolis and his falling in love with the king's daughter Lucina (Thaisa in the play), her childbearing and apparent death at sea, the discovery of her floating casket at Ephesus, her revival by the physician Cerimon and her retirement to the Temple of Diana in Ephesus, her daughter Tharsia's (i.e., Marina's) capture by pirates and enslavement in a brothel, her conversion of Athanagoras (Lysimachus) the governor of Machilenta (Mytilene), and Apollonius' eventual reunion with daughter and wife. Gower's account too is much the same, with slightly differing forms of the proper names: Appolinus' wife is referred to as the king's daughter, Appolinus' daughter is Thaise, the man she marries is Atenagoras of Mitilene, and so on.

Other than changing some proper names, including that of the hero, Shakespeare did not introduce many significant alterations. To be sure, Shakespeare has given a more sordid impression of the brothel in which Marina must dwell, and has contrastingly dignified the character of Lysimachus so as to render him worthy of marrying Marina. In Twine's prose account, Athanagoras actually tries to buy Tharsia from the pirates at an auction; when he is outbid by a bawd, he resolves to be the first to visit Tharsia in her new residence. Shakespeare has cleaned this up, although traces of the older and more licentious character occasionally show through and create the impression of inconsistency. For the most part, however, Shakespeare's play stays unusually close to the episodic narrative structure of his sources.

The relationship of George Wilkins' *The Painfull Aduentures of Pericles Prince of Tyre* (1608) to Shakespeare's play is complex and uncertain. Beyond doubt, Wilkins' prose account is based in part on a *Pericles* play; Wilkins acknowledges in his Argument that this same story has been recently presented "by the Kings Majesties Players." The play he used may, however, not have been the *Pericles* we know from the corrupt 1609 quarto. Parts of Wilkins' narrative are very close to the earlier *Patterne of Painefull Aduentures* by Twine. Could these parts be inventions on Wilkins' part? Kenneth Muir prefers to think (*Shakespeare's Sources*, 1957) that because Wilkins' novel is closer to the first two acts of the play than to the last three acts, Wilkins may have been using an older play that Shakespeare then revised, substantially rewriting the last three acts but changing little in the first two. Whether the presumed *Ur-Pericles* might have been Wilkins' own play is a matter of conjecture. The very existence of an *Ur-Pericles* is by no means universally accepted, but cannot be ruled out as a possibility.

Cymbeline

Cymbeline deals with legendary and romantic history, in which traces of historical event can still be dimly perceived. A Cunobelinus or Cymbeline was in fact leader of the Celtic chieftains in southeast England during the period of Roman hegemony there, following Julius Caesar's invasion of the island in 54 B.C. Cunobelinus ruled from about 5 to 40 A.D., with his capital at Camulodunum (Colchester). He was a friend and ally of Augustus Caesar and enjoyed a peaceful reign. When the kingdom had passed to his sons (one of whom apparently was Caractacus), the Romans under Claudius pursued once again their conquest of England and subdued much of the southeast, though Caractacus escaped to Wales and became a leader of resistance.

Beginning with Geoffrey of Monmouth's *Historia Regum Britanniae* (c. 1136), King Kymbelinus becomes a quasi-legendary figure. Geoffrey adds him to the genealogy of kings (along with Leir, Locrine, etc.) descended from Aeneas' great-grandson Brut, the mythical founder of Britain. Kymbelinus' reign was peaceful, according to Geoffrey, since the king, having been raised in Augustus Caesar's household, willingly paid tribute to Rome without being asked. When Kymbelinus' elder son Guiderius succeeded to the throne, however, said Geoffrey, he defied the Emperor Claudius over the tribute. Guiderius fell in battle and was succeeded by his brother Arviragus, who more than held his own against Claudius, eventually settling matters by negotiation.

By the time of Holinshed's *Chronicles* (1587 edition), the facts are badly confused. Holinshed admits he cannot be sure whether Kymbeline or some other British leader fought against Augustus Caesar, or whether Kymbeline paid tribute; he does report that Guiderius fought Augustus Caesar (rather than Claudius), but is uncertain as to whether the Romans lost or won. Spenser's *The Faerie Queene* II,x,50–51, affirms that Kimbeline fought the Romans over tribute and was slain in battle, whereupon his brother Aviragus took his place and compelled the Roman Claudius to a peace. (In other words, Spenser has conflated Cymbeline and Guiderius.) Shakespeare, like Spenser, imagines the great struggle with Rome and subsequent peace settlement to have taken place during Cymbeline's reign; following Holinshed, he assumes that Rome was then governed by Augustus Caesar. Shakespeare also seems to have consulted a vivid account of the battle in Thomas Blenerhasset's contribution to the *Seconde part of the Myrroure for Magistrates*, 1578, and another account of Cymbeline's reign by John Higgins in the 1587 *Myrroure for Magistrates*. Finally, Shakespeare turned for his background material to quite a different story in Holinshed, concerning a Scottish farmer named Hay who with his two sons helped defend Scotland against the Danes in 976. Shakespeare presumably found this story when reading for *Macbeth*, since it stands between the two accounts—Donwald's murder of Duff and Macbeth's murder of Duncan—that Shakespeare used in writing *Macbeth*. The exploits of Hay and his two sons resemble those of Belarius and the two princes in the final battle of *Cymbeline*.

The quasi-historical setting accounts for only a small part of *Cymbeline*, and Shakespeare had no special reason to set the facts straight. Most of his material is, after all, romantic. The central plot of a wager over a wife's virtue may have come from Boccaccio's *Decameron*, ninth tale of the second day, although as a type this ancient story was widespread and presumably available to Shakespeare in many forms. Earlier versions include the thirteenth-century French *Roi Flore et la belle Jeanne*, the *Roman de la Violette* by Gerbert de Montreuil, a miracle play by Gautier de Coincy, and others. Boccaccio was available to Shakespeare in French translation but not in English.

Boccaccio tells of an Italian merchant, Bernabo of Genoa, who, at a gathering in Paris of fellow merchants discussing the wantonness of their wives, dares to affirm the absolute chastity of his own wife Zinevra. A young merchant, Ambrogiuolo, makes a wager that he can seduce Zinevra and return with proof in three months. Going at once to Genoa, Ambrogiuolo discovers that Zinevra is indeed incorruptible. He therefore bribes an old lady, whom Zinevra has befriended, to convey him hidden in a chest to the lady's bedroom. When the lady is asleep he steals forth from hiding, memorizes details of her room, notes particularly a mole under her left breast, and takes with him a purse, gown, ring, and girdle. Returning to Paris, he convinces his fellow merchants and Bernabo that he has succeeded. Bernabo hereupon travels to within a few miles of Genoa, summons his wife, and secretly orders his servant to kill her on the way. The servant is reluctant to do so, however, and gladly takes only her cloak as evidence of having finished the job. Zinevra now makes her way disguised as a man to Alexandria, and enters the service of the sultan. One day she happens to recognize her own purse and girdle in a Venetian clothes shop in Palestine, inquires as to their owner, meets Ambrogiuolo in this way (who has journeyed to Palestine selling merchandise), and hears from Ambrogiuolo's own boastful lips the story of his treachery. She cannily manages to bring Ambrogiuolo and Bernabo before the sultan, throws off her male disguise, and reveals the whole story. She pardons Bernabo and is reunited with him, but Ambrogiuolo is sentenced by the sultan to be tied to a stake and smeared with honey until the insects devour him.

Shakespeare seems also to have known an English version, *Frederyke of Jennen* (Antwerp, 1518, London 1520 and 1560), translated from the Dutch. In some details it is closer to Shakespeare's play. For example, the merchants who witness the wager include a Spaniard, a Frenchman, a Florentine, and a Genoese (cf. I,iv). Three of these merchants are not present when the villain returns to prove his victory, just as in II,iv of Shakespeare's play. Also, the husband repents even before learning of his wife's innocence, as does Posthumous. Shakespeare greatly accentuates this motif of penance and forgiveness. Another source is a romantic play called *The Rare Triumphs of Love and Fortune*, acted before Elizabeth in 1582, in which the Princess Fidelia is banished by her father for loving Hermione, is betrayed and pursued by her boorish brother Armenio (cf. Cloten), and is hospitably received by a banished courtier named Bomelio who lives hermitlike in a cave. "Fidele" is the disguise name of Shakespeare's Imogen. Folk motifs are particularly dominant in this portion of the story: the cruel queen inevitably reminds us of Snow White's stepmother. Although Shakespeare may not have been acquainted with that particular story, he clearly was interested in folk legend when he wrote *Cymbeline*. One other anonymous romantic play, *Sir Clyomon and Sir Clamydes* (c. 1570–1583), may have given Shakespeare some suggestions for his Welsh scenes.

Beaumont and Fletcher's *Philaster* was written about the same time as *Cymbeline*, and is sometimes thought to resemble Shakespeare's play. Philaster is, like Posthumous, in love with a princess whose father intends her for another suitor. Still, most of the similarities can be attributed to the conventions of the romance genre just then coming into vogue. In any case, no one can be sure whether Shakespeare's play came after or before *Philaster*. It may well be that Shakespeare was the innovator.

The Winter's Tale

Shakespeare based *The Winter's Tale* fairly closely on Robert Greene's romantic novel, *Pandosto: The Triumph of Time*, published in 1588, 1592, and 1595, and then published in 1607 with the title *Dorastus and Fawnia*. Shakespeare changes the names, reverses the two kingdoms of Sicilia and Bohemia, and alters the unhappy ending that afflicts King Pandosto and Queen Bellaria of Bohemia (Leontes and Hermione of Sicilia). Otherwise, the narrative outline remains fairly intact. The story begins with the state visit of King Egistus of Sicilia (Polixenes of Bohemia) to his boyhood companion, Pandosto of Bohemia. Queen Bellaria entertains the guest with such warmth, "oftentimes coming herself into his bed chamber to see that nothing should be amiss to mislike him," that Pandosto understandably grows jealous. He commands his cup-bearer Franion (Camillo) to murder Egistus, and the latter seems to agree but instead warns his victim to flee with him. Their hasty departure appears to confirm Pandosto's worst suspicions. He sends the guard to arrest Bellaria as she plays with her young son Garinter (Mamillius). When the queen gives birth to a daughter in prison, the king orders the child destroyed, but relents upon the insistence of his courtiers and causes the infant to be set adrift in a small boat. The queen nobly defends herself at her trial (in language that Shakespeare has copied in some detail). She herself requests that the oracle at Delphos be consulted. The oracle replies in words that Shakespeare has altered only slightly: "Bellaria is chaste: Egistus blameless: Franion a true subject: Pandosto treacherous: his babe an innocent; and the king shall live without an heir, if that which is lost be not found." Unlike Shakespeare's Leontes, however, Pandosto is immediately stricken with remorse; and when Queen Bellaria collapses at the news of her son Garinter's death, she is truly and irrecoverably dead.

The babe is conveyed by a tempest to the coast of Sicilia and is discovered by an impoverished shepherd named Porrus. He and his wife Mopsa adopt the child, naming her Fawnia. By the age of sixteen, Fawnia's natural beauty rivals that of the goddess Flora. At a meeting of the farmers' daughters of Sicilia, where she is chosen mistress of the feast, Fawnia is espied by the king's son Dorastus on his way home from hawking. She counters his importunate suit with the argument that she is too lowly a match for him, but he replies that the gods themselves sometimes take earthly lovers. Her foster father, distressed by the prince's repeated visits (though he comes in shepherd's costume), resolves to carry the jewels he found with Fawnia to the king and reveal her story, thereby escaping blame for the goings-on. Dorastus escapes with Fawnia to a ship, aided by his servant Capnio (cf. Camillo). Capnio also fulfills a role given by Shakespeare to Autolycus, for he manages to trick the shepherd Porrus into thinking he can see the king if he comes aboard Dorastus' ship. A storm drives these voyagers to Bohemia where, because of the ancient enmity between Egistus and Pandosto, they disguise themselves. Pandosto, happening to hear of Fawnia's beauty, orders her and the others to be arrested as spies and summoned to court, whereupon he falls incestuously in love with the disguised Fawnia. He promises to free "Meleagrus" (Dorastus' disguise name) only if the young man will relinquish his claim to Fawnia. King Egistus meanwhile has discovered his son's whereabouts, and sends ambassadors to Bohemia demanding the return of Dorastus and the execution of Fawnia, Capnio, and Porrus. Pandosto, his love for Fawnia having turned to hate, is about to comply when Porrus reveals the circumstances of

Fawnia's infancy. Overjoyed to rediscover his daughter, Pandosto permits her to marry Dorastus, but then falls into a melancholy fit and commits suicide.

Shakespeare has created some characters almost entirely, such as Paulina, Antigonus, the clownish shepherd's son, and Autolycus, though Capnio does perform one of Autolycus' functions by inveigling the old shepherd aboard ship. Antigonus' journey to the seacoast of Bohemia with the infant Perdita, and his fatal exit "pursued by a bear," are Shakespearean additions. The character of Time is also added, and the shift in tone from tragedy to romance is vastly more pronounced than in Greene. The shepherdesses at the sheepshearing are Shakespearean. The old shepherd has a more substantial and comic role; Camillo is a stronger person than Capnio. Shakespeare omits the incestuous love of Pandosto for his daughter, and brings Hermione back to life. (For this motif of a statue made to breathe, he may well have recalled Ovid's account of Pygmalion in Ovid's *Metamorphoses* Book X.) Shakespeare's Leontes is more irrationally jealous than in Greene's account. Leontes' purgative sorrow is more intense and also more restorative than in the source; he is a truly noble and tragicomic figure, the center of a play about forgiveness and renewal.

Shakespeare may also have known Francis Sabie's *The Fissher-mans Tale* (1595), and its continuation, *Flora's Fortune* (1595). From Greene's cony-catching pamphlets he probably derived many of Autolycus' tricks.

The Tempest

No direct literary source for the whole of *The Tempest* has been found. Shakespeare does seem to have drawn material from various accounts of the shipwreck of the *Sea Venture* in the Bermudas, 1609, although the importance of these materials should not be overstated. Several of the survivors wrote narratives of the shipwreck itself and of their life on the islands for some nine months. Sylvester Jourdain, in *A Discovery of the Barmudas*, published 1610, speaks of miraculous preservation despite the island's reputation for being "a most prodigious and inchanted place." William Strachey's letter, written in July of 1610 and published much later (1625) as *A true Reportory of the Wracke and Redemption . . . from the Ilands of the Bermudas*, describes the panic among the passengers and crew, the much-feared reputation of the island as the habitation of devils and wicked spirits, the actual beauty and fertility of the place with its abundance of wild life (cf. Caliban's descriptions), and the treachery of the Indians they later encounter in Virginia. Shakespeare seems to have read Strachey's letter in manuscript, and may have been acquainted with him. He also kept up with travel accounts of Ralegh and Hariot, and knew various classical evocations of a New World. The name "Setebos" came from Richard Eden's *History of Trauayle* (1577), translated from Peter Martyr's *De Novo Orbe* and from various other travel accounts of the period. All these hints are indeed suggestive, but they are scattered and relate only to the setting and general circumstance of Shakespeare's play.

Shakespeare certainly consulted Montaigne's essay "Of the Caniballes," as translated by John Florio in 1603. Gonzalo's reverie on an ideal commonwealth (II,i) contains many verbal echoes of the essay. Montaigne's point is that supposedly civilized men who condemn as "barbarian" any society not conforming with their own are simply refusing to examine their own shortcomings. A supposedly "primitive" society may well embody perfect religion, justice, and harmony; civilized art can never rival the achievements of nature. The ideal commonwealth has no need of magistrates, riches, poverty, and contracts, all of which breed dissimulation and covetousness. The significance of these ideas for *The Tempest* extends well beyond the particular passage in which they are found. And Caliban himself, whose name is an anagram of "cannibal," illustrates (even though he is not an eater of human flesh) the truth of Montaigne's observation: "I thinke there is more barbarisme in eating men alive, than to feed upon them being dead."

Prospero's famous valedictory speech to "Ye elves of hills, brooks, standing lakes, and groves" (V,i) owes its origin to Medea's similar invocation in Ovid's *Metamorphoses* (Book VII), which Shakespeare knew both in the Latin original and in Golding's translation: "Ye Ayres and windes: ye Elves of Hilles, of B[r]ookes, of Woods alone, Of standing Lakes . . ." Medea also anticipates Shakespeare's Sycorax. Medea thus provides material for the representation of both black and white magic in *The Tempest*, so carefully differentiated by Shakespeare. Ariel is part English fairy, like Puck, and part daemon. The pastoral situation in *The Tempest* is perhaps derived from Spenser's *The Faerie Queene*, Book VI (with its distinctions between savage lust and true courtesy, between nature and art). Italian pastoral drama as practiced by Guarini and (in England) by John Fletcher may also have been an influence. The masque element in *The Tempest*, prominent as in much late Shakespeare, bears the imprint of the courtly masque tradition of Jonson, Beaumont, and Fletcher.

A German play, *Die Schöne Sidea* by Jacob Ayrer, written before 1605, was once thought to have been based on an earlier version of *The Tempest* as performed by English players traveling in Germany. Today the similarities between the two plays are generally attributed to conventions found everywhere in romance.

King Henry the Eighth

Shakespeare's chief source for the first four acts of *Henry VIII*, as for many of his earlier history plays, was Holinshed's *Chronicles* (1587 edition). Holinshed presented him with conflicting views of Cardinal Wolsey, however, and traces of the conflict remain in Shakespeare's play. Much of Holinshed is actually a compilation of the writings of earlier historiographers. In this case, some of Holinshed's material is from the bitterly anti-Wolseyan *Anglica Historia* (1534) of Polydore Vergil. Accordingly, Holinshed gives decidedly unfavorable interpretations of Wolsey's animosity toward the Duke of Buckingham and his unscrupulous meddling in the king's marriage question. Vergil was particularly distressed by the way in which Katharine had been cashiered; he (and Holinshed) report her speeches in her own behalf with manifest approval. Shakespeare preserves this alignment of sympathies in which Katharine is the wrongly accused wife and Wolsey the Machiavel.

Other portions of Holinshed, on the other hand, derive from George Cavendish's *The Life and Death of Thomas Wolsey*, written some time around 1557 and extensively used by the chroniclers, though not separately printed until 1641. Cavendish was a gentleman-usher in the household of Cardinal Wolsey from 1526 to 1530. Although he moralizes about the lesson to be learned from Wolsey's ambitious rise and sudden fall, Cavendish speaks admiringly of the cardinal as an extraordinarily great man. He captures in minutely-observed detail the magnificence of Wolsey's prosperous estate. He gives a moving portrait of Wolsey after his fall, on his sick-bed and near the end, saying to a companion: "if I had served God as diligently as I have done the king, he would not have given me over in my gray hairs." This passage, borrowed verbatim by Holinshed from Cavendish, produces in turn the famous lines from Shakespeare: "Had I but serv'd my God with half the zeal I serv'd my king, he would not in mine age Have left me naked to mine enemies" (III,ii,455–457).

For his fifth act, Shakespeare turned to John Foxe's *Actes and Monuments of Martyrs*. Here he encountered a particularly rabid Protestant point of view, which has left its impression not only on the fifth act but on portrayals of Wolsey (whom Foxe naturally deplored) in earlier scenes. Foxe's hero, Thomas Cranmer, emerges as the victor of Shakespeare's play. Although the triumphantly Protestant ending contrasts oddly with Shakespeare's earlier manifest sympathy for Queen Katharine, the duality of attitudes is somehow plausible and perhaps even typically Elizabethan: Katharine suffered lamentably, and Henry and Wolsey treated her shabbily, but these great events did after all lead to the English Reformation and the rule of Queen Elizabeth. The ambiguity so often noted in *Henry VIII*, then, is an essential part of Shakespeare's sources, not merely because he used conflicting accounts but because many Elizabethan Englishmen necessarily felt mixed emotions toward this chapter of their past.

Shakespeare may also have read in Edward Hall's *The Union of the Two Noble and Illustre Famelies of Lancastre and Yorke*, and in John Speed's *History of Great Britaine* (1611). In addition, he probably knew a dramatic version of the reign of Henry VIII that had appeared about eight years before, *When You See Me You Know Me* by Samuel Rowley (1603–1605).

STAGE HISTORY

Shakespeare belonged to the leading dramatic company of his time, and wrote plays to be acted by men who were his close professional associates. Unfortunately we do not know as much as we would like about the assignment of roles in his plays. The leading actor of the company, Richard Burbage, played Richard III, Hamlet, Othello, and King Lear. Probably he also played such roles as Macbeth, Antony, Coriolanus, and Prospero. In several roles he was impressive enough to have received contemporary mention. Will Kempe was a comic actor who took the part of Dogberry in *Much Ado about Nothing*, Peter in *Romeo and Juliet*, and probably other such buffoonish clowns. His departure from the company in 1599 made room for Robert Armin, a comic actor whose "style" was that of the wise or courtly fool. Shakespeare wrote for him the parts of Touchstone, Feste, Lavatch (in *All's Well*), and the Fool in *King Lear*. Shakespeare wrote his women's parts for boy actors, and was to an extent dependent on their quality and number. The boys, who served as apprentices to the actor-sharers, needed several years of experience before they could handle a demanding part like Juliet or Cleopatra, and yet some boys did manage to reach this remarkable level of proficiency before their voices started changing. The company needed a succession of boys so that they could be replaced in the women's roles when they became young men. (Some of them stayed on as young adult actors.)

Apart from specialized roles for the leading actor, the fool, and the boys, Shakespeare's company was versatile. The actor-sharers, men like John Heminges, Henry Condell, Augustine Phillips, Thomas Pope, Richard Cowley, and William Sly, undertook both major and minor roles as occasion demanded. In about 1603, John Lowin and Alexander Cooke joined the roster of principal actors in the King's company. Phillips died in 1605, making room for Samuel Gilburne. Sly died in 1608, and at this time William Ostler and John Underwood joined the company. Later prominent actors included Joseph Taylor, who played Iago, and Nathan Field. The acting of these men was of high quality. From our point of view today their style would probably seem formal or conventionalized, although considerably less so than that used by actors during Shakespeare's youth. As Hamlet's instructions to the players suggests (*Hamlet*, III,ii), Shakespeare's company put great stress on "naturalness" in acting and clearly believed they had reformed the ranting abuses of the earlier sixteenth century. Even so, Jacobean stage conditions militated against the kind of naturalistic informality we know today. Boys played women's parts; the language of the plays was often poetically quite formal; soliloquies and asides to the audience were common; no scenery existed to create a visual illusion; performance in open daylight on a broad apron stage before large audiences required a declamatory style of elocution; and the absence of artificial lighting precluded the use of night-time effects for ghosts or storms. Costuming ordinarily employed sumptuous Elizabethan dress, although sometimes with special costuming effects for Romans, Jews, sailors, and such.

Shakespeare's first known great success was *1 Henry VI*, in which the heroic role of Lord Talbot made a lasting impression. *Richard III* had a similarly spectacular popularity. Other enduringly popular successes in Shakespeare's own day included *Titus Andronicus*, *Romeo and Juliet*, *Richard II*, *Henry IV*, *Hamlet*, *Othello*, *Pericles*, and many others. On the other hand, *Troilus and Cressida* seems to have been a flop, and *Timon of Athens* probably was never even finished or performed. The history of *All's Well that Ends Well* is a total blank until the publishing of the 1623 Folio. Shakespeare's plays were often in demand at court.

Little is known of Shakespeare's plays in performance from the time of his death until 1642. His reputation was assured, but even as a classic he could not compete with the successful playwrights who succeeded him—notably John Fletcher. To be sure, in a commendatory verse to a collection of Shakespeare's poems in 1640, Leonard Digges asserted that Falstaff, Benedick and Beatrice, and Malvolio still drew fuller houses than Ben Jonson's dramatic creations. Nevertheless, the publication of the First Folio of Shakespeare's works in 1623, including several texts based on the prompt-books which the company had used for its actual performances, suggests that the King's men were no longer interested in guarding the exclusive rights to Shakespeare's plays. In any event, the closing of the theatres in 1642 by a Puritan-dominated Parliament put an end to legitimate theatre in England until the Restoration of 1660. During the interregnum period, Shakespeare lived on in the theatre only through the occasional surreptitious performance of "drolls" or farcical skits derived from *1 Henry IV* ("The Bouncing Knight," or Falstaff), *Hamlet* ("The Grave Makers"), and *A Midsummer Night's Dream* ("The Merry Conceited Humours of Bottom the Weaver").

From the Restoration to Garrick (1660–1742)

The Restoration period saw more adaptations of Shakespeare than performances of anything like the original. The age tended to regard Shakespeare as an untutored "natural" genius who wrote for unrefined audiences in an ignorant time. Any "improvements" to his text would only serve to elevate Shakespeare to the refinement and elegance he deserved. Most "improvements" reduced Shakespeare's sprawling plots to the decorous confines of the classical unities, or gave a new balance and symmetry to the action, or altered the fates of various characters to conform with classical ideas of poetic justice.

In Dryden's and Davenant's version of *The Tempest*

(1670), for example, leaborate symmetry of design is the overriding consideration. The adapters hit on the notion of what they called a "counter plot": since Shakespeare had told the story of a young lady who has never seen a young man, why not provide the play with a young man who has never seen a young lady? Hence the invention of Hippolito, young Duke of Mantua, whom Prospero has brought with him to the island at the time of his banishment and hid in a cave, safe from the fatal gaze of women. Inevitably, however, Hippolito discovers and falls in love with a woman his own age: not Miranda, but Miranda's sister Dorinda. Hippolito must also do battle for a time with Ferdinand, who is unsuccessfully confined to another cave. Eventually each Jack obtains his Jill. Caliban likewise has a sister, Sycorax, and Ariel has a fellow-spirit named Milcha. Milcha's role became much amplified in Thomas Shadwell's operatic version of 1674.

Perhaps the best-known adaptation of Shakespeare in the Restoration period was Nahum Tate's *King Lear*, 1681. This version ends happily, with Lear restored to his throne. The adaptation so satisfied eighteenth-century audiences in their craving for "poetic justice" (that is, a just punishment for villains and a deserved reward for heroes) that Shakespeare's version was banished from the stage until 1838. In Tate's defense, we might point out that prior to Shakespeare the Lear story had always ended with Lear's regaining of his throne; Shakespeare's is the great exception. Tate's version provided a love affair between Edgar and Cordelia. She remains in England rather than going to France, wanders about on the heath during the storm, and is nearly ravished by Edmund until Edgar providentially emerges from his cave and drives off the villain's henchmen. Tate also banished the Fool as offensive to classical ideas of "pure" tragedy unmixed with comedy.

Tate's revision of *Richard II*, called *The Sicilian Usurper*, 1681, ran into political trouble. Despite his changing of the scene to Sicily, and his plaintive insistence afterward that he had intended no offense, his play was seen by the government as a Whig attack on King Charles and was silenced on the third day. Many other Restoration and early eighteenth-century adaptations of Shakespeare had political ramifications: Tate's unsuccessful *Ingratitude of a Commonwealth* (1682) based on *Coriolanus*, John Dennis' *The Invader of His Country* (1719) also based on *Coriolanus*, and others.

One of the earliest Restoration adaptations was Davenant's *The Law Against Lovers*, based on *Measure for Measure* and staged in early 1662. Davenant eliminated virtually all the comic characters, and changed Angelo into a sentimentalized villain who truly loves Isabella, never intends to kill Claudio, and finally wins Isabella's hand in marriage. To this adapted plot Davenant added a subplot of Benedick and Beatrice, with Benedick as Angelo's brother and Beatrice as Angelo's ward. In his *Macbeth* (1674), Davenant stressed operatic splendor, with dancing witches and a ghost of Duncan that continues to haunt Lady Macbeth. This version held the stage until 1744. Thomas Killegrew's company did an adaptation of *The Taming of the Shrew* called *Sauny the Scot*, 1667, written by the actor John Lacy. Sauny is a replacement for Grumio, Petruchio's comic servant. Samuel Pepys disliked the play generally, but did admire the added part of Sauny with his Scottish humours. Thomas Shadwell's *Timon of Athens or the Man-Hater* (1678) gave great prominence to two women: Melissa, whom Timon intends to marry, and Evandra, his mistress whom he intends to leave. Evandra proves, however, to be Timon's only true friend, and they die in one another's arms.

The Restoration impulse to tighten up the classical unities can be seen in Dryden's *Troilus and Cressida, or Truth Found too Late*, 1679, and in his *All for Love, or the World Well Lost*, 1678. The latter is not really an adaptation of Shakespeare so much as a replacement. It tells the story of Antony and Cleopatra with obvious indebtedness to Shakespeare, but confines the action to the very last phase when the lovers are besieged in Alexandria. The cast is limited to about nine named characters as compared with about thirty-one in Shakespeare's play.

Other Restoration and early eighteenth-century adaptations include Thomas Otway's *Caius Marius* (1680), which took the place of Shakespeare's *Romeo and Juliet* until 1744, Tom Durfey's *The Injured Princess, or the Fatal Wager* (1682), based on *Cymbeline*, George Granville's *The Jew of Venice* (1701), which substituted for *The Merchant of Venice* until 1741, and Charles Burnaby's *Love Betrayed* (1703), based on *Twelfth Night*. Perhaps the best-known adaptation of the early eighteenth century is the *Richard III* (1700) of Colley Cibber, manager of the Drury Lane theatre and poet laureate. Some of Cibber's inclusions from *3 Henry VI*, and his added lines—"Off with his head, so much for Buckingham," or "Richard's himself again!"—are still used in modern productions. (See, for example, Laurence Olivier's film version of *Richard III*.)

The stage of the Restoration and early eighteenth century provided a notably different sort of setting for Shakespeare's plays than that of the Globe theatre. The acting companies were restricted in number by royal patent, and played in indoor theatres to a select courtly audience rather than to a cross-section of the London populace. Two companies were established at the beginning of the Restoration. That of Sir William Davenant, the Duke of York's players, began to play at the old theatre in Salisbury Court in 1660, but moved to a new theatre in Lincoln's Inn Fields the following year and to Dorset Garden in 1671. The company under Thomas Killegrew's management, the King's company, moved in 1660 from the Red Bull to a theatre built on Gibbons' Tennis Court in Vere Street and thence to a theatre on Bridges Street, Drury Lane, in 1663. When this first so-called Theatre

Royal was destroyed by fire in 1672, Killegrew's company set up temporarily in Lincoln's Inn Fields, but then moved to the magnificent second Drury Lane theatre, designed by Christopher Wren, in 1674. The two companies united in 1682, chiefly because of insufficiently large audiences to support both. Thereafter they performed chiefly in the Drury Lane theatre, the smaller of the two houses. This single company was the sole source of legitimate drama in London until 1695, when the restiveness of some underpaid actors led to the establishment of a newly patented acting company in Lincoln's Inn Fields. The new company enlisted some impressive talent, notably Thomas Betterton, Elizabeth Barry, and Anne Bracegirdle. Despite such a powerful beginning, and a new theatre in the Haymarket in 1705 designed by Sir John Vanbrugh, however, the project ultimately dwindled into failure and left the field to Colley Cibber at Drury Lane. All the actors united again in one company, and Haymarket became an opera house.

Restoration theatres increasingly made use of the kind of elaborate scenic adornment that, in Shakespeare's time, had been restricted almost entirely to the presentation of courtly masques. The early Restoration also saw use of the proscenium arch with a curtained stage behind it, although a considerable amount of the action still took place on the apron or outer stage. Scenic effects were sometimes lavish, and the tendency toward such spectacle encouraged the production of the operatic versions of Shakespeare already discussed. Artificial lighting was of course necessary for indoor performance, and actresses were used for women's parts in the plays. All these changes moved away from the fluidity and flexibility of the Elizabethan open-air apron stage, devoid of scenery.

The most famous actors of the period from the Restoration in 1660 until the advent of David Garrick in 1742 were Thomas Betterton and Colley Cibber. Betterton was famous for his Macbeth, Bassanio (in *The Merchant of Venice*), Brutus, Othello, and Hamlet. As a director he was responsible for some of the most extensive alterations of Shakespeare that the age witnessed. Cibber too was simultaneously a leading actor, theatre manager, director, and author of many revisions of Shakespeare. Other prominent actors and actresses included Barton Booth and Robert Wilks (who were also joint managers of the Drury Lane theatre), Anne Bracegirdle (who acted Portia, Desdemona, and other Shakespearean roles), and Elizabeth Barry (known for Calpurnia, Lady Macbeth, and Queen Gertrude). The famous Nell Gwyn seemingly did not undertake prominent Shakespearean roles.

The Age of Garrick (1742–1776)

The trend toward dominance of the London stage by a single man, who was manager, director, author, and his own star actor, reached its zenith in the career of David Garrick. His first dramatic season in 1741–1742, at an unlicensed and short-lived theatre in Goodman's Fields, included a resounding success in the role of Richard III. Soon he was hired at an enormous salary to act at Drury Lane. With some fellow actors he made attempts to secure a patent for a new company in 1743, and in 1746–1747 he performed memorably with the actor James Quin at Covent Garden. (The Covent Garden theatre had been providing successful competition for the Drury Lane theatre since its opening in 1732.) In 1747, however, Garrick returned to Drury Lane and became its joint manager and its chief moving spirit until his retirement in 1776.

One of Garrick's achievements during his glorious career was the revival of many Shakespearean plays that had been virtually forgotten. His predecessors had contented themselves with the repetition of a few predictable favorites, such as *Hamlet*, *Othello*, *King Lear* (in Tate's version, naturally), *Macbeth* (with dancing witches), *Julius Caesar*, *Richard III* (as transmuted by Cibber), and *1 Henry IV*. Only toward the end of the period had certain comedies been occasionally revived. Under Garrick, on the other hand, long-neglected comedies took a more regular place in the repertory. Garrick revived *Much Ado about Nothing* in 1748–1749 and *Cymbeline* in 1761–1762, playing the leading roles himself. He also staged lesser-known history plays such as *King John* and *Henry VIII*. His *Antony and Cleopatra* in 1759 was the first since Shakespeare's time. Garrick was his own most brilliant actor in *Hamlet*, *Much Ado about Nothing*, and many others; yet he shied away from certain roles in which other actors excelled. For example, he tended to defer to James Quin and Spranger Barry in *Othello* (at Covent Garden), Charles Macklin as Shylock, Quin as Falstaff, and still others. Garrick also grew too old for Romeo, and so ultimately abandoned that play. The Drury Lane repertory was thus closely tied to his personality and acting style.

Despite the enormous boost Garrick gave to Shakespeare in the theatre, and despite his occasional fidelity to something approaching the texts of the plays as Shakespeare wrote them, Garrick was still the child of his time in his predilection for adapted Shakespeare. His *Macbeth* was closer in some ways to the original than had generally been the case in the preceding century, and yet he omitted the Porter scene as offensive to the decorum of tragedy. His production of *Hamlet* in 1772 rewrote the one great Shakespearean tragedy that had heretofore escaped major revision. His *Romeo and Juliet* (1748) followed Otway's lead in having Juliet awake in the tomb before Romeo dies; and *The Fairies* (1755) entirely omitted the tradesmen of Athens and their performance of "Pyramus and Thisbe." Garrick's version of *The Tempest* was operatic, like Dryden's. *Katharine and Petruchio*, Garrick's adaptation of *The Taming of the Shrew* that included only the wife-taming plot, supplanted the Shakespearean original from 1756 to 1844 and remained popular long afterward. Garrick's *King Lear* (1756) retained Nahum Tate's happy ending, the love affair of Cordelia and Edgar, and the omission of the Fool, even though the actual poetry of some scenes was brought noticeably closer to that of Shakespeare.

Garrick's ability to transform himself in the performing of a role was legendary. He went to hospitals for the insane and studied the behavior of inmates in order to prepare himself for Lear's mad scenes. His passion for a natural style based on observation from life was highly innovative in an age generally devoted to a more formal and rhetorical manner of delivery. Garrick's range of characterization was also extraordinary. He performed low-comedy parts with such verisimilitude that some spectators came away from the theatre convinced that Garrick could be nothing other than a mean-spirited and worthless fellow. Yet his most famous effects were the violent passions: Hamlet's fear and awe in the presence of his father's ghost, Lear's ungovernable fury at his elder daughters' ingratitude, and the like.

One contribution of questionable worth made by Garrick to Shakespearean stage history was his great Shakespeare Jubilee, held at Stratford over a three-day period in the summer of 1769. In its own day the event was both praised as a great honor to Shakespeare's memory and vilified as an ostentatious charade. Its elaborate ceremonies were in fact notably lacking in the performance of Shakespeare's own works. The high point seems instead to have been Garrick's recitation of his "Ode Upon Dedicating the Town Hall, and Erecting a Statue to Shakespeare." Nevertheless, the celebration raised money for the maintenance of various historical monuments in Shakespeare's home town. The whole event did much to establish the vogue of idolatry of Shakespeare that was to be so much a part of nineteenth-century Shakespeare criticism.

Some leading actors from Garrick's time—Charles Macklin, James Quin, Springer Barry—have already been mentioned. Macklin, an older actor than Garrick, never got over his resentment of the younger man's success. Garrick's leading ladies included Hannah Pritchard as Rosalind, Beatrice, and Lady Macbeth; Peg Woffington as Rosalind, Isabella, Viola, Portia, and Mistress Ford; her rival, Anne Bellamy, as Juliet; Mary Ann Yates as Rosalind, Isabella, Cleopatra, and Lady Macbeth; and Susanna Cibber as Juliet. Their acting skill gave impetus to the repeated performances of such comedies as *As You Like It* and *Measure for Measure*.

The Romantic Age: Kemble, Edmund Kean, Macready (1776–1843)

The Romantic Age was generally not a flourishing time for the English theatre. As we have seen in a survey of Shakespeare criticism, Romantic critics such as Lamb and Hazlitt held condescending views of theatrical performances of Shakespeare, and preferred to read Shakespeare's text in the quiet of their own studies. The greatest literary figures of the age did not write for the stage; the occasional dramas written by the Romantic poets are usually "closet" dramas, designed to be read rather than acted. Garrick's huge success in producing Shakespeare proved hard to emulate. One reason for the decline may be that Shakespeare on the stage had been so thoroughly made over into a neoclassical dramatist by Tate, Cibber, and Garrick that he could no longer appeal to the taste of the new age in the outmoded theatrical guise that had been thrust upon him. Many Romantic critics and readers, intent now on the study of Shakespeare's philosophical idealism and of his conceptions of personality or "character," preferred the sublimity of Shakespeare's own poetry to the theatrical spectacle and classical "decorum" they found on the English stage.

Garrick's successor at Drury Lane was John Philip Kemble. Because of strained relations with Richard Brinsley Sheridan, he left Drury Lane in 1802 to undertake the management of Covent Garden, where he achieved a notable success and remained active until his retirement in 1817. Both theatre buildings burned during this period, Covent Garden in 1808 and Drury Lane in 1809, and were splendidly rebuilt. The new Covent Garden enabled Kemble to perform before a large audience of some three thousand spectators, and to indulge in more lavish sets than had heretofore been possible. Kemble was noted for his attention to realistic details in costuming and scenery. His *Henry VIII* (1788–1789) abounded in colorful processions; his *Coriolanus* (1789) was strikingly Roman in costume; his *The Tempest* (produced at this same time) "gave a terrible dance of Furies in one place, and a masque of Neptune and Amphitrite in another." Sarah Siddons, his best-known leading lady, excelled as Rosalind, Queen Katharine, Isabella, Hermione, and Lady Macbeth. Despite Kemble's popularity, however, his productions did not provide a return to Shakespeare's texts; indeed, his desire for spectacle often took him in the other direction. He restored some of Tate's additions to *King Lear* that Garrick had eliminated, and usually performed Shakespearean plays in the altered versions to which the previous age had grown accustomed.

During the years that followed Kemble's retirement in 1817, the English theatre was at a particularly low ebb. Edmund Kean succeeded Kemble as the leading actor of the day, and managed even to impress Romantic critics such as William Hazlitt. He was noted for his Othello and Coriolanus, among other roles. He did make significant restorations in the text of *King Lear* (1823), including the last act with the death of Cordelia; but he still retained the love of Cordelia and Edgar, omitted the Fool, and compromised his task of restoration to such an extent that a contemporary reviewer complained justifiably of too much "plastering." During this period between 1817 and 1837, in fact, the English theatre seems to have been more timid and bound by convention than its public would have desired. Stage traditions are often remarkably persistent, and those established by Tate, Cibber, and Garrick lived well beyond the age for which they were created.

In 1837, however, with the advent of Charles Macready as manager of Covent Garden (from 1837 to 1839) and Drury Lane (from 1841 to 1843), the time for a more thorough restoration of Shakespearean acting texts seemed at hand. Macready was unfortunately not an astute manager and did not achieve a great financial success. Nevertheless, in 1838 he did free *King Lear* "from the interpolations which have disgraced it for nearly two centuries," as a contemporary reviewer put it. Apart from the omission of the blinding of Gloucester, and some minor curtailments and rearrangements of scenes, the play was recognizably as Shakespeare had written it. No less impressively, Macready performed the same service for many other plays. By 1843, in fact, only *Richard III*, *Romeo and Juliet*, and *The Taming of the Shrew* were still being performed in the eighteenth-century versions of Colley Cibber and Garrick.

A reform of equal significance during this period was the abolition, by an act of 1843, of the monopoly on theatrical companies that had been in effect since 1660. The controlling of patents or licenses had had the effect, as we have seen, of limiting the London theatre to at most two companies. After 1843, on the other hand, any company could perform plays in a theatre that met the requirements of public safety. The English theatre, freed of manipulative control and nearly free of the eighteenth-century acting versions of Cibber and Garrick, was in a healthier state than it had been for some time.

The Later Nineteenth Century: Phelps, Charles Kean, Irving (1843–1902)

With the passage of the act in 1843 freeing the theatre from patent control, Drury Lane and Covent Garden fell into an almost immediate and overdue senility. (Drury Lane later recovered and flourished, however.) They were replaced by new theatres and new actors: in particular, Samuel Phelps at the Sadler's Wells theatre, and Charles Kean at the Princess theatre. A third important theatre was the Haymarket, featuring at various times Macready, Charles Kean and his wife, Helen Faucit, and others. All theatres were illuminated with the recently introduced gas lighting. Phelps managed Sadler's Wells until 1862, and presented there a repertory of unparalleled richness including many Elizabethan plays—*The Maid's Tragedy*, *The Duchess of Malfi*, *A New Way to Pay Old Debts*—in addition to those of Shakespeare. His actresses included Isabel Glyn (as Gertrude and Cleopatra) and Laura Addison (as Juliet and Imogen). Some notable revivals were *Timon of Athens*, *2 Henry IV*, and *Pericles*. Charles Kean, the son of Edmund Kean, was noted for his elaborate historical accuracy in the use of costumes and scenery—a trend toward spectacular verisimilitude that John Kemble and Charles Macready had already done much to further.

Under the guidance of Phelps and Kean, and also Ben Webster at the Haymarket, the English theatre continued to restore to Shakespeare his original texts. A Shakespearean *The Taming of the Shrew* appeared at the Haymarket in 1844, *Richard III* at Sadler's Wells in 1845, and *Romeo and Juliet* at the Haymarket in 1845. *King Lear* underwent even further restoration under Phelps' direction, in 1845, than it had received from Macready in 1838. Phelps' *Macbeth* (1847) put aside the musical and spectacular additions that had so long afflicted the witch scenes. During the 1860's, however, the great age of Phelps and Kean suffered a decline. Kean retired in 1859; and F. B. Chatterton at the Drury Lane theatre offered his ominous opinion that "Shakespeare spells ruin." Shakespeare was about to become, in other words, a heavy financial risk for the producer rather than a sure-fire commercial success. This circumstance was the inevitable result of the cumbersome, ornate, and costly productions that were increasingly common in the late nineteenth century.

Shakespearean production during the last decades of the nineteenth century was dominated by Henry Irving, manager of the Lyceum theatre from 1878 until 1902, and by Ellen Terry, his leading lady. Irving was a talented director and producer who enjoyed an enormous success and was eventually rewarded with burial in Westminster Abbey (like Garrick before him). Yet Irving's Shakespearean productions were, from a twentieth-century view at least, overburdened and unwieldy, ingeniously elaborate in unnecessary ways. His stage set for *Henry VIII* in 1892, for example, featured magnificent Tudor interiors with paneled wood ceilings and carved wooden arches, or renditions of Westminster Abbey with tall perpendicular-Gothic stained-glass windows. His striving for elaborate visual effects was the culmination of a trend begun in the Restoration and eighteenth century and perpetuated especially by Kemble, Macready, and Charles Kean. Throughout the entire period from 1660 to 1902, in fact, Shakespearean production never escaped this tendency toward the spectacular. Irving's sets were so massive, and his need for supernumeraries so great, that every Shakespearean production had to be special and costly. Shakespeare was no longer material for a stock repertory, and his plays were produced by Irving with relative infrequency. Because the changing of scenes involved so much time and expense, the texts of the plays had always to be cut and rearranged. Cibber's and Garrick's unreliable revisions were a thing of the past, to be sure, but no actor-producer of the nineteenth century would have thought seriously for a moment of doing Shakespeare uncut.

In America conditions were much the same, and indeed most productions of Shakespeare seen by Americans were either imported from England or inspired by English acting. Macready toured the United States in the 1820's and '40's, and became involved in a celebrated quarrel with the American actor Edwin Forrest. Charles Kean and Irving also acted in America; Kean played opposite Edwin Forrest, whereas Irving performed in 1880 with Edwin Booth. This latter person was the first American actor to win fame abroad. American Shakespeare of the Victorian era was, like its English counterpart, a heavy business. Much of it doubtless deserved the kind of roasting it received in Mark Twain's portrait of two fraudulent strolling Shakespearean actors in *Huckleberry Finn.*

The Twentieth Century: Revival and Adaptation

The early years of the twentieth century saw the continuation and even exaggeration of the opulent style championed by Henry Irving. The foremost actor-manager of the turn-of-the-century era was Herbert Beerbohm Tree, presiding genius at Her Majesty's theatre from its opening in 1897 until his death in 1917. His productions of Shakespeare in this theatre outdid Irving in his own metier, and were indeed lavish on an unprecedented scale. Live rabbits scurried across the stage in his *A Midsummer Night's Dream* (1900). The opening scene of *The Tempest* (1904) revealed a ship magnificently battered by a full-dress storm at sea. Tree's version of *Antony and Cleopatra* (1907) actually staged the meeting of Antony and Cleopatra in Egypt, instead of relying on Enobarbus' description of this event: Cleopatra appeared robed in silver, leading a huge procession through the streets of Alexandria. Such interpretations naturally called for a good deal of rearranging and curtailing of Shakespeare's texts. *King John* (1899) gave its viewers a tableau of Runnymede, even though the play never mentions Magna Carta. Olivia's garden in *Twelfth Night* (1901) revealed to the audience real grass, box hedges, statues, and running fountains. This set was, needless to say, particularly hard to move; scenes located at Duke Orsino's palace had somehow to be worked around the decor of Olivia's garden. Yet Tree was a great success, as Irving had usually been. So too was Johnston Forbes-Robertson, renowned actor of Hamlet and Othello, who expurgated his texts to conform with Victorian standards of decency.

Despite popular fondness for Beerbohm Tree's grand style, however, a movement toward greater stage flexibility and a fidelity to Shakespearean texts was under way. Frank Benson, who brought his repertory company from the provinces to the Lyceum theatre in 1900, offered relatively straightforward productions. Benson produced *Hamlet*, for example, in two sessions (afternoon and evening), from an uncut text of the First Folio. A performance of this sort could not possibly use the unwieldy sets of a Tree production. Benson never could match Tree in popularity, since the times demanded an ornamental style. Even so, his impact was significant. One ingredient of his method was simple economic common sense: he lacked the means to stage Shakespeare as expensively as Tree had done, and needed also to be able to take his flexible productions on tour.

William Poel was more of an idealist and visionary than Benson. His aim in establishing the Elizabethan Stage Society in 1894 was to discover more about Shakespeare's own stage, and to use that knowledge as a means of combating what he viewed as the stifling conventionality of the late Victorian theatre. He was a passionate crusader for swiftly paced acting, continuity of scenes, a fluid stage, and intimacy between actors and audience. His performances were Elizabethan revivals—usually meticulously so, with Elizabethan costuming, an inner stage and open platform, and other aspects of historical reconstruction. Although his audiences were never large, he did prove that Elizabethan staging could work as practical theatre. He performed *The Comedy of Errors* (1895) in Gray's Inn, where it had been performed in 1594 by Shakespeare's company. For his *Romeo and Juliet* (1905) he cast a girl of fourteen as Juliet and a boy of seventeen as Romeo. George Bernard Shaw saw the play and was enormously impressed.

Another believer in Poel's work was Harley Granville-Barker. His productions of Shakespeare at the Savoy theatre in 1912–1914 converted what had heretofore been an experimental movement into successful commercial theatre. In Granville-Barker's view, Poel had gone too far in stripping bare the overornamented stage of Beerbohm Tree. Granville-Barker hit instead upon a format that provided the essential elements of Poel's reform and yet avoided the cult of austerity for its own sake. His opening production in 1912, *The Winter's Tale*, employed three acting areas for the entire play, and stressed above all rapidity of pace and intimacy. He abolished footlights and realistic backdrops. In his *Twelfth Night* of the same year he did away with the tradition of burlesque foolery in which the comic characters had long been played. These innovations naturally caused an uproar, but they also found favor with influential critics. Beerbohm Tree's edifices were soon to become a thing of the past.

The "Old Vic" theatre and its acting company moved toward the new style of acting in the 1910's, mainly under the impetus of the producer Philip Ben Greet, and the theatre's manager, Lilian Baylis. This theatre on London's bankside had been built in 1818 and named the Royal Victoria in 1833. Since 1914 its company has specialized in Shakespearean performance under the direction of Tyrone Guthrie and others. Renamed the National Theatre Company in 1963, this organization continues to be a leader in modern Shakespearean production. Its roster of actors and actresses includes virtually all the great names of twentieth-century Shakespearean acting in Britain: John Gielgud, Ralph Richardson, Laurence Olivier, Michael Redgrave, Edith Evans, Margaret Webster, Charles Laughton, Emlyn Williams, Trevor Howard, Peggy Ashcroft, Maurice Evans, Flora Robson, Vivian Leigh, Cedric Hardwicke, Claire Bloom, Donald

Wolfit, Richard Burton, Wendy Hiller, and many more.

At Stratford, another theatre devoted primarily to "restored" Shakespeare prospered under the management of Frank Benson and then W. Bridges-Adams. A new building for this Memorial Theatre group was erected in 1932. Named the Royal Shakespeare Company since 1961, the organization flourishes today. Indeed, it has spawned a host of imitators in the Western Hemisphere, some of them of high quality: the Canadian Shakespeare Festival at Stratford, Ontario, the American Shakespeare Festival at Stratford, Connecticut, the Great Lakes Festival at Lakewood, Ohio, the Ashland Festival at Ashland, Oregon, and Joseph Papp's Shakespeare Festival in New York's Central Park. All of these Shakespearean repertory companies employ to some extent an open-platform stage, quick shifting of scenery, and the like. In this important sense, Shakespearean production throughout the later twentieth century has remained true to the spirit of Benson, Poel, and Granville-Barker in their rebellion against Victorian embroidery and the constricting proscenium arch.

In another important sense, however, twentieth-century Shakespeare on stage has sometimes returned to the custom of adapting Shakespeare in order to render him more palatable to contemporary tastes. Shakespeare has been remade in the image of modernity. The cant phrase in our day is "relevance," and the themes to which Shakespeare is adapted—alienation, the futility of the political process, the inhumanity of war, the struggles of the oppressed proletariat—are of course new. The occasional stridency of tone and the ideological insistence on a far-out political meaning in Shakespeare are also peculiarly modern, although several eighteenth-century productions of *Richard II* and *Coriolanus* were accused of taking sides in the political controversies of that day. Despite the seeming newness of modern adaptations of Shakespeare, then, the impulse toward updating him in terms of current history is by no means new. Indeed, the belief that Shakespeare ought to belong to our world and speak to its problems is not only a compliment to his universal appeal, but also a natural extention of the theatre's timeless purpose—to interpret Shakespeare. Yet when this purpose leads to the conviction that Shakespeare's texts as written cannot adequately communicate to a modern audience without extensive rearranging or rewriting, the modern director runs the danger of imposing on Shakespeare the same sorts of cultural distortions we have seen in the earlier adaptations of Tate, Cibber, and Garrick.

In some modern adaptations, Shakespeare's plays have become ideological weapons rather than works of art in their own right. Orson Welles' famous production of *Julius Caesar* (1937), for example, drew an analogy between the Caesar of the play and Benito Mussolini. Welles' satire of dictatorship was galvanizing to audiences threatened with the prospect of a Nazi-dominated Europe, but the interpretation of the play was of necessity one-sided; it allowed for no ironic perception of both good and evil in Caesar's one-man rule. Similarly, a production of *Coriolanus* in Paris in the 1930's caused political rioting when the radical left interpreted the play in their terms as an attack on dictatorship, and the extreme right conversely interpreted the play as an indictment of the cowardice and political opportunism of the mob and its leaders. This kind of adaptation of Shakespeare to modern ideological controversy started perhaps with a production of *Troilus and Cressida* in Britain at the close of World War I, in which the mocking of war seemed to capture a current mood of disillusionment. Ever since, it has been fashionable to stage Shakespeare as though he were a fervent opponent of war.

The most influential figures in this movement have included Bertolt Brecht, a leader in the German experimental theatre, and Ian Kott, author of *Shakespeare Our Contemporary*. Kott's book sees Shakespeare as one who speaks with poignant authority to our existentialist world. This view served as the basis, for example, of a Royal Shakespeare Company production of *Macbeth* in the 1960's, starring Alec Guinness and Simone Signoret, in which life was presented as a grotesque and scarifying experience comparable to that of Auschwitz. A production in the 1960's by the same group of the *Henry IV* plays and *Henry V*, under Peter Hall's direction, showed the influence of Brecht in its exaggeratedly squalid tavern scenes and in its terrifying rendition of the Battle of Agincourt—done in total darkness. Other productions of *Henry V* have also made the hero out to be a frightful prig (as George Bernard Shaw interpreted him), by overstating the ironies of Henry's "imperialistic" war against France and by caricaturing his famous speeches as so much cynical rhetoric. On the whole, however, Laurence Olivier's overtly patriotic film version of *Henry V*, produced in wartime England with the sponsorship of the British government, offered considerably less distortion to the text and was indeed a remarkably stirring experience—probably still the finest version of Shakespeare done on film.

Some twentieth-century adaptations of Shakespeare have succeeded in what they did by not pretending to be anything other than lighthearted transmutations of his work into different genres. The American musical comedy version of *The Taming of the Shrew* by Cole Porter, called *Kiss Me, Kate* (1948), featured some delightful songs and did not attempt to take itself too seriously. Equally successful and honest was the rock musical version of *The Two Gentlemen of Verona* in New York, 1972. Leonard Bernstein's *West Side Story* (1957) translated the ancient feud of the Capulets and Montagues from *Romeo and Juliet* into Puerto Rican gang warfare, New York style. The analogy was perhaps a facile and sentimentalized one, but the contemporary music and the frenetic dancing gave a compelling impression of violence and speed. Other musicals have included *The Boys from Syracuse* (1938), based on *The Comedy of Errors*, *Swingin' the Dream* (1939), taken from

A Midsummer Night's Dream, and *Your Own Thing* (1968), a rock adaptation of *Twelfth Night.* Perhaps there is no very great difference between such productions and, say, Dryden's and Davenant's operatic version of *The Tempest*, but at least musical comedy Shakespeare has not attempted to replace the original and banish it entirely from the stage.

On the other hand, adaptations that purport to offer Shakespeare's own plays transmuted into modern settings, or into modern theatrical styles such as the theatre of the absurd, too often succumb to the seeming necessity of rewriting those parts of the plays that no longer fit the new emphasis. Modern dress itself need have no such effect, of course. Despite its controversial beginnings, as, for example in H. K. Ayliff's *Macbeth* at the Royal Court theatre in 1928, Shakespeare in modern dress has successfully made its point that Elizabethan costuming is not necessary to an understanding of Shakespeare. Nor does the use of "period" costuming, as in Tyrone Guthrie's Edwardian version of *All's Well that Ends Well* (Shakespeare Memorial theatre, 1959), necessarily overwhelm the Shakespearean original. When the use of a far-out modern setting becomes a witty contrivance of the director to cover up what he considers an otherwise unintelligible text, however, then a dangerous kind of patronizing (of Shakespeare and of the audience) is at work. The American Shakespeare Festival at Stratford, Connecticut, in a production in the 1960's, transferred *Much Ado about Nothing* to a Texas ranch and portrayed Dogberry as a bumbling sheriff in the fashion of current television and movie westerns. This setting rendered meaningless or anachronistic the various aristocratic relationships and social customs on which Shakespeare's play depends. The analogy may have done something for Dogberry, in other words, but at the expense of the rest of the play. Similar troubles emerge when directors undertake to play *The Merchant of Venice*, for example, as "black" comedy or comedy of the absurd. Portia does have a waspish temper in satirizing her suitors, Bassanio is in part a fortune-hunter, and Shylock does have to endure the taunts of the Christians; but to stress the darker side of the play is to ignore its affirmative poetry about Christian love and to destroy the vision of an ironic balance between human happiness and human inadequacy. The focus on Shakespeare as "our contemporary," in Ian Kott's memorable phrase, is a valuable one so long as one is not trying merely to prove (when necessary, at the expense of Shakespeare's own text) that Shakespeare was a nihilist or Marxist progressive or crusader against war.

The controversy about adaptation of Shakespeare is still very much alive today, and will undoubtedly remain so. The forms of Shakespearean adaptation have altered, but the issues have remained virtually unchanged since 1660. When and to what extent ought the text to be rewritten to conform with the life styles of yesterday or today? Many observers would maintain that the dialogue between purists and adapters is not only inevitable, but healthy. The purist reformer, like William Poel, is needed as a voice of conscience and integrity even though he is perhaps doomed to play the role of lonely visionary. The adapter's goal is, on the other hand, to "interpret" Shakespeare; and, although directors' egos can at times loom larger than the object they would present (a criticism that applies equally to David Garrick and to Peter Brook, a recent Kott disciple), a lively director can certainly generate new interest in a work that might otherwise remain classically "pure" but lifeless. In any case, twentieth-century production has brought us a long way from the Romantic doldrums in which most intelligent readers of Shakespeare could not bear to have their author desecrated by a performance on stage.

SUGGESTIONS FOR READING AND RESEARCH

Abbreviations Used

Shakespeare Newsletter	*ShN*
Shakespeare Quarterly	*SQ*
Shakespeare Studies	*ShakS*
Shakespeare Survey	*ShS*

WORKS OF REFERENCE

Abbott, E. A. *A Shakespearian Grammar*. New edition, London, 1870.

Bartlett, John. *A New and Complete Concordance*. London, 1894, 1953.

Berman, Ronald. *A Reader's Guide to Shakespeare's Plays*. Rev. ed. Glenview, Ill., 1973.

Bullough, Geoffrey. *Narrative and Dramatic Sources of Shakespeare*. 7 vols. London, 1957—.

Campbell, Oscar James, and Edward G. Quinn, eds. *The Reader's Encyclopedia of Shakespeare*. New York, 1966.

Chambers, E. K. *William Shakespeare: A Study of Facts and Problems*. 2 vols. Oxford, 1930.

Ebisch, Walther, in collaboration with L. L. Schücking. *A Shakespeare Bibliography*. Oxford, 1931. *A Supplement for the Years 1930–1935*. Oxford, 1937.

Greg, W. W. *A Bibliography of the English Printed Drama to the Restoration*. 4 vols. London, 1939–1959.

———, ed. *Shakespeare Quarto Facsimiles*. London, 1939—. (An incomplete set; Greg's work is being supplemented by Charlton Hinman.)

Harbage, Alfred. *Annals of English Drama, 975–1700*. Rev. S. Schoenbaum. Philadelphia, 1964.

Hart, Alfred. *Shakespeare and the Homilies*. Melbourne, 1934.

Hinman, Charlton, ed. *The Norton Facsimile: The First Folio of Shakespeare*. New York, 1968.

Hosley, Richard, ed. *Shakespeare's Holinshed*. New York, 1968.

Kökeritz, Helge. *Shakespeare's Names*. New Haven, 1959.

———. *Shakespeare's Pronunciation*. New Haven, 1953.

Long, John. *Shakespeare's Use of Music: Comedies*. Gainesville, Fla., 1955. *Final Comedies*, 1961; *Histories and Tragedies*, 1971.

Muir, Kenneth. *Shakespeare's Sources*. 2 vols. London, 1957.

Muir, Kenneth, and S. Schoenbaum, eds. *A New Companion to Shakespeare Studies*. London and New York, 1971.

Munro, John, ed. *The Shakespeare Allusion Book*. 2 vols. London and New York, 1909; reissued 1932.

Naylor, Edward W. *Shakespeare and Music*. New ed., London, 1931.

Noble, Richmond. *Shakespeare's Biblical Knowledge*. London, 1935.

———. *Shakespeare's Use of Song*. London, 1923.

Onions, C. T. *A Shakespeare Glossary*. 2nd ed. Oxford, 1919.

Publications of the Modern Language Association of America (*PMLA*). Annual Bibliography.

Satin, Joseph, ed. *Shakespeare and His Sources*. Boston, 1966.

Schmidt, Alexander. *Shakespeare-Lexicon*. 5th ed. Berlin, 1962.

Seng, Peter J. *The Vocal Songs in the Plays of Shakespeare*. Cambridge, Mass., 1967.

Shakespeare Newsletter.

Shakespeare Quarterly.

Shakespeare Studies.

Shakespeare Survey.

Shakespearean Research Opportunities.

Spencer, T. J. B., ed. *Shakespeare's Plutarch*. Harmondsworth, Eng., 1964.

Spevack, Marvin. *A Complete and Systematic Concordance to the Works of Shakespeare*. 8 vols. projected. Hildesheim, Germany, 1968—.

Sternfeld, Frederick W. *Music in Shakespearean Tragedy*. London, 1963, 1967.

Studies in Philology. Annual Bibliography.

Taylor, G. Coffin. *Shakespeare's Debt to Montaigne*. Cambridge, Mass., 1925.

Thomson, James A. K. *Shakespeare and the Classics*. London, 1952.

LIFE IN SHAKESPEARE'S ENGLAND

Allen, Don Cameron. *The Star-Crossed Renaissance*. Durham, N.C., 1941.

Baker, Herschel. *The Image of Man: A Study of the Idea of Human Dignity in Classical Antiquity, the Middle Ages and the Renaissance*. Cambridge, Mass., 1961. (First published in 1947 as *The Dignity of Man*.)

———. *The Wars of Truth: Studies in the Decay of Christian Humanism in the Earlier Seventeenth Century*. Cambridge, Mass., 1952.

Bindoff, S. T., et al., eds. *Elizabethan Government and Society*. Essays presented to Sir John Neale. London, 1961.

Bush, Douglas. *The Renaissance and English Humanism.* Toronto, 1939.

Buxton, John. *Elizabethan Taste.* London, 1963.

Byrne, Muriel St. Clare. *Elizabethan Life in Town and Country.* 8th ed. London, 1970.

Caspari, Fritz. *Humanism and the Social Order in Tudor England.* Chicago, 1954.

Cassirer, Ernst. *The Platonic Renaissance in England,* trans. J. E. Pettegrove. Austin, Texas, 1953.

Chambers, R. W. *Thomas More.* London and New York, 1935.

Clapham, John. *A Concise Economic History of Britain from the Earliest Times to 1750.* Cambridge, Eng., 1949.

Craig, Hardin. *The Enchanted Glass.* New York, 1936.

Einstein, Lewis. *Tudor Ideals.* New York, 1921.

Elton, G. R. *The Tudor Revolution in Government.* Cambridge, Eng., 1959.

Ferguson, Arthur B. *The Articulate Citizen and the English Renaissance.* Durham, N.C., 1965.

Fisher, F. J. "Commercial Trends and Policy in Sixteenth-Century England," *The Economic History Review,* X (1940), 95–117.

Harbage, Alfred. *Shakespeare's Audience.* New York, 1941.

Harrison, G. B. *An Elizabethan Journal.* London, 1928; supplements.

———. *A Jacobean Journal . . . 1603–1606.* Lonon, 1941.

———. *A Second Jacobean Journal . . . 1607 to 1610.* Ann Arbor, Mich., 1958.

Haydn, Hiram. *The Counter-Renaissance.* New York, 1950.

Huizinga, Johan. *The Waning of the Middle Ages.* London, 1924; Baltimore, 1955.

Judges, A. V., ed. *The Elizabethan Underworld.* London and New York, 1930.

Kelso, Ruth. *The Doctrine of the English Gentleman in the Sixteenth Century.* Urbana, Ill., 1929.

Knappen, M. M. *Tudor Puritanism.* Chicago, 1939.

Knights, L. C. *Drama and Society in the Age of Jonson.* London, 1937.

Kocher, Paul. *Science and Religion in Elizabethan England.* San Marino, Calif., 1953.

Lovejoy, A. O. *The Great Chain of Being.* Cambridge, Mass., 1936.

Mattingly, Garrett. *The Armada.* Boston, 1959.

Mazzeo, Joseph A. *Renaissance and Revolution.* New York, 1965.

Neale, John E. *Elizabeth I and Her Parliaments.* 2 vols. London and New York, 1953–1958.

———. *The Elizabethan House of Commons.* London, 1949.

———. *Queen Elizabeth I.* London, 1934; New York, 1957.

Nichols, John, ed. *The Progresses and Public Processions of Queen Elizabeth.* 3 vols. London, 1823.

Nicoll, Allardyce, ed. *Shakespeare in His Own Age. ShS 17* (1964).

Ramsey, Peter. *Tudor Economic Problems.* London, 1963.

Read, Conyers. *Lord Burghley and Queen Elizabeth.* New York, 1960.

———. *Mr. Secretary Cecil and Queen Elizabeth.* New York, 1955.

———. *Mr. Secretary Walsingham and the Policy of Queen Elizabeth.* 3 vols. Oxford, 1925.

———. *The Tudors: Personalities and Practical Politics in Sixteenth Century England.* New York, 1936.

Rowse, A. L. *The England of Elizabeth: The Structure of Society.* London, 1951.

Seebohm, Frederic. *The Oxford Reformers.* 3rd ed. London, 1887, 1911.

Spencer, Theodore. *Shakespeare and the Nature of Man.* New York, 1942.

Stone, Lawrence. *The Crisis of the Aristocracy, 1558–1641.* Oxford, 1965.

Stow, John. *Survey of London,* ed. C. L. Kingsford. Oxford, 1971.

Strachey, G. Lytton. *Elizabeth and Essex.* London and New York, 1928.

Tawney, R. H. *Religion and the Rise of Capitalism.* New York, 1926, 1962.

Tayler, Edward W. *Nature and Art in Renaissance Literature.* New York, 1964.

Tillyard, E. M. W. *The Elizabethan World Picture.* London, 1943, 1967.

Wilson, F. P. *Elizabethan and Jacobean.* Oxford, 1945.

Wilson, J. Dover, ed. *Life in Shakespeare's England.* Cambridge, Eng., 1911; 2nd ed., 1926.

Wright, Louis B. *Middle-Class Culture in Elizabethan England.* Chapel Hill, N.C., 1935.

Zeeveld, W. Gordon. *Foundations of Tudor Policy.* Cambridge, Mass., 1948.

THE DRAMA BEFORE SHAKESPEARE

Adams, Henry H. *English Domestic or Homiletic Tragedy, 1575 to 1642.* New York, 1943.

Baskervill, Charles R. *The Elizabethan Jig and Related Song Drama.* Chicago, 1929.

Bevington, David. *From Mankind to Marlowe: Growth of Structure in the Popular Drama of Tudor England.* Cambridge, Mass., 1962.

———. *Tudor Drama and Politics.* Cambridge, Mass., 1968.

Boas, Frederick S. *University Drama in the Tudor Age.* Oxford, 1914.

Bowers, Fredson. *Elizabethan Revenge Tragedy, 1587–1642.* Princeton, 1940.

Bradbrook, Muriel C. *The Growth and Structure of Elizabethan Comedy.* London, 1955.

———. *Themes and Conventions of Elizabethan Tragedy.* Cambridge, Eng., 1935, 1960.

Brooke, C. F. Tucker. *The Tudor Drama.* Boston, 1911.

Brooke, Nicholas. "Marlowe as a Provocative Agent in Shakespeare's Early Plays," *ShS 14* (1961), 34–44.

Chambers, E. K. *The Elizabethan Stage.* 4 vols. Oxford, 1923.

———. *The Mediaeval Stage.* 2 vols. Oxford, 1903.

Clemen, Wolfgang. *English Tragedy before Shakespeare: The Development of Dramatic Speech*, tr. T. S. Dorsch. London, 1961.

Craig, Hardin. *English Religious Drama of the Middle Ages.* Oxford, 1955.

Craik, T. W. *The Tudor Interlude.* Leicester, 1958, 1962.

Cunliffe, J. W. *The Influence of Seneca on Elizabethan Tragedy.* London, 1893.

Doran, Madeleine. *Endeavors of Art: A Study of Form in Elizabethan Drama.* Madison, Wis., 1954, 1972.

Farnham, Willard. *The Medieval Heritage of Elizabethan Tragedy.* Berkeley, 1936.

Freeman, Arthur. *Thomas Kyd: Facts and Problems.* Oxford, 1967.

Gardiner, H. C. *Mysteries' End.* New Haven, 1946.

Greg, W. W. *A Bibliography of the English Printed Drama to the Restoration.* 4 vols. London, 1939–1959.

Harbage, Alfred. *Annals of English Drama, 975–1700.* Rev. S. Schoenbaum. Philadelphia, 1964.

Hardison, O. B., Jr. *Christian Rite and Christian Drama in the Middle Ages.* Baltimore, 1965.

Hogrefe, Pearl. *The Sir Thomas More Circle.* Urbana, Ill., 1959.

Hunter, G. K. *John Lyly: The Humanist as Courtier.* Cambridge, Mass., 1962.

Kocher, Paul H. *Christopher Marlowe: A Study of His Thought, Learning, and Character.* Chapel Hill, N.C., 1946.

Kolve, V. A. *The Play Called Corpus Christi.* Palo Alto and London, 1966.

Levin, Harry. *The Overreacher: A Study of Christopher Marlowe.* Cambridge, Mass., 1952, 1964.

Lucas, F. L. *Seneca and Elizabethan Tragedy.* Cambridge, Eng., 1922.

Margeson, J. M. R. *The Origins of English Tragedy.* Oxford, 1967.

Murray, Peter B. *Thomas Kyd.* New York, 1969.

Nicoll, Allardyce. *Masks, Mimes, and Miracles.* London, 1931.

Reed, A. W. *Early Tudor Drama.* London, 1926.

Ribner, Irving. *The English History Play in the Age of Shakespeare.* Rev. ed. London, 1965.

Rossiter, A. P. *English Drama from Early Times to the Elizabethans.* London, 1950.

Saccio, Peter. *The Court Comedies of John Lyly.* Princeton, 1969.

Salter, F. M. *Medieval Drama in Chester.* Toronto, 1955.

Southern, Richard. *The Medieval Theatre in the Round.* London, 1957.

Spivack, Bernard. *Shakespeare and the Allegory of Evil.* New York, 1958.

Talbert, Ernest William. *Elizabethan Drama and Shakespeare's Early Plays.* Chapel Hill, N.C., 1963.

Thompson, E. N. S. "The English Moral Plays," *Transactions of the Connecticut Academy of Arts and Sciences,* XIV (1910), 291–414.

Welsford, Enid. *The Court Masque.* Cambridge, Eng., 1927.

Wickham, Glynne. *Early English Stages, 1300 to 1660.* London, 1959–1972.

Williams, Arnold. *The Drama of Medieval England.* East Lansing, Mich., 1961.

Wilson, F. P. *Marlowe and the Early Shakespeare.* Oxford, 1953.

Wilson, F. P., and G. K. Hunter. *The English Drama, 1485–1585.* London and New York, 1969.

Collections of Plays

Baskervill, Charles R., et al., eds. *Elizabethan and Stuart Plays.* New York, 1934.

Bevington, David, ed. *Medieval Drama.* Boston, 1973.

Boas, Frederick S., ed. *The Works of Thomas Kyd.* Oxford, 1901.

Bond, R. Warwick, ed. *The Complete Works of John Lyly.* 3 vols. Oxford, 1902.

———, ed. *Early Plays from the Italian.* Oxford, 1911.

Brandl, Alois. *Quellen des weltlichen Dramas in England vor Shakespeare.* Strassburg, 1898.

Case, R. H., gen. ed. *The Works and Life of Christopher Marlowe.* 6 vols. London, 1930–1933.

Cawley, A. C., ed. *The Wakefield Pageants in the Towneley Cycle.* Manchester, 1958.

Creeth, Edmund. *Tudor Plays.* Garden City, N.Y., 1966.

Cunliffe, John W., ed. *Early English Classical Tragedies.* Oxford, 1912.

Dickinson, T. H., ed. *Robert Greene.* London, 1909.

Dodsley, Robert, ed. *A Select Collection of Old English Plays.* 4th ed. by W. Carew Hazlitt. 15 vols. London, 1874–1898.

Early English Text Society. London, 1864—. Publications include the York plays, ed. Lucy Toulmin Smith (1885), the Chester plays, ed. H. Deimling (1892), the Digby plays, ed. F. J. Furnivall (1896), the Towneley plays, ed. G. England (1897), the N Town plays or Ludus Coventriae, ed. K. Block (1922), the Macro plays, ed. Mark Eccles (1969), and the Non-Cycle plays and fragments, ed. Norman Davis (1970). Several are now being reedited.

Farmer, John, ed. *Tudor Facsimile Texts.* London, 1907–1914.

Malone Society Reprints. London, 1907—.

Manly, John M., ed. *Specimens of the Pre-Shakesperean Drama.* 2 vols. Boston, 1897.

Materialien zur Kunde des älteren Englischen Dramas. W. Bang, gen. ed. Louvain, 1902–1914.

Prouty, Charles T., gen. ed. *The Life and Works of George Peele.* 3 vols. New Haven, 1952–1970.

Rose, Martial, ed. *The Wakefield Mystery Plays.* New York, 1962.

Schell, Edgar T., and J. D. Shuchter, *English Morality Plays and Moral Interludes.* New York, 1969.

Young, Karl. *The Drama of the Medieval Church.* 2 vols. Oxford, 1933.

LONDON THEATRES AND DRAMATIC COMPANIES

Adams, John Cranford. *The Globe Playhouse.* Rev. ed. New York, 1961.

Adams, Joseph Quincy. *Shakespearean Playhouses.* Boston, 1917, 1960.

Armstrong, William A. *The Elizabethan Private Theatres: Facts and Problems.* London, 1958.

Baldwin, T. W. *The Organization and Personnel of the Shakespearean Company.* Princeton, 1927.

Beckerman, Bernard. *Shakespeare at the Globe, 1599–1609.* New York, 1962, 1967.

Bentley, Gerald Eades. *The Jacobean and Caroline Stage.* 7 vols. Oxford, 1941–1968.

———. "Shakespeare and the Blackfriars Theatre," *ShS 1* (1948), 38–50.

Brown, John Russell. *Shakespeare's Plays in Performance.* London, 1966.

Campbell, Lily B. *Scenes and Machines on the English Stage During the Renaissance.* Cambridge, Eng., 1923.

Chambers, E. K. *The Elizabethan Stage.* 4 vols. Oxford, 1923.

Feuillerat, Albert, ed. *Documents Relating to the Office of the Revels in the Time of Queen Elizabeth.* Louvain, 1908.

Foakes, R. A., and R. T. Rickert, eds. *Henslowe's Diary.* London, 1961.

Gildersleeve, Virginia C. *Government Regulation of the Elizabethan Drama.* New York, 1908.

Greg, W. W., ed. *Dramatic Documents from the Elizabethan Playhouses; Stage Plots; Actors' Parts; Prompt Books.* 2 vols. Oxford, 1931.

———, ed. *Henslowe Papers.* London, 1907.

Harbage, Alfred. *Theatre for Shakespeare.* Toronto, 1955.

Harrison, G. B. *Elizabethan Plays and Players.* London, 1940, 1956.

Hillebrand, H. N. *The Child Actors.* Urbana, Ill., 1926.

Hodges, C. Walter. *The Globe Restored.* London, 1953.

Hosley, Richard. "The Discovery-space in Shakespeare's Globe," *ShS 12* (1959), 35–46.

———. "The Gallery over the Stage in the Public Playhouse of Shakespeare's Time," *SQ*, VIII (1957), 15–31.

———. "A Reconstruction of the Second Blackfriars," *The Elizabethan Theatre*, ed. David Galloway. Toronto, 1969.

———. "Shakespeare's Use of a Gallery over the Stage," *ShS 10* (1957), 77–89.

———. "Was There a Music-room in Shakespeare's Globe?" *ShS 13* (1960), 113–123.

Joseph, Bertram L. *Acting Shakespeare.* London, 1960.

Kernodle, G. R. *From Art to Theatre: Form and Convention in the Renaissance.* Chicago, 1944.

King, T. J. *Shakespearean Staging, 1599–1642.* Cambridge, Mass., 1971.

Lawrence, W. J. *The Elizabethan Playhouse and Other Studies.* Stratford-upon-Avon, 1912, 1913; New York, 1963.

———. *The Physical Conditions of the Elizabethan Public Playhouse.* Cambridge, Mass., 1927.

———. *Pre-Restoration Stage Studies.* Cambridge, Mass., 1927.

Linthicum, Marie C. *Costume in the Drama of Shakespeare and his Contemporaries.* Oxford, 1936.

Murray, John T. *English Dramatic Companies, 1558–1642.* London and Boston, 1910.

Nagler, Alois M. *Shakespeare's Stage*, tr. R. Manheim. New Haven, 1958.

Nungezer, Edwin. *A Dictionary of Actors.* London and New Haven, 1929.

Reynolds, George F. *The Staging of Elizabethan Plays at the Red Bull Theater, 1605–1625.* New York, 1940.

Seltzer, Daniel. "Elizabethan Acting in *Othello*," *SQ*, X (1959), 201–210.

———. "The Staging of the Last Plays," *Later Shakespeare*, ed. John Russell Brown and Bernard Harris, pp. 127–165. Stratford-upon-Avon Studies 8. London, 1966.

Smith, Irwin. *Shakespeare's Blackfriars Playhouse.* New York, 1964.

———. *Shakespeare's Globe Playhouse.* New York, 1956.

Thompson, Elbert N. S. *The Controversy Between the Puritans and the Stage.* New Haven, 1903, 1966.

Thorndike, Ashley H. *Shakespeare's Theatre.* New York, 1916.

Venezky, Alice. *Pageantry on the Shakespearean Stage.* New York, 1951.

Wallace, C. W. *The Children of the Chapel at Blackfriars, 1597–1603.* Lincoln, Neb., 1908.

Wickham, Glynne. *Early English Stages, 1300 to 1660.* London, 1959–1972.

THE ORDER OF SHAKESPEARE'S PLAYS: HIS DRAMATIC DEVELOPMENT

Bayfield, Matthew A. *A Study of Shakespeare's Versification.* Cambridge, Eng., 1920.

Chambers, E. K. *William Shakespeare: A Study of Facts and Problems.* 2 vols. Oxford, 1930. Appendix H, with bibliographical note.

Clemen, Wolfgang. *The Development of Shakespeare's Imagery.* Cambridge, Mass., 1951.

Cruttwell, Patrick. *The Shakespearean Moment and Its Place in the Poetry of the Seventeenth Century.* London, 1954.

Furnivall, Frederick J., ed. *The Leopold Shakespeare.* London, 1876. The preface contains an explanation of the system of testing and dating plays.

Halliday, F. E. *The Poetry of Shakespeare's Plays.* London, 1954.

König, Goswin. "Der Vers in Shaksperes Dramen," *Quellen und Forschungen*, Vol. LXI, 1888. Contains the most extensive presentation of the numerical results of verse tests.

Monro, John, ed. *The Shakespeare Allusion Book: A Collection of Allusions to Shakspere from 1591 to 1700.* 2 vols. London and New York, 1909. Reissued by E. K. Chambers, London, 1932.

Ness, Frederic W., *The Use of Rhyme in Shakespeare's Plays.* New Haven and London, 1941.

New Shakespeare Society. *Publications*, 1874. Contains Fleay's original tests, Furnivall's discussion, and Ingram on weak endings; *Publications*, 1877–1879. Contains F. S. Pulling's work on the speech-ending test; this work is summarized in Frederick Fleay, *Shakespeare Manual.* London, 1876.

Saintsbury, George. *A History of English Prosody from the Twelfth Century to the Present Day.* London and New York, 1906–1910. Vol. II.

Nearly all modern editions of Shakespeare contain discussions of the dating of his plays.

SHAKESPEARE CRITICISM

Babcock, Robert W. *The Genesis of Shakespeare Idolatry, 1766–1799.* Chapel Hill, N.C., 1931, 1964.

Bentley, Gerald Eades. *Shakespeare and Jonson: Their Reputations in the Seventeenth Century Compared.* 2 vols. Chicago, 1945.

Bradby, Anne, ed. *Shakespeare Criticism, 1919–35.* London, 1936.

Dean, Leonard F., ed. *Shakespeare: Modern Essays in Criticism.* Rev. ed. London and New York, 1967, 1969.

Eastman, Arthur M. *A Short History of Shakespearean Criticism.* New York, 1968.

Eastman, Arthur M., and G. B. Harrison, eds. *Shakespeare's Critics; from Johnson to Auden.* Ann Arbor, 1964.

Halliday, F. E. *Shakespeare and His Critics.* Rev. ed., London and New York, 1958, 1963.

Johnson, Charles F. *Shakespeare and His Critics.* Boston, 1909.

Kermode, Frank, ed. *Four Centuries of Shakespearean Criticism.* New York, 1965.

Lovett, David. *Shakespeare's Characters in Eighteenth-Century Criticism.* Baltimore, 1935.

Monro, John, ed. *The Shakespeare Allusion Book.* 2 vols. London and New York, 1909; reissued 1932.

Muir, Kenneth. "Fifty Years of Shakespearian Criticism: 1900–1950," *ShS 4* (1951), 1–25.

Rabkin, Norman, ed. *Approaches to Shakespeare.* New York, 1964.

Ralli, Augustus. *A History of Shakespearian Criticism.* 2 vols. London, 1932.

Raysor, T. M., ed. *Coleridge's Shakespearean Criticism.* 2 vols. 2nd ed. London, 1960.

Ridler, Anne Bradby, ed. *Shakespeare Criticism, 1935–60.* London, 1963.

Sherbo, Arthur. *Samuel Johnson, Editor of Shakespeare.* Urbana, Ill., 1956.

Siegel, Paul N., ed. *His Infinite Variety: Major Shakespearean Criticism Since Johnson.* Philadelphia, 1964.

Smith, David Nichol, ed. *Shakespeare Criticism: A Selection.* World's Classics, Oxford, 1916.

———, ed. *Shakespeare in the Eighteenth Century.* Oxford, 1928.

Spencer, Hazelton. *Shakespeare Improved.* Cambridge, Mass., 1927.

Spingarn, J. E., ed. *Critical Essays of the Seventeenth Century.* Oxford, 1908–1909.

Westfall, A. V. *American Shakespearean Criticism, 1607–1865.* New York, 1939.

EDITIONS AND EDITORS OF SHAKESPEARE

Alexander, Peter. *Shakespeare's "Henry VI" and "Richard III."* Cambridge, Eng., 1929.

Bowers, Fredson. *Bibliography and Textual Criticism.* Oxford, 1964.

———. *On Editing Shakespeare.* Charlottesville, Va., 1966.

———. *On Editing Shakespeare and the Elizabethan Dramatists.* Philadelphia, 1955.

———. *Textual and Literary Criticism.* Cambridge, Eng., 1959.

Chambers, E. K. *William Shakespeare: A Study of Facts and Problems.* 2 vols. Oxford, 1930.

Craig, Hardin. *A New Look at Shakespeare's Quartos.* Stanford, 1961.

Doran, Madeleine. *"Henry VI," Parts II and III: Their Relation to "The Contention" and "The True Tragedy."* Iowa City, 1928.

Duthie, G. I. *Elizabethan Shorthand and the First Quarto of "King Lear."* Oxford, 1949.

Greg, W. W. *Collected Papers,* ed. J. C. Maxwell. Oxford, 1966.

———. *The Editorial Problem in Shakespeare.* 3rd ed. Oxford, 1954.

———. *Principles of Emendation in Shakespeare.* London, 1928.

———. *The Shakespeare First Folio: Its Bibliographical and Textual History.* Oxford, 1955.

Hart, Alfred. *Stolne and Surreptitious Copies: A Comparative Study of Shakespeare's Bad Quartos.* Melbourne and London, 1942.

Hinman, Charlton. *The Printing and Proof-Reading of the First Folio of Shakespeare.* 2 vols. Oxford, 1963.

Honigmann, E. A. J. *The Stability of Shakespeare's Text.* London and Lincoln, Neb., 1965.

McKerrow, R. B. *An Introduction to Bibliography for Literary Students.* Oxford, 1927.

———. *Prolegomena for the Oxford Shakespeare.* Oxford, 1939.

Pollard, Alfred W. *Shakespeare Folios and Quartos: A Study in the Bibliography of Shakespeare's Plays, 1594–1685.* London, 1909.

———. *Shakespeare's Fight with the Pirates and the Problems of the Transmission of His Text.* Rev. ed. Cambridge, Eng., 1937.

Pollard, Alfred W., and others. *Shakespeare's Hand in the Play of Sir Thomas More.* Cambridge, Eng., 1923.

Sisson, C. J. *New Readings in Shakespeare.* 2 vols. Cambridge, Eng., 1956.

Walker, Alice. *Textual Problems of the First Folio.* Cambridge, Eng., 1953.

Williams, George W., ed. *The Most Excellent and Lamentable Tragedie of Romeo and Juliet: A Critical Edition.* Durham, N.C., 1964.

Wilson, J. Dover. *The Manuscript of Shakespeare's "Hamlet" and the Problems of Its Transmission.* 2 vols. Cambridge, Eng., 1934.

SHAKESPEARE'S ENGLISH

Abbott, E. A. *A Shakespearian Grammar.* New edition, London, 1870.

Barish, Jonas A. *Ben Jonson and the Language of Prose Comedy.* Cambridge, Mass., 1960.

Baugh, Albert C. *A History of the English Language.* 2nd ed. New York, 1957, 1963.

Byrne, Muriel St. Clare, "The Foundations of Elizabethan Language," *ShS 17* (1964), 223–239.

Charney, Maurice. *Shakespeare's Roman Plays: The Function of Imagery in the Drama.* Cambridge, Mass., 1961.

———. *Style in Hamlet.* Princeton, 1969.

Clemen, Wolfgang H. *The Development of Shakespeare's Imagery.* Cambridge, Mass., 1951.

Crane, Milton. *Shakespeare's Prose.* Chicago, 1951.

Dobson, E. J. *English Pronunciation, 1500–1700.* 2 vols. 2nd ed. Oxford, 1968.

Evans, B. Ifor. *The Language of Shakespeare's Plays.* 2nd ed. London, 1959.

Franz, Wilhelm. *Shakespeare-Grammatik.* 3rd ed. Heidelberg, 1924.

Hulme, Hilda M. *Explorations in Shakespeare's Language.* London, 1962.

Jespersen, Otto. *Growth and Structure of the English Language.* 9th ed. New York, 1955.

Joseph, Sister Miriam. *Shakespeare's Use of the Arts of Language.* New York, 1947. Reprinted in part as *Rhetoric in Shakespeare's Time* (1962).

Kökeritz, Helge. *Shakespeare's Names.* New Haven, 1959.

———. *Shakespeare's Pronunciation.* New Haven, 1953.

Mahood, M. M. *Shakespeare's Wordplay.* London, 1957.

Muir, Kenneth. "Shakespeare's Imagery—Then and Now," *ShS 18* (1965), 46–57.

Nares, Robert. *A Glossary . . . of Shakespeare and His Contemporaries.* New ed. by J. O. Halliwell and Thomas Wright. 2 vols. London, 1905. Repr. Detroit, 1966.

Onions, C. T. *A Shakespeare Glossary.* 2nd ed. Oxford, 1919.

Partridge Eric. *Shakespeare's Bawdy.* London, 1947, 1955.

Schmidt, Alexander. *Shakespeare-Lexicon.* 4th ed. Berlin and Leipzig, 1923.

Spurgeon, Caroline. *Shakespeare's Imagery and What It Tells Us.* Cambridge, Eng., 1935.

Vickers, Brian. *The Artistry of Shakespeare's Prose.* London, 1968.

Willcock, Gladys D. "Shakespeare and Elizabethan English," *ShS* 7 (1954), 12–24.

SHAKESPEARE'S CONTEMPORARY DRAMATISTS, AND THE SHAKESPEARE APOCRYPHA

Allen, Morse. *The Satire of John Marston.* Columbus, Ohio, 1920.

Bald, R. C. "*The Booke of Sir Thomas More* and Its Problems," *ShS 2* (1949), 44–61.

Barish, Jonas A., ed. *Ben Jonson: A Collection of Critical Essays.* Englewood Cliffs, N.J., 1963.

Bentley, Gerald Eades. *The Jacobean and Caroline Stage.* 7 vols. Oxford, 1941–1968.

———. "Shakespeare and the Blackfriars Theatre," *ShS 1* (1948), 38–50.

Berringer, Ralph W. "Jonson's *Cynthia's Revels* and the War of the Theatres," *Philological Quarterly,* XXII (1943), 1–22.

Bertram, Paul. *Shakespeare and "The Two Noble Kinsmen."* New Brunswick, N.J., 1965.

Bowers, Fredson T. *Elizabethan Revenge Tragedy, 1587–1642.* Princeton, 1940.

———, ed. *The Dramatic Works of Thomas Dekker.* 4 vols. Cambridge, Eng., 1953–1961.

———, gen. ed. *The Dramatic Works in the Beaumont and Fletcher Canon.* Cambridge, Eng., 1966—.

Brooke, C. F. Tucker, ed. *The Shakespeare Apocrypha.* Oxford, 1908. These plays are currently being re-edited by Richard Proudfoot.

Bullen, A. H., ed. *The Works of Thomas Middleton.* London, 1885–1886.

Caputi, Anthony. *John Marston, Satirist.* Ithaca, N.Y., 1961.

Collins, D. C. "On the Date of *Sir Thomas More,*" *Review of English Studies,* X (1934), 401–411.

Ellis-Fermor, Una. *The Jacobean Drama.* London, 1936.

Gibbons, Brian. *Jacobean City Comedy.* Cambridge, Mass., 1968.

Graves, T. S. "The Political Use of the Stage During the Reign of James I," *Anglia,* XXXVIII (1914), 137–156.

Gregg, Kate L. *Thomas Dekker: A Study in Economic and Social Backgrounds.* Seattle, 1924.

Harbage, Alfred. *Shakespeare and the Rival Traditions.* New York, 1952.

Herford, C. H., and Percy Simpson, eds. *Ben Jonson.* 11 vols. Oxford, 1925–1952.

Heywood, Thomas. *An Apology for Actors.* London, 1612. Ed. Richard H. Perkinson. New York, 1941.

Hunt, Mary L. *Thomas Dekker.* New York, 1911.

Kernan, Alvin. *The Cankered Muse: Satire of the English Renaissance.* New Haven, 1959.

Kirsch, Arthur C. *Jacobean Dramatic Perspectives.* Charlottesville, Va., 1972.

Leech, Clifford. *The John Fletcher Plays.* Cambridge, Mass., 1962.

———. *Shakespeare's Tragedies and Other Studies in Seventeenth Century Drama.* London, 1950.

Leishman, J. B., ed. *The Three Parnassus Plays (1598–1601).* London, 1949.

Lucas, F. L., ed. *The Complete Works of John Webster.* London, 1927.

Malone Society Reprints. Editions of many plays not otherwise represented in this list of books.

Maxwell, Baldwin, *Studies in the Shakespeare Apocrypha.* New York, 1956.

McKeithan, Daniel M. *The Debt to Shakespeare in the Beaumont and Fletcher Plays.* Austin, Texas, 1938.

Morris, Brian. *John Webster.* London, 1970.

Muir, Kenneth. *Shakespeare as Collaborator.* London, 1960.

Nosworthy, J. M. "Shakespeare and *Sir Thomas More,*" *Review of English Studies,* n. s., VI (1955), 12–25.

Ornstein, Robert. *The Moral Vision of Jacobean Tragedy.* Madison, Wis., 1960.

Parrott, T. M., ed. *The Plays and Poems of George Chapman.* 2 vols. London, 1910–1914.

Pettet, E. C. *Shakespeare and the Romance Tradition.* London, 1949.

Price, George R. *Thomas Dekker.* New York, 1969.

Ribner, Irving. *The English History Play in the Age of Shakespeare.* Rev. ed. London, 1965.

Ristine, Frank. *English Tragicomedy.* New York, 1910.

Spivack, Charlotte. *George Chapman.* New York, 1967.

Steele, Mary S. *Plays and Masques at Court During the Reigns of Elizabeth, James, and Charles.* New Haven and London, 1926.

Thorndike, Ashley H. *The Influence of Beaumont and Fletcher on Shakespeare.* Worcester, Mass., 1901.

Waith, Eugene M. *The Herculean Hero in Marlowe, Chapman, Shakespeare, and Dryden.* New York, 1962.

———. *The Pattern of Tragicomedy in Beaumont and Fletcher.* New Haven, 1952.

Welsford, Enid. *The Court Masque.* Cambridge, Eng., 1927.

Wickham, Glynne. *Early English Stages, 1300 to 1660.* London, 1959–1972.

Wilson, F. P. *Elizabethan and Jacobean.* Oxford, 1945.

STAGE HISTORY

Baldwin, T. W. *The Organization and Personnel of the Shakespearean Company.* Princeton, 1927.

Bartholomeusz, Dennis. *Macbeth and the Players.* Cambridge, Eng., 1969.

Brown, Ivor. *Shakespeare and the Actors.* London, 1970.

Brown, John Russell. *Shakespeare's Plays in Performance.* London, 1966.

THE HENRY THE SIXTH PLAYS

Alexander, Peter. *Shakespeare's "Henry VI" and "Richard III."* Cambridge, Eng., 1929.

Berman, Ronald S. "Fathers and Sons in the Henry VI Plays," *SQ*, XIII (1962), 487–497.

Bevington, David. "The Domineering Female in *1 Henry VI*," *ShakS 2* (1966), 51–58.

Brockbank, J. P. "The Frame of Disorder—*Henry VI*," *Early Shakespeare*, ed. John Russell Brown and Bernard Harris, pp. 73–99. Stratford-upon-Avon Studies 3. London, 1961.

Clemen, Wolfgang H. "Anticipation and Foreboding in Shakespeare's Early Histories," *ShS 6* (1953), 23–35.

Doran, Madeleine. *"Henry VI," Parts II and III: Their Relation to "The Contention" and "The True Tragedy."* Iowa City, 1928.

Gaw, Allison. *The Origin and Development of "1 Henry VI" in Relation to Shakespeare, Marlowe, Peele, and Greene.* Los Angeles, 1926.

Kingsford, Charles L. "Fifteenth-Century History in Shakespeare," *Prejudice and Promise in Fifteenth-Century England.* Oxford, 1925.

Law, R. A. "The Chronicles and the *Three Parts* of *Henry VI*," *University of Texas Studies in English*, XXXIII (1954), 13–32.

Leech, Clifford. "The Two-Part Play: Marlowe and the Early Shakespeare," *Shakespeare Jahrbuch*, XCIV (1958), 90–106.

Prouty, Charles T. *"The Contention" and Shakespeare's "2 Henry VI": A Comparative Study.* New Haven, 1954.

Turner, Robert Y. "Characterization in Shakespeare's Early History Plays," *English Literary History*, XXXI (1964), 241–258.

———. "Shakespeare and the Public Confrontation Scene in the Early History Plays," *Modern Philology*, LXXII (1964), 1–12.

Wilson, F. P. *Marlowe and the Early Shakespeare.* Oxford, 1953.

Zeeveld, W. Gordon. "The Influence of Hall on Shakespeare's English Historical Plays," *English Literary History*, III (1936), 317–353.

RICHARD THE THIRD

Brooke, Nicholas. "Reflecting Gems and Dead Bones: Tragedy Versus History in *Richard III*," *Critical Quarterly*, VII (1965), 123–134.

Churchill, George B. *Richard the Third up to Shakespeare. Palaestra*, X. Berlin, 1900.

Clemen, Wolfgang H. *A Commentary on Richard III.* Tr. Jean Bonheim. London, 1968.

———. "Tradition and Originality in Shakespeare's *Richard III*," *SQ*, V (1954), 247–257.

Gerber, Richard. "Elizabethan Convention and Psychological Realism in the Dream and Last Soliloquy of *Richard III*," *English Studies*, XL (1959), 294–300.

Heilman, Robert B. "Satiety and Conscience: Aspects of *Richard III*," *Antioch Review*, XXIV (1964), 57–73.

Kendall, Paul Murray. *Richard the Third.* New York and London, 1956.

Krieger, Murray. "The Dark Generations of *Richard III*," *Criticism*, I (1959), 32–48.

Rossiter, A. P. *Angel with Horns.* London, 1961.

———. "The Structure of *Richard III*," *Durham University Journal*, XXXI (1938), 44–75.

Spivack, Bernard. *Shakespeare and the Allegory of Evil.* New York, 1958.

Stoll, E. E. *Shakespeare Studies.* New York, 1942.

Wood, Alice I. P. *The Stage History of Shakespeare's "King Richard the Third."* New York, 1909.

KING JOHN

Berman, Ronald. "Anarchy and Order in *Richard III* and *King John*," *ShS 20* (1967), 51–59.

Bonjour, Adrien. "The Road to Swinstead Abbey: A Study of the Sense and Structure of *King John*," *English Literary History*, XVIII (1951), 253–274.

Calderwood, James L. "Commodity and Honour in *King John*," *University of Toronto Quarterly*, XXIX (1960), 341–356.

Elliott, John R., Jr., "Shakespeare and the Double Image of King John," *ShakS 1* (1965), 64–84.

Elson, John. "Studies in the *King John* Plays," *J. Q. Adams Memorial Studies*, ed. J. McManaway et al., pp. 183–198. Washington, D.C., 1948.

Harrison, G. B. "Shakespeare's Topical Significances: *I. King John*," *Times Literary Supplement*, 13 Nov. 1930. Reprinted in Anne Bradby, ed., *Shakespeare Criticism, 1919–35.* London, 1936.

Matchett, William H. "Richard's Divided Heritage in *King John*," *Essays in Criticism*, XII (1962), 231–253.

Petit-Dutaillis, Charles. *Le Roi Jean et Shakespeare.* Paris, 1944.

Pettet, E. C. "Hot Irons and Fever: A Note on Some of the Imagery of *King John,*" *Essays in Criticism,* IV (1954), 128–144.

Salter, F. M. "The Problem of *King John,*" *Proceedings and Transactions of the Royal Society of Canada,* XLIII, series III section 2 (1949), 115–136.

Van de Water, Julia C. "The Bastard in *King John,*" *SQ,* XI (1960), 137–146.

Warren, Wilfred L. *King John.* New York, 1961.

TITUS ANDRONICUS

Adams, John C. "Shakespeare's Revisions in *Titus Andronicus,*" *SQ,* XV (1964), 177–190.

Baker, Howard. *Induction to Tragedy.* Baton Rouge, La., 1939.

Barroll, J. Leeds. "Shakespeare and Roman History," *Modern Language Review,* LIII (1958), 327–343.

Bolton, Joseph. "*Titus Andronicus:* Shakespeare at Thirty," *Studies in Philology,* XXX (1933), 208–224.

Bowers, Fredson T. *Elizabethan Revenge Tragedy, 1587–1642.* Princeton, 1940.

Cutts, John P. "Shadow and Substance: Structural Unity in *Titus Andronicus,*" *Comparative Drama,* II (1968), 161–172.

Hamilton, A. C. "*Titus Andronicus:* The Form of Shakespearian Tragedy," *SQ,* XIV (1963), 201–213.

Harris, Bernard. "A Portrait of a Moor," *ShS 11* (1958), 89–97.

Law, R. A. "The Roman Background of *Titus Andronicus,*" *Studies in Philology,* XL (1943), 145–153.

Maxwell, J. C. "Shakespeare's Roman Plays: 1900–1956," *ShS 10* (1957), 1–11.

Price, Hereward T. "The Authorship of *Titus Andronicus,*" *Journal of English and Germanic Philology,* XLII (1943), 55–81.

Sargent, Ralph M. "The Source of *Titus Andronicus,*" *Studies in Philology,* XLVI (1949), 167–183.

Sommers, Alan. " 'Wilderness of Tigers': Structure and Symbolism in *Titus Andronicus,*" *Essays in Criticism,* X (1960), 275–289.

Spencer, Terence. "Shakespeare and the Elizabethan Romans," *ShS 10* (1957), 27–38.

Spivack, Bernard. *Shakespeare and the Allegory of Evil.* New York, 1958.

Thomson, James A. K. *Shakespeare and the Classics.* London, 1952.

Waith, Eugene. "The Metamorphosis of Violence in *Titus Andronicus,*" *ShS 10* (1957), 39–49.

Wilson, J. Dover. "*Titus Andronicus* on the Stage in 1595," *ShS 1* (1948), 17–22.

ROMEO AND JULIET

Adams, Barry B. "The Prudence of Prince Escalus," *English Literary History,* XXXV (1968), 32–50.

Bowling, Lawrence E. "The Thematic Framework of *Romeo and Juliet,*" *PMLA,* LXIV (1949), 208–220.

Brown, John Russell. "S. Franco Zeffirelli's *Romeo and Juliet,*" *ShS 15* (1962), 147–155.

Dickey, Franklin M. *Not Wisely But Too Well.* San Marino, Calif., 1957.

Granville-Barker, Harley. *Prefaces to Shakespeare,* vol. II. Princeton, 1947.

Hill, R. F. "Shakespeare's Early Tragic Mode," *SQ,* IX (1958), 455–469.

Hosley, Richard. "The Use of the Upper Stage in *Romeo and Juliet,*" *SQ,* V (1954), 371–379.

Levin, Harry. "Form and Formality in *Romeo and Juliet,*" *SQ,* XI (1960), 1–11.

Mahood, M. M. *Shakespeare's Wordplay.* London, 1957.

McArthur, Herbert. "Romeo's Loquacious Friend," *SQ,* X (1959), 35–44.

Moore, Olin H. *The Legend of Romeo and Juliet.* Columbus, Ohio, 1950.

Nevo, Ruth. "Tragic Form in *Romeo and Juliet,*" *Studies in English Literature,* IX (1969), 241–258.

Nosworthy, J. M. "The Two Angry Families of Verona," *SQ,* III (1952), 219–226.

Pettet, E. C. "The Imagery of *Romeo and Juliet,*" *English,* VIII (1950), 121–126.

Siegel, Paul N. "Christianity and the Religion of Love in *Romeo and Juliet,*" *SQ,* XII (1961), 371–392.

Tanselle, G. Thomas. "Time in *Romeo and Juliet,*" *SQ,* XV (1964), 349–361.

Williams, George W., ed. *The Most Excellent and Lamentable Tragedie of Romeo and Juliet.* Durham, N.C., 1964.

THE POEMS

Alvarez, A. "William Shakespeare: The Phoenix and the Turtle," *Interpretations*, ed. John Wain. London, 1955.

Beeching, Henry C. *The Sonnets of Shakespeare*. Boston, 1904.

Booth, Stephen. *An Essay on Shakespeare's Sonnets*. New Haven, 1969.

Bradbrook, Muriel C. *Shakespeare and Elizabethan Poetry*. London, 1951.

Bradley, A. C. *Oxford Lectures on Poetry*. London, 1909, 1961.

Bush, Douglas. *Mythology and the Renaissance Tradition in English Poetry*. Minneapolis and London, 1932; rev ed., 1963.

Chambers, E. K. *Shakespearean Gleanings*. London, 1944.

Cruttwell, Patrick. *The Shakespearean Moment and Its Place in the Poetry of the Seventeenth Century*. London, 1954.

Empson, William. "*The Phoenix and the Turtle*," *Essays in Criticism*, XVI (1966), 147–153.

Hamilton, A. C. "*Venus and Adonis*," *Studies in English Literature*, I, no. 1 (1961), 1–15.

Herrnstein, Barbara, ed. *Discussions of Shakespeare's Sonnets*. Boston, 1964.

Hubler, Edward. *The Sense of Shakespeare's Sonnets*. Princeton, 1952.

Hubler, Edward, Northrop Frye, Leslie A. Fiedler, Stephen Spender, and R. P. Blackmur. *The Riddle of Shakespeare's Sonnets*. New York, 1962.

Knight, G. Wilson. *The Mutual Flame: On Shakespeare's Sonnets and The Phoenix and the Turtle*. London, 1955.

Krieger, Murray. *A Window to Criticism: Shakespeare's Sonnets and Modern Poetics*. Princeton, 1964.

Landry, Hilton. *Interpretations in Shakespeare's Sonnets*. Berkeley, 1963.

Leishman, J. B. *Themes and Variations in Shakespeare's Sonnets*. London, 1961.

Lever, J. W. *The Elizabethan Love Sonnet*. London, 1956.

Lewis, C. S. *English Literature in the Sixteenth Century*. Oxford, 1954, 1965.

Matchett, William H. *The Phoenix and the Turtle: Shakespeare's Poems and Chester's Loues Martyr*. The Hague, 1965.

Maxwell, J. C., ed. *The Poems*. The New Cambridge Shakespeare. London, 1969.

Muir, Kenneth. "*A Lover's Complaint:* A Reconsideration," *Shakespeare 1564–1964*, ed. E. A. Bloom, pp. 154–166. Providence, 1964.

Nicoll, Allardyce, ed. *ShS 15* (1962).

Prince, F. T. *William Shakespeare: The Poems*. London, 1963.

Ransom, John Crowe. *The World's Body*. New York and London, 1938, 1968.

Rollins, Hyder E. *A New Variorum Edition of Shakespeare: The Poems*. Philadelphia, 1938. *The Sonnets*. Philadelphia, 1944.

Shakespeare, William. *Shakespeare's Poems: A Facsimile of the Earliest Editions*. New Haven, 1964.

THE PERIOD OF COMEDIES AND HISTORIES

The Comedies

Barber, C. L. *Shakespeare's Festive Comedy*. Princeton, 1959.

Brown, John Russell. *Shakespeare and His Comedies*. London, 1957, 1968.

Campbell, Oscar James. *Shakespeare's Satire*. London and New York, 1943, 1963.

Champion, Larry S. *The Evolution of Shakespeare's Comedy*. Cambridge, Mass., 1970.

Charlton, H. B. *Shakespearian Comedy*. London, 1938.

Evans, Bertrand. *Shakespeare's Comedies*. Oxford, 1960.

Frye, Northrop. "The Argument of Comedy," *English Institute Essays 1948*. New York, 1949.

———. "Characterization in Shakespearian Comedy," *SQ*, IV (1953), 271–277.

———. *A Natural Perspective: The Development of Shakespearean Comedy and Romance*. New York, 1965.

Hunter, Robert G. *Shakespeare and the Comedy of Forgiveness*. New York, 1965.

Muir, Kenneth, ed. *Shakespeare: The Comedies*. Englewood Cliffs, N.J., 1965.

Palmer, John. *Comic Characters of Shakespeare*. London, 1946.

Parrott, T. M. *Shakespearean Comedy*. New York, 1949.

Pettet, E. C. *Shakespeare and the Romance Tradition*. London, 1949.

Phialas, Peter G. *Shakespeare's Romantic Comedies*. Chapel Hill, N.C., 1966.

Sen Gupta, S. C. *Shakespearian Comedy*. London, 1950.

Stevenson, David L. *The Love-Game Comedy*. New York, 1946.

The Histories

Campbell, Lily B. *Shakespeare's "Histories": Mirrors of Elizabethan Policy*. San Marino, Calif., 1947.

Charlton, H. B. *Shakespeare, Politics and Politicians*. Oxford, 1929.

Craig, Hardin. "Shakespeare and the History Play," *J. Q. Adams Memorial Studies*, ed., J. McManaway et al., pp. 55–64. Washington, D.C., 1948.

Dorius, R. J., ed. *Discussions of Shakespeare's Histories*. Boston, 1964.

Ellis-Fermor, Una. *The Frontiers of Drama*, chap. III. 2nd ed. London, 1964.

Jenkins, Harold. "Shakespeare's History Plays: 1900–1951," *ShS 6* (1953), 1–15.
Kelly, Henry A. *Divine Providence in the England of Shakespeare's Histories*. Cambridge, Mass., 1970.
Knights, L. C. "Shakespeare and Political Wisdom," *Sewanee Review*, LXI (1953), 43–55.
———. "Shakespeare's Politics: With Some Reflections on the Nature of Tradition," *Proceedings of the British Academy*, XLIII (1957), 115-132.
Ornstein, Robert. *A Kingdom for a Stage*. Cambridge, Mass., 1972.
Palmer, John. *Political Characters of Shakespeare*. London, 1945.
Pierce, Robert B. *Shakespeare's History Plays: The Family and the State*. Columbus, Ohio, 1971.
Reese, M. M. *The Cease of Majesty*. London and New York, 1961.
Ribner, Irving. *The English History Play in the Age of Shakespeare*. Rev. ed. London, 1965.
Richmond, H. M. *Shakespeare's Political Plays*. New York, 1967.
Rossiter, A. P. "Ambivalence: The Dialectic of the Histories," *Talking of Shakespeare*, ed. John Garrett. London, 1954.
Sen Gupta, S. C. *Shakespeare's Historical Plays*. London, 1964.
Talbert, Ernest William. *The Problem of Order*. Chapel Hill, N.C., 1962.
Tillyard, E. M. W. *Shakespeare's History Plays*. London, 1944, 1961.
Traversi, Derek. *Shakespeare from Richard II to Henry V*. Palo Alto, 1957.
Waith, Eugene M., ed. *Shakespeare: The Histories*. Englewood Cliffs, N.J., 1965.
Wilson, F. P. "The English History Play," *Shakespearian and Other Studies*. Oxford, 1969.

THE MERCHANT OF VENICE

Barnet, Sylvan. "Prodigality and Time in *The Merchant of Venice*," *PMLA*, LXXXVII (1972), 26–30.
———, ed. *Twentieth Century Interpretations of "The Merchant of Venice*." Englewood Cliffs, N.J., 1970.
Freud, Sigmund. "The Theme of the Three Caskets," *Complete Psychological Works of Sigmund Freud*, XII (1911–1913), pp. 291–301. London, 1958.
Graham, Cary B. "Standards of Value in *The Merchant of Venice*," *SQ*, IV (1953), 145–151.
Granville-Barker, Harley. *Prefaces to Shakespeare*, vol. I. Princeton, 1946.
Grebanier, Bernard N. *The Truth about Shylock*. New York, 1962.
Kermode, Frank. "The Mature Comedies," *Early Shakespeare*, ed. John Russell Brown and Bernard Harris. Stratford-upon-Avon Studies 3. London, 1961.
Lelyveld, Toby B. *Shylock on the Stage*. Cleveland, 1960.
Lever, J. W. "Shylock, Portia, and the Values of Shakespearian Comedy," *SQ*, III (1952), 383–386.
Lewalski, Barbara K. "Biblical Allusion and Allegory in *The Merchant of Venice*," *SQ*, XIII (1962), 327–343.
MacKay, Maxine. "*The Merchant of Venice:* A Reflection of the Early Conflict Between Courts of Law and Courts of Equity," *SQ*, XV (1964), 371–375.
Pettet, E. C. "*The Merchant of Venice* and the Problem of Usury," *English Association Essays and Studies*, XXXI (1945), 19–33.
Sinsheimer, Hermann. *Shylock, the History of a Character; or, The Myth of the Jew*. London, 1947.
Stoll, E. E. "Shylock," *Journal of English and Germanic Philology*, X (1911), 236–279. Reprinted in *Shakespeare Studies*. New York, 1942.

MUCH ADO ABOUT NOTHING

Craik, T. W. "*Much Ado about Nothing*," *Scrutiny*, XIX (1953), 297–316.
Davis, Walter R., ed. *Twentieth Century Interpretations of "Much Ado about Nothing*." Englewood Cliffs, N.J., 1969.
Everett, Barbara. "*Much Ado about Nothing*," *Critical Quarterly*, III (1961), 319–335.
Gilbert, Allan. "Two Margarets: The Composition of *Much Ado about Nothing*," *Philological Quarterly*, XLI (1962), 61–71.
Jorgensen, Paul A. "Much Ado about *Nothing*," *SQ*, V (1954), 287–295.
Mulryne, J. R. *Shakespeare: "Much Ado about Nothing*." London, 1965.
Page, Nadine. "The Public Repudiation of Hero," *PMLA*, L (1935), 739–744.
Prouty, Charles T. *The Sources of "Much Ado about Nothing*." New Haven, 1950.
Rossiter, A. P. *Angel with Horns*. London, 1961.
Stoll, E. E. *Shakespeare Studies*. New York, 1942.

THE MERRY WIVES OF WINDSOR

Boughner, D. C. "Traditional Elements in Falstaff," *Journal of English and Germanic Philology*, XLIII (1944), 417–428.

Bradley, A. C. "The Rejection of Falstaff," *Oxford Lectures on Poetry*. London, 1909, 1961.

Campbell, Oscar James. "The Italianate Background of *The Merry Wives of Windsor*," *University of Michigan Essays and Studies in English and Comparative Literature*, VIII (1932), 81–117.

Green, William. *Shakespeare's "Merry Wives of Windsor."* Princeton, 1962.

Hemingway, Samuel B. "On Behalf of That Falstaff," *SQ*, III (1952), 307–311.

Hotson, Leslie. *Shakespeare Versus Shallow*. London, 1931.

Rosenberg, S. L. Millard. "Duke Friedrich of Württemberg," *Shakespeare Association Bulletin*, VIII (1933), 92–93.

Sewell, Sallie. "The Relation between *The Merry Wives of Windsor* and Jonson's *Every Man in His Humour*," *Shakespeare Association Bulletin*, XVI (1941), 175–189.

Steadman, John M. "Falstaff as Actaeon: A Dramatic Emblem," *SQ*, XIV (1963), 231–244.

White, David M. "An Explanation of the *Brooke-Broome* Question in Shakespeare's *Merry Wives*," *Philological Quarterly*, XXV (1946), 280–283.

AS YOU LIKE IT

Babb, Lawrence. *The Elizabethan Malady*. East Lansing, Mich., 1951.

Barnet, Sylvan. "Strange Events: Improbability in *As You Like It*," *ShakS 4* (1968), 119–131.

Campbell, Oscar James. "Jaques," *Huntington Library Bulletin*, VIII (1935), 71–102.

Fink, Z. S. "Jaques and the Malcontent Traveler," *Philological Quarterly*, XIV (1935), 237–252.

Gardner, Helen. "*As You Like It*," *More Talking of Shakespeare*, ed. John Garrett. London and New York, 1959.

Goldsmith, Robert H. *Wise Fools in Shakespeare*. East Lansing, Mich., 1955.

Halio, Jay L. " 'No Clock in the Forest': Time in *As You Like It*," *Studies in English Literature*, II (1962), 197–207.

Harbage, Alfred. *As They Liked It*. New York, 1947.

Hunter, G. K. *William Shakespeare: The Late Comedies*. London, 1962.

Jenkins, Harold. "*As You Like It*," *ShS 8* (1955), 40–51.

Knowles, Richard. "Myth and Type in *As You Like It*," *English Literary History*, XXXIII (1966), 1–22.

Kreider, P. V. "Genial Literary Satire in the Forest of Arden," *Shakespeare Association Bulletin*, X (1935), 212–231.

Lascelles, Mary. "Shakespeare's Pastoral Comedy," *More Talking of Shakespeare*, ed. John Garrett. London and New York, 1959.

Nearing, Homer, Jr. "The Penaltie of Adam," *Modern Language Notes*, LXII (1947), 336–338.

Shaw, John. "Fortune and Nature in *As You Like It*," *SQ*, VI (1955), 45–50.

Staebler, Warren. "Shakespeare's Play of Atonement," *Shakespeare Association Bulletin*, XXIV (1949), 91–105.

Young, David. *The Heart's Forest*. New Haven, 1972.

TWELFTH NIGHT

Barnet, Sylvan. "Charles Lamb and the Tragic Malvolio," *Philological Quarterly*, XXXIII (1954), 178–188.

Downer, Alan S. "Feste's Night," *College English*, XIII (1952), 258–265.

Goldsmith, Robert H. *Wise Fools in Shakespeare*. East Lansing, Mich., 1955.

Hollander, John. "*Twelfth Night* and the Morality of Indulgence," *Sewanee Review*, LXVII (1959), 220–238.

Hotson, Leslie. *The First Night of Twelfth Night*. New York, 1954.

Jenkins, Harold. "Shakespeare's *Twelfth Night*," *Rice Institute Pamphlets*, XLV (1959), iv, 19–42.

King, Walter N., ed. *Twentieth Century Interpretations of "Twelfth Night."* Englewood Cliffs, N.J., 1968.

Knight, G. Wilson. *The Shakespearian Tempest*. London, 1932, 1953.

Leech, Clifford. *"Twelfth Night" and Shakespearian Comedy*. Toronto, 1965.

Lewalski, Barbara K. "Thematic Patterns in *Twelfth Night*," *ShakS 1* (1965), 168–181.

Mueschke, Paul, and Jeannette Fleisher. "Jonsonian Elements in the Comic Underplot of *Twelfth Night*," *PMLA*, XLVIII (1933), 722–740.

Salingar, L. D. "The Design of *Twelfth Night*," *SQ*, IX (1958), 117–139.

Seiden, Melvin. "Malvolio Reconsidered," *University of Kansas City Review*, XXVIII (1961), 105–114.

Summers, Joseph H. "The Masks of *Twelfth Night*," *University of Kansas City Review*, XXII (1955), 25–32. Reprinted in *Shakespeare: Modern Essays in Criticism*, ed. Leonard F. Dean. Rev. ed. London and New York, 1967, 1969.

Tilley, Morris P. "The Organic Unity of *Twelfth Night*," *PMLA*, XXIX (1914), 550–566.

Welsford, Enid. *The Fool*. London, 1935.

Williams, Porter, Jr. "Mistakes in *Twelfth Night* and Their Resolution," *PMLA*, LXXVI (1961), 193–199.

RICHARD THE SECOND

Altick, Richard D. "Symphonic Imagery in *Richard II*," *PMLA*, LXII (1947), 339–365.

Black, Matthew W. "The Sources of Shakespeare's *Richard II*," *J. Q. Adams Memorial Studies*, ed. J. McManaway et al., pp. 199–216. Washington, D.C., 1948.

Bogard, Travis. "Shakespeare's Second Richard," *PMLA*, LXX (1955), 192–209.

Bonnard, Georges A. "The Actor in *Richard II*," *Shakespeare Jahrbuch*, LXXXVII (1952), 87–101.

Dean, Leonard F. "*Richard II:* The State and the Image of the Theater," *PMLA*, LXVII (1952), 211–218.

Dodson, Sarah. "The Northumberland of Shakespeare and Holinshed," *University of Texas Studies in English*, XIX (1939), 74–85.

Doran, Madeleine. "Imagery in *Richard II* and in *Henry IV*," *Modern Language Review*, XXXVII (1942), 113–122.

Dorius, R. J. "A Little More Than a Little," *SQ*, XI (1960), 13–26.

Elliott, John R., Jr., "History and Tragedy in *Richard II*," *Studies in English Literature*, VIII (1968), 253–271.

Forker, Charles R. "Shakespeare's Chronicle Plays as Historical-Pastoral," *ShakS 1* (1965), 85–104.

Kantorowicz, Ernst H. *The King's Two Bodies: A Study in Medieval Political Theology*. Princeton, 1957.

Law, R. A. "Deviations from Holinshed in *Richard II*," *University of Texas Studies in English*, XXIX (1950), 91–101.

———. "Links Between Shakespeare's History Plays," *Studies in Philology*, L (1953), 168–187.

Phialas, Peter G. "The Medieval in *Richard II*," *SQ*, XII (1961), 305–310.

Quinn, Michael. " 'The King Is Not Himself': The Personal Tragedy of *Richard II*," *Studies in Philology*, LVI (1959), 169–186.

Ribner, Irving. "The Political Problem in Shakespeare's Lancastrian Tetralogy," *Studies in Philology*, XLIX (1952), 171–184.

Stirling, Brents. "Bolingbroke's 'Decision'," *SQ*, II (1951), 27–34.

Swinburne, A. C. *Three Plays of Shakespeare*. New York and London, 1909.

Yeats, W. B. "At Stratford-on-Avon," *Ideas of Good and Evil*, collected in *Essays and Introductions*. New York, 1961.

THE HENRY THE FOURTH PLAYS

Barish, Jonas A. "The Turning Away of Prince Hal," *ShakS 1* (1965), 9–17.

Boughner, D. C. "Traditional Elements in Falstaff," *Journal of English and Germanic Philology*, XLIII (1944), 417–428.

———. "Vice, Braggart, and Falstaff," *Anglia*, LXXII (1954), 35–61.

Bradley, A. C. "The Rejection of Falstaff," *Oxford Lectures on Poetry*. London, 1909, 1961.

Bryant, J. A., Jr., "Prince Hal and the Ephesians," *Sewanee Review*, LXVII (1959), 204–219.

Dickinson, Hugh. "The Reformation of Prince Hal," *SQ*, XII (1961), 33–46.

Doran, Madeleine. "Imagery in *Richard II* and in *Henry IV*," *Modern Language Review*, XXXVII (1942), 113–122.

Dorius, R. J., ed. *Twentieth Century Interpretations of "Henry IV Part I."* Englewood Cliffs, N.J., 1970.

Empson, William. "Falstaff and Mr. Dover Wilson," *Kenyon Review*, XV (1953), 213–262.

Fish, Charles. "*Henry IV:* Shakespeare and Holinshed," *Studies in Philology*, LXI (1964), 205–218.

Hunter, G. K. "*Henry IV* and the Elizabethan Two-Part Play," *Review of English Studies*, n. s. V (1954), 236–248.

———. "Shakespeare's Politics and the Rejection of Falstaff," *Critical Quarterly*, I (1959), 229–236.

Jenkins, Harold. *The Structural Problem in Shakespeare's "Henry the Fourth."* London, 1956.

Jorgensen, Paul. "The 'Dastardly Treachery' of Prince John of Lancaster," *PMLA*, LXXVI (1961), 488–492.

Kernan, Alvin. "The Henriad: Shakespeare's Major History Plays," *Yale Review*, LIX (1969), 3–32.

Kleinstück, Johannes. "The Problem of Order in

Shakespeare's Histories," *Neophilologus*, XXXVIII (1954), 268–277.
Knights, L. C. "Notes on Comedy," *Scrutiny*, I (1933), 356–367.
Knowles, Richard. "Unquiet and the Double Plot of *2 Henry IV*," *ShakS 2* (1966), 133–140.
Law, R. A. "Structural Unity in the Two Parts of *Henry the Fourth*," *Studies in Philology*, XXIV (1927), 223–242.
Leech, Clifford. "The Unity of *2 Henry IV*," *ShS 6* (1953), 16–24.
McLuhan, Herbert Marshall. "*Henry IV*, A Mirror of Magistrates," *University of Toronto Quarterly*, XVII (1948), 152–160.
Seng, Peter J. "Songs, Time, and the Rejection of Falstaff," *ShS 15* (1962), 31–40.
Shaaber, M. A. "The Unity of *Henry IV*," *J. Q. Adams Memorial Studies*, ed. J. McManaway et al., pp. 217–228. Washington, D.C., 1948.
Shuchter, J. D. "Prince Hal and Francis: The Imitation of an Action," *ShakS 3* (1967), 129–137.
Spivack, Bernard. "Falstaff and the Psychomachia," *SQ*, VIII (1957), 449–459.
Stewart, J. I. M. "The Birth and Death of Falstaff," *Character and Motive in Shakespeare*. London, 1949.
Stoll, E. E. "Falstaff," *Shakespeare Studies*. New York, 1942.
Tolliver, Harold E. "Falstaff, the Prince, and the History Play," *SQ*, XVI (1965), 63–80.
Williams, Philip. "The Birth and Death of Falstaff Reconsidered," *SQ*, VIII (1957), 359–365.
Wilson, J. Dover. *The Fortunes of Falstaff*. London, 1943.
Young, David P., ed. *Twentieth Century Interpretations of "Henry IV, Part Two."* Englewood Cliffs, N.J., 1968.

HENRY THE FIFTH

Battenhouse, Roy W. "*Henry V* as Heroic Comedy," *Essays . . . in Honor of Hardin Craig*, ed. Richard Hosley. Columbia, Mo., 1962.
Berman, Ronald S., ed. *Twentieth Century Interpretations of "Henry V."* Englewood Cliffs, N.J., 1968.
———. "Shakespeare's Alexander: *Henry V*," *College English*, XXIII (1962), 532–539.
Bethell, S. L. "The Comic Element in Shakespeare's Histories," *Anglia*, LXXI (1952), 82–101.
Burns, Landon C., Jr. "Three Views of *King Henry V*," *Drama Survey*, I (1962), 278–300.
Gilbert, Allan. "Patriotism and Satire in *Henry V*," *Studies in Shakespeare*, ed. A. D. Matthews and C. M. Emery. Coral Gables, Fla., 1953.
Granville-Barker, Harley. "From *Henry V* to *Hamlet*," *Proceedings of the British Academy*, XI (1925), 283–309.
Hobday, C. H. "Imagery and Irony in *Henry V*," *ShS 21* (1968), 107–113.
Jorgensen, Paul A. "Accidental Judgments, Casual Slaughters, and Purposes Mistook: Critical Reactions to Shakspere's *Henry the Fifth*," *Shakespeare Association Bulletin*, XXII (1947), 51–61.
———. *Shakespeare's Military World*. Berkeley and Los Angeles, 1956.
Knights, L. C. *William Shakespeare: The Histories*. London, 1962.
McCloskey, John C. "The Mirror of All Christian Kings," *Shakespeare Association Bulletin*, XIX (1944), 36–40.
Merchant, W. M. "The Status and Person of Majesty," *Shakespeare Jahrbuch*, XC (1954), 285–289.
Webber, Joan. "The Renewal of the King's Symbolic Role: From *Richard II* to *Henry V*," *Texas Studies in Literature and Language*, IV (1963), 530–538.
Williams, Charles. "*Henry V*," *Shakespeare Criticism, 1919–35*, ed. Anne Bradby. London, 1936.

JULIUS CAESAR

Bonjour, Adrien. *The Structure of "Julius Caesar."* Liverpool, 1958.
Burckhardt, Sigurd. *Shakespearean Meanings*. Princeton, 1968.
Charney, Maurice. *Shakespeare's Roman Plays*. Cambridge, Mass., 1961.
Dean, Leonard, ed. *Twentieth Century Interpretations of "Julius Caesar."* Englewood Cliffs, N.J., 1968.
Dorsch, T. S., ed. *Julius Caesar*. The Arden Shakespeare. London and Cambridge, Mass., 1955, 1970.
Foakes, R. A. "An Approach to *Julius Caesar*," *SQ*, V (1954), 259–270.
Granville-Barker, Harley. *Prefaces to Shakespeare*, vol. II. Princeton, 1947.
Hartsock, Mildred E. "The Complexity of *Julius Caesar*," *PMLA*, LXXXI (1966), 56–62.
Knight, G. Wilson. *The Imperial Theme*. London, 1931, 1953.
Knights, L. C. "Shakespeare and Political Wisdom: A Note on the Personalism of *Julius Caesar* and *Coriolanus*," *Sewanee Review*, LXI (1953), 43–55.

MacCallum, M. W. *Shakespeare's Roman Plays and Their Background*. London, 1910.

Mack, Maynard. "Teaching Drama: *Julius Caesar*," *Essays on the Teaching of English*, ed. Edward J. Gordon and Edward S. Noyes. New York, 1960.

Ornstein, Robert. "Seneca and the Political Drama of *Julius Caesar*," *Journal of English and Germanic Philology*, LVII (1958), 51–56.

Palmer, John. *Political Characters of Shakespeare*. London, 1945.

Phillips, James E., Jr. *The State in Shakespeare's Greek and Roman Plays*. New York, 1940.

Ribner, Irving. "Political Issues in *Julius Caesar*," *Journal of English and Germanic Philology*, LVI (1957), 10–22.

Schanzer, Ernest. *The Problem Plays of Shakespeare*. New York, 1963.

Smith, Gordon Ross. "Brutus, Virtue, and Will," *SQ*, X (1959), 367–379.

Stampfer, Judah. *The Tragic Engagement: A Study of Shakespeare's Classical Tragedies*. New York, 1968.

Stirling, Brents. *The Populace in Shakespeare*. New York, 1949.

Traversi, Derek. *Shakespeare: The Roman Plays*. Palo Alto, Calif., 1963.

THE PERIOD OF TRAGEDIES

Bradley, A. C. *Shakespearean Tragedy*. London, 1904. (*Hamlet, Othello, King Lear, Macbeth.*)

Brower, Reuben. *Hero and Saint: Shakespeare and the Græco-Roman Heroic Tradition*. New York and Oxford, 1971.

Campbell, Lily B. *Shakespeare's Tragic Heroes: Slaves of Passion*. Cambridge, Eng., 1930.

Charlton, H. B. *Shakespearian Tragedy*. Cambridge, Eng., 1948.

Cunningham, J. V. *Woe or Wonder: The Emotional Effect of Shakespearean Tragedy*. Denver, 1951. Reprinted in *Tradition and Poetic Structure*. Denver, 1960.

Farnham, Willard. *Shakespeare's Tragic Frontier*. Berkeley, 1950.

Frye, Northrop. *Fools of Time: Studies in Shakespearean Tragedy*. Toronto, 1967.

Harbage, Alfred, ed. *Shakespeare: The Tragedies*. Englewood Cliffs, N.J., 1964.

Holloway, John. *The Story of the Night: Studies in Shakespeare's Major Tragedies*. London and Lincoln, Neb., 1961.

Knight, G. Wilson. *The Wheel of Fire*. London, 1930, 1965.

Lawlor, John. *The Tragic Sense in Shakespeare*. London, 1960.

Leech, Clifford. *Shakespeare's Tragedies and Other Studies in Seventeenth Century Drama*. London, 1950.

———, ed. *Shakespeare: The Tragedies*. Chicago, 1965.

Mack, Maynard. "The Jacobean Shakespeare: Some Observations on the Construction of the Tragedies," *Jacobean Theatre*, ed. John Russell Brown and Bernard Harris. Stratford-upon-Avon Studies 1. London, 1960.

Proser, Matthew N. *The Heroic Image in Five Shakespearean Tragedies*. Princeton, 1965.

Rosen, William. *Shakespeare and the Craft of Tragedy*. Cambridge, Mass., 1960.

Sisson, C. J. *Shakespeare's Tragic Justice*. Scarborough, Ont., 1961.

Speaight, Robert. *Nature in Shakespearian Tragedy*. London, 1955.

Stirling, Brents. *Unity in Shakespearian Tragedy*. New York, 1956.

Whitaker, Virgil. *The Mirror up to Nature*. San Marino, Calif., 1965.

Wilson, Harold S. *On the Design of Shakespearian Tragedy*. Toronto, 1957.

The Greek and Roman Tragedies

Charney, Maurice, ed. *Discussions of Shakespeare's Roman Plays*. Boston, 1964.

———. *Shakespeare's Roman Plays: The Function of Imagery in the Drama*. Cambridge, Mass., 1961.

Knight, G. Wilson. *The Imperial Theme: Further Interpretations of Shakespeare's Tragedies Including the Roman Plays*. London, 1931, 1953.

MacCallum, M. W. *Shakespeare's Roman Plays and Their Background*. London, 1910.

Nicoll, Allardyce, ed., *ShS 10* (1957).

Phillips, James E., Jr. *The State in Shakespeare's Greek and Roman Plays*. New York, 1940.

Spencer, T. J. B. *William Shakespeare: The Roman Plays*. London, 1963.

Stampfer, Judah. *The Tragic Engagement: A Study of Shakespeare's Classical Tragedies*. New York, 1968.

Traversi, Derek. *Shakespeare: The Roman Plays*. Palo Alto, Calif., 1963.

The "Problem" Plays

Campbell, Oscar James. *Shakespeare's Satire*. London and New York, 1943, 1963.

Lawrence, W. W. *Shakespeare's Problem Comedies*. New York, 1931, 1960.

Ornstein, Robert, ed. *Discussions of Shakespeare's Problem Comedies*. Boston, 1961.

Schanzer, Ernest. *The Problem Plays of Shakespeare*. New York, 1963.

Tillyard, E. M. W. *Shakespeare's Problem Plays*. Toronto, 1949.

ALL'S WELL THAT ENDS WELL

Adams, John F. "*All's Well that Ends Well:* The Paradox of Procreation," *SQ*, XII (1961), 261–270.

Arthos, John. "The Comedy of Generation," *Essays in Criticism*, V (1955), 97–117.

Bradbrook, M. C. "Virtue Is the True Nobility," *Review of English Studies*, n. s. I (1950), 289–301.

Calderwood, James L. "Styles of Knowing in *All's Well*," *Modern Language Quarterly*, XXV (1964), 272–294.

Goldsmith, Robert H. *Wise Fools in Shakespeare*. East Lansing, Mich., 1955.

Halio, Jay L. "*All's Well that Ends Well*," *SQ*, XV (1964), 33–43.

Hunter, G. K., ed. *All's Well that Ends Well*. The Arden Shakespeare. 3rd ed. Cambridge, Mass., 1959.

Hunter, Robert G. *Shakespeare and the Comedy of Forgiveness*. New York, 1965.

King, Walter N. "Shakespeare's 'Mingled Yarn,'" *Modern Language Quarterly*, XXI (1960), 33–44.

Knight, G. Wilson. *The Sovereign Flower: On Shakespeare as the Poet of Royalism*. New York, 1958.

Leech, Clifford. "The Theme of Ambition in *All's Well that Ends Well*," *English Literary History*, XXI (1954), 17–29.

Nagarajan, S. "The Structure of *All's Well that Ends Well*," *Essays in Criticism*, X (1960), 24–31.

Price, Joseph G. *The Unfortunate Comedy: A Study of "All's Well that Ends Well" and Its Critics*. Toronto, 1968.

Rossiter, A. P. *Angel with Horns*. London, 1961.

Schoff, Francis G. "Claudio, Bertram, and a Note on Interpretation," *SQ*, X (1959), 11–23.

Stoll, E. E. *From Shakespeare to Joyce*. New York, 1944.

Turner, Robert Y. "Dramatic Conventions in *All's Well that Ends Well*," *PMLA*, LXXV (1960), 497–502.

Wilson, Harold S. "Dramatic Emphasis in *All's Well that Ends Well*," *Huntington Library Quarterly*, XIII (1950), 217–240.

MEASURE FOR MEASURE

Battenhouse, Roy W. "*Measure for Measure* and Christian Doctrine of the Atonement," *PMLA*, LXI (1946), 1029–1059.

Bennett, Josephine W. *"Measure for Measure" as Royal Entertainment*. New York, 1966.

Bradbrook, Muriel C. "Authority, Truth, and Justice in *Measure for Measure*," *Review of English Studies*, XVII (1941), 385–399.

Chambers, R. W. "The Jacobean Shakespeare and *Measure for Measure*," *Proceedings of the British Academy*, XXIII (1937), 135–192.

Coghill, Nevill. "Comic Form in *Measure for Measure*," *ShS 8* (1955), 14–27.

Dickinson, John W. "Renaissance Equity and *Measure for Measure*," *SQ*, XIII (1962), 287–297.

Dunkel, Wilbur. "Law and Equity in *Measure for Measure*," *SQ*, XIII (1962), 275–285.

Empson, William. *The Structure of Complex Words*. London, 1951.

Fairchild, H. "The Two Angelo's," *Shakespeare Association Bulletin*, VI (1931), 53–59.

Fergusson, Francis. *The Human Image in Dramatic Literature*. Garden City, N.Y., 1957.

Geckle, George L., ed. *Twentieth Century Interpretations of "Measure for Measure."* Englewood Cliffs, N.J., 1970.

Holland, Norman. *The Shakespearean Imagination*, New York, 1964.

Knight, G. Wilson. "*Measure for Measure* and the Gospels," *The Wheel of Fire*. London, 1930, 1965.

Knights, L. C. "The Ambiguity of *Measure for Measure*," *Scrutiny*, X (1942), 222–233.

Lascelles, Mary. *Shakespeare's "Measure for Measure."* London, 1953.

Lawrence, W. W. "*Measure for Measure* and Lucio," *SQ*, IX (1958), 443–453.

Leavis, F. R. "The Greatness of *Measure for Measure*," *Scrutiny*, X (1942), 234–247.

Leech, Clifford. "The 'Meaning' of *Measure for Measure*," *ShS 3* (1950), 66–73.

Nagarajan, S. "*Measure for Measure* and Elizabethan Betrothals," *SQ*, XIV (1963), 115–119.

Pope, Elizabeth M. "The Renaissance Background of *Measure for Measure*," *ShS 2* (1949), 66–82.

Schanzer, Ernest. *The Problem Plays of Shakespeare*. New York, 1963.

Sewell, Arthur. *Character and Society in Shakespeare*. London, 1951.

Stead, C. K., ed. *Shakespeare's "Measure for Measure": A Casebook*. London, 1971.

Stevenson, David L. *The Achievement of "Measure for Measure."* Ithaca, N.Y., 1966.

Sypher, Wylie. "Shakespeare as Casuist: *Measure for Measure*," *Sewanee Review*, LVIII (1950), 262–280.

Traversi, Derek. "*Measure for Measure*," *Scrutiny*, XI (1943), 40–58.

TROILUS AND CRESSIDA

Bradbrook, Muriel C. "What Shakespeare Did to Chaucer's *Troilus and Criseyde*," *SQ*, IX (1958), 311–319.

Campbell, Oscar James. *Comicall Satyre and Shakespeare's "Troilus and Cressida."* San Marino, Calif., 1938.

Charlton, H. B. "The Dark Comedies," *Bulletin of the John Rylands Library*, XXI (1937), 78–128.

Dickey, Franklin. *Not Wisely But Too Well*. San Marino, Calif., 1957.

Dunkel, Wilbur D. "Shakespeare's Troilus," *SQ*, II (1951), 331–334.

Foakes, R. A. "*Troilus and Cressida* Reconsidered," *University of Toronto Quarterly*, XXXII (1963), 142–154.

Gérard, Albert. "Meaning and Structure in *Troilus and Cressida*," *English Studies*, XL (1959), 144–157.

Harrier, R. C. "Troilus Divided," *Studies in the English Renaissance Drama in Memory of Karl Julius Holzknecht*, ed. Josephine W. Bennett et al. New York, 1959.

Kaula, David. "Will and Reason in *Troilus and Cressida*," *SQ*, XII (1961), 271–283.

Kimbrough, Robert. *Shakespeare's "Troilus and Cressida" and Its Setting*. Cambridge, Mass., 1964.

Knights, L. C. "*Troilus and Cressida* Again," *Scrutiny*, XVIII (1951), 144–157.

Nowottny, Winifred M. T. " 'Opinion' and 'Value' in *Troilus and Cressida*," *Essays in Criticism*, IV (1954), 282–296.

Presson, Robert K. *Shakespeare's "Troilus and Cressida" and the Legends of Troy*. Madison, Wis., 1953.

Rollins, Hyder E. "The Troilus-Cressida Story from Chaucer to Shakespeare," *PMLA*, XXXII (1917), 383–429.

Rossiter, A. P. *Angel with Horns*. London, 1961.

Spencer, Theodore. *Shakespeare and the Nature of Man*. New York, 1942.

HAMLET

Alexander, Peter. *Hamlet: Father and Son*. New York and London, 1955.

Bevington, David, ed. *Twentieth Century Interpretations of "Hamlet."* Englewood Cliffs, N.J., 1968.

Booth, Stephen. "On the Value of *Hamlet*," *Reinterpretations of Elizabethan Drama*, ed. Norman Rabkin. New York, 1969.

Bowers, Fredson T. *Elizabethan Revenge Tragedy, 1587–1642*. Princeton, 1940.

———. "Hamlet as Minister and Scourge," *PMLA*, LXX (1955), 740–749.

Brown, John Russell, and Bernard Harris, eds. *Hamlet*. Stratford-upon-Avon Studies 5. London, 1963.

Charney, Maurice. *Style in "Hamlet."* Princeton, 1969.

Elliott, G. R. *Scourge and Minister: A Study of "Hamlet" as a Tragedy of Revengefulness and Justice*. Durham, N.C., 1951.

Fergusson, Francis. *The Idea of a Theater*. Princeton, 1949.

Granville-Barker, Harley. *Prefaces to Shakespeare*, vol. I. Princeton, 1946.

Grebanier, Bernard D. *The Heart of Hamlet*. New York, 1949, 1967.

James, D. G. *The Dream of Learning*. Oxford, 1951.

Johnson, S. F. "The Regeneration of Hamlet," *SQ*, III (1952), 187–207.

Jones, Ernest. *Hamlet and Oedipus*. Rev. ed. New York, 1949, 1954.

Joseph, Bertram. *Conscience and the King*. London, 1953.

Kitto, H. D. F. *Form and Meaning in Drama*. London, 1956.

Knights, L. C. *An Approach to Hamlet*. London, 1960.

Levin, Harry. *The Question of Hamlet*. New York and London, 1959.

Lewis, C. S. "Hamlet: The Prince or the Poem?" *Proceedings of the British Academy*, XXVIII (1942), 139–154.

Mack, Maynard. "The World of *Hamlet*," *Yale Review*, XLI (1952), 502–523.

Madariaga, Salvador de. *On Hamlet*. London, 1948, 1964.

Nicoll, Allardyce, ed. *ShS 9* (1956).

Prosser, Eleanor. *Hamlet and Revenge*. Stanford, 1967, 1971.

Rose, Mark. "*Hamlet* and the Shape of Revenge," *English Literary Renaissance*, I (1971), 132–143.

Tillyard, E. M. W. *Shakespeare's Problem Plays*. Toronto, 1949.

Walker, Roy. *The Time Is out of Joint: A Study of "Hamlet."* London and New York, 1948.

Wilson, J. Dover. *What Happens in "Hamlet."* London and New York, 1935, 1951.

OTHELLO

Bayley, John. *The Characters of Love*. New York, 1961.
Dean, Leonard, ed. *A Casebook on "Othello."* New York, 1961.
Dickey, Franklin. *Not Wisely But Too Well*. San Marino, Calif., 1957.
Eliot, T. S. "Shakespeare and the Stoicism of Seneca," *Selected Essays, 1917–1932*. London, 1932.
Elliott, G. R. *Flaming Minister: A Study of "Othello" as Tragedy of Love and Hate*. Durham, N.C., 1953.
Gardner, Helen. *The Noble Moor*. London, 1955.
Granville-Barker, Harley. *Prefaces to Shakespeare*, vol. II. Princeton, 1947.
Heilman, Robert B. *Magic in the Web: Action and Language in "Othello."* Lexington, Ky., 1956.
Hyman, Stanley Edgar. *Iago: Some Approaches to the Illusion of His Motivation*. New York, 1970.
Jones, Eldred. *Othello's Countrymen: The African in English Renaissance Drama*. London, 1965.
Kernan, Alvin B., ed. *The Tragedy of Othello*. New York, 1963.
Kirschbaum, Leo. "The Modern *Othello*," *English Literary History*, XI (1944), 283–296.
Leavis, F. R. *The Common Pursuit*. London, 1952.
Muir, Kenneth, ed. *Shakespeare Survey 21* (1968).
Nowottny, Winifred M. T. "Justice and Love in *Othello*," *University of Toronto Quarterly*, XXI (1952), 330–344.
Rosenberg, Marvin. *The Masks of "Othello."* Berkeley and Los Angeles, 1961.
Seltzer, Daniel. "Elizabethan Acting in *Othello*," *SQ*, X (1959), 201–210.
Sewell, Arthur. *Character and Society in Shakespeare*. London, 1951.
Spivack, Bernard. *Shakespeare and the Allegory of Evil*. New York, 1958.
Stoll, E. E. *From Shakespeare to Joyce*. New York, 1944.

KING LEAR

Barnet, Sylvan. "Some Limitations of a Christian Approach to Shakespeare," *English Literary History*, XXII (1955), 81–92.
Danby, John F. *Shakespeare's Doctrine of Nature: A Study of "King Lear."* London, 1949.
Elton, William R. *King Lear and the Gods*. San Marino, Calif., 1966.
Empson, William. *The Structure of Complex Words*. London, 1951.
Felperin, Howard. *Shakespearean Romance*. Princeton, 1972.
Fraser, Russell A. *Shakespeare's Poetics in Relation to "King Lear."* London, 1962.
Freud, Sigmund. "The Theme of the Three Caskets," *Complete Psychological Works of Sigmund Freud*, XII (1911–1913), pp. 291–301. London, 1958.
Granville-Barker, Harley. *Prefaces to Shakespeare*, vol. I. Princeton, 1946.
Heilman, Robert B. *This Great Stage: Image and Structure in "King Lear."* Baton Rouge, La., 1948.
James, D. G. *The Dream of Learning*. Oxford, 1951.
Jorgensen, Paul A. *Lear's Self-Discovery*. Berkeley and Los Angeles, 1967.
Keast, W. "Imagery and Meaning in the Interpretation of *King Lear*," *Modern Philology*, XLVII (1949), 45–64.
Knights, L. C. *Some Shakespearean Themes*. London, 1959.
Lothian, J. M. *"King Lear": A Tragic Reading of Life*. Toronto, 1949.
Mack, Maynard. *King Lear in Our Time*. Berkeley and Los Angeles, 1965.
MacLean, Norman. "Episode, Scene, Speech, and Word: The Madness of Lear," *Critics and Criticism*, ed. R. S. Crane. Chicago, 1952.
Muir, Kenneth, ed. *King Lear*. The Arden Shakespeare. London and Cambridge, Mass., 1952, 1959.
Nicoll, Allardyce, ed. *Shakespeare Survey 13* (1960).
Rosen, William. *Shakespeare and the Craft of Tragedy*. Cambridge, Mass., 1960.
Rosenberg, Marvin. *The Masks of "King Lear."* Berkeley and Los Angeles, 1972.
Sewall, Richard B. *The Vision of Tragedy*. New Haven, 1959.
Sewell, Arthur. *Character and Society in Shakespeare*. London, 1951.
Stoll, E. E. *Art and Artifice in Shakespeare*. Cambridge, Eng., 1933, 1962.

TIMON OF ATHENS

Bradbrook, Muriel C. *Shakespeare the Craftsman*. London and New York, 1969.
Campbell, Oscar James. *Shakespeare's Satire*. London and New York, 1943, 1963.
Collins, A. S. "*Timon of Athens:* A Reconsideration," *Review of English Studies*, XXII (1946), 96–108.
Cook, David. "*Timon of Athens*," *ShS 16* (1963), 83–94.
Ellis-Fermor, Una. "*Timon of Athens:* An Unfinished

Play," *Review of English Studies*, XVIII (1942), 270–283.
Empson, William. *The Structure of Complex Words*. London, 1951.
Farnham, Willard. *Shakespeare's Tragic Frontier*. Berkeley, 1950.
Honigmann, E. A. J. "*Timon of Athens*," *SQ*, XII (1961), 3–20.
Kernan, Alvin B. *The Cankered Muse: Satire of the English Renaissance*. New Haven, 1959.
Lancashire, Anne. "*Timon of Athens:* Shakespeare's Dr. Faustus," *SQ*, XXI (1970), 35–44.
Maxwell, J. C. "Timon of Athens," *Scrutiny*, XV (1948), 195–208.
Merchant, W. M. "*Timon* and the Conceit of Art," *SQ*, VI (1955), 249–257.
Nowottny, Winifred M. T. "Acts IV and V of *Timon of Athens*," *SQ*, X (1959), 493–497.
Oliver, H. J., ed. *Timon of Athens*. The Arden Shakespeare. London and Cambridge, Mass., 1959.
Pettet, E. C. "*Timon of Athens:* The Disruption of Feudal Morality," *Review of English Studies*, XXIII (1947), 321–336.
Williams, Stanley T. "Some Versions of *Timon of Athens* on the Stage," *Modern Philology*, XVIII (1920), 269–285.

MACBETH

Blisset, William. " 'The Secret'st Man of Blood': A Study of Dramatic Irony in *Macbeth*," *SQ*, X (1959), 397–408.
Brooks, Cleanth. *The Well Wrought Urn*. New York, 1947.
Curry, Walter Clyde. *Shakespeare's Philosophical Patterns*. Baton Rouge, La., 1937.
Driver, Tom. *The Sense of History in Greek and Shakespearean Drama*. New York, 1960.
Elliott, G. R. *Dramatic Providence in "Macbeth."* Princeton, 1958.
Gardner, Helen. "Milton's 'Satan' and the Theme of Damnation in Elizabethan Tragedy," *English Association Essays and Studies*, n. s., I (1948), 46–66.
Jorgensen, Paul A. *Our Naked Frailties*. Berkeley and Los Angeles, 1971.
Knights, L. C. *Some Shakespearean Themes*. London, 1959.
Mack, Maynard. "The Jacobean Shakespeare: Some Observations on the Construction of the Tragedies," *Jacobean Theatre*, ed. John Russell Brown and Bernard Harris. Stratford-upon-Avon Studies 1. London, 1960.
Muir, Kenneth, ed. *Macbeth*. The Arden Shakespeare. London and Cambridge, Mass., 1951.
———, ed. *Shakespeare Survey 19* (1966).
Paul, Henry N. *The Royal Play of Macbeth*. New York, 1950.
Rosen, William. *Shakespeare and the Craft of Tragedy*. Cambridge, Mass., 1960.
Sewell, Arthur. *Character and Society in Shakespeare*. London, 1951.
Spender, Stephen. "Time, Violence, and *Macbeth*," *Penguin New Writing*, III. London, 1946.
Stoll, E. E. *From Shakespeare to Joyce*. New York, 1944.
Walker, Roy. *The Time Is Free*. London and New York, 1949.

ANTONY AND CLEOPATRA

Barnet, Sylvan. "Recognition and Reversal in *Antony and Cleopatra*," *SQ*, VIII (1957), 331–334.
Barroll, J. Leeds. "Antony and Pleasure," *Journal of English and Germanic Philology*, LVII (1958), 708–720.
Bethell, S. L. *Shakespeare and the Popular Dramatic Tradition*. London and Durham, N.C., 1944.
Bradley, A. C. *Oxford Lectures on Poetry*. London, 1909, 1961.
Danby, John. *Elizabethan and Jacobean Poets*. London, 1964.
Dickey, Franklin. *Not Wisely But Too Well*. San Marino, Calif., 1957.
Felperin, Howard. *Shakespearean Romance*. Princeton, 1972.
Frost, David L. *The School of Shakespeare*. Cambridge, Eng., 1968.
Granville-Barker, Harley. *Prefaces to Shakespeare*, vol. I. Princeton, 1946.
Kaula, David. "The Time Sense of *Antony and Cleopatra*," *SQ*, XV (1964), 211–223.
Knights, L. C. *Some Shakespearean Themes*. London, 1959.
Leavis, F. R. "*Antony and Cleopatra* and *All for Love:* A Critical Exercise," *Scrutiny*, V (1936–1937), 158–169.
Lloyd, Michael. "Cleopatra as Isis," *ShS 12* (1959), 88–94.
Mack, Maynard, ed. *Antony and Cleopatra*. Pelican Shakespeare. Baltimore, 1960.

Markels, Julian. *The Pillar of the World.* Columbus, Ohio, 1968.

Maxwell, J. C. "Shakespeare's Roman Plays: 1900–1956," *ShS 10* (1957), 1–11.

Ornstein, Robert. "The Ethic of the Imagination: Love and Art in *Antony and Cleopatra*," *Later Shakespeare*, ed. John Russell Brown and Bernard Harris, pp. 31–46. Stratford-upon-Avon Studies 8. London, 1966.

Palmer, John. *Political Characters of Shakespeare.* London, 1945.

Rackin, Phyllis. "Shakespeare's Boy Cleopatra, the Decorum of Nature, and the Golden World of Poetry," *PMLA*, LXXXVII (1972), 201–212.

Schanzer, Ernest. *The Problem Plays of Shakespeare.* New York, 1963.

Spencer, Terence. "Shakespeare and the Elizabethan Romans," *ShS 10* (1957), 27–38.

Stempel, Daniel. "The Transmigration of the Crocodile," *SQ*, VII (1956), 59–72.

Stewart, J. I. M. *Character and Motive in Shakespeare.* London, 1949.

Waith, Eugene. *The Herculean Hero in Marlowe, Chapman, Shakespeare, and Dryden.* New York, 1962.

CORIOLANUS

Bradley, A. C. *A Miscellany.* London, 1929.

Browning, I. R. "Coriolanus—'Boy of Tears,' " *Essays in Criticism*, V (1955), 18–31.

Burke, Kenneth. "Coriolanus—and the Delights of Faction," *Hudson Review*, XIX (1966–1967), 185–202.

Ellis-Fermor, Una. *Shakespeare the Dramatist.* New York, 1961.

Granville-Barker, Harley. *Prefaces to Shakespeare*, vol. II. Princeton, 1947.

Heuer, Hermann. "From Plutarch to Shakespeare: A Study of *Coriolanus*," *ShS 10* (1957), 50–59.

Knights, L. C. "Shakespeare and Political Wisdom: A Note on the Personalism of *Julius Caesar* and *Coriolanus*," *Sewanee Review*, LXI (1953), 43–55.

———. *Some Shakespearean Themes.* London, 1959.

MacLure, Millar. "Shakespeare and the Lonely Dragon," *University of Toronto Quarterly*, XXIV (1955), 109–120.

Maxwell, J. C. "Animal Imagery in *Coriolanus*," *Modern Language Review*, XLII (1947), 417–421.

Oliver, H. J. "Coriolanus as Tragic Hero," *SQ*, X (1959), 53–60.

Palmer, John. *Political Characters of Shakespeare.* London, 1945.

Phillips, James E., Jr. *Twentieth Century Interpretations of "Coriolanus."* Englewood Cliffs, N.J., 1970.

Rabkin, Norman. "*Coriolanus:* The Tragedy of Politics," *SQ*, XVII (1966), 195–212.

Stirling, Brents. *The Populace in Shakespeare.* New York, 1949.

Traversi, Derek. "*Coriolanus*," *Scrutiny*, VI (1937), 43–58.

Waith, Eugene. *The Herculean Hero in Marlowe, Chapman, Shakespeare, and Dryden.* New York, 1962.

THE PERIOD OF ROMANCES

Bentley, Gerald Eades. "Shakespeare and the Blackfriars Theatre," *ShS 1* (1948), 38–50.

Danby, John F. *Poets on Fortune's Hill.* London, 1952.

Edwards, Philip. "Shakespeare's Romances: 1900–1957," *ShS 11* (1958), 1–18. See also other articles in this issue.

Felperin, Howard. *Shakespearean Romance.* Princeton, 1972.

Foakes, R. A. *Shakespeare: From the Dark Comedies to the Last Plays.* London and Charlottesville, Va., 1971.

Frye, Northrop. *Anatomy of Criticism.* Princeton, 1957.

———. *A Natural Perspective: The Development of Shakespearean Comedy and Romance.* New York, 1965.

James, D. G. "The Failure of the Ballad-Makers," *Scepticism and Poetry.* London, 1937.

Kermode, Frank. *William Shakespeare: The Final Plays.* London, 1963.

Knight, G. Wilson. *The Crown of Life.* London, 1947, 1966.

———. *The Shakespearian Tempest.* London, 1932, 1953.

Leavis, F. R. "A Criticism of Shakespeare's Last Plays," *Scrutiny*, X (1942), 339–345; reprinted in *The Common Pursuit.* London, 1952.

Marsh, D. R. C. *The Recurring Miracle: A Study of "Cymbeline" and the Last Plays.* Pietermaritzburg, Natal, 1962, 1964.

Pettet, E. C. *Shakespeare and the Romance Tradition.* London, 1949.

Seltzer, Daniel. "The Staging of the Last Plays," *Later Shakespeare*, ed. John Russell Brown and Bernard Harris, pp. 127–165. Stratford-upon-Avon Studies 8. London, 1966.

Smith, Hallett. *Shakespeare's Romances.* San Marino, Calif., 1972.

Spencer, Theodore. "Appearance and Reality in Shakespeare's Last Plays," *Modern Philology*, XXXIX (1942), 265–274.

Strachey, Lytton. "Shakespeare's Final Period," *Books and Characters*. London, 1922.

Tillyard, E. M. W. *Shakespeare's Last Plays*. London, 1938, 1964.

Traversi, Derek. *Shakespeare: The Last Phase*. New York, 1954.

Wells, Stanley. "Shakespeare and Romance," *Later Shakespeare*, ed. John Russell Brown and Bernard Harris, pp. 49–79. Stratford-upon-Avon Studies 8. London, 1966.

PERICLES

Arthos, John. "*Pericles, Prince of Tyre:* A Study in the Dramatic Use of Romantic Narrative," *SQ*, IV (1953), 257–270.

Barker, Gerard A. "Themes and Variations in Shakespeare's *Pericles*," *English Studies*, XLIV (1963), 401–414.

Berry, Francis. "Word and Picture in the Final Plays," *Later Shakespeare*, ed. John Russell Brown and Bernard Harris, pp. 81–101. Stratford-upon-Avon Studies 8. London, 1966.

Bland, D. S. "The Heroine and the Sea: An Aspect of Shakespeare's Last Plays," *Essays in Criticism*, III (1953), 39–44.

Craig, Hardin. "*Pericles* and *The Painfull Adventures*," *Studies in Philology*, XLV (1948), 600–605.

Danby, John F. "Sidney and the Late-Shakespearian Romance," *Poets on Fortune's Hill*. London, 1952.

Edwards, Philip. "An Approach to the Problem of *Pericles*," *ShS 5* (1952), 25–49.

Hoeniger, F. D., ed. *Pericles*. The Arden Shakespeare. London and Cambridge, Mass., 1963.

Muir, Kenneth. *Shakespeare as Collaborator*. London, 1960.

Tompkins, J. M. S. "Why *Pericles?*" *Review of English Studies*, n. s., III (1952), 315–324.

CYMBELINE

Brockbank, J. P. "History and Histrionics in *Cymbeline*," *ShS 11* (1958), 42–49.

Gesner, Carol. "*Cymbeline* and the Greek Romance: A Study in Genre," *Studies in English Renaissance Literature*, ed. Waldo F. McNeir. Baton Rouge, La., 1962.

Granville-Barker, Harley. *Prefaces to Shakespeare*, vol. I. Princeton, 1946.

Harris, Bernard. " 'What's past is prologue': *Cymbeline* and *Henry VIII*," *Later Shakespeare*, ed. John Russell Brown and Bernard Harris, pp. 203–233. Stratford-upon-Avon Studies 8. London, 1966.

Hoeniger, F. D. "Irony and Romance in *Cymbeline*," *Studies in English Literature*, II (1962), 219–228.

Jones, Emrys. "Stuart *Cymbeline*," *Essays in Criticism*, XI (1961), 84–99.

Kirsch, Arthur C. "*Cymbeline* and Coterie Dramaturgy," *English Literary History*, XXXIV (1967), 285–306.

Lawrence, W. W. *Shakespeare's Problem Comedies*. New York, 1931, 1960.

Nosworthy, J. M. "The Integrity of Shakespeare: Illustrated from *Cymbeline*," *ShS 8* (1955), 52–56.

Ribner, Irving. "Shakespeare and Legendary History: *Lear* and *Cymbeline*," *SQ*, VII (1956), 47–52.

Stephenson, A. A. "The Significance of *Cymbeline*," *Scrutiny*, X (1942), 329–338.

Wilson, Harold S. "*Philaster* and *Cymbeline*," *English Institute Essays 1951*, ed. Alan Downer, pp. 146–167. New York, 1952.

THE WINTER'S TALE

Bethell, S. L. *The Winter's Tale: A Study*. London, 1947.

Bryant, J. A., Jr. "Shakespeare's Allegory: *The Winter's Tale*," *Sewanee Review*, LXIII (1955), 202–222.

Coghill, Nevill. "Six Points of Stage-Craft in *The Winter's Tale*," *ShS 11* (1958), 31–41.

Ewbank, Inga-Stina. "The Triumph of Time in *The Winter's Tale*," *Review of English Literature*, V, no. 2 (April 1964), 83–100.

Frye, Northrop. "Recognition in *The Winter's Tale*," *Essays on Shakespeare and Elizabethan Drama in Honor of Hardin Craig*, ed. R. Hosley, pp. 235–246. Columbia, Mo., 1962.

Hoeniger, F. D. "The Meaning of *The Winter's Tale*," *University of Toronto Quarterly*, XX (1950), 11–26.

Lawlor, John. "*Pandosto* and the Nature of Dramatic Romance," *Philological Quarterly*, XLI (1962), 96–113.

Pyle, Fitzroy. *The Winter's Tale: A Commentary on the Structure*. London, 1968.

Schanzer, Ernest. "The Structural Pattern of *The Winter's Tale*," *Review of English Literature*, V, no. 2 (April 1964), 72–82.

Tayler, Edward W. *Nature and Art in Renaissance Literature*, New York, 1964.

Tinkler, F. C. "*The Winter's Tale*," *Scrutiny*, V (1937), 344–364.

Young, David. *The Heart's Forest*. New Haven, 1972.

THE TEMPEST

Allen, Don Cameron. *Image and Meaning*. Baltimore, 1960.

Auden, W. H. "The Sea and the Mirror," *The Collected Poetry*. New York, 1945.

Brockbank, Philip. "*The Tempest:* Conventions of Art and Empire," *Later Shakespeare*, ed. John Russell Brown and Bernard Harris, pp. 183–201. Stratford-upon-Avon Studies 8. London, 1966.

Brower, Reuben. "The Mirror of Analogy," *The Fields of Light*. New York, 1951.

Coleridge, S. T. "Lectures on Shakespeare and Milton: The Ninth Lecture," *Shakespearean Criticism*, 2 vols., ed. T. M. Raysor, II, 121–140. 2nd ed. London, 1960.

Curry, Walter Clyde. *Shakespeare's Philosophical Patterns*. Baton Rouge, La., 1937.

Frye, Northrop, ed. *The Tempest*. Pelican Shakespeare. Baltimore, 1959.

Hoeniger, F. D. "Prospero's Storm and Miracle," *SQ*, VII (1956), 33–38.

James, D. G. *The Dream of Prospero*. Oxford, 1967.

Johnson, W. Stacy. "The Genesis of Ariel," *SQ*, II (1951), 205–210.

Kermode, Frank, ed. *The Tempest*. The Arden Shakespeare. London, 1958.

Knox, Bernard. "*The Tempest* and the Ancient Comic Tradition," *English Stage Comedy*, ed. W. K. Wimsatt. *English Institute Essays 1954*. New York, 1955.

McPeek, James. "The Genesis of Caliban," *Philological Quarterly*, XXV (1946), 378–381.

Palmer, D. J., ed. *Shakespeare, "The Tempest": A Casebook*. London, 1968.

Reed, Robert R., Jr. "The Probable Origin of Ariel," *SQ*, XI (1960), 61–65.

Smith, Hallett, ed. *Twentieth Century Interpretations of "The Tempest."* Englewood Cliffs, N.J., 1969.

Still, Colin. *The Timeless Theme*. London, 1936, 1947. Originally published as *Shakespeare's Mystery Play: A Study of "The Tempest,"* 1921.

William, David. "*The Tempest* on the Stage," *Jacobean Theatre*, ed. John Russell Brown and Bernard Harris, pp. 133–157. Stratford-upon-Avon Studies 1. London, 1960.

Wilson, J. Dover. *The Meaning of "The Tempest."* Newcastle, 1936.

Young, David. *The Heart's Forest*. New Haven, 1972.

HENRY THE EIGHTH

Alexander, Peter. "Conjectural History, or Shakespeare's *Henry VIII*," *English Association Essays and Studies*, XVI (1930), 85–120.

Berman, Ronald. "*King Henry the Eighth:* History and Romance," *English Studies*, XLVIII (1967), 112–121.

Bertram, Paul. "*Henry VIII:* The Conscience of the King," *In Defense of Reading*, ed. Reuben A. Brower and R. Poirier. New York, 1962.

Byrne, Muriel St. Claire. "A Stratford Production: *Henry VIII*," *ShS 3* (1950), 120–129.

Clark, Cumberland. A Study of Shakespeare's "*Henry VIII*." London, 1931.

Felperin, Howard. "Shakespeare's *Henry VIII:* History as Myth," *Studies in English Literature*, VI (1966), 225–246.

Kermode, Frank. "What is Shakespeare's *Henry VIII* About?" *Durham University Journal*, IX (1948), 48–55.

Knight, G. Wilson. "*Henry VIII* and the Poetry of Conversion," *The Crown of Life*. London, 1947, 1966.

Nicolson, Marjorie. "The Authorship of *Henry the Eighth*," *PMLA*, XXXVII (1922), 484–502.

Partridge, A. C. *The Problem of Henry VIII Reopened*. Cambridge, Eng., 1949.

Richmond, H. M. "Shakespeare's *Henry VIII:* Romance Redeemed by History," *ShakS 4* (1968), 334–349.

Wasson, John. "In Defense of *King Henry VIII*," *Research Studies*, Washington State University, XXXII (1964), 261–276.

Wiley, Paul L. "Renaissance Exploitation of Cavendish's *Life of Wolsey*," *Studies in Philology*, XLIII (1946), 121–146.

GLOSSARY

Shakespearean Words and Meanings of Frequent Occurrence

A

'A: he (unaccented form).

Abate: lessen, diminish; blunt, reduce; deprive; bar, leave out of account, except; depreciate; humble.

Abuse (N): insult, error, misdeed, offense, crime; imposture, deception; also the modern sense.

Abuse (V): deceive, misapply, put to a bad use; maltreat; frequently the modern sense.

Addition: something added to one's name to denote his rank; mark of distinction; title.

Admiration: wonder; object of wonder.

Admire: wonder at.

Advantage (N): profit, convenience, benefit; opportunity, favorable opportunity; pecuniary profit; often shades toward the modern sense.

Advantage (V): profit, be of benefit to, benefit; augment.

Advice: reflection, consideration, deliberation, consultation.

Affect: aim at, aspire to, incline toward; be fond of, be inclined; love; act upon contagiously (as a disease). (PAST PART.) *Affected:* disposed, inclined, in love, loved.

Affection: passion, love; emotion, feeling, mental tendency, disposition; wish, inclination; affectation.

An: if; but; *an if:* if, though, even if.

Anon: at once, soon; presently, by and by.

Answer: return, requite; atone for; render an account of, account for; obey, agree with; also the modern sense.

Apparent: evident, plain; seeming.

Argument: subject, theme, reason, cause; story; excuse.

As: according as; as far as; namely; as if; in the capacity of; that; so that; that is, that they.

Assay: try, attempt; accost, address; challenge.

Atone: reconcile; set at one.

Attach: arrest, seize.

Awful: commanding reverential fear or respect; profoundly respectful or reverential.

B

Band: bond, fetters, manacle (leash for a dog). *Band* and *bond* are etymologically the same word; *band* was formerly used in both senses.

Basilisk: fabulous reptile said to kill by its look. The basilisk of popular superstition was a creature with legs, wings, a serpentine and winding tail, and a crest or comb somewhat like a cock (Sir Thomas Browne). It was the offspring of a cock's egg hatched under a toad or serpent.

Bate: blunt, abate, reduce; deduct, except.

Battle: army; division of an army.

Beshrew: curse, blame; used as a mild curse, "Bad or ill luck to."

Bias: tendency, bent, inclination, swaying influence; term in bowling applied to the form of the bowl, the oblique line in which it runs, and the kind of impetus given to cause it to run obliquely.

Blood: nature, vigor; supposed source of emotion; passion; spirit, animation; one of the four humours (see *humour*).

Boot (N): advantage, profit; something given in addition to the bargain; booty, plunder.

Boot (V): profit, avail.

Brave (ADJ.): fine, gallant; splendid, finely arrayed, showy; ostentatiously defiant.

Brave (V): challenge, defy; make splendid.

Brook: tolerate, endure.

C

Can: can do; know; be skilled; sometimes used for "did."

Capable: comprehensive; sensible, impressible, susceptible; capable of; gifted, intelligent.

Careful: anxious, full of care; provident; attentive.

Carry: manage, execute; be successful, win; conquer; sustain; endure.

Censure (N): judgment, opinion; critical opinion, unfavorable opinion.

Censure (V): judge, estimate; pass sentence or judgment.

Character (N): writing, printing, record; handwriting; cipher; face, features (bespeaking inward qualities).

Character (V): write, engrave, inscribe.

Check (N): reproof; restraint.

Check (V): reprove, restrain, keep from; control.

Circumstance: condition, state of affairs, particulars; adjunct details; detailed narration, argument, or discourse; formality, ceremony.

Clip: embrace; surround.

Close: secret, private; concealed; uncommunicative; enclosed.

Cog: cheat.

Coil: noise, disturbance, turmoil; fuss, to-do, bustle.

Colour: appearance; pretext, pretense; excuse.

Companion: fellow (used contemptuously).

Complete: accomplished, fully endowed; perfect, perfect in quality; also frequently the modern sense.

Complexion: external appearance; temperament, disposition; the four complexions—sanguine, choleric, phlegmatic, and melancholy—correspond to the four humours (see *humour*); also the modern sense.

Composition: compact, agreement, constitution.

Compound: settle, agree.

Conceit: conception, idea, thought; mental faculty, wit; fancy, imagination; opinion, estimate; device, invention, design.

Condition: temperament, disposition; characteristic, property, quality; social or official position, rank or status; covenant, treaty, contract.

Confound: waste, spend, invalidate, destroy; undo, ruin; mingle indistinguishably, mix, blend.

Confusion: destruction, overthrow, ruin; mental agitation.

Continent: that which contains or encloses; earth, globe; sum, summary.

Contrive: plot; plan; spend or pass (time).

Conversation: conduct, deportment; social intercourse, association.

Converse: hold intercourse; associate with, have to do with.

Cope: encounter, meet; have to do with.
Copy: model, pattern; example; minutes or memoranda.
Cousin: any relative not belonging to one's immediate family.
Cry you mercy: beg your pardon.
Cuckold: husband whose wife is unfaithful.
Curious: careful, fastidious; anxious, concerned; made with care, skillfully, intricately or daintily wrought; particular.
Cursed, curst: shrewish, perverse, spiteful.

D

Dainty: minute; scrupulous, particular; particular about (with *of*); refined, elegant; also the modern sense.
Date: duration, termination, term of existence; limit or end of a term or period, term.
Dear: precious; best; costly; important; affectionate; hearty; grievous, dire; also the modern sense.
Debate: discuss; fight.
Decay (N): downfall, ruin; cause of ruin.
Decay (V): perish, be destroyed; destroy.
Defeat (N): destruction, ruin.
Defeat (V): destroy, disfigure, ruin.
Defy: challenge, challenge to a fight; reject; despise.
Demand (N): inquiry; request.
Demand (V): inquire, question; request.
Deny: refuse (to do something); refuse permission; refuse to accept; refuse admittance; disown.
Depart (N): departure.
Depart (V): part; go away from, leave, quit; take leave (of one another); *depart with, withal:* part with, give up.
Derive: gain, obtain; draw upon, direct (to); descend; pass by descent, be descended or inherited; trace the origin of (refl.).
Difference: diversity of opinion, disagreement, dissension, dispute; characteristic or distinguishing feature; alteration or addition to a coat of arms to distinguish a younger or lateral branch of a family.
Digest: arrange, perfect; assimilate, amalgamate; disperse, dissipate; comprehend, understand; put up with (fig. from the physical sense of digesting food).
Discourse (N): reasoning, reflection; talk, act of conversing, conversation; faculty of conversing; familiar intercourse; relating (as by speech).
Discourse (V): speak, talk, converse; pass (the time) in talk; say, utter, tell, give forth; narrate, relate.
Discover: uncover, expose to view; divulge, reveal, make known; spy out, reconnoiter; betray; distinguish, discern; also the modern sense.
Dispose (N): disposal; temperament, bent of mind, disposition; external manner.
Dispose (V): distribute, manage, make use of; deposit, put or stow away; regulate, order, direct; come to terms. (PAST PART.) *Disposed:* in a good frame of mind; inclined to be merry.
Dispute: discuss, reason; strive against, resist.
Distemper: disturb; disorder, ill humor; illness.
Doit: old Dutch coin, one-half an English farthing.
Doubt (N): suspicion, apprehension; fear, danger, risk; also the modern sense.
Doubt (V): suspect, apprehend; fear; also the modern sense.
Doubtful: inclined to suspect, suspicious, apprehensive; not to be relied on; almost certain.
Duty: reverence, respect, expression of respect; submission to authority, obedience; due.

E

Earnest: money paid as an instalment to secure a bargain; partial payment; often used with quibble in the modern sense.
Ease: comfort, assistance, leisure; idleness, sloth, inactivity; also the modern sense.
Ecstasy: frenzy, madness, state of being beside oneself, excitement, bewilderment; swoon; rapture.
Element: used to refer to the simple substances of which all material bodies were thought to be composed; specifically earth, air, fire, and water, corresponding to the four humors (see *humour*); atmosphere, sky; atmospheric agencies or powers; that one of the four elements which is the natural abode of a creature; hence, natural surroundings, sphere.
Engage: pledge, pawn, mortgage; bind by a promise, swear to; entangle, involve; enlist; embark on an enterprise (refl.).
Engine: mechanical contrivance; artifice, device, plot.
Enlarge: give free scope to; set at liberty, release.
Entertain: keep up, maintain, accept; take into one's service; treat; engage (someone's) attention or thoughts; occupy, while or pass away pleasurably; engage (as an enemy); receive.
Envious: malicious, spiteful, malignant.
Envy: ill-will, malice; hate; also the modern sense.
Even: uniform; direct, straightforward; exact, precise; equable, smooth, comfortable; equal, equally balanced.
Event: outcome; affair, business; also frequently the modern sense.
Exclaim: protest, rail; accuse, blame (with *on*), reproach.
Excursion: stage battle or skirmish (in stage directions).
Excuse: seek to extenuate (a fault); maintain the innocence of; clear oneself, justify or vindicate oneself; decline (refl.).

F

Fact: deed, act; crime.
Faction: party, class, group, set (of persons); party strife, dissension; factious quarrel, intrigue.
Fail: die, die out; err, be at fault; omit, leave undone.
Fair (N): fair thing; one of the fair sex; someone beloved; beauty (the abstract concept).
Fair (ADJ.): just; clear, distinct; beautiful.
Fair (ADV.): fairly (q.v.).
Fairly: beautifully, handsomely; courteously, civilly; properly, honorably, honestly; becomingly, appropriately; favorably, fortunately; softly, gently, kindly.
Fall: let fall, drop; happen, come to pass; befall; shades frequently toward the modern senses.
Falsely: wrongly; treacherously; improperly.
Fame: report; rumor; reputation.
Familiar (N): intimate friend; familiar or attendant spirit, demon associated with and obedient to a person.
Familiar (ADJ.): intimate, friendly; belonging to

household or family, domestic; well-known; habitual, ordinary, trivial; plain, easily understood.

Fancy: fantasticalness; imaginative conception, flight of imagination; amorous inclination or passion, love; liking, taste.

Fantasy: fancy, imagination; caprice, whim.

Favour: countenance, face; complexion; aspect, appearance; leave, permission, pardon; attraction, charm, good will; *in favour,* benevolently.

Fear (N): dread, apprehension; dreadfulness; object of dread or fear.

Fear (V): be apprehensive or concerned about, mistrust, doubt; frighten, make afraid.

Fearful: exciting or inspiring fear, terrible, dreadful; timorous, apprehensive, full of fear.

Feature: shape or form of body, figure; shapeliness, comeliness.

Fellow: companion; partaker, sharer (of); equal, match; customary form of address to a servant or an inferior (sometimes used contemptuously or condescendingly).

Fine (N): end, conclusion; *in fine:* finally.

Fine (ADJ.): highly accomplished or skillful; exquisitely fashioned, delicate; refined, subtle; frequently the modern sense.

Flaw: fragment; crack, fissure; tempest, squall, gust of wind; outburst of passion.

Flesh: reward a hawk or hound with a piece of flesh of the game killed to excite its eagerness of the chase (Onions); hence to inflame by a foretaste of success; initiate or inure to bloodshed (used for a first time in battle); harden, train.

Flourish: fanfare of trumpets (in stage directions).

Fond: foolish, doting; *fond of:* eager for; also the modern sense.

Fool: term of endearment and pity; frequently the modern sense.

For that, for why: because.

Forfend: forbid, avert.

Free: generous, magnanimous; candid, open; guiltless, innocent.

Front: forehead, face; foremost line of battle; beginning.

Furnish: equip, fit out (furnish forth); endow; dress, decorate, embellish.

G

Gear: apparel, dress; stuff, substance, thing, article; discourse, talk; matter, business, affair.

Get: beget.

Gloss: specious fair appearance; lustrous surface.

Go to: expression of remonstrance, impatience, disapprobation, or derision.

Grace (N): kindness, favor, charm, divine favor; fortune, luck; beneficent virtue; sense of duty or propriety; mercy, pardon; embellish; *do grace:* reflect credit on, do honor to, do a favor for.

Grace (V): gratify, delight; honor, favor.

Groat: coin equal to four pence.

H

Habit: dress, garb, costume; bearing, demeanor, manner; occasionally in the modern sense.

Happily: haply, perchance, perhaps.

Hardly: with difficulty.

Have at: I shall come at (you) (i.e., listen to me), I shall attack (a person or thing); let me at.

Have with: I shall go along with; let me go along with; come along.

Having: possession, property, wealth, estate; endowments, accomplishments.

Head: armed force.

Hind: servant, slave; rustic, boor, clown.

His: its. *His* was historically the possessive form of both the masculine and neuter pronouns. *Its,* although not common in Shakespeare's time, occurs in the plays occasionally.

Holp: helped (archaic past tense).

Home: fully, satisfactorily, thoroughly, plainly, effectually; to the quick.

Honest: holding an honorable position, honorable, respectable; decent, kind, seemly, befitting, proper; chaste; genuine; loosely used as an epithet of approbation.

Humour: mood, temper, cast of mind, temperament, disposition; vagary, fancy, whim; moisture (the literal sense); a physiological, and by transference, a psychological term applied to the four chief fluids of the human body—phlegm, blood, choler, and melancholy (the last also called black choler). A person's disposition and his temporary state of mind were determined according to the relative proportions of these fluids in his body; consequently a person was said to be phlegmatic, sanguine, choleric, or melancholy.

I

Image: likeness; visible form; representation; embodiment, type; mental picture, creation of the imagination.

Influence: supposed flowing from the stars or heavens of an ethereal fluid, acting upon the characters and destinies of men (used metaphorically).

Inform: take shape, give form to, imbue, inspire; instruct, teach; charge (against).

Instance: evidence, proof, sign, confirmation; motive, cause.

Invention: power of mental creation, the creative faculty; work of the imagination, artistic creation, premeditated design; device, plan, scheme.

J

Jar (N): discord in music; quarrel, discord.

Jar (V): be out of tune; be discordant, quarrel.

Jump: agree, tally, coincide, fit exactly; risk, hazard.

K

Keep: continue, carry on; dwell, lodge, guard, defend, care for, employ, be with; restrain, control (refl.); confine in prison.

Kind (N): nature, established order of things; manner, fashion, respect; race, class, kindred, family; *by kind:* naturally.

Kind (ADJ.): natural; favorable; affectionate.

Kindly (ADJ.): natural, appropriate; agreeable; innate; benign.

Kindly (ADV.): naturally; gently, courteously.

L

Large: liberal, bounteous, lavish; free, unrestrained; *at large,* at length, in full; in full detail, as a whole, in general.
Late: lately.
Learn: teach; inform (someone of something); also the modern sense.
Let: hinder.
Level: aim; also shades toward the modern sense.
Liberal: possessed of the characteristics and qualities of gentlemen, genteel, becoming in a gentleman, refined; free in speech; unrestrained by prudence or decorum; licentious.
Lie: be in bed; be still; be confined, be kept in prison; dwell, sojourn, reside, lodge.
Like: please, feel affection; liken, compare.
List (N): strip of cloth, selvedge; limit, boundary; desire.
List (V): choose, desire, please; listen to.
'Long of: owing to, on account of.
Look: power to see; take care, see to it; expect; seek, search for.

M

Make: do; have to do (with); consider; go; be effective, make up, complete; also the modern sense.
Manage: management, conduct, administration; action and paces to which a horse is trained; short gallop at full speed.
Marry: mild interjection equivalent to "Indeed!" Originally an oath by the Virgin Mary.
May: can; also frequently the modern sense to denote probability; *might* has corresponding meanings and uses.
Mean (N): instrument, agency, method (also frequent in the plural); effort; opportunity (for doing something); something interposed or intervening; middle position, medium; tenor or alto parts in singing; money, wealth (usually plural form).
Mean (ADJ.): average, moderate, middle; of low degree, station, or position; undignified, base.
Measure (N): grave or stately dance, graceful motion; tune, melody, musical accompaniment; treatment meted out; moderation, proportion; limit; distance, reach.
Measure (V): judge, estimate; traverse.
Mere: absolute, sheer; pure, unmixed; downright, sincere.
Mew (up): coop up (as used of a hawk), shut up, imprison, confine.
Mind (N): thoughts, judgment, opinion, message; purpose, intention, desire; disposition; also the modern sense of the mental faculty.
Mind (V): remind; perceive, notice, attend; intend.
Minion: saucy woman, hussy; follower; favorite, favored person, darling (often used contemptuously).
Misdoubt (N): suspicion.
Misdoubt (V): mistrust, suspect.
Model: pattern, replica, likeness.
Modern: ordinary, commonplace, everyday.
Modest: moderate, marked by moderation, becoming; characterized by decency and propriety; chaste.
Moe: more.
Moiety: half; share; small part, lesser share; portion, part of.
Mortal: fatal; deadly, of or for death; belonging to mankind; human, pertaining to human affairs.
Motion: power of movement; suggestion, proposal; movement of the soul; impulse, prompting; also the modern sense.
Move: make angry; urge, incite, instigate, arouse, prompt; propose, make a proposal to, apply to, appeal to, suggest; also the modern sense.
Muse: wonder, marvel; grumble, complain.

N

Napkin: handkerchief.
Natural: related by blood; having natural or kindly feeling; also the modern sense.
Naught: useless, worthless; wicked, naughty.
Naughty: wicked; good for nothing, worthless.
Nice: delicate; fastidious, dainty, particular, scrupulous; minute, subtle; shy, coy; reluctant, unwilling; unimportant, insignificant, trivial; accurate, precise; wanton, lascivious.
Nothing: not at all.

O

Of: from, away from; during; on; by; as regards; instead of; *out of,* compelled by; made from.
Offer: make an attack; menace; venture, dare, presume.
Opinion: censure; reputation or credit; favorable estimate of oneself; self-conceit, arrogance; self-confidence; public opinion, reputation; also the modern sense.
Or: before; also used conjunctively where no alternative is implied; *or . . . or:* either . . . or; whether . . . or.
Out (ADV.): without, outside; abroad; fully, quite; at an end, finished; at variance, aligned the wrong way.
Out (INTERJ.): an expression of reproach, impatience, indignation, or anger.
Owe: own; also the modern sense.

P

Pack: load; depart, begone; conspire.
Pageant: show, spectacle, spectacular entertainment; device on a moving carriage.
Pain: punishment, penalty; labor, trouble, effort; also frequently the modern sense.
Painted: specious, unreal, counterfeit.
Parle: parley, conference, talk; bugle call for parley.
Part: depart, part from; divide.
Particular: detail; personal interest or concern; details of a private nature; single person.
Party: faction, side, part, cause; partner, ally.
Pass: pass through, traverse; exceed; surpass; pledge.
Passing (ADJ. and ADV.): surpassing, surpassingly, exceedingly.
Passion (N): powerful or violent feeling, violent sorrow or grief; painful affection or disorder of the body; sorrow; feelings or desires of love; passionate speech or outburst.
Passion (V): sorrow, grieve.

Peevish: silly, senseless, childish; perverse, obstinate, stubborn; sullen.
Perforce: by violence or compulsion; forcibly; necessarily.
Physic: medical faculty; healing art, medical treatment; remedy, medicine, healing property.
Pitch: height; specifically, the height to which a falcon soars before stooping on its prey (often used figuratively).
Policy: conduct of affairs (especially public affairs); prudent management; stratagem, trick; contrivance; craft, cunning.
Port: bearing, demeanor; state, style of living, social station; gate.
Possess: have or give possession or command (of something); inform, acquaint; also the modern sense.
Post (N): courier, messenger; post-horse; haste.
Post (V): convey swiftly; hasten, ignore through haste (with *over* or *off*).
Practice: execution; exercise (especially for instruction); stratagem, intrigue; conspiracy, plot, treachery.
Practise: perform, take part in; use stratagem, craft, or artifice; scheme, plot; play a joke on.
Pregnant: resourceful; disposed, inclined; clear, obvious.
Present (ADJ.): ready, immediate, prompt, instant.
Present (V): represent.
Presently: immediately, at once.
Prevent: forestall, anticipate, foresee; also the modern sense.

Process: drift, tenor, gist; narrative, story; formal command, mandate.
Proof: test, trial, experiment; experience; issue, result; proved or tested strength of armor or arms; also the modern sense.
Proper: (one's or its) own; peculiar, exclusive; excellent; honest, respectable; handsome, elegant, fine, good-looking.
Proportion: symmetry; size; form, carriage, appearance, shape; portion, allotment; rhythm.
Prove: make trial of; put to test; show or find out by experience.
Purchase (N): acquisition; spoil, booty.
Purchase (V): acquire, gain, obtain; strive, exert oneself; redeem, exempt.

Q

Quaint: skilled, clever; pretty, fine, dainty; handsome, elegant; carefully or ingeniously wrought or elaborated.
Quality: that which constitutes (something); essential being; good natural gifts; accomplishment, attainment, property; art, skill; rank, position; profession, occupation, business; party, side; manner, style; cause, occasion.
Quick: living (used substantively to mean "living flesh"); alive; lively, sharp, piercing; hasty, impatient; with child.
Quillets: verbal niceties, subtle distinctions.
Quit: requite, reward; set at liberty; acquit, remit; pay for, clear off.

R

Rack (V): stretch or strain beyond normal extent or capacity to endure; strain oneself; distort.
Rage (N): madness, insanity; vehement pain; angry disposition; violent passion or appetite; poetic enthusiasm; warlike ardor or fury.
Rage (V): behave wantonly or riotously; act with fury or violence; enrage; pursue furiously.
Range: extend or lie in the same plane (with); occupy a position; rove, roam; be inconstant; traverse.
Rank: coarsely luxuriant; puffed up, swollen, fat, abundant; full, copious; rancid; lustful; corrupt, foul.
Rate (N): estimate; value or worth; estimation, consideration; standard, style.
Rate (V): allot; calculate, estimate, compute; reckon, consider; be of equal value (with); chide, scold, berate; drive away by chiding or scolding.
Recreant: traitor, coward, cowardly wretch.
Remorse: pity, compassion; also the modern sense.
Remove: removal, absence; period of absence; change.
Resolve: dissolve, melt, dissipate; answer; free from doubt or uncertainty, convince; inform; decide; also the modern sense.
Respect (N): consideration, reflection, act of seeing, view; attention, notice; decency, modest deportment; also the modern sense.
Respect (V): esteem, value, prize; regard, consider; heed, pay attention to; also the modern sense.
Round: spherical; plain, direct, brusque; fair; honest.
Roundly: plainly, unceremoniously.
Rub: obstacle (a term in the game of bowls); unevenness; inequality.

S

Sack: generic term for Spanish and Canary wines; sweet white wine.
Sad: grave, serious; also the modern sense.
Sadness: seriousness; also the modern sense.
Sans: without (French preposition).
Scope: object, aim, limit; freedom, license; free play.
Seal: bring to completion or conclusion, conclude, confirm, ratify, stamp; also the modern sense.
Sennet: a series of notes sounded on a trumpet to herald the approach or departure of a procession (used in stage directions).
Sense: mental faculty, mind; mental perception, import, rational meaning; physical perception; sensual nature; *common sense:* ordinary or untutored perception, observation or knowledge.
Sensible: capable of physical feeling or perception, sensitive; capable of or exhibiting emotion; rational; capable of being perceived.
Serve: be sufficient; be favorable; succeed; satisfy the need for; serve a turn; answer the purpose.
Several: separate, distinct, different; particular, private; various.
Shadow: shade, shelter; reflection; likeness, image; ghost; representation, picture of the imagination, phantom; also the modern sense.
Shift: change; stratagem, strategy, trick, contrivance, device to serve a purpose; *make shift*, manage.
Shrewd: malicious, mischievous, ill-natured; shrewish; bad, of evil import, grievous; severe.
Sirrah: ordinary or customary form of address to inferiors or servants; disrespectful form of address.
Sith: since.

Smock: woman's undergarment; used typically for "a woman."
Something: somewhat.
Sometime: sometimes, from time to time; once, formerly; at times, at one time.
Speed (N): fortune, success; protecting and assisting power; also the modern sense.
Speed (V): fare (well or ill); succeed; be successful; assist, guard, favor.
Spleen: the seat of emotions and passions; violent passion; fiery temper; malice; anger, rage; impulse, fit of passion; caprice; impetuosity.
Spoil: destruction, ruin; plunder; slaughter, massacre.
Starve: die of cold or hunger; be benumbed with cold; paralyze, disable; allow or cause to die.
State: degree, rank; social position, station; pomp, splendor, outward display, clothes; court, household of a great person; shades into the modern sense.
Stay: wait, wait for; sustain; stand; withhold, withstand; stop.
Stead: assist; be of use to, benefit, help.
Still: always, ever, continuously or continually, constant or constantly; silent, mute; also modern senses.
Stomach: appetite, inclination, disposition; resentment; angry temper, resentful feeling; proud spirit, courage.
Straight: immediately.
Strange: belonging to another country or person, foreign, unfriendly; new, fresh; ignorant; estranged.
Success: issue, outcome (good or bad); sequel, succession, descent (as from father to son).
Suggest: tempt; prompt; seduce.
Suggestion: temptation.

T

Table: memorandum, tablet; surface on which something is written or drawn.
Take: strike; bewitch; charm; infect; destroy; repair to for refuge; modern senses.
Tall: goodly, fine; strong in fight, valiant.
Target: shield.
Tax: censure, blame, accuse.
Tell: count; relate.
Thorough: through.
Throughly: thoroughly.
Toward: in preparation; forthcoming, about to take place.
Toy: trifle, idle fancy; folly.
Train: lure, entice, allure, attract.
Trencher: wooden dish or plate.
Trow: think, suppose, believe; know.

U

Undergo: undertake, perform; modern sense.
Undo: ruin.
Unfold: disclose, tell, make known, reveal; communicate.
Unhappy: evil, mischievous; fatal, ill-fated; miserable.
Unjust: untrue, dishonest; unjustified, groundless; faithless, false.
Unkind: unnatural, cruel, faulty; cf. *kind.*
Use (N): custom, habit; interest paid.
Use (V): make practice of; be accustomed; put out at interest.

V

Vail: lower, let fall.
Vantage: advantage; opportunity; benefit, profit; superiority.
Virtue: general excellence; valor, bravery; merit, goodness, honor; good accomplishment, excellence in culture; power; essence, essential part.

W

Want: lack; be in need of; be without.
Watch: be awake, lie awake, sit up at night, lose sleep; keep from sleep (trans.).
Weed: garment, clothes.
Welkin: sky, heavens.
Wink: close the eyes; close the eyes in sleep; have the eyes closed; seem not to see.
Withal: with; with it, this, or these; together with this; at the same time.
Wot: know.

THE ROYAL GENEALOGY OF ENGLAND, 1154–1625

THE PLANTAGENET KINGS

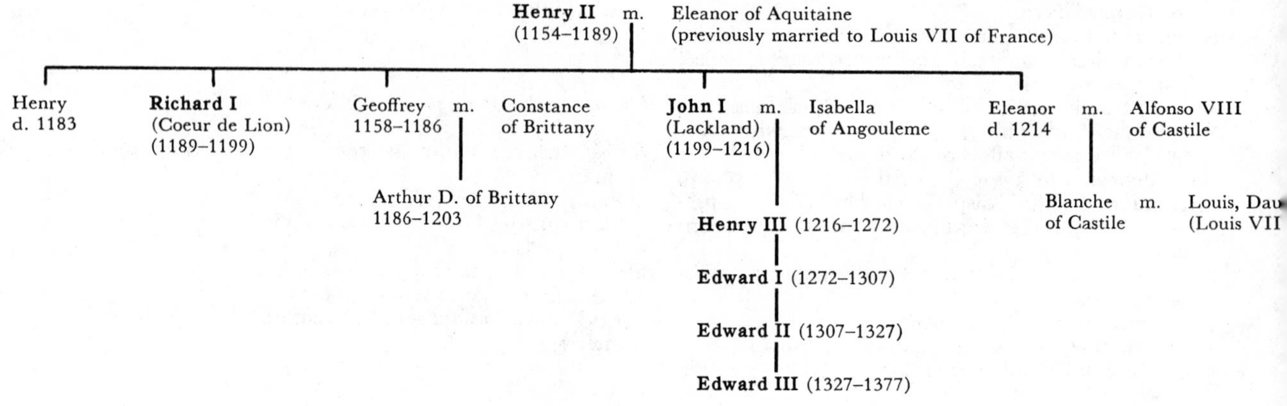

THE LANCASTRIAN KINGS

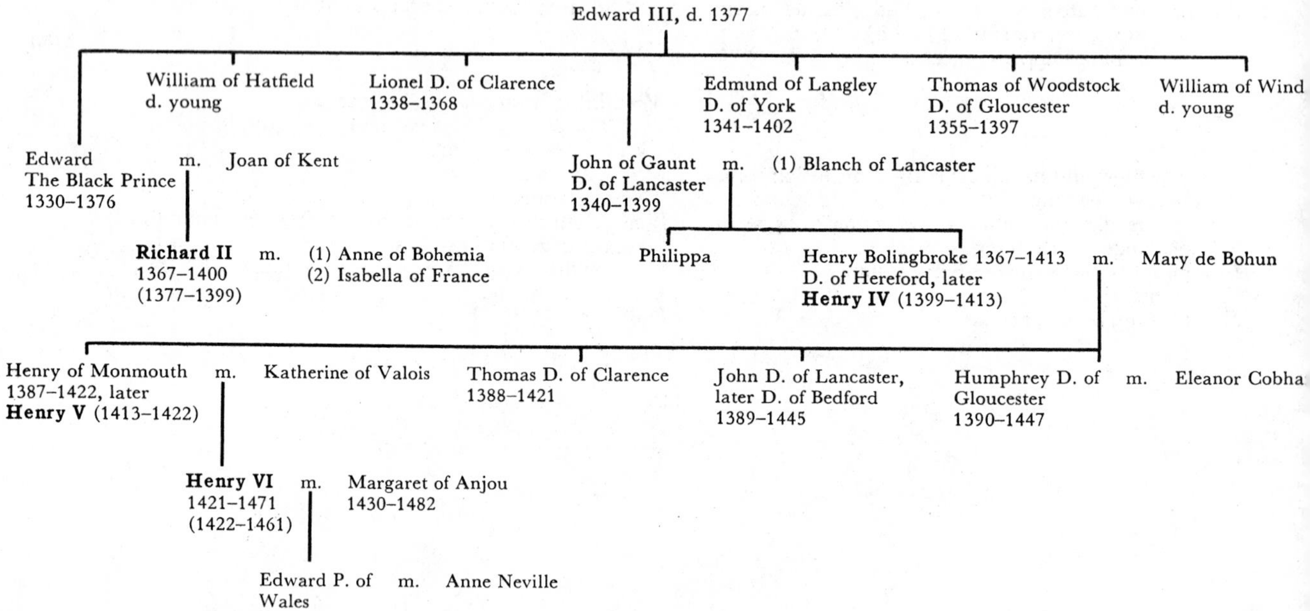

In these diagrams, reigning dates are given in parentheses; other dates indicate life span. Abbreviations: P. Prince, D. Duke, E. Earl, b. born, d. died, m. married. English monarchs are printed in boldface type. The spatial arrangement of names in a family usually but not always indicates order of birth.

In *1 Henry IV*, Shakespeare confuses the Edmund Mortimer who married Glendower's daughter, and died in 1409, with his nephew Edmund, fifth Earl of March, who asserted a claim to the English throne (see "The Yorkist Kings"). Shakespeare also refers to Henry Percy's (Hotspur's) wife as "Kate," though historically she was named Elizabeth.

Catherine Swynford, third wife of John of Gaunt (see "The Tudor Kings"), bore him children before their eventual marriage. These Beauforts, although later legitimized, were specifically barred from any claim to the English throne.

THE YORKIST KINGS

Edward III m. Philippa of Hainault
Edward
William
Lionel D. of Clarence m. Elizabeth de Burgh
John of Gaunt
Edmund Langley 1st D. of York m. Isabel of Castile
Thomas
Philippa m. Edmund Mortimer 3rd E. of March 1351–1381
Edward D. of Aumerle, later D. of York 1373–1415
Roger Mortimer 4th E. of March 1374–1398 m. Eleanor Holland
Edmund d. 1409 m. Daughter of Owen Glendower
Elizabeth m. Henry Percy (Hotspur)
Edmund Mortimer 5th E. of March 1391–1425
Anne Mortimer m. Richard E. of Cambridge 1375–1415
Richard Plantagenet E. of Cambridge, later D. of York 1411–1460 m. Cecily Neville
Edward, E. of March 1422–1483 Edward IV (1461–1483) m. Elizabeth Woodville Lady Grey
Edmund, E. of Rutland 1443–1460
George D. of Clarence 1449–1478 m. Isabell Neville, daughter of Richard E. of Warwick
Richard D. of Gloucester 1452–1485 Richard III (1483–1485)
Elizabeth b. 1465 m. Henry Tudor (Henry VII)
Edward V 1470–1483 (1483)
Richard k. 1483
Edward
Margaret

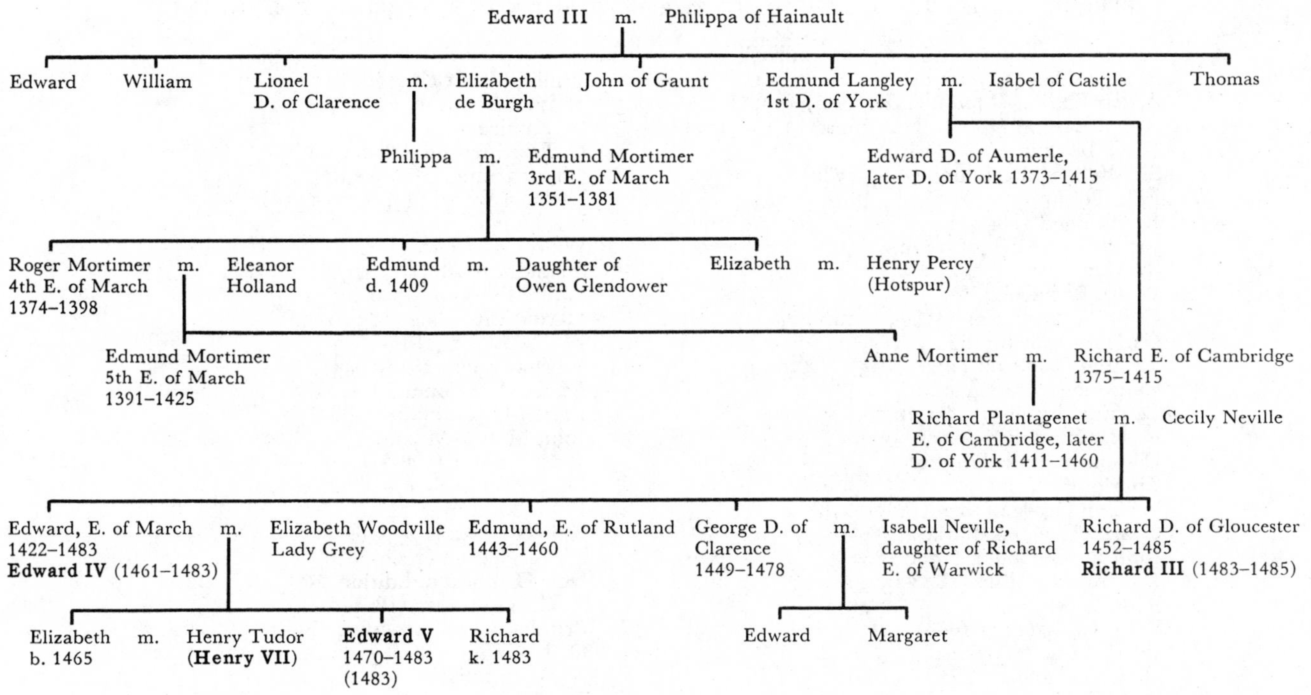

THE TUDOR KINGS

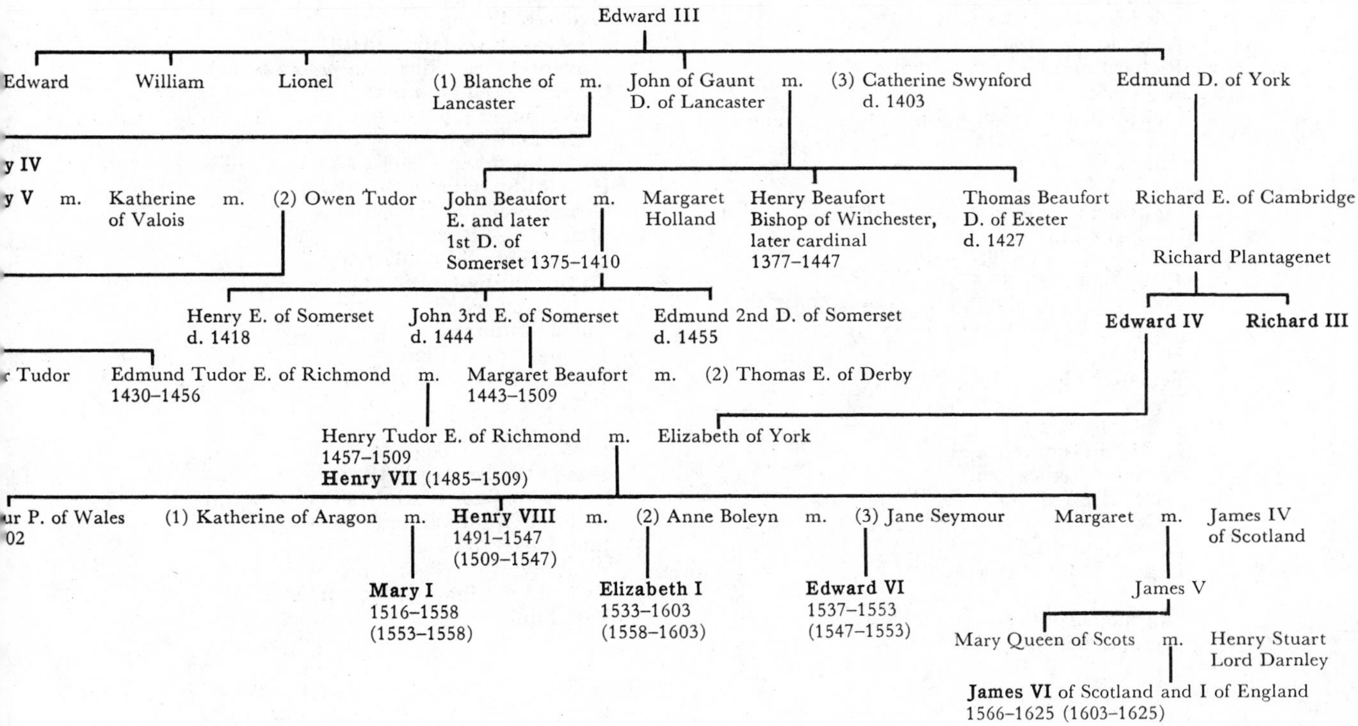

Edward III
Edward
William
Lionel
(1) Blanche of Lancaster m. John of Gaunt D. of Lancaster m. (3) Catherine Swynford d. 1403
Edmund D. of York
y IV
y V m. Katherine of Valois m. (2) Owen Tudor
John Beaufort E. and later 1st D. of Somerset 1375–1410 m. Margaret Holland
Henry Beaufort Bishop of Winchester, later cardinal 1377–1447
Thomas Beaufort D. of Exeter d. 1427
Richard E. of Cambridge
Richard Plantagenet
Henry E. of Somerset d. 1418
John 3rd E. of Somerset d. 1444
Edmund 2nd D. of Somerset d. 1455
Edward IV
Richard III
r Tudor
Edmund Tudor E. of Richmond 1430–1456 m. Margaret Beaufort 1443–1509 m. (2) Thomas E. of Derby
Henry Tudor E. of Richmond 1457–1509 Henry VII (1485–1509) m. Elizabeth of York
ur P. of Wales 02
(1) Katherine of Aragon m. Henry VIII 1491–1547 (1509–1547) m. (2) Anne Boleyn m. (3) Jane Seymour
Margaret m. James IV of Scotland
Mary I 1516–1558 (1553–1558)
Elizabeth I 1533–1603 (1558–1603)
Edward VI 1537–1553 (1547–1553)
James V
Mary Queen of Scots m. Henry Stuart Lord Darnley
James VI of Scotland and I of England 1566–1625 (1603–1625)

LIST OF EDITORS, EDITIONS, TEXTUAL CRITICS, AND COMMENTATORS

REFERRED TO IN THE FOOTNOTES TO THE TEXT BUT NOT ENTERED IN THE INDEX:

R. M. Alden (1873-1924)
Arden Edition (Methuen, London)
Arden Edition (Heath, New York)
H. C. Beeching (1859-1919)
Sir William Blackstone (1723-1780)
F. S. Boas
R. W. Bond (1857-1943)
James Boswell (1778-1822)
Sir Denys Bray
W. O. Brigstock
C. F. Tucker Brooke (1883-1946)
Carleton Brown (1869-1941)
Thomas Caldecott (1744-1833)
Cambridge Edition
Edward Capell (1713-1781)
R. H. Case (1857-1944)
Clarendon Press Edition
Charlotte Clark
William George Clark (1821-1878)
Charles Cowden Clarke (1789-1877)
John Payne Collier (1789-1883)
J. Churton Collins (1848-1908)
R. P. Cowl
W. J. Craig (1843-1906)
W. L. Cross (1862-1948)
Henry Cuningham
P. A. Daniel (*fl.* 1870-1877)
Kenneth Deighton
Nikolaus Delius (1813-1888)
Edward Dowden (1843-1913)
W. H. Durham
Alexander Dyce (1798-1869)
Friedrich Karl Elze (1821-1889)
A. H. R. Fairchild
Richard Farmer (1735-1779)
A. Feuillerat
H. H. Furness (1833-1912)
F. J. Furnivall (1825-1910)
Allison Gaw
Globe Edition
Sir Israel Gollancz (1849-1930)
G. S. Gordon
Zachery Grey (1688-1766)
J. W. Hales (1836-1914)
J. O. Halliwell (-Phillipps) (1820-1889)
Sir Thomas Hanmer (1677-1746)
H. C. Hart
Benjamin Heath (1704-1766)
W. E. Henley (1849-1903)
C. H. Herford (1853-1931)
H. N. Hudson (1814-1886)
William Hughes
Joseph Hunter (1783-1861)
C. M. Ingleby (1823-1886)
Alfred Jackson
Charles Jennens (1700-1773)
I. B. John
Dr. Samuel Johnson (1709-1784)
Thomas Keightley (1789-1872)
William Kenrick (1725?-1779)
F. W. Kilbourne
G. Kinnaer
G. L. Kittredge (1860-1941)
Charles Knight (1791-1873)
Richard Koppel (*fl.* 1877-1919)
Ida Langton
W. W. Lawrence
Sir Sidney Lee (1859-1926)
W. N. Lettsom (1796-1865)
Harold Littledale (1853-1930)
W. W. Lloyd (1813-1899)
Morton Luce (1849-1943)
Edmund Malone (1741-1812)
F. A. Marshall (1840-1889)
John Monck Mason (1726-1809)
John Mitford (1781-1859)
G. C. Moore-Smith (1858-1940)
F. W. Moorman
Robert Nares (1753-1829)
W. A. Neilson (1869-1946)
New Cambridge Edition
A. G. Newcomer (1864-1913)
Brinsley Nicholson (1824-1892)
C. T. Onions (*Shakespeare Glossary*)
N. B. Paradise
T. M. Parrott
Bishop Thomas Percy (1729-1811)
C. Knox Pooler
Alexander Pope (1688-1744)
William Ridgeway (1853-1926)
W. J. Rolfe (1827-1910)
Hyder E. Rollins
Nicholas Rowe (1674-1718)
Alexander Schmidt (*Shakespeare Lexicon*)
George Sewell (*fl.* 1725)
S. W. Singer (1783-1858)
J. C. Smith (b. 1867)
James Spedding (1808-1881)
Howard Staunton (1810-1874)
George Steevens (1736-1800)
Mrs. C. C. Stopes
Lewis Theobald (1688-1744)
Styan Thirlby (1686?-1753)
T. G. Tucker
Tudor Edition
Thomas Tyler (1826-1902)
Thomas Tyrwhit (1730-1785)
John Upton (1707-1760)
H. H. Vaughan
A. W. Verity (1863-1927)
Sidney Walker (1795-1846)
Bishop William Warburton (1698-1779)
Richard Grant White (1822-1885)
John Dover Wilson
W. A. Wright (1836?-1914)
George Wyndham (1863-1913)
Yale Edition

TEXTUAL NOTES

The most usual sort of entry in these notes gives first the *adopted* reading (*in italics*), followed by the rejected reading of the original Folio or quarto text. For instance, the entry "66 *clock* cooke" from I,i of *The Comedy of Errors* means that the original Folio reading in line 66, "cooke," has been emended to "clock" in Craig's edition of the Globe text and in this present edition.

These textual notes also list the departures of this present edition from Craig's edition of the Globe text [C]. In nearly all instances, these changes represent a return to the original Folio or quarto reading. For instance, the entry "4 *ruinate* [F] ruinous [C]" in III,ii of *The Comedy of Errors* means that the Craig-Globe emendation, "ruinous," has been rejected in favor of the original Folio reading, "ruinate." When, on the other hand, the reading adopted by this edition is an emendation not found in the Craig-Globe text, the entry reads typically as follows: "127 *assistance* assistants [Q, C]." This entry from V,i of *Love's Labour's Lost* means that the original quarto reading, "assistants," though retained in Craig's edition of the Globe text, has been emended to "assistance" in this present edition.

Each dramatic text in this present edition is based on a single original copy text, and follows that copy text closely except for the actual emendations listed in these notes. For a discussion of the reasons lying behind the choice of copy text in each instance, see Appendix I, "Canon, Dates, and Early Texts."

The Comedy of Errors

Copy text: the First Folio [F].

I,i,42 (and elsewhere) *Epidamnum* Epidamium 43 *the* he *random* randone 55 *meaner* meane 103 *upon* vp 117 *bark* backe 124 *thee* they 152 *life* helpe

I,ii,S.D. *Antipholus* [*of Syracuse*] Antipholus Erotes 4 *arrival* a riuall 32 S.D. *Exit* Exeunt 40 *unhappy* vnhappie a 65 *score* scoure 66 *clock* cooke 93 *God's* God 94 S.D. *Exit* Exeunt

II,i,S.D. *Antipholus* [*of Ephesus*] Antipholus Sereptus 11 *o' door* adore 12 *ill* thus 20 *Men* Man *masters* Master 21 *Lords* Lord 61 *thousand* hundred 72 *errand* arrant 107 *alone, alone* alone, a loue 112 *Wear* Where

II,ii,S.D. *Antipholus* [*of Syracuse*] Antipholis Errotis 12 *didst* did didst 81 *men* them 99 *tiring* trying 103 *e'en* in [F; omitted in C] 148 *distain'd* [F] unstain'd [C] 177 *stronger* stranger 188 *offer'd* free'd 196 *drone* Dromio

III,i,48 S.D. *Within* Enter Luce 61 S.D. *Within* Enter Adriana 75 *you* your 89 *her* your 91 *her* your

III,ii,S.D. *Luciana* Iuliana 1 *Luc.* Iulia 4 *building* buildings *ruinate* [F] ruinous [C] 16 *attaint* attaine 20 *is* [F] are [C] 21 *but* not 26 *wife* wise 46 *sister's* sister 49 *bed* bud *them* thee 57 *where* when 111 *and* is 130 *chalky* chalkle 171 *here is* here's

IV,i,17 *her* their 28 *carat* charect 60 *whe'r* [F] whether [C] 85 there's [F] there is [C]

IV,ii,6 *Of* Oh 34 *One* On 35 *fury* Fairie 45 *he's* is 48 *That* Thus 61 *'a* I [F] Time [C] 66 S.D. *Exeunt* Exit

IV,iii,35 *ship* ships 61 *you do* do

V,i,33 *God's* God 67 *vile* vilde 121 *death* depth 236 *vile* vilde 402 *ne'er* are 406 *nativity* [F] festivity [C]

Love's Labour's Lost

Copy text: the quarto of 1598 [Q].

I,i,S.D. (and throughout) *Berowne* [Q] Biron [C] *Dumaine* [Q] Dumain [C] 18 *schedule* sedule 24 *three* thee 27 *bankrout* [Q] bankrupt [C] 31 *pomp* pome 62 *feast* fast 114 *swore* sworne 129 *Ber.* [not in Q] 131 *public* publibue 132 *possibly* possible 191 *contempts* Contempls 221 *welkin's* welkis 283 *worst* wost 296 *King* Ber.

I,ii,14 *epitheton* apethaton 106 *blushing* blush-in 150 *Dull* Clo.

II,i,32 *Importunes* Importuous 34 *visag'd* visage 39 *First Lord. Lord* Lor. 40 *Mar.* 1. Lady 44 *parts* peerelsse 56 *Kath.* 2 Lad. 61 *Alencon's* Alansoes 64 *Ros.* 3. Lad. 88 *unpeopled* vnpeeled 115–127 *Ros.* Kather. 131 *half of an* halfe of, of an 143 *demand* pemaund 145 *On* One 180 *mine own* my none 195 *Katharine* Rosalin 210 *Rosaline* Katherin 213 *You* O you 219 *Mar.* Lady Ka. 246 *quote* coate

III,i,14 *as if* if 16 *through the nose* through: nose 19 *thin-belly* thinbellies 28 *penny* [Globe] penne [Q] pen [C] 74 *the mail* thee male *plain* pline 136 *ounce* ouce 139 *remuneration* remuration 148 *What* O what ("O" also omitted at 150, 156, 158, 175) 182 *senior-junior* signior Iunios 192 *clock* Cloake 206 *sue* shue

IV,i,6 *On* Ore 70–71 *saw . . . saw* See . . . see *overcame* couercame 76 *king's* King 109 *suitor . . . suitor* shooter . . . shooter 132 *hit it* hit 136 *ne'er* neare 138 *pin* is in 146 *o' th' one* ath toothen 150 *is a* is 151 S.D. *Shout* Shoot *Exit* Exeunt

IV,ii,29 *of taste* taste 31 *indiscreet* indistreell 37 *Dictynna . . . Dictynna* Dictisima . . . dictisima 38 *Dictynna* dictima 52 *call I* cald 55 *scurrility* squirilitie 62 *one* o 67 *Hol.* Nath. [the subsequent speech prefixes in this scene of Holofernes and Nathaniel are reversed in Q, except at line 109] 72 *pia mater* primater 74 *in whom* whom 82 *sapit* sapis 89 *Of piercing* Of persing [Q] Piercing [C] 95 *Fauste* Facile *pecus* pecas *omne* omnia 99–100 *Venetia . . . pretia* vemchie, vencha, que non te vnde, que non te perreche 124 *canzonet* cangenet 137 *writing* written 140 *Sir Nathaniel* Ped. Sir Holofernes 164 *ben* bien

IV,iii,15,16 *melancholy* mallicholie 38 *wilt* will 49 *King* Long. 53 *triumviry* triumpherie 59 *shop* [Q] slop [C] 75 *idolatry* ydotarie 87 *quoted* coted 93 *And I mine* And mine 99 *ode* Odo 112 *thorn* throne 146 *so infringed* infringed 155 *coaches* couches 161 *mote . . . mote* Moth . . . Moth 180 *like you* like [Q, C] 182 *love* Ione 248 *wood* word 255 *school* [Q] suit [C] 259 *and usurping* vsurping 289 *O! 'tis* [Q] 'Tis [C] 305 *poisons* [Q, Globe] prisons [C] 316 *ladies' eyes* Ladies eyes, With our selues 359 *authors* authour 361 *Let* Lets 383 *Allons! allons!* Alone alone 385 *forsworn* forsorne

V,i,10 *hominem* hominum 28 *insanie* infamie 31 *Bone . . . Priscian* Bome boon for boon prescian 53 *silly* seely 61 *wave* wane 62 *venue* vene we 70 *disputes* [Q] disputest [C] 73 *circum circa* vnum cita 105 *importunate* importunt 116 *secrecy* secretie 125 *Sir Nathaniel* Sir Holofernes [Q] Sir [C] 126 *rendered* rended 127 *assistance* assistants [Q, C] 159 *Allons* Alone

V,ii,13 *ne'er* neare 17 *ha' been a* a bin 28 *cure . . . care* care . . . cure 43 *pencils, ho* pensalls, How 46 *Kath.* Quee. 47 *Prin.* [not in Q] 53 *pearls* Pearle 65 *hests* deuice 74 *wantonness* wantons be 80 *stabb'd* stable 89 *sycamore* Siccamone 96 *they* thy 148 *her* his 152 *ne'er* ere 159 *Boyet.* Berow. 163 *ever* euen 174 *strangers* stranges 208 *requests* [Q] request'st [C] 216 *The . . . it* [assigned in Q to Ros.] 224 *Price* Prise [Q] Prize [C] 232 *and* an 242–255 *Kath.* Mar. 273 *O, they* They 279 *perhaps* perhapt 297 *vailing* varling 299 *woo* woe 309 *run* runs 341 *Construe* Consture 352 *unsullied* vnsallied 373 *Fair gentle* gentle 407 *affectation* affection 463 *zany* saine 472 *it is* tis 482 *manage* nuage 503 *they* thy 517 *least* best 534 *della guerra* delaguar 550 *Boyet.* Bero. 569 *this* his 590 [Q has "Exit Curat."] 593 *canus* [Q] canis [C] 604 *proved* proud 652 *gilt* gift 670 [Q has "Berowne steps foorth"] 678 *The . . . gone* [Q prints as S.D. or as part of Armado's speech] 695 *on! stir* or stir 721 S.D. *Marcade* [Q] Mercade [C] 788 *the ambassadors* embassadours 792 *this in our* this our 797 *quote* cote 817 *instant* instance 822 *intitled* intiled 826 *hermit* herrite [Q] ever [F, C] 834 *A wife* [assigned to Kath. in Q] 855 *estates* estetes 904–905 [the second and third lines of the song are transposed in Q] 926 *foul* full 940–941 *The . . . Apollo* [printed in larger type in Q without speech prefix; F adds speech prefix "Brag." and "You that way: we this way," thus incorporating the ending into the text.]

The Two Gentlemen of Verona

Copy text: the First Folio [F].

I,i,65 *leave* love 77 *I a* I 152 *testerned* cestern'd

I,ii,96 *your* you

I,iii,50 [F repeats speech prefix "Pro."] 88 *father calls* Fathers call's 91 [F has "Finis" at the scene's end]

I,i,119 *stead* steed

II,ii,18 S.D. (and elsewhere) *Panthino* Panthion

II,iii,29 *wood* would 42 *tied* Tide 55 *my* thy

II,iv,50 *father's* father is 62 *know* knew 108 *mistress* a Mistresse 164 *braggardism* Bragadisme 166 *makes* make 196 *mine eye* mine [F, C] 214 S.D. *Exit* Exeunt

II,v,1 *Milan* Padua 43 *that my* that that my

II,vii,52 *likes* [F] likest [C]

III,i,281 *master's ship* Mastership 326 *kissed fasting* fasting 394 S.D. *Exit* Exeunt

IV,i,10 *he is* [F] he's [C] 35 *been* beene often 49 *An* And *near* Neece

IV,ii,17 S.D. *Musicians* Musitian 114 *his* her

IV,iii,17 *abhors* abhor'd 40 *Recking* Wreaking

IV,iv,75 *thou* thee 79 *to leave* not leaue 210 S.D. *Exit* Exeunt

V,ii,7 *Jul.* Pro. 13 *Jul.* Thu. 18 *your* you 56 S.D. *Exit* Exeunt

V,iv,33 *seized* ceazed 67 *one's right* [F] one's own right [C]

The Taming of the Shrew

Copy text: the First Folio [F].

Ind.,i,S.D. *Christophero Sly* [printed at the end of the stage direction in F] 12 *third-borough* Head-borough 88 *A Player* Sincklo

Ind.,ii,2 *lordship* Lord 19 *Sly's* Sies 75 *Christophero* Christopher

I,i,13 *Vincentio* Vincentio's 14 *brought* brough 24 *satiety* sacietie 25 *Mi perdonato* Me Pardonato 47 S.D. *suitor* sister 68 *Hush* Husht 167 *captum* captam 175 *strand* strond 212 *colour'd* Conlord 249 *your* you 253 S.D. *speak* speakes

I,ii,17 S.D. *wrings* rings 18 *masters* mistris 24 *Con . . . trovato* Contutti le core bene trobatto 25 *ben* bene *molto* multo 33 *pip* peepe 46 *this 's* this 73 *she* she is 121 *me and other* me. Other 173 *help me* helpe one 191 *Antonio's* Butonios 214 *ours* yours 267 *feat* seeke 282 *ben* Been

II,i,3 *gawds* goods 8 *thee, tell* tel 76 *Neighbour* neighbors 79 *unto you* vnto 159 *vile* vilde 169 S.D. *Exeunt* Exit *I'll* [F] I will [C] 187 *bonny* bony 249 *askance* a sconce 326 S.D. *Exeunt* Exit 332 *in* me 356 *Valance* Vallens 377 *Marseilles'* Marcellus

III,i,28 *Sigeia* sigeria (also at ll. 32 and 42) 48 [*Aside*] Luc. 51 *Bian.* [not in F] 52 *Luc.* Bian. 54 *Bian.* Hort. 77 *clef* Cliffe 81 *change* charge 82 *Serv.* Nicke.

III,ii,29 *of thy* of 30 *news, old news* newes 33 *hear* heard 56 *swayed* Waid 58 *cheeked* chekt 130 *to her* sir 132 *As I* As

IV,i,44 *wilt thou* [F] will thaw [C] 65 *is* 'tis 183 S.D. *Enter Curtis* Enter Curtis a Seruant

IV,ii,4 *Hor.* Luc. 6 *Luc.* Hor. (also line 8) 13 *none* me 31 *her* them 71 *Take . . . alone* [assigned to "Par." in F] *in* me

IV,iii [F has "Actus Quartus. Scena Prima" here] 63 *Hab.* Fel. 68 *Come, let* [F] let [C] 81 *is a* is 88 *like a* like 183 *account'st* accountedst

IV,iv,1 *Sir* Sirs 5 *Where* Tra. Where 19 *Signior* Tra. Signior 68 [F adds a stage direction: "Enter Peter"] 88 *of* at

IV,v,18 *is* in 35 *make a* make the 38 *where* whether 41 *Allot* A lots 78 *she be* she

V,i,2 [F has "Exit" here] 6 *master's* mistris 54 *master's* Mistris 115 S.D. *Exeunt* Exit 151 *No* Mo 155 *never* ueuer

V,ii [F has "Actus Quintus" here] 2 *done* come 37 *thee* the 45 *better* bitter 52 *Tra.* Tri. 57 *ho* oh 65 *for* sir 93 *vile* vilde 128 *an hundred* fiue hundred 132 *you're* your

A Midsummer Night's Dream

Copy text: the first quarto of 1600 [Q].

I,i,4 *wanes* waues 10 *New-bent* Now bent 19 s.d. *Lysander* Lysander and Helena 24 *stand forth, Demetrius* [printed as a stage direction in Q] 26 *stand forth, Lysander* [printed as a stage direction in Q] 74 *their* there 136 *low* loue 187 *Yours would* Your words 191 *I'ld* ile 216 *sweet* sweld 219 *stranger companies* strange companions

II,i,61 *Fairy* [Q] Fairies [C] 69 *steep* steppe 79 *Ægles* Eagles [Q] Ægle [C] 109 *thin* chinne 158 *the west* west 190 *slay* stay *slayeth* stayeth 201 *not, nor* not, not

II,ii,4 *leathern* lethten 39 *Be* Bet 43 *good* god 47 *is* it

III,i,30 *yourselves* your selfe 57 *Bot.* Cet. 71 *and* or 85 *Odours, odours* Odours, odorous 90 *Puck.* Quin. 200 *you of* you [Q] your [C] 206 *lover's* [Q] love's [C] 206 s.d. *Exeunt* Exit

III,ii,s.d. Q: Enter King of Fairies, and Robin goodfellow 19 *mimic* Minnick 80 *I so* I 85 *bankrout* [Q] bankrupt [C] *sleep* slippe 213 *like* life 220 *passionate words* words 250 *prayers* praise 260 *off* of 264 *O hated* [Q] hated [C] 299 *gentlemen* gentleman 323 *she's* she is 338 *jowl* [Q] jole [C] 344 s.d. *Exit* Exeunt 426 *shalt* shat 451 *To your* your

IV,i,58 *flouriets'* [Q] flowerets' [C] 76 *o'er* or 85 *five* fine 86 *ho!* howe 121 *Seem'd* Seeme 132 *is my* my 143 *Good* The. Good 176 *saw* see 195 *found* fonnd 203 *let us* lets 212 *to expound* expound 214 *a patched* patcht a

IV,ii,s.d. Q reads: Enter Quince, Flute, Thisby and the rabble 3 *Star.* Flut. 5 *Flu.* Thys. (and at ll. 9, 13, 19)

V,i,34 *our* Or 122 *his* this 152 s.d. *Exeunt* Exit 157 *Snout* Flute 193 *up in thee* now againe 202 *vile* vilde 208 *mural down* Moon vsed 226 *as* [Q] one [C] 275–276 *And . . . vanished* [so Q; these lines are transposed in C] 279 *gleams* beames 325 *mote* moth 357 *Bot.* Lyon. 378 *lion* Lyons 379 *behowls* beholds 426–427 *And . . . rest* [these lines are transposed in Q]

1 Henry VI

Copy text: the First Folio [F].

I,i,49 *moist'ned* [F] moist [C] 65 *Rouen* Roan 83 *her* [F] their [C] 94 *Reignier* Reynold 124 *slew* [F] flew [C] 131 (and elsewhere) *Falstaff* [F] Fastolfe [C] 176 *steal* send

I,ii,30 *bred* breed 86 *may see* [F] see [C] 99 *five* fine 103 s.d. (and elsewhere) *La* de 125 *o'er* [F] over [C] 131 *halcyon* Halcyons

I,iii,20 *commandement* [F] commandment [C] 29 *Humphrey* Vmpheir

I,iv,10 *Wont* went 25 *gots* [F] got'st [C] 27 *Duke* Earle 33 *vile* pil'd 50 *were* [F] was [C] 66 *stands* [F] stand [C] 69 s.d. *shoot* shot *fall* falls 95 *thee* [F] thee, Nero [C]

II,i,77 s.d. [F has *Exeunt* preceding this stage direction]

II,ii,20 *Arc* Acre

II,iii,73 *misconster* [F] misconstrue [C]

II,iv,117 *wip'd* whipt 132 *gentle sir* gentle

II,v,75 *third* [F] the third [C] 121 s.d. *Exeunt* Exit 129 *will* [F] ill [C]

III,i,52 *Som.* [not in F] 53 *War.* Som. 54 *Som.* [not in F] 163 *alone* all alone

III,ii,12 *Qui est* Che 13 *pauvres* la pouure 28 *Talbotites* Talbonites 73 *b' uy* [F] be wi' you [C] 103 s.d. *Exeunt* Exit 123 *gleeks* glikes

IV,i,s.d. *Exeter, Governor* and Gouernor Exeter 19 *Patay* Poictiers 173 s.d. *Flourish* [in F, this word appears at l. 181 s.d.] 180 *wist* wish

IV,ii,3 *calls* call 15 *Gen.* Cap.

IV,iii,17 (and throughout) *Lucy* 2 Mes.

IV,iv,16 *legions* Regions

IV,v,55 s.d. *Exeunt* Exit (also at IV,vi,57 s.d.)

IV,vii,89 *'em* him (also at l. 94) 96 s.d. *Exeunt* Exit

V,iii,57 *her* his 85 *random* randon 179 *modestly* modestie 192 *And* Mad

V,iv,49 *Arc* Aire 149 *compromise* compremize

V,v,60 *It most* Most 82 *love* Ioue

2 Henry VI

Copy text: the First Folio [F]. Q = the quarto of 1594.

I,i,37 s.d. *kneeling* kneel 58 *duchies* Dutchesse 93 *had* hath 178 *protector* [Q] Protectors 179 s.d. *Exeunt* Exit 213 s.d. *Exeunt* Exit 256 *in* [Q] in in

I,ii,22 *dream* dreames 38 *are* wer

I,iii,33 *master* Mistresse 44 s.d. *Exeunt* Exit 103 [F has "Exit" here] 145 *I'ld* [Q] I could 215–216 *Then . . . French* [not in F]

I,iv,65 *Aio te* Aio *posse* posso 78 *go* goes

II,i,30 *lord* Lords 47 *Car.* [not in F] 48 *Glou.* [not in F] 91 *Simon* [F] Simpcox [C] 108 *Alban* Albones 132 *his* [Q] it

II,ii,45 *was son* was 46 *son* Sonnes Sonne

III,i,78 *wolves* [F] wolf [C] 140 *suspect* suspence 222 s.d. *Exeunt* Exit 328 *Bristow* [F] Bristol [C]

III,ii,14 s.d. *Somerset* Suffolke, Somerset 26 *Meg* Nell 32 s.d. *swoons* sounds 79 *Margaret* Elianor 100 *Margaret* Elianor 116 *witch* watch 120 *Margaret* Elinor 265 *whe'r* [F] whether [C] (also at III,iii,10) 270 *Commons* [not in F] 327 *consort* [F] concert [C] 332 *turn* turnes

IV,i,1 (and throughout this scene) *Lieut.* [F] Cap. [C] 6 *Clip* Cleape 48 *Jove . . . I* [Q; not in F] 50 *Suf.* [at l. 51 in F] 70 *Yes . . . lord* Poole, Sir Poole? Lord 85 *mother's bleeding* Mother-bleeding 93 *are* and 117 *Paene* Pine (F; C omits) 132 *Suf.* [at l. 133 in F] 134 *vile* vilde 141 s.d. *Exeunt* Exit

IV,ii,37 *fall* faile 191 s.d. *Exeunt* Exit

IV,iv,43 *hate* hateth 58 *you be* you

IV,v,s.d. *enter* enters

IV,vii,75 *But* Kent 95 *caudle* Candle 145 s.d. *Exeunt* Exit

IV,viii,12 *rebel* rabble

IV,ix,33 *calm'd* calme

IV,x,22 *waning* warning 30 *I'll* He 62 *God* [Q] Ioue

V,i,6 *know* knowes 109 *these* thee 111 *sons* [Q] sonne 113 *for* of 130 *mistakes* [F] mistakest [C] 149 *bear 'ard* [F] bear-ward [C] (also at l. 210) 194 *or* and 201 *household* housed

V,ii,28 *œuvres* eumenes

V,iii,29 *faith* [Q] hand 32 *drum* [F] drums [C]

3 Henry VI

Copy text: the First Folio [F]. O = the octavo of 1595.

I,i,11 *dangerously* dangerous 69 *Exe.* [O] Westm. 78 *It was* [F] 'Twas [C] 83 *and that's* that's 105 *Thy* [O] My 259 *stay with* stay 261 *from* [O] to 273 S.D. *Exeunt* Exit

I,ii,47 S.D. *Enter a Messenger* [O] Enter Gabriel. 49 *Mess.* [O] Gabriel 75 S.D. *Exeunt* Exit

I,iv,50 *buckle* [O] buckler 180 S.D. *Exeunt* Exit

II,i,55 *Hew* Hews *fell* fells 113 *And . . . thought* [O; omitted in F] 131 *an idle* [O] a lazie 158 *makes* make 182 *march amain* [O] march

II,ii,89 *Since* Cla. Since 133 *Rich.* [O] War. 172 *deniest* [O] denied'st

II,v,26 *make* makes 54 S.D. [followed in F by "and a Father that hath kill'd his Sonne at another doore"] 78 S.D. [F reads: "Enter Father, bearing of his Sonne"] 87 *kill* killes 119 *Even* Men

II,vi,6 *commixture* [O] Commixtures 8 *The . . . flies* [O; omitted in F] 42 Edw. [O] Rich. 43 *Rich.* [O; not in F] 44 Edw. [so O; in F, follows "it is"] 60 *his* [O] is

III,i,S.D. *two keepers* [O] Sinklo, and Humfrey (and throughout scene in speech prefixes) 7 *scare* scarre 17 *wast* was 24 *thee, sour adversity* the sower Aduersaries 30 *Is* I: 55 *thou that* [O] thou

III,ii,3 *lands* [O] Land 112 *who* [F] whom [C] 123 *honourably* [O] honourable 175 *rends* rents

III,iii,124 *eternal* [O] externall 228 *I'll* [O] I

IV,i,93 *thy* [O] the

IV,ii,15 *towns* Towne

IV,iii,27 S.D. *fly* flyes 59 S.D. *Exit* Exeunt 64 S.D. *Exeunt* exit

IV,iv,17 *wean* waine

IV,v,4 *stands* stand 8 *Comes* Come 21 *ship* shipt

IV,vi,55 *goods be* Goods

IV,viii,S.D. *Exeter* Somerset

V,i,78 *an* in 91 *Jephthah's* Iephah

V,v,38 *thou* the 50 *The Tower* [O] Tower 77 *butcher* [O] butcher Richard 90 S.D. *Exeunt* Exit

V,vi,7 *reckless* wreaklesse

V,vii,5 *renown'd* [O] Renowne 25 *thou* [O] that 30 *Q. Eliz.* [O] Cla. *Thanks* [O] Thank 38 *Reignier* Reynard

Richard III

Copy text: the First Folio [F]. Unless otherwise indicated, the adopted readings are from the first quarto of 1597 [Q1]. The following collation does not list departures from the Globe-Craig text.

I,i,26 *spy* see 41 S.D. *Enter . . . Brackenbury* [eds.] Enter Clarence, and Brackenbury guarded 45 *the* th' 52 *for* but 65 *tempers him to this* tempts him to this harsh 75 *to her for his* for her 88 *an 't* [eds.] and 103 *I* I do 124 *the* this 133 *prey* play 142 *What* Where

I,ii,27 *life* [eds.] death 39 *stand* Stand'st 60 *deed* Deeds 78 *of a* of 138 *thee* the 155 *aspect* Aspects 169 *words* word 202 *Glou.* [not in F] 203 *Anne. To . . . give* [not in F] 225 S.D. *Exeunt* [eds.] Exit (also at l. 227) 226 *Glou. Sirs . . . corse* [not in F]

I,iii,17 *come* comes *lords* Lord 44 *That* Thar 68–69 so Q1. F: Makes him to send, that he may learne the ground 113 *Tell . . . said* [not in F] 160 *of* off 304 *on* an 309 *Q. Eliz.* Mar. 342 *First Murd.* [eds.] Vil. (also at ll. 350, 356)

I,iv,13 *thence* There 87 *First Murd.* [eds.] 2 Mur. 90 *Sec. Murd.* [eds.] 1 128 *'Zounds* Come 137–138 *it is a dangerous thing* [not in F] 149 *'Zounds* [not in F] 177 *Both.* 2 194–195 *I charge . . . sins* I charge you, as you hope for any goodnesse 218 *Why, sirs* [not in F] 243 *And . . . other* [not in F] 273 *As . . . distress* [in F, printed after l. 267]

II,i,S.D. *Buckingham* [eds.] Buckingham, Wooduill 5 *in* to 7 *Rivers and Hastings* Dorset and Riuers 39 *God* heauen 56 *unwittingly* vnwillingly 58 *By* To 67 *on me* [F follows with a line: "Of you Lord Wooduill, and Lord Scales of you"] 84 *this* the 92 *but* and 107 *at* and

II,ii,3 *do you* do 47 *have I* haue 83 *weep* weepes 84–85 *and so . . . weep* [not in F] 87 *Pour* Power 142 *Ludlow* London (also at l. 154) 145 *With all our hearts* [not in F] 147 *God's* God

II,iii,43 *Ensuing* Pursuing (but the catchword on p. 184 in F is "Ensuing")

II,iv,1 *hear* heard 9 *young* good 20 *this* his 21 *Arch.* Car. [Q1] Yor. [F] 65 *death* earth

III,i,9 *Nor* No 40 *in heaven* [not in F] 43 *deep* great 60 S.D. *Exeunt* [eds.] Exit 63 *seems* think'st 78 *all-ending* ending 87 *this* his 96 *loving* Noble 97 *dread* deare 120 *heavy* weightie 123 *as* as, as 141 *needs will* will 150 S.D. *Hastings* [eds.] Hastings, and Dorset 154 *parlous* [eds.] perillous 167 *what will he?* Will not hee?

III,ii,60–62 *I tell . . . elder* Well, Catesby, ere a fort-night make me older 80 *as you do* as 113 *you* [F follows with a line: "Priest. Ile wait vpon your Lordship"]

III,iii,1 *Rat. Come . . . prisoners* [not in F] 16 *When . . . I* [so F; not in the Globe text, and hence not included in the Globe line numbering]

III,iv,4 *that* the 10 *Who I, my lord!* [not in F] 11 *But* [not in F] 32–33 *Hast. I thank . . . Holborn* My Lord of Ely, when I was last in Holborne 60 *Der. I . . . say* [not in F] 84 *raze* rowse 85 *But* And

III,v,4 *wert* were 69 *But* Which 74 *meet'st advantage* meetest vantage 104 *Penker* [eds.] Peuker 105 S.D. *Exeunt* [eds.] Exit 109 S.D. *Exit* Exeunt

III,vi,12 *who's* who

III,vii,43 *Buck. No . . . lord* [not in F] 54 *we'll* we 57

Here . . . how [not in F] 83 *My lord* [not in F] 125 *This* the *her* his (also at 126 and 127) 219 *'zounds! I'll* we will 220 *Glou. O . . . Buckingham* [not in F] 221 *them* him 247 *cousin* Cousins

IV,i,s.d. F: Enter the Queene, Anne Duchesse of Glou-cester, the Duchesse of Yorke, and Marquesse Dorset

IV,ii,36 *My lord* [not in F] 47 *those* the *beyond the sea* [not in F] *sea* [eds.] seas [Q] 49–50 *Catesby! Cate. My lord?* Come hither Catesby 73 *there* then 78 *I'll* He 84–85 *K. Rich. Shall . . . lord* [not in F] 93 *Hereford* Hertford 101–119 *perhaps,— . . . to-day* [not in F] 121 *Tut, tut* [not in F]

IV,iii,13 *Which* And 15 *once* one 31 *at* and 33 *thee* the 40 *Breton* [eds.] Britaine (and elsewhere) 53 *leads* leds

IV,iv,10 *unblown* vnblowed 39 *Tell . . . mine* [not in F] 41 *Harry* [eds.] Husband 45 *holp'st* [eds.] hop'st 52–53 *That excellent . . . souls* [lines reversed in F] 64 *Thy* The 118 *nights* night *days* day 127 *client* Clients 128 *intestate* intestine 141 *Where* Where't 224 *lanc'd* [eds.] lanch'd 238 *or* and 268 *would I* I would 284 *this is* this 323 *loan* [eds.] Loue 324 *Of ten* [eds.] Often 348 *wail* vaile 364–365 *Harp not . . . break* [these lines are reversed in F, and the speech prefix "Q. Eliz." is missing] 366 *K. Rich.* [not in F] 377 *God* Heauen *God's* Heanens 392 *in* with 396 *o'erpast* repast 417 *fond* found 444 *Ratcliffe* [eds.] Catesby 495 *Well* [not in F]

V,i,11 *my lord* [not in F] 25 *Now* Thus

V,ii,11 *centre* Centry 12 *Near* Ne're

V,iii,28 *you* [eds.] your 58 *Catesby* Ratcliffe 59 *Cate.* Rat. 68 *Saw'st thou* Saw'st 82 *loving* Noble 104 *thoughts* noise 114 *the* thy 125 *deadly holes* holes 130 *thy sleep* sleepe 131 *on* [eds.] in (also at l. 139) 152 *lead* laid 154 *souls bid* [eds.] soule bids 176 *falls* fall 180 *now* not 196 *Perjury, perjury* Periurie 199 *to the* all to' th' 208 *'Zounds! who is* Who's 212–214 *K. Rich. O Ratcliffe . . . lord* [not in F] 221 *eaves* [eds.] Ease 222 *see* heare 223 *Lords.* Richm. 224 *Richm.* [eds.] Rich. (and at ll. 227 and 236) 250 *foil* soyle 255 *sweat* sweare 270 s.d. *Ratcliffe* [eds.] Ratcliffe, and Catesby 293 *out all in* in 297 *this* the 304 *K. Rich.* [at l. 306 in F] 307 *unto* to 309 *Conscience is but* For Conscience is 319 *ventures* [eds.] Aduentures 320 *to you* you to 335 *in* on 338 *Fight* Right *bold* boldly 351 *helms* helpes

V,v,4 *this* these *royalty* Royalties 7 *enjoy it, and* and 11 *if . . . now* (if you please) we may 13 *Ferrers* [eds.] Ferris 15 *becomes* [eds.] become 32 *their* thy

King John

Copy text: the First Folio [F].

I,i,s.d. *Chatillon* the Chattylion 30 s.d. *Exeunt* Exit 49 *expedition's* expeditious 147 *I* It 208 *smack* smoake 220 *'tis* [F] it is [C] 237 *he get* get 257 *Thou* That

II,i,1 *K. Phi.* Lewis. 18 *Lew.* [F] K. Phi. [C] 63 *Ate* Ace 113 *breast* beast 144 *shows* shooes 149 *K. Phi. Lewis* King Lewis 152 *Anjou* Angiers 156 *Brittaine* Britaine [F] Bretagne [C] (also at ll. 301, 311, and elsewhere) 215 *Confronts your* Comfort yours 252 *invulnerable* involuerable 259 *roundure* rounder 289 *on's* [F] on his [C] 325 *First Cit.* Hubert (also at ll. 363, 416, 423, 480) 335 *run* rome 368 *First Cit.* Fra. 371 *King'd of our fears* Kings of our feare 424 *niece* neere 487 *Anjou* Angiers

III,i,74 [here F reads: "Actus Tertius, Scæna prima"] 110 *day* daies 148 *task* tast 165 *vile* vilde (and elsewhere) 259 *chafed* cased

III,ii,10 *Exeunt* Exit

III,iii,26 *tune* [F] time [C]

III,iv,44 *not holy* holy 64 *friends* fiends 110 *world's* words

IV,i,92 *mote* moth

IV,ii,1 *again* against 73 *Does* Do

IV,iii,33 *man* mans 41 *have you* you haue 48 *vilest* vildest 155 *cincture* center 159 *Exeunt* Exit

V,ii,26 *Were* Was 36 *cripple* [F] grapple [C] 43 *hast thou* hast 133 *unhair'd* vn-heard 135 *these* this

V,v,7 *wound* woon'd

V,vi,12 *eyeless* endles 22 *swoon* swound

V,vii,17 *mind* winde 21 *cygnet* Symet 108 *give you* giue

Titus Andronicus

Copy text: the first quarto of 1594 [Q]. F = the First Folio.

I,i,55 s.d. *Exeunt* Exit 69 s.d. *three Sons* two sonnes 71 *her* his 98 *manes* manus 122 *your* [Q] you [C] 129 s.d. *Exeunt* Exit 154 *drugs* [Q] grudges [C] 157 *Lav.* [not in Q] 206 *wert* [Q] were [C] 226 *Titan's* Tytus 242 *Pantheon* Pathan 280 *cuique* cuiqum 316 *Phœbe* Thebe 358 *Quin. Mart.* Titus two sonnes speakes 360 *Quin.* Titus sonne speakes 368 *Mart.* 3 Sonne. 369 *Quin.* 2 Sonne. 388 s.d. *They all kneel* they all kneele and say 390 [Q follows with a stage direction: "Exit all but Marcus and Titus"] 398 *Yes . . . remunerate* [F; not in Q] 474 *Luc.* [F; not in Q] 475 *mildly* mi'd ie

II,i,110 *than* this 135 *Stygia* [Q] Styga [C]

II,ii,1 *morn* Moone 11 *Many* Titus. Many 24 *run* runnes

II,iii,13 *snake* snakes 69 *try* trie thy 153 *Some* So me 160 *ears* yeares 192 *Aar.* [not in Q] 210 *unhallowed* vnhollow 222 *beray'd in blood* bereaud in blood [Q, with marginal correction in contemporary hand-writing: "heere reau'd of lyfe"] embrewed here [C] 231 *Pyramus* Priamus 236 *Cocytus'* Ocitus 291 *fault* faults

II,iv,21 *have* halfe 27 *him* them 30 *three* their 38 *why she* [Q] she [C]

III,i,17 *urns* ruines 21 *on thy* out hy 34 *or if* if 146 *his* her 149 s.d. *Moor* Moore alone 215 *possibility* [Q] possibilities [C] 226 *doth flow* [Q] do blow [C] 282 *And Lavinia . . . in these* [Q] Lavinia . . . these [C] 287 *ye* [Q] you [C] (also at IV,i,97)

III,ii [the entire scene is missing in Q; copy text is F] 39 *complainer* complaynet 52 *thy knife* knife 53 *fly* Flys 54 *thee* the 55 *are cloy'd* cloi'd 72 *myself* my selfes

IV,i,15 *Marc.* [not in Q] 50 *quotes* coats 53 *Forc'd* Frocd 70 *I have* [Q] when I have [C] 77 *Tit.* [not in

Q] 88 *hope* hop (?) I op (?) 101 *let alone* [Q] let it alone [C] 109 *base* [Q] bad [C]

IV,ii,13 *bid* [Q] bade [C] 95 *Alcides* Alciades 152 *Muliteus* [Q] Muli lives [C]

IV,iii,56 *Saturn* Saturnine, to 77 *News* Clowne. Newes 94 *emperial's* Emperals 118 *to the* [Q] the [C]

IV,iv,5 *know, as know* know 24, 25 *he* [Q] she [C] 49 *by'r* be 61 *What* Satur. What 62 *Arm* [Q] Arm, arm [C] 93 *feed* seede 98 *ears* yeares

V,i,3 *signifies* [Q] signify [C] 17 *All the Goths* [not in Q] 53 *Get me a ladder* [assigned to Aaron in Q] 96 *which* [Q] that [C] 107 *that* [Q] the [C] 113 *extreme* extreanie 141 *Tut* But 151 S.D. *Enter Æmilius* [Q] Enter a Goth [C]

V,ii,18 *that accord* [Q] it action [C] 49 *globe* Globes 52 *murd'rers* murder *caves* cares 56 *Hyperion's* Epeons 61 *these* them 62 *Rapine* Rape 65 *worldly* wordlie 103 *he is* [Q] he's [C] 106 *shalt* [Q] mayst [C] 155 *Chiron and* Chiron 157 *and Rape* [Q] Rape [C] 173 *vile* vild

V,iii,17 *mo* [Q] more [C] 73 *Lest* Romane Lord. Let 119 *the* [Q] this [C] 125 *cause* course 141 *All.* Marcus. 142 *Marc.* [not in Q] 144 *adjudg'd* adiudge 146 *All.* [not in Q] 154 *blood-stain'd* blood slaine 163 *Sung* Song 170 *him* [Q] them [C] 176 *Roman.* [Q] Æmie. [C] 184 *Ah* [Q] O [C] [For Mr. Craig's textual notes on this play, see *passim* in the glosses below the text.]

Romeo and Juliet

Copy text: the second quarto of 1599 [Q2]. Q1 = the first quarto of 1597.

Chorus, 8 *Doth* [Q2] do [C]

I,i,i *on* [Q2] o' [C] 5 *out of* [Q2] out o' the [C] 19 *'Tis true* [Q2] True [C] 27 *civil* [Q2] cruel [C] 28 *I will* [Q2] and [C] 32 *it in* [Q1] it 38 *comes two* [Q1] comes 50 *disgrace* [Q2] a disgrace [C] 61 *But if* [Q2] If [C] 70 *swashing* washing 87 *one* [Q2] a [C] 127 *drave* drive 129 *city's* [Q1] Citie 134 *Which . . . self* [Q2] That most are busied when they're most alone [C] 141 *farthest* [Q2] furthest [C] 153 *his* is 159 *sun* same 183 *create* [Q1] created 185 *well-seeming* [Q1] welseeing 196 *rais'd* [Q1] made 198 *lovers'* [Q1] loving 208 *Bid a* [Q1] A *make* [Q1] makes 217 *unharm'd* [Q1] vncharmd 224 *makes* make

I,ii,14 *The earth* Earth 15 *She is* Shees 29 *fennel* [Q2] female [C] 32 *on* one 47 *One* [Q1] on 77–78 *Rom. Whither . . . house* [Q2] Rom. Whither? Serv. To supper; to our house [C] 88 *loves* [Q2] lovest [C] 94 *fires* fier

I,iii,36 *high lone* hylone [Q2] alone [C] 54 *perilous* perillous [Q2] parlous [C] 66, 67 *honour* [Q1] houre 99 *it fly* [Q1] flie

I,iv,7–8 *Nor . . . entrance* [Q1; not in Q2] 23 *Mer.* Horatio. 31 *quote* cote 39 *done* [Q1] dum 42 *Of this sir* [Q1] Or saue you 45 *like lamps* [Q1] lights lights 47 *five* fine 58 *Over* [Q2] Athwart [C] 61 *Her* [Q2] The [C] *spider* [Q2] spider's [C] 62 *Her* [Q2] The [C] 63 *film* Philome 66 *maid* [Q1] man 72 *O'er* [Q1] On 76 *breaths* [Q1] breath 81 *dreams he* [Q1] he dreams 103 *side* [Q2] face [C] 111 *forfeit* [Q1] fofreit 113 *sail* [Q1] sute

I,v,1 [Q2 has stage direction here: "Enter Romeo"] 9 *loves* [Q2] lovest [C] 19 *walk* [Q2] have [C] 20 *Ah ha* [Q1] Ah 43 *lady's* [Q2] lady is [C] 48 *As* [Q2] Like [C] 68 *'A* [Q2] He [C] 71 *this* [Q2] the [C] 94 *bitt'rest* [Q2] bitter [C] 96 *sin* [Q2] fine [C] 97 *ready* [Q1] did readie 109 *thine* [Q2] yours [C] 134 *there* [Q1] here 144 *this . . . this* tis . . . tis

II, Chorus, 4 *match'd* match

II,i,6 *Nay . . . too* [assigned to Benvolio in Q2] 9 *one* [Q1] on 10 *pronounce* [Q1] prouaunt *dove* [Q1] day 12 *heir* [Q1] her 13 *Abraham* [Q2] Adam [C] *true* [Q2] trim [C] 28 *in* [Q2] and in [C] 38 *et cætera* [Q1] or

II,ii,16 *do* [Q1] to 20 *eyes* [Q1] eye 31 *pacing* [Q1] puffing 41–42 *nor any . . . name* o be some other name / Belonging to a man 44 *name* [Q1] word 45 *were* [Q1] wene 59 *uttering* [Q2] utterance [C] 61 *maid* [Q2] saint [C] 69 *let* [Q2] stop [C] 75 *eyes* [Q2] sight [C] 80 *that* [Q2] who [C] 83 *wash'd* [Q1] washeth 84 *should* [Q2] would [C] 99 *'haviour* [Q1] behauior 101 *more cunning* [Q1] coying 104 *true-love* [Q2] true love's [C] 107 *vow* [Q2] swear [C] 110 *circled* [Q1] circle 153 *suit* strife 163 *than mine* then 164 *"my Romeo"* [Q2] my Romeo's name [C] 168 *dear* Neece *What* [Q2] At what [C] 169 *By* [Q2] At [C] 178 *farther* [Q2] further [C] 179 *That* [Q2] Who [C] *her* his 180 *gyves* giues 181 *silken* [Q2] silk [C] 187 *Sleep . . . breast* [Q1; assigned in Q2 to Juliet] 189–190 *Hence . . . tell* [preceded in Q2 by four lines of the next scene] *father's* [Q1] Friers close

II,iii,2 *Chequ'ring* [Q1] Checking 3 *flecked* [Q1] fleckeld 4 *fiery* [Q1] burning 16 *plants, herbs* [Q2] herbs, plants [C] 22 *sometime* [Q2] sometimes [C] 23 *weak* [Q2] small [C] 40 *with* [Q2] by [C] 66 *that* [Q2] whom [C] 74 *ring yet* [Q1] yet ringing *mine* [Q2] my [C] 85 *chide not; she whom* [Q1] chide me not, her 88 *that* [Q2] and [C]

II,iv,4 *Why* [Q2] Ah [C] 6 *to* [Q2] of [C] 14 *run* [Q2] shot [C] *through* [Q2] thorough [C] 18 *Ben.* [Q1] Ro. 19 *I can tell you* [Q1; not in Q2] *he's* [Q2] he is [C] 23 *he rests . . . rests* [Q2] rests me . . . rest [C] 30 *fantasticoes* [Q1] phantacies 35 *perdona-mi's* pardons mees 65 *Sure wit* [Q2] Well said [C] 67 *solely* [Q2] sole [C] 72 *faint* faints 73 *Swits . . . swits* [Q2] Switch . . . switch [C] 75 *am* [Q2] have [C] 85 *not, then* [Q2] not [C] 108 *A sail, a sail* [assigned in C to Mer.] 109 *Two . . . smock* [assigned in C to Ben.] 121 *for himself* [Q1] himself 152 *Marry, farewell* [Q1; not in Q2] 172, 173 *bid* [Q2] bade [C] 176 *into* [Q1] in 210 *I warrant* Warrant 223 *dog's* dog 232 *Peter . . . go* [Q1; not in Q2] S.D. *Exeunt* Exit

II,v,5 *glide* glides 11 *three* there 15 *And* M. And 26 *I had* [Q1] I 51 *ah* a [Q2] O [C] 53 *jauncing* [Q2] jaunting [C]

II,vi,18 *gossamer* gossamours 19 *idles* ydeles 27 *music's* musicke

III,i,2 *Capulets* Capels 9 *him* [Q2] it [C] 37 S.D. *Tybalt,*

Tybalt, Petruchio 38 *come* comes 55 *Or* [Q2] And [C] 63 *love* [Q2] hate [C] 71 *injur'd* iniuried 92 *Forbid this* [Q2] Forbidden [C] 93 S.D. *Tybalt [etc.]* Away Tybalt 94 *your houses* houses 115 *this* [Q2] his [C] 118 *cousin* [Q2] kinsman [C] 121 *Mercutio is* [Q2] Mercutio's [C] 127 *Alive* [Q1] He gan 129 *fire-ey'd* [Q1] fier end 171 *agile* [Q1] aged 193 *hate's* [Q1] hearts 197 *I* [Q1] It 200 *he is* [Q2] he's [C] 202 S.D. *Exeunt* Exit

III,ii,9 *By* And by 15 *grown* grow 19 *upon* [Q2] on [C] 21 *he* I 37 *weraday* [Q2] well-a-day [C] 49 *shut* shot 51 *of my* my 56 *swounded* sounded 57 *bankrout* [Q2] bankrupt [C] 60 *one* on 66 *dearest* [Q2] dear-loved [C] 72 *Nurse.* [Q1; not in Q2] 73 *Jul.* [Q1] Nur. 74 [Q2 has "Iu." here] 76 *Dove-feather'd* Rauenous douefeatherd 79 *damned* dimme 143 S.D. *Exeunt* Exit

III,iii,15 *Hence* [Q1] Here 39 [Q2 follows with a line: "This may flyes do, when I from this must flie"] 43 [printed in Q2 before l. 40] 52 *Thou* [Q1] Then *a little speak* [Q2] but speak a word [C] 61 *madmen* [Q1] mad man 70 S.D. *Knock* Enter Nurse, and knocke 73 S.D. *Knock* They knocke 75 S.D. *Knock* Slud knock 82 *Where is* [Q1] Where's 92 *Well, death's* [Q1] deaths 94 *not she* [Q2] she not [C] 110 *denote* [Q1] deuote 113 *And* [Q2] Or [C] 117 *that in thy life lives* that in thy life lies [Q2] too that lives in thee [C] 138 *happy* [Q2] happy too [C] 143 *misbehav'd* mishaued 144 *pout'st upon* puts vp 168 *disguis'd* disguise

III,iv,8 *times to* [Q2] time to [C] 11 *she's* [Q2] she is [C] 20 *A . . . a* [Q2] O' . . . o' [C] (also elsewhere) 34 *very very* [Q1] very

III,v,13 *exhales* [Q1] exhale 36 S.D. *Nurse* Madame and Nurse 53 *times* [Q2] time [C] 54 *Jul.* Ro. 55 *so low* [Q2] below [C] 66 *It is* [Q2] is it [C] 83 *pardon him* padon 107 *beseech* [Q2] I beseech [C] 111 *expects* [Q2] expect'st [C] 127 *earth* [Q2] air [C] 132 *counterfeits* [Q2] counterfeit'st [C] 140 *gives* giue 146 *bridegroom* Bride 150 *How . . . how* [Q2] How now, now now [C] 173 *God ye god-den* Godigeden 182 *train'd* [Q1] liand 229 *Else* [Q2] Or else [C]

IV,i,7 *talk'd* [Q1] talke 10 *do* [Q2] doth [C] 45 *cure* [Q1] care 46 *Ah* [Q1] O 72 *slay* [Q1] stay 78 *off* [Q1] of *any* [Q2] yonder [C] 81 *hide* [Q2] shut [C] 83 *chapless* [Q1] chapels 85 *his shroud* his 92 *thy nurse* [Q1] the nurse 94 *distilling* [Q2] distilled [C] 98 *breath* [Q1] breast 100 *paly* many 110 *In* Is [Q2 follows with a line: "Be borne to buriall in thy kindreds graue"] 111 *shalt* shall 116 *waking* walking 126 *Exeunt* Exit

IV,ii,14 *will'd* wield 21 *To* [Q2] And [C] 47 *Exeunt* Exit

IV,iii,40 *this* [Q2] these [C] 49 *wake* walke 58 *Romeo . . . do* [Q1] Romeo, Romeo, Romeo, heeres drinke

IV,iv,12 S.D. *Exeunt* Exit 20 *faith* father

IV,v,15 *weraday* [Q2] well-a-day [C] 41 *long* [Q1] loue 65 *cure* care 81 *In all* [Q1] And in 82 *fond* some 100 *by* [Q1] my 101 [Q2 has stage direction here: "Exit omnes"] S.D. *Enter Peter* Enter Will Kemp 107 *full of woe* full 124 *Pet.* [in Q2, before "I will dry-beat"] 128 *grief* [Q1] griefes 129 *And . . . oppress* [Q1; not in Q2] 135, 139 *Pretty* [Q1] Prates 148 *Exeunt* Exit

V,i,15 *fares my* [Q1] doth my lady 25 *e'en* in [Q2] even [Q1, C] *defy* [Q1] denie 38 *'a* [Q2] he [C] 76 *pay* [Q1] pray 81 *murder* [Q2] murders [C]

V,iii,3 *yew* [Q1] young 21 S.D. *Balthasar* [Q1] Peter 40 *you* [Q1] ye 67 *bid* [Q2] bade [C] 68 *conjurations* [Q1] commiration 71 *Page.* Boy. [Q1; not in Q2] 102 *fair?* faire? I will beleeue 107 *pallet* [Q2] palace [C] 108 [Q2 has four undeleted lines here: "Depart againe, come lye thou in my arme, / Heer's to thy health, where ere thou tumblest in. / O true Appothecarie! / Thy drugs are quicke. Thus with a kisse I die"] 136 *unthrifty* [Q2] unlucky [C] 137 *yew* yong 186 *churchyard* Church-yards 187 *too* too too 189 S.D. *Enter . . . others* Enter Capels 190 *is so shriek'd* is so shrike [Q2] they so shriek [C] 191 *O, the* [Q2] The [C] 194 *our* your 199 *slaughter'd* Slaughter 201 *tombs* [Q2 has a stage direction here: "Enter Capulet and his wife"] 209 *more early* [Q1] now earling 232 *that* thats 258 *awakening* [Q2] awaking [C] 299 *raise* raie 300 *whiles* [Q2] while [C]

Venus and Adonis

Copy text: the quarto of 1593 [Q].

19 *satiety* sacietie 223, 225 *Sometime* [Q] Sometimes [C] 304 *whe'r* [Q] whether [C] 466 *bankrout* [Q] bankrupt [C] 545 *He* Ho 601 *as* so 616 *javelin's* iauelings 628 *venter* [Q] venture [C] 680 *overshoot* ouer-shut 748 *th'* the th' 940 *randon* [Q] random [C] 1002 *decease* decesse 1027 *falcon* Faulcons 1031 *as* are 1054 *was* had 1095 *sung* song

The Rape of Lucrece

Copy text: the corrected quarto of 1594 [Q].

50 *Collatium* Colatia 124 *life's* liues 135 *For* That 140 *bankrout* [Q] bankrupt [C] (also at l. 711) 324 *consters* [Q] construes [C] 530 *sometime* [Q] sometimes [C] 550 *blows* blow 555 *panteth* pateth 560 *wear* were 782 *musty* mustie [Q] misty [C] 812 *quote* cote 1126 *Relish* Ralish 1129 *hair* heare 1134 *descants* [Q] descant'st [C] 1167, 1169 *peel'd* pild 1310 *tenour* tenure 1345 *seely* seelie [Q] silly [C] (also at l. 1812) 1386 *off* of 1416 *ear* care 1436 *strond* [Q] strand [C] 1486 *swounds* sounds 1500 *who* [Q] whom [C] 1544 *so* to 1549 *sheeds* [Q] sheds [C] 1648 *forbod* [Q] forbade [C] 1662 *wreathed* wretched [Q, C] 1680 *one woe* on woe 1713 *in it* it in

The Passionate Pilgrim

Copy text: the octavo of 1599 [O].

47 *ear* eares 95 *midst* mids 138, 139 *left'st* lefts 168 *stay'st* staies 179 *once 's* once 188 *conster* [O] construe [C] 200 *dismal-dreaming* dreaming 203 *and solace* [O] solace [C] 204 *sigh'd* sight 207 *a moon* an houre 249 *Love's denying* Loue is dying 251 *renying* nenying 275 *With* [O] My [C] 287 *back* blacke 293 *lass* loue 295 *moan* woe 302 *partial* partyall 310 *thy* her *sell*

sale 312, 315 *ere* yer 349 *ear* are 356 *yields* yeeld 394 *beasts* Beares 399–400 [not in O; supplied from *England's Helicon*]

A Lover's Complaint

Copy text: the Sonnet quarto of 1609 [Q].

14 *lattice* lettice 37 *beaded* bedded 51 *'gan* gaue 80 *Of* O 95 *wear* were 118 *Came* Can 164 *seem* seemes 182 *woo* vovv 198 *pallid* palyd 251 *immur'd* enur'd 252 *procur'd* procure 260 *nun* Sunne 293 *O* Or 305 *sounding* [Q] swooning [C]

The Sonnets

Copy text: the quarto of 1609 [Q].

2.4 *totter'd* [Q] tatter'd [C] (also at 26.11) 12.4 *all* or 13.7 *Yourself* You selfe 17.12 *metre* miter 19.5 *fleets* fleet'st 20.7 *hues* Hows 23.14 *with* wit *wit* wiht 25.9 *fight* worth 26.12 *thy* their (also at 27.10, 35.8 [twice], 37.7, 43.11, 45.12, 46.3, 46.8, 46.13, 46.14, 69.5, 70.6, 128.11, 128.14) 28.12 *gild'st the* guil'st th' 28.14 *strength* length 31.8 *thee* there 34.12 *cross* losse 34.13 *sheeds* [Q] sheds [C] 39.12 *doth* dost 40.7 *this self* [Q] thyself [C] 41.8 *she* he 44.13 *nought* naughts 47.11 *not* nor 49.10 *desart* [Q] desert [C] 50.6 *dully* duly 54.14 *vade, by* [Q] fade, my [C] 55.1 *monuments* monument 56.13 *Else* As 59.11 *whe'r* where [Q] whether [C] 65.12 *of* or 67.9 *bankrout* [Q] bankrupt [C] 69.3 *due* end 70.1 *art* are 71.4 *vilest* vildest 76.7 *tell* fel 77.10 *blanks* blacks 90.11 *shall* stall 91.9 *better* bitter 95.12 *turn* turnes 110.13 *best* bes 112.14 *are* y'are 113.6 *latch* lack 113.14 *mak'th mine eye* maketh mine [Q] makes mine eye [C] 126.8 *minutes* mynuit 129.11 *prov'd a* proud and 132.2 *torments* torment 144.6 *side* sight 144.9 *fiend* finde 146.2 *Thrall to* My sinfull earth 147.12 *random* randon 153.14 *eyes* eye

The Merchant of Venice

Copy text: the first quarto of 1600 [Q1].

I,i,S.D. *Salerio, and Solanio* Salaryno, and Salanio (and so throughout) 19 *Peering* Piring 24 *might do at sea* [Q1] at sea might do [C] 27 *dock'd* docks 87 *'tis* [Q1] it is [C] 113 *Is* It is 151 *back* bake 171 *strond* [Q1] strand [C]

I,ii,18 *than to be* [Q1] than be [C] 25 *who . . . who* [Q1] whom . . . whom [C] 36 *who you* [Q1] who [C] 50 *An* [Q1] If [C]64 *throstle* Trassell 92 (and elsewhere) *vilely* vildlie 106 *I will* [Q1] I'll [C] 128 *so was he* [Q1] he was so [C]

I,iii,15 *Oh* Ho 70 *Methoughts* [Q1] Methought [C] 85 *pill'd* pyld [Q1] peel'd [C] 113 *spit* spet (also at l. 127 and II,vii,45) 153 *in* [Q1] i' [C] 178 *I'll* Ile [Q1] I will [C]

II,i,S.D. *Morocco* Morochus 27 *o'erstare* ore-stare [Q1] outstare [C] 31 *thee* the 35 *page* rage

II,ii,3 (and elsewhere in this scene) *Gobbo* Iobbe 10 *Via* fia 27 *incarnation* [Q1] incarnal [C] 32 *commandment* commaundement [Q1] command [C] 54 *say 't* [Q1] say it [C] 83 *murder* muder 84 *in the end* [Q1] at the length [C] 101 *fill-horse* philhorse 105 *last* lost 177 *the twinkling* [Q1] the twinkling of an eye [C] 183 *Where's* [Q1] Where is [C] 197 *misconst'red* [Q1] misconstrued [C]

II,iii,11 *did* doe

II,iv,40 S.D. *Exeunt* Exit

II,v,8 *I* [Q1] that I [C]

II,vi,14 *younker* younger 25 *Ho* Howe 50 *moe* [Q1] more [C] 51 *Gentile* gentle

II,vii,69 *tombs* timber

II,viii,8 *gondola* Gondylo 39 *Slubber* slumber

II,ix,64 *judgement* iudement 73 *Still* Arrag. Still 84 *Mess.* [Q1] Serv. [C]

III,i,40 *my blood* [Q1] blood [C] 46 (and elsewhere) *bankrout* [Q1] bankrupt [C] 51 *cursy* cursie [Q1] courtesy [C] 81 S.D. *Exeunt gentlemen* [Q repeats the stage direction "Enter Tuball"] 100 *o'* a [Q1] on [C] 112 *heard* heere [Q1] where [C] 114 *one* [Q1] in one [C] 126 *turquoise* Turkies 134 *Go* [Q1] Go, go [C]

III,ii,14 (and elsewhere) *Beshrew* Beshrow 23 *eke* ech 67 *eyes* eye 81 *vice* voyce 84 *stairs* stayers 93 *make* maketh 173 *lord's* Lords [Q1] lord [C] 206 *roof* rough 240, 246 *yond* [Q1] yon [C] 270 *Hath* [Q1] Have [C] 318 *Bass.* [not in Q] 330 *Nor* [Q1] No [C]

III,iii,S.D. *Solanio* Salerio

III,iv,21 *cruelty* [Q1] misery [C] 40 *So fare you well* [Q1] And so farewell [C] 49 *Padua* Mantua 50 *cousin's* cosin 81 *my* my my

III,v,3 *you, I* [Q1] ye, I [C] 24 *e'en* in 30 *comes* come 34 *there's* [Q1] there is [C] 82 *merit it* meane it, it [Q1] mean it, then [C] 89 *a wife* wife 94 *howsoe'er* how so mere 95 S.D. *Exeunt* Exit

IV,i,30 *his state* this states 31 *flint* flints 51 *Mistress* Maisters 73 *You may as* [not in Q1] 74 *Why he hath made* [not in Q] *bleat* bleake 75 *pines* of Pines 100 *'tis* as 113 *lose* loose [Q, C] 150 *Clerk.* [not in Q] 230 *No, not* Not not 235 *tenure* [Q1] tenour [C] 272 *off* of 324 *off* of 326 *tak'st* [Q1] cut'st [C] 368 *spirit* [Q1] spirits [C] 379 *God's* God 398 *Gra.* Shy. 407 S.D. *Exeunt* Exit

V,i,41 *Lorenzo?* Lorenzo, & 49 *Sweet soul* [assigned in Q1 to Launcelot] 51 *Stephano* Stephen 59 *patens* pattens [Q1] patines [C] 87 *Erebus* Terebus 109 *ho* how 152 *it you* you 233 *my* mine

Much Ado about Nothing

Copy text: the quarto of 1600 [Q].

I,i,S.D. *Messina, Hero* Messina, Innogen his wife, Hero 42 *bird-bolt* Burbolt 96 *are you* [Q] you are [C] 144 *a* [Q] i' [C] 205 S.D. *Enter Don Pedro* Enter don Pedro, Iohn the bastard 267 (and elsewhere) *vilely* vildly

I,ii,7 *event* euents 25 *Cousin* coosins 28 *skill* shill

I,iii,56 *one* [Q] on [C] 76 *o'* a [Q] of [C] 77 S.D. *Exeunt* exit

II,i,S.D. *Hero* his wife, Hero *Niece* neece, and a kinsman 42 *bear-ward* Berrord 88 S.D. *Don John* or dumb Iohn 104–110 *Balth.* Bene. 217 S.D. *Leonato*

Leonato, Iohn and Borachio, and Conrade 403 *Exeunt* exit
II,iii,38 S.D. *Claudio* Claudio, Musicke 54 *Nay* [Q] Now [C] 64 *Balth.* [not in Q] 141 *us of* of us
III,i,12 *propose* [Q] purpose [C] 58 *she'll* [Q] she [C]
III,ii,28 *can* cannot 54 *D. Pedro* Bene.
III,iii,82 *statutes* [Q] statues [C] 188 *First Watch* [not in Q]
III,iv,18 *in* it
III,v,11 *off* of 57 *suffigance* suffigance. (exit
IV,i,169 *tenour* tenure 204 *princes* princesse 256 *Exeunt* exit 272 *loved* [Q] love [C] 303 *'a* [Q] he [C] 321 *courtesies* cursies
IV,ii,S.D. [in Q, "Borachio" is named after "Constables"] 1 *Dog.* Keeper 2 *Verg.* Cowley (and elsewhere in this scene) 4 *Dog.* Andrew 9 *Dog.* Kemp (and elsewhere) 53 *Verg.* Const. 71 *Con. Off, coxcomb* of Coxcombe 75 *Con.* Couley 90 *Exeunt* exit
V,i,16 *Bid* And 96 *anticly* antiquely, and 98 *off* of 115 *liked* likt [Q] like [C] 184 *on* one 220 *untruths* [Q] untruth [C]
V,ii,105 S.D. *Exeunt* exit
V,iii,3 *Claud.* [not in Q] 10 *dumb* dead 22 *Claud.* Lo.
V,iv,7 *sort* sorts 54 *Ant.* Leo. 98 *Bene.* Leon.

The Merry Wives of Windsor

Copy text: the First Folio [F]. Q = the quarto of 1602.
I,i,45 *George* Thomas [F, C] 60, 62 *Shal.* Slen. [F, C] 259 *contempt* content
I,iii,15 *lime* [Q] liue 60 *legion* [Q: legians] legend 68 *œillades* illiads 77 *cheater* Cheaters 91 *o' the* ith' 92 *humour* [Q] honor 104 *Page* [Q] Ford (also at line 109) 105 *Ford* [Q] Page
I,iv,46 *boitier* boyteene 53 *fort chaud* for chando 92 *baille* ballow
II,i,1 *have I* haue 58 *praised* praise 63 *Hundredth Psalm* hundred Psalms 141 *and there's the humour of it* [Q; not in F] 221 *cavaleiro* Caualeire [F] cavaleire [C] 222 *Ford.* [Q] Shal. 224 *Brook* [Q] Broome (and elsewhere) 228 *mynheers* An-heires [F, C]
II,ii,24 *God* [Q] heauen (also at lines 53, 325) 157 *o'erflow* oreflowes
II,iii,39 *he* rhe 59 *A word* [Q] a 92 *game* [F] I aim [C]
III,i,90 urinals [Q] Vrinal 91–92 *for missing . . . appointments* [Q; not in F] 108–109 *Give . . . terrestrial; so* [Q; not in F]
III,iii,64 *By the Lord* [Q; not in F] *tyrant* [F] traitor [Q, C] 205 *foolish* foolishion
III,iv,12 *Fent.* [not in F] 32 *vile* vilde (and elsewhere) 61 *God* [Q] heaven [F, C] 115 *Exit* Exeunt
III,v,90 *By the Lord* [Q] Yes 155 *Exit* Exeunt
IV,i,49 *hung* hing 71 *lunatics* Lunaties
IV,ii,22 *lunes* lines 59 *Mrs Page* [not in F; C follows F] 68 *Mrs Page* [Q] Mist. Ford. 77 (and elsewhere) *Brainford* [F] Brentford [C] 101 *direct* direct direct 105 *misuse him* misuse 190 *not strike* strike 194 *hag* Ragge 202 *Jeshu* [Q] yea, and no [F, C]
IV,III,1 *Germans desire* Germane desires 9 *them* [Q] him 11 *house* [Q] houses
IV,iv,7 *cold* gold 33 *makes* make 42a *Disguis'd . . . head* [Q, reading "Horne" for "Herne;" not in F] 60 *Mrs Ford.* Ford. 73 *tire* time [F, C]
IV,v,45 *Sim.* Fal. 58 *Thou art* [Q] Thou are 105 *to say my prayers* [Q; not in F]
IV,vi,27 *ever* euen 39 *denote* deuote
V,ii,3 *daughter* [not in F]
V,iii,13 *Hugh* Herne
V,v,2 *hot-blooded* hot-bloodied 26 *bribed* [F] bribe [C] 72 *More* Mote 210 *white* greene 215, 221 *green* white

As You Like It

Copy text: the First Folio [F].
I,i,114 *she* hee 121 *there they* [F] they there [C] 172 *Oli.* [not in F]
I,ii,3 *I were* were 56 *goddesses and hath* goddesses, hath 89 *Cel.* [so Globe] Ros. [F, C] 97 *Le* the 111 *decree* decrees 176 *princess calls* [F] princesses call [C] 220 *An you* You 277 *misconsters* [F] misconstrues [C] 284 *taller* [F] lesser [C]
I,iii,80 *her* per
II,i,5 *not* [F] but [C] 18 *Ami. I would not change it* [so F; assigned to Duke S. in C] 49 *much* must 50 *friends* friend 59 *of the* of
II,iii,10 *some* seeme 16 *Orl.* [not in F] 29 *Orl.* Ad. 71 *seventeen* seauentie
II,iv,1 *weary* merry 33 *ne'er* neuer 38 *Wearing* [F] Wearying [C] 44 *thy wound* they would 50 *batler* [F] batlet [C] 69 *you* your
II,v,51 *Jaq.* Amy.
II,vii,S.D. *Lords* Lord 38 *brain* braiue 55 *Not to seem* Seeme 87 *comes* come 182 *Then* The 198 *master* masters
III,ii,17 (and elsewhere) *vile* vild 29 *good* pood 99 *face* [F] fair [C] 111 *Wint'red* [F] Winter [C] 133 *a desert* Desert 153 *her* his 163 *pulpiter* Iupiter 250 *such fruit* fruite 258 *thy* the 380 *deifying* defying
III,iv,32 *a lover* Louer
III,v,17 *swoon* swound 22 *but upon* vpon 98 *art* [F] are [C] 105 *erewhile* yerewhile 128 *I have* Haue
IV,i,1 *me be* me 19 *my* by 217 *it* in
IV,iii,7 *bid* did bid 11 *tenour* tenure 105 *old oak* [F] oak [C] 143 *In* I 156 *his* this
V,i,41 *sir* sit 62 *policy* police
V,ii,7 *nor her* nor 30 *swoon* sound 35 *overcame* ouercome 115 *Who* Why *to* too
V,iii,20 *ring* rang 31–33 *And . . . prime* [this stanza is printed as the second stanza of the song in F]
V,iv,21 *you your* [F] your [C] 85 *lie* [F] lied [C] 86 *so to the* so ro 120 *her* his 170 *them* him 177 *were* vvete 203 *we'll* [F] we will [C]

Twelfth Night

Copy text: the First Folio [F].
I,ii,15 *Arion* Orion 40 *sight* [F] company [C] 41 *company* [F] sight [C]
I,iii,55 *Sir And.* Ma. 104–105 *curl by* coole my 106 *me*

we 145 *flame* dam'd *set* sit 148 *That's* That

I,v,176 s.d. *Viola* Uiolenta 320 *county's* Countes 330 s.d. [F adds "Finis, Actus primus"]

II,ii,21 *That sure* That 32 *our* O 33 *of* if

II,iii,2 *diluculo* Deliculo 9 *lives* [F] life [C] 26 *leman* Lemon 146 *a nayword* an ayword

II,iv,54 *Fly . . . fly* Fye . . . fie 56 *yew* Ew 91 *I* It

II,v,17 *metal* Mettle 124 *staniel* stallion 157 *born* become *achieve* atcheeues 193 *dear* deero 228 [F adds "Finis Actus secundus"]

III,i,9 *king* Kings 39 *pilchers* [F] pilchards [C] 64 *conster* [F] construe [C] 75 *wise men* wisemens 133 *Hides* [F] Hideth [C]

III,ii,9 *thee the* the

III,iv,25 *Oli.* Mal. 78 *tang* langer 190 *You* Yon 197 *oft* [F] off [C] 222 *on 't* [F] out [C] 227 *griefs* [F] grief [C] 270 *competent* computent 305 *hit* hits 399 *vile* vilde 432 s.d. *Exeunt* Exit

IV,ii,7 *in* in in 41 *clerestories* cleere stores [F] clearstores [C] 56 *haply* happily 77 *sport to* sport

IV,iii,35 [F adds "Finis Actus Quartus"]

V,i,117 *have* [F] hath [C] 178 *H' as* [F] He has [C] 207 *pavin* panyn [F, C] 415 *With hey* hey

Richard II

Copy text: the first quarto of 1597 as press-corrected in all four extant copies [Q1]; and, for the deposition scene, IV,i,154–320, the First Folio [F].

I,i,118 *by my* by 163 *Obedience bids* [repeated in error in Q1]

I,ii,42 *alas, may* [F] may 47 *sit* set 58 *it* is 59 *empty* [F] emptines 60 *begun* begone 70 *hear* [F] cheere

I,iii,15 *thee* the 33 *comest* comes 58 *thee* the 84 *innocency* innocence 108 *his God* [F] God 128 *civil* [F] cruell 133 *Draws* Draw 136 *wrathful iron* [F] harsh resounding 172 *then but* but 180 *you owe* y'owe 193 *far* fare 222 *night* nightes 239 *had it* had't 289 *strew'd* strowd

I,iv, s.d. *Bagot* [F] Bushie 20 *our cousin* our Coosens 23 *Bagot here and Green* [Q6; not in Q1] 27 *What* With 52 s.d. *Enter Bushy* Enter Bushie with news 53 *Bushy, what news* [F; not in Q1]

II,i,15 *life's* liues 18 *fond* found 48 *as a* a 102 *incaged* inraged 113 *not* not, not 124 *brother* brothers 151 *bankrout* [Q1] bankrupt [C] (and elsewhere) 156 *kerns* kerne 177 *the* a 209 *seize* cease 252 *hath* [Q1] have [C] 257 *king's* King 277 *Le Port Blanc* le Port Blan [Q1] Port le Blanc [C] 278 *Brittaine* [Q1] Brittany [C] 284 *Quoint* Coines 285 *Brittaine* [Q1] Bretagne [C] 292 *drooping* drowping

II,ii,16 *eye* eyes 25 *more's* more is 31 *though* thought 59 *broken* [Q1] broke [C] 110 *disorderly thrust* [Q1] thrust disorderly [C] 112 *Th'* T [Q1] The [C] 129 *that's* that is 138 *The . . . will* Will the hatefull commons

II,iii,9 *Cotshall* [Q1] Cotswold [C] 30 *Lordship* Lo: 36 *Hereford* Herefords 75 *rase* race [Q1] raze [C] 99 *the lord* lord 151 *never* [Q1] ne'er [C] 164 *Bristow* [Q1] Bristol [C] (and elsewhere)

III,i,25 *Ras'd* Rac't [Q1] Razed [C]

III,ii,29 *heaven yields* heauens yeeld 30 *else, if* else 32 *succour* succors 40 *boldly* bouldy 72 *O'erthrows* Ouerthrowes 134 *this offence* [F] this 170 *through* thorough

III,iii,13 *brief with you* [F] briefe 17 *over* [Q1] o'er [C] 52 *tattered* tottered 91 *yon* [Q1] yond [C] 119 *a prince, is* princesse

III,iv,11 *joy* griefe 26 *pins* pines 27 *They will* [Q1] They'll [C] 29 *yon* yong 55 *seiz'd* ceasde 57 *We at* at 67 *you* [Q1] you then [C] 80 *Cam'st* Canst

IV,i,22 *him* them 43 *Fitzwater* Fitzwaters 54 *As may* As it may 55 *sun to sun* sinne to sinne 76 *my bond* bond 89 *he is* [Q1] he's [C] 109 *thee* the 145 *you* yon 154–320 [This deposition scene is based on the First Folio text; Q1 has only: "Let it be so, and loe on wednesday next, / We solemnly proclaime our Coronation, / Lords be ready all". Unless otherwise indicated all the new readings in lines 154–320 are taken from Q4.] 165 *limbs* knee 183 *and on* on *yours* thine 229 *folly* follyes 237 *upon* vpon me 250 *To undeck* T'vndeck 251 *and* a 255 *Nor* No, nor 267 *bankrout* [Q4] bankrupt [C, F] 270 *torments* [F] torment'st [C] 276 *the* that 285 *Was* Is *that* which 286 *And* That 289 *a* an 296 *manners* manner 333 *and I'll* Ile

V,i,25 *stricken* [F] throwne 32 *thy* the 34 *the* [F] a [C] 37 *sometime* sometimes 41 *thee* the 43 *quite* [F] quit [C] 62 *And he* He

V,ii,2 *off* of 11 *thee* the (also at lines 17 and 94) 52 *Do these . . . hold* [Q1] hold these justs and triumphs [C] 65 *bond* band 116 *And* An

V,iii,36 *I may* May 68 *And* An 75 *voic'd* voice 106 *shall* still 111 *Boling.* yorke 122 *sets* [Q1] set'st [C] 135–136 *With . . . him* I pardon him with al my heart 144 *cousin too* cousin

V,iv, s.d. *Enter* Manet *and* & 6 *wishtly* [Q1] wistly [C]

V,v,20 *through* thorow 25 *seely* [Q1] silly [C] 27 *sit* set 76 *ern'd* [Q1] yearn'd [C] 94 *Spurr'd, gall'd* [Q1] Spur-gall'd [C]

V,vi,12 s.d. *Fitzwater* Fitzwaters 43 *thorough* through

1 Henry IV

Copy text: the first complete quarto of 1598 [Q1]; and, for I,iii,201 through II,ii,118, the fragment of an earlier quarto [Q0].

I,i,4 *stronds* [Q1] strands [C] 62 *a dear* deere 76–77 *In faith, It is* [assigned in Q1 to King]

I,ii,68 *fubbed* fubd [Q1] fobbed [C] 89 *similes* smiles 177 *thou* the 182 *Bardolph, Peto* Haruey, Rossill

I,iii,84 *that* [Q1] the [C] 201 *Hot.* [missing in Q0–Q4] 239 *whipp'd* whipt [Q1] whip [Q0] 267 *Bristow* [Q0] Bristol [C]

II,ii,17 *two and twenty* xxii 21 *Bardolph* Bardol (and thus, or "Bardoll," throughout the play) 38 *mine* [Q1] my [Q0] 46 *Go hang* Hang [Q0, Q1] 89 *ah!* a 118 *fat rogue* [Q0] rogue [Q1]

II,iii,4 *In respect* in the respect 51 *thee* the 72 *a roan* Roane

II,iv,37 *precedent* present 39 *Poins.* Prin. 144 *lives* [Q1]

live [C] 172 *All's* All is 192 *Prince.* Gad 193, 195, 199 *Gads.* Ross. 363 *talent* [Q1] talon [C] 374 *Owen* O [Q1, C] 434 *tristful* trustfull 521 *lean* lane 540 *mad* made 572 *Good* God (and at l. 573) 580 s.d. *pockets* pocket 584 *Peto.* [not in Q1] 591 *Prince.* [not in Q1]

III,i,70 *here is* [Q1] here's [C] 100 *cantle* scantle 130 *metre* miter 179 *besides* [Q1] beside [C] 194 *she will* sheele

III,ii,38 *do* [Q1] doth [C] 107 *renowned* renowmed 145 *northern* Northren

III,iii,39 *that's* that 66 *tithe* tight 80 *wives* [Q1] wives, and [C] 101 s.d. *them* him 194 *guests* ghesse 224 *o' clock* of clocke

IV,i,20 *lord* mind 55 *Is* tis 99 *Bated* Baited [Q1, C] 108 *dropp'd* drop 116 *altar* altars 126 *cannot* can 127 *yet* it

IV,ii,3 *Sutton Co' fil'* Sutton cophill 34 *fac'd* fazd 37 *tattered* tottered 45 *but* not 79 *in* [Q1] on [C] 86 s.d. *Exit* Exeunt

IV,iii,21 *horse* horses 28 *ours* our 82 *country's* Countrey 110 *mine* [Q1] my [C]

IV,iv,18 *o'er-rul'd* ouerrulde

V,i,25 *I do* I 88 *off* of 114 s.d. *Exeunt* Exit 140 *will it* wil

V,ii,3 *undone* vnder one 8 *Supposition* [Q1] Suspicion [C] 10 *ne'er* neuer 25 s.d. *Hotspur* Percy 72 *libertine* libertie

V,iii,1 *the battle* battell 41 *stand'st* stands 52 *get'st* gets

V,iv,34 *so* and 68 *Nor* Now 76 s.d. *who* he 92 *thee* the 163 *ours* our

V,v,29–30 *valours . . . Have* [Q1] valour . . . Hath [C]

2 Henry IV

Copy text: the quarto of 1600 [Q], of which II,iv,370 through III,ii,113 exists in two states: the original printing by Valentine Sims [Qa], and a second version with six reset pages [Qb] that had been expanded to include III,i, inadvertently omitted from Qa. Qa is the copy text for those portions that were reset, Qb for III,i itself. In addition, the First Folio [F] is copy text for certain passages excised from Q, as indicated below. A number of the emendations adopted here throughout the play follow the suggestion of F, even though its text is to be regarded as the primary authority only for those passages not found in Q.

The Actors' Names [taken from F, at the end of the play]

Induction 35 *hold* hole 36 *Where* [F] When 40 s.d. *Rumour* Rumours

I,i,28 *whom* [F] who 62 *strond* [Q] strand [C] 96 *slain, say so* [F] slain [C] 126 *Too* [F] So 161 *Tra.* Vmfr. 164 *Lean on your* [F] Leaue on you 166–179 *You . . . be* [from F; not in Q] 167 *account* accompt 178 *brought* bring 189–209 *The . . . him* [from F; not in Q]

I,ii,6 *moe* [Q] more [F, C] 10 *intends* [Q] tends [F, C] 24 *fledge* [Q] fledged [F, C] 41 *rascally* [F] rascall 43 *smooth* [F] smoothy 55 *Where's Bardolph* [F; in Q, follows "through it" in line 53] 56 *into* [F] in 111 *hath* [F] haue *age* [F] an ague 112 *time* [F] time in you 127 *as I take it, is* [Q] is, as I take it [F, C] 138 *Fal.* [F] Old. 175 *smell* [Q] to smell [F, C] 191 *costermonger's* [Q] costermonger [C] 192 *bear-herd* [F] Berod 193 *hath his* [F] his 195 *this* [F] his *them, are* [F] the one 227 *you and Prince Harry* [F] you

I,iii, s.d. *Hastings* Hastings, Fauconbridge 21–24 *Till . . . admitted* [from F; not in Q] 26 *case* [F] cause 28 *on* [F] and 36–55 *Yes . . . else* [from F; not in Q] 59 *through* [F] thorough 66 *a* [F] so 71 *Are* [F] And 79 *He . . . Welsh* [F] French and Welch he leaues his back vnarmde, they 84 *'gainst* [F] against 85–108 *Let . . . worst* [from F; not in Q] 109 *Mowb.* [F] Bish.

II,i,15 *and that most* [F] most 24 *vice* [F] view 29 *continuantly* [F] continually 48 *Sir John, I* [F] I 65 *Fal.* Boy. 74 *thou upon* [Q] upon [F, C] 79 *all, all* [F] all 87 *Fie! what* [F] what 158 *German* Iarman 159 *bed-hangers* [Q] bed-hangings [F, C] 160 *tapestries* [F] tapestrie 178 s.d. *Exeunt* exit 181 *to-night* [Q] last night [F, C] 182 *Basingstoke* [F] Billingsgate

II,ii, s.d. *Poins* Poynes, sir Iohn Russel *others* other 7 *vilely* vildly (and elsewhere) 18 *viz.* [F] with 19 *ones* [F] once 23 *thy low* [F] the low 24 *made a shift to eat* [F] eat 80 *Poins.* [Q, F] Bard. [C] 84 *e'en now* euen now [F] enow [Q] 88 *new petticoat* [F] peticote 91 *rabbit* [F] rabble 101 *good blossom* [F] blossome 125 *borrower's* borrowed 128 *to the* [F] the 129–141 [as in Q, F; C assigns the reading of the remainder of the letter to Poins] 144 *familiars* [F] family

II,iii,11 *endear'd* [F] endeere 23–45 *He . . . grave* [from F; not in Q]

II,iv,1 *Fran.* [Q] First Draw. [F, C] 4 *Sec. Draw.* Draw. 15 *Third Draw.* Dra. [speech assigned to First Drawer in C; also at l. 21] 17 *Fran.* [Q] Sec. Draw. [F, C] 23 *Sec. Draw.* [F] Francis 43 *A pox damn you, you* [Q] You [F, C] 47 *them; I* [F] I 74 *Draw.* [Q] First Draw. [C] 125 *shall* [F] shall not 188 *Die men* [F] Men 198 *nothing* [F] no things 276 *the scales* [F] scales 289 *master's* [F] master 299 *it* [F] a 302 *so* [F] to 327 *even now* [F] now 347 *him* [F] thee 365 *blinds* [Q] outbids [F, C] 367 *she's* [Q] she is [F, C] 370–421 [copy text for this passage is Qa] 411 *Exit* [Qb; not in Qa] 421 s.d. *She comes blubbered* [Qa, Qb; printed in C as a stage direction]

III,i [this scene appears in Qb, not in Qa] 22 *billows* [F] pillowes 24 *deafening* [F] deaffing 26 *thy* [F] them 31 s.d. *Sir John Blunt* [Qb; omitted in F, C] 36 *letters* [F] letter 51 *mock* mockes 81 *nature of* [F] natures or 85 *beginnings* [F] beginning 87 *of* [F] or

III,ii,1–113 [copy text for this passage is Qa] 1 *on* [Qa] on, sir [Qb, C] 10 *no* [Qa, Qb] nay [F, C] 42 *Stamford* [F] Samforth 49 *fine* [Qb, F] fiue 61 *Shal.* [not in Qa or Qb; C assigns this and the following speech to Bardolph] 72 *accommodated* [F] accommodate 80 *Pardon* [Qa] Pardon me [Qb, C] 95 *Surecard* [F] Soccard 121 *Fal. Prick him* [Q prints as s.d.: Iohn prickes him] 145 *to fill* [F] fill 153 *him* [Q] him down [F, C] 154 *for his* [F] for 187 *prick me* [F] prick 208–209 *good . . . that* [F] master Shallow 222 *Clement's Inn* [F] Clemham 245 *dame's* [Q] old dame's [F, C] 253 *man's* [Q] man is [F, C] 307 *will* wooll 317

I . . . Shallow [F] would you would 320 *On . . . away* [assigned in Q to Shal.] S.D. *Exeunt* exit 340 *ever* [F] ouer 350 *skin* [F] shin 352 *be* [F] he 353 *'t* [Q] it [F, C] 354 *I'll* [Q] I will [F, C]

IV,i,S.D. *Mowbray* Mowbray, Bardolfe 9 *tenour* tenure (and elsewhere) 12 *could* [F] would [in some copies of Q] 30 *Then, my lord* [F; not in Q] 34 *rags* rage 36 *appear'd* appeare 45 *figure* [F] figures [in some copies of Q] 55–79 *And . . . wrong* [from F; not in Q] 103–139 *O, my . . . king* [from F; not in Q] 116 *force* forc'd 139 *indeed* and did 175 *to our* [F] our 180 *And* At

IV,ii,8 *Than* [F] That *man* [F] man talking 19 *imagin'd* imagine 24 *Employ* [F] Imply 48 *this* [F] his 67 *Lan.* [F; not in Q] 69 *Hast.* [F] Prince 117 *and such acts as yours* [F; not in Q] 122 *these traitors* [F] this traitour

IV,iii,2 *I pray* [F; not in Q] 46 *I came* [so F; Q precedes with "there cosin,"] 89 *lord, pray* [F] lord

IV,iv,S.D. *Warwick* Warwike, Kent 33 *he is* [Q] he's [F, C] 52 *canst thou tell that* [F; not in Q] 77 *others* [F] other 94 *heaven* [F] heauens 104 *write* [F] wet *letters* [F] termes 120 *and will break out* [F; not in Q] 132 *Softly, pray* [F; not in Q]

IV,v,13 *alter'd* [F] vttred [in some copies of Q] 31 *scald'st* [Q, F] scalds [C] 50 *How fares your grace* [F; not in Q] 76 *The virtuous sweets* [F; not in Q] 77 *thighs* [F] thigh 82 *hath* [F] hands 108 *Which* [F] Whom 161 *worst of* [F] worse then 162 *carat, is* [F] karrat 165 *Hast* [Q] Hath [C] 178 *O my son* [F; not in Q] 179 *it in* [F] in 200 *mood* [Q] mode [C] 205 *my* thy 221 *My gracious liege* [F; not in Q] 234 *swoon* swound

V,i,26 *the other day* [F; not in Q] *Hinckley* [F] Hunkly 54 *but a very little* [F] litle 74 *of him* [F] him

V,ii,S.D. Q: Enter Warwike, duke Humphrey, L. chiefe Iustice, Thomas Clarence, Prince, Iohn Westmerland 46 *mix* mist 62 *otherwise* [Q] other [F, C] 127 *rase* race [Q] raze [C] 145 S.D. *Exeunt* exit

V,iii,2 *mine* [Q] my [F, C] 5–6 *here a . . . and a* [F] here . . . and 37 *wag* [F] wags 63 *cabileros* [Q] cavaleros [F, C] 71 *'a; 'tis* [Q] he [F, C] 96 *i' thy* ith thy 116 *conceal* [Q] to conceal [F, C] 133 *knighthood* [F] Knight [Q] 148 S.D. *Exeunt* exit

V,iv,S.D. *Beadle* Sincklo 4 *First Bead.* Sincklo (and throughout scene) 5 *cheer enough* [F] cheere 6 *lately killed* [F] kild 8 *Dol.* [F] Whoore (and throughout scene) 13 *he* [F] I

V,v,5 *Robert Shallow* [F] Shallow 16, 18, 20 *Shal.* Pist. 25 *Fal.* [F; not in Q] 31 *all in* [F] in 71 *evils* [Q] evil [F, C] 86 *cannot well* [F] cannot 87 *should give* [F] giue

Epilogue 1 *courtesy* cursie 34 *died a* [F] died 38 *and so . . . queen* [F; in Q this appears after line 18]

Henry V

Copy text; the First Folio [F], sparingly corrected with reference to the bad quarto of 1600 [Q].

Prologue, 9 *hath* [F] have [C]

I,ii,27 *gives* [F] give [C] 28 *makes* [F] make [C] 38 *succedant* succedaul 45 *Elbe* Elue (also at l. 52) 74 *heir* th'Heire 131 *blood* Bloods 163 *her* their 166 *Ely.* [F] West. [C] 173 *tame* [F] tear [C] 197 *majesty* Maiesties 212 *End* [Q] And 243 *is* [F] are [C]

II,i,25 *mare* [Q] name 29 *Nym* [Q; F assigns speech to Bardolph, and C follows] 39 *drawn* hewne 44, 45 *Iceland* Island 76 *thee defy* [Q] defie thee 83 *enough* enough to 87 *you* your 110–111 *Nym. I . . . betting* [Q; not in F] 121 *that's* that 122 *came* come

II,ii,75 *hath* [Q] haue 87 *furnish him* furnish 107 *a* an 114 *All* And 139 *mark the* make thee 147 *Henry* [Q] Thomas 148 *Masham* [Q] Marsham 159 *Which I* Which 176 *have sought* [Q] sought 181 S.D. *Exeunt* Exit

II,iii,3 *earn* erne [F] yearn [C] (also at l. 6) 15 *ends* [Q] end 18 *'a babbled* a Table 26–27 *knees, and so* [F] knees, and they were as cold as any stone, and so [C] 27 *upward and* [Q] vp-peer'd, and 51 *word* world

II,iv,75 *of England* [F] England [Q, C] (also at l. 115) 107 *pining* [Q] priuy

III,Chorus,4 *Hampton* Douer 6 *fanning* fayning 17 *Harfleur* Harflew (and elsewhere)

III,i,7 *summon* commune 17 *noblest* Noblish 24 *men* me 32 *Straining* Straying

III,iii,32 *heady* headly 35 *Defile* Desire 43 [Here F has a stage direction: "Enter Gouernour"]

III,iv,i *parles bien* bien parlas [throughout the play, the French has been somewhat modernized, besides the emendations listed here] 8 *Et les doigts* [assigned to Alice in F] 9 *Alice.* Kat. 10 *souviendrai* souemeray 12 *Kath.* Alice. 16 *nous* [not in F] 44 *pas déjà* y desia 45 *Non* Nome 50 *Sauf* Sans 54 *ce* il

III,v,S.D. *Brittaine* [F] Bourbon [C] (also at ll. 10 and 32) 11 *de* du 43 *Vaudemont* Vandemont 44 *Faulconbridge* [F] Fauconberg [C] 45 *Foix* Loys 46 *knights* Kings

III,vi,32 *her* [Q] his 119 *lenity* Leuitie

III,vii,12 *pasterns* postures 62 *lief* liue 69 *truie* leuye

IV,Chorus,16 *name* nam'd 20 *cripple* creeple 27 *Presenteth* Presented

IV,i,3 *Good* God 35 *Qui va* Che vous 95 *Thomas* Iohn 152 *who* [F] whom [C] 246 S.D. *Exeunt* Exit (at l. 241) 262 *adoration* Odoration 270 *Think'st* Thinks 308 *if* of 326 *friends* friend

IV,ii, *à cheval* Cheual 4 *la terre* terre 5 *le feu* feu *Ciel* cein 25 *'gainst* against 43 *bankrout* [F] bankrupt [C] 49 *gimmal'd* Iymold [F] gimmal [C] 60 *guard. On* [F] guidon [C]

IV,iii,12 [placed after line 14 in F] 44 *see . . . live* [F] live . . . see [C] 48 *And . . . day* [Q; not in F] 105 *grazing* crasing 124 *'em* vm 128 *thou wilt* [F] thou'lt [C] *for a* [F] for [C]

IV,iv,2 *êtes* estes le 14 *Or* for 36 *de* a 38 *à cette heure* asture 43 *suis* suis le 55 *l'avez* layt a *de* a 59 *suis tombé* intombe 61 *distingué* distinie 70 *Suivez* Saaue

IV,v,2 *perdu . . . perdu* perdia . . . perdie 3 *de* Dieu 11 *honour* [Q; not in F] 15 *by a* [Q] a base 23 S.D. *Exeunt* Exit

IV,vi,15 *And* [Q] He *dear* [Q] my 34 *mistful* mixtfull

IV,vii,60 *yond* [F] yon [C] 81 *their* with 115 *countryman*

[Q] Countrymen 121 *God* [Q] Good 131 *'a live* alive [F, C]

IV,viii,10 *any 's* anyes [F] any is [C] 104 *Faulconbridge* [F] Fauconberg [C] *Foix* Foyes 105 *Vaudemont* Vandemont 118 *we* me

V,Chorus,29 *but* but by

V,i,73 *begun* began 86 *Nell* Doll 87 *Of* of a 94 *swear* swore

V,ii,50 *all* withall 54 *as* all 61 *diffus'd* defused [F, C] 77 *cursitory* curselarie [F] cursorary [C] 275 *de votre seigneurie* nostre Seigneur 290 *the fashion* a fashion

Julius Caesar

Copy text: the First Folio [F].

I,i,S.D. *Marullus* Murellus (and elsewhere) 6 *First Com.* Car. 10 *Sec. Com.* Cobl. (and elsewhere) 16 *Mar.* Fla. 26 *withal* [F] with awl [C] 66 *whe'r* where [F] whether [C] (and elsewhere)

I,ii,1 *Calpurnia* Calphurnia (and elsewhere) 3 *Antonius'* Antonio's (and elsewhere) 155 *walks* [F] walls [C]

I,iii,21 *glaz'd* [F] glared [C] 65 *fools* [F] fool [C] 129 *In* Is

II,i,40 *ides* first 119 *each* [F] every [C] 166 *Let's* [F] Let us [C] 213 *eighth* eight 267 *his* hit

II,ii,19 *fought* fight 23 *did neigh* do neigh 46 *are* heare 129 *earns* earnes [F] yearns [C]

III,i,39 *law* lane 113 *states* State 115 *lies* lye 275 S.D. *Octavius'* Octauio's 283 *for* from

III,ii,109 *art* are 208–209 *Revenge . . . live* [assigned in F to Sec. Plebeian] 225 *wit* writ 264 S.D. *Exeunt* Exit

IV,i,37 *objects, arts* [F] abjects, orts [C]

IV,ii,34–36 *First, Sec., Third Sol.* [not in F]

IV,iii,102 *Pluto's* [F] Plutus' [C] 133 *vilely* vildely 171 *tenure* [F] tenour [C] 242 *Claudius* Claudio (and elsewhere) 244 *Varro* Varrus (and elsewhere) 250 *will* will it

V,i,41 *teeth* teethes 66 S.D. *Exeunt* Exit 69 S.D. *Stands forth* [F: "Lucillius and Messala stand forth"]

V,iii,18 *yond* [F] yon [C] 101 *moe* [F] more [C] 104 *Thasos* Tharsus 108 *Flavius* Flauio

V,iv,7 *Lucil.* [not in F; C assigns to Brutus] 9 *O* Luc. O 17 *the news* thee newes

All's Well that Ends Well

Copy text: the First Folio [F].

I,i,S.D. *Lafew* [F] Lafeu [C] (and throughout) 115 *Look* Lookes 140 *got* goe 159 *ten* two 171 *wear* were

I,ii,3 *First Lord.* 1. Lo. G. (and elsewhere) 15 *Sec. Lord.* 2. Lo. E. (and elsewhere) 18 *Rousillon* Rosignoll 67 *You're* [F] You are [C] 76 S.D. *Exeunt* Exit

I,iii,21 *I* w 91 *one* ore 119 *Dian no queen* Queene 136 *rightly* righlie 177 *loneliness* louelinesse 183 *th' one* on tooth 208 *intenible* intemible 241 *Happily* [F] Haply [C] 255 *and* an

II,i,18 *Sec. Lord.* L. G. 43 *with his cicatrice, an* his sicatrice, with an 64 *fee* see 147 *fits* shifts 158 *impostor* Impostrue 167 *her* [F] his [C] 176 *nay ne* of *worst* [F] if worse [C] 177 *vilest* vildest 195 *heaven* helpe 213 *meed* deed S.D. *Exeunt* Exit

II,ii,23 *taffety* [F] taffeta [C]

II,iii,12 *Laf.* [not in F; speech assigned to Parolles] 13 *Par. So I say* [not in F] 38–43 *And . . . to be* [assigned in C to Lafew] 82 S.D. *She . . . a lord* [in F, at line 68] 100 *her* heere 102 *Hel.* La. 132 *when* whence 137 *it is* is is 308 *war* Warres 309 *detested* detected

II,iv,16 *fortunes* fortune

II,v,29 *End* And 31 *one* on 94 *Ber.* [at line 95 in F]

III,i,23 *to the* to'th the

III,ii,10 *sold* hold 14 *ling* Lings 20 *E'en* In 47 *First Gent.* French E. (and throughout scene except at line 65, assigned to 1. G.) 49 *Sec. Gent.* French G. (throughout scene)

III,v,26 *threatens* [F] threaten [C] 37 *le* la 69 *warrant* write 95 S.D. *Exeunt* Exit

III,vi,37 *his* this 38 *ore* ours 116 *Sec. Lord.* Cap. G. 120, 127 *First Lord.* Capt. E.

III,vii,19 *Resolv'd* Resolue 34 *after this* after

IV,i,98 *art* are 105 S.D. *Exeunt* Exit

IV,ii,25 *Jove's* [F] God's [C] 38 *may rope's . . . snare* make rope's . . . scarre [F] make ropes . . . scarre [C]

IV,iii,95–97 *They . . . midnight* [assigned in F to Bertram] 104 *effected* affected 136 *Hush, hush* [assigned in F and C to Bertram] 158 *All's one to him* [assigned in F to Parolles] 186, 187 *fifty* [F] and fifty [C] 222 *lordship* Lord 268 *our* your [F] the [C] 310 *cardecue* [F] quart d'écu [C] (also at V,ii,35)

IV,iv,16 *you* your

IV,v,15 *sallets* [F] salads [C] (also at line 18) 22 *grass* grace 41 *name* maine

V,i,6 S.D. *a Gentleman* a gentle Astringer

V,ii,1 *Lavatch* [F] Lavache [C] 27 *similes* smiles 34 *under her* vnder

V,iii,6 *blaze* blade 49 *warp'd* warpe 71–72 *Which . . . cesse* [assigned in F to King] 122 *tax* taze 155 *sith* sir 157 S.D. *Diana* Diana, and Parrolles 195 *hit* [F] it [C] 216 *infinite* insuite 314 *are* is 324 *curtsies* [F] courtesies [C]

Measure for Measure

Copy text: the First Folio [F]

I,ii,120 [F begins "Scena Tertia" here] 138 *morality* mortality

I,iii,21 *fourteen* [F] nineteen [C] 27 *Becomes more* More 43 *it* in 47 *bear* [F] bear me [C]

I,iv,54 *givings-out* giving-out 74 *for 's* [F] for his [C] 78 *make* makes

II,i,12 *your* our 39 *breaks of ice* brakes of Ice [F] brakes of vice [C] 248 *is* [F] are [C]

II,ii,25 *'Save* [F] God save [C] 58 *back again* again 96 *new* now 99 *ere* here 111 *ne'er* never 116 *Splits* [F] Split'st [C] 122 *makes* [F] make [C] 149 *sicles* Sickles [F] shekels [C] 150 *rates* rate

II,iv,9 *sere* feard [F, C] 24 *swoons* swounds 53 *or* and 76 *me be* be 94 *all-binding* all-building [F, C] 143 *for 't* [F] for it [C]

III,i,4 *I have* [F] I've [C] 20 *exists* [F] exist'st [C] 29 *sire* fire 52 *me to hear them* them to heare me 69 *Though* Through 130 *penury* periury 222 *her by oath* her oath

III,ii,26 *array* away 50 *it clutched* clutch'd 160 *dearer* deare 193 *not* now 237 *and it* and as it

IV,i,62 *quest* [F] quests [C] 64 *dreams* dreame

IV,ii,48–51 *if . . . thief* [assigned in F to clown] 103 *lordship's* Lords

IV,iii,93 *the under* yond 104 *well* weale 133 *covent* [F] convent [C]

IV,iv,6 *redeliver* reliuer

IV,v,5 *Flavius'* Flauia's 8 *Valencius* [F] Valentinus [C]

V,i,13 *me* we 95 *vile* vild 131 *this 's a* this 'a [F] this is a [C] 168 *her* your 200 *moe* [F] more [C] 428 *confiscation* confutation 545 *that's* that

Troilus and Cressida

Copy text: the quarto of 1609 [Q], which may represent Shakespeare's revision of the play, although the First Folio text [F] represents an independent and valuable textual authority. All adopted readings are from F unless otherwise indicated; [eds.] means that the reading is that of some editor since the First Folio.

Prologue [F; not in Q] 12 *barks* [eds.] Barke 19 *Sperr* [eds.] Stirre

I,i,24 *of the* the 25 *you* yea *to burn* burne 31 *When she* [eds.] then she 37 *a-scorn* [Q, F] a storm [C] 66 *in 't* in it 72 *on of you* of you 77 *not kin* kin 78 *on Friday* a Friday 79 *care I* I

I,ii,17 *they* the 49 *ye* [eds.] yea 92 *wit* [eds.] will 128 *lift* liste 136 *valiantly* valianty 142 *the* [eds.] thee 150 *marvell's* [Q, F] marvellous [C] 194 *Ilium* Ilion 207 *a man* man 221 *man's* man 261 *come* comes 263 *i'* in 281 *date is* [Q] date's [F, C] 292 *too* two 304 *I'll* I wil

I,iii,2 *the jaundice* the Iaundies [F] these Iaundies [Q] 8 *Infects* [Q] Infect [F, C] 13 *every* euer 31 *thy* the 36 *patient* ancient 54 *Retorts* [eds.] Retires 55 *nerve* nerues 56 *spirit* spright 61 *thy* the 70–74 *Agam. Speak . . . oracle* [F; not in Q] 75 *basis* bases 92 *ill . . . evil* influence of euill Planets 106 *primogenity* [Q] primogenitive [F, C] 110 *meets* melts 119 *includes* include 149 *awkward* sillie 159 *unsquar'd* vnsquare 164 *just* right 195 *and* our 219 *ears* eyes 238 *Jove's* great Ioues 247 *affair* affaires 250 *him* with him 252 *the* that 257 *loud* alowd 262 *this* his 263 *rusty* restie 267 *That seeks* And feeds 276 *compass* couple 289 *or means* a meanes 294 *One* A *one* no 297 *this wither'd brawn* my withered braunes 298 *will tell* tell 302 *forfend* [Q] forbid [F, C] *youth* men 304 *Agam.* [F, not in Q] 315 *This 'tis* [F; not in Q] 324 *True . . . perspicuous* [Q] The purpose is perspicuous even [F, C] 327 *were* weare 334 *his honour* those honours 340 *wild* vilde 354–356 *Which . . . limbs* [F; not in Q] 354 *his* [eds.] in his 359 *show our foulest* First shew foule 361–362 *yet . . . better* shall exceed, By shewing the worse first 370 *we* it 373 *did* do 387–388 *Now, Ulysses* [Q, F] Ulysses, Now [C] 389 *thereof* [Q] of it [F, C] 392 *tarre* arre

II,i,15 *vinewedst* [eds.] whinid'st [F] vnsalted [Q] 18 *than* without booke, then 20 *learn a* learn 26 *fool* [Q] a fool [F, C] 42, 44, 45 *Ther., Ajax., Ther.* [F; not in Q] 49 *asinico* [Q,F] assinego [C] *thou* you 60 *you* yee 70 *whosomever* [Q, F] whosoever [C] 76 *I will* It will 81 *I'll* I 111 *if he* and *out* at 115 *your* [eds.] their *on their toes* [F; not in Q] 125 *brach* [eds.] brooch 133 *fifth* first

II,ii,3 *damage* domage 14, 15 *surety* surely 27 *father* fathers 28 *counters* Compters 33 *at* of 35 *reasons* reason 47 *Let's* Sets 52 *holding* keeping *What's* [Q, F] What is [C] 64 *shores* shore 79 *stale* pale 86 *he* be *worthy* [Q] noble [F, C] 90 *never fortune* [Q] fortune never [F, C] 104 *eld* old [F] elders [Q] 149 *off* of 210 *strike* shrike

II,iii,19 *the Neapolitan* [Q] the [F, C] 26 *'a* [Q] have [F, C] 21 *dependant* depending 27 *wouldst* couldst 35 *art* art not 40 *me* [Q follows with a line: "*Patro.* Amen," not in F] 43 *O where?* [Q; not in F, C] 50 *thyself* Thersites 53 *mayst* must 59–63 *You . . . fool* [F; not in Q] 68 *of Agamemnon* [F; not in Q] 70 *Patroclus* this Patroclus 72 *Creator* Prouer [Q, C] 74 *Patroclus* Come Patroclus 78 *whore and a cuckold* [Q] cuckold and a whore [F, C] 80–81 *Now . . . all* [F; not in Q] *serpigo* [eds.] Suppeago 86 *shent* [eds.] sent [F] sate [Q] 87 *appertainments* appertainings 98 *A word, my lord* [F; not in Q] 139 *His pettish lunes* [eds.] His pettish lines [F] His course, and time [Q] *as* and 140 *carriage of this action* streame of his commencement 150 *enter you* entertaine 169 *I hate* I do hate 171 *And yet* [Q] Yet [F, C] 197 *do* doth 201 *Shall* [Q] Must [F, C] 203 *titled* liked 211 *this* his 213 *pash* push 215 *'a* he 222 *let* tell *humours* humorous 224 *'o* of 230 *Ulyss.* [F; speech assigned in Q to Ajax] 232 *He's . . . warm* [assigned in F, Q to Ajax] 233 *praises* praiers *in; his* his 238 *You* Yon 252 *got* gat 254 *all* all thy 255 *thine* [Q] thy [F, C] 260 *bourn* boord 261 *Thy* This 275 *cull* call

III,i,6 *noble* notable 27 *friend* [F; not in Q] 30 *thou too* [Q] thou art too [F, C] 33 *who is* [Q] who's [F, C] 38 *not you* [Q] you not [F, C] 40 *thou* [Q] that thou [F, C] 41 *Cressid* [Q] Cressida [F, C] 94 *Helen.* [so Q, F; C assigns speech to Pandarus] 99 *make 's* [Q] make [F, C] 101 *your poor* your 116 *lord* lad 123 *In . . . so* [F, not in Q] 124 *still love still more* [Q] still more [F, C] 128 *shaft confounds* shafts confound 161 *from* from the 164 *these* this 172 *thee* her

III,ii,3 *he stays* stays 10 *a* to a 12 *those* these 14 *Pandar* [Q] Pandarus [F, C] 22 *palates taste* [Q, F] palate tastes [C] 24 *Sounding* [Q, F] Swooning [C] 40 *unawares* vnwares 66 *Cressid* [Q] Cressida [F, C] 72 *fears* [eds.] teares 88 *This is* This 99 *crown it: no perfection* louer part no affection 118 *be wooed* [Q] are wooed [F, C] 128 *not, till now* till now not 140 *Cunning* [eds.] Comming 167 *aye* age 183 *Want* [eds.] Wants 187 *Yet, after* After 192 *and* or 198 *th' have* [Q] they 've [C] 200 *as* or 207 *pains* paine 215 *with a bed* [eds.; not in Q, F]

III,iii,1 *done* [Q] done you [F, C] 3 *your mind* mind 4 *come* [eds.] loue 29 *off* of 39 *to pass* pass 43 *unplausive* vnpaulsiue *on* [eds.] why turnd on 82 *and favour*

[Q, F] favour [C] 86 *Doth* [Q, F] Do [C] 100 *aiming* [Q] shining [F, C] 102 *giver* giuers 110 *mirror'd* [eds.] married 120 *reverb'rate* [Q, F] reverberates [C] 123 *rapt* [Q, F] wrapt [C] 128 *abject* obiect 140 *on* one 141 *shrieking* [eds.] shriking [Q] shrinking [F] 155 *one* on 158 *hedge* turn 160 *hindmost* him, most 161–163 *Or . . . on* [F; not in Q] *rear* [eds.] neere 164 *past* passe 168 *the welcome* [Q, F] welcome [C] 169 *Let* [Q] O let [F, C] 178 *give* [eds.] goe 184 *Than* That *not stirs* stirs not 197 *every . . . gold* euery thing *Pluto's* [F] Plutus' [C] 198 *deeps* depth 200 *Does* [eds.] do 224 *a dew* dew 233 *we* they 236 *T' invite* [Q, F] To invite [C] 251 *'a* [Q] he [F, C] 267 *to him* [F; not in Q] 275 *the most* the 279 *Grecian* [F; not in Q] *et cetera* [F; not in Q] 296 *of the* [Q] o' [F, C] 300 *you* yee 302 *of* [Q] o' [F, C]

IV,i,4 *you* your 16 *But* Lul'd 40 *do think* beleeue 52 *the soul* soule 53 *merits* deserues 56 *soilure* soyle 76 *you* they 78 *not* [Q, F] but [C]

IV,ii,17 *off* of 32 *capoccia* [eds.] chipochia 53 *'tis* its 65 *us; and for him* him, and 74 *nature* neighbor Pandar 89 *Prithee* Pray thee 94 *knees I beseech you* knees

IV,iii,2 *For* [Q] Of [F, C]

IV,iv,6 *affection* affections 34 *Is 't* [Q, F] Is it [C] 52 *Genius* [Q] Genius so [F, C] 53 *so* [Q] come [F, C] 56 *the root* my throate 60 *my love* loue 66 *there's* there is 72 *Wear* were 79 *They're . . . nature* [F; not in Q] *They're* [eds.] Their *gifts* [eds.] guift 80 *And swelling* [Q] Flowing and swelling [F, C] 81 *person* portion 108 *wear* were 137 *I'll* I 146–150 *Dei. Let . . . chivalry* [F; not in Q] *Dei.* [eds.] Dio.

IV,v,41 *You are* [Q, F] You're [C] 59 *a coasting* [Q, F] accosting [C] 94 *Ulyss. They . . . already* [F; not in Q] 95 *Agam.* Vlises 98 *in deeds* deeds 132 *Of our rank feud* [F; not in Q] 133 *drop* day 161 *my* [Q] mine [F, C] 163 *all* [Q] of [F, C] 165–170 *But . . . integrity* [F; not in Q] 178 *that I* thy *oath* earth 188 *thy* th' 193 *hemm'd* shrupd 199 *Let* O let 206 *As . . . courtesy* [F; not in Q] 220 *Yon* [Q] Yond [F, C] 275 *Beat loud the tabourines* To taste your bounties 287 *As* But 292 *she lov'd* my Lord

V,i,14 *need these* needs this 16 *boy* box 21 *catarrhs* [F; not in Q] 23 *wheezing* [eds.] whissing 24 *limekilns* [eds.] lime-kills 30 *meanest* meanes 36 *sarcenet* sacenet 37 *tassel* toslell 59 *brother* be 61 *hanging* [F; not in Q] 63 *forced* faced 64 *he is* her's 66 *dog* day *mule* Moyle 67 *fitchew* Fichooke 71 *not* [F; not in Q] 73 *Hey-day* [Q] Hoy-day [F, C] *spirits* sprites 78 *good* God 83 *sewer* [eds.] sure 84 *at once* [F; not in Q]

V,ii,13 *Cres.* [eds.] Cal. 16 *should* shall 35 *pray you* pray 40 *Nay* Now 41 *distraction* distruction 42 *prithee* [Q] pray thee [F, C] 46 *How now, my* [Q] Why, how now [F, C] 48 *adieu* [F; not in Q] 57 *these* [F; not in Q] 59 *la* [eds.] lo 68 *Tro. I . . . will* [F;not in Q] 69 *Cres.* Troy. 72 *ha 't* [Q] have 't [F, C] 78 *in* on 81 *Nay . . . me* [assigned in Q, F to Diomedes] 85 *Cres.* [F; not in Q] 89 *one's* [eds.] on's [Q] one [F] 91 *By* And by 118 *co-act* Court 123 *had* were 134 *soil* spoile 136 *'a* [Q] he [F, C] 157 *five* finde 160 *bound* giuen 167 *as I* [eds.] I

V,iii,14 *Cas.* Cres. 20–22 *To . . . charity* [F; not in Q] *give* [eds.] count giue *use* [eds.] as 23 *Cas.* [F; not in Q] 45 *mothers* Mother 58 *But by my ruin* [F; not in Q] 85 *distraction* destruction 104 *these* [eds.] th's

V,iv,4 *young knave's* knaues 17 *begin* [eds.] began 27 *What art thou* What art

V,v,11 *Cedius* [eds.] Cedus 12 *Thoas* [eds.] Thous 22 *scaled* scaling 41 *luck* lust 42 *Ajax.* [F; not in Q]

V,vi,1 *Ajax.* [F; not in Q] 2 *Dio.* [F; not in Q] 13 *Achil.* [F; not in Q] 26 *reck* [eds.] wreake 31 S.D. *Exeunt* [eds.] Exit

V,vii,1 *Achil.* [F; not in Q] 8 S.D. *Exeunt* [eds.] Exit 10 *'Loo* [eds.] lowe 11 *double-horned Spartan* [eds.] double hen'd spartan [Q] double-henned sparrow [F, C] 12 *Exeunt* S.D. [eds.] Exit 17 *a bastard begot* bastard begot

V,viii,7 *dark'ning* [Q] darking [F, C] 15 *part* prat 16 *Troyan trumpets* Troyans trumpet

V,ix,1 *shout is that* is this

V,x,2 *Never . . . night* [F; assigned in Q to Troilus] 21–22 *But . . . dead* [F; not in Q] 23 *vile* proud 24 *pight* pitcht 33 *ignomy and* ignomyny 51 *your* my . . . 52 *door* ore

Hamlet

Copy text: the second quarto of 1604–1605 [Q2]. The First Folio text [F] also represents an independently authoritative text; although seemingly not as close to Shakespeare's own draft as Q2, the Folio text is considerably less marred by typographical errors than is Q2. The adopted readings in these notes are from F unless otherwise indicated; [eds.] means that the adopted reading was first proposed by some editor since the time of F. Some readings are also supplied from the pirated first quarto of 1603 [Q1].

I,i,14 *Who is* [Q2] Who's [F, C] 16 *soldier* [Q1, F] souldiers 17 *hath* [Q2] has [F, C] 43 *'a* [Q2] it [F, C] 44 *harrows* horrowes 45 *Speak to* [Q2] Question [F, C] 63 *Polacks* [eds.] pollax 68 *my* mine 73 *why* [Q1, F] with 87 *heraldry* [Q1, F] heraldy *cast* cost 88 *those* these 91 *return'd* returne 93 *comart* [Q2] covenant [F, C] 94 *design'd* [eds.] desseigne 121 *fear'd* [eds.] feare 138 *you* [Q1, F] your 140 *at it* it 164 *that* [Q2] the [F, C] 175 *conveniently* [Q1, F] conuenient

I,ii,S.D. *Councilors* [eds.] Counsaile: as 21 *this* [Q2] the [F, C] 23 *bands* [Q2] Bonds [F, C] 58 *He hath* [Q1, F] Hath 67 *so* so much *in* [Q2] i' [F, C] 77 *good* coold 82 *shapes* [Q4] chapes 85 *passeth* passes 96 *a* or 129 *sullied* [eds.] sallied [Q2] solid [F] 132 *self* seale 133 *weary* wary 137 *to this* thus 143 *would* [Q1, F] should 149 *even she* [F; not in Q2] 171 *my* [Q2] mine [F, C] 175 *to drink deep* for to drinke 177 *prithee* [Q2] pray thee [F, C] 178 *to see* [Q1, F] to 186 *'a* [Q2] he [F, C; and so throughout the play] 198 *waste* [eds.] wast [Q2, F] vast [C] 213 *watch'd* watch 223 *Indeed, indeed* [Q1, F] Indeede 237 *Very like, very like* [Q1, F] Very like 238 *hundred* hundreth 249 *whatsoever* what someuer 251 *fare* farre 257 *foul* [Q1, F] fonde

I,iii,3 *convoy is* conuay, in 12 *bulk* bulkes 18 *For . . . birth* [F; not in Q2] 21 *safety* [Q2] sanctity [F] sanity [C] 49 *like a* a 63 *to* vnto 65 *comrade* courage 74 *Are* Or 75 *be* boy 76 *loan* loue 77 *dulleth* [Q2] dulls the [F, C] 83 *invites* inuests 105 *I will* [Q2] I'll [F, C] 109 *Running* [eds.] Wrong [Q2] Roaming [F] 115 *springes* springs 123 *parley* parle 125 *tether* tider 129 *implorators* imploratotors 130 *bawds* [eds.] bonds 131 *beguile* beguide

I,iv,2 *is a* is 6 S.D. *go* [eds.] goes 17 *revel* [Q4] reueale 27 *the* [eds.] their 33 *Their* [eds.] His 53 *Revisits* [Q2, F] Revisit'st [C] 82 *artere* [eds.] arture [Q2] artery [C] 86 S.D. *Exeunt* Exit 87 *imagination* imagion

I,v,3 *sulphurous* sulphrus 20 *fretful* [Q1, F] fearefull 42 *wit* [eds.] wits 47 *what a* what 55 *lust* [Q1, F] but 56 *sate* [Q1, F] sort 62 *hebona* [Q2] hebanon [F, C] 68 *posset* possesse 84 *howsomever* [Q2] howsoever [F, C] *pursues* [Q2] pursuest [F, C] 91 *adieu, adieu* [Q2] adieu, Hamlet [F, C] 95 *stiffly* swiftly 96 *whiles* [Q2] while [F, C] 109 *I am* [Q2] I'm [F, C] 113 *Heavens* [Q2] Heaven [F, C] 115 *bird* and 119 *you will* [Q2] you'll [F, C] 122 *my lord* [Q1, F; not in Q2] 126 *in* [Q2] i' [F, C] 131 *my* [Q2] mine [F, C] 132 *Look you, I'll* I will 134 *I am* [Q2] I'm [F, C] 150 *Ah ha* Ha, ha 170 *soe'er* so mere 179 *not to do* doe sweare 181 *Swear* [F; not in Q2]

II,i,S.D. *man* [eds.] man or two 3 *marvellous* [eds.] meruiles 28 *no* [F; not in Q2] 39 *sullies* sallies 40 *i' th'* with 52–53 *at 'friend . . . 'gentleman'* [F; not in Q2] 63 *takes* take 69 *bye ye* [eds.] buy ye [Q2] be wi' you [C] *fare ye* [Q2] fare you [F, C] 105 *passion* passions 112 *quoted* coted 119 *Come* [Q2; not in F, C]

II,ii,20 *are* is 57 *o'erhasty* hastie 90 *since* [F; not in Q2] 97 *he is* hee's 126 *above* about 137 *winking* working 143 *his* her 148 *watch* wath 149 *to a* to 151 *'tis this* this 153 *I would* [Q2] I'd [F, C] 169 S.D. *Exeunt* [eds.] Exit 182 *good* [Q2, F] god [C] 186 *but* [Q2] but not [F, C] 190 *far gone, far gone* far gone [Q2, C] 206 *should be* shall growe 211 *that's out of* [Q2] that is out o' [F, C] 214 *sanity* sanctity 215–216 *suddenly . . . him and* [F; not in Q2] 216 *honourable* [F; not in Q2] 217 *most humbly* [F; not in Q2] 218 *sir* [F; not in Q2] 219 *more* not more 228 *excellent* extent 230 *ye* you 232 *over* euer 233 *cap* lap 240 *What's the* What 241 *that* [F; not in Q2] 244–277 *Let me . . . attended* [F; not in Q2] 280 *even* euer 284 *Come, come* [Q2] Come [F, C] 286 *Why, any* Any 297 *could* can 314 *appeareth nothing to me but* [Q2] appears no other thing to me than [F, C] 315 *a piece* peece 317 *faculties* [Q2] faculty [F, C] 322 *no, nor* nor *woman* [Q1, F] women 326 *you* ye 333 *of* on 337–338 *the clown . . . sere* [F; not in Q2] 339 *blank* black 352–379 *Ham. How . . . too* [F; not in Q2] 358 *berattle* [eds.] be-ratled [F] 366 *most like* [eds.] like most [F] 380 *my* [Q2] mine [F, C] 381 *mows* [Q1, F] mouths 383 *a* [Q2] an [F, C] 390 *lest my* let me 394 *outwards* [Q2] outward [F, C] 402 *he is* [Q2] he's [F, C] 407 *then* [Q2] so [F, C] 413 *my* [Q2] mine [F, C] 416–417 *tragical-historical . . . -pastoral* [F; not in Q2] 441–442 *O, old friend! why* [Q2] O, my old friend! [F, C] 445 *By'r* by 450 *French falconers* friendly Fankners 453 *good lord* [Q2] lord [F, C] 457 *caviary* [Q2] caviare [C] 465 *affectation* affection 467 *in 't* [Q2] in it [F, C] 468 *tale* talke 469 *where* when 473 *'tis* [Q2] it is [F, C] 478 *heraldry* heraldy 482 *and a* [Q2] and [F, C] 496 *Then senseless Ilium* [F; not in Q2] 503 *And like* Like 517 *fellies* [eds.] follies [Q2] Fallies [F] 521 *to* [Q2, F] be to [C] 524 *ah woe* [Q2] O who [F, C] 527 *'mobled queen' is good* [F; not in Q2; F reads "Inobled"] 529 *bisson* Bison 537 *husband's* [Q1, F] husband 542 *whe'r* [Q2, F] whether [C] 543 *Prithee* [Q2] Pray you [F, C] 555 *shall* [Q2] should [F, C] 566 *for a* for 567 *or* [Q1, F] lines, or 572 *till* tell 580 *his* the 581 *in 's* in his 582 *and* an 585 *Hecuba* [Q1, F] her 587 *the cue* that 607 *have* a 610 *O, vengeance* [F; not in Q] 612 *father* [Q1, Q4; not in Q2, F] 615 *stallion* [Q2] scullion [F, C] 616 *brains! Hum, I* [Q2] brain! I [F, C] 626 *'a do* [Q2] he but [F, C] 628 *the devil* a deale

III,i,1 *And* An 19 *here about* [Q2] about [F, C] 27 *into* [Q2] on to [F, C] 28 *too* two 32 *lawful espials* [F; not in Q2] 33 *Will* Wee'le 46 *loneliness* lowlines 55 *let's* [F; not in Q2] 83 *of us all* [Q1, F; not in Q2] 85 *sicklied* sickled 92 *well, well, well* well 99 *the* these 107 *your honesty* you 122 *to a* a 132 *all* [Q1, F; not in Q2] 142 *go* [Q1, F; not in Q2] 147 *O* [F; not in Q2] 148 *too* [F; not in Q2] 149 *hath* [Q2] has [F, C] 151 *you amble* [Q1, F] & amble *lisp* list *you nick-name* [Q2] and nickname [F, C] 153 *your ignorance* ignorance *Go to, I'll* Ile 155 *moe marriage* [Q2] more marriages [F, C] 160 *Th' expectancy* Th' expectation 164 *music* musickt 165 *that* what 166 *time* [Q2] tune [F, C] 167 *feature* stature 169 [Q2 has "Exit" at the end of this line] 196 *unwatch'd* vnmatcht

III,ii,3 *your* our *lief* [eds.] liue 7 *whirlwind* [Q2] the whirlwind [F, C] 11 *tatters* totters *split* [Q1, F] spleet 22 *overdone* ore-doone 26 *virtue her own* vertue her 29 *it make* it makes 30 *of the* of 34 *praise* praysd 42 *sir* [F; not in Q2] 56 *We will* Ay 85 *my* [Q2] mine [F, C] 94 *detecting* detected 121–122 *Ham. I . . . lord* [F; not in Q2] 135 *within 's* [Q2, F] within these [C] 137 *devil* deule [Q2] Diuel [F] 145 S.D. *sound* [Q4] sounds *comes* [Q2] come [F, C] 147 *is miching* [Q1, F] munching 153 *counsel* [Q1, F; not in Q2] 155 *you'll* [Q1, F] you will 166 *orbed* orb'd the 174 *your* our 176 [Q2 follows here with an extraneous unrhymed line: "For women feare too much, euen as they loue"] 177 *For* And *holds* hold 178 *In* Eyther none, in 179 *love* Lord 191 *Wormwood* That's 200 *like* the 209 *joys* ioy 233 *a* [Q1, F] I be a 238 S.D. *Exit* [Q1, F] Exeunt 250 *o'* [Q1, F] of 252 *winch* [Q2, F] wince [C] 259 *my* mine 262 *mistake* [Q2, F] must take [Q1, C] 263 *pox* [F; not in Q2] 267 *Confederate* [Q1, F] Considerat 269 *infected* [Q1, Q4] inuected 271 *usurp* vsurps 272 *for his* [Q2] for 's [F, C] 273 *written* [Q2] writ [F, C] *very* [Q2; not in F, C] 277 *Ham. What . . . fire* [F; not in Q2] 281 *Pol.* [Q2] All. [F, C] 282 *strucken* [F, Q2] stricken [C] 285 *Thus* [Q2] So [F, C] 287 *with two* with 289 *sir* [F; not in Q2] 315 *rather with* with 317 *his* the 318 *far more* more 321 *start* stare 330 *of my* of 332 *Guil.* Ros. 340 *'stonish* [Q2] astonish [F, C] 349 *And* [Q2] So I [F, C] 373 *thumb* the vmber 384 *the top of* [F; not in Q2] 388 *can fret me* [F] fret me not [Q2] can fret me, yet [Q1, C] 405 *Leave me, friends* [so F; Q2 places before "I will say so" and assigns both to Hamlet] 407 *breaths* breakes 409 *bitter . . . day* busines as the bitter day 414 *daggers* dagger 416 *somever* [Q2, F] soever [C]

III,iii,6 *near us* [eds.] near's 7 *brows* [Q2] lunacies [F, C] 15 *cess* [Q2] cease [F, C] 17 *it is* or it is 19 *huge* hough 22 *ruin* raine 23 *but with* but 50 *pardon'd* pardon 58 *shove* showe 73 *pat . . . praying* but now a is a praying 79 *Why* [Q2] O [F, C] *hire and salary* base and silly 91 *game, a-swearing* [Q2] gaming, swearing [F, C]

III,iv,4 *sconce* [eds.] silence 5–6 *with him . . . mother* [F; not in Q2] 6 *warrant* wait 20 *inmost* most 23 *help, ho* how 24 *help, help, help* help 30 *it was* [Q2] 'twas [F, C] 37 *braz'd* [F] brasd [Q2] brass'd [C] 48 *does* [Q2] doth [F, C] 49 *O'er* [Q2] Yea [F, C] 52 *That . . . index* [so F; assigned in Q2 to Hamlet] 59 *heaven-kissing* heaue, a kissing 88 *pandars* pardons 89 *mine . . . soul* my very eyes into my soule 90 *grained* greeued 91 *not leave* leaue there 95 *mine* my 97 *tithe* kyth 139 *Ecstasy* [F; not in Q2] 143 *I the* the 158 *live* leaue 159 *my* [Q2] mine [F, C] 165 *Refrain to-night* to refrain night 178 *Thus* This 186 *ravel* rouell 215 *a* a most 217 S.D. *Exeunt* [eds.] Exit

IV,ii,1 S.D. [so F; Q2 reads, "Enter Hamlet, Rosencraus, and others"] 2 *Ros. Guil. . . . Hamlet* [F; not in Q2] 4 S.D. [F; not in Q2] 6 *Compounded* Compound 19 *ape an apple* [eds.] apple [Q2] Ape [F] 32 *Hide . . . after* [F; not in Q2]

IV,iii,16 *Ho! bring in the* [Q2] Ho, Guildenstern! bring in my [F, C] 37 *if indeed* [Q2] indeed, if [F, C] 45 *With fiery quickness* [F; not in Q2] 54 *and so* so 70 *were* will *begun* begin

IV,v,16 *Let . . . in* [assigned in Q2 to Horatio] 33 O ho! [Q2; not in F, C] 38 *grave* ground 46 *Pray* [Q2] Pray you [F, C] 57 *la* [F; not in Q2] 65 *So* (He answers) So 70 *would* [Q2] should [F, C] 73 *Good* God 77 *O* and now behold, O 82 *in their* in 89 *his* this 100 *impiteous* [Q2, F] impetuous [C] 96 *Queen. Alack . . . this* [F; not in Q2] 97 *Where* Attend, where *are* is 106 *They* The 137 *world's* [Q2] world [F, C] 141 *father* [Q2] father's death [F, C] 142 *swoopstake* [eds.] soopstake 152 S.D. *Let her come in* [so F; Q2 assigns to Laertes] 157 *Till* Tell 160 *an old* a poore 161–163 *Nature . . . loves* [F; not in Q2] 165 *Hey . . . nonny* [F; not in Q2] 176 *pray you* [Q2] pray [F, C] 182 *O you must* you may 188 *affliction* afflictions 196 *All flaxen* Flaxen 200 *Christian* Christians *I pray God* [F; not in Q2] *you* [Q2] ye [F, C] 201 *you see* you

IV,vi,2 *Sea-faring men* [Q2] Sailors [F, C] 8 *an 't* and 22 *good turn* turn 27 *bore* bord 31 *He* So 32 *will give* [F] will [Q2] will make [C]

IV,vii,6 *proceeded* proceede 8 *safety* safetie, greatnes 11 *th' are* [Q2] they are [F, C] 14 *She's so conjunctive* She is so concliue 20 *Would* Worke 21 *gyves* Giues 22 *loud a wind* loued Arm'd 24 *And* But *had* haue 36 *How . . . Hamlet* [F; not in Q2] 37 *These* [Q2] This [F, C] 46 *your pardon* you pardon 48 *and more strange* [F; not in Q2] 54 *devise* [Q2] advise [F, C] 57 *I shall* I 63 *checking* the King 84 *I have* [Q2] I've [F, C] 89 *my* me 93 *Lamord* [Q2] Lamond [F, C] 106 *you* [Q2] him [F, C] 116 *wick* [eds.] weeke 123 *spendthrift* [eds.] spend thirfts 124 *'o* [eds.] of 126 *your . . . deed* indeede your fathers sonne 135 *on* ore 139 *pass* pace 141 *for that* for 155 *should* did 160 *prepar'd* prefard 163 *But stay, what noise* [Q2] how sweet Queene [F] How now, sweet queen [C]· 167 *askant the* [Q2] aslant a [F, C] 168 *hoar* horry 172 *cold* cull-cold 173 *crownet* [Q2] coronet [F, C] 178 *lauds* [Q2] tunes [F, C] 192 *drowns* [Q2] douts [F, C]

V,i,1 *when she* [Q2] that [F, C] 3 *therefore* [Q2] and therefore [F, C] 9 *se offendendo* so offended 13 *and to* to *argal* or all 39–42 *Sec. Clo. Why . . . arms* [F; not in Q2] 49 *frame* [F; not in Q2] 66 *he* [Q2] that he [F, C] *lasts* [Q2, F] last [Q1, C] 68 *stoup* [Q1, F] soope 73 *that* [F; not in Q2] 74 *at* in 85 *'twere* [Q2] it were [F, C] *This* [Q2] It [F, C] 91 *thou, sweet* [Q2] thou, good [F, C] 93 *meant* went 98 *mazzard* massene 100 *'em* them 108 *quillities* [Q2] quillets [F, C] 109 *mad* [Q2] rude [F, C] 114–115 *in this . . . recoveries* [F; not in Q2] 116 *his* [F; not in Q2] 118 *double ones too* doubles 120 *scarcely* [Q2] hardly [F, C] 124 *calf-skins* Calues-skinnes 129 *O* Or 130 *For . . . meet* [F; not in Q2] 132 *'tis* [Q2] it is [F, C] 133 *yet* [Q2] and yet [F, C] 150 *taken* tooke 154 *been* a been 155 *all* [F; not in Q2] 160 *the* that 165 *'tis* [Q2] it's [F, C] 180 *Faith* [Q2] I' faith [F, C] 182 *now-a-days* [F; not in Q2] 199 *Yorick's* sir Yoricks 202 *Let me see* [F; not in Q2] 204 borne bore 230 *as thus* [F; not in Q2] 232 *into* to 239 *winter's* waters 240 *awhile* [Q2] aside [F, C] 252 *have* been 254 *Shards* [F; not in Q2] 270 *treble* double 284 *and rash* rash 286 *wisdom* [Q2] wiseness [F, C] 300 *thou* [F; not in Q2] 308 *thus* this 316 *thee* [Q2] you [F, C] 321 *shortly* thereby 322 *Till* Tell

V,ii,5 *methought* my thought 6 *bilboes* bilbo 8 *sometime* [Q2] sometimes [F, C] 9 *pall* fall *learn* [Q2] teach [F, C] 17 *unseal* vnfold 19 *O* A 27 *me* now 30 *Ere* Or 43 *'As'es* as sir 46 *the* those 51 *in the* [Q2] in [F, C] 52 *Subscrib'd* Subscribe 57 *Ham. Why . . . employment* [F; not in Q2] 63 *think* [Q2] think'st [F, C] 68–80 *To . . . here* [F; not in Q2] 73 *interim is* [eds.] interim's [F] 78 *court* [eds.] count 83 *humbly* humble 95 *Put* [F; not in Q2] 101 *sultry* sully *for* or 104 *But* [F; not in Q2] 109 *mine* my 111 *gentleman* [eds.] gentlemen 114 *feelingly* [Q4] fellingly 119 *dozy* [eds.] dazzie [Q2] dizzy [C] 120 *yaw* [eds.] raw 148 *his* [eds.] this 155 *impawned* [Q2] imponed [F, C] 157 *hangers* hanger 164 *carriages* carriage 166 *cannon* a cannon 167 *might be* be might 170 *'impawned,' as* [eds.] all [Q2] 'imponed,' as [F, C] 172 *laid* layd sir 181 *it is* [Q2] 't is [F, C] 186 *re-deliver you e'en* deliver you 190 *yours. He* [F; not in Q2] 195 *comply* so *sir* [Q2; not in F, C] 199 *yesty* histy 200 *fann'd* [eds.] prophane [Q2] fond [F] *winnowed* trennowed 219 *this wager* [F; not in Q2] 222 *But* [F; not in Q2] 230 *there's a* there is 231 *be now* be 233 *will come* well come 234 *of aught he leaves knows* [Q2] has aught of what he leaves [F, C] 237 *I have* [Q2] I've [F, C] 241 *a sore* [Q2] sore [F, C] 251 *Sir . . . audience* [F; not in Q2] 261 *keep* [F; not in Q2] *till* all 265 *Come on* [F; not in Q2] 272 *has* [Q2] hath [F, C] 274 *better'd* better 283 *union* Vnice ("Onixe" in some copies) 288 *heavens* [eds.] heauen 297 *A touch, a touch* [F; not in Q2] 307 *'t is almost 'gainst* it is almost against 308 *you* you doe 310 *afeard* sure 319 *swounds* [eds.] sounds 324 *Hamlet: Hamlet* Hamlet 326 *hour of* houres 327 *thy* [Q1, F] my 336 *murd'rous* [F; not in Q2] 337 *off* of *thy union* [Q1, F] the Onixe 353 *th' art* [Q2, F] thou'rt [C] 354 *ha 't* [eds.] hate [Q2] have 't [F, C] 356 *live* I leaue 361 *Osr.* [Qq, F provide a stage direction here: "Enter Osrick"] 373 *you* [Q2] ye [F, C] 390 *th' yet* yet 394 *forc'd* for no 403 *on* no 410 *rites* right

Othello

Copy text: the First Folio [F]. Some readings are supplied from the quarto of 1622 [Q]. The adopted readings in the following list of emendations are all from Q unless otherwise indicated; [eds.] means that the adopted reading was first proposed by some editor subsequent to the First Folio.

The Names of the Actors [from F, at the end of the play; F adds, "Gentlemen of Cyprus"]

I,i,1 *Tush, never* Neuer 4 *'Sblood, but* But *you'll* [F] you will [Q, C] 15 *And, in conclusion* [Q; not in F] 25 *toged* Tongued 29 *other* others 30 *Christian* Christen'd 33 *God bless* blesse 66 *full* fall *thick-lips* Thicks-lips 72 *changes* chances 79 *thieves! thieves! thieves!* Theeues, Theeues , 86 *'Zounds, sir* Sir (also at line 108) 103 *spirit* spirits *them* their 117 *are now* are 134 *spake* spoke 147 *produc'd* producted 152 *stand* [eds.] stands 155 *pains* apines 167 *moe* [F] more [Q, C] 183 *night* might 184 *I will* [F] I'll [Q, C]

I,ii,4 *Sometime* [F] Sometimes [Q, C] 15 *and* or 34 *duke* Dukes 68 *darlings* Deareling 75 *weaken* [eds.] weakens 84 *Whither* [F] Where [Q, C]

I,iii,1 *There is* There's *these* this 4 *forty* [F] and forty [Q, C] 34 *toward* [Q, F] towards [C] 87 *broil* Broiles 99 *maim'd* main'd 106 *Duke.* [Q; not in F] 107 *overt* ouer 122 *till* tell 130 *battles* Battaile *fortunes* Fortune 139 *travels'* Trauellours 141 *rocks and* Rocks *heads* head 142 *the* my 143 *other* others 145 *Do grow* Grew *This* These things 147 *thence* hence 155 *intentively* instinctiuely 159 *sighs* kisses 189 *be with* [F] bu'y [Q] be wi' [C] 201 *Into your favour* [Q; not in F] 219 *ear* eares 226 *sovereign* more soueraigne 231 *couch* [eds.] Coach [F] Cooch [Q] 235 *These* [eds.] This 240–241 *If . . . I'll* Why at her Fathers? / *Bra.* I will 242 *Nor I; I would not* Nor would I 249 *did love* loue 258 *why* [F] which [Q, C] 261 *voices* voice 265 *me* [eds.] my 269 *When* [F] For [Q, C] 271 *instruments* Instrument 283 *With* And 294 S.D. *Exeunt* Exit 300 *matters* matter 330 *balance* braine 336 *our unbitted* or vnbitted 337 *scion* [eds.] Seyen 348 *be . . . long* be long that Desdemona should continue 350 *in her* [F; not in Q, C] 357 *error* errors 357–358 *she must . . . purse* [Q; not in F] 363 *a super-subtle* super-subtle 386–388 *What . . . chang'd* [Q; not in F] *I'll go* [eds.] Ile 391 *a snipe* Snpe 394 *H' as* She ha's 401 *ears* [F] ear [Q, C]

II,i,19 *they* to 33 *prays* praye 40 *Third Gent.* Gent. 42 *arrivance* Arriuancie 43 *this* the 53 *Fourth Gent.* [eds.] Gent. 56, 59, 66 *Sec. Gent.* [Q] Gent. 70 *clog* enclogge 82 *And . . . comfort* [Q; not in F] 84 *You* [F] Ye [Q, C] 88 *tell me* tell 92 *the sea* Sea 94 *Sec. Gent.* Gent. *their* this 103 *You would* [F] You'ld [Q, C] 105 *list* leaue 110 *doors* doore 118 *thou write* write 127 *frieze* Freeze [Q, F] frize [C] 159 *such wight* such wightes 171 *gyve* [eds.] giue [F] catch [Q] 214 S.D. *Exeunt* [eds.] Exit 216 *hither* thither 226 *and will she* To 231 *again* a game 244 *compassing* compasse 246 *occasions* occasion 247 *has* he's 267 *mutualities* mutabilities 295 *'t* [F] it [Q, C] 308 *for wife* for wift 315 *rank* right 316 *cap* Cape

II,ii,6 *addiction* [eds.] addition 12 *Heaven bless* Blesse

II,iii,42 *unfortunate* unfortunate 57 *lads* else 62 *to put* put to 67, 77 *God* heauen 74 *A life's* Oh, mans life's 82 *Englishman* Englishmen *expert* exquisite 92 *a* and a 99 *Then . . . auld* And take thy awl'd 105 *God's* heau'ns 115 *God* [Q; not in F, C] 120 *speak* I speake 127 *He's* [F] He is [Q, C] 150 *'Zounds* [Q; not in F, C] 158 *God's will* [Q] Alas 159 *Montano,—sir;—* Montano 162 *God's . . . hold* Fie, fie Lieutenant 163 *You'll be asham'd* [F] You will be shamed [Q, C] 164 *'Zounds* [Q; not in F] *He dies* [F; not in Q, C] 167 *sense of place* [eds.] place of sense 168 *hold* [F] hold, hold [Q, C] 177 *looks* [Q, F] look'st [C] 183 *breast* breastes 190 *be* to be 218 *leagu'd* [eds.] league 224 *Thus* This 233 *the* then 251 *What's* [eds.] What is *matter* matter (Deere?) 252 *well now* well 256 *vile* vil'd 261 *God* [Q] heaven [F, C] 267 *thought* had thought 273 *ways* more wayes 290 *O God* Oh 319 *I'll* I 322 *denotement* [eds.] deuotement 338 *me here* me 349 *were 't* were 360 *fortunes* Fortune 381 *hast* hath 384 *By th' mass* Introth 391 *the* [eds.] a

III,i,S.D. *Musicians* [eds.] Musicians, and Clowne 21 S.D. *Exeunt* Exit 22 *hear, my* hear me, mine 27 *general's wife* Generall 32 *Cas. So . . . friend* [Q; not in F] 52 *To . . . front* [Q; not in F] 56 *Desdemon* Desdemona

III,iii,12 *farther* [Q, F] further [C] 16 *circumstance* Circumstances 55 *Desdemon* [F] Desdemona [Q, C] 60 *or* on 65 *examples* example 66 *their* [eds.] her 94 *you* he 106 *By heaven, he echoes* Alas, thou ecchos't 107 *his* thy 109 *lik'st* [Q, F] likedst [C] 112 *In* Of 135 *free to* free 136 *vile* vild 138 *a* that 139 *But some* Wherein 140 *sessions* [F] session [Q, C] 147 *oft* of 148 *yet* [eds; not in F] 153 *or* and 162 *By heaven* [Q; not in F] 170 *strongly* soundly 175 *God* heaven [F, C] 180 *Is once* Is 182 *blown* blow'd 185 *dances well* Dances 193 *this* [F] it [Q, C] 198 *eye* eyes 204 *keep 't* keepe [Q] kept [F] 215 *I' faith* Trust me 217 *my* your 223 *As* Which *aim not at* aym'd not 233 *disproportion* disproportions 245 *farther* [F] further [Q, C] 246 *Although 'tis* [F] Though it be [Q, C] 248 *to hold to* 259 *qualities* Quantities 273 *of* to 277 *Look where she* [F] Desdemona [Q, C] 278 *O, then* [Q; not in F] *mocks* mock'd 285 *'Faith* Why 302 *A thing* You haue a thing 311 *'faith* but 313 *it is* 'tis 315 *what is* [F] what's [Q, C] 338 *of* in 340 *fed well* [F; not in Q, C] 349 *troop* Throopes 361 *mine* [F] man's [Q, C] 376 *liv'st* [eds.] lou'st [F] liuest [Q] 386 *Her* [eds.] My 391 *see, sir* see 393 *I* and I 395 *supervisor* super-vision 408 *may* might 422 *and then* then 424 *then laid* laid 425 *Over* ore *sigh'd* sigh *kiss'd* kisse 426 *Cried* cry 432 *but* yet 440 *that was* [eds.] it was 447 *the hollow hell* [F] thy hollow cell [Q, C] 452 *perhaps* [Q; not in F] 455 *feels* [eds.] keepes 476 *O, damn her! damn her!* [F] O damn her [Q, C]

III,iv,6 *is* 'tis 23 *that* the 37 *It yet* It 54 *That's* [Q, F] That is [C] 64 *wive* Wiu'd 77 *God* Heauen 80 *is it* is 't 81 *Heaven* [Q; not in F] 86 *can, sir* can 92–93 *Des. I . . . handkerchief* [Q; not in F] 100 *ne'er* neu'r 137 *can he* is 147 *a* [F] that [Q, C] 149 *observancy* [F] observances [Q, C] 150 *fits* [Q, F] fit [C] 161 *they are* they're *'tis* It is 163 *that* the 170 *is 't* [F] is it [Q, C] 171 *I' faith* Indeed 188 *sweet* neither 190 *I would* [F] I'ld [Q, C]

IV,i,9 *So* If 21 *infected* infectious 32 *'Faith* Why 42 *shakes* [F] shake [C] 46 *work* workes 53 *No, forbear* [Q; not in F] 61 *no* not 78 *unsuiting* resulting 80 *'scuse* scuses 89 *y' are* [F] you are [Q, C] 96 *clothes* Cloath 99 *refrain* restraine 102 *conster* [Q] conserue [F] construe [C] 103 *behaviour* behauiours 104 *you now* you 108 *power* dowre 112 *i' faith* indeed 121 *Do you* Do ye 122 *marry her* marry 126 *win* [eds.] winnes 127 *'Faith* Why *you shall* you 134 *beckons* becomes 138 *by this hand, she* [Q; not in F] 144 *shakes* [F] hales [Q, C] 166–167 *An . . . an* If . . . if 171 *'Faith, I* I *street* streets 173 *Yes* [F] 'Faith [Q, C] 203 *thousand thousand* thousand, a thousand 227 *I . . . Venice* [F] Something from Venice, sure [Q, C] 228 *This comes* [F] Come [Q, C] *and* [Q; not in F] *wife's* [F] wife is [Q, C] 229 *God* [Q; not in F, C] 230 *the senators* [F] senators [Q, C] 259 *an* [Q; not in F] 287 *this* his 290 *denote* deonte

IV,ii,24 *Pray* Pray you 30 *nay* May 31 *knees* knee 33 *But not the words* [Q; not in F] 41 *Desdemon* [F] Desdemona [Q, C] 47 *Why, I* I 49 *kinds* kind 54 *A* The 55 *unmoving* and mouing 64 *Ay, there* [eds.] I heere 80 *hear it* [eds.] hear 't 81 *Impudent strumpet* [Q; not in F] 92 *keep* [eds.] keepes 103 *answers* [F] answer [Q, C] 114 *What is* [Q, F] What's [C] 117 *As* That *bear* beare it 119 *said* [F] says [Q, C] 133 *I will* [F] I'll [Q, C] 141 *heaven* Heauens 148 *Alas* [F] O good [Q, C] 155 *in* [eds.] or 168 *'Tis* It is 170 *stay* staies 184 *'Faith, I* I *for* and 189 *deliver to* deliuer 229 *takes* taketh 234 *of him* him

IV,iii,9 *'t* [F] it [Q, C] 13 *He* And 14 *bade* bid 21 *in them* [Q; not in F] 23 *faith* Father 24 *thee* [Q; not in F] 25 *those* these 26 *Barbary* [Q, F] Barbara [C] 33 *Barbary* Brabarie [F] Barbara [C] 41 *sighing* [eds.] singing 74 *for all* [F] for [Q, C]

V,i,1 *bulk* Barke 22 *hear* heard 35 *Forth* For 38 *cry* voyce 42 *it is a* 'Tis 49 *Did* Do 50 *heaven's* heauen 60 *here* there 90 *O heaven* Yes, 'tis 93 *your* [F] you [Q, C] 104 *out o'* o' 111 *'Las, what's . . . what's* Alas, what is . . . What is 114 *dead* quite dead 121 *Fie* Oh 123 *foh! fie* Fie 128 *afore* [F] I pray [Q, C]

V,ii,S.D. *Desdemona* [eds.] and Desdemona 13 *the* thy 15 *needs must* [F] must needs [Q, C] *thee* [F] it [Q, C] 16 *O* [F] A [Q] Ah [C] 19 *that's* [F] this [Q, C] 25 *Desdemon* [F] Desdemona [Q, C] 29 *Alack* [F] Alas [Q, C] *may* [Q, F] do [C] 32 *heaven* Heauens 35 *say so* say 37 *you're* [F] you are [Q, C] 52 *Yes* [Q; not in F] 57 *Then Lord* O Heauen 64 *makes* [F] makest [Q, C] 93 *here* high 101 *Should* Did 127 *heard* heare 143 *Nay, had* had 147 *me* me on her 150 *iterance* [F] iteration [Q, C] 152 *that she* [eds.] she 204 *Desdemon* [F] Desdemona [Q, C] 209 *reprobation* Reprobance 234 *wife* [F] woman [Q, C] 240 *have here* haue 251 *I die, I die* alas, I dye 253 *is* was 276 *cursed, cursed* [F] cursed [Q, C] 281–282 *O . . . Oh* [F] O Desdemona! Desdemona! dead! Oh! Oh! Oh! [Q, C] 291 *wert* was 292 *damned* cursed 318 *thou* [F] the [Q, C] 321 *but* [eds.] it but [F] it [Q] 347 *Judean* Iudean [F] Indian [Q, C] 350 *Drop* [eds.] Drops 357 *that is* [F] that's [Q, C]

King Lear

Copy text: the First Folio [F], except for those 300 or so lines found only in the first quarto of 1608 [Q]. Unless otherwise indicated, readings from Q are from the corrected state of that quarto. A few readings are supplied from the second quarto of 1619 [Q2]. All readings subsequent to F are marked as supplied by "eds."

I,i,5 *equalities* [Q] qualities 19 *sir, by* [F] sir, a son by [Q, C] 22 *to* [F] into [Q, C] 36 *lord* [F] liege [Q, C] 56 *word* [F] words [Q, C] 63 *speak* [F] do [Q, C] 67 *issue* [Q] issues 69 *of* [F] to [Q, C] *Speak* [Q; not in F] 70 *Sir, I* [Q] I 71 *that . . . sister* [F] the self-same metal that my sister is [Q, C] 76 *possesses* [Q] professes 80 *ponderous* [F] richer [Q, C] 85 *our last and* [F] the last, not [Q, C] 95 *no* [F] nor [Q, C] 97 *you* [F] it [Q, C] 106 *To . . . all* [Q; not in F] 107 *my good* [F] good my [Q, C] 112 *mysteries* [eds.] miseries [F] mistresse [Q] 137 *turns* turne *shall* [F] still [Q, C] 148 *wouldst* [F] wilt [Q, C] 151 *falls* [F] stoops [Q, C] *Reserve thy state* [F] Reverse thy doom [Q, C] 155 *sounds* [F] sound [Q, C] 156 *Reverb* [F] Reverbs [Q, C] 157 *as a* [Q] as 158 *thine* [F] thy [Q, C] *nor* [Q] nere 159 *motive* [F] the motive [Q, C] 162 *Lear.* [Q] Kear. *Kent.* [Q] Lent. 165 *Do* [Q; not in F] 166 *the* [Q] thy 167 *gift* [F] doom [Q, C] 171 *That* [F] Since [Q, C] *vows* [F] vow [Q, C] 173 *betwixt* [F] between [Q, C] *sentence* [Q] sentences 177 *disasters* [F] diseases [Q, C] 191 *Glou.* [Q] Cor. 193 *toward* [F] towards [Q, C] 197 *hath* [F] what [Q, C] 209 *on* [Q] in 217 *whom* [F] that [Q, C] *best object* [Q] obiect 219 *The best, the* [F] Most best, most [Q, C] 224 *Fall'n* [Q] Fall 226 *Should* [F] Could [Q, C] 228 *well* [Q] will 235 *As* [Q] That 242 *stands* [Q, F] stand [C] 244 *king*

[F] Lear [Q, C] 251 *respects of fortune* [Q] respect and Fortunes 274 *Love* [F] Use [Q, C] 279 *duty* [F] duties [Q, C] 283 *plighted* [F] pleated [Q] plaited [C] 284 *covers* [Q, F] cover [C] *shame them* [Q] with shame 285 S.D. *Exeunt* [eds.] Exit 286 *little* [F] a little [Q, C] 292 *not been* [Q] beene 299 *from . . . receive* [F] to receive from his age [Q, C] 307 *let us* [F] let's [Q, C] *hit* [Q] sit 309 *disposition* [F] dispositions [Q, C] 311 *of it* [F] on 't [Q, C]

I,ii,21 *top* [eds.] to' 24 *prescrib'd* [F] subscribed [Q, C] 59 *waked* [Q] wake 62 *this to you* [Q] you to this 74 *Has* [F] Hath [Q, C] *before* [F] heretofore [Q, C] 78 *declined* [F] declining [Q, C] 89 *should* [F, Q] shall [C] 93 *writ* [F] wrote [Q, C] 94 *other* [F] further [Q, C] 103–105 *Edm. Nor . . . earth* [Q; not in F] 129 *surfeits* [F] surfeit [Q, C] 131 *stars* [F] the stars [Q, C] 132 *on* [F] by [Q, C] 139 *on* [F] to [Q, C] 142 *Fut* [Q; not in F] Tut [C] 144 *Edgar* [Q; not in F] 145 *and pat* [eds.] Pat [F] and out [Q] 154 *with* [F] about [Q, C] 156–167 *as of . . . come* [Q; not in F] 168 *Why, the* [Q] The 172 *nor* [F] or [Q, C] 176 *until* [F] till [Q, C] 187 *go armed* [Q; not in F]

I,iii,14 *distaste* [F] dislike [Q, C] 16–20 *Not . . . abus'd* [Q; not in F] 21 *have said* [F] tell you [Q, C] 24–25 *I . . . speak* [Q; not in F] 26 *very course* [Q] course

I,iv,1 *well* [Q] will 22 *be'st* [F] be [Q, C] *he's* [F] he is [Q, C] 54 *daughter* [Q] Daughters 93 *strucken* [F] struck [Q, C] 110 *Kent. Why, Fool?* [Q] Lear. Why my Boy? 125 *Lady the* [eds.] the Lady 152 *one* [F] fool [Q, C] 154–170 *Fool. That . . . snatching* [Q; not in F] 169 *the fool* [Q] fool [C] 170 *Give . . . nuncle* [Q] Nunckle, giue me an egge 175 *crown* [Q] Crownes 176 *thine* [F] thy [Q, C] 181 *grace* [F] wit [Q, C] 183 *And* [F] They [Q, C] 188 *e'er* [F] ever [Q, C] 189 *mothers* [F] mother [Q, C] 194 *fools* [Q] Foole 209 *Methinks you* [Q] You 236 *it had* [Q] it's had 239 *Come, sir* [Q; not in F] 240 *your* [F] that [Q, C] 242 *which of late transport* [F] that of late transform [Q, C] 246, 247 *Does* [F] Doth [Q, C] 252–256 *Lear. I . . . father* [Q; not in F] 261 *should* [Q, F] you should [C] 266 *Makes* [F] Make [Q, C] 271 *remainders* [F] remainder [Q, C] 273 *Which* [F] That [Q] And [C] 279 *O . . . come* [Q; not in F] 313 *more of it* [F] the cause [Q, C] 325 *loose* [F] lose [C] 326 *Yea . . . this* [Q; not in F] *is it* [eds.] is 't [Q] 327 *Ha! let* [F] Let [C] *I have another* [F] yet have I left a [Q, C] 332 *thou . . . thee* [Q; not in F] 333 *my lord* [Q; not in F] 358 *Ay* [F] Yes [Q, C] 366 *You* [eds.] Your *attask'd* [Q] at task

I,v,S.D. *Kent* Kent, Gentleman 11 *not* [F] ne'er [Q, C] 17 *What canst tell* [F] Why, what canst thou tell, my [Q, C] 32 *put 's* [F] put his [Q, C] 38 *moe* [F] more [Q, C] 51 S.D. ["Gentleman" enters at line 1 in F]

II,i,2 *you* [Q] your 9 *ear-kissing* [F] ear-bussing [Q, C] 48 *the thunder* [F] their thunders [Q, C] 54 *latch'd* [F] lancht [Q] lanced [C] 55 *But* [Q] And 64 *coward* [F, Globe] caitiff [Q, F] 70 *would the reposal* [F, Globe] could the reposure [Q, C] 72 *I should* [Q] should I 73 *ay, though* [Q] though 78 *spirits* [F] spurs [Q, C] 79 *O strange* [F] Strong [Q, C] 80 *said he* [F; not in Q, C] *I never got him* [Q; not in F] 81 *why* [Q] wher 89 *strange news* [Q] strangenesse 92 *it 's* [F] is [Q, C] 97 *tended* [F] tends [Q] tend [C] 102 *expense and waste* [F, Globe] waste and spoil [Q, C] 108 *It was* [F] 'Twas [Q, C] 122 *prize* [F] poise [Q, C] 129 *businesses* [F] business [Q, C]

II,ii,17 *whoreson* [F] knave, a whoreson [Q, C] 25 *clamorous* [Q] clamours 31 *since* [F] ago since [Q, C] 35 *you: draw* [Q] you 48 *Part* [F; not in Q, C] 63 *A* [F] Ay, a [Q, C] 64 *they* [F] he [Q, C] 65 *years o'* [F] hours at [Q, C] 81 *too* [Q] t' 83 *Bring . . . their* [Q] Being . . . the 84 *Renege* [Q] Reuenge 85 *gale* [Q] gall 95 *What is his fault* [F] what's his offence [Q, C] 111 *faith* [F] sooth [Q, C] 113 *flick'ring* [eds.] flicking [F] fliker-ing [C] 125 *compact* [F] conjunct [Q, C] 130 *dread* [Q] dead 133 *reverent* [Q, F] reverend [C] 137 *respect* [Q] respects 148–152 *His . . . with* [Q; not in F] *contemned'st* [eds.] temnest [Q] 152 *king* [Q] King his Master, needs 153 *he* [F] he's [Q, C] 157 *For . . . legs* [Q; not in F] 158 *Come . . . away* [F assigns to Cornwall] 159 *duke's* [Q] Duke

II,iii,10 *hairs* [F] hair [Q, C] 15 *bare arms* [Q] Armes 18 *sheep* [Q] Sheeps 19 *Sometime* [Q] Sometimes

II,iv,2 *messenger* [Q] messengers 9 *man's* [Q] man 19–20 *No, no . . . have* [Q; not in F] 31 *panting* [Q] painting 34 *whose* [Q] those 40 *which* [F] that [Q, C] 64 *the* [Q] the the *number* [F] train [Q, C] 66 *thou'dst* [F] thou hadst [Q, C] 75 *following* [F] following it [Q, C] *upward* [F] up the hill [Q, C] 77 *have* [Q] hause 103 *her* [Q] tends 133 *mother's* [Q] Mother 150 *her* [Q] his 154 *her, sir* [Q] her 170 *blast her pride* [Q] blister 189 *fickle* [Q] sickly 194 *if you* [F] if [Q, C] 197 *will you* [F] wilt thou [Q, C] 227 *or* [F] an [Q, C] 248 *ye* [F] you [Q, C] 270 *life is* [F] life as [Q] life's as [C] 277 *stirs* [Q, F] stir [C] 303 high [F] bleak [Q, C]

III,i,4 *elements* [F] element [Q, C] 7–15 *tears . . . all* [Q; not in F] 20 *is* [F] be [Q, C] 27 *have* [eds.] hath 30–42 *But . . . you* [Q; not in F] 48 *that* [F] your [Q, C]

III,ii,3 *drown'd* [Q] drown 5 *of* [F] to [Q, C] 7 *Strike* [F] Smite [Q, C] 12 *in* [F] in and [Q, C] 13 *men nor fools* [F] man nor fool [Q, C] 22 *will . . . join* [F] have . . . join'd [Q, C] 50 *pudder* [F] pother [Q, C] 54 *of* [F] man of [Q, C] 57 *Hast* [Q] Ha's 71 *That* [Q] And 78 *True, boy* [F] True, my good boy [Q, C]

III,iii,4 *of* [F] of their [Q, C] 6 *or* [F] nor [Q, C] 8 *There is* [F] There's a [Q, C] 9 *between* [F] betwixt [Q, C] 13 *there is* [F] there's [Q, C] 15 *look* [F] seek [Q, C] 18 *If* [F] Though [Q, C] 20 *is* [F] is some [Q, C] *things* [F] thing [Q, C]

III,iv,10 *thy* [Q] they *roaring* [Q, F] raging [C] 38 S.D. *Enter Fool* [F, at line 36: "Enter Edgar, and Foole"] 47 *blows the cold wind* [Q] blow the windes 48 *bed* [F] cold bed [Q, C] 49 Didst . . . thy [F] Hast thou given all to thy two [Q, C] 53 *ford* [Q] Sword 59 *Bless* [Q] Blisse 65 *What, have* [eds.] Ha's [F] What [Q] 66 *Wouldst . . . 'em* [F] Didst . . . them [Q, C] 83 *word's justice* [F] words justly [Q] word justly [C] 93 *deeply* [Q] deerely 103 *mun* [F] mun, ha, no [C] 104 *boy, boy* [F] boy, my boy [Q, C] *sessa* [eds.] Sesey 105 *Thou*

[F] Why, thou [Q, C] *a* [F] thy [Q, C] 120 *foul* [F] foul fiend [Q, C] 121 *till the* [Q] at 141 *stock-punished* [Q] stockt, punish'd *hath had* [Q] hath 150 *my . . . vile* is grown so vile, my lord [Q, C]

III,v,11 *letter* [Q] letter which 26 *dearer* [Q] deere

III,vi,17 *hizzing* [F] hissing [C] 18–59 *Edgar. The . . . 'scape* [Q; not in F] 23 *justice* [Q] justicer [C] 24 *Now* [Q2] No [Q] 27 *bourn* [eds.] broome [Q] 32 *Hoppedance* [Q] Hopdance [C] 36 *cushions* [eds.] cushings [Q] 37 *the* [eds.] their [Q] 49 *she kicked* [Q2] kickt [Q] 53 *joint* [eds.] ioyne [Q] 57 *on* [eds.] an [Q] 72 *lym* [eds.] Hym 73 *tike* [Q] tight *trundle* [Q] Troudle 74 *him* [F] them [Q, C] 76 *leap'd* [F] leap [Q, C] 82 *makes* [Q] make 86 *Persian* [F] Persian attire [Q, C] 91 *So, so, so* [Q; not in F] 98 *toward* [F] towards [Q, C] 104–108 *Oppressed . . . behind* [Q; not in F] 109–122 *Edg. When . . . lurk* [Q; not in F] 119 *thoughts defile* [Q] thought defiles [C]

III,vii,3 *traitor* [F] villain [Q, C] 10 *festinate* [eds.] festiuate 19 *toward* [F] towards [Q, C] 30 *means* [Q, F] mean [C] 43 *answer'd* [F] answerer [Q, C] 46 *you have* [F, Q] have you [C] 53 *answer* [F] first answer [Q, C] 55 *Dover* [F] Dover, sir [Q, C] 65 *subscribe* [F] subscribed [Q, C] 99–107 *Sec. Serv. . . . him* [Q; not in F] *Sec. Serv.* [eds.] Seruant [Q] *Third Serv.* [eds.] 2 Seruant [Q] 105 *roguish* [Q2; not in Q]

IV,i,19 *You* [F] Alack, sir, you [Q, C] 43 *Then . . . gone* [Q] Get thee away 47 *Which* [F] Who [Q, C] 61–67 *five . . . master* [Q; not in F] 63 *Flibbertigibbet* [eds.] Stiberdigebit [Q] 64 *mopping and mowing* [eds.] Mobing, & Mohing [Q] 72 *does* [Q, F] doth [C]

IV,ii,s.d. *Bastard* [Q] Bastard, and Steward 17 *names* [F] arms [Q, F] 31–50 *I fear . . . deep* [Q; not in F] 32 *its* [eds.] ith [Q] it [C] 38, 48 *vile* [eds.] vild [Q] (and elsewhere) 47 *these* [eds.] this [Q] 53–59 *that . . . so* [Q; not in F] 57 *to threat* [eds.] thereat [Q] 58 *Whilst* [Q corrected] Whil's [Q uncorrected] Whiles [C] *sits . . . cries* [Q] sit'st . . . criest [C] 68 *mew* [Q corrected] now [Q uncorrected, C] 75 *thereat enrag'd* [Q] threat-enrag'd 79 *justicers* [Q corrected] Iustices

IV,iii,1–57 [Q; not in F] 2 *no* [Q] the [C] 13 *sir* [eds.] say [Q] 18 *strove* [eds.] streme [Q] 22 *seem'd* [eds.] seeme [Q] 33 *moisten'd* [eds.] moystened her [Q] 36 *mate and make* [Q] mate and mate [C] 57 s.d. *Exeunt* [eds.] Exit [C]

IV,iv,s.d. *Doctor* [Q] Gentlemen 3 *fumiter* [eds.] femiter [Q] Fenitar [F] 4 *har-docks* [F] hor-docks [Q] burdocks [C] 18 *distress* [Q] desires 26 *importun'd* [F] important [Q, C]

IV,v,21 *Something* [Q] Some thingso · 25 *œillades* [eds.] Eliads 28 *y' are* [F] you are [C] 39 *meet him* [Q] meet

IV,vi,1 *I* [F] we [Q, C] 9, 10 *Y' are* [Q, F] You're [C] 17 *walk* [Q] walk'd 30 *further* [F] farther [Q, C] 32 *ye* [F] you [Q, C] 71 *enridged* [Q] enraged 83 *coining* [Q] crying 98 *white* [Q] the white 129 *there is* [F] there 's [Q, C] 133 *to sweeten* [Q] sweeten 143 *thy* [F] the [Q, C] *see one* [Q] see 165 *thy* [F] thine [Q, C] 166 *lusts* [Q, F] lust'st [C] 168 *Through* [Q] Thorough *small* [Q] great 169 *Plate sin* [eds.] Place sinnes 190 *son-in-laws* [Q, F] sons-in-law [C] 201 *Ay . . . dust* [Q; not in F] *Gent. Good sir* [Q2; not in F, Q] 202 *a smug* [F] a [Q, C] 204 *Masters* [F] My masters [Q, C] 206 *Come, an* [F] Nay, and [Q] Nay, if [C] 207 *by* [F] with [Q, C] 209 *one* [Q] a 256 *English* [F] British [Q, C] *death* [eds.] death, death 265 *we* [F] we'ld [Q, C] 278 *indistinguish'd* [Q] undinguish'd [F] undistinguish'd [C]

IV,vii,8 *Pardon* [F] Pardon me [Q, C] 13 *Doct.* [Q] Gent. (and at lines 17, 43, 51, 78) 21 *sleep* [F] his sleep [Q, C] 23 *Doct.* [not in F; Q has "Gent."] 24 *doubt not* [Q] doubt 24–25 *Cor. Very . . . there* [Q; not in F] 31 *Did challenge* [F] Had challenged [Q, C] 32 *warring* [Q] iarring 33–36 *To stand . . . helm* [Q; not in F] 49 *when* [eds.] where 58 *hand* [F] hands [Q, C] 59 *You* [F] No, sir, you [Q, C] 79–80 *and yet . . . lost* [Q; not in F] 85–99 *Gent. Holds . . . fought* [Q; not in F]

V,i,11–13 *Edm. That . . . hers* [Q; not in F] 16 *me not* [Q] not 18–19 *Gon. I . . . me* [Q; not in F] 21 *hear* [Q] heard 23–28 *Where . . . nobly* [Q; not in F] 25 *touches* [Q] toucheth [C] 32 *proceeding* [F] proceedings [Q, C] 33 *Edm. I . . . tent* [Q; not in F] 36 *pray you* [Q] pray 46 *love* [Q] loues

V,ii,8 *further* [F] farther [Q, C]

V,iii,35 *th'* [F] thou [Q, C] 38–39 *Capt. I . . . it* [Q; not in F] 39 *do 't* [Q] do it [C] 40 *show'd* [Q, F] shown [C] 42 *Who* [F] That [Q, C] 43 *I* [F] We [Q, C] 47 *and appointed guard* [Q corrected; not in F] 48 *had* [F] has [Q, C] 54–59 *At . . . place* [Q; not in F] 55 *We* [Q corrected] mee [Q uncorrected] 57 *sharpness* [Q corrected] sharpes [Q uncorrected] 70 *Gon.* [Q] Alb. 76 *is* [F] are [Q, C] 83 *attaint* [Q] arrest 84 *sister* [Q] Sisters 85 *bar* [eds.] bare 87 *banes* [Q, F] bans [C] 91 *person* [F] head [Q, C] 93 *make* [F] prove [Q, C] 97 *he is* [Q] hes 99 *the* [F] thy [Q, C] 102 *Edm. A . . . herald* [Q; not in F] 109 *Capt. Sound, trumpet* [Q; not in F] 115 *Edm. Sound* [Q; not in F] 129 *is the* [Q] is my priuiledge, The 131 *place, youth* [F] youth, place [Q, C] 152 *war* [F] arms [Q, C] 160 *Gon.* [Q] Bast. 168 *th'* [F] thou [Q, C] (also at line 173) 196 *our* [F] my [Q, C] 204–221 *Edg. This . . . slave* [Q; not in F] 213 *him* [eds.] me [Q] 223 *this* [F] that [Q, C] 227 *confesses* [F] hath confess'd [Q, C] 230 *the* [F] their [Q, C] 238 *Goneril's* [eds.] Gonerill [at line 230] 248 *has* [F] hath [Q, C] 251 *Edg.* [F] Alb. [Q, C] 257 *Howl, howl, howl, howl* [Q] Howle, howle, howle *you* [Q] your 277 *them* [Q] him 289 *You are* [eds.] Your are [F] You'r [Q] 294 s.d., 295 *Messenger* [F] Captain [Q, C] 313 *hates him* [Q, F] hates him much [C] 323 *Edg.* [F] Alb. [Q, C]

Timon of Athens

Copy text: the First Folio [F].

The Actors' Names [Printed in F at the end of the play, and including reference to "Certaine Senatours, Certaine Maskers, Certaine Theeues," "With diuers other Seruants."]

I,i,s.d. *Merchant* Merchant, and Mercer 21 *gum, which oozes* Gowne, which vses 25 *chafes* chases 40 *man* men 41 *moe* [F] more [C] (and elsewhere) 87 *hands* hand *slip* sit 218 *cost* cast 229 *feigned* fegin'd 258 *'mongst* amongest 283 *Come* Comes 294 *First Lord* [not in F]

I,ii,29 *ever* verie 41 *eats* [F] eat [C] 103 *keeps* [F] keep [C] 110 *joy's* [F] joy [C] 119 S.D. *Sound Tucket* [F continues: "Enter the Maskers of Amazons with Lutes in their hands, dauncing and playing"] 127 S.D. *Enter Cupid* [F continues: "with the Maske of Ladies"] 131 *th' ear* There 132 *and smell* all 150 S.D. *single* [F] singles [C] 218 *'tis* [F] it is 219 *Sec. Lord.* 1. L.

II,i,35 *compt* Come

II,ii,4 *resumes* resume 38 *date-broke* debt, broken 74, 107 *mistress'* Masters 137 *propos'd* propose 194 *Flamineus* Flauius

III,ii,72 *spirit* sport

III,iii,5 *Owe* Owes 21 *I be* be

III,iv,S.D. *Men* man *Titus* Lucius 88 *Hor.* 1 Var. 89 *Both Bar. Serv.* 2 Var. 112 *Sempronius* Sempronius Vllorxa 113 *All* [F] All, sirrah, all [C] 116 *There's* [F] There is [C] 117 *Be it* [F] Be 't [C]

III,v,1 *to 't* [F] to it [C] 4 *him* 'em 22 *behave* behooue 49 *felon* fellow 63 *I* Why *h' as* [F] he has 67 *'em* him 82 *honours* Honour

III,vi,91 *lag* legge 101 *with your* [Globe] you with [F, C] 125 *Third Lord.* 2 126 *Sec. Lord.* 3

IV,i,2 *girdles* [F] girdlest [C] 13 *Son* Some 21 *let* yet

IV,ii,41 *does* do

IV,iii,10 *senator* Senators 12 *pasture* Pastour *rother's* Brothers 13 *lean* leaue 42 *puts* [F] put'st [C] 87 *tub-fast* Fubfast 116 *bars* Barne 121 *thy* the 156 *scolds* scold'st 185 *thy* the *doth* do 204 *fortune* future 215 *bade* [F] bid [C] 223 *moss'd* moyst 225 *when* [F] where [C] 255 *command* command'st 283 *my* thy 398 *Apem.* [so F; speech assigned in C to Timon] *them* then 437 *villany* Villaine 447 *Has* [F] Have [C] 451 *less* [F] no less [C] 462 S.D. *Exeunt* Exit 481 *grant'st* grunt'st 487 Nev'r [F] Ne'er [C] 499 *mild* wilde 532 *Have* Ha's

V,i,55 *worship* worshipt 74 *men* man 117 *payment* [F] payment for you [C] 119 *in vain* vaine 129 *chance* chanc'd 150 *sense* since 151 *fail* fall 185 *reverend'st* reuerends

V,iii,4 *read* [F] rear'd [C]

V,iv,2 S.D. *Sound* Sounds 24 *griefs* greefe 55 *Descend* Defend 62 *render'd* remedied

Macbeth

Copy text: the First Folio [F].

I,i,9–10 *Sec. Witch . . . Anon* [F attributes to all the witches]

I,ii,S.D. *Captain* [F] Sergeant [C; and so throughout the scene] 13 *gallowglasses* Gallowgrosses 14 *quarrel* Quarry 21 *ne'er* neu'r 22 *chops* [F] chaps [C] 26 *thunders break* Thunders

I,iii,18 *I'll* [F] I will [C] 22 *sev'nights* [F] se'nnights [C] 32 *weird* weyward [elsewhere in F spelled "weyward" or "weyard"] 39 *Forres* Soris 97 *tale* [F] hail [C] 98 *Came* Can

I,iv,1 *Are* Or

I,v,6 *the wonder* [F] wonder [C] 48 *it* hit

I,vi,4 *martlet* Barlet 9 *most* must

I,vii,6 *shoal* Schoole 47 *do* no 68 *lie* lyes

II,i,55 *strides* sides 56 *sure* sowre 57 *way they* they may

II,iv,6 *Threatens* [F] Threaten [C]

III,i,70 *seeds* [F] seed [C] 75 *Murderers.* Murth. [F] First Mur. [C] 110 *Hath* [F] Have [C]

III,ii,13 *scorch'd* [F] scotch'd [C]

III,iii,7 *and* end

III,iv,78 *time* times 121 S.D. *Exeunt* Exit

III,vi,24 *son* Sonnes 38 *the* their

IV,i,38 S.D. *to* and 59 *germans* Germaine 93 *Dunsinane* Dunsmane 94 S.D. *Descends* Descend 97 *Rebellion's head* Rebellious dead 98 *Birnam* Byrnan (also spelled "Birnan," "Byrnane," and "Birnane" in Act V) 119 *eighth* eight

IV,ii,83 *shag-ear'd* [F] shag-hair'd [C]

IV,iii,4 *down-fall'n* downfall 15 *deserve* discerne 107 *accurs'd* accust 113 *Hath* [F] Have [C] 133 *thy* they 235 *tune* time

V,i,29 *are* [F] is [C]

V,iii,39 *Cure her* Cure 52 *pristine* pristiue 55 *senna* Cyme

V,v,39 *shalt* shall

Antony and Cleopatra

Copy text: the First Folio [F].

I,i,39 *On* One 50 *whose* who

I,ii,4 *charge* change 39 *fertile* foretell 64 *Alexas* [printed in F as speech-prefix] 84 *Saw* Saue 114 *minds* windes 116 *Exit Mess.* [F adds: "Enter another Messenger"] 118 *First Att.* 1 Mes. 119 *Sec. Att.* 2 Mes. 122 *Sec. Mess.* 3 Mes. 127 *contempts* [F] contempt [C] 141 *occasion* an occasion 186 *leave* loue 191 *Hath* Haue 202 *place is* places *requires* require

I,iii,43 *services* Seruicles 71 *affects* [F] affect'st [C] 82 *by my* by

I,iv,3 *Our* One 8 *Vouchsaf'd* vouchsafe 9 *the abstract* th' abstracts 21 *smell* smels 24 *foils* [F] soils [C] 44 *dear'd* fear'd 46 *lackeying* lacking 49 *Make* Makes 56 *wassails* Vassailes 57 *Was* [F] Wast [C] 66 *brows'd* [F] browsed'st [C] 75 *we* me

I,v,34 S.D. *Alexas* Alexas from Cæsar 50 *dumb'd* dumbe 61 *man* mans

II,i,16, 18, 38 *Men.* Mene. 41 *warr'd* wan'd

II,ii,53 *have not* haue 122 *so* say 123 *reproof* proofe 151 *There's* [F] There is [C] 163 *Mesena* [F] Misenum [C] 173 S.D. *Exeunt* Exit omnes 211 *gentlewomen* Gentlewoman 228 *heard* hard 243 *vilest* vildest (and elsewhere)

II,iii,30 *away* alway

II,iv,6 *Mount* [F] the Mount [C]

II,v,2 *All.* Omnes [F] Attend. [C] 12 *finn'd* fine 26 *Antonio's* [F] Antonius [C] 43 *is* 'tis

II,vi,S.D. *Agrippa* Agrippa, Menas 16 *Made* [F] Made the [C] 19 *is* his 54 *There's* [F] There is [C] 59 *composition* composion 67 *meanings* meaning 70 *more of* more 84 *Show 's* [F] Show us [C]

II,vii,98 *is* he is 106 *grows* grow 118 *bear* beate 127 *off* of 131 *Splits* Spleet's 135 *father's* Father 137 *Men.* [not in F]

III,i,5 *Sil.* Romaine (and so throughout scene)

III,ii,10 *Agr.* Ant. 16 *figures* figure 49 *full* the full 59 *wept* weepe

III,iii,21 *look'dst* look'st

III,iv,8 *them* then 9 *took't* look't 24 *yours* your 30 *Your* You 38 *has* he's

III,v,14 *world* would *hast* hadst 16 *the one the* the

III,vi,13 *he there* hither *the kings* the King 22 *knows* [F] know [C] 61 *abstract* [F] obstruct [C] 74 *Comagene* Comageat 75 *Lycaonia* Licoania 78 *do* does 87 *makes his* [F] make them [C]

III,vii,4 *it is* it it 19 S.D. *Canidius* Camidias (also spelled "Camidius" in this scene and elsewhere) 24 *Toryne* Troine 36 *muleters* Militers 42 *Actium* Action 67 S.D. *Exeunt* exit 73 *Can.* Ven. 81 *throws* [F] throes [C]

III,x,S.D. *Enobarbus* Enobarbus and Scarus 14 *June* Inne 28 *he* his

III,xi,19 *that* them 44 *He is* Hee's 47 *seize* cease 58 *tow* stowe 59 *Thy* The

III,xii,S.D. *Thidias* [F] Thyreus [C; and so throughout] 6 S.D. *Ambassador* [so F; named "Euphronius" in C throughout]

III,xiii,55 *Cæsar* Cæsars 74 *deputation* disputation 103 *this* the 162 *smite* smile 165 *discandying* discandering 168 *sits* sets 199 *on* in 201 S.D. *Exit* Exeunt

IV,ii,1 *Domitius* Domitian

IV,iii,8 *Third Sold.* 1 9 *Fourth Sold.* 2 11 *Third Sold.* 1 12 *Fourth Sold.* 2

IV,iv,5 *too* too, Anthony 6 *Ant.* [not in F, or mistakenly placed in line 5 as part of Cleopatra's speech] 8 *Cleo.* [not in F] 24 *Capt.* Alex.

IV,v,1, 3, 6 *Sold.* Eros.

IV,vi,9 *vant* [F] van [C] 13 *dissuade* [F] persuade [C] 20 *more* mote

IV,viii,18 *My* Mine 23 *favouring* sauouring

IV,ix,1 *First Sold.* Cent. (and accordingly, Sec. Sold. is 1 Watch in F, Third Sold. is 2.)

IV,xii,4 *augurers* Auguries 14 *Hast* [F] Hath [C] 21 *spaniel'd* pannelled 37 *dolts* [F] doits [C]

IV,xiii,1 *he's* [F] he is [C]

IX,xiv,4 *tower'd* toward 10 *dislimns* dislimes 18 *moe* [F] more [C] 19 *Cæsar* Cæsars 111 *Decr.* Dercetus (elsewhere in F spelled "Decretas") 140 S.D. *Exeunt* Exit

IV,xv,38 *when* [F] where [C] 44 *huswife* [F] housewife [C] 72 *e'en* in 87 *do 't* [F] do it [C]

V,i,S.D. *Mecænas* Menas 28 *Agr.* Dol. 31 *Agr.* Dola. 36 *launch* [F] lance [C] 59 *live* leaue

V,ii,7 *dung* [F] dug [C] 26 *dependency* dependacie 35 *You . . . surpris'd* [assigned in F to Proculeius, in C to Gallus] 56 *varletry* Varlotarie 81 *O, the* o' th' 87 *autumn 'twas* Anthony it was 96 *nor* [F] or [C] 104 *smites* suites 208 *shall* [F] shalt [C] 216 *Ballad* Ballads 223 *my* mine 317 *wild* [F] vile [C] 321 *awry* away 322 S.D. *in* in, and Dolabella 323 *Where is* Where's

Coriolanus

Copy text: the First Folio [F].

I,i,7 *Marcius* Martius (and so throughout play) 16 *on* one 35 *Sec. Cit.* All. 58 *First Cit.* 2 Cit. (and so throughout scene) 95 *stale 't* scale 't 114 *tauntingly* taintingly 188 *vile* vilde (and elsewhere) 218 *Shouting* Shooting 222 *unroof'd* vnroo'st 230 S.D. *Junius* Annius 243 *Lartius* Lucius 248, 252 *First Sen.* Sen. (and elsewhere)

I,ii,S.D. *Corioles* Coriolus 4 *on* one 27 *Corioles* [F] Corioli [C; and so throughout play)

I,iii,39 *that's* that 50 S.D. *and* and a 91 *Vir.* Vlug. 93 *yarn* yearne 94 *Ithaca* Athica

I,iv,31 *Boils* Byles 42 *Follow 's* followes [F] followed [C] 45 S.D. *and is shut in* [in F, this is part of the stage direction at line 42] 54 *stand'st* [F] stands [C] 56 *Were* Weare 57 *Cato's* Calues

I,vi,6 *Ye* The 53 *Antiates* Antients 70 *Lesser* Lessen

I,vii,7 S.D. *Exeunt* Exit

I,ix,50 *shout* shoot 65 *Caius Marcius* Marcus Caius (and so reversed throughout play) 68, 79, 82, 90 *Cor.* Martius

II,i,46 *Both.* [F] Bru. [C] 62 *can't* can 66 *you you* you 70 *bisson* beesome 79 *forset-seller* [F] fosset-seller [C] 157 *wow* [F] waw [C] 182 *Coriolanus* Martius Caius Coriolanus 195 *wear* were 197 *Cor.* Com. 203 *You* Yon 220 S.D. *Brutus* Enter Brutus 267 *the* their 271 *touch* teach

II,ii,28 *ascent* assent 85 *one on 's* on ones 95 *chin* Shinne 96 *bristled* brizled

II,iii,20 *abram* [F] auburn [C] 30 *wedged* wadg'd 73 *but not* but 94, 97, 113 *Fourth Cit.* 1. 111 *Fifth Cit.* 2. 121 *hire* higher 122 *toge* tongue 123 *does* [F] do [C] 139 *Sixth Cit.* 1. Cit. 141 *Seventh Cit.* 2. Cit. 251–252 *Censorinus . . . by the people chosen* [bracketed words not in F; based on Plutarch]

III,i,66 *many* Meynie 91 *good* God! 129 *native* [F] motive [C] 131 *bosom multiplied* [F] bisson multitude [C] 143 *Where one* Whereon 184, 193, etc. *Citizens.* All. 185 *Sec. Sen.* [F] Senators, &c. [C] 215 *Citizens.* All Ple. 229 *Down . . . him* [followed in F by "Exeunt"] 230 *your* our 237 *Com.* Corio. 238 *Cor.* Mene. 240 *Men.* [not in F] 261 *A Patrician.* Patri. [F] Sec. Patr. [C] 324 *bring him* bring him in peace

III,ii,21 *thwartings* things 24 *Vol.* [F] A Patrician. [C] 32 *herd* heart 99 *sconce? Must I* [F] sconce? [C] 100 *With . . . heart* [F] Must I with base tongue give my noble heart [C] 115 *lulls* lull 129 *suck'dst* suck'st

III,iii,32 *for th'* fourth 36 *Throng* Through 55 *accents* Actions 99 *doth* [F] do [C] 110 *for* from 130 *but* [F] not [C] 135 S.D. *Cominius* Cominius, with Cumalijs

IV,i,4 *extremities* [F] extremity [C] 24 *thee* the 34 *wilt* will

IV,ii,36 *let's* [F] let us [C] 44 *Exeunt* Exit 54 *Exeunt* [in F, "Exeunt" at line 53 and "Exit" at line 54]

IV,iii,9 *appeared* [F] approved [C] 36 *will* well

IV,iv,13 *seems* [F] seem [C] 23 *hate* haue

IV,v,84 *Whoop'd* Hoop'd 133 *no other* [F] no [C] 137

o'erbeat [F] o'erbear [C] 213 *sowl* sole 238 *waking* walking 239 *sleepy* sleepe 242 *war* warres 251 *All.* Both.

IV,vi,2 *the* [F] i' the [C] 12 *Hail, sir!* [F] Both Tri. Hail, sir! [C] 34 *lamentation* Lamention 50 *hath* [F] have [C] 98 *He'll* [F] He will [C] 103 *resists* [F] resist [C] 120 *So incapable* S'incapeble 121 *Was 't* [F] Was it [C] 157 *Exeunt* Exit 161 *let's* [F] let us [C]

IV,vii,15 *Had* haue 28 *yield* yeelds 34 *osprey* Aspray 37 *'twas* 'was 39 *defect* detect 49 *virtues* Vertue 55 *falter* fouler

V,ii,S.D. *on* or 1 *Sentinal* 1 Wat. (and so throughout scene) 65 *errand* arrant 68 *but by* but 73 *swoon* swoond (also at line 107)

V,iii,48 *prate* pray 56 *What 's* [F] What is [C] 63 *holp* hope 115 *through* [F] thorough [C] 149 *fine* fiue 152 *charge* change 163 *cluck'd* clock'd 169 *with our* with him with our 192 *stead* steed

V,iv,47 *is 't* [F] is it [C] 64 *We'll* [F] We will [C]

V,v,4 *Unshout* Vnshoot

V,vi,49 S.D. *sound* sounds 100 *other* others 116 *Flutter'd* Flatter'd 132 S.D. *Draw* Draw both *kill* kils

Pericles

Textual Notes

1420

Copy text: the first quarto of 1609 [Q].

I Chorus, 6 *holy-ales* Holy dayes 11 *these* those 21 *peer* [Q] fere [C] 30 *account'd* [Q] account [C] 39 *a* of

I,i,6 *Music* [Q; not in C] 7 *For the* For 17 *ras'd* racte 33 *the* [Q] thy [C] 56 *Ant.* [not in Q] 111 *our* your 113 *cancel* counsell 127 *you're* you 129 *pleasures fits a* [Q] pleasure fits an [C] 152 *chamber, Thaliard* [Q] chamber [C] 165 *ne'er* neuer 170 *Ant.* [not in Q]

I,ii,S.D. *Pericles* Pericles with his Lords 3 *Be my* By me 20 *honour him* honour 25 *th' ostent* the stint 30 *am* once 41 *blast* sparke 44 *a peace* peace 56 *dares* [Q] dare [C] 61 *for 't* [Q] for it [C] 64 *makes* [Q] makest [C] 68 *ministers* [Q] minister'st [C] 79 *seem* seemes 83 *Bethought me* Bethought 84 *fears* feare 86 *doubt it* doo't 95 *for 't* [Q] for it [C] 100 *them* [Globe] for them [Q, C] 115 *Tarsus* Tharsus (and so throughout) 121 *will sure* will 124 S.D. *Exeunt* Exit

I,iii,9 *Husht* [Q] Hush [C] 10 *comes* [Q] come [C] 14 *Does* [Q] Doth [C] 22 *lest* [Q] lest that [C] 28 *ears it* seas [Q, C] 29 *seas* sea [Q, C] 31 *Hel.* [not in Q] 35 *betook* betake 40 S.D. *Exeunt* Exit

I,iv,8 *they are* [Q] they're [C] 13, 14 *do* to 15 *lungs* toungs [Q, C] 17 *helps* helpers 23 *her* [Q] the [C] 36 *they* thy 39 *two summers* too sauers 58 *thou* thee 67 *Hath* That *these* the 77 *fear* leaue 78 *The* our

II Chorus, 11 *Tarsus* Tharstill 12 *speken* spoken 22 *Sends word* Sau'd one 24 *had* hid *murder* murdred (some corrected copies of Q have "had . . . murder") 36 *escapend* [Q] escapen [C]

II,i,5 *seas* [Q] sea [C] 6 *left me* left my 12 *ho* to *Pilch* pelch 18 *thee* 'th 26 *porpoise* Porpas [Q] porpus [C] 34 *devours* deuowre 36 *they've* they 43 *Third Fish.* 1. 52 *finny* fenny 81 *pray you* [Q] pray [C] 82 *quoth-a* ke-tha *forbid 't! And I* [Q] forbid! I [C] 85 *holidays* all day 94 *all your* you 102 *is* I 105 *The good* [Q] The good King [C] 135 *from* Fame 137 *spares* [Q] spare [C] 140 *gave in his* [Q] gift in 's [C]

II,ii,4 *daughter* daughter heere 27 *Piu . . . fuerza* Pue Per doleera kee per forsa 28 *what's* with 29 *chivalry* Chiually 30 *pompæ* Pompey 33 *Quod* Qui

II,iii,3 *To* I 13 *yours* your 25 *Have* [Q] That [C] 26 *Envied* Enuies [Q] Envy [C] *shall* [Q] do [C] 37 *Yon* You 38 *tells me* tels 43 *son 's* sonne 50 *stor'd* stur'd 51 *you do* do you 57 *is 't* [Q] is it [C] 60 *come* [Q] comes [C] 95 *very well* well 101 *Here's* [Q] Here is 111 *to be* be 113 *Sim.* [not in Q]

II,iv,10 *Their* those 34 *death's indeed* death in deed [Q] death indeed's [C] 41 *For* Try 46 *To* [in C, printed at end of previous line] 56 *it* [not in Q] us [C]

II,v,6 *Which* [Q] Which yet [C] 83 *I'll* [Q] I will [C] 87 *for* [Q] for a [C] 91 *if 't* [Q] if it [C]

III Chorus, 2 *the house about* about the house 6 *fore* from 7 *crickets* Cricket 8 *E'er* Are 17 *coigns* Crignes 29 *appease* oppress [Q, C] 35 *Y-ravished* Iranyshed

III,i,S.D. *on* a 1 *Thou* The 7 *Thou stormest* then storme 8 *spit* speat 11 *midwife* my wife 52 *custom* easterne 53 *her* 'er *for . . . straight* [printed in Q as part of the next line, assigned to Pericles] 61 *in the ooze* in oare 63 *And* The *e'er* ayre 66 *paper* Taper 82 S.D. *Exeunt* Exit

III,ii,37 *I can* can 41 *treasure* pleasure 48 *never raze* neuer [Q] ne'er decay [C] 49 *What's* [Q] What is [C] 56 *bitumed* bottomed 69 *drives* [Q] drive [C] 77 *even* euer 94 *Breathes* breath 97 *set* sets 103 *Doth* [Q] Do [C]

III,iii,6 *shafts* shakes *hurt* hant 29 *Unscissar'd* vnsisterd 30 *ill* will

III,iv,2 *are* [Q] are now [C] 6 *eaning* learning 10 *vestal* vastall 18 S.D. *Exeunt* Exit

IV Chorus, 4 *there* ther's 8 *music* Musicks 10 *her* hie *heart* art 14 *Seeks* Seeke 15 *hath our Cleon* our Cleon hath 16 *wench full grown* full growne wench 17 *ripe* right *rite* sight 21 *she* they 26 *bird* bed 32 *With* [in Q, after "might"] 48 *on* one

IV,i,5 *love i' thy bosom* thy loue bosome 18 *doth* [Q] do [C] 20 *like a* a 24 *have you* [Q] you have [C] 53 *says* [Q] said [C] 62 *wolt* [Q] wilt [C] 64 *stem* sterne 84 *do 't* [Q] do it [C] 96 S.D. *Exeunt* Exit

IV,ii,4 *much* much much 21 *they're too* ther's two 39 *o'er* [Q] over [C] 46 *First Pirate.* Sayler. 52 *farther* [Q] further [C] 55 *It* I [Q, C] 62 *her age* [Q] age [C] 80 *was like* was 98 *must stir* stir 113 *i' the* ethe 137 *Bawd.* Mari. 155 *stirs* [Q] stir [C] 163 S.D. *Exeunt* Exit

IV,iii,1 *are* ere 12 *fact* face 15 *nor* not 17 *pious* impious 21 *thinks* [Q] think [C] 27 *prime* prince 28 *sources* courses 34 *malkin* Mawkin 48 *talents* [Q] talons [C] 49 *Ye're* [Q] You are [C]

IV,iv,1 *long* [Q] longest [C] 3 *your* our 7 *seem* seemes 8 *i' th'* with 10 *the* thy 13–16 [So Q; in C, these lines are in order as follows: 15, 16, 14, 13] 14 *you bear* [Q] Bear you [C] 18 *his* this 19 *grow on* grone 29 *puts* put 48 *scene* Steare

IV,v,10 s.d. *Exeunt* Exit

IV,vi,s.d. *three Bawds* Bawdes 3. 12 *cavaliers* Caualereea 32 *deed* deedes 42 *dignifies* dignities 75 *name 't* name 87 *you're* [Q] you are [C] 94 *aloof* aloft 106 *O, that* that (also at line 190) 138 *ways* way 139 s.d. *Bawd* Bawdes 144 *She* He 161 *ways* way 176 *Coistrel* custerell 196 *I will* will 205 *women* woman

V Chorus, 5 *neele* [Q] neeld [C] 8 *twin* Twine 13 *lost* left 14 *Whence* Where 20 *fervour* [corrected Q] former [uncorrected Q]

V,i,1 *Tyr. Sail.* 1 Say. 7 *Tyr. Sail.* 2 Say. 9 *there is* [Q] there's [C] 10 *pray, greet him* [Q] pray ye, greet them [C] 11 *Tyr. Sail.* 1 Say. [corrected Q] Hell. [uncorrected Q] 15 *you, sir* you 35 *Lys.* [not in Q] 36 *Hel.* Lys. 37 *Till* Hell. Till *night* wight 50 *And, with* And *is now* now 59 *gods* God 61 *inflict* [Q] afflict [C] 64 *here's* [Q] here is [C] 66 *presence* present 69 *I'ld* I do *wed* to wed 70 *one* on *bounty* beautie 72 *feat* fate 81 *Mark'd* Marke 103 *You are* your *countrywoman* Countrey women 104 *shores? . . . shores* shewes? . . . shewes 112 *cas'd* caste 122 *palace* Pallas 124 *make my* make 127 *say* stay 132 *thought'st* thoughts 136 *thousandth* thousand 141 *thou them* thou 163 *dull* duld 165 *daughter's* daughter 179 *impostor* imposture 182 *Per.* Hell. 188 *Here's* [Q] Here is [C] 215 *thou art* th' art 227 *doubt* doat 233 *Music, my lord?* [Q] My lord, I hear 234 *I hear* [assigned in Q as part of Lysimachus' previous speech] 247 *life* like 249 *Do 't* [Q] Do it [C] 262 *suit* sleight

V,ii,8 *Mytilin* Metalin [Q] Mytilene [C] 20 *fancies'* [Q] fancy's [C]

V,iii,6 *who* whom 15 *nun* mum 50 *Per.* Hell. 69 *I* and 89 *preserv'd* preferd 90 *Led* Lead 96 *their* his *the* [Q] and [C] 100 *punish them* punish

Cymbeline

Copy text: the First Folio [F].

I,i,3 *king's* [F] king [C] 69 [F begins "Scena Secunda" here] 139 *blessed* [F] blest [C] 143 *vile* vilde (and elsewhere) 177 *I pray* Pray

I,iii,9 *this* his

I,iv,50 *offend not* offend 78 *Britain* Britanie 80 *but believe* beleeue 90 *or if* [F] if [C] 91 *purchase* purchases 125 *y' are* [F] you're [C] 146 *a friend* [F] afraid [C] 148 *preserve* preseure

I,v,3 s.d. *Exeunt* Exit 65 *farther* [F] further [C] 85 s.d. *Exeunt* Exit

I,vi,7 *desire* desires *blessed* [F] blest [C] 28 *takes* take 43 *nor* [F] not [C] 54 *He's* [F] he Is [C] 61 *Briton* Britaine (and elsewhere) 72 *will 's* [F] will his [C] 84 *wrack* [F] wreck [C] 104 *Fixing* Fiering 109 *illustrous* illustrious [F] unlustrous [C] 147 *Solicits* [F] Solicit'st [C] 168 *men's* men 169 *descended* defended

II,i,15 *gave* [F] give [C] 29 *your* you 36 *to-night* night 56 s.d. *Exeunt* Exit 70 s.d. *Exit* Exeunt

II,ii,49 *bare* beare [F] have [C] 51 s.d. *Exeunt* Exit

II,iii,31 *Clo.* [not in F] 32 *vice* voyce 35 *amend* amed 44 *musics* [F] music [C] 48 *out* on 't 52 *solicits* solicity [F] soliciting [C] 142 *garment* Garments 159 *you* your

II,iv,6 *hopes* hope 18 *legions* Legion 24 *mingled* wing-led 34 *through* thorough 36 *tenour* tenure 37 *Phi.* Post. 41 *had* haue 47 *not* note 57 *you* yon 116 *one of* one 135 *the* her

II,v,16 *German one* Iarmen on 27 *may be nam'd* name

III,i,12 *Britain's* [F] Britain is [C] 20 *rocks* Oakes 54 *Clo. and Lords. We do* [assigned in F to Cymbeline] 64 *moe* [F] more [C]

III,ii,2 *monsters her accuse* [F] monster's her accuser [C] 67 *ere* [F] e'er [C] 69 *score* store *rid* [F] ride [C] 80 *here, nor* heere, not

III,iii,2 *Stoop* Sleepe 23 *bauble* Babe 28 *know* knowes 34 *for* or 83 *wherein they* whereon the

III,iv,22 *lie* lyes 81 *afore 't* a-foot 92 *make* makes 104 *blind first* first 150 *haply* happily 177 *will* [F] you'll [C]

III,v,9 *Queen. And you* [assigned in F to Lucius] 17 s.d. *Exeunt* Exit 32 *looks* looke 40 *strokes* stroke 41 s.d. *Enter* Enter a 44 *loudest* lowd of 145 *insultment* insulment

III,vi,27 [F begins "Scena Septima" here] 71 *I'ld* I do 89 *Leonatus's* Leonatus

IV,i,16 *imperceiverant,* imperseuerant 22 *her face* thy face [F, C]

IV,ii,35 *breed* breeds 48–51 *he . . . dieter* [assigned in F to Arviragus] 58 *patience* patient 101 *company's* Companie's [F] companies [C] 111 *the effect* defect 122 *thank* thanks 132 *humour* Honor 186 *ingenious* ingenuous 205 *crare* care 206 *Might* Might'st 224 *ruddock* Raddocke 290 *is* are 316 *Hast* Hath 329 *Cloten* [F] Cloten's [C] 332 s.d. *to them* [in F and C, treated as the beginning of the Captain's speech in the next line] 336 *are* are heere 366 *came 't* [F] came it [C] *is 't* [F] is it [C] 400 *he 's* [F] he is [C]

IV,iii,40 *betid* betide

IV,iv,2 *find we* we finde 17 *the* their 27 *hard* heard 35 *is 't* [F] is it [C]

V,i,1 *wish'd* am wisht

V,iii,24 *harts* hearts 42 *stoop'd* stopt 43 *they* the 72 *more* [F] moe [C]

V,iv,1 *First Gaol.* Gao. 50 *deserv'd* seru'd 81 *look* looke, looke

V,v,62 *Ladies. La.* [F] First Lady. [C] 64 *heard* heare 126 *saw* see 134 *On* one 205 *got it* got 297 *sorry* sorrow 334 *mere* neere 378 *ye* we 386 *brothers* Brother 387 *whither* whether

The Winter's Tale

Copy text: the First Folio [F].

The Names of the Actors [printed in F at the end of the play]

I,i,30 *have* hath

I,ii,50 *'Verily' is* [F] 'Verily' 's [C] 104 *And* A 148 *What . . . brother* [assigned in F to Leontes] 158 *do* do's 200 *there's* [F] there is [C] 208 *you, they* you 276 *hobby-horse* Holy-Horse

II,i,11 *taught'* [F] taught you [C] 32 s.d. [appears in F at line 1; other stage directions throughout the play are similarly "massed" at the beginning of scenes] 92 *vile* vild (and elsewhere)

II,ii,4 S.D. *Gaoler* [appears in F at line 1; also "Emilia," at line 20] 6 *who* [F] whom [C]

II,iii,S.D. *Servants* Seruants, Paulina 31 *Sec. Serv.* Ser. 39 *What* Who 53 *professes* [F] profess [C] 148 *beseech* [F] beseech you [C] 198 *account* accompt

III,ii,10, 124 S.D. [appear in F at line 1] 10 *Silence* [printed in F as a stage direction] 34 *Who* Whom 52 *bound* [F] bond [C] 157 *woo* woe 166 *doing it* [F] doing 't [C] 172 *Through* [F] Thorough [C] 244 *To* [F] Unto [C]

III,iii,58 S.D. *Shepherd* [appears in F at line 1] 123 *made* mad

IV,iii,7 *on* an 10 *With heigh! with heigh!* With heigh 38 *counters* Compters 40 *currents* Currence 59 *offends* offend

IV,iv,2 *Do* Do's 12 *Digest it* Digest 54 S.D. [appears in F at line 1] 98 *your* you 108 *Y' are* [F] You're [C] 145 *deeds* [F] deed [C] 160 *out* on 't 248 *kiln-hole* kill-hole *off* of 303 *A.* [in F, "Aut." appears at line 304] 371 *who* whom 429 *acknowledg'd* acknowledge 430 *affects* [F] affect'st [C] 433 *who* whom 438 *see* neuer see 449 *hoop* hope 477 *your* my 500 *hide* hides 509 *who* [F] whom [C] 510 *our* her 559 *the* there 590 *She 's* [F] She is [C] *o' our* 'our 623 *could* would *filed* fill'd *off* of 654 *flayed* fled 759 *or toaze* at toaze

V,i,S.D. *Servants* Seruants: Florizel, Perdita 12 *True* [assigned in F to Leontes] 61 *just* just such 75 *I have done* [assigned in F to Cleomenes] 85 *Serv.* [F] Gent. [C] (and so throughout scene)

V,ii,99 *swooned* swounded 121 S.D. *Exeunt* Exit

V,iii,S.D. *Paulina* Paulina: Hermione (like a Statue) 18 *Lonely* Louely 67 *fixture* fixure 114 *it* [F] 't [C] 149 *This* [F] This is [C] 150 *whom* [F] who [C]

The Tempest

Copy text: the First Folio [F].

Names of the Actors [printed in F at the end of the play]

I,i,36 S.D. *Exeunt* Exit 59 *chapp'd* chopt

I,ii,26 *wrack* [F] wreck [C] (and elsewhere) 146 *butt* [F] boat [C] 173 *princesses* Princesse 200 *boresprit* [F] bowsprit [C] 201 *lightnings* Lightning 271 *wast* was 282 *she* he 333 *made* [F] madest [C] 346 *humane* [F] human [C] 351 *Mir.* [F] Pro. [C] 358 *vile* vild 375, 396 *Ariel's* Ariel 381 *the burthen bear* beare the burthen

II,i,36 *So, you're paid* [assigned in F to Antonio] 86 *His . . . harp* [assigned in F to Antonio] 168 *'Save* [F] God save [C]

II,ii,187 *trenchering* [F] trencher [C] 190 *hey-day* high-day

III,i,2 *sets* set

III,ii,92 *further* [F] farther [C] 130 *scout* cout

III,iii,2 *ache* akes 18 S.D. [*Enter*] and 29 *islanders* Islands 65 *plume* plumbe 81 *heart's sorrow* hearts-sorrow [F] heart-sorrow [C]

IV,i,3 *third* [F] thrid [C] 9 *off* of 13 *gift* guest 110 *Cer.* [not in F] 163 S.D. *Exeunt* Exit 193 *them on* on them 264 *Lies* [F] Lie [C]

V,i,16 *runs* [F] run [C] 39 *mushrumps* [F] mushrooms [C] 60 *boil'd* boile 72 *Didst* Did 75 *entertain'd* entertaine 76 *who* whom 82 *lies* ly 111 *Whe'r* Where [F] Whether [C] 136 *who* whom 157 *howsoev'r* [F] howsoe'er [C] 199 *remembrance* remembrances 236 *her* our

Henry VIII

Copy text: the First Folio [F].

I,i,42–45 *All . . . function* [assigned in F to Buckingham] 47 *as you guess* [assigned in F to Norfolk] 63 *'a* O [F] he [C] 80 *he* [F] the [C] 120 *venom* venom'd 167 *wrenching* [F] rinsing [C] 183 *he privily* Priuily 200 *Hereford* Hertford 211 *Aberga'ny* [F] Abergavenny [C] (and elsewhere) 219 *chancellor* Councellour 221 *Nicholas* Michaell 226 *lord* Lords

I,ii,8 S.D. *Enter . . . Suffolk* vsher'd by the Duke of Norfolke. Enter the Queene, Norfolke and Suffolke 67 *business* basenesse 156 *fear'd* feare 164 *confession's* Commissions 170 *To gain* To 179 *him* this 190 *Bulmer* Blumer [F] Blomer [C]

I,iii,S.D. *Sands* Sandys (and sometimes elsewhere, but also "Sands" in F] 12 *saw* see 13 *Or* A 14 *to 't* [F] too [C] 15 *th' have* [F] they've [C] (and elsewhere) 34 *'oui'* wee [F] wear [C]

I,iv,S.D. *Guildford* Guilford (and so elsewhere) 7 *y' are* [F] you're [C] (and elsewhere)

II,i,18 *have* him 53 S.D. *Walter* [F] William [C] 86 *mark* make

II,iii,61 *of you* of you, to you

II,iv,127 *Grif.* Gent. Ush. 133 S.D. *Exeunt* Exit 174 *A* And 183 *spitting* [F] splitting [C]

III,i,23 S.D. *Campeius* Campian 61 *your* our

III,ii,142 *glad* gald 171 *fil'd* fill'd 210 *accompt* [F] account [C] 292 *Who* Whom 339 *legative* [F] legatine [C] 343 *Chattels* Castles

IV,i,20 *Sec. Gent.* 1. 34 *Kimbolton* Kymmalton 55 *First Gent.* 2 101 *Stokesly* Stokeley

IV,ii,7 *think* thanke

V,i,37 *time* Lime 55 S.D. *Exeunt* Exit 139 *precipice* Precepit 140 *woo* woe 175 *I'll* [F] I will [C] 176 *'tis* [F] it is [C]

V,ii,8 *piece* Peere

V,iii,85, 87 *Chan.* Cham. 125 *bare* base 133 *this* his 175 *heart* hearts

V,iv,2 *Parish* [F] Paris [C]

V,v,38 *ways* way *your* you

INDEX

The letter n *following a reference indicates a footnote*

A

B

C

D

Dethick, William (*fl.* 1596), deviser of coat of arms, 499
Deucalion, the Noah of classical mythology, 1121 n., 1237 n.
Devonshire, Earl of, *see* Mountjoy
De Witt, Johannes (*fl.* 1596), Dutch traveler, 32
Diana, goddess of chastity, the hunt, the moon, etc. (Cynthia, Phoebe, Luna), 65–66, 114 n., 159 n., 167 n., 182, 187 n., 199 n., 204 n., 294 n., 373 n., 376 n., 377 n., 414 n., 434 n., 488 n., 496 n., 529 n., 549 n., 600 n., 605 n., 608 n., 678 n., 893 n., 898 n., 1101 n., 1114 n., 1325, 1332
Diana, daughter to the Widow (*All's Well*), 804–805, 1339
Dick the Butcher (*2 Hen. VI*), 262 n.
Dido Queen of Carthage, deserted by Aeneas, 161 n., 187 n., 255 n., 367, 505, 918 n., 1073, 1101 n., 1197 n., 1256 n.
Digges, Leonard (1588–1635), poet and translator, 1354
Dighton, John, murderer of the little princes (*Rich III.*), 327 n.
Diomedes, Grecian prince (*T. and C.*), 290 n., 745 n., 802, 1340–1341
Dion Cassius (155–230?), historian of Rome, 787 n.
Dionysius the Areopagite (5th c.), author *On the Heavenly Hierarchy,* 13
Dionyza, wife to Cleon (*Per.*), 1153, 1155
Doctor Caius, a French physician (*Mer. Wives*), 559–560
Dogberry, a constable (*Much Ado*), 2, 102, 531–532, 797, 834, 1312, 1332, 1340, 1354
Doll Tearsheet, a whore (*2 Hen. IV*), 676, 1336
Donalbain, son to Duncan (*Macb.*), 1046
Don John, bastard brother of Don Pedro (*Much Ado*), 369, 532, 945, 1180, 1332
Donne, John (1571 or 1572–1631), poet, 13, 468
Don Pedro, Prince of Arragon (*Much Ado*), 530, 532, 1331
Doran, Madeleine (1905—), scholar and critic, 59
Dorset, Marquis of, son to the Queen (*Rich. III*), 331 n.
Douglas, Archibald, Earl of (*1 Hen. IV*), 675, 705 n.
Dowdall, John (1563–1636?), traveler, 76
Dowden, Edward (1843–1913), critic and editor, 42, 46
Dowland, John (1563–1626), lutanist and composer, 460 n.
Drake, Sir Francis (1540?–1596), explorer and naval commander, 10, 1170 n.
Drayton, Michael (1573–1631), poet, 66, 501, 653 n., 1150, 1311; *Endimion and Phoebe,* 425, 1330; *Idea's Mirror,* 468, 470; *see also Sir John Oldcastle*
Droeshout engraving, 1151
Dromio of Ephesus, twin brother of Dromio of Syracuse (*Com. Er.*), 81, 82, 1322
Dromio of Syracuse, twin brother of Dromio of Ephesus, 80, 81, 1322
Drummond, William, of Hawthornden (1585–1649), 43–44
Dryden, John (1631–1700), poet, dramatist, and critic, 44, 46, 64, 862, 1071, 1354–1355, 1360
Duchess of Gloucester, *see* Gloucester, Duchess of (*Rich. II*)
Duchess of York, *see* York, Duchess of (*Rich. II* and *Rich. III*)
Du Bellay, Joachim (c. 1522–1560), French sonneteer, 469
Duke, living in banishment (*A.Y.L.*), 586–589
Duke of Ephesus (*Com. Er.*), 81
Duke Vincentio of Vienna (*Meas. Meas.*), 50, 802, 833–834, 1316
Duke of Milan (*Two Gent.*), 136 n., 144 n., 1324
Duke of Venice (*Oth.*), 943–944
Dull, a constable (*L.L.L.*), 102, 531
Dumaine, lord attending on King (*L.L.L.*), 101
Duncan, King of Scotland (*Macb.*), 802, 1043–1046, 1346–1347
Durfey, Thomas (1653–1723), dramatist and critic, 1355
Duthie, G. I., modern editor and scholar, 59
Dyce, Alexander (1798–1869), editor, 58

E

Eastward Ho, comedy by Chapman, Marston, and Jonson, 66, 801
Economics, *see* England, Life in Shakespeare's
Eden, Richard (1521?–1576), translator *History of Trauayle,* 1254 n., 1352
Edgar, son to Gloucester (*K. Lear*), 979–982, 1345
Edmund, bastard son to Gloucester (*K. Lear*), 16, 21, 48, 300, 341, 369, 380 n., 532, 945, 979–982, 1180, 1345
Edmund, Earl of Rutland, *see* Rutland, Earl of (*3 Hen. VI*)
Edmund of Langley, Duke of York, *see* York, Duke of (*Rich. II*)
Education, *see* England, Life in Shakespeare's
Edward I, King of England (reigned 1272–1307), 216 n., 503, 1056 n.
Edward II, see Marlowe
Edward III, King of England (reigned 1327–1377), 221 n., 514 n., 647 n., 649 n., 741 n., 742 n., 748 n.
Edward III, The Reign of King, anonymous play, 67, 259 n., 487 n., 501
Edward the Black Prince, son of Edward III, 643, 828 n.
Edward IV, son to Richard Duke of York (*2* and *3 Henry VI* and *Rich. III*), 8, 206, 208–210, 259 n., 301, 720 n., 1327
Edward, Prince of Wales, afterwards Edward V (*Rich. III*), 210, 300–301
Edward, Prince of Wales, son to Henry VI (*3 Hen. VI*), 206, 210, 301, 310 n., 311 n., 328 n., 1326
Edward VI, King of England (reigned 1547–1553), 8
Edward the Confessor (1002?–1066), King of England, 1046, 1061 n.
Edwards, Richard (1523?–1566), poet and dramatist, contributor to the *Paradise of Dainty Devices,* 420 n.; author *Damon and Pythias,* 23, 1323
Egeus, father to Hermia (*Mids. Dr.*), 182–183
Eglamour, agent for Silvia's escape (*Two Gent.*), 134 n.
Elbow, a simple constable (*Meas. Meas.*), 102, 834, 1340
Eld, G. (*fl.* 1604–1618), printer, 66
Eleanor, Duchess of Gloucester (*2 Hen. VI*), 209
Elements, the four, 14
Elector Palatinate, 1272
Elinor, Queen, mother to King John (*K. John*), 339
Eliot, Sir John (1592–1632), patriot and member of

F

G

H

I

J

K

L

M

N

Nessus, a centaur, 826 n., 1100 n.
Nestor, Grecian prince (*T. and C.*), 117 n., 221 n., 286 n., 506 n., 863, 870 n., 1340
Newcastle-on-Tyne, religious drama at, 19
New Custom, anonymous morality play, 20
Newington Butts, playhouse at, 38, 78
Nice Wanton, anonymous boys' play, 22
Nicolai, Otto (1810–1849), operatic composer, 558
Nine Worthies, 120 n., 126 n., 127 n., 717 n.
Niobe, story of, 898 n., 907 n.
Norfolk, Thomas Howard, second Duke of (*Hen. VIII*), 5, 1274 n.
Norfolk, Thomas Mowbray, first Duke of (*Rich. II*), 643–645, 665 n., 666 n., 720 n., 1335
North, Sir Thomas (1535?–1601), translator of Plutarch's *Lives* (1579), *see* Plutarch
Northumberland, Henry Percy, first Earl of (*Rich. II, 1* and *2 Hen. IV*), 222 n., 645, 674–675, 1335, 1336
Northumberland, Henry Percy, third Earl of, killed 1461; mentioned in *3 Hen. VI* and *Rich. III,* 270 n., 306 n.
Norton, Thomas (1532–1584), author with Thomas Sackville, *Gorboduc,* 24, 25, 66, 207, 637 n., 1344
Norwich, religious drama at, 19
Nurse to Juliet (*R. and J.*), 394, 1310, 1329
Nym (*Mer. Wives* and *Hen. V*), 559–560, 744 n.

O

Oberon, king of the fairies (*Mids. Dr.*), 182–184, 1325
Octavia, sister to Caesar and wife to Antony (*Ant. and Cleo.*), 1071–1072, 1348
Octavius Caesar, one of the triumvirs after Caesar's death, later Augustus, emperor of Rome (*J.C.* and *Ant. and Cleo.*), 604 n., 770–772, 1071–1073, 1338, 1348
Odysseus, *see* Ulysses
Oedipus, King of Thebes, 49
Oldcastle, Sir John (1377?–1417), Lollard leader; also, name of a character in *The Famous Victories of Henvy V,* and an early name for Falstaff, 498, 678 n., 679 n., 720 n., 736 n., 1314, 1315, 1336, 1337
Oldcastle, Sir John, play by Drayton et al., *see Sir John Oldcastle*
Oldys, William (1696–1761), antiquary, 70
Oliver, hero of Charlemagne romances, 213 n., 605 n.
Oliver, elder brother of Orlando (*A.Y.L.*), 587
Oliver Martext, Sir, a vicar (*A.Y.L.*), 605 n., 1334
Olivia (*12th Night*), 616–618, 1323, 1334
Olivier, Sir Laurence, modern actor and director, 367, 738, 1355, 1359–1360
Olson, Elder (1909—), critic, 50
Omphale, Queen of Lydia, 539 n., 546 n.
Ophelia, daughter to Polonius (*Ham.*), 33, 66, 899–903, 1341–1342
Orestes, son of Agamemnon, 49
Orlando, son of Sir Rowland de Boys (*A.Y.L.*), 182, 587–589, 1333
Orleans, Duke of (*Hen. V*), 759 n.
Orodes, King of Parthia, 1075 n., 1087 n.
Orpheus and Eurydice, story of, 202 n., 367, 379 n., 445 n., 528 n.
Orsino, Duke of Illyria (*12th Night*), 616–617
Osric, a courtier (*Ham.*), 6
Ostler, William (d. 1614), actor, 1354
Oswald, steward to Goneril (*K. Lear*), 981, 994 n., 1344
Othello, 16, 21, 25, 30, 45, 46, 118 n., 360 n., 369, 381 n., 393, 427 n., 476 n., 478 n., 494 n., 532, 770, 798, 802, 833, 943–946, **947–979**, 980, 982, 1017–1018, 1022 n., 1043, 1071, 1108, 1148, 1179–1180; date and publication, 51, 54–56, 1317–1318; sources, 1343–1344; stage history, 1356
Othello, a Moor (*Oth.*), 46, 47, 943–946, 1044, 1179–1180, 1216, 1343–1344
Otway, Thomas (1652–1685), dramatist, author *The History and Fall of Caius Marius,* 1355, 1356
Overbury, Sir Thomas (1581–1613), author *Characters,* 1227 n.
Overdone, Mistress, a bawd (*Meas. Meas.*), 2, 834, 1316
Ovid (43 B.C.–18 A.D.), Roman poet, 27, 43, 79, 80, 114 n., 144 n., 257 n., 497, 528 n., 870 n.; *Amores,* 427 n.; *Ars Amandi,* 174 n.; *Fasti,* 439, 1330; *Heroides,* 169 n., 274 n.; *Metamorphoses,* 73, 76, 160 n., 161 n., 182, 191 n., 202 n., 367 n., 375 n., 376 n., 386 n., 425–426, 459 n., 463 n., 482 n., 527 n., 537 n., 567 n., 604 n., 619 n., 1099 n., 1234 n., 1267 n., 1325 n., 1328, 1329, 1330, 1332, 1340, 1352
Oxford, Edward de Vere, seventeenth Earl of (1550–1604), 74
Oxford, John de Vere, thirteenth Earl of (*3 Hen. VI*), 313 n.
Oxford's men, 36

P

Pace, Richard (1482?–1536), English diplomatist, 1284 n.
Pacorus, Parthian prince, 1087 n.
Page, Anne, daughter to Master and Mistress Page (*Mer. Wives*), 559–560, 1332
Page, Master, a gentleman dwelling at Windsor (*Mer. Wives*), 559–560
Page, Mistress (*Mer. Wives*), 559–560
Painter (*Timon*), 1017
Painter, William (1540?–1594), translator *The Palace of Pleasure,* 439, 804, 1329, 1330, 1338, 1339
Palamon and Arcite, story of, 65–66
Palatine Anthology, 496 n.
Palsgrave, John (c. 1483?–1554), translator *Acolastus,* 22
Pandarus, uncle to Cressida (*T. and C.*), 564 n., 630 n., 812 n., 862–863, 1340
Pandion, King, father to Philomela and Procne, 463 n.
Pandulph, Cardinal, Papal legate (*K. John*), 12, 340
Panecia, lost play, 1332
Papp, Joseph, modern director, 1360
Paracelsus (c. 1493–1541), 14, 814 n.
Paris, Count, suitor to Juliet (*R. and J.*), 394–395
Paris, son to Priam (*T. and C.*), 439, 802, 863–864
Paris, Matthew (d. 1259), author *Historia Maior,* 1328
Parnassus plays, 498, 797–798, 1017
Parolles, a follower of Bertram (*All's Well*), 283 n., 803–805, 1339
Parzival, hero of medieval romance, 1181
Pasqualigo, Luigi (*fl.* 1579), author *Il Fedele,* 1332

Q

R

Reynaldo, servant to Polonius (*Ham.*), 912 n.
Reynard the Fox, medieval beast epic, 406 n., 1226 n.
Rhetoric, 62–63
Rhodope, Greek courtesan, 217 n.
Ribner, Irving, modern scholar and editor, 48
Richard, Duke of Gloucester, afterwards King Richard III (*2* and *3 Hen. VI* and *Rich. III*), 8, 11, 18, 48, 79, 206, 208, 210, 267 n., 299–301, 369, 380 n., 498, 643, 945
Richard, Duke of York, son to Edward IV (*Rich. III*), 300
Richard I, King of England, surnamed Coeur-de-Lion (reigned 1189–1199), 225 n., 339–340, 342 n., 343 n., 344 n.
Richard II, King of England (*Rich. II*), 12, 50, 52, 136 n., 206, 232 n., 259 n., 340, 643–646, 674, 681 n., 693 n., 707 n., 758 n., 770, 1335
Richard II, The Tragedy of King, 11, 12, 29, 30, 40, 43, 67, 283 n., 296 n., 339, 358 n., 364 n., 464 n., 500, 643–646, **646–674**, 719 n., 720 n., 724 n., 770, 800, 862, 1110, 1271; date and composition, 51, 52, 54–56, 1305, 1308–1310, 1313–1315; sources, 1334–1336; stage history, 1355, 1360
Richard III, The Tragedy of King, 8, 20, 21, 36, 40, 41, 43, 78, 206–208, 210, 248 n., 276 n., 285 n., 299 n., 299–301, **302–339**, 500, 737, 770, 1271, 1273; date and composition, 54–56, 59, 1305, 1309; sources, 1326–1327; stage history, 1354, 1355, 1358
Richardson, Ralph, twentieth-century actor, 1359
Richardson, William (1743–1814), author *Philosophical Analysis and Illustration of Some of Shakespeare's Remarkable Characters,* 45
Riche, Barnabe (1540?–1617), author *Riche his Farewell to Militarie Profession,* 559, 616, 1332, 1334
Richmond, Margaret Beaufort, Countess of (1443–1509), mother to Henry Tudor, 307 n., 333 n., 338 n.
Righter, Anne, modern scholar and critic, 48
Rivers, Anthony Woodvile, second Earl, brother to Queen Elizabeth (*3 Hen. VI* and *Rich. III*), 1327
Rizzio, David (1533?–1566), secretary to Mary Queen of Scots, 10
Robert Earl of Huntingdon plays, *see* Munday, Anthony
Roberts, James (*fl.* 1600–1608), printer, 53, 862, 1311, 1312, 1316, 1317
Robin Hood, 28, 501, 562 n., 586, 587, 734 n., 1333
Robinson, Clement (*fl.* 1584), author *A Handefull of Pleasant Delites,* 1325
Robson, Flora, twentieth-century actress, 1271, 1359
Roderigo, a Venetian gentleman (*Oth.*), 944, 946, 1344
Roland, hero of medieval romance, 213 n.
Romance, Shakespearean, 501, 1148–1149, 1153, 1179, 1216, 1273
Romances, medieval, *Bevis of Hampton,* 1274 n.; *Gamelyn,* 587, 1333; *Guy of Warwick,* 344 n., 1302 n.; *The Squire of Low Degree,* 766 n.
Romano, Julio (*fl.* 16th c.), Italian artist, 1245 n.
Romeo, son to Montague (*R. and J.*), 393–395, 1329
Romeo and Juliet, 6, 12, 25, 33, 39, 40, 43, 78, 79, 129 n., 163 n., 183, 256–257 n., 292 n., 367, 393–395, **395–424**, 460 n., 486 n., 494 n., 497, 498, 646, 671 n., 802, 809 n., 862, 893 n., 1071, 1186; date and publication, 51, 54, 55, 59, 1305, 1306, 1308, 1310, 1316, 1319, 1320; sources, 1329; stage history, 1355, 1356, 1358–1360
Ronsard, Pierre de (1524–1585), French poet, 469, 1038 n.
Rosalind, daughter to the banished Duke (*A.Y.L.*), 182, 587–589, 617, 1333
Rosaline, lady attending on the Princess (*L.L.L.*), 113 n., 122 n., 531
Rosaline, beloved of Romeo (*R. and J.*), 394
Roscius (d. 62 B.C.), famed Roman comic actor, 298 n., 917 n.
Rose, The, playhouse, 37, 78, 498, 797, 1315, 1344
Rosencrantz, courtier (*Ham.*), 899–901, 1341
Ross, nobleman of Scotland (*Macb.*), 1048 n.
Rotherham, Thomas, Archbishop of York, *see* York, Archbishop of (*Rich. III*)
Rouillet, Claude (*fl.* 1556), author *Philanira,* 1339
Rowe, Nicholas (1674–1718), editor, 44, 57, 70, 72, 76, 440 n., 558
Rowley, Samuel (d. c. 1624), dramatist, author *When You See Me You Know Me,* 67, 1152, 1353; *see also* Middleton, Thomas
Roydon, Matthew (*fl.* 1580–1622), poet, 1306
Rumour, the Presenter (*2 Henry IV*), 676, 705 n.
Rutland, Edmund, Earl of, son to Richard Plantagenet (*3 Hen. VI*), 210, 305 n., 329 n.
Rymer, Thomas (1641–1713), critic, author *A Short View of Tragedy,* 45

S

Sabie, Francis (*fl.* 1595), poet, author *The Fissher-mans Tale* and *Flora's Fortune,* 1352
Sackville, Thomas, Baron Buckhurst (1536–1608), author with Thomas Norton *Gorboduc, see* Norton, Thomas
Sacrament, Play of the, 503
St. Alban, 246 n.
St. Anne, 626 n.
St. David (St. David's Day), 738, 757 n.
St. Denis, 122 n., 217 n., 768 n.
St. George, 72, 213 n., 230 n., 259 n., 332 n., 347 n., 559
St. Helena, 214 n.
St. James of Compostella, 820 n., 931 n.
St. Katharine, 19
St. Laurence, 19
St. Martin (St. Martin's Day, Nov. 11), 214 n., 713 n.
St. Nicholas, St. Nicholas Plays, 17, 19, 145 n., 683 n., 704 n., 921 n.
St. Patrick, 654 n., 912 n.
St. Paul, St. Paul's Cathedral, 17, 35, 304 n., 674 n., 690 n., 708 n., 1148, 1302 n.
St. Philip, 214 n., 850 n.
St. Valentine, 200 n.
Sts. Crispinus and Crispianus, third-century martyrs, 760 n.
Saints' Play, The, 19, 21, 22, 34
Salisbury, John de Montacute, third Earl of (*Rich. II*), 662 n.

T

U

V

W

1305, 1320; sources, 1351–1352; stage history, 1359
Wise, Andrew (*fl.* 1597–1600), publisher, 1309, 1313, 1314
Witches or Weird Sisters, Three (*Macb.*), 1044–1046
Woffington, Margaret (1720–1760), actress, 1357
Wolfit, Donald, twentieth-century actor, 1359–1360
Wolsey, Thomas, Cardinal (1475?–1530), statesman, 5, 10, 20, 23; in *Hen. VIII,* 12, 1271–1273, 1353
Woodes, Nathaniel (*fl.* 1572), clergyman, author *The Conflict of Conscience,* 20
Woodstock, Thomas of, or *1 Richard II,* 646, 1335, 1336
Woodvile, Lieutenant of the Tower (*1 Hen. VI*), 215 n.
Worcester, Thomas Percy, Earl of, brother to Northumberland (*1 Hen. IV*), 657 n., 674–675
Worcester's men, company of players, 36
Worthies, the Nine, 120–121 n., 717 n.
Wotton, Henry (*fl.* 1578), translator *A Courtlie Controversie of Cupids Cautels,* 1323
Wotton, Sir Henry (1568–1639), poet, 1321
Wright, John (*fl.* 1631), bookseller and publisher, 1311
Wyatt, Sir Thomas (1503?–1542), 470, 471
Wycliffe, John (d. 1384), religious reformer, translator of the Bible, 679 n.

X

Xanthippe, wife of Socrates, 163 n.
Xenophon of Ephesus (*fl.* 4th c.), Greek writer of fiction, reputed author *Ephesiaca,* 1329

Y

Yates, Mary Ann (1728–1787), actress, 1357
Yeats, William Butler (1865–1939), poet, 645
Yonge, Bartholomew (*fl.* 1579–1598), translator Montemayor's *Diana,* 1323
York, Archbishop of, Richard Scroop (*1* and *2 Hen. IV*), 676, 705
York, Archbishop of, Thomas Rotherham (*Rich. III*), 316 n.
York, Duchess of, mother to King Edward IV (*Rich. III*), 325 n.
York, Duchess of, widow of Thomas of Woodstock (*Rich. II*), 644, 670 n., 1335
York, Edmund of Langley, first Duke of (*Rich. II*), 8, 220 n., 643–645, 738, 1110, 1335
York, House of, a genealogy, 1362–1363
York, religious drama at, 17–19
York, Richard, Duke of, son of Edward IV, *see* Richard, Duke of York (*Rich. III*)
York, Richard Plantagenet, Duke of (*1, 2,* and *3 Hen. VI*), 206, 208–210, 322 n., 329 n., 1326
Yorkshire Tragedy, A, perhaps by George Wilkins, 54, 57, 66, 801
Young, David, modern scholar and critic, 51
Youth, The Interlude of, anonymous morality play, 20

Z

Zeuxis (*fl.* 5th c. B.C.), Greek painter, 433 n.